Congressional Quarterly's

Guide to
U.S.
Elections

Second Edition

Congressional Quarterly's

Guide to U.S. Elections

Second Edition

Congressional Quarterly Inc.
1414 22nd St., N.W., Washington, D.C. 20037

Ref.
JK
1967
.C662
1985

Congressional Quarterly Inc.

Congressional Quarterly Inc., an editorial research service and publishing company, serves clients in the fields of news, education, business and government. It combines Congressional Quarterly's specific coverage of Congress, government and politics with the more general subject range of an affiliated service, Editorial Research Reports.

Congressional Quarterly publishes the *Congressional Quarterly Weekly Report* and a variety of books, including college political science textbooks under the CQ Press imprint and public affairs paperbacks designed as timely reports to keep journalists, scholars and the public abreast of developing issues and events. CQ also publishes information directories and reference books on the federal government, national elections and politics, including the *Guide to Congress*, the *Guide to the Supreme Court*, the *Guide to U.S. Elections* and *Politics in America*. The *CQ Almanac*, a compendium of legislation for one session of Congress, is published each year. *Congress and the Nation*, a record of government for a presidential term, is published every four years.

CQ publishes *The Congressional Monitor*, a daily report on current and future activities of congressional committees, and several newsletters including *Congressional Insight*, a weekly analysis of congressional action, and *Campaign Practices Reports*, a semimonthly update on campaign laws.

The online delivery of CQ's Washington Alert Service provides clients with immediate access to Congressional Quarterly's institutional information and expertise.

Copyright © 1985 Congressional Quarterly Inc.

All rights reserved. No part of this publication may be reproduced or transmitted in any form or by any means, electronic or mechanical, including photocopy, recording, or any information storage and retrieval system, without permission in writing from the publisher.

Printed in the United States of America

Library of Congress Cataloging in Publication Data

Main entry under title:

Congressional Quarterly's Guide to U.S. elections

Includes bibliography and indexes.
1. Elections — United States — History — Statistics.
2. Political conventions — United States — History.
3. Political parties — United States — History.
I. Congressional Quarterly, inc. II. Title: Guide to U.S. elections. III. Title: Guide to U.S. elections.
JK1967.C662   1985   324.973   85-6912
ISBN 0-87187-339-7

CANISIUS COLLEGE LIBRARY
BUFFALO, N. Y.

Editor: John L. Moore

Assistant Editors: Mary Ames Booker, H. Amy Stern

Major Contributors: Rhodes Cook, Alan Ehrenhalt, Warden Moxley (1939-1984), Matt Pinkus

Contributors: Martha Bomgardner Alito, Irwin B. Arieff, Betsey Bancroft, Nancy Blanpied, Elizabeth Bowman, Christopher Buchanan, Nadine Cohodas, Harrison Donnelly, John Felton, Stephen P. Gasteyer, Kathryn Waters Gest, Diane Granat, Peter A. Harkness, Keith Head, Catherine P. Jaskowiak, Faith Keenan, Nancy Lammers, Larry Light, Andy Plattner, Beth Prather, Renee S. Reiner, Susanna Spencer, Margaret C. Thompson, James R. Wagner, Wayne Walker, Elizabeth Wehr

Graphics: Patrick Murphy, Kathleen A. Ossenfort, Robert Redding

Dust Jacket: Design—Richard A. Pottern; photograph—Ricardo Ferro, *St. Petersburg Times*

Indexes: Jennifer Adams, Judith Leckrone, Jodean Marks

Congressional Quarterly Inc.

Eugene Patterson   *Editor and President*
Wayne P. Kelley   *Publisher*
Peter A. Harkness   *Deputy Publisher and Executive Editor*
Robert C. Hur   *General Manager*
Robert E. Cuthriell   *Director, Research and Development*
I. D. Fuller   *Production Manager*
Maceo Mayo   *Assistant Production Manager*
Sydney E. Garriss   *Computer Services Manager*

Book Department

David R. Tarr   *Director*
Joanne D. Daniels   *Director, CQ Press*
John L. Moore   *Assistant Director*
Kathryn C. Suárez   *Book Marketing Manager*
Mary W. Cohn   *Associate Editor*
Nola Healy Lynch   *Developmental Editor, CQ Press*
Nancy Blanpied, Carolyn Goldinger, Carolyn McGovern, Colleen McGuiness, Susanna Spencer   *Project Editors*
Bryan Daves, Linda M. Pompa, Renee S. Reiner, Maria J. Sayers   *Editorial Assistants*

To
Warden Moxley

He enriched these pages
with his love for knowledge

Summary Table of Contents

Table of Contents

Introduction

Part I
Political Parties

Part II
Presidential Elections

Part III
Gubernatorial Elections

Part IV
Senate Elections

Part V
House Elections

Part VI
Southern Primaries

Appendix

Indexes

Editor's Note: How to Use the Guide to U.S. Elections

The *Guide to U.S. Elections, Second Edition,* contains even more information than the 1975 edition, which was generally regarded as the most comprehensive published collection of data on elections for president, governor, senator and representative. Besides returns for those elections through 1984, this edition contains new sections on gubernatorial and Senate primaries since 1956 and pre-1824 outcomes of the first contests for American state governorships.

This note explains the organization of that material and helps users find the specific facts they want in the updated and expanded *Guide*. There are three key aids to locating information in these pages. The Table of Contents offers an overall view of the book's scope and allows quick access to major sections. Candidate Indexes pinpoint the returns for the more than 65,000 candidates listed in the *Guide*. The General Index spans the broad range of subjects covered and contains references to all sections of the book except those covered by the Candidate Indexes.

Table of Contents

The Summary Table of Contents *(p. vii)* shows at a glance the book's organization. The detailed Table of Contents *(pp. ix-xii)* outlines the seven major parts of the *Guide* — Introduction: Change and Stability in U.S. Elections; Part I: Political Parties; Part II: Presidential Elections; Part III: Gubernatorial Elections: Part IV: Senate Elections; Part V: House Elections and Part VI: Southern Primaries.

Part I contains primarily narrative material — Pre-Convention Politics, 1789-1828; Functions of Party Conventions; a Chronology of Nominating Conventions, 1831-1984; and Historical Profiles of American Political Parties.

Readers of the convention chronology will find the results of important balloting from presidential nominating conventions broken down by state delegations in Key Nominating Convention Ballots *(pp. 161-224)*.

Parts II through VI have a basically parallel structure and contain common elements. Each part begins with an introductory section explaining the origins and development of election procedures for the office covered in that part of the *Guide*. Thus, "The Electoral College" *(pp. 253-266)*, the introduction to the Presidential Elections section, presents a comprehensive dis-

cussion of the constitutional origins and historical development of the Electoral College, details complex and little-known methods used in the various states through the first third of the 19th century to choose presidential electors, recounts historical anomalies in the functioning of the Electoral College and explains why a state's electoral votes frequently have been divided among several presidential candidates. The section covers the two occasions when a president was elected by the House of Representatives, the procedures for counting and challenging electoral votes in Congress and major points of the famous Hayes-Tilden contest in 1876. It concludes with a discussion of instances of presidential disability and ratification of the 25th Amendment. In a similar fashion, the introductions to Parts III through VI trace historical developments in election procedures for governors, senators, representatives and for Southern primary candidates for governor and the Senate.

Popular Election Returns. The major sections of Parts II through VI are listings of popular vote returns — since 1787 for gubernatorial elections; since 1824 for presidential and House elections; since 1913 for Senate elections; since 1919 for Southern primaries; and since 1956 for gubernatorial and Senate primaries outside the 11 states of the Old South.

Special research materials unique to Part II include maps displaying presidential Electoral College results since 1789, presidential primary returns from 1912 to 1984 and a Biographical Directory of Candidates. Part III contains a complete listing of all governors since 1789 and Part IV a complete listing of all senators since 1789. The lists are valuable complements to the gubernatorial and Senate election returns because they contain dates of service and footnotes explaining disputed elections and instances of succession to office by appointment or other non-elective procedures.

Candidate Indexes

Separate Candidate Indexes for the popular election returns appear on pages 1147 to 1273. The eight indexes are: Presidential Candidates Index *(p. 1147)*, Gubernatorial Candidates Index *(p. 1148)*, Gubernatorial Primary Candidates Index *(p. 1160)*, Senate Candidates Index *(p. 1164)*, Senate Primary Candidates Index *(p. 1170)*, Southern Gubernatorial Primary Candidates Index *(p. 1175)*, Southern Senate Primary Can-

ICPSR Historical Election Returns File

The election returns obtained from the Inter-University Consortium for Political and Social Research for the *Guide to U.S. Elections* represent constituency-level totals for candidates appearing in elections for the offices of president, governor and U.S. representative from 1824 to 1973 and for U.S. senator from 1913 to 1973. Congressional Quarterly obtained returns for 1974-85 elections from secretaries of state.

The 1824 starting point for the ICPSR Historical Election Returns File was based on consideration of factors such as the pronounced trend by that year toward popular election of presidential electors, as well as the availability, accessibility and quality of the returns for presidential, gubernatorial and House elections.

Collection of the Data

The original data collection effort, begun in 1962, was supported by the Social Science Research Council and the National Science Foundation. The continuing addition of contemporary election returns is supported by the annual membership fee of more than 300 colleges and universities affiliated with the consortium.

As in the case with any enterprise of the magnitude represented by this data collection, many individuals contributed to its development and growth. Those who provided the initial impetus for the project include Lee Benson, Allan G. Bogue, Dewey Grantham Jr., Samuel P. Hays, Morton P. Keller, V. O. Key, Richard P. McCormick, Phillip Mason, Warren E. Miller, Thomas J. Pressly, William H. Riker and Charles G. Sellers Jr. The ad hoc Committee to Collect the Basic Quantitative Data for American Political History of the American Historical Association had the assistance of more than 100 archivists, historians and political scientists in the collection of the data.

Through the efforts of Warren E. Miller, then executive director of the consortium, financial support was obtained for completion of the data collection, conversion to computer-readable form and the extensive data processing that followed. The data collection and processing effort was successively directed by Walter Dean Burnham, Howard W. Allen and Jerome M. Clubb at the Survey Research Center, and more recently the Center for Political Studies, in the Institute for Social Research, the University of Michigan.

The initial data collection was conducted by scholars in the various states who volunteered their time and effort in locating little-known publications, searching state and local archives for unpublished data, exploring newspaper files, and evaluating the accuracy and reliability of these sources. In as many cases as possible, multiple sources were consulted. While general preference was given to official sources, these scholars were charged with the task of evaluating all available sources in terms of their quality and completeness. While the complete source annotations for the collection are too extensive to publish here, information on the sources for returns from specific elections can be obtained from the ICPSR.

The result of this initial effort, and subsequent work by the ICPSR staff, was the recovery of returns for more than 90 percent of all the elections to these four offices. This estimate is based upon a review of the periodicity of elections by state and office, indicating where elections apparently occurred but no returns could be located. Such hypotheses were confirmed by reference to state manuals and histories or the *Biographical Directory of the United States Congress, 1774-1971*, U.S. Government Printing Office, Washington, D.C. 1971, which indicates the changes in the membership of state delegations. A continuing effort is being made to locate the remaining fugitive returns.

Format of the Election Returns File

In the computer-readable format in which these materials are stored and retrieved by the ICPSR, an election is defined as a set of returns by party or candidate for a specified office in a specified state at a specified time. As a result, the collection now includes returns for more than 25,000 individual elections and records the names of almost 115,000 candidates.

A decision was reached early in the process of conversion of the data to machine-readable form to preserve the original party designations appearing on each original source. Consequently, almost 1,700 unique partisan labels appear in the collection, most of which, of course, represent short-lived or localized minor parties and the combinations and permutations of multi-party support received by individual candidates. In the ICPSR data collection, separate vote totals are recorded for candidates who appeared more than once on a ballot with different and distinct party designations. In short, the data appear in the collection virtually as they appeared in the original sources, with no combinations of either candidate or party totals. *(For details on presentation of these data in the* Guide to U.S. Elections, *Second Edition, see pages 328, 489, 608, 700, 1074.)*

A comprehensive series of manual and machine-aided error-checking procedures has been carried out on these data, and errors discovered through them have been corrected. The ICPSR maintains returns for these elections at the county level in separate and larger computer-readable files. Using these data, it was possible to ascertain that the individual candidate returns summed to the total number of votes cast in the county. Subsequently, county returns were summed as a check against the state or congressional district level returns, both by candidate and in terms of the total number of votes cast. All discrepancies encountered in this process were resolved where possible and appropriate corrections to the machine-readable files were made. No further systematic error checks are planned, although errors discovered through the use of the data are corrected as they are reported to the ICPSR.

Requests for Computer-Readable Data. Requests for data from the Historical Election Returns File in machine-readable form should be addressed to: Executive Director, Inter-University Consortium for Political and Social Research, Box 1248, Ann Arbor, Mich. 48106.

didates Index *(p. 1178)* and the House Candidates Index *(p. 1180)*. Each Candidate Index lists the *years* of candidacy for each candidate. Instructions for use of the candidate indexes appear on the first page of each index.

General Index

The General Index, *(pp. 1275-1308)*, provides page references for all sections of the *Guide to U.S. Elections, Second Edition*, except the popular returns, which are indexed in the special Candidate Indexes described above. The General Index can be used independently as a source of information; for example, the index entry for Herbert C. Hoover *(p. 1289)* indicates that Hoover received votes in presidential primaries in 1920, 1928, 1932, 1936 and 1940; received votes at the 1920, 1928, 1932 and 1940 Republican nominating conventions and was a presidential candidate in 1928 and 1932.

ICPSR Election Data

Except where noted, the returns through 1972 for presidential, gubernatorial, Senate, House and Southern primary elections were obtained from the Inter-University Consortium for Political and Social Research. *(Description of ICPSR Historical Election Returns File, p. xiv; details on the presentation of these returns in this book, pp. 328, 489, 608, 700, 1074)*

Congressional Quarterly is grateful to the ICPSR staff for its assistance and advice in supplementing this information for the second edition of the *Guide*. We thank especially Jerome M. Clubb, executive director; Michael W. Traugott, director, resource development and special projects; and Erik W. Austin, director, archival development.

Other Sources

Major sources used to update or supplement the ICPSR data are identified at the beginning of each section of the *Guide*. Those cited most often are the biennial *America Votes* series compiled by Richard M. Scammon and Alice V. McGillivray (Washington, D.C.: Congressional Quarterly) and *American State Governors, 1776-1976*, vol. 1, by Joseph E. Kallenbach and Jessamine S. Kallenbach (Dobbs Ferry, N.Y.: Oceana Publishing, 1977).

Kenneth C. Martis, author and editor of *The Historical Atlas of United States Congressional Districts 1789-1983* (New York: The Free Press, 1982), provided information on several missing House elections that were verified for inclusion in this edition.

The help of these authors is gratefully acknowledged.

The Writers

Introductions to major sections of the *Guide* have been updated and revised for this edition. Original writers of that material were Rhodes Cook — political parties, convention functions and histories, party profiles (with Elizabeth Wehr); Warden Moxley — presi-

dential, gubernatorial and House elections, reapportionment and redistricting, Southern primaries, Senate elections (with Matt Pinkus). Other contributors to this edition are listed on p. v.

Acknowledgements

Congressional Quarterly expresses appreciation to the following copyright owners for permission to use material from their books in the *Guide to U.S. Elections, Second Edition*:

● Brookings Institution, Washington, D.C.: *Convention Decisions and Voting Records*, by Richard C. Bain and Judith H. Parris. Copyright 1973.

● James W. Davis: *Presidential Primaries: Road to the White House*, Greenwood Press, Westport, Conn., and London, England, reprint. Copyright 1967, 1980.

● Joseph E. Kallenbach and Jessamine S. Kallenbach: *American State Governors, 1776-1976*, vol. 1, Oceana Publications, Dobbs Ferry, N.Y. Copyright 1977.

● Svend Petersen: *A Statistical History of the American Presidential Elections, With Supplementary Tables Covering 1968-1980*, Greenwood Press, Westport, Conn., and London, England, reprint. Copyright 1963, 1968, 1981.

Most of the photographs and engravings appearing in the *Guide to U.S. Elections, Second Edition* were obtained from the collection of the Library of Congress. The National Portrait Gallery, Smithsonian Institution, Washington, D.C., provided the photographs of William Wirt on page 31, Rutherford B. Hayes on page 54, William Jennings Bryan on pages 66, 68, 72, Alton B. Parker on page 70, William Howard Taft on pages 72, 74, the 1888 Republican convention on page 251 and the ballot-counting scene on page 451. Other photos and their sources were: Thomas E. Dewey, pp. 96, 99 — New York State Historical Society; Harry S Truman, p. 99, and Adlai E. Stevenson Jr., pp. 103, 106 — George Tames, *The New York Times;* Eugene Talmadge, p. 1065 — Wide World Photos Inc.

Invariably in a project of this scope — particularly one involving the publication of a large computer data file — there will be some omissions or errors. There were some in the first edition and your letters helped us to correct them for the new volume. Undoubtedly there are others, and to pinpoint them Congressional Quarterly again invites comments and suggestions from scholars and other users of the *Guide to U.S. Elections*.

John L. Moore
August 1985

Introduction

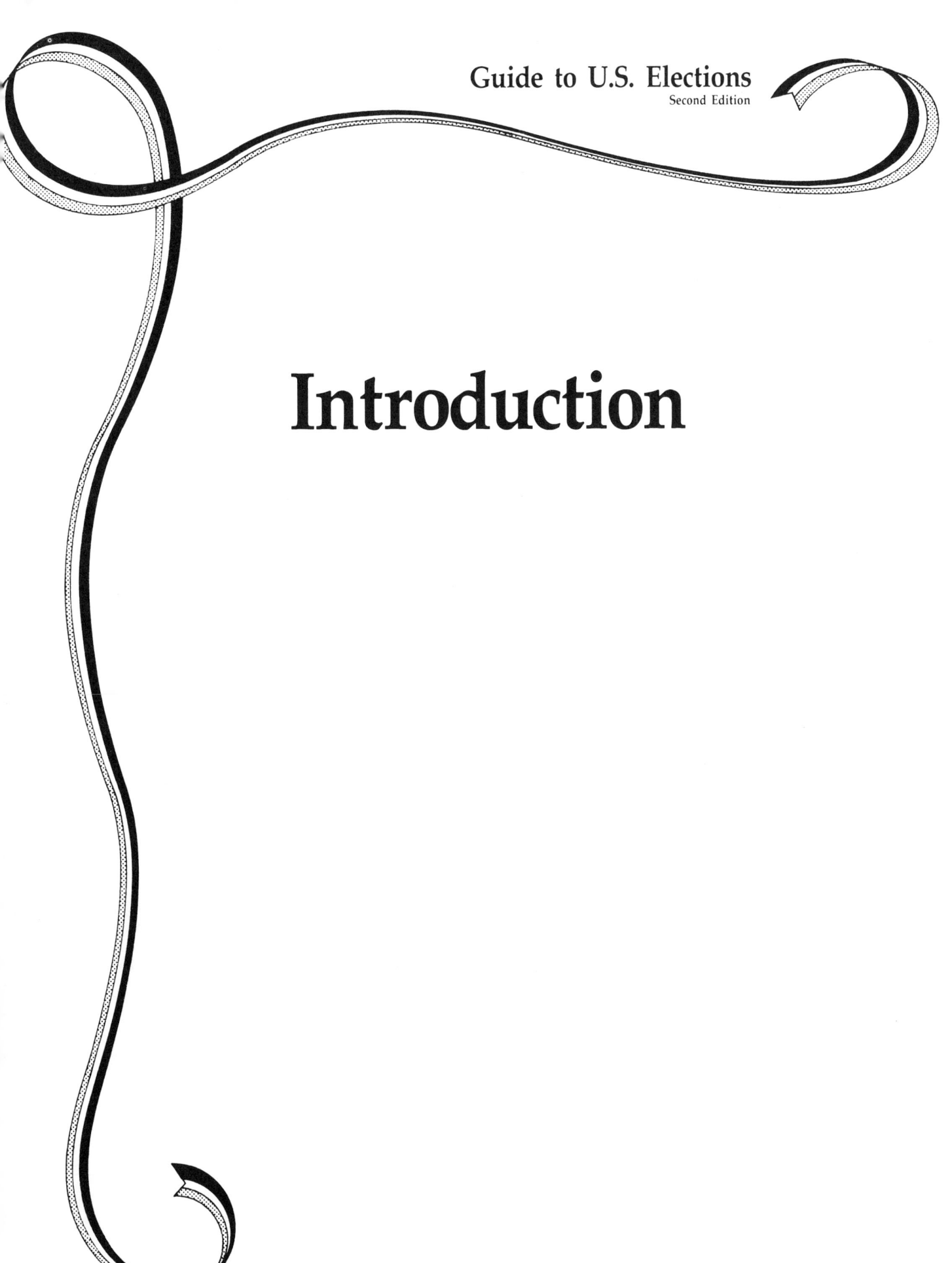

Introduction

Change and Stability in U.S. Elections

By Alan Ehrenhalt
Congressional Quarterly Political Editor

Voters in Virginia's 5th District faced a difficult choice as they went to the polls in February of 1789 to pick a representative for the 1st Congress, scheduled to convene a few months later.

One of their candidates had been an activist in colonial politics for 15 years and a member of the Continental Congress; the other was not only a longtime legislator but a genuine war hero. In the end, though, activist James Madison had an issue on his side that war hero James Monroe could not match. He was the principal author of the U.S. Constitution. One wonders what a modern campaign consultant might have done with that credential.

The candidates spent two weeks debating face to face in the courthouses of the district's eight rural counties, Madison defending the document he had written and Monroe attacking it as a usurpation of states' rights. Madison won that contest of future presidents by 336 votes and went on to serve four terms in the U.S. House. Monroe's congressional ambitions had to be put aside until the next year, when he was elected to fill a vacancy in the Senate.

There is a certain 18th century remoteness about this episode from the birth of the Republic. The electorate to which Madison and Monroe appealed consisted of a few thousand wealthy white male landowners; no one who did not own property was allowed to participate. The city of Washington did not exist; the 1st Congress met in lower Manhattan, and it had only 59 House members when it convened. The idea of two of the Founding Fathers slugging it out in a House race seems incongruous in itself.

But as remote as that election may seem, it is remarkably easy to understand in contemporary terms. There still is a 5th District of Virginia, and — while it has grown, changed its shape and moved south over the course of two centuries — it is roughly the same sort of political entity that it was in 1789.

Voters in Fluvanna County had to make the choice between Madison and Monroe that year; in 1984, still resi-

dents of the 5th District, they helped return conservative Democrat Dan Daniel to the House without opposition. Virginia had 10 House seats in the first Congress, and it has the same number today, although that represents considerably less influence in a chamber of 435 members than it did in a chamber of 59.

Voters in that first election divided between supporters and opponents of the Constitution, but parties did not exist — Madison himself considered them a menace to good government. Nowadays, all members of Congress run as members of one party or the other, but partisan affiliation has never determined elections in the way that it does in most of the free countries of the world. Dan Daniel seeks re-election as a Democrat every two years and votes with Republicans most of the time on the House floor. That is a sort of independence that would have made sense to the people who ran for Congress in the first campaign nearly 200 years ago.

The two-year terms that Madison and his cohorts insisted upon for House members remain with us today, despite numerous attempts to lengthen them, and they define the schedule according to which representatives think. Members of the modern House live from one even-numbered year to the next, as the first congressional generation did and as Madison wanted them to do.

Gerrymandering is a fact of 20th century congressional life, but it was a fact in the 18th century as well. To win his seat in the 1st Congress, Madison had to overcome the handicap of a district that his enemy Patrick Henry had drawn to include every available pocket of opposition to the Constitution Madison wrote. Then, as now, strong candidates had a way of winning in districts where the odds were against them.

It is worthwhile to recall all this to make the point that congressional elections in America are essentially a story of stability and continuity. There have been important alterations over the years — gradual expansion of the franchise

1

in the 19th and early 20th centuries, the arrival of one-person, one-vote in the 1960s — but the underlying system has remained intact. Individual candidates compete in individual districts for what is deemed to be the endorsement of the general public. We have kept doing essentially the same thing while other democratic countries have tinkered with their rules time and again.

It is not possible, of course, to talk about the Senate in exactly the same terms as the House. In the case of the Senate, a great deal has changed. James Monroe made it there in 1790 by a vote of his state Legislature, and that was the way all U.S. senators were chosen until 1914, when the country began operating under the 17th Amendment to the Constitution, which requires election of senators by direct popular vote.

That was a dramatic change, but not a very exotic one. What its authors did was take the method of election that seemed to work successfully for one chamber of Congress and apply it to the other. Since 1914, Senate elections have become more like House elections. What we have been doing at the congressional district level in most places since 1789, we have been doing at the statewide level since 1914.

It is the combination of stability and novelty that makes watching congressional elections such an addictive enterprise for those who develop an interest in it. People change, issues change, campaign styles change; and all of the sound and fury can be measured in the context of an underlying system that is largely what it was when Monroe fought Madison in 1789.

A decade has passed since Congressional Quarterly first published its *Guide to U.S. Elections*, with virtually complete returns for all House and Senate elections since 1824, plus gubernatorial returns and detailed information on all presidential elections and nominating conventions.

This year, CQ is updating the *Guide* to include material on all federal and gubernatorial elections 1974 through 1984 and previously unavailable gubernatorial data covering the period all the way back to the start of the Republic in 1788.

Ten years seems like a long time in presidential politics and in the history of the country. Gerald R. Ford was in office when the *Guide* was first published. Since then, we have witnessed his defeat at the hands of Jimmy Carter, Carter's loss to Ronald Reagan, and Reagan's overwhelming victory for a second term. Each of those elections seemed in some way to mark the end of one chapter of modern presidential history and the beginning of another.

Congress is different. Ten years — five congressional elections — represents an incremental addition to two centuries' worth of data, rather than a few epochal events. Nevertheless, the past decade has brought its share of interesting developments at the congressional level, and

they are all recorded here for scholars and amateur politics buffs to ponder.

When the first *Guide* came out, Democrats had controlled both chambers of Congress for 20 years, and it seemed reasonable to predict that their dominance would stretch on toward the end of the century. That still sounds like a reasonable prophecy for the House, where a decade has seen the Democratic majority remain comfortable even in hard times for the party. But the Senate changed overnight in 1980, when the Reagan presidential landslide eliminated a 59-41 Democratic advantage and replaced it with a Republican majority of 53-47.

It was not only Democratic Senate seats that began to seem endangered in the late 1970s — it was seats held by incumbents of either party. When the first *Guide* was published, it was thought that a place in the Senate was a relatively secure possession. In 1974, a year of considerable political upheaval, only four senators were unseated.

Then came a period in which senators began meeting defeat in surprising numbers. There were nine in 1976, 10 in 1978, and a remarkable 13 in 1980, the year of the Republican accession.

But those who forecast a period of prolonged upheaval and heavy Senate turnover were wrong. In 1982, only two senators were turned out of office; in 1984, just three. The stubbornness of the unfolding electoral history is one thing that makes it so much fun to study. The more sense a theory seems to make, the more likely the next election is to refute it.

House elections have been more stable in recent years, but the election returns presented in this book still suggest a fascinating variety of information about the way American politics is developing, both nationally and at the congressional district level.

As a tantalizing example, I might offer a string of numbers relating to a single constituency, the current 10th District of Massachusetts. The numbers are these: zero, 50, 50, 75, 100, 100, 73, 69 and 56. They represent the percentage of the vote won by the Democratic candidate in the district for the last nine elections.

Imbedded in the figures is an interesting story — of the party's moribund condition in southeastern Massachusetts in the late 1960s; of its sudden rise to competitiveness in 1970 behind a dynamic young candidate, Gerry E. Studds; of Studds' near-miss that year and narrow victory in 1972; of his rise to invincibility, symbolized by the absence of any GOP candidate at all in 1976 and 1978; and finally of his problems in 1984, when he had to seek re-election following his House censure on charges of sexual misconduct.

There are all sorts of stories in the pages of statistics that make up most of this volume. The *Guide to U.S. Elections* is not exactly a novel, but for those who have learned how enjoyable it can be to coax meaning out of election returns, it is surprisingly difficult to put down.

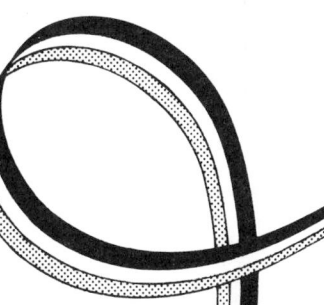

Political Parties

"Interior of Tammany Hall, New York — The Democratic Convention in Session." *Harper's*, July 1868.

Library of Congress Photo No. USZ62-32017

Pre-Convention Politics, 1789-1828

For nearly a century and a half the United States has had an established two-party system. Yet such a system was never envisioned by the Founding Fathers, who viewed the existence of political parties with suspicion.

In his Farewell Address, written in 1796, President George Washington warned the American people of "the danger of parties." He went on to state:

> There is an opinion that parties in free countries are useful checks upon the administration of the government, and serve to keep alive the spirit of liberty. This within certain limits is probably true; and in governments of a monarchical cast patriotism may look with indulgence, if not with favor, upon the spirit of party. But in those of the popular character, in governments purely elective, it is a spirit not to be encouraged.... A fire not to be quenched, it demands a uniform vigilance to prevent its bursting into a flame, lest, instead of warming, it should consume.

Washington's suspicion of parties was shared by other early American leaders. Alexander Hamilton, in 1787, remarked that "[N]othing could be more illjudged than that intolerant spirit which has at all times characterized political parties." Two years later Thomas Jefferson declared: "If I could not go to heaven but with a party, I would not go there at all." Even a generation later, after the establishment of an U.S. party system, two early 19th-century presidents continued to speak out against the existence of political parties. Andrew Jackson, 12 years before he was elected president, wrote in 1816: "Now is the time to exterminate the monster called party spirit." In 1822, after his unopposed 1820 election victory, President James Monroe characterized parties as "the curse of the country."

Early American leaders were heavily influenced in their attitude by a dominant anti-party theme in European political philosophy, which equated parties with factions and viewed both negatively. Thomas Hobbes (1588-1679), David Hume (1711-1776) and Jean Jacques Rousseau (1712-1778) — three European philosophers whose views strongly influenced the Founding Fathers — regarded parties as threats to state government. In England there was no formal party system until the 1820s, several decades after the formation of parties in the United States. In colonial America there were no parties, and there were none in the Continental Congress or under the Articles of Confederation.

The Constitution did not provide authority for political parties or prohibitions against them. Historians have pointed out that most of the Founding Fathers had only a dim understanding of the function of political parties and thus were ambivalent, if not hostile, toward parties when they laid down the framework of the new government. Nevertheless, the delegates to the Constitutional Convention and their successors in Congress ensured a role for parties in the government when they gave protection to civil rights and the right to organize. The Founders set up what they regarded as safeguards against excesses of party activity by providing an elaborate governmental system of checks and balances. The prevailing attitude of the convention was summed up by James Madison, who wrote in *The Federalist* that the "great object" of the new government was "to secure the public good and private rights against the danger of such a faction [party], and at the same time to preserve the spirit and the form of popular government."

Madison's greatest fear was that a party would become a tyrannical majority. This could be avoided, he believed,

Sources

Chambers, William N. *Political Parties in a New Nation: The American Experience, 1776-1809.* New York: Oxford University Press, 1963.

Key, V. O., Jr. *Politics, Parties and Pressure Groups.* 5th ed. New York: Thomas Y. Crowell, 1964.

Nichols, Roy F. *The Invention of the American Political Parties.* New York: Free Press, 1972.

Roseboom, Eugene H. *A History of Presidential Elections: From George Washington to Jimmy Carter.* New York: Macmillan, 1979.

Schlesinger, Arthur M., Jr. *History of U.S. Political Parties.* vol. 1. 1973. Reprint. New York: Chelsea House, 1981.

Stanwood, Edward. *A History of the Presidency from 1788 to 1897.* Boston: Houghton-Mifflin, 1898.

Stimpson, George W. *A Book about American Politics.* New York: Harper, 1952.

"If I could not go to heaven but with a party, I would not go there at all."

—Thomas Jefferson, 1789

through the republican form of government that the proponents of the Constitution advocated. In *The Federalist* Madison wrote that "Among the numerous advantages promised by a well-constructed Union, none deserved to be more accurately developed than its tendency to break and control the violence of faction." A republic, as understood by Madison, was an elected body of wise, patriotic citizens, while a democracy was equated with mob rule. Madison dismissed the democratic form of government as a spectacle of "turbulence and contention."

Ironically, in this setting two competing parties grew up quickly. They developed as a result of public sentiment for and against adoption of the Constitution. The Federalist Party — a loose coalition of merchants, shippers, financiers and other business interests — favored the strong central government provided by the Constitution, while their opponents (at first called Anti-Federalists) were intent upon preservation of sovereignty of the states. Underlying the controversy was the desire of the interests represented by the Federalists to create a government with power to guarantee the value of the currency (and thus protect the position of creditors) and the desire of the agrarians and frontiersmen who made up the Anti-Federalists to maintain easy credit conditions and the power of state legislatures to fend off encroachments by a remote federal government.

Unlike the Federalist Party, which was never more than a loose alliance of particular interests, the Anti-Federalists achieved a high degree of organization. The Federalists, in fact, never considered themselves a political party but rather a gentlemanly coalition of interests representing respectable society. What party management there was, they kept clandestine, a reflection of their own fundamental suspicion of parties.

There is no precise date for the beginning of parties, although both Thomas Jefferson and Alexander Hamilton (a Federalist) referred to the existence of a Jeffersonian republican "faction" in Congress as early as 1792.

While party organization became more formalized in the 1790s and early 1800s, particularly among the Jeffersonians, they never acquired a nationally accepted name. The Jeffersonians most commonly referred to themselves as Republicans. Their opponents labeled the Republicans as Anti-Federalists, disorganizers, Jacobins and Democrats — the latter an unflattering term in the early years of the Republic. To many Americans in the late 18th century, a democrat was considered a supporter of mob rule and revolution and often ideologically identified with the bloody French Revolution.

The designation Democrat-Republican was used by the Jeffersonians in several states but was never widely accepted as a party label. However, historians often refer to the Jeffersonians as the Democratic-Republicans, to avoid confusion with the later and unrelated Republican Party, founded in 1854.

Although the early American political leaders acknowledged the development of parties, they did not foresee the emergence of a two-party system. Rather, they often justified the existence of their own party as a reaction to an unacceptable opposition. Jefferson defended his party involvement as a struggle between good and evil: "[When] the principle of difference is as substantial and as strongly pronounced as between the republicans and the Monocrats of our country, I hold it as honorable to take a firm and decided part, and as immoral to pursue a middle line, as between the parties of Honest men, and Rogues, into which every country is divided."

Presidential Politics

The rise of parties forced an alteration in the presidential selection method envisioned by the creators of the Constitution. Delegates to the Constitutional Convention of 1787 had sought a presidential selection method in which the "spirit of party" would play no part. The Electoral College system they finally settled on was a compromise born of a basic distrust in the political abilities of the populace, the complexities of the separation of powers system and the diversity in the states — slavery in the South and rivalries between the big and small states.

Rather than have the people vote directly for president, the choice was to be entrusted to presidential "electors," who the Founding Fathers hoped would be wise leaders in the separate states, able to choose the one person best qualified to be president.

Caucus System

Strong political parties soon developed and quickly removed the presidential nomination from the hands of state electors. The parties created the first informal nominating device for choosing a president: a caucus of each party's members in Congress.

From 1796 until 1824, congressional caucuses — when a party had enough representatives to form one — chose almost all the candidates for president; the electors then chose from the party nominees. Only twice — in 1800 and 1824 — as a result of a failure of any candidate to receive a majority of electoral votes, were presidential elections decided by the House of Representatives, and even in those two cases political parties were instrumental in the election of the president.

Election of 1789

In the first presidential election, held in 1789 shortly after the ratification of the Constitution, the nominating and electing process centered in the Electoral College. Electors chosen in the various states were, under the Constitution, entitled to cast two votes and required to cast each vote for a different person. The individual receiving votes of a majority of the electors was named president and the person receiving the second highest total was named vice president.

There were no formal nominations in 1789, but public opinion centered on George Washington of Virginia for president. He received 69 electoral votes, the maximum possible. John Adams of Massachusetts was the leading second choice, although he did not enjoy the degree of unanimity that surrounded Washington. Adams easily won the vice presidency, receiving 34 electoral votes.

Presidents, 1789-1829

Term	President	Vice President
1789-93	George Washington (Fed.)	John Adams (Fed.)
1793-97	George Washington (Fed.)	John Adams (Fed.)
1797-1801	John Adams (Fed.)	Thomas Jefferson (D-R)
1801-05	Thomas Jefferson (D-R)	Aaron Burr (D-R)
1805-09	Thomas Jefferson (D-R)	George Clinton (D-R)
1809-13	James Madison (D-R)	George Clinton (D-R)
1813-17	James Madison (D-R)	Elbridge Gerry (D-R)
1817-21	James Monroe (D-R)	Daniel D. Tompkins (D-R)
1821-25	James Monroe (D-R)	Daniel D. Tompkins (D-R)
1825-29	John Q. Adams (D-R)	John C. Calhoun (D-R)

Fed. - Federalist;   D-R - Democratic-Republican

Election of 1792

The Federalists and Democratic-Republicans were emerging as competitive parties by the election of 1792. As a result, the Republic experienced the first modification in the presidential nominating process. No attempt was made to displace President Washington, but the Democratic-Republicans mounted a challenge to Vice President Adams. Meeting in Philadelphia in October 1792, a group of Democratic-Republican leaders from the Middle Atlantic states and South Carolina endorsed Gov. George Clinton of New York for the vice presidency, bypassing Sen. Aaron Burr of the same state. While Adams emerged victorious in the Electoral College, Clinton's endorsement by a meeting of party politicians was a milestone in the evolution of the presidential nominating process and a step away from the original Electoral College system.

Election of 1796

The election of 1796 brought further modifications in the nominating method, evidenced by the appearance of the congressional caucus.

There was no opposition to Thomas Jefferson as the Democratic-Republican presidential candidate, and he was considered the party's standard-bearer by a consensus of party leaders. However, a caucus of Democratic-Republican senators was unable to agree on a running mate, producing a tie vote between Burr and Sen. Pierce Butler of South Carolina that ended with a walk-out by Butler's supporters. As a result, there was no formal Democratic-Republican candidate to run with Jefferson.

The Federalists held what historian Roy F. Nichols described as a "quasi caucus" of the party's members of Congress in Philadelphia in May 1796. The gathering chose Vice President Adams and Minister to Great Britain Thomas Pinckney of South Carolina as the Federalist candidates.

Election of 1800

The election of 1800 was the first where both parties used the congressional caucus as the nominating body. Neither party, however, desired much publicity for the process, gathering in secret to deliberate. The proceedings were sketchily described by private correspondence and occasionally referred to in newspapers of the day. Unlike the public national conventions of later years, privacy was a hallmark of the early caucuses.

Although the actual dates of the 1800 caucuses are hazy, it is believed that both were held in May. The Demo-cratic-Republican caucus was held in Marache's boarding-house in Philadelphia, where 43 of the party's members of Congress selected Aaron Burr to run with Thomas Jefferson, the latter again the presidential candidate by consensus and not formally nominated by the caucus.

Federalist members of Congress met in the Senate chamber in Philadelphia and nominated President Adams and Gen. Charles Cotesworth Pinckney of South Carolina. Pinckney, the elder brother of the Federalist vice presidential candidate in 1796, was placed on the ticket at the insistence of Alexander Hamilton, who believed one of the South Carolina Pinckneys could win. Although the deliberations of the Federalist caucus were secret, the existence of the meeting was not. It was described by the local Democratic-Republican paper, the *Philadelphia Aurora*, as a "Jacobinical conclave." Further denunciations by the paper's author, Benjamin F. Bache, earned him a personal rebuke from the U. S. Senate.

Election of 1804

The 1804 election was the first one held after the 12th Amendment to the Constitution went into effect, requiring electors to cast separate votes for president and vice president. The amendment was designed to avoid the unwieldy situation that had developed in 1800, when the leading two Democratic-Republican candidates, Jefferson and Burr, both received the same number of electoral votes. The unexpected tie vote threw the presidential election into the House of Representatives, where it took 36 ballots before Jefferson finally won. With ratification of the amendment, parties in 1804 and thereafter specifically designated their presidential and vice presidential candidates.

The Democratic-Republicans retained the caucus system of nomination in 1804, as they did for the next two decades, and for the first time they publicly reported their deliberations. The party caucus was held in February and attracted 108 of the party's senators and representatives. President Jefferson was renominated by acclamation, but Vice President Burr was not considered for a second term. On the first nominating roll call publicly reported in American political history, New York's Gov. Clinton was chosen to run for vice president. He received 67 votes to easily defeat Sen. John Breckinridge of Kentucky, who collected 20 votes. To "avoid unpleasant discussions" no names were placed in nomination, and the vote was taken by written ballot.

Before adjourning, the caucus appointed a 13-member committee to conduct the campaign. A forerunner of party national committees, the new campaign group included members of both the House and Senate, but with no two individuals from the same state.

The Federalists dropped the congressional caucus as

"[N]othing could be more illjudged than that intolerant spirit which has at all times characterized political parties."
—Alexander Hamilton, 1787

"Among the numerous advantages promised by a well-constructed Union, none deserves to be more accurately developed than its tendency to break and control the violence of faction."
—James Madison, 1787

their nominating method. Federalist leaders in 1804 informally chose Charles Cotesworth Pinckney for president and Rufus King of New York for vice president. But the details of how they formulated this ticket are not known. There is no record in 1804 of any Federalist meeting to nominate candidates.

Election of 1808

The Democratic-Republican caucus was held in January 1808. For the first time a formal call was issued. Sen. Stephen R. Bradley of Vermont, the chairman of the 1804 caucus, issued the call to all 146 Democratic-Republicans in Congress and several Federalists sympathetic to the Democratic-Republican cause. His authority to call the caucus was questioned by several party leaders, but various reports indicate that 89 to 94 members of Congress attended.

As in 1804 the balloting was done without the formal placing of names in nomination. For president, Jefferson's handpicked successor, Secretary of State James Madison of Virginia, was an easy winner with 83 votes. Vice President Clinton and James Monroe of Virginia each received three votes. For vice president the caucus overwhelmingly renominated Clinton. He received 79 votes, while runner-up John Langdon of New Hampshire collected five. Even after the Democratic-Republicans renominated him for vice president, Clinton's supporters continued to hope that the Federalists would nominate their man for president later in the year. But their hopes were dashed when the nomination ultimately went to Pinckney.

As in 1804 the Democratic-Republican caucus appointed a committee to conduct the campaign. Membership was expanded to 15 House and Senate members and it was formally called the "committee of correspondence and arrangement." The committee was authorized to fill any vacancies on the national ticket, should any occur.

Before adjournment a resolution was approved defending the caucus system as "the most practicable mode of consulting and respecting the interest and wishes of all." Later caucuses adopted similar resolutions throughout the history of the system.

The resolution was meant to stem the rumblings of opposition to the caucus system. Seventeen Democratic-Republican members of Congress signed a protest against Madison's selection and questioned the authority of the caucus as a nominating body. Vice President Clinton, himself selected by the caucus, wrote of his disapproval of the caucus system.

The Federalists in 1808 again altered their presidential selection process, holding a secret meeting of party leaders in August of that year to choose the ticket. The meeting, held in New York City, was initially called by the Federalist members of the Massachusetts Legislature. Twenty-five

to 30 party leaders from seven states, all north of the Potomac River except South Carolina, attended the national meeting. There was some discussion of choosing Vice President George Clinton, a dissident Democratic-Republican, for the presidency, but the meeting ultimately selected the Federalist candidates of 1804: Charles Cotesworth Pinckney and Rufus King.

Election of 1812

The Democratic-Republicans held their quadrennial nominating caucus in May 1812. Eighty-three of the party's 138 members of Congress attended, with the New England and New York delegations poorly represented. The New York delegation was sympathetic to the candidacy of the state's lieutenant governor, De Witt Clinton, who was maneuvering for the Federalist nomination, while New England was noticeably upset with the Madison foreign policy that was leading to war with England. President Madison was renominated with a near-unanimous total, receiving 82 votes. John Langdon of New Hampshire was chosen for vice president by a wide margin, collecting 64 votes to 16 for Gov. Elbridge Gerry of Massachusetts. But Langdon declined the nomination, citing his age (70) as the reason. In a second caucus, held in June, Gerry was a runaway winner with 74 votes.

In 1812, as four years earlier, the Federalists held a secret meeting in New York City. It was more than twice the size of the 1808 gathering, with 70 representatives from 11 states attending the three-day meeting in September. Delegates were sent to the conference by Federalist general committees, with all but nine of the delegates coming from the New England and Middle Atlantic states.

Debate centered on whether to run a separate Federalist ticket or to endorse the candidacy of De Witt Clinton, the nephew of George Clinton. The younger Clinton already had been nominated for the presidency by the New York Democratic-Republican caucus, and the Federalists ultimately adopted a resolution approving his candidacy and that of Jared Ingersoll. Ingersoll was a Pennsylvania Federalist who was initially nominated for vice president by a party legislative caucus in that state.

Election of 1816

The Federalist Party was nearly extinct by 1816 and did not hold any type of meeting to nominate candidates for president and vice president. As a result, nomination by the Democratic-Republican caucus was tantamount to election. Only 58 members of Congress attended the first caucus in the House chamber. With the expectation of better attendance, a second caucus was held several days later in mid-March 1816 and drew 119 senators and representatives. By a vote of 65 to 54, Secretary of State James Monroe was nominated for president, defeating Secretary of War William H. Crawford of Georgia. Forty of Crawford's votes came from five states: Georgia, Kentucky, New Jersey, New York and North Carolina. The vice presidential nomination went to New York governor Daniel D. Tompkins, who easily outdistanced Pennsylvania governor Simon Snyder, 85 to 30. The nominations of Monroe and Tompkins revived a Virginia-New York alliance that extended back to the late 18th century. With the lone exception of 1812, every Democratic-Republican ticket from 1800 until 1824 was composed of a candidate from Virginia and a vice presidential candidate from New York.

While the collapse of the Federalists ensured Democratic-Republican rule, it also increased intraparty friction

and spurred further attacks on the caucus system. Twenty-two Democratic-Republican members of Congress were absent from the second party caucus, and at least 15 were known to be opposed to the system. Historian Edward Stanwood wrote that there were mass meetings around the country to protest the caucus system. Opponents claimed that the writers of the Constitution did not envision the caucus, that presidential nominating should not be a function of Congress and that the caucus system encouraged candidates to curry the favor of Congress.

Election of 1820

The 1820 election came during the "Era of Good Feelings," a phrase coined by a Boston publication, the *Columbian Centinel,* to describe a brief period of virtual one-party rule in the United States. With only one candidate, President James Monroe, there was no need for a caucus. One was called, but fewer than 50 of the Democratic-Republican's 191 members of Congress attended. The caucus voted unanimously to make no nominations and passed a resolution explaining that it was inexpedient to do so. Despite the fact that Monroe and Tompkins were not formally renominated, electoral slates were filed on their behalf. They both received nearly unanimous Electoral College victories.

Demise of the Caucus

In 1824 there was still only one party, but within this party there was an abundance of candidates for the presidency: Secretary of State John Quincy Adams of Massachusetts, Sen. Andrew Jackson of Tennessee, Secretary of War John C. Calhoun of South Carolina, House Speaker Henry Clay of Kentucky and Secretary of the Treasury William H. Crawford. It was generally assumed that Crawford was the strongest candidate among members of Congress and would win a caucus if one were held; therefore, Crawford's opponents joined the growing list of caucus opponents.

In early February 1824, 11 Democratic-Republican members of Congress issued a call for a caucus to be held in the middle of the month. Their call was countered by 24 other members of Congress from 15 states who deemed it "inexpedient under existing circumstances" to hold a caucus. They claimed that 181 members of Congress were resolved not to attend if a caucus were held.

When the caucus convened in mid-February, only 66 members of Congress were present, with three-quarters of those attending from just four states — Georgia, New York, North Carolina and Virginia. As expected, Crawford won the presidential nomination, receiving 64 votes. Selected for vice president was Albert Gallatin of Pennsylvania, who received 57 votes. The caucus adopted a resolution defending its actions as "the best means of collecting and concentrating the feelings and wishes of the people of the Union upon this important subject." A committee was appointed to write an address to the people. As written, the text of the address viewed with alarm the "dismemberment" of the Democratic-Republican Party.

The caucus nomination proved to be an albatross for Crawford as his opponents denounced him as the candidate of "King Caucus." Reflecting the increasing democratization of American politics, other presidential candidates relied on nominations by state legislatures to legitimize their presidential ambitions. However, in an attempt to narrow the field, the candidates had to negotiate among themselves. Calhoun alone withdrew to become the vice

presidential candidate of all the anti-caucus entries. Adams offered the vice presidency to Jackson as "an easy and dignified retirement to his old age." Jackson refused. Other maneuvers were equally unsuccessful, so that four presidential candidates remained in the field to collect electoral votes, subsequently throwing the election into the House of Representatives, where Adams won.

The election of 1828 proved to be a transitional one in the development of the presidential nominating process. The caucus was dead, but the national nominating convention was not yet born. Jackson was nominated by the Legislature of his native Tennessee and in October 1825, three years before the election, accepted the nomination in a speech before the Legislature. He accepted Vice President Calhoun as his running mate, after it was proposed in January 1827 by the *United States Telegraph,* a pro-Jackson paper in Washington. A Pennsylvania state convention paired President Adams with Secretary of the Treasury Richard Rush of Pennsylvania, a ticket that Adams' supporters in other states accepted. Both Jackson and Adams were endorsed by other legislatures, conventions and meetings.

Trend Toward Conventions

The birth of the national convention system came in 1831, seven years after the death of the caucus. The caucus system collapsed when a field of candidates appeared who would not acquiesce to the choice of one caucus-approved candidate. But other factors were present to undermine the caucus system. These included changes in voting procedures and an expansion of suffrage. Between 1800 and 1824 the proportion of states in which the electors were chosen by popular vote rather than by the state legislature increased from 4 out of 16 to 18 out of 24. In 1828 the popular vote reached 1.1 million, compared with fewer than 400,000 in 1824. A broader base of support than the congressional caucus became essential for presidential aspirants.

State legislatures, state conventions and mass meetings all emerged in the 1820s to challenge the caucus. The trend to democratization of the presidential nominating process, as evidenced by the expansion of suffrage and increased importance of the popular vote for president, led shortly to creation of the national nomination convention. The convention system, initiated by the Anti-Masons in 1831, subsequently was adopted by the major parties before the end of the decade.

The birth of the national nominating convention was a milestone in the evolution of the presidential nominating process. Political scientist V. O. Key Jr. summarized some of the major forces that brought about the rise of the convention system:

"We must always have party distinctions."
—Martin Van Buren, 1827

The destruction of the caucus represented more than a mere change in the method of nomination. Its replacement by the convention was regarded as the removal from power of self-appointed oligarchies that had usurped the right to nominate. The new system, the convention, gave, or so it was supposed, the mass of party members an opportunity to participate in nominations. These events occurred as the domestic winds blew in from the growing West, as the suffrage was being broadened, and as the last vestiges of the early aristocratic leadership were disappearing. Sharp alterations in the distribution of power were taking place, and they were paralleled by the shifts in methods of nomination.

With the establishment of the national convention came the re-emergence of the two-party system. Unlike the Founding Fathers, who were suspicious of competitive parties, some political leaders in the late 1820s and 1830s favorably viewed the existence of opposing parties. One of the most prominent of these men, Martin Van Buren, a leading organizer of Jackson's 1828 election victory and himself president after Jackson, had written in 1827: "We must always have party distinctions. . . ."

Bibliography

Books

Arnett, A. M. *The Populist Movement in Georgia.* 1922. Reprint. New York: Columbia University Press, 1971.

Blue, Frederick J. *The Free Soilers: Third Party Politics, 1848-1854.* Urbana, Ill.: University of Illinois Press, 1973.

Borden, Morton. *Parties and Politics in the Early Republic, 1789-1815.* Arlington Heights, Ill.: Davidson, Harlan, 1967.

Brock, William. *Parties and Political Conscience: American Dilemmas, 1840-1850.* Millwood, N.Y.: Kraus International Publications, 1979.

Brown, Stuart G. *First Republicans: Political Philosophy and Public Policy in the Party of Jefferson and Madison.* 1954. Reprint. Westport, Conn.: Greenwood Press, 1977.

Burner, David. *The Politics of Provincialism: The Democratic Party in Transition, 1918-1932.* 1968. Reprint. New York: Alfred A. Knopf, 1981.

Cannon, James P. *The History of American Trotskyism from Its Origin in 1928 to the Founding of the Socialist Labor Workers Party.* New York: Pathfinders Press, 1972.

Carroll, E. Malcolm. *Origins of the Whig Party.* Durham, N.C.: Duke University Press, 1925.

Chambers, W. N., and Walter D. Burnham, eds. *The American Party System.* 2nd ed. New York: Oxford University Press, 1975.

Charles, Joseph. *Origins of the American Party System.* New York: Harper and Row.

Cole, Arthur E. *The Whig Party in the South.* 1914. Reprint. Magnolia, Mass.: Peter Smith, 1959.

Congressional Quarterly. *Presidential Elections Since 1789.* 3rd ed. Washington, D.C.: Congressional Quarterly, 1983.

Crandall, Andrew. *Early History of the Republican Party, 1854-1856.* Magnolia, Mass.: Peter Smith, 1960.

Cunningham, Noble E. *Jeffersonian Republicans, 1789-1801.* Chapel Hill, N.C.: University of North Carolina Press, 1967.

Curtis, Francis. *The Republican Party: A History of Its Fifty Years.* New York: G. P. Putnam and Sons, 1904.

Dinkin, Robert J. *Voting in Revolutionary America: A Study of Elections in the Original Thirteen States, 1776-1789.* Westport, Conn.: Greenwood Press, 1982.

Fairlie, Henry. *The Parties: Republicans and Democrats in this Century.* New York: St. Martin's Press, 1978.

Foner, Eric. *Free Soil, Free Labor, Free Men: The Ideology of the Republican Party Before the Civil War.* New York: Oxford University Press, 1971.

Hicks, John D. *The Populist Revolt: A History of the Farmer's Alliance in the People's Party.* Minneapolis, Minn.: University of Minnesota Press, 1961.

Hofstadter, Richard. *The Idea of a Party System: The Rise of Legitimate Opposition in the United States, 1780-1840.* Berkeley, Calif.: University of California Press, 1969.

Holcombe, Arthur N. *Political Parties of Today: A Study in Republican and Democratic Politics.* New York: Harper and Row, 1974.

Jones, Charles O. *The Republican Party in American Politics.* New York: Macmillan, 1965.

Kent, Frank R. *The Democratic Party: A History.* 1928. Reprint. New York: Johnson Reprint, 1968.

Kipnis, Ira. *American Socialist Movement, 1897-1912.* Westport, Conn.: Greenwood Press, 1968.

Kraut, Alan M., ed. *Crusaders and Compromisers: Essays on the Relationship of Antislavery Struggle to the Antebellum Party System.* Westport, Conn.: Greenwood Press, 1983.

Ladd, Everett C., Jr., and Charles D. Hadley. *Transformations of the American Party System: Political Coalitions from the New Deal to the 1970s.* 2nd ed. New York: W. W. Norton, 1978.

Ladd, Everett C., Jr. *Where Have All the Voters Gone? The Fracturing of American Political Parties.* New York: W. W. Norton, 1978.

Lee, John H. *The Origin and Progress of the American Party in Politics: Embracing a Complete History of the Philadelphia Riots in May and July, 1844.* Salem, N.H.: Ayer, 1970.

Livermore, Shaw, Jr. *Twilight of Federalism: The Disintegration of the Federalist Party, 1815-1830.* Staten Island, N.Y.: Gordian Press, 1972.

McKay, Kenneth. *The Progressive Movement of 1924.* New York: Octagon Books, 1966.

Main, Jackson T. *Political Parties Before the Constitution.* New York: W. W. Norton, 1974.

Nash, Howard P., Jr. *Third Parties in American Politics.* Washington, D.C.: Public Affairs Press, 1958.

Nichols, Roy F. *The Invention of the American Political Parties: A Study of Political Improvisation.* New York: Free Press, 1972.

Pinchot, Amos R. E. *History of the Progressive Party, 1912-1916.* 1958. Reprint. New York: New York University Press, 1978.

Rosenstone, Steven J., Roy L. Behr, and Edward H. Lazarus. *Third Parties in America: Citizen Response to Major Party Failure.* Princeton, N.J.: Princeton University Press, 1984.

Ross, Earle D. *The Liberal Republican Movement.* New York: AMS Press, 1971.

Schlesinger, Arthur M., Jr., ed. *History of U.S. Political*

Parties. 4 vols. 1973. Reprint. New York: Chelsea House, 1981.

Schnapper, Morris B. *Grand Old Party: The First One Hundred Years of the Republican Party.* Washington, D.C.: Public Affairs Press, 1955.

Shannon, David A. *The Decline of American Communism: A History of the Communist Party in the United States Since 1945.* Chatham, N.J.: Chatham Booksellers, 1971.

Smallwood, Frank. *The Other Candidates: Third Parties in Presidential Elections.* Hanover, N.H.: University Press of New England, 1983.

Smith, Theodore C. *Liberty and Free Soil Parties in the Northwest.* New York: Arno Press, 1969.

Stedman, Murray S., Jr., and Susan W. Stedman. *Discontent at the Polls: A Study of Farmer and Labor Parties, 1827-1948.* New York: Russell and Russell Publishers, 1967.

Sundquist, James L. *Dynamics of the Party System: Alignment and Realignment of Political Parties in the United States.* rev. ed. Washington, D.C.: Brookings Institution, 1983.

Timberlake, James H. *Prohibition and the Progressive Movement, 1912-1925.* New York: Random House, 1969.

Tocqueville, Alexis de. *Democracy in America.* New York: Vintage Books, 1971.

Wattenberg, Martin P. *The Decline of the American Political Parties 1952 to 1984.* Boston: Harvard University Press, 1984.

Functions of Party Conventions

Although the presidential nominating convention has been a target of criticism throughout its existence, it has survived to become a traditional fixture of American politics. The longevity and general acceptance of the convention in large part is due to its multiplicity of functions — functions that the convention uniquely combines.

The convention is a nominating body, used by the Democrats, Republicans and most of the principal third parties during the past 150 years. The convention produces a platform, which contains the positions of the party on issues of the campaign. As the supreme governing body of the political party, those attending the convention make major decisions on party affairs. Between conventions such decisions are made by the national committee with the guidance of the party chairman. The convention provides a forum for compromise among the diverse elements within a party, allowing the discussion and often the satisfactory solution of differing points of view. As the ultimate campaign rally, the convention also gathers together thousands of party leaders and rank-and-file members from across the country in an atmosphere that varies widely, sometimes encouraging sober discussion but often resembling a carnival. But even though the process has drawn heavy criticism, the convention has endured because it successfully combines a multiplicity of functions.

The convention is an outgrowth of the American political experience. Nowhere is it mentioned in the Constitution nor has the authority of the convention ever been a subject of congressional legislation. Rather, the convention has evolved along with the presidential selection process. The convention has been the accepted nominating method of the major political parties since the election of 1832, but internal changes within the convention system have been massive since the early, formative years.

Convention Sites

Before the Civil War, conventions frequently were held in small buildings, even churches, and attracted only several hundred delegates and a minimum of spectators. Transportation and communications were slow, so most conventions were held in the late spring in a city with a central geographical location. Baltimore, Md., was the most popular convention city in this period, playing host to the first six Democratic conventions (1832 through 1852), two Whig conventions, one National Republican convention,

and the 1831 Anti-Masonic gathering — America's first national nominating convention. With the nation's westward expansion, the heartland city of Chicago, Ill., emerged as the most frequent convention center. Since its first one in 1860, Chicago has been the site of 24 major party conventions (14 Republican, 10 Democratic).

Since 1976 presidential elections have been publicly funded and parties have depended on host cities to supplement the money ($6.1 million in 1984) the parties could legally spend on their conventions. The Federal Election Commission has ruled that such payments are not prohibited contributions. In 1984 San Francisco provided almost $9 million, including $4.5 million in municipal funds, for the Democratic convention and Dallas privately raised more than $3 million for the GOP event. Adequate hotel and convention hall facilities are another major factor in site selection, as modern-day conventions attract thousands of delegates, party officials, spectators and media representatives. And convention security has become increasingly important. Miami, Fla., reportedly was chosen by the Republicans in 1968 and by both major parties in 1972 largely because the city's island location made it easier to contain protest demonstrations. For the party that controls the White House, often the overriding factor in site selection is the president's personal preference.

The convention sites are selected by the national committees of the two parties about one year before the convention is to take place. This first major step in the quadrennial convention process is followed several months later by announcement of the convention call, the establishment of the major convention committees — credentials, rules, and platform (resolutions) — the appointment of convention officers and finally the holding of the convention itself. While these basic steps have undergone little change during the past 150 years, there have been major alterations within the nominating convention system.

The call to the convention sets the date and site of the meeting and is issued early in each election year, if not before. The call to the first Democratic convention, held in 1832, was issued by the New Hampshire Legislature. Early Whig conventions were called by party members in Congress. With the establishment of national committees later in the 19th century, the function of issuing the convention call fell to these new party organizations. Each national committee currently has the responsibility for allocating delegates to each state.

Democratic Conventions, 1832-1984

Year	City	Dates	Presidential Nominee	Vice Presidential Nominee	No. of Pres. Ballots
1832	Baltimore	May 21-23	Andrew Jackson	Martin Van Buren	1
1835	Baltimore	May 20-23	Martin Van Buren	Richard M. Johnson	1
1840	Baltimore	May 5-6	Martin Van Buren	—[1]	1
1844	Baltimore	May 27-29	James K. Polk	George M. Dallas	9
1848	Baltimore	May 22-25	Lewis Cass	William O. Butler	4
1852	Baltimore	June 1-5	Franklin Pierce	William R. King	49
1856	Cincinnati	June 2-6	James Buchanan	John C. Breckinridge	17
1860	Charleston	April 23-May 3	Deadlocked		57
	Baltimore	June 18-23	Stephen A. Douglas	Benjamin Fitzpatrick Herschel V. Johnson[2]	2
1864	Chicago	August 29-31	George B. McClellan	George H. Pendleton	1
1868	New York	July 4-9	Horatio Seymour	Francis P. Blair	22
1872	Baltimore	July 9-10	Horace Greeley	Benjamin G. Brown	1
1876	St. Louis	June 27-29	Samuel J. Tilden	Thomas A. Hendricks	2
1880	Cincinnati	June 22-24	Winfield S. Hancock	William H. English	2
1884	Chicago	July 8-11	Grover Cleveland	Thomas A. Hendricks	2
1888	St. Louis	June 5-7	Grover Cleveland	Allen G. Thurman	1
1892	Chicago	June 21-23	Grover Cleveland	Adlai E. Stevenson	1
1896	Chicago	July 7-11	William J. Bryan	Arthur Sewall	5
1900	Kansas City	July 4-6	William J. Bryan	Adlai E. Stevenson	1
1904	St. Louis	July 6-9	Alton S. Parker	Henry G. Davis	1
1908	Denver	July 7-10	William J. Bryan	John W. Kern	1
1912	Baltimore	June 25-July 2	Woodrow Wilson	Thomas R. Marshall	46
1916	St. Louis	June 14-16	Woodrow Wilson	Thomas R. Marshall	1
1920	San Francisco	June 28-July 6	James M. Cox	Franklin D. Roosevelt	43
1924	New York	June 24-July 9	John W. Davis	Charles W. Bryan	103
1928	Houston	June 26-29	Alfred E. Smith	Joseph T. Robinson	1
1932	Chicago	June 27-July 2	Franklin D. Roosevelt	John N. Garner	4
1936	Philadelphia	June 23-27	Franklin D. Roosevelt	John N. Garner	Acclamation
1940	Chicago	July 15-18	Franklin D. Roosevelt	Henry A. Wallace	1
1944	Chicago	July 19-21	Franklin D. Roosevelt	Harry S Truman	1
1948	Philadelphia	July 12-14	Harry S Truman	Alben W. Barkley	1
1952	Chicago	July 21-26	Adlai E. Stevenson	John J. Sparkman	3
1956	Chicago	Aug. 13-17	Adlai E. Stevenson	Estes Kefauver	1
1960	Los Angeles	July 11-15	John F. Kennedy	Lyndon B. Johnson	1
1964	Atlantic City	Aug. 24-27	Lyndon B. Johnson	Hubert H. Humphrey	Acclamation
1968	Chicago	Aug. 26-29	Hubert H. Humphrey	Edmund S. Muskie	1
1972	Miami Beach	July 10-13	George McGovern	Thomas F. Eagleton R. Sargent Shriver[3]	1
1976	New York	July 12-15	Jimmy Carter	Walter F. Mondale	1
1980	New York	Aug. 11-14	Jimmy Carter	Walter F. Mondale	1
1984	San Francisco	July 16-19	Walter F. Mondale	Geraldine A. Ferraro	1

1. The 1840 Democratic convention did not nominate a candidate for vice president.

2. The 1860 Democratic convention nominated Benjamin Fitzpatrick, who declined the nomination shortly after the convention adjourned. On June 25 the Democratic National Committee selected Herschel V. Johnson as the party's candidate for vice president.

3. The 1972 Democratic convention nominated Thomas F. Eagleton, who withdrew from the ticket on July 31. On Aug. 8 the Democratic National Committee selected R. Sargent Shriver as the party's candidate for vice president.

Delegate Selection

Both parties have modified the method of allocating delegates to the individual states and territories. From the beginning of the convention system in the 19th century, both the Democrats and Republicans distributed votes to the states based on their Electoral College strength. The first major deviation from this procedure was made by the Republicans after their divisive 1912 convention, in which President William Howard Taft won renomination over former president Theodore Roosevelt. Taft's nomination was due largely to almost solid support from the South — a region vastly over-represented in relation to its number of Republican voters. Before their 1916 convention the Re-

Republican Conventions, 1856-1984

Year	City	Dates	Presidential Nominee	Vice Presidential Nominee	No. of Pres. Ballots
1856	Philadelphia	June 17-19	John C. Fremont	William L. Dayton	2
1860	Chicago	May 16-18	Abraham Lincoln	Hannibal Hamlin	3
1864	Baltimore	June 7-8	Abraham Lincoln	Andrew Johnson	1
1868	Chicago	May 20-21	Ulysses S. Grant	Schuyler Colfax	1
1872	Philadelphia	June 5-6	Ulysses S. Grant	Henry Wilson	1
1876	Cincinnati	June 14-16	Rutherford B. Hayes	William A. Wheeler	7
1880	Chicago	June 2-8	James A. Garfield	Chester A. Arthur	36
1884	Chicago	June 3-6	James G. Blaine	John A. Logan	4
1888	Chicago	June 19-25	Benjamin Harrison	Levi P. Morton	8
1892	Minneapolis	June 7-10	Benjamin Harrison	Whitelaw Reid	1
1896	St. Louis	June 16-18	William McKinley	Garret A. Hobart	1
1900	Philadelphia	June 19-21	William McKinley	Theodore Roosevelt	1
1904	Chicago	June 21-23	Theodore Roosevelt	Charles W. Fairbanks	1
1908	Chicago	June 16-19	William H. Taft	James S. Sherman	1
1912	Chicago	June 18-22	William H. Taft	James S. Sherman Nicholas Murray Butler[1]	1
1916	Chicago	June 7-10	Charles E. Hughes	Charles W. Fairbanks	3
1920	Chicago	June 8-12	Warren G. Harding	Calvin Coolidge	10
1924	Cleveland	June 10-12	Calvin Coolidge	Charles G. Dawes	1
1928	Kansas City	June 12-15	Herbert Hoover	Charles Curtis	1
1932	Chicago	June 14-16	Herbert Hoover	Charles Curtis	1
1936	Cleveland	June 9-12	Alfred M. Landon	Frank Knox	1
1940	Philadelphia	June 24-28	Wendell L. Willkie	Charles L. McNary	6
1944	Chicago	June 26-28	Thomas E. Dewey	John W. Bricker	1
1948	Philadelphia	June 21-25	Thomas E. Dewey	Earl Warren	3
1952	Chicago	July 7-11	Dwight D. Eisenhower	Richard M. Nixon	1
1956	San Francisco	Aug. 20-23	Dwight D. Eisenhower	Richard M. Nixon	1
1960	Chicago	July 25-28	Richard Nixon	Henry Cabot Lodge	1
1964	San Francisco	July 13-16	Barry Goldwater	William E. Miller	1
1968	Miami Beach	Aug. 5-8	Richard Nixon	Spiro T. Agnew	1
1972	Miami Beach	Aug. 21-23	Richard Nixon	Spiro T. Agnew	1
1976	Kansas City	Aug. 16-19	Gerald R. Ford	Robert Dole	1
1980	Detroit	July 14-17	Ronald Reagan	George Bush	1
1984	Dallas	Aug. 20-23	Ronald Reagan	George Bush	1

1. The 1912 Republican convention nominated James S. Sherman, who died on Oct. 30. The Republican National Committee subsequently selected Nicholas Murray Butler to receive the Republican electoral votes for vice president.

publicans reduced the allocation of votes to the Southern states. At their 1924 convention the Republicans applied the first bonus system, by which states were awarded extra votes for supporting the Republican presidential candidate in the previous election. The concept of bonus votes, applied as a reward to the states for supporting the party ticket, has been used and expanded by both parties since that time.

The Democrats first used a bonus system in 1944, completing a compromise arrangement with Southern states for abolishing the party's controversial two-thirds nominating rule. Since then both parties have used various delegate-allocation formulas. At their 1972 convention the Republicans revised the formula and added more than 900 new delegate slots. The Ripon Society, an organization of liberal Republicans, sued to have the new rules overturned. They argued that, because of the extra delegates awarded to states that voted Republican in the previous presidential election, small Southern and Western states were favored

at the expense of the more populous but less Republican Eastern states. The challenge failed when the Supreme Court in February 1976 refused to hear the case and thus let stand a U.S. Court of Appeals decision upholding the rules.

Only 116 delegates from 13 states attended the initial national nominating convention held by the Anti-Masons in 1831, but with the addition of more states and the adoption of increasingly complex voting-allocation formulas by the major parties, the size of conventions spiraled. The 1976 Republican convention had 2,259 delegates, while the Democrats in the same year had 3,075 delegates (casting 3,008 votes). The expanded size in part reflected the democratization of the conventions, with less command by a few party leaders and the dramatic growth of youth, women and minority delegations. Increased representation by such groups was one of the major reasons given by the Republicans for the 60 percent increase in delegate strength authorized by the 1972 convention (and effective

Democrats' Two-Thirds Rule

At their first convention in 1832, the Democrats adopted a rule requiring a two-thirds majority for nomination. Two presidential candidates — Martin Van Buren in 1844 and Champ Clark in 1912 — received majorities but failed to attain the two-thirds requirement.

On the first ballot in 1844 Van Buren received 146 of the 266 convention votes, 54.9 percent of the total. His total fell under a simple majority on succeeding roll calls and on the ninth ballot the nomination went to a dark-horse candidate, former governor James K. Polk of Tennessee.

From the 10th through the 16th ballots in 1912 Clark recorded a simple majority. He reached his peak on the 10th ballot, receiving 556 of the 1,094 convention votes, 50.8 percent of the total. The nomination, however, ultimately went to New Jersey governor Woodrow Wilson, who was selected on the 46th ballot.

At their 1936 convention, the Democrats voted to end the requirement for a two-thirds majority for nomination.

for the 1976 gathering). The Democrats adopted new rules in June 1978 expanding the number of delegates by 10 percent to provide extra representation for state and local officials. The new rules also required that women account for at least 50 percent of the delegates to the 1980 convention.

With the increased size of conventions has come a formalization in the method of delegate selection. In the formative years of the convention system delegate selection was often haphazard and informal. At the Democratic convention in 1835, for example, the state of Maryland had 188 delegates to cast the state's 10 votes. In contrast, the 15 votes for the state of Tennessee were cast by a traveling businessman who happened to be in the convention city at the time of the meeting. While the number of delegates and the number of votes allocated tended to be equal or nearly so later in the 19th century, domination of national conventions was exercised frequently by a few party bosses.

Two basic methods of delegate selection were employed in the 19th century and continued to be used into the 20th: the caucus method, by which delegates were chosen by meetings at the local or state level, and the appointment method, by which delegates were appointed by the governor or a powerful state leader.

Presidential Primaries

A revolutionary new mechanism for delegate selection emerged during the early 1900s: the presidential primary election in which the voters directly elected convention delegates.

Initiated in Florida in 1904, the presidential primary by 1912 was used by 13 states. In his first annual message to Congress the following year, President Woodrow Wilson advocated the establishment of a national primary to select presidential candidates: "I feel confident that I do not misinterpret the wishes or the expectations of the country when I urge the prompt enactment of legislation which will provide for primary elections throughout the country at which the voters of several parties may choose their nomi-

nees for the presidency without the intervention of nominating conventions." Wilson went on to suggest the retention of conventions for the purpose of declaring the results of the primaries and formulating the parties' platforms.

Before any action was taken on Wilson's proposal, the progressive spirit that spurred the growth of presidential primaries died out. Not until after World War II, when widespread pressures for change touched both parties but especially the Democratic, was there a rapid growth in presidential primaries. By 1984 the number of presidential primaries had fallen from its 1980 peak of 37 as six states reverted to the caucus method of delegate selection. *(Selection by caucus method, box, p. 382)*

In most states participation in the presidential primary is restricted to voters belonging to the party holding the primary. In some states, however, participation by voters outside the party is allowed. New rules adopted by the Democrats in 1978 prohibited this practice in Democratic primaries.

1984 Democratic Rules

In June 1982 the Democratic National Committee (DNC) adopted several changes in the presidential nominating process recommended by the party's Commission on Presidential Nominations, chaired by Gov. James B. Hunt Jr. of North Carolina. The Hunt Commission, as it came to be known, suggested revisions to increase the power of party regulars and give the convention more freedom to act on its own. It was the fourth time in 12 years that the Democrats, struggling to repair their nominating process without repudiating earlier reforms, had rewritten their party rules. *(Changes in Democrats' nominating rules, box, p. 21)*

One major change in the Democrats' rules was the creation of a new group of "superdelegates," party and elected officials who would go to the 1984 convention uncommitted and would cast about 14 percent of the ballots. The DNC also adopted a Hunt Commission proposal to weaken the rule binding delegates to vote for their original presidential preference on the first convention ballot. The new rule allowed a presidential candidate to replace any disloyal delegate with a more faithful one.

One of the most significant revisions was the Democrats' decision to relax proportional representation at the convention and end the ban on the "loophole" primary — winner take all by district. Proportional representation is the distribution of delegates among candidates to reflect their share of the primary or caucus vote. Mandated by party rules in 1980, it was blamed by some Democrats for the protracted primary fight between President Jimmy Carter and Sen. Edward M. Kennedy of Massachusetts. Because candidates needed only about 20 percent of the vote in most places to qualify for a share of the delegates, Kennedy was able to remain in contention. But while the system kept Kennedy going, it did nothing to help his chances of winning the nomination.

Although the Democrats' 1984 rules permitted states to retain proportional representation, they also allowed states to take advantage of two options that could help a front-running candidate build the momentum to wrap up the nomination early in the year.

One was a winner-take-more system. States could elect to keep proportional representation but adopt a winner bonus plan that would award the top vote-getter in each district one extra delegate.

The other option was a return to the loophole primary,

Notable Credentials Fights

1848, Democratic. Two rival New York state factions, known as the Barnburners and the Hunkers, sent separate delegations. By a vote of 126 to 125, the convention decided to seat both delegations and split New York's vote between them. This compromise suited neither faction: the Barnburners bolted the convention; the Hunkers remained but refused to vote.

1860, Democratic. Dissatisfaction with the slavery plank in the party platform spurred a walkout by several dozen Southern delegates from the Charleston convention. When the tumultuous convention reconvened in Baltimore six weeks later, a credentials controversy developed on the status of the bolting delegates. The majority report of the credentials committee recommended that the delegates in question, except those from Alabama and Louisiana, be reseated. The minority report recommended that a larger majority of the withdrawing Charleston delegates be allowed to return. The minority report was defeated, 100-1/2 to 150, prompting a walkout by the majority of delegates from nine states.

1880, Republican. Factions for and against the candidacy of former president Ulysses S. Grant clashed on the credentials of the Illinois delegation. By a margin of 353 to 387, the convention rejected a minority report that proposed seating pro-Grant delegates elected at the state convention over other delegates elected at a congressional district caucus. Three other votes were taken on disputed credentials from different Illinois districts, but all were decided in favor of the anti-Grant forces by a similar margin. The votes indicated the weakness of the Grant candidacy. The nomination went to a dark-horse candidate on the 36th ballot, Rep. James A. Garfield of Ohio.

1912, Republican. The furious struggle between President William Howard Taft and Theodore Roosevelt for the presidential nomination centered on credentials. The Roosevelt forces brought 72 delegate challenges to the floor of the convention, but the test of strength between the two candidates came on a procedural motion. By a vote of 567 to 507, the convention tabled a motion presented by the Roosevelt forces barring any of the delegates under challenge from voting on any of the credentials contests. This procedural vote clearly indicated Taft's control of the convention. All the credentials cases were settled in favor of the Taft delegates and the presidential nomination ultimately went to the incumbent president.

1932, Democratic. Two delegations favorable to the front-runner for the presidential nomination, Franklin D. Roosevelt, came under challenge. However, in a show of strength, the Roosevelt forces won both contests: seating a Louisiana delegation headed by Sen. Huey P. Long by a vote of 638-3/4 to 514-1/4 and a Roosevelt delegation from Minnesota by an even wider margin, 658-1/4 to 492-3/4. Roosevelt won the nomination on the fourth ballot.

1952, Democratic. The refusal of three Southern states — Louisiana, South Carolina and Virginia — to agree to a party loyalty pledge, brought their credentials into question. The Virginia delegation argued that the problem prompting the loyalty pledge was covered by state law. By a vote of 650-1/2 to 518, the convention approved the seating of the Virginia delegation. After Louisiana and South Carolina took positions similar to that of Virginia, they were seated by a voice vote.

1952, Republican. Sixty-eight delegates from three Southern states (Georgia, Louisiana and Texas) were the focal point of the fight for the presidential nomination between Gen. Dwight D. Eisenhower and Sen. Robert A. Taft of Ohio. The national committee, controlled by forces favorable to Taft, had voted to seat delegations friendly to the Ohio senator from these three states. But by a vote of 607 to 531 the convention seated the Georgia delegation favorable to Eisenhower and without roll calls seated the Eisenhower delegates from Louisiana and Texas. The general went on to win the presidential nomination on the first ballot.

1968, Democratic. A struggle between the anti-Vietnam war forces, led by Sen. Eugene J. McCarthy of Minnesota, and the party regulars, headed by Vice President Hubert H. Humphrey, dominated the 17 cases considered by the credentials committee. Three of the cases, involving the Texas, Georgia and Alabama delegations, required roll calls on the convention floor. All were won by the Humphrey forces. By a vote of 1,368-1/4 to 956-3/4, the regular Texas delegation headed by Gov. John B. Connally was seated. A minority report to seat the entire Georgia delegation led by black leader Julian Bond was defeated, 1,043.55 to 1,415.45. And a minority report to seat a McCarthy-backed, largely black delegation from Alabama was also rejected, 880-3/4 to 1,607. Humphrey, having shown his strength during the credentials contests, went on to win an easy first ballot nomination.

1972, Democratic. The first test of strength at the convention between South Dakota senator George McGovern's delegates and party regulars came over credentials. Key challenges brought to the convention floor concerned the South Carolina, California and Illinois delegations. The South Carolina challenge was brought by the National Women's Political Caucus in response to alleged underrepresentation of women in the delegation. Although the caucus' position was supposedly supported by the McGovern camp, votes were withheld to avoid jeopardizing McGovern's chances of winning the important California contest. The caucus' challenge lost 1,429.05 to 1,555.75. The California challenge was of crucial importance to McGovern, since it involved 151 delegates initially won by the South Dakota senator in the state's winner-take-all primary, but stripped from him by the credentials committee. By a vote of 1,618.28 to 1,238.22, McGovern regained the contested delegates, thereby nailing down his nomination. With victory in hand, the dominant McGovern camp sought a compromise on the Illinois case, which pitted a delegation headed by Chicago's powerful mayor Richard Daley against an insurgent delegation composed of party reformers. Compromise was unattainable and with the bulk of McGovern delegates voting for the reformers, a minority report to seat the Daley delegates was rejected.

GOP Primary Rules

Any discussion of the 1984 nominating process necessarily focused on the Democrats. One reason was obvious. There was no contest on the Republican side. No one was challenging President Reagan for the GOP nomination. Another reason was almost as apparent: the Democrats were doing all the rules writing.

The Republican Party, wrote political scientist Nelson W. Polsby, "in many respects remains unreformed." Virtually anything was permitted as long as it was not baldly discriminatory. And that was the way GOP leaders wanted it. "We're happy with the rules we have," said Ernie Angelo, head of the GOP's rules review panel. "The process works. The longer it stays the same, the fairer it is."

While state Democratic parties had to adhere to strict standards in devising delegate selection plans, their Republican counterparts were given wide latitude by the Republican National Committee.

The result was a nominating procedure with a simplicity and continuity that the Democrats lacked. A more homogeneous party than the Democrats, the Republicans did not feel the pressure for rules reform that had engulfed the Democrats. No major rules changes were made by the Republicans between 1974 and 1984.

Republicans, however, had not been able to operate totally in their own world. Campaign finance laws and the rising influence of mass media affected Republicans as well as Democrats. And in states where legislatures accommodated the Democrats and created a presidential primary, the Republicans were dragged along.

By an ironic turn of events, the GOP had been less hasty than the Democrats in abandoning primaries. "One of the major ironies of 1984," contended Angelo, was that "Democrats fostered primaries on the grounds that they would give more people a chance to participate. But now that they don't like the results, they're running away from them." There were a number of states, including Texas and Wisconsin, where the GOP in 1984 elected delegates through primaries while the Democrats reverted to the caucus process.

which party rules outlawed in 1980 (with exemptions allowing Illinois and West Virginia to maintain their loophole voting system)s. In the loophole states, voters ballot directly for delegates, with each delegate candidate identified by presidential preference. Sometimes several presidential contenders win at least a fraction of the delegates in a given district, but the most common result is a sweep by the presidential front-runner, even if he has less than an absolute majority. Loophole primaries aid the building of a consensus behind the front-runner, while still giving other candidates a chance to inject themselves back into the race by winning a major loophole state decisively.

The DNC retained the delegate-selection season adopted in 1978, a three-month period stretching from the second Tuesday in March to the second Tuesday in June. But, in an effort to reduce the growing influence of early states in the nominating process, the Democrats required Iowa and New Hampshire to move their highly publicized elections to late winter. Party rules maintained the privileged status of Iowa and New Hampshire before other states but mandated that their initial nominating rounds be held only eight days apart in 1984. Five weeks intervened between the Iowa caucuses and New Hampshire primary in 1980.

The DNC also retained rules requiring primary states to set candidate filing deadlines 30 to 90 days before the election and limiting participation in the delegate selection process to Democrats only. This last rule eliminated crossover primaries where voters could participate in the Democratic primary without designating their party affiliation. Blacks and Hispanics won continued endorsement of affirmative action in the new party rules. Women gained renewed support for the equal division rule, which required state delegations at the national convention to be divided equally between men and women.

During the 1970s and early 1980s the Republican Party followed an entirely different approach and made few changes in its nominating rules. While the Democratic rules were revised somewhat for each presidential cycle, the GOP rules remained stable. *(GOP rules, box, this page)*

Credentials Disputes

Before the opening of a convention the national committee compiles a temporary roll of delegates. The roll is referred to the convention's credentials committee, which holds hearings on the challenges and makes recommendations to the convention, the final arbiter of all disputes.

Some of the most bitter convention battles have concerned the seating of contested delegations. In the 20th century most of the heated credentials fights have concerned delegations from the South. In the Republican Party the challenges focused on the power of the Republican state organizations to dictate the selection of delegates. The issue was hottest in 1912 and 1952, when the party throughout most of the South was a skeletal structure whose power was restricted largely to selection of convention delegates. Within the Democratic Party the question of Southern credentials emerged after World War II on the volatile issues of civil rights and party loyalty. Important credentials challenges on these issues occurred at the 1948, 1952, 1964 and 1968 Democratic conventions.

There were numerous credentials challenges at the 1972 Democratic convention, but, unlike those at its immediate predecessors, the challenges involved delegations from across the nation and focused on violations of the party's newly adopted guidelines.

After their 1952 credentials battle, the Republicans established a contest committee within the national committee to review credentials challenges before the convention. After their divisive 1968 convention the Democrats also created a formal credentials procedure within the national committee to review all challenges before the opening of the convention.

Equally important to the settlement of credentials challenges are the rules under which the convention operates. The Republican Party adopts a completely new set of rules at every convention. Although large portions of the existing rules are enacted each time, general revision is always possible.

After its 1968 convention the Democratic Party set out to reform itself and the convention system. The Commission on Rules and the Commission on Party Structure and Delegate Selection, both created by the 1968 convention, proposed many changes that were accepted by the national

Major Platform Fights

1860, Democratic. A minority report on the slavery plank, stating that the decision on allowing slavery in the territories should be left to the Supreme Court, was approved, 165 to 138. The majority report (favored by the South) declared that no government — local, state or federal — could outlaw slavery in the territories. The acceptance of the minority report precipitated a walkout by several dozen Southern delegates and the eventual sectional split in the party.

1896, Democratic. The monetary plank of the platform committee, favoring free and unlimited coinage of silver at a ratio of 16 to 1 with gold, was accepted by the convention, which defeated a proposed gold plank, 303 to 626. During debate William Jennings Bryan made his famous "Cross of Gold" speech supporting the platform committee plank, bringing him to the attention of the convention and resulting in his nomination for president.

1908, Republican. A minority report, proposing a substitute platform, was presented by Sen. Robert M. LaFollette (Wis.). Minority proposals included increased antitrust activities, enactment of a law requiring publication of campaign expenditures, and popular election of senators. All the proposed planks were defeated by wide margins; the closest vote, on direct election of senators, was 114 for, 866 against.

1924, Democratic. A minority plank was presented that condemned the activities of the Ku Klux Klan, then enjoying a resurgence in the South and some states in the Midwest. The plank was defeated 542-7/20 to 543-3/20, the closest vote in Democratic convention history.

1932, Republican. A minority plank favoring repeal of the 18th Amendment (Prohibition) in favor of a state-option arrangement was defeated, 460-2/9 to 690-19/36.

1948, Democratic. An amendment to the platform, strengthening the civil rights plank by guaranteeing full and equal political participation, equal employment opportunity, personal security and equal treatment in the military service, was accepted, 651-1/2 to 582-1/2.

1964, Republican. An amendment offered by Sen. Hugh Scott (Pa.) to strengthen the civil rights plank by including voting guarantees in state as well as in federal elections and by eliminating job bias was defeated, 409 to 897.

1968, Democratic. A minority report on Vietnam called for cessation of the bombing of North Vietnam, halting of offensive and search-and-destroy missions by American combat units, a negotiated withdrawal of American troops and establishment of a coalition government in South Vietnam. It was defeated, 1,041-1/4 to 1,567-3/4.

1972, Democratic. By a vote of 999.34 to 1,852.86, the convention rejected a minority report proposing a government guaranteed annual income of $6,500 for a family of four. By a vote of 1,101.37 to 1,572.80, a women's rights plank focusing on the issue of abortion was defeated.

1980, Democratic. The platform battle, one of the longest in party history, pitted President Jimmy Carter against his persistent rival, Sen. Edward M. Kennedy (Mass.). Stretching over 17 hours, the debate focused on Kennedy's economics plank, which finally was defeated by a voice vote. Yet Carter was forced to concede on so many specific points, including Kennedy's $12 billion anti-recession jobs programs, that the final document bore little resemblance to the draft initially drawn up by Carter's operatives.

---

committee. As a result, a formal set of rules was adopted for the first time at the party's 1972 convention.

Controversial Rules

Although it did not have a formal set of rules before 1972, the Democratic Party throughout the bulk of its history operated with two critical and controversial rules never used by the Republicans: the unit rule and the two-thirds nominating rule. The unit rule enabled the majority of a delegation, if authorized by its state party, to cast the entire vote of the delegation for one candidate or position. In use since the earliest Democratic conventions, the unit rule was abolished by the 1968 convention.

From its first convention in 1832 until its elimination over a century later at the 1936 convention, the Democrats employed the two-thirds nominating rule, which required any candidate for president or vice president to win not just a simple majority but a two-thirds majority. Viewed as a boon to the South since it allowed that region a virtual veto power over any possible nominee, the rule was abolished with the stipulation that the South would receive an increased vote allocation at later conventions.

In its century of use the two-thirds rule frequently produced protracted, multi-ballot conventions, often giving the Democrats a degree of turbulence the Republicans, requiring only a simple majority, did not have. Between 1832 and 1932, seven Democratic conventions took more than 10 ballots to select a presidential candidate. In contrast, in their entire convention history (1856 through 1984), the Republicans have had just one convention that required more than 10 ballots to select a presidential candidate. *(Democrats' two-thirds rule, box, p. 17)*

One controversy that surfaced during the 1980 Democratic Party convention concerned a rule that bound delegates to vote on the first ballot for the candidates under whose banner they had been elected. Supporters of Senator Kennedy had devoted their initial energies to prying the nomination from incumbent president Jimmy Carter by trying unsuccessfully to open the convention by defeating that rule. The final tally on the rule showed 1,936.42 delegates favoring the binding rule and 1,390.58 opposing it. Passage of the binding rule ensured Carter's renomination, and shortly after the vote Kennedy ended his nine-month challenge to the president by announcing that his name would not be placed in nomination.

Changes in Democrats' Nominating Rules

Between 1968 and 1984 Democrats tinkered with their nominating rules every four years, producing a system that, if not better than before, was always differ-ent. The following chart shows the ebb and flow of the Democratic Party's rules changes, with a "✔" indicating the years these major rules were in effect.

	1972	1976	1980	1984
Timing: Restrict delegate-selection events to a 3-month period (the "window").			✔	✔
Conditions of Participation: Restrict participation in delegate-selection events to Democrats.		✔	✔	✔
Proportional Representation: Ban all types of winner-take-all contests.			✔	
Delegate Loyalty: Give candidates the right to approve delegates identifying with their candidacy.		✔	✔	✔
Bind delegates to vote for their original presidential preference at convention on first ballot.			✔	
Party and Elected Officials: Expand each delegation by 10 percent to include pledged party and elected officials.			✔	✔
Further expand each delegation to include uncommitted party and elected officials ("superdelegates").				✔
Demographic Representation: Encourage participation and representation of minorities and traditionally under-represented groups (affirmative action).	✔	✔	✔	✔
Require delegations to be equally divided between men and women.			✔	✔

Convention Officers

Credentials, rules and platform are the major convention committees, but each party has additional committees, including one in charge of convention arrangements. Within the Republican Party the arrangements committee recommends a slate of convention officers to the national committee, which in turn refers the names to the committee on permanent organization for confirmation. The people the committee chooses are subject to the approval of the convention.

In the Democratic Party, this function is performed by the rules committee.

Both in the Democratic and Republican parties, the presiding officer during the bulk of the convention is the permanent chairman. Over the past quarter century the position usually has gone to the party's leader in the House of Representatives.

However, this loose precedent was broken in the Democratic Party by a rule adopted at the 1972 convention requiring that the position alternate every four years between the sexes.

Party Platforms

The adoption of a party platform is one of the principal functions of a convention. The platform committee is charged with the responsibility of writing a party platform to be presented to the convention for its approval.

The main challenge before the platform committee is to write a platform all party candidates can use in their campaigns. For this reason, platforms often fit the description given them by Wendell L. Willkie, Republican presidential candidate in 1940: "fusions of ambiguity."

Despite the best efforts of platform-builders to resolve their differences in the comparative privacy of the committee room, they sometimes encounter so controversial a subject that it cannot be compromised. Under these conditions dissident committee members often submit a minority report to the convention floor. Open floor fights are not unusual and, like credentials battles, often reflect the strength of the various candidates.

When the party has an incumbent president, the platform often is drafted in the White House or at least has the approval of the president. Rarely does a party adopt a

Third Parties Usually Fade Rapidly

Most third-party movements are like shooting stars, shining brightly in one election and then quickly disappearing. In the last century and a half, 10 third parties — plus independent John B. Anderson in 1980 — have drawn at least 5 percent of the popular vote in a presidential election. But not one of the third parties was able to maintain its foothold in the electoral process. Four had disappeared by the next election, four others drew a smaller vote total and two merged with one of the major parties.

Each of these significant third parties, except the Socialists in 1912, made its best showing in its first election. (The Socialists, led by Eugene V. Debs, first ran in 1900, winning just 0.62 percent of the vote.) The following chart lists each party's presidential candidate and the percentage of the vote the party received in that race and in the following election. A dash (—) indicates that the party had disappeared.

	Year	Percentage of Vote	Next Election
Anti-Masonic (William Wirt)	1832	7.8%	endorsed Whig
Free Soil (Martin Van Buren)	1848	10.1	4.9%
Whig-American (Millard Fillmore)	1856	21.5	—
Southern Democrats (John C. Breckinridge)	1860	18.1	—
Constitutional Union (John Bell)	1860	12.6	—
Populist (James B. Weaver)	1892	8.5	endorsed Democrat
Progressive (Bull Moose) (Theodore Roosevelt)	1912	27.4	0.2
Socialist (Eugene V. Debs)	1912	6.0	3.2
Progressive (Robert M. La Follette)	1924	16.6	—
American Independent (George C. Wallace)	1968	13.5	1.4
John B. Anderson	1980	6.6	endorsed Democrat

platform critical of an incumbent president of the same party.

The first platform was adopted by the Democrats in 1840. It was a short document, fewer than 1,000 words. Since then the platforms with few exceptions have grown longer and longer, covering more issues and appealing to more and more interest groups. The Democratic platform for 1984 epitomized this trend: reflecting the wishes of countless interest groups, the document was about 45,000 words long.

Third Parties: Radical Ideas

Throughout American history, many daring and controversial political platforms adopted by third parties have been rejected as too radical by the major parties. Yet many of these proposals later have won popular acceptance, made their way into the major party platforms — and into law.

Ideas such as the graduated income tax, popular election of senators, women's suffrage, minimum wages, Social Security and the 18-year-old vote were advocated by Populists, Progressives and other independents long before they were finally accepted by the nation as a whole.

The radical third parties and their platforms have been anathema to the established wisdom of the day, de-

nounced as impractical, dangerous, destructive of moral virtues and even traitorous. They have been anti-establishment and more far-reaching in their proposed solutions to problems than the major parties have dared to be.

Major Parties: Broader Appeal

In contrast with the third parties, Democrats and Republicans traditionally have been much more chary of adopting radical platform planks. Trying to appeal to a broad range of voters, the two major parties have tended to compromise differences or to reject controversial platform planks.

The Democratic Party has been more ready than the Republicans to adopt once-radical ideas, but there is usually a considerable time lag between their origin in third parties and their eventual adoption in Democratic platforms. For example, while the Democrats by 1912 had adopted many of the Populist planks of the 1890s, the Bull Moose Progressives of that year already were way ahead of them in proposals for social legislation. Not until 1932 were many of the 1912 Progressive planks adopted by the Democrats.

Similarly, not until the 1960s did Democratic platforms incorporate many of the more far-reaching proposals put forward by the 1948 Progressives.

Communications and the Media

Major changes in the national nominating convention have resulted from the massive advances in transportation and communication technologies during the 20th century.

The revolution in transportation has affected the scheduling of conventions. In the 19th century conventions were sometimes held a year or more before the election and at the latest were completed by late spring of the election year. With the ability of people to assemble quickly, conventions in recent years have been held later in the election year, usually in July or August. Advances in transportation also have affected site location. Geographic centrality is no longer the primary consideration in the selection of a convention city. Increasingly, coastal cities have been chosen as convention hosts.

The invention of new means of communication, particularly television, has had a further impact on the convention system. The changes spurred by the media have been primarily cosmetic ones, designed to give the convention a look of efficiency that was not so necessary in earlier days. As the conduct of the convention has undergone closer scrutiny by the American electorate, both parties have made major efforts to cut back the frivolity and hoopla and to accentuate the more sober aspects of the convention process.

Radio coverage of conventions began in 1924, television coverage 16 years later. One of the first changes inspired by the media age was the termination of the custom that a presidential candidate not appear at the convention but accept his nomination in a ceremony several weeks later. Franklin D. Roosevelt was the first major party candidate to break this tradition when in 1932 he delivered his acceptance speech in person before the Democratic convention. Twelve years later Thomas E. Dewey became the first Republican nominee to give his acceptance speech to the convention. Since then the final activity of both the Democratic and Republican conventions has been the delivery of the acceptance speeches by the vice presidential and presidential nominees.

In addition to curbing the circus-like aspects of the convention, party leaders in recent years have streamlined the schedule, with the assumption that the interest level of most of the viewing public for politics is limited. The result has been shorter speeches and generally fewer roll calls than at those conventions in the pre-television era.

Party leaders desire to put on a good show for the viewing public with the hope of winning votes for their party in November. The convention is a showcase, designed to present the party as both a model of democracy and an efficient, harmonious body. The schedule of convention activities is drawn up with an eye on the peak evening television viewing hours. There is an attempt to put the party's major selling points — the highly partisan keynote speech, the nominating ballots, and the candidates' acceptance speeches — on in prime time. Party leaders often try to keep evidence of bitter party factionalism — such as explosive credentials and platform battles — out of the peak viewing period.

In the media age the appearance of fairness is important, and in a sense this need to look fair and open has assisted the movement for party reform. Some influential party leaders, skeptical of reform of the convention, have found resistance difficult in the glare of television.

Before the revolution in the means of transportation and communication, conventions met in relative anonymity. Today conventions are held in all the privacy of a fishbowl, with every action and every rumor closely scrutinized. They have become media events and as such targets for political demonstrations that can be not only an embarrassment to the party but a security problem as well.

In spite of its difficulties, the convention system has survived. As the nation has developed during the past century and a half, the convention has evolved as well, changing its form but retaining its variety of functions. Criticism has been leveled at the convention, but no substitute has yet been offered that would nominate a presidential ticket, adopt a party platform, act as the supreme governing body of the party and serve as a massive campaign rally and propaganda forum. In addition to these functions, a convention is a place where compromise can take place — compromise often mandatory in a major political party that combines varying viewpoints.

Bibliography

Books

Bain, Richard C., and Judith H. Parris. *Convention Decisions and Voting Records.* Washington, D. C.: Brookings Institution, 1973.

Blue, Frederick J. *The Free Soilers: Third Party Politics, 1848-1854.* Urbana, Ill.: University of Illinois Press, 1973.

Byrne, Gary C., and Paul Marx. *The Great American Convention: A Political History of Presidential Elections.* Palo Alto, Calif.: Pacific Books, 1981.

David, Paul T. *The Politics of National Party Conventions.* Washington, D.C.: Brookings Institution, 1960.

Davis, James W. *National Conventions: Nominations Under the Big Top.* Woodbury, N. Y.: Barron Educational Series, 1973.

———. *National Conventions in an Age of Party Reform.* Westport, Conn.: Greenwood Press, 1983.

Farley, James A. *Behind the Ballots.* 1938. Reprint. New York: Da Capo Press, 1973.

Fleischman, Harry. *Norman Thomas: A Biography.* New York: W. W. Norton, 1969.

Halstead, Murat. *Trimmers, Truckers and Temporizers: Notes of Murat Halstead from the Political Convention of 1856.* Madison, Wis.: Society Press, 1961.

Jones, Chester L. *Readings on Parties and Elections.* Westport, Conn.: Greenwood Press, 1970.

Kane, Joseph Nathan. *Famous First Facts.* 4th ed. New York: H. W. Wilson, 1981.

Keech, William R., and Donald R. Matthews. *The Party's Choice with an Epilogue on the 1976 Nominations.* Washington, D. C.: Brookings Institution, 1976.

Lorant, Stefan. *The Glorious Burden: The American Presidency.* New York: Harper and Row, 1976.

McKee, Thomas H. *The National Conventions and Platforms of All Political Parties, 1789-1905: Convention, Popular and Electoral Vote.* New York: AMS Press, 1971.

Matthews, Donald R. *Perspectives on Presidential Selection.* Washington, D. C.: Brookings Institution, 1973.

Morgan, Wayne. *From Hayes to McKinley: National Party Politics, 1877-1896.* Syracuse, N. Y.: Syracuse University Press, 1969.

Morris, Richard B., ed. *Encyclopedia of American History.* 5th ed. New York: Harper and Row, 1976.

Nash, Howard P., Jr. *Third Parties in American Politics.*

Washington, D.C.: Public Affairs Press, 1958.

Parris, Judith H. *The Convention Problem: Issues in Reform of Presidential Procedures.* Washington, D. C.: Brookings Institution, 1972.

Pomper, Gerald M. *Nominating the President: The Politics of Convention Choice.* New York: Dodd and Mead, 1975.

Porter, Kirk H., and Donald Bruce. *National Party Platforms, 1840-1968.* Urbana: University of Illinois Press, 1972.

Reeves, Richard. *Convention.* New York: Harcourt, Brace, Jovanovich, 1977.

Roseboom, Eugene H. *A History of Presidential Elections: From George Washington to Jimmy Carter.* New York: Macmillan Publishers, 1979.

Rosenstone, Steven J., Roy L. Behr and Edward H. Lazarus. *Third Parties in America: Citizen Response to Major Party Failure.* Princeton, N.J.: Princeton University Press, 1984.

Sanford, Terry. *A Danger of Democracy: The Presidential Nominating Process.* Boulder, Colo.: Westview Press, 1981.

Schlesinger, Arthur M. Jr., ed. *The Coming to Power: Critical Presidential Elections in American History.* New York: Chelsea House, 1981.

Schlesinger, Arthur M. Jr. *History of U.S. Political Parties.* 4 vols. 1973. Reprint. New York: Chelsea House, 1981.

Smallwood, Frank. *The Other Candidates: Third Parties in Presidential Elections.* Hanover, N.H.: University Press of New England, 1983.

Thompson, Kenneth W., and Burkett White. *The Presidential Nominating Process: The George Gund Lectures.* Lanham, Md.: University Press of America, 1983.

White, Theodore H. *America in Search of Itself: The Making of the President, 1956-1980.* New York: Harper and Row, 1982.

———. *The Making of the President, 1960.* New York: Atheneum Publishers, 1961.

———. *The Making of the President, 1964.* New York: Atheneum Publishers, 1965.

———. *The Making of the President, 1968.* New York: Atheneum Publishers, 1969.

———. *The Making of the President, 1972.* New York: Atheneum Publishers, 1973.

Articles

Adkinson, Denny M. "The Electoral Significance of the Vice Presidency." *Presidential Studies Quarterly* 12 (Summer 1982): 330-336.

Angle, Paul M. "The Republican Convention of 1860." *Chicago History* (Spring 1960): 341.

Aldrich, John H. "A Dynamic Model of Presidential Nomination Campaigns." *American Political Science Review* 74 (September 1980): 651-669.

Beckley, C. "Unit Rule in National Nominating Conventions." *American Historical Review* (October 1899): 64-82.

Carleton, William. "The Revolution in the Presidential Convention." *Political Science Quarterly* (June 1957): 224-240.

Cone, S. W. "Dangers of the Conventions." *Democratic Review* (December 1855): 453.

Cooke, Edward F. "Drafting the 1952 Platforms." *Western Political Quarterly* (September 1956): 699-712.

Goldman, Ralph M. "Presidential Nominating Patterns." *Western Political Quarterly* (September 1955): 465-480.

Hoar, George F. "Four National Conventions: 1876, 1880, 1884, and 1888." *Scribner's* (February 1899): 152-174.

Hoxie, R. F. "Convention of the Socialist Party, 1908." *Journal of Political Economy* (July 1908): 442-450.

Jameson, J. F. "Early Political Use of the Word Convention." *American Historical Review* (April 1898): 477-487.

Julian, George W. "The First Republican Convention." *American Historical Review* (January 1899): 318.

McNitt, Andrew D. "The Effect of Preprimary Endorsement on Competition for Nominations: An Examination of Different Nominating Systems." *Journal of Politics* 42 (February 1980): 257-266.

Morgan, J. T. "Party Conventions." *North American Review* (August 1892): 237-244.

Morison, S. E. "The First National Nominating Convention." *American Historical Review* (July 1912): 744-763.

Murdock, J. S. "First National Nominating Convention." *American Historical Review* 1 (1896): 688.

"National Political Conventions of the Last Twelve Years." *World's Work* (June 1916): 167-172.

Nicholas, H. G. "American Political Conventions." *Fortnightly* (September 1948): 154-160.

Polsby, Nelson W. "Decision Making at the National Conventions." *Western Political Quarterly* (September 1960): 609-619.

Potts, C. S. "Unit Rule and Two-Thirds Rule." *Review of Reviews* (June 1912): 705-710.

"Republican Conventions of 1900 and 1904." *Review of Reviews* (July 1904): 3-15.

Rosewater, V. "Nominating a President." *Review of Reviews* (March 1908): 331-335.

Wildavsky, Aaron B. "On the Superiority of National Conventions." *Review of Politics* (July 1962): 307-319.

Williams, D. C. "Choosing the Presidential Candidates." *Political Quarterly* (October 1952): 368-379.

Wilbur, H. W. "Convention and the Caucus." *Gunton's Magazine* (January 1902): 65-72.

Wilson, Woodrow. "There Ought Never to Be Another Presidential Nominating Convention: Excerpts from a Letter, February 5, 1913." *U.S. News & World Report,* Oct. 23, 1967, 124.

Highlights of National Party Conventions, 1831-1984

1831 First national political convention was held in Baltimore by Anti-Masonic Party. Second such convention was held several months later by National Republican Party (no relation to modern Republicans).

1832 Democratic Party met in Baltimore for its first national political convention and nominated Andrew Jackson. The rule requiring a two-thirds majority for nominations was initiated.

1835 President Jackson called his party's convention more than a year before the election to prevent build-up of opposition to his choice of successor, Martin Van Buren.

1839 Whig Party held its first convention and chose the winning slate of William Henry Harrison and John Tyler. Party adopted unit rule for casting state delegations' votes.

1840 To avoid bitter battle over vice presidential nomination, Democratic Party set up a committee to select nominees, subject to approval of convention. In accordance with committee recommendations, Van Buren was nominated for president and no one for vice president.

1844 Democrats nominated James K. Polk — first "dark horse" or compromise candidate — after nine ballots. Silas Wright, convention's choice for vice president, declined the nomination. First time a convention nominee refused nomination. Convention subsequently nominated George M. Dallas.

1848 Democratic convention voted to establish continuing committee, known as "Democratic National Committee."

1852 Democrats and Whigs both adopted platforms before nominating candidates for president, setting precedent followed almost uniformly ever since.

1854 First Republican state convention held in Jackson, Mich., to nominate candidate slate. Platform denounced slavery.

1856 First Republican national convention held in Philadelphia. Kentucky sent the only Southern delegation. Nominated John C. Fremont for president.

1860 One of the longest, most turbulent and mobile conventions in Democratic history. Democrats met in Charleston, S.C., April 23. After 10 days and no agreement on a presidential nominee, delegates adjourned and reconvened in Baltimore in mid-July, for what turned out to be another disorderly meeting. Delegates finally nominated Stephen A. Douglas for president.

Benjamin Fitzpatrick, the convention's choice for vice president, became the first candidate to withdraw after convention adjournment and be replaced by a selection of the national committee. Delegates who bolted the original convention later joined Baltimore dissidents to nominate Vice President John C. Breckinridge for president.

Republicans nominated Abraham Lincoln for the presidency. First Republican credentials dispute took place over seating delegates from slave states and over voting strength of delegates from states where party was comparatively weak. Party rejected unit rule for first time.

Constitutional Union Party running on a platform of national unity nominated John Bell for president.

1864 Civil War led to bitter debate within Democratic Party over candidates, including Gen. George B. McClellan, presidential nominee.

In attempt to close ranks during war, Republicans used the name "Union Party" at convention. Renominated Lincoln. Platform called for constitutional amendment outlawing slavery.

1868 Susan B. Anthony urged Democratic support for women's suffrage.

For the first time, Republicans gave a candidate (Ulysses S. Grant) 100 percent of vote on first ballot. Incumbent Andrew Johnson, who succeeded the assassinated Lincoln, sought nomination unsuccessfully. First Republican convention with full Southern representation.

1872 Republicans renominated Grant at Philadelphia. Dissident liberal Republicans nominated Horace Greeley in Cincinnati. Democrats also nominated Greeley. Victoria Clafin Woodhull, nominated by the Equal Rights Party, was first woman presidential candidate. Black leader Frederick Douglass was her running mate.

1876 First time either party nominated incumbent governor for president; both major parties did so that year with Rutherford B. Hayes, R-Ohio, and Samuel J. Tilden, D-N.Y. Republican convention rejected unit rule for second time.

1880 Republicans nominated James A. Garfield for president on 36th ballot — party's all-time record number of ballots. Unit rule was rejected for third and final time. Republican convention passed loyalty pledge for nominee, binding each delegate to his support.

1884 Democrats turned back Tammany Hall challenge to unit rule.

Republicans nominated James G. Blaine, Maine, for president and John Logan, Illinois, for vice president, reversing 24-year pattern of seeking presidential candidate from the Midwest and vice presidential candidate from the East. John Roy Lynch, three-term U.S. representative from Mississippi, became first black elected temporary chairman of national nominating convention.

1888 Frederick Douglass was first black to receive a vote in presidential balloting at political convention. He received one vote on fourth ballot at Republican convention. Nineteen names were entered into Republican balloting. Benjamin Harrison won nomination on eighth ballot.

1892 Democrat Grover Cleveland broke convention system tradition by receiving third presidential nomination. People's Party (Populists) held first national nominating convention in Omaha, Neb., and adopted first platform.

1896 Democrats, divided over silver-gold question, repudiated Cleveland administration and nominated William Jennings Bryan.

Thirty-four Republican delegates against free silver walked out of convention.

1900   Each party had one woman delegate.

1904   Florida Democrats elected national convention delegates in public primary, under first legislation permitting any recognized party to hold general primary elections.

Republicans nominated Theodore Roosevelt, first time a vice president who had succeeded a deceased president went on to be nominated in his own right.

1908   Democrats, calling for legislation terminating what they called "partnership" between Republicans and corporations, pledged to refuse campaign contributions from corporations.

Call to Republican convention provided for election of delegates by primary method introduced in some states for first time.

1912   Increasing numbers of delegates were selected in primaries held in 13 states.

First time Republicans renominated entire ticket — William Howard Taft and James S. Sherman. Malapportionment of convention seats as result of Republican decline in South killed Theodore Roosevelt's chances of nomination. Taft renominated but 349 delegates protested his nomination by refusing to vote. Roosevelt nominated for president on Progressive ticket at separate convention.

1916   Democrats renominated entire ticket — Woodrow Wilson and Thomas R. Marshall — for first time.

Hopes of reuniting Republicans diminished when Roosevelt could not secure their nomination and refused Progressive renomination.

1920   For first time, women attended conventions in significant numbers.

1924   Republicans adopted bonus votes for first time — three bonus delegates at large allotted to each state carried by party in preceding presidential election. Republican convention was first to be broadcast on radio.

John W. Davis was nominated by Democrats on record 103rd ballot.

Three Democratic women received one or more votes for presidential nomination.

1928   Democrat Alfred E. Smith, governor of New York, was first Roman Catholic nominated for president by a major party.

1932   Republicans began tradition of appointing party leader from House of Representatives as permanent convention chairman.

Franklin D. Roosevelt appeared before Democratic convention to accept presidential nomination, the first major party candidate to do so.

1936   Democratic Party voted to end requirement of two-thirds delegate majority for nomination, a rule adopted at party's first convention and one that sometimes had led to lengthy balloting and selection of dark-horse slates.

Republicans nominated Alfred M. Landon and Frank Knox in vain effort to break new Democratic coalition.

1940   Franklin D. Roosevelt was nominated for unprecedented third term. He then wrote out a refusal of his renomination because of opposition to his vice presidential choice, Henry A. Wallace. Opposition deferred and Wallace was nominated.

Republicans held first political convention to be televised.

1944   Franklin D. Roosevelt, already having broken tradition by winning third term, was nominated for fourth time. Democrats put system of bonus votes into effect for states that voted Democratic in previous presidential election.

Thomas E. Dewey became first Republican candidate to accept nomination in appearance before the convention.

1948   After Democratic convention adopted strong civil rights plank, entire Mississippi delegation and 13 of Alabama's 26 delegates walked out.

Dissidents from 13 Southern states met several days later and nominated Gov. Strom Thurmond of South Carolina for president.

Democrats began appointing Speaker of the House as permanent chairman. Practice followed through 1968, with exception of 1960 when Sam Rayburn declined. Since 1948 conventions, presidential nominees of both parties have appeared at their conventions. Republicans renominated Thomas E. Dewey — first time party renominated a defeated presidential candidate.

1952   Adlai E. Stevenson, who did not seek the nomination, was chosen as Democratic nominee in one of few genuine "drafts" in history of either political party.

Republicans nominated Dwight D. Eisenhower. Women delegates wanted to nominate Sen. Margaret Chase Smith, Maine, for vice president, but Smith requested her name not be put in nomination.

1956   Democratic nominee Stevenson left choice of running mate to convention. Winner of open race was Sen. Estes Kefauver of Tennessee. First time a party loyalty provision was put into effect during delegate selection.

Dwight D. Eisenhower renominated unanimously on first ballot at Republican convention.

1960   Democrats adopted civil rights plank that was strongest in party history. Presidential nominee John F. Kennedy was second Catholic to receive presidential nomination of major party.

Republican nominee Richard Nixon was party's first vice president nominated for president at completion of his term.

1964   Democratic President Lyndon B. Johnson was nominated for second term by acclamation. Fight over credentials of Alabama and Mississippi delegations was overriding issue at the convention.

Sen. Margaret Chase Smith's name was placed in nomination for presidency at Republican convention — first time a woman placed in nomination by a major party. Sen. Barry Goldwater, Ariz., won the nomination.

1968   Democratic delegates voted to end unit rule and to eliminate it from all levels of party politics for 1972 convention. Vice President Hubert H. Humphrey nominated for president.

Republicans nominated Richard Nixon, who had made one of most remarkable political comebacks in American history.

1972   With newly adopted party reform guidelines, the Democratic convention included a record number of women, youth and minorities. Open debate on many issues occurred with an unprecedented 23 credentials challenges brought to the floor. George McGovern, who built up following as an anti-war candidate,

27

nominated for president on first ballot. His choice for vice president, Sen. Thomas F. Eagleton, Mo., became second candidate in American history to withdraw. National committee chose R. Sargent Shriver as replacement.

In harmonious convention Republicans renominated Richard Nixon and Spiro T. Agnew with nearly unanimous votes.

1976 Democrats in unified convention nominated Jimmy Carter. Gathering was notable for lack of bitter floor fights and credentials challenges that had characterized some recent conventions.

Incumbent president Gerald R. Ford received Republican nomination, narrowly surviving a challenge from former governor of California Ronald Reagan.

1980 Democrats renominated President Jimmy Carter in convention marked by bitter contests over party platform and rules binding delegates to vote on first ballot for candidates under whose banner they were elected. The struggle pitted Carter forces against supporters of Sen. Edward M. Kennedy, Mass., who were trying to pry nomination away from the president and alter party platform. While the Carter camp prevailed on delegate-binding rule, Kennedy managed to force major concessions in Democratic platform.

In contrast, a harmonious and unified Republican convention nominated Ronald Reagan. Rumors abounded during convention that former president Gerald R. Ford would serve as Reagan's vice presidential candidate. After it became obvious that efforts to persuade Ford to join the ticket had failed, Reagan chose George Bush as his running mate.

1984 Democrats nominated Walter F. Mondale, Jimmy Carter's vice president, for presidential slot and in a historic move accepted Rep. Geraldine A. Ferraro of New York as his running mate. Ferraro was first woman placed on national ticket by a major party.

A jubilant Republican Party wound up its convention confident that President Ronald Reagan and Vice President George Bush would win in November. With the ticket's renomination certain beforehand, convention was more a celebration than a business meeting of GOP activists.

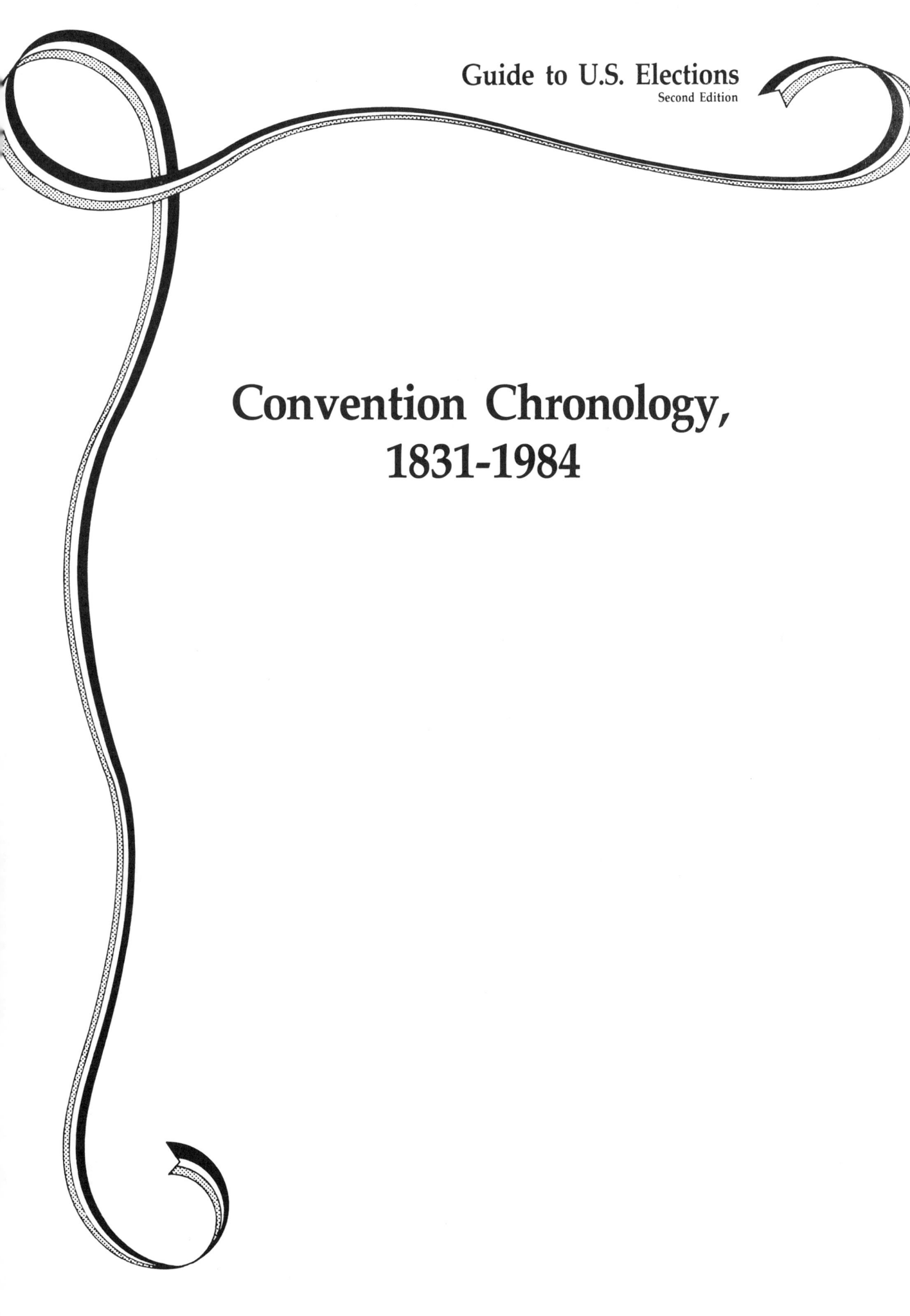

Convention Chronology,
1831-1984

Sources: Convention Chronology

This section (pages 31 to 159) contains brief descriptions of all presidential nominating conventions of major American political parties and excerpts from party platforms. The chronology begins in 1831, when the Anti-Masonic Party held the first nominating convention in American history, and concludes with the Democratic and Republican party conventions of 1984.

The narrative includes conventions for all parties receiving at least 2 percent of the popular vote in the presidential election *(see pages 329 to 365).* Thus, conventions for the Socialist Party, which received at least 2 percent of the presidential popular vote in 1904, 1908, 1912, 1920 and 1932, are included. Socialist Party conventions for other presidential election years when the party received less than 2 percent of the popular vote do not appear.

The source most frequently consulted in preparing the narrative was *Convention Decisions and Voting Records,* Brookings Institution, Washington, D.C., 1973, by Richard C. Bain and Judith H. Parris.

Ballot Vote Totals

Throughout the narrative, vote totals appear for significant ballots on platform disputes and procedural issues and for presidential and vice presidential balloting. The source used for 1835-1972 vote totals was *Convention Decisions and Voting Records.* The sources for the 1976, 1980 and 1984 vote totals were *The Official Proceedings of the Democratic National Convention* and the Republican National Committee. Charts showing state-by-state voting on selected ballots appear in a separate section, "Key Convention Ballots," pages 163 to 221. *(See p. 162 for details on these charts.)*

Platform Excerpts

The source for the party platform excerpts that appear in the convention chronology was *National Party Platforms, 1840-1968,* University of Illinois Press, 1972, compiled by Kirk H. Porter and Donald Bruce Johnson. For the 1972, 1976, 1980 and 1984 Democratic and Republican platforms, the official texts of the platforms adopted by the two parties were used.

In adopting the material from *National Party Platforms, 1840-1968,* Congressional Quarterly has added boldface subheadings to highlight the organization of the texts. For example, excerpts from the 1844 Democratic Party platform appear on page 36. The boldface headings — **Appeal to the Masses, Strict Construction, Internal Improvements,** etc. — do not appear in the text of the party platform as it was published in *National Party Platforms, 1840-1968.* In all other respects, Congressional Quarterly has followed the style and typography of the platform texts appearing in *National Party Platforms, 1840-1968.*

1831-32 Conventions

Presidential Candidates

William Wirt
Anti-Mason

Henry Clay
National Republican

Andrew Jackson
Democrat

Anti-Masons

In September 1831, the Anti-Masonic Party held the first national nominating convention in American history. One hundred sixteen delegates from 13 states, none south of Maryland, gathered in Baltimore. They selected the party's presidential and vice presidential candidates, adopted an address to the people (a precursor of the party platform) and established a national corresponding committee that created the framework for a national campaign organization.

Ironically, the Anti-Masons, whose keystone was opposition to Masonry, nominated a former Mason, William Wirt of Maryland, as their presidential standard-bearer. In spite of a rule requiring a three-fourths nominating majority, Wirt was an easy first-ballot winner and the nearly unanimous nominee of the convention.

He was not, however, the first choice of party leaders, who had been rebuffed in their earlier efforts to persuade Henry Clay and later Supreme Court Justice John McLean to take the presidential nomination. Wirt himself was not an enthusiastic candidate, stating that he saw nothing repugnant about Masonry and that if his views did not suit the convention, he would willingly withdraw from the ticket. The delegates supported Wirt and chose Amos Ellmaker of Pennsylvania as his vice presidential running mate.

National Republicans

In December 1831 the National Republicans held their national convention in Baltimore. The National Republicans were united primarily in their opposition to incumbent President Andrew Jackson. The idea of a convention had been proposed by an anti-Jackson committee in New York City and approved by the leading National Republican newspaper, the *National Intelligencer*. There was no uniform method of delegate selection, with state conventions, legislative caucuses and local meetings all being used.

One hundred sixty-eight delegates from 18 states attended the National Republican convention, although nearly one-quarter were late in arriving due to inclement winter weather. Without any pre-established rules, it was agreed that the roll calls would be taken by announcing each delegate's name. Henry Clay of Kentucky was the convention's unanimous choice for president, and former representative John Sergeant of Pennsylvania was selected without opposition for vice president. Letters accepting their nominations were received from both candidates.

There was no formal platform, although the convention adopted an address to the people that criticized Jackson for dividing a previously harmonious country.

In May 1832 a convention of young National Republicans met in Washington, D.C., and passed a series of resolutions calling for a protective tariff, federal support of

internal improvements and recognition of the Supreme Court as the ultimate authority on constitutional questions. The last was a rebuke of Jackson for disregarding Supreme Court decisions concerning the Cherokee Indians. Other resolutions criticized Jackson's use of the spoils system in distributing patronage and his handling of foreign policy with Great Britain. Although not a formal platform, the resolutions adopted by the convention of young National Republicans were the most definitive discussion of issues during the 1832 campaign.

Democrats

The Democrats held their first national convention in Baltimore in late May 1832. Representatives from 23 states attended. The call for a Democratic national convention had been made by Jacksonian members of the New Hampshire Legislature, and their proposal was approved by prominent members of President Andrew Jackson's administration. The convention was called to order by a member of the New Hampshire Legislature, who explained the intent of the gathering in these words:

"...[The] object of the people of New Hampshire who called this convention was, not to impose on the people, as candidates for either of the two first offices of the government, any local favorite; but to concentrate the opinions of all the states.... They believed that the example of this convention would operate favorably in future elections; that

the people would be disposed, after seeing the good effects of this convention in conciliating the different and distant sections of the country, to continue this mode of nomination." *(Reprinted from* Convention Decisions and Voting Records, *by Richard C. Bain, p. 17.)*

The convention adopted two rules that Democratic conventions retained well into the 20th century. One based each state's convention vote on its electoral vote, an apportionment method unchanged until 1940.

A second rule established a two-thirds nominating majority, a controversial measure that remained a feature of Democratic conventions until 1936. The 1832 convention also adopted the procedure of having one person from each delegation announce the vote of his state.

The delegates did not formally nominate Jackson for the presidency. Instead they concurred in the various nominations he had received earlier from state legislatures. Jackson's choice for vice president, Martin Van Buren of New York, was easily nominated on the first ballot, receiving 208 of the 283 votes cast.

Instead of adopting a platform or address to the people, the convention decided that each state delegation should write its own report to its constituents. The convention also determined to establish in each state general corresponding committees that together would provide a nationwide organization for the campaign.

1835-36 Conventions

Presidential Candidates

Martin Van Buren
Democrat

William Henry Harrison
Whig

Daniel Webster
Whig

Hugh L. White
Whig

Democrats

The Democrats held their second national convention in Baltimore in May 1835. The early date had been set by President Jackson to prevent the emergence of opposition to his hand-picked successor, Vice President Martin Van Buren. Delegates from 22 states and two territories attended, and the size of the delegations was generally related to their distance from Baltimore. One hundred eighty-eight individuals were on hand from Maryland to cast the state's 10 votes, but only one person attended from Tennessee — a visiting businessman who cast 15 votes. Alabama, Illinois and South Carolina were unrepresented.

Two rival Pennsylvania delegations arrived, precipitating the first credentials dispute in convention history. It was decided to seat both delegations and let them share the Pennsylvania vote.

An effort to eliminate the rule requiring a two-thirds nominating majority initially passed by a margin of 231 to 210 (apparently counting individual delegates instead of state convention votes), but the two-thirds rule was reimposed by a voice vote. A question developed whether the nominating majority should be based on only the states represented or on all the states in the union. It was decided to base the majority on only those present.

Martin Van Buren won the presidential nomination, winning all 265 votes. Richard M. Johnson of Kentucky barely reached the necessary two-thirds majority on the first vice presidential ballot, receiving 178 votes, just one vote more than the required minimum. *(Chart, p. 163)*

Johnson, famous as the alleged slayer of the Indian chief Tecumseh, had aroused some disapproval because of his personal life. Johnson had lived with a mulatto mistress by whom he had two daughters.

Once again the Democrats did not write a formal platform, although an address to the people was published in the party newspaper, *The Washington Globe.* Van Buren wrote a letter of acceptance in which he promised to "tread generally in the footsteps of President Jackson."

Whigs

During Jackson's second term, a new party, the Whigs, emerged as the Democrats' primary opposition. It contained remnants of the short-lived National Republican Party, as well as anti-Jackson elements in the Democratic and Anti-Masonic parties. Although the Whigs were a rising political force, the party lacked national cohesion in 1836. Instead of holding a convention and nominating national candidates, the Whigs ran regional candidates nominated by state legislatures. It was the hope of Whig strategists that the regional candidates would receive enough electoral votes to throw the election into the House of Representatives, where the party could unite behind the leading prospect.

Sen. Daniel Webster of New Hampshire ran as the Whig candidate in Massachusetts; Sen. Hugh L. White of Tennessee was the party standard-bearer in the South; Gen. William Henry Harrison of Ohio was the Whig candidate in the rest of the country. The Whigs chose Francis Granger of New York as Harrison and Webster's running mate and John Tyler of Virginia to run with White.

1839-40 Conventions

Presidential Candidates

William Henry Harrison
Whig

Martin Van Buren
Democrat

Whigs

By 1839 the Whigs had established themselves as a powerful opposition party, unified enough to run a national candidate against the Democratic president, Martin Van Buren. The call for the Whigs' first national convention was issued by a group of party members in Congress. Nearly 250 delegates responded, gathering in Harrisburg, Pa., in December 1839.

Three candidates were in contention for the presidential nomination: Generals William Henry Harrison of Ohio and Winfield Scott of Virginia and Sen. Henry Clay of Kentucky. After long debate, it was decided that each state would ballot separately, then select representatives who would meet and discuss the views and results of their delegation meetings with representatives of the other states. The unit rule would be in effect, binding the entire vote of each state to the candidate who received a majority of the state's delegates.

The nominating rules agreed to by the convention strongly favored the forces opposed to Clay. First, they negated substantial Clay strength in state delegations in which he did not hold a majority of the vote. Second, they permitted balloting in relative anonymity, so that delegates would be more likely to defect from the popular Kentuckian than they would if the balloting were public.

Clay led on the first ballot, but switches by Scott delegates on subsequent roll calls gave the nomination to Harrison. On the final ballot, Harrison received 148 votes to 90 for Clay and 16 for Scott. Harrison's vote was short of a two-thirds majority, but under Whig rules only a simple majority was needed to nominate.

To give the ticket factional and geographic balance, a friend of Clay, former Democrat John Tyler of Virginia, was the unanimous selection for vice president. The convention did not risk destruction of the tenuous unity of its anti-Democratic coalition by adopting a party platform or statement of principles.

Democrats

In May 1840 the Democrats held their national convention in Baltimore. The call once again was initiated by members of the New Hampshire Legislature. Delegates

from 21 states attended, while five states were unrepresented. Again, the size of the state delegations was largely determined by their distance from Baltimore. New Jersey sent 59 people to cast the state's eight votes, while only one delegate came from Massachusetts to decide that state's 14 votes.

To avoid a bitter dispute over the vice presidential nomination, the convention appointed a committee to recommend nominees for both spots on the ticket. The committee's recommendation that Van Buren be renominated for president was passed by acclamation. On the touchier problem of the vice presidency, the committee recommended that no nomination be made, a suggestion that was also agreed to by the convention. Dissatisfaction with the personal life of Vice President Johnson had increased, leading to the decision that state Democratic leaders determine who would run as the vice presidential candidate in their own states.

Before the nominating process had begun, the convention had approved the first party platform in American history. A platform committee was appointed "to prepare resolutions declaratory of the principles of the . . . party." The committee report was approved without discussion.

The first Democratic platform was a short document, fewer than 1,000 words long. Although brief by modern standards, the platform clearly emphasized the party's belief in a strict reading of the Constitution. It began by stating "that the federal government is one of limited powers" and spelled out in detail what the federal government could not do. The platform stated that the federal government did not have the power to finance internal improvements, assume state debts, charter a national bank or interfere with the rights of the states, especially relating to slavery. The platform criticized the abolitionists for stirring up the explosive slavery question. The Democrats urged the government to practice economy, supported President Van Buren's independent treasury plan and affirmed their belief in the principles expressed in the Declaration of Independence.

In addition to the platform, the convention adopted an address to the people, which was written by a separate committee. Much longer than the platform, the address discussed party principles, lauded Van Buren and Jackson for following these principles and warned of dire consequences if the opposition should be elected.

Following are excerpts from the Democratic platform of 1840:

Strict Construction. That the federal government is one of limited powers, derived solely from the constitution, and the grants of power shown therein, ought to be strictly construed by all the departments and agents of the government, and that it is inexpedient and dangerous to exercise doubtful constitutional powers.

Internal Improvements. That the constitution does not confer upon the general government the power to commence and carry on, a general system of internal improvements.

State Debts. That the constitution does not confer authority upon the federal government, directly or indirectly, to assume the debts of the several states, contracted for local internal improvements, or other state purposes; nor would such assumption be just or expedient.

Equality of Rights. That justice and sound policy forbid the federal government to foster one branch of industry to the detriment of another, or to cherish the interests of one portion to the injury of another portion of our common country — that every citizen and every section of the country, has a right to demand and insist upon an equality of rights and privileges, and to complete and ample protection of person and property from domestic violence, or foreign aggression.

Government Spending. That it is the duty of every branch of the government, to enforce and practice the most rigid economy, in conducting our public affairs, and that no more revenue ought to be raised, than is required to defray the necessary expenses of the government.

National Bank. That congress has no power to charter a national bank; that we believe such an institution one of deadly hostility to the best interests of the country, dangerous to our republican institutions and the liberties of the people, and calculated to place the business of the country within the control of a concentrated money power, and above the laws and the will of the people.

States' Rights, Slavery. That congress has no power, under the constitution, to interfere with or control the domestic institutions of the several states, and that such states are the sole and proper judges of everything appertaining to their own affairs, not prohibited by the constitution; that all efforts by abolitionists or others, made to induce congress to interfere with questions of slavery, or to take incipient steps in relation thereto, are calculated to lead to the most alarming and dangerous consequences, and that all such efforts have an inevitable tendency to diminish the happiness of the people, and endanger the stability and permanency of the union, and ought not to be countenanced by any friend to our political institutions.

Independent Treasury. That the separation of the moneys of the government from banking institutions, is indispensable for the safety of the funds of the government, and the rights of the people.

Democratic Principles. That the liberal principles embodied by Jefferson in the Declaration of Independence, and sanctioned in the constitution, which makes ours the land of liberty, and the asylum of the oppressed of every nation, have ever been cardinal principles in the democratic faith; and every attempt to abridge the present privilege of becoming citizens, and the owners of soil among us, ought to be resisted with the same spirit which swept the alien and sedition laws from our statute-book.

1843-44 Conventions

Presidential Candidates

James G. Birney
Liberty

Henry Clay
Whig

James K. Polk
Democrat

Liberty Party

The Liberty Party held its second national convention in Buffalo, N.Y., in August 1843. The party, born of the failure of the Whigs and the Democrats to make a strong appeal to abolitionist voters, had held its first national convention in April 1840 in Albany, N.Y. James G. Birney of Michigan, a former slave owner, was nominated for president and Thomas Earle of Ohio was chosen as his running mate. In the 1840 election the party polled 0.29 percent of the national popular vote.

At the 1843 convention, 148 delegates from 12 states assembled in Buffalo and renominated Birney for the presidency and chose Thomas Morris of Ohio as his running mate. The party platform was more than 3,000 words long, the lengthiest platform written by any party in the 19th century. In spite of its length, the platform discussed only one issue, slavery. In the 1844 election, the party received 2.3 percent of the national popular vote, its highest total in any presidential election. By 1848, most members of the party joined the newly formed Free Soil Party.

Following are excerpts from the Liberty Party platform of 1844:

Resolved. That the Liberty party ... will demand the absolute and unqualified divorce of the General Government from Slavery, and also the restoration of equality of rights, among men, in every State where the party exists, or may exist.

Therefore, Resolved, That we hereby give it to be distinctly understood, by this nation and the world, that, as abolitionists, considering that the strength of our cause lies in its righteousness — and our hope for it in our conformity to the LAWS of GOD, and our respect for the RIGHTS OF MAN, we owe it to the Sovereign Ruler of the Universe, as a proof of our allegiance to Him, in all our civil relations and offices, whether as private citizens, or as public functionaries sworn to support the Constitution of the United States, to regard and to treat the third clause of the second section of the fourth article of that instrument, whenever applied to the case of a fugitive slave, as utterly null and void, and consequently as forming no part of the Constitution of the United States, whenever we are called upon, or sworn, to support it.

Whigs

In a harmonious one-day session, the Whigs' national convention nominated for the presidency the party's former leader in Congress, Henry Clay. It was a final rebuff for President John Tyler from the party that had nominated him for the second spot on its ticket in 1840. Three years of bickering between the White House and Whig leaders in Congress had made Tyler, former Democrat, persona non grata in the Whig Party.

Delegates from every state were represented at the Whig convention, held in Baltimore on May 1, 1844. Clay was the unanimous nominee, and it was proposed that he be invited to address the convention the next day. However, the Kentuckian declined this opportunity to make the first acceptance speech in American political history, stating in a letter that he was unable to reconcile an appearance with his "sense of delicacy and propriety." *(Chart, p. 164)*

Three potential candidates for the vice presidency sent letters of withdrawal before balloting for second place on the ticket began. Unlike the convention four years earlier, the Whigs abandoned their relatively secret state caucus method of voting and adopted a public roll call, with the chair calling the name of each delegate. Theodore Frelinghuysen of New Jersey won a plurality of the convention vote for vice president on the first ballot and went on to gain, on the third ballot, the required majority.

After the nominations, several resolutions were adopted, including one that defined Whig principles and served as the party's first platform. It was a brief document, fewer than 100 words long, and the only clear difference between it and the platform adopted later by the Democratic convention was on the issue of distributing proceeds from the sale of public land. The Whigs favored distribution of these revenues to the states; the Democrats opposed it believing the proceeds should be retained by the federal government. In a continued reaction to the Jackson administration, the Whigs criticized "executive usurpations" and proposed a single-term presidency. The rest of the Whig platform called for government efficiency, "a

well-regulated currency" and a tariff for revenue and the protection of American labor.

Westward territorial expansion, particularly the annexation of Texas, was not mentioned in the Whig platform, but it was an explosive issue by 1844 which made a significant impact on the Democratic convention.

Following are excerpts from the Whig platform of 1844:

Resolved, That these principles may be summed as comprising, a well-regulated currency; a tariff for revenue to defray the necessary expenses of the government, and discriminating with special reference to protection of the domestic labor of the country; the distribution of the proceeds of the sales of the public lands; a single term for the presidency; a reform of executive usurpations; — and, generally — such an administration of the affairs of the country as shall impart to every branch of the public service the greatest practicable efficiency, controlled by a well regulated and wise economy.

Democrats

Delegates from every state except South Carolina assembled in Baltimore in late May 1844 for the Democratic convention. The front-runner for the presidential nomination was Martin Van Buren, whose status was threatened on the eve of the convention by his statement against the annexation of Texas. Van Buren's position jeopardized his support in the South, and with a two-thirds majority apparently necessary, dimmed his chances of obtaining the presidential nomination. The question of requiring a two-thirds nominating majority was debated in the early sessions of the convention, and by a vote of 148 to 118 the two-thirds majority rule, initially adopted by the party in 1832, was ratified. *(Chart, p. 163)*

Van Buren led the early presidential balloting, actually receiving a simple majority of the vote on the first ballot. On succeeding roll calls, however, his principal opponent, Lewis Cass of Michigan, gained strength and took the lead. But neither candidate approached the 178 votes needed for nomination.

With a deadlock developing, sentiment for a compromise candidate appeared. James K. Polk, former Speaker of the Tennessee House and former governor of Tennessee, emerged as an acceptable choice and won the nomination on the ninth ballot. It marked the first time in American history that a dark-horse candidate won a presidential nomination. *(Chart, p. 163)*

A friend of Van Buren, Sen. Silas Wright of New York, was the nearly unanimous nominee of the convention for vice president. But Wright refused the nomination, quickly notifying the delegates by way of Samuel Morse's new invention, the telegraph. After two more ballots, George M. Dallas of Pennsylvania was chosen as Polk's running mate.

Among its final actions, the convention appointed a central committee and recommended that a nationwide party organization be established — a forerunner of the national committee. The delegates did not adopt a platform but appointed a committee to draft resolutions.

The resulting document contained the same resolutions included in the party's 1840 platform, plus several new planks. The Democrats opposed the distribution of the proceeds from the sale of public lands; were against placing any restrictions on the executive veto power; and, to alleviate the sectional bitterness aroused by the prospect of Western expansion, recommended the annexation of both Texas and Oregon.

President Tyler, although abandoned by the major parties, wanted to remain in office. Friends and federal officeholders gathered in Baltimore at the same time as the Democrats and nominated Tyler. However, it became apparent that the president's national vote-getting appeal was limited, and he withdrew from the race in favor of the Democrat, Polk.

Following are excerpts from the Democratic platform of 1844:

Appeal to the Masses. That the American Democracy place their trust, not in factitious symbols, not in displays and appeals insulting to the judgment and subversive of the intellect of the people, but in a clear reliance upon the intelligence, patriotism, and the discriminating justice of the American masses.

That we regard this as a distinctive feature of our political creed, which we are proud to maintain before the world, as the great moral element in a form of government springing from and upheld by the popular will; and we contrast it with the creed and practice of Federalism, under whatever name or form, which seeks to palsy the will of the constituent, and which conceives no imposture too monstrous for the popular credulity.

Internal Improvements. That the Constitution does not confer upon the General Government the power to commence or carry on a general system of internal improvements.

State Debts. That the Constitution does not confer authority upon the Federal Government, directly or indirectly, to assume the debts of the several states.

Government Spending. That it is the duty of every branch of the government to enforce and practice the most rigid economy in conducting our public affairs, and that no more revenue ought to be raised than is required to defray the necessary expenses of the government.

National Bank. That Congress has no power to charter a United States Bank, that we believe such an institution one of deadly hostility to the best interests of the country, dangerous to our republican institutions and the liberties of the people.

States' Rights. That Congress has no power, under the Constitution, to interfere with or control the domestic institutions of the several States; and that such States are the sole and proper judges of everything pertaining to their own affairs, not prohibited by the Constitution; that all efforts, by abolitionists or others, made to induce Congress to interfere with questions of slavery, or to take incipient steps in relation thereto, are calculated to lead to the most alarming and dangerous consequences.

Public Lands. That the proceeds of the Public Lands ought to be sacredly applied to the national objects specified in the Constitution, and that we are opposed to the laws lately adopted, and to any law for the distribution of such proceeds among the States, as alike inexpedient in policy and repugnant to the Constitution.

Executive Veto Power. That we are decidedly opposed to taking from the President the qualified veto power by which he is enabled, under restrictions and responsibilities amply sufficient to guard the public interest.

Western Expansion. That our title to the whole of the Territory of Oregon is clear and unquestionable; that no portion of the same ought to be ceded to England or any other power, and that the reoccupation of Oregon and the reannexation of Texas at the earliest practicable period are great American measures, which this Convention recommends to the cordial support of the Democracy of the Union.

1848 Conventions

Presidential Candidates

Lewis Cass
Democrat

Zachary Taylor
Whig

Martin Van Buren
Free Soil

Democrats

Delegates from every state gathered in Baltimore in May 1848 for the Democratic Party's fifth national convention. A seating dispute between two rival New York delegations enlivened the early convention sessions. The conflict reflected a factional fight in the state Democratic Party between a more liberal anti-slavery faction, known as the Barnburners, and a more conservative faction, known as the Hunkers. By a vote of 126 to 125, the convention adopted a compromise by which both delegations were seated and shared New York's vote. However, this compromise satisfied neither of the contesting delegations. The Barnburners bolted the convention. The Hunkers remained but refused to vote. *(Chart, p. 164)*

Before the presidential balloting could begin, the convention had to decide whether to use the controversial two-thirds rule. Consideration of the rule preceded the credentials controversy, which brought an objection from New York delegates who wanted their seating dispute settled first. But, by a vote of 133 to 121, the convention refused to table the issue. A second vote on adoption of the two-thirds rule was approved, 176 to 78. *(Chart, p. 164)*

The front-runner for the presidential nomination was Sen. Lewis Cass of Michigan. Although Cass was from the North, his view that the existence of slavery in the territories should be determined by their inhabitants (a forerunner of Stephen Douglas' "popular sovereignty") was a position acceptable to the South.

Cass received 125 votes on the first ballot, more than double the total of his two principal rivals, James Buchanan of Pennsylvania and Levi Woodbury of New Hampshire. Cass' vote total steadily increased during the next three roll calls, and on the fourth ballot he received 179 votes and was nominated. His vote was actually short of a two-thirds majority of the allotted convention votes, but the chair ruled that, with New York not voting, the required majority was reduced. *(Chart, p. 164)*

The vice presidential nomination went on the second ballot to Gen. William O. Butler of Kentucky, who had 169 of the 253 votes cast. As in the earlier presidential balloting, Butler's two-thirds majority was based on votes cast rather than votes allotted. Butler's primary rival for the nomination was a military colleague, Gen. John A. Quitman of Mississippi.

One of the most significant acts of the convention was the formation of a national committee, with one member from each state, that would handle party affairs until the next convention four years later.

As in 1840 and 1844, the heart of the Democratic platform was a series of resolutions describing the party's concept of a federal government with limited powers. New resolutions emphasized Democratic opposition to a national bank and the distribution of land sales to the states, while applauding the independent treasury plan, the lower tariff bill passed in 1846 and the successful war against Mexico. An effort by William L. Yancey of Alabama to insert in the platform a plank on slavery that would prevent interference with the rights of slaveholders in states or territories was defeated, 216 to 36. The slavery plank written in the platform had the same wording as earlier versions in the 1840 and 1844 Democratic platforms. The plank was milder than Yancey's proposal, stating simply that Congress did not have the power to interfere with slavery in the states. The convention adopted the complete platform by a vote of 247 to 0.

Following are excerpts from the 1848 Democratic platform:

Mexican War. That the war with Mexico, provoked on her part by years of insult and injury, was commenced by her army crossing the Rio Grande, attacking the American troops, and invading our sister State of Texas; and that, upon all the principles of patriotism and laws of nations, it is a just and necessary war on our part, in which every American citizen should have shown himself on the side of his country, and neither morally nor physically, by word or by deed, have given "aid and comfort to the enemy."

Democratic Accomplishments. That the fruits of the great political triumph of 1844, which elected James K. Polk and George M. Dallas President and Vice President of the United States, have fulfilled the hopes of the Democracy of the Union — in defeating the declared purposes of their opponents to create a national bank; in preventing the corrupt and unconstitutional distribution of the land pro-

ceeds, from the common treasury of the Union, for local purposes; in protecting the currency and the labor of the country from ruinous fluctuations, and guarding the money of the people for the use of the people, by the establishment of the constitutional treasury; in the noble impulse given to the cause of free trade, by the repeal of the tariff in 1842 and the creation of the more equal, honest, and productive tariff of 1846.

Whigs

Whig delegates from every state except Texas gathered in Philadelphia in June 1848. Although the Lone Star state was unrepresented, a Texas Whig state convention had earlier given a proxy for their votes to the Louisiana delegates. There was debate in the convention about the legality of the proxy, but it was ultimately accepted by the delegates.

The battle for the Whig's presidential nomination involved three major contenders, the party's respected aging statesman, Henry Clay of Kentucky; and two generals — Zachary Taylor and Winfield Scott, both of Virginia — whose political appeal was significantly increased by their military exploits in the recently completed Mexican War. Taylor led throughout the balloting, taking the lead on the first ballot with 111 votes, compared with 97 for Clay and 43 for Scott. Taylor increased his lead on subsequent roll calls, winning the nomination on the fourth ballot with 171 of the 280 votes cast. *(Chart, p. 165)*

Millard Fillmore of New York and Abbott Lawrence of Massachusetts were the prime contenders for the vice presidential nomination. Fillmore led Lawrence, 115 to 109, on the first ballot and pulled away to win on the second ballot with 173 of the 266 votes cast.

A motion to make the presidential and vice presidential nominations unanimous failed when several delegates objected, doubting Taylor's support of Whig principles.

The Whig convention did not formally adopt a party platform, although a ratification meeting held in Philadelphia after the convention adopted a series of resolutions. The resolutions avoided a discussion of issues, instead lauding the party's presidential nominee, Zachary Taylor, and affirming his faithfulness to the tenets of the party.

Free Soilers

Anti-slavery Whigs, New York Barnburners and members of the Liberty Party gathered in Buffalo, N.Y., in August 1848 to form a new third party, the Free Soilers. While opposition to slavery was a common denominator of the various elements in the new party, the dissident Democrats and Whigs also were attracted to the Free Soil Party by the lack of influence they exerted in their former parties. The call for a Free Soil convention was made by the New York Barnburners at their state conclave in June 1848 and by a non-partisan gathering in Columbus, Ohio, the same month. The latter assembly, organized by Salmon P. Chase, was entitled a People's Convention of Friends of Free Territory and was designed to set the stage for a national Free Soil convention.

Four hundred sixty-five delegates from 18 states (including representatives from the slave states of Delaware, Maryland and Virginia) assembled in Buffalo for the birth of the Free Soil Party. Because of the large number of delegates, convention leaders determined that delegates from each state would select several members to form a Committee on Conference, which would conduct conven-

tion business. The rest of the delegates would sit in a large tent and listen to campaign oratory.

Martin Van Buren, the former Democratic president and a favorite of the Barnburners, was chosen as the new party's standard-bearer on the first ballot. Van Buren received 244 votes to defeat John P. Hale of New Hampshire, who had 181 votes. Hale had been nominated by the Liberty Party in October 1847, but with Van Buren's nomination he withdrew from the race. The vice presidential nomination went to a former Whig, Charles Francis Adams of Massachusetts.

The platform adopted by the Free Soil Party focused on the slavery issue, but its opposition to slavery was milder than earlier Liberty Party platforms. The Free Soilers also declared themselves on other issues besides slavery, further distinguishing themselves from the single-minded Liberty Party.

While the Free Soilers opposed the extension of slavery into the territories, they did not feel the federal government had the power to interfere with slavery in the states. Although this position was significantly stronger than the position adopted by the Democrats, it was milder than the all-out opposition to slavery expressed by the Liberty Party four years earlier.

The Free Soilers also adopted positions on a variety of other issues, supporting free land for settlers, a tariff for revenue purposes, cheap postage and federal spending for river and harbor improvements. Basically, the Free Soil platform expressed belief in a federal government with broader powers than that conceived by the Democrats.

Following are excerpts from the 1848 Free Soil Party platform:

Slavery. That Slavery in the several States of this Union which recognize its existence, depends upon the State laws alone, which cannot be repealed or modified by the Federal Government, and for which laws that Government is not responsible. We therefore propose no interference by Congress with Slavery within the limits of any State.

Resolved, THAT IT IS THE DUTY OF THE FEDERAL GOVERNMENT TO RELIEVE ITSELF FROM ALL RESPONSIBILITY FOR THE EXISTENCE OR CONTINUANCE OF SLAVERY WHEREVER THAT GOVERNMENT POSSESS CONSTITUTIONAL POWER TO LEGISLATE ON THAT SUBJECT, AND IS THUS RESPONSIBILE FOR ITS EXISTENCE.

Resolved, That the true, and, in the judgment of this Convention, the *only* safe means of preventing the extension of Slavery into territory now free, is to prohibit its existence in all such territory by *an act of Congress.*

Government Administration. That we demand CHEAP POSTAGE for the people; a retrenchment of the expenses and patronage of the Federal Government; the *abolition* of all *unnecessary* offices and salaries; and the election by the People of all civil officers in the service of the Government, so far as the same may be practicable.

Internal Improvements. That *river and harbor improvements,* when demanded by the safety and convenience of commerce with foreign nations, or among the several States, are objects of *national concern;* and that it is the duty of Congress, in the exercise of its constitutional powers, to provide therefor.

Homesteading. That the FREE GRANT TO ACTUAL SETTLERS, in consideration of the expenses they incur in making settlements in the wilderness, which are usually fully equal to their actual cost, and of the public benefits resulting therefrom, of reasonable portions of the public lands, under suitable limitations, is a wise and just

measure of public policy, which will promote, in various ways, the interest of all the States of this Union; and we therefore recommend it to the favorable consideration of the American People.

Tariff. That the obligations of honor and patriotism require the earliest practical payment of the national debt,

and we are therefore in favor of such a tariff of duties as will raise revenue adequate to defray the necessary expenses of the Federal Government, and to pay annual installments of our debt and the interest thereon.

Party Motto. *Resolved,* That we inscribe on our banner, "FREE SOIL, FREE SPEECH, FREE LABOR, AND FREE MEN."

1852 Conventions

Presidential Candidates

Franklin Pierce
Democrat

Winfield Scott
Whig

John P. Hale
Free Soil

Democrats

In spite of the efforts of the major politicians of both parties, the explosive slavery question was fast becoming the dominant issue in American politics and was threatening the tenuous intersectional alliances that held together both the Democratic and Whig parties. Under the cloud of this volatile issue, the Democratic convention convened in Baltimore in June 1852.

The delegates were called to order by the party's first national chairman, Benjamin F. Hallett of Massachusetts. Hallett's first action was to limit the size of each state delegation to its electoral vote, dispatching members of oversized delegations to the rear of the hall. Retention of the two-thirds rule provoked little opposition, unlike the disputes at the 1844 and 1848 conventions, and an effort to table the rule was soundly beaten, 269 to 13.

With a degree of orderliness, the convention disposed of procedural matters, clearing the way for the presidential balloting. There were four major contenders for the nomination: Sen. Lewis Cass of Michigan, James Buchanan of Pennsylvania and William L. Marcy of New York — all three over 60 years old — and the rising young senator from Illinois, Stephen A. Douglas, 39. Each of the four challengers led at one point during the numerous ballots that followed.

Cass jumped in front initially, receiving 116 votes on the first ballot. Buchanan trailed with 93, while Marcy and Douglas were far back with 27 and 20 votes, respectively. Cass' vote dropped after the first few roll calls, but he was able to hold the lead until the 20th ballot, when Buchanan moved in front. Buchanan led for several roll calls, followed by Douglas, who edged into the lead on the 30th ballot,

only to be quickly displaced by Cass on the 32nd ballot. Marcy made his spurt between the 36th and 46th ballots, and took the lead on the 45th and 46th ballots. But in spite of the quick changes in fortune, none of the four contenders could win a simple majority of the votes, let alone the two-thirds required. *(Chart, p. 166)*

With a deadlock developing, on the 35th ballot the Virginia delegation introduced a new name, Franklin Pierce of New Hampshire. Although formerly a member of both houses of Congress, Pierce was little known nationally and not identified with any party faction. Pierce's relative anonymity made him an acceptable alternative in the volatile convention. Pierce received 15 votes on the 35th ballot and gradually gained strength on subsequent ballots, with the big break coming on the 49th roll call. Nearly unanimous votes for Pierce in the New England states created a bandwagon effect that resulted in his nomination on this ballot with 279 of the 288 votes cast. The 49 ballots took two days.

Beginning the vice presidential roll call, a spokesman for the Maine delegation suggested that second place on the ticket go to a representative of the South, specifically mentioning Sen. William R. King of Alabama. King moved into a strong lead on the first ballot with 125 votes and easily won nomination on the second roll call with 277 of the 288 votes cast.

The platform adopted by the Democratic convention contained the same nine resolutions that had been in all party platforms since 1840, detailing the Democratic concept of a limited federal government. The platform included a plank supporting the Compromise of 1850, the congressional solution to the slavery question. Actually,

both the Whigs and Democrats endorsed the compromise of 1850. The major point of dispute between the two parties was over the issue of internal improvements, with the Whigs taking a broader view of federal power in this sphere.

Following are excerpts from the Democratic platform of 1852:

> **Compromise of 1850.** *Resolved,* ... the democratic party of the Union, standing on this national platform, will abide by and adhere to a faithful execution of the acts known as the compromise measures settled by the last Congress — "the act for reclaiming fugitives from service or labor" included; which act, being designed to carry out an express provision of the constitution, cannot, with fidelity thereto be repealed nor so changed as to destroy or impair its efficiency.
>
> *Resolved,* That the democratic party will resist all attempts at renewing, in congress or out of it, the agitation of the slavery question, under whatever shape or color the attempt may be made.
>
> **Democratic Principles.** That, in view of the condition of popular institutions in the Old World, a high and sacred duty is devolved, with increased responsibility upon the democratic party of this country, as the party of the people, to uphold and maintain the rights of every State, and thereby the Union of the States, and to sustain and advance among us constitutional liberty, by continuing to resist all monopolies and exclusive legislation for the benefit of the few at the expense of the many, and by a vigilant and constant adherence to those principles and compromises of the constitution, which are broad enough and strong enough to embrace and uphold the Union as it was, the Union as it is, and the Union as it shall be, in the full expansion of the energies and capacity of this great and progressive people.

Whigs

Although in control of the White House, the Whigs were more sharply divided by the Compromise of 1850 than were the Democrats. The majority of Northern Whigs in Congress opposed the Compromise, while most Southern members of the party favored it. Faced with widening division in their ranks, Whig delegates convened in Baltimore in June 1852. The call for this national convention had been issued by Whig members of Congress, and delegates from all 31 states attended.

The convention sessions were often lively and sometimes raucous. When asked to present its report the first day, the credentials committee responded that it was not ready to report and "didn't know when — maybe for days." A minister, invited to the hall to deliver a prayer to the convention, never had his chance. The delegates debated when the prayer should be delivered and finally decided to omit it.

A heated debate occurred on how many votes each state would be apportioned on the platform committee. By a vote of 149 to 144, the delegates adopted a plan whereby each state's vote on the committee would reflect its strength in the electoral college. Strong protests from Southern and small Northern states, however, brought a reversal of this decision, and although no formal vote was recorded, representation on the platform committee was changed so that each state received one vote.

The Northern and Southern wings of the Whig Party were nearly equally represented at the Baltimore convention, and the close split produced a prolonged battle for the party's presidential nomination. The two major rivals for the nomination, President Millard Fillmore and Winfield Scott, had nearly equal strength. Ironically, the basic appeal of Fillmore of New York was among Southern delegates, who appreciated his support of the Compromise of 1850.

Although a native of Virginia, Scott was not popular in the South because of his ambivalence on the Compromise and the active support given him by a leading anti-slavery Northerner, Sen. William H. Seward of New York. Scott's strength was in the Northern and Western states. A third candidate in the field was Daniel Webster, the party's elder statesman, whose appeal was centered in his native New England.

On the first ballot, Fillmore received 133 votes, Scott had 132 and Webster collected 29. This nearly equal distribution of the vote between Fillmore and Scott continued with little fluctuation through the first two days of balloting. Midway through the second day, after the 34th ballot, a motion was made to adjourn. Although defeated by a vote of 126 to 76, other motions were made to adjourn throughout the rest of the session. Finally, amid increasing confusion, after the 46th ballot, delegates voted by a margin of 176 to 116 to adjourn. *(Chart, p. 167)*

Commotion continued the next day, with Southern delegates trying unsuccessfully to expel Henry J. Raymond, the editor of the *New York Times,* who was also a delegate by proxy. In an article, Raymond had charged collusion between party managers and Southern delegates, with the South getting its way on the platform while Scott received the presidential nomination.

Amid this uproar, the leaders of the Fillmore and Webster forces were negotiating. Fillmore was willing to release his delegates to Webster, if Webster could muster 41 votes on his own. As the balloting continued, it was apparent that Webster could not; and enough delegates defected to Scott to give the Mexican War hero a simple majority and the nomination on the 53rd ballot. On the final roll call, Scott received 159 votes, compared with 112 for Fillmore and 21 for Webster.

Several individuals placed in nomination for the vice presidency refused it immediately. The chairman of the convention finally declared Secretary of the Navy William A. Graham of North Carolina to be the unanimous selection. No formal roll-call vote was recorded.

For only the second time in their history, the Whigs adopted a party platform. Like their Democratic adversaries, the Whigs supported the Compromise of 1850 and perceived the federal government as having limited powers. Additional planks called for a tariff on imports to raise revenue and for an isolationist foreign policy that avoided "entangling alliances." The platform was adopted by a vote of 227 to 66, with all the dissenting votes cast by delegates from the North and West.

Following are excerpts from the Whig platform of 1852:

> **Strict Construction.** The Government of the United States is of a limited character, and it is confined to the exercise of powers expressly granted by the Constitution, and such as may be necessary and proper for carrying the granted powers into full execution, and that all powers not granted or necessarily implied are expressly reserved to the States respectively and to the people.
>
> **Foreign Policy.** That while struggling freedom everywhere enlists the warmest sympathy of the Whig party, we still adhere to the doctrines of the Father of his Country, as announced in his Farewell Address, of keeping ourselves free from all entangling alliances with foreign countries, and

of never quitting our own to stand upon foreign ground, that our mission as a republic is not to propagate our opinions, or impose on other countries our form of government by artifice or force; but to teach, by example, and show by our success, moderation and justice, the blessings of self-government, and the advantages of free institutions.

Tariff. Revenue sufficient for the expenses of an economical administration of the Government in time of peace ought to be derived from a duty on imports, and not from direct taxation.

Internal Improvements. The Constitution vests in Congress the power to open and repair harbors, and remove obstructions from navigable rivers, whenever such improvements are necessary for the common defense, and for the protection and facility of commerce with foreign nations, or among the States, said improvements being, in every instance, national and general in their character.

Compromise of 1850. That the series of acts of the Thirty-first Congress, — the act known as the Fugitive Slave Law, included — are received and acquiesced in by the Whig Party of the United States as a settlement in principle and substance, of the dangerous and exciting question which they embrace; and, so far as they are concerned, we will maintain them, and insist upon their strict enforcement, until time and experience shall demonstrate the necessity of further legislation.

Free Democrats (Free Soilers)

After the 1848 election, the New York Barnburners returned to the Democratic Party, and the rest of the Free Soilers were ready to coalesce with either the Democrats or the Whigs. But the process of absorption was delayed by the Compromise of 1850. It was viewed as a solution to the slavery question by the two major parties but was regarded as a sellout by most anti-slavery groups.

Responding to a call for a national convention issued by a Cleveland, Ohio, anti-slavery meeting, delegates gathered in Pittsburgh in August 1852. Anti-slavery Whigs and remnants of the Liberty Party were in attendance at what was termed the Free Soil Democratic Convention.

John P. Hale of New Hampshire unanimously won the presidential nomination, and George W. Julian of Indiana was selected as his running mate.

Although the platform covered a number of issues, the document focused on the slavery question. The Free Soil Democrats opposed the Compromise of 1850 and called for the abolition of slavery. Like both major parties, the Free Democrats expressed the concept of a limited federal government, but they agreed with the Whigs that the government should undertake certain river and harbor improvements. The Free Democrats went beyond the other parties in advocating a homestead policy, extending a welcome to immigrants and voicing support for new republican governments in Europe and the Caribbean.

Following are excerpts from the Free Democratic platform of 1852:

Strict Construction. That the Federal Government is one of limited powers, derived solely from the Constitution, and the grants of power therein ought to be strictly construed by all the departments and agents of the Government, and it is inexpedient and dangerous to exercise doubtful constitutional powers.

Compromise of 1850. That, to the persevering and importunate demands of the slave power for more slave States, new slave Territories, and the nationalization of slavery, our distinct and final answer is — no more slave States, no slave Territory, no nationalized slavery, and no national legislation for the extradition of slaves.

That slavery is a sin against God and a crime against man, which no human enactment nor usage can make right; and that Christianity, humanity, and patriotism, alike demand its abolition.

That the Fugitive Slave Act of 1850 is repugnant to the Constitution, to the principles of the common law, to the spirit of Christianity, and to the sentiments of the civilized world. We therefore deny its binding force upon the American People, and demand its immediate and total repeal.

Homesteading. That the public lands of the United States belong to the people, and should not be sold to individuals nor granted to corporations, but should be held as a sacred trust for the benefit of the people, and should be granted in limited quantities, free of cost, to landless settlers.

Internal Improvements. That river and harbor improvements, when necessary to the safety and convenience of commerce with foreign nations or among the several States, are objects of national concern, and it is the duty of Congress in the exercise of its constitutional powers to provide for the same.

1856 Conventions

Presidential Candidates

John C. Fremont
Republican

Millard Fillmore
Know Nothing

James Buchanan
Democrat

Republicans

With the decline of the Whigs and the increasing importance of the slavery issue, there was room for a new political party. Officially born in 1854, the new Republican Party moved to fill the vacuum.

The party's first meeting was held in Pittsburgh in February 1856, with delegates from 24 states attending. United in their opposition to the extension of slavery and the policies of the Pierce administration, the gathering selected a national committee (with one representative from each state), which was empowered to call the party's first national convention.

The subsequent call was addressed not to Republicans but "to the people of the United States" who were opposed to the Pierce administration and the congressional compromises on slavery. Each state was allocated six delegates at the forthcoming convention, with three additional delegates for each congressional district.

When the first Republican National Convention assembled in Philadelphia in June 1856, the gathering was clearly sectional. There were nearly 600 delegates present, representing all the Northern states, the Border slave states of Delaware, Maryland, Virginia and Kentucky, and the District of Columbia. The territory of Kansas, symbolically important in the slavery struggle, was treated as a state and given full representation. There were no delegations from the remaining Southern slave states.

Under convention rules, the roll call was to proceed in alphabetical order, with each state allocated three times its electoral vote. In response to a question, the chair decided that a simple majority would be required and not the two-thirds majority mandated by the Democratic convention. This was an important rule that distinguished the conventions of the two major parties well into the 20th century.

Two major contenders for the Republican presidential nomination, Salmon P. Chase of Ohio and William H. Seward of New York, both withdrew before the balloting began. Another contender, Supreme Court Justice John McLean of Ohio, withdrew briefly, but then re-entered the race. However, McLean could not catch the front-runner, John C. Fremont of California. Although briefly a U.S.

senator, Fremont was most famous as an explorer, and he benefited from being free of any ideological identification.

The other contenders were all identified with one of the factions that had come to make up the new party. Fremont won a preliminary, informal ballot, receiving 359 votes to 190 for McLean. On the formal roll call, Fremont won easily, winning 520 of the 567 votes. *(Chart, p. 168)*

A preliminary, informal ballot was taken for the vice presidency as well. William L. Dayton, a former senator from New Jersey, led with 253 votes, more than twice the total received by an Illinois lawyer, Abraham Lincoln, who had served in the House of Representatives 1846-48. On the formal ballot, Dayton swept to victory with 523 votes. His nomination was quickly made unanimous.

The Republican platform was approved by a voice vote. It was a document with sectional appeal, written by Northern delegates for the North. Unlike the Democrats, the Republicans opposed the concept of popular sovereignty and believed that slavery should be prohibited in the territories. Specifically, the platform called for the admission of Kansas as a free state.

The Republicans also differed with the Democrats on the question of internal improvements, supporting the view that Congress should undertake river and harbor improvements. The Republican platform denounced the Ostend Manifesto, a document secretly drawn up by three of Pierce's ambassadors in Europe, that suggested the United States either buy or take Cuba from Spain. The Republicans termed the manifesto a "highwayman's plea, that 'might makes right.'"

Both parties advocated the building of a transcontinental transportation system, with the Republicans supporting the construction of a railroad.

Following are excerpts from the Republican platform of 1856:

> **Slavery.** This Convention of Delegates, assembled in pursuance of a call addressed to the people of the United States, without regard to past political differences or divisions, who are opposed to the repeal of the Missouri Compromise; to the policy of the present Administration; to the extension of Slavery into Free Territory; in favor of the

admission of Kansas as a Free State; of restoring the action of the Federal Government to the principles of Washington and Jefferson....

That the Constitution confers upon Congress sovereign powers over the Territories of the United States for their government; and that in the exercise of this power, it is both the right and the imperative duty of Congress to prohibit in the Territories those twin relics of barbarism — Polygamy, and Slavery.

Cuba. That the highwayman's plea, that "might makes right," embodied in the Ostend Circular, was in every respect unworthy of American diplomacy, and would bring shame and dishonor upon any Government or people that gave it their sanction.

Transcontinental Railroad. That a railroad to the Pacific Ocean by the most central and practicable route is imperatively demanded by the interests of the whole country.

Internal Improvements. That appropriations by Congress for the improvement of rivers and harbors, of a national character, required for the accommodation and security of our existing commerce, are authorized by the Constitution, and justified by the obligation of the Government to protect the lives and property of its citizens.

American (Know-Nothings)

In addition to the Republicans, the American Party or Know-Nothings aspired to replace the Whigs as the nation's second major party. However, unlike the Republicans, the Know-Nothings were a national political organization, and the slavery issue that helped unite the Republicans divided the Know-Nothings. The main Know-Nothing concern was to place restrictions on the large number of European immigrants who arrived in the 1840s and 1850s.

The party held its first and only national convention in Philadelphia in February 1856. Several days before the convention began, the American Party's national council met and drew up the party platform. When the convention assembled, anti-slavery delegates objected to the platform, with its espousal of popular sovereignty, and called for the nomination of candidates who would outlaw slavery in the new territories. When their resolution was defeated, 141 to 59, these anti-slavery delegates — mainly from New England and Ohio — bolted the convention.

The remaining delegates nominated former president Millard Fillmore (1850-53) of New York for president. Fillmore was popular in the South for his support of compromise slavery measures during his administration, and was nominated on the second ballot. Andrew Jackson Donelson of Tennessee was chosen as the vice presidential candidate.

In June 1856 several days before the Republican convention was scheduled to begin, the anti-slavery Know-Nothings assembled in New York and nominated Speaker of the House Nathaniel P. Banks of Massachusetts for the presidency and former governor William F. Johnston of Pennsylvania as his running mate. Banks, who actually favored Fremont's nomination, withdrew from the race when Fremont was chosen as the Republican candidate. Johnston bowed out in favor of Fremont's running mate, William L. Dayton, later in the campaign.

The Know-Nothing convention that had met earlier in Philadelphia adopted a platform similar to that of the Democrats on the slavery question. The document advocated non-interference in the affairs of the states and the concept of popular sovereignty for deciding slavery in the territories. Although also calling for economy in government spending, the bulk of the Know-Nothing platform dealt with restricting immigrants. Among the nativistic planks were proposals that native-born citizens be given the first chance for all government offices, that the naturalization period for immigrants be extended to 21 years and that paupers and convicted criminals be kept from entering the United States.

Following are excerpts from the Know-Nothing platform of 1856:

Slavery, States' Rights. The unequalled recognition and maintenance of the reserved rights of the several states, and the cultivation of harmony and fraternal good-will between the citizens of the several states, and to this end, non-interference by Congress with questions appertaining solely to the individual states, and non-intervention by each state with the affairs of any other state.

The recognition of the right of the native-born and naturalized citizens of the United States, permanently residing in any territory thereof, to frame their constitutions and laws, and to regulate their domestic and social affairs in their own mode, subject only to the provisions of the federal Constitution, with the right of admission into the Union whenever they have the requisite population for one representative in Congress.

Nativism. *Americans must rule America;* and to this end, *native*-born citizens should be selected for all state, federal, or municipal offices of government employment, in preference to naturalized citizens....

No person should be selected for political station (whether of native or foreign birth), who recognizes any alliance or obligation of any description to any foreign prince, potentate or power, who refuses to recognize the federal and state constitutions (each within its own sphere), as paramount to all other laws, as rules of particular [political] action.

A change in the laws of naturalization, making a continued residence of twenty-one years, of all not heretofore provided for, an indispensable requisite for citizenship hereafter, and excluding all paupers or persons convicted of crime from landing upon our shores.

Democrats

In June 1856 delegates from all 31 states gathered in Cincinnati, Ohio, for the party's seventh quadrennial convention. It was the first Democratic convention to be held outside Baltimore.

Roll-call votes were taken during the first two days on the establishment of a platform committee and on the method of ticket allocation for the galleries. The first close vote came on the credentials committee report concerning the seating of two contesting New York delegations. By a vote of 136 to 123, the convention agreed to a minority report seating both contending factions and splitting the state's vote between them.

Three men were in contention for the party's presidential nomination: President Franklin Pierce of New Hampshire, James Buchanan of Pennsylvania and Sen. Stephen A. Douglas of Illinois. All three had actively sought the nomination before. Ironically, Buchanan, who had spent the previous three years as ambassador to Great Britain, was in the most enviable position. Having been abroad, Buchanan had largely avoided the increasing slavery controversy that bedeviled his major rivals.

Buchanan led on the first ballot with 135-1/2 votes, with Pierce receiving 122-1/2 and Douglas 33. As the balloting continued, Pierce lost strength, while both Buchanan and Douglas gained. After the 15th roll call, the vote stood:

Buchanan, 168-1/2, Douglas, 118-1/2, Pierce 3-1/2. *(Chart, p. 168)*

While the two front-runners had substantial strength, neither of them was a sectional candidate. Both received votes from Northern and Southern delegations. With the possibility of a stalemate looming, Douglas withdrew after the 16th ballot. On the 17th roll call, Buchanan received all 296 votes, and the nomination.

On the first ballot for the vice presidency, 11 different individuals received votes. Rep. John A. Quitman of Mississippi led with 59 votes, followed by Rep. John C. Breckinridge of Kentucky, with 50. At the beginning of the second ballot, the New England delegations cast a nearly unanimous vote for Breckinridge, creating a bandwagon effect that resulted in the nomination of the Kentuckian. Ironically, before the vice presidential balloting began, Breckinridge had asked that his name be withdrawn from consideration. Believing himself too young (he was 35), Breckinridge stated that "promotion should follow seniority."

In spite of his earlier demurrer, Breckinridge was in the convention hall and announced his acceptance of the nomination. It marked one of the few times in American political history that a candidate was present for his own nomination.

The party platform was considered in two segments, with the domestic and foreign policy sections debated separately. The theme of the domestic section, as in past platforms, was the Democrats' concept of a limited federal government. The unconstitutionality of a national bank, federal support for internal improvements and distribution of proceeds from the sale of public land were again mentioned.

Nearly one-third of the entire platform was devoted to the slavery question, with support for the various congressional compromise measures stressed. The Democratic position was underscored in a passage that was capitalized in the convention *Proceedings:* "non-interference by Congress with slavery in state and territory, or in the District of Columbia."

In another domestic area, the Democrats denounced the Know-Nothings for being un-American. The convention approved the domestic policy section of the platform by a vote of 261 to 35, with only the New York delegation voting in opposition.

The foreign policy section expressed a nationalistic and expansionist spirit that was absent from previous Democratic platforms.

There were six different foreign policy planks, each voted on separately. The first plank, calling for free trade, passed 210 to 29. The second, favoring implementation of the Monroe Doctrine, passed 240 to 21. The third plank, backing westward continental expansion, was approved 203 to 56. The fourth plank, which expressed sympathy with the people of Central America, grew out of the United States' dispute with Great Britain over control of that area. The plank was approved, 221 to 38. The fifth plank, calling for United States "ascendency in the Gulf of Mexico," passed 229 to 33. A final resolution, presented separately, called for the construction of roads to the Pacific Ocean. The resolution was at first tabled, 154 to 120, and a second vote to reconsider failed, 175 to 121. But when the resolution was raised a third time after the presidential nomination, it passed, 205 to 87.

Following are excerpts from the Democratic platform of 1856:

Slavery. That claiming fellowship with, and desiring the co-operation of all who regard the preservation of the Union under the Constitution as the paramount issue — and repudiating all sectional parties and platforms concerning domestic slavery, which seek to embroil the States and incite to treason and armed resistance to law in the Territories; and whose avowed purposes, if consummated, must end in civil war and disunion, the American Democracy recognize and adopt the principles contained in the organic laws establishing the Territories of Kansas and Nebraska as embodying the only sound and safe solution of the "slavery question" upon which the great national idea of the people of this whole country can repose in its determined conservatism of the Union — NON-INTERFERENCE BY CONGRESS WITH SLAVERY IN STATE AND TERRITORY, OR IN THE DISTRICT OF COLUMBIA.

Know-Nothings. ...the liberal principles embodied in the Declaration of Independence ... makes ours the land of liberty and the asylum of the oppressed ... every attempt to abridge the privilege of becoming citizens ... ought to be resisted....

Since the foregoing declaration was uniformly adopted by our predecessors in National Conventions, an adverse political and religious test has been secretly organized by a party claiming to be exclusively American, it is proper that the American Democracy should clearly define its relation thereto, and declare its determined opposition to all secret political societies, by whatever name they may be called.

Free Trade. That there are questions connected with the foreign policy of this country, which are inferior to no domestic question whatever. The time has come for the people of the United States to declare themselves in favor of free seas and progressive free trade....

Latin America. [W]e should hold as sacred the principles involved in the Monroe Doctrine: their bearing and import admit of no misconstruction; they should be applied with unbending rigidity.

Gulf of Mexico. That the Democratic party will expect of the next Administration that every proper effort be made to insure our ascendency in the Gulf of Mexico.

Transcontinental Roads. That the Democratic party recognizes the great importance, in a political and commercial point of view, of a safe and speedy communication, by military and postal roads, through our own territory, between the Atlantic and Pacific coasts....

Whigs

On the verge of extinction, the Whig Party held its last national convention in September 1856. Delegates assembled in Baltimore from 21 states and endorsed the Know-Nothing ticket of Fillmore and Donelson.

However, the Whigs adopted their own platform. It avoided specific issues, instead calling for preservation of the Union. The platform criticized both the Democrats and Republicans for appealing to sectional passions and argued for the presidential candidacy of the former Whig, Millard Fillmore.

Following are excerpts from the Whig platform of 1856:

Preserving the Union. That the Whigs of the United States are assembled here by reverence for the Constitution, and unalterable attachment to the National Union, and a fixed determination to do all in their power to preserve it for themselves and posterity. They have no new principles to announce — no new platform to establish, but are content broadly to rest where their fathers have rested upon the Constitution of the United States, wishing no safer guide, no higher law.

1860 Conventions

Presidential Candidates

Stephen A. Douglas
Democrat

John C. Breckinridge
Southern Democrat

Abraham Lincoln
Republican

John Bell
Constitutional Union

Democrats

Rarely in American history has there been a convention as tumultuous as the one that assembled in Charleston, S.C., in April 1860. The Democrats met at a time when their party was threatened by sectional division, caused by the explosive slavery question. The issue had grown increasingly inflammatory during the 1850s, and, because of rising emotions, the chances of a successful compromise solution decreased.

From the outset of the convention, there was little visible effort to obtain party unity. Parliamentary squabbling with frequent appeals to the chair marked the early sessions. Before the presidential balloting even began, 27 separate roll calls on procedural and platform matters were taken.

A bitter dispute between Northern and Southern delegates over the wording of the platform's slavery plank precipitated a walkout by several dozen Southern delegates. Both the majority and minority reports submitted to the convention called for a reaffirmation of the Democratic platform of 1856. In addition, however, the majority report (favored by the South) declared that no government — local, state or federal — could outlaw slavery in the territories. The minority report took a more moderate position, stating that the decision on allowing slavery in the territories should be left to the Supreme Court.

After a day of debate, the convention agreed, by a vote of 152 to 151, to recommit both reports to the platform committee. Basically, the vote followed sectional lines, with Southern delegates approving recommittal. However, the revised majority and minority reports subsequently presented to the convention were similar to the originals.

An amendment by Benjamin F. Butler of Massachusetts, to endorse the 1856 platform without any mention of slavery, was defeated, 198 to 105. After two procedural roll calls, the delegates voted, 165 to 138, to accept the minority report. The vote followed sectional lines, with the Northern delegates victorious. *(Chart, p. 169)*

Unhappy with the platform and unwilling to accept it, 45 delegates from nine states bolted the convention. The majority of six Southern delegations withdrew (Alabama, Mississippi, Florida, Texas, South Carolina and Louisiana), along with scattered delegates from three other states (Arkansas, Delaware and North Carolina).

With the size of the convention reduced, chairman Caleb Cushing of Massachusetts made an important decision. He ruled that the two-thirds nominating majority would be based on the total votes allocated (303) rather than the number of delegates present and voting. Although Cushing's ruling was approved by a vote of 141 to 112, it countered precedents established at the 1840 and 1848 Democratic conventions, when the nominating majority was based on those present and voting.

Cushing's ruling made it nearly impossible for any candidate to amass the necessary two-thirds majority. Particularly affected was the front-runner, Sen. Stephen A. Douglas of Illinois, whose standing in the South had diminished with his continued support of popular sovereignty. Douglas moved into a big lead on the first ballot, received 145-1/2 votes to 42 for Sen. Robert M. T. Hunter of Virginia and 35-1/2 for James Guthrie of Kentucky. Despite his large lead over the rest of the field, Douglas was well short of the 202 votes needed for nomination and, with his limited sectional appeal, had little chance of gaining the needed delegates.

After three days of balloting and 57 presidential roll calls, the standing of the three candidates had undergone little change. Douglas led with 151-1/2 votes, followed by Guthrie with 65-1/2 and Hunter with 16. The delegates, in session for 10 days and wearied by the presidential deadlock, voted 194-1/2 to 55-1/2 to recess for six weeks and reconvene in Baltimore. This marked the first and only time that a major party adjourned its convention and moved it from one city to another.

Reconvening in Baltimore in June, the delegates were faced with another sticky question: whether or not to seat the delegates who had bolted the Charleston convention. The majority report presented by the credentials committee reviewed each case individually and recommended that the bolting Southern delegates, except those from Alabama and Louisiana, be reseated. The minority report recommended that a larger majority of the withdrawing Charles-

ton delegates be reseated. The minority report was defeated, 150 to 100-1/2. Ten more roll calls followed on various aspects of the credentials dispute, but they did not change the result of the first vote. *(Chart, p. 169)*

The convention vote on credentials produced a new walkout, involving the majority of delegates from Virginia, North Carolina, Tennessee, Maryland, Kentucky, Missouri, Arkansas, California and Oregon, and anti-Douglas delegates from Massachusetts. With the presidential balloting ready to resume, less than two-thirds of the original convention was present.

On the first ballot, Douglas received 173-1/2 of the 190-1/2 votes cast. On the second ballot, his total increased to 190-1/2, but it was obviously impossible for him to gain two-thirds (202) of the votes allocated (303). After the second roll call, a delegate moved that Douglas, having obtained a two-thirds majority of the votes cast, be declared the Democratic presidential nominee. The motion passed unanimously on a voice vote. *(Chart, p. 169)*

The convention left the selection of the vice presidential candidate to a caucus of the remaining Southern delegates. They chose Sen. Benjamin Fitzpatrick of Alabama, who received all 198-1/2 votes cast on the vice presidential roll call.

Shortly after the convention adjourned, Fitzpatrick declined the nomination. For the first time in American history, a national committee was called upon to fill a vacancy on the ticket. By a unanimous vote of committee members, the former governor of Georgia, Herschel V. Johnson, was chosen to be Douglas' running mate.

The Democratic platform, in addition to the controversial slavery plank, provided a reaffirmation of the 1856 platform, with its proposals for a limited federal government but an expansionist foreign policy. The 1860 platform added planks that continued the expansionist spirit, calling for the construction of a transcontinental railroad and acquisition of the island of Cuba.

Following are excerpts from the 1860 Democratic platform:

Slavery. Inasmuch as difference of opinion exists in the Democratic party as to the nature and extent of the powers of a territorial legislature, and as to the powers and duties of Congress, under the Constitution of the United States, over the institution of slavery within the Territories,

Resolved, That the Democratic party will abide by the decision of the Supreme Court of the United States upon these questions of Constitutional law.

Transcontinental Railroad. That one of the necessities of the age, in a military, commercial, and postal point of view, is speedy communication between the Atlantic and Pacific States; and the Democratic party pledge such Constitutional Government aid as will insure the construction of a Railroad to the Pacific coast, at the earliest practicable period.

Cuba. That the Democratic party are in favor of the acquisition of the Island of Cuba on such terms as shall be honorable to ourselves and just to Spain.

Southern Democrats (Breckinridge Faction)

A small group of Southern delegates that bolted the Charleston convention met in Richmond, Va., in early June. They decided to delay action until after the resumed Democratic convention had concluded. In late June they met in Baltimore with bolters from the regular Democratic convention. There were representatives from 19 states among the more than 200 delegates attending, but most of

the 58 Northern delegates were officeholders in the Buchanan administration. Vice President John C. Breckinridge of Kentucky won the presidential nomination, and Sen. Joseph Lane of Oregon was chosen as his running mate.

The platform adopted by the Southern Democrats was similar to the one approved by the Democratic convention at Charleston. The bolters reaffirmed the Democrats' 1856 platform, called for the construction of a transcontinental railroad and acquisition of Cuba. But on the controversial slavery issue, the rump assemblage adopted the Southerners' plank defeated at the Charleston convention. The failure to reach agreement on this one issue, the most disruptive sectional split in the history of American political parties, presaged the Civil War.

Following are excerpts from the platform adopted by the Southern (or Breckinridge faction) Democrats in 1860:

Resolved, that the platform adopted by the Democratic party at Cincinnati be affirmed, with the following explanatory resolutions:

1. That the Government of a Territory organized by an act of Congress is provisional and temporary, and during its existence all citizens of the United States have an equal right to settle with their property in the Territory, without their rights, either of person or property, being destroyed or impaired by Congressional or Territorial legislation.

2. That it is the duty of the Federal Government, in all its departments, to protect, when necessary, the rights of persons and property in the Territories, and wherever else its constitutional authority extends.

Republicans

With their major opposition split along sectional lines, the Republicans gathered for their convention in Chicago in a mood of optimism. The Democrats had already broken up at Charleston before the Republican delegates convened in May 1860.

The call for the convention was addressed not only to faithful party members but to other groups that shared the Republicans' dissatisfaction with the policies of the Buchanan administration. The call to the convention particularly emphasized the party's opposition to any extension of slavery into the territories.

Delegates from all the Northern states and the territories of Kansas and Nebraska, the District of Columbia, and the slave states of Maryland, Delaware, Virginia, Kentucky, Missouri and Texas assembled at Chicago's new 10,000-seat convention hall, known as the Wigwam. A carnival-like atmosphere enveloped Chicago, with bands marching through the streets and thousands of enthusiastic Republicans ringing the overcrowded convention hall.

Inside, the delegates' first debate concerned the credentials report. The question was raised whether the represented Southern states should be allocated votes reflecting their electoral college strength, when there were very few Republicans in these states. By a vote of 275-1/2 to 171-1/2, the convention recommitted the credentials report for the purpose of scaling down the vote allocation of the Southern states.

A second debate arose over what constituted a nominating majority. The rules committee recommended that the nominating majority reflect the total electoral vote of all the states in the Union. The minority report argued that, since all the states were not represented, the nominating majority suggested by the rules committee would in fact require nearly a two-thirds majority. The minority report recommended instead that nominations be based on

a simple majority of votes allocated for the states represented. The minority report passed, 349-1/2 to 88-1/2.

Sen. William H. Seward of New York was the front-runner for the presidential nomination and led on the first ballot. Seward received 173-1/2 votes to lead runner-up Abraham Lincoln of Illinois, who had 102. Sen. Simon Cameron of Pennsylvania followed with 50-1/2 votes, Salmon P. Chase of Ohio with 49 and Edward Bates of Missouri with 48. *(Chart, p. 170)*

With the packed galleries cheering their native son, Lincoln closed the gap on the second roll call. After two ballots, the voting stood: Seward, 184-1/2; Lincoln, 181; Chase, 42-1/2; Bates, 35. Lincoln, who had gained national prominence two years earlier as a result of his debates on slavery with Democrat Stephen A. Douglas in the 1858 campaign for the U.S. Senate, emerged as the candidate of the anti-Seward forces. On the third ballot, he won the nomination. When the third roll call was completed, Lincoln's vote total stood at 231-1/2, 1-1/2 votes short of a majority. But Ohio quickly shifted four votes to Lincoln, giving him the nomination. After changes by other states, the final vote was Lincoln, 340; Seward, 121-1/2.

The primary contenders for the vice presidential nomination were Sen. Hannibal Hamlin of Maine and Cassius M. Clay of Kentucky. Hamlin assumed a strong lead on the first ballot, receiving 194 votes to 100-1/2 for Clay. On the second roll call, an increased vote for Hamlin from states in his native New England created a bandwagon for the Maine senator. Hamlin won the nomination on the second ballot with 367 votes, far outdistancing Clay, who received 86. After the roll call was completed, Hamlin's nomination was declared unanimous.

About half of the platform adopted by the Republican convention dealt with the slavery question. Unlike the Democrats, the Republicans clearly opposed the extension of slavery into the territories. However, the Republican platform also expressed support for states' rights, which served as a rebuke to radical abolitionism.

The Republican and Democratic platforms again were opposed on the question of internal improvements. The Republicans supported river and harbor improvements, while the Democrats, by reaffirming their 1856 platform, opposed any federal support for internal improvements. Both parties favored construction of a transcontinental railroad and opposed restrictions on immigration.

However, on two major issues, the Republicans went beyond the Democrats, advocating a protective tariff and homestead legislation.

Following are excerpts from the 1860 Republican platform:

Slavery. That the new dogma that the Constitution, of its own force, carries slavery into any or all of the territories of the United States, is a dangerous political heresy, at variance with the explicit provisions of that instrument itself, with contemporaneous exposition, and with legislative and judicial precedent; is revolutionary in its tendency, and subversive of the peace and harmony of the country.

That the normal condition of all the territory of the United States is that of freedom. . . . we deny the authority of Congress, of a territorial legislature, or of any individuals, to give legal existence to slavery in any territory of the United States.

States' Rights. That the maintenance inviolate of the rights of the states, and especially the right of each state to order and control its own domestic institutions according to its own judgment exclusively, is essential to that balance of powers on which the perfection and endurance of our political fabric depends; and we denounce the lawless invasion by armed force of the soil of any state or territory, no matter under what pretext, as among the gravest of crimes.

Tariff. That, while providing revenue for the support of the general government by duties upon imports, sound policy requires such an adjustment of these imports as to encourage the development of the industrial interests of the whole country.

Transcontinental Railroad. That a railroad to the Pacific Ocean is imperatively demanded by the interests of the whole country; that the federal government ought to render immediate and efficient aid in its construction; and that, as preliminary thereto, a daily overland mail should be promptly established.

Constitutional Union

At the invitation of a group of Southern Know-Nothing congressmen, the remnants of the 1856 Fillmore campaign, conservative Whigs and Know-Nothings, met in Baltimore in May 1860 to form the Constitutional Union Party.

The chief rivals for the presidential nomination were former Sen. John Bell of Tennessee and Gov. Sam Houston of Texas. Bell won on the second ballot, and Edward Everett of Massachusetts was selected as his running mate.

The Constitutional Union Party saw itself as a national unifying force in a time of crisis. The brief platform did not discuss issues, instead denouncing the sectionalism of the existing parties and calling for national unity.

Following are excerpts from the 1860 Constitutional Union platform:

Whereas, Experience has demonstrated that Platforms adopted by the partisan Conventions of the country have had the effect to mislead and deceive the people, and at the same time to widen the political divisions of the country, by the creation and encouragement of geographical and sectional parties; therefore

Resolved, that it is both the part of patriotism and of duty to *recognize* no political principle other than THE CONSTITUTION OF THE COUNTRY, THE UNION OF THE STATES, AND THE ENFORCEMENT OF THE LAWS.

1864 Conventions
Presidential Candidates

Abraham Lincoln
Republican

George McClellan
Democrat

Republicans (Union Party)

Although elements in the Republican Party were dissatisfied with the conduct of the Civil War, President Lincoln was in firm control of his party's convention, which met in Baltimore in June 1864. As with previous Republican conventions, the call was not limited to the party faithful. Democrats in support of the Lincoln war policy were encouraged to attend, and the name "Union Party" was used to describe the wartime coalition.

Delegates were present from all the Northern states, the territories, the District of Columbia and the slave states of Arkansas, Florida, Louisiana, Tennessee, South Carolina and Virginia. Credentials disputes occupied the early sessions. The credentials committee recommended that all the Southern states except South Carolina be admitted, but denied the right to vote. A minority report, advocating voting privileges for the Tennessee delegation, was passed, 310 to 151. A second minority report favoring voting privileges for Arkansas and Louisiana was approved, 307 to 167. However, the credentials committee recommendation that Florida and Virginia be denied voting rights, and South Carolina be excluded entirely, were accepted without a roll call.

Although dissatisfaction with the administration's war policy had spawned opposition to Lincoln, the boomlets for such presidential hopefuls as Treasury Secretary Salmon P. Chase had petered out by convention time. The Lincoln forces controlled the convention, and the president was easily renominated on the first ballot. Lincoln received 494 of the 516 votes cast, losing only Missouri's 22 votes, which were committed to Gen. Ulysses S. Grant. After the roll call, Missouri moved that the vote be made unanimous.

Lincoln did not publicly declare his preference for a vice presidential running mate, leaving the selection to the convention. The main contenders included the incumbent vice president, Hannibal Hamlin of Maine; the former senator and military governor of Tennessee, Democrat Andrew Johnson; and former senator Daniel S. Dickinson of New York. Johnson led on the first ballot with 200 votes, followed by Hamlin with 150 and Dickinson with 108. After completion of the roll call, a switch to Johnson by the

Kentucky delegation ignited a surge to the Tennesseean that delivered him 492 votes and the nomination.

The Republican (Union) platform was approved without debate. Unlike the Democrats, who criticized the war effort and called for a quick, negotiated peace, the Republicans favored a vigorous prosecution of the war until the South surrendered unconditionally. The Republicans called for the eradication of slavery, with its elimination embodied in a constitutional amendment.

Although the Republican document focused on the Civil War, it also included planks encouraging immigration, urging the speedy construction of a transcontinental railroad and reaffirming the Monroe Doctrine.

Following are excerpts from the Republican (Union) platform of 1864:

Resolved ... we pledge ourselves, as Union men, animated by a common sentiment and aiming at a common object, to do everything in our power to aid the Government in quelling by force of arms the Rebellion now raging against its authority, and in bringing to the punishment due to their crimes the Rebels and traitors arrayed against it.

Resolved, That we approve the determination of the Government of the United States not to compromise with Rebels, or to offer them any terms of peace, except such as may be based upon an unconditional surrender of their hostility and a return to their just allegiance to the Constitution and laws of the United States, and that we call upon the Government to maintain this position and to prosecute the war with the utmost possible vigor to the complete suppression of the Rebellion, in full reliance upon the self-sacrificing patriotism, the heroic valor and the undying devotion of the American people to the country and its free institutions.

Resolved, That as slavery was the cause, and now constitutes the strength of this Rebellion, and as it must be, always and everywhere, hostile to the principles of Republican Government, justice and the National safety demand its utter and complete extirpation from the soil of the Republic ... we are in favor, furthermore, of such an amendment to the Constitution, to be made by the people in conformity with its provisions, as shall terminate and forever prohibit the existence of Slavery within the limits of the jurisdiction of the United States.

Resolved, That the thanks of the American people are due to the soldiers and sailors of the Army and Navy, who have periled their lives in defense of the country and in vindication of the honor of its flag.

Democrats

The Democrats originally scheduled their convention for early summer but postponed it until late August to gauge the significance of military developments.

The party, badly split during the 1860 campaign, no longer had the Southern faction with which to contend. But while there was no longer a regional split, new divisions arose over the continuing war. There was a large peace faction, known as the Copperheads, that favored a quick, negotiated peace with the South. Another faction supported the war but criticized its handling by the Lincoln administration. A third faction supported Lincoln's conduct of the war and defected to support the Republican president.

Although factionalized, the Democratic delegates that assembled in Chicago were optimistic about their party's chances. The war-weary nation, they thought, was ready to vote out the Lincoln administration if there was not a quick change in Northern military fortunes.

Although the border states were represented at the Democratic convention, the territories and seceded Southern states were not. In spite of the party's internal divisions, there was little opposition to the presidential candidacy of Gen. George B. McClellan of New Jersey. The former commander of the Union Army won on the first ballot, receiving 174 of the 226 votes cast. Former governor Thomas H. Seymour of Connecticut trailed with 38 votes. A switch to McClellan by several Ohio delegates prompted shifts by other delegations and brought his total to 202-1/2. Clement Vallandigham, a leader of the Copperhead faction, moved that McClellan's nomination be made unanimous.

Eight candidates were placed in nomination for the vice presidency. James Guthrie of Kentucky led Rep. George H. Pendleton of Ohio, the favorite of the Copperheads, on the first ballot, 65-1/2 to 55. However, shifts to Pendleton by Illinois, Kentucky and New York after completion of the roll call created a bandwagon that led quickly to his unanimous nomination. In the convention hall at the time of his selection, Pendleton made a short speech of acceptance.

The platform adopted by the Democrats reflected the views of the Copperhead faction. The Lincoln administration's conduct of the Civil War was denounced, with particular criticism of the use of martial law and the abridgement of state and civil rights. The platform called for an immediate end to hostilities and a negotiated peace. The "sympathy" of the party was extended to soldiers and sailors involved in the war. Besides a criticism of the war and its conduct by the Lincoln administration, there were no other issues discussed in the platform.

Following are excerpts from the Democratic platform of 1864:

Resolved, That this convention does explicitly declare, as the sense of the American people, that after four years of failure to restore the Union by the experiment of war, during which, under the pretense of a military necessity of war-power higher than the Constitution, the Constitution itself has been disregarded in every part, and public liberty and private right alike trodden down, and the material prosperity of the country essentially impaired, justice, humanity, liberty, and the public welfare demand that immediate efforts be made for a cessation of hostilities, with a view of an ultimate convention of the States, or other peaceable means, to the end that, at the earliest practicable moment, peace may be restored on the basis of the Federal Union of the States.

Resolved, That the sympathy of the Democratic party is heartily and earnestly extended to the soldiery of our army and sailors of our navy, who are and have been in the field and on the sea under the flag of our country, and, in the events of its attaining power, they will receive all the care, protection, and regard that the brave soldiers and sailors of the republic have so nobly earned.

1868 Conventions
Presidential Candidates

Ulysses S. Grant
Republican

Horatio Seymour
Democrat

Republicans

The "National Union Republican Party," as the political organization was termed in its platform, held its first postwar convention in Chicago in May 1868. Delegations from the states of the old Confederacy were accepted; several included blacks.

The turbulent nature of postwar politics was evident in the fact that Gen. Ulysses S. Grant, the clear front-runner for the Republican nomination, had been considered a possible contender for the Democratic nomination barely a year earlier. Less than six months before the convention, the basically apolitical Grant had broken with Andrew Johnson, who had become president following the assassination of Abraham Lincoln in 1865.

Grant's was the only name placed in nomination, and on the ensuing roll call he received all 650 votes.

While the presidential race was cut and dried, the balloting for vice president was wide open, with 11 candidates receiving votes on the initial roll call. Sen. Benjamin F. Wade of Ohio led on the first ballot with 147 votes, followed by Gov. Reuben E. Fenton of New York with 126, Sen. Henry Wilson of Massachusetts with 119 and Speaker of the House Schuyler Colfax of Indiana with 115.

Over the next four ballots, Wade and Colfax were the front-runners, with Colfax finally moving ahead on the fifth ballot. His lead over Wade at this point was only 226 to 207, but numerous vote shifts after the roll call quickly pushed the Indiana representative over the top and gave him the nomination. After all the vote changes, Colfax's total stood at 541, followed by Fenton with 69 and Wade with 38.

Not surprisingly, the platform adopted by the Republicans differed sharply with the Democrats over reconstruction and Johnson's presidency. The Republican platform applauded the radical reconstruction program passed by Congress and denounced Johnson as "treacherous" and deserving of impeachment. The Republican platform approved of voting rights for black men in the South but determined that this was a subject for each state to decide in the rest of the nation.

The two parties also differed on their response to the currency question. While the Democrats favored a "soft-money" policy, the Republicans supported a continued "hard-money" approach, rejecting the Democratic proposal that the economic crisis could be eased by an increased supply of greenbacks.

Following are excerpts from the Republican platform of 1868:

Reconstruction. We congratulate the country on the assured success of the reconstruction policy of Congress, as evinced by the adoption, in the majority of the States lately in rebellion, of constitutions securing equal civil and political rights to all, and regard it as the duty of the Government to sustain those constitutions, and to prevent the people of such States from being remitted to a state of anarchy or military rule.

The guaranty by Congress of equal suffrage to all loyal men at the South was demanded by every consideration of public safety, of gratitude, and of justice, and must be maintained; while the question of suffrage in all the loyal States properly belongs to the people of those States.

President Andrew Johnson. We profoundly deplore the untimely and tragic death of Abraham Lincoln, and regret the accession of Andrew Johnson to the Presidency, who has acted treacherously to the people who elected him and the cause he was pledged to support; has usurped high legislative and judicial functions; has refused to execute the laws; has used his high office to induce other officers to ignore and violate the laws; has employed his executive powers to render insecure the property, the peace, the liberty, and life of the citizen; has abused the pardoning power; has denounced the National Legislature as unconstitutional; has persistently and corruptly resisted, by every means in his power, every proper attempt at the reconstruction of the States lately in rebellion; has perverted the public patronage into an engine of wholesale corruption; and has been justly impeached for high crimes and misdemeanors, and properly pronounced guilty thereof by the vote of thirty-five senators.

Currency. We denounce all forms of repudiation as a national crime; and national honor requires the payment of the public indebtedness in the utmost good faith to all creditors at home and abroad, not only according to the letter, but the spirit of the laws under which it was contracted.

Democrats

Reunited after the Civil War, the Democratic Party held its first postwar convention in New York's newly constructed Tammany Hall. It was no accident that convention proceedings began on July 4, 1868. The Democratic National Committee had set the date, and its chairman, August Belmont of New York, opened the first session with a harsh criticism of Republican reconstruction policy and the abridgement of civil rights.

Delegates from Southern states were voting members of the convention, but an effort to extend representation to the territories was defeated, 184 to 106.

Before the presidential balloting began, the convention chairman ruled that, as at the 1860 Charleston assembly, a nominating majority would be based on two-thirds of the total votes allocated (317) and not votes cast. On the opening ballot, the party's vice presidential candidate four years earlier, George H. Pendleton of Ohio, took the lead. Pendleton, although popular in the economically depressed Midwest because of his plan to inflate the currency by printing more greenbacks, had little appeal in the Eastern states. Nonetheless, he led on the first ballot with 105 votes. President Andrew Johnson was next, with 65 votes. Johnson's vote was largely complimentary and declined after the first roll call. Pendleton, however, showed increased strength, rising to a peak of 156-1/2 votes on the eighth ballot. But Pendleton's total was well short of the 212 votes required to nominate, and his total steadily decreased after the eighth roll call. *(Chart, p. 172)*

The collapse of the Pendleton and Johnson candidacies produced a boom for Gen. Winfield Scott Hancock of Pennsylvania. Opponents of Hancock attempted to break his surge by calling for adjournment after the 16th ballot. Although the move for adjournment was defeated, 174-1/2 to 142-1/2, the Hancock boom began to lose momentum. The Civil War general peaked at 144-1/2 votes on the 18th ballot, well short of a two-thirds majority.

With Hancock stymied, a new contender, Sen. Thomas A. Hendricks of Indiana, gained strength. Hendricks' vote rose to 132 on the 21st ballot, and the trend to the Indiana senator continued on the 22nd ballot until the roll call reached Ohio. However, Ohio shifted its entire vote to Horatio Seymour, the permanent chairman of the convention and a former governor of New York. Seymour declined to be a candidate, and so announced to the convention, but Ohio did not change its vote, and friends of Seymour hustled the reluctant candidate from the hall. The bandwagon had begun, and when the vote switches were completed, Seymour had received all 317 votes.

The vice presidential nomination went to Gen. Francis P. Blair Jr. of Missouri, a former Republican, who was unanimously selected on the first ballot. The names of several other candidates were placed in nomination, but the announcement of Blair's candidacy created a bandwagon that led to the withdrawal of the others.

The Democratic platform was accepted by a voice vote without debate. The platform began by declaring the questions of slavery and secession to be permanently settled by the Civil War. Several planks criticized the Republican reconstruction program, passed by the party's Radical wing in Congress. The Radicals themselves were scathingly denounced for their "unparalleled oppression and tyranny." The Democratic platform expressed its support for Andrew Johnson's conduct as president and decried the attempts to impeach him.

For the first time, the question of the coinage and printing of money was discussed in the party platform. Two planks were included that could be generally interpreted as supporting Pendleton's inflationary greenback plan.

On the tariff issue, the Democrats called for a tariff that would primarily raise revenue but also protect American industry.

Following are excerpts from the Democratic platform of 1868:

> **Reconstruction.** . . . we arraign the Radical party for its disregard of right, and the unparalleled oppression and tyranny which have marked its career.
>
> Instead of restoring the Union, it has, so far as in its power, dissolved it, and subjected ten States, in time of profound peace, to military despotism and negro supremacy.
>
> **President Andrew Johnson.** That the President of the United States, Andrew Johnson, in exercising the power of his high office in resisting the aggressions of Congress upon the Constitutional rights of the States and the people, is entitled to the gratitude of the whole American people; and in behalf of the Democratic party, we tender him our thanks for his patriotic efforts in that regard.
>
> **Currency.** . . . where the obligations of the government do not expressly state upon their face, or the law under which they were issued does not provide, that they shall be paid in coin, they ought, in right and in justice, to be paid in the lawful money of the United States. . . . One currency for the government and the people, the laborer and the officeholder, the pensioner and the soldier, the producer and the bond-holder.

CANISIUS COLLEGE LIBRARY
BUFFALO, N. Y.

1872 Conventions
Presidential Candidates

Horace Greeley
Liberal Republican, Democrat

Ulysses S. Grant
Republican

Liberal Republicans

The short-lived Liberal Republican Party grew out of grievances that elements in the Republican Party had with the policies of the Grant administration. There was particular dissatisfaction with the "carpetbag" governments in the South, support for extensive civil service reform and a general distaste for the corrupt administration of President Ulysses S. Grant.

The idea for the Liberal Republican movement originated in Missouri, where, in the 1870 state elections, a coalition of reform Republicans and Democrats swept to victory. In January 1872 a state convention of this new coalition issued the call for a national convention to be held that May in Cincinnati, Ohio.

Without a formal, nationwide organization, the delegate selection process was haphazard. Some of the delegates were self-appointed, but generally the size of each delegation reflected twice a state's electoral vote.

Three separate groups — reformers, anti-Grant politicians and a coalition of four influential newspaper editors known as "the Quadrilateral" — vied for control of the convention. For the presidential nomination, the reformers favored either Charles Francis Adams of Massachusetts or Sen. Lyman Trumbull of Illinois. The professional politicians were inclined to Supreme Court Justice David Davis of Illinois or Horace Greeley of New York. The newspaper editors opposed Davis.

On the first ballot, Adams led with 203 votes, followed by Greeley with 147, Trumbull with 110, Gov. B. Gratz Brown of Missouri with 95 and Davis with 92-1/2. After the roll call, Brown announced his withdrawal from the race and his support for Greeley. For the next five ballots, Greeley and Adams battled for the lead. But on the sixth ballot, the professional politicians were able to ignite a stampede for Greeley that resulted in his nomination.

Many of the reform-minded delegates, disgusted with the selection of the New York editor, left the convention. The vice presidential nomination went on the second ballot to a Greeley supporter, Gov. Brown of Missouri.

The platform adopted by the Liberal Republicans differed with the one later accepted by the Republicans on three main points: reconstruction, civil service reform and the tariff.

The Liberal Republicans called for an end to reconstruction with its "carpetbag" governments, a grant of universal amnesty to southern citizens and a return to home rule in the South. The Liberal Republicans sharply criticized the corruption of civil service under the Grant administration and labeled its reform one of the leading issues of the day. The civil service plank advocated a one-term limit on the presidency.

The presence of delegates supporting both protection and free trade led to a tariff plank that frankly stated the party's position on the issue should be left to local determination.

Following are excerpts from the Liberal Republican platform of 1872:

> **Reconstruction.** We demand the immediate and absolute removal of all disabilities imposed on account of the Rebellion, which was finally subdued seven years ago, believing that universal amnesty will result in complete pacification in all sections of the country.
>
> Local self-government, with impartial suffrage, will guard the rights of all citizens more securely than any centralized power. The public welfare requires the supremacy of the civil over the military authority, and freedom of person under the protection of the *habeas corpus.*
>
> **Civil Rights.** We recognize the equality of all men before the law, and hold that it is the duty of Government in its dealings with the people to mete out equal and exact justice to all of whatever nativity, race, color, or persuasion, religious or political.
>
> **Civil Service Reform.** The Civil Service of the Government has become a mere instrument of partisan tyranny and personal ambition and an object of selfish greed. It is a scandal and reproach upon free institutions and breeds a demoralization dangerous to the perpetuity of republican government. We therefore regard such thorough reforms of the Civil Service as one of the most pressing necessities of the hour; that honesty, capacity, and fidelity constitute the only valid claim to public employment; that the offices of the Government cease to be a matter of arbitrary favoritism and patronage, and that public station become again a post of honor. To this end it is imperatively

required that no President shall be a candidate for re-election.

Tariff.. . . . recognizing that there are in our midst honest but irreconcilable differences of opinion with regard to the respective systems of Protection and Free Trade, we remit the discussion of the subject to the people in their Congress Districts, and to the decision of Congress thereon, wholly free of Executive interference or dictation.

Homesteading. We are opposed to all further grants of lands to railroads or other corporations. The public domain should be held sacred to actual settlers.

Democrats

The Democratic convention that met in Baltimore in July 1872 was one of the most bizarre in American political history. In sessions totaling only six hours, the delegates endorsed the decisions on candidates and platform made at a convention one month earlier by the Liberal Republicans. The Democratic convention merely rubber-stamped the creation of a coalition of Liberal Republicans and the core of the Democratic Party. *(Chart, p. 173)*

This new coalition was established with little dissent. When it came time for the presidential balloting, nominating speeches were not allowed. On the subsequent roll call, Greeley, the nominee of the Liberal Republicans, received 686 of the allotted 732 votes. It was an ironic choice, because in earlier decades Greeley, as editor of *The New York Tribune,* had been a frequent critic of the Democratic Party. More than anything else, however, Greeley's selection underscored the lack of strong leadership in the post-Civil War Democratic Party.

In similar fashion, the convention endorsed the nomination of B. Gratz Brown for vice president. Brown, the governor of Missouri and the choice of the Liberal Republicans, was the early unanimous nominee of the Democrats, with 713 votes.

By a vote of 574 to 158, the delegates agreed to limit debate on the platform to one hour. Except for a brief introduction, the Democrats approved the same platform that had been adopted by the Liberal Republicans a month earlier. Key planks called for an end to reconstruction and complete amnesty for Southern citizens, a return to a federal government with limited powers, civil service reform and the halt of grants of public land to railroads and other corporations. Ironically, the platform also favored a hard-money policy, a reversal of the Democrats' soft-money stand in 1868. Although there was some objection to the point-by-point acceptance of the Liberal Republican platform, it was adopted by a vote of 671 to 62. *(For platform excerpts, see the Liberal Republican section, p. 52.)*

Republicans

With the reform wing of the Republican Party already having bolted, the remaining elements of the party gathered in relative harmony in Philadelphia in June 1872. President Ulysses S. Grant was renominated without opposition, receiving all 752 votes cast. *(Chart, p. 173)*

The only contest at the convention centered around the vice presidential nomination, with the incumbent, Schuyler Colfax of Indiana, and Sen. Henry Wilson of Massachusetts the two major rivals. Wilson took a slim plurality over Colfax on the first roll call, 364-1/2 to 321-1/2, but a vote shift by Virginia after completion of the roll gave Wilson the necessary majority with 399-1/2 votes.

Without debate or opposition, the platform was adopted. It lauded the 11 years of Republican rule, noting the success of reconstruction, the hard-money policy and the homestead program. A tariff plank called for a duty on imports to raise revenue as well as to protect American business.

The platform also included several progressive planks, including a recommendation that the franking privilege be abolished, an extension of rights to women and a call for federal and state legislation that would ensure equal rights for all races throughout the nation. The last plank was a significant change from the 1868 platform, which called for black suffrage in the South but left the decision on black voting rights to the individual states elsewhere.

Following are excerpts from the Republican platform of 1872:

Reconstruction. We hold that Congress and the President have only fulfilled an imperative duty in their measures for the suppression of violent and treasonable organizations in certain lately rebellious regions, and for the protection of the ballot-box, and therefore they are entitled to the thanks of the nation.

Civil Rights. Complete liberty and exact equality in the enjoyment of all civil, political, and public rights should be established and effectually maintained throughout the Union, by efficient and appropriate State and Federal legislation. Neither the law nor its administration should admit any discrimination in respect of citizens by reason of race, creed, color, or previous condition of servitude.

Civil Service Reform. Any system of the civil service under which the subordinate positions of the government are considered rewards for mere party zeal is fatally demoralizing, and we therefore favor a reform of the system by laws which shall abolish the evils of patronage, and make honesty, efficiency, and fidelity the essential qualifications for public positions, without practically creating a life-tenure of office.

Tariff.. . . .revenue . . . should be raised by duties upon importations, the details of which should be so adjusted as to aid in securing remunerative wages to labor, and to promote the industries, prosperity, and growth of the whole country.

Homesteading. We are opposed to further grants of the public lands to corporations and monopolies, and demand that the national domain be set apart for free homes for the people.

Women's Rights. The Republican party is mindful of its obligations to the loyal women of America for their noble devotion to the cause of freedom. Their admission to wider fields of usefulness is viewed with satisfaction, and the honest demand of any class of citizens for additional rights should be treated with respectful consideration.

1876 Conventions
Presidential Candidates

Rutherford B. Hayes
Republican

Samuel J. Tilden
Democrat

Republicans

The Republican convention assembled in Cincinnati, Ohio, in mid-June 1876. The call to the convention extended the olive branch to the dissident Liberal Republicans, who in large measure had rejoined their original party.

One of the highlights of the early sessions was a speech by the prominent black leader, Frederick Douglass, who lambasted the Republicans for freeing the slaves without providing means for their economic or physical security.

A dispute developed over the seating of two contesting Alabama delegations. It was a candidate-oriented dispute, with the majority report favoring a delegation strongly for House Speaker James G. Blaine of Maine. The minority report supported a delegation pledged to Sen. Oliver P. Morton of Indiana. In the subsequent roll call, the convention decided in favor of the Blaine delegation by a vote of 369 to 360.

The presidential race was contested by the champions of the three nearly equal wings of the party. The Radicals were led by senators Roscoe Conkling of New York and Morton; the Half-Breeds, by Blaine, and the reformers by former treasury secretary Benjamin H. Bristow of Kentucky.

A fiery nominating speech for Blaine, delivered by Col. Robert G. Ingersoll, referred to the House Speaker as the "plumed knight," an appellation that stuck with Blaine the rest of his political career. Although it was a compelling speech, its effect was reduced by a failure in the hall's lighting system, which forced an early adjournment.

Nonetheless, when balloting commenced the next morning, Blaine had a wide lead, receiving 285 votes on the first ballot, compared with 124 for Morton, 113 for Bristow and 99 for Conkling. *(Chart, p. 175)*

In the middle of the second ballot, a procedural dispute arose over the legality of the unit rule. Three delegates in the Pennsylvania delegation wished to vote for another candidate and appealed to the chair. The chair ruled that their votes should be counted, even though Pennsylvania was bound by the state convention to vote as a unit. The ruling of the chair was upheld on a voice vote, but subsequent debate brought a roll call on reconsidering

the decision. The motion to reconsider passed, 381 to 359. However, by a margin of 395 to 353, another roll call upheld the power of the convention chairman to abolish the unit rule.

Although the vote had long-range significance for future Republican conventions, in the short run it provided a slight boost for Blaine, who gained several delegates in Pennsylvania. On the next four ballots, Blaine retained his large lead but could not come close to the necessary 379 votes needed for nomination. The only candidate to show increased strength was Gov. Rutherford B. Hayes of Ohio, who jumped from 68 votes on the fourth roll call to 104 on the fifth.

On the sixth ballot, however, Blaine showed renewed strength, rising to 308 votes, while Hayes assumed second place with 113. The House Speaker continued to gain on the seventh ballot, but the anti-Blaine forces quickly and successfully united behind Hayes. The Ohio governor, a viable compromise choice who had not alienated any of the party factions, won the nomination with 384 votes to 351 for Blaine.

Five candidates were placed in nomination for the vice presidency. However, Rep. William A. Wheeler of New York was so far in the lead that the roll call was suspended after South Carolina voted, and Wheeler was declared the nominee by acclamation.

Platform debate centered on the party's immigration plank. A Massachusetts delegate proposed deletion of the plank, which called for a congressional investigation of oriental immigration. The delegate argued that the plank was inconsistent with the Republican principle that favored the equality of all races. However, by a vote of 518 to 229, the plank was retained as written.

The Republican platform included a scathing denunciation of the Democratic Party, but only on the issues of currency and tariff was it markedly different from the opposition. The Republicans, unlike the Democrats, favored complete payment of Civil War bonds in hard money as quickly as possible. While the Democrats supported a tariff for revenue purposes only, the Republicans implied that the tariff should protect American industry as well as raise revenue.

As in past platforms, the Republicans called for the extension of civil rights, civil service reform, increased rights for women, the abolition of polygamy and the distribution of public land to homesteaders. A new plank proposed that a constitutional amendment be passed forbidding the use of federal funds for non-public schools.

Following are excerpts from the Republican platform of 1876:

> **Currency.** In the first act of congress, signed by President Grant, the national government ... solemnly pledged its faith "to make provisions at the earliest practicable period, for the redemption of the United States notes in coin." Commercial prosperity, public morals, and the national credit demand that this promise be fulfilled by a continuous and steady progress to specie payment.
>
> **Tariff.** The revenue necessary for current expenditures and the obligations of the public debt must be largely derived from duties upon importations, which, so far as possible, should be so adjusted as to promote the interests of American labor and advance the prosperity of the whole country.
>
> **Immigration.** It is the immediate duty of congress fully to investigate the effects of the immigration and importation of Mongolians on the moral and material interests of the country.
>
> **Education.** The public school system of the several states is the bulwark of the American republic; and, with a view to its security and permanence, we recommend an amendment to the constitution of the United States, forbidding the application of any public funds or property for the benefit of any school or institution under sectarian control.
>
> **Democratic Party.** We therefore note with deep solicitude that the Democratic party counts, as its chief hope of success, upon the electoral vote of a united South, secured through the efforts of those who were recently arrayed against the nation; and we invoke the earnest attention of the country to the grave truth, that a success thus achieved would reopen sectional strife and imperil national honor and human rights.
>
> We charge the Democratic party with being the same in character and spirit as when it sympathized with treason; with making its control of the house of representatives the triumph and opportunity of the nation's recent foes; with reasserting and applauding in the national capitol the sentiments of unrepentant rebellion; with sending Union soldiers to the rear, and promoting Confederate soldiers to the front; with deliberately proposing to repudiate the plighted faith of the government; with being equally false and imbecile upon the over-shadowing financial question; with thwarting the ends of justice, by its partisan mismanagements and obstruction of investigation; with proving itself, through the period of its ascendency in the lower house of Congress, utterly incompetent to administer the government; — and we warn the country against trusting a party thus alike unworthy, recreant, and incapable.

Democrats

America's rapid westward expansion was typified by the site of the Democratic Party's 1876 convention — St. Louis, Mo. It marked the first time that a national convention was held west of the Mississippi River.

The Democratic delegates assembled in late June. The one procedural matter debated was a proposal that the two-thirds rule be abolished at the 1880 convention and that the Democratic National Committee include such a recommendation in its next convention call. A move to table the proposal was defeated, 379 to 359. However, the national committee took no action on the proposal.

Two governors, Samuel J. Tilden of New York and Thomas A. Hendricks of Indiana, were the principal contenders for the presidential nomination, with Tilden having a substantial lead in delegates as the convention opened. Ironically, Tilden's most vocal opposition came from his own New York delegation, where John Kelly of Tammany Hall spearheaded an effort to undermine Tilden's candidacy. Tilden's reform moves as governor had alienated Tammany Hall, and several times during the convention, Kelly took the floor to denounce Tilden.

Nonetheless, Tilden had a substantial lead on the first ballot, receiving 401-1/2 votes to 140-1/2 for Hendricks. Although short of the 492 votes needed to nominate, Tilden moved closer when Missouri switched its votes to him after the first roll call. The movement to Tilden continued on the second ballot, and he finished the roll call with 535 votes, more than enough to assure his nomination. *(Chart, p. 174)*

Hendricks, the runner-up for the presidential nomination, was the nearly unanimous choice of the delegates for the vice presidency. Hendricks received 730 votes, with the other eight votes not being cast.

The Democratic platform was an unusual one. Rather than being arranged in usual fashion with a series of numbered planks, it was written in paragraph form in language unusually powerful for a party platform. The theme of the document was the need for reform, and nearly half the paragraphs began with the phrase, "Reform is necessary. . . ."

Debate focused on the party's stand on the currency issue. The majority report proposed repeal of the Resumption Act of 1875, a hard-money measure that called for the payment of Civil War bonds in coin. A minority report sponsored by delegates from five eastern states proposing deletion of this position was defeated, 550 to 219. A second minority report, introduced by Midwestern delegates, favored a more strongly worded opposition to the Resumption Act. It too was defeated, 505 to 229, with Midwestern delegations providing the bulk of the minority vote. The platform as a whole was approved, 651 to 83, again with most of the dissenting votes coming from the Midwest.

Besides the currency proposal, the platform called for extensive civil service reform, a tariff for revenue purposes only, restrictions on Chinese immigration and a new policy on the distribution of public land that would benefit the homesteaders and not the railroads. In addition to its reform theme, the platform was filled with sharp criticisms of Republican rule.

Following are excerpts from the Democratic platform of 1876:

> **Civil Service Reform.** Reform is necessary in the civil service. Experience proves that efficient economical conduct of the government is not possible if its civil service be subject to change at every election, be a prize fought for at the ballot-box, be an approved reward of party zeal instead of posts of honor assigned for proved competency and held for fidelity in the public employ; that the dispensing of patronage should neither be a tax upon the time of our public men nor an instrument of their ambition. Here again, profession falsified in the performance attest that the party in power can work out no practical or salutary reform. Reform is necessary even more in the higher grades of the public service. President, Vice-President, judges, senators, representatives, cabinet officers — these and all others in authority are the people's servants. Their offices are not a private perquisite; they are a public trust. When the annals of this Republic show disgrace and censure of a Vice-

President; a late Speaker of the House of Representatives marketing his rulings as a presiding officer; three Senators profiting secretly by their votes as law-makers; five chairmen of the leading committees of the late House of Representatives exposed in jobbery; a late Secretary of the Treasury forcing balances in the public accounts; a late Attorney-General misappropriating public funds; a Secretary of the Navy enriched and enriching friends by a percentage levied off the profits of contractors with his department; an Ambassador to England censured in a dishonorable speculation; the President's Private Secretary barely escaping conviction upon trial for guilty complicity in frauds upon the revenue; a Secretary of War impeached for high crimes and misdemeanors — the demonstration is complete, that the first step in reform must be the people's choice of honest men from another party, lest the disease of one political organization infect the body politic, and lest by making no change of men or parties, we get no change of measures and no real reform.

Currency. We denounce the improvidence which, in eleven years of peace, has taken from the people in Federal taxes thirteen times the whole amount of the legal-tender notes and squandered four times their sum in useless expense, without accumulating any reserve for their redemption. We denounce the financial imbecility and immorality of that party, which, during eleven years of peace, has made no advance toward resumption, no preparation for resumption, but instead has obstructed resumption by wasting our resources and exhausting all our surplus income, and while annually professing to intend a speedy return to specie payments, has annually enacted fresh hindrances thereto. As such hindrance we denounce the resumption clause of the act of 1875 and we here demand its repeal.

Tariff. We denounce the present tariff levied upon nearly four thousand articles as a masterpiece of injustice, inequality and false pretense, which yields a dwindling and not a yearly rising revenue, has impoverished many industries to subsidize a few.... We demand that all custom-house taxation shall be only for revenue.

Homesteading. Reform is necessary to put a stop to the profligate waste of public lands and their diversion from actual settlers by the party in power, which has squandered two hundred millions of acres upon railroads alone, and out of more than thrice that aggregate has disposed of less than a sixth directly to the tillers of the soil.

Immigration. ... we denounce the policy which thus discards the liberty-loving German and tolerates the revival of the coolie-trade in Mongolian women for immoral purposes, and Mongolian men held to perform servile labor contracts, and demand such modification of the treaty with the Chinese Empire, or such legislation within constitutional limitations, as shall prevent further importation or immigration of the Mongolian race.

1880 Conventions

Presidential Candidates

James A. Garfield
Republican

James B. Weaver
Greenback

Winfield Hancock
Democrat

Republicans

The Republicans gathered in Chicago beginning June 2, 1880, for their seventh quadrennial nominating convention. For the first time, the convention call was addressed only to Republicans and not more broadly to others who sympathized with party principles.

The convention was divided into two factions. One, headed by Sen. Roscoe Conkling of New York, favored the nomination of former president Ulysses S. Grant for a third term. The anti-Grant faction, although not united around one candidate, included the eventual nominee, Rep. James A. Garfield of Ohio, among its leaders.

Pre-convention skirmishing focused on the selection of a temporary chairman. The Grant forces desired one from their own ranks who would uphold the unit rule — a rule important to Grant, because he had the support of a majority of delegates in several large states. However, the Grant strategy was blocked, and a temporary chairman neutral to both sides was chosen by the Republican National Committee, leaving the ultimate decision on the unit rule to the convention.

A test of strength between the two factions came early in the convention on an amended motion by Conkling directing the credentials committee to report to the convention prior to the rules committee. Conkling's amended motion was defeated, 406 to 318.

In spite of the defeat of the amended motion, much time was spent debating delegate credentials. More than 50

cases were presented in committee, and seven of them came to the floor for a vote. Five of the cases featured seating disputes among delegates selected in district caucuses and those chosen for the same seats in state conventions. In each case — involving delegates from the states of Illinois, Kansas and West Virginia — the convention supported the claim of the delegates elected at the district level.

The Illinois credentials fight produced the only candidate-oriented division, with the Grant forces favoring the seating of the delegates selected at the state convention. But by a margin of 387 to 353, the convention voted to seat the delegates selected in the district caucuses. Three other votes were taken on disputed credentials from different Illinois districts, but all were decided in favor of the anti-Grant forces by a similar margin. *(Chart, p. 177)*

The majority report of the rules committee advocated that the controversial unit rule not be used. A motion by the Grant forces that the presidential nominations begin without passage of the rules committee report was defeated, 479 to 276. The vote was a key setback for the supporters of the former president, as the majority report was subsequently adopted by acclamation.

While the Grant forces suffered defeat on adoption of the unit rule, their candidate assumed the lead on the first ballot for president, with 304 votes. Sen. James G. Blaine of Maine followed closely with 284, and Treasury Secretary John Sherman of Ohio, the candidate nominated by Rep. Garfield, trailed with 93 votes.

Ballot after ballot was taken throughout the day, but after the 28th roll call, the last of the night, there was little change in the vote totals of the leading candidates. Grant led with 307 votes; Blaine had 279, and Sherman, 91.

When balloting resumed the next morning, Sherman's vote total jumped to 116, the biggest gain among the contenders, but still well behind Grant and Blaine. Grant gained votes on the 34th ballot, rising to a new high of 312, but on the same roll call a boom for Garfield began, with the Ohio representative collecting 16 votes from Wisconsin. Garfield protested that he was not a candidate but was ruled out of order by the chairman.

The Ohio representative continued to gain on the 35th ballot, his vote total rising to 50. On the next ballot, Garfield won the nomination, receiving the votes of nearly all the anti-Grant delegates. At the end of the roll call, Garfield had 399 votes; Grant, 306, and Blaine, 42, with nine votes distributed among other candidates.

Four men were placed in nomination for the vice presidency, but Chester A. Arthur of New York was the easy winner on the first ballot. Arthur, the former collector of the port of New York, received 468 votes to 193 for former representative Elihu B. Washburne of Illinois. Most of Arthur's support came from delegates who had backed Grant.

The Republican platform was passed by a voice vote without debate. For the first time, the platform included planks that clearly called for the exercise of federal power, emphasizing that the Constitution was "a supreme law, and not a mere contract." This philosophy contrasted with the Democratic platform, which favored home rule and government decentralization.

The two parties also differed on the tariff issue. The Republicans favored a revenue tariff that would also protect American industry, while the Democrats explicitly called for a revenue tariff only.

In its original form, the Republican platform did not include a civil service plank. An amendment from the floor, however, calling for a "thorough, radical and complete" reform of the civil service, was passed by a voice vote.

Following are excerpts from the Republican platform of 1880:

Federal Power. The Constitution of the United States is a supreme law, and not a mere contract. Out of confederated States it made a sovereign nation. Some powers are denied to the Nation, while others are denied to the States; but the boundary between the powers delegated and those reserved is to be determined by the National and not by the State tribunal.

The work of popular education is one left to the care of the several States, but it is the duty of the National Government to aid that work to the extent of its constitutional power. The intelligence of the Nation is but the aggregate of the intelligence in the several States, and the destiny of the Nation must be guided, not by the genius of any one State, but by the aggregate genius of all.

Tariff. We affirm the belief, avowed in 1876, that the duties levied for the purpose of revenue should so discriminate as to favor American labor. . . .

Civil Service Reform. The Republican party, . . . adopts the declaration of President Hayes that the reform of the civil service should be thorough, radical and complete.

Chinese Immigration. . . . the Republican party, regarding the unrestricted immigration of the Chinese as a matter of grave concernment . . . would limit and restrict that immigration by the enactment of such just, humane and reasonable laws and treaties as will produce that result.

Greenback Party

A coalition of farmer and labor groups met in Chicago beginning June 9, 1880, to hold the second national Greenback Party convention. The party's first convention was held four years earlier, but it was not until 1880 that the Greenback Party received more than 2 percent of the popular vote. The party held its third and final convention four years later, but was unable in 1884 to attain 2 percent of the popular vote.

The 1880 convention attracted representatives of the various Greenback Party factions, as well as 44 delegates from the Socialist Labor Party. Rep. James B. Weaver of Iowa was nominated for the presidency, and B. J. Chambers of Texas was chosen as his running mate.

The platform adopted was far broader than the one conceived by the Greenbacks at their first convention in 1876. That year they focused solely on the currency issue. For the agrarian interests, currency planks remained that called for the unlimited coinage of silver and gold and the issuance of currency by the federal government and not private banks. Also adopted for the farm elements were planks advocating increased public land for settlers, denouncing large monopolies and proposing that Congress control passenger and freight rates.

Included for the labor groups were proposals for an eight-hour day, the abolition of child labor, the improvement of working conditions and the curtailment of Chinese immigration.

The Greenback platform also included planks that favored a graduated income tax and women's suffrage.

Following are excerpts from the Greenback platform of 1880:

Currency. . . . All money, whether metallic or paper, should be issued and its volume controlled by the Government, and not by or through banking corporations, and

when so issued should be a full legal-tender for all debts, public and private.

That the bonds of the United States should not be refunded, but paid as rapidly as practicable, according to contract. To enable the Government to meet these obligations, legal-tender currency should be substituted for the notes of the National banks, the National banking system abolished, and the unlimited coinage of silver, as well as gold, established by law.

Labor. That labor should be so protected by National and State authority as to equalize the burdens and insure a just distribution of its results; the eight-hour law of Congress should be enforced, the sanitary condition of industrial establishments placed under rigid control; the competition of contract labor abolished, a bureau of labor statistics established, factories, mines, and workshops inspected, the employment of children under fourteen years of age forbidden, and wages paid in cash.

Chinese Immigration. Slavery being simply cheap labor, and cheap labor being simple slavery, the importation and presence of Chinese serfs necessarily tends to brutalize and degrade American labor.

Homesteading. Railroad and land grants forfeited by reason of non-fulfillment of contract should be immediately reclaimed by the Government, and henceforth the public domain reserved exclusively as homes for actual settlers.

Regulation of Monopolies. It is the duty of Congress to regulate inter-state commerce. All lines of communication and transportation should be brought under such legislative control as shall secure moderate, fair and uniform rates for passenger and freight traffic.

We denounce as destructive to prosperity and dangerous to liberty, the action of the old parties in fostering and sustaining gigantic land, railroad, and money corporations and monopolies, invested with, and exercising powers belonging to the Government, and yet not responsible to it for the manner of their exercise.

Income Tax. All property should bear its just proportion of taxation, and we demand a graduated income tax.

Women's Suffrage. That every citizen of due age, sound mind, and not a felon, be fully enfranchised, and that this resolution be referred to the States, with recommendation for their favorable consideration.

Democrats

The Democrats held their 13th quadrennial nominating convention in Cincinnati, Ohio, in late June 1880. Credentials disputes enlivened the early sessions, with two competing New York delegations the focus of attention. The challenging group, controlled by Tammany Hall, requested 20 of New York's 70 votes. But by a margin of 457 to 205-1/2, the convention refused the request.

Samuel J. Tilden, the Democratic standard-bearer in 1876 and the narrow loser in that controversial election, was not a candidate in 1880, although he did not officially notify his supporters of this fact until the presidential balloting had begun. Tilden's indecision, however, had long before opened the door for other prospective candidates.

On the first ballot, Gen. Winfield Scott Hancock of Pennsylvania, a candidate for the nomination in both 1868 and 1876, led with 171 votes, followed by Sen. Thomas F. Bayard of Delaware with 153-1/2 and former representative

Henry G. Payne of Ohio (who served as a stalking horse for the Tilden forces), with 81.

Tilden's declaration of non-candidacy was announced before the second ballot, and the Tilden forces shifted their strength to House Speaker Samuel J. Randall of Pennsylvania. Nonetheless, Hancock was the big gainer on the second ballot, his vote total jumping to 320. Randall followed with 128-1/2, and Bayard slipped to third place with 112. Although Hancock was well short of the 492 votes needed for nomination, Wisconsin began a string of vote switches to Hancock that resulted in the military leader's selection. After all the changes, Hancock received 705 of the 738 votes cast.

The vice presidential nomination went by acclamation to former representative William H. English of Indiana, the only candidate.

The platform was accepted without debate or opposition. Its style of short, sharp phrases contrasted with the 1876 platform, which was written in flowing sentences built around the theme of the necessity of reform.

The 1880 platform called for decentralization of the federal government with increased local government, currency based on hard money, a tariff for revenue only, civil service reform and an end to Chinese immigration. The platform saved its harshest language to describe the party's reaction to the controversial election of 1876, which it labeled "the great fraud."

Following are excerpts from the Democratic platform of 1880:

Government Centralization. Opposition to centralization and to that dangerous spirit of encroachment which tends to consolidate the powers of all departments in one, and thus to create whatever be the form of government, a real despotism. No sumptuary laws; separation of Church and State, for the good of each; common schools fostered and protected.

Currency. Home rule; honest money, consisting of gold and silver, and paper convertible into coin on demand.

Tariff. . . . a tariff for revenue only.

Civil Service Reform. We execrate the course of this administration in making places in the civil service a reward for political crime, and demand a reform by statute which shall make it forever impossible for a defeated candidate to bribe his way to the seat of the usurper by billeting villains upon the people.

Chinese Immigration. No more Chinese immigration, except for travel, education, and foreign commerce, and that even carefully guarded.

Election of 1876. The great fraud of 1876-77, by which, upon a false count of the electoral voters of two States, the candidate defeated at the polls was declared to be President, and for the first time in American history, the will of the people was set aside under a threat of military violence, struck a deadly blow at our system of representative government. The Democratic party, to preserve the country from the horrors of a civil war, submitted for the time in firm and patriotic faith that the people would punish this crime in 1880. This issue precedes and dwarfs every other. It imposes a more sacred duty upon the people of the Union than ever addressed the conscience of a nation of free men.

1884 Conventions

Presidential Candidates

James G. Blaine
Republican

Grover Cleveland
Democrat

Republicans

The Republicans gathered in Chicago in June 1884 for their convention. For the first time, the call to the convention prescribed how and when delegates should be selected, an effort to avoid the credentials disputes that had besieged the convention four years earlier.

The assassination of President James A. Garfield three years earlier had opened up the Republican presidential race, and the party war horse, James G. Blaine of Maine, emerged as the front-runner for the nomination. However, there was strong opposition to Blaine from several candidates, including the incumbent president, Chester A. Arthur of New York.

The first test between the two sides was over the choice of a temporary chairman. The Blaine forces supported former senator Powell Clayton of Arkansas, while the anti-Blaine coalition favored a black delegate from Mississippi, John R. Lynch. Lynch won by a vote of 424 to 384.

A motion by the Blaine forces to adjourn after the presidential nominating speeches was also beaten, 412 to 391. But on the first ballot Blaine assumed the lead with 334-1/2 votes, followed by President Arthur with 278 and Sen. George F. Edmunds of Vermont with 93. Most of Arthur's strength was in the South, where the administration's patronage power had great effect.

Blaine gained votes on the next two ballots, his total rising to 375 on the third ballot, while Arthur dropped slightly to 274. After this roll call, the anti-Blaine forces tried to force adjournment but were defeated, 458 to 356. On the fourth ballot, Blaine received the nomination, winning 541 votes to 207 for Arthur and 41 for Edmunds.

Sen. John A. Logan of Illinois was the only person placed in nomination for vice president. Logan, who earlier had been in contention for the presidential nomination, received 779 of the 820 votes in the convention for second place on the ticket.

The party platform was adopted without dissent, and on major issues was little different from the planks presented by the Democrats. The Republicans proposed a tariff that would both protect American industry and raise revenue, called for civil service reform, advocated restric-

tions on Chinese immigration and favored increased availability of public lands for settlers. In addition, the Republicans adopted features of the Greenback Party platform, calling for government regulation of railroads and an eight-hour work day.

Following are excerpts from the Republican platform of 1884:

> **Tariff.** We . . . demand that the imposition of duties on foreign imports shall be made, not "for revenue only," but that in raising the requisite revenues for the government, such duties shall be so levied as to afford security to our diversified industries and protection to the rights and wages of the laborer; to the end that active and intelligent labor, as well as capital, may have its just reward, and the laboring man his full share in the national prosperity.

> **Chinese Immigration.** . . . we denounce the importation of contract labor, whether from Europe or Asia, as an offense against the spirit of American institutions; and we pledge ourselves to sustain the present law restricting Chinese immigration, and to provide such further legislation as is necessary to carry out its purposes.

> **Labor.** We favor the establishment of a national bureau of labor; the enforcement of the eight hour law.

> **Regulation of Railroads.** The principle of public regulation of railway corporations is a wise and salutary one for the protection of all classes of the people; and we favor legislation that shall prevent unjust discrimination and excessive charges for transportation, and that shall secure to the people, and the railways alike, the fair and equal protection of the laws.

Democrats

The 1884 Democratic convention was held in Chicago in July. For the first time, the party extended delegate voting rights to the territories and the District of Columbia.

A debate over the unit rule highlighted the first day of the convention. Delegates from Tammany Hall, a minority of the New York delegation, presented an amendment to the temporary rules designed to abolish the unit rule. All the New York delegates were bound by their state convention to vote as a unit. However, the national convention

defeated the amendment by a vote of 463 to 332, thus limiting the power of the Tammany delegates.

A resolution was passed opening the position of party chairman to individuals who were not members of the Democratic National Committee. Another resolution, to eliminate the two-thirds rule at future conventions, was put to a vote, but the roll call was suspended when it became apparent the resolution would not pass.

Several peculiarities were evident during the presidential nominating speeches. Sen. Thomas A. Hendricks of Indiana, the favorite of the Hoosier delegation, nominated former senator Joseph E. McDonald as the state's favorite son in a speech listing attributes that easily could have described Hendricks. Two seconding speeches for Gov. Grover Cleveland of New York were delivered by Tammany delegates who actually used the time to denounce him.

In spite of the opposition within his own delegation, Cleveland was the front-runner for the nomination and had a big lead on the first ballot. Cleveland received 392 votes, easily outdistancing Sen. Thomas F. Bayard of Delaware, who had 170. Former senator Allen G. Thurman of Ohio was next, with 88. Hendricks received one vote but protested to the convention that he was not a candidate.

A boom for Hendricks was undertaken on the second ballot, with the Indiana delegation shifting its support from McDonald to Hendricks. However, Cleveland also gained and continued to hold a large lead over the rest of the field. After two roll calls, these vote totals stood: Cleveland, 475; Bayard, 151-1/2; Hendricks, 123-1/2; Thurman, 60. With the New York governor holding a majority of the vote, North Carolina switched to Cleveland, and this started a bandwagon that gave him the required two-thirds majority. After the shifts, Cleveland received 683 of the 820 votes in the convention.

Over the objections of the Indiana delegation, Hendricks was nominated for the vice presidency. The Indiana leaders were a bit upset that Hendricks did not receive the presidential nomination but did contribute to his nearly unanimous total for second place on the ticket. When the roll call was completed, Hendricks had received all but four votes.

The Democratic platform of 1884 was one of the longest documents adopted by the party in the 19th century. The platform was about 3,000 words long, with the first third devoted to a description of alleged Republican failures.

The platform straddled the increasingly important tariff issue. In 1880 the Democrats clearly favored a revenue tariff only, but the 1884 document called for both revenue and protection of American industry.

A minority report introduced by Benjamin F. Butler, former governor of Massachusetts, focused on the tariff issue. Butler advocated a duty on imports that would hit harder at luxury items and less on necessities than the tariff favored by the majority report and would ensure more protection for American labor. The minority report was defeated, 721-1/2 to 96-1/2.

Butler, a former Republican and, earlier in 1884, nominated for president by the Greenback and Anti-Monopoly parties, also introduced substitute planks on labor, monopoly, public corporations, currency and civil service reform. These other planks were defeated by a voice vote, and the platform as written was adopted by acclamation.

Following are excerpts from the Democratic platform of 1884:

Tariff. Knowing full well, . . . that legislation affecting the operations of the people should be cautious and conservative in method, not in advance of public opinion, but reponsive to its demands, the Democratic party is pledged to revise the tariff in a spirit of fairness to all interests.

But in making reduction in taxes, it is not proposed to injure any domestic industries, but rather to promote their healthy growth. From the foundation of this Government, taxes collected at the Custom House have been the chief source of Federal Revenue. Such they must continue to be. Moreover, many industries have come to rely upon legislation for successful continuance, so that any change of law must be at every step regardful of the labor and capital thus involved. The process of reform must be subject in the execution to this plain dictate of justice. . . .

Sufficient revenue to pay all the expenses of the Federal Government . . . can be got, under our present system of taxation, from the custom house taxes on fewer imported articles, bearing heaviest on articles of luxury, and bearing lightest on articles of necessity.

Civil Liberties — Civil Service Reform. We oppose sumptuary laws which vex the citizen and interfere with individual liberty; we favor honest Civil Service Reform, and the compensation of all United States officers by fixed salaries; the separation of Church and State; and the diffusion of free education by common schools, so that every child in the land may be taught the rights and duties of citizenship.

Chinese Immigration. [W]e . . . do not sanction the importation of foreign labor, or the admission of servile races, unfitted by habits, training, religion, or kindred, for absorption into the great body of our people, or for the citizenship which our laws confer. American civilization demands that against the immigration or importation of Mongolians to these shores our gates be closed.

1888 Conventions

Presidential Candidates

Clinton B. Fisk
Prohibitionist

Grover Cleveland
Democrat

Benjamin Harrison
Republican

Prohibition

The Prohibition Party held its fifth national convention in Indianapolis in late May 1888. The party had held conventions since the 1872 campaign, but not until 1888 did the Prohibitionists receive at least 2 percent of the popular vote. *(Prohibition Party, p. 234)*

The 1888 convention selected Clinton B. Fisk of New Jersey for president and John A. Brooks of Missouri as his running mate. While the platform focused on the need for prohibition, planks were included that covered other issues. The Prohibition Party favored a tariff that would both protect American industry and raise revenue, supported the extension of voting rights, favored immigration restrictions and proposed the abolition of polygamy.

Following are excerpts from the Prohibition Party platform of 1888:

Prohibition. That the manufacture, importation, exportation, transportation and sale of alcoholic beverages should be made public crimes, and prohibited as such.

Tariff. That an adequate public revenue being necessary, it may properly be raised by import duties; but import duties should be so reduced that no surplus shall be accumulated in the Treasury, and that the burdens of taxation shall be removed from foods, clothing and other comforts and necessaries of life, and imposed on such articles of import as will give protection both to the manufacturing employer and producing laborer against the competition of the world.

Democrats

When the Democratic convention assembled in St. Louis in early June 1888, the party, for the first time since the outset of the Civil War, was in control of the White House. There was no contest for the presidential nomination, with the incumbent, Grover Cleveland, renominated by acclamation. However, the death of Vice President Thomas A. Hendricks in 1885 left open the second place on the ticket.

Former senator Allen G. Thurman of Ohio was the favorite for the vice presidential nomination and won easily on the first ballot with 684 votes. Gov. Isaac P. Gray of

Indiana had 101 votes, and Gen. John C. Black of Illinois trailed with 36. After the nomination of the 75-year-old Thurman, red bandannas were strung up around the hall. The bandanna was Thurman's political symbol, used extensively in his public habit of pinching snuff.

The platform was adopted by acclamation. It reaffirmed the Democratic platform written four years earlier, but in addition lauded the policies of President Cleveland and the achievements of Democratic rule, opposed the existing protective tariff and supported legislation to modify it and proposed a reformation of tax laws. A plank introduced from the floor favoring Irish home rule was included in the platform.

Following are excerpts from the Democratic platform of 1888:

Tariff. The Democratic party of the United States, in National Convention assembled, renews the pledge of its fidelity to Democratic faith and reaffirms the platform adopted by its representatives in the Convention of 1884, and indorses the views expressed by President Cleveland in his last annual message to Congress as the correct interpretation of that platform upon the question of Tariff reduction; and also indorses the efforts of our Democratic Representatives in Congress to secure a reduction of excessive taxation....

Resolved, That this convention hereby indorses and recommends the early passage of the bill for the reduction of the revenue now pending in the House of Representatives.

Tax Reform. All unnecessary taxation is unjust taxation.... Every Democratic rule of governmental action is violated when through unnecessary taxation a vast sum of money, far beyond the needs of an economical administration, is drawn from the people and the channels of trade, and accumulated as a demoralizing surplus in the National Treasury.... The Democratic remedy is to enforce frugality in public expense and abolish needless taxation.

Federal Power. Chief among its principles of party faith are the maintenance of an indissoluble Union of free and indestructible States, now about to enter upon its second century of unexampled progress and renown; devotion to a plan of government regulated by a written Con-

stitution, strictly specifying every granted power and expressly reserving to the States or people the entire ungranted residue of power.

Republicans

The Republicans assembled for their convention in Chicago in late June 1888. Not only was the party out of the White House for the first time since the Civil War, but a perennial contender for the presidential nomination, James G. Blaine, had taken himself out of the running. Although this encouraged a number of candidates to seek the nomination, none came near to mustering the needed majority as the balloting for president began.

The 832 convention votes were distributed among 14 candidates, with Sen. John Sherman of Ohio leading the field with 229 votes. Circuit Judge Walter Q. Gresham of Indiana followed with 107 votes, while four other candidates received more than 70 votes. During the rest of the day, two more ballots were taken, with little appreciable change in the strength of the candidates. After the third roll call, Sherman led with 244 votes, followed by Gresham with 123 and former governor Russell A. Alger of Michigan with 122.

The unexpected withdrawal from the race of Chauncey Depew of New York, the favorite of that state's delegation, prompted a call for adjournment after the third ballot. The motion passed, 531 to 287.

When balloting resumed the next morning, the biggest gainer was former Sen. Benjamin Harrison of Indiana. Although Sherman still held the lead with 235 votes on the fourth ballot, Harrison's vote total had leaped from 94 votes on the third to 216 on the fourth. There was little change on the fifth ballot, taken on a Saturday, and after the roll call the delegates approved, 492 to 320, a motion to adjourn until Monday. The motion was generally supported by delegates opposed to Harrison.

When the convention reconvened, both Sherman and Harrison showed small gains — Sherman rising to 244 votes and Harrison to 231. On the next roll call, the seventh, Harrison took the lead for the first time, thanks largely to a shift of votes from delegates previously holding out for Blaine. Harrison led, 279 to 230, and the trend to the Indianan accelerated to a bandwagon the next ballot. Harrison easily achieved a majority on the eighth roll call, winning 544 votes to 118 for Sherman.

Three individuals were placed in nomination for vice president, but former representative Levi P. Morton of New York was the runaway winner on the first ballot. Morton received 592 votes to easily outdistance Rep. William Walter Phelps of New Jersey, 119 votes, and William O. Bradley of Kentucky, 103.

The platform sharply differed from that of the Democrats on the important tariff issue, strongly supporting the protective tariff and opposing the legislation favored by the Democrats. Like the Democrats, the Republicans called for a reduction in taxes, specifically recommending repeal of taxes on tobacco and on alcohol used in the arts and for mechanical purposes. In other areas, the Republicans favored the use of both gold and silver as currency, strongly opposed the Mormon practice of polygamy and called for veterans' pensions.

Following are excerpts from the Republican platform of 1888:

Tariff. We are uncompromisingly in favor of the American system of protection; we protest against its destruction as proposed by the President and his party. They serve the interests of Europe; we will support the interests of America.... The protective system must be maintained. Its abandonment has always been followed by general disaster to all interests, except those of the usurer and the sheriff. We denounce the Mills bill as destructive to the general business, the labor and the farming interests of the country, and we heartily indorse the consistent and patriotic action of the Republican Representatives in Congress in opposing its passage.

Tax Reform. The Republican party would effect all needed reduction of the National revenue by repealing the taxes upon tobacco, which are an annoyance and burden to agriculture, and the tax upon spirits used in the arts, and for mechanical purposes, and by such revision of the tariff laws as will tend to check imports of such articles as are produced by our people, the production of which gives employment to our labor, and releases from import duties those articles of foreign production (except luxuries), the like of which cannot be produced at home. If there shall remain a larger revenue than is requisite for the wants of the government we favor the entire repeal of internal taxes rather than the surrender of any part of our protective system at the joint behests of the whiskey trusts and the agents of foreign manufacturers.

Currency. The Republican party is in favor of the use of both gold and silver as money, and condemns the policy of the Democratic Administration in its efforts to demonetize silver.

Veterans' Benefits. The gratitude of the Nation to the defenders of the Union cannot be measured by laws.... We denounce the hostile spirit shown by President Cleveland in his numerous vetoes of measures for pension relief, and the action of the Democratic House of Representatives in refusing even a consideration of general pension legislation.

Polygamy. The political power of the Mormon Church in the Territories as exercised in the past is a menace to free institutions too dangerous to be longer suffered. Therefore we pledge the Republican party to appropriate legislation asserting the sovereignty of the Nation in all Territories where the same is questioned, and in furtherance of that end to place upon the statute books legislation stringent enough to divorce the political from the ecclesiastical power, and thus stamp out the attendant wickedness of polygamy.

1892 Conventions

Presidential Candidates

Benjamin Harrison
Republican

Grover Cleveland
Democrat

James B. Weaver
Populist

Republicans

Although President Benjamin Harrison was unpopular with various elements in the Republican Party, administration forces were in control of the convention that assembled in early June 1892 in Minneapolis, Minn. A Harrison supporter, former representative William McKinley of Ohio, was elected without opposition as the convention's permanent chairman.

A question concerning the credentials of six Alabama delegates resulted in a protracted debate on whether the six delegates in question could vote on their own case. The situation was resolved when the Alabama delegates voluntarily abstained from voting. The minority report, which proposed seating the six Alabama delegates on the original roll, was defeated, 463 to 423-1/2, and the majority report was subsequently adopted, 476 to 365-1/2. The two votes were candidate-oriented, with the winning side in each case composed largely of Harrison voters.

Harrison's chances of renomination were so strong that two other possibilities, James G. Blaine and William McKinley, never publicly announced as candidates for the presidency. Harrison won easily on the first ballot, receiving 535-1/6 votes to 182-1/6 for Blaine and 182 for McKinley. McKinley was in the ironic position of presiding over the convention at the same time he was receiving votes on the presidential ballot. The Ohioan withdrew briefly as permanent chairman and moved that Harrison's nomination be made unanimous. The motion was withdrawn after objections but placed McKinley publicly on the Harrison bandwagon. *(Chart, p. 181)*

While the Republican Party had an incumbent vice president in Levi P. Morton, the New York delegation supported Whitelaw Reid, the former editor of *The New York Tribune* and ambassador to France. With Morton making little effort to retain his position, Reid was nominated by acclamation, the first time a Republican convention had dispensed with a roll call in choosing a member of its national ticket.

The platform was adopted by a voice vote, and on only two major issues did it differ from that of the Democrats. The Republicans supported a protective tariff, clearly di-verging from the Democrats, who supported import duties for revenue only. The Republicans also included a plank that sympathized with the prohibition effort, while the Democrats announced their opposition "to all sumptuary laws."

Both parties favored a bimetallic currency, with gold and silver of equal value, and supported the construction of a canal across Nicaragua. In addition, the Republicans advocated an expansionist foreign policy.

Following are excerpts from the Republican platform of 1892:

Tariff. We reaffirm the American doctrine of protection. We call attention to its growth abroad. We maintain that the prosperous condition of our country is largely due to the wise revenue legislation of the Republican congress.

We believe that all articles which cannot be produced in the United States, except luxuries, should be admitted free of duty, and that on all imports coming into competition with the products of American labor, there should be levied duties equal to the difference between wages abroad and at home.

Currency. The American people, from tradition and interest, favor bi-metallism, and the Republican party demands the use of both gold and silver as standard money, with such restrictions and under such provisions, to be determined by legislation, as will secure the maintenance of the parity of values of the two metals so that the purchasing and debt-paying power of the dollar, whether of silver, gold, or paper, shall be at all times equal. The interests of the producers of the country, its farmers and its workingmen, demand that every dollar, paper or coin, issued by the government, shall be as good as any other.

Foreign Policy. We reaffirm our approval of the Monroe doctrine and believe in the achievement of the manifest destiny of the Republic in its broadest sense.

Central American Canal. The construction of the Nicaragua Canal is of the highest importance to the American people, both as a measure of National defense and to build up and maintain American commerce, and it should be controlled by the United States Government.

Prohibition. We sympathize with all wise and legitimate efforts to lessen and prevent the evils of intemperance and promote morality.

Democrats

One of the strangest conventions in party annals was held by the Democrats in Chicago in late June 1892. Much of the disturbance was due to stormy weather, with the accompanying noise and leaks in the roof frequently interrupting the proceedings. Inside the hall, the discomfort of the delegates was increased by the vocal opposition of 600 Tammany Hall workers to the renomination of former president Grover Cleveland of New York.

Although Cleveland was a solid favorite for renomination, he was opposed by his home state delegation. The Tammany forces engineered an early state convention that chose a delegation committed to Gov. David B. Hill. But in spite of the hostility of the New York delegation, Cleveland was able to win renomination on the first ballot, receiving 617-1/3 votes to 114 for Hill and 103 for Gov. Horace Boles of Iowa. *(Chart, p. 181)*

Four individuals were placed in nomination for the vice presidency, with Adlai E. Stevenson of Illinois assuming the lead on the first ballot. Stevenson, a former representative and later assistant postmaster general during Cleveland's first administration, led former governor Isaac P. Gray of Indiana, 402 to 343. After the first roll call was completed, Iowa switched to Stevenson, starting a bandwagon that led quickly to his nomination. After all the switches had been tallied, Stevenson was the winner with 652 votes, followed by Gray with 185.

The platform debate centered around the tariff plank. The plank, as originally written, straddled the issue. But a sharply worded substitute proposed from the floor, calling for a tariff for revenue only, passed easily, 564 to 342. The currency section called for stable money, with the coinage of both gold and silver in equal amounts. The platform also included a plank that called for the construction of a canal through Nicaragua.

Following are excerpts from the Democratic platform of 1892:

Tariff. We denounce Republican protection as a fraud, a robbery of the great majority of the American people for the benefit of the few. We declare it to be a fundamental principle of the Democratic party that the Federal Government has no constitutional power to impose and collect tariff duties, except for the purpose of revenue only, and we demand that the collection of such taxes shall be limited to the necessities of the Government when honestly and economically administered.

Currency. ... We hold to the use of both gold and silver as the standard money of the country, and to the coinage of both gold and silver without discriminating against either metal or charge for mintage, but the dollar unit of coinage of both metals must be of equal intrinsic and exchangeable value, or be adjusted through international agreement or by such safeguards of legislation as shall insure the maintenance of the parity of the two metals and the equal power of every dollar at all times in the markets and in the payment of debts; and we demand that all paper currency shall be kept at par with and redeemable in such coin.

Central American Canal. For purposes of national defense and the promotion of commerce between the States, we recognize the early construction of the Nicaragua Canal and its protection against foreign control as of great importance to the United States.

Prohibition. We are opposed to all sumptuary laws, as an interference with the individual rights of the citizen.

Federal Power. ... we solemnly declare that the need of a return to these fundamental principles of free popular government, based on home rule and individual liberty, was never more urgent than now, when the tendency to centralize all power at the Federal capital has become a menace to the reserved rights of the States that strikes at the very roots of our Government under the Constitution as framed by the fathers of the Republic.

Prohibition

The Prohibition Party's sixth convention was held in Cincinnati in late June 1892 and nominated John Bidwell of California for president and James B. Cranfill of Texas as his running mate. While the Prohibition Party continued to run a national ticket through the 1972 election, 1892 marked the last year that the party received more than 2 percent of the popular vote.

Although beginning and ending with calls for prohibition, the 1892 platform as a whole was a reform-minded document, favoring women's suffrage and equal wages for women, an inflated currency and the nationalization of railroad, telegraph, and other public corporations.

Following are excerpts from the Prohibition platform of 1892:

Prohibition. ... We declare anew for the entire suppression of the manufacture, sale, importation, exportation and transportation of alcoholic liquors as a beverage by Federal and State legislation, and the full powers of Government should be exerted to secure this result. Any party that fails to recognize the dominant nature of this issue in American politics is undeserving of the support of the people.

Women's Rights. No citizen should be denied the right to vote on account of sex, and equal labor should receive equal wages, without regard to sex.

Currency. The money of the country should consist of gold, silver, and paper, and be issued by the General Government only, and in sufficient quantity to meet the demands of business and give full opportunity for the employment of labor. To this end an increase in the volume of money is demanded, and no individual or corporation should be allowed to make any profit through its issue. It should be made a legal tender for the payment of all debts, public and private. Its volume should be fixed at a definite sum per capita and made to increase with our increase in population.

Tariff. Tariff should be levied only as a defense against foreign governments which levy tariff upon or bar out our products from their markets, revenue being incidental.

Government Nationalization. Railroad, telegraph, and other public corporations should be controlled by the Government in the interest of the people.

People's Party (Populists)

The most successful of the 19th century farmer-labor coalitions was the People's Party, commonly known as the Populists, which formally organized as a political party at a convention in Cincinnati in May 1891. Further organization was accomplished at a convention in St. Louis the next February, from which emanated the call to the party's first national nominating convention, to be held that summer in Omaha, Neb. The election of 1892 was the only one in which the Populists received more than 2 percent of the national vote. Four years later the party endorsed the Democratic ticket, and from 1900 through 1908 the Populists ran separate tickets, but failed to receive 2 percent of the popular vote. *(Populist Party, p, 232)*

The call to the 1892 convention specified procedures

for the selection of delegates and set the size of the convention at 1,776 delegates. Thirteen hundred to fourteen hundred delegates actually assembled in Omaha for the Populist convention, which opened July 2. The field for the presidential nomination was reduced by the death early in 1892 of the Southern agrarian leader, Leonidas L. Polk of North Carolina, and the refusal of Judge Walter Q. Gresham of Indiana to seek the nomination. First place on the ticket went to former representative James B. Weaver of Iowa, who defeated Sen. James H. Kyle of South Dakota, 995 to 275.

James G. Field of Virginia won the vice presidential nomination over Ben Terrell of Texas by a vote of 733 to 554. The ticket bridged any sectional division, pairing a former Union general (Weaver) with a former Confederate major (Field).

On July 4 the delegates enthusiastically adopted the platform. It contained few ideas that were not contained in the earlier platforms of other farmer-labor parties. But the document adopted by the Populists brought these proposals together into one forcefully written platform. More than half the platform was devoted to the preamble, which demanded widespread reform and sharply criticized the two major parties. It attacked the Democrats and Republicans for waging "a sham battle over the tariff," while ignoring more important issues.

The remainder of the platform was divided into three major parts that discussed finance, transportation and land policy. The Populists proposed that the currency be inflated, with the unlimited coinage of silver and a substantial increase in the circulating medium to at least $50 per capita. The Populists' currency plank was sharply different from those of the two major parties, which favored a stable, bimetallic currency.

The Populists also went well beyond the two major parties in advocating the nationalization of the railroads and telegraph and telephone companies. Both the Populists and Democrats advocated land reform, although the proposals received greater emphasis in the Populist platform.

The Populists included a call for a graduated income tax and expanded government power.

Although not considered part of the platform, supplementary resolutions were passed that favored the initiative and referendum, a limit of one term for the president, the direct election of senators, the secret ballot and additional labor-oriented proposals that called for improvement in working conditions.

Following are excerpts from the Populist platform of 1892:

Preamble. The conditions which surround us best justify our co-operation; we meet in the midst of a nation brought to the verge of moral, political, and material ruin. Corruption dominates the ballot-box, the Legislatures, the Congress, and touches even the ermine of the bench. The

people are demoralized; most of the states have been compelled to isolate the voters at the polling places to prevent universal intimidation and bribery. The newspapers are largely subsidized or muzzled, public opinion silenced, business prostrated, homes covered with mortgages, labor impoverished, and the land concentrating in the hands of capitalists. The urban workmen are denied the right to organize for self-protection; imported pauperized labor beats down their wages, a hireling standing army, unrecognized by our laws, is established to shoot them down, and they are rapidly degenerating into European conditions. The fruits of the toil of millions are boldly stolen to build up colossal fortunes for a few, unprecedented in the history of mankind; and the possessors of these, in turn despise the Republic and endanger liberty. From the same prolific womb of governmental injustice we breed the two great classes — tramps and millionaires. . . .

We have witnessed for more than a quarter of a century the struggles of the two great political parties for power and plunder, while grievous wrongs have been inflicted upon the suffering people. We charge that the controlling influence dominating both these parties have permitted the existing dreadful conditions to develop without serious effort to prevent or restrain them. Neither do they now promise us any substantial reform. They have agreed together to ignore, in the coming campaign, every issue but one. They propose to drown the outcries of a plundered people with the uproar of a sham battle over the tariff, so that capitalists, corporations, national banks, rings, trusts, watered stock, the demonetization of silver and the oppressions of the usurers may all be lost sight of. They propose to sacrifice our homes, lives, and children on the altar of mammon; to destroy the multitude in order to secure corruption funds from the millionaires.

. . . We believe that the power of government — in other words, of the people — should be expanded (as in the case of the postal service) as rapidly and as far as the good sense of an intelligent people and the teachings of experience shall justify, to the end that oppression, injustice and poverty, shall eventually cease in the land.

While our sympathies as a party of reform are naturally upon the side of every proposition which will tend to make men intelligent, virtuous and temperate, we nevertheless regard these questions, important as they are, as secondary to the great issues now pressing for solution, and upon which not only our individual prosperity, but the very existence of free institutions depend; and we ask all men to first help us to determine whether we are to have a republic to administer, before we differ as to the conditions upon which it is to be administered, believing that the forces of reform this day organized will never cease to move forward, until every wrong is remedied, and equal rights and equal privileges securely established for all the men and women of this country.

Currency. We demand free and unlimited coinage of silver and gold at the present legal ratio of 16 to 1.

We demand that the amount of circulating medium be speedily increased to not less than $50 per capita.

We demand that postal savings banks be established by the government for the safe deposit of the earnings of the

---

Explanatory Note

This section on the history of party nominating conventions includes party conventions for parties receiving at least 2 percent of the popular vote in the presidential election. The Socialist Party, for example, received at least 2 percent of the popular vote in 1904, 1908, 1912, 1916, 1920 and 1932; the Socialist Party conventions for these years are included in this section. The Socialist Party conventions for other years when the party received less than 2 percent of the vote are not included. (*Additional details on this section, p. 30*)

people and to facilitate exchange.

Transportation. Transportation being a means of exchange and a public necessity, the government should own and operate the railroads in the interest of the people. The telegraph and telephone, like the post office system, being a necessity for the transmission of news, should be owned and operated by the government in the interest of the people.

Land. The land, including all the natural sources of wealth, is the heritage of the people, and should not be monopolized for speculative purposes, and alien ownership of land should be prohibited. All land now held by railroad and other corporations in excess of their actual needs, and all lands now owned by aliens, should be reclaimed by the government and held for actual settlers only.

1896 Conventions

Presidential Candidates

William McKinley
Republican

William J. Bryan
Democrat

Republicans

The currency issue, which spawned several third-party efforts in the late 19th century, emerged as the dominant issue of contention between the Republican and Democratic parties in the campaign of 1896. The forces in favor of the gold standard were firmly in control of the Republican convention that was held in St. Louis in early June 1896.

Actually, the convention was less a forum for the discussion of issues than a showcase for the political acumen of Mark Hanna of Ohio. Hanna, William McKinley's campaign manager, had been intensely courting delegates across the country, especially in the South, for more than a year before the convention. Before the rap of the opening gavel, Hanna had amassed a majority of the delegates for the popular Ohio governor.

The first evidence of McKinley strength came on a credentials question. A minority report was introduced claiming the credentials committee had held hearings on only two of 160 cases and proposing that the committee resume hearings. A maneuver to squelch the minority report was made when a delegate moved to cut off debate. With the McKinley forces providing most of the majority, the motion passed, 551-1/2 to 359-1/2.

Four other candidates in addition to McKinley were in contention for the presidential nomination, but McKinley was the runaway winner on the first ballot. He received 661-1/2 votes to 84-1/2 for the runner-up, House Speaker Thomas B. Reed of Maine. *(Chart, p. 183)*

There were two serious contenders for the vice presidential nomination: Garret A. Hobart, a McKinley sup-

porter and former state legislator from New Jersey, and Henry Clay Evans, a former candidate for governor of Tennessee. Hobart won, winning 523-1/2 votes on the first ballot to 287-1/2 for Evans.

As at the Democratic convention, the platform debate centered around the currency issue. The gold forces, firmly in control of the Republican convention, produced a majority report that called for maintenance of the gold standard until the time when bimetallism could be effected by an international agreement. This plank did not satisfy the silver minority. Led by Sen. Henry M. Teller of Colorado, a minority plank was introduced favoring the unlimited coinage of silver and gold at the ratio of 16 to 1. Teller's plank, similar to the currency plank adopted later by the Democrats, was defeated, 818-1/2 to 105-1/2. A second roll call on adoption of the majority plank resulted in another decisive defeat for the silver forces. The majority plank carried, 812-1/2 to 110-1/2.

With the decisive defeat of the minority plank, Teller led a walkout by 24 silver delegates, including the entire Colorado and Idaho delegations and members of the Montana, South Dakota and Utah delegations. The rest of the platform was adopted by a voice vote.

The currency plank that caused the commotion was buried deep in the middle of the Republican platform. The document began with a denunciation of Democratic rule and proceeded into a discussion of the merits of a protective tariff. A tariff for revenue purposes only was advocated in the Democratic platform, but the issue in the Republican document was clearly considered to be of secondary importance.

The Republican platform was also distinguishable from that of the Democrats in recommending a more expansionistic foreign policy, proposing stricter immigration restrictions and, for the first time, specifically denouncing the practice of lynching.

Following are excerpts from the Republican platform of 1896:

Currency. The Republican party is unreservedly for sound money.... We are unalterably opposed to every measure calculated to debase our currency or impair the credit of our country. We are therefore opposed to the free coinage of silver, except by international agreement with the leading commercial nations of the earth, which agreement we pledge ourselves to promote, and until such agreement can be obtained the existing gold standard must be maintained.

Tariff. We renew and emphasize our allegiance to the policy of protection, as the bulwark of American industrial independence, and the foundation of American development and prosperity.... Protection and Reciprocity are twin measures of American policy and go hand in hand. Democratic rule has recklessly struck down both, and both must be re-established. Protection for what we produce; free admission for the necessaries of life which we do not produce; reciprocal agreement of mutual interests, which gain open markets for us in return for our open markets for others. Protection builds up domestic industry and trade and secures our own market for ourselves; reciprocity builds up foreign trade and finds an outlet for our surplus.

Foreign Policy. Our foreign policy should be at all times firm, vigorous and dignified, and all our interests in the western hemisphere should be carefully watched and guarded.

The Hawaiian Islands should be controlled by the United States, and no foreign power should be permitted to interfere with them. The Nicaragua Canal should be built, owned and operated by the United States. And, by the purchase of the Danish Islands we should secure a much needed Naval station in the West Indies.... We therefore, favor the continued enlargement of the navy, and a complete system of harbor and sea-coast defenses.

Immigration. For the protection of the equality of our American citizenship and of the wages of our workingmen, against the fatal competition of low priced labor, we demand that the immigration laws be thoroughly enforced, and so extended as to exclude from entrance to the United States those who can neither read nor write.

Lynching. We proclaim our unqualified condemnation of the uncivilized and preposterous [barbarous] practice well known as lynching, and the killing of human beings suspected or charged with crime without process of law.

Democrats

The Democratic convention that assembled in Chicago in July 1896 was dominated by one issue — currency. A delegate's viewpoint on this single issue influenced his position on every vote taken. Generally, the party was split along regional lines, with Eastern delegations favoring a hard-money policy with maintenance of the gold standard, and most Southern and Western delegations supporting a soft-money policy with the unlimited coinage of silver.

Division in the convention was apparent on the first day, when the silver forces challenged the national committee's selection of Gov. David B. Hill of New York as temporary chairman. The pro-silver delegates put up Sen. John W. Daniel of Virginia for the post, and Daniel won easily, 556 to 349. His victory indicated the dominance of the silver forces and presaged their ability to control the convention.

Two sets of credentials challenges were next on the agenda. By a voice vote, the convention agreed to seat a Nebraska delegation headed by a young silver supporter, William Jennings Bryan. And, by a vote of 558 to 368, the convention defeated a recommendation to seat Michigan delegates supported by the hard-money-dominated national committee.

With their lack of strength apparent, the gold forces declined to run a candidate for president. However, the silver delegates could not initially coalesce behind one candidate, and 14 individuals received votes on the first ballot. Rep. Richard P. "Silver Dick" Bland of Missouri was the pacesetter, with 235 votes, followed by Bryan, a former House member, with 137 and Robert E. Pattison, former Pennsylvania governor, with 97. Bryan, 36 years old, earlier had electrified the convention during the platform debate on currency, with his memorable "Cross of Gold" speech, which had elevated him to the position of a major contender. *(Chart, p. 182)*

On the next two roll calls, both candidates showed gains. Bland's total climbed to 291 on the third ballot and Bryan's rose to 219. Bryan continued to gain on the next ballot and assumed the lead over Bland, 280 to 241. The movement to Bryan accelerated on the fifth ballot, and he won the nomination easily, receiving 652 of the 930 convention votes. Although Bryan was the nearly unanimous choice of the silver forces, 162 gold delegates indicated their dissatisfaction with the proceedings by refusing to vote.

With Bryan declining to indicate a preference for vice president, 16 candidates received votes for the office on the first ballot. The Nebraska delegation, following Bryan's example, declined to participate in the vice-presidential balloting.

Former representative John C. Sibley of Pennsylvania took the lead on the first ballot with 163 votes, followed by Ohio editor and publisher John R. McLean with 111, and Maine shipbuilder Arthur Sewall with 100.

Bland spurted into the lead on the second ballot with 294 votes, followed by McLean and Sibley. After the roll call, Sibley withdrew, and on the third ballot the race between Bland and McLean tightened. The Missourian led, 255 to 210, but he too withdrew after the roll call. Sewall emerged as McLean's major competitor on the fourth ballot, and with the withdrawal of the Ohio journalist from the race, the nomination was Sewall's on the fifth ballot. Actually, Sewall's vote total of 602 on the final roll call was less than two-thirds of the convention vote, but with 251 disgruntled gold delegates refusing to vote, the required majority was reduced to only those voting.

Not surprisingly, the platform debate centered around the currency plank. The Eastern delegations proposed that, until silver coinage could be arranged by international agreement, the gold standard should be maintained. The Southern and Western delegations countered by demanding that the unlimited coinage of silver should begin without requiring a delay to reach an international agreement. Bryan managed the platform debate for the silver forces and scheduled himself as the final speaker, an enviable position from which to make a deep impression on the emotion-packed convention.

Bryan made the most of his opportunity, ending his dramatic speech with the famous peroration: "You shall not press down upon the brow of labor this crown of thorns,

you shall not crucify mankind upon a cross of gold." The gold plank was defeated, 626 to 303. Although the speech was a key factor in Bryan's nomination, it was not influential in defeating the gold plank, which was already doomed for defeat. *(Chart, p. 182)*

A resolution commending the Cleveland administration was also defeated, 564 to 357, and after several attempts to modify the currency plank were rejected by voice votes, the platform as a whole was adopted, 622 to 307.

Following are excerpts from the Democratic platform of 1896:

Currency. We demand the free and unlimited coinage of both silver and gold at the present legal ratio of 16 to 1 without waiting for the aid or consent of any other nation.

Railroads. The absorption of wealth by the few, the consolidation of our leading railroad systems, and the formation of trusts and pools require a stricter control by the Federal Government of those arteries of commerce. We demand the enlargement of the powers of the Interstate Commerce Commission and such restriction and guarantees in the control of railroads as will protect the people from robbery and oppression.

No Third Term. We declare it to be the unwritten law of this Republic, established by custom and usage of 100 years, and sanctioned by the examples of the greatest and wisest of those who founded and have maintained our Government that no man should be eligible for a third term of the Presidential office.

Federal Power. During all these years the Democratic Party has resisted the tendency of selfish interests to the centralization of governmental power, and steadfastly maintained the integrity of the dual scheme of government established by the founders of this Republic of republics. Under its guidance and teachings the great principle of local self-government has found its best expression in the maintenance of the rights of the States and in its assertion of the necessity of confining the general government to the exercise of the powers granted by the Constitution of the United States.

1900 Conventions

Presidential Candidates

William McKinley
Republican

William J. Bryan
Democrat

Republicans

Surface harmony was the hallmark of the Republican conclave held in Philadelphia in June 1900. The Colorado delegation, which had walked out of the 1896 convention, was honored by having one of its members, Sen. Edward O. Wolcott, chosen as temporary chairman.

There was no opposition to President William McKinley, and he won all 926 votes on the first roll call. However, the death of Vice President Garret A. Hobart in 1899 had left the second spot on the ticket open. McKinley did not have a preference and asked his campaign manager, Mark Hanna, not to influence the convention. McKinley's hands-off policy worked to the advantage of the popular governor of New York and hero of the Spanish-American War, Theodore Roosevelt, whom Hanna disliked. *(Chart, p. 184)*

Roosevelt's popularity, coupled with the desire of New York boss Thomas C. Platt to eliminate a powerful state rival, enabled the 41-year-old governor to clinch the nomination before balloting began. On the vice presidential roll call, Roosevelt received all but one vote. The single uncast vote came from Roosevelt's New York delegation, which cast 71 of its 72 votes for Roosevelt.

The Republicans adopted a platform that applauded the four years of Republican rule and credited McKinley's policies with improving business conditions and winning the Spanish-American War. The platform defended postwar expansionism and called for increased foreign trade and the creation of a Department of Commerce.

As in 1896, the Republican platform opposed the unlimited coinage of silver and supported maintenance of the gold standard. On the tariff issue, the Republicans continued to laud the protective duty on imports.

Following are excerpts from the Republican platform of 1900:

Foreign Trade, Panama Canal. We favor the construction, ownership, control and protection of an Isthmian Canal by the Government of the United States. New markets are necessary for the increasing surplus of our farm products. Every effort should be made to open and obtain new markets, especially in the Orient, and the Administration is warmly to be commended for its successful efforts to commit all trading and colonizing nations to the policy of the open door in China.

International Expansion. In accepting by the Treaty of Paris the just responsibility of our victories in the Spanish war, the President and the Senate won the undoubted approval of the American people. No other course was possible than to destroy Spain's sovereignty throughout the West Indies and in the Philippine Islands. That course created our responsibility before the world, and with the unorganized population whom our intervention had freed from Spain, to provide for the maintenance of law and order, and for the establishment of good government and for the performance of international obligations. Our authority could not be less than our responsibility; and whenever sovereign rights were extended it became the high duty of the Government to maintain its authority, to put down armed insurrection and to confer the blessings of liberty and civilization upon all the rescued peoples.

Antitrust. We recognize the necessity and propriety of the honest co-operation of capital to meet new business conditions and especially to extend our rapidly increasing foreign trade, but we condemn all conspiracies and combinations intended to restrict business, to create monopolies, to limit production, or to control prices; and favor such legislation as will effectively restrain and prevent all such abuses, protect and promote competition and secure the rights of producers, laborers, and all who are engaged in industry and commerce.

Currency. We renew our allegiance to the principle of the gold standard and declare our confidence in the wisdom of the legislation of the Fifty-sixth Congress, by which the parity of all our money and the stability of our currency upon a gold basis has been secured. . . .

We declare our steadfast opposition to the free and unlimited coinage of silver.

Tariff. We renew our faith in the policy of Protection to American labor. In that policy our industries have been established, diversified and maintained. By protecting the home market competition has been stimulated and production cheapened.

Democrats

The Democrats opened their 1900 convention in Kansas City, Mo., on July 4, and showed a degree of party harmony not evident at their convention four years earlier. After the party factionalism of 1896, the delegates made a conscious effort to display a unified front — an effort aided by the decline of the controversial silver issue. The discovery of new gold deposits in North America and the subsequent increase in currency had lessened the divisive impact of the silver issue.

William Jennings Bryan, the Democratic standard-bearer in 1896, was renominated without opposition, receiving all 936 votes. The harmony in the convention was evident when former New York senator David B. Hill, a leader of the gold forces four years earlier, gave a seconding speech for Bryan. *(Chart, p. 184)*

Seven names were placed in nomination for the vice presidency. However, two withdrew before the balloting began. Adlai E. Stevenson of Illinois, vice president under Grover Cleveland, led on the first roll call with 559-1/2 votes, followed by Hill, who received 200 votes in spite of withdrawing from the race before the voting started. After completion of the ballot, a series of vote switches resulted in Stevenson's unanimous nomination.

The platform was adopted without floor debate. The major theme of the document was anti-imperialism, although an attack on trusts and a discussion of the currency question also were emphasized.

The anti-imperialism section was placed at the beginning of the platform and was labeled the most important issue of the campaign. The delegates enthusiastically accepted the plank, which forcefully criticized American international expansion after the Spanish-American War. The platform asserted "that no nation can long endure half republic and half empire" and denounced increasing U.S. militarism. The Democratic position sharply differed from the one advocated by the Republicans, whose platform defended postwar expansionism.

After the anti-imperialism section was a sharp attack on monopolies, the most detailed antitrust section that had yet appeared in a Democratic platform. The plank called for more comprehensive antitrust legislation and more rigid enforcement of the laws already enacted. Although the Republicans also condemned monopolies, the issue received a mere one-sentence mention in their platform.

With the decline of the silver issue, the necessity of a pro-silver plank was a matter of debate in the resolutions committee. However, Bryan threatened to withdraw his candidacy if a plank calling for the unlimited coinage of silver was not included in the platform. By a majority of one vote, the resolutions committee included the silver plank, and it was accepted without dissent by the convention. The Democratic position set up another distinction with the Republicans, who, as four years earlier, favored maintenance of the gold standard.

In addition to the anti-imperialism, antitrust and currency sections of the platform, the Democrats proposed the creation of a Department of Labor, favored the direct election of senators and, unlike the Republicans, supported the construction and ownership of a Nicaraguan canal. The Republican platform advocated construction and ownership of a canal across the Isthmus of Panama.

Following are excerpts from the Democratic platform of 1900:

Anti-imperialism. We hold that the Constitution follows the flag, and denounce the doctrine that an Executive or Congress deriving their existence and their powers from the Constitution can exercise lawful authority beyond it or in violation of it. We assert that no nation can long endure half republic and half empire, and we warn the American people that imperialism abroad will lead quickly and inevitably to despotism at home. . . .

We are not opposed to territorial expansion when it takes in desirable territory which can be erected into States in the Union, and whose people are willing and fit to become American citizens. We favor trade expansion by every peaceful and legitimate means. But we are unalterably opposed to seizing or purchasing distant islands to be governed outside the Constitution, and whose people can never become citizens. . . .

The importance of other questions, now pending before the American people is no wise diminished and the Democratic party takes no backward step from its position on them, but the burning issue of imperialism growing out of the Spanish war involves the very existence of the Republic and the destruction of our free institutions. We regard it as the paramount issue of the campaign. . . .

We oppose militarism. It means conquest abroad and intimidation and oppression at home. It means the strong arm which has ever been fatal to free institutions. . . . This republic has no place for a vast military establishment, a sure forerunner of compulsory military service and conscription. When the nation is in danger the volunteer soldier is his country's best defender.

Antitrust. We pledge the Democratic party to an unceasing warfare in nation, State and city against private monopoly in every form. Existing laws against trusts must be enforced and more stringent ones must be enacted. . . .

Tariff laws should be amended by putting the products of trusts upon the free list, to prevent monopoly under the plea of protection.

Currency. We reaffirm and indorse the principles of the National Democratic Platform adopted at Chicago in 1896, and we reiterate the demand of that platform for an

American financial system made by the American people for themselves, and which shall restore and maintain a bimetallic price-level, and as part of such system the immediate restoration of the free and unlimited coinage of silver and gold at the present legal ratio of 16 to 1, without waiting for the aid or consent of any other nation.

1904 Conventions

Presidential Candidates

Eugene V. Debs
Socialist

Theodore Roosevelt
Republican

Alton B. Parker
Democrat

Socialists

The Socialist Party held its first national nominating convention in Chicago in early May 1904 and nominated Eugene V. Debs of Indiana for president and Benjamin Hanford of New York as his running mate. Debs ran in 1900 as the presidential candidate of two socialist groups, the Social Democratic Party and a moderate faction of the Socialist Labor Party.

The bulk of the platform was devoted to the philosophy of the international Socialist movement, with its belief in the eventual demise of capitalism and the ultimate achievement of a classless, worker-oriented society. To hasten the creation of a Socialist society, the platform favored many reforms advocated by the Populists and earlier agrarian-labor movements: the initiative, referendum and recall; women's suffrage; tax reform, including the graduated income tax; the public ownership of transportation, communication and exchange; and various labor benefits, including higher wages and shorter hours.

Following are excerpts from the Socialist platform of 1904:

> To the end that the workers may seize every possible advantage that may strengthen them to gain complete control of the powers of government, and thereby the sooner establish the cooperative commonwealth, the Socialist Party pledges itself to watch and work, in both the economic and the political struggle, for each successive immediate interest of the working class; for shortened days of labor and increases of wages; for the insurance of the workers against accident, sickness and lack of employment; for pensions for aged and exhausted workers; for the public ownership of the means of transportation, communication and exchange; for the graduated taxation of incomes, inheritances, franchises and land values, the proceeds to be

applied to the public employment and improvement of the conditions of the workers; for the complete education of children, and their freedom from the workshop; for the prevention of the use of the military against labor in the settlement of strikes; for the free administration of justice; for popular government, including initiative, referendum, proportional representation, equal suffrage of men and women, municipal home rule, and the recall of officers by their constituents; and for every gain or advantage for the workers that may be wrested from the capitalist system, and that may relieve the suffering and strengthen the hands of labor. We lay upon every man elected to any executive or legislative office the first duty of striving to procure whatever is for the workers' most immediate interest, and for whatever will lessen the economic and political powers of the capitalist, and increase the like powers of the worker.

Republicans

President Theodore Roosevelt was totally in command of the Republican convention held in Chicago in June 1904. His most dangerous potential rival for the nomination, Sen. Mark Hanna of Ohio, had died in February, leaving the field clear for Roosevelt.

The rather trivial matter of most interest before the presidential balloting began was Hawaii's vote allocation. The rules committee recommended that the vote of the territory be reduced from six to two. A substitute amendment proposed that Hawaii retain its six votes for the 1904 convention but that its vote allocation be reviewed by the national committee for future conventions. The substitute was accepted by the narrow margin of 495 to 490.

Roosevelt's nomination caused less commotion. On the first ballot, he received all 994 votes. The party leadership favored Sen. Charles W. Fairbanks of Indiana for the vice presidency. Although the Georgia, Illinois, Missouri and

Nebraska delegations noted that they preferred other candidates, Fairbanks was nominated by acclamation.

The party platform was adopted without dissent. In the document the Republicans charted little new ground, instead detailing the benefits of Republican rule and restating old positions. America's expansionistic foreign policy was praised, as was the protective tariff and the gold standard.

A display of Roosevelt theatrics followed the adoption of the platform. The convention chairman was instructed to read a message from the secretary of state to the American consul in Morocco: "We want either Perdicaris alive or Raisuli dead." The message referred to an alleged American citizen, Ion Perdicaris, who had been captured by the Moroccan chieftain, Raisuli. The American ultimatum read to the convention followed the dispatch of several ships to Morocco. The reading of the message roused the delegates, as it was no doubt intended to do.

Following are excerpts from the Republican platform in 1904:

Shipbuilding. We ... favor legislation which will encourage and build up the American merchant marine, and we cordially approve the legislation of the last Congress which created the Merchant Marine Commission to investigate and report upon this subject.

Monopoly. Combinations of capital and of labor are the results of the economic movement of the age, but neither must be permitted to infringe upon the rights and interests of the people. Such combinations, when lawfully formed for lawful purposes, are alike entitled to the protection of the laws, but both are subject to the laws and neither can be permitted to break them.

Democrats

William Jennings Bryan, after two unsuccessful campaigns for the presidency, was not a candidate for the Democratic nomination in 1904. However, he was present at the party's convention in St. Louis that July and was a prominent factor in the proceedings.

Bryan's first appearance before the convention came during a credentials dispute, featuring a challenge by Bryan supporters in Illinois to the state delegation approved by the credentials committee. Bryan spoke in behalf of his supporters, but their minority report was beaten, 647 to 299.

Bryan appeared again to second the presidential nomination of Sen. Francis M. Cockrell of Missouri, one of eight candidates nominated. Much of his speech, however, was devoted to criticizing the conservative front-runner, Alton B. Parker, chief justice of the New York Court of Appeals, while boosting more progressive candidates. In spite of Bryan's opposition, Parker came within nine votes of receiving the necessary two-thirds majority on the first ballot. Parker had 658 votes, followed by Rep. William Randolph Hearst of New York, with 200, and Cockrell, who trailed with 42. Although Hearst had progressive credentials, Bryan hesitated to support him and jeopardize his own leadership of the progressive wing of the party.

With Parker so close to victory, Idaho shifted its votes to the New York judge, prompting enough switches by other states to give Parker 679 votes and the nomination. Hearst, with his strength in the Middle West and West, finished with 181 votes. *(Chart, p. 185)*

With the nomination in hand, Parker stunned the convention by sending a telegram to the New York delega-

tion, announcing his support of the gold standard and advising the convention to select a new candidate if they found his position unacceptable. Parker supporters drafted a response stating that there was nothing to preclude his nomination, because the platform was silent on the currency issue.

Bryan, ill with a fever in his hotel but still a supporter of the silver cause, rose from his sickbed to join several Southern leaders on the floor of the convention in denouncing Parker's telegram and the drafted response. Nonetheless, the response recommended by the Parker forces was approved, 794 to 191, with opposition principally from the Middle West and West.

For vice president, the convention chose former West Virginia senator Henry G. Davis. He nearly achieved a two-thirds majority on the first ballot, receiving 654 votes. With Davis' nomination so near, a motion to declare him the vice presidential candidate was approved. Davis, at age 80, was the oldest candidate ever put on a national ticket by a major party. He was a man of great wealth, and the Democrats hoped that he would give freely to their campaign.

Although the platform was accepted without debate by a voice vote, there was maneuvering behind the scenes to meet the objections of Bryan. The initial platform draft before the resolutions committee included a plank that declared that recent gold discoveries had removed the currency question as a political issue. Bryan found this plank objectionable and successfully fought in the resolutions committee for its deletion. Bryan was less successful in having an income tax plank included but was able to get a more strongly worded antitrust resolution.

Unlike the Democratic platform of 1900, which focused on anti-imperialism, anti-monopoly and currency, the 1904 platform covered about two dozen topics with nearly equal emphasis.

The Democrats and Republicans disagreed on one new issue: federal support for private shipping firms. The Democrats opposed government assistance; the Republicans favored it. But on other issues the platform of the Democrats, like that of the Republicans, broke little new ground, instead restating positions that had been included in earlier Democratic platforms. There was a continued attack on American imperialism and a call for a smaller Army. There were planks that urged less international involvement and more emphasis on domestic improvements.

Following are excerpts from the Democratic platform of 1904:

Roosevelt Administration. The existing Republican administration has been spasmodic, erratic, sensational, spectacular and arbitrary. It has made itself a satire upon the Congress, courts, and upon the settled practices and usages of national and international law ... the necessity of reform and the rescue of the administration of Government from the headstrong, arbitrary and spasmodic methods which distract business by uncertainty, and pervade the public mind with dread, distrust and perturbation.

Shipbuilding. We denounce the ship subsidy bill recently passed by the United States Senate as an iniquitous appropriation of public funds for private purposes and a wasteful, illogical and useless attempt to overcome by subsidy the obstructions raised by Republican legislation to the growth and development of American commerce on the sea.

We favor the upbuilding of a merchant marine without new or additional burdens upon the people and without bounties from the public treasury.

1908 Conventions
Presidential Candidates

Eugene V. Debs
Socialist

William H. Taft
Republican

William J. Bryan
Democrat

Socialists

The Socialists met in Chicago in May 1908 and re-nominated the ticket that had represented the party four years earlier: Eugene V. Debs of Indiana for president and Benjamin Hanford of New York as his running mate.

The platform was divided into several major sections, including a discussion of principles, and topics entitled general demands, industrial demands and political demands. The Socialists' goal was the creation of a classless society, and in pursuance of this goal the movement was identified as a party of the working class.

Among the general demands were proposals for public works programs to aid the unemployed and public ownership of land, means of transportation and communication and monopolies.

Industrial demands included calls for reduced working hours, the abolition of child labor and more effective inspections of working areas.

The section on political demands began with a restatement of earlier positions, with a call for tax reform, women's suffrage and the initiative, referendum and recall. However, the section also included more radical demands, such as the abolition of the Senate, the amendment of the Constitution by popular vote, the direct election of all judges and the removal of power from the Supreme Court to declare legislation passed by Congress unconstitutional.

Following are excerpts from the Socialist platform of 1908:

Public Works Projects. The immediate government relief for the unemployed workers by building schools, by reforesting of cutover and waste lands, by reclamation of arid tracts, and the building of canals, and by extending all other useful public works. All persons employed on such works shall be employed directly by the government under an eight hour work day and at the prevailing union wages. The government shall also loan money to states and municipalities without interest for the purpose of carrying on public works. It shall contribute to the funds of labor organizations for the purpose of assisting their unemployed members, and shall take such other measures within its power as will lessen the widespread misery of the workers caused by the misrule of the capitalist class.

Public Ownership. The collective ownership of railroads, telegraphs, telephones, steamship lines and all other means of social transportation and communication, and all land.

The collective ownership of all industries which are organized on a national scale and in which competition has virtually ceased to exist.

Labor. The improvement of the industrial condition of the workers.

(a) By shortening the workday in keeping with the increased productiveness of machinery.

(b) By securing to every worker a rest period of not less than a day and a half in each week.

(c) By securing a more effective inspection of workshops and factories.

(d) By forbidding the employment of children under sixteen years of age.

(e) By forbidding the interstate transportation of the products of child labor, of convict labor and of all uninspected factories.

(f) By abolishing official charity and substituting in its place compulsory insurance against unemployment, illness, accident, invalidism, old age and death.

Tax Reform. The extension of inheritance taxes, graduated in proportion to the amount of the bequests and the nearness of kin.

A graduated income tax.

Women's Suffrage. Unrestricted and equal suffrage for men and women....

Senate. The abolition of the senate.

Constitutional and Judicial Reforms. The abolition of the power usurped by the supreme court of the United States to pass upon the constitutionality of legislation enacted by Congress. National laws to be repealed or abrogated only by act of Congress or by a referendum of the whole people.

That the constitution be made amendable by majority vote.

That all judges be elected by the people for short terms, and that the power to issue injunctions shall be curbed by immediate legislation.

Republicans

The Republicans held their convention in Chicago in June 1908. Although President Roosevelt declined to be a candidate for re-election, his choice for the presidency, Secretary of War William Howard Taft, was assured of nomination before the convention began.

Two hundred and twenty-three of the 980 seats at the convention were contested, but all the challenges were settled before the convention assembled. However, a dispute arose over the vote-allocation formula for the next convention. An amendment to the rules committee report proposed that the vote allocation be based on population rather than the electoral vote, as was currently in effect. Essentially, the amendment would have reduced the power of the Southern delegations. But a combination of Southern delegates and Taft supporters from other states defeated the amendment, 506 to 471. *(Chart, p. 187)*

Seven names were placed in nomination for the presidency, but Taft was a landslide winner on the first ballot, receiving 702 votes. Sen. Philander C. Knox of Pennsylvania was a distant runner-up with 68 votes.

For vice president, the convention selected Rep. James S. Sherman, a conservative New Yorker. Sherman won 816 votes on the first ballot, easily outdistancing former New Jersey governor Franklin Murphy, who had 77 votes.

The Wisconsin delegation, led by Sen. Robert M. La Follette, introduced a detailed minority report to the party platform. The Wisconsin proposals were considered in several separate sections. The first section included proposals for the establishment of a permanent tariff commission, the creation of a Department of Labor and the limitation of an eight-hour day for government workers. It was defeated, 952 to 28.

The second section recommended legislation to require the publication of campaign contributions. It was defeated, 880 to 94. Further sections of the minority report proposed the physical valuation of railroad property to help determine reasonable rates, and the direct election of senators. The railroad reform plank was beaten, 917 to 63, while the senatorial election plank was rejected, 866 to 114. After these votes, the majority report on the platform was adopted by a voice vote.

The platform approved by the delegates applauded the benefits of Republican rule, noting that under the party's guidance the United States had become the wealthiest nation on Earth. The principle of a protective tariff was applauded, as was the gold standard, an expansionist foreign policy and support for America's merchant marine.

Following are excerpts from the Republican platform of 1908:

> **Party Differences.** In history, the difference between Democracy and Republicanism is that the one stood for debased currency, the other for honest currency; the one for free silver, the other for sound money; the one for free trade, the other for protection; the one for the contraction of American influence, the other for its expansion; the one has been forced to abandon every position taken on the great issues before the people, the other has held and vindicated all.
>
> The present tendencies of the two parties are even more marked by inherent differences. The trend of Democracy is toward socialism, while the Republican party stands for a wise and regulated individualism.... Ultimately Democracy would have the nation own the people, while Republicanism would have the people own the nation.

Democrats

The Democratic convention of 1908 was held in July in Denver, Colo. — the first convention held by a major party in a Western state. The convention was dominated by the Bryan forces, who regained control of the party after the conservative Alton B. Parker's landslide defeat in 1904.

Bryan's strength was evident on the first roll-call vote, concerning a Pennsylvania credentials dispute. The majority report claimed there were voting irregularities in five Philadelphia districts and urged the seating of Bryan delegates in place of those elected. By a vote of 604-1/2 to 386-1/2, the convention defeated the minority report, which argued for the delegates initially elected in the primary, and then passed the majority report by a voice vote.

Bryan's presidential nomination was never in doubt. He was an easy winner on the first ballot, receiving 888-1/2 votes to 59-1/2 for Judge George Gray of Delaware and 46 for Gov. John A. Johnson of Minnesota. *(Chart, p. 186)*

Bryan left the choice of his running mate to the delegates. Although four names were placed in nomination, former Indiana gubernatorial candidate John W. Kern was chosen by acclamation. *The New York Times* sarcastically described the consistency of the Bryan-Kern ticket: "For a man twice defeated for the Presidency was at the head of it, and a man twice defeated for governor of his state was at the tail of it."

The platform adopted by the convention was tailored to Bryan's liking and had as its theme, "Shall the people rule?" The first portion of the document criticized Republican rule, specifically denouncing government overspending, a growing Republican-oriented bureaucracy and an unethical link between big business and the Republican Party characterized by large, unreported campaign contributions.

Meeting three weeks after the Republicans, the Democrats adopted most of the minority planks rejected earlier by the Republicans. Included in the Democratic platform were calls for the physical valuation of railroads, the creation of a Department of Labor, eight-hour work days for government employees, the direct election of senators and a prohibition against corporate campaign contributions and individual contributions over "a reasonable amount." The two parties continued to disagree on support of the American merchant marine, the nature of tariff revision and the direction of foreign policy, particularly regarding the lands acquired after the Spanish-American War.

The Democratic platform restated the party's support of a lower tariff, more extensive antitrust legislation with more rigid enforcement, a graduated income tax, increased power for the Interstate Commerce Commission to regulate railroads, telephone and telegraph companies, and a recommendation of prompt independence for the Philippines.

The Democrats included a plank abhorring Roosevelt's attempt to create a "dynasty," a direct reference to the outgoing president's hand-picking his war secretary, William Howard Taft, as next Republican presidential candidate.

Following are excerpts from the Democratic platform of 1908:

> **Appeal to the Masses.** The conscience of the nation is now aroused to free the Government from the grip of those who have made it a business asset of the favor-seeking corporations. It must become again a people's government, and be administered in all its departments according to the Jeffersonian maxim, "equal rights to all; special privileges to none."

"Shall the people rule?" is the overshadowing issue which manifests itself in all the questions now under discussion.

Campaign Contributions. We demand Federal legislation forever terminating the partnership which has existed between corporations of the country and the Republican party under the expressed or implied agreement that in return for the contribution of great sums of money wherewith to purchase elections, they should be allowed to continue substantially unmolested in their efforts to encroach upon the rights of the people....

We pledge the Democratic party to the enactment of a law prohibiting any corporation from contributing to a campaign fund and any individual from contributing an amount above a reasonable maximum, and providing for the publication before election of all such contributions.

Labor. Questions of judicial practice have arisen especially in connection with industrial disputes. We deem that the parties to all judicial proceedings should be treated with rigid impartiality, and that injunctions should not be issued in any cases in which injunctions would not issue if no industrial dispute were involved....

We favor the eight hour day on all Government work.

We pledge the Democratic party to the enactment of a law by Congress, as far as the Federal jurisdiction extends, for a general employer's liability act covering injury to body or loss of life of employes.

We pledge the Democratic party to the enactment of a law creating a Department of Labor, represented separately in the President's Cabinet, in which Department shall be included the subject of mines and mining.

1912 Conventions

Presidential Candidates

| Eugene V. Debs | William H. Taft | Woodrow Wilson | Theodore Roosevelt |
| Socialist | Republican | Democrat | Progressive |

Socialists

Eugene V. Debs of Indiana was nominated by the Socialists in 1912 to make his fourth run for the presidency. The convention, which met in Indianapolis in May, chose Emil Seidel of Wisconsin as his running mate.

The platform adopted by the Socialists was similar to the one written four years earlier, with calls for increased worker benefits, public works jobs for the unemployed, public ownership of land and the means of transportation and communication, tax reform, widespread political reform and a social insurance program.

The Socialists also added new proposals, advocating public ownership of the banking and currency system, the introduction of minimum wage scales, the elimination of the profit system in government contracts, an increase in corporation taxes and the direct election of the president and vice president.

Following are excerpts from the Socialist platform of 1912:

Social Insurance. By abolishing official charity and substituting a non-contributory system of old age pensions, a general system of insurance by the State of all its members against unemployment and invalidism and a system of compulsory insurance by employers of their workers, without cost to the latter, against industrial diseases, accidents and death.

Government Contracts. By abolishing the profit system in government work and substituting either the direct hire of labor or the awarding of contracts to cooperative groups of workers.

Minimum Wage. By establishing minimum wage scales.

Tax Reform. The adoption of a graduated income tax, the increase of the rates of the present corporation tax and the extension of inheritance taxes, graduated in proportion to the value of the estate and to nearness of kin — the proceeds of these taxes to be employed in the socialization of industry.

Banking and Currency. The collective ownership and democratic management of the banking and currency system.

Direct Election of President. The election of the President and Vice-President by direct vote of the people.

Republicans

The 1912 Republican convention was one of the most tumultuous ever. It was held in Chicago in June and served as a fiery culmination to the bitter contest between President William Howard Taft and former president Theodore Roosevelt for the party's presidential nomination.

Roosevelt had overwhelmed Taft in the presidential primaries, but Roosevelt's popular strength was more than offset by Taft's control of the national committee and Southern delegations. Taft supporters held 37 of 53 seats on the national committee, an edge that the incumbent president's managers used to advantage in settling seating disputes. Two hundred and fifty-four of the 1,078 convention seats were contested before the national committee, and 235 were settled in favor of Taft delegates. Although a number of Roosevelt challenges were made with little justification, the dispensation of the challenges showed Taft's control of the convention organization.

With the conservative Republicans united behind Taft, Roosevelt faced the additional problem of sharing support from the progressive wing of the party with another candidate, Sen. Robert M. La Follette of Wisconsin. La Follette had only 41 delegates; but, angered by Roosevelt's bid to control the progressive forces, refused to withdraw as a candidate.

The first skirmish at the convention was over the choice of a temporary chairman. The Taft forces favored Sen. Elihu Root of New York, while the Roosevelt delegates supported Gov. Francis E. McGovern of Wisconsin. On a prolonged roll call, during which the vote of each delegate was taken individually, Root defeated McGovern, 558 to 501. *(Chart, p. 189)*

With the contest for the temporary chairmanship settled, the battle shifted to credentials. Virtually shut out in the settlement of credentials cases by the national committee, the Roosevelt forces brought 72 delegate challenges to the floor of the convention. Before consideration of the cases, the Roosevelt leaders moved that none of the challenged delegates (favorable to Taft) be allowed to vote on any of the credentials contests. However, a motion to table this proposal carried, 567 to 507, and the challenged delegates were allowed to vote on all cases except their own. Although the Taft forces were clearly in control of the convention, four credentials cases were presented for a vote, and all were decided in favor of the Taft delegates. The rest of the contests were settled by voice votes.

At this point, Roosevelt, who had dramatically come to Chicago to direct his forces, advised his delegates to abstain from voting but to remain in the convention as a silent protest to what he regarded as steamroller tactics. In the convention hall itself, the pro-Roosevelt galleries emphasized the feelings of their leader by rubbing sandpaper and blowing horns to imitate the sounds of a steamroller.

Only two names were placed in nomination for the presidency — Taft's and La Follette's. Taft was nominated by Warren G. Harding of Ohio, who himself would be president less than a decade later but at the time was merely a former lieutenant governor. With most of the Roosevelt delegates abstaining, Taft won easily on the first ballot with 556 votes. Roosevelt received 107 votes and La Follette 41, while 348 delegates were present and did not vote.

Vice President James S. Sherman was easily renominated, collecting 596 votes to 21 for the runner-up, Sen. William E. Borah of Idaho. However, 352 delegates were present but refused to vote, and 72 others were absent. In recognition of Sherman's failing health, the convention passed a resolution empowering the national committee to fill any vacancy on the ticket that might occur.

Although the Roosevelt delegates had remained in the convention hall as a silent protest to the renomination of Taft and Sherman, the groundwork for the creation of a Roosevelt-led third party had begun as soon as the credentials contests were settled in favor of Taft. Before the Republican convention even began its presidential balloting, Roosevelt announced that he would accept the nomination of the "honestly elected majority" of the Republican convention or a new progressive party. The next day, June 22, after final adjournment of the Republican convention, many of the Roosevelt delegates assembled in a Chicago auditorium to hear their leader announce his availablity as a candidate of an honestly elected progressive convention. Gov. Hiram Johnson of California was named temporary chairman of the new party, and planning was begun to hold a national convention later in the summer.

As in 1908, a progressive minority report to the platform was submitted. However, instead of taking individual votes on the various planks, the convention tabled the whole report by a voice vote. Subsequently, the majority report was accepted by a vote of 666 to 53, with 343 delegates present but not voting.

The platform lauded the accomplishments of the McKinley, Roosevelt and Taft administrations but contained few major positions different from the Democrats'. The Republican platform included, however, new planks favoring judicial reform and legislation publicizing campaign contributions and outlawing corporate campaign donations.

Following are excerpts from the Republican platform of 1912:

Tariff. The protective tariff is so woven into the fabric of our industrial and agricultural life that to substitute for it a tariff for revenue only would destroy many industries and throw millions of our people out of employment. The products of the farm and of the mine should receive the same measure of protection as other products of American labor.

Campaign Contributions. We favor such additional legislation as may be necessary more effectually to prohibit corporations from contributing funds, directly or indirectly, to campaigns for the nomination or election of the President, the Vice-President, Senators, and Representatives in Congress.

We heartily approve the recent Act of Congress requiring the fullest publicity in regard to all campaign contributions, whether made in connection with primaries, conventions, or elections.

Judicial Reform. That the Courts, both Federal and State, may bear the heavy burden laid upon them to the complete satisfaction of public opinion, we favor legislation to prevent long delays and the tedious and costly appeals which have so often amounted to a denial of justice in civil cases and to a failure to protect the public at large in criminal cases.

Democrats

For the first time since 1872, the Democratic convention was held in Baltimore. The delegates, who assembled in the Maryland city in June, one week after the Republicans began their convention in Chicago, had a number of presidential candidates to choose from, although House Speaker Champ Clark of Missouri and Gov. Woodrow Wilson of New Jersey were the major contenders.

Once again, William Jennings Bryan had a major impact on the proceedings of a Democratic convention. His first appearance came in opposition to the national committee's selection of Judge Alton B. Parker of New York, the party's standard-bearer in 1904, as temporary chairman. Bryan nominated Sen. John W. Kern of Indiana for the post. In declining to be a candidate for temporary chairman, Kern recommended that Parker also withdraw as a candidate. But when Parker refused, Kern nominated Bryan for the post. Parker won on the roll call that followed, 579 to 508, with most of the Wilson delegates voting for Bryan, the Clark delegates splitting their support and delegates for other candidates favoring Parker. *(Chart, p. 188)*

The defeat of Bryan produced an avalanche of telegrams from across the country, with a contemporary estimate of more than 100,000 flooding the delegates in Baltimore. Most of the telegrams were written by progressives and served to weaken the candidacy of the more conservative Clark.

In an attempt to appease Bryan, Parker urged members of the platform committee to select the Nebraskan as their chairman. Bryan, however, refused this overture. Subsequently, the platform committee announced that, by a margin of 41 to 11, the committee had voted to delay presentation of the platform until after selection of the candidates.

The Wilson forces won their first key vote on a question involving the unit rule. The vote specifically concerned the Ohio delegation, where district delegates, elected for Wilson, were bound by the state convention to vote for Gov. Judson Harmon of Ohio. By a vote of 565-1/2 to 491-1/3, the convention approved the right of the district delegates to vote for Wilson.

The Wilson forces won another test on a credentials dispute concerning the South Dakota delegation. The credentials committee recommended seating a delegation pledged to Clark; but the convention, by a vote of 639-1/2 to 437, supported the minority report, which called for seating delegates pledged to Wilson.

Bryan reappeared before the presidential balloting and introduced a resolution opposing the nomination of any candidate "who is the representative of or under obligation to J. Pierpont Morgan, Thomas F. Ryan, August Belmont, or any other member of the privilege-hunting and favor-seeking class." Bryan's resolution passed easily, 883 to 202-1/2.

Six names were placed in nomination for the presidency. Clark led on the first ballot with 440-1/2 votes, followed by Wilson with 324, Harmon with 148 and Rep. Oscar W. Underwood of Alabama with 117-1/2. Seven hundred and twenty-six votes were needed to nominate. *(Chart, p. 189)*

For nine ballots, there was little change in the vote totals, but on the 10th roll call New York shifted its 90 votes from Harmon to Clark. Expecting a quick triumph, the Clark forces unleashed an hour-long demonstration. However, their celebration was premature. While Clark had 556 votes, a majority, his total was well short of the two-thirds majority (730 votes) required by the rules.

The 10th ballot proved to be the high-water mark for Clark. On succeeding roll calls, he slowly began to lose strength. During the 14th ballot, Bryan received permission to address the convention again, this time to explain his vote. "The Great Commoner" announced that he could not support a candidate endorsed by the Tammany-con-trolled New York delegation and, although bound earlier by state primary results to support Clark, was now switching his vote to Wilson. Most of the Nebraska delegation followed Bryan in voting for Wilson. After the 14th ballot, the vote totals stood: Clark, 553; Wilson, 361; Underwood, 111.

There were long intervals between other major vote switches. On the 20th ballot, Kansas shifted 20 of its votes from Clark to Wilson. On the 28th ballot, after a weekend recess, Indiana's favorite son, Gov. Thomas R. Marshall, withdrew in favor of Wilson. The slow trend in favor of the New Jersey governor finally enabled Wilson to pass Clark on the 30th roll call, 460 to 455; Underwood remained a distant third with 121-1/2 votes. *(Chart, p. 188)*

The convention adjourned for the evening after the 42nd ballot, but the Wilson momentum continued the next day. Illinois switched its 58 votes to Wilson on the 43rd ballot, giving him a simple majority with 602 votes. Clark continued to decline, slipping to 329 votes.

Wilson showed slight gains on the next two ballots, but the big break came on the 46th roll call, when Underwood withdrew. This was followed by the withdrawal of Clark and the other remaining candidates. Wilson received 990 votes on the 46th ballot, followed by Clark with 84.

Clark's failure to win the nomination marked the first occasion since 1844 that a candidate achieved a simple majority of the votes, without subsequently winning the necessary two-thirds majority. The 46 roll calls also represented the highest number of presidential ballots taken at any convention, Republican or Democratic, since 1860.

Wilson preferred Underwood as his running mate, but the Alabama representative was not interested in second place on the ticket. On the vice presidential roll call that followed, nine candidates received votes, led by Marshall with 389 votes and Gov. John Burke of North Dakota with 304-2/3. Marshall lengthened his lead over Burke on the second ballot, 644-1/2 to 386-1/3. After the roll call was completed, a New Jersey delegate moved that Marshall's nomination be made unanimous, and the motion passed.

The Democratic platform was approved without debate before selection of the vice presidential candidate. The platform restated a number of positions included in earlier party documents. It blamed the high cost of living on the protective tariff and the existence of trusts, and it called for a lower, revenue-only tariff and the passage of stronger antitrust legislation. The tariff issue was one of the major areas on which there was a marked difference between the parties, as the Republicans continued to support a protective tariff.

As in 1908, planks were included favoring the publicizing of campaign contributions and calling for the prohibition of corporate contributions and a limit on individual contributions.

The Democrats' labor plank was also virtually a restatement of the party's position four years earlier, supporting creation of a Department of Labor, a more limited use of injunctions, the guaranteed right of workers to organize and passage of an employers' compensation law. In contrast to the Democrats' support of employers' liability, the Republicans advocated workmen's compensation legislation.

Unlike the Republicans, the Democrats called for federal legislation to regulate the rates of railroad, telegraph, telephone and express companies based on valuation by the Interstate Commerce Commission. A plank was also included in the Democratic platform calling for the ratifica-

tion of constitutional amendments establishing a graduated income tax and the direct election of senators — issues on which the Republican platform was silent. Imperialism was again denounced, as it had been in every Democratic platform since 1900.

New planks advocated a single-term presidency, the extension of presidential primaries to all states, reform of the judicial system to eliminate delays and cut expenses in court proceedings, and the strengthening of the government's pure food and public health agencies.

Following are excerpts from the Democratic platform of 1912:

Single-term Presidency. We favor a single Presidential term, and to that end urge the adoption of an amendment to the Constitution making the President of the United States ineligible to reelection, and we pledge the candidates of this Convention to this principle.

Presidential Primaries. The movement toward more popular government should be promoted through legislation in each State which will permit the expression of the preference of the electors for national candidates at presidential primaries.

Judicial Reform. We recognize the urgent need of reform in the administration of civil and criminal law in the United States, and we recommend the enactment of such legislation and the promotion of such measures as will rid the present legal system of the delays, expense, and uncertainties incident to the system as now administered.

States' Rights. Believing that the most efficient results under our system of government are to be attained by the full exercise by the States of their reserved sovereign powers, we denounce as usurpation the efforts of our opponents to deprive the States of any of the rights reserved to them, and to enlarge and magnify by indirection the powers of the Federal government.

Progressives

Early in August 1912 the bolting Roosevelt forces assembled in Chicago and nominated their leader to guide a new party, the Progressives. More than 2,000 delegates, representing every state except South Carolina, gathered for the three-day convention. It was a diverse assembly that matched the Populists in crusading idealism and included, for the first time, women as well as men politicians and social workers as well as businessmen.

While the delegates enthusiastically sang "Onward, Christian Soldiers" and "The Battle Hymn of the Republic" and cheered the appearance of Roosevelt before the convention, there was some dissension caused by the party's racial policy.

During the campaign for the Republican presidential nomination, Taft had the support of party organizations in the South, which included blacks. As a result, Roosevelt directed his appeal strictly to white leaders in the region. Describing Southern black delegates as uneducated and purchasable, Roosevelt insisted that only "lily white" delegations from the South be seated at the Progressive convention, but he allowed blacks to be included in delegations from other states. Although there was no floor debate on this policy, a number of liberal delegates were dissatisfied with Roosevelt's decision.

Both Roosevelt and his handpicked choice for vice president, Gov. Hiram W. Johnson of California, were nominated by acclamation. Jane Addams, a Chicago social worker and leader in the women's rights movement, gave evidence of the role of women in the Progressive Party by delivering a seconding speech for Roosevelt.

Like the nominations of the Progressive standard-bearers, the party platform was adopted by acclamation. But the voice vote hid the dissatisfaction felt by Midwestern and Western Progressives over the antitrust plank. Most of the Progressives from these regions favored the busting of trusts through enforcement of the Sherman Anti-trust Act. Roosevelt, however, favored government regulation rather than trust-busting.

The platform approved by the convention included the trust-busting position. However, Roosevelt and his close advisers deleted the section in the official report. While there was obvious disagreement in the party on this issue, there was no floor debate or roll-call vote on the subject.

With the theme "A Covenant with the People," the platform argued for increased democratization coupled with more people-oriented federal programs. The party favored nationwide presidential primaries, the direct election of senators, the initiative, referendum and recall and women's suffrage. Additionally, the Progressives proposed that state laws ruled unconstitutional be submitted to a vote of the state electorate.

The platform also advocated congressional reforms: the registration of lobbyists; the publicizing of committee hearings except in foreign affairs, and the recording of committee votes.

Like the Democrats, the Progressives favored creation of a Department of Labor and a more limited use of labor injunctions, but additionally the new party called for a prohibition of child labor and convict contract labor.

The Progressives went beyond both major parties in proposing the union of government health agencies into a single national health service and the creation of a social insurance system that would assist both the elderly and workers who were ill or unemployed. To help support their proposed federal programs, the Progressives recommended passage of the income tax amendment and establishment of a graduated inheritance tax.

Having adopted their platform and selected their candidates, the delegates to the Progressive convention adjourned by singing the "Doxology."

Following are excerpts from the Progressive platform of 1912:

Electoral Reform. In particular, the party declares for direct primaries of the nomination of State and National officers, for nation-wide preferential primaries for candidates for the presidency; for the direct election of United States Senators by the people; and we urge on the States the policy of the short ballot, with responsibility to the people secured by the initiative, referendum and recall.

Women's Suffrage. The Progressive party, believing that no people can justly claim to be a true democracy which denies political rights on account of sex, pledges itself to the task of securing equal suffrage to men and women alike.

Judicial Reform. That when an Act, passed under the police power of the State, is held unconstitutional under the State Constitution, by the courts, the people, after an ample interval for deliberation, shall have an opportunity to vote on the question whether they desire the Act to become law, notwithstanding such decision.

Campaign Contributions. We pledge our party to legislation that will compel strict limitation of all campaign contributions and expenditures, and detailed publicity of both before as well as after primaries and elections.

Congressional Reform. We pledge our party to

legislation compelling the registration of lobbyists; publicity of committee hearings except on foreign affairs, and recording of all votes in committee....

National Health Service. We favor the union of all the existing agencies of the Federal Government dealing with the public health into a single national health service without discrimination against or for any one set of therapeutic methods, school of medicine, or school of healing with such additional powers as may be necessary to enable it to perform efficiently such duties in the protection of the public from preventable diseases as may be properly undertaken by the Federal authorities, including the executing of existing laws regarding pure food, quarantine and cognate subjects, the promotion of vital statistics and the extension of the registration area of such statistics, and cooperation with the health activities of the various States and cities of the Nation.

Social Insurance. The protection of home life against the hazards of sickness, irregular employment and old age through the adoption of a system of social insurance adapted to American use....

Antitrust Action. We therefore demand a strong National regulation of inter-State corporations . . . we urge the establishment of a strong Federal administrative commission of high standing, which shall maintain permanent active supervision over industrial corporations engaged in inter-State commerce, or such of them as are of public importance, doing for them what the Government now does for the National banks, and what is now done for the railroads by the Inter-State Commerce Commission.

Income and Inheritance Taxes. We believe in a graduated inheritance tax as a National means of equalizing the obligations of holders of property to Government, and we hereby pledge our party to enact such a Federal law as will tax large inheritances, returning to the States an equitable percentage of all amounts collected.

We favor the ratification of the pending amendment to the Constitution giving the Government power to levy an income tax.

Tariff. We demand tariff revision because the present tariff is unjust to the people of the United States. Fair dealing toward the people requires an immediate downward revision of those schedules wherein duties are shown to be unjust or excessive....

The Democratic party is committed to the destruction of the protective system through a tariff for revenue only — a policy which would inevitably produce widespread industrial and commercial disaster.

Republicans and Democrats. Political parties exist to secure responsible government and to execute the will of the people.

From these great tasks both of the old parties have turned aside. Instead of instruments to promote the general welfare, they have become the tools of corrupt interests which use them impartially to serve their selfish purposes. Behind the ostensible government sits enthroned an invisible government owing no allegiance and acknowledging no responsibility to the people.

To destroy this invisible government, to dissolve the unholy alliance between corrupt business and corrupt politics is the first task of the statesmanship of the day.

States' Rights. The extreme insistence on States' rights by the Democratic party in the Baltimore platform demonstrates anew its ability to understand the world into which it has survived or to administer the affairs of a union of States which have in all essential respects become one people.

1916 Conventions

Presidential Candidates

Charles E. Hughes
Republican

Woodrow Wilson
Democrat

Republicans

The Republicans and Progressives both held their conventions in Chicago in early June 1916. Leaders of both parties were ready to negotiate to heal the split that had divided the Republican Party in 1912.

Before the convention began, the Republican National Committee already had effected reform in the vote-allocation formula. To meet the objection raised in 1912 that the South was overrepresented, the national committee adopted a new method of vote allocation that considered a state's Republican voting strength as well as its electoral vote. Under the new formula, the Southern states lost 78 delegate seats, or more than a third of their 1912 total.

But while the Republicans were willing to make some

internal reforms, most party leaders were adamantly opposed to nominating the hero of the Progressives, Theodore Roosevelt. Before the presidential balloting began, the Republican convention approved by voice vote the selection of a five-man committee to meet jointly with representatives of the Progressive convention, with the hope of finding a course of action that would unify the two parties.

However, the Republican representatives reported back that the Progressives, while desiring unity with the Republicans, firmly favored the nomination of Roosevelt. The Republican convention chairman, Sen. Warren G. Harding of Ohio, instructed the conferees to continue negotiations but allowed the presidential balloting to begin.

Charles Evans Hughes, a Supreme Court justice and former governor of New York, was the front-runner for the Republican nomination. Hughes did not actively seek the nomination and remained on the Supreme Court during the pre-convention period. But he was viewed by many party leaders as an ideal compromise candidate, because of his progressive credentials and lack of involvement in the divisive 1912 campaign.

However, some conservative party leaders felt Hughes was too progressive and sought other candidates. Seventeen men received votes on the first ballot, led by Hughes with 253-1/2. Next were Sen. John W. Weeks of Massachusetts with 105 votes and former senator Elihu Root of New York with 103. Five of the other vote recipients had at least 65 votes each. The justice widened his lead on the second ballot, receiving 328-1/2 votes to 98-1/2 for Root. After the second roll call the convention voted 694-1/2 to 286-1/2 to recess for the evening. Most of the votes for adjournment came from delegates outside the Hughes column. *(Chart, p. 191)*

While the Republican convention was in recess, the joint committee of Republicans and Progressives continued to negotiate. The Republican members proposed Hughes as a compromise candidate, but in a message from his home in Oyster Bay, N.Y., Roosevelt stunned both parties by suggesting the name of Henry Cabot Lodge, a conservative senator from Massachusetts.

The Progressive delegates reacted defiantly to this recommendation by nominating Roosevelt by acclamation and selecting John M. Parker of Louisiana as his running mate. Roosevelt, however, immediately scotched the enthusiasm of the Progressive delegates by conditionally declining the nomination. Roosevelt informed the convention that he would support Hughes if the latter's positions on major issues were acceptable.

When the Republican convention reconvened the next day, the opposition to Hughes had evaporated. The New Yorker received 949-1/2 of the 987 convention votes on the third ballot, and his nomination was subsequently declared unanimous.

Charles W. Fairbanks of Indiana, vice president under Roosevelt, was the convention's choice to fill out the Republican ticket. Fairbanks won on the first ballot by 863 votes to 108 for former Nebraska senator Elmer J. Burkett.

The Wisconsin delegation again presented its own minority platform report, which included planks that denounced "dollar diplomacy" and called for women's suffrage, a referendum before any declaration of war and constitutional amendments to establish the initiative, referendum and recall. The minority report was defeated and the majority report was approved by voice votes.

The adopted platform harshly criticized the policies of the Wilson administration. In foreign policy, the Republicans denounced the Wilson government for "shifty expedients" and "phrase making" and promised "strict and honest neutrality." The platform condemned the administration for its intervention in Mexico and non-involvement in the Philippines. The Republicans also called for a stronger national defense.

The two parties continued to disagree on the tariff issue, with the Republicans criticizing the lower (Democratic-passed) Underwood tariff and arguing for a higher, protective tariff. The Republican platform lauded the party's efforts in passing antitrust and transportation rate regulation, but it criticized the Democrats for harassing business.

Following are excerpts from the Republican platform of 1916:

Foreign Policy. We desire peace, the peace of justice and right, and believe in maintaining a strict and honest neutrality between the belligerents in the great war in Europe. We must perform all our duties and insist upon all our rights as neutrals without fear and without favor. We believe that peace and neutrality, as well as the dignity and influence of the United States, cannot be preserved by shifty expedients, by phrase making, by performances in language, or by attitudes ever changing in an effort to secure votes or voters.

National Defense. We must have a Navy so strong and so well proportioned and equipped, so thoroughly ready and prepared, that no enemy can gain command of the sea and effect a landing in force on either our Western or our Eastern coast. To secure these results we must have a coherent continuous policy of national defense, which even in these perilous days the Democratic party has utterly failed to develop, but which we promise to give to the country.

Merchant Marine. We are utterly opposed to the Government ownership of vessels as proposed by the Democratic party, because Government-owned ships, while effectively preventing the development of the American Merchant Marine by private capital, will be entirely unable to provide for the vast volume of American freights and will leave us more helpless than ever in the hard grip of foreign syndicates.

Tariff. The Republican party stands now, as always, in the fullest sense for the policy of tariff protection to American industries and American labor.

Business. The Republican party firmly believes that all who violate the laws in regulation of business, should be individually punished. But prosecution is very different from persecution, and business success, no matter how honestly attained, is apparently regarded by the Democratic party as in itself a crime. Such doctrines and beliefs choke enterprise and stifle prosperity. The Republican party believes in encouraging American business as it believes in and will seek to advance all American interests.

Women's Suffrage. The Republican party, reaffirming its faith in government of the people, by the people, for the people, as a measure of justice to one-half the adult people of this country, favors the extension of the suffrage to women, but recognizes the right of each state to settle this question for itself.

Democrats

The Democratic convention of 1916 was held in St. Louis in mid-June. The delegates were nearly unanimous in their support for President Woodrow Wilson, who was renominated by the vote of 1,092 to 1 — the lone dissenting vote coming from an Illinois delegate who disapproved of a motion to nominate Wilson by acclamation. With Wilson's

approval, Vice President Thomas R. Marshall was renominated by acclamation.

For the first time in more than two decades, William Jennings Bryan was not a major convention force. Bryan was defeated in his bid to be a delegate-at-large from Nebraska and attended the convention as a reporter. He was invited to address the delegates and echoed the theme stressed by other speakers, that Wilson would keep the nation out of war.

Wilson was the recognized leader of the Democratic Party, but the pacifistic theme, emphasized by Bryan and other convention orators, struck a responsive chord among the delegates that was mildly alarming to Wilson and his managers. They initially had planned to accent the theme of Americanism and national unity.

The wording of the national unity plank was a matter of debate within the platform committee. The Democratic senators from Missouri warned that Wilson's strongly worded plank might offend German-American citizens. Nonetheless, the Wilson plank was retained and placed prominently near the beginning of the platform.

The only section of the platform brought to a floor vote was the plank on women's suffrage. The majority plank favored extending the vote to women, while a minority plank advocated leaving the matter to the individual states. The minority plank was defeated, 888-1/2 to 181-1/2. The rest of the platform was then adopted by a voice vote. The Democratic position on women's suffrage contrasted with that of the Republicans, who proposed leaving the matter up to the individual states. *(Chart, p. 190)*

The platform's inclusion of national unity and military preparedness planks was a contrast with earlier Democratic platforms around the turn of the century, which had consistently denounced imperialism and denied the need for a stronger military. Even though spurred by the war in Europe, the new planks were a notable change.

The rest of the platform focused on the progressive reforms of the Wilson administration, particularly in tariff, banking, labor and agriculture. Wilson himself was lauded as "the greatest American of his generation."

Noticeably absent from the platform were two planks in the party's document four years earlier: a call for a single-term presidency and a defense of states' rights.

Following are excerpts from the Democratic platform of 1916:

National Unity. In this day of test, America must show itself not a nation of partisans but a nation of patriots. There is gathered here in America the best of the blood, the industry and the genius of the whole world, the elements of a great race and a magnificent society to be welded into a mighty and splendid Nation. Whoever, actuated by the purpose to promote the industry of a foreign power, in disregard of our own country's welfare or to injure this government in its foreign relations or cripple or destroy its industries at home, and whoever by arousing prejudices of a racial, religious or other nature creates discord and strife among our people so as to obstruct the wholesome process of unification, is faithless to the trust which the privileges of citizenship repose in him and is disloyal to his country.

Military Preparedness. We therefore favor the maintenance of an army fully adequate to the requirements of order, of safety, and of the protection of the nation's rights, the fullest development of modern methods of seacoast defence and the maintenance of an adequate reserve of citizens trained to arms and prepared to safeguard the people and territory of the United States against any danger of hostile action which may unexpectedly arise; and a fixed policy for the continuous development of a navy, worthy to support the great naval traditions of the United States and fully equal to the international tasks which this Nation hopes and expects to take a part in performing.

Tariff. We reaffirm our belief in the doctrine of a tariff for the purpose of providing sufficient revenue for the operation of the government economically administered, and unreservedly endorse the Underwood tariff law as truly exemplifying that doctrine.

Women's Suffrage. We recommend the extension of the franchise to the women of the country by the States upon the same terms as to men.

Socialists

The Socialists did not hold a convention in 1916 but did nominate candidates and adopt a platform. The candidates were chosen in a unique mail referendum. With Eugene V. Debs' refusal to run, the presidential nomination went to Allan L. Benson of New York. George R. Kirkpatrick of New Jersey was selected as his running mate.

More than half of the Socialist platform was devoted to criticizing the United States' preparations for war. The Socialists opposed the war in Europe and viewed the American drive for preparedness as an effort by ruling capitalists to protect the system and their profits.

The Socialist platform specifically advocated no increase in military appropriations, a national referendum on any declaration of war, the shifting of the power to make foreign policy from the president to Congress, the abandonment of the Monroe Doctrine and immediate independence for the Philippines.

The rest of the platform was divided into sections entitled political demands, industrial demands and collective ownership. The proposals in these sections paralleled earlier Socialist platforms, although there was a new plank, advocating lending by the federal government to local governments, which was an early expression of the concept of revenue-sharing.

Following are excerpts from the Socialist platform of 1916:

Militarism and Preparedness. The working class must recognize militarism as the greatest menace to all efforts toward industrial freedom, and regardless of political or industrial affiliations must present a united front in the fight against preparedness and militarism.... The war in Europe, which diminished and is still diminishing the remote possibility of European attack upon the United States, was nevertheless seized upon by capitalists and by unscrupulous politicians as a means of spreading fear throughout the country, to the end that, by false pretenses, great military establishments might be obtained. We denounce such "preparedness" as both false in principle, unnecessary in character and dangerous in its plain tendencies toward militarism.

Foreign Policy. We, therefore, demand that the power to fix foreign policies and conduct diplomatic negotiations shall be lodged in congress and shall be exercised publicly, the people reserving the right to order congress, at any time, to change its foreign policy.

Referendum on War. That no war shall be declared or waged by the United States without a referendum vote of the entire people, except for the purpose of repelling invasion.

Federal Loans to Local Governments. The government shall lend money on bonds to counties and municipalities at a nominal rate of interest for the purpose of taking over or establishing public utilities and for building or maintaining public roads or highways and public schools.

1920 Conventions

Presidential Candidates

Eugene V. Debs
Socialist

Warren G. Harding
Republican

James M. Cox
Democrat

Socialists

The Socialists held their convention in New York in May and for the fifth time nominated Eugene V. Debs of Indiana for president. It was one of the strangest candidacies in American political history, because at the time Debs was serving a 10-year prison term in the Atlanta federal penitentiary for his outspoken opposition to the American war effort. Seymour Stedman of Ohio was chosen as his running mate.

The Socialist platform was again a distinctive document, going far beyond the platforms of the two major parties in the radical nature of the reforms proposed. The platform characterized the war policies and peace proposals of the Wilson administration as "despotism, reaction and oppression unsurpassed in the annals of the republic." It called for the replacement of the "mischievous" League of Nations with an international parliament. It favored recognition of both the newly established Irish Republic and the Soviet Union.

The Socialists continued to advocate extensive tax reform and included new calls for a tax on unused land and a progressive property tax on wartime profits that would help pay off government debts. The platform warned that the continuing militaristic mood of both major parties could lead to another war.

The Socialists continued to recommend extensive labor benefits, but for the first time they specifically mentioned migratory workers as needing government assistance.

Following are excerpts from the Socialist platform of 1920:

League of Nations. The Government of the United States should initiate a movement to dissolve the mischievous organization called the "League of Nations" and to create an international parliament, composed of democratically elected representatives of all nations of the world based upon the recognition of their equal rights, the principles of self determination, the right to national existence of colonies and other dependencies, freedom of international trade and trade routes by land and sea, and universal disarmament, and be charged with revising the Treaty of Peace on the principles of justice and conciliation.

Labor. Congress should enact effective laws to abolish child labor, to fix minimum wages, based on an ascertained cost of a decent standard of life, to protect migratory and unemployed workers from oppression, to abolish detective and strike-breaking agencies and to establish a shorter work-day in keeping with increased industrial productivity.

Blacks. Congress should enforce the provisions of the Thirteenth, Fourteenth and Fifteenth Amendments with reference to the Negroes, and effective federal legislation should be enacted to secure the Negroes full civil, political, industrial and educational rights.

Republicans

In mid-June, Republicans met for the fifth straight time in Chicago for their quadrennial convention. For the first time, women were on the floor in large numbers as delegates. With the constitutional amendment granting women the vote on the verge of passage, Republicans, especially in the Midwest and West, were quick to include women in their delegations.

The Republicans, like the Democrats two weeks later, entered their convention with no clear front-runner for the presidential nomination. Three candidates were at the top of the list, but two of them, Maj. Gen. Leonard Wood of New Hampshire and Sen. Hiram Johnson of California, split the party's progressive wing, while the third entry, Gov. Frank Lowden of Illinois, ran poorly in the presidential primaries and was accused of campaign spending irregularities.

The names of 11 men were placed in nomination for the presidency, but none came close during the first day of balloting to the 493 votes needed to nominate. Wood led on the initial roll call with 287-1/2 votes, trailed by Lowden with 211-1/2 and Johnson with 133-1/2. Sen. Warren G. Harding of Ohio, who had not campaigned for the nomination as extensively as the three pacesetters, placed sixth with 65-1/2 votes. Wood, Lowden and Johnson all gained strength during the first three ballots. *(Chart, p. 193)*

After the third roll call, the Johnson delegates moved for adjournment but were defeated, 701-1/2 to 275-1/2. On the fourth ballot, Wood's vote total rose to 314-1/2, well short of a majority but the highest mark attained yet by

any candidate. At this point, Harding stood in fifth place with 61-1/2 votes. Although a motion to adjourn had been soundly defeated after the previous roll call, the permanent chairman, Sen. Henry Cabot Lodge of Massachusetts, entertained a new motion to adjourn and declared it passed on a closely divided voice vote.

The adjournment gave Republican leaders a chance to confer and discuss the various presidential possibilities. Much is made in history books about Harding's selection that night in the legendary "smoke-filled room," when Harding was allegedly interviewed at 2 o'clock by Republican leaders and, answering their questions satisfactorily, was chosen as the nominee. The authenticity of the meeting has been questioned, as has the power of the politicians who made the designation. But, nonetheless, it was clear that Harding was a viable compromise choice who was both acceptable to the conservative party leadership and could be nominated by the delegates.

Harding's vote total rose slowly in the next day's balloting until the ninth ballot, when a large shift, primarily of Lowden delegates, boosted the Ohio senator's vote from 133 to 374-1/2. This was the highest total for any candidate to this point and started a bandwagon that produced Harding's nomination on the 10th ballot. After the various switches, the final vote stood: Harding, 692-1/5; Wood, 156, and Johnson, 80-4/5, with the rest of the vote scattered.

Immediately after Harding's nomination, the vice presidential balloting began. After the nomination of Sen. Irvine L. Lenroot of Wisconsin, a delegate from Oregon rose and, standing on his chair, nominated Gov. Calvin Coolidge of Massachusetts. An enthusiastic demonstration followed, showing the wide delegate support for Coolidge. The governor, who had risen to national prominence less than a year earlier with his handling of a Boston police strike, was a runaway winner on the one vice presidential ballot. Coolidge received 674-1/2 votes to Lenroot's 146-1/2.

The Wisconsin delegation again presented a detailed minority report to the platform. It included planks that opposed entry into the League of Nations under the terms of the proposed treaty, objected to compulsory military service, called for the quick conclusion of peace negotiations and normalization of foreign relations and recommended a bonus for servicemen to match the wages of wartime civilian workers.

In domestic reforms, the Wisconsin report advocated the election of federal judges and the passage of a constitutional amendment that would establish the initiative, referendum and recall. The entire minority report was rejected by a voice vote, and the platform as written was adopted in a similar manner.

The platform began by denouncing the Wilson administration for being completely unprepared for both war and peace. It went on to criticize Wilson for establishing an "executive autocracy" by arrogating to himself power that belonged to other branches of government.

The platform included a League of Nations plank that intentionally straddled the controversial issue, applauding the Republican-controlled Senate for defeating Wilson's League but pledging the party "to such agreements with the other nations of the world as shall meet the full duty of America to civilization and humanity. . . ."

To help cut federal spending, the Republicans favored consolidating some departments and bureaus and establishing an executive budget.

Both parties continued to differ on the tariff, with the

Democrats reiterating their belief in a revenue tariff and the Republicans restating their support of a protective tariff.

Following are excerpts from the Republican platform of 1920:

> **League of Nations.** The Republican party stands for agreement among the nations to preserve the peace of the world. . . .
>
> The covenant signed by the President at Paris failed signally . . . and contains stipulations, not only intolerable for an independent people, but certain to produce the injustice, hostility and controversy among nations which it proposed to prevent.
>
> . . . we pledge the coming Republican administration to such agreements with the other nations of the world as shall meet the full duty of America to civilization and humanity, in accordance with American ideals, and without surrendering the right of the American people to exercise its judgment and its power in favor of justice and peace.

Democrats

San Francisco was the host city for the 1920 Democratic convention, marking the first time a convention of one of the major parties was held west of the Rockies. Not only was the site a new one, but when the convention opened in late June, for the first time in a generation the Democratic Party had no recognized leader such as Cleveland, Bryan or Wilson.

President Woodrow Wilson had some hope of a third nomination, but his failing health and skidding popularity made this an unrealistic prospect. But Wilson's refusal to endorse another candidate prevented the emergence of any presidential hopeful as a front-runner for the nomination. In all, 24 candidates received votes on the first presidential roll call, but none approached the 729 votes needed for nomination. William Gibbs McAdoo, Wilson's son-in-law and former treasury secretary, led with 266 votes, in spite of having withdrawn from the race several days before the convention began. Attorney General A. Mitchell Palmer, famed for his efforts during the "Red Scare," followed closely with 254 votes. Two governors, Ohio's James M. Cox and New York's Alfred E. Smith, trailed with 134 and 109 votes, respectively. *(Chart, p. 192)*

Another ballot was taken before evening adjournment, with the top four candidates retaining the same order and nearly the same vote.

During the next day's balloting, Cox gained steadily and passed both McAdoo and Palmer. When the majority of McAdoo and Palmer delegates successfully carried a motion to recess after the 16th ballot, Cox held the lead with 454-1/2 votes. McAdoo was next with 337 votes and Palmer trailed with 164-1/2.

Six more ballots were taken during the evening session, and although Cox's lead narrowed, he still led McAdoo after the 22nd ballot, 430 to 372-1/2. In the next day's balloting, McAdoo gradually gained ground until he finally passed Cox on the 30th ballot, 403-1/2 to 400-1/2. After completion of the roll call, the motion was made to eliminate the lowest candidate on each succeeding ballot until a nominee had been selected. This drastic proposal to shorten the convention was defeated, 812-1/2 to 264.

Balloting continued without interruption through the 36th roll call. McAdoo still led with 399 votes, but his margin over Cox was reduced to 22 votes, and Palmer with 241 votes achieved his highest total since the 11th ballot.

A candidate was finally nominated during the evening session of the convention's third day of presidential ballot-

ing. The Palmer revival fizzled quickly, with most of his delegates going to either McAdoo or Cox. The Ohio governor regained the lead on the 39th ballot, when the majority of the Indiana delegation shifted from McAdoo to Cox. After this roll call, Cox led McAdoo, 468-1/2 to 440, Palmer having slipped to 74. Cox continued to gain, and a last-ditch effort by McAdoo delegates to force an adjournment failed, 637 to 406. Cox's vote total reached 699-1/2 votes on the 44th ballot, and, with victory imminent, a motion was adopted to declare the Ohio governor the unanimous nominee of the convention. *(Chart, p. 192)*

Cox's choice for the vice presidential nomination was Franklin Delano Roosevelt of New York, the 38-year-old assistant secretary of the Navy. Roosevelt was nominated by acclamation.

William Jennings Bryan attended the convention and proposed five planks as amendments to the platform. Only his plank endorsing prohibition, however, was submitted for a roll-call vote, and it was soundly beaten, 929-1/2 to 155-1/2. A counterproposal by a New York delegate, recognizing the legality of the prohibition amendment to the Constitution but favoring the manufacture of beer and light wines for home use, was also defeated, 724-1/2 to 356. The platform finally adopted did not discuss the prohibition question.

Bryan's four other planks covered a wide range of issues. He favored establishing a national newspaper, reducing from two-thirds to a simple majority the vote needed to approve treaties in the Senate, expressed opposition to peacetime universal compulsory military training and recommended that interstate companies reveal the difference between the cost and selling price of their products. All four planks were defeated by voice votes.

One other amendment, calling for the recognition of Irish independence, came to the floor for a roll-call vote. It was beaten, 674 to 402-1/2. Included instead was a milder plank sympathizing with the Irish struggle for indepen-

dence. Subsequently, the delegates approved by voice vote the entire platform as it was first written.

Although the delegates were unwilling to renominate Wilson, the platform was largely devoted to praise of his leadership and legislation passed during his presidency. The platform reflected Wilson's thinking by placing the League of Nations plank prominently at the beginning and supporting the president's call for American membership. The plank did allow for reservations to the treaty, but none that would prevent American participation in the League.

Following are excerpts from the Democratic platform of 1920:

League of Nations. The Democratic Party favors the League of Nations as the surest, if not the only, practicable means of maintaining the permanent peace of the world and terminating the insufferable burden of great military and naval establishments....

We commend the President for his courage and his high conception of good faith in steadfastly standing for the covenant agreed to by all the associated and allied nations at war with Germany, and we condemn the Republican Senate for its refusal to ratify the treaty merely because it was the product of Democratic statesmanship, thus interposing partisan envy and personal hatred in the way of the peace and renewed prosperity of the world....

We advocate the immediate ratification of the treaty without reservations which would impair its essential integrity, but do not oppose the acceptance of any reservations making clearer or more specific the obligations of the United States to the league associates.

Irish Independence. The great principle of national self-determination has received constant reiteration as one of the chief objectives for which this country entered the war and victory established this principle.

Within the limitations of international comity and usage, this Convention repeats the several previous expressions of the sympathy of the Democratic Party of the United States for the aspirations of Ireland for self-government.

1924 Conventions

Presidential Candidates

Calvin Coolidge
Republican

John W. Davis
Democrat

Robert M. La Follette
Progressive

Republicans

The Republicans gathered for their convention in Cleveland, Ohio, in June. For the first time, a convention was broadcast by radio. Also for the first time, Republican Party rules were changed to elect women to the national committee, with one man and one woman to be chosen from each state and territory.

Unlike the Democratic marathon that began two weeks later in New York, there was surface harmony at the Republican convention. President Calvin Coolidge's success in the spring primaries, and his ability to defuse the corruption issue, eliminated any major opposition. Coolidge was easily nominated on the first ballot, receiving 1,065 votes. Sen. Robert M. La Follette of Wisconsin was a distant second with 34 votes, while Sen. Hiram W. Johnson of California collected the remaining 10. *(Chart, p. 195)*

The vice presidential nomination was a confused matter. Eight candidates were nominated, and on the first ballot former Illinois governor Frank O. Lowden led with 222 votes. Although Lowden publicly stated that he would not accept the nomination, he received a majority of the vote on the second roll call. A recess was taken to see if Lowden had changed his mind, but when it was certain that he had not the delegates resumed balloting.

On the third roll call, former budget bureau director Charles G. Dawes received 682-1/2 votes to win nomination. Secretary of Commerce Herbert Hoover was second with 234-1/2 votes.

As was its custom throughout the early 20th century, the Wisconsin delegation proposed a detailed minority report to the platform. Proposals included government ownership of railroads and water power, an increased excess profits tax and reduced taxes on individuals with low incomes. The Wisconsin platform was rejected without a roll-call vote.

The platform that was adopted lauded the economy in government shown by the Republican administration and promised a reduction in taxes.

The Democrats and Republicans continued to differ on the tariff issue, with the Republicans again defending the protective tariff. The Ku Klux Klan was not mentioned in the Republican platform, nor was it discussed on the floor. The controversial organization was the subject of a divisive floor fight at the Democratic convention.

The Republican platform criticized the corruption found to exist in the Harding administration, but it also denounced efforts "to besmirch the names of the innocent and undermine the confidence of the people in the government under which they live."

In the area of foreign policy, the Republicans opposed membership in the League of Nations, although favoring participation in the World Court. While applauding the return of peace and reflecting the nation's increasing mood of isolationism, the Republicans opposed cutbacks in the Army and Navy.

Following are excerpts from the Republican platform of 1924:

Corruption. We demand the speedy, fearless and impartial prosecution of all wrong doers, without regard for political affiliations; but we declare no greater wrong can be committed against the people than the attempt to destroy their trust in the great body of their public servants. Admitting the deep humiliation which all good citizens share that our public life should have harbored some dishonest men, we assert that these undesirables do not represent the standard of our national integrity.

Taxes. We pledge ourselves to the progressive reduction of taxes of all the people as rapidly as may be done with due regard for the essential expenditures for the government administered with rigid economy and to place our tax system on a sound peace time basis.

League of Nations. This government has definitely refused membership in the league of nations or to assume any obligations under the covenant of the league. On this we stand.

Military. There must be no further weakening of our regular army and we advocate appropriations sufficient to provide for the training of all members of the national guard, the citizens' military training camps, the reserve officers' training camps and the reserves who may offer themselves for service. We pledge ourselves for service. We pledge ourselves to round out and maintain the navy to the full strength provided the United States by the letter and spirit of the limitation of armament conference.

War Profiteering. . . .should the United States ever again be called upon to defend itself by arms the president be empowered to draft such material resources and such services as may be required, and to stabilize the prices of services and essential commodities, whether used in actual warfare or private activities.

Republican Philosophy. The prosperity of the American nation rests on the vigor of private initiative which has bred a spirit of independence and self-reliance. The republican party stands now, as always, against all attempts to put the government into business.

American industry should not be compelled to struggle against government competition. The right of the government to regulate, supervise and control public utilities and public interests, we believe, should be strengthened, but we are firmly opposed to the nationalization or government ownership of public utilities.

Democrats

The 1924 Democratic convention in New York's old Madison Square Garden was the longest in American history. From the opening gavel on June 24 through final adjournment on July 10, the convention spanned 17 days. The reason for the convention's unprecedented length was an almost unbreakable deadlock between the party's rural and urban factions that extended the presidential balloting for a record 103 roll calls. *(Chart, pp. 194-195)*

Gov. Alfred E. Smith of New York was the candidate of the urban delegates, while William Gibbs McAdoo of California led the rural forces. But beyond any ideological differences between the two candidates was a bitter struggle between the urban and rural wings for control of the party. Smith, a Roman Catholic of Irish ancestry and an opponent of Prohibition and the Ku Klux Klan, embodied characteristics loathed by the rural leaders. McAdoo, a Protestant, a supporter of Prohibition and tolerant of the Ku Klux Klan, was equally unacceptable to the urban forces. Without a strong leader to unite the two factions, and with the two-thirds rule in effect, a long deadlock was inevitable.

Besides Smith and McAdoo, 14 other candidates were nominated. The most memorable speech was delivered by Franklin Delano Roosevelt, who, in nominating Smith, referred to him as "the happy warrior," a description that remained with Smith the rest of his career.

Presidential balloting commenced on Monday, June 30. McAdoo led on the first roll call with 431-1/2 votes, followed by Smith with 241, with 733 votes needed for nomination. Through the week, 77 ballots were taken, but none of the candidates approached the required two-thirds majority. At the end of the week, after the 77th ballot, McAdoo led with 513 votes; Smith had 367; John W. Davis of West Virginia, the eventual nominee, was a distant third with 76-1/2, an improvement of 45-1/2 votes over his first-ballot total. McAdoo had reached the highest total for any candidate, 530 votes, on the 69th ballot.

William Jennings Bryan, making his last appearance at a Democratic convention, as a delegate from Florida, was given permission to explain his opposition to Smith during the 38th ballot. But Bryan's final convention oration was lost in a chorus of boos from the urban forces who found his rural philosophy increasingly objectionable.

After the 66th ballot, the first of a series of proposals was introduced to break the deadlock. It was recommended that the convention meet in executive session and listen to each of the candidates. This received majority approval, 551 to 538, but a two-thirds majority was needed to change the rules. A second proposal, to invite Smith alone to address the convention, also fell short of the necessary two-thirds, although achieving a majority, 604-1/2 to 473.

After the 73rd ballot, it was recommended that the lowest vote-getter be dropped after each roll call until only five candidates remained, a proposal to be in effect for one day only. This recommendation was defeated, 589-1/2 to 496. A more drastic motion, to adjourn after the 75th ballot and reconvene two weeks later in Kansas City, was decisively beaten, 1,007.3 to 82.7. The delegates did agree, however, to have representatives of each candidate hold a conference over the weekend.

Balloting resumed on Monday, July 7, with the 78th roll call. After the 82nd ballot, a resolution was passed, 985 to 105, releasing all delegates from their commitments.

McAdoo's vote dropped sharply as the balloting progressed, and for the first time, on the 86th roll call, Smith passed him, 360 to 353-1/2. A boom for Sen. Samuel M. Ralston of Indiana, which had begun on the 84th ballot, petered out on the 93rd roll call when Ralston quit the race. At the time of his withdrawal, Ralston was in third place with 196-1/4 votes.

After the ballot, Roosevelt announced that Smith was willing to withdraw from the race if McAdoo would also. McAdoo rejected this suggestion. McAdoo did regain the lead from Smith on the 94th ballot, 395 to 364-1/2, but with victory beyond reach, released his delegates after the 99th ballot.

Davis was the principal beneficiary of the McAdoo withdrawal, moving into second place on the 100th ballot and gaining the lead on the next roll call with 316 votes. Most of Smith's strength moved to Alabama's anti-Klan, anti-Prohibition senator, Oscar W. Underwood, who took second place on the 101st ballot with 229-1/2 votes. Underwood, however, could not keep pace with Davis, who stretched his lead on the next two ballots. After the 103rd ballot, Davis' total stood at 575-1/2 votes to 250-1/2 for the Alabama senator.

Before the next ballot could begin, Iowa switched its vote to Davis, causing other shifts that brought Davis the nomination. After the changes had been recorded, Davis had 844 votes to 102-1/2 for Underwood. The West Virginian's nomination was then declared unanimous.

The core of Davis' vote had come from the rural delegates; urban delegates gave him the necessary votes to win the nomination. After nine days of balloting, the Democrats had a presidential candidate.

The party leadership preferred Gov. Charles W. Bryan of Nebraska, William Jennings Bryan's younger brother, as Davis' running mate. Bryan trailed Tennessee labor leader George L. Berry on the first ballot, 263-1/2 to 238, but vote switches begun by Illinois after the roll call brought Bryan the nomination. After the changes Bryan had 740 votes, barely beyond the two-thirds majority necessary.

The discord evident in the presidential and vice presidential balloting had its roots in the spirited platform battle that preceded the nominations. The first subject of debate was the League of Nations, with the majority report recommending that American entry be determined by a national referendum. The minority plank argued that this was an unwieldy solution that would put the issue aside. Instead, the minority report favored entry into the League of Nations and World Court without reservation. The minority position was rejected, 742-1/2 to 353-1/2. Nonetheless, the Democrats differed markedly in their position from the Republicans, who flatly opposed membership in

the League, although favoring participation in the World Court.

The League of Nations debate proved to be merely a warmup for the controversial religious liberties plank. The focus of debate was the Ku Klux Klan, which was opposed by name in the minority report but was not mentioned in the majority report. In one of the closest votes in convention history, the minority plank was defeated, 543-3/20 to 543-7/20. The vote closely followed factional lines, with most rural delegates opposing condemnation of the Klan and urban delegates supporting the minority plank.

The rest of the platform stressed Democratic accomplishments during the Wilson presidency, in contrast to Republican corruption. Democratic links with the common man were emphasized, while the Republicans were denounced as the party of the rich. The Democratic platform advocated increased taxes on the wealthy in contrast to the Republicans, who promised a reduction in taxes.

The Democrats continued to advocate a low tariff that would encourage competition. A plank demanding states' rights appeared in the platform, but there were also calls for government regulation of the anthracite coal industry, federal support of the American merchant marine and legislation that would restrict and publicize individual campaign contributions.

There were planks favoring a cutback in the American military, a national referendum before any declaration of war (except outright aggression against the United States) and the drafting of resources as well as men during wartime. The anti-militaristic planks were a return to the position the party had held earlier in the 20th century.

Following are excerpts from the Democratic platform of 1924:

Republican Corruption. Such are the exigencies of partisan politics that republican leaders are teaching the strange doctrine that public censure should be directed against those who expose crime rather than against criminals who have committed the offenses. If only three cabinet officers out of ten are disgraced, the country is asked to marvel at how many are free from taint. Long boastful that it was the only party "fit to govern," the republican party has proven its inability to govern even itself. It is at war with itself. As an agency of government it has ceased to function.

Income Tax. The income tax was intended as a tax upon wealth. It was not intended to take from the poor any part of the necessities of life. We hold that the fairest tax with which to raise revenue for the federal government is the income tax. We favor a graduated tax upon incomes, so adjusted as to lay the burdens of government upon the taxpayers in proportion to the benefits they enjoy and their ability to pay.

Campaign Contributions. We favor the prohibition of individual contributions, direct and indirect, to the campaign funds of congressmen, senators or presidential candidates, beyond a reasonable sum to be fixed in the law, for both individual contributions and total expenditures, with requirements for full publicity.

States' Rights. We demand that the states of the union shall be preserved in all their vigor and power. They constitute a bulwark against the centralizing and destructive tendencies of the republican party.

Anti-militarism. We demand a strict and sweeping reduction of armaments by land and sea, so that there shall be no competitive military program or naval building. Until international agreements to this end have been made we advocate an army and navy adequate for our national safety....

War is a relic of barbarism and it is justifiable only as a measure of defense.

War Profiteering. In the event of war in which the manpower of the nation is drafted, all other resources should likewise be drafted. This will tend to discourage war by depriving it of its profits.

Progressives

Under the sponsorship of the Conference of Progressive Political Action, representatives of various liberal, labor and agrarian groups met in Cleveland on July 4 to launch the Progressive Party and ratify the ticket of Wisconsin senator Robert M. La Follette for president and Montana senator Burton K. Wheeler for vice president. The conference earlier had designated La Follette as its presidential nominee and had given him the power to choose his running mate. The national ticket of the Progressives crossed party lines, joining a Republican, La Follette, with a Democrat, Wheeler. The ticket was endorsed by the Socialists, who supported the Progressive candidates rather than run a separate national ticket.

In large part the Progressive platform advocated measures that had been proposed earlier by the Populists, Socialists and Progressives before World War I. The key issue, as viewed by the La Follette Progressives, was "the control of government and industry by private monopoly." The platform favored the government ownership of railroads and water power, rigid federal control over natural resources, the outlawing of injunctions in labor disputes, a cutback in military spending, tax reform and political reform — including the direct election of the president, a national referendum before a declaration of war (except in cases of invasion), election of federal judges and congressional power to override the Supreme Court.

Following are excerpts from the Progressive platform of 1924:

Anti-monopoly. The great issue before the American people today is the control of government and industry by private monopoly.

For a generation the people have struggled patiently, in the face of repeated betrayals by successive administrations, to free themselves from this intolerable power which has been undermining representative government.

Through control of government, monopoly has steadily extended its absolute dominion to every basic industry.

In violation of law, monopoly has crushed competition, stifled private initiative and independent enterprise....

The equality of opportunity proclaimed by the Declaration of Independence and asserted and defended by Jefferson and Lincoln as the heritage of every American citizen has been displaced by special privilege for the few, wrested from the government of the many.

Tax Reform. We ... favor a taxation policy providing for immediate reductions upon moderate incomes, large increases in the inheritance tax rates upon large estates to prevent the indefinite accumulation by inheritance of great fortunes in a few hands, taxes upon excess profits to penalize profiteering, and complete publicity, under proper safeguards, of all Federal tax returns.

Court Reform. We favor submitting to the people, for their considerate judgment, a constitutional amendment providing that Congress may by enacting a statute make it effective over a judicial vote.

We favor such amendment to the constitution as may be necessary to provide for the election of all Federal

Judges, without party designation, for fixed terms not exceeding ten years, by direct vote of the people.

National Referendums. Over and above constitutions and statutes and greater than all is the supreme sovereignty of the people, and with them should rest the final decision of all great questions of national policy. We favor such amendments to the Federal Constitution as may be necessary to provide for the direct nomination and election of the President, to extend the initiative and referendum to the federal government, and to insure a popular referendum for or against war except in cases of actual invasion.

1928 Conventions

Presidential Candidates

Herbert Hoover
Republican

Alfred E. Smith
Democrat

Republicans

The Republicans held their convention in Kansas City, Mo., in mid-June 1928. Nearly a year earlier, President Calvin Coolidge had declared his intention not to seek re-election with a typically brief statement: "I do not choose to run for President in 1928." While some business leaders hoped that Coolidge would be open to a draft, the taciturn incumbent made no effort to encourage them. The vacuum caused by Coolidge's absence was quickly filled by Commerce Secretary Herbert Hoover of California, whose success in the spring primaries solidified his position as the front-runner.

Hoover's strength was evident on the first roll call of the convention, a credentials challenge to 18 Hoover delegates from Texas. In a vote that revealed candidate strength, the move to unseat the Hoover delegates was defeated, 659-1/2 to 399-1/2. In the presidential balloting that followed, he gained more votes to win the nomination easily on the first ballot. Hoover's vote total was swelled before the balloting began by the withdrawal of his principal opponent, former Illinois governor Frank O. Lowden, who declared in a letter that he could not accept the party platform's stand on agriculture. Six names were placed in nomination, but Hoover was a landslide winner, receiving 837 of the 1,089 convention votes. Lowden finished second with 74 votes. *(Chart, p. 197)*

Sen. Charles Curtis of Kansas was virtually unopposed for the vice presidential nomination, receiving 1,052 votes.

Although Wisconsin's prominent progressive leader, Robert M. La Follette, had died in 1925, his state's delegation again presented a minority platform. The report was presented by Sen. Robert M. La Follette Jr., who had taken over his father's Senate seat. Among the planks of the Wisconsin report were proposals favoring enactment of the McNary-Haugen farm bill, government operation of major water power projects, increased income taxes on the rich and liberalization of Prohibition. No vote was taken on the Wisconsin proposals.

A resolution favoring repeal of Prohibition was tabled by a voice vote.

A separate agricultural resolution was proposed that advocated the basic provisions of the McNary-Haugen bill (twice vetoed by Coolidge), without mentioning the controversial bill by name. On a roll-call vote, the resolution was defeated, 807 to 277, with support centered in the farm states but with most Hoover delegates voting against it.

The platform as originally written was adopted by a voice vote. The platform promised continued prosperity and government economy. The belief in a protective tariff was reiterated. The document concluded with a plank entitled "home rule," which expressed the party's belief in self-reliance and strong local government.

Following are excerpts from the Republican platform of 1928:

Tariff. We reaffirm our belief in the protective tariff as a fundamental and essential principle of the economic life of this nation.... However, we realize that there are certain industries which cannot now successfully compete with foreign producers because of lower foreign wages and a lower cost of living abroad, and we pledge the next Republican Congress to an examination and where necessary a revision of these schedules to the end that American labor in these industries may again command the home market, may maintain its standard of living, and may count upon steady employment in its accustomed field.

Outlaw War. We endorse the proposal of the Secretary of State for a multilateral treaty proposed to the principal powers of the world and open to the signatures of all nations, to renounce war as an instrument of national policy

and declaring in favor of pacific settlement of international disputes, the first step in outlawing war.

Agriculture. We promise every assistance in the re-organization of the market system on sounder and more economical lines and, where diversification is needed, Government financial assistance during the period of transition.

The Republican Party pledges itself to the enactment of legislation creating a Federal Farm Board clothed with the necessary powers to promote the establishment of a farm marketing system of farmer-owned and controlled stabilization corporations or associations to prevent and control surpluses through orderly distribution. . . .

We favor, without putting the Government into business, the establishment of a Federal system of organization for co-operative and orderly marketing of farm products.

Prohibition. The people through the method provided by the Constitution have written the Eighteenth Amendment into the Constitution. The Republican Party pledges itself and its nominees to the observance and vigorous enforcement of this provision of the Constitution.

Republican Philosophy. There is a real need of restoring the individual and local sense of responsibility and self-reliance; there is a real need for the people once more to grasp the fundamental fact that under our system of government they are expected to solve many problems themselves through their municipal and State governments, and to combat the tendency that is all too common to turn to the Federal Government as the easiest and least burdensome method of lightening their own responsibilities.

Democrats

The Democratic convention was held in late June in Houston, Texas, the first time since 1860 that the party's nominating convention had been conducted in a Southern city. The rural and urban wings of the party, which had produced the fiasco in Madison Square Garden four years earlier, wanted no more bloodletting. This explained the acceptance of Houston as the convention site by the urban forces, whose presidential candidate, Gov. Alfred E. Smith of New York, was the front-runner for the nomination. Smith's path to the nomination was largely unobstructed, thanks to the decision of William Gibbs McAdoo not to run. McAdoo, the rural favorite in 1924, feared the possibility of another bitter deadlock that would destroy party unity.

The convention broke with tradition by bypassing politicians and selecting Claude G. Bowers of Indiana, a historian and an editorial writer for *The New York World*, as temporary chairman.

When it came time for the selection of a presidential candidate, Franklin Delano Roosevelt once again placed Smith's name in nomination. On the roll call that followed, the New York governor came within 10 votes of the required two-thirds. Ohio quickly switched 44 of its votes to Smith, and the switch pushed "the happy warrior" over the top. When the vote switches were completed, Smith had received 849-1/6 of the 1,100 convention votes. No other candidate's vote had totaled more than 100. *(Chart, p. 197)*

Senate Minority Leader Joseph T. Robinson of Arkansas had little opposition for the vice presidency and was nominated on the first ballot with 914-1/6 votes. Sen. Alben W. Barkley of Kentucky finished a distant second with 77 votes. After a vote switch, Robinson had 1,035-1/6 votes. As a "dry" Protestant from the South, Robinson balanced the ticket. He was the first Southerner to be nominated for national office by either major party since the Civil War.

For the first time since 1912, there were no roll-call votes on amendments to the Democratic platform. A minority plank was introduced calling for the party's complete support of Prohibition, but there was no effort to force a roll-call vote. The platform included a milder Prohibition plank that promised "an honest effort to enforce the 18th Amendment (Prohibition)." On the surface there was little difference from the Republican plank, which pledged "vigorous enforcement" of Prohibition. But in a telegram read to the convention shortly before its final adjournment, Smith negated the effect of the milder plank by declaring there should be "fundamental changes in the present provisions for national Prohibition." Smith's statement was disappointing to many "dry" delegates and lessened whatever enthusiasm they felt for the New York governor. No other issues were discussed, and the platform as written was approved by a voice vote.

Agriculture, the most depressed part of the economy in the 1920s, received more space in the platform than any other issue. The Democrats opposed federal subsidies to farmers, but they advocated government loans to cooperatives and the creation of a federal farm board that would operate similarly to the Federal Reserve Board. While the Republican platform also favored creation of a farm board, as a whole it called for more initiative by the farmers themselves and less direct government help than did the Democratic platform.

Since the late 19th century, Democratic platforms had favored a low tariff. The 1928 tariff plank represented a change, expressing as much interest in ensuring competition and protecting the American wage-earner as in raising revenue. Instead of being consistently low, tariff rates were to be based on the difference between the cost of production in the United States and abroad. As a result of the Democrats' altered stand on the tariff, the positions of the two parties on this issue were the closest they had been in a generation.

The Democrats' 1928 platform did not mention the League of Nations, in contrast to the Republicans, who restated their opposition to the League. Both parties called for maintenance of American military strength until international disarmament agreements could be reached. A section of the Democratic foreign policy plank questioned the extent of presidential power in the area of international affairs. President Coolidge was specifically criticized for authorizing American military intervention in Nicaragua without congressional approval.

An unemployment plank was included in the Democratic platform that proposed the creation of public works jobs in times of economic hardship.

As was the case with most Democratic platforms since the early 19th century, there was a defense of states' rights and a plank that recognized education as an area of state responsibility. The Democrats made no mention of civil rights in contrast to the Republicans, who, as in 1920, proposed federal anti-lynching legislation.

Following are excerpts from the Democratic platform of 1928:

Prohibition. Speaking for the national Democracy, this convention pledges the party and its nominees to an honest effort to enforce the eighteenth amendment.

Agriculture. Farm relief must rest on the basis of an economic equality of agriculture with other industries. To give this equality a remedy must be found which will include among other things:

(a) Credit aid by loans to co-operatives on at least as

favorable a basis as the government aid to the merchant marine.

(b) Creation of a federal farm board to assist the farmer and stock raiser in the marketing of their products, as the Federal Reserve Board has done for the banker and business man.

Presidential War Power. Abolition of the practice of the president of entering into and carrying out agreements with a foreign government, either de facto or de jure, for the protection of such government against revolution or foreign attack, or for the supervision of its internal affairs, when such agreements have not been advised and consented to by the Senate, as provided in the Constitution of the United States, and we condemn the administration for carrying out such an unratified agreement that requires us to use our armed forces in Nicaragua.

Tariff. Duties that will permit effective competition, insure against monopoly and at the same time produce a

fair revenue for the support of government. Actual difference between the cost of production at home and abroad, with adequate safeguard for the wage of the American laborer must be the extreme measure of every tariff rate.

Unemployment and Public Works. We favor the adoption by the government, after a study of this subject, of a scientific plan whereby during periods of unemployment appropriations shall be made available for the construction of necessary public works and the lessening, as far as consistent with public interests, of government construction work when labor is generally and satisfactorily employed in private enterprise.

Education. We believe with Jefferson and other founders of the Republic that ignorance is the enemy of freedom and that each state, being responsible for the intellectual and moral qualifications of its citizens and for the expenditure of the moneys collected by taxation for the support of its schools, shall use its sovereign right in all matters pertaining to education.

1932 Conventions

Presidential Candidates

Norman Thomas
Socialist

Herbert Hoover
Republican

Franklin D. Roosevelt
Democrat

Socialists

The Socialist Party held its convention in Milwaukee, Wis., in May and renominated the same ticket that had represented the party in 1928: Norman Thomas of New York for president and James H. Maurer of Pennsylvania for vice president. Aided by the deepening economic depression, the Socialists received more than 2 percent of the popular vote for the first time since 1920. The party continued to run a national ticket until 1956, but 1932 was the last election in which the Socialists received at least 2 percent of the vote.

By a vote of 117 to 64, the convention adopted a resolution supporting the efforts of the Soviet Union to create a Socialist society. An attempt to oust Morris Hillquit as national chairman of the party was beaten, 108 to 81.

The Socialist platform of 1932 contained a number of proposals that had been set forth in earlier party platforms, such as public ownership of natural resources and the means of transportation and communication, increased

taxes on the wealthy, an end to the Supreme Court's power to rule congressional legislation unconstitutional and a reduction in the size and expenditures of the military.

The platform also advocated United States recognition of the Soviet Union and American entry into the League of Nations. Repeal of Prohibition was recommended, as was the creation of a federal marketing system that would buy and market farm commodities.

To meet the hardship of the Depression, the Socialists listed a series of proposals, which included the expenditure of $10 billion for unemployment relief and public works projects.

Following are excerpts from the Socialist platform of 1932:

Unemployment Relief. 1. A Federal appropriation of $5,000,000,000 for immediate relief for those in need to supplement State and local appropriations.

2. A Federal appropriation of $5,000,000,000 for public works and roads, reforestation, slum clearance, and decent homes for the workers, by Federal Government, States and cities.

3. Legislation providing for the acquisition of land, buildings, and equipment necessary to put the unemployed to work producing food, fuel, and clothing and for the erection of houses for their own use.

4. The 6-hour day and the 5-day week without reduction of wages.

5. A comprehensive and efficient system of free public employment agencies.

6. A compulsory system of unemployment compensation with adequate benefits, based on contributions by the Government and by employers.

7. Old-age pensions for men and women 60 years of age and over.

8. Health and maternity insurance.

Republicans

As the incumbent party during the outset of the Depression, the Republicans bore the major political blame for the worsening economy. In a subdued mood, the party gathered in Chicago in June 1932 for its national convention.

Republican leaders did not view their electoral prospects optimistically for the fall election, but saw no realistic alternative to President Herbert Hoover.

Hoover was easily if unenthusiastically renominated, receiving 1,126-1/2 of the 1,154 convention votes. The highlight of the presidential balloting was the attempt by former Maryland senator Joseph I. France, who ran in several spring primaries, to gain the rostrum and nominate former president Coolidge. France's dramatic plan, however, was foiled by convention managers, who refused him permission to speak and had him escorted from the hall. *(Chart, p. 199)*

Vice President Charles Curtis had stiff opposition in his bid for renomination. The incumbent was seriously challenged by Maj. Gen. James G. Harbord of New York and the national commander of the American Legion, Hanford MacNider of Iowa. Curtis was short of a majority after the first ballot, but Pennsylvania quickly shifted its 75 votes to the vice president and this pushed him over the top. With the vote standing at Curtis, 634-1/4; MacNider, 182-3/4, and Harbord, 161-3/4, Curtis' renomination was made unanimous.

The major platform controversy surrounded the Prohibition plank. The majority plank, supported by Hoover, was ambiguous. It called for the enforcement of Prohibition but advocated a national referendum that would permit each state to determine whether or not it wanted Prohibition. A more clear-cut minority plank favored repeal of Prohibition. The minority proposal was defeated, however, 690-19/36 to 460-2/9. Following this roll call, the rest of the platform was approved by a voice vote.

The document approved by the Republicans was the longest in the party's history — nearly 9,000 words. It blamed the United States' continued economic problems on a worldwide depression, but lauded Hoover's leadership in meeting the crisis. The Republicans saw reduced government spending and a balanced budget as keys to ending the Depression. The party platform viewed unemployment relief as a matter for private agencies and local governments to handle.

The Republicans continued their support of a protective tariff. On the agricultural issue, the party proposed acreage controls to help balance supply and demand.

The final plank of the Republican platform urged party members in Congress to demonstrate party loyalty by supporting the Republican program. The plank warned that the party's strength was jeopardized by internal dissent.

Following are excerpts from the Republican platform of 1932:

Unemployment Relief. The people themselves, by their own courage, their own patient and resolute effort in the readjustments of their own affairs, can and will work out the cure. It is our task as a party, by leadership and a wise determination of policy, to assist that recovery....

True to American traditions and principles of government, the administration has regarded the relief problem as one of State and local responsibility. The work of local agencies, public and private has been coordinated and enlarged on a nation-wide scale under the leadership of the President.

Government Spending. We urge prompt and drastic reduction of public expenditure and resistance to every appropriation not demonstrably necessary to the performance of government, national or local.

Agriculture. The fundamental problem of American agriculture is the control of production to such volume as will balance supply with demand. In the solution of this problem the cooperative organization of farmers to plan production, and the tariff, to hold the home market for American farmers, are vital elements. A third element equally as vital is the control of the acreage of land under cultivation, as an aid to the efforts of the farmer to balance production.

Prohibition. We ... believe that the people should have an opportunity to pass upon a proposed amendment the provision of which, while retaining in the Federal Government power to preserve the gains already made in dealing with the evils inherent in the liquor traffic, shall allow the States to deal with the problem as their citizens may determine, but subject always to the power of the Federal Government to protect those States where prohibition may exist and safeguard our citizens everywhere from the return of the saloon and attendant abuses.

Democrats

With the nation in the midst of the Great Depression, the Democratic Party had its best chance for victory since 1912. The delegates assembled in Chicago in late June 1932, confident that the convention's nominee would defeat President Hoover.

Gov. Franklin D. Roosevelt of New York entered the convention with a majority of the votes, but was well short of the two-thirds majority needed for nomination. Ironically, his principal opponent was the man he had nominated for the presidency three times, former New York governor Alfred E. Smith.

Roosevelt's strength was tested on several key roll calls before the presidential balloting began. Two of the votes involved credentials challenges to Roosevelt delegations from Louisiana and Minnesota. By a vote of 638-3/4 to 514-1/4, the delegates seated the Roosevelt forces from Louisiana, headed by Sen. Huey P. Long. And by a wider margin of 658-1/4 to 492-3/4 the convention seated the Roosevelt delegates from Minnesota. *(Chart, p. 198)*

After settlement of the credentials cases, the battleground shifted to the selection of the permanent convention chairman. The Roosevelt forces backed Sen. Thomas J. Walsh of Montana, who was recommended by the committee on permanent organization. The Smith and other anti-Roosevelt factions coalesced behind Jouett Shouse of Kansas, chairman of the executive committee of the Democratic National Committee, who was recommended for per-

manent chairman by the national committee. But by a vote of 626 to 528, the Roosevelt forces won again, and Walsh assumed the gavel as permanent chairman.

The Roosevelt managers considered challenging the two-thirds rule; but, realizing that a bruising fight could alienate some of their own delegates, particularly in the South, they dropped the idea. Instead, the report of the rules committee recommended that a change in the two-thirds rule be delayed until the 1936 convention.

The presidential balloting began in the middle of an all-night session. After a motion to adjourn was defeated, 863-1/2 to 281-1/2, the first roll call began at 4:30 a.m. Roosevelt received a clear majority of 666-1/4 votes on the first ballot, compared with 201-3/4 for Smith and 90-1/4 for House Speaker John Nance Garner of Texas. Seven hundred and seventy votes were necessary for nomination. *(Chart, p. 198)*

Roosevelt gained slightly on the second ballot, advancing to 677-3/4 votes, while Smith dropped to 194-1/4 and Garner remained constant. Of side interest was the shift of Oklahoma's votes from its governor to Will Rogers, the state's famous humorist.

There were few changes on the next roll call, and at 9:15 a.m. the delegates agreed to adjourn. The vote totals after three ballots: Roosevelt, 682.79; Smith, 190-1/4; Garner, 101-1/4.

When balloting resumed the next evening, William Gibbs McAdoo of California quickly launched the bandwagon for Roosevelt by announcing that his state's 44 votes were switching from Garner to the New York governor. Other states followed California's lead, and when the fourth ballot was completed Roosevelt had 945 votes and the nomination. With the Smith vote holding at 190-1/2, no effort was made to make the nomination unanimous.

Although it is not clear whether there was a formal deal struck before the fourth ballot between the Garner and Roosevelt forces, the Texas representative was the unanimous choice of the convention for vice president. Forty states seconded his nomination, and no roll call was taken.

In an effort to break what he described as "absurd traditions," Roosevelt flew from Albany to Chicago to accept the presidential nomination personally. (Previously, a major party candidate would be formally notified of his nomination in a ceremony several weeks after the convention.) In his speech of acceptance, Roosevelt struck a liberal tone and issued his memorable pledge of "a new deal for the American people."

The platform adopted by the convention was not a blueprint for the New Deal to follow. It was fewer than 2,000 words long, the party's shortest platform since 1888, and less than one-fourth as long as the document adopted by the Republicans. It blamed the Depression on the "disastrous policies" practiced by the Republicans but made few new proposals, instead forcefully restating positions that had appeared in earlier party platforms.

The Democrats advocated a balanced budget with a cut of at least 25 percent in federal spending and called for removal of the federal government from competition with private enterprise in all areas except public works and natural resources.

The Democratic platform, unlike its Republican counterpart, advocated extensive unemployment relief and public works projects, regulation of holding companies and securities exchanges, "a competitive tariff for revenue" and the extension of farm cooperatives.

The plank that sparked the most enthusiasm among the delegates was the call for the repeal of Prohibition. A milder plank favored by "dry" delegates was resoundingly defeated, 934-3/4 to 213-3/4.

The only measure added from the floor of the convention favored "continuous responsibility of government for human welfare, especially for the protection of children." It was approved by a standing vote.

Following are excerpts from the Democratic platform of 1932:

Government Spending. We advocate an immediate and drastic reduction of governmental expenditures by abolishing useless commissions and offices, consolidating departments and bureaus, and eliminating extravagance to accomplish a saving of not less than twenty-five percent in the cost of the Federal Government. And we call upon the Democratic Party in the states to make a zealous effort to achieve a proportionate result.

We favor maintenance of the national credit by a federal budget annually balanced on the basis of accurate executive estimates within revenues, raised by a system of taxation levied on the principle of ability to pay.

Unemployment Relief, Public Works Projects. We advocate the extension of federal credit to the states to provide unemployment relief wherever the diminishing resources of the states makes it impossible for them to provide for the needy; expansion of the federal program of necessary and useful construction effected with a public interest, such as adequate flood control and waterways.

We advocate the spread of employment by a substantial reduction in the hours of labor, the encouragement of the shorter week by applying that principle in government service; we advocate advance planning of public works.

We advocate unemployment and old-age insurance under state laws.

Prohibition. We advocate the repeal of the Eighteenth Amendment. To effect such repeal we demand that the Congress immediately propose a Constitutional Amendment to truly represent the conventions in the states called to act solely on that proposal; we urge the enactment of such measures by the several states as will actually promote temperance, effectively prevent the return of the saloon, and bring the liquor traffic into the open under complete supervision and control by the states.

Agriculture. Extension and development of the Farm Cooperative movement and effective control of crop surpluses so that our farmers may have the full benefit of the domestic market.

The enactment of every constitutional measure that will aid the farmers to receive for their basic farm commodities prices in excess of cost.

1936 Conventions

Presidential Candidates

Alfred M. Landon
Republican

Franklin D. Roosevelt
Democrat

William Lemke
Union

Republicans

The Republican convention, held in Cleveland in early June, was an unusually harmonious gathering for a party out of power. There were only two roll-call votes on the convention floor, for president and vice president, and both were one-sided.

The only matter of debate was the vote allocation for Alaska, Hawaii and the District of Columbia. By a voice vote, the convention approved the minority report of the rules committee, which sliced the vote for these three from six to three votes apiece.

Former president Herbert Hoover received an enthusiastic reception when he spoke, but by that time Kansas governor Alfred M. Landon had the presidential nomination sewed up. Landon, one of the few Republican governors to be re-elected during the Depression, received 984 votes on the first ballot, compared with 19 for Sen. William E. Borah of Idaho. *(Chart, p. 200)*

Before the balloting began, Landon had sent a telegram to the convention that expressed his agreement with the "word and spirit" of the party platform but elaborated his position on several points. The Kansan advocated the passage of a constitutional amendment to ensure women and children safe working conditions and to establish guidelines for wages and hours in the event that legislation passed by Congress was ruled unconstitutional. Landon's message also proposed extending the civil service to include all workers in federal departments and agencies below the rank of assistant secretary, and it defined "sound currency" as currency that could be exchanged for gold. Landon's pronouncements were met with 30 minutes of cheering.

For vice president, the convention selected Col. Frank Knox of Illinois, publisher of *The Chicago Daily News.* Knox, who earlier had campaigned energetically, if not successfully, for the presidential nomination, received all 1,003 votes on the first ballot.

The Republican platform, which began with the sentence, "America is in peril," focused on the alleged threat of New Deal policies to American constitutional govern-

ment. The platform assailed the Roosevelt administration for "dishonoring American traditions" and promised to protect local self-government and the power of the Supreme Court.

The Republicans promised a balanced budget, reduced federal expenditures, a "sound currency," a more discriminating public works program and the administration of unemployment relief by "non-political local agencies" that would be financed jointly by the various states and the federal government.

The Republicans shared with the Democrats the belief in an isolationist foreign policy and the concepts of social security, unemployment insurance and crop control.

Following are excerpts from the Republican platform of 1936:

Roosevelt's 'New Deal.' America is in peril. The welfare of American men and women and the future of our youth are at stake. We dedicate ourselves to the preservation of their political liberty, their individual opportunity and their character as free citizens, which today for the first time are threatened by Government itself....

The powers of Congress have been usurped by the President.

The integrity and authority of the Supreme Court have been flouted.

The rights and liberties of American citizens have been violated.

Regulated monopoly has displaced free enterprise.

The New Deal Administration constantly seeks to usurp the rights reserved to the States and to the people.

Unemployment Relief. The return of responsibility for relief administration to nonpolitical local agencies familiar with community problems....

Undertaking of Federal public works only on their merits and separate from the administration of relief.

Government Spending, Currency. Balance the budget — not by increasing taxes but by cutting expenditures, drastically and immediately....

We advocate a sound currency to be preserved at all hazards.

The first requisite to a sound and stable currency is a balanced budget.

Foreign Policy. We pledge ourselves to promote and maintain peace by all honorable means not leading to foreign alliances or political commitments.

Obedient to the traditional foreign policy of America and to the repeatedly expressed will of the American people, we pledge that America shall not become a member of the League of Nations nor of the World Court nor shall America take on any entangling alliances in foreign affairs.

Democrats

The 1936 Democratic convention, held in Philadelphia in late June, was one of the most harmonious in party history. There were no floor debates, and, for the first time since 1840, there were no roll-call votes.

The only matter that required discussion — elimination of the century-old two-thirds rule — was settled in the rules committee. There, by a vote of 36 to 13, the committee agreed to abrogate the rule, which had been a controversial part of Democratic conventions since 1832. To mollify the South, which was particularly threatened by elimination of the two-thirds rule, the rules committee added a provision that would include consideration of a state's Democratic voting strength in determining its future convention vote allocation. The rules committee report was approved by a voice vote.

Both President Franklin D. Roosevelt and Vice President John Nance Garner were renominated by acclamation, but more than a full day of oratory was expended in eulogizing the Democratic standard-bearers. Roosevelt was seconded by delegates from each of the states and territories — more than 50 separate speakers. Seventeen delegates spoke on behalf of Garner.

Both Roosevelt and Garner personally accepted their nominations in ceremonies at the University of Pennsylvania's Franklin Field. Before a crowd estimated as large as 100,000, Roosevelt electrified his listeners with a speech that blasted his adversaries among the rich as "economic royalists" and included the sentence: "This generation of Americans has a rendezvous with destiny."

As in 1932 the platform adopted by the Democrats was a short one, about 3,000 words. The document paid lip service to the concept of a balanced budget and reduced government spending, but it supported continuation of the extensive federal programs undertaken by the Roosevelt administration.

The platform did not, as many in past years had, mention states' rights; this reflected the party's changing view toward federal power. To counter what was viewed as obstructionism by the Supreme Court, the Democrats suggested the possibility of passing a "clarifying amendment" to the Constitution that would enable Congress and state legislatures to enact bills without the fear of an unfavorable decision from the Supreme Court.

The foreign policy plank recognized the isolationist mood of the period, calling for neutrality in foreign disputes and the avoidance of international commitments that would draw the United States into war.

Following are excerpts from the Democratic platform of 1936:

Federal Power. The Republican platform proposes to meet many pressing national problems solely by action of the separate States. We know that drought, dust storms, floods, minimum wages, maximum hours, child labor, and working conditions in industry, monopolistic and unfair business practices cannot be adequately handled exclusively by 48 separate State legislatures, 48 separate State administrations, and 48 separate State courts. Transactions and

activities which inevitably overflow State boundaries call for both State and Federal treatment.

We have sought and will continue to seek to meet these problems through legislation within the Constitution.

If these problems cannot be effectively solved by legislation within the Constitution, we shall seek such clarifying amendment as will assure to the legislatures of the several States and to the Congress of the United States, each within its proper jurisdiction, the power to enact those laws which the State and Federal legislatures, within their respective spheres, shall find necessary, in order adequately to regulate commerce, protect public health and safety and safeguard economic security. Thus we propose to maintain the letter and spirit of the Constitution.

Government Spending. We are determined to reduce the expenses of government. We are being aided therein by the recession in unemployment. As the requirements of relief decline and national income advances, an increasing percentage of Federal expenditures can and will be met from current revenues, secured from taxes levied in accordance with ability to pay. Our retrenchment, tax and recovery programs thus reflect our firm determination to achieve a balanced budget and the reduction of the national debt at the earliest possible moment.

Foreign Policy. We reaffirm our opposition to war as an instrument of national policy, and declare that disputes between nations should be settled by peaceful means. We shall continue to observe a true neutrality in the disputes of others; to be prepared resolutely to resist aggression against ourselves; to work for peace and to take the profits out of war; to guard against being drawn, by political commitments, international banking or private trading, into any war which may develop anywhere.

Union Party

With the support of Father Charles E. Coughlin and his National Union for Social Justice, on June 19, 1936, Rep. William Lemke of North Dakota, a Republican, declared his presidential candidacy on the newly formed Union Party ticket. Thomas O'Brien, a Boston railroad union lawyer, was announced as Lemke's running mate. The fledgling political organization had a brief existence, running a national ticket only in the 1936 election. *(Union Party profile, p. 236)*

The Union Party was basically an extension of Coughlin's organization, and the Lemke-O'Brien ticket was endorsed at the National Union for Social Justice convention in August by a vote of 8,152 to 1.

The Union Party platform reportedly was written by Coughlin, Lemke and O'Brien at the Roman Catholic priest's church in Royal Oak, Mich. It was a brief document, fewer than 1,000 words, that contained 15 points similar to the 16-point program favored by Coughlin's National Union. The primary distinctions between the Union Party and the two major parties were in currency expansion, civil service reform and restrictions on wealth. The Union Party called for the creation of a central bank, regulated by Congress, that would issue currency to help pay off the federal debt and refinance agricultural and home mortgage indebtedness. The Union Party platform also proposed extending the civil service to all levels of the federal government and advocated placing restrictions on annual individual income coupled with a ceiling on gifts and inheritances. The new party differed from the Socialists by emphasizing that private property should not be confiscated.

Following are excerpts from the Union Party platform of 1936:

Currency Expansion. Congress and Congress alone shall coin and issue the currency and regulate the value of all money and credit in the United States through a central bank of issue.

Immediately following the establishment of the central bank of issue Congress shall provide for the retirement of all tax-exempt, interest-bearing bonds and certificates of indebtedness of the Federal Government and shall refinance all the present agricultural mortgage indebtedness for the farmer and all the home mortgage indebtedness for the farmer and all the home mortgage indebtedness for the city owner by the use of its money and credit which it now gives to the private bankers.

Civil Service Reform. Congress shall so legislate that all Federal offices and positions of every nature shall be distributed through civil-service qualifications and not through a system of party spoils and corrupt patronage.

Restrictions on Wealth. Congress shall set a limitation upon the net income of any individual in any one year and a limitation of the amount that such an individual may receive as a gift or as an inheritance, which limitation shall be executed through taxation.

Foreign Policy. Congress shall establish an adequate and perfect defense for our country from foreign aggression either by air, by land, or by sea, but with the understanding that our naval, air, and military forces must not be used under any consideration in foreign fields or in foreign waters either alone or in conjunction with any foreign power. If there must be conscription, there shall be a conscription of wealth as well as a conscription of men.

1940 Conventions

Presidential Candidates

Wendell L. Willkie
Republican

Franklin D. Roosevelt
Democrat

Republicans

The Republican convention was held in Philadelphia in late June, and it culminated one of the most successful of all campaign blitzes. Wendell L. Willkie, an Indiana native who had never before run for public office, was nominated by the Republicans to run for president. A Democrat until 1938, Willkie had gained fame as a defender of private enterprise in opposition to Roosevelt's public power projects. Although Willkie had broad personal appeal, he and his well-financed group of political "amateurs" did not launch their presidential bid until late spring and missed the presidential primaries. Willkie's momentum came from his rapid rise in the Republican preference polls, as he soared from only 3 percent in early May to 29 percent six weeks later.

At the Republican convention, 10 names were placed in nomination for the presidency. Willkie's principal rivals were Manhattan District Attorney Thomas E. Dewey, making his first presidential bid at age 38, and Sen. Robert A. Taft of Ohio. On the first ballot, Dewey led with 360 votes, followed by Taft with 189 and Willkie with 105. Five hundred and one votes were needed for nomination. *(Chart, p. 201)*

After the first roll call, Dewey steadily lost strength, while Willkie and Taft gained. Willkie assumed the lead on the fourth ballot, passing both Dewey and Taft. Willkie's vote was 306, while Taft moved into second place with 254. Dewey dropped to third with 250.

On the fifth ballot, the contest narrowed to just Willkie and Taft, as both candidates continued to gain — Willkie jumping to 429 votes and Taft to 377. The shift of Michigan's votes to Willkie on the sixth ballot started a bandwagon for the Indianan which pushed him over the top. When the roll call was completed, Willkie was nominated with 655 votes, and a motion to make his nomination unanimous was adopted.

As his running mate, Willkie favored Senate Minority Leader Charles L. McNary of Oregon. McNary, a supporter of some New Deal measures, was opposed by Rep. Dewey Short of Missouri, a vocal anti-New Dealer. McNary, however, was able to win easily on a single ballot, receiving 890 votes to 108 for Short.

The Republican platform was adopted without debate, although an Illinois member of the platform committee commented that his state would have preferred a stronger anti-war plank. As it was, the Republican foreign policy plank sharply criticized the Roosevelt administration for not adequately preparing the nation's defense. However, the rest of the plank was similar to the one adopted three weeks later by the Democrats at the convention: opposing involvement in war but stressing national defense, and advocating aid to the Allies that would not be "inconsistent

with the requirements of our own national defense."

In domestic affairs, the Republicans lambasted the extension of federal power under the New Deal and promised cuts in government spending and the reduction of federal competition with private enterprise. The Republican platform agreed with the concept of unemployment relief and social security initiated by the Roosevelt administration, but it proposed the administration of these programs by the states and not the federal government.

The Republicans attacked Roosevelt's monetary measures and advocated currency reforms that included congressional control.

The platform also proposed new amendments to the Constitution that would provide equal rights for men and women and would limit a president to two terms in office.

Following are excerpts from the Republican platform of 1940:

Foreign Policy. The Republican Party is firmly opposed to involving this Nation in foreign war....

The Republican Party stands for Americanism, preparedness and peace. We accordingly fasten upon the New Deal full responsibility for our unpreparedness and for the consequent danger of involvement in war....

Our sympathies have been profoundly stirred by invasion of unoffending countries and by disaster to nations whole [whose] ideals most closely resemble our own. We favor the extension to all peoples fighting for liberty, or whose liberty is threatened, of such aid as shall not be in violation of international law or inconsistent with the requirements of our own national defense.

Unemployment Relief. We shall remove waste, discrimination, and politics from relief — through administration by the States with federal grants-in-aid on a fair and nonpolitical basis, thus giving the man and woman on relief a larger share of the funds appropriated.

Currency. The Congress should reclaim its constitutional powers over money, and withdraw the President's arbitrary authority to manipulate the currency, establish bimetallism, issue irredeemable paper money, and debase the gold and silver coinage. We shall repeal the Thomas Inflation Amendment of 1933 and the (foreign) Silver Purchase Act of 1934, and take all possible steps to preserve the value of the Government's huge holdings of gold and reintroduce gold into circulation.

Women's Rights. We favor submission by Congress to the States of an amendment to the Constitution providing for equal rights for men and women.

No Third Term. To insure against the overthrow of our American system of government we favor an amendment to the Constitution providing that no person shall be President of the United States for more than two terms.

Democrats

At the time of both major party conventions in the summer of 1940, Hitler's forces were moving quickly and relentlessly across Western Europe. International events assumed a major importance in political decisions. President Franklin D. Roosevelt, who gave evidence before 1940 that he would not seek a third term, became increasingly receptive to the idea of a draft as the Democratic convention drew nearer. The threat to American security caused by the awesomely successful Nazi military machine, coupled with Roosevelt's inability to find an adequate New Deal-style successor, seemed to spur F.D.R.'s decision to accept renomination.

The Democratic convention was held in Chicago in mid-July. On the second night of the convention, a message from Roosevelt was read stating that he did not desire to run for re-election and urging the delegates to vote for any candidate they wished. Although worded in a negative way, the message did not shut the door on a draft. The delegates reacted, however, by sitting in stunned silence until a Chicago city official began shouting over the public address system, "We want Roosevelt." The cheerleading galvanized the delegates into an hour-long demonstration.

Presidential balloting was held the next day. Roosevelt won easily on the first roll call, although two members of his administration, Vice President John Nance Garner and Postmaster General James A. Farley of New York, ran against him. Roosevelt received 946-13/30 of the 1,100 votes. Farley had 72-9/10 and Garner had 61. *(Chart, p. 200)*

While the delegates were satisfied to have Roosevelt at the top of the ticket again, many balked at his choice for vice president, Agriculture Secretary Henry A. Wallace of Iowa. Wallace, a leading liberal in the administration and a former Republican, was particularly distasteful to conservative Democrats. Many delegates were expecting Roosevelt to leave the vice presidential choice to the convention and were unhappy to have the candidate dictated to them.

It took a personal appearance at the convention by the president's wife, Eleanor Roosevelt, and a threat by F.D.R. that he would not accept the presidential nomination without his hand-picked running mate, to steer the delegates toward Wallace. In spite of the pressure by the Roosevelt forces, the vote was scattered among 13 candidates on the vice presidential ballot. Wallace, though, was able to obtain a slim majority, 626-11/30 votes to 329-3/5 for the runner-up, House Speaker William B. Bankhead of Alabama. Because of the displeasure of many of the delegates, Wallace was asked not to address the convention.

The convention closed by hearing a radio address by Roosevelt, who stated that he had not wanted the nomination but accepted it because the existing world crisis called for personal sacrifice.

The party platform was adopted without a roll call, although there was an amendment presented by a Minnesota representative that opposed any violation of the two-term tradition. It was rejected by a voice vote. The platform as adopted was divided into three sections. The first discussed American military preparedness and foreign policy; the second detailed the New Deal's benefits for various segments of the economy (agriculture, labor, business); the third listed New Deal welfare measures, ranging from unemployment relief to low-cost housing.

As a concession to the party's isolationist wing, the first section contained the administration's promise not to participate in foreign wars or fight in foreign lands, except in case of an attack on the United States. The plank stressed the need of a strong national defense to discourage aggression, but also pledged to provide to free nations (such as Great Britain) material aid "not inconsistent with the interests of our own national self-defense."

An electric power plank was included in the second section of the platform as a direct result of the Republicans' selection of Wendell L. Willkie, a former utilities executive, as their presidential candidate. The Democrats argued in favor of the massive public power projects constructed during the New Deal and criticized private utilities such as the one formerly headed by Willkie.

The third section of the platform drew a sharp distinction from the Republicans on the issue of unemployment relief, opposing any efforts to turn the administration of relief over to the states or local governments.

Following are excerpts from the Democratic platform of 1940:

Democratic Achievements. Toward the modern fulfillment of the American ideal, the Democratic Party, during the last seven years, has labored successfully:

1. *To strengthen democracy by defensive preparedness against aggression, whether by open attack or secret infiltration;*

2. *To strengthen democracy by increasing our economic efficiency; and*

3. *To strengthen democracy by improving the welfare of the people.*

Foreign Policy. We will not participate in foreign wars, and we will not send our army, naval or air forces to fight in foreign lands outside of the Americas, except in case of attack. . . .

Weakness and unpreparedness invite aggression. We must be so strong that no possible combination of powers would dare to attack us. We propose to provide America with an invincible air force, a navy strong enough to protect all our seacoasts and our national interests, and a fully-equipped and mechanized army.

Unemployment Relief. We shall continue to recognize the obligation of Government to provide work for deserving workers who cannot be absorbed by private industry.

We are opposed to vesting in the states and local authorities the control of Federally-financed work relief. We believe that this Republican proposal is a thinly disguised plan to put the unemployed back on the dole.

Electric Power. The nomination of a utility executive by the Republican Party as its presidential candidate raises squarely the issue, whether the nation's water power shall be used for all the people or for the selfish interests of a few. We accept that issue.

1944 Conventions

Presidential Candidates

Thomas E. Dewey
Republican

Franklin D. Roosevelt
Democrat

Republicans

For the first time since 1864, the nation was at war during a presidential election year. The Republicans held their convention first, meeting in Chicago in late June 1944. With a minimum of discord, the delegates selected a national ticket and adopted a platform. Gov. Thomas E. Dewey of New York, the front-runner for the presidential nomination, was the nearly unanimous selection when his last two rivals, Gov. John W. Bricker of Ohio and former Minnesota governor Harold E. Stassen, both withdrew from the race before the roll call. On the single ballot, Dewey received 1,056 of the 1,057 votes cast. The one dissenting vote was cast by a Wisconsin delegate for Gen. Douglas MacArthur. *(Chart, p. 202)*

As Dewey's running mate, the delegates unanimously selected Gov. Bricker, an isolationist and party regular, who received all 1,057 votes cast. During the nominating speeches, Rep. Charles A. Halleck of Indiana made the unusual move of recommending his state's first choice for vice president, William L. Hutcheson, for secretary of labor.

Dewey came to Chicago personally to accept the nomination, becoming the first Republican presidential candidate to break the tradition of waiting to accept the nomination in a formal notification ceremony. The thrust of Dewey's speech was an attack on the Roosevelt administration, which he referred to as "stubborn men grown old and tired and quarrelsome in office."

The platform was approved without dissent. The international section was written in a guarded tone. It favored "responsible participation by the United States in post-war cooperative organization" but declared that any agreement must be approved by a two-thirds vote of the Senate. The Republicans favored the establishment of a postwar Jewish state in Palestine.

The domestic section of the platform denounced the New Deal's centralization of power in the federal government, with its increased government spending and deficits. The Republicans proposed to stabilize the economy through the encouragement of private enterprise.

The platform restated several of the planks included four years earlier, among which were the call for an equal rights amendment, a two-term limitation on the president and the return of control over currency matters from the president to Congress.

The Republicans adopted a civil rights plank that

called for a congressional investigation of the treatment of blacks in the military, passage of a constitutional amendment to eliminate the poll tax and legislation that would outlaw lynching and permanently establish a Fair Employment Practice Commission.

Following are excerpts from the Republican platform of 1944:

Postwar International Organization. We favor responsible participation by the United States in post-war cooperative organization among sovereign nations to prevent military aggression and to attain permanent peace with organized justice in a free world.

Such organization should develop effective cooperative means to direct peace forces to prevent or repel military aggression. Pending this, we pledge continuing collaboration with the United Nations to assure these ultimate objectives....

We shall sustain the Constitution of the United States in the attainment of our international aims; and pursuant to the Constitution of the United States any treaty or agreement to attain such aims made on behalf of the United States with any other nation or any association of nations, shall be made only by and with the advice and consent of the Senate of the United States provided two-thirds of the Senators present concur.

Israel. In order to give refuge to millions of distressed Jewish men, women and children driven from their homes by tyranny, we call for the opening of Palestine to their unrestricted immigration and land ownership, so that in accordance with the full intent and purpose of the Balfour Declaration of 1917 and the Resolution of a Republican Congress in 1922, Palestine may be constituted as a free and democratic Commonwealth. We condemn the failure of the President to insist that the mandatory of Palestine carry out the provision of the Balfour Declaration and of the mandate while he pretends to support them.

New Deal. Four more years of New Deal policy would centralize all power in the President, and would daily subject every act of every citizen to regulation by his henchmen; and this country could remain a Republic only in name. No problem exists which cannot be solved by American methods. We have no need of either the communistic or the fascist technique.

...The National Administration has become a sprawling, overlapping bureaucracy. It is undermined by executive abuse of power, confused lines of authority, duplication of effort, inadequate fiscal controls, loose personnel practices and an attitude of arrogance previously unknown in our history.

Economy. We reject the theory of restoring prosperity through government spending and deficit financing.

We shall promote the fullest stable employment through private enterprise.

Civil Rights. We pledge an immediate Congressional inquiry to ascertain the extent to which mistreatment, segregation and discrimination against Negroes who are in our armed forces are impairing morale and efficiency, and the adoption of corrective legislation.

We pledge the establishment by Federal legislation of a permanent Fair Employment Practice Commission.

The payment of any poll tax should not be a condition of voting in Federal elections and we favor immediate submission of a Constitutional amendment for its abolition.

We favor legislation against lynching and pledge our sincere efforts in behalf of its early enactment.

Agriculture. An American market price to the American farmer and the protection of such price by means of support prices, commodity loans, or a combination thereof, together with such other economic means as will assure an income to agriculture that is fair and equitable in comparison with labor, business and industry. We oppose subsidies as a substitute for fair markets.

Serious study of and search for a sound program of crop insurance with emphasis upon establishing a self-supporting program.

Democrats

President Franklin Delano Roosevelt, who four years earlier did not make a final decision about accepting a third nomination until the last moment, clearly stated his intention to run for a fourth term a week before the 1944 convention was to open in Chicago. In a message to Democratic National Chairman Robert E. Hannegan of Missouri released July 11, Roosevelt declared that while he did not desire to run, he would accept renomination reluctantly as a "good soldier."

The early sessions of the convention were highlighted by approval of the rules committee report and settlement of a credentials challenge. The rules committee mandated the national committee to revamp the convention's vote-allocation formula in a way that would take into account Democratic voting strength. This measure was adopted to appease Southern delegates, who in 1936 were promised an increased proportion of the convention vote in return for elimination of the two-thirds rule. No action had been taken to implement the pledge in the intervening eight years.

The credentials dispute involved the Texas delegation, which was represented by two competing groups. By a voice vote, the convention agreed to seat both groups.

Vice President Henry A. Wallace enlivened the presidential nominations by appearing before the convention to urge Roosevelt's renomination. Wallace termed the president the "greatest liberal in the history of the U.S." In the balloting that followed, Roosevelt easily defeated Sen. Harry F. Byrd of Virginia, who was supported by some conservative Southern delegates unhappy with the domestic legislation favored by the New Deal. The final tally: Roosevelt, 1,086; Byrd, 89; former postmaster general James A. Farley, 1. *(Chart, p. 202)*

Roosevelt accepted the nomination in a radio address delivered from the San Diego Naval Base, where he had stopped off en route to a wartime conference.

The real drama of the convention, the selection of the vice presidential nominee, came next. Roosevelt had been ambivalent about the choice of his running mate, encouraging several people to run but not publicly endorsing any of them. The president wrote an ambiguous letter to the convention chairman, which was read to the delegates. Roosevelt stated that if he were a delegate himself he would vote for Wallace's renomination, but that the ultimate choice was the convention's and it must consider the pros and cons of its selection.

In another message, written privately for National Chairman Hannegan, Roosevelt declared that he would be happy to run with either Missouri senator Harry S Truman or Supreme Court Justice William O. Douglas. Most of the party bosses preferred Truman to the more liberal alternatives, Wallace and Douglas. Truman originally was slated to nominate former South Carolina senator and Supreme Court Justice James F. Byrnes for vice president. But, spurred by his political advisers, Roosevelt telephoned Truman in Chicago and urged him to accept the nomination. Truman reluctantly agreed.

Roosevelt's final preference for Truman was not publicly announced, and 12 names were placed before the convention. Wallace led on the first roll call with 429-1/2

votes, followed by Truman with 319-1/2. Favorite sons and other hopefuls shared the remaining votes cast.

Truman passed Wallace on the second ballot, 477-1/2 to 473, and, immediately after completion of the roll call, Alabama began the bandwagon for the Missouri senator by switching its votes to him. When all the shifts had been made, Truman was an easy winner with 1,031 votes, while Wallace finished with 105.

The platform adopted by the convention was a short one, only 1,360 words. The first third of the platform lauded the accomplishments of Roosevelt's first three terms. The rest of the document outlined the party's proposals for the future. In foreign affairs, the Democrats advocated the creation of a postwar international organization that would have adequate forces available to prevent future wars. The party also called for American membership in an international court of justice. The Democrats joined their Republican opponents in favoring the establishment of an independent Jewish state in Palestine.

The domestic section of the platform proposed a continuation of New Deal liberalism, with passage of an equal rights amendment for women, price guarantees and crop insurance for farmers and the establishment of federal aid to education that would be administered by the states.

A minority report concerning foreign policy called for the establishment of an international air force to help keep peace. The proposal was rejected, however, when the platform committee chairman indicated that the existence of an air force was included in the majority report's call for "adequate forces" to be at the disposal of the proposed international organization.

Following are excerpts from the Democratic platform of 1944:

Postwar International Organizations. That the world may not again be drenched in blood by international outlaws and criminals, we pledge:

To join with the other United Nations in the establishment of an international organization based on the principle of the sovereign equality of all peace-loving states, open to membership by all such states, large and small, for the prevention of aggression and the maintenance of international peace and security.

To make all necessary and effective agreements and arrangements through which the nations would maintain adequate forces to meet the needs of preventing war and of making impossible the preparation for war and which would have such forces available for joint action when necessary.

Such organization must be endowed with power to employ armed forces when necessary to prevent aggression and preserve peace.

Israel. We favor the opening of Palestine to unrestricted Jewish immigration and colonization, and such a policy as to result in the establishment there of a free and democratic Jewish commonwealth.

Women's Rights. We favor legislation assuring equal pay for equal work, regardless of sex.

We recommend to Congress the submission of a Constitutional amendment on equal rights for women.

Education. We favor Federal aid to education administered by the states without interference by the Federal Government.

Agriculture. Price guarantees and crop insurance to farmers with all practical steps:

To keep agriculture on a parity with industry and labor.

To foster the success of the small independent farmer.

To aid the home ownership of family-sized farms.

To extend rural electrification and develop broader domestic and foreign markets for agricultural products.

Civil Rights. We believe that racial and religious minorities have the right to live, develop and vote equally with all citizens and share the rights that are guaranteed by our Constitution. Congress should exert its full constitutional powers to protect those rights.

1948 Conventions

Presidential Candidates

Thomas E. Dewey
Republican

Harry S Truman
Democrat

J. Strom Thurmond
States' Rights

Henry A. Wallace
Progressive

Republicans

The Republican convention was held in Philadelphia in late June. As in 1944, New York governor Thomas E. Dewey entered the convention as the front-runner for the nomination. But unlike four years earlier, when he was virtually handed the nomination, Dewey was contested by several candidates, including Ohio senator Robert A. Taft and former Minnesota governor Harold E. Stassen.

In all, seven names were placed in nomination, with 548 votes needed to determine a winner. Dewey led on the first roll call with 434 votes, followed by Taft with 224 and Stassen with 157. Each of the other candidates received fewer than 100 votes. *(Chart, p. 204)*

On the second roll call, Dewey moved closer to the nomination, receiving 515 votes. Taft and Stassen continued to trail, with 274 and 149 votes respectively. At this point, the anti-Dewey forces requested a recess, which was agreed to by the confident Dewey organization.

Unable to form a coalition that could stop Dewey, all his opponents withdrew before the third ballot. On the subsequent roll call, the New York governor was the unanimous choice of the convention, receiving all 1,094 votes.

Dewey's choice for vice president was California governor Earl Warren, who was nominated by acclamation. Warren had been a favorite-son candidate for the presidency and agreed to take second place on the ticket only after receiving assurances that the responsibilities of the vice presidency would be increased if Dewey were elected.

The Republican platform was adopted without dissent. The wording of the platform was unusually positive for a party out of the White House. The failures of the Truman administration were dismissed in a short paragraph, with the rest of the document praising the accomplishments of the Republican 80th Congress and detailing the party's proposals for the future.

One of the major issues of the 1948 campaign was the controversial Taft-Hartley labor law, a measure supported by the Republicans, but which most Democratic leaders felt should be repealed. The Republicans were silent on national health insurance, and the party's housing position stressed private initiative rather than federal legislation. As in 1944 the Republicans opposed the poll tax and segregation in the military and favored legislation to outlaw lynching.

The Republican platform accepted the concept of a bipartisan foreign policy. Paragraphs were inserted that supported the Marshall Plan for European recovery, the United Nations and recognition of Israel.

Following are excerpts from the Republican platform of 1948:

Civil Rights. This right of equal opportunity to work and to advance in life should never be limited in any individual because of race, religion, color, or country of origin. We favor the enactment and just enforcement of such Federal legislation as may be necessary to maintain this right at all times in every part of this Republic....

Lynching or any other form of mob violence anywhere is a disgrace to any civilized state, and we favor the prompt enactment of legislation to end this infamy....

We favor the abolition of the poll tax as a requisite to voting.

We are opposed to the idea of racial segregation in the armed services of the United States.

Housing. Housing can best be supplied and financed by private enterprise; but government can and should encourage the building of better homes at less cost. We recommend Federal aid to the States for local slum clearance and low-rental housing programs only where there is a need that cannot be met either by private enterprise or by the States and localities.

Labor. Here are some of the accomplishments of this Republican Congress: a sensible reform of the labor law, protecting all rights of Labor while safeguarding the entire community, against those breakdowns in essential industries which endanger the health and livelihood of all....

We pledge continuing study to improve labor-management legislation in the light of experience and changing conditions....

We favor equal pay for equal work regardless of sex.

Internal Security. We pledge a vigorous enforcement of existing laws against Communists and enactment of such new legislation as may be necessary to expose the treasonable activities of Communists and defeat their objec-

tive of establishing here a godless dictatorship controlled from abroad.

Foreign Policy. We are proud of the part that Republicans have taken in those limited areas of foreign policy in which they have been permitted to participate. We shall invite the Minority Party to join us under the next Republican Administration in stopping partisan politics at the water's edge.

United Nations. We believe in collective security against aggression and in behalf of justice and freedom. We shall support the United Nations as the world's best hope in this direction, striving to strengthen it and promote its effective evolution and use. The United Nations should progressively establish international law, be freed of any veto in the peaceful settlement of international disputes, and be provided with the armed forces contemplated by the Charter.

Israel. We welcome Israel into the family of nations and take pride in the fact that the Republican Party was the first to call for the establishment of a free and independent Jewish Commonwealth.

Democrats

The Democratic delegates were in a melancholy mood when they gathered in Philadelphia in mid-July 1948. Franklin D. Roosevelt was dead; the Republicans had regained control of Congress in 1946; Roosevelt's successor, Harry S Truman, appeared unable to stem massive defections of liberals and Southern conservatives from the New Deal coalition.

The dissatisfaction of Southern delegates with policies of the national party was a prominent feature of the 1948 convention. Although the national committee had been mandated by the 1944 convention to devise a new vote allocation procedure that would appease the South, the redistribution of votes for the 1948 convention merely added two votes to each of the 36 states that backed Roosevelt in the 1944 election. This did not appreciably bolster Southern strength.

As the convention progressed, Southern displeasure focused on the civil rights issue. The Mississippi delegation included in its credentials anti-civil-rights resolutions that bound the delegation to bolt the convention if a states' rights plank was not included in the platform. The Mississippi resolutions also denied the power of the national convention to require the Democratic Party of Mississippi to support any candidate who favored President Truman's civil rights program or any candidate who failed to denounce that program.

A minority report was introduced that recommended the Mississippi delegation not be seated. This proposal was defeated by a voice vote, and, in the interest of party harmony, no roll-call vote was taken. However, in an unusual move, several delegations, including those of California and New York, asked that they be recorded in favor of the minority report.

Joined by several other Southern states, Texas presented a minority proposal to the rules committee report, which favored re-establishment of the two-thirds rule. The minority proposal, however, was beaten by a voice vote.

When the presidential balloting began, the entire Mississippi delegation and 13 members of the Alabama delegation withdrew in opposition to the convention's stand on civil rights. However, their withdrawal in no way jeopardized the nomination of Truman. Some party leaders had earlier flirted with the possibility of drafting Gen. Dwight D. Eisenhower or even Supreme Court Justice William O.

Douglas. But the lack of interest of these two men in the Democratic nomination left the field clear for Truman.

The incumbent won a clear majority on the first ballot, receiving 926 votes to 266 for Georgia senator Richard B. Russell, who received the votes of more than 90 percent of the remaining Southern delegates. Among the states of the Old Confederacy, Truman received only 13 votes, all from North Carolina. After several small vote switches, the final tally stood: Truman, 947-1/2; Russell, 263. *(Chart, p. 203)*

Veteran Kentucky senator Alben W. Barkley, the convention's keynoter, was nominated by acclamation for vice president.

Truman appeared before the convention to accept the nomination and aroused the dispirited delegates with a lively speech attacking the Republican Congress. Referring to it as the "worst 80th Congress," Truman announced that he would call a special session so that the Republicans could pass the legislation they said they favored in their platform.

The Democratic platform was adopted by a voice vote, after a heated discussion of the civil rights section. As presented to the convention by the platform committee, the plank favored equal rights for all citizens but was couched in generalities such as those in the 1944 plank. Southern delegates wanted a weaker commitment to civil rights, and various Southern delegations offered three different amendments.

One, presented by former governor Dan Moody of Texas and signed by 15 members of the platform committee, was a broadly worded statement that emphasized the power of the states. A second amendment, sponsored by two Tennessee members of the platform committee, was a brief, emphatic statement declaring the rights of the states. The third amendment, introduced by the Mississippi delegation as a substitute for the Moody amendment, specifically listed the powers of the states to maintain segregation. The Moody amendment was beaten, 924 to 310, with nearly all the support limited to the South. The other two amendments were rejected by voice vote. *(Chart, p. 203)*

Northern liberals countered by proposing to strengthen the civil rights plank. Introduced by former representative Andrew J. Biemiller of Wisconsin and championed by Mayor Hubert H. Humphrey of Minneapolis, the amendment commended Truman's civil rights program and called for congressional action to guarantee equal rights in voting participation, employment opportunity, personal security and military service. The Biemiller amendment was passed, 651-1/2 to 582-1/2, with delegations from the larger Northern states supporting it. Delegations from the South were in solid opposition and were joined by delegates from border and small Northern states. *(Chart, p. 203)*

The rest of the platform lauded Truman's legislative program and blamed the Republican Congress for obstructing beneficial legislation. In the New Deal tradition, the platform advocated the extension of social security, raising of the minimum wage, establishment of national health insurance and the creation of a permanent flexible price support system for farmers. Congress was blamed for obstructing passage of federal aid to education, comprehensive housing legislation and funding for the Marshall Plan to help rebuild Europe. The Republicans were also criticized for crippling reciprocal trade agreements, passage of the Taft-Hartley Act and even the rising rate of inflation.

The development of the Cold War with the communist world produced a new issue, internal security, on which the two major parties differed sharply. While the Republican

position stressed the pursuit of subversives, the Democrats placed more emphasis on the protection of individual rights.

In foreign affairs, the Democratic platform called for the establishment of a United Nations military force, international control of the atomic bomb and recognition of the state of Israel.

Following are excerpts from the Democratic platform of 1948:

Civil Rights. We highly commend President Harry S Truman for his courageous stand on the issue of civil rights.

We call upon the Congress to support our President in guaranteeing these basic and fundamental American Principles: (1) the right of full and equal political participation; (2) the right to equal opportunity of employment; (3) the right of security of person; (4) and the right of equal treatment in the service and defense of our nation.

Housing. We shall enact comprehensive housing legislation, including provisions for slum clearance and low-rent housing projects initiated by local agencies. This nation is shamed by the failure of the Republican 80th Congress to pass the vitally needed general housing legislation as recommended by the President. Adequate housing will end the need for rent control. Until then, it must be continued.

Social Security, Health Insurance. We favor the extension of the Social Security program established under Democratic leadership, to provide additional protection against the hazards of old age, disability, disease or death. We believe that this program should include:

Increases in old-age and survivors' insurance benefits by at least 50 percent, and reduction of the eligibility age for women from 65 to 60 years; extension of old-age and survivors' and unemployment insurance to all workers not now covered; insurance against loss of earnings on account of illness or disability; improved public assistance for the needy.

Labor. We advocate the repeal of the Taft-Hartley Act. It was enacted by the Republican 80th Congress over the President's veto. . . .

We favor the extension of the coverage of the Fair Labor Standards Act as recommended by President Truman, and the adoption of a minimum wage of at least 75 cents an hour in place of the present obsolete and inadequate minimum of 40 cents an hour.

We favor legislation assuring that the workers of our nation receive equal pay for equal work, regardless of sex.

United Nations. We will continue to lead the way toward curtailment of the use of the veto. We shall favor such amendments and modifications of the charter as experience may justify. We will continue our efforts toward the establishment of an international armed force to aid its authority. We advocate the grant of a loan to the United Nations recommended by the President, but denied by the Republican Congress, for the construction of the United Nations headquarters in this country.

Disarmament. We advocate the effective international control of weapons of mass destruction, including the atomic bomb, and we approve continued and vigorous efforts within the United Nations to bring about the successful consummation of the proposals which our Government has advanced.

Israel. We pledge full recognition to the State of Israel. We affirm our pride that the United States under the leadership of President Truman played a leading role in the adoption of the resolution of November 29, 1947, by the United Nations General Assembly for the creation of a Jewish State.

Internal Security. We shall continue vigorously to enforce the laws against subversive activities, observing at all times the constitutional guarantees which protect free speech, the free press and honest political activity. We shall strengthen our laws against subversion to the full extent necessary, protecting at all times our traditional individual freedoms.

States' Rights (Dixiecrats)

Provoked by the Democratic convention's adoption of a strong civil rights plank, Gov. Fielding L. Wright of Mississippi invited other Southern Democrats to meet in Birmingham, Ala., on July 17 to select a regional ticket that would reflect Southern views.

It was a disgruntled group that gathered in Birmingham, just three days after the close of the Democratic convention. Placards on the floor of the convention hall identified 13 states, yet there were no delegates from Georgia, Kentucky or North Carolina, and Virginia was represented by four University of Virginia students and an Alexandria woman who was returning home from a trip south. Most major Southern politicians shied away from the bolters, fearing that involvement would jeopardize their standing with the national party and their seniority in Congress.

Former Alabama governor Frank M. Dixon vocalized the anti-civil-rights mood of the gathering with a keynote address charging that Truman's civil rights program would "reduce us to the status of a mongrel, inferior race, mixed in blood, our Anglo-Saxon heritage a mockery."

As its standard-bearers, the convention chose Gov. J. Strom Thurmond of South Carolina for president and Gov. Wright for vice president. Thurmond's acceptance speech touched on another grievance of bolting Southern Democrats: their decreasing power within the Democratic Party. Thurmond warned: "If the South should vote for Truman this year, we might just as well petition the Government to give us a colonial status."

The platform adopted by the Dixiecrats was barely 1,000 words long, but it forcefully presented the case for states' rights. The platform warned that the tendency toward greater federal power ultimately would establish a totalitarian police state.

The Dixiecrats saved their most vitriolic passages to describe the civil rights plank adopted by the Democratic convention. They declared their support for segregation and charged that the plank adopted by the Democrats was meant "to embarrass and humiliate the South."

The platform also charged the national Democratic Party with ingratitude, claiming that the South had supported the Democratic ticket with "clock-like regularity" for nearly 100 years, but that now the national party was being dominated by states controlled by the Republicans.

Following are excerpts from the States' Rights platform of 1948:

States' Rights. We believe that the protection of the American people against the onward march of totalitarian government requires a faithful observance of Article X of the American Bill of Rights which provides that: "The powers not delegated to the United States by the Constitution, nor prohibited by it to the states, are reserved to the states respectively, or to the people."

Civil Rights. We stand for the segregation of the races and the racial integrity of each race; the constitutional right to choose one's associates; to accept private employment without governmental interference, and to earn one's living in any lawful way. We oppose the elimination of segregation employment by Federal bureaucrats called for by the misnamed civil rights program. We favor home rule, local self-

government and a minimum interference with individual rights.

We oppose and condemn the action of the Democratic convention in sponsoring a civil rights program calling for the elimination of segregation, social equality by Federal fiat, regulation of private employment practices, voting and local law enforcement.

We affirm that the effective enforcement of such a program would be utterly destructive of the social, economic and political life of the Southern people, and of other localities in which there may be differences in race, creed or national origin in appreciable numbers.

Progressives

On Dec. 29, 1947, former vice president Henry A. Wallace announced his presidential candidacy at the head of a new liberal party. Officially named the Progressive Party at its convention in Philadelphia in late July 1948, the new party was composed of some liberal Democrats as well as more radical groups and individuals that included some communists.

Nearly 3,200 delegates nominated Wallace for the presidency and Democratic senator Glen H. Taylor of Idaho as his running mate. The colorful Taylor and his family regaled the delegates with their rendition of "When You Were Sweet Sixteen."

On the final night of the convention, 32,000 spectators assembled to hear Wallace deliver his acceptance speech at Shibe Park. The Progressive standard-bearer expressed his belief in "progressive capitalism," which would place "human rights above property rights," and envisioned "a new frontier . . . across the wilderness of poverty and sickness."

Former Roosevelt associate Rexford G. Tugwell chaired the 74-member platform committee that drafted a detailed platform, about 9,000 words in length, that was adopted by the convention. The platform denounced the two major parties as champions of big business and claimed the new party to be the true "political heirs of Jefferson, Jackson and Lincoln." However, many political observers and opponents of the Progressives dismissed the new party as a Communist-front organization.

Although numerous positions taken by the Progressives in 1948 were considered radical, many were later adopted or seriously considered by the major parties.

The foreign policy plank advocated negotiations between the United States and the Soviet Union ultimately leading to a peace agreement, and it sharply criticized the "anti-Soviet hysteria" of the period. The platform called for repeal of the draft, repudiation of the Marshall Plan, worldwide disarmament featuring abolition of the atomic bomb, amnesty for conscientious objectors imprisoned in World War II, recognition and aid to Israel, extension of United Nations humanitarian programs and the establishment of a world legislature.

In the domestic area, the Progressives opposed internal security legislation, advocated the 18-year-old vote, favored the creation of a Department of Culture, called for food stamp and school hot lunch programs and proposed a federal housing plan that would build 25 million homes in 10 years and subsidize low-income housing.

The Progressives also reiterated the proposals of earlier third parties by favoring the direct election of the president and vice president, extensive tax reform, stricter control of monopolies and the nationalization of the principal means of communication, transportation and finance.

The Progressives joined the Democrats and Republicans in proposing strong civil rights legislation and an equal rights amendment for women.

Following are excerpts from the Progressive platform of 1948:

Soviet Union. The Progressive Party . . . demands negotiation and discussion with the Soviet Union to find areas of agreement to win the peace.

Disarmament. The Progressive Party will work through the United Nations for a world disarmament agreement to outlaw the atomic bomb, bacteriological warfare, and all other instruments of mass destruction; to destroy existing stockpiles of atomic bombs and to establish United Nations controls, including inspection, over the production of atomic energy; and to reduce conventional armaments drastically in accordance with resolutions already passed by the United Nations General Assembly.

World Legislation. The only ultimate alternative to war is the abandonment of the principle of the coercion of sovereignties by sovereignties and the adoption of the principle of the just enforcement upon individuals of world federal law, enacted by a world federal legislature with limited but adequate powers to safeguard the common defense and the general welfare of all mankind.

Draft. The Progressive Party calls for the repeal of the peacetime draft and the rejection of Universal Military Training.

Amnesty. We demand amnesty for conscientious objectors imprisoned in World War II.

Internal Security. We denounce anti-Soviet hysteria as a mask for monopoly, militarism, and reaction. . . .

The Progressive Party will fight for the constitutional rights of Communists and all other political groups to express their views as the first line in the defense of the liberties of a democratic people.

Civil Rights. The Progressive Party condemns segregation and discrimination in all its forms and in all places. . . .

We call for a Presidential proclamation ending segregation and all forms of discrimination in the armed services and Federal employment.

We demand Federal anti-lynch, anti-discrimination, and fair-employment-practices legislation, and legislation abolishing segregation in interstate travel.

We call for immediate passage of anti-poll tax legislation, enactment of a universal suffrage law to permit all citizens to vote in Federal elections, and the full use of Federal enforcement powers to assure free exercise of the right to franchise.

Food Stamps, School Lunches. We also call for assistance to low-income consumers through such programs as the food stamp plan and the school hot-lunch program.

Housing. We pledge an attack on the chronic housing shortage and the slums through a long-range program to build 25 million new homes during the next ten years. This program will include public subsidized housing for low-income families.

Nationalization. As a first step, the largest banks, the railroads, the merchant marine, the electric power and gas industry, and industries primarily dependent on government funds or government purchases such as the aircraft, the synthetic rubber and synthetic oil industries must be placed under public ownership.

Youth Vote. We call for the right to vote at eighteen.

1952 Conventions

Presidential Candidates

Dwight D. Eisenhower
Republican

Adlai E. Stevenson
Democrat

Republicans

For the third straight time, both major parties held their conventions in the same city. In 1952 the site was Chicago; the Republicans met there in early July two weeks before the Democrats. The battle for the presidential nomination pitted the hero of the party's conservative wing, Sen. Robert A. Taft of Ohio, against the favorite of most moderate and liberal Republicans, Gen. Dwight D. Eisenhower. The general, a Texas native, had resigned as supreme commander of the North Atlantic Treaty Organization (NATO) less than six weeks before the convention to pursue the nomination actively.

As in 1912, when Taft's father had engaged in a bitter struggle with Theodore Roosevelt for the nomination, the outcome of the presidential race was determined in preliminary battles over convention rules and credentials.

The first confrontation came on the issue of the voting rights of challenged delegates. The Taft forces proposed adoption of the 1948 rules, which would have allowed contested delegates to vote on all credentials challenges except their own. The Eisenhower forces countered by proposing what they called a "fair play amendment," which would seat only those contested delegates who were approved by at least a two-thirds vote of the national committee. At stake were a total of 68 delegates from Georgia, Louisiana and Texas, with the large majority of the challenged delegates in favor of Taft. The Taft forces introduced a substitute to the "fair play amendment," designed to exempt seven delegates from Louisiana. On the first test of strength between the two candidates, the Eisenhower forces were victorious, as the substitute amendment was defeated, 658 to 548. The "fair play amendment" was subsequently approved by a voice vote. *(Chart, p. 206)*

The second confrontation developed with the report of the credentials committee. The Eisenhower forces presented a minority report concerning the contested Georgia, Louisiana and Texas seats. After a bitter debate, a roll-call vote was taken on the Georgia challenge, with the Eisenhower forces winning again, 607 to 531.

The Louisiana and Texas challenges were settled in favor of the Eisenhower forces without a roll-call vote. The favorable settlement of the credentials challenges increased the momentum behind the Eisenhower candidacy.

Before the presidential balloting began, a non-partisan debate was held on a proposal to add state chairmen to the national committee from states recording Republican electoral majorities and to remove the requirement that women hold one of each state's seats on the national committee. The proposal was primarily intended to decrease Southern influence on the national committee. But the major opposition was raised by a number of women delegates who objected to the rule change; however, their effort to defeat it was rejected by voice vote.

Five men were nominated for the presidency, but on completion of the first roll call Eisenhower had 595 votes and was within nine votes of victory. Taft was a strong second with 500 votes. However, before a second ballot could begin, Minnesota switched 19 votes from favorite son Harold E. Stassen to Eisenhower, giving the latter the nomination. After a series of vote changes, the final tally stood: Eisenhower, 845; Taft, 280; other candidates, 81. The general's nomination was subsequently made unanimous.

Eisenhower's choice as a running mate, 39-year-old senator Richard M. Nixon of California, was nominated by acclamation. Eisenhower promised in his acceptance speech to lead a "crusade" against "a party too long in power."

The 6,000-word platform was adopted by a voice vote. The document included a sharp attack on the Democrats, charging the Roosevelt and Truman administrations with "violating our liberties ... by seizing powers never granted," "shielding traitors" and attempting to establish "national socialism." The foreign policy section, written by John Foster Dulles, supported the concept of collective security but denounced the Truman policy of containment and blamed the administration for the communist takeover of China. The Republican platform advocated increased national preparedness.

As well as castigating the Democrats for an incompe-

tent foreign policy, the Republicans denounced their opposition for laxness in maintaining internal security. A plank asserted: "There are no Communists in the Republican Party."

On most domestic issues the platform advocated a reduction in federal power. The civil rights plank proposed federal action to outlaw lynching, poll taxes and discriminatory employment practices. However, unlike the plank four years earlier, the Republican position included a paragraph that declared the individual states had primary responsibility for their own domestic institutions. On a related issue of states' rights, the Republicans, as in 1948, favored state control of tideland resources.

Following are excerpts from the Republican platform of 1952:

Democratic Failures. We charge that they have arrogantly deprived our citizens of precious liberties by seizing powers never granted.

We charge that they work unceasingly to achieve their goal of national socialism....

We charge that they have shielded traitors to the Nation in high places, and that they have created enemies abroad where we should have friends.

We charge that they have violated our liberties by turning loose upon the country a swarm of arrogant bureaucrats and their agents who meddle intolerably in the lives and occupations of our citizens.

We charge that there has been corruption in high places, and that examples of dishonesty and dishonor have shamed the moral standards of the American people.

We charge that they have plunged us into war in Korea without the consent of our citizens through their authorized representatives in the Congress, and have carried on the war without will to victory....

Tehran, Yalta and Potsdam were the scenes of those tragic blunders with others to follow. The leaders of the Administration in power acted without the knowledge or consent of Congress or of the American people. They traded our overwhelming victory for a new enemy and for new oppressions and new wars which were quick to come.

...And finally they denied the military aid that had been authorized by Congress and which was crucially needed if China were to be saved. Thus they substituted on our Pacific flank a murderous enemy for an ally and friend.

Internal Security. By the Administration's appeasement of Communism at home and abroad it has permitted Communists and their fellow travelers to serve in many key agencies and to infiltrate our American life....

There are no Communists in the Republican Party. We have always recognized Communism to be a world conspiracy against freedom and religion. We never compromised with Communism and we have fought to expose it and to eliminate it in government and American life.

Civil Rights. We believe that it is the primary responsibility of each State to order and control its own domestic institutions, and this power, reserved to the states, is essential to the maintenance of our Federal Republic. However, we believe that the Federal Government should take supplemental action within its constitutional jurisdiction to oppose discrimination against race, religion or national origin.

We will prove our good faith by:

Appointing qualified persons, without distinction of race, religion or national origin, to responsible positions in the Government.

Federal action toward the elimination of lynching.

Federal action toward the elimination of poll taxes as a prerequisite to voting.

Appropriate action to end segregation in the District of Columbia.

Enacting Federal legislation to further just and equita-

ble treatment in the area of discriminatory employment practices. Federal action should not duplicate state efforts to end such practices; should not set up another huge bureaucracy.

Labor. We favor the retention of the Taft-Hartley Act.

...We urge the adoption of such amendments to the Taft-Hartley Act as time and experience show to be desirable, and which further protect the rights of labor, management and the public.

Democrats

The Democrats held their 1952 convention in Chicago in late July. The convention lasted six days, the longest by either party in the post-World War II years. The proceedings were enlivened by disputes over credentials and a party loyalty pledge and a wide-open race for the presidential nomination.

The legitimately selected Texas delegation, dominated by the Dixiecrat wing of the state party, was challenged by a delegation loyal to the national party, but chosen in a rump assembly. Without a roll-call vote, the convention approved the credentials of the Dixiecrat-oriented delegates, although their seating was protested by Northern liberals.

The Dixiecrat bolt of 1948 resulted in the introduction of a party loyalty pledge at the 1952 convention. The resolution, introduced by Sen. Blair Moody of Michigan, proposed that no delegate be seated who would not assure the credentials committee that he would work to have the Democratic national ticket placed on the ballot in his state under the party's name. This resolution was aimed at several Southern states that had listed the Thurmond-Wright ticket under the Democratic Party label on their state ballots in 1948.

Sen. Spessard L. Holland of Florida introduced a substitute resolution that simply declared it would be "honorable" for each delegate to adhere to the decisions reached in the convention. Holland's resolution, however, was defeated and Moody's was approved, both by voice votes.

The report of the credentials committee listed three Southern states — Louisiana, South Carolina and Virginia — that declined to abide by the Moody resolution. The question of their seating rights came to a head during the roll call for presidential nominations, when Virginia questioned its own status in the convention. A motion to seat the Virginia delegation in spite of its non-observance of the resolution was presented for a vote. Although not agreeing to the pledge, the chairman of the Virginia delegation indicated that the problem prompting the Moody resolution was covered by state law. After a long, confusing roll call, interrupted frequently by demands to poll individual delegates, the motion to seat the Virginia delegation passed, 650-1/2 to 518. *(Chart, p. 205)*

After efforts to adjourn were defeated, the Louisiana and South Carolina delegations offered assurances similar to those presented by Virginia and were seated by a voice vote.

Eleven names were placed in nomination for the presidency, although the favorite of most party leaders, Illinois governor Adlai E. Stevenson, was a reluctant candidate. Stevenson expressed interest only in running for re-election as governor, but a draft-Stevenson movement developed and gained strength quickly as the convention proceeded.

Sen. Estes Kefauver of Tennessee, a powerful vote-getter in the primaries, was the leader on the first ballot,

with 340 votes. He was followed by Stevenson with 273, Sen. Richard B. Russell of Georgia, the Southern favorite, with 268, and W. Averell Harriman of New York with 123-1/2.

The second ballot saw gains by the three front-runners, with Kefauver's vote rising to 362-1/2, Stevenson's to 324-1/2 and Russell's to 294. A recess was taken during which Harriman and Massachusetts' favorite son, Gov. Paul A. Dever, both withdrew in favor of Stevenson.

The Illinois governor won a narrow majority on the third ballot, receiving 617-1/2 of the 1,230 convention votes. Kefauver finished with 275-1/2 and Russell with 261. The selection of Stevenson represented the first success for a presidential draft movement of a reluctant candidate since the nomination of James A. Garfield by the Republicans in 1880. *(Chart, p. 205)*

For vice president, Stevenson chose Sen. John J. Sparkman of Alabama, who was nominated by acclamation.

Although a reluctant candidate, Stevenson promised the delegates a fighting campaign but warned: "Better we lose the election than mislead the people; and better we lose than misgovern the people."

The Democratic platform was adopted without the rancor that had accompanied consideration of the party platform four years earlier. The document was approved by a voice vote, although both the Georgia and Mississippi delegations asked that they be recorded in opposition.

The platform promised extension and improvement of New Deal and Fair Deal policies that had been proposed and enacted over the previous 20 years. The party's foremost goal was stated to be "peace with honor," which could be achieved by support for a strengthened United Nations, coupled with the policy of collective security in the form of American assistance for allies around the world. The peaceful use of atomic energy was pledged, as were efforts to establish an international control system. However, the platform also promised the use of atomic weapons, if needed, for national defense.

The civil rights plank was nearly identical to the one that appeared in the 1948 platform. Federal legislation was called for to guarantee equal rights in voting participation, employment opportunity and personal security.

The platform called for extending and changing the social security system. A plank favored elimination of the work clause so that the elderly could collect benefits and still work.

Political reform was recommended that would require the disclosure of campaign expenses in federal elections.

The Democrats and Republicans took different stands on several major domestic issues. The Democrats favored repeal of the Taft-Hartley Act; the Republicans proposed to retain the act but make modifications where necessary. The Democrats advocated closing tax loopholes and, after defense needs were met, reducing taxes. The Republicans called for tax reduction based on a cut in government spending. In education, the Democrats favored federal assistance to state and local units; the Republicans viewed education solely as the responsibility of local and state governments.

The Democrats favored continuation of federal power projects, while the Republicans opposed "all-powerful federal socialistic valley authorities."

Both parties favored a parity price program for farmers. The Democrats advocated a mandatory price support program for basic agricultural products at not less than 90 percent of parity, and the Republicans proposing a program that would establish "full parity prices for all farm products."

Following are excerpts from the Democratic platform of 1952:

Atomic Energy. In the field of atomic energy, we pledge ourselves:

(1) to maintain vigorous and non-partisan civilian administrations, with adequate security safeguards:

(2) to promote the development of nuclear energy for peaceful purposes in the interests of America and mankind;

(3) to build all the atomic and hydrogen firepower needed to defend our country, deter aggression, and promote world peace;

(4) to exert every effort to bring about bona fide international control and inspection of all atomic weapons.

Civil Rights. We will continue our efforts to eradicate discrimination based on race, religion or national origin....

We are proud of the progress that has been made in securing equality of treatment and opportunity in the Nation's armed forces and the civil service and all areas under Federal jurisdiction....

At the same time, we favor Federal legislation effectively to secure these rights to everyone:

(1) the right to equal opportunity for employment;

(2) the right to security of persons;

(3) the right to full and equal participation in the Nation's political life, free from arbitrary restraints.

Agriculture. We will continue to protect the producers of basic agricultural commodities under the terms of a mandatory price support program at not less than ninety percent of parity. We continue to advocate practical methods for extending price supports to other storables and to the producers of perishable commodities, which account for three-fourths of all farm income.

Campaign Finance. We advocate new legislation to provide effective regulation and full disclosure of campaign expenditures in elections to Federal office, including political advertising from any source.

Labor. We strongly advocate the repeal of the Taft-Hartley Act.

Tax Reform. We believe in fair and equitable taxation. We oppose a Federal general sales tax. We adhere to the principle of ability to pay. We have enacted an emergency excess profits tax to prevent profiteering from the defense program and have vigorously attacked special tax privileges.... As rapidly as defense requirements permit, we favor reducing taxes, especially for people with lower incomes....

Justice requires the elimination of tax loopholes which favor special groups. We pledge continued efforts to the elimination of remaining loopholes.

Social Security. We favor the complete elimination of the work clause for the reason that those contributing to the Social Security program should be permitted to draw benefits, upon reaching the age of eligibility, and still continue to work.

Education. Local, State and Federal governments have shared responsibility to contribute appropriately to the pressing needs of our educational system. We urge that Federal contributions be made available to State and local units which adhere to basic minimum standards.

The Federal Government should not dictate nor control educational policy.

1956 Conventions

Presidential Candidates

Adlai E. Stevenson
Democrat

Dwight D. Eisenhower
Republican

Democrats

Both parties held their conventions in August, the latest date ever for the Republicans and the latest for the Democrats since the wartime convention of 1864. For the first time since 1888 the date of the Democratic convention preceded that of the Republicans. The Democrats met in mid-August in Chicago with an allotment of 1,372 votes, the largest in party history. The increased allotment was the result of a new distribution formula, which for the first time rewarded states for electing Democratic governors and senators in addition to supporting the party's presidential candidate.

A provision of the convention call handled the party loyalty question, a thorny issue at the 1952 convention, by assuming that, in the absence of a challenge, any delegate would be understood to have the best interests of the party at heart. Another provision of the call threatened any national committeeman who did not support the party's national ticket with removal from the Democratic National Committee.

In an unusual occurrence, nominating speeches were delivered by a past and a future president for men who would not attain the office themselves. Sen. John F. Kennedy of Massachusetts placed Adlai E. Stevenson's name in nomination, while former president Harry S Truman seconded the nomination of New York governor W. Averell Harriman. Truman criticized Stevenson as a "defeatist," but was countered by Eleanor Roosevelt, who appeared before the convention in support of the former Illinois governor.

In spite of the oratorical byplay, Stevenson was in good position to win the nomination before the convention even began, having eliminated his principal rival, Sen. Estes Kefauver of Tennessee, in the primaries. Stevenson won a majority on the first ballot, receiving 905-1/2 votes to easily defeat Harriman, who had 210. Sen. Lyndon B. Johnson of Texas finished third, with 80 votes. Upon completion of the roll call, a motion was approved to make Stevenson's nomination unanimous. *(Chart, p. 207)*

In an unusual move, Stevenson announced that he would not personally select his running mate but would leave the choice to the convention. Stevenson's desire for an open selection was designed to contrast with the expected cut-and-dried nature of the upcoming Republican convention. But the unusual move caught both delegates and prospective candidates off guard.

Numerous delegations passed on the first ballot, and upon completion of the roll call votes were scattered among 13 different candidates. When the vote totals were announced at the end of the roll call, Kefauver led with 483-1/2 votes, followed by Kennedy with 304, Sen. Albert A. Gore of Tennessee with 178, Mayor Robert F. Wagner of New York City with 162-1/2 and Sen. Hubert H. Humphrey of Minnesota with 134-1/2. Six hundred eighty-seven votes were needed to nominate.

With a coalition that included most of the Southern and Eastern delegates, Kennedy drew into the lead on the second ballot. After the roll call but before the chair recognized vote changes, the totals stood: Kennedy, 618; Kefauver, 551-1/2; Gore, 110-1/2. Kentucky, the first state to be recognized, shifted its 30 votes to Kennedy, leaving the 39-year-old senator fewer than 40 votes short of the nomination.

But Gore was recognized next and began a bandwagon for Kefauver by withdrawing in favor of his Tennessee colleague. Other states followed Gore's lead, and at the conclusion of the vote shifts Kefauver had a clear majority. The final tally was Kefauver, 755-1/2 and Kennedy, 589. Kennedy moved that his opponent's nomination be made unanimous.

Ironically, Kefauver won a majority of the votes in only two states in his home region, Tennessee and Florida. His strength lay in Midwestern and Western delegations.

As in 1948 platform debate focused on the civil rights issue. A Minnesota member of the platform committee introduced a minority report that advocated a civil rights plank stronger than that in the majority report. The plank presented by the platform committee pledged to carry out Supreme Court decisions on desegregation, but not through the use of force. The party promised to continue to work for equal rights in voting, employment, personal security and education. The Minnesota substitute was more spe-

cific, as it favored federal legislation to achieve equal voting rights and employment opportunities and to guarantee personal safety. The minority plank also favored more rigid enforcement of civil rights legislation. Although several states clamored for a roll-call vote, the chair took a voice vote, which went against the Minnesota substitute.

The entire platform was the longest yet approved by a Democratic convention, about 12,000 words. The document was divided into 11 sections, the first dealing with defense and foreign policy and the remainder with domestic issues.

The platform described President Eisenhower as a "political amateur . . . dominated . . . by special privilege." It applauded the legislative accomplishments of the Democratic Congress elected in 1954 and proposed a continuation of the social and economic legislation begun during the New Deal.

The foreign policy of the Eisenhower administration was criticized in a plank that accused the Republicans of cutting funds for the military in an attempt to balance the budget. The Democrats declared that the United States must have the strongest military in the world to discourage aggression by America's enemies. The foreign policy plank also pledged to strengthen the United Nations as a peacekeeping organization and promised to work diligently for worldwide disarmament.

The platform blamed the Republicans for allowing big business to dominate the economy and promised tax relief and other government assistance to help small business. The Democrats advocated repeal of the Taft-Hartley Act, as the party had done in every platform since 1948, and favored an increase in the minimum wage. Tax reductions were proposed for lower-income taxpayers, and an increase of at least $200 in the personal tax exemption was recommended.

For farmers, the Democrats proposed price supports at 90 percent of parity on basic crops, as opposed to the Republican program of flexible price supports.

For the first time since the beginning of the New Deal, the Democratic platform mentioned the importance of states' rights. The party also reiterated its position on education, which advocated federal assistance, but stated that ultimate control of the schools lay in the hands of state and local governments.

In political reform the platform proposed restrictions on government secrecy and repeated the party's call for the passage of an equal rights amendment.

Following are excerpts from the Democratic platform of 1956:

Foreign Policy. *The Failure at Home.* Political considerations of budget balancing and tax reduction now come before the wants of our national security and the needs of our Allies. The Republicans have slashed our own armed strength, weakened our capacity to deal with military threats, stifled our air force, starved our army and weakened our capacity to deal with aggression of any sort save by retreat or by the alternatives, "massive retaliation" and global atomic war. Yet, while our troubles mount, they tell us our prestige was never higher, they tell us we were never more secure.

Disarmament. To eliminate the danger of atomic war, a universal, effective and enforced disarmament system must be the goal of responsible men and women everywhere. So long as we lack enforceable international control of weapons, we must maintain armed strength to avoid war. But technological advances in the field of nuclear weapons make disarmament an ever more urgent problem. Time and distance can never again protect any nation of the world.

Labor. We unequivocally advocate repeal of the Taft-Hartley Act. The Act must be repealed because State "right-to-work" laws have their genesis in its discriminatory anti-labor provisions. . . .

The Taft-Hartley Act has been proven to be inadequate, unworkable and unfair. It interferes in an arbitrary manner with collective bargaining, causing imbalance in the relationship between management and labor.

Agriculture. Undertake immediately by appropriate action to endeavor to regain the full 100 percent of parity the farmers received under the Democratic Administrations. We will achieve this by means of supports on basic commodities at 90 percent of parity and by means of commodity loans, direct purchases, direct payments to producers, marketing agreements and orders, production adjustments, or a combination of these, including legislation, to bring order and stability into the relationship between the producer, the processor and the consumer.

Education. We are now faced with shortages of educational facilities that threaten national security, economic prosperity and human well-being. The resources of our States and localities are already strained to the limit. Federal aid and action should be provided, within the traditional framework of State and local control.

Tax Reform. We favor realistic tax adjustments, giving first consideration to small independent business and the small individual taxpayer. Lower-income families need tax relief; only a Democratic victory will assure this. We favor an increase in the present personal tax exemption of $600 to a minimum of at least $800.

Government Secrecy. *Freedom of Information.* During recent years there has developed a practice on the part of Federal agencies to delay and withhold information which is needed by Congress and the general public to make important decisions affecting their lives and destinies. We believe that this trend toward secrecy in Government should be reversed and that the Federal Government should return to its basic tradition of exchanging and promoting the freest flow of information possible in those unclassified areas where secrets involving weapons development and bona fide national security are not involved.

States' Rights. While we recognize the existence of honest differences of opinion as to the true location of a Constitutional line of demarcation between the Federal Government and the States, the Democratic Party expressly recognizes the vital importance of the respective States in our Federal Union. The Party of Jefferson and Jackson pledges itself to continued support of those sound principles of local government which will best serve the welfare of our people and the safety of our democratic rights.

Civil Rights. We are proud of the record of the Democratic Party in securing equality of treatment and opportunity in the nation's armed forces, the Civil Service, and in all areas under Federal jurisdiction. The Democratic Party pledges itself to continue its efforts to eliminate illegal discriminations of all kinds, in relation to (1) full rights to vote, (2) full rights to engage in gainful occupations, (3) full rights to enjoy security of the person, and (4) full rights to education in all publicly supported institutions.

Recent decisions of the Supreme Court of the United States relating to segregation in publicly supported schools and elsewhere have brought consequences of vast importance to our Nation as a whole and especially to communities directly affected. We reject all proposals for the use of force to interfere with the orderly determination of these matters by the courts.

Republicans

The Republicans opened their convention in San Francisco three days after the close of the Democratic

convention in Chicago. In contrast to the turbulent convention of their adversaries, the Republicans' renomination of Dwight D. Eisenhower and Richard M. Nixon was a formality. The only possible obstacle to Eisenhower's candidacy was his health, but by August 1956 his recovery from a heart attack and an ileitis operation was complete enough to allow him to seek a second term. On the convention's single roll call for president, Eisenhower received all 1,323 votes.

What drama occurred at the Republican convention surrounded the vice presidential nomination. Several weeks before the opening of the convention, former Minnesota governor Harold Stassen, the disarmament adviser to Eisenhower, had begun a movement to replace Vice President Nixon with Massachusetts governor Christian A. Herter. However, with lack of interest from party leaders, this movement petered out. At the convention both Herter and Stassen gave nominating speeches for Nixon. During the roll call, a commotion was caused by a Nebraska delegate, who attempted to nominate "Joe Smith." After some discussion, it was determined that "Joe Smith" was a fictitious individual, and the offending delegate was escorted from the hall. On the one ballot for vice president, a unanimous vote was recorded for Nixon.

While no opposition to the platform was expressed on the floor of the convention, several Southern delegates were unhappy with the civil rights plank and withdrew from the convention. The plank in question listed advances in desegregation under the Republican administration, voiced acceptance of the Supreme Court ruling on school desegregation and pledged to enforce existing civil rights statutes.

The platform as a whole was slightly longer than the Democratic document and was dedicated to Eisenhower and "the youth of America." Unlike the Democratic platform, which began with a discussion of foreign policy and national defense, the first issue pursued by the Republicans was the economy.

The Eisenhower administration was praised for balancing the budget, reducing taxes and halting inflation. The platform promised continued balanced budgets, gradual reduction of the national debt and cuts in government spending consistent with the maintenance of a strong military. Two measures favored by the Democrats, tax relief for small businesses and tax reductions for low-income and middle-income families, were both mentioned as secondary economic goals in the Republican platform.

The labor plank advocated revision but not repeal of the Taft-Hartley Act. The agricultural section favored elimination of price-depressing surpluses and continuation of the flexible price-support program. As they had for the past quarter century, the Republicans joined the Democrats in recommending passage of an equal rights amendment.

The foreign policy section of the Republican platform praised the Eisenhower administration for ending the Korean War, stemming the worldwide advance of communism and entering new collective security agreements. The plank also emphasized the necessity of a bipartisan foreign policy. The "preservation" of Israel was viewed as an "important tenet of American foreign policy," a notable difference from the Democratic platform, which took a more even-handed approach toward both Israel and the Arab states.

The national defense section emphasized the United States' possession of "the strongest striking force in the world," a rebuttal to Democratic charges that the Republicans had jeopardized the efficiency of the armed forces in an effort to balance the budget.

Following are excerpts from the Republican platform of 1956:

Economy. We pledge to pursue the following objectives:

Further reductions in Government spending as recommended in the Hoover Commission Report, without weakening the support of a superior defense program or depreciating the quality of essential services of government to our people.

Continued balancing of the budget, to assure the financial strength of the country which is so vital to the struggle of the free world in its battle against Communism; and to maintain the purchasing power of a sound dollar, and the value of savings, pensions and insurance.

Gradual reduction of the national debt.

Then, insofar as consistent with a balanced budget, we pledge to work toward these additional objectives:

Further reductions in taxes with particular consideration for low and middle income families.

Initiation of a sound policy of tax reductions which will encourage small independent businesses to modernize and progress.

Labor. Revise and improve the Taft-Hartley Act so as to protect more effectively the rights of labor unions, management, the individual worker, and the public. The protection of the right of workers to organize into unions and to bargain collectively is the firm and permanent policy of the Eisenhower Administration.

Agriculture. This program must be versatile and flexible to meet effectively the impact of rapidly changing conditions. It does not envision making farmers dependent upon direct governmental payments for their incomes. Our objective is markets which return full parity to our farm and ranch people when they sell their products.

Civil Rights. The Republican Party accepts the decision of the U.S. Supreme Court that racial discrimination in publicly supported schools must be progressively eliminated. We concur in the conclusion of the Supreme Court that its decision directing school desegregation should be accomplished with "all deliberate speed" locally through Federal District Courts. The implementation order of the Supreme Court recognizes the complex and acutely emotional problems created by its decision in certain sections of our country where racial patterns have been developed in accordance with prior and longstanding decisions of the same tribunal.

We believe that true progress can be attained through intelligent study, understanding, education and good will. Use of force or violence by any group or agency will tend only to worsen the many problems inherent in the situation. This progress must be encouraged and the work of the courts supported in every legal manner by all branches of the Federal Government to the end that the constitutional ideal of equality before the law, regardless of race, creed or color, will be steadily achieved.

Foreign Policy. The advance of Communism has been checked, and, at key points, thrown back. The once-monolithic structure of International Communism, denied the stimulant of successive conquests, has shown hesitancy both internally and abroad.

National Defense. We *have* the strongest striking force in the world — in the air — on the sea — and a magnificent supporting land force in our Army and Marine Corps.

Israel. We regard the preservation of Israel as an important tenet of American foreign policy. We are determined that the integrity of an independent Jewish State shall be maintained. We shall support the independence of

Israel against armed aggression. The best hope for peace in the Middle East lies in the United Nations. We pledge our

continued efforts to eliminate the obstacles to a lasting peace in this area.

1960 Conventions

Presidential Candidates

John F. Kennedy
Democrat

Richard M. Nixon
Republican

Democrats

For the first time, a national political convention was held in Los Angeles. More than 4,000 delegates and alternates converged on the California metropolis in July to select the Democratic standard-bearers for 1960. The delegate allocation method had been changed since 1956 by the Democratic National Committee, from a formula that included Democratic voting strength to a system that emphasized population only. No states lost seats, but the new formula tended to strengthen populous Northern states.

The early sessions of the convention dealt with rules and credentials. The convention rules, approved without debate, included the compromise loyalty pledge adopted by the 1956 convention. The only credentials dispute involved two contesting delegations from the Commonwealth of Puerto Rico. By a voice vote, the convention agreed to seat both delegations while splitting the vote of the Commonwealth.

The front-runner for the presidential nomination was Massachusetts senator John F. Kennedy, whose success in the primaries and support from many of the party's urban leaders put him on the verge of a nominating majority. His principal rival was Senate Majority Leader Lyndon B. Johnson of Texas, although the favorite of the convention galleries was Adlai E. Stevenson, the party's unsuccessful standard-bearer in 1952 and 1956. Johnson challenged Kennedy to a debate, which was held before a joint gathering of the Massachusetts and Texas delegations. Coming the day before the balloting, the debate had little effect on the ultimate outcome.

Nine men were nominated, but Kennedy received a clear majority on the first ballot. At the end of the roll call, the Massachusetts senator had 806 votes, to easily outdistance Johnson, who received 409. Sen. Stuart Symington of Missouri was a distant third with 86 votes, and Stevenson followed with 79-1/2. A motion to make Kennedy's nomination unanimous was approved by a voice vote. Kennedy's selection marked the first time since 1920 that a senator

had been nominated for the presidency by Democrats or Republicans and the first time since 1928 that a Roman Catholic had been represented on a national ticket of one of the two major parties. *(Chart, p. 208)*

Kennedy surprised some supporters and political observers by choosing his erstwhile adversary, Lyndon Johnson, as his running mate. A motion to nominate Johnson by acclamation was approved by a voice vote.

Kennedy delivered his acceptance speech to 80,000 spectators at the Los Angeles Coliseum. He envisioned the United States as "on the edge of a new frontier — the frontier of the 1960s — a frontier of unknown opportunities and perils — a frontier of unfulfilled hopes and threats," adding that this "new frontier . . . is not a set of promises — it is a set of challenges."

The Democratic platform was easily the longest yet written by the party, about 20,000 words. The platform itself was approved by a voice vote, although the civil rights and fiscal responsibility planks were debated on the convention floor, and roll-call votes had been taken in committee.

Regional hearings had been held by subcommittees of the 108-member platform committee in the spring, but votes on controversial issues were not taken by the full committee until the convention. A plank that urged elimination of the immigration quota system was approved, 66 to 28, with opposition led by Sen. James O. Eastland of Mississippi. An agricultural plank recommending price supports at 90 percent of parity was passed, 66 to 22, with opponents claiming that it was a restatement of the liberal program proposed by the National Farmers Union. A motion to reconsider the plank was defeated, 38 to 32. An Eastland motion to delete condemnation of "right-to-work" laws was defeated without a recorded vote.

The civil rights plank caused the greatest controversy. Sen. Sam J. Ervin Jr. of North Carolina introduced motions to delete portions that proposed establishing a Fair Employment Practices Commission, continuing the Civil

Rights Commission as a permanent agency, granting the attorney general the power to file civil injunction suits to prevent desegregation, and setting 1963 as the deadline for the initiation of school desegregation plans. Ervin's motions were defeated by a voice vote, and the entire plank was approved, 66 to 24.

Delegates from nine Southern states signed a statement that repudiated the civil rights plank. Led by Georgia Democratic Chairman James H. Gray and Ervin, these nine states introduced a minority report on the convention floor calling for elimination of the platform's civil rights plank. After an hour's debate, the minority report was rejected by a voice vote.

A minority amendment introduced by the Virginia delegation, proposing that the fiscal responsibility plank include a planned schedule for reduction of the national debt, also was rejected by a voice vote.

As approved by the convention, the platform began with a discussion of foreign policy. The Democrats blamed the Republican administration for allowing the United States military strength to deteriorate. The national defense plank declared there was a "missile gap, space gap, and limited-war gap," and promised to improve America's military position so that it would be second to none. The Democrats recommended creation of "a national peace agency for disarmament planning and research." The money saved by international disarmament, the plank stated, could be used to attack world poverty.

Foreign military aid was viewed as a short-range necessity that should be replaced by economic aid "as rapidly as security considerations permit." At the same time, the platform proposed that development programs be placed on a "long-term basis to permit more effective planning."

The Democrats' economic plank called for an average national growth rate of 5 percent annually. Economic growth at this rate would create needed tax revenue, the Democrats believed, which — coupled with cuts in government waste, closing of tax loopholes and more extensive efforts to catch tax evaders — would help balance the budget. The Democrats promised to use measures such as public works projects and temporary tax cuts to combat recessions or depressions.

The platform promised an increase in the minimum wage to $1.25 an hour and pledged to extend coverage to include more workers. There was a pledge to amend the Social Security program so the elderly could continue working without sacrificing basic benefits.

Equal rights legislation was favored, although the platform did not call for passage of a constitutional amendment of 1960.

Following are excerpts from the Democratic platform of 1960:

National Defense. Our military position today is measured in terms of gaps — missile gap, space gap, limited-war gap....

This is the strength that must be erected:

1. Deterrent military power such that the Soviet and Chinese leaders will have no doubt that an attack on the United States would surely be followed by their own destruction.

2. Balanced conventional military forces which will permit a response graded to the intensity of any threats of aggressive force.

3. Continuous modernization of these forces through intensified research and development, including essential programs now slowed down, terminated, suspended or neglected for lack of budgetary support.

Disarmament. This requires a national peace agency for disarmament planning and research to muster the scientific ingenuity, coordination, continuity, and seriousness of purpose which are now lacking in our arms control efforts....

As world-wide disarmament proceeds, it will free vast resources for a new international attack on the problem of world poverty.

Immigration. The national-origins quota system of limiting immigration contradicts the founding principles of this nation. It is inconsistent with our belief in the rights of man. This system was instituted after World War I as a policy of deliberate discrimination by a Republican Administration and Congress....

Foreign Aid. Where military assistance remains essential for the common defense, we shall see that the requirements are fully met. But as rapidly as security considerations permit, we will replace tanks with tractors, bombers with bulldozers, and tacticians with technicians.

Civil Rights. We believe that every school district affected by the Supreme Court's school desegregation decision should submit a plan providing for at least first-step compliance by 1963, the 100th anniversary of the Emancipation Proclamation....

For this and for the protection of all other Constitutional rights of Americans, the Attorney General should be empowered and directed to file civil injunction suits in Federal courts to prevent the denial of any civil right on grounds of race, creed or color.

Economy. We Democrats believe that our economy can and must grow at an average rate of 5 percent annually, almost twice as fast as our average annual rate since 1953. We pledge ourselves to policies that will achieve this goal without inflation....

The policies of a Democratic Administration to restore economic growth will reduce current unemployment to a minimum.

Tax Reform. We shall close the loopholes in the tax laws by which certain privileged groups legally escape their fair share of taxation.

Among the more conspicuous loopholes are depletion allowances which are inequitable, special consideration for recipients of dividend income, and deductions for extravagant "business expenses" which have reached scandalous proportions.

Labor. We pledge to raise the minimum wage to $1.25 an hour and to extend coverage to several million workers not now protected.

Agriculture. The Democratic Administration will work to bring about full parity income for farmers in all segments of agriculture by helping them to balance farm production with the expanding needs of the nation and the world.

Measures to this end include production and marketing quotas measured in terms of barrels, bushels and bales, loans on basic commodities at not less than 90 percent of parity, production payments, commodity purchases, and marketing orders and agreements.

Government Spending. The Democratic Party believes that state and local governments are strengthened — not weakened — by financial assistance from the Federal Government. We will extend such aid without impairing local administration through unnecessary Federal interference or red tape.

Republicans

On July 25, 10 days after the close of the Democratic convention, the Republican convention opened in Chicago.

Although Vice President Richard M. Nixon had a lock on the presidential nomination, the party's two major figures four years later, Arizona senator Barry Goldwater and New York governor Nelson A. Rockefeller, both had major roles in convention activities.

Both Goldwater and Rockefeller announced that they did not want their names placed in nomination, but the Arizona delegation disregarded Goldwater's request and nominated him anyway. In a convention speech, the Arizona senator withdrew his name and went on to advise conservative Republicans to work within the party: "Let's grow up conservatives.... If we want to take this party back — and I think we can someday — let's get to work."

On the roll call that followed, Nixon was a nearly unanimous choice, receiving 1,321 votes to 10 for Goldwater (all from Louisiana). On a voice vote, Nixon's nomination was made unanimous.

Nixon reportedly wanted Rockefeller as his running mate, but was unable to persuade the New Yorker to join the ticket. The Republican standard-bearer subsequently turned to United Nations Ambassador Henry Cabot Lodge Jr., a former senator from Massachusetts who had been beaten for re-election by John Kennedy in 1952. On the vice presidential ballot, Lodge received all but one vote. The lone dissenter, a Texas delegate, initially abstained but switched his vote to Lodge at the end of the roll call.

In his acceptance speech, Nixon promised to campaign in all 50 states and rebutted a theme in Kennedy's acceptance speech. "Our primary aim must be not to help government, but to help people — to help people attain the life they deserve," said Nixon.

Much of the drama of the 1960 Republican convention surrounded the party platform. And the highlight of the platform maneuvering was a late-night meeting involving Nixon and Rockefeller, held at Rockefeller's New York City apartment two days before the opening of the convention. The meeting, a secret to most of Nixon's closest aides, resulted in a 14-point agreement between the two Republican leaders on major issues contained in the platform. The agreement, informally dubbed the "compact of Fifth Avenue," was issued by Rockefeller, who declared that the meeting was held at Nixon's insistence.

Half of the 14 points dealt with national security and foreign policy. The other half discussed domestic issues, including government reorganization, civil rights, agriculture, economic growth and medical care for the elderly. Although not markedly different in wording from the draft of the platform committee, the "compact" expressed a tone of urgency that was not evident in the draft.

The Nixon-Rockefeller agreement was made with the knowledge of the platform committee chairman, Charles H. Percy of Illinois, but was greeted with hostility by many members of the committee and by party conservatives. Goldwater termed the "compact" a "surrender" and the "Munich of the Republican Party" that would ensure the party's defeat that fall.

The two issues of greatest controversy were civil rights and national defense. The original civil rights plank, drafted by the platform committee, did not express support for civil rights demonstrations or promise federal efforts to gain job equality for blacks. The Nixon-Rockefeller agreement did both. Nixon threatened to wage a floor fight if the stronger civil rights plank was not inserted in the platform. By a vote of 50 to 35, the platform committee agreed to reconsider the original civil rights plank; by a margin of 56 to 28, the stronger plank was approved.

With the approval of both Rockefeller and President Dwight D. Eisenhower, several changes were made in the national security plank that emphasized the necessity of quickly upgrading America's armed forces. The platform committee approved reconsideration of the original defense plank by a voice vote, and the whole platform was adopted unanimously.

With disagreements resolved in the committee, there were neither minority reports nor floor fights. The convention approved the platform by a voice vote.

In its final form, the Republican platform was shorter than its Democratic counterpart, although still nearly 15,000 words in length. The foreign policy section asserted that the nation's greatest task was "to nullify the Soviet conspiracy." The platform claimed that America's military strength was second to none but, in line with the Nixon-Rockefeller "compact," indicated that improvements were needed in some parts of the armed forces.

The Republicans joined their Democratic opposition in favoring a workable disarmament program but did not advocate a phaseout of foreign military aid, as did the Democrats. However, the Republicans proposed a change in the funding of foreign aid that emphasized "the increasing use of private capital and government loans, rather than outright grants."

The Republicans agreed with the Democrats that the nation should experience more rapid economic growth but did not adopt the 5 percent annual growth rate favored by the Democrats. The Republicans stressed the virtues of a balanced budget and regarded free enterprise, rather than massive government programs, as the key to economic growth.

As in 1956, the two parties differed on farm price supports. The Republicans supported a program of flexible support payments, while the Democrats recommended setting price supports at 90 percent of parity.

Both parties proposed allowing individuals to work beyond their mandatory retirement age, although the Democrats tied their proposal to amendment of the Social Security program.

The Republicans did not urge elimination of the immigration quota system, as did their opponents, but they favored overhaul of the system to allow an increase in immigration.

On the issue of equal rights, the Republicans continued to favor passage of a constitutional amendment. The Democrats had backed away from this position, which they had held in earlier platforms, instead proposing the passage of equal rights legislation in Congress.

As they had since the beginning of the New Deal, the Republican and Democratic platforms differed noticeably as to the extent and desirability of federal spending. The Democrats viewed federal assistance to state and local governments as beneficial. The Republicans believed the federal government could help meet the problems of urban growth, but that state and local governments should administer all the programs they could best handle.

Following are excerpts from the Republican platform of 1960:

National Defense. The future of freedom depends heavily upon America's military might and that of her allies. Under the Eisenhower-Nixon Administration, our military might has been forged into a power second to none....

The strategic imperatives of our national defense policy are these:

A second-strike capability, that is, a nuclear retaliatory power that can survive surprise attack, strike back, and destroy any possible enemy.

Highly mobile and versatile forces, including forces deployed, to deter or check local aggressions and "brush fire wars" which might bring on all-out nuclear war.

National determination to employ all necessary military capabilities so as to render any level of aggression unprofitable. Deterrence of war since Korea, specifically, has been the result of our firm statement that we will never again permit a potential aggressor to set the ground rules for his aggression; that we will respond to aggression with the full means and weapons best suited to the situation....

Disarmament. We are similarly ready to negotiate and to institute realistic methods and safeguards for disarmament, and for the suspension of nuclear tests. We advocate an early agreement by all nations to forego nuclear tests in the atmosphere, and the suspension of other tests as verification techniques permit.

Immigration. The annual number of immigrants we accept be at least doubled.

Obsolete immigration laws be amended by abandoning the outdated 1920 census data as a base and substituting the 1960 census.

The guidelines of our immigration policy be based upon judgment of the individual merit of each applicant for admission and citizenship.

Foreign Aid. Agreeable to the developing nations, we would join with them in inviting countries with advanced economies to share with us a proportionate part of the capital and technical aid required. We would emphasize the increasing use of private capital and government loans, rather than outright grants, as a means of fostering independence and mutual respect.

Civil Rights. *Voting.* We pledge:

Continued vigorous enforcement of the civil rights laws to guarantee the right to vote to all citizens in all areas of the country....

Public Schools. We pledge:

The Department of Justice will continue its vigorous support of court orders for school desegregation....

We oppose the pretense of fixing a target date 3 years from now for the mere submission of plans for school desegregation. Slow-moving school districts would construe it as a three-year moratorium during which progress would cease, postponing until 1963 the legal process to enforce compliance. We believe that each of the pending court actions should proceed as the Supreme Court has directed and that in no district should there be any such delay.

Employment. We pledge:

Continued support for legislation to establish a Commission on Equal Job Opportunity to make permanent and to expand with legislative backing the excellent work being performed by the President's Committee on Government Contracts....

Housing. We pledge:

Action to prohibit discrimination in housing constructed with the aid of federal subsidies.

Public Facilities and Services. We pledge:

Removal of any vestige of discrimination in the operation of federal facilities or procedures which may at any time be found....

Economy. We reject the concept of artificial growth forced by massive new federal spending and loose money policies. The only effective way to accelerate economic growth is to increase the traditional strengths of our free economy — initiative and investment, productivity and efficiency....

Agriculture. Use of price supports at levels best fitted to specific commodities, in order to widen markets, ease production controls, and help achieve increased farm family income.

Government Reorganization. The President must continue to be able to reorganize and streamline executive operations to keep the executive branch capable of responding effectively to rapidly changing conditions in both foreign and domestic fields....

Two top positions should be established to assist the President in, (1) the entire field of National Security and International Affairs, and (2) Governmental Planning and Management, particularly in domestic affairs.

Government Spending. Vigorous state and local governments are a vital part of our federal union. The federal government should leave to state and local governments those programs and problems which they can best handle and tax sources adequate to finance them. We must continue to improve liaison between federal, state and local governments. We believe that the federal government, when appropriate, should render significant assistance in dealing with our urgent problems of urban growth and change. No vast new bureaucracy is needed to achieve this objective.

1964 Conventions

Presidential Candidates

Barry Goldwater
Republican

Lyndon B. Johnson
Democrat

Republicans

Division between the party's conservative and moderate wings, muted during the Eisenhower administration, exploded at the Republicans' July 13-16 convention in San Francisco.

Although Sen. Barry Goldwater of Arizona, the hero of Republican conservatives, had a commanding lead as the convention opened, he was vigorously challenged by Pennsylvania governor William W. Scranton, the belated leader of the moderate forces. Two days before the presidential balloting, a letter in Scranton's name was sent to Goldwater. It charged the Goldwater organization with regarding the delegates as "little more than a flock of chickens whose necks will be wrung at will." The message continued, describing Goldwater's political philosophy as a "crazy-quilt collection of absurd and dangerous positions." The letter concluded by challenging the Arizona senator to a debate before the convention. Although the message was written by Scranton's staff without his knowledge, the Pennsylvania governor supported the substance of the letter. Goldwater declined the invitation to debate.

Although seven names were placed in nomination for the presidency, the outcome was a foregone conclusion. Goldwater was an easy winner on the first ballot, receiving 883 of the 1,308 votes. Scranton was a distant second with 214 votes; New York governor Nelson A. Rockefeller followed with 114. Scranton moved that Goldwater's nomination be made unanimous, and his motion was approved by a voice vote. Support for the major moderate candidates, Scranton and Rockefeller, was centered in the Northeast. Goldwater had an overwhelming majority of the delegates from other regions. *(Chart, p. 209)*

As his running mate, Goldwater selected the Republican national chairman, Rep. William E. Miller of New York. On disclosing his choice of Miller, Goldwater stated that "one of the reasons I chose Miller is that he drives Johnson nuts." On the vice presidential roll call, the conservative New York representative received 1,305 votes, with three delegates from Tennessee abstaining. A Roman Catholic, Miller became the first member of that faith ever to run on a Republican national ticket.

Goldwater's acceptance speech was uncompromising and did not attempt to dilute his conservatism in an effort to gain votes: "Anyone who joins us in all sincerity we welcome. Those who do not care for our cause, we don't expect to enter our ranks in any case. And let our Republicanism so focused and so dedicated not be made fuzzy and futile by unthinking and stupid labels. I would remind you that extremism in the defense of liberty is no vice. And let me remind you also that moderation in the pursuit of justice is no virtue."

By a voice vote, the convention adopted the party platform, but not before the moderate forces waged floor fights on three issues — extremism, civil rights and control of nuclear weapons. Within the platform committee, 70 to 80 different amendments were presented, but when the platform reached the floor the moderates concentrated on these three specific issues.

Extremism was the first issue considered, with Sen. Hugh Scott of Pennsylvania introducing an amendment that specifically denounced efforts of the John Birch Society, the Ku Klux Klan and the Communist Party to infiltrate the Republican Party. Rockefeller spoke on behalf of the amendment but was booed throughout his speech. Rockefeller argued that a "radical, high-financed, disciplined minority" was trying to take over the Republican Party, a minority "wholly alien to the middle course . . . the mainstream." The amendment was rejected on a standing vote, by a margin estimated at two to one.

A second amendment on extremism, proposed by Michigan governor George W. Romney, condemned extremist groups but not by name. The Romney amendment was similarly rejected on a standing vote by about the same margin. Scott introduced a civil rights amendment adding additional pledges to the existing plank, including more manpower for the Justice Department's Civil Rights Division; a statement of pride in Republican support of the 1964 Civil Rights Act; requirements for first-step compliance with school desegregation by all school districts in one year; voting guarantees to state as well as federal elections, and promises to eliminate job bias. The platform's brief plank on civil rights called for "full implementation and

faithful execution" of the 1964 act, but it also stated that "the elimination of any such discrimination is a matter of heart, conscience and education as well as of equal rights under law." On a roll-call vote, the Scott amendment was defeated, 897 to 409. The pattern of the vote closely followed the presidential ballot, with support for the amendment centered in the Northeast. *(Chart, p. 209)*

Romney offered a brief, alternative civil rights plank that pledged action at the state, local and private levels to eliminate discrimination in all fields. It was defeated by a voice vote.

Scott proposed another amendment, declaring the president to have sole authority to control the use of nuclear weapons. This contrasted with Goldwater's position advocating that North Atlantic Treaty Organization (NATO) commanders be given greater authority in the use of tactical nuclear weapons. The Scott amendment was rejected on a standing vote.

In its final form, the Republican platform was barely half as long as its Democratic counterpart. The Republican platform was divided into four sections, the first two enumerating Democratic failures in foreign policy and domestic affairs. The last two sections detailed Republican proposals.

The Republicans were suspicious of any détente with the communist world, instead calling for "a dynamic strategy of victory . . . for freedom." The platform contended that American military strength was deteriorating and promised the establishment of a military force superior to that of the nation's enemies. The Republicans expressed distrust of the 1963 nuclear test ban treaty and vowed to "never unilaterally disarm America." The platform promised to revitalize NATO, which was viewed as a keystone of Republican foreign policy.

Concerning specific trouble spots around the world, the platform demanded removal of the Berlin Wall, pledged to "move decisively to assure victory in South Vietnam" and promised to recognize a Cuban government in exile as well as to supply assistance to Cuban guerrilla freedom fighters.

Coupled with the anti-communism of the foreign policy sections was the central theme of the domestic sections — the need to trim the power of the federal government and to relocate it in state and local governments. This conservative philosophy was evident in various domestic planks.

The Republicans promised a reduction of at least $5 billion in federal spending and pledged to end budget deficits. A proposal was made to cut federal income taxes and to transfer the excise tax and several other federal tax sources from the federal government to state and local governments. The Republicans also recommended that state and local tax payments be credited against federal income taxes.

The platform favored a reduction of federal involvement in school financing and advocated passage of a constitutional amendment to allow prayer in public schools. A plank was included that urged passage of legislation to curb the flow of obscene materials through the mails.

The "one person, one vote" ruling of the Supreme Court brought the recommendation by the Republicans that a constitutional amendment be passed to allow states with bicameral legislatures to use a measurement other than population.

Following are excerpts from the Republican platform of 1964:

Peace. This Administration has sought accommodations with Communism without adequate safeguards and compensating gains for freedom. It has alienated proven allies by opening a "hot line" first with a sworn enemy rather than with a proven friend, and in general pursued a risky path such as began at Munich a quarter century ago. . . .

The supreme challenge to this policy is an atheistic imperialism — Communism.

Our nation's leadership must be judged by — indeed, American independence and even survival are dependent upon — the stand it takes toward Communism.

That stand must be: victory for freedom. There can be no peace, there can be no security, until this goal is won.

National Defense. This Administration has adopted policies which will lead to a potentially fatal parity of power with Communism instead of continued military superiority for the United States.

It has permitted disarmament negotiations to proceed without adequate consideration of military judgment — a procedure which tends to bring about, in effect, a unilateral curtailment of American arms rendered the more dangerous by the Administration's discounting known Soviet advances in nuclear weaponry.

It has failed to take minimum safeguards against possible consequences of the limited nuclear test ban treaty, including advanced underground tests where permissible and full readiness to test elsewhere should the need arise. . . .

. . . we will regularly review the status of nuclear weaponry under the limited nuclear test ban to assure this nation's protection. We shall also provide sensible, continuing reviews of the treaty itself. . . .

We will maintain a superior, not merely equal, military capability as long as the Communist drive for world domination continues. It will be a capability of balanced force, superior in all its arms, maintaining flexibility for effective performance in the rapidly changing science of war.

Republicans will never unilaterally disarm America.

Berlin. We will demand that the Berlin Wall be taken down prior to the resumption of any negotiations with the Soviet Union on the status of forces in, or treaties affecting, Germany.

Cuba. We Republicans will recognize a Cuban government in exile; we will support its efforts to regain the independence of its homeland; we will assist Cuban freedom fighters in carrying on guerrilla warfare against the Communist regime; we will work for an economic boycott by all nations of the free world in trade with Cuba; and we will encourage free elections in Cuba after liberty and stability are restored.

Vietnam. We will move decisively to assure victory in South Vietnam. While confining the conflict as closely as possible, America must move to end the fighting in a reasonable time and provide guarantees against further aggression. We must make it clear to the Communist world that, when conflict is forced with America, it will end only in victory for freedom.

United Nations. This Administration has failed to provide forceful, effective leadership in the United Nations.

It has weakened the power and influence of this world organization by failing to demand basic improvements in its procedures and to guard against its becoming merely a form of anti-Western insult and abuse.

Federal Power. Humanity is tormented once again by an age-old issue — is man to live in dignity and freedom under God to be enslaved — are men in government to serve, or are they to master, their fellow men? . . .

1. Every person has the right to govern himself, to fix his own goals, and to make his own way with a minimum of governmental interference.

2. It is for government to foster and maintain an

environment of freedom encouraging every individual to develop to the fullest his God-given powers of mind, heart and body; and, beyond this, government should undertake only needful things, rightly of public concern, which the citizen cannot himself accomplish.

We Republicans hold that these two principles must regain their primacy in our government's relations, not only with the American people, but also with nations and peoples everywhere in the world.

Economy. In furtherance of our faith in the individual, we also pledge prudent, responsible management of the government's fiscal affairs to protect the individual against the evils of spendthrift government — protecting most of all the needy and fixed-income families against the cruelest tax, inflation — and protecting every citizen against the high taxes forced by excessive spending, in order that each individual may keep more of his earning for his own and his family's use.

Tax Reform. In furtherance of our faith in limited, frugal and efficient government we also pledge: credit against Federal taxes for specified State and local taxes paid, and a transfer to the States of excise and other Federal tax sources, to reinforce the fiscal strength of State and local governments so that they may better meet rising school costs and other pressing urban and suburban problems such as transportation, housing water systems and juvenile delinquency....

Civil Rights. Full implementation and faithful execution of the Civil Rights Act of 1964, and all other civil rights statutes, to assure equal rights and opportunities guaranteed by the Constitution to every citizen; ... continued opposition to discrimination based on race, creed, national origin or sex. We recognize that the elimination of any such discrimination is a matter of heart, conscience, and education, as well as of equal rights under law.

Education. To continue the advancement of education on all levels, through such programs as selective aid to higher education, strengthened State and local tax resources, including tax credits for college education, while resisting the Democratic efforts which endanger local control of schools; to help assure equal opportunity and a good education for all, while opposing Federally-sponsored "inverse discrimination," whether by the shifting of jobs, or the abandonment of neighborhood schools, for reasons of race;....

School Prayer. Support of a Constitutional amendment permitting those individuals and groups who choose to do so to exercise their religion freely in public places, provided religious exercises are not prepared or prescribed by the state or political subdivision thereof and no person's participation therein is coerced, thus preserving the traditional separation of church and state;....

Obscenity. Enactment of legislation, despite Democratic opposition, to curb the flow through the mails of obscene materials which has flourished into a multimillion dollar obscenity racket;....

Medical Care for Elderly. Full coverage of all medical and hospital costs for the needy elderly people, financed by general revenues through broader implementation of Federal-State plans, rather than the compulsory Democratic scheme covering only a small percentage of such costs, for everyone regardless of need;....

Reapportionment. Support of a Constitutional amendment, as well as legislation, enabling States having bicameral legislatures to apportion one House on bases of their choosing, including factors other than population;....

Democrats

In late August in Atlantic City, N.J., the Democratic convention nominated President Lyndon B. Johnson for a full term in the White House. The proceedings were stage-managed by the president and were met with little visible dissent on the convention floor. The four-day event Aug. 24-27 was a political triumph for the veteran politician from Texas, who less than a year earlier had been the assassinated John F. Kennedy's vice president.

The Democratic convention was larger than any previous convention of an American political party, with 5,260 delegates and alternates. A new vote-allocation formula was in effect that combined consideration of a state's electoral vote with its support for the Kennedy-Johnson ticket in 1960. While no states lost votes from four years earlier, many of the larger states gained significantly. As a result, there were 2,316 votes at the 1964 convention, compared with 1,521 in 1960.

With no controversy surrounding either the party nominee or platform, attention focused on the credentials challenge brought by the integrated Mississippi Freedom Democratic Party against the all-white delegation sent by the regular state party. By a voice vote, the convention approved a compromise negotiated by Minnesota senator Hubert H. Humphrey. The settlement called for seating of the Mississippi regulars, provided they signed a written pledge to back the national ticket and urged the state's presidential electors to do likewise. It also proposed the Democrats as delegates at large, and the remainder of the delegation as honored guests; and it stipulated that at future conventions delegations would be barred from states that allowed racial discrimination in voting. Although the convention approved this solution, the Freedom Democrats rejected the compromise, and all but four members of the regular Mississippi delegation refused to sign the pledge and left the convention.

The convention also approved a recommendation requiring the Alabama delegation to sign a personal loyalty oath, the result of the state party's placing "unpledged" (anti-Johnson) electors on the Alabama ballot. Eleven Alabama members signed the loyalty oath; the remaining 42 delegates and alternates withdrew from the convention.

The roll-call vote for president was dispensed with, and Johnson was nominated by acclamation. Immediately after his selection, Johnson made the unprecedented move of appearing before the delegates to announce his choice for vice president, Humphrey. Johnson had tried to make his selection as suspenseful and dramatic as possible. Although most observers felt Humphrey would be the choice, earlier that day Johnson had called both the Minnesota senator and Connecticut senator Thomas J. Dodd to the White House. However, at this meeting Johnson invited Humphrey to be on the ticket, and later that night the delegates nominated Humphrey by acclamation. (The 1964 Democratic convention was only the second in party history in which there were no roll-call votes — the other time was 1936.)

On the final day of the convention, the two nominees delivered their acceptance speeches. Humphrey frequently referred to the Republican candidate, Sen. Goldwater, as "the temporary Republican spokesman," and listed major legislation supported by a majority of both parties in the Senate, "but not Sen. Goldwater."

The emotional highlight of the convention was the appearance of Attorney General Robert F. Kennedy, who introduced a film about the presidency of his late brother.

By a voice vote, the convention approved the party platform. Following the trend toward longer and longer documents, the platform was 22,000 words in length. Al-

though the document was adopted without debate on the convention floor, several roll-call votes were taken in the platform committee. By a vote of 53 to 16, the committee rejected a proposal by Sen. Joseph S. Clark of Pennsylvania to strengthen the disarmament plank. Clark's proposal called for further disarmament "under world law," wording that the committee majority did not want to include.

By a margin of 39 to 38, the platform committee pledged to support a constitutional amendment giving the District of Columbia representation in Congress. On another roll-call vote (52 to 19), the committee promised to repeal the Taft-Hartley Act provision permitting state right-to-work laws.

Without a recorded vote, the committee adopted another provision by Sen. Clark proposing revision of congressional rules and procedures to "assure majority rule after reasonable debate and to guarantee that major legislative proposals of the President can be brought to a vote after reasonable consideration in committee." The proposal was a reference to the Senate cloture rule, requiring a two-thirds vote to cut off debate, and to the power of the House Rules Committee to keep legislation from the floor.

The entire platform was a wide-ranging document designed to appeal to as many segments of the electorate as possible. Self-described as a "covenant of unity," the platform was written in a moderate tone to contrast with the unqualified conservatism expressed in the Republican platform.

The latter three-quarters of the Democratic platform was a section entitled "An Accounting of Stewardship, 1961-1964," which described the accomplishments of the Kennedy-Johnson administration in 38 areas of public policy. The first quarter of the platform discussed the party's position on major issues of the day, from peace and national defense to civil rights, the economy, agriculture, natural resources, urban affairs, federal power and government reform, and extremism.

In view of the militant anti-communism of Sen. Goldwater and the Republican platform, the Democrats viewed peace and national defense as winning issues with a majority of the electorate. The Democrats claimed that the world was closer to peace than in 1960, due in part to the United States' overwhelming nuclear superiority and internal splits in the communist world, as well as the success of international negotiations such as those resulting in the nuclear test ban treaty. But, in an allusion to Goldwater's stance, the platform warned that recklessness by a president in foreign policy could result in nuclear disaster. The Democratic platform included a provision rejected by the Republicans, insisting that control of nuclear weapons must be kept in the hands of the president.

While peace and national defense were stressed by the Democrats, the Republican platform concentrated on the need to limit the power of the federal government. On this issue, the Democratic platform contained a recommendation to help state and local governments develop new revenue sources. But the Democratic plank also included an assertion that contradicted the Republicans' criticism of expanding federal power: "No government at any level can properly complain of violation of its power, if it fails to meet its responsibilities."

Neither party had a civil rights plank containing specifics. The difference was wording, with the Democrats promising "fair, effective enforcement" of the 1964 Civil Rights Act, but precluding the use of quotas in combating racial discrimination. The Republicans pledged "full implementation and faithful execution" of civil rights laws.

An effort at the Republican convention to have the party platform condemn specific "extremist" groups failed, although the issue was hotly debated on the convention floor. Without dissent, the Democratic platform included a provision that condemned extremism of the right and left, especially the Communist Party, the Ku Klux Klan and the John Birch Society.

The two parties differed in their opinion of the health of the economy. The Republicans blamed their opposition for inflation and continuing unemployment and promised a reduction of at least $5 billion in federal spending. The Democrats countered by claiming the Kennedy-Johnson administration had engineered "the longest and strongest peacetime prosperity in modern history."

Following are excerpts from the Democratic platform of 1964:

Peace. At the start of the third decade of the nuclear age, the preservation of peace requires the strength to wage war and the wisdom to avoid it. The search for peace requires the utmost intelligence, the clearest vision, and a strong sense of reality.... Battered by economic failures, challenged by recent American achievements in space, torn by the Chinese-Russian rift, and faced with American strength and courage — international Communism has lost its unity and momentum.

National Defense. Specifically, we must and we will:
—Continue the overwhelming supremacy of our Strategic Nuclear Forces.
—Strengthen further our forces for discouraging limited wars and fighting subversion.
—Maintain the world's largest research and development effort, which has initiated more than 200 new programs since 1961, to ensure continued American leadership in weapons systems and equipment....
Control of the use of nuclear weapons must remain solely with the highest elected official in the country — the President of the United States....
The complications and dangers in our restless, constantly changing world require of us consummate understanding and experience. One rash act, one thoughtless decision, one unchecked reaction — and cities could become smouldering ruins and farms parched wasteland.

Civil Rights. The Civil Rights Act of 1964 deserves and requires full observance by every American and fair, effective enforcement if there is any default....
True democracy of opportunity will not be served by establishing quotas based on the same false distinctions we seek to erase, nor can the effects of prejudice be neutralized by the expedient of preferential practices.

Extremism. We condemn extremism, whether from the Right or Left, including the extreme tactics of such organizations as the Communist Party, the Ku Klux Klan and the John Birch Society.

Federal Power. The Democratic Party holds to the belief that government in the United States — local, state and federal — was created in order to serve the people. Each level of government has appropriate powers and each has specific responsibilities. The first responsibility of government at every level is to protect the basic freedoms of the people. No government at any level can properly complain of violation of its power, if it fails to meet its responsibilities.
The federal government exists not to grow larger, but to enlarge the individual potential and achievement of the people.
The federal government exists not to subordinate the states, but to support them.

Economy. In 42 months of uninterrupted expansion

under Presidents Kennedy and Johnson, we have achieved the longest and strongest peacetime prosperity in modern history. . . .

It is the national purpose, and our commitment, that every man or woman who is willing and able to work is entitled to a job and to a fair wage for doing it.

1968 Conventions

Presidential Candidates

Richard M. Nixon
Republican

Hubert H. Humphrey
Democrat

George C. Wallace
American Independent

Republicans

The Republican convention, held in Miami Beach, Fla., Aug. 5-8, had a surface tranquility that the later Democratic convention lacked. Only two roll-call votes were taken on the convention floor, to nominate presidential and vice presidential candidates.

There was only one challenge seriously considered by the credentials committee, and that involved a single delegate. By a 32-32 vote, the committee defeated an unexpectedly strong attempt to overturn the preconvention decision to seat Rep. H. R. Gross of Iowa rather than a Des Moines housewife. The full convention approved the report of the credentials committee without a roll-call vote.

The report of the rules committee was approved without comment. It contained recommendations to prohibit discrimination in the selection of future convention delegates and to add the Republican state chairmen as members of the Republican National Committee.

Twelve names were placed in nomination for the presidency, although the contest was clearly among three candidates: the front-runner, former vice president Richard M. Nixon, and two governors, Nelson A. Rockefeller of New York and Ronald Reagan of California. The ideological gulf between the more liberal Rockefeller and the more conservative Reagan made it difficult for them to agree on a common strategy to stop Nixon, even when Reagan abandoned his favorite-son status for active candidacy two days before the balloting.

To head off the defection to Reagan of his more conservative supporters, Nixon seemed to take a sharp tack to the right the day before the balloting. He told Southern delegations he would not run an administration that would "ram anything down your throats," that he opposed school busing, that he would appoint "strict constitutionalists" to the Supreme Court and that he was critical of federal intervention in local school board affairs.

Nixon won the nomination on the first ballot, receiving 692 votes (25 more than necessary) to easily outdistance

Rockefeller, who had 277, and Reagan, who had 182. After vote switches, the final totals were Nixon, 1,238, Rockefeller, 93, and Reagan, 2. In a brief speech to the convention, Reagan moved that Nixon's nomination be made unanimous, but his motion was never put to a vote. *(Chart, p. 211)*

In his selection of a running mate, Nixon surprised many observers by tapping Maryland governor Spiro T. Agnew. Agnew, who had delivered the major nominating speech for Nixon, had, ironically, been one of Rockefeller's earliest and strongest supporters. But the Maryland governor ceased his active support of Rockefeller in March, irked by the New York governor's indecision about entering the race, and, at the beginning of convention week, announced his support for Nixon.

In addition to Agnew, the name of Michigan governor George Romney also was placed in nomination for vice president. Agnew was an easy winner, receiving 1,119 votes to 186 for Romney, who made no effort to withdraw his name. After completion of the roll call, a Romney motion to make Agnew's nomination unanimous was approved.

The delegates approved without debate the 1968 Republican platform, which steered a careful middle course between conservatives and liberals on domestic policy and between "doves" and "hawks" on the touchy Vietnam issue. The 11,500-word document was somewhat more liberal in tone than that of 1960 and was far removed from the militantly conservative tone of the 1964 document.

A major floor fight on the platform was averted when platform committee members, led by Senate Minority Leader Everett McKinley Dirksen of Illinois, substituted for the original hard-line war plank new language stressing the need for de-Americanization of both the military and civilian efforts in Vietnam. Both "hawks" and "doves" decided to go along with the revised version.

As originally written, the plank criticized the Johnson administration for not leaving key Vietnam decisions to the military and for the administration's policy of military

gradualism. Both Nixon and Rockefeller backers opposed the strong language, and a compromise Vietnam plank was accepted. As well as advocating the de-Americanization of the war, it proposed concentrating on protection of the South Vietnamese population rather than on capturing territory, and on efforts to strengthen local forces and responsibility.

While the platform endorsed continued negotiations with Hanoi, it remained silent on the important issues of a bombing pause and of a possible Saigon coalition that would include the communists. During platform committee deliberations, Sen. Jacob K. Javits of New York offered a plank to bring the National Liberation Front into the negotiations, but the suggestion was rejected overwhelmingly.

In its discussion of national defense, the platform criticized the administration for failure to develop superior new weaponry. The document indicated that, when the Vietnam War was over, a reduced defense budget might make possible increased federal spending on social welfare programs. But it neither suggested how much more spending nor recommended any substantial increases in the near future.

The platform treated rioting and crime in militant fashion: "We will not tolerate violence!" The crime plank criticized the Johnson administration for not taking effective action against crime and pledged "an all-out federal-state-local crusade."

It was in the cities plank that the party, in a short statement, mentioned civil rights legislation. The statement simply pledged: "Energetic, positive leadership to enforce statutory and constitutional protections to eliminate discrimination." It was seen as an endorsement of the recently enacted open housing law, in addition to other federal civil rights statutes. The platform did not endorse any new civil rights legislation. However, the Republicans endorsed high-priority objectives of civil rights groups, such as increased food for the poor and job-training programs.

In its youth plank, the Republicans made two specific proposals. First, the party urged the states to lower the voting age to 18 but did not endorse proposals for a constitutional amendment similarly to lower the federal voting age. Second, the plank advocated action to shorten the period in which young men were eligible for the draft and proposed to develop eventually a voluntary force.

Following are excerpts from the Republican platform of 1968:

> **Vietnam.** The Administration's Vietnam policy has failed — militarily, politically, diplomatically, and with relation to our own people.
>
> We condemn the Administration's breach of faith with the American people respecting our heavy involvement in Vietnam. Every citizen bitterly recalls the Democrat campaign oratory of 1964: "We are not about to send American boys 9-10,000 miles away from home to do what Asian boys ought to be doing for themselves." The Administration's failure to honor its own words has led millions of Americans to question its credibility.
>
> The entire nation has been profoundly concerned by hastily-extemporized, undeclared land wars which embroil massive U.S. Army forces thousands of miles from our shores. It is time to realize that not every international conflict is susceptible of solution by American ground forces....
>
> We pledge to adopt a strategy relevant to the real problems of the war, concentrating on the security of the population, on developing a greater sense of nationhood,

and on strengthening the local forces. It will be a strategy permitting a progressive de-Americanization of the war, both military and civilian....

> We pledge a program for peace in Vietnam — neither peace at any price nor a camouflaged surrender of legitimate United States or allied interests — but a positive program that will offer a fair and equitable settlement to all, based on the principle of self-determination, our national interests and the cause of long-range world peace.
>
> We will sincerely and vigorously pursue peace negotiations as long as they offer any reasonable prospect for a just peace. We pledge to develop a clear and purposeful negotiating position.
>
> **National Defense.** Grave errors, many now irretrievable, have characterized the direction of our nation's defense.
>
> A singular notion — that salvation for America lies in standing still — has pervaded the entire effort. Not retention of American superiority but parity with the Soviet Union has been made the controlling doctrine in many critical areas. We have frittered away superior military capabilities, enabling the Soviets to narrow their defense gap, in some areas to outstrip us, and to move to cancel our lead entirely by the early Seventies.
>
> **China.** Improved relations with Communist nations can come only when they cease to endanger other states by force or threat. Under existing conditions, we cannot favor recognition of Communist China or its admission to the United Nations.
>
> **Israel.** The fact of a growing menace to Israel is undeniable. Her forces must be kept at a commensurate strength both for her protection and to help keep the peace of the area. The United States, therefore, will provide countervailing help to Israel, such as supersonic fighters, as necessary for these purposes.
>
> **Crime.** Fire and looting, causing millions of dollars of property damage, have brought great suffering to home owners and small businessmen, particularly in black communities least able to absorb catastrophic losses. The Republican Party strongly advocates measures to alleviate and remove the frustrations that contribute to riots. We simultaneously support decisive action to quell civil disorder, relying primarily on state and local governments to deal with these conditions.
>
> America has adequate peaceful and lawful means for achieving even fundamental social change if the people wish it. *We will not tolerate violence!*
>
> Lawlessness is crumbling the foundations of American society....
>
> We must re-establish the principle that men are accountable for what they do, that criminals are responsible for their crimes, that while the youth's environment may help to explain the man's crime, it does not excuse that crime.
>
> The present Administration has:
>
> —Refused to sanction the use of either the court-supervised wiretapping authority to combat organized crime or the revised rules of evidence, both made available by Congress.
>
> —Failed to deal effectively with threats to the nation's internal security by not prosecuting identified subversives....
>
> For the future, we pledge an all-out, federal-state-local crusade against crime, including:
>
> —Leadership by an Attorney General who will restore stature and respect to that office....
>
> —Enactment of legislation to control indiscriminate availability of firearms, safeguarding the right of responsible citizens to collect, own and use firearms for legitimate purposes, retaining primary responsibility at the state level, with such federal laws as necessary to better enable the states to meet their responsibilities.

Economy. Under the Johnson-Humphrey Administration we have had economic mismanagement of the highest order....

Such funds as become available with the termination of the Vietnam war and upon recovery from its impact on our national defense will be applied in a balanced way to critical domestic needs and to reduce the heavy tax burden.

Democrats

While violence flared in the streets and thousands of police and guards imposed security precautions unprecedented at presidential nominating conventions, the 1968 Democratic convention met Aug. 26-29 in Chicago to nominate Hubert H. Humphrey of Minnesota for the presidency and to endorse the controversial Vietnam policies of the Johnson-Humphrey administration.

Twin themes — physical force to keep order and political force to overrule minority sentiment in the Democratic Party — were apparent throughout the convention.

The physical force, supplied by 11,900 Chicago police, 7,500 Army regulars, 7,500 Illinois National Guardsmen and 1,000 FBI and Secret Service agents, was exerted to keep vociferous Vietnam War critics away from the convention headquarters hotels and the International Amphitheatre where official sessions were held. A security ring several blocks wide guarded the amphitheatre, itself surrounded by a barbed wire fence and multiple security checkpoints for entering delegates, newsmen and guests. No violence erupted in the amphitheatre area, but near the downtown hotels there were days of bitter demonstrations that ended with repeated police use of tear gas. At the end of convention week, the Chicago police announced that 589 persons had been arrested during the disturbances, with more than 119 police and 100 demonstrators injured.

The political force was exerted by the Johnson administration organization backing Vice President Humphrey, whose supporters enjoyed clear control of convention proceedings from start to end. In a distinct minority were the anti-war factions that rallied around the candidacies of Senators Eugene J. McCarthy of Minnesota and George McGovern of South Dakota. The McCarthy forces mounted a series of challenges to the Humphrey faction — on credentials, rules, the platform and finally the nomination itself.

In the first business of the convention, the Humphrey and McCarthy forces joined to ban the unit rule, rejecting by voice vote a motion by the Texas delegation to retain the rule through the 1968 convention.

However, as expected, the brief moments of unity between the opposing sides ended when the convention moved on to consider credentials challenges. The two sides split on the question of adjournment, with the Humphrey forces defeating by a vote of 1,701-1/2 to 875 a motion to delay consideration of credentials until the second session.

The credentials committee had considered an unprecedented number of challenges, involving delegates from 15 states. Although McCarthy supported almost all the challenges, his candidacy was not always the paramount issue. In the case of the disputed Southern delegations, racial imbalance, the party loyalty issue, or a combination of both, were more important. Of the 17 different challenges, McCarthy supported all but one (in Wisconsin); McGovern backed all the Southern challenges; Humphrey supported only the Mississippi challenge publicly.

In a historic move, the convention by a voice vote seated a new loyalist Democratic faction from Mississippi and unseated the delegation of the traditionally segregationist, conservative regular party.

The credentials committee decided all other challenges in favor of the regular delegations, but minority reports were filed for the Alabama, Georgia, North Carolina and Texas challengers. The North Carolina case was decided by a voice vote supporting the regular delegation, but the other three cases were settled by roll-call votes.

The first state to be considered was Texas, and, by a vote of 2,368-1/4 to 956-3/4, the convention approved the seating of the regular delegation led by Gov. John B. Connally. The rival McCarthy-supported Texas faction was led by Sen. Ralph W. Yarborough. *(Chart, p. 210)*

The Georgia case was considered next, with the credentials committee recommending that both rival delegations be seated and the Georgia vote split evenly between them. However, both delegations found this to be an unsatisfactory solution and presented reports to have their entire delegation seated alone. A minority report to seat the challenging Loyal National Democrats, led by black state representative Julian Bond, was defeated 1,415.45 to 1,043.55. A minority report to seat the regular delegation, hand-picked by Gov. Lester G. Maddox and Democratic state chairman James H. Gray, was rejected by a voice vote. The solution recommended by the credentials committee was subsequently approved by a voice vote.

The Alabama case involved three competing factions: the regulars, the largely black National Democratic Party of Alabama (NDPA) and the integrated Alabama Independent Democratic Party (AIDP), created solely to run a slate of presidential electors loyal to the national party against the third-party candidacy of Alabama governor George C. Wallace. The credentials committee proposed seating all members of the regular delegation who would sign a loyalty pledge and replacing those who would not sign with loyal members of the AIDP delegation. However, the McCarthy-backed NDPA introduced a minority report to seat its entire delegation. By a vote of 1,607 to 880-3/4, the convention rejected this minority report and by a voice vote approved the recommendation of the credentials committee.

The remainder of the credentials committee report was approved, including a resolution instructing the Democratic National Committee to include, in the call for the 1972 convention, encouragement to state parties to ensure that all Democrats in each state have a "meaningful and timely" opportunity to participate in delegate selection.

McCarthy, McGovern and other liberal factions won their greatest breakthrough on convention rules, obtaining abolition of a mandatory unit rule for the 1968 convention, and, by a vote of 1,351-1/4 to 1,209, obtaining elimination of the unit rule at every level of party activity leading up to and including the 1972 convention. Many Humphrey-pledged delegates also backed the unit rule change. Also a part of this successful minority report was the requirement that the delegate-selection process in 1972 be public and held within the calendar year of the convention.

A proposal to add state chairmen and state Young Democrat presidents to the Democratic National Committee was defeated, 1,349-1/4 to 1,125-3/4.

On Wednesday night, on the third day of the convention, while nominations and balloting for president took place at the amphitheatre, the worst violence of the convention broke out downtown, and television screens carried pictures of phalanxes of Chicago police advancing on demonstrators.

At the same time, hundreds of Chicago mayor Richard

J. Daley's workers were brought into the galleries with apparent improper credentials. Some delegates, apparently refusing to show their credentials to the omnipresent security guards, were physically ejected from the convention floor. The McCarthy and McGovern forces charged "atrocities" and tried to adjourn the convention for two weeks. House Majority Leader Carl Albert of Oklahoma, the convention chairman, refused to accept their motions.

In addition to Humphrey, McCarthy and McGovern, only two other candidates were placed in nomination — the Rev. Channing E. Phillips of the District of Columbia, who became the first black ever nominated for the presidency at a national convention, and North Carolina governor Dan K. Moore. Telegrams were read from President Johnson and Massachusetts senator Edward M. Kennedy, each stating that he did not choose to be nominated.

The emotional highlight of the session was provided by McGovern's nominator, Connecticut senator Abraham A. Ribicoff, who charged that "with George McGovern as president of the United States we wouldn't have to have Gestapo tactics in the streets of Chicago."

Humphrey was an easy winner on the first ballot, receiving 1,759-1/4 votes to 601 for McCarthy, 146-1/2 for McGovern and 67-1/2 for Phillips. Humphrey's winning majority included the bulk of party moderates, big-city organizations of the North (including Daley's) and Southern conservatives. In a tumultuous ending to one of the wildest nights in American politics, Chairman Albert gaveled through a motion to make the nomination unanimous (despite major opposition on the floor) and adjourned the session. *(Chart, p. 210)*

As his running mate, Humphrey chose Maine senator Edmund S. Muskie. Julian Bond's name also was placed in nomination, but Bond, then 28, withdrew, explaining that he was under the "legal age" to be president (the constitutional minimum is 35). Before the end of the first ballot, Albert recognized Mayor Daley, who moved that Muskie be declared the vice presidential nominee by acclamation. With the convention in a particularly unruly state, the Daley motion was quickly adopted. At the time the roll call was suspended, Muskie already had received 1,942-1/2 votes, a majority. Bond was a distant second with 48-1/2.

A filmed tribute to the late New York senator Robert F. Kennedy preceded the vice presidential nomination. Kennedy had been a presidential candidate until his assassination in June after winning the California primary. The tribute to Kennedy evoked a long, standing ovation and the singing of "The Battle Hymn of the Republic."

The 18,000-word platform, adopted by a voice vote, was a document that met the demands of the Democratic Party's liberals word for word in almost every section except that which dealt with United States policy in Vietnam. At one point during the platform-writing sessions, it appeared that Humphrey might assent to a plank calling for a halt in U.S. bombing of North Vietnam. But President Johnson reportedly sent personal instructions that the plank should support administration policy.

The administration plank, approved by a 62-35 vote in the platform committee, supported a bombing halt only when it "would not endanger the lives of our troops in the field," did not call for a reduction in search-and-destroy missions or a withdrawal of troops until the end of the war, and advocated a new government in Saigon only after the war had ended. The minority plank, drafted by McCarthy and McGovern, called for an immediate halt to the bombing, reduction of offensive operations in the South Vietnamese countryside, a negotiated troop withdrawal and

encouragement of the South Vietnamese government to negotiate with communist insurgents.

The bitterness created by the Vietnam issue and Humphrey's march toward the nomination finally erupted when the convention managers attempted to force debate and voting on the Vietnam plank at 2 a.m., when most television viewers were already asleep. Albert, in violation of convention rules, refused to recognize a motion from a McCarthy backer to adjourn. But a few minutes later, when the convention could not be brought to order, Albert recognized a similar motion from Mayor Daley.

Nearly three hours of debate were held the next afternoon. On the subsequent roll call, the minority plank was defeated, 1,567-3/4 to 1,041-1/4. After the result was announced, members of the New York delegation and others slipped on black armbands and sang "We Shall Overcome." *(Chart, p. 210)*

Unlike the Republican platform, which called for decreased United States involvement in Vietnam, Democrats adopted a plan that called for a continued strong American war effort. Although the Democrats agreed with Republicans that the South Vietnamese eventually should take over their nation's defense, they gave no indication that an expanded Vietnamese role could lead to U.S. troop reductions in the near future.

While promising to reduce waste in military spending, the Democrats stated that the nation "must and will maintain a strong and balanced defense establishment adequate to the task of security and peace." The platform said there "must be no doubt" about U.S. capability to meet either nuclear or more limited challenges.

Crime was one of the leading domestic issues. The platform contained a strongly worded but rather unspecific plank on crime, a plank containing fewer detailed proposals than its Republican counterpart. The Democratic crime plank was entitled "Justice and Law," in a deliberate effort to avoid use of such phrases as "law and order," which were in the Republican plank and which some observers felt had connotations of overly suppressive tactics, particularly in black ghettos.

The Democratic plank did not mention the role of the attorney general. The Republicans said they would seek an attorney general who would "restore stature and respect to that office." Nor did the Democrats, unlike the Republicans, mention implementation of the federal wiretapping authority granted by the Safe Streets Act, or prosecution of subversives.

Both parties pledged further efforts to control the indiscriminate sale of firearms, but neither party was specific. Democratic liberals had tried unsuccessfully within the platform committee to strengthen the gun control section.

The Democratic platform contained a more specific endorsement of open housing than did the Republican document. Both platforms urged better job opportunities, housing and food programs for the poor, and the Democrats also promised reforms in existing welfare programs.

The Democrats, like the Republicans, called for tax reform, but their goals were more pointed. The platform asked for a minimum income tax for wealthy persons based on total income regardless of source and committed the party to seeking decreased rates for lower-income families and an increase in the minimum standard deduction.

The Democrats supported a constitutional amendment to permit 18-year-old voting and recommended a draft lottery and better community representation on draft boards.

Reform of the electoral college was favored, so that it would accurately reflect the will of the voters.

Following are excerpts from the Democratic platform of 1968:

Vietnam. Recognizing that events in Vietnam and the negotiations in Paris may affect the timing and the actions we recommend we would support our Government in the following steps:

Bombing — Stop all bombing of North Vietnam when this action would not endanger the lives of our troops in the field; this action should take into account the response from Hanoi.

Troop Withdrawal — Negotiate with Hanoi an immediate end or limitation of hostilities and the withdrawal from South Vietnam of all foreign forces — both United States and allied forces, and forces infiltrated from North Vietnam.

Election of Postwar Government — Encourage all parties and interests to agree that the choice of the postwar government of South Vietnam should be determined by fair and safeguarded elections, open to all major political factions and parties prepared to accept peaceful political processes. We would favor an effective international presence to facilitate the transition from war to peace and to assure the protection of minorities against reprisal.

Interim Defense and Development Measures — Until the fighting stops, accelerate our efforts to train and equip the South Vietnamese army so that it can defend its own country and carry out cutbacks of U.S. military involvement as the South Vietnamese forces are able to take over their larger responsibilities. We should simultaneously do all in our power to support and encourage further economic, political and social development and reform in South Vietnam, including an extensive land reform program. We support President Johnson's repeated offer to provide a substantial U.S. contribution to the post-war reconstruction of South Vietnam as well as to the economic development of the entire region, including North Vietnam. Japan and the European industrial states should be urged to join in this post-war effort.

National Defense. We must and will maintain a strong and balanced defense establishment adequate to the task of security and peace. There must be no doubt about our strategic nuclear capacity, our capacity to meet limited challenges, and our willingness to act when our vital interests are threatened. . . .

We face difficult and trying times in Asia and in Europe. We have responsibilities and commitments we cannot escape with honor.

China. The immediate prospects that China will emerge from its self-imposed isolation are dim. But both Asians and Americans will have to coexist with the 750 million Chinese on the mainland. We shall continue to make it clear that we are prepared to cooperate with China whenever it is ready to become a responsible member of the international community. We would actively encourage economic, social and cultural exchange with mainland China as a means of freeing that nation and her people from their narrow isolation.

Israel. As long as Israel is threatened by hostile and well-armed neighbors, we will assist her with essential military equipment needed for her defense, including the most advanced types of combat aircraft.

Crime. In fighting crime we must not foster injustice. Lawlessness cannot be ended by curtailing the hard-won liberties of all Americans. The right of privacy must be safeguarded. Court procedures must be expedited. Justice delayed is justice denied.

A respect for civil peace requires also a proper respect for the legitimate means of expressing dissent. A democratic society welcomes criticism within the limits of the law.

Freedom of speech, press, assembly and association, together with free exercise of the franchise, are among the legitimate means to achieve change in a democratic society. But when the dissenter resorts to violence, he erodes the institutions and values which are the underpinnings of our democratic society. We must not and will not tolerate violence.

Tax Reform. We support a proposal for a minimum income tax for persons of high income based on an individual's total income regardless of source, in order that wealthy persons will be required to make some kind of income tax contribution, no matter how many tax shelters they use to protect their incomes.

We also support a reduction of the tax burden on the poor by lowering the income tax rates at the bottom of the tax scale and increasing the minimum standard deduction. No person or family below the poverty level should be required to pay federal income taxes.

Electoral Reform. We fully recognize the principle of one man, one vote in all elections. We urge that due consideration be given to the question of Presidential primaries throughout the nation. We urge reform of the electoral college and election procedures to assure that the votes of the people are fully reflected.

American Independent Party

Former Alabama governor George C. Wallace declared his third-party presidential candidacy on Feb. 8, 1968. The vehicle for his candidacy was his personally created American Independent Party. No convention was held by the party to ratify his selection. (A descendant of the 1968 Wallace campaign, the American Party ran a national ticket in 1972 but received less than 2 percent of the vote.)

On Feb. 14 Wallace announced the choice of former Georgia governor Marvin Griffin as his "interim" vice presidential running mate, but he made clear that an official candidate would be chosen later in the campaign. Griffin's tentative candidacy was necessary to allow the American Independent Party to get on the ballot in several states.

On Oct. 3 Wallace announced his choice of retired Air Force general Curtis E. LeMay, an Ohio native, as his official running mate.

Ten days later, Wallace released the text of his party's platform. The document generally took a harder line toward domestic and international problems than did the Democratic and Republican platforms.

Wallace favored termination of the Vietnam War through negotiations but added that, if negotiations failed, the United States should seek a military solution.

As expected, the emphasis of the platform on domestic issues centered on returning control of local affairs to the states and communities, with the federal government serving in an assisting role rather than an authoritarian manner.

To curb the interference of the federal government in local affairs, Wallace advocated adoption of a constitutional amendment under which federal district judges would stand for election periodically and higher judges, including Supreme Court justices, would be required to be periodically reconfirmed by the Senate. Wallace further proposed, in essence, repeal of the open housing provision of the 1968 Civil Rights Act and to "absolutely prohibit the agencies and agents of the Federal Government from intruding into and seeking to control the affairs of the local school systems of the states, counties and cities of the nation." He further pledged to "cooperate with the administrators of our institutions of higher learning now in the

hands of revolutionaries. We must support these officials in the restoration of order on their campuses and we must assure that no assistance, financial or otherwise, from the federal level be given to those seeking to disrupt and destroy these great institutions."

In a section entitled "Crime and Disorder," Wallace pledged to give his full support to law enforcement agencies at every level of government, to "insist on fair and equal treatment for all persons before the bar of justice," to appoint an attorney general "interested in the enforcement rather than the disruption of the legal processes," and to oppose federal legislation requiring gun registration.

Wallace also promised to seek an immediate increase in Social Security benefits, to increase agricultural support prices to 90 percent of parity and to seek legislation increasing maximum support to 100 percent of parity.

Following are excerpts from the American Independent Party platform of 1968:

Vietnam. We earnestly desire that the conflict be terminated through peaceful negotiations and we will lend all aid, support, effort, sincerity and prayer to the efforts of our negotiators. Negotiation will be given every reasonable and logical chance for success and we will be patient to an extreme in seeking an end to the war through this means. If it becomes evident that the enemy does not desire to negotiate in good faith, that our hopes of termination of hostilities are not being realized and that the lives and safety of our committed troops are being further endangered, we must seek a military conclusion.

National Defense. We propose an intensive and immediate review of the policies, practices and capabilities of the Department of Defense with a view to reestablishing sound principles of logic and reasoning to the decisions and directives of that agency and to eliminating from its ranks all of those who have been party to the dissemination and promulgation of the false doctrines of security and the coercion, intimidation and punishment of all who would oppose or disagree with them.

Middle East. Should arms continue to be introduced ... by foreign powers to such an extent as to endanger the peace in this part of the world, we must take steps to assure that a balance of force is brought to exist. We will join with other nations of the free world in providing the means whereby this balance of force will continue and the threat of aggression of one nation against another is made less likely.

United Nations. We will not abandon the United Nations Organization unless it first abandons us. It should be given fair opportunity at resolving international disputes, however, we will not subordinate the interest of our nation to the interest of any international organization. We feel that in this organization, as in any other, participating members should bear proportionate shares of the cost of operation and we will insist on financial responsibility on the part of the member nations.

Crime. Lawlessness has become commonplace in our present society. The permissive attitude of the executive and judiciary at the national level sets the tone for this moral decay. The criminal and anarchist who preys on the decent law abiding citizen is rewarded for his misconduct through never ending justification and platitudes from those in high places who seem to have lost their concern for that vast segment of America that so strongly believes in law and order....

We will appoint as Attorney General a person interested in the enforcement rather that the disruption of legal processes and restore that office to the dignity and stature it deserves and requires.

Economy. We will review and propose revisions to our present tax structure so as to ease the load of the small income citizen and to place upon all their rightful share of the tax burden....

We will eliminate the favorable treatment now accorded the giant, non-tax paying foundations and institutions and require these organizations to assume their rightful responsibility as to the operation of our government....

We propose to rely heavily upon a competitive market structure rather than upon prices administered or fixed by bureaucratic procedures.

Federal Power. The Federal Government, in derogation and flagrant violation of this Article [X] of the Bill of Rights, has in the past three decades seized and usurped many powers not delegated to it, such as, among others: the operation and control of the public school system of the several states; the power to prescribe the eligibility and qualifications of those who would vote in our state and local elections; the power to intrude upon and control the farmer in the operation of his farm; the power to tell the property owner to whom he can and cannot sell or rent his property; and, many other rights and privileges of the individual citizen, which are properly subject to state or local control, as distinguished from federal control. The Federal Government has forced the states to reapportion their legislatures, a prerogative of the states alone. The Federal Government has attempted to take over and control the seniority and apprenticeship lists of the labor unions; the Federal Government has adopted so-called "Civil Rights Acts," particularly the one adopted in 1964, which have set race against race and class against class, all of which we condemn.

The Judiciary. In the period of the past three decades, we have seen the Federal judiciary, primarily the Supreme Court, transgress repeatedly upon the prerogatives of the Congress and exceed its authority by enacting judicial legislation, in the form of decisions based upon political and sociological considerations, which would never have been enacted by the Congress. We have seen them, in their solicitude for the criminal and lawless element of our society, shackle the police and other law enforcement agencies; and, as a result, they have made it increasingly difficult to protect the law-abiding citizen from crime and criminals. This is one of the principal reasons for the turmoil and the near revolutionary conditions which prevail in our country today, and particularly in our national capital. The Federal judiciary, feeling secure in their knowledge that their appointment is for life, have far exceeded their constitutional authority, which is limited to interpreting or construing the law.

It shall be our policy and our purpose, at the earliest possible time, to propose and advocate and urge the adoption of an amendment to the United States Constitution whereby members of the Federal judiciary at District level be required to face the electorate on his record at periodical intervals; and, in the event he receives a negative vote upon such election, his office shall thereupon become vacant, and a successor shall be appointed to succeed him.

With respect to the Supreme Court and the Courts of Appeals I would propose that this amendment require reconfirmation of the office holder by the United States Senate at reasonable intervals.

1972 Conventions

Presidential Candidates

George McGovern
Democrat

Richard M. Nixon
Republican

Democrats

Massive reforms in convention rules and delegate selection procedures made the 1972 Democratic convention, held in Miami Beach, Fla., July 10-13, significantly different from the violence-plagued assembly in Chicago four years earlier.

Two special commissions created by the 1968 convention drafted the reforms. The Commission on Rules, chaired by Rep. James G. O'Hara of Michigan, composed the first set of rules ever written on Democratic convention procedure. Among the reforms that the Democratic National Committee adopted were:

● A new vote-allocation formula based nearly equally on electoral college strength and the Democratic vote in recent presidential elections.

● An expansion of the convention rules, platform and credentials committees so that their make-up would reflect state population differences rather than the previous method of allocating two seats to each state.

● The assurance that women and men be equally represented on committees and among convention officers.

● The requirement that the meetings and votes of all convention committees be open to the public.

● The requirement that the reports and minority views of all the committees be released at specified dates before the opening of the convention.

● The banning of floor demonstrations for candidates.

● The arrangement of the states and territories for roll calls in random sequence determined by lot rather than in the traditional alphabetical order.

The Commission on Party Structure and Delegate Selection, first chaired by Sen. George McGovern of South Dakota and later by Rep. Donald M. Fraser of Minnesota, formulated 18 guidelines to be met by the states in the delegate-selection process. With the approval of these guidelines by the Democratic National Committee, they became part of the 1972 convention call, thus requiring the states to be in full compliance with the guidelines before they would be seated.

Among the important features of the 18 guidelines were the elimination of the unit rule; the restriction that no

more than 10 percent of a state's delegation be named by its state committee; the requirement that all steps in the delegate-selection process be publicly advertised and held in easily accessible public places within the calendar year of the convention; the requirement that women, youth and minority groups be included in delegations "in reasonable relationship" to their presence in the state's population; and the establishment of a detailed, public method of hearing delegate challenges.

The reforms encouraged an unprecedented number of challenges. The credentials committee opened hearings in Washington, D.C., two weeks before the start of the convention, faced with 82 challenges from 30 states and one territory. A total of 1,289 delegates were challenged, representing more than 40 percent of the convention delegates. More than four-fifths of the challenges were filed on grounds of non-compliance with reform commission guidelines regarding adequate representation of women, youth and minorities.

The most controversial challenges involved the California delegation and the part of the Illinois delegation controlled by Mayor Richard J. Daley of Chicago.

The credentials committee, in a move that surprised supporters of McGovern, a candidate for the presidential nomination, upheld a challenge of California's winner-take-all primary law, stripping McGovern of 151 of the 271 delegate votes he had won in the primary.

The committee voted 72 to 66 to award the 151 convention seats to Sen. Hubert H. Humphrey of Minnesota and seven other candidates in proportion to their share of the popular ballots cast in the state's June primary. Although McGovern was clearly the front-runner for the nomination, the decision, if not overturned by the full convention, threatened his chances of being selected.

In a tense and dramatic balloting session the next day, the committee voted 71 to 61 to unseat Daley and 58 of his Chicago delegates. The committee decided to replace the 59 delegates on grounds that the procedures under which the Daley delegates had been selected violated five of the party's reform guidelines. Most of the Illinois delegates challenging Daley supported McGovern.

Although the losing sides in both the California and Illinois decisions appealed their cases, the courts ruled that the party conventions decide their claims.

The emotional credentials challenges were considered on the first night of the convention. Twenty-three challenges from 15 states were brought to the convention floor, but the spotlight was on the California and Illinois cases. A key preliminary vote took place on a challenge to the South Carolina delegation brought by the National Women's Political Caucus. The challenge, seeking to increase the number of women in the state delegation, was rejected by a vote of 1,555.75 to 1,429.05. *(Chart, p. 212)*

The outcome of the vote could have set an important precedent on what constituted a majority on subsequent challenges. Anti-McGovern forces had hoped to get a ruling from the chair allowing an absolute majority of 1,509 delegates to prevail rather than a simple majority of delegates actually voting.

Convention Chairman Lawrence F. O'Brien (also chairman of the Democratic National Committee) had announced earlier that a majority would consist of one-half plus one of the number of eligible voters. The rules provided that no delegates could vote on their own credentials challenges.

Because the winning total on the South Carolina vote exceeded by a wide margin both the eligible majority and the absolute majority of the convention's 3,016 votes, the anti-McGovern coalition was unable to force a test of what constituted a majority. Thus the vote, although it rejected the position of South Carolina challengers favorable to McGovern, set the stage for returning the 151 California delegates to McGovern. The McGovern forces subsequently won the crucial California challenge, 1,618.28 to 1,238.22.

Immediately after the vote on the California challenge, a Wallace delegate from Florida appealed the ruling of the chair that allowed 120 McGovern delegates from California to vote on their state's other 151 delegates. The appeal was rejected, 1,689.52 to 1,162.23.

Former Nebraska governor Frank B. Morrison, a McGovern supporter, proposed a compromise solution for the Illinois case that would seat both the Daley delegates and the insurgent challengers, while splitting the vote between them. The Morrison proposal asked for suspension of the rules — a parliamentary procedure requiring a two-thirds majority. The motion to suspend the rules was rejected by 1,473.08 nays to 1,411.05 yeas.

The minority report, which asked for seating of the Daley delegates alone, was defeated 1,486.04 to 1,371.56. The vote seated a group, a majority of which supported McGovern, headed by Chicago alderman William Singer and black activist Jesse Jackson. *(Chart, p. 212)*

No other roll-call votes were needed to resolve the remaining credentials challenges. After the settlement of all the delegate contests, the convention had a composition unlike that of any previous major party convention. The 1972 Democratic assembly was the largest in major party history, with 3,203 delegates casting 3,016 votes. Unlike the situation in 1968, most delegates were chosen in state primary elections rather than in state conventions or caucuses. Nearly two-thirds of the delegates to the 1972 convention were selected in primaries, while only 41 percent had been elected by the primary system four years earlier.

There were also large increases in the number of women, youth and racial minorities at the 1972 convention. The proportion of women delegates rose from 13 percent in 1968 to 40 percent in 1972; the number of youth delegates

(30 and under) dramatically jumped from 2.6 percent in 1968 to 21 percent four years later; and black delegates made up 15 percent of the 1972 convention, compared with 5.5 percent in 1968. But while women, youth and blacks were better represented than at earlier conventions, there was a lower level of participation by elected party officials. Only 30 of the 255 Democratic U.S. House members were present in Miami Beach.

The report of the rules committee was approved on the second day of the convention by a voice vote. The report proposed the abolition of winner-take-all primaries in 1976; the abolition of cross-over voting by Republicans in future Democratic presidential primaries; the selection of a woman as chairman of the 1976 convention, with the job rotating between the sexes thereafter; the creation of a special fund in the Democratic National Committee to subsidize the expenses of poor delegates at future national conventions and other party councils, and the appointment of a commission to make "appropriate revisions" in the reform guidelines.

Although the delegates overwhelmingly accepted these reforms, they balked at approving the party charter drafted by the rules committee. The new charter, the first ever written for a major party, was intended to free the national party of four-year presidential election cycles and to broaden public involvement in major national policy questions. But the charter was opposed by some party leaders, particularly members of Congress, who viewed the document as shifting power from elected politicians to the grass-roots level. By a vote of 2,408.45 to 195.10, the convention approved a compromise resolution to delay consideration of the charter until a proposed midterm policy conference in 1974. The compromise also enlarged the Democratic National Committee and revised its membership to reflect Democratic strength in the various states.

The settlement of the California challenge on the opening night of the convention in favor of the McGovern forces effectively locked up the presidential nomination for the South Dakota senator. The next day, two of his major rivals in the primaries, Senators Humphrey and Muskie, withdrew from the race. In the balloting on the third day of the convention, McGovern was an easy winner on the first roll call. Before switches, McGovern had received 1,728.35 votes to 525 for Sen. Henry M. Jackson of Washington, 381.7 for Gov. Wallace of Alabama and 151.95 for Rep. Shirley Chisholm of New York. After vote changes, McGovern's vote total rose to 1,864.95, but no attempt was made to make his nomination unanimous. *(Chart, p. 212)*

With McGovern's first choice for vice president, Sen. Edward M. Kennedy of Massachusetts, rebuffing all overtures, McGovern selected Sen. Thomas F. Eagleton of Missouri. The vice presidential balloting was prolonged by the nomination of six other candidates, and, by the time the roll call was suspended, votes were distributed among more than 70 different "candidates." Eagleton received 1,741.81 votes, a majority. He was followed by Frances T. "Sissy" Farenthold, a women's rights leader from Texas, who had 404.04 votes, Sen. Mike Gravel of Alaska with 225.38 and former Massachusetts governor Endicott Peabody with 107.26. On the motion of Farenthold, the roll call was suspended and Eagleton was nominated by acclamation.

Because of the long vice presidential roll call, it was nearly 3 a.m. before McGovern was able to deliver his acceptance speech. In it he stressed the anti-war theme that was a basic part of his campaign and implored the nation to "come home" to its founding ideals.

Barely 10 days after selection of the Democratic ticket,

on July 25, Eagleton disclosed that he voluntarily had hospitalized himself three times between 1960 and 1966 for "nervous exhaustion and fatigue." McGovern strongly supported his running mate at the time, but in the following days, his support for the Missouri senator began to wane. After a meeting with McGovern on July 31, Eagleton withdrew from the ticket. It marked the first time since 1860 that a major party candidate had withdrawn from a national ticket after the convention had adjourned.

On Aug. 5 McGovern announced that his choice to replace Eagleton was R. Sargent Shriver of Maryland, U.S. ambassador to France and the former director of the Peace Corps and the Office of Economic Opportunity. The newly enlarged Democratic National Committee formally nominated Shriver in an Aug. 8 meeting in Washington. The new vice presidential candidate received 2,936 of the 3,013 votes cast, with the Missouri vote going to Eagleton and four of Oregon's votes to former senator Wayne Morse.

The 1972 Democratic platform was probably the most liberal and the longest (about 25,000 words) ever offered by a major political party. The platform was more a collection of independent reform proposals than a unified plan of action. Its recommendations, largely written by separate subject-area task forces, did not translate into a compact program for Congress to consider or for a president to propose. But the platform's common themes reflected the changes in the party since 1968 and set it off from all other Democratic platforms of the previous generation.

The convention made no concessions to the views of Wallace, even though he made a dramatic appearance at the podium in a wheelchair to urge adoption of minority planks his supporters had offered. Wallace was partially paralyzed from gunshot wounds he had received two months earlier in Laurel, Md., while campaigning for the Democratic presidential nomination.

The Wallace-supported planks called for a constitutional amendment to outlaw busing, tax reform, reintroduction of the death penalty, cutbacks in foreign aid, popular election of federal judges and Senate reconfirmation of Supreme Court justices, a school prayer amendment and support for the right to own guns. They were rejected by voice votes.

Twenty separate minority planks were considered by the convention, but only two were adopted, both by voice vote. One strengthened the American commitment to Israel by adding language promising "a military force in Europe and at sea in the Mediterranean ample to deter the Soviet Union from putting unbearable pressure on Israel." The second endorsed "allocation of federal surplus lands to American Indians on a priority basis."

Two roll-call votes were taken on other planks. The National Welfare Rights Organization sponsored a measure requiring the federal government to guarantee every family of four an annual income of $6,500. This proposal lost, 1,852.86 to 999.34. The other roll call was on a minority plank supporting the right of women to control their reproductive lives without legal interference. Offered by pro-abortion groups, it was defeated 1,572.80 to 1,101.37.

Two other significant minority planks were rejected by voice votes. One was a tax reform measure pushed by Sen. Fred Harris of Oklahoma, which had the slogan, "Take the rich off welfare." The other was a "gay rights" plank endorsing the repeal of all laws regarding voluntary sex acts performed by adults in private.

The platform session demonstrated the firm control McGovern had over the proceedings of the convention. The two minority planks added to the platform were the only proposed additions that McGovern did not specifically oppose. He asked his delegates to support the pro-Israel plank and told them to vote their consciences on the Indian issue.

Planks dealing with domestic issues composed more than four-fifths of the platform. The domestic planks recommended little significant expansion of the size and scope of the federal government. With the major exception of health insurance, the platform sought to restructure society by shifting money and political power to the underprivileged, not by developing federal agencies to alter their lives.

The platform endorsed income redistribution through tax reforms and a guaranteed annual income. It sought expansion of minority-group rights in all political and federal government affairs. To solve the financial crisis at local levels, it endorsed general revenue sharing with local control over use of the money. All this represented a departure from the statist liberalism that had dominated Democratic platforms since the New Deal of the 1930s.

The foreign policy planks broke with the Cold War rhetoric of 1968 and previous years. While endorsing the concept of a strong national defense, the platform devoted more space to peace in Indochina, improved relations with the communist world and less help for non-communist totalitarian regimes. Only four years earlier, the Democrats had given considerable space to warnings against Soviet and Chinese expansion and to praise for the North Atlantic Treaty Organization. The 1968 platform called for scrutiny of wasteful defense spending practices, but the 1972 document made military cuts a major campaign promise and a source of financing for domestic programs.

The platform's position on the Vietnam War was blunt and unequivocal. As "the first order of business" of a Democratic administration, the platform pledged "immediate and complete withdrawal of all U.S. forces in Indochina." The plank also promised an end to military aid to the Saigon regime but pledged economic assistance to Vietnam to help the nation emerge from the war. Amnesty for war resisters was recommended after the return of American prisoners of war.

Following are excerpts from the Democratic platform of 1972:

Foreign Policy. The next Democratic Administration should:

●End American participation in the war in Southeast Asia.

●Re-establish control over military activities and reduce military spending, where consistent with national security.

●Defend America's real interests and maintain our alliances, neither playing world policeman nor abandoning old and good friends.

●Not neglect America's relations with small third-world nations in placing reliance on great power relationships.

●Return to Congress, and to the people, a meaningful role in decisions on peace and war, and

●Make information public, except where real national defense interests are involved.

Vietnam. We believe that war is a waste of human life. We are determined to end forthwith a war which has cost 50,000 American lives, $150 billion of our resources, that has divided us from each other, drained our national will and inflicted incalculable damage to countless people. We will end that war by a simple plan that need not be kept secret: The immediate total withdrawal of all Americans from Southeast Asia.

Military Spending. Military strength remains an essential element of a responsible international policy.

America must have the strength required for effective deterrence.

But military defense cannot be treated in isolation from other vital national concerns. Spending for military purposes is greater by far than federal spending for education, housing, environmental protection, unemployment insurance or welfare. Unneeded dollars for the military at once add to the tax burden and pre-empt funds from programs of direct and immediate benefit to our people. Moreover, too much that is now spent on defense not only adds nothing to our strength but makes us less secure by stimulating other countries to respond.

Vietnam Amnesty. To those who for reasons of conscience refused to serve in this war and were prosecuted or sought refuge abroad, we state our firm intention to declare an amnesty, on an appropriate basis, when the fighting has ceased and our troops and prisoners of war have returned.

Federal Power. The new Democratic Administration can begin a fundamental re-examination of all federal domestic social programs and the patterns of service delivery they support. Simply advocating the expenditure of more funds is not enough, although funds are needed, for billions already have been poured into federal government programs like urban renewal, current welfare and aid to education, with meager results. The control, structure and effectiveness of every institution and government grant system must be fully examined and these institutions must be made accountable to those they are supposed to serve.

Economy. The heart of a program of economic security based on earned income must be creating jobs and training people to fill them. Millions of jobs — real jobs, not make-work — need to be provided. Public service employment must be greatly expanded in order to make the government the employer of last resort and guarantee a job for all.

Tax Reform. The cost of government must be distributed more fairly among income classes. We reaffirm the long-established principle of progressive taxation — allocating the burden according to ability to pay — which is all but a dead letter in the present tax code.

Poverty. The next Democratic Administration must end the present welfare system and replace it with an income security program which places cash assistance in an appropriate context with all of the measures outlined above, adding up to an earned income approach to ensure each family an income substantially more than the poverty level defined in the area. Federal income assistance will supplement the income of working poor people and assure an adequate income for those unable to work.

Crime. There must be laws to control the improper use of hand guns. Four years ago a candidate for the presidency was slain by a hand gun. Two months ago, another candidate for that office was gravely wounded. Three out of four police officers killed in the line of duty are slain with hand guns. Effective legislation must include a ban on sale of hand guns known as Saturday night specials which are unsuitable for sporting purposes.

Free Expression and Privacy. The new Democratic Administration should bring an end to the pattern of political persecution and investigation, the use of high office as a pulpit for unfair attack and intimidation and the blatant efforts to control the poor and to keep them from acquiring additional economic security or political power.

The epidemic of wiretapping and electronic surveillance engaged in by the Nixon Administration and the use of grand juries for purposes of political intimidation must be ended. The rule of law and the supremacy of the Constitution, as these concepts have traditionally been understood, must be restored.

Rights of Women. Women historically have been denied a full voice in the evolution of the political and social institutions of this country and are therefore allied with all underrepresented groups in a common desire to form a more humane and compassionate society. The Democratic Party pledges the following:

●A priority effort to ratify the Equal Rights Amendment. . . .

●Appointment of women to positions of top responsibilities in all branches of the federal government, to achieve an equitable ratio of women and men.

School Busing. We support the goal of desegregation as a means to achieve equal access to quality education for all our children. There are many ways to desegregate schools: School attendance lines may be redrawn; schools may be paired; larger physical facilities may be built to serve larger, more diverse enrollments; magnet schools or educational parks may be used. Transportation of students is another tool to accomplish desegregation. It must continue to be available according to Supreme Court decisions to eliminate legally imposed segregation and improve the quality of education for all children.

Agriculture. We will resist a price ceiling on agriculture products until farm prices reach 110 percent of parity, based on the 1910-14 ratios, and we will conduct a relationship between the prices of raw commodities and retail prices;

We will end farm program benefits to farm units larger than family-size. . . .

Presidential Elections. We favor a Constitutional change to abolish the Electoral College and to give every voter a direct and equal voice in Presidential elections. The amendment should provide for a runoff election, if no candidate received more than 40 percent of the popular vote.

Republicans

Six weeks after the Democratic convention, the Republicans gathered in the same Miami Beach convention hall. The Aug. 21-23 convention, precisely programmed to make the most of free prime time, was a gigantic television spectacular from start to finish. The main business of the convention, the nomination of President Richard Nixon and Vice President Spiro T. Agnew to a second term, was a carefully planned ritual.

The selection of Miami Beach as the convention city provided as much drama as the convention itself. Initially the Republicans had chosen San Diego, Calif., as the host city, but the reluctance of that city to provide necessary facilities on schedule, coupled with the revelation that the International Telephone and Telegraph Corp. had pledged as much as $400,000 in local contributions, led the Republican National Committee to move the convention to Miami Beach.

Despite the preliminary organizational problems, the atmosphere of the convention itself was almost euphoric, and the sessions proceeded with dispatch. The five sessions lasted only 16 hours and 59 minutes, compared with the 32 hours and 18 minutes of the Democratic convention.

The one debate, which lasted only an hour, occurred over the adoption of new procedures for selecting national convention delegates. The Republican National Committee's preconvention rules committee approved a 1976 delegate-allocation plan initiated by Sen. John G. Tower of Texas and Rep. Jack F. Kemp of New York. The plan emphasized a state's Republican presidential vote in awarding bonus delegates. It was viewed as especially beneficial to small Southern and Western states. The conven-

tion rules committee amended the Tower-Kemp plan to make it more palatable to larger states by adding some bonus delegates for states electing Republican governors and members of Congress.

However, Rep. William A. Steiger of Wisconsin introduced a different plan, weighted more toward states electing Republican governors and members of Congress — a plan that would work to the advantage of the larger states. The debate on the contrasting plans focused on the question of whether states should be rewarded chiefly for delivering their electoral votes to a Republican presidential candidate or whether the bonus should be based to some extent on gubernatorial and congressional contests.

The dispute was in part a battle between liberals and conservatives. Final victory for the conservatives was achieved on a 910-to-434 roll-call vote that defeated the Steiger amendment. The reallocation formula adopted by the delegates would expand the 1976 convention to more than 2,000 delegates, compared with the 1,348 who went to Miami Beach in 1972.

The struggle over the delegate-allocation formula was the only sign of party division at the convention. Nixon was renominated on the third night of the convention, receiving 1,347 of the 1,348 votes. The only opposing vote was cast reluctantly by a delegate from New Mexico for Rep. Paul N. McCloskey Jr. of California, whose anti-war challenge of the president had fizzled after the year's first primary in New Hampshire. *(Chart, p. 214)*

One measure of the unity that surrounded the festive proceedings was the appearance of Gov. Nelson A. Rockefeller of New York to deliver Nixon's nominating speech. Rockefeller had become a loyal supporter of the president after having been his chief rival for the Republican nomination in 1960 and 1968.

Agnew was nominated the next night with 1,345 votes. There were two abstentions and one waggish vote for newscaster David Brinkley.

In his acceptance speech, Nixon combined a review of his first four years with promises for the next four and indirect but highly partisan attacks on his Democratic opponent, George McGovern. Nixon stressed that the choice in the upcoming election was "not between radical change and no change, the choice . . . is between change that works and change that won't work."

The Republican platform provoked little discussion on the convention floor and was approved by a voice vote. Two amendments were offered. The first, which would have pledged a prohibition on deficit federal spending, was defeated by voice vote. The second, advocating self-determination for American Indians, was approved by voice vote with the consent of the platform committee chairman, Rep. John J. Rhodes of Arizona.

The document, approximately 20,000 words long, was generally moderate in its proposals and conservative in language, in contrast to the Democrats' liberal platform.

The actual drafting of the Republican platform was heavily influenced by the White House, and platform committee sessions were held behind closed doors. In contrast, the Democrats held 10 regional hearings around the country, drafted their platform in public and were required by party rules to produce a final version at least 10 days before the convention opened.

The Republican platform was sharply critical not only of McGovern's new leadership of the Democratic Party but also of the Kennedy and Johnson administrations of the "nightmarish" 1960s.

The contrast with the Democratic platform on domestic affairs was stark. The Democrats advocated income redistribution through tax reform and a guaranteed annual income. The Republicans mentioned tax reform but did not include specifics. They rejected the guaranteed income plan.

Both parties called for a reduction in property taxes, although the Republicans made no mention of the value-added tax, a revenue measure the Nixon administration was said to be considering.

The Democrats advocated an immediate end to economic controls; the Republicans proposed to remove the controls "once the economic distortions spawned in the late 1960s are repaired."

The Democrats supported a federally financed and administered national health insurance system, while the Republicans supported a national health insurance plan financed by employers and employees as well as the federal government.

The Republicans opposed busing children to achieve racial balance in schools. The Democrats, however, viewed busing as "another tool" to bring about desegregation. The Republicans supported voluntary school prayer, an issue the Democrats did not mention.

The Republicans opposed legislation on gun control, while the Democrats endorsed a ban on the sale of handguns. The Republicans opposed the legalization of marijuana; the Democrats did not mention the subject in their platform.

Both parties took similar positions on several controversial social issues. The Republicans and Democrats both supported the Equal Rights Amendment to the Constitution, but neither platform specifically mentioned abortion or the rights of homosexuals.

Major differences between the parties were evident in national defense and foreign affairs. The Republicans chided the Democrats for proposing "meat-ax slashes" in the defense budget and charged that their proposals were "worse than misguided; they are dangerous." The Republicans rejected what they described as "a whimpering 'come back America' retreat to isolationism."

The continuing Vietnam War highlighted the foreign policy section. The Republican platform took a swipe at the Democrats by promising that the Nixon administration would not abandon the South Vietnamese or "go begging to Hanoi." If negotiations with North Vietnam failed, the platform promised continuation of the administration's Vietnamization program, gradually phasing out American involvement in the war. But before the remaining United States troops would be withdrawn, the Republicans declared, there must be a return of prisoners of war and an accounting of those missing in action. The Republicans opposed any form of amnesty.

The Republicans pledged to maintain an adequate nuclear deterrent, to help other nations develop the capability to defend themselves, to honor treaty commitments and to defend American interests but limit involvement when American interests were not involved.

The Democrats had taken a stronger stand than in previous platforms against what they considered misguided American support for repressive regimes throughout the world. In addition, the Democrats argued for re-examination of the hostile United States policy toward Cuba.

Following are excerpts from the Republican platform of 1972:

Foreign Policy. Historians may well regard these years as a golden age of American diplomacy. Never before

has our country negotiated with so many nations on so wide a range of subjects — and never with greater success.

Vietnam. We will continue to seek a settlement of the Vietnam War which will permit the people of Southeast Asia to live in peace under political arrangements of their own choosing. We take specific note of the remaining major obstacle to settlement — Hanoi's demand that the United States overthrow the Saigon government and impose a Communist-dominated government on the South Vietnamese. We stand unequivocally at the side of the President in his effort to negotiate honorable terms, and in his refusal to accept terms which would dishonor this country.

Military Spending. To the alarm of free nations everywhere, the New Democratic Left now would undercut our defenses and have America retreat into virtual isolation, leaving us weak in a world still not free of aggression and threats of aggression. We categorically reject this slash-now, beg-later approach to defense policy....

We draw a sharp distinction between prudent reductions in defense spending and the meat-ax slashes with which some Americans are not beguiled by the political opposition.

Vietnam Amnesty. We are proud of the men and women who wear our country's uniform, especially of those who have borne the burden of fighting a difficult and unpopular war. Here and now we reject all proposals to grant amnesty to those who have broken the law by evading military service. We reject the claim that those who fled are more deserving, or obeyed a higher morality, than those next in line who served in their places.

Economy. We have already removed some temporary controls on wages and prices and will remove them all once the economic distortions spawned in the late 1960s are repaired. We are determined to return to an unfettered economy at the earliest possible moment.

We affirm our support for the basic principles of capitalism which underline the private enterprise system of the United States. At a time when a small but dominant faction of the opposition Party is pressing for radical economic schemes which so often have failed around the world, we hold that nothing has done more to help the American people achieve their unmatched standard of living than the free enterprise system.

Tax Reform. We reject the deceitful tax "reform" cynically represented as one that would soak the rich, but in fact one that would sharply raise the taxes of millions of families in middle-income brackets as well. We reject as well the lavish spending promised by the opposition Party which would more than double the present budget of the United States Government. This, too, would cause runaway inflation or force heavy increases in personal taxes.

Gun Control. [We pledge to] safeguard the right of responsible citizens to collect, own and use firearms for legitimate purposes, including hunting, target shooting and self-defense. We will strongly support efforts of all law enforcement agencies to apprehend and prosecute to the limit of the law all those who use firearms in the commission of crimes.

Women's Rights. Continued ... support of the Equal Rights Amendment to the Constitution, our Party being the first national party to back this Amendment.

School Busing. We are irrevocably opposed to busing for racial balance. Such busing fails its stated objective — improved learning opportunities — while it achieves results no one wants — division within communities and hostility between classes and races. We regard it as unnecessary, counter-productive and wrong.

School Prayer. We reaffirm our view that voluntary prayer should be freely permitted in public places — particularly, by school children while attending public schools — provided that such prayers are not prepared or prescribed by the state or any of its political subdivisions and that no person's participation is coerced, thus preserving the traditional separation of church and state.

Education. Our efforts to remedy ancient neglect of disadvantaged groups will continue in universities as well as in society at large, but we distinguish between such efforts and quotas. We believe the imposition of arbitrary quotas in the hiring of faculties or the enrollment of students has no place in our universities; we believe quotas strike at the essence of the university.

Health. To assure access to basic medical care for all our people, we support a program financed by employers, employees and the Federal Government to provide comprehensive health insurance coverage, including insurance against the cost of long-term and catastrophic illnesses and accidents and renal failure which necessitates dialysis, at a cost which all Americans can afford....

We oppose nationalized compulsory health insurance. This approach would at least triple in taxes the amount the average citizen now pays for health and would deny families the right to choose the kind of care they prefer. Ultimately it would lower the overall quality of health care for all Americans.

Welfare. Perhaps nowhere else is there a greater contrast in policy and philosophy than between the Administration's remedy for the welfare ills and the financial orgy proposed by our political opposition....

We flatly oppose programs or policies which embrace the principle of a government-guaranteed income. We reject as unconscionable the idea that all citizens have the right to be supported by the government, regardless of their ability or desire to support themselves and their families.

1976 Conventions

Presidential Candidates

Jimmy Carter
Democrat

Gerald R. Ford
Republican

Democrats

Jimmy Carter, whose presidential primary campaign flouted Democratic Party regulars, brought the party's diverse elements together July 12-15 in a show of unaccustomed unity. The four-day 1976 convention in New York City was the party's most harmonious in 12 years and a stark contrast to the bitter and divisive conventions of 1968 and 1972.

The spirit of harmony was evident in the committee reports. No credentials challenges were carried to the convention floor and just one minority plank to the platform was offered. Only the rules committee report sparked much debate, and it was muted compared with the emotional struggles in the previous two conventions.

The lack of a spirited competition for the presidential nomination was an important factor in the absence of credentials challenges. However, the groundwork for the harmonious atmosphere had been established months earlier, when the Democratic National Committee adopted new delegate-selection and convention rules.

The delegate-selection rules abolished the implicit quota system that had been the basis of most challenges in 1972. The only basis for a challenge in 1976 was the violation of a state's delegate selection or affirmative action plan to ensure the fair representation of minorities. Since all states had their plans approved by the national committee's compliance review commission, the credentials committee was not weighing the fairness of the plan, but merely whether the state party had implemented it. In reverse of the 1972 system, the burden of proof was on the challenging individual or group, not on the state parties.

The task of challengers was further impeded by the action of the national committee in October 1975, raising the petition requirement for convention minority reports from 10 percent to 25 percent of credentials committee members.

The stringent new rules had an effect on the demographic composition of the convention. A post-convention survey by the national committee indicated that 36 percent of the delegates in 1976 were women, compared with 38 percent in 1972; 7 percent were black compared with 15 percent four years earlier and 14 percent were youths,

compared with 21 percent in 1972.

The first roll call of the convention came on a rules committee minority report that would have permitted extended debate on the platform. The measure was promoted by party liberals, who complained that the restrictive convention rules cut off their chance for full debate. They urged platform debate on a maximum of three issues for a total of one hour, if at least 300 delegates from 10 states signed a petition for such issues. The proposal called for debate only; no votes would have been taken.

Carter delegates, though, were nearly unanimous in their opposition, fearing that adoption of the minority report would unduly lengthen the proceedings. The convention rejected the minority report by a vote of 735 to 1,957-1/2. *(Chart, p. 215)*

Liberals had better luck when the rules relating to future conventions were considered. By voice votes, they won approval of majority reports to establish the party's new Judicial Council as an arbiter of party rules and to eliminate the controversial loophole primary.

A loophole primary permitted election of delegates on a winner-take-all basis at the congressional district level. Carter and Democratic National Chairman Robert S. Strauss both favored the minority report, which called simply for review of the loophole primary by the newly established Commission on the Role and Future of Presidential Primaries, headed by Michigan state chairman Morley Winograd.

Liberals argued that this was not enough. They claimed that the loophole primary violated the party charter, which required proportional representation. Their position prevailed in the rules committee by a razor-thin margin of 58-1/2 to 58-1/4. Although Carter managers were unhappy with the majority report, they did not press for a roll call and it was approved by voice vote.

But the convention rejected on roll-call votes liberal amendments to mandate the size and agenda of the party's 1978 mid-term conference and to lower the minority report requirement at future conventions.

The minority report on the 1978 conference would have required a prescribed agenda that included the dis-

cussion of policy matters. It also would have mandated a conference of at least 2,000 delegates, two-thirds of them elected at the congressional district level. On the roll call the proposal ran ahead 1,240 to 1,128, but it failed because of convention rules requiring a constitutional majority of 1,505 votes.

Another roll call came on the unsuccessful attempt by liberal delegates to have the minority report requirement at future conventions lowered from 25 percent to 15 percent of convention committee members. It was rejected, 1,249 to 1,354-1/2. *(Chart, p. 215)*

Potentially the most explosive of the rules issues, regarding a "female quota" at future conventions, was settled in behind-the-scenes meetings between Carter and representatives of the women's caucus.

At a rules committee meeting in Washington, D.C., in late June, the women's caucus had demanded equal representation with men in state delegations at future conventions. The Carter forces balked at this. Carter's views prevailed in the rules committee, which urged each state to promote equal division between the sexes but left the implementation of the rule to each state party. The women's caucus filed a minority report.

Both sides expressed a willingness to compromise, and in New York City July 11 and 12 Carter met with representatives of the women's caucus. They reached a compromise that encouraged — but did not require — equal representation for women at the party's mid-term conference and at future conventions. Language was inserted calling for the national committee to "encourage and assist" state parties in achieving equal division.

The compromise also included agreements between Carter and the women on other questions. Carter promised to establish an independent women's division in the party outside the realm of the chairman and pledged full party representation for women. He promised to work for the ratification of the Equal Rights Amendment and pledged high government positions for women.

With acceptance of this compromise by the women's caucus, the minority report was withdrawn and the compromise language on equal division was worked into the majority report.

Balloting for president came on July 14, the third day of the convention, but it was merely a formality. Carter had locked up the nomination over a month earlier when he won the June 8 Ohio primary, a victory that prompted a cascade of endorsements and stymied his remaining opposition. Besides Carter, three other names were placed in nomination: Rep. Morris K. Udall of Arizona, Carter's most persistent primary challenger; Gov. Edmund G. Brown Jr. of California; and anti-abortion crusader Ellen McCormack. The proceedings, though, turned into a love-feast as Udall before the balloting and Brown afterwards appeared at the convention to declare their support for Carter.

On the presidential roll call, Carter received 2,238-1/2 of the convention's 3,008 votes, topping the needed majority little more than halfway through the balloting with the vote from Ohio. Udall finished second with 329-1/2 votes, followed by Brown with 300-1/2, Gov. George C. Wallace of Alabama with 57 and McCormack with 22. The rest of the vote was scattered. After completion of the roll call — and vote switches in California, Rhode Island and Louisiana — a motion to make the nomination unanimous was approved by voice vote. *(Chart, p. 215)*

The following morning Carter announced that his choice for vice president was Sen. Walter F. Mondale of Minnesota. Carter noted that it was a difficult decision, admitting that he had changed his mind three times in the previous 30 days.

In explaining his choice, Carter cited Mondale's experience and political philosophy, his concept of the presidency and the preparation Mondale had made for his interview with Carter. Most of all, Carter emphasized compatibility, saying, "It's a very sure feeling that I have."

Mondale was one of seven prospective running mates Carter had personally interviewed. At his home in Plains, Ga., Carter had interviewed, besides Mondale, Sens. Edmund S. Muskie (Maine) and John Glenn (Ohio). At the New York convention he interviewed Sens. Henry M. Jackson (Wash.), Frank Church (Idaho) and Adlai E. Stevenson III (Ill.) and Rep. Peter W. Rodino Jr. (N.J.). Rodino withdrew his name from consideration shortly after his interview.

Like the presidential roll call the previous night, the balloting for vice president on July 15 was a formality. Mondale had only one declared opponent, Gary Benoit, a Massachusetts college student and a Wallace delegate. Two others were nominated but withdrew — Rep. Ronald V. Dellums of California and Vietnam War resister Fritz Efaw of Oklahoma.

Dellums, a black legislator from Berkeley, appeared personally to withdraw his name and used the opportunity to plead with Carter to pay attention to the needs of minorities at home and to Third World aspirations abroad.

On the roll call, Mondale swamped his rivals, receiving 2,817 votes, more than 90 percent of the convention total. Retiring House Speaker Carl Albert (Okla.) finished a distant second with 36 votes, all cast as a complimentary gesture by his home state delegation. Rep. Barbara C. Jordan (Texas), the black congresswoman from Houston, followed with 24-1/2 votes, an apparent tribute to her dramatic keynote address.

Following the balloting, Mondale delivered his acceptance speech and succeeded in arousing the delegates with a partisan oratorical style reminiscent of his Minnesota mentor, Sen. Hubert H. Humphrey.

"We have just lived through the worst scandal in American history," Mondale declared, "and are now led by a president who pardoned the person who did it." His reference to the Watergate affair and to the Nixon pardon brought the delegates to their feet.

Carter's acceptance speech, unlike Mondale's, was not a rousing one in the traditional sense. But Carter was able to begin his address before 11 p.m., in the prime television slot that Strauss had promised as a contrast to George McGovern's nearly unheard 3 a.m. acceptance speech in 1972. Carter's speech ranged across a variety of issues and featured at least a few lines for those at different ends of the political spectrum.

The 1976 platform had been carefully constructed by the Carter forces at platform committee meetings in Washington, D.C., in June. The 90-page document was something of a throwback to earlier years — a broad statement of party goals rather than a list of legislative programs and controversial stands on issues.

The platform and the care with which it was written reflected the Democrats' determination to avoid the platform fights and issues that proved costly to the party in the previous two elections. The 1968 Vietnam plank approved on the convention floor had split the party so badly that many anti-war Democrats refused to support nominee Hubert H. Humphrey. The 1972 platform, probably the longest (about 25,000 words) and most liberal ever offered by a major party, covered too many issues in elaborate detail. It

provided Republicans with free ammunition, such as the damaging charge that Democrats in 1972 favored "amnesty, acid and abortion."

Unlike 1972, when there was sharp, divisive debate on 20 minority planks, only one minority plank — on revising the 1939 Hatch Act to allow federal employees to run for political office and participate in partisan activity campaigns — was presented to the delegates in Madison Square Garden. It was approved by the Carter forces and was adopted by a voice vote after minimal debate.

Major goals outlined in the rest of the platform:

● A target of 3 percent unemployment within four years.

● A phased-in national health insurance system to be supported through payroll deductions and other federal tax revenues.

● Gradual replacement of federal-state welfare systems with a federal system of income maintenance for recipients who accepted jobs or job training.

● "Full and complete pardon" for Vietnam War resisters, and case-by-case judgment for military deserters.

● Prohibitions against control of multiple energy resources by major oil companies.

● Strategic arms limitation agreements with the Soviet Union "emphasizing mutual reductions."

Following are excerpts from the Democratic platform of 1976:

Full Employment. We have met the goals of full employment with stable prices in the past and can do it again. The Democratic Party is committed to the right of all adult Americans willing, able and seeking work to have opportunities for useful jobs at living wages. To make that commitment meaningful, we pledge ourselves to the support of legislation that will make every responsible effort to reduce adult unemployment to 3 percent within 4 years.

Consistent and coherent economic policy required federal anti-recession grant programs to state and local government, accompanied by public employment, public works projects and direct stimulus to the private sector. In each case, the programs should be phased in automatically when unemployment rises and phased out as it declines.

Inflation. At times, direct government involvement in wage and price decisions may be required to ensure price stability. But we do not believe that such involvement requires a comprehensive system of mandatory controls at this time.

Government Reform. The Democratic Party is committed to the adoption of reforms such as zero-based budgeting, mandatory reorganization timetables, and sunset laws which do not jeopardize the implementation of basic human and political rights.

An Office of Citizen Advocacy should be established as part of the executive branch, independent of any agency, with full access to agency records and with both the power and the responsibility to investigate complaints.

We support the revision of the Hatch Act so as to extend to federal workers the same political rights enjoyed by other Americans as a birthright, while still protecting the Civil Service from political abuse.

We call for legislative action to provide for partial public financing on a matching basis of the congressional elections, and the exploration of further reforms to insure the integrity of the electoral process.

Health. We need a comprehensive national health insurance system with universal and mandatory coverage. Such a national health insurance system should be financed by a combination of employer-employee shared payroll taxes and general tax revenues. Consideration should be given to developing a means of support for national health insurance that taxes all forms of economic income.

Welfare Reform. We should move toward replacement of our existing inadequate and wasteful system with a simplified system of income maintenance, substantially financed by the federal government, which includes a requirement that those able to work be provided with appropriate available jobs or job training opportunities. Those persons who are physically able to work (other than mothers with dependent children) should be required to accept appropriate available jobs or job training.

As an interim step, and as a means of providing immediate federal fiscal relief to state and local governments, local governments should no longer be required to bear the burden of welfare costs. Further, there should be a phased reduction in the states' share of welfare costs.

Civil Rights and Liberties. .... [W]e pledge vigorous federal programs and policies of compensatory opportunity to remedy for many Americans the generations of injustice and deprivation; and full funding of programs to secure the implementation and enforcement of civil rights.

We seek ratification of the Equal Rights Amendment, to insure that sex discrimination in all its forms will be ended, implementation of Title IX, and elimination of discrimination against women in all federal programs.

We pledge effective and vigorous action to protect citizens' privacy from bureaucratic and technological intrusions, such as wiretapping and bugging without judicial scrutiny and supervision; and a full and complete pardon for those who are in legal or financial jeopardy because of their peaceful opposition to the Vietnam War, with deserters to be considered on a case-by-case basis.

We fully recognize the religious and ethical nature of the concerns which many Americans have on the subject of abortion. We feel, however, that it is undesirable to attempt to amend the U.S. Constitution to overturn the Supreme Court decision in this area.

Education. Mandatory transportation of students beyond their neighborhoods for the purpose of desegregation remains a judicial tool of last resort for the purpose of achieving school desegregation. The Democratic Party will be an active ally of those communities which seek to enhance the quality as well as the integration of educational opportunities. We encourage a variety of other measures, including the redrawing of attendance lines, pairing of schools, use of the "magnet school" concept, strong fair housing enforcement, and other techniques for the achievement of racial and economic integration.

The Party reaffirms its support of public school education. The Party also renews its commitment to the support of a constitutionally acceptable method of providing tax aid for the education of all pupils in non-segregated schools in order to insure parental freedom in choosing the best education for their children.

Gun Control. Handguns simplify and intensify violent crime. Ways must be found to curtail the availability of these weapons. The Democratic Party must provide the leadership for a coordinated federal and state effort to strengthen the presently inadequate controls over the manufacture, assembly, distribution and possession of handguns and to ban Saturday night specials.

Furthermore, since people and not guns commit crimes, we support mandatory sentencing for individuals convicted of committing a felony with a gun.

The Democratic Party, however, affirms the right of sportsmen to possess guns for purely hunting and target-shooting purposes.

Energy. The Democratic energy platform begins with a recognition that the federal government has an important role to play in insuring the nation's energy future, and that it must be given the tools it needs to protect the economy and the nation's consumers from arbitrary and excessive energy price increases and help the nation embark on a

massive domestic energy program focusing on conservation, coal conversion, exploration and development of new technologies to insure an adequate short-term and long-term supply of energy for the nation's needs.

The pricing of new natural gas is in need of reform. We should narrow the gap between oil and natural gas prices with new natural gas ceiling prices that maximize production and investment while protecting the economy and the consumer.

Strip mining legislation designed to protect and restore the environment, while ending the uncertainty over the rules governing future coal mining, must be enacted.

The huge reserves of oil, gas and coal on federal territory, including the outer continental shelf, belong to all the people. The Republicans have pursued leasing policies which give the public treasury the least benefit and the energy industry the most benefit from these public resources. Consistent with environmentally sound practices, new leasing procedures must be adopted to correct these policies, as well as insure the timely development of existing leases.

U.S. dependence on nuclear power should be kept to the minimum necessary to meet our needs. We should apply stronger safety standards as we regulate its use. And we must be honest with our people concerning its problems and dangers as well as its benefits.

When competition inadequate to insure free markets and maximum benefit to American consumers exists, we support effective restrictions on the right of major companies to own all phases of the oil industry.

We also support the legal prohibition against corporate ownership of competing types of energy, such as oil and coal. We believe such "horizontal" concentration of economic power to be dangerous both to the national interest and to the functioning of the competitive system.

Establishment of a more orderly system for setting energy goals and developing programs for reaching those goals should be undertaken. The current proliferation of energy jurisdictions among many executive agencies underscores the need for a more coordinated system. Such a system should be undertaken, and provide for centralization of overall energy planning in a specific executive agency and an assessment of the capital needs for all priority programs to increase production and conservation of energy.

Environment. The Democratic Party's strong commitment to environmental quality is based on its conviction that environmental protection is not simply an aesthetic goal, but is necessary to achieve a more just society. Cleaning up air and water supplies and controlling the proliferation of dangerous chemicals is a necessary part of a successful national health program. Protecting the worker from workplace hazards is a key element of our full employment program.

Federal environmental anti-pollution requirement programs should be as uniform as possible to eliminate economic discrimination. A vigorous program with national minimum environmental standards fully implemented, recognizing basic regional differences, will ensure that states and workers are not penalized by pursuing environmental programs.

Foreign Policy. Eight years of Nixon-Ford diplomacy have left our nation isolated abroad and divided at home. Policies have been developed and applied secretly and arbitrarily by the executive department from the time of secret bombing in Cambodia to recent covert assistance in Angola. They have been policies that relied on ad hoc, unilateral maneuvering, and a balance-of-power diplomacy suited better to the last century than to this one. They have disdained traditional American principles which once earned the respect of other peoples while inspiring our own. Instead of efforts to foster freedom and justice in the world, the Republican administration has built a sorry record of disregard for human rights, manipulative interference in the

internal affairs of other nations, and, frequently, a greater concern for our relations with totalitarian adversaries than with our democratic allies...

We will...actively seek to limit the dangers inherent in the international development of atomic energy and in the proliferation of nuclear weapons.

The United States should not provide aid to any government — anywhere in the world — which uses secret police, detention without charges, and torture to enforce its powers. Exceptions to this policy should be rare, and the aid provided should be limited to that which is absolutely necessary. The United States should be open and unashamed in its exercise of diplomatic efforts to encourage the observance of human rights in countries which receive American aid.

National Defense. To this end, our strategic nuclear forces must provide a strong and credible deterrent to nuclear attack and nuclear blackmail. Our conventional forces must be strong enough to deter aggression in areas whose security is vital to our own. In a manner consistent with these objectives, we should seek those disarmament and arms control agreements which will contribute to mutual reductions in both nuclear and conventional arms.

... [W]ith the proper management, with the proper kind of investment of defense dollars, and with the proper choice of military programs, we believe we can reduce present defense spending by about $5-billion to $7-billion.

In order to provide for a comprehensive review of the B1 test and evaluation program, no decision regarding B-1 production should be made prior to February 1977.

Détente. Our task is to establish U.S.-U.S.S.R. relations on a stable basis, avoiding excesses of both hope and fear. Patience, a clear sense of our own priorities, and a willingness to negotiate specific firm agreements in areas of mutual interest can return balance to relations between the United States and the Soviet Union.

However, in the area of strategic arms limitation, the U.S. should accept only such agreements that would not over-all limit the U.S. to levels of intercontinental strategic forces inferior to the limits provided for the Soviet Union.

Middle East. We shall continue to seek a just and lasting peace in the Middle East. The cornerstone of our policy is a firm commitment to the independence and security of the State of Israel.

We will continue our consistent support of Israel, including sufficient military and economic assistance to maintain Israel's deterrent strength in the region, and the maintenance of U.S. military forces in the Mediterranean adequate to deter military intervention by the Soviet Union.

We will avoid efforts to impose on the region an externally devised formula for settlement, and will provide support for initiatives toward settlement, based on direct face-to-face negotiation between the parties and normalization of relations and a full peace within secure and defensible boundaries.

Asia. We remain a Pacific power with important stakes and objectives in the region, but the Vietnam War has taught us the folly of becoming militarily involved where our vital interests were not at stake.

We reaffirm our commitment to the security of the Republic of Korea, both in itself and as a key to the security of Japan. However, on a prudent and carefully planned basis, we can redeploy, and gradually phase out, the U.S. ground forces, and can withdraw the nuclear weapons now stationed in Korea without endangering that support, as long as our tactical air and naval forces in the region remain strong.

Latin America. We must make clear our revulsion at the systematic violations of basic human rights that have occurred under some Latin American military regimes.

We pledge support for a new Panama Canal treaty, which insures the interests of the United States in that waterway, recognizes the principles already agreed upon, takes into account the interests of the Canal work force, and which will have wide hemispheric support.

Relations with Cuba can only be normalized if Cuba refrains from interference in the internal affairs of the United States, and releases all U.S. citizens currently detained in Cuban prisons and labor camps for political reasons. We can move towards such relations if Cuba abandons its provocative international actions and policies.

Republicans

After four boisterous, raucous and sometimes tearful days, Republicans ended their 1976 national convention on a positive note absent during most of a gathering characterized by strident attacks on the Democrats and the Congress they controlled.

The Republican delegates arrived in Kansas City for the Aug. 16-19 convention more evenly split than they had been since 1952, when Dwight D. Eisenhower edged Sen. Robert A. Taft of Ohio (1939-53) for the GOP nomination. Both President Gerald R. Ford, breaking with tradition, and former California governor Ronald Reagan arrived in town three days before the balloting to continue their pursuit of delegates.

Ford, relying heavily on the prestige of the presidency that sometimes had failed to produce results during the seven-month campaign, invited a number of wavering delegates to his hotel suite in the new Crown Center Hotel while Reagan also courted delegates personally.

Campaign strategists and conservative supporters pursued other maneuvers that either fizzled or could not break Ford's scanty but solid delegate margin. Early in the week, conservative House members tried unsuccessfully to convince New York's senator James L. Buckley, Cons-R, to seek the nomination in an effort to draw off enough votes to deny Ford a first-ballot victory.

By a margin of 111 votes on Aug. 17, the Reagan forces lost the first and probably the most important roll call of the convention. The vote came on a Reagan-sponsored amendment to the rules committee report that would have required all presidential candidates to name their running mates before the presidential balloting the next night.

The idea of a test vote on the vice presidential question was sprung by Reagan's campaign manager, John Sears, barely a week before the convention, when on Aug. 9 he appeared before the rules committee and urged that the proposal be included as Section C of Rule 16. The amendment was clearly aimed at throwing Ford on the defensive, because Reagan had designated Sen. Richard S. Schweiker of Pennsylvania as his running mate on July 26. Under the proposal, failure of a candidate to comply would have freed all delegates from any commitments to vote for him.

The Reagan proposal was handily defeated in the preconvention rules committee, where Ford supporters predominated. But Sears was publicly confident that the Reagan forces could carry the issue on the convention floor. Victory on the rules question, he predicted, would be a steppingstone to Reagan's nomination.

The convention debate and vote on Rule 16C was the focal point of the Aug. 17 session and was treated as such by many in the gallery and on the floor, who interrupted the proceedings several times with loud chanting. Vociferous cheers and boos erupted from the Ford and Reagan sections of the hall as speeches were delivered for or against their positions.

Supporters of the proposals characterized it as a "right-to-know" amendment. "A presidential candidate must tell us who's on his team before we are expected to join him," argued former Missouri representative Thomas B. Curtis, the sponsor of the amendment. "The delegates have the right to be consulted for a day of decision that will have an impact for years to come."

Speakers against the amendment countered that it was solely a maneuver of the Reagan forces and that any vice presidential selection reform should be deliberately considered on its merits.

Reagan forces held the lead throughout the early going on the roll-call vote, but they lost the advantage about halfway through when New York voted against the amendment. The final count stood at 1,069 in favor of the amendment and 1,180 against, with 10 abstentions. The vote was the first tangible evidence of Ford strength at the convention and paved the way for his nomination. *(Chart, p. 216)*

None of the other parts of the rules committee report were debated, including the controversial "justice resolution" (Rule 18) that bound delegates elected in primary states according to state law. Fearing a defection of "closet" Reagan delegates in several primary-state delegations, Ford leaders had pushed for the amendment. In contrast to their attitude toward Rule 16C, the Reagan forces did not order a fight on the "justice resolution," although it was extensively debated in committee deliberations. After the roll-call vote on Rule 16C, the rules committee report was adopted by a voice vote.

Whatever enthusiasm the Reagan supporters had lost after their defeat on the vice presidential rule had returned by presidential nominating night, Aug. 18.

Two and one-half hours of the six-hour session were consumed in demonstrations. Reagan's supporters were by far the most boisterous. But it was the Californian's last hurrah of the 1976 Republican convention. On the presidential roll call, Reagan, bolstered by the votes in California and some Deep South states, took a healthy lead. But, as everyone expected, Ford's strength in the big Northeastern states — New York, New Jersey, Pennsylvania, Connecticut, Ohio — and others such as Minnesota and Illinois pushed Ford ahead.

There was a pause as the Virginia delegation was individually polled. Then West Virginia, voting 20 to 8 in favor of Ford, put the president over the top.

The final vote was 1,187 for Ford, 1,070 for Reagan, one vote from the New York delegation for Commerce Secretary Elliot L. Richardson and one abstention. *(Chart, p. 216)*

On a voice vote the convention made the nomination unanimous.

Ford added to the partisan style of the Republican ticket the next day by selecting Sen. Robert Dole of Kansas as his running mate after Reagan ruled out his acceptance of the second spot. While little mentioned during speculation about Ford's vice presidential choice, Dole, a former chairman of the Republican National Committee, was seen as an effective gut fighter who would allow Ford to keep his campaign style presidential in the battle against Carter.

Vice President Nelson A. Rockefeller nominated his own potential successor, telling the crowd that the Kansas senator not only could stand the heat of political battle, but also could "really dole it out." Rockefeller, unpopular with conservatives, had not sought to continue in the job he had gained through appointment in 1974.

On the vice presidential roll call, Dole received 1,921 of

the convention's 2,259 votes. Sen. Jesse A. Helms of North Carolina, a hero of the conservatives, finished a distant second with 103 votes. The remaining votes were scattered among 29 other "candidates."

Ford's acceptance speech concentrated on his record since taking office in mid-1974 and his future goals. The president took credit for cutting inflation in half, increasing employment to a record level and bringing the country to peace.

He touched several times on the restoration of confidence in the White House and the return of personal integrity to the executive branch of government. His administration, Ford said, had been "open, candid and forthright" from the beginning.

Needling his Democratic challenger, Jimmy Carter, Ford asserted to applause: "My record is one of specifics, not smiles." For the future, Ford promised continued economic recovery, less "impudence" from bureaucracy and a balanced federal budget by 1978. He listed a host of other proposals ranging from tax reform to a sane nuclear policy.

"We will build on performance, not promises; experiences, not expediency; real progress instead of mysterious plans to be revealed in some dim and distant future," Ford said in another reference to Carter.

While primarily positive in tone, Ford's speech did rebuke the Democratic Congress for its passage of bills he had vetoed and its obstruction of his proposals to revise tax rules, restrict busing and overhaul criminal laws.

"My friends, Washington is not the problem — their Congress is the problem," he argued.

Ford diverged from his prepared text to issue a direct challenge to Carter. "I'm ready, eager to go before the American people and debate the real issues face to face with Jimmy Carter," the president said. "The American people have the right to know first-hand exactly where both of us stand."

The 1976 Republican platform was a conservative document, combining restrained compliments toward the Ford administration with frequent and slashing attacks on the Democratic Congress.

Ford and Reagan both praised the platform. Although neither side was entirely happy with the final document, both sides were willing to compromise to avoid splitting the party.

By the time the convention got around to debating the platform the night of Aug. 17, an expected bitter struggle between Ford and Reagan forces had been deflated by the earlier vote on rules. The arena, which had been packed two hours earlier, held a somewhat smaller crowd after midnight. Many Ford delegates in particular, confident that they had won the main event, left while members of the platform committee presented the 65-page document.

Two minority planks were offered, in accordance with platform committee rules that required petitions signed by 25 percent of the members. The first, sponsored by Ann F. Peckham of Wisconsin, called for deleting all platform references to abortion. The committee-approved section supported a constitutional amendment "to restore protection of the right to life of unborn children."

The 12-minute debate on the abortion plank did not split along Ford-Reagan lines. Supporters of the minority report argued that abortion was not a suitable topic for a party document. Opponents insisted that the anti-abortion language should be retained. The minority report was defeated clearly by voice vote, and the language stayed in.

The second minority report, a six-paragraph addition to the foreign policy section, was sponsored by 34 Reagan supporters on the platform committee. Without mentioning names, it criticized President Ford and Secretary of State Henry A. Kissinger for losing public confidence, making secret international agreements and discouraging the hope of freedom for those who do not have it — presumably captive nations.

Many of Ford's supporters, including Rep. John B. Anderson (Ill.) and Senate Minority Leader Hugh Scott (Pa.), earlier had expressed strong opposition to the "morality in foreign policy" plank, as it came to be called. Ford's floor leader, Sen. Robert P. Griffin (Mich.), and Rep. David C. Treen (La.) sought compromise language in informal negotiations on the floor. But the Reagan forces, led by Sen. Helms, were adamant.

Not wishing to offend the Reagan contingent further, Ford's supporters decided not to fight. Sen. Roman L. Hruska (Neb.), chairman of the foreign policy subcommittee announced from the podium that there would be no organized opposition to the plank. It was passed by voice vote. The convention then approved the platform, as amended.

The document reflected the nearly equal influence of President Ford and Ronald Reagan at the convention. It was a traditional Republican blueprint for limited government — a clear contrast with the Democratic platform.

Ordinarily, the platform of the party holding the White House heaps praise on the incumbent president and boasts of the way he has led the nation. The Republican platform did not go that far. With Ford embroiled in a contest for the nomination, the platform writers chose to mention him by name only a few times. Richard Nixon was never mentioned. There were only vague references to Watergate.

The platform's foreign policy planks, over which Ford and Reagan clashed most strongly, praised the record of "two Republican administrations." But they also repeated some of Reagan's campaign criticisms of current foreign policy. Kissinger, a favorite target of the party's conservative wing, was not mentioned.

The domestic planks boasted of reductions in inflation and steered clear of direct government initiatives to reduce unemployment. The president was commended for vetoing 40 bills that would have increased federal spending.

The platform concentrated most of its fire on Congress. The Republicans barely acknowledged their opponent for national leadership, Jimmy Carter. The platform mentioned Carter only once, on the first page.

Following are excerpts from the Republican Party platform of 1976:

Republican Philosophy. — As a general rule we believe that government action should be taken first by the government that resides as close to you as possible. Governments tend to become less responsive to your needs the farther away they are from you. Thus, we prefer local and state government to national government, and decentralized national government wherever possible. The Democrats' Platform repeats the same thing on every page: More government, more spending, more inflation. Compare. This Republican Platform says exactly the opposite — less government, less spending, less inflation. In other words, we want you to retain more of your own money; money that represents the worth of your labors, to use as you see fit for the necessities and conveniences of life.

Economy. We believe it is of paramount importance that the American people understand that the number one destroyer of jobs is inflation.

Republicans hope every American realizes that if we are to permanently eliminate high unemployment, it is

essential to protect the integrity of our money. That means putting an end to deficit spending.

Wage and price controls are not the solution to inflation. They attempt to treat only the symptom — rising prices — not the cause. Historically, controls have always been a dismal failure, and in the end they create only shortages, black markets and higher prices. For these reasons the Republican Party strongly opposes any reimposition of such controls, on a standby basis or otherwise.

Sound job creation can only be accomplished in the private sector of the economy. Americans must not be fooled into accepting government as the employer of last resort.

No nation can spend its way into prosperity; a nation can only spend its way into bankruptcy.

Tax Reform. Simplification should be a major goal of tax reform.

When balanced by expenditure reductions, the personal exemption should be raised to $1,000.

Agriculture. We oppose government-controlled grain reserves, just as we oppose federal regulations that are unrealistic in farm practices, such as those imposed by the Occupational Safety and Health Administration (OSHA) and the Environmental Protection Agency (EPA).

We firmly believe that when the nation asks our farmers to go all out to produce as much as possible for world-wide markets, the government should guarantee them unfettered access to those markets. Our farmers should not be singled out by export controls.

Government Reform. There must be functional realignment of government, instead of the current arrangement by subject areas or constituencies.

Revenue Sharing is an effort to reverse the trend toward centralization. Revenue Sharing must continue without unwarranted federal strictures and regulations.

Block grant programs should be extended to replace many existing categorical health, education, child nutrition and social programs.

While we oppose a uniform national primary, we encourage the concept of regional presidential primaries, which would group those states which voluntarily agree to have presidential primaries in a geographical area on a common date.

. . . [W]e oppose "federal post card registration." The possibilities could not only cheapen our ballot, but in fact threaten the entire electoral process.

We offer these proposals of far-reaching reform:

Public accountability demands that [congressmen] publicly vote on increases on the expenses of their office.

—Elimination of proxy voting which allows Members [of Congress] to record votes in committee without being present for the actual deliberations or vote on a measure.

—Full public disclosure of financial interests by Members [of Congress] and divestiture of those interests which present conflicts of interest.

—Improved lobby disclosure legislation so that the people will know how much money is being spent to influence public officials.

Criminal Justice. Each state should have the power to decide whether it wishes to impose the death penalty for certain crimes. All localities are urged to tighten their bail practices and to review their sentencing and parole procedures.

Gun Control. We support the right of citizens to keep and bear arms. We oppose federal registration of firearms. Mandatory sentences for crimes committed with a lethal weapon are the only effective solution to this problem.

Education. We believe that segregated schools are morally wrong and unconstitutional. However, we oppose forced busing to achieve racial balances in our schools. We believe there are educational advantages for children in attending schools in their own neighborhoods and that the Democrat-controlled Congress has failed to enact legislation to protect this concept.

If Congress continues to fail to act, we would favor consideration of an amendment to the Constitution forbidding the assignment of children to schools on the basis of race.

Local communities wishing to conduct non-sectarian prayers in their public schools should be able to do so. We favor a constitutional amendment to achieve this end.

Health. We support extension of catastrophic illness protection to all who cannot obtain it. We should utilize our private health insurance system to assure adequate protection for those who do not have it. Such an approach will eliminate the red tape and high bureaucratic costs inevitable in a comprehensive national program.

The Republican Party opposes compulsory national health insurance.

Civil Rights and Liberties. The Republican Party reaffirms its support for ratification of the Equal Rights Amendment. Our Party was the first national party to endorse the E.R.A. in 1940. We continue to believe its ratification is essential to insure equal rights for all Americans.

The Republican Party favors a continuance of the public dialogue on abortion and supports the efforts of those who seek enactment of a constitutional amendment to restore protection of the right to life for unborn children.

Labor. Union membership as a condition of employment has been regulated by state law under Section 14(b) of the Taft-Hartley Act. This basic right should continue to be determined by the states. We oppose strikes by federal employees, the unionization of our military forces and the legalization of common-situs picketing.

Employees of the federal government should not engage in partisan politics. The Civil Service System must remain nonpartisan and nonpolitical. The Hatch Act now protects federal employees; we insist that it be uniformly administered.

Welfare Reform. We oppose federalizing the welfare system; local levels of government are most aware of the needs of their communities.

We also oppose the guaranteed annual income concept or any programs that reduce the incentive to work.

Those features of the present law, particularly the food stamp program, that draw into assistance programs people who are capable of paying for their own needs should be corrected. The humanitarian purpose of such programs must not be corrupted by eligibility loopholes.

Transportation. In keeping with the local goal setting in transportation, the Republican Party applauds the system under which state and local governments can divert funds from interstate highway mileage not essential to interstate commerce or national defense to other, more pressing community needs, such as urban mass transit.

Energy. One fact should now be clear: We must reduce sharply our dependence on other nations for energy and strive to achieve energy independence at the earliest possible date. We cannot allow the economic destiny and international policy of the United States to be dictated by the sovereign powers that control major portions of the world's petroleum supplies.

We must immediately eliminate price controls on oil and newly-discovered natural gas in order to increase supply, and to provide the capital that is needed to finance further exploration and development of domestic hydrocarbon reserves.

At this critical time, the Democrats have characteristically resorted to political demagoguery seeking short-term political gain at the expense of the long-term national interest. They object to the petroleum industry making any

profit. The petroleum industry is an important segment of our economy and is entitled to reasonable profits to permit further exploration and development.

Now, the Democrats proposed to dismember the American oil industry. We vigorously oppose such divestiture of oil companies — a move which would surely result in higher energy costs, inefficiency and under-capitalization of the industry.

The uncertainties of governmental regulation regarding the mining, transportation and use of coal must be removed and a policy established which will assure that governmental restraints, other than proper environmental controls, do not prevent the use of coal. Mined lands must be returned to beneficial use.

Uranium offers the best intermediate solution to America's energy crisis. We support accelerated use of nuclear energy through processes that have been proven safe.

Environment. We are in complete accord with the recent Supreme Court decision on air pollution that allows the level of government closest to the problem and the solution to establish and apply appropriate air quality standards.

We are determined to preserve land use planning as a unique responsibility of state and local government.

Foreign Policy. We recognize and commend that great beacon of human courage and morality, Alexander Solzhenitsyn, for his compelling message that we must face the world with no illusions about the nature of tyranny. Ours will be a foreign policy that keeps this ever in mind.

Ours will be a foreign policy which recognizes that in international negotiations we must make no undue concessions; that in pursuing détente we must not grant unilateral favors with only the hope of getting future favors in return.

Agreements that are negotiated, such as the one signed in Helsinki, must not take from those who do not have freedom the hope of one day gaining it.

Finally, we are firmly committed to a foreign policy in which secret agreements, hidden from our people, will have no part.

National Defense. A superior national defense is the fundamental condition for a secure America and for peace and freedom for the world. Military strength is the path to peace. A sound foreign policy must be rooted in a superior defense capability, and both must be perceived as a deterrent to aggression and supportive of our national interests.

As a necessary component of our long-range strategy, we will produce and deploy the B-1 bomber in a timely manner, allowing us to retain air superiority.

Security assistance programs are important to our allies and we will continue to strengthen their efforts at self-defense.

Asia. The United States is indisputably a Pacific power. Japan will remain the main pillar of our Asian policy. United States troops will be maintained in Korea so long as there exists the possibility of renewed aggression from North Korea.

We recognize that there is a wide divergence of opinion concerning Vietnam, but we pledge that American troops will never again be committed for the purpose of our own defense, or the defense of those to whom we are committed by treaty or other solemn agreements, without the clear purpose of achieving our stated diplomatic and military objectives.

The United States will fulfill and keep its commitments, such as the mutual defense treaty with the Republic of China.

Latin America. By continuing its policies of exporting subversion and violence, Cuba remains outside the Inter-American family of nations. We condemn attempts by the Cuban dictatorship to intervene in the affairs of other nations; and, as long as such conduct continues, it shall remain ineligible for admission to the Organization of American States.

The United States intends that the Panama Canal be preserved as an international waterway for the ships of all nations. This secure access is enhanced by a relationship which commands the respect of Americans and Panamanians and benefits the people of both countries. In any talks with Panama, however, the United States negotiators should in no way cede, dilute, forfeit, negotiate or transfer any rights, power, authority, jurisdiction, territory or property that are necessary for the protection and security of the United States and the entire Western Hemisphere.

Middle East. Our policy must remain one of decisive support for the security and integrity of Israel.

At the same time, Republican Administrations have succeeded in reestablishing communication with the Arab countries, and have made extensive progress in our diplomatic and commercial relations with the more moderate Arab nations.

Because we have such fundamental interests in the Middle East, it will be our policy to continue our efforts to maintain the balance of power in the Mediterranean region.

Détente. American foreign policy must be based upon a realistic assessment of the Communist challenge in the world. It is clear that the perimeters of freedom continue to shrink throughout the world in the face of the Communist challenge.

Thus our relations with the Soviet Union will be guided by solid principles. We will maintain our strategic and conventional forces; we will oppose the deployment of Soviet power for unilateral advantages or political and territorial expansion; we will never tolerate a shift against us in the strategic balance; and we will remain firm in the face of pressure, while at the same time expressing our willingness to work on the basis of strict reciprocity toward new agreements which will help achieve peace and stability.

United Nations. The political character of the United Nations has become complex. With 144 sovereign members, the U.N. experiences problems associated with a large, sometimes cumbersome and diverse body.

The United States does not wish to dictate to the U.N., yet we do have every right to expect and insist that scrupulous care be given to the rights of all members. Steamroller techniques for advancing discriminatory actions will be opposed.

The United States will continue to be a firm supporter and defender of any nation subjected to such outrageous assaults. We will not accept ideological abuses in the United States.

1980 Conventions

Presidential Candidates

Jimmy Carter
Democrat

Ronald Reagan
Republican

John B. Anderson
Independent

Republicans

Ronald Reagan, the 69-year-old former California governor, was installed as the Republican presidential nominee at the party's national convention in Detroit, but his moment of glory nearly was overshadowed by an unusual flap over the number-two spot. The choosing of Reagan's running mate provided the only suspense at the GOP convention, held July 14-17, 1980, in Detroit's Joe Louis Arena.

Who would fill the number-one spot had been determined long before when Reagan won 28 out of the 34 Republican presidential primaries and eliminated all of his major rivals. The last to withdraw — George Bush — was tapped by Reagan July 16 as his ticket mate in a dramatic post-midnight appearance before the delegates.

For most of the evening of July 16, it looked as though Gerald R. Ford would occupy the second spot on the ticket, which would have made him the first former president to run for vice president. Private polls reportedly had shown that Ford was the only Republican who would enhance Reagan's chances in November. And a number of Republicans had described the combination as a "dream ticket." Groups described as "friends of Ronald Reagan" and "friends of Gerald Ford" had met four times to "discuss" the possibility of forging a Reagan-Ford ticket.

The Ford group consisted of former secretary of state Henry A. Kissinger, former chairman of the Council of Economic Advisers Alan Greenspan, and Ford aides Robert Barnett and John Marsh. The Reagan group was the nucleus of his primary campaign staff: Edwin Meese, campaign director, and Richard Wirthlin, Reagan's pollster. Reagan and Ford first discussed Ford's joining the ticket at a meeting July 15, although no formal offer was made, according to a source close to Reagan. " 'I want you to think this over and then we'll discuss it tomorrow,' " the source quoted Reagan as telling Ford.

The pair met again the following day to continue their discussions, but nothing was resolved. When the convention reconvened at 6:30 p.m., reports began swirling about the floor, many of them spawned by Ford himself, who in two televised interviews gave strong indications that he

would accept the second spot if certain conditions were met.

In an interview with Walter Cronkite of CBS about 7:30 p.m., Ford said, "I would not go to Washington and be a figurehead vice president. If I go to Washington I have to be there in the belief that I would play a meaningful role." Later, in an interview with Barbara Walters of ABC, Ford said he did not want the job unless his role would be "nonceremonial, constructive and responsive." Such an arrangement, he said, would require a "far different structure" from the duties performed by other vice presidents. Asked whether it would be difficult to be a vice president again after having had the top job, Ford said, "Not at all. I'd be more interested in substance than glamor."

Ford declined to spell out what his conditions for taking the job would be, but descriptions of his requirements would have made him in effect co-president with Reagan. The discussions reportedly centered around providing a role for Ford somewhat akin to the White House chief of staff's. In this kind of post he would have had responsibility for agencies such as the Office of Management and Budget, the National Security Council, the domestic policy staff and the Council of Economic Advisers.

Ford further fed the speculation, offering a simple solution to the temporary problem that would have been posed by the 12th Amendment to the Constitution. The amendment would have had the effect of prohibiting the members of the electoral college from California from voting for both Reagan and Ford because both were California residents. The amendment says that the electors from any state must vote for at least one person who is not from that state.

However, nothing in the Constitution would have excluded two residents of the same state from serving as president and vice president or prevented electors from states other than their home state from voting for those two individuals. Ford said Reagan's lawyers had researched the residency question and determined that legally there would be no problem if the former president changed his residence to Michigan, which he represented in the House for 25 years, or to Colorado, where he owned a home.

But Ford expressed reservations about how such a move might be interpreted. "I think it could create in the minds of the American people that we're trying to do something a little cute," he said. "Well, I've never done that in politics. I've got a good reputation and I'm worried about it.... I think it would be construed to be to some extent a gimmick."

As the evening of July 16 wore on, the speculation heightened. "The expectation, as it is presently being reported is it's going through," Gov. William G. Milliken of Michigan said of the Ford candidacy. "I have it on very reliable sources within the Ford camp that it is put together," said Gov. Pierre S. "Pete" du Pont of Delaware.

About 9:15 p.m. Reagan telephoned Ford to ask him to make up his mind whether he wanted the vice president's job. Meanwhile, convention officials proceeded to call the roll of the states. When Reagan received enough votes to become the official nominee, the arena erupted into a cheering, hornblowing, flag-waving, foot-stomping, band-playing demonstration. The noise abated a bit while the roll call was finished, but continued for more than an hour.

But at about 11:15 p.m. the Reagan-Ford arrangement fell apart. Ford went to Reagan's suite in the Detroit Plaza Hotel and the two men agreed that it would be better for Ford to campaign for the GOP ticket rather than be a member of it. "His [Ford's] instinct told him it was not the thing to do," Reagan said later.

When it became apparent that efforts to persuade Ford to join the ticket had failed, Reagan turned to Bush, a moderate with proven vote-getting ability. The Reagan camp refused to acknowledge that Bush was the second choice, even though it was widely perceived that way. "There was everybody else and then the Ford option," Edwin Meese, Reagan's chief of staff, said later.

Bush had been Reagan's most persistent competitor through the long primary season, but he won only six primaries — Michigan, Massachusetts, Connecticut, Pennsylvania, the District of Columbia and Puerto Rico. Bush was one of the vice presidential possibilities favored by those in the party who believed that Reagan had to reach outside the GOP's conservative wing if he were to have broad appeal in November.

Bush supporters said that his background would balance the ticket geographically and that his extensive government service would overcome criticism that Reagan did not have any Washington experience. Bush served from 1967 to 1971 in the U.S. House from Texas and had been ambassador to the United Nations, head of the U.S. liaison office in Peking and director of the Central Intelligence Agency.

Bush's first appearance at the convention earlier had produced a rousing demonstration from supporters throughout the hall, but his strongest support on the floor was in delegations from the Midwest and Northeast, such as New Jersey and the states where he won primary victories.

Reagan's choice of the moderate George Bush was viewed as his first major choice between political pragmatism and ideological purity. Throughout the primary season, Reagan had drawn a large measure of his support from the right wing of the Republican Party and had pledged himself to support conservative economic, social and defense policies. During the convention, Sen. Jesse Helms of North Carolina, the most vocal leader of the GOP's right wing, masterminded the rightward tilt of the party platform to reflect conservative viewpoints. Helms, concerned about the nomination of a moderate such as Bush, threat-ened to place his own name in nomination to put pressure on the GOP standardbearers to abide by conservative and "moral" principles. In the end, Helms supported the Reagan-Bush ticket but warned that it had better support the party's conservative platform. Though Helms was not nominated for vice president, his supporters nonetheless gave him 54 votes. He finished second behind Bush, who got 1,832 votes.

The Republican Party's 1980 platform was more a blueprint for victory in November than a definitive statement of party views. Rather than slug it out over specifics, the party's moderate and conservative wings agreed to blur their differences to appear united, to broaden the party's appeal and to smooth Reagan's way to the White House.

Platform writers veered from traditional Republican positions on a few issues. On others they went out of their way to embrace policies that meshed with Reagan's views more than their own. For the most part, they managed to fashion a policy statement that pleased no party faction entirely but with which all could live reasonably.

Overwhelmingly, platform committee members agreed the document should be basically consistent with Reagan's positions. Thus, though one media poll found delegates overwhelmingly in favor of resuming a peacetime draft, the platform bowed to the view of its nominee and stated its opposition to a renewal of the draft "at this time." In the same manner, the party's platform took no position on ratification of the Equal Rights Amendment (ERA) to the Constitution. Since 1940 Republican platforms had supported an ERA amendment. Reagan, however, opposed ratification, and ERA opponents far outnumbered the amendment's supporters on the platform committee. Yet Reagan, in a gesture to moderates, suggested that the platform not take a position on the issue, and the committee agreed.

Most of the platform document consisted of policy statements on which most Republicans agreed. There were calls for tax cuts, pleas for less government regulation and harsh criticisms of the Carter administration. In two areas, however, the platform took a particularly hard-line position. The platform supported a constitutional amendment that would outlaw abortion and called on a Reagan administration to appoint federal judges who opposed abortion. On defense, platform writers took an already hard-line plank that had been drafted by party staff and moved it sharply to the right. The platform called for massive increases in defense spending and scoffed at the Carter administration's proposed strategic arms limitation treaty (SALT II).

On the other hand, to pick up votes from organized labor, blacks and the poor, the platform made some new overtures to those traditionally non-Republican groups. It pledged to strengthen enforcement of the civil rights laws, made overtures to U.S. workers put out of their jobs by competition from foreign imports and promised to save America's inner cities.

The platform was adopted by the convention July 15 without change, but not before an attempt was made to reopen on the floor one of its more controversial sections. Although party moderates such as Sens. Charles H. Percy, Ill., Charles McC. Mathias Jr., Md., and Jacob K. Javits, N.Y., made little secret of their unhappiness with the platform's failure to reaffirm the party's support for ratification of the ERA, they were particularly chagrined by the section suggesting that Reagan appoint federal judges who oppose abortion. Percy called the section "the worst plank I have ever seen in any platform by the Republican Party."

The moderates July 14 sought to round up support for reopening the platform on the floor, but their efforts failed. In caucuses held early July 15, a number of state delegations including New York and Illinois voted down motions to change the platform's position on abortion.

Nonetheless, as Chairman John J. Rhodes, Ariz., proposed that the convention adopt the platform, Hawaii delegate John Leopold leaped onto a chair to seek Rhodes' recognition. When Rhodes ordered the Hawaii delegation's microphone turned on, Leopold said the group unanimously proposed a motion to suspend the convention rules to permit delegates to "discuss" the platform on the floor. If the rules were suspended, Leopold told reporters, he intended to propose that the language on federal judges be deleted. Not to allow floor discussion of the platform, he said, would be to "railroad" the document through the convention.

Rhodes explained that under convention rules a majority of the members of six state delegations was required to bring a motion to suspend the rules to a vote. He asked if a majority of the delegates from any other state supported Leopold's motion. Only Rep. Silvio O. Conte, chairman of the Massachusetts delegation, rose. But rather than announce support for Leopold's motion, Conte stated only that a majority of his delegation supported a recorded vote on the platform, something Leopold had not proposed. To the applause of many of the delegates, Rhodes then declared that Leopold's motion had failed. The platform subsequently was approved by voice vote.

Ronald Reagan received the Republican nomination on the first ballot. *(Chart, p. 218)*

In his acceptance speech, Reagan combined sharp jabs at the alleged shortcomings of the Carter administration with a reaffirmation of his own conservative credo. Reagan cited three grave threats to the nation's existence — "a disintegrating economy, a weakened defense and an energy policy based on the sharing of scarcity." The culprits, Reagan contended, were President Carter and the Democratic Congress. He said they had preached that the American people needed to tighten their belts. "I utterly reject that view," he declared. Reagan was especially critical of the Democratic administration's conduct of foreign policy. He ridiculed it as weak, vacillating and transparently hypocritical.

Following are excerpts from the Republican Party platform of 1980:

Taxes. . . . [W]e believe it is essential to cut personal tax rates out of fairness to the individual. . . .

Therefore, the Republican Party supports across-the-board reductions in personal income tax rates, phased in over three years, which will reduce tax rates in the range of 14 to 70 percent to a range of from 10 to 50 percent.

. . . Republicans will move to end tax bracket creep caused by inflation. We support tax indexing to protect taxpayers from the automatic tax increases caused when cost-of-living wage increases move them into higher tax brackets.

Welfare. We pledge a system that will:

● provide adequate living standards for the truly needy;

● end welfare fraud by removing ineligibles from the welfare rolls, tightening food stamp eligibility requirements, and ending aid to illegal aliens and the voluntarily unemployed;

● strengthen work incentives, particularly directed at the productive involvement of able-bodied persons in useful community work projects;

● provide educational and vocational incentives to allow recipients to become self-supporting; and

● better coordinate federal efforts with local and state social welfare agencies and strengthen local and state administrative functions.

We oppose federalizing the welfare system; local levels of government are most aware of the needs in their communities. We support a block grant program that will help return control of welfare programs to the states.

Black Americans. During the next four years we are committed to policies that will:

● encourage local governments to designate specific enterprise zones within depressed areas that will promote new jobs, new and expanded businesses and new economic vitality;

● open new opportunities for black men and women to begin small businesses of their own by, among other steps, removing excessive regulations, disincentives for venture capital and other barriers erected by the government;

● bring strong, effective enforcement of federal civil rights statutes, especially those dealing with threats to physical safety and security which have recently been increasing; and

● ensure that the federal government follows a non-discriminatory system of appointments . . . with a careful eye for qualified minority aspirants.

Women's Rights. We acknowledge the legitimate efforts of those who support or oppose ratification of the Equal Rights Amendment.

We reaffirm our Party's historic commitment to equal rights and equality for women.

We support equal rights and equal opportunities for women, without taking away traditional rights of women such as exemption from the military draft. We support the enforcement of all equal opportunity laws and urge the elimination of discrimination against women.

We reaffirm our belief in the traditional role and values of the family in our society. . . . The importance of support for the mother and homemaker in maintaining the values of this country cannot be over-emphasized.

Abortion. While we recognize differing views on this question among Americans in general — and in our own Party — we affirm our support of a constitutional amendment to restore protection of the right to life for unborn children. We also support the Congressional efforts to restrict the use of taxpayers' dollars for abortion.

Education. . . . [T]he Republican Party supports deregulation by the federal government of public education, and encourages the elimination of the federal Department of Education.

We support Republican initiatives in the Congress to restore the right of individuals to participate in voluntary, non-denominational prayer in schools and other public facilities.

. . . [W]e condemn the forced busing of school children to achieve arbitrary racial quotas. . . . It [busing] has failed to improve the quality of education, while diverting funds from programs that could make the difference between success and failure for the poor, the disabled, and minority children.

[W]e reaffirm our support for a system of educational assistance based on tax credits that will in part compensate parents for their financial sacrifices in paying tuition at the elementary, secondary, and post-secondary level.

Health. Republicans unequivocally oppose socialized medicine, in whatever guise it is presented by the Democratic Party. We reject the creation of a national health service and all proposals for compulsory national health insurance.

Older Americans. Social Security is one of this nation's most vital commitments to our senior citizens. We commit the Republican Party to first save, and then strengthen, this fundamental contract between our government and its productive citizens.

... [W]e proudly reaffirm our opposition to mandatory retirement and our long-standing Republican commitment to end the Democrats' earnings limitation upon Social Security benefits. In addition, the Republican Party is strongly opposed to the taxation of Social Security benefits and we pledge to oppose any attempts to tax these benefits.

Crime. We believe that the death penalty serves as an effective deterrent to capital crime and should be applied by the federal government and by states which approve it as an appropriate penalty for certain major crimes.

We believe the right of citizens to keep and bear arms must be preserved. Accordingly, we oppose federal registration of firearms. Mandatory sentences for commission of armed felonies are the most effective means to deter abuse of this right.

Foreign Competition. The Republican Party recognizes the need to provide workers who have lost their jobs because of technological obsolescence or imports the opportunity to adjust to changing economic conditions. In particular, we will seek ways to assist workers threatened by foreign competition.

The Republican Party believes that protectionist tariffs and quotas are detrimental to our economic well-being. Nevertheless, we insist that our trading partners offer our nation the same level of equity, access, and fairness that we have shown them.

Training and Skills. ... [T]he success of federal employment efforts is dependent on private sector participation. It must be recognized as the ultimate location for unsubsidized jobs, as the provider of means to attain this end, and as an active participant in the formulation of employment and training policies on the local and national level.

We urge a reduction of payroll tax rates, a youth differential for the minimum wage, and alleviation of other costs of employment until a young person can be a productive employee.

Fairness to the Employer. The Republican Party declares war on government overregulation.

While we recognize the role of the federal government in establishing certain minimum standards designed to improve the quality of life in America, we reaffirm our conviction that these standards can best be attained through innovative efforts of American business without the federal government mandating the methods of attainment.

OSHA. OSHA should concentrate its resources on encouraging voluntary compliance by employers and monitoring situations where close federal supervision is needed and serious hazards are most likely to occur. OSHA should be required to consult with, advise, and assist businesses in coping with the regulatory burden before imposing any penalty for non-compliance. Small businesses and employers with good safety records should be exempt from safety inspections, and penalties should be increased for those with consistently poor performance.

Agriculture. Republicans will ensure that:
● international trade is conducted on the basis of fair and effective competition and that all imported agricultural products meet the same standards of quality that are required of American producers....
● the future of U.S. agricultural commodities is protected from the economic evils of predatory dumping by other producing nations and that the domestic production of these commodities ... is preserved.
... We believe that agricultural embargoes are only symbolic and are ineffective tools of foreign policy.... The Carter grain embargo should be terminated immediately.

Energy. We are committed to ... a strategy of aggressively boosting the nation's energy supplies; stimulating new energy technology and more efficient energy use; re-storing maximum feasible choice and freedom in the marketplace for energy consumers and producers alike; and eliminating energy shortages and disruptions....

Republicans support a comprehensive program of regulatory reform, improved incentives, and revision of cumbersome and overly stringent Clean Air Act regulations.

We support accelerated use of nuclear energy through technologies that have been proven efficient and safe.

We reject unequivocally punitive gasoline and other energy taxes designed to artificially suppress energy consumption.

A Republican policy of decontrol, development of our domestic energy resources, and incentives for new supply and conservation technologies will substantially reduce our dependence on imported oil.

Republicans will move toward making available all suitable federal lands for multiple use purposes including exploration and production of energy resources.

Environment. We believe that a healthy environment is essential to the present and future well-being of our people, and to sustainable national growth.

At the same time, we believe that it is imperative that environmental laws and regulations be reviewed, and where necessary, reformed to ensure that the benefits achieved justify the costs imposed.

Balanced Budget. If federal spending is reduced as tax cuts are phased in, there will be sufficient budget surpluses to fund the tax cuts, and allow for reasonable growth in necessary program spending.

... We believe a Republican President and a Republican Congress can balance the budget and reduce spending through legislative actions, eliminating the necessity for a Constitutional amendment to compel it. However, if necessary, the Republican Party will seek to adopt a Constitutional amendment to limit federal spending and balance the budget, except in time of national emergency as determined by a two-thirds vote of Congress.

National Security. Republicans commit themselves to an immediate increase in defense spending to be applied judiciously to critically needed programs. We will build toward a sustained defense expenditure sufficient to close the gap with the Soviets. Republicans approve and endorse a national strategy of peace through strength.... The general principles and goals of this strategy would be:
● to inspire, focus, and unite the national will and determination to achieve peace and freedom;
● to achieve overall military and technological superiority over the Soviet Union;
● to create a strategic and civil defense which would protect the American people against nuclear war at least as well as the Soviet population is protected;
● to accept no arms control agreement which in any way jeopardizes the security of the United States or its allies, or which locks the United States into a position of military inferiority;
● to reestablish effective security and intelligence capabilities;
● to pursue positive nonmilitary means to roll back the growth of communism;
● to help our allies and other non-Communist countries defend themselves against Communist aggression; and
● to maintain a strong economy and protect our overseas sources of energy and ... raw materials.

Nuclear Forces. ... We reject the mutual-assured-destruction (MAD) strategy of the Carter Administration.... We propose, instead, a credible strategy which will deter a Soviet attack by the clear capability of our forces to survive and ultimately to destroy Soviet military targets.

A Republican Administration will strive for early modernization of our theater nuclear forces so that a seamless web of deterrence can be maintained against all levels of

attack, and our credibility with our European allies is restored.

National Intelligence. A Republican Administration will seek adequate safeguards to ensure that past abuses will not recur, but we will seek the repeal of ill-considered restrictions sponsored by Democrats, which have debilitated U.S. intelligence capabilities while easing the intelligence collection and subversion efforts of our adversaries.

Arms Control. The Republican approach to arms control has been . . . based on three fundamental premises:

• first, before arms control negotiations may be undertaken, the security of the United States must be assured by the funding and deployment of strong military forces sufficient to deter conflict at any level or to prevail in battle should aggression occur;

• second, negotiations must be conducted on the basis of strict reciprocity of benefits — unilateral restraint by the U.S. has failed to bring reductions by the Soviet Union; and

• third, arms control negotiations, once entered, represent an important political and military undertaking that cannot be divorced from the broader political and military behavior of the parties.

U.S.-Soviet Relations. Republicans believe that the United States can only negotiate with the Soviet Union from a position of unquestioned principle and unquestioned strength.

A Republican Administration will continue to seek to negotiate arms reductions in Soviet strategic weapons, in Soviet bloc force levels in Central Europe, and in other areas that may be amenable to reductions or limitations. We will pursue hard bargaining for equitable, verifiable, and enforceable agreements.

We reaffirm our commitment to press the Soviet Union to implement the United Nations Declaration on Human Rights and the Helsinki Agreements which guarantee rights such as the free interchange of information and the right to emigrate.

Middle East, Persian Gulf. With respect to an ultimate peace settlement, Republicans reject any call for involvement of the PLO as not in keeping with the long-term interests of either Israel or the Palestinian Arabs. The imputation of legitimacy to organizations not yet willing to acknowledge the fundamental right to existence of the State of Israel is wrong.

The sovereignty, security, and integrity of the State of Israel is a moral imperative and serves the strategic interests of the United States. Republicans reaffirm our fundamental and enduring commitment to this principle.

While reemphasizing our commitment to Israel, a Republican Administration will pursue close ties and friendship with moderate Arab states.

The Americas. We deplore the Marxist Sandinista takeover of Nicaragua and the Marxist attempts to destabilize El Salvador, Guatemala, and Honduras. We do not support United States assistance to any Marxist government in this hemisphere and we oppose the Carter Administration aid program for the government of Nicaragua. However, we will support the efforts of the Nicaraguan people to establish a free and independent government.

China. We will strive for the creation of conditions that will foster the peaceful elaboration of our relationship with the People's Republic of China.

At the same time, we deplore the Carter Administration's treatment of Taiwan, our long-time ally and friend. We pledge that our concern for the safety and security of the 17 million people of Taiwan will be constant.

Foreign Aid. No longer should American foreign assistance programs seek to force acceptance of American governmental forms. The principal consideration should be whether or not extending assistance to a nation or group of nations will advance America's interests and objectives.

Decisions to provide military assistance should be made on the basis of U.S. foreign policy objectives. Such assistance to any nation need not imply complete approval of a regime's domestic policy.

Democrats

President Jimmy Carter emerged victorious from a deeply divided Democratic National Convention unsure whether his plea for unity to supporters of rival Sen. Edward M. Kennedy of Massachusetts had succeeded. Kennedy had been Carter's main opponent in his quest for renomination throughout the spring primary season. When it became apparent that Kennedy had not won in the primaries and caucuses the delegate support he needed, he turned his efforts to prying the nomination away from the president at the convention.

Kennedy's presence was strong throughout the convention week and expressions of support for the senator sometimes upstaged those for the incumbent president. Chants of "We want Ted" rocked off the walls of New York's Madison Square Garden during the convention's four days, Aug. 11-14. And their echo faintly followed the president as he left the podium following his acceptance speech. It was a stark reminder that Carter, even though he had captured the nomination and engaged in a series of reconciliation gestures with his rival, still faced the difficult task of rallying a divided party behind his candidacy.

Kennedy's efforts to wrest the nomination from Carter centered around a convention rule that bound delegates to vote on the first ballot for the candidates under whose banner they were elected. When the convention opened, Carter could count 315 more votes than he needed for the nomination — votes that he had won in nominating caucuses and presidential primaries. As a result, Kennedy's only chance to gain the nomination was to defeat the binding rule.

In the week before the convention, negotiators for Carter and Kennedy agreed to one hour of debate on the rules question to begin at 6:30 p.m. Monday, Aug. 11. Kennedy forces had wanted a Tuesday night rules vote, which would have given them an extra day to lobby delegates. But they settled instead for the Monday night debate, which enabled them to argue their case before a prime-time nationwide television audience.

Opponents of the binding rule tried to present a broad-based front. Arguing against the rule on the convention floor were a Carter delegate, two Kennedy backers and two leading uncommitted delegates — New York governor Hugh L. Carey and prominent Washington attorney Edward Bennett Williams, the chief spokesman of the Committee for an Open Convention.

They argued that political conditions had changed since the delegates were elected months earlier and that to bind them would break with a century and a half of Democratic tradition. "For the first time in 150 years, delegates to the national convention are being asked to deliver their final freedom of choice, and to vote themselves into bondage to a candidate," Williams contended. To adopt the binding rule, other speakers added, would make the delegates little more than robots.

But most Carter supporters scoffed at that contention, stressing that delegates were free to vote their conscience on all roll calls but the one for president. Passage of the rule was simply fair play, they added. It had been adopted

in 1978 without opposition by the party's last rules review commission and the Democratic National Committee. Only when it was apparent that Carter was winning, claimed Atlanta mayor Maynard Jackson, did the Kennedy camp want to change the rules to allow a "fifth ball, a fourth out or a tenth inning."

When the measure finally came to a vote, Carter forces turned back the attempt to overturn the proposed rule. The vote was 1,390.580 to 1,936.418 against Kennedy's position. *(Chart p. 217)*

Shortly after the vote, Kennedy ended his nine-month challenge to the president by announcing that his name would not be placed in nomination Aug. 13. Passage of the binding rule assured Carter's renomination.

In addition to its binding-rule objection, the Kennedy camp filed four other minority rules reports, but all were withdrawn before the Aug. 11 session. Three originally had been filed in response to Carter efforts to streamline the convention schedule. At its July meeting in Washington, D.C., the convention rules committee approved proposals to increase the number of signatures required on nominating petitions for president, vice president and convention chairman; to limit to two the number of speakers on each side of each issue of debate; and to allow every roll call, except for president and vice president, to be conducted by telephone while convention business proceeded.

In return for Kennedy's withdrawal of the minority reports, the Carter camp did consent to raise the number of speakers on each issue to three. They also agreed to a Kennedy proposal to add a platform accountability rule that would require each presidential candidate to submit his written views on the party platform along with his pledge to carry it out. The statement would have to be presented shortly after convention consideration of the platform was completed. The Kennedy proposal also called for the candidates' statements to be distributed and read to the delegates.

Despite the loss on the binding rule, the Kennedy camp succeeded in molding the party platform more to their liking. The final document was filled with so many concessions to the Kennedy forces that it won only a half-hearted endorsement from the president. The platform battle, one of the longest in party history, filled 17 hours of debate and roll calls that stretched over two days, Aug. 12 and 13.

Most of Carter's concessions and outright defeats came on the economic and human needs sections of the 40,000-word document. It was these revisions that Carter rejected — as diplomatically as possible — in a statement issued several hours after the debate wound to a close.

In the debate on social issues, Carter lost two roll-call votes — one on adoption of Kennedy's plank calling for jobs to be "our single highest domestic priority," and the other supporting Medicaid funding for abortions. The president also lost a voice vote on a minority report to withhold all party funds and campaign assistance to candidates who did not support the then-pending Equal Rights Amendment to the Constitution.

The only victory posted by Carter in the human needs chapter was over a Kennedy minority report calling for a single, comprehensive national health insurance plan with gradually phased-in benefits. That report was defeated on a 1,409.9-to-1,623.8 vote that came at the start of the platform debate.

It had been clear since the platform was drafted in late June that the economic plank, which contained the major Carter-Kennedy differences, would be the focus of dispute.

When the hour for debate arrived, it was evident that the control Carter had exercised the previous evening on the question of binding delegates had evaporated.

Before the convention began, Carter had yielded to Kennedy language on several issues, including one of the senator's four minority economic reports. That report asserted that a policy of high interest rates and unemployment should not be used to fight inflation. White House domestic affairs adviser Stuart E. Eizenstat announced Aug. 10 that Carter would go along with that amendment — but none of the others in the economy section — because it stated a broad goal while the others called for specific legislation.

The marathon platform debate reached its high point on Tuesday evening, Aug. 12, when Kennedy addressed the delegates on behalf of his minority report on the economic chapter. Kennedy's speech provided the Democratic convention with its most exciting moments. The address, which sparked a 40-minute emotional demonstration when it was over, called for Democratic unity and laced into the Republican nominee, Ronald Reagan.

Kennedy defended his liberal ideology, supporting national health insurance and federal spending to restore deteriorated urban areas. He lashed out at Reagan's proposal for a massive tax cut, labeling it as beneficial only to the wealthy. "For all those whose cares have been our concern the work goes on, the cause endures, the hope still lives and the dream shall never die," concluded Kennedy. Buoyed by the Kennedy oratory, the convention went on to pass by voice vote three liberal Kennedy platform planks on the economy, thereby rejecting the more moderate versions favored by Carter.

The first of the Kennedy-sponsored planks was a statement pledging that fairness would be the overriding principle of the Democrats' economic policy and that no actions would be taken that would "significantly increase" unemployment. The convention next approved a Kennedy plank seeking a $12 billion anti-recession jobs program, a $1 billion rail renewal plan and an expanded housing program for low- and moderate-income families. The final Kennedy economic plank was a statement of opposition to fighting inflation through a policy of high interest rates and unemployment. Carter had agreed to this plank the day before the convention opened.

Carter floor managers realized that it would be difficult to block passage of the Kennedy economic proposals. After the senator's emotion-filled speech, Carter advisers — realizing their position could not prevail — quickly sought to change from a roll call to a voice vote on the economic planks.

During the floor demonstration that followed Kennedy's speech, a series of telephone calls ricocheted between the podium and the senator's campaign trailer located off the convention floor. The negotiations involved how many elements of the Kennedy program would be accepted by voice vote. In the end, Carter prevailed on only one of Kennedy's economic minority reports, the call for an immediate wage and price freeze followed by controls.

Prior to the 1980 convention, Democratic presidential nominees had been able to gloss over their distaste for objectionable portions of the platform. But Kennedy made that difficult to do. In his carefully worded statement following the platform debate, Carter did not flatly reject any of Kennedy's amendments, but he did not embrace them either.

Of Kennedy's $12 billion anti-recession jobs program, Carter said he would "accept and support the intent" of

the program but he refused to commit himself to a specific dollar amount. Responding to Kennedy language that placed a jobs program above all other domestic priorities, Carter wrote, "We must make it clear that to achieve full employment, we must also be successful in our fight against inflation."

Carter treated two women's issues the same way. Responding to adopted language that endorsed federal funding for abortion, the president repeated his personal opposition but said he would be guided by court decisions on the questions. He also reiterated his support for ratification of the Equal Rights Amendment but did not directly comment on the platform language adopted on the floor that prevented the Democratic Party from giving campaign funds to candidates who did not back the amendment.

Carter concluded his statement with the unity refrain that had become the hallmark of every official White House comment on the platform since the drafting process began: "The differences within our party on this platform are small in comparison with the differences between the Republican and Democratic Party platforms." Kennedy apparently agreed. And shortly after Carter's renomination Aug. 13, Kennedy issued a statement endorsing the platform and pledging his support for Carter. In the final moments before adjournment, Kennedy made a stiff and brief appearance on the platform with Carter, Vice President Walter F. Mondale and a host of Democratic officeholders. But the coolness of his appearance — accompanied by the warmest reception of the night — left questionable the commitment of the senator and his supporters to work strenuously for Carter's re-election.

Carter won the Democratic nomination with 2,123 votes compared with Kennedy's 1,150.5. Other candidates split 54.5 votes. *(Chart p. 217)*

In his acceptance speech, Carter alluded to the convention's divisions. He led off with praise for Kennedy's tough campaign, thanks for his concessions during the convention and an appeal for future help. "Ted, your party needs — and I need — you, and your idealism and dedication working for us." Carter spent much of the speech characterizing Reagan's programs as a disastrous "fantasy world" of easy answers. He avoided detailed comments on the economic issues over which he and Kennedy had split, confining himself to statements that he wanted jobs for all who needed them.

As expected, Mondale was renominated for vice president. Two other party members had their names placed in nomination so they could raise the issues of homosexual rights and Carter's decision to reinstitute draft registration. Activist Patricia Simon of Newton, Mass., withdrew after delivering a plea that "we be known as a party of peace." The other candidate was Melvin Boozer of Washington, D.C. Boozer, a number of favorite sons and others received only a smattering of votes and Mondale was nominated by acclamation before that roll call had been completed.

The vice president's acceptance speech set delegates chanting "Not Ronald Reagan" as Mondale reeled off a list of liberal values and programs that, he said, most Americans agreed with. Mondale was one of the few speakers to unequivocally praise Carter's record, which he did at some length. The speech ended with a warning not to "let anyone make us less than what we can be."

Following are excerpts from the Democratic Party platform of 1980:

Employment. We specifically reaffirm our commit-

ment to achieve all the goals of the Humphrey-Hawkins Full Employment Act within the currently prescribed dates in the Act, especially those relating to a joint reduction in unemployment and inflation. Full employment is important to the achievement of a rising standard of living, to the pursuit of sound justice, and to the strength and vitality of America.

Anti-Recession Assistance. A Democratic anti-recession program must recognize that Blacks, Hispanics, other minorities, women, and older workers bear the brunt of recession. We pledge a $12 billion anti-recession jobs program, providing at least 800,000 additional jobs, including full funding of the counter-cyclical assistance program for the cities, a major expansion of the youth employment and training program to give young people in our inner cities new hope, expanded training programs for women and displaced homemakers to give these workers a fair chance in the workplace, and new opportunities for the elderly to contribute their talents and skills.

Tax Reductions. We commit ourselves to targeted tax reductions designed to stimulate production and combat recession as soon as it appears so that tax reductions will not have a disproportionately inflationary effect. We must avoid untargeted tax cuts which would increase inflation.

Federal Spending. Spending restraint must be sensitive to those who look to the federal government for aid and assistance, especially to our nation's workers in times of high unemployment. At the same time, as long as inflationary pressures remain strong, fiscal prudence is essential to avoid destroying the progress made to date in reducing the inflation rate.

Fiscal policy must remain a flexible economic tool. We oppose a Constitutional amendment requiring a balanced budget.

Interest Rates. . . . [W]e must continue to pursue a tough anti-inflationary policy which will lead to an across-the-board reduction in interest rates on loans.

In using monetary policy to fight inflation, the government should be sensitive to the special needs of areas of our economy most affected by high interest rates.

Worker Protection. The Democratic Party will not pursue a policy of high interest rates and unemployment as the means to fight inflation. We will take no action whose effect will be a significant increase in unemployment, no fiscal action, no monetary action, no budgetary action. The Democratic Party remains committed to policies that will not produce high interest rates or high unemployment.

OSHA protections should be properly administered, with the concern of the worker being the highest priority; legislative or administrative efforts to weaken OSHA's basic worker protection responsibilities are unacceptable.

We will continue to oppose a sub-minimum wage for youth and other workers and to support increases in the minimum wage so as to ensure an adequate income for all workers.

Women and the Economy. The Democratic Party . . . commits itself to strong steps to close the wage gap between men and women, to expand child care opportunities for families with working parents, to end the tax discrimination that penalizes married working couples, and to ensure that women can retire in dignity.

We will strictly enforce existing anti-discrimination laws with respect to hiring, pay and promotions. We will adopt a full employment policy, with increased possibilities for part-time work. . . . [W]e will ensure that women in both the public and private sectors are not only paid equally for work which is identical to that performed by men, but are also paid equally for work which is of comparable value to that performed by men.

Human Needs. While we recognize the need for fiscal

restraint ... we pledge as Democrats that for the sole and primary purpose of fiscal restraint alone, we will *not* support reductions in the funding of any program whose purpose is to serve the basic human needs of the most needy in our society — programs such as unemployment, income maintenance, food stamps, and efforts to enhance the educational, nutritional or health needs of children.

Health. The answer to runaway medical costs is not, as Republicans propose, to pour money into a wasteful and inefficient system. The answer is not to cut back on benefits for the elderly and eligibility for the poor. The answer is to enact a comprehensive, universal national health insurance plan.

To meet the goals of a program that will control costs and provide health coverage to every American, the Democratic Party pledges to seek a national health insurance program....

Social Security. The Democratic Party will oppose any effort to tamper with the Social Security system by cutting or taxing benefits as a violation of the contract the American government has made with its people. We hereby make a covenant with the elderly of America that as we have kept the Social Security trust fund sound and solvent in the past, we shall keep it sound and solvent in the years ahead.... We oppose efforts to raise the age at which Social Security benefits will be provided.

Finally, the Democratic Party vehemently opposes all forms of age discrimination and commits itself to eliminating mandatory retirement.

Welfare Reform. As a means of providing immediate federal fiscal relief to state and local governments, the federal government will assume the local government's burden of welfare costs. Further, there should be a phased reduction in the states' share of welfare costs in the immediate future.

We strongly reject the Republican Platform proposal to transfer the responsibility for funding welfare costs entirely to the states. Such a proposal would not only worsen the fiscal situation of state and local governments, but would also lead to reduced benefits and services to those dependent on welfare programs. The Democratic policy is exactly the opposite — to provide greater assistance to state and local governments for their welfare costs and to improve benefits and services....

Education. ... [W]e will continue to support the Department of Education and assist in its all-important educational enterprise....

... The federal government and the states should be encouraged to equalize or take over educational expenses, relieving the overburdened ... taxpayer.

The Democratic Party continues to support programs aimed at achieving communities integrated both in terms of race and economic class.... Mandatory transportation of students beyond their neighborhoods for the purpose of desegregation remains a judicial tool of last resort.

The Party reaffirms its support of public school education and would not support any program or legislation that would create or promote economic, sociological or racial segregation.

The Party accepts its commitment to the support of a constitutionally acceptable method of providing tax aid for the education of all pupils in schools which do not racially discriminate, and excluding so-called segregation academies.

Equal Rights Amendment. ... [T]he Democratic Party must ensure that ERA at last becomes the 27th Amendment to the Constitution. We oppose efforts to rescind ERA in states which have already ratified the amendment, and we shall insist that past rescisions are invalid.

Civil Rights and Liberties. We oppose efforts to undermine the Supreme Court's historic mandate of school desegregation, and we support affirmative action goals to overturn patterns of discrimination in education and employment.

Our commitment to civil rights embraces not only a commitment to legal equality, but a commitment to economic justice as well. It embraces a recognition of the right of every citizen ... to a fair share in our economy.

We call for passage of legislation to charter the purposes, prerogatives, and restraints on the Federal Bureau of Investigation, the Central Intelligence Agency, and other intelligence agencies of government with full protection for the civil rights and liberties of American citizens living at home or abroad. Under no circumstances should American citizens be investigated because of their beliefs.

Abortion. The Democratic Party recognizes reproductive freedom as a fundamental human right. We therefore oppose government interference in the reproductive decisions of Americans, especially those government programs or legislative restrictions that deny poor Americans their right to privacy by funding or advocating one or a limited number of reproductive choices only. Specifically, the Democratic Party opposes ... restrictions on funding for health services for the poor that deny poor women especially the right to exercise a constitutionally-guaranteed right to privacy.

Gun Control. The Democratic Party affirms the right of sportsmen to possess guns for purely hunting and target-shooting purposes. However, handguns simplify and intensify violent crime.... The Democratic Party supports enactment of federal legislation to strengthen the presently inadequate regulations over the manufacture, assembly, distribution, and possession of handguns and to ban "Saturday night specials."

Energy. We must make energy conservation our highest priority, not only to reduce our dependence on foreign oil, but also to guarantee that our children and grandchildren have an adequate supply of energy.

Major new efforts must be launched to develop synthetic and alternative renewable energy sources.

The Democratic Party regards coal as our nation's greatest energy resource. It must play a decisive role in America's energy future.

Oil exploration on federal lands must be accelerated, consistent with environmental protections.

Offshore energy leasing and development should be conditioned on full protection of the environment and marine resources.

Solar energy use must be increased, and strong efforts, including continued financial support, must be undertaken to make certain that we achieve the goal of having solar energy account for 20% of our total energy by the year 2000.

A stand-by gasoline rationing plan must be adopted for use in the event of a serious energy supply interruption.

... Through the federal government's commitment to renewable energy sources and energy efficiency, and as alternative fuels become available in the future, we will retire nuclear power plants....

We must give the highest priority to dealing with the nuclear waste disposal problem.... [E]fforts to develop a safe, environmentally sound nuclear waste disposal plan must be continued and intensified.

Environment. We must move decisively to protect our countryside and our coastline from overdevelopment and mismanagement. ... [P]rotection must be balanced with the need to properly manage and utilize our land resources during the 1980s.

We must develop new and improved working relationships among federal, state, local, tribal, and territorial governments and private interests, to manage effectively our programs for increased domestic energy production and their impact on people, water, air, and the environment in general.

Grain Embargo. Recognizing the patriotic sacrifices made by the American farmer during the agricultural embargo protesting the invasion of Afghanistan, we commend the agricultural community's contribution in the field of foreign affairs. Except in time of war or grave threats to national security, the federal government should impose no future embargoes on agricultural products.

Foreign Policy. The Democratic Administration sought to reconcile ... two requirements of American foreign policy — principle and strength.... We have tried to make clear the continuing importance of American strength in a world of change. Without such strength, there is a genuine risk that global change will deteriorate into anarchy to be exploited by our adversaries' military power. Thus, the revival of American strength has been a central pre-occupation of the Democratic Administration.

The use of American power is necessary as a means of shaping not only a more secure, but also a more decent world.... [W]e must pursue objectives that are moral, that make clear our support for the aspirations of mankind and that are rooted in the ideals of the American people.

That is why the Democrats have stressed human rights. That is why America once again has supported the aspirations of the vast majority of the world's population for greater human justice and freedom.

.. In meeting the dangers of the coming decade the United States will consult closely with our Allies to advance common security and political goals. As a result of annual summit meetings, coordinated economic policies and effective programs of international energy conservation have been fashioned.

... [W]e must continue to improve our relations with the Third World by being sensitive to their legitimate aspirations. The United States should be a positive force for peaceful change in responding to ferment in the Third World.

Our third objective must be peace in the Middle East.... Our nation feels a profound moral obligation to sustain and assure the security of Israel.... Israel is the single democracy, the most stable government, the most strategic asset and our closest ally in the region.

National Security. Our fourth major objective is to strengthen the military security of the United States and our Allies at a time when trends in the military balance have become increasingly adverse. America is now, and will continue to be, the strongest power on earth. It was the Democratic Party's greatest hope that we could, in fact, reduce our military effort. But realities of the world situation, including the unremitting buildup of Soviet military forces, required that we begin early to reverse the decade-long decline in American defense efforts.

Arms Control. ... [T]he Democrats have been and remain committed to arms control, especially to strategic arms limitations, and to maintain a firm and balanced relationship with the Soviet Union.

To avoid the danger to all mankind from an intensification of the strategic arms competition, and to curb a possible acceleration of the nuclear arms race while awaiting the ratification of the SALT II Treaty, we endorse the policy of continuing to take no action which would be inconsistent with its object and purpose, so long as the Soviet Union does likewise.

Arms control and strategic arms limitation are of crucial importance to us and to all other people. The SALT II Agreement is a major accomplishment of the Democratic Administration. It contributes directly to our national security, and we will seek its ratification at the earliest feasible time.

National Unity Campaign

Rep. John B. Anderson of Illinois, a Republican, de-

clared himself an independent candidate for the presidency April 24, 1980, after it became clear that he could not obtain his party's presidential nomination. Anderson created the National Unity Campaign as the vehicle for his third-party candidacy. No party convention was held to select Anderson or to ratify the selection.

On Aug. 25 Anderson announced he had tapped former Wisconsin governor Patrick J. Lucey, a Democrat, to be his running mate. The selection of Lucey was seen as a move by Anderson to attract liberal Democrats disgruntled by President Jimmy Carter's renomination. Anderson's choice of a running mate and the Aug. 30 release of a National Unity Campaign platform helped establish him as a genuine contender in the presidential race.

The 317-page platform put forth specific proposals on a variety of national issues, emphasizing domestic questions. The positions taken generally were fiscally conservative and socially liberal, remaining true to Anderson's "wallet on the right, heart on the left" philosophy.

The platform made clear that Anderson's primary goal was to restore the nation's economic health by adopting fiscal and tax policies that would "generate a substantial pool of investment capital," which then would be used to increase productivity and create jobs. Anderson proposed countercyclical revenue sharing to direct federal funds to areas hardest hit by the election year recession. He rejected mandatory wage and price controls as a cure for inflation, proposing instead a program under which the government would encourage labor and management to work toward agreement on proper levels for wages and prices and use tax incentives to encourage compliance with the standards set. In contrast to both Carter and Reagan, Anderson opposed tax cuts for individuals. He also criticized constitutional amendments to balance the federal budget, saying that while the budget should be balanced "in ordinary times," it could be expected to run a deficit in times of "economic difficulty."

Anderson's energy policy made reducing oil imports the top priority. His platform proposed a 50-cent-a-gallon excise tax on gasoline to discourage consumption, with the revenue to be used to cut Social Security taxes. Anderson favored the decontrol of oil prices begun under Carter and proposed a 40-mile-per-gallon fuel economy standard for new autos.

For American cities, Anderson proposed using about 90 percent of alcohol and tobacco taxes to help build mass transit systems and fight deterioration of public facilities. He also favored offering tax incentives to encourage businesses to locate in blighted urban areas.

In foreign policy, Anderson emphasized strengthening alliances with Western Europe and Japan, resisting Soviet expansion while negotiating "whenever possible" and respecting the sovereignty of Third World nations. His platform supported human rights and humanitarian aid for refugees and disaster victims abroad. He pledged to support the Middle East peace process but opposed the creation of a Palestinian state between Israel and Jordan or U.S. recognition of the Palestine Liberation Organization until the PLO recognized Israel's right to exist.

On defense issues, Anderson opposed development of the MX missile, B-1 bomber and neutron bomb, criticized the arms race and opposed a peacetime draft registration. He pledged to seek ratification of the SALT II treaty negotiated with the Soviet Union, saying that "essential equivalence" existed between U.S. and Soviet missile forces. He opposed a strategy of nuclear superiority,

emphasizing instead the beefing up of conventional military forces.

Following are excerpts from the National Unity Campaign platform of 1980:

Economy. We will construct a Wage-Price Incentives Program. Our administration will invite labor and management leaders to agree upon fair and realistic guidelines and to determine appropriate tax-based incentives to encourage compliance....

In the absence of sharp and prolonged increases in the rate of inflation, we will oppose mandatory wage and price standards.

Youth Unemployment. To deal with the critical problem of youth unemployment, particularly among minorities, we propose: enactment of the proposed Youth Act of 1980 to provide over $2 billion a year for job training and state and local educational programs designed to improve the employability of disadvantaged and out-of-school youth; increased funding for youth career intern programs; a youth opportunity wage incentive that would exempt eligible youths and employers from Social Security taxes during the first months of employment.

Gasoline Tax. We would couple decontrol of oil and gas prices with an excise tax of 50 cents per gallon on gasoline, the full revenues of that tax being returned to individuals through reductions in payroll taxes and increased Social Security benefits.... We will employ tax credits and other incentives to promote substitution of non-petroleum energy for oil, adoption of energy-efficient systems in industry and elsewhere, improvements in transportation and energy production technologies, and development of less wasteful structures for home and commerce.

Nuclear Power. ... [W]e will act on the recommendations of the Rogovin and Kemeny Commissions to make certain that installation of any future plants is preceded by demonstration of satisfactory standards and action on the nuclear waste question. We will assess nuclear power in light of its dependence on public subsidy and of the possibility that slower growth in demand may enable us to phase in other energy supplies in preference to nuclear systems.

Cities. ... [A]n Anderson-Lucey Administration will propose an Urban Reinvestment Trust Fund. Funded through ... revenues from the Federal alcohol and tobacco excise taxes and phased in over three years, it will disburse approximately $3.9 billion annually. It will be used for upgrading, repair and replacement of [urban] capital plant and equipment.

Within our distressed older cities, there are zones of devastation, blighted by crime, arson and population flight.... We favor legislation that would create "enterprise zones" in these areas, by lowering corporate, capital gains, payroll and property taxes and by furnishing new tax incentives....

Environment. We will guard and consolidate the achievements in every field of environmental protection and preservation. We will insist, however, that economic impact studies, assessing not only direct costs but employment and energy implications, accompany proposals for major changes in environmental standards.

Social Issues. We are committed to ratification of the Equal Rights Amendment. We oppose government intrusion in the most intimate of family decisions — the right to bear or not to bear children — and will fight against any constitutional amendment prohibiting abortion. We support public funding of family planning services and other efforts to enable women to find ... alternatives to abortion.

National Defense and Arms Control. In strategic forces, we will maintain a stable balance by preserving essential equivalence with the Soviet Union. To meet an evolving threat to our deterrent, we will modernize and diversify our strategic arsenal.

The growing concern over the threat to fixed, land-based missiles poses an urgent problem to both the United States and the Soviet Union. Economically, environmentally and strategically, the ... cure proposed by the Carter Administration — the MX system — is unsound.

Arms control agreements must enhance our basic security and must not compromise our ability to protect our national interests. Agreements must preserve and reinforce the stability of the strategic balance.... Arms control must be based on adequate, effective verification.

The Western alliance should proceed with its plans to modernize its theater nuclear arsenal; at the same time, we should keep open the possibility of negotiations with the Soviet Union to limit theater nuclear forces.

We favor ... a short-term ... nuclear test ban treaty between the United States, the Soviet Union and the United Kingdom....

For a more effective defense, we will rely heavily on collective security arrangements with our principal allies in NATO and Japan. We will work to reinforce and enhance our historic partnership with our Western European allies.

We will propose to Moscow supplementary measures that could make possible the ratification of the SALT II Treaty and the start of SALT III negotiations. These proposals will respond to concerns expressed in the U.S. Senate regarding such issues as verification and future force reductions.

Middle East. The establishment and maintenance of peace in the Middle East will be an urgent objective.... A lasting settlement must encompass the principles affirmed in the Camp David accords.

Our administration will support the recognition of Palestinian rights as embodied in the Camp David accords, but will oppose the creation of a Palestinian state between Israel and Jordan.

The United States will not recognize or negotiate with the Palestine Liberation Organization unless that organization repudiates terrorism, explicitly recognizes Israel's right to exist in peace and accepts U.N. Security Council Resolutions 242 and 338....

China. ... [T]he Anderson-Lucey Administration would work to discourage antagonism between Russia and China. We should not become an arms supplier to China. We should work for better understanding by China's leaders of the consequences of nuclear war, of measures that should be taken to guard against accidental war and of ways to make the nuclear balance more stable.

Finally, our administration would abide by both the letter and spirit of the Taiwan Relations Act. We would maintain our contacts with Taiwan but would not establish official relations with its government.

1984 Conventions

Presidential Candidates

Walter F. Mondale
Democrat

Ronald Reagan
Republican

Democrats

Ending a long and difficult nomination campaign with a display of party unity and a historic vice presidential choice, Walter F. Mondale used the 1984 Democratic convention to sound the opening themes of his challenge to President Ronald Reagan: family, fairness, the flag and the future.

Accepting their nominations July 19 before cheering, flag-waving delegates at the San Francisco convention, the presidential candidate and his running mate, Rep. Geraldine A. Ferraro of New York, served notice that they would hold Reagan to account for his policies in their uphill battle to capture the White House. "Here is the truth about the [nation's] future," Mondale told the Democrats as they wrapped up their four-day convention. "We are living on borrowed money and borrowed time."

The spectacle of Mondale and Ferraro, with their families, celebrating with delegates in the jammed Moscone Center capped a week in which the Democrats came together to choose their ticket and shore up party unity. Toward that end, the convention succeeded to a greater degree than had seemed possible when the former vice president was battling Sen. Gary Hart of Colorado and the Rev. Jesse Jackson in the primaries and caucuses. There was little acrimony over consideration of the party platform. And, once Mondale was nominated, the three rivals seemed to put aside their most visible differences.

The 56-year-old Minnesotan had been the apparent winner since the final round of primaries on June 5, when he took New Jersey, which gave him the 1,967 pledged delegates needed to take the nomination. Mondale finished the convention balloting with nearly 1,000 votes more than Hart, his closest competitor, yet he was by no means the overwhelming choice. He polled 2,191 votes — about 55 percent of a possible 3,933. *(Chart, p. 220)*

Fears that radical and homosexual elements in San Francisco would stage massive confrontations in the streets outside the convention center — evoking memories of the party's 1968 catastrophe in Chicago — did not materialize. Except for a few minor clashes between crowds and the police, there were no violent incidents. Several hundred thousand homosexuals and labor union members marched

peacefully in separate demonstrations July 15, and protestors representing a variety of causes gathered throughout convention week in the giant parking lot across the street from the convention center.

The Democratic unity displayed in San Francisco — so different from the 1980 convention, when the struggle between President Jimmy Carter and Sen. Edward M. Kennedy of Massachusetts left the party torn and battered — was due largely to delegates' deeply felt antipathy to the policies of the Reagan administration. The unusual harmony was also due, at least in part, to Gov. Mario M. Cuomo of New York, who electrified delegates with his keynote address on the opening night, July 16. In an eloquent appeal for family values and compassion for the poor, he set the tone for the rest of the convention. His speech was rivaled in intensity only by Ferraro's nomination by acclamation July 19 and an impassioned speech given by Jackson on July 17.

Speaking forcefully but without dramatic oratorical flourishes, and repeatedly interrupted by emotional applause, Cuomo combined an appeal to Democratic traditions with specific attacks on the domestic and foreign policies of the Reagan administration. Noting Reagan's reference to America as "a shining city on a hill," Cuomo said that "the hard truth is that not everyone is sharing in this city's splendor and glory. There is despair, Mr. President, in the faces that you don't see, in the places that you don't visit in your shining city."

The product of weeks of intensive work by the candidate and a team of advisers, Mondale's acceptance speech July 19 was a carefully drawn outline for his campaign against Reagan. Although the former vice president had been criticized for lacking speech-making flair during the nomination campaign, he repeatedly brought delegates to their feet during his address.

To introduce Mondale, the party turned to Kennedy, one of its most effective practitioners of rousing oratory. Kennedy's booming voice filled the hall with denunciations of Reagan and the Republican Party, which he called a "cold citadel of privilege."

"By his choice of Geraldine Ferraro, Walter Mondale has already done more for this country in one short day

than Ronald Reagan has done in four long years in office," he said, as delegates cheered and stomped their feet.

Shortly before Mondale's address, aides had passed out thousands of small American flags to delegates, so the crowd was a sea of red, white and blue when the former vice president arrived on the podium.

Pledging a government of "new realism" that would combine strong but conciliatory foreign policies with tough economic initiatives, Mondale vowed in his address to squeeze the budget and raise taxes to reduce soaring deficits, then approaching $200 billion a year. "Let's tell the truth. . . . Mr. Reagan will raise taxes, and so will I," Mondale said. "He won't tell you. I just did."

To Ferraro, the first woman put on the national ticket by a major party, her nomination by acclamation was a special honor. Quoting the late Rev. Martin Luther King Jr., she said that " 'Occasionally in life there are moments which cannot be completely explained in words. Their meaning can only be articulated by the inaudible language of the heart.' Tonight is such a moment for me. My heart is filled with pride."

The platform adopted at the convention created few divisions in the party, but few candidates were enthusiastic about using it in their fall campaigns. Adopted in an emphatic but seldom angry four-hour debate July 17, the platform drew heavily from Mondale's campaign themes. It also contained significant contributions from Hart and Jackson.

The process of assembling the platform was an important exercise for the party. In four months of hearings and drafting sessions, the Democrats invited dozens of interest groups to weave their goals and ideals into the platform. The variegated document became a symbol of the party's all-inclusive philosophy, as it grew to roughly 45,000 words after countless pressure groups had their say.

The final draft was loyal to traditional Democratic ideology, with commitments to unions, blacks, feminists, the poor, environmentalists and other liberal constituencies. But it also included new ideas from the party's younger generation, especially on economic policy. The platform did not call for major new social spending, making it economically more conservative than Democratic documents of the previous 50 years. But in its support for homosexual rights, the availability of abortions and other social issues, it was more liberal than earlier platforms.

The platform's central theme was an attack on the Reagan administration. The document indicted the president's record on topics ranging from budget deficits to civil rights to arms control, and it laid out what Democrats proposed as an alternative.

Besides giving a voice to the various interest groups that composed the Democratic Party, the 1984 platform also was a vehicle designed to unite the three presidential contenders. Negotiations continued up to the last minute on the five minority planks presented to the convention delegates July 17 by Jackson and Hart. But Mondale's forces demonstrated a firm grip on the delegates, soundly defeating Jackson planks on defense spending, "no first use" of nuclear weapons and runoff primaries. Mondale accepted Hart's plank restricting the use of U.S. troops overseas. Mondale also compromised on a Jackson plank outlining the party's affirmative action policy.

One person conspicuously absent from the convention platform debate was Ferraro, who chaired the committee that produced the document. Ferraro was to run the program July 17 — until Mondale asked her to be his running mate. When asked why Ferraro was not handling the plat-

form, Mondale quipped, "There's been a somewhat altered change in Mrs. Ferraro's professional plans over the next eight years."

The debate on the five minority planks was lackluster compared with the heated platform struggles between Carter and Kennedy at the 1980 convention. The first sign that Mondale would surmount the Jackson challenges came on the "no-first-use" plank. After a brief debate, it was defeated, with 1,405.7 delegates voting for it and 2,216.3 against. *(Chart, p. 219)*

As adopted by the platform committee June 23, the document said a Democratic president would "move toward" a policy in which the United States would not initiate a nuclear attack. Jackson supporters said it was "morally and militarily insane" even to consider using nuclear weapons, but Mondale's backers said the arms control language in the platform was strong enough. Also, Mondale argued that the North Atlantic Treaty Organization's conventional forces needed to be strengthened before the United States could adopt a "no-first-use" stance.

In contrast to the opposition to Jackson's national security planks, Hart's "peace plank" was readily accepted by Mondale. Delegates adopted it, 3,271.8 to 351.2. The plank delineated conditions under which a Democratic president would not "hazard American lives or engage in unilateral military involvement" abroad. It was dubbed the Persian Gulf—Central America plank, because the underlying message was that U.S. troops should not be sent to those regions unless American objectives were clear and diplomatic efforts had been exhausted.

Mondale's supporters opposed the plank when the platform committee considered it in June. At that time they said the plank would put a Democratic president "in a political or diplomatic straitjacket." But Mondale softened his stand in San Francisco. By accepting the plank, Mondale also hoped to distinguish Democratic foreign policy from Reagan's "saber-rattling" international agenda, as one Mondale supporter put it.

Jackson's two other minority reports dealt with issues of special interest to his black constituency: runoff primaries in the South and affirmative action. His call to abolish runoff primaries was defeated, but a compromise version of the affirmative action plank was accepted.

Ten Southern states used runoff primaries when no candidate received a majority in the first primary. Jackson claimed these second elections diluted minority voting strength because white voters often reverted to racial loyalty when a runoff choice was between a white and a black candidate. Supporters of second primaries argued that they prevented the nomination of fringe candidates who could receive a plurality in first-round primaries when more credible candidates split the vote. There also was strong sentiment against Jackson's plank from conservative Southerners who did not want the national party dictating their state election procedures.

Mondale's language pledged to eliminate discriminatory barriers to full voting rights. It also promised an indepth study of runoff primaries and other voting practices that could discriminate against minorities.

The other dispute was whether the platform should reject the use of quotas to overturn discrimination in employment and education. As adopted in June, the platform specifically rejected quotas but called for affirmative action goals and timetables to end discrimination in hiring, promotions and education.

Following are excerpts from the Democratic platform of 1984:

Budget Deficits. . . . The Democratic Party is pledged to reducing these intolerable deficits. We will reassess defense expenditures; create a tax system that is both adequate and fair; control skyrocketing health costs without sacrificing quality of care; and eliminate other unnecessary expenditures.

We oppose the artificial and rigid Constitutional restraint of a balanced budget amendment. Further we oppose efforts to call a federal constitutional convention for this purpose.

Defense Spending. . . . As Democrats, we believe in devoting the needed resources to ensure our national security. But military might cannot be measured solely by dollars spent. American military strength must be secured at an affordable cost. We will reduce the rate of increase in defense spending. Through careful reevaluation of proposed and existing weapons, we will stop throwing away money on unworkable or unnecessary systems; through military reform we will focus defense expenditure on the most cost-effective military policies. We will insist that our allies contribute fairly to our collective security, and that the Department of Defense reduces its scandalous procurement waste.

Tax Reform. We will cap the effect of the Reagan tax cuts for wealthy Americans and enhance the progressivity of our personal income tax code, limiting the benefits of the third year of the Reagan tax cuts to the level of those with incomes of less than $60,000. We will partially defer indexation while protecting average Americans. We will close loopholes, eliminate the preferences and write-offs, exemptions, and deductions which skew the code toward the rich and toward unproductive tax shelters. Given the fact that there has been a veritable hemorrhage of capital out of the federal budget, reflected in part by the huge budget deficit, there must be a return to a fair tax on corporate income. Under the Reagan Administration, the rate of taxation on corporations has been so substantially reduced that they are not contributing their fair share to federal revenues. We believe there should be a 15% minimum corporate tax. In addition, our tax code has facilitated the transfer of capital from the United States to investments abroad, contributing to plant closing without notice in many communities and loss of millions of jobs. We will toughen compliance procedures to reduce the $100 billion annual tax evasion. . . .

Controlling Domestic Spending. Social Security is one of the most important and successful initiatives in the history of our country, and it is an essential element of the social compact that binds us together as a community. There is no excuse — as the Reagan Administration has repeatedly suggested — for slashing Social Security to pay for excesses in other areas of the budget. We will steadfastly oppose such efforts, now and in the future.

It is rather in the area of health care costs that reform is urgently needed. By 1988, Medicare costs will rise to $106 billion; by the turn of the century, the debt of the trust fund may be as great as $1 trillion. In the Republican view, the problem is the level of benefits which senior citizens and the needy receive. As Democrats, we will protect the interests of health care beneficiaries. The real problem is the growing cost of health care services.

We propose to control these costs, and to demand that the health care industry become more efficient in providing care to all Americans, both young and old. We will limit what health care providers can receive as reimbursement, and spur innovation and competition in health care delivery. . . .

Education. We call for the immediate restoration of the cuts in funding of education programs by the Reagan Administration, and for a major new commitment to education. We will create a partnership for excellence among federal, state and local governments. We will provide incen-

tives to local school districts to concentrate on science, math, communications and computer literacy; to provide access to advanced technology. . . .

Vocational education should be overhauled to bring instructional materials, equipment, and staff up to date with the technology and practices for the workplace and target assistance to areas with large numbers of disadvantaged youth. We will pay special attention to the needs of the handicapped. . . .

Bilingual education enables children to achieve full competence in the English language and the academic success necessary to their full participation in the life of our nation. . . .

We will make certain that higher education does not become a luxury affordable only by the children of the rich. In our America, no qualified student should be deprived of the ability to go on to college because of financial circumstance.

Job Training. The Democratic Party must give our young people new skills and new hope; we must work hand in hand with the private sector if job training is to lead to jobs. Specifically, targeted efforts are needed to address the urgent problem of unemployment among minority teenagers. We must provide job training for those who have dropped out of school, and take every step to expand educational opportunity for those still in school. We must recognize the special needs of the over-age 50 worker and the displaced homemaker. Through education, training and retraining we must reduce these dangerously high levels of unemployment.

We must provide an opportunity for workers, including those dislocated by changing technologies, to adapt to new opportunities; we must provide workers with choices as to which skills they wish to acquire. We know that Americans want to work. We are committed to ensuring that meaningful job training is available — for our students, for housewives returning to the workplace, and for those displaced by changing patterns of technology or trade. . . .

Housing. First, we must intensify our commitment to the adequate operation, management, and rehabilitation of the current inventory of government-assisted housing. This housing stock is not one, but the only option for the least fortunate among our lower income families and senior citizens. It is the right thing to do and it makes economic sense to preserve our own economic investment.

Second, we must maintain and expand the flow of mortgage capital. The American dream of home ownership will fall beyond the reach of this generation and future ones if government fails to help attract new sources of capital for housing. . . .

Trade. . . . The reality of the 1980s is that the international economy is the arena in which we must compete. The world economy is an integrated economy; the challenge for our political leadership is to assure that the new arena is in fact a fair playing field for American businesses and consumers. We are committed to pursuing industrial strategies that effectively and imaginatively blend the genius of the free market with vital government partnership and leadership. As Democrats, we will be guided by the following principles and policies.

— We need a vigorous, open and fair trade policy that builds America's competitive strength and that allows our nation to remain an advanced, diversified economy while promoting full employment and raising living standards in the United States and other countries of the world; opens overseas markets for American products; strengthens the international economic system; assists adjustment to foreign competition; and recognizes the legitimate interests of American workers, farmers and businesses.

— We will pursue international negotiations to open markets and eliminate trade restrictions, recognizing

149

that the growth and stability of the Third World depends on its ability to sell its products in international markets. High technology, agriculture and other industries should be brought under the General Agreement on Trade and Tariffs. Moreover, the developing world is a major market for U.S. exports, particularly capital goods. As a result, the U.S. has a major stake in international economic institutions that support growth in the developing world.

— We recognize that the growth and development of the Third World is vital both to global stability and to the continuing expansion of world trade. The U.S. presently sells more to the Third World than to the European Community and Japan combined. If we do not buy their goods, they cannot buy ours, nor can they service their debt. Consequently, it is important to be responsive to the issues of the North/South dialogue such as volatile commodity prices, inequities in the functioning of the international financial and monetary markets, and removal of barriers to the export of Third World goods.

— If trade has become big business for the country, exports have become critical to the economic health of a growing list of American industries. In the future, national economic policy will have to be set with an eye to its impact on U.S. exports. The strength of the dollar, the nature of the U.S. tax system, and the adequacy of export finance all play a role in making U.S. exports internationally competitive.

— The United States continues to struggle with trade barriers that affect its areas of international strength. Subsidized export financing on the part of Europe and Japan has also created problems for the United States, as has the use of industrial policies in Europe and Japan. In some cases, foreign governments target areas of America's competitive strength. In other cases, industrial targeting has been used to maintain industries that cannot meet international competition — often diverting exports to the American market and increasing the burden of adjustment for America's import-competing industries. We will ensure that timely and effective financing can be obtained by American businesses through the Export-Import Bank, so that they can compete effectively against subsidized competitors from abroad.

— A healthy U.S. auto industry is essential to a strong trade balance and economy. That industry generates a large number of American jobs and both develops and consumes new technology needed for economic vitality. We believe it is a sound principle of international trade for foreign automakers which enjoy substantial sales in the United States to invest here and create jobs where their markets are. We also believe U.S. automakers need to maintain high volume small car production in the U.S. With the U.S. auto companies' return to profitability (despite continued unemployment in the auto sector), we urge expanded domestic investment to supply consumers with a full range of competitive vehicles. We support efforts by management and labor to improve auto quality and productivity, and to restrain prices.

— Where foreign competition is fair, American industry should compete without government assistance. Where competition is unfair, we must respond powerfully. We will use trade law and international negotiations to aid U.S. workers, farmers, and business injured by unfair trade practices.

Agriculture. . . . The Democratic Party pledges action. We must solve the immediate farm crisis through a combination of humanitarian aid programs abroad, aggressive promotion of farm exports, and a fair moratorium on farm debt and foreclosure by federal credit agencies to family farm borrowers being forced out of business through no fault of their own, until a long-term program addressing the farm credit crisis can be put into place. Beginning next January with the writing of a new long-term farm bill, the Democratic Party pledges to rebuild a prosperous system of family farms and ranches. We will forge a new agreement on a farm and food policy that assures a fair deal for family farmers, consumers, taxpayers, conservationists, and others with a direct stake in the organizational structure of the food economy. . . .

Finally, we must reverse the annual decrease in the value and volume of U.S. farm exports which has occurred in each year of Ronald Reagan's term. Our farm exports are vital to the nation's prosperity and provide a major part of total farm income. We must restore the ability of U.S. farm products to compete in world markets, and increase worldwide demand for American agricultural products. To do this, we must make major changes in Ronald Reagan's economic policies, and correct his grossly distorted currency exchange rates, which have caused American competitiveness in international trade to decline. We must also resist efforts to lower commodity price supports; such action would only lower farm income without addressing the economic policies which are the root cause of declining competitiveness of U.S. farm products in world markets.

Energy. . . . America is blessed with abundant coal and natural gas, substantial supplies of oil, and plentiful reserves of uranium. Although very costly to process, vast supplies of oil shales and tar sands represent future energy sources. Significant contributions to our energy supply can be made by utilizing renewable resources and indigenous energy, such as active and passive solar systems, windpower, geothermal and ocean thermal power, and the recovery of gas from agricultural waste, coal mines, and garbage dumps. These proven energy sources, as well as more experimental energy systems, should be encouraged for the positive environmental and economic contribution they can make to our energy security.

We will insist on the highest possible standards of safety and protection of public health with respect to nuclear power, including siting, design, operation, evacuation plans, and waste disposal procedures. We will require nuclear power to compete fairly in the marketplace. We will reexamine and review all federal subsidies to the nuclear industry, including the Price-Anderson Act's limits on the liability of the industry which will be considered for reauthorization in the next Congress. A Democratic Administration will give the Nuclear Regulatory Commission the integrity, competence, and credibility it needs to carry out its mandate to protect the public health and safety. We will expand the role of the public in NRC procedures.

We will ensure that no offshore oil and gas exploration will be taken up that is inconsistent with the protection of our fisheries and coastal resources.

Hazardous Wastes. Thousands of dump sites across America contain highly dangerous poisons that can threaten the health and safety of families who live nearby or who depend on water supplies that could be contaminated by the poisons. Although Congress has established the Superfund for emergency cleanup of these dangerous sites, President Reagan refuses to use it vigorously. The Democratic Party is committed to enforcing existing laws, to dramatically increasing Superfund resources to clean up all sites that threaten public health, and to assuring that everyone whose health or property is damaged has a fair opportunity to force the polluters to pay for the damage. This increased support should be financed at least in part through new taxes on the generation of hazardous wastes, so companies have an economic incentive to reduce the volume and toxicity of their dangerous wastes. . . .

Clean Air and Water. The Democratic Party supports a reauthorized and strengthened Clean Air Act. Statutory requirements for the control of toxic air pollutants should be strengthened, with the environmental agency required to identify and regulate within three years priority air pollutants known or anticipated to cause cancer and other serious diseases. The Democratic Party calls for an immediate program to reduce sulfur dioxide emissions by 50% from 1980 levels within the next decade. Our effort should be designed to reduce environmental and economic damage from acid rain while assuring such efforts do not cause regional economic dislocations....

The Democratic Party is committed to strengthening the Clean Water Act to curb both direct and indirect discharge of toxic pollutants into our nation's waters, and supports a strengthened Environmental Protection Agency to assure help to American cities in providing adequate supplies of drinking water free of toxic chemicals and other contaminants....

Environmental Protection Agency. The Democratic Party opposes the Reagan Administration's budget cuts, which have severely hampered the effectiveness of our environmental programs. The Environmental Protection Agency should receive a budget that exceeds in real dollars the agency's purchasing power when President Reagan took office, since the agency's workload has almost doubled in recent years.

Public Lands. The Democratic Party believes in retaining ownership and control of our public lands, and in managing those lands according to the principles of multiple use and sustained yield, with appropriate environmental standards and mitigation requirements to protect the public interest. The Democratic Party supports the substantial expansion of the National Wilderness Preservation System, with designations of all types of ecosystems, including coastal areas, deserts, and prairies as well as forest and alpine areas.

Separation of Church and State. The current Administration has consistently sought to reverse in the courts or overrule by constitutional amendment a long line of Supreme Court decisions that preserve our historic commitment to religious tolerance and church/state separation. The Democratic Platform affirms its support of the principles of religious liberty, religious tolerance and church/state separation and of the Supreme Court decisions forbidding violation of those principles. We pledge to resist all efforts to weaken those decisions....

Affirmative Action. The Democratic Party firmly commits itself to protect the civil rights of every citizen and to pursue justice and equal treatment under the law for all citizens. The Party reaffirms its longstanding commitment to the eradication of discrimination in all aspects of American life through the use of affirmative action, goals, timetables, and other verifiable measurements to overturn historic patterns and historic burdens of discrimination in hiring, training, promotions, contract procurement, education, and the administration of all Federal programs....

Equal Rights for Women. A top priority of a Democratic Administration will be ratification of the unamended Equal Rights Amendment.... The Democratic Party defines nondiscrimination to encompass both equal pay for equal work *and* equal pay for work of comparable worth, and we pledge to take every step, including enforcement of current law and amending the Constitution to include the unamended ERA, to close the wage gap.

Abortion. The Democratic Party recognizes reproductive freedom as a fundamental human right. We therefore oppose government interference in the reproductive decisions of Americans, especially government interference which denies poor Americans their right to privacy by funding or advocating one or a limited number of reproductive choices only....

Unions. This nation established a labor policy more than a generation ago whose purpose is to encourage collective bargaining and the right of workers to organize to obtain this goal. The Democratic Party is committed to extending the benefit of this policy to all workers and to removing the barriers to its administration. To accomplish this, the Democratic Party supports: the repeal of Section 14B of the National Labor Relations Act; labor law reform legislation; a prohibition on the misuse of federal bankruptcy law to prevent the circumvention of the collective bargaining process and the destruction of labor-management contracts; and legislation to allow building trades workers the same peaceful picketing rights currently afforded industrial workers....

Voting Rights Act. A Democratic President and Administration pledge to eliminate any and all discriminatory barriers to full voting rights, whether they be at-large requirements, second-primaries, gerrymandering, annexation, dual registration, dual voting or other practices. Whatever law, practice, or regulation discriminates against the voting rights of minority citizens, a Democratic President and Administration will move to strike it down....

Homosexual Rights. ...All groups must be protected from discrimination based on race, color, sex, religion, national origin, language, age, or sexual orientation. We will support legislation to prohibit discrimination in the workplace based on sexual orientation. We will assure that sexual orientation *per se* does not serve as a bar to participation in the military....

National Health Insurance. ...As Democrats we believe that quality health care is a necessity for everyone. We reaffirm our commitment to the long-term goal of comprehensive national health insurance and view effective health care cost containment as an essential step toward that goal. Health cost containment must be based on a strong commitment to quality of service delivery and care. We also pledge to return to a proper emphasis on basic scientific research and meeting the need for health professionals — areas devastated by the Reagan Administration.

Gun Control. We support tough restraints on the manufacture, transportation, and sale of snubnosed handguns, which have no legitimate sporting use and are used in a high proportion of violent crimes.

Arms Control. ...A Democratic President will propose an early summit with regular, annual summits to follow, with the Soviet leaders, and meetings between senior civilian and military officials, in order to reduce tensions and explore possible formal agreements.... A new Democratic Administration will implement a strategy for peace which makes arms control an integral part of our national security policy. We must move the world back from the brink of nuclear holocaust and set a new direction toward an enduring peace, in which lower levels of military spending will be possible. Our ultimate aim must be to abolish all nuclear weapons in a world safe for peace and freedom....

The first practical step is to take the initiative, on January 20, 1985, to challenge the Soviets to halt the arms race quickly. As President Kennedy successfully did in stopping nuclear explosions above ground in 1963, a Democratic President will initiate temporary, verifiable, and mutual moratoria, to be maintained for a fixed period during negotiations so long as the Soviets do the same, on the testing of underground nuclear weapons and anti-satellite weapons; on the testing and deployment of all weapons in space; on the testing and deployment of new strategic ballistic missiles now under development; and on the deployment of nuclear-armed, sea-launched cruise missiles.

These steps should lead promptly to the negotiation of a comprehensive, mutual and verifiable freeze on the testing, production, and deployment of all nuclear weapons. Building on this initiative, the Democratic President will

update and resubmit the SALT II Treaty to the Senate for its advice and consent. . . .

Defense Policy. The Reagan Administration measures military might by dollars spent. The Democratic Party seeks prudent defense based on sound planning and a realistic assessment of threats. In the field of defense policy, the Democratic Administration will work with our NATO and other allies to ensure our collective security, especially by strengthening our conventional defenses so as to reduce our need to rely on nuclear weapons, and to achieve this at increased spending levels, with funding to continue at levels appropriate to our collective security, with the firm hope that successful steps to reduce tensions and to obtain comprehensive and verifiable arms control agreements will guarantee our nation both military security and budgetary relief . . . [and] oppose a peacetime military draft or draft registration. . . .

A Democratic President will be prepared to apply military force when vital American interests are threatened, particularly in the event of an attack upon the United States or its immediate allies. But he or she will not hazard American lives or engage in unilateral military involvement:

● Where our objectives are not clear;

● Until all instruments of diplomacy and non-military leverage, as appropriate, have been exhausted;

● Where our objectives threaten unacceptable costs or unreasonable levels of military force;

● Where the local forces supported are not working to resolve the causes of conflict;

● Where multilateral or allied options for the resolution of conflict are available. . . .

The Middle East. The Democratic Party believes that the security of Israel and the pursuit of peace in the Middle East are fundamental priorities for American foreign policy. Israel remains more than a trusted friend, a steady ally, and a sister democracy. Israel is strategically important to the United States, and we must enter into meaningful strategic cooperation.

The Democratic Party opposes this Administration's sales of highly advanced weaponry to avowed enemies of Israel, such as AWACS aircraft and Stinger missiles to Saudi Arabia. While helping to meet the legitimate defensive needs of states aligned with our nation, we must ensure Israel's military edge over any combination of Middle East confrontation states. The Democratic Party opposes any consideration of negotiations with the PLO, unless the PLO abandons terrorism, recognizes the state of Israel, and adheres to U.N. Resolutions 242 and 338.

Jerusalem should remain forever undivided with free access to the holy places for people of all faiths. As stated in the 1976 and 1980 platforms, the Democratic Party recognizes and supports the established status of Jerusalem as the capital of Israel. As a symbol of this stand, the U.S. Embassy should be moved from Tel Aviv to Jerusalem.

Central America. . . . A Democratic President . . . will approach Central American policy in the following terms:

— First, there must be unequivocal support for the Contadora process and for the efforts by those countries to achieve political solutions to the conflicts that plague the Central American region.

— Second, there must be a commitment on the part of the United States to reduce tensions in the region. We must terminate our support for the *contras* and other paramilitary groups fighting in Nicaragua. We must halt those U.S. military exercises in the region which are being conducted for no other real purpose than to intimidate or provoke the Nicaraguan government or which may be used as a pretext for deeper U.S. military involvement in the area. And, we must evidence our firm willingness to work for a demilitarized Central America, including the mutual withdrawal of all foreign forces and military advisers from the region. A Democratic President will

seek a multilateral framework to protect the security and independence of the region which will include regional agreements to bar new military bases, to restrict the numbers and sophistication of weapons being introduced into Central America, and to permit international inspection of borders. This diplomatic effort can succeed, however, only if all countries in Central America, including Nicaragua, will agree to respect the sovereignty and integrity of their neighbors, to limit their military forces, to reject foreign military bases (other than those provided for in the Panama Canal Treaties), and to deny any external force or power the use of their territories for purposes of subversion in the region. The viability of any security agreement for Central America would be enhanced by the progressive development of pluralism in Nicaragua. To this end, the elections proposed for November [1984] are important; how they are conducted will be an indication of Nicaragua's willingness to move in the direction of genuine democracy.

— Third, there must be a clear, concise signal to indicate that we are ready, willing and able to provide substantial economic resources, through the appropriate multilateral channels, to the nations of Central America, as soon as the Contadora process achieves a measure of success in restoring peace and stability in the region. In the meantime, of course, we will continue to provide humanitarian aid and refugee relief assistance. The Democratic Administration will work to help churches and universities which are providing sanctuary and assistance to Guatemalan, Haitian, and Salvadoran refugees, and will give all assistance to such refugees as is consistent with U.S. law.

— Fourth, a Democratic President will support the newly elected President of El Salvador in his efforts to establish civilian democratic control, by channeling U.S. aid through him and by conditioning it on the elimination of government-supported death squads and on progress toward his objectives of land reform, human rights, and serious negotiations with contending forces in El Salvador, in order to achieve a peaceful democratic political settlement of the Salvadoran conflict.

— Fifth, a Democratic President will not use U.S. armed forces in or over El Salvador or Nicaragua for the purpose of engaging in combat unless:

1) Congress has declared war or otherwise authorized the use of U.S. combat forces, or

2) the use of U.S. combat forces is necessary to meet a clear and present danger of attack upon the U.S., its territories or possessions or upon U.S. embassies or citizens, consistent with the War Powers Act.

Republicans

A jubilant Republican Party wound up its Aug. 20-23 convention in Dallas, Texas, confident that President Ronald Reagan and Vice President George Bush would be the "winning team" in November. With the ticket's renomination certain beforehand, the 33rd Republican National Convention was more a celebration than a business meeting of GOP activists. Behind the cheering and display of party unity, however, ran a current of dissent: Moderates, who were greatly outnumbered, voiced unhappiness with the party's direction and its platform.

During convention week, speaker after speaker criticized the Democrats, saying they represented a legacy of "malaise" from Jimmy Carter's administration and promised only a future of fear. Reagan, too, emphasized that theme in his 55-minute acceptance speech. To repeated interruptions of applause and cheers, he drew sharp differences between Republicans and Democrats and between himself and the Democratic presidential nominee, Walter F. Mondale. "The choices this year are not just between two different personalities or between two political parties," Reagan said. "They are between two different visions

of the future, two fundamentally different ways of governing — their government of pessimism, fear and limits . . . or ours of hope, confidence and growth."

In his acceptance speech, Bush vigorously touted the Reagan administration's record. "Under this president, more lands have been acquired for parks, more for wilderness," he said. "The quality of life is better — and that's a fact." In foreign affairs, Bush said, ". . . there is new confidence in the U.S. leadership around the world. . . . Because our president stood firm in defense of freedom, America has regained respect throughout the world. . . ."

Speakers in previous sessions had sought to make the same points. They tried to link former vice president Mondale to the policies and problems of the administration in which he had served. "Carter-Mondale" became their shorthand for a list of evils: inflation, high interest rates, foreign policy failures and sagging national spirit.

GOP leaders also were anxious to portray the Democratic ticket and the party's leadership as out of step with most Democrats. They gave the spotlight to Democrats-turned-Republicans and issued one of their warmest welcomes to Jeane J. Kirkpatrick, the U.S. representative to the United Nations, whom one party leader referred to as an "enlightened Democrat." Kirkpatrick delivered a foreign policy speech during the opening session.

Yet this convention was clearly a Republican event, with the administration firmly in control and many of its members on hand. The party's leaders also made clear they were making a pitch for women voters, in response to the candidacy of Rep. Geraldine A. Ferraro, D-N.Y., Mondale's running mate.

Conditions outside the hall were almost as controlled as events inside. Police were ever present, but demonstrations by and large were tepid. One major reason was the record-breaking heat: It prompted some protesters to leave town and delegates and the press to stay in the air-conditioned indoors.

The opening ceremonies Aug. 20 were a mix of the patriotic and the political. About 50 young people carrying flags and wearing smocks decorated with red, white and blue elephants lined the interior of the hall; delegates then sang "The Star-Spangled Banner" and recited the pledge of allegiance.

The evening session was the GOP's "ladies' night." Four of the six speakers were women, including Katherine D. Ortega, the U.S. treasurer, and Kirkpatrick. Although Ortega was billed as the keynote speaker, it was Democrat Kirkpatrick who received the most sustained and vigorous applause from the delegates. Kirkpatrick had harsh words for her fellow Democrats, charging that they "treat foreign affairs as an afterthought." She asserted that the Carter administration "did not seem to notice much, care much, or do much" about a host of international problems.

The highlight of the Aug. 21 evening session was a speech by former president Gerald R. Ford. Delegates gave Ford and his wife, Betty, a rousing welcome. Ford wasted no time attacking the Democratic nominee, telling delegates: "Mondale wants this election to be a 'referendum on the future.' I can't blame him for wanting to forget the past, the four years of Carter-Mondale from 1977 through 1980. Who wants to remember four years of roaring inflation, skyrocketing interest rates and so-called 'malaise?'"

Before Reagan and Bush were renominated on the evening of Aug. 22, Sen. Barry Goldwater of Arizona addressed the convention. Goldwater, the party's presidential nominee in 1964, said he wanted to talk to the delegates about "freedom." He opened his speech with a slogan from

his campaign 20 years earlier: "Let me remind you," he said, "extremism in the defense of liberty is no vice." Goldwater charged that the Democrats at their convention "turned their backs on our own heritage. Indeed, they would have us ashamed of our freedom and our ability to defend it. To me, the worst part was that they said nicer things about the Soviet Union than about our own military services."

The delegates moved to renominate Reagan and Bush. Although the outcome came as no surprise, there was an unusual joint roll call on the nominations, with Reagan receiving 2,233 votes and Bush, 2,231. *(Chart, p. 221)*

On the final night of the convention, Reagan and Bush came to the hall to claim their nominations. With standing room only in the 17,000-seat arena, guests were lined up three deep in some places for an evening of balloons, speeches and patriotic music.

Earlier, after spirited debate, the 106-member platform committee adopted a 1984 campaign document that conformed in virtually all respects to the themes Reagan had sounded during his first term in office. The convention itself ratified the 30,000-word platform with no debate Aug. 21. On almost every aspect of public policy, the document stood in stark contrast to the platform the Democrats had adopted in San Francisco.

However, in its strong stand against tax increases and its criticism of the independent Federal Reserve Board, the Republican platform went further than the White House wanted. Administration representatives led by former transportation secretary Drew Lewis sought to soften the tax plank, but, while they succeeded in modifying some of the language, they were unable to alter it substantially. The tax section of the Republican platform pledged that the party would continue efforts to lower tax rates and would support tax reform that "will lead to a fair and simple tax system." The platform said the party believed that a "modified flat tax — with specific exemptions for such items as mortgage interest — is a most promising approach."

Taxes had mushroomed as an election issue when Democratic presidential nominee Walter F. Mondale said in his acceptance speech at the Democratic National Convention that, regardless of who won in November, tax increases would be necessary in 1985 to combat record federal budget deficits. Mondale also accused Reagan of having a secret plan to raise taxes.

Despite a vigorous hour-long debate, the GOP platform committee had refused to endorse either the proposed Equal Rights Amendment (ERA) — which Reagan opposed — or compromise language stating that the Republican Party respected those who supported the amendment. The committee also turned aside challenges by party moderates to language endorsing voluntary prayer in public schools and opposing federal financing for abortions under any circumstances. Some moderate delegates had considered trying to offer a minority plank on the ERA stating respect for differing Republican views on the issue. But moderates determined that they lacked support to bring a floor challenge.

The platform included the following major points:

● Unqualified opposition to tax increases, which were dismissed as a "misguided effort to balance the budget."

● A call for passage by Congress of a constitutional amendment to require a balanced federal budget.

● Support for a constitutional convention to write a balanced budget amendment if Congress failed to act on the issue.

● Criticism of Federal Reserve Board policies as "destabilizing," and a suggestion that the gold standard "may be a useful mechanism" for achieving the goal of stable prices.

● Support for the administration's policy in Central America, specifically its support of the government in El Salvador.

● A pledge of party support for putting the United States in a superior military position in the world, although the term "military superiority" that appeared in the 1980 platform was not used in 1984.

● A call for repealing the windfall profits tax on oil.

● Support for abolition of the Department of Energy.

● Opposition to quotas to remedy discrimination because they "are the most insidious form of discrimination against the innocent."

● Support for a constitutional amendment to ban abortion and reaffirmation of a statement in the 1980 platform that Reagan should appoint federal judges who opposed abortion.

● Support for the right of students to engage in voluntary school prayer.

A multi-section chapter entitled "Security for the Individual" covered the environment, education, individual rights and "our constitutional system." On the environment, the platform said the party "endorses a strong effort to control and clean up toxic wastes." It asserted further that the GOP "supports the continued commitment to clean air and clean water. This support includes the implementation of meaningful clean air and clean water acts."

The 1980 platform had called for abolition of the Department of Education, which Congress created in 1979 at the urging of President Carter. The 1984 GOP platform stated that education was a "local function, a state responsibility and a federal concern. The federal role should be limited." However, it stopped short of urging that the federal department be disbanded.

In the section on individual rights, the platform devoted several paragraphs to GOP support for women's rights. In one section, the document stated, "President Reagan believes, as do we, that all members of our party are free to work individually for women's progress." At another point, the platform called for "assuring that women have equal opportunity, security and real choices for the promising future." But while it called for "equal pay for equal work," the document said that "with equal emphasis, we oppose the concept of 'comparable worth.' We believe that the free-market system can determine the value of jobs better than any government authority."

On the issue of abortion, the platform picked up language from the 1980 document advocating a constitutional amendment to ban abortion and supporting a ban on federal funding for abortion. An amendment that called for support of federal funding for abortions in the case of rape or incest was rejected.

In the foreign affairs area, the Republicans took dead aim at the Democrats. The platform declared that the Soviet Union's "globalist ideology and its leadership obsessed with military power make it a threat to freedom and peace on every continent. The Carter-Mondale Administration ignored that threat, and the Democratic candidates underestimate it today. The Carter-Mondale illusion that the Soviet leaders share our ideals and aspirations is not only false but a profound danger to world peace." The platform added that Republicans "reaffirm our belief that

Soviet behavior at the negotiating table cannot be divorced from Soviet behavior elsewhere."

This section was similar in tone to the 1980 platform, which declared "the premier challenge facing the United States, its allies and the entire globe is to check the Soviet Union's global ambitions." Although the 1984 campaign document did not contain the call for outright U.S. "military superiority" that appeared in the 1980 platform, the notion that the United States should be the superior power in the world ran through the chapter. The platform also stated that the Republicans "enthusiastically" supported the development of "non-nuclear, space-based defensive systems" designed to protect the United States from incoming missiles, as proposed by Reagan in 1983.

Following are excerpts from the Republican platform of 1984:

Economic Policy. Our most important economic goal is to expand and continue the economic recovery and move the nation to full employment without inflation. We therefore oppose any attempts to increase taxes, which would harm the recovery and reverse the trend to restoring control of the economy to individual Americans. We favor reducing deficits by continuing and expanding the strong economic recovery brought about by the policies of this Administration and by eliminating wasteful and unnecessary government spending. . . .

To assure workers and entrepreneurs the capital required to provide jobs and growth, we will further expand incentives for personal saving. We will expand coverage of the Individual Retirement Account, especially to homemakers, and increase and index the annual limits on IRA contributions. We will increase the incentives for savings by moving toward the reduction of taxation of interest income. We will work for indexation of capital assets and elimination of the double taxation of dividends to increase the attractiveness of equity investments for small investors.

We oppose withholding on dividend and interest income. It would discourage saving and investment, create needless paperwork, and rob savers of their due benefits. A higher personal savings rate is key to deficit control. We therefore oppose any disincentives to thrift.

History has proven again and again that wage and price controls will not stop inflation. Such controls only cause shortages, inequities, and ultimately high prices. We remain firmly opposed to the imposition of wage and price controls.

We are committed to bringing the benefits of economic growth to all Americans. Therefore, we support policies which will increase opportunities for the poorest in our society to climb the economic ladder. We will work to establish enterprise zones in urban and rural America; we will work to enable those living in government-owned or subsidized housing to purchase their homes. . . .

Tax Policy. The Republican Party pledges to continue our efforts to lower tax rates, change and modernize the tax system, and eliminate the incentive-destroying effects of graduated tax rates. We therefore support tax reform that will lead to a fair and simple tax system and believe a modified flat tax — with specific exemptions for such items as mortgage interest — is a most promising approach.

For families, we will restore the value of personal exemptions, raising it to a minimum of $2,000 and indexing to prevent further erosion. We will preserve the deduction for mortgage interest payments. We will propose an employment income exclusion to assure that tax burdens are not shifted to the poor. . . .

Balancing the Budget. The congressional budget process is bankrupt. Its implementation has not brought spending under control, and it must be thoroughly reformed. We will work for the constitutional amendment

requiring a balanced federal budget passed by the Republican Senate but blocked by the Democrat-controlled House and denounced by the Democrat Platform. If Congress fails to act on this issue, a constitutional convention should be convened to address only this issue in order to bring deficit spending under control.

The President is denied proper control over the federal budget. To remedy this, we support enhanced authority to prevent wasteful spending, including a line-item veto....

Monetary Policy. Just as our tax policy has only laid the groundwork for a new era of prosperity, reducing inflation is only the first step in restoring a stable currency. A dollar now should be worth a dollar in the future. This allows real economic growth without inflation and is the primary goal of our monetary policy.

The Federal Reserve Board's destabilizing actions must therefore stop. We need coordination between fiscal and monetary policy, timely information about Fed decisions, and an end to the uncertainties people face in obtaining money and credit. The Gold Standard may be a useful mechanism for realizing the Federal Reserve's determination to adopt monetary policies needed to sustain price stability.

Minimum Wage. There are still federal statutes that keep Americans out of the workforce. Arbitrary minimum wage rates, for example, have eliminated hundreds of thousands of jobs and, with them, the opportunity for young people to get productive skills, good work habits, and a weekly paycheck. We encourage the adoption of a youth opportunity wage to encourage employers to hire and train inexperienced workers....

Energy. We will complete America's energy agenda. Natural gas should be responsibly decontrolled as rapidly as possible so that families and businesses can enjoy the full benefits of lower prices and greater production, as with decontrolled oil. We are committed to the repeal of the confiscatory windfall profits tax, which has forced the American consumer to pay more for less and left us vulnerable to the energy and economic stranglehold of foreign producers.

While protecting the environment, we should permit abundant American coal to be mined and consumed. Environmentally sound development of oil and natural gas on federal properties (which has brought the taxpayers $20 billion in revenue in the last four years) should continue. We believe that as controls have been lifted from the energy marketplace, conservation and alternative sources of energy, such as solar, wind, and geothermal, have become increasingly cost-effective....

We now have a sound, long-term program for disposal of nuclear waste. We will work to eliminate unnecessary regulatory procedures so that nuclear plants can be brought on line quickly, efficiently, and safely. We call for an energy policy, the stability and continuity of which will restore and encourage public confidence in the fiscal stability of the nuclear industry.

We are committed to the termination of the Department of Energy. President Reagan has succeeded in abolishing that part which was telling Americans what to buy, where to buy it, and at what price — the regulatory part of DOE. Then he reduced the number of bureaucrats by 25 percent. Now is the time to complete the job.

Agriculture Policy. ... Republicans are very much aware of the devastating impact which high interest rates have had, and continue to have, on the viability of America's farmers and ranchers. We also realize that, unless interest rates decline significantly in the near future, the character of American agriculture and rural life will be tragically changed. For these reasons, we pledge to pursue every possible course of action, including the consideration of temporary interest rate reductions, to ensure the Ameri-

can farmer or rancher is not a patient that dies in the course of a successful economic operation....

Republicans are cognizant that there are many well-managed, efficient, farm and ranch operations which face bankruptcy and foreclosure. The foreclosures and resulting land sales will jeopardize the equity positions of neighboring farms and ranches, compounding financial problems in agriculture. Republicans pledge to implement comprehensive Farmers Home Administration and commercial farm and ranch debt restructuring procedures, including the establishment of local community farm and ranch finance committees, which shall advise borrowers, lenders, and government officials regarding debt restructuring alternatives and farmer and rancher eligibility....

Our farmers and ranchers must have full access to world markets and should not have to face unfair export subsidies and predatory dumping by other producing nations without redress. Republicans believe that unfair trade practices and non-tariff barriers are so serious that a comprehensive renegotiation of multilateral trade arrangements must be undertaken to revitalize the free, fair, and open trade critical to worldwide economic growth.

The Republican Party is unalterably opposed to the use of embargoes of grain or other agricultural products as a tool of foreign policy....

Trade Policy. ... We are committed to a free and open international trading system. All Americans benefit from the free flow of goods, services and capital, and the efficiencies of a vigorous international market. We will work with all of our international trading partners to eliminate barriers to trade, both tariff and non-tariff. As a first step, we call on our trading partners to join in a new round of trade negotiations to revise the General Agreement on Tariffs and Trade in order to strengthen it. And we further call on our trading partners to join us in reviewing trade with totalitarian regimes....

Housing. We reaffirm our commitment to the federal-tax deductibility of mortgage interest payments. In the States, we stand with those working to lower property taxes that strike hardest at the poor, the elderly, and large families. We stand, as well, with Americans earning possession of their homes through "sweat-equity" programs.

We will, over time, replace subsidies and welfare projects with a voucher system, returning public housing to the free market.

Despite billions of dollars poured into public housing developments, conditions remain deplorable for many low-income Americans who live in them. These projects have become breeding grounds for the very problems they were meant to eliminate. Their dilapidated and crumbling structures testify to decades of corrupt or incompetent management by poverty bureaucrats.

Some residents of public housing developments have reversed these conditions by successfully managing their own housing units through creative self-help efforts.... The Republican Party therefore supports the development of programs which will lead to homeownership of public housing developments by current residents.

We strongly believe in open housing. We will vigorously enforce all fair housing laws and will not tolerate their distortion into quotas and controls.

Welfare. ... Because there are different reasons for poverty, our programs address different needs and must never be replaced with a unitary income guarantee. That would betray the interests of the poor and the taxpayers alike.

We will employ the latest technology to combat welfare fraud in order to protect the needy from the greedy.

Whenever possible, public assistance must be a transition to the world of work, except in cases, particularly with the aged and disabled, where that is not appropriate. In other cases, it is long overdue.

Remedying poverty requires that we sustain and broaden economic recovery, hold families together, get government's hand out of their pocketbooks, and restore the work ethic.

Environment. . . . The Republican Party endorses a strong effort to control and clean up toxic wastes. We have already tripled funding to clean up hazardous waste dumps, quadrupled funding for acid rain research, and launched the rebirth of the Chesapeake Bay.

. . . The Republican Party supports the continued commitment to clean air and clean water. This support includes the implementation of meaningful clean air and clean water acts. We will continue to offer leadership to reduce the threat to our environment and our economy from acid rain, while at the same time preventing economic dislocation. . . .

We will be responsible to future generations, but at the same time, we must remember that quality of life means more than protection and preservation. Quality of life also means a good job, a decent place to live, accommodation for a growing population, and the continued economic and technological development essential to our standard of living. . . .

Education. We believe that education is a local function, a State responsibility, and a federal concern. The federal role in education should be limited. It includes helping parents and local authorities ensure high standards, protecting civil rights, and ensuring family rights. . . .

We have enacted legislation to guarantee equal access to school facilities by student religious groups. Mindful of our religious diversity, we reaffirm our commitment to the freedoms of religion and speech guaranteed by the Constitution of the United States and firmly support the rights of students to openly practice the same, including the right to engage in voluntary prayer in schools. . . .

While much has been accomplished, the agenda is only begun. We must complete the block-grant process begun in 1981. We will return revenue sources to State and local governments to make them independent of federal funds and of the control that inevitably follows.

The Republican Party believes that developing the individual dignity and potential of disabled Americans is an urgent responsibility. To this end, the Republican Party commits itself to prompt and vigorous enforcement of the rights of disabled citizens, particularly those rights established under the Education for All Handicapped Children Act, Section 504 of the Rehabilitation Act of 1973, and the Civil Rights of Institutionalized Persons Act. We insist on the highest standards of quality for services supported with federal funds.

In education, as in other activities, competition fosters excellence. We therefore support the President's proposal for tuition tax credits. We will convert the Chapter One grants to vouchers, thereby giving poor parents the ability to choose the best schooling available. Discrimination cannot be condoned, nor may public policies encourage its practice. Civil rights enforcement must not be twisted into excessive interference in the education process.

Crime and Gun Control. . . . Republicans respect the authority of State and local law enforcement officials. The proper federal role is to provide strong support and coordination for their efforts and to vigorously enforce federal criminal laws. By concentrating on repeat offenders, we are determined to take career criminals off the street.

The best way to deter crime is to increase the probability of detection and to make punishment certain and swift. As a matter of basic philosophy, we advocate preventive rather than merely corrective measures. Republicans advocate sentencing reform and secure, adequate prison construction. We concur with the American people's approval of capital punishment where appropriate and will ensure that it is carried out humanely.

Republicans will continue to defend the constitutional right to keep and bear arms. When this right is abused and armed felonies are committed, we believe in stiff, mandatory sentencing. . . .

Discrimination. Just as we must guarantee opportunity, we oppose attempts to dictate results. We will resist efforts to replace equal rights with discriminatory quota systems and preferential treatment. Quotas are the most insidious form of discrimination: reverse discrimination against the innocent. We must always remember that, in a free society, different individual goals will yield different results. . . .

Women's Rights. The Republican Party has an historic commitment to equal rights for women. Republicans pioneered the right of women to vote, and our party was the first major party to advocate equal pay for equal work, regardless of sex.

President Reagan believes, as do we, that all members of our party are free to work individually for women's progress. As a party, we demand that there be no detriment to that progress or inhibition of women's rights to full opportunity and advancement within this society.

With women comprising an increasing share of the work force, it is essential that the employment opportunities created by our free market system be open to individuals without regard to their sex, race, religion, or ethnic origin. We firmly support an equal opportunity approach which gives women and minorities equal access to all jobs — including the traditionally higher-paying technical, managerial, and professional positions — and which guarantees that workers in those jobs will be compensated in accord with the laws requiring equal pay for equal work under Title VII of the Civil Rights Act.

We are creating an environment in which individual talents and creativity can be tapped to the fullest, while assuring that women have equal opportunity, security, and real choices for the promising future. For all Americans, we demand equal pay for equal work. With equal emphasis, we oppose the concept of "comparable worth." We believe that the free market system can determine the value of jobs better than any government authority.

Protecting the Handicapped. We are committed to enforcing statutory prohibitions barring discrimination against any otherwise qualified handicapped individuals, in any program receiving federal financial assistance, solely by reason of their handicap.

We recognize the need for watchful care regarding the procedural due process rights of persons with handicaps both to prevent their placement into inappropriate programs or settings and to ensure that their rights are represented by guardians or other advocates, if necessary.

For handicapped persons who need care, we favor family-based care where possible, supported by appropriate and adequate incentives. We increased the tax credit for caring for dependents or spouses physically or mentally unable to care for themselves. We also provided a deduction of up to $1,500 per year for adopting a child with special needs that may otherwise make adoption difficult.

Labor Unions. We reaffirm the right of all individuals freely to form, join, or assist labor organizations to bargain collectively, consistent with State laws and free from unnecessary government involvement. We support the fundamental principle of fairness in labor relations. We will continue the Reagan Administration's "open door" policy toward organized labor and its leaders. We reaffirm our long-standing support for the right of States to enact "Right-to-Work" laws under section 14(b) of the Taft-Hartley Act.

Campaign Reform. The holding of public office in our country demands the highest degree of commitment to integrity, openness, and honesty by candidates running for all elective offices. Without such a commitment, public

confidence rapidly erodes. Republicans, therefore, reaffirm our commitment to the fair and consistent application of financial disclosure laws. We will continue our support for full disclosure by all high officials of the government and candidates in positions of public trust. This extends to the financial holdings of spouses or dependents, of which the official has knowledge, financial interest, or benefit. We will continue to hold all public officials to the highest ethical standards and will oppose the inconsistent application of those standards on the basis of gender....

...In light of the inhibiting role federal election laws and regulations have had, Congress should consider abolishing the Federal Election Commission....

Abortion. The unborn child has a fundamental individual right to life which cannot be infringed. We therefore reaffirm our support for a human life amendment to the Constitution, and we endorse legislation to make clear that the Fourteenth Amendment's protections apply to unborn children. We oppose the use of public revenues for abortion and will eliminate funding for organizations which advocate or support abortions....

We applaud President Reagan's fine record of judicial appointments, and we reaffirm our support for the appointment of judges at all levels of the judiciary who respect traditional family values and the sanctity of innocent human life....

Foreign Policy. The supreme purpose of our foreign policy must be to maintain our freedom in a peaceful international environment in which the United States and our allies and friends are secure against military threats, and democratic governments are flourishing in a world of increasing prosperity.

This we pledge to our people and to future generations: we shall keep the peace by keeping our country stronger than any potential adversary....

Central America. Today, democracy is under assault throughout [Central America]. Marxist Nicaragua threatens not only Costa Rica and Honduras, but also El Salvador and Guatemala. The Sandinista regime is building the largest military force in Central America, importing Soviet equipment, Eastern bloc and PLO advisers, and thousands of Cuban mercenaries. The Sandinista government has been increasingly brazen in its embrace of Marxism-Leninism. The Sandinistas have systematically persecuted free institutions, including synagogue and church, schools, the private sector, the free press, minorities, and families and tribes throughout Nicaragua. We support continued assistance to the democratic freedom fighters in Nicaragua. Nicaragua cannot be allowed to remain a Communist sanctuary, exporting terror and arms throughout the region. We condemn the Sandinista government's smuggling of illegal drugs into the United States as a crime against American society and international law.

The heroic effort to build democracy in El Salvador has been brutally attacked by Communist guerrillas supported by Cuba and the Sandinistas. Their violence jeopardizes improvements in human rights, delays economic growth, and impedes the consolidation of democracy. El Salvador is nearer to Texas than Texas is to New England, and we cannot be indifferent to its fate. In the tradition of President Truman's postwar aid to Europe, President Reagan has helped the people of El Salvador defend themselves. Our opponents object to that assistance, citing concern for human rights. We share that concern, and more than that, we have taken steps to help curb abuses. We have firmly and actively encouraged human rights reform, and results have been achieved. In judicial reform, the murderers of the American nuns in 1980 have been convicted and sentenced; and in political reform, the right to vote has been exercised by 80 percent of the voters in the fair, open elections of 1982 and 1984. Most important, if the Communists seize power there, human rights will be extinguished, and tens of thousands will be driven from their homes. We, therefore, support the President in his determination that the Salvadoran people will shape their own future.

The Soviet Union. Stable and peaceful relations with the Soviet Union are possible and desirable, but they depend upon the credibility of American strength and determination.... Our policy of peace through strength encourages freedom-loving people everywhere and provides hope for those who look forward one day to enjoying the fruits of self-government....

We hold a sober view of the Soviet Union. Its globalist ideology and its leadership obsessed with military power make it a threat to freedom and peace on every continent.... Republicans reaffirm our belief that Soviet behavior at the negotiating table cannot be divorced from Soviet behavior elsewhere. Over-eagerness to sign agreements with the Soviets at any price, fashionable in the Carter-Mondale Administration, should never blind us to this reality. Any future agreement with the Soviets must require full compliance, be fully verifiable, and contain suitable sanctions for non-compliance.... We insist on full Soviet compliance with all treaties and executive agreements.

We seek to deflect Soviet policy away from aggression and toward peaceful international conduct. To that end, we will seek substantial reductions in nuclear weapons, rather than merely freezing nuclear weapons at their present dangerous level. We will continue multilateral efforts to deny advanced Western technology to the Soviet war machine.

Europe. ... We would be in mortal danger were Western Europe to come under Soviet domination. Fragmenting NATO is the immediate objective of the Soviet military buildup and Soviet subversion.... To keep the peace, the Reagan-Bush Administration is offsetting the Soviet military threat with the defensive power of the Alliance. We are deploying Pershing II and Cruise missiles. Remembering the Nazi Reich, informed voters on both sides of the Atlantic know they cannot accept Soviet military superiority in Europe.

The Middle East. ... Lebanon is still in turmoil, despite our best efforts to foster stability in that unhappy country. With the Syrian leadership increasingly subject to Soviet influence, and the Palestine Liberation Organization and its homicidal subsidiaries taking up residence in Syria, U.S. policy toward the region must remain vigilant and strong. Republicans reaffirm that the United States should not recognize or negotiate with the PLO so long as that organization continues to promote terrorism, rejects Israel's right to exist, and refuses to accept U.N. Resolutions 242 and 338.

The bedrock of that protection remains, as it has for over three decades, our moral and strategic relationship with Israel. We are allies in the defense of freedom. Israel's strength, coupled with United States assistance, is the main obstacle to Soviet domination of the region. The sovereignty, security, and integrity of the state of Israel are moral imperatives. We pledge to help maintain Israel's qualitative military edge over its adversaries.

We recognize that attacks in the U.N. against Israel are but thinly disguised attacks against the United States, for it is our shared ideals and democratic way of life that are their true target. Thus, when a U.N. agency denied Israel's right to participate, we withheld our financial support until that action was corrected. And we have worked behind the scenes and in public in other international organizations to defeat discriminatory attacks against our ally.

...We pledge continued support to Egypt and other moderate regimes against Soviet and Libyan subversion, and we look to them to contribute to our efforts for a long-term settlement of the region's destructive disputes.

We believe that Jerusalem should remain an undivided

city with free and unimpeded access to all holy places by people of all faiths.

China and Taiwan. . . . In keeping with the pledge of the 1980 Platform, President Reagan has continued the process of developing our relationship with the People's Republic of China. We commend the President's initiatives to build a solid foundation for the long-term relations between the United States and the People's Republic, emphasizing peaceful trade and other policies to promote regional peace. Despite fundamental differences in many areas, both nations share an important common objective: opposition to Soviet expansionism.

At the same time, we specifically reaffirm our concern for, and our moral commitment to, the safety and security of the 18 million people on Taiwan. We pledge that this concern will be constant, and we will continue to regard any attempt to alter Taiwan's status by force as a threat to regional peace. We endorse, with enthusiasm, President Reagan's affirmation that it is the policy of the United States to support and fully implement the provisions of the Taiwan Relations Act. In addition, we fully support self determination for the people of Hong Kong.

South Africa. . . . We reaffirm our commitment to the rights of all South Africans. Apartheid is repugnant. In South Africa, as elsewhere on the continent, we support well-conceived efforts to foster peace, prosperity, and stability.

International Organizations. . . . We will not support international organizations inconsistent with our interests. In particular, we will work to eliminate their funding of Communist states.

Prominent among American ideals is the sanctity of the family. Decisions on family size should be made freely by each family. We support efforts to enhance the freedom of such family decisions. We will endeavor to assure that those who are responsible for our programs are more sensitive to the cultural needs of the countries to which we give assistance.

As part of our commitment to the family and our opposition to abortion, we will eliminate all U.S. funding for organizations which in any way support abortion or research on abortion methods. . . .

Americans cannot count on the international organizations to guarantee our security or adequately protect our interests. The United States hosts the headquarters of the United Nations, pays a fourth of its budget, and is proportionally the largest contributor to most international organizations; but many members consistently vote against us. As Soviet influence in these organizations has grown, cynicism and the double standard have become their way of life.

This is why President Reagan announced that we will leave the worst of these organizations, UNESCO. He has put the U.N. on notice that the U.S. will strongly oppose the use of the U.N. to foster anti-semitism, Soviet espionage, and hostility to the United States. The President decisively rejected the U.N. Convention on the Law of the Sea and embarked instead on a dynamic national oceans policy, animated by our traditional commitment to freedom of the seas. That pattern will be followed with regard to U.N. meddling in Antarctica and outer space. Enthusiastically endorsing those steps, we will apply the same standards to all international organizations. We will monitor their votes and activities, and particularly the votes of member states which receive U.S. aid. Americans will no longer silently suffer the hypocrisy of many of these organizations.

Human Rights. The American people believe that United States foreign policy should be animated by the cause of human rights for all the world's peoples.

A well-rounded human rights policy is concerned with specific individuals whose rights are denied by governments of the right or left, and with entire peoples whose Communist governments deny their claim to human rights as

individuals and acknowledge only the "rights" derived from membership in an economic class. Republicans support a human rights policy which includes both these concerns. . . .

By focusing solely on the shortcomings of non-Communist governments, Democrats have missed the forest for the trees, failing to recognize that the greatest threat to human rights is the Communist system itself. . . .

Arms Control. The prospect for peace is excellent because America is strong again. America's defenses have only one purpose: to assure that our people and free institutions survive and flourish.

Our security requires both the capability to defend against aggression and the will to do so. Together, will and capability deter aggression. That is why the danger of war has grown more remote under President Reagan. . . .

We are proud of a strong America. Our military strength exists for the high moral purpose of deterring conflict, not initiating war. The deterrence of aggression is ethically imperative. . . . We reaffirm the principle that the national security policy of the United States should be based upon a strategy of peace through strength, a goal of the 1980 Republican Platform.

Maintaining a technological superiority, the historical foundation of our policy of deterrence, remains essential. In other areas, such as our maritime forces, we should continue to strive for qualitative superiority.

President Reagan committed our nation to a modernized strategic and theater nuclear force sufficient to deter attack against the United States and our allies, while pursuing negotiations for balanced, verifiable reductions of nuclear weapons under arms control agreements. . . .

We will continue to modernize our deterrent capability while negotiating for verifiable arms control. We will continue the policies that have given fresh confidence and new hope to freedom-loving people everywhere. . . .

The Soviet Union has rejected every invitation by President Reagan to resume talks, refusing to return unless we remove the Pershing II and Cruise missiles which we have placed in Europe at the request of our NATO allies. Soviet intransigence is designed to force concessions from the United States even before negotiations begin. We will not succumb to this strategy. The Soviet Union will return to the bargaining table only when it recognizes that the United States will not make unilateral concessions or allow the Soviet Union to achieve nuclear superiority. . . .

To deter Soviet violations of arms control agreements, the United States must maintain the capability to verify, display a willingness to respond to Soviet violations which have military significance, and adopt a policy whereby the defense of the United States is not constrained by arms control agreements violated by the Soviet Union.

We support the President's efforts to curb the spread of nuclear weapons and to improve international controls and safeguards over sensitive nuclear technologies. The President's non-proliferation policy has emphasized results, rather than rhetoric, as symbolized by the successful meeting of nuclear supplier states in Luxembourg in July of this year. We endorse the President's initiative on comprehensive safeguards and his efforts to encourage other supplier states to support such measures.

The first duty of government is to provide for the common defense. . . . We must continue to devote the resources essential to deter a Soviet threat — a threat which has grown and should be met by an improved and modernized U.S. defense capability. . . .

We will continue to strengthen our intelligence services. We will remove statutory obstacles to the effective management, performance, and security of intelligence sources and methods. We will further improve our ability to influence international events in support of our foreign policy objectives, and we will strengthen our counterintelligence facilities. . . .

. . . Republicans understood that our nuclear deterrent

forces are the ultimate military guarantor of America's security and that of our allies. That is why we will continue to support the programs necessary to modernize our strategic forces and reduce the vulnerabilities. This includes the earliest possible deployment of a new small mobile ICBM. . . .

President Reagan has launched a bold new Strategic Defense Initiative to defend against nuclear attack. We enthusiastically support President Reagan's Strategic Defense Initiative. We enthusiastically support the development of non-nuclear, space-based defensive systems to protect the United States by destroying incoming missiles.

Recognizing the need for close consultation with our allies, we support a comprehensive and intensive effort to render obsolete the doctrine of Mutual Assured Destruction (MAD). The Democratic Party embraces Mutual Assured Destruction. The Republican Party rejects the strategy of despair and supports instead the strategy of hope and survival.

We will begin to eliminate the threat posed by strategic nuclear missiles as soon as possible. Our only purpose (one all people share) is to reduce the danger of nuclear war. To that end, we will use superior American technology to achieve space-based and ground-based defensive systems as soon as possible to protect the lives of the American people and our allies.

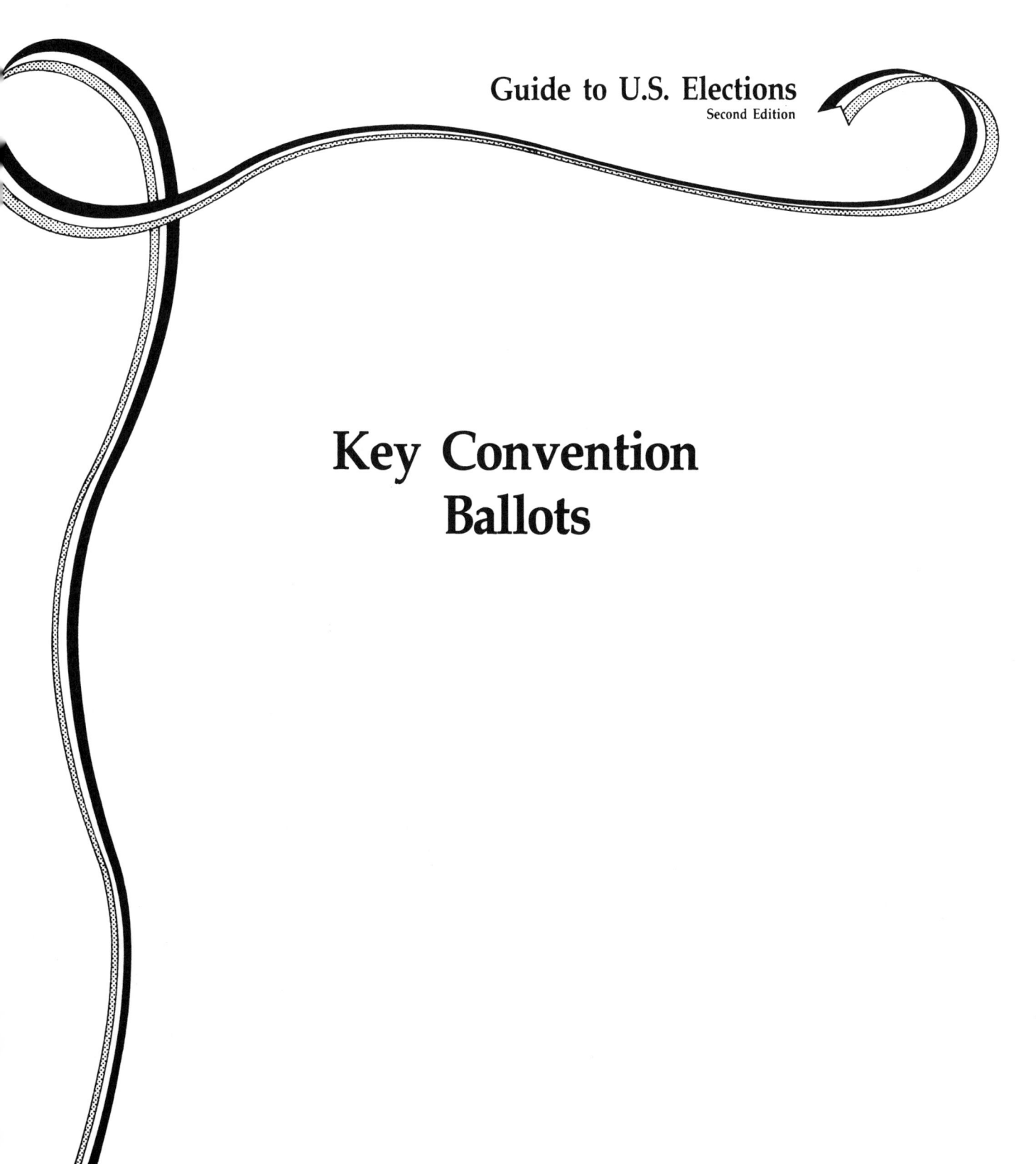

Key Convention Ballots

Sources: Key Convention Ballots

This section (pages 163-221) presents the results of important balloting from the presidential nominating conventions of three major American political parties from 1835 to 1984. The balloting results are arranged in chronological order by convention year. Each table contains a reference indicating the page in the preceding section, "Convention Chronology," where brief descriptions of each convention and key balloting appear.

The source for the balloting results for the 1835-1972 conventions is *Convention Decisions and Voting Records,* Brookings Institution, Washington, D.C., 1973, by Richard C. Bain and Judith H. Parris. Permission to use this material was granted by the Brookings Institution, which holds the copyright. The sources for the 1976, 1980 and 1984 vote totals are *The Official Proceedings of the Democratic National Convention* and the Republican National Committee.

Convention Decisions and Voting Records contains ballots for three major parties in American history — the Democrats, the Whigs and the modern Republicans. This section includes ballots from conventions of these three parties alone.

In selecting ballots to include in the *Guide to U.S. Elections, Second Edition,* Congressional Quarterly followed several criteria:

● To include all initial and deciding presidential

nominating ballots and selected other critical presidential ballots. The Democratic Party conventions of 1832, 1840, 1888, 1916, 1936 and 1964 nominated presidential candidates by acclamation without balloting.

● To include key ballots on important procedural issues, credentials contests and platform disputes.

● To exclude all ballots for vice presidential candidates.

Vote Total Discrepancies

Bain and Parris note frequent discrepancies between totals given in the published proceedings of the party conventions and the totals reached by adding up the state-by-state delegation votes. They state: "Wherever the discrepancy was obvious and the correct figure could be clearly derived, the record has been printed in corrected form. When the added totals of detailed figures listed differ from the sums printed in the proceedings, both totals are given."

Congressional Quarterly has followed this same procedure. For example, on page 166, the 49th presidential ballot of the 1852 Democratic Party convention appears. Franklin Pierce is listed as receiving 279 votes, the sum of the column. A footnote, however, indicates that the convention proceedings recorded Pierce as receiving 283 votes. Similar examples appear on pages 169, 170 and 210.

1844 Democratic

(Narrative, p. 36)

Delegation	Total Votes	Amendment Ratifying Two-Thirds Rule		First Pres. Ballot [1]		Fifth Pres. Ballot [2]		Ninth Pres. Ballot (Before shift)[3]		Ninth Pres. Ballot (After shift)
		Yea	Nay	Van Buren	Cass	Van Buren	Cass	Polk	Cass	Polk
Alabama	9	9	—	1	8	1	8	9	—	9
Arkansas	3	3	—	—	—	—	—	3	—	3
Connecticut	6	3	3	6	—	—	—	6	—	6
Delaware	3	3	—	—	3	—	3	3	—	3
Georgia	10	10	—	—	9	—	9	9	—	10
Illinois	9	9	—	5	2	2	4	9	—	9
Indiana	12	12	—	3	9	1	11	12	—	12
Kentucky	12	12	—	—	—	—	—	12	—	12
Louisiana	6	6	—	—	—	—	—	6	—	6
Maine	9	—	9	8	—	8	1	7	1	9
Maryland	8	6	2	2	4	2	6	7	1	8
Massachusetts	12	5	7	8	1	7	3	10	2	12
Michigan	5	5	—	1	4	—	5	—	5	5
Mississippi	6	6	—	—	6	—	6	6	—	6
Missouri	7	—	7	7	—	7	—	7	—	7
New Hampshire	6	—	6	6	—	2	—	6	—	6
New Jersey	7	7	—	3	2	—	4	2	5	7
New York	36	—	36	36	—	36	—	35	—	36
North Carolina	11	5	5	2	4	—	7	11	—	11
Ohio	23	—	23	23	—	20	3	18	2	23
Pennsylvania	26	12	13	26	—	16	—	19	7	26
Rhode Island	4	2	2	4	—	1	1	4	—	4
Tennessee	13	13	—	—	13	—	13	13	—	13
Vermont	6	3	3	5	1	—	6	—	6	6
Virginia	17	17	—	—	17	—	17	17	—	17
Total	**266**	**148**	**118**	**146**	**83**	**103**	**107**	**231**	**29**	**266**

1. Other candidates: Richard M. Johnson, 24; John C. Calhoun, 6; James Buchanan, 4; Levi Woodbury, 2; Commodore Stewart, 1.
2. Other candidates: Johnson, 29; Buchanan, 26, not voting, 1.
3. Not voting, 6.

1835 Democratic

(Narrative, p. 32)

Delegation	Total Votes	First Pres. Ballot Van Buren
Connecticut	8	8
Delaware	3	3
Georgia	11	11
Indiana	9	9
Kentucky	15	15
Louisiana	5	5
Maine	10	10
Maryland	10	10
Massachusetts	14	14
Mississippi	4	4
Missouri	4	4
New Hampshire	7	7
New Jersey	8	8
New York	42	42
North Carolina	15	15
Ohio	21	21
Pennsylvania	30	30
Rhode Island	4	4
Tennessee	15	15
Vermont	7	7
Virginia	23	23
Total	**265**	**265**

1844 Whig
(Narrative, p. 35)

Delegation	Total Votes	First Pres. Ballot Clay	Delegation	Total Votes	First Pres. Ballot Clay
Alabama	9	9	Missouri	7	7
Arkansas	3	3	New Hampshire	6	6
Connecticut	6	6	New Jersey	7	7
Delaware	3	3	New York	36	36
Georgia	10	10	North Carolina	11	11
Illinois	9	9	Ohio	23	23
Indiana	12	12	Pennsylvania	26	26
Kentucky	12	12	Rhode Island	4	4
Louisiana	6	6	South Carolina	9	9
Maine	9	9	Tennessee	13	13
Maryland	8	8	Vermont	6	6
Massachusetts	12	12	Virginia	17	17
Michigan	5	5			
Mississippi	6	6	Total	275	275

1848 Democratic
(Narrative, p. 37)

Delegation	Total Votes	Adoption of Two-Thirds Rule Yea	Nay	Not Voting	Amendment on N.Y. Credentials Yea	Nay	Not Voting	First Pres. Ballot[1] Cass	Buchanan	Woodbury	Fourth Pres. Ballot[2] Cass	Buchanan	Woodbury
Alabama	9	9	—	—	—	9	—	—	4	5	—	4	5
Arkansas	3	3	—	—	—	3	—	3	—	—	3	—	—
Connecticut	6	6	—	—	6	—	—	—	—	6	—	—	6
Delaware	3	2	1	—	1	2	—	3	—	—	3	—	—
Florida	3	3	—	—	—	3	—	—	—	—	—	—	3
Georgia	10	10	—	—	—	10	—	—	2	5	10	—	—
Illinois	9	9	—	—	9	—	—	9	—	—	9	—	—
Indiana	12	3	9	—	7	5	—	12	—	—	12	—	—
Iowa	4	4	—	—	4	—	—	1	3	—	4	—	—
Kentucky	12	12	—	—	10	2	—	7	1	1	8	1	1
Louisiana	6	6	—	—	—	6	—	6	—	—	6	—	—
Maine	9	9	—	—	9	—	—	—	—	9	—	—	9
Maryland	8	7	1	—	2	5	1	6	—	2	6	—	2
Massachusetts	12	10	2	—	11	1	—	—	—	12	8	—	4
Michigan	5	5	—	—	—	5	—	5	—	—	5	—	—
Mississippi	6	6	—	—	—	6	—	6	—	—	6	—	—
Missouri	7	1	6	—	1	4	2	7	—	—	7	—	—
New Hampshire	6	6	—	—	6	—	—	—	—	6	—	—	6
New Jersey	7	7	—	—	7	—	—	—	7	—	7	—	—
New York	36	—	—	36	—	—	36	—	—	—	—	—	—
North Carolina	11	11	—	—	—	11	—	—	10	1	11	—	—
Ohio	23	—	23	—	14	9	—	23	—	—	23	—	—
Pennsylvania	26	—	26	—	19	7	—	—	26	—	—	26	—
Rhode Island	4	3	1	—	2	2	—	1	—	3	4	—	—
South Carolina	9	9	—	—	—	9	—	—	—	—	9	—	—
Tennessee	13	13	—	—	9	4	—	7	2	1	7	2	2
Texas	4	4	—	—	4	—	—	4	—	—	4	—	—
Vermont	6	1	5	—	5	1	—	4	—	2	6	—	—
Virginia	17	17	—	—	—	17	—	17	—	—	17	—	—
Wisconsin	4	—	4	—	—	4	—	4	—	—	4	—	—
Total	290	176	78	36	126	125	39	125	55	53	179	33	38

1. Other candidates: John C. Calhoun, 9; W. J. Worth, 6; George M. Dallas, 3; not voting, 39.

2. Other candidates: William O. Butler, 4; Worth, 1; not voting, 35.

1848 Whig

(Narrative, p. 38)

Delegation	Total Votes	First Pres. Ballot[1]			Fourth Pres. Ballot[2]		
		Taylor	Clay	Scott	Taylor	Clay	Scott
Alabama	7	6	1	—	6	1	—
Arkansas	3	3	—	—	3	—	—
Connecticut	6	—	6	—	3	3	—
Delaware	3	—	—	—	2	—	1
Florida	3	3	—	—	3	—	—
Georgia	10	10	—	—	10	—	—
Illinois	8	4	3	1	8	—	—
Indiana	12	1	2	9	7	1	4
Iowa	4	2	1	—	4	—	—
Kentucky	12	7	5	—	11	1	—
Louisiana	6	5	1	—	6	—	—
Maine	9	5	1	—	5	—	3
Maryland	8	—	8	—	8	—	—
Massachusetts	12	—	—	—	1	—	2
Michigan	5	—	3	2	2	—	3
Mississippi	6	6	—	—	6	—	—
Missouri	7	6	—	—	7	—	—
New Hampshire	6	—	—	—	2	—	—
New Jersey	7	3	4	—	4	3	—
New York	36	—	29	5	6	13	17
North Carolina	11	6	5	—	10	1	—
Ohio	23	1	1	20	1	1	21
Pennsylvania	26	8	12	6	12	4	10
Rhode Island	4	—	4	—	4	—	—
South Carolina	2	1	1	—	1	1	—
Tennessee	13	13	—	—	13	—	—
Texas	4	4	—	—	4	—	—
Vermont	6	1	5	—	2	2	2
Virginia	17	15	2	—	16	1	—
Wisconsin	4	1	3	—	4	—	—
Total	280	111	97	43	171	32	63

1. Other candidates: Daniel Webster, 22; John McLean, 2; John M. Clayton, 4.
2. Other candidate: Webster, 14.

1852 Democratic

(Narrative, p. 39)

Delegation	Total Votes	First Pres. Ballot[1] Cass	First Pres. Ballot[1] Buchanan	Twentieth Pres. Ballot[2] Buchanan	Twentieth Pres. Ballot[2] Cass	Twentieth Pres. Ballot[2] Douglas	Thirtieth Pres. Ballot[3] Douglas	Thirtieth Pres. Ballot[3] Buchanan	Thirtieth Pres. Ballot[3] Cass	Thirty-Fifth Pres. Ballot[4] Cass	Thirty-Fifth Pres. Ballot[4] Douglas	Thirty-Fifth Pres. Ballot[4] Marcy	Thirty-Fifth Pres. Ballot[4] Buchanan	Forty-Eighth Pres. Ballot[5] Marcy	Forty-Eighth Pres. Ballot[5] Cass	Forty-Eighth Pres. Ballot[5] Pierce	Forty-Eighth Pres. Ballot[5] Douglas	Forty-ninth Pres. Ballot[6] Pierce
Alabama	9	—	9	9	—	—	—	9	—	—	—	—	9	9	—	—	—	9
Arkansas	4	—	4	—	—	4	4	—	—	—	4	—	—	—	—	—	4	4
California	4	—	2	1	—	3	3	1	—	2	1	—	1	—	4	—	—	4
Connecticut	6	2	2	2	2	1	6	—	—	3	3	—	—	6	—	—	—	6
Delaware	3	3	—	—	3	—	—	—	—	3	—	—	—	—	3	—	—	3
Florida	3	—	—	—	—	2	2	—	—	—	2	—	—	—	—	—	2	3
Georgia	10	—	10	10	—	—	—	10	—	—	10	—	—	10	—	—	—	10
Illinois	11	—	—	—	—	11	11	—	—	—	11	—	—	—	—	—	11	11
Indiana	13	—	—	—	—	—	—	—	—	13	—	—	—	—	13	—	—	13
Iowa	4	2	—	—	1	3	4	—	—	2	2	—	—	—	2	—	2	4
Kentucky	12	12	—	—	12	—	—	—	—	12	—	—	—	—	—	12	—	12
Louisiana	6	6	—	—	6	—	6	—	—	6	—	—	—	—	6	—	—	6
Maine	8	5	3	1	4	3	5	2	—	2	5	—	1	—	—	8	—	8
Maryland	8	8	—	—	8	—	—	—	8	8	—	—	—	1	1	5	—	5
Massachusetts	13	9	—	—	1	7	7	—	1	7	1	5	—	6	—	6	1	13
Michigan	6	6	—	—	6	—	—	—	6	6	—	—	—	—	6	—	—	6
Mississippi	7	—	7	7	—	—	—	7	—	—	—	7	—	7	—	—	—	7
Missouri	9	9	—	—	—	9	9	—	—	9	—	—	—	—	9	—	—	9
New Hampshire	5	4	—	—	5	—	—	2	—	5	—	—	—	—	—	5	—	5
New Jersey	7	7	—	7	—	—	—	7	—	7	—	—	—	7	—	—	—	7
New York	35	11	—	—	12	—	1	—	11	12	1	22	—	24	10	—	1	35
North Carolina	10	—	10	9	—	1	4	6	—	—	—	10	—	10	—	—	—	10
Ohio	23	16	—	—	13	6	9	—	7	18	3	—	—	—	15	—	4	17
Pennsylvania	27	—	27	27	—	—	—	27	—	—	—	—	27	—	—	—	—	27
Rhode Island	4	3	—	—	—	4	4	—	—	4	—	—	—	—	—	4	—	4
Tennessee	12	6	6	4	5	3	7	5	—	9	2	—	1	9	—	—	1	12
Texas	4	—	—	—	—	—	—	—	—	—	—	—	—	—	—	—	—	4
Vermont	5	5	—	—	—	5	5	—	—	—	5	—	—	—	—	—	5	5
Virginia	15	—	15	15	—	—	—	15	—	—	—	—	—	—	—	15	—	15
Wisconsin	5	2	—	—	3	2	5	—	—	3	2	—	—	—	3	—	2	5
Total	288	116	93	92	81	64	92	91	33	131	52	44	39	89	72	55	33	279[a]

a. Sum of column; proceedings record 283.
1. Other candidates: William L. Marcy, 27; Stephen A. Douglas, 20; Joseph Lane, 13; Samuel Houston, 8; J. B. Weller, 4; Henry Dodge, 3; William O. Butler, 2; Daniel S. Dickinson, 1; not voting, 1.
2. Other candidates: Marcy, 26; Lane, 13; Houston, 10; Butler, 1; Dickinson, 1.
3. Other candidates: Marcy, 26; Butler, 20; Lane, 13; Houston, 12; Dickinson, 1.
4. Other candidates: Franklin Pierce, 15; Houston, 5; Butler, 1; Dickinson, 1.
5. Other candidates: Buchanan, 28; Houston, 6; Linn Boyd, 2; Butler, 1; R. J. Ingersoll, 1; Dickinson, 1.
6. Other candidates: Cass, 2; Douglas, 2; Butler, 1; Houston, 1; not voting, 3.

1852 Whig

(Narrative, p. 40)

Delegation	Total Votes	First Pres. Ballot			50th Pres. Ballot			52nd Pres. Ballot			53rd Pres. Ballot		
		Scott	Fillmore	Webster	Scott	Fillmore	Webster	Scott	Fillmore	Webster	Scott	Fillmore	Webster
Alabama	9	—	9	—	—	9	—	—	9	—	—	9	—
Arkansas	4	—	4	—	—	4	—	—	4	—	—	4	—
California	4	2	1	1	3	1	—	3	—	1	3	—	1
Connecticut	6	2	1	3	2	1	3	2	1	3	2	1	3
Delaware	3	3	—	—	3	—	—	3	—	—	3	—	—
Florida	3	—	3	—	—	3	—	—	3	—	—	3	—
Georgia	10	—	10	—	—	10	—	—	10	—	—	10	—
Illinois	11	11	—	—	11	—	—	11	—	—	11	—	—
Indiana	13	13	—	—	13	—	—	13	—	—	13	—	—
Iowa	4	—	4	—	1	3	—	1	3	—	1	3	—
Kentucky	12	—	12	—	—	12	—	—	12	—	—	11	—
Louisiana	6	—	6	—	—	6	—	—	6	—	—	6	—
Maine	8	8	—	—	8	—	—	8	—	—	8	—	—
Maryland	8	—	8	—	—	8	—	—	8	—	—	8	—
Massachusetts	13	2	—	11	2	—	11	2	—	11	2	—	11
Michigan	6	6	—	—	6	—	—	6	—	—	6	—	—
Mississippi	7	—	7	—	—	7	—	—	7	—	—	7	—
Missouri	9	—	9	—	3	6	—	1	6	—	3	6	—
New Hampshire	5	1	—	4	1	—	4	1	—	4	5	—	—
New Jersey	7	7	—	—	7	—	—	7	—	—	7	—	—
New York	35	24	7	2	25	7	1	25	7	1	25	7	1
North Carolina	10	—	10	—	—	10	—	—	10	—	—	10	—
Ohio	23	22	1	—	23	—	—	23	—	—	23	—	—
Pennsylvania	27	26	1	—	26	1	—	27	—	—	27	—	—
Rhode Island	4	1	1	2	2	—	2	2	—	2	3	—	1
South Carolina	8	—	8	—	—	8	—	—	8	—	—	8	—
Tennessee	12	—	12	—	—	12	—	4	8	—	3	9	—
Texas	4	—	4	—	—	4	—	—	4	—	—	4	—
Vermont	5	1	1	3	2	—	3	2	2	1	5	—	—
Virginia	15	1	13	—	3	10	—	3	10	—	8	6	—
Wisconsin	5	1	1	3	1	1	3	2	—	2	1	—	4
Total	296	132[a]	133	29	142	122[a]	27	148[a]	118	25	159	112	21

a. The sum of the column for Scott on the first ballot is 131 votes, for Fillmore on the 50th ballot 123 votes and for Scott on the 52nd ballot is 146 votes. The source for these discrepancies is the Baltimore *Sun* for June 19, 1852 and June 22, 1852. The *Sun* reported June 19, 1852, total votes for Scott on the first ballot as 132 votes; however, the column of figures for the state-by-state ballots reported in the *Sun* add up to 131 votes. Similarly, on June 22, 1852 the *Sun* reported 122 votes for Fillmore on the 50th ballot and 148 for Scott on the 52nd ballot, but the state-by-state ballots reported in the *Sun* add up to 123 votes and 146 votes, respectively. Bain's *Convention Decisions and Voting Records* used the Baltimore *Sun* as its source for the 1852 Whig convention ballots.

1856 Democratic

(Narrative, p. 43)

Delegation	Total Votes	First Pres. Ballot				Tenth Pres. Ballot				Fifteenth Pres. Ballot			17th Pres. Ballot
		Buchanan	Pierce	Douglas	Other	Buchanan	Pierce	Douglas	Other	Buchanan	Douglas	Other	Buchanan
Alabama	9	—	9	—	—	—	9	—	—	—	9	—	9
Arkansas	4	—	4	—	—	—	—	4	—	—	4	—	4
California	4	—	—	—	4	—	—	—	4	—	—	4	4
Connecticut	3	6	—	—	—	6	—	—	—	6	—	—	6
Delaware	3	3	—	—	—	3	—	—	—	3	—	—	3
Florida	3	—	3	—	—	—	3	—	—	—	3	—	3
Georgia	10	—	10	—	—	3	—	7	—	3	7	—	10
Illinois	11	—	—	11	—	—	—	11	—	—	11	—	11
Indiana	13	13	—	—	—	13	—	—	—	13	—	—	13
Iowa	4	—	—	4	—	2	—	2	—	2	2	—	4
Kentucky	12	4	5	3	—	4½	—	7½	—	4	7	1	12
Louisiana	6	6	—	—	—	6	—	—	—	6	—	—	6
Maine	8	5	3	—	—	6	2	—	—	7	—	1	8
Maryland	8	6	2	—	—	7	1	—	—	8	—	—	8
Massachusetts	13	4	9	—	—	6	7	—	—	10	3	—	13
Michigan	6	6	—	—	—	6	—	—	—	6	—	—	6
Mississippi	7	—	7	—	—	—	7	—	—	—	7	—	7
Missouri	9	—	—	9	—	—	—	9	—	—	9	—	9
New Hampshire	5	—	5	—	—	—	5	—	—	—	5	—	5
New Jersey	7	7	—	—	—	7	—	—	—	7	—	—	7
New York	35	17	18	—	—	18	17	—	—	17	18	—	35
North Carolina	10	—	10	—	—	—	10	—	—	—	10	—	10
Ohio	23	13½	4½	4	1	13	3½	5	1½	13½	6½	3	23
Pennsylvania	27	27	—	—	—	27	—	—	—	27	—	—	27
Rhode Island	4	—	4	—	—	—	4	—	—	4	—	—	4
South Carolina	8	—	8	—	—	—	8	—	—	—	8	—	8
Tennessee	12	—	12	—	—	—	—	12	—	12	—	—	12
Texas	4	—	4	—	—	—	4	—	—	—	4	—	4
Vermont	5	—	5	—	—	—	—	5	—	—	5	—	5
Virginia	15	15	—	—	—	15	—	—	—	15	—	—	15
Wisconsin	5	3	—	2	—	5	—	—	—	5	—	—	5
Total	**296**	**135½**	**122½**	**33**	**5[1]**	**147½**	**80½**	**62½**	**5½[2]**	**168½**	**118½**	**9[3]**	**296**

1. Other candidate: Lewis Cass, 5.
2. Other candidate: Cass, 5½.
3. Other candidates: Cass, 4½; Pierce, 3½; not voting, 1.

1856 Republican

(Narrative, p. 42)

Delegation	Total Votes	Informal Pres. Ballot[1]		Formal Pres. Ballot[2]	Delegation	Total Votes	Informal Pres. Ballot[1]		Formal Pres. Ballot[2]
		Fremont	McLean	Fremont			Fremont	McLean	Fremont
California	12	12	—	12	Minnesota	2	—	—	—
Connecticut	18	18	—	18	New Hampshire	15	15	—	15
Delaware	9	—	9	9	New Jersey	21	7	14	21
Illinois	34	14	19	33	New York	105	93	3	105
Indiana	39	18	21	39	Ohio	69	30	39	55
Iowa	12	12	—	12	Pennsylvania	81	10	71	57
Kansas	10	9	—	9	Rhode Island	12	12	—	12
Kentucky	5	5	—	5	Vermont	15	15	—	15
Maine	24	13	11	24	Wisconsin	15	15	—	15
Maryland	9	4	3	7	District of Columbia	3	—	—	—
Massachusetts	39	39	—	39	**Total**	**567**	**359**	**190**	**520**
Michigan	18	18	—	18					

1. Other candidates: Nathaniel Banks, 1; Charles Sumner, 2; William Seward, 1; absent or not voting, 14.
2. Other candidates: John McLean, 37; Seward, 1; absent or not voting, 9.

1860 Democratic

(Narrative, p. 45)

Charleston Convention   ## Baltimore Convention

Delegation	Total Votes	Butler Amend. on 1856 platform Yea	Nay	Minority Report on platform Yea	Nay	First Pres. Ballot[1] Douglas	Hunter	Guthrie	57th Pres. Ballot[2] Douglas	Guthrie	Minority Report on Credentials Yea	Nay	Not Voting	Reconsider Louisiana Credentials Yea	Nay	Not Voting	First Pres. Ballot[3] Douglas	Second Pres. Ballot[4] Douglas
Alabama	9	—	9	—	9	—	—	—	—	—	—	—	9	—	—	9	9	9
Arkansas	4	—	4	—	4	—	1	—	—	—	½	½	3	½	½	3	1	1½
California	4	—	4	—	4	—	—	—	—	—	4	—	—	—	4	—	—	—
Connecticut	6	2½	3½	6	—	3½	—	—	3½	2½	2½	3½	—	3½	2½	—	3½	3½
Delaware	3	3	—	—	3	—	2	—	—	—	2	—	1	—	2	1	—	—
Florida	3	—	3	—	3	—	—	—	—	—	—	—	3	—	—	3	—	—
Georgia	10	10	—	—	10	—	—	—	—	—	—	—	10	—	—	10	—	—
Illinois	11	—	11	11	—	11	—	—	11	—	—	11	—	11	—	—	11	11
Indiana	13	—	13	13	—	13	—	—	13	—	—	13	—	13	—	—	13	13
Iowa	4	—	4	4	—	4	—	—	4	—	—	4	—	4	—	—	4	4
Kentucky	12	9	3	2½	9½	—	—	12	—	12	10	2	—	2	10	—	—	3
Louisiana	6	—	6	—	6	—	—	—	—	—	—	—	6	—	—	6	6	6
Maine	8	3	5	8	—	5	—	3	5	3	2½	5½	—	5½	2½	—	5½	7
Maryland	8	5½	2½	3½	4½	2	5	—	4	4	5½	2	½	2	6	—	2½	2½
Massachusetts	13	8	5	7	6	5½	6	—	6	6	8	5	—	5	8	—	10	10
Michigan	6	—	6	6	—	6	—	—	6	—	—	6	—	6	—	—	6	6
Minnesota	4	1½	2½	4	—	4	—	—	—	3	1½	2½	—	2½	1½	—	2½	4
Mississippi	7	—	7	—	7	—	—	—	—	—	—	—	7	—	—	7	—	—
Missouri	9	4½	4½	4	5	4½	—	4½	4½	4½	5	4	—	4½	4½	—	4½	4½
New Hampshire	5	—	5	5	—	5	—	—	5	—	½	4½	—	4½	½	—	5	5
New Jersey	7	5	2	5	2	—	—	7	2	5	4	3	—	2½	4½	—	2½	2½
New York	35	—	35	35	—	35	—	—	35	—	—	35	—	35	—	—	35	35
North Carolina	10	10	—	—	10	1	9	—	1	—	9	1	—	1	8½	½	1	1
Ohio	23	—	23	23	—	23	—	—	23	—	—	23	—	23	—	—	23	23
Oregon	3	3	—	—	3	—	—	—	—	—	3	—	—	—	3	—	—	—
Pennsylvania	27	16½	10½	12	15	9	3	9	9½	17½	17	10	—	10	17	—	10	19
Rhode Island	4	—	4	4	—	4	—	—	4	—	—	4	—	4	—	—	4	4
South Carolina	8	—	8	—	8	—	1	—	—	—	—	—	8	—	—	8	—	—
Tennessee	12	11	1	1	11	—	—	—	1	11	10	1	1	2	10	—	3	3
Texas	4	—	4	—	4	—	—	—	—	—	—	—	4	—	—	4	—	—
Vermont	5	—	5	5	—	5	—	—	—	5	1½	3½	—	4½	½	—	5	5
Virginia	15	12½	2½	1	14	—	15	—	1	—	14	1	—	—	15	—	1½	3
Wisconsin	5	—	5	5	—	5	—	—	5	—	—	5	—	5	—	—	5	5
Total	303	105	198	165	138	145½	42	35½[a]	151½	65½	100½	150	52½	151[b]	100½[c]	51½	173½	190½[d]

a. Sum of column; proceedings record 35.

b. Sum of column; proceedings record 150½.

c. Sum of column, proceedings record 99.

d. Sum of column; proceedings record 181½.

1. Other candidates: Andrew Johnson, 12; Daniel S. Dickenson, 7; Joseph Lane, 6; Isaac Toucey, 2½; Jefferson Davis, 1½; James A. Pearce, 1; not voting, 50.

2. Other candidates: Robert M. T. Hunter, 16; Lane, 14; Dickinson, 4; Davis, 1; not voting, 51.

3. Other candidates: James Guthrie, 9; John C. Breckinridge, 5; Thomas S. Bocock, 1; Horatio Seymour, 1; Henry A. Wise, ½; Dickinson, ½; not voting 112½.

4. Other candidates: Breckinridge, 7½; Guthrie, 5½; not voting, 99½.

1860 Republican

(Narrative, p. 46)

Delegation	Total Votes	First Pres. Ballot [1] Seward	Lincoln	Cameron	Bates	Chase	Second Pres. Ballot [2] Seward	Lincoln	Third Pres. Ballot [3] (Before shift) Seward	Lincoln	Third Pres. Ballot [4] (After shift) Seward	Lincoln
California	8	8	—	—	—	—	8	—	8	—	3	5
Connecticut	12	—	2	—	7	2	—	4	1	4	1	8
Delaware	6	—	—	—	6	—	—	6	—	6	—	6
Illinois	22	—	22	—	—	—	—	22	—	22	—	22
Indiana	26	—	26	—	—	—	—	26	—	26	—	26
Iowa	8	2	2	1	1	1	2	5	2	5½	—	8
Kansas	6	6	—	—	—	—	6	—	6	—	—	6
Kentucky	23	5	6	—	—	8	7	9	6	13	—	23
Maine	16	10	6	—	—	—	10	6	10	6	—	16
Maryland	11	3	—	—	8	—	3	—	2	9	2	9
Massachusetts	26	21	4	—	—	—	22	4	18	8	18	8
Michigan	12	12	—	—	—	—	12	—	12	—	12	—
Minnesota	8	8	—	—	—	—	8	—	8	—	—	8
Missouri	18	—	—	—	18	—	—	—	—	—	—	18
Nebraska	6	2	1	1	—	2	3	1	3	1	—	6
New Hampshire	10	—	—	—	—	1	1	9	1	9	—	10
New Jersey	14	1	7	—	—	—	4	—	5	8	5	8
New York	70	70	—	—	—	—	70	—	70	—	70	—
Ohio	46	—	8	—	—	34	—	14	—	29	—	46
Oregon	5	—	—	—	5	—	—	—	1	4	—	5
Pennsylvania	54	1½	4	47½	—	—	2½	48	—	52	½	53
Rhode Island	8	—	—	—	1	1	—	3	1	5	—	8
Texas	6	4	—	—	2	—	6	—	6	—	—	6
Vermont	10	—	—	—	—	—	—	10	—	10	—	10
Virginia	23	8	14	1	—	—	8	14	8	14	—	23
Wisconsin	10	10	—	—	—	—	10	—	10	—	10	—
District of Columbia	2	2	—	—	—	—	2	—	2	—	—	2
Total	**466**	**173½**	**102**	**50½**	**48**	**49**	**184½**	**181**	**180**	**231½**	**121½**	**340** [a]

a. Sum of column; proceedings record 364.
1. Other candidates: Benjamin F. Wade, 3; John McLean, 12; John M. Reed, 1; William L. Dayton, 14; Charles Sumner, 1; John C. Fremont, 1; Jacob Collamer, 10; absent and not voting, 1.
2. Other candidates: Edward Bates, 35; Simon Cameron, 2; John McLean, 8; Salmon P. Chase, 42½; William L. Dayton, 10; Cassius M. Clay, 2; absent and not voting, 1.
3. Other candidates: Edward Bates, 22; Salmon P. Chase, 24½; John McLean, 5; William L. Dayton, 1; Cassius M. Clay, 1; absent and not voting, 1.
4. Other candidates: Salmon P. Chase, 2; Dayton, 1; Cassius M. Clay, 1; McLean, ½.

1864 Democratic

(Narrative, p. 49)

Delegation	Total Votes	First Pres. Ballot[1] (Before shift)		First Pres. Ballot (After shift)	
		McClellan	Seymour	McClellan	Seymour
California	5	2½	2½	5	—
Connecticut	6	5½	—	6	—
Delaware	3	—	3	—	3
Illinois	16	16	—	16	—
Indiana	13	9½	3½	9½	3½
Iowa	8	3	—	8	—
Kansas	3	3	—	3	—
Kentucky	11	5½	5½	11	—
Maine	7	4	3	7	—
Maryland	7	—	7	—	7
Massachusetts	12	11½	—	12	—
Michigan	8	6½	—	8	—
Minnesota	4	4	—	4	—
Missouri	11	6½	—	7	4
New Hampshire	5	5	—	5	—
New Jersey	7	7	—	7	—
New York	33	33	—	33	—
Ohio	21	8½	10½	15	6
Oregon	3	2	1	3	—
Pennsylvania	26	26	—	26	—
Rhode Island	4	4	—	4	—
Vermont	5	4	1	5	—
Wisconsin	8	7	1	8	—
Total	226	174	38	202½	23½ [a]

1. Other candidates: Horatio Seymour, 12; Charles O'Connor, ½; blank, 1½.
a. Sum of column; proceedings record 28½.

1864 Republican

(Narrative, p. 48)

Delegation	Total Votes	First Pres. Ballot[1]	
		Lincoln	Grant
Arkansas	10	10	—
California	10	7	—
Colorado	6	6	—
Connecticut	12	12	—
Delaware	6	6	—
Illinois	32	32	—
Indiana	26	26	—
Iowa	16	16	—
Kansas	6	6	—
Kentucky	22	22	—
Louisiana	14	14	—
Maine	14	14	—
Maryland	14	14	—
Massachusetts	24	24	—
Michigan	16	16	—
Minnesota	8	8	—
Missouri	22	—	22
Nebraska	6	6	—
Nevada	6	6	—
New Hampshire	10	10	—
New Jersey	14	14	—
New York	66	66	—
Ohio	42	42	—
Oregon	6	6	—
Pennsylvania	52	52	—
Rhode Island	8	8	—
Tennessee	15	15	—
Vermont	10	10	—
West Virginia	10	10	—
Wisconsin	16	16	—
Total	519	494 [b]	22

1. Not voting, 3.
b. Sum of column; proceedings record 484.

1868 Democratic

(Narrative, p. 51)

| Delegation | Total Votes | First Pres. Ballot [1] | | | | 22nd Pres. Ballot [2] (Before shift) | | 22nd Pres. Ballot (After shift) |
		Pendleton	Hancock	Church	Johnson	Hancock	Hendricks	Seymour
Alabama	8	—	—	—	8	8	—	8
Arkansas	5	—	—	—	—	—	5	5
California	5	2	—	—	—	—	5	5
Connecticut	6	—	—	—	—	—	—	6
Delaware	3	3	—	—	—	3	—	3
Florida	3	—	—	—	3	—	3	3
Georgia	9	—	—	—	9	9	—	9
Illinois	16	16	—	—	—	—	16	16
Indiana	13	13	—	—	—	—	13	13
Iowa	8	8	—	—	—	—	8	8
Kansas	3	2	—	—	—	1	2	3
Kentucky	11	11	—	—	—	—	—	11
Louisiana	7	—	7	—	—	7	—	7
Maine	7	1½	4½	—	1	4½	2½	7
Maryland	7	4½	—	—	2½	6	1	7
Massachusetts	12	1	11	—	—	—	—	12
Michigan	8	—	—	—	—	—	8	8
Minnesota	4	4	—	—	—	—	4	4
Mississippi	7	—	7	—	—	7	—	7
Missouri	11	5	2	1	½	2	8	11
Nebraska	3	3	—	—	—	—	3	3
Nevada	3	—	—	—	—	—	3	3
New Hampshire	5	2	2	—	—	4½	½	5
New Jersey	7	—	—	—	—	—	7	7
New York	33	—	—	33	—	—	33	33
North Carolina	9	—	—	—	9	—	9	9
Ohio	21	21	—	—	—	—	—	21
Oregon	3	3	—	—	—	—	3	3
Pennsylvania	26	—	—	—	—	26	—	26
Rhode Island	4	—	—	—	—	—	—	4
South Carolina	6	—	—	—	6	6	—	6
Tennessee	10	—	—	—	10	3½	1½	10
Texas	6	—	—	—	6	6	—	6
Vermont	5	—	—	—	—	—	5	5
Virginia	10	—	—	—	10	10	—	10
West Virginia	5	5	—	—	—	—	5	5
Wisconsin	8	—	—	—	—	—	—	8
Total	317	105	33½	34	65	103½	145½	317

1. Other candidates: James E. English, 16; Joel Parker, 13; Asa Packer, 26; James R. Doolittle, 13; Thomas A. Hendricks, 2½; Frank P. Blair, ½; Reverdy Johnson, 8½.

2. Other candidates: Horatio Seymour, 22; English, 7; Doolittle, 4; Johnson, 4; not voting, 31.

1868 Republican

(Narrative, p. 50)

Delegation	Total Votes	First Pres. Ballot Grant		Delegation	Total Votes	First Pres. Ballot Grant		Delegation	Total Votes	First Pres. Ballot Grant
Alabama	18	18		Maine	14	14		Ohio	42	42
Arkansas	10	10		Maryland	14	14		Oregon	6	6
California	10	10		Massachusetts	24	24		Pennsylvania	52	52
Colorado	6	6		Michigan	16	16		Rhode Island	8	8
Connecticut	12	12		Minnesota	8	8		South Carolina	12	12
Delaware	6	6		Mississippi	14	14		Tennessee	20	20
Florida	6	6		Missouri	22	22		Texas	12	12
Georgia	18	18		Montana	2	2		Vermont	10	10
Idaho	2	2		Nebraska	6	6		Virginia	20	20
Illinois	32	32		Nevada	6	6		West Virginia	10	10
Indiana	26	26		New Hampshire	10	10		Wisconsin	16	16
Iowa	16	16		New Jersey	14	14		District of Columbia	2	2
Kansas	6	6		New York	66	66		**Total**	650	650
Kentucky	22	22		North Carolina	18	18				
Louisiana	14	14		North Dakota [a]	2	2				

a. Dakota Territory. includes North and South Dakota.

1872 Democratic

(Narrative, p. 53)

Delegation	Total Votes	First Pres. Ballot[1] Greeley
Alabama	20	20
Arkansas	12	12
California	12	12
Connecticut	12	12
Delaware	6	—
Florida	8	6
Georgia	22	18
Illinois	42	42
Indiana	30	30
Iowa	22	22
Kansas	10	10
Kentucky	24	24
Louisiana	16	16
Maine	14	14
Maryland	16	16
Massachusetts	26	26
Michigan	22	22
Minnesota	10	10
Mississippi	16	16
Missouri	30	30
Nebraska	6	6
Nevada	6	6
New Hampshire	10	10
New Jersey	18	9
New York	70	70
North Carolina	20	20
Ohio	44	44
Oregon	6	6
Pennsylvania	58	35
Rhode Island	8	8
South Carolina	14	14
Tennessee	24	24
Texas	16	16
Vermont	10	10
Virginia	22	22
West Virginia	10	8
Wisconsin	20	20
Total	**732**	**686**

1. Other candidates: Thomas F. Bayard, 15; Jeremiah S. Black. 21; William S. Groesbeck, 2; blank, 8.

1872 Republican

(Narrative, p. 53)

Delegation	Total Votes	First Pres. Ballot Grant
Alabama	20	20
Arizona	2	2
Arkansas	12	12
California	12	12
Colorado	2	2
Connecticut	12	12
Delaware	6	6
Florida	8	8
Georgia	22	22
Idaho	2	2
Illinois	42	42
Indiana	30	30
Iowa	22	22
Kansas	10	10
Kentucky	24	24
Louisiana	16	16
Maine	14	14
Maryland	16	16
Massachusetts	26	26
Michigan	22	22
Minnesota	10	10
Mississippi	16	16
Missouri	30	30
Montana	2	2
Nebraska	6	6
Nevada	6	6
New Hampshire	10	10
New Jersey	18	18
New Mexico	2	2
New York	70	70
North Carolina	20	20
North Dakota [a]	2	2
Ohio	44	44
Oregon	6	6
Pennsylvania	58	58
Rhode Island	8	8
South Carolina	14	14
Tennessee	24	24
Texas	16	16
Utah	2	2
Vermont	10	10
Virginia	22	22
Washington	2	2
West Virginia	10	10
Wisconsin	20	20
Wyoming	2	2
District of Columbia	2	2
Total	**752**	**752**

a. Dakota Territory. includes North and South Dakota.

1876 Democratic

(Narrative, p. 55)

Delegation	Total Votes	First Pres. Ballot[1]			Second Pres. Ballot[2]	
		Tilden	Hendricks	Hancock	Tilden	Hendricks
Alabama	20	13	5	2	20	—
Arkansas	12	12	—	—	12	—
California	12	12	—	—	12	—
Colorado	6	—	6	—	6	—
Connecticut	12	12	—	—	12	—
Delaware	6	—	—	—	6	—
Florida	8	8	—	—	8	—
Georgia	22	5	—	1	22	—
Illinois	42	19	23	—	26	16
Indiana	30	—	30	—	—	30
Iowa	22	14	6	2	22	—
Kansas	10	—	10	—	2	8
Kentucky	24	24	—	—	24	—
Louisiana	16	9	—	5	16	—
Maine	14	14	—	—	14	—
Maryland	16	11	3	—	14	2
Massachusetts	26	26	—	—	26	—
Michigan	22	14	8	—	19	3
Minnesota	10	10	—	—	10	—
Mississippi	16	16	—	—	16	—
Missouri	30	—	14	—	30	—
Nebraska	6	6	—	—	6	—
Nevada	6	3	3	—	4	—
New Hampshire	10	10	—	—	10	—
New Jersey	18	—	—	—	18	—
New York	70	70	—	—	70	—
North Carolina	20	9	4	5	20	—
Ohio	44	—	—	—	—	—
Oregon	6	6	—	—	6	—
Pennsylvania	58	—	—	58	—	—
Rhode Island	8	8	—	—	8	—
South Carolina	14	14	—	—	14	—
Tennessee	24	—	24	—	—	24
Texas	16	10½	2½	2	16	—
Vermont	10	10	—	—	10	—
Virginia	22	17	1	—	17	1
West Virginia	10	—	—	—	—	—
Wisconsin	20	19	1	—	19	1
Total	**738**	**401½** [a]	**140½**	**75**	**535**	**85**

a. Sum of column; proceedings record 404½.
1. Other candidates: William Allen, 54; Allen G. Thurman, 3; Thomas F. Bayard, 33; Joel Parker, 18; James O. Broadhead, 16.
2. Other candidates: Allen, 54; Bayard, 4; Hancock, 58; Thurman, 2.

1876 Republican

(Narrative, p. 54)

Delegation	Total Votes	First Pres. Ballot[1]				Abolish Unit Rule			Fifth Pres. Ballot[2]					Sixth Pres. Ballot[3]					Seventh Pres. Ballot[4]	
		Blaine	Morton	Conkling	Bristow	Yea	Nay	Not Voting	Blaine	Bristow	Conkling	Hayes	Morton	Blaine	Morton	Conkling	Bristow	Hayes	Blaine	Hayes
Ala.	20	10	—	—	7	20	—	—	16	4	—	—	—	15	—	—	4	1	17	—
Ariz.	2	2	—	—	—	2	—	—	2	—	—	—	—	2	—	—	—	—	2	—
Ark.	12	—	12	—	—	4	8	—	1	—	—	—	11	1	11	—	—	—	11	1
Calif.	12	9	—	1	2	11	1	—	6	—	3	3	—	6	—	2	—	4	6	6
Colo.	6	6	—	—	—	6	—	—	6	—	—	—	—	6	—	—	—	—	6	—
Conn.	12	—	—	—	2	3	9	—	2	8	—	2	—	2	—	—	7	3	2	3
Del.	6	6	—	—	—	5	1	—	6	—	—	—	—	6	—	—	—	—	6	—
Fla.	8	1	4	3	—	4	4	—	2	—	—	—	3	4	4	—	—	—	8	—
Ga.	22	5	6	8	3	9	13	—	8	2	6	—	5	9	4	6	2	—	14	7
Idaho	2	2	—	—	—	2	—	—	2	—	—	—	—	2	—	—	—	—	2	—
Ill.	42	38	—	—	3	38	4	—	33	5	—	3	—	32	—	—	5	3	35	2
Ind.	30	—	30	—	—	1	29	—	—	—	—	—	30	—	30	—	—	—	—	25
Iowa	22	22	—	—	—	22	—	—	21	—	1	—	—	21	—	—	—	1	22	—
Kan.	10	10	—	—	—	10	—	—	10	—	—	—	—	10	—	—	—	—	10	—
Ky.	24	—	—	—	24	1	23	—	—	24	—	—	—	—	—	—	24	—	—	24
La.	16	2	14	—	—	6	10	—	5	—	—	—	11	6	10	—	—	—	14	2
Maine	14	14	—	—	—	14	—	—	14	—	—	—	—	14	—	—	—	—	14	—
Md.	16	16	—	—	—	16	—	—	16	—	—	—	—	16	—	—	—	—	16	—
Mass.	26	6	—	—	17	15	7	4	5	19	—	—	—	5	—	—	19	—	5	21
Mich.	22	8	—	1	9	3	19	—	—	—	—	—	22	—	—	—	—	22	—	22
Minn.	10	10	—	—	—	7	3	—	9	—	—	—	—	9	—	—	—	—	9	1
Miss.	16	—	11	1	3	9	6	1	—	8	2	2	4	1	5	2	4	4	—	16
Mo.	30	14	12	1	2	25	5	—	20	3	—	2	5	18	7	—	3	2	20	10
Mont.	2	2	—	—	—	2	—	—	1	—	—	1	—	1	—	—	—	1	—	2
Neb.	6	6	—	—	—	6	—	—	6	—	—	—	—	6	—	—	—	—	6	—
Nev.	6	—	—	2	3	—	6	—	—	1	2	1	—	—	—	2	2	1	—	6
N.H.	10	7	—	—	3	10	—	—	7	3	—	—	—	7	—	—	3	—	7	3
N.J.	18	13	—	—	—	15	3	—	12	—	—	6	—	12	—	—	—	6	12	6
N.M.	2	2	—	—	—	2	—	—	2	—	—	—	—	2	—	—	—	—	2	—
N.Y.	70	—	—	69	1	15	54	1	—	2	68	—	—	—	—	68	2	—	9	61
N.C.	20	9	2	7	1	6	13	1	—	—	—	12	1	12	1	—	—	1	—	20
N.D.[a]	2	2	—	—	—	2	—	—	2	—	—	—	—	2	—	—	—	—	2	—
Ohio	44	—	—	—	—	14	30	—	—	—	—	—	44	—	—	—	—	44	—	44
Oregon	6	6	—	—	—	6	—	—	6	—	—	—	—	6	—	—	—	—	6	—
Pa.	58	—	—	—	—	1	57	—	5	—	—	—	—	14	—	—	—	—	30	28
R.I.	8	2	—	—	6	1	7	—	2	6	—	—	—	2	—	—	6	—	2	6
S.C.	14	—	13	—	1	2	12	—	5	3	—	1	5	10	2	—	1	1	7	7
Tenn.	24	4	10	—	10	19	5	—	7	10	—	—	7	7	1	—	12	4	6	18
Texas	16	2	5	3	6	4	12	—	3	3	—	1	8	2	4	1	1	7	1	15
Utah	2	2	—	—	—	2	—	—	2	—	—	—	—	2	—	—	—	—	2	—
Vt.	10	1	—	—	8	5	5	—	—	8	—	—	—	—	—	—	8	2	—	10
Va.	22	16	3	3	—	19	2	1	16	—	—	—	3	13	4	—	3	2	14	8
Wash.	2	2	—	—	—	2	—	—	2	—	—	—	—	2	—	—	—	—	2	—
W.Va.	10	8	—	—	—	10	—	—	7	—	—	—	2	6	—	—	—	4	6	4
Wis.	20	20	—	—	—	17	3	—	16	3	—	—	1	16	1	—	3	—	16	4
Wyo.	2	—	—	—	2	—	2	—	—	2	—	—	—	—	—	—	2	—	—	2
D.C.	2	—	2	—	—	2	—	—	1	—	—	—	1	1	1	—	—	—	2	—
Total	**756**	**285**	**124**	**99**	**113**	**395**	**353**	**8**	**286**	**114**	**82**	**104**	**95**	**308**	**85**	**81**	**111**	**113**	**351**	**384**

1. Other candidates: Rutherford B. Hayes, 61; John F. Hartranft, 58; Marshall Jewell, 11; William A. Wheeler, 3; not voting, 2.

2. Other candidates: Hartranft, 69; Elihu B. Washburne, 3; Wheeler, 2; not voting, 2.

3. Other candidates: Hartranft, 50; Washburne, 4; Wheeler, 2; not voting, 2.

4. Other candidates: Benjamin H. Bristow, 21.

a. Dakota Territory, includes North and South Dakota.

1880 Democratic

(Narrative, p. 58)

Delegation	Total Vote	First Pres. Ballot [1]			Second Pres. Ballot [2] (Before shift)			Second Pres. Ballot [3] (After shift)
		Bayard	Hancock	Payne	Hancock	Bayard	Randall	Hancock
Alabama	20	7	7	—	11	5	—	20
Arkansas	12	—	—	—	—	—	—	12
California	12	—	—	—	5	—	—	12
Colorado	6	—	—	—	—	—	—	6
Connecticut	12	4	—	2	—	1	—	12
Delaware	6	6	—	—	—	6	—	6
Florida	8	8	—	—	—	8	—	8
Georgia	22	5	8	—	7	5	—	22
Illinois	42	—	—	—	42	—	—	42
Indiana	30	—	—	—	—	—	—	—
Iowa	22	3	7	2	9	1	12	21
Kansas	10	—	—	—	10	—	—	10
Kentucky	24	6	1	—	8	7	—	24
Louisiana	16	—	16	—	16	—	—	16
Maine	14	—	14	—	14	—	—	14
Maryland	16	16	—	—	—	16	—	14
Massachusetts	26	11½	6	—	11	7	3½	26
Michigan	22	2	5	1	14	4	1	22
Minnesota	10	—	10	—	10	—	—	10
Mississippi	16	8	5	—	6	8	—	16
Missouri	30	4	12	—	28	2	—	30
Nebraska	6	—	—	6	—	—	6	6
Nevada	6	—	—	—	—	—	1	6
New Hampshire	10	3	4	—	5	—	5	10
New Jersey	18	10	—	—	7	4	4	18
New York	70	—	—	70	—	—	70	70
North Carolina	20	7	9	—	20	—	—	20
Ohio	44	—	—	—	—	—	—	44
Oregon	6	—	—	—	—	—	—	6
Pennsylvania	58	7	28	—	32	—	25	58
Rhode Island	8	2	2	—	6	—	1	8
South Carolina	14	14	—	—	—	14	—	14
Tennessee	24	9	11	—	14	8	—	24
Texas	16	5	9	—	11	5	—	16
Vermont	10	—	10	—	10	—	—	10
Virginia	22	10	3	—	7	8	—	22
West Virginia	10	—	3	—	7	1	—	10
Wisconsin	20	6	1	—	10	2	—	20
Total	738	153½	171	81	320	112	128½	705

1. Other candidates: Allen G. Thurman, 68½; Stephen J. Field, 65; William R. Morrison, 62; Thomas A. Hendricks, 49½; Samuel J. Tilden, 38; Horatio Seymour, 8; W. A. H. Loveland, 5; Samuel J. Randall, 6; Thomas Ewing, 10; Joseph E. McDonald, 3; George B. McClellan, 2; Joel Parker, 1; Jeremiah Black, 1; Hugh J. Jewett, 1; James E. English, 1; Lothrop, 1; not voting, 10½.

2. Other candidates: Hendricks, 31; English, 19; Tilden, 6; Thurman, 50; Parker, 2; Field, 65½; Jewett, 1; not voting, 3.

3. Other candidates: Hendricks, 30; Bayard, 2; Tilden, 1.

1880 Republican

(Narrative, p. 56)

Delegation	Total Votes	Minority Report Illinois 1st Dist.			First Pres. Ballot[1]				34th Pres. Ballot[2]				35th Pres. Ballot[3]					36th Pres. Ballot[4]			
		Yea	Nay	Not Voting	Grant	Blaine	Sherman	Other	Grant	Blaine	Sherman	Other	Grant	Blaine	Sherman	Garfield	Other	Grant	Blaine	Garfield	Other
Ala.	20	16	4	—	16	1	3	—	16	4	—	—	16	4	—	—	—	16	4	—	—
Ariz.	2	—	2	—	—	2	—	—	—	2	—	—	—	2	—	—	—	—	—	2	—
Ark.	12	12	—	—	12	—	—	—	12	—	—	—	12	—	—	—	—	12	—	—	—
Calif.	12	—	12	—	—	12	—	—	—	12	—	—	—	12	—	—	—	—	12	—	—
Colo.	6	6	—	—	6	—	—	—	6	—	—	—	6	—	—	—	—	6	—	—	—
Conn.	12	—	10	2	—	3	—	9	—	3	—	9	—	3	—	—	9	—	1	11	—
Del.	6	—	6	—	—	6	—	—	—	6	—	—	—	6	—	—	—	—	6	—	—
Fla.	8	8	—	—	8	—	—	—	8	—	—	—	8	—	—	—	—	8	—	—	—
Ga.	22	6	16	—	6	8	8	—	8	9	5	—	8	9	5	—	—	8	10	1	3
Idaho	2	—	2	—	—	2	—	—	—	2	—	—	—	2	—	—	—	—	2	—	—
Ill.	42	40	—	2	24	10	—	8	24	10	—	8	24	10	—	—	8	24	6	7	5
Ind.	30	5	25	—	1	26	2	1	2	20	2	6	1	2	—	27	—	1	—	29	—
Iowa	22	—	22	—	—	22	—	—	—	22	—	—	—	22	—	—	—	—	—	22	—
Kan.	10	—	—	10	4	6	—	—	4	6	—	—	4	6	—	—	—	4	—	6	—
Ky.	24	21	3	—	20	1	3	—	20	1	3	—	20	1	3	—	—	20	1	3	—
La.	16	8	8	—	8	2	6	—	8	4	4	—	8	4	4	—	—	8	—	8	—
Maine	14	—	14	—	—	14	—	—	—	14	—	—	—	14	—	—	—	—	—	14	—
Md.	16	8	8	—	7	7	2	—	7	2	7	—	7	3	2	4	—	6	—	10	—
Mass.	26	4	22	—	3	—	2	21	4	—	21	1	4	—	21	—	1	4	—	22	—
Mich.	22	1	21	—	1	21	—	—	1	21	—	—	1	21	—	—	—	1	—	21	—
Minn.	10	4	6	—	—	—	—	10	—	6	—	4	1	6	—	—	3	2	—	8	—
Miss.	16	11	5	—	6	4	6	—	8	4	3	1	8	4	3	1	—	7	—	9	—
Mo.	30	29	1	—	29	—	—	1	29	—	—	1	29	—	—	—	1	29	—	1	—
Mont.	2	—	2	—	—	2	—	—	—	2	—	—	—	2	—	—	—	—	—	2	—
Neb.	6	—	6	—	—	6	—	—	—	6	—	—	—	6	—	—	—	—	—	6	—
Nev.	6	—	6	—	—	6	—	—	—	6	—	—	—	6	—	—	—	2	1	3	—
N.H.	10	—	10	—	—	10	—	—	—	10	—	—	—	10	—	—	—	—	—	10	—
N.J.	18	—	18	—	—	16	—	2	—	14	2	2	—	14	2	—	2	—	—	18	—
N.M.	2	—	2	—	—	2	—	—	—	2	—	—	—	2	—	—	—	—	—	2	—
N.Y.	70	47	22	1	51	17	2	—	50	18	2	—	50	18	2	—	—	50	—	20	—
N.C.	20	19	1	—	6	—	14	—	6	—	14	—	6	—	13	1	—	5	—	15	—
N.D.[a]	2	1	1	—	1	1	—	—	1	1	—	—	1	1	—	—	—	—	—	2	—
Ohio	44	16	28	—	—	9	34	1	—	9	34	1	—	9	34	—	1	—	—	43	1
Ore.	6	—	6	—	—	6	—	—	—	6	—	—	—	6	—	—	—	—	—	6	—
Pa.	58	34	24	—	32	23	3	—	35	22	—	1	36	20	—	1	1	37	—	21	—
R.I.	8	—	8	—	—	8	—	—	—	8	—	—	—	8	—	—	—	—	—	8	—
S.C.	14	10	4	—	13	—	1	—	11	1	2	—	11	1	2	—	—	8	—	6	—
Tenn.	24	16	8	—	16	6	1	1	17	4	3	—	17	4	3	—	—	15	1	8	—
Texas	16	11	4	1	11	2	2	1	13	1	1	1	13	1	1	—	1	13	—	3	—
Utah	2	—	2	—	1	1	—	—	1	1	—	—	1	1	—	—	—	—	—	2	—
Vt.	10	4	6	—	—	—	—	10	—	—	—	10	—	—	—	—	10	—	—	10	—
Va.	22	13	9	—	18	3	1	—	16	3	3	—	16	3	3	—	—	19	—	3	—
Wash.	2	—	2	—	—	2	—	—	—	2	—	—	—	2	—	—	—	—	—	2	—
W.Va.	10	—	10	—	1	8	—	1	1	8	1	—	1	8	1	—	—	1	—	9	—
Wis.	20	1	19	—	1	7	3	9	2	1	—	17	2	2	—	16	—	—	—	20	—
Wyo.	2	1	1	—	1	1	—	—	1	1	—	—	1	1	—	—	—	—	—	2	—
D.C.	2	1	1	—	1	1	—	—	1	1	—	—	1	1	—	—	—	—	—	2	—
Total	756	353	387	16	304	284	93	75	312	275	107	62	313	257	99	50	37	306	42	399	9

1. Other candidates: George F. Edmunds, 34; Elihu B. Washburne, 30; William Windom, 10; not voting, 1.
2. Other candidates: Washburne, 30; James A. Garfield, 17; Edmunds, 11; Windom, 4.
3. Other candidates: Washburne, 23; Edmunds, 11; Windom, 3.
4. Other candidates: Washburne, 5; Sherman, 3; not voting, 1.
a. Dakota Territory, includes North and South Dakota.

1884 Democratic

(Narrative, p. 59)

Delegation	Total Votes	Unit Rule: Amendment to Permit Polling of Delegates			First Pres. Ballot[1]			Second Pres. Ballot[2] (Before shift)			Second Pres. Ballot[3] (After shift)	
		Yea	Nay	Not Voting	Cleveland	Bayard	Thurman	Cleveland	Bayard	Hendricks	Cleveland	Bayard
Alabama	20	15	5	—	4	14	1	5	14	—	5	14
Arizona	2	—	—	2	2	—	—	2	—	—	2	—
Arkansas	14	—	14	—	14	—	—	14	—	—	14	—
California	16	16	—	—	—	—	16	—	—	—	16	—
Colorado	6	4	2	—	—	—	1	6	—	—	6	—
Connecticut	12	2	10	—	12	—	—	12	—	—	12	—
Delaware	6	6	—	—	—	6	—	—	6	—	—	6
Florida	8	2	6	—	8	—	—	6	2	—	8	—
Georgia	24	12	12	—	10	12	—	14	10	—	22	2
Idaho	2	—	—	2	2	—	—	2	—	—	2	—
Illinois	44	22	22	—	28	2	1	38	3	1	43	—
Indiana	30	30	—	—	—	—	—	—	—	30	30	—
Iowa	26	6	20	—	23	1	1	22	—	4	26	—
Kansas	18	3	15	—	11	5	2	12	4	—	17	1
Kentucky	26	20	6	—	—	—	—	3	7	15	4	21
Louisiana	16	—	16	—	13	1	1	15	—	—	15	—
Maine	12	2	10	—	12	—	—	12	—	—	12	—
Maryland	16	—	16	—	6	10	—	10	6	—	16	—
Massachusetts	28	21	7	—	5	21	2	8	7½	12½	8	7½
Michigan	26	12	12	2	14	1	11	13	—	13	23	—
Minnesota	14	—	14	—	14	—	—	14	—	—	14	—
Mississippi	18	18	—	—	1	15	1	2	14	2	2	14
Missouri	32	8	24	—	15	10	3	21	5	6	32	—
Montana	2	—	—	2	2	—	—	2	—	—	2	—
Nebraska	10	5	5	—	8	1	1	9	1	—	9	1
Nevada	6	6	—	—	—	—	6	—	—	5	—	—
New Hampshire	8	—	8	—	8	—	—	8	—	—	8	—
New Jersey	18	14	4	—	4	3	—	5	2	11	5	2
New Mexico	2	—	—	2	2	—	—	1	—	—	2	—
New York	72	—	72	—	72	—	—	72	—	—	72	—
North Carolina	22	10	12	—	—	22	—	—	22	—	22	—
Dakota a	2	—	—	2	2	—	—	2	—	—	2	—
Ohio	46	25	21	—	21	—	23	21	—	1	46	—
Oregon	6	—	6	—	2	4	—	2	2	2	6	—
Pennsylvania	60	21	39	—	5	—	—	42	2	11	42	2
Rhode Island	8	—	8	—	8	—	—	6	2	—	7	1
South Carolina	18	3	14	1	8	10	—	8	9	1	10	8
Tennessee	24	17	7	—	2	8	9	2	10	1	24	—
Texas	26	12	10	4	11	10	4	12	12	1	26	—
Utah	2	—	—	2	—	—	—	1	—	1	2	—
Vermont	8	—	8	—	8	—	—	8	—	—	8	—
Virginia	24	6	18	—	13	9	1	13	8	2	23	—
Washington	2	—	—	2	1	—	—	2	—	—	2	—
West Virginia	12	9	3	—	7	2	2	6	3	—	10	2
Wisconsin	22	5	17	—	12	1	2	20	—	2	22	—
Wyoming	2	—	—	2	2	—	—	2	—	—	2	—
District of Columbia	2	—	—	2	2	—	—	—	—	2	2	—
Total	820	332	463	25	392	170	88	475	151½	123½	683	81½

a. Dakota Territory, includes North and South Dakota.

1. Other candidates: Joseph E. McDonald, 56; Samuel J. Randell, 78; John G. Carlisle, 27; George Hoadly, 3; Thomas A. Hendricks, 1; Samuel J. Tilden, 1; Roswell P. Flower. 4.

2. Other candidates: Allen G. Thurman, 60; Randell, 5; McDonald, 2; Tilden, 2; not voting, 1.

3. Other candidates: Hendricks, 45½; Thurman, 4; Randall, 4; McDonald, 2.

1884 Republican

(Narrative, p. 59)

Delegation	Total Vote	Temporary Chairman[1]		First Pres. Ballot[2]			Third Pres. Ballot[3]		Fourth Pres. Ballot[4]	
		Lynch	Clayton	Arthur	Blaine	Edmunds	Arthur	Blaine	Arthur	Blaine
Alabama	20	19	1	17	1	—	17	2	12	8
Arizona	2	—	2	—	2	—	—	2	—	2
Arkansas	14	1	13	4	8	2	3	11	3	11
California	16	—	16	—	16	—	—	16	—	16
Colorado	6	—	6	—	6	—	—	6	—	6
Connecticut	12	6	6	—	—	—	—	—	—	—
Delaware	6	1	5	1	5	—	1	5	1	5
Florida	8	7	1	7	1	—	7	1	5	3
Georgia	24	24	—	24	—	—	24	—	24	—
Idaho	2	2	—	2	—	—	1	1	—	2
Illinois	44	16	28	1	3	—	1	3	3	34
Indiana	30	10	20	9	18	1	10	18	—	30
Iowa	26	3	23	—	26	—	—	26	2	24
Kansas	18	4	14	4	12	—	—	15	—	18
Kentucky	26	20	6	16	5½	—	16	6	15	9
Louisiana	16	11	4	10	2	—	9	4	7	9
Maine	12	—	12	—	12	—	—	12	—	12
Maryland	16	6	10	6	10	—	4	12	1	15
Massachusetts	28	24	4	2	1	25	3	1	7	3
Michigan	26	12	14	2	15	7	4	18	—	26
Minnesota	14	6	8	1	7	6	2	7	—	14
Mississippi	18	16	2	17	1	—	16	1	16	2
Missouri	32	14	16	10	5	6	11	12	—	32
Montana	2	1	1	—	1	1	—	1	—	2
Nebraska	10	2	8	2	8	—	—	10	—	10
Nevada	6	—	6	—	6	—	—	6	—	6
New Hampshire	8	8	—	4	—	4	5	—	2	3
New Jersey	18	9	9	—	9	6	1	11	—	17
New Mexico	2	2	—	2	—	—	2	—	2	—
New York	72	46	26	31	28	12	32	28	30	29
North Carolina	22	17	3	19	2	—	18	4	12	8
Dakota[a]	2	—	2	—	2	—	—	2	—	2
Ohio	46	22	23	—	21	—	—	25	—	46
Oregon	6	—	6	—	6	—	—	6	—	6
Pennsylvania	60	13	45	11	47	1	8	50	8	51
Rhode Island	8	8	—	—	—	8	—	—	1	7
South Carolina	18	18	—	17	1	—	16	2	15	2
Tennessee	24	21	2	16	7	—	17	7	12	11
Texas	26	12	12	11	13	—	11	14	8	15
Utah	2	—	2	2	—	—	2	—	—	2
Vermont	8	8	—	—	—	8	—	—	—	—
Virginia	24	20	4	21	2	—	20	4	20	4
Washington	2	1	1	—	2	—	—	2	—	2
West Virginia	12	—	12	—	12	—	—	12	—	12
Wisconsin	22	11	10	6	10	6	10	11	—	22
Wyoming	2	2	—	2	—	—	2	—	—	2
District of Columbia	2	1	1	1	1	—	1	1	1	1
Total	820	424	384	278	334½	93	274	375	207	541

1. Not voting, 12.
2. Other candidates: John A. Logan, 63½; John Sherman, 30; Joseph R. Hawley, 13; Robert T. Lincoln, 4; William T. Sherman, 2; not voting, 2.
3. Other candidates: George F. Edmunds, 69; Logan, 53; John Sherman, 25; Hawley, 13; Lincoln, 8; William T. Sherman, 3; not voting, 1.
4. Other candidates: Edmunds, 41; Hawley, 15; Logan, 7; Lincoln, 2; not voting, 7.
a. Dakota Territory, includes North and South Dakota.

1888 Republican

(Narrative, p. 62)

Delegation	Total Votes	First Pres. Ballot[1] Alger	Allison	Depew	Gresham	Harrison	Sherman	Sixth Pres. Ballot[2] Alger	Allison	Gresham	Harrison	Sherman	Seventh Pres. Ballot[3] Alger	Allison	Gresham	Harrison	Sherman	Eighth Pres. Ballot[4] Alger	Gresham	Harrison	Sherman
Ala.	20	6	—	1	—	1	12	6	—	—	1	12	6	—	—	12	—	10	—	3	5
Ariz.	2	2	—	—	—	—	—	2	—	—	—	—	2	—	—	—	—	—	—	2	—
Ark.	14	—	—	—	1	1	2	14	—	—	—	—	14	—	—	—	—	14	—	—	—
Calif.	16	—	—	—	—	—	—	—	—	—	—	—	1	—	—	15	—	—	—	15	—
Colo.	6	—	1	—	3	2	—	—	—	—	5	—	—	6	—	—	—	—	—	6	—
Conn.	12	—	—	—	—	—	—	2	4	—	—	6	2	—	—	4	5	—	—	12	—
Del.	6	—	—	—	—	6	—	—	—	1	5	—	—	—	1	5	—	—	—	6	—
Fla.	8	—	—	—	—	1	4	5	—	—	1	1	3	—	—	4	1	4	—	2	2
Ga.	24	—	—	—	1	2	19	—	—	1	2	19	1	—	1	3	17	3	1	10	9
Idaho	2	—	1	—	1	—	—	—	—	—	2	—	—	—	2	—	—	—	—	2	—
Ill.	44	—	—	—	44	—	—	—	—	41	3	—	1	—	40	3	—	—	40	4	—
Ind.	30	—	—	—	1	29	—	—	—	1	29	—	—	—	1	29	—	—	1	29	—
Iowa	26	—	26	—	—	—	—	—	26	—	—	—	—	26	—	—	—	1	3	22	—
Kan.	18	—	—	—	—	—	—	2	3	3	6	1	1	3	—	12	1	1	—	16	—
Ky.	26	4	—	1	5	4	12	6	—	2	7	9	3	—	2	10	9	1	2	15	7
La.	16	2	3	1	1	—	9	3	2	2	—	9	3	2	2	—	9	4	—	9	3
Maine	12	3	2	3	1	2	1	2	1	2	1	3	1	2	2	2	1	—	1	5	3
Md.	16	—	2	1	1	5	5	—	1	—	6	6	—	—	—	9	6	—	—	11	4
Mass.	28	6	2	1	2	4	9	8	2	1	5	11	2	3	1	9	11	1	—	25	2
Mich.	26	26	—	—	—	—	—	26	—	—	—	—	26	—	—	—	—	26	—	—	—
Minn.	14	1	—	2	11	—	—	3	—	5	6	—	2	—	4	8	—	1	—	13	—
Miss.	18	—	—	1	3	—	14	—	—	3	—	14	—	—	3	—	14	—	3	4	11
Mo.	32	6	3	2	11	3	6	15	1	11	2	2	14	—	12	3	2	15	8	7	2
Mont.	2	—	1	—	1	—	—	—	—	1	1	—	—	1	1	—	—	—	—	2	—
Neb.	10	2	3	—	1	—	3	2	5	—	—	3	2	5	—	2	1	1	—	9	—
Nev.	6	3	3	—	—	—	—	5	—	—	—	—	—	6	—	—	—	2	—	4	—
N.H.	8	—	—	4	—	4	—	—	1	—	6	1	—	—	—	8	—	—	—	8	—
N.J.	18	—	—	—	—	—	—	—	—	1	14	—	1	—	1	10	1	—	—	18	—
N.M.	2	1	—	—	—	—	—	1	—	—	—	1	1	—	—	—	1	—	—	2	—
N.Y.	72	—	—	71	—	—	1	—	—	—	72	—	—	—	—	72	—	—	—	72	—
N.C.	22	2	—	1	2	1	15	9	—	—	2	11	7	—	—	3	12	3	—	8	11
N.D.[a]	10	1	1	2	1	1	1	—	—	—	10	—	—	—	—	10	—	—	—	10	—
Ohio	46	—	—	—	—	—	46	—	—	—	1	45	—	—	—	1	45	—	—	1	45
Ore.	6	—	—	—	4	1	—	—	—	5	—	—	—	—	6	—	—	—	—	6	—
Pa.	60	1	—	5	—	—	29	—	—	—	6	54	—	—	—	9	51	—	—	59	1
R.I.	8	—	8	—	—	—	—	—	8	—	—	—	—	6	—	2	—	—	—	8	—
S.C.	18	3	—	1	—	—	11	11	—	—	1	6	11	—	—	1	6	10	—	4	4
Tenn.	24	9	1	2	1	1	7	6	1	—	1	8	9	1	—	3	5	3	—	20	—
Texas	26	2	7	—	5	1	7	3	8	3	1	7	2	8	1	3	7	—	—	26	—
Utah	2	—	2	—	—	—	—	—	2	—	—	—	—	2	—	—	—	—	—	2	—
Vt.	8	—	—	—	—	8	—	—	—	—	8	—	—	—	—	8	—	—	—	8	—
Va.	24	3	3	—	1	5	11	3	5	—	6	10	3	5	—	6	10	—	—	15	9
Wash.	6	—	1	—	3	1	—	1	—	4	1	—	1	—	4	1	—	—	—	6	—
W.Va.	12	1	—	—	2	2	5	1	—	1	2	5	—	—	5	3	1	—	—	12	—
Wis.	22	—	—	—	—	—	—	—	—	1	21	—	—	—	2	20	—	—	—	22	—
Wyo.	2	—	2	—	—	—	—	—	—	—	—	2	—	—	—	—	2	—	—	2	—
D.C.	2	—	—	—	—	—	—	1	—	—	—	—	1	—	—	—	—	—	—	2	—
Total	**832**	**84**	**72**	**99**	**107**	**85**	**229**	**137**	**73**	**91**	**231**	**244**	**120**	**76**	**91**	**279**	**230**	**100**	**59**	**544**	**118**

1. Other candidates: James G. Blaine, 35; John J. Ingalls, 28; William W. Phelps, 25; Jeremiah M. Rusk, 25; Edwin H. Fitler, 24; Joseph R. Hawley, 13; Robert T. Lincoln, 3; William McKinley, 2; not voting, 1.

2. Other candidates: Blaine, 40; McKinley, 12; Foraker, 1; Frederick D. Grant, 1; not voting, 2.

3. Other candidates: McKinley, 16; Blaine, 15; Lincoln, 2; Foraker, 1; Creed Haymond, 1; not voting, 1.

4. Other candidates: Blaine, 5; McKinley, 4; not voting, 2.

a. Dakota Territory includes North and South Dakota.

1892 Democratic

(Narrative, p. 64)

First Pres. Ballot [1]

Delegation	Total Votes	Cleveland	Boies	Hill
Alabama	22	14	1	2
Arizona	6	5	—	—
Arkansas	16	16	—	—
California	18	18	—	—
Colorado	8	—	5	3
Connecticut	12	12	—	—
Delaware	6	6	—	—
Florida	8	5	—	—
Georgia	26	17	—	5
Idaho	6	—	6	—
Illinois	48	48	—	—
Indiana	30	30	—	—
Iowa	26	—	26	—
Kansas	20	20	—	—
Kentucky	26	18	2	—
Louisiana	16	3	11	1
Maine	12	9	—	1
Maryland	16	6	—	—
Massachusetts	30	24	1	4
Michigan	28	28	—	—
Minnesota	18	18	—	—
Mississippi	18	8	3	3
Missouri	34	34	—	—
Montana	6	—	6	—
Nebraska	16	15	—	—
Nevada	6	—	4	—
New Hampshire	8	8	—	—
New Jersey	20	20	—	—
New Mexico	6	4	1	1
New York	72	—	—	72
North Carolina	22	3 1/3	1	—
North Dakota	6	6	—	—
Ohio	46	14	16	6
Oklahoma [a]	4	4	—	—
Oregon	8	8	—	—
Pennsylvania	64	64	—	—
Rhode Island	8	8	—	—
South Carolina	18	2	13	3
South Dakota	8	7	1	—
Tennessee	24	24	—	—
Texas	30	23	6	1
Utah	2	2	—	—
Vermont	8	8	—	—
Virginia	24	12	—	11
Washington	8	8	—	—
West Virginia	12	7	—	1
Wisconsin	24	24	—	—
Wyoming	6	3	—	—
Alaska	2	2	—	—
District of Columbia	2	2	—	—
Total	910	617 1/3	103	114

1892 Republican [a]

(Narrative, p. 63)

First Pres. Ballot [1]

Delegation	Total Votes	Harrison	Blaine	McKinley
Alabama	22	15	—	7
Arizona	2	1	1	—
Arkansas	16	15	—	1
California	18	8	9	1
Colorado	8	—	8	—
Connecticut	12	4	—	8
Delaware	6	4	1	1
Florida	8	8	—	—
Georgia	26	26	—	—
Idaho	6	—	6	—
Illinois	48	34	14	—
Indiana	30	30	—	—
Iowa	26	20	5	1
Kansas	20	11	—	9
Kentucky	26	22	2	1
Louisiana	16	8	8	—
Maine	12	—	12	—
Maryland	16	14	—	2
Massachusetts	30	18	1	11
Michigan	28	7	2	19
Minnesota	18	8	9	1
Mississippi	18	13½	4½	—
Missouri	34	28	4	2
Montana	6	5	1	—
Nebraska	16	15	—	1
Nevada	6	—	6	—
New Hampshire	8	4	2	—
New Jersey	20	18	2	—
New Mexico	6	6	—	—
New York	72	27	35	10
North Carolina	22	17 2/3	2 2/3	1
North Dakota	6	2	4	—
Ohio	46	1	—	45
Oklahoma	2	2	—	—
Oregon	8	1	—	7
Pennsylvania	64	19	3	42
Rhode Island	8	5	1	1
South Carolina	18	13	3	2
South Dakota	8	8	—	—
Tennessee	24	17	4	3
Texas	30	22	6	—
Utah	2	2	—	—
Vermont	8	8	—	—
Virginia	24	9	13	2
Washington	8	1	6	1
West Virginia	12	12	—	—
Wisconsin	24	19	2	3
Wyoming	6	4	2	—
Alaska	2	2	—	—
District of Columbia	2	—	2	—
Indian Territory	2	1	1	—
Total	906	535 1/6	182 1/6	182

a. Includes Indian territory, 2 votes.
1. Other candidates: Arthur P. Gorman, 36½; John G. Carlisle, 14; Adlai E. Stevenson, 16 2/3; James E. Campbell, 2; William R. Morrison, 3; William E. Russell, 1; William C. Whitney, 1; Robert E. Pattison, 1; not voting, ½.

a. Source: Official Proceeding, 10th Republican Convention, p. 114.
1. Other candidates: Thomas B. Reed, 4; Robert T. Lincoln, 1; not voting, 1 2/3.

1896 Democratic

(Narrative, p. 67)

Delegation	Total Votes	Minority Gold Standard Plank			First Pres. Ballot [1]			Fourth Pres. Ballot [2]			Fifth Pres. Ballot [3]	
		Yea	Nay	Not voting	Bryan	Bland	Pattison	Bryan	Bland	Pattison	Bryan	Pattison
Alabama	22	—	22	—	—	—	—	22	—	—	22	—
Arizona	6	—	6	—	—	6	—	—	6	—	6	—
Arkansas	16	—	16	—	—	16	—	—	16	—	16	—
California	18	—	18	—	4	—	—	12	2	—	18	—
Colorado	8	—	8	—	—	—	—	8	—	—	8	—
Connecticut	12	12	—	—	—	—	—	—	—	2	—	2
Delaware	6	5	1	—	1	—	3	1	—	3	1	3
Florida	8	3	5	—	1	2	1	5	—	—	8	—
Georgia	26	—	26	—	26	—	—	26	—	—	26	—
Idaho	6	—	6	—	—	6	—	6	—	—	6	—
Illinois	48	—	48	—	—	48	—	—	48	—	48	—
Indiana	30	—	30	—	—	—	—	—	—	—	30	—
Iowa	26	—	26	—	—	—	—	—	—	—	26	—
Kansas	20	—	20	—	—	20	—	20	—	—	20	—
Kentucky	26	—	26	—	—	—	—	—	—	—	26	—
Louisiana	16	—	16	—	16	—	—	16	—	—	16	—
Maine	12	10	2	—	2	2	5	2	2	5	4	4
Maryland	16	12	4	—	4	—	11	5	—	10	5	10
Massachusetts	30	27	3	—	1	2	3	1	2	3	6	3
Michigan	28	—	28	—	9	4	—	28	—	—	28	—
Minnesota	18	11	6	1	2	—	2	10	1	—	11	—
Mississippi	18	—	18	—	18	—	—	18	—	—	18	—
Missouri	34	—	34	—	—	34	—	—	34	—	34	—
Montana	6	—	6	—	—	4	—	—	6	—	6	—
Nebraska	16	—	16	—	16	—	—	16	—	—	16	—
Nevada	6	—	6	—	—	—	—	6	—	—	6	—
New Hampshire	8	8	—	—	—	—	1	—	—	1	—	1
New Jersey	20	20	—	—	—	—	—	—	—	2	—	2
New Mexico	6	—	6	—	—	6	—	—	6	—	6	—
New York	72	72	—	—	—	—	—	—	—	—	—	—
North Carolina	22	—	22	—	22	—	—	22	—	—	22	—
North Dakota	6	—	6	—	—	—	—	—	—	—	4	—
Ohio	46	—	46	—	—	—	—	—	—	—	46	—
Oklahoma	12	—	12	—	—	12	—	—	12	—	12	—
Oregon	8	—	8	—	—	—	—	8	—	—	8	—
Pennsylvania	64	64	—	—	—	—	64	—	—	64	—	64
Rhode Island	8	8	—	—	—	—	6	—	—	6	—	6
South Carolina	18	—	18	—	—	—	—	18	—	—	18	—
South Dakota	8	8	—	—	6	—	1	7	—	1	8	—
Tennessee	24	—	24	—	—	24	—	—	24	—	24	—
Texas	30	—	30	—	—	30	—	—	30	—	30	—
Utah	6	—	6	—	—	6	—	—	6	—	6	—
Vermont	8	8	—	—	4	—	—	4	—	—	4	—
Virginia	24	—	24	—	—	—	—	—	24	—	24	—
Washington	8	3	5	—	1	7	—	2	6	—	4	—
West Virginia	12	—	12	—	—	—	—	1	10	—	2	—
Wisconsin	24	24	—	—	4	—	—	5	—	—	5	—
Wyoming	6	—	6	—	—	—	—	6	—	—	6	—
Alaska	6	6	—	—	—	6	—	—	6	—	6	—
District of Columbia	6	2	4	—	—	—	—	5	—	—	6	—
Total	930	303	626	1	137	235	97	280	241	97	652	95

1. Other candidates: Horace Boies, 67; Claude Matthews, 37; John R. McLean, 54; Joseph S. C. Blackburn, 82; Adlai E. Stevenson, 6; Henry M. Teller, 8; William E. Russell, 2; Benjamin R. Tillman, 17; James E. Campbell, 1; Sylvester Pennoyer, 8; David B. Hill, 1; not voting, 178.

2. Other candidates: Boies, 33; Mathews, 36; Blackburn, 27; McLean, 46; Stevenson, 8; Hill, 1; not voting, 161.

3. Other candidates: Richard P. Bland, 11; Stevenson, 8; Hill, 1; David Turpie, 1; not voting, 162.

1896 Republican

(Narrative, p. 66)

Delegation	Total Votes	First Pres. Ballot [1]				
		McKinley	Reed	Morton	Allison	Quay
Alabama	22	19	2	1	—	—
Arizona	6	6	—	—	—	—
Arkansas	16	16	—	—	—	—
California	18	18	—	—	—	—
Colorado	8	—	—	—	—	—
Connecticut	12	7	5	—	—	—
Delaware	6	6	—	—	—	—
Florida	8	6	—	2	—	—
Georgia	26	22	2	—	—	2
Idaho	6	—	—	—	—	—
Illinois	48	46	2	—	—	—
Indiana	30	30	—	—	—	—
Iowa	26	—	—	—	26	—
Kansas	20	20	—	—	—	—
Kentucky	26	26	—	—	—	—
Louisiana	16	11	4	—	½	½
Maine	12	—	12	—	—	—
Maryland	16	15	1	—	—	—
Massachusetts	30	1	29	—	—	—
Michigan	28	28	—	—	—	—
Minnesota	18	18	—	—	—	—
Mississippi	18	17	—	—	—	1
Missouri	34	34	—	—	—	—
Montana	6	1	—	—	—	—
Nebraska	16	16	—	—	—	—
Nevada	6	3	—	—	—	—
New Hampshire	8	—	8	—	—	—
New Jersey	20	19	1	—	—	—
New Mexico	6	5	—	—	1	—
New York	72	17	—	55	—	—
North Carolina	22	19½	2½	—	—	—
North Dakota	6	6	—	—	—	—
Ohio	46	46	—	—	—	—
Oklahoma	12 [a]	10	1	—	1	—
Oregon	8	8	—	—	—	—
Pennsylvania	64	6	—	—	—	58
Rhode Island	8	—	8	—	—	—
South Carolina	18	18	—	—	—	—
South Dakota	8	8	—	—	—	—
Tennessee	24	24	—	—	—	—
Texas	30	21	5	—	3	—
Utah	6	3	—	—	3	—
Vermont	8	8	—	—	—	—
Virginia	24	23	1	—	—	—
Washington	8	8	—	—	—	—
West Virginia	12	12	—	—	—	—
Wisconsin	24	24	—	—	—	—
Wyoming	6	6	—	—	—	—
Alaska	4	4	—	—	—	—
District of Columbia	2	—	1	—	1	—
Total	924	661½	84½	58	35½	61½

1. Other candidates: J. Donald Cameron, 1; not voting, 22.
a. Including Indian Territory, 6 votes.

1900 Democratic

(Narrative, p. 69)

Delegation	Total Votes	First Pres. Ballot Bryan
Alabama	22	22
Arizona	6	6
Arkansas	16	16
California	18	18
Colorado	8	8
Connecticut	12	12
Delaware	6	6
Florida	8	8
Georgia	26	26
Idaho	6	6
Illinois	48	48
Indiana	30	30
Iowa	26	26
Kansas	20	20
Kentucky	26	26
Louisiana	16	16
Maine	12	12
Maryland	16	16
Massachusetts	30	30
Michigan	28	28
Minnesota	18	18
Mississippi	18	18
Missouri	34	34
Montana	6	6
Nebraska	16	16
Nevada	6	6
New Hampshire	8	8
New Jersey	20	20
New Mexico	6	6
New York	72	72
North Carolina	22	22
North Dakota	6	6
Ohio	46	46
Oklahoma	12[a]	12
Oregon	8	8
Pennsylvania	64	64
Rhode Island	8	8
South Carolina	18	18
South Dakota	8	8
Tennessee	24	24
Texas	30	30
Utah	6	6
Vermont	8	8
Virginia	24	24
Washington	8	8
West Virginia	12	12
Wisconsin	24	24
Wyoming	6	6
Alaska	6	6
District of Columbia	6	6
Hawaii	6	6
Total	**936**	**936**

a. *Including Indian Territory, 6 votes.*

1900 Republican

(Narrative, p. 68)

Delegation	Total Votes	First Pres. Ballot McKinley
Alabama	22	22
Arizona	6	6
Arkansas	16	16
California	18	18
Colorado	8	8
Connecticut	12	12
Delaware	6	6
Florida	8	8
Georgia	26	26
Idaho	6	6
Illinois	48	48
Indiana	30	30
Iowa	26	26
Kansas	20	20
Kentucky	26	26
Louisiana	16	16
Maine	12	12
Maryland	16	16
Massachusetts	30	30
Michigan	28	28
Minnesota	18	18
Mississippi	18	18
Missouri	34	34
Montana	6	6
Nebraska	16	16
Nevada	6	6
New Hampshire	8	8
New Jersey	20	20
New Mexico	6	6
New York	72	72
North Carolina	22	22
North Dakota	6	6
Ohio	46	46
Oklahoma	12[a]	12
Oregon	8	8
Pennsylvania	64	64
Rhode Island	8	8
South Carolina	18	18
South Dakota	8	8
Tennessee	24	24
Texas	30	30
Utah	6	6
Vermont	8	8
Virginia	24	24
Washington	8	8
West Virginia	12	12
Wisconsin	24	24
Wyoming	6	6
Alaska	4	4
District of Columbia	2	2
Hawaii	2	2
Total	**926**	**926**

a. *Including Indian Territory, 6 votes.*

1904 Democratic *(Narrative, p. 71)*

Delegation	Total Votes	First Pres. Ballot[1] (Before shift)		First Pres. Ballot[2] (After shift)		Sending Telegram to Parker		
		Parker	Hearst	Parker	Hearst	Yea	Nay	Not Voting
Alabama	22	22	—	22	—	22	—	—
Arizona	6	—	6	—	6	—	6	—
Arkansas	18	18	—	18	—	18	—	—
California	20	—	20	—	20	16	4	—
Colorado	10	4	5	4	5	4	6	—
Connecticut	14	14	—	14	—	14	—	—
Delaware	6	—	—	—	—	6	—	—
Florida	10	6	4	6	4	6	4	—
Georgia	26	26	—	26	—	26	—	—
Idaho	6	—	6	6	—	—	6	—
Illinois	54	—	54	—	54	54	—	—
Indiana	30	30	—	30	—	30	—	—
Iowa	26	—	26	—	26	—	26	—
Kansas	20	7	10	7	10	—	20	—
Kentucky	26	26	—	26	—	26	—	—
Louisiana	18	18	—	18	—	18	—	—
Maine	12	7	1	7	1	7	2	3
Maryland	16	16	—	16	—	16	—	—
Massachusetts	32	—	—	—	—	32	—	—
Michigan	28	28	—	28	—	28	—	—
Minnesota	22	9	9	9	9	9	13	—
Mississippi	20	20	—	20	—	20	—	—
Missouri	36	—	—	—	—	—	36	—
Montana	6	6	—	6	—	—	6	—
Nebraska	16	—	4	—	4	—	16	—
Nevada	6	—	6	2	4	2	4	—
New Hampshire	8	8	—	8	—	8	—	—
New Jersey	24	24	—	24	—	24	—	—
New Mexico	6	—	6	—	6	6	—	—
New York	78	78	—	78	—	78	—	—
North Carolina	24	24	—	24	—	24	—	—
North Dakota	8	—	—	—	—	—	8	—
Ohio	46	46	—	46	—	31	6	9
Oklahoma	12[a]	7	3	7	3	7	5	—
Oregon	8	4	2	4	2	4	4	—
Pennsylvania	68	68	—	68	—	68	—	—
Rhode Island	8	2	6	2	6	2	5	1
South Carolina	18	18	—	18	—	18	—	—
South Dakota	8	—	8	—	8	—	8	—
Tennessee	24	24	—	24	—	24	—	—
Texas	36	36	—	36	—	36	—	—
Utah	6	6	—	6	—	6	—	—
Vermont	8	8	—	8	—	8	—	—
Virginia	24	24	—	24	—	24	—	—
Washington	10	—	10	10	—	10	—	—
West Virginia	14	10	2	13	1	14	—	—
Wisconsin	26	—	—	—	—	26	—	—
Wyoming	6	—	6	—	6	2	2	2
Alaska	6	6	—	6	—	6	—	—
District of Columbia	6	6	—	6	—	6	—	—
Hawaii	6	—	6	—	6	2	4	—
Puerto Rico	6	2	—	2	—	6	—	—
Total	1000	658	200	679	181	794	191	15

a. Including Indian Territory, 6 votes.

1. Other candidates: George Gray, 12; Nelson A. Miles, 3; Francis M. Cockrell, 42; Richard Olney, 38; Edward C. Wall, 27; George B. McClellan, 3; Charles A. Towne, 2; Robert E. Pattison, 4; John S. Williams, 8; Bird S. Coler, 1; Arthur P. Gorman, 2.

2. Other candidates: Gray, 12; Miles, 3; Cockrell, 42; Olney, 38; Wall, 27; McClellan, 3; Towne, 2; Pattison, 4; Williams, 8; Coler, 1.

1904 Republican

(Narrative, p. 70)

1908 Democratic

(Narrative, p. 73)

Delegation	Total Votes	First Pres. Ballot Roosevelt
Alabama	22	22
Arizona	6	6
Arkansas	18	18
California	20	20
Colorado	10	10
Connecticut	14	14
Delaware	6	6
Florida	10	10
Georgia	26	26
Idaho	6	6
Illinois	54	54
Indiana	30	30
Iowa	26	26
Kansas	20	20
Kentucky	26	26
Louisiana	18	18
Maine	12	12
Maryland	16	16
Massachusetts	32	32
Michigan	28	28
Minnesota	22	22
Mississippi	20	20
Missouri	36	36
Montana	6	6
Nebraska	16	16
Nevada	6	6
New Hampshire	8	8
New Jersey	24	24
New Mexico	6	6
New York	78	78
North Carolina	24	24
North Dakota	8	8
Ohio	46 [a]	46
Oklahoma	12	12
Oregon	8	8
Pennsylvania	68	68
Rhode Island	8	8
South Carolina	18	18
South Dakota	8	8
Tennessee	24	24
Texas	36	36
Utah	6	6
Vermont	8	8
Virginia	24	24
Washington	10	10
West Virginia	14	14
Wisconsin	26	26
Wyoming	6	6
Alaska	6	6
District of Columbia	2	2
Hawaii	6	6
Philippine Islands	2	2
Puerto Rico	2	2
Total	**994**	**994**

a. Including Indian Territory, 6 votes.

Delegation	Total Votes	First Pres. Ballot[1] Bryan
Alabama	22	22
Arizona	6	6
Arkansas	18	18
California	20	20
Colorado	10	10
Connecticut	14	9
Delaware	6	—
Florida	10	10
Georgia	26	4
Idaho	6	6
Illinois	54	54
Indiana	30	30
Iowa	26	26
Kansas	20	20
Kentucky	26	26
Louisiana	18	18
Maine	12	10
Maryland	16	7
Massachusetts	32	32
Michigan	28	28
Minnesota	22	—
Mississippi	20	20
Missouri	36	36
Montana	6	6
Nebraska	16	16
Nevada	6	6
New Hampshire	8	7
New Jersey	24	—
New Mexico	6	6
New York	78	78
North Carolina	24	24
North Dakota	8	8
Ohio	46	46
Oklahoma	14	14
Oregon	8	8
Pennsylvania	68	49½
Rhode Island	8	5
South Carolina	18	18
South Dakota	8	8
Tennessee	24	24
Texas	36	36
Utah	6	6
Vermont	8	7
Virginia	24	24
Washington	10	10
West Virginia	14	14
Wisconsin	26	26
Wyoming	6	6
Alaska	6	6
District of Columbia	6	6
Hawaii	6	6
Puerto Rico	6	6
Total	**1002**	**888½**

1. Other candidates: John A. Johnson, 46; George Gray, 59½; not voting, 8.

1908 Republican

(Narrative, p. 73)

Delegation	Total Votes	Minority Report on Changing Delegate Apportionment Formula			Minority Plank for Direct Election of Senators		First Pres. Ballot [1]
		Yea	Nay	Not Voting	Yea	Nay	Taft
Alabama	22	—	22	—	—	22	22
Arizona	2	—	2	—	—	2	2
Arkansas	18	—	18	—	—	18	18
California	20	—	20	—	—	20	20
Colorado	10	10	—	—	—	10	10
Connecticut	14	14	—	—	—	14	14
Delaware	6	—	6	—	—	6	6
Florida	10	—	10	—	—	10	10
Georgia	26	—	26	—	—	26	17
Idaho	6	—	6	—	3	3	6
Illinois	54	54	—	—	1	53	3
Indiana	30	30	—	—	11	19	—
Iowa	26	6	20	—	1	25	26
Kansas	20	—	20	—	—	20	20
Kentucky	26	1	25	—	2	24	24
Louisiana	18	—	18	—	—	18	18
Maine	12	12	—	—	—	12	12
Maryland	16	—	16	—	1	15	16
Massachusetts	32	32	—	—	—	32	32
Michigan	28	18	10	—	5	23	27
Minnesota	22	10	11	1	—	22	22
Mississippi	20	—	20	—	—	20	20
Missouri	36	12	24	—	4	32	36
Montana	6	—	6	—	—	6	6
Nebraska	16	7	9	—	16	—	16
Nevada	6	—	6	—	—	6	6
New Hampshire	8	8	—	—	—	8	5
New Jersey	24	23	1	—	—	24	15
New Mexico	2	—	—	2	—	2	2
New York	78	78	—	—	—	78	10
North Carolina	24	—	24	—	—	24	24
North Dakota	8	—	8	—	—	8	8
Ohio	46	8	38	—	2	44	42
Oklahoma	14	—	14	—	14	—	14
Oregon	8	3	5	—	—	8	8
Pennsylvania	68	68	—	—	13	55	1
Rhode Island	8	8	—	—	—	8	8
South Carolina	18	—	18	—	—	18	13
South Dakota	8	8	—	—	8	—	8
Tennessee	24	—	24	—	—	24	24
Texas	36	—	36	—	—	36	36
Utah	6	6	—	—	2	4	6
Vermont	8	8	—	—	—	8	8
Virginia	24	—	24	—	—	24	21
Washington	10	4	6	—	—	10	10
West Virginia	14	14	—	—	5	9	14
Wisconsin	26	26	—	—	25	1	1
Wyoming	6	—	6	—	—	6	6
Alaska	2	2	—	—	—	2	2
District of Columbia	2	1	1	—	—	2	1
Hawaii	2	—	2	—	1	1	2
Philippine Islands	2	—	2	—	—	2	2
Puerto Rico	2	—	2	—	—	2	2
Total	980	471	506	3	114	866	702

1. Other candidates: Philander C. Knox, 68; Charles E. Hughes, 67; Joseph G. Cannon 58; Charles W. Fairbanks, 40; Robert M. LaFollette. 25; Joseph B. Foraker. 16; Theodore Roosevelt, 3; not voting. 1.

1912 Democratic (Narrative, p. 75)

Delegation	Total Votes	Temporary Chairman[1] Bryan	Parker	First Pres. Ballot[2] Clark	Wilson	Harmon	Underwood	Tenth Pres. Ballot[3] Clark	Wilson	Underwood	Thirtieth Pres. Ballot[4] Clark	Wilson	Underwood	43rd Pres. Ballot[5] Clark	Wilson	45th Pres. Ballot[6] Clark	Wilson	46th Pres. Ballot[7] Wilson
Ala.	24	1½	22½	—	—	—	24	—	—	24	—	—	24	—	—	—	—	24
Ariz.	6	4	2	6	—	—	—	6	—	—	4	2	—	3	2	3	3	6
Ark.	18	—	18	18	—	—	—	18	—	—	18	—	—	18	—	18	—	18
Calif.	26	7	18	26	—	—	—	26	—	—	26	—	—	26	—	26	—	2
Colo.	12	6	6	12	—	—	—	12	—	—	12	—	—	11	1	2	10	12
Conn.	14	2	12	—	—	—	—	7	—	7	7	3	4	1	5	2	5	14
Del.	6	6	—	—	6	—	—	—	6	—	—	6	—	—	6	—	6	6
Fla.	12	1	11	—	—	—	12	—	—	12	—	—	12	—	2	—	3	7
Ga.	28	—	28	—	—	—	28	—	—	28	—	—	28	—	—	—	—	28
Idaho	8	8	—	8	—	—	—	8	—	—	2½	5½	—	1	7	1½	6½	8
Ill.	58	—	58	58	—	—	—	58	—	—	58	—	—	—	58	—	58	58
Ind.	30	8	21	—	—	—	—	—	—	—	1	28	—	1	28	—	30	30
Iowa	26	13	13	26	—	—	—	26	—	—	12	14	—	11½	14½	9	17	26
Kan.	20	20	—	20	—	—	—	20	—	—	—	20	—	—	20	—	20	20
Ky.	26	7½	17½	26	—	—	—	26	—	—	26	—	—	26	—	26	—	26
La.	20	10	10	11	9	—	—	10	10	—	7	12	—	6	14	5	15	18
Maine	12	1	11	1	9	—	2	1	11	—	1	9	2	1	11	1	11	12
Md.	16	1½	14½	16	—	—	—	16	—	—	11	4½	—	9	5½	8½	7	16
Mass.	36	18	15	36	—	—	—	33	1	2	—	7	—	—	9	—	9	36
Mich.	30	9	21	12	10	7	—	18	9	—	18	12	—	2	28	2	28	30
Minn.	24	24	—	—	24	—	—	—	24	—	—	24	—	—	24	—	24	24
Miss.	20	—	20	—	—	—	20	—	—	20	—	—	20	—	—	—	—	20
Mo.	36	14	22	36	—	—	—	36	—	—	36	—	—	36	—	36	—	—
Mont.	8	7	1	8	—	—	—	8	—	—	2	6	—	1	7	1	7	8
Neb.	16	13	3	12	—	4	—	13	3	—	3	13	—	3	13	3	13	16
Nev.	6	6	—	6	—	—	—	6	—	—	6	—	—	6	—	6	—	—
N.H.	8	5	3	8	—	—	—	5	3	—	3	5	—	3	5	3	5	8
N.J.	28	24	4	2	24	—	2	4	24	—	4	24	—	4	24	4	24	24
N.M.	8	8	—	8	—	—	—	8	—	—	8	—	—	8	—	8	—	8
N.Y.	90	—	90	—	—	90	—	90	—	—	90	—	—	90	—	90	—	90
N.C.	24	9	15	—	16½	½	7	—	18	6	—	17½	6½	—	22	—	22	24
N.D.	10	10	—	—	10	—	—	—	10	—	—	10	—	—	10	—	10	10
Ohio	48	19	29	1	10	35	—	6	11	—	—	19	10	—	20	—	23	33
Okla.	20	20	—	10	10	—	—	10	10	—	10	10	—	10	10	10	10	20
Ore.	10	9	1	—	10	—	—	—	10	—	—	10	—	—	10	—	10	10
Pa.	76	67	9	—	71	5	—	5	71	—	4	72	—	2	74	—	76	76
R.I.	10	—	10	10	—	—	—	10	—	—	10	—	—	10	—	10	—	10
S.C.	18	18	—	—	18	—	—	—	18	—	—	18	—	—	18	—	18	18
S.D.	10	10	—	—	10	—	—	—	10	—	—	10	—	—	10	—	10	10
Tenn.	24	7	17	6	6	6	6	13	7½	3½	13½	8	2½	10	8	8	10	24
Texas	40	40	—	—	40	—	—	—	40	—	—	40	—	—	40	—	40	40
Utah	8	4	4	1½	6	½	—	1½	6½	—	1½	6½	—	1½	6½	—	8	8
Vt.	8	—	8	—	—	—	—	—	—	—	—	8	—	—	8	—	8	8
Va.	24	10	14	—	9½	—	14½	½	9½	14	3	9½	11½	—	24	—	24	24
Wash.	14	14	—	14	—	—	—	14	—	—	14	—	—	14	—	14	—	14
W.Va.	16	4½	10½	16	—	—	—	16	—	—	16	—	—	—	16	—	16	16
Wis.	26	26	—	6	19	—	—	6	20	—	6	19	—	4	22	—	26	26
Wyo.	6	6	—	6	—	—	—	6	—	—	6	—	—	—	6	—	6	6
Alaska	6	2	4	4	—	—	—	3	3	—	6	—	—	1	5	—	6	6
D.C.	6	—	6	6	—	—	—	6	—	—	6	—	—	6	—	6	—	—
Hawaii	6	2	4	2	3	—	1	2	3	—	2	3	1	2	4	2	4	6
Phil. Is.	6	2	4	—	—	—	—	—	—	—	—	—	—	—	—	—	—	—
P.R.	6	4	2	2	3	—	1	2	4	—	1½	4½	—	1	4½	1	4½	6
Total	**1094**	**508**	**579**	**440½**	**324**	**148**	**117½**	**556**	**350½**	**117½**	**455**	**460**	**121½**	**329**	**602**	**306**	**633**	**990**

1. Other candidates: James A. O'Gorman, 4; John W. Kern, 1; not voting, 2.
2. Other candidates: Simeon E. Baldwin, 22; Thomas R. Marshall, 31; William J. Bryan, 1; William Sulzer, 2; not voting, 8.
3. Other candidates: Harmon, 31; Marshall, 31; Kern, 1; Bryan, 1; not voting, 6.
4. Other candidates: Foss, 30; Harmon, 19; Kern, 2; not voting, ½.
5. Other candidates: Underwood, 98½; Harmon, 28; Foss, 27; Bryan, 1; Kern, 1; not voting, 7½.
6. Other candidates: Underwood, 97; Foss, 27; Harmon, 25; not voting, 6.
7. Other candidates: Clark, 84; Harmon, 12; not voting, 8.

1912 Republican

(Narrative, p. 75)

Delegation	Total Votes	Temporary Chairman[1]		Table Motion Prohibiting Challenged Taft Delegates from Voting			First Pres. Ballot[2]		
		Root	McGovern	Yea	Nay	Not voting	Taft	Roosevelt	Present, Not voting
Alabama	24	22	2	22	2	—	22	—	2
Arizona	6	6	—	6	—	—	6	—	—
Arkansas	18	17	1	17	1	—	17	—	1
California	26	2	24	2	24	—	2	—	24
Colorado	12	12	—	12	—	—	12	—	—
Connecticut	14	14	—	14	—	—	14	—	—
Delaware	6	6	—	6	—	—	6	—	—
Florida	12	12	—	12	—	—	12	—	—
Georgia	28	22	6	24	4	—	28	—	—
Idaho	8	—	8	—	8	—	1	—	—
Illinois	58	9	49	7	51	—	2	53	1
Indiana	30	20	10	20	9	1	20	3	7
Iowa	26	16	10	16	10	—	16	—	—
Kansas	20	2	18	2	18	—	2	—	18
Kentucky	26	23	3	24	2	—	24	2	—
Louisiana	20	20	—	20	—	—	20	—	—
Maine	12	—	12	—	12	—	—	—	12
Maryland	16	8	8	9	7	—	1	9	5
Massachusetts	36	18	18	18	18	—	15	—	21
Michigan	30	19	10	20	10	—	20	9	1
Minnesota	24	—	24	—	24	—	—	—	24
Mississippi	20	16	4	16	4	—	17	—	3
Missouri	36	16	20	16	20	—	16	—	20
Montana	8	8	—	8	—	—	8	—	—
Nebraska	16	—	16	—	16	—	—	2	14
Nevada	6	6	—	6	—	—	6	—	—
New Hampshire	8	8	—	8	—	—	8	—	—
New Jersey	28	—	28	—	28	—	—	2	26
New Mexico	8	6	2	7	1	—	7	1	—
New York	90	76	13	75	15	—	76	8	6
North Carolina	24	3	21	2	22	—	1	1	22
North Dakota	10	—	9	2	8	—	—	—	—
Ohio	48	14	34	14	34	—	14	—	34
Oklahoma	20	4	16	4	16	—	4	1	15
Oregon	10	3	6	5	5	—	—	8	2
Pennsylvania	76	12	64	12	64	—	9	2	62
Rhode Island	10	10	—	10	—	—	10	—	—
South Carolina	18	11	7	11	6	1	16	—	1
South Dakota	10	—	10	—	10	—	—	5	—
Tennessee	24	23	1	23	1	—	23	1	—
Texas	40	31	8	29	9	2	31	—	8
Utah	8	7	1	7	1	—	8	—	—
Vermont	8	6	2	6	2	—	6	—	2
Virginia	24	22	2	21	3	—	22	—	1
Washington	14	14	—	14	—	—	14	—	—
West Virginia	16	—	16	—	16	—	—	—	16
Wisconsin	26	—	12	—	26	—	—	—	—
Wyoming	6	6	—	6	—	—	6	—	—
Alaska	2	2	—	2	—	—	2	—	—
District of Columbia	2	2	—	2	—	—	2	—	—
Hawaii	6	—	6	6	—	—	6	—	—
Philippine Islands	2	2	—	2	—	—	2	—	—
Puerto Rico	2	2	—	2	—	—	2	—	—
Total	**1078**	**558**	**501**	**567**	**507**	**4**	**556**[a]	**107**	**348**[b]

a. Sum of column; proceedings record 561.
b. Sum of column; proceedings record 349.
1. Other candidates: W. S. Lauder, 12; Asle J. Gronna, 1; not voting, 6.
2. Other candidates: Robert M. La Follette, 41; Albert B. Cummins, 17; Charles E. Hughes, 2; absent and not voting, 7.

1916 Democratic

(Narrative, p. 79)

Delegation	Total Votes	Minority Plank on Women's Suffrage		
		Yea	Nay	Not Voting
Alabama	24	1	23	—
Arizona	6	—	6	—
Arkansas	18	—	18	—
California	26	—	26	—
Colorado	12	—	12	—
Connecticut	14	1	13	—
Delaware	6	—	6	—
Florida	12	4	8	—
Georgia	28	23½	4½	—
Idaho	8	—	8	—
Illinois	58	1	57	—
Indiana	30	24	6	—
Iowa	26	—	26	—
Kansas	20	—	20	—
Kentucky	26	—	26	—
Louisiana	20	8	12	—
Maine	12	—	6	6
Maryland	16	16	—	—
Massachusetts	36	6	30	—
Michigan	30	—	30	—
Minnesota	24	9	15	—
Mississippi	20	—	20	—
Missouri	36	4	24	8
Montana	8	—	8	—
Nebraska	16	—	16	—
Nevada	6	—	6	—
New Hampshire	8	1	7	—
New Jersey	28	10	11	7
New Mexico	6	—	6	—
New York	90	—	90	—
North Carolina	24	11	13	—
North Dakota	10	—	10	—
Ohio	48	20	28	—
Oklahoma	20	—	20	—
Oregon	10	—	10	—
Pennsylvania	76	—	76	—
Rhode Island	10	1	9	—
South Carolina	18	—	18	—
South Dakota	10	—	10	—
Tennessee	24	—	24	—
Texas	40	32	8	—
Utah	8	—	8	—
Vermont	8	—	8	—
Virginia	24	—	24	—
Washington	14	—	14	—
West Virginia	16	8	8	—
Wisconsin	26	—	26	—
Wyoming	6	—	6	—
Alaska	6	—	6	—
District of Columbia	6	—	6	—
Hawaii	6	—	6	—
Philippine Islands	6	1	4	1
Puerto Rico	6	—	6	—
Total	1092	181½	888½	22

1916 Republican

(Narrative, p. 78)

Delegation	Total Votes	First Pres. Ballot[1]			Second Pres. Ballot[2]		Third Pres. Ballot[3]
		Hughes	Root	Weeks	Hughes	Root	Hughes
Alabama	16	8	—	3	9	—	16
Arizona	6	4	—	—	4	—	6
Arkansas	15	1	3	3	—	2	15
California	26	9	8	3	11	12	26
Colorado	12	—	5	—	—	5	12
Connecticut	14	5	5	1	5	7	14
Delaware	6	—	—	—	—	—	6
Florida	8	8	—	—	8	—	8
Georgia	17	5	—	6	6	—	17
Idaho	8	4	—	—	4	1	8
Illinois	58	—	—	—	—	—	58
Indiana	30	—	—	—	—	—	30
Iowa	26	—	—	—	—	—	26
Kansas	20	10	2	3	10	2	20
Kentucky	26	10	—	—	11	—	26
Louisiana	12	4	1	3	6	1	12
Maine	12	6	1	3	8	1	12
Maryland	16	7	1	5	7	1	15
Massachusetts	36	4	—	28	12	—	32
Michigan	30	—	—	—	28	—	30
Minnesota	24	—	—	—	—	—	24
Mississippi	12	4	—	1½	4	—	8½
Missouri	36	18	—	8	22	—	34
Montana	8	—	—	—	—	—	7
Nebraska	16	—	—	—	2	—	16
Nevada	6	4	2	—	4	2	6
New Hampshire	8	—	—	8	3	3	8
New Jersey	28	12	12	1	16	3	27
New Mexico	6	2	—	2	2	—	5
New York	87	42	43	—	43	42	87
North Carolina	21	6	2	3	6	2	14
North Dakota	10	—	—	—	—	—	10
Ohio	48	—	—	—	—	—	48
Oklahoma	20	5	1	6	5	1	19
Oregon	10	10	—	—	10	—	10
Pennsylvania	76	2	—	—	8	1	72
Rhode Island	10	10	—	—	10	—	10
South Carolina	11	2	1	3	4	—	6
South Dakota	10	—	—	—	—	—	10
Tennessee	21	9	—	3½	8	½	18
Texas	26	1	1	1	3	3	26
Utah	8	4	3	—	5	2	7
Vermont	8	8	—	—	8	—	8
Virginia	15	5½	3	6	8½	5	15
Washington	14	5	8	—	5	—	14
West Virginia	16	1	—	5	4	1	16
Wisconsin	26	11	—	—	11	—	23
Wyoming	6	6	—	—	6	—	6
Alaska	2	1	—	1	1	—	2
Hawaii	2	—	—	1	1	—	2
Philippine Islands	2	—	1	—	—	1	2
Total	**987**	**253½**	**103**	**105**	**328½**	**98½**	**949½**

1. Other candidates: Albert B. Cummins, 85; Theodore E. Burton, 77½; Charles W. Fairbanks, 74½; Lawrence Y. Sherman, 66; Theodore Roosevelt, 65; Philander C. Knox, 36; Henry Ford, 32; Martin G. Brumbaugh, 29; Robert M. La Follette, 25; William H. Taft, 14; Coleman du Pont, 12; Frank B. Willis, 4; William E. Borah, 2; Samuel W. McCall, 1; not voting, 2½.
2. Other candidates: Fairbanks, 88½; Cummins, 85; Roosevelt, 81; Burton 76½; Sherman, 65; Knox, 36; La Follette, 25; du Pont, 13; John Wanamaker, 5; Willis, 1; Leonard Wood, 1; Warren G. Harding, 1; McCall, 1; not voting 2.
3. Other candidates: Roosevelt, 18½; La Follette, 3; du Pont, 5; Henry Cabot Lodge, 7; Weeks, 3; not voting, 1.

1920 Democratic *(Narrative, p. 82)*

Delegation	Total Votes	First Pres. Ballot[1]				Thirtieth Pres. Ballot[2]			39th Pres. Ballot[3]		44th Pres. Ballot[4]	
		McAdoo	Cox	Palmer	Smith	McAdoo	Cox	Palmer	McAdoo	Cox	McAdoo	Cox
Alabama	24	9	3	6	2	12	7	—	8	—	8	13
Arizona	6	4	1	—	—	3	2	—	4	2	2½	3½
Arkansas	18	3	7	2	—	3	14	1	4	14	—	18
California	26	10	4	3	1	10	13	1	14	12	13	13
Colorado	12	3	—	8	—	5	6	—	4	7	3	9
Connecticut	14	—	—	—	—	1	6	4	3	10	2	12
Delaware	6	4	—	—	—	4	2	—	4	2	3	3
Florida	12	1	—	8	—	3	9	—	3	9	—	12
Georgia	28	—	—	28	—	—	—	28	28	—	—	28
Idaho	8	8	—	—	—	8	—	—	8	—	8	—
Illinois	58	9	9	35	5	21	36	1	18	38	13	44
Indiana	30	—	—	—	—	29	—	—	11	19	—	30
Iowa	26	—	—	—	—	—	26	—	—	26	—	26
Kansas	20	20	—	—	—	20	—	—	20	—	20	—
Kentucky	26	3	23	—	—	5	20	—	5	20	—	26
Louisiana	20	5	2	2	—	4	14	—	7	12	—	20
Maine	12	5	—	5	—	7	—	5	12	—	5	5
Maryland	16	5½	5½	—	—	5½	8½	—	5½	8½	—	13½
Massachusetts	36	4	4	17	7	2	15	16	1	33	—	35
Michigan	30	15	—	12	—	15	6	9	14	12	—	—
Minnesota	24	10	2	7	—	14	4	4	16	7	15	8
Mississippi	20	—	—	—	—	—	20	—	—	20	—	20
Missouri	36	15½	2½	10	—	18	6	5	20½	11½	17	18
Montana	8	1	—	—	—	8	—	—	8	—	2	6
Nebraska	16	—	—	—	—	7	—	—	7	—	2	5
Nevada	6	—	6	—	—	—	6	—	—	6	—	6
New Hampshire	8	4	—	1	—	5	2	1	5	2	6	2
New Jersey	28	—	—	—	—	—	28	—	—	28	—	28
New Mexico	6	2	—	1	—	6	—	—	6	—	6	—
New York	90	—	—	—	90	20	70	—	20	70	20	70
North Carolina	24	—	—	—	—	24	—	—	24	—	24	—
North Dakota	10	6	1	2	—	8	2	—	9	1	4	2
Ohio	48	—	48	—	—	—	48	—	—	48	—	48
Oklahoma	20	—	—	—	—	—	—	—	—	—	—	—
Oregon	10	10	—	—	—	10	—	—	10	—	10	—
Pennsylvania	76	2	—	73	—	2	1	73	2	1	4	68
Rhode Island	10	2	—	5	2	3	4	3	1	7	1	9
South Carolina	18	18	—	—	—	18	—	—	18	—	18	—
South Dakota	10	—	—	—	—	6	4	—	6	3	3	5
Tennessee	24	2	8	9	—	—	—	—	—	—	—	—
Texas	40	40	—	—	—	40	—	—	40	—	40	—
Utah	8	8	—	—	—	8	—	—	8	—	7	1
Vermont	8	4	2	1	1	1	6	1	4	4	—	8
Virginia	24	—	—	—	—	—	—	—	10	11	2½	18½
Washington	14	10	—	—	—	14	—	—	11	2½	—	13
West Virginia	16	—	—	--	—	—	—	—	--	—	—	—
Wisconsin	26	11	5	3	1	19	7	—	19	7	3	23
Wyoming	6	6	—	—	—	6	—	—	6	—	3	3
Alaska	6	2	1	3	—	2	1	3	4	2	—	6
Canal Zone	2	1	—	1	—	1	—	1	2	—	2	—
District of Columbia	6	—	—	6	—	—	—	6	—	6	—	6
Hawaii	6	2	—	4	—	1	5	—	1	5	—	6
Philippine Islands	6	—	—	—	—	3	2	1	3	2	2	4
Puerto Rico	6	1	—	2	—	2	—	2	6	—	1	5
Total	1094	266	134	254[a]	109	403½	400½	165	440	468½	270	699½

a. Sum of column; proceedings record 256.

1. Other candidates: Homer S. Cummings, 25; James W. Gerard, 21; Robert L. Owen, 33; Gilbert M. Hitchcock, 18; Edwin T. Meredith, 27; Edward I. Edwards, 42; John W. Davis, 32; Carter Glass, 26½; Furnifold M. Simmons, 24; Francis B. Harrison, 6; John S. Williams, 20; Thomas R. Marshall, 37; Champ Clark, 9; Oscar W. Underwood, ½; William R. Hearst, 1; William J. Bryan, 1; Bainbridge Colby, 1; Josephus Daniels, 1; Wood, 4.

2. Other candidates: Cummings, 4; Owen, 33; Davis, 58; Glass, 24; Clark, 2; Underwood, 2; not voting, 2.

3. Other candidates: Palmer, 74; Davis, 71½; Owen, 32; Cummings, 2; Clark, 2; Colby, 1; not voting, 3.

4. Other candidates: Palmer, 1; Davis, 52; Owen, 34; Glass, 1½; Colby, 1; not voting, 36.

1920 Republican

(Narrative, p. 81)

Delegation	Total Votes	First Pres. Ballot[1] Wood	Lowden	Johnson	Fourth Pres. Ballot[2] Wood	Lowden	Johnson	Eighth Pres. Ballot[3] Wood	Lowden	Harding	Ninth Pres. Ballot[4] Wood	Lowden	Harding	Tenth Pres. Ballot[5] (Before shift) Wood	Harding	Tenth Pres. Ballot[6] (After shift) Wood	Harding
Alabama	14	4	6	3	4	6	4	4	6	4	4	6	4	3	8	3	8
Arizona	6	6	—	—	6	—	—	6	—	—	6	—	—	6	—	—	6
Arkansas	13	6	6	—	2½	10½	—	1½	11½	—	1½	10½	1	—	13	—	13
California	26	—	—	26	—	—	26	—	—	—	—	—	—	—	—	—	—
Colorado	12	9	2	—	9	2	—	6	3	3	6	1	5	6	5	—	12
Connecticut	14	—	14	—	—	13	1	1	11	—	—	—	13	—	13	—	13
Delaware	6	—	—	—	—	2	—	—	—	3	—	—	3	—	6	—	6
Florida	8	4½	2½	—	6½	1½	—	7	1	—	1	—	7	½	7½	½	7½
Georgia	17	8	9	—	8	9	—	8	9	—	8	8	1	7	10	7	10
Idaho	8	5	—	1	5	1	1	4	2	1	5	1	1	3	2	3	2
Illinois	58	14	41	3	—	41	17	—	41	—	—	41	—	—	22.2	—	38.2
Indiana	30	22	—	8	18	3	6	15	4	11	15	4	11	8	20	9	21
Iowa	26	—	26	—	—	26	—	—	26	—	—	26	—	—	26	—	26
Kansas	20	14	6	—	14	6	—	10	6	4	—	—	20	1	18	1	18
Kentucky	26	—	20	1	—	26	—	—	26	—	—	—	26	—	26	—	26
Louisiana	12	3	3	1	3	6	—	3	7	2	—	—	12	—	12	—	12
Maine	12	11	—	—	11	—	—	12	—	—	12	—	—	12	—	12	—
Maryland	16	16	—	—	16	—	—	16	—	—	16	—	—	10	5	10	5
Massachusetts	35	7	—	—	16	—	—	11	—	—	11	1	1	17	17	17	17
Michigan	30	—	—	30	—	—	30	13	7	—	15	6	1	1	25	1	25
Minnesota	24	19	3	2	17	5	2	16	5	—	17	5	—	21	2	21	2
Mississippi	12	4½	2	2	7½	2½	—	8½	1½	2	7½	—	4½	2½	9½	—	12
Missouri	36	4½	18	3	8½	19	1	2½	15½	17	—	—	36	—	36	—	36
Montana	8	—	—	8	—	—	8	—	—	—	—	—	—	—	—	—	—
Nebraska	16	3	—	13	6	—	10	14	—	—	16	—	—	5	4	5	4
Nevada	6	2	1½	2	2½	2	1½	1½	—	3½	1½	—	3½	—	3½	—	3½
New Hampshire	8	8	—	—	8	—	—	8	—	—	8	—	—	8	—	8	—
New Jersey	28	17	—	11	17	—	11	16	—	2	15	—	4	15	5	15	5
New Mexico	6	6	—	—	6	—	—	6	—	—	6	—	—	6	—	—	6
New York	88	10	2	—	20	32	5	23	45	8	5	4	66	6	68	6	68
North Carolina	22	—	—	1	3	15	2	2	16	4	3	—	18	2	20	2	20
North Dakota	10	2	—	8	3	1	6	3	4	—	3	4	—	1	9	—	10
Ohio	48	9	—	—	9	—	—	9	—	39	9	—	39	—	48	—	48
Oklahoma	20	1½	18½	—	2	18	—	2	18	—	½	—	18	½	18	½	18
Oregon	10	1	—	9	5	—	5	4	—	1	4	—	1	3	2	3	2
Pennsylvania	76	—	—	—	—	—	—	—	—	—	—	—	—	14	60	14	60
Rhode Island	10	10	—	—	10	—	—	10	—	—	10	—	—	—	10	—	10
South Carolina	11	—	8	—	—	11	—	—	11	—	—	—	11	—	11	—	11
South Dakota	10	10	—	—	10	—	—	10	—	—	10	—	—	6	4	6	4
Tennessee	20	20	—	—	19	1	—	10	7	3	6	1	13	—	20	—	20
Texas	23	8½	5	1½	8	9½	1	5	8½	8½	1	1	19½	—	23	—	23
Utah	8	5	2	—	5	2	—	4	2	2	2	2	4	1	5	1	5
Vermont	8	8	—	—	8	—	—	8	—	—	8	—	—	8	—	8	—
Virginia	15	3	12	—	3	12	—	3	10	2	4	—	11	1	14	1	14
Washington	14	—	—	—	—	—	—	—	—	—	—	—	—	5	6	—	14
West Virginia	16	—	—	—	8	—	1	9	—	7	8	—	7	—	16	—	16
Wisconsin	26	1	—	—	1	—	2	1	—	—	1	—	—	—	1	—	1
Wyoming	6	—	3	—	3	3	—	—	—	6	—	—	6	—	6	—	6
Alaska	2	—	—	—	1	—	—	1	—	—	1	—	—	—	2	—	2
District of Columbia	2	2	—	—	2	—	—	2	—	—	2	—	—	—	2	—	2
Hawaii	2	—	—	—	—	2	—	—	2	—	—	2	—	—	2	—	2
Philippine Islands	2	2	—	—	2	—	—	2	—	—	2	—	—	2	—	2	—
Puerto Rico	2	1	1	—	1	1	—	1	1	—	—	—	2	—	2	—	2
Total	984	287½	211½	133½	314½	289	140½	299	307	133[a]	249	121½	374½	181½	644.7	156	692.2

a. Sum of column; proceedings record 133½.

1. Other candidates: Warren G. Harding, 65½; William C. Sproul, 84; Calvin Coolidge, 34; Herbert Hoover, 5½; Coleman du Pont, 7; Jeter C. Pritchard, 21; Robert M. La Follette, 24; Howard Sutherland, 17; William E. Borah, 2; Charles B. Warren, 1; Miles Poindexter, 20; Nicholas M. Butler, 69½; not voting, 1.

2. Other candidates: Harding, 61½; Sproul, 79½; Coolidge, 25; Hoover, 5; du Pont, 2; La Follette, 22; Sutherland, 3; Borah, 1; Poindexter, 15; Butler, 20; James E. Watson, 4; Knox, 2.

3. Other candidates: Johnson, 87; Coolidge, 30; du Pont, 3; Kellogg, 1; La Follette, 24; Poindexter, 15; Irving L. Lenroot, 1; Hoover, 5; Butler, 2; Philander C. Knox, 1; Sproul, 76.

4. Other candidates: Johnson, 82; Sproul, 78; Coolidge, 28; Hoover, 6; Lenroot, 1; Butler, 2; Knox, 1; La Follette, 24; Poindexter, 14; Will H. Hays, 1; H. F. MacGregor, 1; not voting, 1.

5. Other candidates: Lowden, 28; Johnson 80 4/5; Hoover, 10½; Coolidge, 5; Butler, 2; Lenroot, 1; Hays, 1; Knox, 1; La Follette, 24; Poindexter, 2; not voting, 2½.

6. Other candidates: Lowden, 11; Johnson, 80 4/5; Hoover, 9½; Coolidge, 5; Butler, 2; Lenroot, 1; Hays, 1; Knox, 1; La Follette, 24; not voting, ½.

1924 Democratic

(Narrative, p. 85)

Delegation	Total Votes	Minority Report on League of Nations			Minority Report on Ku Klux Klan			First Pres. Ballot[1]		Fiftieth Pres. Ballot[2]		Ninetieth Pres. Ballot[3]		
		Yea	Nay	Not voting	Yea	Nay	Not voting	McAdoo	Smith	McAdoo	Smith	McAdoo	Smith	Ralston
Alabama	24	12½	11½	—	24	—	—	—	—	—	—	—	—	—
Arizona	6	1½	4½	—	1	5	—	4½	—	3½	—	3½	—	—
Arkansas	18	3	15	—	—	18	—	—	—	—	—	—	—	—
California	26	4	22	—	7	19	—	26	—	26	—	26	—	—
Colorado	12	9½	2½	—	6	6	—	—	—	4	3	1	3	½
Connecticut	14	5	9	—	13	1	—	—	6	4	10	2	12	—
Delaware	6	6	—	—	6	—	—	—	—	—	—	—	—	—
Florida	12	5	7	—	1	11	—	12	—	10	1	9	—	3
Georgia	28	—	28	—	1	19½	7½	28	—	28	—	28	—	—
Idaho	8	8	—	—	—	8	—	8	—	8	—	8	—	—
Illinois	58	10	48	—	45	13	—	12	15	13	20	12	36	6
Indiana	30	—	30	—	5	25	—	—	—	—	—	—	—	30
Iowa	26	—	26	—	13½	12½	—	26	—	26	—	—	—	—
Kansas	20	—	20	—	—	20	—	—	—	20	—	—	—	—
Kentucky	26	9½	16½	—	9½	16½	—	26	—	26	—	26	—	—
Louisiana	20	—	20	—	—	20	—	—	—	—	—	—	—	—
Maine	12	11	1	—	8	4	—	2	3½	2½	4½	1½	4½	—
Maryland	16	—	16	—	16	—	—	—	—	—	—	—	—	—
Massachusetts	36	8	28	—	35½	½	—	1½	33	2½	33½	2½	33½	—
Michigan	30	6	24	—	12½	16½	1	—	—	15	15	—	10	20
Minnesota	24	10	14	—	17	7	—	5	10	6	15	6	15	—
Mississippi	20	—	20	—	—	20	—	—	—	—	—	—	—	20
Missouri	36	2	34	—	10½	25½	—	36	—	36	—	—	—	36
Montana	8	—	8	—	1	7	—	7	1	7	—	7	1	—
Nebraska	16	—	16	—	3	13	—	1	—	13	3	1	—	—
Nevada	6	—	6	—	—	6	—	6	—	6	—	—	—	6
New Hampshire	8	8	—	—	2½	5½	—	—	—	4½	3½	3	3½	—
New Jersey	28	—	28	—	28	—	—	—	—	—	28	—	28	—
New Mexico	6	—	6	—	1	5	—	6	—	6	—	6	—	—
New York	90	35	55	—	90	—	—	—	90	2	88	2	88	—
North Carolina	24	6	18	—	3 17/20	20 3/20	—	24	—	17	—	3	—	—
North Dakota	10	1	9	—	10	—	—	10	—	5	5	5	5	—
Ohio	48	48	—	—	32½	15½	—	—	—	—	—	—	20½	17
Oklahoma	20	—	20	—	—	20	—	20	—	20	—	—	—	20
Oregon	10	1	9	—	—	10	—	10	—	10	—	10	—	—
Pennsylvania	76	52	22	2	49½	24½	2	25½	35½	25½	38½	25½	39½	—
Rhode Island	10	—	10	—	10	—	—	—	10	—	10	—	10	—
South Carolina	18	18	—	—	—	18	—	18	—	18	—	18	—	—
South Dakota	10	—	10	—	6	4	—	10	—	9	—	9	—	—
Tennessee	24	15	9	—	3	21	—	24	—	24	—	24	—	—
Texas	40	—	40	—	—	40	—	40	—	40	—	40	—	—
Utah	8	5½	2½	—	4	4	—	8	—	8	—	8	—	—
Vermont	8	2	6	—	8	—	—	1	7	1	7	—	—	—
Virginia	24	24	—	—	2½	21½	—	—	—	—	—	—	—	—
Washington	14	—	14	—	—	14	—	14	—	14	—	14	—	—
West Virginia	16	16	—	—	7	9	—	—	—	—	—	—	—	1
Wisconsin	26	4	22	—	25	1	—	3	23	3	23	1	23	—
Wyoming	6	3	3	—	2	4	—	—	—	1	4½	—	3	—
Alaska	6	—	5	—	6	—	—	1	3	1	3	—	5	—
Canal Zone	6	—	6	—	2	4	—	6	—	6	—	3	3	—
District of Columbia	6	—	6	—	6	—	—	6	—	6	—	6	—	—
Hawaii	6	—	6	—	4	2	—	1	1	1	1	1	—	—
Philippine Islands	6	2	4	—	2	2	2	3	3	3	3	2	2	—
Puerto Rico	6	1	5	—	2	4	—	—	—	—	—	—	1	—
Virgin Islands	—	—	—	—	—	—	—	—	—	—	—	—	—	—
Total	1098	353½	742½	2	542 7/20	543 3/20	12½	431½	241	461½	320½	314	354½	159½

1. *Other candidates: Oscar W. Underwood, 42½; Joseph T. Robinson, 21; Willard Saulsbury, 7; Samuel M. Ralston, 30; Jonathan M. Davis, 20; Albert C. Ritchie, 22½; Woodbridge N. Ferris, 30; James M. Cox, 59; Charles W. Bryan, 18; Fred H. Brown, 17; George S. Silzer, 38; Carter Glass, 25; John W. Davis, 31; William E. Sweet, 12; Patrick Harrison, 43½; Houston Thompson, 1; John B. Kendrick, 6.*

2. *Other candidates: John W. Davis, 64; Ralston, 58; Underwood, 42½; Robinson, 44; Glass, 24; Cox, 54; Ritchie, 16½; Saulsbury, 6; Walsh, 1; Jonathan M. Davis, 2; Owen, 4.*

3. *Other candidates: Underwood, 42½; Robinson 20; John W. Davis, 65½; Glass, 30½; Ritchie, 16½; Saulsbury, 6; Walsh, 5; Bryan, 15; Jonathan M. Davis, 22; Daniels, 19; Meredith, 26; not voting, 2.*

1924 Democratic

(Narrative, p. 85)

Delegation	100th Pres. Ballot[4]			101st Pres. Ballot[5]				102nd Pres. Ballot[6]			103rd Pres. Ballot[7] (Before shift)		103rd Pres. Ballot[8] (After shift)	
	McAdoo	Smith	Davis	Underwood	Smith	Davis	Meredith	Underwood	Davis	Walsh	Underwood	Davis	Underwood	Davis
Alabama	—	—	—	24	—	—	—	24	—	—	24	—	—	24
Arizona	3	—	—	3	—	—	—	3	—	—	3	—	3	—
Arkansas	—	—	—	—	—	—	—	—	—	—	—	—	—	—
California	16½	—	—	—	1	—	3	—	—	26	2	2	—	26
Colorado	½	3½	1½	1	3	2½	1	6½	1½	—	5	3	5	3
Connecticut	2	12	—	11	—	1	—	11	—	3	11	—	—	14
Delaware	—	—	—	—	—	6	—	—	—	—	6	—	6	—
Florida	9	—	3	—	—	3	—	—	5	4	—	6	—	6
Georgia	28	—	—	—	—	5	12	1	13	—	—	27	—	27
Idaho	—	—	—	—	—	—	—	—	—	8	—	8	—	8
Illinois	—	35	6	20	—	4	13	20	3	13	19	19	—	58
Indiana	—	—	14	3	—	10	6	10	10	—	5	25	5	25
Iowa	—	—	—	—	—	—	26	—	—	—	—	—	—	26
Kansas	—	—	20	—	—	20	—	—	20	—	—	20	—	20
Kentucky	12	—	8½	1	1	9	½	1	9	6½	1	22½	—	26
Louisiana	—	—	20	—	—	20	—	—	20	—	—	20	—	20
Maine	1	2	8	5	—	6	—	8	4	—	10	2	10	2
Maryland	—	—	—	—	—	16	—	—	16	—	—	16	—	16
Massachusetts	2½	33½	—	—	33	—	—	8	½	2	23½	2	23½	2
Michigan	—	10	15	10	—	12	1	14	16	—	—	29½	—	29½
Minnesota	6	15	1	—	15	1	—	14	2	1	16	3	16	3
Mississippi	—	—	—	—	—	20	—	—	20	—	—	20	—	20
Missouri	—	—	36	—	—	36	—	—	36	—	—	36	—	36
Montana	1	—	—	—	—	—	—	—	—	8	—	—	—	—
Nebraska	—	2	—	—	1	—	11	2	—	4	2	1	2	1
Nevada	—	6	—	—	—	—	—	—	—	6	—	6	—	6
New Hampshire	—	1	2	—	1	1	1½	—	3½	4½	—	3½	—	3½
New Jersey	—	28	—	16	—	—	—	16	2	—	16	1	16	1
New Mexico	6	—	—	—	1½	1	1	—	2½	—	—	2	—	2
New York	2	88	—	86½	—	—	—	84	1	1	44	4	—	60
North Carolina	—	—	—	1	—	20	1	—	23	—	5½	18½	—	24
North Dakota	3	5	—	—	5	—	1	5	—	5	—	—	—	—
Ohio	—	15	23	5	10	23	5	7	25	—	4	41	1	46
Oklahoma	—	—	—	—	—	—	—	—	20	—	—	20	—	20
Oregon	10	—	—	1	—	2	1	1	2	—	1	5	1	5
Pennsylvania	17½	39½	9	6	36½	19½	1	32½	29½	4	31½	37½	—	76
Rhode Island	—	10	—	10	—	—	—	10	—	—	—	10	—	10
South Carolina	18	—	—	—	—	18	—	—	18	—	—	18	—	18
South Dakota	—	—	—	—	—	—	—	2	—	—	2	—	—	—
Tennessee	6	—	8	1	—	15	—	—	19	—	—	19	—	19
Texas	40	—	—	—	—	—	40	—	40	—	—	40	—	40
Utah	—	—	4	—	—	—	—	—	4	4	—	8	—	8
Vermont	—	8	—	4	—	4	—	4	4	—	—	8	—	8
Virginia	—	—	—	—	—	12	—	—	12	—	—	12	—	24
Washington	—	—	—	—	—	—	—	—	—	14	—	14	—	14
West Virginia	—	—	16	—	—	16	—	—	16	—	—	16	—	16
Wisconsin	—	22	—	8	9	—	1	11	—	9	8	1	1	22
Wyoming	—	3	½	—	3	3	—	—	6	—	—	6	—	6
Alaska	—	6	—	6	—	—	—	6	—	—	2	4	2	4
Canal Zone	3	3	—	—	—	1	3	3	3	—	—	6	—	6
District of Columbia	—	—	—	—	—	—	—	6	—	—	6	—	6	—
Hawaii	1	1	3	1	1	4	—	1	4	—	1	4	1	4
Philippine Islands	2	2	—	5	—	—	1	5	—	—	1	4	1	4
Puerto Rico	—	1	5	1	—	5	—	1	5	—	1	5	1	5
Virgin Islands	—	—	—	—	—	—	—	—	—	—	—	—	—	—
Total	190	351½	203½	229½	121	316	130	317	415½	123	250½	575½	102½	844

4. *Other candidates: Underwood, 41½; Robinson 46; Bryan, 2; Saulsbury, 6; Walsh, 52½; Owen, 20; Ritchie, 17½; Meredith, 75½; David F. Houston, 9; Glass, 35; Daniels, 24; Baker, 4; Berry, 1; James W. Gerard, 10; not voting, 9.*

5. *Other candidates: Robinson, 22½; McAdoo, 52; Walsh, 98; Ritchie, ½; Berry, 1; A. A. Murphree, 4; Houston, 9; Owen, 23; Cummings. 9; Glass, 59; Gerard, 16; Baker, 1; Daniels, 1; Cordell Hull, 2; not voting, 3½.*

6. *Other candidates: Robinson, 21; McAdoo, 21; Smith, 44; Thompson, 1; Ritchie, ½; Bryan, 1; Gerard, 7; Glass, 67; Daniels, 2; Berry 1½; Meredith, 66½; Henry T. Allen, 1; Hull, 1; not voting, 8.*

7. *Other candidates: McAdoo, 14½; Robinson, 21; Meredith, 42½; Glass, 79; Hull, 1; Smith, 10½; Daniels, 1; Gerard, 8; Thompson, 1; Walsh, 84½; not voting, 9.*

8. *Other candidates: Robinson, 20; McAdoo, 11½; Smith, 7½; Walsh, 58; Meredith, 15½; Glass, 23; Gerard, 7; Hull, 1; not voting, 8.*

1924 Republican

(Narrative, p. 84)

Delegation	Total Votes	First Pres. Ballot[1] Coolidge
Alabama	16	16
Arizona	9	9
Arkansas	14	14
California	29	29
Colorado	15	15
Connecticut	17	17
Delaware	9	9
Florida	10	10
Georgia	18	18
Idaho	11	11
Illinois	61	61
Indiana	33	33
Iowa	29	29
Kansas	23	23
Kentucky	26	26
Louisiana	13	13
Maine	15	15
Maryland	19	19
Massachusetts	39	39
Michigan	33	33
Minnesota	27	27
Mississippi	12	12
Missouri	39	39
Montana	11	11
Nebraska	19	19
Nevada	9	9
New Hampshire	11	11
New Jersey	31	31
New Mexico	9	9
New York	91	91
North Carolina	22	22
North Dakota	13	7
Ohio	51	51
Oklahoma	23	23
Oregon	13	13
Pennsylvania	79	79
Rhode Island	13	13
South Carolina	11	11
South Dakota	13	3
Tennessee	27	27
Texas	23	23
Utah	11	11
Vermont	11	11
Virginia	17	17
Washington	17	17
West Virginia	19	19
Wisconsin	29	1
Wyoming	9	9
Alaska	2	2
District of Columbia	2	2
Hawaii	2	2
Philippine Islands	2	2
Puerto Rico	2	2
Total	1109	1065

1. Other candidates: Robert M. La Follette, 34; Hiram W. Johnson, 10.

1928 Democratic

(Narrative, p. 88)

Delegation	Total Votes	First Pres. Ballot[1] (Before shift) Smith	First Pres. Ballot[2] (After shift) Smith
Alabama	24	1	1
Arizona	6	6	6
Arkansas	17	17	17
California	26	26	26
Colorado	12	12	12
Connecticut	14	14	14
Delaware	6	6	6
Florida	12	—	—
Georgia	28	—	—
Idaho	8	8	8
Illinois	58	56	56
Indiana	30	—	25
Iowa	26	26	26
Kansas	20	—	11½
Kentucky	26	26	26
Louisiana	20	20	20
Maine	12	12	12
Maryland	16	16	16
Massachusetts	36	36	36
Michigan	30	30	30
Minnesota	24	24	24
Mississippi	20	—	9½
Missouri	36	—	—
Montana	8	8	8
Nebraska	16	—	12
Nevada	6	6	6
New Hampshire	8	8	8
New Jersey	28	28	28
New Mexico	6	6	6
New York	90	90	90
North Carolina	24	4²/₃	4²/₃
North Dakota	10	10	10
Ohio	48	1	45
Oklahoma	20	10	10
Oregon	10	10	10
Pennsylvania	76	70½	70½
Rhode Island	10	10	10
South Carolina	18	—	—
South Dakota	10	10	10
Tennessee	24	—	23
Texas	40	—	—
Utah	8	8	8
Vermont	8	8	8
Virginia	24	6	6
Washington	14	14	14
West Virginia	16	10½	10½
Wisconsin	26	26	26
Wyoming	6	6	6
Alaska	6	6	6
Canal Zone	6	6	6
District of Columbia	6	6	6
Hawaii	6	6	6
Philippine Islands	6	6	6
Puerto Rico	6	6	6
Virgin Islands	2	2	2
Total	1100	724²/₃	849¹/₆

1. Other candidates: Cordell Hull, 71 and five-sixths; Walter F. George, 52½; James A. Reed, 48; Atlee Pomerene, 47; Jesse H. Jones, 43; Evans Woollen, 32; Patrick Harrison, 20; William A. Ayres, 20; Richard C. Watts, 18; Gilbert M. Hitchcock, 16; Vic Donahey, 5; Houston Thompson, 2.
2. Other candidates: George, 52½; Reed, 52; Hull, 50 and five-sixths; Jones, 43; Watts, 18; Harrison, 8½; Woollen, 7; Donahey, 5; Ayres, 3; Pomerene, 3; Hitchcock, 2; Thompson, 2; Theodore G. Bilbo, 1; not voting, 2½.

1928 Republican

(Narrative, p. 87)

Delegation	Total Votes	First Pres. Ballot[1] Hoover
Alabama	15	15
Arizona	9	9
Arkansas	11	11
California	29	29
Colorado	15	15
Connecticut	17	17
Delaware	9	9
Florida	10	9
Georgia	16	15
Idaho	11	11
Illinois	61	24
Indiana	33	—
Iowa	29	7
Kansas	23	—
Kentucky	29	29
Louisiana	12	11
Maine	15	15
Maryland	19	19
Massachusetts	39	39
Michigan	33	33
Minnesota	27	11
Mississippi	12	12
Missouri	39	28
Montana	11	10
Nebraska	19	11
Nevada	9	9
New Hampshire	11	11
New Jersey	31	31
New Mexico	9	7
New York	90	90
North Carolina	20	17
North Dakota	13	4
Ohio	51	36
Oklahoma	20	—
Oregon	13	13
Pennsylvania	79	79
Rhode Island	13	12
South Carolina	11	11
South Dakota	13	2
Tennessee	19	19
Texas	26	26
Utah	11	9
Vermont	11	11
Virginia	15	15
Washington	17	17
West Virginia	19	1
Wisconsin	26	9
Wyoming	9	9
Alaska	2	2
District of Columbia	2	2
Hawaii	2	2
Philippine Islands	2	2
Puerto Rico	2	2
Total	1089	837

1. Other candidates: Frank O. Lowden, 74; Charles Curtis, 64; James E. Watson, 45; George W. Norris, 24; Guy D. Goff, 18; Calvin Coolidge, 17; Charles G. Dawes, 4; Charles E. Hughes, 1; not voting, 5.

1932 Democratic *(Narrative, p. 90)*

Delegation	Total Votes	Louisiana Credentials			Minnesota Credentials			Permanent Organization		First Pres. Ballot[1]		Second Pres. Ballot[2]		Third Pres. Ballot[3]		Fourth Pres. Ballot[4]	
		Yea	Nay	Not voting	Yea	Nay	Not voting	Yea	Nay	Roosevelt	Smith	Roosevelt	Smith	Roosevelt	Smith	Roosevelt	Smith
Alabama	24	—	24	—	—	24	—	4½	19½	24	—	24	—	24	—	24	—
Arizona	6	—	6	—	—	6	—	—	6	6	—	6	—	6	—	6	—
Arkansas	18	—	18	—	—	18	—	—	18	18	—	18	—	18	—	18	—
California	44	44	—	—	44	—	—	44	—	—	—	—	—	—	—	44	—
Colorado	12	—	12	—	—	12	—	—	12	12	—	12	—	12	—	12	—
Connecticut	16	9½	6½	—	9¼	6¾	—	9½	6½	—	16	—	16	—	16	—	16
Delaware	6	1	5	—	—	6	—	1	5	6	—	6	—	6	—	6	—
Florida	14	3	11	—	—	14	—	—	14	14	—	14	—	14	—	14	—
Georgia	28	—	28	—	—	28	—	—	28	28	—	28	—	28	—	28	—
Idaho	8	—	8	—	—	8	—	—	8	8	—	8	—	8	—	8	—
Illinois	58	50¼	7¾	—	48	10	—	42	16	15¼	2¼	15¼	2¼	15¼	2¼	58	—
Indiana	30	30	—	—	30	—	—	30	—	14	2	16	2	16	2	30	—
Iowa	26	13	13	—	—	26	—	10	16	26	—	26	—	26	—	26	—
Kansas	20	—	20	—	—	20	—	6½	13½	20	—	20	—	20	—	20	—
Kentucky	26	—	26	—	—	26	—	—	26	26	—	26	—	26	—	26	—
Louisiana	20	—	20	—	—	20	—	—	20	20	—	20	—	20	—	20	—
Maine	12	6	6	—	6	6	—	7	5	12	—	12	—	12	—	12	—
Maryland	16	16	—	—	16	—	—	16	—	—	—	—	—	—	—	16	—
Massachusetts	36	36	—	—	36	—	—	36	—	—	36	—	36	—	36	—	36
Michigan	38	—	38	—	—	38	—	—	38	38	—	38	—	38	—	38	—
Minnesota	24	1	23	—	1	23	—	3	21	24	—	24	—	24	—	24	—
Mississippi	20	—	20	—	—	20	—	—	20	20	—	20	—	20	—	20	—
Missouri	36	19½	19½	—	16½	19½	—	16½	10½	12	—	18	—	20½	—	36	—
Montana	8	—	8	—	—	8	—	—	8	8	—	8	—	8	—	8	—
Nebraska	16	—	16	—	—	16	—	1	15	16	—	16	—	16	—	16	—
Nevada	6	—	6	—	—	6	—	—	6	6	—	6	—	6	—	6	—
New Hampshire	8	—	8	—	—	8	—	—	8	8	—	8	—	8	—	8	—
New Jersey	32	32	—	—	32	—	—	32	—	—	32	—	32	—	32	—	32
New Mexico	6	—	6	—	—	6	—	3	3	6	—	6	—	6	—	6	—
New York	94	65	29	—	65	29	—	67	27	28½	65½	29½	64½	31	63	31	63
North Carolina	26	20½	5½	—	—	26	—	4	22	26	—	26	—	25 4/100	—	26	—
North Dakota	10	—	10	—	2½	7½	—	1	9	9	—	10	—	9	—	10	—
Ohio	52	40	11	1	48½	2½	1	49½	2½	—	—	½	—	2½	—	29	17
Oklahoma	22	22	—	—	22	—	—	22	—	—	—	—	—	—	—	22	—
Oregon	10	—	10	—	—	10	—	1	9	10	—	10	—	10	—	10	—
Pennsylvania	76	20½	55½	—	25	49	2	27½	48½	44½	30	44½	23½	45½	21	49	14½
Rhode Island	10	10	—	—	10	—	—	10	—	—	10	—	10	—	10	—	10
South Carolina	18	—	18	—	—	18	—	—	18	18	—	18	—	18	—	18	—
South Dakota	10	—	10	—	—	10	—	—	10	10	—	10	—	10	—	10	—
Tennessee	24	—	24	—	—	24	—	—	24	24	—	24	—	24	—	24	—
Texas	46	46	—	—	46	—	—	46	—	—	—	—	—	—	—	46	—
Utah	8	—	8	—	—	8	—	—	8	8	—	8	—	8	—	8	—
Vermont	8	—	8	—	—	8	—	—	8	8	—	8	—	8	—	8	—
Virginia	24	24	—	—	24	—	—	24	—	—	—	—	—	—	—	24	—
Washington	16	—	16	—	—	16	—	—	16	16	—	16	—	16	—	16	—
West Virginia	16	—	16	—	3	13	—	—	16	16	—	16	—	16	—	16	—
Wisconsin	26	2	24	—	2	24	—	2	24	24	2	24	2	24	2	24	2
Wyoming	6	—	6	—	—	6	—	—	6	6	—	6	—	6	—	6	—
Alaska	6	—	6	—	—	6	—	6	—	5	—	6	—	6	—	6	—
Canal Zone	6	—	6	—	—	6	—	—	6	6	—	6	—	6	—	6	—
District of Columbia	6	—	6	—	—	6	—	—	6	6	—	6	—	6	—	6	—
Hawaii	6	—	6	—	—	6	—	—	6	6	—	6	—	6	—	6	—
Philippine Islands	6	6	—	—	6	—	—	6	—	—	6	—	6	—	6	6	—
Puerto Rico	6	—	6	—	—	6	—	—	6	6	—	6	—	6	—	6	—
Virgin Islands	2	—	2	—	—	2	—	—	2	2	—	2	—	2	—	2	—
Total	1154	514¼	638¾	1	492¾	658¼	3	528	626	666¼	201¾	677¾	194¼	682 29/100	190¼	945	190½

1. *Other candidates: John N. Garner, 90 and one-fourth; Harry F. Byrd, 25; Melvin A. Traylor, 42 and one-fourth; Albert C. Ritchie, 21; James A. Reed, 24; George White, 52; William H. Murray, 23; Newton D. Baker, 8½.*

2. *Other candidates: Garner, 90 and one-fourth; Byrd, 24; Traylor, 40 and one-fourth; Ritchie, 23½; Reed, 18; White, 50½; Baker, 8; Will Rogers, 22; not voting, 5½.*

3. *Other candidates: Garner, 101 and one-fourth; Byrd, 24 and ninety-six-hundredths; Traylor, 40 and one-fourth; Ritchie, 23½; Reed, 27½; White, 52½; Baker, 8½; not voting, 2½.*

4. *Other candidates: Ritchie, 3½; White, 3; Baker, 5½; James M. Cox, 1; not voting, 5½.*

1932 Republican

(Narrative, p. 90)

Delegation	Total Votes	Repeal of Prohibition Plank		First Pres. Ballot [1]
		Yea	Nay	Hoover
Alabama	19	—	19	19
Arizona	9	9	—	9
Arkansas	15	—	15	15
California	47	6	41	47
Colorado	15	1	14	15
Connecticut	19	19	—	19
Delaware	9	—	9	9
Florida	16	—	16	16
Georgia	16	2	14	16
Idaho	11	—	11	11
Illinois	61	45	15½	54½
Indiana	31	28	3	31
Iowa	25	3	22	25
Kansas	21	4	17	21
Kentucky	25	15	10	25
Louisiana	12	—	12	12
Maine	13	5	8	13
Maryland	19	—	19	19
Massachusetts	34	16	17	34
Michigan	41	25½	15½	41
Minnesota	25	—	25	25
Mississippi	11	11	—	11
Missouri	33	8½	23¾	33
Montana	11	—	11	11
Nebraska	17	1	16	17
Nevada	9	8	1	9
New Hampshire	11	—	11	11
New Jersey	35	35	—	35
New Mexico	9	2	7	8
New York	97	76	21	97
North Carolina	28	3	25	28
North Dakota	11	—	11	9
Ohio	55	12 2/9	42 2/9	55
Oklahoma	25	—	25	25
Oregon	13	3	10	9
Pennsylvania	75	51	23	73
Rhode Island	8	8	—	8
South Carolina	10	—	10	10
South Dakota	11	3	8	11
Tennessee	24	1	23	24
Texas	49	—	49	49
Utah	11	1	10	11
Vermont	9	9	—	9
Virginia	25	—	25	25
Washington	19	11	8	19
West Virginia	19	4	15	19
Wisconsin	27	22	5	15
Wyoming	9	9	—	9
Alaska	2	—	2	2
District of Columbia	2	—	2	2
Hawaii	2	2	—	2
Philippine Islands	2	1	1	2
Puerto Rico	2	—	2	2
Total	1154	460 2/9	690 19/36	1126½

1. Other candidates: John J. Blaine, 13; Calvin Coolidge, 4½; Joseph I. France, 4; Charles G. Dawes, 1; James W. Wadsworth, 1; not voting, 4.

1936 Republican

(Narrative, p. 92)

Delegation	Total Votes	First Pres. Ballot[1] Landon
Alabama	13	13
Arizona	6	6
Arkansas	11	11
California	44	44
Colorado	12	12
Connecticut	19	19
Delaware	9	9
Florida	12	12
Georgia	14	14
Idaho	8	8
Illinois	57	57
Indiana	28	28
Iowa	22	22
Kansas	18	18
Kentucky	22	22
Louisiana	12	12
Maine	13	13
Maryland	16	16
Massachusetts	33	33
Michigan	38	38
Minnesota	22	22
Mississippi	11	11
Missouri	30	30
Montana	8	8
Nebraska	14	14
Nevada	6	6
New Hampshire	11	11
New Jersey	32	32
New Mexico	6	6
New York	90	90
North Carolina	23	23
North Dakota	8	8
Ohio	52	52
Oklahoma	21	21
Oregon	10	10
Pennsylvania	75	75
Rhode Island	8	8
South Carolina	10	10
South Dakota	8	8
Tennessee	17	17
Texas	25	25
Utah	8	8
Vermont	9	9
Virginia	17	17
Washington	16	16
West Virginia	16	15
Wisconsin	24	6
Wyoming	6	6
Alaska	3	3
District of Columbia	3	3
Hawaii	3	3
Philippine Islands	2	2
Puerto Rico	2	2
Total	**1003**	**984**

1. Other candidates: William E. Borah, 19.

1940 Democratic

(Narrative, p. 95)

Delegation	Total Votes	First Pres. Ballot[1] Roosevelt
Alabama	22	20
Arizona	6	6
Arkansas	18	18
California	44	43
Colorado	12	12
Connecticut	16	16
Delaware	6	6
Florida	14	12½
Georgia	24	24
Idaho	8	8
Illinois	58	58
Indiana	28	28
Iowa	22	22
Kansas	18	18
Kentucky	22	22
Louisiana	20	20
Maine	10	10
Maryland	16	7½
Massachusetts	34	21½
Michigan	38	38
Minnesota	22	22
Mississippi	18	18
Missouri	30	26½
Montana	8	8
Nebraska	14	13
Nevada	6	2
New Hampshire	8	8
New Jersey	32	32
New Mexico	6	6
New York	94	64½
North Carolina	26	26
North Dakota	8	8
Ohio	52	52
Oklahoma	22	22
Oregon	10	10
Pennsylvania	72	72
Rhode Island	8	8
South Carolina	16	16
South Dakota	8	3
Tennessee	22	22
Texas	46	—
Utah	8	8
Vermont	6	6
Virginia	22	5 14/15
Washington	16	15
West Virginia	16	12
Wisconsin	24	21
Wyoming	6	6
Alaska	6	—
Canal Zone	6	—
District of Columbia	6	6
Hawaii	6	6
Philippine Islands	6	6
Puerto Rico	6	3
Virgin Islands	2	2
Total	**1100**	**946 13/30**

1. Other candidates: James A. Farley, 72 and nine-tenths; John N. Garner, 61; Millard E. Tydings, 9½; Cordell Hull, 5 and two-thirds; not voting, 4½.

1940 Republican

(Narrative, p. 94)

Delegation	Total Votes	First Pres. Ballot[1]			Fourth Pres. Ballot[2]			Fifth Pres. Ballot[3]		Sixth (before shift)[4]		Sixth (after shift)[5]
		Dewey	Taft	Willkie	Dewey	Taft	Willkie	Taft	Willkie	Taft	Willkie	Willkie
Alabama	13	7	6	—	7	5	1	7	5	7	6	13
Arizona	6	—	—	—	—	—	6	—	6	—	6	6
Arkansas	12	2	7	2	3	7	2	10	2	10	2	12
California	44	7	7	7	9	11	10	12	9	22	17	44
Colorado	12	1	4	3	1	4	3	4	4	6	5	12
Connecticut	16	—	—	16	—	—	16	—	16	—	16	16
Delaware	6	—	1	3	—	—	6	—	6	—	6	6
Florida	12	6	1	—	9	2	—	3	7	2	10	12
Georgia	14	7	3	—	6	3	2	7	6	7	6	14
Idaho	8	8	—	—	8	—	—	7	—	6	2	8
Illinois	58	52	2	4	17	27	10	30	17	33	24	58
Indiana	28	7	7	9	5	6	15	7	20	5	23	28
Iowa	22	—	—	—	2	—	—	13	7	15	7	22
Kansas	18	—	—	—	11	2	5	—	18	—	18	18
Kentucky	22	12	8	—	9	13	—	22	—	22	—	22
Louisiana	12	5	5	—	6	6	—	12	—	12	—	12
Maine	13	—	—	—	2	2	9	—	13	—	13	13
Maryland	16	16	—	—	—	—	14	1	14	1	15	16
Massachusetts	34	—	—	1	—	2	28	2	28	2	30	34
Michigan	38	—	—	—	2	—	—	—	—	2	35	38
Minnesota	22	3	4	6	2	9	9	12	9	11	10	22
Mississippi	11	3	8	—	2	9	—	11	—	9	2	11
Missouri	30	10	3	6	4	3	18	7	21	4	26	30
Montana	8	8	—	—	3	3	2	4	4	4	4	8
Nebraska	14	14	—	—	2	5	5	9	5	6	8	14
Nevada	6	—	2	2	—	1	4	2	4	2	4	6
New Hampshire	8	—	—	—	—	—	4	2	6	2	6	8
New Jersey	32	20	—	12	6	1	23	1	26	—	32	32
New Mexico	6	3	1	2	1	1	4	2	4	1	5	6
New York	92	61	—	8	48	5	35	10	75	7	78	92
North Carolina	23	9	7	2	6	6	9	11	12	8	15	23
North Dakota	8	2	1	1	2	1	3	4	4	4	4	8
Ohio	52	—	52	—	—	52	—	52	—	52	—	52
Oklahoma	22	22	—	—	10	6	3	18	4	5	17	22
Oregon	10	—	—	—	1	—	1	—	1	3	7	10
Pennsylvania	72	1	—	1	—	—	19	—	21	—	72	72
Rhode Island	8	1	3	3	—	4	4	4	4	3	5	8
South Carolina	10	10	—	—	8	—	2	—	9	—	10	10
South Dakota	8	—	—	—	4	1	—	7	1	2	6	8
Tennessee	18	8	3	2	5	6	5	9	6	5	10	17
Texas	26	—	26	—	—	26	—	26	—	26	—	26
Utah	8	2	2	1	2	2	1	3	5	1	7	8
Vermont	9	1	3	3	1	3	5	3	6	2	7	9
Virginia	18	2	9	5	—	7	11	7	11	2	16	18
Washington		13	3	—	12	3	—	16	—	4	10	16
West Virginia	16	8	5	3	6	3	7	9	6	—	15	15
Wisconsin	24	24	—	—	24	—	—	—	—	2	20	24
Wyoming	6	1	1	2	3	2	1	3	3	—	6	6
Alaska	3	1	2	—	—	2	1	3	—	1	2	3
District of Columbia	3	2	1	—	—	1	2	1	2	—	3	3
Hawaii	3	—	—	—	—	—	—	1	1	—	3	3
Philippine Islands	2	—	1	1	—	1	1	1	1	—	2	2
Puerto Rico	2	1	1	—	1	1	—	2	—	—	2	2
Total	1000	360	189	105	250	254	306	377	429	318	655	998

1. Other candidates: Arthur H. Vandenberg, 76; Arthur H. James, 74; Joseph W. Martin, 44; Hanford MacNider, 34; Frank E. Gannett, 33; Styles Bridges, 28; Arthur Capper, 18; Herbert Hoover, 17; Charles L. McNary, 13; Harlan F. Bushfield, 9.

2. Other candidates: Vandenberg, 61; James, 56; Hoover, 31; MacNider, 26; McNary, 8; Gannett, 4; Bridges, 1; not voting, 3.

3. Other candidates: James, 59; Dewey, 57; Vandenberg, 42; Hoover, 20; McNary, 9; MacNider, 4; Gannett, 1; not voting, 2.

4. Other candidates: Dewey, 11; Hoover, 10; Gannett, 1; McNary, 1; not voting, 4.

5. Not voting, 2.

1944 Democratic

(Narrative, p. 97)

Delegation	Total Votes	First Pres. Ballot [1] Roosevelt
Alabama	24	22
Arizona	10	10
Arkansas	20	20
California	52	52
Colorado	12	12
Connecticut	18	18
Delaware	8	8
Florida	18	14
Georgia	26	26
Idaho	10	10
Illinois	58	58
Indiana	26	26
Iowa	20	20
Kansas	16	16
Kentucky	24	24
Louisiana	22	—
Maine	10	10
Maryland	18	18
Massachusetts	34	34
Michigan	38	38
Minnesota	24	24
Mississippi	20	—
Missouri	32	32
Montana	10	10
Nebraska	12	12
Nevada	8	8
New Hampshire	10	10
New Jersey	34	34
New Mexico	10	10
New York	96	94½
North Carolina	30	30
North Dakota	8	8
Ohio	52	52
Oklahoma	22	22
Oregon	14	14
Pennsylvania	72	72
Rhode Island	10	10
South Carolina	18	14½
South Dakota	8	8
Tennessee	26	26
Texas	48	36
Utah	10	10
Vermont	6	6
Virginia	24	—
Washington	18	18
West Virginia	18	17
Wisconsin	26	26
Wyoming	8	8
Alaska	6	6
Canal Zone	6	6
District of Columbia	6	6
Hawaii	6	6
Philippine Islands	6	6
Puerto Rico	6	6
Virgin Islands	2	2
Total	1176	1086

1. Other candidates: Harry F. Byrd, 89; James A. Farley, 1.

1944 Republican

(Narrative, p. 96)

Delegation	Total Votes	First Pres. Ballot [1] Dewey
Alabama	14	14
Arizona	8	8
Arkansas	12	12
California	50	50
Colorado	15	15
Connecticut	16	16
Delaware	9	9
Florida	15	15
Georgia	14	14
Idaho	11	11
Illinois	59	59
Indiana	29	29
Iowa	23	23
Kansas	19	19
Kentucky	22	22
Louisiana	13	13
Maine	13	13
Maryland	16	16
Massachusetts	35	35
Michigan	41	41
Minnesota	25	25
Mississippi	6	6
Missouri	30	30
Montana	8	8
Nebraska	15	15
Nevada	6	6
New Hampshire	11	11
New Jersey	35	35
New Mexico	8	8
New York	93	93
North Carolina	25	25
North Dakota	11	11
Ohio	50	50
Oklahoma	23	23
Oregon	15	15
Pennsylvania	70	70
Rhode Island	8	8
South Carolina	4	4
South Dakota	11	11
Tennessee	19	19
Texas	33	33
Utah	8	8
Vermont	9	9
Virginia	19	19
Washington	16	16
West Virginia	19	19
Wisconsin	24	23
Wyoming	9	9
Alaska	3	3
District of Columbia	3	3
Hawaii	5	5
Philippine Islands	2	—
Puerto Rico	2	2
Total	1059	1056

1. Other candidates: Douglas MacArthur, 1; absent, 2.

1948 Democratic

(Narrative, p. 100)

Delegation	Total Votes	Pro-Southern Amendment to Civil Rights Plank		Plank Endorsing Truman's Civil Rights Policy		First Pres. Ballot [1] (Before shift)		First Pres. Ballot [2] (After shift)	
		Yea	Nay	Yea	Nay	Truman	Russell	Truman	Russell
Alabama	26	26	—	—	26	—	26	—	26
Arizona	12	—	12	—	12	12	—	12	—
Arkansas	22	22	—	—	22	—	22	—	22
California	54	1½	52½	53	1	53½	—	54	—
Colorado	12	3	9	10	2	12	—	12	—
Connecticut	20	—	20	20	—	20	—	20	—
Delaware	10	—	10	—	10	10	—	10	—
Florida	20	20	—	—	20	—	19	—	20
Georgia	28	28	—	—	28	—	28	—	28
Idaho	12	—	12	—	12	12	—	12	—
Illinois	60	—	60	60	—	60	—	60	—
Indiana	26	—	26	17	9	25	—	26	—
Iowa	20	—	20	18	2	20	—	20	—
Kansas	16	—	16	16	—	16	—	16	—
Kentucky	26	—	26	—	26	26	—	26	—
Louisiana	24	24	—	—	24	—	24	—	24
Maine	10	—	10	3	7	10	—	10	—
Maryland	20	—	20	—	20	20	—	20	—
Massachusetts	36	—	36	36	—	36	—	36	—
Michigan	42	—	42	42	—	42	—	42	—
Minnesota	26	—	26	26	—	26	—	26	—
Mississippi	22	22	—	—	22	—	—	—	—
Missouri	34	—	34	—	34	34	—	34	—
Montana	12	—	12	1½	10½	12	—	12	—
Nebraska	12	—	12	3	9	12	—	12	—
Nevada	10	—	10	—	10	10	—	10	—
New Hampshire	12	—	12	1	11	11	—	11	—
New Jersey	36	—	36	36	—	36	—	36	—
New Mexico	12	—	12	—	12	12	—	12	—
New York	98	—	98	98	—	83	—	98	—
North Carolina	32	32	—	—	32	13	19	13	19
North Dakota	8	—	8	—	8	8	—	8	—
Ohio	50	—	50	39	11	50	—	50	—
Oklahoma	24	—	24	—	24	24	—	24	—
Oregon	16	3	13	7	9	16	—	16	—
Pennsylvania	74	—	74	74	—	74	—	74	—
Rhode Island	12	—	12	—	12	12	—	12	—
South Carolina	20	20	—	—	20	—	20	—	20
South Dakota	8	—	8	8	—	8	—	8	—
Tennessee	28	28	—	—	28	—	28	—	28
Texas	50	50	—	—	50	—	50	—	50
Utah	12	—	12	—	12	12	—	12	—
Vermont	6	—	6	6	—	5½	—	5½	—
Virginia	26	26	—	—	26	—	26	—	26
Washington	20	—	20	20	—	20	—	20	—
West Virginia	20	—	20	7	13	15	4	20	—
Wisconsin	24	—	24	24	—	24	—	24	—
Wyoming	6	1½	4½	4	2	6	—	6	—
Alaska	6	3	3	2	4	6	—	6	—
Canal Zone	2	—	2	—	2	2	—	2	—
District of Columbia	6	—	6	6	—	6	—	6	—
Hawaii	6	—	6	6	—	6	—	6	—
Puerto Rico	6	—	6	6	—	6	—	6	—
Virgin Islands	2	—	2	2	—	2	—	2	—
Total	1234	310 [a]	924 [b]	651½	582½	926	266	947½	263

a. Sum of column; proceedings record 309.
b. Sum of column; proceedings record 925.
1. Other candidates: Paul V. McNutt, 2½; James A. Roe, 15; Alben W. Barkley, 1; not voting, 23½.
2. Other candidates: McNutt, ½; not voting, 23.

1948 Republican

(Narrative, p. 99)

Delegation	Total Votes	First Pres. Ballot[1]			Second Pres. Ballot[2]			Third Pres. Ballot
		Dewey	Stassen	Taft	Dewey	Stassen	Taft	Dewey
Alabama	14	9	—	5	9	—	5	14
Arizona	8	3	2	3	4	2	2	8
Arkansas	14	3	4	7	3	4	7	14
California	53	—	—	—	—	—	—	53
Colorado	15	3	5	7	3	8	4	15
Connecticut	19	—	—	—	—	—	—	19
Delaware	9	5	1	2	6	1	2	9
Florida	16	6	4	6	6	4	6	16
Georgia	16	12	1	—	13	1	—	16
Idaho	11	11	—	—	11	—	—	11
Illinois	56	—	—	—	5	—	50	56
Indiana	29	29	—	—	29	—	—	29
Iowa	23	3	13	5	13	7	2	23
Kansas	19	12	1	2	14	1	2	19
Kentucky	25	10	1	11	11	1	11	25
Louisiana	13	6	—	7	6	—	7	13
Maine	13	5	4	1	5	7	—	13
Maryland	16	8	3	5	13	—	3	16
Massachusetts	35	17	1	2	18	1	3	35
Michigan	41	—	—	—	—	—	—	41
Minnesota	25	—	25	—	—	25	—	25
Mississippi	8	—	—	8	—	—	8	8
Missouri	33	17	6	8	18	6	7	33
Montana	11	5	3	3	6	2	3	11
Nebraska	15	2	13	—	6	9	—	15
Nevada	9	6	1	2	6	1	2	9
New Hampshire	8	6	2	—	6	2	—	8
New Jersey	35	—	—	—	24	6	2	35
New Mexico	8	3	2	3	3	2	3	8
New York	97	96	—	1	96	—	1	97
North Carolina	26	16	2	5	17	2	4	26
North Dakota	11	—	11	—	—	11	—	11
Ohio	53	—	9	44	1	8	44	53
Oklahoma	20	18	—	1	19	—	1	20
Oregon	12	12	—	—	12	—	—	12
Pennsylvania	73	41	1	28	40	1	29	73
Rhode Island	8	1	—	1	4	—	2	8
South Carolina	6	—	—	6	—	—	6	6
South Dakota	11	3	8	—	7	4	—	11
Tennessee	22	6	—	—	8	—	13	22
Texas	33	2	1	30	2	2	29	33
Utah	11	5	2	4	6	2	3	11
Vermont	9	7	2	—	7	2	—	9
Virginia	21	10	—	10	13	—	7	21
Washington	19	14	2	1	14	2	3	19
West Virginia	16	11	5	—	13	3	—	16
Wisconsin	27	—	19	—	2	19	—	27
Wyoming	9	4	3	2	6	3	—	9
Alaska	3	2	—	1	3	—	—	3
District of Columbia	3	2	—	—	3	—	—	3
Hawaii	5	3	—	1	3	—	2	5
Puerto Rico	2	—	—	2	1	—	1	2
Total	1094	434	157	224	515	149	274	1094

1. Other candidates: Arthur H. Vandenberg, 62; Earl Warren, 59; Dwight H. Green, 56; Alfred E. Driscoll, 35; Raymond E. Baldwin, 19; Joseph W. Martin, 18; B. Carroll Reece, 15; Douglas MacArthur, 11; Everett M. Dirksen, 1; not voting, 3.

2. Other candidates: Vandenberg, 62; Warren, 57; Baldwin, 19; Martin, 10; MacArthur, 7; Reece, 1.

1952 Democratic

(Narrative, p. 104)

Delegation	Total Votes	Seating Virginia Delegation — Yea	Nay	Not voting	Table Motion to Adjourn — Yea	Nay	Not voting	First Pres. Ballot[1] — Harriman	Kefauver	Russell	Stevenson	Second Pres. Ballot[2] — Harriman	Kefauver	Russell	Stevenson	Third Pres. Ballot[3] — Kefauver	Russell	Stevenson
Alabama	22	22	—	—	13½	8½	—	—	8	13	½	—	7½	14	½	7½	14	½
Arizona	12	12	—	—	12	—	—	—	—	—	—	—	—	12	—	—	12	—
Arkansas	22	22	—	—	19	3	—	—	—	—	—	1	1½	18	1½	1½	—	20½
California	68	4	61	3	—	68	—	—	68	—	—	—	68	—	—	68	—	—
Colorado	16	4½	11½	—	4	12	—	5	2	8½	½	5	5	2½	3½	4	3½	8½
Connecticut	16	—	16	—	16	—	—	—	—	—	16	—	—	—	16	—	—	16
Delaware	6	6	—	—	6	—	—	—	—	—	6	—	—	—	6	—	—	6
Florida	24	24	—	—	19	5	—	—	5	19	—	—	5	19	—	5	19	—
Georgia	28	28	—	—	28	—	—	—	—	28	—	—	—	28	—	—	28	—
Idaho	12	12	—	—	—	12	—	3½	3	1	1½	—	—	—	12	—	—	12
Illinois	60	52	8	—	53	7	—	1	3	—	53	—	3	—	54	3	—	54
Indiana	26	14½	6½	5	25	1	—	—	1	—	25	—	1	—	25	1	—	25
Iowa	24	17	7	—	8	15	1	½	8	2	8	½	8½	3	9½	8	3	10
Kansas	16	—	16	—	16	—	—	—	—	—	16	—	—	—	16	—	—	16
Kentucky	26	26	—	—	26	—	—	—	—	—	—	—	—	—	—	—	—	—
Louisiana	20	20	—	—	20	—	—	—	—	20	—	—	—	20	—	—	20	—
Maine	10	2½	7½	—	4½	5½	—	1½	1½	2½	3½	1	1	2½	4½	½	2½	7
Maryland	18	18	—	—	18	—	—	—	18	—	—	—	15½	2	—	8½	2½	6
Massachusetts	36	16	19	1	30	4½	1½	—	—	—	—	—	2½	—	—	5	1	25
Michigan	40	—	40	—	—	40	—	—	40	—	—	—	40	—	—	--	—	40
Minnesota	26	—	26	—	—	26	—	—	—	—	—	1½	17	—	7½	13	—	13
Mississippi	18	18	—	—	18	—	—	—	—	18	—	—	—	18	—	—	18	—
Missouri	34	34	—	—	29	5	—	1½	2	—	18	1½	2	—	19½	2	—	22
Montana	12	—	12	—	12	—	—	—	—	—	—	3	3	3	—	—	—	12
Nebraska	12	8	3	1	—	12	—	—	5	1	2	—	5	1	2	3	1	8
Nevada	10	10	—	—	9½	½	—	—	½	8	1	—	½	7½	2	½	7½	2
New Hampshire	8	1	7	—	—	8	—	—	8	—	—	—	8	—	—	8	—	—
New Jersey	32	—	32	—	24	8	—	1	3	—	28	—	4	—	28	4	—	28
New Mexico	12	12	—	—	12	—	—	1	1½	4	1	—	1½	6	4½	1½	3½	7
New York	94	7	87	—	5	89	—	83½	1	—	6½	84½	—	1	6½	4	—	86½
North Carolina	32	32	—	—	32	—	—	—	—	26	5½	—	—	24	7	—	24	7½
North Dakota	8	8	—	—	8	—	—	—	2	2	2	—	—	—	—	—	—	8
Ohio	54	33½	14½	6	26	28	—	1	29½	7	13	1	27½	8	17½	27	1	26
Oklahoma	24	24	—	—	24	—	—	—	—	—	—	—	—	—	—	—	—	—
Oregon	12	4	8	—	—	12	—	—	12	—	—	—	12	—	—	11	—	1
Pennsylvania	70	57	13	—	35	35	—	4½	22½	—	36	2½	21½	—	40	—	—	70
Rhode Island	12	10	2	—	10	2	—	1½	3½	—	5½	—	4	—	8	—	—	12
South Carolina	16	—	—	16	—	—	16	—	—	16	—	—	—	16	—	—	16	—
South Dakota	8	—	8	—	—	8	—	—	8	—	—	—	8	—	—	8	—	—
Tennessee	28	—	28	—	—	28	—	—	28	—	—	—	28	—	—	28	—	—
Texas	52	52	—	—	52	—	—	—	—	52	—	—	—	52	—	—	52	—
Utah	12	3	9	—	—	12	—	6½	½	2	½	9	1½	—	½	—	—	12
Vermont	6	—	6	—	6	—	—	—	½	—	5	—	½	½	5	—	½	5½
Virginia	28	—	—	28	28	—	—	—	28	—	—	—	28	—	—	28	—	—
Washington	22	12½	9½	—	3	10	—	12	½	—	6	2	12½	½	6	11	½	10½
West Virginia	20	13½	5	1½	10	9	1	—	5½	7	1	—	7½	6½	5½	7½	3½	9
Wisconsin	28	1	27	—	—	28	—	—	28	—	—	—	28	—	—	28	—	—
Wyoming	10	5½	4½	—	2½	7½	—	3½	1½	½	3	2½	3	—	4½	—	—	10
Alaska	6	—	6	—	—	6	—	—	6	—	—	—	6	—	—	6	—	—
Canal Zone	2	2	—	—	2	—	—	—	—	2	—	—	—	2	—	—	—	2
District of Columbia	6	—	6	—	—	6	—	6	—	—	—	6	—	—	—	—	—	6
Hawaii	6	—	6	—	4	2	—	1	1	—	2	—	1	—	5	1	—	5
Puerto Rico	6	2	4	—	1	5	—	—	—	—	6	—	—	—	6	—	—	6
Virgin Islands	2	—	2	—	—	2	—	—	—	—	1	—	1	—	1	—	—	2
Total	**1230**	**650½**	**518**	**61½**	**671**	**539½**[a]	**19½**	**123½**	**340**	**268**	**273**	**121**	**362½**	**294**	**324½**	**275½**	**261**	**617½**

a. Sum of column; proceedings record 534.
1. Other candidates: Alben W. Barkley, 48½; Robert S. Kerr, 65; J. William Fulbright, 22; Paul H. Douglas, 3; Oscar R. Ewing, 4; Paul A. Dever, 37½; Hubert H. Humphrey, 26; James E. Murray, 12; Harry S Truman, 6; William O. Douglas, ½; not voting, 1.
2. Other candidates: Barkley, 78½; Paul H. Douglas, 3; Kerr, 5½; Ewing, 3; Dever, 30½; Truman, 6; not voting, 1½.
3. Other candidates: Barkley, 67½; Paul H. Douglas, 3; Dever, ½; Ewing, 3; not voting, 2.

1952 Republican

(Narrative, p. 103)

Delegation	Total Votes	Pro-Taft Amendment on Louisiana Delegates		Pro-Eisenhower Report on Georgia Delegates		First Pres. Ballot[1] (Before shift)		First Pres. Ballot[2] (After shift)	
		Yea	Nay	Yea	Nay	Eisenhower	Taft	Eisenhower	Taft
Alabama	14	9	5	5	9	5	9	14	—
Arizona	14	12	2	3	11	4	10	4	10
Arkansas	11	11	—	3	8	4	6	11	—
California	70	—	70	62	8	—	—	—	—
Colorado	18	1	17	17	1	15	2	17	1
Connecticut	22	2	20	21	1	21	1	22	—
Delaware	12	5	7	8	4	7	5	12	—
Florida	18	15	3	5	13	6	12	18	—
Georgia	17	17	—	—	—	14	2	16	1
Idaho	14	14	—	—	14	—	14	14	—
Illinois	60	58	2	1	59	1	59	1	59
Indiana	32	31	1	3	29	2	30	2	30
Iowa	26	11	15	16	10	16	10	20	6
Kansas	22	2	20	20	2	20	2	22	—
Kentucky	20	18	2	2	18	1	19	13	7
Louisiana	15	13	2	—	2	13	2	15	—
Maine	16	5	11	11	5	11	5	15	1
Maryland	24	5	19	15	9	16	8	24	—
Massachusetts	38	5	33	33	5	34	4	38	—
Michigan	46	1	45	32	14	35	11	35	11
Minnesota	28	—	28	28	—	9	—	28	—
Mississippi	5	5	—	—	5	—	5	5	—
Missouri	26	4	22	21	5	21	5	26	—
Montana	8	7	1	1	7	1	7	1	7
Nebraska	18	13	5	7	11	4	13	7	11
Nevada	12	7	5	2	10	5	7	10	2
New Hampshire	14	—	14	14	—	14	—	14	—
New Jersey	38	5	33	32	6	33	5	38	—
New Mexico	14	8	6	5	9	6	8	6	8
New York	96	1	95	92	4	92	4	95	1
North Carolina	26	14	12	10	16	12	14	26	—
North Dakota	14	11	3	3	11	4	8	5	8
Ohio	56	56	—	—	56	—	56	—	56
Oklahoma	16	10	6	4	12	4	7	8	4
Oregon	18	—	18	18	—	18	—	18	—
Pennsylvania	70	13	57	52	18	53	15	70	—
Rhode Island	8	2	6	6	2	6	1	8	—
South Carolina	6	5	1	1	5	2	4	6	—
South Dakota	14	14	—	—	14	—	14	7	7
Tennessee	20	20	—	—	20	—	20	20	—
Texas	38	22	16	—	—	33	5	38	—
Utah	14	14	—	—	14	—	14	14	—
Vermont	12	—	12	12	—	12	—	12	—
Virginia	23	13	10	7	16	9	14	19	4
Washington	24	4	20	19	5	20	4	21	3
West Virginia	16	15	1	1	15	1	14	3	13
Wisconsin	30	24	6	6	24	—	24	—	24
Wyoming	12	8	4	4	8	6	6	12	—
Alaska	3	3	—	—	3	1	2	3	—
Canal Zone	—	—	—	—	—	—	—	—	—
District of Columbia	6	6	—	—	6	—	6	6	—
Hawaii	8	7	1	3	5	3	4	4	4
Puerto Rico	3	2	1	1	2	—	3	1	2
Virgin Islands	1	—	1	1	—	1	—	1	—
Total	1206	548	658	607	531	595	500	845	280

1. Other candidates: Earl Warren, 81; Harold E. Stassen, 20; Douglas MacArthur, 10.
2. Other candidates: Warren, 77; MacArthur, 4.

1956 Democratic

(Narrative, p. 106)

Delegation	Total Votes	First Pres. Ballot[1]		
		Stevenson	Harriman	Other
Alabama	26	15½	—	10½
Arizona	16	16	—	—
Arkansas	26	26	—	—
California	68	68	—	—
Colorado	20	13½	6	½
Connecticut	20	20	—	—
Delaware	10	10	—	—
Florida	28	25	—	3
Georgia	32	—	—	32
Idaho	12	12	—	—
Illinois	64	53½	8½	2
Indiana	26	21½	3	1½
Iowa	24	16½	7	½
Kansas	16	16	—	—
Kentucky	30	—	—	30
Louisiana	24	24	—	—
Maine	14	10½	3½	—
Maryland	18	18	—	—
Massachusetts	40	32	7½	½
Michigan	44	39	5	—
Minnesota	30	19	11	—
Mississippi	22	—	—	22
Missouri	38	—	—	38
Montana	16	10	6	—
Nebraska	12	12	—	—
Nevada	14	5½	7	1½
New Hampshire	8	5½	1½	1
New Jersey	36	36	—	—
New Mexico	16	12	3½	½
New York	98	5½	92½	—
North Carolina	36	34½	1	½
North Dakota	8	8	—	—
Ohio	58	52	½	5½
Oklahoma	28	—	28	—
Oregon	16	16	—	—
Pennsylvania	74	67	7	—
Rhode Island	16	16	—	—
South Carolina	20	2	—	18
South Dakota	8	8	—	—
Tennessee	32	32	—	—
Texas	56	—	—	56
Utah	12	12	—	—
Vermont	6	5½	½	—
Virginia	32	—	—	32
Washington	26	19½	6	½
West Virginia	24	24	—	—
Wisconsin	28	22½	5	½
Wyoming	14	14	—	—
Alaska	6	6	—	—
Canal Zone	3	3	—	—
District of Columbia	6	6	—	—
Hawaii	6	6	—	—
Puerto Rico	6	6	—	—
Virgin Islands	3	3	—	—
Total	**1372**	**905½**	**210**	**256½**

1. Other candidates: Lyndon B. Johnson, 80; James C. Davis, 33; Albert B. Chandler, 36½; John S. Battle, 32½; George B. Timmerman, 23½; W. Stuart Symington, 45½; Frank Lausche, 5½.

1956 Republican

(Narrative, p. 107)

Delegation	Total Votes	First Pres. Ballot Eisenhower
Alabama	21	21
Arizona	14	14
Arkansas	16	16
California	70	70
Colorado	18	18
Connecticut	22	22
Delaware	12	12
Florida	26	26
Georgia	23	23
Idaho	14	14
Illinois	60	60
Indiana	32	32
Iowa	26	26
Kansas	22	22
Kentucky	26	26
Louisiana	20	20
Maine	16	16
Maryland	24	24
Massachusetts	38	38
Michigan	46	46
Minnesota	28	28
Mississippi	15	15
Missouri	32	32
Montana	14	14
Nebraska	18	18
Nevada	12	12
New Hampshire	14	14
New Jersey	38	38
New Mexico	14	14
New York	96	96
North Carolina	28	28
North Dakota	14	14
Ohio	56	56
Oklahoma	22	22
Oregon	18	18
Pennsylvania	70	70
Rhode Island	14	14
South Carolina	16	16
South Dakota	14	14
Tennessee	28	28
Texas	54	54
Utah	14	14
Vermont	12	12
Virginia	30	30
Washington	24	24
West Virginia	16	16
Wisconsin	30	30
Wyoming	12	12
Alaska	4	4
District of Columbia	6	6
Hawaii	10	10
Puerto Rico	3	3
Virgin Islands	1	1
Total	**1323**	**1323**

1960 Democratic

(Narrative, p. 109)

Delegation	Total Votes	First Pres. Ballot[1]			
		Kennedy	Johnson	Stevenson	Symington
Alabama	29	3½	20	½	3½
Alaska	9	9	—	—	—
Arizona	17	17	—	—	—
Arkansas	27	—	27	—	—
California	81	33½	7½	31½	8
Colorado	21	13½	—	5½	2
Connecticut	21	21	—	—	—
Delaware	11	—	11	—	—
Florida	29	—	—	—	—
Georgia	33	—	33	—	—
Hawaii	9	1½	3	3½	1
Idaho	13	6	4½	½	2
Illinois	69	61½	—	2	5½
Indiana	34	34	—	—	—
Iowa	26	21½	½	2	½
Kansas	21	21	—	—	—
Kentucky	31	3½	25½	1½	½
Louisiana	26	—	26	—	—
Maine	15	15	—	—	—
Maryland	24	24	—	—	—
Massachusetts	41	41	—	—	—
Michigan	51	42½	—	2½	6
Minnesota	31	—	—	—	—
Mississippi	23	—	—	—	—
Missouri	39	—	—	—	39
Montana	17	10	2	2½	2½
Nebraska	16	11	½	—	4
Nevada	15	5½	6½	2½	½
New Hampshire	11	11	—	—	—
New Jersey	41	—	—	—	—
New Mexico	17	4	13	—	—
New York	114	104½	3½	3½	2½
North Carolina	37	6	27½	3	—
North Dakota	11	11	—	—	—
Ohio	64	64	—	—	—
Oklahoma	29	—	29	—	—
Oregon	17	16½	—	½	—
Pennsylvania	81	68	4	7½	—
Rhode Island	17	17	—	—	—
South Carolina	21	—	21	—	—
South Dakota	11	4	2	1	2½
Tennessee	33	—	33	—	—
Texas	61	—	61	—	—
Utah	13	8	3	—	1½
Vermont	9	9	—	—	—
Virginia	33	—	33	—	—
Washington	27	14½	2½	6½	3
West Virginia	25	15	5½	3	1½
Wisconsin	31	23	—	—	—
Wyoming	15	15	—	—	—
Canal Zone	4	—	4	—	—
District of Columbia	9	9	—	—	—
Puerto Rico	7	7	—	—	—
Virgin Islands	4	4	—	—	—
Total	1521	806	409	79½	86

1. Other candidates:
   Barnett, 23 (Mississippi); Smathers, 30 (29 in Florida, ½ in Alabama, ½ in North Carolina); Humphrey, 41½ (31 in Minnesota, 8 in Wisconsin, 1½ in South Dakota, ½ in Nebraska, ½ in Utah); Meyner, 43 (41 in New Jersey, 1½ in Pennsylvania, ½ in Alabama); Loveless, 1½ (Iowa); Faubus, ½ (Alabama); Brown, ½ (California); Rosellini, ½ (Washington).

1960 Republican

(Narrative, p. 110)

Delegation	Total Votes	First Pres. Ballot	
		Nixon	Goldwater
Alabama	22	22	—
Alaska	6	6	—
Arizona	14	14	—
Arkansas	16	16	—
California	70	70	—
Colorado	18	18	—
Connecticut	22	22	—
Delaware	12	12	—
Florida	26	26	—
Georgia	24	24	—
Hawaii	12	12	—
Idaho	14	14	—
Illinois	60	60	—
Indiana	32	32	—
Iowa	26	26	—
Kansas	22	22	—
Kentucky	26	26	—
Louisiana	26	16	10
Maine	16	16	—
Maryland	24	24	—
Massachusetts	38	38	—
Michigan	46	46	—
Minnesota	28	28	—
Mississippi	12	12	—
Missouri	26	26	—
Montana	14	14	—
Nebraska	18	18	—
Nevada	12	12	—
New Hampshire	14	14	—
New Jersey	38	38	—
New Mexico	14	14	—
New York	96	96	—
North Carolina	28	28	—
North Dakota	14	14	—
Ohio	56	56	—
Oklahoma	22	22	—
Oregon	18	18	—
Pennsylvania	70	70	—
Rhode Island	14	14	—
South Carolina	13	13	—
South Dakota	14	14	—
Tennessee	28	28	—
Texas	54	54	—
Utah	14	14	—
Vermont	12	12	—
Virginia	30	30	—
Washington	24	24	—
West Virginia	22	22	—
Wisconsin	30	30	—
Wyoming	12	12	—
District of Columbia	8	8	—
Puerto Rico	3	3	—
Virgin Islands	1	1	—
Total	1331	1321	10

1964 Republican

(Narrative, p. 113)

Delegation	Total Votes	Minority Amendment on Civil Rights[1]		First Pres. Ballot[2] (Before shift)			First Pres. Ballot[3] (After shift)		
		Yea	Nay	Goldwater	Rockefeller	Scranton	Goldwater	Rockefeller	Scranton
Alabama	20	—	20	20	—	—	20	—	—
Alaska	12	12	—	—	—	8	—	—	8
Arizona	16	—	16	16	—	—	16	—	—
Arkansas	12	—	12	9	1	2	12	—	—
California	86	—	86	86	—	—	86	—	—
Colorado	18	—	18	15	—	3	18	—	—
Connecticut	16	11	5	4	—	12	16	—	—
Delaware	12	11	1	7	—	5	10	—	2
Florida	34	—	34	32	—	2	34	—	—
Georgia	24	—	24	22	—	2	24	—	—
Hawaii	8	4	4	4	—	—	8	—	—
Idaho	14	—	14	14	—	—	14	—	—
Illinois	58	4	54	56	2	—	56	2	—
Indiana	32	—	32	32	—	—	32	—	—
Iowa	24	2	22	14	—	10	24	—	—
Kansas	20	2	18	18	—	1	18	—	1
Kentucky	24	1	23	21	—	3	22	—	2
Louisiana	20	—	20	20	—	—	20	—	—
Maine	14	11	3	—	—	—	—	—	—
Maryland	20	17	3	6	1	13	7	1	12
Massachusetts	34	27	7	5	—	26	34	—	—
Michigan	48	37	9	8	—	—	48	—	—
Minnesota	26	17	9	8	—	—	26	—	—
Mississippi	13	—	13	13	—	—	13	—	—
Missouri	24	1	23	23	—	1	24	—	—
Montana	14	—	14	14	—	—	14	—	—
Nebraska	16	—	16	16	—	—	16	—	—
Nevada	6	—	6	6	—	—	6	—	—
New Hampshire	14	14	—	—	—	14	—	—	14
New Jersey	40	40	—	20	—	20	38	—	2
New Mexico	14	—	14	14	—	—	14	—	—
New York	92	86	6	5	87	—	87	—	—
North Carolina	26	—	26	26	—	—	26	—	—
North Dakota	14	1	13	7	1	—	14	—	—
Ohio	58	—	58	57	—	—	58	—	—
Oklahoma	22	—	22	22	—	—	22	—	—
Oregon	18	10	8	—	18	—	16	—	—
Pennsylvania	64	62	2	4	—	60	64	—	—
Rhode Island	14	11	3	3	—	11	14	—	—
South Carolina	16	—	16	16	—	—	16	—	—
South Dakota	14	—	14	12	—	2	14	—	—
Tennessee	28	—	28	28	—	—	28	—	—
Texas	56	—	56	56	—	—	56	—	—
Utah	14	—	14	14	—	—	14	—	—
Vermont	12	8	4	3	2	2	3	2	2
Virginia	30	—	30	29	—	1	30	—	—
Washington	24	1	23	22	—	1	22	—	1
West Virginia	14	4	10	10	2	2	12	1	1
Wisconsin	30	—	30	30	—	—	30	—	—
Wyoming	12	—	12	12	—	—	12	—	—
District of Columbia	9	7	2	4	—	5	4	—	5
Puerto Rico	5	5	—	—	—	5	5	—	—
Virgin Islands	3	3	—	—	—	3	3	—	—
Total	1308	409	897	883	114	214	1220	6	50

1. Not voting, 2.

2. Other candidates: George Romney, 41 (40 in Michigan, 1 in Kansas); Margaret C. Smith, 27 (14 in Maine, 5 in Vermont, 3 in North Dakota, 2 in Alaska, 1 in Massachusetts, 1 in Ohio, 1 in Washington); Walter H. Judd, 22 (18 in Minnesota, 3 in North Dakota, 1 in Alaska); Hiram L. Fong, 5 (4 in Hawaii, 1 in Alaska); Henry C. Lodge, 2 (Massachusetts).

3. Other candidates: Smith, 22 (14 in Maine, 5 in Vermont, 2 in Alaska, 1 in Washington): Fong, 1 (Alaska); Judd, 1 (Alaska); Romney, 1 (Kansas): not voting, 7 (5 in New York, 2 in Oregon).

1968 Democratic

(Narrative, p. 119)

Delegation	Total Votes	Texas Credentials[1]		Georgia Credentials[2]		Alabama Credentials[3]		End Unit Rule[4]		Report on Vietnam[5]		First Pres. Ballot[6]			
		Yea	Nay	Yea	Nay	Yea	Nay	Yea	Nay	Yea	Nay	Humphrey	McCarthy	McGovern	Phillips
Alabama	32	32	—	10	22	—	—	5½	24½	1½	30½	23	—	—	—
Alaska	22	17	5	5	17	14	8	22	—	10	12	17	2	3	—
Arizona	19	1½	17	17	2	7½	11½	—	19	6½	12½	14½	2½	2	—
Arkansas	33	33	—	3	29	8	23	—	32	7	25	30	2	—	—
California	174	1	173	173	1	173	1	173	1	166	6	14	91	51	17
Colorado	35	—	35	30	5	34	1	35	—	21	14	16½	10	5½	3
Connecticut	44	30	12	13	27	21	21	9	30	13	30	35	8	—	1
Delaware	22	21	—	3	18	2	19	—	21	—	21	21	—	—	—
Florida	63	58	4	9	54	6	57	11	52	7	56	58	5	—	—
Georgia	43	—	—	—	—	25	17½	39	4	19½	23½	19½	13½	1	3
Hawaii	26	26	—	4	22	—	26	3	23	—	26	26	—	—	—
Idaho	25	22½	2½	4½	20½	2	23	1	24	10	15	21	3½	½	—
Illinois	118	114	4	12	83	18	100	3	115	13	105	112	3	3	—
Indiana	63	34	10	25	38	13	41½	63	—	15	47½	49	11	2	1
Iowa	46	37½	8½	32	12	24½	21½	46	—	36	10	18½	19½	5	—
Kansas	38	38	—	3½	34½	5½	31½	6	20	4½	33½	34	1	3	—
Kentucky	46	40½	5½	6	40	6½	39½	6½	39½	7	39	41	5	—	—
Louisiana	36	32	4	7	29	—	36	—	36	2½	33½	35	—	—	—
Maine	27	25	1	5	22	—	26	27	—	4½	22½	23	4	—	—
Maryland	49	46	3	3	46	2	47	49	—	12	37	45	2	2	—
Massachusetts	72	16	47	39	24	29	29	37	31	56	16	2	70	—	—
Michigan	96	70	23	35	58	26	67	43½	44½	52	44	72½	9½	7½	6½
Minnesota	52	34½	14½	16	33	23½	28½	16	33½	16½	34½	38	11½	—	2½
Mississippi	24	2	18½	18	2	12½	8½	21½	½	19½	2½	9½	6½	4	2
Missouri	60	48	12	12	48	8	52	60	—	10	50	56	3½	—	½
Montana	26	20	4	2½	21½	3½	22½	12½	12	6	20	23½	2½	—	—
Nebraska	30	12	16	11	18	13	15	26	2	19	11	15	6	9	—
Nevada	22	13	7	14	8	12½	9½	22	—	3½	18½	18½	2½	1	—
New Hampshire	26	6	20	23	2	25	—	23	3	23	3	6	20	—	—
New Jersey	82	43	25	22	51	21	61	21	61	24	57	62	19	—	1
New Mexico	26	13	13	11	15	11	15	11	15	11½	14½	15	11	—	—
New York	190	—	190	190	—	80[e]	82[e]	190	—	148	42	96½	87	1½	2
North Carolina	59	54½	4½	3½	55½	1	58	2	57	7	51	44½	2	½	—
North Dakota	25	17	5	5	17	7	18	17	5	6	19	18	7	—	—
Ohio	115	37½	27	21	80	30½	65	23	92	48	67	94	18	2	—
Oklahoma	41	40	1	1	40	6½	34	6	35	4	37	37½	2½	½	½
Oregon	35	10	23	32	—	31	3	31	—	29	6	—	35	—	—
Pennsylvania	130	80¾	42¼	31½	90½	22¼	100½	39¾	79½	35¼	92¼	103¾	21½	2½	1½
Rhode Island	27	24½	2½	12	11	2½	24½	3½	23½	5	22	23½	2½	—	—
South Carolina	28	28	—	4	22	—	28	4½	23½	1	27	28	—	—	—
South Dakota	26	1	25	26	—	24	2	26	—	26	—	2	—	24	—
Tennessee	51	48½	1	—	51	½	49½	2½	46½	2	49	49½	½	1	—
Texas	104	—	—	2.55	101.45	—	104	5	99	—	104	100½	2½	—	1
Utah	26	18	8	7	19	5	21	26	—	6	20	23	2	—	1
Vermont	22	5	13	17	4	14	7	22	—	17	5	8	6	7	—
Virginia	54	21½	22½	8½	35½	1	53	9½	43½	8	46	42½	5½	—	2
Washington	47	31½	15½	18	29	16	28	21½	25½	15½	31½	32½	8½	6	—
West Virginia	38	19	12	8	22	9	29	38	—	8	30	34	3	—	—
Wisconsin	59	5	54	52	7	54	4	58	1	52	7	8	49	1	1
Wyoming	22	18½	3½	2	20	6½	15½	3	19	3½	18½	18½	3½	—	—
Canal Zone	5	4	—	2	3	—	4	1	4	1½	3½	4	—	1	—
District of Columbia	23	—	22	22	—	23	—	23	—	21	2	2	—	—	21
Guam	5	4½	½	—	5	—	5	½	4½	½	4½	5	—	—	—
Puerto Rico	8	8	—	7½	—	—	8	1	7	—	8	8	—	—	—
Virgin Islands	5	5	—	2½	—	—	5	5	—	—	5	5	—	—	—
Total	**2622**	1368¼[a]	956¾[b]	1043.55[c]	1415.45[d]	880¾[f]	1607[g]	1351¼[h]	1209[i]	1041¼	1567¾	1759¼[j]	601	146½	67½

1. Not voting, 297.
2. Not voting, 163.
3. Not voting, 134½.
4. Not voting, 61¾.
5. Not voting, 13.
6. Other candidates: Moore, 17½ (12 in North Carolina, 3 in Virginia, 2 in Georgia, ½ in Alabama); Kennedy, 12¾ (proceedings record, 12½) (3½ Alabama, 3 in Iowa, 3 in New York, 1 in Ohio, 1 in West Virginia, ¾ in Pennsylvania, ½ in Georgia); Bryant, 1½ (Alabama); Wallace, ½ (Alabama); Gray, ½ (Georgia). Not voting, 15 (3 in Alabama, 3 in Georgia, 2 in Mississippi, 1 in Arkansas, 1 in California, 1 in Delaware, 1 in Louisiana, 1 in Rhode Island, 1 in Vermont, 1 in Virginia).

a. Sum of column; proceedings record, 1368.
b. Sum of column; proceedings record, 955.
c. Sum of column; proceedings record, 1041½.
d. Sum of column; proceedings record, 1413.
e. New York vote announced after outcome of roll call.
f. Sum of column; proceedings record (without New York vote), 801½.
g. Sum of column; proceedings record (without New York), 1525.
h. Sum of column; proceedings record, 1350.
i. Sum of column; proceedings record, 1206.
j. Sum of column; proceedings record, 1761¾.

1968 Republican

(Narrative, p. 117)

Delegation	Total Votes	First Pres. Ballot[1] (Before shift)			First Pres. Ballot (After shift)		
		Nixon	Rockefeller	Reagan	Nixon	Rockefeller	Reagan
Alabama	26	14	—	12	26	—	—
Alaska	12	11	1	—	12	—	—
Arizona	16	16	—	—	16	—	—
Arkansas	18	—	—	—	18	—	—
California	86	—	—	86	86	—	—
Colorado	18	14	3	1	18	—	—
Connecticut	16	4	12	—	16	—	—
Delaware	12	9	3	—	12	—	—
Florida	34	32	1	1	34	—	—
Georgia	30	21	2	7	30	—	—
Hawaii	14	—	—	—	14	—	—
Idaho	14	9	—	5	14	—	—
Illinois	58	50	5	3	58	—	—
Indiana	26	26	—	—	26	—	—
Iowa	24	13	8	3	24	—	—
Kansas	20	—	—	—	19	1	—
Kentucky	24	22	2	—	24	—	—
Louisiana	26	19	—	7	26	—	—
Maine	14	7	7	—	14	—	—
Maryland	26	18	8	—	26	—	—
Massachusetts	34	—	34	—	34	—	—
Michigan	48	4	—	—	48	—	—
Minnesota	26	9	15	—	26	—	—
Mississippi	20	20	—	—	20	—	—
Missouri	24	16	5	3	24	—	—
Montana	14	11	—	3	14	—	—
Nebraska	16	16	—	—	16	—	—
Nevada	12	9	3	—	12	—	—
New Hampshire	8	8	—	—	8	—	—
New Jersey	40	18	—	—	40	—	—
New Mexico	14	8	1	5	14	—	—
New York	92	4	88	—	4	88	—
North Carolina	26	9	1	16	26	—	—
North Dakota	8	5	2	1	8	—	—
Ohio	58	2	—	—	58	—	—
Oklahoma	22	14	1	7	22	—	—
Oregon	18	18	—	—	18	—	—
Pennsylvania	64	22	41	1	64	—	—
Rhode Island	14	—	14	—	14	—	—
South Carolina	22	22	—	—	22	—	—
South Dakota	14	14	—	—	14	—	—
Tennessee	28	28	—	—	28	—	—
Texas	56	41	—	15	54	—	2
Utah	8	2	—	—	8	—	—
Vermont	12	9	3	—	12	—	—
Virginia	24	22	2	—	24	—	—
Washington	24	15	3	6	24	—	—
West Virginia	14	11	3	—	13	1	—
Wisconsin	30	30	—	—	30	—	—
Wyoming	12	12	—	—	12	—	—
District of Columbia	9	6	3	—	6	3	—
Puerto Rico	5	—	5	—	5	—	—
Virgin Islands	3	2	1	—	3	—	—
Total	**1333**	**692**	**277**	**182**	**1238**	**93**	**2**

1. Other candidates: James A. Rhodes, 55 (Ohio); George Romney, 50 (44 in Michigan, 6 in Utah); Clifford P. Case, 22 (New Jersey); Frank Carlson, 20 (Kansas); Winthrop Rockefeller, 18 (Arkansas); Hiram L. Fong, 14 (Hawaii); Harold Stassen, 2 (1 in Minnesota, 1 in Ohio); John V. Lindsay, 1 (Minnesota).

1972 Democratic
(Narrative, p. 123)

Delegation[1]	Total Votes	Minority Report South Carolina Credentials			Minority Report California Credentials			Minority Report Illinois Credentials		
		Yea	Nay	Not voting	Yea	Nay	Not voting	Yea	Nay	Not voting
California	271	120	151	—	120	—	151	84	136	51
South Carolina	32	—	9	23	3	29	—	31	1	—
Ohio	153	63	87	3	75	78	—	69	70	14
Canal Zone	3	1.50	1.50	—	3	—	—	1	2	—
Utah	19	10	8	1	13	6	—	5	14	—
Delaware	13	5.85	7.15	—	6.50	6.50	—	6.50	6.50	—
Rhode Island	22	20	2	—	22	—	—	7.09	14.91	—
Texas	130	34	96	—	34	96	—	96	34	—
West Virginia	35	13	22	—	15	20	—	24	11	—
South Dakota	17	17	—	—	17	—	—	—	17	—
Kansas	35	17	18	—	18	17	—	18	17	—
New York	278	269	9	—	267	11	—	20	256	2
Virginia	53	34.50	18.50	—	38.50	14.50	—	16.50	35.50	1
Wyoming	11	2.20	8.80	—	4.40	6.60	—	7.70	3.30	—
Arkansas	27	13	14	—	8	19	—	13	14	—
Indiana	76	18	58	—	33	43	—	53	23	—
Puerto Rico	7	6.50	0.50	—	6.50	0.50	—	0.50	6.50	—
Tennessee	49	22	27	—	23	26	—	20	29	—
Pennsylvania	182	55.50	126	0.50	72	105	5	106.50	62	13.50
Mississippi	25	20	5	—	19	6	—	—	25	—
Wisconsin	67	39	28	—	55	12	—	12	55	—
Illinois	170	79	90	1	114.50	55.50	—	76	30	64
Maine	20	1	19	—	—	20	—	13	7	—
Florida	81	1	80	—	3	78	—	80	1	—
New Hampshire	18	13.50	4.50	—	9.90	8.10	—	9	8.10	0.90
Arizona	25	15	10	—	12	13	—	4	21	—
North Carolina	64	6	58	—	21	43	—	39	23	2
Massachusetts	102	97	5	—	97	5	—	11	91	—
Nebraska	24	14	9	1	20	4	—	13	11	—
Georgia	53	5.50	47.50	—	21.75	31.25	—	24	27.50	1.50
North Dakota	14	7	6.30	0.70	8.40	5.60	—	2.10	11.90	—
Maryland	53	24	29	—	27.83	25.17	—	28.67	24.33	—
New Jersey	109	79	29	1	85.50	22.50	1	30	75.50	3.50
Vermont	12	7	5	—	11	1	—	2	10	—
Nevada	11	5.75	5.25	—	5.75	5.25	—	6.75	4.25	—
Michigan	132	51	81	—	55	76	1	85	47	—
Iowa	46	23	23	—	27	19	—	20	26	—
Colorado	36	23	13	—	27	9	—	5	31	—
Alabama	37	1	36	—	1	36	—	32	5	—
Alaska	10	6.75	3.25	—	7.25	2.75	—	4.75	5.25	—
Hawaii	17	2	15	—	7	10	—	17	—	—
Washington	52	—	52	—	—	52	—	52	—	—
Minnesota	64	56	8	—	29	35	—	32	32	—
Louisiana	44	25	19	—	22.50	21.50	—	9.50	32.50	2
Idaho	17	12.50	4.50	—	11.50	5.50	—	4	13	—
Montana	17	10	7	—	14.50	1	1.50	2.50	14.50	—
Connecticut	51	8	43	—	21	30	—	40	11	—
District of Columbia	15	12	3	—	13.50	1.50	—	1.50	13.50	—
Virgin Islands	3	1	2	—	2.50	0.50	—	3	—	—
Kentucky	47	10	37	—	11	36	—	36	10	1
Missouri	73	13.50	59.50	—	22.50	50.50	—	59	13	1
New Mexico	18	10	8	—	10	8	—	8	10	—
Guam	3	1.50	1.50	—	1.50	1.50	—	—	3	—
Oregon	34	16	18	—	33	1	—	2	32	—
Oklahoma	39	11	28	—	11	28	—	29	9	1
Total	3016	1429.05	1555.75	31.20	1618.28	1238.22	159.50	1371.56[a]	1486.04[b]	158.40

1. Delegations at this convention are listed in the order in which they voted. All fractional votes are expressed in decimals for consistency.
  a. Sum of column; proceedings record, 1371.55.
  b. Sum of column; proceedings record, 1486.05.

1972 Democratic

(Narrative, p. 123)

Minority Report Guaranteed Income			First Presidential[2] (Before shift)					First Presidential[3] (After shift)				
Yea	Nay	Not voting	McGovern	Jackson	Wallace	Chisholm	Sanford	McGovern	Jackson	Wallace	Chisholm	Sanford
131	114	26	271	—	—	—	—	271	—	—	—	—
4	21	7	6	10	6	4	6	10	9	6	—	6
39	86	28	77	39	—	23	3	77	39	—	23	3
2.50	0.50	—	3	—	—	—	—	3	—	—	—	—
8	11	—	14	1	—	—	3	14	1	—	—	3
4.55	8.45	—	5.85	6.50	—	0.65	—	5.85	5.85	—	0.65	—
10.86	11.14	—	22	—	—	—	—	22	—	—	—	—
15	115	—	54	23	48	4	—	54	23	48	4	—
3	32	—	16	14	1	—	4	16	14	1	—	4
1	16	—	17	—	—	—	—	17	—	—	—	—
5	30	—	20	10	—	2	1	20	10	—	2	1
152	118	8	263	9	—	6	—	278	—	—	—	—
30	21	2	33.50	4	1	5.50	9	37	5	—	2.50	8.50
0.55	10.45	—	3.30	6.05	—	1.10	—	3.30	6.05	—	1.10	—
10	16	1	1	1	—	—	—	1	1	—	—	—
17	56	3	26	20	26	1	—	28	19	25	—	—
4	3	—	7	—	—	—	—	7	—	—	—	—
21	27	1	—	—	33	10	—	5	—	32	7	—
49.50	117.50	15	81	86.50	2	9.50	1	81	86.50	2	9.50	1
22	—	3	10	—	—	12	3	23	—	—	2	—
29	38	—	55	3	—	5	—	55	3	—	5	—
59	95	16	119	30.50	0.50	4.50	2	155	6	—	1	—
1	19	—	5	—	—	—	—	5	—	—	—	—
4	77	—	2	—	75	2	—	4	—	75	1	—
0.90	14.40	2.70	10.80	5.40	—	—	—	10.80	5.40	—	—	—
6	19	—	21	3	—	—	1	22	3	—	—	—
17	47	—	—	—	37	—	27	—	—	37	—	27
60	40	2	102	—	—	—	—	102	—	—	—	—
2	22	—	21	3	—	—	—	21	3	—	—	—
10.50	34	8.50	14.50	14.50	11	12	1	14.50	14.50	11	12	1
1.40	10.50	2.10	8.40	2.80	0.70	0.70	—	10.50	2.10	—	0.70	—
14.33	38.67	—	13	—	38	2	—	13	—	38	2	—
61.50	35.50	12	89	11.50	—	4	1.50	92.50	11	—	3.50	—
4	8	—	12	—	—	—	—	12	—	—	—	—
2.75	8.25	—	5.75	5.25	—	—	—	5.75	5.25	—	—	—
30.50	96.50	5	50.50	7	67.50	3	1	51.50	7	67.50	2	1
6	39	1	35	—	—	3	4	35	—	—	3	4
15	21	—	27	—	—	7	—	29	2	—	5	—
10	27	—	9	1	24	—	1	9	1	24	—	1
3	5.50	1.50	6.50	3.25	—	—	—	6.50	3.25	—	—	—
1.50	15.50	—	6.50	8.50	—	1	—	6.50	8.50	—	1	—
1	51	—	—	52	—	—	—	—	52	—	—	—
28	33	3	11	—	—	6	—	43	—	—	4	1
22	20	2	10.25	10.25	3	18.50	2	25.75	5.25	3	4	1
5	12	—	12.50	2.50	—	2	—	12.50	2.50	—	2	—
2	14	1	16	—	—	1	—	16	—	—	1	—
22	29	—	30	20	—	—	1	30	20	—	—	1
15	—	—	13.50	1.50	—	—	—	13.50	1.50	—	—	—
2.50	0.50	—	1	1.50	—	0.50	—	1	1.50	—	0.50	—
1	41	5	10	35	—	—	2	10	35	—	—	2
12	55	6	24.50	48.50	—	—	—	24.50	48.50	—	—	—
3	15	—	10	—	8	—	—	10	—	8	—	—
—	3	—	1.50	1.50	—	—	—	1.50	1.50	—	—	—
11	23	—	34	—	—	—	—	34	—	—	—	—
5.50	31.50	2	10.50	23.50	—	1	4	9.50	23.50	—	2	4
999.34	**1852.86**	**163.80**	**1728.35**	**525.00**	**381.70**	**151.95**	**77.50**	**1864.95**	**485.65**	**377.50**	**101.45**	**69.50**

2. Humphrey, 66.70 (46 in Minnesota, 4 in Ohio, 4 in Wisconsin, 3 in Michigan, 2 in Indiana, 2 in Pennsylvania, 2 in Florida, 1 in Utah, 1 in Colorado, 1 in Hawaii, 0.70 in North Dakota); Mills, 33.80 (25 in Arkansas, 3 in Illinois, 3 in New Jersey, 2 in Alabama, 0.55 in Wyoming, 0.25 in Alaska); Muskie, 24.30 (15 in Maine, 5.50 in Illinois, 1.80 in New Hampshire, 1 in Texas, 1 in Colorado); Kennedy, 12.70 (4 in Iowa, 3 in Illinois, 2 in Ohio, 1 in Kansas, 1 in Indiana, 1 in Tennessee, 0.70 in North Dakota); Hays, 5 (Ohio); McCarthy, 2 (Illinois); Mondale, 1 (Kansas); Clark, 1 (Minnesota); not voting, 5 (Tennessee).

3. Humphrey, 35 (16 in Minnesota, 4 in Ohio, 4 in Wisconsin, 3 in Indiana, 3 in Michigan, 2 in Pennsylvania, 1 in Utah, 1 in Florida, 1 in Hawaii); Mills, 32.80 (25 in Arkansas, 2 in Illinois, 2 in New Jersey, 2 in Alabama, 1 in South Carolina, 0.55 in Wyoming, 0.25 in Alaska); Muskie, 20.80 (15 in Maine, 3 in Illinois, 1.80 in New Hampshire, 1 in Texas); Kennedy, 10.65 (4 in Iowa, 2 in Ohio, 1 in Kansas, 1 in Indiana, 1 in Tennessee, 1 in Illinois, 0.65 in Delaware); Hays, 5 (Ohio); McCarthy, 2 (Illinois); Mondale, 1 (Kansas).

1972 Republican

(Narrative, p. 126)

Delegation	Total Votes	First Pres. Ballot	
		Nixon	McCloskey
Alabama	18	18	—
Alaska	12	12	—
Arizona	18	18	—
Arkansas	18	18	—
California	96	96	—
Colorado	20	20	—
Connecticut	22	22	—
Delaware	12	12	—
Florida	40	40	—
Georgia	24	24	—
Hawaii	14	14	—
Idaho	14	14	—
Illinois	58	58	—
Indiana	32	32	—
Iowa	22	22	—
Kansas	20	20	—
Kentucky	24	24	—
Louisiana	20	20	—
Maine	8	8	—
Maryland	26	26	—
Massachusetts	34	34	—
Michigan	48	48	—
Minnesota	26	26	—
Mississippi	14	14	—
Missouri	30	30	—
Montana	14	14	—
Nebraska	16	16	—
Nevada	12	12	—
New Hampshire	14	14	—
New Jersey	40	40	—
New Mexico	14	13	1
New York	88	88	—
North Carolina	32	32	—
North Dakota	12	12	—
Ohio	56	56	—
Oklahoma	22	22	—
Oregon	18	18	—
Pennsylvania	60	60	—
Rhode Island	8	8	—
South Carolina	22	22	—
South Dakota	14	14	—
Tennessee	26	26	—
Texas	52	52	—
Utah	14	14	—
Vermont	12	12	—
Virginia	30	30	—
Washington	24	24	—
West Virginia	18	18	—
Wisconsin	28	28	—
Wyoming	12	12	—
District of Columbia	9	9	—
Guam	3	3	—
Puerto Rico	5	5	—
Virgin Islands	3	3	—
Total	1348	1347	1

1976 Democratic

(Narrative, p. 129)

Delegation	Total Votes	First Pres. Ballot[1] (Before shift)				First Pres. Ballot[2] (After shift)			
		Carter	Udall	Brown	Wallace	Carter	Udall	Brown	Wallace
Alabama	35	30	—	—	5	30	—	—	5
Alaska	10	10	—	—	—	10	—	—	—
Arizona	25	6	19	—	—	6	19	—	—
Arkansas	26	25	1	—	—	25	1	—	—
California	280	73	2	205	—	278	2	—	—
Colorado	35	15	6	11	—	15	6	11	—
Connecticut	51	35	16	—	—	35	16	—	—
Delaware	12	10.50	—	1.50	—	10.50	—	1.50	—
Florida	81	70	—	1	10	70	—	1	10
Georgia	50	50	—	—	—	50	—	—	—
Hawaii	17	17	—	—	—	17	—	—	—
Idaho	16	16	—	—	—	16	—	—	—
Illinois	169	164	1	2	1	164	1	2	1
Indiana	75	72	—	—	3	72	—	—	3
Iowa	47	25	20	1	—	25	20	1	—
Kansas	34	32	2	—	—	32	2	—	—
Kentucky	46	39	2	—	5	39	2	—	5
Louisiana	41	18	—	18	5	35	—	1	5
Maine	20	15	5	—	—	15	5	—	—
Maryland	53	44	6	3	—	44	6	3	—
Massachusetts[3]	104	65	21	—	11	65	21	—	11
Michigan	133	75	58	—	—	75	58	—	—
Minnesota	65	37	2	1	—	37	2	1	—
Mississippi	24	23	—	—	—	23	—	—	—
Missouri	71	58	4	2	—	58	4	2	—
Montana	17	11	2	—	—	11	2	—	—
Nebraska	23	20	—	3	—	20	—	3	—
Nevada	11	3	—	6.50	—	3	—	6.50	—
New Hampshire	17	15	2	—	—	15	2	—	—
New Jersey	108	108	—	—	—	108	—	—	—
New Mexico	18	14	4	—	—	14	4	—	—
New York	274	209.50	56.50	4	—	209.50	56.50	4	—
North Carolina	61	56	—	—	3	56	—	—	3
North Dakota	13	13	—	—	—	13	—	—	—
Ohio	152	132	20	—	—	132	20	—	—
Oklahoma	37	32	1	—	—	32	1	—	—
Oregon	34	16	—	10	—	16	—	10	—
Pennsylvania	178	151	21	6	—	151	21	6	—
Rhode Island	22	14	—	8	—	22	—	—	—
South Carolina	31	28	—	1	2	28	—	1	2
South Dakota	17	11	5	—	—	11	5	—	—
Tennessee	46	45	—	—	1	45	—	—	1
Texas	130	124	—	4	1	124	—	4	1
Utah	18	10	—	5	—	10	—	5	—
Vermont	12	5	4	3	—	5	4	3	—
Virginia	54	48	6	—	—	48	6	—	—
Washington	53	36	11	3	—	36	11	3	—
West Virginia	33	30	1	—	—	30	1	—	—
Wisconsin	68	29	25	—	10	29	25	—	10
Wyoming	10	8	1	1	—	8	1	1	—
District of Columbia	17	12	5	—	—	12	5	—	—
Puerto Rico	22	22	—	—	—	22	—	—	—
Canal Zone	3	3	—	—	—	3	—	—	—
Guam	3	3	—	—	—	3	—	—	—
Virgin Islands	3	3	—	—	—	3	—	—	—
Democrats Abroad	3	2.50	—	0.50	—	2.50	—	0.50	—
Total	**3,008**	**2,238.50**	**329.50**	**300.50**	**57.00**	**2,468.50**	**329.50**	**70.50**	**57.00**

1. Other candidates: Ellen McCormack, 22 (1 in Illinois, 2 in Massachusetts, 11 in Minnesota, 7 in Missouri, 1 in Wisconsin); Frank Church, 19 (3 in Colorado, 4 in Montana, 1 in Nevada, 8 in Oregon, 1 in Utah, 2 in Washington); Hubert H. Humphrey, 10 (9 in Minnesota, 1 in South Dakota); Henry M. Jackson, 10 (2 in Massachusetts, 4 in New York, 1 in Washington, 3 in Wisconsin); Fred Harris, 9 (2 in Massachusetts, 4 in Minnesota, 3 in Oklahoma); Milton J. Shapp, 2 (1 in Massachusetts, 1 in Utah); receiving one vote each: Robert C. Byrd (West Virginia); Cesar Chavez (Utah); Leon Jaworski (Texas); Barbara C. Jordan (Oklahoma); Edward M. Kennedy (Iowa); Jennings Randolph (West Virginia); Fred Stover (Minnesota); "nobody," (0.50 in Nevada); not voting, 3 (1 in Mississippi, 2 in North Carolina).

2. The rules were suspended after the switches and Carter was nominated by acclamation.

3. Massachusetts passed when originally called on and cast its votes at the end of the roll call, after vote switches.

1976 Republican

(Narrative, p. 133)

Delegation	Total Votes	Rule 16C[1]		First Pres. Ballot[2]	
		Yea	Nay	Ford	Reagan
Alabama	37	37	—	—	37
Alaska	19	2	17	17	2
Arizona	29	25	4	2	27
Arkansas	27	17	10	10	17
California	167	166	1	—	167
Colorado	31	26	5	5	26
Connecticut	35	—	35	35	—
Delaware	17	1	16	15	2
Florida	66	28	38	43	23
Georgia	48	39	7	—	48
Hawaii	19	1	18	18	1
Idaho	21	17	4	4	17
Illinois	101	20	79	86	14
Indiana	54	27	27	9	45
Iowa	36	18	18	19	17
Kansas	34	4	30	30	4
Kentucky	37	26	10	19	18
Louisiana	41	34	6	5	36
Maine	20	5	15	15	5
Maryland	43	8	35	43	—
Massachusetts	43	15	28	28	15
Michigan	84	29	55	55	29
Minnesota	42	5	35	32	10
Mississippi	30	—	30	16	14
Missouri	49	30	18	18	31
Montana	20	20	—	—	20
Nebraska	25	18	7	7	18
Nevada	18	15	3	5	13
New Hampshire	21	3	18	18	3
New Jersey	67	4	62	63	4
New Mexico	21	20	1	—	21
New York	154	20	134	133	20
North Carolina	54	51	3	25	29
North Dakota	18	6	12	11	7
Ohio	97	7	90	91	6
Oklahoma	36	36	—	—	36
Oregon	30	14	16	16	14
Pennsylvania	103	14	89	93	10
Rhode Island	19	—	19	19	—
South Carolina	36	25	11	9	27
South Dakota	20	11	9	9	11
Tennessee	43	17	26	21	22
Texas	100	100	—	—	100
Utah	20	20	—	—	20
Vermont	18	—	18	18	—
Virginia	51	36	15	16	35
Washington	38	31	7	7	31
West Virginia	28	12	16	20	8
Wisconsin	45	—	45	45	—
Wyoming	17	9	8	7	10
District of Columbia	14	—	14	14	—
Puerto Rico	8	—	8	8	—
Guam	4	—	4	4	—
Virgin Islands	4	—	4	4	—
Total	**2,259**	**1,069**	**1,180**	**1,187**	**1,070**

1. Not voting, 10.
2. Other candidate: Elliot L. Richardson, 1 (New York); not voting, 1 (Illinois). The nomination was made unanimous at the end of the balloting.

1980 Democratic

(Narrative, p. 141)

Delegation	Total Votes	Minority Rule #5[1]		First Pres. Ballot[3] (Before shift)		First Pres. Ballot[4] (After shift)	
		Yea	Nay	Carter	Kennedy	Carter	Kennedy
Alabama	45	3	42	43	2	43	2
Alaska	11	6.11	4.89	8.40	2.60	8.40	2.60
Arizona	29	16	13	13	16	13	16
Arkansas	33	9	24	25	6	25	6
California	306	171	132[2]	140	166	140	166
Colorado	40	24	16	27	10	27	10
Connecticut	54	28	26	26	28	26	28
Delaware	14	6.50	7.50	10	4	14	—
District of Columbia	19	12	7	12	5	12	5
Florida	100	25	75	75	25	75	25
Georgia	63	1	62	62	—	62	—
Hawaii	19	4	15	16	2	16	2
Idaho	17	9	8	9	7	9	7
Illinois	179	26	153	163	16	163	16
Indiana	80	27	53	53	27	53	27
Iowa	50	21	29	31	17	33	17
Kansas	37	17	20	23	14	23	14
Kentucky	50	12	38	45	5	45	5
Louisiana	51	15	36	50	1	50	1
Maine	22	12	10	11	11	11	11
Maryland	59	27	32	34	24	34	24
Massachusetts	111	81	30	34	77	34	77
Michigan	141	71	70	102	38	102	38
Minnesota	75	30	45	41	14	41	14
Mississippi	32	—	32	32	—	32	—
Missouri	77	20	57	58	19	58	19
Montana	19	9	10	13	6	13	6
Nebraska	24	11	13	14	10	14	10
Nevada	12	6.47	5.53	8.12	3.88	8.12	3.88
New Hampshire	19	9	10	10	9	10	9
New Jersey	113	68	45	45	68	45	68
New Mexico	20	11	9	10	10	10	10
New York	282	163	118	129	151	129	151
North Carolina	69	13	56	66	3	66	3
North Dakota	14	10	4	5	7	5	7
Ohio	161	81	80	89	72	89	72
Oklahoma	42	9	33	36	3	36	3
Oregon	39	14	25	26	13	26	13
Pennsylvania	185	102	83	95	90	95	90
Puerto Rico	41	20	21	21	20	21	20
Rhode Island	23	17	6	6	17	6	17
South Carolina	37	6	31	37	—	37	—
South Dakota	19	10	9	9	10	9	10
Tennessee	55	8	47	51	4	51	4
Texas	152	47	105	108	38	108	38
Utah	20	12	8	11	4	11	4
Vermont	12	7.50	4.50	5	7	5	7
Virginia	64	7	57	59	5	59	5
Washington	58	24	34	36	22	36	22
West Virginia	35	16	19	21	10	21	10
Wisconsin	75	26	49	48	26	48	26
Wyoming	11	3.50	7.50	8	3	8	3
Virgin Islands	4	—	4	4	—	4	—
Guam	4	—	4	4	—	4	—
Latin America	4	4	—	4	—	4	—
Democrats Abroad	4	2.50	1.50	1.50	2	1.50	2
Total	**3,331**	**1,390.58**	**1,936.42**	**2,123.02**	**1,150.48**	**2,129.02**	**1,150.48**

1. The vote was on a minority report by supporters of Sen. Edward M. Kennedy to overturn a proposed rule that would bind all delegates to vote on the first ballot for the presidential candidate under whose banner they were elected. A "yes" vote supported the Kennedy position while a "no" supported the Carter view that delegates should be bound.

2. Not voting, 1.

3. Other candidates: William Proxmire, 10 (Minnesota); Scott M. Matheson, 5 (Utah); Koryne Horbal, 5 (Minnesota); Ronald V. Dellums, 2.5 (2 in New York, 0.5 from Democrats Abroad); receiving 2 votes each: John C.

Culver (Iowa); Warren Spannous (Minnesota); Alice Tripp (Minnesota); Kent Hance (Texas); Robert C. Byrd (West Virginia); receiving 1 vote each: Dale Bumpers (Arkansas); Edmund S. Muskie (Colorado); Walter F. Mondale (Minnesota); Hugh L. Carey (Oklahoma); Tom Steed (Oklahoma); Edmund G. Brown (Wisconsin); uncommitted, 10; not voting, 5; absent, 2.

4. Votes for other candidates remained the same except that Iowa switched its 2 votes for Culver to Carter. After the switches Carter was nominated by acclamation.

1980 Republican

(Narrative, p. 137)

Delegation	Total Votes	First Pres. Ballot[5]		
		Reagan	Anderson	Bush
Alabama	27	27	—	—
Alaska	19	19	—	—
Arizona	28	28	—	—
Arkansas	19	19	—	—
California	168	168	—	—
Colorado	31	31	—	—
Connecticut	35	35	—	—
Delaware	12	12	—	—
District of Columbia	14	14	—	—
Florida	51	51	—	—
Georgia	36	36	—	—
Guam	4	4	—	—
Hawaii	14	14	—	—
Idaho	21	21	—	—
Illinois	102	81	21	—
Indiana	54	54	—	—
Iowa	37	37	—	—
Kansas	32	32	—	—
Kentucky	27	27	—	—
Louisiana	31	31	—	—
Maine	21	21	—	—
Maryland	30	30	—	—
Massachusetts	42	33	9	—
Michigan	82	67	—	13
Minnesota	34	33	—	—
Mississippi	22	22	—	—
Missouri	37	37	—	—
Montana	20	20	—	—
Nebraska	25	25	—	—
Nevada	17	17	—	—
New Hampshire	22	22	—	—
New Jersey	66	66	—	—
New Mexico	22	22	—	—
New York	123	121	—	—
North Carolina	40	40	—	—
North Dakota	17	17	—	—
Ohio	77	77	—	—
Oklahoma	34	34	—	—
Oregon	29	29	—	—
Pennsylvania	83	83	—	—
Puerto Rico	14	14	—	—
Rhode Island	13	13	—	—
South Carolina	25	25	—	—
South Dakota	22	22	—	—
Tennessee	32	32	—	—
Texas	80	80	—	—
Utah	21	21	—	—
Vermont	19	19	—	—
Virginia	51	51	—	—
Virgin Islands	4	4	—	—
Washington	37	36	1	—
West Virginia	18	18	—	—
Wisconsin	34	28	6	—
Wyoming	19	19	—	—
Total	1,994	1,939	37	13

5. Other candidates: Anne Armstrong, 1 (Michigan); not voting, 4.

1984 Democratic

(Narrative, p. 147)

Delegation	Total Votes	No First Use of Nuclear Weapons Yea	Nay	Not Voting	Defense Spending Yea	Nay	Not Voting	Dual Primaries Yea	Nay	Not Voting	Military Force Restrictions Yea	Nay	Not Voting
Alabama	62	15	46	1	11	49	2	13	49	—	61	1	—
Alaska	14	7	7	—	1	13	—	2	12	—	13	1	—
Arizona	40	20	19	—	18	21	—	20	19	—	39	—	—
Arkansas	42	13	29	—	12	30	—	7	33	2	39	2	1
California	345	149	84	—	99	170	—	129	128	—	285	31	—
Colorado	51	31	16	4	5	45	1	26	24	1	51	—	—
Connecticut	60	28	24	8	32	27	1	27	33	—	60	—	—
Delaware	18	1	17	—	1	17	—	1	17	—	18	—	—
D.C.	19	15	4	—	17	2	—	14	5	—	6	12	—
Florida	143	47	76	20	42	81	20	27	110	6	95	25	23
Georgia	84	40	33	—	38	45	—	39	42	—	67	1	2
Hawaii	27	1	26	—	—	27	—	—	27	—	—	—	—
Idaho	22	9	—	—	10	11	—	9	13	—	22	—	—
Illinois	194	42	145	—	40	147	—	48	143	—	191	—	3
Indiana	88	31	46	—	18	64	—	23	64	—	88	—	—
Iowa	58	22	36	—	7	51	—	5	53	—	58	—	—
Kansas	44	14	29	1	6	38	—	10	34	—	44	—	—
Kentucky	63	14	48	—	10	52	—	15	47	—	55	8	—
Louisiana	69	24	32	—	30	39	—	44	22	—	44	22	—
Maine	27	7	16	—	3	23	—	10	16	—	23	1	—
Maryland	74	20	51	3	20	54	—	18	56	—	51	19	4
Massachusetts	116	89	24	—	69	43	1	82	31	1	112	—	—
Michigan	155	43	105	7	32	118	5	37	111	7	137	—	18
Minnesota	86	37	41	8	30	48	8	25	57	4	73	2	11
Mississippi	43	15	26	2	16	26	1	13	29	1	33	8	2
Missouri	86	20	62	4	22	62	2	24	61	1	70	—	16
Montana	25	8	15	2	4	21	—	5	20	—	25	—	—
Nebraska	30	2	25	3	2	25	3	10	17	3	24	—	6
Nevada	20	6	14	—	3	17	—	5	15	—	19	—	—
New Hampshire	22	10	12	—	5	17	—	1	21	—	22	—	—
New Jersey	122	9	113	—	9	113	—	7	115	—	116	6	—
New Mexico	28	7	19	2	2	26	—	3	25	—	27	1	—
New York	285	134	140	—	131	139	7	125	146	3	196	57	—
North Carolina	88	28	56	—	19	66	—	32	55	—	73	3	—
North Dakota	18	13	5	—	8	10	—	8	10	—	18	—	—
Ohio	175	71	103	—	47	122	6	40	133	2	173	—	2
Oklahoma	53	16	35	2	3	47	3	3	49	1	49	3	1
Oregon	50	32	13	5	26	21	3	24	24	2	49	—	1
Pennsylvania	195	42	153	—	39	156	—	53	142	—	195	—	—
Puerto Rico	53	—	53	—	—	53	—	—	53	—	10	43	—
Rhode Island	27	11	15	1	11	15	1	8	18	1	24	—	2
South Carolina	48	21	23	4	23	19	6	21	25	2	21	19	8
South Dakota	19	7	12	—	7	12	—	7	12	—	—	6	—
Tennessee	76	31	41	4	29	41	6	34	39	3	72	1	3
Texas	200	53	137	10	47	141	12	39	150	11	152	38	10
Utah	27	17	10	—	11	15	1	13	14	—	19	7	1
Vermont	17	11	4	—	10	4	—	10	4	—	12	3	—
Virginia	78	29	48	—	29	48	—	33	43	—	50	23	4
Washington	70	49	18	—	29	39	1	35	35	—	67	—	—
West Virginia	44	12	27	5	12	29	3	17	24	3	—	—	—
Wisconsin	89	28	45	16	26	57	6	31	54	4	83	6	—
Wyoming	15	2	12	—	2	12	—	13	1	—	13	1	—
Latin America	5	—	5	—	.5	4.5	—	—	5	—	5	—	—
Democrats Abroad	5	1.5	3.5	—	1.5	3.5	—	—	5	—	5	—	—
Virgin Islands	6	1.2	4.8	—	2.6	2.6	.6	1.2	4.8	—	4.8	1.2	—
American Samoa	6	—	6	—	—	6	—	—	6	—	6	—	—
Guam	7	—	7	—	—	7	—	7	—	—	7	—	—
Total	**3,933**	**1,405.7**	**2,216.3**	**112**	**1,127.6**	**2,591.6**	**99.6**	**1,253.2**	**2,500.8**	**58**	**3,271.8**	**351.2**	**118**

1984 Democratic

(Narrative, p. 147)

First Pres. Ballot[1]

Delegation	Total Votes	Mondale	Hart	Jackson
Alabama	62	39	13	9
Alaska	14	9	4	1
Arizona	40	20	16	2
Arkansas	42	26	9	7
California	345	95	190	33
Colorado	51	1	42	1
Connecticut	60	23	36	1
Delaware	18	13	5	0
D.C.	19	5	—	14
Florida	143	82	55	3
Georgia	84	40	24	20
Hawaii	27	27	—	0
Idaho	22	10	12	0
Illinois	194	114	41	39
Indiana	88	42	38	8
Iowa	58	37	18	2
Kansas	44	25	16	3
Kentucky	63	51	5	7
Louisiana	69	26	19	24
Maine	27	13	13	0
Maryland	74	54	3	17
Massachusetts	116	59	49	5
Michigan	155	96	49	10
Minnesota	86	63	3	4
Mississippi	43	26	4	13
Missouri	86	55	14	16
Montana	25	11	13	1
Nebraska	30	12	17	1
Nevada	20	9	10	1
New Hampshire	22	12	10	0
New Jersey	122	115	—	7
New Mexico	28	13	13	2
New York	285	156	75	52
North Carolina	88	53	19	16
North Dakota	18	10	5	1
Ohio	175	84	80	11
Oklahoma	53	24	26	3
Oregon	50	16	31	2
Pennsylvania	195	177	—	18
Puerto Rico	53	53	—	0
Rhode Island	27	14	12	0
South Carolina	48	16	13	19
South Dakota	19	9	10	0
Tennessee	76	39	20	17
Texas	200	119	40	36
Utah	27	8	19	0
Vermont	17	5	8	3
Virginia	78	34	18	25
Washington	70	31	36	3
West Virginia	44	30	14	0
Wisconsin	89	58	25	6
Wyoming	15	7	7	0
Latin America	5	5	—	0
Democrats Abroad	5	3	1.5	0.5
Virgin Islands	6	4	—	2
American Samoa	6	6	—	0
Guam	7	7	—	0
Total	**3,933**	**2,191**	**1,200.5**	**465.5**

1. *Other candidates: Thomas F. Eagleton, 18 (16 in Minnesota, 2 in North Dakota); George McGovern, 4 (3 in Massachusetts, 1 in Iowa); John Glenn, 2 (Texas); Joseph R. Biden Jr., 1 (Maine); Martha Kirkland, 1 (Alabama); not voting, 40 (27 in California, 7 in Connecticut, 2 in Arizona, 2 in Florida, 1 in Vermont, 1 in Wyoming); absent, 10.*

1984 Republican

(Narrative, p. 152)

Delegation	Total Votes	First Pres. Ballot[2] Reagan
Alabama	38	38
Alaska	18	18
Arizona	32	32
Arkansas	29	29
California	176	176
Colorado	35	35
Connecticut	35	35
Delaware	19	19
District of Columbia	14	14
Florida	82	82
Georgia	37	37
Guam	4	4
Hawaii	14	14
Idaho	21	21
Illinois	93	92
Indiana	52	52
Iowa	37	37
Kansas	32	32
Kentucky	37	37
Louisiana	41	41
Maine	20	20
Maryland	31	31
Massachusetts	52	52
Michigan	77	77
Minnesota	32	32
Mississippi	30	30
Missouri	47	47
Montana	20	20
Nebraska	24	24
Nevada	22	22
New Hampshire	22	22
New Jersey	64	64
New Mexico	24	24
New York	136	136
North Carolina	53	53
North Dakota	18	18
Ohio	89	89
Oklahoma	35	35
Oregon	32	32
Pennsylvania	98	97
Puerto Rico	14	14
Rhode Island	14	14
South Carolina	35	35
South Dakota	19	19
Tennessee	46	46
Texas	109	109
Utah	26	26
Vermont	19	19
Virginia	50	50
Virgin Islands	4	4
Washington	44	44
West Virginia	19	19
Wisconsin	46	46
Wyoming	18	18
Total	**2,235**	**2,233**

2. Not voting, 2.

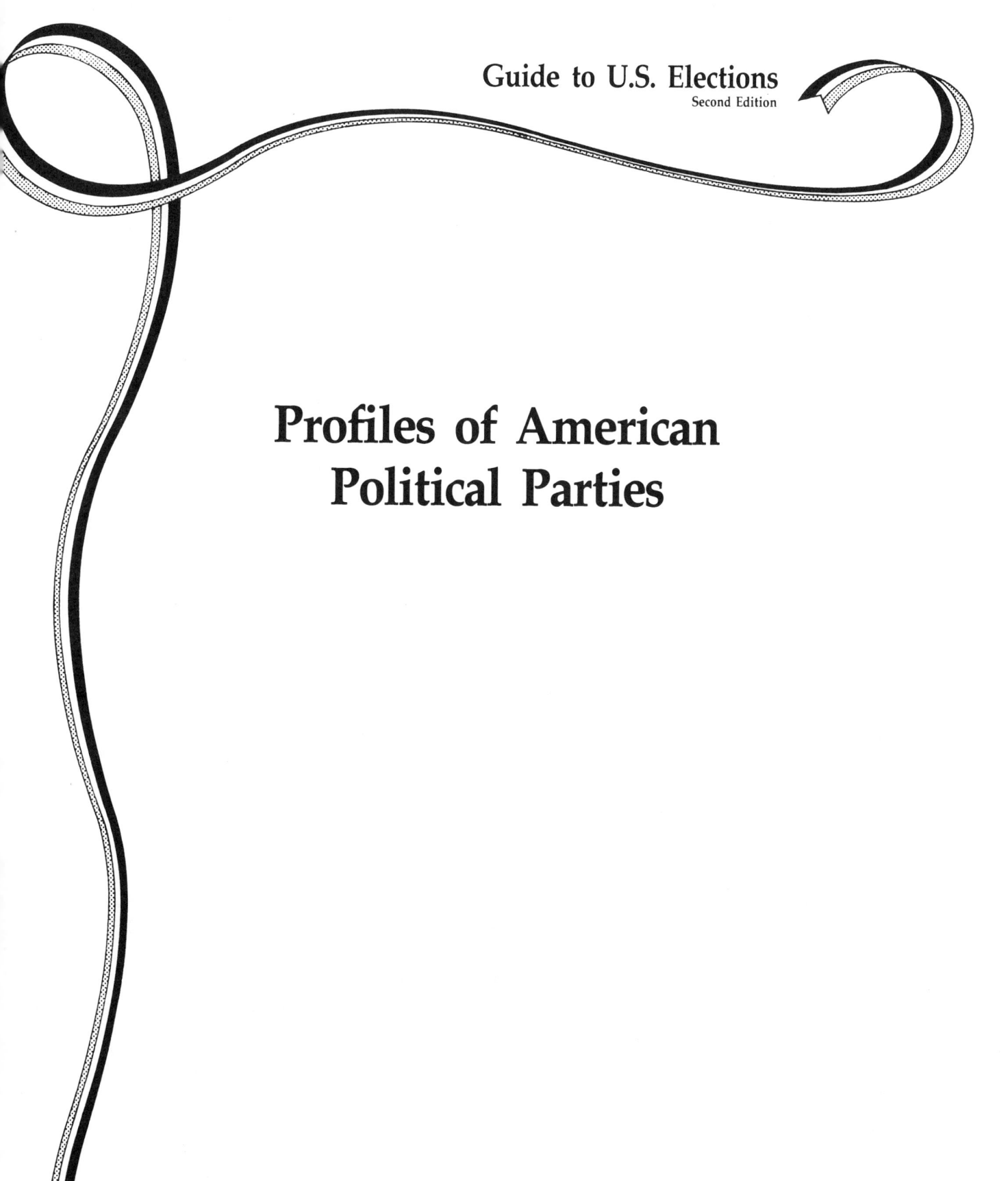

Profiles of American
Political Parties

American Political Parties Since 1789

Major Parties ——————— Third Parties ———————

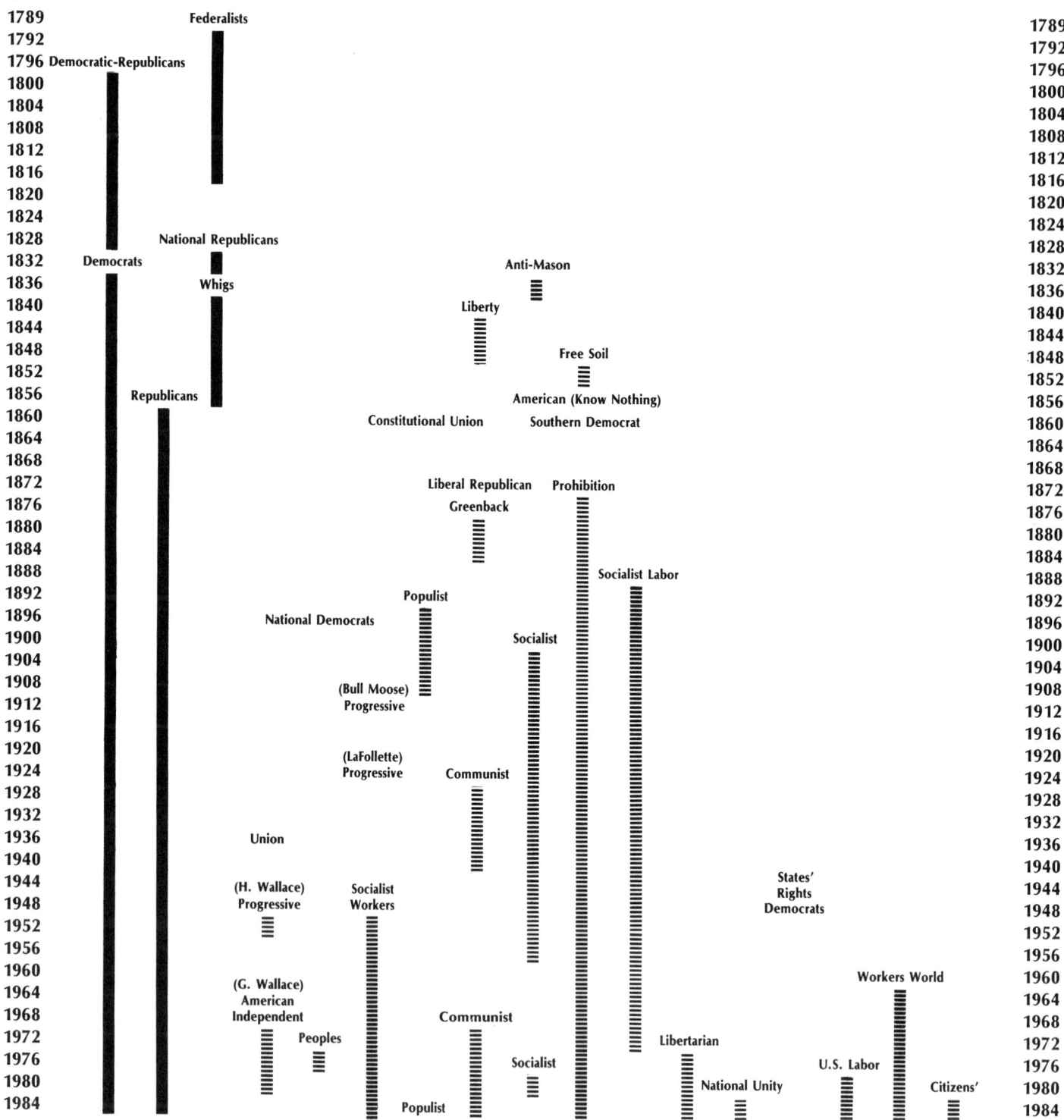

The chart indicates the years parties either ran presidential candidates or held national conventions. The lifespan for many political parties can only be approximated because parties existed at the state or local level before they ran candidates in presidential elections, and parties continued to exist at local levels long after they ceased running presidential candidates.

Historical Profiles
Of American Political Parties

American Party (1968-) and
American Independent Party (1972-)

Both the American Party and the American Independent Party descended from the American Independent Party that served as the vehicle for George C. Wallace's third-party presidential candidacy in 1968.

Wallace, governor of Alabama (1963-67; 1971-79), burst onto the national scene in 1964 as a Democratic presidential candidate opposed to the 1964 Civil Rights Act. Entering three Northern primaries — Wisconsin, Indiana and Maryland — he surprised political observers by winning between 30 percent and 43 percent of the popular vote in the three primaries. His unexpectedly strong showing brought the term "white backlash" into the political vocabulary as a description of the racial undertone of the Wallace vote.

In 1968 Wallace broke with the Democrats and embarked on his second presidential campaign as a third-party candidate under the American Independent Party label. His candidacy capitalized on the bitter reactions of millions of voters, especially whites and blue-collar workers, to the civil rights activism, urban riots, anti-war demonstrations and heavy federal spending on Johnson administration "Great Society" programs that marked the mid-1960s. With the help of his Alabama advisers and volunteer groups, Wallace was able to get his party on the ballot in all 50 states.

The former governor did not hold a convention for his party, but in October he announced his vice presidential running mate (retired Air Force General Curtis LeMay) and released a platform. In the November election the Wallace ticket received 9,901,151 votes (13.5 percent of the popular vote), carried five Southern states and won 46 electoral votes. The party's showing was the best by a third party since 1924, when Robert M. La Follette collected 16.6 percent of the vote on the Progressive Party ticket.

After his defeat in that election, Wallace returned to the Democratic Party, competing in Democratic presidential primaries in 1972 and 1976. Wallace's American Independent Party began to break into factions after the 1968 election but in 1972 united behind John G. Schmitz, a Republican U.S. representative from Southern California (1970-73), as its presidential nominee. Thomas J. Anderson, a farm magazine and syndicated news features publisher from Tennessee, was the candidate for vice president. In many states, the party shortened its name to American Party. In the November election, the Schmitz ticket won 1,090,673 votes (1.4 percent of the popular vote)

but failed to win any electoral votes.

In December 1972 a bitter fight occurred for the chairmanship of the American Independent Party between Anderson and William K. Shearer, the California chairman of the party. Anderson defeated Shearer, retaining control of the party but renaming it the American Party. Shearer, over the following four years, expanded his California-based group into a new national party. He had kept the name American Independent Party in California and made that the name of the new nationwide group.

Thus, by 1976, there were two distinct entities — the American Party headed by Anderson and the American Independent Party headed by Shearer.

The 1976 American Party convention was held in Salt Lake City, Utah, from June 17 to 20. Anderson was nominated for president and Rufus Shackleford of Florida for vice president.

The party's nomination of Anderson followed its failure to enlist a prominent conservative to lead the ticket. Both Gov. Meldrim Thomson Jr. of New Hampshire and Sen. Jesse Helms of North Carolina were approached, but both decided to remain in the Republican Party. With well-known conservatives declining the party's overtures, the convention turned to Anderson. He easily won the nomination on the first ballot by defeating six party workers.

Anderson's campaign stressed the "permanent principles" of the party, augmented by the 1976 platform. These principles included opposition to foreign aid, U.S. withdrawal from the United Nations and an end to trade with or recognition of communist nations. The platform in-

Sources

Congressional Quarterly. *Congressional Quarterly Weekly Report*. Washington, D.C.: Congressional Quarterly.

Dictionary of American History. 8 vols. New York: Charles Scribner's Sons, 1976.

Encyclopedia Americana. 30 vols. Danbury, Conn.: Grolier Education, 1982.

Encyclopaedia Britannica. Chicago: Encyclopaedia Britannica, 1980.

Schlesinger, Arthur M., Jr. *History of U.S. Political Parties*. 1973. Reprint. New York: Chelsea House, 1981.

Stimpson, George W. *A Book About American Politics*. New York: Harper, 1952.

cluded planks opposing abortion, gun control, the Equal Rights Amendment and government-sponsored health care and welfare programs. In general, the party favored limits on federal power and was against budget deficits except in wartime.

The American Party was on the ballot in 18 states, including eight states where the American Independent Party was also. In seven of those eight states, Anderson ran ahead of the American Independent Party ticket. Anderson's strength was spread fairly evenly across the country. His best showings were in Utah (2.5 percent of the vote) and Montana (1.8 percent). He received more than 0.5 percent of the vote in Virginia (1.0), Mississippi (0.9), Minnesota (0.7) and Kentucky (0.7). Anderson's total of 160,773 popular votes (0.2 percent) placed him almost 10,000 votes behind the American Independent Party candidate nationally.

The American Independent Party convention met in Chicago, Aug. 24-27, 1976, and chose former Georgia governor Lester Maddox (1967-71), a Democrat, as its presidential nominee and former Madison, Wis., mayor William Dyke, a Republican, as its vice presidential candidate. Maddox won a first-ballot nomination over Dallas columnist Robert Morris and former representative John R. Rarick, a Democrat of Louisiana (1967-75).

At the convention, a group of nationally prominent conservatives made a bid to take over the party and use it as a vehicle to build a new conservative coalition. Richard Viguerie, a fund raiser for Wallace and a nationally known direct mail expert, was the leader of the group. He was joined at the convention by two leading conservatives — William Rusher, publisher of the *National Review*, and Howard Phillips, the former head of the Office of Economic Opportunity (1973) and leader of the Conservative Caucus, an activist conservative group. Viguerie, Phillips and Rusher all argued that the American Independent Party should be overhauled, changed from a fringe group to a philosophical home for believers in free enterprise and traditional moral values. They also hoped they could attract Sen. Helms, Gov. Thomson or Rep. Philip M. Crane, R-Ill. When none of these men agreed to run on the American Independent Party ticket, Viguerie and his allies found themselves unable to promote successfully Morris, a lesser-known substitute.

Many American Independent Party members favored Maddox because they saw him as a colorful personality, one capable of drawing media attention and perhaps of picking up the 5 percent of the national vote needed to qualify the party for federal funding. Maddox never came close to that goal, however, achieving only 0.2 percent of the national vote (170,531). It was 51,098 votes in California, where American Party nominee Anderson was not on the ballot, that enabled Maddox to run slightly ahead of Anderson nationally.

Despite the power struggle between Anderson and Shearer, there was little difference between their two party platforms. Like the American Party, the American Independent Party opposed abortion, gun control, forced busing, foreign aid and membership in the United Nations.

By 1980 neither party was much of a force in American politics. Both retained the same basic platforms, but each was on the ballot in only a handful of states. The American Independent Party's nominee, former Democratic representative John R. Rarick of Louisiana (1967-75), ran in only eight states. Economist Percy L. Greaves Jr., the American Party candidate, was listed in just seven.

Fielding no candidate, by 1984 the American Independent Party appeared to have dropped out of the presidential contest. The American Party placed Delmar Davis, a book publisher from Pigeon Forge, Tenn., on the ballot in six states.

American Party-'Know-Nothings' (1856)

The American Party politicized the nativist, anti-immigrant movement in the mid-1850s, a peak period of European immigration to the United States in the pre-Civil War years. In the decade before the rise of a formal party, the movement took the form of local, secret organizations whose members were sworn to secrecy about their elaborate rituals. To questions about their affiliation, they pleaded ignorance. Hence, the party's popular name: the Know-Nothings.

Many of the millions of immigrants in the mid-19th century were Catholic, and the Know-Nothings were hostile to Catholics. They advocated nominating only native American Protestants for political office and requiring a 21-year waiting period before naturalization.

In addition to the great waves of immigrants, the party's meteoric rise was spurred by the increasing polarization of the Democrats and Whigs over the volatile slavery issue. The Know-Nothings benefited from the political situation and attracted members from both of the older parties. In the party's peak years 1854 and 1855, the Know-Nothings elected governors in California, Connecticut, Delaware, Kentucky, Massachusetts, New Hampshire and Rhode Island, and elected five senators and 43 members of the House.

But as a national party the Know-Nothings, like the Democrats and Whigs, were split eventually by the slavery issue. When a party convention in June 1855 adopted a pro-Southern position on slavery, anti-slavery elements bolted, dividing the party and setting the stage for its downfall.

The Know-Nothings held their first and only national nominating convention in February 1856 and selected as their candidate the former Whig, President Millard Fillmore (1850-53). The anti-slavery wing of the party convened separately and endorsed the Republican nominee, John C. Fremont. Fillmore finished third in the three-way race, receiving 21.5 percent of the popular vote and carrying only one state, Maryland.

Within a year, the bulk of the Northern Know-Nothings had joined the Republican Party. By the end of the decade, the party existed only in the Border States, where it formed the basis for the unsuccessful, anti-war Constitutional Union Party. (*Constitutional Union Party*, p. 228)

Anti-Federalists (1789-96)

Never a formal party, the Anti-Federalists were a loosely organized group opposed to ratification of the Constitution. With the adoption of the Constitution in 1788, the Anti-Federalists served as the opposition to the Federalists in the early years of Congress.

Anti-Federalists were primarily rural, agrarian interests from inland regions, who favored individual freedom and states' rights, which they felt would be jeopardized by the new Constitution. After ratification, the efforts of the Anti-Federalists led to adoption of the first 10 amendments, the Bill of Rights, which spelled out the major limitations of federal power.

As the opposition faction in Congress during the formative years of the Republic, the Anti-Federalists basically held to a strict interpretation of the Constitution, particularly in regard to the various economic proposals of Treasury Secretary Alexander Hamilton to centralize more power in the federal government.

Although never the majority faction in Congress, the Anti-Federalists were a forerunner of Jefferson's Democratic-Republican Party, which came into existence in the 1790s and dominated American politics for the first quarter of the 19th century. (*Democratic-Republican Party, p. 229*)

Anti-Masonic Party (1832-36)

Born in the late 1820s in upstate New York, the Anti-Masonic Party focused the strong, anti-elitist mood of the period on a conspicuous symbol of privilege, the Masons. The Masons were a secret, fraternal organization with membership drawn largely from the upper class. Conversely, the appeal of the Anti-Masonic movement was to the common man — poor farmers and laborers especially — who resented the secrecy and privilege of the Masons.

The spark that created the party came in 1826, when William Morgan, a dissident Mason from Batavia, N.Y., allegedly on the verge of exposing the inner workings of the order, mysteriously disappeared and never was seen again. Refusal of Masonic leaders to cooperate in the inconclusive investigation of Morgan's disappearance led to suspicions that Masons had kidnapped and murdered him and were suppressing the inquiry.

From 1828 through 1831, the new Anti-Masonic Party spread through New England and the Middle Atlantic states, in many places establishing itself as the primary opposition to the Democrats. In addition to its appeal to the working classes, particularly in Northern rural areas, and its opposition to Masonry, the Anti-Masons displayed a fervor against immorality, as seen not only in secret societies but also in slavery, intemperance and urban life.

In September 1831 the party held the first national nominating convention in American history. One hundred and sixteen delegates from 13 states gathered in Baltimore, Maryland, and nominated former attorney general William Wirt of Maryland for the presidency. While Wirt received only 100,712 votes (7.8 percent of the popular vote) and carried just one state, Vermont, the Anti-Masons did reasonably well at other levels: winning two governorships and 53 House seats.

But the decline of Masonry, especially in New York, where the number of lodges dropped from 507 in 1826 to 48 six years later, robbed the Anti-Masons of an emotional issue and hastened their decline. The 1832 election was the high point for the Anti-Masons as a national party. In the 1836 campaign the party endorsed Whig candidate William Henry Harrison. Subsequently, the bulk of the Anti-Masonic constituency moved into the Whig Party.

Citizens Party (1979-)

Organized in 1979 as a coalition of dissident liberals and populists, the first Citizens Party convention chose author and environmental scientist Barry Commoner as its 1980 presidential candidate and La Donna Harris, wife of former Democratic senator Fred R. Harris of Oklahoma, as his running mate. The Citizens Party ticket ran on the central theme that major decisions in America were made to benefit corporations and not the average citizen. The party proposed public control of energy industries and multinational corporations, a halt to the use of nuclear power, a sharp cut in military spending and price controls on food, fuel, housing and health care.

Commoner ran in all of the large electoral vote states except Florida and Texas. He made his biggest push in California, Illinois, Michigan, New York and Pennsylvania, where party leaders believed they could tap a "sophisticated working-class population" and appeal to political activists who had been involved in the environmental and anti-nuclear movements that sprang up in the late 1970s.

The Commoner/Harris ticket was on the ballot in 29 states and the District of Columbia in 1980. Party leaders asserted that it was the largest number of ballot positions attained by any third party in its first campaign. In addition to its presidential ticket, the Citizens Party also fielded 22 candidates for other offices, including two for the U.S. Senate and seven for the House.

The Citizens Party won 234,294 votes in the 1980 presidential election, or 0.3 percent of the vote.

As its 1984 presidential nominee the Citizens Party chose outspoken feminist Sonia Johnson of Virginia. Johnson first attracted national attention in 1979, when the Mormon Church excommunicated her for supporting the Equal Rights Amendment. In 1982 she staged a 37-day hunger strike in an unsuccessful effort to pressure the Illinois Legislature to approve the ERA. The Citizens Party selected party activist Richard J. Walton of Rhode Island to accompany Johnson on the ticket. Winning 72,200 votes in 1984, the ticket garnered 0.1 percent of the vote.

Communist Party (1924-)

In 1919, shortly after the Russian Revolution, Soviet communists encouraged American left-wing groups to withdraw from the Socialist Party and to form a Communist Party in the United States. After several years of internal dissension, a new political organization named the Workers' Party of America was established in 1921 at the insistence of Moscow. The goal of the new party was revolutionary — to overthrow capitalism and to create a communist state with rule by the working classes.

William Z. Foster, a labor organizer, was the party's first presidential candidate, in 1924. National tickets were run every four years through 1940 and again in 1968, 1972, 1976, 1980 and 1984, but the party's peak year at the polls was 1932, when Foster received 102,221 votes (0.3 percent of the popular vote).

The Communists have a distinctive place in American political history as the only party to have had international ties. In 1929 a party split brought the formal creation of the Communist Party of the United States, with acknowledged status as a part of the worldwide communist movement (the Communist International).

The Communist International terminated during World War II, and in 1944 the party's leader in America, Earl Browder, dissolved the party and committed the movement to operate within the two-party system. In the 1944 campaign the communists endorsed President Franklin D. Roosevelt, who repudiated their support.

However, with the breakup of the U.S.-Soviet alliance after World War II, the Communists reconstituted themselves as a political party. They supported Henry Wallace's Progressive Party candidacy in 1948, but they were limited in the Cold War period of the 1950s by restrictive federal

and state legislation that virtually outlawed the party.

With the gradual easing of restrictive measures, the Communist Party resumed electoral activities in the late 1960s. In a policy statement written in 1966, the party described itself as "a revolutionary party whose aim is the fundamental transformation of society."

The party's success at the polls, however, continued to be minimal. Its presidential candidates in 1968, 1972, 1976, 1980 and 1984 each received less than one-tenth of 1 percent of the vote.

Constitutional Union Party (1860)

The short-lived Constitutional Union Party was formed in 1859 to promote national conciliation in the face of rampant sectionalism, which included Southern threats of secession. The party appealed to conservative remnants of the American (Know-Nothing) and Whig parties, who viewed preservation of the Union as their primary goal.

The Constitutional Union Party held its first and only national convention in Baltimore in May 1860. For president the party nominated John Bell of Tennessee, a former senator and Speaker of the House of Representatives, who previously had been both a Democrat and a Whig. The convention adopted a short platform, which intentionally avoided controversial subjects, most notably the divisive slavery issue. Instead, the platform simply urged support for "the Constitution, the Union and the Laws."

In the fall election, Bell received 590,901 votes (12.6 percent of the popular vote) and won three states — Kentucky, Tennessee and Virginia. However, the Bell ticket finished last in the four-way presidential race and, together with the sectional split in the Democratic Party, was a prominent factor in the victory of Republican Abraham Lincoln.

In the months after the 1860 election the Constitutional Union Party continued to urge national conciliation, but with the outbreak of the Civil War the party disappeared.

Democratic Party (1832-)

There is no precise birth date for the Democratic Party. It developed as an outgrowth of Thomas Jefferson's Democratic-Republican Party, which splintered into factions in the 1820s. The faction led by Andrew Jackson took the name Democratic-Republican, but after 1830 dropped the last half of this label and became simply the Democratic Party. The new party encouraged and benefited from the increasing democratization of American politics that began in the 1820s. Andrew Jackson became a symbol of this mass democracy, and when he was elected in 1828 a period of Democratic dominance began that lasted until the Civil War.

The Democrats were a national party, with a particular appeal among workingmen, immigrants and settlers west of the Alleghenies. The success of the party in the pre-Civil War period was due in part to a national organization stronger than that of its rivals. In 1832 the Democrats were the first major party to hold a national nominating convention and in 1848 became the first party to establish an ongoing national committee.

Between 1828 and 1860, the party held the White House for 24 of the 32 years, controlled the Senate for 26 years and the House of Representatives for 24. Leadership in the party generally resided in Congress. The Democrats'

two-thirds nominating rule, adopted at the 1832 convention and retained for a century, gave the South a veto power over the choice of a national ticket. The result, not only in the pre-Civil War years but until the rule was eliminated in 1936, was the frequent selection of conservative candidates for president.

The early philosophy of the Democratic Party stressed a belief in a strict interpretation of the Constitution, states' rights and limited spending by the federal government. While party members throughout the nation accepted these basic tenets, there was no national consensus on the volatile slavery issue, which strained the party in the mid-19th century and finally divided it geographically in 1860. Two separate Democratic tickets were run in the 1860 election — one Northern, one Southern. The party division aided the election of the candidate of the new anti-slavery Republican Party, Abraham Lincoln, who received less than 40 percent of the popular vote.

During the Civil War the Northern wing of the party was factionalized, with one wing, the Copperheads, hostile to the Union war effort and favoring a negotiated peace with the Confederacy. The stance of the Copperheads, coupled with the involvement of many Southern Democrats in the Confederate government, enabled the Republicans for a generation after the Civil War to denounce the reunified Democratic Party as the "party of treason."

The Democrats were a national party after the Civil War, but they were displaced as the majority party by the Republicans. The strength of the Democrats was in the South, which voted in large majorities for Democratic candidates. Party strength outside the South was scattered, being most noticeable among urban ethnics and voters in the Border States. The period of Republican dominance lasted for nearly three-quarters of a century, 1860 to 1932. The Democrats occupied the White House for 16 of the 72 years, controlled the House of Representatives for 26 years and the Senate for 10.

The Depression, which began in 1929, dramatically altered American politics and provided the opportunity for the Democrats to re-emerge as the majority party. The Democrats swept to victory behind Franklin D. Roosevelt in 1932 and with widespread popular acceptance of his New Deal programs a new coalition was formed, which has remained largely intact. The new majority coalition combined the bulk of the black electorate, the academic community and organized labor with the party's core strength among urban ethnic and Southern voters.

Between 1932 and 1978, the Democrats occupied the presidency 30 of 46 years and controlled both houses of Congress for 42 years. The acceptance of Roosevelt's New Deal, coupled with the abolishment of the two-thirds rule for nominating candidates and decline of Southern power, resulted in more liberal party leadership. The liberal stance of the party included the belief by most party leaders in a broad interpretation of the Constitution, increased use of federal power and government spending to combat the problems of society. This basic philosophy has been maintained by Democratic presidential candidates since 1932.

While the years since 1932 have been the longest period of Democratic control in American history, the party's unity at times has been threatened. The party includes diverse elements across the political spectrum, and its strength at the congressional level frequently has been undermined by a loose alliance of Republicans and Southern Democrats. At the national level the party has been internally divided by explosive, controversial issues —

most notably in the late 1960s and early 1970s — such as the war in Vietnam.

In spite of the impact of divisive issues and inroads in the conservative sector of the party by the Republicans, particularly in presidential elections, the Roosevelt coalition continued basically intact and the Democrats remained the majority party in the 1970s. The 1980 election brought signs of a power shift, however, as the Republicans regained the presidency and won control of the Senate for the first time in 28 years. The 1982 mid-term elections swept 26 new Democrats in the House and strengthened the Democrats' control of that chamber. According to a Gallup Poll taken in spring 1983, when the nation was beginning to recover from the most serious recession since the Great Depression of the 1930s, more than twice as many people described themselves as Democrats (46 percent) than as Republicans (23 percent).

As the economy rebounded under the leadership of Republican president Ronald Reagan, the Democratic Party lost ground, according to a Gallup Poll taken in August 1984. By this time the percentage of people who identified themselves as Democrats had dropped to 42 percent, while the Republican share increased to 28 percent.

Democratic-Republican Party (1796-1828)

The Democratic-Republican Party developed in the early 1790s as the organized opposition to the incumbent Federalists and successor to the Anti-Federalists, who were a loose alliance of elements initially opposed to the ratification of the Constitution and subsequently the policies of the Washington administration designed to centralize power in the federal government.

Thomas Jefferson was the leader of the new party, which as early as 1792 referred to themselves as Republicans. This remained the party's primary name throughout its history, although in some states it became known as the Democratic-Republicans, the label used frequently by historians to refer to Jefferson's party to avoid confusing it with the later Republican Party, which began in 1854. Party members were called Jeffersonian Republicans as well.

The Democratic-Republicans favored states' rights, a literal interpretation of the Constitution, and expanded democracy through extension of suffrage and popular control of the government. The Democratic-Republicans were dominated by rural, agrarian interests, intent on maintaining their dominance over the growing commercial and industrial interests of the Northeast. The principal strength of the party came from the Southern and Middle Atlantic states.

The Democratic-Republicans first gained control of the federal government in 1800, when Jefferson was elected president and the party won majorities in both houses of Congress. For the next 24 years the party controlled both the White House and Congress, the last eight years virtually without opposition. For all but four years during this 24-year period, there was a Virginia-New York alliance controlling the executive branch, with all three presidents from Virginia — Jefferson, James Madison and James Monroe — and three of the four vice presidents from New York. Lacking an opposition party, the Democratic-Republicans in the 1820s became increasingly divided in 1824, when four party leaders ran for president. John Quincy Adams won the election in the House of Representatives, although Andrew Jackson had received more popular votes.

The deep factionalism evident in the 1824 election doomed the Democratic-Republican Party. The two-party system revived shortly thereafter with the emergence of the National Republican Party, an outgrowth of the Adams faction, and the Democratic-Republican Party, the political organization of the Jackson faction. After 1830 the Jacksonians adopted the name Democratic Party.

Federalist Party (1789-1816)

The Federalist Party grew out of the movement that drafted and worked for the ratification of the Constitution of 1787, which established a stronger national government than that in operation under the existing Articles of Confederation. Supporters of the new constitutional government were known as Federalists, and in the formative first decade of the Republic they controlled the national government. With President George Washington staying aloof from the development of political parties, leadership of the Federalists was exercised by Alexander Hamilton and John Adams. The party's basic strength was among urban, commercial interests, who were particularly drawn to the Federalists by the party's belief in a strong federal economic policy and the maintenance of domestic order — viewpoints based on a broad interpretation of the Constitution.

The Federalists were perceived widely as a party of the aristocracy, a decided liability in the late 18th and early 19th centuries when the right to vote was being widely extended to members of the middle and lower classes. Never as well organized as the Democratic-Republicans, the Federalists were unable to compete for support of the important rural, agrarian elements that composed a majority of the electorate.

The election of Jefferson in 1800 ended Federalist control of both the White House and Congress. After 1800 the Federalists did not elect a president or win a majority in either house of Congress. The party's strength was largely limited to commercial New England, where Federalists advocated states' rights and were involved in threats of regional secession in 1808 and again during the War of 1812.

In 1812 the Federalists held their last meeting of party leaders to field a presidential ticket. Four years later there were no nominations, but Federalist electors were chosen in three states. Although this marked the last appearance of the party at the national level, the Federalists remained in existence at the local level until the mid-1820s.

Free Soil Party (1848-1852)

Born as a result of opposition to the extension of slavery into the newly acquired Southwest territories, the Free Soil Party was launched formally at a convention in Buffalo, N.Y., in August 1848. The Free Soilers were composed of anti-slavery elements from the Democratic and Whig parties as well as remnants of the Liberal Party. Representatives from all the Northern states and three Border States attended the Buffalo convention, where the slogan "free soil, free speech, free labor and free men" was adopted. This slogan expressed the anti-slavery sentiment of the Free Soilers as well as the desire for cheap Western land.

Former Democratic president Martin Van Buren (1837-41) was selected by the convention as the party's presidential candidate and Charles Francis Adams, the son of President John Quincy Adams (1825-29), was chosen as his running mate.

In the 1848 election the Free Soil ticket received 291,501 votes (10.1 percent of the popular vote) but was unable to carry a single state. The party did better at the congressional level, winning nine House seats and holding the balance of power in the organization of the closely divided new Congress.

The 1848 election marked the peak of the party's influence. With the passage of compromise legislation on slavery in 1850, the Free Soilers lost their basic issue and began a rapid decline. The party ran its second and last national ticket in 1852, headed by John Hale, who received 155,210 votes (4.9 percent of the popular vote). As in 1848 the Free Soil national ticket failed to carry a single state.

Although the party went out of existence shortly thereafter, its program and constituency were absorbed by the Republican Party, whose birth and growth dramatically paralleled the resurgence of the slavery issue in the mid-1850s.

Greenback Party (1876-1884)

The National Independent or Greenback-Labor Party, commonly known as the Greenback Party, was launched in Indianapolis, Ind., in November 1874 at a meeting organized by the Indiana Grange. The party grew out of the Panic of 1873, a post-Civil War economic depression, which was felt particularly hard by farmers and industrial workers. Currency was the basic issue of the new party, which opposed return to the gold standard and favored retention of the inflationary paper money (known as greenbacks), first introduced as an emergency measure during the Civil War.

In the 1876 presidential election the party ran Peter Cooper, a New York philanthropist, and drafted a platform that focused entirely on the currency issue. Cooper received 75,973 votes (0.9 percent of the popular vote), mainly from agrarian voters. Aided by the continuing depression, a Greenback national convention in 1878 effected the merger of the party with various labor reform groups and a platform was adopted that addressed labor and currency issues. Showing voting strength in the industrial East as well as in the agrarian South and Midwest, the Greenbacks polled more than one million votes in the 1878 congressional races and won 14 seats in the House of Representatives. It marked the high point of the party's strength.

Returning prosperity, the prospect of fusion with one of the major parties and a split between the party's agrarian and labor leadership served to undermine the Greenback Party. In the 1880 election the party elected only eight representatives and its presidential candidate, Rep. James B. Weaver of Iowa, received 305,997 votes (3.3 percent of the popular vote), far less than party leaders expected.

The party slipped further four years later, when the Greenbacks' candidate for president, former Massachusetts governor Benjamin F. Butler, received 175,096 votes (1.7 percent of the popular vote). With the demise of the Greenbacks, most of the party's constituency moved into the Populist Party, the agrarian reform movement that swept the South and Midwest in the 1890s.

Liberal Republican Party (1872)

A faction of the Republican Party, dissatisfied with President Ulysses S. Grant's first term in office, withdrew from the party in 1872 to form its own party. Composed of party reformers, as well as anti-Grant politicians and news-paper editors, the new party focused on the corruption of the Grant administration, the need for civil service reform and for an end to the Reconstruction policy in the South.

The call for the Liberal Republican national convention came from the state party in Missouri, the birthplace of the reform movement. The convention, meeting in Cincinnati, Ohio, in May 1872, nominated Horace Greeley, editor of the *New York Tribune,* for president and Missouri governor B. Gratz Brown as his running mate. Greeley, the choice of anti-Grant politicians but suspect among reformers, was not popular among many Democrats either, who recalled his longtime criticism of the Democratic Party.

However, with the hope of victory in the fall election, the Democratic national convention, meeting in July, endorsed the Liberal Republican ticket and platform. The coalition was an unsuccessful one, as many Democrats refused to vote for Greeley. He received 2,833,711 votes (43.8 percent of the popular vote) but carried only six states and lost to Grant by more than 750,000 votes out of nearly 6.5 million cast. Greeley died shortly after the election.

Underfinanced, poorly organized and dependent on the Democrats' for their success, the Liberal Republicans went out of existence after the 1872 election.

Libertarian Party (1971-)

In the brief period of four years, the Libertarian Party leaped from a fledgling organization on the presidential ballot in only two states to the nation's largest third party.

Formed in Colorado in 1971, the party nominated John Hospers of California for president in 1972. On the ballot only in Colorado and Washington, Hospers garnered 3,671 votes. But he received a measure of national attention when a Republican presidential elector from Virginia, Roger MacBride, cast his electoral vote for the Libertarian presidential nominee.

MacBride's action made him a hero in Libertarian circles, and the party chose him as its 1976 standard-bearer at its August 1975 convention in New York City. MacBride had served in the Vermont Legislature in the 1960s and was defeated for the Republican gubernatorial nomination in that state in 1964. In the 1970s he settled on a farm near Charlottesville, Va., and devoted himself to writing and party affairs. He was co-creator of the television series "Little House on the Prairie."

Making a major effort in 1976, the Libertarians got on the ballot in 32 states, more than Eugene J. McCarthy — who ran independent of any political party — or any other third-party candidate. The reward was a vote of 173,011, more than any other minor party candidate, but far below McCarthy's total and only 0.2 percent of the national vote. MacBride's strength was centered in the West, where he received 5.5 percent of the vote in Alaska and 1.0 percent or more in Arizona, Hawaii and Idaho. He also ran well ahead of his national average in California (0.7 percent) and Nevada (0.8 percent). His running mate was David P. Bergland, a California lawyer.

In 1980 the Libertarian Party appeared on the ballot in all 50 states and the District of Columbia for the first time. The party also fielded about 550 candidates for other offices, a number that dwarfed other third-party efforts. The party nominees, Edward E. Clark of California for president and David Koch of New York for vice president, garnered 921,299 votes or 1.1 percent of the vote nationwide. Again the major support for the Libertarians came

from Western states. Of all minor party presidential candidates running in 1984, the Libertarians appeared on the greatest number of ballots: 38 states and the District of Columbia. Bergland, who had run in 1976 for the second slot, was the party's presidential candidate, and Jim Lewis, a Connecticut business executive, his running mate.

Individual responsibility and minimal government interference were the hallmarks of the Libertarian philosophy. The party favored repeal of laws against so-called victimless crimes — such as those involving pornography, drug use and homosexual activity — the abolition of all federal police agencies, and the elimination of all government subsidies to private enterprise. In foreign and military affairs, the Libertarians advocated the removal of U.S. troops from abroad, a cut in the defense budget and the emergence of the United States as a "giant Switzerland," with no international treaty obligations. MacBride commented that it was his party's intention to "reduce the Pentagon to a trigon."

Libertarians also favored repeal of legislation that they believe hindered individual or corporate action. They opposed gun control, civil rights laws, price controls on oil and gas, labor protection laws, federal welfare and poverty programs, forced busing, compulsory education, Social Security, national medical care, federal land-use restrictions and the 55-miles-per-hour speed limit.

Liberty Party (1840-48)

Born in 1839, the Liberty Party was the product of a split in the anti-slavery movement between a faction led by William Lloyd Garrison that favored action outside the political process and a second led by James G. Birney that proposed action within the political system through the establishment of an independent, anti-slavery party. The Birney faction launched the Liberty Party in November 1839 and the following April a national convention with delegates from six states nominated Birney for the presidency.

Although the Liberty Party was the first political party to take an anti-slavery position, and the only one at the time to do so, most abolitionist voters in the 1840 election supported the Democratic or Whig presidential candidates. Birney received only 6,797 votes (0.3 percent of the popular vote).

Aided by the controversy over the annexation of slaveholding Texas, the Liberty Party's popularity increased in 1844. Birney, again the party's presidential nominee, received 62,103 votes (2.3 percent of the popular vote) but again as in 1840 carried no states. The peak strength of the party was reached two years later in 1846, when in various state elections Liberty Party candidates received 74,017 votes.

In October 1847 the party nominated New Hampshire senator John P. Hale for the presidency, but his candidacy was withdrawn the following year when the Liberty Party joined the broader-based Free Soil Party. *(Free Soil Party, p. 229)*

National Democratic Party (1896)

A conservative party faction in favor of the gold standard, the National Democrats bolted from the Democratic Party after the 1896 convention adopted a pro-silver platform and nominated William Jennings Bryan, who opposed the gold standard. With the nation in the midst of a de-

pression and the Populists in the agrarian Midwest and South demanding monetary reform, currency was the dominant issue of the 1896 campaign. This produced a brief realignment in American politics.

The Republican Party was controlled by leaders who favored maintenance of the gold standard, a non-inflationary currency. Agrarian Midwestern and Southern Democrats, reflecting a Populist philosophy, gained control of the Democratic Party in 1896 and committed it to the free coinage of silver, an inflationary currency demanded by rural elements threatened by debts. The Democrats attracted pro-silver bolters from the Republican Party, but gold standard Democrats, opposed to the Republicans' protectionist position on the tariff issue, established an independent party.

Meeting in Indianapolis, Ind., in September 1896, the National Democrats adopted a platform favoring maintenance of the gold standard and selected a ticket headed by 79-year-old Illinois senator John M. Palmer.

Democratic president Grover Cleveland and leading members of his administration, repudiated by the convention that chose Bryan, supported the National Democrats. During the campaign the National Democrats encouraged conservative Democrats to vote either for the National Democratic ticket or for the Republican candidate, William McKinley. The Palmer ticket received 133,435 votes (1.0 percent of the popular vote), and McKinley defeated Bryan.

With prosperity returning and the Spanish-American War in the late 1890s occurring, the currency issue was overshadowed and the intense Democratic Party factionalism that produced the National Democratic Party ended.

National Republican Party (1828-32)

The Democratic-Republican Party splintered after the 1824 election into two factions. The group led by Andrew Jackson retained the name Democratic-Republican, which eventually was shortened to Democrats; the other faction headed by President John Quincy Adams assumed the name National Republicans. The new party reflected the belief of President Adams in the establishment of a national policy by the federal government: supporting a protective tariff, the Bank of the United States, federal administration of public lands and national programs of internal improvements. However, Adams' belief in a strong national government contrasted with the period's prevailing mood of populism and states' rights.

The Adams forces controlled Congress for two years, 1825 to 1827, but as party structures formalized the National Republicans became a minority in Congress and suffered a decisive loss in the 1828 presidential election. Running for re-election, Adams was beaten by Jackson. Adams received 43.6 percent of the popular vote and carried eight states, none in the South. Henry Clay, the party's candidate against Jackson four years later, had even less success. He received only 37.4 percent of the popular vote and carried just six states, again none of which were in the South.

Poorly organized, with dwindling support and a heritage of defeat, the National Republicans went out of existence after the 1832 election, but their members provided the base for a new anti-Jackson party, the Whigs, which came into being in 1834. *(Whig Party, p. 237)*

National Unity Party (1983-   )

Republican representative John B. Anderson of Illinois formed the National Unity Campaign as the vehicle for his independent presidential campaign in 1980. Anderson began his quest for the presidency by trying to win the Republican Party nomination. But, as a liberal in a party coming under conservative control, he won no primaries and could claim only 57 convention delegates by April 1980. Anderson withdrew from the Republican race and declared his independent candidacy.

Anderson focused his campaign on the need to establish a viable third party as an alternative to domination of the political scene by the Republican and Democratic parties. The National Unity Campaign platform touted the Anderson program as a "new public philosophy" — more innovative than that of the Democrats, who "cling to the policies of the New Deal," and more enlightened than that of the Republicans, who talk "incessantly about freedom, but hardly ever about justice." Generally the group took positions that were fiscally conservative and socially liberal. Anderson and his running mate, former Democratic Wisconsin governor Patrick J. Lucey, tried to appeal to Republican and Democratic voters disenchanted with their parties and to the growing bloc of voters who classified themselves as independents.

The National Unity Campaign ticket was on the ballot in all 50 states in 1980, although Anderson had to wage costly legal battles in some states to ensure that result. In the end, the party won 6.6 percent of the presidential vote, well over the 5 percent necessary to qualify for retroactive federal campaign funding.

In April 1984 Anderson announced that he would not seek the presidency in that year. He said that instead he would focus his energies on building the National Unity Party, which he established officially in December 1983. He planned to concentrate initially on running candidates at the local level. On Aug. 28 Anderson endorsed Walter F. Mondale, the Democratic nominee for president, and his running mate, Geraldine A. Ferraro.

People's Party (1971-   )

Delegates from activist and peace groups established the People's Party at a November 1971 convention held in Dallas, Texas. The initial co-chairmen were pediatrician Dr. Benjamin Spock and author Gore Vidal.

The People's Party first ran a presidential candidate in 1972. They chose Dr. Spock for president and black activist Julius Hobson of Washington, D.C., for vice president. Despite hopes for widespread backing from the poor and social activists, the ticket received only 78,751 votes, 0.1 percent of the national total. A total of 55,167 of those votes came from California alone.

At its 1975 convention, held in St. Louis, Mo., Aug. 31, the People's Party chose black civil rights activist Margaret Wright of California for president and Maggie Kuhn of Pennsylvania, a leader in the Gray Panthers movement for rights for the elderly, for vice president. Kuhn, however, declined the nomination and was replaced on the ticket by Spock.

The party platform focused on cutting the defense budget, closing tax loopholes and making that money available for social programs. Other planks included redistribution of land and wealth; unconditional amnesty for war objectors; and free health care. In her campaign, Wright stressed the necessity for active participation by citizens in the governmental process, so that institutions and programs could be run from the roots up rather than from the top down.

As in 1972 the party's main backing came in California, where it was supported by the state Peace and Freedom Party. Wright's total national vote was 49,024, and 85.1 percent (41,731 votes) of those votes came from California. The party did not field presidential tickets in 1980 and 1984.

People's Party-Populists (1892-1908, 1983-   )

The People's Party, also called the Populist Party, was organized at a convention in Cincinnati, Ohio, in May 1891 and climaxed several decades of farm protest against deteriorating economic conditions. Chronically depressed commodity prices, caused by over-production and world competition, had spurred the politicization of farmers.

Most of the Populist leaders came from the defunct Greenback movement and Southern and Midwestern farm cooperative associations. The Populists tended to blame their problems on the most visible causes, primarily the high railroad rates and shrinking currency supply, but the platform they adopted at their first national nominating convention in 1892 was a wide-reaching one. As well as advocating the government ownership of railroads and the free coinage of silver, the Populists proposed institution of a graduated income tax and the direct election of senators. Although the Populists proposed labor reforms, such as reducing the working day to eight hours, the party never gained appreciable support among industrial workers.

The Populists ran James B. Weaver, the former Greenback candidate, as their presidential nominee in 1892. Weaver received 1,024,280 votes (8.5 percent of the popular vote) and carried five states in the Midwest and Far West. Increasingly tied to the silver issue, the party showed growing strength in the 1894 congressional races. Especially strong west of the Mississippi River, party congressional candidates polled nearly 1.5 million votes. After the election the Populists had six senators and seven representatives in Congress.

The Democrats surprised Populist leaders in 1896 by writing a free silver platform and nominating a free silver candidate, William Jennings Bryan. The Populists were faced with the dilemma of either endorsing Bryan and losing their party identity or of running a separate ticket and splitting the free silver vote. The Populist convention endorsed Bryan but ran a separate candidate for vice president, Thomas E. Watson.

After this initial fusion with the Democrats, most Populists remained within the Democratic Party after the 1896 election. The Populist Party remained in existence, running presidential candidates until 1908, but never received more than 0.8 percent of the popular vote. The party did not expand its voter appeal beyond an agrarian reform movement, but many of its proposals, particularly in the areas of government and electoral reform, were espoused by progressive politicians in the early 20th century and enacted into law.

After being absent from the political scene for nearly three-quarters of a century, the Populist Party revived in early 1984 to place a candidate on the presidential ballot in 14 states. Backers of the new party advocated wiping out the Federal Reserve System, repealing the federal income tax, and protecting U.S. industry from imports.

Progressive Party-Bull Moose (1912)

A split in Republican ranks, spurred by the bitter personal and ideological dispute between President William Howard Taft (1909-13) and former president Theodore Roosevelt (1901-09), resulted in the withdrawal of the Roosevelt forces from the Republican Party after the June 1912 convention and the creation of the Progressive Party two months later. The new party was known popularly as the Bull Moose Party, a name resulting from Roosevelt's assertion early in the campaign that he felt as fit as a bull moose. While the Taft-Roosevelt split was the immediate reason for the new party, the Bull Moosers were an outgrowth of the progressive movement that was a powerful force in both major parties in the early years of the 20th century.

Although in 1908 Roosevelt had handpicked Taft as his successor, his disillusionment with Taft's conservative philosophy came quickly, and with the support of progressive Republicans Roosevelt challenged the incumbent for the 1912 Republican presidential nomination. Roosevelt outpolled Taft in the presidential primary states. Taft nevertheless won the nomination with nearly solid support in the South and among party conservatives, providing the narrow majority of delegates that enabled him to win the bulk of the key credentials challenges.

Although few Republican politicians followed Roosevelt in his bolt, the new party demonstrated a popular base at its convention in Chicago in August 1912. Thousands of delegates, basically middle- and upper-class reformers from small towns and cities, attended the convention that launched the party and nominated Roosevelt for president and California governor Hiram Johnson as his running mate. Roosevelt appeared in person to deliver his "Confession of Faith," a speech detailing his nationalistic philosophy and progressive reform ideas. The Bull Moose platform reflected key tenets of the Progressive movement, calling for more extensive government antitrust action and labor, social, government and electoral reform.

Roosevelt was wounded in an assassination attempt while campaigning in Milwaukee, Wis., in October, but he finished the campaign. In the general election Roosevelt received more than 4 million votes (27.4 percent of the popular vote) and carried six states. His percentage of the vote was the highest ever received by a third-party candidate in American history, but his candidacy split the Republican vote and enabled the Democrats' nominee, Woodrow Wilson, to win the election. The Progressive Party had minimal success at the state and local level, winning approximately 13 House seats but electing no senators or governors.

Roosevelt declined the Progressive nomination in 1916 and endorsed the Republican candidate, Charles Evans Hughes. With the defection of its leader, the decline of the Progressive movement, and the lack of an effective party organization, the Bull Moose Party ceased to exist.

Progressive Party (1924)

Like the Bull Moose Party of Theodore Roosevelt, the Progressive Party that emerged in the mid-1920s was a reform effort led by a Republican. Wisconsin senator Robert M. La Follette led the new Progressive Party, a separate entity from the Bull Moosers, which, unlike the middle- and upper-class Roosevelt party of the previous decade, had its greatest appeal among farmers and organized labor.

The La Follette Progressive Party grew out of the Conference for Progressive Political Action (CPPA), a coalition of railway union leaders and a remnant of the Bull Moose effort that was formed in 1922. The Socialist Party joined the coalition the following year. Throughout 1923 the Socialists and labor unions argued over whether their coalition should form a third party, with the Socialists in favor and the labor unions against it. It was finally decided to run an independent presidential candidate, La Follette, in the 1924 election but not to field candidates at the state and local levels. La Follette was given the power to choose his own running mate and selected Montana senator Burton K. Wheeler, a Democrat.

Opposition to corporate monopolies was the major issue of the La Follette campaign, although the party advocated various other reforms, particularly aimed at farmers and workers, which were proposed earlier by either the Populists or Bull Moosers. But the Progressive Party itself was a major issue in the 1924 campaign, as the Republicans attacked the alleged radicalism of the party.

Although La Follette had its endorsement, the American Federation of Labor (AFL) provided minimal support. The basic strength of the Progressives, like that of the Populists in the 1890s, derived from agrarian voters west of the Mississippi River. La Follette received 4,814,000 votes (16.6 percent of the popular vote) but carried just one state, his native Wisconsin. When La Follette died in 1925, the party collapsed as a national force. It was revived by La Follette's sons on a statewide level in Wisconsin in the mid-1930s.

Progressive Party (1948)

Henry A. Wallace's Progressive Party resulted from the dissatisfaction of liberal elements in the Democratic Party with the leadership of President Harry S Truman, particularly in the realm of foreign policy. The Progressive Party was one of two bolting groups from the Democratic Party in 1948; conservative Southern elements withdrew to form the States' Rights Party.

Henry Wallace, the founder of the Progressive Party, was secretary of agriculture, vice president and finally secretary of commerce under President Franklin D. Roosevelt. He carried the reputation of one of the most liberal idealists in the Roosevelt administration. Fired from the Truman Cabinet in 1946 after breaking with administration policy and publicly advocating peaceful coexistence with the Soviet Union, Wallace began to consider the idea of a liberal third-party candidacy. Supported by the American Labor Party, the Progressive Citizens of America and other progressive organizations in California and Illinois, Wallace announced his third-party candidacy in December 1947.

The Progressive Party was launched formally the following July at a convention in Philadelphia, which ratified the selection of Wallace for president and Sen. Glen H. Taylor, D-Idaho, as his running mate. The party adopted a platform that emphasized foreign policy — opposing the Cold War anti-communism of the Truman administration and specifically urging abandonment of the Truman Doctrine and the Marshall Plan. These measures were designed to contain the spread of communism and bolster non-communist nations. On domestic issues the Progressives stressed humanitarian concerns and equal rights for different sexes and races.

Minority groups — women, youth, blacks, Jews, Spanish-Americans — were active in the new party, but the openness of the Progressives brought Wallace a damaging endorsement from the Communist Party. Believing the two

parties could work together, Wallace accepted the endorsement while characterizing his own philosophy as "progressive capitalism."

The Progressives appeared on the ballot in 45 states, but the Communist endorsement helped keep the party on the defensive the entire campaign. In the November election Wallace received only 1,157,057 votes (2.4 percent of the popular vote), with nearly half of the votes from the state of New York. Not only were the Progressives unable to carry a single state, but in spite of their defection from the Democratic Party President Truman won re-election. The Progressives had poor results in the congressional races, failing to elect one representative or senator.

The Progressive Party's opposition to the Korean War in 1950 drove many moderate elements out of the party, including Henry Wallace. The party ran a national ticket in 1952, but its presidential candidate received only 0.2 percent of the popular vote. The party crumbled completely after the election.

Prohibition Party (1869-   )

The Prohibition Party existed longer than any third party in American history. It was formed in September 1869 at a convention in Chicago, which attracted approximately 500 delegates from 20 states. For the first time in U.S. politics, women had equal status with men as delegates. By a narrow majority the convention decided to form an independent party, and three years later the new party put forth its first national ticket. The party's basic goal was enactment of laws prohibiting the manufacture and sale of intoxicating liquor, but their platforms have included other reform proposals. The 1872 Prohibition Party platform included the first women's suffrage plank.

For all but one election between 1884 and 1916, the party's presidential candidate received at least 1 percent of the popular vote. The party's best showing came in 1892, when its presidential nominee, John Bidwell, received 270,770 votes (2.2 percent of the popular vote). The party has run a national ticket in every presidential election since 1872, but its candidates have never carried a single state. After the 1976 election the Prohibitionist Party changed its name to the National Statesman Party, and its 1980 candidate registered using that party name. The 1984 candidate, Earl F. Dodge of Colorado, emphasized that his party — on the ballots once again as Prohibitionists — no longer focused on a single issue: the party backed religious liberty and an anti-abortion amendment.

The temperance movement succeeded in gaining prohibition legislation in numerous states in the late 19th and early 20th centuries, and its efforts were capped in 1919 by passage of national prohibition legislation (the 18th amendment to the U.S. Constitution, repealed 14 years later by the 21st amendment). The achievements of the temperance movement were due as much to independent organizations, such as the Women's Christian Temperance Union (WCTU) and the Anti-Saloon League, as to the Prohibition Party, which had limited success at the polls. These organizations allowed active Democrats and Republicans to remain in their own parties while working for prohibition.

Republican Party (1854-   )

Born in 1854 in the upper Midwest, the Republican Party grew out of the anti-slavery forces' bitter dissatisfaction with the Kansas-Nebraska Act. The bill overturned earlier legislation (the Missouri Compromise of 1820 and the Compromise of 1850), which limited the extension of slavery into the territories, and instituted the concept of popular sovereignty, by which each territory decided its own position on slavery. While historians generally credit residents of Ripon, Wis., with holding the party's first organizational meeting in March 1854 and citizens of Jackson, Mich., with running the party's first electoral ticket in July 1854, the birth of the party was nearly simultaneous in many communities throughout the Northern states. The volatile slavery issue was the catalyst that brought the party's birth, but the political vacuum caused by the decline of the Whigs and the failure of the Know-Nothing and Free Soil parties to gain a stable national following allowed the Republicans to grow with dramatic rapidity.

The constituency of the new party was limited to the Northern states, since opposition to slavery was the basic issue of the Republicans. But the party did attract diverse elements in the political spectrum — former Whigs, Know-Nothings, Free Soilers and dissident Democrats.

In its first year the party took the name Republican. Horace Greeley is credited with initiating the name in a June 1854 issue of his newspaper, the *New York Tribune*. In pushing the name, he referred to the Jeffersonian Republicans of the early 19th century and Henry Clay's National Republican Party of the 1830s, which was an early rival of the Democrats.

The Republicans ran candidates throughout the North in 1854, and in combination with other candidates opposed to the Kansas-Nebraska Act won a majority in the House of Representatives. Two years later the Republicans ran their first national ticket, and although their presidential candidate John C. Fremont did not win he polled one-third of the vote in a three-man race and carried 11 states. The Republicans were established as a major party.

While the party was built on the slavery question, the Republicans were far from a one-issue party. They presented a nationalistic platform with appeal to business and commercial interests as well as rural anti-slavery elements. The Republicans proposed legislation for homesteading (free land), the construction of a transcontinental railroad, and the institution of a protective tariff.

Firmly established by the late 1850s, the Republican Party benefited from the increasing sectional factionalism in the Democratic Party over the slavery issue. In 1858 the party won control of the House of Representatives. Two years later, with Abraham Lincoln as its candidate, the Republicans won the White House and retained control of the House. Lincoln, benefiting from a sectional split in the Democratic Party, won an unusual four-way race and captured the presidency with 39.8 percent of the popular vote.

Lincoln was a wartime president, and his success in preserving the Union helped the party for the next generation. After the Civil War the Republicans projected a patriotic image, which, coupled with the party's belief in national expansion and limited federal involvement in the free enterprise system, helped make it the dominant party over the next three-quarters of a century. For most of the period between 1860 and 1932, the Republicans were the majority party: occupying the White House for 56 of the 72 years, controlling the Senate for 60 years and the House for 50. Except for the South, where the party basically was limited to the small number of black voters, the Republicans were strong throughout the nation.

Congressional leaders exercised the dominant power

during this period of Republican hegemony. Presidents had little success in challenging the authority wielded by the GOP's congressional leadership.

Just as the party vaulted to power on the divisive slavery issue, its history was altered by another traumatic event — the Great Depression, which began in 1929. As the incumbent party during the economic collapse, the Republicans suffered the political blame; their fall from power was rapid. In 1928 the Republican presidential candidate (Herbert Hoover) carried 40 states; in 1936, during Franklin D. Roosevelt's New Deal days, the Republican standard-bearer (Alfred M. Landon) won just two states. In 1928 the party held a clear majority of seats in both the House and Senate, 267 and 56 respectively; but eight years later the party's numbers had shrunk dramatically, the Republicans holding only 89 seats in the House and 17 in the Senate.

The party eventually made a comeback from this low point but remained the minority party in Congress through the 1978 elections. Between 1932 and 1984 the Republicans won six of 14 presidential elections but controlled both chambers of Congress for just four years. In 1984 the party kept control of the Senate, which it had gained in 1980, but the House remained in Democratic hands.

While the Republicans struggled to find the formula for a new majority, the party's basic conservatism made it increasingly appealing, especially in presidential races, to segments of the electorate that previously were firm parts of the Democratic coalition — notably blue-collar workers and the once-Democratic South. Beginning in 1952, the party was able to attract a winning combination when it ran presidential candidates with a moderate conservative image, such as Dwight D. Eisenhower, Richard Nixon or Ronald Reagan. However, the GOP enjoyed less success at the state and local levels where Democratic majorities, established during the New Deal, remained largely intact.

The Republican difficulties in establishing a new majority were compounded after the 1972 election by the Watergate scandal, which brought down the Nixon administration. Gerald R. Ford, who became president after Nixon resigned Aug. 9, 1974, lost his 1976 election bid to former Georgia governor Jimmy Carter, giving the Democrats control of the White House as well as both houses of Congress.

Republican fortunes improved dramatically in 1980 when former California governor Reagan won a landslide electoral vote victory over Carter. Republicans also took control of the Senate for the first time in 28 years and made substantial gains in the House. Although a resurgence of Democratic political strength in the 1982 midterm elections swept more Democrats into the House, the Republicans retained control of the Senate.

In a Gallup Poll taken shortly before the 1984 national elections, 28 percent of the respondents identified themselves as Republicans. Although Republicans remained the minority party (the Democrats had captured 42 percent of the voters in this survey), the party clearly was recovering from the lows it had experienced during the Watergate era. Not since the Eisenhower presidency had more voters identified themselves as Republicans.

Socialist Labor Party (1888-)

The Socialist Labor Party, the first national Socialist party in the United States, ranks second only to the Prohibitionists among third parties in longevity. Formed in 1874 by elements of the Socialist International in New York, it was first known as the Social Democratic Workingmen's Party. In 1877 the group adopted the name Socialist Labor Party. Throughout the 1880s the party worked in concert with other left-wing third parties, including the Greenbacks.

The Socialist Labor Party ran national tickets in every presidential election from 1892 through 1976. The party collected its highest proportion of the national vote in 1896, when its candidate received 36,356 votes (0.3 percent of the popular vote).

Led by the autocratic Daniel DeLeon (1852-1914), a former Columbia University law lecturer, the Socialist Labor Party became increasingly militant and made its best showing in local races in 1898. But DeLeon's insistence on rigid party discipline and his opposition to the organized labor movement alienated many members. Moderate elements in the party bolted, eventually joining the Socialist Party of Eugene V. Debs, which formed in 1901.

The Socialist Labor Party continued as a small, tightly organized far-left group bound to DeLeon's uncompromising belief in revolution. As late as 1970 the party advocated direct worker action to take over control of production and claimed 5,000 members nationwide.

Socialist Party (1901-)

The Socialist Party was born officially in July 1901 at a convention in Indianapolis, Ind., which joined together former American Railway Union president Eugene V. Debs' Social Democratic Party with a moderate faction of the Socialist Labor Party. The two groups had begun discussions a year before and in the 1900 presidential campaign jointly supported a ticket headed by Debs that received 86,935 votes (0.6 percent of the popular vote).

The 1901 unity convention identified the new Socialist Party with the working class and described the party's goal as "collective ownership . . . of the means of production and distribution." The party grew rapidly in the early 20th century, reaching a peak membership of approximately 118,000 in 1912. That year also proved to be the party's best at the polls. Debs, a presidential candidate five times between 1900 and 1920, received 900,369 votes (6.0 percent of the popular vote). The Socialists elected 1,200 candidates to local offices, including 79 candidates for mayor.

With the outbreak of World War I, the party became a vehicle for anti-war protest. In 1917 pacifist Socialists converted a number of mayoral elections into referendums on the war, winning 34 percent of the vote in Chicago, more than 25 percent in Buffalo and 22 percent in New York City.

The following year Debs was convicted of sedition for making an anti-war speech and was sentenced to a term in the Atlanta federal penitentiary, from which he ran for president in 1920 and received 913,664 votes (3.4 percent of the popular vote).

Four years later the Socialists endorsed Wisconsin senator Robert M. La Follette's presidential candidacy, an unsuccessful attempt to establish a farm-labor coalition. In 1928 the Socialists resumed running their own presidential ticket. With the death of Debs in 1926, the party selected Norman Thomas, a former minister and social worker, to be the party's standard-bearer for the next six elections. The Depression brought a brief surge for the Socialists in 1932, with Thomas polling 883,990 votes (2.2 percent of the popular vote).

But 1932 proved to be only a temporary revival for the Socialists. Roosevelt's New Deal stole their thunder, and the Socialist Party failed to attract even one-half of 1 percent of the vote in any succeeding presidential election. In 1976 the party ran its first presidential ticket in two decades. The candidates received 6,038 votes, .01 percent of the popular vote. Although Socialist Party candidates received a few more votes in the 1980 elections, 6,898, their percentage share of the total vote remained .01 percent. By 1984 it appeared that the old-line Socialist Party had faded again from the presidential candidate scene.

Socialist Workers Party (1938-   )

The Socialist Workers Party was formed in 1938 by followers of the Russian revolutionary Leon Trotsky. Originally a faction within the U.S. Communist Party, the Trotskyites were expelled in 1936 on instructions from Soviet leader Joseph Stalin. A brief Trotskyite coalition with the Socialist Party ended in 1938 when the dissidents decided to organize independently as the Socialist Workers Party.

Since 1948 the party has run a presidential candidate, but its entries have never received more than 0.1 percent of the popular vote. Through its youth arm, the Young Socialist Alliance, the Socialist Workers Party was active in the anti-Vietnam War movement and contributed activists to civil rights protests.

Southern Democrats (1860)

Agitation over the slavery issue, building for a generation, reached a climax in 1860 and produced a sectional split in the Democratic Party. Throughout the mid-19th century the Democrats had remained unified by supporting the various pieces of compromise legislation that both protected slavery in the Southern states and endorsed the policy of popular sovereignty in the territories. But in 1860 Southern Democrats wanted the Democratic convention (meeting in Charleston, S. C.) to insert a plank specifically protecting slavery in the territories. When their plank was defeated, delegates from most of the Southern states walked out.

The Charleston convention stalemated over a presidential choice and, after recessing for six weeks, reconvened in Baltimore where Illinois senator Stephen A. Douglas was nominated. Most of the Southern delegates, plus those from California and Oregon, bolted the convention and nominated their own ticket in a rump convention held after Douglas' selection. Vice President John C. Breckinridge of Kentucky was chosen for president, and Joseph Lane, a states' rights advocate from Oregon, was selected as his running mate. A platform was adopted that recognized the right of slavery to exist in the territories. After the formation of the two sectional tickets, two separate Democratic national committees operated in Washington, D.C., to oversee their campaigns.

Although in the 1860 election the combined Douglas-Breckinridge vote comprised a majority of the ballots cast, the split in Democratic ranks was a boon to the campaign of the Republican candidate, Abraham Lincoln, who won with a plurality of the vote. The Breckinridge ticket received 848,019 votes (18.1 percent of the popular vote) and carried nine Southern and border states.

During the Civil War the Southern Democrats provided much of the leadership for the Confederate government, including its president, Jefferson Davis. At the end of the conflict the Southern Democrats made no attempt to continue as a separate sectional entity and rejoined the national Democratic Party.

States' Rights Democratic Party (1948)

The States' Rights Democratic Party was a conservative Southern faction that bolted from the Democrats in 1948. The immediate reason for the new party, popularly known as the Dixiecrats, was dissatisfaction with President Harry S Truman's civil rights program. But the Dixiecrat effort to maintain a segregated way of life was also an attempt to demonstrate the political power of the 20th century Southern Democrats and to re-establish their importance in the Democratic Party.

The Mississippi Democratic Party's state executive committee met in Jackson in May 1948 to lay the groundwork for the Dixiecrat secession. The meeting called for a bolt by Southern delegates if the Democratic National Convention endorsed Truman's civil rights program. When the convention did approve a strong civil rights plank, the entire Mississippi delegation and half the Alabama delegation left the convention. Gov. Fielding L. Wright of Mississippi invited all anti-Truman delegates to meet in Birmingham three days after the close of the Democratic convention to select a states' rights ticket.

Most Southern Democrats with national prominence and with seniority in Congress and patronage privileges to protect shunned the new Dixiecrat Party. The party's leaders came from the ranks of Southern governors and other state and local officials. The Birmingham convention chose two governors to lead the party: J. Strom Thurmond of South Carolina for president and Wright of Mississippi for vice president.

Other than the presidential ticket, the Dixiecrats did not run candidates for any office. Rather than try to develop an independent party organization, the Dixiecrats, whenever possible, used existing Democratic Party apparatus.

The party was on the ballot in only one state outside the South and in the November election received only 1,169,134 votes (2.4 percent of the popular vote). The Thurmond ticket carried four Deep South states where it ran under the Democratic Party label, but it failed in its basic objective to prevent the re-election of President Truman.

After the election the party ceased to exist almost as abruptly as it had begun, with most of its members returning to the Democratic Party. In a statement upon re-entering the Democratic fold, Thurmond characterized the Dixiecrat episode as "a fight within our family." (While serving in the U.S. Senate 16 years later, Thurmond switched to the Republican Party.)

Union Party (1936)

Advocating more radical economic measures, several early supporters of President Franklin D. Roosevelt broke with him and ran their own ticket in 1936 under the Union Party label. Largely an outgrowth of the Rev. Charles E. Coughlin's National Union for Social Justice, the new party also had the support of Dr. Francis E. Townsend, leader of a movement for government-supported old-age pensions, and Gerald L. K. Smith, self-appointed heir of Louisiana senator Huey P. Long's share-the-wealth program.

Father Coughlin was the keystone of the Union Party and was instrumental in choosing its presidential ticket in June 1936 — Rep. William Lemke, R-N.D., for president and Thomas O'Brien, a Massachusetts railroad union lawyer, for vice president. The new party did not hold a convention. The party's platform reportedly was written by Coughlin, Lemke and O'Brien and was similar to the program espoused by Coughlin's National Union. Among the features of the Union Party platform were proposals for banking and currency reform, a guaranteed income for workers, restrictions on wealth and an isolationist foreign policy.

Lacking organization and finances during the campaign, the party further suffered from the increasingly violent and often anti-Semitic tone of the oratory of both Coughlin and Smith.

The Union Party failed miserably in its primary goal of defeating Roosevelt. Roosevelt won a landslide victory and the Lemke ticket received only 892,492 votes (2 percent of the popular vote). The party standard-bearers were unable to carry a single state, and the Union Party's candidates for the House and Senate all were defeated. The party continued on a local level until it was finally dissolved in 1939.

U.S. Labor Party (1973-   )

Formed in 1973 as the political arm of the National Caucus of Labor Committees (NCLC), the U.S. Labor Party made its debut in national politics in 1976. The NCLC was organized in 1968 by splinters of the radical movements of the 1960s. It is a Marxist group. New Yorker Lyndon LaRouche, the party's chairman and a self-taught economist who worked in the management and computer fields, became its 1976 presidential nominee and Wayne Evans, a Detroit steelworker, his running mate.

The party directed much of its fire at the Rockefeller family. It charged that banks controlled by the Rockefellers were strangling the U.S. and world economies. In an apocalyptic vein, the party predicted a world monetary collapse by Election Day and the destruction of the country by thermonuclear war by the summer of 1977.

LaRouche's party developed a reputation for harassment because of its shouted interruptions and demonstrations against its political foes, including the Communist Party and the United Auto Workers. It accused some left-wing organizations and individuals, such as linguist Noam Chomsky and Marcus Raskin and his Institute for Policy Studies, of conspiring with the Rockefellers and the Central Intelligence Agency.

During the 1976 campaign, LaRouche was more critical of Carter than Ford. He depicted Ford as a well-meaning man out of his depth in the presidency, but Carter as a pawn of nuclear war advocates and a disgracefully unqualified presidential candidate. LaRouche captured only 40,043 votes, less than 0.1 percent of the national vote. He was on the ballot in 23 states and the District of Columbia.

Although the U.S. Labor Party did not run a presidential candidate in the 1980 election, LaRouche ran a strident campaign — as a Democrat. By this time, LaRouche's politics had shifted to the right, and his speeches were fraught with warnings of conspiracy.

He continued his crusade in 1984 but as an "independent Democrat," dismissing Democratic presidential nominee Walter F. Mondale as an "agent of Soviet influence." LaRouche received 78,807 votes and 0.1 percent of the vote.

Whig Party (1834-1856)

Organized in 1834 during the administration of President Andrew Jackson, the Whig Party was an amalgam of forces opposed to Jackson administration policies. Even the name "Whig" was symbolic of the intense anti-Jackson feeling among the party's adherents. The name was taken from the earlier British Whig Party, founded in the 17th century in opposition to the tyranny of the Stuart monarchs. Likewise, the term was popular during the American Revolution, as the colonists opposed what they considered the tyranny of King George III. The new Whig Party was opposed to "King Andrew," the Whig characterization of President Jackson and his strong executive actions.

Southerners, enraged over Jackson's stand against states' rights in the South Carolina nullification dispute, joined the coalition early. Then came businessmen, merchants and conservatives, shocked and fearful of Jackson's war on the Bank of the United States. This group, basically a remnant of the National Republican Party, espoused Henry Clay's American Plan, a program of federal action to aid the economy and tie together the sections of the country. The plan included tariff protection for business, a national bank, public works and distribution to the states of money received for the sale of public lands. The Clay plan became the basis for the Whigs' nationalistic economic program.

Another influential group joining the Whig coalition was the Anti-Masons, an egalitarian movement strong in parts of New England, New York and Pennsylvania.

Throughout its life, the Whig Party was plagued by factionalism and disunity. In 1836, the first presidential election in which the Whigs took part, the party had no national presidential candidate. Rather, three different candidates ran in different parts of the country — Gen. William Henry Harrison, Hugh L. White and Daniel Webster — each hoping to carry Whig electors in states where they were popular. Then the Whig electors, if a majority, could combine in the Electoral College on one candidate or, if that proved impossible, throw the election into the House. But Van Buren, the Democratic nominee, won a majority of the electors.

Befitting their lack of unity, the Whigs adopted no platform in 1840 and nominated Harrison, a military hero, for the presidency. His campaign, emphasizing an apocryphal log cabin and hard cider home life in Ohio, resulted in a landslide victory.

But Harrison died only a month after taking office (April 4, 1841). The new president, John Tyler of Virginia, proceeded to veto most elements of the Whig economic program, including the tariff and re-establishment of the national bank. Given Tyler's well-known states' rights position — ignored by the Whigs in 1840 when they capitalized on his Southern appeal — the vetoes were inevitable. Tyler's outraged Cabinet resigned, and for the rest of his term he remained a president without a party. Since his first two years in office were the only ones in which the Whigs controlled the presidency and both houses of Congress, Tyler's vetoes spoiled the only chance the Whigs ever had of implementing their program.

The Whigs won the White House for the second and last time in 1848 by running another military hero, Gen. Zachary Taylor. Like Harrison, Taylor was a non-ideological candidate who died in office. He was succeeded by Vice President Millard Fillmore.

The development of the slavery question in the 1840s

and its intensification in the 1850s proved to be the death knell for the Whig Party. A party containing anti-slavery New Englanders and Southern plantation owners was simply unable to bridge the gap between them. The Compromise of 1850, forged by Clay, only briefly allayed the controversy over extension of slavery into the Western territories. Many Southern Whigs gravitated toward the Democrats, whom they believed more responsive to their interests. In the North, new parties specifically dedicated to opposing the expansion of slavery (Free Soilers, Anti-Nebraskans, Republicans) attracted Whig voters.

The last Whig national convention, in 1856, adopted a platform but endorsed former president Millard Fillmore, already the nominee of the Know-Nothing Party. The Whig platform deplored sectional strife and called for compromise to save the Union. But it was a futile campaign, with Fillmore carrying only Maryland and winning only 21 percent of the national vote.

Workers World Party (1959-   )

With the Hungarian citizen revolt and other developments in Eastern Europe providing some impetus, the Workers World Party in 1959 split off from the Socialist Workers Party. The party theoretically supports worker uprisings in all parts of the world. Yet it backed the communist governments that put down rebellions in Hungary during the 1950s, Czechoslovakia in the 1960s and Poland in the 1980s. Workers World is an activist revolutionary group that, up until 1980, concentrated its efforts on specific issues, such as the anti-war and civil rights demonstrations during the 1960s and 1970s. The party has an active youth organization, Youth Against War and Fascism.

In 1980 party leaders saw an opportunity, created by the weakness of the U.S. economy and the related high unemployment, to interest voters in its revolutionary ideas. That year it placed Deirdre Griswold, the editor of the party's newspaper and one of its founding members, on the presidential ballot in 10 states. Together with her running mate Larry Holmes, a 27-year-old black activist, Griswold received 13,300 votes. In 1984 Holmes ran as the presidential candidate for the Workers World Party, getting on the ballot in eight states and receiving 15,329 votes.

Bibliography

Books

Bryce, James. *The American Commonwealth*. New York: Macmillan Publishers, 1922.

Duverger, Maurice. *Political Parties: Their Organization and Activity in the Modern State*. 3rd ed. New York: John Wiley and Sons, 1964.

Eldersveld, Samuel J. *Political Parties in American Society*. New York: Basic Books, 1985.

Fleishman, Joel L. *The Future of American Political Parties*. Englewood Cliffs, N.J.: Prentice-Hall, 1982.

Hofstadter, Richard. *The Idea of a Party System: The Rise of Legitimate Opposition in the United States, 1780-1840*. Berkeley: University of California Press, 1969.

Ladd, Everett. *American Political Parties*. New York: W. W. Norton, 1970.

La Palombara, Joseph, and M. Weiner. *Political Parties and Political Development*. Princeton, N.J.: Princeton University Press, 1966.

McCormick, Richard P. *The Second American Party System: Party Formulation in the Jacksonian Era*. Chapel Hill: University of North Carolina Press, 1973.

Main, Jackson. *Political Parties Before the Constitution*. Chapel Hill: University of North Carolina Press, 1973.

Merriam, Charles E. *The American Party System: An Introduction to the Study of Political Parties in the United States*. New York: Macmillan, 1969.

Nichols, Roy F. *The Invention of the American Political Parties*. New York: Free Press, 1972.

Ostrogorski, Moisei. *Democracy and the Organization of Political Parties: The United States*. Brooklyn, N.Y.: Haskell Booksellers, 1970.

Robinson, Edgar E. *The Evolution of American Political Parties*. 1924. Reprint. New York: Harcourt, Brace, Jovanovich, 1971.

Roseboom, Eugene H. *A History of Presidential Elections: From George Washington to Jimmy Carter*. New York: Macmillan, 1979.

Rosenstone, Steven J., Roy L. Behr and Edward H. Lazarus. *Third Parties in America: Citizen Response to Major Party Failure*. Princeton, N.J.: Princeton University Press, 1984.

Rossiter, Clinton. *Parties and Politics in America*. Ithaca, N.Y.: Cornell University Press, 1960.

Schattschneider, E. E. *Party Government*. 1942. Reprint. Westport, Conn.: Greenwood Press, 1977.

Schlesinger, Arthur M. Jr. *History of U.S. Political Parties*. 4 vols. 1973. Reprint. New York: Chelsea House, 1981.

Smallwood, Frank. *The Other Candidates: Third Parties in Presidential Elections*. Hanover, N.H.: University Press of New England, 1983.

Van Buren, Martin. *Inquiry into the Origin and Course of Political Parties in the United States*. New York: A. M. Kelley, 1867.

Political Party Nominees, 1831-1984

The following pages contain a comprehensive list of major and minor party nominees for president and vice president since 1831 when the first nominating convention was held by the Anti-Masonic Party.

In many cases, minor parties made only token efforts at a presidential campaign. Often, third party candidates declined to run after being nominated by the convention, or their names appeared on the ballots of only a few states. In some cases the names of minor candidates did not appear on any state ballots and they received only a scattering of write-in votes, if any.

The basic source used to compile the list was Joseph Nathan Kane's *Facts About the Presidents,* 3rd edition, The H. W. Wilson Co., New York, 1974. To verify the names appearing in Kane, Congressional Quarterly consulted the following additional sources: Richard M. Scammon's *America at the Polls,* University of Pittsburgh Press, 1965; *America Votes 8* (1968), Congressional Quarter-

ly, 1969; *America Votes 10* (1972), Congressional Quarterly, 1973; *Encyclopedia of American History,* edited by Richard B. Morris, Harper and Row, New York, 1965; *Dictionary of American Biography,* Charles Scribner's Sons, 1928-1936; *Facts on File,* Facts on File Inc., New York 1945-75; *History of U.S. Political Parties,* Vols. I-IV, edited by Arthur M. Schlesinger, Bowker, New York, 1973; *History of American Presidential Elections, 1789-1968,* edited by Arthur M. Schlesinger, McGraw Hill, New York, 1971; and *Who Was Who in America,* Vol. I-V (1607-1968), Marquis Who's Who, Chicago. The source for the 1976, 1980 and 1984 candidates was Richard M. Scammon's *America Votes 12* (1977), *America Votes 14* (1981) and *America Votes 16* (1985).

When these sources contained information in conflict with Kane, the conflicting information is included in a footnote. Where a candidate appears in Kane, *but could not be verified in another source,* an asterisk appears beside the candidate's name on the list.

Election of 1832

Democratic Party
President: Andrew Jackson, Tennessee
Vice President: Martin Van Buren, New York
National Republican Party
President: Henry Clay, Kentucky
Vice President: John Sergeant, Pennsylvania
Independent Party
President: John Floyd, Virginia
Vice President: Henry Lee, Massachusetts
Anti-Masonic Party
President: William Wirt, Maryland
Vice President: Amos Ellmaker, Pennsylvania

Election of 1836

Democratic Party
President: Martin Van Buren, New York
Vice President: Richard Mentor Johnson, Kentucky
Whig Party
President: William Henry Harrison, Hugh Lawson White, Daniel Webster
Vice President: Francis Granger, John Tyler.

The Whigs nominated regional candidates in 1836 hoping that each candidate would carry his region and deny Democrat Van Buren an electoral vote majority. Webster was the Whig candidate in Massachusetts; Harrison in the rest of New England, the middle Atlantic states and the West; and White in the South.

Granger was the running mate of Harrison and Webster. Tyler was White's running mate.

Election of 1840

Whig Party
President: William Henry Harrison, Ohio
Vice President: John Tyler, Virginia
Democratic Party
President: Martin Van Buren, New York

The Democratic convention adopted a resolution which left the choice of vice presidential candidates to the states. Democratic electors divided their vice presidential votes among incumbent Richard M. Johnson (48 votes), Littleton W. Tazewell (11 votes) and James K. Polk (1 vote).
Liberty Party
President: James Gillespie Birney, New York
Vice President: Thomas Earle, Pennsylvania

Election of 1844

Democratic Party
President: James Knox Polk, Tennessee
Vice President: George Mifflin Dallas, Pennsylvania
Whig Party
President: Henry Clay, Kentucky
Vice President: Theodore Frelinghuysen, New Jersey
Liberty Party
President: James Gillespie Birney, New York
Vice President: Thomas Morris, Ohio
National Democratic
President: John Tyler, Virginia
Vice President: None
Tyler withdrew from the race in favor of the Democrat, Polk.

Election of 1848

Whig Party
President: Zachary Taylor, Louisiana
Vice President: Millard Fillmore, New York
Democratic Party
President: Lewis Cass, Michigan
Vice President: William Orlando Butler, Kentucky
Free Soil Party
President: Martin Van Buren, New York
Vice President: Charles Francis Adams, Massachusetts
Free Soil (Barnburners—Liberty Party)
President: John Parker Hale, New Hampshire
Vice President: Leicester King, Ohio
Later John Parker Hale relinquished the nomination.

National Liberty Party
President: Gerrit Smith, New York
Vice President: Charles C. Foote, Michigan

Election of 1852

Democratic Party
President: Franklin Pierce, New Hampshire
Vice President: William Rufus De Vane King, Alabama

Whig Party
President: Winfield Scott, New Jersey
Vice President: William Alexander Graham, North Carolina

Free Soil
President: John Parker Hale, New Hampshire
Vice President: George Washington Julian, Indiana

Election of 1856

Democratic Party
President: James Buchanan, Pennsylvania
Vice President: John Cabell Breckinridge, Kentucky

Republican Party
President: John Charles Fremont, California
Vice President: William Lewis Dayton, New Jersey

American (Know-Nothing) Party
President: Millard Fillmore, New York
Vice President: Andrew Jackson Donelson, Tennessee

Whig Party (the "Silver Grays")
President: Millard Fillmore, New York
Vice President: Andrew Jackson Donelson, Tennessee

North American Party
President: Nathaniel Prentice Banks, Massachusetts
Vice President: William Freame Johnson, Pennsylvania
Banks and Johnson declined the nominations and gave their support to the Republicans.

Election of 1860

Republican Party
President: Abraham Lincoln, Illinois
Vice President: Hannibal Hamlin, Maine

Democratic Party
President: Stephen Arnold Douglas, Illinois
Vice President: Herschel Vespasian Johnson, Georgia

Southern Democratic Party
President: John Cabell Breckinridge, Kentucky
Vice President: Joseph Lane, Oregon

Constitutional Union Party
President: John Bell, Tennessee
Vice President: Edward Everett, Massacusetts

Election of 1864

Republican Party
President: Abraham Lincoln, Illinois
Vice President: Andrew Johnson, Tennessee

Democratic Party
President: George Brinton McClellan, New York
Vice President: George Hunt Pendleton, Ohio

Independent Republican Party
President: John Charles Fremont, California
Vice President: John Cochrane, New York
Fremont and Cochrane declined and gave their support to the Republican Party nominees

Election of 1868

Republican Party
President: Ulysses Simpson Grant, Illinois
Vice President: Schuyler Colfax, Indiana

Democratic Party
President: Horatio Seymour, New York
Vice President: Francis Preston Blair, Jr., Missouri

Election of 1872

Republican Party
President: Ulysses Simpson Grant, Illinois
Vice President: Henry Wilson, Massachusetts

Liberal Republican Party
President: Horace Greeley, New York
Vice President: Benjamin Gratz Brown, Missouri

Independent Liberal Republican Party (Opposition Party)
President: William Slocum Groesbeck, Ohio
Vice President: Frederick Law Olmsted, New York

Democratic Party
President: Horace Greeley, New York
Vice President: Benjamin Gratz Brown, Missouri

Straight-out Democratic Party
President: Charles O'Conor, New York
Vice President: John Quincy Adams, Massachusetts

Prohibition Party
President: James Black, Pennsylvania
Vice President: John Russell, Michigan

People's Party (Equal Rights Party)
President: Victoria Claflin Woodhull, New York
Vice President: Frederick Douglass

Labor Reform Party
President: David Davis, Illinois
Vice President: Joel Parker, New Jersey

Liberal Republican Party of Colored Men
President: Horace Greeley, New York
Vice President: Benjamin Gratz Brown, Missouri

National Working Men's Party
President: Ulysses Simpson Grant, Illinois
Vice President: Henry Wilson, Massachusetts

Election of 1876

Republican Party
President: Rutherford Birchard Hayes, Ohio
Vice President: William Almon Wheeler, New York

Democratic Party
President: Samuel Jones Tilden, New York
Vice President: Thomas Andrews Hendricks, Indiana

Greenback Party
President: Peter Cooper, New York
Vice President: Samuel Fenton Cary, Ohio

Prohibition Party
President: Green Clay Smith, Kentucky
Vice President: Gideon Tabor Stewart, Ohio

American National Party
President: James B. Walker, Illinois
Vice President: Donald Kirkpatrick, New York*

Election of 1880

Republican Party
President: James Abram Garfield, Ohio
Vice President: Chester Alan Arthur, New York

Democratic Party
President: Winfield Scott Hancock, Pennsylvania
Vice President: William Hayden English, Indiana

Greenback Labor Party
President: James Baird Weaver, Iowa
Vice President: Benjamin J. Chambers, Texas

Prohibition Party
President: Neal Dow, Maine
Vice President: Henry Adams Thompson, Ohio

American Party
President: John Wolcott Phelps, Vermont
Vice President: Samuel Clarke Pomeroy, Kansas*

Election of 1884

Democratic Party
President: Grover Cleveland, New York
Vice President: Thomas Andrews Hendricks, Indiana

Republican Party
President: James Gillespie Blaine, Maine
Vice President: John Alexander Logan, Illinois

Anti-Monopoly Party
President: Benjamin Franklin Butler, Massachusetts
Vice President: Absolom Madden West, Mississippi

Greenback Party
President: Benjamin Franklin Butler, Massachusetts
Vice President: Absolom Madden West, Mississippi

Prohibition Party
President: John Pierce St. John, Kansas
Vice President: William Daniel, Maryland
American Prohibition Party
President: Samuel Clarke Pomeroy, Kansas
Vice President: John A. Conant, Connecticut
Equal Rights Party
President: Belva Ann Bennett Lockwood, District of Columbia
Vice President: Marietta Lizzie Bell Stow, California

Election of 1888

Republican Party
President: Benjamin Harrison, Indiana
Vice President: Levi Parsons Morton, New York
Democratic Party
President: Grover Cleveland, New York
Vice President: Allen Granberry Thurman, Ohio
Prohibition Party
President: Clinton Bowen Fisk, New Jersey
Vice President: John Anderson Brooks, Missouri*
Union Labor Party
President: Alson Jenness Streeter, Illinois
Vice President: Charles E. Cunningham, Arkansas*
United Labor Party
President: Robert Hall Cowdrey, Illinois
Vice President: William H. T. Wakefield, Kansas*
American Party
President: James Langdon Curtis, New York
Vice President: Peter Dinwiddie Wigginton, California*
Equal Rights Party
President: Belva Ann Bennett Lockwood, District of Columbia
Vice President: Alfred Henry Love, Pennsylvania*
Industrial Reform Party
President: Albert E. Redstone, California*
Vice President: John Colvin, Kansas*

Election of 1892

Democratic Party
President; Grover Cleveland, New York
Vice President: Adlai Ewing Stevenson, Illinois
Republican Party
President: Benjamin Harrison, Indiana
Vice President: Whitelaw Reid, New York
People's Party of America
President: James Baird Weaver, Iowa
Vice President: James Gaven Field, Virginia
Prohibition Party
President: John Bidwell, California
Vice President: James Britton Cranfill, Texas
Socialist Labor Party
President: Simon Wing, Massachusetts
Vice President: Charles Horatio Matchett, New York*

Election of 1896

Republican Party
President: William McKinley, Ohio
Vice President: Garret Augustus Hobart, New Jersey
Democratic Party
President: William Jennings Bryan, Nebraska
Vice President: Arthur Sewall, Maine
People's Party (Populist)
President: William Jennings Bryan, Nebraska
Vice President: Thomas Edward Watson, Georgia
National Democratic Party
President: John McAuley Palmer, Illinois
Vice President: Simon Bolivar Buckner, Kentucky
Prohibition Party
President: Joshua Levering, Maryland
Vice President: Hale Johnson, Illinois*
Socialist Labor Party
President: Charles Horatio Matchett, New York
Vice President: Matthew Maguire, New Jersey
National Party
President: Charles Eugene Bentley, Nebraska
Vice President: James Haywood Southgate, North Carolina*

National Silver Party (Bi-Metallic League)
President: William Jennings Bryan, Nebraska
Vice President: Arthur Sewall, Maine

Election of 1900

Republican Party
President: William McKinley, Ohio
Vice President: Theodore Roosevelt, New York
Democratic Party
President: William Jennings Bryan, Nebraska
Vice President: Adlai Ewing Stevenson, Illinois
Prohibition Party
President: John Granville Wooley, Illinois
Vice President: Henry Brewer Metcalf, Rhode Island
Social-Democratic Party
President: Eugene Victor Debs, Indiana
Vice President: Job Harriman, California
People's Party (Populist—Anti-Fusionist faction)
President: Wharton Barker, Pennsylvania
Vice President: Ignatius Donnelly, Minnesota
Socialist Labor Party
President: Joseph Francis Malloney, Massachusetts
Vice President: Valentine Remmel, Pennsylvania
Union Reform Party
President: Seth Hockett Ellis, Ohio
Vice President: Samuel T. Nicholson, Pennsylvania
United Christian Party
President: Jonah Fitz Randolph Leonard, Iowa
Vice President: David H. Martin, Pennsylvania
People's Party (Populist—Fusionist faction)
President: William Jennings Bryan, Nebraska
Vice President: Adlai Ewing Stevenson, Illinois
Silver Republican Party
President: William Jennings Bryan, Nebraska
Vice President: Adlai Ewing Stevenson, Illinois
National Party
President: Donelson Caffery, Louisiana
Vice President: Archibald Murray Howe, Massachusetts*

Election of 1904

Republican Party
President: Theodore Roosevelt, New York
Vice President: Charles Warren Fairbanks, Indiana
Democratic Party
President: Alton Brooks Parker, New York
Vice President: Henry Gassaway Davis, West Virginia
Socialist Party
President: Eugene Victor Debs, Indiana
Vice President: Benjamin Hanford, New York
Prohibition Party
President: Silas Comfort Swallow, Pennsylvania
Vice President: George W. Carroll, Texas
People's Party (Populists)
President: Thomas Edward Watson, Georgia
Vice President: Thomas Henry Tibbles, Nebraska
Socialist Labor Party
President: Charles Hunter Corregan, New York
Vice President: William Wesley Cox, Illinois
Continental Party
President: Austin Holcomb
Vice President: A. King, Missouri

Election of 1908

Republican Party
President: William Howard Taft, Ohio
Vice President: James Schoolcraft Sherman, New York
Democratic Party
President: William Jennings Bryan, Nebraska
Vice President: John Worth Kern, Indiana
Socialist Party
President: Eugene Victor Debs
Vice President: Benjamin Hanford
Prohibition Party
President: Eugene Wilder Chafin, Illinois
Vice President: Aaron Sherman Watkins, Ohio

Independence Party
President: Thomas Louis Hisgen, Massachusetts
Vice President: John Temple Graves, Georgia
People's Party (Populist)
President: Thomas Edward Watson, Georgia
Vice President: Samuel Williams, Indiana
Socialist Labor Party
President: August Gillhaus, New York
Vice President: Donald L. Munro, Virginia
United Christian Party
President: Daniel Braxton Turney, Illinois
Vice President: Lorenzo S. Coffin, Iowa

Election of 1912

Democratic Party
President: Woodrow Wilson, New Jersey
Vice President: Thomas Riley Marshall, Indiana
Progressive Party ("Bull Moose" Party)
President: Theodore Roosevelt, New York
Vice President: Hiram Warren Johnson, California
Republican Party
President: William Howard Taft, Ohio
Vice President: James Schoolcraft Sherman, New York
Sherman died Oct. 30; replaced by Nicholas Murray
Butler, New York
Socialist Party
President: Eugene Victor Debs, Indiana
Vice President: Emil Seidel, Wisconsin
Prohibition Party
President: Eugene Wilder Chafin, Illinois
Vice President: Aaron Sherman Watkins, Ohio
Socialist Labor Party
President: Arthur Elmer Reimer, Massachusetts
Vice President: August Gillhaus, New York [1]

Election of 1916

Democratic Party
President: Woodrow Wilson, New Jersey
Vice President: Thomas Riley Marshall, Indiana
Republican Party
President: Charles Evans Hughes, New York
Vice President: Charles Warren Fairbanks, Indiana
Socialist Party
President: Allan Louis Benson, New York
Vice President: George Ross Kirkpatrick, New Jersey
Prohibition Party
President: James Franklin Hanly, Indiana
Vice President: Ira Landrith, Tennessee
Socialist Labor Party
President: Arthur Elmer Reimer, Massachusetts*
Vice President: Caleb Harrison, Illinois*
Progressive Party
President: Theodore Roosevelt, New York
Vice President: John Milliken Parker, Louisiana

Election of 1920

Republican Party
President: Warren Gamaliel Harding, Ohio
Vice President: Calvin Coolidge, Massachusetts
Democratic Party
President: James Middleton Cox, Ohio
Vice President: Franklin Delano Roosevelt, New York
Socialist Party
President: Eugene Victor Debs, Indiana
Vice President: Seymour Stedman, Illinois
Farmer Labor Party
President: Parley Parker Christensen, Utah
Vice President: Maximilian Sebastian Hayes, Ohio
Prohibition Party
President: Aaron Sherman Watkins, Ohio
Vice President: David Leigh Colvin, New York
Socialist Labor Party
President: William Wesley Cox, Missouri
Vice President: August Gillhaus, New York
Single Tax Party
President: Robert Colvin Macauley, Pennsylvania
Vice President: R. G. Barnum, Ohio

American Party
President: James Edward Ferguson, Texas
Vice President: William J. Hough

Election of 1924

Republican Party
President: Calvin Coolidge, Massachusetts
Vice President: Charles Gates Dawes, Illinois
Democratic Party
President: John William Davis, West Virginia
Vice President: Charles Wayland Bryan, Nebraska
Progressive Party
President: Robert La Follette, Wisconsin
Vice President: Burton Kendall Wheeler, Montana
Prohibition Party
President: Herman Preston Faris, Missouri
Vice President: Marie Caroline Brehm, California
Socialist Labor Party
President: Frank T. Johns, Oregon
Vice President: Verne L. Reynolds, New York
Socialist Party
President: Robert La Follette, New York
Vice President: Burton Kendall Wheeler, Montana
Workers Party (Communist Party)
President: William Zebulon Foster, Illinois
Vice President: Benjamin Gitlow, New York
American Party
President: Gilbert Owen Nations, District of Columbia
Vice President: Charles Hiram Randall, California [2]
Commonwealth Land Party
President: William J. Wallace, New Jersey
Vice President: John Cromwell Lincoln, Ohio
Farmer Labor Party
President: Duncan McDonald, Illinois*
Vice President: William Bouck, Washington*
Greenback Party
President: John Zahnd, Indiana*
Vice President: Roy M. Harrop, Nebraska*

Election of 1928

Republican Party
President: Herbert Clark Hoover, California
Vice President: Charles Curtis, Kansas
Democratic Party
President: Alfred Emanuel Smith, New York
Vice President: Joseph Taylor Robinson, Arkansas
Socialist Party
President: Norman Mattoon Thomas, New York
Vice President: James Hudson Maurer, Pennsylvania
Workers Party (Communist Party)
President: William Zebulon Foster, Illinois
Vice President: Benjamin Gitlow, New York
Socialist Labor Party
President: Verne L. Reynolds, Michigan
Vice President: Jeremiah D. Crowley, New York
Prohibition Party
President: William Frederick Varney, New York
Vice President: James Arthur Edgerton, Virginia
Farmer Labor Party
President: Frank Elbridge Webb, California
Vice President: Will Vereen, Georgia [3]
Greenback Party
President: John Zahnd, Indiana*
Vice President: Wesley Henry Bennington, Ohio*

Election of 1932

Democratic Party
President: Franklin Delano Roosevelt, New York
Vice President: John Nance Garner, Texas
Republican Party
President: Herbert Clark Hoover, California
Vice President: Charles Curtis, Kansas
Socialist Party
President: Norman Mattoon Thomas, New York
Vice President: James Hudson Maurer, Pennsylvania

Communist Party
President: William Zebulon Foster, Illinois
Vice President: James William Ford, New York
Prohibition Party
President: William David Upshaw, Georgia
Vice President: Frank Stewart Regan, Illinois
Liberty Party
President: William Hope Harvey, Arkansas
Vice President: Frank B. Hemenway, Washington
Socialist Labor Party
President: Verne L. Reynolds, New York
Vice President: John W. Aiken, Massachusetts
Farmer Labor Party
President: Jacob Sechler Coxey, Ohio
Vice President: Julius J. Reiter, Minnesota
Jobless Party
President: James Renshaw Cox, Pennsylvania
Vice President: V. C. Tisdal, Oklahoma
National Party
President: Seymour E. Allen, Massachusetts

Election of 1936
Democratic Party
President: Franklin Delano Roosevelt, New York
Vice President: John Nance Garner, Texas
Republican Party
President: Alfred Mossman Landon, Kansas
Vice President: Frank Knox, Illinois
Union Party
President: William Lemke, North Dakota
Vice President: Thomas Charles O'Brien, Massachusetts
Socialist Party
President: Norman Mattoon Thomas, New York
Vice President: George A. Nelson, Wisconsin
Communist Party
President: Earl Russell Browder, Kansas
Vice President: James William Ford, New York
Prohibition Party
President: David Leigh Colvin, New York
Vice President: Alvin York, Tennessee
Socialist Labor Party
President: John W. Aikin, Massachusetts
Vice President: Emil F. Teichert, New York
National Greenback Party
President: John Zahnd, Indiana*
Vice President: Florence Garvin, Rhode Island*

Election of 1940
Democratic Party
President: Franklin Delano Roosevelt, New York
Vice President: Henry Agard Wallace, Iowa
Republican Party
President: Wendell Lewis Willkie, New York
Vice President: Charles Linza McNary, Oregon
Socialist Party
President: Norman Mattoon Thomas, New York
Vice President: Maynard C. Krueger, Illinois
Prohibition Party
President: Roger Ward Babson, Massachusetts
Vice President: Edgar V. Moorman, Illinois
Communist Party (Workers Party)
President: Earl Russell Browder, Kansas
Vice President: James William Ford, New York
Socialist Labor Party
President: John W. Aiken, Massachusetts
Vice President: Aaron M. Orange, New York
Greenback Party
President: John Zahnd, Indiana*
Vice President: James Elmer Yates, Arizona*

Election of 1944
Democratic Party
President: Franklin Delano Roosevelt, New York
Vice President: Harry S Truman, Missouri
Republican Party
President: Thomas Edmund Dewey, New York

Vice President: John William Bricker, Ohio
Socialist Party
President: Norman Mattoon Thomas, New York
Vice President: Darlington Hoopes, Pennsylvania
Prohibition Party
President: Claude A. Watson, California
Vice President: Andrew Johnson, Kentucky
Socialist Labor Party
President: Edward A. Teichert, Pennsylvania
Vice President: Arla A. Albaugh, Ohio
America First Party
President: Gerald Lyman Kenneth Smith, Michigan
Vice President: Henry A. Romer, Ohio

Election of 1948
Democratic Party
President: Harry S Truman, Missouri
Vice President: Alben William Barkley, Kentucky
Republican Party
President: Thomas Edmund Dewey, New York
Vice President: Earl Warren, California
States' Rights Democratic Party
President: James Strom Thurmond, South Carolina
Vice President: Fielding Lewis Wright, Mississippi
Progressive Party
President: Henry Agard Wallace, Iowa
Vice President: Glen Hearst Taylor, Idaho
Socialist Party
President: Norman Mattoon Thomas, New York
Vice President: Tucker Powell Smith, Michigan
Prohibition Party
President: Claude A. Watson, California
Vice President: Dale Learn, Pennsylvania
Socialist Labor Party
President: Edward A. Teichert, Pennsylvania
Vice President: Stephen Emery, New York
Socialist Workers Party
President: Farrell Dobbs, New York
Vice President: Grace Carlson, Minnesota
Christian Nationalist Party
President: Gerald Lyman Kenneth Smith, Missouri
Vice President: Henry A. Romer, Ohio
Greenback Party
President: John G. Scott, New York
Vice President: Granville B. Leeke, Indiana*
Vegetarian Party
President: John Maxwell, Illinois
Vice President: Symon Gould, New York*

Election of 1952
Republican Party
President: Dwight David Eisenhower, New York
Vice President: Richard Milhous Nixon, California
Democratic Party
President: Adlai Ewing Stevenson, Illinois
Vice President: John Jackson Sparkman, Alabama
Progressive Party
President: Vincent William Hallinan, California
Vice President: Charlotta A. Bass, New York
Prohibition Party
President: Stuart Hamblen, California
Vice President: Enoch Arden Holtwick, Illinois
Socialist Labor Party
President: Eric Hass, New York
Vice President: Stephen Emery, New York
Socialist Party
President: Darlington Hoopes, Pennsylvania
Vice President: Samuel Herman Friedman, New York
Socialist Workers Party
President: Farrell Dobbs, New York
Vice President: Myra Tanner Weiss, New York
America First Party
President: Douglas MacArthur, Wisconsin
Vice President: Harry Flood Byrd, Virginia

American Labor Party
President: Vincent William Hallinan, California
Vice President: Charlotta A. Bass, New York
American Vegetarian Party
President: Daniel J. Murphy, California
Vice President: Symon Gould, New York*
Church of God Party
President: Homer Aubrey Tomlinson, New York
Vice President: Willie Isaac Bass, North Carolina*
Constitution Party
President: Douglas MacArthur, Wisconsin
Vice President: Harry Flood Byrd, Virginia
Greenback Party
President: Frederick C. Proehl, Washington
Vice President: Edward J. Bedell, Indiana
Poor Man's Party
President: Henry B. Krajewski, New Jersey
Vice President: Frank Jenkins, New Jersey

Election of 1956

Republican Party
President: Dwight David Eisenhower, Pennsylvania
Vice President: Richard Milhous Nixon, California
Democratic Party
President: Adlai Ewing Stevenson, Illinois
Vice President: Estes Kefauver, Tennessee
States' Rights Party
President: Thomas Coleman Andrews, Virginia
Vice President: Thomas Harold Werdel, California
Ticket also favored by Constitution Party.
Prohibition Party
President: Enoch Arden Holtwick, Illinois
Vice President: Edward M. Cooper, California
Socialist Labor Party
President: Eric Hass, New York
Vice President: Georgia Cozzini, Wisconsin
Texas Constitution Party
President: William Ezra Jenner, Indiana*
Vice President: Joseph Bracken Lee, Utah*
Socialist Workers Party
President: Farrell Dobbs, New York
Vice President: Myra Tanner Weiss, New York
American Third Party
President: Henry Krajewski, New Jersey
Vice President: Ann Marie Yezo, New Jersey
Socialist Party
President: Darlington Hoopes, Pennsylvania
Vice President: Samuel Herman Friedman, New York
Pioneer Party
President: William Langer, North Dakota*
Vice President: Burr McCloskey, Illinois*
American Vegetarian Party
President: Herbert M. Shelton, California*
Vice President: Symon Gould, New York*
Greenback Party
President: Frederick C. Proehl, Washington
Vice President: Edward Kirby Meador, Massachusetts*
States' Rights Party of Kentucky
President: Harry Flood Byrd, Virginia
Vice President: William Ezra Jenner, Indiana
South Carolinians for Independent Electors
President: Harry Flood Byrd, Virginia
Christian National Party
President: Gerald Lyman Kenneth Smith
Vice President: Charles I. Robertson

Election of 1960

Democratic Party
President: John Fitzgerald Kennedy, Massachusetts
Vice President: Lyndon Baines Johnson, Texas

Republican Party
President: Richard Milhous Nixon, California
Vice President: Henry Cabot Lodge, Massachusetts
National States' Rights Party
President: Orval Eugene Faubus, Arkansas
Vice President: John Geraerdt Crommelin, Alabama
Socialist Labor Party
President: Eric Hass, New York
Vice President: Georgia Cozzini, Wisconsin
Prohibition Party
President: Rutherford Losey Decker, Missouri
Vice President: Earle Harold Munn, Michigan
Socialist Workers Party
President: Farrell Dobbs, New York
Vice President: Myra Tanner Weiss, New York
Conservative Party of New Jersey
President: Joseph Bracken Lee, Utah
Vice President: Kent H. Courtney, Louisiana
Conservative Party of Virginia
President: C. Benton Coiner, Virginia
Vice President: Edward M. Silverman, Virginia
Constitution Party (Texas)
President: Charles Loten Sullivan, Mississippi
Vice President: Merritt B. Curtis, District of Columbia
Constitution Party (Washington)
President: Merritt B. Curtis, District of Columbia
Vice President: B. N. Miller
Greenback Party
President: Whitney Hart Slocomb, California*
Vice President: Edward Kirby Meador, Massachusetts*
Independent Afro-American Party
President: Clennon King, Georgia
Vice President: Reginald Carter
Tax Cut Party (America First Party; American Party)
President: Lar Daly, Illinois
Vice President: Merritt Barton Curtis, District of Columbia
Theocratic Party
President: Homer Aubrey Tomlinson, New York
Vice President: Raymond L. Teague, Alaska*
Vegetarian Party
President: Symon Gould, New York
Vice President: Christopher Gian-Cursio, Florida

Election of 1964

Democratic Party
President: Lyndon Baines Johnson, Texas
Vice President: Hubert Horatio Humphrey, Minnesota
Republican Party
President: Barry Morris Goldwater, Arizona
Vice President: William Edward Miller, New York
Socialist Labor Party
President: Eric Hass, New York
Vice President: Henning A. Blomen, Massachusetts
Prohibition Party
President: Earle Harold Munn, Michigan
Vice President: Mark Shaw, Massachusetts
Socialist Workers Party
President: Clifton DeBerry, New York
Vice President: Edward Shaw, New York
National States' Rights Party
President: John Kasper, Tennessee
Vice President: J. B. Stoner, Georgia
Constitution Party
President: Joseph B. Lightburn, West Virginia
Vice President: Theodore C. Billings, Colorado
Independent States' Rights Party
President: Thomas Coleman Andrews, Virginia
Vice President: Thomas H. Werdel, California*
Theocratic Party
President: Homer Aubrey Tomlinson, New York
Vice President: William R. Rogers, Missouri*
Universal Party
President: Kirby James Hensley, California
Vice President: John O. Hopkins, Iowa

Election of 1968

Republican Party
President: Richard Milhous Nixon, New York
Vice President Spiro Theodore Agnew, Maryland

Democratic Party
President: Hubert Horatio Humphrey, Minnesota
Vice President: Edmund Sixtus Muskie, Maine

American Independent Party
President: George Corley Wallace, Alabama
Vice President: Curtis Emerson LeMay, Ohio
LeMay replaced S. Marvin Griffin, who originally had been selected.

Peace and Freedom Party
President: Eldridge Cleaver
Vice President: Judith Mage, New York

Socialist Labor Party
President: Henning A. Blomen, Massachusetts
Vice President: George Sam Taylor, Pennsylvania

Socialist Workers Party
President: Fred Halstead, New York
Vice President: Paul Boutelle, New Jersey

Prohibition Party
President: Earle Harold Munn, Sr., Michigan
Vice President: Rolland E. Fisher, Kansas

Communist Party
President: Charlene Mitchell, California
Vice President: Michael Zagarell, New York

Constitution Party
President: Richard K. Troxell, Texas
Vice President: Merle Thayer, Iowa

Freedom and Peace Party
President: Dick Gregory (Richard Claxton Gregory), Illinois

Patriotic Party
President: George Corley Wallace, Alabama
Vice President: William Penn Patrick, California

Theocratic Party
President: William R. Rogers, Missouri

Universal Party
President: Kirby James Hensley, California
Vice President: Roscoe B. MacKenna

Election of 1972

Republican Party
President: Richard Milhous Nixon, California
Vice President: Spiro Theodore Agnew, Maryland

Democratic Party
President: George Stanley McGovern, South Dakota
Vice President: Thomas Francis Eagleton, Missouri
Eagleton resigned and was replaced on August 8, 1972, by Robert Sargent Shriver, Maryland, selected by the Democratic National Committee.

American Independent Party
President: John George Schmitz, California
Vice President: Thomas Jefferson Anderson, Tennessee

Socialist Workers Party
President: Louis Fisher, Illinois
Vice President: Genevieve Gunderson, Minnesota

Socialist Labor Party
President: Linda Jenness, Georgia
Vice President: Andrew Pulley, Illinois

Communist Party
President: Gus Hall, New York
Vice President: Jarvis Tyner

Prohibition Party
President: Earle Harold Munn, Sr., Michigan
Vice President: Marshall Uncapher

Libertarian Party
President: John Hospers, California
Vice President: Theodora Nathan, Oregon

People's Party
President: Benjamin McLane Spock
Vice President: Julius Hobson, District of Columbia

America First Party
President: John V. Mahalchik
Vice President: Irving Homer

Universal Party
President: Gabriel Green
Vice President: Daniel Fry

Election of 1976

Democratic Party
President: Jimmy Carter, Georgia
Vice President: Walter F. Mondale, Minnesota

Republican Party
President: Gerald R. Ford, Michigan
Vice President: Robert Dole, Kansas

Independent Candidate
President: Eugene J. McCarthy, Minnesota
Vice President: none[4]

Libertarian Party
President: Roger MacBride, Virginia
Vice President: David P. Bergland, California

American Independent Party
President: Lester Maddox, Georgia
Vice President: William Dyke, Wisconsin

American Party
President: Thomas J. Anderson, Tennessee
Vice President: Rufus Shackleford, Florida

Socialist Workers Party
President: Peter Camejo, California
Vice President: Willie Mae Reid, California

Communist Party
President: Gus Hall, New York
Vice President: Jarvis Tyner, New York

People's Party
President: Margaret Wright, California
Vice President: Benjamin Spock, New York

U.S. Labor Party
President: Lyndon H. LaRouche, New York
Vice President: R. W. Evans, Michigan

Prohibition Party
President: Benjamin C. Bubar, Maine
Vice President: Earl F. Dodge, Colorado

Socialist Labor Party
President: Jules Levin, New Jersey
Vice President: Constance Blomen, Massachusetts

Socialist Party
President: Frank P. Zeidler, Wisconsin
Vice President: J. Quinn Brisben, Illinois

Restoration Party
President: Ernest L. Miller
Vice President: Roy N. Eddy

United American Party
President: Frank Taylor
Vice President: Henry Swan

Election of 1980[5]

Republican Party
President: Ronald Reagan, California
Vice President: George Bush, Texas

Democratic Party
President: Jimmy Carter, Georgia
Vice President: Walter F. Mondale, Minnesota

National Unity Campaign
President: John B. Anderson, Illinois
Vice President: Patrick J. Lucey, Wisconsin

Libertarian Party
President: Edward E. Clark, California
Vice President: David Koch, New York

Citizens Party
President: Barry Commoner, New York
Vice President: LaDonna Harris, New Mexico

Communist Party
President: Gus Hall, New York
Vice President: Angela Davis, California

American Independent Party
President: John R. Rarick, Louisiana
Vice President: Eileen M. Shearer, California

Socialist Workers Party
President: Andrew Pulley, Illinois
Vice President: Matilde Zimmermann

President: Clifton DeBerry, California
Vice President: Matilde Zimmermann

President: Richard Congress, Ohio
Vice President: Matilde Zimmermann

Right to Life Party
President: Ellen McCormack, New York
Vice President: Carroll Driscoll, New Jersey

Peace and Freedom Party
President: Maureen Smith, California
Vice President: Elizabeth Barron

Workers World Party
President: Deirdre Griswold, New Jersey
Vice President: Larry Holmes, New York

Statesman Party
President: Benjamin 'C. Bubar, Maine
Vice President: Earl F. Dodge, Colorado

Socialist Party
President: David McReynolds, New York
Vice President: Diane Drufenbrock, Wisconsin

American Party
President: Percy L. Greaves, New York
Vice President: Frank L. Varnum, California

President: Frank W. Shelton, Utah
Vice President: George E. Jackson

Middle Class Party
President: Kurt Lynen, New Jersey
Vice President: Harry Kieve, New Jersey

Down With Lawyers Party
President: Bill Gahres, New Jersey
Vice President: J. F. Loghlin, New Jersey

Independent Party
President: Martin E. Wendelken
(no vice presidential candidate)

Natural Peoples Party
President: Harley McLain, North Dakota
Vice President: Jewelie Goeller, North Dakota

Election of 1984[6]

Republican Party
President: Ronald Reagan, California
Vice President: George Bush, Texas

Democratic Party
President: Walter F. Mondale, Minnesota
Vice President: Geraldine A. Ferraro, New York

Libertarian Party
President: David Bergland, California
Vice President: Jim Lewis, Connecticut

Independent Party
President: Lyndon H. LaRouche Jr., Virginia
Vice President: Billy Davis, Mississippi

Citizens Party
President: Sonia Johnson, Virginia
Vice President: Richard Walton, Rhode Island

Populist Party
President: Bob Richards, Texas
Vice President: Maureen Kennedy Salaman, California

Independent Alliance Party
President: Dennis L. Serrette, New Jersey
Vice President: Nancy Ross, New York

Communist Party
President: Gus Hall, New York
Vice President: Angela Davis, California

Socialist Workers Party
President: Mel Mason, California
Vice President: Andrea Gonzalez, New York

Workers World Party
President: Larry Holmes, New York
Vice President: Gloria La Riva, California

President: Gavrielle Holmes, New York
Vice President: Milton Vera

American Party
President: Delmar Davis, Tennessee
Vice President: Traves Brownlee, Delaware

Workers League Party
    President: Ed Winn, New York
    Vice Presidents: Jean T. Brust, Helen Halyard, Edward Bergonzi

Prohibition Party
    President: Earl F. Dodge, Colorado
    Vice President: Warren C. Martin, Kansas

Candidates appeared in Kane's Facts About the Presidents *but could not be verified in another source.*

1. 1912: Schlesinger's History of Presidential Elections *lists the Socialist Labor Party vice presidential candidates as Francis. No first name is given for Francis.*
2. 1924: Scammon's America at the Polls *lists the American Party vice presidential candidate as Leander L. Pickett.*
3. 1928: America at the Polls *lists the Farmer Labor Party vice presidential candidate as L. R. Tillman.*
4. 1976: McCarthy, who ran as an independent with no party designation, had no national running mate, favoring the elimination of the office. But as various state lawsrequired a running mate, he had different ones in different states, amounting to nearly two dozen, all political unknowns.

5. 1980: In several cases vice presidential nominees were different from those listed for most states, and the Socialist Workers and American Party nominees for president varied from state to state. For example, because Pulley, the major standard bearer for the Socialist Workers Party was only 29 years old, his name was not allowed on the ballot on some states (the Constitution requires presidential candidates to be at least 35 years old). Hence, the party ran other candidates in those states. In a number of states candidates appeared on the ballot with variants of the party designations listed, without any party designation, or with entirely different party names.
6. 1984: Both Larry Holmes and Gavrielle Holmes were standard bearers of the Workers World Party. Of the two, Larry Holmes was listed on more state ballots. Milton Vera was Gavrielle Holmes' vice presidential running mate in Ohio and Rhode Island. The Workers League party had three vice presidential running mates: Jean T. Brust in Illinois; Helen Halyard in Michigan, New Jersey and Pennsylvania; and Edward Bergonzi in Minnesota and Ohio.

Presidential Elections

"The Republican National Convention in Session in the Auditorium Building, Chicago." *Harper's,* June 30, 1888.

Smithsonian Institution Photo No. 71828

Presidents and Vice Presidents of the United States

President and Political Party	Born	Died	Age at inauguration	Native of—	Elected from—	Term of Service	Vice President
George Washington (F)*	1732	1799	57	Va.	Va.	April 30, 1789-March 4, 1793	John Adams
George Washington (F)			61			March 4, 1793-March 4, 1797	John Adams
John Adams (F)	1735	1826	61	Mass.	Mass.	March 4, 1797-March 4, 1801	Thomas Jefferson
Thomas Jefferson (D-R)	1743	1826	57	Va.	Va.	March 4, 1801-March 4, 1805	Aaron Burr
Thomas Jefferson (D-R)			61			March 4, 1805-March 4, 1809	George Clinton
James Madison (D-R)	1751	1836	57	Va.	Va.	March 4, 1809-March 4, 1813	George Clinton
James Madison (D-R)			61			March 4, 1813-March 4, 1817	Elbridge Gerry
James Monroe (D-R)	1758	1831	58	Va.	Va.	March 4, 1817-March 4, 1821	Daniel D. Tompkins
James Monroe (D-R)			62			March 4, 1821-March 4, 1825	Daniel D. Tompkins
John Q. Adams (N-R)	1767	1848	57	Mass.	Mass.	March 4, 1825-March 4, 1829	John C. Calhoun
Andrew Jackson (D)	1767	1845	61	S.C.	Tenn.	March 4, 1829-March 4, 1833	John C. Calhoun
Andrew Jackson (D)			65			March 4, 1833-March 4, 1837	Martin Van Buren
Martin Van Buren (D)	1782	1862	54	N.Y.	N.Y.	March 4, 1837-March 4, 1841	Richard M. Johnson
W. H. Harrison (W)	1773	1841	68	Va.	Ohio	March 4, 1841-April 4, 1841	John Tyler
John Tyler (W)	1790	1862	51	Va.	Va.	April 6, 1841-March 4, 1845	
James K. Polk (D)	1795	1849	49	N.C.	Tenn.	March 4, 1845-March 4, 1849	George M. Dallas
Zachary Taylor (W)	1784	1850	64	Va.	La.	March 4, 1849-July 9, 1850	Millard Fillmore
Millard Fillmore (W)	1800	1874	50	N.Y.	N.Y.	July 10, 1850-March 4, 1853	
Franklin Pierce (D)	1804	1869	48	N.H.	N.H.	March 4, 1853-March 4, 1857	William R. King
James Buchanan (D)	1791	1868	65	Pa.	Pa.	March 4, 1857-March 4, 1861	John C. Breckinridge
Abraham Lincoln (R)	1809	1865	52	Ky.	Ill.	March 4, 1861-March 4, 1865	Hannibal Hamlin
Abraham Lincoln (R)			56			March 4, 1865-April 15, 1865	Andrew Johnson
Andrew Johnson (R)	1808	1875	56	N.C.	Tenn.	April 15, 1865-March 4, 1869	
Ulysses S. Grant (R)	1822	1885	46	Ohio	Ill.	March 4, 1869-March 4, 1873	Schuyler Colfax
Ulysses S. Grant (R)			50			March 4, 1873-March 4, 1877	Henry Wilson
Rutherford B. Hayes (R)	1822	1893	54	Ohio	Ohio	March 4, 1877-March 4, 1881	William A. Wheeler
James A. Garfield (R)	1831	1881	49	Ohio	Ohio	March 4, 1881-Sept. 19, 1881	Chester A. Arthur
Chester A. Arthur (R)	1830	1886	50	Vt.	N.Y.	Sept. 20, 1881-March 4, 1885	
Grover Cleveland (D)	1837	1908	47	N.J.	N.Y.	March 4, 1885-March 4, 1889	Thomas A. Hendricks
Benjamin Harrison (R)	1833	1901	55	Ohio	Ind.	March 4, 1889-March 4, 1893	Levi P. Morton
Grover Cleveland (D)	1837	1908	55			March 4, 1893-March 4, 1897	Adlai E. Stevenson
William McKinley (R)	1843	1901	54	Ohio	Ohio	March 4, 1897-March 4, 1901	Garret A. Hobart
William McKinley (R)			58			March 4, 1901-Sept. 14, 1901	Theodore Roosevelt
Theodore Roosevelt (R)	1858	1919	42	N.Y.	N.Y.	Sept. 14, 1901-March 4, 1905	
Theodore Roosevelt (R)			46			March 4, 1905-March 4, 1909	Charles W. Fairbanks
William H. Taft (R)	1857	1930	51	Ohio	Ohio	March 4, 1909-March 4, 1913	James S. Sherman
Woodrow Wilson (D)	1856	1924	56	Va.	N.J.	March 4, 1913-March 4, 1917	Thomas R. Marshall
Woodrow Wilson (D)			60			March 4, 1917-March 4, 1921	Thomas R. Marshall
Warren G. Harding (R)	1865	1923	55	Ohio	Ohio	March 4, 1921-Aug. 2, 1923	Calvin Coolidge
Calvin Coolidge (R)	1872	1933	51	Vt.	Mass.	Aug. 3, 1923-March 4, 1925	
Calvin Coolidge (R)			52			March 4, 1925-March 4, 1929	Charles G. Dawes
Herbert Hoover (R)	1874	1964	54	Iowa	Calif.	March 4, 1929-March 4, 1933	Charles Curtis
Franklin D. Roosevelt (D)	1882	1945	51	N.Y.	N.Y.	March 4, 1933-Jan. 20, 1937	John N. Garner
Franklin D. Roosevelt (D)			55			Jan. 20, 1937-Jan. 20, 1941	John N. Garner
Franklin D. Roosevelt (D)			59			Jan. 20, 1941-Jan. 20, 1945	Henry A. Wallace
Franklin D. Roosevelt (D)			63			Jan. 20, 1945-April 12, 1945	Harry S Truman
Harry S Truman (D)	1884	1972	60	Mo.	Mo.	April 12, 1945-Jan. 20, 1949	
Harry S Truman (D)			64			Jan. 20, 1949-Jan. 20, 1953	Alben W. Barkley
Dwight D. Eisenhower (R)	1890	1969	62	Texas	N.Y.	Jan. 20, 1953-Jan. 20, 1957	Richard M. Nixon
Dwight D. Eisenhower (R)			66		Pa.	Jan. 20, 1957-Jan. 20, 1961	Richard M. Nixon
John F. Kennedy (D)	1917	1963	43	Mass.	Mass.	Jan. 20, 1961-Nov. 22, 1963	Lyndon B. Johnson
Lyndon B. Johnson (D)	1908	1973	55	Texas	Texas	Nov. 22, 1963-Jan. 20, 1965	
Lyndon B. Johnson (D)			56			Jan. 20, 1965-Jan. 20, 1969	Hubert H. Humphrey
Richard M. Nixon (R)	1913		56	Calif.	N.Y.	Jan. 20, 1969-Jan. 20, 1973	Spiro T. Agnew
Richard M. Nixon (R)			60		Calif.	Jan. 20, 1973-Aug. 9, 1974	Spiro T. Agnew, Gerald R. Ford
Gerald R. Ford (R)			61	Neb.	Mich.	Aug. 9, 1974-Jan. 20, 1977	Nelson A. Rockerfeller
Jimmy Carter (D)			52	Ga.	Ga.	Jan. 20, 1977-Jan. 20, 1981	Walter F. Mondale
Ronald Reagan (R)			69	Ill.	Calif.	Jan. 20, 1981-Jan. 20, 1985	George Bush
Ronald Reagan (R)			73			Jan. 20, 1985-	George Bush

*Key to abbreviations: (D) Democrat, (D-R) Democrat-Republican, (F) Federalist, (N-R) National Republican, (R) Republican, (W) Whig

The Electoral College

For almost two centuries, Americans have been electing their presidents through the Electoral College. Conceived by the Founding Fathers as a compromise between electing presidents by Congress or by direct popular vote, the system has continued to function even while the United States has undergone radical transformation from an agricultural seaboard nation to a world power.

Under the Electoral College system, each state is entitled to electoral votes equal in number to its congressional delegation — that is, the number of representatives from the state, plus two for the state's two senators. Whichever party receives a plurality of the popular vote in a state usually wins that state's electoral votes. However, there have been numerous exceptions to that rule, including choosing of electors by district, statewide votes for each individual elector and selection of electors by state legislatures.

Constitutional Background

The method of selecting a president was the subject of long debate at the Constitutional Convention of 1787. Several plans were proposed and rejected before a compromise solution, which was modified only slightly in later years, was adopted (Article II, Section I, Clause 2).

Facing the convention when it convened May 25 was the question of whether the chief executive should be chosen by direct popular election, by the Congress, by state legislatures or by intermediate electors. Direct election was opposed, because it was felt generally that the people lacked sufficient knowledge of the character and qualifications of possible candidates to make an intelligent choice. Many delegates also feared that the people of the various states would be unlikely to agree on a single person, usually casting their votes for favorite-son candidates well known to them.

The possibility of giving Congress the power to choose the president also received consideration. However, this plan was rejected, largely because of fear that it would jeopardize the principle of executive independence. Similarly, a plan favored by many delegates, to let state legislatures choose the president, was turned down because it was feared that the president might feel so indebted to the states as to allow them to encroach on federal authority.

Unable to agree on a plan, the convention on Aug. 31 appointed a "Committee of 11" to propose a solution to the problem. The committee on Sept. 4 suggested a compromise under which each state would appoint presidential electors equal to the total number of its representatives and senators. The electors, chosen in a manner set forth by each state legislature, would meet in their own states and each cast votes for two persons. The votes would be counted in Congress, with the candidate receiving a majority elected president and the second-highest candidate becoming vice president.

No distinction was made between ballots for president and vice president. Moreover, the development of national political parties and the nomination of tickets for president and vice president created further confusion in the electoral system. All the electors of one party tended to cast ballots for their two party nominees. But with no distinction between the presidential and vice presidential nominees, the danger arose of a tie vote between the two. That actually happened in 1800, leading to a change in the original electoral system with ratification of the 12th Amendment in 1804.

The committee's compromise plan constituted a great concession to the less populous states, since they were assured of three votes (two for their two senators and at least one for their representative) however small their populations might be. The plan also left important powers with the states by giving complete discretion to state legislatures to determine the method of choosing electors.

The only part of the committee's plan that aroused serious opposition was a provision giving the Senate the right to decide presidential elections in which no candidate

Sources

Petersen, Svend. *A Statistical History of the American Presidential Elections.* Westport, Conn.: Greenwood Press, 1981.

Schlesinger, Arthur M., Jr., ed. *History of American Presidential Elections.* 4 vols. New York: McGraw-Hill, 1971.

Stanwood, Edward. *History of the Presidency, 1788-1916.* 2 vols. rev. ed. New York: Kelley, 1921.

U.S. Bureau of the Census. *Historical Statistics of the United States, Colonial Times to 1970.* 2 vols. Washington, D.C.: Government Printing Office, 1975.

received a majority of electoral votes. Some delegates feared that the Senate, which already had been given treaty ratification powers and the responsibility to "advise and consent" on all important executive appointments, might become too powerful. Therefore, a counterproposal was made and accepted to let the House decide in instances when the electors failed to give a majority of their votes to a single candidate. The interests of the small states were preserved by giving each state's delegation only one vote in the House on roll calls to elect a president.

The system adopted by the Constitutional Convention was a compromise born out of problems involved in diverse state voting requirements, the slavery problem, big-state vs. small-state rivalries and the complexities of the balance of power among different branches of the government. It also apparently was as close to a direct popular election as the men who wrote the Constitution thought possible and appropriate at the time.

The 12th Amendment

Only once since ratification of the Constitution has an amendment been adopted that substantially altered the method of electing the president. In the 1800 presidential election, the Democratic-Republican electors inadvertently caused a tie in the Electoral College by casting equal numbers of votes for Thomas Jefferson, whom they wished to be elected president, and Aaron Burr, whom they wished to elect vice president. The election was thrown into the House of Representatives, and 36 ballots were required before Jefferson was finally elected president. The 12th Amendment, ratified in 1804, sought to prevent a recurrence of this incident by providing that the electors should vote separately for president and vice president. *(Text, Appendix, p. 1127)*

Other changes in the system evolved over the years. The authors of the Constitution, for example, had intended that each state should choose its most distinguished citizens as electors and that they would deliberate and vote as individuals in electing the president. But as strong political parties began to appear, the electors came to be chosen merely as representatives of the parties; independent voting by electors disappeared almost entirely.

Methods of Choosing Electors

In the early years of the Republic, states chose a variety of methods to select presidential electors. For the first presidential election, in 1789, four states held direct popular elections to choose their electors: Pennsylvania and Maryland (at large) as well as Virginia and Delaware (by district). In five states — Connecticut, Georgia, New Jersey, New York and South Carolina — the state legislatures were to make the choice.

Two states, New Hampshire and Massachusetts, adopted a combination of the legislative and popular methods. New Hampshire held a statewide popular vote for presidential electors with the stipulation that any elector would have to win a majority of the popular vote to be elected; otherwise, the Legislature would choose.

In Massachusetts the arrangement was for the people in each congressional district to vote for the two persons they wanted to be presidential electors. From the two persons in each district having the highest number of votes, the Legislature, by joint ballot of both houses, was to choose one. In addition, the Legislature was to choose two additional electors at large.

In a dispute between the two houses of the state Legislature in New York, that state failed to choose electors. The state Senate insisted on full equality with the Assembly (lower house); that is, the Senate wanted each house to take a separate ballot and to resolve any differences between them by agreement rather than by having one house impose its will on the other. The Assembly, on the other hand, wanted a joint ballot, on which the lower house's larger numbers would prevail, or it was willing to divide the electors with the Senate. The failure to compromise cost the state its vote in the first presidential election.

The 12th and 13th states — North Carolina and Rhode Island — had not ratified the Constitution by the time the electors were chosen, and so they did not participate.

Generally similar arrangements prevailed for the election of 1792. Massachusetts, while continuing the system of choosing electors by district, changed the system somewhat to provide for automatic election of any candidate for elector who received a majority of the popular vote. New Hampshire continued the system of popular election at large, but substituted a popular runoff election in place of legislative choice, if no candidate received a majority of the popular vote.

Besides Massachusetts and New Hampshire, electors were chosen in 1792 by popular vote in Maryland and Pennsylvania (at large) and Virginia and Kentucky (by district). State legislatures chose electors in Connecticut, Delaware, Georgia, New Jersey, New York, North Carolina, Rhode Island, South Carolina and Vermont.

By 1796 several changes had occurred. New Hampshire switched back to legislative choice for those electors who failed to receive a majority of the popular vote. Tennessee entered the Union (1796) with a unique system for choosing presidential electors: the state Legislature appointed three persons in each county, who in turn chose the presidential electors. Massachusetts retained the system used in 1792. Other states chose their electors as follows: popular vote, at large: Georgia, Pennsylvania; popular vote, by district: Kentucky, Maryland, North Carolina, Virginia; state legislature: Connecticut, Delaware, New Jersey, New York, Rhode Island, South Carolina, Vermont.

Political Parties and Electors: 1800

As political parties gained power, manipulation of the system of choosing electors became increasingly widespread. For example, in 1800 Massachusetts switched from popular voting to legislative selection of electors because of recent successes by the Democratic-Republican Party in that state. The Federalists, still in firm control of the Legislature, sought to secure the state's entire electoral vote for its presidential candidate, native son John Adams. New Hampshire did likewise.

The Democratic-Republicans were not innocent of this kind of political maneuver. In Virginia, where that party was in control, the Legislature changed the system for choosing electors from districts to a statewide at-large ballot. That way, the expected statewide Democratic-Republican majority could overcome Federalist control in some districts and garner a unanimous vote for Democratic-Republican presidential candidate Thomas Jefferson.

In Pennsylvania, the two houses of the state Legislature could not agree on legislation providing for popular ballots, the system used in the first three elections, so the Legislature itself chose the electors, dividing them between the parties.

In other changes in 1800, Rhode Island switched to popular election and Georgia reverted to legislative elections. The 16 states thus used the following methods of choosing presidential electors in 1800:

- By popular vote: Kentucky, Maryland, North Carolina (by district); Rhode Island, Virginia (at large).
- By the legislature: Connecticut, Delaware, Georgia, Massachusetts, New Hampshire, New Jersey, New York, Pennsylvania, South Carolina, Tennessee (indirectly, as in 1796), Vermont.

Trend to Winner-Take-All System

For the next third of a century, the states moved slowly but inexorably toward a standard system of choosing presidential electors — the statewide, winner-take-all popular ballot. The development of political parties resulted in the adoption of party slates of electors pledged to vote for the parties' presidential candidates. Each party organization saw a statewide ballot as being in its best interest, with the hope of sweeping in all its electors and preventing the opposition group from capitalizing on local areas of strength (which could result in winning only part of the electoral vote under the districting system).

From 1804 to 1832 there were three basic methods used by the states in choosing presidential electors — popular vote, at large; popular vote, by district; and election by the state legislature. The following list shows the changing methods of choosing presidential electors for each state from 1804 to 1932:

1804

Popular vote, at large: New Hampshire, New Jersey, Ohio, Pennsylvania, Rhode Island, Virginia.

Popular vote, by district: Kentucky, Maryland, Massachusetts, North Carolina, Tennessee.

State legislature: Connecticut, Delaware, Georgia, New York, South Carolina, Vermont.

1808

Popular vote, at large: New Hampshire, New Jersey, Ohio, Pennsylvania, Rhode Island, Virginia.

Popular vote, by district: Kentucky, Maryland, North Carolina, Tennessee.

State legislature: Connecticut, Delaware, Georgia, Massachusetts, New York, South Carolina, Vermont.

1812

Popular vote, at large: New Hampshire, Ohio, Pennsylvania, Rhode Island, Virginia.

Popular vote, by district: Kentucky, Maryland, Massachusetts, Tennessee.

State legislature: Connecticut, Delaware, Georgia, Louisiana, New Jersey, New York, North Carolina, South Carolina, Vermont.

1816

Popular vote, at large: New Hampshire, New Jersey, North Carolina, Ohio, Pennsylvania, Rhode Island, Virginia.

Popular vote, by district: Kentucky, Maryland, Tennessee.

State legislature: Connecticut, Delaware, Georgia, Indiana, Louisiana, Massachusetts, New York, South Carolina, Vermont.

Methods of Selecting Electors: Sources

Information on the methods of selecting presidential electors for the period 1789-1836 appears in several sources, and the sources in a number of instances are in conflict. Among the sources are *Historical Statistics of the United States, Colonial Times to 1970*, prepared by the Bureau of the Census with the cooperation of the Social Science Research Council, Washington, D.C.: Government Printing Office, 1975; Edward Stanwood's *A History of the Presidency, 1788-1916*, 2 vols. rev. ed. New York: Kelley, 1921; Svend Petersen's *A Statistical History of the American Presidential Elections*, Westport, Conn.: Greenwood Press, 1981; and Neil R. Peirce's *The People's President: The Electoral College in American History and the Direct Vote Alternative*, New York: Simon and Schuster, 1968.

Congressional Quarterly used the Census Bureau's *Historical Statistics of the United States* as its basic source.

1820

Popular vote, at large: Connecticut, Mississippi, New Hampshire, New Jersey, North Carolina, Ohio, Pennsylvania, Rhode Island, Virginia.

Popular vote, by district: Illinois, Kentucky, Maine, Maryland, Massachusetts, Tennessee.

State legislature: Alabama, Delaware, Georgia, Indiana, Louisiana, Missouri, New York, South Carolina, Vermont.

1824

Popular vote, at large: Alabama, Connecticut, Indiana, Massachusetts, Mississippi, New Hampshire, New Jersey, North Carolina, Ohio, Pennsylvania, Rhode Island, Virginia.

Popular vote, by district: Illinois, Kentucky, Maine, Maryland, Missouri, Tennessee.

State legislature: Delaware, Georgia, Louisiana, New York, South Carolina, Vermont.

1828

Popular vote, at large: Alabama, Connecticut, Georgia, Illinois, Indiana, Kentucky, Louisiana, Massachusetts, Mississippi, Missouri, New Hampshire, New Jersey, North Carolina, Ohio, Pennsylvania, Rhode Island, Vermont, Virginia.

Popular vote, by district: Maine, Maryland, New York, Tennessee.

State legislature: Delaware, South Carolina.

1832

Popular vote, at large: All states except Maryland and South Carolina.

Popular vote, by district: Maryland.

State legislature: South Carolina.

By 1836 Maryland switched to the system of choosing its electors statewide, by popular vote. This left only South Carolina selecting its electors through the state legislature. The state continued this practice through the election of 1860. Only after the Civil War was popular voting for presidential electors instituted in South Carolina.

Thus, since 1836 the statewide, winner-take-all popular vote for electors has been the almost universal practice. Exceptions include the following:

Massachusetts, 1848. Three slates of electors ran — Whig, Democratic and Free Soil — none of which received a majority of the popular vote. Under the law then in force, the state Legislature was to choose in such a case. It chose the Whig electors.

Florida, 1868. The state Legislature chose the electors.

Colorado, 1876. The state Legislature chose the electors because the state had just been admitted to the Union, had held state elections in August and did not want to go to the trouble and expense of holding a popular vote for the presidential election so soon thereafter.

Michigan, 1892. Republicans had been predominant in the state since the 1850s. However, in 1890 the Democrats managed to gain control of the Legislature and the governorship. They promptly enacted a districting system of choosing presidential electors in the expectation that the Democrats could carry some districts and thus win some electoral votes in 1892. The result confirmed their expectations, with the Republicans winning nine and the Democrats five electoral votes that year. But the Republicans soon regained control of the state and re-enacted the at-large system for the 1896 election.

Maine, 1972. In 1969 the Maine Legislature enacted a district system for choosing presidential electors. Two of the state's four electors were selected on the basis of the statewide vote, while the other two were determined by which party carried each of the state's two congressional districts. The system is still in force.

Historical Anomalies

The complicated and indirect system of electing the president has led to anomalies from time to time. In 1836, for example, the Whigs sought to take advantage of the electoral system by running different presidential candidates in different parts of the country. William Henry Harrison ran in most of New England, the mid-Atlantic states and the Midwest; Daniel Webster ran in Massachusetts; Hugh White of Tennessee ran in the South.

The theory was that each candidate could capture electoral votes for the Whig Party in the region where he was strongest. Then the Whig electors could combine on one candidate or, alternatively, throw the election into the House, whichever seemed to their advantage. However, the scheme did not work because Martin Van Buren, the Democratic nominee, captured a majority of the electoral vote.

Another quirk in the system surfaced in 1872. The Democratic presidential nominee, Horace Greeley, died between the popular vote and the meeting of the presidential electors. Thus the Democratic electors had no party nominee to vote for, and each was left to his own judgment. Forty-two of the 66 Democratic electors chose to vote for the Democratic governor-elect of Indiana, Thomas Hendricks. The rest of the electors split their votes among three other politicians: 18 for B. Gratz Brown of Missouri, the Democratic vice presidential nominee; two for Charles J. Jenkins of Georgia, and one for David Davis of Illinois. Three Georgia electors insisted on casting their votes for Greeley, but Congress refused to count them.

The provision that the Electoral College, not the people directly, is to choose the president has led to three presidents assuming the office even though they ran behind their opponents in the popular vote. In two of these instances — Republican Rutherford B. Hayes in 1876 and Republican Benjamin Harrison in 1888 — the winning candidate carried a number of key states by close margins, while losing other states by wide margins. In the third instance — Democratic-Republican John Quincy Adams in 1824 — the House chose the new president after no candidate had achieved a majority in the Electoral College.

Election by Congress

Under the Constitution, Congress has two key responsibilities relating to the election of the president and vice president. First, it is directed to receive and in joint session count the electoral votes certified by the states. Second, if no candidate has a majority of the electoral vote, the House of Representatives must elect the president and the Senate the vice president.

Although many of the framers of the Constitution apparently thought that most elections would be decided by Congress, the House actually has chosen a president only twice, in 1801 and 1825. But a number of campaigns have been deliberately designed to throw elections into the House, where each state has one vote and a majority of states is needed to elect.

In modern times the formal counting of electoral votes has been largely a ceremonial function, but the congressional role can be decisive when votes are contested. The pre-eminent example is the Hayes-Tilden contest of 1876, when congressional decisions on disputed electoral votes from four states gave the election to Republican Rutherford B. Hayes despite the fact that Democrat Samuel J. Tilden had a majority of the popular vote. *(Tilden-Hayes election, p. 261)*

From the beginning, the constitutional provisions governing the selection of the president have had few defenders, and many efforts at Electoral College reform have been undertaken. Although prospects for reform seemed favorable after the close 1968 presidential election, the 91st Congress (1969-71) did not take final action on a proposed constitutional amendment that would have provided for direct popular election of the president and eliminated the existing provision for contingent election by the House. Reform legislation was reintroduced in the Senate during the 94th Congress (1975-77) and 95th Congress (1977-79).

In addition to its role in electing the president, Congress bears responsibility in the related areas of presidential succession and disability. The 20th Amendment empowers Congress to decide what to do if the president-elect and the vice president-elect both fail to qualify by the date prescribed for commencement of their terms; it also gives Congress authority to settle problems arising from the death of candidates in cases where the election devolves upon Congress. Under the 25th Amendment, Congress has ultimate responsibility for resolving disputes over presidential disability. It also must confirm presidential nominations to fill a vacancy in the vice presidency.

Jefferson-Burr Deadlock

The election of 1800 was the first in which the contingent election procedures of the Constitution were put to the test and the president was elected by the House.

The Federalists, a declining but still potent political force, nominated John Adams for a second term and chose Charles Cotesworth Pinckney as his running mate. A Democratic-Republican congressional caucus chose Vice President Thomas Jefferson for president and Aaron Burr, who had been instrumental in winning the New York Legislature for the Democratic-Republicans earlier in 1800, for vice president.

Presidential Election by the House

The following rules, reprinted from Hinds' Prece-dents of the House of Representatives, were adopted by the House in 1825 for use in deciding the presidential election of 1824. They would provide a precedent for any future House election of a president, although the House could change them.

1. In the event of its appearing, on opening all the certificates, and counting the votes given by the electors of the several States for President, that no person has a majority of the votes of the whole number of electors appointed, the same shall be entered on the Journals of this House.

2. The roll of the House shall then be called by States; and, on its appearing that a Member or Members from two-thirds of the States are present, the House shall immediately proceed, by ballot, to choose a Presi-dent from the persons having the highest numbers, not exceeding three, on the list of those voted for as Presi-dent; and, in case neither of those persons shall receive the votes of a majority of all the states on the first ballot, the House shall continue to ballot for a Presi-dent, without interruption by other business, until a President be chosen.

3. The doors of the Hall shall be closed during the balloting, except against the Members of the Senate, stenographers, and the officers of the House.

4. From the commencement of the balloting until an election is made no proposition to adjourn shall be received, unless on the motion of one State, seconded by another State, and the question shall be decided by States. The same rule shall be observed in regard to any motion to change the usual hour for the meeting of the House.

5. In balloting the following mode shall be ob-served, to wit:

The Representatives of each State shall be arranged and seated together, beginning with the seats at the right hand of the Speaker's chair, with the Members from the State of Maine; thence, proceeding with the Members from the States, in the order the States are usually named for receiving petitions* around the Hall of the House, until all are seated.

A ballot box shall be provided for each State.

The Representatives of each State shall, in the first instance, ballot among themselves, in order to ascertain the vote of their State; and they may, if necessary, appoint tellers of their ballots.

After the vote of each State is ascertained, dupli-cates thereof shall be made out; and in case any one of the persons from whom the choice is to be made shall receive a majority of the votes given, on any one ballot-ing by the Representatives of a State, the name of that person shall be written on each of the duplicates; and in case the votes so given shall be divided so that neither of said persons shall have a majority of the whole num-ber of votes given by such State, on any one ballot-

ing, then the word "divided" shall be written on each duplicate.

After the delegation from each State shall have ascertained the vote of their State, the Clerk shall name the States in the order they are usually named for receiving petitions; and as the name of each is called the Sergeant-at-Arms shall present to the delegation of each two ballot boxes, in each of which shall be deposited, by some Representative of the State, one of the duplicates made as aforesaid of the vote of said State, in the presence and subject to the examination of all the Members from said State then present; and where there is more than one Representative from a State, the duplicates shall not both be deposited by the same person.

When the votes of the States are thus all taken in, the Sergeant-at-Arms shall carry one of said ballot boxes to one table and the other to a separate and distinct table.

One person from each State represented in the bal-loting shall be appointed by the Representatives to tell off said ballots; but, in case the Representatives fail to appoint a teller, the Speaker shall appoint.

The said tellers shall divide themselves into two sets, as nearly equal in number as can be, and one of the said sets of tellers shall proceed to count the votes in one of said boxes, and the other set the votes in the other box.

When the votes are counted by the different sets of tellers, the result shall be reported to the House; and if the reports agree, the same shall be accepted as the true votes of the States; but if the reports disagree, the States shall proceed, in the same manner as before, to a new ballot.

6. All questions arising after the balloting commences, requiring the decision of the House, which shall be decided by the House, voting per capita, to be incidental to the power of choosing a President, shall be decided by States without debate; and in case of an equal division of the votes of States, the question shall be lost.

7. When either of the persons from whom the choice is to be made shall have received a majority of all the States, the Speaker shall declare the same, and that that person is elected President of the United States.

8. The result shall be immediately communicated to the Senate by message, and a committee of three persons shall be appointed to inform the President of the United States and the President-elect of said elec-tion.

On February 9, 1825, the election of John Quincy Adams took place in accordance with these rules.

---

* Petitions are no longer introduced in this way. This old procedure of calling the states beginning with Maine proceeded through the original 13 states and then through the remaining states in the order of their admission to the Union.

Splitting of States' Electoral Votes . . .

Throughout the history of presidential elections, there have been numerous cases where a state's electoral votes have been divided between two candidates. The split electoral votes occurred for a variety of reasons.

Electoral Vote Splits, 1789-1836

Splits of a state's electoral votes cast for president before 1836 occurred for these reasons:

● For the first four presidential elections (1789-1800) held under Article II, Section 1 of the Constitution, each elector cast two votes without designating which vote was for president and which for vice president. As a result, electoral votes for each state were often scattered among several candidates. The 12th Amendment, ratified in 1804, required electors to vote separately for president and vice president.

● The district system of choosing electors, in which different candidates each could carry several districts. This system is the explanation for the split electoral votes in Maryland in 1804, 1808, 1812, 1824, 1828 and 1832; North Carolina in 1808; Illinois in 1824; Maine in 1828; and New York in 1828.

● The selection of electors by the legislatures of some states. This system sometimes led to party factionalism or political deals that resulted in the choice of electors loyal to more than one candidate. This was the cause for the division of electoral votes in New York in 1808 and 1824, Delaware in 1824 and Louisiana in 1824.

● The vote of an individual elector for someone other than his party's candidate. This happened in New Hampshire in 1820 when one Democratic-Republican elector voted for John Quincy Adams instead of the party nominee, James Monroe.

Voting for Individual Electors

By 1836 all states except South Carolina, which selected its electors by the state legislature until after the Civil War, had established a system of statewide popular election of electors. The new system limited the frequency of electoral vote splits. Nevertheless, a few states on occasion still divided their electoral votes among different presidential candidates. This occurred because of the practice of listing on the ballot the names of all electors and allowing voters to cross off the names of any particular electors they did not like, or, alternatively, requiring voters to vote for each individual elector. In a close election, electors of different parties sometimes were chosen. An example occurred in California in 1880, when one Democratic elector ran behind the Republican thus:

Winning Votes	Party	Losing Electors	Party
80,443	Democratic	80,282	Republican
80,426	Democratic	80,252	Republican
80,420	Democratic	80,242	Republican
80,413	Democratic	80,228	Republican
80,348	Republican	79,885	Democratic

Other similar occurrences include the following:

New Jersey, 1860. Four Republican and three Douglas Democratic electors won.

California, 1892. Eight Democratic electors and one Republican won.

The electors met in each state on Dec. 4, and the results gradually became known throughout the country: Jefferson and Burr, 73 electoral votes each; Adams, 65; Pinckney, 64; John Jay, 1. The Federalists had lost, but because the Democratic-Republicans had neglected to withhold one electoral vote from Burr, their presidential and vice presidential candidates were tied and the election was thrown into the House.

The lame-duck Congress, with a partisan Federalist majority, was still in office for the electoral count, and the possibilities for intrigue were only too apparent. After toying with and rejecting a proposal to block any election until March 4, when Adams' term expired, the Federalists decided to support Burr and thus elect a relatively pliant politician over a man they considered a "dangerous radical." Alexander Hamilton opposed this move. "I trust the Federalists will not finally be so mad as to vote for Burr," he wrote. "I speak with intimate and accurate knowledge of his character. His elevation can only promote the purposes of the desperate and the profligate. If there be a man in the world I ought to hate, it is Jefferson. With Burr I have always been personally well. But the public good must be paramount to every private consideration."

On Feb. 11, 1801 Congress met in joint session — with Jefferson, the outgoing vice president, in the chair — to count the electoral vote. This ritual ended, the House retired to its own chamber to elect a president. When the House met, it became apparent that the advice of Hamilton had been rejected. A majority of Federalists in the House insisted on backing Burr over Jefferson, the man they despised more. Indeed, if Burr had given clear assurances that he would run the country as a Federalist, he might have been elected. But Burr was unwilling to make those assurances; and, as one chronicler put it, "No one knows whether it was honor or a wretched indecision which gagged Burr's lips."

In all, there were 106 members of the House at the time, 58 Federalists and 48 Democratic-Republicans. If the ballots had been cast per capita Burr would have been elected, but the Constitution provided that each state should cast a single vote and that a majority of states was necessary for election.

On the first ballot Jefferson received the votes of eight states, one short of a majority of the 16 states then in the Union. Six states backed Burr, while the representatives of Vermont and Maryland were equally divided, so they lost their votes. By midnight of the first day of voting, 19 ballots had been taken, and the deadlock remained.

In all, 36 ballots were taken before the House came to a decision on Feb. 17. Predictably, there were men who sought to exploit the situation for personal gain. Jefferson wrote: "Many attempts have been made to obtain terms

... Factionalism and 'Faithless Electors'

North Dakota, 1892. Two Fusionists (Democrats and Populists) and one Republican won. One of the Fusion electors voted for Democrat Grover Cleveland and the other voted for Populist James B. Weaver, while the Republican elector voted for Benjamin Harrison, thus splitting the state's electoral vote three ways.

Ohio, 1892. Twenty-two Republicans and one Democratic elector won.

Oregon, 1892. Three Republicans and one Populist with Democratic support won.

California, 1896. Eight Republicans and one Democratic elector won.

Kentucky, 1896. Twelve Republicans and one Democratic elector won.

Maryland, 1904. Seven Democratic electors and one Republican won.

Maryland, 1908. Six Democratic and two Republican electors won.

California, 1912. Eleven Progressive and two Democratic electors won.

West Virginia, 1916. Seven Republicans and one Democratic elector won.

The increasing use of voting machines and straight-ticket voting — where the pull of a lever or the marking of an "X" results in automatically casting a vote for every elector — led to the decline in split electoral votes.

'Faithless Electors'

Yet another cause for occasional splits in a state's electoral vote is the so-called "faithless elector." Legally, no elector is bound to vote for any particular candidate; he may cast his ballot for whom he chooses. But in reality electors are almost always faithful to the candidate of the party with which they are affiliated.

But at times in American political history an elector has broken ranks to vote for a candidate other than his party's. In 1796 a Pennsylvania Federalist elector voted for Democratic-Republican Thomas Jefferson instead of Federalist John Adams. And some historians and political scientists claim that three Democratic-Republican electors voted for Adams. However, the fluidity of political party lines at that early date and the well-known personal friendship between Adams and at least one of the electors make the claim of their being faithless electors one of continuing controversy. In 1820 a New Hampshire Democratic-Republican elector voted for John Quincy Adams instead of the party nominee, James Monroe.

There was no further occurrence until 1948, when Preston Parks, a Truman elector in Tennessee, voted for Gov. Strom Thurmond of South Carolina, the States Rights Democratic Party (Dixiecrat) presidential nominee. Since then, there have been the following additional instances:

- In 1956, when W. F. Turner, a Stevenson elector in Alabama, voted for a local judge, Walter B. Jones.
- In 1960, when Henry D. Irwin, a Nixon elector in Oklahoma, voted for Sen. Harry F. Byrd, D-Va.
- In 1968, when Dr. Lloyd W. Bailey, a Nixon elector in North Carolina, voted for George C. Wallace, the American Independent Party candidate.
- In 1972, when Roger L. MacBride, a Nixon elector in Virginia, voted for John Hospers, the Libertarian Party candidate.
- In 1976, when Mike Padden, a Ford elector in the state of Washington, voted for former governor Ronald Reagan of California.

and promises from me. I have declared to them unequivocally that I would not receive the Government on capitulation; that I would not go in with my hands tied."

The impasse was broken finally when Vermont and Maryland switched to support Jefferson. Delaware and South Carolina also withdrew their support from Burr by casting blank ballots. The final vote: 10 states for Jefferson, four (all in New England) for Burr. Thus Jefferson became president, and Burr, under the Constitution as it then stood, automatically became vice president.

Federalist James A. Bayard of Delaware, who had played a key role in breaking the deadlock, wrote to Hamilton: "The means existed of electing Burr, but this required his cooperation. By deceiving one man (a great blockhead) and tempting two (not incorruptible), he might have secured a majority of the states. He will never have another chance of being president of the United States; and the little use he has made of the one which has occurred gives me but an humble opinion of the talents of an unprincipled man."

The Jefferson-Burr contest clearly illustrated the dangers of the double-balloting system established by the original Constitution, and pressure began to build for an amendment requiring separate votes for president and vice president. Congress approved the 12th Amendment in December 1803, and the states — acting with unexpected

speed — ratified it in time for the 1804 election.

John Quincy Adams Election

The only other time a president was elected by the House of Representatives occurred in 1825. There were many contenders for the presidency in the 1824 election, but four predominated: John Quincy Adams, Henry Clay, William H. Crawford and Andrew Jackson. Crawford, secretary of the Treasury under President James Monroe, was the early front-runner, but his candidacy faltered after he suffered an incapacitating illness in 1823.

When the electoral votes were counted, Jackson had 99, Adams 84, Crawford 41 and Clay 37. With 18 of the 24 states choosing their electors by popular vote, Jackson also led in the popular voting, although the significance of the popular vote was open to challenge. Under the 12th Amendment, the names of the three top contenders — Jackson, Adams and the ailing Crawford — were placed before the House. Clay's support was vital to either of the two front-runners.

From the start, Clay apparently intended to support Adams as the lesser of two evils. But before the House voted, a great scandal erupted. A Philadelphia newspaper published an anonymous letter alleging that Clay had agreed to support Adams in return for being made secretary of state. The letter alleged also that Clay would have

been willing to make the same deal with Jackson. Clay immediately denied the charge and pronounced the writer of the letter "a base and infamous character, a dastard and a liar."

When the House met to vote, Adams was supported by the six New England states and New York and, in large part through Clay's backing, by Maryland, Ohio, Kentucky, Illinois, Missouri and Louisiana. Thus a majority of 13 delegations voted for him — the bare minimum he needed for election, since there were 24 states in the Union at the time. The election was accomplished on the first ballot, but Adams took office under a cloud from which his administration never emerged.

Jackson had believed the charges and found his suspicions vindicated when Adams, after the election, did appoint Clay as secretary of state. "Was there ever witnessed such a bare-faced corruption in any country before?" Jackson wrote to a friend. Jackson's successful 1828 campaign made much of his contention that the House of Representatives had thwarted the will of the people by denying him the presidency in 1825, even though he had been the leader in popular and electoral votes.

Other Anomalies

On only one occasion has the Senate chosen the vice president. That was in 1837, when Martin Van Buren was elected president with 170 of the 294 electoral votes while his vice presidential running mate, Richard M. Johnson, received only 147 electoral votes — one less than a majority. This discrepancy occurred because Van Buren electors from Virginia boycotted Johnson, reportedly in protest against his social behavior. The Senate elected Johnson, 33-16, over Francis Granger of New York, the runner-up in the electoral vote for vice president.

Although only two presidential elections actually have been decided by the House, a number of others — including those of 1836, 1856, 1860, 1892, 1948, 1960 and 1968 — could have been thrown into the House by only a small shift in the popular vote.

The threat of House election was most clearly evident in 1968, when Democrat George C. Wallace of Alabama ran as a strong third-party candidate. Wallace frequently asserted that he could win an outright majority in the Electoral College by the addition of key Midwestern and Mountain states to his hoped-for base in the Deep South and Border states. In reality, the Wallace campaign had a narrower goal: to win the balance of power in Electoral College voting, thus depriving either major party of the clear electoral majority required for election. Wallace made it clear that he then would expect one of the major party candidates to make concessions in return for enough votes from Wallace electors to win the election. Wallace indicated that he expected the election to be settled in the Electoral College and not in the House of Representatives. At the end of the campaign it was disclosed that Wallace had obtained written affidavits from all of his electors in which they promised to vote for Wallace "or whomsoever he may direct" in the Electoral College.

In response to the Wallace challenge, both major party candidates, Republican Richard Nixon and Democrat Hubert H. Humphrey, maintained that they would refuse to bargain with Wallace for his electoral votes. Nixon asserted that the House, if the decision rested there, should elect the popular-vote winner. Humphrey said the representatives should select "the president they believe would be best for the country." Bipartisan efforts to obtain advance agreements from House candidates to vote for the national popular-vote winner if the election should go to the House ended in failure. Neither Nixon nor Humphrey replied to suggestions that they pledge before the election to swing enough electoral votes to the popular-vote winner to ensure his election without help from Wallace.

In the end Wallace received only 13.5 percent of the popular vote and 46 electoral votes (including the vote of one Republican defector), all from Southern states. He failed to win the balance of power in the Electoral College, which he had hoped to use to wring policy concessions from one of the major party candidates. If Wallace had won a few Border states, or if a few thousand more Democratic votes had been cast in Northern states barely carried by Nixon, thus reducing Nixon's electoral vote below 270, Wallace would have been in a position to bargain off his electoral votes or to throw the election into the House for final settlement.

Counting the Electoral Vote

Congress has mandated a variety of dates for the casting of popular votes, the meeting of the electors to cast ballots in the various states and the official counting of the electoral votes before both houses of Congress.

The Continental Congress made the provisions for the first election. On Sept. 13, 1788, the Congress directed that each state choose its electors on the first Wednesday in January 1789. It further directed these electors to cast their ballots on the first Wednesday in February 1789.

In 1792 the 2nd Congress passed legislation setting up a permanent calendar for choosing electors. Allowing some flexibility in dates, the law directed that states choose their electors within the 34 days preceding the first Wednesday in December of each presidential election year. Then the electors would meet in their various states and cast their ballots on the first Wednesday in December. On the second Wednesday of the following February, the votes were to be opened and counted before a joint session of Congress. Provision also was made for a special presidential election in case of the removal, death, resignation or disability of both the president and vice president.

Under that system states chose presidential electors at various times. For instance, in 1840 the popular balloting for electors began in Pennsylvania and Ohio on Oct. 30 and ended in North Carolina on Nov. 12. South Carolina, the only state still choosing presidential electors through the state Legislature, appointed its electors on Nov. 26.

Congress modified the system in 1845, providing that each state choose its electors on the same day — the Tuesday next after the first Monday in November — a provision that still remains in force. Otherwise, the days for casting and counting the electoral votes remained the same.

The next change occurred in 1887, when Congress provided that electors were to meet and cast their ballots on the second Monday in January instead of the first Wednesday in December. Congress also dropped the provision for a special presidential election.

In 1934 Congress again revised the law. The new arrangements, still in force, directed the electors to meet on the first Monday after the second Wednesday in December. The ballots are opened and counted before Congress on Jan. 6 (the next day if Jan. 6 falls on a Sunday).

The Constitution states: "The President of the Senate shall, in the presence of the Senate and House of Representatives, open all the certificates, and the votes shall then be

Law for Counting Electoral Votes in Congress

Following is the complete text of Title 3, section 15 of the U.S. Code, enacted originally in 1887, governing the counting of electoral votes in Congress:

Congress shall be in session on the sixth day of January succeeding every meeting of the electors. The Senate and House of Representatives shall meet in the Hall of the House of Representatives at the hour of 1 o'clock in the afternoon on that day, and the President of the Senate shall be their presiding officer. Two tellers shall be previously appointed on the part of the Senate and two on the part of the House of Representatives, to whom shall be handed, as they are opened by the President of the Senate, all the certificates and papers purporting to be certificates of the electoral votes, which certificates and papers shall be opened, presented, and acted upon in the alphabetical order of the States, beginning with the letter A; and said tellers, having then read the same in the presence and hearing of the two Houses, shall make a list of the votes as they shall appear from the said certificates; and the votes having been ascertained and counted according to the rules in this subchapter provided, the result of the same shall be delivered to the President of the Senate, who shall thereupon announce the state of the vote, which announcement shall be deemed a sufficient declaration of the persons, if any, elected President and Vice President of the United States, and, together with a list of votes, be entered on the Journals of the two Houses. Upon such reading of any such certificate or paper, the President of the Senate shall call for objections, if any. Every objection shall be made in writing, and shall state clearly and concisely, and without argument, the ground thereof, and shall be signed by at least one Senator and one Member of the House of Representatives before the same shall be received. When all objections so made to any vote or paper from a State shall have been received and read, the Senate shall thereupon withdraw, and such objections shall be submitted to the Senate for its decision; and the Speaker of the House of Representatives shall, in like manner, submit such objections to the House of Representatives for its decision; and no electoral vote or votes from any State which shall have been regularly given by electors whose appointment has been lawfully certified to according to section 6* of this title from which but one return has been received shall be rejected, but the two Houses concurrently may reject the vote or votes when they agree that such vote or votes have not been so regularly given by electors whose appointment has been so certified. If more than one return or paper purporting to be a return from a State shall have been received by the President of the Senate, those votes, and those only, shall be counted which shall have been regularly given by the electors who are shown by the determination mentioned in section 5† of this title to have been appointed, if the determination in said section provided for shall have been made, or by such successors or substitutes, in case of a vacancy in the board of electors so ascertained, as have been appointed to fill such vacancy in the mode provided by the laws of the State; but in case there shall arise the question which of two or more of such State authorities determining what electors have been appointed, as mentioned in section 5 of this title, is the lawful tribunal of such State, the votes regularly given of those electors, and those only, of such State shall be counted whose title as electors the two Houses, acting separately, shall concurrently decide is supported by the decision of such State so authorized by its law; and in such case of more than one return or paper purporting to be a return from a State, if there shall have been no such determination of the question in the State aforesaid, then those votes, and those only, shall be counted which the two Houses shall concurrently decide were cast by lawful electors appointed in accordance with the laws of the State, unless the two Houses, acting separately, shall concurrently decide such votes not to be the lawful votes of the legally appointed electors of such State. But if the two Houses shall disagree in respect of the counting of such votes, then, and in that case, the votes of the electors whose appointment shall have been certified by the executive of the State, under the seal thereof, shall be counted. When the two Houses have voted, they shall immediately again meet, and the presiding officer shall then announce the decision of the questions submitted. No votes or papers from any other State shall be acted upon until the objections previously made to the votes or papers from any State shall have been finally disposed of.

* Section 6 provides for certification of votes by electors by state governors.

†Section 5 provides that if state law specifies a method for resolving disputes concerning the vote for presidential electors, Congress must respect any determination so made by a state.

counted." It gives no guidance on disputed ballots.

Before counting the electoral votes in 1865, Congress adopted the 22nd Joint Rule, which provided that no electoral votes objected to in joint session could be counted except by the concurrent votes of both the Senate and House. The rule was pushed by congressional Republicans to ensure rejection of the electoral votes from the newly reconstructed states of Louisiana and Tennessee. Under this rule, Congress in 1873 also threw out the electoral votes of Louisiana and Arkansas and three from Georgia.

However, the rule lapsed at the beginning of 1876, when the Senate refused to readopt it because the House was in Democratic control. Thus, following the 1876 elec-

tion, when it became apparent that for the first time the outcome of an election would be determined by decisions on disputed electoral votes, Congress had no rules to guide it.

Hayes-Tilden Contest

The 1876 campaign pitted Republican Rutherford B. Hayes against Democrat Samuel J. Tilden. Early election-night returns indicated that Tilden had been elected. He had won the swing states of Indiana, New York, Connecticut and New Jersey; those states plus his expected Southern support would give him the election. However, by the following morning it became apparent that if the Republi-

cans could hold South Carolina, Florida and Louisiana, Hayes would be elected with 185 electoral votes to 184 for Tilden. But if a single elector in any of these states voted for Tilden, he would throw the election to the Democrats. Tilden led in the popular-vote count by more than a quarter million votes.

The situation was much the same in each of the three contested states. Historian Eugene H. Roseboom described it as follows: "The Republicans controlled the state governments and the election machinery, had relied upon the Negro masses for votes, and had practiced frauds as in the past. The Democrats used threats, intimidation, and even violence when necessary, to keep Negroes from the polls; and where they were in a position to do so they resorted to fraud also. The firm determination of the whites to overthrow carpetbag rule contributed to make a full and fair vote impossible; carpetbag hold on the state governments made a fair count impossible. Radical reconstruction was reaping its final harvest."

Both parties pursued the votes of the three states with a fine disregard for propriety or legality, and in the end double sets of elector returns were sent to Congress from all three. Oregon also sent two sets of returns. Although Hayes carried that state, the Democratic governor discovered that one of the Hayes electors was a postmaster and therefore ineligible to be an elector under the Constitution, so he certified the election of the top-polling Democratic elector. However, the Republican electors met, received the resignation of their ineligible colleague, then reappointed him to the vacancy since he had in the meantime resigned his postmastership.

Had the 22nd Joint Rule remained in effect, the Democratic House of Representatives could have objected to any of Hayes' disputed votes. But since the rule had lapsed, Congress had to find some new method of resolving electoral disputes. A joint committee was created to work out a plan, and the resulting Electoral Commission Law was approved by large majorities and signed into law Jan. 29, 1877 — only a few days before the date scheduled for counting the electoral votes.

The law, which applied only to the 1876 electoral vote count, established a 15-member electoral commission that was to have final authority over disputed electoral votes, unless both houses of Congress agreed to overrule it. The commission was to consist of five senators, five representatives and five Supreme Court justices. Each chamber was to select its own members of the commission, with the understanding that the majority party would have three members and the minority two. Four justices, two from each party, were named in the bill, and these four were to select the fifth. It was expected that they would choose Justice David Davis, who was considered a political independent, but he disqualified himself when the Illinois Legislature named him to a seat in the Senate. Justice Joseph P. Bradley, a Republican, then was named to the 15th seat on the commission. The Democrats supported his selection, because they considered him the most independent of the remaining justices, all of whom were Republicans. However, he was to vote with the Republicans on every dispute and thus ensure the victory of Hayes.

The electoral count began in Congress Feb. 1 (moved up from the second Wednesday in February for this one election), and the proceedings continued until March 2. States were called in alphabetical order, and as each disputed state was reached objections were raised to both the Hayes and Tilden electors. The question was then referred to the electoral commission, which in every case voted 8-7 for Hayes. In each case, the Democratic House rejected the commission's decision, but the Republican Senate upheld it, so the decision stood.

As the count went on, Democrats in the House threatened to launch a filibuster to block resumption of joint sessions so that the count could not be completed before Inauguration Day. The threat was never carried out, because of an agreement reached between the Hayes forces and Southern conservatives. The Southerners agreed to let the electoral count continue without obstruction. In return Hayes agreed that, as president, he would withdraw federal troops from the South, end Reconstruction and make other concessions. The Southerners, for their part, pledged to respect Negro rights, a pledge they did not carry out.

Thus, at 4 a.m. March 2, 1877, the president of the Senate was able to announce that Hayes had been elected president with 185 electoral votes, as against 184 for Tilden. Later that day Hayes arrived in Washington. The next evening he took the oath of office privately at the White House, because March 4 fell on a Sunday. His formal inauguration followed on Monday. The country acquiesced. Thus ended a crisis that could have resulted in civil war.

Not until 1887 did Congress enact permanent legislation on the handling of disputed electoral votes. The Electoral Count Act of that year gave each state final authority in determining the legality of its choice of electors and required a concurrent majority of both the Senate and House to reject any electoral votes. It also established procedures for counting electoral votes in Congress. *(Text, p. 261)*

Application of 1887 Law in 1969

The procedures relating to disputed electoral votes were utilized for the first time after the election of 1968. When Congress met in joint session Jan. 6, 1969, to count the electoral votes, Sen. Edmund S. Muskie, D-Maine, and Rep. James G. O'Hara, D-Mich., joined by six other senators and 37 other representatives, filed a written objection to the vote cast by a North Carolina elector, Dr. Lloyd W. Bailey of Rocky Mount. He had been elected as a Republican but chose to vote for George C. Wallace and Curtis LeMay, the presidential and vice presidential candidates of the American Independent Party, instead of Republicans Richard Nixon and Spiro T. Agnew.

Acting under the 1887 law, Muskie and O'Hara objected to Bailey's vote on the grounds that it was "not properly given" because a plurality of the popular votes in North Carolina were cast for Nixon-Agnew and the state's voters had chosen electors to vote for Nixon and Agnew only. Muskie and O'Hara asked that Bailey's vote not be counted at all by Congress.

The 1887 statute, incorporated in the U.S. Code, Title 3, Section 15, stipulated that "no electoral vote or votes from any state which shall have been regularly given by electors whose appointment has been lawfully certified ... from which but one return has been received shall be rejected, but the two Houses concurrently may reject the vote or votes when they agree that such vote or votes have not been so regularly given by electors whose appointment has been so certified." The statute did not define the term "regularly given," although at the time of its adoption chief concern centered on problems of dual sets of electoral vote returns from a state, votes cast on an improper day or votes disputed because of uncertainty about whether a state lawfully was in the Union when the vote was cast.

The 1887 statute provided that if written objection to any state's vote was received from at least one member of both the Senate and House, the two legislative bodies were to retire immediately to separate sessions, debate for two hours with a five-minute limitation on speeches, and that each chamber was to decide the issue by vote before resuming the joint session. The statute made clear that both the Senate and House had to reject a challenged electoral vote (or votes) for such action to prevail.

At the Jan. 6 joint session, in the House chamber with Senate President Pro Tempore Richard B. Russell, D-Ga., presiding, the counting of the electoral vote proceeded smoothly through the alphabetical order of states until the North Carolina result was announced, at which time O'Hara rose to announce filing of the complaint. The two houses then reassembled in joint session at which the results of the separate deliberations were announced and the count of the electoral vote by state proceeded without event. At the conclusion, Russell announced the vote and declared Nixon and Agnew elected.

Although Congress did not sustain the challenge to Bailey's vote, the case of the "faithless" elector led to increased pressure for changes in the procedures. However, no reforms had cleared Congress by early 1985.

Reform Proposals

Since Jan. 6, 1797, when Rep. William L. Smith, F-S.C., introduced in Congress the first proposed constitutional amendment for reform of the Electoral College system, hardly a session of Congress has passed without the introduction of one or more resolutions of this nature. But only one — the 12th Amendment, ratified in 1804 — ever has been approved.

In recent years, public interest in a change in the Electoral College system was spurred by the close 1960 and 1968 elections, by a series of Supreme Court rulings relating to apportionment and districting and by introduction of unpledged elector systems in the Southern states.

House Approval of Amendment

Early in 1969, President Nixon asked Congress to take prompt action on Electoral College reform. He said he would support any plan that would eliminate individual electors and distribute among the presidential candidates the electoral vote of every state and the District of Columbia in a manner more closely approximating the popular vote.

Later that year the House approved, 338-70, a resolution proposing a constitutional amendment to eliminate the Electoral College and to provide instead for direct popular election of the president and vice president. The measure set a minimum of 40 percent of the popular vote as sufficient for election and provided for a runoff election between the two top candidates for the presidency if no candidate received 40 percent. Under this plan the House of Representatives could no longer be called upon to select a president. The proposed amendment also authorized Congress to provide a method of filling vacancies caused by the death, resignation or disability of presidential nominees before the election and a method of filling post-election vacancies caused by the death of the president-elect or vice president-elect.

Nixon, who previously had favored a proportional plan of allocating each state's electoral votes, endorsed the House resolution and urged the Senate to adopt it. To become effective, the proposed amendment had to be approved by a two-thirds majority in both the Senate and House and be ratified by the legislatures of three-fourths of the states.

When the proposal reached the Senate floor in September 1970, small-state and Southern senators succeeded in blocking final action on it. The resolution was laid aside Oct. 5, after two unsuccessful efforts to cut off debate by invoking cloture.

Carter Endorsement of Plan

Another major effort to eliminate the Electoral College occurred in 1977, when President Jimmy Carter included such a proposal in his election reform package, unveiled March 22.

Carter endorsed the amendment approved by the House in 1969 to replace the Electoral College with direct popular election of the president and vice president, and provide for a runoff if no candidate received at least 40 percent of the vote. Because the Senate again was seen as the major stumbling block, the House waited to see what the Senate would do before beginning any deliberation of its own.

After several months of deadlock, the Senate Judiciary Committee approved Sept. 15 the direct presidential election plan by a vote of 9 to 8. But Senate opponents of the measure promised another filibuster and the Senate leadership decided it could not spare the time or effort to try to break it. The measure was never brought to the floor and died when the 95th Congress adjourned in 1978.

On Jan. 15, 1979, the opening day of the 96th Congress, Sen. Birch Bayh, D-Ind., began another effort to abolish the Electoral College through a constitutional amendment. In putting off action in the previous Congress, Senate leaders had agreed to try for early action in the 96th.

A proposed constitutional amendment to abolish the Electoral College and elect the president by popular vote did reach the Senate floor in July 1979. The Senate voted in favor of the measure, 51-48 — 15 votes short of the required two-thirds majority of those present and voting needed to approve a constitutional amendment.

Supporters of the resolution blamed defections by several Northern liberals for the margin of defeat. Major Jewish and black groups extensively lobbied the Northern senators, arguing that the voting strength of black and Jewish voters is maximized under the Electoral College system because both groups are concentrated in urban areas of the large electoral vote states.

As of early 1985 no further efforts to change the Electoral College system had made headway in Congress.

Presidential Disability

A decade of congressional concern over the question of presidential disability was eased in 1967 by ratification of the 25th Amendment to the Constitution. The amendment for the first time provided for continuity in carrying out the functions of the presidency in the event of presidential disability and for filling a vacancy in the vice presidency.

Congressional consideration of the problem of presidential disability had been prompted by President Dwight D. Eisenhower's heart attack in 1955. The ambiguity of the language of the disability clause (Article II, Section 1, Clause 5) of the Constitution had provoked occasional debate ever since the Constitutional Convention of 1787. But

it never had been decided how far the term "disability" extended or who would be the judge of it.

Clause 5 provided that Congress should decide who was to succeed to the presidency if both the president and the vice president died, resigned or became disabled. Congress enacted succession laws three times. By the Act of March 1, 1792, it provided for succession (after the vice president) of the president pro tempore of the Senate, then of the House Speaker; if those offices were vacant, states were to send electors to Washington to choose a new president.

That law stood until passage of the Presidential Succession Act of Jan. 19, 1886, which changed the line of succession to run from the vice president to the secretary of state, secretary of the Treasury and so on through the Cabinet in order of rank. Sixty-one years later the Presidential Succession Act of July 18, 1947, (still in force) placed the Speaker of the House and the president pro tempore of the Senate ahead of Cabinet officers in succession after the vice president.

Before ratification of the 25th Amendment in 1967, no procedures had been laid down to govern situations arising in the event of presidential incapacity or of a vacancy in the office of vice president. Two presidents had had serious disabilities — James A. Garfield, shot in 1881 and confined to his bed until he died 2-1/2 months later, and Woodrow Wilson, who suffered a stroke in 1919. In each case the vice president did not assume any duties of the presidency for fear he would appear to be usurping the powers of that office. As for a vice presidential vacancy, the United States has been without a vice president 18 times for a total of 40 years through 1980, after the elected vice president succeeded to the presidency, died or resigned.

Ratification of the 25th Amendment established procedures that clarified these areas of uncertainty in the Constitution. The amendment provided that the vice president should become acting president under either one of two circumstances. If the president informed Congress that he was unable to perform his duties, the vice president would become acting president until the president could resume his responsibilities. If the vice president and a majority of the Cabinet, or another body designated by Congress, found the president to be incapacitated, the vice president would become acting president until the president informed Congress that his disability had ended. Congress was given 21 days to resolve any dispute over the president's disability; a two-thirds vote of both chambers was required to overrule the president's declaration that he was no longer incapacitated.

Whenever a vacancy occurred in the office of the vice president, either by death, succession to the presidency or resignation, the president was to nominate a vice president, and the nomination was to be confirmed by a majority vote of both houses of Congress.

The proposed 25th Amendment was approved by the Senate and House in 1965. It took effect Feb. 10, 1967, after ratification by 38 states. *(Text, Appendix, p. 1128)*

Within only eight years, the power of the president to appoint a new vice president under the terms of the 25th Amendment was used twice. In 1973 when Vice President Agnew resigned, President Nixon nominated Gerald R. Ford as the new vice president. Ford was confirmed by both houses of Congress and sworn in Dec. 6, 1973. On Nixon's resignation Aug. 9, 1974, Ford succeeded to the presidency, becoming the first president in American history who was elected neither to the presidency nor to the vice presidency. President Ford chose as his new vice president Nelson A. Rockefeller, former governor of New York, who was sworn in Dec. 19, 1974.

With both the president and vice president holding office through appointment rather than election, members of Congress and the public expressed concern about the power of a president to appoint, in effect, his own successor. Accordingly, Sen. John O. Pastore, D-R.I., introduced a proposed constitutional amendment on Feb. 3, 1975, to provide for a special national election for president with more than one year remaining in a presidential term. Hearings were held before the Senate Judiciary Subcommittee on Constitutional Amendments, but no action was taken on the measure.

Confusion After Reagan Shooting

In the aftermath of the attempted assassination of President Ronald Reagan in 1981, there was no need to invoke the presidential disability provisions of the 25th Amendment. However, some of the public statements made by administration officials immediately after the shooting reflected continuing confusion over the issue of who is in charge when the president temporarily is unable to function. Soon after word of the shooting became known, the members of the Reagan Cabinet gathered in the White House, ready to invoke the amendment's procedures, if necessary. Vice President George Bush was on an Air Force jet returning to Washington from Texas.

At a televised press briefing later that afternoon, Secretary of State Alexander M. Haig Jr. confirmed that Reagan was in surgery and under anesthesia. It was clear that he temporarily was unable to make presidential decisions should the occasion — such as a foreign attack or other national emergency — require them. Attempting to reassure the country, Haig stated that he was in control in the White House pending the return of Vice President Bush, with whom he was in contact.

This assertion was followed by a question from the press about who was making administration decisions. Haig responded, "Constitutionally, gentlemen, you have the president, the vice president and the secretary of state in that order, and should the president decide he wants to transfer the helm to the vice president, he will do so. He has not done that."

Haig's response reflected the law in effect before the Presidential Succession Act of 1947. The law applicable in the 1981 shooting incident was the 1947 act (PL 80-199), which specifies that the line of succession is the vice president, the Speaker of the House, the president pro tempore of the Senate, the secretaries of state, Treasury, defense, the attorney general, the secretaries of interior, agriculture, commerce, labor, health and human services, housing and urban development, transportation, energy and education.

Bibliography

Books

Asher, Herbert. *Presidential Elections and American Politics.* Homewood, Ill.: Dow Jones-Irwin, 1980.

Bagby, Wesley. *The Road to Normalcy: The Presidential Campaign and Election of 1920.* New York: AMS Press, 1962.

Barber, James D. *The Presidential Character: Predicting Performance in the White House.* 2nd ed. Englewood Cliffs, N. J.: Prentice-Hall, 1977.

Best, Judith. *The Case Against Direct Election of the President: A Defense of the Electoral College.* Ithaca, N. Y.: Cornell University Press, 1975.

Brams, Steven J. *The Presidential Election Game.* New Haven, Conn.: Yale University Press, 1978.

Burnham, Walter D. *Critical Elections and the Mainsprings of American Politics.* New York: W. W. Norton, 1971.

Clancy, Herbert J. *Presidential Election of 1880.* Chicago, Ill.: Loyola University Press, 1958.

Di Clerico, Robert E., and Eric M. Uslaner. *Few Are Chosen: Problems in Presidential Selection.* New York: McGraw-Hill, 1983.

Drew, Elizabeth. *Portrait of an Election: The 1980 Presidential Campaign.* New York: Simon and Schuster, 1981.

Ewing, Cortez A. M. *Presidential Elections from Abraham Lincoln to Franklin Roosevelt.* 1940. Reprint. Westport, Conn.: Greenwood Press, 1972.

Flanigan, William H., and Nancy H. Zingale. *Political Behavior of the American Electorate.* 5th ed. Newton, Mass.: Allyn and Bacon, 1983.

Gammon, Samuel R., Jr. *The Presidential Election of 1832.* Saint Clair Shores, Mich.: Scholarly Press, 1972.

Germond, Jack W., and Jules Witcover. *Blue Smoke and Mirrors: How Reagan Won and Why Carter Lost the Election of 1980.* New York: Viking Press, 1981.

Gray, Lee L. *How We Chose a President.* 5th ed. New York: St. Martin's Press, 1980.

Gunderson, Robert G. *The Log Cabin Campaign.* 1957. Reprint. Westport, Conn.: Greenwood Press, 1977.

Haworth, Paul L. *The Hayes-Tilden Disputed Presidential Election of 1876.* New York: AMS Press, 1906.

Hess, Stephen. *The Presidential Campaign.* rev. ed. Washington, D. C.: Brookings Institution, 1978.

Hill, David B., and Norman R. Luttberg. *Trends in American Electoral Behavior.* Itasca, Ill.: Peacock, 1980.

Hirschfield, Robert S., ed. *Selection-Election: A Forum on the American Presidency.* Hawthorne, N. Y.: Hawthorne, 1982.

Hoyt, Edwin P. *Jumbos and Jackasses: A Popular History of the Political Wars.* Garden City, N. Y.: Doubleday, 1960.

Jamieson, Kathleen Hall. *Packaging the Presidency: A History and Criticism of Presidential Campaign Advertising.* New York: Oxford University Press, 1984.

Joint Center for Political Studies. *Picking a President: A Guide to Delegate Selection in the United States.* Washington, D. C.: Joint Center for Political Studies, 1980.

Keech, William R., ed. *Winners Take All: Report of the Twentieth Century Task Force on Reform of the Presidential Election Process.* New York: Holmes and Meier, 1978.

Kessel, John H. *Presidential Campaign Politics.* Homewood, Ill.: Dow Jones-Irwin, 1980.

Kirkpatrick, Samuel A., ed. *American Electoral Behavior: Change and Stability.* Beverly Hills, Calif.: Sage, 1976.

Kleppner, Paul, and Walter D. Burnham. *The Evolution of American Electoral Systems.* Westport, Conn.: Greenwood Press, 1982.

Lazarsfeld, Paul F., et al. *The People's Choice: How the Voter Makes Up His Mind in a Presidential Campaign.* New York: Columbia University Press.

Longley, Lawrence D. *The Politics of Electoral College Reform.* New Haven, Conn.: Yale University Press, 1972.

Maisel, Louis, and Joseph Cooper, eds. *The Impact of the Electoral Process.* Beverly Hills, Calif.: Sage, 1977.

Mazmanian, Daniel A. *Third Parties in Presidential Elections.* Washington, D. C.: Brookings Institution, 1974.

Michener, James A. *Presidential Lottery: The Reckless Gamble in Our Electoral System.* New York: Random House, 1969.

Page, Benjamin I. *Choices and Echoes in Presidential Elections: Rational Man and Electoral Democracy.* Chicago: University of Chicago Press, 1978.

Peel, Roy V. *The 1928 Campaign: An Analysis.* 1931. Reprint. Salem, N. H.: Ayer, 1974.

———. *The 1932 Campaign: An Analysis.* 1935. Reprint. New York: Da Capo Press, 1973.

Peirce, Neal. *The People's President: The Electoral College and the Emerging Consensus for a Direct Vote.* New Haven, Conn.: Yale University Press, 1981.

Petersen, Svend. *A Statistical History of the American Presidential Elections.* Westport, Conn.: Greenwood Press, 1981.

Polsby, Nelson, and Aaron Wildavsky. *Presidential Elections: Strategies of American Electoral Politics.* New York: Charles Scribner's Sons, 1980.

Robinson, Edgar E. *The Presidential Vote, 1896-1932.* New York: Octagon Books, 1970.

———. *They Voted for Roosevelt: The Presidential Vote, 1932-1944.* 1947. Reprint. New York: Octagon Books, 1970.

Roseboom, Eugene H. *A History of Presidential Elections: From George Washington to Jimmy Carter.* New York: Macmillan, 1979.

Rosenstone, Steven J., Roy L. Behr and Edward Lazarus. *Third Parties in America: Citizen Response to Major Party Failure.* Princeton, N. J.: Princeton University Press, 1984.

Runyon, John H. *Source Book of American Presidential Campaign and Election Statistics, 1948-1968.* New York: Ungar, 1971.

Sayre, Wallace S. *Voting for President: The Electoral College and the American Political System.* Washington, D. C.: Brookings Institution, 1970.

Scammon, Richard M. *America Votes: A Handbook of Contemporary Election Statistics.* vols. 1 and 2. New York: Macmillan, 1956, 1958. *America Votes.* vols. 3-5. Pittsburgh: University of Pittsburgh, 1959, 1962, and 1964. *America Votes.* vols. 6-11. Washington, D. C.: Congressional Quarterly, 1966-1975.

———, and Alice McGillivray. *America Votes.* vols. 12-15. Washington, D.C.: Congressional Quarterly, 1977-1983. 1983.

Schlesinger, Arthur M., Jr., ed. *History of American Presidential Elections.* 4 vols. New York: McGraw Hill, 1971.

———. *The Coming to Power: Critical Presidential Elections in American History.* New York: Chelsea House, 1981.

Singer, Aaron, ed. *Campaign Speeches of American Presidential Candidates, 1928-1972.* New York: Ungar, 1976.

Smith, Jeffrey A. *American Presidential Elections: Trust and the Rational Voter.* New York: Praeger Publishers, 1980.

Stanwood, Edward. *History of the Presidency.* 2 vols. rev. ed. New York: Kelley, 1921.

Weinbaum, M. G., and L. H. Gold. *Presidential Elections: A Simulation of Readings.* New York: Irvington Publishers, 1982.

White, Theodore H. *America in Search of Itself: The Making of the President, 1956-1980*. New York: Harper and Row, 1982.

———. *The Making of the President, 1960*. New York: Atheneum Publishers, 1961.

———. *The Making of the President, 1964*. New York: Atheneum Publishers, 1965.

———. *The Making of the President, 1968*. New York: Atheneum Publishers, 1969.

———. *The Making of the President, 1972*. New York: Atheneum Publishers, 1973.

Articles

"American Presidential Elections." *Current History* (October 1964): 193-235.

Bayh, Birch. "Electing a President: The Case for Direct Popular Election." *Harvard Journal on Legislation* (January 1969): 1-12.

Blaine, J. G. "Presidential Election of 1892." *North American Review* (November 1892): 513-525.

Branch, L. C. "Making a President in the Electoral College, 1880." *Overland* (November 1896): 551-556.

Brody, Richard, and Lee Sigelman. "Presidential Popularity and Presidential Elections: An Update and Extension." *Public Opinion Quarterly* 47 (Fall 1983): 325-329.

Brunk, Gregory G., and Paul A. Gough. "State Economic Conditions and the 1980 Presidential Election." *Presidential Studies Quarterly* 13 (Winter 1983): 62-69.

Bryan, William J. "Election of 1900." *North American Review* (December 1900): 788-801.

Cohen, Jeffrey Elliot, and David C. Nice. "Party Unity and Presidential Election Performance: 1936-1980." *Presidential Studies Quarterly* 12 (Summer 1982): 317-329.

Courtney, L. H. C. "Recent Presidential Elections." *Nineteenth Century* (January 1897): 1-16.

Crabites, P. "American Presidential Elections." *Nineteenth Century* (November 1924): 719-726.

Eshelman, Edwin D. "Congress and Electoral Reform: An Analysis of Proposals for Changing Our Method of Selecting a President." *Christian Century*, Feb. 5, 1969, 178-181.

Feerick, John D. "The Electoral College: Why It Ought to Be Abolished." *Fordham Law Review* (October 1968): 43.

Freund, Paul A. "Direct Election of the President: Issues and Answers." *American Bar Association Journal* (August 1970): 733.

Gardner, J. W. "Should the Presidential Electoral System Be Abolished?" *Independent*, Jan. 27, 1910, 191-195.

Goldman, Ralph M. "Hubert Humphrey's S. J. Res. 152: A Proposal for Electoral College Reform." *Midwest Journal of Political Science* (February 1958): 89-96.

Gossett, William T. "Direct Popular Election of the President." *American Bar Association Journal* (March 1970): 230.

Huddle, F. P. "Electoral College: Historical Review and Proposals for Reforms." *Editorial Research Reports*, Aug. 18, 1944, 99-144.

Kellenback, J. E. "Recent Proposals to Reform the Electoral College System." *American Political Science Review* (October 1936): 924-929.

Kessel, John H. "The Seasons of Presidential Politics." *Social Science Quarterly* 58 (December 1977): 418-435.

Kirkpatrick, Samuel A., William Lyons and Michael R. Fitzgerald. "Candidates, Parties, and Issues in the American Electorate: Two Decades of Change." *American Politics Quarterly* 3 (July 1975): 247-283.

Lechner, Alfred J. "Direct Election of the President: The Final Step in the Constitutional Evolution of the Right to Vote." *Notre Dame Lawyer* (October 1971): 122-152.

Livingston, James. "The Presidency and the People." *Democracy* 3 (Summer 1983): 41-49.

McLean, S. J. "Presidential Election of 1908." *Quarterly Review* (October 1908): 448-475.

McPherson, J. M. "Grant or Greeley? The Abolitionist Dilemma in the Election of 1872." *American Historical Review* (October 1965): 43-61.

"The 1968 American Presidential Election." *External Affairs Review* (November 1968): 3-11.

Monroe, Kristen R., and Dona Laughlin Metcalf. "Economic Influences of Presidential Popularity Among Key Political and Socioeconomic Groups: A Review of the Evidence and Some New Findings." *Political Behavior* 5 (1983): 309-345.

Ogburn, W. F. "A Measurement of the Factors in the Presidential Election of 1928." *Social Forces* (December 1929): 175-183.

Peck, H. T. "Election of 1896." *Bookman* (December 1905): 334-358.

Pomper, Gerald M. "The 1972 Presidential Election in the USA." *International Problems* (July 1972): 44-54.

———. "The Southern 'Free-Elector Plan'." *Southwestern Social Science Quarterly* (June 1964): 16-25.

"Presidential Election Plan of 1928." *Congressional Digest* (August 1928): 219-250.

"Proposals to Change the Method of Electing the President: A Pro and Con Discussion on the Various Proposals for Change." *Congressional Digest* (August 1928): 219-250.

Roettger, Walter B., and Hugh Winebrenner. "The Voting Behavior of American Political Scientists: The 1980 Presidential Election." *Western Political Quarterly* 36 (March 1983): 134-148.

"Proposed Abolition of the Electoral College: A Pro and Con Discussion." *Congressional Digest* (March 1941): 67-96.

Rubin, Richard L. "The Presidency in the Age of Television." *Proceedings of the Academy of Political Science* 34 (1981): 138-152.

Shogan, R. "1948 Election." *American Heritage* (June 1968): 22-31.

Sievers, H. J. "Reform of the Electoral College." *America*, Nov. 16, 1968, 465.

Silva, Ruth C. "Lodge-Gossett Resolution: A Critical Analysis." *American Political Science Review* (March 1950): 92.

———. "Reform of the Electoral College." *Review of Politics* (July 1952): 397.

Strong, Donald S. "The Presidential Election in the South. 1952." *Journal of Politics* (August 1955): 343-389.

Wechsler, Herbert. "The Lodge-Gossett Plan." *Fortune*, June 1949, 138-146.

———. "Presidential Elections and the Constitution: A Comment on Proposed Amendment." *American Bar Association Journal* (March 1949): 181-184.

West, H. L. "Election of 1904." *Forum* (July 1903): 3-15.

Wilmerding, Lucius, Jr. "Reform of the Electoral System." *Political Science Quarterly* 64 (1949): 1-23.

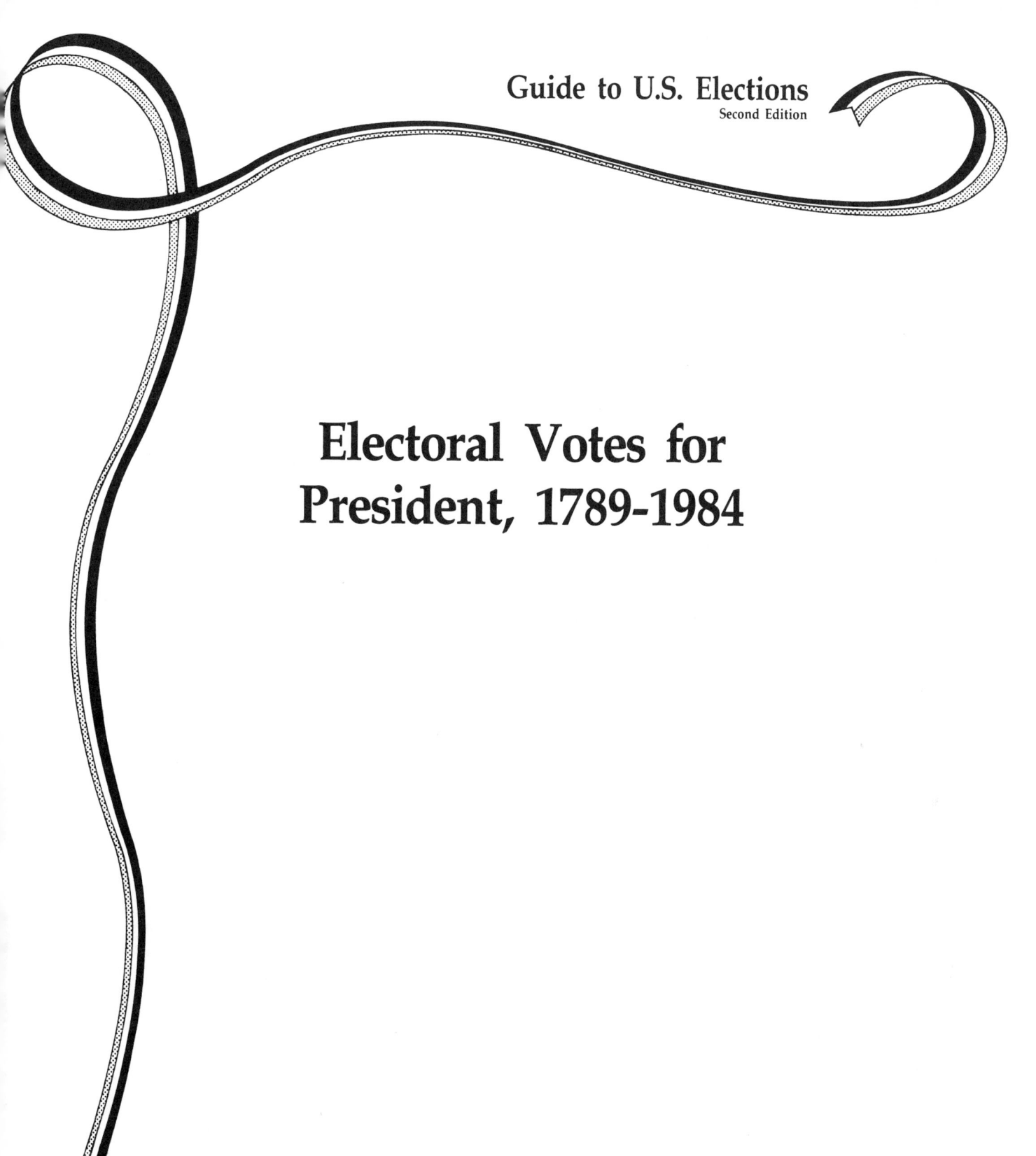

Electoral Votes for President, 1789-1984

Sources: Electoral College Votes

Electoral votes cast for presidential candidates were listed in the *Senate Manual*, Washington, D.C., U.S. Government Printing Office, 1979, pp. 779-812. Figures for 1980 are from *America Votes 14*, ed. Richard M. Scammon and Alice V. McGillivray (Washington, D.C.: Congressional Quarterly, 1981). Figures for 1984 are from *Congressional Quarterly Weekly Report*, Nov. 10, 1984, p. 2931.

Total electoral votes for each state through the 1970 census were compiled from a chart of each apportionment of the House of Representatives, published in the *Biographical Directory of the American Congress,* Washington, D.C., U.S. Government Printing Office, 1971, p. 47. The source for apportionment after the 1980 census was the Bureau of the Census.

Article II, Section 1 of the Constitution gives each state a number of electors equal to the number of senators and representatives to which it is entitled.

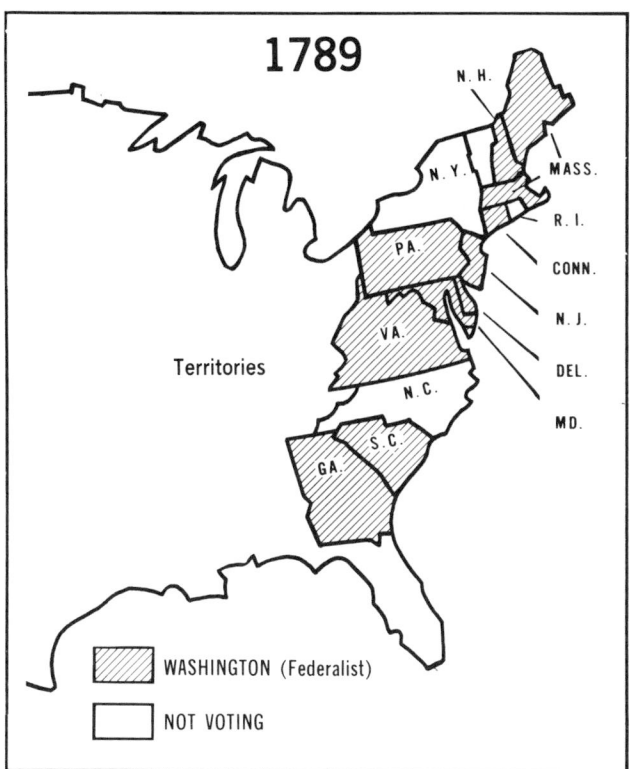

1789

N.H.

N.Y.

MASS.

R.I.

CONN.

PA.

N.J.

VA.

DEL.

Territories

N.C.

MD.

S.C.

GA.

WASHINGTON (Federalist)

NOT VOTING

Electoral Votes 1789-1800

Under Article II section 1 of the Constitution, each presidential elector had two votes and was required to cast each vote for a different person. The person receiving the highest number of votes from a majority of electors was elected president; the person receiving the second highest total became vice president. Since there were 69 electors in 1789, Washington's 69 votes constituted a unanimous election. After ratification of the 12th Amendment in 1804, electors were required to designate which of their two votes was for president and which was for vice president. The Electoral College tables on pages 269 to 272 show *all* electoral votes cast in the elections of 1789, 1792, 1796 and 1800; the charts for 1804 and thereafter show electoral votes cast only for president. For electoral vote totals for vice president, see table page 314.

States	Electoral Votes[6]	Washington	Adams	Jay	Harrison	Rutledge	Hancock	Clinton	Huntington	Milton	Armstrong	Lincoln	Telfair
Connecticut[1]	(14)	7	5	-	-	-	-	-	2	-	-	-	-
Delaware	(6)	3	-	3	-	-	-	-	-	-	-	-	-
Georgia[1]	(10)	5	-	-	-	-	-	-	-	2	1	1	1
Maryland[2]	(16)	6	-	-	6	-	-	-	-	-	-	-	-
Massachusetts	(20)	10	10	-	-	-	-	-	-	-	-	-	-
New Hampshire	(10)	5	5	-	-	-	-	-	-	-	-	-	-
New Jersey[1]	(12)	6	1	5	-	-	-	-	-	-	-	-	-
New York[3]	(16)	-	-	-	-	-	-	-	-	-	-	-	-
North Carolina[4]	(14)	-	-	-	-	-	-	-	-	-	-	-	-
Pennsylvania[1]	(20)	10	8	-	-	-	2	-	-	-	-	-	-
Rhode Island[4]	(6)	-	-	-	-	-	-	-	-	-	-	-	-
South Carolina[1]	(14)	7	-	-	-	6	1	-	-	-	-	-	-
Virginia[5]	(24)	10	5	1	-	-	1	3	-	-	-	-	-
Totals		69	34	9	6	6	4	3	2	2	1	1	1

1. For explanation of split electoral votes, see p. 258.
2. Two Maryland electors did not vote.
3. Not voting. For explanation, see p. 254.
4. Not voting because had not yet ratified Constitution.
5. Two Virginia electors did not vote. For explanation of split electoral votes, see p. 258.
6. Two votes for each elector, see text above.

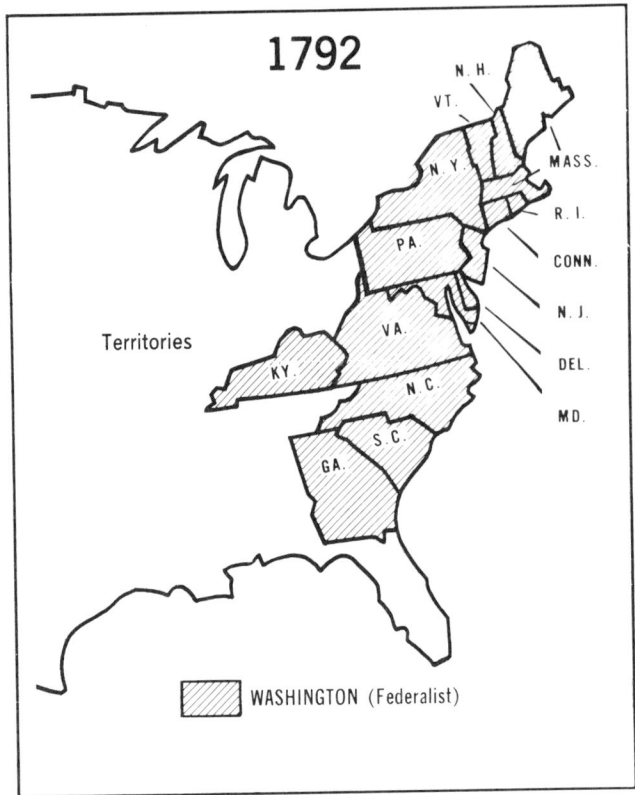

States	Electoral Votes [3]	Washington	Adams	Clinton	Jefferson	Burr
Connecticut	(18)	9	9	-	-	-
Delaware	(6)	3	3	-	-	-
Georgia	(8)	4	-	4	-	-
Kentucky	(8)	4	-	-	4	-
Maryland[1]	(20)	8	8	-	-	-
Massachusetts	(32)	16	16	-	-	-
New Hampshire	(12)	6	6	-	-	-
New Jersey	(14)	7	7	-	-	-
New York	(24)	12	-	12	-	-
North Carolina	(24)	12	-	12	-	-
Pennsylvania[2]	(30)	15	14	1	-	-
Rhode Island	(8)	4	4	-	-	-
South Carolina[2]	(16)	8	7	-	-	1
Vermont[1]	(8)	3	3	-	-	-
Virginia	(42)	21	-	21	-	-
Totals	(270)	132	77	50	4	1

1. Two Maryland electors and one Vermont elector did not vote.
2. For explanation of split electoral votes, see p. 258.
3. Two votes for each elector, see text p. 269.

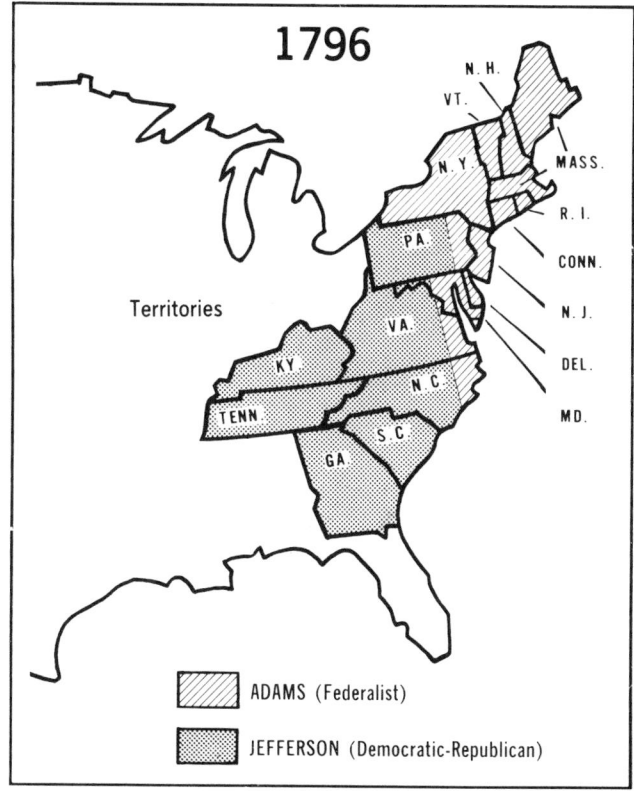

1796

ADAMS (Federalist)

JEFFERSON (Democratic-Republican)

States	Electoral Votes[2]	J. Adams	Jefferson	T. Pinckney	Burr	S. Adams	Ellsworth	Clinton	Jay	Iredell	Henry	Johnston	Washington	C. Pinckney
Connecticut[1]	(18)	9	-	4	-	-	-	-	5	-	-	-	-	-
Delaware	(6)	3	-	3	-	-	-	-	-	-	-	-	-	-
Georgia	(8)	-	4	-	-	-	-	4	-	-	-	-	-	-
Kentucky	(8)	-	4	-	4	-	-	-	-	-	-	-	-	-
Maryland[1]	(20)	7	4	4	3	-	-	-	-	-	2	-	-	-
Massachusetts[1]	(32)	16	-	13	-	-	1	-	-	-	-	2	-	-
New Hampshire	(12)	6	-	-	-	-	6	-	-	-	-	-	-	-
New Jersey	(14)	7	-	7	-	-	-	-	-	-	-	-	-	-
New York	(24)	12	-	12	-	-	-	-	-	-	-	-	-	-
North Carolina[1]	(24)	1	11	1	6	-	-	-	-	3	-	-	1	1
Pennsylvania[1]	(30)	1	14	2	13	-	-	-	-	-	-	-	-	-
Rhode Island	(8)	4	-	-	-	-	4	-	-	-	-	-	-	-
South Carolina	(16)	-	8	8	-	-	-	-	-	-	-	-	-	-
Tennessee	(6)	-	3	-	3	-	-	-	-	-	-	-	-	-
Vermont	(8)	4	-	4	-	-	-	-	-	-	-	-	-	-
Virginia[1]	(42)	1	20	1	1	15	-	3	-	-	-	-	1	-
Totals	**(276)**	**71**	**68**	**59**	**30**	**15**	**11**	**7**	**5**	**3**	**2**	**2**	**2**	**1**

1. For explanation of split electoral votes, see p. 258.
2. Two votes for each elector, see text p. 269.

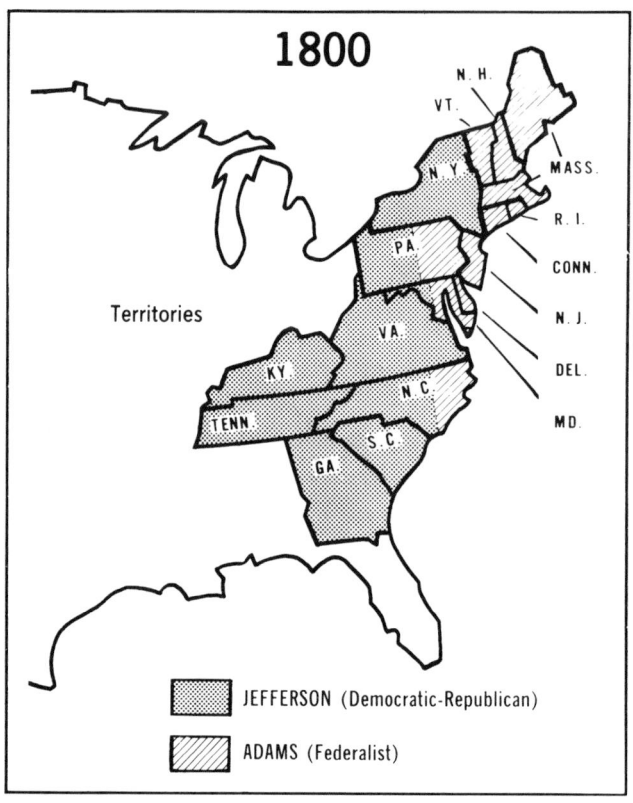

States	Electoral Votes[2]	Jefferson[3]	Burr[3]	Adams	Pinckney	Jay
Connecticut	(18)	-	-	9	9	-
Delaware	(6)	-	-	3	3	-
Georgia	(8)	4	4	-	-	-
Kentucky	(8)	4	4	-	-	-
Maryland[1]	(20)	5	5	5	5	-
Massachusetts	(32)	-	-	16	16	-
New Hampshire	(12)	-	-	6	6	-
New Jersey	(14)	-	-	7	7	-
New York	(24)	12	12	-	-	-
North Carolina[1]	(24)	8	8	4	4	-
Pennsylvania[1]	(30)	8	8	7	7	-
Rhode Island[1]	(8)	-	-	4	3	1
South Carolina	(16)	8	8	-	-	-
Tennessee	(6)	3	3	-	-	-
Vermont	(8)	-	-	4	4	-
Virginia	(42)	21	21	-	-	-
Totals	(276)	73	73	65	64	1

1. For explanation of split electoral votes, see p. 258.
2. Two votes for each elector, see text p. 269.
3. For explanation and result of tie vote, see p. 256.

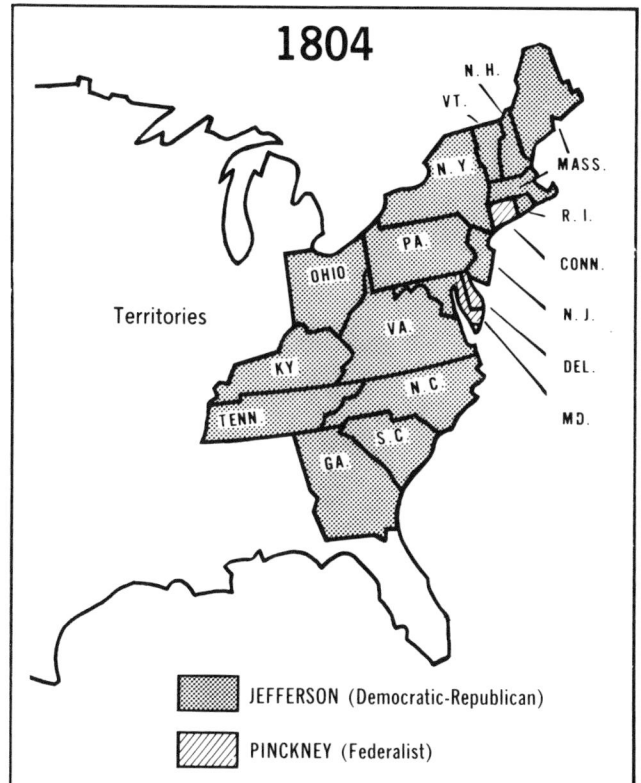

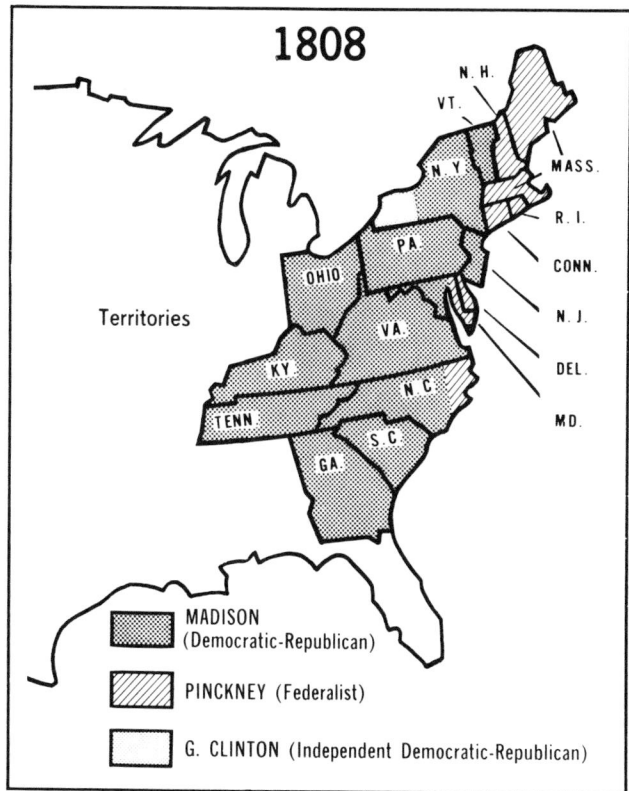

States	Electoral Votes	Jefferson	Pinckney
Connecticut	(9)	-	9
Delaware	(3)	-	3
Georgia	(6)	6	-
Kentucky	(8)	8	-
Maryland[1]	(11)	9	2
Massachusetts	(19)	19	-
New Hampshire	(7)	7	-
New Jersey	(8)	8	-
New York	(19)	19	-
North Carolina	(14)	14	-
Ohio	(3)	3	-
Pennsylvania	(20)	20	-
Rhode Island	(4)	4	-
South Carolina	(10)	10	-
Tennessee	(5)	5	-
Vermont	(6)	6	-
Virginia	(24)	24	-
Totals	(176)	162	14

1. For explanation of split electoral votes, see p. 258.

States	Electoral Votes	Madison	Pinckney	Clinton
Connecticut	(9)	-	9	-
Delaware	(3)	-	3	-
Georgia	(6)	6	-	-
Kentucky[1]	(8)	7	-	-
Maryland[2]	(11)	9	2	-
Massachusetts	(19)	-	19	-
New Hampshire	(7)	-	7	-
New Jersey	(8)	8	-	-
New York[2]	(19)	13	-	6
North Carolina[2]	(14)	11	3	-
Ohio	(3)	3	-	-
Pennsylvania	(20)	20	-	-
Rhode Island	(4)	-	4	-
South Carolina	(10)	10	-	-
Tennessee	(5)	5	-	-
Vermont	(6)	6	-	-
Virginia	(24)	24	-	-
Totals	(176)	122	47	6

1. One Kentucky elector did not vote.
2. For explanation of split electoral votes, see p. 258.

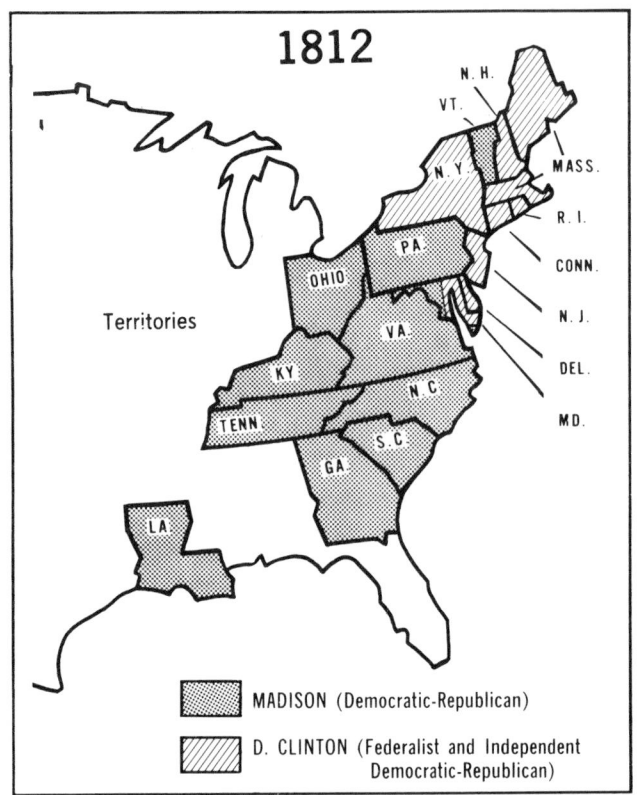

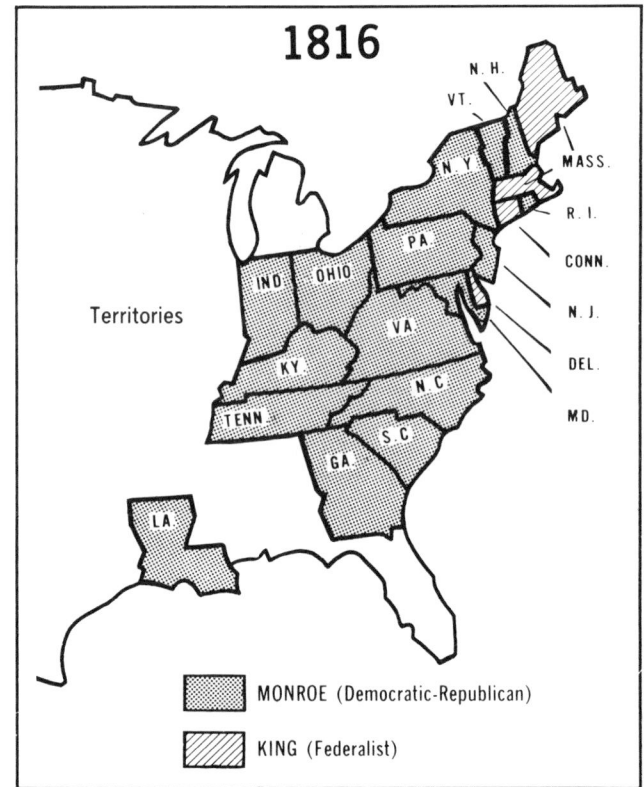

States	Electoral Votes	Madison	Clinton
Connecticut	(9)	-	9
Delaware	(4)	-	4
Georgia	(8)	8	-
Kentucky	(12)	12	-
Louisiana	(3)	3	-
Maryland [1]	(11)	6	5
Massachusetts	(22)	-	22
New Hampshire	(8)	-	8
New Jersey	(8)	-	8
New York	(29)	-	29
North Carolina	(15)	15	-
Ohio [2]	(8)	7	-
Pennsylvania	(25)	25	-
Rhode Island	(4)	-	4
South Carolina	(11)	11	-
Tennessee	(8)	8	-
Vermont	(8)	8	-
Virginia	(25)	25	-
Totals	**(218)**	**128**	**89**

States	Electoral Votes	Monroe	King
Connecticut	(9)	-	9
Delaware [1]	(4)	-	3
Georgia	(8)	8	-
Indiana	(3)	3	-
Kentucky	(12)	12	-
Louisiana	(3)	3	-
Maryland [1]	(11)	8	-
Massachusetts	(22)	-	22
New Hampshire	(8)	8	-
New Jersey	(8)	8	-
New York	(29)	29	-
North Carolina	(15)	15	-
Ohio	(8)	8	-
Pennsylvania	(25)	25	-
Rhode Island	(4)	4	-
South Carolina	(11)	11	-
Tennessee	(8)	8	-
Vermont	(8)	8	-
Virginia	(25)	25	-
Totals	**(221)**	**183**	**34**

1. *For explanation of split electoral votes, see p. 258.*
2. *One Ohio elector did not vote.*

1. *One Delaware and three Maryland electors did not vote.*

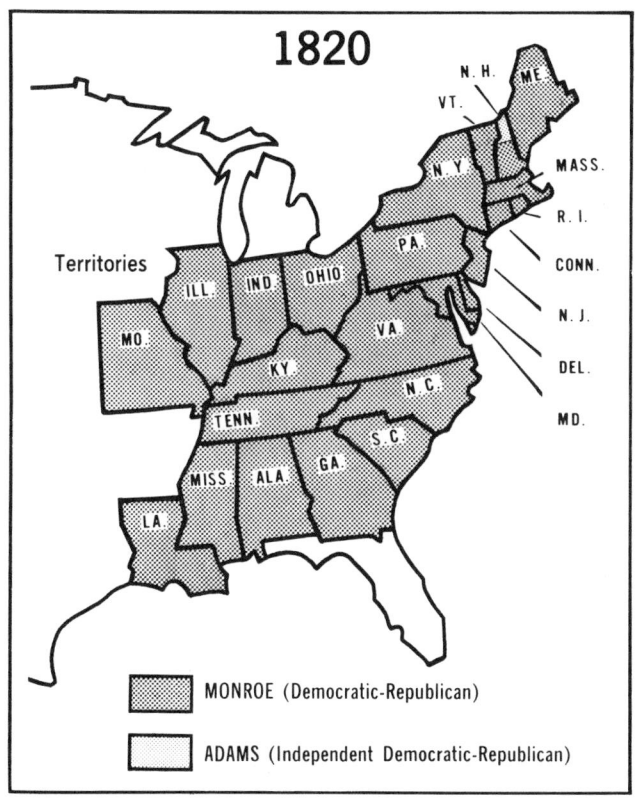

1820

MONROE (Democratic-Republican)

ADAMS (Independent Democratic-Republican)

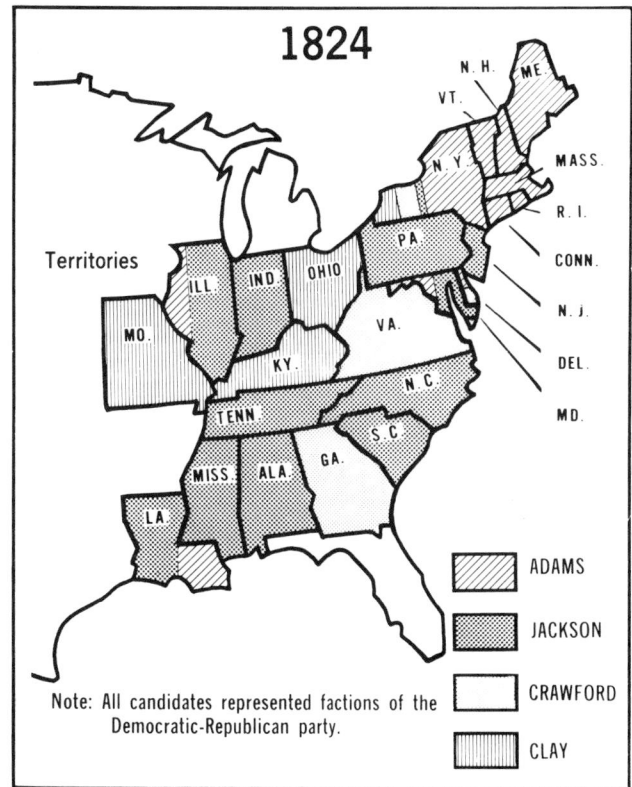

1824

ADAMS

JACKSON

CRAWFORD

CLAY

Note: All candidates represented factions of the Democratic-Republican party.

States	Electoral Votes	Monroe	Adams
Alabama	(3)	3	-
Connecticut	(9)	9	-
Delaware	(4)	4	-
Georgia	(8)	8	-
Illinois	(3)	3	-
Indiana	(3)	3	-
Kentucky	(12)	12	-
Louisiana	(3)	3	-
Maine	(9)	9	-
Maryland	(11)	11	-
Massachusetts	(15)	15	-
Mississippi [1]	(3)	2	-
Missouri	(3)	3	-
New Hampshire [2]	(8)	7	1
New Jersey	(8)	8	-
New York	(29)	29	-
North Carolina	(15)	15	-
Ohio	(8)	8	-
Pennsylvania [1]	(25)	24	-
Rhode Island	(4)	4	-
South Carolina	(11)	11	-
Tennessee [1]	(8)	7	-
Vermont	(8)	8	-
Virginia	(25)	25	-
Totals	**(235)**	**231**	**1**

1. One elector each from Mississippi, Pennsylvania and Tennessee did not vote.
2. For explanation of split electoral votes, see p. 258.

States	Electoral Votes	Jackson	Adams	Crawford	Clay
Alabama	(5)	5	-	-	-
Connecticut	(8)	-	8	-	-
Delaware [1]	(3)	-	1	2	-
Georgia	(9)	-	-	9	-
Illinois [1]	(3)	2	1	-	-
Indiana	(5)	5	-	-	-
Kentucky	(14)	-	-	-	14
Louisiana [1]	(5)	3	2	-	-
Maine	(9)	-	9	-	-
Maryland [1]	(11)	7	3	1	-
Massachusetts	(15)	-	15	-	-
Mississippi	(3)	3	-	-	-
Missouri	(3)	-	-	-	3
New Hampshire	(8)	-	8	-	-
New Jersey	(8)	8	-	-	-
New York [1]	(36)	1	26	5	4
North Carolina	(15)	15	-	-	-
Ohio	(16)	-	-	-	16
Pennsylvania	(28)	28	-	-	-
Rhode Island	(4)	-	4	-	-
South Carolina	(11)	11	-	-	-
Tennessee	(11)	11	-	-	-
Vermont	(7)	-	7	-	-
Virginia	(24)	-	-	24	-
Totals	**(261)**	**99** [2]	**84**	**41**	**37**

1. For explanation of split electoral votes, see p. 258.
2. As no candidate received a majority of the electoral votes, the election was decided by the House of Representatives. See p. 259.

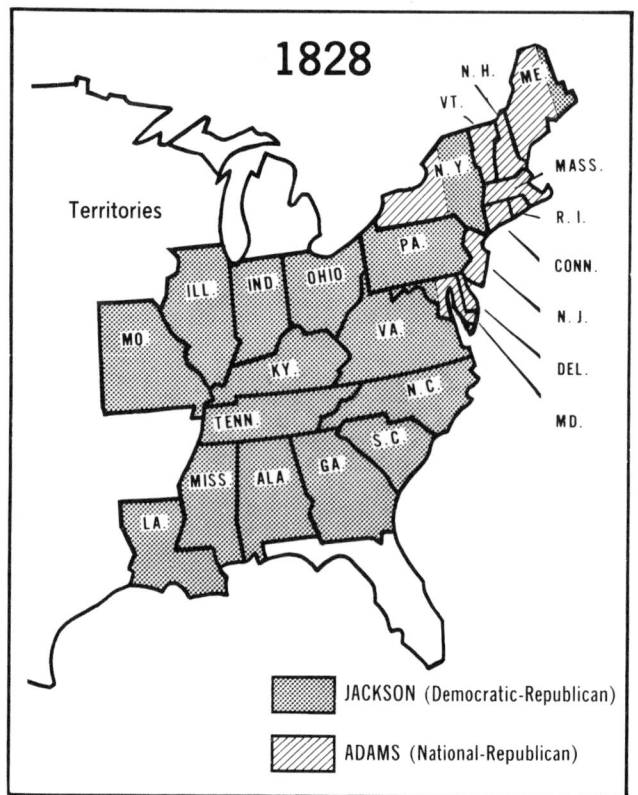

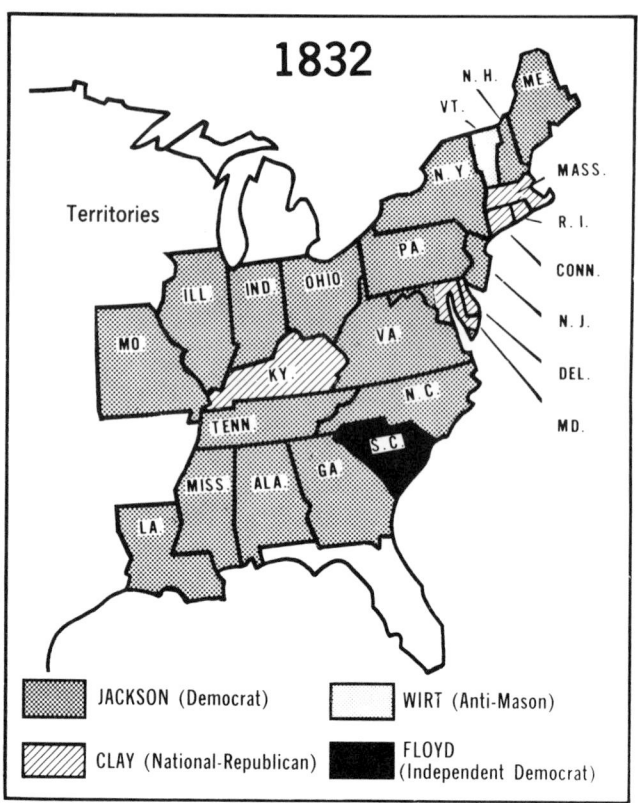

States	Electoral Votes	Jackson	Adams
Alabama	(5)	5	-
Connecticut	(8)	-	8
Delaware	(3)	-	3
Georgia	(9)	9	-
Illinois	(3)	3	-
Indiana	(5)	5	-
Kentucky	(14)	14	-
Louisiana	(5)	5	-
Maine[1]	(9)	1	8
Maryland[1]	(11)	5	6
Massachusetts	(15)	-	15
Mississippi	(3)	3	-
Missouri	(3)	3	-
New Hampshire	(8)	-	8
New Jersey	(8)	-	8
New York[1]	(36)	20	16
North Carolina	(15)	15	-
Ohio	(16)	16	-
Pennsylvania	(28)	28	-
Rhode Island	(4)	-	4
South Carolina	(11)	11	-
Tennessee	(11)	11	-
Vermont	(7)	-	7
Virginia	(24)	24	-
Totals	**(261)**	**178**	**83**

1. For explanation of split electoral votes, see p. 258.

States	Electoral Votes	Jackson	Clay	Floyd	Wirt
Alabama	(7)	7	-	-	-
Connecticut	(8)	-	8	-	-
Delaware	(3)	-	3	-	-
Georgia	(11)	11	-	-	-
Illinois	(5)	5	-	-	-
Indiana	(9)	9	-	-	-
Kentucky	(15)	-	15	-	-
Louisiana	(5)	5	-	-	-
Maine	(10)	10	-	-	-
Maryland[1]	(10)	3	5	-	-
Massachusetts	(14)	-	14	-	-
Mississippi	(4)	4	-	-	-
Missouri	(4)	4	-	-	-
New Hampshire	(7)	7	-	-	-
New Jersey	(8)	8	-	-	-
New York	(42)	42	-	-	-
North Carolina	(15)	15	-	-	-
Ohio	(21)	21	-	-	-
Pennsylvania	(30)	30	-	-	-
Rhode Island	(4)	-	4	-	-
South Carolina	(11)	-	-	11	-
Tennessee	(15)	15	-	-	-
Vermont	(7)	-	-	-	7
Virginia	(23)	23	-	-	-
Totals	**(288)**	**219**	**49**	**11**	**7**

1. Two Maryland electors did not vote. For explanation of split electoral votes, see p. 258.

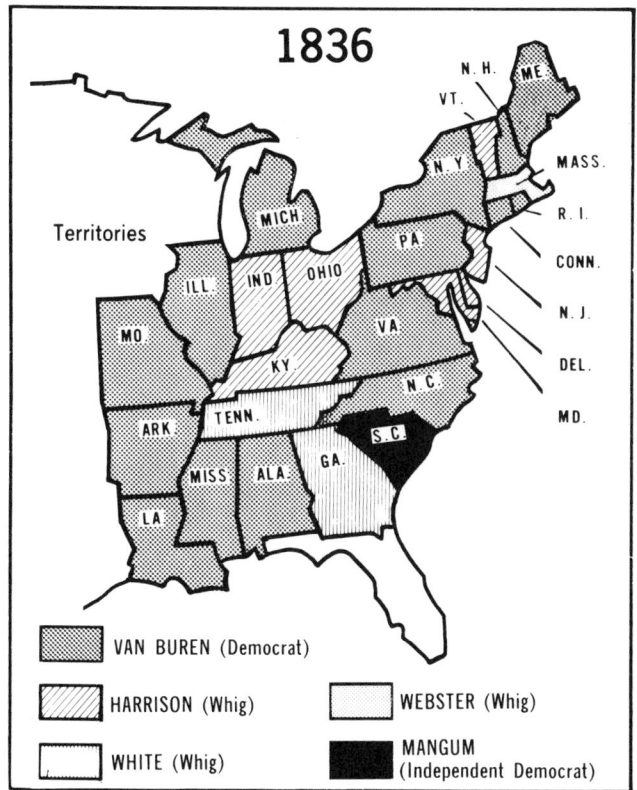

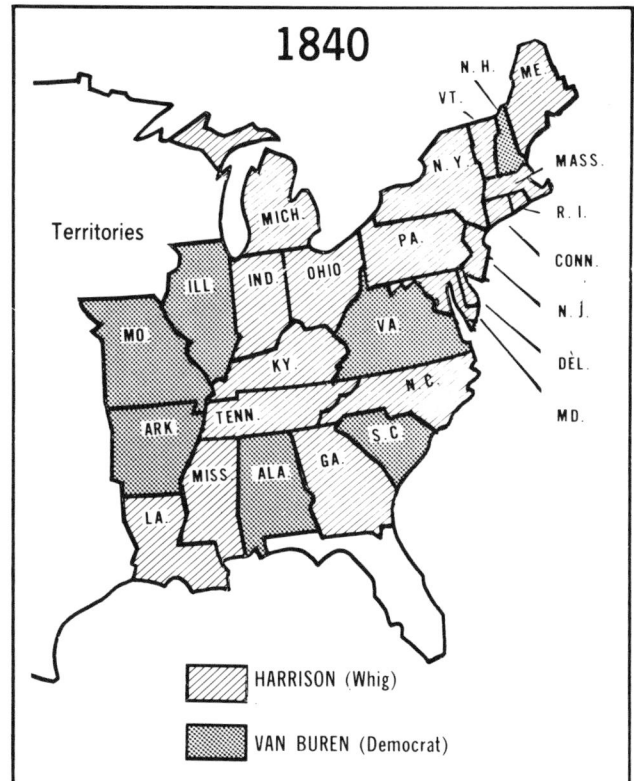

States	Electoral Votes	Van Buren	Harrison[1]	White[1]	Webster[1]	Mangum
Alabama	(7)	7	-	-	-	-
Arkansas	(3)	3	-	-	-	-
Connecticut	(8)	8	-	-	-	-
Delaware	(3)	-	3	-	-	-
Georgia	(11)	-	-	11	-	-
Illinois	(5)	5	-	-	-	-
Indiana	(9)	-	9	-	-	-
Kentucky	(15)	-	15	-	-	-
Louisiana	(5)	5	-	-	-	-
Maine	(10)	10	-	-	-	-
Maryland	(10)	-	10	-	-	-
Massachusetts	(14)	-	-	-	14	-
Michigan	(3)	3	-	-	-	-
Mississippi	(4)	4	-	-	-	-
Missouri	(4)	4	-	-	-	-
New Hampshire	(7)	7	-	-	-	-
New Jersey	(8)	-	8	-	-	-
New York	(42)	42	-	-	-	-
North Carolina	(15)	15	-	-	-	-
Ohio	(21)	-	21	-	-	-
Pennsylvania	(30)	30	-	-	-	-
Rhode Island	(4)	4	-	-	-	-
South Carolina	(11)	-	-	-	-	11
Tennessee	(15)	-	-	15	-	-
Vermont	(7)	-	7	-	-	-
Virginia	(23)	23	-	-	-	-
Totals	(294)	170	73	26	14	11

States	Electoral Votes	Harrison	Van Buren
Alabama	(7)	-	7
Arkansas	(3)	-	3
Connecticut	(8)	8	-
Delaware	(3)	3	-
Georgia	(11)	11	-
Illinois	(5)	-	5
Indiana	(9)	9	-
Kentucky	(15)	15	-
Louisiana	(5)	5	-
Maine	(10)	10	-
Maryland	(10)	10	-
Massachusetts	(14)	14	-
Michigan	(3)	3	-
Mississippi	(4)	4	-
Missouri	(4)	-	4
New Hampshire	(7)	-	7
New Jersey	(8)	8	-
New York	(42)	42	-
North Carolina	(15)	15	-
Ohio	(21)	21	-
Pennsylvania	(30)	30	-
Rhode Island	(4)	4	-
South Carolina	(11)	-	11
Tennessee	(15)	15	-
Vermont	(7)	7	-
Virginia	(23)	-	23
Totals	(294)	234	60

1. For explanation of three Whig presidential candidates, see p. 256.

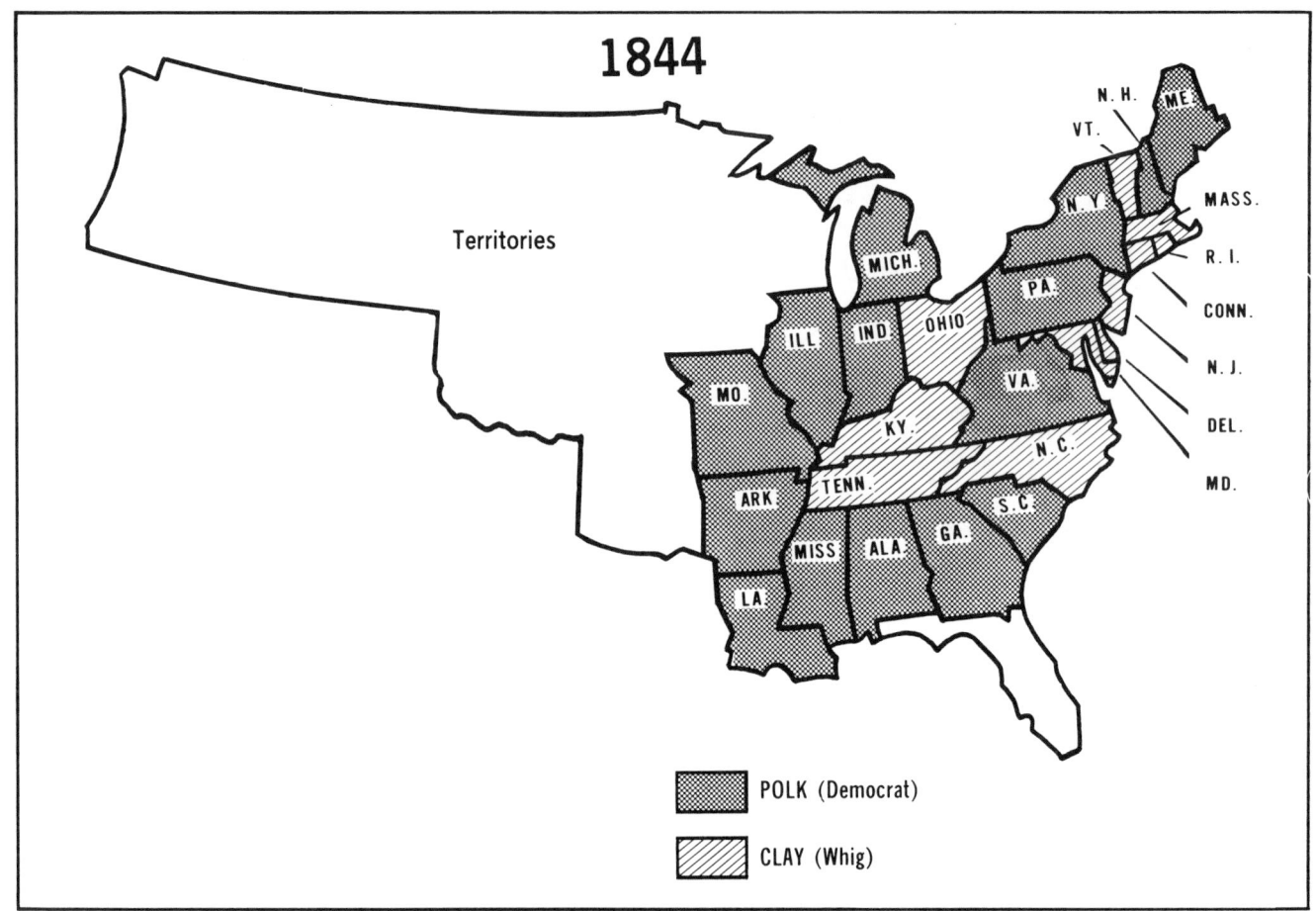

States	Electoral Votes	Polk	Clay
Alabama	(9)	9	-
Arkansas	(3)	3	-
Connecticut	(6)	-	6
Delaware	(3)	-	3
Georgia	(10)	10	-
Illinois	(9)	9	-
Indiana	(12)	12	-
Kentucky	(12)	-	12
Louisiana	(6)	6	-
Maine	(9)	9	-
Maryland	(8)	-	8
Massachusetts	(12)	-	12
Michigan	(5)	5	-
Mississippi	(6)	6	-
Missouri	(7)	7	-
New Hampshire	(6)	6	-
New Jersey	(7)	-	7
New York	(36)	36	-
North Carolina	(11)	-	11
Ohio	(23)	-	23
Pennsylvania	(26)	26	-
Rhode Island	(4)	-	4
South Carolina	(9)	9	-
Tennessee	(13)	-	13
Vermont	(6)	-	6
Virginia	(17)	17	-
Totals	**(275)**	**170**	**105**

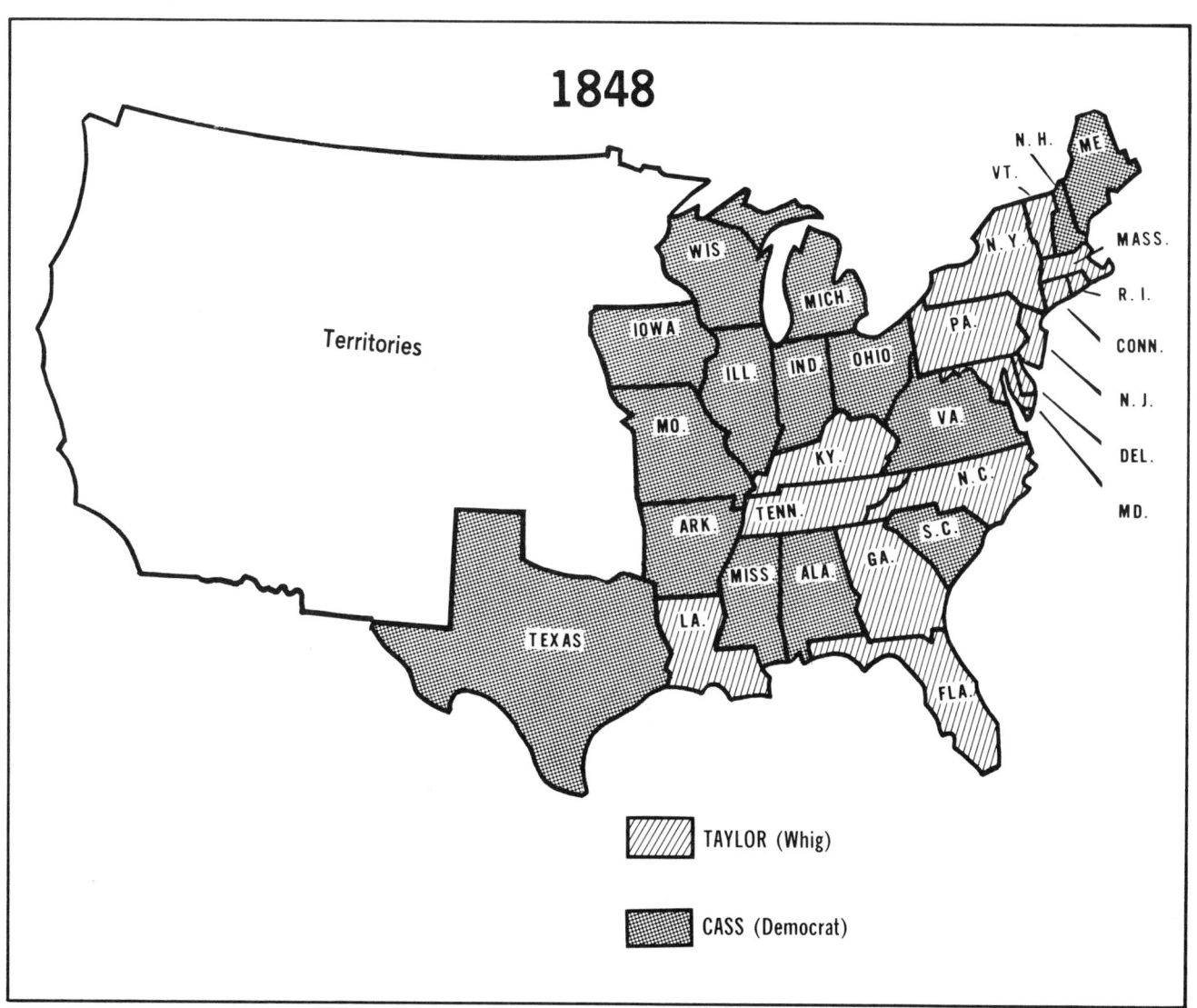

1848

Territories

WIS.
MICH.
IOWA
ILL.
IND.
OHIO
MO.
KY.
ARK.
TENN.
MISS.
ALA.
LA.
TEXAS
GA.
S.C.
N.C.
VA.
PA.
N.Y.
N.H.
VT.
ME.
MASS.
R.I.
CONN.
N.J.
DEL.
MD.
FLA.

TAYLOR (Whig)

CASS (Democrat)

States	Electoral Votes	Taylor	Cass	States	Electoral Votes	Taylor	Cass
Alabama	(9)	-	9	Mississippi	(6)		
Arkansas	(3)	-	3	Missouri	(7)	-	7
Connecticut	(6)	6	-	New Hampshire	(6)	-	6
Delaware	(3)	3	-	New Jersey	(7)	7	-
Florida	(3)	3	-	New York	(36)	36	-
Georgia	(10)	10	-	North Carolina	(11)	11	-
Illinois	(9)	-	9	Ohio	(23)	-	23
Indiana	(12)	-	12	Pennsylvania	(26)	26	-
Iowa	(4)	-	4	Rhode Island	(4)	4	-
Kentucky	(12)	12	-	South Carolina	(9)	-	9
Louisiana	(6)	6	-	Tennessee	(13)	13	-
Maine	(9)	-	9	Texas	(4)	-	4
Maryland	(8)	8	-	Vermont	(6)	6	-
Massachusetts	(12)	12	-	Virginia	(17)	-	17
Michigan	(5)	-	5	Wisconsin	(4)	-	4
				Totals	**(290)**	**163**	**127**

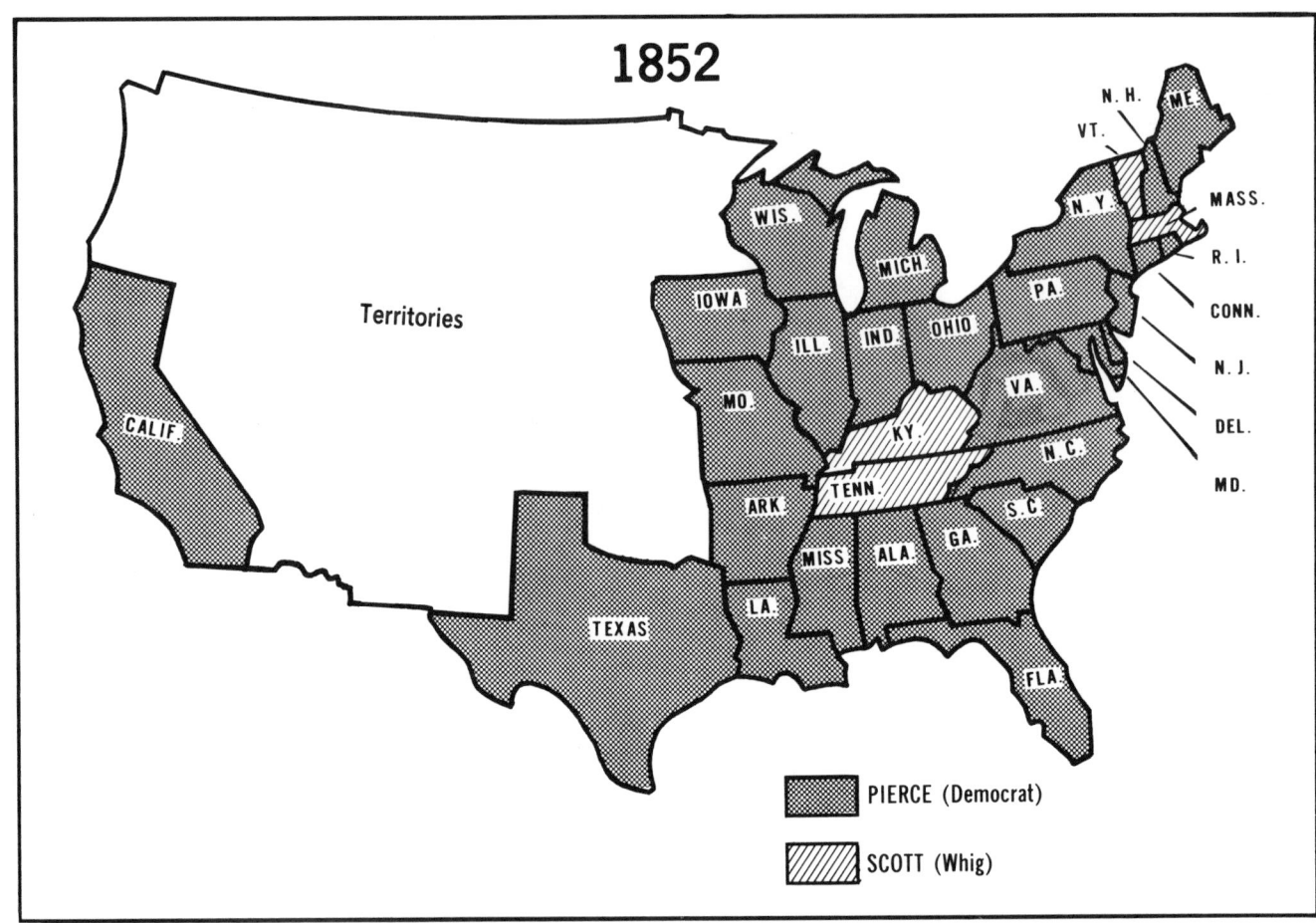

1852

PIERCE (Democrat)

SCOTT (Whig)

States	Electoral Votes	Pierce	Scott	States	Electoral Votes	Pierce	Scott
Alabama	(9)	9	-	Mississippi	(7)	7	-
Arkansas	(4)	4	-	Missouri	(9)	9	-
California	(4)	4	-	New Hampshire	(5)	5	-
Connecticut	(6)	6	-	New Jersey	(7)	7	-
Delaware	(3)	3	-	New York	(35)	35	-
Florida	(3)	3	-	North Carolina	(10)	10	-
Georgia	(10)	10	-	Ohio	(23)	23	-
Illinois	(11)	11	-	Pennsylvania	(27)	27	-
Indiana	(13)	13	-	Rhode Island	(4)	4	-
Iowa	(4)	4	-	South Carolina	(8)	8	-
Kentucky	(12)	-	12	Tennessee	(12)	-	12
Louisiana	(6)	6	-	Texas	(4)	4	-
Maine	(8)	8	-	Vermont	(5)	-	5
Maryland	(8)	8	-	Virginia	(15)	15	-
Massachusetts	(13)	-	13	Wisconsin	(5)	5	-
Michigan	(6)	6	-	**Totals**	**(296)**	**254**	**42**

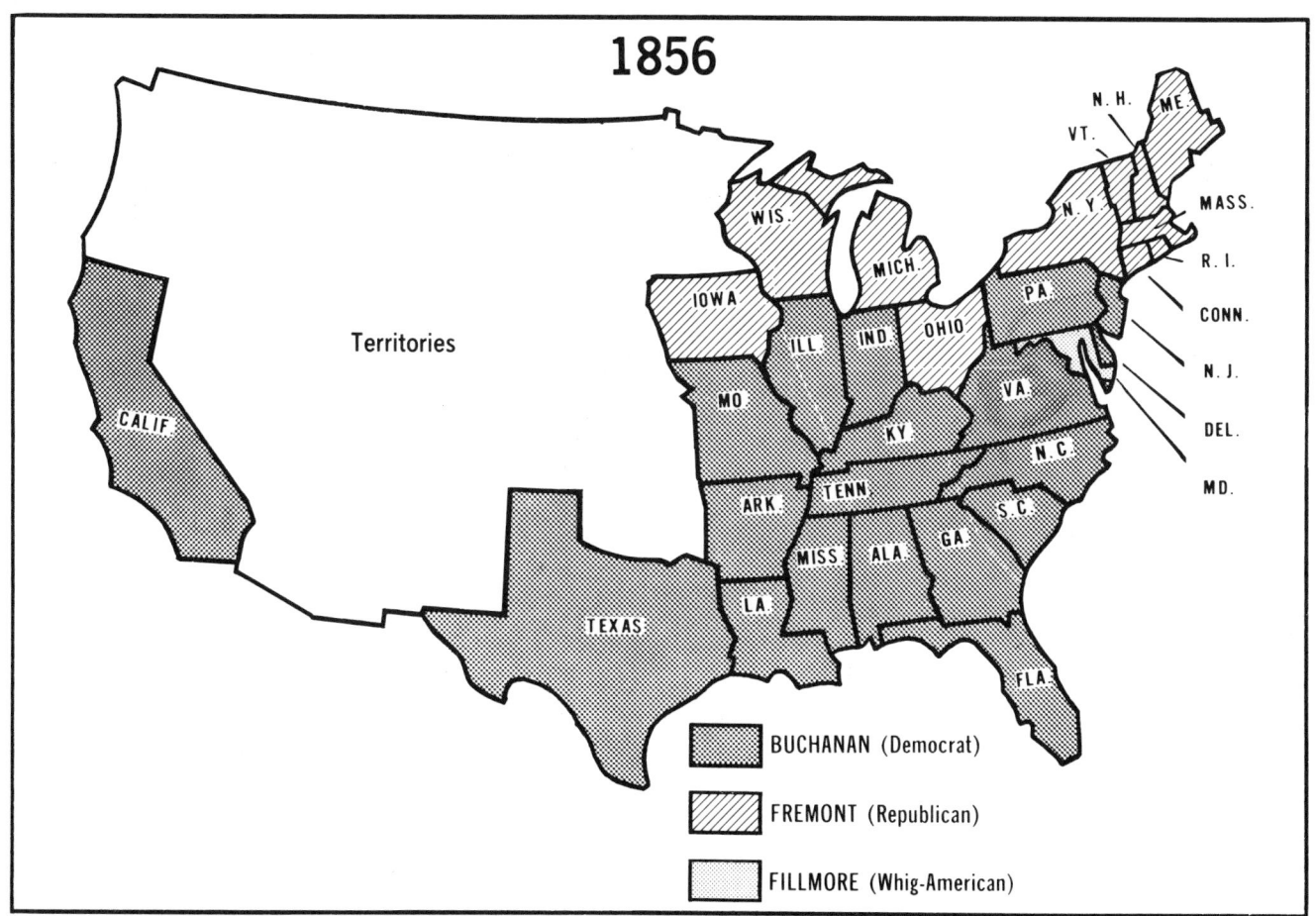

1856

Territories

CALIF.

TEXAS

WIS. IOWA ILL. MO. IND. OHIO KY. TENN. ARK. MISS. ALA. GA. S.C. LA. FLA. N.C. VA. PA. MICH.

N.H. ME. VT. N.Y. MASS. R.I. CONN. N.J. DEL. MD.

BUCHANAN (Democrat)

FREMONT (Republican)

FILLMORE (Whig-American)

States	Electoral Votes	Buchanan	Fremont	Fillmore	States	Electoral Votes	Buchanan	Fremont	Fillmore
Alabama	(9)	9	-	-	**Mississippi**	(7)	7	-	-
Arkansas	(4)	4	-	-	**Missouri**	(9)	9	-	-
California	(4)	4	-	-	**New Hampshire**	(5)	-	5	-
Connecticut	(6)	-	6	-	**New Jersey**	(7)	7	-	-
Delaware	(3)	3	-	-	**New York**	(35)	-	35	-
Florida	(3)	3	-	-	**North Carolina**	(10)	10	-	-
Georgia	(10)	10	-	-	**Ohio**	(23)	-	23	-
Illinois	(11)	11	-	-	**Pennsylvania**	(27)	27	-	-
Indiana	(13)	13	-	-	**Rhode Island**	(4)	-	4	-
Iowa	(4)	-	4	-	**South Carolina**	(8)	8	-	-
Kentucky	(12)	12	-	-	**Tennessee**	(12)	12	-	-
Louisiana	(6)	6	-	-	**Texas**	(4)	4	-	-
Maine	(8)	-	8	-	**Vermont**	(5)	-	5	-
Maryland	(8)	-	-	8	**Virginia**	(15)	15	-	-
Massachusetts	(13)	-	13	-	**Wisconsin**	(5)	-	5	-
Michigan	(6)	-	6	-	**Totals**	**(296)**	**174**	**114**	**8**

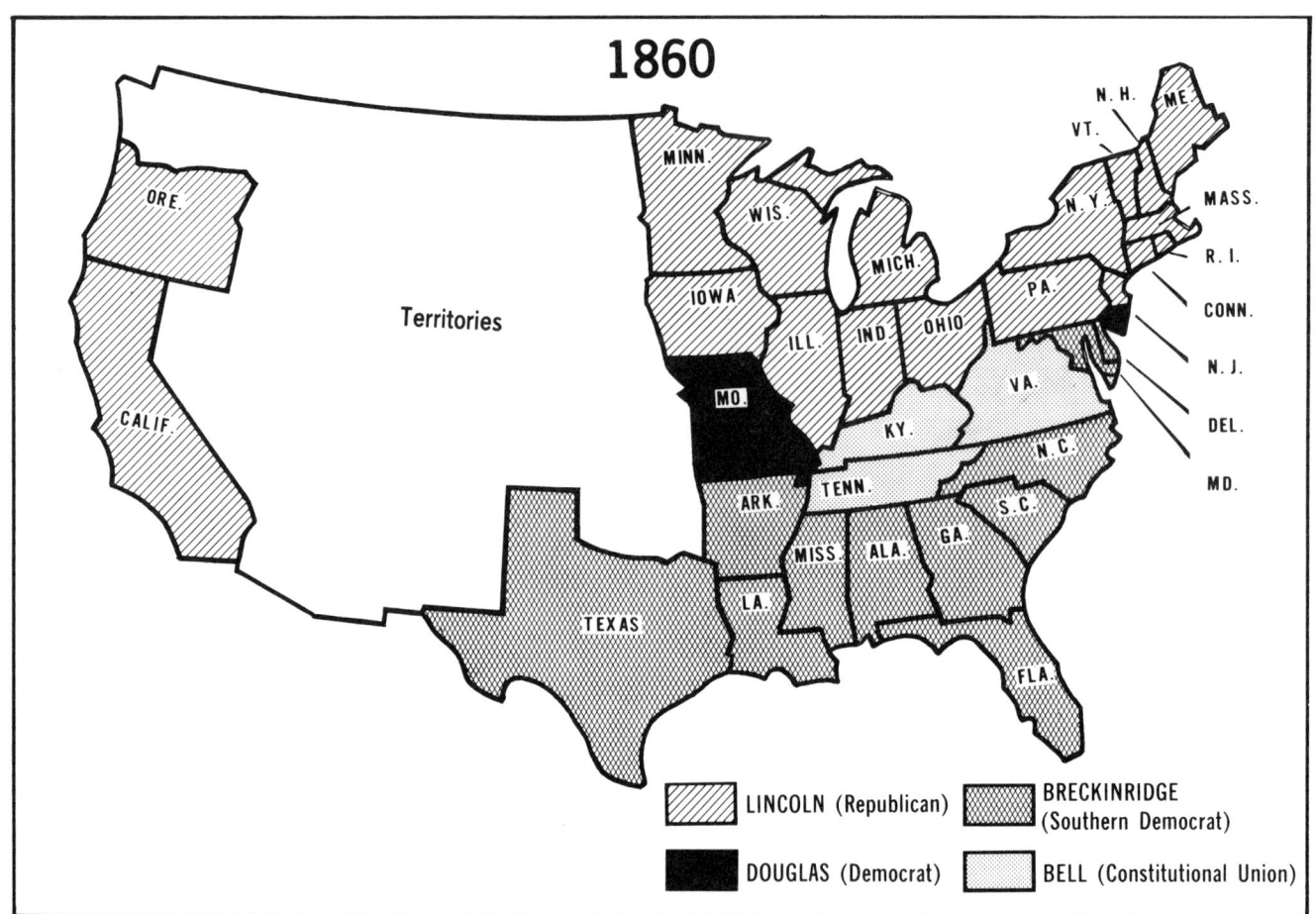

States	Electoral Votes	Lincoln	Breckinridge	Bell	Douglas
Alabama	(9)	-	9	-	-
Arkansas	(4)	-	4	-	-
California	(4)	4	-	-	-
Connecticut	(6)	6	-	-	-
Delaware	(3)	-	3	-	-
Florida	(3)	-	3	-	-
Georgia	(10)	-	10	-	-
Illinois	(11)	11	-	-	-
Indiana	(13)	13	-	-	-
Iowa	(4)	4	-	-	-
Kentucky	(12)	-	-	12	-
Louisiana	(6)	-	6	-	-
Maine	(8)	8	-	-	-
Maryland	(8)	-	8	-	-
Massachusetts	(13)	13	-	-	-
Michigan	(6)	6	-	-	-
Minnesota	(4)	4	-	-	-
Mississippi	(7)	-	7	-	-
Missouri	(9)	-	-	-	9
New Hampshire	(5)	5	-	-	-
New Jersey[1]	(7)	4	-	-	3
New York	(35)	35	-	-	-
North Carolina	(10)	-	10	-	-
Ohio	(23)	23	-	-	-
Oregon	(3)	3	-	-	-
Pennsylvania	(27)	27	-	-	-
Rhode Island	(4)	4	-	-	-
South Carolina	(8)	-	8	-	-
Tennessee	(12)	-	-	12	-
Texas	(4)	-	4	-	-
Vermont	(5)	5	-	-	-
Virginia	(15)	-	-	15	-
Wisconsin	(5)	5	-	-	-
Totals	**(303)**	**180**	**72**	**39**	**12**

1. *For explanation of split electoral votes, see p. 258.*

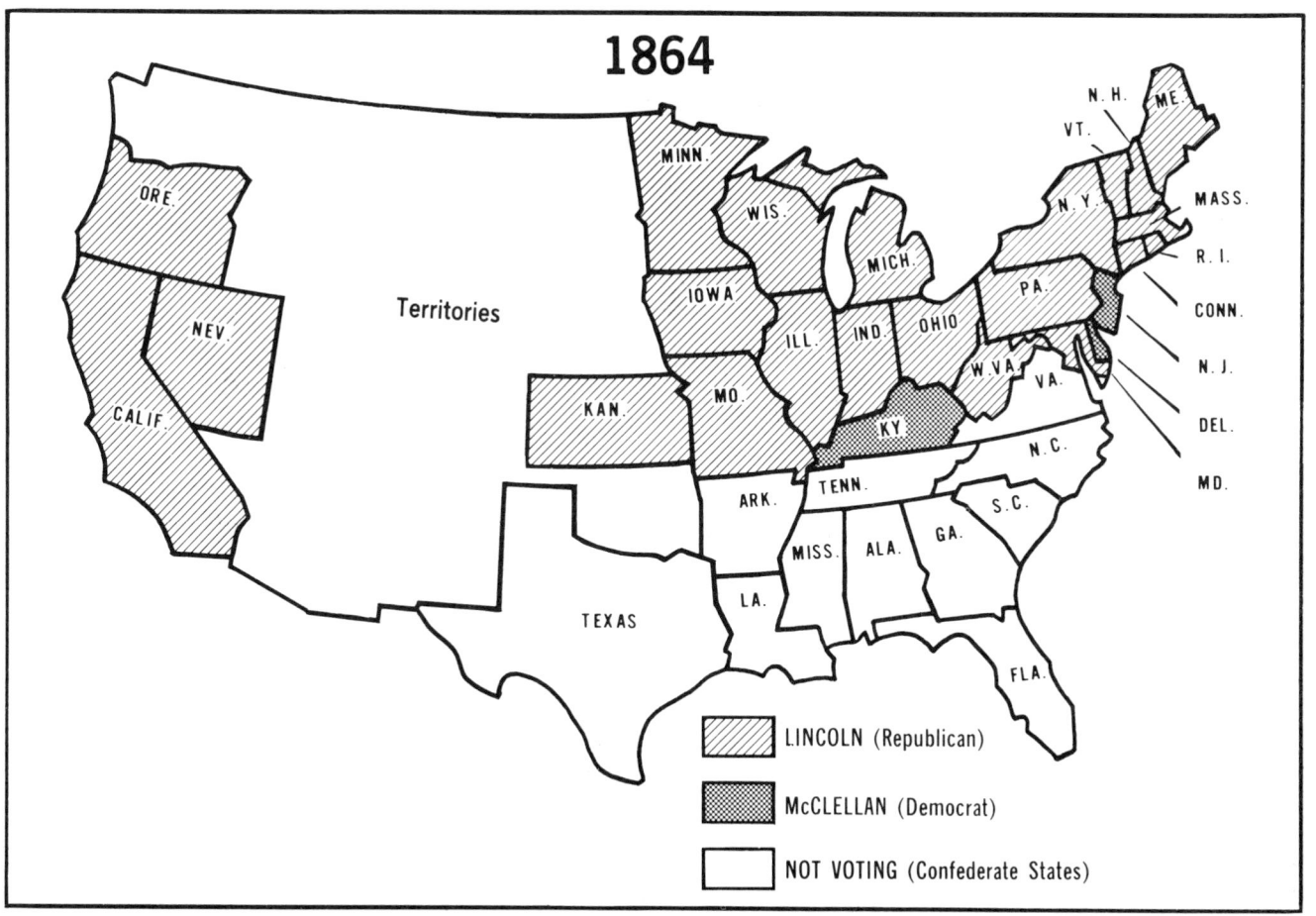

1864

States[1]	Electoral Votes	Lincoln	McClellan
California	(5)	5	-
Connecticut	(6)	6	-
Delaware	(3)	-	3
Illinois	(16)	16	-
Indiana	(13)	13	-
Iowa	(8)	8	-
Kansas	(3)	3	-
Kentucky	(11)	-	11
Maine	(7)	7	-
Maryland	(7)	7	-
Massachusetts	(12)	12	-
Michigan	(8)	8	-
Minnesota	(4)	4	-

States[1]	Electoral Votes	Lincoln	McClellan
Missouri	(11)	11	-
Nevada[2]	(3)	2	-
New Hampshire	(5)	5	-
New Jersey	(7)	-	7
New York	(33)	33	-
Ohio	(21)	21	-
Oregon	(3)	3	-
Pennsylvania	(26)	26	-
Rhode Island	(4)	4	-
Vermont	(5)	5	-
West Virginia	(5)	5	-
Wisconsin	(8)	8	-
Totals	(234)	212	21

1. Eleven Southern States—Alabama, Arkansas, Florida, Georgia, Louisiana, Mississippi, North Carolina, South Carolina, Tennessee, Texas and Virginia—had seceded from the Union and did not vote.
2. One Nevada elector did not vote.

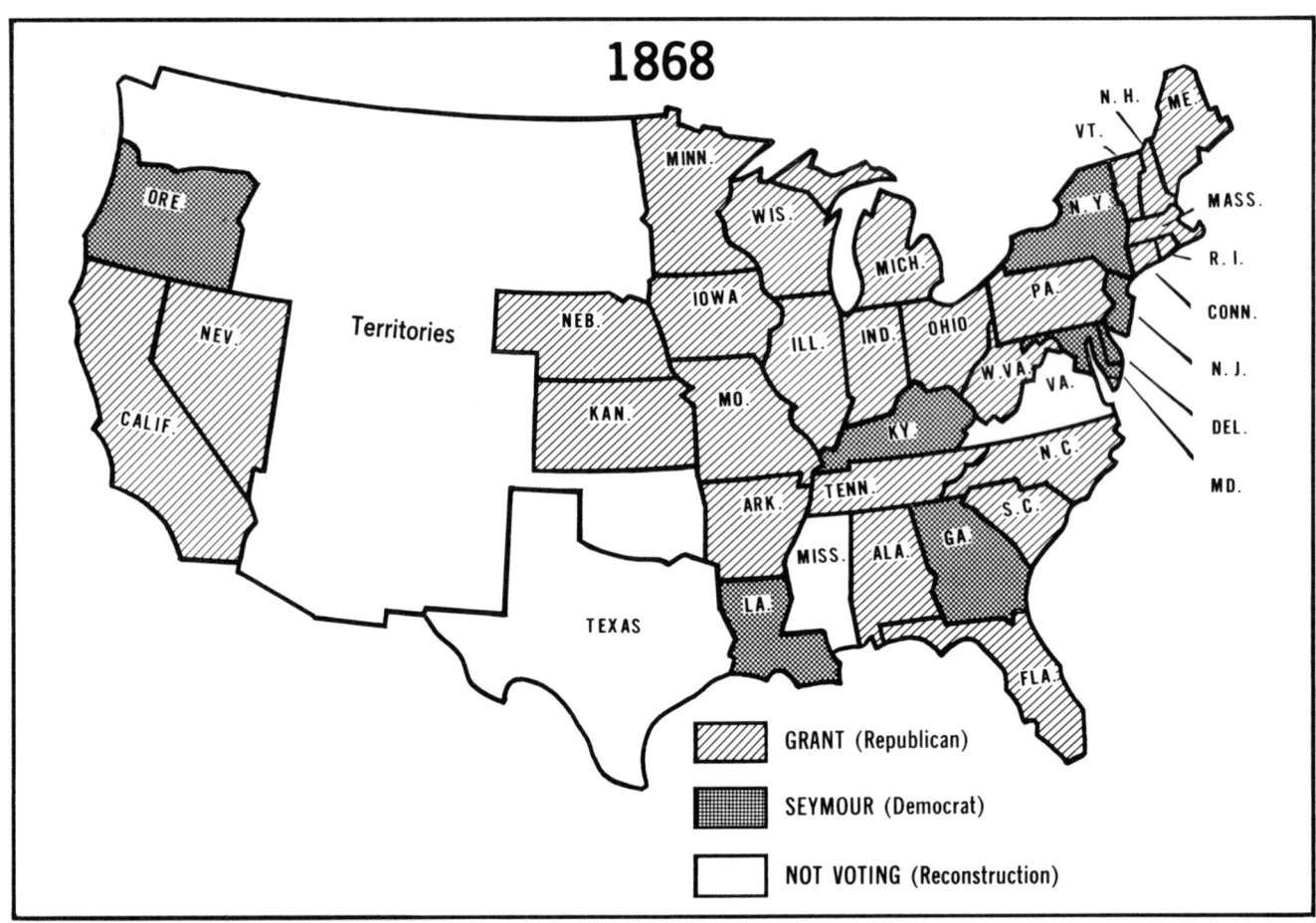

States [1]	Electoral Votes	Grant	Seymour	States [1]	Electoral Votes	Grant	Seymour
Alabama	(8)	8	-	Missouri	(11)	11	-
Arkansas	(5)	5	-	Nebraska	(3)	3	-
California	(5)	5	-	Nevada	(3)	3	-
Connecticut	(6)	6	-	New Hampshire	(5)	5	-
Delaware	(3)	-	3	New Jersey	(7)	-	7
Florida	(3)	3	-	New York	(33)	-	33
Georgia	(9)	-	9	North Carolina	(9)	9	-
Illinois	(16)	16	-	Ohio	(21)	21	-
Indiana	(13)	13	-	Oregon	(3)	-	3
Iowa	(8)	8	-	Pennsylvania	(26)	26	-
Kansas	(3)	3	-	Rhode Island	(4)	4	-
Kentucky	(11)	-	11	South Carolina	(6)	6	-
Louisiana	(7)	-	7	Tennessee	(10)	10	-
Maine	(7)	7	-	Vermont	(5)	5	-
Maryland	(7)	-	7	West Virginia	(5)	5	-
Massachusetts	(12)	12	-	Wisconsin	(8)	8	-
Michigan	(8)	8	-				
Minnesota	(4)	4	-	**Totals**	**(294)**	**214**	**80**

1. Mississippi, Texas and Virginia were not yet readmitted to the Union and did not participate in the election.

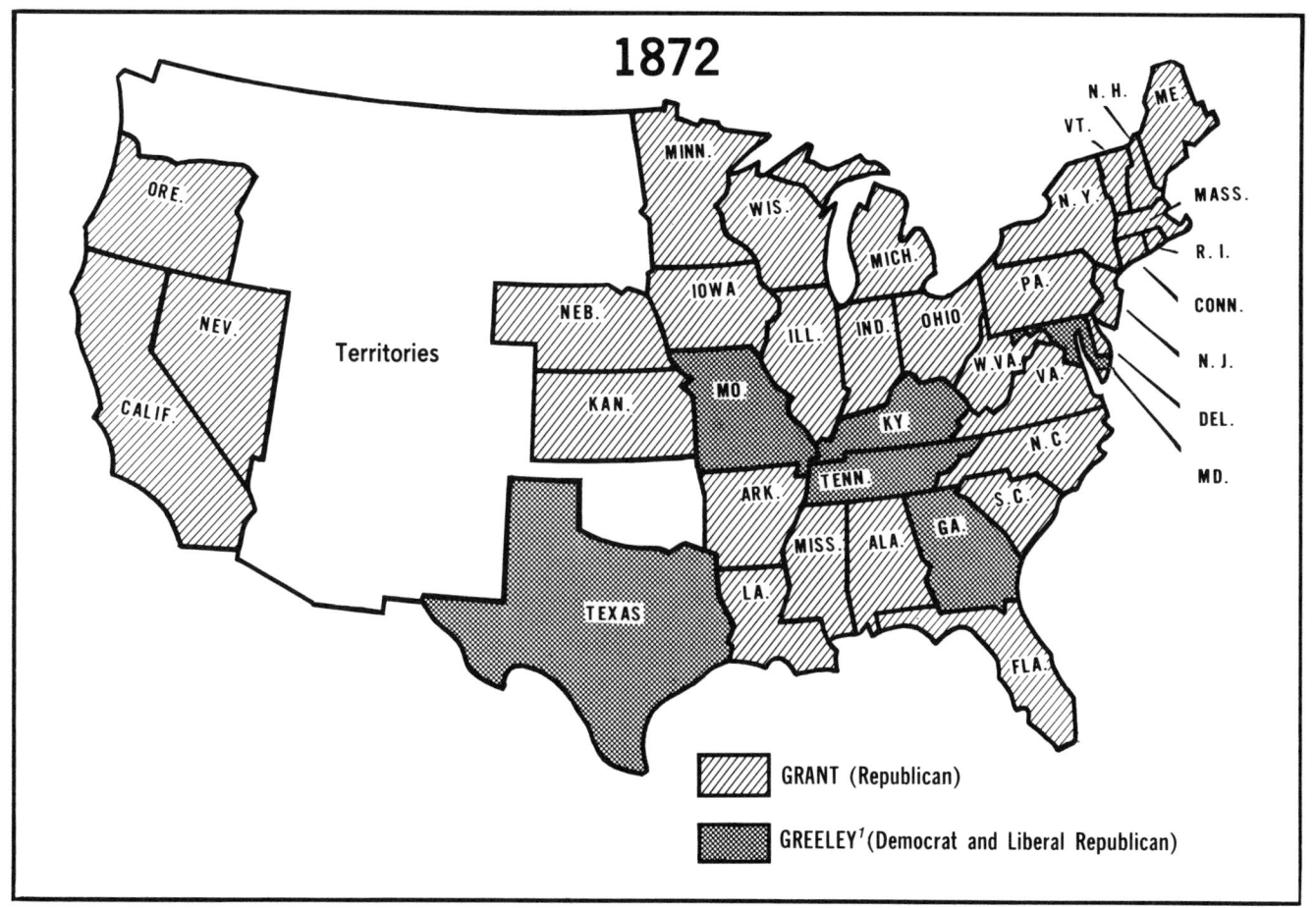

1872

GRANT (Republican)

GREELEY[1] (Democrat and Liberal Republican)

States	Electoral Votes	Grant	Hendricks[1]	Brown[1]	Jenkins[1]	Davis[1]
Alabama	(10)	10	-	-	-	-
Arkansas[2]	(6)	-	-	-	-	-
California	(6)	6	-	-	-	-
Connecticut	(6)	6	-	-	-	-
Delaware	(3)	3	-	-	-	-
Florida	(4)	4	-	-	-	-
Georgia[3]	(11)	-	-	6	2	-
Illinois	(21)	21	-	-	-	-
Indiana	(15)	15	-	-	-	-
Iowa	(11)	11	-	-	-	-
Kansas	(5)	5	-	-	-	-
Kentucky	(12)	-	8	4	-	-
Louisiana[2]	(8)	-	-	-	-	-
Maine	(7)	7	-	-	-	-
Maryland	(8)	-	8	-	-	-
Massachusetts	(13)	13	-	-	-	-
Michigan	(11)	11	-	-	-	-
Minnesota	(5)	5	-	-	-	-
Mississippi	(8)	8	-	-	-	-
Missouri	(15)	-	6	8	-	1

States	Electoral Votes	Grant	Hendricks[1]	Brown[1]	Jenkins[1]	Davis[1]
Nebraska	(3)	3	-	-	-	-
Nevada	(3)	3	-	-	-	-
New Hampshire	(5)	5	-	-	-	-
New Jersey	(9)	9	-	-	-	-
New York	(35)	35	-	-	-	-
North Carolina	(10)	10	-	-	-	-
Ohio	(22)	22	-	-	-	-
Oregon	(3)	3	-	-	-	-
Pennsylvania	(29)	29	-	-	-	-
Rhode Island	(4)	4	-	-	-	-
South Carolina	(7)	7	-	-	-	-
Tennessee	(12)	-	12	-	-	-
Texas	(8)	-	8	-	-	-
Vermont	(5)	5	-	-	-	-
Virginia	(11)	11	-	-	-	-
West Virginia	(5)	5	-	-	-	-
Wisconsin	(10)	10	-	-	-	-
Totals		286	42	18	2	1

1. For explanation of Democratic electoral vote, cast after Greeley's death, see p. 256.

2. Congress refused to accept electoral votes of Arkansas and Louisiana because of disruptive conditions during Reconstruction.

3. Three Georgia electoral votes cast for Greeley were not counted.

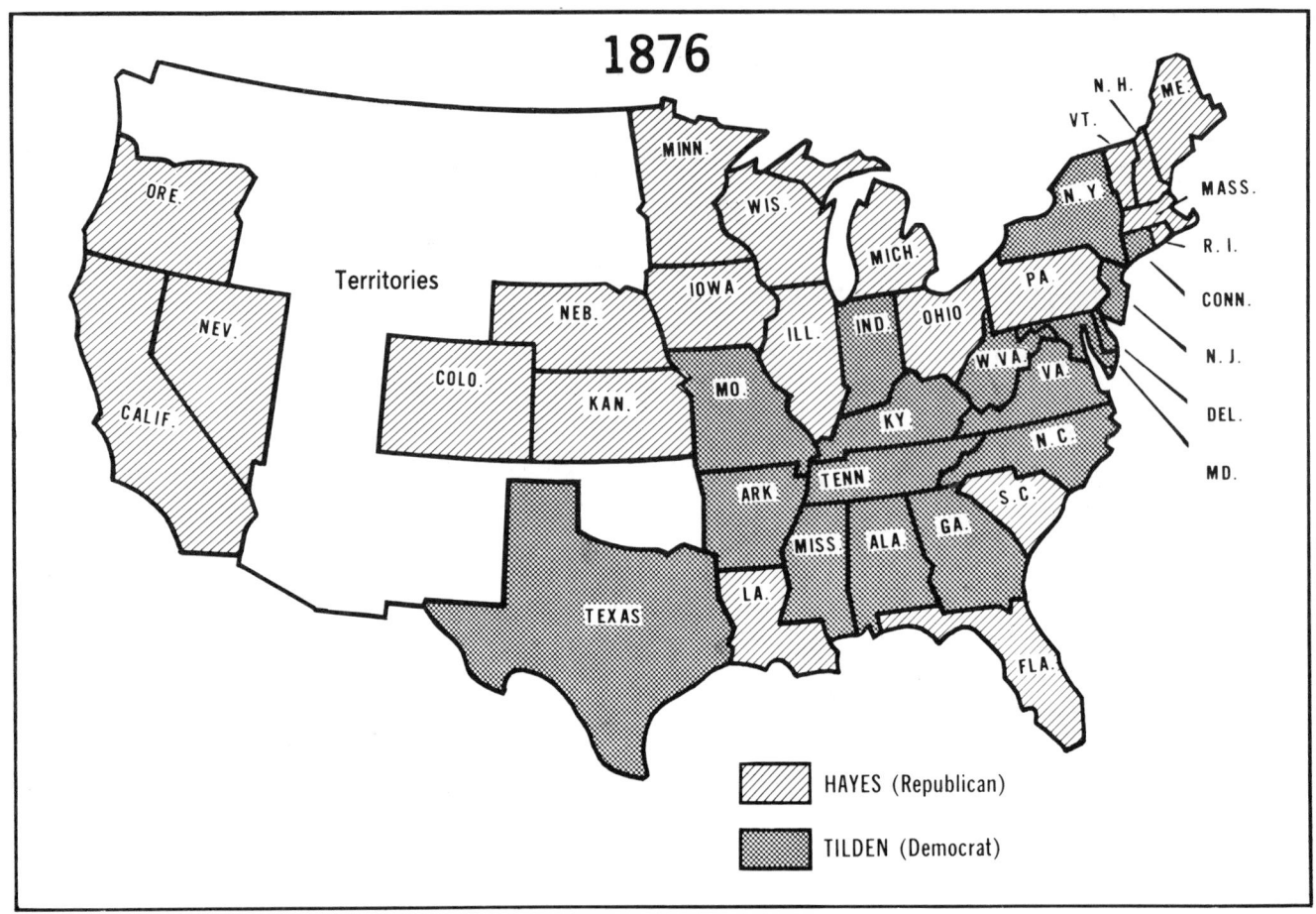

States	Electoral Votes	Hayes	Tilden	States	Electoral Votes	Hayes	Tilden
Alabama	(10)	-	10	Missouri	(15)	-	15
Arkansas	(6)	-	6	Nebraska	(3)	3	-
California	(6)	6	-	Nevada	(3)	3	-
Colorado	(3)	3	-	New Hampshire	(5)	5	-
Connecticut	(6)	-	6	New Jersey	(9)	-	9
Delaware	(3)	-	3	New York	(35)	-	35
Florida[1]	(4)	4	-	North Carolina	(10)	-	10
Georgia	(11)	-	11	Ohio	(22)	22	-
Illinois	(21)	21	-	Oregon[1]	(3)	3	-
Indiana	(15)	-	15	Pennsylvania	(29)	29	-
Iowa	(11)	11	-	Rhode Island	(4)	4	-
Kansas	(5)	5	-	South Carolina[1]	(7)	7	-
Kentucky	(12)	-	12	Tennessee	(12)	-	12
Louisiana[1]	(8)	8	-	Texas	(8)	-	8
Maine	(7)	7	-	Vermont	(5)	5	-
Maryland	(8)	-	8	Virginia	(11)	-	11
Massachusetts	(13)	13	-	West Virginia	(5)	-	5
Michigan	(11)	11	-	Wisconsin	(10)	10	-
Minnesota	(5)	5	-				
Mississippi	(8)	-	8	**Totals**	**(369)**	**185**	**184**

1. For explanation of disputed electoral votes of Florida, Louisiana, Oregon and South Carolina, see p. 261.

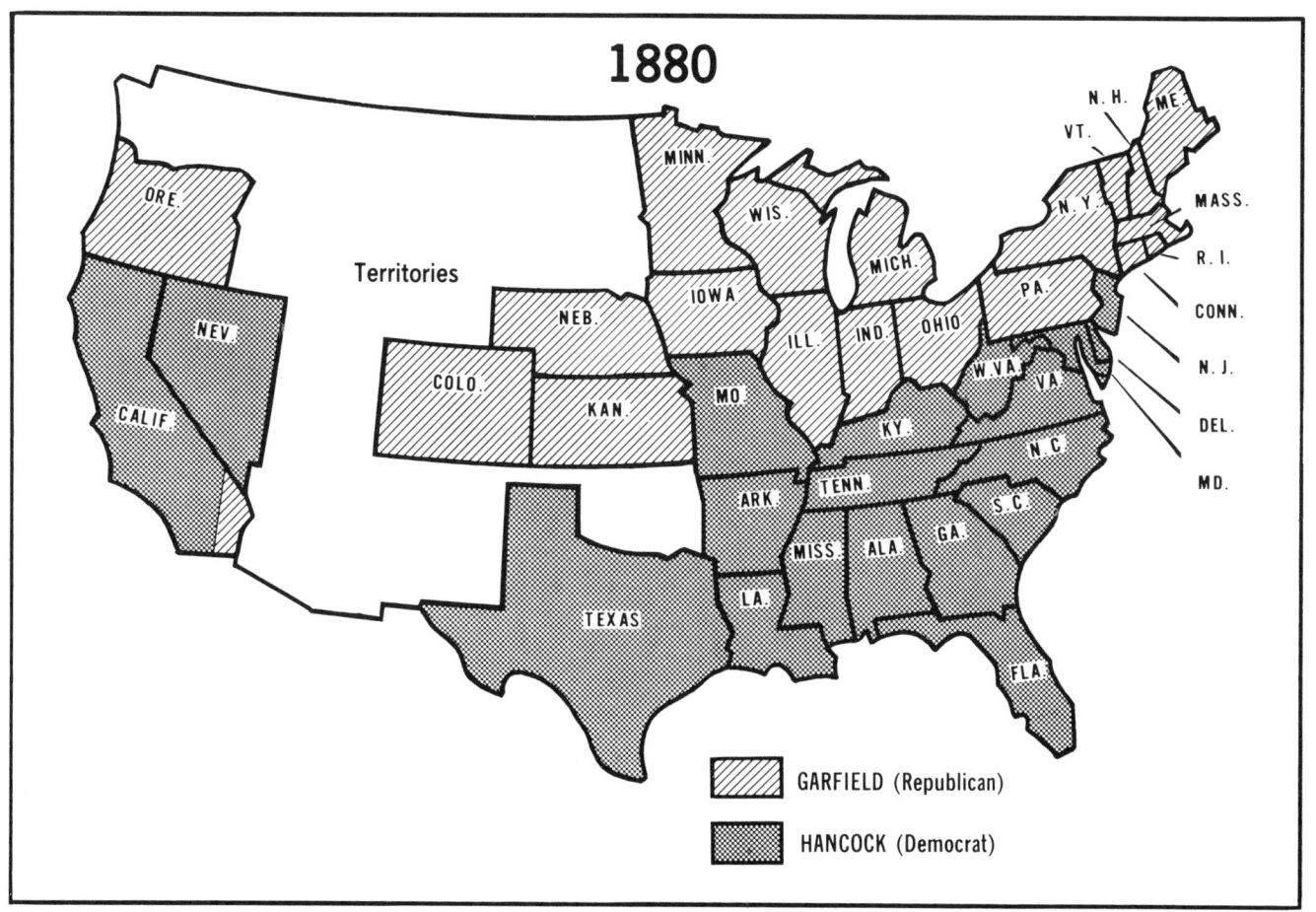

States	Electoral Votes	Garfield	Hancock	States	Electoral Votes	Garfield	Hancock
Alabama	(10)	-	10	Mississippi	(8)	-	8
Arkansas	(6)	-	6	Missouri	(15)	-	15
California[1]	(6)	1	5	Nebraska	(3)	3	-
Colorado	(3)	3	-	Nevada	(3)	-	3
Connecticut	(6)	6	-	New Hampshire	(5)	5	-
Delaware	(3)	-	3	New Jersey	(9)	-	9
Florida	(4)	-	4	New York	(35)	35	-
Georgia	(11)	-	11	North Carolina	(10)	-	10
Illinois	(21)	21	-	Ohio	(22)	22	-
Indiana	(15)	15	-	Oregon	(3)	3	-
Iowa	(11)	11	-	Pennsylvania	(29)	29	-
Kansas	(5)	5	-	Rhode Island	(4)	4	-
Kentucky	(12)	-	12	South Carolina	(7)	-	7
Louisiana	(8)	-	8	Tennessee	(12)	-	12
Maine	(7)	7	-	Texas	(8)	-	8
Maryland	(8)	-	8	Vermont	(5)	5	-
Massachusetts	(13)	13	-	Virginia	(11)	-	11
Michigan	(11)	11	-	West Virginia	(5)	-	5
Minnesota	(5)	5	-	Wisconsin	(10)	10	-
				Totals	**(369)**	**214**	**155**

1. For explanation of split electoral votes, see p. 258.

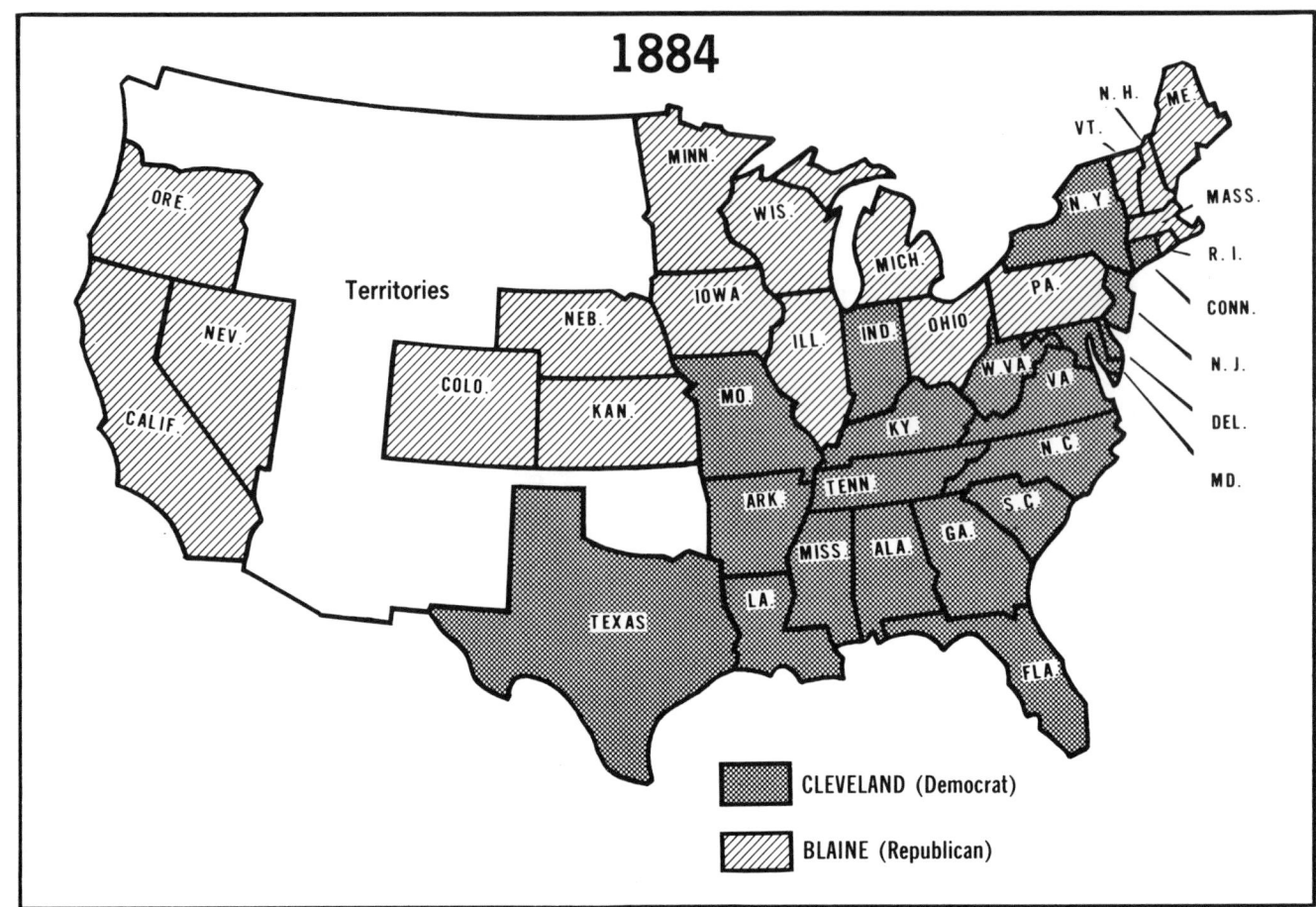

1884

CLEVELAND (Democrat)

BLAINE (Republican)

States	Electoral Votes	Cleveland	Blaine	States	Electoral Votes	Cleveland	Blaine
Alabama	(10)	10	-	**Mississippi**	(9)	9	-
Arkansas	(7)	7	-	**Missouri**	(16)	16	-
California	(8)	-	8	**Nebraska**	(5)	-	5
Colorado	(3)	-	3	**Nevada**	(3)	-	3
Connecticut	(6)	6	-	**New Hampshire**	(4)	-	4
Delaware	(3)	3	-	**New Jersey**	(9)	9	-
Florida	(4)	4	-	**New York**	(36)	36	-
Georgia	(12)	12	-	**North Carolina**	(11)	11	-
Illinois	(22)	-	22	**Ohio**	(23)	-	23
Indiana	(15)	15	-	**Oregon**	(3)	-	3
Iowa	(13)	-	13	**Pennsylvania**	(30)	-	30
Kansas	(9)	-	9	**Rhode Island**	(4)	-	4
Kentucky	(13)	13	-	**South Carolina**	(9)	9	-
Louisiana	(8)	8	-	**Tennessee**	(12)	12	-
Maine	(6)	-	6	**Texas**	(13)	13	-
Maryland	(8)	8	-	**Vermont**	(4)	-	4
Massachusetts	(14)	-	14	**Virginia**	(12)	12	-
Michigan	(13)	-	13	**West Virginia**	(6)	6	-
Minnesota	(7)	-	7	**Wisconsin**	(11)	-	11
				Totals	**(401)**	**219**	**182**

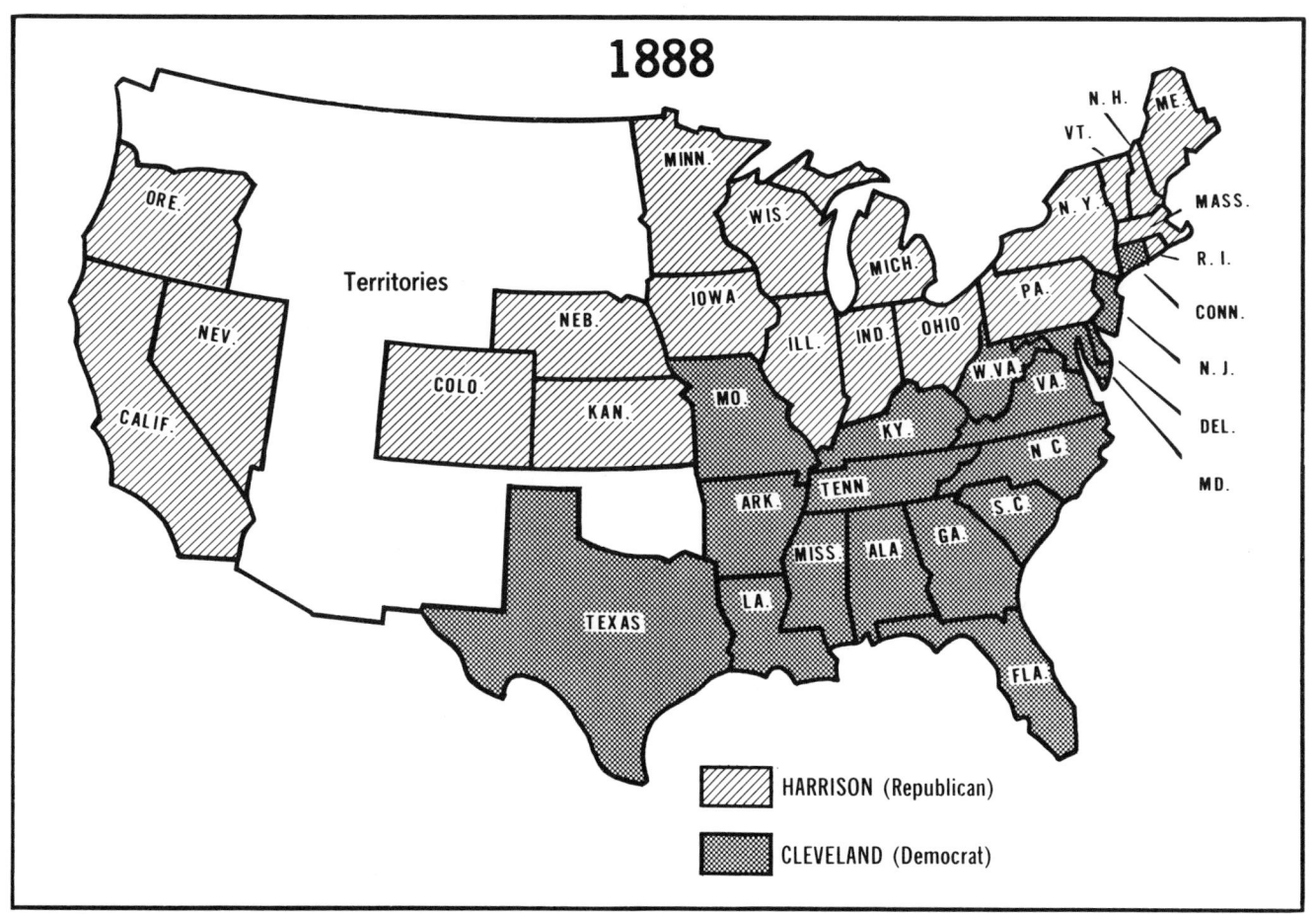

1888

HARRISON (Republican)

CLEVELAND (Democrat)

States	Electoral Votes	Harrison	Cleveland	States	Electoral Votes	Harrison	Cleveland
Alabama	(10)	-	10	**Mississippi**	(9)	-	9
Arkansas	(7)	-	7	**Missouri**	(16)	-	16
California	(8)	8	-	**Nebraska**	(5)	5	-
Colorado	(3)	3	-	**Nevada**	(3)	3	-
Connecticut	(6)	-	6	**New Hampshire**	(4)	4	-
Delaware	(3)	-	3	**New Jersey**	(9)	-	9
Florida	(4)	-	4	**New York**	(36)	36	-
Georgia	(12)	-	12	**North Carolina**	(11)	-	11
Illinois	(22)	22	-	**Ohio**	(23)	23	-
Indiana	(15)	15	-	**Oregon**	(3)	3	-
Iowa	(13)	13	-	**Pennsylvania**	(30)	30	-
Kansas	(9)	9	-	**Rhode Island**	(4)	4	-
Kentucky	(13)	-	13	**South Carolina**	(9)	-	9
Louisiana	(8)	-	8	**Tennessee**	(12)	-	12
Maine	(6)	6	-	**Texas**	(13)	-	13
Maryland	(8)	-	8	**Vermont**	(4)	4	-
Massachusetts	(14)	14	-	**Virginia**	(12)	-	12
Michigan	(13)	13	-	**West Virginia**	(6)	-	6
Minnesota	(7)	7	-	**Wisconsin**	(11)	11	-
				Totals	**(401)**	233	168

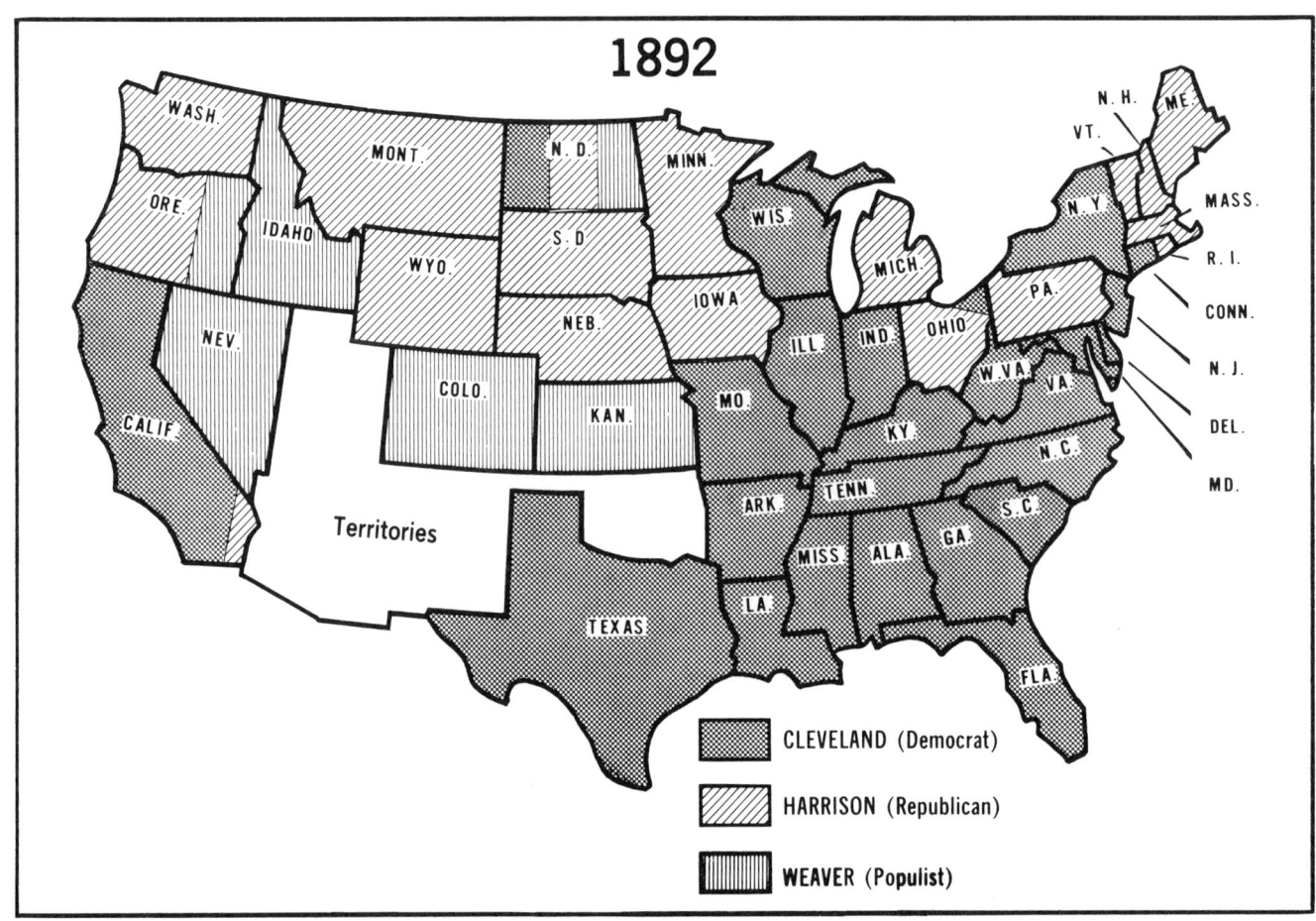

1892

| CLEVELAND (Democrat) |
| HARRISON (Republican) |
| WEAVER (Populist) |

States	Electoral Votes	Cleveland	Harrison	Weaver	States	Electoral Votes	Cleveland	Harrison	Weaver
Alabama	(11)	11	-	-	Montana	(3)	-	3	-
Arkansas	(8)	8	-	-	Nebraska	(8)	-	8	-
California[1]	(9)	8	1	-	Nevada	(3)	-	-	3
Colorado	(4)	-	-	4	New Hampshire	(4)	-	4	-
Connecticut	(6)	6	-	-	New Jersey	(10)	10	-	-
Delaware	(3)	3	-	-	New York	(36)	36	-	-
Florida	(4)	4	-	-	North Carolina	(11)	11	-	-
Georgia	(13)	13	-	-	North Dakota[1]	(3)	1	1	1
Idaho	(3)	-	-	3	Ohio[1]	(23)	1	22	-
Illinois	(24)	24	-	-	Oregon[1]	(4)	-	3	1
Indiana	(15)	15	-	-	Pennsylvania	(32)	-	32	-
Iowa	(13)	-	13	-	Rhode Island	(4)	-	4	-
Kansas	(10)	-	-	10	South Carolina	(9)	9	-	-
Kentucky	(13)	13	-	-	South Dakota	(4)	-	4	-
Louisiana	(8)	8	-	-	Tennessee	(12)	12	-	-
Maine	(6)	-	6	-	Texas	(15)	15	-	-
Maryland	(8)	8	-	-	Vermont	(4)	-	4	-
Massachusetts	(15)	-	15	-	Virginia	(12)	12	-	-
Michigan[1]	(14)	5	9	-	Washington	(4)	-	4	-
Minnesota	(9)	-	9	-	West Virginia	(6)	6	-	-
Mississippi	(9)	9	-	-	Wisconsin	(12)	12	-	-
Missouri	(17)	17	-	-	Wyoming	(3)	-	3	-
					Totals	**(444)**	**277**	**145**	**22**

1. For explanation of split electoral votes, see p. 258.

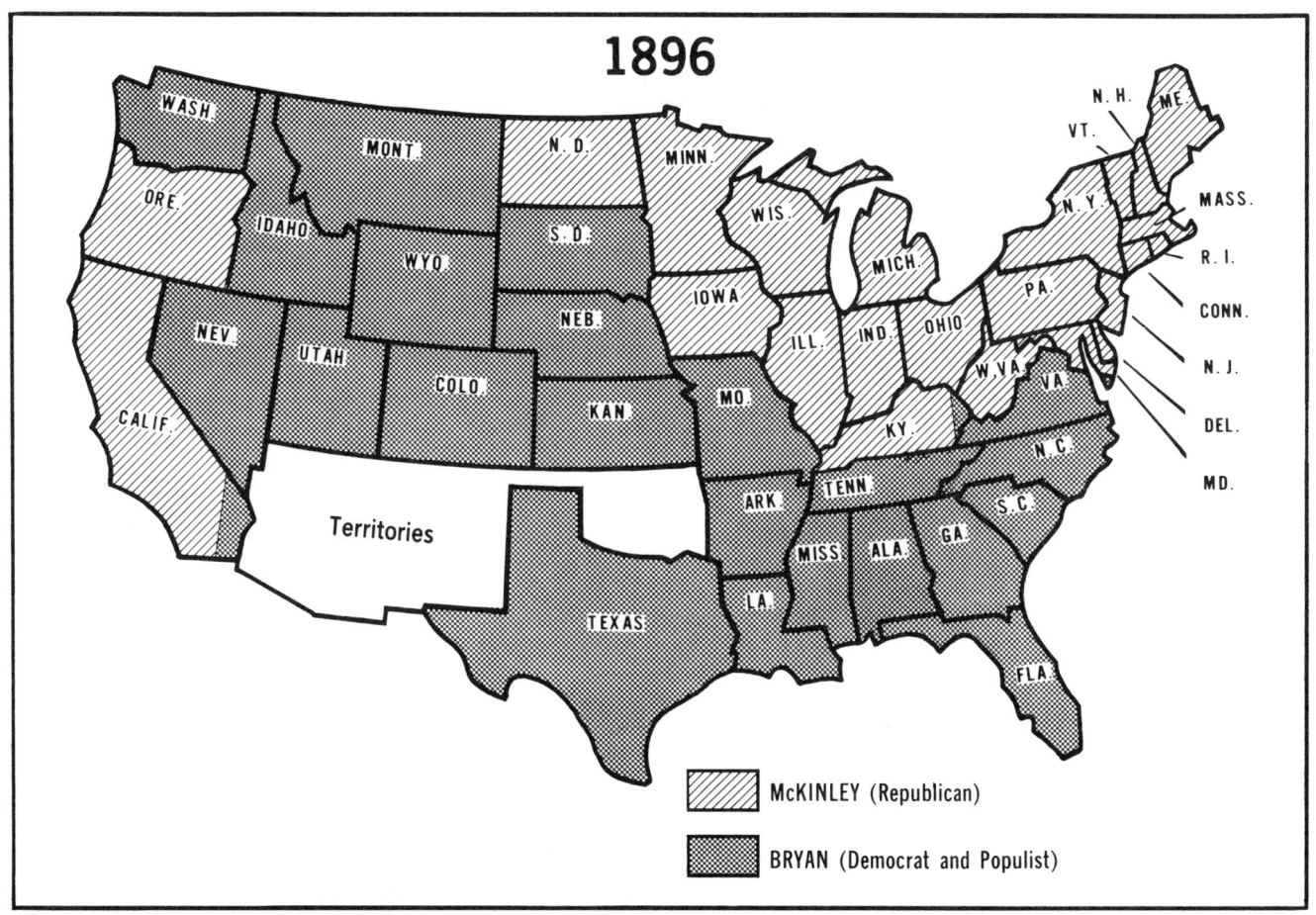

1896

McKINLEY (Republican)

BRYAN (Democrat and Populist)

States	Electoral Votes	McKinley	Bryan	States	Electoral Votes	McKinley	Bryan
Alabama	(11)	-	11	Nebraska	(8)	-	8
Arkansas	(8)	-	8	Nevada	(3)	-	3
California[1]	(9)	8	1	New Hampshire	(4)	4	-
Colorado	(4)	-	4	New Jersey	(10)	10	-
Connecticut	(6)	6	-	New York	(36)	36	-
Delaware	(3)	3	-	North Carolina	(11)	-	11
Florida	(4)	-	4	North Dakota	(3)	3	-
Georgia	(13)	-	13	Ohio	(23)	23	-
Idaho	(3)	-	3	Oregon	(4)	4	-
Illinois	(24)	24	-	Pennsylvania	(32)	32	-
Indiana	(15)	15	-	Rhode Island	(4)	4	-
Iowa	(13)	13	-	South Carolina	(9)	-	9
Kansas	(10)	-	10	South Dakota	(4)	-	4
Kentucky[1]	(13)	12	1	Tennessee	(12)	-	12
Louisiana	(8)	-	8	Texas	(15)	-	15
Maine	(6)	6	-	Utah	(3)	-	3
Maryland	(8)	8	-	Vermont	(4)	4	-
Massachusetts	(15)	15	-	Virginia	(12)	-	12
Michigan	(14)	14	-	Washington	(4)	-	4
Minnesota	(9)	9	-	West Virginia	(6)	6	-
Mississippi	(9)	-	9	Wisconsin	(12)	12	-
Missouri	(17)	-	17	Wyoming	(3)	-	3
Montana	(3)	-	3	**Totals**	**(447)**	**271**	**176**

1. For explanation of split electoral votes, see p. 258.

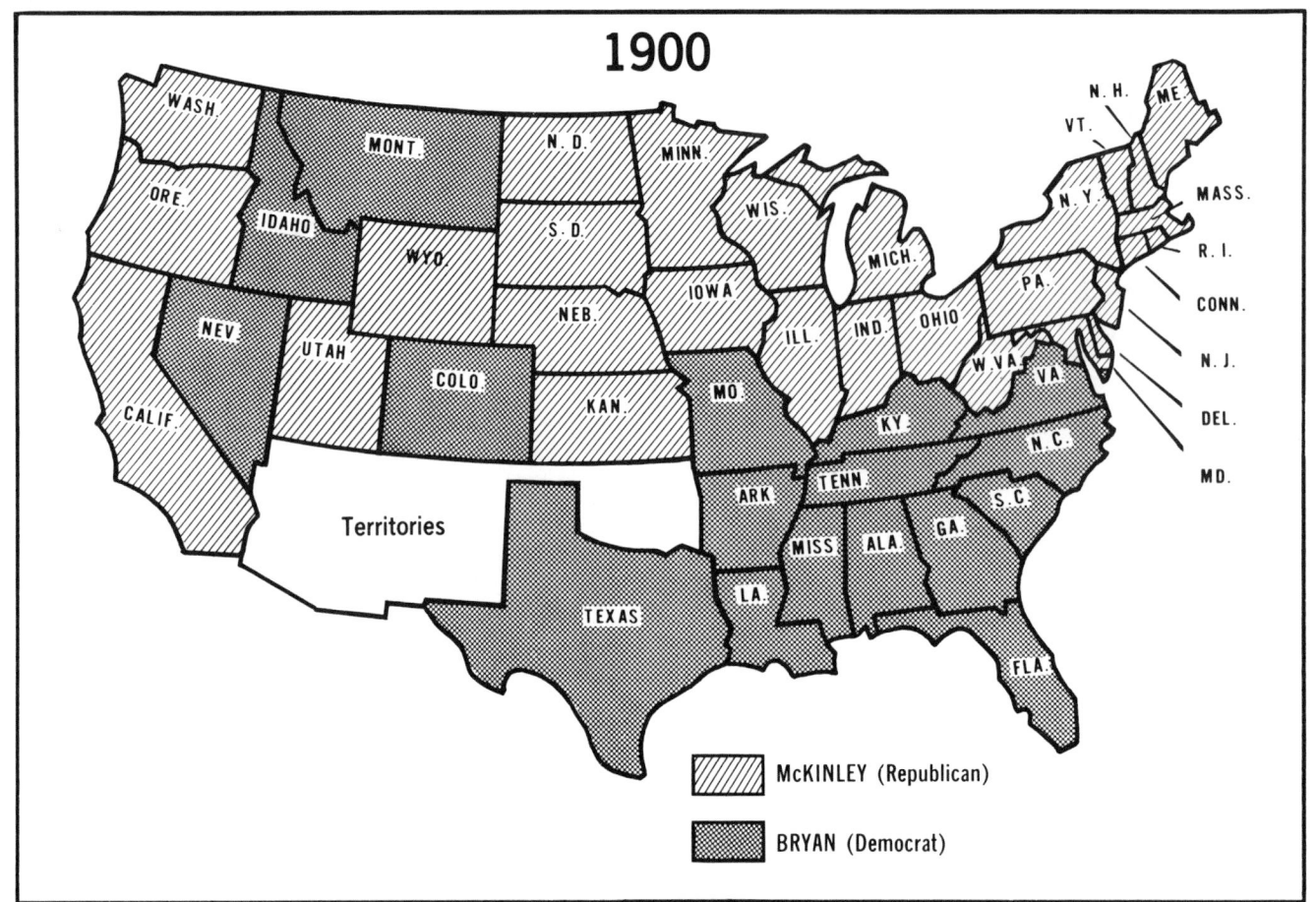

1900

States	Electoral Votes	McKinley	Bryan
Alabama	(11)	-	11
Arkansas	(8)	-	8
California	(9)	9	-
Colorado	(4)	-	4
Connecticut	(6)	6	-
Delaware	(3)	3	-
Florida	(4)	-	4
Georgia	(13)	-	13
Idaho	(3)	-	3
Illinois	(24)	24	-
Indiana	(15)	15	-
Iowa	(13)	13	-
Kansas	(10)	10	-
Kentucky	(13)	-	13
Louisiana	(8)	-	8
Maine	(6)	6	-
Maryland	(8)	8	-
Massachusetts	(15)	15	-
Michigan	(14)	14	-
Minnesota	(9)	9	-
Mississippi	(9)	-	9
Missouri	(17)	-	17
Montana	(3)	-	3
Nebraska	(8)	8	-
Nevada	(3)	-	3
New Hampshire	(4)	4	-
New Jersey	(10)	10	-
New York	(36)	36	-
North Carolina	(11)	-	11
North Dakota	(3)	3	-
Ohio	(23)	23	-
Oregon	(4)	4	-
Pennsylvania	(32)	32	-
Rhode Island	(4)	4	-
South Carolina	(9)	-	9
South Dakota	(4)	4	-
Tennessee	(12)	-	12
Texas	(15)	-	15
Utah	(3)	3	-
Vermont	(4)	4	-
Virginia	(12)	-	12
Washington	(4)	4	-
West Virginia	(6)	6	-
Wisconsin	(12)	12	-
Wyoming	(3)	3	-
Totals	**(447)**	**292**	**155**

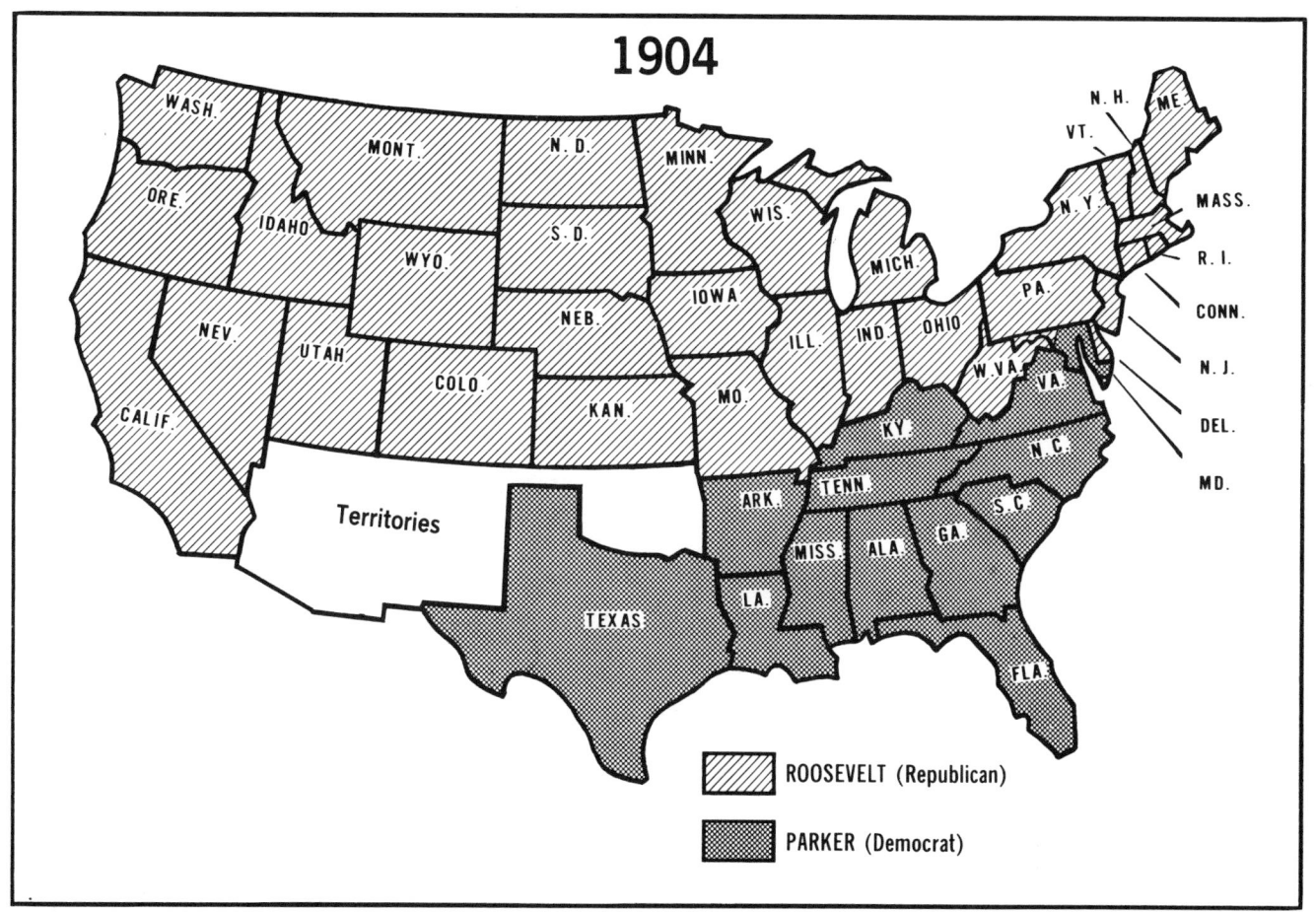

States	Electoral Votes	Roosevelt	Parker	States	Electoral Votes	Roosevelt	Parker
Alabama	(11)	-	11	**Nebraska**	(8)	8	-
Arkansas	(9)	-	9	**Nevada**	(3)	3	-
California	(10)	10	-	**New Hampshire**	(4)	4	-
Colorado	(5)	5	-	**New Jersey**	(12)	12	-
Connecticut	(7)	7	-	**New York**	(39)	39	-
Delaware	(3)	3	-	**North Carolina**	(12)	-	12
Florida	(5)	-	5	**North Dakota**	(4)	4	-
Georgia	(13)	-	13	**Ohio**	(23)	23	-
Idaho	(3)	3	-	**Oregon**	(4)	4	-
Illinois	(27)	27	-	**Pennsylvania**	(34)	34	-
Indiana	(15)	15	-	**Rhode Island**	(4)	4	-
Iowa	(13)	13	-	**South Carolina**	(9)	-	9
Kansas	(10)	10	-	**South Dakota**	(4)	4	-
Kentucky	(13)	-	13	**Tennessee**	(12)	-	12
Louisiana	(9)	-	9	**Texas**	(18)	-	18
Maine	(6)	6	-	**Utah**	(3)	3	-
Maryland[1]	(8)	1	7	**Vermont**	(4)	4	-
Massachusetts	(16)	16	-	**Virginia**	(12)	-	12
Michigan	(14)	14	-	**Washington**	(5)	5	-
Minnesota	(11)	11	-	**West Virginia**	(7)	7	-
Mississippi	(10)	-	10	**Wisconsin**	(13)	13	-
Missouri	(18)	18	-	**Wyoming**	(3)	3	-
Montana	(3)	3	-	**Totals**	(476)	336	140

1. For explanation of split electoral votes, see p. 258.

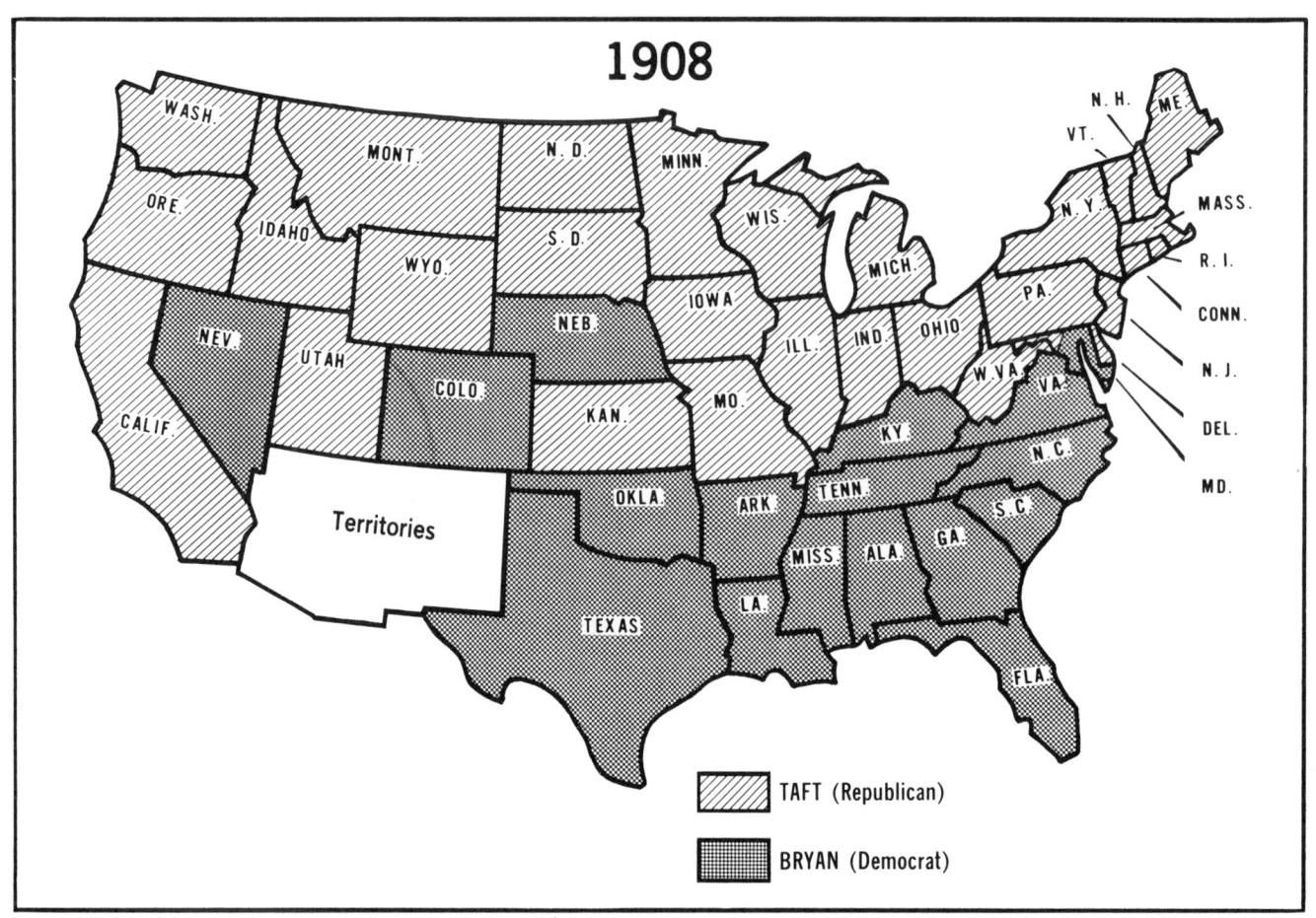

1908

TAFT (Republican)

BRYAN (Democrat)

States	Electoral Votes	Taft	Bryan	States	Electoral Votes	Taft	Bryan
Alabama	(11)	-	11	**Nebraska**	(8)	-	8
Arkansas	(9)	-	9	**Nevada**	(3)	-	3
California	(10)	10	-	**New Hampshire**	(4)	4	-
Colorado	(5)	-	5	**New Jersey**	(12)	12	-
Connecticut	(7)	7	-	**New York**	(39)	39	-
Delaware	(3)	3	-	**North Carolina**	(12)	-	12
Florida	(5)	-	5	**North Dakota**	(4)	4	-
Georgia	(13)	-	13	**Ohio**	(23)	23	-
Idaho	(3)	3	-	**Oklahoma**	(7)	-	7
Illinois	(27)	27	-	**Oregon**	(4)	4	-
Indiana	(15)	15	-	**Pennsylvania**	(34)	34	-
Iowa	(13)	13	-	**Rhode Island**	(4)	4	-
Kansas	(10)	10	-	**South Carolina**	(9)	-	9
Kentucky	(13)	-	13	**South Dakota**	(4)	4	-
Louisiana	(9)	-	9	**Tennessee**	(12)	-	12
Maine	(6)	6	-	**Texas**	(18)	-	18
Maryland[1]	(8)	2	6	**Utah**	(3)	3	-
Massachusetts	(16)	16	-	**Vermont**	(4)	4	-
Michigan	(14)	14	-	**Virginia**	(12)	-	12
Minnesota	(11)	11	-	**Washington**	(5)	5	-
Mississippi	(10)	-	10	**West Virginia**	(7)	7	-
Missouri	(18)	18	-	**Wisconsin**	(13)	13	-
Montana	(3)	3	-	**Wyoming**	(3)	3	-
				Totals	**(483)**	321	162

1. *For explanation of split electoral votes, see p. 258.*

1912

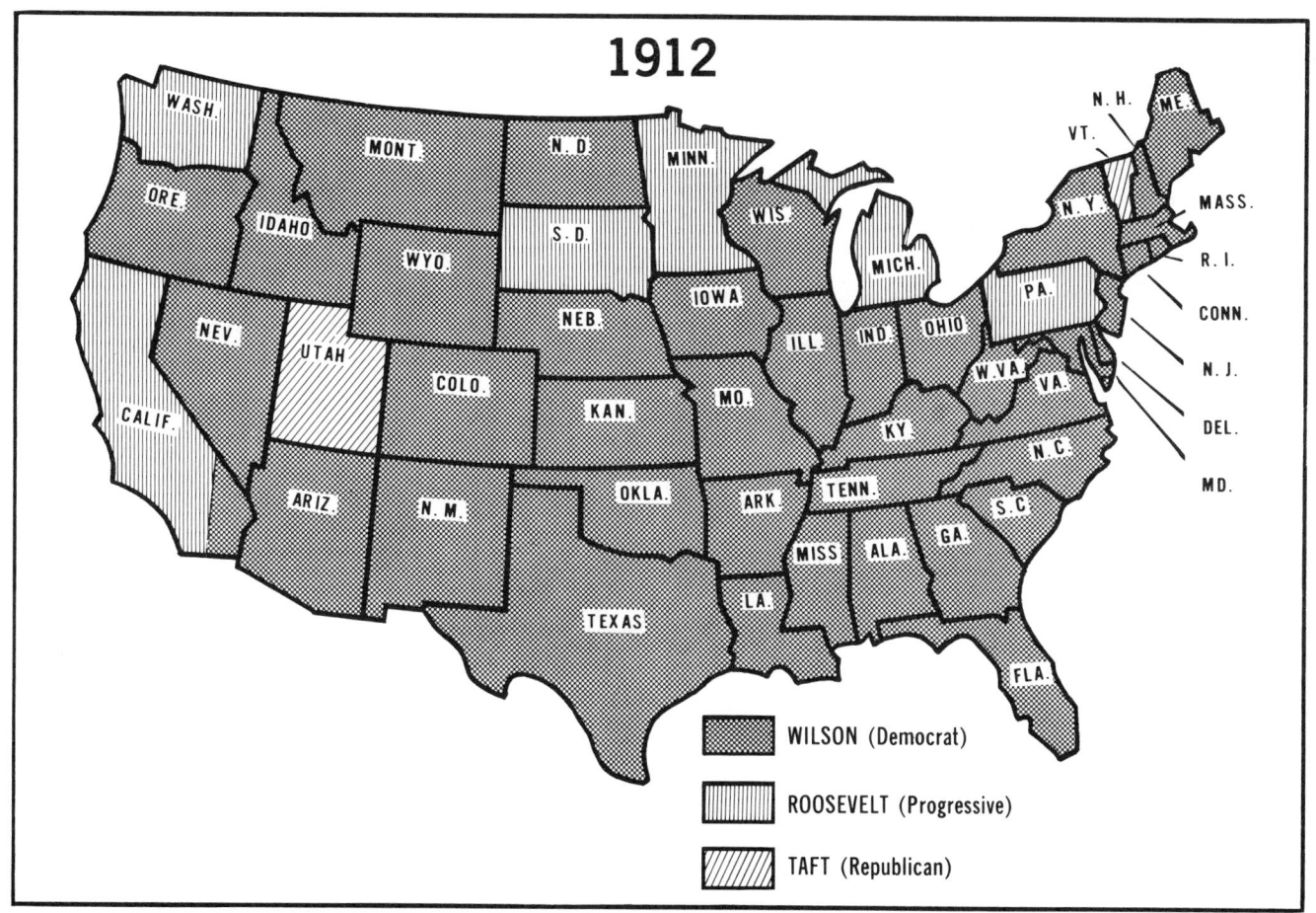

WILSON (Democrat)

ROOSEVELT (Progressive)

TAFT (Republican)

States	Electoral Votes	Wilson	Roosevelt	Taft	States	Electoral Votes	Wilson	Roosevelt	Taft
Alabama	(12)	12	-	-	Nebraska	(8)	8	-	-
Arizona	(3)	3	-	-	Nevada	(3)	3	-	-
Arkansas	(9)	9	-	-	New Hampshire	(4)	4	-	-
California[1]	(13)	2	11	-	New Jersey	(14)	14	-	-
Colorado	(6)	6	-	-	New Mexico	(3)	3	-	-
Connecticut	(7)	7	-	-	New York	(45)	45	-	-
Delaware	(3)	3	-	-	North Carolina	(12)	12	-	-
Florida	(6)	6	-	-	North Dakota	(5)	5	-	-
Georgia	(14)	14	-	-	Ohio	(24)	24	-	-
Idaho	(4)	4	-	-	Oklahoma	(10)	10	-	-
Illinois	(29)	29	-	-	Oregon	(5)	5	-	-
Indiana	(15)	15	-	-	Pennsylvania	(38)	-	38	-
Iowa	(13)	13	-	-	Rhode Island	(5)	5	-	-
Kansas	(10)	10	-	-	South Carolina	(9)	9	-	-
Kentucky	(13)	13	-	-	South Dakota	(5)	-	5	-
Louisiana	(10)	10	-	-	Tennessee	(12)	12	-	-
Maine	(6)	6	-	-	Texas	(20)	20	-	-
Maryland	(8)	8	-	-	Utah	(4)	-	-	4
Massachusetts	(18)	18	-	-	Vermont	(4)	-	-	4
Michigan	(15)	-	15	-	Virginia	(12)	12	-	-
Minnesota	(12)	-	12	-	Washington	(7)	-	7	-
Mississippi	(10)	10	-	-	West Virginia	(8)	8	-	-
Missouri	(18)	18	-	-	Wisconsin	(13)	13	-	-
Montana	(4)	4	-	-	Wyoming	(3)	3	-	-
					Totals	**(531)**	**435**	**88**	**8**

1. For explanation of split electoral votes, see p. 258.

1916

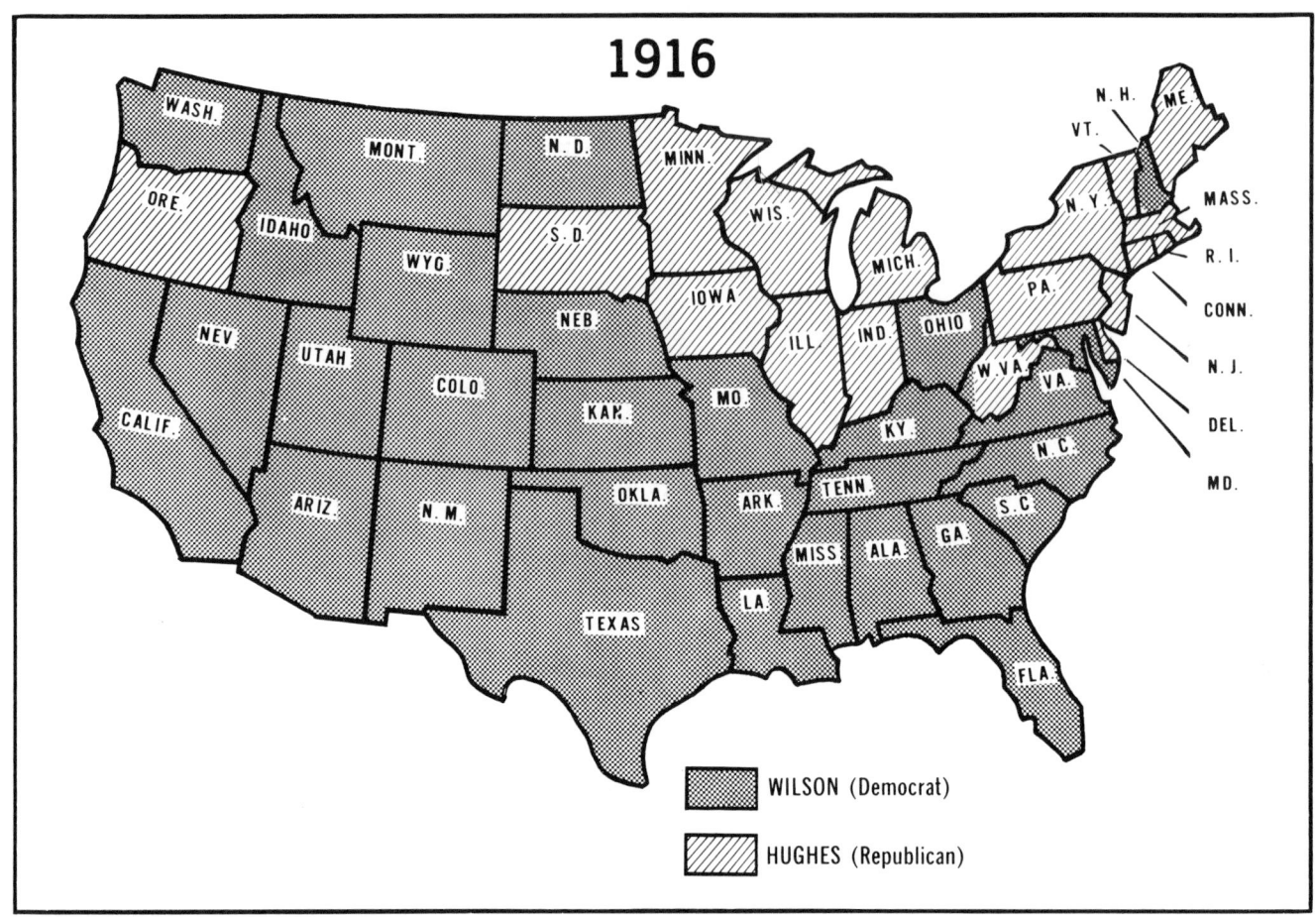

WILSON (Democrat)

HUGHES (Republican)

States	Electoral Votes	Wilson	Hughes	States	Electoral Votes	Wilson	Hughes
Alabama	(12)	12	-	**Nebraska**	(8)	8	-
Arizona	(3)	3	-	**Nevada**	(3)	3	-
Arkansas	(9)	9	-	**New Hampshire**	(4)	4	-
California	(13)	13	-	**New Jersey**	(14)	-	14
Colorado	(6)	6	-	**New Mexico**	(3)	3	-
Connecticut	(7)	-	7	**New York**	(45)	-	45
Delaware	(3)	-	3	**North Carolina**	(12)	12	-
Florida	(6)	6	-	**North Dakota**	(5)	5	-
Georgia	(14)	14	-	**Ohio**	(24)	24	-
Idaho	(4)	4	-	**Oklahoma**	(10)	10	-
Illinois	(29)	-	29	**Oregon**	(5)	-	5
Indiana	(15)	-	15	**Pennsylvania**	(38)	-	38
Iowa	(13)	-	13	**Rhode Island**	(5)	-	5
Kansas	(10)	10	-	**South Carolina**	(9)	9	-
Kentucky	(13)	13	-	**South Dakota**	(5)	-	5
Louisiana	(10)	10	-	**Tennessee**	(12)	12	-
Maine	(6)	-	6	**Texas**	(20)	20	-
Maryland	(8)	8	-	**Utah**	(4)	4	-
Massachusetts	(18)	-	18	**Vermont**	(4)	-	4
Michigan	(15)	-	15	**Virginia**	(12)	12	-
Minnesota	(12)	-	12	**Washington**	(7)	7	-
Mississippi	(10)	10	-	**West Virginia**[1]	(8)	1	7
Missouri	(18)	18	-	**Wisconsin**	(13)	-	13
Montana	(4)	4	-	**Wyoming**	(3)	3	-
				Totals	(531)	277	254

1. For explanation of split electoral votes, see p. 258.

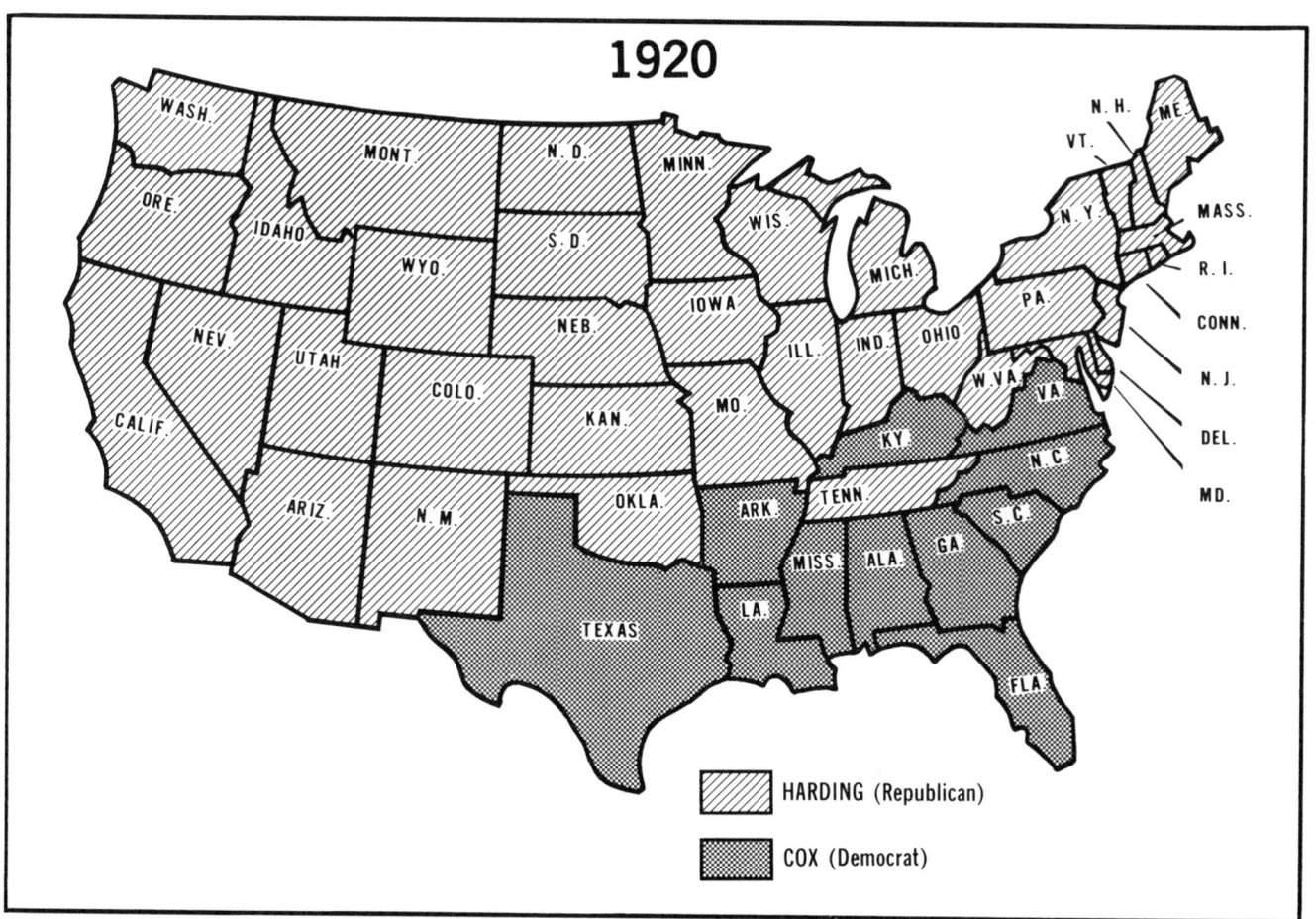

1920

HARDING (Republican)

COX (Democrat)

States	Electoral Votes	Harding	Cox	States	Electoral Votes	Harding	Cox
Alabama	(12)	-	12	Nebraska	(8)	8	-
Arizona	(3)	3	-	Nevada	(3)	3	-
Arkansas	(9)	-	9	New Hampshire	(4)	4	-
California	(13)	13	-	New Jersey	(14)	14	-
Colorado	(6)	6	-	New Mexico	(3)	3	-
Connecticut	(7)	7	-	New York	(45)	45	-
Delaware	(3)	3	-	North Carolina	(12)	-	12
Florida	(6)	-	6	North Dakota	(5)	5	-
Georgia	(14)	-	14	Ohio	(24)	24	-
Idaho	(4)	4	-	Oklahoma	(10)	10	-
Illinois	(29)	29	-	Oregon	(5)	5	-
Indiana	(15)	15	-	Pennsylvania	(38)	38	-
Iowa	(13)	13	-	Rhode Island	(5)	5	-
Kansas	(10)	10	-	South Carolina	(9)	-	9
Kentucky	(13)	-	13	South Dakota	(5)	5	-
Louisiana	(10)	-	10	Tennessee	(12)	12	-
Maine	(6)	6	-	Texas	(20)	-	20
Maryland	(8)	8	-	Utah	(4)	4	-
Massachusetts	(18)	18	-	Vermont	(4)	4	-
Michigan	(15)	15	-	Virginia	(12)	-	12
Minnesota	(12)	12	-	Washington	(7)	7	-
Mississippi	(10)	-	10	West Virginia	(8)	8	-
Missouri	(18)	18	-	Wisconsin	(13)	13	-
Montana	(4)	4	-	Wyoming	(3)	3	-
				Totals	(531)	404	127

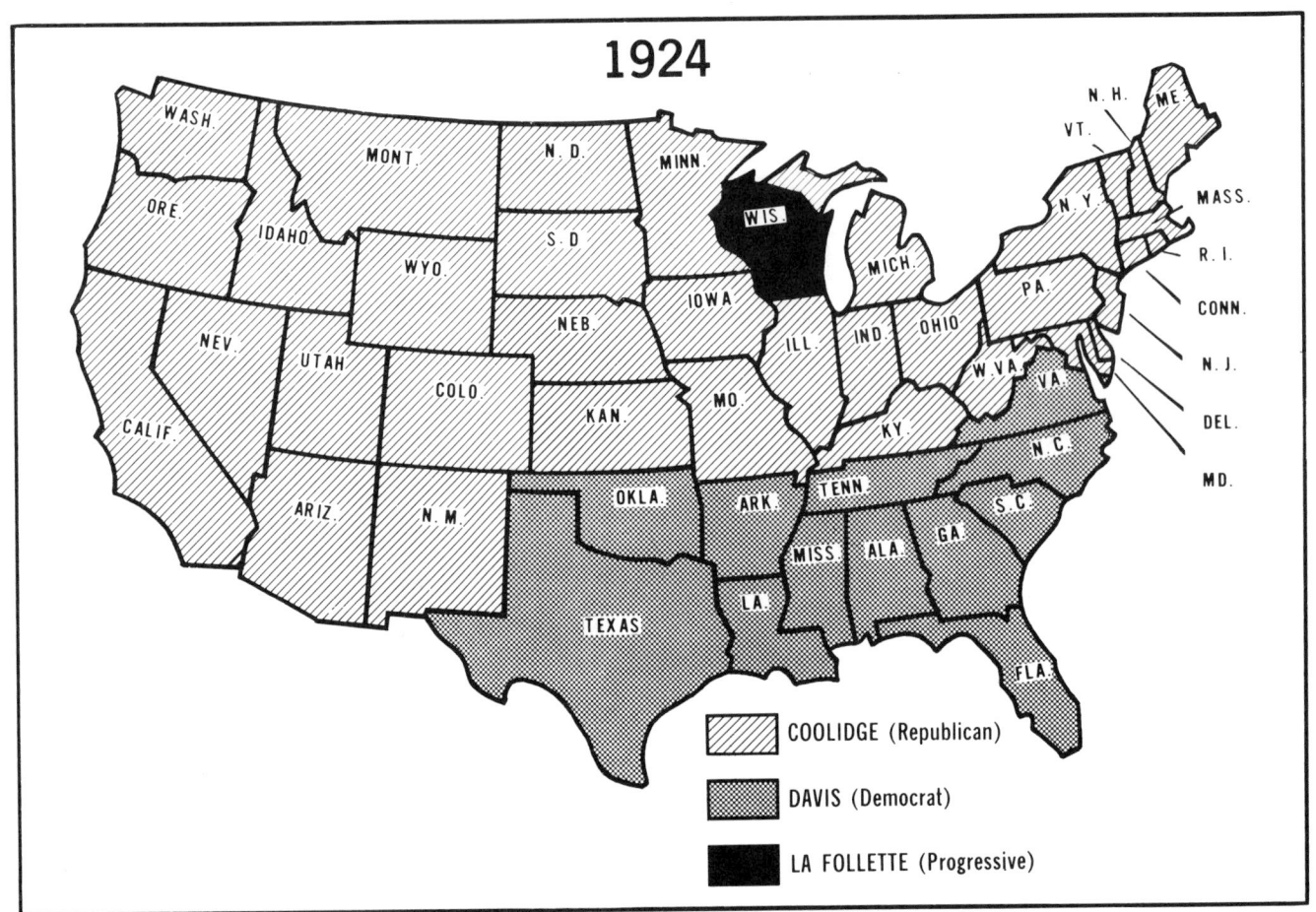

1924

COOLIDGE (Republican)

DAVIS (Democrat)

LA FOLLETTE (Progressive)

States	Electoral Votes	Coolidge	Davis	La Follette	States	Electoral Votes	Coolidge	Davis	La Follette
Alabama	(12)	-	12	-	**Nebraska**	(8)	8	-	-
Arizona	(3)	3	-	-	**Nevada**	(3)	3	-	-
Arkansas	(9)	-	9	-	**New Hampshire**	(4)	4	-	-
California	(13)	13	-	-	**New Jersey**	(14)	14	-	-
Colorado	(6)	6	-	-	**New Mexico**	(3)	3	-	-
Connecticut	(7)	7	-	-	**New York**	(45)	45	-	-
Delaware	(3)	3	-	-	**North Carolina**	(12)	-	12	-
Florida	(6)	-	6	-	**North Dakota**	(5)	5	-	-
Georgia	(14)	-	14	-	**Ohio**	(24)	24	-	-
Idaho	(4)	4	-	-	**Oklahoma**	(10)	-	10	-
Illinois	(29)	29	-	-	**Oregon**	(5)	5	-	-
Indiana	(15)	15	-	-	**Pennsylvania**	(38)	38	-	-
Iowa	(13)	13	-	-	**Rhode Island**	(5)	5	-	-
Kansas	(10)	10	-	-	**South Carolina**	(9)	-	9	-
Kentucky	(13)	13	-	-	**South Dakota**	(5)	5	-	-
Louisiana	(10)	-	10	-	**Tennessee**	(12)	-	12	-
Maine	(6)	6	-	-	**Texas**	(20)	-	20	-
Maryland	(8)	8	-	-	**Utah**	(4)	4	-	-
Massachusetts	(18)	18	-	-	**Vermont**	(4)	4	-	-
Michigan	(15)	15	-	-	**Virginia**	(12)	-	12	-
Minnesota	(12)	12	-	-	**Washington**	(7)	7	-	-
Mississippi	(10)	-	10	-	**West Virginia**	(8)	8	-	-
Missouri	(18)	18	-	-	**Wisconsin**	(13)	-	-	13
Montana	(4)	4	-	-	**Wyoming**	(3)	3	-	-
					Totals	(531)	382	136	13

1928

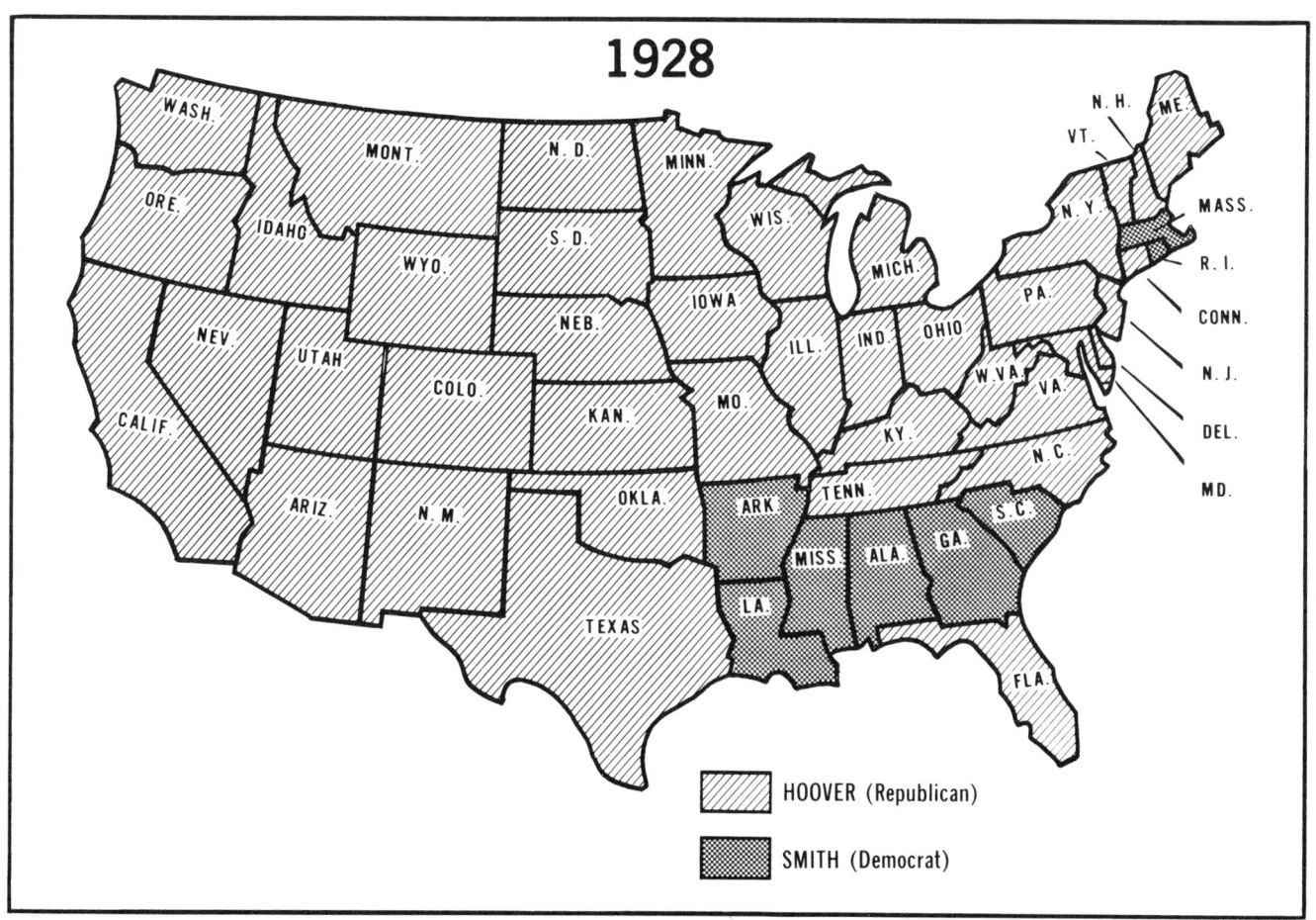

HOOVER (Republican)

SMITH (Democrat)

States	Electoral Votes	Hoover	Smith	States	Electoral Votes	Hoover	Smith
Alabama	(12)	-	12	Nebraska	(8)	8	-
Arizona	(3)	3	-	Nevada	(3)	3	-
Arkansas	(9)	-	9	New Hampshire	(4)	4	-
California	(13)	13	-	New Jersey	(14)	14	-
Colorado	(6)	6	-	New Mexico	(3)	3	-
Connecticut	(7)	7	-	New York	(45)	45	-
Delaware	(3)	3	-	North Carolina	(12)	12	-
Florida	(6)	6	-	North Dakota	(5)	5	-
Georgia	(14)	-	14	Ohio	(24)	24	-
Idaho	(4)	4	-	Oklahoma	(10)	10	-
Illinois	(29)	29	-	Oregon	(5)	5	-
Indiana	(15)	15	-	Pennsylvania	(38)	38	-
Iowa	(13)	13	-	Rhode Island	(5)	-	5
Kansas	(10)	10	-	South Carolina	(9)	-	9
Kentucky	(13)	13	-	South Dakota	(5)	5	-
Louisiana	(10)	-	10	Tennessee	(12)	12	-
Maine	(6)	6	-	Texas	(20)	20	-
Maryland	(8)	8	-	Utah	(4)	4	-
Massachusetts	(18)	-	18	Vermont	(4)	4	-
Michigan	(15)	15	-	Virginia	(12)	12	-
Minnesota	(12)	12	-	Washington	(7)	7	-
Mississippi	(10)	-	10	West Virginia	(8)	8	-
Missouri	(18)	18	-	Wisconsin	(13)	13	-
Montana	(4)	4	-	Wyoming	(3)	3	-
				Totals	**(531)**	**444**	**87**

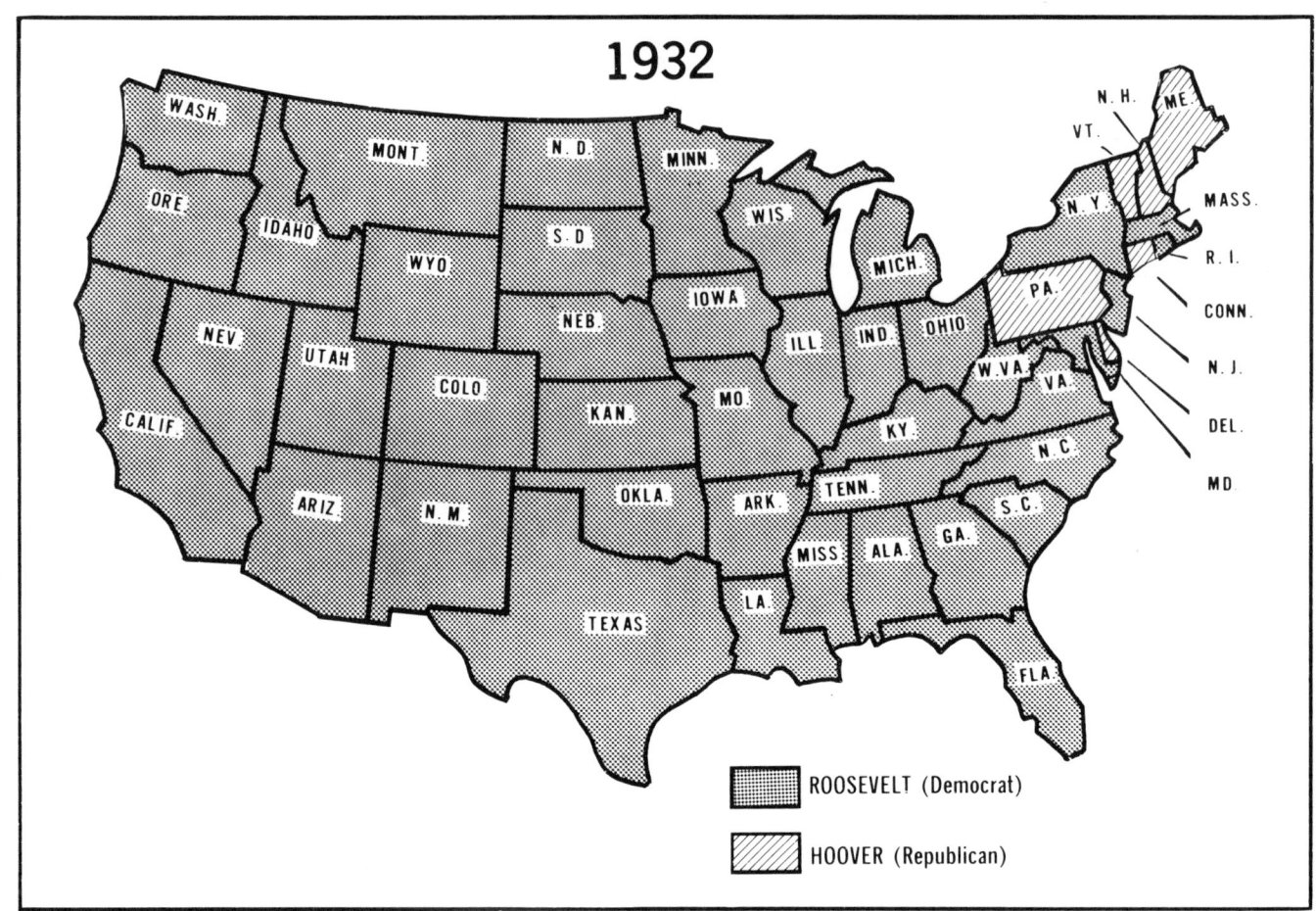

1932

ROOSEVELT (Democrat)

HOOVER (Republican)

States	Electoral Votes	Roosevelt	Hoover	States	Electoral Votes	Roosevelt	Hoover
Alabama	(11)	11	-	Nebraska	(7)	7	-
Arizona	(3)	3	-	Nevada	(3)	3	-
Arkansas	(9)	9	-	New Hampshire	(4)	-	4
California	(22)	22	-	New Jersey	(16)	16	-
Colorado	(6)	6	-	New Mexico	(3)	3	-
Connecticut	(8)	-	8	New York	(47)	47	-
Delaware	(3)	-	3	North Carolina	(13)	13	-
Florida	(7)	7	-	North Dakota	(4)	4	-
Georgia	(12)	12	-	Ohio	(26)	26	-
Idaho	(4)	4	-	Oklahoma	(11)	11	-
Illinois	(29)	29	-	Oregon	(5)	5	-
Indiana	(14)	14	-	Pennsylvania	(36)	-	36
Iowa	(11)	11	-	Rhode Island	(4)	4	-
Kansas	(9)	9	-	South Carolina	(8)	8	-
Kentucky	(11)	11	-	South Dakota	(4)	4	-
Louisiana	(10)	10	-	Tennessee	(11)	11	-
Maine	(5)	-	5	Texas	(23)	23	-
Maryland	(8)	8	-	Utah	(4)	4	-
Massachusetts	(17)	17	-	Vermont	(3)	-	3
Michigan	(19)	19	-	Virginia	(11)	11	-
Minnesota	(11)	11	-	Washington	(8)	8	-
Mississippi	(9)	9	-	West Virginia	(8)	8	-
Missouri	(15)	15	-	Wisconsin	(12)	12	-
Montana	(4)	4	-	Wyoming	(3)	3	-
				Totals	**(531)**	**472**	**59**

1936

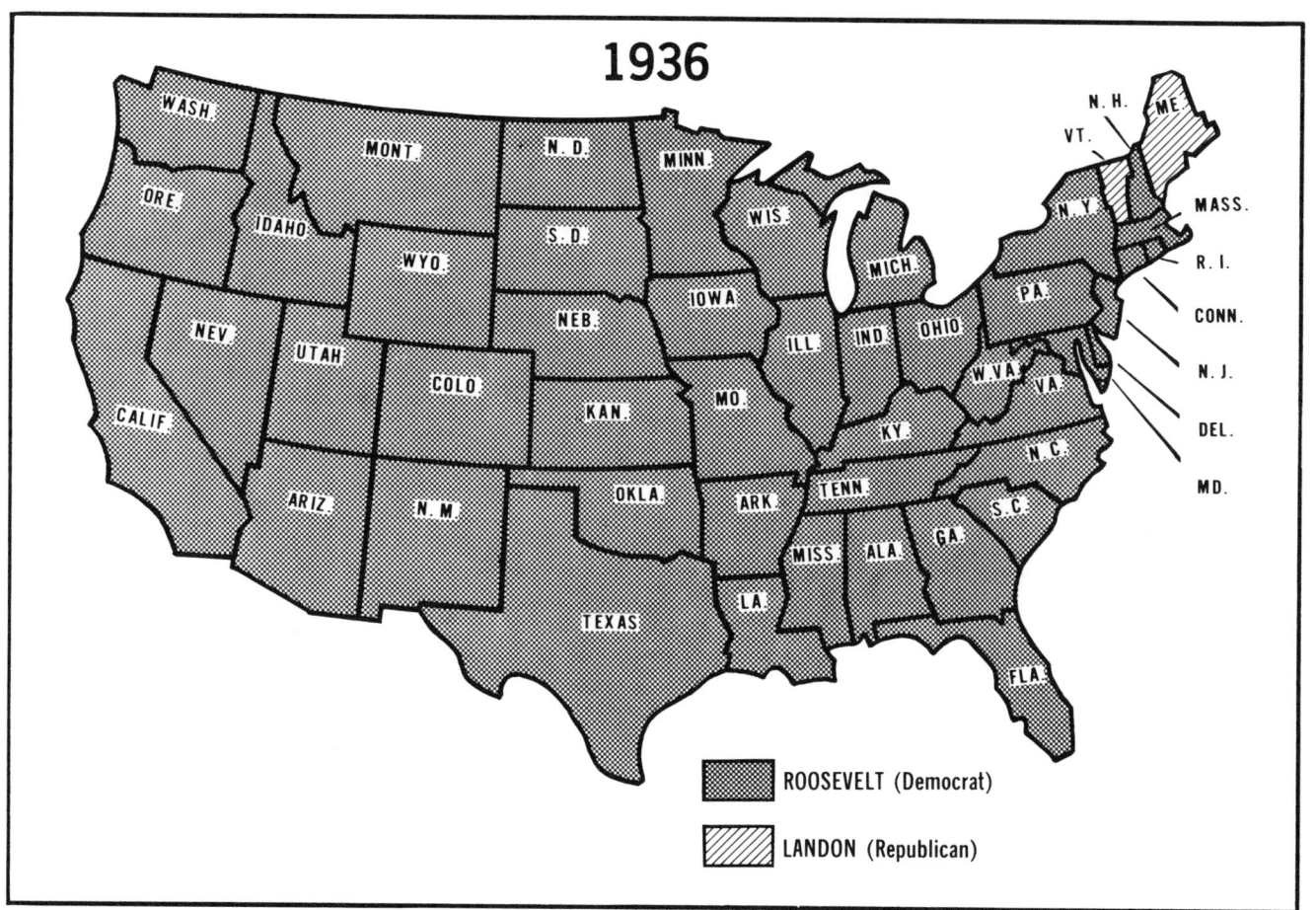

■ ROOSEVELT (Democrat)

▨ LANDON (Republican)

States	Electoral Votes	Roosevelt	Landon	States	Electoral Votes	Roosevelt	Landon
Alabama	(11)	11	-	Nebraska	(7)	7	-
Arizona	(3)	3	-	Nevada	(3)	3	-
Arkansas	(9)	9	-	New Hampshire	(4)	4	-
California	(22)	22	-	New Jersey	(16)	16	-
Colorado	(6)	6	-	New Mexico	(3)	3	-
Connecticut	(8)	8	-	New York	(47)	47	-
Delaware	(3)	3	-	North Carolina	(13)	13	-
Florida	(7)	7	-	North Dakota	(4)	4	-
Georgia	(12)	12	-	Ohio	(26)	26	-
Idaho	(4)	4	-	Oklahoma	(11)	11	-
Illinois	(29)	29	-	Oregon	(5)	5	-
Indiana	(14)	14	-	Pennsylvania	(36)	36	-
Iowa	(11)	11	-	Rhode Island	(4)	4	-
Kansas	(9)	9	-	South Carolina	(8)	8	-
Kentucky	(11)	11	-	South Dakota	(4)	4	-
Louisiana	(10)	10	-	Tennessee	(11)	11	-
Maine	(5)	-	5	Texas	(23)	23	-
Maryland	(8)	8	-	Utah	(4)	4	-
Massachusetts	(17)	17	-	Vermont	(3)	-	3
Michigan	(19)	19	-	Virginia	(11)	11	-
Minnesota	(11)	11	-	Washington	(8)	8	-
Mississippi	(9)	9	-	West Virginia	(8)	8	-
Missouri	(15)	15	-	Wisconsin	(12)	12	-
Montana	(4)	4	-	Wyoming	(3)	3	-
				Totals	**(531)**	**523**	**8**

1940

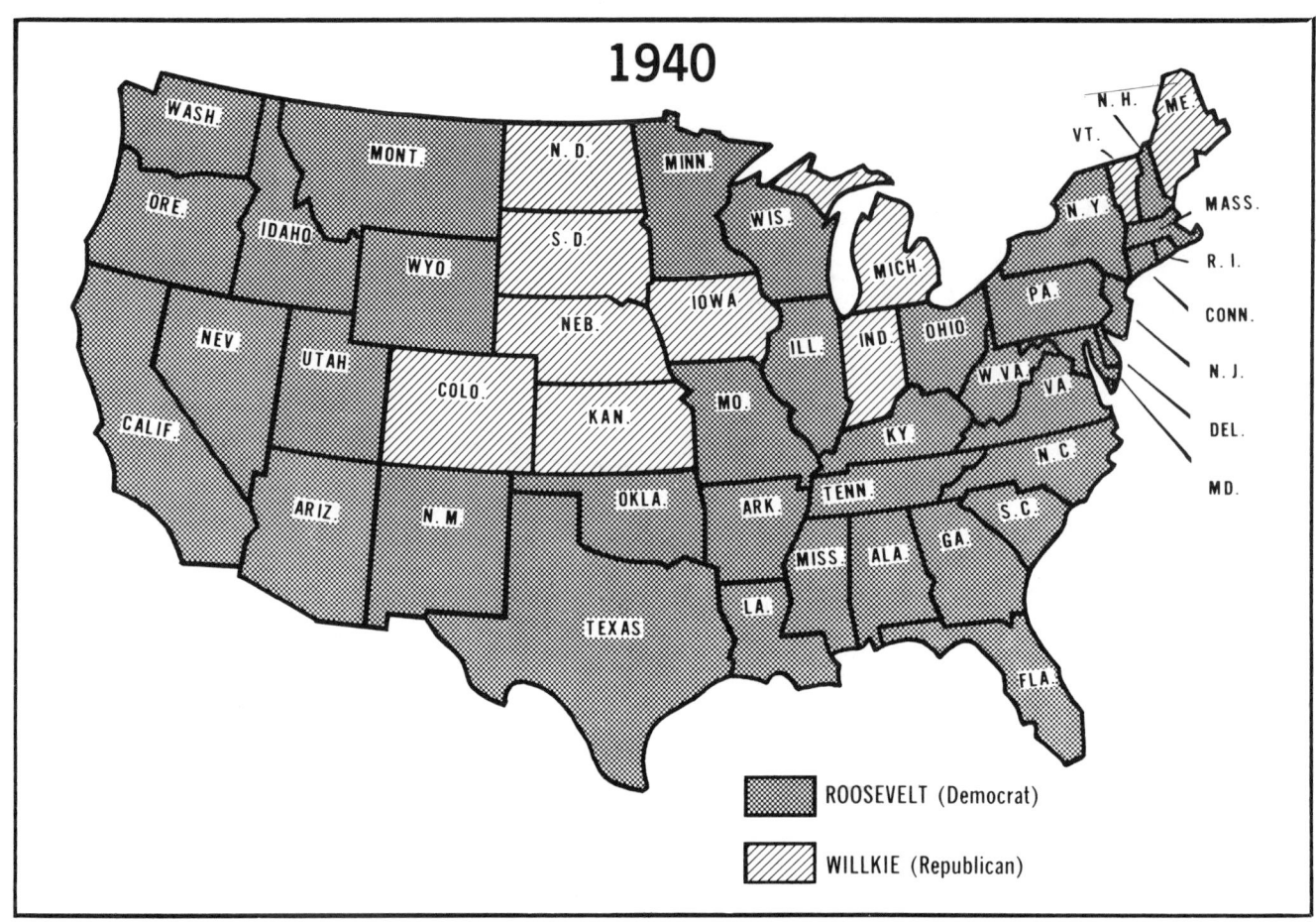

ROOSEVELT (Democrat)

WILLKIE (Republican)

States	Electoral Votes	Roosevelt	Willkie	States	Electoral Votes	Roosevelt	Willkie
Alabama	(11)	11	-	Nebraska	(7)	-	7
Arizona	(3)	3	-	Nevada	(3)	3	-
Arkansas	(9)	9	-	New Hampshire	(4)	4	-
California	(22)	22	-	New Jersey	(16)	16	-
Colorado	(6)	-	6	New Mexico	(3)	3	-
Connecticut	(8)	8	-	New York	(47)	47	-
Delaware	(3)	3	-	North Carolina	(13)	13	-
Florida	(7)	7	-	North Dakota	(4)	-	4
Georgia	(12)	12	-	Ohio	(26)	26	-
Idaho	(4)	4	-	Oklahoma	(11)	11	-
Illinois	(29)	29	-	Oregon	(5)	5	-
Indiana	(14)	-	14	Pennsylvania	(36)	36	-
Iowa	(11)	-	11	Rhode Island	(4)	4	-
Kansas	(9)		9	South Carolina	(8)	8	-
Kentucky	(11)	11	-	South Dakota	(4)	-	4
Louisiana	(10)	10	-	Tennessee	(11)	11	-
Maine	(5)	-	5	Texas	(23)	23	-
Maryland	(8)	8	-	Utah	(4)	4	-
Massachusetts	(17)	17	-	Vermont	(3)	-	3
Michigan	(19)	-	19	Virginia	(11)	11	-
Minnesota	(11)	11	-	Washington	(8)	8	-
Mississippi	(9)	9	-	West Virginia	(8)	8	-
Missouri	(15)	15	-	Wisconsin	(12)	12	-
Montana	(4)	4	-	Wyoming	(3)	3	-
				Totals	**(531)**	**449**	**82**

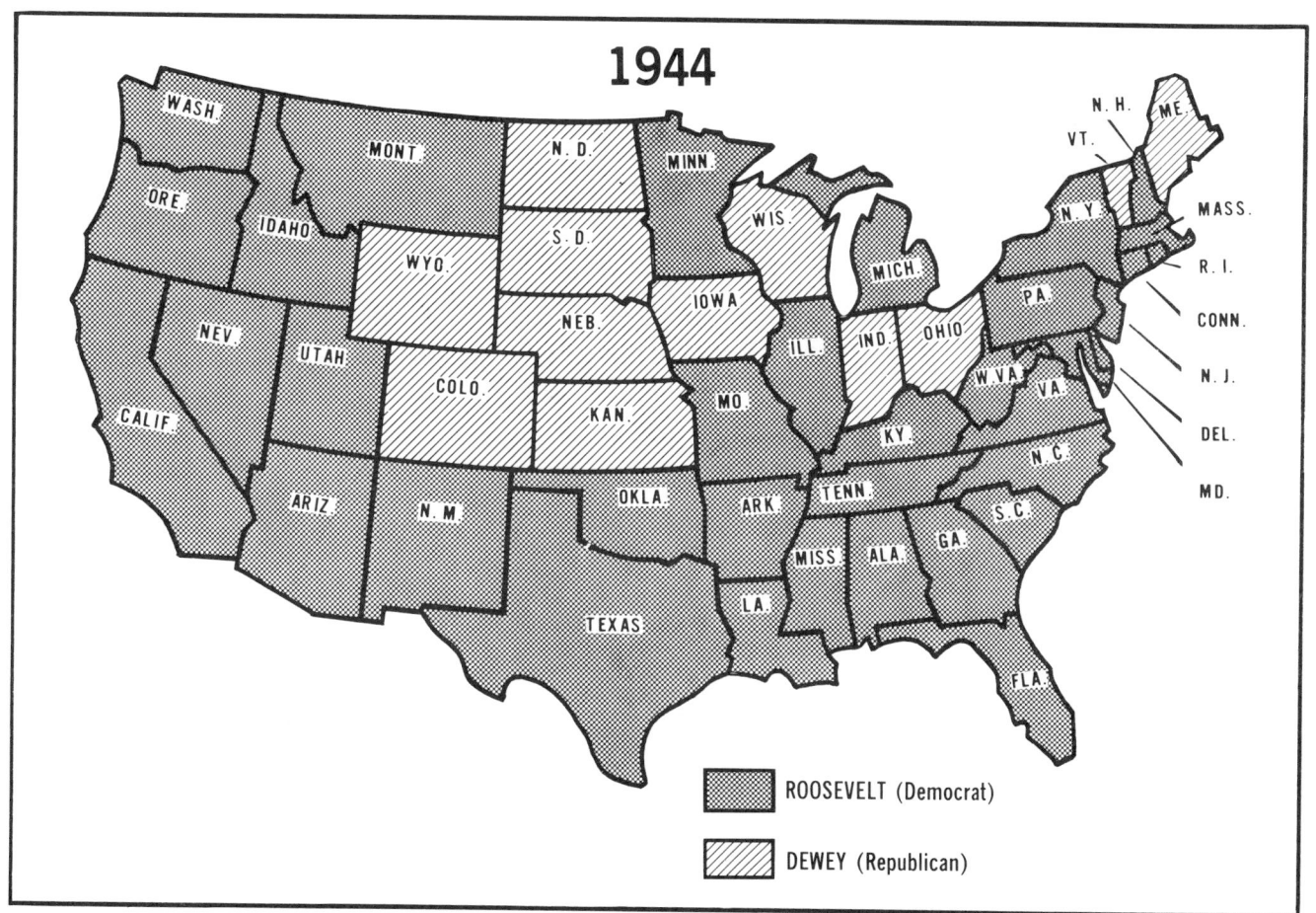

1944

ROOSEVELT (Democrat)

DEWEY (Republican)

States	Electoral Votes	Roosevelt	Dewey	States	Electoral Votes	Roosevelt	Dewey
Alabama	(11)	11	-	**Nebraska**	(6)	-	6
Arizona	(4)	4	-	**Nevada**	(3)	3	-
Arkansas	(9)	9	-	**New Hampshire**	(4)	4	-
California	(25)	25	-	**New Jersey**	(16)	16	-
Colorado	(6)	-	6	**New Mexico**	(4)	4	-
Connecticut	(8)	8	-	**New York**	(47)	47	-
Delaware	(3)	3	-	**North Carolina**	(14)	14	-
Florida	(8)	8	-	**North Dakota**	(4)	-	4
Georgia	(12)	12	-	**Ohio**	(25)	-	25
Idaho	(4)	4	-	**Oklahoma**	(10)	10	-
Illinois	(28)	28	-	**Oregon**	(6)	6	-
Indiana	(13)	-	13	**Pennsylvania**	(35)	35	-
Iowa	(10)	-	10	**Rhode Island**	(4)	4	-
Kansas	(8)	-	8	**South Carolina**	(8)	8	-
Kentucky	(11)	11	-	**South Dakota**	(4)	-	4
Louisiana	(10)	10	-	**Tennessee**	(12)	12	-
Maine	(5)	-	5	**Texas**	(23)	23	-
Maryland	(8)	8	-	**Utah**	(4)	4	-
Massachusetts	(16)	16	-	**Vermont**	(3)	-	3
Michigan	(19)	19	-	**Virginia**	(11)	11	-
Minnesota	(11)	11	-	**Washington**	(8)	8	-
Mississippi	(9)	9	-	**West Virginia**	(8)	8	-
Missouri	(15)	15	-	**Wisconsin**	(12)	-	12
Montana	(4)	4	-	**Wyoming**	(3)	-	3
				Totals	**(531)**	**432**	**99**

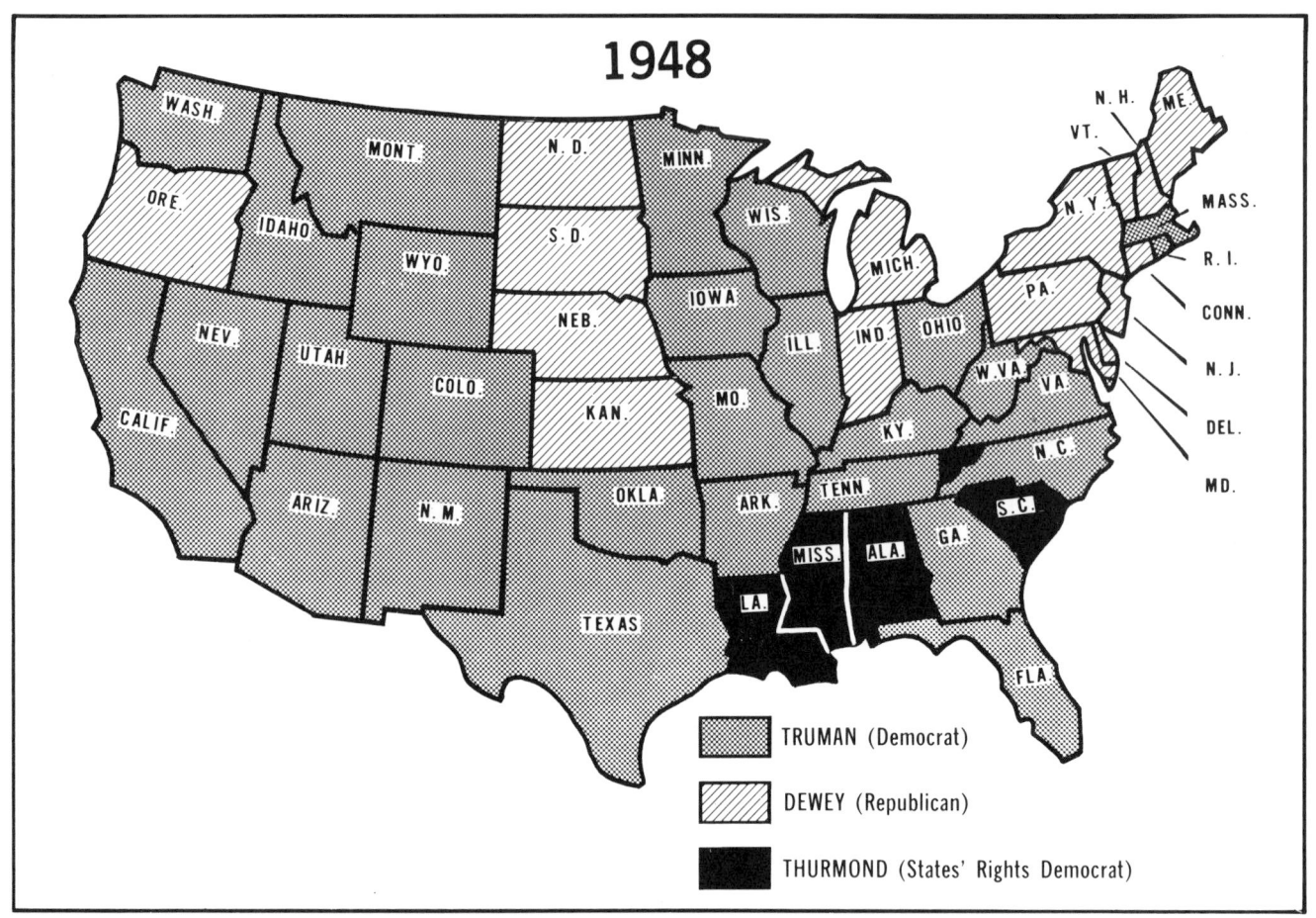

1948

TRUMAN (Democrat)

DEWEY (Republican)

THURMOND (States' Rights Democrat)

States	Electoral Votes	Truman	Dewey	Thurmond	States	Electoral Votes	Truman	Dewey	Thurmond
Alabama	(11)	-	-	11	Nebraska	(6)	-	6	-
Arizona	(4)	4	-	-	Nevada	(3)	3	-	-
Arkansas	(9)	9	-	-	New Hampshire	(4)	-	4	-
California	(25)	25	-	-	New Jersey	(16)	-	16	-
Colorado	(6)	6	-	-	New Mexico	(4)	4	-	-
Connecticut	(8)	-	8	-	New York	(47)	-	47	-
Delaware	(3)	-	3	-	North Carolina	(14)	14	-	-
Florida	(8)	8	-	-	North Dakota	(4)	-	4	-
Georgia	(12)	12	-	-	Ohio	(25)	25	-	-
Idaho	(4)	4	-	-	Oklahoma	(10)	10	-	-
Illinois	(28)	28	-	-	Oregon	(6)	-	6	-
Indiana	(13)	-	13	-	Pennsylvania	(35)	-	35	-
Iowa	(10)	10	-	-	Rhode Island	(4)	4	-	-
Kansas	(8)	-	8	-	South Carolina	(8)	-	-	8
Kentucky	(11)	11	-	-	South Dakota	(4)	-	4	-
Louisiana	(10)	-	-	10	Tennessee [1]	(12)	11	-	1
Maine	(5)	-	5	-	Texas	(23)	23	-	-
Maryland	(8)	-	8	-	Utah	(4)	4	-	-
Massachusetts	(16)	16	-	-	Vermont	(3)	-	3	-
Michigan	(19)	-	19	-	Virginia	(11)	11	-	-
Minnesota	(11)	11	-	-	Washington	(8)	8	-	-
Mississippi	(9)	-	-	9	West Virginia	(8)	8	-	-
Missouri	(15)	15	-	-	Wisconsin	(12)	12	-	-
Montana	(4)	4	-	-	Wyoming	(3)	3	-	-
					Totals	**(531)**	**303**	**189**	**39**

1. For explanation of split electoral votes, see p. 258.

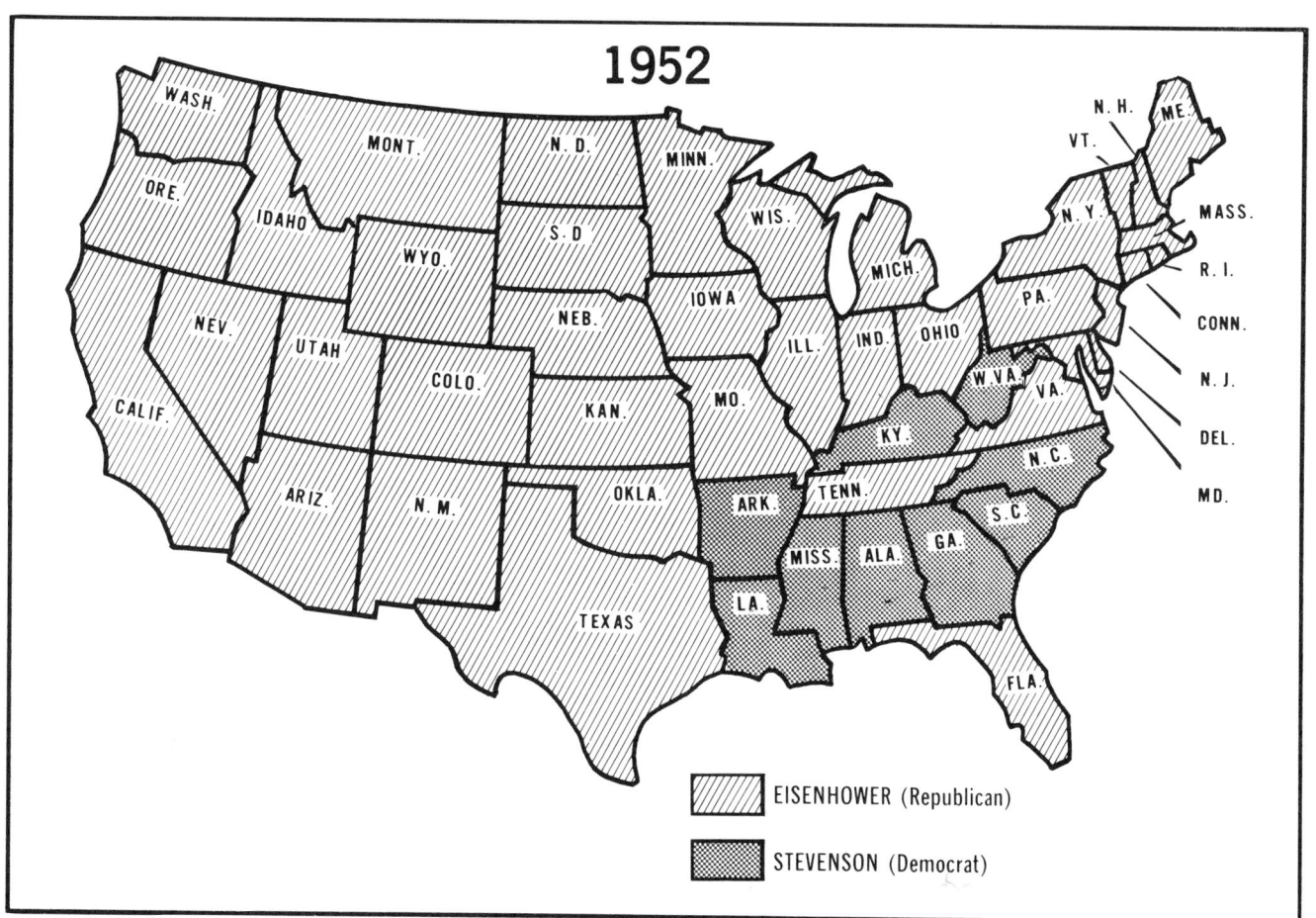

1952

EISENHOWER (Republican)

STEVENSON (Democrat)

States	Electoral Votes	Eisenhower	Stevenson	States	Electoral Votes	Eisenhower	Stevenson
Alabama	(11)	-	11	Nebraska	(6)	6	-
Arizona	(4)	4	-	Nevada	(3)	3	-
Arkansas	(8)	-	8	New Hampshire	(4)	4	-
California	(32)	32	-	New Jersey	(16)	16	-
Colorado	(6)	6	-	New Mexico	(4)	4	-
Connecticut	(8)	8	-	New York	(45)	45	-
Delaware	(3)	3	-	North Carolina	(14)	-	14
Florida	(10)	10	-	North Dakota	(4)	4	-
Georgia	(12)	-	12	Ohio	(25)	25	-
Idaho	(4)	4	-	Oklahoma	(8)	8	-
Illinois	(27)	27	-	Oregon	(6)	6	-
Indiana	(13)	13	-	Pennsylvania	(32)	32	-
Iowa	(10)	10	-	Rhode Island	(4)	4	-
Kansas	(8)	8	-	South Carolina	(8)	-	8
Kentucky	(10)	-	10	South Dakota	(4)	4	-
Louisiana	(10)	-	10	Tennessee	(11)	11	-
Maine	(5)	5	-	Texas	(24)	24	-
Maryland	(9)	9	-	Utah	(4)	4	-
Massachusetts	(16)	16	-	Vermont	(3)	3	-
Michigan	(20)	20	-	Virginia	(12)	12	-
Minnesota	(11)	11	-	Washington	(9)	9	-
Mississippi	(8)	-	8	West Virginia	(8)	-	8
Missouri	(13)	13	-	Wisconsin	(12)	12	-
Montana	(4)	4	-	Wyoming	(3)	3	-
				Totals	**(531)**	**442**	**89**

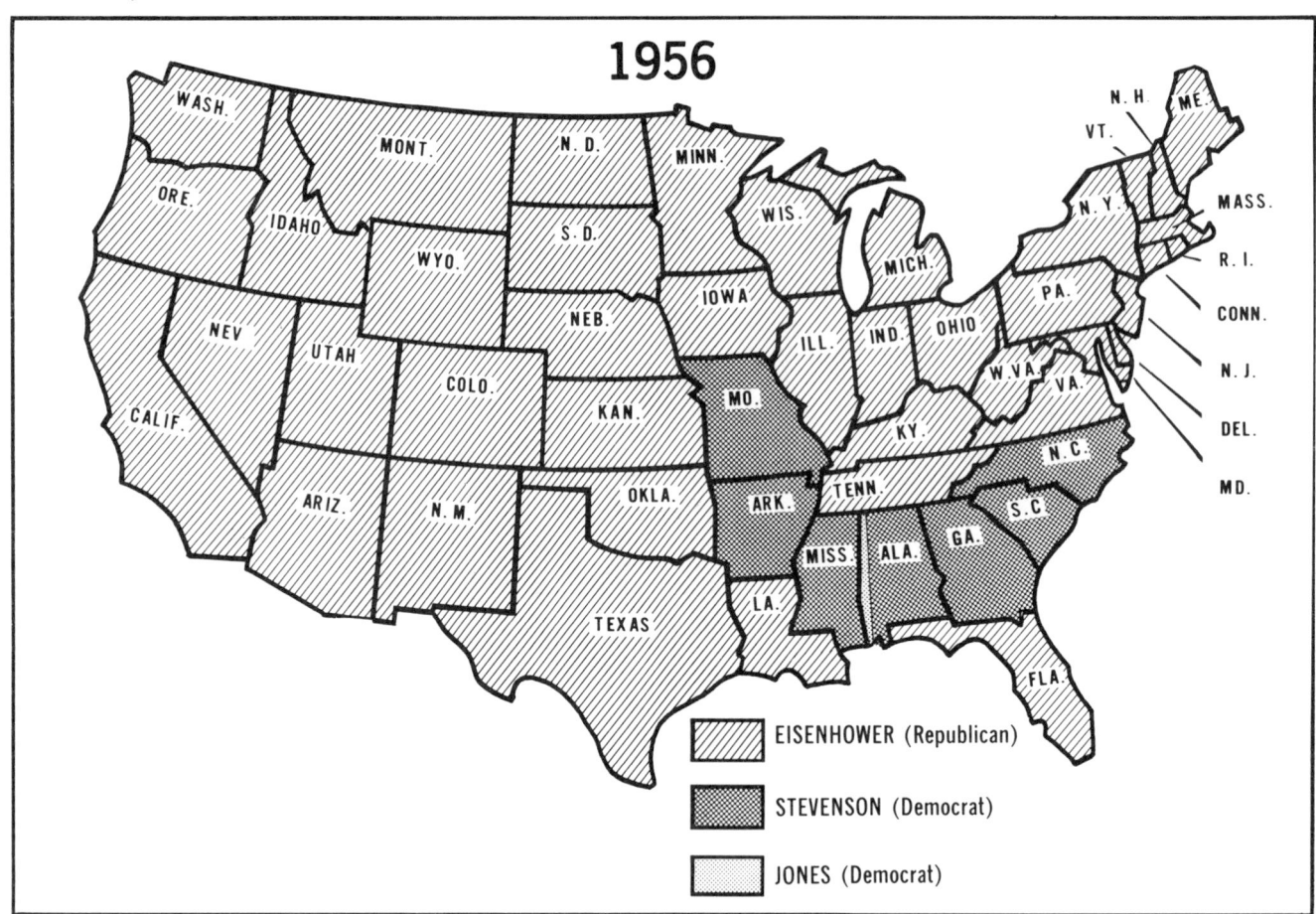

States	Electoral Votes	Eisenhower	Stevenson	Jones	States	Electoral Votes	Eisenhower	Stevenson	Jones
Alabama[1]	(11)	-	10	1	**Nebraska**	(6)	6	-	-
Arizona	(4)	4	-	-	**Nevada**	(3)	3	-	-
Arkansas	(8)	-	8	-	**New Hampshire**	(4)	4	-	-
California	(32)	32	-	-	**New Jersey**	(16)	16	-	-
Colorado	(6)	6	-	-	**New Mexico**	(4)	4	-	-
Connecticut	(8)	8	-	-	**New York**	(45)	45	-	-
Delaware	(3)	3	-	-	**North Carolina**	(14)	-	14	-
Florida	(10)	10	-	-	**North Dakota**	(4)	4	-	-
Georgia	(12)	-	12	-	**Ohio**	(25)	25	-	-
Idaho	(4)	4	-	-	**Oklahoma**	(8)	8	-	-
Illinois	(27)	27	-	-	**Oregon**	(6)	6	-	-
Indiana	(13)	13	-	-	**Pennsylvania**	(32)	32	-	-
Iowa	(10)	10	-	-	**Rhode Island**	(4)	4	-	-
Kansas	(8)	8	-	-	**South Carolina**	(8)	-	8	-
Kentucky	(10)	10	-	-	**South Dakota**	(4)	4	-	-
Louisiana	(10)	10	-	-	**Tennessee**	(11)	11	-	-
Maine	(5)	5	-	-	**Texas**	(24)	24	-	-
Maryland	(9)	9	-	-	**Utah**	(4)	4	-	-
Massachusetts	(16)	16	-	-	**Vermont**	(3)	3	-	-
Michigan	(20)	20	-	-	**Virginia**	(12)	12	-	-
Minnesota	(11)	11	-	-	**Washington**	(9)	9	-	-
Mississippi	(8)	-	8	-	**West Virginia**	(8)	8	-	-
Missouri	(13)	-	13	-	**Wisconsin**	(12)	12	-	-
Montana	(4)	4	-	-	**Wyoming**	(3)	3	-	-
					Totals	(531)	457	73	1

1. For explanation of split electoral votes, see p. 258.

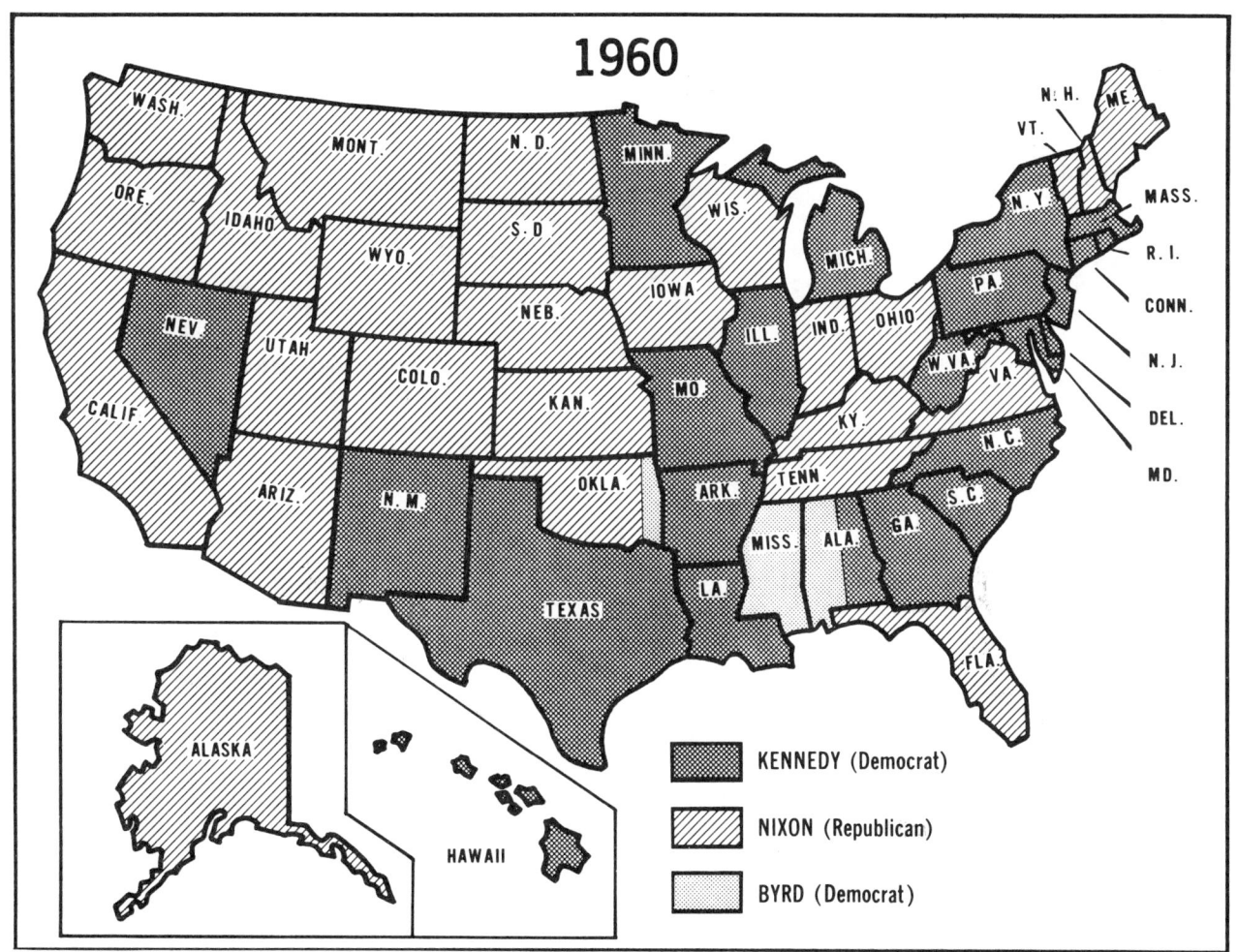

1960

	KENNEDY (Democrat)
	NIXON (Republican)
	BYRD (Democrat)

States	Electoral Votes	Kennedy	Nixon	Byrd	States	Electoral Votes	Kennedy	Nixon	Byrd
Alabama[1]	(11)	5	-	6	Montana	(4)	-	4	-
Alaska	(3)	-	3	-	Nebraska	(6)	-	6	-
Arizona	(4)	-	4	-	Nevada	(3)	3	-	-
Arkansas	(8)	8	-	-	New Hampshire	(4)	-	4	-
California	(32)	-	32	-	New Jersey	(16)	16	-	-
Colorado	(6)	-	6	-	New Mexico	(4)	4	-	-
Connecticut	(8)	8	-	-	New York	(45)	45	-	-
Delaware	(3)	3	-	-	North Carolina	(14)	14	-	-
Florida	(10)	-	10	-	North Dakota	(4)	-	4	-
Georgia	(12)	12	-	-	Ohio	(25)	-	25	-
Hawaii	(3)	3	-	-	Oklahoma[1]	(8)	-	7	1
Idaho	(4)	-	4	-	Oregon	(6)	-	6	-
Illinois	(27)	27	-	-	Pennsylvania	(32)	32	-	-
Indiana	(13)	-	13	-	Rhode Island	(4)	4	-	-
Iowa	(10)	-	10	-	South Carolina	(8)	8	-	-
Kansas	(8)	-	8	-	South Dakota	(4)	-	4	-
Kentucky	(10)	-	10	-	Tennessee	(11)	-	11	-
Louisiana	(10)	10	-	-	Texas	(24)	24	-	-
Maine	(5)	-	5	-	Utah	(4)	-	4	-
Maryland	(9)	9	-	-	Vermont	(3)	-	3	-
Massachusetts	(16)	16	-	-	Virginia	(12)	-	12	-
Michigan	(20)	20	-	-	Washington	(9)	-	9	-
Minnesota	(11)	11	-	-	West Virginia	(8)	8	-	-
Mississippi	(8)	-	-	8	Wisconsin	(12)	-	12	-
Missouri	(13)	13	-	-	Wyoming	(3)	-	3	-
					Totals	**(537)**	**303**	**219**	**15**

1. For explanation of split electoral votes, see p. 258.

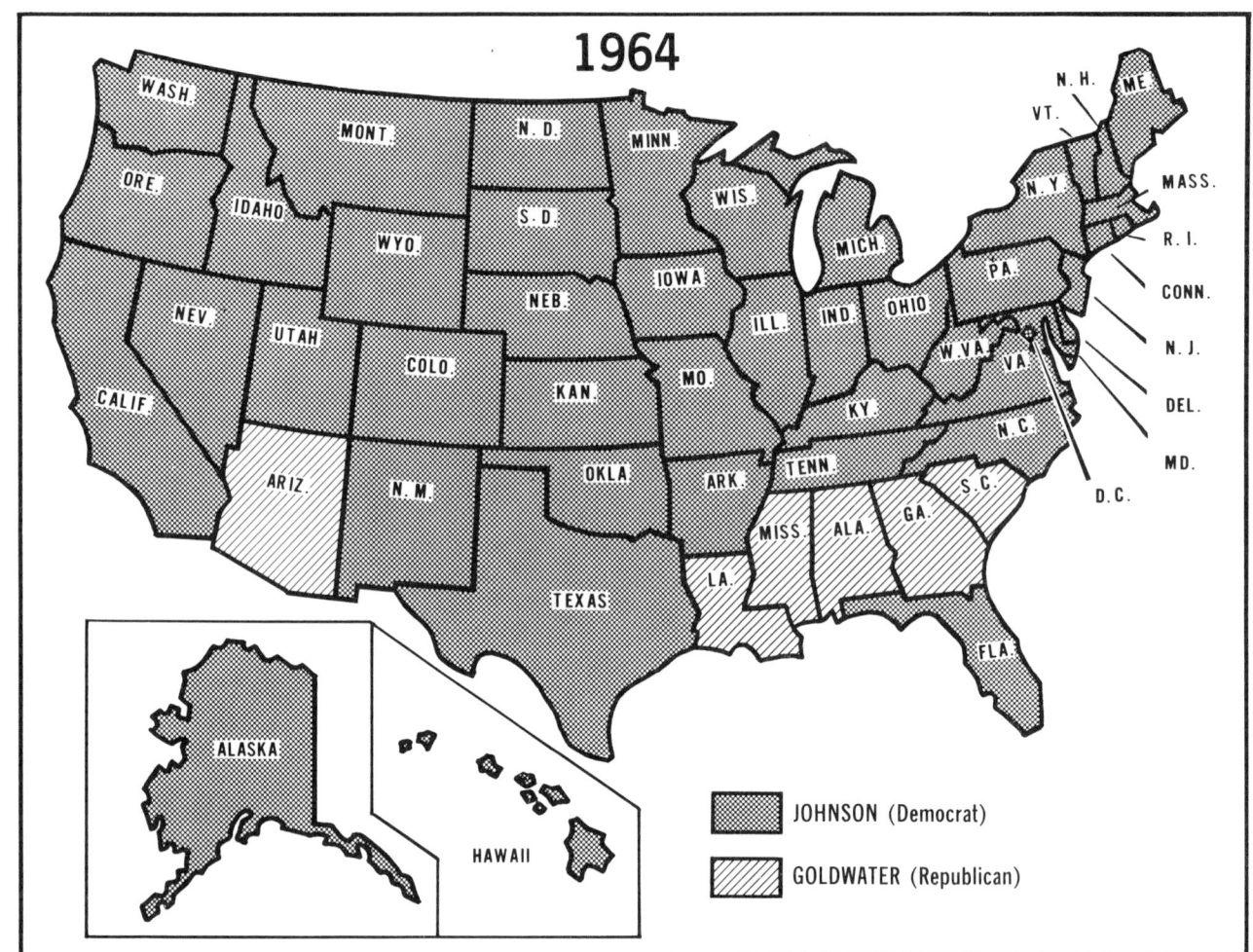

1964

	JOHNSON (Democrat)
	GOLDWATER (Republican)

States	Electoral Votes	Johnson	Goldwater	States	Electoral Votes	Johnson	Goldwater
Alabama	(10)	-	10	Montana	(4)	4	-
Alaska	(3)	3	-	Nebraska	(5)	5	-
Arizona	(5)	-	5	Nevada	(3)	3	-
Arkansas	(6)	6	-	New Hampshire	(4)	4	-
California	(40)	40	-	New Jersey	(17)	17	-
Colorado	(6)	6	-	New Mexico	(4)	4	-
Connecticut	(8)	8	-	New York	(43)	43	-
Delaware	(3)	3	-	North Carolina	(13)	13	-
District of Columbia	(3)	3	-	North Dakota	(4)	4	-
Florida	(14)	14	-	Ohio	(26)	26	-
Georgia	(12)	-	12	Oklahoma	(8)	8	-
Hawaii	(4)	4	-	Oregon	(6)	6	-
Idaho	(4)	4	-	Pennsylvania	(29)	29	-
Illinois	(26)	26	-	Rhode Island	(4)	4	-
Indiana	(13)	13	-	South Carolina	(8)	-	8
Iowa	(9)	9	-	South Dakota	(4)	4	-
Kansas	(7)	7	-	Tennessee	(11)	11	-
Kentucky	(9)	9	-	Texas	(25)	25	-
Louisiana	(10)	-	10	Utah	(4)	4	-
Maine	(4)	4	-	Vermont	(3)	3	-
Maryland	(10)	10	-	Virginia	(12)	12	-
Massachusetts	(14)	14	-	Washington	(9)	9	-
Michigan	(21)	21	-	West Virginia	(7)	7	-
Minnesota	(10)	10	-	Wisconsin	(12)	12	-
Mississippi	(7)	-	7	Wyoming	(3)	3	-
Missouri	(12)	12	-	**Totals**	**(538)**	**486**	**52**

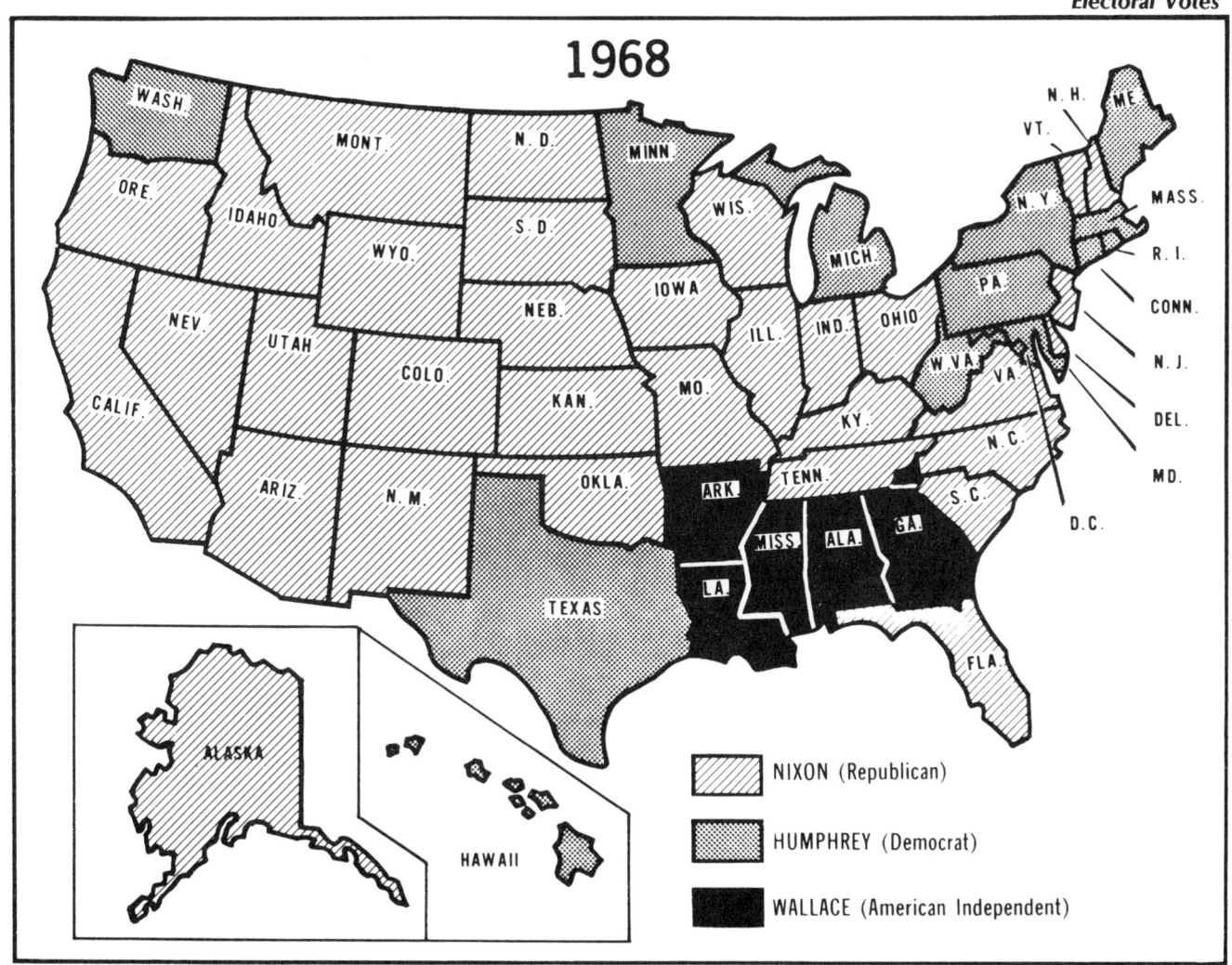

1968

		NIXON (Republican)
		HUMPHREY (Democrat)
		WALLACE (American Independent)

States	Electoral Votes	Nixon	Humphrey	Wallace	States	Electoral Votes	Nixon	Humphrey	Wallace
Alabama	(10)	-	-	10	Montana	(4)	4	-	-
Alaska	(3)	3	-	-	Nebraska	(5)	5	-	-
Arizona	(5)	5	-	-	Nevada	(3)	3	-	-
Arkansas	(6)	-	-	6	New Hampshire	(4)	4	-	-
California	(40)	40	-	-	New Jersey	(17)	17	-	-
Colorado	(6)	6	-	-	New Mexico	(4)	4	-	-
Connecticut	(8)	-	8	-	New York	(43)	-	43	-
Delaware	(3)	3	-	-	North Carolina[1]	(13)	12	-	1
District of Columbia	(3)	-	3	-	North Dakota	(4)	4	-	-
Florida	(14)	14	-	-	Ohio	(26)	26	-	-
Georgia	(12)	-	-	12	Oklahoma	(8)	8	-	-
Hawaii	(4)	-	4	-	Oregon	(6)	6	-	-
Idaho	(4)	4	-	-	Pennsylvania	(29)	-	29	-
Illinois	(26)	26	-	-	Rhode Island	(4)	-	4	-
Indiana	(13)	13	-	-	South Carolina	(8)	8	-	-
Iowa	(9)	9	-	-	South Dakota	(4)	4	-	-
Kansas	(7)	7	-	-	Tennessee	(11)	11	-	-
Kentucky	(9)	9	-	-	Texas	(25)	-	25	-
Louisiana	(10)	-	-	10	Utah	(4)	4	-	-
Maine	(4)	-	4	-	Vermont	(3)	3	-	-
Maryland	(10)	-	10	-	Virginia	(12)	12	-	-
Massachusetts	(14)	-	14	-	Washington	(9)	-	9	-
Michigan	(21)	-	21	-	West Virginia	(7)	-	7	-
Minnesota	(10)	-	10	-	Wisconsin	(12)	12	-	-
Mississippi	(7)	-	-	7	Wyoming	(3)	3	-	-
Missouri	(12)	12	-	-	**Totals**	**(538)**	**301**	**191**	**46**

1. For explanation of split electoral votes, see p. 258.

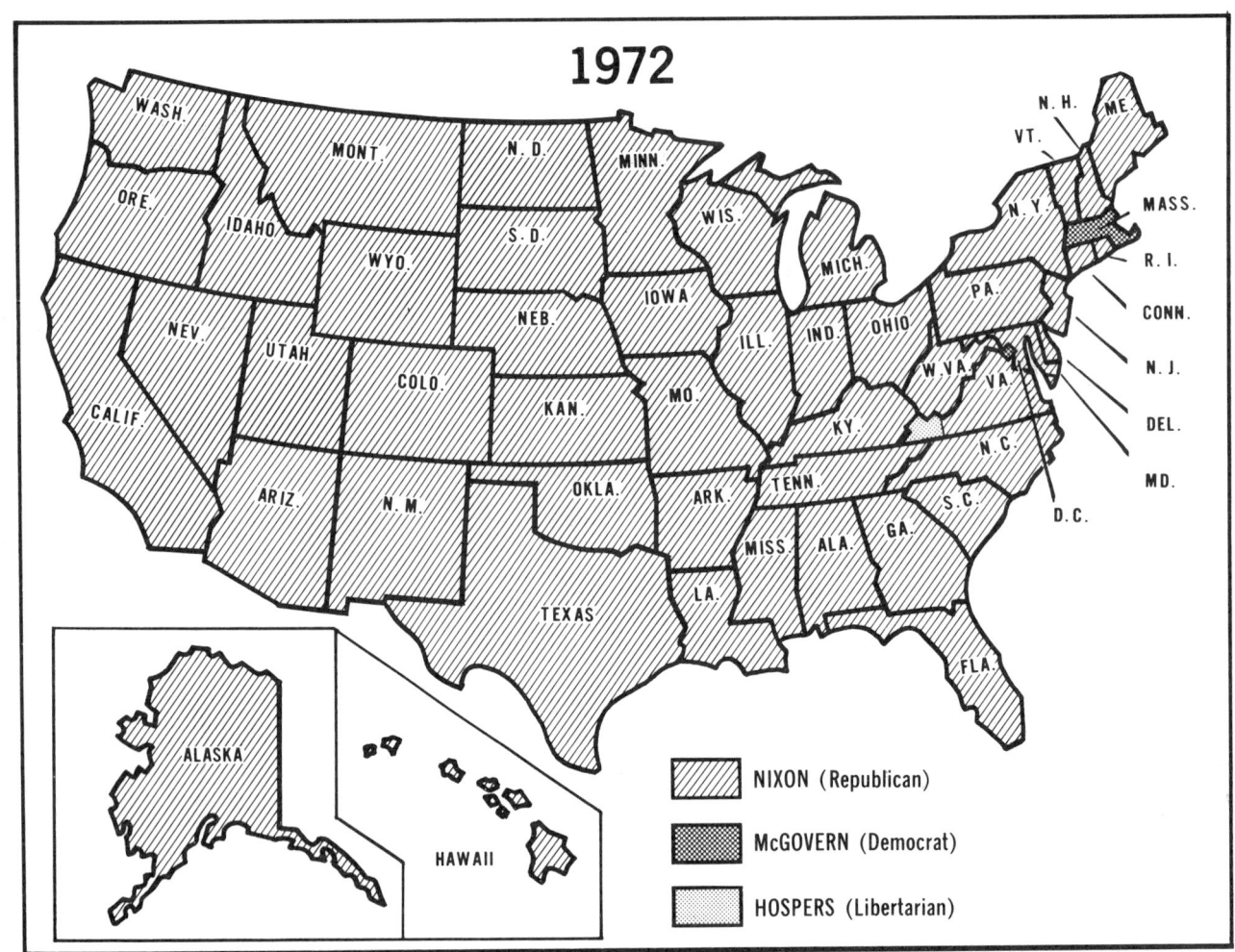

1972

	NIXON (Republican)
	McGOVERN (Democrat)
	HOSPERS (Libertarian)

States	Electoral Votes	Nixon	McGovern	Hospers
Alabama	(9)	9	-	-
Alaska	(3)	3	-	-
Arizona	(6)	6	-	-
Arkansas	(6)	6	-	-
California	(45)	45	-	-
Colorado	(7)	7	-	-
Connecticut	(8)	8	-	-
Delaware	(3)	3	-	-
District of Columbia	(3)	-	3	-
Florida	(17)	17	-	-
Georgia	(12)	12	-	-
Hawaii	(4)	4	-	-
Idaho	(4)	4	-	-
Illinois	(26)	26	-	-
Indiana	(13)	13	-	-
Iowa	(8)	8	-	-
Kansas	(7)	7	-	-
Kentucky	(9)	9	-	-
Louisiana	(10)	10	-	-
Maine	(4)	4	-	-
Maryland	(10)	10	-	-
Massachusetts	(14)	-	14	-
Michigan	(21)	21	-	-
Minnesota	(10)	10	-	-
Mississippi	(7)	7	-	-
Missouri	(12)	12	-	-
Montana	(4)	4	-	-
Nebraska	(5)	5	-	-
Nevada	(3)	3	-	-
New Hampshire	(4)	4	-	-
New Jersey	(17)	17	-	-
New Mexico	(4)	4	-	-
New York	(4)	41	-	-
North Carolina	(13)	13	-	-
North Dakota	(3)	3	-	-
Ohio	(25)	25	-	-
Oklahoma	(8)	8	-	-
Oregon	(6)	6	-	-
Pennsylvania	(27)	27	-	-
Rhode Island	(4)	4	-	-
South Carolina	(8)	8	-	-
South Dakota	(4)	4	-	-
Tennessee	(10)	10	-	-
Texas	(26)	26	-	-
Utah	(4)	4	-	-
Vermont	(3)	3	-	-
Virginia[1]	(12)	11	-	1
Washington	(9)	9	-	-
West Virginia	(6)	6	-	-
Wisconsin	(11)	11	-	-
Wyoming	(3)	3	-	-
Totals	(538)	520	17	1

1. For explanation of split electoral votes, see p. 258.

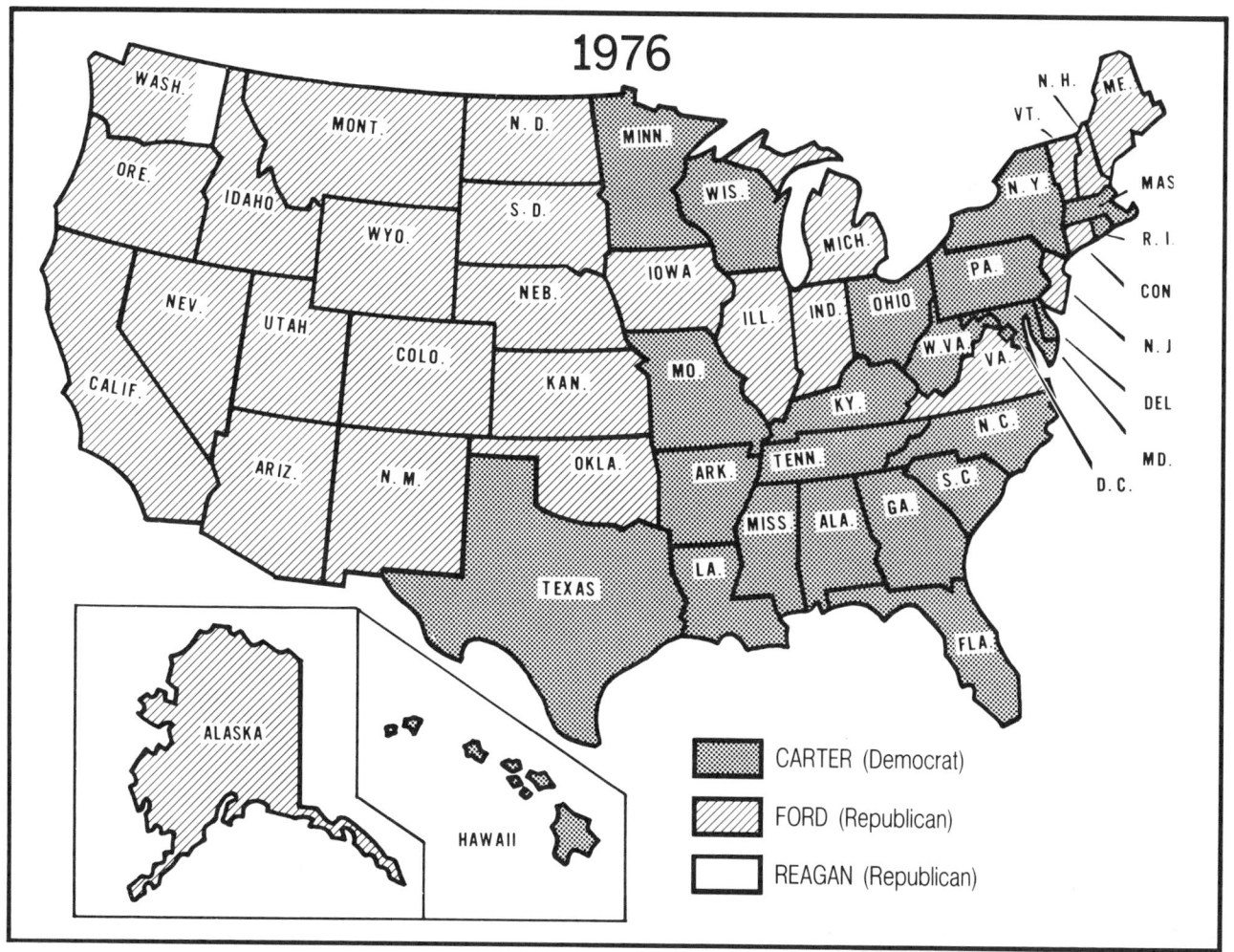

1976

	CARTER (Democrat)
	FORD (Republican)
	REAGAN (Republican)

States	Electoral Votes	Carter	Ford	Reagan	States	Electoral Votes	Carter	Ford	Reagan
Alabama	(9)	9	—	—	Montana	(4)	—	4	—
Alaska	(3)	—	3	—	Nebraska	(5)	—	5	—
Arizona	(6)	—	6	—	Nevada	(3)	—	3	—
Arkansas	(6)	6	—	—	New Hampshire	(4)	—	4	—
California	(45)	—	45	—	New Jersey	(17)	—	17	—
Colorado	(7)	—	7	—	New Mexico	(4)	—	4	—
Connecticut	(8)	—	8	—	New York	(41)	41	—	—
Delaware	(3)	3	—	—	North Carolina	(13)	13	—	—
District of Columbia	(3)	3	—	—	North Dakota	(3)	—	3	—
Florida	(17)	17	—	—	Ohio	(25)	25	—	—
Georgia	(12)	12	—	—	Oklahoma	(8)	—	8	—
Hawaii	(4)	4	—	—	Oregon	(6)	—	6	—
Idaho	(4)	—	4	—	Pennsylvania	(27)	27	—	—
Illinois	(26)	—	26	—	Rhode Island	(4)	4	—	—
Indiana	(13)	—	13	—	South Carolina	(8)	8	—	—
Iowa	(8)	—	8	—	South Dakota	(4)	—	4	—
Kansas	(7)	—	7	—	Tennessee	(10)	10	—	—
Kentucky	(9)	9	—	—	Texas	(26)	26	—	—
Louisiana	(10)	10	—	—	Utah	(4)	—	4	—
Maine	(4)	—	4	—	Vermont	(3)	—	3	—
Maryland	(10)	10	—	—	Virginia	(12)	—	12	—
Massachusetts	(14)	14	—	—	Washington [1]	(9)	—	8	1
Michigan	(21)	—	21	—	West Virginia	(6)	6	—	—
Minnesota	(10)	10	—	—	Wisconsin	(11)	11	—	—
Mississippi	(7)	7	—	—	Wyoming	(3)	—	3	—
Missouri	(12)	12	—	—	**Totals [2]**	**(538)**	**297**	**240**	**1**

1. One Washington State Republican elector voted for Ronald Reagan instead of Ford.

2. The electoral vote for vice president was Walter F. Mondale (D), 297; Robert Dole (R), 241.

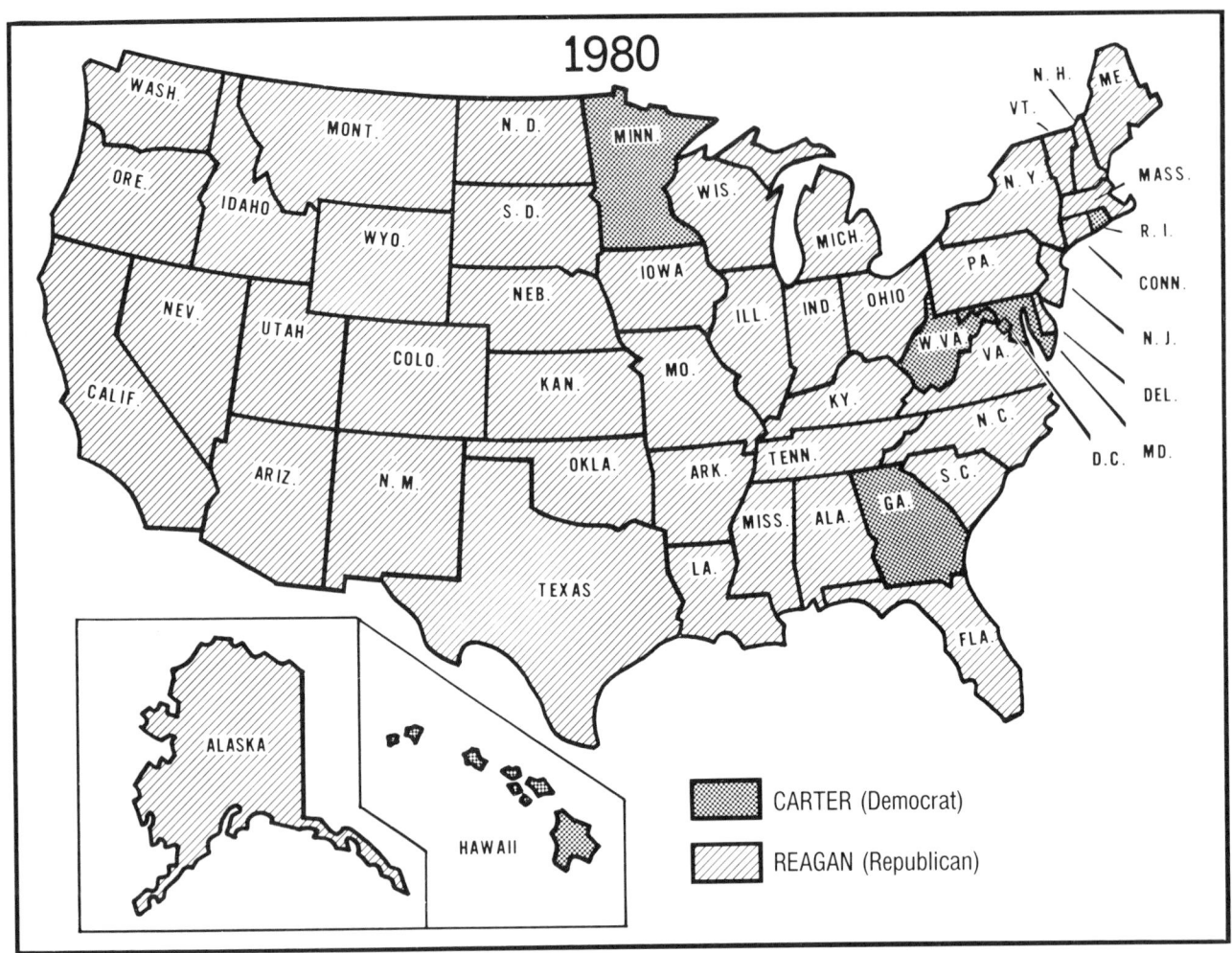

1980

States	Electoral Votes	Carter	Reagan
Alabama	(9)	—	9
Alaska	(3)	—	3
Arizona	(6)	—	6
Arkansas	(6)	—	6
California	(45)	—	45
Colorado	(7)	—	7
Connecticut	(8)	—	8
Delaware	(3)	—	3
District of Columbia	(3)	3	—
Florida	(17)	—	17
Georgia	(12)	12	—
Hawaii	(4)	4	—
Idaho	(4)	—	4
Illinois	(26)	—	26
Indiana	(13)	—	13
Iowa	(8)	—	8
Kansas	(7)	—	7
Kentucky	(9)	—	9
Louisiana	(10)	—	10
Maine	(4)	—	4
Maryland	(10)	10	—
Massachusetts	(14)	—	14
Michigan	(21)	—	21
Minnesota	(10)	10	—
Mississippi	(7)	—	7
Missouri	(12)	—	12

States	Electoral Votes	Carter	Reagan
Montana	(4)	—	4
Nebraska	(5)	—	5
Nevada	(3)	—	3
New Hampshire	(4)	—	4
New Jersey	(17)	—	17
New Mexico	(4)	—	4
New York	(41)	—	41
North Carolina	(13)	—	13
North Dakota	(3)	—	3
Ohio	(25)	—	25
Oklahoma	(8)	—	8
Oregon	(6)	—	6
Pennsylvania	(27)	—	27
Rhode Island	(4)	4	—
South Carolina	(8)	—	8
South Dakota	(4)	—	4
Tennessee	(10)	—	10
Texas	(26)	—	26
Utah	(4)	—	4
Vermont	(3)	—	3
Virginia	(12)	—	12
Washington	(9)	—	9
West Virginia	(6)	6	—
Wisconsin	(11)	—	11
Wyoming	(3)	—	3
Totals	**(538)**	**49**	**489**

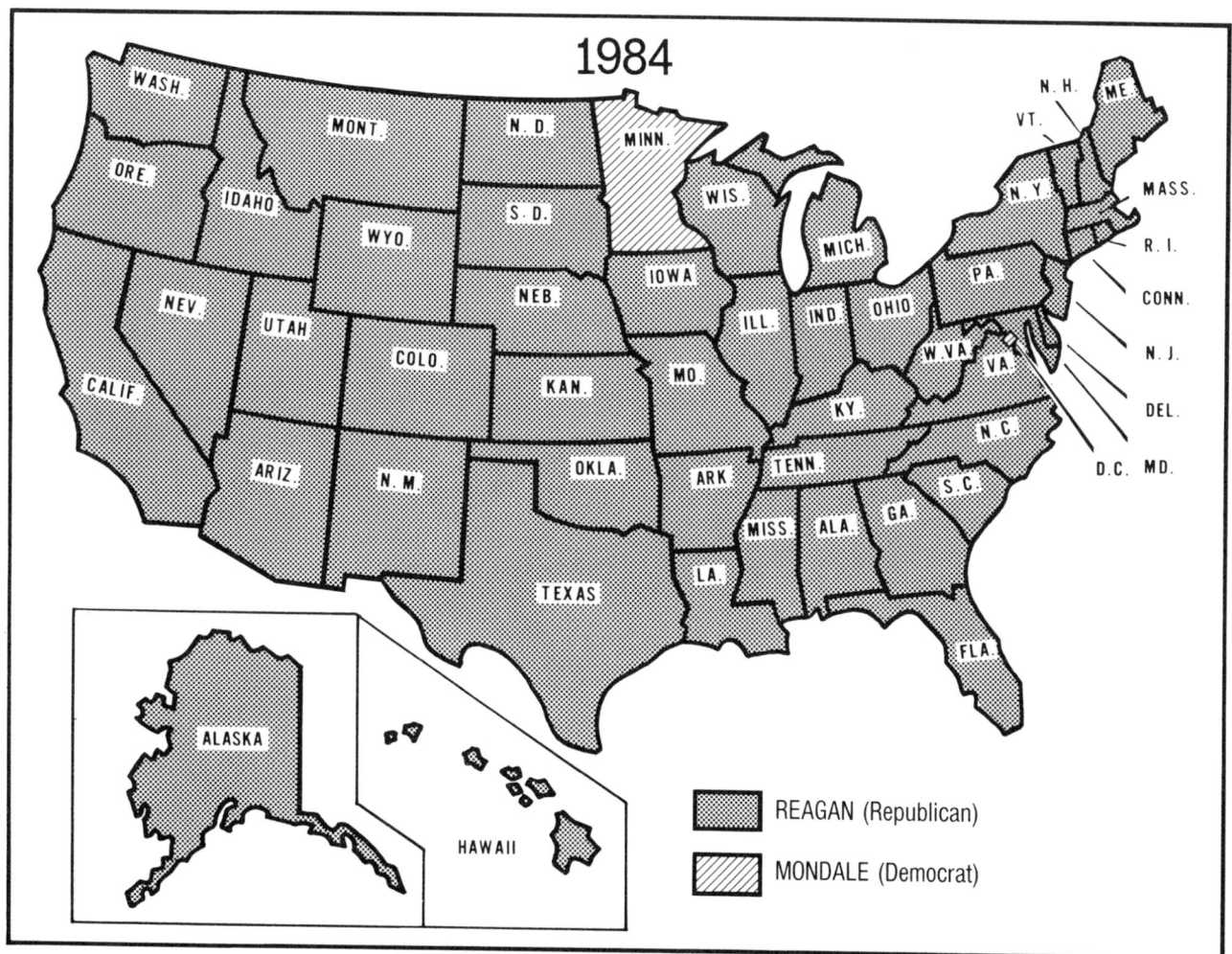

1984

	REAGAN (Republican)
	MONDALE (Democrat)

States	Electoral Votes	Reagan	Mondale
Alabama	(9)	9	—
Alaska	(3)	3	—
Arizona	(7)	7	—
Arkansas	(6)	6	—
California	(47)	47	—
Colorado	(8)	8	—
Connecticut	(8)	8	—
Delaware	(3)	3	—
District of Columbia	(3)	—	3
Florida	(21)	21	—
Georgia	(12)	12	—
Hawaii	(4)	4	—
Idaho	(4)	4	—
Illinois	(24)	24	—
Indiana	(12)	12	—
Iowa	(8)	8	—
Kansas	(7)	7	—
Kentucky	(9)	9	—
Louisiana	(10)	10	—
Maine	(4)	4	—
Maryland	(10)	10	—
Massachusetts	(13)	13	—
Michigan	(20)	20	—
Minnesota	(10)	—	10
Mississippi	(7)	7	—
Missouri	(11)	11	—

States	Electoral Votes	Reagan	Mondale
Montana	(4)	4	—
Nebraska	(5)	5	—
Nevada	(4)	4	—
New Hampshire	(4)	4	—
New Jersey	(16)	16	—
New Mexico	(5)	5	—
New York	(36)	36	—
North Carolina	(13)	13	—
North Dakota	(3)	3	—
Ohio	(23)	23	—
Oklahoma	(8)	8	—
Oregon	(7)	7	—
Pennsylvania	(25)	25	—
Rhode Island	(4)	4	—
South Carolina	(8)	8	—
South Dakota	(3)	3	—
Tennessee	(11)	11	—
Texas	(29)	29	—
Utah	(5)	5	—
Vermont	(3)	3	—
Virginia	(12)	12	—
Washington	(10)	10	—
West Virginia	(6)	6	—
Wisconsin	(11)	11	—
Wyoming	(3)	3	—
Totals	**(538)**	**525**	**13**

Electoral Votes for Vice President, 1804-1984

The following list gives the electoral votes for vice president from 1804 to 1984. Unless indicated by a note, the state-by-state breakdown of electoral votes for each vice presidential candidate was the same as for his or her party's presidential candidate. *(Notes, next page)*

Prior to 1804, under Article II, Section 1 of the Constitution, each elector cast two votes — each vote for a different person. The electors did not distinguish between votes for president and vice president.

The candidate receiving the second highest total became vice president. The 12th Amendment, ratified in 1804, required electors to vote separately for president and vice president.

Candidates

In some cases, persons had received electoral votes although they had never been formally nominated. The word *candidate* is used in this section to designate persons receiving electoral votes.

Sources: Votes and Parties

The *Senate Manual* (Washington, D.C.: Government Printing Office, 1977) was the source used for vice presidential electoral votes.

For political party designation, the basic source was *A Statistical History of the American Presidential Elections* (Westport, Conn.: Greenwood Press, 1981) by Svend Petersen; Petersen gives the party designation of *presidential candidates only.* Congressional Quarterly adopted Petersen's party designations for the running mates of presidential candidates.

To supplement Petersen, Congressional Quarterly consulted the *Biographical Directory of the American Congress, 1774-1971* (Washington, D.C.: Government Printing Office, 1971); the *Dictionary of American Biography,* (New York: Charles Scribner's, 1928-36); the *Encyclopedia of American Biography* (New York: Harper and Row, 1974), and *Who Was Who in America, 1607-1968* (Chicago: Marquis Co., 1943-68).

Year	Candidate	Electoral Votes
1804	George Clinton (Democratic-Republican)	162
	Rufus King (Federalist)	14
1808	George Clinton (Democratic-Republican) [1]	113
	John Langdon (Democratic-Republican)	9
	James Madison (Democratic-Republican)	3
	James Monroe (Democratic-Republican)	3
	Rufus King (Federalist)	47
1812	Elbridge Gerry (Democratic-Republican) [2]	131
	Jared Ingersoll (Federalist)	86
1816	Daniel D. Tompkins (Democratic-Republican)	183
	John E. Howard (Federalist) [3]	22
	James Ross (Federalist)	5
	John Marshall (Federalist)	4
	Robert G. Harper (Federalist)	3
1820	Daniel D. Tompkins (Democratic-Republican) [4]	218
	Richard Rush (Democratic-Republican)	1
	Richard Stockton (Federalist)	8
	Daniel Rodney (Federalist)	4
	Robert G. Harper (Federalist)	1
1824	John C. Calhoun (Democratic-Republican) [5]	182
	Nathan Sanford (Democratic-Republican)	30
	Nathaniel Macon (Democratic-Republican)	24
	Andrew Jackson (Democratic-Republican)	13
	Martin Van Buren (Democratic-Republican)	9
	Henry Clay (Democratic-Republican)	2
1828	John C. Calhoun (Democratic-Republican) [6]	171
	William Smith (Independent Democratic-Republican)	7
	Richard Rush (National Republican)	83
1832	Martin Van Buren (Democratic) [7]	189
	William Wilkins (Democratic)	30
	Henry Lee (Independent Democratic)	11
	John Sergeant (National Republican)	49
	Amos Ellmaker (Anti-Masonic)	7
1836	Richard M. Johnson (Democratic) [8]	147
	William Smith (Independent Democratic)	23
	Francis Granger (Whig)	77
	John Tyler (Whig)	47
1840	John Tyler (Whig)	234
	Richard M. Johnson (Democratic) [9]	48
	L. W. Tazewell (Democratic)	11
	James K. Polk (Democratic)	1
1844	George M. Dallas (Democratic)	170

Year	Candidate	Electoral Votes
	Theodore Frelinghuysen (Whig)	105
1848	Millard Fillmore (Whig)	163
	William O. Butler (Democratic)	127
1852	William R. King (Democratic)	254
	William A. Graham (Whig)	42
1856	John C. Breckinridge (Democratic)	174
	William L. Dayton (Republican)	114
	Andrew J. Donelson (American)	8
1860	Hannibal Hamlin (Republican)	180
	Joseph Lane (Southern Democratic)	72
	Edward Everett (Constitutional Union)	39
	Herschel V. Johnson (Democratic)	12
1864	Andrew Johnson (Republican)	212
	George H. Pendleton (Democratic)	21
1868	Schuyler Colfax (Republican)	214
	Francis P. Blair (Democratic)	80
1872	Henry Wilson (Republican)	286
	Benjamin G. Brown (Democratic) [10]	47
	Alfred H. Colquitt (Democratic)	5
	John M. Palmer (Democratic)	3
	Thomas E. Bramlette (Democratic)	3
	William S. Groesbeck (Democratic)	1
	Willis B. Machen (Democratic)	1
	George W. Julian (Liberal Republican)	5
	Nathaniel P. Banks (Liberal Republican)	1
1876	William A. Wheeler (Republican)	185
	Thomas A. Hendricks (Democratic)	184
1880	Chester A. Arthur (Republican)	214
	William H. English (Democratic)	155
1884	Thomas A. Hendricks (Democratic)	219
	John A. Logan (Republican)	182
1888	Levi P. Morton (Republican)	233
	Allen G. Thurman (Democratic)	168
1892	Adlai E. Stevenson (Democratic)	277
	Whitelaw Reid (Republican)	145
	James G. Field (Populist)	22
1896	Garret A. Hobart (Republican)	271
	Arthur Sewall (Democratic) [11]	149
	Thomas E. Watson (Populist)	27
1900	Theodore Roosevelt (Republican)	292
	Adlai E. Stevenson (Democratic)	155
1904	Charles W. Fairbanks (Republican)	336
	Henry G. Davis (Democratic)	140

Year	Candidate	Electoral Votes
1908	James S. Sherman (Republican)	321
	John W. Kern (Democratic)	162
1912	Thomas R. Marshall (Democratic)	435
	Hiram W. Johnson (Progressive)	88
	Nicholas M. Butler (Republican)	8
1916	Thomas R. Marshall (Democratic)	277
	Charles W. Fairbanks (Republican)	254
1920	Calvin Coolidge (Republican)	404
	Franklin D. Roosevelt (Democratic)	127
1924	Charles G. Dawes (Republican)	382
	Charles W. Bryan (Democratic)	136
	Burton K. Wheeler (Progressive)	13
1928	Charles Curtis (Republican)	444
	Joseph T. Robinson (Democratic)	87
1932	John N. Garner (Democratic)	472
	Charles Curtis (Republican)	59
1936	John N. Garner (Democratic)	523
	Frank Knox (Republican)	8
1940	Henry A. Wallace (Democratic)	449
	Charles L. McNary (Republican)	82
1944	Harry S Truman (Democratic)	432
	John W. Bricker (Republican)	99
1948	Alben W. Barkley (Democratic)	303
	Earl Warren (Republican)	189

Year	Candidate	Electoral Votes
	Fielding L. Wright (States' Rights Democratic)	39
1952	Richard Nixon (Republican)	442
	John J. Sparkman (Democratic)	89
1956	Richard Nixon (Republican)	457
	Estes Kefauver (Democratic)	73
	Herman Talmadge (Democratic)	1
1960	Lyndon B. Johnson (Democratic)	303
	Strom Thurmond (Democratic) [12]	14
	Henry Cabot Lodge (Republican)	219
	Barry Goldwater (Republican)	1
1964	Hubert H. Humphrey (Democratic)	486
	William E. Miller (Republican)	52
1968	Spiro T. Agnew (Republican)	301
	Edmund S. Muskie (Democratic)	191
	Curtis E. LeMay (American Independent)	46
1972	Spiro T. Agnew (Republican)	520
	R. Sargent Shriver (Democratic)	17
	Theodora Nathan (Libertarian)	1
1976	Walter F. Mondale (Democratic)	297
	Robert Dole (Republican) [13]	241
1980	George Bush (Republican)	489
	Walter F. Mondale (Democratic)	49
1984	George Bush (Republican)	525
	Geraldine A. Ferraro (Democratic)	13

1. New York cast 13 presidential electoral votes for Democratic-Republican James Madison and 6 votes for Clinton; for vice president, New York cast 13 votes for Clinton, 3 votes for Madison and 3 votes for Monroe.

Langdon received Ohio's 3 votes and Vermont's 6 votes.

2. The state-by-state vote for Gerry was the same as for Democratic-Republican presidential candidate Madison, except for Massachusetts and New Hampshire. Massachusetts cast 2 votes for Gerry and 20 votes for Ingersoll; New Hampshire cast 1 vote for Gerry and 7 votes for Ingersoll.

3. Four Federalists received vice presidential electoral votes: Howard — Massachusetts, 22 votes; Ross — Connecticut, 5 votes; Marshall — Connecticut, 4 votes; Harper — Delaware, 3 votes.

4. The state-by-state vote for Tompkins was the same as for Democratic-Republican presidential candidate Monroe, except for Delaware, Maryland and Massachusetts. Delaware cast 4 votes for Rodney; Maryland cast 10 votes for Tompkins and 1 for Harper; Massachusetts cast 7 votes for Tompkins and 8 for Stockton.

New Hampshire, which cast 7 presidential electoral votes for Monroe and 1 vote for John Quincy Adams, cast 7 vice presidential electoral votes for Tompkins and 1 vote for Rush.

5. The state-by-state vice presidential electoral vote was as follows:

Calhoun — Alabama, 5 votes; Delaware, 1 vote; Illinois, 3 votes; Indiana, 5 votes; Kentucky, 7 votes; Louisiana, 5 votes; Maine, 9 votes; Maryland, 10 votes; Massachusetts, 15 votes; Mississippi, 3 votes; New Hampshire, 7 votes; New Jersey, 8 votes; New York, 29 votes; North Carolina, 15 votes; Pennsylvania, 28 votes; Rhode Island, 3 votes; South Carolina, 11 votes; Tennessee, 11 votes; Vermont, 7 votes.

Sanford — Kentucky, 7 votes; New York, 7 votes; Ohio, 16 votes.

Macon — Virginia, 24 votes.

Jackson — Connecticut, 8 votes; Maryland, 1 vote; Missouri, 3 votes; New Hampshire, 1 vote.

Van Buren — Georgia, 9 votes.

Clay — Delaware, 2 votes.

6. The state-by-state vote for Calhoun was the same as for Democratic-Republican presidential candidate Jackson, except for Georgia, which cast 2 votes for Calhoun and 7 votes for Smith.

7. The state-by-state vote for Van Buren was the same as for Democratic-Republican presidential candidate Jackson, except for Pennsylvania, which cast 30 votes for Wilkins.

South Carolina cast 11 presidential electoral votes for Independent Democratic presidential candidate Floyd and 11 votes for Independent Democratic vice presidential candidate Lee.

Vermont cast 7 presidential electoral votes for Anti-Masonic candidate Wirt and 7 vice presidential electoral votes for Wirt's running mate, Ellmaker.

8. The state-by-state vote for Johnson was the same as for Democratic presidential candidate Van Buren, except for Virginia, which cast 23 votes for Smith.

Granger's state-by-state vote was the same as for Whig presidential candidate Harrison, except for Maryland and Massachusetts. Maryland cast 10 presidential elec-

toral votes for Harrison and 10 vice presidential votes for Tyler; Massachusetts cast 14 presidential electoral votes for Whig candidate Webster and 14 vice presidential votes for Granger.

Tyler received 11 votes from Georgia, 10 from Maryland, 11 from South Carolina and 15 from Tennessee.

No vice presidential candidate received a majority of the electoral vote. As a result, the Senate, for the only time in history, selected the vice president under the provisions of the 12th Amendment. Johnson was elected vice president by a vote of 33 to 16 for Granger.

9. The Democratic Party did not nominate a vice presidential candidate in 1840. Johnson's state-by-state vote was the same as for presidential candidate Van Buren, except for South Carolina and Virginia.

South Carolina cast 11 votes for Tazewell.

Virginia cast 23 presidential electoral votes for Van Buren, 22 vice presidential votes for Johnson and 1 vice presidential vote for Polk.

10. Liberal Republican and Democratic presidential candidate Horace Greeley died Nov. 29, 1872. As a result, 18 electors pledged to Greeley cast their presidential electoral votes for Brown, Greeley's running mate.

The vice presidential vote was as follows:

Brown — Georgia, 5 votes; Kentucky, 8 votes; Maryland, 8 votes; Missouri, 6 votes; Tennessee, 12 votes; Texas, 8 votes.

Colquitt — Georgia, 5 votes.

Palmer — Missouri, 3 votes.

Bramlette — Kentucky, 3 votes.

Groesbeck — Missouri, 1 vote.

Machen — Kentucky, 1 vote.

Julian — Missouri, 5 votes.

Banks — Georgia, 1 vote.

11. The state-by-state vote for Sewell was the same as for Democratic-Populist candidate William Jennings Bryan, except for the following states, which cast electoral votes for Watson: Arkansas, 3 votes; Louisiana, 4 votes; Missouri, 4 votes; Montana, 1 vote; Nebraska, 4 votes; North Carolina, 5 votes; South Dakota, 2 votes; Utah, 1 vote; Washington, 2 votes; Wyoming, 1 vote.

12. Democratic electors carried Alabama's 11 electoral votes. Five of the electors were pledged to the national Democratic ticket of Kennedy and Johnson. Six electors ran unpledged and voted for Harry F. Byrd for president and Strom Thurmond for vice president.

Mississippi's 8 electors voted for Byrd and Thurmond.

In Oklahoma, the Republican ticket of Nixon and Lodge carried the state, but 1 of the state's 8 electors voted for Byrd for president and Goldwater for vice president.

13. One Republican elector from the state of Washington cast his presidential electoral vote for Reagan instead of the Republican nominee, Ford. But he voted for Dole, Ford's running mate, for vice president. Dole thus received one more electoral vote than Ford.

Popular Vote Returns, 1824-1984

The Popular Vote

Few elements of the American political system have changed so markedly over the years as has the electorate. Since the early days of the nation, when the voting privilege was limited to the upper economic class of males, one voting barrier after another has fallen to pressures for wider suffrage. First non-property-holding males, then women, then black Americans and finally young people pushed for the franchise. By the early 1970s almost every restriction on voting had been removed, and virtually every adult citizen 18 years of age and older had won the right to vote.

Actions to expand the electorate have taken place at both the state and federal levels. Voting qualifications have varied widely in the states because of a provision of the federal Constitution (Article I, Section 2) permitting the states to set their own voting standards. Early in the nation's history, the states dropped their property qualifications for voting but some retained literacy tests as late as 1970.

On the federal level the Constitution has been amended five times to circumvent state qualifications denying the franchise to certain categories of persons. The 14th Amendment, ratified in 1868, directed Congress to reduce the number of representatives from any state that disfranchised adult male citizens for any reason other than commission of a crime. However, no such reduction was ever made. The 15th Amendment, ratified in 1870, prohibited denial of the right to vote "on account of race, color or previous condition of servitude," while the 19th Amendment in 1920 prohibited denial of that right "on account of sex." The 24th Amendment, which came into effect in 1964, barred denial of the right to vote in any federal election "by reason of failure to pay any poll tax or other tax." Finally, in 1971 the 26th Amendment lowered the voting age to 18 in federal, state and local elections.

Congress in the 1950s and 1960s enacted a series of statutes to enforce the 15th Amendment's guaranty against racial discrimination in voting. A law passed in 1970 nullified state residence requirements of longer than 30 days for voting in presidential elections, suspended literacy tests for a five-year period (the suspension was made permanent in 1975) and lowered the minimum voting age from 21 years, the requirement then in effect in most states, to 18. Subsequently, a Supreme Court ruling upheld the voting-age change for federal elections but invalidated it for state and local elections. In the same decision (Oregon v.

Mitchell, 400 U.S. 112, 1970) the court upheld the provision on residence requirements and sustained the suspension of literacy tests with respect to both state and local elections. The 26th Amendment was ratified six months after the court's decision.

The right to vote in presidential elections was extended to citizens of the District of Columbia by the 23rd Amendment, ratified in 1961. District residents had been disfranchised from national elections except for a brief period in the 1870s when they elected a non-voting delegate to the House of Representatives. In 1970 Congress took another step toward full suffrage for District residents by again authorizing the election of a non-voting delegate to the House, beginning in 1971.

Voting Trends

Statistics show that each major liberalization of election laws has resulted in a sharp increase in the number of persons voting. From 1824 to 1856, a period in which states gradually relaxed their property and taxpaying qualifications for voting, voter participation in presidential elections increased from 3.8 percent to 16.7 percent of the total population. In 1920, when the 19th Amendment giving women the franchise went into effect, voter participation increased to 25.1 percent of the population.

Between 1932 and 1976 both the number of voters in presidential elections and the voting-age population almost doubled. Except for the 1948 presidential election, when barely more than half the voting-age population was estimated to have gone to the polls, the turnout in the postwar years through 1968 was approximately 60 percent, according to Census Bureau surveys. This relatively high percentage was due largely to passage of new civil rights laws encouraging blacks to vote.

Despite a steady increase in the number of persons voting in the 1970s, voter turnout actually declined as a percentage of eligible voters who voted. Voter participation reached a modern peak of 63.1 percent in the 1960 presidential election. It declined steadily over the next decade, falling to 61.8 percent in 1964, 60.7 percent in 1968 and 55.4 percent in 1972. Voting in the off-year congressional elections, always lower than in presidential years, also declined during this period. (Growing franchise, table, p. 320)

According to the Census Bureau, 54.4 percent of the voting-age population went to the polls in 1976. In 1980

Growing Franchise in the United States, 1930-84

Year	Estimated Population of Voting Age	Vote Cast for Presidential Electors		Vote Cast for U.S. Representatives	
		Number	Percent	Number	Percent
1930	73,623,000	—	—	24,777,000	33.7
1932	75,768,000	39,732,000	52.4	37,657,000	49.7
1934	77,997,000	—	—	32,256,000	41.4
1936	80,174,000	45,643,000	56.9	42,886,000	53.5
1938	82,354,000	—	—	36,236,000	44.0
1940	84,728,000	49,900,000	58.9	46,951,000	55.4
1942	86,465,000	—	—	28,074,000	32.5
1944	85,654,000	47,977,000	56.0	45,103,000	52.7
1946	92,659,000	—	—	34,398,000	37.1
1948	95,573,000	48,794,000	51.1	45,933,000	48.1
1950	98,134,000	—	—	40,342,000	41.1
1952	99,929,000	61,551,000	61.6	57,571,000	57.6
1954	102,075,000	—	—	42,580,000	41.7
1956	104,515,000	62,027,000	59.3	58,428,000	55.9
1958	106,447,000	—	—	45,818,000	43.0
1960	109,672,000	68,838,000	63.1	64,133,000	58.7
1962	112,952,000	—	—	51,261,000	46.3
1964	114,090,000	70,645,000	61.8	65,886,000	57.8
1966	116,638,000	—	—	52,900,000	45.4
1968	120,285,000	73,212,000	60.7	66,109,000	55.2
1970	124,498,000	—	—	54,173,000	43.8
1972	140,068,000	77,625,000	55.4	71,188,000	50.9
1974	145,035,000	—	—	52,397,000	36.1
1976	150,127,000	81,603,000	54.4	74,419,000	49.6
1978	155,712,000	—	—	54,680,000	35.1
1980	162,761,000	86,515,221	53.2	72,796,000	45.4
1982	169,342,000	—	—	63,852,938	37.7
1984	173,936,000	92,652,793	53.3	82,404,820	47.4

Source: Bureau of the Census, *Statistical Abstracts of the United States;* Congressional Quarterly, *Congress and the Nation* vol. 5; *Congressional Quarterly Weekly Report,* Oct. 30, 1982, p. 2749; Feb. 19, 1983, p. 387; and April 13, 1985, p. 687.

voting declined further, with only 53.2 percent of the 162.8 million Americans of voting age bothering to vote. This was the fifth consecutive presidential election in which the voter turnout decreased. (Census Bureau surveys, it should be pointed out, are based on polls of eligible voters rather than on actual counts of the voting-age population or of registered voters. The bureau defines "eligible" voters as all adult civilians of voting age — 18 and older and registered or not — except persons in penal or other institutions. The number of registered voters nationwide at any given time is impossible to calculate. States have different registration deadlines before an election; persons who move may be registered in more than one state at the same time or temporarily may not be recorded in any state; and some states do not require pre-registration before voting, while others do not require towns and municipalities to keep

registration records. Thus in a few states without registration requirements, the Census Bureau considers all eligible voters as registered voters as well.)

Changes in the age distribution of the electorate figured prominently in the 1970s decline. Due to the surge in the birth rate beginning in 1947, the youth population has been the most rapidly growing group. However, young adults have tended to vote in much smaller proportions than the rest of the voting-age population. Approximately 11 million young voters entered the electorate in 1972 when the voting age was lowered to 18; even though the total number of voters who cast ballots for president rose to 77,625,000, 4.4 million more than in 1968, the percentage of eligible Americans who voted dropped sharply.

In addition to changes in the composition of the electorate, political scientists have attributed the decline in the

percentage of Americans voting to several factors: long periods of political stability, the predictable outcome of many races and the lack of appeal of some candidates.

Studies by the Census Bureau have shown a marked difference in participation among various classes of voters. In general, the studies have found higher participation rates among whites, persons 45 to 65 years of age, non-Southerners, persons with higher family incomes and white-collar employees and professionals. Private studies have shown repeatedly that higher voter turnout in an election generally favors Democrats while a lower one favors Republicans. Far more voters are registered as Democrats.

As the voting population grew, political parties became increasingly important in the electoral process in the 19th century. As the power of the individual's vote became more and more diluted, voters found parties a convenient mechanism for defining political issues and mobilizing the strength to push a particular policy through to enactment and execution. After the rise and fall of numerous different political parties during the first half of the 19th century, most voting strength became and remained polarized in two major parties — the Republican and the Democratic. This changed somewhat in the 20th century. The Progressive movement won a sizable following in the early years of the century, and Americans who refused to register in either of the major parties — the independent voters — increased appreciably in the post-World War II years.

Broadening the Franchise

During the first few decades of the Republic, all 13 of the original states limited the franchise to property holders and taxpayers. Seven of the states required ownership of land or a life estate as opposed to a leased estate as a qualification for voting, while the other six permitted persons to substitute either evidence of ownership of certain amounts of personal property or payment of taxes as a prerequisite to vote.

The framers of the Constitution apparently were content to have the states limit the right to vote to adult males who had a real stake in good government. This meant, in most cases, persons in the upper economic levels. Not wishing to discriminate against any particular type of property owner (uniform federal voting standards inevitably would have conflicted with some of the state standards), the Constitutional Convention adopted without dissent the recommendation of its Committee of Detail providing that qualifications for the electors of the House of Representatives "shall be the same . . . as those of the electors in the several states of the most numerous branch of their own legislatures."

Under this provision fewer than one-half of the adult white men in the United States were eligible to vote at the outset in federal elections. Because no state made women eligible (although states were not forbidden to do so), only one white adult in four qualified to go to the polls. Slaves, both blacks and Indians, were ineligible, and they comprised almost one-fifth of the American population as enumerated in the census of 1790. Also ineligible were white indentured servants, whose status was little better than that of the slaves.

Actually, these early state practices represented a liberalization of restrictions on voting that had prevailed at one time in the colonial period. Roman Catholics had been disfranchised in almost every colony, Jews in most colonies, Quakers and Baptists in some. In Rhode Island Jews re-

'Minority' Presidents

Under the U.S. electoral system, 15 presidents have been elected, either by the Electoral College itself or by the House of Representatives, who did not receive a majority of the popular votes cast in the election. Three of them — John Quincy Adams, Rutherford B. Hayes and Benjamin Harrison — actually trailed their opponents in the popular vote.

The following table shows the percentage of the popular vote received by candidates in the 15 elections in which a "minority" president (designated by boldface type) was elected:

Year Elected				
1824	Jackson 41.34	**Adams** 30.92	Clay 12.99	Crawford 11.17
1844	**Polk** 49.54	Clay 48.08	Birney 2.30	
1848	**Taylor** 47.28	Cass 42.49	Van Buren 10.12	
1856	**Buchanan** 45.28	Fremont 33.11	Fillmore 21.53	
1860	**Lincoln** 39.82	Douglas 29.46	Breckenridge 18.09	Bell 12.61
1876	Tilden 50.97	**Hayes** 47.95	Cooper .97	
1880	**Garfield** 48.27	Hancock 48.25	Weaver 3.32	Others .15
1884	**Cleveland** 48.50	Blaine 48.25	Butler 2.74	St. John 1.47
1888	Cleveland 48.62	**Harrison** 47.82	Fisk 2.19	Streeter 1.29
1892	**Cleveland** 46.05	Harrison 42.96	Weaver 8.50	Others 2.25
1912	**Wilson** 41.84	T. Roosevelt 27.39	Taft 23.18	Debs 5.99
1916	**Wilson** 49.24	Hughes 46.11	Benson 3.18	Others 1.46
1948	**Truman** 49.52	Dewey 45.12	Thurmond 2.40	Wallace 2.38
1960	**Kennedy** 49.72	Nixon 49.55	Others .72	
1968	**Nixon** 43.42	Humphrey 42.72	Wallace 13.53	Others .33

Statesmen, Military Leaders Displaced...

As a nation the United States has never made up its mind what background a president ought to have. Most presidents have come to the White House with long careers of public service behind them. Yet there have been notable exceptions. A look back to the 18th century shows just how often the fashion has changed.

The earliest tradition developed around the secretary of state, who was considered the pre-eminent Cabinet officer and thus the most important man in the executive branch after the president. Washington's first secretary of state was Thomas Jefferson. Although Jefferson left the Cabinet early in Washington's second term, he went on to become leader of the newly formed Democratic Republican Party and its candidate for president in 1796, 1800 and 1804. Losing to John Adams in 1796, Jefferson came back to win four years later.

In turn, Jefferson's secretary of state for two terms, James Madison, won the presidency in 1808. During his first term, President Madison appointed fellow Virginian James Monroe as his secretary of state. And following in what was rapidly becoming a tradition, Monroe went on to the presidency in 1816, serving two terms (1817-25).

Throughout Monroe's terms, the secretary of state was John Quincy Adams, son of former President John Adams. When Monroe's second term was nearing its end, five major candidates, including Adams, entered the race to succeed him. None of the candidates managed to acquire a majority in the Electoral College, and the House then chose Secretary of State Adams.

Adams was the last secretary of state to go directly from his Cabinet post to the White House. After him, only two secretaries of state made it to the White House at all — Martin Van Buren and James Buchanan.

Another institution died at approximately the same time as the Cabinet tradition. "King Caucus" was a derogatory reference to the congressional party caucuses that met throughout the early 1800s to designate presidential nominees. During its heyday, the Washington-centered mentality of the caucus had virtually guaranteed that Cabinet officers should be among those most often nominated by the party in power. But the caucus came under attack as being undemocratic and unrepresentative and ceased to function as a presidential nominating mechanism after 1824. It was replaced by the national conventions, bodies that are not connected with Congress and that as of 1984 had never met in the national capital.

Men on Horseback

The next cycle of American politics, from the presidency of Andrew Jackson (1829-37) to the Civil War, saw a variety of backgrounds qualify candidates for the presidency. One of the most prevalent was the military. Andrew Jackson, who ran in 1824 (unsuccessfully), 1828 and 1832, was a general in the War of 1812, gaining near-heroic stature by his defeat of the British at the Battle of New Orleans in January 1815. Like most military officers who have risen to the presidency, however, Jackson was only a part-time military man.

Other candidates during this era who were or had been military officers included William Henry Harrison, a Whig candidate in 1836 and 1840; Zachary Taylor, the Whig candidate in 1848; Winfield Scott, the 1852 Whig candidate; Franklin Pierce, the Democratic nominee in 1852; and John Charles Fremont in 1856, the Republican Party's first presidential candidate. Thus, from 1824 through 1856, all but one presidential election featured a major candidate with a military background.

The smoldering political conflicts of the 1840s and 1850s probably contributed to the naming of military men for the presidency. Generals had usually escaped involvement in national politics and had avoided taking stands on the issues that divided the country — slavery, expansion, the currency and the tariff.

Later on, the nature of the Civil War almost automatically led at least one of the parties to choose a military officer as presidential standard-bearer every four years. To have been on the "right" side during the war — fighting to save the Union and destroy slavery — was a major political asset in the North and Middle West, where tens of thousands of war veterans were effectively organized in the Grand Army of the Republic (GAR). The GAR became part of the backbone of the Republican Party during the last third of the 19th century.

Consequently, it became customary for Republicans to have a Civil War officer at the head of their ticket. Except for James G. Blaine in 1884, every Republican presidential nominee from 1868 to 1900 had served as an officer in the Union Army during the Civil War. Of all the Republican nominees, however, only Ulysses S. Grant, who was elected president in 1868 and 1872, was a professional military man. The others — Rutherford B. Hayes in 1876, James A. Garfield in 1880, Benjamin Harrison in 1888 and 1892 and William McKinley in 1896 and 1900 — were civilians who volunteered for service in the Civil War.

The Democrats, who had been split over the war, had few prominent military veterans to choose from. Only twice between 1860 and 1900 did the Democrats pick a Civil War officer as their nominee. In 1864, during the Civil War, the Democrats nominated Gen. George B. McClellan, the Union military commander who had fallen out with President Abraham Lincoln. And in 1880 Gen. Winfield Scott Hancock of Pennsylvania was the Democrats' choice.

The Empire State

Otherwise, Democrats tended to favor governors or former governors of New York. Their 1868 nominee was Horatio Seymour, who had been governor of New York in 1853-55 and again 1863-65. In 1876 they chose Samuel J. Tilden, New York's reform governor who was battling Tammany Hall. And in 1884 Grover Cleveland, another New York reform governor, captured the Democratic

. . . At Head of Long Road to Presidency

nomination. He went on to become the first Democrat to win the White House in 28 years. Cleveland was again the Democratic nominee in 1888 and 1892.

Besides being the most populous state, New York was a swing state in presidential politics. During the period from Reconstruction through the turn of the century, most Southern states voted Democratic, while the Republicans usually carried Pennsylvania, the Midwest and New England. A New Yorker appeared as the nominee for president or vice president of at least one of the major parties in every single election from 1868 through 1892.

This general tradition was maintained through the candidacy of Thomas E. Dewey, Republican governor of New York, in 1948. Only twice between 1868 and 1948 was there no New Yorker on the national ticket of at least one of the major parties — for president or vice president. Once, in 1944, both major party presidential nominees, Democrat Franklin D. Roosevelt and Republican Dewey, were selected from New York.

From 1948 to 1984, however, no New Yorkers were nominated by a major party for president and only two for vice president. The latter two were Rep. William E. Miller, R (1951-65), in 1964 and Rep. Geraldine A. Ferraro, D, in 1984. Eisenhower in 1952 and Richard Nixon in 1968 were technically residents of New York, but they were generally identified with other states. Gerald R. Ford's vice president, Nelson Rockefeller, was a former governor of New York, but he was appointed to the vice presidency. He was not asked to be on the ticket when Ford ran in 1976.

Another major swing state in the years from the Civil War through World War I was Indiana. And, in most elections, a prominent Indianan found his way onto one of the major party's national tickets. In the 13 presidential elections between 1868 and 1916, an Indianan appeared 10 times on at least one of the major parties' national tickets. However, since 1916 only one Indianan, Wendell Willkie in 1940, has been a major party's nominee.

The Governors

From 1900 to 1956, Democrats tended to favor governors for the presidential nomination. Democratic governors who received their party's presidential nomination included Woodrow Wilson of New Jersey in 1912, James M. Cox of Ohio in 1920, Alfred E. Smith of New York in 1928, Franklin D. Roosevelt of New York in 1932 and Adlai E. Stevenson of Illinois in 1952.

During the same period, 1900 to 1956, Republican presidential nominees had a wide variety of backgrounds. There were two Cabinet officers, a Supreme Court justice, a U.S. senator, two governors, a private lawyer and a general. Calvin Coolidge of Massachusetts, the 1924 nominee, and Theodore Roosevelt of New York, the 1904 nominee, both of whom succeeded to the presidency from the vice presidency, had been governors of their respective states.

Former Vice Presidents

A sudden change took place in 1960 with the nomination of John F. Kennedy, a senator, and Nixon, a former senator and sitting vice president. It was the first time since 1860 and only the second time in the history of party nominating conventions that an incumbent vice president was chosen for the presidency. And it was only the second time in the 20th century that an incumbent U.S. senator was nominated for the presidency. In the 19th century the phenomenon was also rare, with National Republican Henry Clay in 1832, Democrat Lewis Cass in 1848 and Democrat Stephen A. Douglas in 1860 the only incumbent senators nominated for president by official party conventions. Republican James A. Garfield was a senator-elect at the time of his election in 1880.

The nomination of Nixon, like the nomination of Kennedy, was a sign of things to come. Beginning in 1960 the vice presidency, like the Senate, became a presidential training ground. Vice President Hubert H. Humphrey was chosen by the Democrats for president in 1968. Vice President Spiro T. Agnew was the leading contender for the 1976 Republican presidential nomination before his resignation in October 1973. Former vice president Walter F. Mondale, who had served under Jimmy Carter, emerged as the Democratic choice for the presidential nomination in 1984. Even defeated vice presidential nominees have been considered for the nomination — witness Henry Cabot Lodge Jr. of Massachusetts in 1964, Edmund S. Muskie of Maine in 1972, Sargent Shriver of Maryland in 1976, and Robert Dole of Kansas in 1980.

Governors Making a Comeback?

The field of candidates for the 1980 presidential nomination continued a trend that first appeared in the 1976 campaign — the re-emergence of governors as leading contenders in the nomination sweepstakes. For 16 years, beginning with Kennedy's ascension from the Senate to the White House in 1960, until 1976, senators dominated presidential campaigns. During that time every single major party nominee was a senator or former senator. This trend represented an about-face from earlier times. In the 36 years before Kennedy, the two major parties nominated only one man who ever had served in the Senate.

Yet, while there was no shortage of senators in the 1976 campaign, it was the governors who attracted the most attention. Former California governor Ronald Reagan came close to depriving incumbent Gerald R. Ford of the Republican presidential nomination. The Democratic nominee and eventual winner, former Georgia governor Jimmy Carter, faced a dramatic last-minute challenge from the governor of California at the time, Jerry Brown. Reagan (successfully), Carter and Brown were candidates again in 1980; Reagan again in 1984.

Presidents' Re-election Chances

The record of 20th century U.S. presidential elections indicates that a smooth path to renomination is essential for incumbents seeking re-election.

Every president who actively sought renomination this century was successful. And those who were virtually unopposed within their own party won another term. But all of the presidents who faced significant opposition for renomination ended up losing in the general election.

The following chart shows: the presidents who sought re-election to a second term since 1900, whether they had "clear sailing" or "tough sledding" for renomination and their fate in the general election.

A president with an asterisk (*) next to his name was, like Ronald Reagan in 1984, completing his first full four-year term when he sought re-election. A dash (—) indicates there were no presidential preference primaries. The primary vote for President Lyndon B. Johnson in 1964 included the vote for favorite sons and uncommitted delegate slates.

| | Incumbent's Percentage of: | | |
	Primary Vote	Convention Delegates	General Election Result
'Clear Sailing'			
William McKinley (1900) *	—	100%	Won
Theodore Roosevelt (1904)	—	100	Won
Woodrow Wilson (1916) *	99%	99	Won
Calvin Coolidge (1924)	68	96	Won
Franklin D. Roosevelt (1936) *	93	100	Won
" " (1940)	72	86	Won
" " (1944)	71	92	Won
Harry S Truman (1948)	64	75	Won
Dwight D. Eisenhower (1956) *	86	100	Won
Lyndon B. Johnson (1964)	88	100	Won
Richard Nixon (1972) *	87	99	Won
Ronald Reagan (1984) *	99	100	Won
'Tough Sledding'			
William H. Taft (1912) *	34%	52%	Lost
Herbert Hoover (1932) *	33	98	Lost
Gerald R. Ford (1976)	53	53	Lost
Jimmy Carter (1980) *	51	64	Lost

mained legally ineligible to vote until 1842.

For half a century before the Civil War there was a steady broadening of the electorate. The new Western settlements supplied a stimulus to the principle of universal manhood suffrage, and Jacksonian democracy encouraged its acceptance. Gradually, the seven states making property ownership a condition for voting substituted a taxpaying requirement: Delaware in 1792, Maryland in 1810, Connecticut in 1818, Massachusetts in 1821, New York in 1821, Rhode Island in 1842, and Virginia in 1850. By the mid-19th century most states had removed even the taxpaying qualifications, although some jurisdictions persisted in this practice into the 20th century.

The trend toward a broadened franchise continued in the 20th century with women obtaining the vote and racial barriers to black voting slowly eliminated. Once Congress acted the Supreme Court steadily backed its power to ensure the right to vote. In general by the 200th anniversary of the nation the only remaining restrictions prevented voting by the insane, convicted felons and otherwise eligible voters who were unable to meet short residence requirements for voting.

Voting Behavior

A precise breakdown that shows which groups of voters (such as blacks or women) have higher turnout rates has never been possible. It would require an elaborate questionnaire for every eligible voter asking whether the person had participated in the election and an honest answer from the voter.

In place of a complete survey, the Census Bureau has attempted to measure voting behavior by taking a random sample of the electorate in every election year since 1964. The Survey Research Center-Center for Political Studies at the University of Michigan also analyzes voting behavior. Again, these surveys cannot be precise because they are based on people's responses. Estimates made from the survey differ from the actual ballot count because people frequently report that they or members of their families voted when in fact they did not.

The Census Bureau reported that its preliminary survey following the 1980 election showed that the proportion of the voting-age population who said they were registered to vote (67 percent) was the same as in 1976. This was a decrease from 1968 when 74 percent of the voting-age population reported being registered. Sixty-one percent of the white population of voting age reported they voted in 1980 compared with only 51 percent of the black population and 30 percent of the Hispanic population. However, the report noted that the differences in voter turnout were almost entirely the result of differences in the proportion of the population who were registered — ranging from a high of 68 percent of the white population to 60 percent of the black population and only 36 percent of the Hispanic population.

There was little difference in voter participation for men and women. In 1964 the reported voting rate for men (72 percent) had been about 5 percent higher than for women.

The largest decline in voter turnout in the elections since 1964 occurred in the North and West where voter participation declined by 12 percentage points for whites and 19 percentage points for blacks. In the South there were relatively smaller changes in voter turnout between 1964 and 1980. Although there was an increase in the voter turnout rate for blacks from 44 percent in 1964 to 48 percent in 1980, there was a decrease for whites from 60 percent to 57 percent.

Several reasons were given for the low voter turnout in 1980. Various surveys pointed to a growing sense of powerlessness among the electorate, a feeling that one person's vote was not important and a belief that it made no difference which party won.

Another reason for declining turnouts was that voting could be a time-consuming process. Citizens first had to register. Though requirements had been eased, only five states — Maine, Minnesota, North Dakota, Oregon and Wisconsin — permitted election-day registration in 1980.

Voter turnout varies according to region. Fewer voters go to the polls in one-party regions, especially in the South. And, as mentioned earlier, the actual turnout always is lower than the numbers obtained from surveys since people are reluctant to admit they did not vote. Ironically, in 1912, 1924, 1948 and 1980 — when there were major third-party

candidates — turnout was lower than in the previous election.

Party Affiliation

According to a Gallup Poll released in August 1984, 42 percent of voting-age Americans considered themselves Democrats, 28 percent Republicans and 30 percent independents.

The percentage of GOP voters had not been higher since the presidency of Dwight D. Eisenhower. Neverthe-less, according to the poll, the GOP remained the minority party in major demographic groups except the traditional bastions of Republican support: college graduates, business executives and professionals, farmers and individuals with total family income exceeding $40,000 a year. Proportionately more Democrats were found among blacks, Hispanics, those 50 years and older, those with little education or low incomes, Jews and unskilled workers. More women (43 percent) than men (38 percent) called themselves Democrats.

What They Did Before They Became President

Following are the terms of office for each president and the public jobs each held before becoming president:

George Washington: 1759-74, Virginia House of Burgesses; 1774-75, delegate to Continental Congress; 1775, commander of colonial Army; 1787, delegate to constitutional convention; 1789-97, president.

John Adams: 1771, Massachusetts colonial legislature; 1774-75, Continental Congress; 1778, minister to France; 1779, delegate to Massachusetts constitutional convention; 1780, minister to the Netherlands; 1785, minister to Great Britain; 1785-97, vice president; 1797-1801, president.

Thomas Jefferson: 1769-74, Virginia House of Burgesses; 1775, delegate to Continental Congress; 1775, delegate to Virginia Convention; 1776, delegate to Continental Congress; 1776-79, Virginia House of Delegates; 1779-81, governor of Virginia; 1784-89, envoy and minister to France; 1789-93, secretary of state; 1797-1801, vice president; 1801-09, president.

James Madison: 1774, Colonial Committee of Safety; 1776, delegate to Virginia Convention; 1776-77, Virginia House of Delegates; 1777, Virginia State Council; 1778, Virginia Executive Council; 1779-83, Continental Congress; 1784-86, Virginia House of Delegates; 1786-88, Continental Congress; 1787, delegate to constitutional convention; 1789-97, U.S. House of Representatives (Va.); 1801-09, secretary of state; 1809-17, president.

James Monroe: 1780, Virginia House of Delegates; 1781-83, governor's council; 1783-86, Continental Congress; 1786, Virginia House of Delegates; 1787, delegate to constitutional convention; 1790-94, U.S. Senate (Va.); 1794-96, minister to France; 1799-1803, governor of Virginia; 1803, minister to England and France; 1804, minister to Spain; 1810, Virginia House of Delegates; 1811-17, secretary of state; 1814-15, secretary of war; 1817-25, president.

John Quincy Adams: 1794, minister to Netherlands; 1796, minister to Portugal; 1797, minister to Prussia; 1802, Massachusetts Senate; 1803-08, U.S. Senate (Mass.); 1809-14, minister to Russia; 1815-17, minister to England; 1817-25, secretary of state; 1825-29, president.

Andrew Jackson: 1788, solicitor for western North Carolina; 1796, delegate to Tennessee constitutional convention; 1796-97, U.S. House (Tenn.); 1797-98, U.S. Senate (Tenn.); 1798-1804, Tennessee Supreme Court; 1807, Tennessee Senate; 1812, commander, U.S. militia; 1814, general U.S. Army; 1821, governor of Florida; 1823-25, U.S. Senate (Tenn.); 1829-37, president.

Martin Van Buren: 1813-20, New York Senate; 1815-19, New York attorney general; 1821-28, U.S. Senate; 1829, governor of New York; 1829, secretary of state; 1831, minister to Great Britain; 1833-37, vice president; 1837-41, president.

William Henry Harrison: 1798-99, secretary of Northwest Territory; 1799-1800, U.S. House (territorial delegate); 1801-13, territorial governor of Indiana; 1812-14, general, U.S. Army; 1816-19, U.S. House (Ohio); 1819-21, Ohio Senate; 1825-28, minister to Colombia; 1841, president.

John Tyler: 1811-16, Virginia House of Delegates; 1816, Virginia State Council; 1817-21, U.S. House (Va.); 1823-25, Virginia House of Delegates; 1825-27, governor of Virginia; 1827-36, U.S. Senate (Va.); 1829, Virginia House of Delegates; 1841, vice president; 1841-45, president.

James Knox Polk: 1821-23, chief clerk, Tennessee Senate; 1823-25, Tennessee House; 1825-39, U.S. House (Tenn.); 1839-41, governor of Tennessee; 1841-45, president.

Zachary Taylor: 1808-49, U.S. Army; 1849-50, president.

Millard Fillmore: 1828-31, New York Assembly; 1833-35, U.S. House (N.Y.); 1837-43, U.S. House (N.Y.); 1848-49, New York controller; 1849-50, vice president; 1850-53, president.

Franklin Pierce: 1829-33, New Hampshire House; 1833-37, U.S. House (N.H.); 1837-42, U.S. Senate (N.H.); 1850, New Hampshire constitutional convention; 1853-57, president.

James Buchanan: 1814-15, Pennsylvania House; 1821-31, U.S. House (Pa.); 1832-33, minister to Russia; 1834-45, U.S. Senate (Pa.); 1845-49, secretary of state; 1853, minister to Great Britain; 1857-61, president.

Abraham Lincoln: 1833, postmaster, New Salem, Illinois; 1835-36, Illinois General Assembly; 1847-49, U.S. House (Ill.); 1861-65, president.

Andrew Johnson: 1828-29, alderman, Greeneville, Tenn.; 1830-33, mayor, Greeneville, Tenn.; 1835-37, Tennessee House; 1839-41, Tennessee House; 1841, Tennessee Senate; 1843-53, U.S. House (Tenn.); 1853-57, governor of

Tennessee; 1857-62, U.S. Senate (Tenn.); 1862-65, military governor of Tennessee; 1865, vice president; 1865-69, president.

Ulysses S. Grant: 1843-54, U.S. Army; 1861-65, general, U.S. Army; 1867-68, secretary of war; 1869-77, president.

Rutherford B. Hayes: 1857-59, Cincinnati city solicitor; 1865-67, U.S. House (Ohio); 1868, governor of Ohio; 1876-77, governor of Ohio; 1877-81, president.

James A. Garfield: 1859, Ohio Senate; 1863-80, U.S. House (Ohio); 1881, president.

Chester A. Arthur: 1871-78, collector for Port of New York; 1881, vice president; 1881-85, president.

Grover Cleveland: 1863-65, assistant district attorney of Erie County, N.Y.; 1871-73, sheriff of Erie County, N.Y.; 1882, mayor of Buffalo, N.Y.; 1883-85, governor of New York; 1885-89, president; 1893-97, president.

Benjamin Harrison: 1864-68, reporter of decisions, Indiana Supreme Court; 1879, member, Mississippi River Commission; 1881-87, U.S. Senate (Ind.); 1889-93, president.

William McKinley: 1869-71, prosecutor, Stark County, Ohio; 1877-83, U.S. House (Ohio); 1885-91, U.S. House (Ohio); 1892-96, governor of Ohio; 1897-1901, president.

Theodore Roosevelt: 1882-84, New York State Assembly; 1889-95, U.S. Civil Service Commission; 1895, president of New York City board of police commissioners; 1897, assistant secretary of the Navy; 1898, U.S. Army; 1899-1901, governor of New York; 1901, vice president; 1901-09, president.

William Howard Taft: 1881-82, assistant prosecutor, Cincinnati; 1887, assistant city solicitor, Cincinnati; 1887-90, Cincinnati Superior Court; 1890-92, U.S. solicitor general; 1892-1900, U.S. Circuit Court; 1900-01, president of Philippines Commission; 1901, governor general, Philippine Islands; 1904-08, secretary of war; 1907, provisional governor of Cuba; 1909-13, president.

Woodrow Wilson: 1911-13, governor of New Jersey; 1913-21, president.

Warren G. Harding: 1895, auditor of Marion County, Ohio; 1899-1903, Ohio Senate; 1904-05, lieutenant governor of Ohio; 1915-21, U.S. Senate (Ohio); 1921-23, president.

Calvin Coolidge: 1899, city council of Northampton, Mass.; 1900-01, city solicitor of Northampton, Mass.: 1903-04, clerk of the courts, Hampshire County, Mass.; 1907-08, Massachusetts House; 1910-11, mayor of Northampton, Mass.; 1912-15, Massachusetts Senate; 1916-18, lieutenant governor of Massachusetts; 1919-20, governor of Massachusetts; 1921-23, vice president; 1923-29, president.

Herbert Hoover: 1914-15, chairman of American Relief Committee in London; 1915-18, chairman, Commission for the Relief of Belgium; 1917-19, U.S. food administrator; 1919, chairman, Supreme Economic Conference in Paris; 1920, chairman, European Relief Council; 1921-28, secretary of commerce; 1929-33, president.

Franklin D. Roosevelt: 1911-13, New York Senate; 1913-20, assistant secretary of the Navy; 1929-33, governor of New York; 1933-45, president.

Harry S Truman: 1926-34, administrative judge, court of Jackson County, Missouri; 1935-45, U.S. Senate; 1945, vice president; 1945-53, president.

Dwight D. Eisenhower: 1915-48, U.S. Army; 1950-52, commander of NATO forces in Europe; 1953-61, president.

John F. Kennedy: 1947-53, U.S. House (Mass.); 1953-61, U.S. Senate (Mass.); 1961-63, president.

Lyndon B. Johnson: 1935-37, Texas director of National Youth Administration; 1937-48, U.S. House (Texas); 1949-61, U.S. Senate (Texas); 1961-63, vice president; 1963-69, president.

Richard M. Nixon: 1947-51, U.S. House (Calif.); 1951-53, U.S. Senate (Calif.); 1953-61, vice president; 1969-74, president.

Gerald R. Ford: 1949-73, U.S. House (Mich.); 1973-74, vice president; 1974-77, president.

Jimmy Carter: 1955-62, chairman, Sumter County (Ga.) Board of Education; 1963-67, Georgia Senate; 1971-75, governor of Georgia; 1977-81, president.

Ronald Reagan: 1942-46, Army Air Corps; 1967-75, governor of California; 1981- , president.

Victorious Party in Presidential Races, 1860-1984

State	1860	1864	1868	1872	1876	1880	1884	1888	1892	1896	1900	1904	1908	1912	1916	1920	1924	1928	1932	1936	1940	1944	1948	1952	1956	1960	1964	1968	1972	1976	1980	1984	No. of Times Parties Won: Dem.	Rep.	Other
Ala.	SD	[2]	R	R	D	D	D	D	D	D	D	D	D	D	D	D	D	D	D	D	D	D	SR	D	D[18]	D[19]	R	AI	R	D	R	R	22	6	3
Alaska																										R	D	R	R	R	R	R	1	6	0
Ariz.														D	D	R	R	R	D	D	D	D	D	R	R	R	R	R	R	R	R	R	7	12	0
Ark.	SD	[2]	R	[4]	D	D	D	D	D	D	D	D	D	D	D	D	D	D	D	D	D	D	D	D	D	D	D	AI	R	D	R	R	24	4	2
Calif.	R	R	R	R	R	D[6]	R	R	D[7]	R[12]	R	R	R	PR	D	R	R	R	D	D	D	D	D	R	R	R	D	R	R	R	R	R	9	22	1
Colo.					R	R	R	R	PP	D	D	R	D	D	D	R	R	R	D	D	R	R	D	R	R	R	D	R	R	R	R	R	9	18	1
Conn.	R	R	R	R	D	R	D	D	D	R	R	R	R	D	R	R	R	R	R	D	D	D	R	R	R	D	D	D	R	R	R	R	11	21	0
Del.	SD	D	D	R	D	D	D	D	D	R	R	R	R	D	R	R	R	R	R	D	D	D	R	R	R	D	D	R	R	D	R	R	14	17	1
D.C.																											D	D	D	D	D	D	6	0	0
Fla.	SD	[2]	R	R	R	D	D	D	D	D	D	D	D	D	D	D	D	R	D	D	D	D	D	R	R	R	D	R	R	D	R	R	19	11	1
Ga.	SD	[2]	D	D[5]	D	D	D	D	D	D	D	D	D	D	D	D	D	D	D	D	D	D	D	D	D	D	R	AI	R	D	D	R	26	3	2
Hawaii																										D	D	D	R	D	D	R	5	2	0
Idaho									PP	D	D	R	R	D	D	R	R	R	D	D	D	D	D	R	R	R	D	R	R	R	R	R	10	13	1
Ill.	R	R	R	R	R	R	R	R	D	R	R	R	R	D	R	R	R	R	D	D	D	D	D	R	R	D	D	R	R	R	R	R	9	23	0
Ind.	R	R	R	R	D	R	D	R	D	R	R	R	R	D	R	R	R	R	D	D	R	R	R	R	R	R	D	R	R	R	R	R	7	25	0
Iowa	R	R	R	R	R	R	R	R	R	R	R	R	R	D	R	R	R	R	D	D	R	R	D	R	R	R	D	R	R	R	R	R	5	27	0
Kan.		R	R	R	R	R	R	R	PP	D	R	R	R	D	D	R	R	R	D	D	R	R	R	R	R	R	D	R	R	R	R	R	6	24	1
Ky.	CU	D	D	D	D	D	D	D	D	R[13]	D	D	D	D	D	D	R	R	D	D	D	D	D	D	R	R	D	R	R	D	R	R	22	9	1
La.	SD	[2]	D	[4]	R	D	D	D	D	D	D	D	D	D	D	D	D	D	D	D	D	D	SR	D	R	D	R	AI	R	D	R	R	21	6	3
Maine	R	R	R	R	R	R	R	R	R	R	R	R	R	D	R	R	R	R	R	R	R	R	R	R	R	R	D	D	R	R	R	R	3	29	0
Md.	SD	R	D	D	D	D	D	D	D	R	R	D[14]	D[15]	D	D	R	R	R	D	D	D	D	R	R	R	D	D	D	R	D	D	R	20	11	1
Mass.	R	R	R	R	R	R	R	R	R	R	R	R	R	D	R	R	R	D	D	D	D	D	D	R	R	D	D	D	D	D	R	R	12	20	0
Mich.	R	R	R	R	R	R	R	R	R[8]	R	R	R	R	PR	R	R	R	R	D	D	R	D	R	R	R	D	D	D	R	R	R	R	6	25	1
Minn.	R	R	R	R	R	R	R	R	R	R	R	R	R	PR	R	R	R	R	D	D	D	D	D	R	R	D	D	D	R	D	D	D	11	20	1
Miss.	SD	[2]	[3]	R	D	D	D	D	D	D	D	D	D	D	D	D	D	D	D	D	D	D	SR	D	D	[20]	R	AI	R	D	R	R	21	5	3
Mo.	D	R	R	D	D	D	D	D	D	D	D	R	R	D	D	R	R	R	D	D	D	D	D	R	D	D	D	R	R	D	R	R	20	12	0
Mont.									R	D	D	R	R	D	D	R	R	R	D	D	D	D	D	R	R	R	D	R	R	R	R	R	10	14	0
Neb.			R	R	R	R	R	R	R	D	R	R	D	D	D	R	R	R	D	D	R	R	R	R	R	R	D	R	R	R	R	R	7	23	0
Nev.		R	R	R	R	D	R	R	PP	D	D	R	D	D	D	R	R	R	D	D	D	D	D	R	R	D	D	R	R	R	R	R	13	17	1
N.H.	R	R	R	R	R	R	R	R	R	R	R	R	R	D	D	R	R	R	R	D	D	D	R	R	R	R	D	R	R	R	R	R	6	26	0
N.J.	R[1]	D	D	R	D	D	D	D	D	R	R	R	R	D	R	R	R	R	D	D	D	D	R	R	R	D	D	R	R	R	R	R	14	18	0
N.M.														D	D	R	R	R	D	D	D	D	D	R	R	D	D	R	R	R	R	R	9	10	0
N.Y.	R	R	D	R	D	R	D	R	D	R	R	R	R	D	R	R	R	R	D	D	D	D	R	R	R	D	D	D	R	D	R	R	13	19	0
N.C.	SD	[2]	R	R	D	D	D	D	D	D	D	D	D	D	D	D	D	R	D	D	D	D	D	D	D	D	D	R[22]	R	D	R	R	23	7	1
N.D.									[9]	R	R	R	R	D	D	R	R	R	D	D	R	R	R	R	R	R	D	R	R	R	R	R	5	18	1
Ohio	R	R	R	R	R	R	R	R	R[10]	R	R	R	R	D	D	R	R	R	D	D	D	R	D	R	R	R	D	R	R	D	R	R	8	24	0
Okla.													D	D	D	R	D	R	D	D	D	D	D	R	R	R[21]	D	R	R	R	R	R	10	10	0
Ore.	R	R	D	R	R	R	R	R	R[11]	R	R	R	R	D	R	R	R	R	D	D	D	D	R	R	R	R	D	R	R	R	R	R	7	25	0
Pa.	R	R	R	R	R	R	R	R	R	R	R	R	R	PR	R	R	R	R	R	D	D	D	R	R	R	D	D	D	R	D	R	R	7	24	1
R.I.	R	R	R	R	R	R	R	R	R	R	R	R	R	D	R	R	R	D	D	D	D	D	D	R	R	D	D	D	R	D	D	R	12	20	0
S.C.	SD	[2]	R	R	R	D	D	D	D	D	D	D	D	D	D	D	D	D	D	D	D	D	SR	D	D	D	R	R	R	D	R	R	21	8	2
S.D.									R	D	R	R	R	PR	R	R	R	R	D	D	R	R	R	R	R	R	D	R	R	R	R	R	4	19	1
Tenn.	CU	[2]	R	D	D	D	D	D	D	D	D	D	D	D	D	R	D	R	D	D	D	D	D[17]	R	R	R	D	R	R	D	R	R	20	10	1
Texas	SD	[2]	[3]	D	D	D	D	D	D	D	D	D	D	D	D	D	D	R	D	D	D	D	D	R	R	D	D	D	R	D	R	R	23	6	1
Utah										D	R	R	R	R	D	R	R	R	D	D	D	D	D	R	R	R	D	R	R	R	R	R	8	15	0
Vt.	R	R	R	R	R	R	R	R	R	R	R	R	R	R	R	R	R	R	R	R	R	R	R	R	R	R	D	R	R	R	R	R	1	31	0
Va.	CU	[2]	[3]	R	D	D	D	D	D	D	D	D	D	D	D	D	D	R	D	D	D	D	D	R	R	R	D	R	R[23]	R	R	R	19	10	1
Wash.									R	D	R	R	R	PR	D	R	R	R	D	D	D	D	D	R	R	R	D	D	R	R[24]	R	R	9	14	1
W.Va.		R	R	R	D	D	D	D	D	R	R	R	R	D	R[16]	R	R	R	D	D	D	D	D	D	R	D	D	D	R	D	D	R	17	14	0
Wis.	R	R	R	R	R	R	R	R	D	R	R	R	R	D	R	R	PR	R	D	D	D	R	D	R	R	R	D	R	R	D	R	R	8	23	1
Wyo.									R	D	R	R	R	D	D	R	R	R	D	D	D	R	D	R	R	R	D	R	R	R	R	R	8	16	0
Winning Party	R	R	R	R	R	R	D	R	D	R	R	R	R	D	D	R	R	R	D	D	D	D	D	R	R	D	D	R	R	D	R	R	12	20	0

[1] *Four electors voted Republican; three Democratic.*
[2] *Confederate States did not vote in 1864.*
[3] *Did not vote in 1868.*
[4] *Votes were not counted.*
[5] *Three votes for Greeley not counted.*
[6] *Five electors voted Democratic; one Republican.*
[7] *Eight electors voted Democratic; one Republican.*
[8] *Nine electors voted Republican; five Democratic.*
[9] *One vote each for Democratic, Republican and People's Party.*
[10] *Twenty-two electors voted Republican, one Democratic.*
[11] *Three electors voted Republican; one People's Party.*
[12] *Eight electors voted Republican; one Democratic.*
[13] *Twelve electors voted Republican; one Democratic.*
[14] *Seven electors voted Democratic; one Republican.*
[15] *Six electors voted Democratic; two Republican.*
[16] *Seven electors voted Republican; one Democratic.*
[17] *Eleven electors voted Democratic; one States' Rights.*
[18] *One elector voted for Walter Jones.*
[19] *Six of 11 electors voted for Harry F. Byrd.*
[20] *Eight independent electors voted for Byrd.*
[21] *One vote cast for Byrd.*
[22] *Twelve electors voted Republican; one American Independent.*
[23] *One elector voted for Libertarian.*
[24] *One elector voted for Ronald Reagan.*

With the exception of the District of Columbia, blanks indicate states not yet admitted to the Union. The District of Columbia received the presidential vote in 1961.

A — American Party
AI — American Union Party
CU — Constitutional Union Party
D — Democratic Party
PP — People's Party
PR — Progressive (Bull Moose) Party
R — Republican Party
SD — Southern Democratic Party
SR — States' Rights Party

Sources for Presidential Returns

The presidential election popular returns presented in this section (pages 329-366) were obtained, except for 1976, 1980 and 1984 or where indicated by a footnote, from the Inter-University Consortium for Political and Social Research (ICPSR) at the University of Michigan. The 1976 and 1980 returns and party designations were taken from Richard M. Scammon and Alice V. McGillivray's *America Votes 12* (Washington, D.C.: Congressional Quarterly, 1977) and *America Votes 14* (Washington, D.C.: Congressional Quarterly, 1981). The official 1984 results were obtained from the Federal Election Commission, the Elections Research Center and individual state secretaries of state.

The 1824 starting date for the ICPSR collection was based on factors such as the pronounced trend by 1824 for the election of presidential electors by popular vote, as well as the availability, accessibility and quality of the returns. The bulk of the ICPSR election data collection consists of returns at the county level in computer-readable form.

The collection of ICPSR presidential returns — part of a larger project involving gubernatorial, House and Senate returns — began in 1962 under grants from the Social Science Research Council and the National Science Foundation. Scholars searched state and local archives, newspaper files and other sources for the data. In as many cases as possible, multiple sources were consulted. Although general preference was given to official sources, these scholars were charged with evaluating the quality and completeness of all available sources.

While the complete source annotations for the collection are too extensive to publish here, information on the sources for returns from specific elections can be obtained through the ICPSR. *(Details on ICPSR collection, box, p. xiv)*

For each presidential election from 1824 to 1984, the following information is provided in the tables for the popular returns:

● The total nationwide popular vote and the plurality of the candidate who received the greatest number of votes.
● Names and party affiliations of major candidates.
● State-by-state breakdown of the popular vote and the percentage of the vote received by each candidate.
● The plurality received by the candidate who carried each state.
● The total national popular vote and percentage of the vote received by each candidate.
● The aggregate vote and percentage of the total vote received in each state by minor party candidates, minor parties running unpledged electors or unidentified votes. These figures appear in the column designated "Other." A complete breakdown of the votes included in the "Other" column appears on pages 367-377. The general index contains entries for all candidates.

The omission of popular vote returns for a state *after 1824* indicates an absence of popular voting for that election. The South Carolina Legislature, for example, chose the state's presidential electors until 1860 and the state did not participate in the 1864 presidential election because of the Civil War. Thus, the first popular vote returns shown for South Carolina are for the 1868 election.

Party Designation

In the ICPSR data the distinct — and in many cases *multiple* — party designations appearing in the original sources are preserved. Thus, in the ICPSR returns for 1968, George C. Wallace ran for president under a variety of party designations in different states — "Democratic," "American," "American Independent," "Independent," "George Wallace Party," "Conservative," "American Party of Missouri," "Independent American," "Courage" and "George Wallace and Independent."

To provide one party designation for presidential candidates, Congressional Quarterly has aggregated under a *single party designation* the votes of candidates who are listed in the ICPSR data as receiving votes under more than one party designation. Two sources were used for assigning party designation. For the elections 1824 through 1964, the source for party designation is Svend Petersen's *A Statistical History of the American Presidential Elections* (Westport, Conn.: Greenwood Press, 1981).

For the 1968, 1972, 1976 and 1980 elections, the source for party designation is Scammon's *America Votes 8* (Washington, D.C.: Congressional Quarterly, 1970), *America Votes 10* (1973), *America Votes 12* (1977) and *America Votes 14* (1981). For 1968, Scammon lists Wallace as an "American Independent," and Congressional Quarterly follows this usage. For 1984, party designations were obtained from the Federal Election Commission, the Elections Research Center and individual state secretaries of state.

Vote Totals and Percentages

The total popular vote for each candidate in a given election was determined by adding the votes received by that candidate in each state (including write-in votes where available), even though the vote totals for some states may have come from sources other than ICPSR.

The percentage of the vote received in each state by any candidate or party has been calculated to two decimal places and rounded to one place; thus, 0.05 percent is listed as 0.1 percent. The percentage of the nationwide vote was calculated to three decimal places and rounded to two; thus, 0.005 percent is listed as 0.01 percent. Due to rounding, state percentages and national percentages do not always equal 100 percent.

Pluralities

The plurality column represents the difference between the vote received by the first- and second-place finishers in each state. In a few cases, votes included in the "Other" column were needed to calculate the plurality. In these cases a footnote provides an explanation. *(See, for example, Georgia in the 1916 election, p. 349.)*

1824 Presidential Election

Total Popular Votes: 365,833
Jackson's Plurality: 38,149

STATE	JOHN Q. ADAMS (Democratic-Republican)		ANDREW JACKSON (Democratic-Republican)		HENRY CLAY (Democratic-Republican)		WILLIAM H. CRAWFORD (Democratic-Republican)		OTHER[1]		PLURALITY
	Votes	%	Votes	%	Votes	%	Votes	%	Votes	%	
Alabama	2,422	17.8	9,429	69.3	96	.2	1,656	12.2			7,007
Connecticut	7,494	70.4					1,965	18.5	1,188	11.2	5,529
Illinois	1,516	32.5	1,272	27.2	1,036	22.2	847	18.1			244
Indiana	3,071	19.4	7,444	47.0	5,316	33.6			7		2,128
Kentucky			6,356	27.2	16,982	72.8					10,626
Maine[2]	10,289	81.5					2,336	18.5			7,953
Maryland[2]	14,632	44.1	14,523	43.7	695	2.1	3,364	10.1			109
Massachusetts	30,687	73.0							11,369	27.0	24,071[3]
Mississippi	1,654	33.8	3,121	63.8			119	2.4			1,467
Missouri	159	4.6	1,166	34.0	2,042	59.5	32	.9	33	1.0	876
New Hampshire[2]	9,389	93.6					643	6.4			8,746
New Jersey	8,309	41.9	10,332	52.1			1,196	6.0			2,023
North Carolina			20,231	56.0			15,622	43.3	256	.7	4,609
Ohio[2]	12,280	24.5	18,489	37.0	19,255	38.5					766
Pennsylvania	5,441	11.6	35,736	75.9	1,690	3.6	4,206	8.9			30,295
Rhode Island	2,144	91.5							200	8.5	1,944
Tennessee[2]	216	1.0	20,197	97.5			312	1.5			19,885
Virginia	3,419	22.2	2,975	19.4	419	2.7	8,558	55.7			5,139
Totals	**113,122**	**30.92**	**151,271**	**41.34**	**47,531**	**12.99**	**40,856**	**11.17**	**13,053**	**3.57**	

1828 Presidential Election

Total Popular Votes: 1,148,018
Jackson's Plurality: 141,656

STATE	ANDREW JACKSON (Democratic-Republican)		JOHN Q. ADAMS (National-Republican)		OTHER[1]		PLURALITY
	Votes	%	Votes	%	Votes	%	
Alabama	16,736	89.9	1,878	10.1	4		14,858
Connecticut	4,448	23.0	13,829	71.4	1,101	5.7	9,381
Georgia[2]	19,362	96.8	642	3.2			18,720
Illinois	9,560	67.2	4,662	32.8			4,898
Indiana	22,201	56.6	17,009	43.4			5,192
Kentucky	39,308	55.5	31,468	44.5			7,840
Louisiana	4,605	53.0	4,082	47.0			523
Maine	13,927	40.0	20,773	59.7	89	.3	6,846
Maryland	22,782	49.8	23,014	50.3			232
Massachusetts	6,012	15.4	29,836	76.4	3,226	8.3	23,824
Mississippi	6,763	81.1	1,581	19.0			5,182
Missouri	8,232	70.6	3,422	29.4			4,810
New Hampshire	20,212	45.9	23,823	54.1			3,611
New Jersey	21,809	47.9	23,753	52.1	8		1,944
New York	139,412	51.5	131,563	48.6			7,849
North Carolina	37,814	73.1	13,918	26.9	15		23,896
Ohio	67,596	51.6	63,453	48.4			4,143
Pennsylvania	101,457	66.7	50,763	33.4			50,694
Rhode Island	820	22.9	2,755	77.0	5	.1	1,935
Tennessee[4]	44,293	95.2	2,240	4.8			42,053
Vermont	8,350	25.4	24,363	74.2	120	.4	16,013
Virginia	26,854	69.0	12,070	31.0			14,784
Totals	**642,553**	**55.97**	**500,897**	**43.63**	**4,568**	**.40**	

1. For breakdown of "Other" votes, see minor candidate vote totals, p. 367.
2. Figures from Svend Petersen, *A Statistical History of the American Presidential Elections*, (Westport, Conn., 1981), p. 18.

3. Plurality of 24,071 votes is calculated on the basis of 6,616 for unpledged electors.
4. Figures from Petersen, op. cit., p. 20.

1832 Presidential Election

Total Popular Votes: 1,293,973
Jackson's Plurality: 217,575

STATE	ANDREW JACKSON (Democrat)		HENRY CLAY (National-Republican)		WILLIAM WIRT (Anti-Masonic)		OTHER[1]		PLURALITY
	Votes	%	Votes	%	Votes	%	Votes	%	
Alabama	14,286	99.9	5	.1					14,281
Connecticut	11,269	34.3	18,155	55.3	3,409	10.4			6,886
Delaware	4,110	49.0	4,276	51.0					166
Georgia[2]	20,750	100.0							20,750
Illinois	14,609	68.0	6,745	31.4	97	.5	30	.1	7,864
Indiana	31,652	55.4	25,473	44.6	27	.1			6,179
Kentucky	36,292	45.5	43,449	54.5					7,157
Louisiana	3,908	61.7	2,429	38.3					1,479
Maine	33,978	54.7	27,331	44.0	844	1.4			6,647
Maryland	19,156	50.0	19,160	50.0					4
Massachusetts	13,933	20.6	31,963	47.3	14,692	21.7	7,031	10.4	17,271
Mississippi	5,750	100.0							5,750
Missouri[2]	5,192	100.0							5,192
New Hampshire	24,855	56.8	18,938	43.2					5,917
New Jersey	23,826	49.9	23,466	49.1	468	1.0			360
New York	168,497	52.1	154,896	47.9					13,601
North Carolina	25,261	84.8	4,538	15.2					20,723
Ohio	81,246	51.3	76,566	48.4	538	.3			4,680
Pennsylvania	90,973	57.7			66,706	42.3			24,267
Rhode Island	2,051	35.7	2,871	50.0	819	14.3	6	.1	820
Tennessee	28,078	95.4	1,347	4.6					26,731
Vermont	7,865	24.3	11,161	34.5	13,112	40.5	206	.6	1,951
Virginia	34,243	75.0	11,436	25.0	3				22,807
Totals	**701,780**	**54.23**	**484,205**	**37.42**	**100,715**	**7.78**	**7,273**	**.56**	

1836 Presidential Election

Total Popular Votes: 1,503,534
Van Buren's Plurality: 213,360

STATE	MARTIN VAN BUREN (Democrat)		WILLIAM H. HARRISON (Whig)		HUGH L. WHITE (Whig)		DANIEL WEBSTER (Whig)		OTHER[1]		PLURALITY
	Votes	%	Votes	%	Votes	%	Votes	%	Votes	%	
Alabama	20,638	55.3			16,658	44.7					3,980
Arkansas	2,380	64.1			1,334	35.9					1,046
Connecticut	19,294	50.7	18,799	49.4							495
Delaware	4,154	46.7	4,736	53.2					5	.1	582
Georgia	22,778	48.2			24,481	51.8					1,703
Illinois	18,369	54.7	15,220	45.3							3,149
Indiana	33,084	44.5	41,339	55.6							8,255
Kentucky	33,229	47.4	36,861	52.6							3,632
Louisiana	3,842	51.7			3,583	48.3					259
Maine	22,825	58.9	14,803	38.2					1,112	2.9	8,022
Maryland	22,267	46.3	25,852	53.7							3,585
Massachusetts	33,486	44.8					41,201	55.1	45	.1	7,715
Michigan	6,507	54.0	5,545	46.0							962
Mississippi	10,297	51.3			9,782	48.7					515
Missouri[3]	10,995	60.0			7,337	40.0					3,658
New Hampshire	18,697	75.0	6,228	25.0							12,469
New Jersey	25,592	49.5	26,137	50.5							545
New York	166,795	54.6	138,548	45.4							28,247
North Carolina	26,631	53.1			23,521	46.9			1		3,110
Ohio	97,122	47.9	105,809	52.1							8,687
Pennsylvania	91,466	51.2	87,235	48.8							4,231
Rhode Island	2,962	52.2	2,710	47.8					1		252
Tennessee	26,170	42.1			36,027	57.9					9,857
Vermont	14,040	40.0	20,994	59.8					65	.2	6,954
Virginia	30,556	56.6			23,384	43.4			5		7,172
Totals	**764,176**	**50.83**	**550,816**	**36.63**	**146,107**	**9.72**	**41,201**	**2.74**	**1,234**	**.08**	

1. For breakdown of "Other" vote, see minor candidate vote totals, p. 367.
2. Figures from Petersen, op. cit., p. 21.
3. Figures from Petersen, op. cit., p. 22.

1840 Presidential Election

Total Popular Votes: 2,411,808
Harrison's Plurality: 146,536

STATE	WILLIAM H. HARRISON (Whig)		MARTIN VAN BUREN (Democrat)		JAMES G. BIRNEY (Liberty)		OTHER[1]		PLURALITY
	Votes	%	Votes	%	Votes	%	Votes	%	
Alabama	28,515	45.6	33,996	54.4					5,481
Arkansas	5,160	43.6	6,679	56.4					1,519
Connecticut	31,598	55.6	25,281	44.5					6,317
Delaware	5,967	55.0	4,872	44.9			13	.1	1,095
Georgia	40,339	55.8	31,983	44.2					8,356
Illinois	45,574	48.9	47,441	50.9	160	.2			1,867
Indiana	65,280	55.5	51,696	44.0	30		599	.5	13,584
Kentucky	58,488	64.2	32,616	35.8					25,872
Louisiana	11,296	59.7	7,616	40.3					3,680
Maine	46,612	50.2	46,190	49.8					422
Maryland	33,528	53.8	28,752	46.2					4,776
Massachusetts	72,852	57.4	52,355	41.3	1,618	1.3			20,497
Michigan	22,933	52.1	21,096	47.9					1,837
Mississippi	19,515	53.4	17,010	46.6					2,505
Missouri	22,954	43.4	29,969	56.6					7,015
New Hampshire	26,310	43.9	32,774	54.7	872	1.5			6,464
New Jersey	33,351	51.7	31,034	48.2	69	.1			2,317
New York	226,001	51.2	212,733	48.2	2,809	.6			13,268
North Carolina	46,567	57.7	34,168	42.3					12,399
Ohio	148,043	54.3	123,944	45.4	903	.3			24,099
Pennsylvania	144,023	50.1	143,672	49.9					351
Rhode Island	5,213	60.4	3,263	37.8	19	.2	136	1.6	1,950
Tennessee	60,194	55.7	47,951	44.3					12,243
Vermont	32,440	63.9	18,006	35.5	317	.6	19		14,434
Virginia	42,637	49.4	43,757	50.7					1,120
Totals	**1,275,390**	**52.88**	**1,128,854**	**46.81**	**6,797**	**.28**	**767**	**.03**	

1844 Presidential Election

Total Popular Votes: 2,703,659
Polk's Plurality: 39,490

STATE	JAMES K. POLK (Democrat)		HENRY CLAY (Whig)		JAMES G. BIRNEY (Liberty)		OTHER[1]		PLURALITY
	Votes	%	Votes	%	Votes	%	Votes	%	
Alabama	37,401	59.0	26,002	41.0					11,399
Arkansas	9,546	63.0	5,604	37.0					3,942
Connecticut	29,841	46.2	32,832	50.8	1,943	3.0			2,991
Delaware	5,970	48.8	6,271	51.2			6	.1	301
Georgia	44,147	51.2	42,100	48.8					2,047
Illinois	58,795	53.9	45,854	42.1	3,469	3.2	939	.9	12,941
Indiana	70,183	50.1	67,866	48.4	2,108	1.5			2,317
Kentucky	51,988	45.9	61,249	54.1					9,261
Louisiana	13,782	51.3	13,083	48.7					699
Maine	45,719	53.8	34,378	40.5	4,836	5.7			11,341
Maryland	32,706	47.6	35,984	52.4					3,278
Massachusetts	53,039	40.2	67,062	50.8	10,830	8.2	1,106	.8	14,023
Michigan	27,737	49.9	24,185	43.5	3,638	6.6			3,552
Mississippi	25,846	57.4	19,158	42.6					6,688
Missouri	41,322	57.0	31,200	43.0					10,122
New Hampshire	27,160	55.2	17,866	36.3	4,161	8.5			9,294
New Jersey	37,495	49.4	38,318	50.5	131	.2			823
New York	237,588	48.9	232,482	47.9	15,812	3.3			5,106
North Carolina	39,287	47.6	43,232	52.4			2		3,945
Ohio	149,127	47.8	155,091	49.7	8,082	2.6			5,964
Pennsylvania	167,311	50.5	161,195	48.6	3,139	1.0			6,116
Rhode Island	4,867	39.9	7,322	60.1			5		2,455
Tennessee	59,917	50.0	60,040	50.1					123
Vermont	18,041	37.0	26,770	54.9	3,954	8.1			8,729
Virginia	50,679	53.1	44,860	47.0					5,819
Totals	**1,339,494**	**49.54**	**1,300,004**	**48.08**	**62,103**	**2.30**	**2,058**	**.08**	

1. For breakdown of ''Other'' vote, see minor candidate vote totals, p. 367.

1848 Presidential Election

Total Popular Votes: 2,879,184
Taylor's Plurality: 137,933

STATE	ZACHARY TAYLOR (Whig)		LEWIS CASS (Democrat)		MARTIN VAN BUREN (Free Soil)		OTHER [1]		PLURALITY
	Votes	%	Votes	%	Votes	%	Votes	%	
Alabama	30,482	49.4	31,173	50.6			4		691
Arkansas	7,587	44.9	9,301	55.1					1,714
Connecticut	30,318	48.6	27,051	43.4	5,005	8.0	24		3,267
Delaware	6,440	51.8	5,910	47.5	82	.7			530
Florida	4,120	57.2	3,083	42.8					1,037
Georgia	47,532	51.5	44,785	48.5					2,747
Illinois	52,853	42.4	55,952	44.9	15,702	12.6	89	.1	3,099
Indiana	69,668	45.7	74,695	49.0	8,031	5.3			5,027
Iowa	9,930	44.6	11,238	50.5	1,103	5.0			1,308
Kentucky	67,145	57.5	49,720	42.5					17,425
Louisiana	18,487	54.6	15,379	45.4					3,108
Maine	35,273	40.3	40,195	45.9	12,157	13.9			4,922
Maryland	37,702	52.1	34,528	47.7	129	.2			3,174
Massachusetts	61,072	45.3	35,281	26.2	38,333	28.5	62	.1	22,739
Michigan	23,947	36.8	30,742	47.2	10,393	16.0			6,795
Mississippi	25,911	49.4	26,545	50.6					634
Missouri	32,671	44.9	40,077	55.1					7,406
New Hampshire	14,781	29.5	27,763	55.4	7,560	15.1			12,982
New Jersey	40,015	51.5	36,901	47.5	829	1.1			3,114
New York	218,583	47.9	114,319	25.1	120,497	26.4	2,545	.6	98,086
North Carolina	44,054	55.2	35,772	44.8					8,282
Ohio	138,656	42.2	154,782	47.1	35,523	10.8	26		16,126
Pennsylvania	185,730	50.3	172,186	46.7	11,176	3.0			13,544
Rhode Island	6,705	60.7	3,613	32.7	726	6.6	5	.1	3,092
Tennessee	64,321	52.5	58,142	47.5					6,179
Texas	5,281	31.1	11,644	68.5			75	.4	6,363
Vermont	23,117	48.3	10,943	22.9	13,837	28.9			9,280
Virginia	45,265	49.2	46,739	50.8					1,474
Wisconsin	13,747	35.1	15,001	38.3	10,418	26.6			1,254
Totals	1,361,393	47.28	1,223,460	42.49	291,501	10.12	2,830	.10	

1. For breakdown of "Other" vote, see minor candidate vote totals, p. 367.

1852 Presidential Election

Total Popular Votes: 3,161,830
Pierce's Plurality: 220,568

STATE	FRANKLIN PIERCE (Democrat)		WINFIELD SCOTT (Whig)		JOHN P. HALE (Free Soil)		OTHER[1]		PLURALITY
	Votes	%	Votes	%	Votes	%	Votes	%	
Alabama	26,881	60.9	15,061	34.1			2,205	5.0	11,820
Arkansas	12,173	62.2	7,404	37.8					4,769
California	40,721	53.0	35,972	46.8	61	.1	56	.1	4,749
Connecticut	33,249	49.8	30,359	45.5	3,161	4.7	12		2,890
Delaware	6,318	49.9	6,293	49.7	62	.5			25
Florida	4,318	60.0	2,875	40.0					1,443
Georgia [2]	40,516	64.7	16,660	26.6			5,450	8.7	23,856
Illinois	80,378	51.9	64,733	41.8	9,863	6.4			15,645
Indiana	95,340	52.1	80,907	44.2	6,929	3.8			14,433
Iowa	17,763	50.2	15,856	44.8	1,606	4.5	139	.4	1,907
Kentucky	53,949	48.3	57,428	51.4	266	.2			3,479
Louisiana	18,647	51.9	17,255	48.1					1,392
Maine	41,609	50.6	32,543	39.6	8,030	9.8			9,066
Maryland	40,022	53.3	35,077	46.7	21				4,945
Massachusetts	44,569	35.1	52,683	41.5	28,023	22.1	1,828	1.4	8,114
Michigan	41,842	50.5	33,860	40.8	7,237	8.7			7,982
Mississippi	26,896	60.5	17,558	39.5					9,338
Missouri	38,817	56.4	29,984	43.6					8,833
New Hampshire	28,503	56.4	15,486	30.6	6,546	13.0			13,017
New Jersey	44,301	52.8	38,551	45.9	336	.4	738	.9	5,750
New York	262,083	50.2	234,882	45.0	25,329	4.9			27,201
North Carolina	39,788	50.4	39,043	49.5			60	.1	745
Ohio	169,193	47.9	152,577	43.2	31,133	8.8			16,616
Pennsylvania	198,568	51.2	179,182	46.2	8,500	2.2	1,670	.4	19,386
Rhode Island	8,735	51.4	7,626	44.9	644	3.8			1,109
Tennessee	56,900	49.3	58,586	50.7					1,686
Texas	14,857	73.5	5,356	26.5			10	.1	9,501
Vermont	13,044	29.8	22,173	50.6	8,621	19.7			9,129
	73,872	55.7	58,732	44.3					15,140
	33,658	52.0	22,240	34.4	8,842	13.7			11,418
Totals	**1,607,510**	**50.84**	**1,386,942**	**43.87**	**155,210**	**4.91**	**12,168**	**.38**	

1. For breakdown of "Other" vote, see minor candidate vote totals, p. 367.
2. Figures from Petersen, op. cit., 31.

1856 Presidential Election

Total Popular Votes: 4,054,647
Buchanan's Plurality: 493,727

STATE	JAMES BUCHANAN (Democrat)		JOHN C. FREMONT (Republican)		MILLARD FILLMORE (Whig-American)		OTHER[1]		PLURALITY
	Votes	%	Votes	%	Votes	%	Votes	%	
Alabama	46,739	62.1			28,552	37.9			18,187
Arkansas	21,910	67.1			10,732	32.9			11,178
California	53,342	48.4	20,704	18.8	36,195	32.8	14		17,147
Connecticut	35,028	43.6	42,717	53.2	2,615	3.3			7,689
Delaware	8,004	54.8	310	2.1	6,275	43.0	9	.1	1,729
Florida	6,358	56.8			4,833	43.2			1,525
Georgia	56,581	57.1			42,439	42.9			14,142
Illinois	105,528	44.1	96,275	40.2	37,531	15.7			9,253
Indiana	118,670	50.4	94,375	40.1	22,356	9.5			24,295
Iowa	37,568	40.7	45,073	48.8	9,669	10.5			7,505
Kentucky	74,642	52.5			67,416	47.5			7,226
Louisiana	22,164	51.7			20,709	48.3			1,455
Maine	39,140	35.7	67,279	61.3	3,270	3.0			28,139
Maryland	39,123	45.0	285	.3	47,452	54.6			8,329
Massachusetts	39,244	23.1	108,172	63.6	19,626	11.5	3,006	1.8	68,928
Michigan	52,136	41.5	71,762	57.2	1,660	1.3			19,626
Mississippi	35,456	59.4			24,191	40.6			11,265
Missouri	57,964	54.4			48,522	45.6			9,442
New Hampshire	31,891	45.7	37,473	53.7	410	.6			5,582
New Jersey	46,943	47.2	28,338	28.5	24,115	24.3			18,605
New York	195,878	32.8	276,004	46.3	124,604	20.9			80,126
North Carolina	48,243	56.8			36,720	43.2			11,523
Ohio	170,874	44.2	187,497	48.5	28,121	7.3	148		16,623
Pennsylvania	230,772	50.1	147,963	32.1	82,202	17.8			82,809
Rhode Island	6,680	33.7	11,467	57.9	1,675	8.5			4,787
Tennessee	69,704	52.2			63,878	47.8			5,826
Texas	31,995	66.7			16,010	33.4			15,985
Vermont	10,569	20.9	39,561	78.1	545	1.1			28,992
Virginia	90,083	60.0			60,150	40.0			29,933
Wisconsin	52,843	43.9	67,090	55.7	580	.5			14,247
Totals	1,836,072	45.28	1,342,345	33.11	873,053	21.53	3,177	.08	

1. For breakdown of "Other" vote, see minor candidate vote totals, p. 367.

1860 Presidential Election

Total Popular Vote: 4,685,561
Lincoln's Plurality: 485,706

STATE	ABRAHAM LINCOLN (Republican)		STEPHEN A. DOUGLAS (Democrat)		JOHN C. BRECKINRIDGE (Southern Democrat)		JOHN BELL (Constitutional Union)		OTHER[1]		PLURALITY
	Votes	%	Votes	%	Votes	%	Votes	%	Votes	%	
Alabama			13,618	15.1	48,669	54.0	27,835	30.9			20,834
Arkansas			5,357	9.9	28,732	53.1	20,063	37.1			8,669
California	38,733	32.3	37,999	31.7	33,969	28.4	9,111	7.6	15		734
Connecticut	43,488	58.1	15,431	20.6	14,372	19.2	1,528	2.0			28,057
Delaware	3,822	23.7	1,066	6.6	7,339	45.5	3,888	24.1			3,451
Florida			223	1.7	8,277	62.2	4,801	36.1			3,476
Georgia			11,581	10.9	52,176	48.9	42,960	40.3			9,216
Illinois	172,171	50.7	160,215	47.2	2,331	.7	4,914	1.5	35		11,956
Indiana	139,033	51.1	115,509	42.4	12,295	4.5	5,306	2.0			23,524
Iowa	70,302	54.6	55,639	43.2	1,035	.8	1,763	1.4			14,663
Kentucky[2]	1,364	.9	25,651	17.5	53,143	36.3	66,058	45.2			12,915
Louisiana			7,625	15.1	22,681	44.9	20,204	40.0			2,477
Maine	62,811	62.2	29,693	29.4	6,368	6.3	2,046	2.0			33,118
Maryland	2,294	2.5	5,966	6.5	42,482	45.9	41,760	45.1			722
Massachusetts	106,684	62.8	34,370	20.2	6,163	3.6	22,331	13.2	328	.2	72,314
Michigan	88,481	57.2	65,057	42.0	805	.5	415	.3			23,424
Minnesota	22,069	63.4	11,920	34.3	748	2.2	50	.1	17	.1	10,149
Mississippi			3,282	4.8	40,768	59.0	25,045	36.4			15,723
Missouri	17,028	10.3	58,801	35.5	31,362	18.9	58,372	35.3			429
New Hampshire	37,519	56.9	25,887	39.3	2,125	3.2	412	.6			11,632
New Jersey[2]	58,346	48.1	62,869	51.9							4,523
New York	362,646	53.7	312,510	46.3							50,136
North Carolina			2,737	2.8	48,846	50.5	45,129	46.7			3,717
Ohio	231,709	52.3	187,421	42.3	11,406	2.6	12,194	2.8	136		44,288
Oregon	5,329	36.1	4,136	28.0	5,075	34.4	218	1.5			254
Pennsylvania	268,030	56.3	16,765	3.5	178,871	37.5	12,776	2.7			89,159
Rhode Island	12,244	61.4	7,707	38.6							4,537
Tennessee			11,281	7.7	65,097	44.6	69,728	47.7			4,631
Texas			18		47,454	75.5	15,383	24.5			32,071
Vermont	33,808	75.7	8,649	19.4	218	.5	1,969	4.4			25,159
Virginia	1,887	1.1	16,198	9.7	74,325	44.5	74,481	44.6			156
Wisconsin	86,110	56.6	65,021	42.7	887	.6	161	.1			21,089
Totals	**1,865,908**	**39.82**	**1,380,202**	**29.46**	**848,019**	**18.09**	**590,901**	**12.61**	**531**	**.01**	

1. For breakdown of "Other" vote, see minor candidate vote totals, p. 367.
2. Figures from Petersen, op. cit. p. 37.

1864 Presidential Election

Total Popular Votes: 4,031,887
Lincoln's Plurality: 405,581

STATE[2]	ABRAHAM LINCOLN (Republican)		GEORGE B. MCCLELLAN (Democrat)		OTHER[1]		PLURALITY
	Votes	%	Votes	%	Votes	%	
California	62,053	58.6	43,837	41.4			18,216
Connecticut	44,673	51.4	42,285	48.6			2,388
Delaware	8,155	48.2	8,767	51.8			612
Illinois	189,512	54.4	158,724	45.6			30,788
Indiana	149,887	53.5	130,230	46.5			19,657
Iowa	83,858	63.1	49,089	36.9			34,769
Kansas	17,089	79.2	3,836	17.8	655	3.0	13,253
Kentucky	27,787	30.2	64,301	69.8			36,514
Maine	67,805	59.1	46,992	40.9			20,813
Maryland	40,153	55.1	32,739	44.9			7,414
Massachusetts	126,742	72.2	48,745	27.8	6		77,997
Michigan	91,133	55.1	74,146	44.9			16,987
Minnesota	25,031	59.0	17,376	41.0	26	.1	7,655
Missouri	72,750	69.7	31,596	30.3			41,154
Nevada	9,826	59.8	6,594	40.2			3,232
New Hampshire	36,596	52.6	33,034	47.4			3,562
New Jersey	60,724	47.2	68,020	52.8			7,296
New York	368,735	50.5	361,986	49.5			6,749
Ohio	265,674	56.4	205,609	43.6			60,065
Oregon	9,888	53.9	8,457	46.1	5		1,431
Pennsylvania	296,292	51.6	277,443	48.4			18,849
Rhode Island	14,349	62.2	8,718	37.8			5,631
Vermont	42,419	76.1	13,321	23.9			29,098
West Virginia	23,799	68.2	11,078	31.8			12,721
Wisconsin	83,458	55.9	65,884	44.1			17,574
Totals	2,218,388	55.02	1,812,807	44.96	692	.02	

1. For breakdown of "Other" vote, see minor candidate vote totals, p. 367.
2. Eleven Confederate states did not participate in election because of the Civil War.

1868 Presidential Election

Total Popular Votes: 5,722,440
Grant's Plurality: 304,906

STATE[2]	ULYSSES S. GRANT (Republican)		HORATIO SEYMOUR (Democrat)		OTHER[1]		PLURALITY
	Votes	%	Votes	%	Votes	%	
Alabama	76,667	51.3	72,921	48.8	6		3,746
Arkansas	22,112	53.7	19,078	46.3			3,034
California	54,588	50.2	54,068	49.8			520
Connecticut	50,789	51.5	47,781	48.5			3,008
Delaware	7,614	41.0	10,957	59.0			3,343
Georgia	57,109	35.7	102,707	64.3			45,598
Illinois	250,304	55.7	199,116	44.3			51,188
Indiana	176,548	51.4	166,980	48.6			9,568
Iowa	120,399	61.9	74,040	38.1			46,359
Kansas	30,027	68.8	13,600	31.2	3		16,427
Kentucky	39,566	25.5	115,889	74.6			76,323
Louisiana	33,263	29.3	80,225	70.7			46,962
Maine	70,502	62.4	42,460	37.6			28,042
Maryland	30,438	32.8	62,357	67.2			31,919
Massachusetts	136,379	69.8	59,103	30.2	26		77,276
Michigan	128,563	57.0	97,069	43.0			31,494
Minnesota	43,545	60.8	28,075	39.2			15,470
Missouri	86,860	57.0	65,628	43.0			21,232
Nebraska	9,772	63.9	5,519	36.1			4,253
Nevada	6,474	55.4	5,215	44.6			1,259
New Hampshire	37,718	55.2	30,575	44.8	11		7,143
New Jersey	80,132	49.1	83,001	50.9			2,869
New York	419,888	49.4	429,883	50.6			9,995
North Carolina	96,939	53.4	84,559	46.6			12,380
Ohio	280,159	54.0	238,506	46.0			41,653
Oregon	10,961	49.6	11,125	50.4			164
Pennsylvania	342,280	52.2	313,382	47.8			28,898
Rhode Island	13,017	66.7	6,494	33.3			6,523
South Carolina	62,301	57.9	45,237	42.1			17,064
Tennessee	56,628	68.4	26,129	31.6			30,499
Vermont	44,173	78.6	12,051	21.4			32,122
West Virginia	29,015	58.8	20,306	41.2			8,709
Wisconsin	108,920	56.3	84,708	43.8			24,212
Totals	**3,013,650**	**52.66**	**2,708,744**	**47.34**	**46**		

1. For breakdown of "Other" vote, see minor candidate vote totals, p. 367.
2. Mississippi, Texas and Virginia did not participate in the election due to Reconstruction. In Florida the state Legislature cast the electoral vote.

1872 Presidential Election

Total Popular Votes: 6,467,679
Grant's Plurality: 763,474

STATE	ULYSSES S. GRANT (Republican)		HORACE GREELEY (Democrat, Liberal Republican)		CHARLES O'CONOR (Straight Out Democrat)		OTHER[1]		PLURALITY
	Votes	%	Votes	%	Votes	%	Votes	%	
Alabama	90,272	53.2	79,444	46.8					10,828
Arkansas	41,373	52.2	37,927	47.8					3,446
California	54,007	56.4	40,717	42.5	1,061	1.1			13,290
Connecticut	50,307	52.4	45,685	47.6					4,622
Delaware	11,129	51.0	10,205	46.8	488	2.2			924
Florida	17,763	53.5	15,427	46.5					2,336
Georgia	62,550	45.0	76,356	55.0					13,806
Illinois	241,936	56.3	184,884	43.0	3,151	.7			57,052
Indiana	186,147	53.2	163,632	46.8					22,515
Iowa	131,566	60.8	71,189	32.9	2,221	1.0	11,389	5.2	60,377
Kansas	66,805	66.5	32,970	32.8	156	.2	581	.5	33,835
Kentucky	88,766	46.4	99,995	52.3	2,374	1.2			11,229
Louisiana	71,663	55.7	57,029	44.3					14,634
Maine	61,426	67.9	29,097	32.1					32,329
Maryland	66,760	49.7	67,687	50.3					927
Massachusetts	133,455	69.3	59,195	30.7					74,260
Michigan	138,768	62.6	78,651	35.5	2,879	1.3	1,271	.6	60,117
Minnesota	56,040	61.4	35,131	38.5			168	.2	20,909
Mississippi	82,175	63.5	47,282	36.5					34,893
Missouri	119,196	43.7	151,434	55.5	2,429	.9			32,238
Nebraska	18,329	70.7	7,603	29.3					10,726
Nevada	8,413	57.4	6,236	42.6					2,177
New Hampshire	37,168	53.9	31,425	45.6			313	.5	5,743
New Jersey	91,656	54.5	76,456	45.5					15,200
New York	440,738	53.2	387,282	46.8					53,456
North Carolina	94,772	57.4	70,130	42.5	261	.2			24,642
Ohio	281,852	53.2	244,320	46.2	1,163	.2	2,100	.4	37,532
Oregon	11,818	58.8	7,742	38.5	547	2.7			4,076
Pennsylvania	349,589	62.3	212,040	37.8					137,549
Rhode Island	13,665	71.9	5,329	28.1					8,336
South Carolina	72,290	75.7	22,699	23.8	204	.2	259	.3	49,591
Tennessee	85,655	47.8	93,391	52.2					7,736
Texas	47,910	41.4	67,675	58.5	115	.1			19,765
Vermont	41,481	79.2	10,927	20.9					30,554
Virginia	93,463	50.5	91,647	49.5			85	.1	1,816
West Virginia	32,320	51.7	29,532	47.3	615	1.0			2,788
Wisconsin	105,012	54.6	86,390	44.9	853	.4			18,622
Totals	3,598,235	55.63	2,834,761	43.83	18,602	.29	16,081	.25	

1. For breakdown of "Other" vote, see minor candidate vote totals, p. 367.

1876 Presidential Election[2]

Total Popular Votes: 8,413,101
Tilden's Plurality: 254,235

STATE	RUTHERFORD B. HAYES[2] (Republican)		SAMUEL J. TILDEN[2] (Democrat)		PETER COOPER (Greenback)		OTHER[1]		PLURALITY
	Votes	%	Votes	%	Votes	%	Votes	%	
Alabama	68,708	40.0	102,989	60.0			2		34,281
Arkansas	38,649	39.9	58,086	59.9	211	.2			19,437
California	79,258	50.9	76,460	49.1	47		19		2,798
Connecticut	59,033	48.3	61,927	50.7	774	.6	400	.3	2,894
Delaware	10,752	44.6	13,381	55.5					2,629
Florida	23,849	51.0	22,927	49.0					922
Georgia	50,533	28.0	130,157	72.0					79,624
Illinois	278,232	50.2	258,611	46.7	17,207	3.1	318	.1	19,621
Indiana	208,011	48.3	213,529	49.5	9,533	2.2			5,518
Iowa	171,326	58.4	112,121	38.2	9,431	3.2	520	.2	59,205
Kansas	78,324	63.1	37,902	30.5	7,770	6.3	138	.1	40,422
Kentucky	97,568	37.4	160,060	61.4			2,998	1.2	62,492
Louisiana	75,315	51.7	70,508	48.4					4,807
Maine	66,300	56.6	49,917	42.7			828	.7	16,383
Maryland	71,980	44.0	91,779	56.1					19,799
Massachusetts	150,063	57.8	108,777	41.9			779	.3	41,286
Michigan	166,901	52.4	141,665	44.5	9,023	2.8	837	.3	25,236
Minnesota	72,962	58.8	48,799	39.3	2,399	1.9			24,163
Mississippi	52,603	31.9	112,173	68.1					59,570
Missouri	145,027	41.4	202,086	57.6	3,497	1.0			57,059
Nebraska	31,915	64.8	17,343	35.2					14,572
Nevada	10,383	52.7	9,308	47.3					1,075
New Hampshire	41,540	51.8	38,510	48.1			93	.1	3,030
New Jersey	103,517	47.0	115,962	52.7	714	.3			12,445
New York	489,207	48.2	521,949	51.4	1,978	.2	2,369	.2	32,742
North Carolina	108,484	46.4	125,427	53.6					16,943
Ohio	330,698	50.2	323,182	49.1	3,058	.5	1,712	.3	7,516
Oregon	15,207	50.9	14,157	47.4	509	1.7			1,050
Pennsylvania	384,157	50.6	366,204	48.3	7,209	1.0	1,403	.2	17,953
Rhode Island	15,787	59.6	10,712	40.4					5,075
South Carolina	91,786	50.2	90,897	49.8					889
Tennessee	89,566	40.2	133,177	59.8					43,611
Texas	45,013	29.7	106,372	70.2			46		61,359
Vermont	44,092	68.4	20,254	31.4			114	.2	23,838
Virginia	95,518	40.4	140,770	59.6					45,252
West Virginia	41,997	42.2	56,546	56.8	1,104	1.1			14,549
Wisconsin	130,050	50.6	123,922	48.2	1,509	.6	1,695	.7	6,128
Totals	4,034,311	47.95	4,288,546	50.97	75,973	.90	14,271	.17	

1. For breakdown of "Other" vote, see minor candidate vote totals, p. 367.
2. For resolution of disputed 1876 election, see introduction, p. 261.

1880 Presidential Election

Total Popular Votes: 9,210,420
Garfield's Plurality: 1,898

STATE	JAMES A. GARFIELD (Republican)		WINFIELD S. HANCOCK (Democrat)		JAMES B. WEAVER (Greenback)		OTHER[1]		PLURALITY
	Votes	%	Votes	%	Votes	%	Votes	%	
Alabama	56,350	37.1	91,130	60.0	4,422	2.9			34,780
Arkansas	41,661	38.7	60,489	56.1	4,079	3.8	1,543	1.4	18,828
California	80,282	48.9	80,426	49.0	3,381	2.1	129	.1	144
Colorado	27,450	51.3	24,647	46.0	1,435	2.7	14		2,803
Connecticut	67,071	50.5	64,411	48.5	868	.7	448	.3	2,660
Delaware	14,148	48.0	15,181	51.5	129	.4			1,033
Florida	23,654	45.8	27,964	54.2					4,310
Georgia	54,470	34.6	102,981	65.4					48,511
Illinois	318,036	51.1	277,321	44.6	26,358	4.2	590	.1	40,715
Indiana	232,169	49.3	225,523	47.9	13,066	2.8			6,646
Iowa	183,904	56.9	105,845	32.8	32,327	10.0	1,064	.3	78,059
Kansas	121,520	60.4	59,789	29.7	19,710	9.8	35		61,731
Kentucky	106,490	39.9	148,875	55.7	11,506	4.3	233	.1	42,385
Louisiana	38,978	37.3	65,047	62.3	437	.4			26,069
Maine	74,052	51.5	65,211	45.3	4,409	3.1	231	.2	8,841
Maryland	78,515	45.6	93,706	54.4					15,191
Massachusetts	165,198	58.5	111,960	39.6	4,548	1.6	799	.3	53,238
Michigan	185,335	52.5	131,596	37.3	34,895	9.9	1,250	.4	53,739
Minnesota	93,939	62.3	53,314	35.4	3,267	2.2	286	.2	40,625
Mississippi	34,844	29.8	75,750	64.7	5,797	5.0	677	.6	40,906
Missouri	153,647	38.7	208,600	52.5	35,042	8.8			54,953
Nebraska	54,979	62.9	28,523	32.7	3,853	4.4			26,456
Nevada	8,732	47.6	9,611	52.4					879
New Hampshire	44,856	51.9	40,797	47.2	528	.6	180	.2	4,059
New Jersey	120,555	49.0	122,565	49.8	2,617	1.1	191	.1	2,010
New York	555,544	50.3	534,511	48.4	12,373	1.1	1,517	.1	21,033
North Carolina	115,616	48.0	124,204	51.6	1,126	.5			8,588
Ohio	375,048	51.7	340,867	47.0	6,456	.9	2,613	.4	34,181
Oregon	20,619	50.5	19,955	48.9	267	.7			664
Pennsylvania	444,704	50.8	407,428	46.6	20,667	2.4	1,984	.2	37,276
Rhode Island	18,195	62.2	10,779	36.9	236	.8	25	.1	7,416
South Carolina	57,954	34.1	111,236	65.5	567	.3	36		53,282
Tennessee	107,677	44.3	129,569	53.3	6,017	2.5			21,892
Texas	50,217	21.5	156,010	66.8	27,405	11.7			105,793
Vermont	45,567	70.0	18,316	28.1	1,215	1.9			27,251
Virginia	83,533	39.5	128,083	60.5					44,550
West Virginia	46,243	41.1	57,390	51.0	9,008	8.0			11,147
Wisconsin	144,406	54.0	114,650	42.9	7,986	3.0	160	.1	29,756
Totals	**4,446,158**	**48.27**	**4,444,260**	**48.25**	**305,997**	**3.32**	**14,005**	**.15**	

1. For breakdown of "Other" vote, see minor candidate vote totals, p. 367.

1884 Presidential Election

Total Popular Votes: 10,049,754
Cleveland's Plurality: 25,685

STATE	GROVER CLEVELAND (Democrat)		JAMES G. BLAINE (Republican)		BENJAMIN F. BUTLER (Greenback)		JOHN P. ST. JOHN (Prohibition)		OTHER[1]		PLURALITY
	Votes	%	Votes	%	Votes	%	Votes	%	Votes	%	
Alabama	92,736	60.4	59,444	38.7	762	.5	610	.4	72	.1	33,292
Arkansas	72,734	57.8	51,198	40.7	1,847	1.5					21,536
California	89,288	45.3	102,369	52.0	2,037	1.0	2,965	1.5	329	.2	13,081
Colorado	27,723	41.7	36,084	54.3	1,956	2.9	756	1.1			8,361
Connecticut	67,167	49.0	65,879	48.0	1,682	1.2	2,493	1.8			1,288
Delaware	16,957	56.6	12,953	43.2	10		64	.2			4,004
Florida	31,769	53.0	28,031	46.7			72	.1	118	.2	3,738
Georgia	94,667	65.9	48,603	33.8	145	.1	195	.1			46,064
Illinois	312,351	46.4	337,469	50.2	10,776	1.6	12,074	1.8			25,118
Indiana	244,989	49.8	238,466	48.5	8,194	1.7					6,523
Iowa	177,316	47.0	197,089	52.3			1,499	.4	1,297	.3	19,773
Kansas	90,111	33.9	154,410	58.1	16,341	6.2	4,311	1.6	468	.2	64,299
Kentucky	152,961	55.3	118,690	42.9	1,691	.6	3,139	1.1			34,271
Louisiana	62,594	57.2	46,347	42.4	120	.1	338	.3			16,247
Maine	52,153	40.0	72,217	55.3	3,955	3.0	2,160	1.7	6		20,064
Maryland	96,866	52.1	85,748	46.1	578	.3	2,827	1.5			11,118
Massachusetts	122,352	40.3	146,724	48.4	24,382	8.0	9,923	3.3	2		24,372
Michigan	149,835	37.2	192,669	47.8	42,252	10.5	18,403	4.6			42,834
Minnesota	70,065	36.9	111,685	58.8	3,583	1.9	4,684	2.5			41,620
Mississippi	77,653	64.3	43,035	35.7							34,618
Missouri	236,023	53.5	203,081	46.0			2,164	.5			32,942
Nebraska	54,391	40.5	76,912	57.3			2,899	2.2			22,521
Nevada	5,577	43.6	7,176	56.2	26	.2					1,599
New Hampshire	39,198	46.3	43,254	51.1	554	.7	1,580	1.9			4,056
New Jersey	127,747	49.0	123,436	47.3	3,486	1.3	6,156	2.4	28		4,311
New York	563,048	48.3	562,001	48.2	16,955	1.5	24,999	2.1			1,047
North Carolina	142,905	53.3	125,021	46.6			430	.2			17,884
Ohio	368,280	46.9	400,092	51.0	5,179	.7	11,069	1.4			31,812
Oregon	24,598	46.7	26,845	51.0	726	1.4	479	.9	35	.1	2,247
Pennsylvania	394,772	43.9	472,792	52.6	16,992	1.9	15,154	1.7			78,020
Rhode Island	12,391	37.8	19,030	58.1	422	1.3	928	2.8			6,639
South Carolina	69,845	75.3	21,730	23.4					1,237	1.3	48,115
Tennessee	133,770	51.5	124,101	47.7	957	.4	1,150	.4			9,669
Texas	223,209	69.5	91,234	28.4	3,310	1.0	3,489	1.1			131,975
Vermont	17,331	29.2	39,514	66.5	785	1.3	1,752	3.0	27	.1	22,183
Virginia	145,491	51.1	139,356	48.9			130	.1			6,135
West Virginia	67,311	50.9	63,096	47.8	799	.6	939	.7			4,215
Wisconsin	146,447	45.8	161,155	50.4	4,594	1.4	7,651	2.4			14,708
Totals	**4,874,621**	**48.50**	**4,848,936**	**48.25**	**175,096**	**1.74**	**147,482**	**1.47**	**3,619**	**.04**	

1. For breakdown of "Other" vote, see minor candidate vote totals, p. 367.

1888 Presidential Election

Total Popular Votes: 11,383,320
Cleveland's Plurality: 90,596[2]

STATE	BENJAMIN HARRISON (Republican)		GROVER CLEVELAND (Democrat)		CLINTON B. FISK (Prohibition)		ALSON J. STREETER (Union Labor)		OTHER[1]		PLURALITY
	Votes	%	Votes	%	Votes	%	Votes	%	Votes	%	
Alabama	57,177	32.7	117,314	67.0	594	.3					60,137
Arkansas	59,752	38.0	86,062	54.8	614	.4	10,630	6.8			26,310
California	124,816	49.7	117,729	46.8	5,761	2.3			3,033	1.2	7,087
Colorado	50,772	55.2	37,549	40.8	2,182	2.4	1,266	1.4	177	.2	13,223
Connecticut	74,584	48.4	74,920	48.7	4,234	2.8	240	.2			336
Delaware	12,950	43.5	16,414	55.2	399	1.3			1		3,464
Florida	26,529	39.9	39,557	59.5	414	.6					13,028
Georgia	40,499	28.3	100,493	70.3	1,808	1.3	136	.1			59,994
Illinois	370,475	49.5	348,351	46.6	21,703	2.9	7,134	1.0	150		22,124
Indiana	263,366	49.1	260,990	48.6	9,939	1.9	2,693	.5			2,376
Iowa	211,607	52.3	179,876	44.5	3,550	.9	9,105	2.3	556	.1	31,731
Kansas	182,845	55.2	102,739	31.0	6,774	2.1	37,838	11.4	937	.3	80,106
Kentucky	155,138	45.0	183,830	53.3	5,223	1.5	677	.2			28,692
Louisiana	30,660	26.5	85,032	73.4	160	.1	39				54,372
Maine	73,730	57.5	50,472	39.4	2,691	2.1	1,344	1.1	16		23,258
Maryland	99,986	47.4	106,188	50.3	4,767	2.3					6,202
Massachusetts	183,892	53.4	151,590	44.0	8,701	2.5			60		32,302
Michigan	236,387	49.7	213,469	44.9	20,945	4.4	4,555	1.0			22,918
Minnesota	142,492	54.2	104,372	39.7	15,201	5.8	1,097	.4			38,120
Mississippi	30,095	26.0	85,451	73.8	240	.2					55,356
Missouri	236,252	45.3	261,943	50.2	4,539	.9	18,625	3.6			25,691
Nebraska	108,417	53.5	80,552	39.8	9,435	4.7	4,226	2.1			27,865
Nevada	7,229	57.5	5,303	42.2	41	.3					1,926
New Hampshire	45,734	50.4	43,382	47.8	1,596	1.8			58	.1	2,352
New Jersey	144,347	47.5	151,493	49.9	7,794	2.6					7,146
New York	650,338	49.3	635,965	48.2	30,231	2.3	627	.1	2,587	.2	14,373
North Carolina	134,784	47.2	147,902	51.8	2,840	1.0			37		13,118
Ohio	416,054	49.6	395,456	47.1	24,356	2.9	3,491	.4			20,598
Oregon	33,291	53.8	26,518	42.9	1,676	2.7			404	.7	6,773
Pennsylvania	526,091	52.7	446,633	44.8	20,947	2.1	3,873	.4	24		79,458
Rhode Island	21,969	53.9	17,530	43.0	1,251	3.1	18		7		4,439
South Carolina	13,736	17.2	65,824	82.3					437	.6	52,088
Tennessee	138,978	45.8	158,699	52.3	5,969	2.0	48				19,721
Texas	88,604	25.0	232,189	65.5	4,739	1.3	28,880	8.2			143,585
Vermont	45,193	71.2	16,788	26.5	1,460	2.3			35	.1	28,405
Virginia	150,399	49.5	152,004	50.0	1,684	.6					1,605
West Virginia	78,171	49.0	78,677	49.4	1,084	.7	1,508	1.0			506
Wisconsin	176,553	49.8	155,232	43.8	14,277	4.0	8,552	2.4			21,321
Totals	5,443,892	47.82	5,534,488	48.62	249,813	2.19	146,602	1.29	8,519	.07	

1. For breakdown of "Other" vote, see minor candidate vote totals, p. 367.
2. Harrison won the election. See p. 256.

1892 Presidential Election

Total Popular Votes: 12,056,097
Cleveland's Plurality: 372,639

STATE	GROVER CLEVELAND (Democrat)		BENJAMIN HARRISON (Republican)		JAMES B. WEAVER (Populist)		JOHN BIDWELL (Prohibition)		OTHER[1]		PLURALITY
	Votes	%	Votes	%	Votes	%	Votes	%	Votes	%	
Alabama	138,135	59.4	9,184	4.0	84,984	36.6	240	.1			53,151
Arkansas	87,834	59.3	47,072	31.8	11,831	8.0	113	.1	1,267	.9	40,762
California	118,151	43.8	118,027	43.8	25,311	9.4	8,096	3.0			124
Colorado			38,620	41.1	53,584	57.1	1,677	1.8			14,964
Connecticut	82,395	50.1	77,030	46.8	809	.5	4,026	2.5	333	.2	5,365
Delaware	18,581	49.9	18,077	48.6			564	1.5	13		504
Florida	30,153	85.0			4,843	13.7	475	1.3			25,310
Georgia	129,446	58.0	48,408	21.7	41,939	18.8	988	.4	2,345	1.1	81,038
Idaho			8,599	44.3	10,520	54.2	288	1.5			1,921
Illinois	426,281	48.8	399,308	45.7	22,207	2.5	25,871	3.0			26,973
Indiana	262,740	47.5	255,615	46.2	22,208	4.0	13,050	2.4			7,125
Iowa	196,367	44.3	219,795	49.6	20,595	4.7	6,402	1.4			23,428
Kansas			156,134	48.3	162,888	50.3	4,569	1.4			6,754
Kentucky	175,461	51.5	135,462	39.7	23,500	6.9	6,441	1.9			39,999
Louisiana	87,926	76.5	26,963	23.5							60,963
Maine	48,049	41.3	62,936	54.1	2,396	2.1	3,066	2.6	4		14,887
Maryland	113,866	53.4	92,736	43.5	796	.4	5,877	2.8			21,130
Massachusetts	176,813	45.2	202,814	51.9	3,210	.8	7,539	1.9	652	.2	26,001
Michigan	202,396	43.4	222,708	47.7	20,031	4.3	20,857	4.5	925	.2	20,312
Minnesota	100,589	37.6	122,736	45.8	30,399	11.3	14,117	5.3			22,147
Mississippi	40,030	76.2	1,398	2.7	10,118	19.3	973	1.9			29,912
Missouri	268,400	49.6	227,646	42.0	41,204	7.6	4,333	.8			40,754
Montana	17,690	39.8	18,871	42.4	7,338	16.5	562	1.3			1,181
Nebraska	24,956	12.5	87,213	43.6	83,134	41.5	4,902	2.5			4,079
Nevada	703	6.5	2,811	26.0	7,226	66.8	86	.8			4,415
New Hampshire	42,081	47.1	45,658	51.1	292	.3	1,297	1.5			3,577
New Jersey	170,987	50.7	156,059	46.2	969	.3	8,133	2.4	1,337	.4	14,928
New York	654,868	49.0	609,350	45.6	16,429	1.2	38,190	2.9	17,956	1.3	45,518
North Carolina	132,951	47.4	100,346	35.8	44,336	15.8	2,637	.9			32,605
North Dakota[2]			17,519	48.5	17,700	49.0	899	2.5			181
Ohio	404,115	47.5	405,187	47.7	14,850	1.8	26,012	3.1			1,072
Oregon	14,243	18.2	35,002	44.7	26,875	34.3	2,258	2.9			8,127
Pennsylvania	452,264	45.1	516,011	51.5	8,714	.9	25,123	2.5	888	.1	63,747
Rhode Island	24,336	45.8	26,975	50.7	228	.4	1,654	3.1	3		2,639
South Carolina	54,680	77.6	13,345	18.9	2,407	3.4			72	.1	41,335
South Dakota	8,894	12.7	34,714	49.5	26,552	37.8					8,162
Tennessee	136,468	51.4	100,537	37.8	23,918	9.0	4,809	1.8			35,931
Texas	236,979	57.7	70,982	17.3	96,649	23.5	2,164	.5	4,086	1.0	140,330
Vermont	16,325	29.3	37,992	68.1	42	.1	1,424	2.6	10		21,667
Virginia	164,136	56.2	113,098	38.7	12,275	4.2	2,729	.9			51,038
Washington	29,802	33.9	36,459	41.5	19,165	21.8	2,542	2.9			6,657
West Virginia	84,467	49.4	80,292	46.9	4,167	2.4	2,153	1.3			4,175
Wisconsin	177,325	47.7	171,101	46.1	9,919	2.7	13,136	3.5			6,224
Wyoming			8,454	50.6	7,722	46.2	498	3.0	29	.2	732
Totals	**5,551,883**	**46.05**	**5,179,244**	**42.96**	**1,024,280**	**8.50**	**270,770**	**2.25**	**29,920**	**.25**	

1. For breakdown of "Other" vote, see minor candidate vote totals, p. 367.
2. Figures from Petersen, op. cit., p. 60.

1896 Presidential Election

Total Popular Votes: 13,935,738
McKinley's Plurality: 596,985

STATE	WILLIAM McKINLEY (Republican) Votes	%	WILLIAM J. BRYAN (Democrat, Populist) Votes	%	JOHN M. PALMER (National Democrat) Votes	%	JOSHUA LEVERING (Prohibition) Votes	%	OTHER[1] Votes	%	PLURALITY
Alabama	55,673	28.6	130,298	67.0	6,375	3.3	2,234	1.2			74,625
Arkansas	37,512	25.1	110,103	73.7			889	.6	892	.6	72,591
California	146,756	49.2	144,877	48.5	1,730	.6	2,573	.9	2,662	.9	1,879
Colorado	26,271	13.9	161,005	84.9	1		1,717	.9	545	.3	134,734
Connecticut	110,285	63.2	56,740	32.5	4,336	2.5	1,806	1.0	1,227	.7	53,545
Delaware	20,450	53.2	16,574	43.1	966	2.5	466	1.2			3,876
Florida	11,298	24.3	32,756	70.4	1,778	3.8	656	1.4			21,458
Georgia	59,395	36.6	93,885	57.8	3,670	2.3	5,483	3.4	47		34,490
Idaho	6,324	21.3	23,135	78.1			172	.6			16,811
Illinois	607,130	55.7	465,593	42.7	6,307	.6	9,796	.9	1,940	.2	141,537
Indiana	323,754	50.8	305,538	48.0	2,145	.3	3,061	.5	2,591	.4	18,216
Iowa	289,293	55.5	223,744	42.9	4,516	.9	3,192	.6	805	.2	65,549
Kansas	159,484	47.5	173,049	51.5	1,209	.4	1,723	.5	620	.2	13,565
Kentucky	218,171	48.9	217,894	48.9	5,084	1.1	4,779	1.1			277
Louisiana	22,037	21.8	77,175	76.4	1,834	1.8					55,138
Maine	80,403	67.9	34,587	29.2	1,867	1.6	1,562	1.3			45,816
Maryland	136,959	54.7	104,150	41.6	2,499	1.0	5,918	2.4	723	.3	32,809
Massachusetts	278,976	69.5	105,414	26.3	11,749	2.9	2,998	.8	2,132	.5	173,562
Michigan	293,336	53.8	237,164	43.5	6,923	1.3	4,978	.9	3,182	.6	56,172
Minnesota	193,503	56.6	139,735	40.9	3,222	.9	4,348	1.3	954	.3	53,768
Mississippi	4,819	6.9	63,355	91.0	1,021	1.5	396	.6			58,536
Missouri	304,940	45.2	363,667	54.0	2,365	.4	2,169	.3	891	.1	58,727
Montana	10,509	19.7	42,628	79.9			193	.4			32,119
Nebraska	103,064	46.2	115,007	51.5	2,885	1.3	1,242	.6	983	.4	11,943
Nevada	1,938	18.8	8,348	81.2							6,410
New Hampshire	57,444	68.7	21,650	25.9	3,520	4.2	779	.9	277	.3	35,794
New Jersey	221,367	59.7	133,675	36.0	6,373	1.7			9,599	2.6	87,692
New York	819,838	57.6	551,369	38.7	18,950	1.3	16,052	1.1	17,667	1.2	268,469
North Carolina	155,122	46.8	174,408	52.6	578	.2	635	.2	594	.2	19,286
North Dakota	26,335	55.6	20,686	43.7			358	.8	12		5,649
Ohio	525,991	51.9	477,497	47.1	1,858	.2	5,068	.5	3,881	.4	48,494
Oregon	48,700	50.0	46,739	48.0	977	1.0	919	.9			1,961
Pennsylvania	728,300	61.0	433,228	36.3	11,000	.9	19,274	1.6	2,553	.2	295,072
Rhode Island	37,437	68.3	14,459	26.4	1,166	2.1	1,160	2.1	563	1.0	22,978
South Carolina	9,313	13.5	58,801	85.3	824	1.2					49,488
South Dakota	41,040	49.5	41,225	49.7			672	.8			185
Tennessee	148,683	46.3	167,168	52.1	1,953	.6	3,099	1.0			18,485
Texas	163,894	30.3	370,308	68.4	5,022	.9	1,794	.3			206,414
Utah	13,491	17.3	64,607	82.7							51,116
Vermont	51,127	80.1	10,367	16.7	1,341	2.1	733	1.2			40,490
Virginia	135,379	45.9	154,708	52.5	2,129	.7	2,350	.8	108		19,329
Washington	39,153	41.8	53,314	57.0			968	1.0	148	.2	14,361
West Virginia	105,379	52.2	94,480	46.8	678	.3	1,220	.6			10,899
Wisconsin	268,135	59.9	165,523	37.0	4,584	1.0	7,507	1.7	1.660	.4	102,612
Wyoming	10,072	47.8	10,862	51.6			133	.6			790
Totals	**7,108,480**	*51.01*	**6,511,495**	*46.73*	**133,435**	*.96*	**125,072**	*.90*	**57,256**	*.41*	

1. For breakdown of "Other" vote, see minor candidate vote totals, p. 367.

1900 Presidential Election

Total Popular Votes: 13,970,470
McKinley's Plurality: 859,694

STATE	WILLIAM McKINLEY (Republican)		WILLIAM J. BRYAN (Democrat)		JOHN G. WOOLEY (Prohibition)		EUGENE V. DEBS (Socialist)		OTHER[1]		PLURALITY
	Votes	%	Votes	%	Votes	%	Votes	%	Votes	%	
Alabama	55,612	34.8	97,129	60.8	2,763	1.7			4,188	2.6	41,517
Arkansas	44,800	35.0	81,242	63.5	584	.5			1,340	1.1	36,442
California	164,755	54.5	124,985	41.3	5,024	1.7			7,554	2.5	39,770
Colorado	92,701	42.0	122,705	55.6	3,790	1.7	686	.3	1,013	.5	30,004
Connecticut	102,572	56.9	74,014	41.1	1,617	.9	1,029	.6	963	.5	28,558
Delaware	22,535	53.7	18,852	44.9	546	1.3	56	.1			3,683
Florida	7,355	18.6	28,273	71.3	2,244	5.7	634	1.6	1,143	2.9	20,918
Georgia	34,260	28.2	81,180	66.9	1,402	1.2			4,568	3.8	46,920
Idaho	27,198	46.9	29,484	50.9	857	1.5			445	.8	2,286
Illinois	597,985	52.8	503,061	44.4	17,626	1.6	9,687	.9	3,539	.3	94,924
Indiana	336,063	50.6	309,584	46.6	13,718	2.1	2,374	.4	2,355	.4	26,479
Iowa	307,799	58.0	209,261	39.5	9,502	1.8	2,743	.5	1,040	.2	98,538
Kansas[2]	185,955	52.6	162,601	46.0	3,605	1.0	1,605	.5			23,534
Kentucky	227,132	48.5	235,126	50.2	2,890	.6	766	.2	2,351	.5	7,994
Louisiana	14,234	21.0	53,668	79.0					4		39,434
Maine	65,412	61.9	36,822	34.8	2,581	2.4	878	.8			28,590
Maryland	136,151	51.5	122,237	46.2	4,574	1.7	900	.3	524	.2	13,914
Massachusetts	238,866	57.6	156,997	37.9	6,202	1.5	9,607	2.3	3,132	.8	81,869
Michigan	316,014	58.1	211,432	38.9	11,804	2.2	2,820	.5	1,719	.3	104,582
Minnesota	190,461	60.2	112,901	35.7	8,555	2.7	3,065	1.0	1,329	.4	77,560
Mississippi	5,707	9.7	51,706	87.6					1,642	2.8	45,999
Missouri	314,092	45.9	351,922	51.5	5,965	.9	6,139	.9	5,540	.8	37,830
Montana	25,409	39.8	37,311	58.4	306	.5	711	1.1	119	.2	11,902
Nebraska	121,835	50.5	114,013	47.2	3,655	1.5	823	.3	1,104	.5	7,822
Nevada	3,849	37.8	6,347	62.3							2,498
New Hampshire	54,799	59.3	35,489	38.4	1,270	1.4	790	.9	16		19,310
New Jersey	221,707	55.3	164,808	41.1	7,183	1.8	4,609	1.2	2,743	.7	56,899
New York	822,013	53.1	678,462	43.8	22,077	1.4	12,869	.8	12,622	.8	143,551
North Carolina	132,997	45.5	157,733	53.9	990	.3			798	.3	24,736
North Dakota	35,898	62.1	20,524	35.5	735	1.3	517	.9	109	.2	15,374
Ohio	543,918	52.3	474,882	45.7	10,203	1.0	4,847	.5	6,223	.6	69,036
Oregon	46,172	55.5	32,810	39.4	2,536	3.1	1,464	1.8	269	.3	13,362
Pennsylvania	712,665	60.7	424,232	36.2	27,908	2.4	4,831	.4	3,574	.3	288,433
Rhode Island	33,784	59.7	19,812	35.0	1,529	2.7			1,423	2.5	13,972
South Carolina	3,525	7.0	47,173	93.1							43,648
South Dakota	54,574	56.8	39,538	41.1	1,541	1.6	176	.2	340	.4	15,036
Tennessee	123,108	45.0	145,240	53.0	3,844	1.4	346	.1	1,322	.5	22,132
Texas	131,174	30.9	267,945	63.1	2,642	.6	1,846	.4	20,727	4.9	136,771
Utah	47,089	50.6	44,949	48.3	205	.2	717	.8	111	.1	2,140
Vermont	42,569	75.7	12,849	22.9	383	.7	39	.1	372	.7	29,720
Virginia	115,769	43.8	146,079	55.3	2,130	.8			230	.1	30,310
Washington	57,455	53.4	44,833	41.7	2,363	2.2	2,006	1.9	866	.8	12,622
West Virginia	119,829	54.3	98,807	44.8	1,628	.7	286	.1	246	.1	21,022
Wisconsin	265,760	60.1	159,163	36.0	10,027	2.3	7,048	1.6	503	.1	106,597
Wyoming	14,482	58.6	10,164	41.1			21	.1	41	.2	4,318
Totals	**7,218,039**	**51.67**	**6,358,345**	**45.51**	**209,004**	**1.50**	**86,935**	**.62**	**98,147**	**.70**	

1. For breakdown of "Other" vote, see minor candidate vote totals, p. 367.
2. Figures from Petersen, op. cit., p. 67.

1904 Presidential Election

Total Popular Votes: 13,518,964
Roosevelt's Plurality: 2,543,695

STATE	THEODORE ROOSEVELT (Republican)		ALTON PARKER (Democrat)		EUGENE V. DEBS (Socialist)		SILAS C. SWALLOW (Prohibition)		OTHER[1]		PLURALITY
	Votes	%	Votes	%	Votes	%	Votes	%	Votes	%	
Alabama	22,472	20.7	79,797	73.4	853	.8	612	.6	5,051	4.6	57,325
Arkansas	46,760	40.2	64,434	55.4	1,816	1.6	992	.9	2,326	2.0	17,674
California	205,226	61.9	89,294	26.9	29,535	8.9	7,380	2.2	333	.1	115,932
Colorado	134,661	55.3	100,105	41.1	4,304	1.8	3,438	1.4	1,159	.5	34,556
Connecticut	111,089	58.1	72,909	38.2	4,543	2.4	1,506	.8	1,089	.6	38,180
Delaware	23,705	54.1	19,347	44.1	146	.3	607	1.4	51	.1	4,358
Florida	8,314	21.5	26,449	68.3	2,337	6.0			1,605	4.2	18,135
Georgia	24,004	18.3	83,466	63.7	196	.2	685	.5	22,635	17.3	59,462
Idaho	47,783	65.8	18,480	25.5	4,949	6.8	1,013	1.4	352	.5	29,303
Illinois	632,645	58.8	327,606	30.4	69,225	6.4	34,770	3.2	12,249	1.1	305,039
Indiana	368,289	54.0	274,356	40.2	12,023	1.8	23,496	3.4	4,042	.6	93,933
Iowa	307,907	63.4	149,141	30.7	14,847	3.1	11,601	2.4	2,207	.5	158,766
Kansas	213,455	64.9	86,164	26.2	15,869	4.8	7,306	2.2	6,253	1.9	127,291
Kentucky	205,457	47.1	217,170	49.8	3,599	.8	6,603	1.5	3,117	.7	11,713
Louisiana	5,205	9.7	47,708	88.5	995	1.9					42,503
Maine	65,432	67.4	27,642	28.5	2,102	2.2	1,510	1.6	337	.4	37,790
Maryland	109,497	48.8	109,446	48.8	2,247	1.0	3,034	1.4	5		51
Massachusetts	257,813	57.9	165,746	37.2	13,604	3.1	4,279	1.0	3,658	.8	92,067
Michigan	361,863	69.5	134,163	25.8	8,942	1.7	13,312	2.6	2,163	.4	227,700
Minnesota	216,651	74.0	55,187	18.8	11,692	4.0	6,253	2.1	3,077	1.1	161,464
Mississippi	3,280	5.6	53,480	91.1	462	.8			1,499	2.6	50,200
Missouri	321,449	49.9	296,312	46.0	13,009	2.0	7,191	1.1	5,900	.9	25,137
Montana	33,994	53.5	21,816	34.3	5,675	8.9	339	.5	1,744	2.8	12,178
Nebraska	138,558	61.4	52,921	23.4	7,412	3.3	6,323	2.8	20,518	9.1	85,637
Nevada	6,864	56.7	3,982	32.9	925	7.6			344	2.8	2,882
New Hampshire	54,157	60.1	34,071	37.8	1,090	1.2	750	.8	83	.1	20,086
New Jersey	245,164	56.7	164,566	38.1	9,587	2.2	6,845	1.6	6,085	1.4	80,598
New York	859,533	53.1	683,981	42.3	36,883	2.3	20,787	1.3	16,581	1.0	175,552
North Carolina	82,442	39.7	124,091	59.7	124	.1	342	.2	819	.4	41,649
North Dakota	52,595	75.1	14,273	20.4	2,009	2.9	1,137	1.6			38,322
Ohio	600,095	59.8	344,674	34.3	36,260	3.6	19,339	1.9	4,027	.4	255,421
Oregon	60,309	67.3	17,327	19.3	7,479	8.3	3,795	4.2	746	.8	42,982
Pennsylvania	840,949	68.0	337,998	27.3	21,863	1.8	33,717	2.7	2,211	.2	502,951
Rhode Island	41,605	60.6	24,839	36.2	956	1.4	768	1.1	488	.7	16,766
South Carolina	2,570	4.6	53,320	95.4							50,750
South Dakota	72,083	71.1	21,969	21.7	3,138	3.1	2,965	2.9	1,240	1.2	50,114
Tennessee	105,363	43.4	131,653	54.2	1,354	.6	1,889	.8	2,491	1.0	26,290
Texas	51,307	22.0	167,088	71.5	2,788	1.2	3,933	1.7	8,493	3.6	115,781
Utah	62,446	61.5	33,413	32.9	5,767	5.7					29,033
Vermont	40,459	78.0	9,777	18.8	859	1.7	792	1.5	1		30,682
Virginia	48,180	37.0	80,649	61.8	202	.2	1,379	1.1			32,469
Washington	101,540	70.0	28,098	19.4	10,023	6.9	3,229	2.2	2,261	1.6	73,442
West Virginia	132,620	55.3	100,855	42.0	1,573	.7	4,599	1.9	339	.1	31,765
Wisconsin	280,314	63.2	124,205	28.0	28,240	6.4	9,872	2.2	809	.2	156,109
Wyoming	20,489	66.9	8,930	29.2	987	3.2	208	.7			11,559
Totals	7,626,593	56.41	5,082,898	37.60	402,489	2.98	258,596	1.91	148,388	1.10	

1. For breakdown of "Other" vote, see minor candidate vote totals, p. 367.

1908 Presidential Election

Total Popular Votes: 14,882,734
Taft's Plurality: 1,269,457

STATE	WILLIAM H. TAFT (Republican)		WILLIAM J. BRYAN (Democrat)		EUGENE V. DEBS (Socialist)		EUGENE W. CHAFIN (Prohibition)		OTHER[1]		PLURALITY
	Votes	%	Votes	%	Votes	%	Votes	%	Votes	%	
Alabama	25,561	24.3	74,391	70.8	1,450	1.4	690	.7	3,060	2.9	48,830
Arkansas	56,684	37.3	87,020	57.3	5,842	3.9	1,026	.7	1,273	.8	30,336
California	214,398	55.5	127,492	33.0	28,659	7.4	11,770	3.0	4,306	1.1	86,906
Colorado	123,693	46.9	126,644	48.0	7,960	3.0	5,559	2.1	2		2,951
Connecticut	112,815	59.4	68,255	35.9	5,113	2.7	2,380	1.3	1,340	.7	44,560
Delaware	25,014	52.1	22,055	45.9	239	.5	670	1.4	29		2,959
Florida	10,654	21.6	31,104	63.0	3,747	7.6	1,356	2.8	2,499	5.1	20,450
Georgia	41,355	31.2	72,350	54.6	584	.4	1,452	1.1	16,763	12.7	30,995
Idaho	52,621	54.1	36,162	37.2	6,400	6.6	1,986	2.0	124	.1	16,459
Illinois	629,932	54.5	450,810	39.0	34,711	3.0	29,364	2.5	10,437	.9	179,122
Indiana	348,993	48.4	338,262	46.9	13,476	1.9	18,036	2.5	2,350	.3	10,731
Iowa	275,210	55.6	200,771	40.6	8,287	1.7	9,837	2.0	665	.1	74,439
Kansas	197,316	52.5	161,209	42.9	12,420	3.3	5,030	1.3	68	.2	36,107
Kentucky	235,711	48.0	244,092	49.7	4,093	.8	5,885	1.2	938	.2	8,381
Louisiana	8,958	11.9	63,568	84.6	2,514	3.4			77	.1	54,610
Maine	66,987	63.0	35,403	33.3	1,758	1.7	1,487	1.4	700	.7	31,584
Maryland	116,513	48.9	115,908	48.6	2,323	1.0	3,302	1.4	485	.2	605
Massachusetts	265,966	58.2	155,533	34.0	10,778	2.4	4,373	1.0	20,255	4.4	110,433
Michigan	333,313	61.9	174,619	32.5	11,527	2.1	16,785	3.1	1,880	.4	158,694
Minnesota	195,843	59.3	109,401	33.1	14,472	4.4	10,114	3.1	424	.1	86,442
Mississippi	4,363	6.5	60,287	90.1	978	1.5			1,276	1.9	55,924
Missouri	347,203	48.5	346,574	48.4	15,431	2.2	4,209	.6	2,424	.3	629
Montana	32,471	46.9	29,511	42.6	5,920	8.6	838	1.2	493	.7	2,960
Nebraska	126,997	47.6	131,099	49.1	3,524	1.3	5,179	1.9			4,102
Nevada	10,775	43.9	11,212	45.7	2,103	8.6			436	1.8	437
New Hampshire	53,144	59.3	33,655	37.6	1,299	1.5	905	1.0	592	.7	19,489
New Jersey	265,298	56.8	182,522	39.1	10,249	2.2	4,930	1.1	4,112	.9	82,776
New York	870,070	53.1	667,468	40.7	38,451	2.4	22,667	1.4	39,694	2.4	202,602
North Carolina	114,887	45.5	136,928	54.2	372	.2	354	.1	13		22,041
North Dakota	57,680	61.0	32,884	34.8	2,421	2.6	1,496	1.6	43	.1	24,796
Ohio	572,312	51.0	502,721	44.8	33,795	3.0	11,402	1.0	1,322	.1	69,591
Oklahoma	110,473	43.5	122,362	48.1	21,425	8.4					11,889
Oregon	62,454	56.5	37,792	34.2	7,322	6.6	2,682	2.4	289	.3	24,662
Pennsylvania	745,779	58.8	448,782	35.4	33,914	2.7	36,694	2.9	2,281	.2	296,997
Rhode Island	43,942	60.8	24,706	34.2	1,365	1.9	1,016	1.4	1,288	1.8	19,236
South Carolina	3,945	5.9	62,288	93.8	100	.2			46	.1	58,343
South Dakota	67,536	58.8	40,266	35.1	2,846	2.5	4,039	3.5	88	.1	27,270
Tennessee	117,977	45.9	135,608	52.7	1,870	.7	301	.1	1,424	.6	17,631
Texas	65,605	22.4	216,662	74.0	7,779	2.7	1,626	.6	1,241	.4	151,057
Utah	61,165	56.2	42,610	39.2	4,890	4.5			92	.1	18,555
Vermont	39,552	75.1	11,496	21.8			799	1.5	833	1.6	28,056
Virginia	52,572	38.4	82,946	60.5	255	.2	1,111	.8	181	.1	30,374
Washington	106,062	57.8	58,383	31.8	14,177	7.7	4,700	2.6	248	.1	47,679
West Virginia	137,869	53.4	111,410	43.2	3,679	1.4	5,140	2.0		.1	26,459
Wisconsin	247,744	54.5	166,662	36.7	28,147	6.2	11,565	2.5	320	.1	81,082
Wyoming	20,846	55.4	14,918	39.7	1,715	4.6	66	.2	63	.2	5,928
Totals	7,676,258	51.58	6,406,801	43.05	420,380	2.82	252,821	1.70	126,474	.85	

1. For breakdown of "Other" vote, see minor candidate vote totals, p. 367.

1912 Presidential Election

Total Popular Votes: 15,040,963
Wilson's Plurality: 2,173,945

STATE	WOODROW WILSON (Democrat)		THEODORE ROOSEVELT (Progressive)		WILLIAM H. TAFT (Republican)		EUGENE V. DEBS (Socialist)		OTHER[1]		PLURALITY
	Votes	%	Votes	%	Votes	%	Votes	%	Votes	%	
Alabama	82,438	69.9	22,680	19.2	9,807	8.3	3,029	2.6	5		59,758
Arizona	10,324	43.6	6,949	29.3	2,986	12.6	3,163	13.4	265	1.1	3,375
Arkansas	68,814	55.0	21,644	17.3	25,585	20.5	8,153	6.5	908	.7	43,229
California	283,436	41.8	283,610	41.8	3,847	.6	79,201	11.7	27,783	4.1	174
Colorado	113,912	42.8	71,752	27.0	58,386	22.0	16,366	6.2	5,538	2.1	42,160
Connecticut	74,561	39.2	34,129	17.9	68,324	35.9	10,056	5.3	3,334	1.8	6,237
Delaware	22,631	46.5	8,886	18.3	15,997	32.9	556	1.1	620	1.3	6,634
Florida	35,343	69.5	4,555	9.0	4,279	8.4	4,806	9.5	1,854	3.7	30,537
Georgia	93,087	76.6	21,985	18.1	5,191	4.3	1,058	.9	149	.1	71,102
Idaho	33,921	32.1	25,527	24.1	32,810	31.0	11,960	11.3	1,536	1.5	1,111
Illinois	405,048	35.3	386,478	33.7	253,593	22.1	81,278	7.1	19,776	1.7	18,570
Indiana	281,890	43.1	162,007	24.8	151,267	23.1	36,931	5.6	22,379	3.4	119,883
Iowa	185,322	37.6	161,819	32.9	119,805	24.3	16,967	3.5	8,440	1.7	23,503
Kansas	143,663	39.3	120,210	32.9	74,845	20.5	26,779	7.3	63		23,453
Kentucky	219,484	48.5	101,766	22.5	115,510	25.5	11,646	2.6	4,308	1.0	103,974
Louisiana	60,871	76.8	9,283	11.7	3,833	4.8	5,261	6.6			51,588
Maine	51,113	39.4	48,495	37.4	26,545	20.5	2,541	2.0	947	.7	2,618
Maryland	112,674	48.6	57,789	24.9	54,956	23.7	3,996	1.7	2,566	1.1	54,885
Massachusetts	173,408	35.5	142,228	29.1	155,948	32.0	12,616	2.6	3,856	.8	17,460
Michigan	150,201	27.4	213,243	38.9	151,434	27.6	23,060	4.2	10,033	1.8	61,809
Minnesota	106,426	31.8	125,856	37.7	64,334	19.3	27,505	8.2	10,098	3.0	19,430
Mississippi	57,324	88.9	3,549	5.5	1,560	2.4	2,050	3.2			53,775
Missouri	330,746	47.4	124,375	17.8	207,821	29.8	28,466	4.1	7,158	1.0	122,925
Montana	28,129	35.1	22,709	28.3	18,575	23.1	10,811	13.5	32		5,420
Nebraska	109,008	43.7	72,681	29.1	54,226	21.7	10,185	4.1	3,383	1.4	36,327
Nevada	7,986	39.7	5,620	27.9	3,196	15.9	3,313	16.5			2,366
New Hampshire	34,724	39.5	17,794	20.2	32,927	37.4	1,981	2.3	535	.6	1,797
New Jersey	178,638	41.2	145,679	33.6	89,066	20.5	15,948	3.7	4,332	1.0	32,959
New Mexico	20,437	41.9	8,347	17.1	17,164	35.2	2,859	5.9			3,273
New York	655,573	41.3	390,093	24.6	455,487	28.7	63,434	4.0	23,728	1.5	200,086
North Carolina	144,407	59.2	69,135	28.4	29,129	12.0	987	.4	118	.1	75,272
North Dakota	29,549	34.2	25,726	29.8	22,990	26.6	6,966	8.1	1,243	1.4	3,823
Ohio	424,834	41.0	229,807	22.2	278,168	26.8	90,164	8.7	14,141	1.4	146,666
Oklahoma	119,143	47.0			90,726	35.8	41,630	16.4	2,195	.9	28,417
Oregon	47,064	34.3	37,600	27.4	34,673	25.3	13,343	9.7	4,360	3.2	9,464
Pennsylvania	395,637	32.5	444,894	36.5	273,360	22.5	83,614	6.9	20,231	1.7	49,257
Rhode Island	30,412	39.0	16,878	21.7	27,703	35.6	2,049	2.6	852	1.1	2,709
South Carolina	48,355	95.9	1,293	2.6	536	1.1	164	.3	55	.1	47,062
South Dakota	48,942	42.1	58,811	50.6			4,664	4.0	3,910	3.4	9,869
Tennessee	133,021	52.8	54,041	21.5	60,475	24.0	3,564	1.4	832	.3	72,546
Texas	218,921	72.7	26,715	8.9	28,310	9.4	24,884	8.3	2,131	.7	190,611
Utah	36,576	32.6	24,174	21.5	42,013	37.4	8,999	8.0	510	.5	5,437
Vermont	15,350	24.4	22,129	35.2	23,303	37.1	928	1.5	1,094	1.7	1,174
Virginia	90,332	66.0	21,776	15.9	23,288	17.0	820	.6	759	.6	67,044
Washington	86,840	26.9	113,698	35.2	70,445	21.8	40,134	12.4	11,682	3.6	26,858
West Virginia	113,097	42.1	79,112	29.4	56,754	21.1	15,248	5.7	4,517	1.7	33,985
Wisconsin	164,230	41.1	62,448	15.6	130,596	32.7	33,476	8.4	9,225	2.3	33,634
Wyoming	15,310	36.2	9,232	21.8	14,560	34.4	2,760	6.5	421	1.0	750
Totals	6,293,152	41.84	4,119,207	27.39	3,486,333	23.18	900,369	5.99	241,902	1.61	

1. For breakdown of "Other" vote, see minor candidate vote totals, p. 367.

1916 Presidential Election

Total Popular Votes: 18,535,022
Wilson's Plurality: 579,511

STATE	WOODROW WILSON (Democrat) Votes	%	CHARLES E. HUGHES (Republican) Votes	%	ALLAN L. BENSON (Socialist) Votes	%	J. FRANK HANLY (Prohibition) Votes	%	OTHER[1] Votes	%	PLURALITY
Alabama	99,116	76.0	28,662	22.0	1,916	1.5	741	.6			70,454
Arizona	33,170	57.2	20,522	35.4	3,174	5.5	1,153	2.0			12,648
Arkansas	112,211	66.0	48,879	28.7	6,999	4.1	2,015	1.2			63,332
California	465,936	46.6	462,516	46.3	42,898	4.3	27,713	2.8	187		3,420
Colorado	177,496	60.8	101,388	34.7	9,951	3.4	2,793	1.0	409	.1	76,108
Connecticut	99,786	46.7	106,514	49.8	5,179	2.4	1,789	.8	606	.3	6,728
Delaware	24,753	47.8	26,011	50.2	480	.9	566	1.1			1,258
Florida	55,984	69.3	14,611	18.1	5,353	6.6	4,786	5.9			41,373
Georgia	127,754	79.5	11,294	7.0	941	.6			20,692	12.9	107,062[2]
Idaho	70,054	52.0	55,368	41.1	8,066	6.0	1,127	.8			14,686
Illinois	950,229	43.3	1,152,549	52.6	61,394	2.8	26,047	1.2	2,488	.1	202,320
Indiana	334,063	46.5	341,005	47.4	21,860	3.0	16,368	2.3	5,557	.8	6,942
Iowa	221,699	42.9	280,439	54.3	10,976	2.1	3,371	.7	2,253	.1	58,740
Kansas	314,588	50.0	277,658	44.1	24,685	3.9	12,882	2.1			36,930
Kentucky	269,990	51.9	241,854	46.5	4,734	.9	3,039	.6	461	.1	28,136
Louisiana	79,875	85.9	6,466	7.0	284	.3			6,349	6.8	73,409
Maine	64,033	47.0	69,508	51.0	2,177	1.6	596	.4			5,475
Maryland	138,359	52.8	117,347	44.8	2,674	1.0	2,903	1.1	756	.3	21,012
Massachusetts	247,885	46.6	268,784	50.5	11,058	2.1	2,993	.6	1,102	.2	20,899
Michigan	283,993	43.9	337,952	52.2	16,012	2.5	8,085	1.3	831	.1	53,959
Minnesota	179,155	46.3	179,544	46.4	20,117	5.2	7,793	2.0	758	.2	389
Mississippi	80,422	93.3	4,253	4.9	1,484	1.7			520		76,169
Missouri	398,032	50.6	369,339	46.9	14,612	1.9	3,887	.5	903	.1	28,693
Montana	101,104	56.8	66,933	37.6	9,634	5.4			338	.2	34,171
Nebraska	158,827	55.3	117,771	41.0	7,141	2.5	2,952	1.0	624	.2	41,056
Nevada	17,776	53.4	12,127	36.4	3,065	9.2	346	1.0			5,649
New Hampshire	43,781	49.1	43,725	49.1	1,318	1.5	303	.3			56
New Jersey	211,018	42.7	268,982	54.4	10,405	2.1	3,182	.6	855	.2	57,964
New Mexico	33,693	50.4	31,097	46.5	1,977	3.0	112	.2			2,596
New York	759,426	44.5	879,238	57.5	45,944	2.7	19,031	1.1	2,666	.2	119,812
North Carolina	168,383	58.1	120,890	41.7	509	.2	55				47,493
North Dakota	55,206	47.8	53,471	46.3	5,716	5.0	997	.9			1,735
Ohio	604,161	51.9	514,753	44.2	38,092	3.3	8,085	.7			89,408
Oklahoma	148,123	50.7	97,233	33.3	45,091	15.4	1,646	.6	234	.1	50,890
Oregon	120,087	45.9	126,813	48.5	9,711	3.7	4,729	1.8	310	.1	6,726
Pennsylvania	521,784	40.2	703,823	54.3	42,638	3.3	28,525	2.2	419		182,039
Rhode Island	40,394	46.0	44,858	51.1	1,914	2.2	470	.5	180	.2	4,464
South Carolina	61,845	96.7	1,550	2.4	135	.2			420	.7	60,295
South Dakota	59,191	45.9	64,217	49.8	3,760	2.9	1,774	1.4			5,026
Tennessee	153,280	56.3	116,223	42.7	2,542	.9	145	.1			37,057
Texas	287,415	77.0	64,999	17.4	18,960	5.1	1,936	.5			222,416
Utah	84,145	58.8	54,137	37.8	4,460	3.1	149	.1	254	.2	30,008
Vermont	22,708	35.2	40,250	62.4	798	1.2	709	1.1	10		17,542
Virginia	101,840	67.0	48,384	31.8	1,056	.7	678	.5	67		53,456
Washington	183,388	48.1	167,208	43.9	22,800	6.0	6,868	1.8	730	.2	16,180
West Virginia	140,403	48.5	143,124	49.4	6,144	2.1					2,721
Wisconsin	191,363	42.8	220,822	49.4	27,631	6.2	7,318	1.6			29,459
Wyoming	28,376	54.7	21,698	41.8	1,459	2.8	373	.7			6,678
Totals	**9,126,300**	**49.24**	**8,546,789**	**46.11**	**589,924**	**3.18**	**221,030**	**1.19**	**50,979**	**.28**	

1. For breakdown of "Other" vote, see minor candidate vote totals, p. 367.
2. Plurality of 107,062 votes is calculated on the basis of 20,692 votes cast for the Progressive Party.

1920 Presidential Election

Total Popular Votes: 26,753,786
Harding's Plurality: 6,992,430

STATE	WARREN G. HARDING (Republican) Votes	%	JAMES M. COX (Democrat) Votes	%	EUGENE V. DEBS (Socialist) Votes	%	PARLEY P. CHRISTENSEN (Farmer-Labor) Votes	%	OTHER[1] Votes	%	PLURALITY
Alabama	74,719	31.9	156,064	66.7	2,402	1.0			766	.3	81,345
Arizona	37,016	55.6	29,546	44.4							7,470
Arkansas	71,107	38.7	107,406	58.5	5,108	2.8					36,299
California	624,992	66.2	229,191	24.3	64,076	6.8			25,672	2.7	395,801
Colorado	171,709	59.4	103,721	35.9	7,860	2.7	2,898	1.0	2,807	1.0	67,988
Connecticut	229,238	62.7	120,721	33.0	10,350	2.8	1,947	.5	3,262	.9	108,517
Delaware	52,858	55.7	39,911	42.1	988	1.0	82	.1	1,025	1.1	12,947
Florida[2]	44,853	30.8	90,515	62.0	5,189	3.6			5,124	3.5	45,662
Georgia	42,981	28.7	106,112	70.9	558	.4					63,131
Idaho	88,975	65.6	46,579	34.3	38				32		42,396
Illinois	1,420,480	67.8	534,395	25.5	74,747	3.6	49,632	2.4	15,461	.8	886,085
Indiana	696,370	55.1	511,364	40.5	24,713	2.0	16,499	1.3	14,028	1.1	185,006
Iowa	634,674	70.9	227,924	25.5	16,981	1.9	10,321	1.2	5,185	.6	406,750
Kansas	369,268	64.8	185,464	32.5	15,511	2.7			75		183,804
Kentucky	451,480	49.2	457,203	49.8	6,409	.7			3,250	.4	5,723
Louisiana	38,539	30.5	87,355	69.2					342	.3	48,816
Maine	136,355	65.5	69,306	33.3	2,210	1.1			310	.2	67,049
Maryland	236,117	55.1	180,626	42.2	8,876	2.1	1,645	.4	1,186	.3	55,491
Massachusetts	681,153	68.6	276,691	27.8	32,265	3.3			3,607	.4	404,462
Michigan	755,941	72.8	231,046	22.3	28,446	2.7	10,163	1.0	12,385	1.2	524,895
Minnesota	519,421	70.6	142,994	19.4	56,106	7.6			17,317	2.4	376,427
Mississippi	11,527	14.0	69,252	84.0	1,639	2.0					57,725
Missouri	727,252	54.6	574,799	43.2	20,342	1.5	3,108	.2	6,739	.5	152,453
Montana	109,680	61.0	57,746	32.1			12,283	6.8			51,934
Nebraska	247,498	64.7	119,608	31.3	9,600	2.5			6,037	1.6	127,890
Nevada	15,479	56.9	9,851	36.2	1,864	6.9					5,628
New Hampshire	95,196	59.8	62,662	39.4	1,234	.8					32,534
New Jersey	611,541	67.7	256,887	28.4	27,141	3.0	2,200	.2	6,114	.7	354,654
New Mexico	57,634	54.7	46,668	44.3			1,097	1.0			10,966
New York	1,871,167	64.6	781,238	27.0	203,201	7.0	18,413	.6	24,494	.9	1,089,929
North Carolina	232,819	43.2	305,367	56.7	446	.1			17		72,548
North Dakota	158,997	77.7	37,409	18.3	8,273	4.0					121,588
Ohio	1,182,022	58.5	780,037	38.6	57,147	2.8			2,447	.1	401,985
Oklahoma	243,465	50.2	215,798	44.5	25,698	5.3					27,667
Oregon	143,592	60.2	80,019	33.6	9,801	4.1			5,110	2.2	63,573
Pennsylvania	1,218,216	65.8	503,843	27.2	70,571	3.8	15,705	.9	44,282	2.4	714,373
Rhode Island	107,463	64.0	55,062	32.8	4,351	2.6			1,105	.7	52,401
South Carolina	2,244	3.4	64,170	96.1	28				366	.6	61,926
South Dakota	109,874	60.7	35,938	19.8			34,406	19.0	900	.5	73,936
Tennessee	219,229	51.2	206,558	48.3	2,249	.5					12,671
Texas	114,384	23.5	288,933	59.4	8,122	1.7			75,010	15.4	174,549
Utah	81,555	55.9	56,639	38.8	3,159	2.2	4,475	3.1			24,916
Vermont	67,964	75.8	20,884	23.3					818	.9	47,080
Virginia	87,456	37.9	141,670	61.3	808	.4	240	.1	826	.4	54,214
Washington	223,137	56.0	84,298	21.1	8,913	2.2	77,246	19.4	5,111	1.3	138,839
West Virginia	282,010	55.3	220,789	43.3	5,609	1.1			1,526	.3	61,221
Wisconsin	498,576	71.1	113,196	16.2	80,635	11.5			8,648	1.2	385,380
Wyoming	35,091	64.2	17,429	31.9			2,180	4.0			17,662
Totals	16,133,314	60.30	9,140,884	34.17	913,664	3.42	264,540	.99	301,384	1.13	

1. For breakdown of "Other" vote, see minor candidate vote totals, p. 367.
2. Figures from Petersen, op. cit., p. 83.

1924 Presidential Election

Total Popular Votes: 29,075,959
Coolidge's Plurality: 7,331,384

STATE	CALVIN COOLIDGE (Republican)		JOHN W. DAVIS (Democrat)		ROBERT M. LAFOLLETTE (Progressive)		HERMAN P. FARIS (Prohibition)		OTHER[1]		PLURALITY
	Votes	%	Votes	%	Votes	%	Votes	%	Votes	%	
Alabama	40,615	25.0	113,138	69.7	8,040	5.0	562	.4			72,523
Arizona	30,516	41.3	26,235	35.5	17,210	23.3					4,281
Arkansas	40,518	29.3	84,759	61.2	13,146	9.5			10		44,241
California	733,196	57.2	105,514	8.2	424,649	33.1	18,436	1.4	122		308,547
Colorado	193,956	59.4	75,238	23.0	57,368	17.6					118,718
Connecticut	246,322	61.5	110,184	27.5	42,416	10.6			1,373	.3	136,138
Delaware	52,441	57.7	33,445	36.8	4,979	5.5			16		18,996
Florida	30,633	28.1	62,083	56.9	8,625	7.9	5,498	5.0	2,315	2.1	31,450
Georgia	30,300	18.2	123,260	74.1	12,687	7.6					92,960
Idaho	72,084	48.1	24,217	16.2	53,664	35.8					18,420
Illinois	1,453,321	58.8	576,975	23.4	432,027	17.5	2,367	.1	5,377	.2	876,346
Indiana	703,042	55.3	492,245	38.7	71,700	5.6	4,416	.4	987	.1	210,797
Iowa	537,458	55.0	160,382	16.4	274,448	28.1			4,482	.5	263,010
Kansas	407,671	61.5	156,320	23.6	98,462	14.9			3		251,351
Kentucky	396,758	48.8	375,543	46.1	38,465	4.7			3,093	.4	21,215
Louisiana	24,670	20.2	93,218	76.4					4,063	3.3	68,548
Maine	138,440	72.0	41,964	21.8	11,382	5.9			406	.2	96,476
Maryland	162,414	45.3	148,072	41.3	47,157	13.2			987	.3	14,342
Massachusetts	703,476	62.3	280,817	24.9	141,225	12.5			4,304	.4	422,659
Michigan	874,631	75.4	152,359	13.1	122,014	10.5	6,085	.5	5,330	.5	722,272
Minnesota	420,759	51.2	55,913	6.8	339,192	41.3			6,282	.8	81,567
Mississippi	8,384	7.5	100,057	89.4	3,448	3.1					91,673
Missouri	648,486	49.6	572,962	43.8	83,996	6.4	1,418	.1	1,231	.1	75,524
Montana	74,246	42.5	33,867	19.4	65,985	37.8			370	.2	8,261
Nebraska	218,985	47.2	137,299	29.6	105,681	22.8	1,594	.3			81,686
Nevada	11,243	41.8	5,909	22.0	9,769	36.3					1,474
New Hampshire	98,575	59.8	57,201	34.7	8,993	5.5					41,374
New Jersey	675,162	62.2	297,743	27.4	108,901	10.0	1,337	.1	2,936	.3	377,419
New Mexico	54,745	48.5	48,542	43.0	9,543	8.5					6,203
New York	1,820,058	55.8	950,796	29.1	474,913	14.6			18,172	.6	869,262
North Carolina	190,754	39.6	284,190	59.0	6,651	1.4	13				93,436
North Dakota	94,931	47.7	13,858	7.0	89,922	45.2			370	.2	5,009
Ohio	1,176,130	58.3	477,888	23.7	358,008	17.8			4,271	.2	698,242
Oklahoma	225,756	42.8	255,798	48.5	41,142	7.8			5,134	1.0	30,042
Oregon	142,579	51.0	67,589	24.2	68,403	24.5			908	.3	74,176
Pennsylvania	1,401,481	65.4	409,192	19.1	307,567	14.3	9,779	.5	16,700	.8	992,289
Rhode Island	125,286	59.6	76,606	36.5	7,628	3.6			595	.3	48,680
South Carolina	1,123	2.2	49,008	96.6	623	1.2			1		47,885
South Dakota	101,299	49.7	27,214	13.4	75,200	36.9					26,099
Tennessee	130,831	43.5	159,339	52.9	10,666	3.5	94		100		28,508
Texas	130,794	19.8	485,443	73.7	42,879	6.5					354,649
Utah	77,327	49.3	46,908	29.9	32,662	20.8					30,419
Vermont	80,498	78.2	16,124	15.7	5,943	5.8	316	.3	5		64,374
Virginia	73,328	32.8	139,717	62.5	10,369	4.6			189	.1	66,389
Washington	220,224	52.3	42,842	10.2	150,727	35.8			7,709	1.8	69,497
West Virginia	288,635	49.5	257,232	44.1	36,723	6.3			1,072	.2	31,403
Wisconsin	311,614	37.1	68,096	8.1	453,678	54.0	2,918	.4	4,441	.5	142,064
Wyoming	41,858	52.4	12,868	16.1	25,174	31.5					16,684
Totals	**15,717,553**	**54.06**	**8,386,169**	**28.84**	**4,814,050**	**16.56**	**54,833**	**.19**	**103,354**	**.36**	

1. For breakdown of "Other" vote, see minor candidate vote totals, p. 367.

1928 Presidential Election

Total Popular Votes: 36,790,364
Hoover's Plurality: 6,411,806

STATE	HERBERT C. HOOVER (Republican)		ALFRED E. SMITH (Democrat)		NORMAN M. THOMAS (Socialist)		WILLIAM Z. FOSTER (Communist)		OTHER[1]		PLURALITY
	Votes	%	Votes	%	Votes	%	Votes	%	Votes	%	
Alabama	120,725	48.5	127,796	51.3	460	.2					7,071
Arizona	52,533	57.6	38,537	42.2			184	.2			13,996
Arkansas	77,785	39.3	119,195	60.3	434	.2	317	.2			41,410
California	1,147,929	63.9	614,365	34.2	19,595	1.1	112		14,655	.8	533,564
Colorado	252,924	64.8	132,747	34.0	2,630	.7	675	.2	1,092	.3	120,177
Connecticut	296,614	53.6	252,040	45.6	3,019	.6	730	.1	622	.1	44,574
Delaware	68,860	65.8	35,354	33.8	329	.3	58	.1			33,506
Florida	144,168	57.1	100,721	39.9	4,036	1.6	3,704	1.5			43,447
Georgia	99,368	43.4	129,602	56.6	124	.1	64				30,234
Idaho	97,322	64.2	52,926	34.9	1,293	.9					44,396
Illinois	1,770,723	57.0	1,312,235	42.2	19,138	.6	3,581	.1	1,812	.1	458,488
Indiana	848,290	59.7	562,691	39.6	3,871	.3	321		6,141	.4	285,599
Iowa	623,570	61.8	379,011	37.6	2,960	.3	328		3,320	.3	244,559
Kansas	513,672	72.0	193,003	27.1	6,205	.9	319				320,669
Kentucky	558,064	59.3	381,060	40.5	846	.1	307		354		177,004
Louisiana	51,160	23.7	164,655	76.3							113,495
Maine	179,923	68.6	81,179	31.0	1,065	.4					98,744
Maryland	301,479	57.1	223,626	42.3	1,701	.3	636	.1	906	.2	77,853
Massachusetts	775,566	49.2	792,758	50.2	6,262	.4	2,461	.2	776	.1	17,192
Michigan	965,396	70.4	396,762	28.9	3,516	.3	2,881	.2	3,527	.3	568,634
Minnesota	560,977	57.8	396,451	40.8	6,774	.7	4,853	.5	1,921	.2	164,526
Mississippi	26,202	17.3	124,445	82.2					788	.5	98,243
Missouri	834,080	55.6	662,684	44.2	3,739	.3			342		171,396
Montana	113,472	58.4	78,638	40.5	1,690	.9	577	.3			34,834
Nebraska	345,745	63.2	197,950	36.2	3,433	.6					147,795
Nevada	18,327	56.5	14,090	43.5							4,237
New Hampshire	115,404	58.7	80,715	41.0	465	.2	173	.1			34,689
New Jersey	925,285	59.8	616,162	39.8	4,866	.3	1,240	.1	642		309,123
New Mexico	69,708	59.0	48,211	40.8			158	.1			21,497
New York	2,193,344	49.8	2,089,863	47.4	107,332	2.4	10,876	.3	4,211	.1	103,481
North Carolina	348,923	54.9	286,227	45.1							62,696
North Dakota	131,419	54.8	106,648	44.5	842	.4	936	.4			24,771
Ohio	1,627,546	64.9	864,210	34.5	8,683	.4	2,836	.1	5,071	.2	763,336
Oklahoma	394,046	63.7	219,174	35.4	3,924	.6			1,283	.2	174,872
Oregon	205,341	64.2	109,223	34.1	2,720	.9	1,094	.3	1,564	.5	96,118
Pennsylvania	2,055,382	65.2	1,067,586	33.9	18,647	.6	4,726	.2	4,271	.1	987,796
Rhode Island	117,522	49.6	118,973	50.2			283	.1	416	.2	1,451
South Carolina	5,858	8.5	62,700	91.4	47	.1					56,842
South Dakota	157,603	60.2	102,660	39.2	443	.2	224	.1	927	.4	54,943
Tennessee	195,195	55.5	156,169	44.4	590	.2	70				39,026
Texas	367,036	51.7	341,458	48.1	641	.1	209				25,578
Utah	94,485	53.5	80,985	45.9	954	.5	46				13,500
Vermont	90,404	66.9	44,440	32.9					347	.3	45,964
Virginia	164,609	53.9	140,146	45.9	250	.1	179	.1	180	.1	24,463
Washington	335,503	67.1	156,772	31.4	2,615	.5	1,083	.2	4,068	.8	178,731
West Virginia	375,551	58.4	263,784	41.0	1,313	.2	401	.1	1,703	.3	111,767
Wisconsin	544,205	53.5	450,259	44.3	18,213	1.8	1,528	.2	2,626	.3	93,946
Wyoming	52,748	63.7	29,299	35.4	788	1.0					23,449
Totals	21,411,991	58.20	15,000,185	40.77	266,453	.72	48,170	.13	63,565	.17	

1. For breakdown of "Other" vote, see minor candidate vote totals, p. 367.

1932 Presidential Election

Total Popular Votes: 39,749,382
Roosevelt's Plurality: 7,066,619

STATE	FRANKLIN D. ROOSEVELT (Democrat) Votes	%	HERBERT C. HOOVER (Republican) Votes	%	NORMAN M. THOMAS (Socialist) Votes	%	WILLIAM Z. FOSTER (Communist) Votes	%	OTHER[1] Votes	%	PLURALITY
Alabama	207,732	84.7	34,647	14.1	2,060	.8	676	.3	13		173,085
Arizona	79,264	67.0	36,104	30.5	2,618	2.2	256	.2	9		43,160
Arkansas	186,829	86.3	27,465	12.7	1,166	.5	157	.1	952	.4	159,364
California	1,324,157	58.4	847,902	37.4	63,299	2.8			30,464	1.3	476,255
Colorado	250,151	54.9	188,364	41.3	13,591	3.0	758	.2	2,824	.6	61,787
Connecticut	281,632	47.4	288,420	48.5	20,480	3.5	1,364	.2	2,287	.4	6,788
Delaware	54,319	48.1	57,073	50.6	1,376	1.2	133	.1			2,754
Florida	206,307	74.9	69,170	25.1							137,137
Georgia	234,118	91.6	19,863	7.8	461	.2	23		1,125	.4	214,255
Idaho	109,479	58.7	71,312	38.2	526	.3	491	.3	4,660	2.5	38,167
Illinois	1,882,304	55.2	1,432,756	42.0	67,258	2.0	15,582	.5	10,026	.3	449,548
Indiana	862,054	54.7	677,184	42.9	21,388	1.4	2,187	.1	14,084	.9	184,870
Iowa	598,019	57.7	414,433	40.0	20,467	2.0	559	.1	3,209	.3	183,586
Kansas	424,204	53.6	349,498	44.1	18,276	2.3					74,706
Kentucky	580,574	59.1	394,716	40.2	3,858	.4	275		3,663	.4	185,858
Louisiana	249,418	92.8	18,853	7.0					533	.2	230,565
Maine	128,907	43.2	166,631	55.8	2,489	.8	162	.1	255	.1	37,724
Maryland	314,314	61.5	184,184	36.0	10,489	2.1	1,031	.2	1,036	.2	130,130
Massachusetts	800,148	50.6	736,959	46.6	34,305	2.2	4,821	.3	3,881	.2	63,189
Michigan	871,700	52.4	739,894	44.4	39,205	2.4	9,318	.6	4,648	.3	131,806
Minnesota	600,806	59.9	363,959	36.3	25,476	2.5	6,101	.6	6,501	.7	236,847
Mississippi	140,168	96.0	5,170	3.5	675	.5					134,998
Missouri	1,025,406	63.7	564,713	35.1	16,374	1.0	568		2,833	.2	460,693
Montana	127,476	58.8	78,134	36.0	7,902	3.7	1,801	.8	1,461	.7	49,342
Nebraska	359,082	63.0	201,177	35.3	9,876	1.7					157,905
Nevada	28,756	69.5	12,622	30.5							16,134
New Hampshire	100,680	49.0	103,629	50.4	947	.5	264	.1			2,949
New Jersey	806,394	49.5	775,406	47.6	42,981	2.6	2,908	.2	1,811	.1	30,988
New Mexico	95,089	62.8	54,146	35.7	1,771	1.2	133	.1	389	.3	40,943
New York	2,534,959	54.1	1,937,963	41.3	177,397	3.8	27,956	.6	10,339	.2	596,996
North Carolina	497,566	69.9	208,344	29.3	5,585	.8					289,222
North Dakota	178,350	69.6	71,772	28.0	3,521	1.4	830	.3	1,817	.7	106,578
Ohio	1,301,695	49.9	1,227,319	47.0	64,094	2.5	7,231	.3	9,389	.4	74,376
Oklahoma	516,468	73.3	188,165	26.7							328,303
Oregon	213,871	58.0	136,019	36.9	15,450	4.2	1,681	.5	1,730	.5	77,852
Pennsylvania	1,295,948	45.3	1,453,540	50.8	91,223	3.2	5,659	.2	12,807	.5	157,592
Rhode Island	146,604	55.1	115,266	43.3	3,138	1.2	546	.2	616	.2	31,338
South Carolina	102,347	98.0	1,978	1.9	82	.1			4		100,369
South Dakota	183,515	63.6	99,212	34.4	1,551	.5	364	.1	3,796	1.3	84,303
Tennessee	259,463	66.5	126,752	32.5	1,796	.5	254	.1	1,998	.5	132,711
Texas	767,585	88.2	97,852	11.2	4,416	.5	204		387	.1	669,733
Utah	116,749	56.6	84,513	41.0	4,087	2.0	946	.5			32,236
Vermont	56,266	41.1	78,984	57.7	1,533	1.1	195	.1	2		22,718
Virginia	203,979	68.5	89,634	30.1	2,382	.8	86		1,858	.6	114,345
Washington	353,260	57.5	208,645	33.9	17,080	2.8	2,972	.5	32,844	5.3	144,615
West Virginia	405,124	54.5	330,731	44.5	5,133	.7	444	.1	2,342	.3	74,393
Wisconsin	707,410	63.5	347,741	31.2	53,379	4.8	3,105	.3	3,165	.3	359,669
Wyoming	54,370	56.1	39,583	40.8	2,829	2.9	180	.2			14,787
Totals	**22,825,016**	**57.42**	**15,758,397**	**39.64**	**883,990**	**2.22**	**102,221**	**.26**	**179,758**	**.45**	

1. For breakdown of "Other" vote, see minor candidate vote totals, p. 367.

1936 Presidential Election

Total Popular Votes: 45,642,303
Roosevelt's Plurality: 11,068,093

STATE	FRANKLIN D. ROOSEVELT (Democrat)		ALFRED M. LANDON (Republican)		WILLIAM LEMKE (Union)		NORMAN M. THOMAS (Socialist)		OTHER[1]		PLURALITY
	Votes	%	Votes	%	Votes	%	Votes	%	Votes	%	
Alabama	238,131	86.4	35,358	12.8	543	.2	242	.1	1,397	.5	202,773
Arizona	86,722	69.9	33,433	26.9	3,307	2.7	317	.3	384	.3	53,289
Arkansas	146,756	81.8	32,049	17.9			446	.3	167	.1	114,707
California	1,766,836	67.0	836,431	31.7			11,325	.4	23,794	.9	930,405
Colorado	294,599	60.3	181,267	37.1	9,962	2.0	1,594	.3	824	.2	113,332
Connecticut	382,129	55.3	278,685	40.4	21,805	3.2	5,683	.8	2,421	.4	103,444
Delaware	69,702	54.6	54,014	42.3	442	.4	172	.1	3,273	2.5	15,688
Florida	249,117	76.1	78,248	23.9							170,869
Georgia	255,364	87.1	36,943	12.6	136	.1	68		660	.2	218,421
Idaho	125,683	63.0	66,232	33.2	7,677	3.9					59,451
Illinois	2,282,999	57.7	1,570,393	39.7	89,430	2.3	7,530	.2	5,362	.1	712,606
Indiana	934,974	56.6	691,570	41.9	19,407	1.2	3,856	.2	1,090	.1	243,404
Iowa	621,756	54.4	487,977	42.7	29,887	2.6	1,373	.1	1,944	.2	133,779
Kansas	464,520	53.7	397,727	46.0	497	.1	2,770	.3			66,793
Kentucky	541,944	58.5	369,702	39.9	12,532	1.4	649	.1	1,472	.2	172,242
Louisiana	292,802	88.8	36,697	11.1					93		256,105
Maine[2]	126,333	41.6	168,823	55.6	7,581	2.5	783	.3	720	.2	42,490
Maryland	389,612	62.4	231,435	37.0			1,629	.3	2,220	.4	158,177
Massachusetts	942,716	51.2	768,613	41.8	118,639	6.5	5,111	.3	5,278	.3	174,103
Michigan	1,016,794	56.3	699,733	38.8	75,795	4.2	8,208	.5	4,568	.3	317,061
Minnesota	698,811	61.8	350,461	31.0	74,296	6.6	2,872	.3	3,535	.3	348,350
Mississippi	157,333	97.0	4,467	2.8			342	.2			152,866
Missouri	1,111,043	60.8	697,891	38.2	14,630	.8	3,454	.2	1,617	.1	413,152
Montana	159,690	69.3	63,598	27.6	5,539	2.4	1,066	.5	609	.3	96,092
Nebraska	347,445	57.1	247,731	40.7	12,847	2.1					99,714
Nevada	31,925	72.8	11,923	27.2							20,002
New Hampshire	108,460	49.7	104,642	48.0	4,819	2.2			193	.1	3,818
New Jersey	1,083,549	59.6	719,421	39.6	9,405	.5	3,892	.2	2,860	.2	364,128
New Mexico	105,848	62.7	61,727	36.5	924	.6	343	.2	104	.1	44,121
New York	3,293,222	58.8	2,180,670	39.0			86,897	1.6	35,609	.6	1,112,552
North Carolina	616,141	73.4	223,294	26.6							392,847
North Dakota	163,148	59.6	72,751	26.6	36,708	13.4	552	.2	557	.2	90,397
Ohio	1,747,140	58.0	1,127,855	37.4	132,212	4.4			5,251	.2	619,285
Oklahoma	501,069	66.8	245,122	32.7			2,211	.3	1,328	.2	255,947
Oregon	266,733	64.4	122,706	29.6	21,831	5.3	2,143	.5	608	.2	144,027
Pennsylvania	2,353,987	56.9	1,690,200	40.8	67,478	1.6	14,599	.4	12,172	.3	663,787
Rhode Island	164,338	53.0	125,031	40.3	19,569	6.3			1,340	.4	39,307
South Carolina	113,791	98.6	1,646	1.4							112,145
South Dakota	160,137	54.0	125,977	42.5	10,338	3.5					34,160
Tennessee	328,083	68.9	146,520	30.8	296	.1	692	.2	960	.2	181,563
Texas	730,843	86.9	104,728	12.5	3,193	.4	1,067	.1	772	.1	626,115
Utah	150,248	69.3	64,555	29.8	1,121	.5	432	.2	323	.2	85,693
Vermont	62,124	43.2	81,023	56.4					542	.4	18,899
Virginia	234,980	70.2	98,336	29.4	233	.1	313	.1	728	.2	136,644
Washington	459,579	66.4	206,885	29.9	17,463	2.5	3,496	.5	4,908	.7	252,694
West Virginia	502,872	60.6	325,486	39.2			832	.1	1,173	.1	177,386
Wisconsin	802,984	63.8	380,828	30.3	60,297	4.8	10,626	.8	3,825	.3	422,156
Wyoming	62,624	60.6	38,739	37.5	1,653	1.6	200	.2	166	.2	23,885
Totals	27,747,636	60.79	16,679,543	36.54	892,492	1.96	187,785	.41	134,847	.30	

1. For breakdown of "Other" vote, see minor candidate vote totals, p. 367.
2. Figures from Petersen, op. cit., p. 94.

354

1940 Presidential Election

Total Popular Votes: 49,840,443
Roosevelt's Plurality: 4,927,188

STATE	FRANKLIN D. ROOSEVELT (Democrat)		WENDELL WILLKIE (Republican)		NORMAN M. THOMAS (Socialist)		ROGER W. BABSON (Prohibition)		OTHER[1]		PLURALITY
	Votes	%	Votes	%	Votes	%	Votes	%	Votes	%	
Alabama	250,723	85.2	42,167	14.3	100		698	.2	509	.2	208,556
Arizona	95,267	63.5	54,030	36.0			742	.5			41,237
Arkansas	157,258	78.4	42,122	21.0	301	.2	793	.4			115,136
California	1,877,618	57.4	1,351,419	41.3	16,506	.5	9,400	.3	13,848	.4	526,199
Colorado	265,364	48.4	279,022	50.9	1,899	.4	1,597	.3	378	.1	13,658
Connecticut	417,621	53.4	361,819	46.3					2,062	.3	55,802
Delaware	74,599	54.7	61,440	45.1	110	.1	187	.1			13,159
Florida	359,334	74.0	126,158	26.0							233,176
Georgia	265,194	84.8	46,495	14.9			983	.3	14		218,699
Idaho	127,842	54.4	106,509	45.3					276	.1	21,333
Illinois	2,149,934	51.0	2,047,240	48.5	10,914	.3	9,190	.2			102,694
Indiana	874,063	49.0	899,466	50.5	2,075	.1	6,437	.4	706		25,403
Iowa	578,802	47.6	632,370	52.0			2,284	.2	1,976	.2	53,568
Kansas	364,725	42.4	489,169	56.9	2,347	.3	4,056	.5			124,444
Kentucky	557,312	57.4	410,384	42.3	1,062	.1	1,465	.2			146,928
Louisiana	319,751	85.9	52,446	14.1					108		267,305
Maine	156,478	48.8	163,951	51.1					411	.1	7,473
Maryland	384,552	58.3	269,534	40.8	4,093	.6	11		1,940	.3	115,018
Massachusetts	1,076,522	53.1	939,700	46.4	4,091	.2	1,370	.1	5,310	.3	136,822
Michigan	1,032,991	49.5	1,039,917	49.9	7,593	.4	1,795	.1	3,633	.2	6,926
Minnesota	644,196	51.5	596,274	47.7	5,454	.4			5,264	.4	47,922
Mississippi	168,267	95.7	7,363	4.2	193	.1					160,904
Missouri	958,476	52.3	871,009	47.5	2,226	.1	1,809	.1	209		87,467
Montana	145,698	58.8	99,579	40.2	1,443	.6	664	.3	489	.2	46,119
Nebraska	263,677	42.8	352,201	57.2							88,524
Nevada	31,945	60.1	21,229	39.9							10,716
New Hampshire	125,292	53.2	110,127	46.8							15,165
New Jersey	1,016,404	51.5	944,876	47.9	2,823	.1	852		9,260	.5	71,528
New Mexico	103,699	56.6	79,315	43.3	143	.1	100	.1			24,384
New York	3,251,918	51.6	3,027,478	48.0	18,950	.3	3,250	.1			224,440
North Carolina	609,015	74.0	213,633	26.0							395,382
North Dakota	124,036	44.2	154,590	55.1	1,279	.5	325	.1	545	.2	30,554
Ohio	1,733,139	52.2	1,586,773	47.8							146,366
Oklahoma	474,313	57.4	348,872	42.2			3,027	.4			125,441
Oregon	258,415	53.7	219,555	45.6	398	.1	154		2,678	.6	38,860
Pennsylvania	2,171,035	53.2	1,889,848	46.3	10,967	.3			6,864	.2	281,187
Rhode Island	182,182	56.7	138,653	43.2			74		239	.1	43,529
South Carolina	95,470	95.6	4,360	4.4							91,110
South Dakota	131,362	42.6	177,065	57.4							45,703
Tennessee	351,601	67.3	169,153	32.4	463	.1	1,606	.3			182,448
Texas	861,390	80.9	201,866	19.0	628	.1	928	.1	215		659,524
Utah	153,833	62.2	92,973	37.6	198	.1			191	.1	60,860
Vermont	64,269	44.9	78,371	54.8					422	.3	14,102
Virginia	235,961	68.1	109,363	31.6	282	.1	882	.3	120		126,598
Washington	462,145	58.2	322,123	40.6	4,586	.6	1,686	.2	3,293	.4	140,022
West Virginia	495,662	57.1	372,414	42.9							123,248
Wisconsin	704,811	50.2	679,206	48.3	15,071	1.1	2,148	.2	4,263	.3	25,605
Wyoming	59,287	52.8	52,633	46.9	148	.1	172	.2			6,654
Totals	27,263,448	54.70	22,336,260	44.82	116,827	.23	58,685	.12	65,223	.13	

1. For breakdown of "Other" vote, see minor candidate vote totals, p. 367.

1944 Presidential Election

Total Popular Votes: 47,974,819
Roosevelt's Plurality: 3,598,564

STATE	FRANKLIN D. ROOSEVELT (Democrat) Votes	%	THOMAS E. DEWEY (Republican) Votes	%	NORMAN M. THOMAS (Socialist) Votes	%	CLAUDE A. WATSON (Prohibition) Votes	%	OTHER[1] Votes	%	PLURALITY
Alabama	198,904	81.3	44,478	18.2	189	.1	1,054	.4			154,426
Arizona	80,926	58.8	56,287	40.9			421	.3			24,639
Arkansas	148,965	70.0	63,556	29.8	438	.2					85,409
California	1,988,564	56.5	1,512,965	43.0	2,515	.1	14,770	.4	2,061	.1	475,599
Colorado[2]	234,331	46.4	268,731	53.2	1,977	.4					34,400
Connecticut	435,146	52.3	390,527	46.9	5,097	.6			1,220	.2	44,619
Delaware	68,166	54.4	56,747	45.3	154	.1	294	.2			11,419
Florida	339,377	70.3	143,215	29.7							196,162
Georgia	268,187	81.7	56,507	17.2	6		36		3,373	1.0	211,680
Idaho	107,399	51.6	100,137	48.1	282	.1	503	.2			7,262
Illinois	2,079,479	51.5	1,939,314	48.1	180		7,411	.2	9,677	.2	140,165
Indiana	781,403	46.7	875,891	52.4	2,223	.1	12,574	.8			94,488
Iowa	499,876	47.5	547,267	52.0	1,511	.1	3,752	.4	193		47,391
Kansas	287,458	39.2	442,096	60.3	1,613	.2	2,609	.4			154,638
Kentucky	472,589	54.5	392,448	45.2	535	.1	2,023	.2	317		80,141
Louisiana	281,564	80.6	67,750	19.4					69		213,814
Maine	140,631	47.5	155,434	52.4					335	.1	14,803
Maryland	315,983	52.0	292,150	48.0							23,833
Massachusetts	1,035,296	52.8	921,350	47.0			973	.1	3,046	.1	113,946
Michigan	1,106,899	50.2	1,084,423	49.2	4,598	.2	6,503	.3	2,800	.1	22,476
Minnesota	589,864	52.4	527,416	46.9	5,048	.5			3,176	.3	62,448
Mississippi[3]	168,621	93.6	11,613	6.4							157,008
Missouri	807,804	51.4	761,524	48.4	1,751	.1	1,195	.1	220		46,280
Montana	112,566	54.3	93,163	44.9	1,296	.6	340	.2			19,403
Nebraska	233,246	41.4	329,880	58.6							96,634
Nevada	29,623	54.6	24,611	45.4							5,012
New Hampshire	119,663	52.1	109,916	47.9	46						9,747
New Jersey	987,874	50.3	961,335	49.0	3,358	.2	4,255	.2	6,939	.4	26,539
New Mexico	81,338	53.5	70,559	46.4			147	.1			10,779
New York	3,304,238	52.3	2,987,647	47.3	10,553	.2			14,352	.2	316,591
North Carolina	527,408	66.7	263,155	33.3							264,253
North Dakota	100,144	45.5	118,535	53.8	954	.4	549	.3			18,391
Ohio	1,570,763	49.8	1,582,293	50.2							11,530
Oklahoma	401,549	55.6	319,424	44.2			1,663	.2			82,125
Oregon	248,635	51.8	225,365	46.9	3,785	.8	2,362	.5			23,270
Pennsylvania	1,940,481	51.1	1,835,054	48.4	11,721	.3	5,751	.2	1,789	.1	105,427
Rhode Island	175,356	58.6	123,487	41.3			433	.1			51,869
South Carolina	90,601	87.6	4,617	4.5			365	.4	7,799	7.5	82,802[4]
South Dakota	96,711	41.7	135,365	58.3							38,654
Tennessee	308,707	60.5	200,311	39.2	792	.2	882	.2			108,396
Texas	820,048	71.4	191,372	16.7	592	.1	1,013	.1	135,661	11.8	628,676
Utah	150,088	60.5	97,833	39.4	340	.1					52,255
Vermont	53,806	43.0	71,420	57.0					14		17,614
Virginia	242,276	62.4	145,243	37.4	417	.1	459	.1	90		97,033
Washington	486,774	56.8	361,689	42.2	3,824	.5	2,396	.3	1,645	.2	125,085
West Virginia	392,777	54.9	322,819	45.1							69,958
Wisconsin	650,413	48.6	674,532	50.4	13,205	1.0			1,002	.1	24,119
Wyoming	49,419	48.8	51,921	51.2							2,502
Totals	25,611,936	53.39	22,013,372	45.89	79,000	.16	74,733	.16	195,778	.41	

1. For breakdown of "Other" vote, see minor candidate vote totals, p. 367.
2. Figures from Richard M. Scammon, *America at the Polls*, (Pittsburgh, 1965), p. 71.
3. Ibid., p. 250.
4. Plurality of 82,802 votes is calculated on the basis of 7,799 votes cast for Southern Democratic electors.

1948 Presidential Election

Total Popular Votes: 48,692,442
Truman's Plurality: 2,135,570

STATE	HARRY S TRUMAN (Democrat)		THOMAS E. DEWEY (Republican)		J. STROM THURMOND (States' Rights Democrat)		HENRY A. WALLACE (Progressive)		OTHER[1]		PLURALITY
	Votes	%	Votes	%	Votes	%	Votes	%	Votes	%	
Alabama			40,930	19.0	171,443	79.7	1,522	.7	1,026	.5	130,513
Arizona	95,251	53.8	77,597	43.8			3,310	1.9	907	.5	17,654
Arkansas	149,659	61.7	50,959	21.0	40,068	16.5	751	.3	1,038	.4	98,700
California	1,913,134	47.6	1,895,269	47.1	1,228		190,381	4.7	21,526	.5	17,865
Colorado	267,288	51.9	239,714	46.5			6,115	1.2	2,120	.4	27,574
Connecticut	423,297	47.9	437,754	49.6			13,713	1.6	8,754	1.0	14,457
Delaware	67,813	48.8	69,588	50.0			1,050	.8	622	.5	1,775
Florida	281,988	48.8	194,280	33.6	89,755	15.5	11,620	2.0			87,708
Georgia	254,646	60.8	76,691	18.3	85,135	20.3	1,636	.4	736	.2	169,511
Idaho	107,370	50.0	101,514	47.3			4,972	2.3	960	.4	5,856
Illinois	1,994,715	50.1	1,961,103	49.2					28,228	.7	33,612
Indiana	807,833	48.8	821,079	49.6			9,649	.6	17,653	1.1	13,246
Iowa	522,380	50.3	494,018	47.6			12,125	1.2	9,749	.9	28,362
Kansas	351,902	44.6	423,039	53.6			4,603	.6	9,275	1.2	71,137
Kentucky	466,756	56.7	341,210	41.5	10,411	1.3	1,567	.2	2,714	.3	125,546
Louisiana	136,344	32.8	72,657	17.5	204,290	49.1	3,035	.7	10		67,946
Maine	111,916	42.4	150,234	56.9			1,884	.7			38,318
Maryland	286,521	47.8	294,814	49.2	2,467	.4	9,983	1.7	5,235	.9	8,293
Massachusetts	1,151,788	54.7	909,370	43.2			38,157	1.8	7,832	.4	242,418
Michigan	1,003,448	47.6	1,038,595	49.2			46,515	2.2	21,051	1.0	35,147
Minnesota	692,966	57.2	483,617	39.9			27,866	2.3	7,777	.6	209,349
Mississippi	19,384	10.1	4,995	2.5	167,538	87.2	225	.1			148,154
Missouri	917,315	58.1	655,039	41.5	42		3,998	.3	2,234	.1	262,276
Montana	119,071	53.1	96,770	43.2			7,307	3.3	1,124	.5	22,301
Nebraska	224,165	45.9	264,774	54.2							40,609
Nevada	31,290	50.4	29,357	47.3			1,469	2.4			1,933
New Hampshire	107,995	46.7	121,299	52.4	7		1,970	.9	169	.1	13,304
New Jersey	895,455	45.9	981,124	50.3			42,683	2.2	30,293	1.6	85,669
New Mexico	105,240	56.3	80,303	43.0			1,037	.6	253	.1	24,937
New York	2,780,204	45.0	2,841,163	46.0			509,559	8.3	46,283	.7	60,959
North Carolina	459,070	58.0	258,572	32.7	69,652	8.8	3,915	.5			200,498
North Dakota	95,812	43.4	115,139	52.2	374	.2	8,391	3.8	1,000	.5	19,327
Ohio	1,452,791	49.5	1,445,684	49.2			37,487	1.3			7,107
Oklahoma	452,782	62.8	268,817	37.3							183,965
Oregon	243,147	46.4	260,904	49.8			14,978	2.9	5,051	1.0	17,757
Pennsylvania	1,752,426	46.9	1,902,197	50.9			55,161	1.5	25,564	.7	149,771
Rhode Island	188,736	57.6	135,787	41.4			2,619	.8	560	.2	52,949
South Carolina	34,423	24.1	5,386	3.8	102,607	72.0	154	.1	1		68,184
South Dakota	117,653	47.0	129,651	51.8			2,801	1.1			11,998
Tennessee	270,402	49.1	202,914	36.9	73,815	13.4	1,864	.3	1,288	.2	67,488
Texas	750,700	65.4	282,240	24.6	106,909	9.3	3,764	.3	3,632	.3	468,460
Utah	149,151	54.0	124,402	45.0			2,679	1.0	74		24,749
Vermont	45,557	36.9	75,926	61.5			1,279	1.0	619	.5	30,369
Virginia	200,786	47.9	172,070	41.0	43,393	10.4	2,047	.5	960	.2	28,716
Washington	476,165	52.6	386,315	42.7			31,692	3.5	10,887	1.2	89,850
West Virginia	429,188	57.3	316,251	42.2			3,311	.4			112,937
Wisconsin	647,310	50.7	590,959	46.3			25,282	2.0	13,249	1.0	56,351
Wyoming	52,354	51.6	47,947	47.3			931	.9	193	.2	4,407
Totals	24,105,587	49.51	21,970,017	45.12	1,169,134	2.40	1,157,057	2.38	290,647	.60	

1. For breakdown of "Other" vote, see minor candidate vote totals, p. 367.

1952 Presidential Election

Total Popular Votes: 61,551,118
Eisenhower's Plurality: 6,621,485

STATE	DWIGHT D. EISENHOWER (Republican)		ADLAI E. STEVENSON (Democrat)		VINCENT HALLINAN (Progressive)		STUART HAMBLEN (Prohibition)		OTHER[1]		PLURALITY
	Votes	%	Votes	%	Votes	%	Votes	%	Votes	%	
Alabama	149,231	35.0	275,075	64.6			1,814	.4			125,844
Arizona	152,042	58.4	108,528	41.7							43,514
Arkansas	177,155	43.8	226,300	55.9			886	.2	459	.1	49,145
California	2,897,310	56.3	2,197,548	42.7	24,692	.5	16,117	.3	7,561	.2	699,762
Colorado	379,782	60.3	245,504	39.0	1,919	.3			2,898	.5	134,278
Connecticut	611,012	55.7	481,649	43.9	1,466	.1			2,779	.3	129,363
Delaware	90,059	51.8	83,315	47.9	155	.1	234	.1	262	.1	6,744
Florida	544,036	55.0	444,950	45.0							99,086
Georgia	198,961	30.3	456,823	69.7					1		257,862
Idaho	180,707	65.4	95,081	34.4	443	.2			23		85,626
Illinois	2,457,327	54.8	2,013,920	44.9					9,811	.2	443,407
Indiana	1,136,259	58.1	801,530	41.0	1,222	.1	15,335	.8	979	.1	334,729
Iowa	808,906	63.8	451,513	35.6	5,085	.4	2,882	.2	358		357,393
Kansas	616,302	68.8	273,296	30.5			6,038	.7	530	.1	343,006
Kentucky	495,029	49.8	495,729	49.9	336		1,161	.1	893	.1	700
Louisiana	306,925	47.1	345,027	52.9							38,102
Maine	232,353	66.2	118,806	33.8							113,547
Maryland	499,424	55.4	395,337	43.8	7,313	.8					104,087
Massachusetts	1,292,325	54.2	1,083,525	45.5	4,636	.2	886		2,026	.1	208,800
Michigan	1,551,529	55.4	1,230,657	44.0	3,922	.1	10,331	.4	2,153	.1	320,872
Minnesota	763,211	55.3	608,458	44.1	2,666	.2	2,147	.2	3,001	.2	154,753
Mississippi	112,966	39.6	172,553	60.4							59,587
Missouri	959,429	50.7	929,830	49.1	987	.1	885	.1	931	.1	29,599
Montana	157,394	59.4	106,213	40.1	723	.3	548	.2	159	.1	51,181
Nebraska	421,603	69.2	188,057	30.9							233,546
Nevada	50,502	61.5	31,688	38.6							18,814
New Hampshire	166,287	60.9	106,663	39.1							59,624
New Jersey	1,373,613	56.8	1,015,902	42.0	5,589	.2	989		22,461	.9	357,711
New Mexico	132,170	55.5	105,435	44.2	225	.1	297	.1	250	.1	26,735
New York	3,952,815	55.5	3,104,601	43.6	64,211	.9			6,614	.1	848,214
North Carolina	558,107	46.1	652,803	53.9							94,696
North Dakota	191,712	71.0	76,694	28.4	344	.1	302	.1	1,075	.4	115,018
Ohio	2,100,391	56.8	1,600,367	43.2							500,024
Oklahoma	518,045	54.6	430,939	45.4							87,106
Oregon	420,815	60.5	270,579	38.9	3,665	.5					150,236
Pennsylvania	2,415,789	52.7	2,146,269	46.9	4,222	.1	8,951	.2	5,738	.1	269,520
Rhode Island	210,935	50.9	203,293	49.1	187	.1			83		7,642
South Carolina	168,043	49.3	172,957	50.7			1				4,914
South Dakota	203,857	69.3	90,426	30.7							113,431
Tennessee	446,147	50.0	443,710	49.7	887	.1	1,432	.2	379		2,437
Texas	1,102,818	53.1	969,227	46.7	294		1,983	.1	1,563	.1	133,591
Utah	194,190	58.9	135,364	41.1							58,826
Vermont	109,717	71.5	43,299	28.2	282	.2			203	.1	66,418
Virginia	349,037	56.3	268,677	43.4	311	.1			1,664	.3	80,360
Washington	599,107	54.3	492,845	44.7	2,460	.2			8,296	.8	106,262
West Virginia	419,970	48.1	453,578	51.9							33,608
Wisconsin	979,744	61.0	622,175	38.7	2,174	.1			3,277	.2	357,569
Wyoming	81,049	62.7	47,934	37.1			194	.2	76	.1	33,115
Totals	33,936,137	55.13	27,314,649	44.38	140,416	.23	73,413	.12	86,503	.14	

1. For breakdown of "Other" vote, see minor candidate vote totals, p. 367.

1956 Presidential Election

Total Popular Votes: 62,025,372
Eisenhower's Plurality: 9,555,073

STATE	DWIGHT D. EISENHOWER (Republican)		ADLAI E. STEVENSON (Democrat)		T. COLEMAN ANDREWS (Constitution)		ERIC HASS (Socialist-Labor)		OTHER[1]		PLURALITY
	Votes	%	Votes	%	Votes	%	Votes	%	Votes	%	
Alabama	195,694	39.5	279,542	56.4					20,333	4.1	83,848
Arizona	176,990	61.0	112,880	38.9	303	.1					64,110
Arkansas	186,287	45.8	213,277	52.5	7,008	1.7					26,990
California	3,027,668	55.4	2,420,135	44.3	6,087	.1	300		12,168	.2	607,533
Colorado	394,479	59.5	263,997	39.8	759	.1	3,308	.5	531	.1	130,482
Connecticut	711,837	63.7	405,079	36.3							306,758
Delaware	98,057	55.1	79,421	44.6			110	.1	400	.2	18,636
Florida	643,849	57.2	480,371	42.7					1,542	.1	163,478
Georgia	222,778	33.3	444,688	66.4					2,189	.3	221,910
Idaho	166,979	61.2	105,868	38.8	126	.1			16		61,111
Illinois	2,623,327	59.5	1,775,682	40.3			8,342	.2	56		847,645
Indiana	1,182,811	59.9	783,908	39.7			1,334	.1	6,554	.3	398,903
Iowa	729,187	59.1	501,858	40.7	3,202	.3	125		192		227,329
Kansas	566,878	65.4	296,317	34.2					3,048	.4	270,561
Kentucky[2]	572,192	54.3	476,453	45.2			358		4,802	.5	95,739
Louisiana	329,047	53.3	243,977	39.5					44,520	7.2	85,070
Maine	249,238	70.9	102,468	29.1							146,770
Maryland	559,738	60.0	372,613	40.0							187,125
Massachusetts	1,393,197	59.3	948,190	40.4			5,573	.2	1,546	.1	445,007
Michigan	1,713,647	55.6	1,359,898	44.2					6,923	.2	353,749
Minnesota	719,302	53.7	617,525	46.1			2,080	.2	1,098	.1	101,777
Mississippi	60,683	24.5	144,453	58.2					42,961	17.3	83,770
Missouri	914,289	49.9	918,273	50.1							3,984
Montana	154,933	57.1	116,238	42.9							38,695
Nebraska	378,108	65.5	199,029	34.5							179,079
Nevada	56,049	58.0	40,640	42.0							15,409
New Hampshire	176,519	66.1	90,364	33.8	111						86,155
New Jersey	1,606,942	64.7	850,337	34.2	5,317	.2	6,736	.3	14,980	.6	756,605
New Mexico	146,788	57.8	106,098	41.8	364	.1	69		607	.2	40,690
New York	4,340,340	61.2	2,750,769	38.8							1,589,571
North Carolina	575,069	49.3	590,530	50.7							15,461
North Dakota	156,766	61.7	96,742	38.1	483	.2					60,024
Ohio	2,262,610	61.1	1,439,655	38.9							822,955
Oklahoma	473,769	55.1	385,581	44.9							88,188
Oregon	406,393	55.3	329,204	44.8							77,189
Pennsylvania	2,585,252	56.5	1,981,769	43.3			7,447	.2	2,035		603,483
Rhode Island	225,819	58.3	161,790	41.7							64,029
South Carolina	75,634	25.2	136,278	45.4	2				88,509	29.5	47,769[3]
South Dakota	171,569	58.4	122,288	41.6							49,281
Tennessee	462,288	49.2	456,507	48.6	19,820	2.1			789	.1	5,781
Texas	1,080,619	55.3	859,958	44.0	14,591	.8					220,661
Utah	215,631	64.6	118,364	35.4							97,267
Vermont	110,390	72.2	42,540	27.8					39		67,850
Virginia	386,459	55.4	267,760	38.4	42,964	6.2	351	.1	444	.1	118,699
Washington	620,430	53.9	523,002	45.4			7,457	.7			97,428
West Virginia	449,297	54.1	381,534	45.9							67,763
Wisconsin	954,844	61.6	586,768	37.8	6,918	.5	710	.1	1,318	.1	368,076
Wyoming	74,573	60.1	49,554	39.9							25,019
Totals	35,585,245	57.37	26,030,172	41.97	108,055	.17	44,300	.07	257,600	.42	

1. For breakdown of "Other" vote, see minor candidate vote totals, p. 367.
2. Figures from Petersen, op. cit., p. 109.
3. Plurality of 47,769 votes is calculated on the basis of Stevenson's vote and the 88,509 votes cast for unpledged electors.

1960 Presidential Election

Total Popular Votes: 68,828,960
Kennedy's Plurality: 114,673

STATE	JOHN F. KENNEDY (Democrat) Votes	%	RICHARD M. NIXON (Republican) Votes	%	ERIC HASS (Socialist-Labor) Votes	%	UNPLEDGED Votes	%	OTHER[1] Votes	%	PLURALITY
Alabama	318,303	56.8	236,110	42.1					6,083	1.1	82,193
Alaska	29,809	49.1	30,953	50.9							1,144
Arizona	176,781	44.4	221,241	55.5	469	.1					44,460
Arkansas[2]	215,049	50.2	184,508	43.1					28,952	6.8	30,541
California	3,224,099	49.6	3,259,722	50.1	1,051				21,706	.3	35,623
Colorado	330,629	44.9	402,242	54.6	2,803	.4			563	.1	71,613
Connecticut	657,055	53.7	565,813	46.3							91,242
Delaware	99,590	50.6	96,373	49.0	82				638	.3	3,217
Florida	748,700	48.5	795,476	51.5							46,776
Georgia	458,638	62.5	274,472	37.4					245		184,166
Hawaii	92,410	50.0	92,295	50.0							115
Idaho	138,853	46.2	161,597	53.8							22,744
Illinois	2,377,846	50.0	2,368,988	49.8	10,560	.2			15		8,858
Indiana	952,358	44.6	1,175,120	55.0	1,136	.1			6,746	.3	222,762
Iowa	550,565	43.2	722,381	56.7	230				634	.1	171,816
Kansas	363,213	39.1	561,474	60.5					4,138	.5	198,261
Kentucky	521,855	46.4	602,607	53.6							80,752
Louisiana	407,339	50.4	230,980	28.6					169,572	21.0	176,359
Maine	181,159	43.0	240,608	57.1							59,449
Maryland	565,808	53.6	489,538	46.4					3		76,270
Massachusetts	1,487,174	60.2	976,750	39.6	3,892	.2			1,664	.1	510,424
Michigan	1,687,269	50.9	1,620,428	48.8	1,718	.1			8,682	.3	66,841
Minnesota	779,933	50.6	757,915	49.2	962	.1			3,077	.2	22,018
Mississippi	108,362	36.3	73,561	24.7			116,248[3]	39.0			7,886
Missouri	972,201	50.3	962,218	49.7							9,983
Montana	134,891	48.6	141,841	51.1					847	.3	6,950
Nebraska	232,542	37.9	380,553	62.1							148,011
Nevada	54,880	51.2	52,387	48.8							2,493
New Hampshire	137,772	46.6	157,989	53.4							20,217
New Jersey	1,385,415	50.0	1,363,324	49.2	4,262	.2			20,110	.7	22,091
New Mexico	156,027	50.2	153,733	49.4	570	.2			777	.3	2,294
New York	3,830,085	52.5	3,446,419	47.3					14,319	.2	383,666
North Carolina	713,136	52.1	655,420	47.9							57,716
North Dakota	123,963	44.5	154,310	55.4					158	.1	30,347
Ohio	1,944,248	46.7	2,217,611	53.3							273,363
Oklahoma	370,111	41.0	533,039	59.0							162,928
Oregon	367,402	47.3	408,065	52.6					959	.1	40,663
Pennsylvania	2,556,282	51.1	2,439,956	48.7	7,185	.1			3,118	.1	116,326
Rhode Island	258,032	63.6	147,502	36.4							110,530
South Carolina	198,121	51.2	188,558	48.8					1		9,563
South Dakota	128,070	41.8	178,417	58.2							50,347
Tennessee	481,453	45.8	556,577	52.9					13,746	1.3	75,124
Texas	1,167,935	50.5	1,121,693	48.5					22,213	1.0	46,242
Utah	169,248	45.2	205,361	54.8					100		36,113
Vermont	69,186	41.4	98,131	58.7					7		28,945
Virginia	362,327	47.0	404,521	52.4	397	.1			4,204	.5	42,194
Washington	599,298	48.3	629,273	50.7	10,895	.9			2,106	.2	29,975
West Virginia	441,786	52.7	395,995	47.3							45,791
Wisconsin	830,805	48.1	895,175	51.8	1,310	.1			1,792	.1	64,370
Wyoming	63,331	45.0	77,451	55.0							14,120
Totals	34,221,344	49.72	34,106,671	49.55	47,522	.07	116,248	.17	337,175	.48	

1. For breakdown of "Other" vote, see minor candidate vote totals, p. 367.
2. Figures from Petersen, op. cit., p. 113.
3. Votes for unpledged electors who cast electoral votes for Harry F. Byrd (D Va.), which carried the state.

1964 Presidential Election

Total Popular Votes: 70,641,104
Johnson's Plurality: 15,948,746

STATE	LYNDON B. JOHNSON (Democrat)		BARRY M. GOLDWATER (Republican)		ERIC HASS (Socialist-Labor)		CLIFTON DEBERRY (Socialist Workers)		OTHER[1]		PLURALITY
	Votes	%	Votes	%	Votes	%	Votes	%	Votes	%	
Alabama			479,085	69.5 ς					210,733	30.6	268,353[3]
Alaska	44,329	65.9	22,930	34.1							21,399
Arizona	237,753	49.5	242,535	50.5	482	.1					4,782
Arkansas	314,197	56.1	243,264	43.4					2,965	.5	70,933
California	4,171,877	59.1	2,879,108	40.8	489		378		5,725	.1	1,292,769
Colorado	476,024	61.3	296,767	38.2	302		2,537	.3	1,355	.2	179,257
Connecticut	826,269	67.8	390,996	32.1					1,313	.1	435,273
Delaware	122,704	61.0	78,078	38.8	113	.1			425	.2	44,626
D.C.[2]	169,796	85.5	28,801	14.5							140,995
Florida	948,540	51.2	905,941	48.9 ς							42,599
Georgia	522,163	45.9	616,584	54.1					195		94,421
Hawaii	163,249	78.8	44,022	21.2							119,227
Idaho	148,920	50.9	143,557	49.1							5,363
Illinois	2,796,833	59.5	1,905,946	40.5					62		890,887
Indiana	1,170,848	56.0	911,118	43.6	1,374	.1			8,266	.4	259,730
Iowa	733,030	61.9	449,148	37.9	182		159		2,020	.2	283,882
Kansas	464,028	54.1	386,579	45.1	1,901	.2			5,393	.6	77,449
Kentucky	669,659	64.0	372,977	35.7					3,469	.3	296,682
Louisiana	387,068	43.2	509,225	56.8							122,157
Maine	262,264	68.8	118,701	31.2							143,563
Maryland	730,912	65.5	385,495	34.5							345,417
Massachusetts	1,786,422	76.2	549,727	23.4	4,755	.2			3,894	.2	1,236,695
Michigan	2,136,615	66.7	1,060,152	33.1	1,704	.1	3,817	.1	814		1,076,463
Minnesota	991,117	63.8	559,624	36.0	2,544	.2	1,177	.1			431,493
Mississippi	52,616	12.9	356,512	87.1							303,896
Missouri	1,164,344	64.1	653,535	36.0							510,809
Montana	164,246	59.0	113,032	40.6			332	.1	1,018	.4	51,214
Nebraska	307,307	52.6	276,847	47.4							30,460
Nevada	79,339	58.6	56,094	41.4							23,245
New Hampshire	182,065	63.6	104,029	36.4							78,036
New Jersey	1,867,671	65.6	963,843	33.9	7,075	.3	8,181	.3			903,828
New Mexico	194,015	59.0	132,838	40.4	1,217	.4			543	.2	61,177
New York	4,913,156	68.6	2,243,559	31.3	6,086	.1	3,211		268		2,669,597
North Carolina	800,139	56.2	624,841	43.9							175,298
North Dakota	149,784	58.0	108,207	41.9			224	.1	174	.1	41,577
Ohio	2,498,331	62.9	1,470,865	37.1							1,027,466
Oklahoma	519,834	55.8	412,665	44.3							107,169
Oregon	501,017	63.7	282,779	36.0					2,509	.3	218,238
Pennsylvania	3,130,954	64.9	1,673,657	34.7	5,092	.1	10,456	.2	2,531	.1	1,457,297
Rhode Island	315,463	80.9	74,615	19.1							240,848
South Carolina	215,723	41.1	309,048	58.9					8		93,325
South Dakota	163,010	55.6	130,108	44.4							32,902
Tennessee	635,047	55.5	508,965	44.5					34		126,082
Texas	1,663,185	63.3	958,566	36.5					5,060	.2	704,619
Utah	219,628	54.7	181,785	45.3							37,843
Vermont	108,127	66.3	54,942	33.7					20		53,185
Virginia	558,038	53.5	481,334	46.2	2,895	.3					76,704
Washington	779,699	62.0	470,366	37.4	7,772	.6	537				309,333
West Virginia	538,087	67.9	253,953	32.1							284,134
Wisconsin	1,050,424	62.1	638,495	37.7	1,204	.1	1,692	.1			411,929
Wyoming	80,718	56.6	61,998	43.4							18,720
Totals	**43,126,584**	**61.05**	**27,177,838**	**38.47**	**45,187**	**.06**	**32,701**	**.05**	**258,794**	**.37**	

1. For breakdown of "Other" vote, see minor candidate vote totals, p. 367.
2. Figures from Richard M. Scammon, *America at the Polls*, (Pittsburgh, 1965), p. 521.
3. Plurality of 268,353 votes is calculated on the basis of Goldwater's vote and the 210,732 votes cast for unpledged Democrats.

1968 Presidential Election

Total Popular Votes: 73,203,370
Nixon's Plurality: 510,645

STATE	RICHARD M. NIXON (Republican)		HUBERT H. HUMPHREY (Democrat)		GEORGE C. WALLACE (American Independent)		HENNING A. BLOMEN (Socialist Labor)		OTHER[1]		PLURALITY
	Votes	%	Votes	%	Votes	%	Votes	%	Votes	%	
Alabama	146,591	14.0	195,918	18.8	687,664	65.8			14,332	1.4	491,746
Alaska	37,600	45.3	35,411	42.7	10,024	12.1					2,189
Arizona	266,721	54.8	170,514	35.0	46,573	9.6	75		3,053	.6	96,207
Arkansas[2]	190,759	30.8	188,228	30.4	240,982	38.9					50,223
California	3,467,664	47.8	3,244,318	44.7	487,270	6.7	341		51,994	.7	223,346
Colorado	409,345	50.5	335,174	41.3	60,813	7.5	3,016	.4	2,851	.3	74,171
Connecticut	556,721	44.3	621,561	49.5	76,650	6.1			1,300	.1	64,840
Delaware	96,714	45.1	89,194	41.6	28,459	13.3					7,520
D.C.[3]	31,012	18.2	139,566	81.8							108,554
Florida	886,804	40.5	676,794	30.9	624,207	28.5					210,010
Georgia	380,111	30.4	334,440	26.8	535,550	42.8			173		155,439
Hawaii	91,425	38.7	141,324	59.8	3,469	1.5					49,899
Idaho	165,369	56.8	89,273	30.7	36,541	12.6					76,096
Illinois	2,174,774	47.1	2,039,814	44.2	390,958	8.5	13,878	.3	325		134,960
Indiana	1,067,885	50.3	806,659	38.0	243,108	11.5			5,909	.3	261,226
Iowa	619,106	53.0	476,699	40.8	66,422	5.7	241		5,463	.5	142,407
Kansas	478,674	54.8	302,996	34.7	88,921	10.2			2,192	.3	175,678
Kentucky	462,411	43.8	397,541	37.7	193,098	18.3			2,843	.3	64,870
Louisiana	257,535	23.5	309,615	28.2	530,300	48.3					220,685
Maine	169,254	43.1	217,312	55.3	6,370	1.6					48,058
Maryland	517,995	41.9	538,310	43.6	178,734	14.5					20,315
Massachusetts	766,844	32.9	1,469,218	63.0	87,088	3.7	6,180	.3	2,422	.1	702,374
Michigan	1,370,665	41.5	1,593,082	48.2	331,968	10.0	1,762	.1	8,773	.3	222,417
Minnesota	658,643	41.5	857,738	54.0	68,931	4.3	285		2,909	.2	199,095
Mississippi	88,516	13.5	150,644	23.0	415,349	63.5					264,705
Missouri	811,932	44.9	791,444	43.7	206,126	11.4					20,488
Montana	138,835	50.6	114,117	41.6	20,015	7.3			1,437	.5	24,718
Nebraska	321,163	59.8	170,784	31.8	44,904	8.4					150,379
Nevada	73,188	47.5	60,598	39.3	20,432	13.3					12,590
New Hampshire	154,903	52.1	130,589	43.9	11,173	3.8			633	.2	24,314
New Jersey	1,325,467	46.1	1,264,206	44.0	262,187	9.1	6,784	.2	16,751	.6	61,261
New Mexico	169,692	51.9	130,081	39.8	25,737	7.9			1,771	.5	39,611
New York	3,007,932	44.3	3,378,470	49.8	358,864	5.3	8,432	.1	36,368	.5	370,538
North Carolina	627,192	39.5	464,113	29.2	496,188	31.3					131,004
North Dakota	138,669	55.9	94,769	38.2	14,244	5.8			200	.1	43,900
Ohio	1,791,014	45.2	1,700,586	43.0	467,495	11.8	120		483		90,428
Oklahoma	449,697	47.7	301,658	32.0	191,731	20.3					148,039
Oregon	408,433	49.8	358,866	43.8	49,683	6.1			2,640	.3	49,567
Pennsylvania	2,090,017	44.0	2,259,403	47.6	378,582	8.0	4,977	.1	14,947	.3	169,386
Rhode Island	122,359	31.8	246,518	64.0	15,678	4.1			383		124,159
South Carolina	254,062	38.1	197,486	29.6	215,430	32.3					38,632
South Dakota	149,841	53.3	118,023	42.0	13,400	4.8					31,818
Tennessee	472,592	37.9	351,233	28.1	424,792	34.0					47,800
Texas	1,227,844	39.9	1,266,804	41.1	584,269	19.0			489		38,960
Utah	238,728	56.5	156,665	37.1	26,906	6.4			269	.1	82,063
Vermont	85,142	52.8	70,255	43.5	5,104	3.2			903	.6	14,887
Virginia	590,319	43.4	442,387	32.5	320,272	23.6	4,671	.3	2,281	.2	147,932
Washington	588,510	45.2	616,037	47.3	96,990	7.4	491		2,319	.2	27,527
West Virginia	307,555	40.8	374,091	49.6	72,560	9.6					66,536
Wisconsin	809,997	47.9	748,804	44.3	127,835	7.6	1,338	.1	3,564	.2	61,193
Wyoming	70,927	55.8	45,173	35.5	11,105	8.7					25,754
Totals	31,785,148	43.42	31,274,503	42.72	9,901,151	13.53	52,591	.07	189,977	.26	

1. For breakdown of "Other" vote, see minor candidate vote totals, p. 367.
2. Figures from Richard M. Scammon, *America Votes 8*, (Washington, 1970), p. 26.
3. *Ibid.*, p. 433.

1972 Presidential Election

Total Popular Vote: 77,727,590
Reagan's Plurality: 17,998,388

STATE	RICHARD M. NIXON (Republican)		GEORGE S. McGOVERN (Democrat)		JOHN G. SCHMITZ (American)		BENJAMIN SPOCK (People's)		OTHER [1]		PLURALITY
	Votes	%	Votes	%	Votes	%	Votes	%	Votes	%	
Alabama[2]	654,192	48.8	636,730	47.5	16,481	1.2	13,318	1.0	21,208	1.6	471,778
Alaska	55,349	58.1	32,967	34.6	6,903	7.3					22,382
Arizona	402,812	61.6	198,540	30.4	21,208	3.3			30,945	4.7	204,272
Arkansas	448,541	68.9	199,892	30.7	2,887	.4					248,649
California	4,602,096	55.0	3,475,847	41.5	232,554	2.8	55,167	.7	2,198		1,126,249
Colorado	597,189	62.6	329,980	34.6	17,269	1.8	2,403	.3	7,043	.8	267,209
Connecticut	810,763	58.6	555,498	40.1	17,239	1.3			777	.1	255,265
Delaware	140,357	59.6	92,283	39.2	2,638	1.1			238	.1	48,074
D.C.[3]	35,226	21.6	127,627	78.1					568	.3	92,401
Florida	1,857,759	71.9	718,117	27.8					7,407	.3	1,139,642
Georgia	881,490	75.3	289,529	24.7							591,961
Hawaii	168,933	62.5	101,433	37.5							67,500
Idaho	199,384	64.2	80,826	26.0	28,869	9.3	903	.3	397	.1	118,558
Illinois	2,788,179	59.0	1,913,472	40.5	2,471	.1			19,114	.4	874,707
Indiana	1,405,154	66.1	708,568	33.3			4,544	.2	7,263	.3	696,586
Iowa	706,207	57.6	496,206	40.5	22,056	1.8			1,475	.1	210,001
Kansas	619,812	67.7	270,287	29.5	21,808	2.4			4,188	.5	349,525
Kentucky	676,446	63.4	371,159	34.8	17,627	1.7	1,118	.1	1,149	.1	305,287
Louisiana[4]	686,852	66.0	298,142	28.6	44,127	4.2			12,169	1.2	388,710
Maine	256,458	61.5	160,584	38.5							95,874
Maryland	829,305	61.3	505,781	37.4	18,726	1.4					323,524
Massachusetts	1,112,078	45.2	1,332,540	54.2	1,877	.1	101		11,160	.5	220,462
Michigan	1,961,721	56.2	1,459,435	41.8	63,321	1.8			5,848	.2	502,286
Minnesota	898,269	51.6	802,346	46.1	31,407	1.8	2,805	.2	6,825	.4	95,923
Mississippi	505,125	78.2	126,782	19.6	11,598	1.8			2,458	.4	378,343
Missouri	1,154,058	62.3	698,531	37.7							455,527
Montana	183,976	57.9	120,197	37.9	13,430	4.2					63,779
Nebraska	406,298	70.5	169,991	29.5							236,307
Nevada	115,750	63.7	66,016	36.3							49,734
New Hampshire	213,724	64.0	116,435	34.9	3,386	1.0			510	0.2	97,289
New Jersey	1,845,502	61.6	1,102,211	36.8	34,378	1.2	5,355	.2	9,783	.3	743,291
New Mexico	235,606	61.1	141,084	36.6	8,767	2.3			474	.1	94,522
New York	4,192,778	57.3	2,951,084	40.3					17,968	.3	1,241,694
North Carolina	1,054,889	69.5	438,705	28.9	25,018	1.7					616,184
North Dakota	174,109	62.1	100,384	35.8	5,646	2.0			375	.1	73,725
Ohio	2,441,827	59.6	1,558,889	38.1	80,067	2.0			14,004	.3	882,938
Oklahoma	759,025	73.7	247,147	24.0	23,728	2.3					511,878
Oregon	486,686	52.5	392,760	42.3	46,211	5.0			2,289	.3	93,926
Pennsylvania	2,714,521	59.1	1,796,951	39.1	70,593	1.5			10,040	.2	917,570
Rhode Island	220,383	53.0	194,645	46.8					729	.2	25,738
South Carolina	477,044	70.8	186,824	27.7	10,075	1.5			17		290,220
South Dakota	166,476	54.2	139,945	45.5					994	.3	26,531
Tennessee	813,147	67.7	357,293	29.8	30,373	2.5			369		455,854
Texas	2,298,896	66.2	1,154,289	33.3	6,039	.2			12,057	.4	1,144,607
Utah	323,643	67.6	126,284	26.4	28,549	6.0					197,359
Vermont	117,149	62.9	68,174	36.6	1		1,010	.5			48,975
Virginia	988,493	67.8	438,887	30.1	19,721	1.4			9,918	.7	549,606
Washington	837,135	56.9	568,334	38.6	58,906	4.0	2,644	.2	3,828	.3	268,801
West Virginia	484,964	63.6	277,435	36.4							207,529
Wisconsin	989,430	53.4	810,174	43.7	47,525	2.6	2,701	.2	3,060	.1	179,256
Wyoming	100,464	69.0	44,358	30.5	748	.5					56,106
Totals	**47,170,179**	**60.69**	**29,171,791**	**37.53**	**1,090,673**	**1.40**	**78,751**	**.10**	**216,198**	**.28**	

1. For breakdown of "Other" vote, see minor candidate vote totals, p. 367.
2. Figures from Richard M. Scammon, *America Votes 10* (Washington, 1973), p. 25.
3. *Ibid.*, p. 415.
4. *Ibid.*, p. 156.

1976 Presidential Election

Total Popular Vote: 81,555,889
Carter's Plurality: 1,682,970

STATE	JIMMY CARTER (Democrat)		GERALD R. FORD (Republican)		EUGENE J. McCARTHY (Independent)		ROGER MacBRIDE (Libertarian)		OTHER [1]		PLURALITY
	Votes	%	Votes	%	Votes	%	Votes	%	Votes	%	
Alabama	659,170	55.7	504,070	42.6	99[2]	—	1,481	0.1	18,030	1.5	155,100
Alaska	44,058	35.7	71,555	57.9			6,785	5.5	1,176	1.0	27,497
Arizona	295,602	39.8	418,642	56.4	19,229	2.6	7,647	1.0	1,599	0.2	123,040
Arkansas	498,604	65.0	267,903	34.9	639[2]	0.1			389	0.1	230,701
California	3,742,284	47.6	3,882,244	49.3	58,412[2]	0.7	56,388	0.7	127,789	1.6	139,960
Colorado	460,353	42.6	584,367	54.0	26,107	2.4	5,330	0.5	5,397	0.5	124,014
Connecticut	647,895	46.9	719,261	52.1	3,759[3]	0.3	209[3]	—	10,402	0.8	71,366
Delaware	122,596	52.0	109,831	46.6	2,437	1.0			970	0.4	12,765
D.C.	137,818	81.6	27,873	16.5			274	0.2	2,865	1.7	109,945
Florida	1,636,000	51.9	1,469,531	46.6	23,643	0.8	103[2]	—	21,354	0.7	166,469
Georgia	979,409	66.7	483,743	33.0	991[3]	0.1	175[3]	—	3,140	0.2	495,666
Hawaii	147,375	50.6	140,003	48.1			3,923	1.3			7,372
Idaho	126,549	36.8	204,151	59.3	1,194[2]	0.3	3,558	1.0	8,619	2.5	77,602
Illinois	2,271,295	48.1	2,364,269	50.1	55,939	1.2	8,057	0.2	19,354	0.4	92,974
Indiana	1,014,714	45.7	1,183,958	53.3					21,690	1.0	169,244
Iowa	619,931	48.5	632,863	49.5	20,051	1.6	1,452	0.1	5,009	0.4	12,932
Kansas	430,421	44.9	502,752	52.5	13,185	1.4	3,242	0.3	8,245	0.9	72,331
Kentucky	615,717	52.8	531,852	45.6	6,837	0.6	814	0.1	11,922	1.0	83,865
Louisiana	661,365	51.7	587,446	46.0	6,588	0.5	3,325	0.3	19,715	1.5	73,919
Maine	232,279	48.1	236,320	48.9	10,874	2.3	11[2]	—	3,732	0.8	4,041
Maryland	759,612	52.8	672,661	46.7	4,541[2]	0.3	255[2]	—	2,828	0.2	86,951
Massachusetts	1,429,475	56.1	1,030,276	40.4	65,637	2.6	135[2]	—	22,035	0.9	399,199
Michigan	1,696,714	46.4	1,893,742	51.8	47,905	1.3	5,406	0.1	9,982	0.3	197,028
Minnesota	1,070,440	54.9	819,395	42.0	35,490	1.8	3,529	0.2	21,077	1.1	251,045
Mississippi	381,309	49.6	366,846	47.7	4,074	0.5	2,788	0.4	14,344	1.9	14,463
Missouri	998,387	51.1	927,443	47.5	24,029	1.2			3,741	0.2	70,944
Montana	149,259	45.4	173,703	52.8					5,772	1.8	24,444
Nebraska	233,692	38.5	359,705	59.2	9,409	1.5	1,482	0.2	3,380	0.6	126,013
Nevada	92,479	45.8	101,273	50.2			1,519	0.8	6,605	3.3	8,794
New Hampshire	147,635	43.5	185,935	54.7	4,095	1.2	936	0.3	1,017	0.3	38,300
New Jersey	1,444,653	47.9	1,509,688	50.1	32,717	1.1	9,449	0.3	17,965	0.6	65,035
New Mexico	201,148	48.1	211,419	50.5	1,161[3]	0.3	1,110	0.3	3,571	0.9	10,271
New York	3,389,558	51.9	3,100,791	47.5	4,303[3]	0.1	12,197	0.2	27,321	0.4	288,767
North Carolina	927,365	55.2	741,960	44.2	780[2]	—	2,219	0.1	6,590	0.4	185,405
North Dakota	136,078	45.8	153,470	51.6	2,952	1.0	253	0.1	4,435	1.5	17,392
Ohio	2,011,621	48.9	2,000,505	48.7	58,258	1.4	8,961	0.2	32,528	0.8	11,116
Oklahoma	532,442	48.7	545,708	50.0	14,101	1.3					13,266
Oregon	490,407	47.6	492,120	47.8	40,207	3.9			7,142	0.7	1,713
Pennsylvania	2,328,677	50.4	2,205,604	47.7	50,584	1.1			35,922	0.8	123,073
Rhode Island	227,636	55.4	181,249	44.1	479[2]	0.1	715	0.2	1,091	0.3	46,387
South Carolina	450,807	56.2	346,149	43.1	289[2]	—	53[2]	—	5,285	0.7	104,658
South Dakota	147,068	48.9	151,505	50.4			1,619	0.5	486	0.2	4,437
Tennessee	825,879	55.9	633,969	42.9	5,004	0.3	1,375	0.1	10,118	0.7	191,910
Texas	2,082,319	51.1	1,953,300	48.0	20,118	0.5	189[3]	—	15,958	0.4	129,019
Utah	182,110	33.6	337,908	62.4	3,907	0.7	2,438	0.5	14,835	2.7	155,798
Vermont	80,954	43.1	102,085	54.4	4,001	2.1			725	0.4	21,131
Virginia	813,896	48.0	836,554	49.3			4,648	0.3	41,996	2.5	22,658
Washington	717,323	46.1	777,732	50.0	36,986	2.4	5,042	0.3	18,451	1.2	60,409
West Virginia	435,914	58.0	314,760	41.9	113[3]	—	16[3]	—	161	—	121,154
Wisconsin	1,040,232	49.4	1,004,987	47.8	34,943	1.7	3,814	0.2	20,199	1.0	35,245
Wyoming	62,239	39.8	92,717	59.3	624[2]	0.4	89[2]	0.1	674	0.4	30,478
Totals	40,830,763	50.1	39,147,793	48.0	756,691	0.9	173,011	0.2	647,631	0.8	

1. For breakdown of "Other" vote, see minor candidate vote totals, p. 367.
2. Write-in vote.
3. Write-in vote was not tabulated. Figures from Richard M. Scammon and Alice V. McGillivray, America Votes 14 (Washington, 1981).

1980 Presidential Election

Total Popular Vote: 86,515,221
Reagan's Plurality: 8,420,270

STATE	RONALD REAGAN (Republican)		JIMMY CARTER (Democrat)		JOHN B. ANDERSON (Independent)		ED CLARK (Libertarian)		OTHER		PLURALITY
	Votes	%	Votes	%	Votes	%	Votes	%	Votes	%	
Alabama	654,192	48.8	636,730	47.5	16,481	1.2	13,318	1.0	21,208	1.6	17,462
Alaska	86,112	54.3	41,842	26.4	11,155	7.0	18,479	11.7	857	0.5	44,270
Arizona	529,688	60.6	246,843	28.2	76,952	8.8	18,784	2.2	1,678	0.2	282,845
Arkansas	403,164	48.1	398,041	47.5	22,468	2.7	8,970	1.1	4,939	0.6	5,123
California	4,524,858	52.7	3,083,661	35.9	739,833	8.6	148,434	1.7	90,277	1.1	1,441,197
Colorado	652,264	55.1	367,973	31.1	130,633	11.0	25,744	2.2	7,801	0.7	284,291
Connecticut	677,210	48.2	541,732	38.5	171,807	12.2	8,570	0.6	6,966	0.5	135,478
Delaware	111,252	47.2	105,754	44.8	16,288	6.9	1,974	0.8	632	0.3	5,498
D.C.	23,545	13.4	131,113	74.8	16,337	9.3	1,114	0.6	3,128	1.8	107,568
Florida	2,046,951	55.5	1,419,475	38.5	189,692	5.1	30,524	0.8	288	0.0	627,476
Georgia	654,168	41.0	890,733	55.8	36,055	2.3	15,627	1.0	112	0.0	236,565
Hawaii	130,112	42.9	135,879	44.8	32,021	10.6	3,269	1.1	2,006	0.7	5,767
Idaho	290,699	66.5	110,192	25.2	27,058	6.2	8,425	1.9	1,057	0.2	180,507
Illinois	2,358,049	49.6	1,981,413	41.7	346,754	7.3	38,939	0.8	24,566	0.5	376,636
Indiana	1,255,656	56.0	844,197	37.7	111,639	5.0	19,627	0.9	10,914	0.5	411,459
Iowa	676,026	51.3	508,672	38.6	115,633	8.8	13,123	1.0	4,207	0.3	167,354
Kansas	566,812	57.9	326,150	33.3	68,231	7.0	14,470	1.5	4,132	0.4	240,662
Kentucky	635,274	49.1	616,417	47.6	31,127	2.4	5,531	0.4	6,278	0.5	18,857
Louisiana	792,853	51.2	708,453	45.7	26,345	1.7	8,240	0.5	12,700	0.8	84,400
Maine	238,522	45.6	220,974	42.3	53,327	10.2	5,119	1.0	5,069	1.0	17,548
Maryland	680,606	44.2	726,161	47.1	119,537	7.8	14,192	0.9			45,555
Massachusetts	1,057,631	41.9	1,053,802	41.7	382,539	15.2	22,038	0.9	8,288	0.3	3,829
Michigan	1,915,225	49.0	1,661,532	42.5	275,223	7.0	41,597	1.1	16,148	0.4	253,693
Minnesota	873,268	42.6	954,174	46.5	174,990	8.5	31,592	1.5	17,956	0.9	80,906
Mississippi	441,089	49.4	429,281	48.1	12,036	1.3	5,465	0.6	4,749	0.5	11,808
Missouri	1,074,181	51.2	931,182	44.3	77,920	3.7	14,422	0.7	2,119	0.1	142,999
Montana	206,814	56.8	118,032	32.4	29,281	8.0	9,825	2.7			88,782
Nebraska	419,937	65.9	166,851	26.0	44,993	7.0	9,073	1.4			253,086
Nevada	155,017	62.5	66,666	26.9	17,651	7.1	4,358	1.8	4,193	1.7	88,351
New Hampshire	221,705	57.7	108,864	28.4	49,693	12.9	2,064	0.5	1,664	0.4	112,841
New Jersey	1,546,557	52.0	1,147,364	38.6	234,632	7.9	20,652	0.7	26,479	0.9	399,193
New Mexico	250,779	54.9	167,826	36.7	29,459	6.5	4,365	1.0	4,542	1.0	82,953
New York	2,893,831	46.7	2,728,372	44.0	467,801	7.5	52,648	0.8	59,307	1.0	165,459
North Carolina	915,018	49.3	875,635	47.2	52,800	2.8	9,677	0.5	2,703	0.1	39,383
North Dakota	193,695	64.2	79,189	26.3	23,640	7.8	3,743	1.2	1,278	0.4	114,506
Ohio	2,206,545	51.5	1,752,414	40.9	254,472	5.9	49,033	1.1	21,139	0.5	454,131
Oklahoma	695,570	60.5	402,026	35.0	38,284	3.3	13,828	1.2			293,544
Oregon	571,044	48.3	456,890	38.7	112,389	9.5	25,838	2.2	15,355	1.3	114,154
Pennsylvania	2,261,872	49.6	1,937,540	42.5	292,921	6.4	33,263	0.7	35,905	0.8	324,332
Rhode Island	154,793	37.2	198,342	47.7	59,819	14.4	2,458	0.6	660	0.2	43,549
South Carolina	441,841	49.4	430,385	48.1	14,153	1.6	5,139	0.6	2,553	0.3	11,456
South Dakota	198,343	60.5	103,855	31.7	21,431	6.5	3,824	1.2	250	0.1	94,488
Tennessee	787,761	48.7	783,051	48.4	35,991	2.2	7,116	0.4	3,697	0.2	4,710
Texas	2,510,705	55.3	1,881,147	41.4	111,613	2.5	37,643	0.8	528	0.0	629,558
Utah	439,687	72.8	124,266	20.6	30,284	5.0	7,226	1.2	2,759	0.5	315,421
Vermont	94,628	44.4	81,952	38.4	31,761	14.9	1,900	0.9	3,058	1.4	12,676
Virginia	989,609	53.0	752,174	40.3	95,418	5.1	12,821	0.7	16,010	0.9	237,435
Washington	865,244	49.7	650,193	37.3	185,073	10.6	29,213	1.7	12,671	0.7	215,051
West Virginia	334,206	45.3	367,462	49.8	31,691	4.3	4,356	0.6			33,256
Wisconsin	1,088,845	47.9	981,584	43.2	160,657	7.1	29,135	1.3	13,000	0.6	107,261
Wyoming	110,700	62.6	49,427	28.0	12,072	6.8	4,514	2.6			61,273
Totals	**43,904,153**	**50.7**	**35,483,883**	**41.0**	**5,720,060**	**6.6**	**921,299**	**1.1**	**485,826**	**0.6**	

1. For breakdown of "Other" vote, see minor candidate vote totals, p. 367.

1984 Presidential Election

Total Popular Vote: 92,652,793
Reagan's Plurality: 16,877,937

STATE	RONALD REAGAN (Republican) Votes	%	WALTER F. MONDALE (Democrat) Votes	%	DAVID BERGLAND (Libertarian) Votes	%	LYNDON H. LaROUCHE JR. (Independent) Votes	%	OTHER Votes	%	PLURALITY
Alabama	872,849	60.5	551,899	38.3	9,504	0.7			7,461	0.5	320,950
Alaska	138,377	66.6	62,007	29.9	6,378	3.1			843	0.4	76,370
Arizona	681,416	66.4	333,854	32.5	10,585	1.0			42	—	347,562
Arkansas	534,774	60.5	338,646	38.3	2,221	0.2	1,890	0.2	6,875	0.8	196,128
California	5,467,009	57.5	3,922,519	41.3	49,951	0.5			65,954	0.7	1,544,490
Colorado	821,817	63.4	454,975	35.1	11,257	0.9	4,662	0.4	2,669	0.2	366,842
Connecticut	890,877	60.7	569,597	38.8	204				6,222	0.4	321,280
Delaware	152,190	59.8	101,656	39.9	268	0.1			458	0.2	50,534
D.C.	29,009	13.7	180,408	85.4	279	0.1	127	0.1	1,465	0.7	151,399
Florida	2,730,350	65.3	1,448,816	34.7	754				131	—	1,281,534
Georgia	1,068,722	60.2	706,628	39.8	152		34		584	—	362,094
Hawaii	185,050	55.1	147,154	43.8	2,167	0.6	654	0.2	821	0.2	37,896
Idaho	297,523	72.4	108,510	26.4	2,823	0.7			2,288	0.6	189,013
Illinois	2,707,103	56.2	2,086,499	43.3	10,086	0.2			15,400	0.3	620,604
Indiana	1,377,230	61.7	841,481	37.7	6,741	0.3			7,617	0.3	535,749
Iowa	703,088	53.3	605,620	45.9	1,844	0.1	6,248	0.5	3,005	0.2	97,468
Kansas	677,296	66.3	333,149	32.6	3,329	0.3			8,217	0.8	344,147
Kentucky	821,702	60.0	539,539	39.4			1,776	0.1	6,328	0.5	282,163
Louisiana	1,037,299	60.8	651,586	38.2	1,876	0.1	3,552	0.2	12,509	0.7	385,713
Maine	336,500	60.8	214,515	38.8					2,129	0.4	121,985
Maryland	879,918	52.5	787,935	47.0	5,721	0.3			2,299	0.1	91,983
Massachusetts	1,310,936	51.2	1,239,606	48.4					8,911	0.3	71,330
Michigan	2,251,571	59.2	1,529,638	40.2	10,055	0.3	3,862	0.1	6,532	0.2	721,933
Minnesota	1,032,603	49.5	1,036,364	49.7	2,996	0.1	3,865	0.2	8,621	0.4	3,761
Mississippi	582,377	61.9	352,192	37.4	2,336	0.2	1,001	0.1	3,198	0.3	230,185
Missouri	1,274,188	60.0	848,583	40.0					12	—	425,605
Montana	232,450	60.5	146,742	38.2	5,185	1.3					85,708
Nebraska	460,054	70.6	187,866	28.8	2,079	0.3			2,091	0.3	272,188
Nevada	188,770	65.8	91,655	32.0	2,292	0.8			3,950	1.4	97,115
New Hampshire	267,050	68.6	120,347	30.9	735	0.2	467	0.1	418	0.1	146,703
New Jersey	1,933,630	60.1	1,261,323	39.2	6,416	0.2			16,493	0.5	672,307
New Mexico	307,101	59.7	201,769	39.2	4,459	0.8			1,041	0.2	508,870
New York	3,664,763	53.8	3,119,609	45.8	11,949	0.2			10,489	0.1	545,154
North Carolina	1,346,481	61.9	824,287	37.9	3,794	0.2			799	—	522,194
North Dakota	200,336	64.8	104,429	33.8	703	0.2	1,278	0.4	2,225	0.7	95,907
Ohio	2,678,560	58.9	1,825,440	40.1	5,886	0.1	10,693	0.2	27,040	0.6	853,120
Oklahoma	861,530	68.6	385,080	30.7	9,066	0.7					476,450
Oregon	685,700	55.9	536,479	43.7					4,348	0.3	149,221
Pennsylvania	2,584,323	53.3	2,228,131	46.0	6,982	0.1			25,467	0.5	356,192
Rhode Island	212,080	51.8	197,106	47.9	277	0.1			1,029	0.2	14,974
South Carolina	615,539	63.6	344,459	35.6	4,359	0.4			4,172	0.4	1271,080
South Dakota	200,267	63.0	116,113	36.5					1,487	0.5	84,154
Tennessee	990,212	57.8	711,714	41.6	3,072	0.2	1,852	0.1	5,144	0.3	278,498
Texas	3,433,428	63.6	1,949,276	36.1			14,613	0.3	254	—	1,484,152
Utah	469,105	74.5	155,369	24.7	2,477	0.4			2,735	0.4	313,736
Vermont	135,865	57.9	95,730	40.8	1,002	0.4	423	0.2	1,541	0.6	40,135
Virginia	1,337,078	62.3	796,250	37.1			13,307	0.6			540,828
Washington	1,051,670	56.2	807,352	42.9	8,844	0.5	4,712	0.6	11,332	0.6	244,318
West Virginia	405,483	54.7	328,125	44.3					2,134	0.2	77,358
Wisconsin	1,198,584	54.3	995,740	45.1	4,883	0.2	3,791	2.0	8,691	0.4	202,844
Wyoming	133,241	69.1	53,370	27.7	2,357	1.2					79,871
Totals	**54,455,074**	**58.77**	**37,577,137**	**40.56**	**228,314**	**.25**	**78,807**	**.08**	**241,261**	**.26**	

1. For breakdown of "Other" vote, see minor candidate vote totals, p. 367.

Popular Returns: Minor Candidates and Parties

This section contains popular vote returns for all minor candidates and parties that were aggregated in the columns labeled "Other" in the tables of presidential election returns. The source for these data, except for 1976, 1980, 1984 and where indicated by a footnote, is the Inter-University Consortium for Political and Social Research (ICPSR). For 1976 and 1980 the source was Scammon's *America Votes 12* and *14*. For 1984 the source was the Elections Research Center. Footnotes are on page 377.

The material is presented in the following order:

- Year of presidential election.
- Name of candidate and party, if available from the ICPSR data. "Unknown" is used where ICPSR sources indicated votes but neither candidate nor a party.
- State name, votes and per cent. Statewide percentages were calculated to two decimal places and rounded to one place. Thus, 0.05 per cent is listed as 0.1 per cent.
- Nationwide vote totals and per cent. Totals and percentages were calculated only where a candidate or party received votes in more than one state. Percentages were calculated to three decimal places and rounded to two.

1824

Unpledged Republican

Massachusetts: 6,616 votes, 15.7 per cent of Mass. vote.

Unknown:

Connecticut: 1,188 votes, 11.2 per cent; Indiana: 7; Massachusetts: 4,753, 11.3; Missouri: 33, 1.0; North Carolina: 256, 0.7; Rhode Island: 200, 8.5.

1828

Unknown:

Alabama: 4 votes; Connecticut: 1,101, 5.7 per cent; Maine: 89, 0.3; Massachusetts: 3,226, 8.3; New Jersey: 8; North Carolina: 15; Rhode Island: 5, 0.1; Vermont: 120, 0.4.

1832

Unknown:

Illinois: 30 votes, 0.1 per cent; Massachusetts: 7,031, 10.4; Rhode Island: 6, 0.1; Vermont: 206, 0.6.

1836

Unknown:

Delaware: 5 votes, 0.1 per cent; Maine: 1,112, 2.9; Massachusetts: 45, 0.1; North Carolina; 1; Rhode Island; 1; Vermont: 65, 0.2; Virginia: 5.

1840

Unknown:

Delaware: 13 votes, 0.1 per cent; Indiana: 599, 0.5; Rhode Island: 136, 1.6; Vermont: 19.

1844

Unknown:

Delaware: 6 votes, 0.1 per cent; Illinois, 939, 0.9; Massachusetts: 1,106, 0.8; North Carolina: 2; Rhode Island: 5.

1848

Gerrit Smith (Liberty)

New York: 2,545 votes, 0.6 per cent of N.Y. vote.

In the ICPSR data, the distinct party designations appearing in the original sources are preserved. Thus, in the ICPSR returns for 1880, John W. Phelps received votes under the following four party designations: "Anti-Masonic" — California 5 votes, Illinois 150 votes and Pennsylvania 44 votes; "Anti-Secret" — Kansas 25 votes; "National American" — Michigan 312 votes and "American" — Rhode Island 4 votes and Wisconsin 91 votes.

To provide one party designation for each minor candidate, Congressional Quarterly has aggregated under a single party designation the votes of minor candidates who are listed in the ICPSR data as receiving votes under more than one party designation. The source for the designation is Svend Petersen's *A Statistical History of the American Presidential Elections* (Westport, Conn.: Greenwood Press, 1981) where Petersen gives a party designation. In the 1880 election cited above, Petersen lists John W. Phelps as an "American" party candidate. Where Petersen lists no party designation, Congressional Quarterly selected the party designation for a candidate which appeared most frequently in the ICPSR returns.

Henry Clay (Clay Whig)

Illinois: 89 votes, 0.1 per cent of Ill. vote.

Unknown:

Alabama: 4 votes; Connecticut: 24; Massachusetts: 62, 0.1 per cent; North Carolina: 26; Rhode Island: 5, 0.1; Texas: 75, 0.4.

1852

Daniel Webster (Whig)[1]

Georgia: 5,324 votes, 8.5 per cent; Massachusetts: 1,670 votes, 1.3 per cent.
Totals: 6,994, .22%.

—Broome (Native American)

Massachusetts: 158 votes, 0.1 per cent; New Jersey: 738, 0.9; Pennsylvania: 1,670, 0.4.
Totals: 2,566, 0.08%.

George Michael Troup (Southern Rights)[2]

Alabama: 2,205 votes, 5.0 per cent; Georgia: 126, 0.2.
Totals: 2,331 votes, 0.07%.

Unknown:

California: 56 votes, 0.1 per cent; Connecticut: 12; Iowa: 139, 0.4; North Carolina: 60, 0.1; Texas: 10, 0.1.

1856

Unknown:

California: 14 votes; Delaware: 9, 0.1 per cent; Massachusetts: 3,006, 1.8; Ohio, 148.

1860

Gerrit Smith (Union)

Illinois: 35 votes; Ohio: 136.

Unknown:

California: 15 votes; Massachusetts: 328, 0.2 per cent; Minnesota: 17, 0.1.

1864

E. Cheeseborough

Kansas: 543 votes, 2.5 per cent of Kan. vote.

Unknown:

Kansas: 112 votes, 0.5 per cent; Massachusetts: 6; Minnesota: 26, 0.1; Oregon: 5.

1868

S. J. Crawford
Kansas: 1 vote.

C. B. Lines
Kansas: 1 vote.

Walter Ross
Kansas: 1 vote.

Unknown:
Alabama: 6 votes; Massachusetts: 26; New Hampshire: 11.

1872

James Black (Prohibition)
Michigan: 1,271 votes, 0.6 per cent; Ohio: 2,100, 0.4. Totals: 3,371, 0.05%

George W. Slocum
Iowa: 424 votes, 0.2 per cent of Iowa vote.

James Baird Weaver
Iowa: 309 votes, 0.1 per cent of Iowa vote.

William Palmer
Kansas: 440 votes, 0.4 per cent of Kan. vote.

Liberal Republican Elector
Iowa: 10,447 votes, 4.8 per cent of Iowa vote.

Unknown:
Iowa: 209 votes, 0.1 per cent; Kansas: 141, 0.1; Minnesota: 168, 0.2; New Hampshire: 313, 0.5; South Carolina: 259, 0.3.

1876

Green Clay Smith (Prohibition)
Connecticut: 374 votes, 0.3 per cent; Illinois: 141; Kansas: 110, 0.1; Michigan: 766, 0.2; New York: 2,369, 0.2; Ohio: 1,636, 0.3; Pennsylvania: 1,320, 0.2; Wisconsin: 27. Totals: 6,743; 0.08%

James B. Walker (American)
Illinois: 177 votes; Kansas: 23; Michigan: 71; Ohio: 76; Pennsylvania: 83; Wisconsin: 29. Totals: 459; 0.01%

Louis Brookwater
Iowa: 97 votes.

Communist
Wisconsin: 32 votes.

Unknown:
Alabama: 2 votes; California: 19; Connecticut: 26; Iowa: 423, 0.1 per cent; Kansas: 5; Kentucky: 2,998, 1.2; Maine: 828, 0.7; Massachusetts: 779, 0.3; New Hampshire: 93, 0.1; Texas: 46; Vermont: 114, 0.2; Wisconsin: 1,607, 0.6.

1880

Neal Dow (Prohibition)
California: 54 votes; Connecticut: 409, 0.3 per cent; Illinois: 440, 0.1; Kansas: 10; Kentucky: 233, 0.1; Maine: 92, 0.1; Massachusetts: 682, 0.2; Michigan: 938, 0.3; Minnesota: 286, 0.2; New Hampshire: 180, 0.2; New Jersey: 191, 0.1; New York: 1,517, 0.1; Ohio: 2,613, 0.4; Pennsylvania: 1,940, 0.2; Rhode Island: 20, 0.1; Wisconsin: 69. Totals 9,674, 0.11%

John W. Phelps (American)
California: 5 votes; Illinois: 150; Kansas: 25; Michigan: 312, 0.1 per cent; Pennsylvania: 44; Rhode Island: 4; Wisconsin: 91. Totals 631, 0.01%

A. C. Brewer (Independent Democrat)
Arkansas: 322 votes, 0.3 per cent of Ark. vote.

W. Pitt Norris
Iowa: 433 votes, 0.1 per cent of Iowa vote.

H. Scott Howells
Iowa: 159 votes, 0.1 per cent of Iowa vote.

Unknown:
Arkansas: 1,221 votes, 1.1 per cent; California: 70; Colorado: 14; Connecticut: 39; Iowa: 472, 0.2; Maine: 139, 0.1; Massachusetts: 117; Mississippi: 677, 0.6; Rhode Island: 1; South Carolina: 36.

1884

Unknown:
Alabama: 72 votes, 0.1 per cent; California: 329, 0.2; Florida: 118, 0.2; Iowa: 1,297, 0.3; Kansas: 468, 0.2; Maine: 6; Massachusetts: 2; New Jersey: 28; Oregon: 35, 0.1; South Carolina: 1,237, 1.3; Vermont: 27, 0.1.

1888

Robert H. Cowdrey (United Labor)
Illinois: 150 votes; New York: 519; Oregon: 351; 0.6 per cent. Totals 1,020, 0.01%

Socialist Labor
New York: 2,068 votes, 0.2 per cent. Totals 2,068, 0.02%

James Langdon Curtis (American)
California: 1,591 votes, 0.6 per cent; Pennsylvania: 24. Totals: 1,615, 0.01%

E.W. Perry
Iowa: 399 votes, 0.1 per cent of Iowa vote.

Unknown:
California: 1,442 votes, 0.6 per cent; Colorado: 177, 0.2; Delaware: 1; Iowa: 157; Kansas: 937, 0.3; Maine: 16; Massachusetts: 60; New Hampshire: 58, 0.1; North Carolina: 37; Oregon: 53, 0.1; Rhode Island: 7; South Carolina: 437, 0.6; Vermont: 35, 0.1.

1892

Simon Wing (Socialist Labor)
Connecticut: 333 votes, 0.2 per cent; Massachusetts: 649, 0.2; New Jersey: 1,337, 0.4; New York: 17,956, 1.3; Pennsylvania: 888, 0.1. Totals: 21,163; 0.18%

Unknown:
Arkansas: 1,267 votes, 0.9 per cent; Delaware: 13; Georgia: 2,345, 1.1 Maine: 4; Massachusetts: 3; Michigan: 925, 0.2; Rhode Island: 3; South Carolina: 72, 0.1; Texas: 4,086, 1.0; Vermont: 10; Wyoming: 29, 0.2.

1896

Charles Horatio Matchett (Socialist Labor)
California: 1,611 votes, 0.5 per cent; Colorado: 159, 0.1; Connecticut: 1,223, 0.7; Illinois: 1,147, 0.1; Indiana: 324, 0.1; Iowa: 453, 0.1; Maryland: 587, 0.2; Massachusetts: 2,112, 0.5; Michigan: 293, 0.1; Minnesota: 954, 0.3; Missouri: 599, 0.1; Nebraska: 186, 0.1; New Hampshire: 228, 0.3; New Jersey: 3,985, 1.1; New York: 17,667, 1.2; Ohio: 1,165, 0.1; Pennsylvania: 1,683, 0.1; Rhode Island: 558, 1.0; Virginia: 108; Wisconsin: 1,314, 0.3. Totals: 36,356; 0.26%

Charles Eugene Bentley (National Prohibition)
Arkansas: 892 votes, 0.6 per cent; California: 1,047, 0.4; Colorado: 386, 0.2; Illinois: 793, 0.1; Indiana: 2,267, 0.4; Iowa: 352, 0.1; Kansas: 620, 0.2; Maryland: 136, 0.1; Michigan: 1,816, 0.3; Missouri: 292; Nebraska: 797, 0.4; New Hampshire: 49, 0.1; New Jersey: 5,614, 1.5; North Carolina: 222, 0.1; Ohio: 2,716, 0.3; Pennsylvania: 870, 0.1; Washington: 148, 0.2; Wisconsin: 346, 0.1. Totals: 19,363; 0.14%

W. C. Douglass

North Carolina: 51 votes.

Unknown:

California: 4 votes; Connecticut: 4; Georgia: 47; Massachusetts: 20; Michigan: 1,073, 0.2 per cent; North Carolina: 321, 0.1; North Dakota: 12; Rhode Island: 5.

1900

Wharton Barker (Populist)

Alabama: 4,188 votes, 2.6 per cent; Arkansas: 972, 0.8; Colorado: 333, 0.2; Florida: 1,143, 2.9; Georgia: 4,568, 3.8; Idaho: 445, 0.8; Illinois: 1,141, 0.1; Indiana: 1,438, 0.2; Iowa: 615, 0.1; Kentucky: 1,961, 0.4; Michigan: 889, 0.2; Mississippi: 1,642, 2.8; Missouri: 4,244; 0.6; Nebraska: 1,104, 0.5; New Jersey: 669, 0.2; North Carolina: 798, 0.3; North Dakota: 109, 0.2; Ohio: 251; Oregon: 269, 0.3; Pennsylvania: 638, 0.1; South Dakota: 340, 0.4; Tennessee: 1,322, 0.5; Texas: 20,565, 4.9; Vermont: 367, 0.7; Virginia: 63; West Virginia: 246, 0.1; Wyoming: 20, 0.1.

Totals: 50,340; 0.36%

Joseph F. Malloney (Socialist Labor)

California: 7,554 votes, 2.5 per cent; Colorado: 654, 0.3; Connecticut: 908, 0.5; Illinois: 1,374, 0.1; Indiana: 663, 0.1; Iowa: 259, 0.1; Kentucky: 390, 0.1; Maryland: 382, 0.1; Massachusetts: 2,599, 0.6; Michigan: 830, 0.2; Minnesota: 1,329, 0.4; Missouri: 1,296, 0.2; Montana: 119, 0.2; New Jersey: 2,074, 0.5; New York: 12,622, 0.8; Ohio: 1,688, 0.2; Pennsylvania: 2,936, 0.3; Rhode Island: 1,423, 2.5; Texas: 162; Utah: 102, 0.1; Virginia: 167, 0.1; Washington: 866, 0.8; Wisconsin: 503, 0.1.

Totals: 40,900; 0.29%

Seth Hockett Ellis (Union Reform)

Arkansas: 341 votes, 0.3 per cent; Illinois: 672, 0.1; Indiana: 254; Maryland: 142, 0.1; Ohio: 4,284, 0.4.

Totals: 5,693; 0.04%

Jonah Fitz Randolph Leonard (United Christian)

Illinois: 352 votes; Iowa: 166.

Totals: 518.

E. W. Perrin

Arkansas: 27 votes.

W. J. Palmer

Colorado: 26 votes.

Edward Waldo Emerson

Massachusetts: 342 votes, 0.1 per cent of Mass. vote.

G. W. Pape

Vermont: 1 vote.

S. W. Cook

Wyoming: 21 votes, 0.1 per cent of Wyo. vote.

Anti-Imperialist

Connecticut: 45 votes.

Unknown:

Connecticut: 10 votes; Louisiana: 4; Massachusetts: 191, 0.1; New Hampshire: 16; Utah: 9; Vermont: 4.

1904

Thomas Edward Watson (Populist)

Alabama: 5,051 votes, 4.6 per cent; Arkansas: 2,326, 2.0; Colorado: 824, 0.3; Connecticut: 495, 0.3; Delaware: 51, 0.1; Florida: 1,605, 4.2; Georgia: 22,635, 17.3; Idaho: 352, 0.5; Illinois: 6,725, 0.6; Indiana: 2,444, 0.4; Iowa: 2,207, 0.5; Kansas: 6,253, 1.9; Kentucky: 2,521, 0.6; Maine: 337, 0.4; Maryland: 1; Massachusetts: 1,294, 0.3; Michigan: 1,145, 0.2; Minnesota: 2,103, 0.7; Mississippi: 1,499, 2.6; Missouri: 4,226, 0.7; Montana: 1,531, 2.4; Nebraska: 20,518, 9.1; Nevada: 344, 2.8; New Hampshire: 82, 0.1; New Jersey: 3,705, 0.9; New York: 7,459, 0.5; North Carolina: 819, 0.4; Ohio: 1,392, 0.1; Oregon: 746, 0.8; South

Dakota: 1,240, 1.2; Tennessee: 2,491, 1.0; Texas: 8,062, 3.5; Washington: 669, 0.5; West Virginia: 339, 0.1; Wisconsin: 560, 0.1.

Totals: 114,051; 0.84%

Charles Hunter Corregan (Socialist Labor)

Colorado: 335 votes, 0.1 per cent; Connecticut: 583, 0.3; Illinois: 4,698, 0.4; Indiana: 1,598, 0.2; Kentucky: 596, 0.1; Massachusetts: 2,359, 0.5; Michigan: 1,018, 0.2; Minnesota: 974, 0.3; Missouri: 1,674, 0.3; Montana: 213, 0.3; New Jersey: 2,380, 0.6; New York: 9,122, 0.6; Ohio: 2,635, 0.3; Pennsylvania: 2,211, 0.2; Rhode Island: 488, 0.7; Texas: 431, 0.2; Washington: 1,592, 1.1; Wisconsin: 249, 0.1.

Totals: 33,156; 0.25%

Austin Holcomb (Continental)

Illinois: 826 votes, 0.1 per cent of Ill. vote.

Thomas O. Clark

Maryland: 4 votes.

Unknown:

California: 333 votes, 0.1 per cent; Connecticut: 11; Massachusetts: 5; New Hampshire: 1; Vermont: 1.

1908

Thomas L. Hisgen (Independence)

Alabama: 497 votes, 0.5 per cent; Arkansas: 286, 0.2; California: 4,278, 1.1; Connecticut: 728, 0.4; Delaware: 29, 0.1; Florida: 553, 1.1; Georgia: 76, 0.1; Idaho: 124, 0.1; Illinois: 7,724, 0.7; Indiana: 514, 0.1; Iowa: 404, 0.1; Kansas: 68; Kentucky: 200; Louisiana: 77, 0.1; Maine: 700, 0.7; Maryland: 485; 0.2; Massachusetts: 19,235, 4.2; Michigan: 734, 0.1; Minnesota: 424, 0.1; Missouri: 392, 0.1; Montana: 493, 0.7; Nevada: 436, 1.8; New Hampshire: 584, 0.7; New Jersey: 2,916, 0.6; New York: 35,817, 2.2; North Dakota: 43, 0.1; Ohio: 439; Oregon: 289, 0.3; Pennsylvania: 1,057, 0.1; Rhode Island: 1,105, 1.5; South Carolina: 46, 0.1; South Dakota: 88, 0.1; Tennessee: 332, 0.1; Texas: 106; Utah: 92, 0.1; Vermont: 804, 1.5; Virginia: 51; Washington: 248, 0.1; Wyoming: 63, 0.2.

Totals: 82,537; 0.55%

Thomas Edward Watson (Populist)

Alabama: 1,576 votes, 1.5 per cent; Arkansas: 987, 0.7; Florida: 1,946, 3.9; Georgia: 16,687, 12.6; Illinois: 633, 0.1; Indiana: 1,193, 0.2; Iowa: 261, 0.1; Kentucky: 333, 0.1; Mississippi: 1,276, 1.9; Missouri: 1,165, 0.2; Ohio: 162; Tennessee: 1,092, 0.4; Texas: 960, 0.3; Virginia: 105, 0.1.

Totals: 28,376; 0.19%

August Gillhaus (Socialist Labor)

Connecticut: 608 votes, 0.3 per cent; Illinois: 1,680, 0.2; Indiana: 643, 0.1; Kentucky: 405, 0.1; Massachusetts: 1,011, 0.2; Michigan: 1,085, 0.2; Missouri: 867, 0.1; New Jersey: 1,196, 0.3; New York: 3,877, 0.2; Ohio: 721, 0.1; Pennsylvania: 1,224, 0.1; Rhode Island: 183, 0.3; Texas: 175, 0.1; Virginia: 25; Wisconsin: 318; 0.1.

Totals: 14,018; 0.09%

Daniel Braxton Turney (United Christian)

Illinois: 400 votes; Michigan: 61.

S. H. Lasiter

Colorado: 1 vote.

B. J. McGrue

Colorado: 1 vote.

Edwin H. Lentz

New Hampshire: 8 votes.

Edward Clark

North Carolina: 13 votes.

Republican (Davidson Faction)

Alabama: 987 votes; 0.9 per cent of Ala. vote.

Unknown:

California: 28 votes; Connecticut: 4, Massachusetts: 9; Vermont: 29, 0.1 per cent; Wisconsin: 2.

1912

Eugene W. Chafin (Prohibition)

Arizona: 265 votes, 1.1 per cent; Arkansas: 908, 0.7; California: 23,366, 3.5; Colorado: 5,063, 1.9; Connecticut: 2,068, 1.1; Delaware: 620, 1.3; Florida: 1,854, 3.7; Georgia: 149, 0.1; Idaho: 1,536, 1.5; Illinois: 15,710, 1.4; Indiana: 19,249, 2.9; Iowa: 8,440, 1.7; Kentucky: 3,253, 0.7; Maine: 947, 0.7; Maryland: 2,244, 1.0; Massachusetts: 2,753, 0.6; Michigan: 8,794, 1.6; Minnesota: 7,886, 2.4; Missouri: 5,380, 0.8; Montana: 32; Nebraska: 3,383, 1.4; New Hampshire: 535, 0.6; New Jersey: 2,936, 0.7; New York: 19,455, 1.2; North Carolina: 118, 0.1; North Dakota: 1,243, 1.4; Ohio: 11,511, 1.1; Oklahoma: 2,195, 0.9; Oregon: 4,360, 3.2; Pennsylvania: 19,525, 1.6; Rhode Island: 616, 0.8; South Dakota: 3,910, 3.4; Tennessee: 832, 0.1; Texas: 1,701, 0.6; Vermont: 1,094, 1.7; Virginia: 709, 0.5; Washington: 9,810, 3.0; West Virginia: 4,517, 1.7; Wisconsin: 8,584, 2.2; Wyoming: 421, 1.0.

Totals: 207,972; 1.38%

Arthur E. Reimer (Socialist Labor)

Colorado: 475 votes, 0.2 per cent; Connecticut: 1,260, 0.7; Illinois: 4,066, 0.4; Indiana: 3,130, 0.5; Kentucky: 1,055, 0.2; Maryland: 322, 0.1; Massachusetts: 1,102, 0.2; Michigan: 1,239, 0.2; Minnesota: 2,212; 0.7; Missouri: 1,778, 0.3; New Jersey: 1,396, 0.3; New York: 4,273, 0.3; Ohio: 2,630, 0.3; Pennsylvania: 706, 0.1; Rhode Island: 236, 0.3; Texas: 430, 0.1; Utah: 510, 0.5; Virginia: 50; Washington: 1,872, 0.6; Wisconsin: 632, 0.2.

Totals: 29,374; 0.2%

Independent

Alabama: 5 votes.

Unknown

California: 4,417, 0.7 per cent; Connecticut: 6; Kansas: 63; Massachusetts: 1; South Carolina: 55, 0.1; Wisconsin: 9.

1916

Arthur E. Reimer (Socialist Labor)

Connecticut: 606 votes, 0.3 per cent; Illinois: 2,488, 0.1; Indiana: 1,659, 0.2; Iowa: 460, 0.1; Kentucky: 332, 0.1; Maryland: 756, 0.3; Massachusetts: 1,096, 0.2; Michigan: 831, 0.1; Minnesota: 468, 0.1; Missouri: 903, 0.1; Nebraska: 624, 0.2; New Jersey: 855, 0.2; New York: 2,666, 0.2; Pennsylvania: 419; Rhode Island: 180, 0.2; Utah: 144, 0.1; Virginia: 67; Washington: 730, 0.2.

Totals: 15,284; 0.08%

Progressive [3]

Colorado: 409 votes, 0.1 per cent; Georgia: 20,692, 12.9; Indiana: 3,898, 0.5; Iowa: 1,793, 0.4; Kentucky: 129; Louisiana: 6,349, 6.8; Minnesota: 290, 0.1; Mississippi: 520, 0.6; Montana: 338, 0.2; Oklahoma: 234, 0.1; Oregon: 310, 0.1; South Carolina: 162, 0.3; Utah: 110, 0.1

Totals 35,234; 0.19%

Unknown:

California: 187 votes; Massachusetts: 6; South Carolina: 258, 0.4 per cent; Vermont: 10.

1920

Aaron Sherman Watkins (Prohibition) [4]

Alabama: 766 votes, 0.3 per cent; California: 25,085, 2.7; Colorado: 2,807; 1.0; Connecticut: 1,771; 0.5; Delaware: 986, 1.0; Florida: 5,124, 3.5; Idaho: 32; Illinois: 11,216, 0.5; Indiana: 13,462, 1.1; Iowa: 4,197, 0.5; Kentucky: 3,250, 0.4; Michigan: 9,510, 0.9; Minnesota: 11,489, 1.6; Missouri: 5,152, 0.4; Nebraska: 5,947, 1.6; New Jersey: 4,674, 0.5; New York: 19,653, 0.7; North Carolina: 17; Oregon: 3,595, 1.5; Pennsylvania: 42,696, 2.3; Rhode Island: 510,

0.3; South Dakota: 900, 0.5; Vermont: 762, 0.9; Virginia: 826, 0.4; Washington: 3,790, 1.0; West Virginia: 1,526, 0.3; Wisconsin: 8,648, 1.2.

Totals: 188,391, 0.7%

James Edward Ferguson (American)

Texas: 47,812 votes, 9.8 per cent.

William W. Cox (Socialist Labor)

Connecticut: 1,491 votes, 0.4 per cent; Illinois: 3,471, 0.2; Iowa: 982, 0.1; Maryland: 1,178, 0.3; Massachusetts: 3,583, 0.4; Michigan: 2,450, 0.2; Minnesota: 5,828, 0.8; Missouri: 1,587, 0.1; New Jersey: 923, 0.1; New York: 4,841, 0.2; Oregon: 1,515, 0.6; Pennsylvania: 753; Rhode Island: 495, 0.3; Washington: 1,321, 0.3.

Totals: 30,418; 0.11%

Robert Colvin Macauley (Single Tax)

Delaware: 39 votes; Illinois: 774; Indiana: 566; Maine: 310, 0.2 per cent; Michigan: 425; New Jersey: 517, 0.1; Ohio: 2,153, 0.1; Pennsylvania: 806; Rhode Island: 100, 0.1.

Totals: 5,690; 0.02%

Black and Tan Republican

Texas: 27,198, 5.6 per cent.

Independent Republican

Louisiana: 342 votes, 0.3 percent.

Insurgent Referendum

South Carolina: 366 votes, 0.6 per cent.

Unknown:

California: 587 votes, 0.1 per cent; Iowa: 6; Kansas: 75; Maryland: 8; Massachusetts: 24; Nebraska: 90; Ohio: 294; Pennsylvania: 27; Vermont: 56, 0.1.

1924

Frank T. Johns (Socialist Labor)

Connecticut: 1,373 votes, 0.3 per cent; Illinois: 2,334, 0.1; Kentucky: 1,512, 0.2; Maine: 406, 0.2; Maryland: 987, 0.3; Massachusetts: 1,668, 0.2; Minnesota: 1,855, 0.2; Missouri: 1,066, 0.1; New Jersey: 819, 0.1; New York: 9,928, 0.3; Ohio: 3,025, 0.2; Oregon: 908, 0.3; Pennsylvania: 634; Rhode Island: 268, 0.1; Vermont: 3; Virginia: 189, 0.1; Washington: 982, 0.2; Wisconsin: 411, 0.1.

Totals: 28,368, 0.1%

William Zebulon Foster (Communist)

Illinois: 2,622 votes, 0.1 per cent; Indiana: 987, 0.1; Iowa: 4,037, 0.4; Massachusetts: 2,634, 0.2; Michigan: 5,330, 0.5; Minnesota: 4,427, 0.5; Montana: 370, 0.2; New Jersey: 1,540, 0.1; New York: 8,244, 0.3; North Dakota: 370, 0.2; Pennsylvania: 2,735, 0.1; Rhode Island: 289, 0.1; Washington: 736, 0.2; Wisconsin: 3,759, 0.5.

Totals: 38,080; 0.13%

Gilbert Owen Nations (American)

Arkansas: 10 votes; Florida: 2,315, 2.1 per cent; Kentucky: 1,334, 0.2; New Jersey: 358; Pennsylvania: 13,035, 0.6; Tennessee: 100; Washington: 5,991; 1.4; West Virginia: 1,072, 0.2.

Totals: 24,215; 0.08%.

William J. Wallace (Commonwealth Land)

Delaware: 16 votes; Illinois: 421; Kentucky: 247; Missouri: 165; New Jersey: 219; Ohio: 1,246, 0.1 per cent; Pennsylvania: 296; Rhode Island: 38; Wisconsin: 271.

Totals: 2,919; 0.01%

Andrew Gump

South Carolina: 1 vote.

Socialist

Oklahoma: 5,134 votes, 1.0 percent.

Unknown:

California: 122 votes; Iowa: 445, 0.1 per cent; Kansas: 3; Louisiana: 4,063, 3.3; Massachusetts: 2; Vermont: 2.

1928

Verne L. Reynolds (Socialist Labor)

Connecticut: 622 votes, 0.1 per cent; Illinois: 1,812, 0.1; Indiana: 645, 0.1; Iowa: 230; Kentucky: 354; Maryland: 906, 0.2; Massachusetts: 772, 0.1; Michigan: 799, 0.1; Minnesota: 1,921, 0.2; Missouri: 342; New Jersey: 488; New York: 4,211, 0.1; Ohio: 1,515, 0.1; Oregon: 1,564, 0.5; Pennsylvania: 382; Rhode Island: 416, 0.2; Virginia: 180, 0.1; Washington: 4,068, 0.8; Wisconsin: 381.

Totals: 21,608; 0.6%

William Frederick Varney (Prohibition)

California: 14,394 votes, 0.8 per cent; Indiana: 5,496, 0.4; Michigan: 2,728, 0.2; New Jersey: 154; Ohio: 3,556, 0.1; Pennsylvania: 3,875, 0.1; Vermont: 338, 0.3; West Virginia: 1,703, 0.3; Wisconsin: 2,245, 0.2.

Totals: 34,489; 0.09%.

Frank Elbridge Webb (Farmer Labor)

Colorado: 1,092 votes, 0.3 per cent; Iowa: 3,088, 0.3; Oklahoma: 1,283, 0.2; South Dakota: 927, 0.4.

Totals: 6,390; 0.02%.

Benjamin Gitlow

California: 104 votes.

H. Morgan

California: 6 votes.

W. O. Ligon

Mississippi: 524 votes, 0.4 per cent of Miss. vote.

Z. A. Rogers

Mississippi: 264 votes, 0.2 per cent of Miss. vote.

Unknown:

California: 151 votes; Iowa: 2; Massachusetts: 4; Pennsylvania: 14; Vermont: 9.

1932

William David Upshaw (Prohibition)

Alabama: 13 votes; California: 20,637, 0.9 per cent; Colorado: 1,928, 0.4; Georgia: 1,125, 0.4; Illinois: 6,388, 0.2; Indiana: 10,399, 0.7; Iowa: 2,111, 0.2; Kentucky: 2,263; Massachusetts: 1,142, 0.1; Michigan: 2,893, 0.2; Missouri: 2,429, 0.2; New Jersey: 757, 0.1; Ohio: 7,421, 0.3; Pennsylvania: 11,369, 0.4; Rhode Island: 183, 0.1; South Dakota: 463, 0.2; Tennessee: 1,998, 0.5; Virginia: 1,843, 0.6; Washington: 1,540, 0.3; West Virginia: 2,342, 0.3; Wisconsin: 2,672, 0.2.

Totals: 81,916; 0.21%

William Hope Harvey (Liberty)

Arkansas: 952 votes, 0.4 per cent; California: 9,827, 0.4; Idaho: 4,660, 2.5; Michigan: 217; Montana: 1,461, 0.7; New Mexico: 389, 0.3; North Dakota: 1,817, 0.7; South Dakota: 3,333, 1.2; Texas: 235; Washington: 30,308, 4.9.

Totals: 53,199, 0.13%

Verne L. Reynolds (Socialist Labor)

Colorado: 427 votes, 0.1 per cent; Connecticut: 2,287, 0.4; Illinois: 3,638, 0.1; Indiana: 2,070, 0.1; Kentucky: 1,400, 0.1; Maine: 255, 0.1; Maryland: 1,036, 0.2; Massachusetts: 2,668, 0.2; Michigan: 1,401, 0.1; Minnesota: 770, 0.1; Missouri: 404; New Jersey: 1,054, 0.1; New York: 10,339, 0.2; Ohio: 1,968, 0.1; Oregon: 1,730, 0.5; Pennsylvania: 659; Rhode Island: 433, 0.2; Washington: 996, 0.2; Wisconsin: 493.

Totals: 34,028; 0.09%

Jacob Sechler Coxey (Farmer Labor)

Colorado: 469 votes, 0.1 per cent; Iowa: 1,094, 0.1; Michigan: 137; Minnesota: 5,731, 0.6.

Totals: 7,431; 0.02%

John Zahnd (National)

Indiana: 1,615 votes, 0.1 per cent of Ind. vote.

James R. Cox (Jobless)

Pennsylvania: 726 votes; Virginia: 15.

Totals: 741.

Arizona Progressive Democrat

Arizona: 9 votes.

Independent

Louisiana: 533 votes, 0.2 per cent of La. vote.

Jacksonian

Texas: 152 votes.

Populist

South Carolina: 4 votes.

Unknown:

Iowa: 4 votes; Massachusetts: 71; Pennsylvania: 53; Vermont: 2.

1936

Earl Russell Browder (Communist)[5]

Alabama: 678 votes, 0.3 per cent; Arkansas: 167, 0.1; California: 10,877, 0.4; Colorado: 497, 0.1; Connecticut: 1,193, 0.2; Delaware: 51; Indiana: 1,090, 0.1; Iowa: 506; Kentucky: 210; Maine: 257, 0.1; Maryland: 915, 0.2; Massachusetts: 2,930, 0.2; Michigan: 3,384, 0.2; Minnesota: 2,574, 0.2; Missouri: 417; Montana: 385, 0.2; New Hampshire: 193, 0.1; New Jersey: 1,595, 0.1; New Mexico: 43; New York: 35,609, 0.6; North Dakota: 360, 0.1; Ohio: 5,251, 0.2; Pennsylvania: 4,061, 0.1; Rhode Island: 411, 0.1; Tennessee: 326, 0.1; Texas: 253; Utah: 280, 0.1; Vermont: 405, 0.3; Virginia: 98; Washington: 1,907, 0.3; Wisconsin: 2,197, 0.2; Wyoming: 91, 0.1.

Totals: 79,211; 0.17%

David Leigh Colvin (Prohibition)[5]

Alabama: 719 votes, 0.3 per cent; Arizona: 384, 0.3; California: 12,917, 0.5; Georgia: 660, 0.2; Illinois: 3,438, 0.1; Iowa: 1,182, 0.1; Kentucky: 952, 0.1; Maine: 334, 0.1 ; Massachusetts: 1,032, 0.1; Michigan: 579; Missouri: 908, 0.1; Montana: 224, 0.1; New Jersey: 916, 0.1; New Mexico: 61; North Dakota: 197, 0.1; Oklahoma: 1,328, 0.2; Pennsylvania: 6,687, 0.2; Tennessee: 634, 0.1; Texas: 519, 0.1; Utah: 43; Virginia: 594, 0.2; Washington: 1,041, 0.2; West Virginia: 1,173, 0.1; Wisconsin: 1,071, 0.1; Wyoming: 75, 0.1.

Totals: 37,668; 0.08%

John W. Aiken (Socialist Labor)[5]

Colorado: 327 votes, 0.1 per cent; Connecticut: 1,228, 0.2; Illinois: 1,924, 0.1; Iowa: 252; Kentucky: 310; Maine: 129; Maryland: 1,305, 0.2; Massachusetts: 1,305, 0.1; Michigan: 600; Minnesota: 961, 0.1; Missouri: 292; New Jersey: 349; Oregon: 500, 0.1; Pennsylvania: 1,424; Rhode Island: 929, 0.3; Virginia: 36; Washington: 362, 0.1; Wisconsin: 557.

Totals: 12,790; 0.03%

William Dudley Pelley (Christian)

Washington: 1,598 votes, 0.2 per cent of Wash. vote.

Independent Republican

Delaware: 3,222, 2.5 per cent of Del. vote.

Unknown:

Iowa: 4 votes; Louisiana: 93; Massachusetts: 11; Michigan: 5; Oregon: 108; Vermont: 137, 0.1 per cent.

1940

Earl Russell Browder (Communist)

Alabama: 509 votes, 0.2 per cent; California: 13,586, 0.4; Colorado: 378, 0.1; Connecticut: 1,091, 0.1; Idaho: 276, 0.1; Iowa: 1,524, 0.1; Maine: 411, 0.1; Maryland: 1,274, 0.2; Massachusetts: 3,806, 0.2; Michigan: 2,834, 0.1; Minnesota: 2,711, 0.2; Montana: 489, 0.2; New Jersey: 8,814, 0.5; Oregon: 191; Pennsylvania: 4,519, 0.1; Rhode Island: 239, 0.1; Texas: 215; Utah: 191, 0.1; Vermont: 411, 0.3; Virginia: 72; Washington: 2,626, 0.3; Wisconsin: 2,381, 0.2.

Totals: 48,548; 0.1%

John W. Aiken (Socialist Labor)

Connecticut: 971 votes, 0.1 per cent; Indiana: 706; Iowa: 452; Maryland: 657, 0.1; Massachusetts: 1,492, 0.1; Michigan: 795; Minnesota: 2,553, 0.2; Missouri: 209; New Jersey: 446; Oregon: 2,487, 0.5; Pennsylvania: 1,518; Virginia: 48; Washington: 667, 0.1; Wisconsin: 1,882, 0.1.

Totals: 14,883, 0.03%

Alfred Knutson (Independent)

North Dakota: 545 votes, 0.2 per cent of N.D. vote.

Independent

Louisiana: 108 votes.

Unknown:

California: 262 votes; Georgia: 14; Maryland: 9; Massachusetts: 12; Michigan: 4; Pennsylvania: 827; Vermont: 11.

1944

Edward A. Teichert (Socialist Labor)

California: 180 votes; Connecticut: 1,220, 0.2 per cent; Illinois: 9,677, 0.2; Iowa: 193; Kentucky: 317; Maine: 335, 0.1; Massachusetts: 2,780, 0.1; Michigan: 1,264, 0.1; Minnesota: 3,176, 0.3; Missouri: 220; New Jersey: 6,939, 0.4; New York: 14,352, 0.2; Pennsylvania: 1,789, 0.1; Virginia: 90; Washington: 1,645, 0.2; Wisconsin: 1,002, 0.1.

Totals: 45,179; 0.09%

Gerald L. K. Smith (America First)

Michigan: 1,530 votes, 0.1 per cent; Texas: 250.

Totals: 1,780

Darlington Hoopes (Socialist)

California: 1,408 votes.

Arla A. Albaugh

California: 147 votes.

Independent

Louisiana: 69 votes.

Independent Democrat

Georgia: 3,373 votes, 1.0 per cent of Ga. vote.

Southern Democrat

South Carolina: 7,799, 7.5 per cent of S.C. vote.

Texas Regulars

Texas: 135,411, 11.8 per cent of Texas vote.

Unknown:

California: 326 votes; Massachusetts: 266; Michigan: 6; Vermont: 14.

1948

Norman M. Thomas (Socialist)

Arkansas: 1,037 votes, 0.4 per cent; California: 3,459, 0.1; Colorado: 1,678, 0.3; Connecticut: 6,964, 0.8; Delaware: 250, 0.2; Georgia: 3; Idaho: 332, 0.2; Illinois: 11,522, 0.3; Indiana: 2,179, 0.1; Iowa: 1,829, 0.2; Kansas: 2,807, 0.4; Kentucky: 1,284, 0.2; Maryland: 2,941, 0.5; Michigan: 6,063, 0.3; Minnesota: 4,646, 0.4; Missouri: 2,222, 0.1; Montana: 695, 0.3; New Hampshire: 86; New Jersey: 10,521, 0.5; New Mexico: 80; New York: 40,879, 0.7; North Dakota: 1,000, 0.5; Oregon: 5,051, 1.0; Pennsylvania: 11,325, 0.3; Rhode Island: 429, 0.1; South Carolina: 1; Tennessee: 1,288, 0.2; Texas: 874, 0.1; Vermont: 584, 0.5; Virginia: 726, 0.2; Washington: 3,534, 0.4; Wisconsin: 12,547, 1.0; Wyoming: 137, 0.1.

Totals: 138,973; 0.29%

Claude A. Watson (Prohibition)

Alabama: 1,026 votes, 0.5 per cent, Arizona: 786, 0.4; Arkansas: 1; California: 16,926, 0.4; Delaware: 343, 0.3; Georgia: 732, 0.2; Idaho: 628, 0.3; Illinois: 11,959, 0.3; Indiana: 14,711, 0.9; Iowa: 3,382, 0.3; Kansas: 6,468, 0.8; Kentucky: 1,245, 0.2; Massachusetts: 1,663, 0.1; Michigan: 13,052, 0.6; Missouri: 8;

Montana: 429, 0.2; New Jersey: 10,593, 0.5; New Mexico: 124, 0.1; Pennsylvania: 10,538, 0.3; Texas: 2,758, 0.2; Washington: 6,117, 0.7.

Totals: 103,489; 0.21%

Edward A. Teichert (Socialist Labor)

Arizona: 121 votes, 0.1 per cent; California: 195; Colorado: 214; Connecticut: 1,184, 0.1; Delaware: 29; Illinois: 3,118, 0.1; Indiana: 763, 0.1; Iowa: 4,274, 0.4; Kentucky: 185; Massachusetts: 5,535, 0.3; Michigan: 1,263, 0.1; Minnesota: 2,525, 0.2; Missouri: 3; New Hampshire: 83; New Jersey: 3,354, 0.2; New York: 2,729; Pennsylvania: 1,461; Rhode Island: 131; Virginia: 234, 0.1; Washington: 1,133, 0.1; Wisconsin: 399; Wyoming: 56, 0.1.

Totals: 29,038; 0.06%

Farrell Dobbs (Socialist Workers)

California: 133 votes; Colorado: 228; Connecticut: 606, 0.1 per cent; Iowa: 256; Michigan: 672; Minnesota: 606, 0.1; New Jersey: 5,825, 0.3; New York: 2,675; Pennsylvania: 2,133, 0.1; Utah: 74; Washington: 103; Wisconsin: 303.

Totals: 13,614, 0.03%

Gerald L. K. Smith

California: 42 votes.

John G. Scott (Greenback)

California: 6 votes.

John Maxwell (Vegetarian)

California: 4 votes.

Morgan Blake

Georgia: 1 vote.

Fielding L. Wright

Maryland: 2,294 votes, 0.4 per cent of Md. vote.

Dwight David Eisenhower

Missouri: 1 vote.

Unknown:

California: 761 votes; Illinois: 1,629; Iowa: 8; Louisiana: 10; Massachusetts: 634; Michigan: 1; Pennsylvania: 107; Vermont: 35.

1952

Eric Hass (Socialist Labor)

Arkansas: 1 vote; California: 273; Colorado: 352, 0.1 per cent; Connecticut: 535, 0.1; Delaware: 242, 0.1; Illinois: 9,363, 0.2; Indiana: 979, 0.1; Iowa: 139; Kentucky: 893, 0.1; Massachusetts: 1,957, 0.1; Michigan: 1,495, 0.1; Minnesota: 2,383, 0.2; Missouri: 169; New Jersey: 5,815, 0.2; New Mexico: 35; New York: 1,560; Pennsylvania: 1,377; Rhode Island: 83; Virginia: 1,160, 0.2; Washington: 633, 0.1; Wisconsin: 770, 0.1; Wyoming: 36.

Totals: 30,250; 0.05%

Darlington Hoopes (Socialist)

California: 206 votes; Colorado: 365, 0.1 per cent; Connecticut: 2,244, 0.2; Iowa: 20; Kansas: 530, 0.1; Missouri: 227; Montana: 159, 0.1; New Jersey: 8,593, 0.4; New York: 2,664; Pennsylvania: 2,698, 0.1; Vermont: 185, 0.1; Virginia: 504, 0.1; Washington: 254; Wisconsin: 1,157, 0.1; Wyoming: 40.

Totals: 20,065; 0.03%

Douglas MacArthur (Constitution)

Arkansas: 458 votes, 0.1 per cent; California: 3,504, 0.1; Colorado: 2,181, 0.4: Missouri: 535; New Mexico: 215, 0.1; North Dakota: 1,075, 0.4; Tennessee: 379; Texas: 1,563, 0.1; Washington: 7,290, 0.7.

Totals: 17,200; 0.03%

Farrell Dobbs (Socialist Worker)

Michigan: 655 votes; Minnesota: 618; New Jersey: 3,850, 0.2 per cent; New York: 2,212; Pennsylvania: 1,508; Washington: 119; Wisconsin: 1,350, 0.1.

Totals: 10,312; 0.02%

Henry Krajewski (Poor Man's)

New Jersey: 4,203 votes, 0.2 per cent of N.J. vote.

Unknown:

California: 3,578 votes, 0.1 per cent; Georgia: 1; Idaho: 23; Illinois: 448; Massachusetts: 69; Michigan: 3; New York: 178; Pennsylvania: 155; Vermont: 18.

1956

Harry Flood Byrd (States' Rights)[6]

Kentucky: 2,657 votes, 0.3 per cent of Ky. vote.

Enoch A. Holtwick (Prohibition)[6]

California: 11,119 votes, 0.2 per cent; Delaware: 400, 0.2; Indiana: 6,554, 0.3; Kansas: 3,048, 0.4; Kentucky: 2,145, 0.2; Massachusetts: 1,205, 0.1; Michigan: 6,923, 0.2; New Jersey: 9,147, 0.4; New Mexico: 607, 0.2; Tennessee: 789, 0.1.

Totals: 41,937; 0.07%

Farrell Dobbs (Socialist Workers)

California: 96 votes; Minnesota: 1,098, 0.1 per cent; New Jersey: 4,004, 0.2; Pennsylvania: 2,035; Wisconsin: 564.

Totals: 7,797; 0.01%

Darlington Hoopes (Socialist)

California: 123 votes; Colorado: 531, 0.1 per cent; Iowa: 192; Virginia: 444, 0.1; Wisconsin: 754, 0.1.

Totals: 2,044

Henry Krajewski (American Third Party)

New Jersey: 1,829 votes, 0.1 per cent of N.J. vote.

Gerald L. K. Smith

California: 11 votes.

Independent

Mississippi: 42,961, 17.3 per cent of Miss. vote.

Unpledged

Alabama: 20,323 votes, 4.1 per cent; Louisiana: 44,520, 7.2; South Carolina: 88,509, 29.5.

Unknown:

Alabama: 10 votes; California: 819; Florida: 1,542, 0.1 per cent; Georgia: 2,189, 0.3; Idaho: 16; Illinois: 56; Massachusetts: 341; Vermont: 39.

1960

Rutherford L. Decker (Prohibition)

California: 21,706 votes, 0.3 per cent; Delaware: 284, 0.1; Indiana: 6,746, 0.3; Kansas: 4,138, 0.5; Massachusetts: 1,633, 0.1; Michigan: 2,029, 0.1; Montana: 456, 0.2; New Mexico: 777, 0.3; Tennessee: 2,450, 0.2; Texas: 3,868, 0.2.

Totals: 44,087; 0.06%

Orval E. Faubus (National States Rights)[7]

Alabama: 4,367 votes, 0.8 per cent; Arkansas: 28,952, 6.8; Delaware: 354, 0.2; Louisiana: 169,572, 21.0; Tennessee: 11,296, 1.1.

Totals: 214,541; 0.3%

Farrell Dobbs (Socialist Workers)

Colorado: 563 votes, 0.1 per cent; Iowa: 634, 0.1; Michigan: 4,347, 0.1; Minnesota: 3,077, 0.2; Montana: 391, 0.1; New Jersey: 11,402, 0.4; New York: 14,319, 0.2; North Dakota: 158, 0.1; Pennsylvania: 2,678, 0.1; Utah: 100; Washington: 705, 0.1; Wisconsin: 1,792, 0.1.

Totals: 40,166; 0.06%

Charles Loten Sullivan (Constitutional)

Texas: 18,170 votes, 0.8 per cent.

Total: 0.03%

J. Bracken Lee (Conservative)

New Jersey: 8,708 votes, 0.3 per cent.

Total: 0.01%

C. Benton Coiner (Virginia Conservative)

Virginia: 4,204 votes, 0.5 per cent of Va. vote.

Lar Daly (Tax Cut)

Michigan: 1,767 votes, 0.1 per cent of Mich. vote.

Clennon King (Independent Afro-American Unity)

Alabama: 1,485 votes, 0.3 per cent of Ala. vote.

Merritt B. Curtis (Constitution)

Washington: 1,401 votes, 0.1 per cent of Wash. vote.

T. Coleman Andrews

Maryland: 2 votes.

Barry Goldwater

Maryland: 1 vote.

Stuart Symington

South Carolina: 1 vote.

Independent American

Michigan: 539 votes.

Unknown:

Alabama: 231 votes; Georgia: 245; Illinois: 15; Massachusetts: 31; Oregon: 959, 0.1 per cent; Pennsylvania: 440; Texas: 175; Vermont: 7.

1964

E. Harold Munn (Prohibition)

California: 305 votes; Colorado: 1,355, 0.2 per cent; Delaware: 425, 0.2; Indiana: 8,266, 0.4; Iowa: 1,902, 0.2; Kansas: 5,393, 0.6; Massachusetts: 3,735, 0.2; Michigan: 669; Montana: 499, 0.2; New Mexico: 543, 0.2; North Dakota: 174, 0.1.

Totals: 23,266; 0.03%

John Kasper (National States Rights)

Arkansas: 2,965 votes, 0.5 per cent; Kentucky: 3,469, 0.3; Montana: 519, 0.2.

Totals: 6,953; 0.01%

Joseph B. Lightburn (Constitution)

Texas: 5,060 votes, 0.2 per cent.

Total: 0.01%

James Hensley (Universal Party)

California: 19 votes.

George C. Wallace

Georgia: 60 votes.

Richard B. Russell

Georgia: 50 votes.

Unpledged Democrat

Alabama: 210,732 votes, 30.6 per cent of Ala. vote.

Unknown:

Alabama: 1 vote; California: 5,401, 0.1 per cent; Connecticut: 1,313, 0.1; Georgia: 85; Illinois: 62; Iowa: 118; Massachusetts: 159; Michigan: 145; New York: 268; Oregon: 2,509, 0.3; Pennsylvania: 2,531, 0.1; South Carolina: 8; Tennessee: 34; Vermont: 20.

1968

Dick Gregory (Peace and Freedom)

California: 3,230 votes; Colorado: 1,393, 0.2 per cent; New Jersey: 8,084, 0.3; New York: 24,517, 0.4; Ohio: 372; Pennsylvania: 7,821, 0.2; Virginia: 1,680, 0.1.

Totals: 47,097, 0.06%

Fred Halstead (Socialist Workers)

Arizona: 85 votes; Colorado: 235; Indiana: 1,293, 0.1 per cent; Iowa: 3,377, 0.3; Kentucky: 2,843, 0.3; Michigan: 4,099, 0.1; Minnesota: 807, 0.1; Montana: 457, 0.2; New Hampshire: 104; New Jersey: 8,667, 0.3; New Mexico: 252, 0.1; New York: 11,851, 0.2;

North Dakota: 128, 0.1; Ohio: 69; Pennsylvania: 4,862, 0.1; Rhode Island: 383, 0.1; Utah: 89; Vermont: 295, 0.2; Washington: 272; Wisconsin: 1,222, 0.1.
   Totals: 41,390; 0.06%

Eldridge Cleaver (Peace and Freedom)

Arizona: 217 votes; Iowa: 1,332, 0.1 per cent; Michigan: 4,585, 0.1; Minnesota: 933, 0.1; Washington: 1,669, 0.1.
   Totals: 8,736; 0.01%

Eugene McCarthy

Arizona: 2,751 votes, 0.6 per cent; California: 20,721, 0.3; Minnesota: 584; Oregon: 1,496, 0.2.
   Totals: 25,552; 0.03%

E. Harold Munn (Prohibition)

Alabama: 3,814 votes, 0.4 per cent; California: 59; Colorado: 275; Indiana: 4,616, 0.2; Iowa: 362; Kansas: 2,192, 0.3; Massachusetts: 2,369, 0.1; Michigan: 60: Montana: 510, 0.2; North Dakota: 38; Ohio: 19; Virginia: 601.
   Totals: 14,915; 0.02%

Ventura Chavez (People's Constitution)

New Mexico: 1,519 votes, 0.5 per cent of N.M. vote.

Charlene Mitchell (Communist)

California: 260 votes; Minnesota: 415; Ohio: 23; Washington: 378.

James Hensley (Universal)

Iowa: 142 votes.

Richard K. Troxell (Constitution)

North Dakota: 34 votes.

Kent M. Soeters (Berkeley Defense Group)

California: 17 votes.

Nelson A. Rockefeller

Oregon: 69 votes.

American Independent Democrat

Alabama: 10,518 votes; 1.0 per cent of Ala. vote.

New Party

New Hampshire: 421 votes, 0.1 per cent; Vermont: 579, 0.4.

New Reform

Montana: 470 votes, 0.2 per cent of Mont. vote.

Peace and Freedom

California: 27,707 votes, 0.4 per cent; Utah: 180.
   Totals: 27,887 votes; 0.04%

Unknown:

Colorado: 948 votes, 0.1 per cent; Connecticut: 1,300, 0.1; Georgia: 173; Illinois: 325; Iowa: 250; Massachusetts: 53; Michigan: 29; Minnesota: 170; New Hampshire: 108; Oregon: 1,075, 0.1; Pennsylvania: 2,264, 0.1; Texas: 489; Vermont: 29; Wisconsin: 2,342, 0.1.

1972

Linda Jenness (Socialist Workers)

California: 574 votes; Colorado: 666, 0.1 per cent; Idaho: 397, 0.1; Iowa: 488; Kentucky: 685, 0.1; Massachusetts: 10,600, 0.4; Michigan: 1,603, 0.1; Minnesota: 940, 0.1; Mississippi: 2,458, 0.4; New Hampshire: 368, 0.1; New Jersey: 2,233, 0.1; New Mexico: 474, 0.1; North Dakota: 288, 0.1; Pennsylvania: 4,639, 0.1; Rhode Island: 729, 0.2; South Dakota: 994, 0.3; Texas: 8,664, 0.3; Washington: 623.
   Totals: 37,423; 0.05%

Louis Fisher (Socialist Labor)

California: 197 votes; Colorado: 4,361, 0.5 per cent; Illinois: 12,344, 0.3; Indiana: 1,688, 0.1; Iowa: 195; Massachusetts: 129; Michigan: 2,437, 0.1; Minnesota: 4,261, 0.2; New Jersey: 4,544, 0.2; New York: 4,530, 0.1; Ohio: 7,107, 0.2; Virginia: 9,918, 0.7; Washington: 1,102, 0.1; Wisconsin: 998, 0.1.
   Totals: 53,811, 0.07%

Gus Hall (Communist)

California: 373 votes; Colorado: 432, 0.1 per cent; Illinois: 4,541, 0.1; Iowa: 272; Kentucky: 464; Massachusetts: 46; Michigan: 1,210; Minnesota: 662; New Jersey: 1,263; New York: 5,641, 0.1; North Dakota: 87; Ohio: 6,437, 0.2; Pennsylvania: 2,686, 0.1; Washington: 566; Wisconsin: 663.
   Totals: 25,343; 0.03%

E. Harold Munn (Prohibition)

Alabama: 8,559 votes, 0.9 per cent; California: 53; Colorado: 467, 0.1; Delaware: 238, 0.1; Kansas, 4,188, 0.5.
   Totals: 13,505; 0.02%

John Hospers (Libertarian)

California: 980 votes; Colorado: 1,111, 0.1 per cent; Massachusetts: 43; Washington: 1,537, 0.1.
   Totals: 3,671

John V. Mahalchik (America First)

New Jersey: 1,743 votes, 0.1 per cent of N.J. vote.

Gabriel Green (Universal)

California: 21 votes; Iowa: 199.

John Beno

Colorado: 6 votes.

Evelyn Reed (Socialist Workers)

Indiana: 5,575 votes, 0.3 per cent; New York: 7,797, 0.1; Wisconsin: 506.
   Totals: 13,878; 0.02%

Edward A. Wallace

Ohio: 460 votes.

Socialist Worker

Arizona: 30,945, 4.7 per cent; Louisiana: 12,169, 1.2.

Unknown:

Connecticut: 777 votes, 0.1 per cent; Florida, 7,407, 0.3; Illinois: 2,229, 0.1; Iowa: 321; Massachusetts: 342; Michigan: 598; Minnesota: 962, 0.1; New Hampshire: 142; Oregon: 2,289, 0.3; Pennsylvania: 2,715, 0.1; South Carolina: 17; Tennessee: 369; Texas: 3,393, 0.1; Wisconsin: 893, 0.1; District of Columbia: 568, 0.3.

1976[9]

Lester Maddox (American Independent)

Alabama: 9,198 votes, 0.8 per cent; Arizona: 85; California: 51,098, 0.6; Connecticut: 7,101, 0.5; Georgia: 1,071, 0.1; Idaho: 5,935, 1.7; Kansas: 2,118, 0.2; Kentucky: 2,328, 0.2; Louisiana: 10,058, 0.8; Maine: 8; Maryland: 171; Mississippi: 4,861, 0.6; Nebraska: 3,380, 0.6; Nevada: 1,497, 0.7; New Jersey: 7,716, 0.3; New Mexico: 31; New York: 97; North Dakota: 269, 0.1; Ohio: 15,529, 0.4; Pennsylvania: 25,344, 0.5; Rhode Island: 1; South Carolina: 1,950, 0.2; Tennessee: 2,303, 0.2; Texas: 41; Utah: 1,162, 0.2; Washington: 8,585, 0.6; West Virginia: 12; Wisconsin: 8,552, 0.4; Wyoming: 30.
   Totals: 170,531; 0.2%

Thomas J. Anderson (American)

Alabama: 70 votes; Arizona: 564, 0.1 per cent; Arkansas: 389, 0.1; California: 4,565, 0.1; Colorado: 397; Connecticut: 155; Delaware: 645, 0.3; Florida: 21,325, 0.7; Georgia: 1,168, 0.1; Idaho: 493, 0.1; Illinois: 387; Indiana: 14,048, 0.6; Iowa: 3,040, 0.2; Kansas: 4,724, 0.5; Kentucky: 8,308, 0.7; Maine: 28; Maryland:

321; Massachusetts: 7,555, 0.3; Minnesota: 13,592, 0.7; Mississippi: 6,678, 0.9; Montana: 5,772, 1.8; New Mexico: 106; New York: 451; North Carolina: 5,607, 0.3; North Dakota: 3,796, 1.3; Oregon: 1,035, 0.1; Rhode Island: 24; South Carolina: 2,996, 0.4; Tennessee: 5,769, 0.4; Texas: 11,442, 0.3; Utah: 13,284, 2.5; Virginia: 16,686, 1.0; Washington: 5,046, 0.3; West Virginia: 17; Wyoming: 290, 0.2.

Totals: 160,773; 0.2%.

Peter Camejo (Socialist Workers)

Alabama: 1 vote; Arizona: 928, 0.1 per cent; California: 17,259, 0.2; Colorado: 1,126, 0.1; Connecticut: 42; District of Columbia: 545, 0.3; Georgia: 43; Idaho: 14; Illinois: 3,615, 0.1; Indiana: 5,695, 0.3; Iowa: 267; Kentucky: 350; Louisiana: 2,240, 0.2; Maine: 1; Maryland: 261; Massachusetts: 8,138, 0.3; Michigan: 1,804; Minnesota: 4,149, 0.2; Mississippi: 2,805, 0.4; New Hampshire: 161; New Jersey: 1,184; New Mexico: 2,462, 0.6; New York: 6,996, 0.1; North Dakota: 43; Ohio: 4,717, 0.1; Pennsylvania: 3,009, 0.1; Rhode Island: 462, 0.1; South Carolina: 8; South Dakota: 168, 0.1; Texas: 1,723; Utah: 268; Vermont: 430, 0.2; Virginia: 17,802, 1.0; Washington: 905, 0.1; West Virginia: 2; Wisconsin: 1,691, 0.1.

Totals: 91,314, 0.1%

Gus Hall (Communist)

Alabama: 1,954 votes, 0.2 per cent; California: 12,766, 0.2; Colorado: 403; Connecticut: 186; District of Columbia: 219, 0.1; Georgia: 3; Idaho: 5; Illinois: 9,250, 0.2; Iowa: 554; Kentucky: 426; Louisiana: 7,417, 0.6; Maine: 14; Maryland: 68; Minnesota: 1,092, 0.1; New Jersey: 1,662, 0.1; New Mexico: 19; New York: 10,270, 0.2; North Dakota: 84; Ohio: 7,817, 0.2; Pennsylvania: 1,891; Rhode Island: 334, 0.1; South Carolina: 1; South Dakota: 318, 0.1; Tennessee: 547; Utah: 121; Washington: 817, 0.1; West Virginia: 5; Wisconsin: 749.

Totals: 58,992; 0.07%.

Margaret Wright (People's Party)

California: 41,731 votes, 0.5 per cent; Connecticut: 1; Idaho: 1; Maryland: 8; Massachusetts: 33; Michigan: 3,504, 0.1; Minnesota: 635; New Jersey: 1,044; Washington: 1,124, 0.1; Wisconsin: 943.

Totals: 49,024; 0.06%.

Lyndon H. LaRouche (U.S. Labor)

Alabama: 1 vote; Colorado: 567, 0.1 per cent; Connecticut: 1,789, 0.1; Delaware: 136, 0.1; District of Columbia: 157, 0.1; Georgia: 1; Idaho: 739, 0.2; Illinois: 2,018; Indiana: 1,947, 0.1; Iowa: 241; Kentucky: 510; Maryland: 21; Massachusetts: 4,922, 0.2; Michigan: 1,366; Minnesota: 543; New Hampshire: 186, 0.1; New Jersey: 1,650, 0.1; New Mexico: 1; New York: 5,413, 0.1; North Carolina: 755; North Dakota: 142; Ohio: 4,335, 0.1; Pennsylvania: 2,744, 0.1; South Carolina: 2; Tennessee: 512; Vermont: 196, 0.1; Virginia: 7,508, 0.4; Washington: 903, 0.1; Wisconsin: 738.

Totals: 40,043; 0.05%.

Benjamin C. Bubar (Prohibition)

Alabama: 6,669 votes, 0.6 per cent; California: 34; Colorado: 2,882, 0.3; Delaware: 103; Kansas: 1,403, 0.1; Maine: 3,495, 0.7; Maryland: 2; Massachusetts: 14; New Jersey: 554; New Mexico: 211, 0.1; North Dakota: 63; Ohio: 62; Tennessee: 442.

Totals: 15,934; 0.02%.

Jules Levin (Socialist Labor)

California: 222 votes; Colorado: 14; Connecticut: 1; Delaware: 86; Florida: 19; Georgia: 2; Illinois: 2,422, 0.1 per cent; Iowa: 167; Maine: 1; Maryland: 7; Massachusetts: 19; Michigan: 1,148; Minnesota: 370; New Hampshire: 66; New Jersey: 3,686, 0.1; New York: 28; Ohio: 68; Rhode Island: 188; Washington: 713; Wisconsin: 389.

Totals: 9,616; 0.01%.

Frank P. Zeidler (Socialist)

Connecticut: 5 votes; Florida: 8; Georgia: 2; Idaho: 2; Iowa: 234; Maryland: 16; Minnesota: 354; New Jersey: 469; New Mexico: 240, 0.1 per cent; New York: 14; North Dakota: 38; Washington: 358; Wisconsin: 4,298, 0.2.

Totals: 6,038; 0.01%.

Ernest L. Miller (Restoration)

California: 26 votes; Colorado: 6; Florida: 2; Georgia: 3; Maryland: 8; Tennessee: 316.

Totals: 361.

Frank Taylor (United American)

Arizona: 22 votes; California: 14.

Totals: 36.

Unknown

Alabama: 137 votes; Alaska: 1,176, 1.0 per cent; California: 74; Colorado: 2; Connecticut: 1,122, 0.1; District of Columbia: 1,944, 1.2; Georgia: 847, 0.1; Idaho: 1,430, 0.4; Illinois: 1,662; Iowa: 506; Maine: 185; Maryland: 1,945, 0.1; Massachusetts: 1,354, 0.1; Michigan: 2,160, 0.1; Minnesota: 342; Missouri: 3,741, 0.2; Nevada: 5,108, 2.5; New Hampshire: 604, 0.2; New Mexico: 501, 0.1; New York: 4,052, 0.1; North Carolina: 228; Oregon: 6,107, 0.6; Pennsylvania: 2,934, 0.1; Rhode Island: 82; South Carolina: 328; Tennessee: 229; Texas: 2,752, 0.1; Vermont: 99, 0.1; West Virginia: 125; Wisconsin: 2,839, 0.1; Wyoming: 354, 0.2.

Totals: 44,969; 0.06%.

1980 [10]

Barry Commoner (Citizens)

Alabama: 517 votes; Arizona: 551, 0.1 per cent; Arkansas: 2,345, 0.3; California: 61,063, 0.7; Colorado: 5,614, 0.5; Connecticut: 6,130, 0.4; Delaware, 103; District of Columbia: 1,840, 1.1; Georgia: 104; Hawaii: 1,548, 0.5; Illinois: 10,692, 0.2; Indiana: 4,852, 0.2; Iowa: 2,273, 0.2; Kentucky: 1,304, 0.1; Louisiana: 1,584, 0.1; Maine: 4,394, 0.8; Massachusetts: 2,056, 0.1; Michigan: 11,930, 0.3; Minnesota: 8,407, 0.4; Missouri: 573; New Hampshire: 1,320, 0.4; New Jersey: 8,203, 0.3; New Mexico: 2,202, 0.5; New York: 23,186, 0.4; North Carolina: 2,287, 0.1; North Dakota: 429, 0.2; Ohio: 8,564, 0.2; Oregon: 13,642, 1.2; Pennsylvania: 10,430, 0.2; Rhode Island: 67; Tennessee: 1,112, 0.1; Texas: 453; Utah: 1,009, 0.1; Vermont: 2,316, 1.1; Virginia: 14,024, 0.8; Washington: 9,403, 0.5; Wisconsin: 7,767, 0.3.

Totals: 234,294; 0.3%

Gus Hall (Communist)

Alabama: 1,629 votes, 0.1 per cent; Arizona, 25; Arkansas: 1,244, 0.1; California: 847; Colorado: 487; Delaware: 13; District of Columbia: 371; Florida: 123; Hawaii: 458, 0.2; Illinois: 9,711, 0.2; Indiana: 702; Iowa: 298; Kansas, 967, 0.1; Kentucky: 348; Maine: 591, 0.1; Michigan: 3,262, 0.1; Minnesota: 1,184, 0.1; Missouri: 26; New Hampshire: 129; New Jersey: 2,555, 0.1; New York: 7,414, 0.1; North Dakota: 93; Pennsylvania: 5,184, 0.1; Rhode Island: 218, 0.1; Tennessee: 503; Texas: 49; Utah: 139; Vermont: 118, 0.1; Washington: 834; Wisconsin: 772.

Totals: 45,023; 0.05%

John R. Rarick (American Independent)

Alabama: 15,010 votes, 1.1 per cent; California: 9,856, 0.1; Idaho: 1,057, 0.2; Kansas: 789, 0.1; Louisiana: 10,333, 0.7; Michigan: 5; South Carolina: 2,177, 0.2; Utah: 522, 0.1; Wisconsin: 1,519, 0.1.

Totals: 41,268; 0.05%

Clifton DeBerry (Socialist Workers)

Alabama: 1,303 votes, 0.1 per cent; Arizona: 1,100, 0.1; District of Columbia: 173, 0.1; Florida: 41; Illinois: 1,302; Indiana: 610; Iowa:

244; Louisiana: 783, 0.1; Massachusetts: 5,143, 0.2; Minnesota: 711; Missouri: 1,515, 0.1; New Hampshire: 71; New York: 2,068; North Carolina: 416; North Dakota: 89; Pennsylvania: 20,291, 0.4; Rhode Island: 90; Tennessee: 490; Utah: 124; Vermont: 75; Virginia: 1,986, 0.1; Washington: 1,137, 0.1.

Totals: 38,737; 0.04%

Ellen McCormack (Right to Life)

Delaware: 3 votes; Kentucky: 4,233, 0.3 per cent; Missouri: 5; New Jersey: 3,927, 0.1; New York: 24,159, 0.4; Rhode Island: 1.

Totals: 32,327; 0.04%

Maureen Smith (Peace and Freedom)

California: 18,116 votes, 0.2 per cent.

Deirdre Griswold (Workers World)

California: 15 votes; Delaware: 3; District of Columbia: 52; Florida: 8; Georgia: 1; Illinois: 2,257; Massachusetts: 19; Michigan: 30; Minnesota: 698; Mississippi: 2,402, 0.3 per cent; New Hampshire: 76; New Jersey: 1,288; Ohio: 3,790, 0.1; Rhode Island: 77; Tennessee: 400; Texas: 11; Washington: 341; Wisconsin: 414.

Totals: 13,300; 0.02%

Benjamin C. Bubar (Statesman)

Alabama: 1,743 votes, 0.1 per cent; Arkansas: 1,350, 0.2; California: 36; Colorado, 1,180, 0.1; Delaware: 6; Iowa: 150; Kansas: 821, 0.1; Massachusetts: 34; Michigan: 9; New Mexico: 1,281, 0.3; North Dakota: 54; Ohio: 27; Tennessee: 521.

Totals: 7,212; 0.01%

David McReynolds (Socialist)

Alabama: 1,006 votes, 0.1 per cent; Florida: 116; Iowa: 534; Massachusetts: 62; Minnesota: 536; New Jersey: 1,973, 0.1; North Dakota: 82; Rhode Island: 170; Tennessee: 519; Vermont: 136, 0.1; Washington: 956, 0.1; Wisconsin: 808.

Totals: 6,898; 0.01%

Percy L. Greaves (American)

California: 87 votes: Delaware: 400, 0.2 per cent; Indiana: 4,750, 0.2; Iowa: 189; Michigan: 21; North Dakota: 235, 0.1; Utah: 965, 0.2.

Totals: 6,647; 0.01%

Andrew Pulley (Socialist Workers)

California: 231 votes; Colorado: 520; Delaware: 4; Georgia: 4; Kentucky: 393; Mississippi: 2,347, 0.3 per cent; New Jersey: 2,198, 0.1; New Mexico: 325, 0.1; South Dakota: 250, 0.1.

Totals: 6,272; 0.01%

Richard Congress (Socialist Workers)

Ohio: 4,029 votes, 0.1 per cent.

Kurt Lynen (Middle Class)

New Jersey: 3,694 votes, 0.1 per cent.

Bill Gahres (Down With Lawyers)

New Jersey: 1,718 votes, 0.1 per cent.

Frank W. Shelton (American)

Kansas: 1,555 votes, 0.2 per cent.

Harley McLain (Natural Peoples League)

North Dakota: 296 votes, 0.1 per cent.

Unknown

Alaska: 857 votes, 0.5 per cent; California: 1,242, 0.2; Connecticut: 836, 0.1; Delaware: 101; District of Columbia: 690, 0.4; Georgia: 112; Illinois: 604; Iowa: 519; Maine: 84; Massachusetts: 2,382, 0.1; Michigan: 891; Minnesota: 6,139 (American Party, with no candidate specified), 0.3; Missouri: 604; Nevada: 4,193 (none of the above), 1.7; New Hampshire: 68; New Mexico: 734; New York: 1,064; Oregon: 1,713, 0.1; Rhode Island: 37; South Carolina: 376; Tennessee: 152; Vermont: 413, 0.2; Wisconsin: 1,337, 0.1.

Totals: 23,517; 0.03%.

1984 [11]

Sonia Johnson (Citizens)

Arizona: 18 votes; Arkansas: 960, 0.1 per cent; California: 26,297, 0.3; Colorado: 23; Connecticut: 14; Delaware: 121; Florida: 58; Georgia: 4; Illinois: 2,716, 0.1; Kentucky: 599; Louisiana: 9,502, 0.6; Massachusetts: 18; Michigan: 1,191; Minnesota: 1,219, 0.1; Missouri: 2; New Jersey: 1,247; New Mexico: 455, 0.1; North Dakota: 368, 0.1; Pennsylvania: 21,628, 0.4; Rhode Island: 240; Tennessee: 978, 0.1; Texas: 87; Utah: 844, 0.1; Vermont: 264, 0.1; Washington: 1,891, 0.1; Wisconsin: 1,456, 0.1.

Totals: 72,200; 0.08%.

Bob Richards (Populist)

Alabama: 1,401 votes, 0.1 per cent; Arkansas: 1,461, 0.2; California: 39,265, 0.4; Georgia: 95; Idaho: 2,288, 0.6; Kansas: 3,564, 0.3; Louisiana: 1,310, 0.1; Minnesota: 2,377, 0.1; Mississippi: 641, 0.1; North Dakota: 1,077, 0.3; Rhode Island: 510, 0.1; Tennessee: 1,763, 0.1; Washington: 5,724, 0.3; West Virginia: 996, 0.1; Wisconsin: 3,864, 0.2.

Totals: 66,336; 0.07%

Dennis L. Serrette (Independent Alliance)

Alabama: 659 votes; Arkansas: 1,291, 0.1 per cent; Colorado: 978, 0.1; Connecticut: 1,374, 0.1; Delaware: 68; District of Columbia: 165, 0.1; Georgia: 2; Illinois: 2,386, 0.1; Iowa: 463; Kansas: 2,544, 0.2; Kentucky: 365; Louisiana: 533; Maine: 755, 0.1; Maryland: 656; Massachusetts: 7,998, 0.3; Michigan: 665; Minnesota: 232; Mississippi: 356; Nebraska: 1,025, 0.2; New Hampshire: 305, 0.1; New Jersey: 2,293, 0.1; New Mexico: 155; New York: 3,200; North Dakota: 152; Ohio: 12,090, 0.3; Rhode Island: 49; South Carolina: 682, 0.1; South Dakota: 1,150, 0.4; Tennessee: 524; Texas: 41; Utah: 220; Vermont: 323, 0.1; Washington: 1,654, 0.1; West Virginia: 493, 0.1; Wisconsin: 1,006.

Totals: 46,852; 0.05%.

Gus Hall (Communist)

Alabama: 4,671 votes, 0.3 per cent; Arkansas: 1,499, 0.2; Connecticut: 4,826, 0.3; District of Columbia: 257, 0.1; Georgia: 1; Hawaii: 821, 0.2; Illinois: 4,672, 0.1; Iowa: 286; Kentucky: 328; Maine: 1,292, 0.2; Maryland: 898; Michigan: 1,048; Minnesota: 630; New Jersey: 1,564; New York: 4,226, 0.1; North Dakota: 169, 0.1; Ohio: 4,438, 0.1; Pennsylvania: 1,780; Rhode Island: 75; Tennessee: 1,036, 0.1; Texas: 126; Utah: 184; Vermont: 115, 0.1; Washington: 814; Wisconsin: 596.

Totals: 36,386; 0.04%.

Mel Mason (Socialist Workers)

Alabama: 730 votes, 0.1 per cent; Colorado: 810, 0.1; District of Columbia: 127, 0.1; Florida: 7; Georgia: 10; Illinois: 2,132, 0.1; Iowa: 313; Kentucky: 3,129, 0.1; Louisiana: 1,164, 0.1; Michigan: 1,049; Minnesota: 3,180, 0.1; Mississippi: 1,032, 0.1; Missouri: 8; Nebraska: 1,066, 0.2; New Jersey: 1,264; New Mexico: 224; North Carolina: 799; North Dakota: 239, 0.1; Ohio: 4,344, 0.1; Rhode Island: 61; South Dakota: 337, 0.1; Tennessee: 715; Utah: 142; Vermont: 127, 0.1; Washington: 608; West Virginia: 645, 0.1; Wisconsin: 444.

Totals: 24,706; 0.03%.

Larry Holmes (Workers World)

District of Columbia: 107 votes, 0.1 per cent; Georgia: 2; Maryland: 745; Michigan: 1,416; Mississippi: 1,169, 0.1; New Jersey: 8,404, 0.3; New York: 2,226; Washington: 641; Wisconsin: 619.

Totals: 15,329; 0.02%.

Delmar Davis (American)

Delaware: 269 votes; Georgia: 4; Indiana: 7,617, 0.3 per cent; Kentucky: 428; Missouri: 1; South Carolina: 3,490, 0.4; Tennessee: 7; Utah: 1,345, 0.2.
Totals: 13,161; 0.01%

Ed Winn (Workers League)

Arizona: 3 votes; Illinois: 2,632 ; Michigan: 561; Minnesota: 260; New Jersey: 1,721, 0.1 per cent; Ohio: 3,565, 0.1; Pennsylvania: 2,059.
Totals: 10,801; 0.01%.

Earl F. Dodge (Prohibition)

Arkansas: 842 votes, 0.1 per cent; Colorado: 858, 0.1; Kansas: 2,109, 0.2; Massachusetts: 3; New Mexico: 206; North Dakota: 220, 0.1; Ohio: 4.
Total: 4,242.

Gavrielle Holmes (Workers World)

Ohio: 2,565 votes, 0.1 per cent; Rhode Island: 91.
Total: 2,656.

John B. Anderson (National Unity Party of Kentucky)

Georgia: 3 votes; Kentucky: 1,479; Tennessee: 4.
Total: 1,486.

Gerald Baker (Big Deal)

Iowa: 892 votes.

Arthur J. Lowery (United Sovereign Citizens)

Arkansas: 822 votes, 0.1 per cent; Georgia: 3.
Total: 825.

Unknown

Alaska: 843 votes, 0.4 per cent; Arizona: 21; California: 382; Connecticut, 8; District of Columbia: 809, 0.4; Florida: 32; Georgia: 460; Illinois: 862; Iowa: 1,051, 0.1; Maine: 82; Massachusetts: 892; Michigan: 602; Minnesota: 723; Montana: 1; Nevada: 3,950, 1.4; New Hampshire: 113; New Mexico: 1; New York: 837; Ohio: 34; Oregon: 4,348, 0.4; Rhode Island: 3; Tennessee: 117; Vermont: 712, 0.3; Wisconsin: 706.
Totals: 17,589, 0.02%.

1. Georgia figures for Webster obtained from Petersen, Svend, A Statistical History of the American Presidential Elections, *Westport, Conn.: Greenwood Press, 1981, p. 31.*
2. Troup figures obtained from Petersen, A Statistical History, *ibid.*
3. Iowa and Mississippi figures from Petersen, A Statistical History, *p. 81.* Petersen lists these votes, as well as Progressive votes in all other states, for Theodore Roosevelt. In the ICPSR data for 1916, votes are listed for Progressive electors; Roosevelt's name does not appear. Since Roosevelt declined to be a candidate, Congressional Quarterly followed ICPSR in listing these votes as Progressive.
4. Florida figures for Watkins obtained from Petersen, A Statistical History, *p. 83.*
5. Maine figures for Browder, Colvin and Aiken obtained from Petersen, A

Statistical History, *p. 94.*
6. Kentucky figures for Byrd and Holtwick obtained from Petersen, A Statistical History, *p. 109.*
7. Arkansas figures for Faubus obtained from Petersen, A Statistical History, *p. 113.*
8. Alabama figures for Munn obtained from Scammon, Richard M., America Votes 10, *Washington, D.C.: Congressional Quarterly, 1973, p. 28.*
9. Figures from Scammon, Richard M., and Alice V. McGillivray, America Votes 12, *Washington, D.C.: Congressional Quarterly, 1977.*
10. Figures from Scammon, Richard M., and Alice V. McGillivray, America Votes 14, *Washington, D.C.: Congressional Quarterly, 1981.*
11. Figures from Federal Election Commission and Elections Research Center, Washington, D.C.

Presidential Nomination Campaigns

(Announcement dates of major candidates and length of campaigns since 1972)

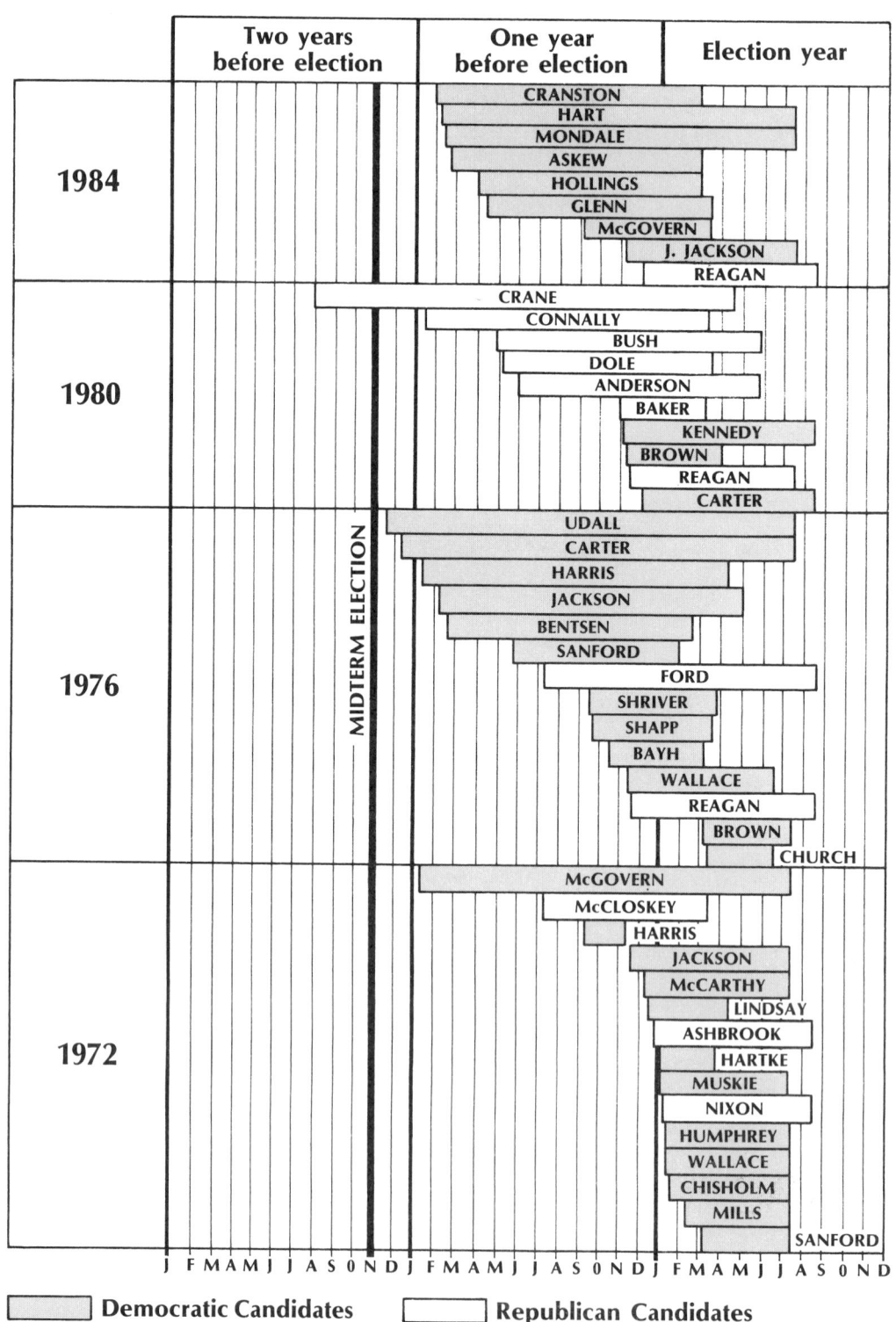

Presidential Primaries

Although they have existed for almost a century, primaries only recently have emerged as a dominant factor in the process by which candidates obtain the presidential nominations of major parties. After many years of ebbing and surging as an alternative to the smoke-filled-room system, presidential primaries flourished in the 1960s and 1970s. They helped to produce a few nominees who otherwise would have been unlikely prospects to capture the highest award a party can bestow.

Partly in reaction against this tendency of primaries to strengthen candidates who may be unpopular with party leaders, state legislatures scheduled fewer primaries in 1984 than in the peak year of 1980. And the caucus system was showing vigor in some states as a superior method of selecting delegates to national party conventions.

'Return to the People'

Presidential primaries originated as an outgrowth of the Progressive movement in the early 20th century. Progressives, populists and reformers in general were fighting state and municipal corruption. They objected to the links between political bosses and big business and advocated returning the government to the people.

Part of this "return to the people" was the inauguration of primary elections, wherein candidates for office would be chosen by the voters of their party rather than by what were looked upon as boss-dominated conventions. It was only a matter of time before the idea spread from state and local elections to presidential contests. Because there was no provision for a nationwide primary, state primaries were initiated to choose delegates to the national party conventions (delegate-selection primaries) and to register voters' preferences on their parties' eventual presidential nominees (preference primaries).

Florida enacted the first presidential primary law in 1901. The law gave party officials an option of holding a party primary to choose any party candidate for public office, as well as delegates to the national conventions. However, there was no provision for placing names of presidential candidates on the ballot — either in the form of a preference vote or with information indicating the preference of the candidates for convention delegates.

Impact of Progressive Movement

Wisconsin's Progressive Republican politician, Gov. Robert M. La Follette, gave a major boost to the presidential primary following the 1904 Republican National Convention. It was at that convention that the credentials of La Follette's Progressive delegation were rejected and a regular Republican delegation was seated from Wisconsin. Angered by what he considered his unfair treatment, La Follette returned to his home state and began pushing for a presidential primary law. The result was the Wisconsin law of 1905 providing for the mandatory direct election of national convention delegates. The law, however, did not including a provision for indicating the presidential preference of the delegates.

Pennsylvania closely followed Wisconsin (in 1906) with a statute providing that each candidate for delegate to a national convention could have printed beside his name on the official primary ballot the name of the presidential candidate he would support at the convention. However, no member of either party exercised this option in the 1908 primary.

La Follette's sponsorship of the delegate-selection primary helped make the concept part of the Progressive political program. The growth of the Progressive movement rapidly resulted in the enactment of presidential primary laws in other states.

The next step in presidential primaries — the preferential vote for president — took place in Oregon. There, in 1910, Sen. Jonathan Bourne, R (1907-13), a Progressive Republican colleague of La Follette (then a senator), sponsored a referendum to establish a presidential preference

Sources

Davis, James W. *Presidential Primaries: Road to the White House.* 1967. Reprint. Westport, Conn.: Greenwood Press, 1980.

Scammon, Richard M. *America Votes 1956-57.* New York: Macmillan, 1958. *America Votes 4.* Pittsburgh: University of Pittsburgh Press, 1962. *America Votes 6, America Votes 8, America Votes 10.* Washington, D.C.: Congressional Quarterly, 1966, 1970, 1973.

——, and Alice V. McGillivray. *America Votes 12, America Votes 14.* Washington, D.C.: Congressional Quarterly, 1977, 1981.

primary, with delegates legally bound to support the winner of the preference primary.

By 1912, with Oregon in the lead, 12 states had enacted presidential primary laws that provided for either direct election of delegates, a preferential vote, or both. The number had expanded to 26 states by 1916.

Primaries and Conventions

The first major test of the impact of presidential primary laws — in 1912 — demonstrated that victories in the primaries did not ensure a candidate's nomination at the convention. Former president Theodore Roosevelt, campaigning in 12 Republican primaries, won nine of them, including a defeat of incumbent Republican president William Howard Taft in Taft's home state of Ohio. Roosevelt lost only three — to Taft by a narrow margin in Massachusetts and to La Follette in North Dakota and in La Follette's home state of Wisconsin.

Despite this impressive string of primary victories, the Republican National Convention rejected Roosevelt in favor of Taft. The Republican National Committee, which organized the convention, and the convention's credentials committee, which ruled on contested delegates, both were dominated by Taft supporters. Moreover, Taft was backed by many state organizations, especially in the South, where most delegates were chosen by caucuses or conventions dominated by party leaders.

On the Democratic side, the convention more closely reflected the results of the primaries. Gov. Woodrow Wilson of New Jersey and Speaker of the House Champ Clark of Missouri were closely matched in total primary votes, with Wilson only 29,632 votes ahead of Clark. Wilson emerged with the nomination after a long struggle with Clark at the convention.

Likewise, in 1916 Democratic primary results foreshadowed the winner of the nomination, although Wilson, who was then the incumbent, had no major opposition for renomination. But once again Republican presidential primaries had little impact upon the nominating process at the convention. The eventual nominee, U.S. Supreme Court Justice Charles Evans Hughes, had won only two primaries.

In 1920 presidential primaries did not play a major role in determining the winner of either party's nomination. Democrat James M. Cox, the eventual nominee, ran in only one primary, his home state of Ohio. Most of the Democratic primaries featured favorite son candidates or write-in votes. And at the convention Democrats took 44 ballots to make their choice.

Similarly, the main entrants in the Republican presidential primaries that year failed to capture their party's nomination. Sen. Warren G. Harding of Ohio, the compromise choice, won the primary in his home state but lost badly in Indiana and garnered only a handful of votes elsewhere. The three leaders in the primaries — Sen. Hiram Johnson of California, Gen. Leonard Wood of New Hampshire and Gov. Frank O. Lowden of Illinois — all lost out in the end.

Revival of Interest

After the first wave of enthusiasm for presidential primaries in the 1910s, interest waned. By 1935 eight states had repealed their presidential primary laws.

The diminution of reform zeal during the 1920s and the preoccupation of the country with depression in the 1930s and war in the 1940s appeared to have been leading factors in this decline. Also, party leaders were not enthusiastic about primaries; the cost of conducting them was relatively high, both for the candidates and the states. Many presidential candidates ignored the primaries, and often voter participation was low.

But after World War II interest picked up again. Some politicians with presidential ambitions, knowing the party leadership was not enthusiastic about their candidacies, entered the primaries to try to generate a bandwagon effect. In 1948 Harold Stassen, Republican governor of Minnesota from 1939 to 1943, entered Republican presidential primaries in opposition to the Republican organization and was able to make some dramatic headway before losing to Gov. Thomas E. Dewey, a Republican of New York, in Oregon. And in 1952 Tennessee senator Estes Kefauver, D (1949-63), riding a wave of public recognition as head of a Senate Organized Crime Investigating Committee, challenged Democratic Party leaders by winning several primaries, including an upset of President Harry S Truman in New Hampshire. The Eisenhower-Taft struggle for the Republican Party nomination that year also stimulated interest in the primaries.

With the growing demand for political reform in the 1960s and early 1970s, the presidential primaries became more attractive as a path to the nomination. John F. Kennedy, then a relatively obscure U.S. senator from Massachusetts, helped to popularize that route with his successful uphill fight for the Democratic nomination in 1960. An unbroken string of Kennedy victories helped force the withdrawal of his chief rival in the primaries, Sen. Hubert H. Humphrey of Minnesota.

Similarly, Sen. Barry M. Goldwater, R-Ariz., in 1964, Richard Nixon, R-Calif., in 1968 and Sen. George S. McGovern, D-S.D., in 1972 — all party presidential nominees — were able to use the primaries to show their vote-getting and organizational abilities.

Democrats Begin to Tinker

Despite the Progressive reforms, party leaders until 1968 remained in firm control of the nominating process. With only a handful of 15 to 20 primaries regularly contested, candidates could count on a short primary season. They began in New Hampshire in March, then tested their appeal during the spring in Wisconsin, Nebraska, Oregon and California before resuming their courtship of party leaders.

But in 1968 the Democrats began tinkering with the nominating rules, resulting in presidential nominating campaigns that were predictable only in their unpredictability. The reforms were launched in an effort to reduce the alienation of liberals and minorities from the Democratic nominating system and to allow the people to choose their own leaders. The Republicans seldom made any changes in their rules. (*GOP rules, box, p. 20; Democratic rules, chart, p. 22*)

This era of grass-roots control produced for the Democrats presidential candidates Sen. George McGovern, a liberal from South Dakota who lost in a landslide to Richard Nixon in 1972, and Jimmy Carter, who beat incumbent president Gerald R. Ford in 1976. For this election, 26 states and the District of Columbia held some variation of the presidential preference primary.

With the record high of 37 primaries held in 1980, the opportunity for mass participation in the nominating process was greater than ever before. President Jimmy Carter and Republican Ronald Reagan were the clear winners of

Types of Primaries and Procedures

Presidential primaries consist of two basic types. One is the presidential preference primary in which voters vote directly for the person they wish to be nominated for president. The second is the type in which voters elect delegates to the national conventions.

States may use various combinations of these methods:

● A state may have a preference vote but choose delegates at party conventions. The preference vote may or may not be binding on the delegates.

● A state may combine the preference and delegate-selection primaries by electing delegates pledged or favorable to a candidate named on the ballot. However, under this system, state party organizations may run unpledged slates of delegates.

● A state may have an advisory preference vote and a separate delegate-selection vote in which delegates may be listed as either pledged to a candidate, favorable or unpledged.

● A state may have a mandatory preference vote with a separate delegate-selection vote. In these cases, the delegates are required to reflect the preference primary vote.

For those primaries in which the preference vote is binding upon delegates, state laws may vary as to the number of ballots through which delegates at the convention may remain committed.

Most primary states hold presidential preference votes, in which voters choose among the candidates who have qualified for the ballot in their states. Although preference votes may be binding or non-binding, in most states the vote is binding on the delegates, who either are elected in the primary itself or chosen outside of it by a caucus process, by a state committee or by the candidates who have qualified to win delegates.

Delegates may be bound for as short as one ballot or as long as a candidate remains in the race. National Democratic rules in effect in 1980 required delegates to be bound for one ballot unless released by the candidate they were elected to support. The rule was repealed for 1984.

Until 1980 the Republicans had a rule requiring delegates bound to a specific candidate by state law in primary states to vote for that candidate at the convention regardless of their personal presidential preferences. That rule was repealed at the July 1980 convention.

Delegates from primary states are allocated to candidates in various ways. Most of the methods are based on the preference vote — proportional representation, statewide winner-take-all (in which the candidate winning the most votes statewide wins all the delegates), congressional district and statewide winner-take-all (in which the high vote-getter in a district wins that district's delegates and the high vote-getter statewide wins all the at-large delegates) or some combination of the three. Still another method is the selection of individual delegates in a "loophole," or direct election, primary. Then the preference vote is either non-binding or there is no preference vote at all.

In the proportional representation system, the qualifying threshold for candidates to win delegates can vary. After a decade of intensive debate, Democratic leaders voted to require proportional representation in all primary and caucus states in 1980. But by 1984, after more rules changes, states were given the right to retain proportional representation only if they wished, awarding delegates to any candidate who drew roughly 20 percent of the vote.

The Republicans allow the primary states to set their own thresholds, which in many states were lower than the Democrats'. In Massachusetts, for example, a GOP candidate in 1980 had to receive only 2.4 percent of the vote to win a delegate.

In nearly half the primary states, major candidates are placed on the ballot by the secretary of state or a special nominating committee. The consent of the candidate is required in only three states — Kentucky, Michigan and North Carolina.

Elsewhere, candidates must take the initiative to get on the ballot. The filing requirements range from sending a letter of candidacy to election officials — the case in Puerto Rico — to filing petitions signed by a specified number of registered voters and paying a filing fee — the case in Alabama.

On many primary ballots, voters have the opportunity to mark a line labeled "uncommitted" if they do not prefer any of the candidates.

---

the long 1980 primary season. Although Carter received a bare majority of the cumulative Democratic primary vote, he amassed a plurality of nearly 2.7 million votes over his major rival, Sen. Edward M. Kennedy, D-Mass. With no opposition in the late primary contests, Reagan emerged as a more one-sided choice of GOP primary voters. He finished nearly 4.6 million votes ahead of George Bush, who eventually withdrew from the race.

Disheartened by their nominee's landslide defeat in 1980, the Democrats revised their nominating rules for the 1984 election. While the revisions of the 1970s were designed to give more influence to grass-roots activists and less to party regulars, these revisions were intended to bring about a deliberative process in which experienced party leaders could help select a consensus Democratic nominee with a strong chance to win the presidency. For the Republicans, the delegate-selection process was pro forma because President Reagan did not face a serious challenge for the Republican nomination.

The Democrats' new rules had some expected, as well as some unexpected, results. For the first time since 1968, the number of mass appeal delegate-selection primaries declined and the number of caucuses increased. The Democrats held only 25 primaries in 1984 to select national convention delegates. Yet, like South Dakota senator George McGovern in 1972 and Jimmy Carter in 1976, Colorado senator Gary Hart used the primaries to vault from the back of the pack, temporarily dislodging former vice president Walter F. Mondale, an early front-runner whose strongest ties were to the party leadership and its tradi-

Selection by Caucus Method

Caucuses, long the quiet backwater of the Democratic nominating process, were washed with controversy in 1984 as they gained in popularity at the expense of presidential primaries.

A strong showing in the caucuses by Walter F. Mondale led many Democrats — and not only supporters of his chief rivals, Colorado senator Gary Hart and black activist Jesse L. Jackson — to conclude that caucuses are inherently unfair.

Mondale's caucus victories might be termed the revenge of the insiders. More so than the primaries, the often-complex, low-visibility world of the caucuses is open to takeover. The mainstream Democratic coalition of party activists, labor union members and teachers was primed to dominate the caucuses in Mondale's behalf. In states with the largest delegate harvests, they did.

Decline in Impact

The impact of caucuses had decreased in the 1970s as the number of primaries grew dramatically. During the 1960s a candidate sought to run well in primary states mainly to have a bargaining chip with which to deal with powerful leaders in the caucus states. Republicans Barry Goldwater in 1964 and Richard Nixon in 1968 and Democrat Hubert H. Humphrey in 1968 all built up solid majorities among caucus state delegates that carried them to their parties' nominations. Humphrey did not even enter a primary in 1968.

But after 1968 candidates placed their principal emphasis on primary campaigning. First Sen. George McGovern, D-S.D. — and then incumbent Republican president Gerald R. Ford and Democratic challenger Jimmy Carter in 1976 — all won their parties' nominations by winning a large majority of the primary state delegates. Neither McGovern nor Ford won a majority of the caucus state delegates. Carter was able to win a majority only after his opponents' campaigns collapsed.

Complex Method

Compared with a primary, the caucus system is complex. Instead of focusing on a single primary election ballot, the caucus presents a multi-tiered system that involves meetings scheduled over several weeks, sometimes even months. There is mass participation at the first level only, with meetings at this step often lasting several hours and attracting only the most enthusiastic and dedicated party members.

The operation of the caucus varies from state to state, and each party has its own set of rules. But most use a process that begins with precinct caucuses or some other type of local mass meeting open to all party voters. Participants, often publicly declaring their votes, elect delegates to the next stage in the process.

In smaller states such as Delaware and Hawaii, delegates are elected directly to a state convention, where the national convention delegates are chosen. In larger states such as Iowa, there is at least one more step. Most frequently, delegates are elected at the precinct caucuses to county conventions, where the national

convention delegates are chosen. In Iowa Democrats hold their district conventions in April and their state convention in mid-June. Iowa Republicans hold district caucuses during the state convention in early June.

Participation, even at the first level of the caucus process, is usually much lower than in primary states. Caucus participants usually are local party leaders and activists, not newcomers to the process. Many rank-and-file voters find a caucus complex and confusing; others find it intimidating.

In a caucus state the focus is on one-on-one campaigning. Time, not money, is the most valuable resource. Because organization and personal campaigning are so important, an early start is far more crucial in a caucus state than in a primary. And because only a small segment of the electorate is targeted in most caucus states, candidates usually use media advertising sparingly. On the average, candidates spend much more money campaigning in primary states than they do in caucus states.

Although the basic steps in the caucus process are the same for both parties, the rules that govern them are vastly different. Democratic rules have been revamped substantially since 1968, establishing national standards for grass-roots participation. Republican rules have remained largely unchanged, with the states given wide latitude in drawing up their delegate-selection plans. Democratic caucuses are open to Democrats only. Republicans allow crossovers where state law permits, creating a wide range of variations. The first step of the Democratic caucus process must be open, well-publicized mass meetings. In most states Republicans do the same. Generally, voters may participate only in the election of local party officials, who meet to begin the caucus process.

Caucus Revival

The most tangible evidence of a revival of the caucus process was the increased percentage of delegates elected from caucus states. For both parties this figure had been on a sharp decline throughout the 1970s. But Democrats broke the downward trend and actually elected more delegates by the caucus process in 1980 than in 1976. The principal reason for the upward swing was that two of the largest delegations — Texas and Michigan — switched from primaries to caucuses to choose delegates. Those two switches more than offset the moves of the Democratic parties in Connecticut, Kansas, Louisiana, New Mexico and Puerto Rico from caucuses to primaries. Between 1980 and 1984 six states switched from a primary to a caucus system, none the other way, and caucuses sent nearly one-third of the delegates to the Democratic convention.

Throughout the 1970s, Republicans elected a larger proportion of their delegates from caucus states than did the Democrats. But that changed in 1980, with only 24 percent of the GOP convention coming from caucus states (compared with 31 percent in 1976 and 53 percent in 1968).

Choosing a Running Mate: The Balancing Act

In modern times veteran political convention-watchers have come to look forward to the almost-traditional night of uncertainty as the new presidential nominee tries to come up with a running mate. But this hectic process is a recent one. During the country's first years the runner-up for the presidency automatically took the second slot.

But that system did not last long. In 1800 Thomas Jefferson and Aaron Burr found themselves in a tie for electoral votes. Neither man's supporters were willing to settle for the lesser office. The deadlock went to the House of Representatives, where Jefferson needed 36 ballots to clinch the presidency. It also led to the 12th Amendment, ratified in 1804, providing for Electoral College balloting for presidents and vice presidents. With the emergence of political parties after 1800, candidates ran as teams. Once party conventions began in 1831, delegates, with the guidance of party bosses, began to do the choosing.

In fact, it was only in 1940 that presidential nominees began regularly hand-picking their running mates. That year, after failing to persuade Secretary of State Cordell Hull to accept the vice presidency, Franklin D. Roosevelt forced Henry A. Wallace on a reluctant Democratic convention by threatening to refuse his own nomination if Wallace was rejected. The only exception to the practice Roosevelt established came in 1956, when Democrat Adlai E. Stevenson left the choice up to the convention.

If the selection of a running mate often has seemed like something of an afterthought, it could be because the position itself is not an especially coveted one. John Adams, the first man to hold the job, once complained, "My country has in its wisdom contrived for me the most insignificant office that ever the intention of man contrived or his imagination conceived."

More than a century later Thomas R. Marshall, Woodrow Wilson's vice president, expressed a similarly dismal view: "Once there were two brothers. One ran away to sea; the other was elected Vice President. And nothing was ever heard of either of them again."

Writing in *The Atlantic* in 1974, historian Arthur Schlesinger Jr. suggested the office be done away with. "It is a doomed office," he commented. "The Vice President has only one serious thing to do: that is, to wait around for the President to die."

But there is a reasonable chance that whoever fills the position will get a chance to move up, either by succession or election. As of September 1984, 13 presidents had held the second-rank,ing post, six in the 20th century. *(See box, opposite.)*

Also, during the 1970s and 1980s the vice presidency evolved from the somnolent office it once was; during this period three vice presidents enjoyed responsibility their predecessors did not. Nelson A. Rockefeller, who served under Gerald R. Ford, was given considerable authority in domestic policy coordination. Vice President Walter F. Mondale was deeply involved in helping President Jimmy Carter set policy, as was George Bush under President Ronald Reagan.

Yet whoever is brought on board is scrutinized not so much as a policy maker, but for how well he or she balances the ticket. One of the most important factors usually is geography, but other traditional factors weighed by nominees are religion and ethnicity. In national politics of the 1980s, however, those considerations seemed to be losing their place to race and sex. While a black candidate for either spot had not been seriously considered as of the 1984 election, the Democrats chose Rep. Geraldine A. Ferraro of New York to be their vice presidential candidate, the first female to receive such an honor.

Thirteen VPs Became President

Thirteen men who served as vice president have become president: John Adams, Thomas Jefferson, Martin Van Buren, John Tyler, Millard Fillmore, Andrew Johnson, Chester A. Arthur, Theodore Roosevelt, Calvin Coolidge, Harry S Truman, Richard Nixon, Lyndon B. Johnson and Gerald R. Ford.

Of those, all but Adams, Jefferson, Van Buren and Nixon first became president on the death or resignation of their predecessor. Seven vice presidents since 1900 have run unsuccessfully for president:

● Thomas R. Marshall, Democratic vice president under Woodrow Wilson from 1913 to 1921, failed to win the nomination in 1920.

● Charles G. Dawes, Republican vice president under Coolidge from 1925 to 1929, unsuccessfully sought the nomination in 1928 and 1932.

● John Nance Garner, Democratic vice president under Franklin D. Roosevelt from 1933 to 1941, ran unsuccessfully for the nomination in 1940.

● Henry A. Wallace, Democratic vice president under Roosevelt from 1941 to 1945, was Progressive Party nominee in 1948.

● Alben W. Barkley, Democratic vice president under Truman from 1949 to 1953, failed to win the 1952 nomination.

● Nixon, Republican vice president under Dwight D. Eisenhower from 1953 to 1961, was the GOP nominee in 1960.

● Hubert H. Humphrey, Democratic vice president under Lyndon Johnson from 1965 to 1969, was the Democratic nominee in 1968.

● Walter F. Mondale, Democratic vice president under Jimmy Carter from 1977 to 1981, was the Democratic nominee in 1984.

tional core elements. Ultimately, Mondale emerged from the primaries with just enough voter support to secure the nomination.

Many observers expressed the view that the Democrats, to guarantee the nomination of a candidate broadly acceptable within the party, would have to make a much stronger break with the concept of mass participation. But the process was expected to be difficult to replace, since there was no consensus among Democrats to give more control to party and elected officials. *(Primary procedures, types, box, p. 381; caucus procedures, box, p. 382)*

Proposals for Reform

In addition to the Democrats' internal party concerns with the nominating process, other critics often cited the length of the primary season (nearly twice as long as the general election campaign), the expense, the physical strain on the candidates and the variations and complexities of state laws as problems of presidential primaries.

To deal with these problems, several states in 1974-75 discussed the feasibility of creating regional primaries, in which individual states within a geographical region would hold their primaries on the same day. Supporters of the concept believed it would reduce candidate expenses and strain and would permit concentration on regional issues.

The idea achieved some limited success when two groups of states — one in the West and the other in the South — decided to organize regional primaries in 1976 in each of their areas. However, the two groups both chose the same day, May 25, to hold their primaries, thus defeating one of the main purposes of the plan by continuing to force candidates to shuttle across the country to cover both areas. The Western states participating in the grouping were Idaho, Nevada and Oregon; the Southern states were Arkansas, Kentucky and Tennessee.

Attempts were also made in New England to construct a regional primary. But jealousy on the part of New Hampshire for its first-in-the-nation primary and hesitancy by the other New England state legislatures defeated the idea. Only Vermont joined Massachusetts, on March 2, in holding a simultaneous presidential primary, although New Hampshire voted only one week earlier.

In 1980 limited regional primaries were held again in several areas of the country — on March 4 in New England (Massachusetts and Vermont), on March 11 in the Southeast (Alabama, Florida and Georgia), and on May 27 in the South (Arkansas and Kentucky) and the West (Idaho and Nevada). In 1984 the so-called Super Tuesday, March 13, produced regional primaries in New England (Massachusetts and Rhode Island) and in the South (Alabama, Florida and Georgia).

Other approaches to changing the primary system have been attempted at the national level. Congressional reform proposals included a single nationwide primary and standardization of the date of primaries to shorten the campaign season.

One suggested change was to establish a direct national primary. But a Democratic study commission as well as several academic groups that examined that idea rejected it. The consensus was that such a process would strip the party leadership of any role in the nominating process, enable presidential candidates to run factional or regional campaigns and increase the primacy of media "image" over serious discussion of the issues. "If you go to a national primary," said Ann Lewis, political director of the Democratic National Committee, "you don't have a political

process anymore, you have the 'Battle of the Network Stars,'..."

Some political scientists longed for the days when the nominees were chosen in large measure by the party leaders. In 1980 Jeane J. Kirkpatrick, then a Georgetown University professor and later the U.S. representative to the United Nations in the Reagan administration, called for the abolition of primaries and creation of a decision-making process restricted to party and elected leaders.

Political scientist Austin Ranney also felt that the power of the party leaders should be restored: "In the old smoke-filled-room days, the people who really chose the presidential nominee were people who knew [the candidates] and saw them in action and had some idea of what they were like." Ranney did not go so far as Kirkpatrick. Instead, he advocated a process in which the consensus of political leaders would be the deciding influence in national conventions. Ranney, however, thought it unlikely that either party would return to the smoke-filled rooms. "I think it's against the whole ethos of our times," he said.

Between 1911 and 1984 hundreds of bills were introduced in Congress to reform the presidential primary system. The biggest batches were introduced during sessions after the 1912, 1952 and 1968 nominating campaigns. All three campaigns produced the feeling among many voters that the will of the electorate, as expressed in the primaries, had been thwarted by national conventions. But since 1911 the only legislation enacted by Congress concerned the presidential primary in the District of Columbia. Rarely did primary reform legislation even reach the hearing stage.

Bibliography

Books

David, Paul T., and James W. Ceasar. *Proportional Representation in Presidential Nominating Politics.* Charlottesville, Va.: University Press of Virginia, 1980.

Davis, James W. *The Presidential Primaries: Road to the White House.* 1967. Reprint. Westport, Conn.: Greenwood Press, 1980.

Link, Arthur. *Wilson: The Road to the White House.* Princeton, N. J.: Princeton University Press, 1947.

Overacker, Louise. *The Presidential Primary.* 1926. Reprint. New York: Arno, 1974.

Page, Benjamin I. *Choices and Echoes in Presidential Elections.* Chicago: University of Chicago Press, 1978.

Ranney, Austin. *Federalization of Presidential Primaries.* Washington, D.C.: American Enterprise Institute, 1978.

Scammon, Richard M. *America Votes: A Handbook of Contemporary Election Statistics.* vols. 1 and 2. New York: Macmillan, 1956, 1958. *America Votes.* vols. 3-5. Pittsburgh: University of Pittsburgh, 1959, 1962 and 1964. *America Votes.* vols. 6-11. Washington, D. C.: Congressional Quarterly, 1966-1975.

——, and Alice V. McGillivray. *American Votes.* vols. 12-15. Washington, D.C.: Congressional Quarterly, 1977-1983.

Stavis, Ben. *We Were the Campaign: New Hampshire to Chicago for McCarthy.* Boston: Beacon Press, 1969.

Articles

Allen, C. D. "The Presidential Primary." *Queens Quarterly* (July-September 1912): 92-99.

Aylesworth, L. R. "Presidential Primary Elections: Legislation of 1910-1912." *American Political Science Review* (August 1912): 429-433.

Barnett, E. D. "Presidential Primary in Oregon." *Political Science Quarterly* (March 1916): 81-104.

Boots, R. S. "Presidential Primary: A Comprehensive Examination of the Presidential Primary at Work and Proposals of Reform." *National Municipal Review* (September 1920): 597-617.

Broder, David S. "Of Presidents and Parties." *Wilson Quarterly* 2 (Fall 1978): 105-114.

Chilton, W. E. "West Virginia and the Primary." *New Leader*, May 23, 1960, 3-18.

Dauer, Manning. "Toward a Model State Presidential Primary Law." *American Political Science Review* (March 1956): 145.

Davenport, F. M. "Pre-Nomination Campaign: The Failure of the Presidential Primary." *Outlook*, April 5, 1916, 807-810

Dickey, Francis J. "The Presidential Preference Primary." *American Political Science Review* (August 1915): 467-487.

Felson, Marcus, and Seymour Sudman. "The Accuracy of Presidential Preference Primary Polls." *Public Opinion Quarterly* 39 (Summer 1975): 232-236.

Hammond, Thomas H. "Another Look at the Role of 'The Rules' in the 1972 Democratic Presidential Primaries." *Western Political Quarterly* 33 (March 1980): 50-72.

Harbison, M. C. "The Presidential Preference Primary." *Tennessee Planner* (April 1953): 131-136.

Harris, J. P. "New Primary System." *State Government* (July 1948): 140.

Holcombe, John W. "Presidential Preference Vote and the Electoral College." *Forum* (December 1912): 681-686.

Kritzer, Herbert M. "The Representativeness of the 1972 Presidential Primaries." *Polity* 10 (Fall 1977): 121-129.

Laprade, William T. "Nominating Primary." *North American Review* (August 1914): 235-243.

Lengle, James I. "Divisive Presidential Primaries and Party Electoral Prospects, 1932-1976." *American Politics Quarterly* 8 (July 1980): 261-277.

Lundeen, Ernest, "Presidential Primaries." *Congressional Record* (March 15, 1919): 5480-5486.

Moran, Jack, and Mark Fenster. "Voter Turnout in Presidential Primaries: A Diachronic Analysis." *American Politics Quarterly* 10 (October 1982): 453-476.

Petrocik, John R., and Dwaine Marvick. "Explaining Party Elite Transformation: Institutional Changes and Insurgent Politics." *Western Political Quarterly* 36 (September 1983): 345-363.

Potts, C. S. "The Convention System and the Presidential Primary." *American Review of Reviews* (May 1912): 561-566.

"Presidential Primaries: Proposals for a New System." *Congressional Quarterly Weekly Report*, July 8, 1972, 1650-1655.

"Presidential Primary System." *Congressional Digest* (August 1928): 221-224.

Rice, Tom W. "The Determinants of Candidate Spending in Presidential Primaries: Advice for the States." *Presidential Studies Quarterly* 12 (Fall 1982): 590-597.

Stoddard, W. L. "Presidential Primary in Oregon." *Political Science Quarterly* (March 1916): 81-104.

"The United States Presidential Elections: Procedures and Prospects, the Primaries and Conventions." *World Today* (July 1952): 278-287.

Sources: Presidential Primary Returns

The main source for the presidential primary returns from 1912 through 1952 was James W. Davis' *Presidential Primaries: Road to the White House,* (Westport, Conn.: Greenwood Press, 1980), excerpted here with permission.

Congressional Quarterly supplemented Davis' material with the following sources: Louise Overacker's *The Presidential Primary,* the source used by Davis for the 1912-1924 returns; "Presidential Preference Primaries, 1928-1956," a 1960 Library of Congress study by Walter Kravitz; the offices of secretaries of state; state handbooks and newspapers. All statistics and footnotes are from Davis, unless otherwise indicated.

The basic source for the primary returns from 1956 through 1980 was Richard M. Scammon's *America Votes* series. For 1984 primaries, Congressional Quarterly obtained the returns from state secretaries of state and the Elections Research Center, Washington, D.C. Statistics and footnotes are from Scammon, unless otherwise indicated.

Figures in the following charts represent one of three types of votes:

- Votes cast directly for a presidential candidate.
- Votes cast for delegates whose candidate preference was indicated on the ballot.
- Votes cast for unpledged delegates. (Included in the "unpledged" category were delegates designated on the ballot as "uninstructed" and "no preference.")

For the delegate-at-large vote in 1912-1924 primaries, Overacker listed the average vote for delegates at large. For the 1928-1952 delegate-at-large, Davis listed the highest vote received by any one delegate at large. Congressional Quarterly followed Davis' style for subsequent years.

Percentages in the following tables have been calculated to two decimal points and then rounded; 0.05 percent appears as 0.1 percent. Therefore, columns of percentages do not always total 100 percent. Presidential candidates, primary winners, favorite sons, members of Congress and prominent national and state political figures are included in the state-by-state primary results; others receiving votes are listed in the footnotes.

1912 Primaries

Republican	Votes	%	Democratic	Votes	%
March 19 North Dakota					
Robert M. LaFollette (Wis.)	34,123	57.2	John Burke (N.D.)[1]	9,357	100.0
Theodore Roosevelt (N.Y.)	23,669	39.7			
William H. Taft (Ohio)	1,876	3.1			
March 26 New York[2]					
April 2 Wisconsin					
LaFollette	133,354	73.2	Woodrow Wilson (N.J.)	45,945	55.7
Taft	47,514	26.1	Champ Clark (Mo.)	36,464	44.2
Roosevelt	628	.3	Others	148	.2
Others	643	.4			
April 9 Illinois					
Roosevelt	266,917	61.1	Clark	218,483	74.3
Taft	127,481	29.2	Wilson	75,527	25.7
LaFollette	42,692	9.8			
April 13 Pennsylvania					
Roosevelt	282,853[3]	59.7	Wilson	98,000[3]	100.0
Taft	191,179[3]	40.3			
April 19 Nebraska					
Roosevelt	45,795	58.7	Clark	21,027	41.0
LaFollette	16,785	21.5	Wilson	14,289	27.9
Taft	13,341	17.1	Judson Harmon (Ohio)	12,454	24.3
Others	2,036	2.6	Others	3,499	6.8
April 19 Oregon					
Roosevelt	28,905	40.2	Wilson	9,588	53.0
LaFollette	22,491	31.3	Clark	7,857	43.4
Taft	20,517	28.5	Harmon	606	3.3
Others	14	—	Others	49	.3
April 30 Massachusetts					
Taft	86,722	50.4	Clark	34,575	68.9
Roosevelt	83,099	48.3	Wilson	15,002	29.9
LaFollette	2,058	1.2	Others	627	1.2
Others	99	.1			
May 6 Maryland					
Roosevelt	29,124	52.8	Clark	34,021	54.4
Taft	25,995	47.2	Wilson	21,490	34.3
			Harmon	7,070	11.3
May 14 California					
Roosevelt	138,563	54.6	Clark	43,163	71.5
Taft	69,345	27.3	Wilson	17,214	28.5
LaFollette	45,876	18.1			
May 21 Ohio					
Roosevelt	165,809	55.3	Harmon	96,164	51.7
Taft	118,362	39.5	Wilson	85,084	45.7
LaFollette	15,570	5.2	Clark	2,428	1.3
			Others	2,440	1.3

Republican

Democratic

	Votes	%		Votes	%

May 28   New Jersey

	Votes	%		Votes	%
Roosevelt	61,297	56.3	Wilson	48,336	98.9
Taft	44,034	40.5	Clark[4]	522	1.1
LaFollette	3,464	3.2			

June 4   South Dakota

	Votes	%		Votes	%
Roosevelt	38,106	55.2	Wilson[5]	4,694	35.2
Taft	19,960	28.9	Clark[5]	4,275	32.0
LaFollette	10,944	15.9	Clark[5]	2,722	20.4
			Others	1,655	12.4

TOTALS

	Votes	%		Votes	%
Roosevelt	1,164,765	51.5	Wilson	435,169	44.6
Taft	766,326	33.9	Clark	405,537	41.6
LaFollette	327,357	14.5	Harmon	116,294	11.9
Others	2,792	.1	Burke	9,357	1.0
			Others	8,418	.9
	2,261,240			974,775	

1. Burke was the "favorite son" candidate, according to the North Dakota secretary of state.
2. Primary law optional in 1912. Republicans elected pledged delegates but figures not available.
3. Unofficial figures.
4. Write-in.

5. No presidential preference. Three sets of delegates ran: one labelled "Wilson-Bryan" which came out openly for Wilson; one "Wilson-Clark-Bryan" which became identified with Clark; one Champ Clark which was accused by the Clark people of being a scheme to split the Clark vote. The "Wilson-Clark-Bryan" list polled 4,275 and the Champ Clark list 2,722. The delegates were given to Wilson by the convention.

1916 Primaries

	Republican			Democratic		
	Votes	%		Votes	%

March 7 Indiana

Charles W. Fairbanks (Ind.)[1]	176,078	100.0	Woodrow Wilson (N.J.)	160,423	100.0

March 14 Minnesota

Albert B. Cummins (Iowa)	54,214	76.8	Wilson	45,136	100.0
Others	16,403	23.2			

March 14 New Hampshire

Unpledged delegates	9,687	100.0	Wilson	5,684	100.0

March 21 North Dakota

Robert M. LaFollette (Wis.)	23,374[2]	70.4	Wilson	12,341	100.0
Others	9,851[2]	29.6			

April 3 Michigan

Henry Ford (Mich.)	83,057	47.4	Wilson	84,972	100.0
William A. Smith (Mich.)	77,872	44.4			
William O. Simpson (Mich.)	14,365	8.2			

April 4 New York

Unpledged delegates	147,038	100.0	Wilson	112,538	100.0

April 4 Wisconsin

LaFollette[1]	110,052	98.8	Wilson	109,462	99.8
Others	1,347	1.2	Others	231	.2

April 11 Illinois

Lawrence Y. Sherman (Ill.)[1]	155,945	90.2	Wilson	136,839	99.8
Theodore Roosevelt (N.Y.)[3]	15,348	8.9	Others	219	.2
Others	1,689	1.0			

April 18 Nebraska

Cummins	29,850	33.7	Wilson	69,506	87.7
Ford	26,884	30.3	Others	9,744	12.3
Charles E. Hughes (N.Y.)[3]	15,837	17.9			
Roosevelt[3]	2,256	2.5			
Others	13,780	15.6			

April 21 Montana

Cummins	10,415	89.9	Wilson	17,960	100.0
Others	1,173	10.1			

April 25 Iowa

Cummins	40,257	100.0	Wilson	31,447	100.0

April 25 Massachusetts

Unpledged delegates at large[4]	60,462	57.3	Wilson	19,580	100.0
Roosevelt[4]	45,117	42.7			

April 25 New Jersey

Roosevelt[3]	1,076	73.7	Wilson	25,407	100.0
Hughes[3]	383	26.3			

Republican

	Votes	%
April 25 Ohio		
Theodore E. Burton (Ohio)[1]	122,165	86.8
Roosevelt[3]	1,932	1.4
Ford[3]	1,683	1.2
Hughes[3]	469	.3
Others	14,428	10.3
May 2 California		
Unpledged delegates	236,277	100.0
May 16 Pennsylvania		
Martin G. Brumbaugh (Pa.)[1]	233,095	86.3
Ford[3]	20,265	7.5
Roosevelt[3]	12,359	4.6
Hughes[3]	1,804	.7
Others	2,682	1.0
May 16 Vermont		
Hughes[3]	5,480	70.0
Roosevelt[3]	1,931	24.6
Others	423	5.4
May 19 Oregon		
Hughes	56,764	59.8
Cummins	27,558	29.0
Others	10,593	11.2
May 23 South Dakota		
Cummins	29,656	100.0
June 6 West Virginia		
[5]		
TOTALS		
Unpledged delegates	453,464	23.6
Brumbaugh	233,095	12.1
Cummins	191,950	10.0
Fairbanks	176,078	9.2
Sherman	155,945	8.1
LaFollette	133,426	6.9
Ford	131,889	6.9
Burton	122,165	6.4
Hughes	80,737	4.2
Roosevelt	80,019	4.2
Smith	77,872	4.0
Simpson	14,365	.7
Others[6]	72,369	3.8
	1,923,374	

Democratic

	Votes	%
April 25 Ohio		
Wilson	82,688	97.2
Others	2,415	2.8
May 2 California		
Wilson	75,085	100.0
May 16 Pennsylvania		
Wilson	142,202	98.7
Others	1,839	1.3
May 16 Vermont		
Wilson	3,711	99.4
Others	23	.6
May 19 Oregon		
Wilson	27,898	100.0
May 23 South Dakota		
Wilson	10,341	100.0
June 6 West Virginia		
[5]		
TOTALS		
Wilson	1,173,220	98.8
Others	14,471	1.2
	1,187,691	

1. *Source for names of "favorite son" candidates:* The New York Times.
2. *Source for vote breakdown: North Dakota secretary of state.*
3. *Write-in.*
4. *No presidential preference vote but one set of delegates at large was for Roosevelt and the other set unpledged.*

5. *Figures not available. Republican winner was Sen. Theodore E. Burton (R Ohio) and Democratic winner was Woodrow Wilson, according to* The New York Times.
6. *In addition to scattered votes, "others" includes Robert G. Ross who received 5,-506 votes in the Nebraska primary; Henry D. Estabrook who received 9,851 in the North Dakota primary and 8,132 in the Nebraska primary.*

1920 Primaries

Republican			Democratic		
	Votes	%		Votes	%

March 9   New Hampshire

Leonard Wood (N.H.)[1]	8,591	53.0	Unpledged delegates[1]	7,103	100.0
Unpledged delegates	5,604	34.6			
Hiram Johnson (Calif.)[1]	2,000	12.3			

March 16   North Dakota

Johnson	30,573	96.1	William G. McAdoo (N.Y.)[2]	49	12.6
Leonard Wood[2]	987	3.1	Others[2]	340	87.4
Frank O. Lowden (Ill.)[2]	265	.8			

March 23   South Dakota

Leonard Wood	31,265	36.5	Others	6,612	100.0
Lowden	26,981	31.5			
Johnson	26,301	30.7			
Others	1,144	1.3			

April 5   Michigan

Johnson	156,939	38.4	McAdoo	18,665	21.1
Leonard Wood	112,568[3]	27.5	Edward I. Edwards (N.J.)	16,642	18.8
Lowden	62,418	15.3	A. Mitchell Palmer (Pa.)	11,187	12.6
Herbert C. Hoover (Calif.)	52,503	12.8	Others	42,000	47.5
Others	24,729	6.0			

April 6   New York

Unpledged delegates	199,149	100.0	Unpledged delegates	113,300	100.0

April 6   Wisconsin [4]

Leonard Wood[2]	4,505	15.0	James M. Cox (Ohio)[2]	76	2.2
Hoover[2]	3,910	13.0	Others	3,391	97.8
Johnson[2]	2,413	8.0			
Lowden[2]	921	3.1			
Others	18,350	60.9			

April 13   Illinois

Lowden	236,802	51.1	Edwards[2]	6,933	32.3
Leonard Wood	156,719	33.8	McAdoo[2]	3,838	17.9
Johnson	64,201	13.8	Cox[2]	266	1.2
Hoover[2]	3,401	.7	Others	10,418	48.6
Others	2,674	.6			

April 20   Nebraska

Johnson	63,161	46.2	Gilbert M. Hitchcock (Neb.)	37,452	67.3
Leonard Wood	42,385	31.0	Others	18,230	32.7
John J. Pershing (Mo.)	27,669	20.3			
Others	3,432	2.5			

April 23   Montana

Johnson	21,034	52.4	Others[2]	2,994	100.0
Leonard Wood	6,804	17.0			
Lowden	6,503	16.2			
Hoover	5,076	12.6			
Warren G. Harding (Ohio)	723	1.8			

April 27   Massachusetts

Unpledged delegates	93,356	100.0	Unpledged delegates	21,226	100.0

Republican   ## Democratic

	Votes	%		Votes	%
April 27 New Jersey					
Leonard Wood	52,909	50.2	Edwards	4,163	91.4
Johnson	51,685	49.0	McAdoo[2]	180	4.0
Hoover	900	.9	Others	213	4.7
April 27 Ohio					
Harding	123,257	47.6	Cox	85,838	97.8
Leonard Wood	108,565	41.9	McAdoo[2]	292	.3
Johnson[2]	16,783	6.5	Others	1,647	1.9
Hoover[2]	10,467	4.0			
May 3 Maryland					
Leonard Wood	15,900	66.4	[5]		
Johnson	8,059	33.6			
May 4 California					
Johnson	369,853	63.9	Unpledged delegates	23,831	100.0
Hoover	209,009	36.1			
May 4 Indiana					
Leonard Wood	85,708	37.9	[5]		
Johnson	79,840	35.3			
Lowden	39,627	17.5			
Harding	20,782	9.2			
May 18 Pennsylvania					
Edward R. Wood (Pa.)	257,841	92.3	Palmer[6]	80,356	73.7
Johnson[2]	10,869	3.8	McAdoo	26,875	24.6
Leonard Wood[2]	3,878	1.4	Edwards[2]	674	.6
Hoover[2]	2,825	1.0	Others	1,132	1.0
Others[2]	4,059	1.5			
May 18 Vermont					
Leonard Wood	3,451	66.1	McAdoo[2]	137	31.4
Hoover[2]	564	10.8	Edwards[2]	58	13.3
Johnson[2]	402	7.7	Cox[2]	14	3.2
Lowden[2]	29	.5	Others	227	52.1
Others	777	14.9			
May 21 Oregon					
Johnson	46,163	38.4	McAdoo	24,951	98.6
Leonard Wood	43,770	36.5	Others	361	1.4
Lowden	15,581	13.0			
Hoover	14,557	12.1			
May 25 West Virginia					
Leonard Wood	27,255	44.6	[5]		
Others	33,849 [7]	55.4			

Republican				**Democratic**		
	Votes	%			Votes	%

June 5   North Carolina

Republican	Votes	%		Democratic	Votes	%
Johnson	15,375	73.3	[5]			
Leonard Wood	5,603	26.7				

TOTALS						
Johnson	965,651	30.3		Unpledged delegates	165,460	28.9
Leonard Wood	710,863	22.3		Palmer	91,543	16.0
Lowden	389,127	12.2		Cox	86,194	15.0
Hoover	303,212	9.5		McAdoo	74,987	13.1
Unpledged delegates	298,109	9.4		Hitchcock	37,452	6.6
Edward R. Wood	257,841	8.1		Edwards	28,470	5.0
Harding	144,762	4.5		Others [9]	87,565	15.3
Pershing	27,669	.9				
Others [8]	89,014	2.8			571,671	
	3,186,248					

1. *Source: Louise Overacker,* The Presidential Primaries *(1926), p. 238-39. There was no preference vote. In the Republican primary, figures given were for delegates at large favoring Wood and Johnson. In the Democratic primary, although delegates were unpledged, the organization (Robert Charles Murchie) group was understood to be for Hoover. The highest Democratic Hoover delegate received 3,714 votes.*

2. *Write-in.*

3. *Source: Overacker, op. cit., p. 238.*

4. *No names entered for presidential preference in the Republican primary. The real contest lay between two lists of delegates, one headed by Robert M. La Follette and the other by Emanuel L. Philipp.*

5. *No names entered and no preference vote recorded.*

6. *Source for name of "favorite son" candidate: The New York Times.*

7. *Most of these votes were received by Sen. Howard Sutherland (R W.Va.). The figure is unofficial.*

8. *In addition to scattered votes, "others" includes Robert G. Ross who received 1,698 votes in the Nebraska primary.*

9. *In addition to scattered votes, "others" includes Robert G. Ross who received 13,179 in the Nebraska primary.*

1924 Primaries

Republican			Democratic		
	Votes	%		Votes	%
March 11 New Hampshire					
Calvin Coolidge (Mass.)	17,170	100.0	Unpledged delegates	6,687	100.0
March 18 North Dakota					
Coolidge	52,815	42.1	William G. McAdoo (Calif.)	11,273	100.0
Robert M. LaFollette (Wis.)	40,252	32.1			
Hiram Johnson (Calif.)	32,363	25.8			
March 25 South Dakota					
Johnson	40,935	50.7	McAdoo[1]	6,983	77.4
Coolidge	39,791	49.3	Unpledged delegates[1]	2,040	22.6
April 1 Wisconsin[2]					
LaFollette[3]	40,738	62.5	McAdoo	54,922	68.2
Coolidge[3]	23,324	35.8	Alfred E. Smith (N.Y.)[3]	5,774	7.2
Johnson[3]	411	.6	Others	19,827	24.6
Others	688	1.1			
April 7 Michigan					
Coolidge	236,191	67.2	Henry Ford (Mich.)[4]	48,567	53.4
Johnson	103,739	29.5	Woodbridge N. Ferris (Mich.)[4]	42,028	46.2
Others	11,312	3.2	Others	435	.5
April 8 Illinois					
Coolidge	533,193	58.0	McAdoo	180,544	98.9
Johnson	385,590	42.0	Smith[3]	235	.1
LaFollette[3]	278	—	Others	1,724	.9
Others	21	—			
April 8 Nebraska					
Coolidge	79,676	63.6	McAdoo[3]	9,342	57.3
Johnson	45,032	35.9	Smith[3]	700	4.3
Others	627	.5	Others[3]	6,268	38.4
April 22 New Jersey					
Coolidge	111,739	89.1	George S. Silzer (N.J.)[5]	35,601	97.7
Johnson	13,626	10.9	Smith[3]	721	2.0
			McAdoo[3]	69	.2
			Others	38	.1
April 22 Pennsylvania					
Coolidge[3]	117,262	87.9	McAdoo[3]	10,376	43.7
Johnson[3]	4,345	3.3	Smith[3]	9,029	38.0
LaFollette[3]	1,224	.9	Others[3]	4,341	18.3
Others	10,523	7.9			
April 29 Massachusetts					
Coolidge	84,840	100.0	Unpledged delegates at large[6]	30,341	100.0
April 29 Ohio					
Coolidge	173,613	86.3	James M. Cox (Ohio)[5]	74,183	71.7
Johnson	27,578	13.7	McAdoo	29,267	28.3

Republican   Democratic

	Votes	%		Votes	%
May 5 Maryland					
Coolidge	19,657	93.7	[7]		
Unpledged delegates	1,326	6.3			
Johnson[3]	3	—			
May 6 California					
Coolidge	310,618	54.3	McAdoo	110,235	85.6
Johnson	261,566	45.7	Unpledged delegates	18,586	14.4
May 6 Indiana					
Coolidge	330,045	84.1	[7]		
Johnson	62,603	15.9			
May 16 Oregon					
Coolidge	99,187	76.8	McAdoo	33,664	100.0
Johnson	30,042	23.2			
May 27 West Virginia					
Coolidge	162,042	100.0	[7]		
May 28 Montana					
Coolidge	19,200	100.0	McAdoo	10,058	100.0
TOTALS					
Coolidge	2,410,363	68.4	McAdoo	456,733	59.8
Johnson	1,007,833	28.6	Cox	74,183	9.7
LaFollette	82,492	2.3	Unpledged delegates	57,654	7.5
Unpledged delegates	1,326	—	Ford	48,567	6.4
Others	23,171	.7	Ferris	42,028	5.5
			Silzer	35,601	4.7
	3,525,185		Smith	16,459	2.2
			Others	32,633	4.3
				763,858	

1. No presidential preference vote, as McAdoo's was the only name entered, but a contest developed between "McAdoo" and "anti-McAdoo" lists of delegates. Figures are average votes cast for these lists.

2. In Wisconsin the real contest in the Republican primary was between two lists of delegates, one led by La Follette and one by Emanuel L. Philipp. In the Democratic primary, the real contest was between two lists of delegates, one favoring Smith and one favoring McAdoo.

3. Write-in.

4. Source for names of "favorite son" candidates: Michigan Manual, 1925.

5. Source for names of "favorite son" candidates: The New York Times.

6. No presidential preference vote provided for. There were nine candidates for the eight places as delegates at large, one of whom announced his preference for Smith during the campaign and received the second highest number of votes.

7. No names entered and no presidential preference vote taken.

1928 Primaries

	Republican			Democratic		
	Votes	%		Votes	%

March 13 New Hampshire

Unpledged delegates at large[1]	25,603	100.0	Unpledged delegates at large[1]	9,716	100.0

March 20 North Dakota

Frank O. Lowden (Ill.)	95,857	100.0	Alfred E. Smith (N.Y.)	10,822	100.0

April 2 Michigan

Herbert C. Hoover (Calif.)	282,809	97.6	Smith	77,276	98.3
Lowden	5,349	1.8	Thomas Walsh (Mont.)	1,034	1.3
Calvin Coolidge (Mass.)	1,666	.6	James A. Reed (Mo.)	324	.4

April 3 Wisconsin

George W. Norris (Neb.)	162,822	87.1	Reed	61,097	75.0
Hoover	17,659	9.4	Smith	19,781	24.3
Lowden	3,302	1.8	Walsh	541	.7
Coolidge	680	.4			
Charles G. Dawes (Ill.)	505	.3			
Others	1,894	1.0			

April 10 Illinois

Lowden	1,172,278	99.3	Smith	44,212	91.7
Hoover	4,368	.4	Reed	3,786	7.9
Coolidge	2,420	.2	William G. McAdoo (Calif.)	213	.4
Dawes	756	.1			
Others	946	.1			

April 10 Nebraska

Norris	96,726	91.8	Gilbert M. Hitchcock (Neb.)	51,019	91.5
Hoover	6,815	6.5	Smith	4,755	8.5
Lowden	711	.7			
Dawes	679	.7			
Coolidge	452	.4			

April 24 Ohio

Hoover	217,430	68.1	Smith	42,365	65.9
Frank B. Willis (Ohio)	84,461	26.5	Atlee Pomerene (Ohio)	13,957	21.7
Dawes	4,311	1.4	Victor Donahey (Ohio)	7,935	12.3
Lowden	3,676	1.2			
Others	9,190	2.9			

April 24 Pennsylvania

[2]			[2]		

April 28 Massachusetts

Hoover[3]	100,279	85.2	Smith	38,081	98.1
Coolidge[3]	7,767	6.6	Walsh	254	.7
Alvan Fuller (Mass.)	1,686	1.4	Others	478	1.2
Lowden[3]	1,040	.9			
Others	6,950	5.9			

May 1 California

Hoover	567,219	100.0	Smith	134,471	54.1
			Reed	60,004	24.1
			Walsh	46,770	18.8
			Others	7,263	2.9

Republican   # Democratic

	Votes	%		Votes	%
May 7 Indiana					
James E. Watson (Ind.)	228,795	53.0	Evans Woollen (Ind.)	146,934	100.0
Hoover	203,279	47.0			
May 7 Maryland[4]					
Hoover	27,128	83.3	[5]		
Unpledged delegates	5,426	16.7			
May 8 Alabama					
[5]			Unpledged delegates at large[6]	138,957	100.0
May 15 New Jersey					
Hoover	382,907	100.0	Smith[3]	28,506	100.0
May 18 Oregon					
Hoover	101,129	98.7	Smith	17,444	48.5
Lowden	1,322	1.3	Walsh	11,272	31.3
			Reed	6,360	17.7
			Others	881	2.5
May 22 South Dakota					
Unpledged delegates at large[7]	34,264	100.0	Unpledged delegates at large[7]	6,221	100.0
May 29 West Virginia					
Guy D. Goff (W.Va.)	128,429	54.0	Smith	81,739	50.0
Hoover	109,303	46.0	Reed	75,796	46.4
			Others	5,789	3.5
June 5 Florida					
[5]			Unpledged delegates at large[8]	108,167	100.00

TOTALS					
Hoover	2,020,325	49.2	Smith	499,452	39.5
Lowden	1,283,535	31.2	Unpledged delegates	263,061	20.8
Norris	259,548	6.3	Reed	207,367	16.4
Watson	228,795	5.6	Woollen	146,934	11.6
Goff	128,429	3.1	Walsh	59,871	4.7
Willis	84,461	2.1	Hitchcock	51,019	4.0
Unpledged delegates	65,293	1.6	Pomerene	13,957	1.1
Coolidge	12,985	.3	Donahey	7,935	.6
Dawes	6,251	.2	McAdoo	213	—
Fuller	1,686	—	Others[10]	14,411	1.1
Others[9]	18,980	.5			
	4,110,288			**1,264,220**	

1. Winning Republican delegates were unofficially pledged to Hoover and winning Democratic delegates were unofficially pledged to Smith, according to Walter Kravitz, "Presidential Preferential Primaries: Results 1928-1956" (1960), p. 4.
2. No figures available.
3. Write-in.
4. Source: Kravitz, op. cit., p. 5.
5. No primary.
6. The Montgomery Advertiser of May 3, 1928, described the delegates as independent and anti-Smith.

7. Winning Republican delegates favored Lowden and winning Democratic delegates favored Smith, according to Kravitz, op. cit., p. 5.
8. The Miami Herald of June 6, 1928, described the delegates as unpledged and anti-Smith.
9. In addition to scattered votes, "others" includes Robert G. Ross who received 8,280 votes in the Ohio primary.
10. In addition to scattered votes, "others" includes Poling who received 7,263 votes in the California primary; and Workman who received 881 in the Oregon primary and 5,-789 in the West Virginia primary.

1932 Primaries

	Republican			Democratic		
		Votes	%		Votes	%
March 8 New Hampshire						
	Unpledged delegates at large[1]	22,903	*100.0*	Unpledged delegates at large[1]	15,401	*100.0*
March 15 North Dakota						
	Joseph I. France (Md.)	36,000[2]	*59.0*	Franklin D. Roosevelt (N.Y.)	52,000[2]	*61.9*
	Jacob S. Coxey (Ohio)	25,000[2]	*41.0*	William H. Murray (Okla.)	32,000[2]	*38.1*
March 23 Georgia						
[3]				Roosevelt	51,498	*90.3*
				Others	5,541	*9.7*
April 5 Wisconsin						
	George W. Norris (Neb.)	139,514	*95.5*	Roosevelt	241,742	*98.6*
	Herbert C. Hoover (Calif.)	6,588	*4.5*	Alfred E. Smith (N.Y.)[4]	3,502	*1.4*
April 12 Nebraska						
	France	40,481	*74.4*	Roosevelt	91,393	*63.5*
	Hoover	13,934	*25.6*	John N. Garner (Texas)	27,359	*19.0*
				Murray	25,214	*17.5*
April 13 Illinois						
	France	345,498	*98.7*	James H. Lewis (Ill.)	590,130	*99.8*
	Hoover	4,368	*1.2*	Roosevelt	1,084	*.2*
	Charles G. Dawes (Ill.)	129	*—*	Smith	266	*—*
				Others[4]	72	*—*
April 26 Massachusetts						
	Unpledged delegates at large[5]	57,534	*100.0*	Smith[5]	153,465	*73.1*
				Roosevelt[5]	56,454	*26.9*
April 26 Pennsylvania						
	France	352,092	*92.9*	Roosevelt	133,002	*56.6*
	Hoover	20,662	*5.5*	Smith	101,227	*43.1*
	Others	6,126	*1.6*	Others	563	*.2*
May 2 Maryland						
	Hoover	27,324	*60.0*	[6]		
	France	17,008	*37.3*			
	Unpledged delegates	1,236	*2.7*			
May 3 Alabama						
[3]				Unpledged delegates[7]	134,781	*100.0*
May 3 California						
	Hoover	657,420	*100.0*	Garner	222,385	*41.3*
				Roosevelt	175,008	*32.5*
				Smith	141,517	*26.3*
May 3 South Dakota						
	Johnson[8]	64,464	*64.7*	Roosevelt	35,370	*100.0*
	Others	35,133	*35.3*			

Republican

	Votes	%

Democratic

	Votes	%

May 10   Ohio

Republican	Votes	%	Democratic	Votes	%
Coxey	75,844	58.9	Murray	112,512	96.4
France	44,853	34.8	Roosevelt[4]	1,999	1.7
Hoover	8,154	6.3	Smith[4]	951	.8
			George White (Ohio)	834	.7
			Newton D. Baker (Ohio)	289	.2
			Garner[4]	72	—

May 10   West Virginia

Republican	Votes	%	Democratic	Votes	%
France	88,005	100.0	Roosevelt	219,671	90.3
			Murray	19,826	8.2
			Others	3,727	1.5

May 17   New Jersey

Republican	Votes	%	Democratic	Votes	%
France	141,330	93.3	Smith	5,234	61.9
Hoover	10,116	6.7	Roosevelt	3,219	38.1

May 20   Oregon

Republican	Votes	%	Democratic	Votes	%
France	72,681	69.0	Roosevelt	48,554	78.6
Hoover	32,599	31.0	Murray	11,993	19.4
			Others	1,214	2.0

June 7   Florida

Republican	Votes	%	Democratic	Votes	%
[3]			Roosevelt	203,372	87.7
			Murray	24,847	10.7
			Others	3,645	1.6

TOTALS

Republican	Votes	%	Democratic	Votes	%
France	1,137,948	48.5	Roosevelt	1,314,366	44.5
Hoover	781,165	33.3	Lewis	590,130	20.0
Norris	139,514	5.9	Smith	406,162	13.8
Coxey	100,844	4.3	Garner	249,816	8.5
Unpledged delegates	81,673	3.5	Murray	226,392	7.7
Johnson	64,464	2.7	Unpledged delegates	150,182	5.1
Dawes	129	—	White	834	—
Others[9]	41,259	1.8	Baker	289	—
			Others[10]	14,762	.5
	2,346,996			2,952,933	

1. Hoover delegates won the Republican primary and Roosevelt delegates won the Democratic primary, according to Kravitz, op. cit., p. 6.

2. Unofficial figures.

3. No primary.

4. Write-in.

5. Delegate-at-large vote in Republican and Democratic primaries. Hoover delegates won the Republican primary, according to Kravitz, op. cit., p. 6. The New York Times of April 28, 1932, also reported that the Republican delegates were pledged to Hoover.

6. No names entered, according to the Maryland Record of Election Returns.

7. These were unpledged delegates who favored Roosevelt, according to Kravitz, op. cit., p. 6.

8. The winning Republican delegation supported Hoover, according to Kravitz, op. cit., p. 7.

9. In addition to scattered votes, "others" includes Bogue who received 35,133 in the South Dakota primary.

10. In addition to scattered votes, "others" includes Leo J. Chassee who received 3,645 in the Florida primary and 3,727 in the West Virginia primary; and Howard who received 5,541 votes in the Georgia primary.

1936 Primaries

	Republican			**Democratic**		
		Votes	%		Votes	%
March 10 New Hampshire						
	Unpledged delegates at large[1]	32,992	100.0	Unpledged delegates at large[1]	15,752	100.0
April 7 Wisconsin						
	William E. Borah (Idaho)	187,334	98.2	Franklin D. Roosevelt (N.Y.)	401,773	100.0
	Alfred M. Landon (Kan.)	3,360	1.8	John N. Garner (Texas)	108	—
				Alfred E. Smith (N.Y.)	46	—
April 14 Illinois						
	Frank Knox (Ill.)	491,575	53.7	Roosevelt	1,416,411	100.0
	Borah	419,220	45.8	Others[2]	411	—
	Landon	3,775	.4			
	Others[2]	205	—			
April 14 Nebraska						
	Borah	70,240	74.5	Roosevelt	139,743	100.0
	Landon	23,117	24.5			
	Others	973	1.0			
April 28 Massachusetts						
	Landon[2]	76,862	80.6	Roosevelt[2]	51,924	85.9
	Herbert C. Hoover (Calif.)[2]	7,276	7.6	Smith[2]	2,928	4.8
	Borah[2]	4,259	4.5	Charles E. Coughlin (Mich.)[2]	2,854	4.7
	Knox[2]	1,987	2.1	Others[2]	2,774	4.6
	Others[2]	5,032	5.3			
April 28 Pennsylvania						
	Borah	459,982	100.0	Roosevelt	720,309	95.3
				Henry Breckinridge (N.Y.)	35,351	4.7
May 4 Maryland						
	[3]			Roosevelt	100,269	83.4
				Breckinridge	18,150	15.1
				Unpledged delegates	1,739	1.4
May 5 California						
	Earl Warren (Calif.)	350,917	57.4	Roosevelt	790,235	82.5
	Landon	260,170	42.6	Upton Sinclair (Calif.)	106,068	11.1
				John S. McGroarty (Calif.)	61,391	6.4
May 5 South Dakota						
	Warren E. Green[4]	44,518	50.1	Roosevelt	48,262	100.0
	Borah	44,261	49.9			
May 12 Ohio						
	Stephen A. Day (Ohio)	155,732	93.4	Roosevelt	514,366	94.0
	Landon	11,015	6.6	Breckinridge	32,950	6.0
May 12 West Virginia						
	Borah	105,855	84.8	Roosevelt	288,799	97.3
	Others	18,986	15.2	Others	8,162	2.7

Republican | # Democratic

	Votes	%		Votes	%
May 15 **Oregon**					
Borah	91,949	90.2	Roosevelt	88,305	99.8
Landon	4,467	4.4	Others	208	.2
Others	5,557	5.4			
May 19 **New Jersey**					
Landon	347,142	79.2	Breckinridge	49,956	81.1
Borah	91,052	20.8	Roosevelt [2]	11,676	18.9
June 6 **Florida**					
[3]			Roosevelt	242,906	89.7
			Others	27,982	10.3
TOTALS					
Borah	1,474,152	44.4	Roosevelt	4,814,978	92.9
Landon	729,908	22.0	Breckinridge	136,407	2.6
Knox	493,562	14.9	Sinclair	106,068	2.0
Warren	350,917	10.6	McGroarty	61,391	1.2
Day	155,732	4.7	Unpledged delegates	17,491	.3
Green	44,518	1.3	Smith	2,974	.1
Unpledged delegates	32,992	1.0	Coughlin	2,854	.1
Hoover	7,276	.2	Garner	108	—
Others [5]	30,753	.9	Others [6]	39,537	.8
	3,319,810			5,181,808	

1. *Delegates favorable to Knox won the Republican primary and Roosevelt delegates won the Democratic primary, according to Kravitz, op. cit., p. 8.*
2. *Write-in.*
3. *No preferential primary held.*
4. *These delegates were unpledged but favored Landon, according to Kravitz, op. cit., p. 9.*

5. *In addition to scattered votes, "others" includes Leo J. Chassee who received 18,986 votes in the West Virginia primary.*
6. *In addition to scattered votes, "others" includes Joseph A. Coutremarsh who received 27,982 votes in the Florida primary and 8,162 votes in the West Virginia primary.*

1940 Primaries

Republican			Democratic		
	Votes	%		Votes	%

March 12 New Hampshire

Unpledged delegates at large	34,616	100.0	Unpledged delegates at large [1]	10,501	100.0

April 2 Wisconsin

Thomas E. Dewey (N.Y.)	70,168	72.6	Franklin D. Roosevelt (N.Y.)	322,991	75.4
Arthur Vandenberg (Mich.)	26,182	27.1	John N. Garner (Texas)	105,662	24.6
Robert A. Taft (Ohio)	341	.4			

April 9 Illinois

Dewey	977,225	99.9	Roosevelt	1,176,531	86.0
Others [2]	552	.1	Garner	190,801	14.0
			Others [2]	35	—

April 9 Nebraska

Dewey	102,915	58.9	Roosevelt	111,902	100.0
Vandenberg	71,798	41.1			

April 23 Pennsylvania

Dewey	52,661	66.7	Roosevelt	724,657	100.0
Franklin D. Roosevelt (N.Y.)	8,294	10.5			
Arthur H. James (Pa.)	8,172	10.3			
Taft	5,213	6.6			
Vandenberg	2,384	3.0			
Herbert C. Hoover (Calif.)	1,082	1.4			
Wendell Willkie (N.Y.)	707	.9			
Others	463	.6			

April 30 Massachusetts

Unpledged delegates at large [3]	98,975	100.0	Unpledged delegates at large [3]	76,919	100.0

May 5 South Dakota

Unpledged delegates	52,566	100.0	Unpledged delegates	27,636	100.0

May 6 Maryland

Dewey	54,802	100.0	[4]		

May 7 Alabama

[4]			Unpledged delegates at large [5]	196,508	100.0

May 7 California

Jerrold L. Seawell [6]	538,112	100.0	Roosevelt	723,782	74.0
			Garner	114,594	11.7
			Unpledged delegates [6]	139,055	14.2

May 14 Ohio

Taft	510,025	99.5	Unpledged delegates at large [7]	283,952	100.0
Dewey [2]	2,059	.4			
John W. Bricker (Ohio)	188	—			
Vandenberg [2]	83	—			
Willkie	53	—			
Others	69	—			

	Republican			Democratic		
	Votes	%		Votes	%
May 14 West Virginia					
R. N. Davis (W.Va.)	106,123	*100.0*	H. C. Allen (W.Va.)	102,729	*100.0*
May 17 Oregon					
Charles L. McNary (Ore.)	133,488	*95.9*	Roosevelt	109,913	*87.2*
Dewey	5,190	*3.7*	Garner	15,584	*12.4*
Taft	254	*.2*	Others	601	*.5*
Willkie	237	*.2*			
Vandenberg	36	*—*			
May 21 New Jersey					
Dewey	340,734	*93.9*	Roosevelt[2]	34,278	*100.0*
Willkie[2]	20,143	*5.6*			
Roosevelt[2]	1,202	*.3*			
Taft[2]	595	*.2*			
Vandenberg[2]	168	*—*			
TOTALS					
Dewey	1,605,754	*49.7*	Roosevelt	3,240,054	*71.7*
Seawell	538,112	*16.7*	Unpledged delegates	734,571	*16.4*
Taft	516,428	*16.0*	Garner	426,641	*9.5*
Unpledged delegates	186,157	*5.8*	Allen	102,729	*2.3*
McNary	133,488	*4.1*	Others	636	*—*
Davis	106,123	*3.3*			
Vandenberg	100,651	*3.1*		4,468,631	
Willkie	21,140	*.7*			
Roosevelt	9,496	*.3*			
James	8,172	*.3*			
Hoover	1,082	*—*			
Bricker	188	*—*			
Others	1,084	*—*			
	3,227,875				

1. Roosevelt delegates won, according to Kravitz, op. cit., p. 10.

2. Write-in.

3. An unpledged Republican slate defeated a slate of delegates pledged to Dewey, according to Kravitz, op. cit., p. 10. Sixty-nine James A. Farley delegates and three unpledged delegates won in the Democratic primary, according to Kravitz, ibid. The New York Times of May 1, 1940, also reported that most Democratic delegates favored Farley.

4. No primary.

5. Winning delegates were pledged to "favorite son" candidate William B. Bankhead,

then Speaker of the U.S. House of Representatives, according to Kravitz, op. cit., p. 10, and the Montgomery Advertiser of May 8, 1940.

6. The Los Angeles Times of May 8, 1940, reported that the Republican delegation was unpledged. In the Democratic primary, according to Davis, p. 293, unpledged slates were headed by Willis Allen, head of the California "Ham and Eggs" pension ticket which received 90,718 votes; and by Lt. Gov. Ellis E. Patterson, whose slate, backed by Labor's Non-Partisan League, received 48,337 votes.

7. Democratic delegates were pledged to Charles Sawyer (Ohio), according to Ohio Election Statistics, 1940, and Kravitz, op. cit., p. 10.

1944 Primaries

	Republican			Democratic	
	Votes	%		Votes	%
March 14 New Hampshire					
Unpledged delegates at large[1]	16,723	100.0	Unpledged delegates at large[1]	6,772	100.0
April 5 Wisconsin					
Douglas MacArthur (Wis.)	102,421	72.6	Franklin D. Roosevelt (N.Y.)	49,632	94.3
Thomas E. Dewey (N.Y.)	21,036	14.9	Others	3,014	5.7
Harold E. Stassen (Minn.)	7,928	5.6			
Wendell Willkie (N.Y.)	6,439	4.6			
Others	3,307	2.3			
April 11 Illinois					
MacArthur	550,354	92.0	Roosevelt	47,561	99.3
Dewey	9,192	1.5	Others	343	.7
Everett M. Dirksen (Ill.)	581	.1			
John W. Bricker (Ohio)	148	—			
Stassen	111	—			
Willkie	107	—			
Others	37,575	6.3			
April 11 Nebraska					
Stassen	51,800	65.7	Roosevelt	37,405	99.2
Dewey	18,418	23.3	Others	319	.8
Willkie	8,249	10.5			
Others	432	.5			
April 25 Massachusetts					
Unpledged delegates at large	53,511	100.0	Unpledged delegates at large	57,299	100.0
April 25 Pennsylvania					
Dewey[2]	146,706	83.8	Roosevelt	322,469	99.7
MacArthur[2]	9,032	5.2	Others	961	.3
Franklin D. Roosevelt (N.Y.)	8,815	5.0			
Willkie[2]	3,650	2.1			
Bricker[2]	2,936	1.7			
Edward Martin (Pa.)	2,406	1.4			
Stassen[2]	1,502	.9			
May 1 Maryland					
Unpledged delegates	17,600	78.9	[3]		
Willkie	4,701	21.1			
May 2 Alabama					
[3]			Unpledged delegates at large[4]	116,922	100.0
May 2 Florida					
[3]			Unpledged delegates at large[5]	118,518	100.0
May 2 South Dakota					
Charles A. Christopherson[6]	33,497	60.2	Fred Hildebrandt (S.D.)[6]	7,414	52.4
Others[6]	22,135	39.8	Others[6]	6,727	47.6

Republican

	Votes	%
May 9 Ohio		
Unpledged delegates at large [7]	360,139	*100.0*
May 9 West Virginia		
Unpledged delegates at large	91,602	*100.0*
May 16 California		
Earl Warren (Calif.)	594,439	*100.0*
May 16 New Jersey		
Dewey	17,393	*86.2*
Roosevelt [2]	1,720	*8.5*
Willkie	618	*3.1*
Bricker	203	*1.0*
MacArthur	129	*.6*
Stassen	106	*.5*
May 19 Oregon		
Dewey [2]	50,001	*78.2*
Stassen [2]	6,061	*9.5*
Willkie [2]	3,333	*5.2*
Bricker [2]	3,018	*4.7*
MacArthur [2]	191	*.3*
Others	1,340	*2.1*
TOTALS		
MacArthur	662,127	*29.1*
Warren	594,439	*26.2*
Unpledged delegates	539,575	*23.8*
Dewey	262,746	*11.6*
Stassen	67,508	*3.0*
Christopherson	33,497	*1.5*
Willkie	27,097	*1.2*
Roosevelt	10,535	*.5*
Bricker	6,305	*.3*
Martin	2,406	*.1*
Dirksen	581	*—*
Others [8]	64,789	*2.9*
	2,271,605	

Democratic

	Votes	%
May 9 Ohio		
Unpledged delegates at large [7]	164,915	*100.0*
May 9 West Virginia		
Claude R. Linger (W.Va.)	59,282	*100.0*
May 16 California		
Roosevelt	770,222	*100.0*
May 16 New Jersey		
Roosevelt	16,884	*99.6*
Thomas E. Dewey (N.Y.)	60	*.4*
May 19 Oregon		
Roosevelt	79,833	*98.7*
Others	1,057	*1.3*
TOTALS		
Roosevelt	1,324,006	*70.9*
Unpledged delegates	464,426	*24.9*
Linger	59,282	*3.2*
Hildebrandt	7,414	*.4*
Dewey	60	*—*
Others [9]	12,421	*.7*
	1,867,609	

1. Nine unpledged and two Dewey delegates won the Republican primary, and Roosevelt delegates won the Democratic primary, according to Kravitz, op. cit., p. 12.
2. Write-in.
3. No primary.
4. The Montgomery Advertiser of May 3, 1944, reported that these delegates were pro-Roosevelt but uninstructed.
5. The New York Times of May 3, 1944, reported that a contest for delegates took place between supporters of Roosevelt and supporters of Sen. Harry F. Byrd (D Va.). A vote breakdown showing Roosevelt and Byrd strength is unavailable.

6. The winning Republican slate was pledged to Stassen, the losing Republican slate to Dewey and the two Democratic slates to Roosevelt, according to the office of the South Dakota secretary of state and Kravitz, op. cit., p. 12.
7. Bricker delegates won the Republican primary and Joseph T. Ferguson delegates won the Democratic primary, according to Kravitz. op. cit., p. 13.
8. In addition to scattered votes, "others" includes Riley A. Bender who received 37,575 votes in the Illinois primary and Joe H. Bottum who received 22,135 in the South Dakota primary.
9. In addition to scattered votes, "others" includes Powell who received 6,727 votes in the South Dakota primary.

1948 Primaries

Republican	Votes	%	Democratic	Votes	%
March 9 New Hampshire					
Unpledged delegates at large[1]	28,854	*100.0*	Unpledged delegates at large[1]	4,409	*100.0*
April 6 Wisconsin					
Harold E. Stassen (Minn.)	64,076	*39.4*	Harry S Truman (Mo.)	25,415	*83.8*
Douglas MacArthur (Wis.)	55,302	*34.0*	Others	4,906	*16.2*
Thomas E. Dewey (N.Y.)	40,943	*25.2*			
Others	2,429	*1.5*			
April 13 Illinois					
Riley A. Bender (Ill.)	324,029	*96.9*	Truman	16,299	*81.7*
MacArthur	6,672	*2.0*	Dwight D. Eisenhower (N.Y.)	1,709	*8.6*
Stassen	1,572	*.5*	Scott Lucas (Ill.)	427	*2.1*
Dewey	953	*.3*	Others[2]	1,513	*7.6*
Robert A. Taft (Ohio)	705	*.2*			
Others[2]	475	*.1*			
April 13 Nebraska					
Stassen	80,979	*43.5*	Truman	67,672	*98.7*
Dewey	64,242	*34.5*	Others	894	*1.3*
Taft	21,608	*11.6*			
Arthur Vandenberg (Mich.)	9,590	*5.2*			
MacArthur	6,893	*3.7*			
Earl Warren (Calif.)	1,761	*.9*			
Joseph W. Martin (Mass.)	910	*.5*			
Others	24	*—*			
April 20 New Jersey[3]					
Dewey	3,714	*41.4*	Truman	1,100	*92.5*
Stassen	3,123	*34.8*	Henry A. Wallace (Iowa)	87	*7.3*
MacArthur	718	*8.0*	Others	2	*.2*
Vandenberg	516	*5.8*			
Taft	495	*5.5*			
Dwight D. Eisenhower (N.Y.)	288	*3.2*			
Joseph W. Martin	64	*.7*			
Alfred E. Driscoll (N.J.)	44	*—*			
Warren	14	*.2*			
April 27 Massachusetts					
Unpledged delegates at large[4]	72,191	*100.0*	Unpledged delegates at large[4]	51,207	*100.0*
April 27 Pennsylvania					
Stassen[2]	81,242	*31.5*	Truman	328,891	*96.0*
Dewey[2]	76,988	*29.8*	Eisenhower	4,502	*1.3*
Edward Martin (Pa.)	45,072	*17.5*	Wallace	4,329	*1.3*
MacArthur[2]	18,254	*7.1*	Harold E. Stassen (Minn.)	1,301	*.4*
Taft[2]	15,166	*5.9*	Douglas MacArthur (Wis.)	1,220	*.4*
Vandenberg	8,818	*3.4*	Others	2,409	*.7*
Harry S Truman (Mo.)	4,907	*1.9*			
Eisenhower	4,726	*1.8*			
Henry A. Wallace (Iowa)	1,452	*.6*			
Others	1,537	*.6*			
May 4 Alabama					
[5]			Unpledged delegates at large[6]	161,629	*100.0*

Republican			Democratic		
	Votes	%		Votes	%

May 4   Florida

| 5 | | | Others [7] | 92,169 | 100.0 |

May 4   Ohio

| Unpledged delegates at large [8] | 426,767 | 100.0 | Unpledged delegates at large [8] | 271,146 | 100.0 |

May 11   West Virginia

| Stassen | 110,775 | 83.2 | Unpledged delegates at large | 157,102 | 100.0 |
| Others | 22,410 | 16.8 | | | |

May 21   Oregon

Dewey	117,554	51.8	Truman	112,962	93.8
Stassen	107,946	47.6	Others	7,436	6.2
Others	1,474	.6			

June 1   California

| Warren | 769,520 | 100.0 | Truman | 811,920 | 100.0 |

June 1   South Dakota

| Hitchcock [9] | 45,463 | 100.0 | Truman [9] | 11,193 | 58.3 |
| | | | Unpledged Delegates [9] | 8,016 | 41.7 |

TOTALS

Warren	771,295	29.1	Truman	1,375,452	63.9
Unpledged delegates	527,812	19.9	Unpledged delegates	653,509	30.4
Stassen	449,713	16.9	Eisenhower	6,211	.3
Bender	324,029	12.2	Wallace	4,416	.2
Dewey	304,394	11.5	Stassen	1,301	.1
MacArthur	87,839	3.3	MacArthur	1,220	.1
Hitchcock	45,463	1.7	Lucas	427	—
Edward Martin	45,072	1.7	Others	109,329	5.1
Taft	37,974	1.4			
Vandenberg	18,924	.7		2,151,865	
Eisenhower	5,014	.2			
Truman	4,907	.2			
Wallace	1,452	.1			
Joseph W. Martin	974	—			
Driscoll	44	—			
Others [10]	28,349	1.1			
	2,653,255				

1. Six unpledged and two Dewey delegates won in the Republican primary, and Truman delegates won in the Democratic primary, according to Kravitz, op. cit., p. 14.

2.   Write-in.

3. Source: Kravitz, op. cit., p. 14.

4. The Boston Globe *of April 28, 1948, reported that the Republican delegation was "generally unpledged" but was expected to support the "favorite son" candidacy of Sen. Leverett Saltonstall (R Mass.) on the first convention ballot. The Globe reported that Democratic delegates were presumed to favor Truman's nomination.*

5. No primary.

6. Unpledged, anti-Truman slate, according to Kravitz, op. cit., p. 15.

7. Unpledged slate, according to Kravitz, ibid.

8. Taft won 44 delegates and Stassen nine in the Republican primary, and W.A. Julian won 55 delegates and Bixler one in the Democratic primary, according to Kravitz., ibid.

9. Republican delegates were unpledged, according to Kravitz, op. cit., p. 15. In the Democratic primary, according to Davis, p. 297, the slate led by South Dakota Democratic Party Chairman Lynn Fellows endorsed Truman and the slate headed by former Rep. Fred Hildebrandt (D S.D.) ran uninstructed.

10. In addition to scattered votes, "others" includes Byer who received 15,675 votes and Vander Pyl who received 6,735 votes in the West Virginia primary.

1952 Primaries

Republican

	Votes	%

Democratic

	Votes	%

March 11   New Hampshire

Republican	Votes	%	Democratic	Votes	%
Dwight D. Eisenhower (N.Y.)	46,661	50.4	Estes Kefauver (Tenn.)	19,800	55.0
Robert A. Taft (Ohio)	35,838	38.7	Harry S Truman (Mo.)	15,927	44.2
Harold E. Stassen (Minn.)	6,574	7.1	Douglas MacArthur (Wis.)	151	.4
Douglas MacArthur (Wis.)[1]	3,227	3.5	James A. Farley (N.Y.)	77	.2
Others	230	.3	Adlai E. Stevenson (Ill.)	40	.1

March 18   Minnesota

Republican	Votes	%	Democratic	Votes	%
Stassen	129,706	44.4	Hubert H. Humphrey (Minn.)	102,527	80.0
Eisenhower[1]	108,692	37.2	Kefauver[1]	20,182	15.8
Taft[1]	24,093	8.2	Truman[1]	3,634	2.8
Earl Warren (Calif.)[1]	5,365	1.8	Dwight D. Eisenhower (N.Y.)	1,753	1.4
MacArthur[1]	1,369	.5			
Estes Kefauver (Tenn.)	386	.1			
Others	22,712	7.8			

April 1   Nebraska

Republican	Votes	%	Democratic	Votes	%
Taft[1]	79,357	36.2	Kefauver	64,531	60.3
Eisenhower[1]	66,078	30.1	Robert S. Kerr (Okla.)	42,467	39.7
Stassen	53,238	24.3			
MacArthur[1]	7,478	3.4			
Warren[1]	1,872	.9			
Others	11,178	5.1			

April 1   Wisconsin

Republican	Votes	%	Democratic	Votes	%
Taft	315,541	40.6	Kefauver	207,520	85.9
Warren	262,271	33.8	Others	34,005	14.1
Stassen	169,679	21.8			
Others	29,133	3.8			

April 8   Illinois

Republican	Votes	%	Democratic	Votes	%
Taft	935,867	73.6	Kefauver	526,301	87.7
Stassen	155,041	12.2	Stevenson	54,336	9.1
Eisenhower[1]	147,518	11.6	Truman	9,024	1.5
MacArthur[1]	7,504	.6	Eisenhower	6,655	1.1
Warren	2,841	.2	Others[1]	3,798	.6
Others	23,550	1.9			

April 15   New Jersey

Republican	Votes	%	Democratic	Votes	%
Eisenhower	390,591	60.7	Kefauver	154,964	100.0
Taft	228,916	35.6			
Stassen	23,559	3.7			

April 22   Pennsylvania

Republican	Votes	%	Democratic	Votes	%
Eisenhower	863,785	73.6	Kefauver[1]	93,160	53.3
Taft[1]	178,629	15.2	Eisenhower[1]	28,660	16.4
Stassen	120,305	10.3	Truman[1]	26,504	15.2
MacArthur[1]	6,028	.5	Robert A. Taft (Ohio)	8,311	4.8
Warren	3,158	.3	Averell Harriman (N.Y.)[1]	3,745	2.1
Harry S Truman (Mo.)	267	—	Stevenson[1]	3,678	2.1
Others	1,121	.1	Richard B. Russell (Ga.)[1]	1,691	1.0
			Others	9,026	5.2

April 29   Massachusetts

Republican	Votes	%	Democratic	Votes	%
Eisenhower[1]	254,898	69.8	Kefauver	29,287	55.7
Taft[1]	110,188	30.2	Eisenhower	16,007	30.5
			Truman	7,256	13.8

	Republican			**Democratic**	
	Votes	%		Votes	%

May 5   Maryland[2]

[3]			Kefauver	137,885	74.8
			Unpledged delegates	46,361	25.2

May 6   Florida

[3]			Russell	367,980	54.5
			Kefauver	285,358	42.3
			Others	21,296	3.2

May 6   Ohio

Taft[4]	663,791	78.8	Kefauver[4]	305,992	62.3
Stassen[4]	178,739	21.2	Robert J. Bulkley (Ohio)[4]	184,880	37.7

May 13   West Virginia

Taft	139,812	78.5	Unpledged delegates at large	191,471	100.0
Stassen	38,251	21.5			

May 16   Oregon

Eisenhower	172,486	64.6	Kefauver	142,440	72.3
Warren	44,034	16.5	William O. Douglas (Wash.)	29,532	15.0
MacArthur	18,603	7.0	Stevenson	20,353	10.3
Taft[1]	18,009	6.7	Eisenhower[1]	4,690	2.4
Wayne L. Morse (Ore.)	7,105	2.7			
Stassen	6,610	2.5			
Others	350	.1			

June 3   California

Warren	1,029,495	66.4	Kefauver	1,155,839	70.4
Thomas H. Werdel (Calif.)	521,110	33.6	Edmund G. Brown (Calif.)	485,578	29.6

June 3   South Dakota

Taft	64,695	50.3	Kefauver	22,812	66.0
Eisenhower	63,879	49.7	Others[5]	11,741	34.0

June 17   District of Columbia[6]

[3]			Harriman	14,075	74.9
			Kefauver	3,377	18.0
			Others[1]	1,329	7.1

TOTALS

Taft	2,794,736	35.8	Kefauver	3,169,448	64.3
Eisenhower	2,114,588	27.1	Brown	485,578	9.9
Warren	1,349,036	17.3	Russell	369,671	7.5
Stassen	881,702	11.3	Unpledged delegates	237,832	4.8
Werdel	521,110	6.7	Bulkley	184,880	3.8
MacArthur	44,209	.6	Humphrey	102,527	2.1
Morse	7,105	.1	Stevenson	78,583	1.6
Kefauver	386	—	Truman	62,345	1.3
Truman	267	—	Eisenhower	57,765	1.2
Others	88,274	1.1	Kerr	42,467	.9
	———		Douglas	29,532	.6
	7,801,413		Harriman	17,820	.4
			Taft	8,311	.2
			MacArthur	151	—
			Farley	77	—
			Others[8]	81,019	1.6
				———	
				4,928,006	

1. Write-in.
2. Source: Kravitz, op. cit., p. 18, and the office of the Maryland secretary of state.
3. No primary.
4. Delegate-at-large vote.
5. These delegates ran on an uninstructed slate, according to Kravitz, op. cit., p. 19.
6. Source: David, Moos, and Goldman, Nominating Politics in 1952, Vol. 2, p. 331-332.
7. In addition to scattered votes, "others" includes Schneider who received 230

received 10,411 in the Nebraska primary; Ritter who received 26,208 and Stearns who received 2,925 in the Wisconsin primary; Slettendahl who received 22,712 in the Minnesota primary and Riley Bender who received 22,321 votes in the Illinois primary.
8. In addition to scattered votes, "others" includes Fox who received 18,322 votes and Charles Broughton who received 15,683 votes in the Wisconsin primary; Compton who received 11,331 and Shaw who received 9,965 in the Florida primary.

1956 Primaries

Republican			Democratic		
	Votes	%		Votes	%

March 13　New Hampshire

	Votes	%		Votes	%
Dwight D. Eisenhower (Pa.)	56,464	98.9	Estes Kefauver (Tenn.)	21,701	84.6
Others	600	1.1	Others	3,945	15.4

March 20　Minnesota

	Votes	%		Votes	%
Eisenhower	198,111	98.4	Kefauver	245,885	56.8
William F. Knowland (Calif.)	3,209	1.6	Adlai E. Stevenson (Ill.)	186,723	43.2
Others	51	—	Others	48	—

April 3　Wisconsin

	Votes	%		Votes	%
Eisenhower	437,089	95.9	Kefauver	330,665[1]	100.0
Others	18,743	4.1			

April 10　Illinois

	Votes	%		Votes	%
Eisenhower	781,710	94.9	Stevenson	717,742	95.3
Knowland	33,534	4.1	Kefauver[2]	34,092	4.5
Others	8,455	1.0	Others	1,640	.2

April 17　New Jersey

	Votes	%		Votes	%
Eisenhower	357,066	100.0	Kefauver	117,056	95.7
Others	23	—	Others	5,230	4.3

April 24　Alaska (Territory)

	Votes	%		Votes	%
Eisenhower	8,291	94.4	Stevenson	7,123	61.1
Knowland	488	5.6	Kefauver	4,536	38.9

April 24　Massachusetts

	Votes	%		Votes	%
Eisenhower[2]	51,951	95.1	John W. McCormack (Mass.)[2]	26,128	47.9
Adlai E. Stevenson (Ill.)[2]	604	1.1	Stevenson[2]	19,024	34.9
Christian A. Herter (Mass.)[2]	550	1.0	Kefauver[2]	4,547	8.3
Richard M. Nixon (N.Y.)[2]	316	.6	Dwight D. Eisenhower (Pa.)[2]	1,850	3.4
John W. McCormack (Mass.)[2]	268	.5	John F. Kennedy (Mass.)[2]	949	1.7
Knowland[2]	250	.5	Averell Harriman (N.Y.)[2]	394	.7
Others[2]	700	1.3	Frank J. Lausche (Ohio)[2]	253	.5
			Others[2]	1,379	2.5

April 24　Pennsylvania

	Votes	%		Votes	%
Eisenhower	951,932	95.5	Stevenson	642,172	93.6
Knowland	43,508	4.4	Kefauver[2]	36,552	5.3
Others	976	.1	Others	7,482	1.1

May 1　District of Columbia[3]

	Votes	%		Votes	%
Eisenhower	18,101	100.0	Stevenson	17,306	66.2
			Kefauver	8,837	33.8

May 7　Maryland

	Votes	%		Votes	%
Eisenhower	66,904	95.5	Kefauver	112,768	65.9
Unpledged delegates	3,131	4.5	Unpledged delegates	58,366	34.1

May 8　Indiana

	Votes	%		Votes	%
Eisenhower	351,903	96.4	Kefauver	242,842[1]	100.0
Others	13,320	3.6			

Republican

	Votes	%

Democratic

	Votes	%

May 8 Ohio

John W. Bricker (Ohio)	478,453[1]	100.0	Lausche	276,670[1]	100.0

May 8 West Virginia

Unpledged delegates at large	111,883[1]	100.0	Unpledged delegates at large	112,832[1]	100.0

May 15 Nebraska

Eisenhower	102,576	99.8	Kefauver	55,265	94.0
Others	230	.2	Others	3,556	6.0

May 18 Oregon

Eisenhower	231,418[1]	100.0	Stevenson[2]	98,131	60.2
			Kefauver[2]	62,987	38.6
			Harriman[2]	1,887	1.2

May 29 Florida

Eisenhower	39,690	92.0	Stevenson	230,285	51.5
Knowland	3,457	8.0	Kefauver	216,549	48.5

June 5 California

Eisenhower	1,354,764[1]	100.0	Stevenson	1,139,964	62.6
			Kefauver	680,722	37.4

June 5 Montana

S.C. Arnold[4]	32,732	85.7	Kefauver	77,228[1]	100.0
Others	5,447	14.3			

June 5 South Dakota

Unpledged delegates[5]	59,374[1]	100.0	Kefauver	30,940[1]	100.0

TOTALS

Eisenhower	5,007,970	85.9	Stevenson	3,051,347	52.3
Bricker	478,453	8.2	Kefauver	2,278,636	39.1
Unpledged delegates	174,388	3.0	Lausche	276,923	4.7
Knowland	84,446	1.4	Unpledged delegates	171,198	2.9
S.C. Arnold	32,732	.6	McCormack	26,128	.4
Stevenson	604	—	Harriman	2,281	—
Herter	550	—	Eisenhower	1,850	—
Nixon	316	—	Kennedy	949	—
McCormack	268	—	Others	23,280	.4
Others[6]	48,545	.8			
	5,828,272			5,832,592	

1. Figures obtained from Scammon's office. In America Votes, Scammon did not record vote totals if a candidate was unopposed or if the primary was strictly for delegate selection.
2. Write-in.
3. Source: Davis, op. cit., pp. 300-301.
4. Voters cast their ballots for S. C. Arnold, "stand-in" candidate for Eisenhower.

5. Slate unofficially pledged to Eisenhower but appeared on the ballot as "No preference."
6. In addition to scattered votes, "others" includes Lar Daly who received 8,364 votes in the Illinois primary, 13,320 votes in the Indiana primary and 5,447 votes in the Montana primary; and John Bowman Chapple who received 18,743 votes in the Wisconsin primary.

1960 Primaries

	Republican			Democratic		
	Votes	%		Votes	%

March 8 New Hampshire

Richard M. Nixon (N.Y.)	65,204	89.3	John F. Kennedy (Mass.)	43,372	85.2
Nelson A. Rockefeller (N.Y.)[1]	2,745	3.8	Others	7,527	14.8
John F. Kennedy (Mass.)[1]	2,196	3.0			
Others	2,886	4.0			

April 5 Wisconsin

Nixon	339,383[2]	100.0	Kennedy	476,024	56.5
			Hubert H. Humphrey (Minn.)	366,753	43.5

April 12 Illinois

Nixon	782,849[2]	99.9	Kennedy[1]	34,332	64.6
Others[1]	442[2]	.1	Adlai E. Stevenson (Ill.)[1]	8,029	15.1
			Stuart Symington (Mo.)[1]	5,744	10.8
			Humphrey[1]	4,283	8.1
			Lyndon B. Johnson (Texas)[1]	442	.8
			Others[1]	337	.6

April 19 New Jersey

Unpledged delegates at large	304,766[2]	100.0	Unpledged delegates at large	217,608[2]	100.0

April 26 Massachusetts

Nixon[1]	53,164	86.0	Kennedy[1]	91,607	92.4
Rockefeller[1]	4,068	6.6	Stevenson[1]	4,684	4.7
Kennedy[1]	2,989	4.8	Humphrey[1]	794	.8
Henry Cabot Lodge (Mass.)[1]	373	.6	Richard M. Nixon (Calif.)[1]	646	.7
Adlai E. Stevenson (Ill.)[1]	266	.4	Symington[1]	443	.4
Barry Goldwater (Ariz.)[1]	221	.4	Johnson[1]	268	.3
Dwight D. Eisenhower (Pa.)[1]	172	.3	Others[1]	721	.7
Others[1]	592	1.0			

April 26 Pennsylvania

Nixon	968,538	98.1	Kennedy[1]	183,073	71.3
Rockefeller[1]	12,491	1.3	Stevenson[1]	29,660	11.5
Kennedy[1]	3,886	.4	Nixon[1]	15,136	5.9
Stevenson[1]	428	—	Humphrey[1]	13,860	5.4
Goldwater[1]	286	—	Symington[1]	6,791	2.6
Others[1]	1,202	.1	Johnson[1]	2,918	1.1
			Rockefeller[1]	1,078	.4
			Others[1]	4,297	1.7

May 3 District of Columbia[3]

Unpledged delegates	9,468	100.0	Humphrey	8,239	57.4
			Wayne L. Morse (Ore.)	6,127	42.6

May 3 Indiana

Nixon	408,408	95.4	Kennedy	353,832	81.0
Others	19,677	4.6	Others	82,937	19.0

May 3 Ohio

Nixon	504,072[2]	100.0	Michael V. DiSalle (Ohio)	315,312[2]	100.0

Republican	Votes	%	Democratic	Votes	%
May 10 Nebraska					
Nixon	74,356	93.8	Kennedy	80,408	88.7
Rockefeller[1]	2,028	2.6	Symington[1]	4,083	4.5
Goldwater[1]	1,068	1.3	Humphrey[1]	3,202	3.5
Others[1]	1,805	2.3	Stevenson[1]	1,368	1.5
			Johnson[1]	962	1.1
			Others[1]	669	.7
May 10 West Virginia					
Unpledged delegates at large	123,756[2]	100.0	Kennedy	236,510	60.8
			Humphrey	152,187	39.2
May 17 Maryland					
[4]			Kennedy	201,769	70.3
			Morse	49,420	17.2
			Unpledged delegates	24,350	8.5
			Others	11,417	4.0
May 20 Oregon					
Nixon	211,276	93.1	Kennedy	146,332	51.0
Rockefeller[1]	9,307	4.1	Morse	91,715	31.9
Kennedy[1]	2,864	1.3	Humphrey	16,319	5.7
Goldwater[1]	1,571	.7	Symington	12,496	4.4
Others[1]	2,015	.9	Johnson	11,101	3.9
			Stevenson[1]	7,924	2.8
			Others[1]	1,210	.4
May 24 Florida					
Nixon	51,036[2]	100.0	George A. Smathers (Fla.)	322,235[2]	100.0
June 7 California					
Nixon	1,517,652[2]	100.0	Edmund G. Brown (Calif.)	1,354,031	67.7
			George H. McLain (Calif.)	646,387	32.3
June 7 South Dakota					
Unpledged delegates	48,461[2]	100.0	Humphrey	24,773[2]	100.0
TOTALS					
Nixon	4,975,938	89.9	Kennedy	1,847,259	32.5
Unpledged delegates	486,451	8.8	Brown	1,354,031	23.8
Rockefeller	30,639	.6	McLain	646,387	11.4
Kennedy	11,935	.2	Humphrey	590,410	10.4
Goldwater	3,146	.1	Smathers	322,235	5.7
Stevenson	694	—	DiSalle	315,312	5.5
Lodge	373	—	Unpledged delegates	241,958	4.3
Eisenhower	172	—	Morse	147,262	2.6
Others[5]	28,619	.5	Stevenson	51,665	.9
			Symington	29,557	.5
	5,537,967		Nixon	15,782	.3
			Johnson	15,691	.3
			Others[6]	109,115	1.9
				5,686,664	

Source: Richard M. Scammon, *America Votes 4*
(Washington, D.C.: Congressional Quarterly Inc., 1962).

1. Write-in.
2. Figures obtained from Scammon's office. In America Votes, Scammon did not record vote totals if a candidate was unopposed or if the primary was strictly for delegate selection.
3. Source: District of Columbia Board of Elections.
4. No primary.
5. In addition to scattered votes, "others" includes Paul C. Fisher who received

2,388 votes in the New Hampshire primary and Frank R. Beckwith who received 19,677 in the Indiana primary.
6. In addition to scattered votes, "others" includes Lar Daly who received 40,853 votes in the Indiana primary and 7,536 in the Maryland primary; Paul C. Fisher who received 6,853 votes in the New Hampshire primary; John H. Latham who received 42,084 in the Indiana primary and Andrew J. Easter who received 3,881 votes in the Maryland primary.

1964 Primaries

Republican			Democratic		
	Votes	%		Votes	%

March 10   New Hampshire

Republican			Democratic		
Henry Cabot Lodge (Mass.)[1]	33,007	35.5	Lyndon B. Johnson (Texas)[1]	29,317	95.3
Barry M. Goldwater (Ariz.)	20,692	22.3	Robert F. Kennedy (N.Y.)[1]	487	1.6
Nelson A. Rockefeller (N.Y.)	19,504	21.0	Henry Cabot Lodge (Mass.)[1]	280	.9
Richard M. Nixon (Calif.)[1]	15,587	16.8	Richard M. Nixon (Calif.)[1]	232	.8
Margaret Chase Smith (Maine)	2,120	2.3	Barry M. Goldwater (Ariz.)[1]	193	.6
Harold E. Stassen (Pa.)	1,373	1.5	Nelson A. Rockefeller (N.Y.)[1]	109	.4
William W. Scranton (Pa.)[1]	105	.1	Others[1]	159	.5
Others	465	.5			

April 7   Wisconsin

Republican			Democratic		
John W. Byrnes (Wis.)	299,612	99.7	John W. Reynolds (Wis.)	522,405	66.2
Unpledged delegate	816	.3	George C. Wallace (Ala.)	266,136	33.8

April 14   Illinois

Republican			Democratic		
Goldwater	512,840	62.0	Johnson[1]	82,027	91.6
Smith	209,521	25.3	Wallace[1]	3,761	4.2
Henry Cabot Lodge[1]	68,122	8.2	Robert F. Kennedy[1]	2,894	3.2
Nixon[1]	30,313	3.7	Others[1]	841	.9
George C. Wallace (Ala.)[1]	2,203	.3			
Rockefeller[1]	2,048	.2			
Scranton[1]	1,842	.2			
George W. Romney (Mich.)[1]	465	.1			
Others[1]	437	.1			

April 21   New Jersey

Republican			Democratic		
Henry Cabot Lodge[1]	7,896	41.7	Johnson[1]	4,863	82.3
Goldwater[1]	5,309	28.0	Wallace[1]	491	8.3
Nixon[1]	4,179	22.1	Robert F. Kennedy[1]	431	7.3
Scranton[1]	633	3.3	Others[1]	124	2.1
Rockefeller[1]	612	3.2			
Others[1]	304	1.6			

April 28   Massachusetts

Republican			Democratic		
Henry Cabot Lodge[1]	70,809	76.9	Johnson[1]	61,035	73.4
Goldwater[1]	9,338	10.1	Robert F. Kennedy[1]	15,870	19.1
Nixon[1]	5,460	5.9	Lodge[1]	2,269	2.7
Rockefeller[1]	2,454	2.7	Edward M. Kennedy (Mass.)[1]	1,259	1.5
Scranton[1]	1,709	1.9	Wallace[1]	565	.7
Lyndon B. Johnson (Texas)[1]	600	.7	Adlai E. Stevenson (Ill.)[1]	452	.5
Smith[1]	426	.5	Hubert H. Humphrey (Minn.)[1]	323	.4
George C. Lodge (Mass.)[1]	365	.4	Others[1]	1,436	1.7
Romney[1]	262	.3			
Others[1]	711	.8			

April 28   Pennsylvania

Republican			Democratic		
Scranton[1]	235,222	51.9	Johnson[1]	209,606	82.8
Henry Cabot Lodge[1]	92,712	20.5	Wallace[1]	12,104	4.8
Nixon[1]	44,396	9.8	Robert F. Kennedy[1]	12,029	4.8
Goldwater[1]	38,669	8.5	William W. Scranton (Pa.)[1]	8,156	3.2
Johnson[1]	22,372	4.9	Lodge[1]	4,895	1.9
Rockefeller[1]	9,123	2.0	Others[1]	6,438	2.5
Wallace[1]	5,105	1.1			
Others[1]	5,269	1.2			

May 2   Texas

Republican			Democratic		
Goldwater	104,137	74.7	[2]		
Henry Cabot Lodge[1]	12,324	8.8			
Rockefeller	6,207	4.5			
Nixon[1]	5,390	3.9			
Stassen	5,273	3.8			
Smith	4,816	3.5			
Scranton[1]	803	.6			
Others[1]	373	.3			

	Republican			Democratic		
	Votes	%			Votes	%

May 5   District of Columbia[3]

[3]			Unpledged delegates		41,095	100.0

May 5   Indiana

Goldwater	267,935	67.0	Matthew E. Welsh (Ind.)		376,023	64.9
Stassen	107,157	26.8	Wallace		172,646	29.8
Others	24,588	6.2	Others		30,367	5.2

May 5   Ohio

James A. Rhodes (Ohio)	615,754 [4]	100.0	Albert S. Porter (Ohio)		493,619 [4]	100.0

May 12   Nebraska

Goldwater	68,050	49.1	Johnson[1]		54,713	89.3
Nixon[1]	43,613	31.5	Robert F. Kennedy[1]		2,099	3.4
Henry Cabot Lodge[1]	22,622	16.3	Wallace[1]		1,067	1.7
Rockefeller[1]	2,333	1.7	Lodge[1]		1,051	1.7
Scranton[1]	578	.4	Nixon[1]		833	1.4
Johnson[1]	316	.2	Goldwater[1]		603	1.0
Others[1]	1,010	.7	Others[1]		904	1.5

May 12   West Virginia

Rockefeller	115,680 [4]	100.0	Unpledged delegates at large		131,432 [4]	100.0

May 15   Oregon

Rockefeller	94,190	33.0	Johnson		272,099 [4]	99.5
Henry Cabot Lodge	79,169	27.7	Wallace[1]		1,365 [4]	.5
Goldwater	50,105	17.6				
Nixon	48,274	16.9				
Smith	8,087	2.8				
Scranton	4,509	1.6				
Others	1,152	.4				

May 19   Maryland

Unpledged delegates	57,004	58.2	Daniel B. Brewster (Md.)		267,106	53.1
Others	40,994	41.8	Wallace		214,849	42.7
			Unpledged delegates		12,377	2.5
			Others		8,275	1.6

May 26   Florida

Unpledged delegates	58,179	57.8	Johnson		393,339 [4]	100.0
Goldwater	42,525	42.2				

June 2   California

Goldwater	1,120,403	51.6	Unpledged delegates[5]		1,693,813	68.0
Rockefeller	1,052,053	48.4	Unpledged delegates[5]		798,431	32.0

June 2   South Dakota

Unpledged delegates	57,653	68.0	Unpledged delegates		28,142 [4]	100.0
Goldwater	27,076	32.0				

Republican

	Votes	%
TOTALS		
Goldwater	2,267,079	*38.2*
Rockefeller	1,304,204	*22.0*
Rhodes	615,754	*10.4*
Henry Cabot Lodge	386,661	*6.5*
Byrnes	299,612	*5.0*
Scranton	245,401	*4.1*
Smith	224,970	*3.8*
Nixon	197,212	*3.3*
Unpledged delegates	173,652	*2.9*
Stassen	113,803	*1.9*
Johnson	23,288	*.4*
Wallace	7,308	*.1*
Romney	727	—
George C. Lodge	365	—
Others6	75,303	*1.3*
	5,935,339	

Democratic

	Votes	%
Unpledged delegates	2,705,290	*43.3*
Johnson	1,106,999	*17.7*
Wallace	672,984	*10.8*
Reynolds	522,405	*8.4*
Porter	493,619	*7.9*
Welsh	376,023	*6.0*
Brewster	267,106	*4.3*
Robert F. Kennedy	33,810	*.5*
Henry Cabot Lodge	8,495	*.1*
Scranton	8,156	*.1*
Edward M. Kennedy	1,259	—
Nixon	1,065	—
Goldwater	796	—
Stevenson	452	—
Humphrey	323	—
Rockefeller	109	—
Others7	48,544	*.8*
	6,247,435	

1. Write-in.

2. No primary authorized.

3. Source: District of Columbia Board of Elections. No figures available for vote for delegates to Republican convention.

4. Figures obtained from Scammon's office. In America Votes, Scammon did not record vote totals if a candidate was unopposed or if the primary was strictly for delegate selection.

5. Gov. Edmund G. Brown (D Calif.) headed the winning slate of delegates and Mayor Sam Yorty of Los Angeles headed the losing slate.

6. In addition to scattered votes, "others" includes Norman LePage who received 82 votes in the New Hampshire primary; Frank R. Beckwith who received 17,884 votes and Joseph G. Ettl who received 6,704 votes in the Indiana primary; John W. Steffey who received 22,135 votes and Robert E. Ennis who received 18,859 votes in the Maryland primary.

7. In addition to scattered votes, "others" includes Lar Daly who received 15,160 votes, John H. Latham who received 8,067 votes and Fay T. Carpenter Swain who received 7,140 votes in the Indiana primary; and Andrew J. Easter who received 8,275 votes in the Maryland primary.

1968 Primaries*

Republican	Votes	%	Democratic	Votes	%

March 12 New Hampshire

Republican	Votes	%	Democratic	Votes	%
Richard M. Nixon (N.Y.)	80,666	77.6	Lyndon B. Johnson (Texas)[1]	27,520	49.6
Nelson A. Rockefeller (N.Y.)[1]	11,241	10.8	Eugene J. McCarthy (Minn.)	23,263	41.9
Eugene J. McCarthy (Minn.)[1]	5,511	5.3	Richard M. Nixon (N.Y.)[1]	2,532	4.6
Lyndon B. Johnson (Texas)[1]	1,778	1.7	Others	2,149	3.9
George W. Romney (Mich.)	1,743	1.7			
Harold E. Stassen (Pa.)	429	.4			
Others	2,570	2.5			

April 2 Wisconsin

Republican	Votes	%	Democratic	Votes	%
Nixon	390,368	79.7	McCarthy	412,160	56.2
Ronald Reagan (Calif.)	50,727	10.4	Johnson	253,696	34.6
Stassen	28,531	5.8	Robert F. Kennedy (N.Y.)[1]	46,507	6.3
Rockefeller[1]	7,995	1.6	Unpledged delegates	11,861	1.6
Unpledged delegates	6,763	1.4	George C. Wallace (Ala.)[1]	4,031	.5
Romney[1]	2,087	.4	Hubert H. Humphrey (Minn.)[1]	3,605	.5
Others	3,382	.7	Others	1,142	.2

April 23 Pennsylvania

Republican	Votes	%	Democratic	Votes	%
Nixon[1]	171,815	59.7	McCarthy	428,259	71.7
Rockefeller[1]	52,915	18.4	Robert F. Kennedy[1]	65,430	11.0
McCarthy[1]	18,800	6.5	Humphrey[1]	51,998	8.7
George C. Wallace (Ala.)[1]	13,290	4.6	Wallace[1]	24,147	4.0
Robert F. Kennedy (N.Y.)[1]	10,431	3.6	Johnson[1]	21,265	3.6
Reagan[1]	7,934	2.8	Nixon[1]	3,434	.6
Hubert H. Humphrey (Minn.)[1]	4,651	1.6	Others[1]	2,556	.4
Johnson[1]	3,027	1.1			
Raymond P. Shafer (Pa.)[1]	1,223	.4			
Others[1]	3,487	1.2			

April 30 Massachusetts

Republican	Votes	%	Democratic	Votes	%
Rockefeller[1]	31,964	30.0	McCarthy	122,697	49.3
John A. Volpe (Mass.)	31,465	29.5	Robert F. Kennedy[1]	68,604	27.6
Nixon[1]	27,447	25.8	Humphrey[1]	44,156	17.7
McCarthy[1]	9,758	9.2	Johnson[1]	6,890	2.8
Reagan[1]	1,770	1.7	Nelson A. Rockefeller (N.Y.)[1]	2,275	1.0
Kennedy[1]	1,184	1.1	Wallace[1]	1,688	.7
Others[1]	2,933	2.8	Others[1]	2,593	1.0

May 7 District of Columbia

Republican	Votes	%	Democratic	Votes	%
Nixon-Rockefeller[2]	12,102	90.1	Robert F. Kennedy[3]	57,555	62.5
Unpledged delegates[2]	1,328	9.9	Humphrey[3]	32,309	35.1
			Humphrey[3]	2,250	2.4

May 7 Indiana

Republican	Votes	%	Democratic	Votes	%
Nixon	508,362[4]	100.0	Robert F. Kennedy	328,118	42.3
			Roger D. Branigin (Ind.)	238,700	30.7
			McCarthy	209,695	27.0

May 7 Ohio

Republican	Votes	%	Democratic	Votes	%
James A. Rhodes (Ohio)	614,492[4]	100.0	Stephen M. Young (Ohio)	549,140[4]	100.0

Republican   # Democratic

	Votes	%		Votes	%

May 14   Nebraska[5]

Nixon	140,336	70.0	Robert F. Kennedy	84,102	51.7
Reagan	42,703	21.3	McCarthy	50,655	31.2
Rockefeller[1]	10,225	5.1	Humphrey[1]	12,087	7.4
Stassen	2,638	1.3	Johnson	9,187	5.6
McCarthy[1]	1,544	.8	Nixon[1]	2,731	1.7
Others	3,030	1.5	Ronald Reagan (Calif.)[1]	1,905	1.2
			Wallace[1]	1,298	.8
			Others	646	.4

May 14   West Virginia

| Unpledged delegates at large | 81,039[4] | 100.0 | Unpledged delegates at large | 149,282[4] | 100.0 |

May 28   Florida

Unpledged delegates	51,509[4]	100.0	George A. Smathers (Fla.)	236,242	46.1
			McCarthy	147,216	28.7
			Unpledged delegates	128,899	25.2

May 28   Oregon

Nixon	203,037	65.0	McCarthy	163,990	44.0
Reagan	63,707	20.4	Robert F. Kennedy	141,631	38.0
Rockefeller[1]	36,305	11.6	Johnson	45,174	12.1
McCarthy[1]	7,387	2.4	Humphrey[1]	12,421	3.3
Kennedy[1]	1,723	.6	Reagan[1]	3,082	.8
			Nixon[1]	2,974	.8
			Rockefeller[1]	2,841	.8
			Wallace[1]	957	.3

June 4   California

Reagan	1,525,091[4]	100.0	Robert F. Kennedy	1,472,166	46.3
			McCarthy	1,329,301	41.8
			Unpledged delegates	380,286	12.0

June 4   New Jersey

Nixon[1]	71,809	81.1	McCarthy[1]	9,906	36.1
Rockefeller[1]	11,530	13.0	Robert F. Kennedy[1]	8,603	31.3
Reagan[1]	2,737	3.1	Humphrey[1]	5,578	20.3
McCarthy[1]	1,358	1.5	Wallace[1]	1,399	5.1
Others[1]	1,158	1.3	Nixon[1]	1,364	5.0
			Others[1]	596	2.2

June 4   South Dakota

Nixon	68,113[4]	100.0	Robert F. Kennedy	31,826	49.5
			Johnson	19,316	30.0
			McCarthy	13,145	20.4

June 11   Illinois

Nixon[1]	17,490	78.1	McCarthy[1]	4,646	38.6
Rockefeller[1]	2,165	9.7	Edward M. Kennedy (Mass.)[1]	4,052	33.7
Reagan[1]	1,601	7.1	Humphrey[1]	2,059	17.1
Others[1]	1,147	5.1	Others[1]	1,281	10.6

Republican

	Votes	%
Reagan	1,696,270	37.9
Nixon	1,679,443	37.5
Rhodes	614,492	13.7
Rockefeller	164,340	3.7
Unpledged delegates	140,639	3.1
McCarthy	44,358	1.0
Stassen	31,598	.7
Volpe	31,465	.7
Robert F. Kennedy	13,338	.3
Wallace	13,290	.3
Nixon-Rockefeller[2]	12,102	.3
Johnson	4,805	.1
Humphrey	4,651	.1
Romney	3,830	.1
Shafer	1,223	—
Others[6]	17,707	.4
	4,473,551	

Democratic

	Votes	%
McCarthy	2,914,933	38.7
Robert F. Kennedy	2,304,542	30.6
Unpledged delegates	670,328	8.9
Young	549,140	7.3
Johnson	383,048	5.1
Branigin	238,700	3.2
Smathers	236,242	3.1
Humphrey	166,463	2.2
Wallace	33,520	.4
Nixon	13,035	.2
Rockefeller	5,116	.1
Reagan	4,987	.1
Edward M. Kennedy	4,052	.1
Others[7]	10,963	.1
	7,535,069	

* Delegate selection primaries were held in Alabama and New York. In America Votes, Scammon did not record vote totals if the primary was strictly for delegate selection and there was no presidential preference voting.

1. Write-in.

2. Prior to the primary, the District Republican organization agreed to divide the nine delegate votes, with six going to Nixon and three going to Rockefeller, according to the 1968 Congressional Quarterly Almanac, Vol. XXIV. Figures obtained from Scammon's office.

3. Figures obtained from Scammon's office. Two slates favored Humphrey; a member of an "independent" Humphrey slate received 2,250 votes.

4. Figures obtained from Scammon's office. In America Votes, Scammon did not record vote totals if a candidate was unopposed or if the primary was strictly for delegate selection.

5. In the American Party presidential primary, Wallace received 493 of the 504 votes cast, or 97.8% of the vote, according to the office of the Nebraska secretary of state.

6. In addition to scattered votes, "others" includes Willis E. Stone who received 527 votes, Herbert F. Hoover who received 247 votes, David Watumull who received 161 votes, William W. Evans who received 151 votes, Elmer W. Coy who received 73 votes and Don DuMont who received 39 votes in the New Hampshire primary; and Americus Liberator who received 1,302 votes in the Nebraska primary.

7. In addition to scattered votes, "others" includes John G. Crommelin who received 186 votes, Richard E. Lee who received 170 votes and Jacob J. Gordon who received 77 votes in the New Hampshire primary.

1972 Primaries*

Republican			**Democratic**		
	Votes	%		Votes	%

March 7 New Hampshire

Richard M. Nixon (Calif.)	79,239	67.6	Edmund S. Muskie (Maine)	41,235	46.4
Paul N. McCloskey (Calif.)	23,190	19.8	George S. McGovern (S.D.)	33,007	37.1
John M. Ashbrook (Ohio)	11,362	9.7	Sam Yorty (Calif.)	5,401	6.1
Others	3,417	2.9	Wilbur D. Mills (Ark.)[1]	3,563	4.0
			Vance Hartke (Ind.)	2,417	2.7
			Edward M. Kennedy (Mass.)[1]	954	1.1
			Hubert H. Humphrey (Minn.)[1]	348	.4
			Henry M. Jackson (Wash.)[1]	197	.2
			George C. Wallace (Ala.)[1]	175	.2
			Others	1,557	1.8

March 14 Florida

Nixon	360,278	87.0	Wallace	526,651	41.6
Ashbrook	36,617	8.8	Humphrey	234,658	18.6
McCloskey	17,312	4.2	Jackson	170,156	13.5
			Muskie	112,523	8.9
			John V. Lindsay (N.Y.)	82,386	6.5
			McGovern	78,232	6.2
			Shirley Chisholm (N.Y.)	43,989	3.5
			Eugene J. McCarthy (Minn.)	5,847	.5
			Mills	4,539	.4
			Hartke	3,009	.2
			Yorty	2,564	.2

March 21 Illinois

Nixon[1]	32,550	97.0	Muskie	766,914	62.6
Ashbrook[1]	170	.5	McCarthy	444,260	36.3
McCloskey[1]	47	.1	Wallace[1]	7,017	.6
Others[1]	802	2.4	McGovern[1]	3,687	.3
			Humphrey[1]	1,476	.1
			Chisholm[1]	777	.1
			Jackson[1]	442	—
			Kennedy[1]	242	—
			Lindsay[1]	118	—
			Others	211	—

April 4 Wisconsin

Nixon	277,601	96.9	McGovern	333,528	29.6
McCloskey	3,651	1.3	Wallace	248,676	22.0
Ashbrook	2,604	.9	Humphrey	233,748	20.7
None of the names shown	2,315	.8	Muskie	115,811	10.3
Others	273	.1	Jackson	88,068	7.8
			Lindsay	75,579	6.7
			McCarthy	15,543	1.4
			Chisholm	9,198	.8
			None of the names shown	2,450	.2
			Yorty	2,349	.2
			Patsy T. Mink (Hawaii)	1,213	.1
			Mills	913	.1
			Hartke	766	.1
			Kennedy[1]	183	—
			Others	559	—

Republican   ## Democratic

	Votes	%		Votes	%
April 25 Massachusetts					
Nixon	99,150	81.2	McGovern	325,673	52.7
McCloskey	16,435	13.5	Muskie	131,709	21.3
Ashbrook	4,864	4.0	Humphrey	48,929	7.9
Others	1,690	1.4	Wallace	45,807	7.4
			Chisholm	22,398	3.6
			Mills	19,441	3.1
			McCarthy	8,736	1.4
			Jackson	8,499	1.4
			Kennedy[1]	2,348	.4
			Lindsay	2,107	.3
			Hartke	874	.1
			Yorty	646	.1
			Others	1,349	.2
April 25 Pennsylvania					
Nixon[1]	153,886	83.3	Humphrey	481,900	35.1
George C. Wallace (Ala.)[1]	20,472	11.1	Wallace	292,437	21.3
Others[1]	10,443	5.7	McGovern	280,861	20.4
			Muskie	279,983	20.4
			Jackson	38,767	2.8
			Chisholm[1]	306	—
			Others	585	—
May 2 District of Columbia					
[2]			Walter E. Fauntroy (D.C.)	21,217	71.8
			Unpledged delegates	8,343	28.2
May 2 Indiana					
Nixon	417,069	100.0	Humphrey	354,244	47.1
			Wallace	309,495	41.2
			Muskie	87,719	11.7
May 2 Ohio					
Nixon	692,828	100.0	Humphrey	499,680	41.2
			McGovern	480,320	39.6
			Muskie	107,806	8.9
			Jackson	98,498	8.1
			McCarthy	26,026	2.1
May 4 Tennessee					
Nixon	109,696	95.8	Wallace	335,858	68.2
Ashbrook	2,419	2.1	Humphrey	78,350	15.9
McCloskey	2,370	2.1	McGovern	35,551	7.2
Others	4	—	Chisholm	18,809	3.8
			Muskie	9,634	2.0
			Jackson	5,896	1.2
			Mills	2,543	.5
			McCarthy	2,267	.5
			Hartke	1,621	.3
			Lindsay	1,476	.3
			Yorty	692	.1
			Others	24	—

Republican

Democratic

	Votes	%		Votes	%
May 6 North Carolina					
Nixon	159,167	94.8	Wallace	413,518	50.3
McCloskey	8,732	5.2	Terry Sanford (N.C.)	306,014	37.3
			Chisholm	61,723	7.5
			Muskie	30,739	3.7
			Jackson	9,416	1.1
May 9 Nebraska					
Nixon	179,464	92.4	McGovern	79,309	41.3
McCloskey	9,011	4.6	Humphrey	65,968	34.3
Ashbrook	4,996	2.6	Wallace	23,912	12.4
Others	801	.4	Muskie	6,886	3.6
			Jackson	5,276	2.7
			Yorty	3,459	1.8
			McCarthy	3,194	1.7
			Chisholm	1,763	.9
			Lindsay	1,244	.6
			Mills	377	.2
			Kennedy[1]	293	.2
			Hartke	249	.1
			Others	207	.1
May 9 West Virginia					
Unpledged delegates at large	95,813[3]	100.0	Humphrey	246,596	66.9
			Wallace	121,888	33.1
May 16 Maryland					
Nixon	99,308	86.2	Wallace	219,687	38.7
McCloskey	9,223	8.0	Humphrey	151,981	26.8
Ashbrook	6,718	5.8	McGovern	126,978	22.4
			Jackson	17,728	3.1
			Yorty	13,584	2.4
			Muskie	13,363	2.4
			Chisholm	12,602	2.2
			Mills	4,776	.8
			McCarthy	4,691	.8
			Lindsay	2,168	.4
			Mink	573	.1
May 16 Michigan					
Nixon	321,652	95.5	Wallace	809,239	51.0
McCloskey	9,691	2.9	McGovern	425,694	26.8
Unpledged delegates	5,370	1.6	Humphrey	249,798	15.7
Others	30	—	Chisholm	44,090	2.8
			Muskie	38,701	2.4
			Unpledged delegates	10,700	.7
			Jackson	6,938	.4
			Hartke	2,862	.2
			Others	51	—
May 23 Oregon					
Nixon	231,151	82.0	McGovern	205,328	50.2
McCloskey	29,365	10.4	Wallace	81,868	20.0
Ashbrook	16,696	5.9	Humphrey	51,163	12.5
Others	4,798	1.7	Jackson	22,042	5.4
			Kennedy	12,673	3.1
			Muskie	10,244	2.5
			McCarthy	8,943	2.2
			Mink	6,500	1.6
			Lindsay	5,082	1.2
			Chisholm	2,975	.7
			Mills	1,208	.3
			Others	618	.2

Republican   # Democratic

May 23 **Rhode Island**	Votes	%		Votes	%
Nixon	4,953	88.3	McGovern	15,603	41.2
McCloskey	337	6.0	Muskie	7,838	20.7
Ashbrook	175	3.1	Humphrey	7,701	20.3
Unpledged delegates	146	2.6	Wallace	5,802	15.3
			Unpledged delegates	490	1.3
			McCarthy	245	.6
			Jackson	138	.4
			Mills	41	.1
			Yorty	6	—
June 6 **California**					
Nixon	2,058,825	90.1	McGovern	1,550,652	43.5
Ashbrook	224,922	9.8	Humphrey	1,375,064	38.6
Others	175	—	Wallace[1]	268,551	7.5
			Chisholm	157,435	4.4
			Muskie	72,701	2.0
			Yorty	50,745	1.4
			McCarthy	34,203	1.0
			Jackson	28,901	.8
			Lindsay	26,246	.7
			Others	20	—
June 6 **New Jersey**					
Unpledged delegates at large	215,719[3]	100.0	Chisholm	51,433	66.9
			Sanford	25,401	33.1
June 6 **New Mexico**					
Nixon	49,067	88.5	McGovern	51,011	33.3
McCloskey	3,367	6.1	Wallace	44,843	29.3
None of the names shown	3,035	5.5	Humphrey	39,768	25.9
			Muskie	6,411	4.2
			Jackson	4,236	2.8
			None of the names shown	3,819	2.5
			Chisholm	3,205	2.1
June 6 **South Dakota**					
Nixon	52,820	100.0	McGovern	28,017	100.0

TOTALS					
Nixon	5,378,704	86.9	Humphrey	4,121,372	25.8
Unpledged delegates	317,048	5.1	McGovern	4,053,451	25.3
Ashbrook	311,543	5.0	Wallace	3,755,424	23.5
McCloskey	132,731	2.1	Muskie	1,840,217	11.5
Wallace	20,472	.3	McCarthy	553,955	3.5
None of the names shown	5,350	.1	Jackson	505,198	3.2
Others[4]	22,433	.4	Chisholm	430,703	2.7
			Sanford	331,415	2.1
	6,188,281		Lindsay	196,406	1.2
			Yorty	79,446	.5
			Mills	37,401	.2
			Fauntroy	21,217	.1
			Unpledged delegates	19,533	.1
			Kennedy	16,693	.1
			Hartke	11,798	.1
			Mink	8,286	.1
			None of the names shown	6,269	—
			Others[5]	5,181	—
				15,993,965	

Delegate selection primaries were held in Alabama and New York. In America Votes, Scammon did not record vote totals if the primary was strictly for delegate selection and there was no presidential preference voting.

1. Write-in.
2. No Republican primary in 1972.

3. Figures obtained from Scammon's office. In America Votes, Scammon did not record vote totals if the primary was strictly for delegate selection.
4. In addition to scattered votes, "others" includes Patrick Paulsen, who received 1,211 votes in the New Hampshire primary.
5. In addition to scattered votes, "others" includes Edward T. Coll, who received 280 votes in the New Hampshire primary and 589 votes in the Massachusetts primary.

1976 Primaries*

Republican | Democratic

	Votes	%		Votes	%
February 24 New Hampshire					
Gerald R. Ford (Mich.)	55,156	49.4	Jimmy Carter (Ga.)	23,373	28.4
Ronald Reagan (Calif.)	53,569	48.0	Morris K. Udall (Ariz.)	18,710	22.7
Others[1]	2,949	2.6	Birch Bayh (Ind.)	12,510	15.2
			Fred R. Harris (Okla.)	8,863	10.8
			Sargent Shriver (Md.)	6,743	8.2
			Hubert H. Humphrey (Minn.)	4,596	5.6
			Henry M. Jackson (Wash.)	1,857	2.3
			George C. Wallace (Ala.)	1,061	1.3
			Ellen McCormack (N.Y.)	1,007	1.2
			Others	3,661	4.8
March 2 Massachusetts					
Ford	115,375	61.2	Jackson	164,393	22.3
Reagan	63,555	33.7	Udall	130,440	17.7
None of the names shown	6,000	3.2	Wallace	123,112	16.7
Others[1]	3,519	1.8	Carter	101,948	13.9
			Harris	55,701	7.6
			Shriver	53,252	7.2
			Bayh	34,963	4.8
			McCormack	25,772	3.5
			Milton J. Shapp (Pa.)	21,693	2.9
			None of the names shown	9,804	1.3
			Humphrey[1]	7,851	1.1
			Edward M. Kennedy (Mass.)[1]	1,623	0.2
			Lloyd Bentsen (Texas)	364	—
			Others	4,905	0.7
March 2 Vermont					
Ford	27,014	84.0	Carter	16,335	42.2
Reagan[1]	4,892	15.2	Shriver	10,699	27.6
Others[1]	251	—	Harris	4,893	12.6
			McCormack	3,324	8.6
			Others	3,463	9.0
March 9 Florida					
Ford	321,982	52.8	Carter	448,844	34.5
Reagan	287,837	47.2	Wallace	396,820	30.5
			Jackson	310,944	23.9
			None of the names shown	37,626	2.9
			Shapp	32,198	2.5
			Udall	27,235	2.1
			Bayh	8,750	.7
			McCormack	7,595	.6
			Shriver	7,084	.5
			Harris	5,397	.4
			Robert C. Byrd (W.Va.)	5,042	.4
			Frank Church (Idaho)	4,906	.4
			Others	7,889	.6
March 16 Illinois					
Ford	456,750	58.9	Carter	630,915	48.1
Reagan	311,295	40.1	Wallace	361,798	27.6
Lar Daly (Ill.)	7,582	1.0	Shriver	214,024	16.3
Others[1]	266	—	Harris	98,862	7.5
			Others[1]	6,315	.5

Republican

Democratic

	Votes	%		Votes	%
March 23 North Carolina					
Reagan	101,468	52.4	Carter	324,437	53.6
Ford	88,897	45.9	Wallace	210,166	34.7
None of the names shown	3,362	1.7	Jackson	25,749	4.3
			None of the names shown	22,850	3.8
			Udall	14,032	2.3
			Harris	5,923	1.0
			Bentsen	1,675	.3
April 6 Wisconsin					
Ford	326,869	55.2	Carter	271,220	36.6
Reagan	262,126	44.3	Udall	263,771	35.6
None of the names shown	2,234	.3	Wallace	92,460	12.5
Others[1]	583	—	Jackson	47,605	6.4
			McCormack	26,982	3.6
			Harris	8,185	1.1
			None of the names shown	7,154	1.0
			Shriver	5,097	.7
			Bentsen	1,730	.2
			Bayh	1,255	.2
			Shapp	596	.1
			Others[1]	14,473	2.0
April 27 Pennsylvania					
Ford	733,472	92.1	Carter	511,905	37.0
Reagan[1]	40,510	5.1	Jackson	340,340	24.6
Others[1]	22,678	2.8	Udall	259,166	18.7
			Wallace	155,902	11.3
			McCormack	38,800	2.8
			Shapp	32,947	2.4
			Bayh	15,320	1.1
			Harris	13,067	.9
			Humphrey[1]	12,563	.9
			Others	5,032	.3
May 4 District of Columbia					
[2]			Carter	10,521	31.6
			Walter E. Fauntroy (unpledged delegates)	10,149	30.5
			Udall	6,999	21.0
			Walter E. Washington (unpledged delegates)	5,161	15.5
			Harris	461	1.4
May 4 Georgia					
Reagan	128,671	68.3	Carter	419,272	83.4
Ford	59,801	31.7	Wallace	57,594	11.5
			Udall	9,755	1.9
			Byrd	3,628	.7
			Jackson	3,358	.7
			Church	2,477	.5
			Shriver	1,378	.3
			Bayh	824	.2
			Harris	699	.1
			McCormack	635	.1
			Bentsen	277	.1
			Shapp	181	—
			Others	2,393	.5

Republican

Democratic

May 4 **Indiana**	Votes	%		Votes	%
Reagan	323,779	51.3	Carter	417,480	68.0
Ford	307,513	48.7	Wallace	93,121	15.2
			Jackson	72,080	11.7
			McCormack	31,708	5.2

May 11 **Nebraska**					
Reagan	113,493	54.5	Church	67,297	38.5
Ford	94,542	45.4	Carter	65,833	37.6
Others	379	.1	Humphrey	12,685	7.2
			Kennedy	7,199	4.1
			McCormack	6,033	3.4
			Wallace	5,567	3.2
			Udall	4,688	2.7
			Jackson	2,642	1.5
			Harris	811	.5
			Bayh	407	.2
			Shriver	384	.2
			Others[1]	1,467	.8

May 11 **West Virginia**					
Ford	88,386	56.8	Byrd	331,639	89.0
Reagan	67,306	43.2	Wallace	40,938	11.0

May 18 **Maryland**					
Ford	96,291	58.0	Edmund G. Brown Jr. (Calif.)	286,672	48.4
Reagan	69,680	42.0	Carter	219,404	37.1
			Udall	32,790	5.5
			Wallace	24,176	4.1
			Jackson	13,956	2.4
			McCormack	7,907	1.3
			Harris	6,841	1.2

May 18 **Michigan**					
Ford	690,180	64.9	Carter	307,559	43.4
Reagan	364,052	34.3	Udall	305,134	43.1
Unpledged delegates	8,473	.8	Wallace	49,204	6.9
Others[1]	109	—	Unpledged delegates	15,853	2.2
			Jackson	10,332	1.5
			McCormack	7,623	1.1
			Shriver	5,738	.8
			Harris	4,081	.6
			Others[1]	3,142	.4

May 25 **Arkansas**					
Reagan	20,628	63.4	Carter	314,306	62.6
Ford	11,430	35.1	Wallace	83,005	16.5
Unpledged delegates	483	1.5	Unpledged delegates	57,152	11.4
			Udall	37,783	7.5
			Jackson	9,554	1.9

May 25 **Idaho**					
Reagan	66,743	74.3	Church	58,570	78.7
Ford	22,323	24.9	Carter	8,818	11.9
Unpledged delegates	727	.8	Humphrey	1,700	2.3
			Brown[1]	1,453	2.0
			Wallace	1,115	1.5
			Udall	981	1.3
			Unpledged delegates	964	1.3
			Jackson	485	.7
			Harris	319	.4

	Republican				Democratic	
	Votes	%			Votes	%

May 25   Kentucky

	Votes	%			Votes	%
Ford	67,976	50.9	Carter		181,690	59.4
Reagan	62,683	46.9	Wallace		51,540	16.8
Unpledged delegates	1,781	1.3	Udall		33,262	10.9
Others	1,088	.8	McCormack		17,061	5.6
			Unpledged delegates		11,962	3.9
			Jackson		8,186	2.7
			Others		2,305	.8

May 25   Nevada

	Votes	%			Votes	%
Reagan	31,637	66.3	Brown		39,671	52.7
Ford	13,747	28.8	Carter		17,567	23.3
None of the names shown	2,365	5.0	Church		6,778	9.0
			None of the names shown		4,603	6.1
			Wallace		2,490	3.3
			Udall		2,237	3.0
			Jackson		1,896	2.5

May 25   Oregon

	Votes	%			Votes	%
Ford	150,181	50.3	Church		145,394	33.6
Reagan	136,691	45.8	Carter		115,310	26.7
Others[1]	11,663	3.9	Brown[1]		106,812	24.7
			Humphrey		22,488	5.2
			Udall		11,747	2.7
			Kennedy		10,983	2.5
			Wallace		5,797	1.3
			Jackson		5,298	1.2
			McCormack		3,753	.9
			Harris		1,344	.3
			Bayh		743	.2
			Others[1]		2,963	.7

May 25   Tennessee

	Votes	%			Votes	%
Ford	120,685	49.8	Carter		259,243	77.6
Reagan	118,997	49.1	Wallace		36,495	10.9
Unpledged delegates	2,756	1.1	Udall		12,420	3.7
Others[1]	97	—	Church		8,026	2.4
			Unpledged delegates		6,148	1.8
			Jackson		5,672	1.7
			McCormack		1,782	.5
			Harris		1,628	.5
			Brown[1]		1,556	.5
			Shapp		507	.2
			Humphrey[1]		109	—
			Others[1]		492	.1

June 1   Montana

	Votes	%			Votes	%
Reagan	56,683	63.1	Church		63,448	59.4
Ford	31,100	34.6	Carter		26,329	24.6
None of the names shown	1,996	2.2	Udall		6,708	6.3
			None of the names shown		3,820	3.6
			Wallace		3,680	3.4
			Jackson		2,856	2.7

June 1   Rhode Island

	Votes	%			Votes	%
Ford	9,365	65.3	Unpledged delegates		19,035	31.5
Reagan	4,480	31.2	Carter		18,237	30.2
Unpledged delegates	507	3.5	Church		16,423	27.2
			Udall		2,543	4.2
			McCormack		2,468	4.1
			Jackson		756	1.3
			Wallace		507	.8
			Bayh		247	.4
			Shapp		132	.2

Republican

Democratic

	Votes	%		Votes	%
June 1 South Dakota					
Reagan	43,068	51.2	Carter	24,186	41.2
Ford	36,976	44.0	Udall	19,510	33.3
None of the names shown	4,033	4.8	None of the names shown	7,871	13.4
			McCormack	4,561	7.8
			Wallace	1,412	2.4
			Harris	573	1.0
June 8 California			Jackson	558	1.0
Reagan	1,604,836	65.5	Brown	2,013,210	59.0
Ford	845,655	34.5	Carter	697,092	20.4
Others[1]	20	—	Church	250,581	7.3
			Udall	171,501	5.0
			Wallace	102,292	3.0
			Unpledged delegates	78,595	2.3
			Jackson	38,634	1.1
			McCormack	29,242	.9
			Harris	16,920	.5
			Bayh	11,419	.3
			Others[1]	215	—
June 8 New Jersey					
Ford	242,122	100.00	Carter	210,655	58.4
			Church	49,034	13.6
			Jackson	31,820	8.8
			Wallace	31,183	8.6
			McCormack	21,774	6.0
			Others	16,373	4.5
June 8 Ohio					
Ford	516,111	55.2	Carter	593,130	52.3
Reagan	419,646	44.8	Udall	240,342	21.2
			Church	157,884	13.9
			Wallace	63,953	5.6
			Gertrude W. Donahey (unpledged delegates)	43,661	3.9
			Jackson	35,404	3.1

TOTALS					
Ford	5,529,899	53.3	Carter	6,235,609	38.8
Reagan	4,758,325	45.9	Brown	2,449,374	15.3
None of the names shown	19,990	0.2	Wallace	1,995,388	12.4
Unpledged delegates	14,727	0.1	Udall	1,611,754	10.0
Daly	7,582	0.1	Jackson	1,134,375	7.1
Others[3]	43,602	0.4	Church	830,818	5.2
			Byrd	340,309	2.1
	10,374,125		Shriver	304,399	1.9
			Unpledged delegates	248,680	1.5
			McCormack	238,027	1.5
			Harris	234,568	1.5
			None of the names shown	93,728	0.6
			Shapp	88,254	0.5
			Bayh	86,438	0.5
			Humphrey	61,992	0.4
			Kennedy	19,805	0.1
			Bentsen	4,046	—
			Others[4]	75,088	0.5
				16,052,652	

Delegate selection primaries were held in Alabama, New York and Texas. In America Votes, Scammon did not record vote totals if the primary was strictly for delegate selection and there was no presidential preference voting.

1. Write-in.

2. Ford unopposed. No primary held.

3. In addition to scattered write-in votes, "others" include Tommy Klein, who received 1,088 votes in Kentucky.

4. In addition to scattered write-in votes, "others" include Frank Ahern who received 1,487 votes in Georgia; Stanley Arnold, 371 votes in New Hampshire; Arthur O. Blessitt, 828 votes in New Hampshire and 7,889 in Georgia; Frank Bona, 135 votes in New Hampshire and 263 in Georgia; Billy Joe Clegg, 174 votes in New Hampshire; Abram Eisenman, 351 votes in Georgia; John S. Gonas, 2,288 votes in New Jersey; Jesse Gray, 3,574 votes in New Jersey; Robert L. Kelleher, 87 votes in New Hampshire, 1,603 in Massachusetts and 139 in Georgia; Rick Loewenherz, 49 votes in New Hampshire; Frank Lomento, 3,555 votes in New Jersey, Floyd L. Lunger, 3,935 votes in New Jersey; H. R. H. "Fifi" Rockefeller, 2,305 votes in Kentucky; George Roden, 153 votes in Georgia; Ray Rollinson, 3,021 votes in New Jersey; Terry Sanford, 53 votes in New Hampshire and 351 votes in Massachusetts; Bernard B. Schechter, 173 votes in New Hampshire.

1980 Primaries[1]

Republican			Democratic		
	Votes	%		Votes	%

February 17 Puerto Rico — — — March 16

Republican	Votes	%	Democratic	Votes	%
George Bush (Texas)[2]	111,940	*60.1*	Jimmy Carter (Ga.)	449,681	*51.7*
Howard H. Baker Jr. (Tenn.)[3]	68,934	*37.0*	Edward M. Kennedy (Mass.)	418,068	*48.0*
Benjamin Fernandez (Calif.)	2,097	*1.1*	Edmund G. Brown Jr. (Calif.)[5]	1,660	*0.2*
John B. Connally (Texas)[4]	1,964	*1.1*	Others	826	*0.1*
Harold Stassen (N.Y.)	672	*0.4*			
Robert Dole (Kan.)	483	*0.3*			
Others	281	*0.1*			

February 26 New Hampshire

Republican	Votes	%	Democratic	Votes	%
Ronald Reagan (Calif.)	72,983	*49.6*	Carter	52,692	*47.1*
Bush	33,443	*22.7*	Kennedy	41,745	*37.3*
Baker	18,943	*12.1*	Brown	10,743	*9.6*
John B. Anderson (Ill.)[6]	14,458	*9.8*	Lyndon LaRouche (N.Y.)	2,326	*2.1*
Philip M. Crane (Ill.)	2,618	*1.8*	Richard Kay (Ohio)	566	*0.5*
Connally	2,239	*1.5*	Others[7]	3,858	*3.4*
Dole	597	*—*			
Others[7]	1,876	*1.3*			

March 4 Massachusetts

Republican	Votes	%	Democratic	Votes	%
Bush	124,365	*31.0*	Kennedy	590,393	*65.1*
Anderson	122,987	*30.7*	Carter	260,401	*28.7*
Reagan	115,334	*28.8*	Brown	31,498	*3.5*
Baker	19,366	*4.8*	Others[7]	5,368	*0.6*
Connally	4,714	*1.2*	No preference	19,663	*2.2*
Crane	4,669	*1.2*			
Gerald R. Ford (Mich.)[7]	3,398	*0.8*			
Dole	577	*—*			
Fernandez	374	*0.1*			
Stassen	218	*0.1*			
Others[7]	2,581	*0.6*			
No preference	2,243	*0.6*			

March 4 Vermont

Republican	Votes	%	Democratic	Votes	%
Reagan	19,720	*30.1*	Carter	29,015	*73.1*
Anderson	19,030	*29.0*	Kennedy	10,135	*25.5*
Bush	14,226	*21.7*	Brown[7]	358	*0.9*
Baker	8,055	*12.3*	LaRouche[7]	6	*—*
Ford[7]	2,300	*3.5*	Others	189	*0.5*
Crane	1,238	*1.9*			
Connally	884	*1.3*			
Stassen	105	*0.2*			
Others[7]	53	*—*			

March 8 South Carolina

Republican	Votes	%
Reagan	79,549	*54.7*
Connally	43,113	*29.6*
Bush	21,569	*14.8*
Baker	773	*0.5*
Fernandez	171	*0.1*
Stassen	150	*0.1*
Dole	117	*0.1*
Nick Belluso	59	*—*

Republican

	Votes	%

Democratic

	Votes	%

March 11 **Alabama**

Republican	Votes	%	Democratic	Votes	%
Reagan	147,352	69.7	Carter	193,734	81.6
Bush	54,730	25.9	Kennedy	31,382	13.2
Crane	5,099	2.4	Brown	9,529	4.0
Baker	1,963	0.9	William L. Nuckols	609	—
Connally	1,077	0.5	Bob Maddox	540	—
Stassen	544	0.3	Unpledged delegates	1,670	0.7
Dole	447	0.2			
Belluso	141	—			

March 11 **Florida**

Republican	Votes	%	Democratic	Votes	%
Reagan	345,699	56.2	Carter	666,321	60.7
Bush	185,996	30.2	Kennedy	254,727	23.2
Anderson	56,636	9.2	Brown	53,474	4.9
Crane	12,000	2.0	Kay	19,160	1.7
Baker	6,345	1.0	No preference	104,321	9.5
Connally	4,958	0.8			
Stassen	1,377	0.2			
Dole	1,086	0.2			
Fernandez	898	0.1			

March 11 **Georgia**

Republican	Votes	%	Democratic	Votes	%
Reagan	146,500	73.2	Carter	338,772	88.0
Bush	25,293	12.6	Kennedy	32,315	8.4
Anderson	16,853	8.4	Brown	7,255	1.9
Crane	6,308	3.2	Cliff Finch (Miss.)	1,378	0.4
Connally	2,388	1.2	Kay	840	0.2
Baker	1,571	0.8	LaRouche	513	0.1
Fernandez	809	0.4	Unpledged delegates	3,707	1.0
Dole	249	0.1			
Stassen	200	0.1			

March 18 **Illinois**

Republican	Votes	%	Democratic	Votes	%
Reagan	547,355	48.4	Carter	780,787	65.0
Anderson	415,193	36.7	Kennedy	359,875	30.0
Bush	124,057	11.0	Brown	39,168	3.3
Crane	24,865	2.2	LaRouche	19,192	1.6
Baker	7,051	0.6	Anderson [7]	1,643	0.1
Connally	4,548	0.4	Others [7]	402	—
V. A. Kelley	3,757	0.3			
Dole	1,843	0.2			
Ford [7]	1,106	0.1			
Others	306	—			

March 25 **Connecticut**

Republican	Votes	%	Democratic	Votes	%
Bush	70,367	38.6	Kennedy	98,662	46.9
Reagan	61,735	33.9	Carter	87,207	41.5
Anderson	40,354	22.1	LaRouche	5,617	2.7
Baker	2,446	1.3	Brown	5,386	2.6
Crane	1,887	1.0	Unpledged delegates	13,403	6.4
Connally	598	0.3			
Dole	333	0.2			
Fernandez	308	0.2			
Unpledged delegates	4,256	2.3			

Republican			Democratic		
	Votes	%		Votes	%

March 25 New York

			Kennedy	582,757	58.9
			Carter	406,305	41.1

April 1 Kansas

Reagan	179,739	63.0	Carter	109,807	56.6
Anderson	51,924	18.2	Kennedy	61,318	31.6
Bush	35,838	12.6	Brown	9,434	4.9
Baker	3,603	1.3	Finch	629	0.3
Connally	2,067	0.7	Maddox	632	0.3
Fernandez	1,650	0.6	Frank Ahern	571	0.2
Crane	1,367	0.5	Ray Rollinson	364	—
R. W. Yeager	1,063	0.4	None of the names shown	11,163	5.8
Alvin G. Carris	483	0.2			
Stassen	383	0.1			
William E. Carlson	311	—			
Donald Badgley	244	—			
None of the names shown	6,726	2.4			

April 1 Wisconsin

Reagan	364,898	40.2	Carter	353,662	56.2
Bush	276,164	30.4	Kennedy	189,520	30.1
Anderson	248,623	27.4	Brown	74,496	11.8
Baker	3,298	0.4	LaRouche	6,896	1.1
Crane	2,951	0.3	Finch	1,842	0.3
Connally	2,312	0.3	Others [7]	509	0.1
Fernandez	1,051	0.1	None of the names shown	2,694	0.4
Stassen	1,010	0.1			
Others [7]	4,951	0.5			
None of the names shown	2,595	0.3			

April 5 Louisiana

Reagan	31,212	74.9	Carter	199,956	55.7
Bush	7,818	18.8	Kennedy	80,797	22.5
Stassen	126	0.3	Brown	16,774	4.7
Belluso	155	0.3	Finch	11,153	3.1
Fernandez	84	0.2	Kay	3,362	0.9
C. Leon Pickett	67	—	Maddox	2,830	0.8
None of the names shown	2,221	5.3	Don Reaux	2,255	0.6
			Unpledged delegates	41,614	11.6

April 22 Pennsylvania

Bush	626,759	50.5	Kennedy	736,854	45.7
Reagan	527,916	42.5	Carter	732,332	45.4
Baker	30,846	2.5	Brown	37,669	2.3
Anderson	26,890	2.1	Anderson [7]	9,182	0.6
Connally	10,656	0.9	Bush [7]	2,074	0.1
Stassen	6,767	0.5	Reagan [7]	1,097	0.1
Alvin J. Jacobson	4,357	0.4	Ford [7]	150	—
Fernandez	2,521	0.2	No preference	93,865	5.8
Others	4,699	0.4			

May 3 Texas

Reagan	268,798	51.0	Carter	770,390	55.9
Bush	249,819	47.4	Kennedy	314,129	22.8
Unpledged delegates	8,152	1.5	Brown	35,585	2.6
			Unpledged delegates	257,250	18.7

Republican

Democratic

	Votes	%		Votes	%

May 6 District of Columbia

	Votes	%		Votes	%
Bush	4,973	66.1	Kennedy	39,561	61.7
Anderson	2,025	26.9	Carter	23,697	36.9
Crane	270	3.6	LaRouche	892	1.4
Stassen	201	2.7			
Fernandez	60	0.8			

May 6 Indiana

	Votes	%		Votes	%
Reagan	419,016	73.7	Carter	398,949	67.7
Bush	92,955	16.4	Kennedy	190,492	32.3
Anderson	56,342	9.9			

May 6 North Carolina

	Votes	%		Votes	%
Reagan	113,854	67.6	Carter	516,778	70.1
Bush	36,631	21.8	Kennedy	130,684	17.7
Anderson	8,542	5.1	Brown	21,420	2.9
Baker	2,543	1.5	No preference	68,380	9.3
Connally	1,107	0.7			
Dole	629	0.4			
Crane	547	0.3			
No preference	4,538	2.7			

May 6 Tennessee

	Votes	%		Votes	%
Reagan	144,625	74.1	Carter	221,658	75.2
Bush	35,274	18.1	Kennedy	53,258	18.1
Anderson	8,722	4.5	Brown	5,612	1.9
Crane	1,574	0.8	Finch	1,663	0.6
Baker [7]	16	—	LaRouche	925	0.3
Ford [7]	14	—	Others [7]	49	—
Connally [7]	1	—	Unpledged delegates	11,515	3.9
Others [7]	8	—			
Unpledged delegates	4,976	2.5			

May 13 Maryland

	Votes	%		Votes	%
Reagan	80,557	48.2	Carter	226,528	47.5
Bush	68,389	40.9	Kennedy	181,091	38.0
Anderson	16,244	9.7	Brown	14,313	3.0
Crane	2,113	1.3	Finch	4,891	1.0
			LaRouche	4,388	0.9
			Unpledged delegates	45,879	9.6

May 13 Nebraska

	Votes	%		Votes	%
Reagan	155,995	76.0	Carter	72,120	46.9
Bush	31,380	15.3	Kennedy	57,826	37.6
Anderson	11,879	5.8	Brown	5,478	3.6
Dole	1,420	0.7	LaRouche	1,169	0.8
Crane	1,062	0.5	Others [7]	1,247	0.8
Stassen	799	0.4	Unpledged delegates	16,041	10.4
Fernandez	400	0.2			
Others [7]	2,268	1.1			

Republican			Democratic		
	Votes	%		Votes	%

May 20 Michigan

Republican			Democratic		
Bush	341,998	57.5	Brown	23,043	29.4
Reagan	189,184	31.8	LaRouche	8,948	11.4
Anderson	48,947	8.2	Others [7]	10,048	12.8
Fernandez	2,248	0.4	Unpledged delegates	36,385	46.4
Stassen	1,938	0.3			
Others [7]	596	0.1			
Unpledged delegates	10,265	1.7			

May 20 Oregon

Republican			Democratic		
Reagan	170,449	54.0	Carter	208,693	56.7
Bush	109,210	34.6	Kennedy	114,651	31.1
Anderson	32,118	10.2	Brown	34,409	9.3
Crane	2,324	0.7	Anderson [7]	5,407	1.5
Others [7]	1,265	0.4	Reagan [7]	2,206	0.6
			Bush [7]	1,838	0.5

May 27 Arkansas

Republican			Democratic		
			Carter	269,375	60.1
			Kennedy	78,542	17.5
			Finch	19,469	4.3
			Unpledged delegates	80,904	18.0

May 27 Idaho

Republican			Democratic		
Reagan	111,868	82.9	Carter	31,383	62.2
Anderson	13,130	9.7	Kennedy	11,087	22.0
Bush	5,416	4.0	Brown	2,078	4.1
Crane	1,024	0.8	Unpledged delegates	5,934	11.8
Unpledged delegates	3,441	2.6			

May 27 Kentucky

Republican			Democratic		
Reagan	78,072	82.4	Carter	160,819	66.9
Bush	6,861	7.2	Kennedy	55,167	23.0
Anderson	4,791	5.1	Kay	2,609	1.1
Stassen	1,223	1.3	Finch	2,517	1.0
Fernandez	764	0.8	Unpledged delegates	19,219	8.0
Unpledged delegates	3,084	3.3			

May 27 Nevada

Republican			Democratic		
Reagan	39,352	83.0	Carter	25,159	37.6
Bush	3,078	6.5	Kennedy	19,296	28.8
None of the names shown	4,965	10.5	None of the names shown	22,493	33.6

June 3 California

Republican			Democratic		
Reagan	2,057,923	80.3	Kennedy slate	1,507,142	44.8
Anderson	349,315	13.6	Carter slate	1,266,276	37.6
Bush	125,113	4.9	Brown slate	135,962	4.0
Crane	21,465	0.8	LaRouche slate	71,779	2.1
Fernandez	10,242	0.4	Others [7]	51	—
Others [7]	14	—	Unpledged slate	382,759	11.4

Republican

	Votes	%

June 3 New Mexico

Reagan	37,982	63.8
Anderson	7,171	12.0
Bush	5,892	9.9
Crane	4,412	7.4
Fernandez	1,795	3.0
Stassen	947	1.6
Unpledged delegates	1,347	2.3

June 3 New Jersey

Reagan	225,959	81.3
Bush	47,447	17.1
Stassen	4,571	1.6

June 3 Montana

Reagan	68,744	86.6
Bush	7,665	9.7
No preference	3,014	3.8

June 3 Ohio

| Reagan | 692,288 | 80.8 |
| Bush | 164,485 | 19.2 |

June 3 Rhode Island

Reagan	3,839	72.0
Bush	993	18.6
Stassen	107	2.0
Fernandez	48	0.9
Unpledged delegates	348	6.5

June 3 South Dakota

Reagan slate	72,861	82.2
Bush	3,691	4.2
Stassen	987	1.1
No preference	5,366	6.1

June 3 West Virginia

Reagan	115,407	83.6
Bush	19,509	14.1
Stassen	3,100	2.2

June 3 Mississippi

Reagan slate	23,028	89.4
Bush slate	2,105	8.2
Unslated	618	2.4

Democratic

	Votes	%

New Mexico

Kennedy	73,721	46.3
Carter	66,621	41.8
LaRouche	4,798	3.0
Finch	4,490	2.8
Unpledged delegates	9,734	6.1

New Jersey

Kennedy	315,109	56.2
Carter	212,387	37.9
LaRouche	13,913	2.5
Unpledged delegates	19,499	3.5

Montana

Carter	66,922	51.5
Kennedy	47,671	36.7
No preference	15,466	11.9

Ohio

Carter	605,744	51.1
Kennedy	523,874	44.4
LaRouche	35,268	3.0
Kay	21,524	1.8

Rhode Island

Kennedy	26,179	68.3
Carter	9,907	25.8
LaRouche	1,160	3.0
Brown	310	0.8
Unpledged delegates	771	2.0

South Dakota

Kennedy slate	33,418	48.6
Carter slate	31,251	45.4
Uncommitted slate	4,094	6.0

West Virginia

| Carter | 197,687 | 62.2 |
| Kennedy | 120,247 | 37.8 |

Republican

	Votes	%
TOTALS [8]		
Reagan	7,709,793	*60.8*
Bush	2,958,093	*23.3*
Anderson	1,572,174	*12.4*
Baker	112,219	*0.9*
Crane	97,793	*0.8*
Connally	80,661	*0.6*
Stassen	24,753	*0.2*
Fernandez	23,423	*0.2*
Dole	7,298	*0.1*
Jacobsen	4,357	—
Kelley	3,757	—
Yeager	1,063	—
Carris	483	—
Belluso	355	—
Carlson	311	—
Badgley	244	—
Pickett	67	—
Unpledged delegates	38,708	*0.3*
No preference	15,161	*0.1*
None of the names shown	14,286	*0.1*
Others	25,452	*0.2*
	12,690,451	

Democratic

	Votes	%
Carter	9,593,335	*51.2*
Kennedy	6,963,625	*37.1*
Brown	573,636	*3.1*
LaRouche	177,784	*1.0*
Kay	48,061	*0.3*
Finch	48,032	*0.3*
Maddox	4,002	—
Reaux	2,255	—
Nuckols	609	—
Ahern	571	—
Rollinson	364	—
Unpledged delegates	950,378	*5.1*
No preference	301,695	*1.6*
None of the names shown	36,350	*0.1*
Others	47,128	*0.2*
	18,747,825	

1. *In 1980, 35 states, the District of Columbia and Puerto Rico held presidential primaries. California Democrats and South Dakota Republicans and Democrats held state-type preference primaries. In New York, Democrats had a presidential preference, but Republicans held primaries for the selection of delegates only, without indication of presidential preference. In Mississippi, Republicans elected delegates by congressional districts pledged to candidates and the vote indicated is for the highest of each slate's candidates in each congressional district. In Arkansas, the Republicans did not hold a primary although Democrats did. In South Carolina, the Democrats did not hold a primary but Republicans did. The vote in Ohio is for at-large delegates pledged to specific candidates and elected as a group. The Republican and Democratic primaries in Puerto Rico were held on two different dates: February 17 and March 16, respectively.*

2. *Bush withdrew May 26.*

3. *Baker withdrew March 5.*

4. *Connally withdrew March 9.*

5. *Brown withdrew April 1.*

6. *Anderson withdrew April 24.*

7. *Write-in vote.*

8. *Totals exclude Puerto Rico, where citizens are unable to vote in the general election.*

1984 Primaries

Republican	Votes	%	Democratic	Votes	%
February 28 New Hampshire					
Ronald Reagan (Calif.)	65,033	86.1	Gary Hart (Colo.)	37,702	37.3
Gary Hart (Colo.)	3,968	5.3	Walter F. Mondale (Minn.)	28,173	27.9
Harold Stassen (Pa.)	1,543	2.0	John Glenn (Ohio)	12,088	12.0
Walter F. Mondale (Minn.) [1]	1,072	1.4	Jesse Jackson (Ill.)	5,311	5.3
John Glenn (Ohio) [1]	1,040	1.4	George McGovern (S.D.)	5,217	5.2
David Kelly (La.)	360	0.5	Ronald Reagan (Calif.) [1]	5,058	5.0
Gary Arnold (Minn.)	252	0.3	Ernest F. Hollings (S.C.)	3,583	3.5
Benjamin Fernandez (Calif.)	202	0.3	Alan Cranston (Calif.)	2,136	2.1
Others	2,100	2.8	Reubin Askew (Fla.)	1,025	1.0
			Gerald Willis (Ala.)	50	0.0
			Others	788	0.8
March 6 Vermont [2]					
Reagan	33,218	98.7	Hart	51,873	70.0
Others	425	1.3	Mondale	14,834	20.0
			Jackson	5,761	7.8
			Askew	444	0.6
			Others	1,147	1.5
13 Alabama					
[3]			Mondale	148,165	34.6
			Glenn	89,286	20.8
			Hart	88,465	20.7
			Jackson	83,787	19.6
			Willis	6,153	1.4
			Hollings	4,759	1.1
			Unpledged delegates	4,464	1.0
			Askew	1,827	0.4
			Cranston	1,377	0.3
March 13 Florida					
Reagan	344,150	100.0	Hart	463,799	39.2
			Mondale	394,350	33.4
			Jackson	144,263	12.2
			Glenn	128,209	10.8
			Askew	26,258	2.2
			McGovern	17,614	1.5
			Hollings	3,115	0.3
			Cranston	2,097	0.2
			Richard B. Kay (Fla.)	1,328	0.1
			Stephen A. Koczak (D.C.)	1,157	0.1
March 13 Georgia					
Reagan	50,793	100.0	Mondale	208,588	30.5
			Hart	186,903	27.3
			Jackson	143,730	21.0
			Glenn	122,744	17.9
			McGovern	11,321	1.7
			Hollings	3,800	0.6
			Unpledged delegates	3,068	0.4
			Willis	1,804	0.3
			Askew	1,660	0.2
			Cranston	923	0.1

Republican

	Votes	%

Democratic

	Votes	%

March 13 Massachusetts

Republican	Votes	%	Democratic	Votes	%
Reagan	58,996	89.5	Hart	245,943	39.0
Unpledged delegates	5,005	7.6	Mondale	160,893	25.5
Others	1,936	2.9	McGovern	134,341	21.3
			Glenn	45,456	7.2
			Jackson	31,824	5.0
			Unpledged delegates	5,080	0.8
			Reagan [1]	3,595	0.6
			Askew	1,394	0.2
			Hollings	1,203	0.2
			Cranston	853	0.1
			Others	380	0.1

March 13 Rhode Island

Republican	Votes	%	Democratic	Votes	%
Reagan	2,028	90.7	Hart	20,011	45.0
Unpledged delegates	207	9.3	Mondale	15,338	34.5
			Jackson	3,875	8.7
			Glenn	2,249	5.0
			McGovern	2,146	4.8
			Unpledged delegates	439	1.0
			Cranston	273	0.6
			Askew	96	0.2
			Hollings	84	0.2

March 18 Puerto Rico

[3]

Democratic	Votes	%
Mondale	141,698	99.1
Hart	874	0.6
Glenn	436	0.3
Sterling P. Davis (Miss.)	31	—

March 20 Illinois

Republican	Votes	%	Democratic	Votes	%
Reagan	594,742	99.9	Mondale	670,951	40.4
Others	336	0.1	Hart	584,579	35.2
			Jackson	348,843	21.0
			McGovern	25,336	1.5
			Glenn	19,800	1.2
			Betty Jean Williams (Ill.)	4,797	0.3
			Cranston	2,786	0.2
			Askew	2,182	0.1
			Others	151	—

March 27 Connecticut

[3]

Democratic	Votes	%
Hart	116,286	52.7
Mondale	64,230	29.1
Jackson	26,395	12.0
Askew	6,098	2.8
McGovern	2,426	1.1
Hollings	2,283	1.0
Unpledged delegates	1,973	0.9
Glenn	955	0.4
Cranston	196	0.1

April 3 New York

[3]

Democratic	Votes	%
Mondale	621,581	44.8
Hart	380,564	27.4
Jackson	355,541	25.6
Glenn	15,941	1.1
Cranston	6,815	0.5
McGovern	4,547	0.3
Askew	2,877	0.2
Others	84	—

Republican

	Votes	%

Democratic

	Votes	%

April 3 **Wisconsin**

Republican			Democratic		
Reagan [4]	280,608	95.2	Hart	282,435	44.4
Others [1]	14,205	4.8	Mondale	261,374	41.1
			Jackson	62,524	9.8
			McGovern	10,166	1.6
			Unpledged delegates	7,036	1.1
			Glenn	6,398	1.0
			Cranston	2,984	0.5
			Hollings	1,650	0.3
			Askew	683	0.1
			Others	518	0.1

April 10 **Pennsylvania**

Republican			Democratic		
Reagan	616,916	99.3	Mondale	747,267	45.1
Others	4,290	0.7	Hart	551,335	33.3
			Jackson	264,463	16.0
			Cranston	22,829	1.4
			Glenn	22,605	1.4
			Lyndon H. LaRouche Jr. (Va.)	19,180	1.2
			McGovern	13,139	0.8
			Robert K. Griser (Pa.)	6,090	0.4
			Askew	5,071	0.3
			Hollings	2,972	0.2
			Others	1,343	0.1

May 1 **District of Columbia**

Republican			Democratic		
Reagan	5,692	100.0	Jackson	69,106	67.3
			Mondale	26,320	25.6
			Hart	7,305	7.1

May 1 **Tennessee**

Republican			Democratic		
Reagan	75,367	90.9	Mondale	132,201	41.0
Unpledged delegates	7,546	9.1	Hart	93,710	29.1
Others	8	—	Jackson	81,418	25.3
			Unpledged delegates	6,682	2.1
			Glenn	4,198	1.3
			McGovern	3,824	1.2
			Others	30	—

May 5 **Louisiana**

Republican			Democratic		
Reagan	14,964	89.7	Jackson	136,707	42.9
Unpledged delegates	1,723	10.3	Hart	79,593	25.0
			Mondale	71,162	22.3
			Unpledged delegates	19,409	6.1
			McGovern	3,158	1.0
			LaRouche	4,970	1.6
			Griser	1,924	0.6
			Kay	1,344	0.4
			Koczak	543	0.2

May 5 **Texas**

Republican			Democratic
Reagan	308,713	96.5	[3]
Unpledged delegates	11,126	3.5	

Republican			**Democratic**		
	Votes	%		Votes	%

May 8 Indiana

Reagan	428,559	100.0	Hart	299,491	41.8
			Mondale	293,413	40.9
			Jackson	98,190	13.7
			Glenn	16,046	2.2
			Bob Brewster (Fla.)	9,815	1.4

May 8 Maryland

Reagan	73,663	100.0	Mondale	215,222	42.5
			Jackson	129,387	25.5
			Hart	123,365	24.3
			Unpledged delegates	15,807	3.1
			LaRouche	7,836	1.5
			Glenn	6,238	1.2
			McGovern	5,796	1.1
			Cranston	1,768	0.3
			Hollings	1,467	0.3

May 8 North Carolina

[3]

			Mondale	342,324	35.6
			Hart	289,877	30.2
			Jackson	243,945	25.4
			Unpledged delegates	44,232	4.6
			Glenn	17,659	1.8
			McGovern	10,149	1.1
			Hollings	8,318	0.9
			Askew	3,144	0.3
			Cranston	1,209	0.1

May 8 Ohio

Reagan	658,169	100.0	Hart	608,528	42.0
			Mondale	583,595	40.3
			Jackson	237,133	16.4
			McGovern	8,991	0.6
			Cranston	4,653	0.3
			LaRouche	4,336	0.3

May 15 Nebraska

Reagan	145,245	99.9	Hart	86,582	58.2
Others	1,403	1.0	Mondale	39,635	26.6
			Jackson	13,495	9.1
			Unpledged delegates	4,631	3.1
			McGovern	1,561	1.0
			LaRouche	1,227	0.8
			Cranston	538	0.4
			Hollings	450	0.3
			Others	736	0.5

May 15 Oregon

Reagan	238,594	98.0	Hart	233,638	58.5
Hart [1]	2,359	.9	Mondale	110,374	27.6
Mondale [1]	477	0.2	Jackson	37,106	9.3
Jackson [1]	412	0.2	Glenn	10,831	2.7
LaRouche [1]	53	—	LaRouche	5,943	1.5
Glenn [1]	52	—	Reagan [1]	1,443	0.4
Others [1]	1,399	.6	Others	344	0.1

<table>
<tr><th colspan="3">Republican</th><th colspan="3">Democratic</th></tr>
<tr><td></td><td>Votes</td><td>%</td><td></td><td>Votes</td><td>%</td></tr>
</table>

May 15 Idaho

Republican	Votes	%	Democratic	Votes	%
Reagan	97,450	92.2	Hart	31,737	58.0
Others	8,237	7.8	Mondale	16,460	30.1
			Jackson	3,104	5.7
			Unpledged delegates	2,225	4.1
			LaRouche	1,196	2.2

June 5 California

Republican	Votes	%	Democratic	Votes	%
Reagan	1,874,897	100.0	Hart	1,155,499	38.9
Others [1]	78		Mondale	1,049,342	35.3
			Jackson	546,693	18.4
			Glenn	96,770	3.3
			McGovern	69,926	2.4
			LaRouche	52,647	1.8

June 5 Montana

Republican	Votes	%	Democratic	Votes	%
Reagan	66,432	92.4	Unpledged delegates	28,385	83.0
Unpledged delegates	5,378	7.5	Hart	3,080	9.0
Others	77	0.1	Mondale	2,026	5.9
			Jackson	388	1.1
			Others	335	1.0

June 5 New Jersey

Republican	Votes	%	Democratic	Votes	%
Reagan	240,054	100.0	Mondale	305,516	45.2
			Hart	200,948	29.7
			Jackson	159,788	23.6
			LaRouche	10,309	1.5

June 5 New Mexico

Republican	Votes	%	Democratic	Votes	%
Reagan	40,805	94.9	Hart	87,610	46.7
Unpledged delegates	2,189	5.1	Mondale	67,675	36.1
			Jackson	22,168	11.8
			McGovern	5,143	2.7
			LaRouche	3,330	1.8
			Unpledged delegates	1,477	0.8

June 5 South Dakota

Republican	Votes	%	Democratic	Votes	%
[3]			Hart	26,641	50.7
			Mondale	20,495	39.0
			Jackson	2,738	5.2
			LaRouche	1,383	2.6
			Unpledged delegates	1,304	2.5

June 5 West Virginia

Republican	Votes	%	Democratic	Votes	%
Reagan	125,790	91.8	Mondale	198,776	53.8
Stassen	11,206	8.2	Hart	137,866	37.3
			Jackson	24,697	6.7
			LaRouche	7,274	2.0
			Alfred Timinski (N.J.)	632	0.2

Republican	Votes	%	**Democratic**	Votes	%

June 12   North Dakota

Republican	Votes	%	Democratic	Votes	%
Reagan	44,109	100.0	Hart	28,603	85.1
			LaRouche	4,018	12.0
			Mondale	934	2.8
			Jackson	51	0.2

TOTALS [5]

Republican	Votes	%	Democratic	Votes	%
Reagan	6,484,987	98.6	Mondale	6,811,214	37.8
Unpledged delegates	22,791	0.3	Hart	6,503,968	36.1
Stassen	12,749	0.2	Jackson	3,282,431	18.2
Hart	6,327	0.1	Glenn	617,473	3.4
Mondale	1,549	—	McGovern	334,801	1.9
Glenn	1,092	—	LaRouche	123,649	0.7
Jackson	412	—	Askew	52,759	0.3
Kelly	360	—	Cranston	51,437	0.3
Arnold	252	—	Hollings	33,684	0.2
Fernandez	202	—	Reagan	10,096	0.1
LaRouche	53	—	Brewster	9,815	0.1
Others	34,494	0.5	Griser	8,014	—
Unpledged delegates	33,174	0.5	Willis	8,007	—
			Williams	4,797	—
	6,575,651		Kay	2,672	—
			Koczak	1,700	—
			Timinski	632	—
			Others	5,856	—
			Unpledged delegates	146,212	0.8
				18,009,217	

1. Write-in vote.
2. In Vermont's Liberty Union presidential primary, Dennis L. Serrette received 276 of the 309 votes cast, or 89.3 percent of the vote.
3. No primary.

4. Delegates could vote for or against Reagan within the Republican ticket.
5. Totals exclude Puerto Rico, where citizens are unable to vote in the general election.

Biographical Directory of Presidential and Vice Presidential Candidates

The names in the directory include all persons who have received electoral votes for president or vice president since 1789. Also included are a number of prominent third-party candidates who received popular votes but no electoral votes. The material is organized as follows: Name, state of residence in the year or years when the individual received electoral votes, party or parties with which the individual was identified when he or she received electoral votes, dates of birth and death (where applicable), major offices held and the year or years when the person received electoral votes. For third-party candidates who received no electoral votes, the dates indicate the year or years in which they were candidates.

For the elections of 1789, 1792, 1796 and 1800, presidential electors did not vote separately for president or vice president. It was, therefore, difficult in many cases to determine whether an individual receiving electoral votes in these elections was a candidate for president or vice president. Where no determination could be made from the sources consulted by Congressional Quarterly, the year in which the individual received electoral votes is given with no specification as to whether the individual was a candidate for president or vice president.

The following sources were used: *Biographical Directory of the American Congress, 1774-1971*, Government Printing Office, Washington, D.C., 1971; *Dictionary of American Biography*, Charles Scribner's Sons, New York, 1928-36; *Encyclopedia of American Biography*, John A. Garraty, editor, Harper and Row, New York, 1974; *Who's Who in American Politics*, 6th edition, 1977-78, edited by Jaques Cattell Press, R. R. Bowker, New York, 1977; *Who Was Who in America, 1607-1968*, Marquis, Chicago, 1943-68; Petersen, Svend, *A Statistical History of the American Presidential Elections*, Greenwood Press, Westport, Conn., 1981; Scammon, Richard M., *America Votes 10* (1972), Governmental Affairs Institute, Congressional Quarterly, Washington, 1973; *America Votes 12* (1976), Governmental Affairs Institute, Congressional Quarterly, Washington, 1977; *America Votes 14* (1980), Elections Research Center, Washington, 1981.

ADAMS, Charles Francis - Mass. (Free Soil) Aug. 18, 1807 - Nov. 21, 1886; House, 1859-61; minister to Great Britain, 1861-68. Candidacy: VP - 1848.

ADAMS, John - Mass. (Federalist) Oct. 30, 1735 - July 4, 1826; Continental Congress, 1774; signer of Declaration of Independence, 1776; minister to Great Britain, 1785; U.S. vice president, 1789-97; U.S. president, 1797-1801. Candidacies: VP - 1789, 1792; P - 1796, 1800.

ADAMS, John Quincy - Mass. (Democratic-Republican, National Republican) July 11, 1767 - Feb. 23, 1848; Senate, 1803-08; minister to Russia, 1809-14; minister to Great Britain, 1815-17; secretary of state, 1817-25; U.S. president, 1825-29; House, 1831-48. Candidacies: P - 1820, 1824, 1828.

ADAMS, Samuel - Mass. (Federalist) Sept. 27, 1722 - Oct. 2, 1803; Continental Congress, 1774-82; signer of Declaration of Independence; governor, 1794-97. Candidacy: 1796.

AGNEW, Spiro Theodore - Md. (Republican) Nov. 9, 1918—; governor, 1967-69; U.S. vice president, 1969-73 (resigned Oct. 10, 1973). Candidacies: VP - 1968, 1972.

ANDERSON, John B. - Ill. (Republican, Independent) Feb. 15, 1922—; state's attorney, 1956-60; House, 1961-80. Candidacy: P - 1980.

ARMSTRONG, James - Pa. (Federalist) Aug. 29, 1748 - May 6, 1828; House, 1793-95. Candidacy: 1789.

ARTHUR, Chester Alan - N.Y. (Republican) Oct. 5, 1830 - Nov. 18, 1886; collector, Port of N.Y., 1871-78; U.S. vice president, 1881; U.S. president, 1881-85 (succeeded James A. Garfield, who was assassinated). Candidacy: VP - 1880.

BANKS, Nathaniel Prentice - Mass. (Liberal Republican) Jan. 30, 1816 - Sept. 1, 1894; House, 1853-57, 1865-73, 1875-79, 1889-91; governor, 1858-61. Candidacy: VP - 1872.

BARKLEY, Alben William - Ky. (Democratic) Nov. 24, 1877 - April 30, 1956; House, 1913-27; Senate, 1927-49, 1955-56; Senate majority leader, 1937-47; Senate minority leader, 1947-49; U.S. vice president, 1949-53. Candidacy: VP - 1948.

BELL, John - Tenn. (Constitutional Union) Feb. 15, 1797 - Sept. 10, 1869; House, 1827-41; Speaker of the House, 1834-35; secretary of war, 1841; Senate, 1847-59. Candidacy: P - 1860.

BENSON, Allan Louis - N.Y. (Socialist) Nov. 6, 1871 - Aug. 19, 1940; writer, editor; founder of *Reconstruction Magazine*, 1918. Candidacy: P - 1916.

BIDWELL, John - Calif. (Prohibition) Aug. 5, 1819 - April 4, 1900; California pioneer; major in Mexican War; House, 1865-67. Candidacy: P - 1892.

BIRNEY, James Gillespie - N.Y. (Liberty) Feb. 4, 1792 - Nov. 25, 1857; Kentucky Legislature, 1816-17; Alabama Legislature, 1819-20. Candidacies: P - 1840, 1844.

BLAINE, James Gillespie - Maine (Republican) Jan. 31, 1830 - Jan. 27, 1893; House, 1863-76; Speaker of the House, 1869-75; Senate, 1876-81; secretary of state, 1881, 1889-92; president, first Pan American Congress, 1889. Candidacy: P - 1884.

BLAIR, Francis Preston Jr. - Mo. (Democratic) Feb. 19, 1821 - July 8, 1875; House, 1857-59, 1860, 1861-62, 1863-64; Senate, 1871-73. Candidacy: VP - 1868.

BRAMLETTE, Thomas E. - Ky. (Democratic) Jan. 3, 1817 - Jan. 12, 1875; governor, 1863-67. Candidacy: VP - 1872.

BRECKINRIDGE, John Cabell - Ky. (Democratic, Southern Democratic) Jan. 21, 1821 - May 17, 1875; House, 1851-55; U.S. vice president, 1857-61; Senate, 1861; major general, Confederacy, 1861-65; secretary of war, Confederacy, 1865. Candidacies: VP - 1856; P - 1860.

BRICKER, John William - Ohio (Republican) Sept. 6, 1893—; attorney general of Ohio, 1933-37; governor, 1939-45; Senate, 1947-59. Candidacy: VP - 1944.

BROWN, Benjamin Gratz - Mo. (Democratic) May 28, 1826 - Dec. 13, 1885; Senate, 1863-67; governor, 1871-73. Candidacy: VP - 1872.

BRYAN, Charles Wayland - Neb. (Democratic) Feb. 10, 1867 - March 4, 1945; governor, 1923-25, 1931-35; Candidacy: VP - 1924.

BRYAN, William Jennings - Neb. (Democratic, Populist) March 19, 1860 - July 26, 1925; House, 1891-95; secretary of state, 1913-15. Candidacies: P - 1896, 1900, 1908.

BUCHANAN, James - Pa. (Democratic) April 23, 1791 - June 1, 1868; House, 1821-31; minister to Russia, 1832-34; Senate, 1834-45; secretary of state, 1845-49; minister to Great Britain, 1853-56; U.S. president, 1857-61. Candidacy: P - 1856.

BURR, Aaron - N.Y. (Democratic-Republican) Feb. 6, 1756 - Sept. 14, 1836; attorney general of N.Y., 1789-90; Senate, 1791-97; U.S. vice president, 1801-05. Candidacies: 1792, 1796, 1800.

BUSH, George - Texas (Republican) June 12, 1924—; House, 1967-70; ambassador to the United Nations, 1971-73; chairman of the Republican National Committee, 1973-74; head of the U.S. liaison office in Peking, 1974-75; director of the Central Intelligence Agency, 1976-77; U.S. vice president, 1981—. Candidacies: VP - 1980, 1984.

BUTLER, Benjamin Franklin - Mass. (Greenback, Anti-Monopoly) Nov. 5, 1818 - Jan. 11, 1893; House, 1867-75, 1877-79; governor, 1883-84. Candidacy: P - 1884.

BUTLER, Nicholas Murray - N.Y. (Republican) April 2, 1862 - Dec. 7, 1947; president, Columbia University, 1901-45; president, Carnegie Endowment for International Peace, 1925-45. Candidacy: VP - 1912. (Substituted as candidate after Oct. 30 death of nominee James S. Sherman.)

BUTLER, William Orlando - Ky. (Democratic) April 19, 1791 - Aug. 6, 1880; House, 1839-43. Candidacy: VP - 1848.

BYRD, Harry Flood - Va. (States' Rights Democratic, Independent Democratic) June 10, 1887 - Oct. 20, 1966; governor, 1926-30; Senate, 1933-65. Candidacies: P - 1956, 1960.

CALHOUN, John Caldwell - S.C. (Democratic-Republican, Democratic) March 18, 1782 - March 31, 1850; House, 1811-17; secretary of war, 1817-25; U.S. vice president, 1825-32; Senate, 1832-43, 1845-50; secretary of state, 1844-45. Candidacies: VP - 1824, 1828.

CARTER, James Earl Jr. - Ga. (Democratic) Oct. 1, 1924—; Georgia Legislature, 1963-67; governor, 1971-75; U.S. president, 1977-81. Candidacies: P - 1976, 1980.

CASS, Lewis - Mich. (Democratic) Oct. 9, 1782 - June 17, 1866; military and civil governor of Michigan Territory, 1813-31; secretary of war, 1831-36; minister to France, 1836-42; Senate, 1845-48, 1849-57; secretary of state, 1857-60. Candidacy: P - 1848.

CLAY, Henry - Ky. (Democratic-Republican, National Republican, Whig) April 12, 1777 - June 29, 1852; Senate, 1806-07, 1810-11, 1831-42, 1849-52; House, 1811-14, 1815-21, 1823-25; Speaker of the House, 1811-14, 1815-20, 1823-25; secretary of state, 1825-29. Candidacies: P - 1824, 1832, 1844.

CLEVELAND, Stephen Grover - N.Y. (Democratic) March 18, 1837 - June 24, 1908; mayor of Buffalo, 1882; governor, 1883-85; U.S. president, 1885-89, 1893-97. Candidacies: P - 1884, 1888, 1892.

CLINTON, De Witt - N.Y. (Independent Democratic-Republican, Federalist) March 2, 1769 - Feb. 11, 1828; Senate, 1802-03; mayor of New York, 1803-07, 1810, 1811, 1813, 1814; governor, 1817-23, 1825-28. Candidacy: P - 1812.

CLINTON, George - N.Y. (Democratic-Republican) July 26, 1739 - April 20, 1812; Continental Congress, 1775-76; governor, 1777-95, 1801-04; U.S. vice president, 1805-12. Candidacies: VP - 1789, 1792, 1796, 1804, 1808.

COLFAX, Schuyler - Ind. (Republican) March 23, 1823 - Jan. 13, 1885; House, 1855-69; Speaker of the House, 1863-69; U.S. vice president, 1869-73. Candidacy: VP - 1868.

COLQUITT, Alfred Holt - Ga. (Democratic) April 20, 1824 - March 26, 1894; House, 1853-55; governor, 1877-82; Senate, 1883-94. Candidacy: VP - 1872.

COOLIDGE, Calvin - Mass. (Republican) July 4, 1872 - Jan. 5, 1933; governor, 1919-21; U.S. vice president, 1921-23; U.S. president, 1923-29. Candidacies: VP - 1920; P - 1924.

COX, James Middleton - Ohio (Democratic) March 31, 1870 - July 15, 1957; House, 1909-13; governor, 1913-15, 1917-21. Candidacy: P - 1920.

CRAWFORD, William Harris - Ga. (Democratic-Republican) Feb. 24, 1772 - Sept. 15, 1834; Senate, 1807-13; president pro tempore of the Senate, 1812-13; secretary of war, 1815-16; secretary of the treasury, 1816-25. Candidacy: P - 1824.

CURTIS, Charles - Kan. (Republican) Jan. 25, 1860 - Feb. 8, 1936; House, 1893-1907; Senate, 1907-13, 1915-29; president pro tempore of the Senate, 1911; U.S. vice president, 1929-33. Candidacies: VP - 1928, 1932.

DALLAS, George Mifflin - Pa. (Democratic) July 10, 1792 - Dec. 31, 1864; Senate, 1831-33; minister to Russia, 1837-39; U.S. vice president, 1845-49; minister to Great Britain, 1856-61. Candidacy: VP - 1844.

DAVIS, David - Ill. (Democratic) March 9, 1815 - June 26, 1886; associate justice of U.S. Supreme Court, 1862-77; Senate, 1877-83. Candidacy: P - 1872.

DAVIS, Henry Gassaway - W.Va. (Democratic) Nov. 16, 1823 - March 11, 1916; Senate, 1871-83; chairman of Pan American Railway Committee, 1901-16. Candidacy: VP - 1904.

DAVIS, John William - W.Va. (Democratic) April 13, 1873 - March 24, 1955; House, 1911-13; solicitor general, 1913-18; ambassador to Great Britain, 1918-21. Candidacy: P - 1924.

DAWES, Charles Gates - Ill. (Republican) Aug. 27, 1865 - April 3, 1951; U.S. comptroller of the currency, 1898-1901; first director of Bureau of the Budget, 1921-22; U.S. vice president, 1925-29; ambassador to Great Britain, 1929-32. Candidacy: VP - 1924.

DAYTON, William Lewis - N.J. (Republican) Feb. 17, 1807 - Dec. 1, 1864; Senate, 1842-51; minister to France, 1861-64. Candidacy: VP - 1856.

DEBS, Eugene Victor - Ind. (Socialist) Nov. 5, 1855 - Oct. 20, 1926; Indiana Legislature, 1885; president, American Railway Union, 1893-97. Candidacies: P - 1900, 1904, 1908, 1912, 1920.

DEWEY, Thomas Edmund - N.Y. (Republican) March 24, 1902 - March 16, 1971; district attorney, New York County, 1937-41; governor, 1943-55. Candidacies: P - 1944, 1948.

DOLE, Robert Joseph - Kan. (Republican) July 22, 1923—; House, 1961-69; Senate, 1969—. Candidacy: VP - 1976.

DONELSON, Andrew Jackson - Tenn. (American "Know-Nothing") Aug. 25, 1799 - June 26, 1871; minister to Prussia, 1846-48; minister to Germany, 1848-49. Candidacy: VP - 1856.

DOUGLAS, Stephen Arnold - Ill. (Democratic) April 23, 1813 - June 3, 1861; House, 1843-47; Senate, 1847-61. Candidacy: P - 1860.

EAGLETON, Thomas Francis - Mo. (Democratic) Sept. 4, 1929—; attorney general

of Missouri, 1961-65; lieutenant governor, 1965-68; Senate, 1968—. Candidacy: VP - 1972. (Resigned from Democratic ticket July 31; replaced by R. Sargent Shriver Jr.)

EISENHOWER, Dwight David - N.Y., Pa. (Republican) Oct. 14, 1890 - March 28, 1969; general of U.S. Army, 1943-48; Army chief of staff, 1945-48; president of Columbia University, 1948-51; commander of North Atlantic Treaty Organization, 1951-52; U.S. president, 1953-61. Candidacies: P - 1952, 1956.

ELLMAKER, Amos - Pa. (Anti-Masonic) Feb. 2, 1787 - Nov. 28, 1851; House, 1815; attorney general of Pennsylvania, 1816-19, 1828-29. Candidacy: VP - 1832.

ELLSWORTH, Oliver - Conn. (Federalist) April 29, 1745 - Nov. 26, 1807; Continental Congress, 1777-84; Senate, 1789-96; chief justice of United States, 1796-1800; minister to France, 1799. Candidacy: 1796.

ENGLISH, William Hayden - Ind. (Democratic) Aug. 27, 1822 - Feb. 7, 1896; House, 1853-61. Candidacy: VP - 1880.

EVERETT, Edward - Mass. (Constitutional Union) April 11, 1794 - Jan. 15, 1865; House, 1825-35; governor, 1836-40; minister to Great Britain, 1841-45; president of Harvard University, 1846-49; secretary of state, 1852-53; Senate, 1853-54. Candidacy: VP - 1860.

FAIRBANKS, Charles Warren - Ind. (Republican) May 11, 1852 - June 4, 1918; Senate, 1897-1905; U.S. vice president, 1905-09. Candidacies: VP - 1904, 1916.

FERRARO, Geraldine A. - N.Y. (Democratic) Aug. 26, 1935—; assistant district attorney, Queens County, 1974-78; House, 1979-85. Candidacy: VP - 1984.

FIELD, James Gaven - Va. (Populist) Feb. 24, 1826 - Oct. 12, 1901; major in the Confederate Army, 1861-65; attorney general of Virginia, 1877-82. Candidacy: VP - 1892.

FILLMORE, Millard - N.Y. (Whig, American "Know-Nothing") Jan. 7, 1800 - March 8, 1874; House, 1833-35, 1837-43; N.Y. comptroller, 1847-49; U.S. vice president, 1849-50; U.S. president, 1850-53. Candidacies: VP - 1848; P - 1856.

FISK, Clinton Bowen - N.J. (Prohibition) Dec. 8, 1828 - July 9, 1890; Civil War brevet major general; founder of Fisk University, 1866; member, Board of Indian Commissioners, 1874, president, 1881-90. Candidacy: P - 1888.

FLOYD, John - Va. (Independent Democratic) April 24, 1783 - Aug. 17, 1837; House, 1817-29; governor, 1830-34. Candidacy: P - 1832.

FORD, Gerald Rudolph Jr. - Mich. (Republican) July 14, 1913—; House, 1949-73; U.S. vice president, 1973-74; U.S. president, 1974-77. Candidacy: P - 1976.

FRELINGHUYSEN, Theodore - N.J. (Whig) March 28, 1787 - April 12, 1862; attorney general of New Jersey, 1817-29; Senate, 1829-35; president of Rutgers College, 1850-62. Candidacy: VP - 1844.

FREMONT, John Charles - Calif. (Republican) Jan. 21, 1813 - July 13, 1890; explorer and Army officer in West before 1847; Senate, 1850-51; governor of Arizona Territory, 1878-81. Candidacy: P - 1856.

GARFIELD, James Abram - Ohio (Republican) Nov. 19, 1831 - Sept. 19, 1881; major general in Union Army during Civil War; House, 1863-80; U.S. president, March 4 - Sept. 19, 1881. Candidacy: P - 1880.

GARNER, John Nance - Texas (Democratic) Nov. 22, 1868 - Nov. 7, 1967; House, 1903-33; Speaker of the House, 1931-33; U.S. vice president, 1933-41. Candidacies: VP - 1932, 1936.

GERRY, Elbridge - Mass. (Democratic-Republican) July 17, 1744 - Nov. 23, 1814; Continental Congress, 1776-81, 1782-85; signer of Declaration of Independence; Constitutional Convention, 1787; House, 1789-93; governor, 1810-12; U.S. vice president, 1813-14. Candidacy: VP - 1812.

GOLDWATER, Barry Morris - Ariz. (Republican) Jan. 1, 1909—; Senate, 1953-65, 1969—. Candidacies: VP - 1960; P - 1964.

GRAHAM, William Alexander - N.C. (Whig) Sept. 5, 1804 - Aug. 11, 1875; Senate, 1840-43; governor, 1845-49; secretary of the Navy, 1850-52; Confederate Senate, 1864. Candidacy: VP - 1852.

GRANGER, Francis - N.Y (Whig) Dec. 1, 1792 - Aug. 31, 1868; House, 1835-37, 1839-41, 1841-43; postmaster general, 1841. Candidacy: VP - 1836.

GRANT, Ulysses Simpson - Ill. (Republican) April 27, 1822 - July 23, 1885; commander-in-chief, Union Army during Civil War; secretary of war, 1867; U.S. president, 1869-77. Candidacies: P - 1868, 1872.

GREELEY, Horace - N.Y. (Liberal Republican, Democratic) Feb. 3, 1811 - Nov. 29, 1872; founder and editor, *New York Tribune*, 1841-72; House, 1848-49. Candidacy: P - 1872.

GRIFFIN, S. Marvin - Ga. (American Independent) Sept. 4, 1907 - June 13, 1982; governor, 1955-59. Candidacy: VP - 1968. (Substituted as candidate until

permanent candidate Curtis LeMay was chosen.)

GROESBECK, William Slocum - Ohio (Democratic) July 24, 1815 - July 7, 1897; House, 1857-59; delegate to International Monetary Conference in Paris, 1878. Candidacy: VP - 1872.

HALE, John Parker - N.H. (Free Soil) March 31, 1806 - Nov. 19, 1873; House, 1843-45; Senate, 1847-53, 1855-65; minister to Spain, 1865-69. Candidacy: P - 1852.

HAMLIN, Hannibal - Maine (Republican) Aug. 27, 1809 - July 4, 1891; House, 1843-47; Senate, 1848-57, 1857-61, 1869-81; governor, Jan. 8 - Feb. 20, 1857; U.S. vice president, 1861-65. Candidacy: VP - 1860.

HANCOCK, John - Mass. (Federalist) Jan. 12, 1737 - Oct. 8, 1793; Continental Congress, 1775-80, 1785-86; president of Continental Congress, 1775-77; governor, 1780-85, 1787-93. Candidacy: 1789.

HANCOCK, Winfield Scott - Pa. (Democratic) Feb. 14, 1824 - Feb. 9, 1886; brigadier general, commander of II Army Corps, Civil War. Candidacy: P - 1880.

HARDING, Warren Gamaliel - Ohio (Republican) Nov. 2, 1865 - Aug. 2, 1923; lieutenant governor, 1904-05; Senate, 1915-21; U.S. president, 1921-23. Candidacy: P - 1920.

HARPER, Robert Goodloe - Md. (Federalist) January 1765 - Jan. 14, 1825; House, 1795-1801; Senate, 1816. Candidacies: VP - 1816, 1820.

HARRISON, Benjamin - Ind. (Republican) Aug. 20, 1833 - March 13, 1901; Union officer in Civil War; Senate, 1881-87; U.S. president, 1889-93. Candidacies: P - 1888, 1892.

HARRISON, Robert H. - Md. 1745 - 1790; chief justice, General Court of Maryland, 1781. Candidacy: 1789.

HARRISON, William Henry - Ohio (Whig) Feb. 9, 1773 - April 4, 1841; delegate to Congress from the Northwest Territory, 1799-1800; territorial governor of Indiana, 1801-13; House, 1816-19; Senate, 1825-28; U.S. president, March 4 - April 4, 1841. Candidacies: P - 1836, 1840.

HAYES, Rutherford Birchard - Ohio (Republican) Oct. 4, 1822 - Jan. 17, 1893; major general in Union Army during Civil War; House, 1865-67; governor, 1868-72, 1876-77; U.S. president, 1877-81. Candidacy: P - 1876.

HENDRICKS, Thomas Andrews - Ind. (Democratic) Sept. 7, 1819 - Nov. 25, 1885; House, 1851-55; Senate, 1863-69;

governor, 1873-77; U.S. vice president, 1885. Candidacies: P - 1872; VP - 1876, 1884.

HENRY, John - Md. (Democratic-Republican) Nov. 1750 - Dec. 16, 1798; Continental Congress, 1778-81, 1784-87; Senate, 1789-97; governor, 1797-98. Candidacy - 1796.

HOBART, Garret Augustus - N.J. (Republican) June 3, 1844 - Nov. 21, 1899; New Jersey Senate, 1876-82; president of New Jersey Senate, 1881-82; Republican National Committee, 1884-96; U.S. vice president, 1897-99. Candidacy: VP - 1896.

HOOVER, Herbert Clark - Calif. (Republican) Aug. 10, 1874 - Oct. 20, 1964; U.S. food administrator, 1917-19; secretary of commerce, 1921-28; U.S. president, 1929-33; chairman, Commission on Organization of the Executive Branch of Government, 1947-49, 1953-55. Candidacies: P - 1928, 1932.

HOSPERS, John - Calif. (Libertarian) June 9, 1918—; director of school of philosophy at University of Southern California. Candidacy: P - 1972.

HOWARD, John Eager - Md. (Federalist) June 4, 1752 - Oct. 12, 1827; Continental Congress, 1784-88; governor, 1788-91; Senate, 1796-1803. Candidacy: VP - 1816.

HUGHES, Charles Evans - N.Y. (Republican) April 11, 1862 - Aug. 27, 1948; governor, 1907-10; associate justice of U.S. Supreme Court, 1910-16; secretary of state, 1921-25; chief justice of United States, 1930-41. Candidacy: P - 1916.

HUMPHREY, Hubert Horatio Jr. - Minn. (Democratic) May 27, 1911 - Jan. 13, 1978; mayor of Minneapolis, 1945-48; Senate, 1949-64, 1971-78; U.S. vice president, 1965-69. Candidacies: VP - 1964; P - 1968.

HUNTINGTON, Samuel - Conn., July 3, 1731 - Jan. 5, 1796; Continental Congress, 1776-84; president of Continental Congress, 1779-81, 1783; governor, 1786-96. Candidacy: 1789.

INGERSOLL, Jared - Pa. (Federalist) Oct. 24, 1749 - Oct. 31, 1822; Continental Congress, 1780-81; Constitutional Convention, 1787. Candidacy: VP - 1812.

IREDELL, James - N.C. (Federalist) Oct. 5, 1751 - Oct. 20, 1799; associate justice of U.S. Supreme Court, 1790-99. Candidacy: 1796.

JACKSON, Andrew - Tenn. (Democratic-Republican, Democratic) March 15, 1767 - June 8, 1845; House, 1796-97; Senate, 1797-98; 1823-25; territorial governor of Florida, 1821; U.S. president, 1829-37. Candidacies: P - 1824, 1828, 1832.

JAY, John - N.Y. (Federalist) Dec. 12, 1745 - May 17, 1829; Continental Congress, 1774-77, 1778-79; president of Continental Congress, 1778-79; minister to Spain, 1779; chief justice of United States, 1789-95; governor, 1795-1801. Candidacies: 1789, 1796, 1800.

JEFFERSON, Thomas - Va. (Democratic-Republican) April 13, 1743 - July 4, 1826; Continental Congress, 1775-76, 1783-85; author and signer of Declaration of Independence, 1776; governor, 1779-81; minister to France, 1784-89; secretary of state, 1789-93; U.S. vice president, 1797-1801; U.S. president, 1801-09. Candidacies: VP - 1792; P - 1796, 1800, 1804.

JENKINS, Charles Jones - Ga. (Democratic) Jan. 6, 1805 - June 14, 1883; governor, 1865-68. Candidacy: P - 1872.

JOHNSON, Andrew - Tenn. (Republican) Dec. 29, 1808 - July 31, 1875; House, 1843-53; governor, 1853-57; Senate, 1857-62, 1875; U.S. vice president, 1865; U.S. president, 1865-69. Candidacy: VP - 1864.

JOHNSON, Herschel Vespasian - Ga. (Democratic) Sept. 18, 1812 - Aug. 16, 1880; Senate, 1848-49; governor, 1853-57; senator, Confederate Congress, 1862-65. Candidacy: VP - 1860.

JOHNSON, Hiram Warren - Calif. (Progressive) Sept. 2, 1866 - Aug. 6, 1945; governor, 1911-17; Senate, 1917-45. Candidacy: VP - 1912.

JOHNSON, Lyndon Baines - Texas (Democratic) Aug. 27, 1908 - Jan. 22, 1973; House, 1937-49; Senate, 1949-61; U.S. vice president, 1961-63; U.S. president, 1963-69. Candidacies: VP - 1960; P - 1964.

JOHNSON, Richard Mentor - Ky. (Democratic) Oct. 17, 1781 - Nov. 19, 1850; House, 1807-19, 1829-37; Senate, 1819-29; U.S. vice president, 1837-41. Candidacies: VP - 1836, 1840.

JOHNSTON, Samuel - N.C. (Federalist) Dec. 15, 1733 - Aug. 18, 1816; Continental Congress, 1780-82; Senate, 1789-93. Candidacy: 1796.

JONES, Walter Burgwyn - Ala. (Independent Democratic) Oct. 16, 1888 - Aug. 1, 1963; Alabama Legislature, 1919-20; Alabama circuit court judge, 1920-35; presiding judge, 1935-63. Candidacy: P - 1956.

JULIAN, George Washington - Ind. (Free Soil, Liberal Republican) May 5, 1817 - July 7, 1899; House, 1849-51, 1861-71. Candidacies: VP - 1852, 1872.

KEFAUVER, Estes - Tenn. (Democratic) July 26, 1903 - Aug. 10, 1963; House, 1939-49; Senate, 1949-63. Candidacy: VP - 1956.

KENNEDY, John Fitzgerald - Mass. (Democratic) May 29, 1917 - Nov. 22, 1963; House, 1947-53; Senate, 1953-60; U.S. president, 1961-63. Candidacy: P - 1960.

KERN, John Worth - Ind. (Democratic) Dec. 20, 1849 - Aug. 17, 1917; Senate, 1911-17. Candidacy: VP - 1908.

KING, Rufus - N.Y. (Federalist) March 24, 1755 - April 29, 1827; Continental Congress, 1784-87; Constitutional Convention, 1787; Senate, 1789-96, 1813-25; minister to Great Britain, 1796-1803, 1825-26. Candidacies: VP - 1804, 1808; P - 1816.

KING, William Rufus de Vane - Ala. (Democratic) April 7, 1786 - April 18, 1853; House, 1811-16; Senate, 1819-44, 1848-52; minister to France, 1844-46; U.S. vice president, March 4 - April 18, 1853. Candidacy: VP - 1852.

KNOX, Franklin - Ill. (Republican) Jan. 1, 1874 - April 28, 1944; secretary of the Navy, 1940-44. Candidacy: VP - 1936.

LA FOLLETTE, Robert Marion - Wis. (Progressive) June 14, 1855 - June 18, 1925; House, 1885-91; governor, 1901-06; Senate, 1906-25. Candidacy: P - 1924.

LANDON, Alfred Mossman - Kan. (Republican) Sept. 9, 1887—; governor, 1933-37. Candidacy: P - 1936.

LANE, Joseph - Ore. (Southern Democratic) Dec. 14, 1801 - April 19, 1881; governor of Oregon Territory, 1849-50, May 16-19, 1853; House (territorial delegate), 1851-59; Senate, 1859-61. Candidacy: VP - 1860.

LANGDON, John - N.H. (Democratic-Republican) June 25, 1741 - Sept. 18, 1819; Continental Congress, 1775-1776, 1783; governor, 1788-89; 1805-09, 1810-12; Senate, 1789-1801; first president pro tempore of the Senate, 1789. Candidacy: VP - 1808.

LEE, Henry - Mass. (Independent Democratic) Feb. 4, 1782 - Feb. 6, 1867; merchant and publicist. Candidacy: VP - 1832.

LeMAY, Curtis Emerson - Ohio (American Independent) Nov. 15, 1906—; Air Force chief of staff, 1961-65. Candidacy: VP - 1968.

LEMKE, William - N.D. (Union) Aug. 13, 1878 - May 30, 1950; House, 1933-41, 1943-50. Candidacy: P - 1936.

LINCOLN, Abraham - Ill. (Republican) Feb. 12, 1809 - April 15, 1865; House, 1847-

49; U.S. president, 1861-65. Candidacies: P - 1860, 1864.

LINCOLN, Benjamin - Mass. (Federalist) Jan. 24, 1733 - May 9, 1810; major general in Continental Army, 1777-81; secretary of war, 1781-83. Candidacy: 1789.

LODGE, Henry Cabot Jr. - Mass. (Republican) July 5, 1902—; Senate, 1937-44, 1947-53; ambassador to United Nations, 1953-60; ambassador to Republic of Vietnam, 1963-64, 1965-67. Candidacy: VP - 1960.

LOGAN, John Alexander - Ill. (Republican) Feb. 9, 1826 - Dec. 26, 1886; House, 1859-62, 1867-71; Senate, 1871-77, 1879-86. Candidacy: VP - 1884.

MACHEN, Willis Benson - Ky. (Democratic) April 10, 1810 - Sept. 29, 1893; Confederate Congress, 1861-65; Senate, 1872-73. Candidacy: VP - 1872.

MACON, Nathaniel - N.C. (Democratic-Republican) Dec. 17, 1757 - June 29, 1837; House, 1791-1815; Speaker of the House, 1801-07; Senate, 1815-28. Candidacy: VP - 1824.

MADISON, James - Va. (Democratic-Republican) March 16, 1751 - June 28, 1836; Continental Congress, 1780-83, 1786-88; Constitutional Convention, 1787; House, 1789-97; secretary of state, 1801-09; U.S. president, 1809-17. Candidacies: P - 1808, 1812.

MANGUM, Willie Person - N.C. (Independent Democrat) May 10, 1792 - Sept. 7, 1861; House, 1823-26; Senate, 1831-36, 1840-53. Candidacy: P - 1836.

MARSHALL, John - Va. (Federalist) Sept. 24, 1755 - July 6, 1835; House 1799-1800; secretary of state, 1800-01; chief justice of United States, 1801-35. Candidacy: VP - 1816.

MARSHALL, Thomas Riley - Ind. (Democratic) March 14, 1854 - June 1, 1925; governor, 1909-13; U.S. vice president, 1913-21. Candidacies: VP - 1912, 1916.

McCARTHY, Eugene Joseph - Minn. (Independent) March 29, 1916—; House, 1949-59; Senate, 1959-71. Candidacy: P - 1976.

McCLELLAN, George Brinton - N.J. (Democratic) Dec. 3, 1826 - Oct. 29, 1885; general-in-chief of Army of the Potomac, 1861; governor, 1878-81. Candidacy: P - 1864.

McGOVERN, George Stanley - S.D. (Democratic) July 19, 1922—; House, 1957-61; Senate, 1963-81. Candidacy: P - 1972.

McKINLEY, William Jr. - Ohio (Republican) Jan. 29, 1843 - Sept. 14, 1901; House, 1877 - May 27, 1884, 1885-91; governor, 1892-96; U.S. president, 1897 - Sept. 14, 1901. Candidacies: P - 1896, 1900.

McNARY, Charles Linza - Ore. (Republican) June 12, 1874 - Feb. 25, 1944; state Supreme Court judge, 1913-15; Senate, 1917 - Nov. 5, 1918, Dec. 18, 1918 - 1944. Candidacy: VP - 1940.

MILLER, William Edward - N.Y. (Republican) March 22, 1914 - June 24, 1983; House, 1951-65; chairman of Republican National Committee, 1961-64. Candidacy: VP - 1964.

MILTON, John - Ga. circa 1740 - circa 1804; secretary of state, Georgia, circa 1778, 1781, 1783. Candidacy: 1789.

MONDALE, Walter Frederick - Minn. (Democratic) Jan. 5, 1928—; Senate, 1964-76; U.S. vice president, 1977-81. Candidacies: VP - 1976, 1980; P - 1984.

MONROE, James - Va. (Democratic-Republican) April 28, 1758 - July 4, 1831; Senate, 1790-94; minister to France, 1794-96, 1803; minister to England, 1803-07; governor, 1799-1802, 1811; secretary of state, 1811-17; U.S. president, 1817-25. Candidacies: VP - 1808; P - 1816, 1820.

MORTON, Levi Parsons - N.Y. (Republican) May 16, 1824 - May 16, 1920; House, 1879-81; minister to France, 1881-85; U.S. vice president, 1889-93; governor, 1895-97. Candidacy: VP - 1888.

MUSKIE, Edmund Sixtus - Maine (Democratic) March 28, 1914—; governor, 1955-59; Senate, 1959-80; secretary of state, 1980-81. Candidacy: VP - 1968.

NATHAN, Theodora Nathalia - Ore. (Libertarian) Feb. 9, 1923—; broadcast journalist; National Judiciary Committee, Libertarian Party, 1972-75; vice chairperson, Oregon Libertarian Party, 1974-75. Candidacy: VP - 1972.

NIXON, Richard Milhous - Calif., N.Y. (Republican) Jan. 9, 1913—; House, 1947-50; Senate, 1950-53; U.S. vice president, 1953-61; U.S. president, 1969-74. Candidacies: VP - 1952, 1956; P - 1960, 1968, 1972.

PALMER, John McAuley - Ill. (Democratic, National Democratic) Sept. 13, 1817 - Sept. 25, 1900; governor, 1869-73; Senate, 1891-97. Candidacies: VP - 1872; P - 1896.

PARKER, Alton Brooks - N.Y. (Democratic) May 14, 1852 - May 10, 1926; chief justice of N.Y. Court of Appeals, 1898-1904. Candidacy: P - 1904.

PENDLETON, George Hunt - Ohio (Democratic) July 19, 1825 - Nov. 24, 1889; House, 1857-65; Senate, 1879-85; minister to Germany, 1885-89. Candidacy: VP - 1864.

PIERCE, Franklin - N.H. (Democratic) Nov. 23, 1804 - Oct. 8, 1869; House, 1833-37; Senate, 1837-42; U.S. president, 1853-57. Candidacy: P - 1852.

PINCKNEY, Charles Cotesworth - S.C. (Federalist) Feb. 25, 1746 - Aug. 16, 1825; president, state senate, 1779; minister to France, 1796. Candidacies: VP - 1800; P - 1804, 1808.

PINCKNEY, Thomas - S.C. (Federalist) Oct. 23, 1750 - Nov. 2, 1828; governor, 1787-89; minister to Great Britain, 1792-96; envoy to Spain, 1794-95; House, 1797-1801. Candidacy: 1796.

POLK, James Knox - Tenn. (Democratic) Nov. 2, 1795 - June 15, 1849; House, 1825-39; Speaker of the House, 1835-39; governor, 1839-41; U.S. president, 1845-49. Candidacies: VP - 1840; P - 1844.

REAGAN, Ronald Wilson - Calif. (Democratic, Republican) Feb. 6, 1911—; governor, 1967-75; U.S. president, 1981—. Candidacies: P - 1980, 1984.

REID, Whitelaw - N.Y. (Republican) Oct. 27, 1837 - Dec. 15, 1912; minister to France, 1889-92; editor-in-chief, *New York Tribune*, 1872-1905. Candidacy: VP - 1892.

ROBINSON, Joseph Taylor - Ark. (Democratic) Aug. 26, 1872 - July 14, 1937; House, 1903-13; governor, Jan. 16 - March 8, 1913; Senate, 1913-37; Senate minority leader, 1923-33; Senate majority leader, 1933-37. Candidacy: VP - 1928.

RODNEY, Daniel - Del. (Federalist) Sept. 10, 1764 - Sept. 2, 1846; governor, 1814-17; House, 1822-23; Senate, 1826-27. Candidacy: VP - 1820.

ROOSEVELT, Franklin Delano - N.Y. (Democratic) Jan. 30, 1882 - April 12, 1945; assistant secretary of the Navy, 1913-20; governor, 1929-33; U.S. president, 1933-45. Candidacies: VP - 1920; P - 1932, 1936, 1940, 1944.

ROOSEVELT, Theodore - N.Y. (Republican, Progressive) Oct. 27, 1858 - Jan. 6, 1919; assistant secretary of the Navy, 1897-98; governor, 1899-1901; U.S. vice president, March 4 - Sept. 14, 1901; U.S. president, 1901-09. Candidacies: VP - 1900; P - 1904, 1912.

ROSS, James - Pa. (Federalist) July 12, 1762 - Nov. 27, 1847; Senate, 1794-1803. Candidacy: VP - 1816.

RUSH, Richard - Pa. (Democratic-Republican, National-Republican) Aug. 29, 1780

- July 30, 1859; attorney general, 1814-17; minister to Great Britain, 1817-24; secretary of the treasury, 1825-28. Candidacies: VP - 1820, 1828.

RUTLEDGE, John - S.C. (Federalist) Sept. 1739 - July 23, 1800; Continental Congress, 1774-76, 1782-83; governor, 1779-82; Constitutional Convention, 1787; associate justice of U.S. Supreme Court, 1789-91. Candidacy: 1789.

SANFORD, Nathan - N.Y. (Democratic-Republican) Nov. 5, 1777 - Oct. 17, 1838; Senate, 1815-21, 1826-31. Candidacy: VP - 1824.

SCHMITZ, John George - Calif. (American Independent) Aug. 12, 1930—; House, 1970-73. Candidacy: P - 1972.

SCOTT, Winfield - N.J. (Whig) June 13, 1786 - May 29, 1866; general-in-chief of U.S. Army, 1841-61. Candidacy: P - 1852.

SERGEANT, John - Pa. (National-Republican) Dec. 5, 1779 - Nov. 23, 1852; House, 1815-23, 1827-29, 1837-41. Candidacy: VP - 1832.

SEWALL, Arthur - Maine (Democratic) Nov. 25, 1835 - Sept. 5, 1900; Democratic National Committee member, 1888-96. Candidacy: VP - 1896.

SEYMOUR, Horatio - N.Y. (Democratic) May 31, 1810 - Feb. 12, 1886; governor, 1853-55, 1863-65. Candidacy: P - 1868.

SHERMAN, James Schoolcraft - N.Y. (Republican) Oct. 24, 1855 - Oct. 30, 1912; House, 1887-91, 1893-1909; U.S. vice president, 1909-12. Candidacies: VP - 1908, 1912. (Died during 1912 campaign; Nicholas Murray Butler replaced Sherman on the Republican ticket.)

SHRIVER, Robert Sargent Jr. - Md. (Democratic) Nov. 9, 1915—; director, Peace Corps, 1961-66; director, Office of Economic Opportunity, 1964-68; ambassador to France, 1968-70. Candidacy: VP - 1972. (Replaced Thomas F. Eagleton on Democratic ticket Aug. 8.)

SMITH, Alfred Emanuel - N.Y. (Democratic) Dec. 30, 1873 - Oct. 4, 1944; governor, 1919-21, 1923-29. Candidacy: P - 1928.

SMITH, William - S.C., Ala. (Independent Democratic-Republican) Sept. 6, 1762 - June 26, 1840; Senate, 1816-23, 1826-31. Candidacies: VP - 1828, 1836.

SPARKMAN, John Jackson - Ala. (Democratic) Dec. 20, 1899—; House, 1937-46; Senate, 1946-79. Candidacy: VP - 1952.

STEVENSON, Adlai Ewing - Ill. (Democratic) Oct. 23, 1835 - June 14, 1914; House, 1875-77, 1879-81; assistant

postmaster general, 1885-89; U.S. vice president, 1893-97. Candidacies: VP - 1892, 1900.

STEVENSON, Adlai Ewing II - Ill. (Democratic) Feb. 5, 1900 - July 14, 1965; assistant to the secretary of Navy, 1941-44; assistant to the secretary of state, 1945; governor, 1949-53; ambassador to United Nations, 1961-65. Candidacies: P - 1952, 1956.

STOCKTON, Richard - N.J. (Federalist) April 17, 1764 - March 7, 1828; Senate, 1796-99; House, 1813-15. Candidacy: VP - 1820.

TAFT, William Howard - Ohio (Republican) Sept. 15, 1857 - March 8, 1930; secretary of war, 1904-08; U.S. president, 1909-13; chief justice of the United States, 1921-30. Candidacies: P - 1908, 1912.

TALMADGE, Herman Eugene - Ga. (Independent Democratic) Aug. 9, 1913—; governor, 1947, 1948-55; Senate, 1957-81. Candidacy: VP - 1956.

TAYLOR, Glen Hearst - Idaho (Progressive) April 12, 1904 - April 28, 1984; Senate, 1945-51. Candidacy: VP - 1948.

TAYLOR, Zachary - La. (Whig) Nov. 24, 1784 - July 9, 1850; major general, U.S. Army; U.S. president, 1849-50. Candidacy: P - 1848.

TAZEWELL, Littleton Waller - Va. (Democratic) Dec. 17, 1774 - May 6, 1860; House, 1800-01; Senate, 1824-32; governor, 1834-36. Candidacy: VP - 1840.

TELFAIR, Edward - Ga. (Democratic-Republican) 1735 - Sept. 17, 1807; Continental Congress, 1778-82, 1784-85, 1788-89; governor, 1786, 1790-93. Candidacy: 1789.

THOMAS, Norman Mattoon - N.Y. (Socialist) Nov. 20, 1884 - Dec. 19, 1968; Presbyterian minister, 1911-31; author and editor. Candidacies: P - 1928, 1932, 1936, 1940, 1944, 1948.

THURMAN, Allen Granberry - Ohio (Democratic) Nov. 13, 1813 - Dec. 12, 1895; House, 1845-47; Ohio Supreme Court, 1851-56; Senate, 1869-81. Candidacy: VP - 1888.

THURMOND, James Strom - S.C. (States' Rights Democrat, Democratic, Republican) Dec. 5, 1902—; governor, 1947-51; Senate, 1954-56, 1956—. Candidacies: P - 1948; VP - 1960.

TILDEN, Samuel Jones - N.Y. (Democratic) Feb. 9, 1814 - Aug. 4, 1886; governor, 1875-77. Candidacy: P - 1876.

TOMPKINS, Daniel D. - N.Y. (Democratic-Republican) June 21, 1774 - June 11,

1825; governor, 1807-17; U.S. vice president, 1817-25. Candidacies: VP - 1816, 1820.

TRUMAN, Harry S - Mo. (Democratic) May 8, 1884 - Dec. 26, 1972; Senate, 1935-45; U.S. vice president, Jan. 20 - April 12, 1945; U.S. president, 1945-53. Candidacies: VP - 1944; P - 1948.

TYLER, John - Va. (Whig) March 29, 1790 - Jan. 18, 1862; governor, 1825-27; Senate, 1827-36; U.S. vice president, March 4 - April 4, 1841; U.S. president, 1841-45. Candidacies: VP - 1836, 1840.

VAN BUREN, Martin - N.Y. (Democratic, Free Soil) Dec. 5, 1782 - July 24, 1862; Senate, 1821-28; governor, January - March 1829; secretary of state, 1829-31; U.S. vice president, 1833-37; U.S. president, 1837-41. Candidacies: VP - 1824, 1832; P - 1836, 1840, 1848.

WALLACE, George Corley - Ala. (American Independent) Aug. 25, 1919—; governor, 1963-67, 1971-79, 1983—. Candidacy: P - 1968.

WALLACE, Henry Agard - Iowa (Democratic, Progressive) Oct. 7, 1888 - Nov. 18, 1965; secretary of agriculture, 1933-40; U.S. vice president, 1941-45; secretary of commerce, 1945-46. Candidacies: VP - 1940; P - 1948.

WARREN, Earl - Calif. (Republican) March 19, 1891 - July 9, 1974; governor, 1943-53; chief justice of United States, 1953-69. Candidacy: VP - 1948.

WASHINGTON, George - Va. (Federalist) Feb. 22, 1732 - Dec. 14, 1799; First and Second Continental Congresses, 1774, 1775; commander-in-chief of armed forces, 1775-83; president of Constitutional Convention, 1787; U.S. president, 1789-97. Candidacies: P - 1789, 1792, 1796.

WATSON, Thomas Edward - Ga. (Populist) Sept. 5, 1856 - Sept. 26, 1922; House, 1891-93; Senate, 1921-22. Candidacies: VP - 1896; P - 1904, 1908.

WEAVER, James Baird - Iowa (Greenback, Populist) June 12, 1833 - Feb. 6, 1912; House, 1879-81, 1885-89; Candidacies: P - 1880, 1892.

WEBSTER, Daniel - Mass. (Whig) Jan. 18, 1782 - Oct. 24, 1852; House, 1813-17, 1823-27; Senate, 1827-41, 1845-50; secretary of state, 1841-43, 1850-52. Candidacy: P - 1836.

WHEELER, Burton Kendall - Mont. (Progressive) Feb. 27, 1882 - Jan. 6, 1975; Senate, 1923-47. Candidacy: VP - 1924.

WHEELER, William Almon - N.Y. (Republican) June 19, 1819 - June 4, 1887; House, 1861-63, 1869-77; U.S. vice

president, 1877-81. Candidacy: VP - 1876.

WHITE, Hugh Lawson - Tenn. (Whig) Oct. 30, 1773 - April 10, 1840; Senate, 1825 - March 3, 1835, Oct. 6, 1835 - 1840. Candidacy: P - 1836.

WILKINS, William - Pa. (Democratic) Dec. 20, 1779 - June 23, 1865; Senate, 1831-34; minister to Russia, 1834-35; House, 1843-44; secretary of war, 1844-45. Candidacy: VP - 1832.

WILLKIE, Wendell Lewis - N.Y. (Republican) Feb. 18, 1892 - Oct. 8, 1944; utility executive, 1933-40. Candidacy: P - 1940.

WILSON, Henry - Mass. (Republican) Feb. 16, 1812 - Nov. 22, 1875; Senate, 1855-73; U.S. vice president, 1873-75. Candidacy: VP - 1872.

WILSON, Woodrow - N.J. (Democratic) Dec. 28, 1856 - Feb. 3, 1924; governor, 1911-13; U.S. president, 1913-21. Candidacies: P - 1912, 1916.

WIRT, William - Md. (Anti-Masonic) Nov. 8, 1772 - Feb. 18, 1834; attorney general, 1817-29. Candidacy: P - 1832.

WRIGHT, Fielding Lewis - Miss. (States' Rights Democratic) May 16, 1895 - May 4, 1956; governor, 1946-52. Candidacy: VP - 1948.

Gubernatorial Elections

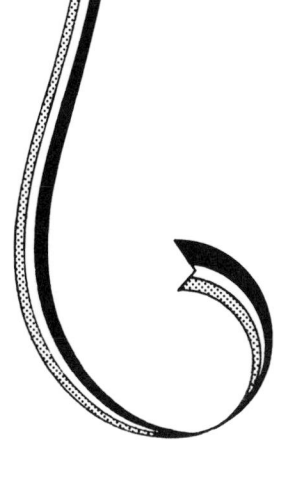

"Counting the Vote on November 7th at 'Elephant Johnnie's.'" From a sketch by S.W. Bennett.

Smithsonian Institution Photo No. 76599-C

Gubernatorial Elections

Governors were not popular during the period of the American Revolution. During the colonial era, the British-appointed governors were the symbols of the mother country's control and, the revolutionaries argued, of tyranny.

During the years before the Revolutionary War, colonial assemblies were able to assert their control over appropriations and thus became the champions of colonial rights against the governors. Thus, when forming their own state constitutions, the newly freed Americans tended to look with suspicion on the office of governor and gave most of the power to the legislative bodies.

For these reasons, early American governors found themselves hemmed in by restrictions. Among such restrictions were both the length of the term of office and the method of election.

Length of Terms

As of 1789 all four New England states — Connecticut, Massachusetts, New Hampshire and Rhode Island (Vermont was admitted in 1791 and Maine in 1820) — held gubernatorial elections every year. Some of the Middle Atlantic states favored somewhat longer terms; New York and Pennsylvania had three-year terms for their governors, although New Jersey instituted a one-year term. The Border and Southern states had a mix: Maryland and North Carolina governors served a one-year term, South Carolina had a two-year term, and Delaware, Virginia and Georgia had three-year terms. No state had a four-year term.

Over the years states have changed the length of gubernatorial terms. With some occasional back and forth movement, the general trend has been toward lengthening terms. New York, for example, has changed the term of office of its governor four times. Beginning in 1777 with a three-year term, the state switched to a two-year term in 1820, back to a three-year term in 1876, back to a two-year term in 1894, and to a four-year term beginning in 1938.

Maryland provides another example of a state that has changed its gubernatorial term several times. Beginning with one year in 1776, the state extended the term to three years in 1838, then to four years in 1851. Regular gubernatorial elections were held every second odd year from then through 1923, when the state had one three-year term so that future elections would be held in even-numbered years, beginning in 1926. Thus, the state held gubernatorial elections in 1919, 1923 and 1926 and then every four years after that.

The trend toward longer gubernatorial terms shows up clearly by comparing the length of terms in 1900 and 1985. Of the 45 states in the Union in 1900, 22, almost half, had two-year terms. One (New Jersey) had a three-year term, while Rhode Island and Massachusetts were the only states left with one-year terms. The remaining 20 states had four-year gubernatorial terms. *(Length of terms, box, p. 454)*

By October 1984, 41 of those same states had four-year terms, and the five states admitted to the Union after 1900 — Oklahoma (1907), Arizona and New Mexico (1912), Alaska and Hawaii (1959) — had four-year gubernatorial terms. This left only four states with two-year terms: Arkansas, New Hampshire, Rhode Island and Vermont.

The elections in November 1984 brought another convert. Voters in Arkansas and New Hampshire were asked to decide whether the governor should serve four years instead of two. In a fairly close ballot New Hampshire rejected the change, which would have required a two-thirds vote to pass, but Arkansas approved it. Rhode Islanders voted for calling a constitutional convention to amend the state constitution. If the legislature decided to call the convention, the delegates were expected to consider lengthening the state's gubernatorial term to four years. Only in Vermont did the two-year term remain firmly entrenched.

Isolation from Presidential Elections

Along with the change to longer terms for governors came another trend — away from holding gubernatorial elections in presidential election years. Except for North Dakota, every state in the 20th century that switched to four-year gubernatorial terms scheduled its elections in non-presidential years. Moreover, Florida, which held its

Sources

The Book of the States, 1984-1985, vol. 25. Lexington, Ky.: Council of State Governments, 1984.

Lipson, Leslie, *The American Governor from Figurehead to Leader.* 1939. Reprint. Westport, Conn.: Greenwood Press, 1969.

Offices of secretaries of state of Connecticut, Georgia, Hawaii, Maine, Massachusetts, New Hampshire, Rhode Island, Vermont, Washington and West Virginia.

Length of Governor Terms

State	1900	1985	Year of change to longer term
Alabama	2	4	—
Alaska*	—	4	—
Arizona*	—	4	1970
Arkansas	2	4	1984
California	4	4	—
Colorado	2	4	1958
Connecticut	2	4	1950
Delaware	4	4	—
Florida	4	4	—
Georgia	2	4	1942
Hawaii*	—	4	—
Idaho	2	4	1946
Illinois	4	4	—
Indiana	4	4	—
Iowa	2	4	1974
Kansas	2	4	1974
Kentucky	4	4	—
Louisiana	4	4	—
Maine	2	4	1958
Maryland	4	4	—
Massachusetts	1	4	1920,1966†
Michigan	2	4	1966
Minnesota	2	4	1962
Mississippi	4	4	—
Missouri	4	4	—
Montana	4	4	—
Nebraska	2	4	1966
Nevada	4	4	—
New Hampshire	2	2	—
New Jersey	3	4	1949
New Mexico*	—	4	1970
New York	2	4	1938
North Carolina	4	4	—
North Dakota	2	4	1964
Ohio	2	4	1958
Oklahoma*	—	4	—
Oregon	4	4	—
Pennsylvania	4	4	—
Rhode Island	1	2	1912
South Carolina	2	4	1926
South Dakota	2	4	1974
Tennessee	2	4	1954
Texas	2	4	1974
Utah	4	4	—
Vermont	2	2	—
Virginia	4	4	—
Washington	4	4	—
West Virginia	4	4	—
Wisconsin	2	4	1970
Wyoming	4	4	—

*Oklahoma was admitted to the Union in 1907, Arizona and New Mexico in 1912, and Alaska and Hawaii in 1959. Oklahoma, Alaska and Hawaii have always had four-year gubernatorial terms; Arizona began with a two-year term and switched to four years in 1970. New Mexico (1912) began with a four-year term, changed to two years in 1916, and back to four years in 1970.

† Massachusetts switched from a one- to a two-year term in 1920 and to a four-year term in 1966.

Source: State secretaries of state; *The Book of the States, 1984-1985*, vol. 25. Lexington, Ky.: The Council of State Governments, 1984.

quadrennial gubernatorial elections in presidential years, changed to non-presidential years in 1966. To make the switch, the state shortened to two years the term of the governor elected in 1964, then resumed the four-year term in 1966. Thus, Florida held gubernatorial elections in 1960, 1964, 1966, 1970 and 1974.

Illinois made a similar switch in 1976-78, leaving only nine states — Delaware, Indiana, Missouri, Montana, North Carolina, North Dakota, Utah, Washington and West Virginia — holding quadrennial gubernatorial elections at the same time as the presidential election. (Louisiana holds its gubernatorial election in presidential years but early in the year instead of November; New Hampshire, Rhode Island and Vermont still had two-year terms, so every other gubernatorial election in these three states occurred in a presidential year. Arkansas, which switched from a two-year to a four-year term in 1984, chose to select its governors in non-presidential election years beginning in 1986.)

Methods of Election

Yet another way in which Americans of the early federal period restricted their governors was by the method of election. In 1789, only in New York and the four New England states did the people directly choose their governors by popular vote. In the remaining eight states, governors were chosen by the state legislatures, thus enhancing the power of the legislatures in their dealing with the governors. But several factors — including the democratic trend to elect public officials directly, the increasing trust in the office of governor and the need for a stronger and more independent chief executive — led to the gradual introduction of popular votes in all the states.

By the 1860s the remaining eight original states all had switched to popular ballots. Pennsylvania was first, in 1790, and was followed by Delaware in 1792, Georgia in 1824, North Carolina in 1835, Maryland in 1838, New Jersey in 1844, Virginia in 1851 and South Carolina in 1865, after the Civil War.

All the states admitted to the Union after the original 13, with one exception, made provision from the very beginning for popular election of their governors. The exception was Louisiana, which from its admission in 1812 until a change in the state constitution in 1845 had a unique system of gubernatorial elections. The people participated by voting in a first-step popular election. In a second step, the Legislature was to select the governor from the two candidates receiving the highest popular vote.

Number of Terms

Another limitation placed on governors is a restriction on the number of terms they are allowed to serve. In the early years at least three states had such limitations: governors of Maryland were eligible to serve three consecutive one-year terms and then were required to retire for at least one year; Pennsylvania allowed its governors three consecutive three-year terms and then forced retirement for at least one term; and in New Jersey, according to the constitution of 1844, a governor could serve only one three-year term before retiring for at least one term.

In 1984 just over half the states — 28 — placed some sort of limitation on the number of consecutive terms their governors could serve. Of these 28, four prohibited their governors from serving more than one term in a row, permitting the governors to serve again after an interim of at least one term. The remaining 24 states allowed their gov-

ernors to seek re-election once but required that they step down after two terms for an interim of at least one term. Three exceptions to that general rule — Delaware, Missouri and North Carolina — imposed an absolute two-term limit. That is, a governor could serve only two terms, however spaced, in his lifetime. The remaining 22 states imposed no limits on the number of consecutive terms a governor could serve. *(Limits on terms, opposite)*

Majority Vote Requirement

A peculiarity of gubernatorial voting that has almost disappeared from the American political scene is the requirement that the winning gubernatorial candidate receive a majority of the popular vote. Otherwise, the choice devolves upon the state legislature or, in one case, a runoff between the two highest candidates is required. Centered in New England, this practice was used mainly in the 19th century. All six New England states (including Vermont and Maine), plus Georgia, had such a provision in their state constitutions at one time. New Hampshire, Vermont, Massachusetts and Connecticut already had the provision when they entered the Union between 1789 and 1791.

Rhode Island required a majority election but did not adopt a provision for legislative election until 1842; Maine adopted a majority provision when it split off from Massachusetts to form a separate state in 1820; and Georgia put the majority provision in its constitution when it switched from legislative to popular election of governors in 1825.

The purpose of the majority provision appears to have been to safeguard against a candidate's winning with a small fraction of the popular vote in a multiple field. In most of New England, the provision was part of the early state constitutions, formed largely in the 1780s, before the development of the two-party system.

The prospect of multiple-candidate fields diminished with the coming of the two-party system. Nevertheless, each of these states had occasion to use the provision at least once. Sometimes, in an extremely close election, minor party candidates received enough of a vote to keep the winner from getting a majority of the total vote. And at other times strong third-party movements or disintegration of the old party structure resulted in the election's being thrown into the state legislature.

Vermont retains the majority vote provision, although its Legislature has not elected a governor since 1912. Georgia maintains the requirement for a majority vote for governor but, instead of legislative election, provides for a runoff between the top two contenders three weeks after the general election. Mississippi has a majority vote provision under the 1890 state constitution, but the provision has not been used because the Democratic Party nominee always has received a majority.

Following are the states that had the majority vote provision for governor (except Mississippi), the years in which the choice devolved on the legislature because of it, and the year, if any, in which the requirement was repealed or changed:

Connecticut. No gubernatorial candidate received a majority of the popular vote, thus throwing the election into the Legislature, in the following years subsequent to 1824: 1833, 1834, 1842, 1844, 1846, 1849, 1850, 1851, 1854, 1855, 1856, 1878, 1884, 1886, 1888 and 1890. Following the election of 1890, the Legislature was unable to choose a new governor, so the outgoing governor, Morgan G. Bulkeley, R, continued to serve through the entire new term (1891-93). The provision was repealed in 1901. The years prior to 1824

Limitations on Governor Terms
(As of 1984)

State	Maximum number of consecutive terms
Alabama	2
Alaska	2
Arizona	No limit
Arkansas	No limit
California	No limit
Colorado	No limit
Connecticut	No limit
Delaware	2*
Florida	2
Georgia	2
Hawaii	2
Idaho	No limit
Illinois	No limit
Indiana	2
Iowa	No limit
Kansas	2
Kentucky	0
Louisiana	2
Maine	2
Maryland	2
Massachusetts	No limit
Michigan	No limit
Minnesota	No limit
Mississippi	0
Missouri	2*
Montana	No limit
Nebraska	2
Nevada	2
New Hampshire	No limit
New Jersey	2
New Mexico	0
New York	No limit
North Carolina	2*
North Dakota	No limit
Ohio	2
Oklahoma	2
Oregon	2
Pennsylvania	2
Rhode Island	No limit
South Carolina	2
South Dakota	2
Tennessee	2
Texas	No limit
Utah	No limit
Vermont	No limit
Virginia	0
Washington	No limit
West Virginia	2
Wisconsin	No limit
Wyoming	No limit

* Indicates an absolute two-term limit. That is, no person may serve more than two gubernatorial terms in his lifetime. In other states with limitations, a governor may serve as many terms as he may be elected to, provided he retires after one, or two, terms, depending on the constitutional provisions of his state, and stays out of office at least one term before running again.

0 Indicates the governor must retire at the end of his first term. After a one-term interim, he may serve again.

2 Indicates the governor must retire after two consecutive terms. After a one-term interim, he may serve again.

Source: *The Book of the States, 1984-1985*, vol. 25. Lexington, Ky.: The Council of State Governments, 1984.

Party Lineup of Governors

The figures below show the number of governorships held by the two parties after each election since 1950.

Year	Democrat	Republican	Independent
1950	23	25	0
1952	18	30	0
1954	27	21	0
1956	29	19	0
1958	35	14	0
1960	34	16	0
1962	34	16	0
1964	33	17	0
1966	25	25	0
1968	19	31	0
1970	29	21	0
1972	31	19	0
1974	36	13	1
1976	37	12	0
1978	32	18	0
1980	26	24	0
1982	34	16	0
1984	34	16	0

SOURCE: Republican National Committee

in which the provision was used, if any, were unavailable from the Connecticut secretary of state's office.

Georgia. Although the majority vote requirement was contained in the constitution as early as 1825, it was not used until the 20th century. In 1966, with an emerging Republican Party, a controversial Democratic nominee and an independent Democrat all affecting the gubernatorial race, no candidate received a majority. The Legislature chose Democrat Lester Maddox. It was the controversy surrounding this experience that led to the change from legislative choice to a runoff between the top two contenders. Earlier, in 1946, the Georgia Legislature also attempted to choose the governor, under unusual circumstances not covered by the majority vote requirement. The governor-elect, Eugene Talmadge, D, died before taking office. When it met, the Legislature chose Talmadge's son, Herman E. Talmadge, as the new governor. Talmadge was eligible for consideration on the basis that he received enough write-in votes in the general election to make him the second-place candidate. But the state Supreme Court voided the Legislature's choice and declared that the lieutenant governor-elect, Melvin E. Thompson, D, should be governor.

Maine. Maine entered statehood in 1820 with a majority vote provision for governor but repealed it in 1880. During this 60-year span, the Legislature was called on to choose the governor nine times, in 1840, 1846, 1848, 1852, 1853, 1854, 1855, 1878 and 1879.

Massachusetts. Like the other New England states, Massachusetts originally had a requirement for majority voting in gubernatorial elections. However, after the Legislature was forced to choose the governor for six straight elections from 1848 to 1853, Massachusetts repealed the provision in 1855. The years in which it was used were 1785, 1833, 1842, 1843, 1845, 1848, 1849, 1850, 1851, 1852 and 1853.

New Hampshire. New Hampshire's mandated majority vote for governor was in force from 1784 through 1912, when it was repealed. The outcome of the following gubernatorial elections was determined by the Legislature: 1785, 1787, 1789, 1790, 1812, 1824, 1846, 1851, 1856, 1863, 1871, 1874, 1875, 1886, 1888, 1890, 1906 and 1912.

Rhode Island. Under the constitution of 1842, Rhode Island required a majority to win the gubernatorial election. Under this mandate, the Legislature chose the governor in the years 1846, 1875, 1876, 1880, 1889, 1890 and 1891. Because of a disagreement between the two houses of the state Legislature, the ballots for governor were not counted in 1893, and Gov. D. Russell Brown, R, continued in office for another term of one year. The provision for majority voting then was repealed.

Before 1842 there was also a requirement for a popular majority, but the Legislature was not allowed to choose a new governor if no candidate achieved a majority. Three times — in 1806, 1832 and 1839 — there was a lack of a majority in a gubernatorial election, with a different outcome each time. In 1806 the lieutenant governor-elect served as acting governor for the term. In 1832 the Legislature mandated a new election, but still no majority choice was reached; three more elections were held, all without a majority being achieved, so the same state officers were continued until the next regular election. And in 1839, when neither the gubernatorial nor lieutenant governor's race yielded a winner by majority, the senior state senator acted as governor for the term.

Vermont. Vermont's provision for majority gubernatorial election resulted in the Legislature's picking the governor 19 times: 1789, 1797, 1813, 1814, 1830, 1831, 1832, 1834, 1841, 1843, 1845, 1846, 1847, 1848, 1849, 1852, 1853, 1902 and 1912. On a 20th occasion, 1835, the Legislature failed to choose a new governor because of a deadlock and the lieutenant governor-elect served as governor for the term. The Vermont provision remains in force.

Bibliography

Books

Book of the States, 1984-1985, vol. 25. Lexington, Ky.: Council of State Governments, 1984.

Haider, Donald H. *When Governments Come to Washington: Governors, Mayors, and Intergovernmental Lobbying*. New York: Free Press, 1974.

Jacob, Herbert. *Politics in the American States*. 3rd ed. Boston: Little, Brown, 1976.

Lipson, Leslie. *The American Governor from Figurehead to Leader*. 1939. Reprint. Westport, Conn.: Greenwood Press, 1969.

Kallenbach, Joseph E., and Jessamine S. Kallenbach. *American State Governors, 1776-1976*. 3 vols. Dobbs Ferry, N.Y.: Oceana Publishing, 1977.

Raimo, John, ed. *Biographical Directory of the Governors of the United States, 1978-1982*. Westport, Conn.: Meckler Publishing, 1983.

Ransone, Coleman B., Jr. *The American Governorship*. Westport, Conn.: Greenwood Press, 1982.

———. *The Office of the Governor in the United States*. 1956. Reprint. Salem, N.C.: Ayer.

Sabato, Larry. *Goodbye to Good-time Charlie: The American Governorship Transformed*. Washington, D.C.: CQ Press, 1983.

Sobel, Robert, ed. *Biographical Directory of the Governors of the United States, 1789-1978.* 4 vols. Westport, Conn.: Meckler Publishing, 1978.

Spence, James R. *The Making of a Governor: The Moore Preyer-Lake Primaries, 1964.* Winston-Salem, N. C.: John F. Blair Publishing, 1968.

Articles

Abrams, Burton A. "Political Power and the Market for Governors." *Public Choice* 37 (1981): 521-529.

Bibby, John F. "Political Parties and Federalism: The Republican National Committee Involvement in Gubernatorial and Legislative Elections." *Publius* 9 (Winter 1979): 229-236.

Bryan, Richard J. "Legislative Election of a Governor." *North Carolina Law Review* (December 1967): 128-142.

Eismeier, Theodore J. "Votes and Taxes: The Political Economy of the American Governorship." *Polity* 15 (Spring 1983): 368-379.

Ewing, Cortez A. M. "Southern Governors." *Journal of Politics* 10 (1948): 385-409.

Fairlie, John A. "The State Governor." *Michigan Law Review* 5 and 6 (March/April 1912).

Jewell, Malcolm E. "Voting Turnout in State Gubernatorial Primaries." *Western Political Quarterly* 30 (June 1977): 236-254.

Kallenbach, Joseph E. "Constitutional Limitations on Reeligibility of National and State Chief Executives." *American Political Science Review* (June 1952): 438-454.

MacDonald, A. F. "American Governors, 1900-1910." *National Municipal Review* (November 1927): 715-719.

Mathews, J. M. "The Role of the Governor." *American Political Science Review* (May 1912): 216-228.

Patterson, Samuel C. "Campaign Spending in Contests for Governor." *Western Political Quarterly* 35 (December 1982): 457-477.

Penning, James M., and Corwin E. Smidt. "Public Funding of Gubernatorial Elections: The Views of State Legislatures." *American Politics Quarterly* 10 (July 1982): 315-332.

Perkins, John A. "American Governors, 1930-1940." *National Municipal Review* (March 1940): 178-184.

Piereson, James E. "Sources of Candidate Success in Gubernatorial Elections, 1910-1970." *Journal of Politics* 39 (November 1977): 939-958.

Reiter, Howard L. "Who Voted for Longley? Maine Elects an Independent Governor." *Polity* 10 (Fall 1977): 65-85.

Solomon, Samuel R. "United States Governors, 1940-1950." *National Municipal Review* (April 1952): 190-197.

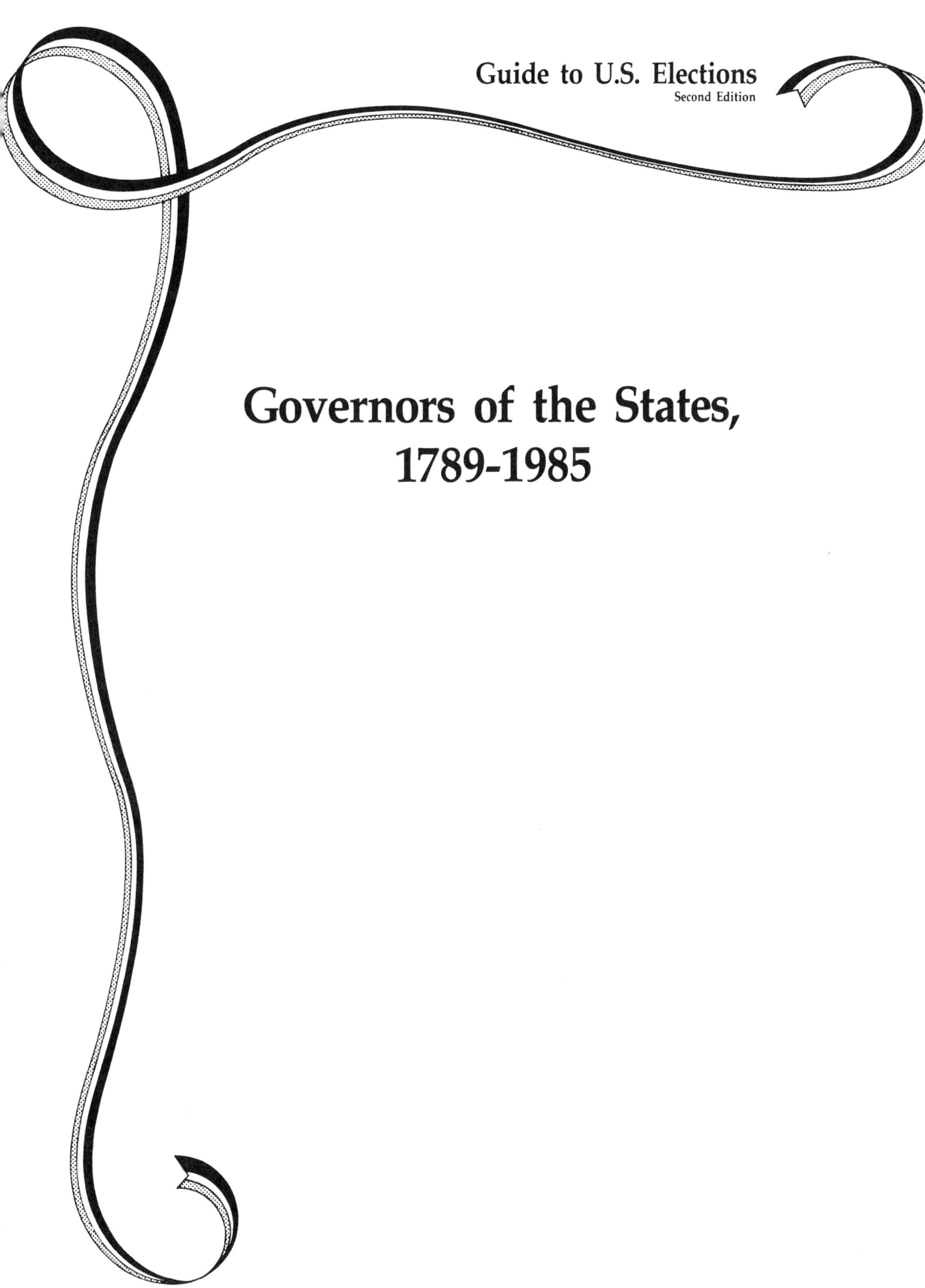

Governors of the States, 1789-1985

Sources: Governors of the States, 1789-1985

This section (pages 461-486) contains a listing of state governors through July 1985. Arranged alphabetically by state, the lists provide the name, political affiliation and dates of service of each state's governors in chronological order.

The following sources were used for the names, party affiliations and dates of service for governors.

● *Governors of the States 1900-1974.* Lexington, Ky.: Council of State Governments, 1974. Compiled by Samuel R. Solomon.

● *The Book of Governors.* Los Angeles: Washington Typographers, 1935. Compiled by William W. Hunt.

● Kallenbach, Joseph E., and Jessamine S. Kallenbach. *American State Governors, 1776-1976.* 3 vols. Dobbs Ferry, N.Y.: Oceana Publishing, 1977.

● State manuals published by the state governments.

● Gubernatorial election returns provided by the Inter-University Consortium for Political and Social Research (ICPSR), appearing on pages 489 to 536.

● *The Encyclopedia Americana.* 30 vols. Danbury, Conn.: Grolier Education, 1982.

Names, Party Affiliation and Dates of Service

For the 20th century, *The Governors of the States 1900-1974* was the primary source for the names of governors and dates of service. The party designations appearing in the ICPSR election returns were used to assign party affiliation. Where the ICPSR returns indicated two or more party designations, only the major party is listed. *(For a list of party abbreviations, see p. 1141; for other references to individual governors, see General Index, p. 1275.)*

For the 18th and 19th centuries, state manuals and Hunt's *The Book of Governors* were used for names and dates of service. Hunt provides the names of state governors and dates of service — in some cases complete dates (month, day and year), in other cases only month and year and in still other cases only the dates of gubernatorial elections. Congressional Quarterly has used the most precise dates available from Hunt and state manuals.

Because political parties did not exist formally in the early years of the Republic, classification of governors by party during this period can be difficult or misleading *("Pre-Convention Politics," p. 7; "Historical Profiles of American Political Parties," p. 225).* In cases where party affiliation was not appropriate or could not be determined, no party designation appears. After 1824, the starting date for the ICPSR gubernatorial election returns, the ICPSR data were used where they provided information on party affiliation. State manuals and *The Encyclopedia Americana*, which gives governors' party affiliation for some states, were also consulted.

Footnotes

Footnotes, based on information from the above sources, have been used to indicate the following circumstances:

● Deaths, resignations or removals from office and succession of lieutenant governors or other officials to governorships.

● Circumstances surrounding disputed elections.

For details on the 20th-century trend toward longer gubernatorial terms and limitations on the number of consecutive terms, as well as unusual gubernatorial election procedures in some states, see "Gubernatorial Elections," pages 453 to 457.

Governors of the States, 1789-1985

ALABAMA

(Became a state Dec. 14, 1819)

Governors	Dates of Service	
William W. Bibb (D-R)	Nov. 9, 1819	July 15, 1820
Thomas Bibb (D-R)	July 15, 1820	Nov. 9, 1821
Israel Pickens (D-R)	Nov. 9, 1821	Nov. 25, 1825
John Murphy (JAC D)	Nov. 25, 1825	Nov. 25, 1829
Gabriel Moore (JAC D)	Nov. 25, 1829	March 3, 1831
Samuel B. Moore (D)	March 3, 1832	Nov. 26, 1831
John Gayle (D)	Nov. 26, 1831	Nov. 21, 1835
Clement C. Clay (D)	Nov. 21, 1835	July 17, 1837
Hugh McVay (D)	July 17, 1837	Nov. 21, 1837
Arthur P. Bagby (D)	Nov. 21, 1837	Nov. 22, 1841
Benjamin Fitzpatrick (D)	Nov. 22, 1841	Dec. 10, 1845
Joshua L. Martin (I)	Dec. 10, 1845	Dec. 16, 1847
Reuben Chapman (D)	Dec. 16, 1847	Dec. 17, 1849
Henry W. Collier (D)	Dec. 17, 1849	Dec. 20, 1853
John A. Winston (D)	Dec. 20, 1853	Dec. 1, 1857
Andrew B. Moore (D)	Dec. 1, 1857	Dec. 2, 1861
John Gill Shorter (D)	Dec. 2, 1861	Dec. 1, 1863
Thomas H. Watts (W)	Dec. 1, 1863	May 1865
Lewis E. Parsons[1]	June 21, 1865	Dec. 20, 1865
Robert M. Patton (W)	Dec. 20, 1865	July 14, 1868
William Hugh Smith (R)	July 14, 1868	Nov. 26, 1870
Robert B. Lindsay (D)	Nov. 26, 1870	Nov. 17, 1872
David P. Lewis (R)	Nov. 17, 1872	Nov. 24, 1874
George S. Houston (D)	Nov. 24, 1874	Nov. 28, 1878
Rufus W. Cobb (D)	Nov. 28, 1878	Dec. 1, 1882
Edward A. O'Neal (D)	Dec. 1, 1882	Dec. 1, 1886
Thomas Seay (D)	Dec. 1, 1886	Dec. 1, 1890
Thomas G. Jones (D)	Dec. 1, 1890	Dec. 1, 1894
William C. Oates (D)	Dec. 1, 1894	Dec. 1, 1896
Joseph F. Johnston (D)	Dec. 1, 1896	Dec. 1, 1900
Wililam D. Jelks (D)[2]	Dec. 1, 1900	Dec. 26, 1900
William J. Samford (D)[3]	Dec. 26, 1900	June 11, 1901
William D. Jelks (D)[4]	June 11, 1901	April 25, 1904
Russell M. Cunningham (D)[5]	April 25, 1904	March 5, 1905
William D. Jelks (D)	March 5, 1905	Jan. 14, 1907
Braxton B. Comer (D)	Jan. 14, 1907	Jan. 17, 1911
Emmet O'Neal (D)	Jan. 17, 1911	Jan. 18, 1915
Charles Henderson (D)	Jan. 18, 1915	Jan. 20, 1919
Thomas E. Kilby (D)	Jan. 20, 1919	Jan. 15, 1923
William W. Brandon (D)	Jan. 15, 1923	Jan. 17, 1927
Bibb Graves (D)	Jan. 17, 1927	Jan. 19, 1931
Benjamin M. Miller (D)	Jan. 19, 1931	Jan. 14, 1935
Bibb Graves (D)	Jan. 14, 1935	Jan. 17, 1939
Frank M. Dixon (D)	Jan. 17, 1939	Jan. 19, 1943
Chauncey M. Sparks (D)	Jan. 19, 1943	Jan. 20, 1947
James E. Folsom (D)	Jan. 20, 1947	Jan. 15, 1951
Gordon Persons (D)	Jan. 15, 1951	Jan. 17, 1955
James E. Folsom (D)	Jan. 17, 1955	Jan. 19, 1959
John M. Patterson (D)	Jan. 19, 1959	Jan. 14, 1963
George C. Wallace (D)	Jan. 14, 1963	Jan. 16, 1967
Lurleen B. Wallace (D)[6]	Jan. 16, 1967	May 7, 1968
Albert P. Brewer (D)[7]	May 7, 1968	Jan. 18, 1971
George C. Wallace (D)	Jan. 18, 1971	Jan. 15, 1979
Forrest (Fob) James (D)	Jan. 15, 1979	Jan. 17, 1983
George C. Wallace (D)	Jan. 17, 1983	

ALASKA

(Became a state Jan. 3, 1959)

Governors	Dates of Service	
William A. Egan (D)	Jan. 3, 1959	Dec. 5, 1966
Walter J. Hickel (R)[1]	Dec. 5, 1966	Jan. 29, 1969
Keith H. Miller (R)[2]	Jan. 29, 1969	Dec. 5, 1970
William A. Egan (D)	Dec. 5, 1970	Dec. 2, 1974
Jay S. Hammond (R)	Dec. 2, 1974	Dec. 6, 1982
Bill Sheffield (D)	Dec. 6, 1982	

ARIZONA

(Became a state Feb. 14, 1912)

Governors	Dates of Service	
George W. P. Hunt (D)	Feb. 14, 1912	Jan. 1, 1917
Thomas E. Campbell (R)[1]	Jan. 1, 1917	Dec. 25, 1917
George W. P. Hunt (D)[2]	Dec. 25, 1917	Jan. 6, 1919
Thomas E. Campbell (R)	Jan. 6, 1919	Jan. 1, 1923
George W. P. Hunt (D)	Jan. 1, 1923	Jan. 7, 1929

Alabama

1. Provisional governor, appointed by president.
2. Jelks, as president of the state Senate, took office as acting governor due to the illness of governor-elect Samford.
3. Died June 11, 1901.
4. As president of the state Senate, Jelks became governor on Samford's death. Subsequently re-elected in 1902.
5. As lieutenant governor, he became acting governor due to the illness of Jelks.
6. Died May 7, 1968.
7. As lieutenant governor, he succeeded to office.

Alaska

1. Resigned Jan. 29, 1969.
2. As secretary of state, he succeeded to office.

Arizona

1. Campbell was initially declared the winner, but the election was contested. After an extended recount, Hunt was declared the winner by 43 votes.
2. Hunt served out the remainder of the term following his successful challenge to Campbell's election.
3. Died May 25, 1948.
4. As secretary of state, he succeeded to office. Subsequently elected.
5. Resigned Oct. 20, 1977, to become ambassador to Argentina.
6. As secretary of state, he succeeded to office. Died March 4, 1978.
7. As attorney general, he succeeded to office. Subsequently elected.

John C. Phillips (R)	Jan. 7, 1929	Jan. 5, 1931
George W. P. Hunt (D)	Jan. 5, 1931	Jan. 2, 1933
Benjamin B. Moeur (D)	Jan. 2, 1933	Jan. 4, 1937
Rawghile C. Stanford (D)	Jan. 4, 1937	Jan. 2, 1939
Robert T. Jones (D)	Jan. 2, 1939	Jan. 6, 1941
Sidney P. Osborn (D)[3]	Jan. 6, 1941	May 25, 1948
Dan E. Garvey (D)[4]	May 25, 1948	Jan. 1, 1951
J. Howard Pyle (R)	Jan. 1, 1951	Jan. 3, 1955
Ernest W. McFarland (D)	Jan. 3, 1955	Jan. 5, 1959
Paul J. Fannin (R)	Jan. 5, 1959	Jan. 4, 1965
Sam Goddard (D)	Jan. 4, 1965	Jan. 2, 1967
Jack Williams (R)	Jan. 2, 1967	Jan. 6, 1975
Raul Castro (D)[5]	Jan. 6, 1975	Oct. 20, 1977
Wesley Bolin (D)[6]	Oct. 20, 1977	March 4, 1978
Bruce Babbitt (D)[7]	March 4, 1978	

ARKANSAS

(Became a state June 15, 1836)

Governors	Dates of Service	
James S. Conway (D)	Sept. 13, 1836	Nov. 4, 1840
Archibald Yell (D)[1]	Nov. 4, 1840	April 29, 1844
Samuel Adams (D)[2]	April 24, 1844	Nov. 5, 1844
Thomas S. Drew (D)[3]	Nov. 5, 1844	Jan. 10, 1849
Richard C. Byrd (D)[4]	Jan. 11, 1849	April 19, 1849
John S. Roane (D)	April 19, 1849	Nov. 15, 1852
Elias N. Conway (D)	Nov. 15, 1852	Nov. 16, 1860
Henry M. Rector (ID)	Nov. 16, 1860	Nov. 4, 1862
Thomas Fletcher[5]	Nov. 4, 1862	Nov. 15, 1862
Harris Flannigan (D)	Nov. 15, 1862	April 18, 1864
Isaac Murphy (UN)	April 18, 1864	July 2, 1868
Powell Clayton (R)[6]	July 2, 1868	March 17, 1871
Ozra A. Hadley (R)[7]	March 17, 1871	Jan. 6, 1873
Elisha Baxter (R)	Jan. 6, 1873	Nov. 12, 1874
A. H. Garland (D)	Nov. 12, 1874	Jan. 11, 1877
William R. Miller (D)	Jan. 11, 1877	Jan. 13, 1881
Thomas J. Churchill (D)	Jan. 13, 1881	Jan. 13, 1883
James H. Berry (D)	Jan. 13, 1883	Jan. 17, 1885
Simon P. Hughes (D)	Jan. 17, 1885	Jan. 1889
James P. Eagle (D)	Jan. 1889	Jan. 1893
William M. Fishback (D)	Jan. 1893	Jan. 1895
James P. Clarke (D)	Jan. 1895	Jan. 12, 1897
Daniel Webster Jones (D)	Jan. 12, 1897	Jan. 8, 1901
Jeff Davis (D)	Jan. 8, 1901	Jan. 8, 1907
John S. Little (D)[8]	Jan. 8, 1907	Feb. 11, 1907
John I. Moore (D)[9]	Feb. 11, 1907	May 11, 1907

Xenophon O. Pindall (D)[10]	May 14, 1907	Jan. 11, 1909
George W. Donaghey (D)	Jan. 11, 1909	Jan. 15, 1913
Joseph T. Robinson (D)[11]	Jan. 15, 1913	March 10, 1913
William K. Oldham (D)[12]	March 10, 1913	March 13, 1913
Junius M. Futrell (D)[13]	March 13, 1913	July 23, 1913
George W. Hays (D)	July 23, 1913	Jan. 9, 1917
Charles H. Brough (D)	Jan. 9, 1917	Jan. 11, 1921
Thomas C. McRae (D)	Jan. 11, 1921	Jan. 13, 1925
Thomas J. Terrall (D)	Jan. 13, 1925	Jan. 11, 1927
John E. Martineau (D)[14]	Jan. 11, 1927	March 4, 1928
Harvey Parnell (D)[15]	March 4, 1928	Jan. 10, 1933
Junius M. Futrell (D)	Jan. 10, 1933	Jan. 12, 1937
Carl E. Bailey (D)	Jan. 12, 1937	Jan. 14, 1941
Homer M. Adkins (D)	Jan. 14, 1941	Jan. 9, 1945
Benjamin T. Laney (D)	Jan. 9, 1945	Jan. 11, 1949
Sidney S. McMath (D)	Jan. 11, 1949	Jan. 13, 1953
Frances A. Cherry (D)	Jan. 13, 1953	Jan. 11, 1955
Orval E. Faubus (D)	Jan. 11, 1955	Jan. 10, 1967
Winthrop Rockefeller (R)	Jan. 10, 1967	Jan. 12, 1971
Dale Bumpers (D)[16]	Jan. 12, 1971	Jan. 3, 1975
Bob Riley (D)[17]	Jan. 3, 1975	Jan. 14, 1975
David Pryor (D)[18]	Jan. 14, 1975	Jan. 3, 1979
Joe Purcell (D)[19]	Jan. 3, 1979	Jan. 9, 1979
Bill Clinton (D)	Jan. 9, 1979	Jan. 19, 1981
Frank D. White (R)	Jan. 19, 1981	Jan. 11, 1983
Bill Clinton (D)	Jan. 11, 1983	

CALIFORNIA

(Became a state Sept. 9, 1850)

Governors	Dates of Service	
Peter H. Burnett (ID)[1]	Dec. 20, 1849	Jan. 9, 1851
John McDougal (ID)[2]	Jan. 9, 1851	Jan. 8, 1852
John Bigler (D)	Jan. 8, 1852	Jan. 9, 1856
J. Neely Johnson (AM)	Jan. 9, 1856	Jan. 8, 1858
John B. Weller (D)	Jan. 8, 1858	Jan. 9, 1860
Milton S. Latham (D)[3]	Jan. 9, 1860	Jan. 14, 1860
John G. Downey (D)[4]	Jan. 14, 1860	Jan. 10, 1862
Leland Stanford (R)	Jan. 10, 1862	Dec. 10, 1863
Frederick F. Low (UN R)	Dec. 10, 1863	Dec. 5, 1867
Henry H. Haight (D)	Dec. 5, 1867	Dec. 8, 1871
Newton Booth (R)[5]	Dec. 8, 1871	Feb. 27, 1875
Romualdo Pacheco (R)[6]	Feb. 27, 1875	Dec. 9, 1875
William Irwin (D)	Dec. 9, 1875	Jan. 8, 1880
George C. Perkins (R)	Jan. 8, 1880	Jan. 10, 1883
George Stoneman (D)	Jan. 10, 1883	Jan. 8, 1887

Arkansas
1. Resigned April 29, 1844.
2. As president of the state Senate, he succeeded to office.
3. Resigned Jan. 10, 1849.
4. As president of the state Senate, he succeeded to office.
5. Acting governor.
6. Resigned March 17, 1871.
7. Succeeded to office.
8. Resigned Feb. 11, 1907.
9. Acting governor.
10. Elected president of the state Senate, he then succeeded to office as governor.
11. Resigned March 10, 1913.
12. As president of the state Senate, he succeeded to office.
13. As president of the state Senate, he succeeded to office.
14. Resigned March 4, 1928.
15. As lieutenant governor, he succeeded to office. Subsequently elected.
16. Resigned Jan. 3, 1975.
17. As lieutenant governor, he succeeded to office.

18. Resigned Jan. 3, 1979.
19. As lieutenant governor, he succeeded to office.

California
1. Resigned Jan. 9, 1851.
2. As lieutenant governor, he succeeded to office.
3. Resigned Jan. 14, 1860.
4. As lieutenant governor, he succeeded to office.
5. Resigned Feb. 27, 1875.
6. As lieutenant governor, he succeeded to office.
7. Died Sept. 13, 1887.
8. As lieutenant governor, he succeeded to office.
9. Resigned March 15, 1917.
10. As lieutenant governor, he succeeded to office. Subsequently elected.
11. Died June 2, 1934.
12. As lieutenant governor, he succeeded to office. Subsequently elected.
13. Resigned Oct. 5, 1953.
14. As lieutenant governor, he succeeded to office. Subsequently elected.

Washington Bartlett (D)[7]	Jan. 8, 1887	Sept. 13, 1887
Robert W. Waterman (R)[8]	Sept. 13, 1887	Jan. 8, 1891
Henry H. Markham (R)	Jan. 8, 1891	Jan. 11, 1895
James H. Budd (D)	Jan. 11, 1895	Jan. 3, 1899
Henry T. Gage (R & UL)	Jan. 3, 1899	Jan. 6, 1903
George C. Pardee (R)	Jan. 6, 1903	Jan. 8, 1907
James N. Gillett (R)	Jan. 8, 1907	Jan. 3, 1911
Hiram W. Johnson (R, PROG)[9]	Jan. 3, 1911	March 15, 1917
William D. Stephens (RP PROG)[10]	March 15, 1917	Jan. 9, 1923
Friend William Richardson (R)	Jan. 9, 1923	Jan. 4, 1927
Clement C. Young (R)	Jan. 4, 1927	Jan. 6, 1931
James Rolph Jr. (R)[11]	Jan. 6, 1931	June 2, 1934
Frank F. Merriam (R)[12]	June 2, 1934	Jan. 2, 1939
Culbert L. Olson (D)	Jan. 2, 1939	Jan. 4, 1943
Earl Warren (R)[13]	Jan. 4, 1943	Oct. 5, 1953
Goodwin J. Knight (R)[14]	Oct. 5, 1953	Jan. 5, 1959
Edmund G. Brown (D)	Jan. 5, 1959	Jan. 2, 1967
Ronald Reagan (R)	Jan. 1, 1967	Jan. 6, 1975
Edmund G. Brown Jr. (D)	Jan. 6, 1975	Jan. 3, 1983
George Deukmejian (R)	Jan. 3, 1983	

COLORADO

(Became a state Aug. 1, 1876)

Governors	Dates of Service	
John L. Routt (R)	Nov. 3, 1876	Jan. 14, 1879
Frederick W. Pitkin (R)	Jan. 14, 1879	Jan. 9, 1883
James B. Grant (D)	Jan. 9, 1883	Jan. 13, 1885
Benjamin H. Eaton (R)	Jan. 13, 1885	Jan. 11, 1887
Alva Adams (D)	Jan. 11, 1887	Jan. 10, 1889
Job A. Cooper (R)	Jan. 10, 1889	Jan. 13, 1891
John L. Routt (R)	Jan. 13, 1891	Jan. 10, 1893
Davis H. Waite (POP & SL, D)	Jan. 10, 1893	Jan. 8, 1895
Albert W. McIntire (R)	Jan. 8, 1895	Jan. 12, 1897
Alva Adams (D)	Jan. 12, 1897	Jan. 10, 1899
Charles S. Thomas (FUS)	Jan. 10, 1899	Jan. 8, 1901
James B. Orman (FUS)	Jan. 8, 1901	Jan. 13, 1903
James H. Peabody (R)	Jan. 13, 1903	Jan. 10, 1905
Alva Adams (D)[1]	Jan. 10, 1905	March 16, 1905
James H. Peabody (R)	March 16, 1905	March 17, 1905
Jesse F. McDonald (R)[2]	March 17, 1905	Jan. 8, 1907
Henry A. Buchtel (R)	Jan. 8, 1907	Jan. 12, 1909
John F. Shafroth (D)	Jan. 12, 1909	Jan. 14, 1913
Elias M. Ammons (D)	Jan. 14, 1913	Jan. 12, 1915
George A. Carlson (R)	Jan. 12, 1915	Jan. 9, 1917

Julius C. Gunter (D)	Jan. 9, 1917	Jan. 14, 1919
Oliver H. Shoup (R)	Jan. 14, 1919	Jan. 9, 1923
William E. Sweet (D)	Jan. 9, 1923	Jan. 13, 1925
Clarence J. Morley (R)	Jan. 13, 1925	Jan. 11, 1927
William H. Adams (D)	Jan. 11, 1927	Jan. 10, 1933
Edwin C. Johnson (D)[3]	Jan. 10, 1933	Jan. 3, 1937
Ray H. Talbot (D)[4]	Jan. 3, 1937	Jan. 12, 1937
Teller Ammons (D)	Jan. 12, 1937	Jan. 10, 1939
Ralph L. Carr (R)	Jan. 10, 1939	Jan. 12, 1943
John C. Vivian (R)	Jan. 12, 1943	Jan. 14, 1947
William L. Knous (D)[5]	Jan. 14, 1947	April 15, 1950
Walter W. Johnson (D)[6]	April 15, 1950	Jan. 9, 1951
Dan Thornton (R)	Jan. 9, 1951	Jan. 11, 1955
Edwin C. Johnson (D)	Jan. 11, 1955	Jan. 8, 1957
Stephen L. R. McNichols (D)	Jan. 8, 1957	Jan. 8, 1963
John A. Love (R)[7]	Jan. 8, 1963	July 16, 1973
John D. Vanderhoof (R)[8]	July 16, 1973	Jan. 14, 1975
Richard D. Lamm (D)	Jan. 14, 1975	

CONNECTICUT

(Ratified the Constitution Jan. 9, 1788)

Governors	Dates of Service	
Samuel Huntington[1]	May 11, 1786	Jan. 5, 1796
Oliver Wolcott (FED)[2]	Jan. 5, 1796	Dec. 1, 1797
Jonathan Trumbull (FED)[3]	Dec. 1, 1797	Aug. 7, 1809
John Treadwell (FED)	Aug. 7, 1809	May 9, 1811
Roger Griswold (FED)[4]	May 9, 1811	Oct. 25, 1812
John Cotton Smith (FED)	Oct. 25, 1812	May 8, 1817
Oliver Wolcott Jr. (D-R)	May 8, 1817	May 2, 1827
Gideon Tomlinson (D-R, NR)[5]	May 2, 1827	March 1831
John S. Peters (NR)	March 1831	May 4, 1833
Henry W. Edwards (D)	May 4, 1833	May 7, 1834
Samuel A. Foote (NR)	May 7, 1834	May 6, 1835
Henry W. Edwards (D)	May 6, 1835	May 2, 1838
William W. Ellsworth (W)	May 2, 1838	May 4, 1842
Chauncey F. Cleveland (D)	May 4, 1842	May 1844
Roger S. Baldwin (W)	May 1844	May 6, 1846
Isaac Toucey (D)	May 6, 1846	May 5, 1847
Clark Bissell (W)	May 5, 1847	May 2, 1849
Joseph Trumbull (W)	May 2, 1849	May 4, 1850
Thomas H. Seymour (D)[6]	May 4, 1850	Oct. 13, 1853
Charles H. Pond (D)[7]	Oct. 13, 1853	May 1854
Henry Dutton (W)	May 1854	May 1855
William T. Minor (AM)	May 1855	May 6, 1857
Alexander H. Holley (R)	May 6, 1857	May 5, 1858

Colorado

1. The 1904 election between Alva Adams (D) and James H. Peabody (R) caused a dispute surrounding charges of fraud which had to be settled by the Legislature. Both contenders were asked to withdraw. Adams served as governor for 66 days and Peabody for one day.
2. As lieutenant governor, he succeeded to office.
3. Resigned Jan. 3, 1937.
4. As lieutenant governor, he succeeded to office.
5. Resigned April 15, 1950.
6. As lieutenant governor, he succeeded to office.
7. Resigned July 16, 1973.
8. As lieutenant governor, he succeeded to office.

Connecticut

1. Died Jan. 5, 1796.
2. Died Dec. 1, 1797.
3. Died Aug. 7, 1809.
4. Died Oct. 25, 1812.
5. Resigned in 1831 to become U.S. senator.
6. Resigned Oct. 13, 1853.
7. As lieutenant governor, he succeeded to office.
8. The 1890 election was disputed, with Democrats claiming that Luzon Morris had won a majority of the popular vote and been elected governor, and Republicans claiming that he had not and demanding an election by the Legislature. Since control of the Legislature was divided, the two houses could not agree on what to do, so Governor Bulkeley remained in office for the term.
9. Died April 21, 1909.
10. As lieutenant governor, he succeeded to office.
11. Resigned Jan. 8, 1925.
12. As lieutenant governor, he succeeded to office. Subsequently elected.
13. Resigned Dec. 27, 1946.
14. As lieutenant governor, he succeeded to office.
15. Died March 7, 1948.
16. As lieutenant governor, he succeeded to office.
17. Resigned Jan. 21, 1961.
18. As lieutenant governor, he succeeded to office. Subsequently elected.
19. Resigned Dec. 31, 1980.
20. As lieutenant governor, he succeeded to office. Subsequently elected.

William A. Buckingham (R)	May 5, 1858	May 2, 1866
Joseph R. Hawley (R)	May 2, 1866	May 1, 1867
James E. English (D)	May 1, 1867	May 5, 1869
Marshall Jewell (R)	May 5, 1869	May 4, 1870
James E. English (D)	May 4, 1870	May 1871
Marshall Jewell (R)	May 16, 1871	May 7, 1873
Charles R. Ingersoll (D)	May 7, 1873	Jan. 3, 1877
Richard D. Hubbard (D)	Jan. 3, 1877	Jan. 9, 1879
Charles B. Andrews (R)	Jan. 9, 1879	Jan. 5, 1881
Hobart B. Bigelow (R)	Jan. 5, 1881	Jan. 3, 1883
Thomas M. Waller (D)	Jan. 3, 1883	Jan. 8, 1885
Henry B. Harrison (R)	Jan. 8, 1885	Jan. 7, 1887
Phineas C. Lounsbury (R)	Jan. 7, 1887	Jan. 10, 1889
Morgan G. Bulkeley (R)[8]	Jan. 10, 1889	Jan. 4, 1893
Luzon B. Morris (D)	Jan. 4, 1893	Jan. 9, 1895
O. Vincent Coffin (R)	Jan. 9, 1895	Jan. 6, 1897
Lorrin A. Cooke (R)	Jan. 6, 1897	Jan. 4, 1899
George E. Lounsbury (R)	Jan. 4, 1899	Jan. 9, 1901
George P. McLean (R)	Jan. 9, 1901	Jan. 7, 1903
Abiram Chamberlain (R)	Jan. 7, 1903	Jan. 4, 1905
Henry Roberts (R)	Jan. 4, 1905	Jan. 9, 1907
Rollin S. Woodruff (R)	Jan. 9, 1907	Jan. 6, 1909
George L. Lilley (R)[9]	Jan. 6, 1909	April 21, 1909
Frank B. Weeks (R)[10]	April 21, 1909	Jan. 4, 1911
Simeon E. Baldwin (D)	Jan. 4, 1911	Jan. 6, 1915
Marcus H. Holcomb (R)	Jan. 6, 1915	Jan. 5, 1921
Everett J. Lake (R)	Jan. 5, 1921	Jan. 3, 1923
Charles A. Templeton (R)	Jan. 3, 1923	Jan. 7, 1925
Hiram Bingham (R)[11]	Jan. 7, 1925	Jan. 8, 1925
John H. Trumbull (R)[12]	Jan. 8, 1925	Jan. 7, 1931
Wilbur L. Cross (D)	Jan. 7, 1931	Jan. 4, 1939
Raymond E. Baldwin (R)	Jan. 4, 1939	Jan. 8, 1941
Robert A. Hurley (D)	Jan. 8, 1941	Jan. 6, 1943
Raymond E. Baldwin (R)[13]	Jan. 6, 1943	Dec. 27, 1946
Wilbert Snow (D)[14]	Dec. 27, 1946	Jan. 8, 1947
James L. McConaughy (R)[15]	Jan. 8, 1947	March 7, 1948
James C. Shannon (R)[16]	March 7, 1948	Jan. 5, 1949
Chester Bowles (D)	Jan. 5, 1949	Jan. 3, 1951
John D. Lodge (R)	Jan. 3, 1951	Jan. 5, 1955
Abraham Ribicoff (D)[17]	Jan. 5, 1955	Jan. 21, 1961
John Dempsey (D)[18]	Jan. 21, 1961	Jan. 6, 1971
Thomas J. Meskill (R)	Jan. 6, 1971	Jan. 8, 1975
Ella T. Grasso (D)[19]	Jan. 8, 1975	Dec. 31, 1980
William A. O'Neill (D)[20]	Dec. 31, 1980	

DELAWARE

(Ratified the Constitution Dec. 7, 1787)

Governors	Dates of Service	
Joshua Clayton (FED)[1]	June 2, 1789	Jan. 13, 1796
Gunning Bedford Sr. (FED)[2]	Jan. 1796	Sept. 28, 1797
Daniel Rogers (FED)[3]	Sept. 28, 1797	Jan. 1799
Richard Bassett (FED)[4]	Jan. 1799	March 1801

James Sykes (FED)[5]	March 1801	Jan. 1802
David Hall (D-R)	Jan. 1802	Jan. 1805
Nathaniel Mitchell (FED)	Jan. 1805	Jan. 1808
George Truitt (FED)	Jan. 1808	Jan. 1811
Joseph Haslet (D-R)	Jan. 1811	Jan. 1814
Daniel Rodney (FED)	Jan. 1814	Jan. 1817
John Clark (FED)	Jan. 1817	Jan. 1820
Henry Molleston[6]		
Jacob Stout (FED)[7]	Jan. 1820	Jan. 1821
John Collins (D-R)[8]	Jan. 1821	April 1822
Caleb Rodney (D-R)[9]	April 1822	Jan. 1823
Joseph Haslet (D-R)[10]	Jan. 1823	June 20, 1823
Charles Thomas (D-R)[11]	June 20, 1823	Jan. 1824
Samuel Paynter (FED)	Jan. 1824	Jan. 1827
Charles Polk (FED)	Jan. 1827	Jan. 1830
David Hazzard (D)	Jan. 1830	Jan. 1833
Caleb P. Bennett (D)[12]	Jan. 1833	April 9, 1836
Charles Polk[13]	April 9, 1836	Jan. 1837
Cornelius P. Comegys (W)	Jan. 1837	Jan. 1841
William B. Cooper (W)	Jan. 1841	Jan. 1845
Thomas Stockton (W)[14]	Jan. 1845	March 2, 1846
Joseph Maull (W)[15]	March 2, 1846	May 1, 1846
William Temple (W)[16]	May 1, 1846	Jan. 1847
William Tharp (D)	Jan. 1847	Jan. 1851
William H. Ross (D)	Jan. 1851	Jan. 1855
Peter F. Causey (AM)	Jan. 1855	Jan. 1859
William Burton (D)	Jan. 1859	Jan. 1863
William Cannon (UN)[17]	Jan. 1863	March 1, 1865
Gove Saulsbury (D)[18]	March 1, 1865	Jan. 1871
James Ponder (D)	Jan. 1871	Jan. 1875
John P. Cochran (D)	Jan. 1875	Jan. 1879
John W. Hall (D)	Jan. 1879	Jan. 1883
Charles C. Stockley (D)	Jan. 1883	Jan. 1887
Benjamin T. Biggs (D)	Jan. 1887	Jan. 1891
Robert J. Reynolds (D)	Jan. 1891	Jan. 1895
Joshua H. Marvel (R)[19]	Jan. 1895	April 8, 1895
William T. Watson (D)[20]	April 8, 1895	Jan. 19, 1897
Ebe W. Tunnell (D)	Jan. 19, 1897	Jan. 15, 1901
John Hunn (R)	Jan. 15, 1901	Jan. 17, 1905
Preston Lea (R)	Jan. 17, 1905	Jan. 19, 1909
Simeon S. Pennewill (R)	Jan. 19, 1909	Jan. 21, 1913
Charles R. Miller (R)	Jan. 21, 1913	Jan. 17, 1917
John G. Townsend Jr. (R)	Jan. 17, 1917	Jan. 18, 1921
William D. Denney (R)	Jan. 18, 1921	Jan. 20, 1925
Robert P. Robinson (R)	Jan. 20, 1925	Jan. 15, 1929
C. Douglass Buck (R)	Jan. 15, 1929	Jan. 19, 1937
Richard C. McMullen (D)	Jan. 19, 1937	Jan. 21, 1941
Walter W. Bacon (R)	Jan. 21, 1941	Jan. 18, 1949
Elbert N. Carvel (D)	Jan. 18, 1949	Jan. 20, 1953
J. Caleb Boggs (R)[21]	Jan. 20, 1953	Dec. 30, 1960
David P. Buckson (R)[22]	Dec. 30, 1960	Jan. 17, 1961
Elbert N. Carvel (D)	Jan. 17, 1961	Jan. 19, 1965
Charles L. Terry Jr. (D)	Jan. 19, 1965	Jan. 21, 1969
Russell W. Peterson (R)	Jan. 21, 1969	Jan. 16, 1973
Sherman W. Tribbitt (D)	Jan. 16, 1973	Jan. 18, 1977
Pierre duPont (R)	Jan. 18, 1977	Jan. 15, 1985
Michael N. Castle (R)	Jan. 15, 1985	

Delaware

1. *Joshua Clayton was president of Delaware from 1789 to 1793 and governor from 1793 to 1796.*
2. *Died Sept. 28, 1797.*
3. *Acting governor.*
4. *Resigned in March 1801.*
5. *Acting governor.*
6. *Died before taking office.*
7. *Acting governor.*
8. *Died in April 1822.*
9. *Acting governor.*
10. *Died June 20, 1823.*
11. *Acting governor.*
12. *Died April 9, 1836.*
13. *Acting governor.*
14. *Died March 2, 1846.*
15. *Acting governor. Died May 1, 1846.*
16. *Acting governor.*
17. *Died March 1, 1865.*
18. *Acting governor. Subsequently elected.*
19. *Died April 8, 1895.*
20. *Acting governor.*
21. *Resigned Dec. 30, 1960.*
22. *As lieutenant governor, he succeeded to office.*

FLORIDA

(Became a state March 3, 1845)

Governors	Dates of Service	
William D. Moseley (D)	June 25, 1845	Oct. 1, 1849
Thomas Brown (W)	Oct. 1, 1849	Oct. 3, 1853
James E. Broome (D)	Oct. 3, 1853	Oct. 5, 1857
Madison S. Perry (D)	Oct. 5, 1857	Oct. 7, 1861
John Milton (D)[1]	Oct. 7, 1861	April 1, 1865
William Marvin[2]	July 13, 1865	Dec. 20, 1865
David S. Walker (C)	Dec. 20, 1865	July 9, 1868
Harrison Reed (R)	July 9, 1868	Jan. 7, 1873
Ossian B. Hart (R)[3]	Jan. 7, 1873	March 18, 1874
Marcellus L. Stearns (R)[4]	March 18, 1874	Jan. 2, 1877
George F. Drew (D)	Jan. 2, 1877	Jan. 4, 1881
William D. Bloxham (D)	Jan. 4, 1881	Jan. 6, 1885
Edward A. Perry (D)	Jan. 6, 1885	Jan. 8, 1889
Francis P. Fleming (D)	Jan. 8, 1889	Jan. 3, 1893
Henry L. Mitchell (D)	Jan. 3, 1893	Jan. 5, 1897
William D. Bloxham (D)	Jan. 5, 1897	Jan. 8, 1901
William S. Jennings (D)	Jan. 8, 1901	Jan. 3, 1905
Napoleon B. Broward (D)	Jan. 3, 1905	Jan. 5, 1909
Albert W. Gilchrist (D)	Jan. 5, 1909	Jan. 7, 1913
Park Trammell (D)	Jan. 7, 1913	Jan. 2, 1917
Sidney J. Catts (IP)	Jan. 2, 1917	Jan. 4, 1921
Cary A. Hardee (D)	Jan. 4, 1921	Jan. 6, 1925
John W. Martin (D)	Jan. 6, 1925	Jan. 8, 1929
Doyle E. Carlton (D)	Jan. 8, 1929	Jan. 3, 1933
David Sholtz (D)	Jan. 3, 1933	Jan. 5, 1937
Frederick P. Cone (D)	Jan. 5, 1937	Jan. 7, 1941
Spessard L. Holland (D)	Jan. 7, 1941	Jan. 2, 1945
Millard F. Caldwell (D)	Jan. 2, 1945	Jan. 4, 1949
Fuller Warren (D)	Jan. 4, 1949	Jan. 6, 1953
Daniel T. McCarty (D)[5]	Jan. 6, 1953	Sept. 28, 1953
Charley E. Johns (D)[6]	Sept. 18, 1953	Jan. 4, 1955
LeRoy Collins (D)[7]	Jan. 4, 1955	Jan. 3, 1961
Farris Bryant (D)	Jan. 3, 1961	Jan. 5, 1965
Haydon Burns (D)	Jan. 5, 1965	Jan. 3, 1967
Claude R. Kirk Jr. (R)	Jan. 3, 1967	Jan. 5, 1971
Reubin Askew (D)	Jan. 5, 1971	Jan. 2, 1979
Robert Graham (D)	Jan. 2, 1979	

GEORGIA

(Ratified the Constitution Jan. 2, 1788)

Governors	Dates of Service	
George Handley	Jan. 26, 1788	Jan. 7, 1789
George Walton (D-R)	Jan. 7, 1789	Nov. 9, 1789
Edward Telfair (D-R)	Nov. 9, 1789	Nov. 7, 1793
George Mathews (D-R)	Nov. 7, 1793	Jan. 15, 1796
Jared Irwin (D-R)	Jan. 15, 1796	Jan. 12, 1798
James Jackson (D-R)	Jan. 12, 1798	March 3, 1801
David Emanuel (D-R)	March 3, 1801	Nov. 7, 1801
Josiah Tattnall Jr. (D-R)	Nov. 7, 1801	Nov. 4, 1802
John Milledge (D-R)	Nov. 4, 1802	Sept. 23, 1806
Jared Irwin (D-R)	Sept. 23, 1806	Nov. 10, 1809
David B. Mitchell (D-R)	Nov. 10, 1809	Nov. 5, 1813
Peter Early (D-R)	Nov. 5, 1813	Nov. 10, 1815
David B. Mitchell (D-R)	Nov. 10, 1815	March 4, 1817
William Rabun (D-R)	March 4, 1817	Oct. 24, 1819
Matthew Talbot (D-R)	Oct. 24, 1819	Nov. 5, 1819
John Clark (D-R)	Nov. 5, 1819	Nov. 7, 1823
George M. Troup (D-R)	Nov. 7, 1823	Nov. 7, 1827
John Forsyth (D-R)	Nov. 7, 1827	Nov. 4, 1829
George R. Gilmer (D)	Nov. 4, 1829	Nov. 9, 1831
Wilson Lumpkin (UN D)	Nov. 9, 1831	Nov. 4, 1835
William Schley (D)	Nov. 4, 1835	Nov. 8, 1837
George R. Gilmer (W)	Nov. 8, 1837	Nov. 6, 1839
Charles J. McDonald (D)	Nov. 6, 1839	Nov. 8, 1843
George W. Crawford (W)	Nov. 8, 1843	Nov. 3, 1847
George W. Towns (D)	Nov. 3, 1847	Nov. 5, 1851
Howell Cobb (UN D)	Nov. 5, 1851	Nov. 9, 1853
Herschel V. Johnson (D)	Nov. 9, 1853	Nov. 6, 1857
Joseph E. Brown (D)	Nov. 6, 1857	June 17, 1865
James Johnson (D)	June 17, 1865	Dec. 14, 1865
Charles J. Jenkins (D)	Dec. 14, 1865	Jan. 13, 1868
Gen. Thomas H. Ruger[1]	Jan. 13, 1868	July 4, 1868
Rufus Brown Bullock (R)[2]	July 4, 1868	Oct. 23, 1871
Benjamin Conley (R)[3]	Oct. 30, 1871	Jan. 12, 1872
James M. Smith (LR)	Jan. 12, 1872	Jan. 12, 1877
Alfred Holt Colquitt (D)	Jan. 12, 1877	Nov. 4, 1882
Alexander H. Stephens (D)[4]	Nov. 4, 1882	March 4, 1883
James H. Boynton (D)[5]	March 5, 1883	May 10, 1883
Henry D. McDaniel (D)	May 10, 1883	Nov. 9, 1886
John B. Gordon (D)	Nov. 9, 1886	Nov. 8, 1890
William J. Northen (D)	Nov. 8, 1890	Oct. 27, 1894
William Y. Atkinson (D)	Oct. 27, 1894	Oct. 29, 1898
Allen D. Candler (D)	Oct. 29, 1898	Oct. 25, 1902
Joseph M. Terrell (D)	Oct. 25, 1902	June 29, 1907
Hoke Smith (D)	June 29, 1907	June 26, 1909
Joseph M. Brown (D)	June 26, 1909	July 1, 1911
Hoke Smith (D)[6]	July 1, 1911	Nov. 16, 1911
John M. Slaton (D)[7]	Nov. 16, 1911	Jan. 25, 1912
Joseph M. Brown (D)	Jan. 25, 1912	June 28, 1913
John M. Slaton (D)	June 28, 1913	June 26, 1915
Nathaniel E. Harris (D)	June 26, 1915	June 30, 1917
Hugh M. Dorsey (D)	June 30, 1917	June 25, 1921
Thomas W. Hardwick (D)	June 25, 1921	June 30, 1923
Clifford M. Walker (D)	June 30, 1923	June 25, 1927
Lamartine G. Hardman (D)	June 25, 1927	June 27, 1931
Richard B. Russell (D)[8]	June 27, 1931	Jan. 10, 1933
Eugene Talmadge (D)	Jan. 10, 1933	Jan. 12, 1937

Florida

1. *Died April 1, 1865.*
2. *Acting governor, appointed by president.*
3. *Died March 18, 1874.*
4. *As lieutenant governor, he succeeded to office.*
5. *Died Sept. 28, 1953.*
6. *As president of the state Senate, he succeeded to office for the remainder of the first half of McCarty's term.*
7. *Elected in a special election to serve the last two years of McCarty's term. Subsequently re-elected.*

Georgia

1. *Military governor.*
2. *Resigned Oct. 23, 1871.*
3. *As president of the state Senate, he succeeded to office.*
4. *Died March 4, 1883.*
5. *As president of the state Senate, he succeeded to office.*
6. *Resigned Nov. 16, 1911.*
7. *As president of the state Senate, he succeeded to office.*
8. *Resigned Jan. 10, 1933.*
9. *Died Dec. 21, 1946, before his inauguration.*
10. *Eugene Talmadge's death led to a famous controversy that lasted several months, during which three different men claimed office as governor. The Talmadge-dominated Legislature elected Herman Talmadge, Eugene's son, to serve out his term, but this action was disputed by outgoing governor Ellis Arnall and Lieutenant Governor-elect Melvin E. Thompson. Herman Talmadge seized the governor's mansion by force, but was thrown out after 67 days in office by the Georgia Supreme Court, which ruled his election by the Legislature unconstitutional. Thompson then assumed office as governor until 1948, when a special election was held. He lost the Democratic nomination to Talmadge, who then won the special election for the remaining two years of the term. Talmadge was re-elected in 1950.*
11. *Republican candidate Howard Callaway led in the popular vote, but failed to win a majority because of write-in votes cast for former governor Ellis Arnall, who had lost the Democratic primary to Lester Maddox. The Legislature elected Maddox as governor.*

Eurith D. Rivers (D)	Jan. 12, 1937	Jan. 14, 1941
Eugene Talmadge (D)	Jan. 14, 1941	Jan. 12, 1943
Ellis G. Arnall (D)	Jan. 12, 1943	Jan. 14, 1947
Eugene Talmadge (D)[9]		
Herman E. Talmadge (D)[10]	Jan. 14, 1947	March 18, 1947
Melvin E. Thompson (D)	March 18, 1947	Nov. 17, 1948
Herman E. Talmadge (D)	Nov. 17, 1948	Jan. 11, 1955
S. Marvin Griffin (D)	Jan. 11, 1955	Jan. 13, 1959
S. Ernest Vandiver Jr. (D)	Jan. 13, 1959	Jan. 15, 1963
Carl Edward Sanders (D)	Jan. 15, 1963	Jan. 10, 1967
Lester G. Maddox (D)[11]	Jan. 10, 1967	Jan. 12, 1971
Jimmy Carter (D)	Jan. 12, 1971	Jan. 14, 1975
George Busbee (D)	Jan. 14, 1975	Jan. 11, 1983
Joe Frank Harris (D)	Jan. 11, 1983	

HAWAII

(Became a state Aug. 21, 1959)

Governors	Dates of Service	
William F. Quinn (R)	Aug. 21, 1959	Dec. 3, 1962
John A. Burns (D)	Dec. 3, 1962	Dec. 2, 1974
George R. Ariyoshi (D)	Dec. 2, 1974	

IDAHO

(Became a state July 3, 1890)

Governors	Dates of Service	
George L. Shoup (R)[1]	1890	Dec. 1890
N. B. Willey (R)[2]	Dec. 1890	Jan. 1893
William J. McConnell (R)	Jan. 1893	Jan. 4, 1897
Frank Steunenberg (D)	Jan. 4, 1897	Jan. 7, 1901
Frank W. Hunt (D-FUS)	Jan. 7, 1901	Jan. 5, 1903
John T. Morrison (R)	Jan. 5, 1903	Jan. 2, 1905
Frank R. Gooding (R)	Jan. 2, 1905	Jan. 4, 1909
James H. Brady (R)	Jan. 4, 1909	Jan. 2, 1911
James H. Hawley (D)	Jan. 2, 1911	Jan. 6, 1913
John M. Haines (R)	Jan. 6, 1913	Jan. 4, 1915
Moses Alexander (D)	Jan. 4, 1915	Jan. 6, 1919
David W. Davis (R)	Jan. 6, 1919	Jan. 1, 1923
Charles C. Moore (R)	Jan. 1, 1923	Jan. 3, 1927
H. Clarence Baldridge (R)	Jan. 3, 1927	Jan. 5, 1931
C. Ben Ross (D)	Jan. 5, 1931	Jan. 4, 1937
Barzilla W. Clark (D)	Jan. 4, 1937	Jan. 2, 1939
Clarence A. Bottolfsen (R)	Jan. 2, 1939	Jan. 6, 1941
Chase A. Clark (D)	Jan. 6, 1941	Jan. 4, 1943
Clarence A. Bottolfsen (R)	Jan. 4, 1943	Jan. 1, 1945
Charles C. Gossett (D)[3]	Jan. 1, 1945	Nov. 17, 1945
Arnold Williams (D)[4]	Nov. 17, 1945	Jan. 6, 1947

Charles A. Robins (R)	Jan. 6, 1947	Jan. 1, 1951
Len B. Jordan (R)	Jan. 1, 1951	Jan. 3, 1955
Robert E. Smylie (R)	Jan. 3, 1955	Jan. 2, 1967
Don Samuelson (R)	Jan. 2, 1967	Jan. 4, 1971
Cecil D. Andrus (D)[5]	Jan. 4, 1971	Jan. 24, 1977
John V. Evans (D)[6]	Jan. 24, 1977	

ILLINOIS

(Became a state Dec. 3, 1818)

Governors	Dates of Service	
Shadrach Bond (D-R)	Oct. 6, 1818	Dec. 5, 1822
Edward Coles (D-R)	Dec. 5, 1822	Dec. 6, 1826
Ninian Edwards (NR)	Dec. 6, 1826	Dec. 6, 1830
John Reynolds (NR)[1]	Dec. 6, 1830	Nov. 17, 1834
William L. D. Ewing[2]	Nov. 17, 1834	Dec. 3, 1834
Joseph Duncan (W)	Dec. 3, 1834	Dec. 7, 1838
Thomas Carlin (D)	Dec. 7, 1838	Dec. 8, 1842
Thomas Ford (D)	Dec. 8, 1842	Dec. 9, 1846
Augustus C. French (D)	Dec. 9, 1846	Jan. 10, 1853
Joel A. Matteson (D)	Jan. 10, 1853	Jan. 12, 1857
William H. Bissell (R)[3]	Jan. 12, 1857	March 18, 1860
John Wood (R)[4]	March 21, 1860	Jan. 14, 1861
Richard Yates (R)	Jan. 14, 1861	Jan. 16, 1865
Richard J. Oglesby (R)	Jan. 16, 1865	Jan. 11, 1869
John M. Palmer (R)	Jan. 11, 1869	Jan. 13, 1873
Richard J. Oglesby (R)[5]	Jan. 13, 1873	Jan. 23, 1873
John L. Beveridge (R)[6]	Jan. 23, 1873	Jan. 8, 1877
Shelby M. Cullom (R)[7]	Jan. 8, 1877	Feb. 8, 1883
John M. Hamilton (R)[8]	Feb. 16, 1883	Jan. 30, 1885
Richard J. Oglesby (R)	Jan. 30, 1885	Jan. 14, 1889
Joseph W. Fifer (R)	Jan. 14, 1889	Jan. 10, 1893
John P. Altgeld (D)	Jan. 10, 1893	Jan. 11, 1897
John R. Tanner (R)	Jan. 11, 1897	Jan. 14, 1901
Richard Yates (R)	Jan. 14, 1901	Jan. 9, 1905
Charles S. Deneen (R)	Jan. 9, 1905	Feb. 3, 1913
Edward F. Dunne (D)	Feb. 3, 1913	Jan. 8, 1917
Frank O. Lowden (R)	Jan. 8, 1917	Jan. 10, 1921
Len Small (R)	Jan. 10, 1921	Jan. 14, 1929
Louis L. Emmerson (R)	Jan. 14, 1929	Jan. 9, 1933
Henry Horner (D)[9]	Jan. 9, 1933	Oct. 6, 1940
John H. Stelle (D)[10]	Oct. 6, 1940	Jan. 13, 1941
Dwight H. Green (R)	Jan. 13, 1941	Jan. 10, 1949
Adlai E. Stevenson (D)	Jan. 10, 1949	Jan. 12, 1953
William G. Stratton (R)	Jan. 12, 1953	Jan. 9, 1961
Otto Kerner (D)[11]	Jan. 9, 1961	May 22, 1968
Samuel H. Shapiro (D)[12]	May 22, 1968	Jan. 13, 1969
Richard B. Ogilvie (R)	Jan. 13, 1969	Jan. 8, 1973
Daniel Walker (D)	Jan. 8, 1973	Jan. 10, 1977
James R. Thompson (R)	Jan. 10, 1977	

Idaho

1. *Resigned in December 1890.*
2. *As lieutenant governor, he succeeded to office.*
3. *Resigned Nov. 17, 1945.*
4. *As lieutenant governor, he succeeded to office.*
5. *Resigned Jan. 24, 1977.*
6. *As lieutenant governor, he succeeded to office. Subsequently elected.*

Illinois

1. *Resigned Nov. 17, 1834.*
2. *Ewing was acting lieutenant governor and succeeded to office as governor follow-*
ing Reynolds' resignation.
3. *Died March 18, 1860.*
4. *As lieutenant governor, he succeeded to office.*
5. *Resigned Jan. 23, 1873.*
6. *As lieutenant governor, he succeeded to office.*
7. *Resigned Feb. 8, 1883.*
8. *As lieutenant governor, he succeeded to office.*
9. *Died Oct. 6, 1940.*
10. *As lieutenant governor, he succeeded to office.*
11. *Resigned May 22, 1968.*
12. *As lieutenant governor, he succeeded to office.*

INDIANA

(Became a state Dec. 11, 1816)

Governors	Dates of Service	
Jonathan Jennings (D-R)[1]	Nov. 7, 1816	Sept. 12, 1822
Ratliff Boon (D-R)[2]	Sept. 12, 1822	Dec. 4, 1822
William Hendricks (D-R)[3]	Dec. 5, 1822	Feb. 12, 1825
James B. Ray (CLAY R)[4]	Feb. 12, 1825	Dec. 7, 1831
Noah Noble (NR, W)	Dec. 7, 1831	Dec. 6, 1837
David Wallace (W)	Dec. 6, 1837	Dec. 9, 1840
Samuel Bigger (W)	Dec. 9, 1840	Dec. 6, 1843
James Whitcomb (D)[5]	Dec. 6, 1843	Dec. 27, 1848
Paris C. Dunning (D)[6]	Dec. 27, 1848	Dec. 5, 1849
Joseph A. Wright (D)	Dec. 5, 1849	Jan. 12, 1857
Ashbel P. Willard (D)[7]	Jan. 12, 1857	Oct. 4, 1860
Abraham A. Hammond (D)[8]	Oct. 4, 1860	Jan. 14, 1861
Henry S. Lane (R)[9]	Jan. 14, 1861	Jan. 16, 1861
Oliver P. Morton (R)[10]	Jan. 16, 1861	Jan. 23, 1867
Conrad Baker (R)[11]	Jan. 24, 1867	Jan. 13, 1873
Thomas A. Hendricks (D)	Jan. 13, 1873	Jan. 8, 1877
James D. Williams (D)[12]	Jan. 8, 1877	Nov. 20, 1880
Isaac P. Gray (D)[13]	Nov. 20, 1880	Jan. 10, 1881
Albert G. Porter (R)	Jan. 10, 1881	Jan. 1885
Isaac P. Gray (D)	Jan. 1885	Jan. 1889
Alvin P. Hovey (R)[14]	Jan. 1889	Nov. 21, 1891
Ira Joy Chase (R)[15]	Nov. 21, 1891	Jan. 1893
Claude Matthews (D)	Jan. 1893	Jan. 11, 1897
James A. Mount (R)	Jan. 11, 1897	Jan. 14, 1901
Winfield T. Durbin (R)	Jan. 14, 1901	Jan. 9, 1905
J. Frank Hanly (R)	Jan. 9, 1905	Jan. 11, 1909
Thomas R. Marshall (D)	Jan. 11, 1909	Jan. 13, 1913
Samuel M. Ralston (D)	Jan. 13, 1913	Jan. 8, 1917
James Putnam Goodrich (R)	Jan. 8, 1917	Jan. 10, 1921
Warren T. McCray (R)[16]	Jan. 10, 1921	April 30, 1924
Emmett F. Branch (R)[17]	April 30, 1924	Jan. 12, 1925
Edward Jackson (R)	Jan. 12, 1925	Jan. 14, 1929
Harry G. Leslie (R)	Jan. 14, 1929	Jan. 9, 1933
Paul V. McNutt (D)	Jan. 9, 1933	Jan. 11, 1937
M. Clifford Townsend (D)	Jan. 11, 1937	Jan. 13, 1941
Henry F. Schricker (D)	Jan. 13, 1941	Jan. 8, 1945
Ralph F. Gates (R)	Jan. 8, 1945	Jan. 10, 1949
Henry F. Schricker (D)	Jan. 10, 1949	Jan. 12, 1953
George N. Craig (R)	Jan. 12, 1953	Jan. 14, 1957
Harold W. Handley (R)	Jan. 14, 1957	Jan. 9, 1961
Matthew E. Welsh (D)	Jan. 9, 1961	Jan. 11, 1965
Roger D. Branigin (D)	Jan. 11, 1965	Jan. 13, 1969
Edgar D. Whitcomb (R)	Jan. 13, 1969	Jan. 8, 1973
Otis R. Bowen (R)	Jan. 8, 1973	Jan. 12, 1981
Robert D. Orr (R)	Jan. 12, 1981	

IOWA

(Became a state Dec. 28, 1846)

Governors	Dates of Service	
Ansel Briggs (D)	Dec. 3, 1846	Dec. 4, 1850
Stephen P. Hempstead (D)	Dec. 4, 1850	Dec. 9, 1854
James W. Grimes (R)	Dec. 9, 1854	Jan. 13, 1858
Ralph P. Lowe (R)	Jan. 13, 1858	Jan. 11, 1860
Samuel J. Kirkwood (R)	Jan. 11, 1860	Jan. 14, 1864
William M. Stone (UN R)	Jan. 14, 1864	Jan. 16, 1868
Samuel Merrill (R)	Jan. 16, 1868	Jan. 11, 1872
Cyrus C. Carpenter (R)	Jan. 11, 1872	Jan. 13, 1876
Samuel J. Kirkwood (R)[1]	Jan. 13, 1876	Feb. 1, 1877
Joshua G. Newbold (R)[2]	Feb. 1, 1877	Jan. 17, 1878
John H. Gear (R)	Jan. 17, 1878	Jan. 12, 1882
Buren R. Sherman (R)	Jan. 12, 1882	Jan. 14, 1886
William Larrabee (R)	Jan. 14, 1886	Feb. 26, 1890
Horace Boies (D)	Feb. 27, 1890	Jan. 11, 1894
Frank D. Jackson (R)	Jan. 11, 1894	Jan. 16, 1896
Francis M. Drake (R)	Jan. 16, 1896	Jan. 13, 1898
Leslie M. Shaw (R)	Jan. 13, 1898	Jan. 16, 1902
Albert B. Cummins (R)[3]	Jan. 16, 1902	Nov. 24, 1908
Warren Garst (R)[4]	Nov. 24, 1908	Jan. 14, 1909
Beryl F. Carroll (R)	Jan. 14, 1909	Jan. 16, 1913
George W. Clarke (R)	Jan. 16, 1913	Jan. 11, 1917
William L. Harding (R)	Jan. 11, 1917	Jan. 13, 1921
Nathan E. Kendall (R)	Jan. 13, 1921	Jan. 15, 1925
John Hammill (R)	Jan. 15, 1925	Jan. 15, 1931
Daniel W. Turner (R)	Jan. 15, 1931	Jan. 12, 1933
Clyde L. Herring (D)	Jan. 12, 1933	Jan. 14, 1937
Nelson G. Kraschel (D)	Jan. 14, 1937	Jan. 12, 1939
George A. Wilson (R)	Jan. 12, 1939	Jan. 14, 1943
Bourke B. Hickenlooper (R)	Jan. 14, 1943	Jan. 11, 1945
Robert D. Blue (R)	Jan. 11, 1945	Jan. 13, 1949
William S. Beardsley (R)[5]	Jan. 13, 1949	Nov. 21, 1954
Leo Elthon (R)[6]	Nov. 22, 1954	Jan. 13, 1955
Leo Arthur Hoegh (R)	Jan. 13, 1955	Jan. 17, 1957
Herschel C. Loveless (D)	Jan. 17, 1957	Jan. 12, 1961
Norman A. Erbe (R)	Jan. 12, 1961	Jan. 17, 1963
Harold E. Hughes (D)[7]	Jan. 17, 1963	Jan. 1, 1969

Indiana
1. Resigned Sept. 12, 1822.
2. Acting governor.
3. Resigned Feb. 12, 1825.
4. Acting governor. Subsequently elected.
5. Resigned Dec. 27, 1848.
6. Acting governor.
7. Died Oct. 4, 1860.
8. Acting governor.
9. Resigned Jan. 16, 1861.
10. Acting governor. Subsequently elected. Resigned in 1867.
11. Acting governor. Subsequently elected.
12. Died Nov. 20, 1880.
13. Acting governor.

14. Died Nov. 21, 1891.
15. Acting governor.
16. Resigned April 30, 1924.
17. As lieutenant governor, he succeeded to office.

Iowa
1. Resigned Feb. 1, 1877.
2. As lieutenant governor, he succeeded to office.
3. Resigned Nov. 24, 1908.
4. As lieutenant governor, he succeeded to office.
5. Died Nov. 21, 1954.
6. As lieutenant governor, he succeeded to office.
7. Resigned Jan. 1, 1969
8. As lieutenant governor, he succeeded to office.

Robert D. Fulton (D)[8]	Jan. 1, 1969	Jan. 16, 1969
Robert D. Ray (R)	Jan. 16, 1969	Jan. 14, 1983
Terry E. Branstad (R)	Jan. 14, 1983	

William H. Avery (R)	Jan. 11, 1965	Jan. 9, 1967
Robert B. Docking (D)	Jan. 9, 1967	Jan. 13, 1975
Robert F. Bennett (R)	Jan. 13, 1975	Jan. 8, 1979
John Carlin (D)	Jan. 8, 1979	

KANSAS

(Became a state Jan. 29, 1861)

Governors	Dates of Service	
Charles Robinson (R)	Feb. 9, 1861	Jan. 12, 1863
Thomas Carney (R)	Jan. 12, 1863	Jan. 9, 1865
Samuel J. Crawford (R)[1]	Jan. 9, 1865	Nov. 4, 1868
Nehemiah Green (R)[2]	Nov. 4, 1868	Jan. 11, 1869
James Madison Harvey (R)	Jan. 11, 1869	Jan. 13, 1873
Thomas A. Osborn (R)	Jan. 13, 1873	Jan. 18, 1877
George T. Anthony (R)	Jan. 18, 1877	Jan. 13, 1879
John P. St. John (R)	Jan. 13, 1879	Jan. 8, 1883
George Washington Glick (D)	Jan. 8, 1883	Jan. 13, 1885
John A. Martin (R)	Jan. 13, 1885	Jan. 14, 1889
Lyman U. Humphrey (R)	Jan. 14, 1889	Jan. 9, 1893
Lorenzo D. Lewelling (POP)	Jan. 9, 1893	Jan. 14, 1895
Edmund N. Morrill (R)	Jan. 14, 1895	Jan. 11, 1897
John W. Leedy (D-PP)	Jan. 11, 1897	Jan. 9, 1899
William E. Stanley (R)	Jan. 9, 1899	Jan. 12, 1903
Willis J. Bailey (R)	Jan. 12, 1903	Jan. 9, 1905
Edward W. Hoch (R)	Jan. 9, 1905	Jan. 11, 1909
Walter R. Stubbs (R)	Jan. 11, 1909	Jan. 13, 1913
George H. Hodges (D)	Jan. 13, 1913	Jan. 11, 1915
Arthur Capper (R)	Jan. 11, 1915	Jan. 13, 1919
Henry J. Allen (R)	Jan. 13, 1919	Jan. 8, 1923
Jonathan McM. Davis (D)	Jan. 8, 1923	Jan. 12, 1925
Ben S. Paulen (R)	Jan. 12, 1925	Jan. 14, 1929
Clyde M. Reed (R)	Jan. 14, 1929	Jan. 12, 1931
Harry W. Woodring (D)	Jan. 12, 1931	Jan. 9, 1933
Alfred M. Landon (R)	Jan. 9, 1933	Jan. 11, 1937
Walter A. Huxman (D)	Jan. 11, 1937	Jan. 9, 1939
Payne H. Ratner (R)	Jan. 9, 1939	Jan. 11, 1943
Andrew F. Schoeppel (R)	Jan. 11, 1943	Jan. 13, 1947
Frank Carlson (R)[3]	Jan. 13, 1947	Nov. 28, 1950
Frank L. Hagaman (R)[4]	Nov. 28, 1950	Jan. 8, 1951
Edward F. Arn (R)	Jan. 8, 1951	Jan. 10, 1955
Frederick L. Hall (R)[5]	Jan. 10, 1955	Jan. 3, 1957
John McCuish (R)[6]	Jan. 3, 1957	Jan. 14, 1957
George Docking (D)	Jan. 14, 1957	Jan. 9, 1961
John Anderson Jr. (R)	Jan. 9, 1961	Jan. 11, 1965

KENTUCKY

(Became a state June 1, 1792)

Governors	Dates of Service	
Isaac Shelby (D-R)	June 4, 1792	June 7, 1796
James Garrard (D-R)	June 7, 1796	June 1, 1804
Christopher Greenup (D-R)	June 1, 1804	June 1, 1808
Charles Scott (D-R)	June 1, 1808	June 1, 1812
Isaac Shelby (D-R)	June 1, 1812	June 1, 1816
George Madison (D-R)[1]	June 1, 1816	Oct. 21, 1816
Gabriel Slaughter (D-R)[2]	Oct. 21, 1816	June 1, 1820
John Adair (D-R)	June 1, 1820	June 1, 1824
Joseph Desha (D-R)	June 1, 1824	June 1, 1828
Thomas Metcalfe (NR)	June 1, 1828	June 1, 1832
John Breathitt (D)[3]	June 1, 1832	Feb. 22, 1834
James Morehead (NR)[4]	Feb. 22, 1834	June 1, 1836
James Clark (W)[5]	June 1, 1836	Oct. 5, 1839
Charles A. Wickliffe (W)[6]	Oct. 5, 1839	June 1, 1840
Robert P. Letcher (W)	June 1, 1840	June 1, 1844
William Owsley (W)	June 1, 1844	June 1, 1848
John J. Crittenden (W)[7]	June 1, 1848	July 31, 1850
John L. Helm (W)[8]	July 31, 1850	Sept. 1851
Lazarus W. Powell (D)	Sept. 1851	Sept. 1855
Charles S. Morehead (AM)	Sept. 1855	Sept. 1859
Beriah Magoffin (D)[9]	Sept. 1859	Aug. 18, 1862
James F. Robinson (UN)[10]	Aug. 18, 1862	Sept. 1863
Thomas E. Bramlette (UN)	Sept. 1863	Sept. 1867
John L. Helm (D)[11]	Sept. 1867	Sept. 13, 1867
John W. Stevenson (D)[12]	Sept. 13, 1867	March 4, 1871
Preston H. Leslie (D)[13]	March 4, 1871	Sept. 1875
James B. McCreary (D)	Sept. 1875	Sept. 1879
Luke P. Blackburn (D)	Sept. 1879	Sept. 1883
J. Procter Knott (D)	Sept. 1883	Sept. 1887
Simon B. Buckner (D)	Sept. 1887	Sept. 1891
John Y. Brown (D)	Sept. 1891	Dec. 1895
William O. Bradley (R)	Dec. 1895	Dec. 12, 1899
William S. Taylor (R)[14]	Dec. 12, 1899	Jan. 31, 1900
William Goebel (D)[15]	Jan. 31, 1900	Feb. 3, 1900
John C. W. Beckham (D)[16]	Feb. 3, 1900	Dec. 10, 1907

Kansas

1. Resigned Nov. 4, 1868.
2. Succeeded to office.
3. Resigned Nov. 28, 1950.
4. As lieutenant governor, he succeeded to office.
5. Resigned Jan. 3, 1957.
6. As lieutenant governor, he succeeded to office.

Kentucky

1. Died Oct. 21, 1816.
2. As lieutenant governor, he succeeded to office.
3. Died Feb. 22, 1834.
4. As lieutenant governor, he succeeded to office.
5. Died Oct. 5, 1839.
6. As lieutenant governor, he succeeded to office.
7. Resigned July 31, 1850.
8. As lieutenant governor, he succeeded to office.

9. Resigned Aug. 18, 1862.
10. As president of the state Senate, he succeeded to office.
11. Died Sept. 13, 1867.
12. As lieutenant governor, he succeeded to office. Subsequently elected. Resigned March 4, 1871.
13. As president of the state Senate, he succeeded to office. Subsequently elected.
14. Taylor was removed by the Legislature following an election challenge by his Democratic opponent, William Goebel.
15. Successfully challenged the election of William S. Taylor. Died Feb. 3, 1900.
16. As lieutenant governor, he succeeded to office. Subsequently elected.
17. Resigned May 19, 1919.
18. As lieutenant governor, he succeeded to office.
19. Resigned Oct. 9, 1939.
20. As lieutenant governor, he succeeded to office. Subsequently elected.
21. Resigned Nov. 27, 1950.
22. As lieutenant governor, he succeeded to office. Subsequently elected.
23. Resigned Dec. 28, 1974.
24. As lieutenant governor, he succeeded to office.

August E. Willson (R)	Dec. 10, 1907	Dec. 12, 1911
James B. McCreary (D)	Dec. 12, 1911	Dec. 7, 1915
Augustus O. Stanley (D)[17]	Dec. 7, 1915	May 19, 1919
James D. Black (D)[18]	May 19, 1919	Dec. 9, 1919
Edwin P. Morrow (R)	Dec. 9, 1919	Dec. 11, 1923
William J. Fields (D)	Dec. 11, 1923	Dec. 13, 1927
Flem D. Sampson (R)	Dec. 13, 1927	Dec. 8, 1931
Ruby Lafoon (D)	Dec. 8, 1931	Dec. 10, 1935
Albert B. (Happy) Chandler (D)[19]	Dec. 10, 1935	Oct. 9, 1939
Keen Johnson (D)[20]	Oct. 9, 1939	Dec. 7, 1943
Simeon S. Willis (R)	Dec. 7, 1943	Dec. 9, 1947
Earle C. Clements (D)[21]	Dec. 9, 1947	Nov. 27, 1950
Lawrence W. Wetherby (D)[22]	Nov. 27, 1950	Dec. 13, 1955
Albert B. (Happy) Chandler (D)	Dec. 13, 1955	Dec. 9, 1959
Bert T. Combs (D)	Dec. 9, 1959	Dec. 10, 1963
Edward T. Breathitt (D)	Dec. 10, 1963	Dec. 12, 1967
Louie B. Nunn (R)	Dec. 12, 1967	Dec. 7, 1971
Wendell H. Ford (D)[23]	Dec. 7, 1971	Dec. 28, 1974
Julian Carroll (D)[24]	Dec. 28, 1974	Dec. 11, 1979
John Y. Brown Jr. (D)	Dec. 11, 1979	Dec. 13, 1983
Martha Layne Collins (D)	Dec. 13, 1983	

LOUISIANA

(Became a state April 30, 1812)

Governors	Dates of Service	
William C. C. Claiborne	July 30, 1812	Dec. 16, 1816
Jacques Philippe Villere	Dec. 17, 1816	Dec. 17, 1820
Thomas B. Robertson[1]	Dec. 18, 1820	Nov. 15, 1824
Henry S. Thibodeaux[2]	Nov. 15, 1824	Dec. 13, 1824
Henry S. Johnson (AM FAC)	Dec. 13, 1824	Dec. 15, 1828
Pierre Derbigny (NR)[3]	Dec. 15, 1828	Oct. 6, 1829
Armand Beauvais[4]	Oct. 6, 1829	Jan. 14, 1830
Jacques Dupre	Jan. 14, 1830	Jan. 31, 1831
Andre B. Roman (NR)	Jan. 31, 1831	Feb. 4, 1835
Edward E. White (W)	Feb. 4, 1835	Feb. 4, 1839
Andre B. Roman (W)	Feb. 4, 1839	Jan. 30, 1843
Alexander Mouton (D)	Jan. 30, 1843	Feb. 11, 1846

Isaac Johnson (D)	Feb. 12, 1846	Jan. 27, 1850
Joseph M. Walker (D)	Jan. 28, 1850	Jan. 17, 1853
Paul O. Hebert (D)	Jan. 18, 1853	Jan. 21, 1856
Robert C. Wickliffe (D)	Jan. 22, 1856	Jan. 22, 1860
Thomas O. Moore (D)	Jan. 23, 1860	Jan. 25, 1864
George F. Shepley[5]	July 2, 1862	March 4, 1864
Henry W. Allen[6]	Jan. 25, 1864	June 2, 1865
Michael Hahn[7]	March 4, 1864	March 4, 1865
James M. Wells (D)[8]	March 4, 1865	June 3, 1867
Benjamin F. Flanders[9]	June 3, 1867	Jan. 8, 1868
Joshua Baker[10]	Jan. 8, 1868	June 27, 1868
Henry C. Warmoth (R)	June 27, 1868	Dec. 9, 1872
Pinckney B. S. Pinchback[11]	Dec. 9, 1872	Jan. 13, 1873
William P. Kellogg (R)[12]	Jan. 13, 1873	Jan. 5, 1877
Francis T. Nicholls (D)[13]	Jan. 8, 1877	Jan. 13, 1880
Louis A. Wiltz (D)[14]	Jan. 14, 1880	Oct. 16, 1881
Samuel D. McEnery (D)[15]	Oct. 16, 1881	May 20, 1888
Francis T. Nicholls (D)	May 21, 1888	May 10, 1892
Murphy J. Foster (A-LOT D, D)	May 10, 1892	May 8, 1900
William W. Heard (D)	May 8, 1900	May 10, 1904
Newton C. Blanchard (D)	May 10, 1904	May 12, 1908
Jared Y. Sanders (D)	May 12, 1908	May 14, 1912
Luther E. Hall (D)	May 14, 1912	May 9, 1916
Ruffin G. Pleasant (D)	May 9, 1916	May 11, 1920
John M Parker (D)	May 11, 1920	May 13, 1924
Henry L. Fuqua (D)[16]	May 13, 1924	Oct. 11, 1926
Oramel H. Simpson(D)[17]	Oct. 11, 1926	May 21, 1928
Huey P. Long Jr. (D)[18]	May 21, 1928	Jan. 25, 1932
Alvin O. King (D)[19]	Jan. 25, 1932	May 10, 1932
Oscar K. Allen (D)[20]	May 10, 1932	Jan. 28, 1936
James A. Noe (D)[21]	Jan. 28, 1936	May 12, 1936
Richard W. Leche (D)[22]	May 12, 1936	June 26, 1939
Earl K. Long (D)[23]	June 26, 1939	May 14, 1940
Sam H. Jones (D)	May 14, 1940	May 9, 1944
James H. Davis (D)	May 9, 1944	May 11, 1948
Earl K. Long (D)	May 11, 1948	May 13, 1952
Robert F. Kennon (D)	May 13, 1952	May 8, 1956
Earl K. Long (D)	May 8, 1956	May 10, 1960
James H. Davis (D)	May 10, 1960	May 12, 1964
John J. McKeithen (D)	May 12, 1964	May 9, 1972
Edwin W. Edwards (D)	May 9, 1972	March 10, 1980
David C. Treen (R)	March 10, 1980	March 12, 1984
Edwin W. Edwards (D)	March 12, 1984	

Louisiana

1. Resigned Nov. 15, 1824.
2. As president of the state Senate, he succeeded to office.
3. Died Oct. 1, 1829.
4. As president of the state Senate, he succeeded to office.
5. Military governor within Union lines.
6. Last elected Confederate governor.
7. Elected within Union lines. Resigned March 4, 1865.
8. As lieutenant governor, he succeeded to office. Subsequently elected. Removed June 3, 1867.
9. Under military authority.
10. Under military authority.
11. Acting governor.
12. The 1872 gubernatorial election in Louisiana set off a bitter dispute between Republicans backing Kellogg and Democrats supporting his opponent, John McEnery. Each side organized its own boards to canvass the vote, resulting in two separate sets of election returns, one showing Kellogg the winner, the other McEnery. To add to the confusion, two rival legislatures assumed office, each claiming legitimacy, and Kellogg and McEnery were both inaugurated as governor by their respective factions. President Ulysses S. Grant (R) finally stepped in and recognized Kellogg as the legitimate governor on May 22, 1873.

13. The 1876 election set off a dispute similar to that of 1872. Nicholls, the Democrat, and Packard, the Republican, each had election returns showing him the winner. There were also two legislatures, each controlled by a different party. Nicholls set up a de facto state government and was recognized by federal authorities.

14. Died in October 1881.
15. As lieutenant governor, he succeeded to office. Subsequently elected.
16. Died Oct. 11, 1926.
17. As lieutenant governor, he succeeded to office.
18. Resigned Jan. 25, 1932.
19. As lieutenant governor, he succeeded to office.
20. Died Jan. 28, 1936.
21. As lieutenant governor, he succeeded to office.
22. Resigned June 26, 1939.
23. As lieutenant governor, he succeeded to office.

MAINE

(Became a state March 15, 1820)

Governors	Dates of Service	
William King (D-R)[1]	May 31, 1820	May 28, 1821
William D. Williamson (D-R)[2]	May 29, 1821	Dec. 25, 1821
Benjamin Ames (D-R)[3]	Dec. 25, 1821	Jan. 2, 1821
Daniel Rose (D-R)[4]	Jan. 2, 1822	Jan. 4, 1822
Albion K. Parris (D-R)	Jan. 5, 1822	Jan. 3, 1827
Enoch Lincoln (D-R)[5]	Jan. 3, 1827	Oct. 8, 1829
Nathan Cutler (D)[6]	Oct. 12, 1829	Feb. 5, 1830
Joshua Hall (D)[7]	Feb. 5, 1830	Feb. 10, 1830
Jonathan G. Hunton (NR)	Feb. 10, 1830	Jan. 5, 1831
Samuel E. Smith (JAC D)	Jan. 5, 1831	Jan. 1, 1834
Robert P. Dunlap (D)	Jan. 1, 1834	Jan. 3, 1838
Edward Kent (W)	Jan. 3, 1838	Jan. 2, 1839
John Fairfield (D)	Jan. 2, 1839	Jan. 6, 1841
Richard H. Vose[8]	Jan. 12, 1841	Jan. 13, 1841
Edward Kent (W)	Jan. 13, 1841	Jan. 5, 1842
John Fairfield (D)[9]	Jan. 5, 1842	March 7, 1843
Edward Kavanagh (D)[10]	March 7, 1843	Jan. 1, 1844
David Dunn (D)	Jan. 2, 1844	Jan. 3, 1844
John W. Dana (D)	Jan. 3, 1844	Jan. 5, 1844
Hugh J. Anderson (D)	Jan. 5, 1844	May 12, 1847
John W. Dana (D)	May 13, 1847	May 8, 1850
John Hubbard (D)	May 9, 1850	Jan. 5, 1853
William G. Crosby (W)	Jan. 5, 1853	Jan. 3, 1855
Anson P. Morrill (R)	Jan. 3, 1855	Jan. 2, 1856
Samuel Wells (D)	Jan. 2, 1856	Jan. 8, 1857
Hannibal Hamlin (R)[11]	Jan. 8, 1857	Feb. 25, 1857
Joseph H. Williams (R)[12]	Feb. 26, 1857	Jan. 8, 1858
Lot M. Morrill (R)	Jan. 8, 1858	Jan. 2, 1861
Israel Washburn Jr. (R)	Jan. 2, 1861	Jan. 7, 1863
Abner Coburn (R)	Jan. 7, 1863	Jan. 6, 1864
Samuel Cony (UN R)	Jan. 6, 1864	Jan. 2, 1867
Joshua L. Chamberlain (R)	Jan. 2, 1867	Jan. 4, 1871
Sidney Perham (R)	Jan. 4, 1871	Jan. 7, 1874
Nelson Dingley Jr. (R)	Jan. 7, 1874	Jan. 5, 1876
Selden Connor (R)	Jan. 5, 1876	Jan. 8, 1879
Alonzo Garcelon (D)	Jan. 8, 1879	Jan. 1880
Daniel F. Davis (R)	Jan. 17, 1880	Jan. 1881
Harris M. Plaisted (D)	Jan. 13, 1881	Jan. 3, 1883
Frederick Robie (R)	Jan. 3, 1883	Jan. 5, 1887
Joseph R. Bodwell (R)[13]	Jan. 5, 1887	Dec. 15, 1887
Sebastian S. Marble (R)[14]	Dec. 16, 1887	Jan. 2, 1889
Edwin C. Burleigh (R)	Jan. 2, 1889	Jan. 4, 1893

Henry B. Cleaves (R)	Jan. 4, 1893	Jan. 6, 1897
Llewellyn Powers (R)	Jan. 6, 1897	Jan. 2, 1901
John F. Hill (R)	Jan. 2, 1901	Jan. 4, 1905
William T. Cobb (R)	Jan. 4, 1905	Jan. 6, 1909
Bert M. Fernald (R)	Jan. 6, 1909	Jan. 4, 1911
Frederick W. Plaisted (D)	Jan. 4, 1911	Jan. 1, 1913
William T. Haines (R)	Jan. 1, 1913	Jan. 6, 1915
Oakley C. Curtis (D)	Jan. 6, 1915	Jan. 3, 1917
Carl E. Milliken (R)	Jan. 3, 1917	Jan. 5, 1921
Frederic H. Parkhurst (R)[15]	Jan. 5, 1921	Jan. 31, 1921
Percival P. Baxter (R)[16]	Jan. 31, 1921	Jan. 8, 1925
Ralph O. Brewster (R)	Jan. 8, 1925	Jan. 2, 1929
William T. Gardiner (R)	Jan. 2, 1929	Jan. 4, 1933
Louis J. Brann (D)	Jan. 4, 1933	Jan. 6, 1937
Lewis O. Barrows (R)	Jan. 6, 1937	Jan. 1, 1941
Sumner Sewall (R)	Jan. 1, 1941	Jan. 3, 1945
Horace A. Hildreth (R)	Jan. 3, 1945	Jan. 5, 1949
Frederick G. Payne (R)[17]	Jan. 5, 1949	Dec. 25, 1952
Burton M. Cross (R)[18]	Dec. 26, 1952	Jan. 5, 1955
Edmund S. Muskie (D)[19]	Jan. 5, 1955	Jan. 3, 1959
Robert N. Haskell (R)[20]	Jan. 3, 1959	Jan. 8, 1959
Clinton A. Clauson (D)[21]	Jan. 8, 1959	Dec. 30, 1959
John H. Reed (R)[22]	Dec. 30, 1959	Jan. 5, 1967
Kenneth M. Curtis (D)	Jan. 5, 1967	Jan. 1, 1975
James B. Longley (I)	Jan. 2, 1975	Jan. 3, 1979
Joseph E. Brennan (D)	Jan. 3, 1979	

MARYLAND

(Ratified the Constitution April 28, 1788)

Governors	Dates of Service	
John Eager Howard (FED)	Nov. 24, 1788	Nov. 14, 1791
George Plater (FED)[1]	Nov. 14, 1791	Feb. 10, 1792
James Brice (FED)[2]	Feb. 13, 1792	April 5, 1792
Thomas Sim Lee (FED)	April 5, 1792	Nov. 14, 1794
John H. Stone (FED)	Nov. 14, 1794	Nov. 17, 1797
John Henry (FED)	Nov. 17, 1797	Nov. 14, 1798
Benjamin Ogle (FED)	Nov. 14, 1798	Nov. 10, 1801
John Francis Mercer (D-R)	Nov. 10, 1801	Nov. 15, 1803
Robert Bowie (D-R)	Nov. 15, 1803	Nov. 10, 1806
Robert Wright (D-R)[3]	Nov. 12, 1806	May 6, 1809
James Butcher (D-R)[4]	May 6, 1809	June 9, 1809
Edward Lloyd (D-R)	June 9, 1809	Nov. 16, 1811
Robert Bowie (D-R)	Nov. 16, 1811	Nov. 25, 1812

Maine

1. *Resigned May 28, 1821.*
2. *Acting governor. Resigned Dec. 25, 1821.*
3. *Acting governor.*
4. *Acting governor.*
5. *Died Oct. 8, 1829.*
6. *Acting governor.*
7. *Acting governor.*
8. *As president of the state Senate, acted as governor while an inconclusive popular election result was being resolved in the Legislature.*
9. *Resigned March 7, 1843.*
10. *Acting governor.*
11. *Resigned Feb. 25, 1857.*
12. *Acting governor.*
13. *Died Dec. 15, 1887.*
14. *Acting governor.*
15. *Died Jan. 31, 1921.*
16. *As president of the state Senate, he succeeded to office. Subsequently elected.*
17. *Resigned Dec. 25, 1952.*
18. *As president of the state Senate, he succeeded to office. Had previously been elected for a two-year term beginning January 1953.*
19. *Resigned Jan. 3, 1959.*
20. *As president of the state Senate, he succeeded to office.*

21. *Died Dec. 30, 1959.*
22. *As president of the state Senate, he succeeded to office. Subsequently elected in a special election for the remainder of Clauson's term. Re-elected in 1962.*

Maryland

1. *Died Feb. 10, 1792.*
2. *Acting governor.*
3. *Resigned May 6, 1809.*
4. *Acting governor.*
5. *Died July 11, 1831.*
6. *Acting governor. Subsequently elected by the Legislature.*
7. *Resigned March 4, 1874.*
8. *Acting governor. Subsequently elected by the Legislature.*
9. *Resigned March 27, 1885.*
10. *Acting governor. Subsequently elected by the Legislature.*
11. *Resigned Jan. 3, 1947.*
12. *Elected by the Legislature to complete the remaining five days of O'Conor's term. Had previously been elected for a four-year term beginning January 8, 1947.*
13. *Resigned Jan. 7, 1969.*
14. *Elected by the Legislature to complete Agnew's term. Subsequently re-elected in 1970 and 1974. Suspended from office Oct. 7, 1977 — Jan. 15, 1979.*
15. *As lieutenant governor, served as acting governor.*

Levin Winder (FED)	Nov. 25, 1812	Jan. 2, 1816
Charles Ridgely (FED)	Jan. 2, 1816	Jan. 8, 1819
Charles Goldsborough (FED)	Jan. 8, 1819	Dec. 20, 1819
Samuel Sprigg (D-R)	Dec. 20, 1819	Dec. 16, 1822
Samuel Stevens Jr. (D-R)	Dec. 16, 1822	Jan. 9, 1826
Joseph Kent (D-R)	Jan. 9, 1826	Jan. 15, 1829
Daniel Martin (A-JAC D)	Jan. 15, 1829	Jan. 15, 1830
Thomas King Carroll (D)	Jan. 15, 1830	Jan. 13, 1831
Daniel Martin (A-JAC D)[5]	Jan. 13, 1831	July 11, 1831
George Howard (A-JAC D)[6]	July 11, 1831	Jan. 17, 1833
James Thomas (A-JAC D)	Jan. 17, 1833	Jan. 14, 1836
Thomas W. Veazey (W)	Jan. 14, 1836	Jan. 7, 1839
William Grason (D)	Jan. 7, 1839	Jan. 3, 1842
Francis Thomas (D)	Jan. 3, 1842	Jan. 6, 1845
Thomas G. Pratt (W)	Jan. 6, 1845	Jan. 3, 1848
Philip Francis Thomas (D)	Jan. 3, 1848	Jan. 6, 1851
Enoch L. Lowe (D)	Jan. 6, 1851	Jan. 11, 1854
Thomas W. Ligon (D)	Jan. 11, 1854	Jan. 13, 1858
Thomas H. Hicks (AM)	Jan. 13, 1858	Jan. 8, 1862
Augustus W. Bradford (UN R)	Jan. 8, 1862	Jan. 10, 1866
Thomas Swann (UN R)	Jan. 10, 1866	Jan. 13, 1869
Oden Bowie (D)	Jan. 13, 1869	Jan. 10, 1872
William P. Whyte (D)[7]	Jan. 10, 1872	March 4, 1874
James B. Groome (D)[8]	March 4, 1874	Jan. 12, 1876
John Lee Carroll (D)	Jan. 12, 1876	Jan. 14, 1880
William T. Hamilton (D)	Jan. 14, 1880	Jan. 9, 1884
Robert M. McLane (D)[9]	Jan. 9, 1884	March 27, 1885
Henry Lloyd (D)[10]	March 27, 1885	Jan. 11, 1888
Elihu E. Jackson (D)	Jan. 11, 1888	Jan. 13, 1892
Frank Brown (D)	Jan. 13, 1892	Jan. 8, 1896
Lloyd Lowndes (R)	Jan. 8, 1896	Jan. 10, 1900
John W. Smith (D)	Jan. 10, 1900	Jan. 13, 1904
Edwin Warfield (D)	Jan. 1, 1904	Jan. 8, 1908
Austin L. Crothers (D)	Jan. 8, 1908	Jan. 10, 1912
Phillips L. Goldsborough (R)	Jan. 10, 1912	Jan. 12, 1916
Emerson C. Harrington (D)	Jan. 12, 1916	Jan. 14, 1920
Albert C. Ritchie (D)	Jan. 14, 1920	Jan. 9, 1935
Harry W. Nice (R)	Jan. 9, 1935	Jan. 11, 1939
Herbert R. O'Conor (D)[11]	Jan. 11, 1939	Jan. 3, 1947
William P. Lane Jr. (D)[12]	Jan. 3, 1947	Jan. 10, 1951
Theodore R. McKeldin (R)	Jan. 10, 1951	Jan. 14, 1959
J. Millard Tawes (D)	Jan. 14, 1959	Jan. 25, 1967
Spiro T. Agnew (R)[13]	Jan. 25, 1967	Jan. 7, 1969
Marvin Mandel (D)[14]	Jan. 7, 1969	Jan. 15, 1979
Blair Lee (D)[15]	Oct. 7, 1977	Jan. 15, 1979
Harry Hughes (D)	Jan. 17, 1979	

MASSACHUSETTS

(Ratified the Constitution Feb. 6, 1788)

Governors	Dates of Service	
John Hancock	May 30, 1787	Oct. 8, 1793
Samuel Adams	Oct. 8, 1793	June 2, 1797
Increase Sumner (FED)	June 2, 1797	June 7, 1799
Moses Gill (FED)[1]	June 7, 1799	May 20, 1800

Caleb Strong (FED)	May 30, 1800	May 29, 1807
James Sullivan (D-R)	May 29, 1807	Dec. 10, 1808
Levi Lincoln (D-R)[2]	Dec. 10, 1808	May 1, 1809
Christopher Gore (FED)	May 1809	June 1810
Elbridge Gerry (D-R)	June 1810	June 1812
Caleb Strong (FED)	June 1812	May 30, 1816
John Brooks (FED)	May 30, 1816	May 31, 1823
William Eustis (D-R)	May 31, 1823	Feb. 6, 1825
Marcus Morton (D-R)[3]	Feb. 6, 1825	May 26, 1825
Levi Lincoln (AR, NR)[4]	May 26, 1825	Jan. 9, 1834
John Davis (NR, W)	Jan. 9, 1834	March 1, 1835
Samuel T. Armstrong (W)[5]	March 1, 1835	Jan. 13, 1836
Edward Everett (W)	Jan. 13, 1836	Jan. 18, 1840
Marcus Morton (D)	Jan. 18, 1840	Jan. 7, 1841
John Davis (W)	Jan. 7, 1841	Jan. 17, 1843
Marcus Morton (D)	Jan. 17, 1843	Jan. 1844
George N. Briggs (W)	Jan. 1844	Jan. 11, 1851
George S. Boutwell (D)	Jan. 11, 1851	Jan. 14, 1853
John H. Clifford (W)	Jan. 14, 1853	Jan. 12, 1854
Emory Washburn (W)	Jan. 12, 1854	Jan. 4, 1855
Henry J. Gardner (AM)	Jan. 4, 1855	Jan. 7, 1858
Nathaniel P. Banks (R)	Jan. 7, 1858	Jan. 3, 1861
John A. Andrew (R)	Jan. 3, 1861	Jan. 4, 1866
Alexander H. Bullock (UN)	Jan. 4, 1866	Jan. 7, 1869
William Claflin (R)	Jan. 7, 1869	Jan. 4, 1872
William B. Washburn (R)[6]	Jan. 4, 1872	April 29, 1874
Thomas Talbot (R)[7]	April 29, 1874	Jan. 7, 1875
William Gaston (D)	Jan. 7, 1875	Jan. 6, 1876
Alexander H. Rice (R)	Jan. 6, 1876	Jan. 2, 1879
Thomas Talbot (R)	Jan. 2, 1879	Jan. 8, 1880
John Davis Long (R)	Jan. 8, 1880	Jan. 4, 1883
Benjamin F. Butler (D)	Jan. 4, 1883	Jan. 3, 1884
George D. Robinson (R)	Jan. 3, 1884	Jan. 6, 1887
Oliver Ames (R)	Jan. 6, 1887	Jan. 7, 1890
John Q. A. Brackett (R)	Jan. 7, 1890	Jan. 8, 1891
William E. Russell (D)	Jan. 8, 1891	Jan. 4, 1894
Frederic T. Greenhalge (R)[8]	Jan. 4, 1894	March 5, 1896
Roger Wolcott (R)[9]	March 5, 1896	Jan. 4, 1900
Winthrop M. Crane (R)	Jan. 4, 1900	Jan. 8, 1903
John L. Bates (R)	Jan. 8, 1903	Jan. 5, 1905
William L. Douglas (D)	Jan. 5, 1905	Jan. 4, 1906
Curtis Guild Jr. (R)	Jan. 4, 1906	Jan. 7, 1909
Eban Sumner Draper (R)	Jan. 7, 1909	Jan. 5, 1911
Eugene N. Foss (D)	Jan. 5, 1911	Jan. 8, 1914
David I. Walsh (D)	Jan. 8, 1914	Jan. 6, 1916
Samuel W. McCall (R)	Jan. 6, 1916	Jan. 2, 1919
Calvin Coolidge (R)	Jan. 2, 1919	Jan. 6, 1921
Channing H. Cox (R)	Jan. 6, 1921	Jan. 8, 1925
Alvan T. Fuller (R)	Jan. 8, 1925	Jan. 3, 1929
Frank G. Allen (R)	Jan. 3, 1929	Jan. 8, 1931
Joseph B. Ely (D)	Jan. 8, 1931	Jan. 3, 1935
James M. Curley (D)	Jan. 3, 1935	Jan. 7, 1937
Charles F. Hurley (D)	Jan. 7, 1937	Jan. 5, 1939
Leverett Saltonstall (R)	Jan. 5, 1939	Jan. 3, 1945
Maurice J. Tobin (D)	Jan. 3, 1945	Jan. 2, 1947
Robert F. Bradford (R)	Jan. 2, 1947	Jan. 6, 1949
Paul A. Dever (D)	Jan. 6, 1949	Jan. 8, 1953
Christian A. Herter (R)	Jan. 8, 1953	Jan. 3, 1957

Massachusetts

1. Acting governor.
2. Acting governor.
3. Acting governor.
4. ICPSR data shows that there were two elections for governor in Massachusetts in 1831 and returns for both have been provided. The winner both times was incumbent Levi Lincoln. An explanation was obtained from Albert Bushnell Hart's Commonwealth of Massachusetts, vol. 4 (New York: States History Company, 1930), p. 82. Massachusetts had a one-year term for its governors during this period. Apparently the state decided in 1831 to move its gubernatorial election from April to November to coincide with presiden-

tial elections in 1832 and succeeding years. As a consequence, Lincoln was required to run twice within the same year to make the adjustment.
5. Acting governor.
6. Resigned May 1, 1874.
7. Acting governor.
8. Died March 5, 1896.
9. As lieutenant governor, he succeeded to office. Subsequently elected.
10. Resigned Jan. 22, 1969.
11. As lieutenant governor, he succeeded to office. Subsequently elected.

Foster J. Furcolo (D)	Jan. 3, 1957	Jan. 5, 1961
John A. Volpe (R)	Jan. 5, 1961	Jan. 3, 1963
Endicott Peabody (D)	Jan. 3, 1963	Jan. 7, 1965
John A. Volpe (R)[10]	Jan. 7, 1965	Jan. 22, 1969
Francis W. Sargent (R)[11]	Jan. 22, 1969	Jan. 2, 1975
Michael S. Dukakis (D)	Jan. 2, 1975	Jan. 4, 1979
Edward J. King (D)	Jan. 4, 1979	Jan. 6, 1983
Michael S. Dukakis (D)	Jan. 6, 1983	

Luren D. Dickinson (R)[9]	March 16, 1939	Jan. 1, 1941
Murray D. Van Wagoner (D)	Jan. 1, 1941	Jan. 1, 1943
Harry F. Kelly (R)	Jan. 1, 1943	Jan. 1, 1947
Kim Sigler (R)	Jan. 1, 1947	Jan. 1, 1949
G. Mennen Williams (D)	Jan. 1, 1949	Jan. 1, 1961
John B. Swainson (D)	Jan. 1, 1961	Jan. 1, 1963
George W. Romney (R)[10]	Jan. 1, 1963	Jan. 22, 1969
William G. Milliken (R)[11]	Jan. 22, 1969	Jan. 1, 1983
James J. Blanchard (D)	Jan. 1, 1983	

MICHIGAN

(Became a state Jan. 26, 1837)

Governors	Dates of Service	
Stevens T. Mason (D)	Nov. 3, 1835	Jan. 7, 1840
Edward Mundy (D)[1]	April 3, 1838	June 12, 1838
William Woodbridge (W)[2]	Jan. 7, 1840	Feb. 23, 1841
James W. Gordon (W)[3]	Feb. 23, 1841	Jan. 3, 1842
John S. Barry (D)	Jan. 3, 1842	Jan. 5, 1846
Alpheus Felch (D)[4]	Jan. 5, 1846	March 3, 1847
William L. Greenly (D)[5]	March 3, 1847	Jan. 3, 1848
Epaphroditus Ransom (D)	Jan. 3, 1848	Jan. 7, 1850
John S. Barry (D)	Jan. 7, 1850	Jan. 1, 1851
Robert McClelland (D)[6]	Jan. 1, 1851	March 7, 1853
Andrew Parsons (D)[7]	March 7, 1853	Jan. 3, 1855
Kinsley S. Bingham (R)	Jan. 3, 1855	Jan. 5, 1859
Moses Wisner (R)	Jan. 5, 1859	Jan. 2, 1861
Austin Blair (R)	Jan. 2, 1861	Jan. 4, 1865
Henry H. Crapo (UN R)	Jan. 4, 1865	Jan. 6, 1869
Henry P. Baldwin (R)	Jan. 6, 1869	Jan. 1, 1873
John J. Bagley (R)	Jan. 1, 1873	Jan. 3, 1877
Charles M. Croswell (R)	Jan. 3, 1877	Jan. 1, 1881
David H. Jerome (R)	Jan. 1, 1881	Jan. 1, 1883
Josiah W. Begole (D)	Jan. 1, 1883	Jan. 1, 1885
Russell A. Alger (R)	Jan. 1, 1885	Jan. 1, 1887
Cyrus G. Luce (R)	Jan. 1, 1887	Jan. 1, 1891
Edward B. Winans (D)	Jan. 1, 1891	Jan. 1, 1893
John T. Rich (R)	Jan. 1, 1893	Jan. 1, 1897
Hazen S. Pingree (R)	Jan. 1, 1897	Jan. 1, 1901
Aaron T. Bliss (R)	Jan. 1, 1901	Jan. 1, 1905
Fred M. Warner (R)	Jan. 1, 1905	Jan. 1, 1911
Chase S. Osborn (R)	Jan. 1, 1911	Jan. 1, 1913
Woodbridge N. Ferris (D)	Jan. 1, 1913	Jan. 1, 1917
Albert E. Sleeper (R)	Jan. 1, 1917	Jan. 1, 1921
Alexander J. Groesbeck (R)	Jan. 1, 1921	Jan. 1, 1927
Fred W. Green (R)	Jan. 1, 1927	Jan. 1, 1931
Wilber M. Brucker (R)	Jan. 1, 1931	Jan. 1, 1933
William A. Comstock (D)	Jan. 1, 1933	Jan. 1, 1935
Frank D. Fitzgerald (R)	Jan. 1, 1935	Jan. 1, 1937
Frank Murphy (D)	Jan. 1, 1937	Jan. 1, 1939
Frank D. Fitzgerald (R)[8]	Jan. 1, 1939	March 16, 1939

MINNESOTA

(Became a state May 11, 1858)

Governors	Dates of Service	
Henry H. Sibley (D)	May 24, 1858	Jan. 2, 1860
Alexander Ramsey (R)[1]	Jan. 2, 1860	July 10, 1863
Henry A. Swift (R)[2]	July 10, 1863	Jan. 11, 1864
Stephen Miller (UN)	Jan. 11, 1864	Jan. 8, 1866
William R. Marshall (R)	Jan. 8, 1866	Jan. 9, 1870
Horace Austin (R)	Jan. 9, 1870	Jan. 7, 1874
Cushman K. Davis (R)	Jan. 7, 1874	Jan. 7, 1876
John S. Pillsbury (R)	Jan. 7, 1876	Jan. 10, 1882
Lucius F. Hubbard (R)	Jan. 10, 1882	Jan. 5, 1887
Andrew R. McGill (R)	Jan. 5, 1887	Jan. 9, 1889
William R. Merriam (R)	Jan. 9, 1889	Jan. 4, 1893
Knute Nelson (R)	Jan. 4, 1893	Jan. 31, 1895
David M. Clough (R)	Jan. 31, 1895	Jan. 2, 1899
John Lind (D & POP)	Jan. 2, 1899	Jan. 7, 1901
Samuel R. Van Sant (R)	Jan. 7, 1901	Jan. 4, 1905
John A. Johnson (D)[3]	Jan. 4, 1905	Sept. 21, 1909
Adolph O. Eberhart (R)[4]	Sept. 21, 1909	Jan. 5, 1915
Winfield S. Hammond (D)[5]	Jan. 5, 1915	Dec. 30, 1915
Joseph A. A. Burnquist (R)[6]	Dec. 30, 1915	Jan. 5, 1921
Jacob A. O. Preus (R)	Jan. 5, 1921	Jan. 6, 1925
Theodore Christianson (R)	Jan. 6, 1925	Jan. 6, 1931
Floyd B. Olson (F-LAB)[7]	Jan. 6, 1931	Aug. 22, 1936
Hjalmar Petersen (F-LAB)[8]	Aug. 22, 1936	Jan. 4, 1937
Elmer A. Benson (F-LAB)	Jan. 4, 1937	Jan. 2, 1939
Harold E. Stassen (R)[9]	Jan. 2, 1939	April 27, 1943
Edward J. Thye (R)[10]	April 27, 1943	Jan. 8, 1947
Luther W. Youngdahl (R)[*1]	Jan. 8, 1947	Sept. 27, 1951
C. Elmer Anderson (R)[12]	Sept. 27, 1951	Jan. 5, 1955
Orville L. Freeman (DFL)	Jan. 5, 1955	Jan. 2, 1961
Elmer L. Andersen (R)[13]	Jan. 2, 1961	March 25, 1963
Karl F. Rolvaag (DFL)[14]	March 25, 1963	Jan. 2, 1967
Harold LeVander (R)	Jan. 2, 1967	Jan. 4, 1971
Wendell R. Anderson (DFL)	Jan. 4, 1971	Dec. 29, 1976
Rudolph G. Perpich (D)	Dec. 29, 1976	Jan. 1, 1979
Albert H. Quie (R)	Jan. 1, 1979	Jan. 3, 1983
Rudolph G. Perpich (D)	Jan. 3, 1983	

Michigan
1. Lieutenant governor, serving as acting governor for several months in 1838.
2. Resigned Feb. 23, 1841.
3. As lieutenant governor, he succeeded to office.
4. Resigned March 3, 1847.
5. As lieutenant governor, he succeeded to office.
6. Resigned March 7, 1853.
7. As lieutenant governor, he succeeded to office.
8. Died March 16, 1939.
9. As lieutenant governor, he succeeded to office.
10. Resigned Jan. 22, 1969.
11. As lieutenant governor, he succeeded to office. Subsequently elected.

Minnesota
1. Resigned July 10, 1863.
2. As lieutenant governor, he succeeded to office.

3. Died Sept. 21, 1909.
4. As lieutenant governor, he succeeded to office. Subsequently elected.
5. Died Dec. 30, 1915.
6. As lieutenant governor, he succeeded to office. Subsequently elected.
7. Died Aug. 22, 1936.
8. As lieutenant governor, he succeeded to office.
9. Resigned April 27, 1943.
10. As lieutenant governor, he succeeded to office.
11. Resigned Sept. 27, 1951.
12. As lieutenant governor, he succeeded to office. Subsequently elected.
13. The 1962 election between incumbent Governor Andersen (R) and Lieutenant Governor Karl Rolvaag (DFL) was disputed. Andersen served for almost three months of the term before the Minnesota Supreme Court ruled that Rolvaag had won by 91 votes.
14. Served the remainder of the four-year term after the removal of Governor Andersen.

MISSISSIPPI

(Became a state Dec. 10, 1817)

Governors	Dates of Service	
David Holmes (D-R)	Dec. 10, 1817	Jan. 5, 1820
George Poindexter (D-R)	Jan. 5, 1820	Jan. 7, 1822
Walter Leake (D-R)[1]	Jan. 7, 1822	Nov. 17, 1825
Gerard C. Brandon (D-R)[2]	Nov. 17, 1825	Jan. 7, 1826
David Holmes (D-R)[3]	Jan. 7, 1826	July 25, 1826
Gerard C. Brandon (D)[4]	July 25, 1826	Jan. 9, 1832
Abram M. Scott (NR)[5]	Jan. 9, 1832	June 12, 1833
Charles Lynch (NR)[6]	June 12, 1833	Nov. 20, 1833
Hiram G. Runnels (D)[7]	Nov. 20, 1833	Nov. 20, 1835
John A. Quitman (W)[8]	Dec. 3, 1835	Jan. 7, 1836
Charles Lynch (W)	Jan. 7, 1836	Jan. 8, 1838
Alexander G. McNutt (D)	Jan. 8, 1838	Jan. 10, 1842
Tilgham M. Tucker (D)	Jan. 10, 1842	Jan. 10, 1844
Albert G. Brown (D)	Jan. 10, 1844	Jan. 10, 1848
Joseph M. Matthews (D)	Jan. 10, 1848	Jan. 10, 1850
John A. Quitman (D)[9]	Jan. 10, 1850	Feb. 3, 1851
John I. Guion (D)[10]	Feb. 3, 1851	Nov. 4, 1851
James Whitfield (D)[11]	Nov. 24, 1851	Jan. 10, 1852
Henry S. Foote (UN)[12]	Jan. 10, 1852	Jan. 5, 1854
John J. Pettus (D)[13]	Jan. 5, 1854	Jan. 10, 1854
John J. McRae (D)	Jan. 10, 1854	Nov. 16, 1857
William McWillie (D)	Nov. 16, 1857	Nov. 21, 1859
John J. Pettus (D)	Nov. 21, 1859	Nov. 16, 1863
Charles Clark (D)[14]	Nov. 16, 1863	May 22, 1865
William L. Sharkey	June 1865	Oct. 16, 1865
Benjamin G. Humphreys[15]	Oct. 16, 1865	June 15, 1868
Adelbert Ames	June 15, 1868	March 10, 1870
James L. Alcorn (R)[16]	March 10, 1870	Nov. 30, 1871
Ridgley C. Powers (R)[17]	Nov. 30, 1871	Jan. 4, 1874
Adelbert Ames (R)[18]	Jan. 4, 1874	March 29, 1876
John M. Stone (D)[19]	March 29, 1876	Jan. 29, 1882
Robert Lowry (D)	Jan. 29, 1882	Jan. 13, 1890
John M. Stone (D)	Jan. 13, 1890	Jan. 20, 1896
Anselm J. McLaurin (D)	Jan. 20, 1896	Jan. 16, 1900
Andrew H. Longino (D)	Jan. 16, 1900	Jan. 19, 1904
James Kimble Vardaman (D)	Jan. 19, 1904	Jan. 21, 1908
Edmond Favor Noel (D)	Jan. 21, 1908	Jan. 16, 1912
Earl LeRoy Brewer (D)	Jan. 16, 1912	Jan. 18, 1916
Theodore Gilmore Bilbo (D)	Jan. 18, 1916	Jan. 20, 1920
Lee Maurice Russell (D)	Jan. 20, 1920	Jan. 22, 1924
Henry Lewis Whitfield (D)[20]	Jan. 22, 1924	March 18, 1927
Dennis Murphree (D)[21]	March 18, 1927	Jan. 17, 1928
Theodore Gilmore Bilbo (D)	Jan. 17, 1928	Jan. 19, 1932
Martin Sennett Conner (D)	Jan. 19, 1932	Jan. 21, 1936
Hugh L. White (D)	Jan. 21, 1936	Jan. 16, 1940
Paul B. Johnson (D)[22]	Jan. 16, 1940	Dec. 26, 1943
Dennis Murphree (D)[23]	Dec. 26, 1943	Jan. 18, 1944
Thomas L. Bailey (D)[24]	Jan. 18, 1944	Nov. 2, 1946
Fielding L. Wright (D)[25]	Nov. 2, 1946	Jan. 22, 1952
Hugh L. White (D)	Jan. 22, 1952	Jan. 17, 1956
J. P. Coleman (D)	Jan. 17, 1956	Jan. 19, 1960
Ross R. Barnett (D)	Jan. 19, 1960	Jan. 21, 1964
Paul B. Johnson Jr. (D)	Jan. 21, 1964	Jan. 16, 1968
John Bell Williams (D)	Jan. 16, 1968	Jan. 18, 1972
William Lowe Waller (D)	Jan. 18, 1972	Jan. 20, 1976
Cliff Finch (D)	Jan. 20, 1976	Jan. 22, 1980
William Winter (D)	Jan. 22, 1980	Jan. 10, 1984
Bill Allain (D)	Jan. 10, 1984	

MISSOURI

(Became a state Aug. 10, 1821)

Governors	Dates of Service	
Alexander McNair (D-R)	Aug. 10, 1821	Nov. 15, 1824
Frederick Bates (AR)[1]	Nov. 15, 1824	Aug. 4, 1825
Abraham J. Williams (D-R)[2]	Aug. 4, 1825	Jan. 20, 1826
John Miller (JAC D)	Jan. 20, 1826	Nov. 14, 1832
Daniel Dunklin (D)	Nov. 14, 1832	Sept. 13, 1836
Lilburn W. Boggs (D)	Sept. 13, 1836	Nov. 16, 1840
Thomas Reynolds (D)[3]	Nov. 16, 1840	Feb. 9, 1844
Meredith M. Marmaduke (D)[4]	Feb. 9, 1844	Nov. 20, 1844
John C. Edwards (D)	Nov. 20, 1844	Dec. 27, 1848
Austin A. King (D)	Dec. 27, 1848	Jan. 3, 1853
Sterling Price (D)	Jan. 3, 1853	Jan. 5, 1857
Trusten Polk (D)[5]	Jan. 5, 1857	Feb. 27, 1857
Hancock Lee Jackson (D)[6]	Feb. 27, 1857	Oct. 22, 1857
Robert Marcellus Stewart (D)	Oct. 22, 1857	Jan. 3, 1861
Claiborne Fox Jackson (D)[7]	Jan. 31, 1861	July 30, 1861
Hamilton R. Gamble (UN)[8]	July 31, 1861	Jan. 31, 1864
Willard Preble Hall (UN)[9]	Jan. 31, 1864	Jan. 2, 1865
Thomas C. Fletcher (UN R)	Jan. 2, 1865	Jan. 12, 1869
Joseph W. McClurg (R)	Jan. 12, 1869	Jan. 9, 1871
Benjamin G. Brown (R)	Jan. 9, 1871	Jan. 8, 1873
Silas Woodson (D)	Jan. 8, 1873	Jan. 12, 1875
Charles Henry Hardin (D)	Jan. 12, 1875	Jan. 8, 1877
John S. Phelps (D)	Jan. 8, 1877	Jan. 10, 1881
Thomas T. Crittenden (D)	Jan. 10, 1881	Jan. 12, 1885
John S. Marmaduke (D)[10]	Jan. 12, 1885	Dec. 28, 1887
Albert P. Morehouse (D)[11]	Dec. 28, 1887	Jan. 14, 1889
David R. Francis (D)	Jan. 14, 1889	Jan. 9, 1893
William J. Stone (D)	Jan. 9, 1893	Jan. 11, 1897

Mississippi
1. Died Nov. 17, 1825.
2. As lieutenant governor, he succeeded to office.
3. Resigned July 25, 1826.
4. As lieutenant governor, he succeeded to office. Subsequently elected.
5. Died June 12, 1833.
6. As president of the state Senate, he succeeded to office.
7. Resigned Nov. 20, 1835.
8. As president of the state Senate, he succeeded to office.
9. Resigned Feb. 3, 1851.
10. As president of the state Senate, he succeeded to office.
11. As president of the state Senate, he succeeded to office.
12. Resigned Jan. 5, 1854.
13. As president of the state Senate, he succeeded to office.
14. Removed from office May 22, 1865.
15. Removed from office June 15, 1868.
16. Resigned Nov. 30, 1871.
17. As lieutenant governor, he succeeded to office.
18. Resigned March 29, 1876.
19. As president of the state Senate, he succeeded to office. Subsequently elected.
20. Died March 18, 1927.
21. As lieutenant governor, he succeeded to office.
22. Died Dec. 26, 1943.
23. As lieutenant governor, he succeeded to office.
24. Died Nov. 2, 1946.
25. As lieutenant governor, he succeeded to office. Subsequently elected.

Missouri
1. Died Aug. 4, 1825.
2. Acting governor.
3. Died in 1844.
4. Acting governor.
5. Resigned Feb. 27, 1857.
6. Acting governor.
7. Removed from office in 1861 by convention.
8. Appointed governor by convention. Died Jan. 31, 1864.
9. Acting governor.
10. Died Dec. 28, 1887.
11. Acting governor.

Lawrence Vest Stephens (D)	Jan. 11, 1897	Jan. 14, 1901
Alexander M. Dockery (D)	Jan. 14, 1901	Jan. 9, 1905
Joseph W. Folk (D)	Jan. 9, 1905	Jan. 11, 1909
Herbert S. Hadley (R)	Jan. 11, 1909	Jan. 13, 1913
Elliot W. Major (D)	Jan. 13, 1913	Jan. 8, 1917
Frederick D. Gardner (D)	Jan. 8, 1917	Jan. 10, 1921
Arthur M. Hyde (R)	Jan. 10, 1921	Jan. 12, 1925
Samuel A. Baker (R)	Jan. 12, 1925	Jan. 14, 1929
Henry S. Caulfield (R)	Jan. 14, 1929	Jan. 9, 1933
Guy B. Park (D)	Jan. 9, 1933	Jan. 11, 1937
Lloyd C. Stark (D)	Jan. 11, 1937	Jan. 13, 1941
Forrest C. Donnell (R)	Jan. 13, 1941	Jan. 8, 1945
Phil M. Donnelly (D)	Jan. 8, 1945	Jan. 10, 1949
Forrest Smith (D)	Jan. 10, 1949	Jan. 12, 1953
Phil M. Donnelly (D)	Jan. 12, 1953	Jan. 14, 1957
James T. Blair Jr. (D)	Jan. 14, 1957	Jan. 9, 1961
John M. Dalton (D)	Jan. 9, 1961	Jan. 11, 1965
Warren E. Hearnes (D)	Jan. 11, 1965	Jan. 8, 1973
Christopher S. Bond (R)	Jan. 8, 1973	Jan. 10, 1977
Joseph P. Teasdale (D)	Jan. 10, 1977	Jan. 12, 1981
Christopher S. Bond (R)	Jan. 12, 1981	Jan. 14, 1985
John Ashcroft (R)	Jan. 14, 1985	

MONTANA

(Became a state Nov. 8, 1889)

Governors	Dates of Service	
Joseph K. Toole (D)	Nov. 8, 1889	Jan. 1, 1893
John E. Rickards (R)	Jan. 2, 1893	Jan. 3, 1897
Robert B. Smith (PP & D)	Jan. 4, 1897	Jan. 7, 1901
Joseph K. Toole (D)[1]	Jan. 7, 1901	April 1, 1908
Edwin L. Norris (D)[2]	April 1, 1908	Jan. 5, 1913
Samuel V. Stewart (D)	Jan. 6, 1913	Jan. 2, 1921
Joseph M. Dixon (R)	Jan. 3, 1921	Jan. 4, 1925
John E. Erickson (D)[3]	Jan. 4, 1925	March 13, 1933
Frank H. Cooney (D)[4]	March 13, 1933	Dec. 15, 1935
William E. Holt (D)[5]	Dec. 16, 1935	Jan. 4, 1937
Roy E. Ayers (D)	Jan. 4, 1937	Jan. 6, 1942
Samuel C. Ford (R)	Jan. 6, 1941	Jan. 3, 1949
John W. Bonner (D)	Jan. 3, 1949	Jan. 4, 1953
J. Hugo Aronson (R)	Jan. 4, 1953	Jan. 4, 1961
Donald G. Nutter (R)[6]	Jan. 4, 1961	Jan. 25, 1962
Tim M. Babcock (R)[7]	Jan. 26, 1962	Jan. 6, 1969
Forrest H. Anderson (D)	Jan. 6, 1969	Jan. 1, 1973

Thomas L. Judge (D)	Jan. 1, 1973	Jan. 5, 1981
Ted Schwinden (D)	Jan. 5, 1981	

NEBRASKA

(Became a state March 1, 1867)

Governors	Dates of Service	
David Butler (R)[1]	March 27, 1867	June 2, 1871
William H. James (R)[2]	June 2, 1871	Jan. 13, 1873
Robert W. Furnas (R)	Jan. 13, 1873	Jan. 1875
Silas Garber (R)	Jan. 1875	Jan. 1879
Albinus Nance (R)	Jan. 1879	Jan. 1883
James W. Dawes (R)	Jan. 1883	Jan. 15, 1887
John M. Thayer (R)	Jan. 15, 1887	Jan. 15, 1891
James E. Boyd (D)[3]	Jan. 15, 1891	May 5, 1891
John M. Thayer (R)[4]	May 5, 1891	Feb. 8, 1892
James E. Boyd (D)[5]	Feb. 8, 1892	Jan. 1893
Lorenzo Crounse (R)	Jan. 1893	Jan. 1895
Silas A. Holcomb (D & PPI)	Jan. 1895	Jan. 5, 1899
William A. Poynter (FUS)[6]	Jan. 5, 1899	Jan. 3, 1901
Charles H. Dietrich (R)[7]	Jan. 3, 1901	May 1, 1901
Ezra P. Savage (R)[8]	May 1, 1901	Jan. 8, 1903
John H. Mickey (R)	Jan. 8, 1903	Jan. 3, 1907
George L. Sheldon (R)	Jan. 3, 1907	Jan. 7, 1909
Ashton C. Shallenberger (D)	Jan. 7, 1909	Jan. 5, 1911
Chester H. Aldrich (R)	Jan. 5, 1911	Jan. 9, 1913
John H. Morehead (D)	Jan. 9, 1913	Jan. 4, 1917
Keith Neville (D)	Jan. 4, 1917	Jan. 9, 1919
Samuel R. McKelvie (R)	Jan. 9, 1919	Jan. 3, 1923
Charles W. Bryan (D)	Jan. 4, 1923	Jan. 8, 1925
Adam McMullen (R)	Jan. 8, 1925	Jan. 3, 1929
Arthur J. Weaver (R)	Jan. 3, 1929	Jan. 8, 1931
Charles W. Bryan (D)	Jan. 8, 1931	Jan. 3, 1935
Robert L. Cochran (D)	Jan. 3, 1935	Jan. 9, 1941
Dwight P. Griswold (R)	Jan. 9, 1941	Jan. 9, 1947
Val Peterson (R)	Jan. 9, 1947	Jan. 8, 1953
Robert Berkey Crosby (R)	Jan. 8, 1953	Jan. 6, 1955
Victor E. Anderson (R)	Jan. 6, 1955	Jan. 8, 1959
Ralph G. Brooks (D)[9]	Jan. 8, 1959	Sept. 9, 1960
Dwight W. Burney (R)[10]	Sept. 9, 1960	Jan. 5, 1961
Frank B. Morrison (D)	Jan. 5, 1961	Jan. 5, 1967
Norbert T. Tiemann (R)	Jan. 5, 1967	Jan. 7, 1971
J. James Exon (D)	Jan. 7, 1971	Jan. 3, 1979
Charles Thone (R)	Jan. 4, 1979	Jan. 6, 1983
Robert Kerrey (D)	Jan. 6, 1983	

Montana

1. Resigned April 1, 1908.
2. As lieutenant governor, he succeeded to office. Subsequently elected.
3. Resigned March 13, 1933.
4. As lieutenant governor, he succeeded to office. Died Dec. 15, 1935.
5. As president of the state Senate, he succeeded to office.
6. Died Jan. 25, 1962.
7. As lieutenant governor, he succeeded to office. Subsequently elected.

Nebraska

1. Impeached. Removed from office June 2, 1871.
2. As lieutenant governor, he succeeded to office.

3. The election of Boyd was challenged by Governor Thayer on the grounds that Boyd had been born in Ireland and was not an American citizen, and was thus ineligible to be governor. Boyd was removed by the Nebraska Supreme Court May 5, 1891.
4. Following the removal of Boyd, Thayer returned to office.
5. U.S. Supreme Court declared that Boyd was a citizen, and he returned to office Feb. 18, 1892, and served out the remainder of his term.
6. Fusion composed of Democrats and Populists.
7. Resigned May 1, 1901.
8. As lieutenant governor, he succeeded to office.
9. Died Sept. 9, 1960.
10. As lieutenant governor, he succeeded to office.

NEVADA

(Became a state Oct. 31, 1864)

Governors	Dates of Service	
H. G. Blasdel (UN R)	Dec. 5, 1864	Jan. 2, 1871
L. R. Bradley (D)	Jan. 3, 1871	Jan. 6, 1879
John H. Kinkead (R)	Jan. 7, 1879	Jan. 1, 1883
Jewett W. Adams (D)	Jan. 2, 1883	Jan. 3, 1887
C. C. Stevenson (R)[1]	Jan. 4, 1887	Sept. 2, 1890
Frank Bell (R)[2]	Sept. 21, 1890	Jan. 5, 1891
R. K. Colcord (R)	Jan. 6, 1891	Jan. 7, 1895
John S. Jones (D SIL)[3]	Jan. 8, 1895	April 10, 1896
Reinhold Sadler (SIL R)[4]	April 10, 1896	Jan. 1, 1903
John Sparks (D & SILVER)[5]	Jan. 1, 1903	May 22, 1908
Denver S. Dickerson (D)[6]	May 22, 1908	Jan. 2, 1911
Tasker L. Oddie (R)	Jan. 2, 1911	Jan. 4, 1915
Emmet D. Boyle (D)	Jan. 4, 1915	Jan. 1, 1923
James G. Scrugham (D)	Jan. 1, 1923	Jan. 3, 1927
Frederick B. Balzar (R)[7]	Jan. 3, 1927	March 21, 1934
Morley I. Griswold (R)[8]	March 21, 1934	Jan. 7, 1935
Richard Kirman Sr. (D)	Jan. 7, 1935	Jan. 2, 1939
Edward P. Carville (D)[9]	Jan. 2, 1939	July 24, 1945
Vail M. Pittman (D)[10]	July 24, 1945	Jan. 1, 1951
Charles H. Russell (R)	Jan. 1, 1951	Jan. 5, 1959
Grant Sawyer (D)	Jan. 5, 1959	Jan. 2, 1967
Paul D. Laxalt (R)	Jan. 2, 1967	Jan. 4, 1971
Mike O'Callaghan (D)	Jan. 4, 1971	Jan. 1, 1979
Robert F. List (R)	Jan. 1, 1979	Jan. 3, 1983
Richard H. Bryan (D)	Jan. 3, 1983	

NEW HAMPSHIRE

(Ratified the Constitution June 21, 1788)

Governors	Dates of Service	
John Sullivan (FED)	June 6, 1789	June 5, 1790
Josiah Bartlett (D-R)	June 5, 1790	June 5, 1794
Joseph T. Gilman (FED)	June 5, 1794	June 6, 1805
John Langdon (D-R)	June 6, 1805	June 8, 1809
Jeremiah Smith (FED)	June 8, 1809	June 7, 1810
John Langdon (D-R)	June 7, 1810	June 5, 1812
William Plumer (D-R)	June 5, 1812	June 3, 1813
John T. Gilman (FED)	June 13, 1813	June 6, 1816
William Plumer (D-R)	June 6, 1816	June 3, 1819
Samuel Bell (D-R)	June 3, 1819	June 5, 1823
Levi Woodbury (D-R)	June 5, 1823	June 2, 1824
David L. Morrill (D-R)	June 3, 1824	June 7, 1827
Benjamin Pierce (D-R)	June 7, 1827	June 5, 1828
John Bell (NR)	June 5, 1828	June 4, 1829
Benjamin Pierce (JAC D)	June 4, 1829	June 3, 1830
Matthew Harvey (JAC D)[1]	June 3, 1830	Feb. 28, 1831
Joseph M. Harper (D)[2]	Feb. 28, 1831	June 2, 1831
Samuel Dinsmoor (JAC D)	June 2, 1831	June 5, 1834

William Badger (D)	June 5, 1834	June 2, 1836
Isaac Hill (D)	June 2, 1836	June 5, 1839
John Page (D)	June 5, 1839	June 2, 1842
Henry Hubbard (D)	June 2, 1842	June 6, 1844
John H. Steele (D)	June 6, 1844	June 4, 1846
Anthony Colby (W)	June 4, 1846	June 3, 1847
Jared W. Williams (D)	June 3, 1847	June 7, 1849
Samuel Dinsmoor (D)	June 7, 1849	June 3, 1852
Noah Martin (D)	June 3, 1852	June 8, 1854
Nathaniel B. Baker (D)	June 8, 1854	June 7, 1855
Ralph Metcalf (AM)	June 7, 1855	June 4, 1857
William Haile (R)	June 4, 1857	June 2, 1859
Ichabod Goodwin (R)	June 2, 1859	June 6, 1861
Nathaniel S. Berry (R)	June 6, 1861	June 3, 1863
Joseph A. Gilmore (R)	June 3, 1863	June 8, 1865
Frederick Smyth (UN)	June 8, 1865	June 6, 1867
Walter Harriman (R)	June 6, 1867	June 2, 1869
Onslow Stearns (R)	June 3, 1869	June 8, 1871
James A. Weston (D)	June 14, 1871	June 6, 1872
Ezekiel A. Straw (R)	June 6, 1872	June 3, 1874
James A. Weston (D)	June 3, 1874	June 10, 1875
Person C. Cheney (R)	June 10, 1875	June 6, 1877
Benjamin F. Prescott (R)	June 7, 1877	June 5, 1879
Natt Head (R)	June 5, 1879	June 2, 1881
Charles H. Bell (R)	June 2, 1881	June 7, 1883
Samuel W. Hale (R)	June 7, 1883	June 4, 1885
Moody Currier (R)	June 4, 1885	June 2, 1887
Charles H. Sawyer (R)	June 2, 1887	June 6, 1889
David H. Goodell (R)	June 6, 1889	Jan. 8, 1891
Hiram A. Tuttle (R)	Jan. 8, 1891	Jan. 5, 1893
John B. Smith (R)	Jan. 5, 1893	Jan. 3, 1895
Charles A. Busiel (R)	Jan. 3, 1895	Jan. 7, 1897
George A. Ramsdell (R)	Jan. 7, 1897	Jan. 5, 1899
Frank W. Rollins (R)	Jan. 5, 1899	Jan. 3, 1901
Chester B. Jordan (R)	Jan. 3, 1901	Jan. 1, 1903
Nahum J. Batchelder (R)	Jan. 1, 1903	Jan. 5, 1905
John McLane (R)	Jan. 5, 1905	Jan. 3, 1907
Charles M. Floyd (R)	Jan. 3, 1907	Jan. 7, 1909
Henry B. Quinby (R)	Jan. 7, 1909	Jan. 5, 1911
Robert P. Bass (R)	Jan. 5, 1911	Jan. 2, 1913
Samuel D. Felker (D)	Jan. 2, 1913	Jan. 7, 1915
Rolland H. Spaulding (R)	Jan. 7, 1915	Jan. 3, 1917
Henry Wilder Keyes (R)[3]	Jan. 3, 1917	Jan. 2, 1919
John H. Bartlett (R)	Jan. 2, 1919	Jan. 6, 1921
Albert O. Brown (R)	Jan. 6, 1921	Jan. 4, 1923
Fred H. Brown (D)	Jan. 4, 1923	Jan. 1, 1925
John G. Winant (R)	Jan. 1, 1925	Jan. 6, 1927
Huntley N. Spaulding (R)	Jan. 6, 1927	Jan. 3, 1929
Charles W. Tobey (R)	Jan. 3, 1929	Jan. 1, 1931
John G. Winant (R)	Jan. 1, 1931	Jan. 3, 1935
H. Styles Bridges (R)	Jan. 3, 1935	Jan. 7, 1937
Francis P. Murphy (R)	Jan. 7, 1937	Jan. 2, 1941
Robert O. Blood (R)	Jan. 2, 1941	Jan. 4, 1945
Charles M. Dale (R)	Jan. 4, 1945	Jan. 6, 1949
Sherman Adams (R)	Jan. 6, 1949	Jan. 1, 1953
Hugh Gregg (R)	Jan. 1, 1953	Jan. 6, 1955
Lane Dwinell (R)	Jan. 6, 1955	Jan. 1, 1959
Wesley Powell (R)	Jan. 1, 1959	Jan. 3, 1963

Nevada
1. Left office due to disability, Sept. 1, 1890. Died Sept. 21, 1890.
2. As lieutenant governor, he succeeded to office.
3. Died April 10, 1896.
4. As lieutenant governor, he succeeded to office. Subsequently elected.
5. Died May 22, 1908.
6. As lieutenant governor, he succeeded to office.
7. Died March 21, 1934.
8. As lieutenant governor, he succeeded to office.
9. Resigned July 24, 1945.
10. As lieutenant governor, he succeeded to office. Subsequently elected.

New Hampshire
1. Resigned Feb. 28, 1831.
2. Acting governor in 1831.
3. Keyes was disqualified at the end of his term by illness and Jesse M. Barton, president of the state Senate, became acting governor.
4. Hospitalized Nov. 20, 1982. Died Dec. 29, 1982.
5. As president of the state Senate, served as acting governor until the Legislature dissolved on Nov. 30, 1982.
6. As secretary of state, served as acting governor until new members of the Legislature were sworn in.
7. As new president of the state Senate, served as acting governor.

John W. King (D)	Jan. 3, 1963	Jan. 2, 1969
Walter Peterson (R)	Jan. 2, 1969	Jan. 4, 1973
Meldrim Thomson Jr. (R)	Jan. 4, 1973	Jan. 4, 1979
Hugh J. Gallen (D)[4]	Jan. 4, 1979	Nov. 11, 1982
Robert B. Monier (D)[5]	Nov. 11, 1982	Nov. 30, 1982
William M. Gardner (D)[6]	Nov. 30, 1982	Dec. 1, 1982
Vesta M. Roy (D)[7]	Dec. 1, 1982	Jan. 6, 1983
John H. Sununu (R)	Jan. 6, 1983	

NEW JERSEY

(Ratified the Constitution Dec. 18, 1787)

Governors	Dates of Service	
William Livingston (FED)[1]	Aug. 27, 1776	July 25, 1790
Elisha Lawrence (FED)[2]	July 25, 1790	Oct. 30, 1790
William Paterson (FED)[3]	Oct. 30, 1790	March 4, 1793
Thomas Henderson (FED)	March 30, 1793	June 3, 1793
Richard Howell (FED)	June 3, 1793	Oct. 31, 1801
Joseph Bloomfield (D-R)	Oct. 31, 1801	Oct. 28, 1802
John Lambert (D-R)[4]	Nov. 15, 1802	Oct. 29, 1803
Joseph Bloomfield (D-R)	Oct. 29, 1803	Oct. 29, 1812
Aaron Ogden (FED)	Oct. 29, 1812	Oct. 29, 1813
William S. Pennington (D-R)[5]	Oct. 29, 1813	June 19, 1815
William Kennedy (D-R)[6]	June 19, 1815	Oct. 25, 1815
Mahlon Dickerson (D-R)[7]	Oct. 26, 1815	Feb. 1, 1817
Isaac H. Williamson (FED)	Feb. 6, 1817	Oct. 30, 1829
Peter D. Vroom (D)	Nov. 6, 1829	Oct. 26, 1832
Samuel L. Southard (W)	Oct. 26, 1832	Feb. 1833
Elias P. Seeley (W)	Feb. 27, 1833	Oct. 23, 1833
Peter D. Vroom (D)	Oct. 25, 1833	Oct. 28, 1836
Philemon Dickerson (D)	Nov. 3, 1836	Oct. 27, 1837
William Pennington (W)	Oct. 27, 1837	Oct. 27, 1843
Daniel Haines (D)	Oct. 27, 1843	Jan. 21, 1845
Charles C. Stratton (W)	Jan. 21, 1845	Jan. 18, 1848
Daniel Haines (D)	Jan. 18, 1848	Jan. 20, 1851
George F. Fort (D)	Jan. 21, 1851	Jan. 17, 1854
Rodman M. Price (D)	Jan. 17, 1854	Jan. 20, 1857
William A. Newell (FUS)	Jan. 20, 1857	Jan. 17, 1860
Charles S. Olden (R)	Jan. 17, 1860	Jan. 20, 1863
Joel Parker (D)	Jan. 20, 1863	Jan. 16, 1866
Marcus L. Ward (UN)	Jan. 16, 1866	Jan. 19, 1869
Theodore F. Randolph (D)	Jan. 19, 1869	Jan. 16, 1872
Joel Parker (D)	Jan. 16, 1872	Jan. 19, 1875
Joseph D. Bedle (D)	Jan. 19, 1875	Jan. 15, 1878
George B. McClellan (D)	Jan. 15, 1878	Jan. 18, 1881
George C. Ludlow (D)	Jan. 18, 1881	Jan. 15, 1884
Leon Abbett (D)	Jan. 15, 1884	Jan. 18, 1887
Robert S. Green (D)	Jan. 18, 1887	Jan. 21, 1890
Leon Abbett (D)	Jan. 21, 1890	Jan. 17, 1893
George T. Werts (D)	Jan. 17, 1893	Jan. 21, 1896
John W. Griggs (R)[8]	Jan. 21, 1896	Jan. 31, 1898

Foster M. Voorhees (R)[9]	Feb. 1, 1898	Oct. 18, 1898
David O. Watkins (R)[10]	Oct. 18, 1898	Jan. 17, 1899
Foster M. Voorhees (R)	Jan. 17, 1899	Jan. 21, 1902
Franklin Murphy (R)	Jan. 21, 1902	Jan. 17, 1905
Edward C. Stokes (R)	Jan. 17, 1905	Jan. 21, 1908
John F. Fort (R)	Jan. 21, 1908	Jan. 17, 1911
Woodrow Wilson (D)[11]	Jan. 17, 1911	March 1, 1913
James F. Fielder (D)[12]	March 1, 1913	Oct. 28, 1913
Leon R. Taylor (D)[13]	Oct. 28, 1913	Jan. 20, 1914
James F. Fielder (D)	Jan. 20, 1914	Jan. 15, 1917
Walter E. Edge (R)[14]	Jan. 15, 1917	May 16, 1919
William N. Runyon (R)[15]	May 16, 1919	Jan. 13, 1920
Clarence E. Case (R)[16]	Jan. 13, 1920	Jan. 20, 1920
Edward I. Edwards (D)	Jan. 20, 1920	Jan. 15, 1923
George S. Silzer (D)	Jan. 15, 1923	Jan. 19, 1926
Arthur Harry Moore (D)	Jan. 19, 1926	Jan. 15, 1929
Morgan F. Larson (R)	Jan. 15, 1929	Jan. 19, 1932
Arthur Harry Moore (D)[17]	Jan. 19, 1932	Jan. 3, 1935
Clifford R. Powell (R)[18]	Jan. 3, 1935	Jan. 8, 1935
Horace G. Prall (R)[19]	Jan. 8, 1935	Jan. 15, 1935
Harold G. Hoffman (R)	Jan. 15, 1935	Jan. 18, 1938
Arthur Harry Moore (D)	Jan. 18, 1938	Jan. 21, 1941
Charles Edison (D)	Jan. 21, 1941	Jan. 18, 1944
Walter E. Edge (R)	Jan. 18, 1944	Jan. 21, 1947
Alfred E. Driscoll (R)	Jan. 21, 1947	Jan. 19, 1954
Robert B. Meyner (D)	Jan. 19, 1954	Jan. 16, 1962
Richard J. Hughes (D)	Jan. 16, 1962	Jan. 20, 1970
William T. Cahill (R)	Jan. 20, 1970	Jan. 15, 1974
Brendan T. Byrne (D)	Jan. 15, 1974	Jan. 19, 1982
Thomas H. Kean (R)	Jan. 19, 1982	

NEW MEXICO

(Became a state Jan. 6, 1912)

Governors	Dates of Service	
William C. McDonald (D)	Jan. 6, 1912	Jan. 1, 1917
Ezequiel C. de Baca (D)[1]	Jan. 1, 1917	Feb. 18, 1917
Washington E. Lindsey (R)[2]	Feb. 19, 1917	Jan. 1, 1919
Octaviano A. Larrazolo (R)	Jan. 1, 1919	Jan. 1, 1921
Merritt C. Mechem (R)	Jan. 1, 1921	Jan. 1, 1923
James F. Hinkle (D)	Jan. 1, 1923	Jan. 1, 1925
Arthur T. Hannett (D)	Jan. 1, 1925	Jan. 1, 1927
Richard C. Dillon (R)	Jan. 1, 1927	Jan. 1, 1931
Arthur Seligman (D)[3]	Jan. 1, 1931	Sept. 25, 1933
Andrew W. Hockenhull (D)[4]	Sept. 25, 1933	Jan. 1, 1935
Clyde Tingley (D)	Jan. 1, 1935	Jan. 1, 1939
John E. Miles (D)	Jan. 1, 1939	Jan. 1, 1943
John J. Dempsey (D)	Jan. 1, 1943	Jan. 1, 1947
Thomas J. Mabry (D)	Jan. 1, 1947	Jan. 1, 1951
Edwin L. Mechem (R)	Jan. 1, 1951	Jan. 1, 1955

New Jersey
1. *Died in office.*
2. *As vice president of the Legislative Council, he succeeded to office.*
3. *Resigned March 4, 1793.*
4. *Acting governor.*
5. *Resigned June 19, 1815.*
6. *As vice president of the Legislative Council, he succeeded to office.*
7. *Resigned Feb. 1, 1817.*
8. *Resigned Jan. 31, 1898.*
9. *Acting governor.*
10. *Acting governor.*
11. *Resigned March 1, 1913, having been elected president of the United States.*
12. *As president of the state Senate, he succeeded to office. Resigned Oct. 28, 1913.*
13. *Acting governor.*
14. *Resigned May 16, 1919.*

15. *As president of the state Senate, he succeeded to office. Service ended Jan. 13, 1920.*
16. *Acting governor.*
17. *Resigned Jan. 3, 1935.*
18. *As president of the state Senate, he succeeded to office. Service ended Jan. 8, 1935.*
19. *Acting governor.*

New Mexico
1. *Died Feb. 18, 1917.*
2. *As lieutenant governor, he succeeded to office.*
3. *Died Sept. 25, 1933.*
4. *As lieutenant governor, he succeeded to office.*
5. *Resigned Nov. 30, 1962.*
6. *As lieutenant governor, he succeeded to office.*

John F. Simms (D)	Jan. 1, 1955	Jan. 1, 1957
Edwin L. Mechem (R)	Jan. 1, 1957	Jan. 1, 1959
John Burroughs (D)	Jan. 1, 1959	Jan. 1, 1961
Edwin L. Mechem (R)[5]	Jan. 1, 1961	Nov. 30, 1962
Tom Bolack (R)[6]	Nov. 30, 1962	Jan. 1, 1963
Jack M. Campbell (D)	Jan. 1, 1963	Jan. 1, 1967
David F. Cargo (R)	Jan. 1, 1967	Jan. 1, 1971
Bruce King (D)	Jan. 1, 1971	Jan. 1, 1975
Jerry Apodaca (D)	Jan. 1, 1975	Jan. 1, 1979
Bruce King (D)	Jan. 1, 1979	Jan. 1, 1983
Toney Anaya (D)	Jan. 1, 1983	

NEW YORK

(Ratified the Constitution July 26, 1788)

Governors	Dates of Service	
George Clinton (D-R)	July 9, 1777	July 1, 1795
John Jay (FED)	July 1, 1795	July 1, 1801
George Clinton (D-R)	July 1, 1801	July 1, 1804
Morgan Lewis (D-R)	July 1, 1804	July 1, 1807
Daniel D. Tompkins (D-R)[1]	July 1, 1807	Feb. 24, 1817
John Tayler (D-R)[2]	Feb. 24, 1817	July 1, 1817
De Witt Clinton (D-R)	July 1, 1817	Jan. 1, 1823
Joseph C. Yates (D-R)	Jan. 1, 1823	Jan. 1, 1825
De Witt Clinton (CLINT R)[3]	Jan. 1, 1825	Feb. 11, 1828
Nathaniel Pitcher (D-R)[4]	Feb. 11, 1828	Jan. 1, 1829
Martin Van Buren (JAC D)[5]	Jan. 1, 1829	March 12, 1829
Enos T. Throop (JAC D)[6]	March 12, 1829	Jan. 1, 1833
William L. Marcy (D)	Jan. 1, 1833	Jan. 1, 1839
William H. Seward (W)	Jan. 1, 1839	Jan. 1, 1843
William C. Bouck (D)	Jan. 1, 1843	Jan. 1, 1845
Silas Wright (D)	Jan. 1, 1845	Jan. 1, 1847
John Young (W)	Jan. 1, 1847	Jan. 1, 1849
Hamilton Fish (W)	Jan. 1, 1849	Jan. 1, 1851
Washington Hunt (W-A-RENT)	Jan. 1, 1851	Jan. 1, 1853
Horatio Seymour (D)	Jan. 1, 1853	Jan. 1, 1855
Myron H. Clark (FUS R)	Jan. 1, 1855	Jan. 1, 1857
John A. King (R)	Jan. 1, 1857	Jan. 1, 1859
Edwin D. Morgan (R)	Jan. 1, 1859	Jan. 1, 1863
Horatio Seymour (D)	Jan. 1, 1863	Jan. 1, 1865
Reuben E. Fenton (UN)	Jan. 1, 1865	Jan. 1, 1869
John T. Hoffman (D)	Jan. 1, 1869	Jan. 1, 1873
John A. Dix (R)	Jan. 1, 1873	Jan. 1, 1875
Samuel J. Tilden (D)	Jan. 1, 1875	Jan. 1, 1877
Lucius Robinson (D)[7]	Jan. 1, 1877	Jan. 1, 1880
Alonzo B. Cornell (R)	Jan. 1, 1880	Jan. 1, 1883
Grover Cleveland (D)[8]	Jan. 1, 1883	Jan. 6, 1885
David B. Hill (D)[9]	Jan. 6, 1885	Jan. 1, 1892

Roswell P. Flower (D)	Jan. 1, 1892	Jan. 1, 1895
Levi P. Morton (R)[10]	Jan. 1, 1895	Jan. 1, 1897
Frank S. Black (R)	Jan. 1, 1897	Jan. 1, 1899
Theodore Roosevelt (R)	Jan. 1, 1899	Jan. 1, 1901
Benjamin B. Odell Jr. (R)	Jan. 1, 1901	Jan. 1, 1905
Frank W. Higgins (R)	Jan. 1, 1905	Jan. 1, 1907
Charles Evans Hughes (R)[11]	Jan. 1, 1907	Oct. 6, 1910
Horace White (R)[12]	Oct. 6, 1910	Jan. 1, 1911
John A. Dix (D)	Jan. 1, 1911	Jan. 1, 1913
William Sulzer (D)[13]	Jan. 1, 1913	Oct. 17, 1913
Martin H. Glynn (D)[14]	Oct. 17, 1913	Jan. 1, 1915
Charles S. Whitman (R)	Jan. 1, 1915	Jan. 1, 1919
Alfred E. Smith (D)	Jan. 1, 1919	Jan. 1, 1921
Nathan L. Miller (R)	Jan. 1, 1921	Jan. 1, 1923
Alfred E. Smith (D)	Jan. 1, 1923	Jan. 1, 1929
Franklin D. Roosevelt (D)	Jan. 1, 1929	Jan. 1, 1933
Herbert H. Lehman (D)[15]	Jan. 1, 1933	Dec. 3, 1942
Charles Poletti (D)[16]	Dec. 3, 1942	Jan. 1, 1943
Thomas E. Dewey (R)	Jan. 1, 1943	Jan. 1, 1955
W. Averell Harriman (D)	Jan. 1, 1955	Jan. 1, 1959
Nelson A. Rockefeller (R)[17]	Jan. 1, 1959	Dec. 18, 1973
Malcolm Wilson (R)[18]	Dec. 18, 1973	Jan. 1, 1975
Hugh Carey (D)	Jan. 1, 1975	Jan. 1, 1983
Mario M. Cuomo (D)	Jan. 1, 1983	

NORTH CAROLINA

(Ratified the Constitution Nov. 21, 1789)

Governors	Dates of Service	
Samuel Johnston	Dec. 20, 1787	Dec. 17, 1789
Alexander Martin (FED)	Dec. 17, 1789	Dec. 14, 1792
Richard D. Spaight (D-R)	Dec. 14, 1792	Nov. 19, 1795
Samuel Ashe (D-R)	Nov. 19, 1795	Dec. 7, 1798
William R. Davie (FED)	Dec. 7, 1798	Nov. 23, 1799
Benjamin Williams (D-R)	Nov. 23, 1799	Dec. 6, 1802
James Turner (D-R)	Dec. 6, 1802	Dec. 10, 1805
Nathaniel Alexander (D-R)	Dec. 10, 1805	Dec. 1, 1807
Benjamin Wiliams (D-R)	Dec. 1, 1807	Dec. 12, 1808
David Stone (D-R)	Dec. 12, 1808	Dec. 5, 1810
Benjamin Smith (D-R)	Dec. 5, 1810	Dec. 9, 1811
William Hawkins (D-R)	Dec. 9, 1811	Nov. 29, 1814
William Miller (D-R)	Dec. 7, 1814	Dec. 3, 1817
John Branch (D-R)	Dec. 6, 1817	Dec. 7, 1820
Jesse Franklin (D-R)	Dec. 7, 1820	Dec. 7, 1821
Gabriel Holmes (D-R)	Dec. 7, 1821	Dec. 7, 1824
Hutchins G. Burton (D-R)	Dec. 7, 1824	Dec. 8, 1827
James Iredell (D-R)	Dec. 8, 1827	Dec. 12, 1828
John Owen (D)	Dec. 12, 1828	Dec. 18, 1830

New York
1. *Resigned Feb. 24, 1817, having been elected vice president of the United States.*
2. *As lieutenant governor, he succeeded to office.*
3. *Died Feb. 11, 1828.*
4. *As lieutenant governor, he succeeded to office.*
5. *Resigned March 12, 1829.*
6. *As lieutenant governor, he succeeded to office. Subsequently elected.*
7. *Term of office changed from two years to three years.*
8. *Resigned Jan. 6, 1885, having been elected president of the United States.*
9. *As lieutenant governor, he succeeded to office. Subsequently elected.*
10. *Term of office changed from three years to two years.*
11. *Resigned Oct. 6, 1910.*
12. *As lieutenant governor, he succeeded to office.*
13. *Impeached; removed from office Oct. 17, 1913.*
14. *As lieutenant governor, he succeeded to office.*
15. *First governor elected to a four-year term (in 1938). Resigned Dec. 3, 1942.*
16. *As lieutenant governor, he succeeded to office.*
17. *Resigned Dec. 18, 1973.*
18. *As lieutenant governor, he succeeded to office.*

North Carolina
1. *Resigned Dec. 6, 1854.*
2. *Acting governor.*
3. *Died July 7, 1861.*
4. *Acting governor.*
5. *Removed from office. Last Confederate governor.*
6. *Provisional governor appointed by President Johnson.*
7. *Removed July 1, 1868.*
8. *Impeached. Removed from office Dec. 15, 1870.*
9. *As lieutenant governor, he succeeded to office. Subsequently elected. Died July 11, 1874.*
10. *As lieutenant governor, he succeeded to office.*
11. *Resigned Feb. 5, 1879.*
12. *As lieutenant governor, he succeeded to office. Subsequently elected.*
13. *Died April 8, 1891.*
14. *As lieutenant governor, he succeeded to office.*
15. *Died Nov. 7, 1954.*
16. *As lieutenant governor, he succeeded to office. Subsequently elected.*

Montfort Stokes (D)	Dec. 18, 1830	Dec. 6, 1832
David L. Swain (D)	Dec. 6, 1832	Dec. 10, 1835
Richard D. Spaight Jr. (D)	Dec. 10, 1835	Dec. 31, 1836
Edward B. Dudley (W)	Dec. 31, 1836	Jan. 1, 1841
John M. Morehead (W)	Jan. 1, 1841	Jan. 1, 1845
William A. Graham (W)	Jan. 1, 1845	Jan. 1, 1849
Charles Manly (W)	Jan. 1, 1849	Jan. 1, 1851
David S. Reid (D)[1]	Jan. 1, 1851	Dec. 6, 1854
Warren Winslow (D)[2]	Dec. 6, 1854	Jan. 1, 1855
Thomas Bragg (D)	Jan. 1, 1855	Jan. 1, 1859
John W. Ellis (D)[3]	Jan. 1, 1859	July 7, 1861
Henry T. Clark (D)[4]	July 7, 1861	Sept. 8, 1862
Zebulon B. Vance (C)[5]	Sept. 8, 1862	May 29, 1865
William W. Holden[6]	May 29, 1865	Dec. 15, 1865
Jonathan Worth (C)[7]	Dec. 15, 1865	July 1, 1868
William W. Holden (R)[8]	July 1, 1868	Dec. 15, 1870
Tod R. Caldwell (R)[9]	Dec. 15, 1870	July 11, 1874
Curtis H. Brogden (R)[10]	July 11, 1874	Jan. 1, 1877
Zebulon B. Vance (D)[11]	Jan. 1, 1877	Feb. 5, 1879
Thomas J. Jarvis (D)[12]	Feb. 5, 1879	Jan. 21, 1885
Alfred M. Scales (D)	Jan. 21, 1885	Jan. 17, 1889
Daniel G. Fowle (D)[13]	Jan. 17, 1889	April 8, 1891
Thomas M. Holt (D)[14]	April 8, 1891	Jan. 18, 1893
Elias Carr (D)	Jan. 18, 1893	Jan. 12, 1897
Daniel L. Russell (D)	Jan. 12, 1897	Jan. 15, 1901
Charles B. Aycock (D)	Jan. 15, 1901	Jan. 11, 1905
R. B. Glenn (D)	Jan. 11, 1905	Jan. 12, 1909
W. W. Kitchin (D)	Jan. 12, 1909	Jan. 15, 1913
Locke Craig (D)	Jan. 15, 1913	Jan. 11, 1917
Thomas W. Bickett (D)	Jan. 11, 1917	Jan. 12, 1921
Carmeron Morrison (D)	Jan. 12, 1921	Jan. 14, 1925
Angus Wilton McLean (D)	Jan. 14, 1925	Jan. 11, 1929
O. Max Gardner (D)	Jan. 11, 1929	Jan. 5, 1933
John C. B. Ehringhaus (D)	Jan. 5, 1933	Jan. 7, 1937
Clyde R. Hoey (D)	Jan. 7, 1937	Jan. 9, 1941
J. Melville Broughton (D)	Jan. 9, 1941	Jan. 4, 1945
R. Gregg Cherry (D)	Jan. 4, 1945	Jan. 6, 1949
W. Kerr Scott (D)	Jan. 6, 1949	Jan. 8, 1953
William B. Umstead (D)[15]	Jan. 8, 1953	Nov. 7, 1954
Luther H. Hodges (D)[16]	Nov. 7, 1954	Jan. 5, 1961
Terry Sanford (D)	Jan. 5, 1961	Jan. 8, 1965
Dan K. Moore (D)	Jan. 8, 1965	Jan. 3, 1969
Robert W. Scott (D)	Jan. 3, 1969	Jan. 5, 1973
James E. Holshouser Jr. (R)	Jan. 5, 1973	Jan. 8, 1977
James B. Hunt Jr. (D)	Jan. 8, 1977	Jan. 5, 1985
James G. Martin (R)	Jan. 5, 1985	

NORTH DAKOTA

(Became a state Nov. 2, 1889)

Governors	Dates of Service	
John Miller (R)	Nov. 4, 1889	Jan. 6, 1891
Andrew H. Burke (R)	Jan. 7, 1891	Jan. 4, 1893
Eli C. D. Shortridge (FUS)	Jan. 4, 1893	Jan. 7, 1895
Roger Allin (R)	Jan. 7, 1895	Jan. 5, 1897
Frank A. Briggs (R)[1]	Jan. 5, 1897	Aug. 9, 1898
Joseph M. Devine (R)[2]	Aug. 9, 1898	Jan. 3, 1899
Frederick B. Fancher (R)	Jan. 3, 1899	Jan. 10, 1901
Frank White (R)	Jan. 10, 1901	Jan. 4, 1905
Elmore Y. Sarles (R)	Jan. 5, 1905	Jan. 9, 1907
John Burke (D)	Jan. 9, 1907	Jan. 8, 1913
Louis B. Hanna (R)	Jan. 8, 1913	Jan. 3, 1917
Lynn J. Frazier (R)[3]	Jan. 3, 1917	Nov. 23, 1921
Ragnvald A. Nestos (R)[4]	Nov. 23, 1921	Jan. 5, 1925
Arthur G. Sorlie (R)[5]	Jan. 7, 1925	Aug. 28, 1928
Walter J. Maddock (R)[6]	Aug. 28, 1928	Jan. 9, 1929
George F. Shafer (R)	Jan. 9, 1929	Dec. 31, 1932
William Langer (R)[7]	Dec. 31, 1932	July 17, 1934
Ole H. Olson (R)[8]	July 17, 1934	Jan. 7, 1935
Thomas H. Moodie (D)[9]	Jan. 7,1935	Feb. 2, 1935
Walter Welford (R)[10]	Feb. 2, 1935	Jan. 6, 1937
William Langer (I)	Jan. 6, 1937	Jan. 5, 1939
John Moses (D)	Jan. 5, 1939	Jan. 4, 1945
Fred G. Aandahl (R)	Jan. 4, 1945	Jan. 3, 1951
C. Norman Brunsdale (R)	Jan. 3, 1951	Jan. 9, 1957
John E. Davis (R)	Jan. 9, 1957	Jan. 4, 1961
William L. Guy (D)	Jan. 4, 1961	Jan. 2, 1973
Arthur A. Link (D)	Jan. 2, 1973	Jan. 7, 1981
Allen I. Olson (R)[11]	Jan. 7, 1981	Jan. 8, 1985
George Sinner (D)[11]	Jan. 8, 1985	

OHIO

(Became a state March 1, 1803)

Governors	Dates of Service	
Edward Tiffin (D-R)[1]	March 3, 1803	March 4, 1807
Thomas Kirker (D-R)[2]	March 4, 1807	Dec. 12, 1808
Samuel Huntington (D-R)	Dec. 12, 1808	Dec. 8, 1810

North Dakota

  1. *Died in 1898.*
  2. *As lieutenant governor, he succeeded to office.*
  3. *Recalled in election of Oct. 28, 1921; removed Nov. 23, 1921.*
  4. *Elected in recall election of 1921, which removed Governor Frazier. Subsequently elected for a full two-year term.*
  5. *Died Aug. 28, 1928.*
  6. *As lieutenant governor, he succeeded to office.*
  7. *Removed by North Dakota Supreme Court July 17, 1934.*
  8. *As lieutenant governor, he succeeded to office.*
  9. *Disqualified by North Dakota Supreme Court Feb. 2, 1935.*
  10. *As lieutenant governor, he succeeded to office.*
  11. *Although Olson relinquished his office on Jan. 5 and Sinner assumed it Jan. 8, the North Dakota Supreme Court held that Sinner's term began Jan. 1.*

Ohio

  1. *Resigned March 4, 1807.*
  2. *As Speaker of the state Senate, he succeeded to office.*

  3. *Resigned March 24, 1814.*
  4. *As Speaker of the state Senate, he succeeded to office.*
  5. *Resigned Jan. 4, 1822.*
  6. *As Speaker of the state Senate, he succeeded to office.*
  7. *Resigned April 15, 1844.*
  8. *As Speaker of the state Senate, he succeeded to office.*
  9. *The election of 1848 was disputed, and Ford's election was delayed until Jan. 22, 1849.*
  10. *Resigned July 13, 1853.*
  11. *As lieutenant governor, he succeeded to office. Subsequently elected.*
  12. *Died Aug. 29, 1865.*
  13. *As lieutenant governor, he succeeded to office.*
  14. *Resigned March 2, 1877, having been elected president of the United States.*
  15. *As lieutenant governor, he succeeded to office.*
  16. *Died June 18, 1906.*
  17. *As lieutenant governor, he succeeded to office.*
  18. *Resigned Jan. 3, 1957.*
  19. *As lieutenant governor, he succeeded to office.*

Return Jonathan Meigs (D-R)[3]	Dec. 8, 1810	March 24, 1814
Othneil Looker (D-R)[4]	March 24, 1814	Dec. 8, 1814
Thomas Worthington (D-R)	Dec. 8, 1814	Dec. 14, 1818
Ethan Allen Brown (D-R)[5]	Dec. 14, 1818	Jan. 4, 1822
Allen Trimble (D-R)[6]	Jan. 4, 1822	Dec. 28, 1822
Jeremiah Morrow (JAC D)	Dec. 28, 1822	Dec. 19, 1826
Allen Trimble (NR)	Dec. 19, 1826	Dec. 18, 1830
Duncan McArthur (NR)	Dec. 18, 1830	Dec. 7, 1832
Robert Lucas (D)	Dec. 7, 1832	Dec. 12, 1836
Joseph Vance (W)	Dec. 12, 1836	Dec. 13, 1838
Wilson Shannon (D)	Dec. 13, 1838	Dec. 16, 1840
Thomas Corwin (W)	Dec. 16, 1840	Dec. 14, 1842
Wilson Shannon (D)[7]	Dec. 14, 1842	April 15, 1844
Thomas W. Bartley (D)[8]	April 15, 1844	Dec. 3, 1844
Mordecai Bartley (W)	Dec. 3, 1844	Dec. 12, 1846
William Bebb (W)	Dec. 12, 1846	Jan. 22, 1849
Seabury Ford (W)[9]	Jan. 22, 1849	Dec. 12, 1850
Reuben Wood (D)[10]	Dec. 12, 1850	July 13, 1853
William Medill (D)[11]	July 13, 1853	Jan. 14, 1856
Salmon P. Chase (R)	Jan. 14, 1856	Jan. 9, 1860
William Dennison Jr. (R)	Jan. 9, 1860	Jan. 13, 1862
David Tod (UN)	Jan. 13, 1862	Jan. 11, 1864
John Brough (UN)[12]	Jan. 11, 1864	Aug. 29, 1865
Charles Anderson (UN)[13]	Aug. 29, 1865	Jan. 8, 1866
Jacob D. Cox (UN)	Jan. 8, 1866	Jan. 13, 1868
Rutherford B. Hayes (R)	Jan. 13, 1868	Jan. 8, 1872
Edward F. Noyes (R)	Jan. 8, 1872	Jan. 12, 1874
William Allen (D)	Jan. 12, 1874	Jan. 10, 1876
Rutherford B. Hayes (R)[14]	Jan. 10, 1876	March 2, 1877
Thomas L. Young (R)[15]	March 2, 1877	Jan. 14, 1878
Richard M. Bishop (D)	Jan. 14, 1878	Jan. 12, 1880
Charles Foster (R)	Jan. 12, 1880	Jan. 14, 1884
George Hoadly (D)	Jan. 14, 1884	Jan. 11, 1886
Joseph B. Foraker (R)	Jan. 11, 1886	Jan. 13, 1890
James E. Campbell (D)	Jan. 13, 1890	Jan. 11, 1892
William McKinley Jr. (R)	Jan. 11, 1892	Jan. 13, 1896
Asa S. Bushnell (R)	Jan. 13, 1896	Jan. 8, 1900
George K. Nash (R)	Jan. 8, 1900	Jan. 11, 1904
Myron T. Herrick (R)	Jan. 11, 1904	Jan. 8, 1906
John M. Pattison (D)[16]	Jan. 8, 1906	June 18, 1906
Andrew L. Harris (R)[17]	June 18, 1906	Jan. 11, 1909
Judson Harmon (D)	Jan. 11, 1909	Jan. 13, 1913
James M. Cox (D)	Jan. 13, 1913	Jan. 11, 1915
Frank B. Willis (R)	Jan. 11, 1915	Jan. 8, 1917
James M. Cox (D)	Jan. 8, 1917	Jan. 10, 1921
Harry L. Davis (R)	Jan. 10, 1921	Jan. 8, 1923
Alvin Victor Donahey (D)	Jan. 8, 1923	Jan. 14, 1929
Myers Y. Cooper (R)	Jan. 14, 1929	Jan. 12, 1931
George White (D)	Jan. 12, 1931	Jan. 14, 1935
Martin L. Davey (D)	Jan. 14, 1935	Jan. 9, 1939
John W. Bricker (R)	Jan. 9, 1939	Jan. 8, 1945
Frank J. Lausche (D)	Jan. 8, 1945	Jan. 13, 1947
Thomas J. Herbert (R)	Jan. 13, 1947	Jan. 10, 1949
Frank J. Lausche (D)[18]	Jan. 10, 1949	Jan. 3, 1957
John W. Brown (R)[19]	Jan. 3, 1957	Jan. 14, 1957

C. William O'Neill (R)	Jan. 14, 1957	Jan. 12, 1959
Michael V. DiSalle (D)	Jan. 12, 1959	Jan. 14, 1963
James A. Rhodes (R)	Jan. 14, 1963	Jan. 11, 1971
John J. Gilligan (D)	Jan. 11, 1971	Jan. 13, 1975
James A. Rhodes (R)	Jan. 13, 1975	Jan. 10, 1983
Richard F. Celeste (D)	Jan. 10, 1983	

OKLAHOMA

(Became a state Nov. 16, 1907)

Governors	Dates of Service	
Charles N. Haskell (D)	Nov. 16, 1907	Jan. 9, 1911
Lee Cruce (D)	Jan. 9, 1911	Jan. 11, 1915
Robert L. Williams (D)	Jan. 11, 1915	Jan. 13, 1919
James B. A. Robertson (D)	Jan. 13, 1919	Jan. 8, 1923
John C. Walton (D)[1]	Jan. 8, 1923	Nov. 19, 1923
Martin E. Trapp (D)[2]	Nov. 19, 1923	Jan. 10, 1927
Henry S. Johnston (D)[3]	Jan. 10, 1927	March 20, 1929
William J. Holloway (D)[4]	March 20, 1929	Jan. 12, 1931
William H. Murray (D)	Jan. 12, 1931	Jan. 14, 1935
Ernest W. Marland (D)	Jan. 14, 1935	Jan. 9, 1939
Leon C. Phillips (D)	Jan. 9, 1939	Jan. 11, 1943
Robert S. Kerr (D)	Jan. 11, 1943	Jan. 13, 1947
Roy J. Turner (D)	Jan. 13, 1947	Jan. 8, 1951
Johnston Murray (D)	Jan. 8, 1951	Jan. 10, 1955
Raymond D. Gary (D)	Jan. 10, 1955	Jan. 12, 1959
J. Howard Edmondson (D)[5]	Jan. 12, 1959	Jan. 6, 1963
George P. Nigh (D)[6]	Jan. 6, 1963	Jan. 14, 1963
Henry L. Bellmon (R)	Jan. 14, 1963	Jan. 9, 1967
Dewey F. Bartlett (R)	Jan. 9, 1967	Jan. 11, 1971
David Hall (D)	Jan. 11, 1971	Jan. 13, 1975
David L. Boren (D)	Jan. 13, 1975	Jan. 3, 1979
George Nigh (D)	Jan. 3, 1979	

OREGON

(Became a state Feb. 14, 1859)

Governors	Dates of Service	
John Whiteaker (D)	March 3, 1859	Sept. 10, 1862
A. C. Gibbs (UN R)	Sept. 10, 1862	Sept. 12, 1866
George L. Woods (R)	Sept. 12, 1866	Sept. 14, 1870
La Fayette Grover (D)[1]	Sept. 14, 1870	Feb. 1, 1877
Stephen F. Chadwick (D)[2]	Feb. 1, 1877	Sept. 11, 1878
William Wallace Thayer (D)	Sept. 11, 1878	Sept. 13, 1882
Zenas F. Moody (R)	Sept. 13, 1882	Jan. 12, 1887
Sylvester Pennoyer (D)	Jan. 12, 1887	Jan. 14, 1895
William P. Lord (R)	Jan. 14, 1895	Jan. 9, 1899
Theodore T. Geer (R)	Jan. 9, 1899	Jan. 14, 1903

Oklahoma

1. Impeached; removed from office, Nov. 19, 1923.
2. As lieutenant governor, he succeeded to office.
3. Impeached; removed from office, March 20, 1929.
4. As lieutenant governor, he succeeded to office.
5. Resigned Jan. 6, 1963.
6. As lieutenant governor, he succeeded to office.

Oregon

1. Resigned Feb. 1, 1877.
2. As secretary of state, he succeeded to office.
3. Resigned March 1, 1909.
4. As secretary of state, he succeeded to office. Resigned June 17, 1910.
5. As president of the state Senate, he succeeded to office.

6. Died March 3, 1919.
7. As secretary of state, he succeeded to office.
8. Died Dec. 21, 1929.
9. As president of the state Senate, he succeeded to office.
10. Died Oct. 28, 1947.
11. As speaker of the House, he succeeded to office for the remainder of the first two years of Snell's term.
12. Elected for the last two years of Snell's term in a special election. Subsequently re-elected. Resigned Dec. 27, 1952.
13. As president of the state senate, he succeeded to office. Subsequently elected. Died Jan. 31, 1956.
14. As president of the state Senate, he succeeded to office for the remainder of the first two years of Patterson's term.
15. Elected in a special election for the last two years of Patterson's term.

George E. Chamberlain (D)[3]	Jan. 14, 1903	March 1, 1909
Frank W. Benson (R)[4]	March 1, 1909	June 17, 1910
Jay Bowerman (R)[5]	June 17, 1910	Jan. 10, 1911
Oswald West (D)	Jan. 10, 1911	Jan. 12, 1915
James Withycombe (R)[6]	Jan. 12, 1915	March 3, 1919
Ben W. Olcott (R)[7]	March 3, 1919	Jan. 8, 1923
Walter M. Pierce (D)	Jan. 8, 1923	Jan. 10, 1927
Isaac L. Patterson (R)[8]	Jan. 10, 1927	Dec. 21, 1929
A. W. Norblad (R)[9]	Dec. 22, 1929	Jan. 12, 1931
Julius L. Meier (I)	Jan. 12, 1931	Jan. 14, 1935
Charles H. Martin (D)	Jan. 14, 1935	Jan. 9, 1939
Charles A. Sprague (R)	Jan. 9, 1939	Jan. 11, 1943
Earl Snell (R)[10]	Jan. 11, 1943	Oct. 28, 1947
John H. Hall (R)[11]	Oct. 30, 1947	Jan. 10, 1949
Douglas McKay (R)[12]	Jan. 10, 1949	Dec. 27, 1952
Paul L. Patterson (R)[13]	Dec. 27, 1952	Jan. 31, 1956
Elmo Smith (R)[14]	Feb. 1, 1956	Jan. 14, 1957
Robert D. Holmes (D)[15]	Jan. 14, 1957	Jan. 12, 1959
Mark O. Hatfield (R)	Jan. 12, 1959	Jan. 9, 1967
Tom McCall (R)	Jan. 9, 1967	Jan. 13, 1975
Robert W. Straub (D)	Jan. 13, 1975	Jan. 8, 1979
Victor Atiyeh (R)	Jan. 8, 1979	

PENNSYLVANIA

(Ratified the Constitution Dec. 12, 1787)

Governors	Dates of Service	
Peter Mulhenberg	Oct. 31, 1787	Oct. 14, 1788
David Redick	Oct. 14, 1788	Nov. 5, 1788
George Ross	Nov. 5, 1788	Dec. 21, 1790
Thomas Mifflin	Dec. 21, 1790	Dec. 17, 1799
Thomas McKean (D-R)	Dec. 17, 1799	Dec. 20, 1808
Simon Snyder (D-R)	Dec. 20, 1808	Dec. 16, 1817
William Findlay (D-R)	Dec. 16, 1817	Dec. 19, 1820
Joseph Hiester (D-R)	Dec. 19, 1820	Dec. 16, 1823
John A. Shulze (JAC D)	Dec. 16, 1823	Dec. 15, 1829
George Wolfe (JAC D)	Dec. 15, 1829	Dec. 15, 1835
Joseph Ritner (D)	Dec. 15, 1835	Jan. 15, 1839
David R. Porter (D)	Jan. 15, 1839	Jan. 21, 1845
Francis R. Shunk (D)[1]	Jan. 21, 1845	July 9, 1848
William F. Johnston (W)[2]	July 26, 1848	Jan. 20, 1852
William Bigler (D)	Jan. 20, 1852	Jan. 16, 1855
James Pollock (W)	Jan. 16, 1855	Jan. 19, 1858
William F. Packer (D)	Jan. 19, 1858	Jan. 15, 1861
Andrew G. Curtin (R)	Jan. 15, 1861	Jan. 15, 1867
John W. Geary (R)	Jan. 15, 1867	Jan. 21, 1873

John F. Hartranft (R)	Jan. 21, 1873	Jan. 18, 1879
Henry M. Hoyt (R)	Jan. 21, 1879	Jan. 16, 1883
Robert E. Pattison (D)	Jan. 16, 1883	Jan. 18, 1887
James A. Beaver (R)	Jan. 18, 1887	Jan. 20, 1891
Robert E. Pattison (D)	Jan. 20, 1891	Jan. 15, 1895
Daniel H. Hastings (R)	Jan. 15, 1895	Jan. 17, 1899
William A. Stone (R)	Jan. 17, 1899	Jan. 20, 1903
Samuel W. Pennypacker (R)	Jan. 20, 1903	Jan. 15, 1907
Edwin S. Stuart (R)	Jan. 15, 1907	Jan. 17, 1911
John K. Tener (R)	Jan. 17, 1911	Jan. 19, 1915
Martin G. Brumbaugh (R)	Jan. 19, 1915	Jan. 21, 1919
William C. Sproul (R)	Jan. 21, 1919	Jan. 16, 1923
Gifford Pinchot (R)	Jan. 16, 1923	Jan. 18, 1927
John S. Fisher (R)	Jan. 18, 1927	Jan. 20, 1931
Gifford Pinchot (R, PROG)	Jan. 20, 1931	Jan. 15, 1935
George H. Earle (D)	Jan. 15, 1935	Jan. 17, 1939
Arthur H. James (R)	Jan. 17, 1939	Jan. 19,1943
Edward Martin (R)[3]	Jan. 19, 1943	Jan. 2, 1947
John C. Bell Jr. (R)[4]	Jan. 2, 1947	Jan. 21, 1947
James H. Duff (R)	Jan. 21, 1947	Jan. 16, 1951
John S. Fine (R)	Jan. 16, 1951	Jan. 18, 1955
George M. Leader (D)	Jan. 18, 1955	Jan. 20, 1959
David L. Lawrence (D)	Jan. 20, 1959	Jan. 15, 1963
William W. Scranton (R)	Jan. 15, 1963	Jan. 17, 1967
Raymond P. Shafer (R)	Jan. 17, 1967	Jan. 19, 1971
Milton J. Shapp (D)	Jan. 19, 1971	Jan. 16, 1979
Richard L. Thornburgh (R)	Jan. 16, 1979	

RHODE ISLAND

(Ratified the Constitution May 29, 1790)

Governors	Dates of Service	
Arthur Fenner (D-R)[1]	May 5, 1790	Oct. 15, 1805
Henry Smith (D-R)[2]	Oct. 15, 1805	May 7, 1806
Isaac Wilbur (D-R)[3]	May 7, 1806	May 6, 1807
James Fenner	May 6, 1807	May 1, 1811
William Jones (FED)	May 1, 1811	May 7, 1817
Nehemiah R. Knight (D-R)[4]	May 7, 1817	Jan. 9, 1821
Edward Wilcox (D-R)[5]	Jan. 9, 1821	May 2, 1821
William C. Gibbs (D-R)	May 2, 1821	May 5, 1824
James Fenner (D-R)	May 5, 1824	May 4, 1831
Lemuel H. Arnold (D)[6]	May 4, 1831	May 1, 1833
John Brown Francis (D)	May 1, 1833	May 2, 1838
William Sprague (W)	May 2, 1838	May 1, 1839
Samuel Ward King (W)[7]	May 2, 1839	May 2, 1843
James Fenner (L & O W)	May 2, 1843	May 6, 1845

Pennsylvania

1. Resigned July 9, 1848.

2. Interregnum from July 9 to July 26, 1848. Johnston became acting governor. Subsequently elected.

3. Resigned Jan. 2, 1947.

4. As lieutenant governor, he succeeded to office.

Rhode Island

1. Died Oct. 15, 1805.

2. Smith, as first senator, served as governor.

3. No governor was elected in 1806. Wilbur, the lieutenant governor, served as acting governor.

4. Resigned Jan. 9, 1821.

5. As lieutenant governor, he succeeded to office.

6. In the 1832 election, no candidate for governor received the majority of the total vote cast which was required for election. Elections were held four more times — on May 16, July 18, August 28 and Nov. 21 — each one resulting without choice. Arnold was continued in office until 1833. (The returns for this election, p. 524, show only the first election.)

7. No governor was elected in 1839, no candidate having received a majority of the vote. In addition, no lieutenant governor was elected. King, as first senator, became acting governor for the term. Subsequently re-elected three times.

8. Resigned July 20, 1853.

9. As lieutenant governor, he succeeded to office.

10. Resigned March 3, 1863.

11. As president of the state Senate, he succeeded to office.

12. No candidate received a majority of the vote in the election of 1893, and under the law the Legislature was required to elect the governor. However, because of a dispute between the two houses no choice was made. Governor Brown continued in office for the term. He was re-elected in 1894. The controversy over the election resulted in repeal of the majority-vote requirement in 1893.

13. Died Dec. 16, 1901.

14. As lieutenant governor, he succeeded to office.

15. Died Feb. 4, 1928.

16. As lieutenant governor, he succeeded to office. Subsequently elected.

17. Resigned Oct. 6, 1945.

18. As lieutenant governor, he succeeded to office. Subsequently elected. Resigned Dec. 19, 1950.

19. As lieutenant governor, he succeeded to office.

Charles Jackson (LIBER W)	May 6, 1845	May 6, 1846
Byron Diman (L & O W)	May 6, 1846	May 4, 1847
Elisha Harris (W)	May 4, 1847	May 1, 1849
Henry B. Anthony (W)	May 1, 1849	May 6, 1851
Philip Allen (D)[8]	May 6, 1851	July 20, 1853
Francis M. Dimond (D)[9]	July 20, 1853	May 2, 1854
William W. Hoppin (W, R)	May 2, 1854	May 26, 1857
Elisha Dyer (R)	May 26, 1857	May 31, 1859
Thomas G. Turner	May 31, 1859	May 29, 1860
William Sprague (FUS, UN)[10]	May 29, 1860	March 3, 1863
William C. Cozzens[11]	March 3, 1863	May 26, 1863
James Y. Smith (UN R)	May 26, 1863	May 29, 1866
Ambrose E. Burnside (R)	May 29, 1866	May 25, 1869
Seth Padelford (R)	May 25, 1869	May 27, 1873
Henry Howard (R)	May 27, 1873	May 25, 1875
Henry Lippitt (R)	May 25, 1875	May 29, 1877
Charles Van Zandt (R & TEMP)	May 29, 1877	May 25, 1880
Alfred H. Littlefield (R)	May 25, 1880	May 29, 1883
Augustus O. Bourn (R)	May 29, 1883	May 26, 1885
George P. Wetmore (R)	May 26, 1885	May 31, 1887
John W. Davis (D)	May 31, 1887	May 29, 1888
Royal C. Taft (R)	May 29, 1888	May 28, 1889
Herbert W. Ladd (R)	May 28, 1889	May 27, 1890
John W. Davis (D)	May 27, 1890	May 26, 1891
Herbert W. Ladd (R)	May 26, 1891	May 31, 1892
D. Russell Brown (R)[12]	May 31, 1892	May 29, 1895
Charles W. Lippitt (R)	May 29, 1895	May 25, 1897
Elisha Dyer (R)	May 25, 1897	May 29, 1900
William Gregory (R)[13]	May 29, 1900	Dec. 16, 1901
Charles D. Kimball (R)[14]	Dec. 16, 1901	Jan. 6, 1903
Lucius F. C. Garvin (D)	Jan. 6, 1903	Jan. 3, 1905
George H. Utter (R)	Jan. 3, 1905	Jan. 1, 1907
James H. Higgins (D)	Jan. 1, 1907	Jan. 5, 1909
Aram J. Pothier (R)	Jan. 5, 1909	Jan. 5, 1915
R. Livingston Beeckman (R)	Jan. 5, 1915	Jan. 4, 1921
Emery J. San Souci (R)	Jan. 4, 1921	Jan. 2, 1923
William S. Flynn (D)	Jan. 2, 1923	Jan. 6, 1925
Aram J. Pothier (R)[15]	Jan. 6, 1925	Feb. 4, 1928
Norman S. Case (R)[16]	Feb. 4, 1928	Jan. 3, 1933
Theodore F. Green (D)	Jan. 3, 1933	Jan. 5, 1937
Robert E. Quinn (D)	Jan. 5, 1937	Jan. 3, 1939
William H. Vanderbilt (R)	Jan. 3, 1939	Jan. 7, 1941
J. Howard McGrath (D)[17]	Jan. 7, 1941	Oct. 6, 1945
John O. Pastore (D)[18]	Oct. 6, 1945	Dec. 19, 1950
John S. McKiernan (D)[19]	Dec. 19, 1950	Jan. 2, 1951
Dennis J. Roberts (D)	Jan. 2, 1951	Jan. 6, 1959
Christopher Del Sesto (R)	Jan. 6, 1959	Jan. 3, 1961
John A. Notte Jr. (D)	Jan. 3, 1961	Jan. 1, 1963
John H. Chafee (R)	Jan. 1, 1963	Jan. 7, 1969
Frank Licht (D)	Jan. 7, 1969	Jan. 2, 1973

Philip W. Noel (D)	Jan. 2, 1973	Jan. 4, 1977
Joseph J. Garrahy (D)	Jan. 4, 1977	Jan. 1, 1985
Edward DiPrete (R)	Jan. 1, 1985	

SOUTH CAROLINA

(Ratified the Constitution May 23, 1788)

Governors	Dates of Service	
Charles Pinckney	Jan. 26, 1789	Dec. 5, 1792
William Moultrie (FED)	Dec. 5, 1792	Dec. 1794
Arnoldus Vander Horst (FED)	Dec. 1794	Dec. 1796
Charles Pinckney (D-R)	Dec. 1796	Dec. 6, 1798
Edward Rutledge (FED)[1]	Dec. 18, 1798	Jan. 23, 1800
John Drayton (D-R)[2]	Jan. 23, 1800	Dec. 1802
James B. Richardson (D-R)	Dec. 1802	Dec. 1804
Paul Hamilton (D-R)	Dec. 1804	Dec. 1806
Charles Pinckney (D-R)	Dec. 1806	Dec. 10, 1808
John Drayton (D-R)	Dec. 10, 1808	Dec. 1810
Henry Middleton (D-R)	Dec. 10, 1810	Dec. 1812
Joseph Alston (D-R)	Dec. 1812	Dec. 1814
David R. Williams (D-R)	Dec. 1814	Dec. 1816
Andrew Pickens (D-R)	Dec. 1816	Dec. 1818
John Geddes (D-R)	Dec. 1818	Dec. 1820
Thomas Bennett (D-R)	Dec. 1820	Dec. 1822
John Lyde Wilson (D-R)	Dec. 1822	Dec. 1824
Richard I. Manning (D-R)	Dec. 1824	Dec. 1826
John Taylor (D-R)	Dec. 1826	Dec. 1828
Stephen D. Miller (D)	Dec. 1828	Dec. 1830
James Hamilton Jr. (D)	Dec. 1830	Dec. 13, 1832
Robert Y. Hayne (D)	Dec. 13, 1832	Dec. 11, 1834
George McDuffie (D)	Dec. 11, 1834	Dec. 1836
Pierce M. Butler (D)	Dec. 1836	Dec. 10, 1838
Patrick Noble (D)[3]	Dec. 10, 1838	April 7, 1840
B. K. Henagan (D)[4]	April 7, 1840	Dec. 10, 1840
John P. Richardson (D)	Dec. 10, 1840	Dec. 1842
James H. Hammond (D)	Dec. 1842	Dec. 1844
William Aiken (D)	Dec. 1844	Dec. 1846
David Johnson (D)	Dec. 1846	Dec. 1848
Whitmarsh B. Seabrook (D)	Dec. 1848	Dec. 1850
John Hugh Means (D)	Dec. 16, 1850	Dec. 1852
John Laurence Manning (D)	Dec. 1852	Dec. 1854
James H. Adams (D)	Dec. 1854	Dec. 1856
Robert F. W. Alston (D)	Dec. 1856	Dec. 1858
William H. Gist (D)	Dec. 1858	Dec. 1860
Francis W. Pickens (D)	Dec. 1860	Dec. 1862
Milledge L. Bonham (D)	Dec. 1862	Dec. 1864

South Carolina

1. *Died Jan. 23, 1800.*
2. *As lieutenant governor, he succeeded to office. Subsequently elected.*
3. *Died April 7, 1840.*
4. *As lieutenant governor, he succeeded to office.*
5. *Last Confederate governor. Removed by federal authorities.*
6. *Provisional governor appointed by President Johnson.*
7. *Deposed by act of Congress.*
8. *There was a dispute between two factions in the House of Representatives over the elections and seating of eight of its members following the 1876 election. The pro-Chamberlain (R) faction declared Chamberlain to have been re-elected and he was re-inaugurated on December 7. The pro-Hampton (D) faction also organized as the House of Representatives and on December 14 declared Hampton to have been elected. He was inaugurated on the same day. For a time there were two rival state governments. In several cases arising later, raising the question of Hampton's authority to act as governor, the Supreme Court of the state declared him to be the lawfully elected chief executive of the state. Chamberlain dropped his claim to the office on April 10, 1877, following the withdrawal of federal troops from the state in March 1877 by President Hayes.*

9. *Resigned Feb. 26, 1879.*
10. *As lieutenant governor, he succeeded to office. Resigned in September 1880.*
11. *As president of the state Senate, he succeeded to office.*
12. *Resigned July 10, 1886.*
13. *As lieutenant governor, he succeeded to office.*
14. *Died June 2, 1899.*
15. *As lieutenant governor, he succeeded to office. Subsequently elected.*
16. *Resigned Jan. 14, 1915.*
17. *As lieutenant governor, he succeeded to office.*
18. *Resigned May 20, 1922.*
19. *As lieutenant governor, he succeeded to office.*
20. *Resigned Nov. 4, 1941.*
21. *As lieutenant governor, he succeeded to office. Died Feb. 27, 1942.*
22. *As president of the state Senate, he succeeded to office.*
23. *Resigned Jan. 2, 1945.*
24. *As lieutenant governor, he succeeded to office.*
25. *Resigned April 22, 1965.*
26. *As lieutenant governor, he succeeded to office. Subsequently elected.*

Andrew G. Magrath (D)[5]	Dec. 20, 1864	May 25, 1865
Benjamin F. Perry[6]	June 30, 1865	Nov. 29, 1865
James L. Orr (C)[7]	Nov. 29, 1865	July 6, 1868
Robert K. Scott (R)	July 9, 1868	Dec. 7, 1872
Franklin J. Moses Jr. (R)	Dec. 7, 1872	Dec. 1, 1874
Daniel H. Chamberlain (R)[8]	Dec. 1, 1874	April 10, 1877
Wade Hampton (D)[9]	Dec. 14, 1876	Feb. 26, 1879
William D. Simpson (D)[10]	Feb. 26, 1879	Sept. 1, 1880
Thomas B. Jeter (D)[11]	Sept. 1, 1880	Nov. 30, 1880
Johnson Hagood (D)	Nov. 30, 1880	Dec. 1882
Hugh Smith Thompson (D)[12]	Dec. 1882	July 10, 1886
John C. Sheppard (D)[13]	July 10, 1886	Nov. 30, 1886
John P. Richardson (D)	Nov. 30, 1886	Dec. 4, 1890
Benjamin Ryan Tillman (D)	Dec. 4, 1890	Dec. 1894
John Gary Evans (D)	Dec. 4, 1894	Jan. 18, 1897
William H. Ellerbe (D)[14]	Jan. 18, 1897	June 2, 1899
Miles B. McSweeney (D)[15]	June 2, 1899	Jan. 20, 1903
Duncan C. Heyward (D)	Jan. 20, 1903	Jan. 15, 1907
Martin F. Ansel (D)	Jan. 15, 1907	Jan. 17, 1911
Coleman L. Blease (D)[16]	Jan. 17, 1911	Jan. 14, 1915
Charles A. Smith (D)[17]	Jan. 14, 1915	Jan. 19, 1915
Richard I. Manning (D)	Jan. 19, 1915	Jan. 21, 1919
Robert A. Cooper (D)[18]	Jan. 21, 1919	May 20, 1922
Wilson G. Harvey (D)[19]	May 20, 1922	Jan. 16, 1923
Thomas G. McLeod (D)	Jan. 16, 1923	Jan. 18, 1927
John G. Richards (D)	Jan. 18, 1927	Jan. 20, 1931
Ibra C. Blackwood (D)	Jan. 20, 1931	Jan. 15, 1935
Olin D. Johnston (D)	Jan. 15, 1935	Jan. 17, 1939
Burnet R. Maybank (D)[20]	Jan. 17, 1939	Nov. 4, 1941
Joseph E. Harley (D)[21]	Nov. 4, 1941	Feb. 27, 1942
Richard M. Jeffries (D)[22]	March 2, 1942	Jan. 19, 1943
Olin D. Johnston (D)[23]	Jan. 19, 1943	Jan. 2, 1945
Ransome J. Williams (D)[24]	Jan. 2, 1945	Jan. 21, 1947
J. Strom Thurmond (D)	Jan. 21, 1947	Jan. 16, 1951
James F. Byrnes (D)	Jan. 16, 1951	Jan. 18, 1955
George Bell Timmerman Jr. (D)	Jan. 18, 1955	Jan. 20, 1959
Ernest F. Hollings (D)	Jan. 20, 1959	Jan. 15, 1963
Donald S. Russell (D)[25]	Jan. 15, 1963	April 22, 1965
Robert E. McNair (D)[26]	April 22, 1965	Jan. 19, 1971
John C. West (D)	Jan. 19, 1971	Jan. 21, 1975
James Edwards (R)	Jan. 21, 1975	Jan. 10, 1979
Richard Riley (D)	Jan. 10, 1979	

SOUTH DAKOTA

(Became a state Nov. 2, 1889)

Governors	Dates of Service	
Arthur C. Melette (R)	Nov. 2, 1889	Jan. 1893
Charles H. Sheldon (R)	Jan. 1893	Jan. 1, 1897
Andrew E. Lee (PP, FUS)	Jan. 1, 1897	Jan. 8, 1901
Charles N. Herreid (R)	Jan. 8, 1901	Jan. 3, 1905
Samuel H. Elrod (R)	Jan. 3, 1905	Jan. 8, 1907
Coe I. Crawford (R)	Jan. 8, 1907	Jan. 5, 1909
Robert S. Vessey (R)	Jan. 5, 1909	Jan. 7, 1913
Frank M. Byrne (R)	Jan. 7, 1913	Jan. 2, 1917

Peter Norbeck (R)	Jan. 2, 1917	Jan. 4, 1921
William H. McMaster (R)	Jan. 4, 1921	Jan. 6, 1925
Carl Gunderson (R)	Jan. 6, 1925	Jan. 4, 1927
William J. Bulow (D)	Jan. 4, 1927	Jan. 6, 1931
Warren E. Green (R)	Jan. 6, 1931	Jan. 3, 1933
Tom Berry (D)	Jan. 3, 1933	Jan. 5, 1937
Leslie Jensen (R)	Jan. 5, 1937	Jan. 3, 1939
Harlan J. Bushfield (R)	Jan. 3, 1939	Jan. 5, 1943
Merrell Q. Sharpe (R)	Jan. 5, 1943	Jan. 7, 1947
George T. Mickelson (R)	Jan. 7, 1947	Jan. 2, 1951
Sigurd Anderson (R)	Jan. 2, 1951	Jan. 4, 1955
Joe Foss (R)	Jan. 4, 1955	Jan. 6, 1959
Ralph E. Herseth (D)	Jan. 6, 1959	Jan. 3, 1961
Archie M. Gubbrud (R)	Jan. 3, 1961	Jan. 5, 1965
Nils A. Boe (R)	Jan. 5, 1965	Jan. 7, 1969
Frank L. Farrar (R)	Jan. 7, 1969	Jan. 5, 1971
Richard F. Kneip (D)[1]	Jan. 5, 1971	July 24, 1978
Harvey L. Wollman (D)[2]	July 24, 1978	Jan. 1, 1979
William J. Janklow (R)	Jan. 1, 1979	

TENNESSEE

(Became a state June 1, 1796)

Governors	Dates of Service	
John Sevier (D-R)	March 30, 1796	Sept. 23, 1801
Archibald Roane (D-R)	Sept. 23, 1801	Sept. 23, 1803
John Sevier (D-R)	Sept. 23, 1803	Sept. 20, 1809
Willie Blount (D-R)	Sept. 20, 1809	Sept. 27, 1815
Joseph McMinn (D-R)	Sept. 27, 1815	Oct. 1, 1821
William Carroll (D-R)	Oct. 1, 1821	Oct. 1, 1827
Sam Houston (D-R)[1]	Oct. 1, 1827	April 16, 1829
William Hall (D-R)[2]	April 16, 1829	Oct. 1, 1829
William Carroll (D)	Oct. 1, 1829	Oct. 12, 1835
Newton Cannon (W)	Oct. 12, 1835	Oct. 14, 1839
James K. Polk (D)	Oct. 14, 1839	Oct. 15, 1841
James C. Jones (W)	Oct. 15, 1841	Oct. 14, 1845
Aaron V. Brown (D)	Oct. 14, 1845	Oct. 17, 1847
Neill S. Brown (W)	Oct. 17, 1847	Oct. 16, 1849
William Trousdale (D)	Oct. 16, 1849	Oct. 16, 1851
William B. Campbell (W)	Oct. 16, 1851	Oct. 17, 1853
Andrew Johnson (D)	Oct. 17, 1853	Nov. 3, 1857
Isham G. Harris (D)	Nov. 3, 1857	March 12, 1862
Andrew Johnson[3]	March 12, 1862	March 4, 1865
William G. Brownlow (W, R)[4]	April 5, 1865	Oct. 1867
DeWitt Clinton Senter (CR)[5]	Oct. 11, 1867	Oct. 10, 1871
John C. Brown (D, LR)	Oct. 10, 1871	Jan. 18, 1875
James D. Porter Jr. (D)	Jan. 18, 1875	Feb. 16, 1879
Albert S. Marks (D)	Feb. 16, 1879	Jan. 17, 1881
Alvin Hawkins (R)	Jan. 17, 1881	Jan. 15, 1883
William B. Bate (LOWTAX D, D)	Jan. 15, 1883	Jan. 17, 1887
Robert L. Taylor (D)	Jan. 17, 1887	Jan. 19, 1891
John P. Buchanan (D)	Jan. 19, 1891	Jan. 16, 1893
Peter Turney (D)[6]	Jan. 16, 1893	Jan. 21, 1897
Robert L. Taylor (D)	Jan. 21, 1897	Jan. 16, 1899
Benton McMillin (D)	Jan. 16, 1899	Jan. 19, 1903
James B. Frazier (D)[7]	Jan. 19, 1903	March 21, 1905

South Dakota

1. Resigned July 24, 1978.
2. As lieutenant governor, he succeeded to office.

Tennessee

1. Resigned April 16, 1829.
2. As Speaker of the state Senate, he succeeded to office.
3. Appointed military governor by President Lincoln.
4. Resigned in October 1867.

5. As Speaker of the state Senate, he succeeded to office. Subsequently elected.
6. Governor Turney ran for re-election in 1894, but his Republican opponent, H. Clay Evans, appeared to have won a narrow victory. There were allegations of fraud, however, resulting in a recount of the votes by the Legislature. The Legislature's count made Turney the winner, and he took office for a second term.
7. Resigned March 21, 1905.
8. As Speaker of the state Senate, he succeeded to office.
9. Died Oct. 2, 1927.
10. As Speaker of the state Senate, he succeeded to office. Subsequently elected.

John I. Cox (D)[8]	March 21, 1905	Jan. 17, 1907
Malcolm R. Patterson (D)	Jan. 17, 1907	Jan. 26, 1911
Ben W. Hooper (R)	Jan. 26, 1911	Jan. 17, 1915
Thomas C. Rye (D)	Jan. 17, 1915	Jan. 15, 1919
Albert H. Roberts (D)	Jan. 15, 1919	Jan. 15, 1921
Alfred A. Taylor (R)	Jan. 15, 1921	Jan. 16, 1923
Austin Peay (D)[9]	Jan. 16, 1923	Oct. 2, 1927
Henry H. Horton (D)[10]	Oct. 3, 1927	Jan. 17, 1933
Hill McAlister (D)	Jan. 17, 1933	Jan. 15, 1937
Gordon Browning (D)	Jan. 15, 1937	Jan. 16, 1939
Prentice Cooper (D)	Jan. 16, 1939	Jan. 16, 1945
James N. McCord (D)	Jan. 16, 1945	Jan. 17, 1949
Gordon Browning (D)	Jan. 17, 1949	Jan. 15, 1953
Frank G. Clement (D)	Jan. 15, 1953	Jan. 19, 1959
Buford Ellington (D)	Jan. 19, 1959	Jan. 15, 1963
Frank G. Clement (D)	Jan. 15, 1963	Jan. 16, 1967
Buford Ellington (D)	Jan. 16, 1967	Jan. 16, 1971
Winfield Dunn (R)	Jan. 16, 1971	Jan. 18, 1975
Ray Blanton (D)	Jan. 18, 1975	Jan. 17, 1979
Lamar Alexander (R)	Jan. 17, 1979	

TEXAS

(Became a state Dec. 29, 1845)

Governors	Dates of Service	
Anson Jones (D)	Dec. 9, 1844	Feb. 19, 1846
J. Pinckney Henderson (D)	Feb. 19, 1846	Dec. 21, 1847
George T. Wood (D)	Dec. 21, 1847	Dec. 21, 1849
P. Hansbrough Bell (D)[1]	Dec. 21, 1849	Nov. 23, 1853
J. W. Henderson (D)[2]	Nov. 23, 1853	Dec. 21, 1853
Elisha M. Pease (D)	Dec. 21, 1853	Dec. 21, 1857
Hardin R. Runnels (D)	Dec. 21, 1857	Dec. 21, 1859
Sam Houston (ID)[3]	Dec. 21, 1859	March 16, 1861
Edward Clark (D)[4]	March 16, 1861	Nov. 7, 1861
Francis R. Lubbock[5]	Nov. 7, 1861	Nov. 5, 1863
Pendleton Murrah[6]	Nov. 5, 1863	June 17, 1865
Andrew J. Hamilton[7]	June 17, 1865	Aug. 9, 1866
J. W. Throckmorton (C)	Aug. 9, 1866	Aug. 8, 1867
Elisha M. Pease[8]	Aug. 8, 1867	Sept. 30, 1869
Edmund J. Davis (R)	Jan. 8, 1870	Jan. 15, 1874
Richard Coke (D)[9]	Jan. 15, 1874	Dec. 1, 1876
Richard B. Hubbard (D)[10]	Dec. 1, 1876	Jan. 21, 1879
Oran M. Roberts (D)	Jan. 21, 1879	Jan. 16, 1883
John Ireland (D)	Jan. 16, 1883	Jan. 18, 1887
Lawrence S. Ross (D)	Jan. 18, 1887	Jan. 20, 1891
James S. Hogg (D)	Jan. 20, 1891	Jan. 15, 1895
Charles A. Culberson (D)	Jan. 15, 1895	Jan. 17, 1899
Joseph D. Sayers (D)	Jan. 17, 1899	Jan. 20, 1903
Samuel W. T. Lanham (D)	Jan. 20, 1903	Jan. 15, 1907
Thomas M. Campbell (D)	Jan. 15, 1907	Jan. 17, 1911
Oscar B. Colquitt (D)	Jan. 17, 1911	Jan. 19, 1915

James E. Ferguson (D)[11]	Jan. 19, 1915	Aug. 25, 1917
William P. Hobby (D)[12]	Aug. 25, 1917	Jan. 18, 1921
Pat M. Neff (D)	Jan. 18, 1921	Jan. 20, 1925
Miriam A. Ferguson (D)	Jan. 20, 1925	Jan. 18, 1927
Dan Moody (D)	Jan. 18, 1927	Jan. 20, 1931
Ross M. Sterling (D)	Jan. 20, 1931	Jan. 17, 1933
Miriam A. Ferguson (D)	Jan. 17, 1933	Jan. 15, 1935
James V. Allred (D)	Jan. 15, 1935	Jan. 17, 1939
W. Lee O'Daniel (D)[13]	Jan. 17, 1939	Aug. 4, 1941
Coke R. Stevenson (D)[14]	Aug. 4, 1941	Jan. 21, 1947
Beauford H. Jester (D)[15]	Jan. 21, 1947	July 11, 1949
Allan Shivers (D)[16]	July 11, 1949	Jan. 15, 1957
Price Daniel (D)	Jan. 15, 1957	Jan. 15, 1963
John B. Connally (D)	Jan. 15, 1963	Jan. 21, 1969
Preston Smith (D)	Jan. 21, 1969	Jan. 16, 1973
Dolph Briscoe (D)	Jan. 16, 1973	Jan. 16, 1979
William P. Clements (R)	Jan. 16, 1979	Jan. 18, 1983
Mark White (D)	Jan. 18, 1983	

UTAH

(Became a state Jan. 4, 1896)

Governors	Dates of Service	
Heber Manning Wells (R)	Jan. 6, 1896	Jan. 2, 1905
John C. Cutler (R)	Jan. 2, 1905	Jan. 4, 1909
William Spry (R)	Jan. 4, 1909	Jan. 1, 1917
Simon Bamberger (D)	Jan. 1, 1917	Jan. 3, 1921
Charles R. Mabey (R)	Jan. 3, 1921	Jan. 5, 1925
George H. Dern (D)	Jan. 5, 1925	Jan. 2, 1933
Henry H. Blood (D)	Jan. 2, 1933	Jan. 6, 1941
Herbert B. Maw (D)	Jan. 6, 1941	Jan. 3, 1949
J. Bracken Lee (R)	Jan. 3, 1949	Jan. 7, 1957
George Dewey Clyde (R)	Jan. 7, 1957	Jan. 4, 1965
Calvin L. Rampton (D)	Jan. 4, 1965	Jan. 3, 1977
Scott M. Matheson (D)	Jan. 3, 1977	Jan. 7, 1985
Norman H. Bangerter (R)	Jan. 7, 1985	

VERMONT

(Became a state March 4, 1791)

Governors	Dates of Service	
Thomas Chittenden[1]	March 4, 1791	Aug. 25, 1797
Paul Brigham[2]	Aug. 25, 1797	Oct. 16, 1797
Isaac Tichenor (FED)	Oct. 16, 1797	Oct. 9, 1807
Israel Smith (D-R)	Oct. 9, 1807	Oct. 14, 1808
Isaac Tichenor (FED)	Oct. 14, 1808	Oct. 14, 1809
Jonas Galusha (D-R)	Oct. 14, 1809	Oct. 23, 1813

Texas
1. Resigned Nov. 23, 1853.
2. As lieutenant governor, he succeeded to office.
3. Resigned March 16, 1861.
4. As lieutenant governor, he succeeded to office.
5. Resigned Nov. 5, 1863.
6. Administration terminated June 17, 1865, due to fall of the Confederacy.
7. Provisional governor appointed by the president.
8. Appointed under martial law. Vacated office Sept. 30, 1869. Governorship is considered to have remained vacant until inauguration of Edmund J. Davis.
9. Resigned Dec. 1, 1876.
10. As lieutenant governor, he succeeded to office.
11. Impeached. Removed from office August 25, 1917.
12. As lieutenant governor, he succeeded to office. Subsequently elected.
13. Resigned Aug. 4, 1941.

14. As lieutenant governor, he succeeded to office. Subsequently elected.
15. Died July 11, 1949.
16. As lieutenant governor, he succeeded to office. Subsequently elected.

Vermont
1. Died Aug. 25, 1797.
2. As lieutenant governor, he succeeded to office.
3. No candidate received a majority of the vote and the Legislature failed to elect a governor in 1835. Silas H. Jennison, the lieutenant governor, served as governor for the term and was subsequently elected.
4. Died Feb. 7, 1870.
5. As lieutenant governor, he succeeded to office.
6. Resigned Jan. 16, 1950.
7. As lieutenant governor, he succeeded to office.

Martin Chittenden (FED)	Oct. 23, 1813	Oct. 14, 1815
Jonas Galusha (D-R)	Oct. 14, 1815	Oct. 13, 1820
Richard Skinner (D-R)	Oct. 13, 1820	Oct. 10, 1823
Cornelius P. Van Ness (D-R)	Oct. 10, 1823	Oct. 13, 1826
Ezra Butler (D-R)	Oct. 13, 1826	Oct. 10, 1828
Samuel C. Crafts (NR)	Oct. 10, 1828	Oct. 18, 1831
William A. Palmer (A-MAS)	Oct. 18, 1831	Nov. 2, 1835
Silas H. Jennison (W)³	Nov. 2, 1835	Oct. 15, 1841
Charles Paine (W)	Oct. 15, 1841	Oct. 13, 1843
John Mattocks (W)	Oct. 13, 1843	Oct. 11, 1844
William Slade (W)	Oct. 11, 1844	Oct. 9, 1846
Horace Eaton (W)	Oct. 9, 1846	Oct. 1848
Carlos Coolidge (W)	Oct. 1848	Oct. 11, 1850
Charles K. Williams (W)	Oct. 11, 1850	Oct. 1852
Erastus Fairbanks (W)	Oct. 1852	Oct. 1853
John S. Robinson (D)	Oct. 1853	Oct. 13, 1854
Stephen Royce (W, R)	Oct. 13, 1854	Oct. 10, 1856
Ryland Fletcher (R)	Oct. 10, 1856	Oct. 10, 1858
Hiland Hall (R)	Oct. 10, 1858	Oct. 12, 1860
Erastus Fairbanks (R)	Oct. 12, 1860	Oct. 11, 1861
Frederick Holbrook (R)	Oct. 11, 1861	Oct. 9, 1863
John Gregory Smith (R)	Oct. 9, 1863	Oct. 13, 1865
Paul Dillingham (R)	Oct. 13, 1865	Oct. 13, 1867
John B. Page (R)	Oct. 13, 1867	Oct. 15, 1869
Peter T. Washburn (R)⁴	Oct. 15, 1869	Feb. 7, 1870
George W. Hendee (R)⁵	Feb. 7, 1870	Oct. 6, 1870
John W. Stewart (R)	Oct. 6, 1870	Oct. 3, 1872
Julius Converse (R)	Oct. 3, 1872	Oct. 8, 1874
Asahel Peck (R)	Oct. 8, 1874	Oct. 5, 1876
Horace Fairbanks (R)	Oct. 5, 1876	Oct. 3, 1878
Redfield Proctor (R)	Oct. 3, 1878	Oct. 7, 1880
Roswell Farnham (R)	Oct. 7, 1880	Oct. 5, 1882
John L. Barstow (R)	Oct. 5, 1882	Oct. 2, 1884
Samuel E. Pingree (R)	Oct. 2, 1884	Oct. 7, 1886
Ebenezer J. Ormsbee (R)	Oct. 7, 1886	Oct. 4, 1888
William P. Dillingham (R)	Oct. 4, 1888	Oct. 2, 1890
Carroll S. Page (R)	Oct. 2, 1890	Oct. 6, 1892
Levi K. Fuller (R)	Oct. 6, 1892	Oct. 4, 1894
Urban A. Woodbury (R)	Oct. 4, 1894	Oct. 8, 1896
Josiah Grout (R)	Oct. 8, 1896	Oct. 6, 1898
Edward C. Smith (R)	Oct. 6, 1898	Oct. 4, 1900
William W. Stickney (R)	Oct. 4, 1900	Oct. 3, 1902
John G. McCullough (R)	Oct. 3, 1902	Oct. 6, 1904
Charles J. Bell (R)	Oct. 6, 1904	Oct. 4, 1906
Fletcher D. Proctor (R)	Oct. 4, 1906	Oct. 8, 1908
George H. Prouty (R)	Oct. 8, 1908	Oct. 5, 1910
John A. Mead (R)	Oct. 5, 1910	Oct. 3, 1912
Allen M. Fletcher (R)	Oct. 3, 1912	Jan. 7, 1915
Charles W. Gates (R)	Jan. 7, 1915	Jan. 4, 1917
Horace F. Graham (R)	Jan. 4, 1917	Jan. 9, 1919
Percival W. Clement (R)	Jan. 9, 1919	Jan. 6, 1921
James Hartness (R)	Jan. 6, 1921	Jan. 4, 1923
Redfield Proctor (R)	Jan. 4, 1923	Jan. 8, 1925
Franklin S. Billings (R)	Jan. 8, 1925	Jan. 6, 1927
John E. Weeks (R)	Jan. 6, 1927	Jan. 8, 1931
Stanley C. Wilson (R)	Jan. 8, 1931	Jan. 10, 1935
Charles M. Smith (R)	Jan. 10, 1935	Jan. 7, 1937
George D. Aiken (R)	Jan. 7, 1937	Jan. 9, 1941

William H. Wills (R)	Jan. 9, 1941	Jan. 4, 1945
Mortimer R. Proctor (R)	Jan. 4, 1945	Jan. 9, 1947
Ernest W. Gibson (R)⁶	Jan. 9, 1947	Jan. 16, 1950
Harold J. Arthur (R)⁷	Jan. 16, 1950	Jan. 4, 1951
Lee E. Emerson (R)	Jan. 4, 1951	Jan. 6, 1955
Joseph B. Johnson (R)	Jan. 6, 1955	Jan. 8, 1959
Robert T. Stafford (R)	Jan. 8, 1959	Jan. 5, 1961
Frank Ray Keyser Jr. (R)	Jan. 5, 1961	Jan. 10, 1963
Philip H. Hoff (D)	Jan. 10, 1963	Jan. 9, 1969
Deane C. Davis (R)	Jan. 9, 1969	Jan. 4, 1973
Thomas P. Salmon (D)	Jan. 4, 1973	Jan. 6, 1977
Richard A. Snelling (R)	Jan. 6, 1977	Jan. 10, 1985
Madeleine M. Kunin (D)	Jan. 10, 1985	

VIRGINIA

(Ratified the Constitution June 25, 1788)

Governors	Dates of Service	
Beverley Randolph	Dec. 3, 1788	Dec. 1, 1791
Henry Lee	Dec. 1, 1791	Dec. 1, 1794
Robert Brooke	Dec. 1, 1794	Dec. 1, 1796
James Wood (D-R)	Dec. 1, 1796	Dec. 1, 1799
James Monroe (D-R)	Dec. 1, 1799	Dec. 1, 1802
John Page (D-R)	Dec. 1, 1802	Dec. 1, 1805
William H. Cabell (D-R)	Dec. 7, 1805	Dec. 1, 1808
John Tyler Sr. (D-R)	Dec. 1, 1808	Jan. 1811
James Monroe (D-R)¹	Jan. 16, 1811	April 5, 1811
George William Smith (D-R)²	April 6, 1811	Dec. 26, 1811
Peyton Randolph (D-R)³	Dec. 27, 1811	Jan. 3, 1812
James Barbour(D-R)	Jan. 3, 1812	Dec. 1, 1814
Wilson Carey Nicholas (D-R)	Dec. 1, 1814	Dec. 1, 1816
James P. Preston (D-R)	Dec. 1, 1816	Dec. 1, 1819
Thomas M. Randolph (D-R)	Dec. 1, 1819	Dec. 1, 1822
James Pleasants (D-R)	Dec. 1, 1822	Dec. 1825
John Tyler Jr. (D-R)	Dec. 10, 1825	March 4, 1827
William B. Giles (D)	March 4, 1827	March 4, 1830
John Floyd (D)	March 4, 1830	March 31, 1834
Littleton W. Tazewell (D)⁴	March 31, 1834	April 30, 1836
Wyndham Robertson (D)⁵	April 30, 1836	March 31, 1837
David Campbell (D)	March 31, 1837	March 31, 1840
Thomas W. Gilmer (W)⁶	March 31, 1840	March 1841
John Mercer Patton (W)⁷	March 18, 1841	March 31, 1841
John Rutherford (W)⁸	March 31, 1841	March 31, 1842
John M. Gregory (W)⁹	March 31, 1842	Jan. 1, 1843
James McDowell (W)	Jan. 1, 1843	Jan. 1, 1846
William Smith (D)	Jan. 1, 1846	Jan. 1, 1849
John B. Floyd (D)	Jan. 1, 1849	Jan. 16, 1852
Joseph Johnson (D)	Jan. 16, 1852	Dec. 31, 1855
Henry A. Wise (D)	Jan. 1, 1856	Dec. 31, 1859
John Letcher (D)	Jan. 1, 1860	Dec. 31, 1863
William Smith (D)¹⁰	Jan. 1, 1864	April 1865
Francis H. Peirpoint¹³	June 20, 1861	April 4, 1868
Henry H. Wells¹²	April 4, 1868	Sept. 21, 1869

Virginia

1. Resigned April 5, 1811.

2. As senior member of the Council of State, became acting governor. Died Dec. 1811.

3. As senior member of the Council of State, became acting governor.

4. Resigned April 30, 1836.

5. As senior member of the Council of State, became acting governor.

6. Resigned in March 1841.

7. As senior member of the Council of State, became acting governor. Following Gilmer's resignation, the Legislature did not elect a new governor for 21 months. Patton,

Rutherford and Gregory took turns as acting governor.

8. As senior member of the Council of State, became acting governor.

9. As senior member of the Council of State, became acting governor.

10. Last Confederate governor.

11. Became Union governor June 20, 1861. Appointed provisional governor May 9, 1865.

12. Provisional governor.

13. Provisional governor from September 1869 to Jan. 1, 1870. Elected to four-year term beginning Jan. 1, 1870.

Gilbert C. Walker (C)[13]	Sept. 21, 1869	Jan. 1, 1874
James Lawson Kemper (D)	Jan. 1, 1874	Jan. 1, 1878
Frederick W. M. Holliday (D)	Jan. 1, 1878	Jan. 1, 1882
William E. Cameron (READJ)	Jan. 1, 1882	Jan. 1, 1886
Fitzhugh Lee (D)	Jan. 1, 1886	Jan. 1, 1890
Philip W. McKinney (D)	Jan. 1, 1890	Jan. 1, 1894
Charles T. O'Ferrall (D)	Jan. 1, 1894	Jan. 1, 1898
James Hoge Tyler (D)	Jan. 1, 1898	Jan. 1, 1902
Andrew J. Montague (D)	Jan. 1, 1902	Feb. 1, 1906
Claude A. Swanson (D)	Feb. 1, 1906	Feb. 1, 1910
William H. Mann (D)	Feb. 1, 1910	Feb. 1, 1914
Henry C. Stuart (D)	Feb. 1, 1914	Feb. 1, 1918
Westmoreland Davis (D)	Feb. 1, 1918	Feb. 1, 1922
E. Lee Trinkle (D)	Feb. 1, 1922	Feb. 1, 1926
Harry F. Byrd (D)	Feb. 1, 1926	Jan. 15, 1930
John G. Pollard (D)	Jan. 15, 1930	Jan. 17, 1934
George C. Peery (D)	Jan. 17, 1934	Jan. 19, 1938
James H. Price (D)	Jan. 19, 1938	Jan. 21, 1942
Colgate W. Darden Jr. (D)	Jan. 21, 1942	Jan. 16, 1946
William M. Tuck (D)	Jan. 16, 1946	Jan. 18, 1950
John S. Battle (D)	Jan. 18, 1950	Jan. 20, 1954
Thomas B. Stanley (D)	Jan. 20, 1954	Jan. 11, 1958
James Lindsay Almond Jr. (D)	Jan. 11, 1958	Jan. 13, 1962
Albertis S. Harrison Jr. (D)	Jan. 13, 1962	Jan. 15, 1966
Mills E. Godwin Jr. (D)	Jan. 15, 1966	Jan. 17, 1970
Linwood Holton (R)	Jan. 17, 1970	Jan. 12, 1974
Mills E. Godwin Jr. (R)	Jan. 12, 1974	Jan. 14, 1978
John Dalton (R)	Jan. 14, 1978	Jan. 16, 1982
Charles S. Robb (D)	Jan. 16, 1982	

WASHINGTON

(Became a state Nov. 11, 1889)

Governors	Dates of Service	
Elisha P. Ferry (R)	Nov. 11, 1889	Jan. 9, 1893
John H. McGraw (R)	Jan. 9, 1893	Jan. 11, 1897
John R. Rogers (PP, D)[1]	Jan. 11, 1897	Dec. 26, 1901
Henry McBride (R)[2]	Dec. 26, 1901	Jan. 9, 1905
Albert E. Mead (R)	Jan. 9, 1905	Jan. 27, 1909
Samuel G. Cosgrove (R)[3]	Jan. 27, 1909	March 28, 1909
Marion E. Hay (R)[4]	March 29, 1909	Jan. 11, 1913
Ernest Lister (D)[5]	Jan. 11, 1913	June 14, 1919
Louis F. Hart (R)[6]	June 14, 1919	Jan. 12, 1925
Roland H. Hartley (R)	Jan. 12, 1925	Jan. 9, 1933
Clarence D. Martin (D)	Jan. 9, 1833	Jan. 13, 1941
Arthur B. Langlie (R)	Jan. 13, 1941	Jan. 8, 1945
Monrad C. Wallgren (D)	Jan. 8, 1945	Jan. 10, 1949
Arthur B. Langlie (R)	Jan. 10, 1949	Jan. 14, 1957
Albert D. Rosellini (D)	Jan. 14, 1957	Jan. 11, 1965

Daniel J. Evans (R)	Jan. 11, 1965	Jan. 12, 1977
Dixy Lee Ray (D)	Jan. 12, 1977	Jan. 14, 1981
John D. Spellman (R)	Jan. 14, 1981	Jan. 16, 1985
Booth Gardner (D)	Jan. 16, 1985	

WEST VIRGINIA

(Became a state June 19, 1863)

Governors	Dates of Service	
Arthur I. Boreman (UN R, R)[1]	June 20, 1863	Feb. 26, 1869
Daniel D. T. Farnsworth (R)[2]	Feb. 27, 1869	March 3, 1869
William E. Stevenson (R)	March 4, 1869	March 3, 1871
John Jeremiah Jacob (D, I)	March 4, 1871	March 3, 1877
Henry Mason Mathews (D)	March 4, 1877	March 3, 1881
Jacob B. Jackson (D)	March 4, 1881	March 3, 1885
Emanuel Willis Wilson (D)[3]	March 4, 1885	Feb. 5, 1890
Aretas Brooks Fleming (D)[4]	Feb. 6, 1890	March 3, 1893
William A. MacCorkle (D)	March 4, 1893	March 3, 1897
George W. Atkinson (R)	March 4, 1897	March 4, 1901
Albert B. White (R)	March 4, 1901	March 4, 1905
William M. O. Dawson (R)	March 4, 1905	March 4, 1909
William E. Glasscock (R)	March 4, 1909	March 4, 1913
Henry D. Hatfield (R)	March 4, 1913	March 4, 1917
John J. Cornwell (D)	March 4, 1917	March 4, 1921
Ephraim F. Morgan (R)	March 4, 1921	March 4, 1925
Howard M. Gore (R)	March 4, 1925	March 4, 1929
William G. Conley (R)	March 4, 1929	March 4, 1933
Herman G. Kump (D)	March 4, 1933	Jan. 18, 1937
Homer A. Holt (D)	Jan. 18, 1937	Jan. 13, 1941
Matthew M. Neely (D)	Jan. 13, 1941	Jan. 15, 1945
Clarence W. Meadows (D)	Jan. 15, 1945	Jan. 17, 1949
Okey L. Patteson (D)	Jan. 17, 1949	Jan. 19, 1953
William C. Marland (D)	Jan. 19, 1953	Jan. 14, 1957
Cecil H. Underwood (R)	Jan. 14, 1957	Jan. 16, 1961
William W. Barron (D)	Jan. 16, 1961	Jan. 18, 1965
Hulett C. Smith (D)	Jan. 18, 1965	Jan. 13, 1969
Arch A. Moore Jr. (R)	Jan. 13, 1969	Jan. 17, 1977
John D. Rockefeller (D)	Jan. 17, 1977	Jan. 14, 1985
Arch A. Moore Jr. (R)	Jan. 14, 1985	

WISCONSIN

(Became a state May 29, 1848)

Governors	Dates of Service	
Nelson Dewey (D)	June 7, 1848	Jan. 5, 1852
Leonard J. Farwell (W)	Jan. 5, 1852	Jan. 2, 1854

Washington
1. Died Dec. 26, 1901.
2. As lieutenant governor, he succeeded to office.
3. Died March 28, 1909.
4. As lieutenant governor, he succeeded to office.
5. Died June 14, 1919.
6. As lieutenant governor, he succeeded to office. Subsequently elected.

West Virginia
1. Resigned Feb. 26, 1869.
2. As president of the state Senate, he succeeded to office.
3. Wilson continued in office for almost one year beyond the expiration of his term pending a settlement of the disputed election of 1888.
4. The 1888 election between Democrat Aretas Brooks Fleming and Republican Nathan Goff was very close, and the final outcome was in dispute. After almost one year of investigation, the West Virginia Legislature declared Fleming the winner, and he took office Feb. 6, 1890.

Wisconsin
1. Barstow's election to a second term in 1855 was disputed by his opponent, Coles Bashford, who charged fraud. Barstow took office, but resigned while the case was pending in court. The office was awarded to Bashford several days later.
2. Acting governor.
3. Successfully contested the election of William Augustus Barstow and served out the remainder of the term.
4. Died April 19, 1862.
5. Acting governor.
6. Resigned Jan. 1, 1906.
7. As lieutenant governor, he succeeded to office. Subsequently elected.
8. Elected in 1942 for a two-year term, but died Dec. 7, 1942, before inauguration.
9. As lieutenant governor, he succeeded to office. Subsequently elected. Died March 12, 1947.
10. As lieutenant governor, he succeeded to office. Subsequently elected.
11. Resigned July 7, 1977.
12. As lieutenant governor, he succeeded to office.

William A. Barstow (D)[1]	Jan. 2, 1854	March 21, 1856
Arthur MacArthur (D)[2]	March 21, 1856	March 25, 1856
Coles Bashford (R)[3]	March 25, 1856	
Alexander W. Randall (R)	Jan. 4, 1858	Jan. 6, 1862
Louis P. Harvey (R)[4]	Jan. 6, 1862	April 19, 1862
Edward Salomon (R)[5]	April 19, 1862	Jan. 4, 1864
James T. Lewis (R)	Jan. 4, 1864	Jan. 1, 1866
Lucius Fairchild (R)	Jan. 1, 1866	Jan. 1, 1872
Cadwallader C. Washburn (R)	Jan. 1, 1872	Jan. 5, 1874
William R. Taylor (D)	Jan. 5, 1874	Jan. 3, 1876
Harrison Ludington (R)	Jan. 3, 1876	Jan. 7, 1878
William E. Smith (R)	Jan. 7, 1878	Jan. 2, 1882
Jeremiah M. Rusk (R)	Jan. 2, 1882	Jan. 7, 1889
William D. Hoard (R)	Jan. 7, 1889	Jan. 5, 1891
George W. Peck (D)	Jan. 5, 1891	Jan. 7, 1895
William H. Upham (R)	Jan. 7, 1895	Jan. 4, 1897
Edward Scofield (R)	Jan. 4, 1897	Jan. 7, 1901
Robert M. LaFollette (R)[6]	Jan. 7, 1901	Jan. 1, 1906
James O. Davidson (R)[7]	Jan. 1, 1906	Jan. 2, 1911
Francis E. McGovern (R)	Jan. 2, 1911	Jan. 4, 1915
Emanuel L. Philipp (R)	Jan. 4, 1915	Jan. 3, 1921
John J. Blaine (R)	Jan. 3, 1921	Jan. 3, 1927
Fred R. Zimmerman (R)	Jan. 3, 1927	Jan. 7, 1929
Walter J. Kohler Sr. (R)	Jan. 7, 1929	Jan. 5, 1931
Philip F. LaFollette (R)	Jan. 5, 1931	Jan. 2, 1933
Albert G. Schmedeman (D)	Jan. 2, 1933	Jan. 7, 1935
Philip F. LaFollette (PROG)	Jan. 7, 1935	Jan. 2, 1939
Julius P. Heil (R)	Jan. 2, 1939	Jan. 4, 1943
Orland S. Loomis (PROG)[8]		
Walter S. Goodland (R)[9]	Jan. 4, 1943	March 12, 1947
Oscar Rennebohm (R)[10]	March 12, 1947	Jan. 1, 1951
Walter J. Kohler Jr. (R)	Jan. 1, 1951	Jan. 7, 1957
Vernon W. Thomson (R)	Jan. 7, 1957	Jan. 5, 1959
Gaylord A. Nelson (D)	Jan. 5, 1959	Jan. 7, 1963
John W. Reynolds (D)	Jan. 7, 1963	Jan. 4, 1965
Warren P. Knowles (R)	Jan. 4, 1965	Jan. 4, 1971
Patrick J. Lucey (D)[11]	Jan. 4, 1971	July 7, 1977
M. J. Schreiber (D)[12]	July 7, 1977	Jan. 1, 1979
Lee S. Dreyfus (R)	Jan. 1, 1979	Jan. 3, 1983
Anthony S. Earl (D)	Jan. 3, 1983	

WYOMING

(Became a state July 10, 1890)

Governors	Dates of Service	
Francis E. Warren (R)[1]	Oct. 11, 1890	Nov. 24, 1890
Amos W. Barber (R)[2]	Nov. 24, 1890	Jan. 2, 1893
John E. Osborne (D)[3]	Jan. 2, 1893	Jan. 7, 1895
William A. Richards (R)	Jan. 7, 1895	Jan. 2, 1899
DeForest Richards (R)[4]	Jan. 2, 1899	April 28, 1903
Fenimore C. Chatterton (R)[5]	April 28, 1903	Jan. 2, 1905
Bryant B. Brooks (R)[6]	Jan. 2, 1905	Jan. 2, 1911
Joseph M. Carey (D)	Jan. 2, 1911	Jan. 4, 1915
John B. Kendrick (D)[7]	Jan. 4, 1915	Feb. 26, 1917
Frank L. Houx (D)[8]	Feb. 26, 1917	Jan. 6, 1919
Robert D. Carey (R)	Jan. 6, 1919	Jan. 1, 1923
William B. Ross (D)[9]	Jan. 1, 1923	Oct. 2, 1924
Frank E. Lucas (R)[10]	Oct. 2, 1924	Jan. 5, 1925
Nellie T. Ross (D)[11]	Jan. 5, 1925	Jan. 3, 1927
Frank C. Emerson (R)[12]	Jan. 3, 1927	Feb. 18, 1931
Alonzo M. Clark (R)[13]	Feb. 18, 1931	Jan. 2, 1933
Leslie A. Miller (D)[14]	Jan. 2, 1933	Jan. 2, 1939
Nels H. Smith (R)	Jan. 2, 1939	Jan. 4, 1943
Lester C. Hunt (D)[15]	Jan. 4, 1943	Jan. 3, 1949
Arthur G. Crane (R)[16]	Jan. 3, 1949	Jan. 1, 1951
Frank A. Barrett (R)[17]	Jan. 1, 1951	Jan. 3, 1953
Clifford Joy Rogers (R)[18]	Jan. 3, 1953	Jan. 3, 1955
Milward L. Simpson (R)	Jan. 3, 1955	Jan. 5, 1959
John J. Hickey (D)[19]	Jna. 5, 1959	Jan. 2, 1961
Jack R. Gage (D)[20]	Jan. 2, 1961	Jan. 6, 1963
Clifford P. Hansen (R)	Jan. 7, 1963	Jan. 2, 1967
Stanley K. Hathaway (R)	Jan. 2, 1967	Jan. 6, 1975
Ed Herschler (D)	Jan. 6, 1975	

Wyoming

1. Resigned Nov. 24, 1890.
2. As secretary of state, he succeeded to office for the remainder of the first half of Gov. Warren's term.
3. Elected in a special election for the second half of Warren's term.
4. Died April 28, 1903.
5. As secretary of state, he succeeded to office for the remainder of the first half of Richards' term.
6. Elected in a special election for second half of Richards' term. Subsequently re-elected.
7. Resigned Feb. 26, 1917.
8. As secretary of state, he succeeded to office.
9. Died Oct. 2, 1924.
10. As secretary of state, he succeeded to office for the remainder of the first half of Ross's term.
11. Elected in a special election for the second half of Ross' (her husband's) term.
12. Died Feb. 18, 1931.
13. As secretary of state, he succeeded to office for the remainder of the first half of Gov. Emerson's term.
14. Elected in a special election for the second half of Emerson's term. Subsequently re-elected.
15. Resigned Jan. 3, 1949.
16. As secretary of state, he succeeded to office.
17. Resigned Jan. 3, 1953.
18. As secretary of state, he succeeded to office.
19. Resigned Jan. 2, 1961.
20. As secretary of state, he succeeded to office.

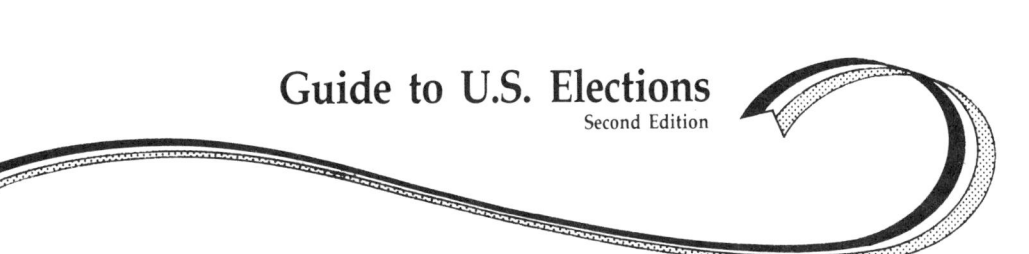

Popular Vote Returns

Sources for Gubernatorial Returns

The gubernatorial popular election returns presented in this section *(pp. 489-536)* for the years 1787 through 1823 were obtained from *American State Governors, 1776-1976*, by Joseph E. Kallenbach and Jessamine S. Kallenbach (Dobbs Ferry, N.Y.: Oceana Publishing, 1977). Those for 1824 through 1973 were obtained from the Inter-University Consortium for Political and Social Research (ICPSR) at the University of Michigan. Major sources for returns since 1973 were Congressional Quarterly, which obtained them from the state secretaries of state, and the *America Votes* series, compiled biennially by Richard M. Scammon and Alice V. McGillivray of the Elections Research Center, Washington, D.C., and published by Congressional Quarterly.

The symbol # next to returns before 1974 indicates that Congressional Quarterly obtained the returns from a source other than Kallenbach or the ICPSR. A complete list of other sources used appears on page 536. A "Gubernatorial Candidates Index" is located on pages 1148-1159.

While complete source annotations for the ICPSR collection are too extensive to publish here, information on the sources for returns from specific elections can be obtained through the ICPSR. *(ICPSR collection, box, p. xiv.)*

Presentation of Returns

The gubernatorial returns are arranged alphabetically by state and in chronological order of election within each state listing. The candidate receiving the greatest number of popular votes is listed first with his or her vote total and percentage of the total vote cast, followed in descending order of votes received by all other candidates receiving *at least 5 percent* of the total vote cast.

Special elections to fill vacancies are designated in the returns.

Vote Totals and Percentages

The ICPSR collection includes all candidates receiving popular votes. In the *Guide to U.S. Elections, Second Edition*, only gubernatorial candidates receiving *at least 5 percent of the total vote* for that election are included. For example, the ICPSR data collection for the 1908 Illinois gubernatorial election shows that 1,154,612 votes were cast, with Republican Charles S. Deneen receiving 550,076 votes (47.64 percent), Democrat Adlai E. Stevenson receiving 526,92 votes (45.64 percent) and four other candidates receiving the remaining 77,624 votes (6.72 percent). These four candidates do not appear on page 499 of this book because none of them received 5 percent or more of the vote.

The percentages used in this section were calculated to two decimal places on the basis of the total number of votes cast in the election and rounded to one place. Thus, on page 499, for the 1908 Illinois election, Deneen's percentage of the total vote is listed as 47.6 percent and Stevenson's as 45.6 percent. The percentages are rounded to one decimal place and do not add to 100 percent because of the scattered votes for the other four candidates.

Names and Party Designations

Names are listed as they were recorded in the official returns or other source documentation. In some instances, particularly in the 19th century, candidate names in the ICPSR file are incomplete. First names were the most commonly missing elements in the original sources consulted by the scholars and archivists who gathered the ICPSR returns. Congressional Quarterly has added full names when they could be determined and has corrected obvious misspellings.

In the ICPSR returns, the distinct — and in many cases, *multiple* — party designations appearing in the original sources are preserved. In many cases party labels represent combinations of multi-party support received by individual candidates. If, for example, on the ballot and official returns more than one party name was listed next to a candidate's name, then the party designation appearing in the election returns for that candidate will be a unique abbreviation for that combination of parties. *(For a list of party abbreviations, see p. 1141.)*

In the special case of a candidate's name listed separately on the original ballot under more than one party — where returns were reported *separately* for each party — Congressional Quarterly has summed the votes recorded under the several parties and that figure appears as the candidate's total vote. Whenever separate party totals have been summed, a *comma* separates the abbreviations of the parties contributing the largest and second largest share of the total vote.

Most cases of this special situation occurred in New York and Pennsylvania during this century. For example, in the original ICPSR returns for New York's 1946 gubernatorial election, James M. Mead received 1,532,161 votes as Democratic Party candidate, 428,903 votes as American Labor Party candidate and 177,418 votes as Liberal Party candidate for a total of 2,138,482 votes.

In organizing the ICPSR data for publication, Congressional Quarterly has summed all votes Mead received from these three parties. Thus, on page 518 only Mead's total vote of 2,138,482 appears.

Congressional Quarterly has also included party abbreviations for the two parties that contributed the most votes to Mead's total — separated by a comma. Thus, immediately following his name appear the abbreviations — D, AM LAB — indicating that Mead was a candidate of at least two parties and that the greatest number of votes he received was as a Democrat.

Gubernatorial Elections:
Popular Vote Returns, 1787-1984

ALABAMA

(Became a state Dec. 14, 1819)

	Candidates	Votes	%
1819	William Wyatt Bibb (D-R)	8,342	53.9
	M. D. Williams	7,140	46.1
1821	Israel Pickens (D-R)	9,616	57.4
	Dr. Henry Chambers	7,129	42.6
1823	Israel Pickens (D-R)	10,534	56.7
	Dr. Henry Chambers	8,035	43.3
1825	John Murphy (JAC D)	12,184	100.0
1827	John Murphy (JAC D)	8,334	99.2
1829	Gabriel Moore (JAC D)	10,956	100.0
1831	John Gayle (D)	15,309	55.5
	Nicholas Davis (NR)	8,923	32.4
	Samuel B. Moore	3,354	12.2
1833	John Gayle (D)	9,750	100.0
1835	Clement Comer Clay (D)	25,491	64.8
	Enoch Parsons (SR W)	13,760	35.0
1837	Arthur P. Bagby (D)	23,902	53.7
	Samuel W. Oliver (A-VB D)	20,605	46.3
1839	Arthur P. Bagby (D)	22,681	89.9
	Arthur F. Hopkins (W)	2,532	10.0
1841	Benjamin Fitzpatrick (D)	31,808	58.3
	James W. McClung (IW)	22,777	41.7
1843	Benjamin Fitzpatrick (D)	✔	
1845	Joshua L. Martin (I)	29,261	52.1
	Nathaniel Terry (D)	25,473	45.3
1847	Reuben Chapman (D)	35,880	55.7
	Nicholas Davis (W)	28,565	44.3
1849	Henry Watkins Collier (D)	37,221	98.1
1851	Henry Watkins Collier (D)	38,517	85.5
	James Shields (W)	5,760	12.8
1853	John A. Winston (D)	30,862	65.0
	Earnest (W)	9,499	20.0
	Nicks (UN D)	7,096	15.0
1855	John A. Winston (D)	43,936	57.2
	Shortridge (AM)	31,864	41.5
1857	Andrew B. Moore (D)	41,871	94.5
1859	Andrew B. Moore (D)	47,293	72.4
	William F. Samford (SO RTS D)	18,070	27.7
1861	John Gill Shorter (D)	38,221	57.5
	Thomas Hill Watts (W)	28,117	42.3
1863	Thomas Hill Watts (W)	28,201	71.7
	John Gill Shorter (D)	9,664	24.6
1865	Robert Miller Patton (W)	20,611	45.2
	Michael J. Bulger (D)	16,380	35.9
	William R. Smith (UN)	8,557	18.8
1868	William Hugh Smith (R)	62,067	100.0
1870	Robert B. Lindsay (D)	77,723	50.5
	William Hugh Smith (R)	76,282	49.5
1872	David P. Lewis (R)	89,868	52.5
	Hendon (LR)	81,371	47.5
1874	George S. Houston (D)	107,118	53.3
	David P. Lewis (R)	93,928	46.7
1876	George S. Houston (D)	96,401	63.4
	Woodruff (R)	55,682	36.6
1878	Rufus W. Cobb (D)	88,255	100.0
1880	Rufus W. Cobb (D)	134,905	76.1
	Pickens (G)	42,363	23.9
1882	Edward A. O'Neal (D)	102,617	68.7

	Candidates	Votes	%
	J. L. Sheffield (R)	46,742	31.3
1884	Edward A. O'Neal (D)	143,229	99.7
1886	Thomas Seay (D)	145,095	79.4
	Arthur Bingham (R)	36,793	20.1
1888	Thomas Seay (D)	155,973	77.6
	W. T. Ewing (R)	44,707	22.2
1890	Thomas G. Jones (D)	139,912	76.1
	Benjamin M. Long (R)	42,391	23.1
1892	Thomas G. Jones (D)	126,955	52.2
	R. F. Kolb (ID)	115,732	47.5
1894	W. C. Oates (D)	110,875	57.1
	R. F. Kolb (POP)	83,292	42.9
1896	Joseph F. Johnston (D)	128,549	59.0
	Albert T. Goodwyn (POP)	89,290	41.0
1898	Joseph F. Johnston (D)	110,551	67.0
	Gilbert B. Dean (POP)	50,052	30.3

Explanation of Symbols

In the returns for gubernatorial elections, *symbols* are used to denote special circumstances. Where no symbol is used, the candidate who received the most votes won the election on the basis of the popular vote and served as governor. The following is a key to the symbols used:

✔ Elected and served as governor, but the number of votes and the percentage of the total received were not available.

† Elected governor by the state legislature because no candidate received a majority of the popular vote as required by state law at the time of the election. *(See p. 455 for an explanation of the election of governors by state legislatures.)*

* Symbol used for two types of situations: (1) the candidate who won the election did not serve as governor because he died before assuming office; (2) none of the candidates running qualified to become governor on the basis of the election returns or action by the state legislature. *(For an explanation of a specific case, consult the appropriate state listed in the section, "Governors of the States, 1787-1985," pp. 461-486.)*

‡ Disputed election. The symbol is used in a variety of circumstances such as an election dispute resulting in the unseating of a governor after he assumed office or resulting in rival governors each claiming to have been legitimately elected. *(For an explanation of a specific case, consult the appropriate state listed in the selection, "Governors of the States, 1787-1985," pp. 461-486.)*

\# Information was obtained from a source other than Congressional Quarterly's basic sources for this volume. *(For a list of the other sources used, see p. 536.)*

	Candidates	Votes	%
1900	William J. Samford (D)	115,167	71.0
	John A. Steele (R)	28,305	17.5
	G. B. Crowe (POP)	17,444	10.8
1902	William D. Jelks (D)	67,748	73.7
	John A. W. Smith (R)	24,150	26.3
1906	B. B. Comer (D)	61,223	85.5
	Asa E. Stratton (R)	9,981	13.9
1910	Emmet O'Neal (D)	77,694	78.7
	Joseph O. Thompson (R)	19,210	19.5
1914	Charles Henderson (D)	61,307	78.7
	John B. Shields (R)	11,773	15.1
1918	Thomas E. Kilby (D)	54,746	80.2
	Smith	13,497	19.8
1922	William W. Brandon (D)	113,605	77.6
	O. D. Street (R)	31,175	21.3
1926	Bibb Graves (D)	93,432	81.2
	J. A. Bingham (R)	21,605	18.8
1930	B. M. Miller (D)	155,034	61.8
	Hugh A. Locke (I)	95,745	38.2
1934	Bibb Graves (D)	155,197	86.9
	Edmund H. Dryer (R)	22,621	12.7
1938	Frank Dixon (D)	115,761	87.4
	W. A. Clardy (R)	16,513	12.5
1942	Chauncey Sparks (D)	69,048	89.0
	Hugh McEniry (R)	8,167	10.5
1946	James E. Folsom (D)	174,959	88.7
	Lyman Ward (R)	22,362	11.3
1950	Gordon Persons (D)	155,414	91.1
	John S. Crowder (R)	15,177	8.9
1954	James E. Folsom (D)	244,401	73.4
	Tom Abernethy (R)	88,688	26.6
1958	John Patterson (D)	239,633	88.4
	William L. Longshore Jr. (R)	30,415	11.2
1962	George C. Wallace (D)	303,987	96.3
1966	Lurleen B. Wallace (D)	537,505	63.4
	James Martin (R)	262,943	31.0
	C. R. Robinson (I)	47,653	5.6
1970	George C. Wallace (D)	637,046	74.5
	John Logan Cashin (NDPA)	125,491	14.7
	A. C. Shelton (I)	75,679	8.9
1974	George C. Wallace (D)	497,574	83.2
	Elvin McCary (R)	88,381	14.8
1978	Forrest H. James (D)	551,886	72.6
	Guy Hunt (R)	196,963	25.9
1982	George C. Wallace (D)	650,538	57.6
	Emory Folmar (R)	440,815	39.1

ALASKA

(Became a state Jan. 3, 1959)

	Candidates	Votes	%
1958	William A. Egan (D)	29,189	59.6
	John Butrovich Jr. (R)	19,299	39.4
1962	William A. Egan (D)	29,627	52.3
	Mike Stepovich (R)	27,054	47.7
1966	Walter J. Hickel (R)	33,145	50.0
	William A. Egan (D)	32,065	48.4
1970	William A. Egan (D)	42,309	52.4
	Keith H. Miller (R)	37,264	46.1
1974	Jay S. Hammond (R)	45,840	47.7
	William A. Egan (D)	45,553	47.4
	Joseph E. Vogler (ALI)	4,770	5.0
1978	Jay S. Hammond (R)	49,580	39.1
	Walter J. Hickel (write-in)	33,555	26.4
	Chancy Croft (D)	25,656	20.2
	Tom Kelly (I)	15,656	12.3

	Candidates	Votes	%
1982	Bill Sheffield (D)	89,918	46.1
	Tom Fink (R)	72,291	37.1
	Richard L. Randolph (LIBERT)	29,067	14.9

ARIZONA

(Became a state Feb. 14, 1912)

	Candidates	Votes	%
1911	George W. P. Hunt (D)	11,123	51.5
	Edward W. Wells (R)	9,166	42.4
	P. W. Gallentine (SOC)	1,247	5.8
1914	George W. P. Hunt (D)	25,226	49.5
	Ralph H. Cameron (R)	17,602	34.5
	George U. Young (PROG)	5,206	10.2
	J. R. Barnette (SOC)	2,973	5.8
1916	Thomas E. Campbell (R)	27,976‡	48.0
	George W. P. Hunt (D)	27,946	47.9
1918	Thomas E. Campbell (R)	25,927	49.9
	Fred T. Colter (D)	25,588	49.3
1920	Thomas E. Campbell (R)	37,060	54.2
	Mit Simms (D)	31,385	45.9
1922	George W. P. Hunt (D)	37,310	54.9
	Thomas E. Campbell (R)	30,599	45.1
1924	George W. P. Hunt (D)	38,372	50.5
	Dwight B. Heard (R)	37,571	49.5
1926	George W. P. Hunt (D)	39,979	50.3
	E. S. Clark (R)	39,580	49.8
1928	John C. Phillips (R)	47,829	51.7
	George W. P. Hunt (D)	44,553	48.2
1930	George W. P. Hunt (D)	48,875	51.4
	John C. Phillips (R)	46,231	48.6
1932	B. B. Moeur (D)	75,314	63.2
	J. C. Kinney (R)	42,202	35.4
1934	B. B. Moeur (D)	61,355	59.7
	Thomas Maddock (R)	39,242	38.2
1936	R. C. Stanford (D)	87,678	70.7
	Thomas E. Campbell (R)	36,114	29.1
1938	R. T. Jones (D)	80,350	68.6
	Jerrie W. Lee (R)	32,022	27.3
1940	Sidney P. Osborn (D)	97,606	65.5
	Jerrie W. Lee (R)	50,358	33.8
1942	Sidney P. Osborn (D)	63,484	72.5
	Jerrie W. Lee (R)	23,562	26.9
1944	Sidney P. Osborn (D)	100,220	77.9
	Jerrie W. Lee (R)	27,261	21.2
1946	Sidney P. Osborn (D)	73,595	60.1
	Bruce D. Brockett (R)	48,867	39.9
1948	Dan E. Garvey (D)	104,008	59.2
	Bruce D. Brockett (R)	70,419	40.1
1950	Howard Pyle (R)	99,109	50.8
	Ana Frohmiller (D)	96,118	49.2
1952	Howard Pyle (R)	156,592	60.2
	Joe C. Haldiman (D)	103,693	39.8
1954	Ernest W. McFarland (D)	128,104	52.5
	Howard Pyle (R)	115,866	47.5
1956	Ernest W. McFarland (D)	171,848	59.6
	Horace B. Griffen (R)	116,744	40.5
1958	Paul Fannin (R)	160,136	55.1
	Robert Morrison (D)	130,329	44.9
1960	Paul Fannin (R)	235,502	59.3
	Lee Ackerman (D)	161,605	40.7
1962	Paul Fannin (R)	200,578	54.8
	Sam Goddard (D)	165,263	45.2
1964	Sam Goddard (D)	252,098	53.2
	Richard Kleindienst (R)	221,404	46.8
1966	Jack Williams (R)	203,438	53.8
	Sam Goddard (D)	174,904	46.2

	Candidates	Votes	%
1968	Jack Williams (R)	279,923	*57.8*
	Sam Goddard (D)	204,075	*42.2*
1970	Jack Williams (R)	209,356	*50.9*
	Raul H. Castro (D)	202,053	*49.1*
1974	Raul H. Castro (D)	278,375	*50.4*
	Russell Williams (R)	273,674	*49.6*
1978	Bruce Babbitt (D)	282,605	*52.5*
	Evan Mecham (R)	241,093	*44.8*
1982	Bruce Babbitt (D)	453,795	*62.5*
	Leo Corbet (R)	235,877	*32.5*
	Sam Steiger (LIBERT)	36,649	*5.0*

ARKANSAS

(Became a state June 15, 1836)

	Candidates	Votes	%
1836	James S. Conway (D)	5,338	*62.2*
	Absalom Fowler (W)	3,222	*37.5*
1840	Archibald Yell (D)	✔	
1844	Thomas S. Drew (D)	8,859	*47.6*
	Gibson (W)	7,244	*38.9*
	Byrd (I)	2,507	*13.5*
1849	John S. Roane (D)	3,290	*50.5*
	Wilson (W)	3,228	*49.5*
1852	Elias N. Conway (D)	15,932	*55.2*
	Smith (W)	12,955	*44.9*
1856	Elias N. Conway (D)	28,159	*64.6*
	Yell (AM)	15,436	*35.4*
1860	Henry M. Rector (ID)	31,578	*52.5*
	R. H. Johnson (D)	28,622	*47.5*
1872	Elisha Baxter (R)	41,808	*51.8*
	Joseph Brooks (D)	38,909	*48.2*
1874	A. H. Garland (D)	76,552	*100.0*
1876	William R. Miller (D)	69,775	*65.6*
	Bishop (R)	36,272	*34.1*
1878	William R. Miller (D)	88,726	*100.0*
1880	Thomas J. Churchill (D)	84,185	*72.8*
	Parks (G)	31,424	*27.2*
1882	James H. Berry (D)	87,669	*59.6*
	W. D. Slack (R)	49,372	*33.5*
	R. K. Garland (G)	10,142	*6.9*
1884	Simon P. Hughes (D)	100,875	*64.6*
	Thomas Boles (R)	55,388	*35.5*
1886	Simon P. Hughes (D)	90,650	*55.3*
	S. Gregg (R)	54,063	*33.0*
	C. E. Cunningham (AG WHEEL)	19,169	*11.7*
1888	James P. Eagle (D)	99,229	*54.1*
	C. M. Norwood (LAB)	84,273	*45.9*
1890	James P. Eagle (D)	106,267	*55.5*
	N. B. Fizer (R)	85,181	*44.5*
1892	W. M. Fishback (D)	90,115	*57.7*
	W. G. Whipple (R)	33,634	*21.5*
	J. P. Carnahan (POP)	31,116	*19.9*
1894	J. P. Clarke (D)	74,809	*59.1*
	H. L. Remmel (R)	26,085	*20.6*
	D. E. Barker (POP)	24,181	*19.1*
1896	Daniel Webster Jones (D)	91,114	*64.3*
	H. L. Remmel (R)	35,837	*25.3*
	A. W. Files (POP)	13,980	*9.9*
1898	Daniel Webster Jones (D)	75,354	*67.4*
	H. F. Auten (R)	27,524	*24.6*
	W. S. Morgan (POP)	8,332	*7.5*
1900	Jefferson Davis (D)	88,636	*66.7*
	H. L. Remmel (R)	40,701	*30.6*
1902	Jefferson Davis (D)	77,354	*64.6*
	Harry H. Meyers (R)	29,251	*24.4*
	Charles D. Greaves (POP)	8,345	*7.0*

	Candidates	Votes	%
1904	Jefferson Davis (D)	90,263	*61.0*
	Harry H. Myers (R)	53,898	*36.4*
1906	John S. Little (D)	105,586	*69.1*
	John I. Worthington (R)	41,689	*27.3*
1908	George W. Donaghey (D)	110,418	*68.1*
	John I. Worthington (R)	44,863	*27.7*
1910	George W. Donaghey (D)	101,612	*67.4*
	Andrew I. Roland (R)	39,870	*26.5*
	Dan Hogan (SOC)	9,196	*6.1*
1912	Joe T. Robinson (D)	109,825	*64.7*
	Andrew I. Roland (R)	46,440	*27.4*
	G. E. Mikel (SOC)	13,384	*7.9*

Special Election

1913	George W. Hays (D)	53,655	*64.3*
	Harry H. Meyers (R)	17,040	*20.4*
	George W. Murphy (PROG)	8,431	*10.1*
	J. Emil Webber (SOC)	4,378	*5.2*

1914	George W. Hays (D)	94,143	*69.5*
	Audrey L. Kinney (R)	30,947	*22.8*
	Dan Hogan (SOC)	10,434	*7.7*
1916	Charles H. Brough (D)	122,041	*69.5*
	Wallace Townsend (R)	43,963	*25.0*
	William Davis (SOC)	9,730	*5.5*
1918	Charles H. Brough (D)	68,192	*93.4*
	Clay Fulks (SOC)	4,792	*6.6*
1920	Thomas C. McRae (D)	123,637	*65.0*
	Wallace Townsend (R)	46,350	*24.4*
	J. H. Blount (NEG I)	15,627	*8.2*
1922	Thomas C. McRae (D)	99,987	*78.1*
	John W. Grabiel (R)	28,055	*21.9*
1924	Thomas J. Terral (D)	99,598	*79.8*
	John W. Grabiel (R)	25,152	*20.2*
1926	John E. Martineau (D)	116,735	*76.5*
	M. D. Bowers (R)	35,969	*23.6*
1928	Harvey J. Parnell (D)	151,743	*77.3*
	M. D. Bowers (R)	44,545	*22.7*
1930	Harvey J. Parnell (D)	112,847	*81.2*
	J. O. Livesay (R)	26,162	*18.8*
1932	Julius M. Futrell (D)	200,096	*90.4*
	J. O. Livesay (R)	19,717	*8.9*
1934	Julius M. Futrell (D)	123,918	*89.2*
	C. C. Ledbetter (R)	13,083	*9.4*
1936	Carl E. Bailey (D)	155,152	*84.9*
	Osro Cobb (R)	26,875	*14.7*
1938	Carl E. Bailey (D)	118,696	*86.3*
	Charles S. Cole (I)	12,077	*8.8*
1940	Homer M. Adkins (D)	184,578	*91.4*
	H. C. Stump (R)	16,600	*8.2*
1942	Homer M. Adkins (D)	98,871	*100.0*
1944	Ben Laney (D)	186,401	*86.0*
	H. C. Stump (R)	30,442	*14.0*
1946	Ben Laney (D)	128,029	*84.1*
	W. T. Mills (R)	24,133	*15.9*
1948	Sidney S. McMath (D)	217,771	*89.2*
	C. R. Black (R)	26,500	*10.9*
1950	Sidney S. McMath (D)	266,778	*84.1*
	Jefferson W. Speck (R)	50,303	*15.9*
1952	Francis Cherry (D)	342,292	*87.4*
	Jefferson W. Speck (R)	49,292	*12.6*
1954	Orval E. Faubus (D)	208,121	*62.1*
	Pratt C. Remmel (R)	127,004	*37.9*
1956	Orval E. Faubus (D)	321,797	*80.7*
	Roy Mitchell (R)	77,215	*19.4*
1958	Orval E. Faubus (D)	236,598	*82.5*
	George W. Johnson (R)	50,288	*17.5*
1960	Orval E. Faubus (D)	292,064	*69.2*
	Henry M. Britt (R)	129,921	*30.8*
1962	Orval E. Faubus (D)	225,743	*73.3*
	Willis Ricketts (R)	82,349	*26.7*

	Candidates	Votes	%
1964	Orval E. Faubus (D)	337,489	*57.0*
	Winthrop Rockefeller (R)	254,561	*43.0*
1966	Winthrop Rockefeller (R)	306,324	*54.4*
	James Johnson (D)	257,203	*45.6*
1968	Winthrop Rockefeller (R)	322,782	*52.4*
	Marion Crank (D)	292,813	*47.6*
1970	Dale Bumpers (D)	375,648	*61.7*
	Winthrop Rockefeller (R)	197,418	*32.4*
	Walter L. Carruth (AM)	36,132	*5.9*
1972	Dale Bumpers (D)	488,892	*75.4*
	Len E. Blaylock (R)	159,177	*24.6*
1974	David H. Pryor (D)	358,018	*65.6*
	Ken Coon (R)	187,872	*34.4*
1976	David H. Pryor (D)	605,083	*83.2*
	Leon Griffith (R)	121,716	*16.7*
1978	Bill Clinton (D)	335,101	*63.4*
	Lynn A. Lowe (R)	193,746	*36.6*
1980	Frank D. White (R)	435,684	*51.9*
	Bill Clinton (D)	403,241	*48.1*
1982	Bill Clinton (D)	431,855	*54.7*
	Frank D. White (R)	357,496	*45.3*
1984	Bill Clinton (D)	554,561	*62.6*
	Woody Freeman (R)	331,987	*37.4*

CALIFORNIA

(Became a state Sept. 9, 1850)

	Candidates	Votes	%
1849	P. H. Burnett (ID)	6,783	*47.4*
	W. S. Sherwood	3,220	*22.7*
	J. A. Sutter	2,201	*15.5*
	J. W. Geary	1,358	*9.6*
1851	John Bigler (D)	23,175	*50.5*
	P. B. Reading (W)	22,732	*49.5*
1853	John Bigler (D)	38,940	*51.0*
	William Walde (W)	37,454	*49.0*
1855	J. N. Johnson (AM)	51,157	*52.5*
	John Bigler (D)	46,225	*47.5*
1857	J. B. Weller (D)	53,122	*56.7*
	Edward Stanly (R)	21,040	*22.5*
	G. W. Bowie (AM)	19,481	*20.8*
1859	M. S. Latham (D)	61,352	*59.7*
	John Currey (A-LEC D)	31,298	*30.5*
	Leland Stanford (R)	10,110	*9.8*
1861	Leland Stanford (R)	56,036	*46.8*
	J. R. McConnell (SEC D)	32,751	*27.4*
	John Conness (UN D)	30,944	*25.8*
1863	Frederick F. Low (UN R)	64,283	*59.0*
	J. G. Downey (D)	44,622	*41.0*
1867	H. H. Haight (D)	49,895	*54.0*
	George C. Gurham (R)	40,359	*43.7*
1871	Newton Booth (R)	62,581	*52.1*
	H. H. Haight (D)	57,520	*47.9*
1875	William Irwin (D)	61,509	*50.0*
	T. G. Phelps (R)	31,322	*25.5*
	John Bidwell (I)	29,752	*24.2*
1879	George C. Perkins (R)	67,965	*42.4*
	Hugh J. Glenn (D)	47,667	*29.8*
	William F. White (WMP/L)	44,482	*27.8*
1882	George Stoneman (D)	90,694	*55.1*
	Morris M. Estee (R)	67,175	*40.8*
1886	Washington Bartlett (D)	84,965	*43.4*
	John F. Swift (R)	84,316	*43.1*
	C. C. O'Donnell (I)	12,227	*6.3*
1890	H. H. Markham (R)	125,129	*49.6*
	E. B. Pond (D)	117,184	*46.4*
1894	James H. Budd (D)	111,944	*39.3*

	Candidates	Votes	%
	Morris M. Estee (R)	110,738	*38.9*
	J. V. Webster (PP)	51,304	*18.0*
1898	Henry T. Gage (R & UL)	148,354	*51.7*
	James G. Maguire (D & POP)	129,261	*45.0*
1902	George C. Pardee (R)	146,332	*48.1*
	Franklin K. Lane (D)	143,783	*47.2*
1906	James N. Gillett (R)	125,887	*40.4*
	Theodore A. Bell (D)	117,590	*37.7*
	W. H. Langdon (I LEAGUE)	45,008	*14.4*
	Austin Lewis (SOC)	16,036	*5.1*
1910	Hiram W. Johnson (R)	177,191	*45.9*
	Theodore A. Bell (D)	154,835	*40.1*
	J. Stitt Wilson (SOC)	47,819	*12.4*
1914	Hiram W. Johnson (PROG)	460,495	*49.7*
	John D. Fredericks (R)	271,990	*29.4*
	J. B. Curtin (D)	116,121	*12.5*
	Noble A. Richardson (SOC)	50,716	*5.5*
1918	William D. Stephens (R P&PROG)	387,547	*56.3*
	Theodore A. Bell (I)	251,189	*36.5*
1922	Friend William Richardson (R)	576,445	*59.7*
	Thomas Lee Woolwine (D)	347,530	*36.0*
1926	C. C. Young (R)	814,815	*71.2*
	Justus S. Wardell (D)	282,451	*24.7*
1930	James Rolph Jr. (R)	999,393	*72.2*
	Milton K. Young (D)	333,973	*24.1*
1934	Frank F. Merriam (R)	1,138,620	*48.9*
	Upton Sinclair (D)	879,537	*37.8*
	Raymond L. Haight (C PROG)	302,519	*13.0*
1938	Culbert L. Olson (D)	1,391,734	*52.5*
	Frank F. Merriam (R)	1,171,019	*44.2*
1942	Earl Warren (R)	1,275,237	*57.1*
	Culbert L. Olson (D)	932,995	*41.8*
1946	Earl Warren (R-D)	2,344,542	*91.6*
	Henry R. Schmidt (P)	180,579	*7.1*
1950	Earl Warren (R)	2,461,754	*64.9*
	James Roosevelt (D)	1,333,856	*35.1*
1954	Goodwin J. Knight (R)	2,290,519	*56.8*
	Richard Perrin Graves (D)	1,739,368	*43.2*
1958	Edmund G. Brown (D)	3,140,076	*59.8*
	William F. Knowland (R)	2,110,911	*40.2*
1962	Edmund G. Brown (D)	3,037,109	*51.9*
	Richard M. Nixon (R)	2,740,351	*46.8*
1966	Ronald Reagan (R)	3,742,913	*57.6*
	Edmund G. Brown (D)	2,749,174	*42.3*
1970	Ronald Reagan (R)	3,439,664	*52.8*
	Jess Unruh (D)	2,938,607	*45.1*
1974	Edmund G. Brown Jr. (D)	3,131,648	*50.1*
	Houston I. Flournoy (R)	2,952,954	*47.3*
1978	Edmund G. Brown Jr. (D)	3,878,812	*56.0*
	Evelle J. Younger (R)	2,526,534	*36.5*
	Ed Clark (I)	377,960	*5.5*
1982	George Deukmejian (R)	3,881,014	*49.3*
	Tom Bradley (D)	3,787,669	*48.1*

COLORADO

(Became a state Aug. 1, 1876)

	Candidates	Votes	%
1876	John L. Routt (R)	14,154	*51.5*
	Hughes (D)	13,316	*48.5*
1878	Frederick W. Pitkin (R)	14,308	*50.0*
	W. A. H. Loveland (D)	11,535	*40.3*
	R. G. Buckingham (G)	2,783	*9.7*
1880	Frederick W. Pitkin (R)	28,465	*53.3*
	John S. Hough (D)	23,547	*44.1*
1882	James B. Grant (D)	31,375	*51.1*
	E. L. Campbell (R)	28,820	*46.9*

	Candidates	Votes	%
1884	Benjamin H. Eaton (R)	33,845	*50.7*
	Alva Adams (D)	30,743	*46.1*
1886	Alva Adams (D)	29,234	*49.7*
	William H. Meyer (R)	26,816	*45.6*
1888	Job A. Cooper (R)	49,490	*53.8*
	T. M. Patterson (D)	39,197	*42.6*
1890	John L. Routt (R)	41,827	*50.1*
	Caldwell Yeaman (D)	35,359	*42.4*
	John G. Coy (F ALNC)	5,199	*6.2*
1892	Davis H. Waite (POP & SL D)	43,342	*46.7*
	Joseph C. Helm (R)	38,806	*41.8*
	Joseph H. Maupin (D)	8,944	*9.6*
1894	Albert W. McIntire (R)	93,502	*52.0*
	Davis H. Waite (POP)	73,894	*41.1*
1896	Alva Adams (D)	87,387	*46.2*
	M. S. Bailey (N SILVER)	71,808	*38.0*
	G. H. Allen (R)	23,945	*12.7*
1898	Charles S. Thomas (FUS)	93,966	*62.8*
	Henry R. Wolcott (R)	51,051	*34.1*
1900	James B. Orman (FUS)	118,647	*53.8*
	Frank C. Goudy (R)	96,027	*43.5*
1902	James H. Peabody (R)	87,684	*46.9*
	E. C. Stimson (D)	80,727	*43.2*
1904	Alva Adams (D)	123,092‡	*50.6*
	James H. Peabody (R)	113,754	*46.8*
1906	Henry A. Buchtel (R)	92,602	*45.6*
	Alva Adams (D)	74,416	*36.6*
	Ben B. Lindsey (I)	18,014	*8.9*
	William D. Haywood (SOC)	16,015	*7.9*
1908	John F. Shafroth (D)	130,141	*49.4*
	Jesse F. McDonald (R)	118,953	*45.2*
1910	John F. Shafroth (D)	114,676	*54.0*
	John B. Stephen (R)	97,691	*46.0*
1912	Elias M. Ammons (D)	114,044	*42.9*
	Edward P. Costigan (PROG-BMR)	66,132	*24.9*
	C. C. Parks (R)	63,061	*23.7*
	Charles A. Ashelstrom (SOC)	16,189	*6.1*
1914	George A. Carlson (R)	129,096	*48.7*
	T. M. Patterson (D)	90,640	*34.2*
	Edward P. Costigan (PROG)	32,920	*12.4*
1916	Julius C. Gunter (D)	151,912	*53.3*
	George A. Carlson (R)	117,723	*41.3*
1918	Oliver H. Shoup (R)	112,693	*51.1*
	Tynan (D)	102,397	*46.5*
1920	Oliver H. Shoup (R)	174,488	*59.6*
	James M. Collins (D)	108,738	*37.1*
1922	William E. Sweet (D)	138,098	*49.6*
	Benjamin Griffith (R)	134,353	*48.3*
1924	Clarence J. Morley (R)	178,078	*51.9*
	William E. Sweet (D)	151,041	*44.0*
1926	William H. Adams (D)	183,342	*59.8*
	Oliver H. Shoup (R)	116,756	*38.1*
1928	William H. Adams (D)	240,160	*61.9*
	William L. Boatright (R)	144,067	*37.1*
1930	William H. Adams (D)	197,067	*60.4*
	Robert F. Rockwell (R)	124,164	*38.1*
1932	Edwin C. Johnson (D)	257,188	*57.2*
	James D. Parriott (R)	183,258	*40.8*
1934	Edwin C. Johnson (D)	237,026	*58.1*
	Nate C. Warren (R)	162,791	*39.9*
1936	Teller Ammons (D)	263,311	*54.6*
	Charles M. Armstrong (R)	210,614	*43.7*
1938	Ralph L. Carr (R)	255,159	*55.8*
	Teller Ammons (D)	199,562	*43.7*
1940	Ralph L. Carr (R)	296,671	*54.4*
	George E. Saunders (D)	245,292	*45.0*
1942	John C. Vivian (R)	193,501	*56.2*
	Homer F. Bedford (D)	149,402	*43.4*
1944	John C. Vivian (R)	259,862	*52.4*
	Roy Best (D)	236,086	*47.6*

	Candidates	Votes	%
1946	William Lee Knous (D)	174,604	*52.1*
	Leon E. Lavington (R)	160,483	*47.9*
1948	William Lee Knous (D)	332,752	*66.3*
	David A. Hamil (R)	168,928	*33.7*
1950	Dan Thornton (R)	236,472	*52.4*
	Walter W. Johnson (D)	212,976	*47.2*
1952	Dan Thornton (R)	349,924	*57.1*
	John W. Metzger (D)	260,044	*42.4*
1954	Edwin C. Johnson (D)	262,205	*53.6*
	Donald G. Brotzman (R)	227,335	*46.4*
1956	Stephen L. R. McNichols (D)	331,283	*51.3*
	Donald G. Brotzman (R)	313,950	*48.7*
1958	Stephen L. R. McNichols (D)	321,165	*58.4*
	Palmer L. Burch (R)	228,643	*41.6*
1962	John A. Love (R)	349,342	*56.7*
	Stephen L. R. McNichols (D)	262,890	*42.6*
1966	John A. Love (R)	356,730	*54.0*
	Robert L. Knous (D)	287,132	*43.5*
1970	John A. Love (R)	350,690	*52.5*
	Mark Hogan (D)	302,432	*45.2*
1974	Richard D. Lamm (D)	441,408	*53.2*
	John D. Vanderhoof (R)	378,698	*45.7*
1978	Richard D. Lamm (D)	483,985	*58.7*
	Ted Strickland (R)	317,292	*38.5*
1982	Richard D. Lamm (D)	627,960	*65.7*
	John D. Fuhr (R)	302,740	*31.7*

CONNECTICUT

(Ratified the Constitution Jan. 9, 1788)

	Candidates	Votes	%
1787-1795	Samuel Huntington	✓	
1796	Oliver Wolcott Sr.	3,805†	*48.8*
	Jonathan Trumbull II	1,187	*15.2*
	Jonathan Ingersoll	937	*12.0*
	Oliver Ellsworth	629	*8.1*
	Richard Law	485	*6.2*
1797	Oliver Wolcott Sr.	✓	
1798-1800	Jonathan Trumbull II	✓	
1801	Jonathan Trumbull II	11,156	*83.8*
	Richard Law	1,056	*7.9*
1802	Jonathan Trumbull II (FED)	11,398	*69.9*
	Ephraim Kirby (D-R)	4,523	*27.7*
1803	Jonathan Trumbull II (FED)	14,375	*64.0*
	Ephraim Kirby (D-R)	7,848	*35.0*
1804	Jonathan Trumbull II (FED)	11,108	*61.8*
	William Hart (D-R)	6,871	*38.2*
1805	Jonathan Trumbull II (FED)	12,700	*61.9*
	William Hart (D-R)	7,810	*38.1*
1806	Jonathan Trumbull II (FED)	13,413	*58.6*
	William Hart (D-R)	9,460	*41.4*
1807	Jonathan Trumbull II (FED)	11,959	*60.0*
	William Hart (D-R)	7,971	*40.0*
1808	Jonathan Trumbull II (FED)	12,146	*61.6*
	William Hart (D-R)	7,566	*38.4*
1809	Jonathan Trumbull II (FED)	14,650	*64.2*
	Asa Spalding (D-R)	8,159	*35.8*
1810	John Treadwell (FED)	10,265†	*49.5*
	Asa Spalding (D-R)	7,185	*34.6*
	Roger Griswold (FED)	3,110	*15.0*
1811	Roger Griswold (FED)	✓	
	John Treadwell (FED)		
1812	Roger Griswold (FED)	11,721	*86.1*
	Elijah Boardman (D-R)	1,487	*10.9*
1813	John C. Smith (FED)	11,893	*59.1*
	Elijah Boardman (D-R)	7,201	*35.8*

	Candidates	Votes	%
1814	John C. Smith (FED)	9,415	72.9
	Elijah Boardman (D-R)	2,619	20.3
1815	John C. Smith (FED)	8,176	59.3
	Elijah Boardman (D-R)	4,876	35.3
1816	John C. Smith (FED)	11,386	52.3
	Oliver Wolcott Jr. (AM, TOL¹)	10,170	46.7
1817	Oliver Wolcott Jr. (TOL¹, REF)	13,655	50.6
	John C. Smith (FED)	13,119	48.6
1818	Oliver Wolcott Jr. (CONST, REF)	16,432	87.0
1819	Oliver Wolcott Jr. (TOL¹, REF)	22,539	86.8
1820	Oliver Wolcott Jr. (D-R)	15,738	78.4
1821	Oliver Wolcott Jr. (D-R)	10,064	86.6
1822	Oliver Wolcott Jr. (D-R)	8,568	85.5
1823	Oliver Wolcott Jr. (D-R)	9,090	88.9
1824	Oliver Wolcott Jr. (D-R)	6,637	92.1
	Timothy Pitkin (OPP R)	466	6.5
1825	Oliver Wolcott Jr. (D-R)	7,147	70.1
	David Daggett (FED)	1,342	13.2
	Nathan Smith (OPP R)	863	8.5
	Timothy Pitkin (OPP R)	525	5.2
1826	Oliver Wolcott Jr. (D-R)	6,780	57.8
	David Daggett (FED)	4,340	37.0
1827	Gideon Tomlinson (OLD R)	7,681	57.7
	Oliver Wolcott (OPP R)	5,295	39.8
1828	Gideon Tomlinson (NR)	9,297	97.3
1829	Gideon Tomlinson (NR)	9,612	95.8
1830	Gideon Tomlinson (NR)	12,988	95.6
1831	John S. Peters (NR)	12,819	65.4
	Zalmon Storrs (A-MASC)	4,778	24.4
1832	John S. Peters (NR)	11,971	70.3
	Calvin Willey (D)	4,463	26.2
1833	John S. Peters (NR)	9,212	42.3
	Henry W. Edwards (D)	9,030†	41.5
	Zalmon Storrs (A-MASC)	3,250	14.9
1834	Samuel A. Foot (NR)	18,411†	49.8
	Henry W. Edwards (D)	15,834	42.9
	Zalmon Storrs (A-MASC)	2,398	6.5
1835	Henry W. Edwards (D)	22,129	51.5
	Samuel A. Foot (W)	20,335	47.3
1836	Henry W. Edwards (D)	20,360	53.6
	Gideon Tomlinson (W)	17,393	45.8
1837	Henry W. Edwards (D)	23,805	52.5
	William W. Ellsworth (W)	21,508	47.5
1838	William W. Ellsworth (W)	27,115	54.1
	S. P. Beers (D)	21,489	42.9
1839	William W. Ellsworth (W)	26,581	51.4
	Niles (D)	24,047	46.5
1840	William W. Ellsworth (W)	30,360	54.0
	Niles (D)	25,782	45.8
1841	William W. Ellsworth (W)	26,078	56.0
	Nicoll (D)	20,458	44.0
1842	Chauncey F. Cleveland (D)	25,564†	49.9
	William W. Ellsworth (W)	23,700	46.2
1843	Chauncey F. Cleveland (D)	27,416	50.1
	Roger S. Baldwin (W)	25,401	46.4
1844	Roger S. Baldwin (W)	30,093†	49.4
	Chauncey F. Cleveland (D)	28,846	47.3
1845	Roger S. Baldwin (W)	29,508	51.0
	Isaac Toucey (D)	26,258	45.3
1846	Clark Bissell (W)	27,822	48.6
	Isaac Toucey (D)	27,203†	47.5
1847	Clark Bissell (W)	30,137	50.5
	Whittlesey (D)	27,402	45.9
1848	Clark Bissell (W)	30,717	50.4
	George S. Catlin (D)	28,525	46.8
1849	Joseph Trumbull (W)	27,300†	48.8
	Thomas H. Seymour (D)	25,106	44.9
	Niles (F SOIL)	3,520	6.3
1850	Thomas H. Seymour (D)	29,022†	48.3
	Foster (W)	28,209	46.9
1851	Thomas H. Seymour (D)	30,077†	49.0

	Candidates	Votes	%
	Foster (W)	28,756	46.9
1852	Thomas H. Seymour (D)	31,624	50.4
	Kendrick (W)	28,241	45.0
1853	Thomas H. Seymour (D)	30,814	51.0
	Dutton (W)	20,671	34.2
	Gillette (F SOIL)	8,926	14.8
1854	Ingham (D)	28,538	48.6
	Henry Dutton (W)	19,465†	33.2
	Chapman (TEMP)	10,672	18.2
1855	William T. Minor (AM)	28,080†	43.5
	Ingham (D)	27,291	42.3
	Henry Dutton (W)	9,162	14.2
1856	Ingham (D)	32,704	49.0
	William T. Minor (AM)	26,008†	39.0
	Wells (R)	6,740	10.1
1857	Alexander H. Holley (R)	31,709	50.4
	Ingham (D)	31,156	49.5
1858	William A. Buckingham (R)	36,298	51.8
	Pratt (D)	33,549	47.8
1859	William A. Buckingham (R)	40,247	51.1
	Pratt (D)	38,369	48.7
1860	William A. Buckingham (R)	44,458	50.3
	Seymour (D)	43,920	49.7
1861	William A. Buckingham (R)	43,012	51.2
	Loomis (D)	40,926	48.8
1862	William A. Buckingham (R)	39,782	56.5
	Loomis (D)	30,634	43.5
1863	William A. Buckingham (R)	41,032	51.6
	Thomas H. Seymour (D)	38,395	48.3
1864	William A. Buckingham (UN R)	39,820	53.8
	Origen S. Seymour (D)	34,162	46.2
1865	William A. Buckingham (UN R)	42,374	57.5
	Origen S. Seymour (D)	31,339	42.5
1866	Joseph R. Hawley (R)	43,974	50.3
	James E. English (D)	43,433	49.7
1867	James E. English (D)	47,565	50.5
	Joseph R. Hawley (R)	46,578	49.5
1868	James E. English (D)	50,541	50.9
	Marshall Jewell (R)	48,777	49.1
1869	Marshall Jewell (R)	45,493	50.2
	James E. English (D)	45,082	49.8
1870	James E. English (D)	44,128	50.5
	Marshall Jewell (R)	43,285	49.5
1871	Marshall Jewell (R)	47,473	50.1
	James E. English (D)	47,370	49.9
1872	Marshall Jewell (R)	46,563	50.0
	Richard D. Hubbard (D)	44,562	47.9
1873	Charles R. Ingersoll (D)	45,060	51.9
	Haven (R)	39,245	45.2
1874	Charles R. Ingersoll (D)	46,755	53.9
	Harrison (R)	39,973	46.1
1875	Charles R. Ingersoll (D)	53,752	53.2
	Greene (R)	44,272	43.9
1876	Richard D. Hubbard (D)	61,934	50.8
	Robinson (R)	58,514	48.0
1878	Charles B. Andrews (R)	48,867†	46.7
	Richard D. Hubbard (D)	46,385	44.3
	Atwater (N)	8,314	7.9
1880	Hobart B. Bigelow (R)	67,070	50.5
	James E. English (D)	64,293	48.4
1882	Thomas M. Waller (D)	59,014	51.0
	Morgan G. Bulkeley (R)	54,853	47.4
1884	Thomas M. Waller (D)	67,910	49.3
	Henry B. Harrison (R)	66,274†	48.1
1886	Cleveland (D)	58,818	47.7
	Phineas C. Lounsbury (R)	56,920†	46.2
1888	Luzon B. Morris (D)	75,074	48.9
	Morgan G. Bulkeley (R)	73,659†	47.9
1890	Luzon B. Morris (D)	67,658*	50.0
	S. E. Merwin (R)	63,975	47.3
1892	Luzon B. Morris (D)	82,787	50.3

	Candidates	Votes	%
	S. E. Merwin (R)	76,745	46.6
1894	O. Vincent Coffin (R)	83,975	54.2
	Cady (D)	66,287	42.8
1896	Lorrin A. Cooke (R)	108,807	62.5
	Sargent (D)	56,524	32.5
1898	George E. Lounsbury (R)	81,015	54.2
	Morgan (D)	64,227	42.9
1900	George P. McLean (R)	95,822	53.0
	S. L. Bronson (D)	81,421	45.1
1902	Abiram Chamberlain (R)	85,338	53.4
	Melbert B. Cary (D)	69,330	43.4
1904	Henry Roberts (R)	104,736	54.9
	A. Heaton Robertson (D)	79,164	41.5
1906	Rollin S. Woodruff (R)	88,384	54.8
	Charles Thayer (D)	67,776	42.1
1908	George L. Lilley (R)	98,179	51.9
	A. Heaton Robertson (D)	82,260	43.5
1910	Simeon E. Baldwin (D)	77,243	46.5
	Goodwin (R)	73,528	44.3
	Hunter (SOC)	12,179	7.3
1912	Simeon E. Baldwin (D)	78,264	41.1
	Studley (R)	67,531	35.5
	Smith (PROG)	31,020	16.3
	Beardsley (SOC)	10,236	5.4
1914	Marcus H. Holcomb (R)	91,262	50.4
	Lyman Tingier (D)	73,888	40.8
1916	Marcus H. Holcomb (R)	109,293	51.1
	Morris Beardsley (D)	96,787	45.3
1918	Marcus H. Holcomb (R)	84,891	50.7
	Thomas Spellacy (D)	76,773	45.9
1920	Everett J. Lake (R)	230,792	63.0
	Rollin U. Tyler (D)	119,912	32.8
1922	Charles A. Templeton (R)	170,231	52.4
	David Fitzgerald (D)	148,641	45.7
1924	Hiram Bingham (R)	246,336	66.2
	Charles Morris (D)	118,676	31.9
1926	John H. Trumbull (R)	192,425	63.6
	Charles Morris (D)	107,045	35.4
1928	John H. Trumbull (R)	296,216	53.6
	Charles Morris (D)	252,209	45.6
1930	Wilbur L. Cross (D)	215,072	49.9
	E. E. Rogers (R)	209,607	48.6
1932	Wilbur L. Cross (D)	288,347	49.0
	John H. Trumbull (R)	277,503	47.1
1934	Wilbur L. Cross (D)	257,996	46.7
	Hugh Meade Alcorn (R)	249,397	45.2
	Jasper McLevy (SOC)	38,438	7.0
1936	Wilbur L. Cross (D)	372,953#	55.3
	Arthur M. Brown (R)	277,190#	41.1
1938	Raymond E. Baldwin (R, UN)	230,237	36.4
	Wilbur L. Cross (D)	227,549	36.0
	Jasper McLevy (SOC)	166,253	26.3
1940	Robert A. Hurley (D)	388,361	49.5
	Raymond E. Baldwin (R, UN)	374,581	47.8
1942	Raymond E. Baldwin (R)	281,362	48.9
	Robert A. Hurley (D)	255,166	44.4
	Jasper McLevy (SOC)	34,537	6.0
1944	Raymond E. Baldwin (R)	418,289	50.5
	Robert A. Hurley (D)	392,417	47.4
1946	James L. McConaughy (R)	371,852	54.4
	Wilbert Snow (D)	276,335	40.4
1948	Chester Bowles (D)	431,746	49.3
	James C. Shannon (R)	429,071	49.0
1950	John D. Lodge (R)	436,418	49.7
	Chester Bowles (D)	419,404	47.7
1954	Abraham A. Ribicoff (D)	463,643	49.5
	John D. Lodge (R)	460,528	49.2
1958	Abraham A. Ribicoff (D)	607,012	62.3
	Fred R. Zeller (R)	360,644	37.0
1962	John N. Dempsey (D)	549,027	53.2
	John Alsop (R)	482,852	46.8

	Candidates	Votes	%
1966	John N. Dempsey (D)	561,599	55.7
	E. Clayton Gengras (R)	446,536	44.3
1970	Thomas J. Meskill (R)	582,160	53.8
	Emilio Q. Daddario (D)	500,561	46.2
1974	Ella T. Grasso (D)	643,490	58.4
	Robert H. Steele (R)	440,169	39.9
1978	Ella T. Grasso (D)	613,109	59.1
	Ronald A. Sarasin (R)	422,316	40.7
1982	William A. O'Neill (D)	578,264	53.3
	Lewis B. Rome (R)	497,773	45.9

1. Toleration Party.

DELAWARE

(Ratified the Constitution Dec. 7, 1787)

	Candidates	Votes	%
1792[1]	Joshua Clayton	2,209	48.3
	Thomas Montgomery	1,902	41.6
	George Mitchell	458	10.0
1795	Gunning Bedford Jr.	2,352	52.3
	Archibald Alexander	2,142	47.7
1798	Richard Bassett (FED)	2,490	52.5
	David Hall (D-R)	2,068	43.6
1801	David Hall (D-R)	3,475	50.1
	Nathanael Mitchell (FED)	3,457	49.9
1804	Nathanael Mitchell (FED)	4,391	52.0
	Joseph Hazlett (D-R)	4,050	48.0
1807	George Truitt (FED)	3,309	51.9
	Joseph Hazlett (D-R)	3,062	48.1
1810	Joseph Hazlett (D-R)	3,664	50.5
	Daniel Rodney (FED)	3,593	49.5
1813	Daniel Rodney (FED)	4,643	55.2
	James Riddle (D-R)	3,768	44.8
1816	John Clarke (FED)	3,998	53.2
	Mansen Bull (D-R)	3,517	46.8
1819	Henry Molleston (FED)	3,823*	54.6
	Mansen Bull (D-R)	3,185	45.4
1820	John Collins (D-R)	3,965	53.1
	Jesse Green (FED)	3,500	46.9
1822	Joseph Hazlett (D-R)	3,784	50.1
	James Booth (FED)	3,762	49.9
1823	Samuel Paynter (FED)	4,348	51.8
	Daniel Hazzard (D-R)	4,051	48.2
1826	Charles Polk (FED)	4,344#	50.6
	David Hazzard (D-R)	4,238#	49.4
1829	David Hazzard (AM D-R)	✔ #	
	A. Thompson (JAC D) #		
1832	Caleb P. Bennett (D)	4,220	50.3
	Arnold Naudain (NR)	4,166	49.7
1836	Cornelius P. Comegys (W)	4,693	52.3
	Nehemiah Clark (D)	4,276	47.7
1840	William B. Cooper (W)	5,855	53.8
	Warren Jefferson (D)	5,024	46.2
1844	Thomas Stockton (W)	6,140	50.2
	William Tharp (D)	6,095	49.8
1846	William Tharp (D)	6,148	50.6
	Peter F. Causey (W)	6,012	49.4
1850	William H. Ross (D)	6,001	48.3
	Peter F. Causey (W)	5,978	48.1
1854	Peter F. Causey (AM)	6,941	52.6
	Barton (D)	6,244	47.4
1858	William Burton (D)	7,758	50.7
	Buckmaster	7,554	49.3
1862	William Cannon (UN)	8,155	50.3
	Jefferson (D)	8,044	49.7
1866	Gove Saulsbury (D)	9,810	53.3
	James Riddle (R)	8,598	46.7
1870	James Ponder (D)	11,464	55.7
	Thomas B. Coursey (R)	9,130	44.3

	Candidates	Votes	%
1874	John P. Cochran (D)	12,488	52.6
	Jump (R)	11,259	47.4
1878	John W. Hall (D)	10,730	79.1
	Stewart (NG)	2,835	20.9
1882	Charles C. Stockley (D)	16,558	53.1
	Curry (R)	14,620	46.9
1886	Benjamin T. Biggs (D)	13,942	63.6
	Hoffecker (TEMP REF)	7,835	35.8
1890	Robert J. Reynolds (D)	17,801	50.4
	Richardson (R)	17,258	48.9
1894	Joshua H. Marvel (R)	19,880	50.8
	Ebe W. Tunnell (D)	18,659	47.7
1896	Ebe W. Tunnell (D)	15,507	44.2
	John H. Hoffecker (R)	11,014	31.4
	John C. Higgins (A-AK R)	7,154	20.4
1900	John Hunn (R)	22,421	53.6
	Peter J. Ford (D)	18,808	44.9
1904	Preston Lea (R)	22,532	51.4
	Caleb S. Pennewill (D)	19,780	45.1
1908	Simeon S. Pennewill (R)	24,905	52.0
	Rowland G. Paynter (D)	22,794	47.6
1912	Charles R. Miller (R & PROG)	22,745	47.0
	Thomas M. Monaghan (D)	21,460	44.3
	George B. Hynson (PROG)	3,019	6.2
1916	John G. Townsend Jr. (R)	26,664	52.1
	James H. Hughes (D)	24,053	47.0
1920	William E. Denney (R)	51,895	55.2
	Andrew J. Lynch (D)	41,038	43.7
1924	Robert P. Robinson (R)	53,046	59.6
	Joseph Bancroft (D)	34,830	39.2
1928	C. Douglass Buck (R)	63,716	61.2
	Charles M. Wharton (D)	40,346	38.8
1932	Clayton Douglass Buck (R)	60,903	54.2
	L. Layton (D)	50,401	44.9
1936	Richard C. McMullen (D)	65,437	51.6
	Harry L. Cannon (R)	52,782	41.6
	Isaac Dolphus Short (IR)	8,400	6.6
1940	Walter W. Bacon (R)	70,629	52.4
	Josiah Marvel Jr. (D)	61,237	45.4
1944	Walter W. Bacon (R)	63,829	50.5
	Isaac J. MacCollum (D)	62,156	49.2
1948	Elbert N. Carvel (D)	75,339	53.7
	Hyland P. George (R)	64,996	46.3
1952	J. Caleb Boggs (R)	88,977	52.1
	Elbert N. Carvel (D)	81,772	47.9
1956	J. Caleb Boggs (R)	91,965	52.0
	J. H. Tyler McConnell (D)	85,047	48.1
1960	Elbert N. Carvel (D)	100,792	51.7
	John W. Rollins (R)	94,043	48.3
1964	Charles L. Terry Jr. (D)	102,797	51.4
	David P. Buckson (R)	97,374	48.7
1968	Russell W. Peterson (R)	104,474	50.5
	Charles L. Terry Jr. (D)	102,360	49.5
1972	Sherman W. Tribbitt (D)	117,274	51.3
	Russell W. Peterson (R)	109,583	47.9
1976	Pierre duPont (R)	130,531	56.9
	Sherman W. Tribbitt (D)	97,480	42.5
1980	Pierre duPont (R)	159,004	70.6
	William J. Gordy (D)	64,217	28.5
1984	Michael N. Castle (R)	132,250	55.5
	William T. Quillen (D)	108,315	44.5

1. *Before 1792 governor chosen by Legislature.*

FLORIDA

(Became a state March 3, 1845)

	Candidates	Votes	%
1845	William D. Moseley (D)	3,292	55.1
	R. K. McCall (W)	2,679	44.9

	Candidates	Votes	%
1848	Thomas S. Brown (W)	4,147	53.3
	W. Bailey (D)	3,636	46.7
1852	James E. Broome (D)	4,628	51.6
	George T. Ward (W)	4,336	48.4
1856	Madison S. Perry (D)	6,208	51.3
	David S. Walker (AM)	5,894	48.7
1860	John Milton (D)	6,937	57.1
	Edward Hopkins (CST U)	5,215	42.9
1865	David S. Walker (D)	5,873#	100.0
1868	Harrison Reed (R)	14,421#	59.1
	George W. Scott (D)	7,731#	31.7
	Samuel Walker (RAD R)	2,251#	9.2
1872	Ossian B. Hart (R)	17,603	52.4
	William D. Bloxham (LR)	16,004	47.6
1876	George F. Drew (D)	24,613	50.5
	Marcellus L. Stearns (R)	24,116	49.5
1880	William D. Bloxham (D)	28,372	54.9
	Simon B. Conover (R)	23,307	45.1
1884	Edward A. Perry (D)	32,096	53.5
	Pope (R)	27,865	46.5
1888	Francis P. Fleming (D)	40,195	60.4
	V. J. Shipman (R)	26,385	39.6
1892	Henry L. Mitchell (D)	32,064	78.7
	Alonzo P. Baskin (FLA PP)	8,379	20.6
1896	William D. Bloxham (D)	27,171	66.6
	E. R. Gunby (R)	8,290	20.3
	W. A. Wicks (POP)	5,370	13.2
1900	William S. Jennings (D)	29,251	82.0
	M. B. MacFarlane (R)	6,438	18.0
1904	Napoleon B. Broward (D)	28,971	79.2
	M. B. MacFarlane (R)	6,357	17.4
1908	Albert W. Gilchrist (D)	33,036	78.8
	John M. Cheney (R)	6,453	15.4
	A. J. Pettigrew (SOC)	2,427	5.8
1912	Park Trammell (D)	38,377	80.2
	Thomas W. Cox (SOC)	3,467	7.2
	William R. O'Neal (R)	2,646	5.5
1916	Sidney J. Catts (IP)	39,546#	47.7
	W. V. Knott (D)	30,343	36.6
	George W. Allen (R)	10,333	12.5
1920	Cary A. Hardee (D)	103,407	77.9
	George E. Gay (R)	23,788	17.9
1924	John W. Martin (D)	84,181	82.8
	W. O'Neal	17,499	17.2
1928	Doyle E. Carlton (D)	148,455	61.0
	W. J. Howey (R)	95,018	39.0
1932	David Sholtz (D)	186,270	66.6
	W. J. Howey (R)	93,323	33.4
1936	Fred P. Cone (D)	253,638	80.9
	E. E. Callaway (R)	59,832	19.1
1940	Spessard L. Holland (D)	334,152	100.0
1944	Millard F. Caldwell (D)	361,077	78.9
	Bert Lee Acker (R)	96,321	21.1
1948	Fuller Warren (D)	381,459	83.4
	Bert Lee Acker (R)	76,153	16.6
1952	Daniel T. McCarty (D)	624,463	74.8
	Harry S. Swan (R)	210,009	25.2

Special Election

1954	Leroy Collins (D)	287,769	80.5
	J. Tom Watson (R)	69,852	19.5

1956	Leroy Collins (D)	747,753	73.7
	William A. Washburn Jr. (R)	266,980	26.3
1960	Farris Bryant (D)	849,407	59.9
	George C. Petersen (R)	569,936	40.2
1964	Haydon Burns (D)	933,554	56.1
	Charles R. Holley (R)	686,297	41.3
1966	Claude R. Kirk Jr. (R)	821,190	55.1
	Robert King High (D)	668,233	44.9

	Candidates	Votes	%
1970	Reubin Askew (D)	984,305	*56.8*
	Claude R. Kirk Jr. (R)	746,243	*43.0*
1974	Reubin Askew (D)	1,118,954	*61.2*
	Jerry Thomas (R)	709,438	*38.8*
1978	Robert Graham (D)	1,406,580	*55.6*
	Jack M. Eckerd (R)	1,123,888	*44.4*
1982	Robert Graham (D)	1,739,553	*64.7*
	L. A. Bafalis (R)	949,013	*35.3*

GEORGIA

(Ratified the Constitution Jan. 2, 1788)

	Candidates	Votes	%
1825[1]	George M. Troup	20,545	*50.9*
	John Clark	19,857	*49.2*
1827	John Forsyth	23,174	*70.6*
1829	George R. Gilmer	27,398	*71.5*
	Joel Crawford	10,946	*28.6*
1831	Wilson Lumpkin	27,224	*51.7*
	George R. Gilmer	25,468	*48.3*
1833	Wilson Lumpkin	30,868	*51.4*
	Joel Crawford	29,186	*48.6*
1835	William Schley (D)	31,190	*52.3*
	Dougherty (W)	28,497	*47.7*
1837	George R. Gilmer (W)	✔	
	William Schley (D)		
1839	Charles James McDonald (D)	34,668	*51.5*
	Dougherty (W)	32,715	*48.6*
1841	Charles James McDonald (D)	38,514	*52.7*
	William C. Dawson (W)	34,511	*47.3*
1843	George Walker Crawford (W)	38,711	*52.3*
	Mark A. Cooper (D)	35,273	*47.7*
1845	George Walker Crawford (W)	41,523	*51.1*
	McAllister (D)	39,753	*48.9*
1847	George Washington Towns (D)	43,219	*50.8*
	Clinch (W)	41,941	*49.3*
1849	George Washington Towns (D)	46,634	*51.8*
	Hill (W)	43,349	*48.2*
1851	Howell Cobb (UN)	57,414	*59.7*
	McDonald (SOR W)	38,824	*40.3*
1853	Hershel Vespasian Johnson (D)	47,638	*50.3*
	Jenkins (W)	47,128	*49.7*
1855	Hershel Vespasian Johnson (D)	54,136	*52.1*
	Andrews (AM)	43,358	*41.8*
	Overby (TEMP)	6,333	*6.1*
1857	Joseph Emerson Brown (D)	57,631	*55.1*
	Hill (AM)	46,889	*44.9*
1859	Joseph Emerson Brown (D)	63,806	*60.2*
	Akin (OPP)	42,195	*39.8*
1868	Rufus B. Bullock (R)	83,107	*52.1*
	Gordon (D)	76,539	*47.9*
1872	James Milton Smith (LR)	104,539	*69.2*
	Walker (R)	46,475	*30.8*
1876	Alfred Holt Colquitt (D)	110,624	*76.2*
	Norcross (R)	34,492	*23.8*
1880	Alfred Holt Colquitt (D)	117,803	*64.9*
	Norwood (ID)	63,631	*35.1*
1882	Alexander H. Stephens (D)	107,649	*70.6*
	Gartrell (ID)	44,893	*29.4*
1884	Henry D. McDaniel (D)	✔	
1886	John B. Gordon (D)	101,159	*99.2*
1888	John B. Gordon (D)	121,999	*100.0*
1890	William J. Northen (D)	105,365	*100.0*
1892	William J. Northen (D)	136,543	*66.7*
	Peck (PP)	68,093	*33.3*
1894	William Y. Atkinson (D)	121,249	*55.6*

	Candidates	Votes	%
	J. K. Hines (POP)	96,990	*44.4*
1896	William Y. Atkinson (D)	123,206	*58.9*
	Seaborn Wright (POP)	85,981	*41.1*
1898	Allen D. Candler (D)	118,028	*69.8*
	Hogan (POP)	51,191	*30.3*
1900	Allen D. Candler (D)	92,729	*78.6*
	George W. Trayler (POP)	25,285	*21.4*
1902	Joseph M. Terrell (D)	81,548	*93.6*
	Hines (POP)	5,566	*6.4*
1904	Joseph M. Terrell (D)	67,523	*100.0*
1906	Hoke Smith (D)	94,223	*99.9*
1908	Joseph M. Brown (D)	112,292	*90.5*
	Yancy Carter (I)	11,746	*9.5*
1910	Hoke Smith (D)	✔	
	Joseph M. Brown		
1912	John M. Slaton (D)	✔	
1914	Nathaniel E. Harris (D)	✔	
1916	Hugh M. Dorsey (D)	✔	
1918	Hugh M. Dorsey (D)	59,536	*100.0*
1920	Thomas W. Hardwick (D)	✔	
1922	Clifford M. Walker (D)	75,000	*100.0*
1924	Clifford M. Walker (D)	152,367	*100.0*
1926	Lamartine G. Hardman (D)	47,300	*100.0*
1928	Lamartine G. Hardman (D)	✔	
1930	Richard B. Russell (D)	✔	
1932	Eugene Talmadge (D)	240,242	*100.0*
1934	Eugene Talmadge (D)	53,101	*100.0*
1936	Eurith D. Rivers (D)	263,140	*99.7*
1938	Eurith D. Rivers (D)	66,863	*94.3*
1940	Eugene Talmadge (D, ID)	286,277	*99.6*
1942	Ellis Arnall (D)	62,220	*96.3*
1946	Eugene Talmadge (D)	144,067*	*99.1*

Special Election

1948	Herman E. Talmadge (D)	354,712	*97.5*

1950	Herman E. Talmadge (D)	230,771	*98.4*
1954	S. Marvin Griffin (D)	331,899	*100.0*
1958	S. Ernest Vandiver (D)	168,414	*100.0*
1962	Carl E. Sanders (D)	311,524	*100.0*
1966	Howard H. Callaway (R)	453,665	*47.8*
	Lester Maddox (D)	450,626†	*47.4*
1970	Jimmy Carter (D)	620,419	*59.3*
	Hal Suit (R)	424,983	*40.6*
1974	George Busbee (D)	646,777	*69.1*
	Ronnie Thompson (R)	289,113	*30.9*
1978	George Busbee (D)	534,572	*80.6*
	Rodney M. Cook (R)	128,139	*19.3*
1982	Joe Frank Harris (D)	734,090	*62.8*
	Robert H. Bell (R)	434,496	*37.2*

1. Before 1825 governor chosen by Legislature.

HAWAII

(Became a state Aug. 21, 1959)

	Candidates	Votes	%
1959	William F. Quinn (R)	86,213	*51.1*
	John A. Burns (D)	82,074	*48.7*
1962	John A. Burns (D)	114,308	*58.3*
	William F. Quinn (R)	81,707	*41.7*
1966	John A. Burns (D)	108,840	*51.1*
	Randolph Crossley (R)	104,324	*48.9*
1970	John A. Burns (D)	137,812	*57.7*
	Sam King (R)	101,249	*42.4*

	Candidates	Votes	%
1974	George R. Ariyoshi (D)	136,262	54.6
	Randolph Crossley (R)	113,388	45.4
1978	George R. Ariyoshi (D)	153,394	54.5
	John Leopold (R)	124,610	44.3
1982	George R. Ariyoshi (D)	141,043	45.2
	Frank F. Fasi (ID)	89,303	28.6
	D. G. Anderson (R)	81,507	26.1

IDAHO

(Became a state July 3, 1890)

	Candidates	Votes	%
1890	G. L. Shoup (R)	10,262	56.4
	Wilson (D)	7,948	43.7
1892	William J. McConnell (R)	8,178	40.7
	John M. Burke (D)	6,769	33.7
	Abraham J. Crook (PP)	4,865	24.2
1894	William J. McConnell (R)	10,208	41.5
	James W. Ballantine (PP)	7,121	29.0
	Edward A. Stevenson (D)	7,057	28.7
1896	Frank Steunenberg (PP-D-S-R)	22,096	76.8
	David H. Budlong (R)	6,441	22.4
1898	Frank Steunenberg (FUS)	19,407	48.8
	A. B. Moss (R)	13,794	34.7
	J. H. Anderson (PP)	5,371	13.5
1900	Frank W. Hunt (D-FUS)	28,628	52.0
	D. W. Standrod (R)	26,468	48.0
1902	John T. Morrison (R)	31,874	52.9
	Frank W. Hunt (D)	26,021	43.2
1904	Frank R. Gooding (R)	41,877	58.7
	Henry Heitfeld (D)	24,252	34.0
	Theodore B. Shaw (SOC)	4,000	5.6
1906	Frank R. Gooding (R)	38,386	52.2
	Charles O. Stockslager (D)	29,496	40.1
	Thomas F. Kelley (SOC)	4,650	6.3
1908	James H. Brady (R)	47,864	49.6
	Moses Alexander (D)	40,145	41.6
	Ernest Untermann (SOC)	6,155	6.4
1910	James H. Hawley (D)	40,856	47.4
	James H. Brady (R)	39,961	46.4
	S. W. Motley (SOC)	5,342	6.2
1912	John M. Haines (R)	35,074	33.2
	James H. Hawley (D)	33,992	32.2
	G. H. Martin (PROG)	24,325	23.1
	L. A. Coblentz (SOC)	11,094	10.5
1914	Moses Alexander (D)	47,618	44.1
	John M. Haines (R)	40,349	37.4
	Hugh E. McElroy (EP)	10,583	9.8
	L. A. Coblentz (SOC)	7,967	7.4
1916	Moses Alexander (D)	63,877	47.5
	David W. Davis (R)	63,305	47.1
	Annie E. Triplow (SOC)	7,321	5.4
1918	David W. Davis (R)	57,626	60.0
	H. F. Samuels (D)	38,499	40.1
1920	David W. Davis (R)	75,748	53.0
	Ted A. Walters (D)	38,509	26.9
	Sherman D. Fairchild (I)	28,752	20.1
1922	Charles C. Moore (R)	50,538	39.5
	H. F. Samuels (PROG)	40,516	31.7
	M. Alexander (D)	36,810	28.8
1924	Charles C. Moore (R)	65,408	43.9
	H. F. Samuels (PROG)	58,163	39.0
	A. L. Freehafer (D)	25,081	16.8
1926	H. C. Baldridge (R)	61,575	51.1
	W. Scott Hall (PROG)	34,208	28.4
	Asher B. Wilson (D)	24,837	20.6
1928	H. C. Baldridge (R)	87,681	57.8

	Candidates	Votes	%
	C. Ben Ross (D)	63,046	41.6
1930	C. Ben Ross (D)	73,896	56.0
	John McMurray (R)	58,002	44.0
1932	C. Ben Ross (D)	116,663	61.7
	Defenbach (R)	68,863	36.4
1934	C. Ben Ross (D)	93,313	54.6
	Frank L. Stephan (R)	75,659	44.3
1936	Barzilla W. Clark (D)	115,098	57.2
	Frank L. Stephan (R)	83,430	41.5
1938	C. A. Bottolfsen (R)	106,268	57.3
	C. Ben Ross (D)	77,697	41.9
1940	Chase A. Clark (D)	120,420	50.5
	C. A. Bottolfsen (R)	118,117	49.5
1942	C. A. Bottolfsen (R)	72,260	50.2
	Chase A. Clark (D)	71,826	49.9
1944	Charles C. Gossett (D)	109,527	52.6
	W. H. Detweiler (R)	98,532	47.4
1946	Charles A. Robins (R)	102,233	56.4
	Arnold Williams (D)	79,131	43.6
1950	Len B. Jordan (R)	107,642	52.6
	Calvin E. Wright (D)	97,150	47.4
1954	Robert E. Smylie (R)	124,038	54.2
	Clark Hamilton (D)	104,647	45.8
1958	Robert E. Smylie (R)	121,810	51.0
	A. M. Derr (D)	117,236	49.0
1962	Robert E. Smylie (R)	139,578	54.6
	Vernon K. Smith (D)	115,876	45.4
1966	Don Samuelson (R)	104,586	41.4
	Cecil D. Andrus (D)	93,744	37.1
	Perry Swisher (I)	30,913	12.2
	Philip W. Jungert (I)	23,139	9.2
1970	Cecil D. Andrus (D)	128,004	52.2
	Don Samuelson (R)	117,108	47.8
1974	Cecil D. Andrus (D)	184,142	70.9
	Jack M. Murphy (R)	68,731	26.5
1978	John V. Evans (D)	169,540	58.8
	Allan Larsen (R)	114,149	39.6
1982	John V. Evans (D)	165,365	50.6
	Philip Batt (R)	161,157	49.4

ILLINOIS

(Became a state Dec. 3, 1818)

	Candidates	Votes	%
1818	Shadrach Bond	3,427	
1822	Edward Coles	2,854	33.2
	Joseph B. Phillips	2,687	31.2
	Thomas C. Browne	2,443	28.4
	James B. Moore	622	7.2
1826	Ninian Edwards (NR)	6,280	49.4
	Thomas Sloo Jr. (JAC D)	5,833	45.9
1830	John Reynolds (NR)	12,837	59.0
	William Kinney (JAC D)	8,938	41.1
1834	Joseph Duncan (W)	17,340	52.9
	William Kinney (D)	10,224	31.2
	Robert H. McLaughlin	4,315	13.2
1838	Thomas Carlin (D)	30,668	50.8
	Cyrus Edwards (W)	29,722	49.2
1842	Thomas Ford (D)	46,502	53.8
	Joseph Duncan (W)	39,030	45.2
1846	Augustus C. French (D)	58,660	58.2
	Thomas M. Kilpatrick (W)	37,033	36.7
	Richard Eels (LIB)	5,154	5.1
1848	Augustus C. French (D)	67,828	86.8
	W. S. D. Morison	5,659	7.2
	Charles V. Dyer	4,692	6.0

	Candidates	Votes	%
1852	Joel A. Matteson (D)	80,789	*52.4*
	E. B. Webb (W)	64,408	*41.8*
	D. A. Knowlton (F SOIL)	9,024	*5.9*
1856	William H. Bissell (R)	111,466	*47.0*
	William A. Richardson (D)	106,769	*45.0*
	Buckner S. Morris (AM)	19,078	*8.0*
1860	Richard Yates (R)	172,218	*51.2*
	James C. Allen (D)	159,293	*47.3*
1864	Richard J. Oglesby (UN R)	190,376	*54.5*
	James C. Robinson (D)	158,711	*45.5*
1868	John M. Palmer (R)	250,467	*55.5*
	John R. Eden (D)	200,813	*44.5*
1872	Richard J. Oglesby (R)	237,777	*54.4*
	Gust Koener (LR)	197,083	*45.1*
1876	Shelby M. Cullom (R)	279,263	*50.6*
	Lewis Steward (D & G)	272,495	*49.4*
1880	Shelby M. Cullom (R)	314,565	*50.4*
	Lyman Trumbull (D)	277,562	*44.5*
1884	Richard J. Oglesby (R)	334,234	*49.6*
	Carter H. Harrison (D)	319,645	*47.5*
1888	Joseph W. Fifer (R)	367,856	*49.2*
	John M. Palmer (D)	355,313	*47.5*
1892	John P. Altgeld (D)	425,498	*48.7*
	Joseph W. Fifer (R)	402,666	*46.1*
1896	John R. Tanner (R)	587,637	*54.1*
	John P. Altgeld (R)	474,256	*43.7*
1900	Richard Yates (R)	580,200	*51.5*
	Samuel Alschuler (D)	518,966	*46.1*
1904	Charles S. Deneen (R)	634,029	*59.1*
	Lawrence B. Stringer (D)	334,880	*31.2*
	John Collins (SOC)	59,062	*5.5*
1908	Charles S. Deneen (R)	550,076	*47.6*
	Adlai E. Stevenson (D)	526,912	*45.6*
1912	Edward F. Dunne (D)	443,120	*38.1*
	Charles S. Deneen (R)	318,469	*27.4*
	Frank H. Funk (PROG)	303,401	*26.1*
	John C. Kennedy (SOC)	78,679	*6.8*
1916	Frank O. Lowden (R)	696,535	*52.7*
	Edward F. Dunne (D)	556,654	*42.1*
1920	Len Small (R)	1,243,148	*58.9*
	James Hamilton Lewis (D)	731,541	*34.6*
1924	Len Small (R)	1,366,436	*56.7*
	Norman L. Jones (D)	1,021,408	*42.4*
1928	Louis L. Emmerson (R)	1,709,818	*56.8*
	Floyd E. Thompson (D)	1,284,897	*42.7*
1932	Henry Horner (D)	1,930,330	*57.6*
	Len Small (R)	1,364,043	*40.7*
1936	Henry Horner (D)	2,067,861	*53.1*
	C. Wayland Brooks (R)	1,682,674	*43.2*
1940	Dwight H. Green (R)	2,197,778	*52.9*
	Harry B. Hershey (D)	1,940,833	*46.7*
1944	Dwight H. Green (R)	2,013,270	*50.8*
	Thomas J. Courtney (D)	1,940,999	*48.9*
1948	Adlai E. Stevenson (D)	2,250,074	*57.1*
	Dwight H. Green (R)	1,678,007	*42.6*
1952	William G. Stratton (R)	2,317,363	*52.5*
	Sherwood Dixon (D)	2,089,721	*47.3*
1956	William G. Stratton (R)	2,171,786	*50.3*
	Richard B. Austin (D)	2,134,909	*49.5*
1960	Otto Kerner (D)	2,594,731	*55.5*
	William G. Stratton (R)	2,070,479	*44.3*
1964	Otto Kerner (D)	2,418,394	*51.9*
	Charles H. Percy (R)	2,239,095	*48.1*
1968	Richard B. Ogilvie (R)	2,307,295	*51.2*
	Samuel H. Shapiro (D)	2,179,501	*48.4*
1972	Daniel Walker (D)	2,371,303	*50.7*
	Richard B. Ogilvie (R)	2,293,809	*49.0*
1976	James R. Thompson (R)	3,000,395	*64.7*
	Michael J. Howlett (D)	1,610,258	*34.7*
1978	James R. Thompson (R)	1,859,684	*59.0*
	Michael Bakalis (D)	1,263,134	*40.1*

	Candidates	Votes	%
1982	James R. Thompson (R)	1,816,101	*49.4*
	Adlai E. Stevenson III (D)	1,811,027	*49.3*

INDIANA

(Became a state Dec. 11, 1816)

	Candidates	Votes	%
1816	Jonathan Jennings	5,211	*57.0*
	Thomas Posey	3,934	*43.0*
1819	Jonathan Jennings	9,168	*81.4*
	Christopher Harrison	2,088	*18.6*
1822	William Hendricks		Unopposed
1825	James Brown Ray (CLAY R)	13,852	*53.2*
	Isaac Blackford (NR)	12,165	*46.8*
1828	James Brown Ray (CLAY R)	15,131	*39.5*
	Israel T. Canby (JAC D)	12,251	*32.0*
	Harbin H. Moore (NR)	10,898	*28.5*
1831	Noah Noble (NR)	23,518	*45.6*
	James G. Read (JAC D)	21,002	*40.7*
	Milton Stapp (I)	6,984	*13.5*
1834	Noah Noble (W)	36,797	*57.4*
	James G. Read (D)	27,276	*42.6*
1837	David Wallace (W)	46,067	*55.5*
	John Dumont (W)	36,915	*44.5*
1840	Samuel Bigger (W)	62,970	*53.7*
	Tilghman A. Howard (D)	54,297	*46.3*
1843	James Whitcomb (D)	60,930	*50.2*
	Samuel Bigger (W)	58,809	*48.4*
1846	James Whitcomb (D)	64,104	*50.7*
	Joseph G. Marshall (W)	60,138	*47.5*
1849	Joseph A. Wright (D)	76,996	*52.3*
	John A. Matson (W)	67,218	*45.6*
1852	Joseph A. Wright (D)	92,959	*54.7*
	Nicholas McCarty (W)	73,647	*43.3*
1856	Ashbel P. Willard (D)	117,981	*51.3*
	Oliver P. Morton (R)	112,039	*48.7*
1860	Henry S. Lane (R)	136,725	*51.9*
	Thomas Andrews Hendricks (D)	126,968	*48.2*
1864	Oliver P. Morton (R)	152,275	*53.7*
	Joseph E. McDonald (D)	131,200	*46.3*
1868	Conrad Baker (R)	171,523	*50.1*
	Thomas Andrews Hendricks (D)	170,602	*49.9*
1872	Thomas Andrews Hendricks (D)	189,424	*50.1*
	Thomas McClelland Browne (R)	188,276	*49.8*
1876	James Douglas Williams (D)	213,164	*49.1*
	Benjamin Harrison (R)	208,080	*47.9*
1880	Albert Gallatin Porter (R)	231,405	*49.2*
	Franklin Landers (D)	224,452	*47.7*
1884	Isaac P. Gray (D)	245,130	*49.5*
	William H. Calkins (R)	237,748	*48.0*
1888	Alvin P. Hovey (R)	263,194	*49.0*
	Courtland C. Matson (D)	260,994	*48.6*
1892	Claude Matthews (D)	260,601	*47.5*
	Ira J. Chase (R)	253,625	*46.2*
1896	James A. Mount (R)	320,936	*50.9*
	Benjamin F. Shively (D)	294,855	*46.8*
1900	Winfield T. Durbin (R)	331,531	*50.5*
	John W. Kern (D)	306,368	*46.7*
1904	J. Frank Hanly (R)	359,362	*53.5*
	John W. Kern (D)	274,998	*41.0*
1908	Thomas R. Marshall (D)	348,843	*49.0*
	James E. Watson (R)	334,040	*46.9*
1912	Samuel M. Ralston (D)	275,357	*43.0*
	Albert J. Beveridge (PROG)	166,654	*26.0*
	Winfield T. Durbin (R)	141,684	*22.1*
	Stephen N. Reynolds (SOC)	35,464	*5.5*

	Candidates	Votes	%
1916	James P. Goodrich (R)	337,831	47.8
	John A. M. Adair (D)	325,060	46.0
1920	Warren T. McCray (R)	683,253	54.6
	Carleton B. McCulloch (D)	515,253	41.2
1924	Ed Jackson (R)	654,184	52.9
	Carleton B. McCulloch (D)	572,303	46.3
1928	Harry G. Leslie (R)	728,203	51.3
	Frank C. Dailey (D)	683,545	48.1
1932	Paul V. McNutt (D)	862,127	55.0
	Raymond S. Springer (R)	669,797	42.8
1936	Maurice Clifford Townsend (D)	908,494	55.4
	Raymond S. Springer (R)	727,526	44.3
1940	Henry F. Schricker (D)	889,620	49.9
	Glenn R. Hillis (R)	885,657	49.7
1944	Ralph F. Gates (R)	849,346	51.0
	Samuel D. Jackson (D)	802,765	48.2
1948	Henry F. Schricker (D)	884,995	53.6
	Hobart Creighton (R)	745,892	45.1
1952	George N. Craig (R)	1,075,685	55.7
	John A. Watkins (D)	841,984	43.6
1956	Harold W. Handley (R)	1,086,868	55.6
	Ralph Tucker (D)	859,393	44.0
1960	Matthew E. Welsh (D)	1,072,717	50.4
	Crawford F. Parker (R)	1,049,540	49.3
1964	Roger D. Branigin (D)	1,164,763	56.2
	Richard O. Ristine (R)	901,342	43.5
1968	Edgar D. Whitcomb (R)	1,080,271	52.7
	Robert L. Rock (D)	965,816	47.1
1972	Otis R. Bowen (R)	1,203,903	56.8
	Matthew E. Welsh (D)	900,489	42.5
1976	Otis R. Bowen (R)	1,236,555	56.8
	Larry A. Conrad (D)	927,243	42.6
1980	Robert D. Orr (R)	1,257,383	57.7
	John A. Hillenbrand (D)	913,116	41.9
1984	Robert D. Orr (R)	1,146,497	52.2
	W. Wayne Townsend (D)	1,036,832	47.2

IOWA

(Became a state Dec. 28, 1846)

	Candidates	Votes	%
1846	Ansel Briggs (ER)	7,626	50.8
	Thomas McKnight (W)	7,379	49.2
1850	Stephen Hempstead (D)	13,486	52.9
	James L. Thompson (W)	11,403	44.8
1854	James W. Grimes (R)	23,325	52.4
	Curtis Bates (NEB)	21,202	47.6
1857	Ralph P. Lowe (R)	38,498	50.9
	Ben M. Samuels (D)	36,088	47.7
1859	Samuel J. Kirkwood (R)	56,502	51.4
	A. C. Dodge (D)	53,332	48.6
1861	Samuel J. Kirkwood (R)	60,303	55.5
	William H. Merritt (D)	43,245	39.8
1863	William M. Stone (UN)	86,118	60.5
	James M. Tuttle (D)	56,169	39.5
1865	William M. Stone (UN R)	70,461	56.4
	Thomas H. Benton (D)	54,090	43.3
1867	Samuel Merrill (R)	90,204	58.9
	Charles Mason (D)	62,966	41.1
1869	Samuel Merrill (R)	97,243	62.9
	George Gillaspie (D)	57,287	37.1
1871	Cyrus Clay Carpenter (R)	109,328	61.6
	J. C. Knapp (D)	68,199	38.4
1873	Cyrus Clay Carpenter (R)	105,132	56.0
	J. G. Vale (A-MONOP)	82,556	44.0
1875	Samuel Jordan Kirkwood (R)	124,855	57.0
	Shepherd Leffler (D)	93,270	42.6

	Candidates	Votes	%
1877	John Henry Gear (R)	121,316	49.4
	John P. Irish (D)	79,304	32.3
	Daniel P. Stubbs (G)	34,316	14.0
1879	John Henry Gear (R)	157,408	53.9
	Henry H. Trimble (D)	85,364	29.3
	Daniel Campbell (G)	45,674	15.7
1881	Buren R. Sherman (R)	133,328	56.7
	L. G. Kinne (D)	73,344	31.2
	D. M. Clark (G)	28,112	12.0
1883	Buren R. Sherman (R)	164,095	50.1
	L. G. Kinne (D)	140,012	42.8
	James B. Weaver (G)	23,089	7.1
1885	William Larrabee (R)	175,605	50.8
	Charles Whiting (D)	168,584	48.7
1887	William Larrabee (R)	169,596	50.1
	T. J. Anderson (D)	153,706	45.4
1889	Horace Boies (D)	180,106	49.9
	Joseph Hutchinson (R)	173,450	48.1
1891	Horace Boies (D)	207,594	49.4
	Herman C. Wheeler (R)	199,381	47.5
1893	Frank D. Jackson (R)	206,821	49.7
	Horace Boies (D)	174,656	42.0
	J. M. Joseph (PP)	23,980	5.8
1895	Francis M. Drake (R)	208,708	52.0
	W. I. Babb (D)	149,428	37.2
	S. B. Crane (PP)	32,189	8.0
1897	Leslie M. Shaw (R)	224,729	51.3
	Fred E. White (D)	194,853	44.5
1899	Leslie M. Shaw (R)	239,464	55.3
	Fred E. White (D)	183,301	42.3
1901	Albert B. Cummins (R)	226,902	58.1
	T. J. Phillips (D)	143,783	36.8
1903	Albert B. Cummins (R)	238,804	57.1
	J. B. Sullivan (D)	159,725	38.2
1906	Albert B. Cummins (R)	216,995	50.2
	Claude R. Porter (D)	196,123	45.4
1908	Beryl F. Carroll (R)	256,980	54.6
	Fred E. White (D)	196,929	41.8
1910	Beryl F. Carroll (R)	205,678	49.8
	Claude R. Porter (D)	187,353	45.4
1912	George W. Clarke (R)	184,150	39.9
	Edward G. Dunn (D)	182,449	39.6
	John L. Stevens (PROG)	71,879	15.6
1914	George W. Clarke (R)	207,881	49.3
	John T. Hamilton (D)	181,036	42.9
1916	William L. Harding (R)	313,586	61.0
	E. T. Meredith (D)	186,832	36.4
1918	William L. Harding (R)	192,662	50.6
	Claude R. Porter (D)	178,815	46.9
1920	Nathan E. Kendall (R)	513,118	58.7
	Clyde L. Herring (D)	338,108	38.7
1922	Nathan E. Kendall (R)	419,648	70.5
	J. R. Files (D)	175,252	29.5
1924	John Hammill (R)	604,624	72.7
	J. C. Murtagh (D)	226,850	27.3
1926	John Hammill (R)	377,330	71.3
	Alex R. Miller (D)	150,374	28.4
1928	John Hammill (R)	591,720	62.8
	L. W. Housel (D)	350,722	37.2
1930	Dan W. Turner (R)	364,036	65.7
	Fred P. Hageman (D)	186,039	33.6
1932	Clyde L. Herring (D)	508,573	52.8
	Dan W. Turner (R)	455,145	47.2
1934	Clyde L. Herring (D)	468,921	54.3
	Dan W. Turner (R)	394,634	45.7
1936	Nelson G. Kraschel (D)	524,178	48.7
	George Wilson (R)	521,747	48.4
1938	George Wilson (R)	447,061	52.7
	Nelson G. Kraschel (D)	387,779	45.7
1940	George Wilson (R)	620,480	52.7
	John Valentine (D)	553,941	47.1

	Candidates	Votes	%
1942	Bourke B. Hickenlooper (R)	438,547	62.8
	Nelson G. Kraschel (D)	258,310	37.0
1944	Robert D. Blue (R)	561,827	56.0
	R. F. Mitchell (D)	437,684	43.6
1946	Robert D. Blue (R)	362,592	57.4
	Frank Miles (D)	266,190	42.1
1948	William Beardsley (R)	553,900	55.7
	Carroll O. Switzer (D)	434,432	43.7
1950	William Beardsley (R)	506,642	59.1
	Lester S. Gillette (D)	347,176	40.5
1952	William Beardsley (R)	638,388	51.9
	Herschel C. Loveless (D)	587,671	47.8
1954	Leo A. Hoegh (R)	435,944	51.4
	Clyde E. Herring (D)	410,255	48.4
1956	Herschel C. Loveless (D)	616,852	51.2
	Leo A. Hoegh (R)	587,383	48.8
1958	Herschel C. Loveless (D)	465,024	54.1
	William G. Murray (R)	394,071	45.9
1960	Norman A. Erbe (R)	645,026	52.1
	E. J. McManus (D)	592,063	47.9
1962	Harold E. Hughes (D)	430,899	52.6
	Norman A. Erbe (R)	388,955	47.4
1964	Harold E. Hughes (D)	794,610	68.1
	Evan Hultman (R)	365,131	31.3
1966	Harold E. Hughes (D)	494,259	55.3
	William G. Murray (R)	394,518	44.2
1968	Robert D. Ray (R)	614,328	54.1
	Paul Franzenburg (D)	521,216	45.9
1970	Robert D. Ray (R)	403,394	51.0
	Robert D. Fulton (D)	368,911	46.6
1972	Robert D. Ray (R)	707,177	58.4
	Paul Franzenburg (D)	487,282	40.3
1974	Robert D. Ray (R)	534,518	58.1
	James F. Schaben (D)	377,553	41.0
1978	Robert D. Ray (R)	491,713	58.3
	Jerome D. Fitzgerald (D)	345,519	41.0
1982	Terry E. Branstad (R)	548,313	52.8
	Roxanne Conlin (D)	483,291	46.5

KANSAS

(Became a state Jan. 29, 1861)

	Candidates	Votes	%
1862	Thomas Carney (R)	9,990	64.7
	W. R. Wagstaff (UN R)	5,456	35.3
1864	Samuel J. Crawford (R)	12,711	60.7
	Solon O. Thacher (R-UNION)	8,244	39.3
1866	Samuel J. Crawford (R)	19,370	70.4
	J. L. McDowell (N UNION)	8,151	29.6
1868	James M. Harvey (R)	29,795	68.2
	George W. Glick (D)	13,881	31.8
1870	James M. Harvey (R)	40,667	66.4
	Isaac Sharp (D)	20,496	33.5
1872	Thomas A. Osborn (R)	66,715	65.8
	Thaddeus H. Walker (LR)	34,698	34.2
1874	Thomas A. Osborn (R)	48,794	56.4
	James C. Cusey (D)	35,301	40.8
1876	George T. Anthony (R)	69,176	56.8
	John Martin (D)	46,201	37.9
1878	John P. St. John (R)	74,020	53.5
	John R. Goodin (D)	37,208	26.9
	D. P. Mitchell (G)	27,057	19.6
1880	John P. St. John (R)	115,144	57.9
	Edmund G. Ross (D)	63,557	32.0
	H. P. Vrooman (G LAB)	19,481	9.8
1882	George W. Glick (D)	83,232	46.4

	Candidates	Votes	%
	John P. St. John (R)	75,158	41.9
	Charles Robinson (G LAB)	20,933	11.7
1884	John A. Martin (R)	146,777	55.3
	George W. Glick (D)	108,284	40.8
1886	John A. Martin (R)	149,715	54.7
	Thomas Moonlight (D)	115,667	42.3
1888	L. U. Humphrey (R)	180,841	54.7
	John Martin (D)	107,582	32.5
	P. P. Elder (UN LAB)	35,847	10.8
1890	L. U. Humphrey (R)	115,024	39.1
	J. F. Willits (ALNC D)	106,945	36.3
	Charles Robinson (D & RESUB)	71,357	24.2
1892	L. D. Lewelling (POP)	162,507	50.0
	Abram W. Smith (R)	158,075	48.7
1894	E. N. Morrill (R)	148,700	49.5
	L. D. Lewelling (D-PP)	118,329	39.4
	David Overmyer (STAL D)	27,709	9.2
1896	John W. Leedy (D-PP)	167,941	50.5
	E. N. Morrill (R)	160,507	48.3
1898	W. E. Stanley (R)	149,312	51.8
	John W. Leedy (D-PP)	134,158	46.6
1900	W. E. Stanley (R)	181,897	51.9
	John W. Breidenthal (D-PP)	164,793	47.0
1902	W. J. Bailey (R)	159,242	55.5
	W. H. Craddock (D)	117,148	40.8
1904	Edward W. Hoch (R)	186,731	57.9
	David M. Dale (D)	116,991	36.3
1906	Edward W. Hoch (R)	152,147	48.2
	William A. Harris (D)	150,024	47.6
1908	W. R. Stubbs (R)	196,692	52.5
	Jeremiah D. Botkin (D)	162,385	43.3
1910	W. R. Stubbs (R)	162,181	49.8
	George H. Hodges (D)	146,014	44.8
1912	George H. Hodges (D)	167,437	46.6
	Arthur Capper (R)	167,408	46.5
	George W. Kleihege (SOC)	24,767	6.9
1914	Arthur Capper (R)	209,543	39.7
	George H. Hodges (D)	161,696	30.6
	Henry J. Allen (PROG)	84,060	15.9
	J. B. Billard (I)	47,201	8.9
1916	Arthur Capper (R)	353,169	60.8
	W. C. Lansdon (D)	192,037	33.1
1918	Henry J. Allen (R)	287,957	66.4
	W. C. Lansdon (D)	133,054	30.7
1920	Henry J. Allen (R)	319,914	58.4
	Jonathan M. Davis (D)	214,940	39.3
1922	Jonathan M. Davis (D)	271,058	50.9
	W. Y. Morgan (R)	252,602	47.4
1924	Ben S. Paulen (R)	323,402	49.0
	Jonathan M. Davis (D)	182,861	27.7
	William Allen White (I)	149,811	22.7
1926	Ben S. Paulen (R)	321,540	63.3
	Jonathan M. Davis (D)	179,308	35.3
1928	Clyde M. Reed (R)	433,395	65.6
	Chauncey B. Little (D)	219,327	33.2
1930	Harry H. Woodring (D)	217,171	35.0
	Frank Haucke (R)	216,920	34.9
	John R. Brinkley (I)	183,278	29.5
1932	Alfred M. Landon (R)	278,581	34.8
	Harry H. Woodring (D)	272,944	34.1
	John R. Brinkley (I)	244,607	30.6
1934	Alfred M. Landon (R)	422,030	53.5
	Omar B. Ketchum (D)	359,877	45.6
1936	Walter A. Huxman (D)	433,319	51.1
	Will G. West (R)	411,446	48.5
1938	Payne Ratner (R)	393,989	52.1
	Walter A. Huxman (D)	341,271	45.1
1940	Payne Ratner (R)	425,928	49.6
	William H. Burke (D)	425,498	49.6
1942	Andrew F. Schoeppel (R)	287,895	56.7
	William H. Burke (D)	212,071	41.8

	Candidates	Votes	%
1944	Andrew F. Schoeppel (R)	463,110	*65.7*
	Robert S. Lemon (D)	231,410	*32.8*
1946	Frank Carlson (R)	309,064	*53.5*
	Harry H. Woodring (D)	254,283	*44.0*
1948	Frank Carlson (R)	433,396	*57.0*
	Randolph Carpenter (D)	307,485	*40.4*
1950	Edward F. Arn (R)	333,001	*53.8*
	Kenneth T. Anderson (D)	275,494	*44.5*
1952	Edward F. Arn (R)	491,338	*56.3*
	Charles Rooney (D)	363,482	*41.7*
1954	Fred Hall (R)	329,868	*53.0*
	George Docking (D)	286,218	*46.0*
1956	George Docking (D)	479,701	*55.5*
	Warren W. Shaw (R)	364,340	*42.1*
1958	George Docking (D)	415,506	*56.5*
	Clyde M. Reed (R)	313,036	*42.5*
1960	John Anderson Jr. (R)	511,534	*55.5*
	George Docking (D)	402,261	*43.6*
1962	John Anderson Jr. (R)	341,257	*53.4*
	Dale E. Saffels (D)	291,285	*45.6*
1964	William H. Avery (R)	432,667	*50.9*
	Harry G. Wiles (D)	400,264	*47.1*
1966	Robert Docking (D)	380,030	*54.8*
	William H. Avery (R)	304,325	*43.9*
1968	Robert Docking (D)	447,269	*51.9*
	Rick Harman (R)	410,673	*47.6*
1970	Robert Docking (D)	404,611	*54.3*
	Kent Frizzell (R)	333,227	*44.7*
1972	Robert Docking (D)	571,256	*62.0*
	Morris Kay (R)	341,440	*37.1*
1974	Robert F. Bennett (R)	387,792	*49.5*
	Vern Miller (D)	384,115	*49.0*
1978	John Carlin (D)	363,835	*49.4*
	Robert F. Bennett (R)	348,015	*47.3*
1982	John Carlin (D)	405,772	*53.2*
	Sam Hardage (R)	339,356	*44.5*

KENTUCKY

(Became a state June 1, 1792)

	Candidates	Votes	%
1800[1]	James Garrard	8,390	*39.4*
	Christopher Greenup	6,745	*31.7*
	Benjamin Logan	3,995	*18.8*
	Thomas Todd	2,166	*10.2*
1804	Christopher Greenup	25,917	
1808	Charles Scott	22,050	*61.3*
	John Allen	8,430	*23.4*
	Green Clay	5,516	*15.3*
1812	Isaac Shelby	30,362	*70.9*
	Gabriel Slaughter	12,464	*29.1*
1816	George Madison		Unopposed
1820	John Adair	20,493	*32.8*
	William Logan	19,947	*32.0*
	Joseph Desha	12,419	*19.9*
	Anthony Butler	9,567	*15.3*
1824	Joseph Desha	38,463	*59.5*
	Christopher Tompkins	22,300	*34.5*
	William Russell	3,899	*6.0*
1828	Thomas Metcalfe (NR)	38,940	*50.5*
	William T. Barry (D)	38,231	*49.5*
1832	John Breathitt (D)	40,780	*50.9*
	Buck (NR)	39,269	*49.1*
1836	James Clark (W)	38,591	*55.8*
	M. Flournoy (D)	30,576	*44.2*
1840	Robert P. Letcher (W)	54,892	*58.4*
	French (D)	39,160	*41.6*

	Candidates	Votes	%
1844	William Owsley (W)	59,792	*52.1*
	Butler (D)	55,089	*48.0*
1848	John J. Crittenden (W)	64,982	*53.4*
	Lazarus W. Powell (D)	56,675	*46.6*
1851	Lazarus W. Powell (D)	54,821	*48.8*
	Archibald Dixon (W)	54,023	*48.1*
1855	Charles S. Morehead (AM)	69,870	*51.6*
	Clark (D)	65,570	*48.4*
1859	Beriah Magoffin (D)	76,631	*53.2*
	Joshua F. Bell (OPP)	67,504	*46.8*
1863	Thomas E. Branlette (UN)	68,422	*79.6*
	Charles A. Wickliffe (D)	17,503	*20.4*
1867	John Larue Helm (D)	90,216	*65.7*
	Sidney M. Barnes (R)	33,939	*24.7*
	William B. Kinkead (C)	13,167	*9.6*

Special Election

1868	John W. Stevenson (D)	115,520	*81.3*
	R. Tarvin Baker (R)	26,610	*18.7*

1871	Preston H. Leslie (D)	126,445	*58.6*
	George M. Thomas (R)	89,298	*41.4*
1875	James B. McCreary (D)	126,976	*58.3*
	John M. Harlan (R)	90,795	*41.7*
1879	Luke P. Blackburn (D)	125,399	*55.4*
	Walter Evans (R)	81,881	*36.2*
	C. W. Cook (G)	18,954	*8.4*
1883	J. Procter Knott (D)	133,615	*60.0*
	Thomas Z. Morrow (R)	89,181	*40.0*
1887	Simon B. Buckner (D)	143,466	*50.7*
	William O. Bradley (R)	126,754	*44.8*
1891	John Young Brown (D)	144,168	*49.9*
	Andrew T. Wood (R)	116,087	*40.1*
	S. B. Erwin (POP)	25,631	*8.9*
1895	William O. Bradley (R)	172,436	*48.3*
	Hardin (D)	163,524	*45.8*
1899	William S. Taylor (R)	193,727‡	*48.1*
	William Goebel (D)	191,331	*47.5*

Special Election

1900	John C. W. Beckham (D)	233,197	*49.9*
	John W. Yerkes (R)	229,468	*49.1*

1903	John C. W. Beckham (D)	229,014	*52.1*
	Belknap (R)	202,862	*46.2*
1907	August E. Willson (R)	214,478	*51.2*
	Hager (D)	196,428	*46.9*
1911	James B. McCreary (D)	226,549	*53.7*
	E. C. Orear (R)	195,672	*46.3*
1915	Augustus Owsley Stanley (D)	219,991	*49.1*
	Edwin P. Morrow (R)	219,520	*49.0*
1919	Edwin P. Morrow (R)	254,472	*53.8*
	J. D. Black (D)	214,134	*45.3*
1923	William J. Fields (D)	356,045	*53.3*
	Charles I. Dawson (R)	306,277	*45.8*
1927	Flem D. Sampson (R)	399,698	*52.1*
	John C. W. Beckham (D)	367,576	*47.9*
1931	Ruby Lafoon (D)	438,513	*54.3*
	William B. Harrison (R)	366,982	*45.4*
1935	Albert B. "Happy" Chandler (D)	556,262	*54.5*
	King Swope (R)	461,104	*45.1*
1939	Keen Johnson (D)	460,834	*56.5*
	King Swope (R)	354,704	*43.5*
1943	Simeon S. Willis (R)	279,144	*50.5*
	J. Lyter Donaldson (D)	270,525	*48.9*
1947	Earle C. Clements (D)	387,795	*57.2*
	Eldon S. Dummit (R)	287,756	*42.5*
1951	Lawrence W. Wetherby (D)	346,345	*54.6*
	Eugene Siler (R)	288,014	*45.4*

	Candidates	Votes	%
1955	Albert B. "Happy" Chandler (D)	451,647	58.0
	Edwin R. Denney (R)	322,671	41.5
1959	Bert T. Combs (D)	516,549	60.6
	John M. Robsion (R)	336,456	39.4
1963	Edward T. Breathitt (D)	449,551	50.7
	Louie B. Nunn (R)	436,496	49.3
1967	Louie B. Nunn (R)	454,123	51.2
	Henry Ward (D)	425,674	48.0
1971	Wendell H. Ford (D)	470,720	50.6
	Tom Emberton (R)	412,653	44.3
1975	Julian Carroll (D)	470,159	62.8
	Robert E. Gable (R)	277,998	37.2
1979	J. Y. Brown Jr. (D)	558,088	59.4
	Louie B. Nunn (R)	381,278	40.6
1983	Martha Layne Collins (D)	561,674	54.6
	Jim Bunning (R)	454,650	44.2

1. Governors were chosen by a specially elected body of electors in 1792 and 1796.

LOUISIANA

(Became a state April 30, 1812)

	Candidates	Votes	%
1812[1]	W. C. C. Claiborne (AM FAC)[2]	2,757	71.2
	Jacques Villeré (CREOLE)	946	24.4
1816[1]	Jacques Villeré (CREOLE)	2,314	51.9
	Joshua Lewis (AM FAC)[2]	2,145	48.1
1820[1]	Thomas B. Robertson (AM FAC)[2]	1,903	40.1
	Pierre Derbigny (CREOLE)	1,187	25.0
	A. L. Duncan (AM FAC)[2]	1,031	21.7
	Jean Noel Destrehan (CREOLE)	627	13.2
1824[1]	Henry Johnson (AM FAC)[2]	2,649	44.9
	Jacques Villeré (CREOLE)	1,773	30.0
	Bernard Marigny (CREOLE)	1,484	25.1
1828[1]	Pierre Derbigny (NR)	3,253	44.2
	Thomas Butler (JAC D)	1,629	22.1
	Bernard Marigny (JAC D)	1,291	17.5
	Philemon Thomas (NR)	1,194	16.2
1831[1]	Andre B. Roman (NR)	3,630	43.6
	W. S. Hamilton (JAC D)	2,730	32.8
	Arnaud Beauvais (NR)	1,502	18.1
	David Randall (JAC D)	456	5.5
1834[1]	Edward D. White (W)	6,018	57.6
	Dawson (D)	4,438	42.4
1838[1]	Andre B. Roman (W)	7,588	52.8
	Prieur (D)	6,776	47.2
1842[1]	Alexander Mouton (D)	9,716	54.2
	Henry Johnson (W)	8,204	45.8
1846	Isaac Johnson (D)	13,353	53.2
	Debuys (W)	11,101	44.2
1849	Joseph Walker (D)	18,459	51.5
	Declouet (W)	17,407	48.5
1852	Paul O. Hebert (D)	17,529	53.0
	Louis Bordelon (W)	15,532	47.0
1855	Robert C. Wickliffe (D)	22,382	53.6
	Derbigny (AM)	19,417	46.5
1859	Thomas O. Moore (D)	25,434	62.0
	Wells (OPP)	15,587	38.0
1864	Henry W. Allen	7,497	87.5
	Stafford	807	9.4
1865	James Madison Wells (D)	22,532	78.2
	Henry W. Allen	6,297	21.8
1868	Henry C. Warmoth (R)	64,271	62.8
	James G. Taliaferro (D)	38,118	37.2
1872	William Pitt Kellogg (R)	72,890‡	57.4
	John McEnery (D)	54,079	42.6

	Candidates	Votes	%
1876	Francis T. Nicholls (D)	84,487‡	52.5
	Stephen B. Packard (R)	76,476	47.5
1879	Louis A. Wiltz (D)	73,623	64.6
	Taylor Beattie (R)	40,415	35.4
1884	Samuel D. McEnery (D)	88,780	67.1
	John A. Stevenson (R)	43,502	32.9
1888	Francis T. Nicholls (D)	136,747	72.5
	Henry C. Warmoth (R)	51,993	27.6
1892	Murphy J. Foster (A-LOT D)	79,407	44.5
	Samuel D. McEnery (D)	47,046	26.4
	A. H. Leonard (R)	29,648	16.6
	John E. Breaux (IR)	12,409	7.0
	R. H. Tannehill (POP)	9,792	5.5
1896	Murphy J. Foster (D)	116,116	56.9
	John N. Pharr (R POP FU)	87,698	43.0
1900	William Wright Heard (D)	60,206	78.3
	Don Caffery Jr. (R FUS, PP)	14,215	18.5
1904	Newton C. Blanchard (D)	47,745	89.0
	W. J. Behan (R)	5,877	11.0
1908	Jared Y. Sanders (D)	60,066	87.1
	Henry N. Pharr (R)	7,617	11.1
1912	Luther E. Hall (D)	50,581	89.5
	H. S. Suthon (R)	4,961	8.8
1916	Ruffin G. Pleasant (D)	80,807	62.5
	John M. Parker (PROG)	48,085	37.2
1920	John M. Parker (D)	53,792#	97.6
1924	Henry L. Fuqua (D)	66,203	97.9
1928	Huey P. Long (D)	92,941	96.1
1932	Oscar K. Allen (D)	110,193	100.0
1936	Richard W. Leche (D)	131,999	100.0
1940	Sam H. Jones (D)	225,841	99.4
1944	Jimmie H. Davis (D)	51,604	100.0
1948	Earl K. Long (D)	76,566	100.0
1952	Robert F. Kennon (D)	118,723	96.0
1956	Earl K. Long (D)	172,291	100.0
1960	Jimmie H. Davis (D)	407,907	80.5
	F. C. Grevemberg (R)	86,135	17.0
1964	John J. McKeithen (D)	469,589	60.7
	Charlton H. Lyons Sr. (R)	297,753	38.5
1968	John J. McKeithen (D)	372,762	100.0
1972	Edwin W. Edwards (D)	641,146	57.2
	David C. Treen (R)	480,424	42.8
1975	Edwin W. Edwards (D)	430,095	100.0
1979	David C. Treen (R)	690,691	50.3
	Louis Lambert (D)	681,134	49.7
1983	Edwin W. Edwards (D)	1,008,282	62.4
	David C. Treen (R)	586,643	36.3

1. Until 1845 the governor was elected by joint vote of the two houses of the Legislature, which could choose one of the two who received the most popular votes. In all nine elections under this system the candidate receiving a popular plurality was subsequently chosen by the Legislature. Thereafter elections were determined by a plurality of the popular vote.
2. Until 1828, contests were essentially between candidates supported by the "American" and "Creole" factions of the Jeffersonian Republican party.

MAINE

(Became a state March 15, 1820)

	Candidates	Votes	%
1820	William King (D-R)	21,083	95.3
1821	Albion K. Parris (D-R)	12,887	52.8
	Ezekiel Whitman (FED)	6,811	27.9
	Joshua Wingate Jr. (D-R)	3,879	15.9
1822	Albion K. Parris (D-R)	15,476	69.8
	Ezekiel Whitman (FED)	5,795	26.1
1823	Albion K. Parris (D-R)	18,550	95.6

	Candidates	Votes	%		Candidates	Votes	%
1824	Albion K. Parris (D-R)	19,759	96.8	1856	Hannibal Hamlin (R)	69,444	57.4
1825	Albion K. Parris (D-R)	14,206	93.1		Samuel Wells (D)	44,912	37.1
1826	Enoch Lincoln (D-R)	20,689	98.2		George F. Patten (W)	6,664	5.5
1827	Enoch Lincoln (D-R)	19,969	97.6	1857	Lot M. Morrill (R)	54,283	56.0
1828	Enoch Lincoln (D-R)	25,755	91.6		Manassah H. Smith (D)	42,647	44.0
1829	Jonathan G. Hunton (NR)	23,315	50.1	1858	Lot M. Morrill (R)	60,599	53.5
	Smith (JAC D)	22,991	49.4		Manassah H. Smith (D)	52,697	46.5
1830	Samuel E. Smith (JAC D)	30,215	51.1	1859	Lot M. Morrill (R)	57,215	55.8
	Jonathan G. Hunton (NR)	28,639	48.5		Manassah H. Smith (D)	45,407	44.3
1831	Samuel E. Smith (D)	28,292	56.3	1860	Israel Washburn Jr. (R)	70,014	56.5
	Daniel Goodenow (NR)	21,821	43.5		E. K. Smart (D)	52,167	42.1
1832	Samuel E. Smith (D)	31,987	52.8	1861	Israel Washburn Jr. (R)	57,475	58.7
	Daniel Goodenow (NR)	27,651	45.6		C. D. Jameson (D)	21,119	21.6
1833	Robert P. Dunlap (D)	25,731	52.1		John W. Dana (OPP D)	19,363	19.8
	Daniel Goodenow (W)	18,112	36.7	1862	Abner Coburn (R)	46,689	53.3
	Samuel E. Smith (DISS D)	3,024	6.1		Bion Bradbury (D)	33,645	38.4
1834	Robert P. Dunlap (D)	38,133	52.1		C. D. Jameson (D)	7,302	8.3
	Peleg Sprague (W)	33,912	46.3	1863	Samuel Cony (UN R)	67,916	57.4
1835	Robert P. Dunlap (D)	27,733	61.4		Bion Bradbury (D)	50,366	42.6
	William King (W)	16,860	37.3	1864	Samuel Cony (UN R)	65,583	58.6
1836	Robert P. Dunlap (D)	31,837	58.2		Joseph Howard (D)	46,403	41.4
	Edward Kent (W)	22,703	41.5	1865	Samuel Cony (UN R)	54,430	63.3
1837	Edward Kent (W)	34,358	50.1		Joseph Howard (D)	31,609	36.7
	Gorham Parks (D)	33,879	49.4	1866	Joshua L. Chamberlain (R)	69,626	62.4
1838	John Fairfield (D)	46,216	51.6		Eben F. Pillsbury (D)	41,939	37.6
	Edward Kent (W)	42,897	47.9	1867	Joshua L. Chamberlain (R)	57,713	55.6
1839	John Fairfield (D)	40,768	53.8		Eben F. Pillsbury (D)	45,990	44.3
	Edward Kent (W)	34,749	45.9	1868	Joshua L. Chamberlain (R)	75,523	57.3
1840	Edward Kent (W)	45,574†	50.0		Eben F. Pillsbury (D)	56,207	42.7
	John Fairfield (D)	45,507	49.9	1869	Joshua L. Chamberlain (R)	50,784	53.3
1841	John Fairfield (D)	47,354	55.0		Franklin Smith (D)	39,428	41.4
	Edward Kent (W)	36,780	42.7		N. G. Hichborn (TEMP)	5,028	5.3
1842	John Fairfield (D)	40,855	56.9	1870	Sidney Perham (R)	54,019	54.1
	Edward Robinson (W)	26,745	37.3		Charles W. Roberts (D)	45,732	45.8
	James Appleton	4,080	5.7	1871	Sidney Perham (R)	58,285	55.1
1843	Hugh J. Anderson (D)	27,631	55.4		Charles P. Kimball (D)	47,538	44.9
	Edward Robinson (W)	17,244	34.6	1872	Sidney Perham (R)	71,883	56.5
	James Appleton (LIB & SC)	4,962	10.0		Charles P. Kimball (D)	55,343	43.5
1844	Hugh J. Anderson (D)	40,540	51.1	1873	Nelson Dingley Jr. (R)	45,239	55.9
	Edward Robinson (W)	33,342	42.0		Joseph Titcomb (D)	32,924	40.7
	James Appleton (LIB & SC)	5,527	7.0	1874	Nelson Dingley Jr. (R)	50,865	53.4
1845	Hugh J. Anderson (D)	31,353	50.7		Joseph Titcomb (D)	41,898	44.0
	Freeman H. Morse (W)	24,880	40.2	1875	Selden Connor (R)	57,782	51.7
1846	John W. Dana (D)	33,805†	46.9		Charles W. Roberts (D)	53,837	48.2
	David Bronson (W)	28,986	40.2	1876	Selden Connor (R)	75,867	55.5
	Samuel Fessenden (LIB & SC)	9,343	13.0		John C. Talbot (D)	60,423	44.2
1847	John W. Dana (D)	33,461	51.3	1877	Selden Connor (R)	53,584	52.5
	David Bronson (W)	24,304	37.2		Joseph H. Williams (D)	42,311	41.5
	Samuel Fessenden (LIB & SC)	7,517	11.5		Henry C. Munson (G)	5,291	5.2
1848	John W. Dana (D)	37,310†	47.0	1878	Selden Connor (R)	56,559	44.8
	Elijah L. Hamlin (W)	30,026	37.9		Joseph L. Smith (G)	41,371	32.8
	Samuel Fessenden (F SOIL)	11,978	15.1		Alonzo Garcelon (D)	28,218†	22.4
1849	John Hubbard (D)	37,534	50.9	1879	Daniel F. Davis (R)	68,527†	49.5
	Elijah L. Hamlin (W)	28,260	38.3		Joseph L. Smith (NG)	47,987	34.7
	George F. Talbot (FS & SC)	8,025	10.9		Alonzo Garcelon (D)	21,525	15.6
1850	John Hubbard (D)	41,220	51.0	1880	Harris M. Plaisted (D & G)	73,713	49.9
	William G. Crosby (W)	32,308	40.0		Daniel F. Davis (R)	73,544	49.8
	George F. Talbot (F SOIL)	7,271	9.0	1882	Frederick Robie (R)	72,481	52.4
1852	John Hubbard (D)	41,616†	44.3		Harris M. Plaisted (FUS)	63,921	46.2
	William G. Crosby (W)	29,129	31.0	1884	Frederick Robie (R)	78,699	55.4
	Anson G. Chandler (A-MAINE)	21,589	23.0		John B. Redman (D)	58,983	41.5
1853	Albert Pillsbury (D)	36,127	43.3	1886	Joseph R. Bodwell (R)	68,850	53.7
	William G. Crosby (W)	27,259†	32.7		Clark S. Edwards (D)	55,289	43.1
	Anson P. Morrill (WILDCAT)	11,012	13.2	1888	Edwin C. Burleigh (R)	79,401	54.6
	Ezekiel Holmes (FS & SC)	9,039	10.8		William L. Putnam (D)	61,348	42.2
1854	Anson P. Morrill (R)	44,817†	49.5	1890	Edwin C. Burleigh (R)	64,264	56.4
	Albion K. Parris (D)	28,285	31.2		William P. Thompson (D)	45,370	39.8
	Isaac Reed (W)	14,014	15.5	1892	Henry B. Cleaves (R)	67,900	52.1
1855	Anson P. Morrill (R)	51,488	46.6		Charles F. Johnson (D)	55,392	42.5
	Samuel Wells (D)	48,367†	43.8	1894	Henry B. Cleaves (R)	69,322	64.3
	Isaac Reed (W)	10,645	9.6		Charles F. Johnson (D)	30,405	28.2

	Candidates	Votes	%
1896	Llewellyn Powers (R)	82,596	66.9
	M. P. Frank (D)	34,350	27.8
1898	Llewellyn Powers (R)	53,900	62.9
	Samuel L. Lord (D)	28,485	33.2
1900	John F. Hill (R)	73,470	62.3
	Samuel L. Lord (D)	40,086	34.0
1902	John F. Hill (R)	65,354	59.5
	Samuel W. Gould (D)	38,107	34.7
1904	William T. Cobb (R)	76,962	58.5
	C. W. Davis (D)	50,146	38.1
1906	William T. Cobb (R)	69,427	52.0
	C. W. Davis (D)	61,363	46.0
1908	Bert M. Fernald (R)	73,537	51.6
	Obadiah Gardner (D)	66,282	46.5
1910	Frederick W. Plaisted (D)	73,304	52.0
	Bert M. Fernald (R)	64,644	45.9
1912	William T. Haines (R)	70,931	50.0
	Frederick W. Plaisted (D)	67,702	47.7
1914	Oakley C. Curtis (D)	62,076	43.8
	William T. Haines (R)	58,887	41.6
	H. P. Gardner (PROG)	18,226	12.9
1916	Carl E. Milliken (R)	81,760	54.0
	Oakley C. Curtis (D)	67,930	44.9
1918	Carl E. Milliken (R)	63,607	52.3
	Bertrand G. McIntire (D)	58,062	47.7
1920	Frederick H. Parkhurst (R)	135,393	65.9
	Bertrand G. McIntire (D)	70,047	34.1
1922	Percival P. Baxter (R)	103,713	58.0
	William R. Pattangall (D)	75,226	42.0
1924	Ralph O. Brewster (R)	145,281	57.2
	William R. Pattangall (D)	108,626	42.8
1926	Ralph O. Brewster (R)	100,776	55.5
	Ernest L. McLean (D)	80,748	44.5
1928	William Tudor Gardiner (R)	148,053	69.3
	Edward C. Moran Jr. (D)	65,572	30.7
1930	William Tudor Gardiner (R)	82,310	55.1
	Edward C. Moran Jr. (D)	67,172	44.9
1932	Louis J. Brann (D)	121,158	50.3
	Burleigh Martin (R)	118,800	49.3
1934	Louis J. Brann (D)	156,917	54.0
	Alfred K. Ames (R)	133,414	45.9
1936	Lewis O. Barrows (R)	173,716	56.0
	F. Harold Dubord (D)	130,466	42.1
1938	Lewis O. Barrows (R)	157,206	52.9
	Louis J. Brann (D)	139,745	47.0
1940	Sumner Sewall (R)	162,719	63.8
	Fulton J. Redman (D)	92,053	36.1
1942	Sumner Sewall (R)	118,047	66.8
	George W. Lane Jr. (D)	58,558	33.2
1944	Horace A. Hildreth (R)	131,849	70.3
	Paul J. Jullien (D)	55,781	29.7
1946	Horace A. Hildreth (R)	110,327	61.3
	F. Davis Clark (D)	69,624	38.7
1948	Frederick G. Payne (R)	145,956	65.6
	Louis B. Lausier (D)	76,544	34.4
1950	Frederick G. Payne (R)	145,823	60.5
	Earle S. Grant (D)	94,304	39.1
1952	Burton M. Cross (R)	128,532	52.1
	James C. Oliver (D)	82,538	33.4
	Neil Bishop (IR)	35,732	14.5
1954	Edmund S. Muskie (D)	135,673	54.5
	Burton M. Cross (R)	113,298	45.5
1956	Edmund S. Muskie (D)	180,254	59.2
	W. A. Trafton Jr. (R)	124,395	40.8
1958	Clinton A. Clauson (D)	145,673	52.0
	Horace A. Hildreth (R)	134,572	48.0

Special Election

1960	John H. Reed (R)	219,768	52.7
	Frank M. Coffin (D)	197,447	47.3

	Candidates	Votes	%
1962	John H. Reed (R)	146,604	50.1
	Maynard C. Dolloff (D)	146,121	49.9
1966	Kenneth M. Curtis (D)	172,036	53.1
	John H. Reed (R)	151,802	46.9
1970	Kenneth M. Curtis (D)	163,138	50.1
	James S. Erwin (R)	162,248	49.9
1974	James B. Longley (I)	142,464	39.1
	George J. Mitchell (D)	132,219	36.3
	James S. Erwin (R)	84,176	23.1
1978	Joseph E. Brennan (D)	176,493	47.7
	Linwood E. Palmer (R)	126,862	34.3
	Herman C. Frankland (I)	65,889	17.8
1982	Joseph E. Brennan (D)	281,066	61.1
	Charles R. Cragin (R)	172,949	37.6

MARYLAND

(Ratified the Constitution April 28, 1788)

	Candidates	Votes	%
1838[1]	William Grayson (D)	27,722	50.3
	John L. Steele (W)	27,409	49.7
1841	Francis Thomas (D)	28,959	50.6
	Johnson (W)	28,320	49.4
1844	Thomas G. Pratt (W)	35,040	50.4
	Carroll (D)	34,495	49.6
1847	Philip Francis Thomas (D)	34,368	50.5
	Goldsborough (W)	33,730	49.5
1850	Enoch L. Lowe (D)	36,340	51.0
	Clark (W)	34,858	49.0
1853	Thomas Watkins Ligon (D)	39,087	52.8
	Richard J. Bowie (W)	34,939	47.2
1857	Thomas Holliday Hicks (AM)	47,141	54.9
	John C. Groome (D)	38,681	45.1
1861	Augustus W. Bradford (UN R)	57,498	68.8
	Howard (PEACE D)	26,086	31.2
1864	Thomas Swann (UN R)	40,579	55.9
	E. F. Chambers (D)	32,068	44.1
1867	Oden Bowie (D)	63,694	74.3
	Hugh L. Bond (R)	22,050	25.7
1871	William P. Whyte (D)	73,959	55.7
	Jacob Tome (R)	58,824	44.3
1875	John Lee Carroll (D)	85,447	54.1
	Harris (R)	72,544	45.9
1879	William T. Hamilton (D)	90,731	56.9
	Garey (R)	68,619	43.1
1883	Robert M. McLane (D)	92,694	53.5
	Holton (R)	80,712	46.6
1887	Elihu E. Jackson (D)	99,038	52.1
	Brooks (R)	86,622	45.6
1891	Frank Brown (D)	108,539	56.5
	Vannort (R)	78,388	40.8
1895	Lloyd Lowndes (R)	124,936	52.0
	John E. Hurst (D)	106,169	44.2
1899	John Walter Smith (D)	128,409	51.1
	Lloyd Lowndes (R)	116,286	46.3
1903	Edwin Warfield (D)	108,548	52.0
	S. A. Williams (R)	95,923	46.0
1907	Austin L. Crothers (D)	102,051	50.7
	Gaither (R)	94,302	46.8
1911	Phillips Lee Goldsborough (R)	106,392	49.3
	Arthur Pue Gorman (D)	103,395	47.9
1915	Emerson C. Harrington (D)	119,317	49.6
	Ovington E. Weller (R)	116,136	48.2
1919	Albert C. Ritchie (D)	112,240	49.1
	Harry W. Nice (R)	112,075	49.0
1923	Albert C. Ritchie (D)	177,871	56.0
	Alexander Armstrong (R)	137,471	43.3

	Candidates	Votes	%
1926	Albert C. Ritchie (D)	207,435	57.9
	Addison E. Mullikin (R)	148,145	41.4
1930	Albert C. Ritchie (D)	283,639	56.0
	William F. Broening (R)	216,864	42.8
1934	Harry W. Nice (R)	253,813	49.5
	Albert C. Ritchie (D)	247,664	48.3
1938	Herbert R. O'Conor (D)	308,372	54.6
	Harry W. Nice (R)	242,095	42.9
1942	Herbert R. O'Conor (D)	198,486	52.6
	Theodore R. McKeldin (R)	179,206	47.5
1946	William Preston Lane Jr. (D)	268,084	54.7
	Theodore R. McKeldin (R)	221,752	45.3
1950	Theodore R. McKeldin (R)	369,807	57.3
	William Preston Lane Jr. (D)	275,824	42.7
1954	Theodore R. McKeldin (R)	381,451	54.5
	Harry Clifton Byrd (D)	319,033	45.5
1958	J. Millard Tawes (D)	485,061	63.6
	James Patrick Devereux (R)	278,173	36.5
1962	J. Millard Tawes (D)	428,071	55.6
	Frank Small Jr. (R)	341,271	44.4
1966	Spiro T. Agnew (R)	455,318	49.5
	George P. Mahoney (D)	373,543	40.6
	Hyman A. Pressman (I)	90,899	9.9
1970	Marvin Mandel (D)	639,579	65.7
	C. Stanley Blair (R)	314,336	32.3
1974	Marvin Mandel (D)	602,648	63.5
	Louise Gore (R)	346,449	36.5
1978	Harry Hughes (D)	718,328	71.0
	J. Glenn Beall Jr. (R)	293,635	29.0
1982	Harry Hughes (D)	705,910	62.0
	Robert A. Pascal (R)	432,826	38.0

1. Before 1838 governor chosen by General Assembly.

MASSACHUSETTS

(Ratified the Constitution Feb. 6, 1788)

	Candidates	Votes	%
1788	John Hancock	17,841	80.5
1789	John Hancock	17,264	80.7
1790	John Hancock	14,283	86.5
1791	John Hancock	15,996	93.9
1792	John Hancock	14,628	86.6
1793	John Hancock	16,428	89.9
1794	Samuel Adams	14,425	61.5
1795	Samuel Adams	15,976	90.2
1796[1]	Samuel Adams	15,195	57.4
	Increase Sumner (FED)	11,298	42.6
1797[1]	Increase Sumner (FED)	14,540	56.7
	James Sullivan (D-R)	11,118	43.3
1798[1]	Increase Sumner (FED)	18,245	75.2
	James Sullivan (D-R)	6,014	24.8
1799	Increase Sumner (FED)	24,073	72.9
1800	Caleb Strong (FED)	19,630	50.3
	Elbridge Gerry (D-R)	17,019	43.6
1801	Caleb Strong (FED)	25,452	55.3
	Elbridge Gerry (D-R)	20,184	43.9
1802	Caleb Strong (FED)	29,983	60.5
	Elbridge Gerry (D-R)	19,443	43.9
1803	Caleb Strong (FED)	29,199	67.3
	Elbridge Gerry (D-R)	13,910	32.3
1804	Caleb Strong (FED)	30,011	55.1
	James Sullivan (D-R)	23,996	44.0
1805	Caleb Strong (FED)	35,204	51.0
	James Sullivan (D-R)	33,518	48.6
1806	Caleb Strong (FED)	37,740	50.2
	James Sullivan (D-R)	37,109	49.4

	Candidates	Votes	%
1807	James Sullivan (D-R)	41,954	51.5
	Caleb Strong (FED)	39,224	48.1
1808	James Sullivan (D-R)	41,193	50.8
	Christopher Gore (FED)	39,643	48.9
1809	Christopher Gore (FED)	47,916	51.3
	Levi Lincoln I (D-R)	45,118	48.3
1810	Elbridge Gerry (D-R)	46,541	51.2
	Christopher Gore (FED)	44,079	48.5
1811	Elbridge Gerry (D-R)	43,328	51.6
	Christopher Gore (FED)	40,142	47.8
1812	Caleb Strong (FED)	52,696	50.6
	Elbridge Gerry (D-R)	51,326	49.3
1813	Caleb Strong (FED)	56,754	56.6
	Joseph B. Varnum (D-R)	42,789	42.7
1814	Caleb Strong (FED)	56,374	55.0
	Lemuel Dexter (D-R)	45,953	44.8
1815	Caleb Strong (FED)	50,921	53.6
	Lemuel Dexter (D-R)	43,938	46.2
1816	John Brooks (FED)	49,527	51.1
	Lemuel Dexter (D-R)	47,321	48.8
1817	John Brooks (FED)	46,160	54.6
	Henry Dearborn (D-R)	38,129	45.1
1818	John Brooks (FED)	39,538	55.7
	Benjamin W. Crowninshield (D-R)	30,041	42.4
1819	John Brooks (FED)	42,875	53.7
	Benjamin W. Crowninshield (D-R)	35,277	44.2
1820	John Brooks (FED)	31,072	58.3
	William Eustis (D-R)	21,927	41.1
1821	John Brooks (FED)	28,608	58.3
	William Eustis (D-R)	20,268	41.3
1822	John Brooks (FED)	28,487	57.1
	William Eustis (D-R)	21,177	42.5
1823	William Eustis (D-R)	34,402	52.7
	Harrison G. Otis (FED)	30,171	46.2
1824	William Eustis (D-R)	38,650	52.9
	Samuel Lathrop (FED)	34,210	46.8
1825	Levi Lincoln (R-FF)	35,221	94.1
1826	Levi Lincoln (AR)	27,884	68.0
	Samuel Hubbard (FED)	9,044	22.1
	James Lloyd (FED)	2,212	5.4
1827	Levi Lincoln (AR)	29,029	74.2
	William C. Jarvis (FB R)	7,130	18.2
1828	Levi Lincoln (AR)	27,981	81.5
	Marcus Morton (JAC R)	4,423	12.9
1829	Levi Lincoln (NR)	25,217	71.6
	Marcus Morton (JAC R)	6,864	19.5
1830	Levi Lincoln (NR)	30,908	65.5
	Marcus Morton (JAC R)	14,440	30.6
1831	Levi Lincoln (NR)	31,875	65.2
	Marcus Morton (JAC R)	12,694	26.0
1831	Levi Lincoln (NR)	28,804	53.9
	Samuel Lathrop (A-MAS)	13,357	25.0
	Marcus Morton (D)	10,975	20.6
1832	Levi Lincoln (NR)	33,946	52.9
	Marcus Morton (D)	15,197	23.7
	Samuel Lathrop (A-MAS)	14,755	23.0
1833	John Davis (NR)	25,149†	40.3
	John Quincy Adams (A-MAS)	18,274	29.3
	Marcus Morton (D)	15,493	24.8
	Samuel L. Allen (WM)	3,459	5.5
1834	John Davis (W)	43,757	58.1
	Marcus Morton (D)	18,683	24.8
	John Bailey (A-MAS)	10,160	13.5
1835	Edward Everett (W)	37,555	57.9
	Marcus Morton (D)	25,227	38.9
1836	Edward Everett (W)	42,160	53.8
	Marcus Morton (D)	35,992	45.9
1837	Edward Everett (W)	50,565	60.3
	Marcus Morton (D)	32,987	39.4
1838	Edward Everett (W)	51,642	55.0
	Marcus Morton (D)	41,795	44.5

	Candidates	Votes	%		Candidates	Votes	%
1839	Marcus Morton (D)	51,034	50.0	1864	John A. Andrew (UN)	125,281	71.8
	Edward Everett (W)	50,725	49.7		Henry W. Paine (D)	49,190	28.2
1840	John Davis (W)	70,884	55.7	1865	Alexander H. Bullock (UN)	69,912	76.6
	Marcus Morton (D)	55,169	43.3		Darius N. Couch (D)	21,245	23.3
1841	John Davis (W)	55,974	50.4	1866	Alexander H. Bullock (R)	91,980	77.5
	Marcus Morton (D)	51,367	46.3		Theodore H. Sweetser (D)	26,671	22.5
1842	Marcus Morton (D)	56,491†	47.9	1867	Alexander H. Bullock (R)	98,306	58.3
	John Davis (W)	54,939	46.6		John Quincy Adams (D)	70,360	41.7
	Samuel E. Sewall (LIB)	6,382	5.4	1868	William Claflin (R)	132,121	67.6
1843	George N. Briggs (W)	57,899†	47.7		John Quincy Adams (D)	63,266	32.4
	Marcus Morton (D)	54,242	44.7	1869	William Claflin (R)	74,106	53.5
	Samuel E. Sewall (LIB)	8,903	7.3		John Quincy Adams (D)	50,735	36.6
1844	George N. Briggs (W)	69,570	51.8		Edwin M. Chamberlain (LAB REF)	13,567	9.8
	George Bancroft (D)	54,714	40.8	1870	William Claflin (R)	79,549	53.0
	Samuel E. Sewall (LIB)	9,734	7.3		John Quincy Adams (D)	48,680	32.3
1845	George N. Briggs (W)	51,638†	48.8		Wendell Phillips (LAB REF & P)	21,946	14.6
	Isaac Davis (D)	37,427	35.3	1871	William B. Washburn (R)	75,129	54.9
	Samuel E. Sewall (LIB)	8,316	7.9		John Quincy Adams (D)	47,725	34.9
	Henry Shaw (AM R)	8,089	7.6		Edwin M. Chamberlain (LAB REF)	6,848	5.0
1846	George N. Briggs (W)	54,813	53.8	1872	William B. Washburn (R)	133,900	69.1
	Isaac Davis (D)	33,199	32.6		Francis W. Bird (LR)	59,626	30.8
	Samuel E. Sewall (LIB)	9,997	9.8	1873	William B. Washburn (R)	72,183	54.6
1847	George N. Briggs (W)	53,742	51.0		William Gaston (D)	59,360	44.9
	Caleb Cushing (D)	39,398	37.4	1874	William Gaston (D)	96,376	51.8
	Samuel E. Sewall (LIB)	9,157	8.7		Thomas Talbot (R)	89,344	48.0
1848	George N. Briggs (W)	61,640†	49.7	1875	Alexander H. Rice (R)	83,639	48.3
	Stephen C. Phillips (F SOIL)	36,011	29.0		William Gaston (D)	78,333	45.2
	Caleb Cushing (D)	25,323	20.4		John I. Baker (TEMP)	9,124	5.3
1849	George N. Briggs (W)	54,009†	49.3	1876	Alexander H. Rice (R)	137,665	53.6
	George S. Boutwell (D)	30,040	27.4		Charles Francis Adams (D)	106,850	41.6
	Stephen C. Phillips (F SOIL)	25,247	23.1	1877	Alexander H. Rice (R)	91,255	49.5
1850	George N. Briggs (W)	56,778	46.8		William Gaston (D)	73,185	39.7
	George S. Boutwell (D)	36,023†	29.7		Robert C. Pitman (P)	16,354	8.9
	Stephen C. Phillips (F SOIL)	27,636	22.8	1878	Thomas Talbot (R)	134,725	52.6
1851	Robert C. Winthrop (W)	64,279	46.9		Benjamin F. Butler (BUT D & R)	109,435	42.7
	George S. Boutwell (D)	43,889†	32.0	1879	John D. Long (R)	122,751	50.4
	John G. Palfrey (F SOIL)	28,560	20.9		Benjamin F. Butler (BUT D & R)	109,149	44.8
1852	John H. Clifford (W)	62,233†	45.0	1880	John D. Long (R)	164,926	58.4
	Henry W. Bishop (D)	38,763	28.0		Charles P. Thompson (D)	111,410	39.5
	Horace Mann (F SOIL)	36,740	26.5	1881	John D. Long (R)	96,609	61.2
1853	Emory Washburn (W)	59,224†	45.9		Charles P. Thompson (D)	54,586	34.6
	Henry W. Bishop (D)	35,086	27.2	1882	Benjamin F. Butler (D-NG LAB)	133,946	52.3
	Henry Wilson (F SOIL)	29,020	22.5		Robert R. Bishop (R)	119,997	46.8
1854	Henry J. Gardner (AM)	81,503	62.6	1883	George D. Robinson (R)	160,092	51.3
	Emory Washburn (W)	27,279	20.9		Benjamin F. Butler (D & G)	150,228	48.1
	Henry W. Bishop (D)	13,742	10.6	1884	George D. Robinson (R)	159,345	52.4
1855	Henry J. Gardner (AM)	51,497	37.7		William C. Endicott (D)	111,829	36.8
	Julius Rockwell (R)	36,715	26.9		Matthew J. McCafferty (G)	24,363	8.0
	Erasmus D. Beach (D)	34,728	25.5	1885	George D. Robinson (R)	112,243	53.5
	Samuel H. Walley (W)	13,296	9.7		Frederick O. Prince (D)	90,346	43.1
1856	Henry J. Gardner (FREM AM)	92,467	58.9	1886	Oliver Ames (R)	122,346	50.2
	Erasmus D. Beach (D)	40,077	25.5		John F. Andrew (D)	112,883	46.3
	George W. Gordon (FILL AM)	10,385	6.6	1887	Oliver Ames (R)	136,000	51.1
1857	Nathaniel P. Banks (R)	60,797	46.6		Henry B. Lovering (D)	118,394	44.5
	Henry J. Gardner (AM)	37,596	28.8	1888	Oliver Ames (R)	180,849	52.7
	Erasmus D. Beach (D)	31,760	24.3		William E. Russell (D)	152,780	44.5
1858	Nathaniel P. Banks (R)	68,700	57.6	1889	John Q. A. Brackett (R)	127,357	48.4
	Erasmus D. Beach (D)	38,298	32.1		William E. Russell (D)	120,582	45.8
	Amos A. Lawrence (AM)	12,084	10.1		John Blackmer (P)	15,108	5.7
1859	Nathaniel P. Banks (R)	58,780	54.0	1890	William E. Russell (D)	140,507	49.2
	Benjamin F. Butler (D)	35,334	32.5		John Q. A. Brackett (R)	131,454	46.0
	George N. Briggs (AM)	14,365	13.2	1891	William E. Russell (D)	157,982	49.1
1860	John A. Andrew (R)	104,527	61.6		Charles H. Allen (R)	151,515	47.1
	Erasmus D. Beach (D)	35,191	20.8	1892	William E. Russell (D)	186,377	49.0
	Amos A. Lawrence (CST U)	23,816	14.0		William H. Haile (R)	183,843	48.4
1861	John A. Andrew (R)	65,261	67.1	1893	Frederic T. Greenhalge (R)	192,613	52.8
	Isaac Davis (D)	31,266	32.1		John E. Russell (D)	156,916	43.0
1862	John A. Andrew (R)	79,835	59.5	1894	Frederic T. Greenhalge (R)	189,307	56.5
	Charles Devens Jr. (PP)	54,167	40.4		John E. Russell (D)	123,930	37.0
1863	John A. Andrew (UN R)	70,483	70.7	1895	Frederic T. Greenhalge (R)	186,280	56.8
	Henry W. Paine (D)	29,207	29.3		George Fred Williams (D)	121,599	37.1

	Candidates	Votes	%
1896	Roger Wolcott (R)	258,204	67.1
	George Fred Williams (D, BRYAN D)	103,662	27.0
1897	Roger Wolcott (R)	165,095	61.2
	George Fred Williams (D)	79,552	29.5
	William Everett (DN)	13,879	5.1
1898	Roger Wolcott (R)	191,146	60.2
	Alexander B. Bruce (D)	107,960	34.0
1899	Winthrop Murray Crane (R)	168,902	56.5
	Robert Treat Paine (D)	103,802	34.7
1900	Winthrop Murray Crane (R)	228,054	59.1
	Robert Treat Paine (D)	130,078	33.7
1901	Winthrop Murray Crane (R)	185,809	57.3
	Josiah Quincy (D)	114,362	35.2
1902	John L. Bates (R)	196,276	49.2
	William A. Gaston (D)	159,156	39.9
	John C. Chase (SOC)	33,629	8.4
1903	John L. Bates (R)	199,684	50.4
	William A. Gaston (D)	163,700	41.3
	John C. Chase (SOC)	25,251	6.4
1904	William L. Douglas (D)	234,670	52.1
	John L. Bates (R)	198,681	44.1
1905	Curtis Guild Jr. (R)	197,469	50.5
	Charles W. Bartlett (D)	174,911	44.7
1906	Curtis Guild Jr. (R)	222,528	52.0
	John B. Moran (D, I LEAGUE)	192,295	44.9
1907	Curtis Guild Jr. (R)	188,068	50.3
	Henry M. Whitney (D, D CIT)	84,379	22.6
	Thomas L. Hisgen (I LEAGUE)	75,499	20.2
1908	Eben S. Draper (R)	228,318	51.6
	James H. Vahey (D)	168,162	38.0
	William N. Osgood (I LEAGUE)	23,101	5.2
1909	Eben S. Draper (R)	190,186	48.6
	James H. Vahey (D)	182,252	46.6
1910	Eugene N. Foss (D, D & PROG)	229,352	52.0
	Eben S. Draper (R)	194,173	44.1
1911	Eugene N. Foss (D, D & PROG)	214,897	48.8
	Louis A. Frothingham (R)	206,795	47.0
1912	Eugene N. Foss (D)	193,184	40.6
	Joseph Walker (R)	143,597	30.2
	Charles S. Bird (PROG)	122,602	25.8
1913	David I. Walsh (D)	183,267	39.8
	Charles S. Bird (PROG)	127,755	27.7
	Augustus P. Gardner (R)	116,705	25.3
1914	David I. Walsh (D)	210,442	45.9
	Samuel W. McCall (R)	198,627	43.4
	Joseph Walker (PROG)	32,145	7.0
1915	Samuel W. McCall (R)	235,863	47.0
	David I. Walsh (D)	229,550	45.7
1916	Samuel W. McCall (R)	276,123	52.5
	Frederick W. Mansfield (D)	229,883	43.7
1917	Samuel W. McCall (R)	226,145	58.3
	Frederick W. Mansfield (D)	135,676	35.0
1918	Calvin Coolidge (R)	214,863	50.9
	Richard H. Long (D)	197,828	46.8
1919	Calvin Coolidge (R)	317,774	60.9
	Richard H. Long (D)	192,673	37.0
1920	Channing H. Cox (R)	643,869	67.0
	John J. Walsh (D)	290,350	30.2
1922	Channing H. Cox (R)	464,873	52.2
	John F. Fitzgerald (D)	404,192	45.4
1924	Alvan T. Fuller (R)	650,817	56.0
	James M. Curley (D)	490,010	42.2
1926	Alvan T. Fuller (R)	595,006	58.8
	William A. Gaston (D)	407,389	40.3
1928	Frank G. Allen (R)	769,372	50.1
	Charles H. Cole (D)	750,137	48.8
1930	Joseph B. Ely (D)	606,902	49.5
	Frank G. Allen (R)	590,238	48.2
1932	Joseph B. Ely (D)	825,479	52.8
	William Sterling Youngman (R)	704,576	45.0
1934	James M. Curley (D)	736,463	49.7

	Candidates	Votes	%
	Gaspar G. Bacon (R)	627,413	42.3
	Frank A. Goodwin (E TAX)	94,141	6.4
1936	Charles F. Hurley (D)	867,743	47.6
	John W. Haigis (R)	839,740	46.1
1938	Leverett Saltonstall (R)	941,465	53.3
	James M. Curley (D)	793,884	45.0
1940	Leverett Saltonstall (R)	999,223	49.7
	Paul A. Dever (D)	993,635	49.5
1942	Leverett Saltonstall (R)	758,402	54.1
	Roger L. Putnam (D)	630,265	45.0
1944	Maurice J. Tobin (D)	1,048,284	53.6
	Horace T. Cahill (R)	897,708	45.9
1946	Robert F. Bradford (R)	911,152	54.1
	Maurice J. Tobin (D)	762,743	45.3
1948	Paul A. Dever (D)	1,239,247	59.0
	Robert F. Bradford (R)	849,895	40.5
1950	Paul A. Dever (D)	1,074,570	56.3
	Arthur W. Coolidge (R)	824,069	43.1
1952	Christian A. Herter (R)	1,175,955	49.9
	Paul A. Dever (D)	1,161,499	49.3
1954	Christian A. Herter (R)	985,339	51.8
	Robert F. Murphy (D)	910,087	47.8
1956	Foster Furcolo (D)	1,234,618	52.8
	Sumner G. Whittier (R)	1,096,759	46.9
1958	Foster Furcolo (D)	1,067,020	56.2
	Charles Gibbons (R)	818,463	43.1
1960	John A. Volpe (R)	1,269,295	52.5
	Joseph D. Ward (D)	1,130,810	46.8
1962	Endicott Peabody (D)	1,053,322	49.9
	John A. Volpe (R)	1,047,891	49.7
1964	John A. Volpe (R)	1,176,462	50.3
	Francis X. Bellotti (D)	1,153,416	49.3
1966	John A. Volpe (R)	1,277,358	62.6
	Edward J. McCormack (D)	752,720	36.9
1970	Francis W. Sargent (R)	1,058,623	56.7
	Kevin H. White (D)	799,269	42.8
1974	Michael S. Dukakis (D)	992,284	53.5
	Francis W. Sargent (R)	784,353	42.3
1978	Edward J. King (D)	1,030,294	52.5
	Francis W. Hatch (R)	926,072	47.2
1982	Michael S. Dukakis (D)	1,219,109	59.5
	John W. Sears (R)	749,679	36.6

1. *Totals for losing candidates in these elections include some votes for other candidates.*

MICHIGAN

(Became a state Jan. 26, 1837)

	Candidates	Votes	%
1835	Stevens T. Mason (D)	7,385	89.2
	John Biddle (W)	815	9.8
1837	Stevens T. Mason (D)	15,318	50.2
	Charles C. Trowbridge (W)	14,884	48.8
1839	William Woodbridge (W)	19,069	51.9
	E. Farnsworth (D)	17,710	48.2
1841	John S. Barry (D)	21,001	55.8
	Philo C. Fuller (W)	15,449	41.1
1843	John S. Barry (D)	21,394	54.6
	Zind Pilcher (W)	15,024	38.3
	James G. Birney (LIB)	2,736	7.0
1845	Alpheus Felch (D)	20,123	50.8
	Stephen Vickery (W)	16,322	41.2
	James G. Birney (LIB)	3,048	7.7
1847	Epaphroditus Ransom (D)	24,639	53.2
	James M. Edmunds (W)	18,990	41.0
	Chester Gurney (LIB)	2,585	5.6

	Candidates	Votes	%		Candidates	Votes	%
1849	John S. Barry (D)	27,845	54.0	1910	Chase S. Osborn (R)	202,803	52.9
	Flavius Littlejohn (W FS)	23,561	45.7		Lawton T. Hemans (D)	159,770	41.6
1851	Robert McClelland (D)	23,827	58.3	1912	Woodbridge N. Ferris (D)	194,017	35.4
	Townsend E. Gidley (W FS)	16,901	41.3		Amos S. Musselman (R)	169,963	31.0
1852	Robert McClelland (D)	42,791	51.4		Lucius W. Watkins (N PROG)	152,909	27.9
	Zacharaiah Chandler (W)	34,662	41.6	1914	Woodbridge N. Ferris (D)	212,063	48.2
	Isaac P. Christiancy (F SOIL)	5,880	7.1		Chase S. Osborn (R)	176,254	40.0
1854	Kinsley S. Bingham (R)	43,652	53.0		Henry R. Pattengill (N PROG)	36,747	8.3
	Barry (NEB D)	38,676	47.0	1916	Albert E. Sleeper (R)	363,724	55.8
1856	Kinsley S. Bingham (R)	71,402	56.9		Edwin F. Sweet (D)	264,440	40.6
	Felch (D)	54,085	43.1	1918	Albert E. Sleeper (R)	266,738	61.4
1858	Moses Wisner (R)	65,201	53.8		John W. Bailey (D)	158,142	36.4
	Stuart (D)	56,060	46.2	1920	Alexander J. Groesbeck (R)	703,180	66.4
1860	Austin Blair (R)	87,780	56.7		Woodbridge N. Ferris (D)	310,566	29.3
	Barry (D)	67,053	43.3	1922	Alexander J. Groesbeck (R)	356,933	61.2
1862	Austin Blair (R)	68,716	52.5		Alva M. Cummins (D)	218,252	37.4
	Stout (D)	62,102	47.5	1924	Alexander J. Groesbeck (R)	799,225	68.8
1864	Henry H. Crapo (UN R)	91,353	55.2		Edward Frensdorf (D)	343,577	29.6
	William H. Fenton (D)	74,293	44.9	1926	Fred W. Green (R)	399,564	63.4
1866	Henry H. Crapo (R)	97,112	58.6		William A. Comstock (D)	227,155	36.0
	Williams (D)	68,650	41.4	1928	Fred W. Green (R)	961,179	69.9
1868	Henry P. Baldwin (R)	128,042	56.8		William A. Comstock (D)	404,546	29.4
	John Moore (D)	97,290	43.2	1930	Wilber M. Brucker (R)	483,990	56.9
1870	Henry P. Baldwin (R)	100,176	53.8		William A. Comstock (D)	357,664	42.0
	Charles C. Comstock (D)	83,391	44.8	1932	William A. Comstock (D)	887,672	54.9
1872	John J. Bagley (R)	137,602	63.0		Wilber M. Brucker (R)	696,935	43.1
	Blair (L)	80,958	37.0	1934	Frank D. Fitzgerald (R)	659,743	52.4
1874	John J. Bagley (R)	111,519	50.5		Arthur J. Lacy (D)	577,044	45.8
	Henry Chamberlain (D)	105,550	47.8	1936	Frank Murphy (D)	892,774	51.0
1876	Charles M. Croswell (R)	165,926	52.3		Frank D. Fitzgerald (R)	843,855	48.2
	Webber (D)	142,493	44.9	1938	Frank D. Fitzgerald (R)	847,245	52.8
1878	Charles M. Croswell (R)	126,280	45.4		Frank Murphy (D)	753,752	47.0
	Barnes (D)	78,503	28.2	1940	Murray D. Van Wagoner (D)	1,077,065	53.1
	Smith (NG)	73,313	26.4		Luren D. Dickinson (R)	945,784	46.6
1880	David H. Jerome (R)	178,944	51.3	1942	Harry F. Kelly (R)	645,335	52.6
	Holloway (D)	137,671	39.4		Murray D. Van Wagoner (D)	573,314	46.7
	Woodman (G)	31,085	8.9	1944	Harry F. Kelly (R)	1,208,859	54.7
1882	Josiah W. Begole (D & G)	154,269	49.5		Edward J. Fry (D)	989,307	44.8
	David H. Jerome (R)	149,697	48.0	1946	Kim Sigler (R)	1,003,878	60.3
1884	Russell A. Alger (R)	190,840	47.7		Murray D. Van Wagoner (D)	644,540	38.7
	Josiah W. Begole (D & G)	186,884	46.7	1948	G. Mennen Williams (D)	1,128,664	53.4
	David Preston (P)	22,307	5.6		Kim Sigler (R)	964,810	45.7
1886	Cyrus G. Luce (R)	181,474	47.7	1950	G. Mennen Williams (D)	935,152	49.8
	George L. Yaple (D)	174,042	45.7		Harry F. Kelly (R)	933,998	49.7
	Samuel Dickie (P)	25,179	6.6	1952	G. Mennen Williams (D)	1,431,893	50.0
1888	Cyrus G. Luce (R)	233,595	49.2		Fred M. Alger Jr. (R)	1,423,275	49.7
	Wellington R. Burt (D)	216,450	45.6	1954	G. Mennen Williams (D)	1,216,308	55.6
1890	Edward B. Winans (D)	183,725	46.2		Donald S. Leonard (R)	963,300	44.1
	James M. Turner (R)	172,205	43.3	1956	G. Mennen Williams (D)	1,666,689	54.7
	Azariah S. Partridge (P)	28,681	7.2		Albert E. Cobo (R)	1,376,376	45.1
1892	John T. Rich (R)	221,228	47.2	1958	G. Mennen Williams (D)	1,225,533	53.0
	Allen B. Morse (D)	205,138	43.8		Paul D. Bagwell (R)	1,078,089	46.6
1894	John T. Rich (R)	237,215	56.9	1960	John B. Swainson (D)	1,643,634	50.5
	Spencer O. Fisher (D)	130,823	31.4		Paul D. Bagwell (R)	1,602,022	49.2
	Alva W. Nichols (PP)	30,008	7.2	1962	George Romney (R)	1,420,086	51.4
1896	Hazen S. Pingree (R)	304,431	55.6		John B. Swainson (D)	1,339,513	48.5
	Charles R. Sligh (D & POP)	225,200	41.1	1964	George Romney (R)	1,764,355	55.9
1898	Hazen S. Pingree (R)	243,239	57.8		Neil Staebler (D)	1,381,442	43.7
	Justin R. Whiting (DPUS)	168,142	39.9	1966	George Romney (R)	1,490,430	60.5
1900	Aaron T. Bliss (R)	305,612	55.8		Zolton A. Ferency (D)	963,383	39.1
	William C. Maybury (D)	226,208	41.3	1970	William G. Milliken (R)	1,338,711	50.4
1902	Aaron T. Bliss (R)	211,261	52.5		Sander Levin (D)	1,294,600	48.7
	Lorenzo T. Durand (D)	174,077	43.3	1974	William G. Milliken (R)	1,356,865	51.1
1904	Fred M. Warner (R)	283,799	54.1		Sander Levin (D)	1,242,247	46.8
	Woodbridge N. Ferris (D)	223,571	42.6	1978	William G. Milliken (R)	1,628,485	56.8
1906	Fred M. Warner (R)	227,567	60.9		William Fitzgerald (D)	1,237,256	43.2
	Charles H. Kimmerle (D)	130,018	34.8	1982	James J. Blanchard (D)	1,561,291	51.4
1908	Fred M. Warner (R)	262,141	48.4		Richard H. Headlee (R)	1,369,582	45.1
	Lawton T. Hemans (D)	252,611	46.6				

MINNESOTA

(Became a state May 11, 1858)

	Candidates	Votes	%
1857	Henry H. Sibley (D)	17,790	50.3
	Alexander Ramsey (R)	17,550	49.7
1859	Alexander Ramsey (R)	21,335	54.8
	George L. Becker (D)	17,583	45.2
1861	Alexander Ramsey (R)	16,274#	60.9
	E. O. Hamlin (D)	10,448#	39.1
1863	Stephen Miller (UN)	19,628	60.6
	Henry T. Wells (D)	12,739	39.4
1865	William R. Marshall (R)	17,308	55.6
	H. M. Rice (D)	13,847	44.5
1867	William R. Marshall (R)	34,874	54.2
	Charles E. Flandrau (D)	29,511	45.8
1869	Horace Austin (R)	27,599	50.4
	George L. Otis (D)	25,390	46.4
1871	Horace Austin (R)	46,669	59.9
	Winthrop Young (D)	31,212	40.1
1873	Cushman K. Davis (R)	40,741#	52.9
	Ara Barton (IR & D)	35,245#	45.8
1875	John S. Pillsbury (R)	45,073#	53.6
	David L. Buell (D)	35,275#	41.9
1877	John S. Pillsbury (R)	57,071#	57.9
	W. L. Banning (D)	39,147#	39.7
1879	John S. Pillsbury (R)	57,522	54.0
	Edmund Rice (D)	41,844	39.3
1881	Lucius F. Hubbard (R)	65,025	63.6
	R. W. Johnson (D)	37,168	36.4
1883	Lucius F. Hubbard (R)	72,462	55.4
	A. Bierman (D)	58,245	44.8
1886	A. R. McGill (R)	106,966	48.5
	A. A. Ames (D)	104,483	47.4
1888	William R. Merriam (R)	134,355	51.3
	Eugene M. Wilson (D)	110,251	42.1
	Hugh Harrison (P)	17,150	6.6
1890	William R. Merriam (R)	88,111	36.6
	Thomas Wilson (D)	85,844	35.6
	Sidney M. Owen (ALNC)	58,513	24.3
1892	Knute Nelson (R)	109,220	42.7
	Daniel W. Lawler (D)	94,600	37.0
	Ignatius Donnelly (PP)	39,860	15.6
1894	Knute Nelson (R)	147,943	49.9
	Sidney M. Owen (PP)	87,898	29.7
	George L. Becker (D)	53,583	18.1
1896	David M. Clough (R)	165,906	49.2
	John Lind (PP & D)	162,254	48.1
1898	John Lind (D & POP)	131,980	52.3
	William H. Eustis (R)	111,796	44.3
1900	Samuel R. Van Sant (R)	152,905	48.7
	John Lind (PP & D)	150,651	48.0
1902	Samuel R. Van Sant (R)	155,849	57.5
	Leonard A. Rosing (D)	99,362	36.7
1904	John A. Johnson (D)	147,992	48.7
	Robert C. Dunn (R)	140,130	46.1
1906	John A. Johnson (D)	168,480	60.9
	A. L. Cole (R)	96,162	34.8
1908	John A. Johnson (D)	175,036	52.2
	Jacob F. Jacobson (R)	147,034	43.8
1910	Adolph O. Eberhart (R)	164,185	55.7
	James Gray (D)	103,779	35.2
1912	Adolph O. Eberhart (R)	129,688	40.7
	Peter M. Ringdal (D)	99,659	31.3
	P. V. Collins (PROG)	33,455	10.5
	E. E. Lobeck (P)	29,876	9.4
	David Morgan (PUB OWN)	25,769	8.1
1914	Winfield S. Hammond (D)	156,304	45.5
	William E. Lee (R)	143,730	41.9
	W. G. Calderwood (P)	18,582	5.4
	Tom J. Lewis (SOC)	17,325	5.1

	Candidates	Votes	%
1916	Joseph A. A. Burnquist (R)	245,841	62.9
	Thomas P. Dwyer (D)	93,112	23.8
	J. O. Bentall (SOC)	26,306	6.7
	Thomas J. Anderson (P)	19,884	5.1
1918	Joseph A. A. Burnquist (R)	166,615	45.1
	David H. Evans (F-LAB)	111,966	30.3
	Fred E. Wheaton (D)	76,838	20.8
1920	Jacob A. O. Preus (R)	415,805	53.1
	Henrik Shipstead (I)	281,406	35.9
	L. C. Hodgson (D)	81,291	10.4
1922	Jacob A. O. Preus (R)	309,756	45.2
	Magnus Johnson (F-LAB)	295,479	43.1
	Edward Indrehus (D)	79,903	11.7
1924	Theodore Christianson (R)	406,692	48.7
	Floyd B. Olson (F-LAB)	366,029	43.8
	Carlos Avery (D)	49,353	5.9
1926	Theodore Christianson (R)	395,779	56.5
	Magnus Johnson (F-LAB)	266,845	38.1
	Alfred Jaques (D)	38,008	5.4
1928	Theodore Christianson (R)	549,857	55.0
	Ernest Lundeen (F-LAB)	227,193	22.7
	Andrew Nelson (D)	213,734	21.4
1930	Floyd B. Olson (F-LAB)	472,354	59.3
	Ray P. Chase (R)	289,528	36.4
1932	Floyd B. Olson (F-LAB)	522,438	50.6
	Earle Brown (R)	334,081	32.3
	John E. Regan (D)	169,859	16.4
1934	Floyd B. Olson (F-LAB)	468,812	44.6
	Martin A. Nelson (R)	396,359	37.7
	John E. Regan (D)	176,928	16.8
1936	Elmer A. Benson (F-LAB)	680,342	60.7
	Martin A. Nelson (R)	431,841	38.6
1938	Harold E. Stassen (R)	678,839	59.9
	Elmer A. Benson (F-LAB)	387,263	34.2
	Thomas Gallagher (D)	65,875	5.8
1940	Harold E. Stassen (R)	654,686	52.1
	Hjalmar Petersen (F-LAB)	459,609	36.5
	Ed Murphy (D)	140,021	11.1
1942	Harold E. Stassen (R)	409,800	51.6
	Hjalmar Petersen (F-LAB)	299,917	37.8
	John D. Sullivan (D)	75,151	9.5
1944	Edward J. Thye (R)	701,185	61.1
	Byron G. Allen (DFL)	440,132	38.3
1946	Luther W. Youngdahl (R)	519,067	59.0
	Harold H. Barker (DFL)	349,565	39.7
1948	Luther W. Youngdahl (R)	643,572	53.2
	Charles L. Halsted (DFL)	545,746	45.1
1950	Luther W. Youngdahl (R)	635,800	60.8
	Harry H. Peterson (DFL)	400,637	38.3
1952	C. Elmer Anderson (R)	785,125	55.3
	Orville L. Freeman (DFL)	624,480	44.0
1954	Orville L. Freeman (DFL)	607,099	52.7
	C. Elmer Anderson (R)	538,865	46.8
1956	Orville L. Freeman (DFL)	731,180	51.4
	Ancher Nelsen (R)	685,196	48.2
1958	Orville L. Freeman (DFL)	658,326	56.8
	George Mackinnon (R)	490,731	42.3
1960	Elmer L. Andersen (R)	783,813	50.6
	Orville L. Freeman (DFL)	760,934	49.1
1962	Karl F. Rolvaag (DFL)	619,842‡	49.7
	Elmer L. Andersen (R)	619,751	49.7
1966	Harold Levander (R)	680,593	52.6
	Karl F. Rolvaag (DFL)	607,943	46.9
1970	Wendell R. Anderson (DFL)	737,921	54.3
	Douglas M. Head (R)	621,780	45.7
1974	Wendell R. Anderson (DFL)	786,787	62.8
	John W. Johnson (R)	367,722	29.3
1978	Albert H. Quie (R)	830,019	52.3
	Rudy Perpich (D)	718,244	45.3
1982	Rudy Perpich (D)	1,049,104	58.6
	Wheelock Whitney (R)	715,796	40.0

MISSISSIPPI

(Became a state Dec. 10, 1817)

	Candidates	Votes	%
1817	David Holmes	4,108	
1819	George Poindexter	2,721	61.5
	Thomas Hinds	1,702	38.5
1821	Walter Leake	4,730	78.8
	Charles B. Green	1,269	21.2
1823	Walter Leake	4,730	51.3
	David Dickson	2,511	27.2
	William Lattimore	1,986	21.5
1825	David Holmes (OLD R)	7,850	84.0
	Cowles Mead (OLD R)	1,499	16.0
1827	Gerard C. Brandon	5,482	51.0
	Daniel Williams	3,392	31.6
	Beverly R. Grayson	1,866	17.4
1829	Gerard C. Brandon (JAC D)	6,052	64.6
	George W. Winchester (NR)	3,310	35.4
1831	Abram M. Scott (NR)	3,953	30.5
	Hiram G. Runnels (JAC D)	3,711	28.6
	Charles Lynch (JAC D)	2,902	22.4
	Wiley Harris (JAC D)	1,899	14.7
1833	Hiram G. Runnels (D)	6,614	52.9
	Abram M. Scott (W)	5,900	47.2
1835	Charles Lynch (W)	9,877	51.1
	Hiram G. Runnels (D)	9,451	48.9
1837	Alexander G. McNutt (D)	12,823	46.4
	Morgan	9,861	35.7
	Grimball (W)	4,951	17.9
1839	Alexander G. McNutt (D)	18,880	54.3
	Edward Turner (W)	15,886	45.7
1841	Tilgham M. Tucker (D)	19,059	53.2
	D. O. Shattuck (W)	16,783	46.8
1843	Albert G. Brown (A-RPT D)	21,115	52.9
	Clayton (W)	17,442	43.7
1845	Albert G. Brown (D)	27,669	64.8
	Coopwood (W)	15,029	35.2
1849	John A. Quitman (D)	33,117	59.0
	Lea (W)	22,996	40.9
1851	Henry S. Foote (UN)	27,836	51.4
	Davis (SO RTS)	26,301	48.6
1853	John J. McCrae (D)	30,460	54.0
	Rogers (W)	25,967	46.0
1855	John J. McCrae (D)	32,669	54.2
	C. D. Fontaine (AM)	27,578	45.8
1857	William McWillie (D)	27,376	66.0
	William Yerger (AM)	14,085	34.0
1859	John J. Pettus (D)	34,559	76.8
	H. W. Walter (OPP)	10,408	23.1
1861	John J. Pettus (D)	29,959	86.9
	Jacob Thompson	3,556	10.3
1863	Charles Clark	16,050	69.8
	A. M. West	4,914	21.4
	Reuben Davis	2,021	8.8
1865	Benjamin G. Humphreys (SEC W)	19,037	42.2
	E. S. Fisher (UN)	15,557	34.5
	W. S. Patton	10,519	23.3
1868	Benjamin G. Humphreys (D)	62,321	52.6
	Beriah B. Eggleston (R)	56,072	47.4
1869	James L. Alcorn (R)	76,186	66.7
	Louis Dent (C)	38,097	33.3
1873	Adelbert Ames (R)	73,324	58.1
	James L. Alcorn (I)	52,857	41.9
1877	John M. Stone (D)	96,376	98.8
1881	Robert Lowry (D)	76,805	59.6
	King (G & R)	51,994	40.4
1885	Robert Lowry (D)	88,783	100.0
1889	John M. Stone (D)	84,929	100.0
1895	Anselm J. McLaurin (D)	46,870	72.1
	Frank Burkitt (PP)	18,167	27.9

	Candidates	Votes	%
1899	Andrew H. Longino (D)	42,273	87.4
	R. K. Prewitt (POP)	6,097	12.6
1903	James K. Vardaman (D)	32,191	100.0
1907	Edmund F. Noel (D)	29,528	100.0
1911	Earl Brewer (D)	40,471	95.2
1915	Theodore G. Bilbo (D)	50,541	92.6
	J. T. Lester (SOC)	4,046	7.4
1919	Lee M. Russell (D)	39,239	96.9
1923	Henry L. Whitfield (D)	29,138	100.0
1927	Theodore G. Bilbo (D)	31,717	100.0
1931	Martin S. Conner (D)	45,942	100.0
1935	Hugh L. White (D)	45,881	100.0
1939	Paul B. Johnson (D)	61,614	100.0
1943	Thomas L. Bailey (D)	50,488	100.0
1947	Fielding L. Wright (D)	161,993	97.5
1951	Hugh L. White (D)	43,422	100.0
1955	J. P. Coleman (D)	40,707	100.0
1959	Ross R. Barnett (D)	57,671	100.0
1963	Paul B. Johnson Jr. (D)	225,456	61.9
	Rubel L. Phillips (R)	138,605	38.1
1967	John Bell Williams (D)	315,318	70.3
	Rubel L. Phillips (R)	133,379	29.7
1971	William L. Waller (D)	601,222	77.0
	James Charles Evers (I)	172,762	22.1
1975	Cliff Finch (D)	369,568	52.2
	Gil Carmichael (R)	319,632	45.1
1979	William F. Winter (D)	413,620	61.1
	Gil Carmichael (R)	263,702	38.9
1983	Bill Allain (D)	409,209#	55.1
	Leon Bramlett (R)	288,764#	38.9

MISSOURI

(Became a state Aug. 10, 1821)

	Candidates	Votes	%
1820	Alexander McNair (D-R)	6,576	72.0
	William Clark (D-R)	2,556	28.0
1824	Frederick Bates (AR)	6,165	57.1
	William H. Ashley (CLAY R)	4,636	42.9
1825	John Miller (JAC D)	2,801	47.9
	Carr (JAC D)	1,622	27.8
	Todd (NR)	1,423	24.3
1828	John Miller	11,043	100.0
1832	Daniel Dunklin (D)	9,141	50.9
	John Bull (A-JAC)	8,132	45.2
1836	Lilburn W. Boggs (D)	14,315	52.3
	Ashley (I)	13,055	47.7
1840	Thomas Reynolds (D)	29,656	57.2
	Clark (W)	22,205	42.8
1844	John Cummins Edwards (D)	36,978	54.1
	Allen (W)	31,357	45.9
1848	Austin A. King (D)	48,921	59.0
	James S. Rollins (W)	33,942	41.0
1852	Sterling Price (D)	46,494	58.7
	James Winston (W)	32,706	41.3
1856	Trusten Polk (D)	47,066	40.8
	R. C. Ewing (AM)	40,620	35.2
	Thomas Hart Benton (BENTON D)	27,615	24.0

Special Election

1857	R. M. Stewart (D)	47,975	50.2
	J. S. Rollins (AM & EMANC)	47,619	49.8

	Candidates	Votes	%
1860	Claiborne Fox Jackson (D)	74,239	47.0
	Sample Orr (OPP)	66,400	42.0
	Hancock Jackson (SOC)	11,362	7.2
1864	Thomas C. Fletcher (UN R)	73,600	70.3
	Thomas L. Price (D)	31,064	29.7
1868	Joseph W. McClurg (R)	82,090	56.7
	John S. Phelps (D)	62,778	43.3
1870	Benjamin Gratz Brown (D)	104,374	62.3
	Joseph W. McClurg (R)	63,235	37.7
1872	Silas Woodson (D & L)	156,767	56.3
	John B. Henderson (R)	121,889	43.7
1874	Charles H. Hardin (D)	149,566	57.2
	William Gentry (R)	112,104	42.8
1876	John S. Phelps (D)	199,583	57.0
	Gustavus A. Finkelnburg (R)	147,684	42.2
1880	Thomas Theodore Crittenden (D)	207,670	52.2
	Dyer (R)	153,636	38.6
	Brown (G)	36,340	9.1
1884	John Sappington Marmaduke (D)	218,885	50.1
	Nicholas Ford (G & R)	207,939	47.5
1888	David Rowland Francis (D)	255,764	49.4
	E. E. Kimball (R)	242,531	46.8
1892	William Joel Stone (D)	265,044	49.0
	William Warner (R)	235,383	43.5
	L. Leonard (PP)	37,262	6.9
1896	Lawrence Vest Stephens (D)	351,062	52.9
	Robert E. Lewis (R)	307,729	46.4
1900	Alexander Monroe Dockery (D)	350,045	51.2
	Flory (R)	317,905	46.5
1904	Joseph Wingate Folk (D)	326,652	50.7
	Cyrus P. Walbridge (R)	296,552	46.1
1908	Herbert Spencer Hadley (R)	355,932	49.7
	Cowherd (D)	340,053	47.5
1912	Elliott Woolfolk Major (D)	337,019	48.2
	John C. McKinley (R)	217,819	31.2
	Albert D. Nortoni (PROG)	109,146	15.6
1916	Frederick Dozier Gardner (D)	382,355	48.7
	Lamm (R)	380,092	48.4
1920	Arthur Mastick Hyde (R)	722,020	54.3
	Atkinson (D)	580,726	43.6
1924	Samuel Aaron Baker (R)	640,135	49.4
	A. T. Nelson (D)	634,263	48.9
1928	Henry Stewart Caulfield (R)	784,311	51.6
	Francis M. Wilson (D)	731,783	48.2
1932	Guy Brasfield Park (D)	968,551	60.2
	Edward H. Winter (R)	629,428	39.1
1936	Lloyd Crow Stark (D)	1,037,133	57.1
	Jesse W. Barrett (R)	772,934	42.5
1940	Forrest C. Donnell (R)	911,530	50.1
	Larry McDaniel (D)	907,917	49.9
1944	Phil M. Donnelly (D)	793,490	50.9
	Jean Paul Bradshaw (R)	762,908	49.0
1948	Forrest Smith (D)	893,092	57.0
	Murray E. Thompson (R)	670,064	42.8
1952	Phil M. Donnelly (D)	983,169	52.6
	Howard Elliott (R)	886,270	47.4
1956	James T. Blair Jr. (D)	941,528	52.1
	Lon Hocker (R)	866,810	47.9
1960	John M. Dalton (D)	1,095,195	58.0
	Edward G. Farmer (R)	792,131	42.0
1964	Warren E. Hearnes (D)	1,110,651	62.1
	Ethan A. H. Shepley (R)	678,949	37.9
1968	Warren E. Hearnes (D)	1,063,495	60.7
	Lawrence K. Roos (R)	688,300	39.3
1972	Christopher S. Bond (R)	1,029,451	55.2
	Edward L. Dowd (D)	832,751	44.6
1976	Joseph P. Teasdale (D)	971,184	50.2
	Christopher S. Bond (R)	958,110	49.6
1980	Christopher S. Bond (R)	1,098,950	52.6
	Joseph P. Teasdale (D)	981,884	47.0
1984	John Ashcroft (R)	1,194,506	56.7
	Kenneth J. Rothman (D)	913,700	43.3

MONTANA

(Became a state Nov. 8, 1889)

	Candidates	Votes	%
1889	Joseph K. Toole (D)	19,735	51.0
	Thomas C. Power (R)	18,991	49.0
1892	John E. Rickards (R)	18,187	41.2
	Timothy E. Collins (D)	17,650	40.0
	William Kennedy (PP)	7,794	17.6
1896	Robert B. Smith (PP & D)	36,688	71.0
	Alexander C. Botkin (R-SIL R)	14,993	29.0
1900	Joseph K. Toole (D)	31,419	49.3
	David S. Folsom (R)	22,691	35.6
	Thomas S. Hogan (ID)	9,188	14.4
1904	Joseph K. Toole (D-LAB-PP)	35,377	53.8
	William Lindsay (R)	26,957	41.0
	Malcolm A. O'Malley (SOC)	3,431	5.2
1908	Edwin L. Norris (D)	32,282	47.3
	Edward Donlan (R)	30,792	45.2
	Harry Hazelton (SOC)	5,112	7.5
1912	Samuel V. Stewart (D)	25,371	31.7
	Harry L. Wilson (R)	22,950	28.7
	Frank J. Edwards (PROG)	18,881	23.6
	Lewis J. Duncan (SOC)	12,766	16.0
1916	Samuel V. Stewart (D)	85,683	49.4
	Frank J. Edwards (R)	76,556	44.1
	Lewis J. Duncan (SOC)	11,342	6.5
1920	Joseph M. Dixon (R)	111,113	59.7
	Burton K. Wheeler (D)	74,875	40.3
1924	John E. Erickson (D)	88,801	51.0
	Joseph M. Dixon (R)	74,126	42.6
	Frank J. Edwards (F-LAB)	10,576	6.1
1928	John E. Erickson (D)	114,256	58.7
	Wellington D. Rankin (R)	79,777	41.0
1932	John E. Erickson (D)	104,949	48.5
	Frank A. Hazelbaker (R)	101,105	46.7
1936	Roy E. Ayers (D)	115,310	51.0
	Frank A. Hazelbaker (R)	108,854	48.1
1940	Samuel C. Ford (R)	124,435	50.7
	Roy E. Ayers (D)	119,453	48.6
1944	Samuel C. Ford (R)	116,461	56.4
	Leif Erickson (D)	89,224	43.2
1948	John W. Bonner (D)	124,267	55.7
	Samuel C. Ford (R)	97,792	43.9
1952	John Hugo Aronson (R)	134,423	51.0
	John W. Bonner (D)	129,369	49.0
1956	John Hugo Aronson (R)	138,878	51.4
	Arnold H. Olsen (D)	131,488	48.6
1960	Donald G. Nutter (R)	154,230	55.1
	Paul Cannon (D)	125,651	44.9
1964	Tim Babcock (R)	144,113	51.3
	Roland Renne (D)	136,862	48.7
1968	Forrest H. Anderson (D)	150,481	54.1
	Tim Babcock (R)	116,432	41.9
1972	Thomas L. Judge (D)	172,523	54.1
	Ed Smith (R)	146,231	45.9
1976	Thomas L. Judge (D)	195,420	61.7
	Robert Woodahl (R)	115,848	36.6
1980	Ted Schwinden (D)	199,574	55.4
	Jack Ramirez (R)	160,892	44.6
1984	Ted Schwinden (D)	266,578	70.3
	Pat M. Goodover (R)	100,070	26.4

NEBRASKA

(Became a state March 1, 1867)

	Candidates	Votes	%
1866	David Butler (R)	4,083	50.4
	J. S. Morton (D)	4,001	49.4

	Candidates	Votes	%		Candidates	Votes	%
1868	David Butler (R)	8,576	57.5	1930	Charles W. Bryan (D)	222,161	50.8
	T. R. Porter (D)	6,349	42.5		Arthur J. Weaver (R)	215,615	49.3
1870	David Butler (R)	11,126	56.3	1932	Charles W. Bryan (D)	296,117	52.5
	J. H. Croxton (D)	8,648	43.7		Dwight Griswold (R)	260,888	46.3
1872	Robert W. Furnas (R)	16,543	59.6	1934	Robert L. Cochran (D)	284,095	50.8
	H. C. Lett (D)	11,227	40.4		Dwight Griswold (R)	266,707	47.7
1874	Silas Garber (R)	21,548	59.9	1936	Robert L. Cochran (D)	333,412	55.9
	Albert Tuxbury (D)	8,946	24.9		Dwight Griswold (R)	257,279	43.1
	J. F. Gardner (PP I)	4,159	11.6	1938	Robert L. Cochran (D)	218,787	44.0
1876	Silas Garber (R)	31,947	61.2		Charles J. Warner (R)	201,898	40.6
	Paren England (D)	17,219	33.0		Charles W. Bryan	76,258	15.4
	J. F. Gardner (G)	3,022	5.8	1940	Dwight Griswold (R)	365,638	60.9
1878	Albinus Nance (R)	29,269	56.1		Terry Carpenter (D)	235,167	39.1
	W. H. Webster (D)	13,471	25.8	1942	Dwight Griswold (R)	283,271	74.8
	Levi G. Todd (G)	9,484	18.2		Charles W. Bryan (D)	95,231	25.2
1880	Albinus Nance (R)	55,237	63.2	1944	Dwight Griswold (R)	410,136	76.1
	T. W. Tipton (D)	28,167	32.3		George W. Olsen (D)	128,760	23.9
1882	James W. Dawes (R)	43,495	48.8	1946	Val Peterson (R)	249,468	65.5
	J. S. Morton (D)	28,562	32.1		Frank Sorrell (D)	131,367	34.5
	E. P. Ingersoll (G)	16,991	19.1	1948	Val Peterson (R)	286,119	60.1
1884	James W. Dawes (R)	72,835	54.5		Frank Sorrell (D)	190,214	39.9
	J. S. Morton (D)	57,634	43.2	1950	Val Peterson (R)	247,089	54.9
1886	John M. Thayer (R)	76,456	55.2		Walter R. Raecke (D)	202,638	45.1
	J. E. North (D)	52,456	37.9	1952	Robert B. Crosby (R)	365,409	61.4
	H. W. Hardy (P)	8,198	5.9		Walter R. Raecke (D)	229,400	38.6
1888	John M. Thayer (R)	103,982	51.3	1954	Victor E. Anderson (R)	250,080	60.3
	J. A. McShane (D)	85,420	42.1		William Ritchie (D)	164,753	39.7
1890	James E. Boyd (D)	71,331‡	33.3	1956	Victor E. Anderson (R)	308,285	54.3
	J. H. Powers (PP I)	70,187	32.8		Frank Sorrell (D)	228,048	40.2
	L. D. Richards (R)	68,878	32.2		George L. Morris	31,583	5.6
1892	Lorenzo Crounse (R)	78,426	39.7	1958	Ralph G. Brooks (D)	211,345	50.2
	Charles Henry Van Wyck (PP I)	68,617	34.8		Victor E. Anderson (R)	209,705	49.8
	J. S. Morton (D)	44,195	22.4	1960	Frank B. Morrison (D)	311,344	52.0
1894	Silas A. Holcomb (D & PPI)	97,825	48.0		John R. Cooper (R)	287,302	48.0
	T. J. Majors (R)	94,613	46.4	1962	Frank B. Morrison (D)	242,669	52.2
1896	Silas A. Holcomb (D & PPI)	116,415	53.5		Fred A. Seaton (R)	221,885	47.8
	J. H. McColl (R)	94,724	43.5	1964	Frank B. Morrison (D)	347,026	60.0
1898	William A. Poynter (FUS)	95,703	50.2		Dwight W. Burney (R)	231,029	40.0
	M. L. Hayward (R)	92,982	48.8	1966	Norbert T. Tiemann (R)	299,245	61.5
1900	Charles H. Dietrich (R)	113,879	48.9		Philip C. Sorensen (D)	186,985	38.5
	William A. Poynter (FUS)	113,018	48.5	1970	J. James Exon (D)	248,552	53.8
1902	John H. Mickey (R)	96,471	49.7		Norbert T. Tiemann (R)	201,994	43.8
	William H. Thompson (FUS)	91,116	46.9	1974	J. James Exon (D)	267,012	59.2
1904	John H. Mickey (R)	111,711	49.7		Richard D. Marvel (R)	159,780	35.4
	George W. Berge (FUS)	102,568	45.6		Ernest W. Chambers (I)	24,320	5.4
1906	George L. Sheldon (R)	97,858	51.3	1978	Charles Thone (R)	275,473	55.9
	Ashton Shallenberger (D & PPI)	84,885	44.5		Gerald T. Whelan (D)	216,754	44.0
1908	Ashton Shallenberger (D & PPI)	132,960	49.9	1982	Robert Kerrey (D)	277,436	50.6
	George L. Sheldon (R)	125,967	47.3		Charles Thone (R)	270,203	49.3
1910	Chester H. Aldrich (R)	123,070	51.9				
	James C. Dahlman (D)	107,760	45.5				
1912	John H. Morehead (D & PPI)	123,997	49.3				
	Chester H. Aldrich (R & PROG)	114,075	45.3				
1914	John H. Morehead (D & PPI)	120,201	50.4				
	R. B. Howell (R)	101,229	42.4				
1916	Keith Neville (D & PPI)	143,564	49.3				
	Abraham L. Sutton (R & PROG)	136,811	47.0				
1918	Samuel R. McKelvie (R)	121,188	54.5				
	Keith Neville (D)	97,886	44.0				
1920	Samuel R. McKelvie (R)	152,863	40.4				
	John H. Morehead (D)	130,433	34.5				
	Arthur G. Wray (NON PL)	88,905	23.5				
1922	Charles W. Bryan (D)	214,070	54.6				
	Charles H. Randall (R)	164,435	42.0				
1924	Adam McMullen (R)	229,067	51.1				
	J. N. Norton (D)	183,709	41.0				
	Dan Butler (PROG)	35,594	7.9				
1926	Adam McMullen (R)	206,120	49.8				
	Charles W. Bryan (D)	202,688	49.0				
1928	Arthur J. Weaver (R)	308,262	57.0				
	Charles W. Bryan (D)	230,640	42.6				

NEVADA

(Became a state Oct. 31, 1864)

	Candidates	Votes	%
1864	Henry G. Blasdel (UN R)	9,834	60.0
	David E. Buell (D)	6,555	40.0
1866	Henry G. Blasdel (R)	5,125	55.5
	John D. Winters (D)	4,105	44.5
1870	L. R. Bradley (D)	7,200	53.9
	F. A. Tritte (R)	6,147	46.1
1874	L. R. Bradley (D)	10,339	57.1
	Hazlett (R)	7,754	42.9
1878	John H. Kinkead (R)	9,678	51.4
	L. R. Bradley (D)	9,151	48.6
1882	Jewett W. Adams (D)	7,770	54.3
	Enoch Strother (R)	6,535	45.7

	Candidates	Votes	%
1886	C. C. Stevenson (R)	6,463	52.4
	Jewett W. Adams (D)	5,869	47.6
1890	R. K. Colcord (R)	6,601	53.3
	Thomas Winters (D)	5,791	46.7
1894	J. S. Jones (D SIL)	5,223	49.9
	A. C. Cleveland (R)	3,861	36.9
	G. E. Peckham (POP)	711	6.8
	Theodore Winters (D)	678	6.5
1898	Reinhold Sadler (SIL R)	3,570	35.7
	William McMillan (R)	3,548	35.5
	George Russell (D)	2,057	20.6
	J. B. McCullough (PP)	833	8.3
1902	John Sparks (D & SILVER)	6,540	57.8
	A. C. Cleveland (R)	4,778	42.2
1906	John Sparks (D & SILVER)	8,686	58.5
	James F. Mitchell (R)	5,336	36.0
	Thomas B. Casey (SOC)	815	5.5
1910	Tasker L. Oddie (R)	10,435	50.6
	D. S. Dickerson (D)	8,798	42.7
	Henry F. Gegax (SOC)	1,393	6.8
1914	Emmet D. Boyle (D)	9,623	44.7
	Tasker L. Oddie (R)	8,537	39.6
	W. A. Morgan (SOC)	3,391	15.7
1918	Emmet D. Boyle (D)	12,875	52.1
	Tasker L. Oddie (R)	11,845	47.9
1922	James G. Scrugham (D)	15,437	53.9
	John H. Miller (R)	13,215	46.1
1926	Fred B. Balzar (R)	16,374	53.0
	James G. Scrugham (D)	14,521	47.0
1930	Fred B. Balzar (R)	18,442	53.3
	C. L. Richards (D)	16,192	46.8
1934	Richard Kirman Sr. (D)	23,088	53.9
	Morley Griswold (R)	14,778	34.5
	L. C. Branson (I)	4,940	11.5
1938	Edward P. Carville (D)	28,528	61.9
	John A. Fulton (R)	17,586	38.1
1942	Edward P. Carville (D)	24,505	60.3
	A. V. Tallman (R)	16,164	39.8
1946	Vail Pittman (D)	28,655	57.4
	Melvin E. Jepson (R)	21,247	42.6
1950	Charles H. Russell (R)	35,609	57.6
	Vail Pittman (D)	26,164	42.4
1954	Charles H. Russell (R)	41,665	53.1
	Vail Pittman (D)	36,797	46.9
1958	Grant Sawyer (D)	50,864	59.9
	Charles H. Russell (R)	34,025	40.1
1962	Grant Sawyer (D)	64,784	66.8
	Oran K. Gragson (R)	32,145	33.2
1966	Paul Laxalt (R)	71,807	52.2
	Grant Sawyer (D)	65,870	47.8
1970	Mike O'Callaghan (D)	70,697	48.1
	Ed Fike (R)	64,400	43.8
1974	Mike O'Callaghan (D)	114,114	67.4
	Shirley Crumpler (R)	28,959	17.1
	James Ray Houston (IA)	26,285	15.5
1978	Robert F. List (R)	108,097	56.2
	Robert E. Rose (D)	76,361	39.7
1982	Richard H. Bryan (D)	128,132	53.4
	Robert F. List (R)	100,104	41.8

NEW HAMPSHIRE

(Ratified the Constitution June 21, 1788)

	Candidates	Votes	%
1788	John Langdon	4,421	50.0
	John Sullivan	3,664	41.5
1789	John Sullivan	3,657†	42.9

	Candidates	Votes	%
	John Pickering	3,488	40.9
	Josiah Bartlett	968	11.3
1790	John Pickering	3,189	41.0
	Joshua Wentworth	2,369	30.4
	Josiah Bartlett	1,676†	21.5
1791	Josiah Bartlett	8,679	96.8
1792	Josiah Bartlett	8,092	96.5
1793	Josiah Bartlett	7,388	75.0
	John Langdon	1,306	13.3
	John T. Gilman	708	7.2
1794	John T. Gilman	7,629	72.9
1795	John T. Gilman	9,340	98.9
1796	John T. Gilman (FED)	7,809	72.5
1797	John T. Gilman (FED)	9,625	88.9
1798	John T. Gilman (FED)	9,397	77.3
	Oliver Peabody (D-R)	1,189	9.8
	Timothy Walker	734	6.0
1799	John T. Gilman (FED)	10,138	86.4
1800	John T. Gilman (FED)	10,362	61.8
	Timothy Walker (D-R)	6,039	36.0
1801	John T. Gilman (FED)	10,898	65.5
	Timothy Walker (D-R)	5,249	31.5
1802	John T. Gilman (FED)	10,377	54.1
	John Langdon (D-R)	8,753	45.7
1803	John T. Gilman (FED)	12,263	57.5
	John Langdon (D-R)	9,011	42.3
1804	John T. Gilman (FED)	12,246	50.4
	John Langdon (D-R)	12,009	49.5
1805	John Langdon (D-R)	16,097	56.6
	John T. Gilman (FED)	12,287	43.2
1806	John Langdon (D-R)	15,277	74.3
	Timothy Farrar (FED)	1,720	8.4
	John T. Gilman (FED)	1,553	7.5
1807	John Langdon (D-R)	13,912	82.5
1808	John Langdon (D-R)	12,641	79.5
	John T. Gilman (FED)	1,261	7.9
1809	Jeremiah Smith (FED)	15,610	50.4
	John Langdon (D-R)	15,241	49.2
1810	John Langdon (D-R)	16,325	51.7
	Jeremiah Smith (FED)	15,166	48.0
1811	John Langdon (D-R)	17,554	54.7
	Jeremiah Smith (FED)	14,477	45.1
1812	John T. Gilman (FED)	15,613	48.8
	William Plumer (D-R)	15,492†	48.4
1813	John T. Gilman (FED)	18,107	50.7
	William Plumer (D-R)	17,410	48.7
1814	John T. Gilman (FED)	19,695	51.1
	William Plumer (D-R)	18,794	48.7
1815	John T. Gilman (FED)	18,357	50.7
	William Plumer (D-R)	17,799	49.2
1816	William Plumer (D-R)	20,338	53.0
	James Sheafe (FED)	17,994	46.9
1817	William Plumer (D-R)	19,088	54.0
	James Sheafe (FED)	12,029	34.0
	Jeremiah Mason (FED)	3,607	10.2
1818	William Plumer (D-R)	18,674	59.3
	Jeremiah Mason (FED)	6,850	21.8
	William Hale (FED)	5,019	16.0
1819	Samuel Bell (D-R)	13,761	56.7
	William Hale (FED)	8,660	35.7
1820	Samuel Bell (D-R)	22,212	89.7
1821	Samuel Bell (D-R)	22,582	92.4
1822	Samuel Bell (D-R)	22,934	95.6
1823	Levi Woodbury (D-R)	16,985	56.7
	Samuel Dinsmoor Sr. (D-R)	12,718	42.5
1824	David L. Morrill	14,429†	49.7
	Levi Woodbury	11,274	38.9
	Jeremiah Smith	2,868	9.9
1825	David L. Morrill	✔	
1826	David L. Morrill	17,528	58.8
	Benjamin Pierce	12,287	41.2

	Candidates	Votes	%		Candidates	Votes	%
1827	Benjamin Pierce	✔		1857	William Haile (R)	34,214	51.9
	David L. Morrill				John S. Wells (D)	31,209	47.4
1828	John Bell (NR)	21,784	52.7	1858	William Haile (R)	36,308	53.4
	Benjamin Pierce (JAC D)	19,562	47.3		Asa P. Cate (D)	31,597	46.5
1829	Benjamin Pierce (JAC D)	21,601	53.6	1859	Ichabod Goodwin (R)	36,296	52.5
	John Bell (NR)	18,708	46.4		Asa P. Cate (D)	32,802	47.5
1830	Matthew Harvey (JAC D)	22,502	54.9	1860	Ichabod Goodwin (R)	38,031	53.1
	Upham (NR)	18,490	45.1		Asa P. Cate (D)	33,543	46.9
1831	Samuel Dinsmoor (JAC D)	23,503	55.6	1861	Nathaniel S. Berry (R)	35,467	52.9
	Ichabod Bartlett (NR)	18,681	44.2		Stark (D)	31,452	46.9
1832	Samuel Dinsmoor (D)	24,175	62.3	1862	Nathaniel S. Berry (R)	32,150	51.5
	Ichabod Bartlett	14,604	37.7		Stark (D)	28,566	45.8
1833	Samuel Dinsmoor (D)	28,270	84.5	1863	Eastman (D)	32,833	49.6
1834	William Badger (D)	✔			Joseph A. Gilmore (R)	29,035†	43.8
1835	William Badger (D)	23,709	63.4		Harriman (UN)	4,372	6.6
	Joseph Healy	13,707	36.6	1864	Joseph A. Gilmore (UN)	37,006	54.2
1836	Isaac Hill (D)	✔			Edward W. Harrington (D)	31,340	45.9
1837	Isaac Hill (D)	✔		1865	Frederick Smyth (UN)	34,145	54.9
1838	Isaac Hill (D)	28,741	52.7		Edward W. Harrington (D)	28,017	45.0
	J. Wilson Jr. (W)	25,565	46.9	1866	Frederick Smyth (R)	35,137	53.5
1839	John Page (D)	30,466	55.9		John G. Sinclair (D)	30,481	46.4
	J. Wilson Jr. (W)	23,925	43.9	1867	Walter Harriman (R)	35,809	52.2
1840	John Page (D)	29,469	58.1		John G. Sinclair (D)	32,663	47.6
	Enos Stevens (W)	20,700	40.8	1868	Walter Harriman (R)	39,785	51.6
1841	John Page (D)	29,453	56.7		John G. Sinclair (D)	37,262	48.3
	Enos Stevens (W)	21,178	40.8	1869	Onslow Stearns (R)	35,777	52.8
1842	Henry Hubbard (D)	26,830	55.8		John Bedell (D)	32,004	47.2
	Enos Stevens (W)	12,364	25.7	1870	Onslow Stearns (R)	34,912	51.0
	John H. White (ID)	5,994	12.5		John Bedell (D)	25,023	36.6
	Daniel Hoit (AB)	2,756	5.7	1871	James A. Weston (D)	34,700†	49.8
1843	Henry Hubbard (D)	23,052	51.7		James Pike (R)	33,892	48.6
	Anthony Colby (W)	12,561	28.2	1872	Ezekiel A. Straw (R)	38,751	50.8
	John H. White (C)	5,497	12.3		James A. Weston (D)	36,584	47.9
	Daniel Hoit (AB)	3,416	7.7	1873	Ezekiel A. Straw (R)	34,023	50.2
1844	John H. Steele (D)	26,155	53.6		James A. Weston (D)	32,016	47.2
	Anthony Colby (W)	14,794	30.3	1874	James A. Weston (D)	35,608†	49.6
	Daniel Hoit (AB)	5,737	11.8		Luther McCutchins (R)	34,143	47.5
1845	John H. Steele (D)	23,298	51.3	1875	Person C. Cheney (R)	39,293†	49.6
	Anthony Colby (FEDL)	15,591	34.4		Hiram R. Roberts (D)	39,121	49.4
	Daniel Hoit (AB)	5,464	12.0	1876	Person C. Cheney (R)	41,761	52.0
1846	Jared W. Williams (D)	26,914	48.6		Marcy (D)	38,133	47.5
	Anthony Colby (W)	17,704†	32.0	1877	Benjamin F. Prescott (R)	40,757	52.3
	Nathaniel S. Berry (AB)	10,406	18.8		Marcy (D)	36,726	47.2
1847	Jared W. Williams (D)	30,806	50.9	1878	Benjamin F. Prescott (R)	39,372	50.6
	Anthony Colby (W)	21,109	34.9		McKean (D)	37,860	48.7
	Nathaniel S. Berry (AB)	8,531	14.1	1879	Natt Head (R)	38,175	50.3
1848	Jared W. Williams (D)	32,193	52.4		McKean (D)	31,135	41.0
	Nathaniel S. Berry (W FS)	28,819	46.9		W. S. Brown (N)	6,507	8.6
1849	Samuel Dinsmoor Jr. (D)	30,107	53.6	1880	Charles H. Bell (R)	44,434	51.6
	Levi Chamberlain (W)	18,764	33.4		Frank Jones (D)	40,815	47.4
	Nathaniel S. Berry (FS & SC)	7,162	12.8	1882	Samuel W. Hale (R)	38,399	50.4
1850	Samuel Dinsmoor Jr. (D)	30,683	55.1		M. V. B. Edgerly (D)	36,879	48.4
	Levi Chamberlain (W)	18,387	33.0	1884	Moody Currier (R)	42,514	50.3
	Nathaniel S. Berry (F SOIL)	6,556	11.8		Hill (D)	39,637	46.9
1851	Samuel Dinsmoor Jr. (D)	27,350†	47.1	1886	Charles H. Sawyer (R)	37,819†	48.9
	Thomas E. Sawyer (W)	18,407	31.7		Cogswell (D)	37,334	48.2
	John Atwood (F SOIL)	12,159	20.9	1888	David H. Goodell (R)	44,809†	49.5
1852	Noah Martin (D)	30,747	51.0		Charles H. Amsden (D)	44,217	48.8
	Thomas E. Sawyer (W)	19,850	32.9	1890	Hiram A. Tuttle (R)	42,479†	49.3
	John Atwood (F SOIL)	9,483	15.7		Charles H. Amsden (D)	42,386	49.2
1853	Noah Martin (D)	30,924	54.7	1892	John B. Smith (R)	43,676	50.2
	James Bell (W)	17,580	31.1		Luther F. McKinney (D)	41,501	47.7
	John H. White (F SOIL)	7,997	14.1	1894	Charles A. Busiel (R)	46,491	56.0
1854	Nathaniel B. Baker (D)	29,788	51.3		Henry O. Kent (D)	33,959	40.9
	James Bell (W)	17,028	29.4	1896	George A. Ramsdell (R)	48,387	61.4
	Jared Perkins (F SOIL)	11,081	19.1		Henry O. Kent (D)	28,333	36.0
1855	Ralph Metcalf (AM)	32,783	50.7	1898	Frank W. Rollins (R)	44,730	54.2
	Nathaniel B. Baker (D)	27,055	41.8		Charles F. Stone (D)	35,653	43.2
	James Bell (W)	3,436	5.3	1900	Chester B. Jordan (R)	53,891	59.4
1856	Ralph Metcalf (AM)	32,119†	48.2		Frederick E. Potter (D)	34,956	38.5
	John S. Wells (D)	32,031	48.0	1902	Nahum J. Bachelder (R)	42,115	53.2

	Candidates	Votes	%
	Henry F. Hollis (D)	33,844	*42.8*
1904	John McLane (R)	51,171	*57.8*
	Henry F. Hollis (D)	35,437	*40.1*
1906	Charles M. Floyd (R)	40,581†	*49.8*
	Nathan C. Jameson (D)	37,672	*46.2*
1908	Henry B. Quinby (R)	44,630	*50.4*
	Clarence E. Carr (D)	41,386	*46.7*
1910	Robert P. Bass (R)	44,908	*53.4*
	Clarence E. Carr (D)	37,737	*44.8*
1912	Samuel D. Felker (D)	34,203†	*41.1*
	Franklin Worcester (R)	32,504	*39.0*
	Winston Churchill (PROG)	14,401	*17.3*
1914	Rolland H. Spaulding (R)	46,413	*55.2*
	Albert W. Noone (D)	33,674	*40.0*
1916	Henry W. Keyes (R)	45,851	*53.2*
	John C. Hutchins (D)	38,853	*45.1*
1918	John H. Bartlett (R)	38,228	*54.1*
	Martin (D)	32,383	*45.9*
1920	Albert O. Brown (R)	93,273	*59.6*
	Charles E. Tilton (D)	62,174	*39.7*
1922	Fred H. Brown (D)	70,160	*53.3*
	Windsor H. Goodnow (R)	61,526	*46.7*
1924	John G. Winant (R)	88,650	*53.9*
	Fred H. Brown (D)	75,691	*46.1*
1926	Huntley N. Spaulding (R)	77,394	*59.7*
	Eaton D. Sargent (D)	52,236	*40.3*
1928	Charles W. Tobey (R)	108,431	*57.5*
	Eaton D. Sargent (D)	79,798	*42.3*
1930	John G. Winant (R)	75,518	*58.0*
	Albert W. Noone (D)	54,441	*41.8*
1932	John G. Winant (R)	106,777	*54.2*
	Henri Ledoux (D)	89,487	*45.4*
1934	H. Styles Bridges (R)	89,481	*50.6*
	John L. Sullivan (D)	87,019	*49.2*
1936	Francis P. Murphy (R)	118,178	*56.6*
	Amos Blandin (D)	89,011	*42.6*
1938	Francis P. Murphy (R)	107,841	*57.1*
	John L. Sullivan (D)	80,847	*42.8*
1940	Robert O. Blood (R)	112,386	*50.7*
	F. Clyde Keefe (D)	109,093	*49.3*
1942	Robert O. Blood (R)	83,766	*52.2*
	William J. Neal (D)	76,782	*47.8*
1944	Charles M. Dale (R)	115,799	*53.1*
	James J. Powers (D)	102,232	*46.9*
1946	Charles M. Dale (R)	103,204	*63.1*
	F. Clyde Keefe (D)	60,247	*36.9*
1948	Sherman Adams (R)	116,212	*52.2*
	Herbert W. Hill (D)	105,207	*47.3*
1950	Sherman Adams (R)	108,907	*57.0*
	Robert P. Bingham (D)	82,258	*43.0*
1952	Hugh Gregg (R)	167,791	*63.2*
	William H. Craig (D)	97,924	*36.9*
1954	Lane Dwinell (R)	107,287	*55.1*
	John Shaw (D)	87,344	*44.9*
1956	Lane Dwinell (R)	141,578	*54.7*
	John Shaw (D)	117,117	*45.3*
1958	Wesley Powell (R)	106,790	*51.7*
	Bernard L. Boutin (D)	99,955	*48.4*
1960	Wesley Powell (R)	161,123	*55.5*
	Bernard L. Boutin (D)	129,404	*44.5*
1962	John W. King (D)	135,481	*58.9*
	John Pillsbury (R)	94,567	*41.1*
1964	John W. King (D)	190,863	*66.8*
	John Pillsbury (R)	94,824	*33.2*
1966	John W. King (D)	125,882	*53.9*
	Hugh Gregg (R)	107,259	*45.9*
1968	Walter Peterson (R)	149,902	*52.5*
	Emile R. Bussiere (D)	135,378	*47.4*
1970	Walter Peterson (R)	102,298	*46.0*
	Roger J. Crowley Jr. (D)	98,098	*44.1*
	Meldrim Thomson Jr. (AM)	22,033	*9.9*

	Candidates	Votes	%
1972	Meldrim Thomson Jr. (R)	133,702	*41.4*
	Roger J. Crowley Jr. (D)	126,107	*39.0*
	Malcolm McLane (I)	63,199	*19.6*
1974	Meldrim Thomson Jr. (R)	115,933	*51.1*
	Richard W. Leonard (D)	110,591	*48.8*
1976	Meldrim Thomson Jr. (R)	197,589	*57.7*
	Harry V. Spanos (D)	145,015	*42.3*
1978	Hugh J. Gallen (D)	133,133	*49.4*
	Meldrim Thomson Jr. (R)	122,464	*45.4*
1980	Hugh J. Gallen (D)	226,436	*59.0*
	Meldrim Thomson Jr. (R)	156,178	*40.7*
1982	John H. Sununu (R)	145,389	*51.4*
	Hugh J. Gallen (D)	132,317	*46.8*
1984	John H. Sununu (R)	256,571	*66.8*
	Chris Spirou (D)	127,156	*33.1*

NEW JERSEY

(Ratified the Constitution Dec. 18, 1787)

	Candidates	Votes	%
1844[1]	Charles C. Stratton (W)	37,949	*50.9*
	Thompson (D)	36,591	*49.1*
1847	Daniel Haines (D)	34,765	*51.9*
	William Wright (W)	32,251	*48.1*
1850	George F. Fort (D)	39,723	*53.8*
	Runk (W)	34,054	*46.2*
1853	Rodman M. Price (D)	38,312	*52.6*
	Haywood (W)	34,530	*47.4*
1856	William A. Newell (FUS)	50,803	*51.3*
	Alexander (D)	48,246	*48.7*
1859	Charles S. Olden (R)	53,315	*50.8*
	Wright (D)	51,714	*49.2*
1862	Joel Parker (D)	61,307	*56.8*
	Marcus L. Ward (UN)	46,710	*43.2*
1865	Marcus L. Ward (UN)	67,525	*51.1*
	Runvon (D)	64,706	*48.9*
1868	Theodore F. Randolph (D)	83,955	*51.4*
	John I. Blair (R)	79,333	*48.6*
1871	Joel Parker (D)	82,362	*51.9*
	Cornelius Walsh (R)	76,383	*48.1*
1874	Joseph D. Bedle (D)	97,283	*53.7*
	Halsey (R)	84,050	*46.4*
1877	George B. McClellan (D)	97,837	*51.7*
	Newell (R)	85,094	*44.9*
1880	George C. Ludlow (D)	121,666	*49.5*
	Potts (R)	121,015	*49.3*
1883	Leon Abbett (D)	103,856	*49.9*
	Dixon (R)	97,047	*46.7*
1886	Robert S. Green (D)	109,939	*47.4*
	Howey (R)	101,919	*44.0*
	Fisk (P)	19,808	*8.6*
1889	Leon Abbett (D)	138,245	*51.4*
	Grubb (R)	123,992	*46.1*
1892	George T. Werts (D)	167,257	*49.7*
	John Kean Jr. (R)	159,632	*47.4*
1895	John W. Griggs (R)	162,900	*52.3*
	McGill (D)	136,000	*43.6*
1898	Foster M. Voorhees (R)	164,051	*48.9*
	Elvin W. Crane (D & CD)	158,552	*47.3*
1901	Franklin Murphy (R)	183,814	*50.9*
	James M. Seymour (D)	166,681	*46.1*
1904	Edward C. Stokes (R)	231,363	*53.5*
	Black (D)	179,719	*41.6*
1907	John Franklin Fort (R)	194,313	*49.3*
	Katzenbach (D)	186,300	*47.3*
1910	Woodrow Wilson (D)	233,682	*53.9*
	Vivian M. Lewis (R)	184,626	*42.6*

	Candidates	Votes	%
1913	James F. Fielder (D)	173,148	*46.1*
	Edward C. Stokes (R)	140,298	*37.4*
	Everett Colby (PROG)	41,132	*11.0*
1916	Walter E. Edge (R)	247,343	*55.4*
	Wittpenn (D)	177,696	*39.8*
1919	Edward I. Edwards (D)	217,486	*49.2*
	Newton A. K. Bugbee (R)	202,976	*45.9*
1922	George S. Silzer (D)	427,206	*52.2*
	Runyon (R)	383,312	*46.8*
1925	Arthur Harry Moore (D)	471,549	*51.9*
	Arthur Whitney (R)	433,121	*47.6*
1928	Morgan F. Larson (R)	824,005	*54.9*
	William L. Dill (D)	671,728	*44.7*
1931	Arthur Harry Moore (D)	735,504	*57.8*
	David Baird Jr. (R)	505,451	*39.7*
1934	Harold G. Hoffman (R)	686,530	*49.9*
	William L. Dill (D)	674,096	*49.0*
1937	Arthur Harry Moore (D)	746,033	*50.8*
	Lester H. Clee (R)	700,767	*47.8*
1940	Charles Edison (D)	984,407	*51.4*
	Robert C. Hendrickson (R)	920,512	*48.0*
1943	Walter E. Edge (R)	634,364	*55.2*
	Vincent J. Murphy (D)	506,604	*44.1*
1946	Alfred E. Driscoll (R)	807,378	*57.1*
	Lewis G. Hansen (D)	585,960	*41.4*
1949	Alfred E. Driscoll (R)	885,882	*51.5*
	Elmer H. Wene (D)	810,022	*47.1*
1953	Robert B. Meyner (D)	962,710	*53.2*
	Paul L. Troast (R)	809,068	*44.7*
1957	Robert B. Meyner (D)	1,101,130	*54.6*
	Malcolm S. Forbes (R)	897,321	*44.5*
1961	Richard J. Hughes (D)	1,084,194	*50.4*
	James P. Mitchell (R)	1,049,274	*48.7*
1965	Richard J. Hughes (D)	1,279,568	*57.4*
	Wayne Dumont Jr. (R)	915,996	*41.1*
1969	William T. Cahill (R)	1,411,905	*59.7*
	Robert B. Meyner (D)	911,003	*38.5*
1973	Brendan T. Byrne (D)	1,397,613	*66.4*
	Charles W. Sandman Jr. (R)	676,235	*32.1*
1977	Brendan T. Byrne (D)	1,184,564	*55.7*
	Raymond H. Bateman (R)	888,880	*41.8*
1981	Thomas H. Kean (R)	1,145,999	*49.5*
	James J. Florio (D)	1,144,202	*49.4*

1. Before 1844 governor chosen by Legislature.

NEW MEXICO

(Became a state Jan. 6, 1912)

	Candidates	Votes	%
1911	W. C. McDonald (D)	31,036	*51.0*
	Holm O. Bursum (R)	28,019	*46.1*
1916	Ezequiel C. deBaca (D)	32,875	*49.4*
	Holm O. Bursum (R)	31,552	*47.4*
1918	Octaviano A. Larrazolo (R)	23,752	*50.5*
	Felix Garcia (D)	22,433	*47.7*
1920	Merritt C. Mechem (R)	54,426	*51.3*
	Richard H. Hanna (D)	50,755	*47.8*
1922	James F. Hinkle (D)	60,317	*54.6*
	C. L. Hill (R)	49,363	*44.7*
1924	Arthur T. Hannett (D)	56,183	*48.8*
	Manuel B. Otero (R)	55,984	*48.6*
1926	Richard C. Dillon (R)	56,294	*51.6*
	Arthur T. Hannett (D)	52,523	*48.2*
1928	Richard C. Dillon (R)	65,967	*55.6*
	Robert C. Dow (D)	52,550	*44.3*
1930	Arthur Seligman (D)	62,789	*53.2*

	Candidates	Votes	%
	Clarence M. Botts (R)	55,026	*46.6*
1932	Arthur Seligman (D)	83,612	*54.8*
	Richard C. Dillon (R)	67,406	*44.2*
1934	Clyde Tingley (D)	78,390	*51.9*
	Jaffa Miller (R)	71,899	*47.6*
1936	Clyde Tingley (D)	97,090	*57.2*
	Jaffa Miller (R)	72,539	*42.8*
1938	John E. Miles (D)	82,344	*52.2*
	Albert K. Mitchell (R)	75,017	*47.6*
1940	John E. Miles (D)	103,035	*55.6*
	Maurice Miera (R)	82,306	*44.4*
1942	John J. Dempsey (D)	59,258	*54.6*
	Joseph F. Tondre (R)	49,380	*45.5*
1944	John J. Dempsey (D)	76,443	*51.8*
	Carroll G. Gunderson (R)	71,113	*48.2*
1946	Thomas J. Mabry (D)	70,055	*52.8*
	Edward L. Safford (R)	62,575	*47.2*
1948	Thomas J. Mabry (D)	103,969	*54.7*
	Manuel Lujan (R)	86,023	*45.3*
1950	Edwin L. Mechem (R)	96,846	*53.7*
	John E. Miles (D)	83,359	*46.3*
1952	Edwin L. Mechem (R)	129,116	*53.8*
	Everett Grantham (D)	111,034	*46.2*
1954	John F. Simms Jr. (D)	110,583	*57.0*
	Alvin Stockton (R)	83,373	*43.0*
1956	Edwin L. Mechem (R)	131,488	*52.2*
	John F. Simms Jr. (D)	120,263	*47.8*
1958	John Burroughs (D)	103,481	*50.5*
	Edwin L. Mechem (R)	101,567	*49.5*
1960	Edwin L. Mechem (R)	153,765	*50.3*
	John Burroughs (D)	151,777	*49.7*
1962	Jack M. Campbell (D)	130,933	*53.0*
	Edwin L. Mechem (R)	116,184	*47.0*
1964	Jack M. Campbell (D)	191,497	*60.2*
	Merle H. Tucker (R)	126,540	*39.8*
1966	David F. Cargo (R)	134,625	*51.7*
	T. E. Lusk (D)	125,587	*48.3*
1968	David F. Cargo (R)	160,140	*50.5*
	Fabian Chavez Jr. (D)	157,230	*49.5*
1970	Bruce King (D)	148,835	*51.3*
	Pete V. Domenici (R)	134,640	*46.4*
1974	Jerry Apodaca (D)	164,172	*49.9*
	Joseph R. Skeen (R)	160,430	*48.8*
1978	Bruce King (D)	174,631	*50.5*
	Joseph R. Skeen (R)	170,848	*49.4*
1982	Toney Anaya (D)	215,840	*53.0*
	John B. Irick (R)	191,626	*47.0*

NEW YORK

(Ratified the Constitution July 26, 1788)

	Candidates	Votes	%
1789	George Clinton	6,391	*51.7*
	Robert Yates	5,962	*48.3*
1792	George Clinton (ANTI-FED)[1]	8,440	*50.3*
	John Jay (FED)	8,332	*49.7*
1795	John Jay (FED)	13,481	*53.1*
	Robert Yates (ANTI-FED)[1]	11,892	*46.9*
1798	John Jay (FED)	16,012	*54.0*
	Robert R. Livingston (ANTI-FED)[1]	13,632	*46.0*
1801	George Clinton (D-R)	24,808	*54.3*
	Stephen Van Rensselaer (FED)	20,843	*45.7*
1804	Morgan Lewis (FED)	30,829	*58.2*
	Aaron Burr (D-R)	22,139	*41.8*
1807	Daniel Tompkins (D-R)	35,074	*53.1*
	Morgan Lewis (ANTI-CLINT)[2]	30,989	*46.9*
1810	Daniel Tompkins (D-R)	43,094	*54.2*
	Jonas Platt (ANTI-CLINT)[2]	36,484	*45.8*

Gubernatorial Elections

	Candidates	Votes	%		Candidates	Votes	%
1813	Daniel Tompkins (D-R)	43,324	52.2	1879	Alonzo B. Cornell (R)	418,567	46.7
	Stephen Van Rensselaer (FED)	39,718	47.8		Lucius Robinson (D)	375,790	41.9
1816	Daniel Tompkins (D-R)	45,412	54.0		John Kelly (TAM D)	77,566	8.7
	Rufus King (FED)	38,647	46.0	1882	Grover Cleveland (D)	535,318	58.5
					Charles J. Folger (R)	341,464	37.3
Special Election				1885	David B. Hill (D)	501,456	48.9
					Ira Davenport (R)	490,331	47.9
1817	De Witt Clinton (D-R)	43,310	96.7	1888	David B. Hill (D)	650,464	49.4
					Warner Miller (R)	631,303	48.0
1820	De Witt Clinton (CLINT R)	47,447	50.8	1891	Roswell P. Flower (D)	582,893	50.1
	Daniel Tompkins (ANTI-CL R)³	45,990	49.2		Jacob Sloat Fassett (R)	534,956	46.0
1822	Joseph C. Yates (D-R)	128,493	97.8	1894	Levi P. Morton (R)	673,818	53.1
1824	De Witt Clinton (CLINT R)	103,684	54.1		David B. Hill (D)	517,710	40.8
	Samuel Young (VB R)	88,037	45.9	1896	Frank S. Black (R)	774,253	55.3
1826	De Witt Clinton (CLINT R)	99,808	51.0		Wilbur E. Porter (D)	561,361	40.1
	William B. Rochester (VB R)	96,080	49.1	1898	Theodore Roosevelt (R)	661,707	49.0
1828	Martin Van Buren (JAC D)	136,795	49.5		Augustus Van Wyck (D)	643,921	47.7
	Smith Thompson (NR)	106,415	38.5	1900	Benjamin B. Odell Jr. (R)	804,859	52.0
	Solomon Southwick (A-MAS)	33,335	12.1		John B. Stanchfield (D)	693,733	44.8
1830	Enos T. Throop (JAC D)	128,947	51.7	1902	Benjamin B. Odell Jr. (R)	665,150	48.1
	Francis Granger (NR)	120,667	48.3		Bird S. Coler (D)	655,398	47.4
1832	William L. Marcy (JAC D)	166,410	51.5	1904	Frank W. Higgins (R)	813,264	50.3
	Francis Granger (NR)	156,672	48.5		D. Cady Herrick (D)	732,704	45.3
1834	William L. Marcy (D)	181,900	51.8	1906	Charles Evans Hughes (R)	749,002	50.5
	William H. Seward (W)	169,008	48.2		William R. Hearst (D, I LEAGUE)	691,105	46.6
1836	William L. Marcy (D)	166,218	54.9	1908	Charles Evans Hughes (R)	804,651	49.1
	Jesse Buel (W)	136,653	45.1		Lewis Stuyvesant Chanler (D)	735,189	44.8
1838	William H. Seward (W)	192,882	51.4	1910	John A. Dix (D)	689,700	48.0
	William L. Marcy (D)	182,461	48.6		Henry L. Stimson (R)	622,299	43.3
1840	Wiliam H. Seward (W)	222,011	50.3	1912	William Sulzer (D)	649,559	41.5
	William C. Bouck (D)	216,726	49.1		Job E. Hedges (R)	444,105	28.3
1842	William C. Bouck (D)	208,062	51.8		Oscar S. Straus (IL & NPR)	393,183	25.1
	Luther Bradish (W)	186,089	46.4	1914	Charles S. Whitman (R)	686,701	47.7
1844	Silas Wright (D)	241,087	49.5		Martin H. Glynn (D, I LEAGUE)	541,269	37.5
	Millard Fillmore (W)	231,060	47.4		William Sulzer (AM, P)	126,270	8.8
1846	John Young (W)	197,627	50.7	1916	Charles S. Whitman (R, N PROG)	850,020	52.6
	Silas Wright (D)	192,361	49.3		Samuel Seabury (D)	686,862	42.5
1848	Hamilton Fish (W)	218,280	47.9	1918	Alfred E. Smith (D)	1,009,936	47.4
	John Dix (F SOIL)	123,360	27.1		Charles S. Whitman (R, P)	995,094	46.6
	Reuben Walworth (D)	114,457	25.1		Charles W. Ervin (SOC)	121,705	5.7
1850	Washington Hunt (W-A-RENT)	214,614	49.6	1920	Nathan L. Miller (R)	1,335,878	46.6
	Horatio Seymour (D)	214,352	49.6		Alfred E. Smith (D)	1,261,812	44.0
1952	Horatio Seymour (D)	264,121	50.3		Joseph D. Cannon (SOC)	159,804	5.6
	Washington Hunt (W)	241,525	46.0	1922	Alfred E. Smith (D)	1,397,657	55.2
1854	Myron H. Clark (FUS R)	156,804	33.4		Nathan L. Miller (R)	1,011,725	40.0
	Horatio Seymour (SOFT D)	156,495	33.3	1924	Alfred E. Smith (D)	1,627,111	50.0
	Daniel Ullman (AM)	122,282	26.1		Theodore Roosevelt Jr. (R)	1,518,552	46.6
	Greene C. Bronson (HARD D)	33,850	7.2	1926	Alfred E. Smith (D)	1,523,813	52.3
1856	John A. King (R)	264,400	44.5		Ogden L. Mills (R)	1,276,137	43.8
	Amasa J. Parker (D)	198,616	33.4	1928	Franklin D. Roosevelt (D)	2,130,238	49.0
	Erastus Brooks (AM)	130,870	22.0		Albert Ottinger (R)	2,104,630	48.4
1858	Edwin D. Morgan (R)	247,868	45.5	1930	Franklin D. Roosevelt (D)	1,770,342	56.1
	Amasa J. Parker (D)	230,329	42.3		Charles H. Tuttle (R)	1,045,231	33.1
	Lorenzo Burrows (AM)	61,137	11.2		Robert P. Carroll (LAW PRES)	191,666	6.1
1860	Edwin D. Morgan (R)	358,002	53.2	1932	Herbert H. Lehman (D)	2,659,597	56.7
	William Kelly (DOUG D)	294,803	43.8		William J. Donovan (R)	1,812,002	38.6
1862	Horatio Seymour (D)	306,649	50.9	1934	Herbert H. Lehman (D)	2,201,727	57.8
	James S. Wadsworth (UN)	295,897	49.1		Robert Moses (R)	1,393,744	36.6
1864	Reuben E. Fenton (UN)	369,557	50.6	1936	Herbert H. Lehman (D, AM LAB)	2,970,595	53.5
	Horatio Seymour (D)	361,264	49.4		William F. Bleakley (R)	2,450,105	44.1
1866	Reuben E. Fenton (UN)	366,315	50.9	1938	Herbert H. Lehman (D, AM LAB)	2,391,331	50.4
	John T. Hoffman (D)	352,526	49.0		Thomas E. Dewey (R, I PROG)	2,326,892	49.0
1868	John T. Hoffman (D)	439,301	51.6	1942	Thomas E. Dewey (R)	2,148,546	52.1
	John A. Griswold (R)	411,355	48.4		John J. Bennett Jr. (D)	1,501,039	36.4
1870	John T. Hoffman (D)	399,552	51.9		Dean Alfange (AM LAB)	403,626	9.8
	Stewart L. Woodford (R)	366,436	47.6	1946	Thomas E. Dewey (R)	2,825,633	56.9
1872	John A. Dix (R)	445,801	53.2		James M. Mead (D, AM LAB)	2,138,482	43.1
	Francis Kernan (LR)	392,350	46.8	1950	Thomas E. Dewey (R)	2,819,523	53.1
1874	Samuel J. Tilden (D)	416,391	52.4		Walter A. Lynch (D, L)	2,246,855	42.3
	John A. Dix (R)	366,074	46.1	1954	Averell Harriman (D, L)	2,560,738	49.6
1876	Lucius Robinson (D)	519,832	51.3		Irving M. Ives (R)	2,549,613	49.4
	Edwin D. Morgan (R)	489,371	48.3				

518

	Candidates	Votes	%
1958	Nelson A. Rockefeller (R)	3,126,929	54.7
	Averell Harriman (D, L)	2,553,895#	44.7
1962	Nelson A. Rockefeller (R)	3,081,587	53.1
	Robert M. Morgenthau (D, L)	2,552,418	44.0
1966	Nelson A. Rockefeller (R)	2,690,626	44.6
	Frank O'Connor (D)	2,298,363	38.1
	Paul L. Adams (C)	510,023	8.5
	Franklin Roosevelt Jr. (L)	507,234	8.4
1970	Nelson A. Rockefeller (R, CSI)	3,151,432	52.4
	Arthur J. Goldberg (D, L)	2,421,426	40.3
	Paul L. Adams (C)	422,514	7.0
1974	Hugh L. Carey (D, L)	3,028,503	57.2
	Malcolm Wilson (R, C)	2,219,667	41.9
1978	Hugh L. Carey (D)	2,429,272	50.9
	Perry B. Duryea (R)	2,156,404	45.2
1982	Mario M. Cuomo (D)	2,675,213	50.9
	Lew Lehrman (R)	2,494,827	47.5

1. Anti-Federalist Party
2. Anti-Clinton Party
3. Anti-Clinton Republican Party

NORTH CAROLINA

(Ratified the Constitution Nov. 21, 1789)

	Candidates	Votes	%
1836[1]	Edward B. Dudley (W)	33,993	53.2
	Richard D. Spaight (D)	29,950	46.8
1838	Edward B. Dudley (W)	38,119	64.2
	John Branch (D)	21,155	35.6
1840	John M. Morehead (W)	44,514	55.0
	Romulus M. Saunders (D)	36,428	45.0
1842	John M. Morehead (W)	39,596	53.1
	Louis D. Henry (D)	35,024	46.9
1844	William A. Graham (W)	42,586	51.9
	Michael Hoke (D)	39,433	48.1
1846	William A. Graham (W)	43,486	55.0
	James B. Shepard (D)	35,627	45.0
1848	Charles Manly (W)	42,536	50.5
	David S. Reid (D)	41,682	49.5
1850	David S. Reid (D)	45,058	51.6
	Charles Manly (W)	42,341	48.5
1852	David S. Reid (D)	48,484	53.0
	John Kerr (W)	42,993	47.0
1854	Thomas Bragg (D)	48,705	51.1
	Alfred Dockery (W)	46,644	48.9
1856	Thomas Bragg (D)	57,698	56.2
	John A. Gilmer (AM)	44,970	43.8
1858	John W. Ellis (D)	56,429	58.5
	Duncan K. McCrae (DISTRIB)	40,036	41.5
1860	John W. Ellis (D)	59,396	52.7
	John Pool (W)	53,303	47.3
1862	Zebulon B. Vance	55,282	72.7
	William J. Johnston	20,813	27.4
1864	Zebulon B. Vance	58,070	80.0
	William W. Holden	14,491	20.0
1865	Jonathan Worth	32,539	55.7
	William W. Holden	25,809	44.2
1866	Jonathan Worth (C)	34,250	75.9
	Alfred Dockery (NC R)	10,759	23.8
1868	William W. Holden (R)	92,235	55.5
	Thomas S. Ashe (C)	73,600	44.3
1872	Tod R. Caldwell (R)	98,630	50.5
	Augustus S. Merrimon (D)	96,731	49.5
1876	Zebulon B. Vance (D)	123,265	52.8
	Thomas Settle (R)	110,061	47.2
1880	Thomas J. Jarvis (D)	121,837	51.3

	Candidates	Votes	%
	Ralph P. Buxton (R)	115,559	48.7
1884	Alfred M. Scales (D)	143,249	53.8
	Tyre York (R)	122,795	46.1
1888	Daniel G. Fowle (D)	148,405	52.0
	Oliver H. Dockery (R)	134,035	46.9
1892	Elias Carr (D)	135,327	48.3
	David M. Furches (R)	94,681	33.8
	Wyatt P. Exum (PP)	47,747	17.0
1896	Daniel L. Russell (R)	154,025	46.5
	Cyrus B. Watson (D)	145,286	43.9
	William A. Guthrie (PP)	30,943	9.4
1900	Charles B. Aycock (D)	186,650	59.6
	Spencer B. Adams (R)	126,296	40.3
1904	R. B. Glenn (D)	128,761	61.7
	C. J. Harris (R)	79,505	38.1
1908	W. W. Kitchin (D)	145,102	57.3
	J. E. Cox (R)	107,760	42.6
1912	Locke Craig (D)	149,972	61.4
	Iredell Meares (PROG)	49,925	20.4
	Thomas Settle (R)	43,627	17.9
1916	Thomas W. Bickett (D)	167,664	58.1
	Frank A. Linney (R)	120,157	41.7
1920	Cameron Morrison (D)	308,151	57.2
	John J. Parker (R)	230,193	42.8
1924	Angus Wilton McLean (D)	294,441	61.3
	I. M. Meekins (R)	185,578	38.7
1928	O. Max Gardner (D)	362,009	55.6
	H. F. Seawell (R)	289,415	44.4
1932	J. C. B. Ehringhaus (D)	497,708	70.1
	Clifford Frazier (R)	212,561	29.9
1936	Clyde R. Hoey (D)	542,139	66.7
	Gilliam Grissom (R)	270,943	33.3
1940	J. Melville Broughton (D)	608,744	75.7
	Robert H. McNeill (R)	195,402	24.3
1944	R. Gregg Cherry (D)	528,995	69.6
	Frank C. Patton (R)	230,968	30.4
1948	W. Kerr Scott (D)	570,995	73.2
	George M. Pritchard (R)	206,166	26.4
1952	William B. Umstead (D)	796,306	67.5
	H. F. Seawell Jr. (R)	383,329	32.5
1956	Luther H. Hodges (D)	760,480	67.0
	Kyle Hayes (R)	375,379	33.1
1960	Terry Sanford (D)	735,248	54.5
	Robert L. Gavin (R)	613,975	45.5
1964	Dan K. Moore (D)	790,343	56.6
	Robert L. Gavin (R)	606,165	43.4
1968	Robert W. Scott (D)	821,232	52.7
	James C. Gardner (R)	737,075	47.3
1972	James C. Holshouser Jr. (R)	767,470	51.0
	Hargrove Bowles Jr. (D)	729,104	48.5
1976	James B. Hunt (D)	1,081,293	65.0
	David T. Flaherty (R)	564,102	33.9
1980	James B. Hunt (D)	1,143,145	61.9
	Beverly Lake (R)	691,449	37.4
1984	James G. Martin (R)	1,208,167	54.3
	Rufus Edmisten (D)	1,011,209	45.4

1. Before 1836 governor chosen by General Assembly.

NORTH DAKOTA

(Became a state Nov. 2, 1889)

	Candidates	Votes	%
1889	John Miller (R)	25,365	66.6
	William Roach (D)	12,733	33.4
1890	Andrew H. Burke (R)	19,053	52.2
	William Roach (D)	12,604	34.6
	Muir (I)	4,821	13.2

	Candidates	Votes	%
1892	Eli C. D. Shortridge (FUS)	18,943	*52.4*
	Andrew H. Burke (R)	17,203	*47.6*
1894	Roger Allin (R)	23,723	*55.8*
	Wallace (POP)	9,354	*22.0*
	Kinter (D)	8,188	*19.2*
1896	Frank A. Briggs (R)	25,918	*55.6*
	R. B. Richardson (FUS)	20,690	*44.4*
1898	Frederick B. Fancher (R)	27,308	*58.4*
	Holmes (FUS)	19,496	*41.7*
1900	Frank White (R)	34,052	*59.2*
	M. A. Wipperman (D & I)	22,275	*38.7*
1902	Frank White (R)	31,613	*62.7*
	Cronan (D)	17,576	*34.9*
1904	Elmore Y. Sarles (R)	48,026	*70.7*
	M. F. Hegge (D)	16,744	*24.7*
1906	John Burke (D)	34,424	*53.2*
	Elmore Y. Sarles (R)	29,309	*45.3*
1908	John Burke (D)	49,398	*51.1*
	C. A. Johnson (R)	46,849	*48.4*
1910	John Burke (D)	47,005	*50.0*
	C. A. Johnson (R)	44,555	*47.4*
1912	Louis B. Hanna (R)	39,811	*45.5*
	F. O. Hellstrom (D)	31,544	*36.0*
	W. D. Sweet (PROG)	9,406	*10.7*
	A. E. Bowen Jr. (SOC)	6,835	*7.8*
1914	Louis B. Hanna (R)	44,279	*49.6*
	F. O. Hellstrom (D)	34,746	*38.9*
	J. A. Williams (SOC)	6,019	*6.7*
1916	Lynn J. Frazier (R)	87,665	*79.2*
	D. H. McArthur (D)	20,351	*18.4*
1918	Lynn J. Frazier (R & NP)	54,517	*59.7*
	S. J. Doyle (D & I)	36,733	*40.3*
1920	Lynn J. Frazier (R & NP)	117,018	*51.0*
	J. F. T. O'Connor (D & I)	112,488	*49.0*

Special Election

1921	Ragnvald A. Nestos (IR)	111,434	*50.9*
	Lynn J. Frazier (R & NP)	107,332	*49.1*
1922	Ragnvald A. Nestos (R)	110,321	*57.7*
	William Lemke (NON PART)	81,048	*42.4*
1924	Arthur G. Sorlie (R)	101,170	*53.9*
	Halvor L. Halvorson (D)	86,414	*46.1*
1926	Arthur G. Sorlie (R)	131,003	*81.7*
	D. M. Holmes (D)	24,287	*15.2*
1928	George F. Shafer (R)	131,193	*56.5*
	Walter Maddock (D)	100,205	*43.2*
1930	George F. Shafer (R)	133,264	*73.6*
	Pierce Blewett (D)	41,988	*23.2*
1932	William Langer (R)	134,231	*54.8*
	Herbert C. Depuy (D)	110,263	*45.0*
1934	Thomas H. Moodie (D)	145,433	*53.0*
	Lydia Langer (R)	127,954	*46.6*
1936	William Langer (I)	98,750	*35.8*
	Walter Welford (R)	95,697	*34.7*
	John Moses (D)	80,726	*29.3*
1938	John Moses (D)	138,270	*52.5*
	John N. Hagan (R)	125,246	*47.5*
1940	John Moses (D)	173,278	*63.1*
	Jack A. Patterson (R)	101,287	*36.9*
1942	John Moses (D)	101,390	*57.6*
	Oscar W. Hagen (R)	74,577	*42.4*
1944	Fred G. Aandahl (R)	107,863	*52.0*
	William T. Depuy (D)	59,961	*28.9*
	Alvin C. Strutz (IR)	38,997	*18.8*
1946	Fred G. Aandahl (R)	116,672	*68.9*
	Quentin Burdick (D)	52,719	*31.1*
1948	Fred G. Aandahl (R)	131,764	*61.3*
	Howard Henry (D)	80,655	*37.5*
1950	Norman Brunsdale (R)	121,822	*66.3*

	Candidates	Votes	%
	Clyde G. Byerly (D)	61,950	*33.7*
1952	Norman Brunsdale (R)	199,944	*78.7*
	Ole S. Johnson (D)	53,990	*21.3*
1954	Norman Brunsdale (R)	124,253	*64.2*
	Cornelius Bymers (D)	69,248	*35.8*
1956	John E. Davis (R)	147,566	*58.5*
	Wallace E. Warner (D)	104,869	*41.5*
1958	John E. Davis (R)	111,836	*53.1*
	John F. Lord (D)	98,763	*46.9*
1960	William L. Guy (D)	136,148	*49.4*
	C. P. Dahl (R)	122,486	*44.5*
	Herschel Lashkowitz (I)	16,741	*6.1*
1962	William L. Guy (D)	115,258	*50.4*
	Mark Andrews (R)	113,251	*49.6*
1964	William L. Guy (D)	146,414	*55.7*
	Don Halcrow (R)	116,247	*44.3*
1968	William L. Guy (D)	135,955	*54.8*
	Robert P. McCarney (R)	108,382	*43.7*
1972	Arthur A. Link (D)	143,899	*51.0*
	Richard Larsen (R)	138,032	*49.0*
1976	Arthur A. Link (D)	153,309	*51.6*
	Richard Elkin (R)	138,321	*46.5*
1980	Allen I. Olson (R)	162,230	*53.6*
	Arthur A. Link (D)	140,391	*46.4*
1984	George Sinner (D)	173,922	*55.3*
	Allen I. Olson (R)	140,460	*44.7*

OHIO

(Became a state March 1, 1803)

	Candidates	Votes	%
1803	Edward Tiffin (D-R)	4,564	
1805	Edward Tiffin (D-R)	4,783	
1807[1]	Return J. Meigs Jr. (D-R)	5,550	*53.8*
	Nathanael Massie (D-R)	4,757	*46.2*
1808	Samuel Huntington (D-R)	7,293	*44.8*
	Thomas Worthington (D-R)	5,601	*34.4*
	Thomas Kirker (D-R)	3,397	*20.9*
1810	Return J. Meigs Jr. (D-R)	9,924	*56.2*
	Thomas Worthington (D-R)	7,731	*43.8*
1812	Return J. Meigs Jr. (FED)	11,859	*60.0*
	Thomas Scott (D-R)	7,903	*40.0*
1814	Thomas Worthington (D-R)	15,879	*72.0*
	Othniel Looker (FED)	6,171	*28.0*
1816	Thomas Worthington (D-R)	22,931	*74.4*
	James Dunlap (D-R)	6,295	*20.4*
	Ethan A. Brown (FED)	1,607	*5.2*
1818	Ethan A. Brown (D-R)	30,194	*78.9*
	James Dunlap (D-R)	8,075	*21.1*
1820	Ethan A. Brown (D-R)	34,836	*71.3*
	Jeremiah Morrow (D-R)	9,426	*19.3*
	William H. Harrison (D-R)	4,348	*8.9*
1822	Jeremiah Morrow (D-R)	26,059	*43.4*
	Allen Trimble (FED)	22,889	*38.1*
	William W. Irwin (D-R)	11,060	*18.4*
1824	Jeremiah Morrow (JAC D)	38,328	*51.0*
	Allen Trimble (NR)	36,869	*49.0*
1826	Allen Trimble (NR)	70,475	*84.2*
	Alex Campbell	4,765	*5.7*
	Benjamin Tappan	4,209	*5.0*
1828	Allen Trimble (NR)	53,971	*51.4*
	John W. Campbell (JAC D)	51,004	*48.5*
1830	Duncan McArthur (NR)	49,677	*50.1*
	Robert Lucas (JAC D)	49,186	*49.6*
1832	Robert Lucas (D)	71,038	*52.9*
	Darius Lyman (NR)	63,213	*47.1*

	Candidates	Votes	%		Candidates	Votes	%
1834	Robert Lucas (D)	70,738	*51.2*	1899	George K. Nash (R)	417,199	*45.9*
	James Findlay (W)	67,414	*48.8*		John R. McLean (D)	368,176	*40.5*
1836	Joseph Vance (W)	92,204	*51.6*		Samuel M. Jones (NON PART)	106,721	*11.8*
	Eli Baldwin (D)	86,158	*48.3*	1901	George K. Nash (R)	436,092	*52.7*
1838	Wilson Shannon (D)	107,884	*51.4*		James Kilbourne (D)	368,525	*44.5*
	Joseph Vance (W)	102,146	*48.6*	1903	Myron T. Herrick (R)	475,560	*54.9*
1840	Thomas Corwin (W)	145,444	*52.9*		Tom L. Johnson (D)	361,748	*41.8*
	Wilson Shannon (D)	129,312	*47.1*	1905	John M. Pattison (D)	473,264	*50.5*
1842	Wilson Shannon (D)	119,774	*49.3*		Myron T. Herrick (R)	430,617	*46.0*
	Thomas Corwin (W)	117,902	*48.6*	1908	Judson Harmon (D)	552,569	*49.2*
1844	Mordecai Bartley (W)	146,333	*48.7*		Andrew L. Harris (R)	533,197	*47.5*
	David Tod (D)	145,062	*48.3*	1910	Judson Harmon (D)	477,077	*51.6*
1846	William Bebb (W)	118,857	*48.3*		Warren G. Harding (R)	376,700	*40.8*
	David Tod (D)	116,554	*47.3*		Tom Clifford (SOC)	60,637	*6.6*
1848	Seabury Ford (W)	148,766‡	*49.9*	1912	James M. Cox (D)	439,023	*42.4*
	John B. Weller (D)	148,452	*49.8*		Robert B. Brown (R)	272,500	*26.3*
1850	Reuben Wood (D)	133,093	*49.7*		Arthur·L. Garford (PROG)	217,903	*21.0*
	William Johnston (W)	121,105	*45.2*		C. E. Ruthenberg (SOC)	87,709	*8.5*
	Edward Smith (F SOIL)	13,747	*5.1*	1914	Frank B. Willis (R)	523,074	*46.3*
1851	Reuben Wood (D)	145,656	*51.6*		James M. Cox (D)	493,804	*43.7*
	Samuel F. Vinton (W)	119,550	*42.4*		James R. Garfield (PROG)	60,904	*5.4*
	Samuel Lewis (F SOIL)	16,910	*6.0*	1916	James M. Cox (D)	568,218	*48.4*
1853	William Medill (D)	147,663	*52.1*		Frank B. Willis (R)	561,602	*47.8*
	Nelson Barrere (W)	85,843	*30.3*	1918	James M. Cox (D)	486,403	*50.6*
	Samuel Lewis (F SOIL)	49,846	*17.6*		Frank B. Willis (R)	474,559	*49.4*
1855	Salmon P. Chase (R)	146,720	*48.6*	1920	Harry L. Davis (R)	1,039,835	*51.9*
	William Medill (D)	131,019	*43.4*		Vic Donahey (D)	918,962	*45.9*
	Allen Trimble (W)	24,276	*8.0*	1922	Vic Donahey (D)	821,948	*50.5*
1857	Salmon P. Chase (R)	160,685	*48.6*		Carmi A. Thompson (R)	804,200	*49.4*
	H. B. Payne (D)	159,294	*48.2*	1924	Vic Donahey (D)	1,065,981	*54.0*
1859	William Dennison Jr. (R)	184,502	*51.9*		Harry L. Davis (R)	888,139	*45.0*
	Rufus P. Ranney (D)	171,266	*48.1*	1926	Vic Donahey (D)	707,733	*50.5*
1861	David Tod (UN)	206,997	*57.7*		Myers Y. Cooper (R)	685,897	*49.0*
	Hugh J. Jewett (D)	151,774	*42.3*	1928	Myers Y. Cooper (R)	1,355,517	*54.8*
1863	John Brough (UN)	288,856	*60.6*		Martin L. Davey (D)	1,106,739	*44.7*
	C. L. Vallandigham (D)	187,728	*39.4*	1930	George White (D)	1,033,168	*52.8*
1865	Jacob D. Cox (UN)	223,642	*53.5*		Myers Y. Cooper (R)	923,538	*47.2*
	George W. Morgan (D)	193,791	*46.4*	1932	George White (D)	1,356,518	*52.8*
1867	Rutherford B. Hayes (R)	243,811	*50.3*		David S. Ingalls (R)	1,151,933	*44.9*
	A. G. Thurman (D)	240,622	*49.7*	1934	Martin L. Davey (D)	1,118,257	*51.1*
1869	Rutherford B. Hayes (R)	236,092	*50.7*		Clarence J. Brown (R)	1,052,851	*48.1*
	George H. Pendleton (D)	228,703	*49.1*	1936	Martin L. Davey (D)	1,539,461	*52.0*
1871	Edward F. Noyes (R)	238,273	*51.8*		John W. Bricker (R)	1,412,773	*47.7*
	George W. McCook (D)	218,105	*47.4*	1938	John W. Bricker (R)	1,265,548	*52.5*
1873	William Allen (D)	214,654	*47.8*		Charles Sawyer (D)	1,147,323	*47.6*
	Edward F. Noyes (R)	213,837	*47.6*	1940	John W. Bricker (R)	1,824,863	*55.6*
1875	Rutherford B. Hayes (R)	297,817	*50.3*		Martin L. Davey (D)	1,460,396	*44.5*
	William Allen (D)	292,279	*49.3*	1942	John W. Bricker (R)	1,086,937	*60.5*
1877	Richard M. Bishop (D)	271,642	*48.9*		John McSweeney (D)	709,599	*39.5*
	William H. West (R)	249,105	*44.9*	1944	Frank J. Lausche (D)	1,603,809	*51.8*
1879	Charles Foster (R)	336,321	*50.3*		James Garfield Stewart (R)	1,491,450	*48.2*
	Thomas Ewing (D)	319,132	*47.7*	1946	Thomas J. Herbert (R)	1,166,550	*50.6*
1881	Charles Foster (R)	312,785	*50.1*		Frank J. Lausche (D)	1,125,997	*48.9*
	John W. Bookwalter (D)	288,426	*46.2*	1948	Frank J. Lausche (D)	1,619,775	*53.7*
1883	George Hoadly (D)	359,693	*50.1*		Thomas J. Herbert (R)	1,398,514	*46.3*
	Joseph B. Foraker (R)	347,164	*48.3*	1950	Frank J. Lausche (D)	1,522,249	*52.6*
1885	Joseph B. Foraker (R)	359,281	*49.1*		Don H. Ebright (R)	1,370,570	*47.4*
	George Hoadly (D)	341,830	*46.8*	1952	Frank J. Lausche (D)	2,015,110	*55.9*
1887	Joseph B. Foraker (R)	356,534	*47.9*		Charles P. Taft (R)	1,590,058	*44.1*
	Thomas E. Powell (D)	333,205	*44.8*	1954	Frank J. Lausche (D)	1,405,262	*54.1*
1889	James E. Campbell (D)	379,423	*48.9*		James A. Rhodes (R)	1,192,528	*45.9*
	Joseph B. Foraker (R)	368,551	*47.5*	1956	C. William O'Neill (R)	1,984,988	*56.0*
1891	William McKinley Jr. (R)	386,739	*48.6*		Michael V. DiSalle (D)	1,557,103	*44.0*
	James E. Campbell (D)	365,228	*45.9*	1958	Michael V. DiSalle (D)	1,869,260	*56.9*
1893	William McKinley Jr. (R)	433,342	*52.6*		C. William O'Neill (R)	1,414,874	*43.1*
	Lawrence T. Neal (D)	352,347	*42.8*	1962	James A. Rhodes (R)	1,836,432	*58.9*
1895	Asa S. Bushnell (R)	427,141	*51.0*		Michael V. DiSalle (D)	1,280,521	*41.1*
	James E. Campbell (D)	334,519	*40.0*	1966	James A. Rhodes (R)	1,795,277	*62.2*
	Jacob S. Coxey (PP)	52,625	*6.3*		Frazier Reams Jr. (D)	1,092,054	*37.8*
1897	Asa S. Bushnell (R)	429,915	*50.3*	1970	John J. Gilligan (D)	1,725,560	*54.2*
	Horace L. Chapman (D)	401,750	*47.0*		Roger Cloud (R)	1,382,659	*43.4*

	Candidates	Votes	%
1974	James A. Rhodes (R)	1,493,679	48.6
	John J. Gilligan (D)	1,482,191	48.2
1978	James A. Rhodes (R)	1,402,167	49.3
	Richard F. Celeste (D)	1,354,631	47.6
1982	Richard F. Celeste (D)	1,981,882	59.0
	Clarence Brown Jr. (R)	1,303,962	38.8

1. The election was challenged by Massie. The Legislature eventually declared Meigs ineligible and arranged for a new election in 1808. Pending the outcome of that election, Speaker of the Senate Thomas Kirker was acting governor.

OKLAHOMA

(Became a state Nov. 16, 1907)

	Candidates	Votes	%
1907	Charles N. Haskell (D)	137,633	53.4
	Frank Frantz (R)	110,296	42.8
1910	Lee Cruce (D)	119,873	48.6
	J. W. McNeal (R)	99,319	40.2
	J. T. Crumbie (SOC)	24,457	9.9
1914	Robert L. Williams (D)	100,596	39.7
	John Fields (R)	95,909	37.8
	Fred W. Holt (SOC)	52,704	20.8
1918	James B. A. Robertson (D)	104,132	53.5
	Horace G. McKeever (R)	82,905	42.6
1922	John C. Walton (D)	280,207	54.5
	John Fields (R)	230,469	44.8
1926	Henry S. Johnston (D)	213,162	54.9
	Omer K. Benedict (R)	171,710	44.2
1930	William H. Murray (D)	301,921	59.1
	Ira A. Hill (R)	208,575	40.8
1934	E. W. Marland (D)	365,992	58.2
	William B. Pine (R)	243,936	38.8
1938	Leon C. Phillips (D)	355,740	70.0
	Ross Rizley (R)	148,861	29.3
1942	Robert S. Kerr (D)	196,565	51.9
	William J. Otjen (R)	180,454	47.6
1946	Roy J. Turner (D)	259,491	52.5
	Olney F. Flynn (R)	227,426	46.0
1950	Johnston Murray (D)	329,308	51.1
	Jo O. Ferguson (R)	313,205	48.6
1954	Raymond Gary (D)	357,386	58.7
	Reuben K. Sparks (R)	251,808	41.3
1958	J. Howard Edmondson (D)	399,504	74.1
	Phil Ferguson (R)	107,495	20.0
	D. A. Jelly Boyce (I)	31,840	5.9
1962	Henry Bellmon (R)	392,316	55.3
	W. P. Atkinson (D)	315,357	44.4
1966	Dewey F. Bartlett (R)	377,078	55.7
	Preston J. Moore (D)	296,328	43.8
1970	David Hall (D)	338,338	48.4
	Dewey F. Bartlett (R)	336,157	48.1
1974	David L. Boren (D)	514,389	63.9
	James M. Inhofe (R)	290,459	36.1
1978	George Nigh (D)	402,240	51.7
	Ron Shotts (R)	367,055	47.2
1982	George Nigh (D)	548,159	62.1
	Tom Daxon (R)	332,207	37.6

OREGON

(Became a state Feb. 14, 1859)

	Candidates	Votes	%
1858	John Whiteaker (D)	5,134	54.7
	E. M. Barnum (OPP)	4,213	44.9

	Candidates	Votes	%
1862	A. C. Gibbs (UN R)	7,039	67.1
	John F. Miller (D)	3,450	32.9
1866	George L. Woods (R)	10,316	50.7
	James K. Kelly (D)	10,039	49.3
1870	La Fayette Grover (D)	11,726	51.4
	Joel Palmer (R)	11,095	48.6
1874	La Fayette Grover (D)	9,713	38.2
	J. C. Tolman (R)	9,163	36.1
	Thomas F. Campbell (I)	6,532	25.7
1878	William Wallace Thayer (D)	15,689	47.9
	C. C. Beekman (R)	15,610	47.7
1882	Zenas F. Moody (R)	21,481	51.8
	Smith (D)	20,029	48.3
1886	Sylvester Pennoyer (D)	27,901	50.9
	T. R. Cornelius (R)	24,199	44.1
1890	Sylvester Pennoyer (D)	38,920	53.6
	D. P. Thompson (R)	33,765	46.5
1894	William P. Lord (R)	41,139	47.2
	Nathan Pierce (PP)	26,125	30.0
	William Galloway (D)	17,865	20.5
1898	Theodore Thurston Geer (R)	45,094	53.2
	W. R. King (D-PP)	34,542	40.8
1902	George E. Chamberlain (D)	41,857	46.2
	W. J. Furnish (R)	41,611	45.9
1906	George E. Chamberlain (D)	46,002	47.6
	James Withycombe (R)	43,508	45.0
	C. W. Barzee (SOC)	4,468	5.0
1910	Oswald West (D)	54,853	46.6
	Jay Bowerman (R)	48,751	41.4
	W. S. Richards (SOC)	8,040	6.8
	A. E. Eaton (P)	6,046	5.1
1914	James Withycombe (R)	121,037	48.8
	C. J. Smith (D)	94,594	38.1
	W. J. Smith (SOC)	14,284	5.8
1918	James Withycombe (R)	81,067	53.0
	Walter M. Pierce (D)	65,440	42.8
1922	Walter M. Pierce (D)	133,392	57.4
	Ben W. Olcott (R)	99,164	42.6
1926	I. L. Patterson (R)	120,073	53.1
	Walter M. Pierce (D)	93,470	41.4
	H. H. Stallard (I)	12,402	5.5
1930	Julius L. Meier (I)	135,608	54.5
	Ed F. Bailey (D)	62,434	25.1
	Phil Metschan (R)	46,840	18.8
1934	Charles H. Martin (D)	116,677	38.6
	Peter Zimmerman (I)	95,519	31.6
	Joe E. Dunne (R)	86,923	28.7
1938	Charles A. Sprague (R)	214,062	57.4
	Henry L. Hess (D)	158,744	42.6
1942	Earl Snell (R)	220,188	77.9
	Lew Wallace (D)	62,561	22.1
1946	Earl Snell (R)	237,681	69.1
	Carl C. Donaugh (D)	106,474	30.9

Special Election

1948	Douglas McKay (R)	271,295	53.2
	Lew Wallace (D)	226,949	44.5

1950	Douglas McKay (R)	334,160	66.1
	Austin F. Flegal (D)	171,750	34.0
1954	Paul Patterson (R)	322,522	56.9
	Joseph K. Carson Jr. (D)	244,179	43.1

Special Election

1956	Robert D. Holmes (D)	369,439	50.5
	Elmo Smith (R)	361,840	49.5

1958	Mark O. Hatfield (R)	331,900	55.3
	Robert D. Holmes (D)	267,934	44.7

	Candidates	Votes	%
1962	Mark O. Hatfield (R)	345,497	*54.2*
	Robert Y. Thornton (D)	265,359	*41.6*
1966	Tom McCall (R)	377,346	*55.3*
	Robert W. Straub (D)	305,008	*44.7*
1970	Tom McCall (R)	369,964	*55.6*
	Robert W. Straub (D)	293,892	*44.2*
1974	Robert W. Straub (D)	444,812	*57.7*
	Victor Atiyeh (R)	324,751	*42.1*
1978	Victor Atiyeh (R)	498,452	*54.9*
	Robert W. Straub (D)	409,411	*44.9*
1982	Victor Atiyeh (R)	639,841	*61.4*
	Ted Kulongoski (D)	374,316	*35.9*

PENNSYLVANIA

(Ratified the Constitution Dec. 12, 1787)

	Candidates	Votes	%
1790	Thomas Mifflin	27,725	*90.8*
	Arthur St. Clair (FED)	2,802	*9.2*
1793	Thomas Mifflin (D-R)	18,590	*63.5*
	Frederick A. Muhlenberg (FED)	10,706	*36.5*
1796	Thomas Mifflin (D-R)	30,020	*96.7*
1799	Thomas McKean (D-R)	38,036	*53.8*
	James Ross (FED)	32,641	*46.2*
1802	Thomas McKean (D-R)	47,849	*73.6*
	James Ross (FED)	17,037	*26.2*
1805	Thomas McKean (I D-R)[1]	43,644	*52.9*
	Simon Snyder (D-R)	38,833	*47.1*
1808	Simon Snyder (D-R)	67,975	*60.9*
	James Ross (FED)	39,575	*35.5*
1811	Simon Snyder (D-R)	52,319	*90.8*
	William Tilghman (FED)	3,609	*6.3*
1814	Simon Snyder (D-R)	51,009	*62.6*
	Isaac Wayne (FED)	29,566	*36.3*
1817	William Findlay (D-R)	66,331	*52.8*
	Joseph Hiester (D-R/FED)	59,272	*47.2*
1820	Joseph Hiester (D-R)	67,905	*50.6*
	William Findlay (D-R)	66,300	*49.4*
1823	John Andrew Schulze (D-R)	89,928	*58.3*
	Andrew Gregg (FED)	64,211	*41.7*
1826	John Andrew Schulze (JAC D)	72,710	*96.9*
1829	George Wolf (JAC D)	78,138	*60.1*
	Joseph Ritner (A-MAS)	51,776	*39.9*
1832	George Wolf (D)	91,385	*50.9*
	Joseph Ritner (A-MAS)	88,115	*49.1*
1835	Joseph Ritner (D)	94,023	*46.9*
	George Wolf (W)	65,804	*32.8*
	Henry Muhlenburgh	40,586	*20.3*
1838	David R. Porter (D)	127,821	*51.1*
	Joseph Ritner (A-MASC)	122,325	*48.9*
1841	David R. Porter (D)	136,504	*54.4*
	John Banks (W)	113,453	*45.3*
1844	Francis R. Shunk (D)	160,322	*50.3*
	Joseph Markle (W)	156,041	*48.9*
1847	Francis R. Shunk (D)	146,081	*50.8*
	James Irwin (W)	128,148	*44.6*
1848	William F. Johnston (W)	168,522	*50.0*
	Morris Longstreth (D)	168,225	*50.0*
1851	William Bigler (D)	186,499	*50.9*
	William F. Johnston (W)	178,034	*48.6*
1854	James Pollock (W)	203,822	*54.6*
	William Bigler (D)	166,991	*44.8*
1857	William F. Packer (D)	188,836	*52.0*
	David Wilmot (R)	146,139	*40.2*
	Isaac Hazlehurst (AM)	28,168	*7.8*
1860	Andrew G. Curtin (R)	262,403	*53.3*

	Candidates	Votes	%
	Henry D. Foster (D)	230,269	*46.7*
1863	Andrew G. Curtin (R)	269,496	*51.5*
	George W. Woodward (D)	254,171	*48.5*
1866	John White Geary (R)	307,274	*51.4*
	Hiester Clymer (D)	290,096	*48.6*
1869	John White Geary (R)	290,552	*50.4*
	Asa Packer (D)	285,956	*49.6*
1872	John Frederick Hartranft (R)	353,387	*52.6*
	Charles B. Buckalew (D)	317,823	*47.3*
1875	John Frederick Hartranft (R)	304,175	*49.9*
	Cyrus L. Pershing (D)	292,136	*47.9*
1878	Henry Martyn Hoyt (R)	319,567	*45.5*
	Andrew H. Dill (D)	297,060	*42.3*
	Samuel R. Mason (G)	81,758	*11.6*
1882	Robert E. Pattison (D)	355,791	*47.8*
	James A. Beaver (R)	315,589	*42.4*
	John Stewart (IR)	43,743	*5.9*
1886	James A. Beaver (R)	412,285	*50.3*
	Chauncey F. Black (D)	369,634	*45.1*
1890	Robert E. Pattison (D)	464,209	*50.0*
	George W. Delamater (R)	447,655	*48.2*
1894	Daniel H. Hastings (R)	574,801	*60.3*
	William M. Singerly (D)	333,404	*35.0*
1898	William A. Stone (R)	476,206	*49.0*
	George A. Jenks (D)	358,300	*36.9*
	Silas C. Swallow (P, HG)	132,931	*13.7*
1902	Samuel W. Pennypacker (R)	592,867	*54.2*
	Robert E. Pattison (D)	436,451	*39.9*
1906	Edwin S. Stuart (R)	506,418	*50.3*
	Lewis Emery Jr. (D, LINCOLN)	458,064	*45.5*
1910	John K. Tener (R)	412,658	*41.3*
	William H. Berry (KEY)	382,127	*38.3*
	Webster Grim (D)	129,395	*13.0*
	John W. Slayton (SOC)	53,055	*5.3*
1914	Martin G. Brumbaugh (R, KEY)	588,705	*53.0*
	Vance C. McCormick (D, WASH)	453,880	*40.8*
1918	William Sproul (R, WASH)	552,537	*61.1*
	Eugene C. Bonniwell (D, F PLAY)	305,315	*33.7*
1922	Gifford Pinchot (R)	831,696	*56.8*
	John A. McSparran (D)	581,625	*39.7*
1926	John S. Fisher (R)	1,102,823	*73.3*
	Eugene C. Bonniwell (D, LAB)	365,280	*24.3*
1930	Gifford Pinchot (R, P)	1,068,874	*50.8*
	John M. Hemphill (D, L)	1,010,204	*47.7*
1934	George H. Earle (D)	1,476,377	*50.0*
	William A. Schnader (R)	1,410,138	*47.8*
1938	Arthur H. James (R)	2,036,345	*53.4*
	Charles Jones (D, ROYAL OAK)	1,756,280	*46.1*
1942	Edward Martin (R)	1,367,531	*53.7*
	F. Clair Ross (D)	1,149,897	*45.1*
1946	James H. Duff (R)	1,828,462	*58.5*
	John S. Rice (D)	1,270,947	*40.7*
1950	John S. Fine (R)	1,796,119	*50.7*
	Richardson Dilworth (D)	1,710,355	*48.3*
1954	George M. Leader (D)	1,996,266	*53.7*
	Lloyd H. Wood (R)	1,717,070	*46.2*
1958	David L. Lawrence (D)	2,024,852	*50.8*
	Arthur T. McGonigle (R)	1,948,769	*48.9*
1962	William W. Scranton (R)	2,424,918	*55.4*
	Richardson Dilworth (D)	1,938,627	*44.3*
1966	Raymond P. Shafer (R)	2,110,349	*52.1*
	Milton Shapp (D)	1,868,719	*46.1*
1970	Milton Shapp (D)	2,043,029	*55.2*
	Raymond J. Broderick (R)	1,542,854	*41.7*
1974	Milton Shapp (D)	1,878,252	*53.8*
	Andrew L. Lewis Jr. (R)	1,578,917	*45.2*
1978	Richard L. Thornburgh (R)	1,966,042	*52.5*
	Peter Flaherty (D)	1,737,888	*46.4*
1982	Richard L. Thornburgh (R)	1,872,784	*50.8*
	Allen E. Ertel (D)	1,772,353	*48.1*

1. Independent Democratic Republican.

RHODE ISLAND

(Ratified the Constitution May 29, 1790)

	Candidates	Votes	%
1790-1796	Arthur Fenner	✓	
1797	Arthur Fenner	1,204	
1798-1800	Arthur Fenner	✓	
1801	Arthur Fenner	3,756	
1802	Arthur Fenner	3,802	66.3
	William Greene	1,934	33.7
1803-1805	Arthur Fenner	✓	
1806	Richard Jackson Jr.	1,662*	43.1
	Henry Smith	1,097	28.4
	Peleg Arnold	1,094	28.3
1807	James Fenner	2,564	65.9
	Seth Wheaton	1,268	32.6
1808-1810	James Fenner	✓	
1811	William Jones (FED)	3,885	51.1
	James Fenner	3,651	48.1
1812	William Jones (FED)	4,122	51.5
	James Fenner	3,874	48.4
1813	William Jones	3,350	
1814	William Jones	2,713	76.6
1815	William Jones (FED)	3,372	56.6
	Peleg Arnold (D-R)	2,588	43.4
1816	William Jones (FED)	3,591	52.4
	Nehemiah R. Knight (D-R)	3,259	47.6
1817	Nehemiah R. Knight (D-R)	3,949	50.4
	William Jones (FED)	3,878	49.5
1818	Nehemiah R. Knight (D-R)	4,509	53.7
	Elisha R. Potter (FED)	3,893	46.3
1819	Nehemiah R. Knight	2,664	
1820	Nehemiah R. Knight	1,981	100.0
1821	William C. Gibbs (D-R)	3,801	57.6
	Samuel W. Bridgham	2,801[1]	
1822	William C. Gibbs	2,092	100.0
1823	William C. Gibbs	1,647	100.0
1824	James Fenner	2,146	78.3
	Wheeler Martin	594	21.7
1825	James Fenner	1,731	100.0
1826	James Fenner	✓	
1827	James Fenner	2,421	100.0
1828	James Fenner	4,233	100.0
1829	James Fenner	3,584	100.0
1830	James Fenner	2,793	63.1
	Asa Messer	1,455	32.9
1831	Lemuel H. Arnold	3,780	56.8
	James Fenner	2,877	43.2
1832	Lemuel H. Arnold	2,711*	48.5
	James Fenner	2,283	40.8
	William Sprague	592	10.6
1833	John Brown Francis	4,025	55.0
	Lemuel H. Arnold	3,292	45.0
1834	John Brown Francis	3,676	51.0
	Nehemiah R. Knight	3,520	48.9
1835	John Brown Francis	3,880	50.7
	Nehemiah R. Knight	3,774	49.3
1836	John Brown Francis	4,020	56.2
	Tristam Burges	2,984	41.7
1837	John Brown Francis	2,716	73.1
	William Peckham	946	25.5
1838	William Sprague	3,984	52.5
	John Brown Francis	3,504	46.2
1839	William Sprague	2,948*	47.4
	Nathaniel Bullock	2,771	44.6
	Tristam Burges	457	7.4
1840	Samuel Ward King (W)	4,797	58.4
	Thomas F. Carpenter	3,418	41.6
1841	Samuel Ward King (W)	2,648	97.7
1842	Samuel Ward King (W)	4,866	67.9
	Thomas F. Carpenter	2,291	32.0

	Candidates	Votes	%
1843	James Fenner (L & O W)	9,140	55.3
	Thomas F. Carpenter (D)	7,393	44.7
1844	James Fenner (LAW ORD)	5,560	96.4
1845	Charles Jackson (LIBER W)	7,900	50.4
	James Fenner (L & O W)	7,699	49.2
1846	Byron Diman (L & O W)	7,477†	49.8
	Charles Jackson (D & LIBN)	7,391	49.2
1847	Elisha Harris (W)	6,300	55.3
	Olney Ballou (D)	4,350	38.2
1848	Elisha Harris (W)	5,695	58.0
	Adnah Sackett (D)	3,683	37.5
1849	Henry B. Anthony (W)	5,081	59.0
	Adnah Sackett (D)	2,964	34.4
	Edward Harris (F SOIL)	458	5.3
1850	Henry B. Anthony (W)	3,629	80.2
	Edward Harris (F SOIL)	761	16.8
1851	Philip Allen (D)	6,958	52.6
	Josiah Chapin (W)	6,071	45.9
1852	Philip Allen (D)	9,184	51.2
	Elisha Harris (W)	8,746	48.8
1853	Philip Allen (D)	10,371	54.2
	William W. Hoppin (W)	8,228	43.0
1854	William W. Hoppin (W)	9,112	58.4
	Francis M. Dimond (D)	6,484	41.6
1855	William W. Hoppin (W & AM)	10,466	81.5
	Americus V. Potter (D)	2,306	18.0
1856	William W. Hoppin (AM & R)	10,035	58.3
	Americus V. Potter (D)	7,158	41.6
1857	Elisha Dyer (R)	9,621	65.3
	Americus V. Potter (D)	5,123	34.8
1858	Elisha Dyer (R)	7,934	69.0
	Elisha R. Potter (D)	3,572	31.0
1859	Thomas G. Turner (R)	8,904	71.3
	Elisha R. Potter (D)	3,567	28.6
1860	William Sprague (FUS)	12,295	52.8
	Seth Padelford (R)	10,835	46.6
1861	William Sprague (UN)	11,844	53.7
	James Y. Smith (R)	10,200	46.3
1862	William Sprague (UN)	11,195	99.5
1863	James Y. Smith (R)	10,828	58.0
	William C. Cozzens (D & CST)	7,537	40.4
1864	James Y. Smith (UN R)	8,840	50.4
	George H. Browne (D)	7,302	41.7
	Amos C. Barstow (CONST)	1,339	7.6
1865	James Y. Smith (UN R)	10,061	93.0
1866	Ambrose E. Burnside (R)	8,197	73.3
	Lymon Pierce (D)	2,816	25.2
1867	Ambrose E. Burnside (R)	7,372	69.9
	Lymon Pierce (D)	3,178	30.1
1868	Ambrose E. Burnside (R)	10,038	63.7
	Lymon Pierce (D)	5,731	36.3
1869	Seth Padelford (R)	7,370	68.5
	Lymon Pierce (D)	3,390	31.5
1870	Seth Padelford (R)	10,493	62.5
	Lymon Pierce (D)	6,295	37.5
1871	Seth Padelford (R)	8,838	62.2
	Thomas Steere (D)	5,367	37.8
1872	Seth Padelford (R)	9,455	53.6
	Olney Arnold (D)	8,193	46.4
1873	Henry Howard (R)	9,656	71.8
	Benjamin G. Chace (D)	3,786	28.2
1874	Henry Howard (R)	12,335	87.5
	Lymon Pierce (D)	1,589	11.3
1875	Rowland Hazard (I)	8,724	39.2
	Henry Lippitt (R)	8,368†	37.6
	Charles R. Cutler (D)	5,166	23.2
1876	Henry Lippitt (R)	8,689†	45.6
	Albert C. Howard (P)	6,733	35.4
	William B. Beach (D)	3,599	18.9
1877	Charles C. Van Zandt (R & TEMP)	12,455	50.9
	Jerothmul B. Barnaby (D)	11,783	48.2

	Candidates	Votes	%
1878	Charles C. Van Zandt (R & TEMP)	11,454	58.1
	Isaac Lawrence (D)	7,639	38.8
1879	Charles C. Van Zandt (R & TEMP)	9,717	62.1
	Thomas W. Segar (D)	5,506	35.2
1880	Alfred H. Littlefield (R)	10,224†	44.8
	Horace A. Kimball (D)	7,440	32.6
	Albert C. Howard (IR & P)	5,047	22.1
1881	Alfred H. Littlefield (R)	10,849	67.0
	Horace A. Kimball (D)	4,756	29.4
1882	Alfred H. Littlefield (R)	10,056	64.8
	Horace A. Kimball (D)	5,311	34.2
1883	Augustus O. Bourn (R)	13,078	54.5
	William Sprague (D)	10,201	42.5
1884	Augustus O. Bourn (R)	15,936	62.4
	Thomas W. Segar (D)	9,592	37.6
1885	George Peabody Wetmore (R)	12,563	56.0
	Ziba O. Slocum (D)	8,674	38.6
	George H. Slade (P)	1,206	5.4
1886	George Peabody Wetmore (R)	14,340	53.4
	Amasa Sprague (D)	9,994	37.0
	George H. Slade (P)	2,585	9.6
1887	John W. Davis (D)	18,095	51.5
	George Peabody Wetmore (R)	15,111	43.0
	Thomas H. Peabody (P)	1,895	5.4
1888	Royal C. Taft (R)	20,744	52.3
	John W. Davis (D)	17,556	44.3
1889	John W. Davis (D)	21,289	49.4
	Herbert W. Ladd (R)	16,870†	39.1
	James H. Chace (LAW ENF)	3,596	8.3
1890	John W. Davis (D)	20,548†	48.8
	Herbert W. Ladd (R)	18,988	45.1
1891	John W. Davis (D)	22,249	49.0
	Herbert W. Ladd (R)	20,995†	46.2
1892	D. Russell Brown (R)	27,461	50.2
	William T. C. Wardwell (D)	25,433	46.5
1893	David S. Baker (D)	22,015*	46.7
	D. Russell Brown (R)	21,830	46.3
	Metcalf (P)	3,265	6.9
1894	D. Russell Brown (R)	29,157	53.2
	David S. Baker Jr. (D)	22,650	41.3
1895	Charles Warren Lippitt (R)	25,098	56.9
	George L. Littlefield (D)	14,289	32.4
	Smith Quimby (P)	2,624	6.0
1896	Charles Warren Lippitt (R)	28,472	56.4
	George L. Littlefield (D)	17,061	33.8
	Thomas H. Peabody (P)	2,950	5.8
1897	Elisha Dyer (R)	24,309	58.1
	Daniel T. Church (D)	13,675	32.7
	Thomas H. Peabody (P)	2,096	5.0
1898	Elisha Dyer (R)	24,743	57.7
	Daniel T. Church (D)	13,224	30.9
	James P. Reid (SOC LAB)	2,877	6.7
1899	Elisha Dyer (R)	24,308	56.4
	George W. Greene (D)	14,602	33.9
	Thomas F. Herrick (SOC LAB)	2,941	6.8
1900	William Gregory (R)	26,043	54.3
	Nathan W. Littlefield (D)	17,184	35.9
	James P. Reid (SOC LAB)	2,858	6.0
1901	William Gregory (R)	25,575	53.6
	Lucius F. C. Garvin (D)	19,038	39.9
1902	Lucius F. C. Garvin (D)	32,279	54.0
	Charles Dean Kimball (R)	24,541	41.0
1903	Lucius F. C. Garvin (D)	30,578	49.3
	Samuel Pomeroy Colt (R)	29,275	47.2
1904	George H. Utter (R)	33,821	48.9
	Lucius F. C. Garvin (D)	32,965	47.7
1905	George H. Utter (R)	31,311	53.3
	Lucius F. C. Garvin (D)	25,816	44.0
1906	James H. Higgins (D)	33,195	49.9
	George H. Utter (R)	31,877	47.9
1907	James H. Higgins (D)	33,300	50.4

	Candidates	Votes	%
	Frederick H. Jackson (R)	31,005	46.9
1908	Aram J. Pothier (R)	38,676	52.6
	Olney Arnold (D)	31,406	42.7
1909	Aram J. Pothier (R)	37,107	57.0
	Olney Arnold (D)	25,338	38.9
1910	Aram J. Pothier (R)	33,540	49.6
	Lewis A. Waterman (D)	32,400	47.9
1911	Aram J. Pothier (R)	37,969	53.4
	Lewis A. Waterman (D)	30,575	43.0
1912	Aram J. Pothier (R)	34,133	43.7
	Theodore Francis Green (D)	32,725	41.9
	Albert H. Humes (PROG)	8,457	10.8
1914	R. Livingston Beeckman (R)	41,996	53.8
	Patrick H. Quinn (D)	32,182	41.3
1916	R. Livingston Beeckman (R)	49,524	55.9
	Addison P. Munroe (D)	36,158	40.8
1918	R. Livingston Beeckman (R)	42,682	53.1
	Alberic A. Archambault (D)	36,031	44.8
1920	Emery J. San Souci (R)	109,138	64.6
	Edward M. Sullivan (D)	55,963	33.2
1922	William S. Flynn (D)	81,935	51.7
	Harold J. Gross (R)	74,724	47.2
1924	Aram J. Pothier (R)	122,749	58.6
	Felix A. Toupin (D)	85,942	41.0
1926	Aram J. Pothier (R)	89,574	53.9
	Joseph H. Gainer (D)	75,882	45.7
1928	Norman S. Case (R)	121,748	51.6
	Alberic A. Archambault (D)	113,594	48.1
1930	Norman S. Case (R)	112,070	50.5
	Theodore Francis Green (D)	108,558	48.9
1932	Theodore Francis Green (D)	146,474	55.2
	Norman S. Case (R)	115,438	43.5
1934	Theodore Francis Green (D)	140,258	56.6
	Luke H. Callan (R)	105,139	42.4
1936	Robert E. Quinn (D)	160,776	53.7
	Charles P. Sisson (R)	137,369	45.9
1938	William H. Vanderbilt (R)	167,003	53.7
	Robert E. Quinn (D)	129,603	41.6
1940	J. Howard McGrath (D)	177,937	55.8
	William H. Vanderbilt (R)	140,480	44.1
1942	J. Howard McGrath (D)	139,407	58.5
	James O. McManus (R)	98,741	41.5
1944	J. Howard McGrath (D)	179,010	60.7
	Norman D. Macleod (R)	116,158	39.4
1946	John O. Pastore (D)	148,885	54.1
	John G. Murphy (R)	126,456	45.9
1948	John O. Pastore (D)	198,056	61.2
	Albert P. Ruerat (R)	124,441	38.4
1950	Dennis J. Roberts (D)	176,125	59.3
	Eugene J. Lachapelle (R)	120,683	40.7
1952	Dennis J. Roberts (D)	215,587	52.6
	Raoul Archambault Jr. (R)	194,102	47.4
1954	Dennis J. Roberts (D)	189,595	57.7
	Dean J. Lewis (R)	137,131	41.7
1956	Dennis J. Roberts (D)	192,315	50.1
	Christopher Del Sesto (R)	191,604	49.9
1958	Christopher Del Sesto (R)	176,505	50.9
	Dennis J. Roberts (D)	170,275	49.1
1960	John A. Notte Jr. (D)	227,318	56.6
	Christopher Del Sesto (R)	174,044	43.4
1962	John H. Chafee (R)	163,952	50.1
	John A. Notte Jr. (D)	163,554	49.9
1964	John H. Chafee (R)	239,501	61.2
	Edward P. Gallogly (D)	152,165	38.9
1966	John H. Chafee (R)	210,202	63.3
	Horace E. Hobbs (D)	121,862	36.7
1968	Frank Licht (D)	195,766	51.0
	John H. Chafee (R)	187,958	49.0
1970	Frank Licht (D)	173,420	50.1
	Herbert F. DeSimone (R)	171,549	49.5
1972	Philip W. Noel (D)	216,953	52.6

	Candidates	Votes	%
1974	Herbert F. DeSimone (R)	194,315	*47.1*
	Philip W. Noel (D)	252,436	*78.5*
1976	James W. Nugent (R)	69,224	*21.5*
	J. Joseph Garrahy (D)	218,561	*54.8*
1978	James L. Taft (R)	178,254	*44.7*
	J. Joseph Garrahy (D)	197,386	*62.8*
	Lincoln Almond (R)	96,596	*30.7*
1980	Joseph A. Doorley Jr. (I)	20,381	*6.5*
	J. Joseph Garrahy (D)	299,174	*73.7*
1982	Vincent A. Cianci (R)	106,729	*26.3*
	J. Joseph Garrahy (D)	247,208	*73.3*
	Vincent Mazullo (R)	79,602	*23.6*
1984	Edward DiPrete (R)	245,059	*60.0*
	Anthony J. Solomon (D)	163,311	*40.0*

1. *Includes votes for other candidates.*

	Candidates	Votes	%
1950	James F. Byrnes (D)	50,633	*100.0*
1954	George Bell Timmerman Jr. (D)	214,204	*100.0*
1958	Ernest F. Hollings (D)	77,714	*100.0*
1962	Donald Russell (D)	253,704	*100.0*
1966	Robert E. McNair (D)	255,854	*58.2*
	Joseph O. Rogers Jr. (R)	184,088	*41.8*
1970	John C. West (D)	250,551	*51.7*
	Albert Watson (R)	221,233	*45.6*
1974	James B. Edwards (R)	266,109	*50.9*
	W. J. Bryan Dorn (D)	248,938	*47.6*
1978	Richard W. Riley (D)	384,898	*61.4*
	Edward L. Young (R)	236,946	*37.8*
1982	Richard W. Riley (D)	468,819	*69.8*
	W. D. Workman (R)	202,806	*30.2*

1. *Before 1865 governor chosen by Legislature.*

SOUTH CAROLINA

(Ratified the Constitution May 23, 1788)

	Candidates	Votes	%
1865[1]	James L. Orr	9,771	*51.8*
	Wade Hampton	9,109	*48.3*
1868	Robert K. Scott (R)	69,693	*75.0*
	W. D. Porter	23,087	*24.8*
1870	Robert K. Scott (R)	85,071	*62.3*
	R. B. Carpenter (D)	51,537	*37.7*
1872	Franklin J. Moses Jr. (R)	69,838	*65.4*
	Reuben Tomlinson (ID)	36,553	*34.2*
1874	Daniel H. Chamberlain (R)	80,403	*53.9*
	John T. Green (I REF D)	68,818	*46.1*
1876	Wade Hampton (D)	92,261	*50.3*
	Daniel H. Chamberlain (R)	91,127	*49.7*
1878	Wade Hampton (D)	119,550	*99.8*
1880	Johnson Hagood (D)	117,432	*96.4*
1882	Hugh S. Thompson (D)	67,158	*79.5*
	McLane (G)	17,319	*20.5*
1884	Hugh S. Thompson (D)	67,895	*100.0*
1886	John P. Richardson (D)	33,114	*100.0*
1888	John P. Richardson (D)	58,730	*100.0*
1890	Benjamin Ryan Tillman (D)	59,159	*79.8*
	A. C. Haskell (ID)	14,828	*20.0*
1892	Benjamin Ryan Tillman (D)	56,673	*99.9*
1894	John Gary Evans (D)	39,507	*69.6*
	Sampson Pope (POP)	17,278	*30.4*
1896	William H. Ellerbe (D)	59,424	*89.1*
	Sampson Pope (LW R)	4,432	*6.7*
1898	William H. Ellerbe (D)	28,225	*100.0*
1900	Miles B. McSweeney (D)	46,457	*100.0*
1902	Duncan C. Heyward (D)	31,817	*100.0*
1904	Duncan C. Heyward (D)	51,917	*100.0*
1906	Martin F. Ansel (D)	30,251	*99.9*
1908	Martin F. Ansel (D)	61,060	*100.0*
1910	Coleman L. Blease (D)	30,739	*99.8*
1912	Coleman L. Blease (D)	44,122	*99.5*
1914	Richard I. Manning (D)	34,600	*99.8*
1916	Richard I. Manning (D)	60,396	*97.9*
1918	Robert A. Cooper (D)	25,267	*100.0*
1920	Robert A. Cooper (D)	58,050	*100.0*
1922	Thomas G. McLeod (D)	34,065	*100.0*
1924	Thomas G. McLeod (D)	53,545	*100.0*
1926	John G. Richards (D)	16,589	*100.0*
1930	Ibra C. Blackwood (D)	17,790	*100.0*
1934	Olin D. Johnston (D)	23,177	*100.0*
1938	Burnet R. Maybank (D)	49,009	*99.4*
1942	Olin D. Johnston (D)	23,859	*100.0*
1946	J. Strom Thurmond (D)	26,520	*100.0*

SOUTH DAKOTA

(Became a state Nov. 2, 1889)

	Candidates	Votes	%
1889	Arthur C. Mellette (R)	53,964	*69.3*
	P. F. McClure (D)	23,840	*30.6*
1890	Arthur C. Mellette (R)	34,487	*44.5*
	H. L. Loucks (I)	24,591	*31.7*
	Maris Taylor (D)	18,484	*23.8*
1892	Charles H. Sheldon (R)	33,214	*47.2*
	A. L. Vanosdel (I)	22,323	*31.7*
	Peter Couchman (D)	14,872	*21.1*
1894	Charles H. Sheldon (R)	40,402	*52.0*
	Isaac Howe (I)	27,568	*35.5*
	James A. Ward (D)	8,756	*11.3*
1896	Andrew E. Lee (PP)	41,177	*49.8*
	A. O. Ringsrud (R)	40,869	*49.4*
1898	Andrew E. Lee (FUS)	37,319	*49.6*
	Kirk G. Phillips (R)	36,980	*49.2*
1900	Charles N. Herreid (R)	53,788	*56.3*
	Burre H. Lien (FUS)	40,091	*42.0*
1902	Charles N. Herreid (R)	48,195	*64.7*
	John W. Martin (D)	21,396	*28.7*
1904	Samuel H. Elrod (R)	68,561	*68.3*
	Louis N. Crill (D)	24,772	*24.7*
1906	Coe I. Crawford (R)	48,709	*65.3*
	John A. Stransky (D)	19,923	*26.7*
1908	Robert S. Vessey (R)	62,989	*55.3*
	Andrew E. Lee (D)	44,876	*39.4*
1910	Robert S. Vessey (R)	61,744	*58.4*
	Chauncey L. Wood (D)	37,983	*35.9*
1912	Frank M. Byrne (R)	57,161	*48.5*
	Edwin S. Johnson (D)	53,850	*45.7*
1914	Frank M. Byrne (R)	49,138	*50.1*
	J. W. McCarter (D)	34,542	*35.2*
	R. O. Richards (I)	9,725	*9.9*
1916	Peter Norbeck (R)	72,789	*56.6*
	Rinehart (D)	50,545	*39.3*
1918	Peter Norbeck (R)	51,175	*53.2*
	Mark P. Bates (NON PART)	25,118	*26.1*
	James B. Bird (D)	17,858	*18.6*
1920	William H. McMaster (R)	103,592	*56.3*
	Mark P. Bates (NON PART)	48,426	*26.3*
	W. W. Howes (D)	31,870	*17.3*
1922	William H. McMaster (R)	78,984	*45.0*
	Louis N. Crill (D)	50,409	*28.7*
	Lorraine Daly (NON PART)	46,033	*26.2*
1924	Carl Gunderson (R)	109,914	*53.9*
	William J. Bulow (D)	46,613	*22.9*
	A. L. Putnam (F-LAB)	27,027	*13.3*

	Candidates	Votes	%
	R. O. Richards (I)	20,359	10.0
1926	William J. Bulow (D)	87,076	47.4
	Carl Gunderson (R)	74,101	40.3
	Tom Ayres (F-LAB)	11,958	6.5
	John E. Hipple (I)	10,637	5.8
1928	William J. Bulow (D)	136,016	52.5
	Buell F. Jones (R)	121,643	46.9
1930	Warren E. Green (R)	107,643	53.0
	D. A. McCullough (D)	93,954	46.2
1932	Tom Berry (D)	158,058	55.6
	Warren E. Green (R)	120,473	42.4
1934	Tom Berry (D)	172,228	58.6
	William C. Allen (R)	119,477	40.7
1936	Leslie Jensen (R)	151,659	51.6
	Tom Berry (D)	142,255	48.4
1938	Harlan J. Bushfield (R)	149,362	54.0
	Oscar Fosheim (D)	127,485	46.1
1940	Harlan J. Bushfield (R)	167,686	55.1
	Lewis W. Bicknell (D)	136,428	44.9
1942	Merrell Q. Sharpe (R)	109,786	61.5
	Lewis B. Bicknell (D)	68,706	38.5
1944	Merrell Q. Sharpe (R)	148,646	65.5
	Lynn Fellows (D)	78,276	34.5
1946	George T. Mickelson (R)	108,998	67.2
	Richard Haeder (D)	53,294	32.8
1948	George T. Mickelson (R)	149,883	61.1
	Harold J. Volz (D)	95,489	38.9
1950	Sigurd Anderson (R)	154,254	60.9
	Joe Robbie (D)	99,062	39.1
1952	Sigurd Anderson (R)	203,102	70.2
	Sherman A. Iverson (D)	86,412	29.9
1954	Joe Foss (R)	133,878	56.7
	Ed C. Martin (D)	102,377	43.3
1956	Joe Foss (R)	158,819	54.4
	Ralph Herseth (D)	133,198	45.6
1958	Ralph Herseth (D)	132,761	51.4
	Phil Saunders (R)	125,520	48.6
1960	Archie M. Gubbrud (R)	154,530	50.7
	Ralph Herseth (D)	150,095	49.3
1962	Archie M. Gubbrud (R)	143,682	56.1
	Ralph Herseth (D)	112,438	43.9
1964	Nils A. Boe (R)	150,151	51.7
	John F. Lindley (D)	140,419	48.3
1966	Nils A. Boe (R)	131,710	57.7
	Robert Chamberlin (D)	96,504	42.3
1968	Frank L. Farrar (R)	159,646	57.7
	Robert Chamberlin (D)	117,260	42.4
1970	Richard F. Kneip (D)	131,616	54.9
	Frank L. Farrar (R)	108,347	45.2
1972	Richard F. Kneip (D)	185,012	60.0
	Carveth Thompson (R)	123,165	40.0
1974	Richard F. Kneip (D)	149,151	53.6
	John E. Olson (R)	129,077	46.4
1978	William J. Janklow (R)	147,116	56.6
	Roger McKellips (D)	112,679	43.4
1982	William J. Janklow (R)	197,426	70.9
	Michael J. O'Connor (D)	81,136	29.1

TENNESSEE

(Became a state June 1, 1796)

	Candidates	Votes	%
1796[1]	John Sevier	✔	
1797	John Sevier	✔	
1799[2]	John Sevier	5,295	99.7
1801	Archibald Roane	8,438	99.9

	Candidates	Votes	%
1803	John Sevier	6,786	58.0
	Archibald Roane	4,923	42.0
1805[2]	John Sevier	10,293	63.7
	Archibald Roane	5,855	36.3
1807	John Sevier		
	William Cocke		
1809	Willie Blount	✔	
	William Cocke		
1811	Willie Blount	✔	
1813	Willie Blount	21,510	
1815[2]	Joseph McMinn	14,873	42.8
	Robert Weakley	7,209	20.7
	Jesse Wharton	6,038	17.4
	Robert C. Foster	3,809	11.0
	Thomas Johnson	2,826	8.1
1817	Joseph McMinn	27,802	64.3
	Robert C. Foster	15,450	35.7
1819	Joseph McMinn	35,244	
	Enoch Parsons		
1821	William Carroll	42,210	79.0
	Edward Ward	11,200	21.0
1823	William Carroll	32,597	
1825	William Carroll	14,807	99.8
1827	Samuel Houston	40,017	54.7
	Newton Cannon	31,244	42.7
1829	William Carroll	59,875	99.8
1831	William Carroll (D)	64,834	97.3
1833	William Carroll (D)	53,224	97.8
1835	Newton Cannon (W)	41,862	50.4
	William Carroll	33,180	40.0
	Humphries	7,999	9.6
1837	Newton Cannon (W)	53,385	60.9
	Armstrong (D)	34,312	39.1
1839	James K. Polk (D)	53,714	51.0
	Newton Cannon (W)	51,624	49.0
1841	James C. Jones (W)	53,829	51.5
	James K. Polk (D)	50,705	48.5
1843	James C. Jones (W)	52,584	51.3
	James K. Polk (D)	49,944	48.7
1845	Aaron V. Brown (D)	58,277	50.6
	Foster (W)	56,805	49.4
1847	Neill S. Brown (W)	61,450	50.4
	Aaron V. Brown (D)	60,454	49.6
1849	William Trousdale (D)	61,740	50.6
	Neill S. Brown (W)	60,340	49.4
1851	William B. Campbell (W)	63,423	50.7
	William Trousdale (D)	61,648	49.3
1853	Andrew Johnson (D)	63,413	50.9
	Henry (W)	61,163	49.1
1855	Andrew Johnson (D)	67,499	50.8
	Gentry (AM)	65,332	49.2
1857	Isham G. Harris (D)	71,539	54.4
	Hatton (AM)	59,867	45.6
1859	Isham G. Harris (D)	76,226	52.8
	Netherland (OPP)	68,218	47.2
1863	Robert L. Caruthers	7,050	98.4
1865	William G. Brownlow (W, R)	22,814	99.9
1867	William G. Brownlow (R)	74,484	76.9
	Emerson Etheridge (C)	22,440	23.2
1869	De Witt Clinton Senter (CR)	120,333	68.6
	William B. Stokes (RAD R)	55,036	31.4
1870	John C. Brown (D)	76,666	65.0
	W. H. Wisener (R)	41,278	35.0
1872	John C. Brown (LR)	97,689	53.7
	Freeman (R)	84,100	46.3
1874	James D. Porter Jr. (D)	103,061	64.9
	Horace Maynard (R)	55,836	35.1
1876	James D. Porter Jr. (D)	123,740	58.8
	Thomas (I)	73,695	35.0
1878	Albert S. Marks (D)	89,097	60.3
	E. M. Wight (R)	43,175	29.2

	Candidates	Votes	%
	R. M. Edwards (G)	15,470	10.5
1880	Alvin Hawkins (R)	103,966	42.6
	Wright (STC D)	79,081	32.4
	Wilson (LOWTAX D)	57,568	23.6
1882	William B. Bate (LOWTAX D)	120,091	52.9
	Alvin Hawkins (R)	93,182	41.0
1884	William B. Bate (D)	132,201	51.3
	Reid (R)	125,276	48.7
1886	Robert L. Taylor (D)	126,491	53.5
	Alfred A. Taylor (R)	109,842	46.5
1888	Robert L. Taylor (D)	156,799	51.8
	Samuel W. Hawkins (R)	139,014	45.9
1890	John P. Buchanan (D)	113,536	56.6
	Baxter (R)	76,071	37.9
	Kelly (P)	11,011	5.5
1892	Peter Turney (D)	126,248	47.9
	George W. Winsted (R)	100,599	38.1
	John P. Buchanan (PP)	31,515	12.0
1894	H. Clay Evans (R)	105,164‡	45.2
	Peter Turney (D)	104,350	44.9
	Mills (POP)	23,129	9.9
1896	Robert L. Taylor (D)	156,227	48.8
	G. N. Tillman (R)	149,374	46.6
1898	Benton McMillin (D)	105,640	57.9
	Fowler (R)	72,611	39.8
1900	Benton McMillin (D)	145,708	53.9
	John E. McCall (R)	119,831	44.3
1902	James B. Frazier (D)	98,951	61.8
	Campbell (R)	59,002	36.8
1904	James B. Frazier (D)	131,503	55.7
	Littleton (R)	103,409	43.8
1906	Malcolm R. Patterson (D)	111,876	54.4
	Evans (R)	92,804	45.2
1908	Malcolm R. Patterson (D)	133,176	53.7
	G. N. Tillman (R)	113,269	45.7
1910	Ben W. Hooper (R)	133,076	51.9
	Robert L. Taylor (D)	121,694	47.5
1912	Ben W. Hooper (R)	124,641	50.2
	Benton McMillin (D)	116,610	46.9
1914	Tom C. Rye (D)	137,636	53.6
	Ben W. Hooper (R)	117,717	45.8
1916	Tom C. Rye (D)	146,759	55.0
	John W. Overall (R)	117,819	44.2
1918	Albert H. Roberts (D)	98,628	62.4
	H. B. Lindsay (R)	59,518	37.6
1920	Alfred A. Taylor (R)	229,133	54.9
	Albert H. Roberts (D)	185,890	44.6
1922	Austin Peay (D)	141,012	57.9
	Alfred A. Taylor (R)	102,586	42.1
1924	Austin Peay (D)	162,002	57.2
	T. F. Peck (R)	121,228	42.8
1926	Austin Peay (D)	84,979	64.7
	Walter White (R)	46,238	35.2
1928	Henry H. Horton (D)	195,546	61.1
	Raleigh Hopkins (R)	124,733	39.0
1930	Henry H. Horton (D)	153,341	63.8
	C. Arthur Bruce (R)	85,558	35.6
1932	Hill McAlister (D)	169,075	42.8
	John E. McCall (R)	117,797	29.8
	Lewis S. Pope (I)	106,990	27.1
1934	Hill McAlister (D)	198,743	61.8
	Lewis S. Pope (FUS)	122,965	38.2
1936	Gordon Browning (D)	332,523	80.4
	P. H. Thach (R)	77,392	18.7
1938	Prentice Cooper (D)	210,567	71.7
	Howard H. Baker (R)	83,031	28.3
1940	Prentice Cooper (D)	323,466	72.1
	C. Arthur Bruce (R)	125,245	27.9
1942	Prentice Cooper (D)	120,148	70.2
	C. N. Frazier (R)	51,120	29.9
1944	James N. McCord (D)	275,746	62.5

	Candidates	Votes	%
	J. W. Kilgo (R)	158,742	36.0
1946	James N. McCord (D)	149,937	65.3
	W. O. Lowe (R)	73,222	31.9
1948	Gordon Browning (D)	363,903	66.9
	Roy Acuff (R)	179,957	33.1
1950	Gordon Browning (D)	184,437	78.1
	John R. Neal (R)	51,757	21.9
1952	Frank G. Clement (D)	640,290	79.4
	R. Beecher Witt (R)	166,377	20.6
1954	Frank G. Clement (D)	281,291	87.2
	John R. Neal (I)	39,574	12.3
1958	Buford Ellington (D)	248,874	57.5
	James N. McCord (I)	136,406	31.5
	Thomas P. Wall (R)	35,938	8.3
1962	Frank G. Clement (D)	315,648	50.9
	William R. Anderson (I)	203,765	32.8
	Hubert D. Patty (R)	99,884	16.1
1966	Buford Ellington (D)	532,998	81.2
	H. L. Crowder (I)	64,602	9.8
	Charles Moffett (I)	50,221	7.7
1970	Winfield Dunn (R)	575,777	52.0
	John J. Hooker Jr. (D)	509,521	46.0
1974	Ray Blanton (D)	576,833	55.4
	Lamar Alexander (R)	455,467	43.8
1978	Lamar Alexander (R)	661,959	55.6
	Jake Butcher (D)	523,495	44.0
1982	Lamar Alexander (R)	737,963	59.6
	Randy Tyree (D)	500,937	40.4

1. Until the 1830s contests were essentially on a personal popularity basis among members of the Democratic Republican Party.
2. Returns are incomplete.

TEXAS

(Became a state Dec. 29, 1845)

	Candidates	Votes	%
1845	J. Pinckney Henderson	7,853#	82.0
	James B. Miller	1,673#	17.5
1847	George T. Wood (D)	6,801	53.5
	J. B. Miller (D)	4,022	31.6
	N. H. Darnell	1,285	10.1
1849	P. Hansbrough Bell (D)	10,226	48.0
	George T. Wood	8,430	39.6
	John T. Mills	2,632	12.4
1851	P. Hansbrough Bell	12,484	47.0
	M. T. Johnson	5,029	18.9
	J. A. Green	3,941	14.8
	B. H. Epperson	2,868	10.8
	J. J. Chambers	2,148	8.1
1853	Elisha M. Pease (D)	13,099	36.2
	W. B. Ochiltree (W)	9,180	25.4
	G. T. Wood (D)	5,983	16.5
	L. D. Evans (D)	4,679	12.9
	T. J. Chambers (D)	2,449	6.8
1855	Elisha M. Pease (D)	20,164	58.4
	D. C. Dickson (KN)	13,081	37.9
1857	Hardin R. Runnels (D)	32,552	57.9
	Sam Houston (AM)	23,628	42.1
1859	Sam Houston (ID)	36,227	56.8
	Hardin R. Runnels (D)	27,500	43.2
1861	Francis R. Lubbock	21,860	38.1
	Edward Clark	21,675	37.8
	T. J. Chambers	13,759	24.0
1863	Pendleton Murrah	17,486	56.6
	T. J. Chambers	12,254	39.7

	Candidates	Votes	%
1865	J. W. Throckmorton (C)	49,277	80.3
	Elisha M. Pease (R)	12,068	19.7
1866	J. W. Throckmorton	48,631	80.1
	Elisha M. Pease (R)	12,051	19.9
1869	Edmund J. Davis (R)	39,838	50.2
	A. J. Hamilton (D)	39,046	49.2
1873	Richard Coke (D)	98,906	66.0
	Edmund J. Davis (R)	51,049	34.0
1875	Richard Coke (D)	149,974	75.0
	William Chambers (R)	49,994	25.0
1878	Oran M. Roberts (D)	158,960	67.1
	William H. Hamman (NG)	55,004	23.2
	A. B. Norton (R)	22,941	9.7
1880	Oran M. Roberts (D)	165,949	62.9
	E. J. Davis (R)	64,372	24.4
	W. H. Hamman (G)	33,699	12.8
1882	John Ireland (D)	150,811	58.0
	George W. Jones (R-G-FUS)	108,988	41.9
1884	John Ireland (D)	210,691	63.2
	George W. Jones (R)	98,031	29.4
	A. B. Norton (G)	23,464	7.0
1886	Lawrence S. Ross (D)	229,806	73.0
	A. M. Cochran (R)	66,456	21.1
	E. L. Dahoney (P)	18,556	5.9
1888	Lawrence S. Ross (D)	249,361	70.8
	Marion Martin (P & F ALNC)	102,807	29.2
1890	James S. Hogg (D)	261,998	76.7
	Webster Flanagan (R)	76,932	22.5
1892	James S. Hogg (D)	190,386	43.7
	George Clark (R)	133,434	30.7
	Thomas L. Nugent (POP)	108,483	24.9
1894	Charles A. Culberson (D)	207,171	48.9
	Thomas L. Nugent (POP)	151,595	35.8
	W. K. Makemson (R)	54,525	12.9
1896	Charles A. Culberson (D)	298,568	55.3
	Jerome C. Kearby (POP)	238,688	44.2
1898	Joseph D. Sayers (D)	291,548	71.2
	Barnett Gibbs (POP)	114,865	28.1
1900	Joseph D. Sayers (D)	303,548	67.6
	R. E. Hannay (R)	112,864	25.1
	T. J. McMinn (POP)	26,579	5.9
1902	Samuel W. T. Lanham (D)	269,076	74.9
	George W. Burkett (R)	65,706	18.3
1904	Samuel W. T. Lanham (D)	204,961	73.6
	J. G. Lowden (R)	56,499	20.3
1906	Thomas M. Campbell (D)	149,263	81.2
	C. A. Gray (R)	23,779	12.9
1908	Thomas M. Campbell (D)	220,996	72.9
	John N. Simpson (R)	73,309	24.2
1910	Oscar B. Colquitt (D)	174,578	79.8
	J. O. Terrell (R)	26,176	12.0
	Reddin Andrews (SOC)	11,536	5.3
1912	Oscar B. Colquitt (D)	233,073	77.8
	Reddin Andrews (SOC)	25,238	8.4
	C. W. Johnson (R)	22,914	7.6
	Ed C. Lasater (PROG)	15,754	5.3
1914	James E. Ferguson (D)	176,601	82.0
	E. R. Meitzen (SOC)	24,977	11.6
	John W. Philip (R)	11,405	5.3
1916	James E. Ferguson (D)	297,177	80.5
	R. B. Creager (R)	49,117	13.3
	E. R. Meitzen (SOC)	19,278	5.2
1918	William P. Hobby (D)	148,982	84.0
	Charles A. Boynton (R)	26,713	15.1
1920	Pat M. Neff (D)	290,672	60.2
	J. G. Culbertson (R)	90,102	18.7
	T. H. McGregor (AM)	69,380	14.4
	H. Capers (B & T R)	26,128	5.4
1922	Pat M. Neff (D)	332,676	81.9
	W. H. Atwell (R)	73,569	18.1
1924	Miriam A. Ferguson (D)	422,563	58.9

	Candidates	Votes	%
	George C. Butte (R)	294,920	41.1
1926	Dan Moody (D)	233,002	87.5
	H. H. Haines (R)	32,434	12.2
1928	Dan Moody (D)	582,897	82.4
	W. H. Holmes (R)	123,337	17.4
1930	Ross Sterling (D)	253,732	80.0
	W. E. Talbot (R)	62,334	19.7
1932	Miriam A. Ferguson (D)	521,395	61.6
	Orville Bullington (R)	322,589	38.1
1934	James V. Allred (D)	428,755	96.4
1936	James V. Allred (D)	780,442	92.9
	C. O. Harris (R)	58,744	7.0
1938	W. Lee O'Daniel (D)	358,943	96.8
1940	W. Lee O'Daniel (D)	1,040,358	94.7
	G. C. Hopkins (R)	57,971	5.3
1942	Coke R. Stevenson (D)	280,735	96.8
1944	Coke R. Stevenson (D)	1,006,778	90.9
	B. J. Peasley (R)	101,110	9.1
1946	Beauford H. Jester (D)	345,507	91.2
	Eugene Nolte Jr. (R)	33,277	8.8
1948	Beauford H. Jester (D)	1,024,160	84.7
	Alvin H. Lane (R)	177,399	14.7
1950	Allan Shivers (D)	367,345	90.2
	Ralph W. Currie (R)	39,793	9.8
1952	Allan Shivers (D, R)	1,853,863	99.9
1954	Allan Shivers (D)	569,533	89.4
	Tod R. Adams (R)	66,154	10.4
1956	Price Daniel (D)	1,433,051	78.4
	William R. Bryant (R)	271,088	14.8
	W. Lee O'Daniel (write-in)	122,103	6.7
1958	Price Daniel (D)	695,035	88.1
	Edwin S. Mayer (R)	94,098	11.9
1960	Price Daniel (D)	1,637,755	72.8
	William M. Steger (R)	612,963	27.2
1962	John B. Connally (D)	847,036	54.0
	Jack Cox (R)	715,025	45.6
1964	John B. Connally (D)	1,877,793	73.8
	Jack Crichton (R)	661,675	26.0
1966	John B. Connally (D)	1,037,517	72.8
	T. E. Kennerly (R)	368,025	25.8
1968	Preston Smith (D)	1,662,019	57.0
	Paul Eggers (R)	1,254,333	43.0
1970	Preston Smith (D)	1,197,726	53.6
	Paul Eggers (R)	1,037,723	46.4
1972	Dolph Briscoe (D)	1,633,493	47.9
	Hank C. Grover (R)	1,533,986	45.0
	Ramsey Muniz (LRU)	214,118	6.3
1974	Dolph Briscoe (D)	1,016,334	61.4
	Jim Granberry (R)	514,725	31.1
	Ramsey Muniz (LRU)	93,295	5.6
1978	William P. Clements (R)	1,183,839	50.0
	John Hill (D)	1,166,979	49.2
1982	Mark White (D)	1,697,870	53.2
	William P. Clements (R)	1,465,937	45.9

UTAH

(Became a state Jan. 4, 1896)

	Candidates	Votes	%
1896	Heber M. Wells (R)	20,833	50.3
	J. T. Caine (D)	18,519	44.7
1900	Heber M. Wells (R)	47,600	51.7
	James H. Moyle (D)	44,447	48.3
1904	John C. Cutler (R)	50,837	50.0
	James H. Moyle (D)	38,047	37.4
	William M. Ferry (AM)	7,959	7.8

	Candidates	Votes	%
1908	William Spry (R)	52,913	*47.5*
	Jesse William Knight (D)	43,266	*38.8*
	James A. Street (AM)	11,404	*10.2*
1912	William Spry (R)	42,552	*38.2*
	John F. Tolton (D)	36,076	*32.4*
	Nephi L. Morris (PROG)	23,590	*21.2*
	Homer P. Burt (SOC)	8,797	*7.9*
1916	Simon Bamberger (D)	78,298	*55.0*
	Nephi L. Morris (R)	59,522	*41.8*
1920	Charles R. Mabey (R)	83,518	*58.2*
	T. N. Taylor (D)	54,913	*38.3*
1924	George H. Dern (D)	81,308	*53.0*
	Charles R. Mabey (R)	72,127	*47.0*
1928	George H. Dern (D)	102,953	*58.5*
	William H. Wattis (R)	72,306	*41.1*
1932	Henry H. Blood (D)	116,031	*56.4*
	William W. Seegmiller (R)	85,913	*41.8*
1936	Henry H. Blood (D)	109,656	*51.0*
	Ray E. Dillman (R)	80,118	*37.2*
	Harman W. Peery	24,754	*11.5*
1940	Herbert B. Maw (D)	128,519	*52.1*
	Don B. Colton (R)	117,713	*47.7*
1944	Herbert B. Maw (D)	123,907	*50.2*
	J. Bracken Lee (R)	122,851	*49.8*
1948	J. Bracken Lee (R)	151,253	*55.0*
	Herbert B. Maw (D)	123,814	*45.0*
1952	J. Bracken Lee (R)	180,516	*55.1*
	Earl J. Glade (D)	147,188	*44.9*
1956	George Dewey Clyde (R)	127,164	*38.2*
	L. C. Romney (D)	111,297	*33.4*
	J. Bracken Lee (I)	94,428	*28.4*
1960	George Dewey Clyde (R)	195,634	*52.7*
	William A. Barlocker (D)	175,855	*47.3*
1964	Calvin L. Rampton (D)	226,956	*57.0*
	Mitchell Melich (R)	171,300	*43.0*
1968	Calvin L. Rampton (D)	289,283	*68.7*
	Carl W. Buehner (R)	131,729	*31.3*
1972	Calvin L. Rampton (D)	331,998	*69.7*
	Nicholas L. Strike (R)	144,449	*30.3*
1976	Scott M. Matheson (D)	280,706	*52.0*
	Vernon B. Romney (R)	248,027	*46.0*
1980	Scott M. Matheson (D)	330,974	*55.2*
	Bob Wright (R)	266,578	*44.4*
1984	Norman H. Bangerter (R)	351,792	*55.9*
	Wayne Owens (D)	275,669	*43.8*

VERMONT

(Became a state March 4, 1791)

	Candidates	Votes	%
1791	Thomas Chittenden	✔	
1792	Thomas Chittenden	✔	
1793	Thomas Chittenden	3,184	*51.7*
	Isaac Tichenor	2,712	*44.1*
1794	Thomas Chittenden	2,643	*52.1*
	Isaac Tichenor	2,000	*39.4*
1795	Thomas Chittenden	4,260	*60.7*
	Isaac Tichenor	2,038	*29.1*
1796	Thomas Chittenden	✔	
1797	Isaac Tichenor (FED)	†	
1798	Isaac Tichenor (FED)	6,211	*66.4*
	Moses Robinson (D-R)	2,805	*30.0*
1799	Isaac Tichenor (FED)	✔	
1800	Isaac Tichenor (FED)	6,444	*64.0*
	Israel Smith (D-R)	3,239	*32.2*
1801	Isaac Tichenor (FED)	✔	
1802	Isaac Tichenor (FED)	7,823	*60.5*

	Candidates	Votes	%
	Israel Smith (D-R)	5,085	*39.3*
1803	Isaac Tichenor (FED)	✔	
1804	Isaac Tichenor (FED)	8,075	*56.6*
	Jonathan Robinson (D-R)	6,184	*43.4*
1805	Isaac Tichenor (FED)	8,682	*60.9*
	Jonathan Robinson (D-R)	5,056	*35.5*
1806	Isaac Tichenor (FED)	8,551	*54.1*
	Israel Smith (D-R)	6,930	*43.9*
1807	Israel Smith (D-R)	9,983	*53.2*
	Isaac Tichenor (FED)	8,571	*45.7*
1808	Isaac Tichenor (FED)	13,634	*50.8*
	Israel Smith (D-R)	12,775	*47.6*
1809	Jonas Galusha (D-R)	14,583	*51.1*
	Isaac Tichenor (FED)	13,467	*47.2*
1810	Jonas Galusha (D-R)	13,810	*57.3*
	Isaac Tichenor (FED)	9,912	*41.2*
1811	Jonas Galusha (D-R)	13,828	*54.0*
	Martin Chittenden (FED)	11,214	*43.8*
1812	Jonas Galusha (D-R)	19,158	*53.6*
	Martin Chittenden (FED)	15,950	*44.6*
1813	Jonas Galusha (D-R)	16,828	*49.5*
	Martin Chittenden (FED)	16,532†	*48.7*
1814	Martin Chittenden (FED)	17,466†	*49.4*
	Jonas Galusha (D-R)	17,411	*49.3*
1815	Jonas Galusha (D-R)	18,055	*52.1*
	Martin Chittenden (FED)	16,032	*46.3*
1816	Jonas Galusha (D-R)	17,262	*55.2*
	Samuel Strong (FED)	13,888	*44.4*
1817	Jonas Galusha (D-R)	13,756	*64.3*
	Isaac Tichenor (FED)	7,430	*34.7*
1818	Jonas Galusha (D-R)	15,243	*95.3*
1819	Jonas Galusha (D-R)	12,268	*81.5*
	William C. Bradley (D-R)	1,035	*6.9*
1820	Richard Skinner (D-R)	13,152	*93.4*
1821	Richard Skinner (D-R)	12,434	*98.7*
1822	Richard Skinner (D-R)	✔	
1823	Cornelius P. Van Ness (D-R)	11,479	*85.6*
	Dudley Chase	1,088	*8.1*
1824	Cornelius P. Van Ness (D-R)	13,428	*85.8*
	Joel Doolittle	1,882	*12.0*
1825	Cornelius P. Van Ness (D-R)	12,229	*98.4*
1826	Ezra Butler (D-R)	8,966	*63.3*
	Joel Doolittle	3,157	*22.3*
1827	Ezra Butler (D-R)	13,699	*85.2*
	Joel Doolittle	1,951	*12.1*
1828	Samuel C. Crafts (NR)	16,285	*91.8*
	Joel Doolittle	933	*5.3*
1829	Samuel C. Crafts (NR)	14,325#	*55.7*
	Heman Allen (A-MASC)	7,376#	*28.7*
	Joel Doolittle (JAC)	3,973#	*15.4*
1830	Samuel C. Crafts (OPP)†	13,476#	*43.9*
	William A. Palmer (A-MAS)	10,923#	*35.6*
	Ezra Meech (JAC)	6,285#	*20.5*
1831	William A. Palmer (A-MAS)†	15,258#	*44.0*
	Heman Allen (NR)	12,990#	*37.5*
	Ezra Meech (JAC)	6,158#	*17.8*
1832	William A. Palmer (A-MAS)	17,318†	*42.2*
	Samuel C. Crafts (NR)	15,499	*37.7*
	Ezra Meech (D)	8,210	*20.0*
1833	William A. Palmer (A-MAS)	20,565	*52.9*
	Ezra Meech (FUS)	15,683	*40.3*
1834	William A. Palmer (A-MAS)	17,131†	*45.4*
	William C. Bradley (D)	10,385	*27.5*
	Horatio Seymour (W)	10,159	*26.9*
1835	William A. Palmer (A-MAS)	16,210*	*46.4*
	William C. Bradley (D)	13,254	*37.9*
	Charles Paine (W)	5,435	*15.6*
1836	Silas H. Jennison (W & A-MASC)	20,371	*55.8*
	William C. Bradley (D)	16,134	*44.2*
1837	Silas H. Jennison (W)	22,257	*55.7*
	William C. Bradley (D)	17,722	*44.3*

	Candidates	Votes	%		Candidates	Votes	%
1838	Silas H. Jennison (W)	22,169	56.0		Charles N. Davenport (D)	11,292	24.9
	William C. Bradley (D)	17,416	44.0	1867	John B. Page (R)	31,694	73.3
1839	Silas H. Jennison (W)	24,621	52.5		John L. Edwards (D)	11,510	26.6
	Nathan Smilie (D)	22,256	47.5	1868	John B. Page (R)	42,615	73.6
1840	Silas H. Jennison (W)	33,653	59.4		John L. Edwards (D)	15,289	26.4
	Paul Dillingham Jr. (D)	23,000	40.6	1869	Peter T. Washburn (R)	31,834	73.5
1841	Charles Paine (W)	23,582†	48.5		Homer W. Heaton (D)	11,455	26.5
	Nathan Smilie (D)	21,693	44.6	1870	John W. Stewart (R)	33,367	73.5
	Titus Hutchinson (LIB)	3,091	6.4		Homer W. Heaton (D)	12,058	26.5
1842	Charles Paine (W)	27,167	50.9	1872	Julius Converse (R)	41,946	71.6
	Nathan Smilie (D)	24,130	45.2		A. B. Gardner (LR)	16,613	28.4
1843	John Mattocks (W)	24,465†	48.7	1874	Asahel Peck (R)	33,582	71.7
	Daniel Kellogg (D)	21,982	43.8		W. H. H. Bingham (D)	13,257	28.3
	Charles K. Williams (LIB)	3,766	7.5	1876	Horace Fairbanks (R)	44,723	68.0
1844	William Slade (W)	28,265	51.5		W. H. H. Bingham (D)	20,988	31.9
	Daniel Kellogg (D)	20,930	38.2	1878	Redfield Proctor (R)	37,312	64.3
	William R. Shafter (LIB)	5,618	10.2		W. H. H. Bingham (D)	17,274	29.8
1845	William Slade (W)	22,770†	47.2	1880	Roswell Farnham (R)	47,848	67.7
	Daniel Kellogg (D)	18,591	38.5		Edward J. Phelps (D)	21,245	30.1
	William R. Shafter (LIB)	6,534	13.5	1882	John L. Barstow (R)	35,839	69.1
1846	Horace Eaton (W)	23,638†	48.5		George E. Eaton (D)	14,466	27.9
	John Smith (D)	17,877	36.7	1884	Samuel E. Pingree (R)	42,524	67.3
	Lawrence Brainerd (F SOIL)	7,118	14.6		Lyman W. Redington (D)	19,820	31.4
1847	Horace Eaton (W)	22,455†	46.7	1886	Ebenezer J. Ormsbee (R)	37,709	66.0
	Paul Dillingham Jr. (D)	18,661	38.8		Stephen C. Shurtleff (D)	17,187	30.1
	Lawrence Brainerd (F SOIL)	6,926	14.4	1888	William P. Dillingham (R)	48,522	69.9
1848	Carlos Coolidge (W)	22,132†	43.7		Stephen C. Shurtleff (D)	19,527	28.1
	Oscar L. Shafter (F SOIL D)	15,018	29.6	1890	Carroll S. Page (R)	33,462	62.1
	Paul Dillingham (CASS D)	13,477	26.6		Herbert F. Brigham (D)	19,299	35.8
1849	Carlos Coolidge (W)	26,443†	49.6	1892	Levi K. Fuller (R)	38,918	65.2
	Horatio Needham (F SOIL D)	23,492	44.1		B. B. Smalley (D)	19,216	32.2
	Jonas Clark (D)	3,357	6.3	1894	Urban A. Woodbury (R)	42,663	73.6
1850	Charles K. Williams (W)	24,809	51.3		George W. Smith (D)	14,142	24.4
	Lucius B. Peck (F SOIL D)	19,189	39.6	1896	Josiah Grout (R)	53,426	76.4
	John Roberts (HUNKER D)	4,379	9.1		J. Henry Jackson (D)	14,855	21.3
1851	Charles K. Williams (W)	22,864	51.0	1898	Edward C. Smith (R)	38,555	71.0
	Timothy B. Redfield (F SOIL)	15,121	33.7		Thomas W. Moloney (D)	14,686	27.0
	John S. Robinson (HUNKER D)	6,790	15.2	1900	William W. Stickney (R)	48,441	72.2
1852	Erastus Fairbanks (W)	23,795†	49.3		John H. Center (D)	17,129	25.5
	John S. Robinson (D)	15,001	31.1	1902	John G. McCullough (R)	31,864†	45.6
	Lawrence Brainerd (F SOIL)	9,445	19.6		Percival W. Clement (H LIC)	28,201	40.3
1853	Erastus Fairbanks (W)	21,118	44.1		Felix W. McGettrick (D)	7,364	10.5
	John S. Robinson (D)	18,287†	38.2	1904	Charles J. Bell (R)	48,115	72.2
	Lawrence Brainerd (F SOIL)	8,370	17.5		Eli H. Porter (D)	16,556	24.9
1854	Stephen Royce (W)	27,811	62.4	1906	Fletcher D. Proctor (R)	42,332	60.1
	Merritt Clark (D)	15,130	33.9		Percival W. Clement (ID)	26,912	38.2
1855	Stephen Royce (R)	25,699#	59.0	1908	George H. Prouty (R)	45,598	70.8
	Merritt Clark (D)	12,800#	29.4		James E. Burke (D)	15,953	24.8
	James M. Slade (AM)	3,631#	8.3	1910	John A. Mead (R)	35,263	64.2
1856	Ryland Fletcher (R)	34,757	74.3		Charles D. Watson (D)	17,425	31.7
	Henry Keyes (D)	11,747	25.1	1912	Allen M. Fletcher (R)	26,237†	40.5
1857	Ryland Fletcher (R)	27,065	67.1		Harland B. Howe (D)	20,001	30.9
	Henry Keyes (D)	12,984	32.2		Frazer Metzger (PROG)	15,629	24.1
1858	Hiland Hall (R)	29,460	68.5	1914	Charles W. Gates (R)	36,972	59.5
	Henry Keyes (D)	13,538	31.5		Harland B. Howe (D)	16,191	26.1
1859	Hiland Hall (R)	31,367	68.4		Walter J. Aldrich (PROG)	6,929	11.2
	John G. Saxe (D)	14,499	31.6	1916	Horace F. Graham (R)	43,265	71.1
1860	Erastus Fairbanks (R)	34,260	71.0		William B. Mayo (D)	15,789	26.0
	John G. Saxe (DOUG D)	11,890	24.6	1918	Percival W. Clement (R)	28,358	67.2
1861	Frederick Holbrook (UN R)	33,155	78.8		William B. Mayo (D, P)	13,859	32.8
	Andrew Tracy (UN D)	5,722	13.6	1920	James Hartness (R, P)	67,674	78.0
	B. H. Smalley (BRECK D)	3,190	7.6		Fred C. Martin (D)	18,917	21.8
1862	Frederick Holbrook (R)	30,032	88.5	1922	Redfield Proctor (R, P)	51,104	74.8
	B. H. Smalley (D)	3,724	11.0		J. Holmes Jackson (D)	17,059	25.0
1863	John Gregory Smith (R)	29,613	71.2	1924	Franklin S. Billings (R)	75,510	79.3
	Timothy P. Redfield (D)	11,962	22.8		Fred C. Martin (D)	18,263	19.2
1864	John Gregory Smith (UN)	31,260	71.8	1926	John E. Weeks (R)	44,564	60.9
	Timothy P. Redfield (D)	12,283	28.2		Herbert C. Comings (D, P)	28,651	39.1
1865	Paul Dillingham (R)	27,586	75.7	1928	John E. Weeks (R)	94,974	73.5
	Charles N. Davenport (D)	8,857	24.3		Harry C. Shurtleff (D)	33,563	26.0
1866	Paul Dillingham (R)	34,117	75.1	1930	Stanley C. Wilson (R)	52,836	71.0

	Candidates	Votes	%
	Park H. Pollard (D)	21,540	*28.9*
1932	Stanley C. Wilson (R)	81,656	*61.7*
	James P. Leamy (D)	49,247	*37.2*
1934	Charles M. Smith (R)	73,620	*57.3*
	James P. Leamy (D)	54,159	*42.1*
1936	George D. Aiken (R)	83,602	*60.9*
	Alfred H. Heininger (D)	53,218	*38.8*
1938	George D. Aiken (R)	75,098	*66.8*
	Fred C. Martin (D)	37,404	*33.3*
1940	William H. Wills (R)	87,346	*64.0*
	John McGrath (D)	49,068	*36.0*
1942	William H. Wills (R)	44,804	*77.9*
	Park H. Pollard (D)	12,708	*22.1*
1944	Mortimer R. Proctor (R)	78,907	*65.9*
	Ernest H. Bailey (D)	40,835	*34.1*
1946	Ernest W. Gibson (R)	57,849	*80.3*
	Berthold C. Coburn (D)	14,096	*19.6*
1948	Ernest W. Gibson (R)	86,394	*71.9*
	Charles F. Ryan (D)	33,588	*28.0*
1950	Lee E. Emerson (R)	64,915	*74.5*
	J. Edward Moran (D)	22,227	*25.5*
1952	Lee E. Emerson (R)	78,338	*51.9*
	Robert W. Larrow (D)	60,051	*39.8*
	Henry W. Vail (IR)	12,447	*8.3*
1954	Joseph B. Johnson (R)	59,778	*52.3*
	E. Frank Branon (D)	54,554	*47.7*
1956	Joseph B. Johnson (R)	88,379	*57.5*
	E. Frank Branon (D)	65,420	*42.5*
1958	Robert T. Stafford (R)	62,222	*50.3*
	Bernard J. Leddy (D)	61,503	*49.7*
1960	F. Ray Keyser Jr. (R)	92,861	*56.4*
	Russell F. Niquette (D)	71,755	*43.6*
1962	Philip H. Hoff (D, I)	61,383	*50.6*
	F. Ray Keyser Jr. (R)	60,035	*49.4*
1964	Philip H. Hoff (D)	106,611	*64.9*
	Ralph A. Foote (R, I)	57,576	*35.1*
1966	Philip H. Hoff (D)	78,669	*57.7*
	Richard A. Snelling (R)	57,577	*42.3*
1968	Deane C. Davis (R)	89,387	*55.5*
	John J. Daley (D)	71,656	*44.5*
1970	Deane C. Davis (R)	87,458	*57.0*
	Leo O'Brien Jr. (D)	66,028	*43.0*
1972	Thomas P. Salmon (D, I VT)	104,533	*55.2*
	Luther F. Hackett (R)	82,491	*43.6*
1974	Thomas P. Salmon (D, I VT)	79,842	*56.6*
	Walter L. Kennedy (R)	53,672	*38.0*
	Martha Abbott (LU)	7,629	*5.4*
1976	Richard A. Snelling (R)	99,268	*53.4*
	Stella B. Hackel (D)	75,262	*40.5*
	Bernard J. Sanders (LU)	11,317	*6.1*
1978	Richard A. Snelling (R)	78,181	*62.8*
	Edwin C. Granai (D)	42,482	*34.1*
1980	Richard A. Snelling (R)	123,229	*58.6*
	J. Jerome Diamond (D)	77,363	*36.8*
1982	Richard A. Snelling (R)	93,111	*55.0*
	Madeleine M. Kunin (D)	74,394	*44.0*
1984	Madeleine M. Kunin (D)	116,938	*50.0*
	John J. Easton (R)	113,264	*48.5*

VIRGINIA

(Ratified the Constitution June 25, 1788)

	Candidates	Votes	%
1851[1]	Joseph Johnson (D)	67,074	*53.0*
	Summers (W)	59,476	*47.0*
1855	Henry A. Wise (D)	83,224	*53.2*
	Flournoy (AM)	73,244	*46.8*
1859	John Letcher (D)	77,112	*51.9*
	Goggin (OPP)	71,543	*48.1*

	Candidates	Votes	%
1861	John Letcher	✔	
1863	William Smith	✔	
	Munford		
	Flournoy		
1869	Gilbert C. Walker (C)	119,535	*54.2*
	H. H. Wells (RAD)	101,204	*45.9*
1873	James L. Kemper (D)	119,672	*56.2*
	Robert E. Hughes (R)	93,413	*43.8*
1877	Frederick W. M. Holliday (D)	101,873	*95.9*
1881	William E. Cameron (READJ)	113,464	*53.0*
	John W. Daniel (D)	100,757	*47.0*
1885	Fitzhugh Lee (D)	152,547	*52.8*
	John S. Wise (R)	136,508	*47.2*
1889	Philip W. McKinney (D)	163,180	*57.2*
	William Mahone (R)	121,240	*42.5*
1893	Charles T. O'Ferrall (D)	128,144	*59.7*
	Edmund R. Cocke (POP)	79,653	*37.1*
1897	James Hoge Tyler (D)	110,253	*64.6*
	Patrick H. McCaull (R)	56,739	*33.2*
1901	A. J. Montague (D)	116,691	*58.2*
	J. Hampton Hoge (R)	81,366	*40.6*
1905	Claude A. Swanson (D)	84,235	*64.5*
	Lunsford L. Lewis (R)	45,815	*35.1*
1909	William Hodges Mann (D)	70,759	*63.4*
	William P. Kent (R)	40,357	*36.1*
1913	Henry C. Stuart (D)	66,518	*91.9*
	C. Campbell (SOC)	3,789	*5.2*
1917	Westmoreland Davis (D)	64,226	*71.5*
	T. J. Muncy (R)	24,957	*27.8*
1921	Elbert Lee Trinkle (D)	139,416	*66.2*
	Henry W. Anderson (R)	65,833	*31.2*
1925	Harry F. Byrd (D)	107,378	*74.1*
	S. Harris Hoge (R)	37,592	*25.9*
1929	John Garland Pollard (D)	169,329	*62.8*
	William Moseley Brown (R)	99,650	*36.9*
1933	George C. Peery (D)	122,820	*73.7*
	Fred W. McWane (R)	40,377	*24.2*
1937	James H. Price (D)	124,145	*82.8*
	J. Powell Royall	23,670	*15.8*
1941	Colgate W. Darden Jr. (D)	98,680	*80.6*
	Muse	21,896	*17.9*
1945	William M. Tuck (D)	112,355	*66.6*
	S. Lloyd Landreth	52,386	*31.0*
1949	John S. Battle (D)	184,772	*70.4*
	Walter Johnson (R)	71,991	*27.4*
1953	Thomas B. Stanley (D)	226,998	*54.8*
	Ted Dalton (R)	183,328	*44.3*
1957	J. Lindsay Almond Jr. (D)	326,921	*63.2*
	Ted Dalton (R)	188,628	*36.4*
1961	Albertis S. Harrison Jr. (D)	251,861	*63.8*
	H. Clyde Pearson (R)	142,567	*36.1*
1965	Mills E. Godwin Jr. (D)	269,526	*47.9*
	Linwood Holton (R)	212,207	*37.7*
	William J. Story Jr. (C)	75,307	*13.4*
1969	Linwood Holton (R)	480,869	*52.5*
	William C. Battle (D)	415,695	*45.4*
1973	Mills E. Godwin Jr. (R)	525,075	*50.7*
	Henry Howell (I)	510,103	*49.3*
1977	John Dalton (R)	699,302	*55.9*
	Henry Howell (D)	541,319	*43.3*
1981	Charles S. Robb (D)	760,357	*53.5*
	J. Marshall Coleman (R)	659,398	*46.4*

1. Before 1851 governor was elected by General Assembly.

WASHINGTON

(Became a state Nov. 11, 1889)

	Candidates	Votes	%
1889	Elisha P. Ferry (R)	33,711	*57.7*
	Eugene Scruple (D)	24,732	*42.3*

	Candidates	Votes	%
1892	John H. McGraw (R)	33,281	*37.0*
	Henry J. Snively (D)	28,959	*32.2*
	C. W. Young (PP)	23,750	*26.4*
1896	John R. Rogers (PP)	50,849	*55.6*
	P. C. Sullivan (R)	38,154	*41.7*
1900	John R. Rogers (D)	52,048	*48.9*
	J. M. Frink (R)	49,860	*46.8*
1904	Albert E. Mead (R)	74,278	*51.3*
	George Turner (D)	59,119	*40.9*
	D. Burgess (SOC)	7,421	*5.1*
1908	Samuel G. Cosgrove (R)	110,190	*62.6*
	John Pattison (D)	58,126	*33.0*
1912	Ernest Lister (D)	97,251	*30.6*
	M. E. Hay (R)	96,629	*30.4*
	Robert T. Hodge (PROG)	77,731	*24.4*
	Anna A. Maley (SOC)	37,155	*11.7*
1916	Ernest Lister (D)	181,745	*48.1*
	Henry McBride (R)	167,809	*44.4*
	L. E. Katterfeld (SOC)	21,117	*5.6*
1920	Louis F. Hart (R)	210,662	*52.7*
	Robert Bridges (F-LAB)	121,371	*30.4*
	W. W. Black (D)	66,079	*16.5*
1924	Roland H. Hartley (R)	220,162	*56.4*
	Ben F. Hill (D)	126,447	*32.4*
	J. R. Oman (F-LAB)	40,073	*10.3*
1928	Roland H. Hartley (R)	281,991	*56.2*
	Scott Bullitt (D)	214,334	*42.7*
1932	Clarence D. Martin (D)	352,215	*57.3*
	John A. Gellatly (R)	207,497	*33.8*
	L. C. Hicks (LIB)	41,710	*6.8*
1936	Clarence D. Martin (D)	466,550	*69.4*
	Roland H. Hartley (R)	189,141	*28.1*
1940	Arthur B. Langlie (R)	392,522	*50.2*
	C. C. Dill (D)	386,706	*49.5*
1944	Monrad C. Wallgren (D)	428,834	*51.5*
	Arthur B. Langlie (R)	400,604	*48.1*
1948	Arthur B. Langlie (R)	445,958	*50.5*
	Monrad C. Wallgren (D)	417,035	*47.2*
1952	Arthur B. Langlie (R)	567,822	*52.7*
	Hugh B. Mitchell (D)	510,675	*47.4*
1956	Albert D. Rosellini (D)	616,773	*54.6*
	Emmett T. Anderson (R)	508,041	*45.0*
1960	Albert D. Rosellini (D)	611,987	*50.3*
	Lloyd Andrews (R)	594,122	*48.9*
1964	Daniel J. Evans (R)	697,256	*55.8*
	Albert D. Rosellini (D)	548,692	*43.9*
1968	Daniel J. Evans (R)	692,378	*54.7*
	John J. O'Connell (D)	560,262	*44.3*
1972	Daniel J. Evans (R)	747,825	*50.8*
	Albert D. Rosellini (D)	630,613	*42.8*
	Vick Gould (TPCT)	86,843	*5.9*
1976	Dixy Lee Ray (R)	821,797	*53.1*
	John D. Spellman (R)	687,039	*44.4*
1980	John D. Spellman (R)	981,083	*56.7*
	James A. McDermott (D)	749,813	*43.3*
1984	Booth Gardner (D)	1,006,993	*53.3*
	John Spellman (R)	881,994	*46.7*

WEST VIRGINIA

(Became a state June 19, 1863)

	Candidates	Votes	%
1863	Arthur I. Boreman (UN R)	25,797	*100.0*
1864	Arthur I. Boreman (UN R)	19,353	*100.0*
1866	Arthur I. Boreman (R)	23,802	*58.1*
	Benjamin H. Smith (D)	17,158	*41.9*
1868	William E. Stevenson (R)	26,935	*54.6*
	James M. Camden (D)	22,358	*45.4*
1870	John J. Jacob (D)	29,097	*51.9*
	William E. Stevenson (R)	26,924	*48.1*

	Candidates	Votes	%
1872	John J. Jacob (I)	42,888	*51.6*
	Johnson N. Camden (D)	40,305	*48.5*
1876	Henry M. Mathews (D)	56,206	*56.2*
	Nathan Goff (R)	43,477	*43.5*
1880	Jacob B. Jackson (D)	60,991	*51.3*
	George C. Sturgiss (R)	44,855	*37.7*
	N. B. French (G)	13,027	*11.0*
1884	E. Willis Wilson (D)	71,408	*52.0*
	Edwin Maxwell (R)	66,059	*48.1*
1888	Nathan Goff (R)	78,904‡	*50.0*
	A. Brooks Fleming (D)	78,798	*50.0*
1892	William A. MacCorkle (D)	84,585	*49.4*
	Thomas E. Davis (R)	80,658	*47.1*
1896	George W. Atkinson (R)	105,588	*52.4*
	Cornelius C. Watts (D)	93,558	*46.4*
1900	A. B. White (R)	118,798	*53.8*
	John H. Holt (D)	100,233	*45.4*
1904	William M. O. Dawson (R)	121,540	*50.8*
	John J. Cornwell (D)	112,538	*47.0*
1908	William E. Glasscock (R)	130,807	*50.7*
	Bennett (D)	118,909	*46.1*
1912	H. D. Hatfield (R)	128,062	*47.7*
	W. R. Thompson (D)	119,292	*44.5*
	Walter B. Hilton (SOC)	15,048	*5.6*
1916	John J. Cornwell (D)	143,324	*49.5*
	Robinson (R)	140,558	*48.6*
1920	Ephraim F. Morgan (R)	242,237	*47.3*
	Arthur B. Koontz (D)	185,662	*36.3*
	S. B. Montgomery (NON PART)	81,330	*15.9*
1924	Howard M. Gore (R)	302,987	*53.0*
	Jake Fisher (D)	261,846	*45.8*
1928	William G. Conley (R)	345,729	*53.7*
	J. Alfred Taylor (D)	296,637	*46.1*
1932	Herman G. Kump (D)	402,316	*53.8*
	T. C. Townsend (R)	342,660	*45.8*
1936	Homer A. Holt (D)	492,333	*59.2*
	Summers H. Sharp (R)	339,890	*40.8*
1940	Matthew M. Neely (D)	496,028	*56.4*
	Daniel Boone Dawson (R)	383,698	*43.6*
1944	Clarence W. Meadows (D)	395,122	*54.4*
	Daniel Boone Dawson (R)	330,649	*45.6*
1948	Okey L. Patteson (D)	438,752	*57.1*
	Herbert S. Boreman (R)	329,309	*42.9*
1952	William C. Marland (D)	454,898	*51.5*
	Rush D. Holt (R)	427,629	*48.5*
1956	Cecil H. Underwood (R)	440,502	*53.9*
	Robert H. Mollohan (D)	377,121	*46.1*
1960	W. W. Barron (D)	446,755	*54.0*
	Harold E. Neely (R)	380,665	*46.0*
1964	Hulett Smith (D)	433,023	*54.9*
	Cecil H. Underwood (R)	355,559	*45.1*
1968	Arch A. Moore Jr. (R)	378,315	*50.9*
	James M. Sprouse (D)	365,530	*49.1*
1972	Arch A. Moore Jr. (R)	423,817	*54.7*
	John D. Rockefeller IV (D)	350,462	*45.3*
1976	John D. Rockefeller (D)	495,661	*66.2*
	Cecil H. Underwood (R)	253,420	*33.8*
1980	John D. Rockefeller (D)	401,863	*54.1*
	Arch A. Moore (R)	337,240	*45.4*
1984	Arch A. Moore, Jr. (R)	394,937	*53.3*
	Clyde M. See, Jr. (D)	346,565	*46.7*

WISCONSIN

(Became a state May 29, 1848)

	Candidates	Votes	%
1848	Nelson Dewey (D)	19,875	*57.6*
	Tweedy (W)	14,621	*42.4*

Gubernatorial Elections

	Candidates	Votes	%
1849	Nelson Dewey (D)	16,701	*52.6*
	Collins (W)	11,317	*35.6*
	Chase (F SOIL)	3,761	*11.8*
1851	Leonard J. Farwell (W)	22,319	*50.6*
	Upham (D)	21,812	*49.4*
1853	William Augustus Barstow (D)	30,455	*54.7*
	Holton (W)	21,886	*39.3*
	Baird (W)	3,318	*6.0*
1855	William Augustus Barstow (D)	36,387‡	*50.1*
	Coles Bashford (R)	36,197	*49.9*
1857	Alexander W. Randall (R)	44,693	*50.3*
	Cross (D)	44,239	*49.7*
1859	Alexander W. Randall (R)	63,466	*51.6*
	Harrison C. Hobart (D)	59,525	*48.4*
1861	Louis P. Harvey (R)	53,777	*54.2*
	Ferguson (D)	45,456	*45.8*
1863	James T. Lewis (R)	78,470	*58.8*
	Henry L. Palmer (D)	55,049	*41.2*
1865	Lucius Fairchild (R)	58,332	*54.7*
	Harrison C. Hobart (D)	48,330	*45.3*
1867	Lucius Fairchild (R)	73,637	*51.7*
	John J. Tallmadge (D)	68,873	*48.3*
1869	Lucius Fairchild (R)	69,502	*53.2*
	Charles D. Robinson (D)	61,239	*46.8*
1871	Cadwallader C. Washburn (R)	78,301	*53.2*
	James R. Doolittle (D)	68,920	*46.8*
1873	William R. Taylor (D)	81,599	*55.2*
	Cadwallader C. Washburn (R)	66,224	*44.8*
1875	Harrison Ludington (R)	85,165	*50.2*
	William R. Taylor (D)	84,374	*49.8*
1877	William E. Smith (R)	78,750	*44.9*
	Mallory (D)	70,486	*40.2*
	Edward P. Allis (G)	26,116	*14.9*
1879	William E. Smith (R)	100,537	*53.2*
	Jenkins (D)	75,030	*39.7*
	May (G)	12,996	*6.9*
1881	Jeremiah M. Rusk (R)	81,754	*47.6*
	Nicholas D. Fratt (D)	69,797	*40.6*
	Theodore D. Kanouse (P)	13,225	*7.7*
1884	Jeremiah M. Rusk (R)	163,210	*51.0*
	Nicholas D. Fratt (D)	143,943	*45.0*
1886	Jeremiah M. Rusk (R)	133,247	*46.5*
	Gilbert M. Woodward (D)	114,525	*40.0*
	John Cochrane (LAB)	21,467	*7.5*
	John M. Olin (P)	17,089	*6.0*
1888	William D. Hoard (R)	175,696	*49.5*
	James Morgan (D)	155,423	*43.8*
1890	George W. Peck (D)	160,388	*51.9*
	William D. Hoard (R)	132,074	*42.7*
1892	George W. Peck (D)	178,135	*47.9*
	John C. Spooner (R)	170,538	*45.9*
1894	William H. Upham (R)	196,151	*52.3*
	George W. Peck (D)	142,250	*37.9*
	D. Frank Powell (PP)	25,604	*6.8*
1896	Edward Scofield (R)	264,981	*59.7*
	Willis C. Silverthorn (D)	169,257	*38.1*
1898	Edward Scofield (R)	173,137	*52.6*
	Hiram Wilson Sawyer (D)	135,353	*41.1*
1900	Robert M. La Follette (R)	264,419	*59.8*
	Louis G. Bomrich (D)	160,674	*36.4*
1902	Robert M. La Follette (R)	193,407	*52.9*
	David S. Rose (D)	145,820	*39.9*
1904	Robert M. La Follette (R)	227,253	*50.6*
	George W. Peck (D)	176,301	*39.2*
	Arnold (SOCIAL D)	24,857	*5.5*
1906	James O. Davidson (R)	183,526	*57.4*
	John A. Aylward (D)	103,114	*32.3*
	Winfield R. Gaylord (SOCIAL D)	24,435	*7.6*
1908	James O. Davidson (R)	242,963	*54.0*
	John A. Aylward (D)	165,977	*36.9*
	Harvey D. Brown (SOCIAL D)	28,583	*6.4*
1910	Francis E. McGovern (R)	161,559	*50.6*
	Schmitz (D)	110,446	*34.6*
	Jacobs (SOCIAL D)	39,539	*12.4*
1912	Francis E. McGovern (R)	179,317	*45.6*
	John C. Karel (D)	167,298	*42.5*
	Carl D. Thompson (SOCIAL D)	34,385	*8.7*
1914	Emanuel L. Philipp (R)	140,835	*43.3*
	John C. Karel (D)	119,567	*36.7*
	John J. Blaine (I)	32,543	*10.0*
	Oscar Ameringer (SOCIAL D)	25,940	*8.0*
1916	Emanuel L. Philipp (R)	227,896	*52.7*
	Burt Williams (D)	164,633	*38.1*
	Rae Weaver (SOC)	30,813	*7.1*
1918	Emanuel L. Philipp (R)	155,799	*47.0*
	Moehlenpah (D)	112,576	*34.0*
	Seidel (SOC)	57,532	*17.4*
1920	John J. Blaine (R)	366,247	*53.0*
	McCoy (D)	247,746	*35.8*
	Coleman (SOC)	71,103	*10.3*
1922	John J. Blaine (R)	367,929	*76.4*
	Arthur A. Bentley (ID)	51,061	*10.6*
	Louis A. Arnold (SOC)	39,570	*8.2*
1924	John J. Blaine (R)	412,255	*51.8*
	Martin L. Lueck (D)	317,550	*39.9*
	William F. Quick (SOC)	45,268	*5.7*
1926	Fred R. Zimmerman (R)	350,927	*63.5*
	Charles B. Perry (I)	76,507	*13.8*
	Virgil H. Cady (I)	72,627	*13.1*
	Herman O. Kent (SOC)	40,293	*7.3*
1928	Walter J. Kohler Sr. (R)	547,738	*55.4*
	Albert G. Schmedeman (D)	394,368	*39.9*
1930	Philip F. La Follette (R)	392,958	*64.8*
	Hammersley (D)	170,020	*28.0*
1932	Albert G. Schmedeman (D)	590,114	*52.5*
	Walter J. Kohler Sr. (R)	470,805	*41.9*
	Metcalfe (SOC)	56,965	*5.1*
1934	Philip F. La Follette (PROG)	373,083	*39.1*
	Albert G. Schmedeman (D)	359,467	*37.7*
	Greene (R)	172,980	*18.1*
1936	Philip F. La Follette (PROG)	573,724	*46.4*
	Alexander Wiley (R)	363,973	*29.4*
	William L. Lueck (D)	268,530	*21.7*
1938	Julius P. Heil (R)	543,675	*55.4*
	Philip F. La Follette (PROG)	353,381	*36.0*
	Bolens (D)	78,446	*8.0*
1940	Julius P. Heil (R)	558,678	*40.7*
	Orland S. Loomis (PROG)	546,436	*39.8*
	McGovern (D)	264,985	*19.3*
1942	Orland S. Loomis (PROG)	397,664*	*49.7*
	Julius P. Heil (R)	291,945	*36.5*
	Sullivan (D)	98,153	*12.3*
1944	Walter S. Goodland (R)	697,740	*52.8*
	Daniel W. Hoan (D)	536,357	*40.6*
	Benz (PROG)	76,028	*5.8*
1946	Walter S. Goodland (R)	621,970	*59.8*
	Daniel W. Hoan (D)	406,499	*39.1*
1948	Oscar Rennebohm (R)	684,839	*54.1*
	Carl W. Thompson (D)	558,497	*44.1*
1950	Walter J. Kohler Jr. (R)	605,649	*53.2*
	Carl W. Thompson (D)	525,319	*46.2*
1952	Walter J. Kohler Jr. (R)	1,009,171	*62.5*
	William Proxmire (D)	601,844	*37.3*
1954	Walter J. Kohler Jr. (R)	596,158	*51.5*
	William Proxmire (D)	560,747	*48.4*
1956	Vernon W. Thomson (R)	808,273	*51.9*
	William Proxmire (D)	749,421	*48.1*
1958	Gaylord A. Nelson (D)	644,296	*53.6*
	Vernon W. Thomson (R)	556,391	*46.3*
1960	Gaylord A. Nelson (D)	890,868	*51.6*
	Philip G. Kuehn (R)	837,123	*48.4*
1962	John W. Reynolds (D)	637,491	*50.4*

	Candidates	Votes	%
	Philip G. Kuehn (R)	625,536	49.4
1964	Warren P. Knowles (R)	856,779	50.6
	John W. Reynolds (D)	837,901	49.4
1966	Warren P. Knowles (R)	626,041	53.5
	Patrick J. Lucey (D)	539,258	46.1
1968	Warren P. Knowles (R)	893,463	52.9
	Bronson C. La Follette (D)	791,100	46.8
1970	Patrick J. Lucey (D)	728,403	54.2
	Jack B. Olson (R)	602,617	44.9
1974	Patrick J. Lucey (D)	628,639	53.2
	William D. Dyke (R)	497,195	42.1
1978	Lee S. Dreyfus (R)	816,056	54.4
	Martin J. Schreiber (D)	673,813	44.9
1982	Anthony S. Earl (D)	896,812	56.7
	Terry J. Kohler (R)	662,838	41.9

WYOMING

(Became a state July 10, 1890)

	Candidates	Votes	%
1890	Francis E. Warren (R)	8,879	55.4
	George W. Baxter (D)	7,153	44.6

Special Election

1892	John E. Osborne (D)	9,290	53.8
	Edward Ivinson (R)	7,509	43.5

1894	William A. Richards (R)	10,149	52.6
	William H. Holliday (D)	6,965	36.1
	Lewis C. Tidball (POP)	2,176	11.3
1898	DeForest Richards (R)	10,383	52.4
	Horace C. Alger (D)	8,989	45.4
1902	DeForest Richards (R)	14,483	57.8
	George T. Beck (D)	10,017	40.0

Special Election

1904	Bryant B. Brooks (R)	17,765	57.5
	John E. Osborne (D)	12,137	39.3

1906	Bryant B. Brooks (R)	16,317	60.2
	Stephen A. D. Keister (D)	9,444	34.8
1910	Joseph M. Carey (D)	21,086	55.6
	W. E. Mullen (R)	15,235	40.2

	Candidates	Votes	%
1914	John B. Kendrick (D)	22,387	51.6
	Hilliard S. Ridgely (R)	19,174	44.2
1918	Robert D. Carey (R)	23,825	56.1
	Frank L. Houx (D)	18,640	43.9
1922	William B. Ross (D)	31,110	50.6
	John W. Hay (R)	30,387	49.4

Special Election

1924	Nellie T. Ross (D)	43,323	55.1
	E. J. Sullivan (R)	35,275	44.9

1926	Frank C. Emerson (R)	35,651	50.9
	Nellie T. Ross (D)	34,286	49.0
1930	Frank C. Emerson (R)	38,058	50.6
	Leslie A. Miller (D)	37,188	49.4

Special Election

1932	Leslie A. Miller (D)	48,130	50.9
	Harry R. Weston (R)	44,692	47.2

1934	Leslie A. Miller (D)	54,305	57.9
	A. M. Clark (R)	38,792	41.4
1938	Nels H. Smith (R)	57,288	59.8
	Leslie A. Miller (D)	38,501	40.2
1942	Lester C. Hunt (D)	39,599	51.3
	Nels H. Smith (R)	37,568	48.7
1946	Lester C. Hunt (D)	43,020	52.9
	Earl Wright (R)	38,333	47.1
1950	Frank A. Barrett (R)	54,441	56.2
	John J. McIntyre (D)	42,518	43.9
1954	Milward L. Simpson (R)	56,275	50.5
	William Jack (D)	55,163	49.5
1958	J. J. Hickey (D)	55,070	48.9
	Milward L. Simpson (R)	52,488	46.6
1962	Clifford P. Hansen (R)	64,970	54.5
	Jack R. Gage (D)	54,298	45.5
1966	Stanley K. Hathaway (R)	65,624	54.3
	Ernest Wilkerson (D)	55,249	45.7
1970	Stanley K. Hathaway (R)	74,249	62.8
	John J. Rooney (D)	44,008	37.2
1974	Ed Herschler (D)	71,741	55.9
	Dick Jones (R)	56,645	44.1
1978	Ed Herschler (D)	69,972	50.9
	John C. Ostlund (R)	67,595	49.1
1982	Ed Herschler (D)	106,427	63.1
	Warren A. Morton (R)	62,128	36.9

See Governor Returns; Other Sources (next page).

Governor Returns: Other Sources

In the preceding pages (489-535), the symbol # is used to denote returns taken from a source other than Congressional Quarterly's two principal sources of historical gubernatorial popular election returns: the Inter-University Consortium for Political and Social Research (ICPSR) for 1824-1974 returns, or Joseph E. Kallenbach and Jessamine S. Kallenbach, *American State Governors, 1776-1976*, vol. 1, Dobbs Ferry, N.Y.: Oceana Publications, 1977, for pre-

1824 returns. Election returns from 1975-83 were taken from the biennial series *America Votes* by Richard M. Scammon and Alice V. McGillivray, Washington, D.C.: Congressional Quarterly. For 1984 elections, Congressional Quarterly obtained the official, final returns from the individual secretaries of state. This page lists the source for elections where the symbol # appears. *(For a description of the ICPSR collection, see pp. xiv, 488.)*

Delaware 1928:
  Secretary of State of Delaware.
Florida 1868:
  Morris, Allen. *The Florida Handbook 1975-76*. Tallahassee, Fla.: Peninsular Publishing, 1975; 532.
Florida 1916:
  Governors of the States 1900-1974. Lexington, Ky.: Council of State Governments; 16.
Louisiana 1920:
  Secretary of State of Louisiana.
Minnesota 1861, 1873, 1875, 1877:
  The Minnesota Legislative Manual 1973-1974. St. Paul, Minn.: State of

Minnesota; 507-508.
Mississippi 1983:
  Secretary of State of Mississippi.
New York 1958:
  Scammon, Richard M. *America Votes 3*. Pittsburgh: University of Pittsburgh, 1959; 272.
Texas 1845:
  Kallenbach, Joseph E., and Jessamine S. Kallenbach. *American State Governors, 1776-1976*. vol. 1, Dobbs Ferry, N.Y.: Oceana Publications, 1977; 572.
Vermont 1829, 1830, 1831, 1855:
  Vermont State Manual and Legislative Directory; 314-315.

Gubernatorial Primary Returns, 1956-1984

(For Southern primary gubernatorial returns, see p. 1075.)

ALASKA

	Candidates	Votes	%
1958	**Republican Primary**		
	John Butrovich (R)		100.0
	Democratic Primary		
	William A. Egan (D)	22,735	61.1
	Victor Rivers (D)	8,845	23.7
	J. G. Williams (D)	5,656	15.2
1962	**Republican Primary**		
	Mike Stepovich (R)	6,415	38.1
	Howard W. Pollock (R)	5,247	31.2
	John B. Coghill (R)	2,295	13.6
	Verne O. Martin (R)	1,504	8.9
	Milo H. Fritz (R)	1,371	8.1
	Democratic Primary		
	William A. Egan (D)	13,698	62.3
	George H. Byer (D)	5,275	24.0
	Warren A. Taylor (D)	2,386	10.8
1966	**Republican Primary**		
	Walter J. Hickel (R)	10,580	55.3
	Bruce Kendall (R)	4,511	23.6
	Mike Stepovich (R)	4,039	21.1
	Democratic Primary		
	William A. Egan (D)	19,801	61.0
	Wendell P. Kay (D)	12,660	39.0
1970	**Republican Primary**		
	Keith Miller (R)	19,153	53.4
	Howard W. Pollock (R)	16,691	46.5
	Democratic Primary		
	William A. Egan (D)	23,973	67.5
	Larry Carr (D)	11,350	31.9
1974	**Republican Primary**		
	Jay S. Hammond (R)	28,602	47.2
	Walter J. Hickel (R)	20,728	34.2
	Keith Miller (R)	10,864	17.9

	Candidates	Votes	%
	Democratic Primary		
	William A. Egan (D)	20,356	91.0
1978 [1]	**Republican Primary**		
	Jay S. Hammond (R)	31,896	39.1
	Walter J. Hickel (R)	31,798	38.9
	Tom Fink (R)	17,487	21.4
	Democratic Primary		
	Chancy Croft (D)	8,911	36.1
	Edward A. Merdes (D)	8,639	35.0
	Jalmar M. Kerttula (D)	7,125	28.9

1. There were recounts of the votes received by the two top finishers in both primaries. In the Republican recount, Hammond's vote was 31,921 (50.0 percent) and Hickel's was 31,823 (49.9 percent). In the Democratic recount, Croft's vote was 8,910 (50.7 percent) and Merdes' was 8,655 (49.3 percent).

Gubernatorial Primary Sources

The major source for this section was the *America Votes* series compiled biennially by Richard M. Scammon and Alice V. McGillivray and published since 1966 by Congressional Quarterly Inc. Other sources were the returns obtained by Congressional Quarterly after each federal and gubernatorial election. In cases of discrepancies, the *Guide to U.S. Elections, Second Edition*, accepted the *America Votes* figure. Candidates are listed only if they received 5 percent or more of the vote.

The first year for which *America Votes* reported primary returns, 1956, was chosen as the starting point for this section because gubernatorial primary votes for earlier years are not readily available. Senate primary returns back to 1919 for 11 Southern states, where victory in the Democratic primary was tantamount to election for many years, may be found on pp. 1075-1090.

Where no primary is indicated for a year in which a state elected a governor, it generally means that party conventions chose the nominees. Notes at the end of a state's listing explain other unusual circumstances.

	Candidates	Votes	%
1982	**Republican Primary**		
	Tom Fink (R)	41,911	*51.3*
	Terry Miller (R)	36,594	*44.8*
	Democratic Primary		
	Bill Sheffield (D)	21,940	*39.7*
	Steve Cowper (D)	21,680	*39.2*
	H. A. Boucher (D)	8,584	*15.5*

ARIZONA

	Candidates	Votes	%
1956	**Republican Primary**		
	Horace B. Griffen (R)	20,471	*46.0*
	O. D. Miller (R)	17,858	*40.1*
	Fred Trump (R)	6,199	*13.9*
	Democratic Primary		
	Ernest W. McFarland (D)		*100.0*
1958	**Republican Primary**		
	Paul Fannin (R)		*100.0*
	Democratic Primary		
	Robert Morrison (D)	77,931	*50.4*
	Dick Searles (D)	58,699	*37.9*
	Marvin L. Burton (D)	18,122	*11.7*
1960	**Republican Primary**		
	Paul Fannin (R)		*100.0*
	Democratic Primary		
	Lee Ackerman (D)		*100.0*
1962	**Republican Primary**		
	Paul Fannin (R)		*100.0*
	Democratic Primary		
	Sam Goddard (D)	91,661	*59.8*
	Joe Haldiman (D)	41,645	*27.2*
	J. M. Morris (D)	19,850	*13.0*
1964	**Republican Primary**		
	Richard Kleindienst (R)	64,310	*62.8*
	Evan Mecham (R)	38,131	*37.2*
	Democratic Primary		
	Sam Goddard (D)	114,377	*60.0*
	Art Brock (D)	57,067	*30.0*
	J. M. Morris (D)	11,303	*5.9*

	Candidates	Votes	%
1966	**Republican Primary**		
	John R. Williams (R)	37,409	*44.3*
	John Haugh (R)	25,905	*30.6*
	Robert W. Pickrell (R)	21,192	*25.1*
	Democratic Primary		
	Sam Goddard (D)	63,180	*45.5*
	Norman Green (D)	53,921	*38.9*
	Andrew J. Gilbert (D)	23,637	*17.0*
1968	**Republican Primary**		
	John R. Williams (R)		*100.0*
	Democratic Primary		
	Sam Goddard (D)	112,948	*73.4*
	Currin V. Shields (D)	30,337	*19.7*
	Jack DeVault (D)	10,613	*6.9*
1970	**Republican Primary**		
	John R. Williams (R)		*100.0*
	Democratic Primary		
	Raul H. Castro (D)	63,294	*52.0*
	Jack Ross (D)	30,921	*25.4*
	George Nader (D)	27,534	*22.6*
1974	**Republican Primary**		
	Russell Williams (R)	53,132	*35.6*
	Evan Mecham (R)	30,266	*20.3*
	William C. Jacquin (R)	27,138	*18.2*
	John R. Driggs (R)	23,519	*15.7*
	Milton H. Graham (R)	15,315	*10.2*
	Democratic Primary		
	Raul H. Castro (D)	115,268	*67.2*
	Jack Ross (D)	31,250	*18.2*
	David R. Moss (D)	19,143	*11.2*
1978	**Republican Primary**		
	Evan Mecham (R)	50,713	*44.1*
	Jack Londen (R)	40,116	*34.9*
	Democratic Primary		
	Bruce Babbitt (D)	108,548	*76.8*
	David R. Moss (D)	32,785	*23.2*
	Libertarian Primary		
	V. Gene Lewter (LIBERT)		*100.0*
	Socialist Worker Primary		
	Jessica Sampson (SOC WORK)		*100.0*
1982	**Republican Primary**		
	Leo Corbet (R)	108,766	*61.7*
	Evan Mecham (R)	67,456	*38.3*

Candidates	Votes	%
Democratic Primary		
Bruce Babbitt (D)	142,559	*85.8*
Steve Jancek (D) [2]	23,492	*14.1*
Libertarian Primary		
Sam Stelger (LIBERT)		*100.0*

CALIFORNIA

	Candidates	Votes	%
1958	**Republican Primary**		
	William F. Knowland (R)	1,290,106	*77.5*
	Edmund G. Brown (D)	374,879	*22.5*
	Democratic Primary		
	Edmund G. Brown (D)	1,890,622	*82.6*
	William F. Knowland (R)	313,385	*13.7*
1962	**Republican Primary**		
	Richard M. Nixon (R)	1,285,151	*65.4*
	Joseph C. Shell (R)	656,542	*33.4*
	Democratic Primary		
	Edmund G. Brown (D)	1,739,792	*81.4*
	Prohibition Primary		
	Robert L. Wyckoff		*100.0*
1966	**Republican Primary**		
	Ronald Reagan (R)	1,417,623	*64.7*
	George Christopher (R)	675,683	*30.8*
	Democratic Primary		
	Edmund G. Brown (D)	1,355,262	*51.9*
	Samuel W. Yorty (D)	981,088	*37.6*
1970	**Republican Primary**		
	Ronald Reagan (R)		*100.0*
	Democratic Primary		
	Jess Unruh (D)	1,602,690	*64.0*
	Samuel W. Yorty (D)	659,494	*26.3*
	American Independent Primary		
	William K. Shearer (AMI)	14,069	*61.4*
	Keith H. Greene (AMI)	8,827	*38.5*
	Peace and Freedom Primary		
	Ricardo Romo (PFP)	6,214	*63.5*
	Warren A. Nielsen (PFP)	3,569	*36.5*

2. *Jancek died before the primary, but his name remained on the ballot.*

	Candidates	Votes	%
1974	**Republican Primary**		
	Houston I. Flournoy (R)	1,164,015	*63.0*
	Ed Reinecke (R)	556,259	*30.1*
	Democratic Primary		
	Edmund G. Brown Jr. (D)	1,085,752	*37.7*
	Joseph L. Alioto (D)	544,007	*18.9*
	Robert Moretti (D)	478,469	*16.6*
	William M. Roth (D)	293,686	*10.2*
	Jerome R. Waldie (D)	227,489	*7.9*
	American Independent Primary		
	Edmon V. Kaiser (AMI)		*100.0*
	Peace and Freedom Primary		
	Elizabeth Keathley (PFP)	2,111	*28.1*
	Lester H. Higby (PFP)	1,855	*24.7*
	C. T. Weber (PFP)	1,822	*24.2*
	Trudy Saposhnek (PFP)	1,417	*18.8*
1978	**Republican Primary**		
	Evelle J. Younger (R)	1,008,087	*40.0*
	Ed Davis (R)	738,741	*29.3*
	Ken Maddy (R)	484,583	*19.2*
	Pete Wilson (R)	230,146	*9.1*
	Democratic Primary		
	Edmund G. Brown Jr. (D)	2,567,067	*77.5*
	American Independent Primary		
	Theresa F. Dietrich (AMI)	12,278	*57.4*
	Laszlo Kecskemethy (AMI)	9,112	*42.6*
	Peace and Freedom Primary		
	Marilyn Seals (PFP)		*100.0*
1982	**Republican Primary**		
	George Deukmejian (R)	1,165,266	*51.1*
	Mike Curb (R)	1,020,935	*44.8*
	Democratic Primary		
	Tom Bradley (D)	1,726,985	*61.1*
	John Garamendi (D)	712,161	*25.2*
	American Independent Primary		
	James C. Griffin (AMI)		*100.0*
	Peace and Freedom Primary		
	Elizabeth Martinez (PFP)	4,353	*55.1*
	Jan B. Tucker (PFP)	3,552	*44.9*
	Libertarian Primary		
	Dan P. Dougherty (LIBERT)		*100.0*

COLORADO

	Candidates	Votes	%
1956	**Republican Primary**		
	Donald G. Brotzman (R)		100.0
	Democratic Primary		
	Stephen McNichols (D)		100.0
1958	**Republican Primary**		
	Palmer L. Burch (R)		100.0
	Democratic Primary		
	Stephen McNichols (D)		100.0
1962	**Republican Primary**		
	John A. Love (R)	66,027	59.6
	David A. Hamil (R)	44,693	40.4
	Democratic Primary		
	Stephen McNichols (D)		100.0
1966	**Republican Primary**		
	John A. Love (R)		100.0
	Democratic Primary		
	Robert L. Knous (D)		100.0
1970	**Republican Primary**		
	John A. Love (R)		100.0
	Democratic Primary		
	Mark Hogan (D)		100.0
1974	**Republican Primary**		
	John D. Vanderhoof (R)	94,334	60.5
	Robert W. Daniels (R)	61,691	39.5
	Democratic Primary		
	Richard D. Lamm (D)	120,452	58.7
	Thomas Farley (D)	84,796	41.3
1978	**Republican Primary**		
	Ted Strickland (R)	87,248	59.0
	Richard Plock (R)	60,597	41.0
	Democratic Primary		
	Richard D. Lamm (D)		100.0
1982	**Republican Primary**		
	John D. Fuhr (R)		100.0
	Democratic Primary		
	Richard D. Lamm (D)		100.0

CONNECTICUT

	Candidates	Votes	%
1970 [3]	**Republican Primary**		
	Thomas J. Meskill (R)	93,419	71.4
	Wallace Barnes (R)	37,383	28.6
1978 [3]	**Republican Primary**		
	Ella T. Grasso (D)	137,904	67.3
	Robert K. Killian (D)	66,924	32.7

DELAWARE

	Candidates	Votes	%
1972 [4]	**Republican Primary**		
	Russell W. Peterson (R)	23,929	54.3
	David P. Buckson (R)	20,138	45.7
1980 [4]	**Republican Primary**		
	Pierre S. (Pete) du Pont IV (R)		100.0
	Democratic Primary		
	William J. Gordy (D)		100.0
1984 [4]	**Republican Primary**		
	Michael N. Castle (R)		100.0
	Democratic Primary		
	William T. Quillen (D)	20,473	59.1
	Sherman W. Tribbitt (D)	14,185	40.9

HAWAII

	Candidates	Votes	%
1959	**Republican Primary**		
	William F. Quinn (R)		100.0
	Democratic Primary		
	John A. Burns (D)	69,152	89.8
	E. D. Hitchcock (D)	7,828	10.2

3. In Connecticut, party conventions nominated candidates subject to a system of "challenge" primaries that allowed defeated candidates to petition for a popular vote if they received at least 20 percent of the convention vote. Returns are given here for challenge primaries held for the governorship nomination between 1956 and 1984.

4. From 1972 through 1978 Delaware used a system of "challenge" primaries, in which a candidate for statewide office who received at least 35 percent of the convention vote could challenge the endorsed candidate in a primary.

Candidates	Votes	%
Commonwealth Primary		
David Kihei (CP)	65	*64.4*
Epifanio Taok (CP)	36	*35.6*
1962 Republican Primary		
William F. Quinn (R)	44,205	*57.1*
James K. Kealoha (R)	33,272	*49.9*
Democratic Primary		
John A. Burns (D)	71,540	*90.2*
Hyman Greenstein (D)	7,781	*9.8*
1966 Republican Primary		
Randolph Crossley (R)	35,311	*98.1*
Democratic Primary		
John A. Burns (D)	86,825	*79.5*
G. J. Fontes (D)	22,401	*20.5*
1970 Republican Primary		
Samuel P. King (R)	20,605	*49.3*
Hebden Porteus (R)	17,880	*42.8*
David Watumull (R)	3,318	*7.9*
Democratic Primary		
John A. Burns (D)	82,441	*53.2*
Thomas P. Gill (D)	69,209	*44.7*
1974 Republican Primary		
Randolph Crossley (R)	25,425	*82.5*
Joseph K. Hao (R)	5,405	*17.5*
Democratic Primary		
George R. Ariyoshi (D)	71,319	*36.2*
Frank F. Fasi (D)	62,023	*31.5*
Thomas P. Gill (D)	59,280	*30.1*
1978 Republican Primary		
John Leopold (R)	20,524	*91.6*
Democratic Primary		
George R. Ariyoshi (D)	130,527	*50.3*
Frank F. Fasi (D)	126,903	*48.9*
Aloha Democrat Primary		
John Moore (A-D)		*100.0*
Libertarian Primary		
Gregory Reeser (LIBERT)		*100.0*
Non-partisan Primary		
Alema Leota (NON-PART)	236	*58.9*
Frank Pore (NON-PART)	165	*41.1*

Candidates	Votes	%
1982 Republican Primary		
D. G. Anderson (R)	11,997	*96.8*
Democratic Primary		
George R. Ariyoshi (D)	128,993	*53.9*
Jean King (D)	106,935	*44.7*
Independent Democratic Primary		
Frank F. Fasi (ID)		*100.0*
Non-partisan Primary		
BraDa Ji Price (NON-PART) [5]		*100.0*

IDAHO

Candidates	Votes	%
1958 Republican Primary		
Robert E. Smylie (R)		*100.0*
Democratic Primary		
A. M. Derr (D)	25,599	*34.5*
H. Max Hanson (D)	25,477	*34.3*
John Glasby (D)	21,207	*28.6*
1962 Republican Primary		
Robert E. Smylie (R)	37,761	*57.2*
Elvin A. Lindquist (R)	16,565	*25.1*
George L. Crookham (R)	11,669	*17.7*
Democratic Primary		
Vernon K. Smith (D)	35,574	*43.1*
Charles Herndon (D)	18,072	*21.9*
John G. Walters (D)	13,186	*16.0*
Howard D. Hechtner (D)	7,952	*9.6*
Conley Ward (D)	5,427	*6.6*
1966 Republican Primary		
Don Samuelson (R)	52,891	*61.0*
Robert E. Smylie (R)	33,753	*39.0*
Democratic Primary		
Charles Herndon (D) [6]	28,926	*40.7*
Cecil D. Andrus (D)	27,649	*39.0*
William J. Dee (D)	14,409	*20.3*
1970 Republican Primary		
Don Samuelson (R)	46,719	*58.4*
Dick Smith (R)	33,339	*41.6*

5. *Price withdrew and no substitution was made.*

6. *Herndon died after the primary and the Democratic state central committee substituted Andrus as the nominee.*

Candidates	Votes	%
Democratic Primary		
Cecil D. Andrus (D)	29,036	*46.0*
Vernon Ravenscroft (D)	23,369	*37.1*
Lloyd Walker (D)	10,664	*16.9*
1974 **Republican Primary**		
Jack M. Murphy (R)		*100.0*
Democratic Primary		
Cecil D. Andrus (D)		*100.0*
1978 **Republican Primary**		
Allan Larsen (R)	33,778	*28.7*
Vernon Ravenscroft (D)	32,455	*27.6*
C. L. Otter (R)	30,523	*26.0*
Larry Jackson (R)	13,510	*11.5*
Democratic Primary		
John V. Evans (D)		*100.0*
American Primary		
Wayne L. Loveless (AM)		*100.0*
1982 **Republican Primary**		
Phillip Batt (R)	63,622	*63.9*
Ralph Olmstead (R)	35,932	*36.1*
Democratic Primary		
John V. Evans (D)		*100.0*

ILLINOIS

Candidates	Votes	%
1956 **Republican Primary**		
William G. Stratton (R)	556,909	*69.8*
Warren E. Wright (R)	187,645	*23.5*
Democratic Primary		
Herbert C. Paschen (D) [7]	475,813	*57.8*
Morris B. Sachs (D)	347,458	*42.2*
1960 **Republican Primary**		
William G. Stratton (R)	499,365	*59.1*
Hayes Robertson (R)	345,340	*40.9*
Democratic Primary		
Otto Kerner (D)	649,253	*60.9*
Joseph D. Lohman (D)	232,345	*21.8*
Stephen A. Mitchell (D)	184,651	*17.3*

Candidates	Votes	%
1964 **Republican Primary**		
Charles H. Percy (R)	626,111	*60.3*
William J. Scott (R)	388,903	*37.4*
Democratic Primary		
Otto Kerner (D)		*100.0*
1968 **Republican Primary**		
Richard B. Ogilvie (R)	335,727	*47.5*
John H. Altofer (R)	288,904	*40.9*
William G. Stratton (R)	50,041	*7.1*
Democratic Primary		
Samuel H. Shapiro (D)		*100.0*
1972 **Republican Primary**		
Richard B. Ogilvie (R)	442,323	*75.5*
John Mathis (D)	143,053	*24.4*
Democratic Primary		
Daniel Walker (D)	735,193	*51.4*
Paul Simon (D)	694,900	*48.6*
1976 **Republican Primary**		
James R. Thompson (R)	625,457	*86.4*
Richard H. Cooper (R)	97,937	*13.5*
Democratic Primary		
Michael J. Howlett (D)	811,721	*53.8*
Daniel Walker (D)	696,380	*46.2*
1978 **Republican Primary**		
James R. Thompson (R)		*100.0*
Democratic Primary		
Michael Bakalis (D)	601,045	*82.8*
W. Dakin Williams (D)	124,406	*17.2*
1982 **Republican Primary**		
James R. Thompson (R)	507,893	*83.7*
John E. Roche (R)	54,858	*9.0*
V. A. Kelley (R)	43,627	*7.2*
Democratic Primary		
Adlai E. Stevenson III (D)		*100.0*

INDIANA

Candidates	Votes	%
1976 [8] **Republican Primary**		
Otis R. Bowen (R)		*100.0*

7. Paschen withdrew after the primary and the Democratic state committee substituted Richard B. Austin as the party's nominee.

8. Until 1976 all nominations for statewide office in Indiana were made by state party conventions.

Candidates	Votes	%
Democratic Primary		
Larry A. Conrad (D)	358,421	64.5
Jack L. New (D)	105,965	19.1
Robert J. Fair (D)	91,606	16.5

1980 **Republican Primary**

Robert D. Orr (R)		100.0

Democratic Primary

John A. Hillenbrand (D)	284,182	52.4
W. Wayne Townsend (D)	257,779	47.6

1984 **Republican Primary**

Robert D. Orr (R)	319,889	71.6
John Snyder (R)	126,778	28.4

Democratic Primary

W. Wayne Townsend (D)	347,948	56.9
Virginia Dill McCarty (D)	219,806	35.9
Donald W. Mantooth (D)	43,507	7.1

IOWA

Candidates	Votes	%
1956 **Republican Primary**		
Leo A Hoegh (R)		100.0
Democratic Primary		
Herschel C. Loveless (D)	77,206	70.0
Lawrence E. Plummer (D)	33,103	30.0

1958 **Republican Primary**

William G. Murray (R)	112,496	56.6
W. H. Nicholas (R)	86,154	43.4

Democratic Primary

Herschel C. Loveless (D)		100.0

1960 **Republican Primary**

Norman A. Erbe (R)	81,869	36.3
Jack Schroeder (R)	75,599	33.5
W. H. Nicholas (R)	68,037	30.2

Democratic Primary

E. J. McManus (D)	74,990	61.7
Harold E. Hughes (D)	46,542	38.3

1962 **Republican Primary**

Norman A. Erbe (R)	134,010	67.7
W. H. Nicholas (R)	63,966	32.3

Democratic Primary

Harold E. Hughes (D)	66,624	78.9
Lewis E. Lint (D)	17,770	21.1

1964 **Republican Primary**

Evan Hultman (R)		100.0

Democratic Primary

Harold E. Hughes (D)		100.0

1966 **Republican Primary**

William G. Murray (R)	87,371	50.5
Robert K. Beck (R)	85,733	49.5

Democratic Primary

Harold E. Hughes (D)		100.0

1968 **Republican Primary**

Robert Ray (R)	108,744	43.2
Donald E. Johnson (R)	77,715	30.8
Robert K. Beck (R)	65,439	26.0

Democratic Primary

Paul Frazenburg		100.0

1970 **Republican Primary**

Robert Ray (R)		100.0

Democratic Primary

Robert Fulton (D)	48,459	46.7
William Gannon (D)	46,524	44.8
Robert L. Nereim (D)	8,796	8.5

1972 **Republican Primary**

Robert Ray (R)		100.0

Democratic Primary

Paul Franzenburg (D)	85,807	57.5
John Tapscott (D)	63,284	42.4

American Independent Primary

Robert D. Dilley (AMI)		100.0

1974 **Republican Primary**

Robert Ray (R)		100.0

Democratic Primary

James F. Schaben (D)	59,840	44.8
William Gannon (D)	52,420	39.3
Clark Rasmussen (D)	21,240	15.9

1978 **Republican Primary**

Robert Ray (R)	136,517	87.5
Donovan D. Nelson (R)	19,486	12.5

Democratic Primary

Jerome D. Fitzgerald (D)	58,039	55.5
Tom Whitney (D)	37,132	35.5
Warren D. Strait (D)	9,443	9.0

543

	Candidates	Votes	%
1982	**Republican Primary**		
	Terry Branstad (R)		*100.0*
	Democratic Primary		
	Roxanne Conlin (D)	94,481	*48.2*
	Jerome D. Fitzgerald (D)	61,340	*31.3*
	Edward L. Campbell (D)	40,233	*20.5*

KANSAS

	Candidates	Votes	%
1956	**Republican Primary**		
	Warren W. Shaw (R)	156,476	*52.7*
	Fred Hall (R)	123,398	*41.5*
	Democratic Primary		
	George Docking (D)	76,544	*50.3*
	Harry H. Woodring (D)	75,548	*49.7*
1958	**Republican Primary**		
	Clyde M. Reed (R)	142,247	*72.6*
	Fred Hall (R)	35,632	*18.2*
	Democratic Primary		
	George Docking (D)		*100.0*
1960	**Republican Primary**		
	John Anderson (R)	128,081	*48.7*
	McDill Boyd (R)	116,725	*44.4*
	William H. Addington (R)	18,169	*6.9*
	Democratic Primary		
	George Docking (D)		*100.0*
1962	**Republican Primary**		
	John Anderson (R)	164,888	*84.1*
	Harvey F. Crouch (R)	31,221	*15.9*
	Democratic Primary		
	Dale E. Saffels (D)	69,728	*59.7*
	George Hart (D)	47,055	*40.3*
1964	**Republican Primary**		
	William H. Avery (R)	85,746	*30.4*
	McDill Boyd (R)	75,451	*26.7*
	Paul R. Wunsch (R)	71,601	*25.4*
	William M. Ferguson (R)	36,622	*13.0*
	Democratic Primary		
	Harry G. Wiles (D)	50,590	*32.4*
	Jules V. Doty (D)	37,305	*23.9*
	George Hart (D)	30,973	*19.8*
	Joseph W. Henkle (D)	21,304	*13.6*
	J. Donald Coffin (D)	9,140	*5.9*

	Candidates	Votes	%
1966	**Republican Primary**		
	William H. Avery (R)	144,842	*75.1*
	Dell Crozier (R)	48,051	*24.9*
	Democratic Primary		
	Robert Docking (D)	96,414	*85.5*
	George Hart (D)	16,385	*14.5*
1968	**Republican Primary**		
	Rick Harman (R)	133,454	*48.9*
	John Crutcher (R)	128,635	*47.1*
	Democratic Primary		
	Robert Docking (D)		*100.0*
1970	**Republican Primary**		
	Kent Frizzell (R)	141,298	*60.5*
	Rick Harman (R)	78,086	*33.4*
	Democratic Primary		
	Robert Docking (D)		*100.0*
1972	**Republican Primary**		
	Morris Kay (R)	138,815	*46.6*
	John Anderson (R)	88,088	*29.6*
	Ray E. Frisbie (R)	46,125	*15.5*
	Reynolds Shultz (R)	24,911	*8.4*
	Democratic Primary		
	Robert Docking (D)		*100.0*
1974	**Republican Primary**		
	Robert F. Bennett (R)	67,347	*32.4*
	Donald O. Concannon (R)	66,817	*32.1*
	Forrest J. Robinson (R)	56,440	*27.2*
	Robert W. Clack (R)	17,333	*8.3*
	Democratic Primary		
	Vern Miller (D)		*100.0*
1978	**Republican Primary**		
	Robert F. Bennett (R)	142,239	*69.2*
	Robert R. Sanders (R)	40,542	*19.7*
	Harold Knight (R)	22,671	*11.1*
	Democratic Primary		
	John Carlin (D)	71,366	*55.2*
	Bert Chaney (D)	34,132	*26.4*
	Harry G. Wiles (D)	23,762	*18.4*
1982	**Republican Primary**		
	Sam Hardage (R)	86,692	*36.8*
	Dave Owen (R)	79,770	*33.8*
	Wendell Lady (R)	61,419	*26.0*
	Democratic Primary		
	John Carlin (D)	103,780	*78.9*
	Jimmy D. Montgomery (D)	27,785	*21.1*

KENTUCKY

	Candidates	Votes	%
1959	**Republican Primary**		
	John M. Robsion (R)	63,130	86.3
	Thurman J. Hamlin (R)	6,019	8.2
	Granville Thomas (R)	3,991	5.5
	Democratic Primary		
	Bert T. Combs (D)	292,462	53.0
	Harry Lee Waterfield (D)	259,461	45.6
1963	**Republican Primary**		
	Louie B. Nunn (R)	77,455	88.5
	J. N. R. Cecil (R)	10,039	11.5
	Democratic Primary		
	Edward T. Breathitt (D)	318,858	53.8
	Albert B. Chandler (D)	256,451	43.2
1967	**Republican Primary**		
	Louie B. Nunn (R)	90,216	50.4
	Marlow W. Cook (R)	86,397	48.3
	Democratic Primary		
	Henry Ward (D)	207,797	52.4
	Albert B. Chandler (D)	111,782	28.2
	Harry Lee Waterfield (D)	42,583	10.7
1971	**Republican Primary**		
	Thomas Emberton (R)	84,863	84.1
	Ried Martin (R)	6,379	6.3
	Thurman J. Hamlin (R)	5,469	5.4
	Democratic Primary		
	Wendell H. Ford (D)	237,815	53.0
	Bert T. Combs (D)	195,678	43.6
1975	**Republican Primary**		
	Robert E. Gable (R)	38,113	51.3
	Elmer Begley (R)	16,885	22.7
	T. William Klein (R)	10,844	14.6
	Granville Thomas (R)	8,426	11.3
	Democratic Primary		
	Julian Carroll (D)	263,965	66.3
	Todd Hollenbach (D)	113,285	28.5
1979	**Republican Primary**		
	Louie B. Nunn (R)	106,006	79.6
	Ray B. White (R)	18,514	13.9
	Democratic Primary		
	John Y. Brown (D)	165,158	29.1
	Harvey Sloane (D)	139,713	24.6
	Terry McBrayer (D)	131,530	23.2
	Carroll Hubbard (D)	68,577	12.1
	Thelma L. Stovall (D)	47,633	8.4

	Candidates	Votes	%
1983	**Republican Primary**		
	Jim Bunning (R)	72,808	74.4
	Lester Burns (R)	7,340	7.5
	Donald Wiggins (R)	5,464	5.6
	Elizabeth Wickham (R)	5,174	5.3
	Democratic Primary		
	Martha Layne Collins (D)	223,692	34.0
	Harvey Sloane (D)	219,160	33.3
	Grady Strumbo (D)	199,795	30.3

MAINE

	Candidates	Votes	%
1956	**Republican Primary**		
	Willis A Trafton (R)	42,901	51.0
	Philip F. Chapman (R)	24,787	29.4
	Alexander A. LaFleur (R)	16,479	19.6
	Democratic Primary		
	Edmund S. Muskie (D)		100.0
1958	**Republican Primary**		
	Horace A. Hildreth (R)	63,424	62.0
	Philip F. Chapman (R)	38,865	38.0
	Democratic Primary		
	Clinton A. Clauson (D)	20,736	51.8
	Maynard C. Dolloff (D)	19,301	48.2
1960	**Republican Primary**		
	John H. Reed (R)		100.0
	Democratic Primary		
	Frank M. Coffin (D)		100.0
1962	**Republican Primary**		
	John H. Reed (R)		100.0
	Democratic Primary		
	Maynard C. Dolloff (D)	18,234	50.3
	Richard J. Dubord (D)	18,007	49.7
1966	**Republican Primary**		
	John H. Reed (R)	55,924	59.7
	James S. Erwin (R)	37,765	40.3
	Democratic Primary		
	Kenneth M. Curtis (D)	30,879	55.6
	Carlton D. Reed (D)	13,839	24.9
	Dana W. Childs (D)	10,793	19.4

Candidates	Votes	%
1970 **Republican Primary**		
James S. Erwin (R)	72,760	*89.1*
Calvin F. Grass (R)	8,898	*10.9*
Democratic Primary		
Kenneth M. Curtis (D)	33,052	*63.2*
Plato Truman (D)	19,266	*36.8*
1974 **Republican Primary**		
James S. Erwin (R)	38,044	*39.3*
Harrison L. Richardson (R)	36,693	*37.9*
Wakine G. Tanous (R)	18,786	*19.4*
Democratic Primary		
George J. Mitchell (D)	33,312	*37.5*
Joseph E. Brennan (D)	23,443	*26.4*
Peter S. Kelley (D)	21,358	*24.1*
Lloyd P. LaFountain (D)	7,954	*9.0*
1978 **Republican Primary**		
Linwood E. Palmer (R)	35,976	*48.7*
Charles L. Cragin (R)	28,244	*38.3*
Jerrold B. Speers (R)	9,603	*13.0*
Democratic Primary		
Joseph E. Brennan (D)	38,361	*52.0*
Philip L. Merrill (D)	26,803	*36.3*
Richard J. Carey (D)	8,588	*11.6*
1982 **Republican Primary**		
Charles L. Cragin (R)	32,235	*38.0*
Sherry F. Huber (R)	27,739	*32.7*
Richard H. Pierce (R)	24,820	*29.3*
Democratic Primary		
Joseph E. Brennan (D)	56,990	*76.8*
Georgette B. Berube (D)	17,219	*23.2*

MARYLAND

Candidates	Votes	%
1958 **Republican Primary**		
James Devereux (R)		*100.0*
Democratic Primary		
J. Millard Tawes (D)	261,594	*82.0*
Bruce S. Campbell (D)	24,953	*7.8*
Morgan L. Amaimo (D)	16,459	*5.2*
Joseph A. Phillips (D)	15,836	*5.0*
1962 **Republican Primary**		
Frank Small (R)	71,791	*77.8*
Karla Balentine (R)	11,504	*12.5*
Joseph L. Pavlock (R)	8,972	*9.7*

Candidates	Votes	%
Democratic Primary		
J. Millard Tawes (D)	178,792	*40.4*
George P. Mahoney (D)	125,966	*28.5*
David Hume (D)	118,295	*26.7*
1966 **Republican Primary**		
Spiro T. Agnew (R)	98,531	*83.2*
Andrew J. Groszer (R)	9,987	*8.4*
Democratic Primary		
George P. Mahoney (D)	148,446	*30.2*
Carlton R. Sickles (D)	146,507	*29.8*
Thomas B. Finan (D)	134,216	*27.3*
Clarence W. Miles (D)	42,304	*8.6*
1970 **Republican Primary**		
C. Stanley Blair (R)	101,541	*81.5*
Peter James (R)	15,790	*12.8*
John C. Webb (R)	7,194	*5.7*
Democratic Primary		
Marvin Mandel (D)	414,160	*89.1*
1974 **Republican Primary**		
Louise Gore (R)	57,626	*53.6*
Lawrence J. Hogan (R)	49,887	*46.4*
Democratic Primary		
Marvin Mandel (D)	254,509	*65.7*
Wilson K. Barnes (D)	96,902	*25.0*
1978 **Republican Primary**		
J. Glenn Beall Jr. (R)	76,011	*57.7*
Carlton Beall (R)	30,119	*22.8*
Louise Gore (R)	20,690	*15.7*
Democratic Primary		
Harry R. Hughes (D)	213,457	*37.2*
Blair Lee (D)	194,236	*33.9*
Theodore G. Venetoulis (D)	140,486	*24.5*
1982 **Republican Primary**		
Robert A. Pascal (R)	113,425	*84.3*
Ross Z. Pierpont (R)	21,165	*15.7*
Democratic Primary		
Harry R. Hughes (D)	393,244	*59.8*
Harry J. McGuirk (D)	129,049	*26.3*
Harry W. Kelley (D)	61,271	*12.5*

MASSACHUSETTS

Candidates	Votes	%
1956 **Republican Primary**		
Sumner G. Whittier (R)		*100.0*

Candidates	Votes	%
Democratic Primary		
Foster Furcolo (D)	358,051	*73.1*
Thomas H. Buckley (D)	131,496	*26.9*

1958 [9]

Candidates	Votes	%
Republican Primary		
Charles Gibbons (R)	158,944	*84.3*
George Fingold (R)	23,031	*12.2*

Democratic Primary		
Foster Furcolo (D)		*100.0*

1960

Republican Primary		
John A. Volpe (R)		*100.0*

Democratic Primary		
Joseph D. Ward (D)	180,848	*30.2*
Endicott Peabody (D)	152,762	*25.5*
Francis E. Kelly (D)	98,107	*16.4*
Robert F. Murphy (D)	76,577	*12.8*
John F. Kennedy (D) [10]	52,972	*8.8*

1962

Republican Primary		
John A. Volpe (R)		*100.0*

Democratic Primary		
Endicott Peabody (D)	596,553	*80.0*
Clement A. Riley (D)	149,499	*20.0*

1964

Republican Primary		
John A. Volpe (R)		*100.0*

Democratic Primary		
Francis X. Bellotti (D)	363,675	*49.6*
Endicott Peabody (D)	336,780	*45.9*

1966

Republican Primary		
John A. Volpe (R)		*100.0*

Democratic Primary		
Edward J. McCormack (D)	343,381	*55.1*
Kenneth P. O'Donnell (D)	279,541	*44.9*

1970

Republican Primary		
Francis W. Sargent (R)		*100.0*

Democratic Primary		
Kevin H. White (D)	231,605	*34.3*
Maurice A. Donahue (D)	218,665	*32.4*
Francis X. Bellotti (D)	164,313	*24.4*
Kenneth P. O'Donnell (D)	59,970	*8.9*

9. Fingold died a few days before the primary. Charles Gibbons, supported by the Republican state committee, polled 158,944 sticker and write-in votes, followed by 23,031 for Fingold, whose name remained on the ballot, and 6,535 other write-ins.

10. John F. Kennedy of Canton, Mass.; not to be confused with Sen. John F. Kennedy, D-Mass., then a candidate for president.

Candidates	Votes	%
1974 **Republican Primary**		
Francis W. Sargent (R)	124,250	*63.3*
Carroll P. Sheehan (R)	71,936	*36.7*

Democratic Primary		
Michael S. Dukakis (D)	444,590	*57.7*
Robert H. Quinn (D)	326,385	*42.3*

1978

Republican Primary		
Francis W. Hatch (R)	141,070	*56.0*
Edward F. King (R)	110,932	*44.0*

Democratic Primary		
Edward J. King (D)	442,174	*51.1*
Michael S. Dukakis (D)	365,417	*42.2*
Barbara Ackermann (D)	58,220	*6.7*

1982

Republican Primary		
John W. Sears (R)	90,617	*50.7*
John R. Lakian (R)	46,675	*26.1*
Andrew H. Card (R)	40,899	*22.9*

Democratic Primary		
Michael S. Dukakis (D)	631,911	*53.5*
Edward J. King (D)	549,335	*46.5*

MICHIGAN

Candidates	Votes	%
1956 **Republican Primary**		
Albert E. Cobo (R)	348,652	*69.0*
Donald S Leonard (R)	156,822	*31.0*

Democratic Primary		
G. Mennen Williams (D)		*100.0*

1958

Republican Primary		
Paul D. Bagwell (R)		*100.0*

Democratic Primary		
G. Mennen Williams (D)	385,864	*85.5*
W. L. Johnson (D)	65,614	*14.5*

1960

Republican Primary		
Paul D. Bagwell (R)		*100.0*

Democratic Primary		
John B. Swainson (D)	274,743	*50.8*
James M. Hare (D)	205,086	*37.9*
Edward Connor (D)	60,895	*11.3*

1962

Republican Primary		
George W. Romney (R)		*100.0*

Gubernatorial Elections

Candidates	Votes	%
Democratic Primary		
John B. Swainson (D)		100.0
1964 Republican Primary		
George W. Romney (R)	583,356	87.9
George N. Higgins (R)	80,608	12.1
Democratic Primary		
Neil Staebler (D)		100.0
1966 Republican Primary		
George W. Romney (R)		100.0
Democratic Primary		
Zoltan A. Ferency (D)		100.0
1970 Republican Primary		
William G. Milliken (R)	416,491	77.8
James C. Turner (R)	119,140	22.2
Democratic Primary		
Sander Levin (D)	304,343	54.1
Zolton A. Ferency (D)	167,442	29.8
George N. Parris (D)	49,559	8.8
George F. Montgomery (D)	41,218	7.3
American Independent Primary		
James L. McCormick (WRITE IN)		
1974 Republican Primary		
William G. Milliken (R)		100.0
Democratic Primary		
Sander M. Levin (D)	445,273	61.3
Jerome P. Cavanagh (D)	199,361	27.4
James E. Wells (D)	81,844	11.3
1978 Republican Primary		
William G. Milliken (R)		100.0
Democratic Primary		
William Fitzgerald (D)	240,641	39.8
Zolton A. Ferency (D)	151,062	25.0
Patrick McCullough (D)	108,742	18.0
William Ralls (D)	104,364	17.2
1982 Republican Primary		
Richard H. Headlee (R)	220,378	34.4
James H. Brickley (R)	194,429	30.3
L. Brooks Patterson (R)	180,065	28.1
Jack Welborn (R)	46,505	7.2
Democratic Primary		
James J. Blanchard (D)	406,941	50.2
William Fitzgerald (D)	138,453	17.1
David A. Plawecki (D)	95,805	11.8
Zolton A. Ferency (D)	85,088	10.5
Edward C. Pierce (D)	44,894	5.5

MINNESOTA[11]

Candidates	Votes	%
1956 Republican Primary		
Ancher Nelsen (IR)	283,844	94.4
Democratic Primary		
Orville L. Freeman (DFL)	269,740	89.5
1958 Republican Primary		
George MacKinnon (IR)	202,833	85.3
Glenn B. Brown (IR)	34,878	14.7
Democratic Primary		
Orville L. Freeman (DFL)	331,822	87.6
Harold Strom (DFL)	47,041	12.4
1960 Republican Primary		
Elmer L. Andersen (IR)		100.0
Democratic Primary		
Orville L. Freeman (DFL)	264,571	88.8
Belmont Tudisco (DFL)	33,452	11.2
1962 Republican Primary		
Elmer L. Andersen (IR)		100.0
Democratic Primary		
Karl F. Rolvaag (DFL)	271,818	92.5
Belmont Tudisco (DFL)	22,042	7.5
1966 Republican Primary		
Harold LeVander (IR)	276,403	97.9
Democratic Primary		
Karl F. Rolvaag (DFL)	336,656	66.3
A. M. Keith (DFL)	157,661	31.0
1970 Republican Primary		
Douglas M. Head (IR)	210,621	87.5
John C. Peterson (IR)	19,737	8.2
Democratic Primary		
Wendell R. Anderson (DFL)		100.0
1974 Republican Primary		
John W. Johnson (IR)		100.0
Democratic Primary		
Wendell R. Anderson (DFL)	254,671	78.2
Thomas E. McDonald (DFL)	70,871	21.8

11. In Minnesota, the Democratic Party is known as the Democratic-Farmer-Labor Party (DFL) and the Republican Party is known as the Independent Republican Party (IR).

Candidates	Votes	%

1978 **Republican Primary**

Albert H. Quie (IR)	174,799	*83.6*
Robert W. Johnson (IR)	34,406	*16.4*

Democratic Primary

Rudy Perpich (DFL)	390,069	*80.0*
Alice Tripp (DFL)	97,247	*20.0*

American Primary

Richard Pedersen (AM)		*100.0*

1982 **Republican Primary**

Wheelock Whitney (IR)	185,801	*60.1*
Lou Wangberg (IR)	105,696	*34.2*
Harold E. Stassen (IR)	17,795	*5.7*

Democratic Primary

Rudy Perpich (DFL)	275,920	*51.2*
Warren Spannaus (DFL)	248,218	*46.1*

MISSOURI

Candidates	Votes	%

1956 **Republican Primary**

Lon Hocker (R)	136,388	*66.9*
Joseph M. Whealen (R)	53,811	*26.4*
Winford Sidebotham (R)	13,710	*6.7*

Democratic Primary

James T. Blair (D)	387,330	*88.1*
Charles A. Lee (D)	34,107	*7.7*

1960 **Republican Primary**

Edward G. Farmer (R)	107,637	*54.1*
William B. Ewald (R)	57,953	*29.1*
Harry C. Timmerman (R)	33,388	*16.8*

Democratic Primary

John M. Dalton (D)	466,984	*86.4*

1964 **Republican Primary**

Ethan Shepley (R)	161,327	*75.7*
Harry C. Timmerman (R)	17,510	*8.2*
William B. Ewald (R)	17,170	*8.1*
Joseph M. Badgett (R)	17,156	*8.0*

Democratic Primary

Warren E. Hearnes (D)	334,708	*51.9*
Hilary A. Bush (D)	283,640	*44.0*

1968 **Republican Primary**

Lawrence K. Roos (R)	170,428	*76.4*
Harry C. Timmerman (R)	41,549	*18.6*
Harvey F. Euge (R)	10,994	*5.0*

Democratic Primary

Warren E. Hearnes (D)	497,056	*85.5*
Robert B. Curtis (D)	42,971	*7.4*
Milton Morris (D)	41,506	*7.1*

1972 **Republican Primary**

Christopher S. (Kit) Bond (R)	265,467	*75.1*
Gene McNary (R)	56,652	*16.0*
R. J. King (R)	21,422	*6.1*

Democratic Primary

Edward L. Dowd (D)	265,011	*40.8*
William S. Morris (D)	152,055	*23.4*
Joseph P. Teasdale (D)	135,965	*20.9*
Earl R. Blackwell (D)	72,212	*11.1*

Non-partisan Primary

Paul J. Leonard (NON-PART)	606	*55.4*
Charles S. Miller (NON-PART)	487	*44.6*

1976 **Republican Primary**

Christopher S. (Kit) Bond (R)	286,377	*92.0*
Harvey F. Euge (R)	24,975	*8.0*

Democratic Primary

Joseph P. Teasdale (D)	419,656	*48.6*
William Cason (D)	340,208	*39.4*

1980 **Republican Primary**

Christopher S. (Kit) Bond (R)	223,678	*63.5*
William Phelps (R)	122,867	*34.9*

Democratic Primary

Joseph P. Teasdale (D)	359,263	*54.0*
James I. Spainhower (D)	294,917	*44.3*

1984 **Republican Primary**

John Ashcroft (R)	245,308	*67.4*
Gene McNary (R)	115,516	*31.8*

Democratic Primary

Kenneth J. Rothman (D)	288,543	*56.0*
Mel Carnahan (D)	104,368	*20.3*
Norman L. Merrell (D)	97,973	*19.0*

MONTANA

Candidates	Votes	%

1956 **Republican Primary**

J. Hugo Aronson (R)		*100.0*

Democratic Primary

Arnold H. Olsen (D)	55,269	*44.9*
John W. Bonner (D)	51,306	*41.7*
Danny O'Neill (D)	14,777	*12.0*

	Candidates	Votes	%
1960	**Republican Primary**		
	Donald G. Nutter (R)	33,099	*50.4*
	Wesley A. D'Ewart (R)	32,538	*49.6*
	Democratic Primary		
	Paul Cannon (D)	44,690	*34.9*
	Jack Toole (D)	40,537	*31.6*
	Mike Kuchera (D)	33,216	*25.9*
	Willard E. Fraser (D)	6,505	*5.1*
1964	**Republican Primary**		
	Tim M. Babcock (R)		*100.0*
	Democratic Primary		
	Roland Renne (D)	71,967	*55.9*
	Mike Kuchera (D)	56,710	*44.1*
1968	**Republican Primary**		
	Tim M. Babcock (R)	50,369	*55.1*
	Ted James (R)	36,664	*40.1*
	Democratic Primary		
	Forrest H. Anderson (D)	39,057	*38.3*
	Eugene H. Mahoney (D)	35,562	*34.9*
	LeRoy Anderson (D)	16,476	*16.2*
	Willard E. Fraser (D)	8,525	*8.3*
1972	**Republican Primary**		
	Ed Smith (R)	39,552	*40.6*
	Frank Dunkle (R)	37,375	*38.4*
	Tom A. Selstad (R)	18,046	*18.5*
	Democratic Primary		
	Thomas L. Judge (D)	75,917	*59.9*
	Dick Dzivi (D)	38,639	*30.5*
1976	**Republican Primary**		
	Robert Woodahl (R)	47,629	*56.7*
	John K. McDonald (R)	36,420	*43.3*
	Democratic Primary		
	Thomas L. Judge (D)		*100.0*
1980	**Republican Primary**		
	Jack Ramirez (R)	48,926	*68.4*
	Al Bishop (R)	14,522	*20.3*
	Florence Haegen (R)	8,118	*11.3*
	Democratic Primary		
	Ted Schwinden (D)	69,051	*50.6*
	Thomas L. Judge (D)	57,946	*42.5*
1984	**Republican Primary**		
	Pat M. Goodover (R)	56,199	*100.0*

	Candidates	Votes	%
	Democratic Primary		
	Ted Schwinden (D)	80,633	*81.4*
	Robert Carlson Kelleher (D)	18,423	*18.6*

NEBRASKA

	Candidates	Votes	%
1956	**Republican Primary**		
	Victor E. Anderson (R)	86,168	*82.6*
	Edwin L. Hart (R)	18,202	*17.4*
	Democratic Primary		
	Frank Sorrell (D)	43,301	*69.9*
	Ted Baum (D)	18,667	*30.1*
1958	**Republican Primary**		
	Victor E. Anderson (R)	90,150	*76.4*
	Louis H. Hector (R)	27,768	*23.5*
	Democratic Primary		
	Ralph G. Brooks (D)	37,816	*54.8*
	Edward A. Dosek (D)	31,221	*45.2*
1960	**Republican Primary**		
	John R. Cooper (R)	61,286	*37.7*
	Hazel Abel (R)	39,109	*24.1*
	Terry Carpenter (R)	25,659	*15.8*
	Dwain Williams (R)	23,545	*14.5*
	Del Lienemann (R)	9,390	*5.8*
	Democratic Primary		
	Frank B. Morrison (D)	51,335	*48.0*
	Robert Conrad (D)	44,486	*41.6*
	Charles A. Bates (D)	5,477	*5.1*
1962	**Republican Primary**		
	Fred A. Seaton (R)	130,816	*85.3*
	George A. Clarke (R)	17,368	*11.3*
	Democratic Primary		
	Frank B. Morrison (D)	78,817	*76.6*
	Mrs. Ralph G. Brooks (D)	15,565	*15.1*
	Tony Mangiamelli (D)	8,464	*8.3*
1964	**Republican Primary**		
	Dwight W. Burney (R)	82,256	*58.8*
	Jack Romans (R)	44,102	*31.5*
	Democratic Primary		
	Frank B. Morrison (D)	83,362	*88.8*
	Charles A. Bates (D)	6,543	*7.0*
1966	**Republican Primary**		
	Norbert T. Tiemann (R)	78,338	*44.0*
	Val Peterson (R)	63,589	*35.7*
	Bruce Hagemeister (R)	22,574	*12.7*
	Henry E. Kuhlmann (R)	12,052	*6.8*

Candidates	Votes	%
Democratic Primary		
Philip C. Sorensen (D)	65,051	*56.8*
J. W. Burbach (D)	35,439	*30.9*
Henry E. Ley (D)	13,819	*12.1*
1970 **Republican Primary**		
Norbert T. Tiemann (R)	97,616	*50.5*
Clifton B. Batchelder (R)	89,355	*46.2*
Democratic Primary		
J. James Exon (D)	54,783	*44.6*
J. W. Burbach (D)	51,760	*42.2*
Richard R. Larsen (D)	15,602	*12.7*
1974 **Republican Primary**		
Richard D. Marvel (R)		*100.0*
Democratic Primary		
J. James Exon (D)	125,690	*87.4*
Richard D. Schmitz (D)	17,889	*12.4*
1978 **Republican Primary**		
Charles Thone (R)	89,378	*45.3*
Robert A. Phares (R)	48,402	*24.5*
Stanley R. Juelfs (R)	43,828	*22.2*
Vance D. Rogers (R)	14,076	*7.1*
Democratic Primary		
Gerald T. Whelan (D)	104,178	*79.4*
Robert V. Hansen (D)	26,509	*20.2*
1982 **Republican Primary**		
Charles Thone (R)	115,750	*62.5*
Stan DeBoer (R)	55,983	*30.2*
Barton E. Chandler (R)	13,086	*7.1*
Democratic Primary		
Bob Kerrey (D)	87,913	*71.0*
George Burrows (D)	35,426	*28.6*

NEVADA

Candidates	Votes	%
1958 **Republican Primary**		
Charles H. Russell (R)		*100.0*
Democratic Primary		
Grant Sawyer (D)	20,711	*46.3*
Harvey Dickerson (D)	13,372	*29.9*
George E. Franklin (D)	10,175	*22.7*

	Candidates	Votes	%
1962	**Republican Primary**		
	Oran K. Gragson (R)	16,538	*64.3*
	H. M. Greenspun (R)	9,176	*35.7*
	Democratic Primary		
	Grant Sawyer (D)	40,168	*81.4*
	Gene Austin (D)	5,017	*10.2*
1966	**Republican Primary**		
	Paul Laxalt (R)	32,768	*94.7*
	John P. Screen (R)	1,834	*5.3*
	Democratic Primary		
	Grant Sawyer (D)	40,982	*58.6*
	Edward G. Marshall (D)	13,858	*19.8*
	Charles E. Springer (D)	13,270	*19.0*
1970	**Republican Primary**		
	Ed Fike (R)	31,931	*88.2*
	Margie Dyer (R)	4,281	*11.8*
	Democratic Primary		
	Mike O'Callgahan (D)	41,185	*68.8*
	Hank Thornley (D)	16,107	*26.9*
1974	**Republican Primary**		
	Shirley Crumpler (R)	17,076	*49.4*
	William Bickerstaff (R)	13,632	*39.5*
	Gilbert D. Buck (R)	2,405	*7.0*
	Democratic Primary		
	Mike O'Callaghan (D)	69,089	*90.8*
1978	**Republican Primary**		
	Robert F. List (R)	39,997	*82.4*
	William C. Allen (R)	3,038	*6.3*
	"None of these Candidates" [12]	3,570	*7.3*
	Democratic Primary		
	Robert E. Rose (D)	41,672	*48.1*
	John Foley (D)	20,186	*23.3*
	Jack Schofield (D)	18,414	*21.3*
1982	**Republican Primary**		
	Robert F. List (R)	39,319	*57.0*
	Mike Moody (R)	13,849	*20.1*
	"None of these Candidates" [12]	13,252	*19.2*
	Democratic Primary		
	Richard H. Bryan (D)	55,261	*51.1*
	Myron E. Leavitt (D)	34,783	*32.1*
	Stan Colton (D)	10,830	*10.0*

12. Nevada provided space on the ballot for a vote against the candidates listed.

NEW HAMPSHIRE

	Candidates	Votes	%
1956	**Republican Primary**		
	Lane Dwinell (R)	38,734	53.1
	Wesley Powell (R)	33,408	45.8
	Democratic Primary		
	John Shaw (D)		100.0
1958	**Republican Primary**		
	Wesley Powell (R)	39,761	47.5
	Hugh Gregg (R)	39,365	47.1
	Democratic Primary		
	Bernard L. Boutin (D)	16,646	47.0
	John Shaw (D)	12,783	36.1
	Alfred J. Champagne (D)	4,586	13.0
1960	**Republican Primary**		
	Wesley Powell (R)	49,119	49.9
	Hugh Gregg (R)	48,108	48.8
	Democratic Primary		
	Bernard L. Boutin (D)	31,650	77.6
	John Shaw (D)	7,151	17.5
1962	**Republican Primary**		
	John Pillsbury (R)	55,784	56.4
	Wesley Powell (R)	42,005	42.4
	Democratic Primary		
	John W. King (D)	27,933	93.2
	Elmer E. Bussey (D)	2,039	6.8
1964	**Republican Primary**		
	John Pillsbury (R)	32,200	51.4
	Wesley Powell (R)	21,764	34.7
	John W. King (WRITE IN)	3,608	5.8
	John C. Mongan (R)	3,532	5.6
	Democratic Primary		
	John W. King (D)		100.0
1966	**Republican Primary**		
	Hugh Gregg (R)	33,946	44.9
	James J. Barry (R)	20,791	27.5
	Alexander M. Taft (R)	14,845	19.6
	Democratic Primary		
	John W. King (D)		100.0
1968	**Republican Primary**		
	Walter R. Peterson (R)	29,262	34.1
	Wesley Powell (R)	26,498	30.9
	Meldrim Thomson (R)	25,275	29.5

	Candidates	Votes	%
	Democratic Primary		
	Emile R. Bussiere (D)	12,021	32.7
	Henry P. Sullivan (D)	10,895	29.6
	Vincent P. Dunn (D)	10,412	28.3
1970	**Republican Primary**		
	Walter R. Peterson (R)	43,667	50.9
	Meldrim Thomson Jr. (R)	41,392	48.2
	Democratic Primary		
	Roger J. Crowley (D)	17,089	47.5
	Charles F. Whittemore (D)	13,354	37.1
	Dennis J. Sullivan (D)	4,747	13.2
1972	**Republican Primary**		
	Meldrim Thomson Jr. (R)	43,611	47.9
	Walter R. Peterson (R)	41,252	45.3
	Democratic Primary		
	Roger J. Crowley (D)	29,326	61.4
	Robert E. Raiche (D)	16,216	33.9
1974	**Republican Primary**		
	Meldrim Thomson Jr. (R)	47,244	54.9
	David L. Nixon (R)	37,286	43.3
	Democratic Primary		
	Richard W. Leonard (D)	16,503	37.8
	Harry V. Spanos (D)	14,149	32.4
	Hugh Gallen (D)	13,030	29.8
1976	**Republican Primary**		
	Meldrim Thomson Jr. (R)	52,968	64.6
	Gerald J. Zeiller (R)	26,728	32.6
	Democratic Primary		
	Harry V. Spanos (D)	21,589	41.3
	James A. Connor (D)	15,758	30.2
	Hugh Gallen (D)	13,629	26.1
1978	**Republican Primary**		
	Meldrim Thomson Jr. (R)	45,069	59.7
	Wesley Powell (R)	28,286	37.4
	Democratic Primary		
	Hugh Gallen (D)	26,217	73.0
	Delbert F. Downing (D)	9,688	27.0
1980	**Republican Primary**		
	Meldrim Thomson Jr. (R)	55,554	56.4
	Louis C. D'Allesandro (R)	40,060	40.7
	Democratic Primary		
	Hugh Gallen (D)	37,786	81.3
	Thomas B. Wingate (D)	8,689	18.7

	Candidates	Votes	%
1982	**Republican Primary**		
	John H. Sununu (R)	26,617	*31.9*
	Robert B. Monier (R)	24,823	*29.7*
	Louis C. D'Allesandro (R)	24,163	*29.0*
	Democratic Primary		
	Hugh Gallen (D)		*100.0*
1984	**Republican Primary**		
	John H. Sununu (R)	52,737	*84.1*
	James F. Fallon (R)	8,994	*14.3*
	Democratic Primary		
	Chris Spirou (D)	22,835	*49.5*
	Paul McEachern (D)	18,460	*40.0*
	Robert L. Dupay (D)	4,060	*8.8*

NEW JERSEY

	Candidates	Votes	%
1957	**Republican Primary**		
	Malcolm S. Forbes (R)	216,677	*63.7*
	Wayne Dumont (R)	123,350	*36.3*
	Democratic Primary		
	Robert B. Meyner (D)		*100.0*
1961	**Republican Primary**		
	James P. Mitchell (R)	202,188	*43.7*
	Walter H. Jones (R)	160,553	*34.7*
	Wayne Dumont (R)	95,761	*20.7*
	Democratic Primary		
	Richard J. Hughes (D)	222,789	*84.2*
	Weldon R. Sheets (D)	21,285	*8.0*
	Eugene E. Demarest (D)	20,487	*7.7*
1965	**Republican Primary**		
	Wayne Dumont (R)	167,402	*50.3*
	Charles W. Sandman (R)	154,491	*46.5*
	Democratic Primary		
	Richard J. Hughes (D)	236,518	*90.9*
	William J. Clark (D)	23,722	*9.1*
1969	**Republican Primary**		
	William T. Cahill (R)	158,980	*39.3*
	Charles W. Sandman (R)	144,877	*35.8*

	Candidates	Votes	%
	Harry L. Sears (R)	46,778	*11.6*
	Francis X. McDermott (R)	35,503	*8.8*
	Democratic Primary		
	Robert B. Meyner (D)	173,801	*44.8*
	William F. Kelly (D)	87,888	*22.6*
	Henry Hellstoski (D)	60,483	*15.6*
	D. Louis Tonti (D)	34,810	*9.0*
	Ned J. Parsekian (D)	24,908	*6.4*
1973	**Republican Primary**		
	Charles W. Sandman (R)	209,657	*57.5*
	William T. Cahill (R)	148,034	*40.6*
	Democratic Primary		
	Brendan T. Byrne (D)	193,120	*45.3*
	Ann Klein (D)	116,705	*27.4*
	Ralph C. DeRose (D)	95,085	*22.3*
1977	**Republican Primary**		
	Raymond H. Bateman (R)	196,592	*54.7*
	Thomas H. Kean (R)	129,982	*36.2*
	C. Robert Sarcone (R)	20,861	*5.8*
	Democratic Primary		
	Brendan T. Byrne (D)	175,448	*30.3*
	Robert A. Roe (D)	134,116	*23.2*
	Ralph C. DeRose (D)	99,948	*17.3*
	James J. Florio (D)	87,743	*15.1*
	Joseph A. Hoffman (D)	58,835	*10.2*
1981	**Republican Primary**		
	Thomas H. Kean (R)	122,512	*30.7*
	Lawrence F. Kramer (R)	83,565	*21.0*
	Joseph Sullivan (R)	67,651	*17.0*
	Jim Wallwork (R)	61,816	*15.5*
	Barry T. Parker (R)	26,040	*6.5*
	Democratic Primary		
	James J. Florio (D)	164,179	*25.9*
	Robert A. Roe (D)	98,660	*15.6*
	Kenneth A. Gibson (D)	95,212	*15.0*
	Joseph P. Merlino (D)	70,910	*11.2*
	John J. Degnan (D)	65,844	*10.4*
	Thomas F. X. Smith (D)	57,479	*9.1*

NEW MEXICO

	Candidates	Votes	%
1956	**Republican Primary**		
	Edwin L. Mechem (R)		*100.0*

Candidates	Votes	%
Democratic Primary		
John F. Simms (D)	46,722	*48.3*
Ingram B. Pickett (D)	43,937	*45.4*
Robert F. Stephens (D)	6,067	*6.3*
1958 Republican Primary		
Edwin L. Mechem (R)		*100.0*
Democratic Primary		
John Burroughs (D)	46,344	*43.8*
Joseph A. Bursey (D)	33,623	*31.7*
Ingram B. Pickett (D)	18,150	*17.1*
Robert C. Dow (D)	5,569	*5.2*
1960 Republican Primary		
Edwin L. Mechem (R)	29,486	*76.0*
Paul W. Robinson (R)	9,331	*24.0*
Democratic Primary		
John Burroughs (D)	66,541	*53.7*
Joseph A. Bursey (D)	48,841	*39.4*
Thomas E. Holland (D)	8,413	*6.8*
1962 Republican Primary		
Edwin L. Mechem (R)		*100.0*
Democratic Primary		
Jack M. Campbell (D)	47,873	*38.7*
Ed V. Mead (D)	44,385	*35.9*
Leo T. Murphy (D)	28,755	*23.3*
1964 Republican Primary		
Merle H. Tucker (R)		*100.0*
Democratic Primary		
Jack M. Campbell (D)		*100.0*
1966 Republican Primary		
David F. Cargo (R)	17,836	*51.8*
Clifford J. Hawley (R)	16,588	*48.2*
Democratic Primary		
Thomas E. Lusk (D)	85,211	*59.9*
John Burroughs (D)	57,143	*40.1*
1968 Republican Primary		
David F. Cargo (R)	28,014	*54.9*
Clifford J. Hawley (R)	23,052	*45.1*
Democratic Primary		
Fabian Chavez (D)	41,348	*30.9*
Bruce King (D)	24,658	*18.4*
Calvin Horn (D)	24,376	*18.2*
Mack Easley (D)	21,436	*16.0*
Bobby M. Mayfield (D)	19,528	*14.6*

	Candidates	Votes	%
1970	**Republican Primary**		
	Peter V. Domenici (R)	25,881	*46.0*
	Stephen C. Helbing (R)	13,265	*23.6*
	Edward M. Hartman (R)	5,309	*9.4*
	Tom Clear (R)	5,262	*9.3*
	Junio Lopez (R)	4,272	*7.6*
	Democratic Primary		
	Bruce King (D)	62,718	*48.9*
	Jack Daniels (D)	47,523	*37.1*
	ALexander F. Sceresse (D)	17,918	*14.0*
1974	**Republican Primary**		
	Joe Skeen (R)	28,227	*55.4*
	John P. Eastham (R)	15,003	*29.5*
	James L. Hughes (R)	4,758	*9.3*
	Walter E. Bruce (R)	2,913	*5.7*
	Democratic Primary		
	Jerry Apodaca (D)	45,447	*30.6*
	Tibo J. Chavez (D)	35,090	*23.6*
	Odis Echols (D)	25,760	*17.3*
	Bobby M. Mayfield (D)	22,806	*15.3*
	Drew Cloud (D)	12,707	*8.6*
1978	**Republican Primary**		
	Joe Skeen (R)	38,638	*81.2*
	Philip R. Grant (R)	8,966	*18.8*
	Democratic Primary		
	Bruce King (D)	92,432	*61.3*
	Robert E. Ferguson (D)	58,334	*38.7*
1982	**Republican Primary**		
	John B. Irick (R)	35,789	*54.5*
	William A. Sego (R)	27,220	*41.5*
	Democratic Primary		
	Toney Anaya (D)	101,077	*56.9*
	Aubrey L. Dunn (D)	60,866	*34.3*
	Fabian Chavez (D)	11,874	*6.7*

NEW YORK

	Candidates	Votes	%
1970 [13]	**Republican Primary**		
	Nelson A. Rockefeller (R)		*100.0*
	Democratic Primary		
	Arthur J. Goldberg (D)	493,295	*52.2*
	Howard J. Samuels (D)	451,703	*47.8*

13. *Until 1970, candidates for state office in New York were nominated by state party conventions or central committees.*

NORTH DAKOTA

Candidates	Votes	%
Liberal Primary		
Arthur J. Goldberg (L)		*100.0*
Conservative Primary		
Paul L. Adams (C)		*100.0*

1974

Candidates	Votes	%
Republican Primary		
Malcolm Wilson (R)		*100.0*
Democratic Primary		
Hugh L. Carey (D)	600,283	*60.8*
Howard J. Samuels (D)	387,369	*39.2*
Liberal Primary		
Edward Morrison (L) [14]		*100.0*
Conservative Primary		
Malcolm Wilson (C)		*100.0*

1978

Candidates	Votes	%
Republican Primary		
Perry B. Duryea (R)		*100.0*
Democratic Primary		
Hugh L. Carey (D)	376,457	*52.0*
Mary Anne Krupsak (D)	244,252	*33.7*
Jeremiah B. Bloom (D)	103,479	*14.3*
Conservative Primary		
Perry B. Duryea (C)		*100.0*
Liberal Primary		
Hugh L. Carey (L)		*100.0*

1982

Candidates	Votes	%
Republican Primary		
Lew Lehrman (R)	464,231	*80.6*
Paul J. Curran (R)	111,814	*19.4*
Democratic Primary		
Mario M. Cuomo (D)	678,900	*52.3*
Edward I. Koch (D)	618,356	*47.7*
Conservative Primary		
Lew Lehrman (R)		*100.0*
Liberal Primary		
Mario M. Cuomo (L)		*100.0*
Right to Life Primary		
Robert J. Bohner (RTL)		*100.0*

14. *Morrison withdrew after the primary and the Liberal state committee substituted Hugh L. Carey as the party's nominee.*

NORTH DAKOTA

	Candidates	Votes	%
1956	**Republican Primary**		
	John E. Davis (R)	55,149	*53.3*
	Ray Schnell (R)	48,296	*46.7*
	Democratic Primary		
	Wallace E. Warner (D)		*100.0*
1958	**Republican Primary**		
	John E. Davis (R)		*100.0*
	Democratic Primary		
	John F. Lord (D)	26,447	*55.4*
	Art Ford (D)	21,271	*44.6*
1960	**Republican Primary**		
	C. P. Dahl (R)	86,900	*77.6*
	Orris G. Nordhougen (R)	25,132	*22.4*
	Democratic Primary		
	William L. Guy (D)		*100.0*
1962	**Republican Primary**		
	Mark Andrews (R)		*100.0*
	Democratic Primary		
	William L. Guy (D)		*100.0*
1964	**Republican Primary**		
	Donald M. Halcrow (R)	43,089	*55.0*
	Robert P. McCarney (R)	35,269	*45.0*
	Democratic Primary		
	William L. Guy (D)		*100.0*
1968	**Republican Primary**		
	Robert P. McCarney (R)	47,324	*52.5*
	Edward W. Doherty (R)	42,845	*47.5*
	Democratic Primary		
	William L. Guy (D)		*100.0*
1972	**Republican Primary**		
	Richard Larsen (R)	66,045	*67.8*
	Robert P. McCarney (R)	31,377	*32.2*
	Democratic Primary		
	Arthur A. Link (D)	29,979	*93.1*
	Edward P. Burns (D)	2,231	*6.9*
1976	**Republican Primary**		
	Richard Elkin (R)	54,427	*81.9*
	Herb Geving (R)	12,013	*18.1*

Candidates	Votes	%
Democratic Primary		
Arthur A. Link (D)		100.0
American Primary		
Martin Vaaler (AM)		100.0
1980 Republican Primary		
Allen I. Olson (R)	60,016	75.7
Orville W. Hagen (R)	19,306	24.3
Democratic Primary		
Arthur A. Link (D)		100.0
1984 Republican Primary		
Allen L. (Al) Olson (R)	41,191	100.0
Democratic Primary		
George A. Sinner (D)	36,461	87.6
Anna Belle Bourgois (D)	5,180	12.4

OHIO

Candidates	Votes	%
1956 Republican Primary		
C. William O'Neill (R)	425,947	72.5
John W. Brown (R)	161,826	27.5
Democratic Primary		
Michael V. DiSalle (D)	279,831	57.4
John E. Sweeney (D)	106,071	21.8
Robert W. Reider (D)	41,224	8.5
Frank X. Kryzan (D)	37,290	7.6
1958 Republican Primary		
C. William O'Neill (R)	346,660	63.6
Charles P. Taft (R)	198,173	36.4
Democratic Primary		
Michael V. DiSalle (D)	242,830	37.7
Anthony J. Celebrezze (D)	140,453	21.8
Albert S. Porter (D)	108,498	16.8
Robert N. Gorman (D)	57,694	9.0
M. E. Sensenbrenner (D)	52,350	8.1
Clingan Jackson (D)	35,175	5.5
1962 Republican Primary		
James A. Rhodes (R)	520,868	89.6
William L. White (R)	59,916	10.3
Democratic Primary		
Michael V. DiSalle (D)	331,463	50.3
Mark McElroy (D)	299,207	45.4

	Candidates	Votes	%
1966	**Republican Primary**		
	James A. Rhodes (R)	577,827	88.7
	William L. White (R)	73,428	11.3
	Democratic Primary		
	Frazier Reams Jr. (D)	326,419	58.5
	Harry H. McIlwain (D)	231,406	41.5
1970	**Republican Primary**		
	Roger Cloud (R)	468,369	50.5
	Donald E. Lukens (R)	283,257	30.5
	Paul W. Brown (R)	164,672	17.7
	Democratic Primary		
	John J. Gilligan (D)	547,675	59.7
	Robert E. Sweeney (D)	216,195	23.6
	Mark McElroy (D)	153,702	16.7
	American Independent Primary		
	Edwin G. Lawton (AMI)	3,463	64.9
	Robert W. Annable (AMI)	1,870	35.1
1974	**Republican Primary**		
	James A. Rhodes (R)	385,669	62.8
	Charles E. Fry (R)	183,899	29.9
	Bert Dawson (R)	44,938	7.3
	Democratic Primary		
	John J. Gilligan (D)	713,488	70.6
	James D. Nolan (D)	297,244	29.4
1978	**Republican Primary**		
	James A. Rhodes (R)	393,632	67.7
	Charles F. Kurfess (R)	187,544	32.3
	Democratic Primary		
	Richard F. Celeste (D)	491,524	84.6
	Dale Reusch (D)	88,314	15.2
1982	**Republican Primary**		
	Clarence Brown Jr. (R)	347,176	51.5
	Seth Taft (R)	153,806	22.8
	Thomas A. Van Meter (R)	136,761	20.3
	Robert W. Teater (R)	35,821	5.3
	Democratic Primary		
	Richard F. Celeste (D)	436,887	42.4
	William J. Brown (D)	383,007	37.2
	Jerry Springer (D)	210,524	20.4
	Libertarian Primary		
	Phyllis Goetz (LIBERT)		100.0

OKLAHOMA

Candidates	Votes	%
1958 **Republican Primary**		
Phil Ferguson (R)	31,602	*51.4*
Clarence E. Barnes (R)	21,075	*34.3*
Carmon C. Harris (R)	5,941	*9.7*
Democratic Primary		
J. Howard Edmondson (D)	108,358	*21.1*
W. P. Atkinson (D)	107,616	*20.9*
George Miskovsky (D)	87,766	*17.1*
William O. Coe (D)	72,763	*14.2*
Bill Doenges (D)	57,990	*11.3*
Jim A. Rinehart (D)	39,279	*7.6*
Democratic Runoff		
J. Howard Edmondson (D)	363,742	*69.6*
W. P. Atkinson (D)	158,780	*30.4*
1962 **Republican Primary**		
Henry Bellmon (R)	56,560	*91.4*
Leslie C. Skoien (R)	5,313	*8.6*
Democratic Primary		
Raymond Gary (D)	176,525	*33.0*
W. P. Atkinson (D)	91,182	*17.1*
Preston J. Moore (D)	85,248	*16.0*
George Nigh (D)	84,404	*15.8*
Fred R. Harris (D)	78,476	*14.7*
Democratic Runoff		
W. P. Atkinson (D)	231,994	*50.0*
Raymond Gary (D)	231,545	*49.9*
1966 **Republican Primary**		
Dewey F. Bartlett (R)	46,053	*49.0*
John N. H. Camp (R)	45,185	*48.1*
Democratic Primary		
Raymond Gary (D)	160,825	*31.6*
Preston J. Moore (D)	104,081	*20.4*
David Hall (D)	94,309	*18.5*
Cleeta J. Rogers (D)	71,248	*14.0*
Charles Nesbitt (D)	26,546	*5.2*
Republican Runoff		
Dewey F. Bartlett (R)	46,916	*55.2*
John N. H. Camp (R)	38,043	*44.8*
Democratic Runoff		
Preston J. Moore (D)	228,625	*53.7*
Raymond Gary (D)	196,835	*46.3*
1970 **Republican Primary**		
Dewey F. Bartlett (R)		*100.0*

Candidates	Votes	%
Democratic Primary		
David Hall (D)	198,976	*49.5*
Bryce Baggett (D)	96,069	*23.9*
Joe Cannon (D)	56,842	*14.1*
Wilburn Cartwright (D)	50,396	*12.5*
Democratic Runoff		
David Hall (D)	179,902	*57.5*
Bryce Baggett (D)	132,952	*42.5*
1974 **Republican Primary**		
James M. Inhofe (R)	88,594	*58.8*
Denzil D. Garrison (R)	62,188	*41.2*
Democratic Primary		
Clem R. McSpadden (D)	238,534	*37.7*
David L. Boren (D)	225,321	*35.6*
David Hall (D)	169,290	*26.7*
Democratic Runoff		
David L. Boren (D)	286,171	*53.5*
Clem R. McSpadden (D)	248,623	*46.5*
1978 **Republican Primary**		
Ron Shotts (R)	82,895	*76.8*
Jerry L. Mash (R)	13,145	*12.2*
Jim Head (R)	11,826	*11.0*
Democratic Primary		
George Nigh (D)	276,910	*49.9*
Larry Derryberry (D)	208,055	*37.5*
Bob Funston (D)	69,475	*12.5*
Democratic Runoff		
George Nigh (D)	269,681	*57.7*
Larry Derryberry (D)	197,457	*42.3*
1982 **Republican Primary**		
Tom Daxon (R)	73,677	*64.7*
Neal A. McCaleb (R)	35,379	*31.1*
Democratic Primary		
George Nigh (D)	379,301	*82.6*
Howard L. Bell (D)	79,735	*17.4*

OREGON

Candidates	Votes	%
1956 **Republican Primary**		
Elmo E. Smith (R)	225,748	*91.0*
Earl L. Dickson (R)	22,306	*9.0*
Democratic Primary		
Robert D. Holmes (D)	112,307	*50.8*
Lew Wallace (D)	108,822	*49.2*

	Candidates	Votes	%
1958	**Republican Primary**		
	Mark O. Hatfield (R)	106,687	*47.9*
	Sig Unander (R)	65,180	*29.2*
	Warren Gill (R)	40,489	*18.2*
	Democratic Primary		
	Robert D. Holmes (D)	129,491	*62.0*
	Lew Wallace (D)	59,992	*28.7*
	Wiley W. Smith (D)	18,484	*8.8*
1962	**Republican Primary**		
	Mark O. Hatfield (R)	174,811	*82.2*
	George Altvater (R)	37,306	*17.5*
	Democratic Primary		
	Robert Y. Thornton (D)	149,000	*66.2*
	Walter J. Pearson (D)	62,331	*27.7*
1966	**Republican Primary**		
	Tom McCall (R)	215,959	*91.4*
	John L. Reynolds (R)	20,286	*8.6*
	Democratic Primary		
	Robert W. Straub (D)	182,697	*72.5*
	Ben Musa (D)	41,610	*16.5*
	Emmet T. Rogers (D)	17,618	*7.0*
1970	**Republican Primary**		
	Tom McCall (R)	183,298	*74.4*
	Robert H. Wampler (R)	38,322	*15.6*
	Andrew R. Gigler (R)	24,797	*10.1*
	Democratic Primary		
	Robert W. Straub (D)	182,683	*65.9*
	Art Pearl (D)	33,716	*12.2*
	Gracie Hansen (D)	20,329	*7.3*
	Al Holdiman (D)	18,180	*6.6*
1974	**Republican Primary**		
	Victor G. Atiyeh (R)	144,454	*60.7*
	Clay Myers (R)	79,003	*33.2*
	Democratic Primary		
	Robert W. Straub (D)	107,205	*33.6*
	Betty Roberts (D)	98,654	*30.9*
	Jim Redden (D)	88,795	*27.8*
1978	**Republican Primary**		
	Victor G. Atiyeh (R)	115,593	*46.4*
	Tom McCall (R)	83,568	*33.5*
	Roger Martin (R)	42,644	*17.1*
	Democratic Primary		
	Robert W. Straub (D)	144,761	*51.0*
	Marvin J. Hollingsworth (D)	52,901	*18.7*
	Emily Ashworth (D)	49,201	*17.3*

	Candidates	Votes	%
1982	**Republican Primary**		
	Victor G. Atiyeh (R)	208,333	*82.4*
	Clif Everett (R)	17,741	*7.0*
	Walter Huss (R)	16,892	*6.7*
	Democratic Primary		
	Ted Kulongoski (D)	186,580	*59.5*
	Don Clark (D)	60,850	*19.4*
	Jerry Rust (D)	22,962	*7.3*

PENNSYLVANIA

	Candidates	Votes	%
1958	**Republican Primary**		
	A. T. McGonigle (R)	578,286	*53.3*
	Harold E. Stassen (R)	344,043	*31.7*
	William S. Livengood (R)	138,284	*12.7*
	Democratic Primary		
	David Lawrence (D)	730,229	*74.4*
	Roy E. Furman (D)	194,464	*19.8*
	Edward P. Lavelle (D)	56,188	*5.7*
1962	**Republican Primary**		
	William W. Scranton (R)	743,785	*78.0*
	J. Collins McSparran (R)	209,041	*21.9*
	Democratic Primary		
	Richardson Dilworth (D)	651,096	*72.9*
	Harvey F. Johnston (D)	143,243	*16.0*
	Charles J. Schmitt (D)	96,899	*10.9*
1966	**Republican Primary**		
	Raymond P. Shafer (R)	835,768	*78.0*
	Harold E. Stassen (R)	172,150	*16.1*
	George J. Brett (R)	63,366	*5.9*
	Democratic Primary		
	Milton Shapp (D)	543,057	*48.6*
	Robert P. Casey (D)	493,886	*44.2*
	Erwin L. Murray (D)	80,803	*7.2*
1970	**Republican Primary**		
	Raymond Broderick (R)		*100.0*
	Democratic Primary		
	Milton Shapp (D)	519,161	*49.1*
	Robert P. Casey (D)	480,944	*45.5*
	American Independent Primary		
	Francis T. McGeever (AMI)		*100.0*
	Constitutional Primary		
	Andrew J. Watson (CST)		*100.0*

	Candidates	Votes	%
1974	**Republican Primary**		
	Andrew L. Lewis (R)	534,637	*76.9*
	Alvin J. Jacobson (R)	97,072	*14.0*
	Leonard M. Strunk (R)	63,868	*9.2*
	Democratic Primary		
	Milton Shapp (D)	729,201	*70.4*
	Martin P. Mullen (D)	199,613	*19.3*
	Harvey F. Johnston (D)	106,474	*10.3*
	Constitutional Primary		
	Stephen Depue (CST)	1,006	*52.8*
	Norah M. Cope (CST)	898	*47.2*
1978	**Republican Primary**		
	Richard L. Thornburgh (R)	325,376	*32.6*
	Arlen Specter (R)	206,802	*20.7*
	Bob Butera (R)	190,653	*19.1*
	David W. Marston (R)	161,813	*16.2*
	Henry Hager (R)	57,119	*5.7*
	Democratic Primary		
	Peter Flaherty (D)	574,889	*44.9*
	Robert P. Casey (D)	445,146	*34.7*
	Ernest P. Kline (D)	223,811	*17.5*
1982	**Republican Primary**		
	Richard L. Thornburgh (R)		*100.0*
	Democratic Primary		
	Allen E. Ertel (D)	436,251	*57.6*
	Steve Douglas (D)	143,762	*19.0*
	Earl S. McDowell (D)	116,880	*15.4*
	Eugene Knox (D)	59,925	*7.9*

RHODE ISLAND

	Candidates	Votes	%
1956	**Republican Primary**		
	Christopher Del Sesto (R)		*100.0*
	Democratic Primary		
	Dennis J. Roberts (D)		*100.0*
1958	**Republican Primary**		
	Christopher Del Sesto (R)		*100.0*
	Democratic Primary		
	Dennis J. Roberts (D)	53,121	*56.1*
	Armand H. Coté (D)	41,536	*43.9*
1960	**Republican Primary**		
	Christopher Del Sesto (R)		*100.0*

	Candidates	Votes	%
	Democratic Primary		
	John A. Notte (D)	73,607	*56.3*
	Armand H. Coté (D)	57,200	*43.7*
1962	**Republican Primary**		
	John H. Chafee (R)	17,756	*62.5*
	Louis Jackvony (R)	10,459	*36.8*
	Democratic Primary		
	John A. Notte (D)	49,204	*53.1*
	Kevin Coleman (D)	41,658	*45.0*
1964	**Republican Primary**		
	John H. Chafee (R)		*100.0*
	Democratic Primary		
	Edward P. Gallogly (D)	55,282	*56.7*
	Alexander R. Walsh (D)	25,457	*26.1*
	John L. Rego (D)	16,715	*17.2*
1966	**Republican Primary**		
	John H. Chafee (R)		*100.0*
	Democratic Primary		
	Horace E. Hobbs (D)		*100.0*
1968	**Republican Primary**		
	John H. Chafee (R)		*100.0*
	Democratic Primary		
	Frank Licht (D)		*100.0*
1970	**Republican Primary**		
	Herbert F. DeSimone (R)	11,826	*96.0*
	Democratic Primary		
	Frank Licht (D)		*100.0*
1972	**Republican Primary**		
	Herbert F. DeSimone (R)		*100.0*
	Democratic Primary		
	Philip W. Noel (D)		*100.0*
1974	**Republican Primary**		
	James W. Nugent (R)		*100.0*
	Democratic Primary		
	Philip W. Noel (D)		*100.0*
1976	**Republican Primary**		
	James L. Taft (R)		*100.0*

Candidates	Votes	%
Democratic Primary		
J. Joseph Garrahy (D)	113,625	*82.4*
Giovani Folcarelli (D)	24,314	*17.6*
1978 **Republican Primary**		
Lincoln Almond (R)		*100.0*
Democratic Primary		
J. Joseph Garrahy (D)		*100.0*
1982 **Republican Primary**		
Vincent Marzullo (R)		*100.0*
Democratic Primary		
J. Joseph Garrahy (D)		*100.0*
1984 **Republican Primary**		
Edward D. DiPrete (R)	245,059	*100.0*
Democratic Primary		
Anthony J. Solomon (D)	73,090	*57.9*
Joseph W. Walsh (D)	53,041	*42.0*

SOUTH DAKOTA

Candidates	Votes	%
1956 **Republican Primary**		
Joe J. Foss (R)		*100.0*
Democratic Primary		
Ralph Herseth (D)		*100.0*
1958 **Republican Primary**		
Phil Saunders (R)	49,746	*61.6*
L. R. Houck (R)	21,621	*26.8*
Charles Lacey (R)	9,384	*11.6*
Democratic Primary		
Ralph Herseth (D)		*100.0*
1960 **Republican Primary**		
Archie M. Gubbrud (R)		*100.0*
Democratic Primary		
Ralph Herseth (D)		*100.0*
1962 **Republican Primary**		
Archie M. Gubbrud (R)		*100.0*
Democratic Primary		
Ralph Herseth (D)		*100.0*

	Candidates	Votes	%
1964	**Republican Primary**		
	Nils A. Boe (R)	50,335	*53.5*
	Sigurd Anderson (R)	43,809	*46.5*
	Democratic Primary		
	John F. Lindley (D)	27,071	*65.8*
	Merton B. Tice (D)	14,051	*34.2*
1966	**Republican Primary**		
	Nils A. Boe (R)		*100.0*
	Democratic Primary		
	Robert Chamberlin (D)		*100.0*
1968	**Republican Primary**		
	Frank Farrar (R)		*100.0*
	Democratic Primary		
	Robert Chamberlin (D)		*100.0*
1970	**Republican Primary**		
	Frank Farrar (R)	48,520	*58.2*
	Frank E. Henderson (R)	34,893	*41.8*
	Democratic Primary		
	Richard F. Kneip (D)		*100.0*
1972	**Republican Primary**		
	Carveth Thompson (R)	65,538	*72.4*
	Simon W. Chance (R)	24,975	*27.6*
	Democratic Primary		
	Richard K. Kneip (D)		*100.0*
1974	**Republican Primary**		
	John E. Olson (R)	49,973	*55.6*
	Ronald F. Williamson (R)	25,509	*28.4*
	Oscar W. Hagen (R)	14,444	*16.1*
	Democratic Primary		
	Richard F. Kneip (D)	45,932	*66.2*
	Bill Dougherty (D)	23,467	*33.8*
1978	**Republican Primary**		
	William J. Janklow (R)	46,423	*50.9*
	LeRoy G. Hoffman (R)	30,026	*32.9*
	Clint Roberts (R)	14,774	*16.2*
	Democratic Primary		
	Roger McKellips (D)	34,160	*49.1*
	Harvey Wollman (D)	32,690	*47.0*
1982	**Republican Primary**		
	William J. Janklow (R)		*100.0*

Candidates	Votes	%
Democratic Primary		
Michael J. O'Connor (D)	24,101	*58.8*
Elvern R. Varilek (D)	16,916	*41.2*

UTAH

	Candidates	Votes	%
1956	**Republican Primary**		
	George D. Clyde (R)	62,811	*53.5*
	J. Bracken Lee (R)	54,544	*46.5*
	Democratic Primary		
	L. C. Romney (D)	40,908	*52.0*
	John S. Boyden (D)	37,798	*48.0*
1960	**Republican Primary**		
	George D. Clyde (R)	50,592	*57.8*
	Lamont B. Gundersen (R)	37,002	*42.2*
	Democratic Primary		
	W. A. Barlocker (D)	74,424	*70.6*
	Ira A. Huggins (D)	31,045	*29.4*
1964	**Republican Primary**		
	Mitchell Melich (R)	63,108	*53.0*
	D. James Cannon (R)	55,938	*47.0*
	Democratic Primary		
	Calvin L. Rampton (D)	57,848	*62.7*
	Ernest Howard Dean (D)	34,470	*37.3*
1968	**Republican Primary**		
	Carl W. Buehner (R)	93,635	*70.1*
	Lamar A. Rawlings (R)	39,907	*29.9*
	Democratic Primary		
	Calvin L. Rampton (D)		*100.0*
1972	**Republican Primary**		
	Nicholas L. Strike (R)		*100.0*
	Democratic Primary		
	Calvin L. Rampton (D)		*100.0*
1976	**Republican Primary**		
	Vernon B. Romney (R)	87,251	*53.4*
	Dixie L. Leavitt (R)	76,139	*46.6*
	Democratic Primary		
	Scott M. Matheson (D)	50,505	*59.0*
	John P. Creer (D)	35,154	*41.0*

	Candidates	Votes	%
1984	**Republican Primary**		
	Norman H. Bangerter (R)	94,347	*56.4*
	Dan Marriott (R)	72,940	*43.6*
	Democratic Primary		
	Wayne Owens (D)	51,302	*62.0*
	Kem C. Gardner (D)	31,421	*38.0*

VERMONT

	Candidates	Votes	%
1956	**Republican Primary**		
	Joseph B. Johnson (R)		*100.0*
	Democratic Primary		
	E. Frank Branon (D)		*100.0*
1958	**Republican Primary**		
	Robert T. Stafford (R)		*100.0*
	Democratic Primary		
	Bernard J. Leddy (D)		*100.0*
1960	**Republican Primary**		
	F. Ray Keyser (R)	17,491	*29.6*
	Robert S. Babcock (R)	16,762	*28.4*
	A. Luke Crispe (R)	14,874	*25.2*
	W. A. Simpson (R)	9,916	*16.8*
	Democratic Primary		
	Russell F. Niquette (D)		*100.0*
1962	**Republican Primary**		
	F. Ray Keyser (R)		*100.0*
	Democratic Primary		
	Philip H. Hoff (D)		*100.0*
1964	**Republican Primary**		
	Ralph A. Foote (R)	19,121	*42.8*
	Robert S. Babcock (R)	16,225	*36.3*
	Roger MacBride (R)	9,265	*20.7*
	Democratic Primary		
	Philip H. Hoff (D)		*100.0*
1966	**Republican Primary**		
	Richard A. Snelling (R)	22,069	*59.0*
	Thomas L. Hayes (R)	15,286	*40.9*
	Democratic Primary		
	Philip H. Hoff (D)		*100.0*

	Candidates	Votes	%
1968	**Republican Primary**		
	Deane C. Davis (R)	36,719	62.7
	James L. Oakes (R)	21,791	37.2
	Democratic Primary		
	John J. Daley (D)		100.0
1970	**Republican Primary**		
	Deane C. Davis (R)	31,549	79.3
	Thomas L. Hayes (R)	8,048	20.2
	Democratic Primary		
	Leo O'Brien (D)	18,058	54.7
	John J. Daley (D)	14,795	44.8
1972	**Republican Primary**		
	Luther F. Hackett (R)	33,323	54.4
	James M. Jeffords (R)	27,902	45.5
	Democratic Primary		
	Thomas P. Salmon (D)		100.0
1974	**Republican Primary**		
	Walter L. Kennedy (R)	23,738	55.5
	Harry R. Montague (R)	13,901	32.5
	T. James Lannon (R)	4,667	10.9
	Democratic Primary		
	Thomas P. Salmon (D)	18,498	83.6
	John F. Reilly (D)	3,537	16.0
1976	**Republican Primary**		
	Richard Snelling (R)	24,279	70.8
	William G. Craig (R)	9,429	27.5
	Democratic Primary		
	Stella B. Hackel (D)	18,522	44.0
	Brian D. Burns (D)	14,725	34.9
	Robert O'Brien (D)	8,809	20.9
	Liberty Union Primary		
	Bernard Sanders (LU)		100.0
1978	**Republican Primary**		
	Richard A. Snelling (R)		100.0
	Democratic Primary		
	Edwin C. Granai (D)	8,572	64.6
	Bernard G. O'Shea (D)	4,570	34.4
	Liberty Union Primary		
	Earl S. Gardner (LU)		100.0

	Candidates	Votes	%
1980	**Republican Primary**		
	Richard A. Snelling (R)	38,228	85.0
	Clifford Thompson (R)	3,432	7.6
	Kirk E. Faryniasz (R)	2,273	5.0
	Democratic Primary		
	M. Jerome Diamond (D)	15,738	50.3
	Timothy J. O'Connor (D)	14,857	47.5
1982	**Republican Primary**		
	Richard A. Snelling (R)		100.0
	Democratic Primary		
	Madeleine M. Kunin (D)	16,002	90.7
	Clifford Thompson (D)	1,433	8.1
	Liberty Union Primary		
	Richard F. Gottlieb (LU)		100.0
1984	**Republican Primary**		
	John J. Easton (R)	30,436	61.3
	Hilton Wick (R)	19,170	38.2
	Democratic Primary		
	Madeleine M. Kunin (D)	17,138	100.0
	Liberty Union Primary		
	Richard F. Gottlieb (LU)		100.0

WASHINGTON[15]

	Candidates	Votes	%
1956	**Republican Primary**		
	Emmett T. Anderson (R)	192,500	59.6
	Don Eastvold (R)	99,020	30.7
	Democratic Primary		
	Albert D. Rosellini (D)	236,291	55.7
	Earl S. Coe (D)	140,882	33.2
	Roderick Lindsay (D)	39,072	9.2
1960	**Republican Primary**		
	Lloyd J. Andrews (R)	263,897	64.6
	Newman Clark (R)	144,440	35.4
	Democratic Primary		
	Albert D. Rosellini (D)	244,579	82.2
	John Patric (D)	28,970	9.7
	Bruce M. Sigman (D)	24,031	8.1

15. In Washington's so-called "jungle" primaries, all candidates for an office appeared together on the same ballot with their parties designated. Nominations went to the Republican and Democrat receiving the most votes for the office. Independents and minor party candidates gained a place on the general election ballot by obtaining at least 1 percent of the total vote cast in the primary. Percentages were calculated here as if candidates had run in separate party primaries.

	Candidates	Votes	%
1964	**Republican Primary**		
	Daniel J. Evans (R)	323,152	59.5
	Richard G. Christensen (R)	213,217	39.5
	Democratic Primary		
	Albert D. Rosellini (D)	243,220	84.9
	Jessop McDonnell (D)	17,262	6.0
1968	**Republican Primary**		
	Daniel J. Evans (R)	305,897	89.4
	Democratic Primary		
	John J. O'Connell (D)	182,969	50.5
	Martin J. Durkan (D)	162,382	44.8
1972	**Republican Primary**		
	Daniel J. Evans (R)	224,953	67.9
	Perry B. Woodall (R)	100,372	30.3
	Democratic Primary		
	Albert D. Rosellini (D)	276,121	47.5
	Martin J. Durkan (D)	195,931	33.7
	James A. McDermott (D)	99,155	17.1
1976	**Republican Primary**		
	John Spellman (R)	185,439	60.5
	Harley Hoppe (R)	111,957	36.5
	Democratic Primary		
	Dixy Lee Ray (D)	205,232	37.6
	Wes Uhlman (D)	198,336	36.4
	Marvin Durning (D)	136,290	25.0
1980	**Republican Primary**		
	John Spellman (R)	162,426	40.6
	Duane Berentson (R)	154,724	38.7
	Bruce Chapman (R)	70,875	17.7
	Democratic Primary		
	James A. McDermott (D)	321,256	56.4
	Dixy Lee Ray (D)	234,252	41.1
1984	**Republican Primary**		
	John Spellman (R)	239,463	95.5
	Democratic Primary		
	Booth Gardner (D)	421,087	64.4
	Jim McDermott (D)	209,435	32.0

WEST VIRGINIA

	Candidates	Votes	%
1956	**Republican Primary**		
	Cecil H. Underwood (R)	98,344	50.5
	John T. Copenhaver (R)	91,088	46.8

	Candidates	Votes	%
	Democratic Primary		
	Robert H. Mollohan (D)	148,557	42.6
	Milton J. Ferguson (D)	95,869	27.5
	J. Howard Myers (D)	75,606	21.7
	Joe F. Burdett (D)	24,913	7.1
1960	**Republican Primary**		
	Harold E. Neely (R)	102,618	55.3
	Chapman Revercomb (R)	83,028	44.7
	Democratic Primary		
	W. W. Barron (D)	187,501	51.0
	Hulett C. Smith (D)	140,079	38.1
	Orel J. Skeen (D)	39,907	10.9
1964	**Republican Primary**		
	Cecil H. Underwood (R)	152,573	89.7
	Harry H. Cupp (R)	11,325	6.7
	Democratic Primary		
	Hulett C. Smith (D)	186,273	53.3
	Bonn Brown (D)	85,527	24.4
	Julius W. Singleton (D)	47,845	13.7
	Harold G. Cutright (D)	30,119	8.6
1968	**Republican Primary**		
	Arch A. Moore Jr. (R)	106,299	57.2
	Cecil H. Underwood (R)	76,659	41.1
	Democratic Primary		
	James M. Sprouse (D)	123,181	37.6
	C. Donald Robertson (D)	118,637	36.2
	Paul J. Kaufman (D)	72,917	22.3
1972	**Republican Primary**		
	Arch A. Moore Jr. (R)		100.0
	Democratic Primary		
	John D. (Jay) Rockefeller IV (D)	262,613	72.2
	Lee M. Kenna (D)	63,514	17.5
	Robert Myers (D)	37,616	10.3
1976	**Republican Primary**		
	Cecil H. Underwood (R)	97,671	64.4
	Ralph D. Albertazzie (R)	44,393	29.3
	Democratic Primary		
	John D. (Jay) Rockefeller IV (D)	206,732	49.7
	James M. Sprouse (D)	118,707	28.5
	Ken Hechler (D)	52,791	12.7
	John G. Hutchinson (D)	26,222	6.3
1980	**Republican Primary**		
	Arch A. Moore Jr. (R)		100.0
	Democratic Primary		
	John D. (Jay) Rockefeller IV (D)	250,550	78.0
	H. John Rogers (D)	70,452	21.9

	Candidates	Votes	%
1984	**Republican Primary**		
	Arch A. Moore (R)	135,887	100.0
	Democratic Primary		
	Clyde M. See (D)	148,049	39.8
	Warren R. McGraw (D)	104,138	28.0
	Chauncey H. Browning (D)	101,712	27.4

WISCONSIN

	Candidates	Votes	%
1956	**Republican Primary**		
	Vernon W. Thomson (R)		100.0
	Democratic Primary		
	William Proxmire (D)		100.0
1958	**Republican Primary**		
	Vernon W. Thomson (R)		100.0
	Democratic Primary		
	Gaylord Nelson (D)		100.0
1960	**Republican Primary**		
	Philip G. Kuehn (R)		100.0
	Democratic Primary		
	Gaylord Nelson (D)		100.0
1962	**Republican Primary**		
	Philip G. Kuehn (R)	250,539	53.8
	Wilbur N. Renk (R)	199,616	42.9
	Democratic Primary		
	John W. Reynolds (D)		100.0
1964	**Republican Primary**		
	Warren P. Knowles (R)	246,760	71.9
	Milo G. Knutson (R)	96,421	28.1
	Democratic Primary		
	John W. Reynolds (D)	241,170	70.3
	Dominic H. Frinzi (D)	102,066	29.7
1966	**Republican Primary**		
	Warren P. Knowles (R)		100.0
	Democratic Primary		
	Patrick J. Lucey (D)	128,359	45.2
	David Carley (D)	95,803	33.7
	Dominic H. Frinzi (D)	44,344	15.6
	Abe L. Swed (D)	15,362	5.4

	Candidates	Votes	%
1968	**Republican Primary**		
	Warren P. Knowles (R)		100.0
	Democratic Primary		
	Bronson C. LaFollette (D)	173,458	84.4
	Floyd L. Wille (D)	31,778	15.5
1970	**Republican Primary**		
	Jack B. Olson (R)	203,434	91.4
	Roman R. Blenski (R)	19,061	8.6
	Democratic Primary		
	Patrick J. Lucey (D)	177,584	60.6
	Donald O. Peterson (D)	105,849	36.1
	American Primary		
	Leo J. McDonald (AM)		100.0
1974	**Republican Primary**		
	William D. Dyke (R)		100.0
	Democratic Primary		
	Patrick J. Lucey (D)	259,001	78.2
	Edmond E. Hou-Seye (D)	72,113	21.8
	American Primary		
	William H. Upham (AM)		100.0
1978	**Republican Primary**		
	Lee Sherman Dreyfus (R)	197,279	57.9
	Bob Kasten (R)	143,361	42.1
	Democratic Primary		
	Martin J. Schreiber (D)	217,572	60.4
	David Carley (D)	132,901	36.9
	Conservative Primary		
	Eugene R. Zimmerman (C)		100.0
1982	**Republican Primary**		
	Terry J. Kohler (R)	227,844	68.2
	Lowell B. Jackson (R)	106,413	31.8
	Democratic Primary		
	Anthony S. Earl (D)	268,857	45.9
	Martin J. Schreiber (D)	245,952	42.0
	James B. Wood (D)	71,282	12.2
	Libertarian Primary		
	Larry Smiley (LIBERT)		100.0
	Constitution Primary		
	James P. Wickstrom (CONST)		100.0

Candidates	Votes	%
Socialist Workers Primary		
Peter Seidman (SOC WORK)		*100.0*

WYOMING

	Candidates	Votes	%
1958	**Republican Primary**		
	Milward L. Simpson (R)	28,749	*77.6*
	Stanley Edwards (R)	8,294	*22.4*
	Democratic Primary		
	J. J. Hickey (D)		*100.0*
1962	**Republican Primary**		
	Clifford P. Hansen (R)	28,494	*57.0*
	Charles M. Crowell (R)	16,906	*33.8*
	R. E. Cheever (R)	4,575	*9.1*
	Democratic Primary		
	Jack R. Gage (D)	21,051	*55.5*
	William Jack (D)	16,875	*44.5*
1966	**Republican Primary**		
	Stan Hathaway (R)	26,110	*55.2*
	Joe Burke (R)	19,815	*41.9*
	Democratic Primary		
	Ernest Wilkerson (D)	13,145	*31.1*
	Bill Nation (D)	9,834	*23.2*
	Jack R. Gage (D)	8,661	*20.5*
	Raymond B. Whitaker (D)	6,238	*14.7*
	Howard L. Burke (D)	4,426	*10.5*

	Candidates	Votes	%
1970	**Republican Primary**		
	Stan Hathaway (R)		*100.0*
	Democratic Primary		
	John J. Rooney (D)		*100.0*
1974	**Republican Primary**		
	Dick Jones (R)	15,502	*26.5*
	Malcolm Wallop (R)	14,688	*25.1*
	Roy Peck (R)	14,217	*24.3*
	Clarence Brimmer (R)	14,014	*24.0*
	Democratic Primary		
	Ed Herschler (D)	19,997	*46.6*
	Harry E. Leimback (D)	15,255	*35.5*
	John J. Rooney (D)	7,674	*17.9*
1978	**Republican Primary**		
	John C. Ostlund (R)	40,251	*58.9*
	Gus Fleischli (R)	24,824	*36.4*
	Democratic Primary		
	Ed Herschler (D)	28,406	*65.3*
	Margaret McKinstry (D)	15,111	*34.7*
1982	**Republican Primary**		
	Warren A. Morton (R)	52,536	*74.3*
	Rex G. Welty (R)	9,106	*12.9*
	Carl A. Johnson (R)	9,025	*12.8*
	Democratic Primary		
	Ed Herschler (D)	44,396	*85.2*
	Pat McGuire (D)	7,720	*14.8*

Senate Elections

"Interior of Polling-Place." *Frank Leslie's Illustrated Newspaper*, Nov. 23, 1889.

Library of Congress Photo No. USZ62-2148

Senate Elections

The creation of the United States Senate was a result of the so-called "great compromise" at the Constitutional Convention in 1787. The small states wanted equal representation in Congress, fearing domination by the larger states under a population formula. The larger states, however, naturally wished for a legislature based on population, where their strength would prevail.

In compromising this dispute, delegates simply split the basis for representation between the two houses — population for the House of Representatives, equal representation by state for the Senate. By the terms of the compromise, each state was entitled to two senators. In a sense, they were conceived to be ambassadors from the states, representing the sovereign interests of the states to the federal government.

Election by State Legislatures

To elect these "ambassadors," the Founding Fathers chose the state legislatures instead of the people themselves. The argument was that legislatures would be able to give more sober and reflective thought than the people at large to the kind of persons needed to represent the states' interests to the federal government. The delegates also thought the state legislatures and thus the states would take a greater interest in the fledgling national government if they were involved in its operations this way. Furthermore, the state legislatures had chosen the members of the Continental Congress (the Congress under the Articles of Confederation), as well as the members of the Constitutional Convention itself, so the procedure was familiar to the delegates.

In choosing the state legislatures as the instruments of election for senators, the Constitutional Convention considered and abandoned several alternatives. Some delegates had suggested that the senators be elected by the House or appointed by the president from a list of nominees selected by the state legislatures. These ideas were discarded as making the Senate too dependent on another part of the federal government. Also turned down was a scheme for a system of electors, similar to presidential electors, to choose the senators in each state. And popular election was rejected as being too radical and inconvenient.

So deeply entrenched was the ambassadorial aspect of a senator's duty that state legislatures sometimes took it upon themselves to instruct senators on how to vote. This occasionally raised severe problems of conscience among senators and resulted in several resignations.

For example, in 1836 future president John Tyler was serving as a U.S. senator from Virginia. That year the Virginia Legislature instructed him to vote for a resolution to expunge the Senate censure of President Andrew Jackson for his removal of the federal deposits from the Bank of the United States. Tyler had voted for the censure resolution and was a bitter opponent of Jackson. He resigned from the Senate rather than comply.

In another instance, Sen. Hugh Lawson White of Tennessee, a Whig, resigned from the Senate in 1840 after being instructed by his state Legislature to vote for the sub-treasury bill, an economic measure supported by the Democratic Van Buren administration.

Another problem for the Founding Fathers was the length of the senatorial term. The framers of the Constitution tried to balance two principles: the belief that relatively frequent elections were necessary to promote good behavior and the need for steadiness and continuity in government.

Delegates proposed terms of three, four, five, six, seven

Sources

Haynes, George H. *The Election of Senators.* New York: Henry Holt, 1906.
——. *The Senate of the United States, Its History and Practice.* Boston: Houghton Mifflin, 1938.
Hupman, Richard D. *Senate Election, Expulsion and Censure Cases from 1793 to 1972.* Compiled by the Senate library under the direction of Francis R. Valeo, secretary of the Senate. Washington, D.C.: Government Printing Office, 1972.
Riddick, Floyd M., Senate parliamentarian. *The Term of a Senator, When Does It Begin and End? Constitution, Laws and Precedents Pertaining to the Term of a Senator.* Prepared under the direction of Emery L. Frazier, secretary of the Senate. Washington, D.C.: Government Printing Office, 1966.
U.S. Senate. Committee on Rules and Administration. *Senate Manual.* 97th Cong., 1st sess., 1981.

and nine years. They finally settled on six-year staggered terms, with one-third of the members coming up for election every two years. *(Classification of senators, terms, p. 574)*

Changing Election Procedures

At first each state made its own arrangements for its state legislature to elect the senators. Many states required an election by the two chambers of the legislature sitting separately.

That is, each chamber had to vote for the same candidate for him to be elected. Other states, however, provided for election by a joint ballot of the two chambers sitting together.

However, the Constitution specifically authorized Congress to regulate senatorial elections if it so chose. Article I, Section 4, Paragraph 1 states, "The times, places and manner of holding elections for Senators and Representatives shall be prescribed in each state by the legislature thereof; but the Congress may at any time by law make or alter such regulations, except as to the places of chusing Senators." *(Constitutional provisions for election to the Senate, Appendix, p. 1126)*

1866 Act of Congress

In 1866 Congress decided to exercise its authority. Procedures in some states, particularly those requiring concurrent majorities in both houses of the state legislature for election to the Senate, had resulted in numerous delays and vacancies.

The new federal law set up the following procedure: The first ballot for senator was to be taken by the two chambers of each state legislature voting separately. If no candidate received a majority of the vote in both houses, then the two chambers were to meet and ballot jointly until a majority choice emerged.

Also included in the 1866 law were provisions for roll-call votes in the state legislatures (secret ballots had been taken in several states) and for a definite timetable. The law directed that the first vote take place on the second Tuesday after the meeting and organization of the legislature, followed by a minimum of a single ballot on every legislative day thereafter until election of a senator resulted.

But the new uniform system did not have the desired effect. The requirement for a majority vote continued the frequency of deadlock. In fact one of the worst deadlocks in senatorial election history happened under the 1866 federal law.

The case occurred in Delaware at the end of the 19th century. In 1899, with the Legislature divided between two factions of the Republican Party and the Democrats in the minority, no majority selection could be made for the senatorial term beginning March 4, 1899. So bitter was the Republican factional dispute that neither side would support a candidate acceptable to the other; nor would the Democrats play kingmaker by siding with one or the other Republican group. The dispute continued throughout the life of the 56th Congress (1899-1901), leaving a seat unfilled.

Furthermore, the term of Delaware's other Senate seat ended in 1901, necessitating another election. The same pattern continued, with the Legislature unable to fill either seat, leaving Delaware totally unrepresented in the Senate from March 4, 1901, until March 1, 1903, when two sena-

tors were finally elected in the closing days of the 57th Congress (1901-03). The deadlock was broken when the two Republican factions split the state's two seats between them.

Abuses of Election by Legislatures

Besides the frequent deadlocks, critics pointed to what they saw as other faults in the system. They charged that the party caucuses in the state legislatures, as well as individual members, were subject to intense and unethical lobbying practices by supporters of various senatorial candidates. The relatively small size of the electing body and the high stakes involved — a seat in the Senate — often tempted the use of questionable methods in conducting the elections.

Allegations that such methods were used involved the Senate itself in election disputes. The Constitution makes Congress the judge of its own members. Article I, Section 5, Paragraph 1 states, "Each House shall be the judge of the elections, returns, and qualifications of its own members...."

One of the most sensational cases concerned the election of William Lorimer, R-Ill. Lorimer won on the 99th ballot taken by the Illinois Legislature in 1909. A year after he had taken his seat, the Senate cleared Lorimer of charges that he had won election by bribery. But the revelation of new evidence prompted another investigation, and in 1912 the Senate voted that Lorimer's election was invalid and that he was not entitled to his seat.

Critics had still another grievance against the legislative method of choosing senators. They contended that elections to the state legislatures were often overshadowed by senatorial contests. Thus when voters went to the polls to choose their state legislators, they sometimes would be urged to disregard state and local issues and vote for a legislator who promised to support a certain candidate for the U.S. Senate. This, the critics said, led to neglect of state government and issues. Moreover, drawn-out Senate contests tended to hold up the consideration of state business.

Demands for Popular Elections

But the main criticism of legislative elections was that they distorted or even blocked the will of the people. Throughout the 19th century, the movement toward popular election had taken away from the legislatures the right to elect government and presidential electors in states that had such provisions. Now attention focused on the Senate.

Five times around the turn of the century the House passed constitutional amendments to provide for Senate elections by popular vote — in the 52nd Congress on Jan. 16, 1893; in the 53rd Congress on July 21, 1894; in the 55th Congress on May 11, 1898; in the 56th Congress on April 13, 1900, and in the 57th Congress on Feb. 13, 1902. But each time the Senate refused to act.

Frustrated in their desire for direct popular elections, reformers began implementing various formulas for preselecting Senate candidates, attempting to reduce the legislative balloting to something approaching a mere formality. In some cases party conventions endorsed nominees for the Senate, allowing the voters at least to know who the members of the legislature were likely to support. Southern states early in the century adopted the party primary to choose Senate nominees. However, legislators never could be legally bound to support anyone because the Constitu-

Senate Appointments and Special Elections

Governors were given specific authority in the Constitution to make temporary appointments to the Senate. Article I, Section 3, Paragraph 2 states: "If vacancies happen by resignation, or otherwise, during the recess of the legislature of any state, the executive thereof may make temporary appointments until the next meeting of the legislature, which shall then fill such vacancies."

The principle was established as early as 1794 that a vacancy created solely because a state legislature had failed to elect a new senator could not be filled by appointment, because the vacancy had not occurred "during the recess of the legislature."

For example, the term of Sen. Matthew Quay, R-Pa. (1887-99, 1901-04) expired March 3, 1899. The Legislature was in session but had not re-elected him. Nor did it elect anyone before adjourning that April 20. Thereupon, the governor appointed Quay to the vacancy; but the Senate did not allow Quay to take the seat, because the vacancy had occurred during the meeting of the Legislature. In 1901 the Legislature elected Quay for the remainder of the term.

On the other hand, if a senator's term expired and the legislature was *not* in session, a governor was able to make an appointment — but only until the legislature either elected a successor or adjourned without electing one. For example, on March 3, 1809, the term of Sen. Samuel Smith, D-R-Md. (1803-15, 1822-33) expired. The Legislature was not then in session and had not elected a successor. Therefore the governor appointed Smith to fill the vacancy until the next meeting of the Legislature, which was scheduled for June 5, 1809. The Senate ruled that he was entitled to the seat. During the subsequent meeting of the state Legislature that year, Smith was elected to a full term.

Whatever the condition under which an appointment had been made, it was to last only through the next state legislative session. Even if a legislature failed to elect a new senator, the appointed senator's service was to expire with the adjournment of the state legislature.

This principle was confirmed in the case of Sen. Samuel Phelps, Whig-Vt. (1839-51, 1853-54). Phelps was appointed in January 1853 to a vacancy caused by the death of Sen. William Upham, Whig-Vt. (1843-53), whose term was to run through March 3, 1855. As the Legislature was in recess, Phelps continued to serve until the expiration of the 32nd Congress on March 3, 1853, and also during a special session of the 33rd Congress in March and April 1853. The Vermont Legislature met during October and December without electing a senator to fill the unexpired term. Phelps then showed up for the regular session of the 33rd Congress in December, but the Senate in March 1854 decided he was not entitled to retain his seat, because the Legislature had met and adjourned without electing a new senator.

17th Amendment and Special Elections

The adoption of the 17th Amendment in 1913, providing for popular election of senators, altered the provision for gubernatorial appointment of senators to fill vacancies. The amendment provided that, in case of a vacancy, "the executive authority of such state shall issue writs of election to fill such vacancies: *Provided*, that the legislature of any state may empower the executive thereof to make temporary appointments until the people fill the vacancies by election as the legislature may direct." Under this provision, state legislatures allowed governors to make temporary appointments until the vacancy could be filled by a special election. Special elections — elections held to fill unexpired terms — were usually held in November of an even-numbered year. Some states, however, provided for special elections to be held within just a few months after the vacancy occurred.

Before ratification of the 17th Amendment the term of an appointee generally ended when a successor was elected to fill the unexpired term or at the end of the six-year term, whichever occurred first. After the ratification of the 17th Amendment but before ratification of the 20th Amendment in 1933, senators who were elected to fill lengthy unexpired terms usually could take office immediately, displacing an appointee. If an appointee was serving near the close of a six-year term, most states would hold simultaneous elections to fill both the six-year term and the four-month "lame-duck" term. Sometimes different persons would be elected to each term.

To eliminate the lame-duck sessions that ran from December of an even-numbered year through March 3 of the next year, the 20th Amendment changed the March 3 beginning date of the terms for Congress and the president to Jan. 3. After the so-called lame-duck amendment took effect, senators elected to fill vacancies in terms that had several years to run would take office immediately, as before, but, if a vacancy occurred near the end of a six-year term, an appointee would often serve until the Jan. 3 expiration date, eliminating the necessity for a special election.

Some states, however, have held elections in November for the remaining two months of a term. Georgia voters in 1972, for example, found on the ballot two Senate elections, one for a six-year term and one for a two-month term to fill the unexpired term of Sen. Richard B. Russell, D (1933-71), who died in office.

Dates of Service

Title II, Section 36 of the U.S. Code sets the dates on which senators appointed or elected to fill unexpired terms formally begin service and go on the payroll. The service of an appointee commences the day of appointment and continues until a successor is elected and qualified. If the Senate is in sine die adjournment when a new senator is elected to succeed an appointee, he will take office and begin receiving his salary on the day after the election.

If the Senate is in session when a new senator is elected to succeed an appointee, the new senator may take office when he presents himself before the Senate to take the oath; the appointee may continue in office until this occurs or the Senate adjourns sine die, whichever happens first. The term of the newly elected senator would then begin at sine die adjournment.

tion gave them the unfettered power of electing to the Senate whomever they chose.

Oregon took the lead in instituting non-binding popular elections. Under a 1901 law, voters expressed their choice for senator in popular ballots. While the election results had no legal force, the law required that the popular returns be formally announced to the state Legislature before it elected a senator.

At first the law did not work — the winner of the informal popular vote in 1902 was not chosen senator by the Legislature. But the reformers increased their pressure, demanding that candidates for the Legislature sign a pledge to vote for the winner of the popular vote. By 1908 the plan was successful. The Republican Legislature elected to the Senate Democrat George Chamberlain, the winner of the popular contest. Several other states — including Colorado, Kansas, Minnesota, Montana, Nevada and Oklahoma — adopted the Oregon method.

The 17th Amendment

Despite these palliatives, pressures continued to mount for a switch to straight popular elections. Frustrated at the failure of the Senate to act, proponents of change began pushing for a convention to propose this and perhaps other amendments to the Constitution. (Article V of the Constitution provides two methods of proposing amendments — either passage by two-thirds of both houses of Congress or through the calling of a special convention if requested by the legislatures of two-thirds of the states. In either case any amendment proposed by Congress or by a special convention must be ratified by three-fourths of the states.)

Conservatives began to fear a convention more than they did popular election of senators. There was no precedent for an amending convention and conservatives worried that it might be dominated by liberals and progressives who would propose numerous amendments and change the very nature of the government. Consequently, their opposition to popular election of senators diminished.

At the same time progressives of both parties made strong gains in the midterm elections of 1910. Some successful Senate candidates had made pledges to work for adoption of a constitutional amendment providing for popular election. In this atmosphere the Senate debated and finally passed the amendment on June 12, 1911, by a vote of 64-24. The House concurred in the Senate version on May 13, 1912, by a vote of 238-39. Ratification of the 17th Amendment was completed by the requisite number of states on April 8, 1913, and was proclaimed a part of the Constitution by Secretary of State William Jennings Bryan on May 31, 1913.

The first popularly elected senator was chosen in a special election in November 1913. He was Sen. Blair Lee, D-Md. (1914-17), elected for the remaining three years of the unexpired term of Sen. Isidor Rayner, D (1905-12), who had died in office.

There was no wholesale changeover in membership when the 17th Amendment became effective. In fact every one of the 23 senators elected by state legislatures for their previous terms, and running for re-election to full terms in November 1914, was successful. Seven had retired or died, and two had been defeated for renomination.

The changeover in method of electing senators ended the frequent legislative stalemates in choosing members of the Senate. Otherwise many things remained the same.

There were still election disputes, including charges of corruption, as well as miscounting of votes.

Election Disputes

Election disputes continued to occupy the Senate. A bitter contest for a New Hampshire Senate seat in 1974 between Republican representative Louis C. Wyman and Democrat John A. Durkin wound up in the Senate after a seesaw battle between New Hampshire authorities over who had won. The state Ballot Law Commission had finally awarded the victory to Wyman by two votes, but Durkin took his case to the Senate. After wrestling with the problem for seven months, the Senate gave up and declared the seat vacant. A new election was held Sept. 16, 1975, which Durkin won decisively.

Senate's Three Classes

The Senate is divided into three classes or groups of members. A member's class depends on the year in which he or she is elected. Article I, Section 3, Paragraph 2 of the Constitution, relating to the classification of senators in the first and succeeding Congresses, provides that "Immediately after they shall be assembled in consequence of the first election, they shall be divided as equally as may be into three classes. The seats of the Senators of the first class shall be vacated at the expiration of the second year, of the second class at the expiration of the fourth year and of the third class at the expiration of the sixth year, so that one-third may be chosen every second year...."

Thus senators belonging to class one began their regular terms in the years 1789, 1791, 1797, 1803, etc., continuing through the present day to 1971, 1977, 1983 and coming up for re-election in 1988. Senators belonging to class two began their regular terms in 1789, 1793, 1799, 1805, etc., continuing through to the present day in 1967, 1973, 1979 and were up for election in 1984. And senators belonging to class three began their regular terms in 1789, 1795, 1801, 1807, etc., continuing through the present day to 1969, 1975, 1981 and coming up for re-election in 1986.

Sessions and Terms

In the fall of 1788, the expiring Continental Congress established a schedule for the incoming government under the new Constitution. The Congress decided that the new government was to commence on the first Wednesday in March 1789 — March 4. Even though the House did not achieve a quorum until April 1 and the Senate April 6, and President Washington was not inaugurated until April 30, Senate, House and presidential terms were still considered to have begun March 4. The term of the first Congress continued through March 3, 1791. Because congressional and presidential terms were fixed at exactly two, four and six years, March 4 became the official date of transition from one administration to another every four years and from one Congress to another every two years.

'Long' and 'Short' Sessions

The Constitution did not mandate a regular congressional session to begin March 4. Instead, Article I, Section 4, Paragraph 2 called for at least one congressional session every year, to convene on the first Monday in December unless Congress by law set a different day. Consequently, except when called by the president for special sessions, or when Congress itself set a different day, Congress convened

in regular session each December, until the passage of the 20th Amendment in 1933.

The December date resulted in a long and short session. The first (long) session would meet in December of an odd-numbered year and continue into the next year, usually adjourning some time the next summer. The second (short) session began in December of an even-numbered year and continued through March 3 of the next year, when its term ran out. It also became customary for the Senate to meet in brief special session on March 4 or March 5, especially in years when a new president was inaugurated, to act on presidential nominations.

To illustrate with an example of a typical Congress, the 29th (1845-47): President James K. Polk, D, was inaugurated on March 4, 1845. The Senate met in special session from March 4 to March 20 to confirm Polk's Cabinet and other appointments. Then the first regular session convened Dec. 1, 1845, working until Aug. 10, 1846, when it adjourned. The second, a short session, lasted from Dec. 7, 1846, through March 3, 1847.

Since it was not clear whether terms of members of Congress ended at midnight March 3 or noon March 4, the custom evolved of extending the legislative day of March 3, in odd-numbered years, to noon March 4.

The 20th Amendment

The political consequence of the short session was to encourage filibusters and other delaying tactics by members determined to block legislation that would die upon the automatic adjournment of Congress on March 3. Moreover, the Congresses that met in short session always included a substantial number of "lame-duck" members who had been defeated at the polls, yet were able quite often to determine the legislative outcome of the session.

Dissatisfaction with the short session began to mount after 1900. During the Wilson administration (1913-21),

each of four such sessions ended with a Senate filibuster and the loss of important bills including several funding bills. Sen. George W. Norris, R-Neb. (1913-43), became the leading advocate of a constitutional amendment to abolish the short session by starting the terms of Congress and the president in January instead of March. The Senate approved the Norris amendment five times during the 1920s, only to see it blocked in the House each time. It was finally approved by both chambers in 1932 and became the 20th Amendment upon ratification by the 36th state in 1933.

The amendment provided that the terms of senators and representatives would begin and end at noon on the third day of January of the year following the election. However, according to the *Senate Manual* (1981 edition, p. 653), "In view of the impracticality of dealing with split days, ... it has been the long established practice for payment of salaries, computation of allowances and recording of service to credit a member for the full day of the third of January he takes office and consider his term as ended at the close of business on the second of January six years later." Congressional Quarterly has retained this convention in the list of senators in this volume, with dates of service shown as beginning on Jan. 3 and ending on Jan. 2.

The 20th Amendment also established noon Jan. 20 as the day on which the president and vice president take office. It provided also that Congress should meet annually on Jan. 3 "unless they shall by law appoint a different day." The second session of the 73rd Congress was the first to convene on the new date, Jan. 3, 1934. Franklin D. Roosevelt was the first president and John N. Garner the first vice president to be inaugurated on Jan. 20, at the start of their second terms in 1937.

The amendment was intended to permit Congress to extend its first session for as long as necessary and to complete the work of its second session before the next election, thereby obviating legislation by a lame-duck body.

Bibliography

Books

Barone, Michael, and Grant Ujifusa. *The Almanac of American Politics: The President, the Senators, the Representatives, the Governors: Their Records and Election Results, Their States and Districts, 1984.* Washington, D.C.: National Journal, 1983.

Bryce, James. *The American Commonwealth.* 1922. Reprint. New York: AMS Press.

Congressional Quarterly. *Guide to Congress.* 3rd ed. Washington, D.C.: Congressional Quarterly, 1982.

Council of State Governments. *State Elective Officials and the Legislatures.* Lexington, Ky.: The Council of State Governments, 1983.

Ehrenhalt, Alan, ed. *Politics in America: Members of Congress in Washington and at Home, 1984.* Washington, D.C.: Congressional Quarterly, 1983.

Falco, Maria J. *Bigotry: Ethnic, Machine and Sexual Politics in a Senatorial Election.* Westport, Conn.: Greenwood Press, 1980.

Farrand, Max. *Records of the Federal Convention of 1787.* 4 vols. rev. ed. New Haven, Conn.: Yale University Press, 1967.

Fenno, Richard F. Jr. *Home Style: House Members in Their Districts.* Boston: Little, Brown, 1978.

Hinckley, Barbara. *Congressional Elections.* Washington, D.C.: CQ Press, 1981.

Huckshorn, Robert J. *Politics of Defeat: Campaigning for Congress.* Amherst, Mass.: University of Massachusetts Press, 1971.

Mann, Thomas E. *Unsafe at Any Margin: Interpreting Congressional Elections.* Washington, D.C.: American Enterprise Institute, 1978.

———, and Norman J. Ornstein. *The American Elections of 1982.* Washington, D.C.: American Enterprise Institute, 1983.

Matteson, David M. *The Organization of the Government under the Constitution.* New York: Da Capo Press, 1970.

Matthews, Donald R. *U.S. Senators and their World.* 1960. Reprint. Westport, Conn.: Greenwood Press, 1980.

Maurine, Christopher. *Black Americans in Congress.* New York: Crowell, 1975.

Miller, Warren, Arthur Miller and Edward Schneider. *American National Election Studies Data Sourcebook, 1952-1978.* Cambridge, Mass.: Harvard University Press, 1980.

Rogers, Lindsay. *The American Senate.* 1926. Reprint. New York: Johnson Reprint.

Scammon, Richard M. *America Votes: A Handbook of Contemporary Election Statistics.* vols. 1 and 2. New York: Macmillan, 1956, 1958. *America Votes.* vols. 3-5.

Pittsburgh: University of Pittsburgh, 1959, 1962 and 1964. *America Votes*. vols. 6-11. Washington, D.C.: Congressional Quarterly, 1966-1975.

———, and Alice McGillivray. *America Votes*. vols. 12-15. Washington, D.C.: Congressional Quarterly, 1977-1983.

Articles

Abramowitz, Alan I. "A Comparison of Voting for U.S. Senator and Representative in 1978." *American Political Science Review* 74 (September 1980): 633-640.

———. "Choices and Echoes in the 1978 U.S. Senate Elections: A Research Note." *American Journal of Political Science* 25 (February 1981): 112-118.

Barkworth, T. E. "Should United States Senators be Elected by the People?" *Michigan Political Science Association* 1 (1893): 78-97.

Baxter, S. "Representative Inequality of Senators." *North American Review* (December 1903): 897-903.

Bernstein, Robert A. "Divisive Primaries Do Hurt: U.S. Senate Races, 1956-1972." *American Political Science Review* 71 (June 1977): 540-545.

Brookshire, Robert G., and Dean F. Duncan III. "Congressional Career Patterns and Party Systems." *Legislative Studies Quarterly* 8 (February 1983): 65-78.

Bullock, Charles S. III, and David W. Brady. "Party Constituency and Roll Call Voting in the U.S. Senate." *Legislative Studies Quarterly* 8 (February 1983): 29-43.

Burgess, J. W. "The Election of United States Senators by Popular Vote." *Political Science Quarterly* (December 1903): 650-663.

Burnstein, Paul. "Party Balance, Replacement of Legislators, and Federal Government Expenditures, 1941-1976." *Western Political Quarterly* 32 (June 1979): 203-208.

Clark, W. "Electing Senators and the President by Popular Vote and the Veto Power." *Arena* (September 1894): 453.

"Direct Election of Senators." *American Monthly Review of Reviews* (December 1902): 644.

Farrand, Max. "Popular Election of Senators." *Yale Review* (January 1913): 234-241.

Fox, C. F. "Popular Election of United States Senators." *Arena* (May 1902): 455.

Haynes, John. "Popular Election of Senators." *Johns Hopkins University Studies in Historical and Political Science* (November/December 1893).

Hoar, George F. "Election of Senators." *Congressional Record* 25 (1893):103.

Kostroski, Warren. "The Effect of Number of Terms on the Re-Election of Senators, 1920-1970." *Journal of Politics* 40 (May 1978): 488-497.

Kuklinski, James H., and Darrell M. West. "Economic Expectations and Voting Behavior in the United States House and Senate Elections." *American Political Science Review* 75 (June 1981): 436-447.

"Let Us Have Popular Election of Senators." *American Monthly Review of Reviews* (February 1903): 219.

Mann, Thomas E., and Raymond E. Wolfinger. "Candidates and Parties in Congressional Elections." *American Political Science Review* 74 (September 1980): 617-632.

Mitchell, J. H. "Election of Senators by Popular Vote." *Forum* (June 1896): 385-397.

Moffett, S. E. "Is the Senate Unfairly Constituted?" *Political Science Quarterly* (June 1895): 248-256.

Northway, Stephen A. "Election of United States Senators by the People." *Congressional Record* 26 (1894): 7763.

Paulin, C. O. "The First Election Under the Constitution." *Iowa Journal of History and Politics* (January 1904): 28.

Platt, Orville H. "Election of United States Senators." *Congressional Record* 35 (1902): 6594.

Strong, M. K. "Post War Congressional Elections: Elections of 1866." *Current History* (May 1946): 41-53.

Tuchel, Peter. "The Initial Re-election Chances of Appointed and Elected United States Senators." *Polity* 16 (Fall 1983): 138-142.

Uslaner, Eric M. "Party Reform and Electoral Disaggregation: A Paradox in Congress?" *Policy Studies Journal* 5 (Summer 1977): 454-459.

Westlye, Mark C. "Competitiveness of Senate Seats and Voting Behavior in Senate Elections." *American Journal of Political Science* 27 (May 1983): 253-283.

Winchester, Boyd. "The House and the Election of Senators." *Arena* (July 1900): 14-20.

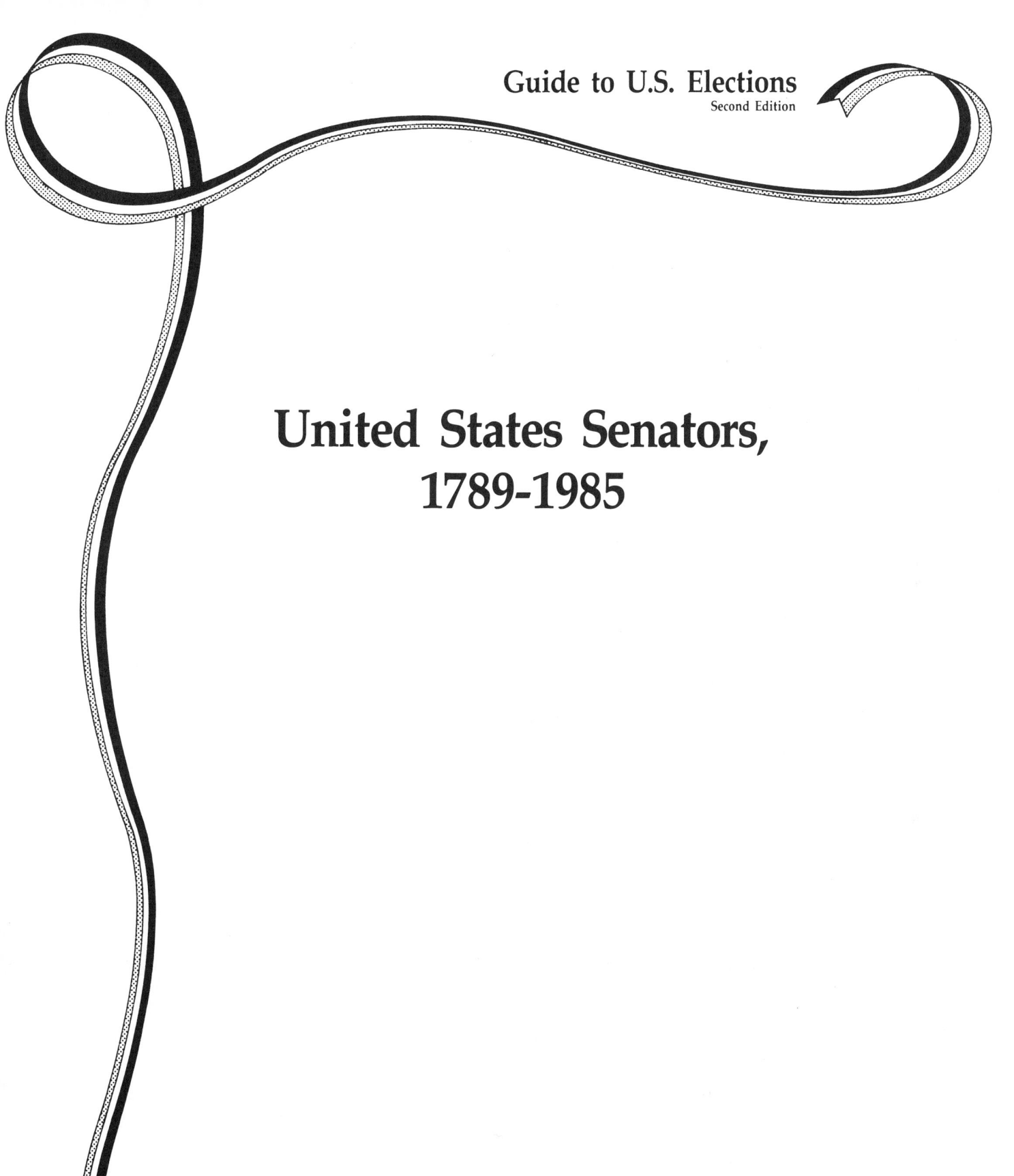

United States Senators,
1789-1985

Sources: U.S. Senators, 1789-1985

This section (pages 579 to 606) contains a listing of United States senators who served from March 4, 1789, through January 1985 — from the 1st Congress to the first session of the 99th Congress. Arranged alphabetically by state, the lists provide the name, political affiliation and dates of service of each senator in chronological order within each class. *(Explanation of Senate classes, p. 574)*

The primary source for the names, classes and dates of service of senators is the *Senate Manual* (U.S. Government Printing Office, Washington, D.C., 1981). Congressional Quarterly obtained additional information in certain cases from the *Biographical Directory of the American Congress, 1774-1971* (U.S. Government Printing Office, Washington, D.C., 1971). Footnotes were derived from both sources.

Party Affiliation

Determinations of senators' party affiliations were based on three sources. From 1913, when the 197th Amendment established popular election of senators, to 1972 party designations were taken from the Inter-University Consortium for Political and Social Research (ICPSR) popular vote returns (pages 609 to 636). However, if a senator was elected in any one election with the support of more than one political party, only the major party is indicated in the listing. For example, Sen. Robert F. Kennedy of New York, who in 1964 was the nominee of both the Democratic and Liberal parties, appears as a Democrat (D).

Also from 1913 on, whenever senators switched parties during their period of service, each party is listed even if the senator was not formally elected as a nominee of the new party. For example, Sen. Wayne Morse of Oregon (1945-69) is listed as a Republican, Independent and Democrat (R,I,D). He was elected twice as a Republican in 1944 and 1950, left that party in 1952 and called himself an Independent until 1955, and then became a Democrat. He was re-elected as a Democrat in 1956 and 1962. *(For a list of party abbreviations, see page 1141; for other references to individual senators, see "General Index," p. 1275.)*

For the period before popular election of senators (1789-1913), party affiliations were taken from the *Biographical Directory of the American Congress, 1774-1971* and the *Dictionary of American Biography* (20 volumes, Charles Scribner's Sons, New York, 1928-58).

Because political parties did not formally exist in the early years of the Republic, classification of senators by party during this period can be difficult or misleading. *(See Pre-Convention Politics, p. 7; Historical Profiles of American Political Parties, p. 225.)* In cases where party affiliation was not appropriate or could not be determined, no party designation appears.

Footnotes

Except where otherwise noted, senators were elected to office by state legislatures or, after ratification of the 17th Amendment in 1913, by popular vote.

Footnotes have been used to indicate the following circumstances:

● The appointment of a senator by the govenor of his state to fill an unexpired term. In such cases the service of an appointee ended at the expiration of the six-year term, or when a new senator was elected, or after the recess of the state legislature. *(For explanation of terms of appointees, see p. 573.)* In many cases, the appointee was elected to the Senate while serving there by appointment. In these cases, the footnote states that the senator was appointed and "subsequently elected."

● The death or resignation of a senator before the expiration of the term for which he was elected or appointed. In a number of instances, retiring or defeated senators resigned shortly before the start of a new congressional session. This enabled the succeeding senator to take office early by appointment, thereby giving him seniority over other newly elected senators. The practice has become less common due to changes in seniority rules. Resignations are footnoted but subsequent appointments are not. However, the dates of service shown in the main listing account for the complete period served.

● The expulsion of a senator by the Senate, and certain cases of disputed elections. Information on these was obtained from *Senate Election, Expulsion and Censure Cases* (S Doc 92-7), a publication prepared in 1972 by the Senate Rules and Administration Committee.

● A change in political party affiliation by a senator, if it could be determined that the senator was elected or appointed as a member of one political party but was subsequently re-elected as a nominee of a different party.

United States Senators, 1789-1985

Note: In the footnotes, "elected" indicates election by the state legislature prior to ratification of the 17th Amendment, April 8, 1913.

ALABAMA

(Became a state Dec. 14, 1819)

Class 2

Senators	Dates of Service	
William R. King (D-R, D)[1]	Dec. 14, 1819	April 15, 1844
Dixon H. Lewis (D)[2]	April 22, 1844	Oct. 25, 1848
Benjamin Fitzpatrick (D)[3]	Nov. 25, 1848	Nov. 30, 1849
Jeremiah Clemens (D)	Nov. 30, 1849	March 3, 1853
Clement Claiborne Clay Jr. (D)[4]	March 4, 1853	March 14, 1861
Willard Warner (R)	July 25, 1868	March 3, 1871
George Goldthwaite (D)[5]	March 4, 1871	March 3, 1877
John T. Morgan (D)[6]	March 4, 1877	June 11, 1907
John H. Bankhead (D)[7]	June 18, 1907	March 1, 1920
Braxton B. Comer (D)[8]	March 5, 1920	Nov. 2, 1920
J. Thomas Heflin (D)	Nov. 2, 1920	March 3, 1931
John H. Bankhead II (D)[9]	March 4, 1931	June 12, 1946
George R. Swift (D)[10]	June 15, 1946	Nov. 5, 1946
John Sparkman (D)	Nov. 6, 1946	Jan. 2, 1979
Howell Heflin (D)	Jan. 3, 1979	

Class 3

John W. Walker (D-R)[11]	Dec. 14, 1819	Dec. 12, 1822
William Kelly (D-R)	Dec. 12, 1822	March 3, 1825
Henry H. Chambers (D-R)[12]	March 4, 1825	Jan. 25, 1826
Israel Pickens (D-R)[13]	Feb. 17, 1826	Nov. 27, 1826
John McKinley (D-R, D)	Nov. 27, 1826	March 3, 1831
Gabriel Moore (D)	March 4, 1831	March 3, 1837
John McKinley (D)[14]	March 4, 1837	April 22, 1837
Clement Comer Clay (D)[15]	June 19, 1837	Nov. 15, 1841
Arthur P. Bagby (D)[16]	Nov. 24, 1841	June 16, 1848

William R. King (D)[17]	July 1, 1848	Dec. 20, 1852
Benjamin Fitzpatrick (D)[18]	Jan. 14, 1853	Jan. 21, 1861
George E. Spencer (R)	July 25, 1868	March 3, 1879
George S. Houston (D)[19]	March 4, 1879	Dec. 31, 1879
Luke Pryor (D)[20]	Jan. 7, 1880	Nov. 23, 1880
James L. Pugh (D)	Nov. 24, 1880	March 3, 1897
Edmund W. Pettus (D)[21]	March 4, 1897	July 27, 1907
Joseph F. Johnston (D)[22]	Aug. 6, 1907	Aug. 8, 1913
Francis S. White (D)	May 11, 1914	March 3, 1915
Oscar W. Underwood (D)	March 4, 1915	March 3, 1927
Hugo Black (D)[23]	March 4, 1927	Aug. 19, 1937
Dixie Bibb Graves (D)[24]	Aug. 20, 1937	Jan. 10, 1938
Lister Hill (D)[25]	Jan. 11, 1938	Jan. 2, 1969
James B. Allen (D)[26]	Jan. 3, 1969	June 1, 1978
Maryon Pittman Allen (D)[27]	June 8, 1978	Nov. 7, 1978
Donald W. Stewart (D)[28]	Nov. 8, 1978	Jan. 1, 1981
Jeremiah Denton (R)	Jan. 2, 1981	

ALASKA

(Became a state Jan. 3, 1959)

Class 2

Senators	Dates of Service	
E. L. Bartlett (D)[1]	Jan. 3, 1959	Dec. 11, 1968
Ted Stevens (R)[2]	Dec. 24, 1968	

Class 3

Ernest Gruening (D)	Jan. 3, 1959	Jan. 2, 1969
Mike Gravel (D)	Jan. 3, 1969	Jan. 2, 1981
Frank H. Murkowski (R)	Jan. 3, 1981	

Alabama

1. Resigned April 15, 1844.
2. Appointed by governor to fill vacancy. Subsequently elected. Died Oct. 25, 1848.
3. Appointed by governor to fill vacancy.
4. Seat declared vacant March 14, 1861. Vacancy lasted until July 25, 1868, because of Civil War.
5. Not sworn in until Jan. 15, 1872, because of protest.
6. Died June 11, 1907.
7. Appointed by governor to fill vacancy. Subsequently elected. Died March 1, 1920.
8. Appointed by governor to fill vacancy.
9. Died June 12, 1946.
10. Appointed by governor to fill vacancy. Resigned Nov. 5, 1946.
11. Resigned Dec. 12, 1822.
12. Died Jan. 25, 1826.
13. Appointed by governor to fill vacancy.
14. Resigned April 22, 1837.
15. Resigned Nov. 15, 1841.
16. Resigned June 16, 1848.

17. Appointed by governor to fill vacancy. Subsequently elected. Resigned Dec. 20, 1852.
18. Appointed by governor to fill vacancy. Subsequently elected. Withdrew from Senate Jan. 21, 1861, because of Civil War. Seat remained vacant until July 25, 1868.
19. Died Dec. 31, 1879.
20. Appointed by governor to fill vacancy.
21. Died July 27, 1907.
22. Died Aug. 8, 1913.
23. Resigned Aug. 19, 1937.
24. Appointed by governor to fill vacancy. Resigned Jan. 10, 1938.
25. Appointed by governor to fill vacancy. Subsequently elected.
26. Died June 1, 1978.
27. Appointed by governor to fill vacancy.
28. Resigned Jan. 1, 1981.

Alaska

1. Died Dec. 11, 1968.
2. Appointed by governor to fill vacancy. Subsequently elected.

ARIZONA

(Became a state Feb. 14, 1912)

Class 1

Senators	Dates of Service	
Henry Fountain Ashurst (D)	March 27, 1912	Jan. 2, 1941
Ernest W. McFarland (D)	Jan. 3, 1941	Jan. 2, 1953
Barry Goldwater (R)	Jan. 3, 1953	Jan. 2, 1965
Paul J. Fannin (R)	Jan. 3, 1965	Jan. 2, 1977
Dennis DeConcini (D)	Jan. 3, 1977	

Class 3

Marcus A. Smith (D)	March 27, 1912	March 3, 1921
Ralph H. Cameron (R)	March 4, 1921	March 3, 1927
Carl Hayden (D)	March 4, 1927	Jan. 2, 1969
Barry Goldwater (R)	Jan. 3, 1969	

ARKANSAS

(Became a state June 15, 1836)

Class 2

Senators	Dates of Service	
William S. Fulton (D)[1]	Sept. 18, 1836	Aug. 15, 1844
Chester Ashley (D)[2]	Nov. 8, 1844	April 29, 1848
William K. Sebastian (D)[3]	May 12, 1848	July 11, 1861
Alexander McDonald (R)	June 23, 1868	March 3, 1871
Powell Clayton (R)	March 14, 1871	March 3, 1877
Augustus H. Garland (D)[4]	March 4, 1877	March 6, 1885
James H. Berry (D)	March 20, 1885	March 3, 1907
Jeff Davis (D)[5]	March 4, 1907	Jan. 3, 1913
John N. Heiskell (D)[6]	Jan. 6, 1913	Jan. 29, 1913
William M. Kavanaugh (D)	Jan. 29, 1913	March 3, 1913
Joseph T. Robinson (D)[7]	March 10, 1913	July 14, 1937
John E. Miller (D)[8]	Nov. 15, 1937	March 31, 1941
Lloyd Spencer (D)[9]	April 1, 1941	Jan. 2, 1943
John L. McClellan (D)[10]	Jan. 3, 1943	Nov. 28, 1977
Kaneaster Hodges Jr. (D)[11]	Dec. 10, 1977	Jan. 2, 1979
David Pryor (D)	Jan. 3, 1979	

Class 3

Ambrose H. Sevier (D)[12]	Sept. 18, 1836	March 15, 1848
Solon Borland (D)[13]	March 30, 1848	April 3, 1853
Robert W. Johnson (D)[14]	July 6, 1853	March 3, 1861
Charles B. Mitchel (D)[15]	March 4, 1861	July 11, 1861
Benjamin F. Rice (R)	June 23, 1868	March 3, 1873
Stephen W. Dorsey (R)	March 4, 1873	March 3, 1879
James D. Walker (D)	March 4, 1879	March 3, 1885
James K. Jones (D)	March 4, 1885	March 3, 1903
James P. Clarke (D)[16]	March 4, 1903	Oct. 1, 1916
William F. Kirby (D)	Nov. 8, 1916	March 2, 1921
Thaddeus H. Caraway (D)[17]	March 4, 1921	Nov. 6, 1931
Hattie W. Caraway (D)[18]	Nov. 13, 1931	Jan. 2, 1945
J. William Fulbright (D)[19]	Jan. 3, 1945	Dec. 31, 1974
Dale Bumpers (D)	Jan. 3, 1975	

CALIFORNIA

(Became a state Sept. 9, 1850)

Class 1

Senators	Dates of Service	
John C. Frémont (D)	Sept. 9, 1850	March 3, 1851
John B. Weller (D)	Jan. 30, 1852	March 3, 1857
David C. Broderick (D)[1]	March 4, 1857	Sept. 16, 1859
Henry P. Haun (D)[2]	Nov. 3, 1859	March 4, 1860
Milton S. Latham (D)	March 5, 1860	March 3, 1863
John Conness (UN R)	March 4, 1863	March 3, 1869
Eugene Casserly (D)[3]	March 4, 1869	Nov. 29, 1873
John S. Hager (A-MON D)	Dec. 23, 1873	March 3, 1875
Newton Booth (A-MONOPT)	March 4, 1875	March 3, 1881
John F. Miller (R)[4]	March 4, 1881	March 8, 1886
George Hearst (D)[5]	March 23, 1886	Aug. 4, 1886
Abram P. Williams (R)	Aug. 4, 1886	March 3, 1887
George Hearst (D)[6]	March 4, 1887	Feb. 28, 1891
Charles N. Felton (R)	March 19, 1891	March 3, 1893
Stephen M. White (D)	March 4, 1893	March 3, 1899
Thomas R. Bard (R)	Feb. 7, 1900	March 3, 1905
Frank P. Flint (R)	March 4, 1905	March 3, 1911
John D. Works (R)	March 4, 1911	March 3, 1917
Hiram W. Johnson (R)[7]	April 2, 1917	Aug. 6, 1945
William F. Knowland (R)[8]	Aug. 26, 1945	Jan. 2, 1959

Arkansas

1. *Died Aug. 15, 1844.*
2. *Died April 29, 1848.*
3. *Appointed by governor to fill vacancy. Subsequently elected. Expelled July 11, 1861. Seat remained vacant until June 23, 1868, because of Civil War.*
4. *Resigned March 6, 1885.*
5. *Died Jan. 3, 1913.*
6. *Appointed by governor to fill vacancy.*
7. *Died July 14, 1937.*
8. *Resigned March 31, 1941.*
9. *Appointed by governor to fill vacancy.*
10. *Died Nov. 28, 1977.*
11. *Appointed by governor to fill vacancy.*
12. *Resigned March 15, 1848.*
13. *Appointed by governor to fill vacancy. Subsequently elected. Resigned April 3, 1853.*
14. *Appointed by governor to fill vacancy. Subsequently elected.*
15. *Expelled July 11, 1861. Vacancy until June 23, 1868, because of Civil War.*
16. *Died Oct. 1, 1916.*
17. *Died Nov. 6, 1931.*
18. *Appointed by governor to fill vacancy. Subsequently elected.*
19. *Resigned Dec. 31, 1974.*

California

1. *Died Sept. 16, 1859.*
2. *Appointed by governor to fill vacancy.*
3. *Resigned Nov. 29, 1873.*
4. *Died March 8, 1886.*
5. *Appointed by governor to fill vacancy.*
6. *Died Feb. 28, 1891.*
7. *Died Aug. 6, 1945.*
8. *Appointed by governor to fill vacancy. Subsequently elected.*
9. *Died July 30, 1964.*
10. *Appointed by governor to fill vacancy. Resigned Dec. 31, 1964.*
11. *Resigned Jan. 2, 1971.*
12. *Resigned Jan. 1, 1977.*
13. *Vacancy from March 4, 1855, to Jan. 12, 1857, because of failure of Legislature to elect.*
14. *Died June 21, 1893.*
15. *Appointed by governor to fill vacancy. Subsequently elected.*
16. *Resigned Nov. 8, 1938.*
17. *Appointed by governor to fill vacancy.*
18. *Resigned Nov. 30, 1950.*
19. *Resigned Jan. 1, 1953, having been elected vice president of the United States.*
20. *Appointed by governor to fill vacancy. Subsequently elected.*

Clair Engle (D)[9]	Jan. 3, 1959	July 30, 1964
Pierre Salinger (D)[10]	Aug. 4, 1964	Dec. 31, 1964
George Murphy (R)[11]	Jan. 1, 1965	Jan. 2, 1971
John V. Tunney (D)[12]	Jan. 2, 1971	Jan. 1, 1977
S. I. Hayakawa (R)	Jan. 2, 1977	Jan. 2, 1983
Pete Wilson (R)	Jan. 3, 1983	

Class 3

William M. Gwin (D)	Sept. 9, 1850	March 3, 1855
William M. Gwin (D)[13]	Jan. 13, 1857	March 3, 1861
James A. McDougall (D)	March 4, 1861	March 3, 1867
Cornelius Cole (R)	March 4, 1867	March 3, 1873
Aaron A. Sargent (R)	March 4, 1873	March 3, 1879
James T. Farley (D)	March 4, 1879	March 3, 1885
Leland Stanford (R)[14]	March 4, 1885	June 21, 1893
George C. Perkins (R)[15]	July 26, 1893	March 3, 1915
James D. Phelan (D)	March 4, 1915	March 3, 1921
Samuel M. Shortridge (R)	March 4, 1921	March 3, 1933
William Gibbs McAdoo (D)[16]	March 4, 1933	Nov. 8, 1938
Thomas M. Storke (D)[17]	Nov. 9, 1938	Jan. 2, 1939
Sheridan Downey (D)[18]	Jan. 3, 1939	Nov. 30, 1950
Richard M. Nixon (R)[19]	Dec. 4, 1950	Jan. 1, 1953
Thomas H. Kuchel (R)[20]	Jan. 2, 1953	Jan. 2, 1969
Alan Cranston (D)	Jan. 3, 1969	

COLORADO

(Became a state Aug. 1, 1876)

Class 2

Senators	Dates of Service	
Henry M. Teller (R)[1]	Nov. 15, 1876	April 17, 1882
George M. Chilcott (R)[2]	April 17, 1882	Jan. 27, 1883
Horace A. W. Tabor (R)	Jan. 27, 1883	March 3, 1883
Thomas M. Bowen (R)	March 4, 1883	March 3, 1889
Edward O. Wolcott (R)	March 4, 1889	March 3, 1901
Thomas M. Patterson (D)	March 4, 1901	March 3, 1907
Simon Guggenheim (R)	March 4, 1907	March 3, 1913
John F. Shafroth (D)	March 4, 1913	March 3, 1919
Lawrence C. Phipps (R)	March 4, 1919	March 3, 1931
Edward P. Costigan (D)	March 4, 1931	Jan. 2, 1937
Edwin C. Johnson (D)	Jan. 3, 1937	Jan. 2, 1955
Gordon Allott (R)	Jan. 3, 1955	Jan. 2, 1973
Floyd K. Haskell (D)	Jan. 3, 1973	Jan. 2, 1979
William L. Armstrong (R)	Jan. 3, 1979	

Class 3

Jerome B. Chaffee (R)	Nov. 15, 1876	March 3, 1879
Nathaniel P. Hill (R)	March 4, 1879	March 3, 1885
Henry M. Teller (R, I SIL R, D)[3]	March 4, 1885	March 3, 1909
Charles J. Hughes Jr. (D)[4]	March 4, 1909	Jan. 11, 1911
Charles S. Thomas (D)	Jan. 15, 1913	March 3, 1921
Samuel D. Nicholson (R)[5]	March 4, 1921	March 24, 1923
Alva B. Adams (D)[6]	May 17, 1923	Nov. 30, 1924
Rice W. Means (R)	Dec. 1, 1924	March 3, 1927
Charles W. Waterman (R)[7]	March 4, 1927	Aug. 27, 1932
Walter Walker (D)[8]	Sept. 26, 1932	Dec. 6, 1932
Karl C. Schuyler (R)	Dec. 7, 1932	March 3, 1933
Alva B. Adams (D)[9]	March 4, 1933	Dec. 1, 1941
Eugene D. Millikin (R)[10]	Dec. 20, 1941	Jan. 2, 1957
John A. Carroll (D)	Jan. 3, 1957	Jan. 2, 1963
Peter H. Dominick (R)	Jan. 3, 1963	Jan. 2, 1975
Gary Hart (D)	Jan. 3, 1975	

CONNECTICUT

(Ratified the Constitution Jan. 9, 1788)

Class 1

Senators	Dates of Service	
Oliver Ellsworth (FED)[1]	March 4, 1789	March 8, 1796
James Hillhouse (FED)[2]	May 12, 1796	June 10, 1810
Samuel W. Dana (FED)	May 10, 1810	March 3, 1821
Elijah Boardman (D-R)[3]	March 4, 1821	Aug. 18, 1823
Henry W. Edwards (D-R)[4]	Dec. 1, 1823	March 3, 1827
Samuel A. Foote (D-R)	March 4, 1827	March 3, 1833
Nathan Smith (W)[5]	March 4, 1833	Dec. 6, 1835
John M. Niles (D)[6]	Dec. 14, 1835	March 3, 1839
Thaddeus Betts (W)[7]	March 4, 1839	April 7, 1840
Jabez W. Huntington (W)[8]	May 4, 1840	Nov. 2, 1847
Roger S. Baldwin (W)[9]	Nov. 11, 1847	March 3, 1851
Isaac Toucey (D)[10]	May 12, 1852	March 3, 1857
James Dixon (R)	March 4, 1857	March 3, 1869
William A. Buckingham (R)[11]	March 4, 1869	Feb. 5, 1875
William W. Eaton (D)[12]	Feb. 5, 1875	March 3, 1881
Joseph R. Hawley (R)	March 4, 1881	March 3, 1905
Morgan G. Bulkeley (R)	March 4, 1905	March 3, 1911
George P. McLean (R)	March 4, 1911	March 3, 1929
Frederic C. Walcott (R)	March 4, 1929	Jan. 2, 1935
Francis Maloney (D)[13]	Jan. 3, 1935	Jan. 16, 1945
Thomas C. Hart (R)[14]	Feb. 15, 1945	Nov. 5, 1946
Raymond E. Baldwin (R)[15]	Dec. 27, 1946	Dec. 17, 1949

Colorado
1. Resigned April 17, 1882.
2. Appointed by governor to fill vacancy.
3. Elected as a Republican in 1885 and 1891, an Independent Silver Republican in 1897 and a Democrat in 1903.
4. Died Jan. 11, 1911. Vacancy until Jan. 15, 1913, because of failure of Legislature to elect.
5. Died March 24, 1923.
6. Appointed by governor to fill vacancy.
7. Died Aug. 27, 1932.
8. Appointed by governor to fill vacancy.
9. Died Dec. 1, 1941.
10. Appointed by governor to fill vacancy. Subsequently elected.

Connecticut
1. Resigned March 8, 1796.
2. Resigned June 10, 1810.
3. Died Aug. 18, 1823.
4. Appointed by governor to fill vacancy. Subsequently elected.
5. Died Dec. 6, 1835.
6. Appointed by governor to fill vacancy. Subsequently elected.
7. Died April 7, 1840.

8. Died Nov. 2, 1847.
9. Appointed by governor to fill vacancy. Subsequently elected.
10. Vacant from March 4, 1851, to May 11, 1852, because of failure of governor to appoint.
11. Died Feb. 5, 1875.
12. Appointed by governor to fill vacancy. Subsequently elected.
13. Died Jan. 16, 1945.
14. Appointed by governor to fill vacancy.
15. Resigned Dec. 17, 1949.
16. Appointed by governor to fill vacancy. Subsequently elected.
17. Resigned March 4, 1791.
18. Died July 23, 1793.
19. Resigned June 10, 1796.
20. Died July 19, 1807.
21. Resigned.
22. Resigned May 24, 1854.
23. Died Nov. 21, 1875.
24. Appointed by governor to fill vacancy.
25. Died April 21, 1905.
26. Died Oct. 14, 1924.
27. Died July 28, 1952.
28. Appointed by governor to fill vacancy.

William Benton (D)[16]	Dec. 17, 1949	Jan. 2, 1953
William A. Purtell (R)	Jan. 3, 1953	Jan. 2, 1959
Thomas J. Dodd (D)	Jan. 3, 1959	Jan. 2, 1971
Lowell P. Weicker Jr. (R)	Jan. 3, 1971	

Class 3

William S. Johnson[17]	March 4, 1789	March 4, 1791
Roger Sherman[18]	June 13, 1791	July 23, 1793
Stephen M. Mitchell	Dec. 2, 1793	March 3, 1795
Jonathan Trumbull[19]	March 4, 1795	June 10, 1796
Uriah Tracy (FED)[20]	Oct. 13, 1796	July 19, 1807
Chauncey Goodrich (FED)[21]	Oct. 25, 1807	May 1813
David Daggett (FED)	May 13, 1813	March 3, 1819
James Lanman (D-R)	March 4, 1819	March 3, 1825
Calvin Willey (D-R)	May 4, 1825	March 3, 1831
Gideon Tomlinson (D)	March 4, 1831	March 3, 1837
Perry Smith (D)	March 4, 1837	March 3, 1843
John M. Niles (D)	March 4, 1843	March 3, 1849
Truman Smith (W)[22]	March 4, 1849	May 24, 1854
Francis Gillette (F SOIL W)	May 25, 1854	March 3, 1855
Lafayette S. Foster (R)	March 4, 1855	March 3, 1867
Orris S. Ferry (R)[23]	March 4, 1867	Nov. 21, 1875
James E. English (D)[24]	Nov. 27, 1875	May 17, 1876
William H. Barnum (D)	May 17, 1876	March 3, 1879
Orville H. Platt (R)[25]	March 4, 1879	April 21, 1905
Frank B. Brandegee (R)[26]	May 10, 1905	Oct. 14, 1924
Hiram Bingham (R)	Dec. 17, 1924	March 3, 1933
Augustine Lonergan (D)	March 4, 1933	Jan. 2, 1939
John A. Danaher (R)	Jan. 3, 1939	Jan. 2, 1945
Brien McMahon (D)[27]	Jan. 3, 1945	July 28, 1952
William A. Purtell (R)[28]	Aug. 29, 1952	Nov. 4, 1952
Prescott Bush (R)	Nov. 5, 1952	Jan. 2, 1963
Abraham Ribicoff (D)	Jan. 3, 1963	Jan. 2, 1981
Christopher J. Dodd (D)	Jan. 3, 1981	

DELAWARE

(Ratified the Constitution Dec. 7, 1787)

Class 1

Senators	Dates of Service	
George Read (FED)[1]	March 4, 1789	Sept. 18, 1793
Henry Latimer (FED)[2]	Feb. 7, 1795	Feb. 28, 1801
Samuel White (FED)[3]	Feb. 28, 1801	Nov. 4, 1809
Outerbridge Horsey (FED)	Jan. 12, 1810	March 3, 1821
Caesar A. Rodney (D-R)[4]	Jan. 10, 1822	Jan. 29, 1823
Thomas Clayton (FED)	Jan. 8, 1824	March 3, 1827
Louis McLane (D-R)[5]	March 4, 1827	April 16, 1829

Arnold Naudain (NR)[6]	Jan. 7, 1830	June 16, 1836
Richard H. Bayard (W)[7]	June 17, 1836	Sept. 19, 1839
Richard H. Bayard (W)	Jan. 12, 1841	March 3, 1845
John M. Clayton (W)[8]	March 4, 1845	Feb. 23, 1849
John Wales (W)	Feb. 23, 1849	March 3, 1851
James A. Bayard Jr. (W, D)[9]	March 4, 1851	Jan. 29, 1864
George Read Riddle (D)[10]	Jan. 29, 1864	March 29, 1867
James A. Bayard Jr. (D)[11]	April 5, 1867	March 3, 1869
Thomas F. Bayard Sr. (D)[12]	March 4, 1869	March 6, 1885
George Gray (D)	March 18, 1885	March 3, 1899
L. Heisler Ball (R)[13]	March 2, 1903	March 3, 1905
Henry A. du Pont (R)[14]	June 13, 1906	March 3, 1917
Josiah O. Wolcott (D)[15]	March 4, 1917	July 2, 1921
T. Coleman du Pont (R)[16]	July 7, 1921	Nov. 6, 1922
Thomas F. Bayard Jr. (D)	Nov. 7, 1922	March 3, 1929
John G. Townsend Jr. (R)	March 4, 1929	Jan. 2, 1941
James M. Tunnell (D)	Jan. 3, 1941	Jan. 2, 1947
John J. Williams (R)[17]	Jan. 3, 1947	Dec. 31, 1970
William V. Roth Jr. (R)	Jan. 1, 1971	

Class 2

Richard Bassett (FED)	March 4, 1789	March 3, 1793
John Vining (FED)[18]	March 4, 1793	Jan. 19, 1798
Joshua Clayton (FED)[19]	Jan. 19, 1798	Aug. 11, 1798
William Hill Wells (FED)[20]	Jan. 17, 1799	Nov. 6, 1804
James A. Bayard Sr. (FED)[21]	Nov. 13, 1804	March 3, 1813
William Hill Wells (FED)	May 28, 1813	March 3, 1817
Nicholas Van Dyke (FED)[22]	March 4, 1817	May 21, 1826
Daniel Rodney (FED)[23]	Nov. 8, 1826	Jan. 12, 1827
Henry M. Ridgeley	Jan. 12, 1827	March 3, 1829
John M. Clayton (NR, W)[24]	March 4, 1829	Dec. 29, 1836
Thomas Clayton (W)	Jan. 9, 1837	March 3, 1847
Presley Spruance (W)	March 4, 1847	March 3, 1853
John M. Clayton (W)[25]	March 4, 1853	Nov. 9, 1856
Joseph P. Comegys (W)[26]	Nov. 19, 1856	Jan. 14, 1857
Martin W. Bates (D)	Jan. 14, 1857	March 3, 1859
Willard Saulsbury Sr. (D)	March 4, 1859	March 3, 1871
Eli Saulsbury (D)	March 4, 1871	March 3, 1889
Anthony Higgins (R)	March 4, 1889	March 3, 1895
Richard R. Kenney (D)[27]	Jan. 19, 1897	March 3, 1901
James F. Allee (R)[28]	March 2, 1903	March 3, 1907
Harry A. Richardson (R)	March 4, 1907	March 3, 1913
Willard Saulsbury Jr. (D)	March 4, 1913	March 3, 1919
L. Heisler Ball (R)	March 4, 1919	March 3, 1925
T. Coleman du Pont (R)[29]	March 4, 1925	Dec. 9, 1928
Daniel O. Hastings (R)[30]	Dec. 10, 1928	Jan. 2, 1937
James H. Hughes (D)	Jan. 3, 1937	Jan. 2, 1943
C. Douglass Buck (R)	Jan. 3, 1943	Jan. 2, 1949
J. Allen Frear Jr. (D)	Jan. 3, 1949	Jan. 2, 1961
J. Caleb Boggs (R)	Jan. 3, 1961	Jan. 2, 1973
Joseph R. Biden Jr. (D)	Jan. 3, 1973	

Delaware
1. *Resigned Sept. 18, 1793.*
2. *Resigned Feb. 28, 1801.*
3. *Appointed by governor to fill vacancy. Subsequently elected. Died Nov. 4, 1809.*
4. *Resigned Jan. 29, 1823.*
5. *Resigned April 16, 1829.*
6. *Resigned June 16, 1836.*
7. *Resigned Sept. 19, 1839. Vacant until Jan. 12, 1841.*
8. *Resigned Feb. 23, 1849.*
9. *Resigned Jan. 29, 1864.*
10. *Died March 29, 1867.*
11. *Appointed by governor to fill vacancy. Subsequently elected.*
12. *Resigned March 6, 1885.*
13. *Vacant until March 2, 1903, because of failure of Legislature to elect.*
14. *Vacant until June 13, 1906, because of failure of Legislature to elect.*
15. *Resigned July 2, 1921.*

16. *Appointed by governor to fill vacancy.*
17. *Resigned Dec. 31, 1970.*
18. *Resigned Jan. 19, 1798.*
19. *Died Aug. 11, 1798.*
20. *Resigned Nov. 6, 1804.*
21. *Resigned March 3, 1813.*
22. *Died May 21, 1826.*
23. *Appointed by governor to fill vacancy.*
24. *Resigned Dec. 29, 1836.*
25. *Died Nov. 9, 1856.*
26. *Appointed by governor to fill vacancy.*
27. *Vacancy until Jan. 19, 1897, because of failure of Legislature to elect.*
28. *Vacancy until March 2, 1903, because of failure of Legislature to elect.*
29. *Resigned Dec. 9, 1928.*
30. *Appointed by governor to fill vacancy. Subsequently elected.*

FLORIDA

(Became a state March 3, 1845)

Class 1

Senators	Dates of Service	
David Levy Yulee (D)	July 1, 1845	March 3, 1851
Stephen R. Mallory (D)[1]	March 4, 1851	March 14, 1861
Adonijah S. Welch (R)	July 2, 1868	March 3, 1869
Abijah Gilbert (R)	March 4, 1869	March 3, 1875
Charles W. Jones (D)	March 4, 1875	March 3, 1887
Samuel Pasco (D)[2]	May 19, 1887	April 18, 1899
James P. Taliaferro (D)[3]	April 19, 1899	March 3, 1911
Nathan P. Bryan (D)[4]	March 4, 1911	March 3, 1917
Park Trammell (D)[5]	March 4, 1917	May 8, 1936
Scott M. Loftin (D)[6]	May 26, 1936	Nov. 3, 1936
Charles O. Andrews (D)[7]	Nov. 4, 1936	Sept. 18, 1946
Spessard L. Holland (D)[8]	Sept. 25, 1946	Jan. 2, 1971
Lawton Chiles (D)	Jan. 3, 1971	

Class 3

Senators	Dates of Service	
James D. Westcott Jr. (D)	July 1, 1845	March 3, 1849
Jackson Morton (W)	March 4, 1849	March 3, 1855
David Levy Yulee (D)[9]	March 4, 1855	Jan. 21, 1861
Thomas W. Osborn (R)	June 30, 1868	March 3, 1873
Simon B. Conover (R)	March 4, 1873	March 3, 1879
Wilkinson Call (D)	March 4, 1879	March 3, 1897
Stephen R. Mallory (D)[10]	May 24, 1897	Dec. 23, 1907
William J. Bryan (D)[11]	Dec. 26, 1907	March 22, 1908
William H. Milton (D)[12]	March 27, 1908	March 3, 1909
Duncan U. Fletcher (D)[13]	March 4, 1909	June 17, 1936
William L. Hill (D)[14]	July 1, 1936	Nov. 3, 1936
Claude Pepper (D)	Nov. 4, 1936	Jan. 2, 1951
George A. Smathers (D)	Jan. 3, 1951	Jan. 2, 1969
Edward J. Gurney (R)[15]	Jan. 3, 1969	Dec. 31, 1974
Richard Stone (D)[16]	Jan. 2, 1975	Dec. 31, 1980
Paula Hawkins (R)	Jan. 1, 1981	

GEORGIA

(Ratified the Constitution Jan. 2, 1788)

Class 2

Senators	Dates of Service	
William Few (D-R)	March 4, 1789	March 3, 1793
James Jackson (D-R)[1]	March 4, 1793	1795
George Walton[2]	Nov. 16, 1795	Feb. 20, 1796
Josiah Tatnall	Feb. 20, 1796	March 3, 1799
Abraham Baldwin (D-R)[3]	March 4, 1799	March 4, 1807
George Jones[4]	Aug. 27, 1807	Nov. 7, 1807
William H. Crawford (D-R)[5]	Nov. 7, 1807	March 23, 1813
William B. Bulloch (D-R)[6]	April 8, 1813	Nov. 6, 1813
William Wyatt Bibb (D-R)[7]	Nov. 6, 1813	Nov. 9, 1816
George M. Troup (D-R)[8]	Nov. 13, 1816	Sept. 23, 1818
John Forsyth (D-R)[9]	Nov. 23, 1818	Feb. 17, 1819
Freeman Walker (D-R)[10]	Nov. 6, 1819	Aug. 8, 1821
Nicholas Ware (D-R)[11]	Nov. 10, 1821	Sept. 7, 1824
Thomas W. Cobb (D-R)[12]	Nov. 7, 1824	1828
Oliver H. Prince (D-R)	Nov. 7, 1828	March 3, 1829
George M. Troup (D)[13]	March 4, 1829	March 2, 1833
John Pendleton King (D)[14]	Nov. 21, 1833	Nov. 1, 1837
Wilson Lumpkin (D)	Nov. 22, 1837	March 3, 1841
John M. Berrien (W)[15]	March 4, 1841	May 1845
John M. Berrien (W)	Nov. 14, 1845	March 3, 1847
John M. Berrien (W)[16]	Nov. 13, 1847	May 28, 1852
Robert M. Charlton[17]	May 31, 1852	March 3, 1853
Robert Toombs (D)[18]	March 4, 1853	March 14, 1861
Homer V. M. Miller (D)	Feb. 24, 1871	March 3, 1871
Thomas M. Norwood (D)	Nov. 14, 1871	March 3, 1877
Benjamin H. Hill (D)[19]	March 4, 1877	Aug. 16, 1882
Pope Barrow (D)	Nov. 15, 1882	March 3, 1883
Alfred H. Colquitt (D)[20]	March 4, 1883	March 26, 1894
Patrick Walsh (D)[21]	April 2, 1894	March 3, 1895
Augustus O. Bacon (D)[22]	March 4, 1895	Feb. 14, 1914
William S. West (D)[23]	March 2, 1914	Nov. 3, 1914
Thomas W. Hardwick (D)	Nov. 4, 1914	March 3, 1919

Florida

1. Seat declared vacant March 14, 1861. Vacancy lasted until July 2, 1868, because of Civil War.
2. Pasco served continuously through this period, twice by appointment of the governor and twice by election.
3. Taliaferro served twice by election and once by appointment during his term of office.
4. Appointed by governor to fill vacancy. Subsequently elected.
5. Died May 8, 1936.
6. Appointed by governor to fill vacancy.
7. Died Sept. 18, 1946.
8. Appointed by governor to fill vacancy. Subsequently elected.
9. Retired from the Senate Jan. 21, 1861, because of Civil War. Seat remained vacant until June 30, 1868.
10. Mallory served twice by election and once by appointment during his term of office. Died Dec. 23, 1907.
11. Appointed by governor to fill vacancy. Died March 22, 1908.
12. Appointed by governor to fill vacancy.
13. Appointed by governor to fill vacancy. Subsequently elected. Died June 17, 1936.
14. Appointed by governor to fill vacancy.
15. Resigned Dec. 31, 1974.
16. Resigned Dec. 31, 1980.

Georgia

1. Resigned.
2. Appointed by governor to fill vacancy.
3. Died March 4, 1807.
4. Appointed by governor to fill vacancy.
5. Resigned March 23, 1813.
6. Appointed by governor to fill vacancy.
7. Resigned Nov. 9, 1816.
8. Resigned Sept. 23, 1818.
9. Resigned Feb. 17, 1819.
10. Resigned Aug. 8, 1821.

11. Died Sept. 7, 1824.
12. Resigned.
13. Resigned March 2, 1833.
14. Resigned Nov. 1, 1837.
15. Resigned in May 1845. Seat vacant until Nov. 14, 1845, because of failure of Legislature to elect.
16. Vacant from March 4, 1847, to Nov. 13, 1847, because of failure of Legislature to elect. Resigned May 28, 1852.
17. Appointed by governor to fill vacancy.
18. Seat declared vacant March 14, 1861. Remained vacant until Feb. 24, 1871, because of Civil War.
19. Died Aug. 16, 1882.
20. Died March 26, 1894.
21. Appointed by governor to fill vacancy. Subsequently elected.
22. Bacon was elected three times and appointed twice during his term of service. Died Feb. 14, 1914.
23. Appointed by governor to fill vacancy.
24. Died April 18, 1932.
25. Appointed by governor to fill vacancy.
26. Died Jan. 21, 1971.
27. Appointed by governor to fill vacancy.
28. Died March 19, 1806.
29. Resigned Nov. 14, 1809.
30. Resigned March 9, 1829.
31. Resigned June 27, 1834.
32. Resigned in February 1848.
33. Appointed by governor to fill vacancy.
34. Retired from Senate Jan. 28, 1861. Vacancy until Feb. 1, 1871, because of Civil War.
35. Resigned May 26, 1880.
36. Appointed by governor to fill vacancy. Subsequently elected.
37. Died Nov. 13, 1910.
38. Appointed by governor to fill vacancy. Resigned July 14, 1911.
39. Died Sept. 26, 1922.
40. Appointed by governor to fill vacancy.

William J. Harris (D)[24]	March 4, 1919	April 18, 1932
John S. Cohen (D)[25]	April 25, 1932	Jan. 11, 1933
Richard B. Russell (D)[26]	Jan. 12, 1933	Jan. 21, 1971
David H. Gambrell (D)[27]	Feb. 1, 1971	Nov. 7, 1972
Sam Nunn (D)	Nov. 8, 1972	

Class 3

James Gunn	March 4, 1789	March 3, 1801
James Jackson (D-R)[28]	March 4, 1801	March 19, 1806
John Milledge (D-R)[29]	June 19, 1806	Nov. 14, 1809
Charles Tait (D-R)	Nov. 27, 1809	March 3, 1819
John Elliott (D-R)	March 4, 1819	March 3, 1825
John M. Berrien (D-R)[30]	March 4, 1825	March 9, 1829
John Forsyth (D)[31]	Nov. 9, 1829	June 27, 1834
Alfred Cuthbert (D)	Jan. 12, 1835	March 3, 1843
Walter T. Colquitt (D)[32]	March 4, 1843	February 1848
Herschel V. Johnson (D)[33]	Feb. 4, 1848	March 3, 1849
William C. Dawson (W)	March 4, 1849	March 3, 1855
Alfred Iverson (D)[34]	March 4, 1855	Jan. 28, 1861
Joshua Hill (UN R)	Feb. 1, 1871	March 3, 1873
John B. Gordon (D)[35]	March 4, 1873	May 26, 1880
Joseph E. Brown (D)[36]	May 26, 1880	March 3, 1891
John B. Gordon (D)	March 4, 1891	March 3, 1897
Alexander S. Clay (D)[37]	March 4, 1897	Nov. 13, 1910
Joseph M. Terrell (D)[38]	Nov. 17, 1910	July 14, 1911
Hoke Smith (D)	Dec. 4, 1911	March 3, 1921
Thomas E. Watson (D)[39]	March 4, 1921	Sept. 26, 1922
Rebecca L. Felton (D)[40]	Oct. 3, 1922	Nov. 21, 1922
Walter F. George (D)	Nov. 22, 1922	Jan. 2, 1957
Herman E. Talmadge (D)	Jan. 3, 1957	Jan. 2, 1981
Mack Mattingly (R)	Jan. 3, 1981	

HAWAII

(Became a state Aug. 21, 1959)

Class 1

Senators	Dates of Service	
Hiram L. Fong (R)	Aug. 21, 1959	Jan. 2, 1977
Spark M. Matsunaga (D)	Jan. 3, 1977	

Class 3

Oren E. Long (D)	Aug. 21, 1959	Jan. 2, 1963
Daniel K. Inouye (D)	Jan. 3, 1963	

IDAHO

(Became a state July 3, 1890)

Class 2

Senators	Dates of Service	
George L. Shoup (R)	Dec. 18, 1890	March 3, 1901
Fred T. Dubois (D)	March 4, 1901	March 3, 1907
William E. Borah (R)[1]	March 4, 1907	Jan. 19, 1940
John Thomas (R)[2]	Jan. 27, 1940	Nov. 10, 1945
Charles C. Gossett (D)[3]	Nov. 17, 1945	Nov. 5, 1946
Henry C. Dworshak (R)	Nov. 6, 1946	Jan. 2, 1949
Bert H. Miller (D)[4]	Jan. 3, 1949	Oct. 8, 1949
Henry C. Dworshak (R)[5]	Oct. 14, 1949	July 23, 1962
Len B. Jordan (R)[6]	Aug. 6, 1962	Jan. 2, 1973
James A. McClure (R)	Jan. 3, 1973	

Class 3

William J. McConnell (R)	Dec. 18, 1890	March 3, 1891
Fred T. Dubois (R)	March 4, 1891	March 3, 1897
Henry Heitfeld (POP)	March 4, 1897	March 3, 1903
Weldon B. Heyburn (R)[7]	March 4, 1903	Oct. 17, 1912
Kirtland I. Perky (D)[8]	Nov. 18, 1912	Feb. 5, 1913
James H. Brady (R)[9]	Feb. 6, 1913	Jan. 13, 1918
John F. Nugent (D)[10]	Jan. 22, 1918	Jan. 14, 1921
Frank R. Gooding (R)[11]	Jan. 15, 1921	June 24, 1928
John Thomas (R)[12]	June 30, 1928	March 3, 1933
James P. Pope (D)	March 4, 1933	Jan. 2, 1939
D. Worth Clark (D)	Jan. 3, 1939	Jan. 2, 1945
Glen H. Taylor (D)	Jan. 3, 1945	Jan. 2, 1951
Herman Welker (R)	Jan. 3, 1951	Jan. 2, 1957
Frank Church (D)	Jan. 3, 1957	Jan. 2, 1981
Steven D. Symms (R)	Jan. 3, 1981	

Idaho

1. *Died Jan. 19, 1940.*
2. *Appointed by governor to fill vacancy. Subsequently elected. Died Nov. 10, 1945.*
3. *Appointed by governor to fill vacancy.*
4. *Died Oct. 8, 1949.*
5. *Appointed by governor to fill vacancy. Subsequently elected. Died July 23, 1962.*
6. *Appointed by governor to fill vacancy. Subsequently elected.*

7. *Died Oct. 17, 1912.*
8. *Appointed by governor to fill vacancy.*
9. *Died Jan. 13, 1918.*
10. *Appointed by governor to fill vacancy. Subsequently elected. Resigned Jan. 14, 1921.*
11. *Appointed by governor to fill vacancy. Subsequently elected. Died June 24, 1928.*
12. *Appointed by governor to fill vacancy. Subsequently elected.*

ILLINOIS

(Became a state Dec. 3, 1818)

Class 2

Senators	Dates of Service	
Jesse B. Thomas (D-R)	Dec. 3, 1818	March 3, 1829
John McLean (D)[1]	March 4, 1829	Oct. 14, 1830
David J. Baker (D)[2]	Nov. 12, 1830	Dec. 11, 1830
John M. Robinson (D)	Dec. 11, 1830	March 3, 1841
Samuel McRoberts (D)[3]	March 4, 1841	March 27, 1843
James Semple (D)[4]	Aug. 16, 1843	March 3, 1847
Stephen A. Douglas (D)[5]	March 4, 1847	June 3, 1861
Orville H. Browning (R)[6]	June 26, 1861	Jan. 12, 1863
William A. Richardson (D)	Jan. 12, 1863	March 3, 1865
Richard Yates (R)	March 4, 1865	March 3, 1871
John A. Logan (R)	March 4, 1871	March 3, 1877
David Davis (I)	March 4, 1877	March 3, 1883
Shelby M. Cullom (R)	March 4, 1883	March 3, 1913
James Hamilton Lewis (D)	March 26, 1913	March 3, 1919
Medill McCormick (R)[7]	March 4, 1919	Feb. 25, 1925
Charles S. Deneen (R)[8]	Feb. 26, 1925	March 3, 1931
James Hamilton Lewis (D)[9]	March 4, 1931	April 9, 1939
James M. Slattery (D)[10]	April 14, 1939	Nov. 21, 1940
C. Wayland Brooks (R)	Nov. 22, 1940	Jan. 2, 1949
Paul H. Douglas (D)	Jan. 3, 1949	Jan. 2, 1967
Charles H. Percy (R)	Jan. 3, 1967	Jan. 2, 1985
Paul Simon (D)	Jan. 3, 1985	

Class 3

Ninian Edwards (D-R)[11]	Dec. 3, 1818	March 4, 1824
John McLean (D-R)	Nov. 23, 1824	March 3, 1825
Elias K. Kane (D)[12]	March 4, 1825	Dec. 11, 1835
William Lee D. Ewing (D)	Dec. 30, 1835	March 3, 1837
Richard M. Young (D)	March 4, 1837	March 3, 1843
Sidney Breese (D)	March 4, 1843	March 3, 1849
James Shields (D)	March 4, 1849	March 15, 1849
James Shields (D)[13]	Dec. 3, 1849	March 3, 1855
Lyman Trumbull (R)	March 4, 1855	March 3, 1873
Richard J. Oglesby (R)	March 4, 1873	March 3, 1879
John A. Logan (R)[14]	March 4, 1879	Dec. 26, 1886
Charles B. Farwell (R)	Jan. 19, 1887	March 3, 1891

John McAuley Palmer (D)	March 4, 1891	March 3, 1897
William E. Mason (R)	March 4, 1897	March 3, 1903
Albert J. Hopkins (R)	March 4, 1903	March 3, 1909
William Lorimer (R)[15]	June 18, 1909	July 13, 1912
Lawrence Y. Sherman (R)	March 26, 1913	March 3, 1921
William B. McKinley (R)[16]	March 4, 1921	Dec. 7, 1926
Frank L. Smith (R)[17]		
Otis F. Glenn (R)	Dec. 3, 1928	March 3, 1933
William H. Dietrich (D)	March 4, 1933	Jan. 2, 1939
Scott W. Lucas (D)	Jan. 3, 1939	Jan. 2, 1951
Everett McKinley Dirksen (R)[18]	Jan. 3, 1951	Sept. 7, 1969
Ralph Tyler Smith (R)[19]	Sept. 17, 1969	Nov. 16, 1970
Adlai E. Stevenson III (D)	Nov. 17, 1970	Jan. 2, 1981
Alan J. Dixon (D)	Jan. 3, 1981	

INDIANA

(Became a state Dec. 11, 1816)

Class 1

Senators	Dates of Service	
James Noble (D-R)[1]	Dec. 11, 1816	Feb. 26, 1831
Robert Hanna (W)[2]	Aug. 19, 1831	Jan. 3, 1832
John Tipton (D)	Jan. 4, 1832	March 3, 1839
Albert S. White (W)	March 4, 1839	March 3, 1845
Jesse D. Bright (D)[3]	March 4, 1845	Feb. 5, 1862
Joseph A. Wright (D)[4]	Feb. 24, 1862	Jan. 14, 1863
David Turpie (D)	Jan. 14, 1863	March 3, 1863
Thomas A. Hendricks (D)	March 4, 1863	March 3, 1869
Daniel D. Pratt (R)	March 4, 1869	March 3, 1875
Joseph E. McDonald (D)	March 4, 1875	March 3, 1881
Benjamin Harrison (R)	March 4, 1881	March 3, 1887
David Turpie (D)	March 4, 1887	March 3, 1899
Albert J. Beveridge (R)	March 4, 1899	March 3, 1911
John W. Kern (D)	March 4, 1911	March 3, 1917
Harry S. New (R)	March 4, 1917	March 3, 1923
Samuel M. Ralston (D)[5]	March 4, 1923	Oct. 14, 1925
Arthur R. Robinson (R)[6]	Oct. 20, 1925	Jan. 2, 1935
Sherman Minton (D)	Jan. 3, 1935	Jan. 2, 1941
Raymond E. Willis (R)	Jan. 3, 1941	Jan. 2, 1947
William E. Jenner (R)	Jan. 3, 1947	Jan. 2, 1959

Illinois

1. Died Oct. 14, 1830.
2. Appointed by governor to fill vacancy.
3. Died March 27, 1843.
4. Appointed by governor to fill vacancy. Subsequently elected.
5. Died June 3, 1861.
6. Appointed by governor to fill vacancy.
7. Died Feb. 25, 1925.
8. Appointed by governor to fill vacancy. Subsequently elected.
9. Died April 9, 1939.
10. Appointed by governor to fill vacancy.
11. Resigned March 4, 1824.
12. Died Dec. 11, 1835.
13. Shields was seated but his election was declared void by the Senate March 15, 1849, because he had not been a citizen of the United States for the requisite number of years prior to his election. Subsequently elected to fill the vacancy and, having in the interim met the constitutional requirement, took his seat Dec. 3, 1849.
14. Died Dec. 26, 1886.
15. Lorimer was accused of bribery and other corrupt practices in securing his election to the Senate. After lengthy investigation, the Senate voted on July 13, 1912, to declare his election invalid.
16. Died Dec. 7, 1926.
17. Smith was appointed by the governor Dec. 6, 1926, to fill the remaining three months of McKinley's term. He had previously been elected for a full six-year term. He was not permitted to take the oath for either term. The Committee on Privileges and Elections recommended on Jan. 17, 1928, that Smith not be allowed to take his seat because of

fraud and corruption during the campaign. The Senate adopted this resolution Jan. 19, 1928, and the seat was declared vacant. According to the Biographical Directory, Smith "resigned Feb. 9, 1928," but since the seat was already vacant, this action was apparently meaningless.
18. Died Sept. 7, 1969.
19. Appointed by governor to fill vacancy.

Indiana

1. Died Feb. 26, 1831.
2. Appointed by governor to fill vacancy.
3. Expelled Feb. 5, 1862, for writing a letter to Jefferson Davis addressing him as "President of the Confederate States." (Biographical Directory, p. 637).
4. Appointed by governor to fill vacancy.
5. Died Oct. 14, 1925.
6. Appointed by governor to fill vacancy. Subsequently elected.
7. Died Oct. 4, 1852.
8. Appointed by governor to fill vacancy.
9. Vacancy from March 4, 1855, to Feb. 4, 1857.
10. Died Nov. 1, 1877.
11. Appointed by governor to fill vacancy. Subsequently elected.
12. Resigned March 3, 1905.
13. Died March 14, 1916.
14. Appointed by governor to fill vacancy.
15. Died Jan. 25, 1944.
16. Appointed by governor to fill vacancy.

Vance Hartke (D)	Jan. 3, 1959	Jan. 2, 1977
Richard G. Lugar (R)	Jan. 3, 1977	

Class 3

Waller Taylor (D-R)	Dec. 11, 1816	March 3, 1825
William Hendricks (D)	March 4, 1825	March 3, 1837
Oliver H. Smith (W)	March 4, 1837	March 3, 1843
Edward A. Hannegan (D)	March 4, 1843	March 3, 1849
James Whitcomb (D)[7]	March 4, 1849	Oct. 4, 1852
Charles W. Cathcart (D)[8]	Nov. 23, 1852	Jan. 11, 1853
John Petit (D)	Jan. 11, 1853	March 3, 1855
Graham N. Fitch (D)[9]	Feb. 4, 1857	March 3, 1861
Henry S. Lane (R)	March 4, 1861	March 3, 1867
Oliver H. P. T. Morton (R)[10]	March 4, 1867	Nov. 1, 1877
Daniel W. Voorhees (D)[11]	Nov. 6, 1877	March 3, 1897
Charles W. Fairbanks (R)[12]	March 4, 1897	March 3, 1905
James A. Hemenway (R)	March 4, 1905	March 3, 1909
Benjamin F. Shively (D)[13]	March 4, 1909	March 14, 1916
Thomas Taggart (D)[14]	March 20, 1916	Nov. 7, 1916
James E. Watson (R)	Nov. 8, 1916	March 3, 1933
Frederick Van Nuys (D)[15]	March 4, 1933	Jan. 25, 1944
Samuel D. Jackson (D)[16]	Jan. 28, 1944	Nov. 13, 1944
William E. Jenner (R)	Nov. 14, 1944	Jan. 2, 1945
Homer E. Capehart (R)	Jan. 3, 1945	Jan. 2, 1963
Birch Bayh (D)	Jan. 3, 1963	Jan. 2, 1981
Dan Quayle (R)	Jan. 3, 1981	

IOWA

(Became a state Dec. 28, 1846)

Class 2

Senators	Dates of Service	
George W. Jones (D)	Dec. 7, 1848	March 3, 1859
James W. Grimes (R)[1]	March 4, 1859	Dec. 6, 1869
James B. Howell (R)	Jan. 18, 1870	March 3, 1871
George G. Wright (R)	March 4, 1871	March 3, 1877
Samuel J. Kirkwood (R)[2]	March 4, 1877	March 7, 1881
James W. McDill (R)[3]	March 8, 1881	March 3, 1883
James F. Wilson (R)	March 4, 1883	March 3, 1895
John H. Gear (R)[4]	March 4, 1895	July 14, 1900
Jonathan P. Dolliver (R)[5]	Aug. 22, 1900	Oct. 15, 1910
Lafayette Young (R)[6]	Nov. 12, 1910	April 11, 1911
William S. Kenyon (R)[7]	April 12, 1911	Feb. 24, 1922

Charles A. Rawson (R)[8]	Feb. 24, 1922	Dec. 1, 1922
Smith W. Brookhart (R)[9]	Dec. 2, 1922	April 12, 1926
Daniel F. Steck (D)[10]	April 12, 1926	March 3, 1931
L. J. Dickinson (R)	March 4, 1931	Jan. 2, 1937
Clyde L. Herring (D)	Jan. 19, 1937	Jan. 2, 1943
George A. Wilson (R)	Jan. 14, 1943	Jan. 2, 1949
Guy M. Gillette (D)	Jan. 3, 1949	Jan. 2, 1955
Thomas E. Martin (R)	Jan. 3, 1955	Jan. 2, 1961
Jack Miller (R)	Jan. 3, 1961	Jan. 2, 1973
Dick Clark (D)	Jan. 3, 1973	Jan. 2, 1979
Roger W. Jepsen (R)	Jan. 3, 1979	Jan. 2, 1985
Tom Harkin (D)	Jan. 3, 1985	

Class 3

Augustus C. Dodge (D)[11]	Dec. 7, 1848	Feb. 22, 1855
James Harlan (R)[12]	March 4, 1855	Jan. 12, 1857
James Harlan (R)[13]	Jan. 29, 1857	May 15, 1865
Samuel J. Kirkwood (R)	Jan. 13, 1866	March 3, 1867
James Harlan (R)	March 4, 1867	March 3, 1873
William B. Allison (R)[14]	March 4, 1873	Aug. 4, 1908
Albert B. Cummins (R)[15]	Nov. 24, 1908	July 30, 1926
David W. Stewart (R)[16]	Aug. 7, 1926	March 3, 1927
Smith W. Brookhart (R)	March 4, 1927	March 3, 1933
Richard Louis Murphy (D)[17]	March 4, 1933	July 16, 1936
Guy M. Gillette (D)	Nov. 4, 1936	Jan. 2, 1945
Bourke B. Hickenlooper (R)	Jan. 3, 1945	Jan. 2, 1969
Harold E. Hughes (D)	Jan. 3, 1969	Jan. 2, 1975
John C. Culver (D)	Jan. 3, 1975	Jan. 2, 1981
Charles E. Grassley (R)	Jan. 3, 1981	

KANSAS

(Became a state Jan. 29, 1861)

Class 2

Senators	Dates of Service	
James H. Lane (R)[1]	April 4, 1861	July 11, 1866
Edmund G. Ross (R)[2]	July 19, 1866	March 3, 1871
Alexander Caldwell (R)[3]	March 4, 1871	March 24, 1873
Robert Crozier (R)[4]	Nov. 24, 1873	Feb. 2, 1874
James M. Harvey (R)	Feb. 2, 1874	March 3, 1877
Preston B. Plumb (R)[5]	March 4, 1877	Dec. 20, 1891
Bishop W. Perkins (R)[6]	Jan. 1, 1892	March 3, 1893

Iowa

1. *Resigned Dec. 6, 1869.*
2. *Resigned March 7, 1881.*
3. *Appointed by governor to fill vacancy. Subsequently elected.*
4. *Died July 14, 1900.*
5. *Appointed by governor to fill vacancy. Subsequently elected. Died Oct. 15, 1910.*
6. *Appointed by governor to fill vacancy.*
7. *Resigned Feb. 24, 1922.*
8. *Appointed by governor to fill vacancy.*
9. *Elected to fill vacancy in term expiring March 3, 1925. Presented credentials for term expiring March 3, 1931, and was seated. Steck challenged Brookhart's right to the seat, alleging that ballots cast for Steck had either been rejected or counted for Brookhart, and that illegal votes had been cast for Brookhart. The Senate voted to unseat Brookhart and award the seat to Steck, who took the oath April 12, 1926, and served for the remainder of the term.*
10. *Successfully contested the election of Smith W. Brookhart.*
11. *Resigned Feb. 22, 1855.*
12. *Harlan was elected by the Legislature for the term beginning March 4, 1855, and took his seat. The Senate voted Jan. 12, 1857, to deny him a seat, following protests that the Legislature that elected him had not been properly constituted.*
13. *Elected to fill the vacancy caused by the Senate's having declared the seat vacant, and took his seat Jan. 29, 1857. Resigned May 15, 1865.*

14. *Died Aug. 4, 1908.*
15. *Died July 30, 1926.*
16. *Appointed by governor to fill vacancy. Subsequently elected.*
17. *Died July 16, 1936.*

Kansas

1. *Died July 11, 1866.*
2. *Appointed by governor to fill vacancy. Subsequently elected.*
3. *Resigned March 24, 1873.*
4. *Appointed by governor to fill vacancy.*
5. *Died Dec. 20, 1891.*
6. *Appointed by governor to fill vacancy.*
7. *Resigned June 4, 1906.*
8. *Appointed by governor to fill vacancy.*
9. *Died Jan. 21, 1962.*
10. *Appointed by governor to fill vacancy. Subsequently elected. Resigned Dec. 23, 1978.*
11. *Resigned March 3, 1929.*
12. *Appointed by governor to fill vacancy.*
13. *Died Nov. 8, 1949.*
14. *Appointed by governor to fill vacancy.*

John Martin (D)	March 4, 1893	March 3, 1895
Lucien Baker (R)	March 4, 1895	March 3, 1901
Joseph R. Burton (R)[7]	March 4, 1901	June 4, 1906
Alfred W. Benson (R)[8]	June 11, 1906	Jan. 23, 1907
Charles Curtis (R)	Jan. 23, 1907	March 3, 1913
William H. Thompson (D)	March 4, 1913	March 3, 1919
Arthur Capper (R)	March 4, 1919	Jan. 2, 1949
Andrew F. Schoeppel (R)[9]	Jan. 3, 1949	Jan. 21, 1962
James B. Pearson (R)[10]	Jan. 31, 1962	Dec. 23, 1978
Nancy Landon Kassebaum (R)	Dec. 23, 1978	

Class 3

Samuel C. Pomeroy (R)	April 4, 1861	March 3, 1873
John J. Ingalls (R)	March 4, 1873	March 3, 1891
William A. Peffer (POP)	March 4, 1891	March 3, 1897
William A. Harris (D)	March 4, 1897	March 3, 1903
Chester I. Long (R)	March 4, 1903	March 3, 1909
Joseph L. Bristow (R)	March 4, 1909	March 3, 1915
Charles Curtis (R)[11]	March 4, 1915	March 3, 1929
Henry J. Allen (R)[12]	April 1, 1929	Nov. 30, 1930
George McGill (D)	Dec. 1, 1930	Jan. 2, 1939
Clyde M. Reed (R)[13]	Jan. 3, 1939	Nov. 8, 1949
Harry Darby (R)[14]	Dec. 2, 1949	Nov. 28, 1950
Frank Carlson (R)	Nov. 29, 1950	Jan. 2, 1969
Robert Dole (R)	Jan. 3, 1969	

KENTUCKY

(Became a state June 1, 1792)

Class 2

Senators	Dates of Service	
John Brown (D-R)	June 18, 1792	March 3, 1805
Buckner Thruston (D-R)[1]	March 4, 1805	Dec. 18, 1809
Henry Clay (D-R)	Jan. 4, 1810	March 3, 1811
George M. Bibb (D-R)[2]	March 4, 1811	Aug. 23, 1814
George Walker (D-R)[3]	Aug. 30, 1814	Dec. 16, 1814
William T. Barry (D-R)[4]	Dec. 16, 1814	May 1, 1816
Martin D. Hardin (D-R)[5]	Nov. 13, 1816	March 3, 1817
John J. Crittenden (D-R)[6]	March 4, 1817	March 3, 1819
Richard M. Johnson (D-R)	Dec. 10, 1819	March 3, 1829
George M. Bibb (D-R)	March 4, 1829	March 3, 1835
John J. Crittenden (W)	March 4, 1835	March 3, 1841
James T. Morehead (W)	March 4, 1841	March 3, 1847
Joseph R. Underwood (W)	March 4, 1847	March 3, 1853

John B. Thompson (W)	March 4, 1853	March 3, 1859
Lazarus W. Powell (D)	March 4, 1859	March 3, 1865
James Guthrie (D)[7]	March 4, 1865	Feb. 7, 1868
Thomas C. McCreery (D)	Feb. 19, 1868	March 3, 1871
John W. Stevenson (D)	March 4, 1871	March 3, 1877
James B. Beck (D)[8]	March 4, 1877	May 3, 1890
John G. Carlisle (D)[9]	May 17, 1890	Feb. 4, 1893
William Lindsay (D)	Feb. 15, 1893	March 3, 1901
Joseph C. S. Blackburn (D)	March 4, 1901	March 3, 1907
Thomas H. Paynter (D)	March 4, 1907	March 3, 1913
Ollie M. James (D)[10]	March 4, 1913	Aug. 28, 1918
George B. Martin (D)[11]	Sept. 7, 1918	March 3, 1919
A. Owsley Stanley (D)	March 4, 1919	March 3, 1925
Fred M. Sackett (R)[12]	March 4, 1925	Jan. 9, 1930
John M. Robsion (R)[13]	Jan. 9, 1930	Nov. 30, 1930
Ben M. Williamson (D)	Dec. 1, 1930	March 3, 1931
Marvel M. Logan (D)[14]	March 4, 1931	Oct. 3, 1939
Albert B. Chandler (D)[15]	Oct. 10, 1939	Nov. 1, 1945
William A. Stanfill (R)[16]	Nov. 19, 1945	Nov. 5, 1946
John Sherman Cooper (R)	Nov. 6, 1946	Jan. 2, 1949
Virgil Chapman (D)[17]	Jan. 3, 1949	March 8, 1951
Thomas R. Underwood (D)[18]	March 19, 1951	Nov. 4, 1952
John Sherman Cooper (R)	Nov. 5, 1952	Jan. 2, 1955
Alben W. Barkley (D)[19]	Jan. 3, 1955	April 30, 1956
Robert Humphreys (D)[20]	June 21, 1956	Nov. 6, 1956
John Sherman Cooper (R)	Nov. 7, 1956	Jan. 2, 1973
Walter D. Huddleston (D)	Jan. 3, 1973	Jan. 2, 1985
Mitch McConnell (R)	Jan. 3, 1985	

Class 3

John Edwards (D-R)	June 18, 1792	March 3, 1795
Humphrey Marshall (FED)	March 4, 1795	March 3, 1801
John Breckinridge (D-R)[21]	March 4, 1801	Aug. 7, 1805
John Adair (D-R)[22]	Nov. 8, 1805	Nov. 18, 1806
Henry Clay (D-R)	Dec. 29, 1806	March 3, 1807
John Pope (D-R)	March 4, 1807	March 3, 1813
Jesse Bledsoe (D-R)[23]	March 4, 1813	Dec. 24, 1814
Isham Talbot (D-R)	Jan. 5, 1815	March 3, 1819
William Logan (D-R)[24]	March 4, 1819	May 28, 1820
Isham Talbot (D-R)	Oct. 19, 1820	March 3, 1825
John Rowan (D-R)	March 4, 1825	March 3, 1831
Henry Clay (NR, W)[25]	Nov. 10, 1831	March 31, 1842
John J. Crittenden (W)[26]	March 31, 1842	June 12, 1848
Thomas Metcalfe[27]	June 23, 1848	March 3, 1849
Henry Clay (W)[28]	March 4, 1849	June 29, 1852
David Meriwether (D)[29]	July 6, 1852	Sept. 1, 1852
Archibald Dixon (W)	Sept. 1, 1852	March 3, 1855
John J. Crittenden (W)	March 4, 1855	March 3, 1861

Kentucky
1. *Resigned Dec. 18, 1809.*
2. *Resigned Aug. 23, 1814.*
3. *Appointed by governor to fill vacancy.*
4. *Resigned May 1, 1816.*
5. *Appointed by governor to fill vacancy. Subsequently elected.*
6. *Resigned March 3, 1819.*
7. *Resigned Feb. 7, 1868.*
8. *Died May 3, 1890.*
9. *Resigned Feb. 4, 1893.*
10. *Died Aug. 28, 1918.*
11. *Appointed by governor to fill vacancy.*
12. *Resigned Jan. 9, 1930.*
13. *Appointed by governor to fill vacancy.*
14. *Died Oct. 3, 1939.*
15. *Appointed by governor to fill vacancy. Subsequently elected. Resigned Nov. 1, 1945.*
16. *Appointed by governor to fill vacancy.*
17. *Died March 8, 1951.*
18. *Appointed by governor to fill vacancy.*

19. *Died April 30, 1956.*
20. *Appointed by governor to fill vacancy.*
21. *Resigned Aug. 7, 1805.*
22. *Resigned Nov. 18, 1806.*
23. *Resigned Dec. 24, 1814.*
24. *Resigned May 28, 1820.*
25. *Resigned March 31, 1842.*
26. *Resigned June 12, 1848.*
27. *Appointed by governor to fill vacancy. Subsequently elected.*
28. *Died June 29, 1852.*
29. *Appointed by governor to fill vacancy.*
30. *Expelled Dec. 4, 1861.*
31. *Died Sept. 22, 1872.*
32. *Appointed by governor to fill vacancy. Subsequently elected.*
33. *Died May 23, 1914.*
34. *Appointed by governor to fill vacancy. Subsequently elected.*
35. *Resigned Jan. 19, 1949, to become vice president of the United States.*
36. *Appointed by governor to fill vacancy.*
37. *Resigned Dec. 16, 1968.*
38. *Resigned Dec. 27, 1974.*

John C. Breckinridge (D)[30]	March 4, 1861	Dec. 4, 1861
Garrett Davis (D)[31]	Dec. 10, 1861	Sept. 22, 1872
Willis B. Machen (D)[32]	Sept. 27, 1872	March 3, 1873
Thomas C. McCreery (D)	March 4, 1873	March 3, 1879
John Stuart Williams (D)	March 4, 1879	March 3, 1885
Joseph C. S. Blackburn (D)	March 4, 1885	March 3, 1897
William J. Deboe (R)	March 4, 1897	March 3, 1903
James B. McCreary (D)	March 4, 1903	March 3, 1909
William O. Bradley (R)[33]	March 4, 1909	May 23, 1914
Johnson N. Camden Jr. (D)[34]	June 16, 1914	March 3, 1915
John C. W. Beckham (D)	March 4, 1915	March 3, 1921
Richard P. Ernst (R)	March 4, 1921	March 3, 1927
Alben W. Barkley (D)[35]	March 4, 1927	Jan. 19, 1949
Garrett L. Withers (D)[36]	Jan. 20, 1949	Nov. 26, 1950
Earle C. Clements (D)	Nov. 27, 1950	Jan. 2, 1957
Thruston B. Morton (R)[37]	Jan. 3, 1957	Dec. 16, 1968
Marlow W. Cook (R)[38]	Dec. 17, 1968	Dec. 27, 1974
Wendell H. Ford (D)	Dec. 28, 1974	

Judah P. Benjamin (W, D)[7]	March 4, 1853	March 14, 1861
John S. Harris (R)	July 17, 1868	March 3, 1871
J. Rodman West (R)	March 4, 1871	March 3, 1877
William P. Kellogg (R)	March 4, 1877	March 3, 1883
Randall L. Gibson (D)[8]	March 4, 1883	Dec. 15, 1892
Donelson Caffery (D)[9]	Dec. 31, 1892	March 3, 1901
Murphy J. Foster (D)	March 4, 1901	March 3, 1913
Joseph E. Ransdell (D)	March 4, 1913	March 3, 1931
Huey P. Long (D)[10]	Jan. 25, 1932	Sept. 10, 1935
Rose McConnell Long (D)[11]	Jan. 31, 1936	Jan. 2, 1937
Allen J. Ellender (D)[12]	Jan. 3, 1937	July 27, 1972
Elaine S. Edwards (D)[13]	Aug. 1, 1972	Nov. 13, 1972
J. Bennett Johnston (D)	Nov. 14, 1972	

LOUISIANA

(Became a state April 30, 1812)

Class 2

Senators	Dates of Service	
John N. Destrehan (D-R)[1]		
Thomas Posey (D-R)[2]	Oct. 8, 1812	Feb. 4, 1813
James Brown (D-R)	Feb. 5, 1813	March 3, 1817
William C. C. Claiborne (D-R)[3]	March 4, 1817	Nov. 23, 1817
Henry Johnson (D-R)[4]	Jan. 12, 1818	May 27, 1824
Dominique Bouligny (D-R)	Nov. 19, 1824	March 3, 1829
Edward Livingston (D)[5]	March 4, 1829	May 24, 1831
George A. Waggaman (NR)	Nov. 15, 1831	March 3, 1835
Robert C. Nicholas (D)	Jan. 13, 1836	March 3, 1841
Alexander Barrow (W)[6]	March 4, 1841	Dec. 29, 1846
Pierre Soulé (D)	Jan. 21, 1847	March 3, 1847
Solomon W. Downs (D)	March 4, 1847	March 3, 1853

Class 3

Allan B. Magruder (D-R)	Sept. 3, 1812	March 3, 1813
Eligius Fromentin (D-R)	March 4, 1813	March 3, 1819
James Brown (D-R)[14]	March 4, 1819	Dec. 10, 1823
Josiah S. Johnston (D-R)[15]	Jan. 15, 1824	May 19, 1833
Alexander Porter (W)[16]	Dec. 19, 1833	Jan. 5, 1837
Alexander Mouton (D)[17]	Jan. 12, 1837	March 1, 1842
Charles M. Conrad (W)	April 14, 1842	March 3, 1843
Henry Johnson (W)[18]	Feb. 12, 1844	March 3, 1849
Pierre Soulé (D)[19]	March 4, 1849	April 11, 1853
John Slidell (D)[20]	April 28, 1853	Feb. 4, 1861
William P. Kellogg (R)[21]	July 17, 1868	Nov. 1, 1872
James B. Eustis (D)	Jan. 12, 1876	March 3, 1879
Benjamin F. Jonas (D)	March 4, 1879	March 3, 1885
James B. Eustis (D)	March 4, 1885	March 3, 1891
Edward D. White (D)[22]	March 4, 1891	March 12, 1894
Newton C. Blanchard (D)[23]	March 12, 1894	March 3, 1897
Samuel D. McEnery (D)[24]	March 4, 1897	June 28, 1910
John R. Thornton (D)	Dec. 7, 1910	March 3, 1915
Robert F. Broussard (D)[25]	March 4, 1915	April 12, 1918
Walter Guion (D)[26]	April 22, 1918	Nov. 5, 1918
Edward J. Gay (D)	Nov. 6, 1918	March 3, 1921
Edwin S. Broussard (D)	March 4, 1921	March 3, 1933
John H. Overton (D)[27]	March 4, 1933	May 14, 1948
William C. Feazel (D)[28]	May 18, 1948	Dec. 30, 1948
Russell B. Long (D)	Dec. 31, 1948	

Louisiana

1. *Elected Sept. 3, 1812, but did not take oath. Resigned Oct. 1, 1812.*
2. *Appointed by governor to fill vacancy.*
3. *Died Nov. 23, 1817.*
4. *Resigned May 27, 1824.*
5. *Resigned May 24, 1831.*
6. *Died Dec. 29, 1846.*
7. *Seat declared vacant March 14, 1861. Vacancy until July 17, 1868, because of Civil War.*
8. *Died Dec. 15, 1892.*
9. *Appointed by governor to fill vacancy. Subsequently elected.*
10. *Elected Nov. 4, 1930, but did not take oath until Jan. 25, 1932. Governor during interim. Died Sept. 10, 1935.*
11. *Appointed by governor to fill vacancy. Subsequently elected.*
12. *Died July 27, 1972.*
13. *Appointed by governor to fill vacancy. Resigned Nov. 13, 1972.*

14. *Resigned Dec. 10, 1823.*
15. *Died May 19, 1833.*
16. *Resigned Jan. 5, 1837.*
17. *Resigned March 1, 1842.*
18. *Vacancy from March 4, 1843, to Feb. 12, 1844.*
19. *Resigned April 11, 1853.*
20. *Retired Feb. 4, 1861. Vacancy until July 17, 1868, because of Civil War.*
21. *Resigned Nov. 1, 1872. Vacancy from Nov. 1, 1872, until Jan. 12, 1876.*
22. *Resigned March 12, 1894.*
23. *Appointed by governor to fill vacancy. Subsequently elected.*
24. *Died June 28, 1910.*
25. *Died April 12, 1918.*
26. *Appointed by governor to fill vacancy.*
27. *Died May 14, 1948.*
28. *Appointed by governor to fill vacancy.*

MAINE

(Became a state March 15, 1820)

Class 1

Senators	Dates of Service	
John Holmes (D-R)	June 13, 1820	March 3, 1827
Albion K. Parris (D-R)[1]	March 4, 1827	Aug. 26, 1828
John Holmes (NR)	Jan. 15, 1829	March 3, 1833
Ether Shepley (D)[2]	March 4, 1833	March 3, 1836
Judah Dana (D)[3]	Dec. 7, 1836	Feb. 22, 1837
Reuel Williams (D)[4]	Feb. 22, 1837	Feb. 15, 1843
John Fairfield (D)[5]	March 3, 1843	Dec. 24, 1847
Wyman B. S. Moor (D)[6]	Jan. 5, 1848	May 26, 1848
Hannibal Hamlin (D)[7]	May 26, 1848	Jan. 7, 1857
Amos Nourse	Jan. 16, 1857	March 3, 1857
Hannibal Hamlin (R)[8]	March 4, 1857	Jan. 17, 1861
Lot Myrick Morrill (R)	Jan. 17, 1861	March 3, 1869
Hannibal Hamlin (R)	March 4, 1869	March 3, 1881
Eugene Hale (R)	March 4, 1881	March 3, 1911
Charles F. Johnson (D)	March 4, 1911	March 3, 1917
Frederick Hale (R)	March 4, 1917	Jan. 2, 1941
Ralph O. Brewster (R)	Jan. 3, 1941	Jan. 2, 1953
Frederick G. Payne (R)	Jan. 3, 1953	Jan. 2, 1959
Edmund S. Muskie (D)[9]	Jan. 3, 1959	May 7, 1980
George J. Mitchell (D)[10]	May 17, 1980	

Class 2

John Chandler (D-R)	June 14, 1820	March 3, 1829
Peleg Sprague (NR)[11]	March 4, 1829	Jan. 1, 1835
John Ruggles (D)	Jan. 20, 1835	March 3, 1841
George Evans (W)	March 4, 1841	March 3, 1847
James W. Bradbury (D)	March 4, 1847	March 3, 1853
William P. Fessenden (R)[12]	Feb. 10, 1854	July 1, 1864
Nathan A. Farwell (R)[13]	Oct. 27, 1864	March 3, 1865
William P. Fessenden (R)[14]	March 4, 1865	Sept. 9, 1869
Lot Myrick Morrill (R)[15]	Oct. 30, 1869	July 7, 1876
James G. Blaine (R)[16]	July 10, 1876	March 5, 1881
William P. Frye (R)[17]	March 18, 1881	Aug. 8, 1911
Obadiah Gardner (D)[18]	Sept. 23, 1911	March 3, 1913
Edwin C. Burleigh (R)[19]	March 4, 1913	June 16, 1916

Bert M. Fernald (R)[20]	Sept. 12, 1916	Aug. 23, 1926
Arthur R. Gould (R)	Nov. 30, 1926	March 3, 1931
Wallace H. White Jr. (R)	March 4, 1931	Jan. 2, 1949
Margaret Chase Smith (R)	Jan. 3, 1949	Jan. 2, 1973
William D. Hathaway (D)	Jan. 3, 1973	Jan. 2, 1979
William S. Cohen (R)	Jan. 3, 1979	

MARYLAND

(Ratified the Constitution April 28, 1788)

Class 1

Senators	Dates of Service	
Charles Carroll (FED)[1]	March 4, 1789	Nov. 30, 1792
Richard Potts (FED)[2]	Jan. 10, 1793	Oct. 24, 1796
John E. Howard (FED)	Nov. 30, 1796	March 3, 1803
Samuel Smith (D-R)[3]	March 4, 1803	March 3, 1815
Robert G. Harper[4]	Jan. 29, 1816	Dec. 6, 1816
Alexander C. Hanson(FED)[5]	Dec. 20, 1816	April 23, 1819
William Pinkney (D-R)[6]	Dec. 21, 1819	Feb. 25, 1822
Samuel Smith (D-R)	Dec. 16, 1822	March 3, 1833
Joseph Kent (NR)[7]	March 4, 1833	Nov. 24, 1837
William D. Merrick (W)	Jan. 4, 1838	March 3, 1845
Reverdy Johnson (W)[8]	March 4, 1845	March 7, 1849
David Stewart (W)[9]	Dec. 6, 1849	Jan. 12, 1850
Thomas G. Pratt (W)	Jan. 12, 1850	March 3, 1857
Anthony Kennedy (UN)	March 4, 1857	March 3, 1863
Reverdy Johnson (D)[10]	March 4, 1863	July 10, 1868
William Pinkney Whyte (D)[11]	July 13, 1868	March 3, 1869
William T. Hamilton (D)	March 4, 1869	March 3, 1875
William Pinkney Whyte (D)	March 4, 1875	March 3, 1881
Arthur P. Gorman (D)	March 4, 1881	March 3, 1899
Louis E. McComas (R)	March 4, 1899	March 3, 1905
Isidor Rayner (D)[12]	March 4, 1905	Nov. 25, 1912
William P. Jackson (R)[13]	Nov. 29, 1912	Jan. 28, 1914
Blair Lee (D)	Jan. 29, 1914	March 3, 1917
Joseph I. France (R)	March 4, 1917	March 3, 1923
William Cabell Bruce (D)	March 4, 1923	March 3, 1929
Phillips Lee Goldsborough (R)	March 4, 1929	Jan. 2, 1935
George W. Radcliffe (D)	Jan. 3, 1935	Jan. 2, 1947

Maine
1. *Resigned Aug. 26, 1828.*
2. *Resigned March 3, 1836.*
3. *Appointed by governor to fill vacancy.*
4. *Resigned Feb. 15, 1843.*
5. *Died Dec. 24, 1847.*
6. *Appointed by governor to fill vacancy.*
7. *Resigned Jan. 7, 1857.*
8. *Resigned Jan. 17, 1861, to become vice president of the United States.*
9. *Resigned May 7, 1980, having been confirmed Secretary of State.*
10. *Appointed by governor to fill vacancy.*
11. *Resigned Jan. 1, 1835.*
12. *Resigned July 1, 1864.*
13. *Appointed by governor to fill vacancy. Subsequently elected.*
14. *Died Sept. 9, 1869.*
15. *Appointed by governor to fill vacancy. Subsequently elected. Resigned July 7, 1876.*
16. *Appointed by governor to fill vacancy. Subsequently elected. Resigned March 5, 1881.*
17. *Died Aug. 8, 1911.*
18. *Appointed by governor to fill vacancy.*
19. *Died June 16, 1916.*
20. *Died Aug. 23, 1926.*

Maryland
1. *Resigned Nov. 30, 1792.*
2. *Resigned Oct. 24, 1796.*
3. *Served continuously during this period, twice by election, once by appointment of the governor.*

4. *Resigned Dec. 6, 1816.*
5. *Died April 23, 1819.*
6. *Died Feb. 25, 1822.*
7. *Died Nov. 24, 1837.*
8. *Resigned March 7, 1849.*
9. *Appointed by governor to fill vacancy.*
10. *Resigned July 10, 1868.*
11. *Appointed by governor to fill vacancy.*
12. *Died Nov. 25, 1912.*
13. *Appointed by governor to fill vacancy.*
14. *Resigned Dec. 10, 1797.*
15. *Resigned Dec. 1, 1800.*
16. *Served first by election and subsequently by appointment of the governor during this period.*
17. *Resigned Nov. 12, 1806.*
18. *Resigned Jan. 14, 1826.*
19. *Resigned Dec. 20, 1834.*
20. *Died Oct. 5, 1836.*
21. *Died Oct. 24, 1840.*
22. *Died Dec. 20, 1862.*
23. *Appointed by governor to fill vacancy. Subsequently elected. Died Feb. 14, 1865.*
24. *Vacancy from March 4, 1867, to March 7, 1868.*
25. *Died Feb. 24, 1891.*
26. *Appointed by governor to fill vacancy. Subsequently elected.*
27. *Died June 4, 1906.*
28. *Appointed by governor to fill vacancy. Subsequently elected. Died March 17, 1908.*

Herbert R. O'Conor (D)	Jan. 3, 1947	Jan. 2, 1953
J. Glenn Beall (R)	Jan. 3, 1953	Jan. 2, 1965
Joseph D. Tydings (D)	Jan. 3, 1965	Jan. 2, 1971
J. Glenn Beall Jr. (R)	Jan. 3, 1971	Jan. 2, 1977
Paul S. Sarbanes (D)	Jan. 3, 1977	

Class 3

John Henry (D-R)[14]	March 4, 1789	Dec. 10, 1797
James Lloyd (D-R)[15]	Dec. 11, 1797	Dec. 1, 1800
William Hindman (FED)[16]	Dec. 12, 1800	Nov. 19, 1801
Robert Wright (D-R)[17]	Nov. 19, 1801	Nov. 12, 1806
Philip Reed (D-R)	Nov. 25, 1806	March 3, 1813
Robert H. Goldsborough (FED)	May 21, 1813	March 3, 1819
Edward Lloyd (D-R)[18]	Dec. 21, 1819	Jan. 14, 1826
Ezekiel F. Chambers (W)[19]	Jan. 24, 1826	Dec. 20, 1834
Robert H. Goldsborough (W)[20]	Jan. 13, 1835	Oct. 5, 1836
John S. Spence (W)[21]	Dec. 31, 1836	Oct. 24, 1840
John Leeds Kerr (W)	Jan. 5, 1841	March 3, 1843
James A. Pearce (W, D)[22]	March 4, 1843	Dec. 20, 1862
Thomas H. Hicks (R)[23]	Dec. 29, 1862	Feb. 14, 1865
John A. J. Creswell (R)	March 9, 1865	March 3, 1867
George Vickers (D)[24]	March 7, 1868	March 3, 1873
George R. Dennis (D)	March 4, 1873	March 3, 1879
James B. Groome (D)	March 4, 1879	March 3, 1885
Ephraim King Wilson (D)[25]	March 4, 1885	Feb. 24, 1891
Charles H. Gibson (D)[26]	Nov. 19, 1891	March 3, 1897
George L. Wellington (R)	March 4, 1897	March 3, 1903
Arthur P. Gorman (D)[27]	March 4, 1903	June 4, 1906
William Pinkney Whyte (D)[28]	June 8, 1906	March 17, 1908
John Walter Smith (D)	March 25, 1908	March 3, 1921
Ovington E. Weller (R)	March 4, 1921	March 3, 1927
Millard E. Tydings (D)	March 4, 1927	Jan. 2, 1951
John Marshall Butler (R)	Jan. 3, 1951	Jan. 2, 1963
Daniel B. Brewster (D)	Jan. 3, 1963	Jan. 2, 1969
Charles McC. Mathias Jr. (R)	Jan. 3, 1969	

MASSACHUSETTS

(Ratified the Constitution Feb. 6, 1788)

Class 1

Senators	Dates of Service	
Tristram Dalton (FED)	March 4, 1789	March 3, 1791
George Cabot (FED)[1]	March 4, 1791	June 9, 1796
Benjamin Goodhue (FED)[2]	June 11, 1796	Nov. 8, 1800
Jonathan Mason (FED)	Nov. 14, 1800	March 3, 1803
John Quincy Adams (FED, D-R)[3]	March 4, 1803	June 8, 1808

James Lloyd (FED)[4]	June 9, 1808	May 1, 1813
Christopher Gore (FED)[5]	May 5, 1813	May 30, 1816
Eli P. Ashmun (FED)[6]	June 12, 1816	May 10, 1818
Prentiss Mellen (FED)[7]	June 5, 1818	May 15, 1820
Elijah H. Mills (FED)	June 12, 1820	March 3, 1827
Daniel Webster (D-R, NR, W)[8]	May 30, 1827	Feb. 22, 1841
Rufus Choate (W)	Feb. 23, 1841	March 3, 1845
Daniel Webster (W)[9]	March 4, 1845	July 22, 1850
Robert C. Winthrop (W)[10]	July 30, 1850	Feb. 1, 1851
Robert Rantoul (D)	Feb. 1, 1851	March 3, 1851
Charles Sumner (F SOIL, R)[11]	March 4, 1851	March 11, 1874
William B. Washburn (R)	April 17, 1874	March 3, 1875
Henry L. Dawes (R)	March 4, 1875	March 3, 1893
Henry Cabot Lodge (R)[12]	March 4, 1893	Nov. 9, 1924
William M. Butler (R)[13]	Nov. 13, 1924	Dec. 5, 1926
David I. Walsh (D)	Dec. 6, 1926	Jan. 2, 1947
Henry Cabot Lodge Jr. (R)	Jan. 3, 1947	Jan. 2, 1953
John F. Kennedy (D)[14]	Jan. 3, 1953	Dec. 22, 1960
Benjamin A. Smith II (D)[15]	Dec. 27, 1960	Nov. 6, 1962
Edward M. Kennedy (D)	Nov. 7, 1962	

Class 2

Caleb Strong (FED)[16]	March 4, 1789	June 1, 1796
Theodore Sedgwick (FED)	June 11, 1796	March 3, 1799
Samuel Dexter (FED)[17]	March 4, 1799	May 30, 1800
Dwight Foster (FED)[18]	June 6, 1800	March 3, 1803
Timothy Pickering (FED)	March 4, 1803	March 3, 1811
Joseph B. Varnum (D-R)	June 8, 1811	March 3, 1817
Harrison Gray Otis (FED)[19]	March 4, 1817	May 30, 1822
James Lloyd (FED)[20]	June 5, 1822	May 23, 1826
Nathaniel Silsbee (D-R, NR)	May 31, 1826	March 3, 1835
John Davis (W)[21]	March 4, 1835	Jan. 5, 1841
Isaac C. Bates (W)[22]	Jan. 13, 1841	March 16, 1845
John Davis (W)	March 24, 1845	March 3, 1853
Edward Everett (W)[23]	March 4, 1853	June 1, 1854
Julius Rockwell[24]	June 3, 1854	Jan. 31, 1855
Henry Wilson (R)[25]	Jan. 31, 1855	March 3, 1873
George S. Boutwell (R)	March 12, 1873	March 3, 1877
George F. Hoar (R)[26]	March 4, 1877	Sept. 30, 1904
Winthrop Murray Crane (R)[27]	Oct. 12, 1904	March 3, 1913
John W. Weeks (R)	March 4, 1913	March 3, 1919
David I. Walsh (D)	March 4, 1919	March 3, 1925
Frederick H. Gillett (R)	March 4, 1925	March 3, 1931
Marcus A. Coolidge (D)	March 4, 1931	March 3, 1937
Henry Cabot Lodge Jr. (R)[28]	Jan. 3, 1937	Feb. 3, 1944
Sinclair Weeks (R)[29]	Feb. 8, 1944	Dec. 19, 1944
Leverett Saltonstall (R)	Jan. 10, 1945	Jan. 2, 1967
Edward W. Brooke (R)	Jan. 3, 1967	Jan. 2, 1979
Paul E. Tsongas (D)[30]	Jan. 3, 1979	Jan. 1, 1985
John F. Kerry (D)	Jan. 2, 1985	

Massachusetts
1. *Resigned June 9, 1796.*
2. *Resigned Nov. 8, 1800.*
3. *Resigned June 8, 1808.*
4. *Resigned May 1, 1813.*
5. *Appointed by governor to fill vacancy. Subsequently elected. Resigned May 30, 1816.*
6. *Resigned May 10, 1818.*
7. *Resigned May 15, 1820.*
8. *Resigned Feb. 22, 1841.*
9. *Resigned July 22, 1850.*
10. *Appointed by governor to fill vacancy.*
11. *Died March 11, 1874.*
12. *Died Nov. 9, 1924.*
13. *Appointed by governor to fill vacancy.*

14. *Resigned Dec. 22, 1960, having been elected president of the United States.*
15. *Appointed by governor to fill vacancy.*
16. *Resigned June 1, 1796.*
17. *Resigned May 30, 1800.*
18. *Resigned March 3, 1803.*
19. *Resigned May 30, 1822.*
20. *Resigned May 23, 1826.*
21. *Resigned Jan. 5, 1841.*
22. *Died March 16, 1845.*
23. *Resigned June 1, 1854.*
24. *Appointed by governor to fill vacancy.*
25. *Resigned March 3, 1873.*
26. *Died Sept. 30, 1904.*
27. *Appointed by governor to fill vacancy. Subsequently elected.*
28. *Resigned Feb. 3, 1944.*
29. *Appointed by governor to fill vacancy.*
30. *Resigned Jan. 1, 1985.*

MICHIGAN

(Became a state Jan. 26, 1837)

Class 1

Senators	Dates of Service	
Lucius Lyon (D)	Jan. 26, 1837	March 3, 1839
Augustus S. Porter (W)	Jan. 20, 1840	March 3, 1845
Lewis Cass (D)[1]	March 4, 1845	May 29, 1848
Thomas Fitzgerald (D)[2]	June 8, 1848	March 3, 1849
Lewis Cass (D)	March 4, 1849	March 3, 1857
Zachariah Chandler (R)	March 4, 1857	March 3, 1875
Isaac P. Christiancy (R)[3]	March 4, 1875	Feb. 10, 1879
Zachariah Chandler (R)[4]	Feb. 19, 1879	Nov. 1, 1879
Henry P. Baldwin (R)[5]	Nov. 17, 1879	March 3, 1881
Omar D. Conger (R)	March 4, 1881	March 3, 1887
Francis B. Stockbridge (R)[6]	March 4, 1887	April 30, 1894
John Patton Jr. (R)[7]	May 5, 1894	Jan. 14, 1895
Julius C. Burrows (R)	Jan. 23, 1895	March 3, 1911
Charles E. Townsend (R)	March 4, 1911	March 3, 1923
Woodbridge N. Ferris (D)[8]	March 4, 1923	March 23, 1928
Arthur H. Vandenberg (R)[9]	March 31, 1928	April 18, 1951
Blair Moody (D)[10]	April 22, 1951	Nov. 4, 1952
Charles E. Potter (R)	Nov. 5, 1952	Jan. 2, 1959
Philip A. Hart (D)[11]	Jan. 3, 1959	Dec. 26, 1976
Donald W. Riegle Jr. (D)	Dec. 30, 1976	

Class 2

Senators	Dates of Service	
John Norvell (D)	Jan. 26, 1837	March 3, 1841
William Woodbridge (W)	March 4, 1841	March 3, 1847
Alpheus Felch (D)	March 4, 1847	March 3, 1853
Charles E. Stuart (D)	March 4, 1853	March 3, 1859
Kinsley S. Bingham (R)[12]	March 4, 1859	Oct. 5, 1861
Jacob M. Howard (R)	Jan. 4, 1862	March 3, 1871
Thomas W. Ferry (R)	March 4, 1871	March 3, 1883
Thomas W. Palmer (R)	March 4, 1883	March 3, 1889
James McMillan (R)[13]	March 4, 1889	Aug. 10, 1902
Russell A. Alger (R)[14]	Sept. 27, 1902	Jan. 24, 1907
William Alden Smith (R)	Feb. 6, 1907	March 3, 1919
Truman H. Newberry (R)[15]	March 4, 1919	Nov. 18, 1922
James Couzens (R)[16]	Nov. 29, 1922	Oct. 22, 1936
Prentiss M. Brown (D)	Nov. 19, 1936	Jan. 2, 1943
Homer Ferguson (R)	Jan. 3, 1943	Jan. 2, 1955
Patrick V. McNamara (D)[17]	Jan. 3, 1955	April 30, 1966
Robert P. Griffin (R)[18]	May 11, 1966	Jan. 2, 1979
Carl Levin (D)	Jan. 3, 1979	

MINNESOTA

(Became a state May 11, 1858)

Class 1

Senators	Dates of Service	
Henry M. Rice (D)	May 11, 1858	March 3, 1863
Alexander Ramsey (R)	March 4, 1863	March 3, 1875
Samuel J. R. McMillan (R)	March 4, 1875	March 3, 1887
Cushman K. Davis (R)[1]	March 4, 1887	Nov. 27, 1900
Charles A. Towne (D)[2]	Dec. 5, 1900	Jan. 23, 1901
Moses E. Clapp (R)	Jan. 23, 1901	March 3, 1917
Frank B. Kellogg (R)	March 4, 1917	March 3, 1923
Henrik Shipstead (F-LAB, R)[3]	March 4, 1923	Jan. 2, 1947
Edward J. Thye (R)	Jan. 3, 1947	Jan. 2, 1959
Eugene J. McCarthy (DFL)	Jan. 3, 1959	Jan. 2, 1971
Hubert H. Humphrey (DFL)[4]	Jan. 3, 1971	Jan. 13, 1978
Muriel Humphrey (DFL)[5]	Jan. 25, 1978	Nov. 7, 1978
Dave Durenberger (IR)	Nov. 8, 1978	

Class 2

Senators	Dates of Service	
James Shields (D)	May 11, 1858	March 3, 1859
Morton S. Wilkinson (R)	March 4, 1859	March 3, 1865
Daniel S. Norton (R)[6]	March 4, 1865	July 13, 1870
William Windom (R)[7]	July 15, 1870	Jan. 22, 1871
Ozora P. Stearns (R)	Jan. 18, 1871	March 3, 1871
William Windom (R)[8]	March 4, 1871	March 4, 1881
A. J. Edgerton (R)[9]	March 12, 1881	Oct. 26, 1881
William Windom (R)	Oct. 27, 1881	March 3, 1883
Dwight M. Sabin (R)	March 4, 1883	March 3, 1889
William D. Washburn (R)	March 4, 1889	March 3, 1895
Knute Nelson (R)[10]	March 4, 1895	April 28, 1923
Magnus Johnson (F-LAB)	July 16, 1923	March 3, 1925
Thomas D. Schall (R)[11]	March 4, 1925	Dec. 22, 1935
Elmer A. Benson (F-LAB)[12]	Dec. 27, 1935	Nov. 3, 1936
Guy V. Howard (R)	Nov. 4, 1936	Jan. 2, 1937
Ernest Lundeen (F-LAB)[13]	Jan. 3, 1937	Aug. 31, 1940
Joseph H. Ball (R)[14]	Oct. 14, 1940	Nov. 17, 1942
Arthur E. Nelson (R)	Nov. 18, 1942	Jan. 2, 1843
Joseph H. Ball (R)	Jan. 3, 1943	Jan. 2, 1949
Hubert H. Humphrey (DFL)[15]	Jan. 3, 1949	Dec. 29, 1964
Walter F. Mondale (DFL)[16]	Dec. 30, 1964	Dec. 30, 1976
Wendell R. Anderson (DFL)[17]	Dec. 30, 1976	Dec. 29, 1978
Rudy Boschwitz (IR)	Dec. 30, 1978	

Michigan
1. Resigned May 29, 1848.
2. Appointed by governor to fill vacancy.
3. Resigned Feb. 10, 1879.
4. Died Nov. 1, 1879.
5. Appointed by governor to fill vacancy. Subsequently elected.
6. Died April 30, 1894.
7. Appointed by governor to fill vacancy.
8. Died March 23, 1928.
9. Appointed by governor to fill vacancy. Subsequently elected. Died April 18, 1951.
10. Appointed by governor to fill vacancy.
11. Died Dec. 26, 1976.
12. Died Oct. 5, 1861.
13. Died Aug. 10, 1902.
14. Appointed by governor to fill vacancy. Subsequently elected. Died Jan. 24, 1907.
15. Resigned Nov. 18, 1922.
16. Appointed by governor to fill vacancy. Subsequently elected. Died Oct. 22, 1936.
17. Died April 30, 1966.
18. Appointed by governor to fill vacancy. Subsequently elected.

Minnesota
1. Died Nov. 27, 1900.
2. Appointed by governor to fill vacancy.
3. Elected as a Farmer-Laborite in 1922, 1928 and 1934, as a Republican in 1940.
4. Died Jan. 13, 1978.
5. Appointed by governor to fill vacancy.
6. Died July 13, 1870.
7. Appointed by governor to fill vacancy.
8. Resigned March 4, 1881.
9. Appointed by governor to fill vacancy.
10. Died April 28, 1923.
11. Died Dec. 22, 1935.
12. Appointed by governor to fill vacancy.
13. Died Aug. 31, 1940.
14. Appointed by governor to fill vacancy.
15. Resigned Dec. 29, 1964, having been elected vice president of the United States.
16. Appointed by governor to fill vacancy. Subsequently elected. Resigned Dec. 30, 1976, having been elected vice president of the United States.
17. Appointed by governor to fill vacancy. Resigned Dec. 29, 1978.

MISSISSIPPI

(Became a state Dec. 10, 1817)

Class 1

Senators	Dates of Service	
Walter Leake (D-R)[1]	Dec. 10, 1817	May 15, 1820
David Holmes (D-R)[2]	Aug. 30, 1820	Sept. 25, 1825
Powhatan Ellis (D-R)[3]	Sept. 28, 1825	Jan. 28, 1826
Thomas B. Reed (D-R)	Jan. 28, 1826	March 3, 1827
Powhatan Ellis (D-R)[4]	March 4, 1827	July 10, 1832
John Black (D, W)[5]	Nov. 12, 1832	Jan. 22, 1838
James F. Trotter (D)[6]	Jan. 22, 1838	July 10, 1838
Thomas Hickman Williams (D)[7]	Nov. 12, 1838	March 3, 1839
John Henderson (W)	March 4, 1839	March 3, 1845
Jesse Speight (D)[8]	March 4, 1845	May 1, 1847
Jefferson Davis (D)[9]	Aug. 10, 1847	Sept. 23, 1851
John J. McRae (D)[10]	Dec. 1, 1851	March 17, 1852
Stephen Adams (D)	March 17, 1852	March 3, 1857
Jefferson Davis (D)[11]	March 4, 1857	March 14, 1861
Adelbert Ames (R)[12]	April 1, 1870	Jan. 10, 1874
Henry R. Pease (R)	Feb. 3, 1874	March 3, 1875
Blanche K. Bruce (R)	March 4, 1875	March 3, 1881
James Z. George (D)[13]	March 4, 1881	Aug. 14, 1897
Hernando D. Money (D)[14]	Oct. 8, 1897	March 3, 1911
John Sharp Williams (D)	March 4, 1911	March 3, 1923
Hubert D. Stephens (D)	March 4, 1923	Jan. 2, 1935
Theodore G. Bilbo (D)[15]	Jan. 3, 1935	Jan. 2, 1947
John C. Stennis (D)	Nov. 5, 1947	

Class 2

Thomas Hill Williams (D-R)	Dec. 10, 1817	March 3, 1829
Thomas B. Reed (D)[16]	March 4, 1829	Nov. 26, 1829
Robert H. Adams (D)[17]	Jan. 6, 1830	July 2, 1830
George Poindexter (D)[18]	Oct. 15, 1830	March 3, 1835
Robert J. Walker (D)[19]	March 4, 1835	March 5, 1845
Joseph W. Chalmers (D)[20]	Nov. 3, 1845	March 3, 1847
Henry Stuart Foote (W)[21]	March 4, 1847	Jan. 8, 1852
Walker Brooke (W)	Feb. 18, 1852	March 3, 1853

Albert G. Brown (D)[22]	March 4, 1853	March 14, 1861
Hiram R. Revels (R)	Feb. 25, 1870	March 3, 1871
James L. Alcorn (R)[23]	Dec. 4, 1871	March 3, 1877
Lucius Q. C. Lamar (D)[24]	March 4, 1877	March 6, 1885
Edward C. Walthall (D)[25]	March 9, 1885	Jan. 24, 1894
Anselm J. McLaurin (D)	Feb. 7, 1894	March 3, 1895
Edward C. Walthall (D)[26]	March 4, 1895	April 21, 1898
William V. Sullivan (D)[27]	May 31, 1898	March 3, 1901
Anselm J. McLaurin (D)[28]	March 4, 1901	Dec. 22, 1909
James Gordon (D)[29]	Dec. 27, 1909	Feb. 22, 1910
Le Roy Percy (D)	Feb. 23, 1910	March 3, 1913
James K. Vardaman (D)	March 4, 1913	March 3, 1919
Pat Harrison (D)[30]	March 4, 1919	June 22, 1941
James O. Eastland (D)[31]	June 30, 1941	Sept. 28, 1941
Wall Doxey (D)	Sept. 29, 1941	Jan. 2, 1943
James O. Eastland (D)[32]	Jan. 3, 1943	Dec. 27, 1978
Thad Cochran (R)	Dec. 27, 1978	

MISSOURI

(Became a state Aug. 10, 1821)

Class 1

Senators	Dates of Service	
Thomas H. Benton (D-R, D)	Aug. 10, 1821	March 3, 1851
Henry S. Geyer (D)	March 4, 1851	March 3, 1857
Trusten Polk (D)[1]	March 4, 1857	Jan. 10, 1862
John B. Henderson (D)[2]	Jan. 17, 1862	March 3, 1869
Carl Schurz (R)	March 4, 1869	March 3, 1875
Francis M. Cockrell (D)	March 4, 1875	March 3, 1905
William Warner (R)	March 18, 1905	March 3, 1911
James A. Reed (D)	March 4, 1911	March 3, 1929
Roscoe C. Patterson (R)	March 4, 1929	Jan. 2, 1935
Harry S Truman (D)[3]	Jan. 3, 1935	Jan. 18, 1945
Frank P. Briggs (D)[4]	Jan. 18, 1945	Jan. 2, 1947
James P. Kem (R)	Jan. 3, 1947	Jan. 2, 1953
Stuart Symington (D)[5]	Jan. 3, 1953	Dec. 27, 1976
John C. Danforth (R)	Dec. 27, 1976	

Mississippi

1. *Resigned May 15, 1820.*
2. *Appointed by governor to fill vacancy. Subsequently elected. Resigned Sept. 25, 1825.*
3. *Appointed by governor to fill vacancy.*
4. *Resigned July 10, 1832.*
5. *Appointed by governor to fill vacancy. Subsequently elected. Resigned Jan. 22, 1838.*
6. *Resigned July 10, 1838.*
7. *Appointed by governor to fill vacancy. Subsequently elected.*
8. *Died May 1, 1847.*
9. *Appointed by governor to fill vacancy. Subsequently elected. Resigned Sept. 23, 1851.*
10. *Appointed by governor to fill vacancy.*
11. *Seat declared vacant March 14, 1861. Vacancy until April 1, 1870, because of Civil War.*
12. *Resigned Jan. 10, 1874.*
13. *Died Aug. 14, 1897.*
14. *Appointed by governor to fill vacancy. Subsequently elected.*
15. *Elected for term beginning Jan. 3, 1947, but was never sworn in. Died Aug. 21, 1947.*
16. *Died Nov. 26, 1829.*
17. *Died July 2, 1830.*
18. *Appointed by governor to fill vacancy. Subsequently elected.*
19. *Resigned March 5, 1845.*
20. *Appointed by governor to fill vacancy. Subsequently elected.*
21. *Resigned Jan. 8, 1852.*
22. *Seat declared vacant March 14, 1861. Vacancy until Feb. 25, 1870, because of Civil War.*
23. *Elected Jan. 18, 1870. Took oath Dec. 4, 1871. Governor during interim.*
24. *Resigned March 6, 1885.*
25. *Appointed by governor to fill vacancy. Subsequently elected. Resigned Jan. 24, 1894.*

26. *Died April 21, 1898.*
27. *Appointed by governor to fill vacancy. Subsequently elected.*
28. *Died Dec. 22, 1909.*
29. *Appointed by governor to fill vacancy.*
30. *Died June 22, 1941.*
31. *Appointed by governor to fill vacancy.*
32. *Resigned Dec. 27, 1978.*

Missouri

1. *Expelled Jan. 10, 1862.*
2. *Appointed by governor to fill vacancy. Subsequently elected.*
3. *Resigned Jan. 18, 1945, having been elected vice president of the United States.*
4. *Appointed by governor to fill vacancy.*
5. *Resigned Dec. 27, 1976.*
6. *Died June 6, 1833.*
7. *Appointed by governor to fill vacancy. Subsequently elected. Died Oct. 3, 1843.*
8. *Appointed by governor to fill vacancy. Subsequently elected.*
9. *Expelled Jan. 10, 1862.*
10. *Appointed by governor to fill vacancy.*
11. *Resigned Dec. 19, 1870.*
12. *Appointed by governor to fill vacancy.*
13. *Died Sept. 20, 1877.*
14. *Appointed by governor to fill vacancy.*
15. *Died April 14, 1918.*
16. *Appointed by governor to fill vacancy.*
17. *Died May 16, 1925.*
18. *Appointed by governor to fill vacancy.*
19. *Resigned Feb. 3, 1933.*
20. *Died Sept. 13, 1960.*
21. *Appointed by governor to fill vacancy. Subsequently elected. Resigned Dec. 27, 1968.*

Class 3

David Barton (D-R)	Aug. 10, 1821	March 3, 1831
Alexander Buckner (D)[6]	March 4, 1831	June 6, 1833
Lewis F. Linn (D)[7]	Oct. 25, 1833	Oct. 3, 1843
David R. Atchison (D)[8]	Oct. 14, 1843	March 3, 1855
James S. Green (D)	Jan. 12, 1857	March 3, 1861
Waldo P. Johnson (D)[9]	March 17, 1861	Jan. 10, 1862
Robert Wilson (UN)[10]	Jan. 17, 1862	Nov. 13, 1863
B. Gratz Brown (D)	Nov. 13, 1863	March 3, 1867
Charles D. Drake (R)[11]	March 4, 1867	Dec. 19, 1870
Daniel T. Jewett (R)[12]	Dec. 19, 1870	Jan. 20, 1871
Francis P. Blair (D)	Jan. 20, 1871	March 3, 1873
Lewis V. Bogy (D)[13]	March 4, 1873	Sept. 20, 1877
David H. Armstrong (D)[14]	Sept. 29, 1877	Jan. 26, 1879
James Shields (D)	Jan. 27, 1879	March 3, 1879
George G. Vest (D)	March 4, 1879	March 3, 1903
William J. Stone (D)[15]	March 4, 1903	April 14, 1918
Xenophon P. Wilfley (D)[16]	April 30, 1918	Nov. 5, 1918
Selden P. Spencer (R)[17]	Nov. 6, 1918	May 16, 1925
George H. Williams (R)[18]	May 25, 1925	Dec. 5, 1926
Harry B. Hawes (D)[19]	Dec. 6, 1926	Feb. 3, 1933
Bennett Champ Clark (D)	Feb. 3, 1933	Jan. 2, 1945
Forrest C. Donnell (R)	Jan. 3, 1945	Jan. 2, 1951
Thomas C. Hennings Jr. (D)[20]	Jan. 3, 1951	Sept. 13, 1960
Edward V. Long (D)[21]	Sept. 23, 1960	Dec. 27, 1968
Thomas F. Eagleton (D)	Dec. 28, 1968	

MONTANA

(Became a state Nov. 8, 1889)

Class 1

Senators	Dates of Service	
Wilbur F. Sanders (R)	Jan. 1, 1890	March 3, 1893
Lee Mantle (R)[1]	Jan. 16, 1895	March 3, 1899
William A. Clark (D)[2]	March 4, 1899	May 15, 1900
Paris Gibson (D)	March 7, 1901	March 3, 1905
Thomas H. Carter (R)	March 4, 1905	March 3, 1911
Henry L. Myers (D)	March 4, 1911	March 3, 1923
Burton K. Wheeler (D)	March 4, 1923	Jan. 2, 1947
Zales N. Ecton (R)	Jan. 3, 1947	Jan. 2, 1953
Mike Mansfield (D)	Jan. 3, 1953	Jan. 2, 1977
John Melcher (D)	Jan. 3, 1977	

Class 2

Thomas C. Power (R)	Jan. 2, 1890	March 3, 1895
Thomas H. Carter (R)	March 4, 1895	March 3, 1901
William A. Clark (D)	March 4, 1901	March 3, 1907
Joseph M. Dixon (R)	March 4, 1907	March 3, 1913

Thomas J. Walsh (D)[3]	March 4, 1913	March 2, 1933
John E. Erickson (D)[4]	March 13, 1933	Nov. 6, 1934
James E. Murray (D)	Nov. 7, 1934	Jan. 2, 1961
Lee Metcalf (D)[5]	Jan. 3, 1961	Jan. 12, 1978
Paul G. Hatfield (D)[6]	Jan. 22, 1978	Dec. 14, 1978
Max Baucus (D)	Dec. 15, 1978	

NEBRASKA

(Became a state March 1, 1867)

Class 1

Senators	Dates of Service	
Thomas W. Tipton (R)	March 1, 1867	March 3, 1875
Algernon S. Paddock (R)	March 4, 1875	March 3, 1881
Charles H. Van Wyck (R)	March 4, 1881	March 3, 1887
Algernon S. Paddock (R)	March 4, 1887	March 3, 1893
William V. Allen (POP)	March 4, 1893	March 3, 1899
Monroe L. Hayward (R)[1]	March 8, 1899	Dec. 5, 1899
William V. Allen (POP)[2]	Dec. 13, 1899	March 28, 1901
Charles H. Dietrich (R)	March 28, 1901	March 3, 1905
Elmer J. Burkett (R)	March 4, 1905	March 3, 1911
Gilbert M. Hitchcock (D)	March 4, 1911	March 3, 1923
Robert B. Howell (R)[3]	March 4, 1923	March 11, 1933
William H. Thompson (D)[4]	May 24, 1933	Nov. 6, 1934
Richard C. Hunter (D)	Nov. 7, 1934	Jan. 2, 1935
Edward R. Burke (D)	Jan. 3, 1935	Jan. 2, 1941
Hugh Butler (R)[5]	Jan. 3, 1941	July 1, 1954
Sam W. Reynolds (R)[6]	July 3, 1954	Nov. 7, 1954
Roman L. Hruska (R)[7]	Nov. 8, 1954	Dec. 27, 1976
Edward Zorinsky (D)	Dec. 28, 1976	

Class 2

John M. Thayer (R)	March 1, 1867	March 3, 1871
Phineas W. Hitchcock (R)	March 4, 1871	March 3, 1877
Alvin Saunders (R)	March 4, 1877	March 3, 1883
Charles F. Manderson (R)	March 4, 1883	March 3, 1895
John M. Thurston (R)	March 4, 1895	March 3, 1901
Joseph H. Millard (R)	March 28, 1901	March 3, 1907
Norris Brown (R)	March 4, 1907	March 3, 1913
George W. Norris (R, I)[8]	March 4, 1913	Jan. 2, 1943
Kenneth S. Wherry (R)[9]	Jan. 3, 1943	Nov. 29, 1951
Fred A. Seaton (R)[10]	Dec. 10, 1951	Nov. 4, 1952
Dwight Griswold (R)[11]	Nov. 5, 1952	Apr. 12, 1954
Eva Bowring (R)[12]	April 16, 1954	Nov. 7, 1954
Hazel H. Abel (R)[13]	Nov. 8, 1954	Dec. 31, 1954
Carl T. Curtis (R)	Jan. 1, 1955	Jan. 2, 1979
J. James Exon (D)	Jan. 3, 1979	

Montana

1. *Vacancy from March 4, 1893, to Jan. 16, 1895, because of failure of Legislature to elect.*
2. *Resigned May 15, 1900.*
3. *Died March 2, 1933.*
4. *Appointed by governor to fill vacancy.*
5. *Died Jan. 12, 1978.*
6. *Appointed by governor to fill vacancy. Resigned Dec. 14, 1978.*

Nebraska

1. *Died Dec. 5, 1899.*
2. *Appointed by governor to fill vacancy.*

3. *Died March 11, 1933.*
4. *Appointed by governor to fill vacancy.*
5. *Died July 1, 1954.*
6. *Appointed by governor to fill vacancy.*
7. *Resigned Dec. 27, 1976.*
8. *Norris elected as Republican in 1912, 1918, 1924 and 1930. Elected as Independent in 1936.*
9. *Died Nov. 29, 1951.*
10. *Appointed by governor to fill vacancy.*
11. *Died April 12, 1954.*
12. *Appointed by governor to fill vacancy.*
13. *Resigned Dec. 31, 1954.*

NEVADA

(Became a state Oct. 31, 1864)

Class 1

Senators	Dates of Service	
William M. Stewart (R)	Dec. 15, 1864	March 3, 1875
William Sharon (R)	March 4, 1875	March 3, 1881
James G. Fair (D)	March 4, 1881	March 3, 1887
William M. Stewart (R)	March 4, 1887	March 3, 1905
George S. Nixon (R)[1]	March 4, 1905	June 5, 1912
William A. Massey (R)[2]	July 1, 1912	Jan. 29, 1913
Key Pittman (D)[3]	Jan. 29, 1913	Nov. 10, 1940
Berkeley L. Bunker (D)[4]	Nov. 27, 1940	Dec. 6, 1942
James G. Scrugham (D)[5]	Dec. 7, 1942	June 23, 1945
E. P. Carville (D)[6]	July 25, 1945	Jan. 2, 1947
George W. Malone (R)	Jan. 3, 1947	Jan. 2, 1959
Howard W. Cannon (D)	Jan. 3, 1959	Jan. 2, 1983
Chic Hecht (R)	Jan. 3, 1983	

Class 3

James W. Nye (R)	Dec. 16, 1864	March 3, 1873
John P. Jones (R)	March 4, 1873	March 3, 1903
Francis G. Newlands (D)[7]	March 4, 1903	Dec. 24, 1917
Charles B. Henderson (D)[8]	Jan. 12, 1918	March 3, 1921
Tasker L. Oddie (R)	March 4, 1921	March 3, 1933
Patrick A. McCarran (D)[9]	March 4, 1933	Sept. 28, 1954
Ernest S. Brown (R)[10]	Oct. 1, 1954	Dec. 1, 1954
Alan Bible (D)[11]	Dec. 2, 1954	Dec. 17, 1974
Paul Laxalt (R)	Dec. 18, 1974	

NEW HAMPSHIRE

(Ratified the Constitution June 21, 1788)

Class 2

Senators	Dates of Service	
Paine Wingate (FED)	March 4, 1789	March 3, 1793
Samuel Livermore[1]	March 4, 1793	June 12, 1801

Simeon Olcott (FED)	June 17, 1801	March 3, 1805
Nicholas Gilman (D-R)[2]	March 4, 1805	May 2, 1814
Thomas W. Thompson	June 24, 1814	March 3, 1817
David L. Morrill (D-R)	March 4, 1817	March 3, 1823
Samuel Bell (D-R, NR, W)	March 4, 1823	March 3, 1835
Henry Hubbard (D)	March 4, 1835	March 3, 1841
Levi Woodbury (D)[3]	March 4, 1841	Nov. 20, 1845
Benning W. Jenness (D)[4]	Dec. 1, 1845	June 13, 1846
Joseph Cilley (D)	June 13, 1846	March 3, 1847
John P. Hale (D)	March 4, 1847	March 3, 1853
Charles G. Atherton (D)[5]	March 4, 1853	Nov. 15, 1853
Jared W. Williams[6]	Nov. 29, 1853	Aug. 3, 1854
John P. Hale (R)	July 30, 1855	March 3, 1865
Aaron H. Cragin (R)	March 4, 1865	March 3, 1877
Edward H. Rollins (R)	March 4, 1877	March 3, 1883
Austin F. Pike (R)[7]	March 4, 1883	Oct. 8, 1886
Person C. Cheney (R)[8]	Nov. 24, 1886	June 14, 1887
William E. Chandler (R)	June 14, 1887	March 3, 1889
Gilman Marston (R)[9]	March 4, 1889	June 18, 1889
William E. Chandler (R)	June 19, 1889	March 3, 1901
Henry E. Burnham (R)	March 4, 1901	March 3, 1913
Henry F. Hollis (D)	March 13, 1913	March 3, 1919
Henry W. Keyes (R)	March 4, 1919	Jan. 2, 1937
Styles Bridges (R)[10]	Jan. 3, 1937	Nov. 26, 1961
Maurice J. Murphy Jr. (R)[11]	Dec. 7, 1961	Nov. 6, 1962
Thomas J. McIntyre (D)	Nov. 7, 1962	Jan. 2, 1979
Gordon J. Humphrey (R)	Jan. 3, 1979	

Class 3

John Langdon (D-R)	March 4, 1789	March 3, 1801
James Sheafe (FED)[12]	March 4, 1801	June 14, 1802
William Plumer (FED)	June 17, 1802	March 3, 1807
Nahum Parker[13]	March 4, 1807	June 1, 1810
Charles Cutts (FED)[14]	June 21, 1810	June 10, 1813
Jeremiah Mason (FED)[15]	June 10, 1813	June 16, 1817
Clement Storer	June 27, 1817	March 3, 1819
John F. Parrott (D-R)	March 4, 1819	March 3, 1825
Levi Woodbury (D-R)	June 16, 1825	March 3, 1831
Isaac Hill (D)[16]	March 4, 1831	May 30, 1836
John Page (D)	June 8, 1836	March 3, 1837
Franklin Pierce (D)[17]	March 4, 1837	Feb. 28, 1842
Leonard Wilcox (D)[18]	March 1, 1842	March 3, 1843
Charles G. Atherton (D)	March 4, 1843	March 3, 1849
Moses Norris Jr. (D)[19]	March 4, 1849	Jan. 11, 1855
John S. Wells [20]	Jan. 16, 1855	March 3, 1855

Nevada
1. Died June 5, 1912.
2. Appointed by governor to fill vacancy.
3. Died Nov. 10, 1940.
4. Appointed by governor to fill vacancy.
5. Died June 23, 1945.
6. Appointed by governor to fill vacancy.
7. Died Dec. 24, 1917.
8. Appointed by governor to fill vacancy. Subsequently elected.
9. Died Sept. 28, 1954.
10. Appointed by governor to fill vacancy.
11. Resigned Dec. 17, 1974.

New Hampshire
1. Resigned June 12, 1801.
2. Died May 2, 1814.
3. Resigned Nov. 20, 1845.
4. Appointed by governor to fill vacancy.
5. Died Nov. 15, 1853.
6. Appointed by governor to fill vacancy. Senate resolution of Aug. 3, 1854, declared that representation under the appointment had expired. Vacancy from Aug. 4, 1854, to July 29, 1855.
7. Died Oct. 8, 1886.
8. Appointed by governor to fill vacancy.
9. Appointed by governor to fill vacancy.
10. Died Nov. 26, 1961.

11. Appointed by governor to fill vacancy.
12. Resigned June 14, 1802.
13. Resigned June 1, 1810.
14. Elected, subsequently appointed by governor to fill vacancy.
15. Resigned June 16, 1817.
16. Resigned May 30, 1836.
17. Resigned Feb. 28, 1842.
18. Appointed by governor to fill vacancy. Subsequently elected.
19. Died Jan. 11, 1855.
20. Appointed by governor to fill vacancy.
21. Died May 26, 1857.
22. Resigned July 27, 1866.
23. Appointed by governor to fill vacancy.
24. Appointed by governor to fill vacancy.
25. Served continuously during this period; twice by election, once by appointment of the governor.
26. Died Aug. 17, 1918.
27. Appointed by governor to fill vacancy.
28. Died July 24, 1953.
29. Appointed by governor to fill vacancy.
30. Resigned Dec. 31, 1974.
31. Appointed by governor to fill vacancy. Wyman and John A. Durkin (D) both claimed to have been elected to the seat for a six-year term beginning Jan. 3, 1975. Neither was seated. After unsuccessfully attempting for seven months to determine the winner, the Senate July 30, 1975, voted to declare the seat vacant effective Aug. 8, 1975.
32. Appointed by governor to fill vacancy.
33. Won special election Sept. 16, 1975. Resigned Dec. 29, 1980.

James Bell (R)[21]	July 30, 1855	May 26, 1857
Daniel Clark (R)[22]	June 27, 1857	July 27, 1866
George G. Fogg (R)[23]	Aug. 31, 1866	March 3, 1867
James E. Patterson (R)	March 4, 1867	March 3, 1873
Bainbridge Wadleigh (R)	March 4, 1873	March 3, 1879
Charles H. Bell (R)[24]	March 13, 1879	June 16, 1879
Henry W. Blair (R)[25]	June 17, 1879	March 3, 1891
Jacob H. Gallinger (R)[26]	March 4, 1891	Aug. 17, 1918
Irving W. Drew (R)[27]	Sept. 2, 1918	Nov. 5, 1918
George H. Moses (R)	Nov. 6, 1918	March 3, 1933
Fred H. Brown (D)	March 4, 1933	Jan. 2, 1939
Charles W. Tobey (R)[28]	Jan. 3, 1939	July 24, 1953
Robert W. Upton (R)[29]	Aug. 14, 1953	Nov. 7, 1954
Norris Cotton (R)[30]	Nov. 8, 1954	Dec. 31, 1974
Louis C. Wyman (R)[31]	Jan. 1, 1975	Jan. 2, 1975
Norris Cotton (R)[32]	Aug. 8, 1975	Sept. 18, 1975
John A. Durkin (D)[33]	Sept. 18, 1975	Dec. 29, 1980
Warren B. Rudman (R)	Dec. 29, 1980	

NEW JERSEY

(Ratified the Constitution Dec. 18, 1787)

Class 1

Senators	Dates of Service	
Jonathan Elmer (FED)	March 4, 1789	March 3, 1791
John Rutherfurd (FED)[1]	March 4, 1791	Nov. 26, 1798
Franklin Davenport[2]	Dec. 5, 1798	March 3, 1799
James Schureman[3]	March 4, 1799	Feb. 16, 1801
Aaron Ogden (FED)	Feb. 28, 1801	March 3, 1803
John Condit (D-R)[4]	Sept. 1, 1803	March 3, 1809
John Lambert	March 4, 1809	March 3, 1815
James J. Wilson (D-R)[5]	March 4, 1815	Jan. 8, 1821
Samuel L. Southard (D-R)[6]	Jan. 26, 1821	March 3, 1823
Joseph McIlvaine (D-R)[7]	Nov. 12, 1823	Aug. 19, 1826
Ephraim Bateman (D-R)[8]	Nov. 10, 1826	Jan. 12, 1829
Mahlon Dickerson (D)	Jan. 30, 1829	March 3, 1833
Samuel L. Southard (NR, W)[9]	March 4, 1833	June 26, 1842
William L. Dayton (W)[10]	July 2, 1842	March 3, 1851
Robert F. Stockton (D)[11]	March 4, 1851	Jan. 10, 1853
John R. Thomson (D)[12]	March 4, 1853	Sept. 12, 1862
Richard S. Field (R)[13]	Nov. 21, 1862	Jan. 14, 1863
James W. Wall (D)	Jan. 14, 1863	March 3, 1863
William Wright (D)[14]	March 4, 1863	Nov. 1, 1866
Frederick T. Frelinghuysen (R)[15]	Nov. 12, 1866	March 3, 1869
John P. Stockton (D)	March 4, 1869	March 3, 1875

Class 2

Theodore F. Randolph (D)	March 4, 1875	March 3, 1881
William J. Sewell (R)	March 4, 1881	March 3, 1887
Rufus Blodgett (D)	March 4, 1887	March 3, 1893
James Smith Jr. (D)	March 4, 1893	March 3, 1899
John Kean (R)	March 4, 1899	March 3, 1911
James E. Martine (D)	March 4, 1911	March 3, 1917
Joseph S. Frelinghuysen (R)	March 4, 1917	March 3, 1923
Edward I. Edwards (D)	March 4, 1923	March 3, 1929
Hamilton F. Kean (R)	March 4, 1929	Jan. 2, 1935
A. Harry Moore (D)[16]	Jan. 3, 1935	Jan. 18, 1938
John Milton (D)[17]	Jan. 18, 1938	Nov. 8, 1938
W. Warren Barbour (R)[18]	Nov. 9, 1938	Nov. 22, 1943
Arthur Walsh (D)[19]	Nov. 26, 1943	Dec. 6, 1944
H. Alexander Smith (R)	Dec. 7, 1944	Jan. 2, 1959
Harrison A. Williams Jr. (D)[20]	Jan. 3, 1959	March 11, 1982
Nicholas F. Brady (R)[21]	April 20, 1982	Dec. 27, 1982
Frank R. Lautenberg (D)	Dec. 27, 1982	

Class 2

William Paterson (FED)[22]	March 4, 1789	Nov. 13, 1790
Philemon Dickinson	Nov. 23, 1790	March 3, 1793
Frederick Frelinghuysen (FED)[23]	March 4, 1793	Nov. 12, 1796
Richard Stockton (FED)	Nov. 12, 1796	March 3, 1799
Jonathan Dayton	March 4, 1799	March 3, 1805
Aaron Kitchell[24]	March 4, 1805	March 12, 1809
John Condit (D-R)[25]	March 21, 1809	March 3, 1817
Mahlon Dickerson (D-R)[26]	March 4, 1817	Jan. 30, 1829
Theodore Frelinghuysen (NR)	March 4, 1829	March 3, 1835
Garret D. Wall (D)	March 4, 1835	March 3, 1841
Jacob W. Miller (W)	March 4, 1841	March 3, 1853
William Wright (D)	March 4, 1853	March 3, 1859
John C. Ten Eyck (R)	March 4, 1859	March 3, 1865
John P. Stockton (D)[27]	March 4, 1865	March 27, 1866
Alexander G. Cattell (R)	Sept. 19, 1866	March 3, 1871
Frederick T. Frelinghuysen (R)	March 4, 1871	March 3, 1877
John R. McPherson (D)	March 4, 1877	March 3, 1895
William J. Sewell (R)[28]	March 4, 1895	Dec. 27, 1901
John F. Dryden (R)	Jan. 29, 1902	March 3, 1907
Frank O. Briggs (R)	March 4, 1907	March 3, 1913
Wiliam Hughes (D)[29]	March 4, 1913	Jan. 30, 1918
David Baird (R)[30]	Feb. 23, 1918	March 3, 1919
Walter E. Edge (R)[31]	March 4, 1919	Nov. 21, 1929
David Baird Jr. (R)[32]	Nov. 30, 1929	Dec. 2, 1930
Dwight W. Morrow (R)[33]	Dec. 3, 1930	Oct. 5, 1931
W. Warren Barbour (R)[34]	Dec. 1, 1931	Jan. 2, 1937
William H. Smathers (D)	April 15, 1937	Jan. 2, 1943
Albert W. Hawkes (R)	Jan. 3, 1943	Jan. 2, 1949
Robert C. Hendrickson (R)	Jan. 3, 1949	Jan. 2, 1955
Clifford P. Case (R)	Jan. 3, 1955	Jan. 2, 1979
Bill Bradley (D)	Jan. 3, 1979	

New Jersey

1. *Resigned Nov. 26, 1798.*
2. *Appointed by governor to fill vacancy.*
3. *Resigned Feb. 16, 1801.*
4. *Appointed by governor to fill vacancy. Subsequently elected.*
5. *Resigned Jan. 8, 1821.*
6. *Appointed by governor to fill vacancy. Subsequently elected. Resigned March 3, 1823.*
7. *Died Aug. 19, 1826.*
8. *Resigned Jan. 12, 1829.*
9. *Died June 26, 1842.*
10. *Appointed by governor to fill vacancy. Subsequently elected.*
11. *Resigned Jan. 10, 1853.*
12. *Died Sept. 12, 1862.*
13. *Appointed by governor to fill vacancy.*
14. *Died Nov. 1, 1866.*
15. *Appointed by governor to fill vacancy. Subsequently elected.*
16. *Resigned Jan. 18, 1938.*

17. *Appointed by governor to fill vacancy.*
18. *Died Nov. 22, 1943.*
19. *Appointed by governor to fill vacancy.*
20. *Resigned March 11, 1982.*
21. *Appointed by governor to fill vacancy. Resigned Dec. 27, 1982.*
22. *Resigned Nov. 13, 1790.*
23. *Resigned Nov. 12, 1796.*
24. *Resigned March 12, 1809.*
25. *Appointed by governor to fill vacancy. Subsequently elected.*
26. *Resigned Jan. 30, 1829.*
27. *Seat declared vacant March 27, 1866.*
28. *Died Dec. 27, 1901.*
29. *Died Jan. 30, 1918.*
30. *Appointed by governor to fill vacancy. Subsequently elected.*
31. *Resigned Nov. 21, 1929.*
32. *Appointed by governor to fill vacancy.*
33. *Died Oct. 5, 1931.*
34. *Appointed by governor to fill vacancy. Subsequently elected.*

NEW MEXICO

(Became a state Jan. 6, 1912)

Class 1

Senators	Dates of Service	
Thomas B. Catron (R)	March 27, 1912	March 3, 1917
Andrieus A. Jones (D)[1]	March 4, 1917	Dec. 20, 1927
Bronson Cutting (R)[2]	Dec. 29, 1927	Dec. 6, 1928
Octaviano A. Larrazolo (R)	Dec. 7, 1928	March 3, 1929
Bronson Cutting (R)[3]	March 4, 1929	May 6, 1935
Dennis Chavez (D)[4]	May 11, 1935	Nov. 18, 1962
Edwin L. Mechem (R)[5]	Nov. 30, 1962	Nov. 3, 1964
Joseph M. Montoya (D)	Nov. 4, 1964	Jan. 2, 1977
Harrison (Jack) Schmitt (R)	Jan. 3, 1977	Jan. 2, 1983
Jeff Bingaman (D)	Jan. 3, 1983	

Class 2

Senators	Dates of Service	
Albert B. Fall (R)[6]	March 27, 1912	March 4, 1921
Holm O. Bursum (R)[7]	March 11, 1921	March 3, 1925
Sam G. Bratton (D)[8]	March 4, 1925	June 24, 1933
Carl A. Hatch (D)[9]	Oct. 10, 1933	Jan. 2, 1949
Clinton P. Anderson (D)	Jan. 3, 1949	Jan. 2, 1973
Pete V. Domenici (R)	Jan. 3, 1973	

NEW YORK

(Ratified the Constitution July 26, 1788)

Class 1

Senators	Dates of Service	
Philip Schuyler (FED)	July 15, 1789	March 3, 1791
Aaron Burr (D-R)	March 4, 1791	March 3, 1797
Philip Schuyler (FED)[1]	March 4, 1797	Jan. 3, 1798
John S. Hobart (FED)[2]	Jan. 11, 1798	April 16, 1798
William North (FED)[3]	May 5, 1798	Aug. 17, 1798
James Watson (FED)[4]	Aug. 17, 1798	March 19, 1800
Gouverneur Morris (FED)	April 3, 1800	March 3, 1803
Theodorus Bailey (D-R)[5]	March 4, 1803	Jan. 16, 1804
John Armstrong (D-R)[6]	Feb. 4, 1804	June 30, 1804

Samuel L. Mitchill (D-R)	Nov. 9, 1804	March 3, 1809
Obadiah German (D-R)	March 4, 1809	March 3, 1815
Nathan Sanford (D-R)	March 4, 1815	March 3, 1821
Martin Van Buren (D-R)[7]	March 4, 1821	Dec. 20, 1828
Charles E. Dudley (D)	Jan. 15, 1829	March 3, 1833
Nathaniel P. Tallmadge (D)[8]	March 4, 1833	June 17, 1844
Daniel S. Dickinson (D)[9]	Nov. 30, 1844	March 3, 1851
Hamilton Fish (W)	March 4, 1851	March 3, 1857
Preston King (R)	March 4, 1857	March 3, 1863
Edwin D. Morgan (R)	March 4, 1863	March 3, 1869
Reuben E. Fenton (R)	March 4, 1869	March 3, 1875
Francis Kernan (D)	March 4, 1875	March 3, 1881
Thomas C. Platt (R)[10]	March 4, 1881	May 16, 1881
Warner Miller (R)	July 16, 1881	March 3, 1887
Frank Hiscock (R)	March 4, 1887	March 3, 1893
Edward Murphy Jr. (D)	March 4, 1893	March 3, 1899
Chauncey M. Depew (R)	March 4, 1899	March 3, 1911
James A. O'Gorman (D)	March 31, 1911	March 3, 1917
William M. Calder (R)	March 4, 1917	March 3, 1923
Royal S. Copeland (D)[11]	March 4, 1923	June 17, 1938
James M. Mead (D)	Dec. 3, 1938	Jan. 2, 1947
Irving M. Ives (R)	Jan. 3, 1947	Jan. 2, 1959
Kenneth B. Keating (R)	Jan. 3, 1959	Jan. 2, 1965
Robert F. Kennedy (D)[12]	Jan. 3, 1965	June 6, 1968
Charles E. Goodell (R)[13]	Sept. 10, 1968	Jan. 2, 1971
James L. Buckley (C-R)	Jan. 3, 1971	Jan. 2, 1977
Daniel Patrick Moynihan (D)	Jan. 3, 1977	

Class 3

Rufus King (FED)[14]	July 16, 1789	May 23, 1796
John Laurance (FED)[15]	Nov. 9, 1796	Aug. 1800
John Armstrong (D-R)[16]	Nov. 6, 1800	Feb. 5, 1802
De Witt Clinton (D-R)[17]	Feb. 9, 1802	Nov. 4, 1803
John Armstrong (D-R)[18]	Nov. 10, 1803	Feb. 4, 1804
John Smith (D-R)	Feb. 4, 1804	March 3, 1813
Rufus King (FED)	March 4, 1813	March 3, 1825
Nathan Sanford (D-R)	Jan. 14, 1826	March 3, 1831
William L. Marcy (D)[19]	March 4, 1831	Jan. 1, 1833
Silas Wright Jr. (D)[20]	Jan. 4, 1833	Nov. 26, 1844
Henry A. Foster (D)[21]	Nov. 30, 1844	Jan. 18, 1845
John A. Dix (D)	Jan. 18, 1845	March 3, 1849
William H. Seward (W)	March 4, 1849	March 3, 1861
Ira Harris (R)	March 4, 1861	March 3, 1867
Roscoe Conkling (R)[22]	March 4, 1867	May 16, 1881
Elbridge G. Lapham (R)	July 22, 1881	March 3, 1885
William M. Evarts (R)	March 4, 1885	March 3, 1891
David B. Hill (D)	Jan. 7, 1892	March 3, 1897

New Mexico

1. *Died Dec. 20, 1927.*
2. *Appointed by governor to fill vacancy.*
3. *Died May 6, 1935.*
4. *Appointed by governor to fill vacancy. Subsequently elected. Died Nov. 18, 1962.*
5. *Appointed by governor to fill vacancy.*
6. *Resigned March 4, 1921.*
7. *Appointed by governor to fill vacancy. Subsequently elected.*
8. *Resigned June 24, 1933.*
9. *Appointed by governor to fill vacancy. Subsequently elected.*

New York

1. *Resigned Jan. 3, 1798.*
2. *Resigned April 16, 1798.*
3. *Appointed by governor to fill vacancy.*
4. *Resigned March 19, 1800.*
5. *Resigned Jan. 16, 1804.*
6. *Resigned June 30, 1804.*

7. *Resigned Dec. 20, 1828.*
8. *Resigned June 17, 1844.*
9. *Appointed by governor to fill vacancy. Subsequently elected.*
10. *Resigned May 16, 1881.*
11. *Died June 17, 1938.*
12. *Died June 6, 1968.*
13. *Appointed by governor to fill vacancy.*
14. *Resigned May 23, 1796.*
15. *Resigned in August 1800.*
16. *Resigned Feb. 5, 1802.*
17. *Resigned Nov. 4, 1803.*
18. *Appointed by governor to fill vacancy.*
19. *Resigned Jan. 1, 1833.*
20. *Resigned Nov. 26, 1844.*
21. *Appointed by governor to fill vacancy.*
22. *Resigned May 16, 1881.*
23. *Resigned June 28, 1949.*
24. *Appointed by governor to fill vacancy.*

Thomas C. Platt (R)	March 4, 1897	March 3, 1909
Elihu Root (R)	March 4, 1909	March 3, 1915
James W. Wadsworth Jr. (R)	March 4, 1915	March 3, 1927
Robert F. Wagner (D)[23]	March 4, 1927	June 28, 1949
John Foster Dulles (R)[24]	July 7, 1949	Nov. 8, 1949
Herbert H. Lehman (D)	Nov. 9, 1949	Jan. 2, 1957
Jacob K. Javits (R)	Jan. 9, 1957	Jan. 2, 1981
Alphonse M. D'Amato (R)	Jan. 3, 1981	

NORTH CAROLINA

(Ratified the Constitution Nov. 21, 1789)

Class 2

Senators	Dates of Service	
Samuel Johnston (FED)	Nov. 27, 1789	March 3, 1793
Alexander Martin (D-R)	March 4, 1793	March 3, 1799
Jesse Franklin (D-R)	March 4, 1799	March 3, 1805
James Turner (D-R)[1]	March 4, 1805	Nov. 21, 1816
Montfort Stokes (D-R)	Dec. 4, 1816	March 3, 1823
John Branch (D-R)[2]	March 4, 1823	March 9, 1829
Bedford Brown (D)[3]	Dec. 9, 1829	Nov. 11, 1840
Willie P. Mangum (W)	Nov. 25, 1840	March 3, 1853
David S. Reid (D)[4]	Dec. 6, 1854	March 3, 1859
Thomas Bragg (D)[5]	March 4, 1859	July 11, 1861
Joseph C. Abbott (R)	July 17, 1868	March 3, 1871
Matt W. Ransom (D)	Jan. 30, 1872	March 3, 1895
Marion Butler (POP)	March 4, 1895	March 3, 1901
Furnifold M. Simmons (D)	March 4, 1901	March 3, 1931
Josiah W. Bailey (D)[6]	March 4, 1931	Dec. 15, 1946
William B. Umstead (D)[7]	Dec. 18, 1946	Dec. 30, 1948
J. Melville Broughton (D)[8]	Dec. 31, 1948	March 6, 1949
Frank P. Graham (D)[9]	March 29, 1949	Nov. 26, 1950
Willis Smith (D)[10]	Nov. 27, 1950	June 23, 1953
Alton A. Lennon (D)[11]	July 10, 1953	Nov. 28, 1954
W. Kerr Scott (D)[12]	Nov. 29, 1954	April 16, 1958
B. Everett Jordan (D)[13]	April 19, 1958	Jan. 2, 1973
Jesse Helms (R)	Jan. 3, 1973	

Class 3

Benjamin Hawkins (FED)	Nov. 27, 1789	March 3, 1795
Timothy Bloodworth (D-R)	March 4, 1795	March 3, 1801
David Stone (D-R)[14]	March 4, 1801	Feb. 17, 1807
Jesse Franklin (D-R)	March 4, 1807	March 3, 1813

David Stone (D-R)[15]	March 4, 1813	Dec. 24, 1814
Francis Locke (D-R)[16]		
Nathaniel Macon (D-R)[17]	Dec. 5, 1815	Nov. 14, 1828
James Iredell (D-R)	Dec. 15, 1828	March 3, 1831
Willie P. Mangum (D)[18]	March 4, 1831	Nov. 26, 1836
Robert Strange (D)[19]	Dec. 5, 1836	Nov. 16, 1840
William A. Graham (W)	Nov. 25, 1840	March 3, 1843
William H. Haywood Jr. (D)[20]	March 4, 1843	July 25, 1846
George E. Badger (W)	Nov. 25, 1846	March 3, 1855
Asa Biggs (D)[21]	March 4, 1855	May 5, 1858
Thomas L. Clingman (D)[22]	May 6, 1858	July 11, 1861
John Pool (R)	July 17, 1868	March 3, 1873
Augustus S. Merrimon (D)	March 4, 1873	March 3, 1879
Zebulon B. Vance (D)[23]	March 4, 1879	April 14, 1894
Thomas J. Jarvis (D)[24]	April 19, 1894	Jan. 23, 1895
Jeter C. Pritchard (R)	Jan. 23, 1895	March 3, 1903
Lee S. Overman (D)[25]	March 4, 1903	Dec. 12, 1930
Cameron Morrison (D)[26]	Dec. 13, 1930	Dec. 4, 1932
Robert R. Reynolds (D)	Dec. 5, 1932	Jan. 2, 1945
Clyde R. Hoey (D)[27]	Jan. 3, 1945	May 12, 1954
Sam J. Ervin Jr. (D)[28]	June 5, 1954	Dec. 31, 1974
Robert Morgan (D)	Jan. 3, 1975	Jan. 2, 1981
John P. East (R)	Jan. 3, 1981	

NORTH DAKOTA

(Became a state Nov. 2, 1889)

Class 1

Senators	Dates of Service	
Lyman R. Casey (R)	Nov. 25, 1889	March 3, 1893
William N. Roach (D)	March 4, 1893	March 3, 1899
Porter J. McCumber (R)	March 4, 1899	March 3, 1923
Lynn J. Frazier (R)	March 4, 1923	Jan. 2, 1941
William Langer (R)[1]	Jan. 3, 1941	Nov. 8, 1959
C. Norman Brunsdale (R)[2]	Nov. 19, 1959	Aug. 7, 1960
Quentin N. Burdick (D)	Aug. 8, 1960	

Class 3

Gilbert A. Pierce (R)	Nov. 21, 1889	March 3, 1891
Henry C. Hansbrough (R)	March 4, 1891	March 3, 1909
Martin N. Johnson (R)[3]	March 4, 1909	Oct. 21, 1909
Fountain L. Thompson (D)[4]	Nov. 10, 1909	Jan. 31, 1910
William E. Purcell (D)[5]	Feb. 1, 1910	Feb. 1, 1911

North Carolina
1. *Resigned Nov. 21, 1816.*
2. *Resigned March 9, 1829.*
3. *Resigned Nov. 11, 1840.*
4. *Vacancy from March 4, 1853, to Dec. 6, 1854.*
5. *Expelled July 11, 1861. Vacancy until July 17, 1868, because of Civil War.*
6. *Died Dec. 15, 1946.*
7. *Appointed by governor to fill vacancy.*
8. *Died March 6, 1949.*
9. *Appointed by governor to fill vacancy.*
10. *Died June 23, 1953.*
11. *Appointed by governor to fill vacancy.*
12. *Died April 16, 1958.*
13. *Appointed by governor to fill vacancy. Subsequently elected.*
14. *Approximate date of resignation, Feb. 17, 1807.*
15. *Resigned Dec. 24, 1814.*
16. *Elected in 1814 but never seated. Did not qualify. Resigned Dec. 5, 1815.*
17. *Resigned Nov. 14, 1828.*
18. *Resigned Nov. 26, 1836.*
19. *Resigned Nov. 16, 1840.*
20. *Resigned July 25, 1846.*

21. *Resigned May 5, 1858.*
22. *Appointed by governor to fill vacancy. Subsequently elected. Expelled July 11, 1861. Vacancy until July 17, 1868, because of Civil War.*
23. *Died April 14, 1894.*
24. *Appointed by governor to fill vacancy.*
25. *Died Dec. 12, 1930.*
26. *Appointed by governor to fill vacancy.*
27. *Died May 12, 1954.*
28. *Appointed by governor to fill vacancy. Subsequently elected. Resigned Dec. 31, 1974.*

North Dakota
1. *Died Nov. 8, 1959.*
2. *Appointed by governor to fill vacancy.*
3. *Died Oct. 21, 1909.*
4. *Appointed by governor to fill vacancy. Resigned Jan. 31, 1910.*
5. *Appointed by governor to fill vacancy.*
6. *Died June 22, 1925.*
7. *Appointed by governor to fill vacancy. Subsequently elected.*
8. *Died March 3, 1945.*
9. *Appointed by governor to fill vacancy. Subsequently elected.*

Asle J. Gronna (R)	Feb. 2, 1911	March 3, 1921
Edwin F. Ladd (R)[6]	March 4, 1921	June 22, 1925
Gerald P. Nye (R)[7]	Nov. 14, 1925	Jan. 2, 1945
John Moses (D)[8]	Jan. 3, 1945	March 3, 1945
Milton R. Young (R)[9]	March 12, 1945	Jan. 2, 1981
Mark Andrews (R)	Jan. 3, 1981	

OHIO

(Became a state March 1, 1803)

Class 1

Senators	Dates of Service	
John Smith (D-R)[1]	April 1, 1803	April 25, 1808
Return J. Meigs Jr. (D-R)[2]	Dec. 12, 1808	May 10, 1810
Thomas Worthington (D-R)[3]	Dec. 15, 1810	Dec. 1, 1814
Joseph Kerr (D-R)	Dec. 10, 1814	March 3, 1815
Benjamin Ruggles (D-R)	March 4, 1815	March 3, 1833
Thomas Morris (D)	March 4, 1833	March 3, 1839
Benjamin Tappan (D)	March 4, 1839	March 3, 1845
Thomas Corwin (W)[4]	March 4, 1845	July 20, 1850
Thomas Ewing (W)[5]	July 20, 1850	March 3, 1851
Benjamin F. Wade (W, R)	March 15, 1851	March 3, 1869
Allen G. Thurman (D)	March 4, 1869	March 3, 1881
John Sherman (R)[6]	March 4, 1881	March 5, 1897
Marcus A. Hanna (R)[7]	March 5, 1897	Feb. 15, 1904
Charles W. F. Dick (R)	March 2, 1904	March 3, 1911
Atlee Pomerene (D)	March 4, 1911	March 3, 1923
Simeon D. Fess (R)	March 4, 1923	Jan. 2, 1935
Vic Donahey (D)	Jan. 3, 1935	Jan. 2, 1941
Harold H. Burton (R)[8]	Jan. 3, 1941	Sept. 30, 1945
James W. Huffman (D)[9]	Oct. 8, 1945	Nov. 5, 1946
Kingsley A. Taft (R)	Nov. 6, 1946	Jan. 2, 1947
John W. Bricker (R)	Jan. 3, 1947	Jan. 2, 1959
Stephen M. Young (D)	Jan. 3, 1959	Jan. 2, 1971
Robert Taft Jr. (R)[10]	Jan. 3, 1971	Dec. 28, 1976
Howard M. Metzenbaum (D)	Dec. 29, 1976	

Class 3

Thomas Worthington (D-R)	April 1, 1803	March 3, 1807
Edward Tiffin (D-R)[11]	March 4, 1807	March 3, 1809
Stanley Griswold (D-R)[12]	May 18, 1809	Dec. 11, 1809
Alexander Campbell (D-R)	Dec. 11, 1809	March 3, 1813
Jeremiah Morrow (D-R)	March 4, 1813	March 3, 1819
William A. Trimble (D-R)[13]	March 4, 1819	Dec. 13, 1821
Ethan Allen Brown (D-R)	Jan. 3, 1822	March 3, 1825
William H. Harrison (D-R)[14]	March 4, 1825	May 20, 1828
Jacob Burnet	Dec. 10, 1828	March 3, 1831
Thomas Ewing (NR, W)	March 4, 1831	March 3, 1837

William Allen (D)	March 4, 1837	March 3, 1849
Salmon P. Chase (F SOIL D)	March 4, 1849	March 3, 1855
George E. Pugh (D)	March 4, 1855	March 3, 1861
Salmon P. Chase (R)[15]	March 4, 1861	March 6, 1861
John Sherman (R)[16]	March 21, 1861	March 8, 1877
Stanley Matthews (R)	March 21, 1877	March 3, 1879
George H. Pendleton (D)	March 4, 1879	March 3, 1885
Henry B. Payne (D)	March 4, 1885	March 3, 1891
Calvin S. Brice (D)	March 4, 1891	March 3, 1897
Joseph B. Foraker (R)	March 4, 1897	March 3, 1909
Theodore E. Burton (R)	March 4, 1909	March 3, 1915
Warren G. Harding (R)[17]	March 4, 1915	Jan. 13, 1921
Frank B. Willis (R)[18]	Jan. 14, 1921	March 30, 1928
Cyrus Locher (D)[19]	April 4, 1928	Dec. 14, 1928
Theodore E. Burton (R)[20]	Dec. 15, 1928	Oct. 28, 1929
Roscoe C. McCulloch (R)[21]	Nov. 5, 1929	Nov. 30, 1930
Robert J. Bulkley (D)	Dec. 1, 1930	Jan. 2, 1939
Robert A. Taft (R)[22]	Jan. 3, 1939	July 31, 1953
Thomas A. Burke (D)[23]	Nov. 10, 1953	Dec. 2, 1954
George H. Bender (R)	Dec. 16, 1954	Jan. 2, 1957
Frank J. Lausche (D)	Jan. 3, 1957	Jan. 2, 1969
William B. Saxbe (R)[24]	Jan. 3, 1969	Jan. 4, 1974
Howard M. Metzenbaum (D)[25]	Jan. 4, 1974	Dec. 23, 1974
John Glenn (D)	Dec. 23, 1974	

OKLAHOMA

(Became a state Nov. 16, 1907)

Class 2

Senators	Dates of Service	
Robert L. Owen (D)	Dec. 11, 1907	March 3, 1925
William B. Pine (R)	March 4, 1925	March 3, 1931
Thomas P. Gore (D)	March 4, 1931	Jan. 2, 1937
Josh Lee (D)	Jan. 3, 1937	Jan. 2, 1943
Edward H. Moore (R)	Jan. 3, 1943	Jan. 2, 1949
Robert S. Kerr (D)[1]	Jan. 3, 1949	Jan. 1, 1963
J. Howard Edmondson (D)[2]	Jan. 7, 1963	Nov. 3, 1964
Fred R. Harris (D)	Nov. 4, 1964	Jan. 2, 1973
Dewey F. Bartlett (R)	Jan. 3, 1973	Jan. 2, 1979
David L. Boren (D)	Jan. 3, 1979	

Class 3

Thomas P. Gore (D)	Dec. 11, 1907	March 3, 1921
John W. Harreld (R)	March 4, 1921	March 3, 1927
Elmer Thomas (D)	March 4, 1927	Jan. 2, 1951
A. S. Mike Monroney (D)	Jan. 3, 1951	Jan. 2, 1969
Henry Bellmon (R)	Jan. 3, 1969	Jan. 2, 1981
Don Nickles (R)	Jan. 3, 1981	

Ohio
1. *Resigned April 25, 1808.*
2. *Resigned May 10, 1810.*
3. *Resigned Dec. 1, 1814.*
4. *Resigned July 20, 1850.*
5. *Appointed by governor to fill vacancy.*
6. *Resigned March 5, 1897.*
7. *Appointed by governor to fill vacancy. Subsequently elected. Died Feb. 15, 1904.*
8. *Resigned Sept. 30, 1945.*
9. *Appointed by governor to fill vacancy.*
10. *Resigned Dec. 28, 1976.*
11. *Resigned March 3, 1809.*
12. *Appointed by governor to fill vacancy.*
13. *Died Dec. 13, 1821.*
14. *Resigned May 20, 1828.*

15. *Resigned March 6, 1861.*
16. *Resigned March 8, 1877.*
17. *Resigned Jan. 13, 1921, to become president of the United States.*
18. *Died March 30, 1928.*
19. *Appointed by governor to fill vacancy.*
20. *Died Oct. 28, 1929.*
21. *Appointed by governor to fill vacancy.*
22. *Died July 31, 1953.*
23. *Appointed by governor to fill vacancy.*
24. *Resigned Jan. 4, 1974.*
25. *Appointed by governor to fill vacancy. Resigned Dec. 23, 1974.*

Oklahoma
1. *Died Jan. 1, 1963.*
2. *Appointed by governor to fill vacancy.*

OREGON

(Became a state Feb. 14, 1859)

Class 2

Senators	Dates of Service	
Delazon Smith (D)	Feb. 14, 1859	March 3, 1859
Edward D. Baker (R)[1]	Oct. 2, 1860	Oct. 21, 1861
Benjamin Stark (D)[2]	Oct. 29, 1861	Sept. 12, 1862
Benjamin F. Harding (R)	Sept. 12, 1862	March 3, 1865
George H. Williams (R)	March 4, 1865	March 3, 1871
James K. Kelly (D)	March 4, 1871	March 3, 1877
La Fayette Grover (D)	March 4, 1877	March 3, 1883
Joseph N. Dolph (R)	March 4, 1883	March 3, 1895
George W. McBride (R)	March 4, 1895	March 3, 1901
John H. Mitchell (R)[3]	March 4, 1901	Dec. 8, 1905
John M. Gearin (D)[4]	Dec. 13, 1905	Jan. 23, 1907
Frederick W. Mulkey (R)	Jan. 23, 1907	March 3, 1907
Jonathan Bourne Jr. (R)	March 4, 1907	March 3, 1913
Harry Lane (D)[5]	March 4, 1913	May 23, 1917
Charles L. McNary (R)[6]	May 29, 1917	Nov. 5, 1918
Frederick W. Mulkey (R)[7]	Nov. 6, 1918	Dec. 17, 1918
Charles L. McNary (R)[8]	Dec. 18, 1918	Feb. 25, 1944
Guy Cordon (R)[9]	March 4, 1944	Jan. 2, 1955
Richard L. Neuberger (D)[10]	Jan. 3, 1955	March 9, 1960
Hall S. Lusk (D)[11]	March 16, 1960	Nov. 8, 1960
Maurine B. Neuberger (D)	Nov. 9, 1960	Jan. 2, 1967
Mark O. Hatfield (R)	Jan. 10, 1967	

Class 3

Joseph Lane (D)	Feb. 14, 1859	March 3, 1861
James W. Nesmith (D)	March 4, 1861	March 3, 1867
Henry W. Corbett (R)	March 4, 1867	March 3, 1873
John H. Mitchell (R)	March 4, 1873	March 3, 1879
James H. Slater (D)	March 4, 1879	March 3, 1885
John H. Mitchell (R)	Nov. 18, 1885	March 3, 1897
Joseph Simon (R)[12]	Oct. 8, 1898	March 3, 1903
Charles W. Fulton (R)	March 4, 1903	March 3, 1909
George E. Chamberlain (D)	March 4, 1909	March 3, 1921
Robert N. Stanfield (R)	March 4, 1921	March 3, 1927
Frederick Steiwer (R)[13]	March 4, 1927	Jan. 31, 1938
Alfred Evan Reames (D)[14]	Feb. 1, 1938	Nov. 8, 1938

Alexander G. Barry (R)	Nov. 9, 1938	Jan. 2, 1939
Rufus C. Holman (R)	Jan. 3, 1939	Jan. 2, 1945
Wayne L. Morse (R, I, D)[15]	Jan. 3, 1945	Jan. 2, 1969
Bob Packwood (R)	Jan. 3, 1969	

PENNSYLVANIA

(Ratified the Constitution Dec. 12, 1787)

Class 1

Senators	Dates of Service	
William Maclay (D-R)[1]	March 4, 1789	March 3, 1791
Albert Gallatin (D-R)[2]	Feb. 28, 1793	Feb. 28, 1794
James Ross (FED)	April 1, 1794	March 3, 1803
Samuel Maclay (D-R)[3]	March 4, 1803	Jan. 4, 1809
Michael Leib (D-R)[4]	Jan. 9, 1809	Feb. 14, 1814
Jonathan Roberts (D-R)	Feb. 24, 1814	March 3, 1821
William Findlay (D-R)	Dec. 10, 1821	March 3, 1827
Isaac D. Barnard[5]	March 4, 1827	Dec. 6, 1831
George M. Dallas (D)	Dec. 13, 1831	March 3, 1833
Samuel McKean (D)	Dec. 7, 1833	March 3, 1839
Daniel Sturgeon (D)	Jan. 14, 1840	March 3, 1851
Richard Brodhead (D)	March 4, 1851	March 3, 1857
Simon Cameron (R)[6]	March 4, 1857	March 4, 1861
David Wilmot (R)	March 14, 1861	March 3, 1863
Charles R. Buckalew (D)	March 4, 1863	March 3, 1869
John Scott (R)	March 4, 1869	March 3, 1875
William A. Wallace (D)	March 4, 1875	March 3, 1881
John I. Mitchell (R)	March 4, 1881	March 3, 1887
Matthew S. Quay (R)[7]	March 4, 1887	March 3, 1899
Matthew S. Quay (R)[8]	Jan. 17, 1901	May 28, 1904
Philander C. Knox (R)[9]	June 10, 1904	March 4, 1909
George T. Oliver (R)	March 17, 1909	March 3, 1917
Philander C. Knox (R)[10]	March 4, 1917	Oct. 12, 1921
William E. Crow (R)[11]	Oct. 24, 1921	Aug. 2, 1822
David A. Reed (R)[12]	Aug. 8, 1922	Jan. 2, 1935
Joseph F. Guffey (D)	Jan. 3, 1935	Jan. 2, 1947
Edward Martin (R)	Jan. 3, 1947	Jan. 2, 1959
Hugh Scott (R)	Jan. 3, 1959	Jan. 2, 1977
John Heinz (R)	Jan. 3, 1977	

Oregon
1. *Vacancy from March 4, 1859, to Oct. 2, 1860. Died Oct. 21, 1861.*
2. *Appointed by governor to fill vacancy.*
3. *Died Dec. 8, 1905.*
4. *Appointed by governor to fill vacancy.*
5. *Died May 23, 1917.*
6. *Appointed by governor to fill vacancy.*
7. *Resigned Dec. 17, 1918.*
8. *Appointed by governor to fill vacancy. Subsequently elected. Died Feb. 25, 1944.*
9. *Appointed by governor to fill vacancy. Subsequently elected.*
10. *Died March 9, 1960.*
11. *Appointed by governor to fill vacancy.*
12. *Vacancy from March 4, 1897, to Oct. 7, 1898, because of failure of Legislature to elect.*
13. *Resigned Jan. 31, 1938.*
14. *Appointed by governor to fill vacancy.*
15. *Elected as a Republican in 1944 and 1950, as a Democrat in 1956 and 1962. Morse was also an Independent from Oct. 24, 1952, to Feb. 17, 1955.*

Pennsylvania
1. *Vacancy from March 4, 1791, to Feb. 28, 1793, because of failure of Legislature to elect.*
2. *Senate resolution of Feb. 28, 1794, declared that Gallatin had not been a citizen for the nine years required by the Constitution for Senate membership.*
3. *Resigned Jan. 4, 1809.*

4. *Resigned Feb. 14, 1814.*
5. *Resigned Dec. 6, 1831.*
6. *Resigned March 4, 1861.*
7. *Quay was elected for two six-year terms, his second term expiring March 3, 1899. The Legislature adjourned without electing a senator for the new term beginning March 4, 1899. Quay was appointed by the governor to fill the vacancy on April 21, 1899. When the Senate convened, he presented his credentials Dec. 25, 1899, but was not permitted to take his seat. On April 24, 1900, the seat was declared vacant. Quay was elected to fill the vacancy and took his seat Jan. 17, 1901.*
8. *Died May 28, 1904.*
9. *Appointed by governor to fill vacancy. Subsequently elected. Resigned March 4, 1909.*
10. *Died Oct. 12, 1921.*
11. *Appointed by governor to fill vacancy. Died Aug. 2, 1922.*
12. *Appointed by governor to fill vacancy. Subsequently elected.*
13. *Resigned June 30, 1801.*
14. *Appointed by governor to fill vacancy. Subsequently elected.*
15. *Resigned June 30, 1834.*
16. *Resigned March 5, 1845.*
17. *Resigned March 3, 1877.*
18. *Died Dec. 31, 1921.*
19. *Appointed by governor to fill vacancy. Subsequently elected.*
20. *Credentials as senator-elect were presented and referred to the Committee on Privileges and Elections. Meanwhile Vare was not permitted to take his seat and on Dec. 6, 1929, was declared not entitled to a seat.*
21. *Appointed by governor to fill vacancy.*

Class 3

Robert Morris (FED)	March 4, 1789	March 3, 1795
William Bingham (FED)	March 4, 1795	March 3, 1801
John P. G. Muhlenberg (D-R)[13]	March 4, 1801	June 30, 1801
George Logan (D-R)[14]	July 13, 1801	March 3, 1807
Andrew Gregg (D-R)	March 4, 1807	March 3, 1813
Abner Lacock (D-R)	March 4, 1813	March 3, 1819
Walter Lowrie (D-R)	March 4, 1819	March 3, 1825
William Marks (D-R)	March 4, 1825	March 3, 1831
William Wilkins (D & A-MAS)[15]	March 4, 1831	June 30, 1834
James Buchanan (D)[16]	Dec. 6, 1834	March 5, 1845
Simon Cameron (D)	March 13, 1845	March 3, 1849
James Cooper (W)	March 4, 1849	March 3, 1855
William Bigler (D)	Jan. 14, 1856	March 3, 1861
Edgar Cowan (R)	March 4, 1861	March 3, 1867
Simon Cameron (R)[17]	March 4, 1867	March 3, 1877
J. Donald Cameron (R)	March 20, 1877	March 3, 1897
Boies Penrose (R)[18]	March 4, 1897	Dec. 31, 1921
George Wharton Pepper (R)[19]	Jan. 9, 1922	March 3, 1927
William S. Vare (R)[20]		
Joseph R. Grundy (R)[21]	Dec. 11, 1929	Dec. 1, 1930
James J. Davis (R)	Dec. 2, 1930	Jan. 2, 1945
Francis J. Myers (D)	Jan. 3, 1945	Jan. 2, 1951
James H. Duff (R)	Jan. 16, 1951	Jan. 2, 1957
Joseph S. Clark (D)	Jan. 3, 1957	Jan. 2, 1969
Richard S. Schweiker (R)	Jan. 3, 1969	Jan. 2, 1981
Arlen Specter (R)	Jan. 3, 1981	

RHODE ISLAND

(Ratified the Constitution May 29, 1790)

Class 1

Senators	Dates of Service	
Theodore Foster (LAW ORD)	June 7, 1790	March 3, 1803
Samuel J. Potter[1]	March 4, 1803	Oct. 14, 1804
Benjamin Howland (D-R)	Oct. 29, 1804	March 3, 1809
Francis Malbone[2]	March 4, 1809	June 4, 1809
Christopher G. Champlin[3]	June 26, 1809	Oct. 2, 1811
William Hunter (FED)	Oct. 28, 1811	March 3, 1821
James De Wolf (D-R)[4]	March 4, 1821	Oct. 31, 1825

Asher Robbins (D-R, NR, W)	Oct. 31, 1825	March 3, 1839
Nathan F. Dixon (W)[5]	March 4, 1839	Jan. 29, 1842
William Sprague (W)[6]	Feb. 5, 1842	Jan. 17, 1844
John B. Francis (LAW ORD)	Jan. 25, 1844	March 3, 1845
Albert C. Greene (W)	March 4, 1845	March 3, 1851
Charles T. James (D)	March 4, 1851	March 3, 1857
James F. Simmons (R)[7]	March 4, 1857	Aug. 15, 1862
Samuel G. Arnold (R)	Sept. 5, 1862	March 3, 1863
Wiliam Sprague (R)[8]	March 4, 1863	March 3, 1875
Ambrose E. Burnside (R)[9]	March 4, 1875	Sept. 13, 1881
Nelson W. Aldrich (R)	Oct. 5, 1881	March 3, 1911
Henry F. Lippitt (R)	March 4, 1911	March 3, 1917
Peter G. Gerry (D)	March 4, 1917	March 3, 1929
Felix Hebert (R)	March 4, 1929	Jan. 2, 1935
Peter G. Gerry (D)	Jan. 3, 1935	Jan. 2, 1947
J. Howard McGrath (D)[10]	Jan. 3, 1947	Aug. 23, 1949
Edward L. Leahy (D)[11]	Aug. 24, 1949	Dec. 18, 1950
John O. Pastore (D)[12]	Dec. 19, 1950	Dec. 28, 1976
John H. Chafee (R)	Dec. 29, 1976	

Class 2

Joseph Stanton Jr. (D-R)	June 7, 1790	March 3, 1793
William Bradford [13]	March 4, 1793	October 1797
Ray Greene (FED)[14]	Nov. 13, 1797	March 5, 1801
Christopher Ellery (D-R)	May 6, 1801	March 3, 1805
James Fenner (D-R)[15]	March 4, 1805	September 1807
Elisha Mathewson (D-R)	Oct. 26, 1807	March 3, 1811
Jeremiah B. Howell (FED)	March 4, 1811	March 3, 1817
James Burrill Jr. (D-R)[16]	March 4, 1817	Dec. 25, 1820
Nehemiah R. Knight (D-R, D)	Jan. 9, 1821	March 3, 1841
James F. Simmons (W)	March 4, 1841	March 3, 1847
John H. Clarke (W)	March 4, 1847	March 3, 1853
Philip Allen (D)	July 20, 1853	March 3, 1859
Henry B. Anthony (R)[17]	March 4, 1859	Sept. 2, 1884
William P. Sheffield (R)[18]	Nov. 19, 1884	Jan. 20, 1885
Jonathan Chace (R)[19]	Jan. 20, 1885	April 9, 1889
Nathan F. Dixon III (R)	April 10, 1889	March 3, 1895
George Peabody Wetmore (R)	March 4, 1895	March 3, 1907
George Peabody Wetmore (R)[20]	Jan. 22, 1908	March 3, 1913
LeBaron B. Colt (R)[21]	March 4, 1913	Aug. 18, 1924
Jesse H. Metcalf (R)	Nov. 5, 1924	Jan. 2, 1937
Theodore F. Green (D)	Jan. 3, 1937	Jan. 2, 1961
Claiborne Pell (D)	Jan. 3, 1961	

Rhode Island
  1. Died Oct. 14, 1804.
  2. Died June 4, 1809.
  3. Resigned Oct. 2, 1811.
  4. Resigned Oct. 31, 1825.
  5. Died Jan. 29, 1842.
  6. Resigned Jan. 17, 1844.
  7. Resigned Aug. 15, 1862.
  8. Nephew of William Sprague, listed above with footnote 6.
  9. Died Sept. 13, 1881.
  10. Resigned Aug. 23, 1949.

  11. Appointed by governor to fill vacancy.
  12. Resigned Dec. 28, 1976.
  13. Resigned in October 1797.
  14. Resigned March 5, 1801.
  15. Resigned in September 1807.
  16. Died Dec. 25, 1820.
  17. Died Sept. 2, 1884.
  18. Appointed by governor to fill vacancy.
  19. Resigned April 9, 1889.
  20. Vacant March 4, 1907 to Jan. 22, 1908, because of failure of Legislature to elect.
  21. Died Aug. 18, 1924.

SOUTH CAROLINA

(Ratified the Constitution May 23, 1788)

Class 2

Senators	Dates of Service	
Pierce Butler (D-R)[1]	March 4, 1789	Oct. 25, 1796
John Hunter (FED)[2]	Dec. 8, 1796	Nov. 26, 1798
Charles Pinckney (D-R)[3]	Dec. 6, 1798	1801
Thomas Sumter (D-R)[4]	Dec. 15, 1801	Dec. 16, 1810
John Taylor (D-R)[5]	Dec. 31, 1810	November 1816
William Smith (D-R)	Dec. 4, 1816	March 3, 1823
Robert Y. Hayne (D-R)[6]	March 4, 1823	Dec. 13, 1832
John C. Calhoun (D)[7]	Dec. 29, 1832	March 3, 1843
Daniel Elliott Huger (D)[8]	March 4, 1843	March 3, 1845
John C. Calhoun (D)[9]	Nov. 26, 1845	March 31, 1850
Franklin H. Elmore (D)[10]	April 11, 1850	May 29, 1850
Robert W. Barnwell (D)[11]	June 4, 1850	Dec. 18, 1850
R. Barnwell Rhett (D)[12]	Dec. 18, 1850	May 7, 1852
William F. DeSaussure (D)[13]	May 10, 1852	March 3, 1853
Josiah J. Evans (D)[14]	March 4, 1853	May 6, 1858
Arthur P. Hayne (D)[15]	May 11, 1858	Dec. 2, 1858
James Chestnut Jr. (D)[16]	Dec. 3, 1858	July 11, 1861
Thomas J. Robertson (R)	July 15, 1868	March 3, 1877
Matthew C. Butler (D)	March 4, 1877	March 3, 1895
Benjamin R. Tillman (D)[17]	March 4, 1895	July 3, 1918
Christie Bénet (D)[18]	July 6, 1918	Nov. 5, 1918
William P. Pollock (D)	Nov. 6, 1918	March 3, 1919
Nathaniel B. Dial (D)	March 4, 1919	March 3, 1925
Coleman L. Blease (D)	March 4, 1925	March 3, 1931
James F. Byrnes (D)[19]	March 4, 1931	July 8, 1941
Alva M. Lumpkin (D)[20]	July 17, 1941	Aug. 1, 1941
Roger C. Peace (D)[21]	Aug. 5, 1941	Nov. 4, 1941
Burnet R. Maybank (D)[22]	Nov. 5, 1941	Sept. 1, 1954
Charles E. Daniel (D)[23]	Sept. 6, 1954	Dec. 23, 1954
Strom Thurmond (D)[24]	Dec. 24, 1954	April 4, 1956
Thomas A. Wofford (D)[25]	April 5, 1956	Nov. 6, 1956
Strom Thurmond (D, R)[26]	Nov. 7, 1956	

Class 3

Ralph Izard (FED)	March 4, 1789	March 3, 1795
Jacob Read (FED)	March 4, 1795	March 3, 1801
John E. Colhoun (D-R)[27]	March 4, 1801	Oct. 26, 1802
Pierce Butler (D-R)[28]	Nov. 4, 1802	Nov. 21, 1804
John Gaillard (D-R)[29]	Dec. 6, 1804	Feb. 26, 1826

William Harper (D-R)[30]	March 8, 1826	Nov. 29, 1826
William Smith (D-R)	Nov. 29, 1826	March 3, 1831
Stephen D. Miller D)[31]	March 4, 1831	March 2, 1833
William C. Preston (D)[32]	Nov. 26, 1833	Nov. 29, 1842
George McDuffie (D)[33]	Dec. 2, 1842	Aug. 17, 1846
Andrew P. Butler (D)[34]	Dec. 4, 1846	May 25, 1857
James H. Hammond (D)[35]	Dec. 7, 1857	Nov. 11, 1860
Frederick A. Sawyer (R)	July 16, 1868	March 3, 1873
John J. Patterson (R)	March 4, 1873	March 3, 1879
Wade Hampton (D)	March 4, 1879	March 3, 1891
John L. M. Irby (D)	March 4, 1891	March 3, 1897
Joseph H. Earle (D)[36]	March 4, 1897	May 20, 1897
John L. McLaurin (D)[37]	May 27, 1897	March 3, 1903
Asbury C. Latimer (D)[38]	March 4, 1903	Feb. 20, 1908
Frank B. Gary (D)	March 6, 1908	March 3, 1909
Ellison D. Smith (D)[39]	March 4, 1909	Nov. 17, 1944
Wilton E. Hall (D)[40]	Nov. 20, 1944	Jan. 2, 1945
Olin D. Johnston (D)[41]	Jan. 3, 1945	April 18, 1965
Donald Russell (D)[42]	April 22, 1965	Nov. 8, 1966
Ernest F. Hollings (D)	Nov. 9, 1966	

SOUTH DAKOTA

(Became a state Nov. 2, 1889)

Class 2

Senators	Dates of Service	
Richard F. Pettigrew (R)	Nov. 2, 1889	March 3, 1901
Robert J. Gamble (R)	March 4, 1901	March 3, 1913
Thomas Sterling (R)	March 4, 1913	March 3, 1925
William H. McMaster (R)	March 4, 1925	March 3, 1931
William J. Bulow (D)	March 4, 1931	Jan. 2, 1943
Harlan J. Bushfield (R)[1]	Jan. 3, 1943	Sept. 27, 1948
Vera C. Bushfield (R)[2]	Oct. 6, 1948	Dec. 26, 1948
Karl E. Mundt (R)	Dec. 31, 1948	Jan. 2, 1973
James Abourezk (D)	Jan. 3, 1973	Jan. 2, 1979
Larry Pressler (R)	Jan. 3, 1979	

Class 3

Gideon C. Moody (R)	Nov. 2, 1889	March 3, 1891
James H. Kyle (I)[3]	March 4, 1891	July 1, 1901
Alfred B. Kittredge (R)[4]	July 11, 1901	March 3, 1909
Coe I. Crawford (R)	March 4, 1909	March 3, 1915
Edwin S. Johnson (D)	March 4, 1915	March 3, 1921

South Carolina
1. Resigned Oct. 25, 1796.
2. Resigned Nov. 26, 1798.
3. Resigned in 1801.
4. Resigned Dec. 16, 1810.
5. Resigned in November 1816.
6. Resigned Dec. 13, 1832.
7. Resigned March 3, 1843.
8. Resigned March 3, 1845. Seat vacant until Nov. 26, 1845.
9. Died March 31, 1850.
10. Appointed by governor to fill vacancy. Died May 29, 1850.
11. Appointed by governor to fill vacancy.
12. Resigned May 7, 1852.
13. Appointed by governor to fill vacancy. Subsequently elected.
14. Died May 6, 1858.
15. Appointed by governor to fill vacancy.
16. Expelled July 11, 1861. Vacancy until July 15, 1868, because of Civil War.
17. Died July 3, 1918.
18. Appointed by governor to fill vacancy.
19. Resigned July 8, 1941.
20. Appointed by governor to fill vacancy. Died Aug. 1, 1941.
21. Appointed by governor to fill vacancy.
22. Died Sept. 1, 1954.
23. Appointed by governor to fill vacancy. Resigned Dec. 23, 1954.
24. Resigned April 4, 1956.
25. Appointed by governor to fill vacancy.
26. Became a Republican on Sept. 16, 1964.

27. Died Oct. 26, 1802.
28. Resigned Nov. 21, 1804.
29. Died Feb. 26, 1826.
30. Appointed by governor to fill vacancy.
31. Resigned March 2, 1833.
32. Resigned Nov. 29, 1842.
33. Resigned Aug. 17, 1846.
34. Died May 25, 1857.
35. Did not attend sessions of the Senate after Nov. 11, 1860. Vacancy until July 16, 1868, because of Civil War.
36. Died May 20, 1897.
37. Appointed by governor to fill vacancy. Subsequently elected.
38. Died Feb. 20, 1908.
39. Died Nov. 17, 1944.
40. Appointed by governor to fill vacancy.
41. Died April 18, 1965.
42. Appointed by governor to fill vacancy.

South Dakota
1. Died Sept. 27, 1948.
2. Appointed by governor to fill vacancy. Resigned Dec. 26, 1948.
3. Died July 1, 1901.
4. Appointed by governor to fill vacancy. Subsequently elected.
5. Died Dec. 20, 1936.
6. Appointed by governor to fill vacancy.
7. Died June 22, 1962.
8. Appointed by governor to fill vacancy.

Peter Norbeck (R)[5]	March 4, 1921	Dec. 20, 1936
Herbert E. Hitchcock (D)[6]	Dec. 29, 1936	Nov. 8, 1938
Gladys Pyle (R)	Nov. 9, 1938	Jan. 2, 1939
J. Chandler Gurney (R)	Jan. 3, 1939	Jan. 2, 1951
Francis Case (R)[7]	Jan. 3, 1951	June 22, 1962
Joe H. Bottum (R)[8]	July 9, 1962	Jan. 2, 1963
George McGovern (D)	Jan. 3, 1963	Jan. 2, 1981
James Abdnor (R)	Jan. 3, 1981	

TENNESSEE

(Became a state June 1, 1796)

Class 1

Senators	Dates of Service	
William Cocke (D-R)	Aug. 2, 1796	March 3, 1797
William Cocke (D-R)[1]	April 22, 1797	Sept. 26, 1797
Andrew Jackson (D-R)[2]	Sept. 26, 1797	April 1798
Daniel Smith (D-R)[3]	Oct. 6, 1798	Dec. 12, 1798
Joseph Anderson (D-R)[4]	March 4, 1799	March 3, 1815
George W. Campbell (D-R)[5]	Oct. 10, 1815	April 20, 1818
John H. Eaton (D-R)[6]	Sept. 5, 1818	March 9, 1829
Felix Grundy (D)[7]	Oct. 19, 1829	July 4, 1838
Ephraim H. Foster (W)[8]	Sept. 17, 1838	March 3, 1839
Felix Grundy (D)[9]	Dec. 14, 1839	Dec. 19, 1840
Alfred O. P. Nicholson (D)[10]	Dec. 25, 1840	Feb. 7, 1942
Ephraim H. Foster (W)	Oct. 17, 1843	March 3, 1845
Hopkins L. Turney (W)	March 4, 1845	March 3, 1851
James C. Jones (W)	March 4, 1851	March 3, 1857
Andrew Johnson (D)[11]	Oct. 8, 1857	March 4, 1862
David T. Patterson (D)	July 28, 1866	March 3, 1869
William G. Brownlow (R)	March 4, 1869	March 3, 1875
Andrew Johnson (D)[12]	March 4, 1875	July 31, 1875
David M. Key (D)[13]	Aug. 18, 1875	Jan. 19, 1877
James E. Bailey (D)	Jan. 19, 1877	March 3, 1881
Howell E. Jackson (D)[14]	March 4, 1881	April 14, 1886
W. C. Whitthorne (D)[15]	April 16, 1886	March 3, 1887
William B. Bate (D)[16]	March 4, 1887	March 9, 1905
James B. Frazier (D)	March 21, 1905	March 3, 1911
Luke Lea (D)	March 4, 1911	March 3, 1917

Kenneth D. McKellar (D)	March 4, 1917	Jan. 2, 1953
Albert Gore (D)	Jan. 3, 1953	Jan. 2, 1971
Bill Brock (R)	Jan. 3, 1971	Jan. 2, 1977
Jim Sasser (D)	Jan. 3, 1977	

Class 2

William Blount (D-R)[17]	Aug. 2, 1796	July 8, 1797
Joseph Anderson (D-R)	Sept. 26, 1797	March 3, 1799
William Cocke (D-R)	March 4, 1799	March 3, 1805
Daniel Smith (D-R)[18]	March 4, 1805	March 31, 1809
Jenkin Whiteside (D-R)[19]	April 11, 1809	Oct. 8, 1811
George W. Campbell (D-R)[20]	Oct. 8, 1811	Feb. 11, 1814
Jesse Wharton (D-R)[21]	March 17, 1814	Oct. 10, 1815
John Williams (D-R)[22]	Oct. 10, 1815	March 3, 1823
Andrew Jackson (D-R)[23]	March 4, 1823	Oct. 14, 1825
Hugh Lawson White (D-R, D)	Oct. 28, 1825	March 3, 1835
Hugh Lawson White (D)[24]	Oct. 6, 1835	Jan. 13, 1840
Alexander Anderson (D)	Jan. 27, 1840	March 4, 1841
Spencer Jarnagin (W)[25]	Oct. 17, 1843	March 3, 1847
John Bell (W)	Nov. 22, 1847	March 3, 1853
John Bell (W)	Oct. 29, 1853	March 3, 1859
Alfred O. P. Nicholson (D)[26]	March 4, 1859	July 11, 1861
Joseph S. Fowler (UN R)	July 25, 1866	March 3, 1871
Henry Cooper (D)	March 4, 1871	March 3, 1877
Isham G. Harris (D)[27]	March 4, 1877	July 8, 1897
Thomas B. Turley (D)[28]	July 20, 1897	March 3, 1901
Edward W. Carmack (D)	March 4, 1901	March 3, 1907
Robert L. Taylor (D)[29]	March 4, 1907	March 31, 1912
Newell Sanders (R)[30]	April 8, 1912	Jan. 24, 1913
William R. Webb (D)	Jan. 24, 1913	March 3, 1913
John K. Shields (D)	March 4, 1913	March 3, 1925
Lawrence D. Tyson (D)[31]	March 4, 1925	Aug. 24, 1929
William E. Brock (D)[32]	Sept. 2, 1929	March 3, 1931
Cordell Hull (D)[33]	March 4, 1931	March 3, 1933
Nathan L. Bachman (D)[34]	March 4, 1933	April 23, 1937
George L. Berry (D)[35]	May 6, 1937	Nov. 8, 1938
Tom Stewart (D)	Jan. 16, 1939	Jan. 2, 1949
Estes Kefauver (D)[36]	Jan. 3, 1949	Aug. 10, 1963
Herbert S. Walters (D)[37]	Aug. 20, 1963	Nov. 3, 1964
Ross Bass (D)	Nov. 4, 1964	Jan. 2, 1967
Howard H. Baker Jr. (R)	Jan. 3, 1967	Jan. 2, 1985
Albert Gore Jr. (D)	Jan. 3, 1985	

Tennessee
1. *Appointed by governor to fill vacancy.*
2. *Resigned in April 1798.*
3. *Appointed by governor to fill vacancy.*
4. *Served twice through election and once by appointment of the governor during this period.*
5. *Resigned April 20, 1818.*
6. *Appointed by governor to fill vacancy. Resigned March 9, 1829.*
7. *Resigned July 4, 1838.*
8. *Appointed by governor to fill vacancy. Subsequently elected for term beginning March 4, 1839, but resigned March 3, 1839. Vacancy until Dec. 14, 1839.*
9. *Died Dec. 19, 1840.*
10. *Appointed by governor to fill vacancy.*
11. *Resigned March 4, 1862. Vacancy until July 28, 1866, because of Civil War.*
12. *Died July 31, 1875.*
13. *Appointed by governor to fill vacancy.*
14. *Resigned April 14, 1886.*
15. *Appointed by governor to fill vacancy.*
16. *Died March 9, 1905.*
17. *Expelled July 8, 1797.*
18. *Resigned March 31, 1809.*

19. *Resigned Oct. 8, 1811.*
20. *Resigned Feb. 11, 1814.*
21. *Appointed by governor to fill vacancy.*
22. *Williams served twice by election and once by appointment of the governor during this period.*
23. *Resigned Oct. 14, 1825.*
24. *White's seat was vacant between March 4, 1835, and Oct. 5, 1835. Resigned Jan. 13, 1840.*
25. *Vacancy from March 4, 1841, to Oct. 17, 1843.*
26. *Expelled July 11, 1861. Vacant until July 25, 1866, because of Civil War.*
27. *Died July 8, 1897.*
28. *Appointed by governor to fill vacancy. Subsequently elected.*
29. *Died March 31, 1912.*
30. *Appointed by governor to fill vacancy.*
31. *Died Aug. 24, 1929.*
32. *Appointed by governor to fill vacancy. Subsequently elected.*
33. *Resigned March 3, 1933.*
34. *Appointed by governor to fill vacancy. Subsequently elected. Died April 23, 1937.*
35. *Appointed by governor to fill vacancy.*
36. *Died Aug. 10, 1963.*
37. *Appointed by governor to fill vacancy.*

TEXAS

(Became a state Dec. 29, 1845)

Class 1

Senators	Dates of Service	
Thomas J. Rusk (D)[1]	Feb. 21, 1846	July 29, 1857
J. P. Henderson (D)[2]	Nov. 9, 1857	June 4, 1858
Matthias Ward (D)[3]	Sept. 27, 1858	Dec. 5, 1859
Louis T. Wigfall (D)[4]	Dec. 5, 1859	July 11, 1861
J. W. Flanagan (R)	March 31, 1870	March 3, 1875
Samuel B. Maxey (D)	March 4, 1875	March 3, 1887
John H. Reagan (D)[5]	March 4, 1887	June 10, 1891
Horace Chilton (D)[6]	June 10, 1891	March 22, 1892
Roger Q. Mills (D)	March 23, 1892	March 3, 1899
Charles A. Culberson (D)	March 4, 1899	March 3, 1923
Earle B. Mayfield (D)	March 4, 1923	March 3, 1929
Tom Connally (D)	March 4, 1929	Jan. 2, 1953
Price Daniel (D)[7]	Jan. 3, 1953	Jan. 14, 1957
William A. Blakley (D)[8]	Jan. 15, 1957	April 28, 1957
Ralph Yarborough (D)	April 29, 1957	Jan. 2, 1971
Lloyd M. Bentsen Jr. (D)	Jan. 3, 1971	

Class 2

Senators	Dates of Service	
Sam Houston (D)	Feb. 21, 1846	March 3, 1859
John Hemphill (D)[9]	March 4, 1859	July 11, 1861
Morgan C. Hamilton (R)	March 31, 1870	March 3, 1877
Richard Coke (D)	March 4, 1877	March 3, 1895
Horace Chilton (D)	March 4, 1895	March 3, 1901
Joseph W. Bailey (D)[10]	March 4, 1901	Jan. 3, 1913
Rienzi M. Johnston (D)[11]	Jan. 4, 1913	Jan. 29, 1913
Morris Sheppard (D)[12]	Jan. 29, 1913	April 9, 1941
Andrew Jackson Houston (D)[13]	April 21, 1941	June 26, 1941
W. Lee O'Daniel (D)	Aug. 4, 1941	Jan. 2, 1949
Lyndon B. Johnson (D)[14]	Jan. 3, 1949	Jan. 3, 1961
William A. Blakley (D)[15]	Jan. 3, 1961	June 14, 1961
John Tower (R)	June 15, 1961	Jan. 2, 1985
Phil Gramm (R)	Jan. 3, 1985	

UTAH

(Became a state Jan. 4, 1896)

Class 1

Senators	Dates of Service	
Frank J. Cannon (R)	Jan. 22, 1896	March 3, 1899
Thomas Kearns (R)[1]	Jan. 23, 1901	March 3, 1905
George Sutherland (R)	March 4, 1905	March 3, 1917
William H. King (D)	March 4, 1917	Jan. 2, 1941
Abe Murdock (D)	Jan. 3, 1941	Jan. 2, 1947
Arthur V. Watkins (R)	Jan. 3, 1947	Jan. 2, 1959
Frank E. Moss (D)	Jan. 3, 1959	Jan. 2, 1977
Orrin G. Hatch (R)	Jan. 3, 1977	

Class 3

Senators	Dates of Service	
Arthur Brown (R)	Jan. 22, 1896	March 3, 1897
Joseph L. Rawlins (D)	March 4, 1897	March 3, 1903
Reed Smoot (R)	March 4, 1903	March 3, 1933
Elbert D. Thomas (D)	March 4, 1933	Jan. 2, 1951
Wallace F. Bennett (R)	Jan. 3, 1951	Dec. 20, 1974
Jake Garn (R)	Dec. 21, 1974	

VERMONT

(Became a state March 4, 1791)

Class 1

Senators	Dates of Service	
Moses Robinson (D-R)[1]	Oct. 17, 1791	Oct. 15, 1796
Isaac Tichenor (FED)[2]	Oct. 18, 1796	Oct. 17, 1797
Nathaniel Chipman (FED)	Oct. 17, 1797	March 3, 1803
Israel Smith (D-R)[3]	March 4, 1803	Oct. 1, 1807
Jonathan Robinson	Oct. 10, 1807	March 3, 1815

Texas
1. Died July 29, 1857.
2. Died June 4, 1858.
3. Appointed by governor to fill vacancy.
4. Expelled July 11, 1861. Vacant until March 31, 1870, because of Civil War.
5. Resigned June 10, 1891.
6. Appointed by governor to fill vacancy.
7. Resigned Jan. 14, 1957.
8. Appointed by governor to fill vacancy.
9. Expelled July 11, 1861. Vacant until March 31, 1870, because of Civil War.
10. Resigned Jan. 3, 1913.
11. Appointed by governor to fill vacancy.
12. Died April 9, 1941.
13. Appointed by governor to fill vacancy. Died June 26, 1941.
14. Resigned Jan. 3, 1961, immediately after taking oath of office, having been elected vice president of the United States.
15. Appointed by governor to fill vacancy.

Utah
1. Vacancy from March 4, 1899, to Jan. 22, 1901, because of failure of Legislature to elect.

Vermont
1. Resigned Oct. 15, 1796.
2. Resigned Oct. 17, 1797.
3. Resigned Oct. 1, 1807.
4. Died March 28, 1866.

5. Appointed by governor to fill vacancy. Subsequently elected. Resigned Nov. 1, 1891.
6. Appointed by governor to fill vacancy. Subsequently elected. Died March 4, 1908.
7. Appointed by governor to fill vacancy.
8. Died Dec. 17, 1930.
9. Appointed by governor to fill vacancy.
10. Resigned Aug. 2, 1946.
11. Appointed by governor to fill vacancy. Subsequently elected.
12. Died Sept. 10, 1971.
13. Appointed by governor to fill vacancy. Subsequently elected.
14. Resigned Sept. 1, 1801.
15. Resigned Nov. 3, 1817.
16. Resigned Jan. 8, 1818.
17. Resigned April 11, 1842.
18. Appointed by governor to fill vacancy. Subsequently elected.
19. Died Jan. 14, 1853.
20. Appointed by governor to fill vacancy. By resolution of March 16, 1854, the Senate declared that he was not entitled to retain his seat. Seat remained vacant until Oct. 14, 1854.
21. Died Nov. 9, 1865.
22. Appointed by governor to fill vacancy. Subsequently elected.
23. Died Dec. 28, 1898.
24. Appointed by governor to fill vacancy.
25. Died July 12, 1923.
26. Died Oct. 6, 1933.
27. Appointed by governor to fill vacancy. Subsequently elected. Died June 20, 1940.
28. Appointed by governor to fill vacancy.

Isaac Tichenor (FED)	March 4, 1815	March 3, 1821
Horatio Seymour (D-R)	March 4, 1821	March 3, 1833
Benjamin Swift (W)	March 4, 1833	March 3, 1839
Samuel S. Phelps (W)	March 4, 1839	March 3, 1851
Solomon Foot (W, R)[4]	March 4, 1851	March 28, 1866
George F. Edmunds (R)[5]	April 3, 1866	Nov. 1, 1891
Redfield Proctor (R)[6]	Nov. 2, 1891	March 4, 1908
John W. Stewart (R)[7]	March 24, 1908	Oct. 20, 1908
Carroll S. Page (R)	Oct. 21, 1908	March 3, 1923
Frank L. Greene (R)[8]	March 4, 1923	Dec. 17, 1930
Frank C. Partridge (R)[9]	Dec. 23, 1930	March 31, 1931
Warren R. Austin (R)[10]	April 1, 1931	Aug. 2, 1946
Ralph E. Flanders (R)[11]	Nov. 1, 1946	Jan. 2, 1959
Winston L. Prouty (R)[12]	Jan. 3, 1959	Sept. 10, 1971
Robert T. Stafford (R)[13]	Sept. 16, 1971	

Class 3

Stephen R. Bradley (D-R)	Oct. 17, 1791	March 3, 1795
Elijah Paine (FED)[14]	March 4, 1795	Sept. 1, 1801
Stephen R. Bradley (D-R)	Oct. 15, 1801	March 3, 1813
Dudley Chase (D-R)[15]	March 4, 1813	Nov. 3, 1817
James Fisk (D-R)[16]	Nov. 4, 1817	Jan. 8, 1818
William A. Palmer (D-R)	Oct. 20, 1818	March 3, 1825
Dudley Chase (D-R)	March 4, 1825	March 3, 1831
Samuel Prentiss (W)[17]	March 4, 1831	April 11, 1842
Samuel C. Crafts (W)[18]	Apr. 23, 1842	March 3, 1843
William Upham (W)[19]	March 4, 1843	Jan. 14, 1853
Samuel S. Phelps (W)[20]	Jan. 17, 1853	March 16, 1854
Lawrence Brainerd	Oct. 14, 1854	March 3, 1855
Jacob Collamer (R)[21]	March 4, 1855	Nov. 9, 1865
Luke P. Poland (R)[22]	Nov. 21, 1865	March 3, 1867
Justin S. Morrill (R)[23]	March 4, 1867	Dec. 28, 1898
Jonathan Ross (R)[24]	Jan. 11, 1899	Oct. 17, 1900
William P. Dillingham (R)[25]	Oct. 18, 1900	July 12, 1923
Porter H. Dale (R)[26]	Nov. 6, 1923	Oct. 6, 1933
Ernest W. Gibson (R)[27]	Nov. 21, 1933	June 20, 1940
Ernest W. Gibson Jr. (R)[28]	June 24, 1940	Jan. 2, 1941
George D. Aiken (R)	Jan. 10, 1941	Jan. 2, 1975
Patrick J. Leahy (D)	Jan. 3, 1975	

VIRGINIA

(Ratified the Constitution June 25, 1788)

Class 1

Senators	Dates of Service	
William Grayson (A-FED)[1]	March 4, 1789	March 12, 1790
John Walker[2]	March 31, 1790	Nov. 9, 1790
James Monroe (D-R)[3]	Nov. 9, 1790	Nov. 18, 1794
Stevens T. Mason (D-R)[4]	Nov. 18, 1794	May 10, 1803
John Taylor (D-R)[5]	June 4, 1803	Dec. 7, 1803
Abraham B. Venable (D-R)[6]	Dec. 7, 1803	June 7, 1804
William B. Giles (D-R)[7]	Aug. 11, 1804	Dec. 4, 1804
Andrew Moore (D-R)	Dec. 4, 1804	March 3, 1809
Richard Brent (D-R)[8]	March 4, 1809	Dec. 30, 1814
James C. Barbour (D-R)[9]	Jan. 2, 1815	March 27, 1825
John Randolph (D-R)	Dec. 9, 1825	March 3, 1827
John Tyler (D-R, D)[10]	March 4, 1827	Feb. 29, 1836
William C. Rives (D)[11]	March 4, 1836	March 3, 1839
William C. Rives (D)	Jan. 18, 1841	March 3, 1845
Isaac S. Pennybacker (D)[12]	Dec. 3, 1845	Jan. 12, 1847
James M. Mason (D)[13]	Jan. 21, 1847	July 11, 1861
Waitman T. Willey (R)[14]	July 13, 1861	March 3, 1863
Lemuel J. Bowden (R)[15]	March 4, 1863	Jan. 2, 1864
John F. Lewis (R)	Jan. 27, 1870	March 3, 1875
Robert W. Withers (C)	March 4, 1875	March 3, 1881
William Mahone (R)	March 4, 1881	March 3, 1887
John W. Daniel (D)[16]	March 4, 1887	June 29, 1910
Claude A. Swanson (D)[17]	Aug. 1, 1910	March 3, 1933
Harry Flood Byrd (D)[18]	March 4, 1933	Nov. 10, 1965
Harry F. Byrd Jr. (D, I)[19]	Nov. 12, 1965	Jan. 2, 1983
Paul S. Trible Jr. (R)	Jan. 3, 1983	

Class 2

Richard Henry Lee (A-FED)[20]	March 4, 1789	Oct. 8, 1792
John Taylor (D-R)[21]	Oct. 18, 1792	May 11, 1794
Henry Tazewell (D-R)[22]	Nov. 18, 1794	Jan. 24, 1799

Virginia

1. *Died March 12, 1790.*
2. *Appointed by governor to fill vacancy.*
3. *Resigned Nov. 18, 1794.*
4. *Died May 10, 1803.*
5. *Appointed by governor to fill vacancy.*
6. *Resigned June 7, 1804.*
7. *Appointed by governor to fill vacancy.*
8. *Died Dec. 30, 1814.*
9. *Resigned March 27, 1825.*
10. *Resigned Feb. 29, 1836.*
11. *The seat was vacant between the expiration of Rives' first term March 3, 1839, and his re-election and subsequent service beginning Jan. 18, 1841.*
12. *Died Jan. 12, 1847.*
13. *Expelled July 11, 1861. Vacant until July 13, 1861.*
14. *Willey was elected by a "rump" state Legislature which supported the Union and represented territory which was later to become West Virginia.*
15. *Died Jan. 2, 1864. Bowden, like Willey, his predecessor, was elected to represent Virginia by a "rump" state Legislature which supported the Union. After his death, the seat remained vacant until Jan. 27, 1870, because of the Civil War.*
16. *Died June 29, 1910.*
17. *Appointed by governor to fill vacancy. Subsequently elected. Resigned March 3, 1933.*
18. *Appointed by governor to fill vacancy. Subsequently elected. Resigned Nov. 10, 1965.*
19. *Appointed by governor to fill vacancy. Subsequently elected as a Democrat in 1966, as an Independent in 1970.*

20. *Resigned Oct. 8, 1792.*
21. *Resigned May 11, 1794.*
22. *Died Jan. 24, 1799.*
23. *Resigned May 22, 1804.*
24. *Appointed by governor to fill vacancy.*
25. *Resigned March 3, 1815.*
26. *Resigned Dec. 4, 1819.*
27. *Resigned Dec. 15, 1822.*
28. *Died Aug. 20, 1824.*
29. *Resigned July 16, 1832.*
30. *Resigned Feb. 22, 1834.*
31. *Resigned July 4, 1836.*
32. *Resigned March 13, 1837.*
33. *Expelled July 11, 1861. Vacant until July 13, 1861.*
34. *Carlile was elected by a "rump" state Legislature which supported the Union and represented territory which was later to become West Virginia. After the expiration of his term, the seat remained vacant until Jan. 28, 1870, because of Civil War.*
35. *The seat was vacant between the expiration of Johnston's first term March 3, 1871, and his re-election and subsequent seating March 15, 1871.*
36. *Died May 14, 1892.*
37. *Appointed by governor to fill vacancy. Subsequently elected.*
38. *Died Nov. 12, 1919.*
39. *Appointed by governor to fill vacancy. Subsequently elected. Died May 28, 1946.*
40. *Appointed by governor to fill vacancy.*
41. *Resigned Dec. 30, 1966.*
42. *Resigned Jan. 1, 1979.*

Wilson C. Nicholas (D-R)[23]	Dec. 5, 1799	May 22, 1804
Andrew Moore (D-R)[24]	Aug. 11, 1804	Dec. 4, 1804
William B. Giles (D-R)[25]	Dec. 4, 1804	March 3, 1815
Armistead T. Mason (D-R)	Jan. 3, 1816	March 3, 1817
John W. Eppes (D-R)[26]	March 4, 1817	Dec. 4, 1819
James Pleasants (D-R)[27]	Dec. 10, 1819	Dec. 15, 1822
John Taylor (D-R)[28]	Dec. 18, 1822	Aug. 20, 1824
Littleton W. Tazewell (D-R, D)[29]	Dec. 7, 1824	July 16, 1832
William C. Rives (D)[30]	Dec. 10, 1832	Feb. 22, 1834
Benjamin W. Leigh (D)[31]	Feb. 26, 1834	July 4, 1836
Richard E. Parker (D)[32]	Dec. 12, 1836	March 13, 1837
William H. Roane (D)	March 14, 1837	March 3, 1841
William S. Archer (W)	March 4, 1841	March 3, 1847
Robert M. T. Hunter (D)[33]	March 4, 1847	July 11, 1861
John S. Carlile (UN)[34]	July 13, 1861	March 3, 1865
John W. Johnston (C)[35]	Jan. 28, 1870	March 3, 1883
H. H. Riddleberger (R)	March 4, 1883	March 3, 1889
John S. Barbour Jr. (D)[36]	March 4, 1889	May 14, 1892
Eppa Hunton (D)[37]	May 28, 1892	March 3, 1895
Thomas S. Martin (D)[38]	March 4, 1895	Nov. 12, 1919
Carter Glass (D)[39]	Feb. 2, 1920	May 28, 1946
Thomas G. Burch (D)[40]	May 31, 1946	Nov. 5, 1946
A. Willis Robertson (D)[41]	Nov. 6, 1946	Dec. 30, 1966
William B. Spong Jr. (D)	Dec. 31, 1966	Jan. 2, 1973
William Lloyd Scott (R)[42]	Jan. 3, 1973	Jan. 1, 1979
John W. Warner (R)	Jan. 2, 1979	

WASHINGTON

(Became a state Nov. 11, 1889)

Class 1

Senators	Dates of Service	
John B. Allen (R)	Nov. 20, 1889	March 3, 1893
John L. Wilson (R)[1]	Feb. 1, 1895	March 3, 1899
Addison G. Foster (R)	March 4, 1899	March 3, 1905
Samuel H. Piles (R)	March 4, 1905	March 3, 1911
Miles Poindexter (R)	March 4, 1911	March 3, 1923
Clarence C. Dill (D)	March 4, 1923	Jan. 2, 1935
L. B. Schwellenbach (D)[2]	Jan. 3, 1935	Dec. 16, 1940
Mon C. Wallgren (D)[3]	Dec. 19, 1940	Jan. 10, 1945
Hugh B. Mitchell (D)[4]	Jan. 10, 1945	Dec. 25, 1946
Harry P. Cain (R)	Dec. 26, 1946	Jan. 2, 1953
Henry M. Jackson (D)[5]	Jan. 3, 1953	Sept. 1, 1983
Daniel J. Evans (R)[6]	Sept. 12, 1983	

Class 3

Watson C. Squire (R)	Nov. 20, 1889	March 3, 1897
George Turner (D)	March 4, 1897	March 3, 1903
Levi Ankeny (R)	March 4, 1903	March 3, 1909

Wesley L. Jones (R)[7]	March 4, 1909	Nov. 19, 1932
Elijah S. Grammer (R)[8]	Nov. 22, 1932	March 3, 1933
Homer T. Bone (D)[9]	March 4, 1933	Nov. 13, 1944
Warren G. Magnuson (D)	Dec. 14, 1944	Jan. 2, 1981
Slade Gorton (R)	Jan. 3, 1981	

WEST VIRGINIA

(Became a state June 19, 1863)

Class 1

Senators	Dates of Service	
Peter G. Van Winkle (R)	Aug. 4, 1863	March 3, 1869
Arthur I. Boreman (R)	March 4, 1869	March 3, 1875
Allen T. Caperton (D)[1]	March 4, 1875	July 26, 1876
Samuel Price[2]	Aug. 26, 1876	Jan. 26, 1877
Frank Hereford (D)	Jan. 26, 1877	March 3, 1881
Johnson N. Camden (D)	March 4, 1881	March 3, 1887
Charles J. Faulkner (D)	March 4, 1887	March 3, 1899
Nathan B. Scott (R)	March 4, 1899	March 3, 1911
William E. Chilton (D)	March 4, 1911	March 3, 1917
Howard Sutherland (R)	March 4, 1917	March 3, 1923
Matthew M. Neely (D)	March 4, 1923	March 3, 1929
Henry D. Hatfield (R)	March 4, 1929	Jan. 2, 1935
Rush D. Holt (D)[3]	June 21, 1935	Jan. 2, 1941
Harley M. Kilgore (D)[4]	Jan. 3, 1941	Feb. 28, 1956
William R. Laird III (D)[5]	March 13, 1956	Nov. 6, 1956
Chapman Revercomb (R)	Nov. 7, 1956	Jan. 2, 1959
Robert C. Byrd (D)	Jan. 3, 1959	

Class 2

Waitman T. Willey (R)	Aug. 4, 1863	March 3, 1871
Henry G. Davis (D)	March 4, 1871	March 3, 1883
John E. Kenna (D)[6]	March 4, 1883	Jan. 11, 1893
Johnson N. Camden (D)	Jan. 25, 1893	March 3, 1895
Stephen B. Elkins (R)[7]	March 4, 1895	Jan. 4, 1911
Davis Elkins (R)[8]	Jan. 9, 1911	Jan. 31, 1911
Clarence W. Watson (D)	Feb. 1, 1911	March 3, 1913
Nathan Goff (R)	March 4, 1913	March 3, 1919
Davis Elkins (R)	March 4, 1919	March 3, 1925
Guy D. Goff (R)	March 4, 1925	March 3, 1931
Matthew M. Neely (D)[9]	March 4, 1931	Jan. 12, 1941
Joseph Rosier (D)[10]	Jan. 13, 1941	Nov. 17, 1942
Hugh Ike Shott (R)	Nov. 18, 1942	Jan. 2, 1943
Chapman Revercomb (R)	Jan. 3, 1943	Jan. 2, 1949
Matthew M. Neely (D)[11]	Jan. 3, 1949	Jan. 18, 1958
John D. Hoblitzell Jr. (R)[12]	Jan. 25, 1958	Nov. 4, 1958
Jennings Randolph (D)	Nov. 5, 1958	Jan. 2, 1985
John D. Rockefeller IV (D)	Jan. 3, 1985	

Washington

  1. *Vacancy from March 4, 1893, to Feb. 1, 1895, because of failure of Legislature to elect. John B. Allen was appointed by governor March 10, 1893, to fill vacancy, but by Senate resolution of Aug. 28, 1893, was declared not entitled to a seat.*
  2. *Resigned Dec. 16, 1940.*
  3. *Resigned Jan. 10, 1945.*
  4. *Appointed by governor to fill vacancy. Resigned Dec. 25, 1946.*
  5. *Died Sept. 1, 1983.*
  6. *Appointed by governor to fill vacancy. Subsequently elected.*
  7. *Died Nov. 19, 1932.*
  8. *Appointed by governor to fill vacancy.*
  9. *Resigned Nov. 13, 1944.*

West Virginia

  1. *Died July 26, 1876.*
  2. *Appointed by governor to fill vacancy.*
  3. *Elected Nov. 6, 1934, to a six-year term, but did not reach the age of 30—required by the Constitution for service in the Senate—until June 19, 1935. Took his seat June 21, 1935.*
  4. *Died Feb. 28, 1956.*
  5. *Appointed by governor to fill vacancy.*
  6. *Died Jan. 11, 1893.*
  7. *Died Jan. 4, 1911.*
  8. *Appointed by governor to fill vacancy.*
  9. *Resigned Jan. 12, 1941.*
  10. *Appointed by governor to fill vacancy.*
  11. *Died Jan. 18, 1958.*
  12. *Appointed by governor to fill vacancy.*

WISCONSIN

(Became a state May 29, 1848)

Class 1

Senators	Dates of Service	
Henry Dodge (D)	June 8, 1848	March 3, 1857
James R. Doolittle (R)	March 4, 1857	March 3, 1869
Matthew H. Carpenter (R)	March 4, 1869	March 3, 1875
Angus Cameron (R)	March 4, 1875	March 3, 1881
Philetus Sawyer (R)	March 4, 1881	March 3, 1893
John L. Mitchell (D)	March 4, 1893	March 3, 1899
Joseph V. Quarles (R)	March 4, 1899	March 3, 1905
Robert M. La Follette (R)[1]	Jan. 4, 1906	June 18, 1925
R. M. La Follette Jr. (R, PROG)[2]	Sept. 30, 1925	Jan. 2, 1947
Joseph R. McCarthy (R)[3]	Jan. 3, 1947	May 2, 1957
William Proxmire (D)	Aug. 28, 1957	

Class 3

Isaac P. Walker (D)	June 8, 1848	March 3, 1855
Charles Durkee (R)	March 4, 1855	March 3, 1861
Timothy O. Howe (R)	March 4, 1861	March 3, 1879
Matthew H. Carpenter (R)[4]	March 4, 1879	Feb. 24, 1881
Angus Cameron (R)	March 10, 1881	March 3, 1885
John Coit Spooner (R)	March 4, 1885	March 3, 1891
William F. Vilas (D)	March 4, 1891	March 3, 1897
John Coit Spooner (R)[5]	March 4, 1897	May 1, 1907
Isaac Stephenson (R)	May 17, 1907	March 3, 1915
Paul O. Husting (D)[6]	March 4, 1915	Oct. 21, 1917
Irvine L. Lenroot (R)	April 18, 1918	March 3, 1927
John J. Blaine (R)	March 4, 1927	March 3, 1933
F. Ryan Duffy (D)	March 4, 1933	Jan. 2, 1939

Alexander Wiley (R)	Jan. 3, 1939	Jan. 2, 1963
Gaylord Nelson (D)	Jan. 8, 1963	Jan. 2, 1981
Bob Kasten (R)	Jan. 3, 1981	

WYOMING

(Became a state July 10, 1890)

Class 1

Senators	Dates of Service	
Francis E. Warren (R)	Nov. 18, 1890	March 3, 1893
Clarence D. Clark (R)[1]	Jan. 23, 1895	March 3, 1917
John B. Kendrick (D)[2]	March 4, 1917	Nov. 3, 1933
Joseph C. O'Mahoney (D)[3]	Jan. 1, 1934	Jan. 2, 1953
Frank A. Barrett (R)	Jan. 3, 1953	Jan. 2, 1959
Gale W. McGee (D)	Jan. 3, 1959	Jan. 2, 1977
Malcolm Wallop (R)	Jan. 3, 1977	

Class 2

Joseph M. Carey (R)	Nov. 15, 1890	March 3, 1895
Francis E. Warren (R)[4]	March 4, 1895	Nov. 24, 1929
Patrick J. Sullivan (R)[5]	Dec. 5, 1929	Nov. 30, 1930
Robert D. Carey (R)	Dec. 1, 1930	Jan. 2, 1937
Harry H. Schwartz (D)	Jan. 3, 1937	Jan. 2, 1943
E. V. Robertson (R)	Jan. 3, 1943	Jan. 2, 1949
Lester C. Hunt (D)[6]	Jan. 3, 1949	June 19, 1954
Edward D. Crippa (R)[7]	June 24, 1954	Nov. 28, 1954
Joseph C. O'Mahoney (D)	Nov. 29, 1954	Jan. 2, 1961
John Joseph Hickey (D)[8]	Jan. 3, 1961	Nov. 6, 1962
Milward L. Simpson (R)	Nov. 7, 1962	Jan. 2, 1967
Clifford P. Hansen (R)[9]	Jan. 3, 1967	Dec. 31, 1978
Alan K. Simpson (R)	Jan. 1, 1979	

Wisconsin

1. Elected Jan. 25, 1905. Took oath Jan. 4, 1906. Governor during interim. Died June 18, 1925. Vacancy from June 19 to Sept. 29, 1925.

2. Elected as a Republican in 1925 and 1928, as a Progressive in 1934 and 1940.

3. Died May 2, 1957.

4. Died Feb. 24, 1881.

5. Resigned effective May 1, 1907.

6. Died Oct. 21, 1917. Seat vacant until April 18, 1918.

Wyoming

1. Vacancy from March 4, 1893, to Jan. 23, 1895, because of failure of Legislature to elect.

2. Died Nov. 3, 1933. Vacancy from Nov. 4, 1933, to Jan. 1, 1934.

3. Appointed by governor to fill vacancy. Subsequently elected.

4. Died Nov. 24, 1929.

5. Appointed by governor to fill vacancy.

6. Died June 19, 1954.

7. Appointed by governor to fill vacancy.

8. Keith Thomson (R), who had been elected Nov. 8, 1960, to a full six-year term beginning Jan. 3, 1961, died Dec. 9, 1960. Hickey, the incumbent governor, resigned and was appointed by his successor to fill the vacancy.

9. Resigned Dec. 31, 1978.

606

Popular Vote Returns

Sources for Senate Popular Returns

The Senate popular election returns presented in this section (pp. 609-637) for the years 1913 through 1973 were obtained from the Inter-University Consortium for Political and Social Research (ICPSR) at the University of Michigan. For Senate elections 1974 through 1982, returns were obtained from Richard M. Scammon and Alice M. McGillivray, *America Votes*, vols. 11-15 (Washington, D.C.: Congressional Quarterly, 1975-83). Returns for the 1975 special election in New Hampshire were obtained from the New Hampshire secretary of state. For 1984 elections, Congressional Quarterly obtained returns from secretaries of state.

The symbol # next to returns before 1974 indicates that Congressional Quarterly obtained the returns from a source other than the ICPSR. A complete list of other sources used appears on page 673. A "Senate Candidates Index" is located on pages 1164 to 1169.

While complete source annotations for the ICPSR collection are too extensive to publish here, information can be obtained through the ICPSR. *(ICPSR collection, box, p. xiv.)*

Presentation of Returns

The Senate returns are arranged alphabetically by state and in chronological order by class of senator within each state listing. *(For an explanation of Senate classes, see p. 574.)* The candidate receiving the greatest number of popular votes is listed first with his or her vote total and percentage of the total vote cast, followed in descending order of votes received by all other candidates receiving *at least 5 percent* of the total vote cast.

Special elections to fill vacancies are designated in the returns. *(For an explanation of special elections, see p. 573.)*

Where a state *simultaneously* held a special election to fill the remaining few months of an unexpired term and a general election for the next full six-year term, the special election is listed *after* the general election. For example, see page 611 where the 1946 California general and special election returns appear.

Where a state had a special election and a general election for the same class in the same year, but not simultaneously, the elections appear in the order they occurred. For example, see page 618 where the 1936 Louisiana special election, held in April, precedes the general election, held in November.

Vote Totals and Percentages

The ICPSR data collection includes all candidates receiving popular votes. In the *Guide to U.S. Elections, Second Edition*, only Senate candidates receiving *at least 5 percent* of the total vote are included. For exam-

ple, in the ICPSR data collection for the 1944 New York senatorial election, 6,209,317 votes were cast, with Robert F. Wagner receiving 3,294,576 votes (53.05 percent), Thomas J. Curran receiving 2,899,497 votes (46.69 percent) and a third candidate, Eric Hass, receiving 15,244 (0.25 percent).

The returns for the 1944 New York Senate election appear on page 626. Returns for Hass are not listed because he received less than 5 percent of the total vote. The percentage listed for Wagner is 53.1 and for Curran is 46.7. The procedure used throughout this section was to calculate percentages to two places on the basis of the *total number of votes cast* and to round each percentage to one decimal place. Due to rounding and scattered votes for other candidates, percentages listed for Senate races may not add to 100 percent.

Party Designation

In the ICPSR returns, the distinct — and in many cases, *multiple* — party designations appearing in the original sources are preserved. In many cases party labels represent combinations of multi-party support received by individual candidates. If, for example, on the ballot and official returns more than one party name was listed next to a candidate's name, then the party designation appearing in the election returns for that candidate will be a unique abbreviation for that combination of parties. *(For a list of party abbreviations, see p. 1141.)*

In the special case of a candidate's name listed separately on the original ballot under more than one party — where returns were reported *separately* for each party — Congressional Quarterly has summed the votes recorded under the several parties and that figure appears as the candidate's total vote. Whenever separate party totals have been summed, a *comma* separates the abbreviations of the parties contributing the largest and second-largest share of the total vote.

Most cases of this special situation occurred in New York and Pennsylvania. For example, in the 1944 New York election cited above, Wagner's total vote of 3,294,576 was comprised of 2,485,735 as the Democratic Party nominee, 483,785 votes as the American Labor Party nominee and 325,056 votes as the Liberal Party nominee. On page 626, only Wagner's total vote of 3,294,576 appears.

Congressional Quarterly also has included party abbreviations for the two parties that contributed the most votes to Wagner's total. Thus, immediately following his name appear the abbreviations — D, AM LAB — indicating that Wagner was a candidate of at least two parties and that the greatest number of votes he received was as a Democrat.

Senate Popular Vote Returns, 1913-1984

Note: Prior to ratification of the 17th Amendment, April 8, 1913, a number of states conducted non-binding popular polls for Senate candidates, designed to guide the state legislatures in choosing between candidates. The Inter-University Consortium for Political and Social Research obtained some of the returns for these polls, and they are published in the following list. *(Explanation of non-binding elections, p. 572)*

ALABAMA

	Candidates	Votes	%
	Class 2		
1918	John H. Bankhead (D)	54,880	100.0

Special Election

1920	J. Thomas Heflin (D)	161,531	71.4
	C. P. Lunsford (R)	62,020	27.4

1924	J. Thomas Heflin (D)	120,017	75.2
	F. H. Lathrop (R)	39,623	24.8
1930	John H. Bankhead II (D)	150,985	59.7
	J. Thomas Heflin (I)	101,862	40.3
1936	John H. Bankhead II (D)	239,632	87.0
	H. E. Berkstresser (R)	33,698	12.2
1942	John H. Bankhead II (D)	69,212	100.0

Special Election

1946	John Sparkman (D)	163,217	100.0

1948	John Sparkman (D)	185,534	84.0
	Paul G. Parsons (R)	35,341	16.0
1954	John Sparkman (D)	259,348	82.5
	J. Foy Guin Jr. (R)	55,110	17.5
1960	John Sparkman (D)	389,196	70.2
	Julian Elgin (R)	164,868	29.8
1966	John Sparkman (D)	482,138	60.1
	John Grenier (R)	313,018	39.0
1972	John Sparkman (D)	654,491	62.3
	Winton M. (Red) Blount (R)	347,523	33.1
1978	Howell Heflin (D)	547,054	94.0
	Jerome B. Couch (P)	34,951	6.0
1984	Howell Heflin (D)	860,535	62.8
	Albert Lee Smith Jr. (R)	498,508	36.3
	Class 3		
1914	Oscar W. Underwood (D)	63,338	78.1
	Alex C. Birch (R)	12,320	15.2
	A. P. Longshore (PROG)	4,263	5.3

Special Election

1914	Frank S. White (D)	102,326	99.9

1920	Oscar W. Underwood (D)	155,664	68.0
	L. H. Reynolds (R)	71,334	31.2
1926	Hugo L. Black (D)	91,843	80.9
	E. H. Dryer (R)	21,722	19.1
1932	Hugo L. Black (D)	209,614	86.3
	J. Theodore Johnson (R)	33,425	13.8

Special Election

1938	Lister Hill (D)		

1938	Lister Hill (D)	113,413#	86.4
	J. M. Pennington (R)	17,885#	13.6
1944	Lister Hill (D)	202,604	81.8
	John A. Posey (R)	41,983	17.0
1950	Lister Hill (D)	125,534	76.5
	John G. Crommelin Jr. (I)	38,477	23.5
1956	Lister Hill (D)	330,182	100.0
1962	Lister Hill (D)	201,937	50.9
	James D. Martin (R)	195,134	49.1
1968	Jim Allen (D)	638,774	70.0
	Perry Hooper (R)	201,227	22.1
	Robert Schwenn (NDPA)	72,699	8.0
1974	Jim Allen (D)	501,541	95.8

Special Election

1978	Donald W. Stewart (D)	401,852	54.9
	James D. Martin (R)	316,170	43.2

1980	Jeremiah Denton (R)	650,362	50.2
	James E. Folsom Jr. (D)	610,175	47.1

Explanation of Symbols

In the returns for Senate elections *symbols* are used to denote special circumstances. In cases where no symbol is used, the candidate who received the most votes won the election to the Senate.

The following is a key to the symbols used:

✔ Elected to the Senate, but the number of votes and the percentage of the total vote received by the winner are not available.

* The symbol is used in two kinds of situations: (1) When the winner of the election died before the term of office was to begin; (2) When the apparent winner was not permitted to take office. *(For an explanation of specific cases, consult the appropriate state in the list of senators, pp. 579-606).*

Information was obtained from a source other than the Inter-University Consortium for Political and Social Research. *(For a listing of other sources, see p. 637).*

ALASKA

Candidates	Votes	%
(Became a state Jan. 3, 1959)		

Class 2

	Candidates	Votes	%
1958	E. L. Bartlett (D)	40,939	83.8
	R. E. Robertson (R)	7,299	15.0
1960	E. L. Bartlett (D)	38,041	63.4
	Lee L. McKinley (R)	21,937	36.6
1966	E. L. Bartlett (D)	49,289	75.5
	Lee L. McKinley (R)	15,961	24.5

Special Election

	Candidates	Votes	%
1970	Ted Stevens (R)	47,908	59.6
	Wendell P. Kay (D)	32,456	40.4
1972	Ted Stevens (R)	74,216	77.3
	Gene Guess (D)	21,791	22.7
1978	Ted Stevens (R)	92,783	75.6
	Donald W. Hobbs (D)	29,574	24.1
1984	Ted Stevens (R)	146,919	71.2
	John E. Havelock (D)	58,804	28.5

Class 3

	Candidates	Votes	%
1958	Ernest Gruening (D)	26,063	52.6
	Mike Stepovich (R)	23,462	47.4
1962	Ernest Gruening (D)	33,827	58.1
	Ted Stevens (R)	24,354	41.9
1968	Mike Gravel (D)	36,527	45.1
	Elmer Rasmuson (R)	30,286	37.4
	Ernest Gruening (I)	14,118	17.4
1974	Mike Gravel (D)	54,361	58.3
	C. R. Lewis (R)	38,914	41.7
1980	Frank H. Murkowski (R)	84,159	53.7
	Clark S. Gruening (D)	72,007	45.9

ARIZONA

	Candidates	Votes	%
	Class 1		
1916	Henry F. Ashurst (D)	29,882	55.4
	Joseph H. Kibbey (R)	21,261	39.4
	W. S. Bradford (SOC)	2,827	5.2
1922	Henry F. Ashurst (D)	39,722	65.0
	James H. McClintock (R)	21,358	35.0
1928	Henry F. Ashurst (D)	47,013	54.3
	Ralph H. Cameron (R)	39,651	45.8
1934	Henry F. Ashurst (D)	67,648	72.0
	J. E. Thompson (R)	24,075	25.6
1940	Ernest W. McFarland (D)	101,495	71.6
	I. A. Jennings (R)	39,657	28.0
1946	Ernest W. McFarland (D)	80,415	69.2
	Ward S. Powers (R)	35,022	30.1
1952	Barry Goldwater (R)	132,063	51.3
	Ernest W. McFarland (D)	125,338	48.7
1958	Barry Goldwater (R)	164,593	56.1
	Ernest W. McFarland (D)	129,030	43.9
1964	Paul Fannin (R)	241,084	51.4
	Roy Elson (D)	227,704	48.6
1970	Paul Fannin (R)	228,284	56.0
	Sam Grossman (D)	179,512	44.0
1976	Dennis DeConcini (D)	400,334	54.0
	Sam Steiger (R)	321,236	43.3
1982	Dennis DeConcini (D)	411,970	56.9
	Pete Dunn (R)	291,749	40.3
	Class 3		
1914	Marcus A. Smith (D)	25,800	53.2

	Candidates	Votes	%
	J. L. Hubbell (R)	9,182	19.0
	Eugene W. Chafin (IP)	7,293	15.1
	Bert Davis (SOC)	3,582	7.4
	J. Bernard Nelson (PROG)	2,606	5.4
1920	Ralph H. Cameron (R)	35,893	55.2
	Marcus A. Smith (D)	29,169	44.8
1926	Carl Hayden (D)	44,591	58.3
	Ralph H. Cameron (R)	31,845	41.7
1932	Carl Hayden (D)	74,310	66.7
	Ralph H. Cameron (R)	35,737	32.1
1938	Carl Hayden (D)	82,714	76.5
	B. H. Clingan (R)	25,378	23.5
1944	Carl Hayden (D)	90,335	69.4
	Fred W. Fickett (R)	39,891	30.6
1950	Carl Hayden (D)	116,246	62.8
	Bruce Brockett (R)	68,846	37.2
1956	Carl Hayden (D)	170,816	61.4
	Ross F. Jones (R)	107,447	38.6
1962	Carl Hayden (D)	199,217	54.9
	Evan Mecham (R)	163,388	45.1
1968	Barry Goldwater (R)	274,607	57.2
	Roy Elson (D)	205,338	42.8
1974	Barry Goldwater (R)	320,396	58.3
	Jonathan Marshall (D)	229,523	41.7
1980	Barry M. Goldwater (R)	432,371	49.5
	Bill Schulz (D)	422,972	48.4

ARKANSAS

	Candidates	Votes	%
	Class 2		
1918	Joseph T. Robinson (D)	78,386	100.0
1924	Joseph T. Robinson (D)	100,408#	73.5
	Charles F. Cole (R)	36,163#	26.5
1930	Joseph T. Robinson (D)	141,806	100.0
1936	Joseph T. Robinson (D)	155,075	81.8
	G. C. Ledbetter (R)	30,997	16.4

Special Election

1937	John E. Miller (I)	66,990	60.7
	Carl E. Bailey (D)	43,406	39.3
1942	John L. McClellan (D)	99,126	100.0
1948	John L. McClellan (D)	216,401	93.3
	R. Walter Tucker (I)	15,521	6.7
1954	John L. McClellan (D)	291,058	100.0
1960	John L. McClellan (D)	✔	
1966	John L. McClellan (D)	✔	
1972	John L. McClellan (D)	386,398	60.8
	Wayne H. Babbitt (R)	248,238	39.1
1978	David H. Pryor (D)	399,916	76.6
	Tom Kelly (R)	84,722	16.2
	John G. Black (I)	37,488	7.2
1984	David Pryor (D)	502,341	57.3
	Ed Bethune (R)	373,615	42.7

Class 3

1914	James P. Clarke (D)	33,449#	74.9
	Meyers (R)	11,222#	25.1

Special Election

1916	William F. Kirby (D)	110,293	69.3
	H. L. Remmel (R)	48,922	30.7
1920	Thaddeus H. Caraway (D)	126,577	65.9
	Charles F. Cole (R)	65,381	34.1
1926	Thaddeus H. Caraway (D)	28,064	82.8
	R. A. Jones (R)	5,848	17.2

	Candidates	Votes	%
Special Election			
1932	Hattie W. Caraway (D)	31,133#	*91.6*
	Rex Floyd (I)	1,752#	*5.2*
1932	Hattie W. Caraway (D)	183,795	*89.5*
	John W. White (R)	21,597	*10.5*
1938	Hattie W. Caraway (D)	122,871	*89.6*
	C. D. Atkinson (R)	14,240	*10.4*
1944	J. William Fulbright (D)	182,529	*85.1*
	Victor M. Wade (R)	31,942	*14.9*
1950	J. William Fulbright (D)	302,582	*100.0*
1956	J. William Fulbright (D)	331,679	*83.0*
	Ben C. Henley (R)	68,016	*17.0*
1962	J. William Fulbright (D)	214,867	*68.7*
	Kenneth Jones (R)	98,013	*31.3*
1968	J. William Fulbright (D)	349,965	*59.2*
	Charles Bernard (R)	241,739	*40.9*
1974	Dale Bumpers (D)	461,056	*84.9*
	John Harris Jones (R)	82,026	*15.1*
1980	Dale Bumpers (D)	477,905	*59.1*
	Bill Clark (R)	330,576	*40.9*

CALIFORNIA

	Candidates	Votes	%
Class 1			
1916	Hiram W. Johnson (R & PROG)	574,667	*61.1*
	George S. Patton (D)	277,852	*29.5*
	Walter Thomas Mills (SOC)	49,341	*5.2*
1922	Hiram W. Johnson (R)	564,422	*62.2*
	William J. Pearson (D)	215,748	*23.8*
	H. Clay Needham (P)	70,748	*7.8*
	Upton Sinclair (SOC)	56,982	*6.3*
1928	Hiram W. Johnson (R)	1,148,397	*74.1*
	Minor Moore (D)	282,411	*18.2*
	Charles H. Randall (P)	92,106	*5.9*
1934	Hiram W. Johnson (R-D-PR-C)	1,946,572	*94.5*
	George R. Kirkpatrick (SOC)	108,748	*5.3*
1940	Hiram W. Johnson (R-D-PROG)	2,238,899	*82.5*
	Fred Dyster (P)	366,044	*13.5*
1946	William F. Knowland (R)	1,428,067	*54.1*
	Will Rogers Jr. (D)	1,167,161	*44.2*
Special Election			
1946	William F. Knowland (R)	425,273	*74.3*
	Will Rogers Jr. (D)	90,723	*15.9*
1952	William F. Knowland (R-D)	3,982,448	*87.7*
	Reuben W. Borough (I PROG)	542,270	*11.9*
1958	Clair Engle (D)	2,927,693	*57.0*
	Goodwin J. Knight (R)	2,204,337	*42.9*
1964	George Murphy (R)	3,628,555	*51.5*
	Pierre Salinger (D)	3,411,912	*48.5*
1970	John V. Tunney (D)	3,496,558	*53.9*
	George Murphy (R)	2,877,617	*44.3*
1976	S. I. Hayakawa (R)	3,748,973	*50.2*
	John V. Tunney (D)	3,502,862	*46.9*
1982	Pete Wilson (R)	4,022,565	*51.5*
	Edmund G. Brown Jr. (D)	3,494,968	*44.8*
Class 3			
1914	James D. Phelan (D)	279,896	*31.6*
	Francis J. Heney (PROG)	255,232	*28.8*
	Joseph R. Knowland (R)	254,159	*28.7*
	Ernest Untermann (SOC)	56,805	*6.4*
1920	Samuel M. Shortridge (R)	447,835	*49.0*
	James D. Phelan (D)	371,580	*40.7*
	James S. Edwards (P)	57,768	*6.3*
1926	Samuel M. Shortridge (R)	670,128	*63.1*
	John B. Elliott (D)	391,599	*36.9*
1932	William Gibbs McAdoo (D)	943,164	*43.4*
	Tallant Tubbs (R)	669,676	*30.8*
	Robert P. Shuler (P)	560,088	*25.8*
1938	Sheridan Downey (D-PRO-TN)	1,372,314	*54.4*
	Philip Bancroft (R)	1,126,240	*44.7*
1944	Sheridan Downey (D)	1,728,155	*52.3*
	Frederick F. Houser (R)	1,576,553	*47.7*
1950	Richard M. Nixon (R)	2,183,454	*59.2*
	Helen Gahagan Douglas (D)	1,502,507	*40.8*
Special Election			
1954	Thomas H. Kuchel (R)	2,090,836	*53.2*
	Samuel William Yorty (D)	1,788,071	*45.5*
1956	Thomas H. Kuchel (R)	2,892,918	*54.0*
	Richard Richards (D)	2,445,816	*45.6*
1962	Thomas H. Kuchel (R)	3,180,483	*56.3*
	Richard Richards (D)	2,452,839	*43.4*
1968	Alan Cranston (D)	3,680,352	*51.8*
	Max Rafferty (R)	3,329,148	*46.9*
1974	Alan Cranston (D)	3,693,160	*60.5*
	H. L. (Bill) Richardson (R)	2,210,267	*36.2*
1980	Alan Cranston (D)	4,705,399	*56.5*
	Paul Gann (R)	3,093,426	*37.1*

COLORADO

	Candidates	Votes	%
Class 2			
1912	John F. Shafroth (D)	118,260	*47.3*
	Clyde C. Dawson (R)	66,949	*26.8*
	Frank D. Catlin (PROG-BMR)	58,649	*23.5*
1918	Lawrence C. Phipps (R)	107,726	*49.5*
	John F. Shafroth (D)	104,347	*47.9*
1924	Lawrence C. Phipps (R)	159,698	*50.2*
	Alva B. Adams (D)	139,660	*43.9*
	Morton Alexander (F-LAB)	16,039	*5.0*
1930	Edward P. Costigan (D)	180,028	*55.9*
	George H. Shaw (R)	137,487	*42.7*
1936	Edwin C. Johnson (D)	299,376	*63.5*
	Raymond L. Sauter (R)	166,308	*35.3*
1942	Edwin C. Johnson (D)	174,612	*50.2*
	Ralph L. Carr (R)	170,970	*49.2*
1948	Edwin C. Johnson (D)	340,719	*66.8*
	Will F. Nicholson (R)	165,069	*32.4*
1954	Gordon Allott (R)	248,502	*51.3*
	John A. Carroll (D)	235,686	*48.7*
1960	Gordon Allott (R)	389,428	*53.5*
	Robert L. Knous (D)	334,854	*46.0*
1966	Gordon Allott (R)	368,307	*58.0*
	Roy Romer (D)	266,198	*41.9*
1972	Floyd K. Haskell (D)	457,545	*49.4*
	Gordon Allott (R)	447,957	*48.4*
1978	William L. Armstrong (R)	480,596	*58.7*
	Floyd K. Haskell (D)	330,247	*40.3*
1984	William L. Armstrong (R)	833,821	*64.2*
	Nancy Dick (D)	449,327	*34.6*
Class 3			
Special Election			
1912	Charles S. Thomas (D)	111,633	*44.9*
	Charles W. Waterman (R)	66,627	*26.8*
	I. N. Stevens (PROG-BMR)	64,405	*25.9*

	Candidates	Votes	%
1914	Charles S. Thomas (D)	102,037	40.3
	Hubert Work (R)	98,728	39.0
	Benjamin Griffith (PROG)	27,072	10.7
	J. C. Griffiths (SOC)	13,943	5.5
1920	Samuel D. Nicholson (R)	156,577	54.5
	Tully Scot (D)	112,890	39.3

Special Election

1924	Rice W. Means (R)	159,353	50.2
	Morrison Shafroth (D)	138,714	43.7
	Charles T. Philp (F-LAB)	17,542	5.5

1926	Charles W. Waterman (R)	149,585	50.3
	William E. Sweet (D)	138,113	46.4
1932	Alva B. Adams (D)	226,516	51.9
	Karl C. Schuyler (R)	198,519	45.5

Special Election

1932	Karl C. Schuyler (R)	207,540	48.8
	Walter Walker (D)	206,475	48.5

1938	Alva B. Adams (D)	262,806	58.2
	Archibald A. Lee (R)	181,297	40.2

Special Election

1942	Eugene D. Millikin (R)	191,517	56.1
	James A. Marsh (D)	143,817	42.1

1944	Eugene D. Millikin (R)	277,410#	56.1
	Barney L. Whatley (D)	214,335#	43.0
1950	Eugene D. Millikin (R)	239,734	53.3
	John A. Carroll (D)	210,442	46.8
1956	John A. Carroll (D)	319,872	50.2
	Dan Thornton (R)	317,102	49.8
1962	Peter H. Dominick (R)	328,655	53.6
	John A. Carroll (D)	279,586	45.6
1968	Peter H. Dominick (R)	459,952	58.6
	Stephen L. R. McNichols (D)	325,584	41.5
1974	Gary Hart (D)	471,691	57.2
	Peter H. Dominick (R)	325,508	39.5
1980	Gary W. Hart (D)	590,501	50.3
	Mary E. Buchanan (R)	571,295	48.7

CONNECTICUT

	Candidates	Votes	%
	Class 1		
1916	George P. McLean (R)	107,020	50.2
	Homer Cummings (D)	98,649	46.2
1922	George P. McLean (R)	169,524	52.3
	Thomas J. Spellacy (D)	147,276	45.5
1928	Frederic C. Walcott (R)	296,958	53.9
	Augustine Lonergan (D)	251,429	45.6
1934	Francis T. Maloney (D)	265,552	51.8
	Frederic C. Walcott (R)	247,623	48.3
1940	Francis T. Maloney (D)	416,740	53.2
	Paul L. Cornell (R, UN)	358,313	45.7
1946	Raymond E. Baldwin (R)	381,328	56.1
	Joseph M. Tone (D)	276,424	40.7

Special Election

1946	Raymond E. Baldwin (R)	378,707	55.8
	Wilbur L. Cross (D)	278,188	41.0

	Candidates	Votes	%
	Special Election		
1950	William Benton (D)	431,413	49.2
	Prescott S. Bush (R)	430,311	49.1

1952	William A. Purtell (R)	573,854	52.5
	William Benton (D)	485,066	44.4
1958	Thomas J. Dodd (D)	554,841	57.5
	William A. Purtell (R)	410,622	42.5
1964	Thomas J. Dodd (D)	781,008	64.6
	John Lodge (R)	426,939	35.3
1970	Lowell P. Weicker Jr. (R)	454,721	41.7
	Joseph D. Duffey (D)	368,111	33.8
	Thomas J. Dodd (DODD I)	266,497	24.5
1976	Lowell P. Weicker Jr. (R)	785,683	57.7
	Gloria Schaffer (D)	561,018	41.2
1982	Lowell P. Weicker Jr. (R)	545,987	50.4
	Anthony T. Moffett (D)	499,146	46.1

	Class 3		
1914	Frank B. Brandegee (R)	89,983	49.8
	Simeon Baldwin (D)	76,081	42.1
1920	Frank B. Brandegee (R)	216,792	59.4
	Augustine Lonergan (D)	131,824	36.1

Special Election

1924	Hiram Bingham (R)	112,400#	60.4
	Hamilton Holt (D)	71,871#	38.6

1926	Hiram Bingham (R)	191,401	63.3
	Rollin U. Tyler (D)	107,753	35.6
1932	Augustine Lonergan (D)	282,327	48.5
	Hiram Bingham (R)	278,061	47.7
1938	John A. Danaher (R)	270,413	42.9
	Augustine Lonergan (D, UN)	252,426	40.0
	Bellani Trombley (SOC)	99,282	15.8
1944	Brien McMahon (D)	430,716	52.0
	John A. Danaher (R)	391,748	47.3
1950	Brien McMahon (D)	453,646	51.7
	Joseph E. Talbot (R)	409,053	46.6

Special Election

1952	Prescott S. Bush (R)	559,465	51.2
	Abraham A. Ribicoff (D)	530,505	48.5

1956	Prescott S. Bush (R)	610,829	54.8
	Thomas J. Dodd (D)	479,460	43.1
1962	Abraham A. Ribicoff (D)	527,522	51.3
	Horace Seely-Brown (R)	501,694	48.8
1968	Abraham A. Ribicoff (D)	655,043	54.3
	Edwin H. May (R)	551,455	45.7
1974	Abraham A. Ribicoff (D)	690,820	63.7
	James H. Brannen III (R)	372,055	34.3
1980	Christopher J. Dodd (D)	763,969	56.3
	James L. Buckley (R)	581,884	42.9

DELAWARE

	Candidates	Votes	%
	Class 1		
1916	Josiah O. Wolcott (D)	25,434	49.7
	Henry A. du Pont (R)	22,925	44.8
1922	Thomas F. Bayard (D)	37,304	49.8
	T. Coleman du Pont (R)	36,979	49.4

Candidates	Votes	%
Special Election		
1922 Thomas F. Bayard (D)	36,954	49.7
T. Coleman du Pont (R)	36,894	49.6
1928 John G. Townsend Jr. (R)	63,725	61.0
Thomas F. Bayard (D)	40,828	39.1
1934 John G. Townsend Jr. (R)	52,829	53.3
Wilbur L. Adams (D)	45,771	46.2
1940 James M. Tunnell (D)	68,294	50.6
John G. Townsend Jr. (R)	63,799	47.3
1946 John J. Williams (R)	62,603	55.2
James M. Tunnell (D)	50,910	44.9
1952 John J. Williams (R)	93,020	54.5
A. I. du Pont Bayard (D)	77,685	45.5
1958 John J. Williams (R)	82,280	53.3
Elbert N. Carvel (D)	72,152	46.7
1964 John J. Williams (R)	103,782	51.7
Elbert N. Carvel (D)	96,850	48.3
1970 William V. Roth Jr. (R)	94,979	58.8
Jacob Zimmerman (D)	64,740	40.1
1976 William V. Roth Jr. (R)	125,502	55.8
Thomas C. Maloney (D)	98,055	43.6
1982 William V. Roth Jr. (R)	105,357	55.2
David N. Levinson (D)	84,413	44.2

Class 2

Candidates	Votes	%
1918 Lewis Heisler Ball (R)	21,519	51.2
Willard Saulsbury (D)	20,113	47.8
1924 T. Coleman du Pont (R)	52,731	59.4
James M. Tunnell (D & PROG)	36,085	40.6
1930 Daniel O. Hastings (R)	47,909	54.5
Thomas F. Bayard (D)	39,881	45.4
Special Election		
1930 Daniel O. Hastings (R)	47,665	54.8
Thomas F. Bayard (D)	39,279	45.1
1936 James H. Hughes (D)	67,136	53.0
Daniel O. Hastings (R)	52,460	41.4
Robert G. Houston (IR)	6,897	5.4
1942 Clayton Douglass Buck (R)	46,210	54.2
E. Ennals Berl (D)	38,322	44.9
1948 J. Allen Frear Jr. (D)	71,888	50.9
Clayton Douglass Buck (R)	68,246	48.3
1954 J. Allen Frear Jr. (D)	82,511	56.9
Herbert B. Warburton (R)	62,389	43.1
1960 J. Caleb Boggs (R)	98,874	50.7
J. Allen Frear Jr. (D)	96,090	49.3
1966 J. Caleb Boggs (R)	97,268	59.1
James M. Tunnell Jr. (D)	67,263	40.9
1972 Joseph R. Biden Jr. (D)	116,006	50.5
J. Caleb Boggs (R)	112,844	49.1
1978 Joseph R. Biden Jr. (D)	93,930	58.0
James H. Baxter (R)	66,479	41.0
1984 Joseph R. Biden Jr. (D)	147,831	60.1
John M. Burris (R)	98,101	39.1

FLORIDA

Candidates	Votes	%
Class 1		
1916 Park Trammell (D)	58,391	82.9
W. R. O'Neal (R)	8,774	12.5
1922 Park Trammell (D)	45,707	88.0
W. C. Lawson (IR)	6,074	11.7
1928 Park Trammell (D)	153,816	68.5
Barclay H. Warburton (R)	70,633	31.5

Candidates	Votes	%
1934 Park Trammell (D)	131,780	100.0
Special Election		
1936 Charles O. Andrews (D)	241,528	80.9
Howard C. Babcock (R)	57,016	19.1
1940 Charles O. Andrews (D)	323,216	100.0
1946 Spessard L. Holland (D)	156,232	78.7
J. Harry Schad (R)	42,413	21.4
1952 Spessard L. Holland (D)	616,665	99.8
1958 Spessard L. Holland (D)	386,113	71.2
Leland Hyzer (R)	155,956	28.8
1964 Spessard L. Holland (D)	997,585	63.9
Claude R. Kirk Jr. (R)	562,212	36.0
1970 Lawton Chiles (D)	902,438	53.9
William C. Cramer (R)	772,817	46.1
1976 Lawton Chiles (D)	1,799,518	63.0
John Grady (R)	1,057,886	37.0
1982 Lawton Chiles (D)	1,637,667	61.7
Van B. Poole (R)	1,015,330	38.3

Class 3

Candidates	Votes	%
1914 Duncan U. Fletcher (D)	22,761	99.5
1920 Duncan U. Fletcher (D)	98,966	74.3
John M. Cheney (R)	27,914	21.0
1926 Duncan U. Fletcher (D)	51,054	77.9
John M. Lindsay (RDC)	8,381	12.8
W. R. O'Neal (R)	6,133	9.4
1932 Duncan U. Fletcher (D)	204,651	99.8
Special Election		
1936 Claude Pepper (D)	246,050	100.0
1938 Claude Pepper (D)	145,757	82.5
Thomas E. Swanson (R)	31,035	17.6
1944 Claude Pepper (D)	335,685	71.3
Miles H. Draper (R)	135,258	28.7
1950 George A. Smathers (D)	238,987	76.2
John P. Booth (R)	74,228	23.7
1956 George A. Smathers (D)	655,418	100.0
1962 George A. Smathers (D)	657,633	70.0
Emerson Rupert (R)	281,381	30.0
1968 Edward J. Gurney (R)	1,131,499	55.9
Leroy Collins (D)	892,637	44.1
1974 Richard Stone (D)	781,031	43.4
Jack Eckerd (R)	736,674	40.9
John Grady (AM)	282,659	15.7
1980 Paula Hawkins (R)	1,822,460	51.7
Bill Gunter (D)	1,705,409	48.3

GEORGIA

Candidates	Votes	%
Class 2		
Special Election		
1914 Thomas W. Hardwick (D)	62,239	68.9
Hutch (PROG)	28,163	31.2
1918 William J. Harris (D)	53,731	88.4
Williams (R)	7,078	11.6
1924 William J. Harris (D)	155,497#	100.0
1930 William J. Harris (D)	55,606	100.0
Special Election		
1932 Richard B. Russell (D)	238,931	100.0

	Candidates	Votes	%
1936	Richard B. Russell (D)	263,468	100.0
1942	Richard B. Russell (D)	59,870	96.9
1948	Richard B. Russell (D)	362,104	99.9
1954	Richard B. Russell (D)	333,917	100.0
1960	Richard B. Russell (D)	576,140	99.9
1966	Richard B. Russell (D)	631,002	100.0
1972	Sam Nunn (D)	635,970	54.0
	Fletcher Thompson (R)	542,331	46.0

Special Election

1972	Sam Nunn (D)	404,890	52.0
	Fletcher Thompson (R)	362,501	46.5
1978	Sam Nunn (D)	536,320	83.1
	John W. Stokes (R)	108,808	16.9
1984	Sam Nunn (D)	1,344,104	79.9
	Jon Michael Hicks (R)	337,196	20.1

Class 3

1914	Hoke Smith (D)	61,489	68.4
	McClure (PROG)	28,435	31.6
1920	Thomas Watson (D)	124,630	94.9
	Harvey S. Edwards (I)	6,700	5.1

Special Election

1922	Walter F. George (D)	75,860	100.0
1926	Walter F. George (D)	47,446	100.0
1932	Walter F. George (D)	234,590	92.8
	James W. Arnold (R)	18,151	7.2
1938	Walter F. George (D)	66,897	95.1
1944	Walter F. George (D)	272,541	100.0
1950	Walter F. George (D)	261,290	100.0
1956	Herman E. Talmadge (D)	541,094	100.0
1962	Herman E. Talmadge (D)	306,250	100.0
1968	Herman E. Talmadge (D)	885,103	77.5
	E. Earl Patton (R)	256,796	22.5
1974	Herman E. Talmadge (D)	627,376	71.7
	Jerry Johnson (R)	246,866	28.2
1980	Mack Mattingly (R)	803,686	50.9
	Herman E. Talmadge (D)	776,143	49.1

HAWAII

	Candidates	Votes	%

(Became a state Aug. 21, 1959)

Class 1

1959	Hiram L. Fong (R)	87,161	52.9
	Frank F. Fasi (D)	77,647	47.1
1964	Hiram L. Fong (R)	110,747	53.0
	Thomas P. Gill (D)	96,789	46.4
1970	Hiram L. Fong (R)	124,163	51.6
	Cecil Heftel (D)	116,597	48.4
1976	Spark M. Matsunaga (D)	162,305	53.7
	William F. Quinn (R)	122,724	40.6
1982	Spark M. Matsunaga (D)	245,386	80.1
	Clarence J. Brown (R)	52,071	17.0

Class 3

1959	Oren E. Long (D)	83,700	51.1
	Wilfred C. Tsukiyama (R)	79,123	48.3
1962	Daniel K. Inouye (D)	136,294	69.4
	Ben Dillingham (R)	60,067	30.6
1968	Daniel K. Inouye (D)	189,248	83.4
	Wayne C. Thiessen (R)	34,008	15.0

	Candidates	Votes	%
1974	Daniel K. Inouye (D)	207,454	82.9
	James D. Kimmel (PP)	42,767	17.1
1980	Daniel K. Inouye (D)	224,485	77.9
	Cooper Brown (R)	53,068	18.4

IDAHO

	Candidates	Votes	%

Class 2

1918	William E. Borah (R)	63,587	67.2
	Frank L. Moore (D)	31,018	32.8
1924	William E. Borah (R)	99,846	79.5
	Frank Martin (D)	25,199	20.1
1930	William E. Borah (R)	94,938	72.4
	Joseph M. Tyler (D)	36,162	27.6
1936	William E. Borah (R)	128,723	63.4
	C. Ben Ross (D)	74,444	36.6

Special Election

1940	John Thomas (R)	124,535	53.0
	Glen H. Taylor (D)	110,664	47.1
1942	John Thomas (R)	73,353	51.5
	Glen H. Taylor (D)	68,989	48.5

Special Election

1946	Henry C. Dworshak (R)	105,523	58.6
	George E. Donart (D)	74,629	41.4
1948	Bert C. Miller (D)	107,000	50.0
	Henry C. Dworshak (R)	103,868	48.5

Special Election

1950	Henry C. Dworshak (R)	104,608	51.9
	Claude J. Burtenshaw (D)	97,092	48.1
1954	Henry C. Dworshak (R)	142,269	62.8
	Glen H. Taylor (D)	84,139	37.2
1960	Henry C. Dworshak (R)	152,648	52.3
	R. F. (Bob) McLaughlin (D)	139,448	47.7

Special Election

1962	Len B. Jordan (R)	131,279	51.0
	Gracie Pfost (D)	126,398	49.1
1966	Len B. Jordan (R)	139,819	55.4
	Ralph R. Harding (D)	112,637	44.6
1972	James A. McClure (R)	161,804	52.3
	William E. (Bud) Davis (D)	140,913	45.5
1978	James A. McClure (R)	194,412	68.4
	Dwight Jensen (D)	89,635	31.6
1984	James A. McClure (R)	293,193	72.2
	Peter M. Busch (D)	105,591	26.0

Class 3

1914	James H. Brady (R)	47,486	43.9
	James H. Hawley (D)	41,266	38.1
	Paul Clagstone (EP)	10,321	9.5
	C. W. Cooper (SOC)	7,888	7.3

Candidates	Votes	%
Special Election		
1918 John F. Nugent (D)	48,467	*50.5*
Frank R. Gooding (R)	47,497	*49.5*
1920 Frank R. Gooding (R)	75,985	*54.1*
John F. Nugent (D)	64,513	*45.9*
1926 Frank R. Gooding (R)	56,847	*45.4*
H. F. Samuels (PROG)	37,047	*29.6*
John F. Nugent (D)	31,285	*25.0*
Special Election		
1928 John Thomas (R)	90,922	*62.6*
Chase Clark (D)	53,399	*36.7*
1932 James Pope (D)	103,020	*55.7*
John Thomas (R)	78,225	*42.3*
1938 D. Worth Clark (D)	99,801	*54.7*
Donald A. Callahan (R)	81,939	*44.9*
1944 Glen H. Taylor (D)	107,096	*51.1*
C. A. Bottolfsen (R)	102,373	*48.9*
1950 Herman Welker (R)	124,237	*61.7*
D. Worth Clark (D)	77,180	*38.3*
1956 Frank Church (D)	149,096	*56.2*
Herman Welker (R)	102,781	*38.7*
Glen H. Taylor (WRITE IN)	13,415	*5.1*
1962 Frank Church (D)	141,657	*54.7*
Jack Hawley (R)	117,129	*45.3*
1968 Frank Church (D)	173,482	*60.3*
George V. Hansen (R)	114,394	*39.7*
1974 Frank Church (D)	145,140	*56.1*
Robert L. Smith (R)	109,072	*42.1*
1980 Steven D. Symms (R)	218,701	*49.7*
Frank Church (D)	214,439	*48.8*

ILLINOIS

Candidates	Votes	%
Class 2		
1918 Medill McCormick (R)	479,957	*50.5*
James Hamilton Lewis (D)	426,943	*44.9*
1924 Charles S. Deneen (R)	1,449,180	*63.5*
Albert A. Sprague (D)	806,702	*35.4*
1930 James Hamilton Lewis (D)	1,432,216	*64.0*
Ruth Hanna McCormick (R)	687,469	*30.7*
1936 James Hamilton Lewis (D)	2,142,887	*56.5*
Otis F. Glenn (R)	1,545,160	*40.7*
Special Election		
1940 C. Wayland Brooks (R)	2,045,924	*50.1*
James M. Slattery (D)	2,025,097	*49.6*
1942 C. Wayland Brooks (R)	1,582,887	*53.2*
Raymond S. McKeough (D)	1,380,011	*46.4*
1948 Paul H. Douglas (D)	2,147,754	*55.1*
C. Wayland Brooks (R)	1,740,026	*44.6*
1954 Paul H. Douglas (D)	1,804,338	*53.6*
Joseph T. Meek (R)	1,563,683	*46.4*
1960 Paul H. Douglas (D)	2,530,943	*54.6*
Samuel W. Witwer (R)	2,093,846	*45.2*
1966 Charles H. Percy (R)	2,100,449	*55.0*
Paul H. Douglas (D)	1,678,147	*43.9*
1972 Charles H. Percy (R)	2,867,078	*62.2*
Roman Pucinski (D)	1,721,031	*37.4*
1978 Charles H. Percy (R)	1,698,711	*53.3*
Alex Seith (D)	1,448,187	*45.5*

	Candidates	Votes	%
1984	Paul Simon (D)	2,397,303	*50.1*
	Charles H. Percy (R)	2,308,039	*48.2*

Class 3

	Candidates	Votes	%
1914	Lawrence Y. Sherman (R)	390,661	*38.5*
	Roger C. Sullivan (D)	373,403	*36.8*
	Raymond Robins (PROG)	203,027	*20.0*
1920	William B. McKinley (R)	1,381,384	*66.8*
	Peter A. Waller (D)	554,372	*26.8*
1926	Frank L. Smith (R)	842,273*	*46.9*
	George E. Brennan (D)	774,943	*43.1*
	Hugh S. Magill (IR)	156,245	*8.7*

Special Election

1928	Otis F. Glenn (R)	1,594,031	*54.5*
	Anton J. Cermak (D)	1,315,338	*44.9*

1932	William H. Dieterich (D)	1,670,466	*52.2*
	Otis F. Glenn (R)	1,471,841	*46.0*
1938	Scott W. Lucas (D)	1,638,162	*51.3*
	Richard J. Lyons (R)	1,542,574	*48.3*
1944	Scott W. Lucas (D)	2,059,023	*52.6*
	Richard J. Lyons (R)	1,841,793	*47.1*
1950	Everett McKinley Dirksen (R)	1,951,984	*53.9*
	Scott W. Lucas (D)	1,657,630	*45.8*
1956	Everett McKinley Dirksen (R)	2,307,352	*54.1*
	Richard Stengel (D)	1,949,883	*45.7*
1962	Everett McKinley Dirksen (R)	1,961,202	*52.9*
	Sidney R. Yates (D)	1,748,007	*47.1*
1968	Everett McKinley Dirksen (R)	2,358,947	*53.0*
	William G. Clark (D)	2,073,242	*46.6*

Special Election

1970	Adlai E. Stevenson III (D)	2,065,054	*57.4*
	Ralph Tyler Smith (R)	1,519,718	*42.2*

1974	Adlai E. Stevenson III (D)	1,811,496	*62.2*
	George M. Burditt (R)	1,084,884	*37.2*
1980	Alan J. Dixon (D)	2,565,302	*56.0*
	David C. O'Neal (R)	1,946,296	*42.5*

INDIANA

	Candidates	Votes	%
	Class 1		
1916	Harry S. New (R)	337,089	*47.8*
	John W. Kern (D)	325,588	*46.1*
1922	Samuel M. Ralston (D)	558,169	*50.9*
	Albert J. Beveridge (R)	524,558	*47.8*

Special Election

1926	Arthur R. Robinson (R)	519,401	*50.6*
	Evans Woollen (D)	496,540	*48.4*

1928	Arthur R. Robinson (R)	782,144	*55.3*
	Albert Stump (D)	623,996	*44.1*
1934	Sherman Minton (D)	758,801	*51.5*
	Arthur R. Robinson (R)	700,103	*47.5*
1940	Raymond E. Willis (R)	888,070	*50.5*
	Sherman Minton (D)	864,803	*49.1*
1946	William E. Jenner (R)	739,809	*54.9*
	M. Clifford Townsend (D)	584,288	*43.4*
1952	William E. Jenner (R)	1,020,605	*52.4*
	Henry F. Schricker (D)	911,169	*46.8*

	Candidates	Votes	%
1958	R. Vance Hartke (D)	973,636	56.5
	Harold W. Handley (R)	731,635	42.4
1964	R. Vance Hartke (D)	1,128,505	54.3
	D. Russell Bontrager (R)	941,519	45.3
1970	R. Vance Hartke (D)	870,990	50.1
	Richard L. Roudebush (R)	866,707	49.9
1976	Richard G. Lugar (R)	1,275,833	58.8
	R. Vance Hartke (D)	878,522	40.5
1982	Richard G. Lugar (R)	978,301	53.8
	Floyd Fithian (D)	828,400	45.6

Class 3

	Candidates	Votes	%
1914	Benjamin F. Shively (D)	272,249	42.1
	Hugh Miller (R)	226,766	35.1
	Albert J. Beveridge (PROG)	108,581	16.8

Special Election

1916	James E. Watson (R)	335,193	47.7
	Thomas Taggart (D)	325,607	46.3

1920	James E. Watson (R)	681,854	54.6
	Thomas Taggart (D)	514,191	41.2
1926	James E. Watson (R)	522,737	50.0
	Albert Stump (D)	511,454	49.0
1932	Frederick Van Nuys (D)	870,053	55.6
	James E. Watson (R)	661,750	42.3
1938	Frederick Van Nuys (D)	788,386	49.8
	Raymond E. Willis (R)	783,189	49.5

Special Election

1944	William E. Jenner (R)	857,250	52.1
	Cornelius O'Brien (D)	775,417	47.1

1944	Homer E. Capehart (R)	829,489	50.2
	Henry F. Schricker (D)	807,766	48.9
1950	Homer E. Capehart (R)	844,303	52.8
	Alex M. Campbell (D)	741,025	46.4
1956	Homer E. Capehart (R)	1,084,262	55.2
	Claude R. Wickard (D)	871,781	44.4
1962	Birch Bayh (D)	905,491	50.3
	Homer E. Capehart (R)	894,547	49.7
1968	Birch Bayh (D)	1,060,456	51.7
	William D. Ruckelshaus (R)	988,571	48.2
1974	Birch Bayh (D)	889,269	50.7
	Richard G. Lugar (R)	814,117	46.4
1980	Dan Quayle (R)	1,182,414	53.8
	Birch Bayh (D)	1,015,962	46.2

IOWA

	Candidates	Votes	%
	Class 2		
1918	William S. Kenyon (R)	230,264	65.4
	Charles R. Keyes (D)	121,830	34.6

Special Election

1922	Smith W. Brookhart (R)	389,751	63.1
	Clyde L. Herring (D)	227,833	36.9

1924[1]	Smith W. Brookhart (R)	447,594	50.0
	Daniel F. Steck (D)	446,840	50.0
1930	Lester J. Dickinson (R)	307,613	56.3
	Daniel F. Steck (D)	235,186	43.0
1936	Clyde L. Herring (D)	539,555	50.5
	Lester J. Dickinson (R)	503,635	47.1

	Candidates	Votes	%
1942	George A. Wilson (R)	410,333	58.0
	Clyde L. Herring (D)	295,194	41.7
1948	Guy M. Gillette (D)	578,226	57.8
	George A. Wilson (R)	415,778	41.6
1954	Thomas E. Martin (R)	442,409	52.2
	Guy M. Gillette (D)	402,712	47.5
1960	Jack Miller (R)	642,463	51.9
	Herschel C. Loveless (D)	595,119	48.1
1966	Jack Miller (R)	522,339	60.9
	E. B. Smith (D)	324,114	37.8
1972	Dick Clark (D)	662,637	55.1
	Jack Miller (R)	530,525	44.1
1978	Roger W. Jepsen (R)	421,598	51.1
	Dick Clark (D)	395,066	47.9
1984	Tom Harkin (D)	716,883	55.5
	Roger W. Jepsen (R)	564,381	43.7

Class 3

1914	Albert B. Cummins (R)	205,832	48.2
	Connolly (D)	167,251	39.2
	Spurgeon (I)	24,490	5.7
1920	Albert B. Cummins (R)	528,499	61.4
	Claude R. Porter (D)	322,015	37.4
1926	Smith W. Brookhart (R)	323,409	56.5
	Claude R. Porter (D)	247,869	43.3

Special Election

1926	David W. Stewart (R)	336,410	100.0

1932	Richard Louis Murphy (D)	538,422	54.9
	Henry Field (R)	399,929	40.8

Special Election

1936	Guy M. Gillette (D)	536,075	51.9
	Berry F. Halden (R)	481,521	46.6

1938	Guy M. Gillette (D)	413,788	49.7
	Lester J. Dickinson (R)	410,983	49.4
1944	Bourke B. Hickenlooper (R)	523,963	51.3
	Guy M. Gillette (D)	494,229	48.4
1950	Bourke B. Hickenlooper (R)	470,613	54.8
	Albert J. Loveland (D)	383,766	44.7
1956	Bourke B. Hickenlooper (R)	635,499	53.9
	R. M. Evans (D)	543,156	46.1
1962	Bourke B. Hickenlooper (R)	431,364	53.4
	E. B. Smith (D)	376,602	46.6
1968	Harold E. Hughes (D)	574,884	50.3
	David M. Stanley (R)	568,469	49.7
1974	John C. Culver (D)	462,947	52.0
	David M. Stanley (R)	420,546	47.3
1980	Charles E. Grassley (R)	683,014	53.5
	John C. Culver (D)	581,545	45.5

1. Disputed election. See list of senators, Iowa, p. 586.

KANSAS

	Candidates	Votes	%
	Class 2		
1912	William H. Thompson (D)	172,601	49.3
	W. R. Stubbs (R)	151,647	43.3
	Allan W. Ricker (SOC)	25,610	7.3
1918	Arthur Capper (R)	281,931	63.7
	William H. Thompson (D)	149,300	33.7
1924	Arthur Capper (R)	428,494	70.1
	James Malone (D)	154,189	25.2

	Candidates	Votes	%
1930	Arthur Capper (R)	364,548	61.1
	Jonathan M. Davis (D)	232,161	38.9
1936	Arthur Capper (R)	417,873	51.0
	Omar B. Ketchum (D)	396,685	48.4
1942	Arthur Capper (R)	284,059	57.1
	George McGill (D)	200,437	40.3
1948	Andrew F. Schoeppel (R)	393,412	54.9
	George McGill (D)	305,987	42.7
1954	Andrew F. Schoeppel (R)	348,144	56.3
	George McGill (D)	258,575	41.8
1960	Andrew F. Schoeppel (R)	485,499	54.6
	Frank Theis (D)	388,895	43.8

Special Election

1962	James B. Pearson (R)	344,689	56.2
	Paul L. Aylward (D)	260,756	42.5
1966	James B. Pearson (R)	350,077	52.2
	J. Floyd Breeding (D)	303,223	45.2
1972	James B. Pearson (R)	622,591	71.4
	Arch Tetzlaff (D)	200,764	23.0
1978	Nancy Landon Kassebaum (R)	403,354	53.9
	William R. Roy (D)	317,602	42.4
1984	Nancy Landon Kassebaum (R)	757,402	76.0
	James R. Maher (D)	211,664	21.2

Class 3

1914	Charles Curtis (R)	180,823	35.5
	George A. Neeley (D)	176,929	34.8
	Victor Murdock (PROG)	116,755	22.9
1920	Charles Curtis (R)	327,072	64.0
	George H. Hodges (D)	170,443	33.4
1926	Charles Curtis (R)	308,222	63.6
	Charles Stephens (D)	168,446	34.7

Special Election

1930	George McGill (D)	288,889	50.0
	Henry J. Allen (R)	276,833	48.0
1932	George McGill (D)	328,992	45.7
	Ben S. Paulen (R)	302,809	42.0
	George Alfred Brown (I)	65,583	9.1
1938	Clyde M. Reed (R)	419,532	56.2
	George McGill (D)	326,774	43.8
1944	Clyde M. Reed (R)	387,090	57.8
	Thurman Hill (D)	272,053	40.7
1950	Frank Carlson (R)	335,880	54.3
	Paul Aiken (D)	271,365	43.8

Special Election

1950	Frank Carlson (R)	321,718	55.2
	Paul Aiken (D)	261,405	44.8
1956	Frank Carlson (R)	477,822	57.9
	George Hart (D)	333,939	40.5
1962	Frank Carlson (R)	388,500	62.4
	K. L. Smith (D)	223,630	35.9
1968	Bob Dole (R)	490,911	60.1
	William I. Robinson (D)	315,911	38.7
1974	Bob Dole (R)	403,983	50.9
	William R. Roy (D)	390,451	49.1
1980	Robert Dole (R)	598,686	63.8
	John Simpson (D)	340,271	36.2

KENTUCKY

Candidates		Votes	%

Class 2

1918	Augustus Owsley Stanley (D)	184,385	50.8
	Ben L. Bruner (R)	178,797	49.2
1924	Frederic M. Sackett (R)	406,123	51.6
	Augustus Owsley Stanley (D)	381,605	48.4
1930	Marvel M. Logan (D)	336,748	52.1
	John M. Robsion (R)	309,180	47.9
1936	Marvel M. Logan (D)	539,968	58.8
	Robert M. Lucas (R)	365,850	39.8

Special Election

1940	Albert B. (Happy) Chandler (D)	561,151	58.3
	Walter B. Smith (R)	401,812	41.7
1942	Albert B. (Happy) Chandler (D)	216,958	55.3
	Richard J. Colbert (R)	175,081	44.7

Special Election

1946	John Sherman Cooper (R)	327,652	53.3
	John Young Brown (D)	285,829	46.5
1948	Virgil Chapman (D)	408,256	51.4
	John Sherman Cooper (R)	383,776	48.3

Special Election

1952	John Sherman Cooper (R)	494,576	51.5
	Thomas R. Underwood (D)	465,652	48.5
1954	Alben W. Barkley (D)	434,109	54.5
	John Sherman Cooper (R)	362,948	45.5

Special Election

1956	John Sherman Cooper (R)	538,505	53.2
	Lawrence W. Wetherby (D)	473,140	46.8
1960	John Sherman Cooper (R)	644,087	59.2
	Keen Johnson (D)	444,290	40.8
1966	John Sherman Cooper (R)	483,805	64.5
	John Young Brown (D)	266,079	35.5
1972	Walter D. Huddleston (D)	528,550	50.9
	Louie B. Nunn (R)	494,337	47.6
1978	Walter D. Huddleston (D)	290,730	61.0
	Louie Guenthner (R)	175,766	36.9
1984	Mitch McConnell (R)	644,990	49.9
	Walter D. Huddleston (D)	639,721	49.5

Class 3

1914	John C. W. Beckham (D)	175,999	51.8
	Willson (R)	144,758	42.6

Special Election

1914	Johnson N. Camden Jr. (D)	177,797	54.0
	Bullitt (R)	133,139	40.4
1920	Richard P. Ernst (R)	454,226	50.3
	John C. W. Beckham (D)	449,244	49.7
1926	Alben W. Barkley (D)	286,997	51.8
	Richard P. Ernst (R)	266,657	48.2
1932	Alben W. Barkley (D)	574,977	59.2
	M. H. Thatcher (R)	393,865	40.5

	Candidates	Votes	%
1938	Alben W. Barkley (D)	346,735	62.0
	John P. Haswell (R)	212,266	38.0
1944	Alben W. Barkley (D)	464,053	54.8
	James Park (R)	380,425	44.9
1950	Earle C. Clements (D)	334,249	54.2
	Charles I. Dawson (R)	278,368	45.1

Special Election

1950	Earle C. Clements (D)	317,320#	54.4
	Charles I. Dawson (R)	265,994#	45.6

1956	Thruston B. Morton (R)	506,903	50.4
	Earle C. Clements (D)	499,922	49.7
1962	Thruston B. Morton (R)	432,648	52.8
	Wilson W. Wyatt (D)	387,440	47.2
1968	Marlow W. Cook (R)	484,260	51.4
	Katherine Peden (D)	448,960	47.6
1974	Wendell H. Ford (D)	399,406	53.5
	Marlow W. Cook (R)	328,982	44.1
1980	Wendell H. Ford (D)	720,861	65.1
	Mary Louise Foust (R)	386,029	34.9

LOUISIANA

	Candidates	Votes	%

Class 2

1918	Joseph E. Ransdell (D)	44,224	100.0
1924	Joseph E. Ransdell (D)	94,939	100.0
1930	Huey P. Long (D)	130,536	100.0

Special Election

1936	Rose McConnell Long (D)	131,930#	100.0

1936	Allen J. Ellender (D)	293,256	100.0
1942	Allen J. Ellender (D)	85,488	100.0
1948	Allen J. Ellender (D)	330,315	100.0
1954	Allen J. Ellender (D)	207,115	100.0
1960	Allen J. Ellender (D)	432,228	79.8
	George W. Reese Jr. (R)	109,698	20.2
1966	Allen J. Ellender (D)	437,695	100.0
1972	J. Bennett Johnston (D)	598,987	55.2
	John J. McKeithen (I)	250,161	23.1
	Ben C. Toledano (R)	206,846	19.1
1978 [2]	J. Bennett Johnston (D)	—	—
1984 [2]	J. Bennett Johnston (D)	—	—

Class 3

1914	Robert F. Broussard (D)	✓	

Special Election

1918	Edward J. Gay (D)	44,345	100.0

1920	Edwin S. Broussard (D)	94,944#	100.0
1926	Edwin S. Broussard (D)	54,180	100.0
1932	John H. Overton (D)	249,189	100.0
1938	John H. Overton (D)	151,585	99.8
1944	John H. Overton (D)	286,365	100.0

Special Election

1948	Russell B. Long (D)	305,346	74.9
	Clem S. Clarke (R)	102,339	25.1

1950	Russell B. Long (D)	220,907	87.7
	Charles S. Gerth (R)	30,931	12.3

	Candidates	Votes	%
1956	Russell B. Long (D)	335,564	100.0
1962	Russell B. Long (D)	318,838	75.6
	Taylor Walters O'Hearn (R)	103,066	24.4
1968	Russell B. Long (D)	518,586	100.0
1974	Russell B. Long (D)	434,643	100.0
1980 [2]	Russell B. Long (D)	—	—

2. Dash (—) in place of 1978, 1980 and 1984 votes indicates elected. Louisiana holds an open-primary election with candidates from all parties running on the same ballot. Any candidate who receives a majority is elected; if no candidate receives 50 percent, there is a runoff election in November between the two top finishers.

MAINE

	Candidates	Votes	%

Class 1

1916	Frederick Hale (R)	79,841	52.8
	Charles Johnson (D)	69,486	46.0
1922	Frederick Hale (R)	101,026	57.5
	Oakley C. Curtis (D)	74,659	42.5
1928	Frederick Hale (R)	145,501	69.6
	Herbert E. Holmes (D)	63,429	30.4
1934	Frederick Hale (R)	139,773	50.1
	F. Harold Dubord (D)	138,573	49.7
1940	Ralph O. Brewster (R)	150,149	58.6
	Louis J. Brann (D)	105,740	41.3
1946	Ralph O. Brewster (R)	111,215	63.6
	Peter M. MacDonald (D)	63,799	36.5
1952	Frederick G. Payne (R)	139,205	58.7
	Roger P. Dube (D)	82,665	34.9
	Earl S. Grant (I)	15,294#	6.4
1958	Edmund S. Muskie (D)	172,842	60.8
	Frederick G. Payne (R)	111,522	39.2
1964	Edmund S. Muskie (D)	253,511	66.6
	Clifford G. McIntire (R)	127,040	33.4
1970	Edmund S. Muskie (D)	199,954	61.9
	Neil S. Bishop (R)	123,906	38.3
1976	Edmund S. Muskie (D)	292,704	60.2
	Robert A. G. Monks (R)	193,489	39.8
1982	George J. Mitchell (D)	279,819	60.9
	David F. Emery (R)	179,882	39.1

Class 2

Special Election

1916	Bert M. Fernald (R)	81,369	54.3
	Kenneth Sills (D)	68,201	45.5

1918	Bert M. Fernald (R)	66,858	55.6
	Earl Newbert (D)	53,460	44.4
1924	Bert M. Fernald (R)	148,783	60.4
	Fulton J. Redman (D)	97,428	39.6

Special Election

1926	Arthur R. Gould (R)	79,498	71.8
	Fulton J. Redman (D)	31,225	28.2

1930	Wallace H. White Jr. (R)	88,262	60.9
	Frank H. Haskell (D)	56,561	39.1
1936	Wallace H. White Jr. (R)	158,068	50.8
	Louis J. Brann (D)	153,420	49.3
1942	Wallace H. White Jr. (R)	111,520	66.7
	Fulton J. Redman (D)	55,754	33.3
1948	Margaret Chase Smith (R)	159,182	71.3
	Adrian H. Scolten (D)	64,074	28.7
1954	Margaret Chase Smith (R)	144,530	58.6
	Paul A. Fullam (D)	102,075	41.4

	Candidates	Votes	%
1960	Margaret Chase Smith (R)	256,890	61.7
	Lucia M. Cormier (D)	159,809	38.4
1966	Margaret Chase Smith (R)	188,291	59.0
	Elmer H. Violette (D)	131,136	41.1
1972	William D. Hathaway (D)	224,270	53.2
	Margaret Chase Smith (R)	197,040	46.8
1978	William S. Cohen (R)	212,294	56.6
	William D. Hathaway (D)	127,327	33.9
	Hayes E. Gahagan (I)	27,824	7.4
1984	William S. Cohen (R)	404,414	73.3
	Elizabeth H. Mitchell (D)	142,626	25.9

MARYLAND

Class 1

Special Election

	Candidates	Votes	%
1913	Blair Lee (D)	112,485#	56.8
	Thomas Parran (R)	73,300#	37.0

1916	Joseph Irwin France (R)	113,662	49.3
	David J. Lewis (D)	109,740	47.6
1922	William Cabell Bruce (D)	160,947	52.6
	Joseph Irwin France (R)	139,581	45.6
1928	Phillips Lee Goldsborough (R)	256,224	54.1
	William Cabell Bruce (D)	214,447	45.2
1934	George L. Radcliffe (D)	264,279	56.1
	Joseph Irwin France (R)	197,643	42.0
1940	George L. Radcliffe (D)	394,239#	64.7
	Harry W. Nice (R)	203,912#	33.5
1946	Herbert R. O'Conor (D)	237,232#	50.2
	David John Markey (R)	235,000#	49.8
1952	J. Glenn Beall (R)	449,823	52.5
	George P. Mahoney (D)	406,370	47.5
1958	J. Glenn Beall (R)	382,021	51.0
	Thomas D'Alesandro Jr. (D)	367,270	49.0
1964	Joseph D. Tydings (D)	678,649	62.8
	J. Glenn Beall (R)	402,393	37.2
1970	J. Glenn Beall Jr. (R)	484,960	50.7
	Joseph D. Tydings (D)	460,442	48.1
1976	Paul S. Sarbanes (D)	772,101	56.5
	J. Glenn Beall Jr. (R)	530,439	38.8
1982	Paul S. Sarbanes (D)	707,356	63.5
	Lawrence J. Hogan (R)	407,334	36.5

Class 3

1914	John Walter Smith (D)	110,204	51.0
	Edward C. Carrington Jr. (R)	94,864	43.9
1920	Ovington E. Weller (R)	184,999	47.3
	John Walter Smith (D)	169,200	43.3
	George D. Iverson Jr. (I)	21,345	5.5
1926	Millard E. Tydings (D)	195,410	57.6
	Ovington E. Weller (R)	139,995	41.3
1932	Millard E. Tydings (D)	293,389	66.2
	Wallace Williams (R)	138,266	31.2
1938	Millard E. Tydings (D)	357,245	68.3
	Oscar Leser (R)	153,253	29.3
1944	Millard E. Tydings (D)	344,725	61.7
	Blanchard Randall Jr. (R)	213,705	38.3
1950	John Marshall Butler (R)	326,291	53.0
	Millard E. Tydings (D)	283,180	46.0
1956	John Marshall Butler (R)	473,059	53.0
	George P. Mahoney (D)	419,108	47.0
1962	Daniel B. Brewster (D)	439,723	62.0
	Edward T. Miller (R)	269,131	38.0
1968	Charles McC. Mathias Jr. (R)	541,893	47.8
	Daniel B. Brewster (D)	443,367	39.1

	Candidates	Votes	%
	George P. Mahoney (I)	148,467	13.1
1974	Charles McC. Mathias Jr. (R)	503,223	57.3
	Barbara Mikulski (D)	374,563	42.7
1980	Charles McC. Mathias Jr. (R)	850,970	66.2
	Edward T. Conroy (D)	435,118	33.8

MASSACHUSETTS

Class 1

	Candidates	Votes	%
1916	Henry Cabot Lodge (R)	267,177	51.7
	John F. Fitzgerald (D)	234,238	45.3
1922	Henry Cabot Lodge (R)	414,130	47.6
	William A. Gaston (D)	406,776	46.8

Special Election

1926	David I. Walsh (D)	525,303	52.0
	William M. Butler (R)	469,989	46.5

1928	David I. Walsh (D)	818,055	53.6
	Benjamin Loring Young (R)	693,563	45.5
1934	David I. Walsh (D)	852,776	59.4
	Robert M. Washburn (R)	536,692	37.4
1940	David I. Walsh (D)	1,088,838	55.6
	Henry Parkman Jr. (R)	838,122	42.8
1946	Henry Cabot Lodge Jr. (R)	989,736	59.6
	David I. Walsh (D)	660,200	39.7
1952	John F. Kennedy (D)	1,211,984	51.4
	Henry Cabot Lodge Jr. (R)	1,141,247	48.4
1958	John F. Kennedy (D)	1,362,926	73.2
	Vincent J. Celeste (R)	488,318	26.2

Special Election

1962	Edward M. Kennedy (D)	1,162,611	55.4
	George C. Lodge (R)	877,669	41.9

1964	Edward M. Kennedy (D)	1,716,907	74.3
	Howard Whitmore Jr. (R)	587,663	25.4
1970	Edward M. Kennedy (D)	1,202,856	62.1
	Josiah A. Spaulding (R)	715,978	37.0
1976	Edward M. Kennedy (D)	1,726,657	69.3
	Michael Robertson (R)	722,641	29.0
1982	Edward M. Kennedy (D)	1,247,084	60.8
	Raymond Shamie (R)	784,602	38.3

Class 2

1918	David I. Walsh (D)	207,478	49.7
	John W. Weeks (R)	188,287	45.1
	Thomas W. Lawson (I)	21,985	5.3
1924	Frederick H. Gillett (R)	566,188	50.3
	David I. Walsh (D)	547,600	48.6
1930	Marcus A. Coolidge (D)	651,939	54.0
	William M. Butler (R)	539,226	44.7
1936	Henry Cabot Lodge Jr. (R)	875,160	48.5
	James M. Curley (D)	739,751	41.0
	Thomas C. O'Brien (UN)	134,245	7.4
1942	Henry Cabot Lodge Jr. (R)	721,239	52.4
	Joseph E. Casey (D)	641,042	46.6

Special Election

1944	Leverett Saltonstall (R)	1,228,754	64.3
	John H. Corcoran (D)	667,086	34.9

1948	Leverett Saltonstall (R)	1,088,475	53.0
	John I. Fitzgerald (D)	954,398	46.4

	Candidates	Votes	%
1954	Leverett Saltonstall (R)	956,605	50.5
	Foster Furcolo (D)	927,899	49.0
1960	Leverett Saltonstall (R)	1,358,556	56.2
	Thomas J. O'Connor Jr. (D)	1,050,725	43.5
1966	Edward W. Brooke (R)	1,213,473	60.7
	Endicott Peabody (D)	774,761	38.7
1972	Edward W. Brooke (R)	1,505,932	63.5
	John J. Droney (D)	823,278	34.7
1978	Paul E. Tsongas (D)	1,093,283	55.1
	Edward W. Brooke (R)	890,584	44.8
1984	John Kerry (D)	1,393,150	55.1
	Raymond Shamie (R)	1,136,913	44.9

MICHIGAN

	Candidates	Votes	%
	Class 1		
1916	Charles E. Townsend (R)	364,657	56.3
	Lawrence Price (D)	257,954	39.9
1922	Woodbridge N. Ferris (D)	294,932	50.6
	Charles E. Townsend (R)	281,843	48.4
1928	Arthur H. Vandenberg (R)	977,893	71.8
	John W. Bailey (D)	376,592	27.7

Special Election

1928	Arthur H. Vandenberg (R)	974,203	72.0
	John W. Bailey (D)	375,673	27.8

1934	Arthur H. Vandenberg (R)	626,017	51.3
	Frank A. Picard (D)	573,574	47.0
1940	Arthur H. Vandenberg (R)	1,053,104	52.7
	Frank Fitzgerald (D)	939,740	47.0
1946	Arthur H. Vandenberg (R)	1,085,570	67.1
	James H. Lee (D)	517,923	32.0
1952	Charles E. Potter (R)	1,428,352	50.6
	Blair Moody (D)	1,383,416	49.0

Special Election

1952	Charles E. Potter (R)	1,417,032	51.2
	Blair Moody (D)	1,347,705	48.7

1958	Philip A. Hart (D)	1,216,966	53.6
	Charles E. Potter (R)	1,046,963	46.1
1964	Philip A. Hart (D)	1,996,912	64.4
	Elly M. Peterson (R)	1,096,272	35.3
1970	Philip A. Hart (D)	1,744,672	66.8
	Lenore Romney (R)	858,438	32.9
1976	Donald W. Riegle Jr. (D)	1,831,031	52.5
	Marvin L. Esch (R)	1,635,087	46.8
1982	Donald W. Riegle Jr. (D)	1,728,793	57.7
	Philip E. Ruppe (R)	1,223,288	40.9

	Class 2		
1918	Truman H. Newberry (R)	220,054	50.2
	Henry Ford (D)	212,487	48.5
1924	James Couzens (R)	858,934	74.3
	Mortimer E. Cooley (D)	284,609	24.6

Special Election

1924	James Couzens (R)	839,569	75.0
	Mortimer E. Cooley (D)	266,851	23.9

1930	James Couzens (R)	634,577	78.2
	Thomas A. E. Weadock (D)	169,757	20.9
1936	Prentiss M. Brown (D)	910,937	53.3

	Candidates	Votes	%
	Wilber M. Brucker (R)	714,602	41.8
1942	Homer Ferguson (R)	589,652	49.6
	Prentiss M. Brown (D)	561,595	47.2
1948	Homer Ferguson (R)	1,045,156	50.7
	Frank E. Hook (D)	1,000,329	48.5
1954	Patrick V. McNamara (D)	1,088,550	50.8
	Homer Ferguson (R)	1,049,420	48.9
1960	Patrick V. McNamara (D)	1,669,179	51.7
	Alvin M. Bentley (R)	1,548,873	48.0
1966	Robert P. Griffin (R)	1,363,530	55.9
	G. Mennen Williams (D)	1,069,484	43.8

Special Election

1966	Robert P. Griffin (R)	1,321,222	56.0
	G. Mennen Williams (D)	1,031,138	43.7

1972	Robert P. Griffin (R)	1,781,065	52.3
	Frank J. Kelley (D)	1,577,178	46.3
1978	Carl Levin (D)	1,484,193	52.1
	Robert P. Griffin (R)	1,362,165	47.9
1984	Carl Levin (D)	1,915,831	51.8
	Jack Lousma (R)	1,745,302	47.2

MINNESOTA

	Candidates	Votes	%
	Class 1		
1916	Frank B. Kellogg (R)	185,159	48.6
	Daniel W. Lawler (D)	117,541	30.8
	W. G. Calderwood (P)	78,425	20.6
1922	Henrik Shipstead (F-LAB)	325,372	47.1
	Frank B. Kellogg (R)	241,833	35.0
	Anna D. Olesen (D)	123,624	17.9
1928	Henrik Shipstead (F-LAB)	665,169	65.4
	Arthur E. Nelson (R)	342,992	33.7
1934	Henrik Shipstead (F-LAB)	503,379	49.9
	Einar Hoidale (D)	294,757	29.2
	N. J. Holmberg (R)	200,083	19.8
1940	Henrik Shipstead (R)	641,049	53.0
	Elmer A. Benson (F-LAB)	310,875	25.7
	John E. Regan (D)	248,658	20.6
1946	Edward J. Thye (R)	517,775	58.9
	Theodore Jorgenson (DFL)	349,520	39.8
1952	Edward J. Thye (R)	785,649	56.6
	William E. Carlson (DFL)	590,011	42.5
1958	Eugene J. McCarthy (DFL)	608,847	52.9
	Edward J. Thye (R)	536,629	46.6
1964	Eugene J. McCarthy (DFL)	931,363	60.3
	Wheelock Whitney (R)	605,933	39.3
1970	Hubert H. Humphrey (DFL)	788,256	57.8
	Clark MacGregor (R)	568,025	41.6
1976	Hubert H. Humphrey (DFL)	1,290,736	67.5
	Gerald W. Brekke (R)	478,611	25.0
	Paul Helm (AM)	125,612	6.6

Special Election

1978	Dave Durenberger (IR)	957,908	61.4
	Robert E. Short (DFL)	538,675	34.5

1982	Dave Durenberger (IR)	949,207	52.6
	Mark Dayton (DFL)	840,401	46.6

	Class 2		
1912	Knute Nelson (R)	173,074	62.8
	Daniel W. Lawler (D)	102,691	37.2
1918	Knute Nelson (R)	206,687	60.1
	W. G. Calderwood (N)	137,294	39.9

Candidates	Votes	%
Special Election		
1923 Magnus Johnson (F-LAB)	290,165#	57.5
J. A. O. Preus (R)	195,319#	38.7
1924 Thomas D. Schall (R)	388,594	46.5
Magnus Johnson (F-LAB)	380,646	45.5
John J. Farrell (D)	53,709	6.4
1930 Thomas D. Schall (R)	293,626	37.6
Einar Hoidale (D)	282,018	36.1
Ernest Lundeen (F-LAB)	178,671	22.9
1936 Ernest Lundeen (F-LAB)	663,363	62.2
Theodore Christianson (R)	402,404	37.8
Special Election		
1936 Guy V. Howard (R)	317,457	42.9
N. J. Holmberg (I)	210,364	28.4
Andrew Olaf Devolt (I PROG)	147,858	20.0
John G. Alexander (I)	64,493	8.7
1942 Joseph H. Ball (R)	356,297	47.0
Elmer A. Benson (F-LAB)	213,965	28.2
Martin A. Nelson (I PROG)	109,231	14.4
Ed Murphy (D)	78,959	10.4
Special Election		
1942 Arthur E. Nelson (R)	372,240	56.1
Al Hansen (F-LAB)	177,008	26.7
John E. O'Rourke (D)	114,086	17.2
1948 Hubert H. Humphrey (DFL)	729,494	59.9
Joseph H. Ball (R)	482,801	39.7
1954 Hubert H. Humphrey (DFL)	642,193	56.4
Val Bjornson (R)	479,619	42.1
1960 Hubert H. Humphrey (DFL)	884,168	57.5
P. Kenneth Peterson (R)	648,586	42.2
1966 Walter F. Mondale (DFL)	685,840	53.9
Robert A. Forsythe (R)	574,868	45.2
1972 Walter F. Mondale (DFL)	981,320	56.7
Phil Hansen (R)	742,121	42.9
1978 Rudy Boschwitz (IR)	894,092	56.6
Wendell R. Anderson (DFL)	638,375	40.4
1984 Rudy Boschwitz (IR)	1,199,926	58.1
Joan Anderson Growe (DFL)	852,844	41.3

MISSISSIPPI

Candidates	Votes	%
Class 1		
1916 John Sharp Williams (D)	74,290	100.0
1922 Hubert D. Stephens (D)	63,636	93.2
1928 Hubert D. Stephens (D)	111,210	100.0
1934 Theodore G. Bilbo (D)	51,709	100.0
1940 Theodore G. Bilbo (D)	143,333	100.0
1946 Theodore G. Bilbo (D)	46,747*	100.0
Special Election		
1947 John C. Stennis (D)	52,068	26.9
William M. Colmer (D)	45,725	23.6
Forrest B. Jackson (D)	43,642	22.5
Paul B. Johnson Jr. (D)	27,159	14.0
John E. Rankin (D)	24,492	12.6
1952 John C. Stennis (D)	233,919	100.0
1958 John C. Stennis (D)	61,039	100.0
1964 John C. Stennis (D)	343,364	100.0

Candidates	Votes	%
1970 John C. Stennis (D)	286,622	88.4
William R. Thompson (I)	37,593	11.6
1976 John C. Stennis (D)	554,433	100.0
1982 John C. Stennis (D)	414,099	64.2
Haley Barbour (R)	230,927	35.8
Class 2		
1918 Pat Harrison (D)	30,055	95.0
1924 Pat Harrison (D)	97,257	100.0
1930 Pat Harrison (D)	33,953	100.0
1936 Pat Harrison (D)	140,570	100.0
Special Election		
1941 Wall Doxey (D)	59,485	50.3
Ross Collins (D)	58,809	49.7
1942 James O. Eastland (D)	51,355	100.0
1948 James O. Eastland (D)	151,478	100.0
1954 James O. Eastland (D)	100,848	95.6
1960 James O. Eastland (D)	244,341	91.8
Joe A. Moore (R)	21,807	8.2
1966 James O. Eastland (D)	258,248	65.5
Prentiss Walker (R)	105,652	26.8
Clifton R. Whitley (I)	30,641	7.8
1972 James O. Eastland (D)	375,102	58.1
Gil Carmichael (R)	249,779	38.7
1978 Thad Cochran (R)	263,089	45.1
Maurice Dantin (D)	185,454	31.8
Charles Evers (I)	133,646	22.9
1984 Thad Cochran (R)	580,314	60.9
William D. Winter (D)	371,926	39.1

MISSOURI

Candidates	Votes	%
Class 1		
1916 James A. Reed (D)	396,166	50.6
Dickey (R)	371,710	47.4
1922 James A. Reed (D)	506,267	51.9
R. R. Brewster (R)	462,009	47.3
1928 Roscoe C. Patterson (R)	787,499	51.9
Charles M. Hay (D)	726,322	47.9
1934 Harry S Truman (D)	787,110	59.5
Roscoe C. Patterson (R)	524,954	39.7
1940 Harry S Truman (D)	930,775	51.2
Manvel H. Davis (R)	886,376	48.7
1946 James P. Kem (R)	572,556	52.7
Frank Briggs (D)	511,544	47.1
1952 Stuart Symington (D)	1,008,523	54.0
James P. Kem (R)	858,170	45.9
1958 Stuart Symington (D)	780,083	66.5
Hazel Palmer (R)	393,847	33.6
1964 Stuart Symington (D)	1,186,666	66.6
Jean Paul Bradshaw (R)	596,377	33.5
1970 Stuart Symington (D)	655,431	51.1
John C. Danforth (R)	617,903	48.2
1976 John C. Danforth (R)	1,090,067	56.9
Warren E. Hearnes (D)	813,571	42.5
1982 John C. Danforth (R)	784,876	50.8
Harriett Woods (D)	758,629	49.1
Class 3		
1914 William J. Stone (D)	311,616	50.4
Thomas J. Akins (R)	257,054	41.6

Candidates	Votes	%
Special Election		
1918 Selden P. Spencer (R)	302,680	*52.4*
Joseph Folk (D)	267,397	*46.3*
1920 Selden P. Spencer (R)	711,161	*53.7*
Breckinridge Long (D)	589,498	*44.5*
1926 Harry B. Hawes (D)	506,015	*51.3*
George H. Williams (R)	470,654	*47.7*
Special Election		
1926 Harry B. Hawes (D)	509,439	*51.9*
George H. Williams (R)	473,128	*48.2*
1932 J. Bennett (Champ) Clark (D)	1,017,046	*63.2*
Henry W. Kiel (R)	577,184	*35.9*
1938 J. Bennett (Champ) Clark (D)	757,587	*60.7*
Henry S. Caulfield (R)	488,687	*39.2*
1944 Forrest C. Donnell (R)	779,029	*50.0*
Roy McKittrick (D)	777,229	*49.9*
1950 Thomas C. Hennings Jr. (D)	685,732	*53.6*
Forrest C. Donnell (R)	593,139	*46.4*
1956 Thomas C. Hennings Jr. (D)	1,015,936	*56.4*
Herbert Douglas (R)	785,048	*43.6*
Special Election		
1960 Edward V. Long (D)	999,656	*53.2*
Lon Hocker (R)	880,576	*46.8*
1962 Edward V. Long (D)	666,929	*54.6*
Crosby Kemper (R)	555,330	*45.4*
1968 Thomas F. Eagleton (D)	887,414	*51.1*
Thoms B. Curtis (R)	850,544	*48.9*
1974 Thomas F. Eagleton (D)	735,433	*60.1*
Thomas B. Curtis (R)	480,900	*39.3*
1980 Thomas F. Eagleton (D)	1,074,859	*52.0*
Gene McNary (R)	985,399	*47.7*

MONTANA

Candidates	Votes	%
Class 1		
1916 Henry L. Myers (D)	85,585	*51.1*
Charles N. Pray (R)	72,753	*43.4*
Henry Labeau (SOC)	9,292	*5.5*
1922 Burton K. Wheeler (D)	88,205	*55.4*
Carl W. Riddick (R)	69,464	*43.6*
1928 Burton K. Wheeler (D)	103,655	*53.2*
Joseph M. Dixon (R)	91,185	*46.8*
1934 Burton K. Wheeler (D)	142,823	*70.1*
George M. Bourquin (R)	58,519	*28.7*
1940 Burton K. Wheeler (D)	176,753	*73.4*
E. K. Cheadle (R)	63,941	*26.6*
1946 Zales N. Ecton (R)	101,901	*53.5*
Leif Erickson (D)	86,476	*45.4*
1952 Mike Mansfield (D)	133,109	*50.8*
Zales N. Ecton (R)	127,360	*48.6*
1958 Mike Mansfield (D)	174,910	*76.2*
Lou W. Welch (R)	54,573	*23.8*
1964 Mike Mansfield (D)	180,643	*64.5*
Alex Blewett (R)	99,367	*35.5*
1970 Mike Mansfield (D)	150,060	*60.5*
Harold E. Wallace (R)	97,809	*39.5*
1976 John Melcher (D)	206,232	*64.2*
Stanley C. Burger (R)	115,213	*35.8*
1982 John Melcher (D)	174,861	*54.5*
Larry Williams (R)	133,789	*41.7*

Candidates	Votes	%
Class 2		
1912 Thomas J. Walsh (D)	28,421	*41.2*
Joseph M. Dixon (PROG)	22,161	*32.1*
Henry C. Smith (R)	18,450	*26.7*
1918 Thomas J. Walsh (D)	46,160	*41.1*
Oscar M. Lanstrum (R)	40,229	*35.8*
Jeanette Rankin (N)	26,013	*23.1*
1924 Thomas J. Walsh (D)	89,681	*52.8*
Frank B. Linderman (R)	72,005	*42.4*
1930 Thomas J. Walsh (D)	106,274	*60.3*
Albert J. Galen (R)	66,724	*37.9*
Special Election		
1934 James E. Murray (D)	116,965	*59.6*
Scott Leavitt (R)	77,370	*39.5*
1936 James E. Murray (D)	121,769	*55.0*
T. O. Larson (R)	60,038	*27.1*
Joseph P. Monaghan (I)	39,655	*17.9*
1942 James E. Murray (D)	83,673	*49.1*
Wellington D. Rankin (R)	82,461	*48.4*
1948 James E. Murray (D)	125,193	*56.7*
Tom J. Davis (R)	94,458	*42.7*
1954 James E. Murray (D)	114,591	*50.4*
Wesley A. D'Ewart (R)	112,863	*49.6*
1960 Lee Metcalf (D)	140,331	*50.7*
Orvin B. Fjare (R)	136,281	*49.3*
1966 Lee Metcalf (D)	138,166	*53.2*
Tim Babcock (R)	121,697	*46.8*
1972 Lee Metcalf (D)	163,609	*52.0*
Henry S. Hibbard (R)	151,316	*48.1*
1978 Max Baucus (D)	160,353	*55.7*
Larry Williams (R)	127,589	*44.3*
1984 Max Baucus (D)	215,704	*56.9*
Chuck Cozzens (R)	154,308	*40.7*

NEBRASKA

Candidates	Votes	%
Class 1		
1916 Gilbert M. Hitchcock (D & PRI)	143,082	*50.0*
John L. Kennedy (R & PROG)	131,359	*45.9*
1922 Robert Beecher Howell (R)	220,350	*56.8*
Gilbert M. Hitchcock (D)	148,265	*38.2*
1928 Robert Beecher Howell (R)	324,014	*61.3*
Richard L. Metcalfe (D)	204,737	*38.7*
1934 Edward R. Burke (D)	305,858	*55.3*
Robert G. Simmons (R)	237,126	*42.9*
Special Election		
1934 Richard C. Hunter (D)	281,421	*56.5*
J. H. Kemp (R)	216,846	*43.5*
1940 Hugh Butler (R)	340,250	*57.0*
R. L. Cochran (D)	247,659	*41.5*
1946 Hugh Butler (R)	271,208	*70.8*
John E. Mekota (D)	111,751	*29.2*
1952 Hugh Butler (R)	408,971	*69.1*
Stanley D. Long (D)	164,660	*27.8*
Special Election		
1954 Roman L. Hruska (R)	250,341	*60.9*
James F. Green (D)	160,881	*39.1*

	Candidates	Votes	%
1958	Roman L. Hruska (R)	232,227	*55.6*
	Frank B. Morrison (D)	185,152	*44.4*
1964	Roman L. Hruska (R)	345,772	*61.4*
	Raymond W. Arndt (D)	217,605	*38.6*
1970	Roman L. Hruska (R)	240,894	*52.5*
	Frank B. Morrison (D)	217,681	*47.4*
1976	Edward Zorinsky (D)	313,809	*52.4*
	John Y. McCollister (R)	284,284	*47.5*
1982	Edward Zorinsky (D)	363,350	*66.6*
	Jim Keck (R)	155,760	*28.5*

Class 2

	Candidates	Votes	%
1918	George W. Norris (R)	119,486	*54.5*
	John H. Morehead (D)	99,696	*45.5*
1924	George W. Norris (R)	274,640	*62.4*
	J. J. Thomas (D & PROG)	165,370	*37.6*
1930	George W. Norris (R)	247,118	*56.8*
	Gilbert M. Hitchcock (D)	172,795	*39.7*
1936	George W. Norris (I)	258,700	*43.8*
	Robert G. Simmons (R)	223,276	*37.8*
	Terry Carpenter (D)	108,391	*18.4*
1942	Kenneth S. Wherry (R)	186,207	*49.0*
	George W. Norris (I)	108,851	*28.6*
	Foster May (D)	83,763	*22.0*
1948	Kenneth S. Wherry (R)	267,575	*56.7*
	Terry Carpenter (D)	204,320	*43.3*

Special Election

1952	Dwight Griswold (R)	369,841	*63.6*
	William Ritchie (D)	211,898	*36.4*

1954	Carl T. Curtis (R)	255,695	*61.1*
	Keith Neville (D)	162,990	*38.9*

Special Election

1954	Hazel H. Abel (R)	233,589	*57.8*
	William H. Meier (D)	170,828	*42.2*

1960	Carl T. Curtis (R)	352,748	*58.9*
	Robert B. Conrad (D)	245,837	*41.1*
1966	Carl T. Curtis (R)	296,116	*61.2*
	Frank B. Morrison (D)	187,950	*38.8*
1972	Carl T. Curtis (R)	301,841	*53.1*
	Terry Carpenter (D)	265,922	*46.8*
1978	J. James Exon (D)	334,276	*67.6*
	Donald Shasteen (R)	159,806	*32.3*
1984	J. James Exon (D)	332,217	*51.9*
	Nancy Hoch (R)	307,147	*48.0*

NEVADA

	Candidates	Votes	%
	Class 1		
1910	George S. Nixon (R)	9,779	*48.0*
	Key Pittman (D)	8,624	*42.4*
	Jud Harris (SOC)	1,959	*9.6*

Special Election

1912	Key Pittman (D)	7,942	*39.8*
	W. A. Massey (R)	7,853	*39.3*
	G. A. Steele (SOC)	2,740	*13.7*
	S. Summerfield (PROG)	1,428	*7.2*

1916	Key Pittman (D)	12,765	*38.8*
	Samuel Platt (R)	10,618	*32.3*

	Candidates	Votes	%
	A. Grant Miller (SOC)	9,507	*28.9*
1922	Key Pittman (D)	18,201	*62.8*
	Charles S. Chandler (R)	10,770	*37.2*
1928	Key Pittman (D)	19,515	*59.3*
	Samuel Platt (R)	13,414	*40.7*
1934	Key Pittman (D)	27,581	*64.5*
	George W. Malone (R)	14,273	*33.4*
1940	Key Pittman (D)	31,351	*60.5*
	Samuel Platt (R)	20,488	*39.5*

Special Election

1942	J. G. Scrugham (D)	23,805	*58.7*
	Cecil W. Creel (R)	16,735	*41.3*

1946	George W. Malone (R)	27,801	*55.2*
	Berkeley L. Bunker (D)	22,553	*44.8*
1952	George W. Malone (R)	41,906	*51.7*
	Thomas B. Mechling (D)	39,184	*48.3*
1958	Howard W. Cannon (D)	48,732	*57.7*
	George W. Malone (R)	35,760	*42.3*
1964	Howard W. Cannon (D)	67,336	*50.0*
	Paul Laxalt (R)	67,288	*50.0*
1970	Howard W. Cannon (D)	85,187	*57.7*
	William J. Raggio (R)	60,838	*41.2*
1976	Howard W. Cannon (D)	127,295	*63.0*
	David Towell (R)	63,471	*31.4*
1982	Chic Hecht (R)	120,377	*50.1*
	Howard W. Cannon (D)	114,720	*47.7*

Class 3

1908	Francis G. Newlands (D)	12,473	*53.4*
	P. L. Flanigan (R)	8,972	*38.4*
	T. C. Lutz (SOC)	1,929	*8.3*
1914	Francis G. Newlands (D)	8,078	*37.5*
	Samuel Platt (R)	8,038	*37.3*
	A. Grant Miller (SOC)	5,451	*25.3*

Special Election

1918	Charles B. Henderson (D)	12,197	*47.7*
	E. E. Roberts (R)	8,053	*31.5*
	Anne Martin (I)	4,603	*18.0*

1920	Tasker L. Oddie (R)	11,550	*42.1*
	Charles B. Henderson (D)	10,402	*37.9*
	Anne Martin (I)	4,981	*18.2*
1926	Tasker L. Oddie (R)	17,430	*55.8*
	Ray T. Baker (D)	13,273	*42.5*
1932	Patrick A. McCarran (D)	21,398	*52.1*
	Tasker L. Oddie (R)	19,706	*47.9*
1938	Patrick A. McCarran (D)	27,406	*59.0*
	Tasker L. Oddie (R)	19,078	*41.0*
1944	Patrick A. McCarran (D)	30,595	*58.4*
	George W. Malone (R)	21,816	*41.6*
1950	Patrick A. McCarran (D)	35,829	*58.0*
	George E. Marshall (R)	25,933	*42.0*

Special Election

1954	Alan Bible (D)	45,043	*58.1*
	Ernest S. Brown (R)	32,470	*41.9*

1956	Alan Bible (D)	50,677	*52.6*
	Cliff Young (R)	45,712	*47.4*
1962	Alan Bible (D)	63,443	*65.3*
	William B. Wright (R)	33,749	*34.7*
1968	Alan Bible (D)	83,622	*54.8*
	Ed Fike (R)	69,068	*45.2*
1974	Paul Laxalt (R)	79,605	*47.0*

	Candidates	Votes	%
1980	Harry Reid (D)	78,981	46.6
	Paul Laxalt (R)	144,224	58.5
	Mary Gojack (D)	92,129	37.4

NEW HAMPSHIRE

	Candidates	Votes	%
	Class 2		
1918	Henry W. Keyes (R)	37,787	53.6
	Eugene E. Reed (D)	32,763	46.4
1924	Henry W. Keyes (R)	94,432	59.8
	George E. Farrand (D)	63,596	40.2
1930	Henry W. Keyes (R)	72,225	57.9
	Albert W. Noone (D)	52,284	41.9
1936	Styles Bridges (R)	107,923	51.9
	William N. Rogers (D)	99,195	47.7
1942	Styles Bridges (R)	88,601	54.6
	Francis P. Murphy (D)	73,656	45.4
1948	Styles Bridges (R)	129,600	58.1
	Alfred E. Fortin (D)	91,760	41.2
1954	Styles Bridges (R)	117,150	60.2
	Gerard L. Morin (D)	77,386	39.8
1960	Styles Bridges (R)	173,521	60.4
	Herbert W. Hill (D)	114,024	39.7

Special Election

1962	Thomas J. McIntyre (D)	117,612	52.3
	Perkins Bass (R)	107,199	47.7
1966	Thomas J. McIntyre (D)	123,888	54.0
	Harrison R. Thyng (R)	105,241	45.9
1972	Thomas J. McIntyre (D)	184,495	56.9
	Wesley Powell (R)	139,852	43.1
1978	Gordon J. Humphrey (R)	133,745	50.7
	Thomas J. McIntyre (D)	127,945	48.5
1984	Gordon J. Humphrey (R)	225,828	58.7
	Norman E. D'Amours (D)	157,447	41.0

	Class 3		
1914	Jacob H. Gallinger (R)	42,113	51.7
	Raymond B. Stevens (D)	36,382	44.6

Special Election

1918	George H. Moses (R)	35,528	50.8
	John B. Jameson (D)	34,459	49.2
1920	George H. Moses (R)	90,173	57.7
	Raymond B. Stevens (D)	65,035	41.6
1926	George H. Moses (R)	79,279	62.3
	Robert C. Murchie (D)	47,935	37.7
1932	Fred H. Brown (D)	98,766	50.4
	George H. Moses (R)	96,649	49.3
1938	Charles W. Tobey (R)	100,633	54.2
	Fred H. Brown (D)	84,920	45.8
1944	Charles W. Tobey (R)	110,549	50.9
	Joseph J. Betley (D)	106,508	49.1
1950	Charles W. Tobey (R)	106,142	55.7
	Emmet J. Kelley (D)	72,473	38.0
	Wesley Powell (I)	11,958	6.3

Special Election

1954	Norris Cotton (R)	114,068	60.2
	Stanley J. Betley (D)	75,490	39.8
1956	Norris Cotton (R)	161,424	64.1

	Candidates	Votes	%
	Laurence M. Pickett (D)	90,519	35.9
1962	Norris Cotton (R)	134,035	59.7
	Alfred Catalfo Jr. (D)	90,444	40.3
1968	Norris Cotton (R)	170,163	59.3
	John W. King (D)	116,816	40.7
1974 [3]	Louis C. Wyman (R)	110,926*	49.7
	John A. Durkin (D)	110,924	49.7

Special Election

1975 [3]	John A. Durkin (D)	140,778	53.6
	Louis C. Wyman (R)	113,007	43.1
	Carmen C. Chimento (AM)	8,787	3.3

1980	Warren B. Rudman (R)	195,563	52.1
	John A. Durkin (D)	179,455	47.8

3. Wyman's two-vote margin was challenged by Durkin. The Senate refused to seat either candidate. After seven months of fruitless efforts to decide a winner, the Senate voted July 30, 1975, to declare the seat vacant effective Aug. 8, 1975. In a special election Sept. 16, 1975, Durkin defeated Wyman.

NEW JERSEY

	Candidates	Votes	%
	Class 1		
1916	Joseph S. Frelinghuysen (R)	244,715	56.0
	James Martine (D)	170,019	38.9
1922	Edward I. Edwards (D)	451,832	54.9
	Joseph S. Frelinghuysen (R)	362,699	44.1
1928	Hamilton F. Kean (R)	841,752	57.9
	Edward I. Edwards (D)	608,623	41.8
1934	A. Harry Moore (D)	785,971	57.9
	Hamilton F. Kean (R)	554,483	40.9

Special Election

1938	W. Warren Barbour (R)	816,667	53.0
	William H. J. Ely (D)	704,159	45.7
1940	W. Warren Barbour (R)	1,029,331	55.1
	James H. R. Cromwell (D)	823,893	44.1

Special Election

1944	H. Alexander Smith (R)	939,987	50.4
	Elmer H. Wene (D)	910,096	48.8
1946	H. Alexander Smith (R)	799,808	58.5
	George E. Brunner (D)	548,458	40.1
1952	H. Alexander Smith (R)	1,286,782	55.5
	Archibald S. Alexander (D)	1,011,187	43.6
1958	Harrison A. Williams Jr. (D)	966,832	51.4
	Robert Winthrop Kean (R)	882,287	46.9
1964	Harrison A. Williams Jr. (D)	1,677,515	61.9
	Bernard M. Shanley (R)	1,011,280	37.3
1970	Harrison A. Williams Jr. (D)	1,157,074	54.0
	Nelson G. Gross (R)	903,026	42.2
1976	Harrison A. Williams Jr. (D)	1,681,140	60.7
	David F. Norcross (R)	1,054,508	38.0
1982	Frank R. Lautenberg (D)	1,117,549	50.9
	Millicent Fenwick (R)	1,047,626	47.8

	Class 2		
1918	Walter E. Edge (R)	179,022	50.3
	George M. Lamonte (D)	153,743	43.2

Candidates	Votes	%
Special Election		
1918 David Baird (R)	170,414	49.2
Charles O'Connor Hennessy (D)	154,734	44.6
1924 Walter E. Edge (R)	608,020	61.8
Frederick W. Donnelly (D)	331,034	33.7
1930 Dwight W. Morrow (R)	601,497	58.5
Alexander Simpson (D)	401,007	39.0
Special Elections		
1930 Dwight W. Morrow (R)	571,006	59.1
Thelma Parkinson (D)	372,739	38.6
1932 W. Warren Barbour (R)	741,734	49.6
Percy H. Stewart (D)	725,511	48.5
1936 William H. Smathers (D)	916,414	54.9
W. Warren Barbour (R)	740,088	44.3
1942 Albert W. Hawkes (R)	648,855	53.1
William H. Smathers (D)	559,851	45.8
1948 Robert C. Hendrickson (R)	934,720	50.0
Archibald S. Alexander (D)	884,414	47.3
1954 Clifford P. Case (R)	861,528	48.7
Charles R. Howell (D)	858,158	48.5
1960 Clifford P. Case (R)	1,483,832	55.7
Thorn Lord (D)	1,151,385	43.2
1966 Clifford P. Case (R)	1,278,843	60.0
Warren W. Wilentz (D)	788,021	37.0
1972 Clifford P. Case (R)	1,743,854	62.5
Paul J. Krebs (D)	963,573	34.5
1978 Bill Bradley (D)	1,082,960	55.3
Jeffrey Bell (R)	844,200	43.1
1984 Bill Bradley (D)	1,986,644	64.2
Mary V. Mochary (R)	1,080,100	35.2

NEW MEXICO

Candidates	Votes	%
Class 1		
1916 Andrieus A. Jones (D)	34,142	51.1
Frank A. Hubbell (R)	30,622	45.8
1922 Andrieus A. Jones (D)	60,969	55.2
S. B. Davis Jr. (R)	48,721	44.1
1928 Bronson M. Cutting (R)	68,070	57.7
Jethro S. Vaught (D)	49,913	42.3
Special Election		
1928 Octaviano A. Larrazolo (R)	64,623	55.7
Juan N. Vigil (D)	51,495	44.4
1934 Bronson M. Cutting (R)	76,228	50.2
Dennis Chavez (D)	74,944	49.4
Special Election		
1936 Dennis Chavez (D)	94,585	55.7
M. A. Otero Jr. (R)	75,030	44.2
1940 Dennis Chavez (D)	103,194	56.0
Albert K. Mitchell (R)	81,257	44.1
1946 Dennis Chavez (D)	68,650	51.5
Patrick J. Hurley (R)	64,632	48.5
1952 Dennis Chavez (D)	122,543	51.1
Patrick J. Hurley (R)	117,168	48.9
1958 Dennis Chavez (D)	127,496	62.7
Forrest S. Atchley (R)	75,827	37.3
1964 Joseph M. Montoya (D)	178,209	54.7

Candidates	Votes	%
Edwin L. Mechem (R)	147,562	45.3
1970 Joseph M. Montoya (D)	151,486	52.3
Anderson Carter (R)	135,004	46.6
1976 Harrison (Jack) Schmitt (R)	234,681	56.8
Joseph M. Montoya (D)	176,382	42.7
1982 Jeff Bingaman (D)	217,682	53.8
Harrison (Jack) Schmitt (R)	187,128	46.2
Class 2		
1918 Albert B. Fall (R)	24,322	51.4
W. B. Walton (D)	22,470	47.5
Special Election		
1921 Holm O. Bursum (R)	36,868	51.4
R. H. Hanna (D)	31,353	43.7
1924 Sam G. Bratton (D)	57,355	49.9
Holm O. Bursum (R)	54,558	47.4
1930 Sam G. Bratton (D)	69,356	58.6
Herbert B. Holt (R)	48,699	41.2
Special Election		
1934 Carl A. Hatch (D)	81,934	54.5
Richard C. Dillon (R)	67,577	45.0
1936 Carl A. Hatch (D)	104,550	61.7
Ernest W. Everly (R)	64,817	38.3
1942 Carl A. Hatch (D)	63,301	59.2
J. Benson Newell (R)	43,704	40.8
1948 Clinton P. Anderson (D)	108,269	57.2
Patrick J. Hurley (R)	80,226	42.4
1954 Clinton P. Anderson (D)	111,351	57.3
Edwin L. Mechem (R)	83,071	42.7
1960 Clinton P. Anderson (D)	190,654	63.4
William Colwes (R)	109,897	36.6
1966 Clinton P. Anderson (D)	137,205	53.1
Anderson Carter (R)	120,988	46.9
1972 Pete V. Domenici (R)	204,253	54.0
Jack Daniels (D)	173,815	46.0
1978 Pete V. Domenici (R)	183,442	53.4
Toney Anaya (D)	160,045	46.6
1984 Pete V. Domenici (R)	361,371	71.9
Judith A. Pratt (D)	141,253	28.1

NEW YORK

Candidates	Votes	%
Class 1		
1916 William M. Calder (R)	839,314	54.3
William F. McCombs (D & AM)	605,933	39.2
1922 Royal S. Copeland (D)	1,276,667	52.6
William M. Calder (R)	995,421	41.0
1928 Royal S. Copeland (D)	2,084,273	49.1
Alanson B. Houghton (R)	2,034,014	47.9
1934 Royal S. Copeland (D)	2,046,377	55.3
E. Harold Cluett (R)	1,363,440	36.9
Norman Thomas (SOC)	194,952	5.3
Special Election		
1938 James M. Mead (D, AM LAB)	2,438,904	53.6
Edward F. Corsi (R, I PROG)	2,083,666	45.8
1940 James M. Mead (D, AM LAB)	3,274,766	53.3
Bruce Barton (R)	2,868,852	46.7
1946 Irving M. Ives (R)	2,559,365	52.6

	Candidates	Votes	%
1952	Herbert H. Lehman (D, AM LAB)	2,308,112	47.4
	Irving M. Ives (R)	3,853,934	55.2
	John Cashmore (D)	2,521,736	36.1
	George S. Counts (L)	489,775	7.0
1958	Kenneth B. Keating (R)	2,842,942	50.8
	Frank S. Hogan (D, L)	2,709,950	48.4
1964	Robert F. Kennedy (D, L)	3,823,749	53.5
	Kenneth B. Keating (R)	3,104,056	43.4
1970	James L. Buckley (C, I ALNC)	2,288,190	38.8
	Richard L. Ottinger (D)	2,171,232	36.8
	Charles E. Goodell (R, L)	1,434,472	24.3
1976	Daniel Patrick Moynihan (D)	3,422,594	54.2
	James L. Buckley (R)	2,836,633	44.9
1982	Daniel Patrick Moynihan (D)	3,232,146	65.1
	Florence M. Sullivan (R)	1,696,766	34.2

Class 3

	Candidates	Votes	%
1914	James W. Wadsworth Jr. (R)	639,112	47.0
	James W. Gerard (D, I LEAGUE)	571,419	42.1
1920	James W. Wadsworth Jr. (R)	1,434,393	52.4
	Harry C. Walker (D)	901,310	32.9
	Jacob Panken (SOC)	208,155	7.6
	Ella A. Boole (P)	159,623	5.8
1926	Robert F. Wagner (D)	1,321,463	46.5
	James W. Wadsworth Jr. (R)	1,205,246	42.4
	F. W. Cristman (IR)	231,906	8.2
1932	Robert F. Wagner (D)	2,532,905	55.8
	George Z. Medalie (R)	1,751,186	38.6
1938	Robert F. Wagner (D, AM LAB)	2,497,029	54.5
	John Lord O'Brian (R, I PROG)	2,058,615	45.0
1944	Robert F. Wagner (D, AM LAB)	3,294,576	53.1
	Thomas J. Curran (R)	2,899,497	46.7

Special Election

1949	Herbert H. Lehman (D, L)	2,582,438	52.0
	John Foster Dulles (R)	2,384,381	48.0

1950	Herbert H. Lehman (D, L)	2,632,313	50.3
	Joe R. Hanley (R)	2,367,353	45.3
1956	Jacob K. Javits (R)	3,723,933	53.3
	Robert F. Wagner Jr. (D, L)	3,265,159	46.7
1962	Jacob K. Javits (R)	3,272,417	57.4
	James B. Donovan (D, L)	2,289,323	40.1
1968	Jacob K. Javits (R, L)	3,269,772	49.7
	Paul O'Dwyer (D)	2,150,695	32.7
	James L. Buckley (C)	1,139,402	17.3
1974	Jacob K. Javits (R, L)	2,340,188	45.3
	Ramsey Clark (D)	1,973,781	38.2
	Barbara A. Keating (C)	822,584	15.9
1980	Alphonse M. D'Amato (R)	2,699,652	44.9
	Elizabeth Holtzman (D)	2,618,661	43.5
	Jacob K. Javits (L)	664,544	11.0

NORTH CAROLINA

	Candidates	Votes	%
	Class 2		
1918	Furnifold M. Simmons (D)	143,519	60.5
	John M. Morehead (R)	93,707	39.5
1924	Furnifold M. Simmons (D)	295,344	61.6
	A. A. Whitener (R)	184,493	38.5
1930	Josiah W. Bailey (D)	324,293	60.6
	George M. Pritchard (R)	210,761	39.4
1936	Josiah W. Bailey (D)	564,088	70.8
	Frank R. Patton (R)	233,000	29.2
1942	Josiah W. Bailey (D)	230,427	65.9
	Sam J. Morris (R)	119,165	34.1
1948	J. Melville Broughton (D)	540,762	70.7

	Candidates	Votes	%
	John A. Wilkinson (R)	220,307	28.8

Special Election

1948	J. Melville Broughton (D)	534,917#	100.0

Special Election

1950	Willis Smith (D)	364,912	67.0
	E. L. Gavin (R)	177,753	32.6
1954	W. Kerr Scott (D)	408,312	65.9
	Paul C. West (R)	211,322	34.1

Special Election

1954	W. Kerr Scott (D)	402,268	100.0

Special Election

1958	B. Everett Jordan (D)	431,492	70.0
	Richard C. Clarke Jr. (R)	184,977	30.0
1960	B. Everett Jordan (D)	793,521	61.4
	Kyle Hayes (R)	497,964	38.6
1966	B. Everett Jordan (D)	501,440	55.6
	John S. Shallcross (R)	400,502	44.4
1972	Jesse Helms (R)	795,248	54.0
	Nick Galifianakis (D)	677,293	46.0
1978	Jesse Helms (R)	619,151	54.5
	John Ingram (D)	516,663	45.5
1984	Jesse Helms (R)	1,156,768	51.7
	James B. Hunt, Jr. (D)	1,070,488	47.8

Class 3

1914	Lee S. Overman (D)	121,342	58.1
	A. A. Whitener (R)	87,101	41.7
1920	Lee S. Overman (D)	310,504	57.5
	A. E. Holton (R)	229,343	42.5
1926	Lee S. Overman (D)	218,934	60.5
	Johnson J. Hayes (R)	142,891	39.5
1932	Robert R. Reynolds (D)	476,048	68.3
	Jake F. Newell (R)	221,392	31.7
1938	Robert R. Reynolds (D)	316,685	63.8
	Charles A. Jonas (R)	179,461	36.2
1944	Clyde R. Hoey (D)	533,813	70.3
	A. I. Ferree (R)	226,037	29.8
1950	Clyde R. Hoey (D)	376,473	68.7
	Halsey B. Leavitt (R)	171,804	31.3

Special Election

1954	Sam J. Ervin Jr. (D)	410,574	100.0
1956	Sam J. Ervin Jr. (D)	731,353	66.6
	Joel A. Johnson (R)	367,475	33.4
1962	Sam J. Ervin Jr. (D)	491,520	60.5
	Claude L. Greene Jr. (R)	321,635	39.6
1968	Sam J. Ervin Jr. (D)	870,406	60.6
	Robert Vance Somers (R)	566,934	39.4
1974	Robert B. Morgan (D)	633,775	62.1
	William E. Stevens (R)	377,618	37.0
1980	John P. East (R)	898,064	50.0
	Robert Morgan (D)	887,653	49.4

NORTH DAKOTA

	Candidates	Votes	%
	Class 1		
1916	Porter J. McCumber (R)	57,714	53.9
	John Burke (D)	40,988	38.2
	E. R. Fry (SOC)	8,472	7.9
1922	Lynn J. Frazier (R & NP)	101,312	52.3
	J. F. T. O'Connor (D & I)	92,464	47.7
1928	Lynn J. Frazier (R)	159,940	79.6
	F. F. Burchard (D)	38,856	19.4
1934	Lynn J. Frazier (R)	151,205	58.2
	Henry Holt (D)	104,477	40.2
1940	William Langer (R)	100,647	38.1
	William Lemke (I)	92,593	35.1
	Charles V. Vogel (D)	69,847	26.5
1946	William Langer (R)	88,210	53.3
	Arthur E. Thompson (I)	38,804	23.5
	Abner B. Larson (D)	38,368	23.2
1952	William Langer (R)	157,907	66.4
	Harold A. Morrison (D)	55,347	23.3
	Fred G. Aandahl (I)	24,741	10.4
1958	William Langer (R)	117,070	57.2
	Raymond Vendsel (D)	84,892	41.5

Special Election

1960	Quentin N. Burdick (D)	104,593	49.7
	John E. Davis (R)	103,475	49.2

1964	Quentin N. Burdick (D)	149,264	57.6
	Thomas S. Kleppe (R)	109,681	42.4
1970	Quentin N. Burdick (D)	134,519	61.3
	Thomas S. Kleppe (R)	82,996	37.8
1976	Quentin N. Burdick (D)	175,772	62.1
	Richard Stroup (R)	103,466	36.6
1982	Quentin N. Burdick (D)	164,873	62.8
	Gene Knorr (R)	89,304	34.0

	Class 3		
1914	Asle J. Gronna (R)	48,732	55.8
	W. E. Purcell (D)	29,640	34.0
	W. H. Brown (SOC)	6,231	7.1
1920	Edwin F. Ladd (R & NP)	130,614	59.8
	H. H. Perry (D & I)	87,765	40.2
1926	Gerald P. Nye (R)	107,921	69.6
	Norris H. Nelson (I)	18,951	12.2
	F. F. Burchard (D)	13,519	8.7
	C. P. Stone (R)	9,738	6.3

Special Election

1926	Gerald P. Nye (R)	79,709	50.2
	L. B. Hanna	59,499	37.5
	C. P. Stone	19,586	12.3

1932	Gerald P. Nye (R)	172,796	72.3
	P. W. Lanier (D)	65,575	27.5
1938	Gerald P. Nye (R)	131,907	50.1
	William Langer (I)	112,007	42.6
	J. J. Nygaard (D)	19,244	7.3
1944	John Moses (D)	95,102	45.2
	Gerald P. Nye (R)	69,530	33.0
	Lynn U. Stambaugh (IR)	44,596	21.2

Special Election

1946	Milton R. Young (R)	75,998	55.5
	William Lanier (D)	37,507	27.4
	Gerald P. Nye (I)	20,848	15.2

1950	Milton R. Young (R)	126,209	67.6
	Harry O'Brien (D)	60,507	32.4
1956	Milton R. Young (R)	155,305	63.6
	Quentin N. Burdick (D)	87,919	36.0
1962	Milton R. Young (R)	135,705	60.7
	William Lanier (D)	88,032	39.4
1968	Milton R. Young (R)	154,968	64.6
	Herschel Lashkowitz (D)	80,815	33.7
1974	Milton R. Young (R)	114,117	48.4
	William L. Guy (D)	113,931	48.3
1980	Mark Andrews (R)	210,347	70.3
	Kent Johanneson (D)	86,658	29.0

OHIO

	Candidates	Votes	%
	Class 1		
1916	Atlee Pomerene (D)	571,488	49.3
	Myron T. Herrick (R)	535,391	46.2
1922	Simeon D. Fess (R)	794,149	50.9
	Atlee Pomerene (D)	744,558	47.7
1928	Simeon D. Fess (R)	1,412,805	60.7
	Charles V. Truax (D)	908,952	39.1
1934	Vic Donahey (D)	1,276,206	60.0
	Simeon D. Fess (R)	839,068	39.4
1940	Harold H. Burton (R)	1,602,567	52.4
	John McSweeney (D)	1,457,359	47.6
1946	John W. Bricker (R)	1,275,774	57.0
	James W. Huffman (D)	947,610	42.4

Special Election

1946	Kingsley A. Taft (R)	1,193,942	56.2
	Henry P. Webber (D)	929,584	43.8

1952	John W. Bricker (R)	1,878,961	54.6
	Michael V. DiSalle (D)	1,563,330	45.4
1958	Stephen M. Young (D)	1,652,211	52.5
	John W. Bricker (R)	1,497,199	47.5
1964	Stephen M. Young (D)	1,923,608	50.2
	Robert Taft Jr. (R)	1,906,781	49.8
1970	Robert Taft Jr. (R)	1,565,682	49.7
	Howard M. Metzenbaum (D)	1,495,262	47.5
1976	Howard M. Metzenbaum (D)	1,941,113	49.5
	Robert A. Taft Jr. (R)	1,823,774	46.5
1982	Howard M. Metzenbaum (D)	1,923,767	56.7
	Paul E. Pfeifer (R)	1,396,790	41.1

	Class 3		
1914	Warren G. Harding (R)	526,115	49.2
	Timothy S. Hogan (D)	423,742	39.6
	Arthur L. Garford (PROG)	67,509	6.3
1920	Frank B. Willis (R)	1,134,953	59.1
	W. A. Julian (D)	782,650	40.8
1926	Frank B. Willis (R)	711,359	53.2
	Atlee Pomerene (D)	623,221	46.6

Special Election

1928	Theodore E. Burton (R)	1,429,534	62.4
	Graham P. Hunt (D)	856,807	37.4

Special Election

1930	Robert J. Bulkley (D)	1,046,561#	54.8
	Roscoe C. McCulloch (R)	863,944#	45.2

	Candidates	Votes	%
1932	Robert J. Bulkley (D)	1,290,175	52.5
	Gilbert Bettman (R)	1,126,830	45.8
1938	Robert A. Taft (R)	1,257,412	53.6
	Robert J. Bulkley (D)	1,086,815	46.4
1944	Robert A. Taft (R)	1,500,809	50.3
	William G. Pickrel (D)	1,483,069	49.7
1950	Robert A. Taft (R)	1,645,643	57.5
	Joseph T. Ferguson (D)	1,214,459	42.5

Special Election

1954	George H. Bender (R)	1,257,874	50.1
	Thomas A. Burke (D)	1,254,899	49.9

1956	Frank J. Lausche (D)	1,864,589	52.9
	George H. Bender (R)	1,660,910	47.1
1962	Frank J. Lausche (D)	1,843,813	61.6
	John Marshall Briley (R)	1,151,292	38.4
1968	William B. Saxbe (R)	1,928,964	51.5
	John J. Gilligan (D)	1,814,152	48.5
1974	John Glenn (D)	1,930,670	64.6
	Ralph J. Perk (R)	918,133	30.7
1980	John Glenn (D)	2,770,786	68.8
	James E. Betts (R)	1,137,695	28.2

OKLAHOMA

	Candidates	Votes	%

Class 2

1912	Robert L. Owen (D)	126,407	50.4
	Dickerson (R)	83,448	33.3
1918	Robert L. Owen (D)	105,050	55.4
	Johnson (R)	77,188	40.7
1924	William B. Pine (R)	341,720	61.6
	John Calloway Walton (D)	196,527	35.4
1930	Thomas P. Gore (D)	255,838	52.3
	William B. Pine (R)	232,589	47.5
1936	Josh Lee (D)	493,407	68.0
	Herbert K. Hyde (R)	229,004	31.6
1942	Edward H. Moore (R)	204,163	54.8
	Josh Lee (D)	166,653	44.8
1948	Robert S. Kerr (D)	441,654	62.3
	Ross Rizley (R)	265,169	37.4
1954	Robert S. Kerr (D)	335,127	55.8
	Fred M. Mock (R)	262,013	43.7
1960	Robert S. Kerr (D)	474,116	54.8
	B. Hayden Crawford (R)	385,646	44.6

Special Election

1964	Fred R. Harris (D)	466,782	51.2
	Bud Wilkinson (R)	445,392	48.8

1966	Fred R. Harris (D)	343,157	53.7
	Pat J. Patterson (R)	295,585	46.3
1972	Dewey F. Bartlett (R)	516,934	51.4
	Ed Edmondson (D)	478,212	47.6
1978	David L. Boren (D)	493,953	65.5
	Robert B. Kamm (R)	247,857	32.9
1984	David L. Boren (D)	906,131	75.6
	Will E. Crozier (R)	280,638	23.4

Class 3

1914	Thomas P. Gore (D)	119,443	48.0
	Burford (R)	73,292	29.4
	P. S. Nagle (SOC)	52,259	21.0

	Candidates	Votes	%
1920	John W. Harreld (R)	247,721	50.6
	Scott Ferris (D)	218,371	44.6
1926	Elmer Thomas (D)	195,307	54.8
	John W. Harreld (R)	159,287	44.7
1932	Elmer Thomas (D)	426,130	65.6
	Wirt Franklin (R)	218,854	33.7
1938	Elmer Thomas (D)	307,936	65.4
	Harry G. Glasser (R)	159,734	33.9
1944	Elmer Thomas (D)	390,851	55.7
	William J. Otjen (R)	309,222	44.0
1950	A. S. Mike Monroney (D)	345,953	54.8
	W. H. Bill Alexander (R)	285,224	45.2
1956	A. S. Mike Monroney (D)	459,996	55.4
	Douglas McKeever (R)	371,146	44.7
1962	A. S. Mike Monroney (D)	353,890	53.2
	B. Hayden Crawford (R)	307,966	46.3
1968	Henry Bellmon (R)	470,120	51.7
	A. S. Mike Monroney (D)	419,658	46.2
1974	Henry Bellmon (R)	390,997	49.4
	Ed Edmondson (D)	387,162	48.9
1980	Don Nickles (R)	587,252	53.5
	Andrew Coats (D)	478,283	43.5

OREGON

	Candidates	Votes	%

Class 2

1912	Harry Lane (D)	40,172	30.1
	Ben Selling (R)	38,453	28.8
	Jonathan Bourne Jr. (POPU GOV)	25,929	19.4
	B. F. Ramp (SOC)	11,093	8.3
	A. E. Clark (PROG)	11,083	8.3
	B. Lee Paget (P)	6,848	5.1
1918	Charles L. McNary (R)	82,360	54.2
	Oswald West (D)	64,303	42.3

Special Election

1918	Fred W. Mulkey (R)	103,913	84.5
	Martha E. Bean (SOC)	19,014	15.5

1924	Charles L. McNary (R)	174,672	66.0
	Milton A. Miller (D)	65,340	24.7
	F. E. Coulter (PROG)	20,379	7.7
1930	Charles L. McNary (R)	137,231	58.1
	Elton Watkins (D)	66,028	27.9
	L. A. Banks (I)	17,488	7.4
1936	Charles L. McNary (R)	199,332	49.7
	Willis Mahoney (D)	193,822	48.3
1942	Charles L. McNary (R)	214,755	77.1
	Walter W. Whitbeck (D)	63,946	22.9

Special Election

1944	Guy Cordon (R)	260,631	57.5
	Willis Mahoney (D)	192,305	42.5

1948	Guy Cordon (R)	299,295	60.0
	Manley J. Wilson (D)	199,275	40.0
1954	Richard L. Neuberger (D)	285,775	50.2
	Guy Cordon (R)	283,313	49.8
1960	Maurine B. Neuberger (D)	412,757	54.6
	Elmo Smith (R)	343,009	45.4

Special Election

1960	Maurine B. Neuberger (D)	422,024	55.0
	Elmo Smith (R)	345,464	45.0

	Candidates	Votes	%
1966	Mark O. Hatfield (R)	354,391	51.7
	Robert B. Duncan (D)	330,374	48.2
1972	Mark O. Hatfield (R)	494,671	53.7
	Wayne Morse (D)	425,036	46.2
1978	Mark O. Hatfield (R)	550,165	61.6
	Vernon Cook (D)	341,616	38.3
1984	Mark O. Hatfield (R)	808,152	66.5
	Margie Hendricksen (D)	406,122	33.4

Class 3

	Candidates	Votes	%
1908	George E. Chamberlain (D)	52,421	46.7
	H. M. Cake (R)	50,899	45.3
1914	George E. Chamberlain (D)	111,748	45.5
	R. A. Booth (R)	88,297	36.0
	William Hanley (PROG)	26,220	10.7
1920	Robert N. Stanfield (R)	116,696	50.7
	George E. Chamberlain (D)	100,124	43.5
1926	Frederick Steiwer (R)	89,007	39.8
	Bert E. Haney (D)	81,301	36.3
	Robert N. Stanfield (I)	50,246	22.5
1932	Frederick Steiwer (R)	186,210	52.7
	Walter B. Gleason (D)	137,237	38.9
1938	Rufus C. Holman (R)	203,120	54.9
	Willis Mahoney (D)	167,135	45.1

Special Election

1938	Alexander G. Barry (R)	180,815	54.2
	Robert A. Miller (D)	152,773	45.8

1944	Wayne Morse (R)	269,095	60.7
	Edgar W. Smith (D)	174,140	39.3
1950	Wayne Morse (R)	376,510	74.8
	Howard Latourette (D)	116,780	23.2
1956	Wayne Morse (D)	396,849	54.2
	Douglas McKay (R)	335,405	45.8
1962	Wayne Morse (D)	344,716	54.2
	Sig Unander (R)	291,587	45.8
1968	Bob Packwood (R)	408,825	50.2
	Wayne Morse (D)	405,380	49.8
1974	Bob Packwood (R)	420,984	54.9
	Betty Roberts (D)	338,591	44.2
1980	Bob Packwood (R)	594,290	52.1
	Ted Kulongoski (D)	501,963	44.0

PENNSYLVANIA

	Candidates	Votes	%
	Class 1		
1916	Philander C. Knox (R, RO PROG)	680,447	56.3
	Ellis L. Orvis (D)	450,112	37.3
1922	David A. Reed (R)	802,146	56.0
	Samuel E. Shull (D)	423,583	29.6
	William J. Burke (PROG)	127,180	8.9

Special Election

1922	David A. Reed (R)	860,483#	86.1
	Rachel C. Robinson (P)	60,390#	6.0
	William J. VanEssen (SOC)	55,703#	5.6

1928	David A. Reed (R)	1,948,646	64.4
	William N. McNair (D)	1,029,055	34.0
1934	Joseph F. Guffey (D)	1,494,001	50.8
	David A. Reed (R)	1,366,877	46.5
1940	Joseph F. Guffey (D)	2,069,980	51.8
	Jay Cooke (R)	1,893,104	47.4
1946	Edward Martin (R)	1,853,458	59.3

	Candidates	Votes	%
	Joseph F. Guffey (D)	1,245,338	39.8
1952	Edward Martin (R)	2,331,034	51.6
	Guy Kurtz Bard (D)	2,168,546	48.0
1958	Hugh Scott (R)	2,042,586	51.2
	George M. Leader (D)	1,929,821	48.4
1964	Hugh Scott (R)	2,429,858	50.6
	Genevieve Blatt (D)	2,359,223	49.1
1970	Hugh Scott (R)	1,874,106	51.4
	William G. Sesler (D)	1,653,774	45.4
1976	John Heinz (R)	2,381,891	52.4
	William J. Green III (R)	2,126,977	46.8
1982	John Heinz (R)	2,136,418	59.3
	Cyril H. Wecht (D)	1,412,965	39.2

Class 3

	Candidates	Votes	%
1914	Boies Penrose (R, PERS LIB)	519,801	46.8
	Gifford Pinchot (WASH, B MOOSE)	269,175	24.2
	A. Mitchell Palmer (D)	266,415	24.0
1920	Boies Penrose (R)	1,068,985	59.9
	John A. Farrell (D)	484,862	27.2
	Leah Cobb Marion (P)	132,610	7.4

Special Election

1922	George Wharton Pepper (R)	819,507	57.6
	Fred B. Kerr (D)	468,330	32.9

1926	William S. Vare (R)	822,187*	54.6
	William B. Wilson (D, LAB)	648,680	43.1

Special Election

1930	James J. Davis (R)	1,462,186	71.5
	Sedgwick Kistler (D)	523,338	25.6

1932	James J. Davis (R)	1,371,844	49.3
	Lawrence H. Rupp (D)	1,200,767	43.2
1938	James J. Davis (R)	2,086,932	54.7
	George H. Earle (D, ROYAL OAK)	1,694,464	44.4
1944	Francis J. Myers (D)	1,864,735	50.0
	James J. Davis (R)	1,840,943	49.4
1950	James H. Duff (R)	1,820,400	51.3
	Francis J. Myers (D)	1,694,076	47.7
1956	Joseph S. Clark (D)	2,268,641	50.1
	James H. Duff (R)	2,250,671	49.7
1962	Joseph S. Clark (D)	2,238,383	51.1
	James E. Van Zandt (R)	2,134,649	48.7
1968	Richard S. Schweiker (R)	2,399,762	51.9
	Joseph S. Clark (D)	2,117,662	45.8
1974	Richard S. Schweiker (R)	1,843,317	53.0
	Peter Flaherty (D)	1,596,121	45.9
1980	Arlen Specter (R)	2,230,404	50.5
	Peter Flaherty (D)	2,122,391	48.0

RHODE ISLAND

	Candidates	Votes	%
	Class 1		
1916	Peter G. Gerry (D)	47,048	52.9
	Henry Lippitt (R)	39,211	44.1
1922	Peter G. Gerry (D)	82,889	52.2
	R. Livingston Beeckman (R)	68,930	43.4
1928	Felix Hebert (R)	119,228	50.6
	Peter G. Gerry (D)	116,234	49.3
1934	Peter G. Gerry (D)	140,700	57.1
	Felix Hebert (R)	105,545	42.9
1940	Peter G. Gerry (D)	173,847	55.2

	Candidates	Votes	%
1946	James O. McManus (R)	141,312	*44.8*
	J. Howard McGrath (D)	150,748	*55.1*
	W. Gurnee Dyer (R)	122,780	*44.9*

Special Election

1950	John O. Pastore (D)	184,520	*61.6*
	Austin T. Levy (R)	114,890	*38.4*
1952	John O. Pastore (D)	225,128	*54.8*
	Bayard Ewing (R, CLEAN GV)	185,850	*45.2*
1958	John O. Pastore (D)	222,166	*64.5*
	Bayard Ewing (R)	122,353	*35.5*
1964	John O. Pastore (D)	319,607	*82.7*
	Ronald R. Lagueux (R)	66,715	*17.3*
1970	John O. Pastore (D)	230,469	*67.5*
	John McLaughlin (R)	107,351	*31.5*
1976	John H. Chafee (R)	230,329	*57.7*
	Richard P. Lorber (D)	167,665	*42.0*
1982	John H. Chafee (R)	175,495	*51.2*
	Julius C. Michaelson (D)	167,283	*48.8*

Class 2

1918	LeBaron B. Colt (R)	42,055	*51.8*
	George O'Shaunessy (D)	37,573	*46.2*
1924	Jesse H. Metcalf (R)	120,815	*57.6*
	William S. Flynn (D)	87,620	*41.8*

Special Election

1924	Jesse H. Metcalf (R)	116,572	*56.4*
	William S. Flynn (D)	88,138	*42.6*
1930	Jesse H. Metcalf (R)	112,202	*50.3*
	Peter G. Gerry (D)	109,687	*49.2*
1936	Theodore F. Green (D)	149,157	*48.6*
	Jesse H. Metcalf (R)	136,174	*44.4*
	Lapointe (UN)	21,501	*7.0*
1942	Theodore F. Green (D)	138,239	*58.0*
	Ira Lloyd Letts (R)	100,236	*42.0*
1948	Theodore F. Green (D)	190,284	*59.3*
	Thomas P. Hazard (R)	130,668	*40.7*
1954	Theodore F. Green (D)	193,654	*59.3*
	Walter I. Sundlun (R)	132,970	*40.7*
1960	Claiborne Pell (D)	275,575	*68.9*
	Raoul Archambault (R)	124,408	*31.1*
1966	Claiborne Pell (D)	219,331	*67.7*
	Ruth M. Briggs (R)	104,838	*32.3*
1972	Claiborne Pell (D)	221,942	*53.7*
	John H. Chafee (R)	188,990	*45.7*
1978	Claiborne Pell (D)	229,557	*75.1*
	James G. Reynolds (R)	76,061	*24.9*
1984	Claiborne Pell (D)	286,780	*72.6*
	Barbara Leonard (R)	108,492	*27.4*

SOUTH CAROLINA

	Candidates	Votes	%
	Class 2		
1918	Nathaniel B. Dial (D)	25,792	*100.0*

Special Election

1918	William P. Pollock (D)	✔	
1924	Coleman L. Blease (D)	49,060	*100.0*
1930	James F. Byrnes (D)	16,213	*100.0*

	Candidates	Votes	%
1936	James F. Byrnes (D)	113,696	*98.6*

Special Election

1941	Burnet R. Maybank (D)	✔	
1942	Burnet R. Maybank (D)	23,356	*100.0*
1948	Burnet R. Maybank (D)	135,998	*96.5*
1954	Strom Thurmond (WRITE IN)	143,442	*63.1*
	Edgar A. Brown (D)	83,525	*36.8*

Special Election

1956	Strom Thurmond (D)	245,371	*100.0*
1960	Strom Thurmond (D)	330,164	*100.0*
1966	Strom Thurmond (R)	271,297	*62.2*
	Bradley Morrah (D)	164,955	*37.8*
1972	Strom Thurmond (R)	415,806	*63.3*
	Eugene N. Zeigler (D)	241,056	*36.7*
1978	Strom Thurmond (R)	351,733	*55.6*
	Charles D. Ravenel (D)	281,119	*44.4*
1984	Strom Thurmond (R)	644,815	*66.8*
	Melvin Purvis Jr. (R)	306,982	*31.8*

Class 3

1914	Ellison D. Smith (D)	32,950	*99.8*
1920	Ellison D. Smith (D)	64,388	*100.0*
1926	Ellison D. Smith (D)	14,560	*100.0*
1932	Ellison D. Smith (D)	104,472	*98.1*
1938	Ellison D. Smith (D)	45,751	*98.9*
1944	Olin D. Johnston (D)	94,556	*92.9*
1950	Olin D. Johnston (D)	50,240	*99.9*
1956	Olin D. Johnston (D)	230,150	*82.2*
	L. P. Crawford (R)	49,695	*17.8*
1962	Olin D. Johnston (D)	178,712	*57.2*
	W. D. Workman Jr. (R)	133,930	*42.8*

Special Election

1966	Ernest F. Hollings (D)	223,790	*51.4*
	Marshall Parker (R)	212,032	*48.7*
1968	Ernest F. Hollings (D)	404,060	*61.9*
	Marshall Parker (R)	248,780	*38.1*
1974	Ernest F. Hollings (D)	356,126	*69.5*
	Gwenyfred Bush (R)	146,645	*28.6*
1980	Ernest F. Hollings (D)	612,554	*70.4*
	Marshall T. Mays (R)	257,946	*29.6*

SOUTH DAKOTA

	Candidates	Votes	%
	Class 2		
1918	Thomas Sterling (R)	51,198	*55.1*
	Rinehart (D)	36,210	*39.0*
	Rafferty (I)	5,560	*6.0*
1924	William H. McMaster (R)	90,006	*44.1*
	U. S. G. Cherry (D)	63,548	*31.2*
	Tom Ayres (F-LAB)	21,136	*10.4*
	George W. Egan (I)	14,484	*7.1*
1930	William J. Bulow (D)	106,317	*51.6*
	William H. McMaster (R)	99,595	*48.4*
1936	William J. Bulow (D)	141,509	*48.8*
	Chandler Gurney (R)	135,461	*46.8*
1942	Harlan J. Bushfield (R)	106,704	*58.7*
	Tom Berry (D)	74,945	*41.3*

	Candidates	Votes	%
1948	Karl E. Mundt (R)	144,084	59.3
	John A. Engel (D)	98,749	40.7
1954	Karl E. Mundt (R)	135,071	57.3
	Kenneth Holum (D)	100,674	42.7
1960	Karl E. Mundt (R)	160,181	52.4
	George McGovern (D)	145,261	47.6
1966	Karl E. Mundt (R)	150,517	66.3
	Donn H. Wright (D)	76,563	33.7
1972	James Abourezk (D)	174,773	57.0
	Robert W. Hirsch (R)	131,613	42.9
1978	Larry Pressler (R)	170,832	66.8
	Don Barnett (D)	84,767	33.2
1984	Larry Pressler (R)	235,176	74.5
	George V. Cunningham (D)	80,537	25.5

Class 3

	Candidates	Votes	%
1914	Edwin S. Johnson (D)	47,668	48.1
	Charles H. Burke (R)	44,244	44.7
1920	Peter Norbeck (R)	92,267	50.1
	Tom Ayres (NON PART)	44,309	24.1
	U. S. G. Cherry (D)	36,833	20.0
	R. O. Richards (I)	10,032	5.5
1926	Peter Norbeck (R)	105,756	59.5
	C. J. Gunderson (D)	59,128	33.3
	Howard Platt (F-LAB)	12,797	7.2
1932	Peter Norbeck (R)	151,845	53.8
	U. S. G. Cherry (D)	125,731	44.6
1938	Chandler Gurney (R)	146,813	52.5
	Tom Berry (D)	133,064	47.5

Special Election

1938	Gladys Pyle (R)	155,292	58.1
	John T. McCullen Sr. (D)	112,177	41.9

1944	Chandler Gurney (R)	145,248	63.9
	George M. Bradshaw (D)	82,199	36.1
1950	Francis Case (R)	160,670	63.9
	John A. Engel (D)	90,692	36.1
1956	Francis Case (R)	147,621	50.8
	Kenneth Holum (D)	143,001	49.2
1962	George McGovern (D)	127,458	50.1
	Joe Bottum (R)	126,861	49.9
1968	George McGovern (D)	158,961	56.8
	Archie Gubbrud (R)	120,951	43.2
1974	George McGovern (D)	147,929	53.0
	Leo K. Thorsness (R)	130,955	47.0
1980	James Abdnor (R)	190,594	58.2
	George McGovern (D)	129,018	39.4

TENNESSEE

	Candidates	Votes	%
	Class 1		
1916	Kenneth D. McKellar (D)	143,718	54.4
	Ben W. Hooper (R)	118,174	44.8
1922	Kenneth D. McKellar (D)	151,523	68.0
	Newell Sanders (R)	71,199	32.0
1928	Kenneth D. McKellar (D)	175,431	59.3
	J. A. Fowler (R)	120,289	40.7
1934	Kenneth D. McKellar (D)	195,430	63.4
	Ben W. Hooper (R)	110,401	35.8
1940	Kenneth D. McKellar (D)	295,440	70.8
	Howard Baker (R)	121,790	29.2
1946	Kenneth D. McKellar (D)	145,654	66.6
	W. B. Ladd (R)	57,237	26.2

	Candidates	Votes	%
	John R. Neal (I)	11,516	5.3
1952	Albert Gore (D)	545,432	74.2
	Hobart F. Atkins (R)	153,479	20.9
1958	Albert Gore (D)	317,324	79.0
	Hobart F. Atkins (R)	76,371	19.0
1964	Albert Gore (D)	570,542	53.6
	Dan H. Kuykendall (R)	493,475	46.4
1970	Bill Brock (R)	562,645	51.3
	Albert Gore (D)	519,858	47.4
1976	Jim Sasser (D)	751,180	52.5
	Bill Brock (R)	673,231	47.0
1982	Jim Sasser (D)	780,113	61.9
	Robin L. Beard (D)	479,642	38.1

Class 2

	Candidates	Votes	%
1918	John K. Shields (D)	98,605	62.2
	H. Clay Evans (R)	59,989	37.8
1924	Lawrence D. Tyson (D)	147,821	57.3
	H. B. Lindsay (R)	109,863	42.6
1930	Cordell Hull (D)	154,071	71.3
	Paul E. Divine (R)	58,550	27.1

Special Election

1930	William E. Brock (D)	144,021	74.4
	F. Todd Meacham (R)	49,634	25.6

Special Election

1934	Nathan L. Bachman (D)	200,249	80.1
	John R. Neal (I)	49,773	19.9
1936	Nathan L. Bachman (D)	273,298	76.4
	Dwayne D. Maddox (R)	67,238	18.8

Special Election

1938	A. Tom Stewart (D)	194,026	70.5
	Harley G. Fowler (R)	72,098	26.2
1942	A. Tom Stewart (D)	109,881	68.9
	F. Todd Meacham (R)	34,324	21.5
	John R. Neal (I)	15,317	9.6
1948	Estes Kefauver (D)	326,062	65.3
	B. Carroll Reece (R)	166,947	33.5
1954	Estes Kefauver (D)	249,121	70.0
	Tom Wall (R)	106,971	30.0
1960	Estes Kefauver (D)	594,460	71.8
	A. Bradley Frazier (R)	234,053	28.3

Special Election

1964	Ross Bass (D)	568,905	52.1
	Howard H. Baker Jr. (R)	517,330	47.4
1966	Howard H. Baker Jr. (R)	483,063	55.7
	Frank G. Clement (D)	383,843	44.3
1972	Howard H. Baker Jr. (R)	716,539	61.6
	Ray Blanton (D)	440,599	37.9
1978	Howard H. Baker Jr. (R)	642,644	55.5
	Jane Eskind (D)	466,228	40.3
1984	Albert Gore, Jr. (D)	1,000,607	60.7
	Victor Ashe (R)	557,016	33.8
	Ed McAteer (I)	87,234	5.3

TEXAS

Candidates	Votes	%
Class 1		
1916 Charles A. Culberson (D)	303,035	81.3
Alex W. Atcheson (R)	48,788	13.1
1922 Earle B. Mayfield (D)	261,063	66.6
George E. B. Peddy (R)	130,731	33.4
1928 Tom Connally (D)	566,139	81.2
T.M. Kennerly (R)	130,172	18.7
1934 Tom Connally (D)	437,254	96.7
1940 Tom Connally (D)	993,974	94.3
George I. Shannon (R)	60,051	5.7
1946 Tom Connally (D)	336,931	88.5
Murray C. Sells (R)	43,619	11.5
1952 Price Daniel (D, R)	1,894,671	100.0

Special Election

1957	Ralph Yarborough (D)	364,878	38.1
	Martin Dies (D)	290,869	30.4
	Thad Hutcheson (R)	219,591	22.9

1958	Ralph Yarborough (D)	587,030	74.6
	Roy Whittenburg (R)	185,926	23.6
1964	Ralph Yarborough (D)	1,463,958	56.2
	George Bush (R)	1,134,337	43.6
1970	Lloyd Bentsen (D)	1,193,814	53.5
	George Bush (R)	1,036,045	46.4
1976	Lloyd Bentsen (D)	2,199,956	56.8
	Alan Steelman (R)	1,636,370	42.2
1982	Lloyd Bentsen (D)	1,818,223	58.6
	James M. Collins (R)	1,256,759	40.5

Class 2

1918	Morris Sheppard (D)	155,178	86.7
	J. Webs Flanagan (R)	22,214	12.4
1924	Morris Sheppard (D)	592,057	85.4
	T. M. Kennerly (R)	101,252	14.6
1930	Morris Sheppard (D)	266,562	86.9
	D. J. Haesly (R)	39,053	12.7
1936	Morris Sheppard (D)	773,574	92.6
	Carlos G. Watson (R)	59,491	7.1

Special Election

1941	W. Lee O'Daniel (D)	175,590	30.5
	Lyndon B. Johnson (D)	174,284	30.3
	Gerald C. Mann (D)	140,807	24.5
	Martin Dies (D)	80,551	14.0

1942	W. Lee O'Daniel (D)	260,629	94.9
1948	Lyndon B. Johnson (D)	702,785	66.2
	Jack Porter (R)	349,665	32.9
1954	Lyndon B. Johnson (D)	539,319	84.7
	Carlos G. Watson (R)	94,131	14.8
1960	Lyndon B. Johnson (D)	1,306,605	58.0
	John G. Tower (R)	926,653	41.1

Special Primary[4]

1961	John G. Tower (R)	327,308#	30.9
	William A. Blakley (D)	190,818#	18.1
	Jim Wright (D)	171,328#	16.2
	Will Wilson (D)	121,961#	11.5
	Maury Maverick Jr. (D)	104,992#	9.9
	Henry B. Gonzalez (D)	97,659#	9.2

Candidates	Votes	%
Special Runoff Election[4]		
1961 John G. Tower (R)	448,217	50.6
William A. Blakley (D)	437,874	49.4

1966	John G. Tower (R)	842,501	56.4
	Waggoner Carr (D)	643,855	43.1
1972	John G. Tower (R)	1,822,877	53.4
	Barefoot Sanders (D)	1,511,985	44.3
1978	John G. Tower (R)	1,151,376	49.8
	Robert Krueger (D)	1,139,149	49.3
1984	Phil Gramm (R)	3,111,348	58.5
	Lloyd Doggett (D)	2,202,557	41.4

4. *Under Texas law passed after the 1957 special election, candidates in special elections for the Senate would all run together in a primary with party affiliation. If none received a majority of the vote in the first primary, a runoff would be held between the top two contenders. (1957 special election, opposite)*

UTAH

Candidates	Votes	%
Class 1		
1916 William H. King (D)	81,057	56.9
George Sutherland (R)	56,862	39.9
1922 William H. King (D)	58,749	48.6
Ernest Bamberger (R)	58,188	48.2
1928 William H. King (D)	97,436	55.5
Ernest Bamberger (R)	77,073	43.9
1934 William H. King (D)	95,931	53.1
Don B. Colton (R)	82,154	45.4
1940 Abe Murdock (D)	155,499	62.9
Philo T. Farnsworth Jr. (R)	91,931	37.2
1946 Arthur V. Watkins (R)	101,142	51.2
Abe Murdock (D)	96,257	48.8
1952 Arthur V. Watkins (R)	177,435	54.3
Walter K. Granger (D)	149,598	45.7
1958 Frank E. Moss (D)	112,827	38.7
Arthur V. Watkins (R)	101,471	34.8
J. Bracken Lee (I)	77,013	26.4
1964 Frank E. Moss (D)	227,822	57.3
Ernest L. Wilkinson (R)	169,562	42.7
1970 Frank E. Moss (D)	210,207	56.2
Laurence J. Burton (R)	159,004	42.5
1976 Orrin G. Hatch (R)	290,221	53.7
Moss E. Frank (D)	241,948	44.8
1982 Orrin G. Hatch (R)	309,332	58.3
Ted Wilson (D)	219,482	41.3

Class 3

1914	Reed Smoot (R)	56,282	49.1
	James H. Moyle (D & PROG)	53,127	46.3
1920	Reed Smoot (R)	82,566	56.6
	Milton H. Welling (D)	56,280	38.6
1926	Reed Smoot (R)	88,101	61.5
	Ashby Snow (D)	53,809	37.6
1932	Elbert D. Thomas (D)	116,909	56.7
	Reed Smoot (R)	86,066	41.7
1938	Elbert D. Thomas (D)	102,353	55.8
	Franklin S. Harris (R)	81,071	44.2
1944	Elbert D. Thomas (D)	148,748	59.9
	Adam S. Bennion (R)	99,532	40.1
1950	Wallace F. Bennett (R)	142,427	53.9
	Elbert D. Thomas (D)	121,198	45.8
1956	Wallace F. Bennett (R)	178,261	54.0
	Alonzo F. Hopkin (D)	152,120	46.0
1962	Wallace F. Bennett (R)	166,755	52.4
	David S. King (D)	151,656	47.6

	Candidates	Votes	%
1968	Wallace F. Bennett (R)	225,075	*53.7*
	Milton L. Weilenmann (D)	192,168	*45.8*
1974	Jake Garn (R)	210,299	*50.0*
	Wayne Owens (D)	185,377	*44.1*
1980	Jake Garn (R)	437,675	*73.6*
	Dan Berman (D)	151,454	*25.5*

VERMONT

	Candidates	Votes	%
	Class 1		
1916	Carroll S. Page (R)	47,362	*74.2*
	Oscar C. Miller (D)	14,956	*23.4*
1922	Frank L. Greene (R)	45,284	*67.9*
	William B. Mayo (D)	21,375	*32.1*
1928	Frank L. Greene (R)	93,136	*71.6*
	Fred C. Martin (D)	37,030	*28.5*

Special Election

1931	Warren R. Austin (R)	27,661#	*64.3*
	Stephen M. Driscoll (D)	15,360#	*35.7*

1934	Warren R. Austin (R)	67,146	*51.0*
	Fred C. Martin (D)	63,632	*48.4*
1940	Warren R. Austin (R)	93,283	*66.5*
	Ona S. Searles (D)	47,101	*33.6*
1946	Ralph E. Flanders (R)	54,729	*74.6*
	Charles P. McDevitt (D)	18,594	*25.4*
1952	Ralph E. Flanders (R)	111,406	*72.3*
	Allan R. Johnston (D)	42,630	*27.7*
1958	Winston L. Prouty (R)	64.900	*52.2*
	Frederick J. Fayette (D)	59,536	*47.8*
1964	Winston L. Prouty (R, I)	87,879	*53.5*
	Frederick J. Fayette (D)	76,457	*46.5*
1970	Winston L. Prouty (R)	91,198	*58.9*
	Philip H. Hoff (D)	62,271	*40.2*

Special Election

1972	Robert T. Stafford (R)	45,888#	*64.3*
	Randolph T. Major (D)	23,842#	*33.4*

1976	Robert T. Stafford (R)	94,481	*50.0*
	Thomas P. Salmon (D)	85,682	*45.3*
1982	Robert T. Stafford (R)	84,450	*50.3*
	James A. Guest (D)	79,340	*47.2*

	Class 3		
1914	William P. Dillingham (R)	35,137	*56.0*
	Charles A. Prouty (PROG D & P)	26,776	*42.7*
1920	William P. Dillingham (R)	69,650	*78.0*
	Howard E. Shaw (D)	19,580	*21.9*

Special Election

1923	Porter H. Dale (R)	30,582	*66.2*
	Park H. Pollard (D)	15,621	*33.8*

1926	Porter H. Dale (R, P)	52,286	*73.4*
	James E. Kennedy (D)	18,878	*26.5*
1932	Porter H. Dale (R)	74,319	*55.1*
	Fred C. Martin (D)	60,453	*44.9*

Special Election

1934	Ernest W. Gibson (R)	28,436#	*58.2*
	Harry W. Witters (D)	20,382#	*41.8*

	Candidates	Votes	%
1938	Ernest W. Gibson (R)	73,990	*65.7*
	John McGrath (D)	38,673	*34.3*

Special Election

1940	George D. Aiken (R)	87,150	*61.6*
	Herbert B. Comings (D)	54,263	*38.4*

1944	George D. Aiken (R)	81,094	*65.8*
	Harry W. Witters (D)	42,136	*34.2*
1950	George D. Aiken (R)	69,543	*78.0*
	James E. Bigelow (D)	19,608	*22.0*
1956	George D. Aiken (R)	103,101	*66.4*
	Bernard G. O'Shea (D)	52,184	*33.6*
1962	George D. Aiken (R)	81,241	*66.9*
	W. Robert Johnson (D)	40,134	*33.1*
1968	George D. Aiken (R, D)	157,154	*99.9*
1974	Patrick J. Leahy (D, I VT)	70,629	*49.5*
	Richard W. Mallary (R)	66,223	*46.4*
1980	Patrick J. Leahy (D)	104,176	*49.8*
	Stewart M. Ledbetter (R)	101,421	*48.5*

VIRGINIA

	Candidates	Votes	%
	Class 1		
1916	Claude A. Swanson (D)	133,091	*99.9*
1922	Claude A. Swanson (D)	116,393	*71.9*
	J. W. McGavock (R)	42,903	*26.5*
1928	Claude A. Swanson (D)	275,425	*99.8*

Special Election

1933	Harry F. Byrd (D)	119,377	*71.3*
	Henry A. Wise (R)	44,648	*26.7*

1934	Harry F. Byrd (D)	109,963	*76.0*
	Lawrence C. Page (R)	30,289	*20.9*
1940	Harry F. Byrd (D)	274,260	*93.3*
1946	Harry F. Byrd (D)	163,960	*64.9*
	Lester S. Parsons (R)	77,005	*30.5*
1952	Harry F. Byrd (D)	398,677	*73.4*
	H. M. Vise Sr. (ID)	69,133	*12.7*
	Clarke T. Robb (SOCIAL D)	67,281	*12.4*
1958	Harry F. Byrd (D)	317,221	*69.3*
	Louise Wensel (I)	120,224	*26.3*
1964	Harry F. Byrd (D)	592,260	*63.8*
	Richard A. May (R)	176,624	*19.0*
	James W. Respess (I)	95,526	*10.3*

Special Election

1966	Harry F. Byrd Jr. (D)	389,028	*53.3*
	Lawrence M. Traylor (R)	272,804	*37.4*
	John W. Carter (C)	57,692	*7.9*

1970	Harry F. Byrd Jr. (I)	506,623	*53.5*
	George C. Rawlings Jr. (D)	295,057	*31.2*
	Ray Garland (R)	145,031	*15.3*
1976	Harry F. Byrd Jr. (I)	890,778	*57.2*
	Elmo R. Zumwalt (D)	596,009	*38.3*
1982	Paul S. Trible Jr. (R)	724,571	*51.2*
	Richard Davis (D)	690,839	*48.8*

	Class 2		
1918	Thomas S. Martin (D)	40,403	*99.7*

Candidates	Votes	%
Special Election		
1920 Carter Glass (D)	184,646#	91.3
J. R. Pollard (R)	17,576#	8.7
1924 Carter Glass (D)	151,498	73.1
Carroll Livingston Ricker (SOC)	50,092	24.2
1930 Carter Glass (D)	112,002	76.7
J. Cloyd Byars (I)	26,091	17.9
Joe C. Morgan (SOC)	7,954	5.4
1936 Carter Glass (D)	244,518	91.7
1942 Carter Glass (D)	79,421	91.1
Lawrence S. Wilkes (SOC)	5,690	6.5
Special Election		
1946 A. Willis Robertson (D)	169,680	68.2
Robert H. Woods (R)	72,253	29.0
1948 A. Willis Robertson (D)	253,865	65.6
Robert H. Woods (R)	119,366	30.8
1954 A. Willis Robertson (D)	244,844	79.9
Charles William Lewis Jr. (ID)	32,681	10.7
Clarke T. Robb (SOCIAL D)	28,922	9.4
1960 A. Willis Robertson (D)	506,169	81.3
Stuart D. Baker (ID)	88,718	14.2
1966 William B. Spong Jr. (D)	429,855	58.6
James P. Ould Jr. (R)	245,681	33.5
F. Lee Hawthorne (C)	58,251	7.9
1972 William Lloyd Scott (R)	718,337	51.5
William B. Spong Jr. (D)	643,963	46.1
1978 John W. Warner (R)	613,232	50.2
Andrew P. Miller (D)	608,511	49.8
1984 John W. Warner (R)	1,406,194	70.0
Edythe C. Harrison (D)	601,142	29.9

WASHINGTON

Candidates	Votes	%
Class 1		
1916 Miles Poindexter (R)	202,287	55.4
George Turner (D)	135,339	37.1
Bruce Rogers (SOC)	21,709	5.9
1922 Clarence C. Dill (D)	130,375	44.2
Miles Poindexter (R)	126,556	43.0
James A. Duncan (F-LAB)	35,352	12.0
1928 Clarence C. Dill (D)	261,524	53.4
Kenneth Mackintosh (R)	227,415	46.5
1934 Lewis B. Schwellenbach (D)	302,606	60.9
Reno Odlin (R)	168,994	34.0
1940 Mon C. Wallgren (D)	404,718	54.2
Stephen F. Chadwick (R)	342,589	45.8
1946 Harry P. Cain (R)	358,847	54.3
Hugh B. Mitchell (D)	298,683	45.2
1952 Henry M. Jackson (D)	595,288	56.2
Harry P. Cain (R)	460,884	43.5
1958 Henry M. Jackson (D)	597,040	67.3
William B. Bantz (R)	278,271	31.4
1964 Henry M. Jackson (D)	875,950	72.2
Lloyd J. Andrews (R)	337,138	27.8
1970 Henry M. Jackson (D)	879,385	82.4
Charles W. Elicker (R)	170,790	16.0
1976 Henry M. Jackson (D)	1,071,219	71.8
George M. Brown (R)	361,546	24.2
1982 Henry M. Jackson (D)	943,655	69.0
Doug Jewett (R)	332,273	24.3
King Lysen (I)	72,297	5.3

Candidates	Votes	%
Special Election		
1983 Daniel J. Evans (R)	617,699	55.4
Mike Lowry (D)	496,393	44.6
Class 3		
1914 Wesley L. Jones (R)	130,479	37.8
W. W. Black (D)	91,733	26.6
Ole Hanson (PROG)	83,282	24.1
Adam H. Barth (SOC)	30,234	8.8
1920 Wesley L. Jones (R)	217,069	56.4
C. L. France (F-LAB)	99,309	25.8
George F. Cotterill (D)	68,488	17.8
1926 Wesley L. Jones (R)	164,130	51.3
A. Scott Bullitt (D)	148,792	46.5
1932 Homer T. Bone (D)	365,949	60.6
Wesley L. Jones (R)	197,450	32.7
1938 Homer T. Bone (D)	371,535	62.6
Ewing D. Colvin (R)	220,204	37.1
1944 Warren G. Magnuson (D)	452,013	55.1
Harry P. Cain (R)	364,356	44.4
1950 Warren G. Magnuson (D)	397,719	53.4
Walter Williams (R)	342,464	46.0
1956 Warren G. Magnuson (D)	685,565	61.1
Arthur B. Langlie (R)	436,652	38.9
1962 Warren G. Magnuson (D)	491,365	52.1
Richard G. Christensen (R)	446,204	47.3
1968 Warren G. Magnuson (D)	796,183	64.4
Jack Metcalf (R)	435,894	35.3
1974 Warren G. Magnuson (D)	611,811	60.7
Jack Metcalf (R)	363,626	36.1
1980 Slade Gorton (R)	936,317	54.2
Warren G. Magnuson (D)	792,052	45.8

WEST VIRGINIA

Candidates	Votes	%
Class 1		
1916 Howard Sutherland (R)	144,243	50.1
William E. Chilton (D)	138,585	48.2
1922 Matthew M. Neely (D)	198,853	51.2
Howard Sutherland (R)	185,046	47.6
1928 Henry D. Hatfield (R)	327,266	50.7
Matthew M. Neely (D)	317,620	49.2
1934 Rush D. Holt (D)	349,882	55.1
Henry D. Hatfield (R)	281,756	44.4
1940 Harley M. Kilgore (D)	492,413	56.3
Thomas Sweeney (R)	381,806	43.7
1946 Harley M. Kilgore (D)	273,151	50.3
Thomas Sweeney (R)	269,617	49.7
1952 Harley M. Kilgore (D)	470,019	53.6
Chapman Revercomb (R)	406,554	46.4
Special Election		
1956 Chapman Revercomb (R)	432,123	53.7
William C. Marland (D)	373,051	46.3
1958 Robert C. Byrd (D)	381,745	59.2
Chapman Revercomb (R)	263,172	40.8
1964 Robert C. Byrd (D)	515,015	67.7
Cooper P. Benedict (R)	246,072	32.3
1970 Robert C. Byrd (D)	345,965	77.6
Elmer H. Dodson (R)	99,658	22.4
1976 Robert C. Byrd (D)	566,423	99.9
1982 Robert C. Byrd (D)	387,170	68.5
Cleveland K. Benedict (R)	173,910	30.8

	Candidates	Votes	%
	Class 2		
1918	David Elkins (R)	115,216	*53.5*
	Clarence W. Watson (D)	97,715	*45.4*
1924	Guy D. Goff (R)	290,004	*50.9*
	William E. Chilton (D)	271,809	*47.7*
1930	Matthew M. Neely (D)	342,467	*61.9*
	James Ellwood Jones (R)	209,427	*37.9*
1936	Matthew M. Neely (D)	488,620	*59.1*
	Hugh Ike Shott (R)	338,363	*40.9*
1942	Chapman Revercomb (R)	256,816	*55.4*
	Matthew M. Neely (D)	207,045	*44.6*

Special Election

1942	Hugh Ike Shott (R)	227,469	*52.3*
	Joseph Rosier (D)	207,678	*47.7*
1948	Matthew M. Neely (D)	435,354	*57.0*
	Chapman Revercomb (R)	328,534	*43.0*
1954	Matthew M. Neely (D)	325,263	*54.8*
	Thomas Sweeney (R)	268,066	*45.2*

Special Election

1958	Jennings Randolph (D)	374,167	*59.3*
	John D. Hoblitzell Jr. (R)	256,510	*40.7*
1960	Jennings Randolph (D)	458,355	*55.3*
	Cecil H. Underwood (R)	369,935	*44.7*
1966	Jennings Randolph (D)	292,325	*59.5*
	Francis J. Love (R)	198,891	*40.5*
1972	Jennings Randolph (D)	486,310	*66.5*
	Louise Leonard (R)	245,531	*33.6*
1978	Jennings Randolph (D)	249,034	*50.5*
	Arch A. Moore (R)	244,317	*49.5*
1984	John D. (Jay) Rockefeller IV (D)	374,233	*51.8*
	John R. Raese (R)	344,680	*47.7*

WISCONSIN

	Candidates	Votes	%
	Class 1		
1916	Robert M. La Follette (R)	251,303	*60.5*
	William F. Wolfe (D)	135,144	*32.5*
	Richard Elsner (SOCIAL D)	28,908	*7.0*
1922	Robert M. La Follette (R)	379,494	*80.6*
	Jessie Jack Hooper (ID)	78,029	*16.6*

Special Election

1925	Robert M. La Follette Jr. (R)	237,719	*67.5*
	Edward F. Dithmar (IR)	91,318	*25.9*
1928	Robert M. La Follette Jr. (R)	635,376	*85.6*
	William H. Markham (IR)	81,302	*11.0*
1934	Robert M. La Follette Jr. (PROG)	440,513	*47.8*
	John M. Callahan (D)	223,438	*24.2*
	John B. Chapple (R)	210,569	*22.8*
1940	Robert M. La Follette Jr. (PROG)	605,609	*45.3*
	Fred H. Clausen (R)	553,692	*41.4*
	James E. Finnegan (D)	176,688	*13.2*
1946	Joseph R. McCarthy (R)	620,430	*61.3*
	Howard J. McMurray (D)	378,772	*37.4*
1952	Joseph R. McCarthy (R)	870,444	*54.2*
	Thomas E. Fairchild (D)	731,402	*45.6*

	Candidates	Votes	%
Special Election			
1957	William Proxmire (D)	435,985	*56.4*
	Walter J. Kohler Jr. (R)	312,931	*40.5*
1958	William Proxmire (D)	682,440	*57.1*
	Roland J. Steinle (R)	510,398	*42.7*
1964	William Proxmire (D)	892,013	*53.3*
	Wilbur N. Renk (R)	780,116	*46.6*
1970	William Proxmire (D)	948,445	*70.8*
	John E. Erickson (R)	381,297	*28.5*
1976	William Proxmire (D)	1,396,970	*72.2*
	Stanley York (R)	521,902	*27.0*
1982	William Proxmire (D)	983,311	*63.6*
	Scott McCallum (R)	527,355	*34.1*

	Class 3		
1914	Paul O. Husting (D)	134,925	*43.8*
	Francis E. McGovern (R)	133,969	*43.5*
	Emil Seidel (SOCIAL D)	29,774	*9.7*

Special Election

1918	Irvine L. Lenroot (R)	163,980#	*38.7*
	John Davies (D)	148,714#	*35.1*
	Victor L. Berger (SOC)	110,487#	*26.1*
1920	Irvine L. Lenroot (R)	281,576	*41.6*
	James Thompson (I)	235,029	*34.7*
	Paul S. Reinsch (D)	89,265	*13.2*
	Frank J. Weber (SOC)	66,172	*9.8*
1926	John J. Blaine (R)	300,759	*55.0*
	Charles D. Rosa (I-PROG-R)	111,122	*20.3*
	Thomas M. Kearney (D)	66,672	*12.2*
	Leo Krzycki (SOC)	31,317	*5.7*
1932	F. Ryan Duffy (D)	610,236	*57.0*
	John B. Chapple (R)	387,668	*36.2*
	Emil Seidel (SOC)	65,807	*6.1*
1938	Alexander Wiley (R)	446,770	*47.7*
	Herman L. Ekern (PROG)	249,209	*26.6*
	F. Ryan Duffy (D)	231,976	*24.7*
1944	Alexander Wiley (R)	634,513	*50.5*
	Howard J. McMurray (D)	537,144	*42.8*
	Harry Sauthoff (PROG)	73,089	*5.8*
1950	Alexander Wiley (R)	595,283	*53.3*
	Thomas E. Fairchild (D)	515,539	*46.2*
1956	Alexander Wiley (R)	892,473	*58.6*
	Henry W. Maier (D)	627,903	*41.2*
1962	Gaylord Nelson (D)	662,342	*52.6*
	Alexander Wiley (R)	594,846	*47.2*
1968	Gaylord Nelson (D)	1,020,931	*61.7*
	Jerris Leonard (R)	633,910	*38.3*
1974	Gaylord Nelson (D)	740,700	*61.8*
	Thomas E. Petri (R)	429,327	*35.8*
1980	Bob Kasten (R)	1,106,311	*50.2*
	Gaylord Nelson (D)	1,065,487	*48.3*

WYOMING

	Candidates	Votes	%
	Class 1		
1916	John B. Kendrick (D)	26,324	*51.5*
	Clarence D. Clark (R)	23,258	*45.5*
1922	John B. Kendrick (D)	35,734	*57.3*
	F. W. Mondell (R)	26,627	*42.7*
1928	John B. Kendrick (D)	43,032	*53.5*
	Charles E. Winter (R)	37,076	*46.1*
1934	Joseph C. O'Mahoney (D)	53,806	*56.6*

Candidates	Votes	%
Vincent Carter (R)	40,819	43.0

Special Election

1934	Joseph C. O'Mahoney (D)	53,859	56.9
	Vincent Carter (R)	40,825	43.1
1940	Joseph C. O'Mahoney (D)	65,022	58.7
	Milward Simpson (R)	45,682	41.3
1946	Joseph C. O'Mahoney (D)	45,843	56.2
	Harry B. Henderson (R)	35,714	43.8
1952	Frank A. Barrett (R)	67,176	51.6
	Joseph C. O'Mahoney (D)	62,921	48.4
1958	Gale McGee (D)	58,035	50.8
	Frank A. Barrett (R)	56,122	49.2
1964	Gale McGee (D)	76,485	54.0
	John S. Wold (R)	65,185	46.0
1970	Gale McGee (D)	67,207	55.8
	John S. Wold (R)	53,279	44.2
1976	Malcolm Wallop (R)	84,810	54.6
	Gale McGee (D)	70,558	45.4
1982	Malcolm Wallop (R)	94,725	56.7
	Rodger McDaniel (D)	72,466	43.3

Class 2

1918	Francis E. Warren (R)	23,975	57.8
	John E. Osborne (D)	17,528	42.2
1924	Francis E. Warren (R)	41,293	55.2
	Robert R. Rose (D)	33,536	44.8
1930	Robert D. Carey (R)	43,626	59.1
	Harry H. Schwartz (D)	30,259	41.0

Special Election

1930	Robert D. Carey (R)	42,726#	58.8
	Harry H. Schwartz (D)	29,904#	41.2
1936	Harry H. Schwartz (D)	53,919	53.8
	Robert D. Carey (R)	45,483	45.4
1942	Edward V. Robertson (R)	41,486	54.6
	Harry H. Schwartz (D)	34,503	45.4
1948	Lester C. Hunt (D)	57,953	57.1
	Edward V. Robertson (R)	43,527	42.9
1954	Joseph C. O'Mahoney (D)	57,845	51.5
	William Henry Harrison (R)	54,407	48.5

Special Election

1954	Joseph C. O'Mahoney (D)	57,163	51.6
	William Henry Harrison (R)	53,705	48.4
1960	Keith Thomson (R)	78,103*	56.4
	Raymond B. Whitaker (D)	60,447	43.6

Special Election

1962	Milward Simpson (R)	69,043	57.8
	J. J. Hickey (D)	50,329	42.2
1966	Clifford P. Hansen (R)	63,548	51.8
	Teno Roncalio (D)	59,141	48.2
1972	Clifford P. Hansen (R)	101,314	71.3
	Mike Vinich (D)	40,753	28.7
1978	Alan K. Simpson (R)	82,908	62.2
	Raymond B. Whitaker (D)	50,456	37.8
1984	Alan K. Simpson (R)	146,373	78.3
	Victor A. Ryan (D)	40,525	21.7

Senate Returns: Other Sources

In the preceding pages of Senate popular election returns (609-636) the symbol # is used to denote 1913-75 returns taken from a source other than the election data provided by the Inter-University Consortium for Political and Social Research (ICPSR). This page lists the source for each of those returns. *(For description of ICPSR data, see pp. xiv, 608.)*

The most frequently used alternative source was *Statistics of the Congressional Elections of —*, published by the Clerk of the House of Representatives for every general election year since 1920.

Alabama
1938: *Statistics of the Congressional Election of Nov. 8, 1938.*

Arkansas
1924: *Statistics of the Congressional and Presidential Election of Nov. 4, 1924.*
1914: 1916 *World Almanac*, published by the *New York World* newspaper.
1932 special election: Alexander Heard and Donald S. Strong, *Southern Primaries and Elections, 1920-1949*, p. 31.

Colorado
1944: *Statistics of the Congressional and Presidential Election of Nov. 7, 1944.*

Connecticut
1924 special election: *Statistics of the Congressional Election of Nov. 4, 1924.*

Georgia
1924: *Statistics of the Congressional and Presidential Election of Nov. 4, 1924.*

Kentucky
1950 special election: *Statistics of the Congressional Election of Nov. 7, 1950.*

Louisiana
1936 special election: Louisiana Secretary of State.
1920: *Statistics of the Congressional and Presidential Election of Nov. 2, 1920.*

Maine
1952: *Statistics of the Congressional and Presidential Election of Nov. 4, 1952.*

Maryland
1913 special election: Maryland Secretary of State.
1940: *Statistics of the Congressional and Presidential Election of Nov. 5, 1940.*
1946: *Statistics of the Congressional Election of Nov. 5, 1946.*

Minnesota
1923 special election: 1924 *World Almanac*, published by the *New York World* newspaper.

North Carolina
1948 special election: *Statistics of Congressional and Presidential Election of Nov. 2, 1948.*

Ohio
1930 special election: *Statistics of Congressional Election of Nov. 4, 1930.*

Pennsylvania
1922 special election: *Statistics of the Congressional Election of Nov. 7, 1922.*

Texas
1961 special primary: Richard M. Scammon (ed.), *America Votes 5,* (Pittsburgh, 1964), p. 401.

Vermont:
1931 special election: Vermont Secretary of State.
1972 special election: Richard M. Scammon (ed.), *America Votes 10,* (Washington, 1973), p. 372.
1934 special election: Vermont Secretary of State.

Virginia
1920 special election: *Statistics of the Congressional and Presidential Election of Nov. 2, 1920.*

Wisconsin
1918 special election: Seward W. Livermore, *Politics is Adjourned: Woodrow Wilson and the War Congress,* (Middletown, Conn.: Wesleyan University Press, 1966), p. 271.

Wyoming
1930 special election: *Statistics of the Congressional Election of Nov. 4, 1930.*

Senate Primary Returns, 1956-1984

(For Southern primary Senate returns, see p. 1090.)

ALASKA

	Candidates	Votes	%
	Class 2		
1958 [1]	**Republican Primary**		
	R. E. Robertson (R)		100.0
	Democratic Primary		
	E. L. Bartlett (D)		100.0
1960	**Republican Primary**		
	Lee L. McKinley (R)	8,867	68.2
	Lawrence M. Brayton (R)	4,131	31.8
	Democratic Primary		
	E. L. Bartlett (D)		100.0
1966	**Republican Primary**		
	Lee L. McKinley (R)	9,310	55.8
	Lawrence M. Brayton (R)	5,492	32.9
	Maxine B. Whaley (R)	1,866	11.2
	Democratic Primary		
	E. L. Bartlett (D)	27,994	87.2
	T. J. Bichsel (D)	1,864	5.8
1970	**Special Republican Primary**		
	Ted Stevens (R)	39,062	96.7
	Special Democratic Primary		
	Wendell P. Kay (R)	16,729	56.8
	Joe Josephson (R)	12,730	43.2
1972	**Republican Primary**		
	Ted Stevens (R)		100.0
	Democratic Primary		
	Gene Guess (D)		100.0

	Candidates	Votes	%
1978	**Republican Primary**		
	Ted Stevens (R)		100.0
	Democratic Primary		
	Donald W. Hobbs (D)	10,589	55.0
	Joe Sonneman (D)	8,662	45.0
1984	**Republican Primary**		
	Ted Stevens (R)	65,552	100.0
	Democratic Primary		
	John E. Havelock (D)	19,074	65.5
	Dave Carlson (D)	4,620	15.9
	Michael Beaseley (D)	2,443	8.4
	Joe Tracanna (D)	1,661	5.7

Senate Primary Sources

The major source for this section was the *America Votes* series compiled biennially by Richard M. Scammon and Alice V. McGillivray and published since 1966 by Congressional Quarterly Inc. Other sources were the returns obtained by Congressional Quarterly after each federal and gubernatorial election. In cases of discrepancies, the *Guide to U.S. Elections, Second Edition*, accepted the *America Votes* figure. Candidates are listed only if they received 5 percent or more of the vote.

The first year for which *America Votes* reported primary returns, 1956, was chosen as the starting point for this section because Senate primary votes for earlier years are not readily available. Senate primary returns back to 1912 for 11 Southern states, where victory in the Democratic primary was tantamount to election for many years, may be found on pp. 1090-1102.

Primary returns are grouped according to the three classes used to stagger the six-year Senate terms. For an explanation of the Senate classes, see p. 574.

Where no primary is indicated for a year in which a state elected a senator, it generally means that party conventions chose the nominees. Notes at the end of a state's listing explain other unusual circumstances.

---

1. Alaska became a state Jan. 3, 1959. The first Senate elections for that state were for unspecified terms. The Senate later determined that Sen. Bartlett would serve two years (Class 2) and Sen. Gruening, four (Class 3).

Candidates	Votes	%

Class 3

1958 [1] **Republican Primary**

Mike Stepovich (R)		100.0

Democratic Primary

Ernest Gruening (D)		100.0

1962 **Republican Primary**

Ted Stevens (R)	11,000	72.5
Frank Cook (R)	4,175	27.5

Democratic Primary

Ernest Gruening (D)	18,525	86.3
R. L. Veach (D)	2,946	13.7

1968 **Republican Primary**

Elmer Rasmuson (R)	10,320	53.1
Ted Stevens (R)	9,111	46.9

Democratic Primary

Mike Gravel (D)	17,971	52.9
Ernest Gruening (D)	16,015	47.1

1974 **Republican Primary**

C. R. Lewis (R)	21,065	52.7
Terry Miller (R)	16,336	40.8
Red Stevens (R)	2,207	5.5

Democratic Primary

Mike Gravel (D)	22,834	54.3
Gene Guess (D)	15,090	35.9
Richard J. Greuel (D)	3,367	8.0

1980 **Republican Primary**

Frank H. Murkowski (R)	16,292	59.0
Arthur R. Kennedy (R)	5,527	20.0
Morris Thompson (R)	3,635	13.2

Democratic Primary

Clark S. Gruening (D)	39,719	54.9
Mike Gravel (D)	31,504	43.5

ARIZONA

Candidates	Votes	%

Class 1

1958 **Republican Primary**

Barry Goldwater (R)		100.0

Democratic Primary

Ernest W. McFarland (D)	111,429	72.5
Stephen W. Langmade (D)	42,199	27.5

Candidates	Votes	%

1964 **Republican Primary**

Paul Fannin (R)		100.0

Democratic Primary

Roy L. Elson (D)	76,697	41.4
Renz L. Jennings (D)	64,331	34.7
Howard V. Peterson (D)	22,424	12.1
George Gavin (D)	10,291	5.6

1970 **Republican Primary**

Paul Fannin (R)		100.0

Democratic Primary

Sam Grossman (D)	78,006	65.2
John Kruglick (D)	27,324	22.8
H. L. Kelly (D)	14,238	11.9

1976 **Republican Primary**

Sam Steiger (R)	102,843	52.5
John B. Conlan (R)	93,033	47.5

Democratic Primary

Dennis DeConcini (D)	121,423	53.4
Carolyn Warner (D)	71,612	31.5
Wade Church (D)	34,266	15.1

Libertarian Primary

Allan Norwitz (LIBERT)		100.0

1982 **Republican Primary**

Pete Dunn (R)	97,391	55.1
Dean Sellers (R)	79,375	44.9

Democratic Primary

Dennis DeConcini (D)	140,328	84.4
Caroline P. Killeen (D)	25,909	15.6

Special Libertarian Primary

Randall Clamons (LIBERT)		100.0

Class 3

1956 **Republican Primary**

Ross F. Jones (R)	31,246	79.3
Albert H. Mackenzie (R)	8,147	20.7

Democratic Primary

Carl Hayden (D)	99,859	82.4
Robert E. Miller (D)	21,370	17.6

1962 **Republican Primary**

Evan Mecham (R)	40,300	59.0
Stephen Shadegg (R)	27,965	41.0

Candidates	Votes	%
Democratic Primary		
Carl Hayden (D)	117,688	*76.5*
W. Lee McLane (D)	36,158	*23.5*
1968 **Republican Primary**		
Barry Goldwater (R)		*100.0*
Democratic Primary		
Roy L. Elson (D)	95,231	*62.8*
Bob Kennedy (D)	41,397	*27.3*
Dick Herbert (D)	15,061	*9.9*
1974 **Republican Primary**		
Barry Goldwater (R)		*100.0*
Democratic Primary		
Jonathan Marshall (D)	79,225	*53.6*
George Oglesby (D)	36,262	*24.5*
William M. Feighan (D)	32,449	*21.9*
1980 **Republican Primary**		
Barry Goldwater (R)		*100.0*
Democratic Primary		
Bill Schulz (D)	97,520	*55.4*
James F. McNulty Jr. (D)	58,894	*33.4*
Frank DePaoli (D)	19,259	*10.9*
Libertarian Primary		
Fred Esser (LIBERT)		*100.0*

CALIFORNIA

Candidates	Votes	%
Class 1		
1958 [2] **Republican Primary**		
Goodwin J. Knight (R)	790,939	*49.1*
George Christopher (R)	558,245	*34.7*
Clair Engle (R)	173,845	*10.8*
Democratic Primary		
Clair Engle (D)	1,558,622	*70.8*
Goodwin J. Knight (R)	385,170	*17.5*
George Christopher (R)	221,783	*10.1*
1964 **Republican Primary**		
George Murphy (R)	1,121,591	*54.1*
Leland M. Kaiser (R)	689,323	*33.3*
Fred Hall (R)	261,036	*12.6*

2. California's cross-filing law permitted a candidate to enter both the Democratic and Republican primaries.

Candidates	Votes	%
Democratic Primary		
Pierre Salinger (D)	1,177,517	*44.3*
Alan Cranston (D)	1,037,748	*39.0*
George McLain (D)	180,405	*6.8*
1970 **Republican Primary**		
George Murphy (R)	1,325,271	*64.3*
Norton Simon (R)	670,702	*32.5*
Democratic Primary		
John V. Tunney (D)	1,010,812	*41.6*
George E. Brown (D)	812,463	*33.4*
Kenneth Hahn (D)	417,970	*17.2*
American Independent Primary		
Charles C. Ripley (AMI)	14,115	*65.0*
John Ortman (AMI)	7,600	*34.9*
Peace and Freedom Primary		
Robert Scheer (PFP)		*100.0*
1976 **Republican Primary**		
S. I. Hayakawa (R)	886,743	*38.2*
Robert H. Finch (R)	614,240	*26.5*
Alphonzo E. Bell (R)	532,969	*23.0*
John L. Harmer (R)	197,252	*8.5*
Democratic Primary		
John V. Tunney (D)	1,774,879	*53.8*
Tom Hayden (D)	1,210,637	*36.7*
American Independent Primary		
Jack McCoy (AMI)		*100.0*
Peace and Freedom Primary		
David Wald (PFP)		*100.0*
1982 **Republican Primary**		
Pete Wilson (R)	851,292	*37.5*
Paul N. McCloskey (R)	577,267	*25.5*
Barry M. Goldwater Jr. (R)	408,308	*18.0*
Robert K. Dornan (R)	181,970	*8.0*
Democratic Primary		
Edmund G. Brown Jr. (D)	1,392,660	*50.7*
Gore Vidal (D)	415,366	*15.1*
Paul B. Carpenter (D)	415,198	*15.1*
Daniel K. Whitehurst (D)	167,574	*6.1*
American Independent Primary		
Theresa Dietrich (AMI)		*100.0*
Peace and Freedom Primary		
David Wald (PFP)		*100.0*

Candidates	Votes	%
Libertarian Primary		
Joseph Fuhrig (LIBERT)		*100.0*

Class 3

1956

Candidates	Votes	%
Republican Primary		
Thomas H. Kuchel (R)	1,332,074	*90.4*
Democratic Primary		
Richard Richards (D)	1,004,336	*53.4*
Thomas H. Kuchel (R)	494,066	*26.2*
Samuel W. Yorty (D)	383,813	*20.4*
Prohibition Party Primary		
Ray Gourley (P)		*100.0*

1962

Candidates	Votes	%
Republican Primary		
Thomas H. Kuchel (R)	1,357,975	*75.0*
Loyd Wright (R)	247,300	*13.7*
Howard Jarvis (R)	180,768	*10.0*
Democratic Primary		
Richard Richards (D)	1,674,563	*82.6*
Gabriel Green (D)	171,379	*8.5*
J. F. Coleman (D)	170,296	*8.4*

1968

Candidates	Votes	%
Republican Primary		
Max Rafferty (R)	1,112,947	*50.1*
Thomas H. Kuchel (R)	1,043,315	*46.9*
Democratic Primary		
Alan Cranston (D)	1,681,825	*59.0*
Anthony C. Beilenson (D)	644,844	*22.6*
Walter R. Buchanan (D)	227,798	*8.0*
William M. Bennett (D)	207,720	*7.3*
Peace and Freedom Primary		
Paul Jacobs (PFP)		*100.0*

1974

Candidates	Votes	%
Republican Primary		
H. L. (Bill) Richardson (R)	1,061,986	*64.6*
Earl W. Brian (R)	273,636	*16.7*
James E. Johnson (R)	118,715	*7.2*
William H. Reinholz (R)	107,217	*6.5*
Democratic Primary		
Alan Cranston (D)	2,262,574	*83.5*
Howard L. Gifford (D)	318,080	*11.7*
American Independent Primary		
Jack McCoy (AMI)		*100.0*
Peace and Freedom Primary		
Gayle M. Justice (PFP)		*100.0*

	Candidates	Votes	%
1980	**Republican Primary**		
	Paul Gann (R)	934,433	*40.0*
	Samuel W. Yorty (R)	668,583	*28.6*
	John G. Schmitz (R)	442,839	*19.0*
	Democratic Primary		
	Alan Cranston (D)	2,608,746	*79.9*
	Richard Morgan (D)	350,394	*10.7*
	American Independent Primary		
	James C. Griffin (AMI)		*100.0*
	Peace and Freedom Primary		
	David Wald (PFP)		*100.0*
	Libertarian Primary		
	David Bergland (LIBERT)		*100.0*

COLORADO

	Candidates	Votes	%
	Class 2		
1960	**Republican Primary**		
	Gordon Allott (R)		*100.0*
	Democratic Primary		
	Robert L. Knous (D)		*100.0*
1966	**Republican Primary**		
	Gordon Allott (R)		*100.0*
	Democratic Primary		
	Roy Romer (D)		*100.0*
1972	**Republican Primary**		
	Gordon Allott (R)		*100.0*
	Democratic Primary		
	Floyd K. Haskell (D)	77,574	*58.8*
	Anthony F. Vollack (D)	54,298	*41.2*
1978	**Republican Primary**		
	William L. Armstrong (R)	108,573	*73.4*
	Jack Swigert (R)	39,247	*26.6*
	Democratic Primary		
	Floyd K. Haskell (D)		*100.0*
1984	**Republican Primary**		
	William L. Armstrong (R)	105,870	*100.0*

Candidates	Votes	%
Democratic Primary		
Nancy Dick (D)	78,248	*51.0*
Carlos F. Lucero (D)	75,277	*49.0*

Class 3

1956

Candidates	Votes	%
Republican Primary		
Dan Thornton (R)		*100.0*
Democratic Primary		
John A. Carroll (D)	62,688	*50.8*
Charles Brannan (D)	60,701	*49.2*

1962

Candidates	Votes	%
Republican Primary		
Peter H. Dominick (R)		*100.0*
Democratic Primary		
John A. Carroll (D)		*100.0*

1968

Candidates	Votes	%
Republican Primary		
Peter H. Dominick (R)		*100.0*
Democratic Primary		
Stephen McNichols (D)	92,250	*58.5*
Kenneth Montfort (D)	65,347	*41.5*

1974

Candidates	Votes	%
Republican Primary		
Peter H. Dominick (R)		*100.0*
Democratic Primary		
Gary Hart (D)	81,161	*39.9*
Herrick S. Roth (D)	66,819	*32.9*
Martin P. Miller (D)	55,339	*27.2*

1980

Candidates	Votes	%
Republican Primary		
Mary E. Buchanan (R)	65,803	*30.8*
Howard W. Callaway (R)	64,256	*30.1*
Sam Zakhem (R)	42,629	*20.0*
John M. Cogswell (R)	40,651	*19.0*
Democratic Primary		
Gary Hart (D)		*100.0*

CONNECTICUT

Candidates	Votes	%
Class 1		

1970 [3]

Candidates	Votes	%
Republican Primary		
Lowell P. Weicker Jr. (R)	77,057	*60.3*
John M. Lupton (R)	50,657	*39.7*
Democratic Primary		
Joseph D. Duffey (D)	79,166	*43.7*

Candidates	Votes	%
Alphonsus J. Donahue (D)	66,916	*36.8*
Edward L. Marcus (D)	35,715	*19.7*

Class 3

1980 [3]

Candidates	Votes	%
Republican Primary		
James L. Buckley (R)	64,962	*56.5*
Richard C. Buzzuto (R)	50,096	*43.5*

DELAWARE

Candidates	Votes	%
Class 1		

1982

Candidates	Votes	%
Republican Primary		
William V. Roth Jr. (R)		*100.0*
Democratic Primary		
David N. Levinson (D)		*100.0*

Class 2

1978 [4]

Candidates	Votes	%
Republican Primary		
James H. Baxter (R)	12,107	*53.7*
James E. Venema (R)	10,422	*46.3*

1984

Candidates	Votes	%
Republican Primary		
John M. Burris (R)		*100.0*
Democratic Primary		
Joseph R. Biden (D)		*100.0*

HAWAII

Candidates	Votes	%
Class 1		

1959 [5]

Candidates	Votes	%
Republican Primary		
Hiram L. Fong (R)		*100.0*
Democratic Primary		
Frank F. Fasi (D)	46,868	*59.9*
William H. Heen (D)	31,317	*40.0*

1964

Candidates	Votes	%
Republican Primary		
Hiram L. Fong (R)	31,770	*95.2*

3. In Connecticut, party conventions nominated candidates subject to a system of "challenge" primaries that allowed defeated candidates to petition for a popular vote if they received at least 20 percent of the convention vote.

4. From 1972 through 1978 Delaware used a system of "challenge" primaries, in which a candidate for statewide office who received at least 35 percent of the convention vote could challenge the endorsed candidate in a primary. There was no Senate election in Delaware in 1980, the first year that the state used the direct primary system.

Candidates	Votes	%
Democratic Primary		
Thomas P. Gill (D)	71,298	64.0
Nadao Yoshinaga (D)	37,253	33.4

1970 **Republican Primary**

Candidates	Votes	%
Hiram L. Fong (R)		100.0

Democratic Primary

Candidates	Votes	%
Cecil Heftel (D)	78,934	62.4
Tony N. Hodges (D)	30,430	24.1
Neil Abercrombie (D)	17,058	13.5

1976 **Republican Primary**

Candidates	Votes	%
William F. Quinn (R)	32,058	93.7
Spencer J. Cabral (R)	2,170	6.3

Democratic Primary

Candidates	Votes	%
Spark M. Matsunaga (D)	105,731	51.0
Patsy Mink (D)	84,732	40.9

Libertarian Primary

Candidates	Votes	%
Rockne Johnson (LIBERT)		100.0

Non-Partisan Primary

Candidates	Votes	%
James D. Kimmel (NON PART)		100.0

People's Primary

Candidates	Votes	%
Anthony N. Hodges (PP)		100.0

1982 **Republican Primary**

Candidates	Votes	%
Clarence J. Brown (R)	6,142	65.2
Arbis D. Shipley (R)	3,279	34.8

Democratic Primary

Candidates	Votes	%
Spark M. Matsunaga (D)		100.0

Independent Democratic Primary

Candidates	Votes	%
E. F. Bernier-Nachtwey (ID)		100.0

Class 3

1959 [5] **Republican Primary**

Candidates	Votes	%
Wilfred C. Tsukiyama (R)		100.0

Democratic Primary

Candidates	Votes	%
Oren E. Long (D)	61,345	83.9
Kenneth E. Young (D)	9,036	12.3

Commonwealth Primary

Candidates	Votes	%
Eugene Ressencourt (CP)		100.0

5. Hawaii became a state Aug. 21, 1959. The first Senate elections for that state were for unspecified terms. The Senate later determined that Sen. Fong would serve the long term (Class 1) and Sen. Long, the short term (Class 3).

Candidates	Votes	%
1962 **Republican Primary**		
Ben F. Dillingham (R)		100.0
Democratic Primary		
Daniel K. Inouye (D)	80,707	93.6
Frank Troy (D)	5,476	6.3

1968 **Republican Primary**

Candidates	Votes	%
Wayne C. Thiessen (R)		100.0

Democratic Primary

Candidates	Votes	%
Daniel K. Inouye (D)	111,135	87.5
William Lampard (D)	14,357	11.3

Peace and Freedom Primary

Candidates	Votes	%
Oliver Lee (PFP)		100.0

1974 **Democratic Primary**

Candidates	Votes	%
Daniel K. Inouye (D)		100.0

Peoples Primary

Candidates	Votes	%
James D. Kimmel (PP)	61	64.9
Floyd Nachtwey (PP)	33	35.1

1980 **Republican Primary**

Candidates	Votes	%
Cooper Brown (R)	3,219	39.0
Lawrence I. Weisman (R)	2,586	31.4
Dan Dew (R)	1,854	22.5
E. F. Bernier-Nachtwey (R)	584	7.1

Democratic Primary

Candidates	Votes	%
Daniel K. Inouye (D)	198,468	87.5
Kamuela Price (D)	15,361	6.8
John P. Fritz (D)	12,929	5.7

Libertarian Primary

Candidates	Votes	%
H. E. Shasteen (LIBERT)		100.0

IDAHO

Candidates	Votes	%
Class 2		

1960 **Republican Primary**

Candidates	Votes	%
Henry C. Dworshak (R)		100.0

Democratic Primary

Candidates	Votes	%
Gregg Potvin (D)	16,524	23.7
Bob McLaughlin (D)	14,694	21.1
Compton White (D)	14,515	20.8
A. W. Brunt (D)	13,015	18.7
Joseph R. Garry (D)	10,899	15.6

Candidates	Votes	%
Democratic Runoff		
R. F. (Bob) McLaughlin	13,117	*51.9*
Gregg Potvin	12,174	*48.1*

1966 Republican Primary

Candidates	Votes	%
Len B. Jordan (R)		*100.0*

Democratic Primary

Candidates	Votes	%
Ralph R. Harding (D)		*100.0*

1972 Republican Primary

Candidates	Votes	%
James A. McClure (R)	46,522	*36.1*
George Hansen (R)	35,412	*27.4*
Glen Wegner (R)	24,582	*19.1*
Robert E. Smylie (R)	22,497	*17.4*

Democratic Primary

Candidates	Votes	%
William E. (Bud) Davis (D)	23,953	*36.1*
W. Anthony Park (D)	17,636	*26.5*
Byron Johnson (D)	15,526	*23.4*
Rose Bowman (D)	9,327	*14.0*

1978 Republican Primary

Candidates	Votes	%
James A. McClure		*100.0*

Democratic Primary

Candidates	Votes	%
Dwight Jensen (D)		*100.0*

1984 Republican Primary

Candidates	Votes	%
James A. McClure (R)	102,125	*100.0*

Democratic Primary

Candidates	Votes	%
Peter M. Busch (D)	27,871	*62.0*
Louis A. Hatheway (D)	17,065	*38.0*

Class 3

1956 Republican Primary

Candidates	Votes	%
Herman Welker (R)	31,399	*42.5*
William S. Holden (R)	21,081	*28.5*
Ray J. Davis (R)	12,349	*16.7*
John C. Sanborn (R)	8,261	*11.2*

Democratic Primary

Candidates	Votes	%
Frank Church (D)	27,942	*37.7*
Glen H. Taylor (D)	27,742	*37.5*
Claude Burtenshaw (D)	11,738	*15.9*
Alvin McCormack (D)	6,596	*8.9*

1962 Republican Primary

Candidates	Votes	%
Jack Hawley (R)	38,210	*60.2*
George Hansen (R)	25,223	*39.8*

Democratic Primary

Candidates	Votes	%
Frank Church (D)		*100.0*

1968 Republican Primary

Candidates	Votes	%
George Hansen (R)		*100.0*

Democratic Primary

Candidates	Votes	%
Frank Church (D)		*100.0*

1974 Republican Primary

Candidates	Votes	%
Robert L. Smith (R)	45,553	*72.0*
Donald L. Winder (R)	13,406	*21.2*
Charles Bolstridge (R)	4,331	*6.8*

Democratic Primary

Candidates	Votes	%
Frank Church (D)	53,659	*85.8*
Leon R. Olson (D)	8,904	*14.2*

American Primary

Candidates	Votes	%
Jean L. Stoddard (AM)		*100.0*

1980 Republican Primary

Candidates	Votes	%
Steven D. Symms (R)		*100.0*

Democratic Primary

Candidates	Votes	%
Frank Church (D)		*100.0*

Libertarian Primary

Candidates	Votes	%
Larry Fullmer (LIBERT)		*100.0*

ILLINOIS

Candidates	Votes	%
Class 2		

1960 Republican Primary

Candidates	Votes	%
Samuel W. Witwer (R)	249,849	*31.5*
Warren E. Wright (R)	226,449	*28.6*
William H. Rentschler (R)	202,600	*25.6*
John W. Lewis (R)	48,989	*6.2*

Democratic Primary

Candidates	Votes	%
Paul H. Douglas (D)		*100.0*

1966 Republican Primary

Candidates	Votes	%
Charles H. Percy (R)	605,815	*90.6*
Howard J. Doyle (R)	38,636	*5.8*

Democratic Primary

Candidates	Votes	%
Paul H. Douglas (D)		*100.0*

1972 Republican Primary

Candidates	Votes	%
Charles H. Percy (R)		*100.0*

Democratic Primary

Candidates	Votes	%
Roman C. Pucinski (D)	859,890	*70.6*
W. Dakin Williams (D)	357,744	*29.4*

	Candidates	Votes	%
1978	**Republican Primary**		
	Charles H. Percy (R)	401,409	*84.2*
	Lar Daly (R)	74,739	*15.7*
	Democratic Primary		
	Alex Seith (D)	483,196	*69.5*
	Anthony R. Martin-Trigona (D)	212,105	*30.5*
1984	**Republican Primary**		
	Charles H. Percy (R)	387,865	*59.3*
	Tom Corcoran (R)	239,847	*36.7*
	Democratic Primary		
	Paul Simon (D)	556,757	*35.6*
	Roland W. Burris (D)	360,182	*23.0*
	Alex Seith (D)	327,125	*20.9*
	Philip J. Rock (D)	303,397	*23.0*

Class 3

	Candidates	Votes	%
1956	**Republican Primary**		
	Everett McKinley Dirksen (R)		*100.0*
	Democratic Primary		
	Richard Stengel (D)		*100.0*
1962	**Republican Primary**		
	Everett McKinley Dirksen (R)	742,973	*87.1*
	Harley D. Jones (R)	109,574	*12.8*
	Democratic Primary		
	Sidney R. Yates (D)	744,128	*77.2*
	Lar Daly (D)	219,169	*22.7*
1968	**Republican Primary**		
	Everett McKinley Dirksen (R)	622,710	*92.1*
	Roy C. Johnson (R)	53,069	*7.8*
	Democratic Primary		
	William G. Clark (D)		*100.0*
1970	**Special Republican Primary**		
	Ralph Tyler Smith (R)	414,489	*58.9*
	William H. Rentschler (R)	271,648	*38.6*
	Special Democratic Primary		
	Adlai E. Stevenson III (D)		*100.0*
1974	**Republican Primary**		
	George M. Burditt (R)	432,796	*84.7*
	Lar Daly (R)	78,146	*15.3*
	Democratic Primary		
	Adlai E. Stevenson III (D)	822,248	*82.9*
	W. Dakin Williams (D)	169,662	*17.1*

	Candidates	Votes	%
1980	**Republican Primary**		
	David C. O'Neal (R)	424,634	*41.5*
	William J. Scott (R)	352,138	*34.4*
	Richard E. Carver (R)	245,668	*24.1*
	Democratic Primary		
	Alan J. Dixon (D)	671,746	*66.9*
	Alex Seith (D)	190,339	*18.9*
	Robert A. Wallace (D)	64,037	*6.4*

INDIANA

Candidates	Votes	%

Class 1

	Candidates	Votes	%
1976 [6]	**Republican Primary**		
	Richard G. Lugar (R)	393,064	*65.5*
	Edgar D. Whitcomb (R)	179,203	*29.8*
	Democratic Primary		
	R. Vance Hartke (D)	304,076	*53.1*
	Philip H. Hayes (D)	268,790	*46.9*
1982	**Republican Primary**		
	Richard G. Lugar (R)		*100.0*
	Democratic Primary		
	Floyd Fithian (D)	262,644	*59.5*
	Michael Kendall (D)	178,702	*40.5*

Class 3

	Candidates	Votes	%
1980	**Republican Primary**		
	Dan Quayle (R)	397,273	*77.1*
	Roger F. Marsh (R)	118,273	*22.9*
	Democratic Primary		
	Birch Bayh (D)		*100.0*

IOWA

Candidates	Votes	%

Class 2

	Candidates	Votes	%
1960 [7]	**Republican Primary**		
	Jack Miller (R)	66,455	*30.8*
	Dayton Countryman (R)	62,500	*29.0*
	Rollo Bergeson (R)	31,559	*14.6*

6. *Before 1976, when Indiana adopted a primary system, party conventions nominated candidates for statewide office.*

7. *Because no candidate in Iowa's 1960 Republican primary received the minimum percentage required for Senate nomination, a state convention was held, resulting in the nomination of Miller.*

Candidates	Votes	%
Ken Stringer (R)	29,927	13.9
Oliver J. Reeve (R)	14,414	6.7
Ernest J. Seemann (R)	10,931	5.1
Democratic Primary		
Herschel C. Loveless (D)		100.0

1966 **Republican Primary**

Jack Miller (R)	141,141	83.9
Herbert H. Hoover (R)	27,007	16.1

Democratic Primary

E. B. Smith (D)	39,870	50.1
Gary L. Cameron (D)	22,650	28.5
Ernest J. Seeman (D)	8,646	10.9
Robert L. Nereim (D)	8,343	10.5

1972 **Republican Primary**

Jack Miller (R)	170,590	84.4
Ralph Scott (R)	31,607	15.6

Democratic Primary

Dick Clark (D)		100.0

American Independent Primary

William A Rocap (AMI)		100.0

1978 **Republican Primary**

Roger W. Jepsen (R)	87,397	57.3
Maurie Van Nostrand (R)	54,189	35.5
Joe Bertroche (R)	10,860	7.1

Democratic Primary

Dick Clark (D)	87,880	80.5
Gerald Baker (D)	13,132	12.0
Robert L. Nereim (D)	8,176	7.5

1984 **Republican Primary**

Roger W. Jepsen (R)	113,996	100.0

Democratic Primary

Tom Harkin (D)	106,005	100.0

Class 3

1956 **Republican Primary**

Bourke B. Hickenlooper (R)	157,652	67.7
Dayton Countryman (R)	75,264	32.3

Democratic Primary

R. M. Evans (D)	64,195	63.1
Lumund Wilcox (D)	37,590	36.9

Candidates	Votes	%

1962 **Republican Primary**

Bourke B. Hickenlooper (R)	164,535	85.4
Herbert H. Hoover (R)	28,095	14.6

Democratic Primary

E. B. Smith (D)		100.0

1968 **Republican Primary**

David M. Stanley (R)	143,854	58.7
James E. Bromwell (R)	65,509	26.7
Dayton Countryman (R)	22,049	9.0
William N. Plymat (R)	13,485	5.5

Democratic Primary

Harold E. Hughes (D)	103,936	86.8
Robert L. Nereim (D)	15,772	13.2

1974 **Republican Primary**

David M. Stanley (R)	87,464	66.9
George F. Milligan (R)	43,206	33.1

Democratic Primary

John C. Culver (D)		100.0

1980 **Republican Primary**

Charles E. Grassley (R)	170,120	66.7
Tom Stoner (R)	89,409	33.3

Democratic Primary

John C. Culver (D)		100.0

KANSAS

Candidates	Votes	%

Class 2

1960 **Republican Primary**

Andrew F. Schoeppel (R)	201,753	80.0
Henry P. Cleaver (R)	50,507	20.0

Democratic Primary

Frank Theis (D)	88,194	59.1
Joseph W. Henkle (D)	60,942	40.9

1962 **Special Republican Primary**

James B. Pearson (R)	124,854	62.3
Edward F. Arn (R)	75,524	37.7

Special Democratic Primary

Paul L. Aylward (D)		100.0

	Candidates	Votes	%
1966	**Republican Primary**		
	James B. Pearson (R)	101,523	*50.3*
	R. F. Ellsworth (R)	83,083	*41.1*
	Ava A. Anderson (R)	10,095	*5.0*
	Democratic Primary		
	J. Floyd Breeding (D)	51,860	*49.9*
	K. L. Smith (D)	19,433	*18.7*
	Harold S. Herd (D)	16,963	*16.3*
	Leigh Warner (D)	15,625	*15.0*
1972	**Republican Primary**		
	James B. Pearson (R)	229,908	*82.2*
	Harlan D. House (R)	49,825	*17.8*
	Democratic Primary		
	Arch O. Tezlaff (D)		*100.0*
1978	**Republican Primary**		
	Nancy Landon Kassebaum (R)	67,324	*30.6*
	Wayne Angell (R)	54,161	*24.6*
	Sam Hardage (R)	30,248	*13.7*
	Jan Meyers (R)	20,933	*9.5*
	Deryl K. Schuster (R)	18,568	*8.5*
	Norman E. Gaar (R)	14,502	*6.6*
	Democratic Primary		
	William R. Roy (D)	100,508	*76.7*
	Dorothy K. White (D)	13,865	*10.6*
	James R. Maher (D)	11,556	*8.8*
1984	**Republican Primary**		
	Nancy Landon Kassebaum (R)	214,429	*100.0*
	Democratic Primary		
	James R. Maher (D)	97,843	*100.0*

Class 3

	Candidates	Votes	%
1956	**Republican Primary**		
	Frank Carlson (R)	215,364	*77.9*
	Walter I. Biddle (R)	61,053	*22.1*
	Democratic Primary		
	George Hart (D)	54,553	*40.4*
	Paul L. Aylward (D)	54,085	*40.0*
	Fred Kilian (D)	16,384	*12.1*
	Marlyn Korf (D)	10,176	*7.5*
1962	**Republican Primary**		
	Frank Carlson (R)	167,498	*86.9*
	Joe Corpstein (R)	25,168	*13.1*
	Democratic Primary		
	K. L. Smith (D)	65,876	*62.5*
	Joseph J. Poizner (D)	39,458	*37.5*

	Candidates	Votes	%
1968	**Republican Primary**		
	Robert Dole (R)	190,782	*68.5*
	William H. Avery (R)	87,801	*31.5*
	Democratic Primary		
	William I. Robinson (D)	56,242	*40.9*
	James K. Logan (D)	50,709	*36.9*
	K. L. Smith (D)	13,698	*10.0*
1974	**Republican Primary**		
	Robert Dole (R)		*100.0*
	Democratic Primary		
	William R. Roy (D)	125,634	*85.0*
	George Hart (D)	22,109	*15.0*
1980	**Republican Primary**		
	Robert Dole (R)	201,484	*81.9*
	Jim H. Grainge (R)	44,674	*18.1*
	Democratic Primary		
	John Simpson (D)	52,004	*35.8*
	James R. Maher (D)	46,322	*31.9*
	John A. Barnes (D)	16,466	*11.3*
	Ken North (D)	14,218	*9.8*
	Ed Phillips (D)	8,838	*6.1*
	Howard C. Lee (D)	7,461	*5.1*

KENTUCKY

	Candidates	Votes	%
	Class 2		
1960	**Republican Primary**		
	John Sherman Cooper (R)	50,896	*96.3*
	Democratic Primary		
	Keen Johnson (D)	112,797	*58.0*
	John Young Brown (D)	75,897	*39.0*
1966	**Republican Primary**		
	John Sherman Cooper (R)	65,023	*92.8*
	Democratic Primary		
	John Young Brown (D)	71,759	*75.6*
	Gaines P. Wilson (D)	12,921	*13.6*
	James Ward Lentz (D)	5,399	*5.7*
	J. N. R. Cecil (D)	4,861	*5.1*
1972	**Republican Primary**		
	Louie B. Nunn (R)	57,348	*69.7*
	Robert E. Gable (R)	18,107	*22.0*

Candidates	Votes	%
Democratic Primary		
Walter D. Huddleston (D)	106,144	71.6
Sandy Hockensmith (D)	14,786	10.0
James E. Wallace (D)	11,290	7.6
Willis V. Johnson (D)	8,727	5.9

1978

Candidates	Votes	%
Republican Primary		
Louie Guenthner (R)	14,218	47.2
Oline Carmical (R)	9,346	31.0
Thurman J. Hamlin (R)	6,550	21.8
Democratic Primary		
Walter D. Huddleston (D)	89,333	75.6
Jack A. Watson (D)	13,177	11.1
William J. Taylor (D)	8,710	7.4
George W. Tolhurst (D)	6,921	5.9

1984

Candidates	Votes	%
Republican Primary		
Mitchell McConnell (R)	39,465	79.2
C. Roger Harker (R)	3,798	7.6
T. William Klein (R)	3,352	6.7
Thurman Hamlin (R)	3,202	6.4
Democratic Primary		
Walter D. Huddleston (D)		100.0

Class 3

1956 [8]

Candidates	Votes	%
Republican Primary		
Thruston B. Morton (R)	42,038	70.6
Julian H. Golden (R)	12,976	21.8
Granville Thomas (R)	4,495	7.6
Democratic Primary		
Earle C. Clements (D)	218,353	60.8
Joe B. Bates (D)	136,533	38.0

1962

Candidates	Votes	%
Republican Primary		
Thruston B. Morton (R)	41,892	91.2
Thurman J. Hamlin (R)	4,048	8.8
Democratic Primary		
Wilson W. Wyatt (D)	127,403	77.0
Marion Vance (D)	28,513	17.2
James L. Delk (D)	9,483	5.7

1968

Candidates	Votes	%
Republican Primary		
Marlow W. Cook (R)	73,171	62.0
Eugene Siler (R)	39,743	33.7
Democratic Primary		
Katherine Peden (D)	86,317	43.8
John Young Brown (D)	51,509	26.2

8. Candidates for the special election to fill the unexpired term of Sen. Alben W. Barkley (D), who died April 30, 1956, were nominated by the Democratic and Republican state committees, not by primaries. The 1956 Senate primary in Kentucky was for the Class 3 seat that was slated to be filled that year.

Candidates	Votes	%
Foster Ockerman (D)	25,602	13.0
Ted Osborn (D)	20,049	10.2

1974

Candidates	Votes	%
Republican Primary		
Marlow W. Cook (R)	35,904	87.6
Thurman J. Hamlin (R)	2,826	6.9
T. William Klein (R)	2,256	5.5
Democratic Primary		
Wendell H. Ford (D)	136,458	84.8
Harvey E. Brazin (D)	24,436	15.2
American Primary		
William E. Parker (AM)		100.0

1980

Candidates	Votes	%
Republican Primary		
Mary Louise Foust (R)	25,717	42.0
Granville Thomas (R)	10,246	16.7
Jackson M. Andrews (R)	8,382	13.7
T. William Klein (R)	6,418	10.5
Yale J. Lubkin (R)	5,669	9.2
DeSota Vaught (R)	4,848	7.9
Democratic Primary		
Wendell H. Ford (D)	188,047	87.0
Flora T. Stuart (D)	28,202	13.0

MAINE

Candidates	Votes	%
Class 1		

1958

Candidates	Votes	%
Republican Primary		
Frederick G. Payne (R)	82,448	83.6
Herman D. Sahagian (R)	16,133	16.4
Democratic Primary		
Edmund S. Muskie (D)		100.0

1964

Candidates	Votes	%
Republican Primary		
Clifford McIntire (R)		100.0
Democratic Primary		
Edmund S. Muskie (D)		100.0

1970

Candidates	Votes	%
Republican Primary		
Neil S. Bishop (R)	45,216	59.8
Abbott O. Greene (R)	30,201	40.0
Democratic Primary		
Edmund S. Muskie (D)		100.0

1976

Candidates	Votes	%
Republican Primary		
Robert A. G. Monks (R)	65,224	83.9
Plato Truman (R)	12,552	16.1

Candidates	Votes	%

Democratic Primary

| Edmund S. Muskie (D) | | 100.0 |

1982

Republican Primary

| David F. Emery (R) | | 100.0 |

Democratic Primary

| George J. Mitchell (D) | | 100.0 |

Class 2

1960

Republican Primary

| Margaret Chase Smith (R) | | 100.0 |

Democratic Primary

| Lucia M. Cormier (D) | | 100.0 |

1966

Republican Primary

| Margaret Chase Smith (R) | | 100.0 |

Democratic Primary

Elmer H. Violette (D)	23,259	45.2
Plato Truman (D)	19,844	38.5
Jack L. Smith (D)	8,386	16.3

1972

Republican Primary

| Margaret Chase Smith (R) | 76,964 | 66.7 |
| Robert A. G. Monks (R) | 38,345 | 33.3 |

Democratic Primary

| William D. Hathaway (D) | 61,921 | 90.8 |
| Jack L. Smith (D) | 6,263 | 9.2 |

1978

Republican Primary

| William S. Cohen (R) | | 100.0 |

Democratic Primary

| William D. Hathaway (D) | | 100.0 |

1984

Republican Primary

| William S. Cohen (R) | | 100.0 |

Democratic Primary

| Elizabeth H. Mitchell (D) | | 100.0 |

MARYLAND

Candidates	Votes	%

Class 1

1958

Republican Primary

| J. Glenn Beall (R) | 67,580 | 89.6 |
| Henry J. Laque (R) | 7,826 | 10.4 |

Candidates	Votes	%

Democratic Primary

Thomas D'Alesandro Jr. (D)	125,408	34.7
George P. Mahoney (D)	119,796	33.2
James Bruce (D)	53,365	14.8
Clarence D. Long (D)	47,290	13.1

1964

Republican Primary

J. Glenn Beall (R)	68,930	59.8
James P. Gleason (R)	35,645	30.9
William A. Albaugh (R)	8,352	7.2

Democratic Primary

Joseph D. Tydings (D)	279,564	64.5
Louis L. Goldstein (D)	155,086	26.6
John J. Harbaugh (D)	22,665	5.2

1970

Republican Primary

J. Glenn Beall Jr. (R)	99,687	83.5
Harry L. Simms (R)	9,927	8.3
Wainwright Dawson (R)	9,786	8.2

Democratic Primary

Joseph D. Tydings (D)	242,874	52.7
George P. Mahoney (D)	173,157	37.6
Walter G. Finch (D)	33,361	7.2

1976

Republican Primary

| J. Glenn Beall Jr. (R) | | 100.0 |

Democratic Primary

| Paul S. Sarbanes (D) | 302,983 | 56.5 |
| Joseph D. Tydings (D) | 191,875 | 35.8 |

1982

Republican Primary

Lawrence J. Hogan (R)	79,375	65.5
Donovan B. Finch (R)	25,290	20.8
William A. Albaugh (R)	16,599	13.7

Democratic Primary

| Paul S. Sarbanes (D) | 432,931 | 81.1 |

Class 3

1956 [9]

Republican Primary

John Marshall Butler (R)	58,642	86.6
Earl E. Knepper (R)	5,376	7.9
Henry J. Laque (R)	3,696	5.5

9. Until 1962 Maryland used a system of convention unit votes, with each county (and each of the six legislative districts into which Baltimore city was divided) being allocated as many unit votes as it had members of the state legislature, ranging from three to seven. These unit votes were automatically credited to the candidate carrying the county or legislative district. In 1956, because Tydings and Mahoney tied in unit votes at 76 each, Tydings won the nomination with the higher popular vote. But illness forced him to retire from the campaign and Mahoney was substituted by the party state committee.

Candidates	Votes	%
Democratic Primary		
Millard E. Tydings (D)	142,238	*47.5*
George P. Mahoney (D)	134,246	*44.8*
1962 **Republican Primary**		
Edward T. Miller (R)	43,437	*48.1*
James P. Gleason (R)	34,523	*38.3*
Harry L. Simms (R)	7,689	*8.5*
Henry J. Laque (R)	4,565	*5.1*
Democratic Primary		
Daniel B. Brewster (D)	182,272	*52.2*
Blair Lee (D)	100,915	*28.9*
Elbert M. Byrd (D)	32,147	*9.2*
Herbert J. Hoover (D)	19,719	*5.6*
1968 **Republican Primary**		
Charles McC. Mathias Jr. (R)	66,777	*80.0*
Harry L. Simms (R)	11,927	*14.3*
Paul F. Wattay (R)	4,790	*5.7*
Democratic Primary		
Daniel B. Brewster (D)	150,481	*67.4*
Ross Z. Pierpont (D)	38,555	*17.3*
Walter G. Finch (D)	19,829	*8.9*
Richard R. Howes (D)	14,224	*6.4*
1974 **Republican Primary**		
Charles McC. Mathias Jr. (R)	79,823	*75.8*
Ross Z. Pierpont (R)	25,512	*24.2*
Democratic Primary		
Barbara A. Mikulski (D)	132,658	*40.9*
Bernard L. Talley (D)	79,080	*24.4*
Walter G. Finch (D)	32,068	*9.9*
Xavier A. Aragona (D)	17,668	*5.4*
1980 **Republican Primary**		
Charles McC. Mathias Jr. (R)	82,430	*55.0*
John M. Brennan (R)	24,848	*16.6*
V. Dallas Merrell (R)	23,073	*15.4*
Roscoe G. Bartlett (R)	10,970	*7.3*
Democratic Primary		
Edward T. Conroy (D)	79,033	*22.4*
Victor L. Crawford (D)	52,803	*15.0*
Robert L. Douglass (D)	43,035	*12.2*
Dennis C. McCoy (D)	40,510	*11.5*
R. Spencer Oliver (D)	35,407	*10.4*
John A. Kennedy (D)	20,255	*5.7*
Frank J. Broschart (D)	19,455	*5.5*

MASSACHUSETTS

Candidates	Votes	%
Class 1		
1958 **Republican Primary**		
Vincent J. Celeste (R)		*100.0*

Candidates	Votes	%
Democratic Primary		
John F. Kennedy (D)		*100.0*
1962 [10] **Special Republican Primary**		
George C. Lodge (R)	244,921	*55.5*
Laurence Curtis (R)	196,444	*44.5*
Special Democratic Primary		
Edward M. Kennedy (D)	559,303	*72.9*
Edward J. McCormack (D)	247,403	*27.1*
1964 **Republican Primary**		
Howard Whitmore (R)		*100.0*
Democratic Primary		
Edward M. Kennedy (D)		*100.0*
1970 **Republican Primary**		
Josiah A. Spaulding (R)	109,306	*57.3*
John J. McCarthy (R)	81,356	*42.7*
Democratic Primary		
Edward M. Kennedy (D)		*100.0*
1976 **Republican Primary**		
Michael Robertson (R)		*100.0*
Democratic Primary		
Edward M. Kennedy (D)	534,725	*73.9*
Robert E. Dinsmore (D)	117,496	*16.2*
Frederick C. Langone (D)	59,315	*8.2*
1982 **Republican Primary**		
Raymond Shamie (R)		*100.0*
Democratic Primary		
Edward M. Kennedy (D)		*100.0*

Class 2

Candidates	Votes	%
1960 **Republican Primary**		
Leverett Saltonstall (R)		*100.0*
Democratic Primary		
Thomas J. O'Connor (D)	270,081	*48.3*
Foster Furcolo (D)	217,939	*39.0*
Edmund C. Buckley (D)	70,744	*12.7*
1966 **Republican Primary**		
Edward W. Brooke (R)		*100.0*

10. A special election was held in Massachusetts in 1962 to fill two years of the four-year unexpired term of Sen. John F. Kennedy (D), who resigned Dec. 22, 1960, after he was elected president. The first two years of the vacancy were filled by an appointee of the governor.

Candidates	Votes	%
Democratic Primary		
Endicott Peabody (D)	320,967	*50.3*
John F. Collins (D)	265,016	*41.6*
Thomas B. Adams (D)	51,435	*8.1*

1972   **Republican Primary**

Candidates	Votes	%
Edward W. Brooke (R)		*100.0*

Democratic Primary

John J. Droney (D)	215,523	*45.1*
Gerald O'Leary (D)	169,876	*35.5*
John P. Lynch (D)	92,979	*19.4*

1978   **Republican Primary**

Edward W. Brooke (R)	146,351	*53.3*
Avi Nelson (R)	128,388	*46.7*

Democratic Primary

Paul E. Tsongas (D)	296,915	*35.6*
Paul Guzzi (D)	258,960	*31.0*
Kathleen Sullivan Alioto (D)	161,036	*19.3*
Howard Phillips (D)	65,397	*7.8*
Elaine Noble (D)	52,464	*6.3*

1984   **Republican Primary**

Raymond Shamie (R)	173,851	*62.4*
Elliot L. Richardson (R)	104,761	*37.6*

Democratic Primary

John F. Kerry (D)	322,470	*40.8*
James M. Shannon (D)	297,941	*37.7*
David M. Bartley (D)	85,910	*10.9*
Michael Joseph Connolly (D)	82,999	*10.5*

MICHIGAN

Candidates	Votes	%
Class 1		

1958   **Republican Primary**

Charles E. Potter (R)		*100.0*

Democratic Primary

Philip A. Hart (D)	297,767	*80.2*
Homer Martin (D)	73,334	*19.8*

1964   **Republican Primary**

Elly M. Peterson (R)	219,883	*39.0*
James F. O'Neil (R)	192,825	*34.2*
Edward A. Meany (R)	151,498	*26.8*

Democratic Primary

Philip A. Hart (D)		*100.0*

	Candidates	Votes	%
1970	**Republican Primary**		
	Lenore Romney (R)	277,086	*51.3*
	Robert J. Huber (R)	262,938	*48.7*

Democratic Primary

Philip A. Hart (D)		*100.0*

1976   **Republican Primary**

Marvin L. Esch (R)	209,250	*44.2*
Thomas E. Brennan (R)	129,917	*27.5*
Robert J. Huber (R)	82,092	*17.3*
Deane Baker (R)	51,852	*11.0*

Democratic Primary

Donald W. Riegle Jr. (D)	325,705	*44.3*
Richard H. Austin (D)	208,310	*28.3*
James G. O'Hara (D)	170,473	*23.2*

1982   **Republican Primary**

Philip E. Ruppe (R)	253,082	*46.0*
William S. Ballenger (R)	122,523	*22.3*
Robert J. Huber (R)	102,693	*18.7*
Deane Baker (R)	71,902	*13.0*

Democratic Primary

Donald W. Riegle Jr. (D)		*100.0*

Class 2

1960   **Republican Primary**

Alvin M. Bentley (R)	344,043	*72.0*
Donald S. Leonard (R)	133,562	*28.0*

Democratic Primary

Patrick V. McNamara (D)		*100.0*

1966 [11]   **Special Republican Primary**

Robert P. Griffin (R)	356,700	*100.0*

Special Democratic Primary

G. Mennen Williams (D)	381,496	*59.6*
Jerome P. Cavanagh (D)	258,822	*40.4*

1966 [11]   **Republican Primary**

Robert P. Griffin (R)	387,892	*100.0*

Democratic Primary

G. Mennen Williams (D)	437,438	*60.1*
Jerome P. Cavanagh (D)	290,465	*39.9*

11. *Robert P. Griffin (R) was appointed in May 1966 to fill the vacancy caused by the death of Sen. Patrick V. McNamara (D) on April 30. On Aug. 2 two Senate primaries were held simultaneously in Michigan, a special primary for the remainder of McNamara's term and a regular primary for the full term beginning in January 1967. Griffin, who was unopposed for the Republican nomination, and G. Mennen Williams (D) won both primaries. In the November general election Griffin defeated Williams for both the short and the full terms. Returns for the short-term primary from Elections Research Center, Washington, D.C.*

	Candidates	Votes	%
1972	**Republican Primary**		
	Robert P. Griffin (R)		*100.0*
	Democratic Primary		
	Frank J. Kelley (D)		*100.0*
1978	**Republican Primary**		
	Robert P. Griffin (R)	322,530	*78.3*
	L. Brooks Patterson (R)	89,383	*21.7*
	Democratic Primary		
	Carl Levin (D)	226,584	*38.9*
	Phil Power (D)	115,117	*19.8*
	Richard F. Vander Veen (D)	89,257	*15.3*
	Anthony Derezinski (D)	53,696	*9.2*
	John Otterbacher (D)	50,860	*8.7*
	Paul Rosenbaum (D)	46,892	*8.1*
1984	**Republican Primary**		
	Jack Lousma (R)	328,002	*62.7*
	Jim Dunn (R)	194,657	*37.2*
	Democratic Primary		
	Carl Levin (D)	376,873	*100.0*

MINNESOTA[12]

	Candidates	Votes	%
	Class 1		
1958	**Republican Primary**		
	Edward J. Thye (R)	202,241	*91.0*
	E. C. Slettedahl (R)	13,734	*6.2*
	Democratic Primary		
	Eugene J. McCarthy (DFL)	279,796	*75.7*
	Hjalmar Petersen (DFL)	76,340	*20.6*
1964	**Republican Primary**		
	Wheelock Whitney (R)		*100.0*
	Democratic Primary		
	Eugene J. McCarthy (DFL)	245,068	*90.5*
	R. H. Underdahl (DFL)	14,562	*5.4*
1970	**Republican Primary**		
	Clark MacGregor (R)	220,353	*93.3*
	John D. Baucom (R)	15,797	*6.7*

	Candidates	Votes	%
	Democratic Primary		
	Hubert H. Humphrey (DFL)	338,705	*79.2*
	Earl D. Craig (DFL)	88,709	*20.8*
1976	**Republican Primary**		
	Gerald W. Brekke (R)	76,183	*54.5*
	Richard Franson (R)	32,115	*23.0*
	John H. Glover (R)	13,014	*9.3*
	Roland Riemers (R)	9,307	*6.7*
	Bea Mooney (R)	9,150	*6.5*
	Democratic Primary		
	Hubert H. Humphrey (DFL)	317,632	*91.3*
	Dick Bullock (DFL)	30,262	*8.7*
1978 [13]	**Special Republican Primary**		
	Dave Durenberger (IR)	139,187	*67.3*
	Malcolm Moos (IR)	32,314	*15.6*
	Ken Nordstrom (IR)	14,635	*7.1*
	Will Lundquist (IR)	12,261	*5.9*
	Special Democratic Primary		
	Robert E. Short (DFL)	257,269	*48.0*
	Donald M. Fraser (DFL)	253,818	*47.4*
	Special American Primary		
	Paul Helm (AM)		*100.0*
1982	**Republican Primary**		
	Dave Durenberger (IR)	287,651	*93.4*
	Mary Jane Rachner (IR)	20,401	*6.6*
	Democratic Primary		
	Mark Dayton (DFL)	359,014	*69.1*
	Eugene J. McCarthy (DFL)	125,229	*24.1*
	Class 2		
1960	**Republican Primary**		
	P. K. Peterson (R)	256,641	*89.5*
	James Malcolm Williams (R)	30,242	*10.5*
	Democratic Primary		
	Hubert H. Humphrey (D)		*100.0*
1966	**Republican Primary**		
	Robert A. Forsythe (R)	211,282	*81.2*
	Henry A. Johnsen (R)	48,941	*18.8*
	Democratic Primary		
	Walter F. Mondale (DFL)	410,841	*91.0*
	Ralph E. Franklin (DFL)	40,785	*9.0*

12. In Minnesota, the Democratic Party is known as the Democratic-Farmer-Labor Party (DFL) and the Republican Party is known as the Independent Republican Party (IR).

13. A special Minnesota election was held, in conjunction with the November general election, to fill the unexpired term of Sen. Hubert H. Humphrey (DFL), who died Jan. 13, 1978.

Candidates	Votes	%

1972 **Republican Primary**

| Philip Hansen (R) | | 100.0 |

Democratic Primary

| Walter F. Mondale (DFL) | 230,679 | 89.9 |

1978 **Republican Primary**

| Rudy Boschwitz (IR) | 185,393 | 86.8 |
| Harold E. Stassen (IR) | 28,170 | 13.2 |

Democratic Primary

| Wendell R. Anderson (DFL) | 286,209 | 56.9 |
| John S. Connolly (DFL) | 159,974 | 31.8 |

American Primary

| Sal Carlone (AM) | | 100.0 |

1984 **Republican Primary**

| Rudy Boschwitz (IR) | 162,555 | 96.6 |

Democratic Primary

| Joan Anderson Growe (DFL) | 238,190 | 75.9 |
| Robert W. (Bob) Mattson (DFL) | 61,489 | 19.6 |

MISSOURI

Candidates	Votes	%

Class 1

1958 **Republican Primary**

Hazel Palmer (R)	61,481	44.6
William M. Thomas (R)	36,438	26.5
Homer S. Cotton (R)	27,023	19.6
Hiram Grosby (R)	12,818	9.3

Democratic Primary

| Stuart Symington (D) | 365,470 | 92.2 |
| Lawrence L. Hastings (D) | 19,954 | 5.0 |

1964 **Republican Primary**

| Jean P. Bradshaw (R) | 165,048 | 78.2 |
| Morris D. Duncan (R) | 46,030 | 21.8 |

Democratic Primary

| Stuart Symington (D) | 563,313 | 92.0 |
| William M. Thomas (D) | 35,509 | 5.8 |

1970 **Republican Primary**

John C. Danforth (R)	165,728	72.6
Doris M. Bass (R)	45,049	19.7
Morris D. Duncan (R)	17,670	7.7

Candidates	Votes	%

Democratic Primary

| Stuart Symington (D) | 392,670 | 89.3 |

American Primary

Gene Chapman (AM)	684	47.1
Lawrence Petty (AM)	400	27.5
Ralph A. DePugh (AM)	368	25.4

1976 **Republican Primary**

| John C. Danforth (R) | 284,025 | 93.5 |
| Gregory Hansman (R) | 19,796 | 6.5 |

Democratic Primary [14]

Jerry Litton (D)	401,822	45.4
Warren E. Hearnes (D)	233,544	26.4
James W. Symington (D)	222,681	25.2

1982 **Republican Primary**

| John C. Danforth (R) | 217,162 | 73.9 |
| Mel Hancock (R) | 61,378 | 20.9 |

Democratic Primary

Harriett Woods (D)	263,259	44.8
Burleigh Arnold (D)	140,446	23.9
Tom Ryan (D)	75,599	12.9
Thomas E. Zych (D)	35,876	6.1

Class 3

1956 **Republican Primary**

Herbert Douglas (R)	83,458	40.8
Albert E. Schoenbeck (R)	78,747	38.5
William M. Thomas (R)	28,924	14.1
William E. Van Taay (R)	13,556	6.6

Democratic Primary

| Thomas C. Hennings Jr. (D) [15] | 389,986 | 95.9 |

1962 **Republican Primary**

Crosby Kemper (R)	119,136	66.6
Duane Cox (R)	23,606	13.2
Morris D. Duncan (R)	15,109	8.5
William M. Thomas (R)	14,131	7.9

Democratic Primary

| Edward V. Long (D) | 370,826 | 86.5 |
| Lewis E. Morris (D) | 37,507 | 8.8 |

1968 **Republican Primary**

| Thomas B. Curtis (R) | 192,028 | 84.5 |
| Morris D. Duncan (R) | 24,418 | 10.8 |

14. Rep. Jerry Litton, the winner of the Democratic Senate primary on Aug. 3, 1976, died the same day and the Missouri Democratic central committee substituted Warren E. Hearnes, the second-place finisher, as the party's nominee.

15. Candidates for the short-term Senate seat vacated by the death of Sen. Thomas C. Hennings Jr. (D) in September 1960 were nominated by the Democratic and Republican state committees of Missouri.

Candidates	Votes	%
Democratic Primary		
Thomas F. Eagleton (D)	224,017	*36.6*
Edward V. Long (D)	198,901	*32.5*
True Davis (D)	178,961	*29.3*

1974   **Republican Primary**

Candidates	Votes	%
Thomas B. Curtis (R)	136,447	*81.9*
Paul M. Robinett (R)	16,882	*10.1*
Gregory Hansman (R)	13,285	*8.0*

Democratic Primary

Candidates	Votes	%
Thomas F. Eagleton (D)	420,681	*87.5*
Pat O'Brien (D)	30,389	*6.3*
Lee C. Sutton (D)	29,835	*6.2*

1980   **Republican Primary**

Candidates	Votes	%
Gene McNary (R)	197,060	*61.5*
David Doctorian (R)	82,332	*25.7*
Morris D. Duncan (R)	21,959	*6.9*
Gregory Hansman (R)	18,893	*5.9*

Democratic Primary

Candidates	Votes	%
Thomas F. Eagleton (D)	553,392	*82.8*
Lee C. Sutton (D)	53,280	*8.2*
Herb Fillmore (D)	38,677	*6.0*

MONTANA

Candidates	Votes	%
Class 1		

1958   **Republican Primary**

Candidates	Votes	%
Lou W. Welch (R)	19,860	*50.8*
Blanche Anderson (R)	19,264	*49.2*

Democratic Primary

Candidates	Votes	%
Mike Mansfield (D)	97,207	*91.7*

1964   **Republican Primary**

Candidates	Votes	%
Alex Blewett (R)	31,934	*59.4*
Lyman Brewster (R)	12,375	*23.0*
Antoinette Rosell (R)	9,480	*17.6*

Democratic Primary

Candidates	Votes	%
Mike Mansfield (D)	109,904	*85.5*
Joseph P. Monaghan (D)	18,630	*14.5*

1970   **Republican Primary**

Candidates	Votes	%
Harold E. Wallace (R)		*100.0*

Democratic Primary

Candidates	Votes	%
Mike Mansfield (D)	68,146	*77.2*
Tom McDonald (D)	10,733	*12.2*
John W. Lawlor (D)	9,384	*10.6*

1976   **Republican Primary**

Candidates	Votes	%
Stanley C. Burger (R)	32,313	*40.4*
Dave Drum (R)	27,257	*34.1*
John F. Tierney (R)	15,129	*18.9*
Larry L. Gilbert (R)	5,258	*6.6*

Democratic Primary

Candidates	Votes	%
John Melcher (D)	84,413	*87.9*
Ray E. Gulick (D)	11,593	*12.1*

1982   **Republican Primary**

Candidates	Votes	%
Larry Williams (R)	49,615	*88.1*
Willie D. Morris (R)	6,696	*11.9*

Democratic Primary

Candidates	Votes	%
John Melcher (D)	83,539	*68.3*
Michael A. Bond (D)	33,565	*27.4*

Class 2

1960   **Republican Primary**

Candidates	Votes	%
Orvin B. Fjare (R)	25,899	*38.5*
Sumner Gerard (R)	17,932	*26.6*
Wayne Montgomery (R)	13,527	*20.1*
James H. Morrow (R)	5,261	*7.8*

Democratic Primary

Candidates	Votes	%
Lee Metcalf (D)	45,339	*35.1*
John W. Bonner (D)	33,246	*25.8*
Le Roy Anderson (D)	26,152	*20.3*
John W. Mahan (D)	24,208	*18.8*

1966   **Republican Primary**

Candidates	Votes	%
Tim M. Babcock (R)		*100.0*

Democratic Primary

Candidates	Votes	%
Lee Metcalf (D)		*100.0*

1972   **Republican Primary**

Candidates	Votes	%
Henry S. Hibbard (R)	43,028	*49.7*
Harold E. Wallace (R)	26,463	*30.6*
Norman C. Wheeler (R)	13,826	*16.0*

Democratic Primary

Candidates	Votes	%
Lee Metcalf (D)	106,491	*86.4*
Jerome Peters (D)	16,729	*13.6*

1978   **Republican Primary**

Candidates	Votes	%
Larry Williams (R)	35,479	*61.6*
Bill Osborne (R)	16,436	*28.6*
Clancy Rich (R)	5,622	*9.8*

Democratic Primary

Candidates	Votes	%
Max Baucus (D)	87,085	*65.3*
Paul Hatfield (D)	25,789	*19.3*
John Driscoll (D)	18,184	*13.6*

1984	Republican Primary		
	Chuck Cozzens (R)	33,661	*50.7*
	Ralph Bouma (R)	17,900	*27.0*
	Aubyn Curtiss (R)	14,729	*22.2*
	Democratic Primary		
	Max Baucus (D)	80,726	*79.4*
	Bob Ripley (D)	20,979	*20.6*

NEBRASKA

Candidates	Votes	%

Class 1

1958	Republican Primary		
	Roman L. Hruska (R)		*100.0*
	Democratic Primary		
	Frank B. Morrison (D)	35,482	*51.9*
	Eugene O'Sullivan (D)	26,436	*38.6*
	Mike F. Kracher (D)	6,500	*9.5*
1964	**Republican Primary**		
	Roman L. Hruska (R)		*100.0*
	Democratic Primary		
	Raymond W. Arndt (D)		*100.0*
1970	**Republican Primary**		
	Roman L. Hruska (R)	159,057	*85.6*
	Otis Glebe (R)	26,627	*14.3*
	Democratic Primary		
	Frank B. Morrison (D)	85,293	*67.2*
	Wallace C. Peterson (D)	34,856	*27.5*
	David J. Thomas (D)	6,610	*5.2*
1976	**Republican Primary**		
	John Y. McCollister (R)	150,732	*78.3*
	Richard F. Proud (R)	41,519	*21.6*
	Democratic Primary		
	Edward Zorinsky (D)	79,988	*48.6*
	Hess Dyas (D)	77,384	*47.0*
1982	**Republican Primary**		
	Jim Keck (R)	104,550	*66.0*
	Ken Cameron (R)	53,453	*33.8*
	Democratic Primary		
	Edward Zorinsky (D)		*100.0*

Class 2

1960	Republican Primary		
	Carl T. Curtis (R)		*100.0*
	Democratic Primary [16]		
	Ralph G. Brooks (D)	41,777	*42.4*
	Clair A. Callan (D)	34,052	*34.5*
	Albert J. Baker (D)	14,355	*14.6*
	Mike F. Kracher (D)	8,424	*8.5*
1966	**Republican Primary**		
	Carl T. Curtis (R)		*100.0*
	Democratic Primary		
	Frank B. Morrison (D)	91,178	*78.0*
	Raymond W. Arndt (D)	25,657	*21.9*
1972	**Republican Primary**		
	Carl T. Curtis (R)	141,213	*74.0*
	Ronald L. Blauvelt (R)	30,138	*15.8*
	Christine M. Kneifl (R)	10,941	*5.7*
	Democratic Primary		
	Terry Carpenter (D)	52,779	*29.0*
	Wallace C. Peterson (D)	49,569	*27.2*
	Wayne W. Ziebarth (D)	42,181	*23.1*
	Donald Searcy (D)	25,854	*14.2*
1978	**Republican Primary**		
	Donald Shasteen (R)	127,525	*78.4*
	Lenore R. Etchison (R)	34,916	*21.5*
	Democratic Primary		
	J. James Exon (D)		*100.0*
1984	**Republican Primary**		
	Nancy Hoch (R)	61,009	*40.5*
	John W. DeCamp (R)	24,730	*16.4*
	Richard N. Thompson (R)	23,720	*15.7*
	Fred A. Lockwood (R)	21,115	*14.0*
	Ken Cameron (R)	16,123	*10.7*
	Democratic Primary		
	J. James Exon (D)	135,242	*100.0*

16. *Gov. Ralph G. Brooks, winner of the Senate primary, died in September 1960 and the Nebraska Democratic state committee substituted Robert Conrad as the party's nominee. Conrad had been a candidate for the Democratic gubernatorial nomination.*

NEVADA

Candidates	Votes	%
Class 1		
1958 **Republican Primary**		
George W. Malone (R)		*100.0*
Democratic Primary		
Howard W. Cannon (D)	22,787	*51.7*
Fred Anderson (D)	21,319	*48.3*
1964 **Republican Primary**		
Paul Laxalt (R)	25,220	*90.3*
Wilford Owen Woodruff (R)	1,433	*5.1*
Democratic Primary		
Howard W. Cannon (D)	36,320	*59.6*
William A. Galt (D)	12,054	*19.8*
Harry Claiborne (D)	10,807	*17.7*
1970 **Republican Primary**		
William J. Raggio (R)	32,816	*90.5*
Wilford O. Woodruff (R)	3,456	*9.5*
Democratic Primary		
Howard W. Cannon (D)	54,320	*89.3*
Walter D. Duesenberg (D)	4,350	*7.1*
1976 [17] **Republican Primary**		
David Towell (R)	25,960	*67.4*
S. M. Cavnar (R)	5,964	*15.5*
"None of these candidates"	5,164	*13.4*
Democratic Primary		
Howard W. Cannon (D)	61,407	*85.8*
"None of these candidates"	4,817	*6.7*
1982 [17] **Republican Primary**		
Chic Hecht (R)	26,940	*39.1*
Rick Fore (R)	17,065	*24.8*
Jack Kenney (R)	12,191	*17.7*
S. M. Cavnar (R)	6,327	*9.2*
"None of these candidates"	5,411	*7.8*
Democratic Primary		
Howard W. Cannon (D)	54,288	*49.7*
James Santini (D)	49,735	*45.5*

Candidates	Votes	%
Class 3		
1956 **Republican Primary**		
Clifton Young		*100.0*

17. In Nevada, primary voters may vote for "None of these candidates." The "None of these candidates" vote is given here only where it amounted to 5 percent or more of the total.

Candidates	Votes	%
Democratic Primary		
Alan Bible (D)	26,784	*68.2*
Mahlon Brown (D)	8,043	*20.5*
Harvey Dickerson (D)	2,436	*6.2*
Jay Sourwine (D)	2,020	*5.1*
1962 **Republican Primary**		
William B. Wright (R)	17,478	*69.7*
Charles B. Grant (R)	6,811	*27.1*
Democratic Primary		
Alan Bible (D)	38,556	*76.2*
Jack Streeter (D)	10,703	*21.1*
1968 **Republican Primary**		
Ed Fike (R)	20,585	*53.0*
William J. Raggio (R)	17,634	*45.4*
Democratic Primary		
Alan Bible (D)		*100.0*
1974 **Republican Primary**		
Paul Laxalt (R)	33,660	*81.3*
Jim Talbert (R)	3,984	*9.6*
S. M. Cavnar (R)	3,752	*9.1*
Democratic Primary		
Harry Reid (D)	44,768	*58.6*
Maya Miller (D)	25,738	*33.7*
Dan Miller (D)	5,869	*7.7*
1980 **Republican Primary**		
Paul Laxalt (R)	45,857	*90.3*
Richard A. Glister (R)	2,509	*5.0*
Democratic Primary		
Mary Gojack (D)		*100.0*

NEW HAMPSHIRE

Candidates	Votes	%
Class 2		
1960 **Republican Primary**		
Styles Bridges (R)	87,629	*92.9*
Albert Levitt (R)	6,681	*7.1*
Democratic Primary		
Herbert W. Hill (D)	16,198	*40.2*
Alphonse Roy (D)	13,782	*34.3*
Frank L. Sullivan (D)	10,266	*25.5*

Candidates	Votes	%

1962 [18]   **Special Republican Primary**

Perkins Bass (R)	31,037	*31.3*
Doloris Bridges (R)	29,345	*29.6*
Maurice J. Murphy (R)	24,204	*24.4*
Chester E. Merrow (R)	14,417	*14.6*

Special Democratic Primary

Thomas J. McIntyre (D)		*100.0*

1966   **Republican Primary**

Harrison R. Thyng (R)	22,741	*29.5*
Wesley Powell (R)	18,145	*23.5*
William R. Johnson (R)	17,410	*22.6*
Lane Dwinell (R)	10,781	*14.0*
Doloris Bridges (R)	7,613	*9.9*

Democratic Primary

Thomas J. McIntyre (D)		*100.0*

1972   **Republican Primary**

Wesley Powell (R)	42,837	*48.0*
Peter J. Booras (R)	19,714	*22.1*
David A. Brock (R)	16,326	*18.3*
Marshall W. Cobleigh (R)	10,106	*11.3*

Democratic Primary

Thomas J. McIntyre (D)		*100.0*

1978   **Republican Primary**

Gordon J. Humphrey (R)	35,503	*50.4*
James A. Masiello (R)	18,371	*26.1*
Alf E. Jacobson (R)	13,619	*19.4*

Democratic Primary

Thomas J. McIntyre (D)	31,796	*80.7*
Raymond J. Coughlan (D)	7,605	*19.3*

1984   **Republican Primary**

Gordon J. Humphrey (R)	57,763	*99.1*

Democratic Primary

Norman E. D'Amours (D)	42,371	*99.3*

Class 3

1956   **Republican Primary**

Norris Cotton (R)	61,673	*89.5*
Joseph Moore (R)	7,264	*10.5*

Democratic Primary

Laurence M. Pickett (D)		*100.0*

18. *A special New Hampshire election was held to fill the unexpired term of Sen. Styles Bridges (R), who died Nov. 26, 1961.*

Candidates	Votes	%

1962   **Republican Primary**

Norris Cotton (R)	87,445	*94.4*
Norman LePage (R)	5,167	*5.6*

Democratic Primary

Alfred Catalfo (D)		*100.0*

1968   **Republican Primary**

Norris Cotton (R)	78,058	*92.4*
John C. Mongan (R)	6,279	*7.4*

Democratic Primary

John W. King (D)		*100.0*

1974   **Republican Primary**

Louis C. Wyman (R)	66,749	*83.0*
Leslie R. Babb (R)	13,670	*17.0*

Democratic Primary

John A. Durkin (D)	22,258	*50.0*
Laurence I. Radway (D)	14,646	*32.9*
Dennis J. Sullivan (D)	6,330	*14.2*

1980   **Republican Primary**

Warren B. Rudman (R)	20,206	*20.3*
John H. Sununu (R)	16,885	*16.9*
Wesley Powell (R)	14,861	*14.9*
Edward B. Hager (R)	9,821	*9.9*
Lawrence J. Brady (R)	9,426	*9.5*
David H. Bradley (R)	9,361	*9.4*
Anthony Campaigne (R)	8,495	*8.6*
George B. Roberts (R)	7,397	*7.4*

Democratic Primary

John A. Durkin (D)	36,933	*79.6*
William F. Sullivan (D)	9,486	*20.4*

NEW JERSEY

Candidates	Votes	%

Class 1

1958   **Republican Primary**

Robert W. Kean (R)	152,884	*43.0*
Bernard M. Shanley (R)	128,990	*36.3*
Robert Morris (R)	73,658	*20.7*

Democratic Primary

Harrison A. Williams Jr. (D)	152,413	*43.1*
John J. Grogan (D)	139,605	*39.5*
Joseph E. McLean (D)	61,478	*17.4*

1964   **Republican Primary**

Bernard M. Shanley (R)		*100.0*

Candidates	Votes	%
Democratic Primary		
Harrison A. Williams Jr. (D)		*100.0*

1970 | **Republican Primary** | | |
Nelson G. Gross (R)	150,662	*65.4*
James A. Quaremba (R)	43,547	*18.9*
Joseph T. Gavin (R)	36,208	*15.7*
Democratic Primary		
Harrison A. Williams Jr. (D)	190,692	*65.6*
Frank J. Guarini (D)	100,045	*34.4*

1976 | **Republican Primary** | | |
David F. Norcross (R)	196,457	*68.3*
Martin E. Wendelken (R)	45,472	*15.8*
James E. Parker (R)	27,672	*9.6*
N. Leonard Smith (R)	17,892	*6.2*
Democratic Primary		
Harrison A. Williams Jr. (D)	378,553	*85.1*
Stephen J. Foley (D)	66,178	*14.9*

1982 | **Republican Primary** | | |
Millicent Fenwick (R)	193,683	*54.3*
Jeffrey Bell (R)	163,145	*45.7*
Democratic Primary		
Frank R. Lautenberg (D)	104,666	*26.0*
Andrew Maguire (D)	92,878	*23.0*
Joseph A. LeFante (D)	81,440	*20.2*
Barbara B. Sigmund (D)	45,708	*11.3*
Howard Rosen (D)	28,427	*7.0*

Class 2

Candidates	Votes	%
1960 **Republican Primary**		
Clifford P. Case (R)	230,802	*63.7*
Robert Morris (R)	120,729	*33.3*
Democratic Primary		
Thorn Lord (D)	177,429	*81.6*
Richard M. Glassner (D)	40,134	*18.4*

1966 | **Republican Primary** | | |
Clifford P. Case (R)		*100.0*
Democratic Primary		
Warren W. Wilentz (D)	197,428	*72.7*
David Frost (D)	31,289	*11.5*
John J. Winberry (D)	19,745	*7.3*
Clarence Coggins (D)	16,775	*6.2*

1972 | **Republican Primary** | | |
Clifford P. Case (R)	187,268	*70.1*
James W. Ralph (R)	79,776	*29.9*

Candidates	Votes	%
Democratic Primary		
Paul J. Krebs (D)	135,000	*43.2*
Daniel M. Gaby (D)	86,213	*27.6*
Joseph T. Karcher (D)	51,321	*16.4*
Henry Kielbasa (D)	40,235	*12.9*

1978 | **Republican Primary** | | |
Jeffrey Bell (R)	118,555	*50.7*
Clifford P. Case (R)	115,082	*49.3*
Democratic Primary		
Bill Bradley (D)	217,502	*58.9*
Richard C. Leone (D)	97,667	*26.4*
Alexander J. Menza (D)	32,386	*8.8*

1984 | **Republican Primary** | | |
Mary V. Mochary (R)	111,851	*61.4*
Robert Morris (R)	70,418	*38.6*
Democratic Primary		
Bill Bradley (D)	404,301	*92.9*
Elliot Greenspan (D)	30,680	*7.0*

NEW MEXICO

Candidates	Votes	%
Class 1		
1958 **Republican Primary**		
Forrest S. Atchley (R)	10,384	*51.3*
Reginaldo Espinoza (R)	9,861	*48.7*
Democratic Primary		
Dennis Chavez (D)	68,689	*65.7*
E. S. Walker (D)	35,927	*34.3*

1964 | **Republican Primary** | | |
Edwin L. Mechem (R)		*100.0*
Democratic Primary		
Joseph M. Montoya (D)		*100.0*

1970 | **Republican Primary** | | |
Anderson Carter (R)	32,122	*57.8*
David F. Cargo (R)	17,951	*32.3*
Harold G. Thompson (R)	5,544	*10.0*
Democratic Primary		
Joseph M. Montoya (D)	85,285	*73.1*
Richard B. Edwards (D)	31,381	*26.9*

1976 | **Republican Primary** | | |
| | | |
| Harrison (Jack) Schmitt (R) | 34,074 | *71.7* |

Candidates	Votes	%
Eugene W. Pierce (R)	10,965	23.1
Arthur A. Lavine (R)	2,481	5.2

Democratic Primary

Joseph M. Montoya (D)	96,063	66.3
Robert R. Sims (D)	48,824	33.7

1982   **Republican Primary**

Harrison (Jack) Schmitt (R)		100.0

Democratic Primary

Jeff Bingaman (D)	91,780	54.4
Jerry Apodaca (D)	66,598	39.4
Virginia R. Keehan (D)	10,466	6.2

Class 2

1960   **Republican Primary**

William F. Colwes (R)	18,884	53.0
Joseph Rendon (R)	11,866	33.3
Frederic W. Airy (R)	4,859	13.6

Democratic Primary

Clinton P. Anderson (D)	98,037	81.3
James P. Speer (D)	9,360	7.8
N. Tito Quintana (D)	8,981	7.4

1966   **Republican Primary**

Anderson Carter (R)		100.0

Democratic Primary

Clinton P. Anderson (D)		100.0

1972   **Republican Primary**

Pete V. Domenici (R)	37,337	63.2
David F. Cargo (R)	12,522	21.2
E. Lee Francis (R)	4,583	7.8

Democratic Primary

Jack Daniels (D)	45,648	29.7
Robert A. Mondragon (D)	29,603	19.3
David L. Norvell (D)	24,917	16.2
Thomas G. Morris (D)	22,849	14.9

1978   **Republican Primary**

Pete V. Domenici (R)		100.0

Democratic Primary

Toney Anaya (D)		100.0

1984   **Republican Primary**

Pete V. Domenici (R)	42,760	100.0

Democratic Primary

Judith A. Pratt (D)	67,722	45.5
Nick Franklin (D)	56,434	37.9
Anselmo A. Chavez (D)	24,694	16.6

NEW YORK

Candidates	Votes	%

Class 1

1970 [19]   **Republican Primary**

Charles E. Goodell (R)		100.0

Democratic Primary

Richard L. Ottinger (D)	366,789	39.6
Paul O'Dwyer (D)	302,438	32.7
Theodore C. Sorensen (D)	154,434	16.7
Richard D. McCarthy (D)	102,224	11.0

Liberal Primary

Charles E. Goodell (L)		100.0

Conservative Primary

James L. Buckley (C)		100.0

1976   **Republican Primary**

James L. Buckley (R)	242,527	70.5
Peter A. Peyser (R)	101,629	29.5

Democratic Primary

Daniel Patrick Moynihan (D)	333,697	36.4
Bella S. Abzug (D)	323,705	35.3
Ramsey Clark (D)	94,191	10.3
Paul O'Dwyer (D)	82,689	9.0
Abraham J. Hirschfeld (D)	82,331	9.0

Conservative Primary

James L. Buckley (C)		100.0

Liberal Primary [20]

Henry S. Stern (L)		100.0

1982   **Republican Primary**

Florence M. Sullivan (R)	216,486	42.4
Muriel Siebert (R)	157,446	30.8
Whitney N. Seymour (R)	136,974	26.8

Democratic Primary

Daniel Patrick Moynihan (D)	922,059	85.1
Melvin Klenetsky (D)	161,012	14.9

Conservative Primary

Florence M. Sullivan (C)		100.0

Liberal Primary

Daniel Patrick Moynihan (L)		100.0

Right to Life Primary

Florence M. Sullivan (RTL)		100.0

19. Until 1968, when New York adopted a primary system, party conventions or state central committees nominated candidates for statewide office.

20. Stern withdrew after the primary and the Liberal Party's state committee substituted Daniel Patrick Moynihan (D) as the Liberal nominee.

Candidates	Votes	%
Class 3		

NORTH DAKOTA

Candidates	Votes	%
Class 1		

1968   **Republican Primary**

Candidates	Votes	%
Jacob K. Javits (R)		100.0

Democratic Primary

Paul O'Dwyer (D)	275,877	36.1
Eugene H. Nickerson (D)	257,639	33.7
Joseph Y. Resnick (D)	229,893	30.1

Liberal Primary

Jacob K. Javits (L)	10,277	72.1
Murray Baron (L)	3,969	27.8

Conservative Primary

James L. Buckley (C)		100.0

1974   **Republican Primary**

Jacob K. Javits (R)		100.0

Democratic Primary

Ramsey Clark (D)	414,327	48.0
Lee Alexander (D)	255,250	29.6
Abraham J. Hirschfeld (D)	194,076	22.5

Liberal Primary

Jacob K. Javits (L)		100.0

Conservative Primary

Barbara A. Keating (C)		100.0

1980   **Republican Primary**

Alfonse M. D'Amato (R)	323,468	55.7
Jacob K. Javits (R)	257,433	44.3

Democratic Primary

Elizabeth Holtzman (D)	378,567	40.7
Bess Myerson (D)	292,767	31.5
John V. Lindsay (D)	146,815	15.8
John Santucci (D)	111,129	12.0

Conservative Primary

Alfonse M. D'Amato (C)		100.0

Liberal Primary

Jacob K. Javits (R)		100.0

Right to Life Primary

Alfonse M. D'Amato (RTL)		100.0

1958   **Republican Primary**

William Langer (R) [21]	68,541	65.5
Clyde Duffy (R)	34,152	32.6

Democratic Primary

Raymond Vendsel (D)	30,775	65.8
Anson Anderson (D)	15,999	34.2

1964   **Republican Primary**

Tom Kleppe (R)		100.0

Democratic Primary

Quentin N. Burdick (D)		100.0

1970   **Republican Primary**

Tom Kleppe (R)		100.0

Democratic Primary

Quentin N. Burdick (D)		100.0

1976   **Republican Primary**

Richard Stroup (R)		100.0

Democratic Primary

Quentin N. Burdick (D)		100.0

American Primary

Clarence Haggard (AM)		100.0

1982   **Republican Primary**

Gene Knorr (R)		100.0

Democratic Primary

Quentin N. Burdick (D)		100.0

Class 3		

1956   **Republican Primary**

Milton R. Young (R)	88,738	88.6
Ray R. Lake (R)	11,398	11.4

Democratic Primary

Quentin N. Burdick (D)		100.0

1962   **Republican Primary**

Milton R. Young (R)	67,938	92.2
Roger Vorachek (R)	5,729	7.8

21. *No primaries were held for the June 1960 special election in North Dakota to fill the vacancy caused by Sen. Langer's death. Nominees were selected by state conventions.*

Candidates	Votes	%
Democratic Primary		
William Lanier (D)		*100.0*

1968   **Republican Primary**

Candidates	Votes	%
Milton R. Young (R)		*100.0*
Democratic Primary		
Herschel Lashkowitz (D)		*100.0*

1974   **Republican Primary**

Candidates	Votes	%
Milton R. Young (R)		*100.0*
Democratic Primary		
William L. Guy (D)	55,269	*83.0*
Robert P. McCarney (D)	11,286	*17.0*

1980   **Republican Primary**

Candidates	Votes	%
Mark Andrews (R)		*100.0*
Democratic Primary		
Kent Johanneson (D)	30,789	*77.4*
Michael P. Saba (D)	9,013	*22.6*

OHIO

Candidates	Votes	%
Class 1		

1958   **Republican Primary**

Candidates	Votes	%
John W. Bricker (R)		*100.0*
Democratic Primary		
Stephen M. Young (D)		*100.0*

1964   **Republican Primary**

Candidates	Votes	%
Robert A. Taft Jr. (R)	606,944	*79.1*
Ted W. Brown (R)	160,263	*20.9*
Democratic Primary		
Stephen M. Young (D)	520,641	*66.5*
John Glenn (D)	206,956	*26.4*

1970   **Republican Primary**

Candidates	Votes	%
Robert A. Taft Jr. (R)	472,202	*50.3*
James A. Rhodes (R)	466,932	*49.7*
Democratic Primary		
Howard M. Metzenbaum (D)	430,469	*46.3*
John Glenn (D)	417,027	*44.9*
Kenneth W. Clement (D)	50,375	*5.4*
American Independent Primary		
Richard B. Kay (AMI)		*100.0*

1976   **Republican Primary**

Candidates	Votes	%
Robert A. Taft Jr. (R)		*100.0*
Democratic Primary		
Howard M. Metzenbaum (D)	576,124	*53.6*
James V. Stanton (D)	400,552	*37.3*
James D. Nolan (D)	62,979	*5.8*

1982   **Republican Primary**

Candidates	Votes	%
Paul E. Pfeifer (R)	364,579	*60.0*
Walter E. Beckjord (R)	180,198	*29.7*
Bill Ress (WRITE IN)	62,446	*10.3*
Democratic Primary		
Howard M. Metzenbaum (D)	810,785	*82.9*
Norbert G. Dennerll (D)	167,778	*17.1*
Libertarian Primary		
Philip Herzing (LIBERT)		*100.0*

Class 3		

1956   **Republican Primary**

Candidates	Votes	%
George H. Bender (R)		*100.0*
Democratic Primary		
Frank J. Lausche (D)		*100.0*

1962   **Republican Primary**

Candidates	Votes	%
John M. Briley (R)	177,987	*35.3*
Charles E. Fry (R)	143,320	*28.4*
John S. Ballard (R)	132,924	*26.3*
Ross Pepple (R)	50,221	*10.0*
Democratic Primary		
Frank J. Lausche (D)	437,902	*74.0*
Albert T. Ball (D)	90,609	*15.3*
Raymond Warren Beringer (D)	63,543	*10.7*

1968   **Republican Primary**

Candidates	Votes	%
William B. Saxbe (R)	575,178	*82.3*
William L. White (R)	71,191	*10.2*
Albert E. Payne (R)	52,393	*7.5*
Democratic Primary		
John J. Gilligan (D)	544,814	*55.4*
Frank J. Lausche (D)	438,588	*44.6*

1974   **Republican Primary**

Candidates	Votes	%
Ralph J. Perk (R)	341,078	*64.8*
Peter E. Voss (R)	185,342	*35.2*
Democratic Primary		
John Glenn (D)	571,871	*54.4*
Howard M. Metzenbaum (D)	480,123	*45.6*

Candidates	Votes	%
1980		
Republican Primary		
James E. Betts (R)		*100.0*
Democratic Primary		
John Glenn (D)	934,230	*85.9*
Frances A. Waterman (D)	88,506	*8.1*
Francis Hunstiger (D)	64,270	*5.9*

OKLAHOMA

Candidates	Votes	%
Class 2		
1960		
Republican Primary		
B. Hayden Crawford (R)	37,508	*70.4*
Herbert K. Hyde (R)	15,743	*29.6*
Democratic Primary		
Robert S. Kerr (D)	300,061	*77.6*
Thomas C. Dunn (D)	65,139	*16.8*
D. R. Condo (D)	21,420	*5.5*
1964 [22]		
Special Republican Primary		
Bud Wilkinson (R)	100,544	*79.2*
Thomas J. Harris (R)	19,170	*15.1*
Forest W. Beall (R)	7,211	*5.7*
Special Democratic Primary		
J. Howard Edmondson (D)	215,455	*36.4*
Fred R. Harris (D)	190,868	*32.3*
Raymond Gary (D)	170,869	*28.9*
Special Democratic Runoff		
Fred R. Harris (D)	277,362	*60.9*
J. Howard Edmondson (D)	178,051	*39.1*
1966		
Republican Primary		
Pat J. Patterson (R)	36,036	*42.5*
Don Kinkaid (R)	32,137	*37.9*
Gustav K. Brandborg (R)	16,617	*19.6*
Republican Runoff		
Pat J. Patterson (R)	42,550	*58.3*
Don Kinkaid (R)	30,452	*41.7*
Democratic Primary		
Fred R. Harris (D)	359,747	*83.6*
W. R. Owens (D)	41,580	*9.7*
Billy E. Brown (D)	29,184	*6.8*
1972		
Republican Primary		
Dewey F. Bartlett (R)	94,935	*93.1*
C. W. Wood (R)	7,029	*6.9*

22. A special election was held in Oklahoma to fill the unexpired term of Sen. Robert S. Kerr (D), who died Jan. 1, 1963.

Candidates	Votes	%
Democratic Primary		
Ed Edmondson (D)	249,729	*56.3*
Charles Nesbitt (D)	92,101	*20.8*
Al Terrill (D)	33,520	*7.6*
Jed Johnson (D)	28,795	*6.5*
1978		
Republican Primary		
Robert B. Kamm (R)		*100.0*
Democratic Primary		
David L. Boren (D)	252,560	*45.8*
Ed Edmondson (D)	155,626	*28.2*
Gene Stipe (D)	114,423	*20.8*
Democratic Runoff		
David L. Boren (D)	281,587	*60.5*
Ed Edmondson (D)	184,175	*39.5*
1984		
Republican Primary		
George L. Mothershed (R)	46,933	*39.3*
Will E. (Bill) Crozier (R)	39,581	*33.1*
Gar Graham (R)	32,901	*27.6*
Democratic Primary		
David L. Boren (D)	432,534	*89.9*
Marshall Luse (D)	48,761	*10.1*
Class 3		
1956		
Republican Primary		
Douglas McKeever (R)	24,447	*55.5*
Paul V. Beck (R)	7,666	*17.4*
Ernest G. Albright (R)	6,539	*14.8*
Dan M. Madrano (R)	5,379	*12.2*
Democratic Primary		
A. S. Mike Monroney (D)	245,572	*71.1*
H. O. Doenges (D)	54,546	*15.8*
Ora J. Fox (D)	29,825	*8.6*
1962		
Republican Primary		
B. Hayden Crawford (R)		*100.0*
Democratic Primary		
A. S. Mike Monroney (D)	335,922	*74.3*
Wilson Wallace (D)	64,996	*14.4*
Billy E. Brown (D)	26,440	*5.8*
Woodrow W. Bussey (D)	24,725	*5.5*
1968		
Republican Primary		
Henry Bellmon (R)		*100.0*
Democratic Primary		
A. S. Mike Monroney (D)	281,697	*76.3*
W. R. Owens (D)	32,823	*8.9*
Jesse L. Leeds (D)	22,843	*6.2*
Billy E. Brown (D)	20,681	*5.6*

	Candidates	Votes	%
	American Primary		
	George Washington (AM)	414	*57.6*
	Landis B. Hiniker (AM)	305	*42.4*
1974	**Republican Primary**		
	Henry Bellmon (R)	132,888	*87.1*
	Warner M. Hornbeck (R)	19,733	*12.9*
	Democratic Primary		
	Ed Edmondson (D)	288,665	*48.7*
	Charles Nesbitt (D)	222,727	*37.5*
	Wilburn Cartwright (D)	35,107	*5.9*
	Democratic Runoff		
	Ed Edmondson (D)	306,178	*58.7*
	Charles Nesbitt (D)	215,685	*41.3*
1980	**Republican Primary**		
	Don Nickles (R)	47,879	*34.7*
	John Zink (R)	45,914	*33.3*
	Ed Noble (R)	39,839	*28.9*
	Republican Runoff		
	Don Nickles (R)	81,697	*65.6*
	John Zink (R)	42,818	*34.4*
	Democratic Primary		
	Robert S. Kerr Jr. (D)	156,666	*34.0*
	Andrew Coats (D)	154,762	*33.6*
	Gene Howard (D)	55,503	*12.1*
	James E. Hamilton (D)	49,369	*10.7*
	Democratic Runoff		
	Andrew Coats (D)	209,952	*53.0*
	Robert S. Kerr Jr. (D)	185,814	*46.9*
	Libertarian Primary		
	Robert Murphy (LIBERT)		*100.0*

OREGON

	Candidates	Votes	%
	Class 2		
1960 [23]	**Special Republican Primary**		
	Elmo E. Smith (R)	201,024	*85.5*
	George Altvater (R)	33,022	*14.0*
	Special Democratic Primary		
	Maurine B. Neuberger (D)	244,865	*99.5*

23. A special Oregon election to fill the unexpired term of Sen. Richard L. Neuberger (D), who died March 9, 1960, was held in conjunction with the election for the full term, beginning Jan. 3, 1961. His widow, Maurine B. Neuberger (D), and Elmo Smith (R), won both primaries and Maurine Neuberger went on to defeat Smith in the November general election for both the short and full terms. The short term had been filled until the election by an interim appointee. Figures for special primary from the Elections Research Center, Washington, D.C.

	Candidates	Votes	%
1960	**Republican Primary**		
	Elmo E. Smith (R)	179,575	*76.5*
	George Altvater (R)	20,438	*8.7*
	R. F. Cook (R)	19,443	*8.3*
	Thomas Killam (R)	14,490	*6.2*
	Democratic Primary		
	Maurine B. Neuberger (D)	211,961	*77.9*
	Harry C. Fowler (D)	28,032	*10.3*
	William B. Murphy (D)	16,245	*6.0*
1966	**Republican Primary**		
	Mark O. Hatfield (R)	178,782	*75.9*
	Walter Huss (R)	30,906	*13.1*
	James Bacaloff (R)	19,699	*8.4*
	Democratic Primary		
	Robert B. Duncan (D)	161,189	*62.2*
	Howard Morgan (D)	89,174	*34.4*
1972	**Republican Primary**		
	Mark O. Hatfield (R)	171,594	*61.1*
	Lynn Engdahl (R)	63,859	*22.8*
	Kenneth A. Brown (R)	30,826	*11.0*
	Democratic Primary		
	Wayne L. Morse (D)	173,147	*43.7*
	Robert B. Duncan (D)	130,845	*33.0*
	Don Willner (D)	74,060	*18.7*
1978	**Republican Primary**		
	Mark O. Hatfield (R)	159,617	*65.7*
	Bert W. Hawkins (R)	43,350	*17.8*
	Robert D. Maxwell (R)	24,294	*10.0*
	Richard L. Schnepel (R)	15,628	*6.4*
	Democratic Primary		
	Vernon Cook (D)	151,754	*58.3*
	John Sweeney (D)	41,599	*16.0*
	Jack A. Brown (D)	35,211	*13.5*
	Steve Anderson (D)	30,066	*11.6*
1984	**Republican Primary**		
	Mark O. Hatfield (R)	214,114	*78.6*
	John T. Schiess (R)	26,848	*9.9*
	Sherry Reynolds (R)	18,590	*6.8*
	Democratic Primary		
	Margie Hendriksen (D)	249,142	*75.8*
	Sam Kahl (D)	79,317	*24.1*

Class 3

	Candidates	Votes	%
1956	**Republican Primary**		
	Douglas McKay (R)	123,281	*49.5*
	Phil Hitchcock (R)	99,296	*39.8*
	Elmer Deetz (R)	23,170	*9.3*

Candidates	Votes	%
Democratic Primary		
Wayne L. Morse (D)	195,784	*83.4*
Woody Smith (D)	38,959	*16.6*

1962 **Republican Primary**

Candidates	Votes	%
Sig Ulander (R)	106,821	*50.1*
Edwin R. Durno (R)	72,955	*34.2*
Harold M. Livingston (R)	16,880	*7.9*
Democratic Primary		
Wayne L. Morse (D)	183,385	*79.8*
Charles E. Gilbert (D)	46,171	*20.1*

1968 **Republican Primary**

Candidates	Votes	%
Bob Packwood (R)	241,464	*88.0*
John S. Boyd (R)	32,807	*12.0*
Democratic Primary		
Wayne L. Morse (D)	185,091	*49.0*
Robert B. Duncan (D)	174,795	*46.3*

1974 **Republican Primary**

Candidates	Votes	%
Bob Packwood (R)		*100.0*
Democratic Primary		
Wayne L. Morse (D) [24]	155,729	*49.0*
Jason Boe (D)	125,055	*39.3*
Robert T. Daly (D)	21,881	*6.9*

1980 **Republican Primary**

Candidates	Votes	%
Bob Packwood (R)	191,127	*62.4*
Brenda Jose (R)	45,973	*15.0*
Kenneth A. Brown (R)	23,599	*7.7*
Rosalie Huss (R)	22,929	*7.5*
Willard D. Severn (R)	22,281	*7.3*
Democratic Primary		
Ted Kulongoski (D)	161,153	*47.7*
Charles O. Porter (D)	69,649	*20.6*
Jack Sumner (D)	46,107	*13.6*
John Sweeney (D)	39,691	*11.7*
Gene Arvidson (D)	20,548	*6.1*

PENNSYLVANIA

Candidates	Votes	%
Class 1		

1958 **Republican Primary**

Candidates	Votes	%
Hugh Scott (R)	766,102	*74.0*
Weldon B. Heyburn (R)	160,857	*15.5*
Harrison A. Moyer (R)	108,179	*10.4*

Candidates	Votes	%
Democratic Primary		
George M. Leader (D)	724,645	*74.2*
Clarence P. Bowers (D)	252,468	*25.8*

1964 **Republican Primary**

Candidates	Votes	%
Hugh Scott (R)	869,774	*88.9*
W. Henry McFarland (R)	106,376	*10.9*
Democratic Primary		
Genevieve Blatt (D)	461,111	*45.4*
Michael A. Musmanno (D)	460,620	*45.4*
David B. Roberts (D)	93,311	*9.2*

1970 **Republican Primary**

Candidates	Votes	%
Hugh Scott (R)		*100.0*
Democratic Primary		
William G. Sesler (D)	477,680	*53.8*
Norval D. Reece (D)	241,731	*27.3*
Frank Mesaros (D)	167,779	*18.9*
American Independent Primary		
W. Henry McFarland (AMI)		*100.0*
Constitution Primary		
Frank W. Gaydosh (CONST)		*100.0*

1976 **Republican Primary**

Candidates	Votes	%
John Heinz (R)	358,715	*37.7*
Arlen Specter (R)	332,513	*35.0*
George R. Packard (R)	160,379	*16.9*
Democratic Primary		
William J. Green III (D)	762,733	*68.8*
Jeanette Reibman (D)	345,264	*31.1*
Constitution Primary		
Andrew J. Watson (CONST)		*100.0*

1982 **Republican Primary**

Candidates	Votes	%
John Heinz (R)		*100.0*
Democratic Primary		
Cyril H. Wecht (D)	426,625	*57.2*
John J. Logue (D)	166,078	*22.3*
Cyril E. Sagan (D)	152,631	*20.5*

Candidates	Votes	%
Class 3		

1956 **Republican Primary**

Candidates	Votes	%
James H. Duff (R)	803,971	*85.0*
Paul E. Sanger (R)	141,820	*15.0*
Democratic Primary		
Joseph S. Clark (D)		*100.0*

24. Sen. Morse died after winning the primary and the Democratic state central committee substituted Betty Roberts as the party's nominee.

Candidates	Votes	%
1962 **Republican Primary**		
James E. Van Zandt (R)		*100.0*
Democratic Primary		
Joseph S. Clark (D)		*100.0*
1968 **Republican Primary**		
Richard S. Schweiker (R)		*100.0*
Democratic Primary		
Joseph S. Clark (D)	460,380	*53.3*
John H. Dent (D)	402,799	*46.7*
1974 **Republican Primary**		
Richard S. Schweiker (R)		*100.0*
Democratic Primary		
Peter Flaherty (D)	485,361	*47.1*
Herbert S. Denenberg (D)	447,081	*43.3*
Frank Mesaros (D)	64,070	*6.2*
Constitution Primary		
George W. Shankey (CONST)		*100.0*
1980 **Republican Primary**		
Arlen Specter (R)	419,372	*36.4*
Bud Haabestad (R)	382,281	*33.2*
Edward L. Howard (R)	148,200	*12.9*
Democratic Primary		
Peter Flaherty (D)	771,119	*53.2*
Joseph Rhodes (D)	179,107	*12.4*
Peter Liacouras (D)	116,975	*8.1*
C. Delores Tucker (D)	107,483	*7.4*
Ed Mezvinsky (D)	100,841	*7.0*
Tom Anderson (D)	89,656	*6.2*

RHODE ISLAND

Candidates	Votes	%
Class 1		
1958 **Republican Primary**		
Bayard Ewing (R)		*100.0*
Democratic Primary		
John O. Pastore (D)		*100.0*
1964 **Republican Primary**		
Ronald R. Lagueux (R)		*100.0*
Democratic Primary		
John O. Pastore (D)		*100.0*

Candidates	Votes	%
1970 **Republican Primary**		
John McLaughlin (R)		*100.0*
Democratic Primary		
John O. Pastore (D)	54,090	*88.1*
John Quattrocchi (D)	7,332	*11.9*
1976 **Republican Primary**		
John H. Chafee (R)		*100.0*
Democratic Primary		
Richard P. Lorber (D)	60,118	*37.8*
Philip W. Noel (D)	60,018	*37.7*
John P. Hawkins (D)	25,456	*16.0*
1982 **Republican Primary**		
John H. Chafee (R)		*100.0*
Democratic Primary		
Julius C. Michaelson (D)	56,800	*82.4*
Helen E. Flynn (D)	12,159	*17.6*
Class 2		
1960 **Republican Primary**		
Raoul Archambault (R)		*100.0*
Democratic Primary		
Claiborne Pell (D)	83,184	*61.3*
Dennis J. Roberts (D)	44,924	*33.1*
Howard McGrath (D)	7,535	*5.6*
1966 **Republican Primary**		
Ruth M. Briggs (R)	15,451	*82.1*
Charles H. Eden (R)	3,363	*17.9*
Democratic Primary		
Claiborne Pell (D)		*100.0*
1972 **Republican Primary**		
John H. Chafee (R)		*100.0*
Democratic Primary		
Claiborne Pell (D)		*100.0*
1978 **Republican Primary**		
James G. Reynolds (R)		*100.0*
Democratic Primary		
Claiborne Pell (D)	69,729	*87.0*
Raymond J. Greiner (D)	6,076	*7.6*
Francis P. Kelley (D)	4,330	*5.4*
1984 **Republican Primary**		
Barbara Leonard (R)	108,492	*100.0*

665

Candidates	Votes	%
Democratic Primary		
Claiborne Pell (D)	82,394	*100.0*

SOUTH DAKOTA

Candidates	Votes	%
Class 2		
1960 **Republican Primary**		
Karl E. Mundt (R)		*100.0*
Democratic Primary		
George McGovern (D)		*100.0*
1966 **Republican Primary**		
Karl E. Mundt (R)	66,758	*82.1*
Richard R. Murphy (R)	14,593	*17.9*
Democratic Primary		
Donn H. Wright (D)		*100.0*
1972 **Republican Primary** [25]		
Robert W. Hirsch (R)	27,322	*27.4*
Gordon Mydland (R)	22,297	*22.3*
Chuck Lien (R)	21,995	*22.0*
Kenneth D. Stofferahn (R)	16,615	*16.6*
Tom Reardon (R)	11,592	*11.6*
Democratic Primary		
James Abourezk (D)	46,931	*79.4*
George Blue (D)	12,163	*20.6*
1978 **Republican Primary**		
Larry Pressler (R)	66,893	*73.9*
Ronald F. Williamson (R)	23,646	*26.1*
Democratic Primary		
Don Barnett (D)	37,319	*55.1*
Kenneth D. Stofferahn (D)	30,384	*44.9*
1984 **Republican Primary**		
Larry Pressler (R)		*100.0*
Democratic Primary		
George V. Cunningham (D)	31,376	*68.1*
Dean L. Sinclair (D)	14,672	*31.8*
Class 3		
1956 **Republican Primary**		
Francis Case (R)		*100.0*

Candidates	Votes	%
Democratic Primary		
Kenneth Holum (D)	23,464	*60.8*
Merton B. Tice (D)	15,099	*39.1*
1962 **Republican Primary** [26]		
Francis Case (R)	57,583	*83.5*
A. C. Miller (R)	11,414	*16.5*
Democratic Primary		
George McGovern (D)		*100.0*
1968 **Republican Primary**		
Archie M. Gubbrud (R)		*100.0*
Democratic Primary		
George McGovern (D)		*100.0*
1974 **Republican Primary**		
Leo K. Thorsness (R)	49,716	*52.3*
Al Schock (R)	35,406	*37.3*
Barbara B. Gunderson (R)	9,852	*10.4*
Democratic Primary		
George McGovern (D)		*100.0*
1980 **Republican Primary**		
James Abdnor (R)	68,196	*72.9*
Dale Bell (R)	25,314	*27.1*
Democratic Primary		
George McGovern (D)	44,822	*62.4*
Larry Schumaker (D)	26,958	*37.6*

UTAH

Candidates	Votes	%
Class 1		
1958 **Republican Primary**		
Arthur V. Watkins (R)	39,593	*68.1*
Carvel Mattsson (R)	18,563	*31.9*
Democratic Primary		
Frank E. Moss (D)	35,862	*59.2*
Brigham E. Roberts (D)	24,736	*40.8*
1964 **Republican Primary**		
Ernest L. Wilkinson (R)	61,167	*50.7*
Sherman P. Lloyd (R)	59,398	*49.3*
Democratic Primary		
Frank E. Moss (D)		*100.0*

25. A state Republican convention was held June 26 because no one received the 35 percent required for nomination under the South Dakota primary law. Hirsch was nominated at this convention.

26. Case died shortly after winning the primary and the Republican state committee substituted Joe H. Bottum as the party's nominee.

Candidates	Votes	%
1970		
Republican Primary		
Laurence J. Burton (R)		*100.0*
Democratic Primary		
Frank E. Moss (D)		*100.0*
1976 [27]		
Republican Primary		
Orrin G. Hatch (R)	104,490	*64.6*
Jack Carlson (R)	57,249	*35.4*
Democratic Primary		
Frank E. Moss (D)		*100.0*

Class 3

Candidates	Votes	%
1956		
Republican Primary		
Wallace F. Bennett (R)		*100.0*
Democratic Primary		
Alonzo F. Hopkin (D)	44,980	*56.8*
Herbert B. Maw (D)	34,246	*43.2*
1962		
Republican Primary		
Wallace F. Bennett (R)	70,519	*59.2*
J. Bracken Lee (R)	48,606	*40.8*
Democratic Primary		
David S. King (D)	55,965	*77.4*
Calvin L. Rampton (D)	16,327	*22.6*
1968		
Republican Primary		
Wallace F. Bennett (R)	81,945	*60.9*
Mark E. Anderson (R)	52,689	*39.1*
Democratic Primary		
Milton Weilenmann (D)	47,908	*50.7*
Phil L. Hansen (D)	46,579	*49.3*
1974		
Republican Primary		
Jake Garn (R)		*100.0*
Democratic Primary		
Wayne Owens (D)		*100.0*
American Primary		
Bruce Bangerter (AM)	2,254	*50.9*
Kenneth R. Larsen (AM)	2,173	*49.1*
1980 [27]		
Democratic Primary		
Dan Berman (D)	28,930	*50.2*
A. Stephen Dirks (D)	28,643	*49.7*

Candidates	Votes	%
American Primary		
George M. Batchelor (AM)	675	*54.5*
Larry Topham (AM)	563	*45.5*

VERMONT

Candidates	Votes	%
Class 1		
1958		
Republican Primary		
Winston L. Prouty (R)	31,866	*64.6*
Lee E. Emerson (R)	17,468	*35.4*
Democratic Primary		
Frederick J. Fayette (D)		*100.0*
1964		
Republican Primary		
Winston L. Prouty (R)		*100.0*
Democratic Primary		
Frederick J. Fayette (D)	12,388	*71.0*
William H. Meyer (D)	4,913	*28.2*
1970		
Republican Primary		
Winston L. Prouty (R)		*100.0*
Democratic Primary		
Philip H. Hoff (D)	23,082	*69.7*
Fiore L. Bove (D)	7,941	*24.0*
William H. Meyer (D)	2,024	*6.1*
1972 [28]		
Special Republican Primary		
Robert T. Stafford (R)		*100.0*
Special Democratic Primary		
Randolph T. Major (D)		*100.0*
1976		
Republican Primary		
Robert T. Stafford (R)	24,338	*68.7*
John J. Welch (R)	10,911	*30.8*
Democratic Primary		
Thomas P. Salmon (D)	21,674	*52.7*
Scott Skinner (D)	19,238	*46.8*
Liberty Union Primary		
Nancy Kaufman (LU)	362	*69.6*
John Medeiros (LU)	146	*28.1*

27. The Republican candidate in 1980 and the Republican and Democratic candidates in 1982 were nominated by convention.

28. A special election was held in 1972 to fill the unexpired term of Sen. Winston L. Prouty (R), who died Sept. 10, 1971. Robert T. Stafford had been appointed to fill the vacancy on an interim basis.

Candidates	Votes	%
1982 **Republican Primary**		
Robert T. Stafford (R)	26,323	*46.2*
Stewart M. Ledbetter (R)	19,743	*34.7*
John M. McClaughry (R)	10,692	*18.8*
Democratic Primary		
James A. Guest (D)	11,352	*67.1*
Thomas E. McGregor (D)	3,749	*22.1*
Earl S. Gardner (D)	1,281	*7.6*
Citizens Primary		
Ion Laskaris (CIT)		*100.0*
Liberty Union Primary		
Jerry Levy (LU)		*100.0*

Class 3

Candidates	Votes	%
1956 **Republican Primary**		
George D. Aiken (R)		*100.0*
Democratic Primary		
Bernard G. O'Shea (D)		*100.0*
1962 **Republican Primary**		
George D. Aiken (R)		*100.0*
Democratic Primary		
W. Robert Johnson (D)	5,718	*54.7*
William H. Meyer (D)	4,741	*45.3*
1968 **Republican Primary**		
George D. Aiken (R)	42,248	*72.8*
William K. Tufts (R)	15,786	*27.2*
Democratic Primary		
George D. Aiken (WRITE IN)	1,354	*61.8*
Others (WRITE IN)	438	*20.0*
Philip H. Hoff (WRITE IN)	400	*18.2*
1974 **Republican Primary**		
Richard W. Mallary (R)	27,221	*59.1*
Charles R. Ross (R)	16,479	*35.8*
Democratic Primary		
Patrick J. Leahy (D)	19,801	*83.9*
Nathaniel Frothingham (D)	3,703	*15.7*
1980 **Republican Primary**		
Stewart M. Ledbetter (R)	16,518	*35.3*
James E. Mullin (R)	12,256	*26.2*
Tom Evslin (R)	8,575	*18.3*
T. Garry Buckley (R)	5,209	*11.1*
Robert Schuettinger (R)	3,450	*7.4*

Candidates	Votes	%
Democratic Primary		
Patrick J. Leahy (D)		*100.0*
Liberty Union Primary		
Earl S. Gardner (LU)		*100.0*

WASHINGTON

Candidates	Votes	%
Class 1		
1958 **Republican Primary**		
William B. Bantz (R)		*100.0*
Democratic Primary		
Henry M. Jackson (D)	334,862	*85.8*
Alice F. Bryant (D)	55,200	*14.1*
1964 **Republican Primary**		
Lloyd J. Andrews (R)	216,616	*81.2*
David J. Williams (R)	37,450	*14.0*
Democratic Primary		
Henry M. Jackson (D)	478,892	*90.6*
Alice F. Bryant (D)	29,052	*5.5*
1970 **Republican Primary**		
Charles W. Elicker (R)	33,262	*37.1*
Howard S. Reed (R)	22,293	*24.9*
R. J. Odman (R)	14,856	*16.6*
William H. Davis (R)	11,207	*12.5*
Bill Patrick (R)	7,976	*8.9*
Democratic Primary		
Henry M. Jackson (D)	497,309	*84.3*
Carl Maxey (D)	79,201	*13.4*
1976 **Republican Primary**		
George M. Brown (R)	51,885	*29.5*
Warren Hanson (R)	43,905	*25.0*
Harry C. Nielsen (R)	28,030	*15.9*
Wilbur R. Parkin (R)	21,639	*12.3*
William H. Davis (R)	16,881	*9.6*
Clarice L. R. Privette (R)	13,526	*7.7*
Democratic Primary		
Henry M. Jackson (D)	549,974	*87.4*
Dennis Kelley (D)	54,470	*8.7*
1982 **Republican Primary**		
Doug Jewett (R)	73,616	*46.3*
Larry Penberthy (R)	46,037	*28.9*
Ken Talbott (R)	15,581	*9.8*
Patrick S. McGowan (R)	13,054	*8.2*

Candidates	Votes	%
Democratic Primary		
Henry M. Jackson (D)	450,580	*94.9*

1983 [29] **Special Republican Primary**

Candidates	Votes	%
Dan Evans (R)	250,046	*64.3*
Lloyd E. Cooney (R)	133,799	*34.4*

Special Democratic Primary

Candidates	Votes	%
Mike Lowry (D)	179,509	*61.5*
Charles Royer (D)	103,304	*35.4*

Class 3

1956 **Republican Primary**

Candidates	Votes	%
Arthur B. Langlie (R)		*100.0*

Democratic Primary

Candidates	Votes	%
Warren G. Magnuson (D)		*100.0*

1962 **Republican Primary**

Candidates	Votes	%
Richard G. Christensen (R)	178,616	*82.1*
Ben Larson (R)	38,759	*17.8*

Democratic Primary

Candidates	Votes	%
Warren G. Magnuson (D)	280,981	*93.7*
John Patric (D)	18,849	*6.3*

1968 **Republican Primary**

Candidates	Votes	%
Jack Metcalf (R)	210,981	*73.6*
Harvey L. Cole (R)	40,844	*14.2*
Ralph O. Westlake (R)	25,756	*9.0*

Democratic Primary

Candidates	Votes	%
Warren G. Magnuson (D)	373,303	*92.9*
Arthur DeWitt (D)	28,683	*7.1*

1974 **Republican Primary**

Candidates	Votes	%
Jack Metcalf (R)	103,616	*61.0*
Jesse Chiang (R)	31,193	*18.4*
Donald C. Knutson (R)	13,738	*8.1*
June Riggs (R)	8,491	*5.0*

Democratic Primary

Candidates	Votes	%
Warren G. Magnuson (D)	288,038	*92.5*
John Patric (D)	23,438	*7.5*

1980 **Republican Primary**

Candidates	Votes	%
Slade Gorton (R)	313,560	*55.6*
Lloyd E. Cooney (R)	229,178	*40.7*

29. A special election was held to fill the five-year unexpired term of Sen. Henry M. Jackson (D), who died Sept. 1, 1983. Under Washington's so-called "jungle" primary, all 33 candidates appeared on the same Oct. 11 ballot with their party designations. The two highest vote getters, Dan Evans (R) and Mike Lowry (D), won ballot positions for the special election. Percentages are calculated here as if candidates had run in separate party primaries.

Candidates	Votes	%
Democratic Primary		
Warren G. Magnuson (D)	348,471	*92.4*

WEST VIRGINIA

Candidates	Votes	%

Class 1

1956 [30] **Special Republican Primary**

Candidates	Votes	%
Chapman Revercomb (R)	79,106	*41.5*
Tom Sweeney (R)	57,556	*30.2*
Philip H. Hill (R)	37,574	*19.7*
A. J. Carey (R)	11,268	*5.9*

Special Democratic Primary

Candidates	Votes	%
William C. Marland (D)	118,159	*37.2*
John G. Fox (D)	104,869	*33.1*
Byron B. Randolph (D)	56,945	*17.9*
Walter G. Crichton (D)	26,972	*8.5*

1958 **Republican Primary**

Candidates	Votes	%
Chapman Revercomb (R)		*100.0*

Democratic Primary

Candidates	Votes	%
Robert C. Byrd (D)	170,686	*80.2*
Fleming N. Alderson (D)	23,915	*11.2*
Jack R. Delligatti (D)	18,235	*8.6*

1964 **Republican Primary**

Candidates	Votes	%
Cooper P. Benedict (R)		*100.0*

Democratic Primary

Candidates	Votes	%
Robert C. Byrd (D)	268,368	*85.4*
William F. Champe (D)	45,738	*14.6*

1970 [31] **Democratic Primary**

Candidates	Votes	%
Robert C. Byrd (D)	195,725	*89.0*
John J. McOwen (D)	24,286	*11.0*

1976 [31] **Democratic Primary**

Candidates	Votes	%
Robert C. Byrd (D)		*100.0*

1982 **Republican Primary**

Candidates	Votes	%
Cleveland K. Benedict (R)	73,638	*80.9*
James A. Washburn (R)	9,877	*10.8*
Frederick A. Weiland (R)	7,531	*8.3*

Democratic Primary

Candidates	Votes	%
Robert C. Byrd (D)		*100.0*

30. A special election was held in West Virginia to fill the seat vacated by the death of Sen. Harley M. Kilgore (D) on Feb. 28, 1956.

31. No Republican candidates entered the 1970 and 1976 Senate primaries in West Virginia. After the primary date in 1970, the party designated Elmer H. Dodson as the Republican candidate. No Republican candidate was designated in 1976.

Candidates	Votes	%

Class 2

1958 [32] **Special Republican Primary**

John D. Hoblitzell (R)		100.0

Special Democratic Primary

Jennings Randolph (D)	102,547	47.2
William C. Marland (D)	77,901	35.8
Arnold M. Vickers (D)	25,439	11.7
W. R. Wilson (D)	11,540	5.3

1960 **Republican Primary**

Cecil H. Underwood (R)		100.0

Democratic Primary

Jennings Randolph (R)		100.0

1966 **Republican Primary**

Francis J. Love (R)	61,479	63.4
Harold G. Cutright (R)	35,530	36.6

Democratic Primary

Jennings Randolph (D)		100.0

1972 **Republican Primary**

Louise Leonard (R)		100.0

Democratic Primary

Jennings Randolph (D)		100.0

1978 **Republican Primary**

Arch A. Moore Jr. (R)	90,406	90.6
Donald G. Michels (R)	9,414	9.4

Democratic Primary

Jennings Randolph (D)	181,480	80.5
Sharon Rogers (D)	43,991	19.5

1984 **Republican Primary**

John R. Raese (R)	61,389	47.8
Samuel N. Kusic (R)	44,820	34.9
J. Frank Deem (R)	13,707	10.7

Democratic Primary

John D. (Jay) Rockefeller IV (D)	240,559	66.3
Lacy Wright (D)	51,591	14.2
Ken Auvil (D)	41,408	11.4
Homer L. Harris (D)	29,138	8.0

WISCONSIN

Candidates	Votes	%

Class 1

1957 [33] **Special Republican Primary**

Walter J. Kohler (R)	109,256	34.4
Glenn R. Davis (R)	100,532	31.7
Alvin E. O'Konski (R)	66,784	21.0
Warren P. Knowles (R)	23,996	7.6

Special Democratic Primary

William Proxmire (D)	86,341	60.3
Clement J. Zablocki (D)	56,817	39.7

1958 **Republican Primary**

Roland J. Steinle (R)		100.0

Democratic Primary

William Proxmire (D)	220,146	85.6
Harry Halloway (D)	20,880	8.1
Arthur J. McGurn (D)	16,014	6.2

1964 **Republican Primary**

Wilbur N. Renk (R)		100.0

Democratic Primary

William Proxmire (D)	295,676	88.8
Kenneth F. Klinkert (D)	20,022	6.0
Arlyn F. Wollenburg (D)	17,333	5.2

1970 **Republican Primary**

John E. Erickson (R)		100.0

Democratic Primary

William Proxmire (D)		100.0

American Primary

Edmond E. Hou-Seye (AM)		100.0

1976 **Republican Primary**

Stanley York (R)		100.0

Democratic Primary

William Proxmire (D)		100.0

1982 **Republican Primary**

Scott McCallum (R)	182,043	67.7
Paul T. Brewer (R)	86,728	32.3

Democratic Primary

William Proxmire (D)	467,214	86.1
Marcel Dandeneau (D)	75,258	13.9

32. A special West Virginia election was held fill the seat of Sen. Matthew M. Neely (D), who died Jan. 18, 1958.

33. A special election was held in Wisconsin to fill the unexpired term of Sen. Joseph R. McCarthy (R), who died May 2, 1957.

WYOMING

Candidates	Votes	%

Candidates	Votes	%

Libertarian Primary

George Liljenfeldt (LIBERT) · · · 100.0

Constitution Primary

Sanford G. Knapp (CONST) · · · 100.0

Class 3

1956 Republican Primary

| Alexander Wiley (R) | 221,042 | 48.9 |
| Glenn R. Davis (R) | 211,016 | 46.7 |

Democratic Primary

| Henry W. Maier (D) | 169,999 | 66.9 |
| Elliot N. Walstead (D) | 83,801 | 33.0 |

1962 Republican Primary

| Alexander Wiley (R) | 347,155 | 80.3 |
| Arlyn F. Wollenburg (R) | 85,044 | 19.7 |

Democratic Primary

Gaylord Nelson (D) · · · 100.0

1968 Republican Primary

Jerris Leonard (R)	133,060	50.7
Robert I. Johnson (R)	73,344	28.0
James J. Donohue (R)	45,523	17.4

Democratic Primary

Gaylord Nelson (D) · · · 100.0

1974 Republican Primary

| Thomas E. Petri (R) | 130,523 | 85.2 |
| James A. Sigl (R) | 22,714 | 14.8 |

Democratic Primary

Gaylord Nelson (D) · · · 100.0

American Primary

Gerald L. McFarren (AM) · · · 100.0

1980 Republican Primary

Bob Kasten (R)	134,586	36.8
Terry J. Kohler (R)	106,270	29.0
Douglass Cofrin (R)	84,355	23.0
Russell A. Olson (R)	40,823	11.1

Democratic Primary

Gaylord Nelson (D) · · · 100.0

Constitution Primary

James P. Wickstrom (CONST) · · · 100.0

Libertarian Primary

Bervin J. Larson (LIBERT) · · · 100.0

Class 1

1958 Republican Primary

Frank A. Barrett (R) · · · 100.0

Democratic Primary

| Gale McGee (D) | 22,098 | 59.5 |
| Hepburn T. Armstrong (D) | 15,024 | 40.5 |

1964 Republican Primary

| John S. Wold (R) | 23,278 | 52.0 |
| K. L. Sailors (R) | 21,522 | 48.0 |

Democratic Primary

| Gale McGee (D) | 39,140 | 89.6 |
| I. Wayne Kinney (D) | 4,535 | 10.4 |

1970 Republican Primary

| John S. Wold (R) | 40,276 | 88.0 |
| Arthur E. Linde (R) | 5,479 | 12.0 |

Democratic Primary

| Gale McGee (D) | 32,956 | 79.6 |
| D. P. Svilar (D) | 8,448 | 20.4 |

1976 Republican Primary

Malcolm Wallop (R)	41,445	76.6
Nels T. Larson (R)	6,965	12.9
Doyle W. Henry (R)	5,727	10.6

Democratic Primary

Gale McGee (D) · · · 100.0

1982 Republican Primary

| Malcolm Wallop (R) | 61,650 | 80.9 |
| Richard Redland (R) | 14,543 | 19.1 |

Democratic Primary

Rodger McDaniel (D) · · · 100.0

Class 2

1960 Republican Primary

| E. Keith Thomson (R) | 31,596 | 69.1 |
| Frank A Barrett (R) | 13,380 | 29.2 |

Democratic Primary

Raymond B. Whitaker (D)	18,031	44.1
Velma Linford (D)	13,792	33.8
Carl A. Johnson (D)	5,370	13.1
Charles B. Chittim (D)	3,653	8.9

	Candidates	Votes	%
1962 [34]	**Special Republican Primary**		
	Milward L. Simpson (R)	30,124	*59.6*
	K. L. Sailors (R)	20,383	*40.4*
	Special Democratic Primary		
	J. J. Hickey (D)		*100.0*
1966	**Republican Primary**		
	Clifford P. Hansen (R)	40,102	*86.1*
	I. Wayne Kinney (R)	6,468	*13.9*
	Democratic Primary		
	Teno Roncalio (D)		*100.0*
1972	**Republican Primary**		
	Clifford P. Hansen (R)		*100.0*

	Candidates	Votes	%
1972	**Democratic Primary**		
	Mike Vinich (D)	16,148	*52.5*
	Doyle W. Henry (D)	5,642	*18.4*
	Patrick E. Shanklin (D)	4,665	*15.2*
	William E. Fritchell (D)	4,281	*13.9*
1978	**Republican Primary**		
	Alan K. Simpson (R)	37,332	*54.7*
	Hugh Binford (R)	20,768	*30.4*
	Gordon H. Barrows (R)	8,494	*12.4*
	Democratic Primary		
	Raymond B. Whitaker (D)	19,854	*47.6*
	Dean M. Larson (D)	11,039	*26.5*
	Charles Carroll (D)	10,797	*25.9*
1984	**Republican Primary**		
	Alan K. Simpson (R)	66,178	*87.9*
	Stephen Tarver (R)	9,137	*12.1*
	Democratic Primary		
	Victor A. Ryan (D)	17,608	*45.3*
	Al Hamburg (D)	12,088	*31.1*
	Michael J. Dee (D)	9,187	*23.6*

34. A special election was held in Wyoming to fill the unexpired term of E. Keith Thomson (R), who died after winning the Senate seat in 1960. J. J. Hickey (D), the incumbent governor, resigned in January 1961 and his successor appointed him to the seat, where he served until after the special election was held, in November 1962.

House Elections

"Interior of a Polling-booth; Arrangements for Receiving and Depositing Votes." *Frank Leslie's Illustrated Newspaper*, Nov. 17, 1860.

Library of Congress Photo No. USZ62-3495

House Elections

The authors of the Constitution of the United States recognized that the new government needed an executive to carry out the laws and a judiciary to resolve conflicts arising from them. But it was Congress, the lawmaking body, that the Founding Fathers designed to be the heart of the new Republic.

There was little question that the new Congress should be bicameral, in accordance with the practice of English Parliament and followed by most of the colonial governments and 10 of the 13 states. As George Mason put it during the Constitutional Convention in 1787, the minds of Americans were settled on two points: "an attachment to republican government [and] an attachment to more than one branch in the Legislature."

But little agreement existed over how the members of each of the houses should be chosen. The nationalists insisted that the new government rest on the consent of the people rather than the state legislatures. So they held it essential that at least "the first branch," or House, be elected popularly. The government "ought to possess . . . the mind or sense of the people at large," said James Wilson. *(Box, p. 679)*

Those who were suspicious of a national government preferred election to the House by the state legislatures. "The people immediately should have as little to do" with electing the government as possible, said Roger Sherman, because "they want information and are constantly liable to be misled." Election by the legislatures was twice defeated, however, and popular election for the House agreed to with only one state dissenting.

There was little support for the view that the people also should elect the Senate. Nor did the delegates to the Constitutional Convention think that the House should choose members of the Senate from among persons nominated by the state legislatures. Election of the Senate by the state legislatures was agreed to with only two states dissenting.

The People's Branch

The House of Representatives was to be the branch of government closest to the people. The members would be popularly elected; the terms of office would be two years so that the representatives would not lose touch with their homes; and the House would be a numerous branch, with members having relatively small constituencies.

The lower houses of the state legislatures served as models for the U.S. House. All the states had at least one chamber elected by popular vote. Ten states had two-house legislatures; Georgia, Pennsylvania and Vermont had popularly elected unicameral legislatures.

Article I, Section 2 of the Constitution set few requirements for election to the House: a representative had to be at least 25 years of age, have been a U.S. citizen for seven years and be an inhabitant of the state from which elected. *(Constitutional provisions for election to Congress, Appendix, p. 1126)*

The Constitution left the qualification of voters to the states, with one overriding principle: the qualifications could be no more restrictive than for the most numerous branch of each of the states' own legislatures. At first, property qualifications for voting were general. Five states required ownership of real estate, five mandated either real estate or other property and three required personal wealth or payment of public taxes. But the democratic trend of the early 19th century swept away most property qualifications, producing practically universal white male suffrage by the 1830s.

Over the years several changes in the Constitution also have broadened the franchise. The 15th Amendment (1870) extended the franchise to newly freed slaves; the 19th Amendment (1920) granted the right of suffrage to women; the 23rd Amendment (1961) extended the presidential vote to the District of Columbia; the 24th Amendment (1964) abolished the poll tax; and the 26th Amendment (1971) lowered the voting age to 18 from 21. In 1965 Congress passed the Voting Rights Act to remove barriers several states and localities had erected to keep blacks and other minorities from voting.

Two-Year Term

Many delegates to the Constitutional Convention preferred annual elections for the House, believing that the

---

Sources

Galloway, George B. *History of the House of Representatives.* 2nd ed. New York: Crowell, 1976.

Jones, Charles O. *Every Second Year.* Washington, D.C.: Brookings Institution, 1967.

body should reflect the wishes of the people as closely as possible. James Madison, however, argued for a three-year term, to allow representatives to gain knowledge and experience in national affairs as well as the affairs of their own localities. The delegates compromised on two-year terms.

The two-year term has not been universally popular. From time to time proposals have been made to extend the term to four years. The movement to extend the House term to four years last gained momentum in 1966 after President Lyndon B. Johnson urged the extension in his State of the Union message Jan. 12. His proposal received more applause than any other part of his speech.

However, the proposed amendment never emerged from committee. Opponents criticized the proposal's provision that the four-year term coincide with the presidential term. This would create a House of "coattail riders," critics said, and end the minority party's traditional gains in non-presidential election years. This fear of diminishing the independence of the House appeared to be the principal factor that killed the proposal. (*Election Results, Congress and the Presidency, 1856-1984, table, p. 1124*)

Size of the House

The size of the original House was written into Article I, Section 2 of the Constitution, along with directions to apportion the House according to population after the first census in 1790. Until the first census and apportionment, the 13 states were to have the following numbers of representatives: Connecticut, 5; Delaware, 1; Georgia, 3; Maryland, 6; Massachusetts, 8; New Hampshire, 3; New Jersey, 4; New York, 6; North Carolina, 5; Pennsylvania, 8; Rhode Island, 1; South Carolina, 5; Virginia, 10. This apportionment of seats — 65 in all — thus mandated by the Constitution remained in effect during the first and second Congresses (1789-93). (Seats allotted to North Carolina and Rhode Island were not filled until 1790, after those states had ratified the Constitution.)

By act of Congress (April 14, 1792), an apportionment measure provided for a ratio of one member for every 33,000 inhabitants and fixed the exact number of representatives to which each state was entitled. Congress enacted a new apportionment measure, including the mathematical formula to be used, every 10 years (except 1920) until a permanent law became effective in 1929. In 1911 Congress set the maximum size of the House at 435 members, which it reached after the 1970 census. (*Reapportionment, p. 683*)

Majority Elections

Five New England states at one time or another had a requirement for majority victory in congressional elections. The requirement provided that, to win a seat in the U.S. House, a candidate had to achieve more than 50 percent of the popular vote. If no candidate gained such a majority, new elections were held until one contender succeeded.

The provision was last invoked in Maine in 1844, in New Hampshire in 1845, in Vermont in 1866, in Massachusetts in 1848 and in Rhode Island in 1892. Sometimes, multiple races were necessary because none of the candidates could achieve the required majority. In the 4th District of Massachusetts in 1848-49, for example, 12 successive elections were held to try to choose a representative. None of them was successful, and the district remained unrepresented in the House during the 31st Congress (1849-51).

Multi-Member Districts

In the early days of the House several states had districts that elected more than one representative. For example, in 1824 Maryland's 5th District chose two representatives, while the remaining seven districts chose one each. And in Pennsylvania two districts (the 4th and 9th) elected three representatives each, and four districts (the 7th, 8th, 11th and 17th) chose two representatives each.

As late as 1838, New York still had as many as five multi-member districts — one (the 3rd) electing four members and four (the 8th, 17th, 22nd and 23rd) choosing two each. But the practice ended in 1842 when Congress enacted a law that "no one district may elect more than one Representative." The provision was a part of the reapportionment legislation following the census of 1840.

Elections in Odd-Numbered Years

Another practice that has faded out over the years was general elections in odd-numbered years for the House. Prior to ratification of the 20th (lame-duck) Amendment in 1933, regular sessions of Congress began in December of odd-numbered years. There were, therefore, 11 months in the odd-numbered years to elect members before the beginning of the congressional session. For example, in 1841 the following states held general elections for representative for the 27th Congress, convening that year: Alabama, Connecticut, Illinois, Indiana, Kentucky, Maryland, Mississippi, New Hampshire, North Carolina, Rhode Island, Tennessee and Virginia.

The practice continued until late in the century. In 1875 four states still chose their representatives in regular odd-year elections: California, Connecticut, Mississippi and New Hampshire. But in 1881 all members of the House were being chosen in even-numbered years (except for special elections to fill vacancies). One major problem encountered by states choosing their representatives in odd-numbered years was the possibility of a special session of the new Congress being called before the states' elections were held. Depending on the date of the election, a state could be unrepresented in the House. For example, California elected its U.S. House delegation to the 40th Congress (1867-69) on Sept. 4, 1867, in plenty of time for the first regular session scheduled for Dec. 2. But the Congress already had met in two special sessions — March 4 to March 20 and July 3 to July 20 — without any representation from California.

Southern Anomalies

Many of the anomalies in election of U.S. representatives occurred in the South. That region's experience with slavery, Civil War, Reconstruction and racial antagonisms created special problems for the regular electoral process.

Article I, Section 2 of the Constitution contained a formula for counting slaves for apportionment purposes: every five slaves would be counted as three persons. Thus, the total population of a state to be used in determining its congressional representation would be the free population plus three-fifths of the slave population.

After the Civil War and the emancipation of the slaves, blacks were fully counted for the purposes of apportionment. The 14th Amendment, ratified in 1868, required that apportionment be based on "the whole number of persons in each State...." On this basis, several Southern states tried to claim immediate additional representation on readmission to the Union. Tennessee, for example, chose an

Congressional Characteristics and Public Opinion

From the early days of the Republic until the present, the American public has criticized the qualifications of members of Congress. Through the years the House has received more criticism than the Senate, perhaps because senators were not elected by popular vote until 1914.

An early but still familiar critique of Congress was written in the 1830s by Alexis de Tocqueville, the French aristocrat, scholar and astute observer of America. After he had seen both chambers in session, Tocqueville wrote the following in his famous book of observations, *Democracy in America*:

> On entering the House of Representatives at Washington, one is struck by the vulgar demeanor of that great assembly. Often there is not a distinguished man in the whole number. Its members are almost all obscure individuals, whose names bring no associations to mind. They are mostly village lawyers, men in trade, or even persons belonging to the lower classes of society. In a country in which education is very general, it is said that the representatives of the people do not always know how to write correctly.
>
> At a few yards' distance is the door of the Senate, which contains within a small space a large proportion of the celebrated men of America. Scarcely an individual is to be seen in it who has not had an active and illustrious career: the Senate is composed of eloquent advocates, distinguished generals, wise magistrates, and statesmen of note, whose arguments would do honor to the most remarkable parliamentary debates of Europe.

Profile of 'Average' Member

A more modern — and charitable — description of the "average" member of Congress was presented in a popular textbook of the 1960s, *American Democracy*:

> He is a little over 50, has served in Congress for a number of years, and has had previous political experience before coming to Congress, such as membership in his state legislature. He has a college degree, is a lawyer by profession, a war veteran, and, before coming to Congress, was a well-known and popular member of the community. He has been reasonably successful in business or the practice of law, although not so successful that he is sacrificing a huge income in giving up his private occupation for a public job. Congress is clearly not an accurate cross section of the American people but neither is it a community of intellectuals and technicians.

The description was accurate, even to the exclusive use of "he." Although the composition had changed some by the mid-1980s, most members of Congress were male Caucasian and Christian, especially Protestant. Of the 535 members of Congress at the beginning of 1985, 24 were women, 20 were black (including the nonvoting delegate from the District of Columbia) and a scattering were of Hispanic, Asian or Middle Eastern heritage. Among religious groups, Protestants have comprised nearly three-fourths of the membership of both houses in recent years, although Roman Catholic members have become more numerous than members belonging to any single Protestant denomination. Catholics took the lead from Methodists in 1965 and retained it 20 years later. At the beginning of the 99th Congress, there were 144 Catholics. More than half of the Protestant members were affiliated with four denominations: Methodists led with 78, followed by 65 Episcopalians, 56 Presbyterians, and 47 Baptists. There were 38 Jewish members.

It was likely that a senator was a former House member but rare that a representative had served earlier in the Senate. Only two former presidents served in Congress after their terms in the White House: John Quincy Adams and Andrew Johnson. *(Members of Congress Who Became President, box, next page)*

Although by the mid-1980s the legal profession long had been dominant among members, most other occupations — including banking, business, journalism, farming and education — had been represented. The principal occupational groups underrepresented were the clergy and blue-collar workers. Scientists and physicians also had been underrepresented in Congress.

Although many members came from established professions, that did little to enhance their public image. Polls indicated that contemporary Americans retained a certain skepticism about the character of their politicians. A Gallup Poll taken in June 1979 found that only 19 percent of Americans approved of the way Congress was doing its job, while 61 percent disapproved. Another Gallup survey released nine months later showed that 78 percent of Americans believed that some members of Congress won election by using "unethical and illegal methods in their campaigns." In addition, four out of 10 persons surveyed believed that at least 20 percent of the members of Congress employed questionable methods to get elected. This poll was taken after disclosure of what came to be known as the Abscam affair, in which a few members were alleged to have taken bribes from undercover FBI agents posing as wealthy Arabs in return for political and legislative favors. Subsequent to the poll, one senator and six members of the House were convicted for their parts in the scandal.

Another Gallup Poll, released in August 1983, offered further evidence of the poor public image of politicians in the United States. When asked how the respondents would rate members of the House and Senate in the areas of honesty and ethical standards, only 17 percent rated senators as having very high or high standards and 14 percent rated members of the House similarly. In contrast, 29 percent of the respondents expressed a low or very low opinion of senators in these areas and 38 percent expressed the same low opinions about House members.

Members of Congress Who Became President

When Gerald R. Ford became president in 1974, he brought to 23 the number of presidents who had served previously in the House of Representatives or the Senate or both.

Following is a list of these presidents and the chambers in which they served. Three other presidents — George Washington, John Adams and Thomas Jefferson — had served in the Continental Congress, as had James Madison and James Monroe.

James A. Garfield was elected to the Senate in January 1880 for a term beginning March 4, 1881, but declined to accept in December 1880 because he had been elected president. John Quincy Adams served in the House for 17 years after his term as president, and Andrew Johnson returned to the Senate five months before he died.

House Only

James Madison
James K. Polk
Millard Fillmore
Abraham Lincoln
Rutherford B. Hayes
James A. Garfield
William McKinley
Gerald R. Ford

Senate Only

James Monroe
John Quincy Adams
Martin Van Buren
Benjamin Harrison
Warren G. Harding
Harry S Truman

Both Chambers

Andrew Jackson
William Henry Harrison
John Tyler
Franklin Pierce
James Buchanan

Andrew Johnson
John F. Kennedy
Lyndon B. Johnson
Richard Nixon

Source: *Biographical Directory of the American Congress, 1774-1971.* Washington, D.C.: Government Printing Office, 1971.

extra U.S. representative, electing him at large in 1868, and claimed that inasmuch as its slaves were now free the state had added to its apportionment population a sufficient number to give it nine instead of eight representatives. Virginia took similar action in 1869 and 1870; South Carolina did it in both 1868 and 1870. But the House declined to seat the additional representatives, declaring that states would have to await the regular reapportionment following the 1870 census for any changes in their representation.

Part of the 14th Amendment ratified in 1868 affected — or was intended to affect — Southern representation in the House. The second paragraph of the amendment states, "When the right to vote at any election for the choice of electors for President and Vice President of the United States, Representatives in Congress, the executive and judicial officers of a State, or the members of the legislature thereof, is denied to any of the male inhabitants of such state, being twenty-one years of age, and citizens of the United States, or in any other way abridged, except for participation in rebellion, or other crime, the basis of representation [in the U.S. House] shall be reduced in the proportion which the number of such male citizens shall bear to the whole number of male citizens twenty-one years of age in such state."

Designed as a club to force the South to accept black voting participation, the provision was incorporated in the reapportionment legislation of 1872. According to the legislation, the number of representatives from any state interfering with the exercise of the right to vote was to be reduced in proportion to the number of inhabitants of voting age whose right to go to the polls was denied or abridged.

But the provision never was put into effect because of the difficulty of determining the exact number of persons whose right to vote was being abridged and also because of the decline of Northern enthusiasm for forcing Reconstruction policies on the South.

As an alternative to invoking the difficult 14th Amendment provision, Congress often considered election challenges filed against members from the South. When Republicans were in control of the House, several Democrats from the former Confederate states found themselves unseated, often on charges that black voting rights were abused in their districts.

During the 47th Congress (1881-83) five Democrats from former Confederate states were unseated; in the 51st Congress (1889-91), six; and in the 54th Congress (1895-97), seven.

Special Elections

When a vacancy occurs in the House, the usual procedure is for the governor of the affected state to call a special election. Such elections may be held at any time throughout the year, and there are usually several during each two-year Congress.

At times there are delays in the calling of special elections. One of the longest periods in recent years when a congressional district went unrepresented occurred in 1959-60. On April 28, 1959, Rep. James G. Polk, D (1931-41, 1949-59), of the Ohio 6th District died. But not until November 1960 was there an election to replace him. It was held simultaneously with the general election, and the winner, Ward M. Miller, R, served only the two months remaining in the term. For the full term, both Republicans and Democrats nominated candidates different from those who ran for the short term.

In the days of the lame-duck sessions of Congress, elections for the remainder of a term quite often were held simultaneously with the general election, because the session following the election was an important working meeting that lasted until March 4.

However, since the passage of the 20th Amendment and the ending of most lame-duck sessions, elections for the remaining two months of a term have become less common. Miller, for example, never was sworn in because Congress was not in session during the period when he was waiting to serve as a representative.

Usually states are more prompt in holding special House elections than was Ohio in 1959-60. One of the most rapid instances of succession occurred in Texas' 10th District in 1963. Democratic representative Homer Thornberry (1949-63) submitted his resignation on Sept. 26, 1963, to take effect Dec. 20. On the strength of Thornberry's post-dated resignation, a special election was held in his district — the first election was held Nov. 9 and the runoff on Dec. 17. The winner, J. J. Pickle, D, was ready to take his seat as soon as Thornberry stepped down. He was sworn in the next day, Dec. 21, 1963.

Bibliography

Books

Bryce, James. *The American Commonwealth.* 1922. Reprint. New York: AMS Press.

Commons, John R. *Proportional Representation.* 2nd ed. Reprint. New York: A. M. Kelley, 1907.

Congressional Quarterly. *Congressional Districts in the 1980s.* Washington, D.C.: Congressional Quarterly, 1983.

Congressional Quarterly. *Guide to Congress.* 3rd ed. Washington, D.C.: Congressional Quarterly, 1982.

Davidson, Roger H., and Walter J. Oleszek. *Congress and Its Members.* 2nd ed. Washington, D.C.: CQ Press, 1985.

Farrand, Max. *Records of the Federal Convention of 1787.* 4 vols. New Haven, Conn.: Yale University Press, 1967.

Galloway, George B. *History of the House of Representatives.* 2nd. ed. New York: Crowell, 1976.

Grofman, Bernard, et al. *Reapportionment Policy.* Urbana, Ill.: Policy Studies Organization, University of Illinois at Urbana-Champagne, 1981.

Hacker, Andrew. *Congressional Districting.* Washington, D.C.: Brookings, 1963.

Luce, Robert. *Legislative Principles.* 1930. Reprint. New York: Da Capo Press, 1971.

McPhee, William N., and William A. Glasser, eds. *Public Opinion and Congressional Elections.* 1962. Reprint. Westport, Conn.: Greenwood Press, 1981.

Martis, Kenneth C. *The Historical Atlas of United States Congressional Districts 1789-1983.* New York: The Free Press, 1982.

Matteson, David M. *The Organization of the Government Under the Constitution.* New York: Da Capo Press, 1970.

O'Rourke, Timothy. *The Impact of Reapportionment.* New Brunswick, N. J.: Transaction Books, 1980.

Polsby, Nelson W., ed. *Reapportionment in the 1970s.* Berkeley, Calif.: University of California Press, 1971.

Scammon, Richard M. *America Votes: A Handbook of Contemporary Election Statistics.* vols. 1 and 2. New York: Macmillan, 1956, 1958. *America Votes.* vols. 3-5. Pittsburgh: University of Pittsburgh, 1959, 1962 and 1964. *America Votes.* vols. 6-11. Washington, D.C.: Congressional Quarterly, 1966-1975.

———, and Alice V. McGillivray. *America Votes.* vols. 12-15. Washington, D.C.: Congressional Quarterly, 1977-1983.

Schmeckebier, Laurence F. *Congressional Apportionment.* 1941. Reprint. Westport, Conn.: Greenwood Press, 1976.

Articles

Abramowitz, Alan I. "A Comparison of Voting for U.S. Senator and Representative in 1978." *American Political Science Review* 74 (September 1980): 633-640.

Alford, John R., and John R. Hibbing. "Increased Incumbency Advantage in the House." *Journal of Politics* 43 (November 1981): 1042-1061.

Baker, Gordon E. "Redistricting in the Seventies: The Political Thicket Deepens." *National Civic Review* (June 1972): 277-285.

Bond, Jon R. "The Influence of Constituency Diversity on Electoral Competition in Voting for Congress, 1974-1978." *Legislative Studies Quarterly* 8 (May 1983): 201-217.

Born, Richard. "Generational Replacement and the Growth of Incumbent Reelection Margins in the U.S. House." *American Political Science Review* 73 (September 1979): 811-817.

———. "House Incumbents and Inter-Election Vote Change." *Journal of Politics* 39 (November 1977): 1008-1034.

———. "The Influence of House Primary Election Divisiveness on General Election Margins, 1962-1976." *Journal of Politics* 43 (August 1981): 640-661.

Brookshire, Robert G., and Dean F. Duncan III. "Congressional Career Patterns and Party Systems." *Legislative Studies Quarterly* 8 (February 1983): 29-43.

Burnstein, Paul. "Party Balance, Replacement of Legislators, and Federal Government Expenditures, 1941-1976." *Western Political Quarterly* 32 (June 1979): 203-208.

Brosius, M. "Should the Number of the Federal House of Representatives Be Limited to Its Present Number?" *Arena* (October 1892): 569-577.

Chafee, Zechariah. "Congressional Reapportionment." *Harvard Law Review* (1929): 1015-1047.

Collie, Melissa P. "Incumbency, Electoral Safety and Turnover in the House of Representatives." *American Political Science Review* 75 (March 1981): 119-131.

"Congress in the Thicket: The Congressional Redistricting Bill of 1967." *George Washington Law Review* 36 (1967): 224-234.

"Congressional Reapportionment." *Forum* (January 1901): 568-577.

"Congressional Redistricting: One Man, One Vote Demands Near Mathematical Precision." *De Paul Law Review* (Autumn 1969): 152-171.

"Constitutional Right to Congressional Districts of Equal Population." *Yale Law Journal* (November 1946): 127-139.

Dixon, Robert G. "Apportionment Standards and Judicial Power." *Notre Dame Lawyer* (June 1963): 367-400.

———. "Reapportionment in the Supreme Court and Congress: The Constitutional Struggle for Fair Representation." *Michigan Law Review* (December 1964): 209-242.

"Equal Representation and the Weighted Vote Alternative." *Yale Law Review* (Spring 1970): 311-321.

Gannett, H. "New Congressional Apportionment." *Forum* (January 1901): 568-577.

Gazell, James A. "One Man, One Vote: Its Long Germination." *Western Political Quarterly* (September 1970): 445-462.

Goodman, Paul. "Social Status of Party Leadership: The House of Representatives, 1779-1804." *William and Mary Quarterly* 25 (1958): 465-474.

Gross, Donald A. "Representative Styles and Legislative Behavior." *Western Political Quarterly* 31 (September 1978): 359-371.

Hazel, H. R. "Reapportionment and Representative Government: Legislative and Congressional Redistricting." *Greater Cleveland* (December 1944): 94-102.

Irwin, William P. "Representation and Apportionment." *Parliamentary Affairs* (Summer 1968): 226-245.

———. "Representation and Election: The Reapportionment Cases in Retrospect." *Michigan Law Review* 67 (1969): 729-754.

James, E. J. "First Apportionment of Federal Representatives in the United States." *Annals of the American Academy of Political and Social Science* (January

1897): 1-41.

Jones, Charles O. "Inter-Party Competition for Congressional Seats." *Western Political Quarterly* (September 1964): 461-476.

Katz, Ellis. "Apportionment and Majority Rule." *Publius* (1971): 141-161.

Keifer, J. W. "Equality of Representation in the Congress." *Independent* (June 21, 1906): 1479.

Kuklinski, James H., and Darrell M. West. "Economic Expectations and Voting Behavior in the United States House and Senate Elections." *American Political Science Review* 75 (June 1981): 436-447.

"Legislative Reapportionment." *Law and Contemporary Problems* (Spring 1952): 253-469.

Lehne, Richard. "Shape of the Future: Suburbs Seen as Biggest Bloc in Congress for the First Time after 1970 Reapportionment." *National Civic Review* (September 1969): 351-355.

Leiserson, Avery. "National Party Organization and Congressional Districts." *Western Political Quarterly* (September 1963): 33-49.

Linton, Robert N. "Further Exploration in the Political Thicket: The Gerrymander and the Constitution." *Loyola Law Review* (October 1973): 1-47.

"The Method and Procedure of the Apportionment of Representatives in the United States Congress." *Estadistica* (June 1943): 94-102.

Mann, Thomas E., and Raymond E. Wolfinger. "Candidates and Parties in Congressional Elections." *American Political Science Review* 74 (September 1980): 617-632.

Meyers, B. F. "Single Vote in Congressional Elections." *North American Review* (June 1890): 782-785.

More, W. "One Man, One Vote: Virginia's Democratic Primary." *America*, July 30, 1966, 110.

Noragon, Jack L. "Congressional Redistricting and Population Composition, 1964-1970." *Midwest Journal of Political Science* (May 1972): 295-302.

"Note on Reapportionment." *Harvard Law Review* (April 1966): 374-379.

Paullin, C. O. "First Elections Under the Constitution." *Iowa Journal of History and Politics* (January 1904): 28.

Payne, James L. "Career Intentions and Electoral Performance of Members of the U.S. House." *Legislative Studies Quarterly* 7 (February 1982): 93-99.

———. "The Personal Electoral Advantage of House Incumbents, 1936-1976." *American Politics Quarterly* 8 (October 1980): 449-464.

Peel, R. V. "Political Implications of the 1950 Census of Population." *Western Political Quarterly* (December 1950): 615-619.

"Reapportionment." *Harvard Law Review* 79 (1966): 1226-1287.

"The Reapportionment of the United States Congress." *American Political Science Review* (March 1951): 153-157.

"Representation in the Federal and State Legislatures: Unequal Voting, A Challenge to Democracy." *Labor's Economic Review* (December 1956): 89-100.

Robeck, Bruce W. "State Legislator Candidacies for the U.S. House: Prospect for Success." *Legislative Studies Quarterly* 7 (November 1982): 507-514.

Rohde, David W. "Risk-Bearing and Progressive Ambition: The Case of the United States House of Representatives." *American Journal of Political Science* 23 (February 1979): 1-26.

Roll, C. W. "We, Some of the People: Apportionment in the Thirteen State Conventions Ratifying the Constitution." *American History* (June 1969): 21-40.

Sigelman, Lee. "Special Elections to the U. S. House: Some Descriptive Generalizations." *Legislative Studies Quarterly* (November 1981): 577-588.

Stone, Walter J. "The Dynamics of Constituency: Electoral Control in the House." *American Politics Quarterly* 8 (October 1980): 399-424.

Sullivan, John L. "Electoral Choice and Popular Control of Policy: The Case of the 1966 House Elections." *American Political Science Review* (December 1972): 1256-1268.

Uslaner, Eric M. "Party Reform and Electoral Disaggregation: A Paradox in Congress." *Policy Studies Journal* 5 (Summer 1977): 454-459.

Willcox, W. F. "Apportionment of Representatives." *American Economic Review* (March 1916): 3-6.

———. "Apportionment of Representatives." *Science* (June 8, 1928): 385-389.

———. "Methods of Apportioning Seats in the House of Representatives." *American Statistical Association Journal* (December 1954): 685-695.

Wattenberg, Martin P. "From Parties to Candidates: Examining the Role of the Media." *Public Opinion Quarterly* 46 (Summer 1982): 216-227.

Wollock, Andrea J. "Reapportionment Now." *State Legislatures* (January 1982): 7-13.

Wright, John R., and Richard G. Niemi. "Perceptions of Candidates' Issue Positions." *Political Behavior* 5 (1983): 209-223.

Reapportionment and Redistricting

Reapportionment, the redistribution of the 435 seats in the U.S. House of Representatives among the states to reflect shifts in population, and redistricting, the redrawing of congressional district lines within each state, are among the most important processes in the U.S. political system. They help determine whether the House will be dominated by Democrats or Republicans, liberals or conservatives, and whether racial or ethnic minorities receive fair representation.

Reapportionment and redistricting occur every 10 years on the basis of the decennial population census. States whose populations grew quickly over the previous 10 years gain congressional seats, while those that lost population or grew much more slowly than the national average lose seats. The number of House delegates for the rest of the states remains the same.

The states that gain or lose seats must make extensive changes in their congressional maps. Even those states with stable delegations must make modifications that account for population shifts within their boundaries in accordance with Supreme Court "one-person, one-vote" rulings.

Despite their importance to the political process, reapportionment and redistricting draw little interest from the general public. This is ironic, wrote Andrea J. Wollock in the January 1982 issue of *State Legislatures*, because reapportionment is not only a "supremely important" political issue but also "a source of unsurpassed political drama and intrigue." Partisan interests are enhanced, personal ambitions of powerful politicians are furthered. Incumbents are protected or politically crippled. Tempers flare and fists fly, as they did during a redistricting debate in the Illinois Legislature in 1981.

Among the many unique features to emerge in the remarkable nation-creating endeavor of 1787 was a national legislative body whose membership was to be elected by the people and apportioned on the basis of population. In keeping with the nature of the Constitution, however, only fundamental rules and regulations were provided. How to interpret and implement the instructions contained in the document were left to future generations.

Within this flexible framework, many questions soon arose concerning the House of Representatives. How large was it to be? What mathematical formula was to be used in calculating the distribution of seats among the various states? Were the representatives to be elected at large or by districts? If by districts, what standards should be used in fixing their boundaries? The Congress and the courts have been wrestling with these questions for almost 200 years.

Until the mid-20th century, such questions generally remained in the hands of the legislators. But with growing concentration of the population in urban areas, variations in population among congressional districts became more pronounced. Efforts to persuade Congress to redress the grievance of heavily populated but under-represented areas proved unsuccessful. Rural legislators were so intent on preventing power from slipping out of their control that they managed to block reapportionment of the House following the census of 1920.

Not long afterward, litigants tried to persuade the Supreme Court to order the states to revise congressional district boundaries in line with population shifts. After initial failure, a breakthrough occurred in 1964 in the case of *Wesberry v. Sanders*. The court declared that the Constitution required that "as nearly as practicable, one man's vote in a congressional election is to be worth as much as another's."

In the years that followed the court repeatedly reaffirmed its "one-person, one-vote" requirement. In *Karcher v. Daggett* in 1983 the court held that no deviation from that principle was permissible unless the state proved that the population variation was necessary to achieve some legitimate goal. This ruling immediately drew fire from those who thought it would allow states to ignore several other traditional factors involved in redistricting — such as compactness of the district or integrity of county and city lines — in their quest for districts of precisely equal populations.

Early History

Modern legislative bodies are descended from the councils of feudal lords and gentry that medieval kings summoned for the purpose of raising revenues and armies. These councils did not represent a king's subjects in any modern sense. They represented certain groups of subjects, such as the nobility, the clergy, the landed gentry and town merchants. Representation was by interest groups and bore no relation to equal representation for equal numbers of people. In England, the king's council became Parliament, with the higher nobility and clergy making up the House of Lords and representatives of the gentry and merchants making up the House of Commons.

Beginning as little more than administrative and advi-

sory arms of the throne, royal councils in time developed into lawmaking bodies and acquired powers that eventually eclipsed those of the monarchs they served. The power struggle in England climaxed during the Cromwellian period when the king was executed and a "benevolent" dictatorship was set up under Oliver Cromwell. By 1800 Parliament was clearly the superior branch of government.

During the 18th and early 19th centuries, as the power of Parliament grew, the English became increasingly concerned about the "representativeness" of their system of apportionment. Newly developing industrial cities had no more representation in the House of Commons than small, almost-deserted country towns. Small constituencies were bought and sold. Men from these empty "rotten boroughs" often were sent to Parliament representing a single "patron" landowner or clique of wealthy men. It was not until the Reform Act of 1832 that Parliament curbed such excesses and turned toward a representative system based on population.

The growth of the powers of Parliament as well as the development of English ideas of representation during the 17th and 18th centuries had a profound effect on the colonists in America. Representative assemblies were unifying forces behind the breakaway of the colonies from England and the establishment of the newly independent country.

Colonists in America, generally modeling their legislatures after England's, used both population and land units as bases for apportionment. Patterns of early representation varied. "Nowhere did representation bear any uniform relation to the number of electors. Here and there the factor of size had been crudely recognized," Robert Luce pointed out in his book *Legislative Principles.*

In New England, the town usually was the basis for representation. In the Middle Atlantic region, the county frequently was used. Virginia used the county with additional representation for specified cities. In many areas, towns and counties were fairly equal in population. Thus territorial representation afforded roughly equal representation for equal numbers of people. Delaware's three counties, for example, were of almost equal population and had the same representation in the Legislature. But in Virginia the disparity was enormous (from 951 people in one county to 22,015 in another). Thomas Jefferson criticized the state's constitution on the ground that "among those who share the representation, the shares are unequal."

The Continental Congress, with representation from every colony, proclaimed in the Declaration of Independence in 1776 that governments derive "their just powers from the consent of the governed" and that "the right of representation in the legislature" is an "inestimable right" of the people. The Constitutional Convention of 1787 included representatives from all the states. However, in neither of these bodies were the state delegations or voting powers proportional to population.

Intentions of Founding Fathers

Andrew Hacker, in his book *Congressional Districting,* said that to understand what the framers of the Constitution had in mind when they drew up the section concerning the House of Representatives, it was necessary to study closely several sources: the Constitution itself, the recorded discussions and debates at the Constitutional Convention, *The Federalist Papers* (essays written by Alexander Hamilton, John Jay and James Madison in defense of the Constitution) and the deliberations of the states' ratifying conventions.

The Constitution declares only that each state is to be allotted a certain number of representatives. It does not state specifically that congressional districts must be equal or nearly equal in population. Nor does it require specifically that a state create districts at all. However, it seems clear that the first clause of Article I, Section 2, providing that House members should be chosen "by the people of the several states," indicated that the House of Representatives, in contrast to the Senate, was to represent people rather than states. "It follows," Hacker wrote, "that if the states are to have equal representation in the upper chamber, then individuals are to be equally represented in the lower body."

The third clause of Article I, Section 2 provided that congressional apportionment among the states must be according to population. But Hacker argued that "there is little point in giving the states congressmen 'according to their respective numbers' if the states do not redistribute the members of their delegations on the same principle. For representatives are not the property of the states, as are the senators, but rather belong to the people who happen to reside within the boundaries of those states. Thus, each citizen has a claim to be regarded as a political unit equal in value to his neighbors." In this and similar ways, constitutional scholars have argued the case for single-member congressional districts deduced from the wording of the Constitution itself.

The issue of unequal representation arose only once during debate in the Constitutional Convention. The occasion was Madison's defense of Article I, Section 4 of the proposed Constitution, giving Congress the power to override state regulations on "the times . . . and manner" of holding elections for members of Congress. Madison's argument related to the fact that many state legislatures of the time were badly malapportioned: "The inequality of the representation in the legislatures of particular states would produce a like inequality in their representation in the national legislature, as it was presumable that the counties having the power in the former case would secure it to themselves in the latter."

The implication was that states would create congressional districts and that unequal districting was undesirable and should be prevented.

Madison made this interpretation even more clear in his contributions to *The Federalist Papers.* Arguing in favor of the relatively small size of the projected House of Representatives, he wrote in *No. 56:* "Divide the largest state into ten or twelve districts and it will be found that there will be no peculiar local interests . . . which will not be within the knowledge of the Representative of the district."

In the same paper, Madison said: "The Representatives of each state will not only bring with them a considerable knowledge of its laws, and a local knowledge of their respective districts, but will probably in all cases have been members, and may even at the very time be members, of the state legislature, where all the local information and interests of the state are assembled, and from whence they may easily be conveyed by a very few hands into the legislature of the United States." And, finally, in *Federalist Paper No. 57* Madison stated that ". . . each Representative of the United States will be elected by five or six thousand citizens." In making these arguments, Madison seems to have assumed that all or most representatives would be elected by districts rather than at large.

In the states' ratifying conventions, the grant to Con-

gress by Article I, Section 4 of ultimate jurisdiction over the "times, places and manner of holding elections" (except the places of choosing senators) held the attention of many delegates. There were differences over the merits of this section, but no justification of unequal districts was prominently used to attack the grant of power. Further evidence that individual districts were the intention of the Founding Fathers was given in the New York ratifying convention, when Alexander Hamilton said: "The natural and proper mode of holding elections will be to divide the state into districts in proportion to the number to be elected. This state will consequently be divided at first into six."

From his study of the sources relating to the question of congressional districting, Hacker concluded: "There is, then, a good deal of evidence that those who framed and ratified the Constitution intended that the House of Representatives have as its constituency a public in which the votes of all citizens were of equal weight.... The House of Representatives was designed to be a popular chamber, giving the same electoral power to all who had the vote. And the concern of Madison ... that districts be equal in size was an institutional step in the direction of securing this democratic principle."

Reapportionment of Seats

Article I, Section 2, Clause 3 of the Constitution laid down the basic rules for apportionment and reapportionment of seats in the House of Representatives: "Representatives ... shall be apportioned among the several States which may be included within this Union, according to their respective Numbers, which shall be determined by adding to the whole Number of free Persons, including those Bound to Service for a Term of Years, and excluding Indians not taxed, three-fifths of all other Persons. The actual Enumeration shall be made within three Years after the first Meeting of the Congress of the United States, and within every subsequent Term of Ten years, in such manner as they shall by Law direct. The number of Representatives shall not exceed one for every thirty Thousand, but each State shall have at least one Representative...." *(Constitutional provisions on elections, Appendix, p. 1126)*

The Constitution made the first apportionment, which was to remain in effect until the first census was taken. No reliable figures on the population were available at the time. The 13 states were allocated the following numbers of representatives: New Hampshire, three; Massachusetts, eight; Rhode Island and Providence Plantations, one; Connecticut, five; New York, six; New Jersey, four; Pennsylvania, eight; Delaware, one; Maryland, six; Virginia, 10; North Carolina, five; South Carolina, five; and Georgia, three. The apportionment of seats — 65 in all — thus mandated by the Constitution remained in effect during the 1st and 2nd Congresses (1789-93).

Apparently realizing that apportionment of the House was likely to become a major bone of contention, the 1st Congress submitted to the states a proposed constitutional amendment containing a formula to be used in future reapportionments. The amendment, which was not ratified, provided that following the taking of a decennial census there would be one representative for every 30,000 persons until the House membership reached 100, "after which the proportion shall be so regulated by Congress that there shall be not less than 100 representatives, nor less than one representative for every 40,000 persons, until the

number of representatives shall amount to 200, after which the proportion shall be so regulated by Congress, that there shall not be less than 200 representatives, nor more than one representative for every 50,000 persons."

First Apportionment by Congress

The states' refusal to ratify the reapportionment-formula amendment forced Congress to enact apportionment legislation after the first census was taken in 1790. The first apportionment bill was sent to the president on March 23, 1792. Washington sent the bill back to Congress without his signature — the first presidential veto.

The bill had incorporated the constitutional minimum of 30,000 as the size of each district. But the population of each state was not a simple multiple of 30,000. Significant fractions were left over when the number of people in each state was divided by 30,000. Thus, for example, Vermont was found to be entitled to 2.851 representatives, New Jersey to 5.98 and Virginia to 21.018. Therefore, a formula had to be found that would deal in the fairest possible manner with unavoidable variations from exact equality.

Accordingly, Congress proposed in the first apportionment bill to distribute the members on a fixed ratio of one representative for each 30,000 inhabitants, and give an additional member to each state with a fraction exceeding one-half. Washington's veto was based on the belief that eight states would receive more than one representative for each 30,000 persons under this formula.

A motion to override the veto was unsuccessful. A new bill meeting the president's objections was introduced April 9, 1792, and approved April 14. The act provided for a ratio of one member for every 33,000 inhabitants and fixed the exact number of representatives to which each state was entitled. The total membership of the House was to be 105. In dividing the population of the various states by 33,000, all remainders were to be disregarded. This was known as the method of rejected fractions; it was devised by Thomas Jefferson.

Reapportionment by Jefferson's Method

Jefferson's method of reapportionment resulted in great inequalities among districts. A Vermont district would contain 42,766 inhabitants, a New Jersey district 35,911 and a Virginia district only 33,187. Emphasis was placed on what was considered the ideal size of a congressional district rather than on what the size of the House ought to be. This method was in use until 1840.

The reapportionment act based on the census of 1800 continued the ratio of 33,000, which provided a House of 141 members. Debate on the third apportionment bill began in the House on Nov. 22, 1811, and the bill was sent to the president on Dec. 21. The ratio was fixed at 35,000, yielding a House of 181 members. Following the 1820 census, Congress approved an apportionment bill providing a ratio of 40,000 inhabitants per district. The sum of the quotas for the various states produced a House of 213 members.

The act of May 22, 1832, fixed the ratio at 47,700, resulting in a House of 240 members. Dissatisfaction with the method in use continued, and Daniel Webster launched a vigorous attack against it. He urged adoption of a method that would assign an additional representative to each state with a large fraction. His approach to the reapportionment process was outlined in a report he submitted to Congress in 1832: "The Constitution, therefore, must be understood not as enjoining an absolute relative equality — because

that would be demanding an impossibility — but as requiring of Congress to make the apportionment of Representatives among the several states according to their respective numbers, *as near as may be*. That which cannot be done perfectly must be done in a manner as near perfection as can be.... In such a case approximation becomes a rule."

Following the 1840 census, Congress adopted a reapportionment method similar to that advocated by Webster. The method fixed a ratio of one representative for every 70,680 persons. This figure was reached by deciding on a fixed size of the House in advance (223), dividing that figure into the total national "representative population" and using the result (70,680) as the fixed ratio. The population of each state was then divided by this ratio to find the number of its representatives and the states were assigned an additional representative for each fraction over one-half. Under this method the actual size of the House dropped. *(Congressional apportionment, box, p. 688)*

The modified reapportionment formula adopted by Congress in 1842 was found to be more satisfactory than the previous method, but another change was made following the census of 1850. The new system was proposed by Rep. Samuel F. Vinton of Ohio and became known as the Vinton method.

Vinton Apportionment Formula

Under the Vinton formula, Congress first fixed the size of the House and then distributed the seats. The total qualifying population of the country was divided by the desired number of representatives, and the resulting number became the ratio of population to each representative. The population of each state was divided by this ratio and each state received the number of representatives equal to the whole number in the quotient for that state. Then, to reach the required size of the House, additional representatives were assigned based on the remaining fractions, beginning with the state having the largest fraction. This procedure differed from the 1842 method only in the last step, which assigned one representative to every state having a fraction larger than one-half.

Proponents of the Vinton method pointed out that it had the distinct advantage of making it possible to fix the size of the House in advance and to take into account at least the largest fractions. The concern of the House turned from the ideal size of a congressional district to the ideal size of the House itself.

Under the 1842 reapportionment formula, the exact size of the House could not be fixed in advance. If every state with a fraction over one-half were given an additional representative, the House might wind up with a few more or a few less than the desired number. However, under the Vinton method, only states with the largest fractions were given additional House members and only up to the desired total size of the House.

Reapportionments by Vinton Method

Six reapportionments were carried out under the Vinton method. The 1850 census Act contained three provisions not included in any previous law. First, it required reapportionment not only after the census of 1850 but also after all the subsequent censuses; second, it purported to fix the size of the House permanently at 233 members; and third, it provided in advance for an automatic apportionment by the secretary of the interior under the method prescribed in the act.

Following the census of 1860, according to the provisions of the act passed a decade before, an automatic reapportionment was to be carried out by the Interior Department. However, because the size of the House was to remain at the 1850 level, some states faced loss of representation and others would gain less than they expected. To avert that possibility, an act was approved March 4, 1862, increasing the size of the House to 241 and giving an extra representative to eight states — Illinois, Iowa, Kentucky, Minnesota, Ohio, Pennsylvania, Rhode Island and Vermont.

Apportionment legislation following the 1870 census contained several new provisions. The act of Feb. 2, 1872, fixed the size of the House at 283, with the proviso that the number should be increased if new states were admitted. A supplemental act of May 30, 1872, assigned one additional representative each to Alabama, Florida, Indiana, Louisiana, New Hampshire, New York, Pennsylvania, Tennessee and Vermont.

Another section of the 1872 act provided that no state should thereafter be admitted "without having the necessary population to entitle it to at least one representative fixed by this bill." That provision was found to be unenforceable because no Congress can bind a succeeding Congress. Moreover, no ratio was fixed by the act, although the basis on which the representatives were assigned was 131,425. In 1890 Idaho was admitted with a population of 84,385 and Wyoming with a population of 60,705.

With the Reconstruction era at its height in the South, the reapportionment legislation of 1872 reflected the desire of Congress to enforce Section 2 of the new 14th Amendment. That section attempted to protect the right of blacks to vote by providing for reduction of representation in the House of a state that interfered with the exercise of that right. The number of representatives of such a state was to be reduced in proportion to the number of inhabitants of voting age whose right to go to the polls was denied or abridged. The reapportionment bill repeated the language of the section, but it never was put into effect because of the difficulty of determining the exact number of persons whose right to vote was being abridged.

The reapportionment act of Feb. 25, 1882, provided for a House of 325 members, with additional members for any new states admitted to the Union. No new apportionment provisions were added. The acts of Feb. 7, 1891, and Jan. 16, 1901, were routine as far as apportionment was concerned. The 1891 measure provided for a House of 356 members, and the 1901 statute increased the number to 386.

Despite the apparent advantages of the Vinton method, certain difficulties revealed themselves as the formula was applied. Zechariah Chafee Jr. of the Harvard Law School summarized these problems in an article in the *Harvard Law Review* in 1929. The method, he pointed out, suffered from what he called the "Alabama paradox." Under that aberration, an increase in the total size of the House might be accompanied by an actual loss of a seat by some states, even though there had been no corresponding change in population. This phenomenon first appeared in tables prepared for Congress in 1881, which gave Alabama eight members in a House of 299 but only seven members in a House of 300. It could even happen that the state which lost a seat was the one state that had expanded in population, while all the others had fewer persons.

Chafee concluded from his study of the Vinton method: "Thus, it is unsatisfactory to fix the ratio of popu-

lation per Representative before seats are distributed. Either the size of the House comes out haphazard, or, if this be determined in advance, the absurdities of the 'Alabama paradox' vitiate the apportionment. Under present conditions, it is essential to determine the size of the House in advance; the problem thereafter is to distribute the required number of seats among the several states as nearly as possible in proportion to their respective populations so that no state is treated unfairly in comparison with any other state."

Maximum Membership of House

On Aug. 8, 1911, the membership of the House was fixed at 433. Provision was made in the reapportionment act of that date for the addition of one representative each from Arizona and New Mexico, which were expected to become states in the near future. Thus, the size of the House reached 435, where it has remained up to the present with the exception of a brief period (1959-63) when the admission of Alaska and Hawaii raised the total temporarily to 437.

Limiting the size of the House amounted to recognition that the body soon would expand to unmanageable proportions if Congress continued the practice of adding new seats every 10 years, to match population gains without depriving any state of its existing representation. Agreement on a fixed number made the task of reapportionment all the more difficult when the population not only increased but became much more mobile. Population shifts brought Congress up hard against the politically painful necessity of taking seats away from slow-growing states to give the fast-growing states adequate representation.

A new mathematical calculation was adopted for the reapportionment following the 1910 census. Devised by W. F. Willcox of Cornell University, the new system established a priority list that assigned seats progressively, beginning with the first seat above the constitutional minimum of at least one seat for each state. When there were 48 states, this method was used to assign the 49th member, the 50th member, and so on, until the agreed-upon size of the House was reached. The method was called major fractions and was used after the censuses of 1910, 1930 and 1940. There was no reapportionment after the 1920 census.

1920s Struggle

The results of the 14th decennial census were announced Dec. 17, 1920, just after the short session of the 66th Congress convened. The 1920 census showed that for the first time in history most Americans were urban residents. This came as a profound shock to persons accustomed to emphasizing the nation's rural traditions and the virtues of life on farms and in small towns. Rural legislators immediately mounted an attack on the census results and succeeded in postponing reapportionment legislation for almost a decade.

Thomas Jefferson once wrote: "Those who labor in the earth are the chosen people of God, if ever He had a chosen people, whose breasts He had made His peculiar deposit for substantial and genuine virtue. . . . The mobs of great cities add just as much to the support of pure government as sores do to the strength of the human body. . . . I think our governments will remain virtuous for many centuries as long as they are chiefly agricultural: and this shall be as long as there shall be vacant lands in any part of America. When they get piled up upon one another in large cities as

in Europe, they will become corrupt as in Europe."

As their power waned throughout the latter part of the 19th century and the early part of the 20th, farmers and their spokesmen clung to the Jeffersonian belief that somehow they were more pure and virtuous than the growing number of urban residents. When finally faced with the fact that they were in the minority, these country residents put up a strong rear-guard action to prevent the inevitable shift of congressional districts to the cities.

Rural representatives insisted that, since the 1920 census was taken as of Jan. 1, the farm population had been under-counted. In support of this contention, they argued that many farm laborers were seasonally employed in the cities at that time of year. Furthermore, mid-winter road conditions probably had prevented enumerators from visiting many farms, they said; and other farmers were said to have been uncounted because they were absent on winter vacation trips. The change of the census date to Jan. 1 in 1920 had been made to conform to recommendations of the Agriculture Department, which had asserted that the census should be taken early in the year if an accurate statistical picture of farming conditions was desired.

Another point raised by rural legislators was that large numbers of unnaturalized aliens were congregated in Northern cities, with the result that these cities gained at the expense of constituencies made up mostly of citizens of the United States. Rep. Homer Hoch, R-Kan., submitted a table showing that, in a House of 435 representatives, exclusion from the census count of persons not naturalized would have altered the allocation of seats to 16 states. Southern and Western farming states would have retained the number of seats allocated to them in 1911 or would have gained, while Northern industrial states and California would have lost or at least would have gained fewer seats.

A constitutional amendment to exclude all aliens from the enumeration for purposes of reapportionment was proposed during the 70th Congress (1927-29) by Rep. Hoch, Sen. Arthur Capper, R-Kan., and others. During the Senate Commerce Committee's hearings on reapportionment, Sen. Frederick M. Sackett, R-Ky., and Sen. Lawrence D. Tyson, D-Tenn., said they too intended to propose amendments to the same effect. But nothing further came of the proposals.

Reapportionment Bills Opposed

The first bill to reapportion the House according to the 1920 census was drafted by the House Census Committee early in 1921. Proceeding on the principle that no state should have its representation reduced, the committee proposed to increase the total number of representatives from 435 to 483. But the House voted 267-76 to keep its membership at 435 and passed the bill so amended on Jan. 19, 1921. Eleven states would have lost seats and eight would have gained. The bill then was blocked by a Senate committee, where it died when the 66th Congress expired March 4, 1921.

Early in the 67th Congress, the House Census Committee again reported a bill, this time fixing the total membership at 460, an increase of 25. Two states — Maine and Massachusetts — would have lost one representative each and 16 states would have gained. On the House floor an unsuccessful attempt was made to fix the number at the existing 435, and the House sent the bill back to committee.

During the 68th Congress (1923-25), the House Census Committee failed to report any reapportionment bill, and

Congressional Apportionment, 1789-1980

Year of Census[1]

	1789†	1790	1800	1810	1820	1830	1840	1850	1860	1870	1880	1890	1900	1910	1930#	1940	1950	1960	1970	1980
Ala.				1*	3	5	7	7	6	8	8	9	9	10	9	9	9	8	7	7
Alaska																	1*	1	1	1
Ariz.														1*	1	2	2	3	4	5
Ark.						1*	1	2	3	4	5	6	7	7	7	7	6	4	4	4
Calif.							2*	2	3	4	6	7	8	11	20	23	30	38	43	45
Colo.										1*	1	2	3	4	4	4	4	4	5	6
Conn.	5	7	7	7	6	6	4	4	4	4	4	4	5	5	6	6	6	6	6	6
Del.	1	1	1	2	1	1	1	1	1	1	1	1	1	1	1	1	1	1	1	1
Fla.							1*	1	1	2	2	2	3	4	5	6	8	12	15	19
Ga.	3	2	4	6	7	9	8	8	7	9	10	11	11	12	10	10	10	10	10	10
Hawaii																	1*	2	2	2
Idaho											1*	1	1	2	2	2	2	2	2	2
Ill.				1*	1	3	7	9	14	19	20	22	25	27	27	26	25	24	24	22
Ind.				1*	3	7	10	11	11	13	13	13	13	13	12	11	11	11	11	10
Iowa							2*	2	6	9	11	11	11	11	9	8	8	7	6	6
Kan.									1	3	7	8	8	8	7	6	6	5	5	5
Ky.		2	6	10	12	13	10	10	9	10	11	11	11	11	9	9	8	7	7	7
La.				1*	3	3	4	4	5	6	6	6	7	8	8	8	8	8	8	8
Maine				7*	7	8	7	6	5	5	4	4	4	4	3	3	3	2	2	2
Md.	6	8	9	9	9	8	6	6	5	6	6	6	6	6	6	6	7	8	8	8
Mass.	8	14	17	13‡	13	12	10	11	10	11	12	13	14	16	15	14	14	12	12	11
Mich.							1*	3	4	6	9	11	12	13	17	17	18	19	19	18
Minn.								2*	2	3	5	7	9	10	9	9	9	8	8	8
Miss.				1*	1	2	4	5	5	6	7	7	8	8	7	7	6	5	5	5
Mo.					1	2	5	7	9	13	14	15	16	16	13	13	11	10	10	9
Mont.											1*	1	1	2	2	2	2	2	2	2
Neb.									1*	1	3	6	6	6	5	4	4	3	3	3
Nev.									1*	1	1	1	1	1	1	1	1	1	1	2
N.H.	3	4	5	6	6	5	4	3	3	3	2	2	2	2	2	2	2	2	2	2
N.J.	4	5	6	6	6	6	5	5	5	7	7	8	10	12	14	14	14	15	15	14
N.M.														1*	1	2	2	2	2	3
N.Y.	6	10	17	27	34	40	34	33	31	33	34	34	37	43	45	45	43	41	39	34
N.C.	5	10	12	13	13	13	9	8	7	8	9	9	10	10	11	12	12	11	11	11
N.D.											1*	1	2	3	2	2	2	2	1	1
Ohio			1*	6	14	19	21	21	19	20	21	21	21	22	24	23	23	24	23	21
Okla.													5*	8	9	8	6	6	6	6
Ore.									1*	1	1	1	2	2	3	3	4	4	4	5
Pa.	8	13	18	23	26	28	24	25	24	27	28	30	32	36	34	33	30	27	25	23
R.I.	1	2	2	2	2	2	2	2	2	2	2	2	2	3	2	2	2	2	2	2
S.C.	5	6	8	9	9	9	7	6	4	5	7	7	7	7	6	6	6	6	6	6
S.D.											2*	2	2	3	2	2	2	2	2	1
Tenn.		1	3	6	9	13	11	10	8	10	10	10	10	10	9	10	9	9	8	9
Texas							2*	2	4	6	11	13	16	18	21	21	22	23	24	27
Utah												1*	1	2	2	2	2	2	2	3
Vt.		2	4	6	5	5	4	3	3	3	2	2	2	2	1	1	1	1	1	1
Va.	10	19	22	23	22	21	15	13	11	9	10	10	10	10	9	9	10	10	10	10
Wash.											1*	2	3	5	6	6	7	7	7	8
W.Va.										3	4	4	5	6	6	6	6	5	4	4
Wis.							2*	3	6	8	9	10	11	11	10	10	10	10	9	9
Wyo.											1*	1	1	1	1	1	1	1	1	1
Total	65	106	142	186	213	242	232	237	243	293	332	357	391	435	435	435	437**	435	435	435

[1] Apportionment effective with congressional election two years after census.

† Constitution ratified. Original apportionment made in Constitution, pending first census.

No apportionment was made in 1920.

* These figures are not based on any census, but indicate the provisional representation accorded newly admitted states by the Congress, pending the next census.

‡ Twenty members were assigned to Massachusetts, but seven of these were credited to Maine when that area became a state.

** Normally 435, but temporarily increased two seats by Congress when Alaska and Hawaii became states.

Source: *Biographical Directory of the American Congress* and Bureau of the Census

midway in the 69th Congress (1925-27) it became apparent that the committee would not produce a reapportionment measure. Accordingly, on April 8, 1926, Rep. Henry E. Barbour, R-Calif., moved that the committee be discharged from further consideration of a bill identical with that passed by the House in 1921 keeping the chamber's membership at 435.

Chairman Bertrand H. Snell, N.Y., of the House Rules Committee, representing the Republican leadership of the House, raised a point of order against Barbour's motion. The Speaker of the House, Nicholas Longworth, R-Ohio, pointed out that decisions of earlier Speakers tended to indicate that reapportionment had been considered a matter of "constitutional privilege" and that Rep. Barbour's motion must be held in order if these precedents were followed. But the Speaker said he doubted whether the precedents had been interpreted correctly. He therefore submitted to the House the question of whether the pending motion should be considered privileged. The House sustained the Rules Committee by voting 87-265 not to consider the question privileged.

Intervention by Coolidge

President Calvin Coolidge, who previously had made no reference to reapportionment in his communications to Congress, announced in January 1927 that he favored passage of a new apportionment bill during the short session of the 69th Congress, which would end in less than two months. The House Census Committee refused to act. Its chairman, Rep. E. Hart Fenn, R-Conn., therefore moved in the House on March 2, 1927, to suspend the rules and pass a bill he had introduced authorizing the secretary of commerce to reapportion the House immediately after the 1930 census. The motion was voted down 183-197.

The Fenn bill was rewritten early in the 70th Congress (1927-29) to give Congress itself a chance to act before the proposed reapportionment by the secretary of commerce should go into effect. The bill was submitted to the House, which on May 18, 1928, voted 186-165 to recommit it to the Census Committee. After minor changes, the Fenn bill was again reported to the House and was passed on Jan. 11, 1929. No record vote was taken on passage of the bill, but a motion to return it to the committee was rejected 134-227.

Four days later, the reapportionment bill was reported by the Senate Commerce Committee. Repeated efforts to bring it up for floor action ahead of other bills failed. Its supporters gave up the fight on Feb. 27, 1929 — five days before the end of the session, when it became evident that senators from states slated to lose representation were ready to carry on a filibuster that would have blocked not only reapportionment but all other measures.

Intervention by Hoover

As the date of the next census became imminent, President Herbert Hoover listed provision for the 1930 census and reapportionment as "matters of emergency legislation" that should be acted upon in the special session of the 71st Congress that was convened on April 15, 1929. In response to this urgent request, the Senate June 13 passed, 48-37, a combined census-reapportionment bill that had been approved by voice vote of the House two days earlier.

The 1929 law established a permanent system of reapportioning the 435 House seats following each census. It provided that immediately after the convening of the 71st Congress for its short session in December 1930, the president was to transmit to Congress a statement showing the population of each state together with an apportionment of representatives to each state based on the existing size of the House. Failing enactment of new apportionment legislation, that apportionment would go into effect without further action and would remain in effect for ensuing elections to the House of Representatives until another census had been taken and another reapportionment made.

Because two decades had passed between reapportionments, a greater shift than usual took place following the 1930 census. California's House delegation was almost doubled, rising from 11 to 20. Michigan gained four seats, Texas three, and New Jersey, New York and Ohio two each. Twenty-one states lost a total of 27 seats; Missouri lost three and Georgia, Iowa, Kentucky and Pennsylvania each lost two.

To test the fairness of two allocation methods — the familiar major fractions and the new equal proportions system — the 1929 act required the president to report the distribution of seats by both methods. But, pending legislation to the contrary, the method of major fractions was to be used.

The two methods gave an identical distribution of seats based on 1930 census figures. However, in 1940 the two methods gave different results: under major fractions, Michigan would have gained a seat lost by Arkansas; under equal proportions, there would have been no change in either state. The automatic reapportionment provisions of the 1929 act went into effect in January 1941. But the House Census Committee moved to reverse the result, favoring the certain Democratic seat in Arkansas over a possible Republican gain if the seat were shifted to Michigan. The Democratic-controlled Congress went along, adopting equal proportions as the method to be used in reapportionment calculations after the 1950 and subsequent censuses, and making this action retroactive to January 1941 to save Arkansas its seat.

While politics doubtless played a part in the timing of the action taken in 1941, the method of equal proportions had come to be accepted as the best available. It had been worked out by Edward V. Huntington of Harvard in 1921. At the request of the Speaker of the House, all known methods of apportionment were considered in 1929 by the National Academy of Sciences Committee on Apportionment. The committee expressed its preference for equal proportions.

Method of Equal Proportions

The method of equal proportions involves complicated mathematical calculations. In brief, each of the 50 states is initially assigned the one seat to which every state is entitled by the Constitution. Then "priority numbers" for states to receive second seats, third seats and so on are calculated by dividing the state's population by the square root of n(n-1), where "n" is the number of seats for that state. The priority numbers are then lined up in order and the seats given to the states with priority numbers until 435 are awarded.

The method is designed to make the *proportional* difference between the average district size in any two states as small as possible. For instance, using 1980 census figures, if New Mexico got three seats and Indiana got 10, as occurred under the method of equal proportions, New Mexico would have an average district size of 433,323, and Indiana would have an average district size of 549,018. That makes Indiana's average district 27 percent larger than New Mexico's. On the other hand, if New Mexico got

two seats and Indiana got 11, as would have happened if the major fractions method had been used in 1980, New Mexico's average district of 649,984 would be 30 percent larger than Indiana's average of 499,107.

Two respected private statisticians, M. L. Balinski and H. P. Young, have argued that the equal proportions method has "cheated the larger states, and given undue representation to the smaller ones," in violation of the Supreme Court's one-person, one-vote rule. They have advocated a return to the Vinton method of apportionment. Such a bill was introduced in Congress in early 1981, but it received little attention and died at the end of the session.

Redistricting: Drawing the Lines

Although the Constitution contained provisions for the apportionment of U. S. House seats among the states, it was silent about how these members should be elected. From the beginning most states divided their territory into geographic districts, permitting only one member of Congress to be elected from each district.

But some states allowed would-be House members to run at large, with voters able to cast as many votes as there were seats to be filled. Still other states created what were known as multi-member districts; in these a single geographic unit would elect two or more members of the House. At various times, some states used combinations of these methods. For example, a state might elect 10 representatives from 10 individual districts and two at large.

In the first few elections to the House, New Hampshire, Pennsylvania, New Jersey and Georgia elected their representatives at large, as did Rhode Island and Delaware, the two states with only a single representative. Districts were used in Massachusetts, New York, Maryland, Virginia and South Carolina. In Connecticut, a preliminary election was held to nominate three times as many persons as the number of representatives to be chosen at large in the subsequent election. In 1840, 22 of the 31 states elected their representatives by districts. New Hampshire, New Jersey, Georgia, Alabama, Mississippi and Missouri, with a combined representation of 33 House seats, elected their representatives at large. Three states, Arkansas, Delaware and Florida, had only one representative each.

Those states that used congressional districts quickly developed what came to be known as the gerrymander. This was the practice of drawing district lines so as to maximize the advantage of a political party or interest group. The name originated from a salamander-shaped congressional district created by the Massachusetts Legislature in 1812 when Elbridge Gerry was governor. *(Box, p. 691)*

Constant efforts had been made during the early 1800s to lay down national rules, by means of a constitutional amendment, for congressional districting. The first resolution proposing a mandatory division of each state into districts was introduced in Congress in 1800. In 1802 the legislatures of Vermont and North Carolina adopted resolutions in support of such action. From 1816 to 1826, 22 state resolutions were adopted proposing the election of representatives by districts.

In Congress, Sen. Mahlon Dickerson of New Jersey proposed such an amendment regularly almost every year from 1817 to 1826. It was adopted by the Senate three times, in 1819, 1820 and 1822, but each time it failed to reach a vote in the House.

Because most states accepted the principle of local representation, congressional efforts to pass a constitutional amendment were unsuccessful. Instead, a law was passed in 1842 that required continuous single-member congressional districts. That law required representatives to be "elected by districts composed of contiguous territory equal in number to the representatives to which said state may be entitled, no one district electing more than one Representative."

When President John Tyler signed the bill, he appended to it a memorandum voicing doubt as to the constitutionality of the districting provisions. The memorandum precipitated a minor constitutional crisis. The House, urged on by Rep. John Quincy Adams of Massachusetts, appointed a select committee to consider the action of the president. Chaired by the aging former president, the committee drew up a resolution protesting Tyler's action as "unwarranted by the Constitution and laws of the United States, injurious to the public interest, and of evil example for the future; and this House do hereby solemnly protest against the said act of the President and against its ever being repeated or adduced as a precedent hereafter." The House took no action on the resolution; several attempts to call it up under suspension of the rules failed to receive the necessary two-thirds vote.

Districting Legislation, 1850-1910

The districting provisions of the 1842 act were not repeated in the legislation that followed the 1850 census. But in 1862 an act separate from the reapportionment act revived the provisions of the act of 1842 requiring districts to be composed of contiguous territory.

The 1872 reapportionment act again repeated the districting provisions and went even further by adding that districts should contain "as nearly as practicable an equal number of inhabitants." Similar provisions were included in the acts of 1881 and 1891. In the act of Jan. 16, 1901, the words "compact territory" were added, and the clause then read "contiguous and compact territory and containing as nearly as practicable an equal number of inhabitants." This requirement appeared also in the legislation of Aug. 8, 1911. (The "contiguous and compact" provisions of the act subsequently lapsed and, as of mid-1985, had not been replaced.)

Several unsuccessful attempts were made to enforce redistricting provisions. Despite the districting requirements of the act of June 25, 1842, New Hampshire, Georgia, Mississippi and Missouri elected their representatives at large that autumn. When the House elected at that time convened for its first session on Dec. 4, 1843, objection was made to seating the representatives of the four states. The dispute was referred to the Committee on Elections. The majority report of the committee, submitted by its chairman, Rep. Stephen A. Douglas, D-Ill., asserted that the act of 1842 was not binding upon the states and that the representatives in question were entitled to their seats. An amendment to the majority report deleted all reference to the apportionment law. A minority report by Rep. Garrett Davis, Whig-Ky., contended that the members had not been elected according to the Constitution and the laws and were not entitled to their seats.

The matter was debated in the House Feb. 6-14, 1844. With the Democratic Party holding a majority of more than 60, and with 18 of the 21 challenged members being Democrats, the House decided to seat the members. However, by 1848 all four states had come around to electing their representatives by districts.

The next challenge a House representative encountered over federal districting laws occurred in 1901. A charge that the existing Kentucky redistricting law did not comply with the redistricting provision of the federal reapportionment law of Jan. 16, 1901, was leveled to prevent the seating of Rep. George G. Gilbert, D, of Kentucky's 8th District. The committee assigned to investigate the matter turned aside the challenge, asserting that the federal act was not binding on the states. The reasons given were practical and political:

"Your committee are therefore of opinion that a proper construction of the Constitution does not warrant the conclusion that by that instrument Congress is clothed with power to determine the boundaries of Congressional districts, or to revise the acts of a State Legislature in fixing such boundaries; and your committee is further of opinion that even if such power is to be implied from the language of the Constitution, it would be in the last degree unwise and intolerable that it should exercise it. To do so would be to put into the hands of Congress the ability to disfranchise, in effect, a large body of the electors. It would give Congress the power to apply to all the States, in favor of one party, a general system of gerrymandering. It is true that the same method is to a large degree resorted to by the several states, but the division of political power is so general and diverse that notwithstanding the inherent vice of the system of gerrymandering, some kind of equality of distribution results."

In 1908 the Virginia Legislature transferred Floyd County from the 5th District to the 6th District. As a result, the population of the 5th District was reduced from 175,579 to 160,191 and that of the 6th District was increased from 181,571 to 196,959. The average for the state was 185,418.

When the newly elected representative from the 5th District, Edward W. Saunders, D, was challenged by his opponent in the election, the majority of the congressional investigating committee upheld the challenge. They concluded that the Virginia law of 1908 was null and void because it did not conform with the federal law of Jan. 16, 1901, or with the constitution of Virginia, and that the district should be regarded as including the counties that were a part of it before enactment of the 1908 state legislation. In that case Saunders' opponent would have had a majority of the votes, so the committee recommended that he be seated. Thus, for the first time, it appeared that the districting legislation would be enforced, but the House did not take action on the committee's report and Saunders' challenger was not seated.

Court Action on Redistricting

After the long and desultory battle over reapportionment in the 1920s, those who were unhappy over the inaction of Congress and the state legislatures began taking their cases to court. At first, the protestors had no luck. But as the population disparity grew in both federal and state legislative districts and the Supreme Court began to show a tendency to intervene, the objectors were more successful.

Finally, in a series of decisions beginning with *Baker v. Carr* in 1962 (369 U.S. 186) the court exerted great influence over the redistricting process, ordering that congressional districts as well as state and local legislative districts be drawn so that their populations would be as nearly equal as possible.

Origins of the Gerrymander

The practice of "gerrymandering" — the excessive manipulation of the shape of a legislative district to benefit a certain incumbent or party — is probably as old as the republic, but the name originated in 1812.

In that year the Massachusetts Legislature carved out of Essex County a district that historian John Fiske said had a "dragonlike contour." When the painter Gilbert Stuart saw the misshapen district, he penciled in a head, wings and claws and exclaimed: "That will do for a salamander!" — to which editor Benjamin Russell replied: "Better say a Gerrymander!" — after Elbridge Gerry, then governor of Massachusetts.

Supreme Court's 1932 Decision

The 1962 ruling essentially reversed the direction the court had taken in 1932. *Wood v. Broom* (287 U.S. 1) was a case challenging the constitutionality of a Mississippi redistricting law. The question was whether the 1911 federal redistricting act — which required that districts be separate, compact, contiguous and equally populated and which had been neither specifically repealed not reaffirmed in the 1929 reapportionment act — was still in effect.

Speaking for the court, Chief Justice Charles Evans Hughes ruled that the 1911 act, in effect, had expired with the approval of the 1929 apportionment act and that the standards of the 1911 act therefore were no longer applicable. The court reversed the decision of a lower federal court, which had permanently enjoined elections under the new Mississippi redistricting act because it violated the standards of the 1911 act.

That the Supreme Court upheld a state law that failed to provide for districts of equal population was almost less important than the minority opinion that the court should not have heard the case. Four justices — Louis D. Brandeis, Harlan F. Stone, Owen J. Roberts and Benjamin N.

Cardozo — while concurring in the majority opinion, said they would have dismissed the Wood suit for "want of equity." The "want-of-equity" phrase in this context suggested a policy of judicial self-limitation with respect to the entire question of judicial involvement in essentially "political" questions.

'Political Thicket'

Not until 1946, in *Colegrove v. Green* (328 U.S. 549, 1946), did the court again rule in a significant case dealing with congressional redistricting. The case was brought by Kenneth Colegrove, a political science professor at Northwestern University, who alleged that Illinois' congressional districts — varying in size between 112,116 and 914,053 in population — were so unequal that they violated the 14th Amendment's guarantee of equal protection of the laws. A seven-man Supreme Court divided 4-3 in dismissing the suit.

Justice Felix Frankfurter gave the opinion of the court, speaking for himself and Justices Stanley F. Reed and Harold H. Burton. Frankfurter's opinion cited *Wood v. Broom* to indicate that Congress had deliberately removed the standard set by the 1911 act. "We also agree," he said, "with the four Justices [Brandeis, Stone, Roberts and Cardozo] who were of the opinion that the bill in *Wood v. Broom* should be 'dismissed for want of equity.' " The issue, Frankfurter said, was "of a peculiarly political nature and therefore not meant for judicial interpretation. . . . The short of it is that the Constitution has conferred upon Congress exclusive authority to secure fair representation by the states in the popular House and has left to that House determination whether states have fulfilled their responsibility. If Congress failed in exercising its powers, whereby standards of fairness are offended, the remedy lies ultimately with the people. . . . To sustain this action would cut very deep into the very being of Congress. Courts ought not to enter this political thicket. The remedy for unfairness in districting is to secure state legislatures that will apportion properly, or to invoke the ample powers of Congress." Frankfurter also said that the court could not affirmatively remap congressional districts and that elections at large would be politically undesirable.

Justice Hugo L. Black, joined by Justices William O. Douglas and Frank Murphy, in a dissenting opinion maintained that the district court did have jurisdiction over congressional redistricting. The three justices cited as evidence a section of the U.S. Code that allowed district courts to redress deprivations of constitutional rights occurring through action of the states. Black's opinion also rested on a previous case in which the court had indicated that federal constitutional questions, unless "frivolous," fall under the jurisdiction of the federal courts. Black asserted that the appellants had standing to sue and that the population disparities did violate the equal protection clause of the 14th Amendment.

With the court split 3-3 on whether the judiciary had or should exercise jurisdiction, Justice Wiley B. Rutledge cast the deciding vote in *Colegrove v. Green*. On the question of justiciability, Rutledge agreed with Black, Douglas and Murphy that the issue could be considered by the federal courts. Thus a majority of the court participating in the *Colegrove* case felt that congressional redistricting cases were justiciable.

Yet on the question of granting relief in this specific instance, Rutledge agreed with Frankfurter, Reed and Burton that the case should be dismissed. He pointed out that four of the nine justices in *Wood v. Broom* had felt that dismissal should be for want of equity. Rutledge saw a "want-of-equity" situation in *Colegrove v. Green* as well. "I think the gravity of the constitutional questions raised [are] so great, together with the possibility of collision [with the political departments of the government], that the admonition [against avoidable constitutional decision] is appropriate to be followed here," Rutledge said. Jurisdiction, he thought, should be exercised "only in the most compelling circumstances." He thought that "the shortness of time remaining [before the forthcoming election] makes it doubtful whether action could or would be taken in time to secure for petitioners the effective relief they seek." Rutledge warned that congressional elections at large would deprive citizens of representation by districts, "which the prevailing policy of Congress demands." In the case of at-large elections, he warned, "the cure sought may be worse than the disease." For all these reasons he concluded that the case was "one in which the Court may properly, and should, decline to exercise its jurisdiction."

Changing Views

In the ensuing years, law professors, political scientists and other commentators expressed growing criticism of the *Colegrove* doctrine and growing impatience with the Supreme Court's reluctance to intervene in redistricting disputes. At the same time, the membership of the court was changing, and the new members were more inclined toward judicial action on redistricting.

In the 1950s the court decided two cases that laid some groundwork for its subsequent reapportionment decisions. The first was *Brown v. Board of Education* (347 U.S. 483, 1954), the historic school desegregation case, in which the court decided that an individual citizen could assert a right to equal protection of the laws under the 14th Amendment, contrary to the "separate but equal" doctrine of public facilities for white and black citizens. Six years later, in *Gomillion v. Lightfoot* (364 U.S. 339, 1960), the court held that the Alabama Legislature could not draw the city limits of Tuskegee so as to exclude nearly every black vote. In his opinion, Justice Frankfurter drew a clear line between redistricting challenges based on the 14th Amendment, such as *Colegrove*, and 15th Amendment challenges to discriminatory redistricting as in *Gomillion*. But Justice Charles E. Whittaker said that the equal protection clause was the proper constitutional basis for the decision. One commentator later remarked that *Gomillion* amounted to a "dragon" in the "political thicket" of *Colegrove*.

By 1962 only three members of the *Colegrove* court remained: Justices Black and Douglas, dissenters in that case, and Justice Frankfurter, aging spokesman for restraint in the exercise of judicial power.

By then it was clear that malapportionment within the states no longer could be ignored. By 1960 not a single state legislative body existed in which there was not at least a 2-to-1 population disparity between the most and the least heavily populated districts. For example, the disparity was 242-1 in the Connecticut House, 223-1 in the Nevada Senate, 141-1 in the Rhode Island Senate and 9-1 in the Georgia Senate. Studies of the effective vote of large and small counties in state legislatures between 1910 and 1960 showed that the effective vote of the large counties had slipped while their percentage of the national population had more than doubled. The most lightly populated counties, on the other hand, advanced from a position of slight over-representation to one of extreme over-representation,

Malapportionment and Gerrymandering

The prevalence of malapportionment in the creation of U.S. congressional districts was, to many observers, one of the chief evils in the American system before the "one-person, one-vote" ruling by the Supreme Court in 1964. On Feb. 17 of that year, the court, in the case of *Wesberry v. Sanders*, declared that "as nearly as is practicable, one man's vote in a congressional election is to be worth as much as another's."

Malapportionment

Malapportionment occurred when districts of grossly unequal populations were created — either through actions of state legislatures in establishing new districts or, as was the more frequent practice in America, simply by failing to redistrict despite major population shifts.

Within a single state, populations in some congressional districts varied by as much as eight to one. Generally, growing urban areas were under-represented, to the advantage of rural areas.

Examples of great disparity in congressional district sizes in modern U.S. history included: New York (1930), 776,425 residents in the largest district and 90,671 in the smallest district; Ohio (1946), 698,650 and 163,561; Illinois (1946), 914,053 and 112,116; Arkansas (1946), 423,152 and 177,476; Texas (1962), 951,527 and 216,371; Michigan (1962), 802,994 and 177,431; Maryland (1962), 711,045 and 243,570; South Dakota (1962), 497,669 and 182,845.

The decennial census and ensuing reapportionment of House seats eventually forced redistricting in most states, although some resorted to the expedient of electing members at large (this occurred in Texas, Hawaii, Ohio, Michigan and Maryland in 1962) rather than face redrawing district lines.

A 1967 law (PL 90-196) banned at-large elections in states with more than one representative. However, that law has been interpreted variously by the states. And where divided states' legislatures have been unable to agree on a redistricting plan, the courts have had to impose their own plan.

Although sizes vary somewhat because of apportionment and inequalities that build between censuses, generally the districts start out nearly equal in population.

In their 1985 book, *Congress and Its Members*, political scientists Roger H. Davidson and Walter J. Oleszek noted:

> Population equality has thus been achieved at the expense of other goals. Parity in numbers of residents makes it hard to respect political divisions such as county lines. It also makes it hard to follow economic, social, or geographic boundaries. The congressional district, therefore, tends to be an artificial creation with little relationship to real communities of interest — economic or geographic or political. This heightens the congressional district's isolation, forcing candidates to forge

their own unique factions and alliances. It also aids incumbents, who have ways of reaching voters without relying on commercial communications media.

Gerrymandering

Gerrymandering was the name given to excessive manipulation of the shape of legislative districts to benefit a particular politician or political party. The gerrymander was named after Democrat Elbridge Gerry, the governor of Massachusetts in 1812 when the Legislature created a peculiar salamander-shaped district to benefit his party. *(Sketch of district, box, p. 691)*

Unlike malapportionment, gerrymandering has not been prohibited by law. It still is used today by both political parties. In 1961 Republican legislators in New York created one gerrymander-like creature stretching across the greater part of upstate New York, his head hanging over Albany in the east and his tail reaching for Rochester in the west. Such salamander, tadpole and fishlike creatures sprang to life on the maps of New York City's boroughs. In North Carolina after the 1960 census, Democratic redistricters formed an almost perfect gerrymander shape to throw the state's sole Republican representative in with a strong Democratic opponent.

After the 1980 census, Democrats in control of California's Legislature drew a district in the San Francisco Bay area in which two segments were linked only by a body of water. New Jersey's map was a gerrymander that boasted some of the most bizarrely shaped districts in the nation. The Supreme Court threw those districts out in 1983 but on the grounds of population inequality, not because they were gerrymandered.

Davidson and Oleszek cite two kinds of gerrymandering: "packing" and "cracking." In the first case, a district line is drawn so as to encompass as many of one party's voters as possible, thus "packing" it with supporters. "Cracking" entails diluting one party's strength by dispersing it among two or more districts.

The intent of practically every gerrymander is political — to create a maximum number of districts that would elect the party candidates or types of candidates favored by the controlling group in the state legislature that did the redistricting, thus increasing, or maintaining, the political power of the already politically dominant group. Concluded Davidson and Oleszek:

> The long-range effects of gerrymanders are not easily measured.... Marginal or competitive districts (those where the winner gains less than 55 percent of the votes) are tougher for a party to capture and hold, but they have the advantage of yielding legislative seats with a modest number of voters (that is, a minimal winning coalition). Safe districts, while naturally preferred by the incumbents, can waste the majority party's votes by furnishing outsized victories.

holding almost twice as many seats as they would be entitled to by population size alone. Predictably, the rural-dominated state legislatures resisted every move toward reapportioning state legislative districts to reflect new population patterns.

Population imbalance among congressional districts was substantially lopsided but by no means so gross. In Texas the 1960 census showed the most heavily populated district had four times as many inhabitants as the most lightly populated. Arizona, Maryland and Ohio each had at least one district with three times as many inhabitants as the least populated. In most cases, rural areas benefited from the population imbalance in congressional districts. As a result of the postwar population movement out of central cities to the surrounding areas, the suburbs were the most under-represented.

Baker v. Carr

It was against this background that a group of Tennessee city dwellers successfully broke the longstanding precedent against federal court involvement in legislative apportionment problems. For more than half a century, since 1901, the Tennessee Legislature had refused to reapportion itself, even though a decennial reapportionment based on population was specifically required by the state's constitution. In the meantime, Tennessee's population had grown and shifted dramatically to urban areas. By 1960 the House legislative districts ranged from 3,454 to 36,031 in population, while the Senate districts ranged from 39,727 to 108,094. Appeals by urban residents to the rural-controlled Tennessee Legislature proved fruitless. A suit brought in the state courts to force reapportionment was rejected on grounds that the courts should stay out of legislative matters.

City dwellers then appealed to the federal courts, stating that they had no redress: the Legislature had refused to act for more than half a century, the state courts had refused to intervene and Tennessee had no referendum or initiative laws. They charged that there was "a debasement of their votes by virtue of the incorrect, obsolete and unconstitutional apportionment" to such an extent that they were being deprived of their right to "equal protection of the laws" under the 14th Amendment. (The 14th Amendment reads, in part: "No state shall ... deny to any person within its jurisdiction the equal protection of the laws.")

The Supreme Court on March 26, 1962, handed down its historic decision in *Baker v. Carr*, ruling in favor of the Tennessee city dwellers by a 6-2 margin. In the majority opinion, Justice William J. Brennan Jr. emphasized that the federal judiciary had the power to review the apportionment of state legislatures under the 14th Amendment's equal protection clause. "The mere fact that a suit seeks protection as a political right," Brennan wrote, "does not mean that it presents a political question" that the courts should avoid.

In a vigorous dissent, Justice Frankfurter said the majority decision constituted "a massive repudiation of the experience of our whole past" and was an assertion of "destructively novel judicial power." He contended that the lack of any clear basis for relief "catapults the lower courts" into a "mathematical quagmire." Frankfurter insisted that "there is not under our Constitution a judicial remedy for every political mischief." Appeal for relief, he maintained, should not be made in the courts, but rather "to an informed civically militant electorate."

The court had abandoned the view that malapportionment questions were outside its competence. But it stopped there and in *Baker v. Carr* did not address the merits of the challenge to the legislative districts.

Gray v. Sanders

The one-person, one-vote rule was set out first by the court almost exactly one year after its decision in *Baker v. Carr*. But the case in which the announcement came did not involve congressional districts.

In the ruling in the case of *Gray v. Sanders*, the court found that Georgia's county-unit primary system for electing state officials — a system that weighted votes to give advantage to rural districts in statewide primary elections — denied voters equal protection of the laws.

All votes in a statewide election must have equal weight, held the court: "How then can one person be given twice or 10 times the voting power of another person in a statewide election merely because he lives in a rural area or because he lives in the smallest rural county? Once the geographical unit for which a representative is to be chosen is designated, all who participate in the election are to have an equal vote — whatever their race, whatever their sex, whatever their occupation, whatever their income, and wherever their home may be in that geographical unit. This is required by the Equal Protection Clause of the Fourteenth Amendment. The concept of 'we the people' under the Constitution visualizes no preferred class of voters but equality among those who meet the basic qualification. The idea that every voter is equal to every other voter in his State, when he casts his ballot in favor of one of several competing candidates, underlies many of our decisions.... The conception of political equality from the Declaration of Independence to Lincoln's Gettysburg Address, to the Fifteenth, Seventeenth, and Nineteenth Amendments can mean only one thing — one person, one vote."

The Rule Applied

The court's rulings in *Baker* and *Gray* concerned the equal weighting and counting of votes cast in state elections. In 1964, deciding the case of *Wesberry v. Sanders*, the court applied the one-person, one-vote principle to congressional districts and set equality as the standard for congressional redistricting.

Shortly after the *Baker* decision was handed down, James P. Wesberry Jr., an Atlanta resident and a member of the Georgia Senate, filed suit in federal court in Atlanta claiming that gross disparity in the population of Georgia's congressional districts violated 14th Amendment rights of equal protection of the laws. At the time, Georgia districts ranged in population from 272,154 in the rural 9th District in the northeastern part of the state to 823,860 in the 5th District in Atlanta and its suburbs. District lines had not been changed since 1931. The state's number of House seats remained the same in the interim, but Atlanta's district population — already high in 1931 compared with the others — had more than doubled in 30 years, making a 5th District vote worth about one-third that of a vote in the 9th.

On June 20, 1962, the three-judge federal court divided 2-1 in dismissing Wesberry's suit. The majority reasoned that the precedent of *Colegrove* still controlled in congressional district cases. The judges cautioned against federal judicial interference with Congress and against "depriving others of the right to vote" if the suit should result in at-large elections. They suggested that the Georgia Legislature (under court order to reapportion itself) or the U.S.

Congress might better provide relief. Wesberry then appealed to the Supreme Court, which heard arguments in the case in November 1963.

On Feb. 17, 1964, the Supreme Court ruled in the case of *Wesberry v. Sanders* (376 U.S. 1) that congressional districts must be substantially equal in population. The court, which upheld Wesberry's challenge by a 6-3 decision, based its ruling on the history and wording of Article I, Section 2 of the Constitution providing that representatives shall be apportioned among the states according to their respective numbers and be chosen by the people of the several states. This language, the court stated, meant that "as nearly as is practicable, one man's vote in a congressional election is to be worth as much as another's."

The majority opinion, written by Justice Black and supported by Chief Justice Earl Warren and Justices Brennan, Douglas, Arthur J. Goldberg and Byron R. White, said that, "While it may not be possible to draw congressional districts with mathematical precision, that is no excuse for ignoring our Constitution's plain objective of making equal representation for equal numbers of people the fundamental goal for the House of Representatives."

In a strongly worded dissent, Justice John M. Harlan asserted that the Constitution did not establish population as the only criterion of congressional districting and that the subject was left by the Constitution to the discretion of the states, subject only to the supervisory power of Congress. "The constitutional right which the court creates is manufactured out of whole cloth," Harlan concluded.

The *Wesberry* opinion established no precise standards for districting beyond declaring that districts must be as nearly equal in population "as is practicable." In his dissent, Harlan suggested that a disparity of more than 100,000 between a state's largest and smallest districts would "presumably" violate the equality standard enunciated by the majority. On that basis, Harlan estimated, the districts of 37 states with 398 representatives would be unconstitutional, "leaving a constitutional House of 37 members now sitting."

Neither did the court's decision make any reference to gerrymandering, since it discussed only the population, not the shape of districts. In a separate districting opinion handed down the same day as *Wesberry,* the court dismissed a challenge to congressional districts in New York City, which had been brought by voters who charged that Manhattan's "silk-stocking" 17th District had been gerrymandered to exclude blacks and Puerto Rican citizens.

Strict Equality

Five years elapsed between the court's admonition in *Wesberry v. Sanders* and the court's next application of constitutional standards to congressional districting.

In 1967 the court hinted at the strict stance it would adopt two years later. With two unsigned opinions, the court sent back to Indiana and Missouri for revision those two states' congressional redistricting plans because they allowed variations of as much as 20 percent from the average district population.

Two years later, Missouri's revised plan returned to the court for full review. With its decision in the case of *Kirkpatrick v. Preisler* (385 U.S. 450), the court by a 6-3 vote rejected the plan. It was unacceptable, held the majority, because it allowed a variation of as much as 3.1 percent from perfectly equal population districts.

The court thus made clear its strict application of "one person, one vote" to congressional redistricting. Minor deviations from the strict equal-population principle were permissible only when the state provided substantial evidence that the variation was unavoidable.

Writing for the court, Justice Brennan declared that there was no "fixed numerical or percentage population variance small enough to be considered *de minimis* and to satisfy without question the 'as nearly as practicable' standard." "Equal representation for equal numbers of people is a principle designed to prevent debasement of voting power and diminution of access to elected Representatives. Toleration of even small deviations detracts from these purposes," Brennan wrote.

The only permissible variances in population, the court ruled, were those that were unavoidable despite the effort to achieve absolute equality or those that could be legally justified. The variances in Missouri could have been avoided, the court said.

None of Missouri's arguments for the plan qualified as "legally acceptable" justifications. The court rejected the argument that population variance was necessary to allow representation of distinct interest groups. It said that acceptance of such variances to produce districts with specific interests was "antithetical" to the basic purpose of equal representation.

Justice Byron R. White dissented from the majority opinion, which he characterized as "an unduly rigid and unwarranted application of the Equal Protection Clause which will unnecessarily involve the courts in the abrasive task of drawing district lines." White added that some "acceptably small" population variance could be established. He indicated that considerations of existing political boundaries and geographical compactness could justify to him some variation from "absolute equality" of population.

Justice Harlan, joined by Justice Potter Stewart, objected that "whatever room remained under this Court's prior decisions for the free play of the political process in matters of reapportionment is now all but eliminated by today's Draconian judgments."

Practical Results

As a result of the court decisions of the 1960s, nearly every state was forced to redraw its congressional district lines — sometimes more than once. By the end of the decade, 39 of the 45 states with more than one representative had made the necessary adjustments.

However, the effect of the one-person, one-vote standard on congressional districts did not bring about immediate equality in districts in the years 1964-70. Most of the new districts were far from equal in population, because the only official population figures came from the 1960 census. Massive population shifts during the decade rendered most post-*Wesberry* efforts to achieve equality useless.

But following redistricting in 1971-72, based on the 1970 census, the result achieved was that House members elected in November 1972 to the 93rd Congress represented districts that differed only slightly in population from the state average. In 385 of the 435 districts, the district's variance was less than 1 percent from the state average district population.

By contrast, only nine of the districts in the 88th Congress (elected in 1962) deviated less than 1 percent from the state average; 81 were between 1 and 5 percent; 87 from 5 to 10 percent; and in 236 districts the deviation was 10 percent or greater. Twenty-two House members were

---

The Voting Rights Act

There is one form of gerrymandering that is expressly forbidden by law: redistricting for the purpose of racial discrimination. The Voting Rights Act of 1965, extended in 1970, 1975 and 1982, banned redistricting plans that diluted the voting strength of black communities. Other minorities, including Hispanics, Asian-Americans, American Indians and native Alaskans subsequently were brought under the protection of the law.

The law originally was aimed at those Southern states where blacks had long been targets of discrimination. At the time the original law was passed, racial redistricting was not a great problem since black voting strength was minimal. However, with the enhancement of registration and voting rights for blacks, lawmakers feared that affected states would, through gerrymandering, divide black communities among several congressional districts and lower the chances of electing black representatives. That concern resulted in Section Five, the pre-clearance provisions of the act under which nine states and parts of 13 others must receive Justice Department approval of their congressional redistricting plans.

The Voting Rights Act is widely considered the most effective civil rights measure ever enacted. The voter registration provisions have been the most successful. Black voter registration in Mississippi increased from 6.7 percent in 1964 to 67.4 percent in 1976. Black representation in state legislatures, which also come under the purview of the Voting Rights Act, increased substantially. But black congressional representation has not expanded as greatly. After the 1964 elections the nine states that now must clear entire state plans (Alabama, Alaska, Arizona, Georgia, Louisiana, Mississippi, South Carolina, Texas and Virginia) had 74 seats and no black congressmen. In 1985 they had 79 seats and just one black representative (Mickey Leland, D-Texas).

elected at large.

The Supreme Court made only one major ruling concerning congressional districts during the 1970s. On June 18, 1973, the court declared the Texas congressional districts, as redrawn in 1971, unconstitutional because of excessive population variance among districts. The variance between the largest and smallest districts was 4.9872 percent. The court returned the case to a three-judge federal panel, which adopted a new congressional district plan, effective Oct. 17, 1973.

Precise Equality

Almost exactly 10 years later, on June 22, 1983, the Supreme Court handed down another redistricting decision with sweeping implications. In a 5-4 decision, the court ruled in *Karcher v. Daggett* that states must adhere as closely as possible to the one-person, one-vote standard and bear the burden of proving that deviations from precise population equality were made in pursuit of a legitimate goal. The decision overturned New Jersey's congressional map because the variation between the most populated and the least populated districts was 0.69 percent.

Brennan, who wrote the court opinion in *Baker* and *Kirkpatrick*, also wrote the opinion in *Karcher*, contending that population differences between districts "could have been avoided or significantly reduced with a good-faith effort to achieve population equality."

"Adopting any standard other than population equality, using the best census data available, would subtly erode the Constitution's ideal of equal representation," Brennan wrote. "If state legislators knew that a certain *de minimis* level of population differences were acceptable, they would doubtless strive to achieve that level rather than equality. Furthermore, choosing a different standard would import a high degree of arbitrariness into the process of reviewing reapportionment plans. In this case, appellants argue that a maximum deviation of approximately 0.7 percent should be considered *de minimis*. If we accept that argument, how are we to regard deviations of 0.8 percent, 0.95 percent, 1.0 percent or 1.1 percent? . . . To accept the legitimacy of unjustified, though small population deviations in this case would mean to reject the basic premise of *Kirkpatrick* and *Wesberry*."

Brennan said that "any number of consistently applied legislative policies might justify" some population variation. These included "making districts compact, respecting municipal boundaries, preserving the cores of prior districts, and avoiding contests between incumbent Representatives." However, he cautioned, the state must show "with some specificity that a particular objective required the specific deviations in its plan, rather than simply relying on general assertions."

In his dissent Justice White criticized the majority for its "unreasonable insistence on an unattainable perfection in the equalizing of congressional districts." He warned that the decision would invite "further litigation of virtually every congressional redistricting plan in the nation"

The court did not address the underlying political issue in the New Jersey case, which was that its map had been drawn to serve Democratic interests. As a partisan gerrymander, the map had few peers, boasting some of the most oddly shaped districts in the country. One constituency, known as "the fishhook" by its detractors, twisted through central New Jersey's industrial landscape, picking up Democratic voters along the way. Another stretched from the suburbs of New York to the fringes of Trenton.

In separate dissents Justices Lewis F. Powell Jr. and John Paul Stevens broadly hinted that they were willing to hear constitutional challenges to instances of partisan gerrymandering. "A legislator cannot represent his constituents properly — nor can voters from a fragmented district exercise the ballot intelligently — when a voting district is nothing more than an artificial unit divorced from, and indeed often in conflict with, the various communities established in the State," wrote Powell.

Congress and Redistricting

Several attempts were made by Congress in the post-World War II period to enact new legislation on redistricting. Only one of these efforts was successful — enactment of a measure barring at-large elections in states with more than one representative.

On Jan. 9, 1951, President Harry S Truman, upon presentation of the official state population figures of the 1950 census, asked for changes in existing law to tighten federal control of state redistricting. Specifically, he asked for a ban on gerrymandering, an end to at-large seats in

states having more than one representative and a sharp reduction in the huge differences in size among congressional districts within most states.

On behalf of the administration, Emanuel Celler, D-N.Y., chairman of the House Judiciary Committee, introduced a bill to require compact and contiguous congressional districts that would not vary by more than 15 percent between districts within a state. The bill also eliminated at-large seats and made redistricting mandatory every 10 years in accordance with population changes. But the House Judiciary Committee took no action on the proposals.

Rep. Celler regularly introduced his bill throughout the 1950s and early 1960s, but it made no headway until the Supreme Court handed down the *Wesberry* decision in 1964. On June 24, 1964, a Celler bill was approved by a House Judiciary subcommittee. But the full committee did not act on the bill before adjournment of Congress.

On March 16, 1965, the House finally passed a redistricting bill. It established 15 percent as the maximum percentage by which a congressional district's population might deviate from the average size of the state's districts; prohibited at-large elections for any state with more than one House seat; required that districts be composed of "contiguous territory in as compact form as practicable," and forbade more than one redistricting of a state between decennial censuses. A major reason for House approval of Celler's bill appeared to be a desire to gain protection from court imposition of even more rigid criteria. But the measure encountered difficulties in the Senate Judiciary Committee. After considerable wrangling over its provisions, the committee voted to report the bill without precise agreement on its wording. No report was ever filed by the committee.

In 1967 a redistricting bill was passed by both the Senate and the House, but not in the same form. And the bill had a different purpose from that of previous bills dealing with the subject. Instead of trying to establish standards of fairness in drawing district lines, the chief purpose in 1967 was to prevent the courts from ordering redistricting of House seats or from ordering any state to hold elections at large — a procedure that many incumbent representatives feared — until after the House had been reapportioned on the basis of the 1970 census.

A combination of liberal Democrats and Republicans in the Senate managed to defeat the conference report Nov. 8, 1967, by a vote of 22-55. Liberals favored court action, which they believed would eliminate many conservative rural districts, while Republicans felt that redistricted areas, especially in the growing suburbs, would elect more Republicans than Democrats.

To avoid at-large elections, the Senate added a rider to a House-passed private bill. Under the rider, at-large elections of U.S. representatives were banned in all states entitled to more than one representative, with the exceptions of New Mexico and Hawaii. Those states had a tradition of electing their two representatives at large. Both of them, however, soon passed districting laws — New Mexico for the 1968 elections and Hawaii for 1970.

In 1971 Celler introduced a new version of his proposed redistricting legislation. Although the House Judiciary Committee reported the measure favorably, no further action was taken on the bill, and it died at the end of the 92nd Congress.

After the 1960 census, an attempt had been made to increase the size of the House to avoid some of the losses of seats that would otherwise be suffered by several states. By a vote of 12-14, the House Judiciary Committee on Sept. 9, 1961, rejected a motion to recommend enlarging the House to 453 seats. And by a vote of 14-15, the same committee rejected a bill reported by a subcommittee that would have increased the permanent size of the House to 438.

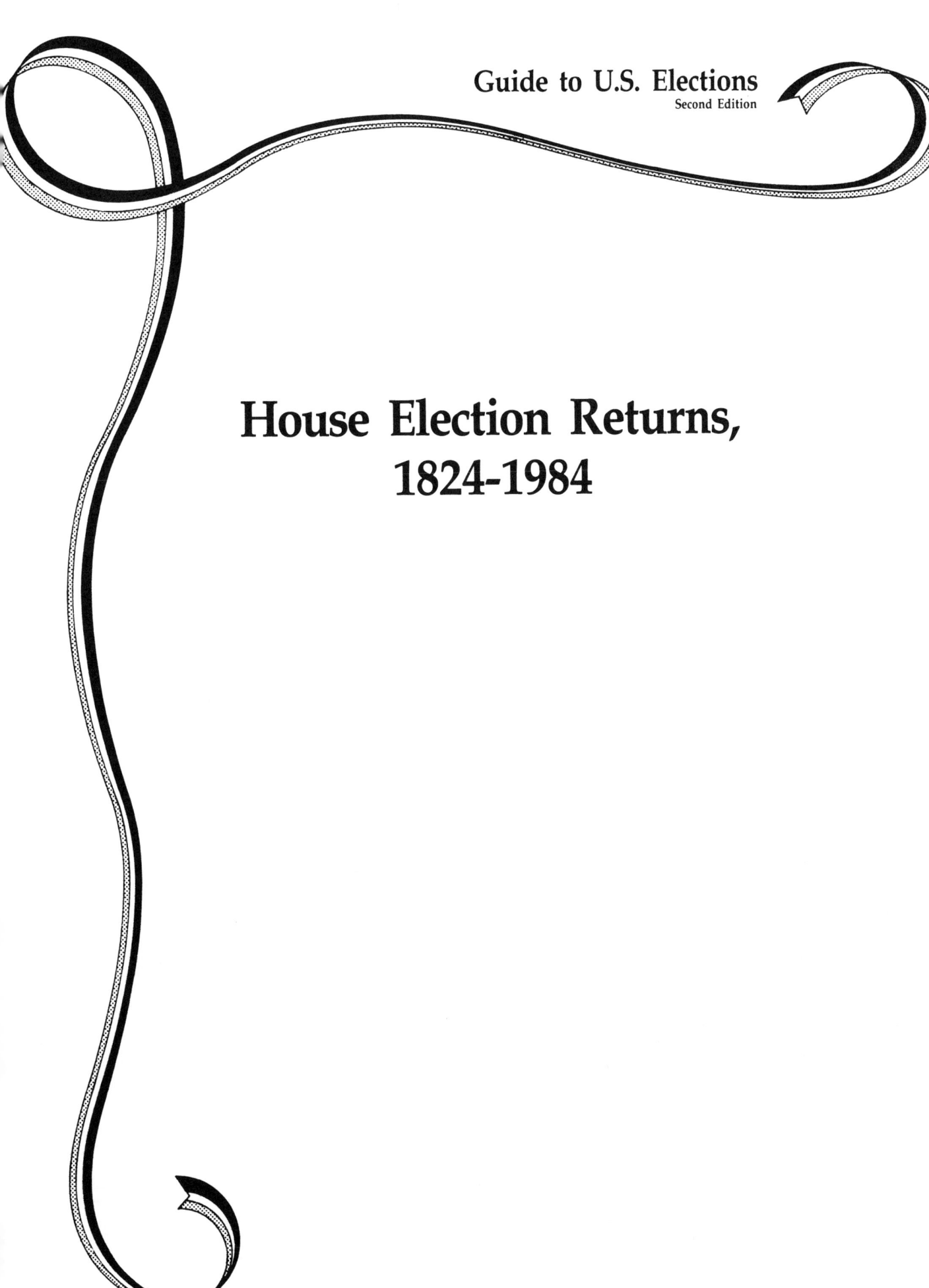

House Election Returns,
1824-1984

Sources for House Popular Returns

The popular election returns for the House of Representatives presented in this section *(pp. 701-1062)* for the years 1824-1973 were obtained from the Inter-University Consortium for Political and Social Research (ICPSR) at the University of Michigan. Major sources for returns since 1973 were Congressional Quarterly, which obtained them from the state secretaries of state, and the *America Votes* series compiled biennially by Richard M. Scammon and Alice V. McGillivray of the Elections Research Center, Washington, D.C.

The symbol # next to returns before 1974 indicates that Congressional Quarterly obtained the returns from a source other than the ICPSR. A complete set of other sources used appears on page 1062. A "House Candidates Index" is located on pages 1180-1273.

While the complete source annotations for the ICPSR collection are too extensive to publish here, information on the sources for specific election returns can be obtained through the ICPSR. *(ICPSR collection, box, p. xiv)*

Presentation of Returns

The House returns are arranged chronologically by year and alphabetically by state for each year. Within each state, single-member districts are listed first in numerical order. At-large seats appear at the end of the single-member districts with "AL" in the district identification column. Multi-member districts, in the few instances in which they appear in the 19th century, are listed in numerical order under the separate heading "Multi-Member Districts." *(For an explanation of multi-member districts, see p. 678.)*

Special election results appear after all general election returns for each state under a separate "Special Elections" heading. Returns for special off-year elections are listed at the end of the preceding year's general election returns.

Names and Party Designations

Candidate names appear to the right of the district number, with the candidate receiving the highest number of votes listed first. Other candidates who received *at least 5 percent* of the total votes cast are listed in descending order. In multi-member districts or at-large districts electing more than one representative, candidates who received fewer than 100 votes were not listed.

In some instances, particularly in the 19th century, names in the ICPSR file are incomplete. First names were the element most commonly missing in the original sources consulted by the scholars and archivists who gathered the ICPSR returns. In cases where a vote total is known but there is no name at all, or the name obviously could not be identified, Congressional Quarterly has labeled the votes as being cast for an "Unidentified Candidate."

In the ICPSR returns, the distinct — and in many cases, *multiple* — party designations appearing in the original sources are preserved. In many cases party labels represent combinations of multi-party support received by individual candidates. If, for example, on the ballot and official returns more than one party name was listed next to a candidate's name, then the party designation appearing in the election returns for that candidate will be a unique abbreviation for that combination of parties. *(For a list of party abbreviations, see p. 1141.)*

In the special case of a candidate's name listed separately on the original ballot under more than one party — where returns were reported *separately* for each party — Congressional Quarterly has summed the votes recorded under the several parties and that figure appears as the candidate's total vote. Whenever separate party totals have been summed, a *comma* separates the abbreviations of the parties contributing the largest and second largest share of the total vote.

Most cases of this special situation occurred in New York and Pennsylvania during this century. For example, in the original ICPSR returns for the House election in New York's 10th District in 1938, Emanuel Celler received 31,645 votes as the Democratic Party candidate, 12,181 votes as the American Labor Party candidate and 55 votes as the City Fusion Party candidate, for a total of 43,881 votes. Congressional Quarterly summed all votes received by Celler from these three parties *(p. 944)*.

Congressional Quarterly indicated the two parties that contributed the most votes to Celler's total — separated by a comma. Thus, immediately following his name appear the abbreviations (D, AM LAB), indicating that Celler was a candidate of two or more parties and that he received most votes as a Democrat.

Vote Totals and Percentages

Each candidate's total vote and percentage of the total vote cast for all candidates appear in columns to the right of the candidate's name and party designation. Percentages have been calculated to two decimal places and rounded to one place. Due to rounding and the scattered votes of minor candidates, percentages in individual House races may not add up to 100.

Only candidates from single-member districts who received *at least 5 percent of the total vote* for that election are included. In multi-member districts or at-large districts electing more than one representative, candidates who received fewer than 100 votes were not listed.

If no vote total is shown for a candidate but the percentage of total vote is listed as 100 percent, in most cases the candidate ran unopposed. State election officials either did not put the candidate's name on the ballot or simply did not make an effort to record the total number of votes.

No percentages of total vote have been computed for multi-member districts or at-large districts electing more than one representative. Candidates in these types of districts did not run against specific opponents, and in most cases the number of votes cast in any one contest could not be determined.

In some cases, percentages do not appear next to candidates in single-member districts because vote totals for all the candidates who ran in the district were not available even though the names of all candidates may appear. In such cases, the symbol ✔ appears in the vote column of the winning candidate.

House Popular Vote Returns, 1824-1985

1824 House Elections

DELAWARE

Candidates	Votes	%
AL Louis McLane (FED)	3,387	51.7
Arnold Naudain (OLD R)	3,163	48.3

GEORGIA

AL Wiley Thompson	10,543	✓
John Forsyth	10,219	✓
Edward F. Tattnall	10,043	✓
Alfred Cuthbert	9,950	✓
George Cary	9,672	✓
James Meriwether	9,491	✓
Charles E. Haynes	8,881	✓

Special Election

AL Richard H. Wilde	5,002	61.0
Lyman	3,194	39.0

ILLINOIS

AL Daniel P. Cook (NR)	7,425	62.6
Shadrack Bond	4,409	37.2

INDIANA

1 Ratliff Boon (JAC D)	4,281	42.1
Jacob Call	3,222	31.7
Thomas H. Blake (NR)	2,661	26.2
2 Jonathan Jennings (CLAY R)	4,680	53.2
Jeremiah Sullivan (NR)	4,119	46.8
3 John Test (NR)	3,434	47.1
James Brown Ray (CLAY R)	2,471	33.9
Daniel J. Caswell	1,388	19.0

Special Election

1 Jacob Call (JAC D)	2,155	50.4
Thomas H. Blake (NR)	2,087	48.8

KENTUCKY

1 David Trimble (D)	✓
2 Thomas Metcalfe (D)	✓
3 Henry Clay	✓
4 Robert P. Letcher (CD)	✓
5 James Johnson (D)	✓
6 Joseph Lecompte (D)	✓
7 Thomas P. Moore (D)	✓
8 Richard A. Buckner (D)	✓
9 Charles A. Wickliffe (D)	✓
10 Francis Johnson (AD)	✓
11 William S. Young (D)	✓
12 Robert P. Henry (CLAY D)	✓

LOUISIANA

1 Edward Livingston (D)	✓
2 Henry H. Gurley (W)	✓
3 William L. Brent (W)	✓

MAINE

1 William Burleigh (AD)	✓
2 John Anderson (JEFF D)	✓
3 Ebenezer Herrick	✓
4 Peleg Sprague	✓
5 Enoch Lincoln	✓
6 Jeremiah O'Brien (D)	✓
7 David Kidder (W)	✓

MARYLAND

Candidates	Votes	%
1 Clement Dorsey	1,824	55.3
Raphael Neale	1,476	44.7
2 Joseph Kent	1,908	52.3
John C. Weems	1,741	47.7
3 George Peter	1,602	52.5
George C. Washington	1,448	47.5

Explanation of Symbols in House Returns

In the returns for House elections *symbols* are used to denote special circumstances. In cases where no symbol is used, the candidate who received the most votes won the election to the House. The following is a key to the symbols used:

✓ Elected to the House. The symbol is used to identify winning candidates in three types of situations: (1) When candidates ran for two or more at-large seats in states which chose all of their at-large representatives in a single election, or ran in a multi-member district; (2) when the vote total and percentage of one or more of the candidates are unavailable and (3) when a candidate who did not receive the highest vote total was seated by the House. *(Explanation of multi-member districts, see p. 678.)*

‡ The symbol is used when an election dispute resulted in the unseating of a representative *after* he was sworn in. *(For discussion of specific cases, consult the* Biographical Directory of the American Congress 1774-1971, *U.S. Government Printing Office, Washington, D.C. 1971; hereafter referred to as the* Biographical Directory.*)*

* The symbol is used for three types of situations: (1) When a representative-elect died or declined his seat before the constitutionally set date for the beginning of his term—March 4 until 1935, and Jan. 3 thereafter; (2) when the House refused to seat any candidate claiming election to a seat and (3) when state law required a candidate to obtain a popular vote majority for election to the House, but the candidate receiving the most votes failed to receive a majority. *(For discussion of specific cases, consult the* Biographical Directory; *explanation of majority vote requirement, see p. 703.)*

Information for 1824-1973 returns was obtained from a source other than the Inter-University Consortium for Political and Social Research. *(For a listing of other sources, see p. 1062.)*

Footnotes. Numbered footnotes are used to explain unusual situations, such as a series of elections in the same year in the same House district, anomalies resulting from reapportionment and special procedures for conducting House elections in certain states.

MARYLAND

	Candidates	Votes	%
4	Thomas Worthington	4,321	55.3
	John Lee	3,491	44.7
6	George Mitchell	2,854	53.9
	Phillip Reed	2,439	46.1
7	John Leeds Kerr	1,950	50.3
	Thomas Emory	1,924	49.7
8	Robert Martin	3,088	51.9
	John Spence	2,858	48.1

Multi-Member District

5	Peter Little	9,686✔	
	John Barney	5,515✔	
	Isaac McKim	5,346	

MASSACHUSETTS

		Votes	%
1	Daniel Webster (AR)	3,669	99.9
2	Benjamin W. Crowninshield (AR)	1,379	58.1
	Frederick Howes	760	32.0
3	John Varnum	1,736	50.2
	John Merrill	1,659	48.0
4	Edward Everett	1,906	57.2
	Unidentified Candidate	1,357	40.7
5	John Locke (AR)	1,524	60.6
	Joseph G. Kendall	423	16.8
	Tomes	186	7.4
6	Samuel C. Allen (AR)	1,726	55.7
	George Grennell Jr	1,335	43.1
7	Henry W. Dwight (AR)	1,742	54.8
	Nathan Willis	1,375	43.3
8	Tom Lathrop (AR)	1,874	58.2
	James Fowler	1,201	37.3
9	John Bailey	1,669	57.3
	Sher Leland	991	34.0
10	Francis Baylies (JAC R)	1,778	54.8
	James L. Hodges	1,363	42.0
11	John Reed (AR)	1,057	58.2
	Barker Burnell	460	25.3
	Walter Folger	297	16.4
12	Aaron Hobart (AR)	1,606	72.3
	Ebenezer Gay	320	14.4
	William Baylies	263	11.9
13	John Davis (AR)	1,262	51.2
	James Libley	1,195	48.5

MISSOURI

		Votes	%
AL	John Scott (CLAY R)	5,022	47.0
	George F. Strother (JAC D)	4,528	42.4
	Robert Wash	1,125	10.5

NEW HAMPSHIRE [1]

AL	Ichabod Bartlett	11,603✔	
	Thomas Whipple Jr.	8,690✔	
	James Miller	6,923*	
	Nehemiah Eastman	6,823✔	
	Jonathan Harvey	6,105✔	
	Ezekiel Webster	5,928	
	Joseph Healy	5,479	
	Phinchas Handerson	5,296	
	Titus Brown	5,222	
	Atkinson	4,670	
	Livermore	3,854	
	(Scattering)	801	
	Evans	672	

NEW JERSEY

AL	George Holcombe (D-R)	17,706✔	
	Samuel Swan (D-R)	17,672✔	
	Lewis Condict (D-R)	17,668✔	
	Daniel Garrison (D-R)	17,595✔	
	George Cassedy (D-R)	17,550✔	
	Ebenezer Tucker (D-R)	17,022✔	

NEW YORK

	Candidates	Votes	%
1	Silas Wood	2,140	60.5
	James Lent	1,398	39.5
2	Joshua Sands	1,683	53.1
	John T. Bergen	1,484	46.9
4	Aaron Ward	1,586	39.0
	Jonathan Ward	1,297	31.9
	John Hunter	1,188	29.2
5	Bartow White	3,596	52.8
	Peter Livingston	3,210	47.2
6	John Hallock Jr	2,103	47.2
	Hector Craig	1,978	44.4
	Walter Case	374	8.4
7	Abraham Hasbrouck	2,916	51.2
	John Lounsberry	2,781	48.8
8	James Strong	3,129	60.0
	Robert Livingston	2,089	40.0
9	William McManus	3,807	56.6
	George R. Davis	2,925	43.5
10	Stephen Van Rensselaer	3,850	100.0
11	Henry Ashley	3,531	58.4
	William Heermance	2,519	41.6
12	William Deitz	2,810	56.9
	Constant Brown	2,129	43.1
13	William G. Angel	3,379	52.2
	William Campbell	3,094	47.8
14	Henry Storrs	4,146	57.3
	James Lynch	3,094	42.7
15	Michael Hoffman	2,410	52.7
	John Herkimer	2,164	47.3
16	Henry Markell	3,114	54.9
	William Dodge	2,562	45.1
17	John W. Taylor	3,858	100.0
18	Henry C. Martindale	3,448	64.6
	John Gale	1,893	35.4
19	Henry Ross	3,209	52.3
	William Hogan	2,932	47.7
21	Elias Whitmore	3,128	50.4
	Lot Clark	3,073	49.6
22	John Miller	3,857	54.3
	John Lynde	3,243	45.7
23	Luther Badger	3,214	50.8
	Elisha Litchfield	3,116	49.2
24	Charles Kellogg	3,372	53.1
	Rowland Day	2,976	46.9
25	Charles Humphrey	3,144	51.2
	David Woodcook	2,999	48.8
27	Moses Hayden	4,456	59.5
	Charles H. Carroll	3,028	40.5
28	Timothy Porter	2,099	35.3
	William Woods	1,937	32.6
	Daniel Cruger	1,693	28.5
29	Parmenio Adams	4,035	57.6
	Isaac Wilson	2,969	42.4
30	Daniel Garnsey	2,387	35.4
	William Hotchkiss	2,235	33.1
	John G. Camp	2,127	31.5

Multi-Member Districts

3	Churchill C. Cambreleng	5,650✔	
	Gulian Verplanck	4,863✔	
	Jeromous Johnson	4,588✔	
	John Rathbone	3,980	
	Charles G. Haines	3,855	
	Peter Sharpe	3,741	
	Henry Wheaton	750	
20	Nicoll Fosdick	5,676✔	
	Egbert Ten Eyck	5,484‡	
	Daniel Hugunin Jr.	5,128	
	Horance Allen	5,466	
26	Dudley Marvin	8,366✔	
	Robert Rose	4,899✔	
	John Maynard	4,438	
	Aaron Remer	2,732	

OHIO [2]

	David Jennings	✔	
	Mordecai Bartley	✔	
	William McLean	✔	
	William Wilson	✔	

Candidates	Votes	%
Philemon Beecher (FED)	✔	
John C. Wright (AD)	✔	
John Sloane (W)	✔	
Elisha Whittlesey (W)	✔	
John Woods (W)	✔	
Samuel F. Vinton (W)	✔	
James Findlay (JAC D)	✔	
John W. Campbell (D)	✔	
John Thomson (D)	✔	
Joseph Vance (D)	✔	

PENNSYLVANIA

1	John Wurts	✔	
2	Joseph Hemphill	✔	
3	Daniel H. Miller	✔	
5	Philip S. Markley	✔	
6	Robert Harris	✔	
	Christian Gleim		
10	James S. Mitchell	✔	
12	John Mitchell	✔	
13	Alexander Thompson	✔	
14	Andrew Stewart	✔	
15	Joseph Lawrence	✔	
16	George Plumer	✔	
	John H. Wise		
18	Patrick Farrelly	✔	

Multi-Member Districts

4	James Buchanan	✔	
	Charles Miner	✔	
	Samuel Edwards	✔	
	William Anderson		
	Isaac D. Barnard		
	Samuel Houston		
7	William Addams	✔	
	Henry Wilson	✔	
	George Keck		
	Daniel Rose		
8	George Wolf	✔	
	Samuel D. Ingham	✔	
9	Samuel McKean	✔	
	George Kremer	✔	
	Espy Van Horne	✔	
	William Cox Ellis		
11	James Wilson	✔	
	John Findlay	✔	
17	James Allison Jr	✔	
	James S. Stevenson	✔	

SOUTH CAROLINA

		Votes	%
1	Joel R. Poinsett (D)	1,474	58.4
	Samuel Warren	1,052	41.7
2	James Hamilton Jr (SR FT)		100.0
3	Thomas R. Mitchell		100.0
4	Andrew R. Govan		100.0
5	Starling Tucker		100.0
6	George McDuffie (D)	✔	
7	Joseph Gist (D)	3,398	54.8
	J. McCreary	1,869	30.2
	F. W. Davie	933	15.1
8	John Wilson	✔	
9	John Carter	1,882	46.3
	Spann	1,132	27.8
	Levy	1,055	25.9

VERMONT

		Votes	%
1	William C. Bradley	✔	
2	Rollin C. Mallary	3,284	95.6
3	George E. Wales	✔	
4	Ezra Meech	3,093	54.6
	Benjamin Swift	1,836	32.4
	Stephen Royce	404	7.1
5	John Mattocks	2,434	52.7
	Daniel A. A. Buck	2,099	45.4

Footnotes, see p. 703.

1825 House Elections

ALABAMA

Candidates	Votes	%
1 Gabriel Moore (JAC D)	5,098	71.1
Clement Comer Clay (JAC D)	2,070	28.9
2 Robert E. B. Baylor (JAC D)	1,687	56.8
John McKee	972✓	31.7
John D. Terrell (NR)	342	11.5
3 George Owen (JAC D)	543	100.0

CONNECTICUT

Candidates	Votes	
AL Gideon Tomlinson	6,263✓	
Elisha Phelps	5,934✓	
Ralph Ingersoll	5,628✓	
Orange Merwin	5,518✓	
Noyes Barber	4,401✓	
John Baldwin	3,653✓	
Daniel Burrows	1,785	
Elisha Tracy	1,491	
Timothy Pitkin	1,293	
Calvin Willey	911	
Samual Foot	574	
Dennis Kimberly	415	
Asa Barron	407	
George Learnid	376	
Samual Church	305	
Robert Fairchild	220	
Roger Sherman	186	
Lyman Law	162	
Calvin Goddard	160	
Thomas Williams	149	

MISSISSIPPI

	Votes	%
AL Christopher Rankin (JAC D)	5,671	99.1

NEW HAMPSHIRE[1]

Special Elections

Candidates	Votes	%
AL Titus Brown	✓	
AL Joseph Healy	13,600	56.4
Ezekiel Webster	10,523	43.6

NORTH CAROLINA

Candidates	Votes	%
1 Lemuel Sawyer (OPP R)	2,483	59.8
Alfred M. Gatlin (OLD R)	1,671	40.2
2 Willis Alston (OPP R)	1,321	42.1
George Outlaw Sr (OLD R)	978	31.2
James Grant	837	26.7
3 Richard Hines (OPP R)	2,607	52.7
Thomas H. Hall (OLD R)	2,343	47.3
4 John H. Bryan (OPP R)	2,488	51.0
Richard D. Spaight (OLD R)	2,392	49.0
5 Gabriel Holmes (OPP R)	3,347	62.8
Charles Hooks (OLD R)	1,982	37.2
6 Weldon N. Edwards (OLD R)		100.0
7 Archibald McNeill (OLD R)	✓	
John Culpepper (OPP R)		
8 Willie P. Mangum (FED)	2,301	50.6
Josiah Crudup	2,243	49.4
9 Romulus M. Saunders (LD R)	✓	
10 John Long Jr	3,252	52.9
John Giles	2,891	47.1
11 Henry W. Conner (OLD R)	✓	
T. Hunt (OPP R)	86	
12 Samuel P. Carson (OPP R)	2,081	35.2
Robert B. Vance (OLD R)	1,924	32.6
James Graham (OLD R)	1,903	32.2
13 Lewis Williams	✓	

RHODE ISLAND[2]

	Votes	
AL Tristam Burges	2,932✓	
Dutee J. Pearce	2,534	
Job Durfee	2,468	
Samuel Eddy	2,121	
William Hunter	364	

Special Election

	Votes	%
AL Dutee J. Pearce	1,960	56.9
Job Durfee	1,482	43.0

TENNESSEE

Candidates	Votes	%
1 John Blair	3,613	51.9
John Tipton	3,348	48.1
2 John Cocke	3,887	56.1
Thomas Arnold	3,044	43.9
3 James Standifer	4,332	53.3
James C. Mitchell	3,793✓	46.7
4 Jacob C. Isacks	✓	
6 James K. Polk	3,659	35.3
Andrew Erwin	2,742	26.5
Lunsford M. Bramlett	2,347	22.7
James Sanford	1,508	14.6

(continued)

Candidates	Votes	%
7 Samuel Houston	5,684	84.8
John Bruce	1,014	15.1
8 John H. Marable	2,177	38.7
James B. Reynolds	1,922	34.1
Willie Blount	1,533	27.2
9 Adam R. Alexander	2,865	42.0
David Crockett	2,594	38.1
James Ferrill	912	13.4
Thomas H. Persons	447	6.6

VIRGINIA

Candidates		
1 Thomas Newton Jr	✓	
2 James Trezvant	✓	
Eppes		
3 William S. Archer	✓	
4 Mark Alexander	✓	
5 John Randolph	✓	
6 Thomas Davenport	✓	
Urquehart		
Lanier		
Graves		
7 Nathaniel H. Claiborne	✓	
J. Leftwich		
8 Burwell Bassett	✓	
S. Jones		
James		
9 Robert S. Garnett	✓	
Upshaw		
10 John Taliaferro	✓	
Hooe		
11 Andrew Stevenson	✓	
12 William C. Rives	✓	
13 Robert Taylor	✓	
14 Charles F. Mercer	✓	
15 William Armstrong	✓	
Colston		
16 William McCoy	✓	
Shetter		
17 John Floyd	✓	
18 Benjamin Estill (AR)	✓	
Graham		
Crockett		
19 William Smith	✓	
Lovell		
20 Alfred H. Powell	✓	
Smith		
Steenberger		
Kercheval		
21 Joseph Johnson	✓	
Doddridge		
22 John S. Barbour	✓	
Maxwell		

1824 Elections

1. New Hampshire was entitled to six representatives in the House for the 19th Congress (1825-27). State law required that to be elected, a candidate had to receive a popular vote majority for any particular House seat. With candidates running at large, as they did in the 1824 election, the determination of what constituted a majority was calculated as follows:

First, the total vote was calculated by summing all votes cast for the House, yielding a figure of 72,066. This figure divided by six, the number of House seats to be filled, equals 12,011. In order to win, a candidate thus needed a majority of the 12,011 votes, that is, one half plus one additional vote. Dividing 12,011 by two equals 6,005.5, which was rounded up to whole votes to 6,006—the vote total needed for election.

Five candidates who were running—Bartlett, Whipple, Miller, Eastman and Harvey—received at least 6,006 votes and thus were elected. Miller did not serve in the House; thus an asterisk appears next to his vote total.

Since none of the other candidates qualified for the sixth seat, it remained vacant until a special election was held in 1825 between Webster and Healy, who finished sixth and seventh in 1824. (See 1825 New Hampshire, this page.)

2. No information available as to whether the Ohio representatives were elected by district or at large.

1825 Elections

1. Brown filed a vacancy left when James Miller was elected in 1824 but did not serve. Healy defeated Webster to fill the state's undecided sixth House seat, which no candidate had won in 1824 due to the majority vote requirement.

2. Rhode Island was entitled to two seats in the 19th Congress (1825-27), but state law required that a candidate receive a popular vote majority for election. Pearce failed to qualify in the general election but won the subsequent special election shown on this page. (Majority Vote Requirement, see box this page.)

Majority Vote Requirement

During part of the 19th century, five New England states—Maine, Massachusetts, New Hampshire, Rhode Island and Vermont—had state laws requiring that candidates win election to the House by a popular vote majority. The specific procedures varied among the five states. The majority vote requirement was last used in 1892 Rhode Island (See p. 678).

The footnote on this page for the 1824 New Hampshire section explains how the majority vote requirement worked in New Hampshire when two or more candidates running at-large could be elected. For the purpose of illustrating how the vote total required for election was determined, Congressional Quarterly has *included all election returns* provided by the ICPSR for this election.

In other at-large elections appearing in this section (pages 701 to 1050), candidates receiving fewer than 100 votes and scattered votes for unidentified candidates are *deleted*. Therefore, the calculation of the vote total needed for election in these five states, in cases where a majority was required, cannot be determined on the basis of the returns published in the *Guide to U.S. Elections, Second Edition*.

1826 House Elections

DELAWARE

	Candidates	Votes	%
AL	Louis McLane (FED)	4,630*	54.1
	Arnold Naudain (OLD R)	3,931	45.9

GEORGIA

1	Edward F. Tattnall	1,623	100.0
2	John Forsyth	2,717	100.0
3	Wiley Thompson	3,042	60.3
	Cleveland	2,001	39.7
4	Wilson Lumpkin	4,070	50.3
	Colquett	4,026	49.7
5	Charles E. Haynes	2,369	78.7
	Longstreet	640	21.3
6	Tomlinson Fort	2,993	54.0
	Cuthbert	2,552	46.0
7	John Floyd	3,971	51.2
	King	3,786	48.8

ILLINOIS

AL	Joseph Duncan (JAC D)	6,322	49.3
	Daniel P. Cook (NR)	5,669	44.2
	James Tumey	824	6.4

INDIANA

1	Thomas H. Blake (NR)	5,223	43.0
	Ratliff Boon (JAC D)	5,202	42.8
	Lawrence S. Shuler	1,723	14.2
2	Jonathan Jennings (CLAY R)	7,913	99.5
3	Oliver H. Smith (JAC D)	6,015	54.9
	John Test (NR)	4,946	45.1

KENTUCKY

Special Elections

5	Robert McHatton (JAC D)	1,479	34.3
	Alfred Sandford	1,167	27.1
	Nicholas D. Coleman	992	23.0
	William Brown	677	15.7
12	John F. Henry (NR)	2,206	51.0
	Chittenden Lyon (JAC D)	2,119	49.0

LOUISIANA

1	Edward Livingston (D)	✔	
2	Henry H. Gurley	✔	
3	William L. Brent	✔	

MAINE

1	William Burleigh (AD)	2,140	60.5
2	John Anderson (JEFF D)	2,399	57.9
3	Joseph F. Wingate (D)	1,531	55.2
4	Peleg Sprague	1,613	97.2
5	James W. Ripley (D)	1,504	52.7
6	Jeremiah O'Brien (D)	1,716	54.4
7	Samuel Butman	✔	
	W. D. Williamson		

MARYLAND

1	Clement Dorsey	1,580	91.1
2	John C. Weems	1,687	50.2
	Regin Estep	1,672	49.8
3	George C. Washington	2,100	53.6
	George Peter	1,815	46.4

	Candidates	Votes	%
4	Michael C. Sprigg	3,085	43.5
	John Lee	2,672	37.7
	T. Kennedy	671	9.5
	S. Hughes	668	9.4
6	Levin Gale	1,204	25.2
	I. Demaulsby	1,145	24.0
	J. Williams	1,008	21.1
	William Colliller	763	16.0
	P. Reed	551	11.5
7	John L. Kerr	1,890	52.9
	P. B. Hopper	1,680	47.1
8	Ephraim K. Wilson	3,514	97.7

Multi-Member District

5	Peter Little	7,017	✔
	John Barney	6,916	✔
	John Kennedy	3,997	

MASSACHUSETTS

1	Daniel Webster (AR)	1,545	92.6
2	Benjamin W. Crowninshield (AR)	234	58.9
	Stephen White	39	9.8
3	John Varnum	1,773	61.0
	Caleb Cushing	916	31.5
4	Edward Everett	1,292	96.4
5	John Locke (AR)	886	55.2
	Joseph Kendall	539	33.6
	Luther Lawrence	140	8.7
6	Samuel C. Allen (AR)	1,227	57.6
	George Grennell	826	38.8
7	Henry W. Dwight (AR)	2,597	58.9
	Nathan Willis	1,082	24.5
	Jon Allen	561	12.7
8	Isaac C. Bates	1,833	60.8
	Samuel C. Lathrop	948	31.4
	James Rowler	220	7.3
9	John Baily (AR)	854	60.0
	William Ellis	331	23.2
10	James L. Hodges	1,551	56.1
	Hercules Cushman	717	25.9
	Francis Bayleys (JACS R)	429	15.5
11	John Reed (AR)	998	81.9
	Walter Folger	201	16.5
12	Joseph Richardson	1,188	58.9
	Thomas L. Beats	670	33.2
13	John Davis (AR)	1,316	90.1
	Jonas Tibley	110	7.5

MISSOURI

AL	Edward Bates (JAC D)	6,636	61.5
	Scott (NR)	4,159	38.5

NEW JERSEY

AL	George Holcombe (JAC&AR)	24,538	✔
	Lewis Condict (AR)	15,615	✔
	Samuel Swan (AR)	14,701	✔
	Isaac Pierson (AR)	14,697	✔
	Hedge Thompson (AR)	14,479	✔
	Ebenezer Tucker (AR)	14,433	✔
	Daniel Garrison (JAC R)	10,166	
	George Cassedy (JAC R)	9,944	
	Isaac G. Farlee (JAC R)	9,752	
	Benjamin B. Cooper (JAC R)	9,512	
	William Kennedy (JAC R)	9,282	
	James Parker	637	
	Ephraim Bateman	297	
	Peter D. Vroom	136	
	Caleb Newbold	110	

NEW YORK

	Candidates	Votes	%
1	Silas Wood	1,485	97.9
2	John Wood	1,335	54.7
	John Smith	1,104	45.3
4	Aaron Ward	2,566	59.6
	John Haff	1,738	40.4
5	Thomas Oakley	3,266	50.8
	Edmund Pendleton	3,159	49.2
6	John Hallock Jr.	2,393	56.8
	Hector Craig	1,817	43.2
7	George Belden	2,677	50.7
	Lemuel Jenkins	2,608	49.4
8	James Strong	2,984	59.9
	Walter Patterson	2,002	40.2
9	John Dickinson	3,339	51.9
	James Hogeboom	3,098	48.1
10	Stephen Van Rensselaer	3,006	100.0
11	Selah Hobbie	4,076	58.9
	Isaac Burr	2,847	41.1
12	John De Graff	3,309	100.0
13	Samuel Chase	2,618	50.9
	George Morell	2,389	46.4
14	Henry Storrs	4,174	69.8
	Ezekiel Bacon	1,808	30.2
15	Michael Hoffman	2,684	59.5
	Daniel Van Horn	1,829	40.5
16	Henry Markell	2,611	51.6
	Aarron Haring	2,445	48.4
17	John W. Taylor	2,910	57.5
	Alphens Goodrich	2,150	42.5
18	Henry Martindale	2,496	51.1
	John Williard	2,392	48.9
19	Richard Keese	3,328	52.4
	Asa Hascall	3,022	47.6
21	John Clark	3,354	52.6
	Robert Monell	3,024	47.4
22	John G. Stower	3,785	55.6
	John Miller	3,024	44.4
23	Jonas Earll Jr	3,420	51.8
	Luther Badger	3,178	48.2
24	Nathaniel Garrow	3,039	54.1
	Elijah Miller	2,575	45.9
25	David Woodcook	3,366	52.3
	Charles Humphrey	3,076	47.8
27	Daniel Barnard	4,299	52.3
	Enos Pomeroy	3,927	47.7
28	John Magee	3,300	40.8
	Timothy Porter	2,331	28.9
	William Woods	1,246	15.4
	Phillip Church	1,203	14.9
29	David Evans	3,843	54.2
	Simeon Cumings	3,251	45.8
30	Daniel Garnsey	4,801	55.1
	Albert Tracy	3,919	44.9

Multi-Member Districts

3	Churchill C. Cambreleng	9,108	✔
	Gulian Verplanck	5,705	✔
	Jeromus Johnson	5,376	✔
	King	3,814	
	Vanwych	3,631	
20	Silas Wright	6,579	✔
	Rudolph Bunner	6,558	✔
	Nicolli Fosdick	6,048	
	Elisha Camp	6,039	
26	Dudley Marvin	8,082	✔
	John Maynard	5,554	✔
	Nathaniel Allen	4,153	
	John Knox	2,631	

OHIO

1	James Findlay (JAC R)	2,954	42.6
	D. Morris (AR)	2,443	35.2
	T. Morris (JAC R)	1,546	22.3
2	John Woods (AR)	✔	
	T. R. Ross (JAC R)		

OHIO

Candidates	Votes	%
3 William McLean (AR)	✔	
4 Joseph Vance (AR)	✔	
5 William Russell (JAC R)	2,111	35.5
Collins (AR)	1,444	24.3
Morris (AR)	1,249	21.0
Shephard (AR)	1,140	19.2
6 William Creighton Jr (AR)	3,652	63.5
John Thompson	2,099	36.5
7 Samuel F. Vinton (AR)	✔	
8 William Wilson (AR)	✔	
9 Philemon Beecher (AR)	3,708	61.3
Mathews (JAC R)	2,346	38.8
10 John Davenport (AR)	✔	
11 John C. Wright (AR)	2,344	35.5
Beebe (AR)	2,136	32.4
John M. Goodenow (JAC R)	2,116	32.1
12 John Sloane (AR)	3,417	50.7
John Tomson (JAC R)	3,319	49.3
13 Elisha Whittlesey (AR)	✔	
14 Mordecai Bartley (AR)	2,500	59.7
Cooke	1,688	40.3

Special Election[1]

Thomas Shannon (D)	✔	

PENNSYLVANIA

Candidates	Votes	%
1 Joel Sutherland (JAC R)	✔	
S. Breck (AR)		
W. Duane		
2 John Sergeant (AR)	✔	
Horn (JAC R)		
Thomas Kittera (UNP R)		
3 Daniel H. Miller (JAC R)	✔	
Harrison		

Candidates	Votes	%
5 John B. Sterigere	✔	
6 Innis Green	✔	
John M. Forster		
10 Adam King	✔	
12 John Mitchell	✔	
13 Chauncy Forward	✔	
14 Andrew Stewart	✔	
15 Joseph Lawrence	✔	
16 Richard Coulter (FED)	✔	
18 Stephan Barlow	✔	

Multi-Member Districts

Candidates	Votes	%
4 Charles Miner (FED)	✔	
James Buchanan (FED)	✔	
Samuel Anderson (FED)	✔	
7 Joseph Fry	✔	
William Addams	✔	
8 Samuel D. Ingham	✔	
George Wolf	✔	
9 Samuel McKean	✔	
Espy Van Horne	✔	
George Kremer	✔	
11 James Wilson	✔	
William Ramsey	✔	
17 James S. Stevenson	✔	
Robert Orr Jr.	✔	

Special Elections

Candidates	Votes	%
2 Thomas Kittera (FED)	✔	
Horn (JAC R)		
13 Chauncy Forward	✔	
William Piper		
18 Thomas H. Sill (FED)	1,812	39.8
Barlow	1,045	23.0
Hays	937	20.6
Herrington	760	16.7

SOUTH CAROLINA

Candidates	Votes	%
1 William Drayton (UN D)		100.0
2 James Hamilton Jr (SR FT)		100.0
3 Thomas R. Mitchell	✔	
Robert B. Campbell		
4 William D. Martin (D)	✔	
Andrew R. Govan		
5 Starling Tucker	✔	
Caldwell		
6 George McDuffie (D)	✔	
7 William T. Nuckolls	✔	
Samuel McCreary		
James McKibbin		
8 Warren R. Davis (SR D)	2,478	50.3
John Wilson	2,453	49.8
9 John Carter		100.0

VERMONT[2]

Candidates	Votes	%
1 Jonathan Hunt (NR)	✔	
2 Rollin C. Mallary	3,050	98.3
3 George E. Wales	2,634	96.2
4 Heman Allen	2,631*	46.5
Benjamin Swift	2,546	45.0
5 Daniel Azro Ashley Buck (D)	4,400	73.0
James Bell (NR)	1,542	25.6

VIRGINIA

Special Election

Candidates	Votes	%
5 George W. Crump (JAC R)	✔	
Giles		

1. No information available as to whether Shannon was elected in a district or at large.

2. In the 4th district, neither candidate received the majority of the vote required to win. In a later election, for which no returns are available, Swift was elected.

House Candidates Index

For an index of all House candidates listed in this section (pages 701 to 1061), see pages 1180-1273. Instructions for use of the House Candidates Index appear on page 1180.

1827 House Elections

ALABAMA

	Candidates	Votes	%
1	Gabriel Moore (JAC D)	846	100.0
2	John McKee	1,140	69.5
	Thomas W. Farrar	500	30.5
3	George Owen (JAC D)		100.0

CONNECTICUT

		Votes	
AL	Ralph Ingersoll	7,838✔	
	Elisha Phelps	6,762✔	
	David Plant	4,890✔	
	Orange Merwin	4,472✔	
	John Baldwin	4,195✔	
	Noyes Barber	3,607✔	
	Alexander Stewart	2,690	
	Ansel Sterling	2,656	
	Andrew Judson	2,509	
	Robert Fairchild	2,451	
	Timothy Pitkin	1,304	
	Lyman Law	1,284	
	Joseph Eaton	1,211	
	Noah Benedict	948	
	Gideon Tomlinson	484	
	Alexander Stewart	474	
	Roger Sherman	448	
	Nathan Pendleton	416	
	Thomas S. Williams	351	

DELAWARE

Special Election

		Votes	%
AL	Kensey Johns Jr (FED)	4,148	52.4
	James A. Bayard (OLD R)	3,753	47.4

GEORGIA

Special Elections

		Votes	%
AL	Richard H. Wilde	✔	
AL	George R. Gilmer	21,008	63.5
	Charlton	12,094	36.5

KENTUCKY

		Votes	%
1	Henry Daniel (JAC D)	4,163	52.2
	David Trimble (JAC D)	3,811	47.8
2	Thomas Metcalfe (JAC D)	2,964	54.9
	Conn	2,436	45.1
3	James Clark (JAC D)	2,914	57.9
	Taylor	2,121	42.1
4	Robert P. Letcher (W)	3,637	53.3
	Rodes	3,182	46.7
5	Robert L. McHatton (JAC D)	3,307	52.5
	Sandford	2,988	47.5
6	Joseph Lecompte (JAC D)	3,546	50.9
	Crittenden	3,183	45.7
7	Thomas P. Moore (JAC D)	3,681	90.5
	Thompson	386	9.5
8	Richard A. Buckner (A-JAC D)	3,527	52.1
	Owens	3,247	47.9
9	Charles A. Wickliffe (JAC D)	3,856	66.1
	White	1,982	34.0
10	Joel Yancey (JAC D)	3,268	50.8
	Johnson	3,169	49.2

	Candidates	Votes	%
11	William S. Young (JAC D)	4,009	56.0
	John Calhoun	3,155	44.0
12	Chittenden Lyon (JAC D)	3,471	52.1
	Henry (NR)	2,070	31.1
	New	1,123	16.9

Special Elections[1]

		Votes	
11	John Calhoon	2,290	*
	Thomas Chilton	1,685	
11	Thomas Chilton	✔	
	John Calhoon		

MAINE

Special Election

		Votes	%
1	Rufus McIntire (JAC D)	2,169	54.5
	John Holmes	1,814	45.5

MISSISSIPPI

		Votes	%
AL	William Haile (JAC D)	1,914	34.6
	John Norton	1,312	23.7
	Beverly R. Grayson	1,204	21.8
	Adam Benjamin (NR)	1,096	19.8

NEW HAMPSHIRE

		Votes	
AL	Ichabod Bartlett (OLD R)	22,680✔	
	Titus Brown (OLD R)	22,354✔	
	Joseph Healy (OLD R)	21,515✔	
	Jonathan Harvey (OLD R)	20,873✔	
	David Barker Jr (OLD R)	14,456✔	
	Thomas Whipple Jr (OLD R)	12,189✔	
	E. Web (AR)		
	S. C. Web		
	Eastman		
	Cartland		

NORTH CAROLINA

		Votes	%
1	Lemuel Sawyer (OLD R)	2,943	65.1
	William B. Shepard (OPP R)	1,579	34.9
2	Willis Alston	✔	
3	Thomas H. Hall (OPP R)	✔	
	Richard Hines (OLD R)		
4	John H. Bryan	✔	
5	Gabriel Holmes	✔	
6	Daniel Turner	1,116	28.5
	Charles A. Hill	1,049	26.8
	Willis Boddie	783	20.0
	William M. Sneed	620	15.8
	Joseph H. Bryan	345	8.8
7	John Culpepper (AR)	2,375	41.2
	John A. Cameron	1,990	34.5
	John Gilchrist	1,387	24.1
8	Daniel L. Barringer (OLD R)	2,398	53.3
	Archibald D. Murphey (OPP R)	2,102	46.7
9	Augustine H. Shepperd (OLD R)	4,304	64.6
	Bedford Brown (OPP R)	2,361	35.4
10	John Long (AR)	✔	
	Asa Eubank		
11	Henry W. Conner (OLD R)	3,182	81.9
	Samuel Henderson (OPP R)	702	18.1
12	Samuel P. Carson (OLD R)	4,187	63.4
	Robert B. Vance (OPP R)	2,419	36.6

	Candidates	Votes	%
13	Lewis Williams (AR)	✔	
	John Mushat		

RHODE ISLAND

		Votes	
AL	Tristam Burges (NR)	2,230✔	
	Dutee J. Pearce (NR)	2,126✔	

TENNESSEE

		Votes	%
1	John Blair	4,216	55.8
	John Tipton	3,208	42.4
2	Pryor Lea	3,688	39.7
	Thomas D. Arnold	3,316	35.7
	William B. Reese	2,272	24.5
3	James C. Mitchell	5,732	55.7
	James Standifer	4,566	44.3
4	Jacob C. Isacks	6,823	100.0
5	Robert Desha	4,509	61.1
	John Hall	1,581	21.4
	William Trousdale	1,292	17.5
6	James K. Polk	6,351	56.6
	Lunsford M. Bramlett	4,878	43.4
7	John Bell	4,889	55.7
	Felix Grundy	3,887	44.3
8	James B. Reynolds	2,609	51.0
	John H. Marable	2,507✔	49.0
9	David Crockett	5,868	49.1
	Adam R. Alexander	3,646	30.5
	William Arnold	2,427	20.3

VIRGINIA

1	Thomas Newton Jr (AR)	✔	
	George Loyall		
2	James Trezvant	✔	
3	William S. Archer	✔	
4	Mark Alexander	✔	
5	John Randolph	✔	
6	Thomas Davenport	✔	
7	Nathaniel H. Claiborne	✔	
	Campbell		
8	Burwell Bassett	✔	
9	John Roane	✔	
10	John Taliaferro	✔	
11	Andrew Stevenson	✔	
12	William C. Rives	✔	
13	Philip P. Barbour (A-A)	✔	
14	Charles F. Mercer	✔	
	Thompson		
15	William Armstrong	✔	
	Peter		
16	William McCoy	✔	
17	John Floyd	✔	
18	Alexander Smyth	✔	
	Sharp		
19	Lewis Maxwell	✔	
	Smith		
	Lovell		
20	Robert Allen	✔	
	Samuel Kercheval		
	Alfred H. Powell		
21	Isaac Leffler (AR)	✔	
	Haymond		
	Johnson (JAC R)		
22	John S. Barbour	✔	
	Hunton		

1. Rep. William S. Young died Sept. 20, 1827, and a special election was held to replace him in November of that year. In initial counting of the returns, Thomas Chilton led John Calhoon 2,704 votes to 2,679. But then returns from Hardin County were thrown out, with Chilton losing 1,019 votes and Calhoon losing only 389 votes, making Calhoon the winner. The returns minus Hardin County are listed in the ICPSR data above.

Calhoon then resigned, never having formally claimed the House seat, and both candidates then petitioned the governor to call a new election. A second special election was held Dec. 20-22, and was won by Chilton. No returns are available.

1828 House Elections

DELAWARE

Candidates	Votes	%
AL Kensey Johns Jr. (FED)	4,769	52.2
James A. Bayard (OLD R)	4,347	47.5

GEORGIA

Candidates	Votes	%
AL George R. Gilmer	*	
Thomas F. Foster	✔	
Richard H. Wilde	✔	
Wilson Lumpkin	✔	
James M. Wayne	✔	
Charles E. Haynes	✔	
Wiley Thompson	✔	

ILLINOIS

Candidates	Votes	%
AL Joseph Duncan (JAC D)	10,447	62.9
George Forquer (NR)	6,158	37.1

INDIANA

Candidates	Votes	%
1 Ratliff Boon (JAC D)	7,272	52.2
Thomas H. Blake (NR)	6,671	47.8
2 Jonathan Jennings (CLAY R)	7,659	73.3
John H. Thompson	2,785	26.7
3 John Test (NR)	6,867	55.8
Jonathan McCarty (JAC D)	5,433	44.2

LOUISIANA

Candidates	Votes	%
1 Edward D. White	✔	
2 Henry H. Gurley	✔	
3 Walter H. Overton (D)	✔	

MAINE[1]

Candidates	Votes	%
1 Rufus McIntire (JAC D)	2,981	66.0
2 John Anderson (JEFF D)	3,189	76.2
3 Joseph F. Wingate (D)	2,086	73.0
4 Peleg Sprague	2,086*	94.4
5 James W. Ripley (JAC R)	2,394	56.9
Reuel Washburn (AR)	1,813	43.1
6 Jeremiah O'Brien (D)	1,709*	48.2
Hathaway	1,119	31.5
7 Samuel Butman	3,336	62.0

MASSACHUSETTS

Candidates	Votes	%
1 Benjamin Gorham	3,234	78.3
William Ingalls	819	19.8
2 Benjamin W. Crowninshield (AR)	1,326	54.0
Leverett Saltonstall	631	25.7
Ezra Mudge	284	11.6
Joseph S. Cabot (JACS R)	186	7.6
3 John Varnum	1,663	72.6
George Savory	379	16.6
Samuel Phillips	149	6.5
4 Edward Everett	3,004	73.9
S. M. Parker	470	11.6
S. Fiske	465	11.4
5 Joseph G. Kendall	1,436	52.7
John Socke (AR)	1,205	44.2
6 George Grennell Jr	2,023	69.7
Elihu Hoyt	456	15.7
Samuel F. Dickinson	277	9.5
7 Henry W. Dwight (AR)	2,237	53.0
George W. Briggs	1,033	24.5
Nathan Willis (JACS R)	922	21.8
8 Isaac C. Bates (AR)	2,133	87.7
John Mills	192	7.9

Candidates	Votes	%
9 John Bailey (AR)	2,047	77.4
William Ellis	375	14.2
Ebenezer Seaver	151	5.7
10 James L. Hodges	1,338	81.5
Francis Baylies	129	7.9
11 John Reed (AR)	1,027	94.3
12 Joseph Richardson	1,114	50.4
Thomas P. Beal	1,003	45.4
13 John Davis (AR)	2,293	89.6
Jonas Sibley (JACS R)	184	7.2

MISSISSIPPI

Special Election

Candidates	Votes	%
AL Thomas Hinds (JAC D)	1,844	89.5

MISSOURI

Candidates	Votes	%
AL Spencer Pettis (JAC D)	7,108	61.0
Edward Bates (NR)	4,539	39.0

NEW JERSEY

Candidates	Votes	%
AL Lewis Condict (NR)	23,783✔	
Richard M. Cooper (NR)	23,737✔	
Isaac Pierson (NR)	23,733✔	
Samuel Swan (NR)	23,709✔	
James F. Randolph (NR)	23,684✔	
Thomas H. Hughes (NR)	23,604✔	
William N. Jeffers (JAC D)	22,014	
James Parker (JAC D)	22,003	
Peter D. Vroom Jr (JAC D)	21,994	
John Clement (JAC D)	21,949	
George Cassedy (JAC D)	21,921	
Samuel Fowler (JAC D)	21,902	

Special Elections

Candidates	Votes	%
AL Thomas Sinnickson (NR)	23,425	51.8
James D. Westcott (JAC D)	21,527	47.6
AL James F. Randolph (NR)	23,388	51.7
James Parker (JAC D)	21,752	48.1

NEW YORK

Candidates	Votes	%
1 James Lent	3,105	52.3
Silas Wood	2,831	47.7
2 Jacob Crocheron	2,885	59.2
Peter Radcliff	1,988	40.8
4 Henry B. Cowles	3,492	51.0
Tompkins	3,352	49.0
5 Abraham Bockee	4,640	58.5
Pendleton	3,293	41.5
6 Hector Craig	3,535	55.7
Wilkin	2,816	44.3
7 Charles G. De Witt	4,203	61.9
Bevier	1,857	27.4
Bogardus	731	10.8
8 James Strong	3,592	50.9
James Vanderpoel	3,459	49.1
9 John Dickinson	4,588	51.6
George Davis	4,302	48.4
10 Ambrose Spencer	4,157	51.0
Charles Dudley	3,889	47.7
11 Perkins King	5,342	61.6
Jacob Haight	3,335	38.4
12 Peter Borst	3,637	57.5
Jacob Livingston	2,688	42.5
13 William Angel	4,474	55.7
Erastus Crafts	3,559	44.3
14 Henry Storrs	5,508	51.1
Greene C. Bronson	5,274	48.9

Candidates	Votes	%
15 Michael Hoffman	3,246	100.0
16 Benedict Arnold	4,064	52.9
William Dodge	3,623	47.1
17 John Taylor	3,533	54.9
John Cramer	2,900	45.1
18 Henry Martindale	3,902	58.0
John Willard	2,823	42.0
19 Isaac Finch	4,682	51.8
William Hogan	4,360	48.2
21 Robert Monell	4,720	63.6
Tilly Lynde	2,704	36.4
22 Thomas Beekman	4,831	53.4
John Stower	4,217	46.6
23 Jonas Earll Jr	4,068	44.9
Daniel Kellogg	3,597	39.7
Parson Shippman	1,402	15.5
24 Gershom Powers	4,098	61.6
Charles Kellogg	1,651	24.8
Moses Dixon	901	13.6
25 Thomas Maxwell	5,462	60.1
Daniel Woodcook	3,623	39.9
27 Timothy Childs	6,520	54.6
Addison Gardiner	4,294	36.0
Danial Barnard	1,125	9.4
28 John Magee	5,390	55.2
Timothy Porter	4,382	44.8
29 Phinehas Tracy	6,924	68.9
Herman Redfield	3,123	31.1
30 Ebenezer Norton	5,226	45.0
John Birdsall	2,820	24.3
John Camp	2,003	17.3
Daniel Garnsey	1,560	13.4

Multi-Member Districts

Candidates	Votes	%
3 Campbell P. White	18,070✔	
Gulian C. Verplanck	14,138✔	
Churchill C. Cambreleng	14,117✔	
Ogden	11,204	
Taylor	10,956	
Lord	6,788	
20 Joseph Hawkins	9,060✔	
George Fisher	8,939‡	
Silas Wright	8,932	
Perley Keyes	8,617	
26 Robert Rose	8,444✔	
Jehiel Halsey	6,833✔	
Phineas Bates	6,651	
Dudley Marvin	5,138	
Isreal Richardson	4,886	

OHIO

Candidates	Votes	%
1 James Findlay (JAC R)	✔	
2 James Shields (JAC R)	✔	
John Woods (AR)		
3 Joseph H. Crane (AR)	✔	
4 Joseph Vance (AR)	✔	
5 William Russell (JAC R)	✔	
6 William Creighton Jr (AR)	✔	
7 Samuel F. Vinton (AR)	✔	
8 William Stanbery (JAC R)	✔	
9 William W. Irvin (JAC R)	✔	
Philemon Beecher (AR)		
10 William Kennon Sr (JAC R)	✔	
John Davenport (AR)	✔	
11 John M. Goodenow (JAC R)	✔	
John C. Wright (AR)		
12 John Thomson (JAC R)	✔	
John Sloane (AR)		
13 Elisha Whittlesey (AR)	✔	
14 Mordecai Bartley (AR)	2,632	50.0
Hunter	1,432	27.2
Wood	1,200	22.8

Special Election

Candidates	Votes	%
6 Francis S. Muhlenberg (JAC R)	✔	

1. In the 6th district, no candidate received the majority of the vote required to win. In a later election, for which no returns are available, Leonard Jarvis (D) was the winner.

PENNSYLVANIA

	Candidates	Votes	%
1	Joel B. Sutherland (JAC R)	✔	
	Peter A. Browne (AR)		
2	Joseph Hemphill (JAC R)	✔	
	John Sergeant (AR)		
3	Daniel H. Miller (JAC R)	✔	
	Samuel Harvey (AR)		
5	John B. Sterigere (JAC R)	✔	
6	Innis Green (JAC R)	✔	
	Valentine Hummel		
10	Adam King (JAC R)	✔	
12	John Scott (JAC R)	✔	
13	Chauncey Forward (JAC R)	✔	
14	Thomas Irwin (JAC R)	✔	
15	William McCreery (JAC R)	✔	
16	Richard Coulter (JAC R)	✔	
18	Thomas H. Sill (AR)	✔	

Multi-Member Districts

	Candidates	Votes	%
4	George C. Leiper (JAC R)	✔	
	James Buchanan (JAC R)	✔	
	Joshua Evans Jr. (JAC R)	✔	
	Anderson		

	Candidates	Votes	%
	Hiester		
	Haines		
7	Henry A. P. Muhlenburg (JAC R)	✔	
	Joseph Fry Jr (JAC R)	✔	
	Henry King		
	William Addams		
8	Samuel Ingham (JAC R)	✔	
	George Wolf (JAC R)	✔	
9	James Ford (JAC R)	✔	
	Alem Marr (JAC R)	✔	
	Philander Stephens (JAC R)	✔	
11	William Ramsey (JAC R)	✔	
	Thomas H. Crawford (JAC R)	✔	
17	John Gilmore (JAC R)	✔	
	William Wilkins	✔	
	James S. Stevenson (JAC R)		
	Moore (AR)		

SOUTH CAROLINA

	Candidates	Votes	%
1	William Drayton (UN D)		100.0
2	Robert W. Barnwell (D)		100.0
3	John Campbell (SR W)	✔	
	Thomas R. Mitchell		
4	William D. Martin (D)		100.0
5	Starling Tucker	✔	
6	George McDuffie (D)	✔	
7	William T. Nuckolls	✔	
8	Warren R. Davis (SR D)	✔	
	Cobb		
9	James Blair (UN D)	✔	
	Richard I. Manning (D)		
	Spann		

VERMONT[1]

	Candidates	Votes	%
1	Jonathan Hunt (NR)	3,028	86.2
	Daniel Kellogg	327	9.3
2	Rollin Carolas Mallary	✔	
3	Horace Everett (W)	✔	
4	Benjamin Swift	4,370	67.5
	Ezra Meech (D)	1,936	29.9
5	Daniel Azro Ashley Buck (D)	1,779*	35.1
	William Cahoon (A-MASC)	1,427	28.1
	Cushman (JAC)	1,303	25.7
	James Bell (NR)	564	11.1

1. No candidate received the majority of the vote in the 5th district required for election. A series of special elections were held in an attempt to meet the requirement and fill the seat. In the eighth special election, William Cahoon was elected. No returns are available for these special elections.

1829 House Elections

ALABAMA

	Candidates	Votes	%
1	Clement C. Clay (JAC D)	4,309	52.1
	Nicholas Davis (NR)	3,960	47.9
2	Robert E. B. Baylor (JAC D)	3,845	54.5
	Seth Barton	1,879	26.6
	Henry W. Ellis (JAC D)	1,335	18.9
3	Dixon Hall Lewis (SR D)	4,227	44.1
	Samuel Oliver	2,908	30.3
	Armstrong	2,449	25.6

CONNECTICUT

		Votes	
AL	Ralph Ingersoll	8,281	✔
	Noyes Barber	7,552	✔
	Ebenezer Young	6,592	✔
	Jabez Huntington	6,285	✔
	William Storrs	5,671	✔
	William Ellsworth	5,588	✔
	David Plant	5,401	
	John Niles	3,189	
	Andrew Judson	3,052	
	Orange Merwin	3,009	
	Elisha Phelps	2,501	
	John Trott	2,278	
	Hinman	2,244	
	Roger Sherman	1,299	
	Daniel Burrows	1,256	
	Joseph Eaton	440	
	Larrd Sherwood	344	
	Timothy Pitkin	290	
	Nathan Smith	241	
	Roger Huntington	204	
	Iriah Isham	144	
	Alex Stewart	130	

GEORGIA

Special Election

		Votes	%
AL	Henry G. Lamar	20,706	57.5
	Charlton	15,296	42.5

KENTUCKY

		Votes	%
1	Henry Daniel (JAC D)	✔	
	Harrison		
2	Nicholas D. Coleman (JAC D)	2,520	45.1
	Adam Beatty (NR)	2,519	45.1
	George M. Bedinger (NR)	461	8.3
3	James Clark	2,605	71.4
	Matthews Flournoy	1,045	28.6
4	Robert P. Letcher (W)	✔	
5	Richard M. Johnson (JAC D)	3,634	55.2
	R. McHatton	2,955	44.9
6	Joseph Lecompte (JAC D)	3,371	51.6
	Thomas P. Wilson	3,167	48.4
7	John Kinkead (D)	3,694	56.3
	William B. Booker	2,872	43.7
8	Nathan Gaither (D)	2,267	34.5
	Martin Beatty	2,168	33.0
	William Owens	988	15.0
	Tunstal Quarles	950	14.5
9	Charles Wickliffe (D)	✔	
10	Joel Yancey (JAC D)	3,235	50.8
	Francis Johnson	3,132	49.2
11	Thomas Chilton	4,185	64.7
	James Crutcher	2,282	35.3
12	Chittenden Lyon		100.0

MARYLAND

	Candidates	Votes	%
1	Clement Dorsey	1,316	88.0
2	Benedict Semmes (D)	1,947	54.2
	John C. Weems	1,625	45.2
3	George C. Washington (W)	3,116	100.0
4	Michael C. Sprigg (D)	4,190	56.0
	William Price	3,293	44.0
6	George E. Mitchell	2,591	53.5
	James W. Williams	2,253	46.5
7	Richard Spencer (D)	1,711	50.3
	John Leeds Kerr (W)	1,692	49.7
8	Ephraim K. Wilson (D)	4,374	98.0

Multi-Member District

		Votes	
5	Benjamin C. Howard (D)	6,297	✔
	Elias Brown (W)	6,153	✔
	P. Little	4,745	
	John Barney	3,763	

MISSISSIPPI

		Votes	%
AL	Thomas Hinds (JAC D)	4,585	42.9
	David Dickson (JAC D)	2,425	22.7
	A. L. Benjamin (NR)	1,920	18.0
	William Haile (JAC D)	1,759	16.5

NEW HAMPSHIRE

		Votes	
AL	John W. Weeks (JAC D)	✔	
	Henry Hubbard (JAC D)	✔	
	Thomas Chandler (JAC D)	✔	
	Jonathan Harvey (JAC D)	✔	
	John Brodhead (JAC D)	✔	
	Joseph Hammons (JAC D)	✔	
	Wallace (NR)		
	Boardman (NR)		
	Webster (NR)		
	Barker (NR)		
	Bell (NR)		
	Lord (NR)		

NORTH CAROLINA

		Votes	%
1	William B. Shepard (D-R)	2,491	54.0
	Lemuel Sawyer (OPP R)	2,121	46.0
2	Willis Alston	✔	
3	Thomas H. Hall (D-R)		100.0
4	Jesse Speight (D-R)	3,137	64.3
	Thomas H. Daves (D-R)	1,282	26.3
	James Manney (OPP R)	459	9.4
5	Gabriel Holmes (D-R)	2,551	52.2
	Edward B. Dudley (D-R)	2,333	47.8
6	Robert Potter (D-R)	2,661	83.9
	Samuel Hillman (OPP R)	396	12.5
7	Edmund Deberry (AR)	3,098	51.9
	John A. Cameron (D-R)	2,869	48.1
8	Daniel L. Barringer (D-R)	2,650	61.7
	James A. Craig (D-R)	1,590	37.0
9	Augustine H. Shepard (D-R)		100.0
10	John Giles (D-R)	3,226*	58.6
	John Long (AR)	2,281	41.4
11	Henry W. Conner	✔	
12	Samuel P. Carson	✔	
13	Lewis Williams (NR)	✔	
	Samuel King (D-R)		

Special Election

		Votes	%
10	Abraham Rencher (NR)	1,972	56.2
	John Long (NR)	1,538	43.8

PENNSYLVANIA

Special Election

	Candidates	Votes	%
17	Harmar Denny (A-MAS)	✔	
	James S. Stevenson (D)		

RHODE ISLAND

		Votes	
AL	Dutee J. Pearce (NR)	4,328	✔
	Tristam Burges (NR)	4,108	✔
	Samuel Eddy (NR)	1,251	
	Job Durfee (NR)	1,126	
	Elisha R. Potter (NR)	518	
	John Dwolf Jr (NR)	208	

TENNESSEE

		Votes	%
1	John Blair	3,899	67.2
	John A. Rogers	1,048	18.1
	William Priestly	856	14.8
2	Pryor Lea	4,813	51.7
	Thomas D. Arnold	4,496	48.3
3	James Standifer	8,383	82.3
	John Lowry	1,802	17.7
4	Jacob C. Isacks	3,869	100.0
5	Robert Desha	4,575	64.2
	William Trousdale	2,547	35.8
6	James K. Polk	9,963	100.0
7	John Bell	5,542	100.0
8	Cave Johnson	3,470	52.9
	John H. Marable	3,085	47.1
9	David Crockett	6,783	64.0
	Adam R. Alexander	3,643	34.4

VIRGINIA

1	Thomas Newton Jr (NR)	‡
	George Loyall (JAC R)	
2	James Trezvant	✔
3	William S. Archer (JAC R)	✔
4	Mark Alexander	✔
5	Thomas T. Bouldin	✔
	Miller	
	George W. Crump	
6	Thomas Davenport	✔
7	Nathaniel H. Claiborne	✔
8	Richard Coke Jr	✔
	Burwell Bassett	
	Braxton	
9	John Roane	✔
10	John Taliaferro (NR)	✔
	Newton	
11	Andrew Stevenson (JAC R)	✔
12	William C. Rives (JAC R)	
13	Philip P. Barbour (JAC R)	✔
14	Charles F. Mercer	✔
	Gibson	
15	William Armstrong	✔
16	William McCoy	✔
17	Robert Craig	✔
	Miller	
18	Alexander Smyth	✔
19	Lewis Maxwell	✔
	Lovell	
	Smith	
20	Robert Allen	✔
	Kercheval	
21	Philip Doddridge	✔
	Johnson	
22	John S. Barbour	✔

Special Election

12	William F. Gordon (JAC R)	✔

1830 House Elections

DELAWARE

Candidates	Votes	%
AL John J. Milligan (NR)	4,267	52.6
Henry M. Ridgely (JAC D)	3,833	47.3

GEORGIA

Candidates	Votes	%
AL Richard H. Wilde	26,313✓	
Wilson Lumpkin	25,896✓	
Daniel Newman	24,459✓	
Henry G. Lamar	22,422✓	
Thomas F. Foster	21,443✓	
James M. Wayne	21,210✓	
Wiley Thompson	20,713✓	
Charles E. Haynes	17,244	
T. U. T. Charlton	15,049	
Roger L. Gamble	14,263	
Seaton Grantland	13,738	
Reuben C. Shorter	5,150	

LOUISIANA

Candidates	Votes	%
1 Edward D. White	✓	
2 Philemon Thomas (D)	✓	
3 Henry A. Bullard	✓	

MAINE

Candidates	Votes	%
1 Rufus McIntire (JAC D)	✓	
2 John Anderson (JEFF D)	✓	
3 Edward Kavanagh (D)	2,169	52.4
Moses Shaw (NR)	1,712	41.4
4 George Evans (NR)	✓	
5 Cornelius Holland (D)	✓	
6 Leonard Jarvis (D)	✓	
7 James Bates (D)	✓	

MASSACHUSETTS

Candidates	Votes	%
1 Nathan Appleton (NR)	3,341	56.3
Henry Lee (A-TARIFF)	2,475	41.7
2 Rufus Choate (NR)	1,740	59.1
Benjamin Crowninshield	767	26.1
Cabot (JAC R)	352	12.0
3 Jeremiah Nelson (NR)	2,952	62.3
Gayton S. Osgood (JACS R)	1,695	35.8
4 Edward Everett (NR)	2,176	82.6
James Russell	427	16.2
5 Joseph G. Kendall (NR)	1,675	97.0
6 George Grennell Jr (NR)	1,515	72.4
Isaac Billings	511	24.4
7 George N. Briggs (NR)	1,707	57.5
Nathan Willis (JACS R)	825	27.8
Henry W. Dwight	222	7.5
8 Isaac C. Bates (NR)	1,827	77.7
John Mills (JACS R)	470	20.0
9 Henry A. S. Dearborn (NR)	1,872	55.0
Moses Thacher (A-MAS)	1,088	32.0
Abel Cushing	239	7.0
10 James L. Hodges (NR)	3,437	50.5
Micah H. Buggles (A-MASDNR)	3,227	47.4
11 John Reed (NR)	949	94.3
12 John Quincy Adams (NR)	1,811	70.7
Arad Thompson	378	14.8
William Baylies	327	12.8
13 John Davis (NR)	2,014	72.7
Dan Thurber (JACS R)	598	21.6
Unidentified Candidate (A-MAS&SC)	160	5.8

NEW JERSEY

Candidates	Votes	%
AL Lewis Condict (NR)	15,268✓	
Thomas H. Hughes (NR)	15,214✓	
Richard M. Cooper (NR)	15,150✓	
Isaac Southard (NR)	15,069✓	
Silas Condit (NR)	14,823✓	
James F. Randolph (NR)	14,513✓	
Parker (D)	14,361	
Wurts (D)	14,054	
Mickle (D)	14,011	
Fowler (D)	13,936	
Travers (D)	13,915	
Jeffers (D)	13,086	

NEW YORK

Candidates	Votes	%
1 James Lent (JAC D)	2,557	54.5
John King	2,138	45.5
2 John Bergen (JAC D)	2,147	50.4
John Wyckoff	2,116	49.6
4 Aaron Ward (JAC D)	2,998	53.6
John Hunter	1,767	31.6
Jonathan Ferris	830	14.8
5 Edmund Pendleton (NR)	3,463	52.3
Stoddard Judd	3,161	47.7
6 Samuel Wilkin (NR)	2,498	50.9
Isaac Vanduzer	2,414	49.1
7 John Brodhead (JAC D)	3,854	59.7
Thomas Lockwood	2,602	40.3
8 John King (JAC D)	3,400	56.8
Robert Leroy Livingston	2,586	43.2
9 Job Pierson (JAC D)	4,453	59.3
John Dickinson	3,052	40.7
10 Gerrit Lansing (JAC D)	3,684	53.0
Ambrose Spencer	3,274	47.1
11 Erastus Root (JAC D)	5,004	61.0
Isaac Ogden	3,201	39.0
12 Joseph Bouck (JAC D)	3,509	64.9
Peter Mann	1,898	35.1
13 William Angel (JAC D)	4,119	50.9
Horace Lathrop	3,969	49.1
14 Samuel Beardsley (JAC D)	5,498	57.3
Simon Dexter	3,850	40.1
15 Michael Hoffman (JAC D)	3,127	60.7
Hiram Nolton	2,024	39.3
16 Nathan Soule (JAC D)	3,399	52.7
Daniel Cady	3,049	47.3
17 John Taylor (NR)	2,597	42.0
Samuel Young	2,350	38.0
David Garnsey	1,238	20.0
18 Nathaniel Pitcher (JAC D)	3,294	52.5
Henry Martindale	2,983	47.5
19 William Hogan (JAC D)	3,621	52.5
Luther Bradish	1,843	26.7
Thomas Gilson	1,434	20.8
21 John Collier (NR)	4,686	58.9
Abial Cook	3,267	41.1
22 Edward C. Reed (JAC D)	4,531	51.7
Eleazer Edgcomb	4,240	48.3
23 Freeborn Jewett (JAC D)	4,539	62.4
William Jerome	2,739	37.6
24 Ulysses Doubleday (JAC D)	3,643	50.1
Josiah Hopkins	3,399	46.8
25 Gamaliel Barstow (NR)	3,805	51.2
Charles Humphrey	3,621	48.8
27 Frederick Whittlesey (NR)	7,410	65.8
Calvin Bryan	3,846	34.2
28 Grattan Wheeler (NR)	5,950	54.5
John Magee	4,961	45.5
29 Phinehas Tracy (NR)	6,802	68.9
Isaac Wilson	3,071	31.1
30 Bates Cooke (NR)	6,997	66.7
Ebenezer Norton	3,093	29.5

Multi-Member Districts

Candidates	Votes	%
3 Churchill G. Cambreleng (JAC D)	10,974✓	
Campbell White (JAC D)	10,801✓	
Gulian Verplanck (JAC D)	10,791✓	
Abraham Lawrence	7,614	
Thomas Smith	7,420	
Adoniram Chandler	7,331	
Thomas Hertell	2,246	
John Frazce	2,158	
Isaac Pierce	2,126	
20 Daniel Wardwell (JAC D)	9,092✓	
Charles Dayan (JAC D)	8,982✓	
Chester Buck	6,172	
George Fisher	6,044	
26 John Dickson (NR)	9,746✓	
William Babcock (NR)	9,560✓	
Jarad Wilson	7,361	
Jehiel Halsey	7,281	

OHIO

Candidates	Votes	%
1 James Findlay (JAC R)	✓	
Benham (NR)		
2 Thomas Corwin (NR)	✓	
James Shields (JAC R)		
3 Joseph H. Crane (NR)	✓	
4 Joseph Vance (NR)	✓	
5 William Russell (JAC R)	✓	
6 William Creighton Jr (NR)	✓	
7 Samuel F. Vinton (NR)	✓	
8 William Stanbery (NR)	✓	
McLean		
9 William W. Irvin (JAC R)	✓	
10 William Kennon Sr (NR)	✓	
11 Humphrey H. Leavitt (JAC R)	✓	
12 John Thomson (JAC R)	✓	
13 Elisha Whittlesey (NR)	4,114	43.6
Sloane (A-MAS)	3,383	35.9
Raven (JAC R)	1,938	20.5
14 Leonard Case (NR)	*	

PENNSYLVANIA

Candidates	Votes	%
1 Joel B. Sutherland (D)	✓	
Simpson (D)		
2 Henry Horn (JAC)	✓	
Coxe (NR)		
3 John G. Watmough (NR)	✓	
Daniel H. Miller (D)		
5 Joel K. Mann	✓	
6 John C. Bucher	✓	
Valentine Hummel		
10 Adam King	✓	
12 Robert Allison	✓	
13 George Burd	✓	
14 Andrew Stewart	✓	
15 Thomas M. T. McKennan	✓	
16 Richard Coulter	✓	
18 John Banks	✓	

Multi-Member Districts

Candidates	Votes	%
4 David Potts Jr	✓	
Joshua Evans Jr	✓	
William Hiester	✓	
7 Henry King	✓	
Henry A. P. Muhlenburg	✓	
8 Samuel A. Smith	✓	
Peter Ihrie Jr	✓	
9 James Ford	✓	
Philander Stephens	✓	
Lewis Dewart	✓	
11 Thomas H. Crawford	✓	
William Ramsey	✓	
17 Harmar Denny	✓	
John Gilmore	✓	

SOUTH CAROLINA

Candidates	Votes	%
1 William Drayton (UN D)		100.0
2 Robert W. Barnwell (D)		100.0
3 Thomas R. Mitchell	2,200	53.8
John Campbell (SR W)	1,893	46.3
5 John K. Griffin (SR W)	✔	
B. Watts		
6 George McDuffie (D)	✔	
7 William T. Nuckolls	✔	

Candidates	Votes	%
8 Warren R. Davis (SR D)	✔	
9 James Blair (D)		100.0

VERMONT [1]

Candidates	Votes	%
1 Jonathan Hunt (NR)	2,735	58.5
Orsamus C. Merrill (D)	1,483	31.7
Samuel Elliott	286	6.1

Candidates	Votes	%
2 Rollin C. Mallary	3,750	84.8
William Slade	484	11.0
3 Horace Everett	2,876	49.0
Royal Ransom	2,038	34.7
Alden Patridge	790	13.5
4 Bailey	2,925*	40.5
Heman Allen	2,613	36.2
Galusha	842	11.7
5 William Cahoon (A-MAS)	4,128	52.6
Israil P. Dana	3,468	44.2

1. No candidate received a majority of the vote in the 4th district required for election.
A series of special elections were held in an attempt to meet the requirement. Herman
Allen was finally elected in the eighth special election. No returns are available for these
special elections.

1831 House Elections

ALABAMA

Candidates	Votes	%
1 Clement Comer Clay (D)	2,770	100.0
2 Samuel W. Mardis (D)	5,400	41.6
Jesse Winston Garth (NR)	4,611	35.5
Robert E. B. Baylor (D)	2,976	22.9
3 Dixon Hall Lewis (SR D)	6,268	59.5
John Murphy (D)	4,270	40.5

CONNECTICUT

Candidates	Votes	%
AL Ebenezer Young (NR)	15,889✔	
Noyes Barber (NR)	11,950✔	
Ralph Ingersoll (NR)	11,938✔	
Jabez Huntington (NR)	10,946✔	
William Ellsworth (NR)	10,931✔	
William Storrs (NR)	10,750✔	
Simeon Miner (D)	6,022	
Isaac Touny (D)	5,784	
Elisha Haley (D)	5,197	
William Hollabird (D)	4,010	
Thaddeus Betts (D)	3,242	

ILLINOIS

Candidates	Votes	%
AL Joseph Duncan (JAC D)	13,052	54.0
Sidney Breese	4,659	19.3
Edward Coles	3,397	14.0
Alexander P. Field	1,844	7.6

INDIANA

Candidates	Votes	%
1 Ratliff Boon (JAC D)	11,280	50.9
John Law (JAC D)	10,868	49.1
2 John Carr (JAC D)	4,854	32.8
William W. Wick (NR)	4,605	31.1
James B. Ray (NR)	1,732	11.7
Jonathan Jennings (NR)	1,680	11.3
John H. Thompson (NR)	1,486	10.0
3 Jonathan McCarty (JAC D)	6,238	42.6
Oliver H. Smith (JAC D)	5,297	36.2
John Test (NR)	3,107	21.2

KENTUCKY[1]

Candidates	Votes	%
Chilton Allan (CLAY D)	✔	
Henry Daniel (JAC D)	✔	
Richard M. Johnson (JAC D)	✔	
Albert G. Hawes (JAC D)	✔	
Nathan Gaither (D)	✔	
Chittenden Lyon (D)	✔	
John Adair (D)	✔	
Charles A. Wickliffe (D)	✔	
Joseph Lecompte (D)	✔	
Robert P. Letcher (W)	✔	
Christopher Tompkins (W)	✔	
Thomas A. Marshall (W)	✔	

MARYLAND

Candidates	Votes	%
1 Daniel Jenifer (NR)	1,717	59.0
John J. Brooke	1,194	41.0
2 Benedict J. Semmes (D)	1,773	62.3
Alexander Keech	1,072	37.7
3 George C. Washington (W)	3,145	100.0
4 Francis Thomas (D)	4,452	53.5
Michael C. Sprigg	3,872	46.5
6 George E. Mitchell	2,770	53.2
James W. Williams	2,438	46.8
7 John Leeds Kerr (W)	1,794	50.5
Richard Spencer (D)	1,756	49.5
8 John S. Spence (D)	3,150	92.5

Multi-Member District

Candidates	Votes	%
5 Benjamin C. Howard (D)	6,160✔	
John T. H. Worthington (D)	5,740✔	
Ebenezer L. Finley	4,973	
Elias Brown (W)	1,997	

MISSISSIPPI

Candidates	Votes	%
AL Franklin E. Plummer (JAC D)	2,922	37.8
David Dickson (JAC D)	1,981	25.7
John N. Norton	979	12.7
James C. Wilkins	958	12.4
William L. Sharkey (NR)	744	9.6

MISSOURI

Candidates	Votes	%
AL Spencer D. Pettis (JAC D)	8,302	63.5
Barton (NR)	4,775	36.5

Special Election

Candidates	Votes	%
AL William H. Ashley (D)	4,897	50.3
Wells (D)	4,841	49.7

NEW HAMPSHIRE

Candidates	Votes	%
AL Joseph Hammons (JAC D)	✔	
Thomas Chandler (JAC D)	✔	
John W. Weeks (JAC D)	✔	
Henry Hubbard (JAC D)	✔	
John Brodhead (JAC D)	✔	
Joseph M. Harper (JAC D)	✔	

NORTH CAROLINA

Candidates	Votes	%
1 William B. Shepard (D-R)	2,872	61.9
John H. Wheeler (OPP R)	1,768	38.1
2 John Branch		100.0
3 Thomas H. Hall (D-R)	2,944	55.6
Joseph R. Lloyd (OPP R)	2,352	44.4

Explanation of Symbols in House Returns

In the returns for House elections *symbols* are used to denote special circumstances. In cases where no symbol is used, the candidate who received the most votes won the election to the House. The following is a key to the symbols used:

✔ Elected to the House. The symbol is used to identify winning candidates in three types of situations: (1) When candidates ran for two or more at-large seats in states which chose all of their at-large representatives in a single election, or ran in a multi-member district; (2) when the vote total and percentage of one or more of the candidates are unavailable and (3) when a candidate who did not receive the highest vote total was seated by the House. *(Explanation of multi-member districts, see p. 678.)*

‡ The symbol is used when an election dispute resulted in the unseating of a representative *after* he was sworn in. *(For discussion of specific cases, consult the* Biographical Directory of the American Congress 1774-1971, *U.S. Government Printing Office, Washington, D.C. 1971; hereafter referred to as the* Biographical Directory.*)*

* The symbol is used for three types of situations: (1) When a representative-elect died or declined his seat before the constitutionally set date for the beginning of his term—March 4 until 1935, and Jan. 3 thereafter; (2) when the House refused to seat any candidate claiming election to a seat and (3) when state law required a candidate to obtain a popular vote majority for election to the House, but the candidate receiving the most votes failed to receive a majority. *(For discussion of specific cases, consult the* Biographical Directory; *explanation of majority vote requirement, see p. 703.)*

Information for 1824-1973 returns was obtained from a source other than the Inter-University Consortium for Political and Social Research. *(For a listing of other sources, see p. 1062.)*

Footnotes. Numbered footnotes are used to explain unusual situations, such as a series of elections in the same year in the same House district, anomalies resulting from reapportionment and special procedures for conducting House elections in certain states.

Footnote, see p. 713.

NORTH CAROLINA

Candidates	Votes	%
4 Jesse Speight (D-R)		100.0
5 James I. McKay		100.0
6 Robert Potter (D-R)		100.0
7 Lauchlin Bethune (D-R)	3,086	50.3
Edmund Deberry (OPP R)	3,049	49.7
8 Daniel L. Barringer (D-R)		100.0
9 Augustine H. Shepperd		100.0
10 Abraham Rencher (OPP R)		100.0
11 Henry W. Conner (D-R)	✔	
Bartlett Shipp (OPP R)		
12 Samuel P. Carson (D-R)	4,422	76.5
Anthony Casey (OPP R)	1,355	23.5
13 Lewis Williams		100.0

Special Election

	Votes	%
6 Micajah T. Hawkins (D-R)	949	35.3
Mann (D-R)	863	32.1
James Wyche (OPP R)	533	19.8
Pope (OPP R)	342	12.7

PENNSYLVANIA

Special Election

	Votes	%
11 Robert McCoy (WOLF D)	2,459	44.4
Mahon (A-WOLF D)	1,931	34.8
McSherry (A-MAS)	1,154	20.8

RHODE ISLAND

	Votes	%
AL Tristam Burges (NR)	2,931✔	
Dutee J. Pearce (NR)	2,727✔	

1. It is not known whether the Kentucky representatives were elected at large or in districts.

TENNESSEE

Candidates	Votes	%
1 John Blair (D)	4,120	50.3
William B. Carter (W)	4,076	49.7
2 Thomas D. Arnold (W)	4,935	51.2
Pryor Lea (D)	4,702	48.8
3 James Standifer (W)	8,906	99.5
4 Jacob C. Isacks	3,538	45.0
John B. McCormick	3,068	39.0
Hopkins L. Turney (D)	1,256	16.0
5 William Hall (D)	4,040	50.7
Robert H. Burton	3,928	49.3
6 James K. Polk (D)	6,993	99.4
7 John Bell (W)	6,934	100.0
8 Cave Johnson (D)	5,111	99.8
9 William Fitzgerald (D)	8,534	51.8
David Crockett (W)	7,948	48.2

VERMONT

Special Election

	Votes	%
2 William Slade (A-MAS)	4,614	49.0
Williams (NR)	3,815	40.5
White (JAC)	838	8.9

VIRGINIA

	Votes	%
1 Thomas Newton Jr (NR)	✔	
George Loyall (D)		
2 John Y. Mason (D)	✔	
Eppes		
3 William S. Archer (D)	✔	
4 Mark Alexander	✔	

Candidates	Votes	%
5 Thomas T. Bouldin	✔	
George W. Crump		
6 Thomas Davenport	✔	
7 Nathaniel H. Claiborne	✔	
8 Richard Coke Jr	✔	
Braxton		
9 John J. Roane	✔	
Upshaw		
Bernard		
10 Joseph W. Chinn (D)	✔	
John Taliaferro (NR)		
11 Andrew Stevenson (D)	✔	
12 William F. Gordon (D)	✔	
13 John M. Patton (D)	✔	
Dade		
14 Charles F. Mercer (NR)	✔	
Gibson (D)		
15 William Armstrong	✔	
Lucas		
16 William McCoy	✔	
Stribling		
17 Robert Craig	✔	
Miller		
18 Charles C. Johnson	✔	
Joseph Draper		
19 Lewis Maxwell (NR)	✔	
Smith (NR)		
Reynolds		
20 Robert Allen	✔	
Mason		
21 Philip Doddridge	✔	
22 John S. Barbour	✔	
Wallace		

1832 House Elections

DELAWARE

	Candidates	Votes	%
AL	John J. Milligan (W)	4,257	50.7
	Martin W. Bates (D)	4,142	49.3

GEORGIA

		Votes	
AL	James M. Wayne	34,010 ✓	
	Richard H. Wilde	29,813 ✓	
	George R. Gilmer	26,061 ✓	
	Augustin S. Clayton	25,854 ✓	
	Thomas F. Foster	25,517 ✓	
	Roger L. Gamble	24,278 ✓	
	Seaborn Jones	22,640 ✓	
	William Schley	22,376 ✓	
	John Coffee	22,284 ✓	
	Haynes	21,638	
	Owens	21,362	
	Terrell	21,361	
	Watson	20,884	
	Branham	20,535	
	Stewart	20,006	
	Harris	19,288	
	Newman	16,278	
	Lamar	16,136	
	Milton	5,157	

Special Election

		Votes	%
AL	Augustin S. Clayton	12,587	52.2
	William Schley	11,541	47.8

ILLINOIS

		Votes	%
1	Charles Slade (D)	2,470	31.3
	Ninian Edwards (NR)	2,078	26.3
	Sidney Breese	1,770	22.4
	Charles Dunn	1,020	12.9
	Henry L. Webb	551	7.0
2	Zadoc Casey (D)	3,208	46.0
	William B. Archer (OPP D)	2,168	31.1
	Wickliff Kitchell	1,593	22.9
3	Joseph Duncan (D)	8,234	76.8
	Jonathan H. Pugh (OPP D)	2,323	21.7

LOUISIANA

1	Edward D. White (W)		✓
2	Philemon Thomas (D)		✓
3	Henry A. Bullard (W)		✓

MISSOURI[1]

		Votes	%
AL	William H. Ashley (A-BANK)	9,498	51.8
	Robert W. Wells (PRO-BANK)	8,836	48.2

NEW JERSEY

		Votes	
AL	William N. Shinn (D)	24,383 ✓	
	Ferdinand S. Schenck (D&A-MASC)	24,288 ✓	
	Thomas Lee (D)	24,265 ✓	
	James Parker (D)	23,903 ✓	
	Philemon Dickerson (D&A-MASC)	23,860 ✓	
	Samuel Fowler (D&A-MASC)	23,808 ✓	
	Condict (NR-A-MAS)	23,784	
	Wright (NR-A-MAS)	23,779	
	Pennington (NR-A-MAS)	23,770	
	Reeves (NR)	23,325	
	Southard (NR)	23,310	
	Budd (NR)	23,257	

NEW YORK

	Candidates	Votes	%
1	Abel Huntington (D)	4,193	59.9
	David Gardiner (NR)	2,806	40.1
2	Isaac Van Houten (D)	3,007	57.5
	John Gurnee (NR)	2,224	42.5
4	Aaron Ward (D)	4,173	57.8
	Henry B. Cowles (NR)	3,051	42.2
5	Abraham Bockee (D)	4,728	52.7
	Edmund Pendleton (NR)	4,241	47.3
6	John Brown (D)	4,200	59.0
	Samuel Wilkin (NR)	2,923	41.0
7	Charles Bodle (D)	5,225	62.3
	Thomas Lockwood (NR)	3,167	37.7
9	Job Pierson (D)	4,849	53.5
	John Dickinson (NR)	4,213	46.5
10	Gerrit Lansing (D)	4,483	51.0
	Ambrose Spencer (NR)	4,302	49.0
11	John Cramer (D)	4,831	51.6
	John Taylor (NR)	4,531	48.4
12	Henry Martindale (NR)	3,037	44.5
	John McIntyre (D)	2,165	31.7
	Samuel Stevens (NR)	1,619	23.7
13	Reuben Whallon (D)	4,251	55.2
	Thomas Gibson (NR)	3,449	44.8
14	Ranson Gillet (D)	3,897	50.5
	Luther Bradish (NR)	3,817	49.5
15	Charles McVean (D)	4,554	56.2
	Howland Fish (NR)	3,546	43.8
16	Abijah Mann Jr (D)	4,964	59.6
	Ela Collins (NR)	3,362	40.4
18	Daniel Wardwell (D)	4,393	50.0
	Daniel Lee (NR)	4,387	50.0
19	Sherman Page (D)	4,914	54.9
	John Morris (NR)	4,039	45.1
20	Noadiah Johnson (D)	4,302	53.8
	John Collier (NR)	3,692	46.2
21	Henry Mitchell (D)	3,719	52.6
	Tilly Lynde (NR)	3,349	47.4
24	Rowland Day (D)	4,456	53.2
	Laban Hoskins (NR)	3,913	46.8
25	Samuel Clark (D)	4,899	52.4
	Joseph Colt (NR)	4,453	47.6
26	John Dickson (NR)	3,903	62.6
	John Price (D)	2,333	37.4
27	Edward Howell (D)	5,748	63.2
	William Woods (NR)	3,349	36.8
28	Frederick Whittlesey (NR)	4,828	58.9
	Isaac Hills (D)	3,374	41.1
29	George Lay (NR)	5,308	70.3
	David Miller (D)	2,248	29.8
30	Philo Fuller (NR)	5,248	57.8
	James Faulkner (D)	3,839	42.3
31	Abner Hazeltine (NR)	5,393	60.7
	Alson Leavenworth (D)	3,494	39.3
32	Millard Fillmore (NR)	4,184	69.6
	Jonathan Hoyt (D)	1,828	30.4
33	Gideon Hard (NR)	3,789	58.6
	Franklin Butterfield (D)	2,678	41.4

Multi-Member Districts

		Votes	
3	Cornelius Lawrence (D)	18,222 ✓	
	Campbell White (D)	18,171 ✓	
	Dudley Selden (D)	18,006 ✓	
	Churchill C. Cambreleng (D)	17,927 ✓	
	David Ogden (NR)	12,334	
	Hubert Van Wagenen (NR)	12,326	
	Jonathan Thompson (NR)	12,176	
	George Talman (NR)	12,158	
8	John Adams (D)	9,677 ✓	
	Aaron Vanderpoel (D)	9,565 ✓	
	Jedediah Miller (NR)	7,743	
	John Martin (NR)	7,642	
17	Samuel Beardsley (D)	9,121 ✓	
	Joel Turrill (D)	8,693 ✓	
	Charles P. Kirkland (NR)	8,487	
	Peter Sken Smith (NR)	8,220	
22	Nicoll Halsey (D)	8,329 ✓	
	Samuel G. Hathaway (D)	8,300 ✓	

	Candidates	Votes	%
	Eleazer W. Edgecomb (NR)	7,026	
	Gamaliel H. Barstow (NR)	7,009	
23	William K. Fuller (D)	8,934 ✓	
	William Taylor (D)	8,933 ✓	
	Elijah Rhoades (NR)	8,295	
	James B. Eldredge (NR)	8,279	

OHIO

		Votes	%
1	Robert T. Lytle (D)	4,458	53.7
	Pendleton	3,847	46.3
2	Taylor Webster (D)	3,635	57.6
	Collins	2,678	42.4
3	Joseph H. Crane	2,821	44.8
	Helfenstein (D)	2,588	41.1
	Young	893	14.2
4	Thomas Corwin	3,756	52.6
	McLean (D)	3,387	47.4
5	Thomas L. Hamer (D)	2,171	32.5
	Fishback	2,069	31.0
	Morris (D)	2,028	30.4
	Russel	403	6.0
6	Samuel F. Vinton	3,065	66.1
	House (D)	1,569	33.9
7	William Allen (D)	3,739	50.0
	McArthur	3,737	50.0
8	Jeremiah McLene (D)	3,769	45.6
	Olds	3,193	38.7
	Parish	1,296	15.7
9	John Chaney (D)	4,235	54.0
	Irvin	3,609	46.0
10	Joseph Vance	4,854	71.9
	Shelby (D)	1,866	27.6
11	James M. Bell	3,131	50.3
	Shannon (D)	3,091	49.7
12	Robert Mitchell (D)	4,002	52.7
	Stanberry	3,591	47.3
13	David Spangler	3,277	43.8
	Colerick (D)	2,170	29.0
	Rigdon (D)	2,038	27.2
14	William Patterson (D)	2,294	54.1
	Cooke	1,944	45.9
15	Jonathan Sloane	3,117	43.5
	Wood (D)	2,439	34.0
	Humphrey	1,614	22.5
16	Elisha Whittlesey	4,281	46.2
	Rayen (D)	2,980	32.2
	Webb	1,997	21.6
17	John Thomson (D)	2,856	55.5
	Potter	2,286	44.5
18	Benjamin Jones (D)	3,037	56.1
	Quimby	2,379	43.9
19	Humphrey H. Leavitt (D)	3,182	50.8
	Stokely	3,085	49.2

PENNSYLVANIA

		Votes	%
1	Joel B. Sutherland (D)	2,366	50.0
	James Gowen (NR)	1,916	40.5
	Samuel B. Davis (UVD)	451	9.5
3	John G. Watnough (NR)	4,041	56.3
	J. R. Burden (D)	2,268	31.6
	Mahon M. Levis (UVD)	869	12.1
5	Joel K. Mann (D)		✓
6	Robert Ramsey (D)		✓
7	David D. Wagener (D)		✓
8	Henry King (D)		✓
9	Henry A. P. Muhlenburg (D)		✓
10	William Clark (NR)		✓
11	Charles A. Barnitz (NR)		✓
12	George Chambers (NR)		✓
13	Jesse Miller (D)		✓
14	Joseph Henderson (D)		✓
15	Andrew Beaumont (D)		✓
16	Joseph B. Anthony (D)		✓

Footnote, see p. 715.

PENNSYLVANIA

Candidates	Votes	%
17 John Laporte (D)	✔	
18 George Burd (D)	✔	
19 Richard Coulter (D)	✔	
20 Andrew Stewart (NR)	✔	
21 Thomas M. T. McKennan (NR)	✔	
22 Harmar Denny (A-MAS)	✔	
23 Samuel S. Harrison (D)	✔	
24 John Banks (A-MAS)	✔	
25 John Galbraith (D)	✔	

Candidates	Votes	%
Multi-Member Districts		
2 Horace Binney (NR)	5,364 ✔	
James Harper (NR)	5,104 ✔	
B. W. Richards (D)	3,396	
Henry Horn (D)	3,191	
4 Edward Darlington (A-MAS)	✔	
William Hiester (A-MAS)	✔	
David Potts Jr (A-MAS)	✔	

VERMONT

Candidates	Votes	%
1 Hiland Hall (W)	✔	
2 William Slade (W)	✔	
3 Horace Everett	✔	
4 Heman Allen (W)	✔	
5 Benjamin F. Deming (W)	✔	

1. Missouri's House representation was raised from one seat to two after the 1830 reapportionment, but in the 1832 general election only one seat was filled. The second representative was elected in 1833. See Missouri 1833, p. 716.

1833 House Elections

ALABAMA

Candidates	Votes	%
1 Clement C. Clay (D)	1,310	100.0
2 John McKinley (D)	3,724	52.5
James Davis	3,369	47.5
3 Samuel W. Mardis (D)	5,242	57.2
Elisha Young (NR)	2,053	22.4
R. E. B. Baylor (D)	1,867	20.4
4 Dixon H. Lewis (SSR D)		100.0
5 John Murphy (D)	✔	
James Dellet (W)		

CONNECTICUT

Candidates	Votes	%
AL Noyes Barber (NR)	10,121✔	
William Ellsworth (NR)	10,064✔	
Ebenezer Young (NR)	10,045✔	
Jabez Huntington (NR)	9,449✔	
Samuel Foot (NR)	8,029✔	
Samuel Tweedy (NR)	7,815✔	
Andrew Judson (D&A-MASC)	7,469	
Epaphias Porter (D&A-MASC)	7,376	
William Hollabird (D&A-MASC)	7,229	
Samuel Simons (D&A-MASC)	6,896	
Gideon Wells (D&A-MASC)	6,842	
Labern Clarke (D&A-MASC)	6,567	
Richard Hubbard	2,143	
Alanson Hamlin	2,021	
Luther Loomis	446	
Zalman Wildman	400	

INDIANA

Candidates	Votes	%
1 Ratliff Boon (D)	3,973	50.6
Dennis Pennington	1,120	14.3
Robert M. Evans	1,069	13.6
James R. E. Goodlet	788	10.0
Seth M. Levenworth	611	7.8
2 John Ewing (W)	1,921	20.9
John W. Davis (D)	1,919	20.9
John Law	1,668	18.2
George Boon	1,459	15.9
William C. Linton	1,183	12.9
Hugh L. Livingston	1,022	11.1
3 John Carr (D)	4,530	58.2
Harbin H. Moore	3,257	41.8
4 Amos Lane (D)	4,262	50.8
John Test (D)	3,455	41.2
Enoch McCarty	676	8.1
5 Jonathan McCarty (W)	4,590	51.8
Oliver H. Smith (D)	4,268	48.2
6 George L. Kinnard (D)	5,412	52.8
William W. Wick (D)	4,818	47.0
7 Edward A. Hannegan (D)	4,794	54.0
Albert S. White (W)	4,056	45.7

KENTUCKY

Candidates	Votes	%
1 Chittenden Lyon	✔	
Linn Boyd		
2 Albert G. Hawes (D)	2,998	50.8
Philip Thompson (OPP)	2,902	49.2
3 Christopher Tompkins (W)	4,074	50.4
Elijah Hise (D)	4,008	49.6
4 Martin Beaty	✔	
Nathan Gaither		
Elisha Smith		
5 Thomas P. Moore (D)	2,626*	51.0
Robert P. Letcher (W)	2,521	49.0
6 Thomas Chilton	✔	
James Allen		
7 Benjamin Hardin (W)	2,826	52.0
C. A. Rudd	2,610	48.0
8 Patrick H. Pope	✔	
Henry Crittenden		

Candidates	Votes	%
9 James Love (D)	2,445	41.3
John White (W)	2,189	37.0
Smith	1,050	17.7
10 Chilton Allen		100.0
11 Amos Davis	2,990✔	
James Crawford	2,372	
Henry Daniel		
Kenaz Farrow		
12 Thomas A. Marshall (W)	2,722	59.2
Adam Beatty	1,874	40.8
13 Richard M. Johnson (D)	4,737	73.6
John P. Gaines (W)	1,702	26.4

MAINE

Candidates	Votes	%
1 Rufus McIntire (JAC D)	✔	
2 Francis O. J. Smith (D)	✔	
3 Edward Kavanagh (D)	✔	
4 George Evans (NR)	3,542	52.1
White (D)	2,693	39.6
5 Moses Mason (D)	✔	
6 Joseph Hall (D)	✔	
7 Leonard Jarvis (D)	✔	
8 Gorham Parks (D)	✔	

MARYLAND

Candidates	Votes	%
1 Littleton P. Dennis (NR)	3,213	51.7
Steuart (D)	3,003	48.3
2 Richard B. Carmichael (D)	3,243	51.9
Hoffer (NR)	3,004	48.1
3 James Turner (NR)	3,049	49.3
Sewell (D)	1,570	25.4
Worthington	1,563	25.3
4 James P. Heath (NR)	2,805	52.0
Howard (D)	2,592	48.0
5 Isaac McKim (D)	3,181	53.3
Stewart (NR)	2,792	46.7
6 William Cost Johnson (NR)	3,063	55.6
Dorsey (D)	2,442	44.4
7 Francis Thomas (D)	4,012	54.0
Dixon (NR)	3,421	46.0
8 John T. Stoddert (D)	2,360	51.3
Genifle (NR)	2,244	48.7

MASSACHUSETTS

Candidates	Votes	%
1 Benjamin Gorham (NR)	2,304	56.1
Theodore Lyman (D)	1,320	32.2
Amasa Walker (A-MAS)	429	10.5
2 Rufus Choate (NR)	2,216	59.0
Joseph S. Cabot (D)	1,204	32.1
William B. Breed	324	8.6
3 Gayton P. Osgood (D&A-MASC)	3,279	51.4
Caleb Cushing (NR)	2,895	45.4
4 Edward Everett (NR)	2,413	77.7
John Wade	667	21.5
5 John Davis (NR)	2,848	85.9
John Spurry	328	9.9
6 George Grennell Jr (NR)	2,521	71.6
William Whitaker	599	17.0
Israel Billings	309	8.8
7 George N. Briggs (NR)	2,705	64.4
Russell Brown	1,273	30.3
8 Isaac C. Bates (NR)	2,168	72.6
William W. Thompson	333	11.1
Samuel Lathrop (A-MAS)	223	7.5
9 William Jackson (A-MAS)	2,869	50.9
Henry A. S. Dearborn (NR)	1,841	32.7
Daniel Thurber (D)	652	11.6
10 William Baylies (NR)	2,899	50.9
Micah H. Ruggles	2,554	44.8
11 John Reed (NR)	1,442	96.9
12 John Quincy Adams (A-MAS)	2,592	75.5
Frederick Lincoln	714	20.8

MISSISSIPPI

Candidates	Votes	%
AL Franklin E. Plummer (W)	7,826✔	
Harry Cage (D)	7,682✔	
John L. Guion (W)	4,523	
Felix H. Walker	2,243	
Nathan Bouldin	1,223	

MISSOURI[1]

Candidates	Votes	%
AL John Bull (W)	3,671	27.7
Strother (JAC D)	3,630	27.4
Shannon (JAC D)	3,430	25.9
Birch (I)	2,130	16.1

NEW HAMPSHIRE

Candidates	Votes	%
AL Henry Hubbard (D)	✔	
Franklin Pierce (D)	✔	
Robert Burns (D)	✔	
Benning M. Bean (D)	✔	
Joseph M. Harper (D)	✔	
Azel Hatch (A-MAS)		
John Gould (A-MAS)		
D. C. Atkinson (A-MAS)		
John Harvey (A-MAS)		
Caleb Emery (A-MAS)		
Samuel E. Cones (NR)		
James Wilson Jr (NR)		
John Wingate (NR)		
Leonard Wilcox (NR)		
Anthony Colby (NR)		

NORTH CAROLINA

Candidates	Votes	%
1 William B. Shepard (W)		100.0
2 Jesse A. Bynum (W)	2,198	59.8
Andrew Joyner	1,476	40.2
3 Thomas H. Hall	✔	
4 Jesse Speight (D)		100.0
5 James I. McKay (D)	2,570	55.6
Lewis Dishongh (W)	2,056	44.4
6 Micajah T. Hawkins (D)	1,694	38.9
Robert P. Gilliam	1,472	33.8
William P. Williams	1,189	27.3
7 Edmund Deberry (W)	3,268	50.3
Lauchlin Bethune (D)	3,231	49.7
8 Daniel L. Barringer (W)	2,497	50.6
John G. A. Williamson (D)	2,436	49.4
9 Augustine H. Shepperd (D)		100.0
10 Abraham Rencher (W)		100.0
11 Henry W. Conner (D)		100.0
12 James Graham (W)	3,272	41.6
Samuel P. Carson (D)	2,402	30.6
David Newland	2,183	27.8
13 Lewis Williams		.0

PENNSYLVANIA[2]

Special Election

Candidates	Votes	%
1 Joel B. Sutherland	2,835	57.0
John Sergeant	2,139	43.0

RHODE ISLAND[3]

Candidates	Votes	%
AL Tristam Burges (W)	3,162✔	
Dutee J. Pearce (D)	2,078	
Updike (W)	1,913	
Sprague (D)	1,499	
Cranston (W)	376	
Greene (W)	364	
Dixon (W)	168	

Special Election

Candidates	Votes	%
AL Dutee J. Pearce (D)	2,152	55.2
Dixon (W)	1,705	43.7

SOUTH CAROLINA

	Candidates	Votes	%
1	Henry L. Pinckney (D)	✓	
	A. M. S. Harris (UN)		
	Joel R. Poinsett (UN)		
2	William J. Grayson (W)	1,282	79.2
	Benjamin Allston (UN)	335	20.7
3	Thomas Singleton (SR)	2,089	55.7
	Thomas R. Mitchell (UN)	1,665	44.4
4	John M. Felder (D)	✓	
5	John K. Griffin (SR W)	✓	
6	George McDuffie (D)	2,991	70.4
	J. Pressley (UN)	1,254	29.5
7	William K. Clowney (SR)	4,514	51.2
	Thomas Williams (UN)	4,309	48.8
8	Warren R. Davis (SR D)	✓	
	Grisham (UN)		
9	James Blair (D)		100.0

TENNESSEE

	Candidates	Votes	%
1	John Blair (D)	3,236	42.4
	William B. Carter (W)	2,642	34.7
	Thomas D. Arnold (W)	1,747	22.9
2	Samuel Bunch (W)	4,319	70.4
	John Cocke (D)	1,815	29.6
3	Luke Lea (UN D)	3,558	46.7
	Joseph Williams (W)	2,145	28.1
	John F. Gillespie	1,921	25.2
4	James Standifer (W)	4,172	57.4
	James Greene	3,100	42.6
5	John B. Forester	3,862	55.9
	Jacob C. Isaacs	3,051	44.1

	Candidates	Votes	%
6	Balie Peyton (W)	4,710	74.4
	Archibald W. Overton	1,621	25.6
7	John Bell (W)	5,951	100.0
8	David W. Dickinson (D)	2,452	42.4
	William Brady	2,209	38.2
	Abraham Maury (W)	1,129	19.5
9	James K. Polk (D)	4,751	68.5
	Thomas Porter	1,512	21.8
	T. F. Bradford	671	9.7
10	William M. Inge (D)	5,013	61.8
	James W. Combs	1,593	19.6
	Thomas D. Davenport	1,508	18.6
11	Cave Johnson (D)	3,386	45.1
	Richard Cheatham (W)	2,468	32.9
	John H. Marable	1,651	22.0
12	David Crockett (W)	3,985	51.1
	William Fitzgerald (D)	3,812	48.9
13	Christopher H. Williams (W)	2,374	34.6
	William C. Dunlap (D)	2,364 ✓	34.5
	Adam R. Alexander	2,123	30.9

VIRGINIA

	Candidates	Votes	%
1	George Loyall (D)	1,428	53.1
	Miles King (NR)	1,261	46.9
2	John Y. Mason (D)	✓	
3	William S. Archer (D)	✓	
4	James H. Gholson (NR)	✓	
	George C. Dromgoole (D)		
	Knox		
	Goode		
5	John Randolph (NR)	✓	

	Candidates	Votes	%
6	Thomas Davenport (NR)	✓	
	Cabell		
7	Nathaniel H. Claiborne (D)		
8	Henry A. Wise (D)	✓	
	Richard Coke Jr (NR)		
9	William P. Taylor (NR)	✓	
	John J. Roane (D)		
	Upshaw		
10	Joseph W. Chinn (D)	✓	
	John Taliaferro (NR)		
11	Andrew Stevenson (D)	✓	
	John Robertson (NR)		
12	William F. Gordon (NR)	✓	
13	John M. Patton (D)	✓	
14	Charles F. Mercer (NR)	✓	
	Mason (D)		
15	Edward Lucas (D)	✓	
	Archer		
	Naylor		
	A. Smith		
16	James M. H. Beale (D)	✓	
	Meyerhoeffer		
	Steele		
17	Samuel McDowell Moore (NR)	✓	
	Craig (D)		
18	John H. Fulton (D)	✓	
	Byars		
19	William McComas (D)	✓	
	Smith		
20	John J. Allen (NR)	✓	
	Maxwell		
21	Edgar C. Wilson (NR)	✓	
	Morgan		

1. *Missouri added a second representative after the 1830 census. See Missouri 1832, p. 714.*

2. *Joel B. Sutherland was elected from Pennsylvania's 1st district in 1832. He subsequently resigned to become an associate judge of the court of common pleas in Philadelphia, but then ran for and won back his House seat in an 1833 special election.*

3. *Rhode Island had two House seats for the 23rd Congress (1833-35). A majority of the vote was required for election. Dutee J. Pearce failed to qualify in the initial election, but was later elected over Dixon in a special election for which no returns are available.*

1834 House Elections

CONNECTICUT

Special Election

Candidates	Votes	%
AL Phineas Miner (W)	17,007✓	
Ebenezer Jackson (W)	16,920✓	
Joseph Trumbull (W)	16,906✓	
Luther Loomis (D)	16,696	
Lancelot Phelps (D)	16,668	
Samuel Ingham (D)	16,464	
Richard Hubbard (A-MASC)	1,186	
Horace Cowles (A-MASC)	1,150	
Sheldon Leavitt (A-MASC)	1,104	
Samuel Ingram	230	

DELAWARE

	Votes	%
AL John J. Milligan (W)	4,779	50.8
Bayard (D)	4,626	49.2

GEORGIA

	Votes	%
AL James M. Wayne (D)	32,933 *	
William Schley (D)	32,852✓	
Charles E. Haynes (D)	32,609✓	
George W. B. Towns (D)	32,603✓	
John Coffee (D)	32,581✓	
George W. Owens (D)	32,530✓	
James C. Terrell (D)	32,493✓	
Seaton Grantland (D)	32,445✓	
John W. A. Sanford (D)	32,412✓	
Gilmer (W)	28,417	
Wilde (W)	28,294	
Foster (W)	28,036	
Gamble (W)	27,835	
Chappell (W)	27,673	
Lamar (W)	27,507	
Beall (W)	27,500	
Newman (W)	27,457	
Daniel (W)	27,447	

ILLINOIS

		Votes	%
1	John Reynolds (D)	4,523	45.9
	Adam W. Snider (D)	3,723	37.8
	Edward Humphrey	1,603	16.3
2	Zadoc Casey (D)	5,647	58.3
	William H. Davidson	4,036	41.7
3	William L. May (D)	6,828	52.8
	Benjamin Mills	6,117	47.3

Special Elections

		Votes	%
1	John Reynolds (D)	1,721	48.0
	Perrie Menard	871	24.3
	William Orr	501	14.0
	H. L. Webb	490	13.7
3	William May (D)	2,705	72.7
	Benjamin Mills	956	25.7

KENTUCKY

Special Election

		Votes	%
5	Robert P. Letcher (W)	3,731	51.9
	Thomas P. Moore (D)	3,461	48.1

LOUISIANA

		Votes	%
1	Henry Johnson (W)	2,417	55.9
	Gayarre	1,384	32.0
	Nicholls	523	12.1
2	Eleazer W. Ripley (D)	1,162	42.2
	Chinn (W)	900	32.7

Candidates		Votes	%
	J. M. Bradford	434	15.8
	Woodroof	258	9.4
3	Rice Garland (W)	1,989	59.1
	Walker	1,378	40.9

MAINE [1]

		Votes	%
1	Jeremiah Goodwin (D)	3,685*	43.9
	Horace Porter (W)	3,511	41.9
	W. A. Hayes	500	6.0
	J. McDonald	492	5.9
2	Francis O. J. Smith (D)	5,262	51.9
	James C. Churchill (W)	4,827	47.7
3	Jeremiah Bailey (W)	4,240	51.7
	Edward Kavanagh (D)	3,778	46.1
4	George Evans (W)	5,134	59.4
	Amos Nourse (D)	3,301	38.2
5	Moses Mason Jr. (D)	4,791	53.8
	Oliver Herrick (W)	3,736	41.9
6	Joseph Hall (D)	4,251	61.9
	Webster Kelly (W)	2,402	35.0
7	Leonard Jarvis (D)	3,742	50.7
	Elijah Hamlin (W)	3,417	46.3
8	Gorham Parks (D)	6,192	55.4
	Edward Kent (W)	4,831	43.3

MASSACHUSETTS

		Votes	%
1	Abbott Lawrence (W)	5,508	64.9
	William Foster (D)	2,528	29.8
2	Stephen C. Phillips (W)	4,230	59.9
	Joseph S. Cabot (D)	2,784	39.4
3	Caleb Cushing (W)	4,353	58.1
	Gayton P. Osgood (D)	2,683	35.8
4	Samuel Hoar (W)	2,153	54.5
	Herman Lincoln	871	22.1
	James Russell	646	16.4
5	Levi Lincoln (W)	4,777	74.1
	Madison S. Fisher (D)	1,653	25.6
6	George Grennell Jr (W)	3,434	65.5
	Israel Billings (A-MAS)	1,520	29.0
7	George N. Briggs (W)	4,229	59.1
	Theodore Sedgwick (D)	2,902	40.6
8	William B. Calhoun (W)	3,839	61.3
	Oliver Warner (D)	2,409	38.4
9	William Jackson (A-MAS)	3,003	67.5
	Daniel Thurber (D)	1,121	25.2
10	Nathaniel B. Borden (D)	4,306	53.5
	William Baylis (W)	3,697	45.9
11	John Reed (A-MAS)	2,352	79.1
	William J. A. Bradford (D)	607	20.4
12	John Quincy Adams (A-MAS)	3,234	86.8

Special Elections

		Votes	%
2	Stephen C. Phillips (W)	4,245	60.1
	Joseph S. Cabot (D)	2,778	39.3
5	Levi Lincoln (W)	4,226	77.3
	Isaac Davis (D)	1,113	20.4

NEW JERSEY

		Votes	%
AL	William N. Shinn (D)	27,413✓	
	Philemon Dickerson (D)	27,404✓	
	Ferdinand S. Schenck (D)	27,398✓	
	Thomas Lee (D)	27,396✓	
	James Parker (D)	27,390✓	
	Samuel Fowler (D)	27,358✓	
	Condict (W)	26,413	
	Randolph (W)	26,393	
	Pennington (W)	26,384	
	Spencer (W)	26,373	
	Ogden (W)	26,372	
	Brick (W)	26,339	

NEW YORK

	Candidates	Votes	%
1	Abel Huntingdon (D)	4,442	58.5
	Abraham T. Rose (W)	3,152	41.5
2	Samuel Barton (D)	3,943	59.9
	Billop B. Seaman (W)	2,642	40.1
4	Aaron Ward (D)	4,527	57.9
	Horace Bailey (W)	3,290	42.1
5	Abraham Rockee (D)	4,948	55.2
	Edmund H. Pendleton (W)	4,022	44.8
6	John W. Brown (D)	4,337	55.7
	Thomas McKissock (W)	3,445	44.3
7	Nicholas Sickles (D)	5,676	62.6
	Jacob D. Dewitt (W)	3,393	37.4
9	Hiram P. Hunt (W)	4,985	50.1
	Job Pierson (D)	4,961	49.9
10	Gerit Y. Lansing (D)	4,944	52.2
	Daniel D. Barnard (W)	4,521	47.8
11	John Cramer (D)	5,160	50.9
	Anson Brown (W)	4,978	49.1
12	David Russell (W)	3,942	59.5
	John McLean (D)	2,681	40.5
13	Henry H. Ross (W)	4,296	50.3
	Dudley Farlin (D)	4,246	49.7
14	Ransom H. Gillet (D)	4,134	53.5
	Joseph W. Smith (W)	3,589	46.5
15	Matthias J. Bovee (D)	4,695	53.4
	Peter J. Waggoner (W)	4,104	46.6
16	Abijah Mann Jr. (D)	5,246	62.3
	Elisha P. Hurlbut (W)	3,175	37.7
18	Daniel Wardwell (D)	4,512	50.3
	Jesse Smith (W)	4,467	49.8
19	Sherman Page (D)	5,122	57.9
	Don F. Herrick (W)	3,719	42.1
20	William Seymour (D)	4,950	58.4
	Erastus Root (W)	3,532	41.6
21	William Mason (D)	3,930	54.2
	Alvah Hunt (W)	3,320	45.8
24	U. F. Doubleday (D)	4,759	55.0
	Laban Hoskins (W)	3,898	45.0
25	Graham H. Chapin (D)	5,183	52.0
	John M. Holley (W)	4,781	48.0
26	Francis Granger (W)	4,378	59.5
	Oliver Phelps (D)	2,986	40.6
27	Joshua Lee (D)	6,077	60.9
	Aaron Remur (W)	3,907	39.1
28	Timothy Childs (W)	5,076	54.9
	Fletcher M. Haight (D)	4,164	45.1
29	George W. Lay (W)	6,409	62.5
	John B. Skinner (D)	3,844	37.5
30	Philo C. Fuller (W)	5,928	56.0
	James McCall (D)	4,658	44.0
31	Abner Hazeltine (W)	6,250	55.8
	Oliver Lee (D)	4,946	44.2
32	Thomas C. Love (W)	4,783	66.0
	George P. Barker (D)	2,468	34.0
33	Gideon Hard (W)	4,156	51.9
	Nathan Dayton (D)	3,854	48.1

Multi-Member Districts

		Votes	%
3	Churchill C. Cambreleng (D)	19,019✓	
	Campbell P. White (D)	18,983✓	
	John McKeon (D)	18,871✓	
	Ely Moore (D)	18,552✓	
	Ogden Hoffman (W)	16,822	
	G. C. Verplanck (W)	16,807	
	James G. King (W)	16,642	
	Dudley Selden (W)	16,578	
8	Aaron Vanderpoel (D)	10,287✓	
	Valentine Efner (D)	10,210✓	
	Killian Miller (W)	8,166	
	Benjamin Pond (W)	8,153	
17	Samuel Beardsley (D)	9,597✓	
	Joel Turrill (D)	9,488✓	
	Joshua A. Spencer (W)	8,665	
	Peter Sken Smith (W)	8,546	
22	Joseph Reynolds (D)	8,870✓	
	Stephen B. Leonard (D)	8,859✓	
	William A. Ely (W)	7,644	

NEW YORK

	Candidates	Votes	%
	John James Speed Jr (W)	7,220	
23	William Taylor (D)	9,466✔	
	William K. Fuller (D)	9,461✔	
	Victory Birdseye (W)	8,045	
	J. D. Ledyard (W)	8,034	

OHIO

	Candidates	Votes	%
1	Bellamy Storer (W)	4,327	50.6
	Lytle (D)	4,231	49.4
2	Taylor Webster (D)	3,328	52.6
	McNutt (W)	3,001	47.4
3	Joseph H. Crane (W)	4,165	52.4
	Helfenstein (D)	3,781	47.6
4	Thomas Corwin (W)	3,847	58.6
	McDowell (D)	2,723	41.5
5	Thomas L. Hamer (D)	3,479	68.7
	Jones (W)	1,586	31.3
6	Samuel F. Vinton (W)	3,825	62.6
	Jolline (D)	2,283	37.4
7	William K. Bond (W)	4,333	51.8
	Allen (D)	4,037	48.2
8	Jeremiah McLene (D)	3,919	51.1
	Olds (W)	3,751	48.9
9	John Chaney (D)	4,447	58.5
	Irvin (W)	3,158	41.5
10	Samson Mason (W)	4,382	66.2
	Ellsbury (D)	1,950	29.5
11	William Kennon Sr (D)	3,496	50.5
	Bell (W)	3,427	49.5
12	Elias Howell (W)	4,294	54.3
	Mitchell (D)	3,610	45.7
13	David Spangler (W)	3,410	56.3
	Colerick (D)	2,644	43.7
14	William Patterson (D)	4,731	52.7
	Bartley (W)	4,243	47.3
15	Jonathan Sloane (W)	5,453	51.6
	Rice (D)	5,116	48.4
16	Elisha Whittlesey (W)	5,616	60.2
	Dart (D)	3,721	39.9
17	John Thompson (D)	2,346	59.8
	Richardson (W)	1,327	33.8
	McCraig (A-MASC)	253	6.4
18	Benjamin Jones (D)	2,739	51.8
	Quinby (W)	2,548	48.2
19	Daniel Kilgore (D)	3,370	51.7
	Stokely (W)	3,143	48.3

PENNSYLVANIA

	Candidates	Votes	%
1	Joel B. Sutherland (D)	3,782	61.7
	Gowen (W)	2,345	38.3
3	Michael W. Ash (D)	5,757	55.6
	Watmough (W)	4,598	44.4
5	Jacob Fry Jr (D)	3,766	55.3
	Royer (W)	3,047	44.7
6	Mathias Morris (W)	3,341	52.4
	Chapman (D)	3,040	47.6
7	David D. Wagener (D)	4,602	72.8
	Brown (W)	1,718	27.2
8	Edward B. Hubley (D)	3,648	59.6
	Livingston (W)	2,478	40.5
9	Henry A. P. Muhlenburg (D)	4,816	69.3
	Kirbey (W)	2,132	30.7
10	William Clark (W)	3,396	54.3
	Bucher (D)	2,859	45.7
11	Henry Logan (D)	3,218	55.1
	Barnitz (W)	2,619	44.9
12	George Chambers (W)	4,085	59.8
	Heck (D)	2,751	40.2
13	Jesse Miller (D)	3,906	51.4
	Whitesides (W)	3,696	48.6
14	Joseph Henderson (D)	4,239	52.5
	Milliken (W)	3,830	47.5
15	Andrew Beaumont (D)	3,902	56.1
	Shoemaker (W)	3,051	43.9
16	Joseph B. Anthony (D)	5,437	62.8
	Packer (W)	3,226	37.2
17	John Laporte (D)	4,264	56.8
	Williston (W)	3,239	43.2
18	Job Mann (D)	3,535	54.6
	Ogle (W)	2,938	45.4
19	John Klingensmith Jr (D)	4,359	59.7
	Coulter (W)	2,939	40.3
20	Andrew Buchanan (D)	3,428	59.0
	Stewart (W)	2,387	41.1
21	Thomas M. T. McKennan (W)	2,703	51.3
	Ringland (D)	2,569	48.7
22	Harmar Denny (W)	3,428	53.5
	Snowden (D)	2,976	46.5
23	Samuel S. Harrison (D)	3,845	69.8
	Gilmore (W)	1,664	30.2
24	John Banks (W)	2,748	52.2
	Power (D)	2,514	47.8
25	John Galbraith (D)	4,642	60.7
	Sill (W)	3,011	39.3

Multi-Member Districts

	Candidates	Votes	%
2	Joseph R. Ingersoll (W)	5,589✔	
	James Harper (W)	5,560✔	
	Linnard (D)	3,710	
	Horn (D)	3,671	
4	David Potts Jr (W)	10,348✔	
	William Heister (W)	10,348✔	
	Edward Darlington (W)	10,329✔	
	Archibald T. Dick (D)	8,477	
	Benjamin Champneys (D)	8,472	
	John Morgan (D)	8,471	

SOUTH CAROLINA

	Candidates	Votes	%
1	Henry L. Pinckney (SR)	1,680	52.8
	Alfred Huger (UN)	1,503	47.2
2	William J. Grayson (SR)	✔	
	Unidentified Candidate (SSR & SC)		
3	Robert B. Campbell (SR)	2,242	53.2
	James C. Postell (UN)	1,948	46.3
4	James H. Hammond (SR)	4,025	100.0
5	John K. Griffin (SR)		100.0
6	Francis W. Pickens (SR)	2,836	74.6
	John S. Pressly (UN)	968	25.5
7	James Rogers (UN)	4,213	51.1
	William K. Clowney (SR)	4,038	48.9
8	Warren R. Davis (SR)	2,925*	50.6
	Perry (UN)	2,855	49.4
9	Richard I. Manning (UN)	1,392	64.5
	Rees (SR)	765	35.5

Special Elections

	Candidates	Votes	%
3	Robert B. Campbell (NULL)	✔	
	James C. Postell (UN)		
6	Francis W. Pickens (SR)	✔	
	John S. Pressly (UN)		

VERMONT

	Candidates	Votes	%
1	Hiland Hall (W)	3,395	50.7
	Robinson (D)	1,872	28.0
2	William Slade (A-MAS)	4,012	55.0
	Jonas Clark (D)	1,494	20.5
	Robert Pierpont (W)	1,491	20.5
3	Horace Everett (W)	3,717	44.6
	Sam C. Loveland (A-MAS)	2,774	33.3
	Alden Partridge (D)	1,768	21.2
4	Heman Allen (W)	2,574	51.2
	Vanness (D)	1,678	33.4
	Smith	778	15.5
5	Henry F. Janes (A-MAS)	3,641	51.5
	Isaac Fletcher (D)	3,398	48.1

VIRGINIA

Special Elections

	Candidates	Votes	%
5	James W. Bouldin (D)	✔	
	Beverly Tucker (W)		
11	John Robertson (W)	689	67.6
	Roane (D)	331	32.5

1. No candidate in Maine's 1st district received the majority vote required for election. At a later special election, Rufus McIntyre was elected. No returns are available for the special election.

1835 House Elections

ALABAMA

	Candidates	Votes	%
1	Reuben Chapman (D)	4,403	47.8
	Clascock (D)	2,993	32.5
	Scott (D)	1,819	19.7
2	Joshua L. Martin (D)	✔	
	Davis		
	Thatch		
3	Joab Lawler (W)	2,498	40.2
	Shortridge (D)	2,362	38.0
	May	1,356	21.8
4	Dixon H. Lewis (SR D)		100.0
5	Francis S. Lyon (W)	✔	
	Baylor (D)		
	Bates		

CONNECTICUT

	Candidates	Votes	
AL	Samuel Ingham (D)	21,286	✔
	Isaac Toucey (D)	21,262	✔
	Zalmon Wildman (D)	21,220	✔
	Andrew T. Judson (D)	21,160	✔
	Lancelot Phelps (D)	21,059	✔
	Elisha Haley (D)	21,019	✔
	John Holley (W)	19,170	
	Noyes Barbor (W)	18,931	
	Ebenezer Young (W)	18,888	
	Samuel Tweedy (W)	18,881	
	Ebenezer Jackson (W)	18,809	
	Joseph Trumbull (W)	18,649	
	Horace Cowles	353	
	Sheldon Leavit	328	
	Elisha Stearns	313	
	Richard Hubbard	313	
	William Waterbury	301	

GEORGIA

Special Election

	Candidates	Votes	
AL	Thomas Glascock (D)	30,540	✔
	Jesse F. Cleveland (D)	30,077	✔
	Jabez Y. Jackson (D)	30,072	✔
	Hopkins Holsey (D)	29,727	✔
	Wilde (W)	27,542	
	Foster (W)	27,525	
	Gamble (W)	27,266	
	Beall (W)	26,871	

INDIANA

	Candidates	Votes	%
1	Ratliff Boon (D)	4,028	51.4
	John G. Clendenin (W)	3,815	48.6
2	John W. Davis (D)	5,499	55.3
	John Ewing (W)	4,440	44.7
3	John Carr (D)	5,048	56.1
	Charles Dewey (W)	3,954	43.9
4	Amos Lane (D)	4,769	50.4
	George H. Dunn (W)	4,687	49.6
5	Jonathan McCarty (W)	4,824	48.9
	James Rariden (W)	2,684	27.2
	John Finley	2,353	23.9
6	George L. Kinnard (D)	7,483	61.6
	Jacob B. Lowe	4,658	38.4
7	Edward A. Hannegan (D)	6,910	66.3
	James Gregory (W)	3,515	33.7

KENTUCKY

	Candidates	Votes	
1	Linn Boyd (D)	✔	
2	Albert G. Hawes (JAC D)		
3	Joseph R. Underwood (W)		

	Candidates	Votes	%
4	Sherrod Williams (W)	✔	
5	James Harlan (W)	✔	
6	John Calhoon (W)	✔	
7	Benjamin Hardin (W)	✔	
8	William J. Graves (W)	✔	
9	John White (W)	✔	
10	Chilton Allan (CLAY D)	✔	
11	Richard French (D)	✔	
12	John Chambers (W)	✔	
13	Richard M. Johnson (JAC D)	✔	

MARYLAND

	Candidates	Votes	%
1	John N. Steele (W)	1,967	100.0
2	James A. Pearce (W)	3,386	50.2
	Unidentified Candidate (D)	3,363	49.8
3	James Turner (W)	2,866	51.1
	Unidentified Candidate (D)	2,748	49.0
5	George C. Washington (W)	1,058	100.0
6	Francis Thomas (D)	3,838	53.0
	Unidentified Candidate (W)	3,405	47.0
7	Daniel Jenifer (W)	1,919	58.7
	Unidentified Candidate (D)	1,352	41.3

Multi-Member District

	Candidates	Votes	
4	Benjamin C. Howard (D)	6,738	✔
	Isaac McKim (D)	6,675	✔
	Unidentified Candidate (W)	6,205	
	Unidentified Candidate (W)	6,111	

MICHIGAN [1]

(Became a state Jan. 26, 1837)

	Candidates	Votes	%
AL	Issac Crary (D)	7,019	94.9

MISSISSIPPI

	Candidates	Votes	
AL	David Dickson (D)	9,387	✔
	John F. H. Claiborne (D)	8,836	✔
	James C. Wilkins (W)	7,445	
	Benjamin W. Edwards (D)	7,396	
	Harry Vose	224	

MISSOURI

	Candidates	Votes	
AL	William H. Ashley (I)	12,825	✔
	Albert G. Harrison (D)	10,856	✔
	Strother (D)	10,677	
	Birch (I)	8,843	

NEW HAMPSHIRE

	Candidates	Votes	
AL	Robert Burns (D)	✔	
	Samuel Cushman (D)	✔	
	Joseph Weeks (D)	✔	
	Franklin Pierce (D)	✔	
	Benning M. Bean (D)	✔	
	Samuel Hale		
	Samuel W. Carr		
	James Wilson Jr		
	Anthony Colby		
	Joseph Bell		

NORTH CAROLINA

	Candidates	Votes	%
1	William B. Shepard (W)	2,534	85.5
	Isaac Pipkin (D)	429	14.5
2	Jesse A. Bynum (D)	2,228	52.9
	William L. Long (W)	1,986	47.1
3	Ebenezer Pettigrew (W)	3,072	54.9
	Thomas H. Hall (D)	2,529	45.2
4	Jesse Speight (D)	3,017	57.3
	John McLeod (W)	2,250	42.7

	Candidates	Votes	%
5	James I. McKay (D)	2,690	63.4
	Lewis Dishongh (W)	1,553	36.6
6	Micajah T. Hawkins (D)	2,540	62.5
	Josiah Crudup (W)	1,522	37.5
7	Edmund Deberry (W)	3,426	53.8
	Lauchlin Bethune (D)	2,940	46.2
8	William Montgomery (D)	2,695	50.4
	Daniel L. Barringer (W)	2,654	49.6
9	Augustine H. Shepperd (W)	✔	
10	Abraham Rencher (SR W)	3,078	51.4
	Burton Craige (W)	1,619	27.0
	Richard M. Pearson (W)	1,297	21.6
11	Henry W. Conner (D)	3,385	63.2
	Bartlett Shipp (W)	1,974	36.8
12	James Graham (W)	3,733‡	48.6
	David Newland (D)	3,726	48.5
13	Lewis Williams (W)	✔	

RHODE ISLAND

	Candidates	Votes	
AL	William Sprague (D)	3,924	✔
	Dutee J. Pearce (D)	3,901	✔
	Burges (W)	3,776	
	Cranston (W)	3,659	
	Ruyers	101	

TENNESSEE

	Candidates	Votes	%
1	William B. Carter (W)	3,696	48.6
	Alexander Anderson (D)	2,054	27.0
	Thomas D. Arnold (W)	1,863	24.5
2	Samuel Bunch (W)	4,370	68.3
	David Adams (D)	2,026	31.7
3	Luke Lea (UN D)	4,250	58.7
	Joseph L. Williams (W)	2,992	41.3
4	James Standifer (W)	4,383	60.1
	William T. Senter (D)	2,915	39.9
5	John B. Forester (W)	5,645	83.5
	Peter Buram (D)	1,112	16.5
6	Balie Peyton (W)	3,530	100.0
7	John Bell (W)	4,832	100.0
8	Abram P. Maury (W)	3,006	60.6
	Robert Jetton (D)	1,956	39.4
9	James K. Polk (D)	5,165	100.0
10	Ebenezer J. Shields (W)	3,217	40.5
	Thomas Porter	2,381	30.0
	A. A. Kincannon	2,344	29.5
11	Cave Johnson (D)	2,714	63.7
	William Turner (W)	1,549	36.3
12	Adam Huntsman (D)	4,652	51.4
	David Crockett (W)	4,400	48.6
13	William C. Dunlap (D)	4,903	63.9
	C. H. Williams (W)	2,770	36.1

VIRGINIA

	Candidates	Votes	%
1	George Loyall (D)	1,625	52.5
	Emmerson (W)	1,471	47.5
2	John Y. Mason (D)	1,193	70.2
	Urquehart (W)	507	29.8
3	John W. Jones (D)	1,566	68.3
	Archer (W)	728	31.7
4	George C. Droomgoole (D)	1,365	55.7
	Gholson (W)	1,088	44.4
5	James W. Bouldin (D)	1,264	59.0
	Bolling (W)	879	41.0
6	Walter Coles (D)	1,728	54.1
	Davenport (W)	1,467	45.9
7	Nathaniel H. Claiborne (D)	1,680	51.3
	Stuart (D)	1,592	48.7
8	Henry A. Wise (W)	1,212	62.9
	Coke (W)	716	37.1
9	John Roane Jr (D)	1,150	50.3
	Taylor (W)	1,138	49.7

1. Crary was elected to the House from Michigan in 1835 in anticipation that admission to the Union would follow soon thereafter. However, Michigan's admission was delayed until Jan. 26, 1837. Crary took his seat the next day. Thus, the 1835 election entitled him to serve just over one month (Jan. 27, 1837-March 3, 1837) in the 24th Congress (1835-37).

VIRGINIA

Candidates	Votes	%
10 John Taliaferro (W)	869	50.5
Chino (D)	852	49.5
11 John Robertson (W)	1,384	53.6
Roane (D)	1,199	46.4
12 James Garland (D)	1,970	55.6
Gordon (W)	1,576	44.4
13 John M. Patton (D)	406	100.0

Candidates	Votes	%
14 Charles F. Mercer (W)	692	83.6
Mason (D)	136	16.4
15 Edward Lucas (D)	1,971	51.6
Cooke (W)	1,849	48.4
16 James M. H. Beale (D)	2,112	93.2
Jones (W)	154	6.8
17 Robert Craig (D)	2,592	50.3
Moore (W)	2,564	49.7

Candidates	Votes	%
18 George W. Hopkins (D)	2,518	64.3
Fulton (W)	1,399	35.7
19 William McComas (W)	2,121	55.0
Smith (D)	1,733	45.0
20 Joseph Johnson (D)	1,858	46.4
Allen (W)	1,809	45.1
Maxwell	342	8.5
21 William S. Morgan (D)	2,311	57.5
Wilson (W)	1,710	42.5

1836 House Elections

ARKANSAS

(Became a state June 15, 1836)

Candidates	Votes	%
AL Archibald Yell (D)	5,420	73.4
William Cummins (W)	1,967	26.6

Special Election

AL Archibald Yell (VB D)	✔	

CONNECTICUT

Special Election

AL Orrin Holt (D)	17,367	51.4
John Brockway (W)	16,431	48.6

DELAWARE

AL John J. Milligan (W)	4,705	52.3
Unidentified Candidate (D)	4,297	47.7

GEORGIA

AL Thomas Glascock (D)	48,448	✔
George W. B. Towns (D)	29,600	✔
Jesse F. Cleveland (D)	29,580	✔
Charles E. Haynes (D)	29,490	✔
Seaton Grantland (D)	29,343	✔
George W. Owens (D)	29,316	✔
Hopkins Holsey (D)	29,227	✔
Jabez Y. Jackson (D)	29,227	✔
William C. Dawson (W)	29,003	✔
Julius C. Alford (W)	28,855	
Colquette (W)	28,677	
Habersham (W)	28,557	
John Coffee (D)	28,543	
King (W)	28,458	
Nesbit (W)	28,419	
Black (W)	28,407	
Joseph Jackson (W)	28,353	

Special Election

AL William C. Dawson (W)	24,239	53.0
John W. A. Sanford (D)	21,472	47.0

ILLINOIS

1 Adam W. Snyder (VB D)	4,552	40.4
John Reynolds (D)	4,441	39.4
William J. Gatewood	2,270	20.2
2 Zadoc Casey (D)	7,142	65.8
Alexander P. Field	3,568	32.9
3 William L. May (D)	11,764	54.1
John T. Stewart	10,001	46.0

LOUISIANA

1 Henry Johnson (W)	✔	
2 Eleazer W. Ripley (D)	*	
3 Rice Garland (W)	✔	

MAINE [1]

1 John Fairfield (D)	✔	
2 Francis O. J. Smith (D)	4,237	52.1
James Brooks	3,583	44.0
3 Jonathan Cilley (D)	2,153	48.6
Jeremiah Bailey (W)	2,048	46.2
4 George Evans (W)	✔	
5 Timothy J. Carter (D)	4,165	59.9
Oliver Herrick (W)	2,397	34.5

Candidates	Votes	%
6 Alfred Marshall	1,387*	45.9
Hugh J. Anderson (D)	854	28.2
Philip Morrill	766	25.3
7 Joseph C. Noyes (W)	✔	
Timothy Pilsbury	1,848	
Frederic Hobbs	1,544	
Anson G. Chandler	895	
8 Thomas Davee (D)	3,498	58.1
John S. Tenney (W)	2,458	40.8

MASSACHUSETTS

1 Richard Fletcher (W)	4,702	61.8
Amasa Walker (D)	2,895	38.0
2 Stephen C. Phillips (W)	3,920	51.1
Joseph S. Cabot (D)	3,749	48.9
3 Caleb Cushing (W)	3,949	57.2
Gayton P. Osgood (D)	2,916	42.2
4 William Parmenter (D)	4,034	56.5
Samuel Hoar (W)	3,097	43.4
5 Levi Lincoln (W)	4,697	65.5
Jubal Harrington (D)	2,443	34.1
6 George Grennell Jr (W)	3,872	69.9
Samuel C. Allen (D)	1,645	29.7
7 George A. Briggs (W)	3,567	54.5
Theodore Sedgwick (D)	2,961	45.2
8 William B. Calhoun (W)	3,798	57.5
George Bancroft (D)	2,794	42.3
9 William S. Hastings (W)	3,137	55.2
Alexander H. Everett (D)	2,495	43.9
10 Nathaniel B. Borden (D)	3,093	68.7
William Baylies (W)	1,399	31.1
11 John Reed (W)	2,628	55.8
Henry Crocker (D)	2,079	44.2
12 John Quincy Adams (W)	3,125	82.6
Solomon Lincoln (D)	260	6.9
John Thomas	222	5.9

MISSOURI

AL Albert G. Harrison (D)	16,468	✔
John Miller (D)	15,129	✔
Birch (WHITE D)	10,007	
Unidentified Candidate	7,533	

NEW JERSEY

AL Charles C. Stratton (W)	✔	
Thomas Jones Yorke (W)	✔	
John B. Aycrigg (W)	✔	
John P. B. Maxwell (W)	✔	
Joseph F. Randolph (W)	✔	
William Halstead (W)	✔	

NEW YORK

1 Thomas Jackson (D)	3,731	61.9
Abraham Rose (W)	2,297	38.1
2 Abraham Vanderveer (D)	3,893	56.3
John Dikeman (W)	3,019	43.7
4 Gouverneur Kemble (D)	2,738	45.9
James Turk	1,962	32.9
Walker Todd	1,265	21.2
5 Obadiah Titus (D)	3,687	63.9
Bartow White (W)	2,082	36.1
6 Nathaniel Jones (D)	3,479	60.3
Samuel Eager	2,289	39.7
7 John Brodhead (D)	3,276	41.5
Benjamin Bevier	2,947	37.3
Steveryn Bruyn	1,669	21.2
9 Henry Vail (D)	4,935	51.1
Hiram Hunt (W)	4,729	48.9

Candidates	Votes	%
10 Albert Gallup (D)	4,882	52.9
Jonathan Jenkins	4,351	47.1
11 John De Graff (D)	5,322	57.0
John Taylor	4,014	43.0
12 David Russell (W)	3,543	57.4
Orville Clark	2,629	42.6
13 John Palmer (D)	4,259	56.8
Reuben Sandford	3,240	43.2
14 James Spencer (D)	3,843	54.5
Asa Hascall (W)	3,212	45.5
15 John Edwards (D)	3,740	51.2
Cornelius Patman	3,571	48.8
16 Arphaxed Loomis (D)	3,410	100.0
18 Isaac Bronson (D)	4,669	56.1
Elisha Camp	3,653	43.9
19 John Prentiss (D)	3,784	54.0
Eben Morehouse	3,229	46.0
20 Amasa Parker (D)	4,501	100.0
21 John Clark (D)	3,701	58.7
Abial Cook	2,602	41.3
24 William Noble (D)	4,303	53.7
Robert Muir	3,715	46.3
25 Samuel Birdsall (D)	4,915	53.9
John Maynard (W)	4,213	46.2
26 Mark Sibley (W)	3,410	55.3
Jared Willson	2,754	44.7
27 John Andrews (D)	5,219	59.3
George Edwards	3,576	40.7
28 Timothy Childs (W)	4,693	53.6
Horace Gay	4,067	46.4
29 William Patterson (W)	5,040	60.6
William Mitchell	3,279	39.4
30 Luther Peck (W)	5,456	53.5
James Faulkner	4,741	46.5
31 Richard Marvin (W)	5,372	52.9
Oliver Lee (D)	4,782	47.1
32 Millard Fillmore (W)	4,475	61.4
Thomas Sherwood	2,810	38.6
33 Charles Mitchell (W)	4,091	50.7
Washington Hunt	3,980	49.3

Multi-Member Districts

3 Edward Curtis (W)	17,524	✔
Ely Moore (D)	16,673	✔
Churchill Cambreleng (D)	16,447	✔
J. Ogden Hoffman (W)	16,441	✔
Gideon Lee (D)	16,198	
John McKeon (D)	15,943	
Ira Wheeler (W)	15,920	
Hubert Wagenen (W)	14,703	
James Monroe (W)	3,144	
Stephen Hasbrook	1,334	
8 Zadock Pratt (D)	9,085	✔
Robert McClellan (D)	8,156	✔
Colba Reed	6,309	
Ambrose Jordan	6,293	
17 Abraham Grant (D)	8,249	✔
Henry Foster (D)	6,878	✔
Joshua Spencer	5,570	
John Grant	5,570	
Israel Stoddard	1,417	
22 Andrew Bruyn (D)	8,151	✔
Hiram Gray (D)	7,779	✔
Charles Cook	7,244	
Benjamin Ferris	6,915	
23 William Taylor (D)	7,665	✔
Bennet Bicknell (D)	7,635	✔
B. Davis Noxon	4,676	
Eliphalet Jackson	4,675	

NORTH CAROLINA

Special Election

12 James Graham (W)	4,791	60.1
David Newland (W)	3,177	39.9

Footnote, see p. 723.

OHIO

	Candidates	Votes	%
1	Alexander Duncan (D)	4,734	52.2
	Bellamy Storer (W)	4,333	47.8
2	Taylor Webster (D)	3,891	52.5
	Jesse Corwin (W)	3,523	47.5
3	Patrick G. Goode (W)	6,300	55.7
	James Brown (D)	5,018	44.3
4	Thomas Corwin (W)	4,770	64.6
	Samuel H. Hale (D)	2,614	35.4
5	Thomas L. Hamer (D)	4,375	57.0
	Owen T. Fishback (W)	3,305	43.0
6	Calvary Morris (W)	3,780	50.4
	Nahum Ward (D)	3,703	49.3
7	William Key Bond (W)	4,844	52.4
	William Allen (D)	4,395	47.6
8	Joseph Ridgway (W)	6,499	56.9
	Jeremiah M. Lene	4,915	43.1
9	John Chaney (D)	5,838	60.7
	Henry Stanberry (W)	3,784	39.3
10	Sampson Mason (W)	6,907	67.8
	John Shelby (D)	3,267	32.1
11	James Alexander Jr. (W)	4,305	51.2
	William Kennon Sr. (D)	4,102	48.8
12	Alex Harper (W)	5,018	52.1
	Jno Hamm (D)	4,619	47.9
13	Daniel P. Leadbetter (D)	5,027	56.9
	Abraham Shane (W)	3,802	43.1
14	William H. Hunter (D)	6,422	52.7
	Jabez Wright (W)	5,766	47.3
15	J. W. Allen (W)	8,206	55.6
	Harvey Rice (D)	6,489	44.0
16	Elisha Whittlesey (W)	7,691	62.8
	Ashbel Dart (D)	4,550	37.2
17	Andrew W. Loomis (D)	3,382	50.2
	George McCook (W)	3,359	49.8
18	Matthias Shepler (D)	4,384	56.9
	Samuel Quinby (W)	3,325	43.1
19	Daniel Kilgore (D)	3,570	61.1
	John B. Bayliss (W)	2,274	38.9

PENNSYLVANIA

	Candidates	Votes	%
1	Lemuel Paynter (D)	2,568	55.3
	Unidentified Candidate (W)	2,074	44.7
3	Francis J. Harper (D)	4,432	50.5
	Unidentified Candidate (W)	4,339	49.5

	Candidates	Votes	%
5	Jacob Fry Jr (D)	3,194	61.9
	Unidentified Candidate (W)	1,963	38.1
6	Mathias Morris (W)	3,260	51.4
	Unidentified Candidate (D)	3,085	48.6
7	David D. Wagener (D)	✔	
	Unidentified Candidate (W)		
8	Edward B. Hubley (D)	2,881	54.3
	Unidentified Candidate (W)	2,430	45.8
9	Henry A. P. Muhlenberg (D)	4,276	57.5
	Unidentified Candidate (W)	3,160	42.5
10	Luther Reily (D)	2,885	50.8
	Unidentified Candidate (W)	2,795	49.2
11	Henry Logan (D)	3,366	58.2
	Unidentified Candidate (W)	2,414	41.8
12	Daniel Sheffer (D)	3,108	50.5
	Unidentified Candidate (W)	3,047	49.5
13	Charles McClure (D)	3,633	57.8
	Unidentified Candidate (W)	2,655	42.2
14	William W. Potter (D)	4,914	61.1
	Unidentified Candidate (W)	3,134	38.9
15	Robert H. Hammond (D)	2,881	52.1
	Unidentified Candidate (W)	2,646	47.9
16	David Petrikin (D)	4,275	58.6
	Unidentified Candidate (W)	3,026	41.5
17	Samuel W. Morris (D)	3,888	60.5
	Unidentified Candidate (W)	2,536	39.5
18	Charles Ogle (W)	✔	
	Unidentified Candidate (D)		
19	John Klingensmith Jr (D)	3,694	58.0
	Unidentified Candidate (W)	2,674	42.0
20	Andrew Buchanan (D)	3,252	100.0
21	Thomas M. T. McKennan (W)	2,766	52.2
	Unidentified Candidate (D)	2,537	47.8
22	Richard Biddle (W)	3,155	51.4
	Unidentified Candidate (D)	2,984	48.6
23	William Beatty (D)	✔	
	Unidentified Candidate (W)		
24	Thomas Henry (W)	✔	
	Unidentified Candidate (D)		
25	Arnold Plummer (D)	4,281	54.4
	Unidentified Candidate (W)	3,582	45.6
	Multi-Member Districts		
2	George W. Toland (W)	✔	
	John Sergeant (W)	5,317✔	
	Unidentified Candidate (D)	3,072	

	Candidates	Votes	%
	Unidentified Candidate (D)		
4	David Potts Jr (W)	✔	
	Edward Davies (W)	✔	
	Edward Darlington (W)	9,916✔	
	Unidentified Candidate (D)	8,561	
	Unidentified Candidate (D)		
	Unidentified Candidate (D)		

Special Elections

13	James Black (D)	✔	
	Robert Elliot (A-MAS)		
24	John James Pearson (W)	✔	

SOUTH CAROLINA

1	Hugh S. Legare (UN D)	✔	
	Henry L. Pinckney (D)		
2	Robert Barnwell Smith (D)	✔	
	William J. Grayson (SR W)		
3	John Campbell (SR D)	✔	
	Thomas Smith		
4	Franklin H. Elmore (SR D)		100.0
5	John K. Griffin (SR W)	✔	
6	Francis W. Pickens (SSR NULL)	✔	
7	William K. Clowney (SR D)	✔	
	James Rogers (D)		
8	Waddy Thompson Jr (W)	✔	
9	John P. Richardson (SR D)	✔	
	J. G. Bowman		

VERMONT

1	Hiland Hall (W)	4,220	57.2
	John S. Robinson	3,023	41.0
2	William Slade (W)	3,918	64.5
	Jonas Clark	1,536	25.3
	E. D. Barber	481	7.9
3	Horace Everett (W)	3,747	47.1
	Alden Partridge	3,180	40.0
	Martin Flint	961	12.1
4	Heman Allen (W)	3,522	60.2
	C. P. Vanness	2,203	37.7
5	Isaac Fletcher (D)	3,765	52.8
	Henry F. Janes (W)	3,324	46.6

1. In Maine's 6th district, no candidate received the required majority. A series of special elections were held in an attempt to meet the requirement. In the 5th special election, Anderson was elected. No returns are available for these special elections.

1837 House Elections

ALABAMA

Candidates	Votes	%
1 Reuben Chapman (D)	7,599	81.4
Gabriel Moore (W)	1,742	18.7
2 Joshua L. Martin (D)	2,496	46.2
David Greenhill Lyon (W)	1,461	27.0
Stone	1,446	26.8
3 Joab Lawler (W)	5,874	52.7
Henry W. Ellis (D)	5,277	47.3
4 Dixon H. Lewis (SR W)		100.0
5 Francis Lyon (W)	3,651	50.3
R. E. B. Baylor (NULL-NR)	3,604	49.7

CONNECTICUT

Candidates	Votes	%
1 Isaac Toucey (D)	4,410	50.4
Joseph Trumbull (W)	4,334	49.6
2 Samuel Ingham (D)	10,194	54.4
Henry Flagg (W)	8,558	45.6
3 Elisha Haley (D)	2,367	51.2
Thomas Williams (W)	2,252	48.8
4 Thomas Whittlesey (D)	3,604	52.7
Gideon Tomlinson (W)	3,239	47.3
5 Lancelot Phelps (D)	3,493	50.7
Phineas Miner (W)	3,391	49.3
6 Orrin Holt (D)	5,301	52.3
John Brockway (W)	4,843	47.7

GEORGIA

Special Election

Candidates	Votes	%
AL Julius C. Alford (W)	17,754	53.4
Liddell (D)	15,480	46.6

INDIANA

Candidates	Votes	%
1 Ratliff Boon (D)	4,534	50.4
John Pitcher (W)	4,467	49.6
2 John Ewing (W)	5,820	54.4
John Law (D)	4,887	45.6
3 William Graham (W)	5,717	56.6
John S. Simonson (D)	4,390	43.4
4 George H. Dunn (W)	6,091	54.6
Amos Lane (D)	5,057	45.4
5 James Rariden (W)	6,599	57.5
Johnathan McCarty (W)	4,845	42.2
6 William Herod (W)	9,635	62.1
James B. Ray (D)	5,888	37.9
7 Albert S. White (W)	10,937	74.2
Nathan Jackson (W)	3,789	25.7

Special Election

Candidates	Votes	%
6 William Herod (W)	3,703	51.5
William W. Wick	3,493	48.5

KENTUCKY

Candidates	Votes	%
1 John L. Murray (D)	2,921	39.7
Linn Boyd (D)	2,547	34.6
Campbell (W)	1,888	25.7
2 Edward Rumsey (W)	4,035	89.1
Jones (D)	496	11.0
3 Joseph R. Underwood (W)	4,589	100.0
4 Sherrod Williams (W)	3,189	47.1
McHenry (D)	1,819	26.9
Monroe (W)	1,764	26.1
5 James Harlan (W)		100.0
6 John Calhoon (W)	3,656	55.7
Vanmetre (D)	2,902	44.2
7 John Pope (I)	3,248	54.4
Hardin (W)	2,728	45.7
8 William J. Graves (W)	5,021	63.0
T. F. Marshall (W)	2,950	37.0

Candidates	Votes	%
9 John White (W)	3,700	60.0
Garrard (D)	2,464	40.0
10 Richard Hawes (W)		100.0
11 Richard H. Menifee (W)	4,084	51.5
French (D)	3,850	48.5
12 John Chambers (W)	2,886	74.5
Leach (D)	989	25.5
13 William W. Southgate (W)	4,457	50.7
Phelps (D)	4,116	46.8

MARYLAND

Candidates	Votes	%
1 John Dennis (W)	2,076	59.6
Handy (D)	1,409	40.4
2 James A. Pearce (W)	2,714	53.2
Evans (D)	2,388	46.8
3 John T. H. Worthington (D)	2,413	53.2
Brown (W)	2,126	46.8
5 William Cost Johnson (I)	1,292	52.8
Kimmell (W)	1,153	47.2
6 Francis Thomas (D)	3,819	52.0
Merrick (W)	3,523	48.0
7 Daniel Jenifer (W)		100.0

Multi-Member District

Candidates	Votes	%
4 Benjamin C. Howard (D)	7,184	✔
Isaac McKim (D)	7,141	✔
Kennedy (W)	6,950	
Ridgely (W)	6,873	

MICHIGAN

Candidates	Votes	%
AL Isaac Crary (D)	11,451	52.6
Hezekiah Wells (W)	10,329	47.4

MISSISSIPPI

Candidates	Votes	%
AL Sergeant S. Prentiss (W)	13,688	‡
Thomas Word (W)	12,374	‡
John F. H. Claiborne (D)	6,206	
Samuel Gholson (D)	5,881	

Special Election

Candidates	Votes	%
AL John F. H. Claiborne (D)	11,198	‡
Samuel Gholson (D)	9,971	‡
Prentiss (W)	7,153	
Acee (W)	6,632	

NEW HAMPSHIRE

Candidates	Votes	%
AL Charles G. Atherton (D)		✔
Jared W. Williams (D)		✔
James Farrington (D)		✔
Samuel Cushman (D)		✔
Joseph Weeks (D)		✔
Charles B. Goodrich		
Joseph Bell		
Richard Bradley		
Anthony Colby		
James Wilson Jr.		

NORTH CAROLINA

Candidates	Votes	%
1 Samuel T. Sawyer (W)	2,111	55.3
G. C. Moore (D)	1,706	44.7
2 Jesse Bynum (D)		✔
William L. Long (W)		
3 Edward Stanly (W)	2,842	56.6
Louis D. Wilson (D)	2,176	43.4
4 Charles Shepard (W)	2,392	55.6
William D. Moseley (D)	1,914	44.5
5 James I. McKay (D)	3,023	81.9
T. C. Miller (D)	668	18.1

Candidates	Votes	%
6 Micajah T. Hawkins (D)	1,949	54.1
Joseph Macklin (D)	894	24.8
John L. Henderson (W)	762	21.1
7 Edmund Deberry (W)	3,323	57.4
Lauchlin Bethune (D)	2,465	42.6
8 William Montgomery (D)	2,591	51.9
William A. Graham (W)	2,400	48.1
9 Augustine H. Shepperd (W)	3,359	50.9
John Hill (D)	3,239	49.1
10 Abraham Rencher (W)	3,041	90.6
Micajah Cox (D)	205	6.1
11 Henry W. Conner (D)		100.0
12 James Graham (W)		✔
13 Lewis Williams (D)		✔
Samuel Patterson		

PENNSYLVANIA

Special Election

Candidates	Votes	%
3 Charles Naylor (W)	2,356	56.0
Ingersoll (D)	1,853	44.0

RHODE ISLAND

Candidates	Votes	%
AL Joseph L. Tillinghast (W)	4,282	✔
Robert B. Cranston (W)	4,221	✔
Dutee J. Pearce (D)	3,261	
Howard (D)	3,201	
Dorr (D)	72	
King (CONST)	25	

TENNESSEE

Candidates	Votes	%
1 William B. Carter (W)	3,994	51.5
Thomas D. Arnold (W)	3,756	48.5
2 Abraham McClellan (D)	3,612	52.9
Samuel Bunch (W)	2,357	34.5
Eliot (W)	865	12.7
3 Joseph L. Williams (W)	6,812	72.0
R. M. Anderson (W)	2,653	28.0
4 James Standifer (W)	5,110	66.4
Stone (D)	2,581	33.6
5 Hopkins L. Turney (D)	3,437	49.9
Coxe (W)	2,984	43.3
Peter Burum (D)	466	6.8
6 William B. Campbell (W)	4,142	60.0
William C. Trousdale (D)	2,760	40.0
7 John Bell (W)	4,639	100.0
8 Abram P. Maury (W)	3,043	55.3
William Crockett (D)	2,458	44.7
9 James K. Polk (D)	4,245	100.0
10 Ebenezer J. Shields (W)	4,432	55.7
A. A. Kincannon (D)	3,521	44.3
11 Richard Cheatham (W)	3,822	50.6
Cave Johnson (D)	3,731	49.4
12 John W. Crockett (W)	8,456	85.7
A. M. Hughes (W)	1,413	14.3
13 Christopher H. Williams (W)	5,360	60.7
William C. Dunlap (D)	3,478	39.4

VIRGINIA

Candidates	Votes	%
1 Francis Mallory (W)		✔
Joel Holleman (D)		
2 Francis E. Rives (D)		✔
William B. Goodyear (D)		
3 John W. Jones (D)		✔
4 George C. Dromgoole (D)		✔
5 James W. Bouldin (D)		✔
6 Walter Coles (D)		✔
J. Kerr (W)		

VIRGINIA

Candidates	Votes	%
7 Archibald Stuart (D)	✔	
Nathaniel H. Claiborne (W)		
8 Henry A. Wise (W)	✔	
9 Robert M. T. Hunter (W)	✔	
Upshaw (D)		
Harwood (D)		
10 John Talliaferro (W)	✔	
J. Gibson		

Candidates	Votes	%
11 John Robertson (W)	✔	
12 James Garland (D)	✔	
13 John M. Patton (D)	✔	
14 Charles F. Mercer (W)	✔	
William T. T. Mason (D)		
15 James M. Mason (D)	✔	
J. B. D. Smith (W)		
16 Isaac S. Pennybacker (D)	✔	
David Steele (W)		

Candidates	Votes	%
17 Robert Craig (D)	✔	
E. Johnston (W)		
18 George W. Hopkins (D)	✔	
John N. Humes (D)		
19 Andrew Beirne (D)	✔	
Andrew Donnally (W)		
20 Joseph Johnson (D)	✔	
John J. Jackson (W)		
21 William S. Morgan (D)	✔	

House Candidates Index

For an index of all House candidates listed in this section (pages 701 to 1061), see pages 1180-1273. Instructions for use of the House Candidates Index appear on page 1180.

1838 House Elections

ARKANSAS

Candidates	Votes	%
AL Edward Cross (D)	6,771	*61.0*
Cummings (W)	4,328	*39.0*

DELAWARE

	Votes	%
AL Thomas Robinson Jr (D)	4,451	*50.3*
John J. Milligan (W)	4,399	*49.7*

GEORGIA

	Votes	
AL William C. Dawson (SR W)	33,278	✓
Julius C. Alford (SR W)	32,320	✓
Walter T.Colquitt (SR W)	32,299	✓
Richard W. Habersham (SR W)	32,282	✓
Thomas Butler King (SR W)	32,213	✓
Lott Warren (SR W)	31,887	✓
Eugenius A. Nisbet (SR W)	31,841	✓
Edward J. Black (SR W)	31,801	✓
Mark A. Cooper (SR W)	31,723	✓
David C. Campbell (D)	31,270	
Alfred Iverson (D)	31,238	
Josiah S. Patterson (D)	31,187	
Graves (D)	31,074	
Robert W. Pooler (D)	31,042	
Junius Hillyer (D)	30,967	
Burney (D)	30,932	
McWhorter (D)	30,796	
Nelson (D)	30,782	

ILLINOIS

	Votes	%
1 John Reynolds (D)	8,029	*61.2*
John Hogan (W)	5,100	*38.9*
2 Zadock Casey (D)	8,367	*94.3*
Samuel McRoberts (W)	501	*5.6*
3 John T. Stuart (W)	18,248	*50.0*
Stephen A. Douglas (D)	18,213	*49.9*

LOUISIANA

	Votes	%
1 Edward D. White (W)	3,351	*57.4*
Slidell (D)	2,486	*42.6*
2 Thomas W. Chinn (W)	1,790	*55.7*
Lawson (D)	1,423	*44.3*
3 Rice Garland (W)		*100.0*

MAINE

	Votes	%
1 Nathan Clifford (D)	5,568	*54.8*
Nathan D. Appleton (W)	4,560	*44.9*
2 Albert Smith (D)	5,709	*50.1*
Ezekiel Whitman (W)	5,623	*49.3*
3 John D. McCrate (D)	4,859	*50.6*
Benjamin Randall (W)	4,652 ✓	*48.5*
4 George Evans (W)	7,143	*60.9*
John Hubbard (D)	4,591	*39.1*
5 Virgil D. Parris (D)	6,765	*57.4*
Zadoc Long (W)	4,999	*42.4*
6 Hugh J. Anderson (D)	5,727	*60.9*
William G. Crosby (W)	3,519	*37.4*
7 Joshua A. Lowell (D)	5,033	*51.8*
Joseph C. Noyes (W)	4,666	*48.1*
8 Thomas Davee (D)	7,839	*51.9*
John S. Tenney (W)	7,042	*46.6*

Special Elections

	Votes	%
3 Edward Robinson (W)	✓	
John D. McCrate (D)		
5 Virgil D. Parris (D)	4,349	*57.4*
Zadoc Long (W)	3,690	*42.4*

MARYLAND

Special Election

Candidates	Votes	%
4 John P. Kennedy (W)	7,153	*53.2*
Marriott (D)	6,291	*46.8*

MASSACHUSETTS[1]

	Votes	%
1 Richard Fletcher (W)	5,145*	*63.1*
Bradford Sumner (D)	2,952	*36.2*
2 Leverett Saltonstall (W)	3,734	*59.1*
Robert Rantoul Jr (D)	2,031	*32.1*
Joseph S. Cabot (D)	536	*8.5*
3 Caleb Cushing (W)	4,762	*61.1*
Gayton P. Osgood (D)	2,730	*35.0*
4 William Parmenter (D)	4,972	*50.1*
Nathan Brooks (W)	4,433	*44.7*
5 Levi Lincoln (W)	4,251	*55.2*
Isaac Davis (D)	2,630	*34.1*
Charles Allen	797	*10.3*
6 James C. Alvord (W)	4,440	*61.8*
Thomas Nims (D)	2,054	*28.6*
Osmyn Baker (W)	653	*9.1*
7 George N. Briggs (W)	4,328	*54.5*
Henry W. Bishop (D)	3,601	*45.3*
8 William B. Calhoun (W)	4,363	*59.4*
William W. Thompson (D)	2,957	*40.3*
9 William S. Hastings (W)	4,049	*56.6*
Alexander H. Everett (D)	3,090	*43.2*
10 Henry Williams (D)	3,306	*51.7*
Nathaniel B. Borden (W)	2,920	*45.7*
11 John Reed (W)	3,519	*56.4*
Henry Crocker (D)	2,703	*43.3*
12 John Quincy Adams (W)	4,100	*59.0*
William M. Jackson (D)	2,822	*40.6*

Special Election

	Votes	%
2 Leverett Saltonstall (W)	3,730	*58.9*
Robert Rantoul Jr (D)	2,034	*32.1*
Joseph S. Cabot (D)	542	*8.6*

MICHIGAN

	Votes	%
AL Isaac E. Crary (D)	16,360	*50.4*
Hezekiah E. Wells (W)	16,099	*49.6*

MISSISSIPPI

Special Election

	Votes	
AL Sergeant S. Prentiss (W)	12,721	✓
Thomas Word (W)	12,077	✓
J. F. H. Claiborne (D)	11,767	
Reuben Davis (D)	11,346	

MISSOURI

	Votes	
AL Albert G. Harrison (D)	23,410	✓
John Miller (D)	23,182	✓
Allen (W)	17,191	
Wilson (W)	16,706	

NEW JERSEY

	Votes	
AL Peter D. Vroom (D)	28,492	✓
William R. Cooper (D)	28,455	✓
Philemon Dickerson (D)	28,453	✓
Daniel B. Ryall (D)	28,441	✓
Joseph Kille (D)	28,426	✓
Joseph Randolph (W)	28,426	✓

Candidates	Votes	%
Strat (W)	28,395	
Max (W)	28,386	
Hal (W)	28,337	
Yorke (W)	28,321	
Force (D)	28,315	
Aigg (W)	28,295	

NEW YORK

	Votes	%
1 Thomas Jackson (D)	4,896	*56.5*
Nathaniel Miller (W)	3,776	*43.5*
2 James De la Montanya (D)	4,405	*55.2*
John Gurnee (W)	3,576	*44.8*
4 Gouverneur Kemble (D)	4,986	*54.3*
Joshua Brown (W)	4,203	*45.7*
5 Charles Johnston (W)	5,262	*53.1*
Obadiah Titus (D)	4,645	*46.9*
6 Nathaniel Jones (D)	4,184	*51.3*
Thomas McKissock (W)	3,978	*48.7*
7 Rufus Palen (W)	5,453	*54.2*
Anthony Hasbrouck (D)	4,615	*45.8*
9 Hiram Hunt (W)	5,483	*52.8*
Henry Vail (D)	4,909	*47.2*
10 Daniel Barnard (W)	5,680	*52.5*
Albert Gallup (D)	5,145	*47.5*
11 Anson Brown (W)	5,401	*51.8*
Nicholas Hill (D)	5,028	*48.2*
12 David Russell (W)	4,346	*61.9*
John Williams (D)	2,671	*38.1*
13 Augustus Hand (D)	4,480	*50.3*
Thomas Tomlinson (W)	4,436	*49.8*
14 John Fine (D)	4,756	*50.5*
Henry Van Rensselaer (W)	4,663	*49.5*
15 Peter Wagner (W)	4,491	*50.3*
David Sacia (D)	4,441	*49.7*
16 Andrew Doig (D)	5,043	*56.8*
Seth Miller (W)	3,835	*43.2*
18 Thomas Chittenden (W)	4,989	*53.7*
Issac Bronson (D)	4,309	*46.3*
19 John Prentiss (D)	4,724	*52.8*
William Averill (W)	4,216	*47.2*
20 Judson Allen (D)	5,072	*54.2*
Erastus Root (W)	4,284	*45.8*
21 John Clark (W)	3,908	*52.3*
John Clapp (D)	3,563	*47.7*
24 Christopher Morgan (W)	4,631	*50.9*
William Noble (D)	4,464	*49.1*
25 Theron Strong (D)	5,824	*50.7*
John Holley (W)	5,670	*49.3*
26 Francis Granger (W)	4,233	*57.9*
Jared Willson (D)	3,083	*42.1*
27 Meredith Mallory (D)	5,438	*51.2*
Thomas Johnson (W)	5,182	*48.8*
28 Thomas Kempshall (W)	5,476	*56.9*
Henry Selden (W)	4,144	*43.1*
29 Seth Gates (W)	6,033	*65.3*
William Mitchell (D)	3,202	*34.7*
30 Luther Peck (W)	6,521	*57.8*
Calvin Chamberlain (D)	4,763	*42.2*
31 Richard Marvin (W)	7,053	*57.6*
Charles Williams (D)	5,198	*42.4*
32 Millard Fillmore (W)	5,414	*65.7*
George Barker (D)	2,831	*34.3*
33 Charles Mitchell (W)	4,690	*55.0*
Henry Curtis (D)	3,840	*45.0*

Multi-Member Districts

	Votes	
3 Ogden Hoffman (W)	20,577	✓
Moses Grinnell (W)	20,563	✓
Edward Curtis (W)	20,458	✓
James Monroe (W)	20,454	✓
John McKeon (D)	19,227	
Isaac Varian (D)	19,206	
Churchill Cambreleng (D)	19,205	
Ely Moore (D)	18,843	
8 John Ely (D)	9,668	✓
Aaron Vanderpoel (D)	9,628	✓

Footnote, see p. 727.

NEW YORK

Candidates	Votes	%
Mitchell Sanford (W)	9,499	
Robert Dorlon (W)	9,469	
17 David Brewster (D)	9,395✔	
John Floyd (D)	9,286✔	
Henry Fitzhugh (W)	8,601	
Charles Kirkland (W)	8,362	
22 Amasa Dana (D)	9,157✔	
Stephen Leonard (D)	9,152✔	
William Ely (W)	8,757	
John Miller (W)	8,725	
23 Nehemiah Earll (D)	9,189✔	
Edward Rogers (D)	9,099✔	
A. Lawrence Foster (W)	9,056	
Victory Birdseye (W)	9,015	

OHIO

	Candidates	Votes	%
1	Alexander Duncan (D)	4,572	51.0
	N. G. Pendleton (W)	4,396	49.0
2	John B. Weller (D)	4,877	54.9
	John Beers (W)	4,010	45.1
3	Patrick G. Goode (W)	7,589	50.7
	William Sawyer (D)	7,368	49.3
4	Thomas Corwin (W)	5,866	99.6
5	William Doan (D)	4,543	56.6
	Daniel Fisher (W)	3,479	43.4
6	Calvery Morris (W)	5,321	55.1
	Joseph Morris (D)	4,337	44.9
7	William K. Bond (W)	4,834	50.9
	Allen Latham (D)	4,658	49.1
8	Joseph Ridgway (W)	6,916	51.4
	John McElvain (D)	6,552	48.7
9	William Medill (D)	6,791	64.6
	John M. Creed (W)	3,729	35.5
10	Samson Mason (W)	6,997	58.1
	Rowland Brown (D)	5,040	41.9
11	Isaac Parrish (D)	4,692	52.7
	James Alexander Jr (W)	4,220	47.4
12	Jonathan Taylor (D)	5,668	51.5
	Alexander Harper (W)	5,347	48.5
13	Daniel P. Leadbetter (D)	7,515	57.5
	James S. Irwin (W)	5,555	42.5
14	George Sweeny (D)	8,601	56.4
	Joseph M. Root (W)	6,654	43.6
15	John W. Allen (W)	8,800	53.8
	John W. Willey (D)	7,558	46.2
16	Joshua R. Giddings (W)	7,581	57.7
	Benjamin Bissell (D)	5,556	42.3
17	John Hastings (D)	4,952	53.2
	Charles D. Coffin (W)	4,349	46.8

	Candidates	Votes	%
18	David A. Starkweather (D)	6,154	60.6
	Hiram B. Wellman (W)	4,010	39.5
19	Henry Swearingen (D)	4,036	52.9
	Samuel Stokely (W)	3,589	47.1

PENNSYLVANIA

	Candidates	Votes	%
1	Lemuel Paynter (D)	3,675	55.1
	J. B. Sutherland (W)	2,994	44.9
3	Charles Naylor (W)	6,670	53.1
	C. J. Ingersoll (D)	5,894	46.9
5	Joseph Fornance (D)	4,527	54.9
	Joseph Royer (W)	3,723	45.1
6	John Davis (D)	4,464	51.9
	Matthew Morris (W)	4,138	48.1
7	David D. Wagener (D)	6,189	62.8
	P. S. Michler (W)	3,672	37.2
8	Peter Newhard (D)	4,636	54.5
	W. C. Livingston (W)	3,876	45.5
9	George M. Keim (D)	7,030	68.6
	D. M. Bieber (W)	3,212	31.4
10	William Simonton (W)	5,000	58.7
	William Reily (D)	3,514	41.3
11	James Gerry (D)	4,197	56.6
	C. A. Barnitz (W)	3,220	43.4
12	James Cooper (W)	5,738	56.0
	Daniel Sheffer (D)	4,503	44.0
13	William S. Ramsey (D)	5,569	57.3
	Frederick Watts (W)	4,145	42.7
14	William W. Potter (D)	6,510	50.9
	William Irvin (W)	6,288	49.1
15	Robert Hammond (D)	5,156	56.7
	James Merrill (W)	3,946	43.4
16	David Petrikin (D)	6,225	53.5
	David Hurley (W)	5,411	46.5
17	Samuel W. Morris (D)	5,147	54.2
	William Willard (W)	4,354	45.8
18	Charles Ogle (W)	5,106	55.1
	Job Mann (D)	4,158	44.9
19	Albert G. Marchand (D)	5,800	60.5
	Joseph Markle (W)	3,784	39.5
20	Enos Hook (D)	4,498	63.0
	H. Oliphant (W)	2,643	37.0
21	Isaac Leet (D)	3,508	50.2
	Joseph Lawrence (W)	3,487	49.9
22	Richard Biddle (W)	6,090	58.1
	James Power (D)	4,391	41.9
23	William Beatty (D)	5,694	61.1
	George W. Smith (W)	3,625	38.9
24	Thomas Henry (W)	5,265	54.9
	James D. White (D)	4,330	45.1

	Candidates	Votes	%
25	John Galbraith (D)	6,208	51.2
	David Dick (W)	5,920	48.8

Multi-Member Districts

	Candidates	Votes	%
2	George W. Toland	✔	
	John Sergeant (W)	7,132✔	
	J. R. Evans (D)	3,152	
	J. Brasnears (D)		
4	John Edwards (W)	✔	
	Francis James (W)	✔	
	Edward Davies (W)	15,192✔	
	R. Frazer (D)	11,353	
	John Evans (D)		
	G. G. Leiper (D)		

Special Election

	Candidates	Votes	%
9	George M. Keim (D)	2,115	89.8

SOUTH CAROLINA[2]

	Candidates	Votes	%
1	Isaac E. Holmes (D)	1,504	63.8
	Hugh S. Legare (UN D)	854	36.2
2	R. Barnwell Rhett (D)		100.0
3	John Campbell (SR D)	1,280	67.4
	Thomas Smith	620	32.6
4	Franklin H. Elmore (SR D)	*	100.0
5	John K. Griffin (SR W)		100.0
6	Francis W. Pickens (NULL)		100.0
7	James Rogers (D)	✔	
	F. W. Davie		
8	Waddy Thompson Jr (W)	3,339	58.9
	J. N. Witner	2,327	41.1
9	John P. Richardson (SR D)	*	100.0

VERMONT

	Candidates	Votes	%
1	Hiland Hall (W)	5,211	53.9
	John Roberts (D)	4,328	44.7
2	William Slade (W)	4,752	68.9
	Charles Linsley (D)	2,095	30.4
3	Horace Everett (W)	5,183	56.8
	Alden Partridge (D)	3,841	42.1
4	John Smith (D)	4,375	49.0
	Heman Allen (W)	4,085	45.8
5	Isaac Fletcher (D)	4,996	52.2
	William Upham (W)	4,515	47.2

VIRGINIA

Special Election

	Candidates	Votes	%
13	Linn Banks (D)	✔	
	Daniel F. Slaughter (W)		

1. Richard Fletcher of the 1st district never served in the 26th Congress (1839-41). In an 1839 special election, Abbott Lawrence was elected to succeed him. *(See p. 728.)*

2. Franklin H. Elmore of the 4th district and John P. Richardson of the 9th district did not serve in the 26th Congress (1839-41). Sampson Butler and Thomas Sumter were later elected to the seats in special elections for which returns are unavailable.

1839 House Elections

ALABAMA

	Candidates	Votes	%
1	Reuben Chapman (D)	7,384	100.0
2	David Hubbard (D)	3,303	56.3
	Lyon (W)	2,561	43.7
3	George W. Crabb (W)	5,927	50.5
	Ellis (D)	5,816	49.5
4	Dixon H. Lewis (SR W)		100.0
5	James Dellet (W)	4,350	52.6
	Murphey (D)	3,927	47.4

CONNECTICUT

	Candidates	Votes	%
1	Joseph Trumbull (W)	5,180	53.2
	Isaac Toucey (D)	4,108	42.2
2	William L. Storrs (W)	10,525	51.5
	Samuel Ingham (D)	9,924	48.5
3	Thomas Williams (W)	3,066	50.7
	Codington Billings (D)	2,978	49.3
4	Thomas B. Osborne (W)	3,968	52.4
	Thomas Whittlesey (D)	3,604	47.6
5	Truman Smith (W)	3,988	53.5
	Charles Phelps (D)	3,466	46.5
6	John Brockway (W)	3,997	52.5
	Chauncey Cleveland (D)	3,565	46.8

INDIANA

	Candidates	Votes	%
1	George H. Proffit (W)	6,008	53.5
	Robert Dale Owen (D)	5,229	46.5
2	John W. Davis (D)	7,516	54.7
	John Ewing (W)	6,217	45.3
3	John Carr (D)	6,998	57.7
	William Graham (W)	5,121	42.3
4	Thomas Smith (D)	6,541	54.1
	George H. Dunn (W)	5,542	45.9
5	James Rariden (W)	6,257	40.2
	William Thompson (D)	5,333	34.3
	Jonathan McCarty (W)	3,961	25.5
6	William W. Wick (D)	9,505	52.8
	William Herod (W)	8,494	47.2
7	Tilghman A. Howard (D)	9,929	55.3
	Thomas J. Evans (W)	8,036	44.7

KENTUCKY

	Candidates	Votes	%
1	Linn Boyd (D)	✔	
2	Phillip Triplett (W)	✔	
3	Joseph R. Underwood (W)	✔	
4	Sherrod Williams (W)	✔	
5	Simeon H. Anderson (W)	✔	
6	Willis Green (W)	✔	
7	John Pope (W)	✔	
8	William J. Graves (W)	✔	
9	John White (W)	✔	
10	Richard Hawes (W)	✔	
11	Landaff W. Andrews (W)	✔	
12	Garrett Davis (HC W)	✔	
13	William O. Butler (D)	✔	

MARYLAND

	Candidates	Votes	%
1	John Dennis (W)	2,062	52.8
	Stewart (D)	1,817	46.5
2	Philip F. Thomas (D)	3,831	51.3
	Pearce (W)	3,643	48.7
3	John T. H. Worthington (D)	3,924	62.3
	Turner (I)	2,378	37.7
5	William Cost Johnson (W)	3,325	56.7
	Duvall (D)	2,535	43.3
6	Francis Thomas (D)	4,279	53.3
	Price (W)	3,704	46.2
7	Daniel Jenifer (W)	1,984	56.1
	Key (D)	1,553	43.9

Multi-Member District

	Candidates	Votes	%
4	James Carroll (D)	8,018 ✔	
	Soloman Hillen Jr (D)	8,011 ✔	

Candidates	Votes	%
Kennedy (W)	7,634	
Pitts (W)	7,629	

MASSACHUSETTS

Special Elections

	Candidates	Votes	%
1	Abbott Lawrence (W)	4,963	57.4
	Bradford Sumner (D)	3,665	42.4
6	Osmyn Baker (W)	2,581	50.8
	Rodolphus Dickinson (D)	2,020	39.8
	Israel Billings (AB-D)	451	8.9

MISSISSIPPI

	Candidates	Votes	%
AL	Albert G. Brown (D)	16,730 ✔	
	Jacob Thompson (D)	16,501 ✔	
	A. L. Benjamin (W)	14,094	
	Reuben Davis (W)	13,808	

NEW HAMPSHIRE

	Candidates	Votes	%
AL	Ira A. Eastman (D)	✔	
	Edmund Burke (D)	✔	
	Tristram Shaw (D)	✔	
	Charles G. Atherton (D)	✔	
	Jared W. Williams (D)	✔	
	P. Handerson (FED)		
	J. Smith (FED)		
	Joel Eastman (FED)		
	A. Colby (FED)		
	I. Bartlett (FED)		
	D. Hoit (FEDL AB)		
	P. P. Woodbury (FEDL AB)		
	J. M. Harper (FEDL AB)		
	Southworth (FEDL AB)		

NORTH CAROLINA

	Candidates	Votes	%
1	Kenneth Rayner (W)	2,635	56.7
	Samuel T. Sawyer (D)	2,009	43.3
2	Jesse A. Bynum (D)	✔	
	William L. Long (W)		
3	Edward Stanly (W)	3,098	54.8
	Thomas H. Hall (D)	2,554	45.2
4	Charles Shepard (D)	2,890	57.1
	Samuel J. Biddle (W)	2,175	42.9
5	James I. McKay (D)	2,360	87.9
	Frederick J. Hill (W)	325	12.1
6	Micajah T. Hawkins (D)	1,625	50.1
	Robert C. Hilliard (D)	1,621	49.9
7	Edmund Deberry (W)	3,649	57.0
	William A. Morris (D)	2,753	43.0
8	William Montgomery (D)	2,916	53.3
	G. W. Haywood (W)	2,553	46.7
9	John Hill (D)	3,743	50.3
	Augustine H. Shepperd (W)	3,696	49.7
10	Charles Fisher (D)	3,539	51.4
	Pleasant Henderson (W)	3,348	48.6
11	Henry W. Conner (D)	3,041	54.8
	Edney (W)	2,504	45.2
12	James Graham (W)	✔	
13	Lewis Williams (W)	2,900	51.5
	Roderick Murchison (W)	2,731	48.5

PENNSYLVANIA

Special Election

	Candidates	Votes	%
14	George McCullough (D)	4,094	50.9
	Irvin (W)	3,956	49.1

RHODE ISLAND

	Candidates	Votes	%
AL	Joseph L. Tillinghast (W)	4,050 ✔	
	Robert B. Cranston (W)	3,912 ✔	

Candidates	Votes	%
Thomas W. Dorr (D)	3,660	
Benjamin B. Thurston (D)	3,595	

TENNESSEE

	Candidates	Votes	%
1	William B. Carter (W)	4,787	59.0
	Joseph Powell (D)	3,334	41.1
2	Abraham M. McClellan (D)	3,363	65.3
	John A. McKenny (W)	1,790	34.7
3	Joseph L. Williams (W)	5,173	99.9
4	Julius W. Blackwell (D)	4,448	61.3
	William Stone (W)	2,806	38.7
5	Hopkins L. Turney (D)	4,953	65.6
	Anthony Dibrell (W)	2,603	34.5
6	William B. Campbell (W)	5,126	60.5
	William Trousdale (D)	3,350	39.5
7	John Bell (W)	3,895	59.4
	Robert M. Burton (D)	2,665	40.6
8	Meredith P. Gentry (W)	3,245	54.2
	William G. Childress (D)	2,744	45.8
9	Harvey M. Watterson (D)	4,521	58.9
	Daniel L. Barenger (W)	3,154	41.1
10	Aaron V. Brown (D)	5,017	57.8
	Ebenezer Shields (W)	3,668	42.2
11	Cave Johnson (D)	4,289	57.9
	Richard Cheatham (W)	3,117	42.1
12	John W. Crockett (W)	5,155	58.1
	Stephen C. Pavatt (D)	3,719	41.9
13	Christopher H. Williams (W)	3,447	55.5
	William C. Dunlap (D)	2,767	44.5

VIRGINIA

	Candidates	Votes	%
1	Joel Holleman (D)	1,920	51.9
	Mallory (W)	1,781	48.1
2	Francis E. Rives (D)	1,334	57.6
	Pegram (W)	982	42.4
3	John W. Jones (D)	409	58.5
	Taylor (W)	290	41.5
4	George C. Dromgoole (D)	1,236	57.1
	Gholson (W)	927	42.9
5	John Hill (W)	835	54.1
	Wilson (D)	708	45.9
6	Walter Coles (D)	1,564	51.6
	Witcher (W)	1,465	48.4
7	William L. Goggin (W)	1,498	52.7
	Stuart (D)	1,347	47.4
8	Henry A. Wise (W)	858	88.4
	Shultice (D)	113	11.6
9	Robert M. T. Hunter (W)	1,203	52.0
	Scott (D)	1,109	48.0
10	John Taliaferro (W)	1,331	51.4
	Grayson (D)	1,258	48.6
11	John M. Botts (W)	1,459	53.8
	Selden (D)	1,251	46.2
12	James Garland (W)	1,638	66.3
	Gordon (D)	831	33.7
13	Linn Banks (D)	1,785	56.1
	Slaughter (W)	1,396	43.9
14	Charles F. Mercer (W)	1,355	59.3
	Mason (D)	932	40.8
15	William Lucas (D)	2,074	50.1
	Barton (W)	2,070	50.0
16	Green B. Samuels (D)	1,826	60.3
	Steele (W)	1,201	39.7
17	Robert Craig (D)	2,336	58.8
	Moore (W)	1,635	41.2
18	George W. Hopkins (W)	2,921	55.9
	George (D)	2,308	44.1
19	Andrew Beirne (D)	2,745	61.5
	Wethered (W)	1,721	38.5
20	Joseph Johnson (D)	2,370	47.2
	Camden (W)	1,967	39.2
	Shinn (D)	682	13.6
21	Lewis Steenrod (D)	2,667	55.8
	Hammond (W)	2,112	44.2

1840 House Elections

ARKANSAS

Candidates	Votes	%
AL Edward Cross (D)	7,876	57.6
Fowler (W)	5,788	42.4

DELAWARE

AL George B. Rodney (W)	5,896	54.2
Thomas Robinson Jr. (D)	4,974	45.8

GEORGIA

AL William C. Dawson (W)	39,299 ✔	
Richard W. Habersham (W)	39,105 ✔	
Eugenius A. Nisbet (W)	39,098 ✔	
Thomas F. Foster (W)	39,004 ✔	
Lott Warren (W)	39,001 ✔	
Julius C. Alford (W)	38,980 ✔	
Roger L. Gamble (W)	38,924 ✔	
Thomas Butler King (W)	38,895 ✔	
James A. Meriwether (W)	38,840 ✔	
Mark A. Cooper (D)	35,922	
Edward J. Black (D)	35,783	
Lumpkin (D)	35,730	
Campbell (D)	35,678	
Hillyer (D)	35,660	
Pooler (D)	35,657	
Patterson (D)	35,615	
Iverson (D)	35,608	

Special Election

AL Hines Holt (W)	✔	#

INDIANA

Special Election

7 Henry S. Lane (W)	11,726	53.1
Edward A. Hannegan (D)	10,376	47.0

LOUISIANA

1 Edward D. White (W)	3,802	68.4
Leonard (D)	1,757	31.6
2 John B. Dawson (D)	1,933	50.2
Morgan (W)	1,920	49.8
3 John Moore (W)	3,427	50.6
Winn (D)	3,353	49.5

MAINE

1 Nathan Clifford (D)	5,428	54.6
Daniel Goodenow (W)	4,516	45.4
2 William Pitt Fessenden (W)	5,794	50.5
Albert Smith (D)	5,659	49.3
3 Benjamin Randall (W)	5,720	54.3
Joseph Sewall (D)	4,769	45.3
4 George Evans (W)	7,430*	62.5
John Hubbard (D)	4,450	37.4
5 Nathaniel S. Littlefield (D)	2,144	47.0
Zadoc Long (W)	2,123	46.6
6 Alfred Marshall (D)	5,805	58.9
Stanford A. Kingsbury (W)	3,965	40.2
7 Joshua A. Lowell (D)	5,194	50.0
Joseph C. Noyes (W)	5,051	48.6
8 Elisha H. Allen (W)	7,738	51.5
Hannibal Hamlin (D)	7,115	47.4

MASSACHUSETTS

1 Robert C. Winthrop (W)	7,286	63.0
Bradford Sumner (D)	4,232	36.6
2 Leverett Saltonstall (W)	6,153	58.4
Robert Rantoul (D)	4,276	40.6
3 Caleb Cushing (W)	6,529	60.9
Gayton P. Osgood (D)	4,047	37.8

Candidates	Votes	%
4 William Parmenter (D)	6,156	50.3
Nathan Brooks (W)	5,912	48.3
5 Levi Lincoln (W)	7,069	62.4
Isaac Davis (D)	4,126	36.4
6 Osmyn Baker (W)	6,167	62.6
Rhodelphius Larkenson (D)	3,537	35.9
7 George N. Briggs (W)	5,447	54.1
Henry W. Bishop (D)	4,561	45.3
8 William B. Calhoun (W)	5,701	56.0
Chester W. Chapin (D)	4,300	42.2
9 William S. Hastings (W)	5,906	57.8
Alexander H. Everett (D)	4,197	41.1
10 Nathaniel B. Borden (W)	4,320	52.4
Henry Williams (D)	3,730	45.2
11 Barker Burnell (W)	5,120	59.5
Henry Crocker (D)	3,378	39.3
12 John Quincy Adams (W)	5,948	54.2
William M. Jackson (D)	4,945	45.0

Special Election

1 Robert C. Winthrop (W)	7,280	62.9
Bradford Sumner (D)	4,239	36.7

MICHIGAN

AL Jacob M. Howard (W)	22,841	51.2
Alpheus Felch (D)	21,464	48.1

MISSOURI

AL John Miller (D)	29,594 ✔	
John C. Edwards (D)	29,382 ✔	
Samuels (W)	21,492	
Sibley (W)	21,331	

NEW JERSEY

AL William Halsted (W)	33,342 ✔	
Joseph F. Randolph (W)	33,321 ✔	
John B. Aycrigg (W)	33,315 ✔	
John P. B. Maxwell (W)	33,315 ✔	
Charles C. Stratton (W)	33,313 ✔	
Thomas Jones Yorke (W)	33,299 ✔	
Peter D. Vroom (D)	31,138	
William R. Cooper (D)	31,109	
Joseph Kille (D)	31,106	
Kennedy (D)	31,103	
Philemon Dickerson (D)	31,101	
Daniel B. Ryall (D)	31,098	

NEW YORK

1 Charles Floyd (D)	6,069	55.4
William Buffett (W)	4,880	44.6
2 Joseph Egbert (D)	5,620	54.0
Lawrence Hillyer (W)	4,780	46.0
4 Aaron Ward (D)	5,949	54.6
Nicholas Cruger (W)	4,955	45.4
5 Richard Davis (D)	5,164	51.1
Charles Johnston (W)	4,947	48.9
6 James Clinton (D)	4,867	52.8
Thomas McKissock (W)	4,343	47.2
7 John Van Buren (D)	6,007	50.3
Benjamin Bevier (W)	5,930	49.7
9 Hiram Hunt (W)	5,732	51.0
Samuel Fowler (D)	5,466	48.7
10 Daniel Barnard (W)	6,351	51.4
James French (D)	5,973	48.3
11 Archibald Linn (W)	6,074	52.1
John Cramer (D)	5,579	47.8
12 Bernard Blair (W)	4,996	61.7
Orville Clark (D)	3,061	37.8

Candidates	Votes	%
13 Thomas Tomlinson (W)	5,906	53.6
Augustus Hand (D)	5,107	46.4
14 Henry Van B. Rensselaer (W)	6,258	51.3
Preston King (D)	5,948	48.7
15 John Sanford (D)	5,341	53.0
Marcellus Weston (W)	4,732	47.0
16 Andrew Doig (D)	5,981	55.2
Harvey Doolittle (W)	4,774	44.1
18 Thomas Chittenden (W)	6,212	51.9
Alpheus Greene (D)	5,750	48.1
19 Samuel Bowne (D)	5,612	53.5
David Hard (W)	4,831	46.0
20 Samuel Gordon (D)	5,976	52.4
Herman Golld (W)	5,434	47.6
21 John Clark (W)	4,306	51.3
John Tacy (D)	4,085	48.7
24 Christopher Morgan (W)	5,148	50.8
Peter Yawger (D)	4,935	48.7
25 John Maynard (W)	6,749	50.6
John Demott (D)	6,551	49.2
26 Francis Granger (W)	4,800	57.1
Jared Willson (D)	3,457	41.1
27 William Oliver (W)	6,949	53.0
Thomas Johnson (W)	6,170	47.0
28 Timothy Childs (W)	6,052	53.9
Lyman Langworthy (D)	5,092	45.4
29 Seth Gates (W)	6,970	63.4
John Skinner (D)	3,881	35.3
30 John Young (W)	7,974	56.7
Leman Gibbs (D)	6,096	43.3
31 Staley Clarke (W)	8,909	60.2
Benjamin Chamberlain (D)	5,789	39.2
32 Millard Fillmore (W)	6,682	63.9
Leader Roberts (D)	3,742	35.8
33 Alfred Babcock (W)	5,524	55.4
Silas Burroughs (D)	4,309	43.2

Multi-Member Districts

3 James Roosevelt (D)	22,010 ✔	
Charles Ferris (D)	21,975 ✔	
John McKeon (D)	21,748 ✔	
Fernando Wood (D)	21,730 ✔	
Moses Grinnell (W)	20,996	
James Monroe (W)	20,862	
Robert Smith (W)	20,862	
Prescott Hall (W)	20,838	
8 Jacob Houck Jr. (D)	11,210 ✔	
Robert McClellan (D)	11,194 ✔	
Jededia Miller (D)	10,143	
Justus McKinstry (W)	10,139	
17 David Brewster (D)	11,837 ✔	
John Floyd (D)	11,775 ✔	
Fortune White (W)	11,364	
Thomas Bond (W)	11,328	
Arba Blair (LIB)	506	
James Brown (LIB)	505	
22 Samuel Partridge (D)	10,374 ✔	
Lewis Riggs (D)	10,363 ✔	
Ezra Sweet (W)	10,245	
James Dunn (W)	10,243	
23 Victory Birdseye (W)	10,854 ✔	
A. Lawrence Foster (W)	10,826 ✔	
Nehemiah Earll (D)	10,772	
William Hough (D)	10,747	
John Pratt (LIB)	274	
Robert Furman (LIB)	233	

OHIO

1 Nathaniel G. Pendleton (W)	6,119	50.7
Alexander Duncan (D)	5,959	49.3
2 John B. Weller (D)	5,730	50.3
Lewis D. Campbell (W)	5,661	49.7
3 Patrick G. Goode (W)	10,438	50.4
William Sawyer (D)	10,275	49.6
4 Jeremiah Morrow (W)	6,796	60.0
Benjamin Baldwin (D)	4,529	40.0

OHIO

	Candidates	Votes	%
5	William Doan (D)	5,671	53.7
	Thomas L. Shields (W)	4,884	46.3
6	Calvary Morris (W)	8,724	55.8
	George House (D)	6,882	44.0
7	William Russell (W)	6,953	56.8
	Allen Latham (D)	5,287	43.2
8	Joseph Ridgway (W)	9,909	57.5
	Henry N. Hedges Sr (D)	7,326	42.5
9	William Medill (D)	8,218	57.1
	George Sanderson (D)	6,163	42.9
10	Sampson Mason (W)	10,055	61.4
	Matthew Bonner (D)	6,317	38.6
11	Benjamin S. Cowan (W)	5,791	53.0
	Isaac Parrish (D)	5,129	47.0
12	Joshua Mathiot (W)	7,540	53.7
	Jonathan Taylor (D)	6,497	46.3
13	James Matthews (D)	8,679	53.6
	Henry B. Curtis (W)	7,508	46.4
14	George Sweeny (D)	11,211	52.3
	James Hedges (W)	10,245	47.8
15	Sherlock J. Andrews (W)	11,874	57.8
	David K. Carter (D)	8,663	42.2
16	Joshua R. Giddings (W)	11,725	66.0
	Thomas J. Mlain (D)	6,033	34.0
17	John Hastings (D)	5,278	50.3
	Charles D. Coffin (W)	5,223	49.7
18	Ezra Dean (D)	6,508	54.7
	Levi Cox (W)	5,399	45.3
19	Samuel Stokely (W)	4,390	51.8
	William C. McAuslen (D)	4,092	48.2

PENNSYLVANIA

	Candidates	Votes	%
1	Charles Brown (D)	✔	
3	Charles J. Ingersoll (D)	✔	
5	Joseph Fornance (D)	4,507	54.9
	Unidentified Candidate (W)	3,704	45.1
6	Robert Ramsey (W)	4,411	50.1
	Unidentified Candidate (D)	4,389	49.9
7	John Westbrook (D)	5,331	64.0
	Unidentified Candidate (W)	3,000	36.0
8	Peter Newhard (D)	4,299	55.7
	Unidentified Candidate (W)	3,415	44.3

	Candidates	Votes	%
9	George M. Keim (D)	4,033	100.0
10	William Simonton (W)	4,525	56.7
	Unidentified Candidate (D)	3,462	43.4
11	James Gerry (D)	3,711	53.3
	Unidentified Candidate (W)	3,248	46.7
12	James Cooper (W)	5,475	55.5
	Unidentified Candidate (D)	4,384	44.5
13	William S. Ramsey (D)	5,311*	56.2
	Unidentified Candidate (W)	4,142	43.8
14	James Irvin (W)	6,762	51.6
	Unidentified Candidate (D)	6,336	48.4
15	Benjamin A. Bidlack (D)	6,040	60.4
	Unidentified Candidate (W)	3,959	39.6
16	John Snyder (D)	5,138	51.6
	Unidentified Candidate (W)	4,813	48.4
17	Davis Dimock Jr (D)	7,054	58.7
	Unidentified Candidate (W)	4,961	41.3
18	Charles Ogle (W)	5,449	56.7
	Unidentified Candidate (D)	4,160	43.3
19	Albert G. Marchand (D)	5,188	59.5
	Unidentified Candidate (W)	3,532	40.5
20	Enos Hook (D)	4,757	56.3
	Unidentified Candidate (W)	3,686	43.7
21	Joseph Lawrence (W)	4,045	52.2
	Unidentified Candidate (D)	3,712	47.9
22	William W. Irwin (W)	6,831	61.4
	Unidentified Candidate (D)	4,287	38.6
23	William Jack (D)	4,414	52.5
	Unidentified Candidate (W)	4,001	47.6
24	Thomas Henry (W)	5,372	56.6
	Unidentified Candidate (D)	4,120	43.4
25	Arnold Plummer (D)	7,906	51.0
	Unidentified Candidate (W)	7,600	49.0

Multi-Member Districts

	Candidates	Votes	%
2	George W. Toland (W)	✔	
	John Sergeant (W)	✔	
4	John Edwards (W)	✔	
	Francis James (W)	✔	
	Jeremiah Brown (W)	15,779 ✔	
	Unidentified Candidate (D)		
	Unidentified Candidate (D)		
	Unidentified Candidate (D)		

Special Elections

	Candidates	Votes	%
13	Charles McClure (D)	3,452	94.7
22	Henry M. Brackenridge (W)	6,858	61.5
	Wilkens (D)	4,297	38.5

SOUTH CAROLINA

	Candidates	Votes	%
1	Isaac E. Holmes (D)	1,413	86.9
	Hugh S. Legare	213	13.1
2	R. Barnwell Rhett (D)		100.0
3	John Campbell (SR D)		100.0
4	Sampson H. Butler (D)		100.0
5	Patrick C. Caldwell (D)	2,040	39.3
	James Irby (W)	1,812	34.9
	S. Barkley (D)	1,340	25.8
6	Francis W. Pickens (NULL D)		100.0
7	James Rogers (D)		100.0
8	William Butler (W)	2,718	46.8
	J. W. Norris (D)	2,571	44.2
	J. Powell (D)	523	9.0
9	Thomas D. Sumter (D)	✔	
	Evans (D)		

VERMONT

	Candidates	Votes	%
1	Hiland Hall (W)	6,923	62.7
	Daniel Kellogg (D)	4,084	37.0
2	William Slade (W)	6,728	68.6
	Charles Lindsley (D)	3,034	30.9
3	Horace Everett (W)	6,729	59.1
	Truman B. Ransom (D)	4,497	39.5
4	Augustus Young (W)	6,148	55.9
	John Smith (D)	4,791	43.6
5	John Mattocks (W)	5,479	50.6
	Isaac Fletcher (D)	5,248	48.4

VIRGINIA

Special Election

	Candidates	Votes	%
14	William M. McCarty (W)	1,033	56.6
	Cuthbert Powell (W)	722	39.6

1841 House Elections

ALABAMA

Candidates	Votes	%
AL Reuben Chapman (D)	23,376✔	
Dixon H. Lewis (D)	23,339✔	
Benjamin Glover Shields (D)	23,092✔	
William Winter Payne (D)	23,090✔	
George Houston (D)	23,036✔	
George Crabb (W)	17,828	
Henry W. Hilliard (W)	17,429	
James Taylor Rather (W)	17,290	
John M. Lewis (W)	17,271	
J. Burke (W)	16,656	
William D. Dunn (W)	627	

CONNECTICUT

	Candidates	Votes	%
1	Joseph Trumbull (W)	5,142	57.1
	Thomas Seymour (D)	3,867	42.9
2	William Boardman (W)	6,225	54.3
	Charles Ingersoll (D)	5,234	45.7
3	Thomas Williams (W)	3,230	55.7
	Erastus Coit (D)	2,565	44.3
4	Thomas Osborne (W)	4,089	55.6
	William Pomeroy (D)	3,269	44.4

	Candidates	Votes	%
5	Truman Smith (W)	3,993	55.9
	John Smith (D)	3,157	44.2
6	John Brockway (W)	4,121	57.3
	Chauncey Cleveland (D)	3,076	42.7

ILLINOIS

		Votes	%
1	John Reynolds (D)	8,046	59.5
	Henry L. Webb (W)	5,313	39.3
2	Zadoc Casey (W)	7,121	50.6
	S. H. Anderson (D)	6,949	49.4
3	John T. Stuart (W)	21,726	52.0
	James H. Ralston (D)	19,562	46.8

INDIANA

		Votes	%
1	George H. Proffit (W)	5,311	57.4
	James Lockhart (D)	3,946	42.6
2	Richard W. Thompson (W)	6,323	52.7
	John W. Davis (D)	5,670	47.3
3	Joseph L. White (W)	5,596	51.6
	John Carr (D)	5,250	48.4

		Votes	%
4	James H. Cravens (W)	6,056	54.4
	Thomas Smith (D)	5,026	45.2
5	Andrew Kennedy (D)	5,664	39.8
	Jonathan McCarty (W)	4,299	30.2
	Caleb B. Smith (W)	4,048	28.5
6	David Wallace (W)	8,206	53.9
	Nathan B. Palmer (D)	7,009	46.1
7	Henry S. Lane (W)	9,477	59.7
	John Bryce (D)	6,392	40.3

KENTUCKY

		Votes	%
1	Linn Boyd (D)	✔	
2	Philip Triplett (W)	✔	
	John H. McHenry (W)		
3	Joseph R. Underwood (W)	3,924	72.7
	J. W. Irwin (W)	1,477	27.4
4	Bryan Y. Owsley (W)	✔	
	Martin Beatty (W)		
	Nathan Gaither (D)		
5	John B. Thompson (W)	2,106	36.6
	Thomas P. Moore (D)	1,939	33.7
	John Kinkead (W)	1,704	29.6
6	Willis Green (W)	2,640	38.2
	John L. Helm (W)	2,298	33.2
	Hough	1,978	28.6
7	John Pope (W)	1,012	87.6
	Gray	58	5.0
8	James C. Sprigg (W)	2,576	66.4
	William H. Field (W)	1,306	33.6
9	John White (W)	1,424	100.0
10	Thomas F. Marshall (W)	✔	
	L. B. Smith (W)		
11	Landaff W. Andrews (W)	✔	
	J. C. Mason (D)		
12	Garret Davis (W)		100.0
13	William O. Butler (D)	4,840	52.8
	W. W. Southgate (W)	4,334	47.2

MAINE

Special Election

4	David Bronson (W)	✔	

MARYLAND

		Votes	%
1	Isaac D. Jones (W)	1,910	50.1
	Cottman (W)	1,904	49.9
2	James Alfred Pearce (W)	1,357	100.0
3	James W. Williams (D)	2,563	68.4
	Orrick (W)	1,187	31.7
5	William Cost Johnson (W)	2,627	68.7
	Kimmell (W)	1,195	31.3
6	John T. Mason (D)	4,130	52.6
	Lynch (W)	3,727	47.4
7	Augustus R. Sollers (W)	✔	
	Somervell (I)		

Multi-Member District

4	Alexander Randall (W)	7,783✔	
	John P. Kennedy (W)	7,733✔	
	Murray (D)	7,657	
	Gallagher (D)	7,654	

MASSACHUSETTS

Special Election

		Votes	%
5	Charles Hudson (W)	3,099	57.8
	Isaac Davis (D)	1,782	33.2
	Cyrus B. Grovesnor	333	6.2

MISSISSIPPI

		Votes	%
AL	William L. Gwin (D)	18,988✔	
	Jacob Thompson (D)	18,956✔	

Explanation of Symbols in House Returns

In the returns for House elections *symbols* are used to denote special circumstances. In cases where no symbol is used, the candidate who received the most votes won the election to the House. The following is a key to the symbols used:

✔ Elected to the House. The symbol is used to identify winning candidates in three types of situations: (1) When candidates ran for two or more at-large seats in states which chose all of their at-large representatives in a single election, or ran in a multi-member district; (2) when the vote total and percentage of one or more of the candidates are unavailable and (3) when a candidate who did not receive the highest vote total was seated by the House. *(Explanation of multi-member districts, see p. 678.)*

‡ The symbol is used when an election dispute resulted in the unseating of a representative *after* he was sworn in. *(For discussion of specific cases, consult the* Biographical Directory of the American Congress 1774-1971, *U.S. Government Printing Office, Washington, D.C. 1971; hereafter referred to as the* Biographical Directory.)

* The symbol is used for three types of situations: (1) When a representative-elect died or declined his seat before the constitutionally set date for the beginning of his term—March 4 until 1935, and Jan. 3 thereafter; (2) when the House refused to seat any candidate claiming election to a seat and (3) when state law required a candidate to obtain a popular vote majority for election to the House, but the candidate receiving the most votes failed to receive a majority. *(For discussion of specific cases, consult the* Biographical Directory; *explanation of majority vote requirement, see p. 703.)*

Information for 1824-1973 returns was obtained from a source other than the Inter-University Consortium for Political and Social Research. *(For a listing of other sources, see p. 1062.)*

Footnotes. Numbered footnotes are used to explain unusual situations, such as a series of elections in the same year in the same House district, anomalies resulting from reapportionment and special procedures for conducting House elections in certain states.

MISSISSIPPI

Candidates	Votes	%
Adam Benjamin (W)	16,593	
William Harley (W)	16,333	

NEW HAMPSHIRE

	Candidates	Votes	%
AL	Charles G. Atherton (D)	✔	
	Edmund Burke (D)	✔	
	John R. Reding (D)	✔	
	Tristram Shaw (D)	28,870 ✔	
	Ira A. Eastman (D)	20,833 ✔	

NORTH CAROLINA

	Candidates	Votes	%
1	Kenneth Rayner (W)	1,593	93.5
2	John R. J. Daniel (D)	✔	
	William W. Cherry (W)		
3	Edward Stanly (W)	✔	
	H. I. Toole (D)		
4	William H. Washington (W)	✔	
	Joshiah O. Watson (D)		
5	James I. McKay (D)	1,706	85.7
	Baker (W)	284	14.3
6	Archibald H. Arrington (D)	1,569	46.6
	Micajah T. Hawkins (D)	1,450	43.0
	William Russell (D)	351	10.4
7	Edmund Deberry (W)	2,769	70.8
	Edward McCollum (D)	1,145	29.3
8	Romulus M. Saunders (D)	2,576	55.2
	James S. Smith (W)	2,090	44.8
9	Augustine H. Shepperd (W)	3,689	52.6
	David S. Reid (D)	3,321	47.4
10	Abraham Rencher (W)	✔	
	Charles Fisher (D)		
	Jonathan Worth (W)		
11	Greene W. Caldwell (D)	3,063	57.2
	Daniel M. Barringer (W)	2,293	42.8
12	James Graham (W)	3,546	61.8
	Thomas L. Clingman (W)	2,188	38.2
13	Lewis Williams (D)	3,373	65.7
	Roderick Murchison (W)	1,760	34.3

PENNSYLVANIA

Special Elections

	Candidates	Votes	%
2	Joseph R. Ingersoll (W)	5,822	55.4
	Pettit (D)	4,596	43.7
18	Henry Black (W)	3,220	68.1
	Philson (D)	1,507	31.9
20	Henry W. Beeson (D)	3,777	56.5
	Andrew Stewart (W)	2,914	43.6

RHODE ISLAND

	Candidates	Votes	%
AL	Robert B. Cranston (W)	2,516 ✔	
	Joseph L. Tillinghast (W)	2,487 ✔	

TENNESSEE

	Candidates	Votes	%
1	Thomas D. Arnold (W)	2,506	88.3
	Robert J. McKinney	157	5.5
2	Abraham McClelland (D)	3,484	53.0
	William T. Senter (W)	3,089	47.0
3	Joseph L. Williams (W)	1,022	99.4
4	Thomas J. Campbell (W)	3,757	49.4
	Julius W. Blackwell (D)	3,699	48.6
5	Hopkins L. Turney (D)	3,974	68.0
	John Goodall (W)	1,872	32.0
6	William B. Campbell (W)	2,207	89.1
	Jesse Skein	271	10.9
7	Robert L. Caruthers (W)	3,211	72.3
	John Hall (D)	1,231	27.7
8	Meredith P. Gentry (W)	2,813	70.1
	Thomas Hogan (D)	1,200	29.9
9	Harvey M. Watterson (D)	3,557	54.8
	Terry H. Cahal (W)	2,933	45.2
10	Aaron V. Brown (D)	3,448	83.7
	Ebenezer J. Shields (W)	670	16.3
11	Cave Johnson (D)	3,264	74.3
	N. H. Allen (W)	1,132	25.8
12	Milton Brown (W)	5,503	63.3
	Stephen C. Davatt (D)	3,195	36.7
13	Christopher H. Williams (W)	4,370	57.9
	Levin H. Coe (D)	3,178	42.1

VIRGINIA

	Candidates	Votes	%
1	Francis Mallory (W)	✔	
	Waltas		
3	George B. Cary (D)	✔	
	Collier		
3	John W. Jones (D)	✔	
	J. Leigh		
4	William O. Goode (D)	✔	
	Baptist		
	Marshall		
5	Edmund W. Hubard (D)	✔	
	John Hill (W)		
6	Walter Coles (D)	✔	
	Witcher (W)		
7	William L. Goggin (W)	✔	
	Stuart (D)		
8	Henry A. Wise (W)	✔	
9	Robert M. T. Hunter (I)	✔	
	Corbin (W)		
	Braxton (D)		
10	John Taliaferro (W)	✔	
	Grayson (D)		
11	John M. Botts (W)	✔	
12	Thomas W. Gilmer (W)	✔	
	Garland		
	Holladay		
13	William Smith (D)	‡	
	Linn Banks (D)		
14	Cuthbert Powell (W)	✔	
	Shreve		
15	Richard W. Barton (W)	✔	
	William Lucas (D)		
16	William A. Harris (D)	✔	
	Samuel C. Williams (D)		
	M. H. Beale		
	G. T. Barbee		
17	Alexander H. H. Stuart (W)	✔	
	McDowell		
18	George W. Hopkins (D)	✔	
	J. Watson (W)		
19	George W. Summers (W)	✔	
	Ellis		
	Caperton		
20	Samuel L. Hayes (D)	✔	
	Augustine J. Smith (W)		
21	Lewis Stennrod (D)	✔	

1842 House Elections

ARKANSAS

Candidates	Votes	%
AL Edward Cross (D)	9,413	57.4
Cummins (W)	5,315	32.4
Evans (I)	1,686	10.3

DELAWARE

Candidates	Votes	%
AL George B. Rodney (W)	5,467	50.0
Jones (D)	5,458	50.0

GEORGIA

Candidates	Votes	%
AL Mark A. Cooper (D)	35,451✔	
John B. Lamar (D)	35,307✔	
Howell Cobb (D)	35,217✔	
Edward J. Black (D)	35,181✔	
William H. Stiles (D)	35,176✔	
Hugh A. Haralson (D)	35,162✔	
Joseph H. Lumpkin (D)	35,159✔	
John Millen (D)	35,026✔	
Richard W. Habersham (W)	33,474	
Roger L. Gamble (W)	33,249	
Augustus R. Wright (W)	33,214	
Richard H. Wilde (W)	32,997	
Absalom H. Chappell (W)	32,980	
Agustus H. Kenan (W)	32,827	
Thomas B. King (W)	32,822	
Henry P. Smead (W)	32,560	

LOUISIANA

Candidates	Votes	%
1 John Slidell (SR D)	✔	
2 Alcee La Branche (D)	✔	
3 John B. Dawson (D)	✔	
4 Pierre E. J. B. Bossier (CALH D)	✔	

MASSACHUSETTS

Candidates	Votes	%
1 Robert C. Winthrop (W)	5,782	53.7
William Washburn (D)	4,473	41.5
2 Daniel P. King (W)	3,711	50.6
J. C. Stickney (D)	2,854	38.9
Moses P. Hanson	660	9.0
3 Amos Abbott (W)	3,932	50.4
Gayton P. Osgood (D)	3,064	39.3
Gardner B. Perry	708	9.1
4 William Parmenter (D)	5,339	52.5
Samuel Hoar (W)	4,010	39.5
Thomas W. Ward	783	7.7
5 Charles Hudson (W)	5,010	50.9
David Henshaw (D)	4,090	41.6
Phineas Crandall	682	6.9
6 Osmyn Baker (W)	5,150	50.1
Chester W. Chapin (D)	4,127	40.2

Candidates	Votes	%
Lucius Boltwood (LIB)	971	9.5
7 Julius Rockwell (W)	4,680	53.6
Brown	3,335	38.2
Joel Hayden	643	7.4
8 John Quincy Adams (W)	5,996	51.8
Ezra Wilkinson (D)	5,418	46.8
9 Henry Williams (D)	6,575	55.0
Seth Sprague (W)	4,510	37.7
Hedges Read	800	6.7
10 Barker Burnell (W)	4,776	52.0
Julius H. Shaw	4,085	44.5

Special Elections [1]

	Votes	%
1 Nathan Appleton (W)	2,753	67.0
William Washburn (D)	1,232	30.0
1 Robert Winthrop (W)	5,781	53.8
William Washburn (D)	4,468	41.6
9 William Jackson (W)	2,775*	48.3
Ezra Wilkinson (D)	2,773	48.2

MISSOURI

Candidates	Votes	%
AL James H. Relfe (D)	✔	
John Jameson (D)	✔	
Gustavus M. Bower (D)	✔	
James B. Bowlin (D)	✔	
James M. Hughes (D)	✔	
John P. Campbell		

NEW YORK

Candidates	Votes	%
1 Selah B. Strong (D)	5,463	61.9
King (W)	3,354	38.0
2 Henry C. Murphy (D)	4,563	51.6
Silliman (W)	4,214	47.7
3 J. Phillips Phoenix (W)	5,084	54.9
Nicoll (W)	4,156	44.8
4 William B. Maclay (D)	5,549	53.7
Williams (W)	4,777	46.2
5 Moses G. Leonard (D)	5,282	54.6
Scoles (W)	4,389	45.4
6 Hamilton Fish (W)	5,904	50.8
McKeon (D)	5,699	49.1
7 Joseph H. Anderson (D)	4,811	58.3
Cruger (W)	3,435	41.7
8 Richard D. Davis (D)	6,069	57.2
Rankin (W)	4,527	42.6
9 James G. Clinton (D)	5,563	55.6
Wheeler (W)	4,439	44.4
10 Jeremiah Russell (D)	7,376	57.6
Elting (W)	5,436	42.4
11 Zadock Pratt (D)	6,967	54.6
Palen (W)	5,772	45.2

Candidates	Votes	%
12 David L. Seymour (D)	5,419	50.0
Stevenson (W)	5,335	49.3
13 Daniel D. Barnard (W)	6,317	51.0
French (D)	5,980	48.3
14 Charles Rogers (W)	6,143	71.0
Hunter (D)	2,263	26.2
15 Lemuel Stetson (D)	4,635	52.1
McDonald (W)	4,092	46.0
16 Chesselden Ellis (D)	7,328	50.4
Linn (W)	7,110	48.9
17 Charles S. Benton (D)	6,750	57.4
Frey (W)	4,870	41.4
18 Preston King (D)	6,578	56.2
Sherman (W)	4,785	40.9
19 Orville Hungerford (D)	5,579	52.3
Merrick (W)	4,810	45.1
20 Samuel Beardsley (D)	6,404	50.5
Kirkland (W)	5,619	44.4
Delong (LIB)	647	5.1
21 Jeremiah Cary (D)	8,085	57.4
Tuckerman (W)	5,893	41.8
22 Smith M. Purdy (D)	8,560	52.4
Hunt (W)	7,597	46.5
23 Orville Robinson (D)	7,819	50.9
Duer (W)	6,598	42.9
Jackson (LIB)	956	6.2
24 Horace Wheaton (D)	6,558	51.1
Granger (W)	6,024	46.9
25 George Rathbun (D)	7,177	50.0
Morgan (W)	6,686	46.6
26 Amasa Dana (D)	7,796	53.0
Woodwh (W)	6,626	45.0
27 Byram Green (D)	6,446	52.3
Adams (W)	5,611	45.5
28 Thomas J. Patterson (W)	5,333	48.9
Sampson (D)	5,298	48.6
29 Charles H. Carroll (W)	6,979	91.8
Pitts (LIB)	623	8.2
30 William S. Hubbell (D)	7,692	51.9
Sherman (W)	6,847	46.2
31 Asher Tyler (W)	7,521	56.0
Tenbrk (D)	5,667	42.2
32 William A. Moseley (W)	4,826	51.9
Vosbgh (D)	4,113	44.2
33 Albert Smith (W)	4,844	53.3
Cooley (D)	3,894	42.9
34 Washington Hunt (W)	4,672	50.5
Piper (D)	4,347	47.0

PENNSYLVANIA

Special Elections

	Votes	%
17 Almon H. Read (D)	4,479	60.1
Kingsbury (W)	2,605	34.9
18 Philson (D)	2,711	50.0
James M. Russell (W)	2,634✔	48.6

1. In the 9th district, William S. Hastings, who had been elected in 1840, died June 17, 1842. In the special election to succeed him for the remainder of the 27th Congress (1841-43), no candidate received the requisite majority. A series of special elections were held, all resulting without choice, so the seat remained vacant for the remainder of the term. No returns are available for these special elections.

1843 House Elections

ALABAMA

	Candidates	Votes	%
1	James Dellet (W)	4,843	50.7
	Goldthwaite (D)	4,708	49.3
2	James E. Belser (D)	3,960	52.2
	Pettit (W)	3,633	47.9
3	Dixon H. Lewis (D)	3,509	52.3
	Lea (W)	3,202	47.7
4	William W. Payne (D)	4,298	51.7
	Young (W)	4,021	48.3
5	George S. Houston (D)	2,518	50.3
	Armstrong (D)	2,488	49.7
6	Reuben Chapman (D)		100.0
7	Felix G. McConnell (D)	4,456	52.4
	Chilton (W)	3,860	45.4

CONNECTICUT

		Votes	%
1	Thomas H. Seymour (D)	7,005	49.1
	T. K. Brace (W)	6,949	48.7
2	John J. Stewart (D)	6,577	48.9
	S. D. Hubbard (W)	6,500	48.3
3	George S. Catlin (D)	5,582	52.8
	E. Eldredge (W)	4,332	41.0
	I. Wilson (LIB)	534	5.1
4	Samuel Simons (D)	8,061	49.2
	T. B. Osborne (W)	7,948	48.5

GEORGIA

Special Election

		Votes	
AL	Alexander H. Stephens (W)	38,471 ✔	
	Absalom H. Chappell (W)	37,463 ✔	
	James H. Stark (D)	34,961	
	Herschel V. Johnson (D)	34,757	

ILLINOIS

		Votes	%
1	Robert Smith (D)	7,347	56.1
	J. L. D. Morrison (W)	5,568	42.5
2	John McClernand (D)	6,364	63.7
	Zadock Casey (W)	3,629	36.3
3	Orlando B. Ficklin (D)	6,425	53.8
	Justin Hardin (W)	5,528	46.3
4	John Wentworth (D)	7,552	51.5
	Giles Spring (W)	5,931	40.5
	John H. Henderson (LIB)	1,167	8.0
5	Stephen A. Douglas (D)	8,641	50.6
	Orville H. Browning (W)	8,180	47.9
6	Joseph P. Hoge (D)	7,796	51.0
	Cyrus Walker (W)	7,222	47.3
7	John J. Hardin (W)	6,230	52.9
	James A. McDougall (D)	5,357	45.4

INDIANA

		Votes	%
1	Robert Dale Owen (D)	6,679	52.2
	John W. Payne (W)	6,127	47.8
2	Thomas J. Henley (D)	7,020	53.6
	Joseph L. White (W)	6,070	46.4
3	Thomas Smith (D)	7,021	50.9
	John A. Matson (W)	6,766	49.1
4	Caleb B. Smith (W)	4,097	49.1
	Charles H. Test	3,442	41.3
	Hiram P. Bennett	749	9.0
5	William J. Brown (D)	7,399	54.0
	David Wallace (W)	6,314	46.0
6	John W. Davis (D)	7,167	53.6
	George G. Dunn (W)	6,205	46.4
7	Joseph A. Wright (D)	5,441	50.0
	Edward W. McGaughey (W)	5,438	50.0
8	John Pettit (D)	6,403	51.7
	James R. M. Bryant (W)	5,985	48.3

	Candidates	Votes	%
9	Samuel C. Sample (W)	5,693	50.8
	Ebenezer M. Chamberlain (D)	5,379	48.0
10	Andrew Kennedy (D)	5,358	51.2
	Lewis G. Thompson (W)	5,098	48.7

KENTUCKY

		Votes	%
1	Linn Boyd (D)	6,097	56.7
	Barbour (W)	4,649	43.3
2	Willis Green (W)	5,236	51.2
	McCreary (D)	4,984	48.8
3	Henry Grider (W)	4,434	51.6
	Irwin (W)	4,167	48.5
4	George A. Caldwell (D)	4,560	45.0
	Owsley (W)	4,066	40.1
	Stone (W)	1,507	14.9
5	James W. Stone (D)	4,872	44.7
	Grigsby (W)	3,701	33.9
	John Pope (W)	2,338	21.4
6	John White (W)	6,850	90.6
	Daniel Garrard (D)	709	9.4
7	William P. Thomasson (W)	4,900	46.5
	Lecompte (D)	4,497	42.6
	Sprigg (W)	1,152	10.9
8	Garrett Davis (W)	5,788	54.1
	C. A. Wickliffe (D)	4,916	45.9
9	Richard French (D)	5,481	51.9
	L. W. Andrews (W)	5,073	48.1
10	John W. Tibbatts (D)	6,507	51.8
	Wall (W)	6,064	48.2

MAINE

		Votes	%
1	Joshua Herrick (D)	4,421	50.6
	Jonathan Tucker	1,142	13.1
	Burleigh Smart	1,114	12.7
	Nathan Clifford	1,063	12.2
2	Robert P. Dunlap (D)	4,837	55.3
	Josiah S. Little	2,790	31.9
	Samuel Fessenden	956	10.9
3	Luther Severance (W)	3,799	53.3
	Samuel Wells (D)	2,700	37.9
	Seth May (LIB)	621	8.7
4	Freeman H. Morse (W)	3,546	50.2
	Charles Andrews (D)	2,701	38.3
5	Benjamin White (D)	6,167	51.2
	William G. Crosby (W)	4,558	37.8
	James Bowen	699	5.8
6	Hannibal Hamlin (D)	4,638	54.5
	Elisha Allen	2,673	31.4
	David Shepherd	1,182	13.9
7	Shepard Cary (D)	5,309	52.9
	Thomas Robinson (W)	4,505	44.9

MARYLAND

		Votes	%
1	John M. S. Causin (W)	3,776	57.9
	Bowie (D)	2,741	42.1
2	Francis Brengle (W)	6,116	51.8
	J. T. Mason (D)	5,694	48.2
3	John Wethered (W)	4,448	52.2
	S. Brady (D)	4,074	47.8
4	John P. Kennedy (W)	5,894	52.7
	J. Legrand (D)	5,299	47.3
5	Jacob A. Preston (W)	4,229	50.1
	A. Constable (D)	4,211	49.9
6	Thomas Spence (W)	2,197	91.1

MASSACHUSETTS

Special Election

		Votes	%
10	Joseph Grinnell (W)	4,943	53.2
	Sampson Perkins	3,927	42.3

MICHIGAN

	Candidates	Votes	%
1	Robert McClelland (D)	7,862	55.3
	Jacob M. Howard (W)	5,495	38.7
	Arthur S. Porter (LIB)	829	5.8
2	Lucius Lyon (D)	7,171	52.6
	Joseph R. Williams (W)	5,202	38.2
	Rufus B. Bement (LIB)	1,246	9.1
3	James B. Hunt (D)	6,209	56.4
	Thomas J. Drake (W)	4,007	36.4
	William Caufield (LIB)	749	6.8

MISSISSIPPI

		Votes	
AL	Jacob Thompson (A-RPT D)	19,861 ✔	
	William H. Hammett (A-RPT D)	18,813 ✔	
	Robert W. Roberts (A-RPT D)	18,518 ✔	
	Tilghman M. Tucker (A-RPT D)	15,923 ✔	
	Howard (REDEM D)	15,468	
	Dunbar (REDEM D)	15,185	
	Gilmer (REDEM D)	14,744	
	Kendall (REDEM D)	14,124	

NEW HAMPSHIRE

	Edmund Burke (D)	✔	
	John R. Reding (D)	✔	
	Moses Norris Jr (D)	✔	
	John P. Hale (D)	✔	

NEW JERSEY

		Votes	%
1	Lucius Q. C. Elmer (D)	5,668	51.3
	Unidentified Candidate (W)	5,374	48.7
2	George Sykes (D)	7,573	52.0
	Unidentified Candidate (W)	6,995	48.0
3	Isaac G. Farlee (D)		100.0
4	Littleton Kirkpatrick (D)	6,207	51.1
	Unidentified Candidate (W)	5,949	48.9
5	William Wright (IRR W)	5,313	52.7
	Unidentified Candidate (W)	4,773	47.3

NORTH CAROLINA

		Votes	%
1	Thomas L. Clingman (W)	3,817	56.9
	James Graham (W)	2,888	43.1
2	Daniel M. Barringer (W)	4,136	52.2
	Burton Craige (D)	3,788	47.8
3	David S. Reid (D)	4,195	52.3
	Anderson Mitchell (W)	3,827	47.7
4	Edmund Deberry (W)	2,042	52.5
	George C. Mendenhall (W)	1,850	47.5
5	Romulus M. Saunders (D)	3,142	51.2
	Henry W. Miller (W)	3,001	48.9
6	James I. McKay (D)	1,737	79.0
	Leach (W)	462	21.0
7	John R. J. Daniel (D)	3,644	51.1
	Henry K. Nash (W)	3,486	48.9
8	Archibald H. Arrington (D)	4,803	53.0
	Edward Stanly (W)	4,264	47.0
9	Kenneth Rayner (W)	3,719	56.4
	Moore (D)	2,879	43.6

OHIO

		Votes	%
1	Alexander Duncan (D)	6,058	52.3
	Haines (I)	5,044	43.6
2	John B. Weller (D)	5,563	50.7
	Campbell (W)	5,308	48.4
3	Robert C. Schenck (W)	7,870	56.9
	Lowe (D)	5,571	40.2
4	Joseph Vance (W)	7,510	61.1
	Hunt (D)	4,552	37.0

OHIO

Candidates	Votes	%
5 Emery D. Potter (D)	4,894	55.9
Tilden (W)	3,856	44.1
6 Henry St. John (D)	4,367	99.0
7 Joseph J. McDowell (D)	5,376	49.9
Thompson (W)	5,052	46.9
8 John I. Vanmeter (W)	5,344	50.5
Lucas (D)	5,142	48.6
9 Elias Florence (W)	5,429	52.7
Medill (D)	4,864	47.3
10 Heman Allen Moore (D)	7,194	49.6
Ridgway (W)	6,939	47.9
11 Jacob Brinckerhoff (D)	5,814	56.3
Irwin (I)	2,520	24.4
Waldan (W)	1,996	19.3
12 Samuel F. Vinton (W)	4,133	54.3
Cleveland (D)	3,269	42.9
13 Perley B. Johnson (W)	4,658	51.0
Barker (D)	4,410	48.3
14 Alexander Harper (W)	5,196	54.7
Jennings (D)	4,002	42.1
15 Joseph Morris (D)	5,321	50.9
Cowen (W)	4,617	44.2
16 James Mathews (D)	4,427	55.7
Douglass (W)	3,524	44.3
17 William C. McCauslin (D)	6,741	51.6
Hanna (W)	5,883	45.1
18 Ezra Dean (D)	3,668	68.5
Wellhouse (W)	1,588	29.7
19 Daniel R. Tilden (W)	6,712	47.9
Luman (D)	6,310	45.1
Hall (LIB)	986	7.0
20 Joshua R. Giddings (W)	6,140	57.4
Ranney (D)	3,757	35.1
Wade (LIB)	797	7.5
21 Henry R. Brinckerhoff (D)	5,949	49.0
Hamlin (W)	5,533	45.6
Parish (LIB)	650	5.4

PENNSYLVANIA

Candidates	Votes	%
1 Edward Joy Morris (W)	2,855	45.3
McCully (D)	2,379	37.7
Croust (D)	1,072	17.0
2 Joseph R. Ingersoll (W)	5,414	63.2
Neal (D)	3,153	36.8
3 John T. Smith (D)	3,997	55.8
Sargent (W)	3,162	44.2
4 Charles J. Ingersoll (D)	3,316	55.5
Conrad (W)	2,664	44.6
5 Jacob S. Yost (D)	4,845	54.6
Huddleson (W)	4,022	45.4
6 Michael H. Jenks (W)	5,750	53.0
Davis (D)	5,101	47.0
7 Abraham R. McIlvaine (W)	4,391	51.7
Allison (D)	4,106	48.3
8 Jeremiah Brown (W)	4,898	47.0
Martin (D)	3,940	37.8
Roberts (A-MAS)	1,582	15.2
9 John Ritter (D)	3,941	69.3
Hehn (W)	1,747	30.7
10 Richard Brodhead (D)	5,049	100.0

Candidates	Votes	%
11 Benjamin A. Bidlack (D)	5,007	64.8
Willits (W)	2,716	35.2
12 Almon H. Read (D)	4,243	56.5
Jones (W)	3,266	43.5
13 Henry Frick (W)	5,430	51.2
Snyder (D)	5,181	48.8
14 Alexander Ramsey (W)	5,893	52.5
Umberger (D)	5,326	47.5
15 Henry Nes (W)	4,016	54.1
Small (D)	3,413	45.9
16 James Black (D)	5,617	52.0
Miller (W)	5,189	48.0
17 James Irvin (W)	5,725	56.6
McCulloh (D)	4,389	43.4
18 Andrew Stewart (W)	5,141	50.7
Clevenger (D)	5,004	49.3
19 Henry D. Foster (D)	6,432	100.0
20 John Dickey (W)	4,962	47.1
Leet (D)	4,903	46.5
Lemoyne (LIB)	681	6.5
21 William Wilkins (D)	4,438	49.7
Craig (W&A-MASC)	2,237	25.0
Breckenridge (W)	1,884	21.1
22 Samuel Hays (D)	5,044	85.0
Doughty (A-MASC)	892	15.0
23 Charles M. Reed (W)	5,073	50.2
Irvine (D)	5,033	49.8
24 Joseph Buffington (W)	5,079	55.4
Lorain (D)	4,082	44.6

RHODE ISLAND

Candidates	Votes	%
1 Henry Y. Cranston (L & O W)	4,078	61.3
John H. Weeden (D)	2,557	38.4
2 Elisha R. Potter (L & O W)	2,917	61.2
Wilmarth N. Aldrich (D)	1,846	38.7

SOUTH CAROLINA

Candidates	Votes	%
1 James A. Black (CALH D)		✔
William K. Clowney (SR D)		
2 Richard F. Simpson (D)		✔
William Butler (W)		
Downs (D)		
3 Joseph A. Woodward (D)		✔
Thomas D. Sumter (D)		
4 John Campbell (SR D)		✔
5 Armistead Burt (D)	2,198	44.1
Patrick C. Caldwell (SSR D)	1,564	31.4
Brooks	1,225	24.6
6 Isaac E. Holmes (D)		✔
James S. Rhett		
7 R. Barnwell Rhett (D)	1,883	58.0
S. Trotti	1,363	42.0

TENNESSEE

Candidates	Votes	%
1 Andrew Johnson (D)	5,495	52.9
Aikin (W)	4,892	47.1
2 William T. Senter (W)	6,310	59.6
Wallace (D)	4,280	40.4

Candidates	Votes	%
3 Julius W. Blackwell (D)	5,793	50.4
Campbell (W)	5,700	49.6
4 Alvan Cullom (D)	5,180	58.7
Bransford (W)	3,650	41.3
5 George M. Jones (D)	5,111	63.5
Long (W)	2,943	36.5
6 Aaron V. Brown (D)	5,259	52.3
N. S. Brown (W)	4,798	47.7
7 David W. Dickerson (W)	6,137	100.0
8 Joseph H. Peyton (W)	4,853	55.6
Donnelson (D)	3,874	44.4
9 Cave Johnson (D)	4,904	51.2
Henry (W)	4,676	48.8
10 John B. Ashe (W)	5,457	50.9
Staunton (D)	5,264	49.1
11 Milton Brown (W)	5,852	61.1
Pavatt (D)	3,723	38.9

VERMONT

Candidates	Votes	%
1 Solomon Foot (W)	6,698	54.9
C. B. Harrington (D)	4,926	40.4
2 Jacob Collamer (W)	5,825	48.9
Truman B. Ransom (D)	4,833	40.5
Titus Hutchinson (LIB)	1,003	8.4
3 George Perkins Marsh (W)	6,254	53.5
John Smith (D)	4,595	39.3
W. H. French (LIB)	718	6.1
4 Paul Dillingham Jr (D)	6,317	50.8
George B. Chandler (W)	4,957	39.8
G. Putnam (LIB)	797	6.4

VIRGINIA

Candidates	Votes	%
1 Archibald Atkinson (D)	1,789	50.2
Langhorne (W)	1,778	49.9
2 George C. Dromgoole (D)	762	80.6
3 Walter Coles (D)	2,017	51.4
Gilmer (W)	1,911	48.7
4 Edmund W. Hubard (D)	2,164	51.5
Toler (W)	2,037	48.5
5 Thomas W. Gilmer (D)	2,361	50.2
Goggin (W)	2,341	49.8
6 John W. Jones (D)	2,368	50.4
Botts (W)	2,335	49.7
7 Henry A. Wise (D)	1,470	57.1
Carter (W)	1,105	42.9
8 Willoughby Newton (W)	1,008	55.2
Hunter (D)	818	44.8
9 Samuel Chilton (W)	1,532	57.1
Smith (D)	1,149	42.9
10 William Lucas (D)	2,698	56.2
Faulkner (W)	2,104	43.8
11 William Taylor (D)	1,979	83.5
Stuart (W)	392	16.5
12 Augustus A. Chapman (D)	2,552	64.5
Watts (W)	1,402	35.5
13 George W. Hopkins (D)	761	57.7
Fulton (W)	558	42.3
14 George W. Summers (W)	3,271	52.7
Hays (D)	2,942	47.4
15 Lewis Steenrod (D)		100.0

1844 House Elections

ALABAMA

Special Election

Candidates	Votes	%
3 William L. Yancey (D)	2,197	50.7
Daniel Watrous (W)	2,137	49.3

ARKANSAS

	Votes	%
AL Archibald Yell (D)	11,112	59.1
Walker (W)	7,576	40.3

DELAWARE

	Votes	%
AL John W. Houston (W)	6,221	50.7
Biddle (D)	6,043	49.3

GEORGIA

	Votes	%
1 Thomas Butler King (W)	3,702	55.9
Spalding (D)	2,918	44.1
2 Seaborn Jones (D)	6,460	51.1
Crawford (W)	6,182	48.9
3 Washington Poe (W)	4,881*	50.7
Chappell (D)	4,741	49.3
4 Hugh A. Haralson (D)	5,771	52.5
Floyd (W)	5,214	47.5
5 John H. Lumpkin (D)	7,720	61.2
Miller (W)	4,889	38.8
6 Howell Cobb (D)	6,306	59.0
Underwood (W)	4,379	41.0
7 Alexander H. Stephens (W)	4,199	57.1
Janes (D)	3,152	42.9
8 Robert Toombs (W)	4,665	58.5
Black (D)	3,309	41.5

Special Election

	Votes	%
AL Duncan L. Clinch (W)	33,506	53.4
Sanford (D)	29,206	46.6

ILLINOIS

	Votes	%
1 Robert Smith (D)	7,966	64.7
John Reynolds (OPP D)	4,146	33.7
2 John A. McClernand (D)	7,968	99.0
3 Orlando B. Ficklin (D)	7,786	57.6
Usher F. Linder (W)	5,311	39.3
4 John Wentworth (D)	9,516	54.9
Buckner S. Morris (W)	5,910	34.1
John H. Henderson (LIB)	1,875	10.8
5 Stephen A. Douglas (D)	9,799	53.9
David M. Woodson (W)	8,043	44.2
6 Joseph P. Hoge (D)	8,752	52.0
Martin P. Sweet (W)	7,563	45.0
7 Edwin D. Baker (W)	6,658	52.4
John Calhoun (D)	5,948	46.9

LOUISIANA

1 John Slidell (SR D)	✔	
2 Bannon G. Thibodeaux (W)	✔	
3 John H. Harmanson (D)	✔	
4 Isaac E. Morse (D)	✔	

MAINE [1]

	Votes	%
1 William A. Hayes	5,321*	46.5
George Scamman	3,377	29.5
Joshua Herrick	2,061	18.0
2 Robert P. Dunlap (D)	✔	
3 Luther Severance (W)	✔	
4 John D. McCrate (D)	7,464	52.8
F. H. Morse	5,948	42.1

Candidates	Votes	%
5 Cullen Sawtelle (D)	6,377	53.2
William G. Crosby	4,625	38.6
Drummond Farnsworth	678	5.7
6 Hannibal Hamlin (D)	✔	
7 Hezekiah Williams (D)	✔	

MASSACHUSETTS

	Votes	%
1 Robert C. Winthrop (W)	8,455	62.7
Benjamin F. Hallett	4,461	33.1
2 Daniel P. King (W)	4,986	57.6
George Herod (D)	2,770	32.0
Henry B. Hanton	886	10.2
3 Amos Abbott (W)	6,315	52.1
George S. Boutwell (D)	4,770	39.4
Abner L. Bailey	1,001	8.3
4 Benjamin Thompson (W)	5,269	51.7
William Parmenter (D)	4,405	43.2
Thomas W. Ward	516	5.1
5 Charles Hudson (W)	5,463	55.8
Isaac Davis (D)	3,518	36.0
Rudolphius B. Hubbard	795	8.1
6 George Ashmun (W)	7,467	51.7
Chester W. Chapin (D)	5,850	40.5
Lucius Boltwood (LIB)	1,014	7.0
7 Julius Rockwell (W)	6,769	51.5
Increase Sumner	5,235	39.8
Joel Hayden	970	7.4
8 John Quincy Adams (W)	8,089	56.6
Isaac H. Wright	5,340	37.4
Appleton Howe	733	5.1
9 Artemas Hale (W)	4,881	50.5
Foster Hooper	3,599	37.2
Laban M. Wheaton	998	10.3
10 Joseph Grinnell (W)	5,924	58.5
Edward W. Greene	3,772	37.3

MICHIGAN

	Votes	%
1 Robert McClelland (D)	10,132	51.2
Edwin Lawrence (W)	8,677	43.9
2 John J. Chipman (D)	9,435	47.7
Henry W. Taylor (W)	8,967	45.4
Edwin A. Atlee (LIB)	1,240	6.3
3 James B. Hunt (D)	8,331	51.3
George W. Wisner (W)	6,967	42.9
William Caufield (LIB)	934	5.8

MISSOURI

	Votes	%
AL John S. Phelps (D)	36,023 ✔	
James B. Bowlin (D)	35,510 ✔	
Sterling Price (D)	35,128 ✔	
James H. Relfe (D)	35,007 ✔	
Leonard H. Sims (W)	29,225 ✔	
Thomas B. Hudson (W)	28,309	
J. Thornton (W)	27,685	
Ratliff Boone (D)	27,263	
A. Jones (W)	27,226	
D. C. M. Parsons (D)	19,123	

NEW JERSEY

	Votes	%
1 James G. Hampton (W)	7,440	54.7
Elmer (D)	6,153	45.3
2 Samuel G. Wright (W)	6,910	51.5
Sykes (D)	6,503	48.5
3 John Runk (W)	8,942	50.0
Isaac G. Farlee (D)	8,926	50.0
4 Joseph E. Edsall (D)	8,779	60.0
Robtsn (W)	5,848	40.0
5 William Wright (W)	9,996	100.0

NEW YORK

Candidates	Votes	%
1 John W. Lawrence (D)	6,132	55.4
Cogswell (W)	4,935	44.6
2 Henry I. Seaman (NAM)	6,164	51.8
Murphy (W)	5,686	47.7
3 William S. Miller (NAM)	6,613	54.7
Nicoll (D)	5,388	44.6
4 William B. Maclay (D)	6,783	51.0
Lawrence (NAM)	6,428	48.4
5 Thomas M. Woodruff (NAM)	6,214	49.7
Leonard (D)	6,009	48.1
6 William W. Campbell (NAM)	7,856	48.8
Moore (W)	7,750	48.2
7 Joseph H. Anderson (D)	6,098	55.8
Barretto (W)	4,807	44.0
8 William W. Woodworth (D)	7,340	52.1
Rankin (W)	6,710	47.6
9 Archibald C. Niven (D)	7,162	52.3
Hasbrouck (W)	6,474	47.3
10 Samuel Gordon (D)	8,645	51.1
Gould (W)	8,121	48.0
11 John F. Collin (D)	8,226	53.1
Sanford (W)	7,254	46.9
12 Richard P. Herrick (W)	6,242	51.6
Seymour (D)	5,692	47.0
13 Bradford R. Wood (D)	7,058	50.0
Wheaton (W)	6,967	49.3
14 Erastus D. Culver (W)	7,512	56.6
Bishop (D)	5,297	39.9
15 Joseph Russell (D)	5,441	50.4
Moore (W)	4,750	44.0
Boardn (LIB)	606	5.6
16 Hugh White (W)	8,423	50.1
Ellis (D)	8,124	48.4
17 Charles S. Benton (D)	7,691	54.7
Alexander (W)	5,706	40.6
18 Preston King (D)	8,145	54.1
Hopkins (W)	6,295	41.8
19 Orville Hungerford (D)	6,304	50.0
Bradley (W)	5,587	44.3
Porter (LIB)	717	5.7
20 Timothy Jenkins (D)	7,617	48.2
White (W)	7,094	44.9
Allen (LIB)	1,086	6.9
21 Charles Goodyear (D)	9,298	52.3
Danforth (W)	7,966	44.8
22 Stephen Strong (D)	9,608	50.9
Sweet (W)	8,818	46.7
23 William J. Hough (D)	8,128	45.6
Ledyd (W)	7,426	41.7
Brown (LIB)	2,268	12.7
24 Horace Wheaton (D)	6,961	49.2
Noxon (W)	6,495	45.9
25 George Rathbun (D)	7,511	48.3
Richardson (W)	7,130	45.8
Stayles (LIB)	921	5.9
26 Samuel S. Ellsworth (D)	8,763	51.5
Judd (W)	7,662	45.0
27 John De Mott (D)	6,581	48.4
Holley (W)	6,387	47.0
28 Elias B. Holmes (W)	6,807	52.7
Selden (D)	5,722	44.3
29 Charles H. Carroll (W)	8,310	53.9
Wadsworth (D)	6,465	42.0
30 Martin Grover (D)	9,115	50.6
Cady (W)	8,893	49.4
31 Abner Lewis (W)	8,299	59.9
Campbell (D)	3,446	24.9
Allen (LIB)	2,114	15.3
32 William A. Moseley (W)	6,910	55.7
Stevens (D)	5,081	41.0
33 Albert Smith (W)	6,366	56.3
Chand (D)	4,215	37.2
McKay (LIB)	736	6.5
34 Washington Hunt (W)	5,733	51.0
Piper (D)	4,948	44.1

Footnote, see p. 737.

OHIO

Candidates	Votes	%
1 James J. Faran (D)	8,760	54.2
George P. Torrence (W)	7,071	43.8
2 Francis A. Cunningham (D)	6,381	51.6
Lewis D. Campbell (W)	5,881	47.5
3 Robert C. Schenck (W)	9,850	55.3
Edward A. King (D)	7,428	41.7
4 Joseph Vance (W)	10,470	60.9
John H. Young (D)	6,413	37.3
5 William Sawyer (D)	5,916	54.6
J. W. Riley (W)	4,901	45.2
6 Henry St. John (D)	6,975	56.8
Abel Rawson (W)	5,278	43.0
7 Joseph J. McDowell (D)	7,004	52.3
James H. Thompson (W)	6,044	45.2
8 Allen G. Thurman (D)	7,039	50.6
John J. Vanmetre (W)	6,707	48.2
9 Augustus L. Perrill (D)	6,475	52.5
Elias Florence (W)	5,797	47.0
10 Columbus Delano (W)	9,297	49.3
Caleb H. McNulty (D)	9,285	49.3
11 Jacob Brinkerhoff (D)	8,466	51.9
William McLaughlin (W)	7,501	46.0
12 Samuel F. Vinton (W)	6,750	58.4
Elisha Morgan (D)	3,753	32.5
Francis Cleveland (ID)	738	6.4
13 Isaac Parrish (D)	5,825	50.3
Perley B. Johnson (W)	5,620	48.5
14 Alexander Harper (W)	6,951	53.0
George W. Manypenny (D)	5,814	44.3
15 Joseph Morris (D)	6,807	50.3
Joseph A. Ramage (W)	6,207	45.9
16 John D. Cummins (D)	6,568	54.6
Christian Deardorff (W)	5,465	45.4
17 George Fries (D)	7,699	50.0
Samuel Stokely (W)	7,236	47.0
18 David A. Starkweather (D)	6,981	55.4
John Augustine (W)	5,449	43.3
19 Daniel R. Tilden (W)	8,744	48.8
William Coolman (D)	7,934	44.3

Candidates	Votes	%
Lyman W. Hall (LIB)	1,229	6.9
20 Joshua R. Giddings (F SOIL W)	10,048	60.3
Samuel Starkweather (D)	5,287	31.7
Edward Wade (LIB)	1,312	7.9
21 Joseph M. Root (W)	7,641	48.6
Richard Warner (D)	7,140	45.4
Joel Tiffany (LIB)	954	6.1

Special Election

Candidates	Votes	%
10 Alfred Parish Stone (D)	✔	#
James R. Stanberry (W)		

PENNSYLVANIA

Candidates	Votes	%
1 Lewis C. Levin (AM)	✔	
2 Joseph R. Ingersoll (W)	✔	
3 John H. Campbell (AM)	✔	
4 Charles J. Ingersoll (D)	✔	
5 Jacob S. Yost (D)	✔	
6 Jacob Erdman (D)	✔	
7 Abraham R. McIlvaine (W)	✔	
8 John Strohm (W)	✔	
9 John Ritter (D)	✔	
10 Richard Brodhead Jr (D)	✔	
11 Owen D. Leib (D)	✔	
12 David Wilmot (D)	✔	
13 James Pollock (W)	✔	
14 Alexander Ramsey (W)	✔	
15 Moses McLean (D)	✔	
16 James Black (D)	✔	
17 John Blanchard (W)	✔	
18 Andrew Stewart (W)	✔	
19 Henry D. Foster (D)	✔	
20 John H. Ewing (W)	✔	
21 Cornelius Darragh (W)	✔	
22 William S. Garvin (D)	✔	
23 James Thompson (D)	✔	
24 Joseph Buffington (W)	✔	

Candidates	Votes	%
Special Elections		
12 George Fuller (D)	✔	
13 James Pollock (W)	✔	
21 Cornelius Darragh (W)	✔	

SOUTH CAROLINA

Candidates	Votes	%
1 James A. Black (CALH D)		100.0
2 Richard F. Simpson (D)	5,162	64.0
William Butler (W)	2,902	36.0
3 Joseph A. Woodward (D)		100.0
4 Alexander D. Sims (D)	2,706	52.5
John McQueen (D)	2,448	47.5
5 Armistead Burt (D)		100.0
6 Isaac E. Holmes (D)		100.0
7 R. Barnwell Rhett (D)	✔	

VERMONT

Candidates	Votes	%
1 Solomon Foot (W)	7,696	56.7
Charles K. Field (D)	4,681	34.5
Oscar L. Shafter (LIB)	1,119	8.2
2 Jacob Collamer (W)	7,108	55.4
Levi B. Vilas (D)	4,527	35.3
Titus Hutchinson (LIB)	1,189	9.3
3 George P. Marsh (W)	6,331	56.9
John Smith (D)	3,423	30.8
William H. French (LIB)	1,357	12.2
4 Paul Dillingham Jr. (D)	6,551	47.9
George B. Chandler (W)	5,696	41.7
George Putnam (LIB)	1,369	10.0

VIRGINIA

Special Elections

Candidates	Votes	%
5 William L. Goggin (W)	✔	
7 Thomas H. Bayly (D)	✔	
Carter (W)		

1. In Maine's 1st district, no candidate received the necessary majority. In a special election for which returns are unavailable, John F. Scamman (D) was chosen to fill the vacancy.

1845 House Elections

ALABAMA

	Candidates	Votes	%
1	Edmund S. Dargan (D)	4,962	*51.6*
	Dunn (W)	4,649	*48.4*
2	Henry W. Hilliard (W)	5,386	*50.6*
	Cochran (D)	5,258	*49.4*
3	William L. Yancey (D)	4,987	*100.0*
4	William W. Payne (D)	4,935	*63.7*
	Erwin (D)	2,818	*36.4*
5	George S. Houston (D)	4,035	*81.4*
	Nool (D)	922	*18.6*
6	Reuben Chapman (D)		*100.0*
7	Felix G. McConnell (D)	3,305	*56.9*
	Rice (D)	2,504	*43.1*

CONNECTICUT

	Candidates	Votes	%
1	James Dixon (W)	7,612	*50.9*
	Seymour (D)	6,941	*46.5*
2	Samuel Hubbard (W)	7,266	*54.2*
	Stewart (D)	5,814	*43.4*
3	John Rockwell (W)	5,734	*48.1*
	Catlin (D)	5,391	*45.3*
	Wilson (LIB)	784	*6.6*
4	Truman Smith (W)	8,957	*51.7*
	J. C. Smith (D)	7,856	*45.3*

FLORIDA

(Became a state Mar. 3, 1845)

	Candidates	Votes	%
AL	Edward C. Cabell (W)	2,523‡	*50.5*
	William H. Brockenbrough (D)	2,472	*49.5*

INDIANA

	Candidates	Votes	%
1	Robert Dale Owen (D)	7,336	*53.7*
	George P. R. Wilson (W)	6,331	*46.3*
2	Thomas J. Henley (D)	7,219	*53.1*
	Roger Martin (W)	6,376	*46.9*
3	Thomas Smith (D)	7,246	*51.1*
	Joseph C. Eggleston (W)	6,706	*47.3*
4	Caleb B. Smith (W)	4,863	*56.4*
	John Finley (D)	3,201	*37.2*
	Matthew R. Hull (LIB)	553	*6.4*
5	William W. Wick (D)	7,459	*54.8*
	James P. Foley (W)	5,883	*43.2*
6	John W. Davis (D)	8,183	*60.9*
	Eli P. Farmer (W)	5,253	*39.1*
7	Edward W. McGaughey (W)	6,192	*50.7*
	Joseph A. Wright (D)	6,023	*49.3*
8	John Pettit (D)	6,260	*51.6*
	Albert L. Holmes (W)	5,771	*47.6*
9	Charles W. Cathcart (D)	6,231	*50.0*
	Samuel C. Sample (W)	5,959	*47.8*
10	Andrew Kennedy (D)	5,837	*50.0*
	Lewis G. Thompson (W)	5,482	*47.0*

KENTUCKY

	Candidates	Votes	%
1	Linn Boyd (D)	6,377	*97.1*
2	John H. McHenry (W)	6,070	*53.0*
	Thomas McCreery (D)	5,385	*47.0*
3	Henry Grider (W)	5,511	*56.0*
	S. A. Atchison (D)	4,338	*44.1*
4	Joshua F. Bell (W)	6,044	*50.3*
	G. A. Caldwell (D)	5,965	*49.7*
5	Bryan R. Young (W)	6,126	*51.1*
	James W. Stone (D)	5,869	*48.9*
6	John P. Martin (D)	4,074	*37.1*
	G. Adams (W)	3,658	*33.3*
	G. R. McKee (W)	3,240	*29.5*
7	William P. Thomasson (W)	6,023	*52.2*
	Elijah Nuttall (D)	5,510	*47.8*
8	Garret Davis (W)	5,819	*53.3*
	T. F. Marshall (D)	5,109	*46.8*
9	Andrew Trumbo (W)	5,741	*51.6*
	Richard French (D)	5,381	*48.4*
10	John W. Tibbatts (D)	7,107	*50.8*
	John P. Gaines (W)	6,875	*49.2*

MARYLAND

	Candidates	Votes	%
1	John G. Chapman (W)	4,238	*52.2*
	Key (D)	3,884	*47.8*
2	Thomas J. Perry (D)	6,789	*52.7*
	Snively (W)	6,095	*47.3*
3	Thomas W. Ligon (D)	5,924	*54.1*
	Wethered (W)	5,030	*45.9*
4	William F. Giles (D)	5,824	*48.8*
	Kennedy (W)	4,962	*41.6*
	Duncan (AM)	1,147	*9.6*
5	Albert Constable (D)	4,631	*51.0*
	Wright (W)	4,444	*49.0*
6	Edward H. C. Long (W)	3,735	*51.1*
	Martin (D)	3,577	*48.9*

MISSISSIPPI

	Candidates	Votes	%
AL	Jacob Thompson (D)	27,423✓	
	Jefferson Davis (D)	27,193✓	
	Stephen Adams (D)	26,836✓	
	Robert W. Roberts (D)	26,059✓	
	Tompkins (W)	18,194	
	Starke (W)	17,452	
	Brooke (W)	17,094	

NEW HAMPSHIRE [1]

	Candidates	Votes	%
AL	Mace Moulton (D)	24,068✓	
	James H. Johnson (D)	24,011✓	
	Moses Norris Jr (D)	23,765✓	
	Woodbury (D)	21,913	
	Edwards (FEDL)	14,692	
	Nesmith (FEDL)	14,690	
	Goodwin (FEDL)	14,562	
	Sawyer (FEDL)	13,833	
	Hale	7,053	
	Porter (AB)	5,272	
	Moore (AB)	4,968	
	Perkins (AB)	4,554	
	Cilley (AB)	4,503	

NORTH CAROLINA

	Candidates	Votes	%
1	James Graham (W)	5,245	*51.6*
	Thomas L. Clingman (W)	4,918	*48.4*
2	Daniel M. Barringer (W)	5,368	*50.1*
	Charles Fisher (D)	5,342	*49.9*
3	David S. Reid (D)	5,133	*54.0*
	Alexander B. McMillan (W)	4,369	*46.0*
4	Alfred Dockery (W)	4,078	*56.5*
	Jonathan Worth (W)	3,135	*43.5*
5	James C. Dobbin (D)	5,242	*61.8*
	John H. Haughton (W)	3,236	*38.2*
6	James I. McKay (D)	5,169	*66.3*
	Thomas D. Meares (W)	2,633	*33.8*
7	John R. J. Daniel (D)	4,872	*64.1*
	Robert C. Bond (W)	2,729	*35.9*
8	Henry S. Clarke (D)	4,654	*53.7*
	Richard S. Donnell (W)	4,009	*46.3*
9	Asa Biggs (D)	3,695	*51.0*
	David Outlaw (W)	3,549	*49.0*

RHODE ISLAND

	Candidates	Votes	%
1	Henry Cranston (W)	4,900	*98.8*
2	Lemuel H. Arnold (LIBER W)	3,202	*51.1*
	Elisha R. Potter (L & O W)	2,995	*47.8*

TENNESSEE

	Candidates	Votes	%
1	Andrew Johnson (D)	6,068	*56.3*
	William B. Brownlow (W)	4,715	*43.7*
2	William M. Cocke (W)	4,884	*45.0*
	George S. Gilbert (D)	3,864	*35.6*
	Lewis Reneau (IW)	2,098	*19.3*
3	John H. Crozier (W)	6,179	*51.4*
	Julius W. Blackwell (D)	5,841	*48.6*
4	Alvin Cullom (D)	6,266	*93.1*
	Isaac Clendenon	467	*6.9*
5	George W. Jones (D)	6,528	*100.0*
6	Barclay Martin (D)	4,476	*59.8*
	William D. Kindrick (W)	3,009	*40.2*
7	Meredith T. Gentry (W)	5,849	*67.9*
	Charles L. Nelson (D)	2,760	*32.1*
8	Edwin Hickman Ewing (W)	✓	#
	Joseph H. Peyton (W)	5,204	*55.3*
	William Trousdale (D)	4,202	*44.7*
9	Lucien B. Chase (D)	4,281	*57.6*
	John J. Mathewson (W)	3,156	*42.4*
10	Frederick P. Stanton (D)	5,901	*52.8*
	Phineas T. Scruggs (W)	5,283	*47.2*
11	Milton Brown (W)	5,166	*59.9*
	Nelson Hess (D)	3,454	*40.1*

VIRGINIA

	Candidates	Votes	%
1	Archibald Atkinson (D)	✓	
	Whitfield		
2	George C. Dromgoole (D)	✓	
3	William M. Tredway (D)	✓	
4	Edmund W. Hubard (D)	✓	
5	Shelton F. Leake (D)	✓	
	Irving		
6	James A. Seddon (D)	✓	
	John M. Botts (W)		
7	Thomas H. Bayly (D)	✓	
	Southall		
8	Robert M. T. Hunter (D)	✓	
	Willoughby Newton (W)		
9	John S. Pendleton (W)	✓	
	McCarty		
10	Henry Bedinger (D)	✓	
	Lucas		
11	William Taylor (D)	✓	
12	Augustus A. Chapman (D)	✓	
13	George W. Hopkins (D)	✓	
14	Joseph Johnson (D)	✓	
	Camden		
15	William G. Brown (D)	✓	
	Allen		

1. New Hampshire was entitled to four seats in the 29th Congress (1845-47), but only elected three representatives. Woodbury did not receive the necessary number of votes to be elected in the 1845 at-large election, and no winner was subsequently chosen in a special election. (See New Hampshire, 1846.) So the fourth seat remained vacant for the entire Congress. (Explanation of New Hampshire majority vote requirement, p. 703.)

1846 House Elections

ALABAMA

Special Elections

	Candidates	Votes	%
3	James L. F. Cottrell (D)	3,299	50.2
	Samuel S. Beeman (W)	3,269	49.8
7	Franklin W. Bowdon (D)	2,704	45.2
	Benjamin Goodman (W)	1,979	33.1
	T. A. Walker (D)	1,303	21.8

ARKANSAS

		Votes	%
AL	Robert W. Johnson (LOCOFOCO)	✔	

Special Election

		Votes	%
AL	Thomas W. Newton (W)	1,753	28.6
	Paschal	1,722	28.1
	Albert Rust (D)	1,654	27.0
	Noland (W)	858	14.0

DELAWARE

		Votes	%
AL	John W. Houston (W)	6,154	50.6
	Dillw (D)	6,007	49.4

FLORIDA

		Votes	%
AL	Edward C. Cabell (W)	✔	

GEORGIA

	Candidates	Votes	%
1	Thomas Butler King (W)	3,274	59.6
	Cohen (D)	2,220	40.4
2	Alfred Iverson (D)	5,599	51.8
	Crawford (W)	5,202	48.2
3	John W. Jones (W)	4,083	51.1
	George W. B. Towns (D)	3,904	48.9
4	Hugh A. Haralson (D)	4,908	50.8
	Mosley (W)	4,756	49.2
5	John H. Lumpkin (D)	5,349	79.4
	Crook (W)	1,263	18.8
6	Howell Cobb (D)	4,368	59.5
	Cleveland (W)	2,968	40.5
7	Alexander H. Stephens (W)	3,507	62.8
	Turner (D)	2,078	37.2
8	Robert Toombs (W)	3,560	65.0
	Unidentified Candidate (D)	1,917	35.0

Special Election

		Votes	%
3	George W. B. Towns (D)	4,026	51.6
	Baber (W)	3,773	48.4

ILLINOIS

		Votes	%
1	Robert Smith (OPP D)	7,068	58.1
	Lyman Trumbull (D)	5,019	41.3
2	John A. McClernand (D)	7,151	97.3
3	Orlando B. Ficklin (D)	6,707	57.1
	Robert K. McLaughlin (I)	5,014	42.7
4	John Wentworth (D)	12,115	55.8
	John Kerr (W)	6,079	28.0
	Owen Lovejoy (LIB)	3,531	16.3
5	Stephen A. Douglas (D)	9,629*	57.0
	Isaac VanderVenter (W)	6,864	40.6
6	Thomas J. Turner (D)	8,843	48.4
	James Knox (W)	8,456	46.3
	Wade Talcott (LIB)	947	5.2
7	Abraham Lincoln (W)	6,340	55.5
	Peter Cartwright (D)	4,829	42.3

IOWA[1]

(Became a state Dec. 28, 1846)

		Votes	%
	S. Clinton Hastings (D)	✔	
	Shepherd Leffler (D)	✔	

MASSACHUSETTS

	Candidates	Votes	%
1	Robert C. Winthrop (W)	5,980	63.9
	Peter F. Homer (D)	1,688	18.1
	Samuel G. Howe (LIB)	1,334	14.3
2	Daniel P. King (W)	3,735	62.6
	George W. Dike (D)	1,621	27.2
	Samuel Gall (LIB)	427	7.2
3	Amos Abbott (W)	4,965	52.5
	George S. Boutwell (D)	3,098	32.7
	Chauncey L. Knapp (LIB)	1,108	11.7
4	John G. Palfrey (W)	4,513	50.6
	Frederick Robinson (D)	3,754	42.1
	James G. Carter (LIB)	544	6.1
5	Charles Hudson (W)	6,068	50.3
	Walter A. Bryant (D)	4,107	34.1
	R. B. Hubbard (LIB)	1,508	12.5
6	George Ashmun (W)	6,628	55.1
	Stephen S. W. Taber (D)	4,245	35.3
	John Dickinson Jr (LIB)	1,021	8.5
7	Julius Rockwell (W)	5,716	53.1
	Heratio Byington (D)	4,138	38.4
	Jasper Bement (LIB)	861	8.0
8	John Quincy Adams (W)	5,765	61.6
	Isaac H. Wright (D)	2,617	28.0
	Appleton Howe (LIB)	882	9.4
9	Artemas Hale (W)	4,937	50.1
	Foster Hooper (D)	3,718	37.7
	Laban M. Wheaton (LIB)	1,023	10.4
10	Joseph Grinnell (W)	3,806	62.8
	Timothy G. Coffin (D)	1,788	29.5

MICHIGAN

		Votes	%
1	Robert McClelland (D)	7,877	52.1
	Edwin Lawrence (W)	6,442	42.6
	Charles H. Stewart (LIB)	791	5.2
2	Edward Bradley (D)	9,517	49.1
	James W. Gordon (W)	8,681	44.8
	Erastus Hussey (LIB)	1,156	6.0
3	Kinsley S. Bingham (D)	6,529	48.9
	George W. Wisner (W)	5,811	43.5
	William Caufield (LIB)	981	7.4

MISSOURI

		Votes	%
1	James B. Bowlin (D)	7,466	52.2
	Uriel Wright (W)	5,268	36.8
	William Milburn	1,572	11.0
2	John Jamison (D)	8,156	80.3
	Preston P. Brickey (W)	1,814	17.9
3	James S. Green (D)	8,624	55.3
	John G. Miller (W)	6,981	44.7
4	Willard P. Hall (D)	8,884	65.0
	James H. Birch (W)	4,789	35.0
5	John S. Phelps (D)	7,195	53.1
	John P. Campbell (W)	6,348	46.9

Special Election

		Votes	%
AL	William McDaniel (D)	9,155	48.6
	William M. Kincaid (W)	8,610	45.7

NEW HAMPSHIRE[2]

Special Election

		Votes	%
AL	Woodbury (D)	26,810*	48.8
	Goodwin (W)	16,567	30.1
	Hale (I)	11,475	20.9

NEW JERSEY

		Votes	%
1	James G. Hampton (W)	✔	
2	William A. Newell (W)	✔	

	Candidates	Votes	%
3	Joseph E. Edsall (D)	✔	
4	John Van Dyke (W)	✔	
5	Dudley S. Gregory (W)	✔	

NEW YORK

		Votes	%
1	Frederick Lord (D)	4,045	54.7
	Abraham Rose (W)	3,353	45.3
2	Henry Murphy (D)	5,267	45.9
	Gerret Van Wagenan (W)	5,070	44.2
	Henry Seaman (AM)	771	6.7
3	Henry Nicoll (D)	4,609	48.6
	Phillip Phoenix (W)	4,560	48.1
4	William Maclay (D)	4,749	46.1
	John Williams (W)	4,057	39.4
	William Picall (AM)	865	8.4
5	Frederick Tallmadge (W)	4,205	42.2
	David Broderick (D)	3,809	38.2
	David Wheeler (AM)	1,493	15.0
6	David S. Jackson (D)	6,071‡	43.3
	James Monroe (W)	5,928	42.3
	William Campbell (AM)	1,841	13.1
7	William Nelson (W)	4,324	51.2
	Edward Suffem (D)	4,099	48.5
8	Cornelius Warren (W)	5,450	45.7
	Henry Delamater (D)	5,221	43.8
	Charles Haight	1,251	10.5
9	Daniel St.John (W)	6,158	56.3
	John Monell (D)	4,719	43.1
10	Eliakim Sherrill (W)	7,967	53.6
	Jeremiah Russell (D)	6,742	45.4
11	Peter Sylvester (W)	6,586	53.3
	Silas Camp (D)	5,770	46.7
12	Gideon Reynold (W)	5,509	52.8
	Nicholas Masters (D)	4,822	46.3
13	John Slingerland (W-A-RENT)	7,155	58.1
	Bradford Wood (D)	5,087	41.3
14	Orlando Kellogg (W)	9,449	67.7
	Winslow Watson (D)	4,020	28.8
15	Sidney Lawrence (D)	5,174	53.4
	William McLean (W)	4,181	43.2
16	Hugh White (W)	7,576	51.3
	Lucio Smith (D)	7,024	47.5
17	George Petrie (ID)	5,532	51.1
	Abraham Van Alstine (D)	4,717	43.6
	John Underwood	576	5.3
18	William Collins (W)	5,878	48.2
	Francis Seger (D-HANKER)	5,732	47.0
19	Joseph Mullin (D)	4,915	46.6
	Orville Hungerford (D)	4,871	46.2
	Hugh Smith	763	7.2
20	Timothy Jenkins (D)	6,018	47.6
	Orsamus Matteson (W)	5,693	45.0
	James Delong	940	7.4
21	George Starkweather (D)	7,209	50.1
	Ebenezer Blakeley (W)	6,889	47.9
22	Ausburn Birdsall (D)	7,904	51.7
	Gideon Chase (BARN D)	6,995	45.8
23	William Duer (W)	6,431	45.0
	Avery Skinner (D)	6,186	43.3
	Cyrus Hawley	1,597	11.2
24	Daniel Gott (W)	5,561	49.2
	William Fuller (D)	5,157	45.6
	Charles Wheaton	569	5.0
25	Harmon Conger (W)	6,253	47.7
	William Shankland (D)	6,036	46.1
	John Boyd	811	6.2
26	William Lawrence (W)	6,753	48.6
	John Wisner (D)	6,739	48.5
27	John Holley (W)	5,468	48.3
	James Wilson (D)	5,180	45.7
	Levi Gaylord	678	6.0
28	Elias Holmes (W)	6,131	54.0
	Maltby Strong (IW)	4,370	38.5
	Samuel Porter	855	7.5

1. Information unavailable as to whether the Iowa elections were at large or by district.

2. Woodbury did not receive the required majority. (See New Hampshire, 1845, p. 738.)

NEW YORK

	Candidates	Votes	%
29	Robert Rose (W)	7,539	55.9
	Peter Mitchel (D)	5,451	40.5
30	David Rumsey Jr (W)	7,034	51.8
	Hugh Magee (D)	6,126	45.1
31	Dudley Marvin (W)	7,022	63.8
	Ebenezer Lester (D)	3,279	29.8
	Constant Allen	711	6.5
32	Nathan Hall (W)	5,660	54.5
	Hiram Barney (D)	4,385	42.2
33	Harvey Putnam (W)	5,628	58.9
	Junius Smith (D)	3,151	33.0
	Ferdinand McKay	559	5.9
34	Washington Hunt (W)	4,992	51.3
	Sanford Church (D)	4,347	44.7

OHIO

	Candidates	Votes	%
1	James J. Faran (D)	7,055	54.1
	Thomas J. Straight (W)	4,301	33.0
	William Green	1,143	8.8
2	David Fisher (W)	7,086	52.7
	Elijah Vance (D)	5,915	44.0
3	Robert C. Schenck (W)	8,863	55.4
	F. A. Cunningham (D)	6,681	41.7
4	Richard S. Canby (W)	7,822	57.5
	William Kershner (D)	5,226	38.4
5	William Sawyer (D)	5,483	53.3
	Morrison R. Waite (W)	4,764	46.3
6	Rodolphus Dickinson (D)	5,802	57.2
	Eli Dresback (D)	4,159	41.0
7	Thomas L. Hamer (D)	6,785*	92.1
	Alex Campbell	384	5.2
8	John L. Taylor (W)	6,127	51.6
	L. Byington (D)	5,465	46.0
9	Thomas O. Edwards (W)	6,030	50.8
	A. L. Perrill (D)	5,779	48.7
10	Daniel Duncan (W)	7,539	49.2
	Samuel Medary (D)	7,239	47.3
11	John K. Miller (D)	7,645	57.8
	W. McLaughlin (W)	2,237	16.9
	J. H. Godman (W)	1,949	14.7
	C. Delano (W)	989	7.5
12	Samuel F. Vinton (W)	3,424	38.8
	Flavius Case (D)	3,245	36.8
	C. Morris	1,240	14.1
	A. Cushing	568	6.4

	Candidates	Votes	%
13	Thomas Ritchey (D)	5,032	48.8
	P. B. Johnson (W)	5,005	48.5
14	Nathan Evans (W)	5,529	52.0
	W. W. Tracy (D)	4,674	44.0
15	William Kennon Jr (D)	5,386	50.1
	B. S. Cowan (W)	4,988	46.4
16	John D. Cummins (D)	5,080	54.0
	John Everhard (W)	4,180	44.4
17	George Fries (D)	5,318	50.4
	Van Brown (W)	4,906	46.5
18	Samuel Lahm (D)	4,651	50.0
	David A. Starkweather (W)	4,530	48.7
19	John Crowell (W)	6,573	48.2
	Rufus P. Ranney (D)	6,041	44.3
	John Hutchins (LIB)	1,016	7.5
20	Joshua R. Giddings (W)	6,548	60.6
	Zenas Blish (D)	2,865	26.5
	Edw. Wade (LIB)	1,398	12.9
21	Joseph M. Root (W)	6,126	48.0
	Josiah Harris (D)	5,160	40.4
	Joel Tiffany (LIB)	1,471	11.5

PENNSYLVANIA

	Candidates	Votes	%
1	Lewis C. Levin (AM)	✔	
2	Joseph R. Ingersoll (W)	✔	
3	Charles Brown (D)	✔	
4	Charles J. Ingersoll (D)	✔	
5	John Freedly (W)	✔	
6	John W. Hornbeck (W)	✔	
7	Abraham R. McIlvaine (W)	✔	
8	John Strohm (W)	✔	
9	William Strong (D)	✔	
10	Richard Brodhead (D)	✔	
11	Chester P. Butler (W)	✔	
12	David Wilmot (D)	✔	
13	James Pollock (W)	✔	
14	George N. Eckert (W)	✔	
15	Henry Nes (W)	✔	
16	Jasper E. Brady (W)	✔	
17	John Blanchard (W)	✔	
18	Andrew Stewart (W)	✔	
19	Job Mann (D)	✔	
20	John Dickey (W)	✔	
21	Moses Hampton (W)	✔	
22	John W. Farrelly (W)	✔	
23	James Thompson (D)	✔	
24	Alexander Irvin (W)	✔	

SOUTH CAROLINA

	Candidates	Votes	%
1	James A. Black (CALH D)	4,364	61.2
	L. P. Herndon	1,665	23.4
	G. A. Alston	1,099	15.4
2	Richard F. Simpson (D)		100.0
3	Joseph A. Woodward (D)	✔	
4	Alexander D. Sims (D)	✔	
5	Armistead Burt (D)		100.0
6	Isaac E. Holmes (D)	✔	
	D. J. Dowling		
7	R. Barnwell Rhett (D)		100.0

TEXAS

(Became a state Dec. 29, 1845)

		Votes	%
1	David Kaufman (D)	589	98.7
2	Timothy Pillsbury (CALH D)	1,751	49.9
	William E. Jones	678	19.3
	S. M. Williams	621	17.7
	R. E. B. Baylor	458	13.0

Special Elections

		Votes	%
1	David S. Kaufman (D)	1,478	58.9
	William R. Scurry	532	21.2
	William B. Ochiltree	497	19.8
2	Timothy Pillsbury (CALH D)	1,276	30.0
	Samuel M. Williams	1,233	29.0
	William G. Cooke	954	22.5
	N. Lewis	423	10.0
	Joseph C. Megginson	253	6.0

VERMONT

		Votes	%
1	William Henry (W)	6,627	54.0
	Bradley (D)	3,071	25.0
	Unidentified Candidate (LIB&SC)	2,580	21.0
2	Jacob Collamer (W)	5,457	49.1
	Hugh H. Henry (D)	3,854	34.7
	Titus Hutchinson (LIB)	1,732	15.6
3	George Perkins Marsh (W)	5,644	53.9
	Homer E. Hubbell (D)	3,207	30.7
	Norris Day (LIB)	1,575	15.1
4	Lucius B. Peck (D)	5,594	44.1
	George B. Chandler (W)	5,059	39.9
	Rowell (LIB)	1,255	9.9

1847 House Elections

ALABAMA

	Candidates	Votes	%
1	John Gayle (W)	5,050	52.9
	John Taylor (D)	4,490	47.1
2	Henry W. Hilliard (W)		100.0
3	Sampson W. Harris (D)		100.0
4	Samuel W. Inge (D)	4,528	51.0
	W. M. Murphy (W)	4,360	49.1
5	George S. Houston (D)	4,476	60.1
	D. Hubbard (D)	2,978	40.0
6	Williamson R. W. Cobb (D)	3,321	45.2
	William Acklen (D)	2,747	37.4
	B. F. Pope (D)	1,284	17.5
7	Franklin W. Bowdon (D)	5,419	52.3
	S. F. Rice (D)	4,024	38.9
	Phillips	793	7.7

CONNECTICUT

		Votes	%
1	James Dixon (W)	7,676	50.5
	William Hammersley (D)	7,167	47.1
2	Samuel D. Hubbard (W)	7,325	50.9
	Samuel Ingham (D)	6,669	46.4
3	John A. Rockwell (W)	6,112	49.5
	Noyes Billings (D)	5,578	45.2
	Increase Wilson (LIB)	653	5.3
4	Truman Smith (W)	9,082	52.0
	George Taylor (D)	7,980	45.7

ILLINOIS

Special Elections

		Votes	%
5	William A. Richardson (D)	11,423	77.5
	Nathaniel G. Wilcox (W)	3,312	22.5
7	John Henry (W)	2,411	56.8
	Issur W. Crosby (D)	1,289	30.3
	Archibald Job (OPP D)	293	6.9

INDIANA

		Votes	%
1	Elisha Embree (W)	7,446	51.4
	Robert Dale Owen (D)	7,054	48.7
2	Thomas J. Henley (D)	7,170	50.1
	John S. Davis (W)	7,130	49.9
3	John L. Robinson (D)	7,908	51.5
	Pleasant A. Hackleman (W)	7,422	48.3
4	Caleb B. Smith (W)	4,988	58.5
	Charles H. Test	3,540	41.5
5	William W. Wick (D)	7,087	50.4
	Nicolas McCarty (W)	6,799	48.4
6	George G. Dunn (W)	7,455	50.0
	David M. Dobson (D)	7,454	50.0
7	Richard W. Thompson (W)	6,402	50.7
	Joseph A. Wright (D)	6,224	49.3
8	John Pettit (D)	6,931	51.0
	David Brier (W)	6,511	47.9
9	Charles W. Cathcart (D)	7,555	51.0
	Daniel D. Pratt (W)	7,063	47.7
10	William Rockhill (D)	6,617	50.4
	William G. Ewing (W)	6,441	49.1

IOWA

		Votes	%
1	William Thompson (D)	5,530	52.6
	Jesse B. Browne (W)	4,986	47.4
2	Shepherd Leffler (D)	5,160	51.4
	Thomas McKnight (W)	4,873	48.6

KENTUCKY

		Votes	%
1	Linn Boyd (D)	7,421	63.9
	Delaney (W)	4,194	36.1
2	Samuel O. Peyton (D)	6,068	50.5
	Waddill (W)	5,958	49.5

	Candidates	Votes	%
3	Beverly L. Clarke (D)	5,291	51.1
	Todd (W)	5,065	48.9
4	Aylett Buckner (W)	6,177	51.6
	James (D)	5,791	48.4
5	John B. Thompson (W)	6,779	53.0
	Wickliffe (D)	6,019	47.0
6	Green Adams (W)	6,303	54.3
	Price (D)	5,307	45.7
7	W. Garnett Duncan (W)	6,760	51.1
	David Meriwether (D)	6,477	48.9
8	Charles S. Morehead (W)	4,348	41.3
	S. F. J. Trabue (AM)	3,143	29.9
	A. K. Marshall (D)	3,037	28.9
9	Richard French (D)	6,473	51.2
	Cox (W)	6,166	48.8
10	John P. Gaines (W)	7,496	50.4
	L. B. Desha (D)	7,372	49.6

LOUISIANA

		Votes	%
1	Emile La Sere (D)	2,813	63.6
	Montegut (W)	1,613	36.4
2	Bannon G. Thibodeaux (W)	4,280	55.1
	Landry (D)	3,489	44.9
3	John H. Harmanson (D)	4,118	54.8
	Saunders (W)	3,399	45.2
4	Isaac E. Morse (D)	4,138	53.9
	Waddell (W)	3,534	46.1

MAINE

		Votes	%
1	David Hammons (D)	5,430	53.6
	Samuel Hopkins (W)	3,521	34.7
	Theodore Stevens Jr (LIB)	1,101	10.9
2	Asa W. H. Clapp (D)	4,369	52.0
	Josiah S. Little (W)	3,023	36.0
	Unidentified Candidate (LIB & SC)	1,010	12.0
3	Hiram Belcher (W)	5,687	51.8
	Cutter (D)	3,487	31.7
	Unidentified Candidate (LIB & SC)	1,812	16.5
4	Franklin Clark (D)	5,266	49.2
	Freeman H. Morse (W)	4,657	43.5
	Unidentified Candidate (LIB & SC)	775	7.2
5	Ephraim K. Smart (D)	4,548	44.2
	Levi Johnson (W)	3,852	37.4
	Unidentified Candidate (LIB & SC)	1,892	18.4
6	James S. Wiley (D)	4,817	48.2
	Sanford Kingsbury (W)	3,615	36.2
	Unidentified Candidate (LIB & SC)	1,560	15.6
7	Hezekiah Williams (D)	5,033	52.0
	Pike (W)	3,740	38.6
	Unidentified Candidate (LIB & SC)	910	9.4

MARYLAND

		Votes	%
1	John G. Chapman (W)		100.0
2	J. Dixon Roman (W)	7,136	51.1
	Shriver (D)	6,820	48.9
3	Thomas W. Ligon (D)	4,202	55.0
	Unidentified Candidate (W)	3,433	45.0
4	Robert M. McLane (D)	10,158	53.8
	Kennedy (W)	8,720	46.2
5	Alexander Evans (W)	4,909	52.5
	Carmichael (D)	4,444	47.5
6	John W. Crisfield (W)	4,497	54.5
	Unidentified Candidate (D)	3,760	45.5

MICHIGAN

Special Election

	Candidates	Votes	%
2	Charles E. Stuart (D)	10,052	52.1
	James W. Gordon (W)	8,455	43.8

MISSISSIPPI

		Votes	%
1	Jacob Thompson (D)	7,191	54.4
	Josselyn (ID)	6,033	45.6
2	Winfield S. Featherston (D)	6,433	53.5
	McClung (W)	5,587	46.5
3	Patrick W. Tompkins (W)	6,939	52.1
	Roberts (D)	6,390	47.9
4	Albert G. Brown (D)	✔	
	John A. Quitman		

NEW HAMPSHIRE

		Votes	%
1	Amos Tuck (I)	5,608	57.7
	Jennes (LOCOFOCO)	4,025	41.4
2	Charles H. Peaslee (D)	8,873	57.2
	Unidentified Candidate	4,275	27.6
	Unidentified Candidate	2,356	15.2
3	James Wilson (W)	5,926	51.2
	Moulton (LOCOFOCO)	5,086	44.0
4	James H. Johnson (LOCOFOCO)	✔	

NORTH CAROLINA

		Votes	%
1	Thomas L. Clingman (W)	4,550	57.1
	John Gray Bynum (W)	3,426	43.0
2	Nathaniel Boyden (W)	3,882	51.7
	Joseph M Bogle (IW)	3,025	40.3
	John N. Vogler (ID)	606	8.1
3	Daniel M. Barringer (W)	3,412	81.2
	Walter F. Leake (D)	792	18.8
4	Augustine H. Shepperd (W)	4,022	60.4
	Junius L. Clemmons (D)	2,634	39.6
5	Abraham W. Venable (D)	4,588	50.9
	John Kerr (W)	4,435	49.2
6	John R. J. Daniel (D)	3,896	51.8
	Archibald H. Arrington (ID)	3,410	45.4
7	James J. McKay (D)	3,894	65.8
	William R. Hall (W)	1,827	30.9
8	Richard S. Donnell (W)	4,293	52.3
	William K. Lane (D)	3,924	47.8
9	David Outlaw (W)	3,795	55.3
	Asa Biggs (D)	3,071	44.7

RHODE ISLAND[1]

		Votes	%
1	Robert B. Cranston (W)	3,303	50.4
	Fenner Brown (D)	2,429	37.0
2	Wilkins Updike (W)	2,035*	44.2
	Benjamin B. Thurston (D)	1,928	41.8
	Lemuel H. Arnold (W)	453	9.8

Special Election

		Votes	%
2	Benjamin B. Thurston (D)	2,415	50.0
	Wilkins Updike (W)	2,350	48.6

TENNESSEE

		Votes	%
1	Andrew Johnson (D)	5,658	51.4
	Oliver P. Temple (W)	5,342	48.6
2	William M. Cocke (W)	7,277	61.0
	Wayne W. Wallace (D)	4,650	39.0
3	John H. Crozier (W)	6,945	51.8
	Samuel S. Smith (D)	6,474	48.3
4	Hugh L. W. Hill (D)	5,604	58.7
	John L. Goodall (W)	3,947	41.3
5	George W. Jones (D)	4,697	98.8

1. In the 1847 general election, no candidate in the 2nd district received the required majority. In a special election for which returns are unavailable, Thurston was the winner.

TENNESSEE

	Candidates	Votes	%
6	James H. Thomas (D)	5,562	55.6
	Boling Gordan (W)	4,443	44.4
7	Meredith P. Gentry (W)	5,989	65.1
	R. G. Ellis (D)	3,207	34.9
8	Washington Barrow (W)	5,544	58.8
	John B. Pittman (D)	3,887	41.2
9	Lucien B. Chase (D)	4,898	53.8
	John T. Swayne (W)	4,205	46.2
10	Frederick P. Stanton (D)	5,564	50.1
	John W. Harris (W)	5,539	49.9
11	William T. Haskell (W)	6,380	57.2
	John Gardner (D)	4,771	42.8

VIRGINIA

	Candidates	Votes	%
1	Archibald Atkinson (D)	2,238	50.8
	Watts (W)	2,166	49.2
2	George C. Dromgoole (D)	1,641	50.2
	Bolling (W)	1,625	49.8
3	Thomas S. Flournoy (W)	650	50.0
	Treadway (D)	649	50.0
4	Thomas S. Bocock (D)	2,263	51.4
	Irving (W)	2,138	48.6
5	William L. Goggin (W)	2,980	50.9
	Leake (D)	2,870	49.1
6	John M. Botts (W)	2,959	54.5
	Leake (D)	2,468	45.5
7	Thomas H. Bayly (D)	1,107	56.1
	Jones (W)	866	43.9
8	Richard L. T. Beale (D)	2,016	51.0
	Newton (W)	1,934	49.0
9	John S. Pendleton (W)	2,861	58.3
	Hunter (D)	2,045	41.7
10	Henry Bedinger (D)	3,053	52.7
	Kennedy (W)	2,746	47.4
11	James McDowell (D)	2,995	58.4
	Gray (W)	2,135	41.6
12	William B. Preston (W)	3,583	52.4
	Chapman (D)	3,257	47.6
13	Andrew S. Fulton (W)	2,094	38.8
	McMullen (D)	2,078	38.5
	Goodson	1,230	22.8
14	Robert A. Thompson (D)	3,290	50.4
	McComas (W)	3,235	49.6
15	William G. Brown (D)	✔	

Special Election

	Candidates	Votes	%
2	Richard K. Meade (D)	✔	

1848 House Elections

ARKANSAS

	Candidates	Votes	%
AL	Robert W. Johnson (D)	14,456	60.8
	Newton (W)	9,328	39.2

DELAWARE

	Candidates	Votes	%
AL	John W. Houston (W)	6,369	51.4
	Whiteley (D)	6,026	48.6

FLORIDA

		Votes	%
AL	Edward Cabell (W)	4,382	53.5
	William P. Duval (D)	3,805	46.5

GEORGIA

		Votes	%
1	Thomas Butler King (W)	3,549	57.0
	Joseph W. Jackson (D)	2,680	43.0
2	Marshall J. Wellborn (D)	6,625	50.3
	James S. Calhoun (W)	6,538	49.7
3	Allen F. Owen (W)	4,754	52.7
	John I. Carey (D)	4,260	47.3
4	Hugh A. Haralson (D)	5,532	50.9
	John A. Williamson (W)	5,341	49.1
5	Thomas C. Hackett (D)	8,767	59.8
	James M. Calhoun (W)	5,904	40.2
6	Howell Cobb (D)	5,891	57.7
	James W. Harris (W)	4,314	42.3
7	Alexander H. Stephens (W)	4,019	60.7
	Joseph (D)	2,602	39.3
8	Robert Toombs (W)	4,232	62.4
	Unindentified Candidate (D)	2,551	37.6

ILLINOIS

		Votes	%
1	William H. Bissell (D)	9,892	97.1
2	John A. McClernand (D)	6,537	65.0
	Samuel Marshall (W)	3,514	34.9
3	Timothy R. Young (D)	8,207	61.3
	George M. Hanson (W)	5,151	38.5
4	John Wentworth (D)	11,857	50.9
	J. Young Scammon (W)	8,302	35.6
	Owen Lovejoy (F SOIL)	3,138	13.5
5	William A. Richardson (D)	11,463	95.9
6	Edward D. Baker (W)	10,325	50.9
	Joseph B. Wells (D)	9,292	45.8
7	Thomas L. Harris (D)	7,201	49.8
	Stephen V. Logan (W)	7,095	49.1

IOWA

		Votes	%
1	William Thompson (D)	6,477	50.3
	Daniel F. Miller (W)	6,091	47.3
2	Shepherd Leffler (D)	5,789	50.9
	Timothy Davis (W)	5,398	47.5

MAINE

		Votes	%
1	Elbridge Gerry (D)	5,897	54.4
	John Jameson	3,984	36.8
	David Gerry	840	7.8
2	Nathaniel S. Littlefield (D)	5,160	46.7
	Isaac Lincoln	4,407	39.9
	Samuel Fessenden	1,438	13.0
3	John Otis (W)	5,274	44.2
	Moses Shelburne	4,132	34.6
	Ezekiel Holmes	2,526	21.2
4	Rufus K. Goodenow (W)	6,582	48.6
	John D. McCrate	5,607	41.4
	William H. Vinton	977	7.2
5	Cullen Sawtelle (D)	5,875	50.4
	Abner Coburn	3,589	30.8

	Candidates	Votes	%
	Cyrus Fletcher	2,063	17.7
6	Charles Stetson (D)	5,095	40.8
	Israel Washburn Jr	4,492	36.0
	Jeremiah Curtis	2,043	16.4
	Samuel Veazie	849	6.8
7	Thomas J. D. Fuller (D)	5,807	53.8
	George Downes	4,269	39.6
	Tristram Redman	661	6.1

MASSACHUSETTS[1]

		Votes	%
1	Robert C. Winthrop (W)	7,726	66.9
	Charles Sumner (F SOIL)	2,336	20.2
	Benjamin F. Hallett (D)	1,460	12.7
2	Daniel P. King (W)	4,201	54.5
	Benjamin F. Newhall	1,903	24.7
	Robert Rantoul Jr. (D)	1,588	20.6
3	James H. Duncan (W)	6,685	53.0
	Chauncey L. Knapp (F SOIL)	3,038	24.1
	George S. Boutwell (D)	2,868	22.8
4	Benjamin Thompson (W)	3,852*	42.6
	John G. Palfrey (F SOIL)	3,038	33.6
	Richard Frothingham Jr.	2,060	22.8
5	Charles Allen (F SOIL)	5,847	58.7
	Charles Hudson (W)	2,868	28.8
	Isaac Davis (D)	1,217	12.2
6	George Ashmun (W)	7,073	52.2
	Muling Guswold	3,766	27.8
	Daniel W.	2,677	19.8
7	Julius Rockwell (W)	5,865	51.3
	Thomas F. Plunkett	3,220	28.2
	Charles Sedgwick	2,325	20.4
8	Horace Mann (W)	11,087	83.9
	Bradford S. Wales	2,027	15.3
9	Orin Fowler (F SOIL W)	3,726	51.2
	Nathaniel Morton	2,128	29.2
	Foster Hooper	1,414	19.4
10	Joseph Grinnell (W)	4,719	56.2
	A. H. Howland	1,504	17.9
	Charles B. H. Fessenden	1,199	14.3
	Simpson Hart	673	8.0

Special Election

		Votes	%
8	Horace Mann (W)	4,357	58.3
	Edgar K. Mutaker	1,952	26.1
	Appleton Howe	944	12.6

MICHIGAN

		Votes	%
1	Alexander W. Buel (D)	10,015	46.7
	George C. Bates (W)	8,747	40.8
	Caleb N. Ormsby (F SOIL)	2,665	12.4
2	William Sprague (W FS)	13,559	53.3
	Charles E. Stuart (D)	11,881	46.7
3	Kinsley S. Bingham (D)	9,348	49.1
	George H. Hazelton (W)	7,802	40.9
	John M. Lamb (F SOIL)	1,899	10.0

MISSOURI

		Votes	%
1	James B. Bowlin (D)	10,312	60.4
	Cook (W)	6,776	39.7
2	William V. N. Bay (D)	8,394	54.6
	Porter (W)	6,968	45.4
3	James S. Green (D)	9,754	56.8
	Wilson (W)	7,417	43.2
4	Willard P. Hall (D)	10,840	71.0
	Samuel (W)	4,418	29.0
5	John S. Phelps (D)	11,062	65.4
	Winston (W)	5,848	34.6

NEW JERSEY

	Candidates	Votes	%
1	Andrew K. Hay (W)	7,052	51.1
	Unidentified Candidate (D)	6,043	43.8
	Unidentified Candidate (AM)	718	5.2
2	William A. Newell (W)	9,877	54.1
	Unidentified Candidate (D)	8,382	45.9
3	Isaac Wildrick (D)	9,215	76.8
	Unidentified Candidate (W)	2,778	23.2
4	John Van Dyke (W)	7,282	54.5
	Unidentified Candidate (D)	6,023	45.1
5	James G. King (W)	9,679	56.7
	Unidentified Candidate (D)	6,716	39.3

NEW YORK

		Votes	%
1	John A. King (W)	4,397	47.9
	Jones (F SOIL)	2,457	26.8
	Brown (D)	2,332	25.4
2	David A. Bokee (W)	8,168	54.2
	Mereac (D)	5,812	38.6
	Crooke (F SOIL)	1,087	7.2
3	J. Phillips Phoenix (W)	5,601	55.0
	Hart (D)	3,788	37.2
	Smith (F SOIL)	793	7.8
4	Walter Underhill (W)	5,649	49.0
	Maclay (D)	3,904	33.9
	Hecker (F SOIL)	1,035	9.0
	Foote (D)	944	8.2
5	George Briggs (W)	5,627	49.1
	Walsh (D)	2,765	24.1
	Hasbrouck (D)	1,602	14.0
	Spencer (F SOIL)	1,476	12.9
6	James Brooks (W)	9,709	51.7
	Law (D)	6,976	37.2
	Field (F SOIL)	2,042	10.9
7	William Nelson (W)	4,948	50.3
	N. C. Blvt (D)	3,133	31.9
	J. C. Blvt (F SOIL)	1,754	17.8
8	Ransom Halloway (W)	6,301	51.2
	Nun (D)	4,333	35.2
	Bailey (F SOIL)	1,681	13.7
9	Thomas McKissock (W)	5,876	47.3
	Woodward (D)	4,667	37.6
	Curtis (D)	1,874	15.1
10	Herman D. Gould (W)	6,267	40.0
	Edgerton (F SOIL)	4,443	28.3
	Fitch (A-RENT)	3,013	19.2
	Wheeler (D)	1,953	12.5
11	Peter H. Silvester (W)	6,621	47.4
	Olney (D)	3,893	27.9
	Beekman (F SOIL)	3,453	24.7
12	Gideon Reynolds (D&A-RENT)	6,055	53.0
	Warren (W)	5,362	47.0
13	John L. Schoolcraft (W)	7,227	53.9
	Bouton (D)	3,876	28.9
	Wood (F SOIL)	2,315	17.3
14	George R. Andrews (W)	7,088	57.0
	Culver (F SOIL)	3,166	25.5
	Cutting (D)	2,186	17.6
15	John R. Thurman (W)	4,670	42.6
	Heding (D)	3,455	31.5
	Lawrence (F SOIL)	2,828	25.8
16	Hugh White (W)	8,183	52.3
	Campbell (D)	4,059	26.0
	Cowen (F SOIL)	3,392	21.7
17	Henry P. Alexander (W)	6,109	47.2
	Nellis (F SOIL)	5,564	43.0
	Samons (D)	1,264	9.8
18	Preston King (F SOIL)	7,309	53.1
	Squire (W)	5,133	37.3
	Dodge (D)	1,325	9.6
19	Charles E. Clarke (W)	4,636	39.7
	Ives (F SOIL)	4,427	37.9
	Dann (D)	2,624	22.5
20	Orsamus B. Matteson (W)	6,094	42.4
	Mann (F SOIL)	5,069	35.3

1. In the 4th district, no candidate received the necessary majority. Twelve elections were held to try to fill the seat, but all of them resulted without choice. The seat was vacant for the entire 31st Congress (1849-51).

NEW YORK

Candidates	Votes	%
Williams (D)	3,214	22.4
21 Hiram Walden (D)	6,636	42.1
Smith (W)	6,330	40.2
Hammond (F SOIL)	2,787	17.7
22 Henry Bennett (W)	8,014	46.5
Mason (D)	6,394	37.1
Smith (F SOIL)	2,839	16.5
23 William Duer (W)	8,107	48.2
Nye (F SOIL)	6,884	41.0
Crouse (D)	1,640	9.8
24 Daniel Gott (W)	5,403	42.2
Sedgwick (F SOIL)	4,906	38.3
Baldwin (D)	2,498	19.5
25 Harmon S. Conger (W)	6,732	46.9
Ballard (F SOIL)	5,747	40.1
Hyde (D)	1,870	13.0
26 William T. Jackson (W)	6,444	40.4
Wisner (F SOIL)	6,396	40.1
Hathaway (D)	3,117	19.5
27 William A. Sackett (W)	5,845	45.2
Bascom (F SOIL)	5,260	40.7
Bigelow (D)	1,802	14.1
28 Abraham M. Schermerhorn (W)	6,611	52.0
Selden (F SOIL)	4,746	37.3
Smith (D)	1,367	10.7
29 Robert L. Rose (W)	7,816	53.4
Garlghse (F SOIL)	4,659	31.8
Parburt (D)	2,166	14.8
30 David Rumsey Jr (W)	7,282	45.0
Grover (F SOIL)	5,938	36.7
Angel (D)	2,982	18.4
31 Elijah Risley (W)	6,946	51.7
Chaffee (D)	3,649	27.2
Colman (F SOIL)	2,832	21.1
32 Elbridge G. Spaulding (W)	7,622	56.9
Clinton (D)	3,408	25.4
Wadsworth (F SOIL)	2,367	17.7
33 Harvey Putnam (W)	5,489	50.6
Smith (F SOIL)	2,780	25.6
Willett (D)	2,575	23.8
34 Lorenzo Burrows (W)	5,372	47.0
Davis (F SOIL)	3,846	33.6
Burroughs (D)	2,214	19.4

Special Elections

	Votes	%
6 Horace Greeley (W)	9,932	53.9
Bradhst	6,826	37.0
Townsend	1,681	9.1
27 Blackmar (W)	5,921	45.6
Smith (F SOIL)	5,308	40.9
Foster (HUNKER)	1,751	13.5

OHIO

	Votes	%
1 David T. Disney (D)	9,292	50.9
Thomas J. Strait (W)	6,297	34.5
Samuel Lewis (F SOIL)	2,158	11.8
2 Lewis D. Campbell (F SOIL W)	6,914	51.6
William H. Baldwin (D)	6,479	48.4
3 Robert C. Schenck (W)	9,289	53.5
Joseph W. McCorkle (D)	8,082	46.5
4 Moses B. Corwin (W)	8,761	54.7
John A. Corwin (D)	6,215	38.8
William A. Rogers (F SOIL)	1,030	6.4
5 Emery D. Potter (D)	7,029	62.2
John Fitch (W)	4,240	37.5
6 Rodolphus Dickinson (D)	7,404	58.8
Cooper K. Watson (W)	5,184	41.2

Candidates	Votes	%
7 Jonathan D. Morris (D)	7,135	59.5
John Joliffe (W)	3,583	29.9
Thomas Gatch (IW)	1,278	10.7
8 John L. Taylor (W)	7,449	52.9
Francis Cleveland (D)	6,624	47.1
9 Edson B. Olds (D)	6,984	50.3
Thomas O. Edwards (W)	6,906	49.7
10 Charles Sweetzer (D)	8,454	49.5
Daniel Duncan (W)	8,438	49.4
11 John K. Miller (D)	9,165	62.6
Jacob Brinkerhoff (W)	5,462	37.3
12 Samuel F. Vinton (W)	5,799	53.3
Simeon W. Tucker (D)	4,416	40.6
David Richmond (ID)	670	6.2
13 William A. Whittlesey (D)	6,375	51.4
William P. Cutler (W)	6,037	48.6
14 Nathan Evans (W)	6,606	53.1
Matthew Gaston (D)	5,840	46.9
15 William F. Hunter (W)	6,711	51.4
William Kennon Jr. (D)	6,338	48.5
16 Moses Hoagland (D)	6,104	54.0
Martin Welker (W)	5,144	45.5
17 Joseph Cable (D)	6,987	50.2
James Mason (W)	6,330	45.5
18 David K. Carter (D)	6,682	60.0
Samuel Hemphill (W)	4,448	40.0
19 John Crowell (W)	9,561	56.0
Rufus P. Ranney (D)	7,507	44.0
20 Joshua R. Giddings (F SOIL W)	5,879	62.7
Bushnell White (D)	3,155	33.6
21 Joseph M. Root (F SOIL W)	8,434	57.8
E. M. Stone (D)	6,077	41.6

PENNSYLVANIA

	Votes	%
1 Lewis C. Levin (AM)	4,897	52.2
Florence (D)	4,228	45.1
2 Joseph R. Chandler (W)	6,656	63.2
Van Dyke (D)	3,874	36.8
3 Henry D. Moore (W)	6,844	52.9
Hallowell (D)	6,098	47.1
4 John Robbins Jr (D)	6,661	51.6
John S. Littell (W)	6,251	48.4
5 John Freedley (W)	6,655	50.7
McKeever (D)	6,474	49.3
6 Thomas Ross (D)	8,036	51.0
Taylor (W)	7,716	49.0
7 Jesse C. Dickey (W)	5,786	52.9
Hemphill (D)	5,160	47.1
8 Thaddeus Stevens (W)	9,565	63.6
Shaffer (D)	5,464	36.4
9 William Strong (D)	8,451	67.8
Adams (W)	4,014	32.2
10 Milo M. Dimmick (D)	7,764	63.6
Wheeler (W)	4,444	36.4
11 Chester P. Butler (W)	5,032	42.4
Wright (D)	4,902	41.3
Collings (ID)	1,938	16.3
12 David Wilmot (F SOIL D)	8,619	60.2
Tracy (D)	4,773	33.3
Brewster (CASS D)	922	6.4
13 Joseph Casey (W)	6,817	51.0
Unidentified Candidate (D)	6,555	49.0
14 Charles W. Pitman (W)	10,203	57.7
Dock (D)	7,472	42.3
15 Henry Nes (W)	6,599	52.4
Joel B. Danner (D)	5,989	47.6
16 James X. McLanahan (D)	8,725	53.9
Brady (W)	7,472	46.1

Candidates	Votes	%
17 Samuel Calvin (W)	8,712	50.2
Parker (D)	8,648	49.8
18 Andrew Jackson Ogle (W)	6,902	50.9
Dawson (D)	6,649	49.1
19 Job Mann (D)	9,110	58.7
Livergood (W)	6,398	41.3
20 Robert R. Reed (W)	6,417	49.5
Hopkins (D)	6,359	49.1
21 Moses Hampton (W)	7,666	50.8
Black (D)	6,613	43.8
22 John W. Howe (F SOIL)	7,509	51.2
McFarland (D)	7,161	48.8
23 James Thompson (D)	7,509	50.9
Campbell (W)	7,026	47.6
24 Alfred Gilmore (D)	7,267	50.2
Smith (W)	7,008	48.4

Special Election

	Votes	%
6 Samuel A. Bridges (D)	6,526	50.5
Lesher Trexler (W)	6,393	49.5

SOUTH CAROLINA[1]

	Votes	%
1 Daniel Wallace (W)	3,369	39.8
Thompson	3,044	35.9
Davie	2,061	24.3
2 James L. Orr (D)	✔	
B. F. Perry (D)		
3 Joseph A. Woodward (D)	✔	
J. O'Hanlon		
4 Alexander D. Sims (D)	*	
John McQueen (D)		
5 Armistead Burt (D)	5,991	84.2
Heller	1,121	15.8
6 Isaac E. Holmes (TAYLOR D)	✔	
Samuel G. Barker (CASS D)		
W. C. Clayton		
7 William F. Colcock (D)	✔	

Special Election

	Votes	%
1 Daniel Wallace (W)	2,139	36.9
Thompson	2,134	36.8
Davis	1,525	26.3

VERMONT

1 William P. Henry (W)	✔	
2 William Hebard (W)	✔	
3 George P. Marsh (W)	✔	
4 Lucius B. Peck (D)	✔	

WISCONSIN

(Became a state May 29, 1848)

	Votes	%
1 Charles Durkee (F SOIL)	5,038	38.5
William P. Lynde (D)	4,436	33.9
Finch (W)	3,615	27.6
2 Orsamus Cole (W)	6,280	45.2
Smith (D)	5,690	41.0
Crabb (F SOIL)	1,916	13.8
3 James Duane Doty (D)	5,746	50.3
Howe (W)	3,338	29.2
Judd (F SOIL)	2,330	20.4

Special Election[2]

Mason C. Darling (D)	✔	
William P. Lynde (D)	✔	

1. *In the South Carolina 4th district, Sims was elected but died Jan. 16, 1848. McQueen was chosen to succeed him in a special election for which no returns are available.*

2. *This was the first House election held by Wisconsin after it achieved statehood. Information is unavailable as to whether the elections were at-large or by district.*

1849 House Elections

ALABAMA

	Candidates	Votes	%
1	William J. Alston (TAYLOR W)	4,922	51.8
	C. C. Sellers (SO RTS D)	4,588	48.2
2	Henry W. Hilliard (W)	6,770	53.1
	J. L. Pugh (IW)	5,975	46.9
3	Sampson W. Harris (D)	5,511	52.6
	John Hunter (W)	4,962	47.4
4	Samuel W. Inge (D)	4,665	52.4
	Joseph Baldwin (W)	4,245	47.6
5	David Hubbard (D)	4,575	49.1
	Wood (W)	3,084	33.1
	O'Neal (D)	1,655	17.8
6	Williamson R. W. Cobb (D)	4,594	53.4
	Jere Clemens (D)	4,005	46.6
7	Franklin W. Bowdon (D)	6,002	55.1
	Bradford (W)	4,895	44.9

CALIFORNIA

(Became a state Sept. 9, 1850)

	Candidates	Votes	%
AL	George W. Wright (I)	5,451✔	
	Edward Gilbert (D)	5,300✔	
	R. M. Price	4,040	
	Lewis Dent	2,129	
	D. A. Morse	2,066	
	E. J. C. Kewen	1,826	
	William M. Shepard	1,773	
	W. E. Shannon	1,327	
	P. O. Halsted	1,271	
	L. W. Hastings	215	

CONNECTICUT

	Candidates	Votes	%
1	Loren P. Waldo (D)	7,444	50.4
	Charles Chapman (W)	7,327	49.6
2	Walter Booth (D)	6,672	50.1
	James F. Babcock (W)	6,532	49.0
3	Chauncey F. Cleveland (D)	6,140	50.6
	John A. Rockwell (W)	5,992	49.4
4	Thomas B. Butler (W)	8,172	51.6
	Nathaniel H. Wildman (D)	7,028	44.4

INDIANA

	Candidates	Votes	%
1	Nathaniel Albertson (D)	8,271	52.1
	Elisha Embree (W)	7,598	47.9
2	Cyrus L. Dunham (D)	7,823	51.6
	William McKee Dunn (W)	7,338	48.4
3	John L. Robinson (D)	8,120	52.5
	Joseph Robinson (W)	7,348	47.5
4	George W. Julian (F SOIL)	4,737	50.8
	Samuel W. Parker (W)	4,583	49.1
5	William J. Brown (D)	8,762	54.7
	William Herod (W)	7,265	45.3
6	Willis A. Gorman (D)	8,466	54.1
	John S. Watts (W)	7,196	45.9
7	Edward W. McGaughey (W)	6,782	58.0
	Grafton F. Cookerly (D)	4,909	42.0
8	Joseph E. McDonald (D)	7,432	51.2
	Henry S. Lane (W)	7,098	48.9
9	Graham N. Fitch (D)	8,800	50.8
	Williamson Wright (W)	8,519	49.2
10	Andrew J. Harlan (D)	7,366	52.1
	David Kilgore (W)	6,777	47.9

KENTUCKY

	Candidates	Votes	%
1	Linn Boyd (D)	5,208	100.0
2	James L. Johnson (W)	8,031	67.4
	Peyton (D)	3,878	32.6
3	Finis E. McLean (W)	5,679	100.0
4	George A. Caldwell (D)	6,719	54.6
	Buckner (W)	5,579	45.4

	Candidates	Votes	%
5	John B. Thompson (W)	6,586	100.0
6	Daniel Breck (W)	6,353	54.7
	Martin (D)	5,271	45.4
7	Humphrey Marshall (W)	6,261	50.3
	Lane (D)	6,197	49.7
8	Charles S. Morehead (W)	5,195	52.7
	Trabue (AM)	4,665	47.3
9	John C. Mason (D)	6,882	52.8
	Houston (W)	6,164	47.3
10	Richard H. Stanton (D)	7,764	51.2
	Gaines (W)	7,400	48.8

LOUISIANA

	Candidates	Votes	%
1	Emile La Sere (D)	3,295	56.3
	Jackson (W)	2,559	43.7
2	Charles M. Conrad (W)	5,092	52.4
	Beatty (D)	4,622	47.6
3	John H. Harmanson (D)	2,464	53.8
	Stewart (W)	2,117	46.2
4	Isaac E. Morse (D)	4,751	51.3
	Ogden (W)	4,516	48.7

MARYLAND

	Candidates	Votes	%
1	Richard J. Bowie (W)	4,283	100.0
2	William T. Hamilton (D)	7,307	50.4
	T. J. McKaig (W)	7,191	49.6
3	Edward Hammond (D)	6,903	60.8
	George W. Gray (W)	4,456	39.2
4	Robert M. McLane (D)	7,277	53.5
	John R. Kenly (W)	6,326	46.5
5	Alexander Evans (W)	4,986	52.6
	S. M. Magraw (D)	4,487	47.4
6	John Bozman Kerr (W)	3,457	100.0

MISSISSIPPI

	Candidates	Votes	%
1	Jacob Thompson (D)	9,109	57.3
	Bradford (W)	6,801	42.8
2	Winfield S. Featherston (D)	7,237	54.0
	Harris (W)	6,170	46.0
3	William McWillie (D)	7,406	52.0
	Gray (W)	6,834	48.0
4	Albert G. Brown (D)	7,980	67.6
	Winans (W)	3,820	32.4

NEW HAMPSHIRE

	Candidates	Votes	%
1	Amos Tuck (F SOIL)	6,971	51.1
	G. W. Kit (D)	6,638	48.6
2	Charles H. Peaslee (D)	8,590	60.6
	Eastman (F SOIL)	3,673	25.9
	Stewart	1,914	13.5
3	James Wilson (F SOIL)	7,766	51.2
	Vose (D)	7,378	48.7
4	Harry Hibbard (D)	7,363	57.8
	J. Kittredge (F SOIL)	3,658	28.7
	Unidentified Candidate	1,712	13.5

NORTH CAROLINA

	Candidates	Votes	%
1	Thomas L. Clingman (W)	7,231	86.3
2	Joseph P. Caldwell (W)	6,353	78.0
	Montford S. Stokes (D)	1,795	22.0
3	Edmund Deberry (W)	4,899	53.3
	Green W. Caldwell (D)	4,299	46.7
4	Augustine H. Shepperd (W)	4,405	58.4
	Thomas W. Keene (D)	3,138	41.6
5	Abraham W. Venable (D)	5,025	53.8
	Henry K. Nash (W)	4,315	46.2
6	John R. J. Daniel (D)	4,413	64.5
	William J. Clarke (D)	2,430	35.5

	Candidates	Votes	%
7	William S. Ashe (D)	5,128	64.6
	David Reid (D)	2,813	35.4
8	Edward Stanly (W)	4,987	50.2
	William K. Lane (D)	4,940	49.8
9	David Outlaw (W)	4,053	53.8
	Thomas Person (D)	3,477	46.2

OHIO

Special Election

6	Amos E. Wood (D)		✔

RHODE ISLAND[1]

		Votes	%
1	George G. King (W)	3,005	67.3
	Fenner Brown (D)	1,250	28.0
2	Benjamin B. Thurston (D)	2,017*	48.5
	Sylvester G. Sherman (W)	1,959	47.1

Special Election

		Votes	%
2	Nathan F. Dixon (W)	2,824	56.1
	Benjamin B. Thurston (FS CLN)	2,209	43.9

TENNESSEE

		Votes	%
1	Andrew Johnson (D)	6,068	54.5
	Taylor (W)	5,060	45.5
2	Albert G. Watkins (W)	7,125	58.9
	Cocke (D)	4,968	41.1
3	Josiah M. Anderson (W)	7,269	54.7
	Lyon (D)	6,018	45.3
4	John H. Savage (D)	4,713	79.2
	Rogs (D)	1,239	20.8
5	George W. Jones (D)	6,736	100.0
6	James H. Thomas (D)	6,135	56.1
	Buchanan (W)	4,802	43.9
7	Meredith P. Gentry (W)	5,766	100.0
8	Andrew Ewing (D)	4,894	50.4
	Cullom (W)	4,816	49.6
9	Isham G. Harris (D)	5,433	55.8
	Morris (W)	4,302	44.2
10	Frederick P. Stanton (D)	6,250	51.9
	Harris (W)	5,799	48.1
11	Christopher H. Williams (W)	8,944	100.0

TEXAS

		Votes	%
1	David S. Kaufman (D)	8,944	96.0
2	Volney E. Howard (D)	4,120	58.1
	Williamson	2,976	41.9

VERMONT

Special Election

		Votes	%
3	James Meacham (W)	6,645	54.5
	Peck (EVA)	4,716	38.7
	Harrington (OPP&SC)	835	6.9

VIRGINIA

		Votes	%
1	John S. Millson (D)	2,736	51.7
	Wats (W)	2,559	48.3
2	Richard K. Meade (D)		100.0
3	Thomas H. Averett (D)	2,113	50.8
	Fly (W)	2,048	49.2
4	Thomas S. Bocock (D)	2,694	53.0
	Irving (W)	2,388	47.0
5	Paulus Powell (D)	3,136	50.9
	Goggin (W)	3,029	49.1

1. *In the second district, no candidate received the required majority. In the subsequent special election shown on this page, Nathan F. Dixon defeated Thurston.*

VIRGINIA

Candidates	Votes	%
6 James A. Seddon (D)	2,844	53.6
Botts (W)	2,458	46.4
7 Thomas H. Bayly (D)	1,653	64.8
Mallory (W)	900	35.3
8 Alexander R. Holladay (D)	2,163	51.0
Forbes (W)	2,078	49.0
9 Jeremiah Morton (D)	2,798	54.0
Pendleton (W)	2,381	46.0

Candidates	Votes	%
10 Richard Parker (D)	3,429	55.2
Far (W)	2,787	44.8
11 James McDowell (D)		100.0
12 Henry A. Edmundson (D)	2,540	54.0
Anderson (W)	2,161	46.0
13 Fayette McMullen (D)	4,421	67.2
George (W)	2,155	32.8
14 James M. H. Beale (D)	4,312	51.3
McComas (W)	4,094	48.7

Candidates	Votes	%
15 Alexander Newman (D)	2,926	53.0
Russell (W)	2,598	47.0

Special Election

Candidates	Votes	%
15 Thomas S. Haymond (W)	2,873	50.6
Thompson (D)	2,807	49.4

House Candidates Index

For an index of all House candidates listed in this section (pages 701 to 1061), see pages 1180-1273. Instructions for use of the House Candidates Index appear on page 1180.

1850 House Elections

DELAWARE

Candidates	Votes	%
AL George Read Riddle (D)	6,055	48.7
Rodney (W)	5,926	47.7

FLORIDA

	Votes	%
AL Edward C. Cabell (W)	4,531	52.8
John Beard (D)	4,050	47.2

ILLINOIS

	Votes	%
1 William H. Bissell (D)	12,841	100.0
2 Willis Allen (D)	5,763	54.5
Thomas G. C. Davis (W)	4,816	45.5
3 Orlando B. Ficklin (D)	7,429	56.3
E. G. Ryan (W)	5,739	43.5
4 Richard S. Molony (D)	11,231	48.9
Churchill Coffing (W)	10,587	46.1
5 William A. Richardson (D)	8,099	53.0
Orville H. Browning (W)	7,197	47.1
6 Thompson Campbell (D)	8,181	50.7
Martin P. Sweet (W)	7,857	48.7
7 Richard Yates (W)	7,008	52.8
Thomas L. Harris (D)	6,254	47.1

IOWA

	Votes	%
1 Bernhart Henn (D)	7,437	50.5
George G. Wright (W)	6,985	47.4
2 Lincoln Clark (D)	5,745	54.0
William H. Henderson (W)	4,725	44.4

Special Election

	Votes	%
1 Daniel F. Miller (W)	5,463	51.3
William Thompson (D)	4,801	45.1

MAINE

	Votes	%
1 Moses MacDonald (D)	5,173	49.6
N. D. Appleton (W)	4,683	44.9
M. Sweat (F SOIL)	530	5.1
2 John Appleton (D)	5,943	50.1
William Pitt Fessenden (W FS)	5,903	49.8
3 Robert Goodenow (W)	4,831	44.7
Lot M. Merrill (D)	4,700	43.5
Seth May (F SOIL)	1,272	11.8
4 Charles Andrews (D)	6,718	49.6
Isaac Reed (W)	6,652	49.1
5 Ephraim K. Smart (D)	5,911	52.5
Theophilus Cushing (W)	5,295	47.0
6 Israel Washburn Jr (W)	5,412	46.3
Strickland (D)	3,696	31.6
Stetson (D)	2,554	21.8
7 Thomas J. D. Fuller (D)	4,814	47.0
James S. Pike (W)	4,629	45.2
S. C. Foster (F SOIL)	716	7.0

MASSACHUSETTS

	Votes	%
1 William Appleton (W)	5,839	65.6
John T. Heard	1,855	20.9
Benjamin B. Mufsey (F SOIL)	1,167	13.1
2 Robert Rantoul Jr (D)	7,183	51.4
Charles W. Upham (W)	6,089	43.6
3 James H. Duncan (W)	4,250	56.8
Alpheus R. Brown	1,764	23.6
Thomas W. Higginson (F SOIL)	1,255	16.8
4 Benjamin Thompson (W)	6,380	47.6
John G. Palfrey (F SOIL)	6,293	47.0
Richard Frothingham Jr.	717	5.4

Candidates	Votes	%
5 Charles Allen (F SOIL)	4,819	51.1
Ira M. Barton (W)	2,620	27.8
I. S. C. Knowlton	1,990	21.1
6 George T. Davis (W)	4,877	51.8
Chester W. Chapin	3,031	32.2
Samuel Williston	1,460	15.5
7 John Z. Goodrich (W)	4,623	52.8
Henry W. Bishop	4,056	46.3
8 Horace Mann (F SOIL)	6,697	50.3
Samuel H. Walley (W)	4,301	32.3
Edgar K. Whittaker	2,262	17.0
9 Orin Fowler (F SOIL W)	6,345	66.1
Edward P. Little (D)	2,795	29.1
10 Zeno Scudder (W)	2,179	55.3
Charles B. H. Fessenden	907	23.0
Simpson Hart (F SOIL)	429	10.9
Daniel Fisher	239	6.1

Special Election

	Votes	%
1 Samuel A. Elliott (W)	2,355	74.9
Charles Sumner (F SOIL)	473	15.0
John T. Heard	297	9.4

MICHIGAN

	Votes	%
1 Ebenezer J. Penniman (W FS)	10,766	54.7
Alexander W. Buel (D)	8,914	45.3
2 Charles E. Stuart (D)	11,929	50.8
Joseph R. Williams (W FS)	11,517	49.0
3 James L. Conger (W FS)	8,646	50.5
Charles C. Hascall (D)	8,427	49.2

MISSOURI

	Votes	%
1 John F. Darby (W)	7,145	39.6
Rozier (BENTON D)	5,600	31.0
Bowlin (A-BEN D)	5,317	29.4
2 Gilchrist Porter (W)	6,889	52.9
Henderson (D)	5,878	45.1
3 John G. Miller (W)	6,578	42.3
Green (A-BEN D)	6,554	42.2
J. Miller (BENTON D)	2,411	15.5
4 Willard P. Hall (A-BEN D)	5,606	37.5
Bowman (D)	5,505	36.9
Gardenhire (BENTON D)	3,826	25.6
5 John S. Phelps (BENTON D)	8,473	52.4
Woodson (W)	5,667	35.0
Shields (A-BEN D)	2,035	12.6

NEW JERSEY

	Votes	%
1 Nathan T. Stratton (D)	6,475	52.7
Whitney (W)	5,824	47.4
2 Charles Skelton (D)	9,259	52.6
Richards (W)	8,358	47.4
3 Isaac Wildrick (D)	9,097	66.9
Edsall (W)	4,498	33.1
4 George H. Brown (W)	6,470	50.9
Vail (D)	6,251	49.1
5 Rodman M. Price (D)	8,286	50.3
Ryerson (W)	8,149	49.5

NEW YORK

	Votes	%
1 John G. Floyd (D)	4,125	53.0
Rose (W)	3,661	47.0
2 Obadiah Bowne (W)	7,728	52.3
Bogardus (D)	6,428	43.5
3 Emanuel B. Hart (D)	3,679	48.4
Rodman (W)	2,164	28.5
Bowen (W)	1,755	23.1
4 J. H. Hobart Haws (W)	4,155	48.8
Marsh (D)	3,824	44.9

Candidates	Votes	%
McGrath (D)	541	6.4
5 George Briggs (W)	4,444	51.9
Arculars (D)	4,114	48.1
6 James Brooks (W)	8,357	54.6
Cochran (D)	6,724	44.0
7 Abraham P. Stevens (D)	4,851	52.6
Gurnee (W)	4,372	47.4
8 Gilbert Dean (D)	6,218	51.1
Cruger (W)	5,942	48.9
9 William Murray (D)	5,810	51.1
McKissock (W)	5,563	48.9
10 Marius Schoonmaker (W)	7,851	52.4
Allaben (D)	7,135	47.6
11 Josiah Sutherland (D)	6,672	52.9
Cowles (W)	5,940	47.1
12 David L. Seymour (D)	5,811	51.0
Sage (W)	5,594	49.1
13 John L. Schoolcraft (W)	7,032	51.0
Corning (W)	6,746	49.0
14 John H. Boyd (W)	6,286	58.7
Thompson (D)	4,415	41.3
15 Joseph Russell (D)	5,506	50.8
Tabor (W)	5,324	49.2
16 John Wells (W)	8,428	53.1
Marvin (D)	7,460	47.0
17 Alexander H. Buel (D)	6,685	52.5
Alexander (W)	6,047	47.5
18 Preston King (D)	7,101	59.2
Grant (W)	4,893	40.8
19 Willard Ives (D)	5,477	52.0
Clarke (W)	5,058	48.0
20 Timothy Jenkins (D)	7,828	50.4
Matteson (W)	7,711	49.6
21 William Snow (D)	7,664	50.2
Chase (W)	7,608	49.8
22 Henry Bennett (W)	9,170	53.0
Taylor (D)	8,131	47.0
23 Leander Babcock (D)	8,423	54.1
Williams (W)	7,136	45.9
24 Daniel T. Jones (D)	6,186	51.7
Smith (W)	5,419	45.3
25 Thomas Y. Howe Jr (D)	7,037	50.1
Morgan (W)	7,011	49.9
26 Henry S. Walbridge (W)	7,700	50.7
Halsey (D)	7,497	49.3
27 William A. Sackett (W)	6,305	52.0
Smith (D)	5,814	48.0
28 Abraham M. Schermerhorn (W)	6,036	51.8
Buchan (D)	5,623	48.2
29 Jeradiah Horsford (W)	7,727	57.9
Wadsworth (D)	5,609	42.1
30 Reuben Robie (D)	8,368	52.6
Church (W)	7,538	47.4
31 Frederick S. Martin (W)	7,210	52.4
Waite (D)	6,549	47.6
32 Soloman G. Haven (W)	6,613	55.2
Stevens (D)	5,365	44.8
33 Augustus P. Hascall (W)	5,715	60.7
Sprague (D)	3,699	39.3
34 Lorenzo Burrows (W)	5,753	51.9
Piper (D)	5,332	48.1

OHIO

	Votes	%
1 David T. Disney (D)	16,640	99.3
2 Lewis D. Campbell (W)	5,992	53.2
Elijah Vance (D)	5,279	46.8
3 Hiram Bell (W)	8,014	53.1
George B. Holt (D)	7,088	46.9
4 Benjamin Stanton (W)	8,110	60.0
John A. Corwin (D)	5,181	38.3
5 Alfred P. Edgerton (D)	7,684	59.2
James W. Riley (W)	5,281	40.7
6 Frederick W. Green (D)	7,224	91.8
John C. Spink	609	7.7

OHIO

	Candidates	Votes	%
7	Nelson Barrere (W)	5,515	51.4
	Enoch M. Ellsberry (D)	5,219	48.6
8	John L. Taylor (W)	5,850	51.9
	Joseph McCormick (D)	5,321	47.2
9	Edson B. Olds (D)	6,283	50.7
	P. Van Trump (W)	6,110	49.3
10	Charles Sweetser (D)	8,579	50.4
	Samuel Galloway (W)	8,442	49.6
11	George H. Busby (D)	7,615	58.6
	Thomas H. Ford (W)	5,037	38.8
12	John Welch (W)	5,261	54.9
	Hiram G. Daniels (D)	4,037	42.1
13	James M. Gaylord (D)	5,744	49.3
	William E. Finck (W)	5,698	48.9
14	Alexander Harper (W)	5,108	50.2
	Thomas Maxfield (D)	4,750	46.7
15	William F. Hunter (W)	5,751	51.1
	Thomas L. Jewett (D)	5,506	48.9
16	John Johnson (W)	5,458	51.4
	Moses Hoagland (D)	5,156	48.6
17	Joseph Cable (D)	6,685	55.8
	Matthew Roberts (W)	5,303	44.2
18	David K. Carter (D)	5,754	62.3
	John Brown (W)	3,477	37.7
19	Eben Newton (W)	8,277	56.5
	Luther Day (D)	6,382	43.5
20	Joshua R. Giddings (F SOIL W)	6,896	77.8
	Irad Kelley	1,716	19.4
21	Norton S. Townshend (D)	6,677	47.6
	Samuel T. Worcester (W)	6,230	44.4
	Joseph Root (F SOIL)	1,120	8.0

PENNSYLVANIA

	Candidates	Votes	%
1	Thomas B. Florence (D)	5,352	52.9
	Levin (AM)	4,164	41.1
	Savery (W)	609	6.0
2	Joseph R. Chandler (W)	5,912	60.7
	Martin (D)	3,714	38.1
3	Henry D. Moore (W)	5,604	51.2
	Lundy (D)	5,333	48.8

	Candidates	Votes	%
4	John Robbins Jr (D)	6,173	57.6
	Littell (W)	4,554	42.5
5	John McNair (D)	5,925	53.3
	Freedley (W)	5,199	46.7
6	Thomas Ross (D)	7,568	50.8
	Taylor (W)	7,328	49.2
7	John A. Morrison (D)	4,671	50.4
	Dickey (W)	4,601	49.6
8	Thaddeus Stevens (W)	5,701	58.4
	Unindentified Candidate (D)	4,069	41.7
9	J. Glancey Jones (D)	5,377	52.6
	Keim (W)	4,847	47.4
10	Milo M. Dimmick (D)	6,400	94.1
11	Henry M. Fuller (W)	6,216	50.2
	Wright (D)	6,157	49.8
12	Galusha A. Grow (D)	6,880	54.6
	Adams (W)	5,730	45.4
13	James Gamble (D)	6,832	52.5
	Armstrong (W)	6,172	47.5
14	Thomas M. Bibighaus (W)	7,048	53.6
	Boas (D)	6,095	46.4
15	William H. Kurtz (D)	5,765	51.8
	Smyser (W)	5,372	48.2
16	James X. McLanahan (D)	7,276	52.0
	Bard (W)	6,705	48.0
17	Andrew Parker (D)	7,270	51.4
	McCulloch (W)	6,863	48.6
18	John L. Dawson (D)	6,404	51.1
	Ogle (W)	6,135	48.9
19	Joseph H. Kuhns (W)	5,745	42.4
	Unindentified Candidate (D)	4,688	34.6
	McKinney (D)	1,716	12.7
	McDonald (D)	1,391	10.3
20	John Allison (W)	5,596	50.5
	Power (D)	5,489	49.5
21	Thomas M. Howe (W)	5,406	51.6
	Salisbery (D)	4,247	40.5
	Cullen (NAM)	539	5.1
22	John W. Howe (W)	6,284	51.7
	Shatk (D)	5,882	48.4
23	Carlton B. Curtis (D)	6,522	50.4
	Walker (W)	6,416	49.6
24	Alfred Gilmore (D)	6,513	53.6
	Taylor (W)	5,644	46.4

Special Election

	Candidates	Votes	%
15	Joel B. Danner (D)	5,970	53.5
	W. McIlwain (W)	5,193	46.5

SOUTH CAROLINA

	Candidates	Votes	%
1	Daniel Wallace (W)		100.0
2	James L. Orr (D)		100.0
3	Joseph A. Woodward (D)		100.0
4	John McQueen (D)		100.0
5	Armistead Burt (D)		100.0
6	William Aiken (D)	1,928	59.2
	Isaac E. Holmes (D)	1,097	33.7
	J. Smith Rhett	232	7.1
7	William F. Colcock (D)		100.0

VERMONT

	Candidates	Votes	%
1	A. L. Miner (W)	4,369	37.5
	A. P. Lyman (W)	4,126	35.4
	D. Roberts Jr (D)	2,689	23.1
2	William Hebard (W)	5,652	55.2
	Jefferson P. Kidder (D)	4,384	42.8
3	James Meacham (W)	5,945	56.5
	Beardsley (D)	2,960	28.1
	Harrington (OPP)	1,521	14.5
4	Thomas Bartlett Jr (D)	7,009	54.9
	B. N. Davis (W)	5,014	39.2
	Willard (OPP)	640	5.0

WISCONSIN

	Candidates	Votes	%
1	Charles Durkee (F SOIL)	7,512	57.4
	Elme (D)	5,574	42.6
2	Ben C. Eastman (D)	7,262	55.4
	Cole (W)	5,852	44.6
3	James Duane Doty (F SOIL)	11,159	67.5
	Hobt (D)	5,372	32.5

1851 House Elections

ALABAMA

	Candidates	Votes	%
1	John Bragg (SO RTS D)	5,372	58.3
	C. C. Langdon (UNT)	3,849	41.7
2	James Abercrombie (UN W)	7,598	56.2
	John Cochran (SEC)	5,911	43.8
3	Sampson W. Harris (SEC D)	4,967	53.1
	W. S. Mudd (UN W)	4,385	46.9
4	William R. Smith (UNT)	4,173	50.4
	John Erwin (SO RTS D)	4,114	49.6
5	George S. Houston (UN D)	✔	
	D. Hubbard (SEC D)		
6	Williamson R. W. Cobb (UN D)	3,708	74.0
	Robert Murphy (SO RTS D)	1,303	26.0
7	Alexander White (UN W)	5,744	51.7
	S. F. Rice (SEC D)	5,371	48.3

ARKANSAS

		Votes	%
AL	Robert W. Johnson (D)	11,970	57.4
	Preston (W)	8,877	42.6

CALIFORNIA

		Votes	%
AL	Edward C. Marshall (D)	24,469✔	
	Joseph W. McCorkle (D)	24,315✔	
	E. J. C. Kewew (W)	21,460	
	B. J. Moore (W)	20,224	

CONNECTICUT

		Votes	%
1	Charles Chapman (W)	7,805	48.8
	Loren P. Waldo (D)	7,759	48.5
2	Colin M. Ingersoll (D)	7,331	50.1
	Babcock (W)	6,786	46.3
3	Chauncey F. Cleveland (D)	6,261	51.0
	Ames (W)	5,810	47.3
4	Origen S. Seymour (D)	8,633	49.3
	Butler (W)	8,485	48.4

GEORGIA

		Votes	%
1	Joseph W. Jackson (SOR W)	4,279	51.6
	Hopkins (UN)	4,011	48.4
2	James Johnson (UN)	8,107	53.7
	Bening (SOR W)	6,985	46.3
3	David J. Bailey (SOR W)	6,011	50.7
	Chappel (UN)	5,853	49.3
4	Charles Murphey (UN)	7,750	58.1
	Stell (SOR W)	5,601	42.0
5	Elijah W. Chastain (UN)	13,882	65.0
	Stiles (SOR W)	7,481	35.0
6	Junius Hillyer (UN)	6,937	71.1
	Jones (SOR W)	2,819	28.9
7	Alexander H. Stephens (UN)	4,744	70.8
	Lewis (SOR W)	1,955	29.2
8	Robert Toombs (UN)	4,704	65.0
	McMillan (SOR W)	2,538	35.1

INDIANA

		Votes	%
1	James Lockhart (D)	8,173	51.0
	Lemuel Debruler (W)	7,855	49.0
2	Cyrus L. Dunham (D)	8,097	53.2
	Roger Martin (W)	7,125	46.8
3	John L. Robinson (D)	8,242	50.2
	Johnson Watts (W)	8,173	49.8
4	Samuel W. Parker (W)	5,102	52.9
	George W. Julian (F SOIL)	4,540	47.1
5	Thomas A. Hendricks (D)	9,062	62.1
	William P. Rush (W)	5,543	38.0
6	Willis A. Gorman (D)	9,474	66.9
	Eli P. Farmer (W)	4,693	33.1
7	John G. Davis (D)	6,076	51.1
	Edward W. McGaughey (W)	5,814	48.9

	Candidates	Votes	%
8	Daniel Mace (D)	7,552	50.8
	David Brier (W)	7,294	49.0
9	Graham N. Fitch (D)	9,356	50.6
	Schuyler Colfax (W)	9,118	49.4
10	Samuel Brenton (W FS)	8,776	50.9
	James W. Borden (D)	8,483	49.2

KENTUCKY

		Votes	%
1	Linn Boyd (D)	6,638	57.5
	H. M. McCarty (W)	3,446	29.9
	Hiram McElroy	1,460	12.7
2	Benjamin E. Grey (W)	5,751	63.5
	Jeff Jennings	3,301	36.5
3	Presley U. Ewing (W)	5,405	52.1
	Beverly L. Clarke	4,978	47.9
4	William T. Ward (W)	4,582	100.0
5	James W. Stone (D)	5,843	51.6
	C. S. Hill	5,480	48.4
6	Addison White (W)	5,846	56.6
	Theodore T. Garrard	4,130	40.0
7	Humphrey Marshall (W)	6,333	50.5
	David Merriwether	6,216	49.5
8	John C. Breckinridge (D)	5,671	52.5
	Leslie Combs (W)	5,141	47.6
9	John C. Mason (D)	5,929	72.1
	Samuel Montgomery (W)	2,236	27.2
10	Richard Stanton (D)	7,649	53.6
	William C. Marshall (W)	6,622	46.4

LOUISIANA

		Votes	%
1	Louis St.Martin (D)	3,199	53.7
	Hagan (W)	2,763	46.3
2	J. Aristide Landry (W)	5,933	56.9
	Vanwinder (D)	4,500	43.1
3	Alexander G. Penn (D)	4,740	56.9
	Upton (W)	3,590	43.1
4	John Moore (W)	5,852	52.9
	Isaac E. Morse (D)	5,214	47.1

MARYLAND

		Votes	%
1	Richard J. Bowie (W)	✔	
	T. F. Bowie (D)		
2	William T. Hamilton (D)	6,863	50.9
	Roman (W)	6,626	49.1
3	Edward Hammond (D)	5,434	64.7
	Lynch (I)	2,968	35.3
4	Thomas Yates Walsh (W)	6,683	50.9
	William P. Whyte (D)	6,453	49.1
5	Alexander Evans (W)	4,992	52.7
	McCullough (D)	4,486	47.3
6	Joseph S. Cottman (IW)	✔	
	Henry (W)		

MISSISSIPPI

		Votes	%
1	Benjamin D. Nabers (UN)	9,659	57.5
	Thompson (SR)	7,155	42.6
2	John A. Wilcox (UN)	6,927	52.8
	Unidentified Candidate (SR)	6,201	47.2
3	John D. Freeman (UN)	7,774	51.8
	Unidentified Candidate (SR)	7,241	48.2
4	Albert G. Brown (SR)	7,010	57.8
	Dawson (UN)	5,119	42.2

NEW HAMPSHIRE

		Votes	%
1	Amos Tuck (W FS)	7,691	51.3
	Kittredge (D)	7,304	48.7
2	Charles H. Peaslee (D)	7,170	55.0
	Colby (W)	3,803	29.2
	Fowler (F SOIL)	2,060	15.8

	Candidates	Votes	%
3	Jared Perkins (W FS)	8,682	52.9
	Morrison (D)	7,741	47.1
4	Harry Hibbard (D)	5,125	61.1
	Kittredge (W)	2,248	26.8
	White (F SOIL)	1,018	12.1

NORTH CAROLINA

		Votes	%
1	Thomas L. Clingman (SEC W)	6,600	70.1
	Burgess S. Gaither (W)	2,819	29.9
2	Joseph P. Caldwell (W)	✔	
3	Alfred Dockery (W)	5,344	55.6
	Green W. Caldwell (D)	4,260	44.4
4	James T. Morehead (W)	2,512	86.4
5	Abraham W. Venable (SEC D)	4,057	60.0
	Calvin Graves (UN D)	2,710	40.1
6	John R. J. Daniel (SEC D)	2,815	72.1
	Henry W. Miller (W)	928	23.8
7	William S. Ashe (D)	✔	
8	Edward Stanly (W)	5,236	51.3
	Thomas Ruffin (SEC D)	4,966	48.7
9	David Outlaw (W)	2,868	61.6
	William F. Martin (D)	1,759	37.8

PENNSYLVANIA

Special Election

		Votes	%
11	John Brisbin (D)	3,625	52.5
	Dana (W)	3,283	47.5

RHODE ISLAND

		Votes	%
1	George G. King (W)	3,486	51.2
	Welcome B. Sayles (D)	3,270	48.0
2	Benjamin B. Thurston (D)	3,335	59.6
	Charles Jackson (W)	2,150	38.4

TENNESSEE

		Votes	%
1	Andrew Johnson (D)	6,538	57.4
	Hayns (D)	4,844	42.6
2	Albert G. Watkins (W)	9,592	81.9
	Hurley (W)	2,125	18.1
3	William M. Churchwell (D)	6,674	50.1
	Anderson (W)	6,658	49.9
4	John H. Savage (D)	5,816	57.2
	Goodpasture (W)	4,352	42.8
5	George W. Jones (D)	5,937	100.0
6	William H. Polk (W)	4,228	53.5
	James H. Thomas (D)	3,672	46.5
7	Meredith P. Gentry (W)	2,572	100.0
8	William Cullom (W)	5,196	55.6
	South (D)	4,145	44.4
9	Isham G. Harris (D)	3,654	56.2
	Hornberger (W)	2,852	43.8
10	Frederick P. Stanton (D)	6,495	51.8
	Coleman (W)	6,042	48.2
11	Christopher H. Williams (W)	10,693	100.0

TEXAS

		Votes	%
1	Richardson Scurry (D)	6,758	53.9
	William B. Ochiltree (W)	4,009	32.0
	B. R. Wallace	1,126	9.0
2	Volney E. Howard (D)	6,724	48.7
	G. K. Lewis	2,904	21.0
	H. McLeod	2,798	20.3
	H. N. Patter	1,200	8.7

VIRGINIA

		Votes	%
1	John S. Millson (D)	2,271	59.6
	Cowper (W)	1,541	40.4

VIRGINIA

Candidates	Votes	%
2 Richard K. Meade (D)		100.0
3 Thomas H. Averett (D)	1,365	57.4
Flournoy (W)	1,014	42.6
4 Thomas S. Bocock (D)	1,596	61.2
Bolling (W)	1,014	38.9
5 Paulus Powell (D)	2,857	51.5
Goggin (W)	2,695	48.5

Candidates	Votes	%
6 John S. Caskie (D)	2,960	54.5
Botts (W)	2,472	45.5
7 Thomas H. Bayly (D)		100.0
8 Alexander R. Holladay (D)		100.0
9 James F. Strother (W)	2,367	55.9
Mton (D)	1,868	44.1
10 Charles J. Faulkner (W)	2,351	53.7
Bedinger (D)	2,031	46.4

Candidates	Votes	%
11 John Letcher (D)		100.0
12 Henry A. Edmundson (D)		100.0
13 Fayette McMullen (D)		100.0
14 James M. H. Beale (D)	4,012	58.8
Smith (W)	2,813	41.2
15 George W. Thompson (D)	4,251	52.5
Haymond (W)	3,850	47.5

1852 House Elections

ARKANSAS

Candidates	Votes	%
1 Alfred B. Greenwood (D)	7,939	100.0
2 Edward A. Warren (D)	3,748	53.2
Unidentified Candidate (W)	3,301	46.8

CALIFORNIA

AL Milton S. Latham (D)	39,881✔	
James A. McDougall (D)	39,387✔	
P. L. Edwards (W)	34,933	
G. B. Tingley (W)	34,299	

DELAWARE

AL George Read Riddle (D)	6,692	50.2
John W. Houston (W)	6,630	49.8

FLORIDA

AL Augustus E. Maxwell (D)	4,637	50.3
Cabell (W)	4,587	49.7

ILLINOIS

1 Elihu B. Washburne (W)	7,392	43.9
Thompson Campbell (D)	7,106	42.2
Newman Campbell (F SOIL)	2,245	13.3
2 John Wentworth (D)	7,538	46.7
Cyrus Aldrich (W)	6,437	39.9
James H. Collins (F SOIL)	2,149	13.3
3 Jesse O. Norton (W)	8,268	46.0
William Reddick (D)	8,092	45.0
J. H. Bryant (F SOIL)	1,603	8.9
4 James Knox (W)	9,871	47.4
Lewis W. Rop (D)	9,684	46.5
L. W. Curtis (F SOIL)	1,290	6.2
5 William A. Richardson (D)	9,018	51.6
O. H. Browning (W)	8,397	48.1
6 Richard Yates (W)	10,105	51.1
John Calhoun (D)	9,675	48.9
7 James C. Allen (D)	8,283	54.1
Charles H. Constable (W)	7,005	45.8
8 William H. Bissell (ID)	5,937	39.8
Joseph Gillespie (W)	4,683	31.4
T. B. Fouke (D)	4,301	28.8
9 Willis Allen (D)	12,100	98.5

INDIANA

1 Smith Miller (D)	9,007	59.0
Kea (W)	6,252	41.0
2 William H. English (D)	8,654	55.0
Fergason (W)	7,094	45.1
3 Cyrus L. Dunham (D)	8,911	52.8
Marshall (W)	7,980	47.2
4 James H. Lane (D)	8,783	53.0
Farquhar (W)	7,789	47.0
5 Samuel W. Parker (W)	7,181	53.9
Grose (D)	6,153	46.2
6 Thomas A. Hendricks (D)	8,240	53.6
Bradley (W)	7,135	46.4
7 John G. Davis (D)	8,607	56.3
Barbour (W)	6,685	43.7
8 Daniel Mace (D)	8,740	54.4
Gregory (W)	7,337	45.6
9 Norman Eddy (D)	8,038	53.7
Biddle (W)	6,930	46.3
10 Ebenezer M. Chamberlain (D)	6,875	53.5
Brenton (W)	5,966	46.5
11 Andrew J. Harlan (D)	7,779	54.1
Wallace (W)	6,608	45.9

IOWA

Candidates	Votes	%
1 Bernhart Henn (D)	9,709	55.2
P. Veile (W)	7,874	44.8
2 John P. Cook (W)	7,777	52.2
L. Clark (D)	7,114	47.8

KENTUCKY

Special Election

7 William Preston (W)	6,560	57.5
Calvin Sanders (D)	4,841	42.5

MAINE

1 Moses MacDonald (D)	9,218	57.8
Appleton (W)	5,333	33.4
Fessenden (F SOIL)	1,358	8.5
2 Samuel Mayall (D)	9,917	52.6
Gilman (W)	7,932	42.0
3 E. Wilder Farley (W)	5,255	36.4
Kimball (D)	4,724	32.7
Smith (D)	3,874	26.8
4 Samuel P. Benson (W)	8,708	54.4
Porter (D)	5,433	33.9
May (F SOIL)	1,580	9.9
5 Israel Washburn Jr (W)	8,227	51.1
Strickland (D)	4,376	27.2
Waterhouse (D)	3,444	21.4
6 Thomas J. D. Fuller (D)	6,283	52.6
Robinson (W)	5,280	44.2

MASSACHUSETTS

1 Zeno Scudder (W)	4,016	61.3
A. H. Howland	2,368	36.2
2 Samuel L. Crocker (W)	3,599	45.8
Geishom Weston (F SOIL)	3,455	44.0
M. Ide (D)	738	9.4
3 J. Wiley Edmands (W)	3,416	48.5
Charles F. Adams (F SOIL)	2,978	42.3
Arthur W. Austin (D)	471	6.7
4 Samuel H. Walley (W)	4,290	60.5
Levi A. Dowley (D)	1,745	24.6
Charles M. Ellis (F SOIL)	1,028	14.5
5 William Appleton (W)	4,672	55.7
Adam W. Thasler Jr. (D)	2,081	24.8
Anson Burlingame (F SOIL)	1,550	18.5
6 Charles W. Upham (W)	4,265	46.6
George Hood (F SOIL)	4,096	44.8
Nathaniel J. Lord	532	5.8
7 Nathaniel P. Banks (D)	4,605	50.1
Luther V. Bell (W)	4,300	46.8
8 Tappan Wentworth (W)	4,411	45.9
Henry Wilson (F SOIL)	4,319	44.9
Benjamin F. Butler (D)	481	5.0
9 Alexander De Witt (F SOIL)	4,039	41.3
Isaac Davis (D)	2,925	29.9
Ira M. Barton (W)	2,796	28.6
10 Edward Dickinson (W)	4,160	56.9
Samuel F. Cutler (D)	1,625	22.2
Eustus Hopkins (F SOIL)	1,507	20.6
11 John Z. Goodrich (W)	5,579	51.9
Whiting Griswold (D)	4,842	45.1

Special Elections

2 Francis Fay (W)	4,989	47.2
George Hood (F SOIL)	4,821	45.6
4 Lorenzo Labine (W)	4,620	50.9
John A. Bolles (F SOIL)	4,055	44.7
9 Edward P. Little (D)	3,711	50.4
Jacob H. Loud (W)	3,595	48.8

MICHIGAN

Candidates	Votes	%
1 David Stuart (D)	10,127	50.4
William A. Howard (W)	9,370	46.6
2 David A. Noble (D)	10,024	51.7
Joseph R. Williams (W FS)	9,367	48.3
3 Samuel Clark (D)	10,765	49.2
Henry R. Williams (W)	9,969	45.6
4 Hestor L. Stevens (D)	10,746	51.8
George Bradley (W)	8,948	43.1
Ephraim Calkins (F SOIL)	1,048	5.1

MISSOURI[1]

1 Thomas H. Benton (BENTON D)	8,437	45.3
Car (W)	7,595	40.7
Bogy (A-BEN D)	2,615	14.0
2 Alfred W. Lamb (D)	7,007	53.0
Por (W)	6,224	47.0
3 John G. Miller (W)	8,297	51.3
Green (D)	7,869	48.7
4 Mordecai Oliver (W)	7,612	46.7
Unidentified Candidate (A-BEN D)	4,452	27.3
King (BENTON D)	4,243	26.0
5 John S. Phelps (D)	11,392	67.6
Price (W)	5,458	32.4

NEW JERSEY

1 Nathan T. Stratton (D)	7,185	51.3
Boyle (W)	6,816	48.7
2 Charles Skelton (D)	10,229	52.6
Brown (W)	9,238	47.5
3 Samuel Lilly (D)	10,193	55.1
Brown (W)	8,315	44.9
4 George Vail (D)	9,247	59.6
Coursen (W)	6,265	40.4
5 Alexander C. M. Pennington (W)	7,636	50.6
Price (D)	7,469	49.5

NEW YORK

1 James Maurice (D)	7,801	53.7
King (W)	6,136	42.3
2 Thomas W. Cumming (D)	7,228	51.5
Sanford (W)	6,789	48.4
3 Hiram Walbridge (D)	5,814	54.4
Bowen (W)	4,797	44.9
4 Mike Walsh (D)	4,802	52.9
Hawes (W)	2,564	28.2
Kly (D)	1,712	18.9
5 William M. Tweed (D)	5,394	51.6
Hoxie (W)	4,243	40.6
Mor (W)	818	7.8
6 John Wheeler (D)	6,354	54.4
Varnum (W)	5,243	44.9
7 William A. Walker (D)	5,801	52.1
Roberts (W)	4,702	42.2
8 Francis B. Cutting (D)	4,414	56.5
Brooks (W)	3,398	43.5
9 Jared V. Peck (D)	8,533	59.4
Clark (W)	5,827	40.6
10 William Murray (D)	7,768	54.8
Farnham (W)	6,407	45.2
11 Theodore R. Westbrook (D)	9,092	53.5
Smith (W)	7,902	46.5
12 Gilbert Dean (D)	9,937	50.4
Cruger (W)	9,798	49.7
13 Russell Sage (W)	6,583	51.0
Seyr (D)	6,185	47.9
14 Rufus W. Peckham (D)	8,363	53.5
Egberts (W)	7,190	46.0
15 Charles Hughes (D)	9,988	49.5
Northrup (W)	9,693	48.0

1. Missouri's House representation rose from five seats to seven following the 1850 reapportionment, but elections to the two additional seats were not held in time for the regular 1852 election. Instead, they were held in 1853. See Missouri 1853, p. 753.

NEW YORK

	Candidates	Votes	%
16	George A. Simmons (W)	7,093	50.9
	Ireland (D)	6,852	49.1
17	Bishop Perkins (D)	10,085	53.2
	Vanrenr (W)	7,274	38.4
	Reddington (F SOIL)	1,601	8.4
18	Peter Rowe (D)	10,916	52.1
	Miller (W)	10,057	48.0
19	George W. Chase (W)	9,550	54.3
	Gordon (D)	8,034	45.7
20	Orsamus B. Matteson (W)	8,530	50.2
	Mouln (D)	6,600	38.9
	Spen (W)	1,542	9.1
21	Henry Bennett (W)	9,876	49.9
	Smith (D)	9,534	48.2
22	Gerrit Smith (ULTRA AB)	8,049	40.5
	Hoh (D)	6,206	31.2
	Tenck (W)	5,620	28.3
23	Caleb Lyon (IW)	8,937	53.1
	Mundy (D)	7,891	46.9
24	Daniel T. Jones (D)	6,605	46.6
	Gott (W)	6,120	43.2
	Ray (F SOIL)	1,458	10.3
25	Edwin B. Morgan (W)	9,150	47.4
	How (D)	8,996	46.6
	Cuyler (F SOIL)	1,147	6.0
26	Andrew Oliver (D)	8,546	49.2
	Woods (W)	8,529	49.1
27	John J. Taylor (D)	9,426	50.4
	Cook (W)	8,410	45.0
28	George Hastings (D)	10,681	53.7
	Irvine (W)	9,225	46.3
29	Azariah Boody (W)	7,290	50.2
	Field (D)	6,578	45.3
30	Benjamin Pringle (W)	9,386	48.7
	Sherman (W)	8,903	46.2
	Landon (F SOIL)	976	5.1
31	Thomas T. Flagler (W)	5,858	46.0
	Woods (D)	5,508	43.3
	Murphy (F SOIL)	1,358	10.7
32	Solomon G. Haven (W)	8,037	51.8
	Verk (D)	7,054	45.4
33	Reuben E. Fenton (D)	8,717	48.8
	Crooker (W)	8,661	48.5

OHIO

	Candidates	Votes	%
1	David T. Disney (D)	5,852	57.1
	Cassilly (W)	4,317	42.1
2	John Scott Harrison (W)	4,780	54.5
	Roll (D)	3,849	43.9
3	Lewis D. Campbell (W)	8,680	50.4
	Vallandigham (D)	8,533	49.6
4	Matthias H. Nichols (D)	7,648	53.8
	Plunkett (W)	6,378	44.9
5	Alfred P. Edgerton (D)	9,072	66.1
	Parker (W)	4,561	33.2
6	Andrew Ellison (D)	7,479	50.6
	Barrere (W)	7,208	48.7
7	Aaron Harlan (W)	7,580	54.7
	Telfair (D)	5,018	36.2
	Nix (F SOIL)	1,252	9.0
8	Moses B. Corwin (W)	8,561	57.9
	Young (D)	5,780	39.1

	Candidates	Votes	%
9	Fred W. Green (D)	8,198	74.1
	Goodman (W)	2,095	18.9
	Sam (F SOIL)	768	6.9
10	John L. Taylor (W)	7,653	53.1
	Sherer (D)	6,763	46.9
11	Thomas Ritchey (D)	9,037	56.3
	Welch (W)	6,681	41.7
12	Edson B. Olds (D)	8,549	49.2
	Galloway (W)	8,480	48.8
13	William D. Lindsley (D)	6,739	44.4
	Saddler (W)	6,035	39.8
	Jacob Brinkerhoff (F SOIL)	2,390	15.8
14	Harvey H. Johnson (D)	7,591	49.3
	Lockwood (W)	4,763	31.0
	Norton S. Townshend (F SOIL)	3,030	19.7
15	William R. Sapp (W)	6,140	38.8
	William Winnell (D)	6,109	38.6
	Rich (F SOIL)	2,650	16.8
	Vance	924	5.8
16	Edward Ball (W)	7,161	52.3
	Gaylord (D)	6,347	46.3
17	Wilson Shannon (D)	7,142	54.1
	Hollister (W)	6,054	45.9
18	George Bliss (D)	6,140	46.7
	Lyman (W)	5,307	40.3
	Earl (F SOIL)	1,708	13.0
19	Edward Wade (F SOIL)	5,274	40.5
	Case (W)	4,046	31.0
	Wilson (D)	3,715	28.5
20	Joshua R. Giddings (F SOIL)	5,752	40.1
	Woods (D)	4,427	30.8
	Newton (W)	4,179	29.1
21	Andrew Stuart (D)	7,423	47.8
	Brewer (W)	6,885	44.3
	Lee (F SOIL)	1,220	7.9

PENNSYLVANIA

	Candidates	Votes	%
1	Thomas B. Florence (D)	4,937	44.5
	Price (W)	3,200	28.9
	Levin (NAM)	2,953	26.6
2	Joseph R. Chandler (W)	6,594	62.4
	Ham (D)	3,556	33.7
3	John Robbins Jr (D)	5,857	51.5
	Sanderson (W)	3,300	29.0
	Painter (NAM)	2,206	19.4
4	William H. Witte (D)	5,843	46.9
	Lambert (W)	4,546	36.5
	Cornman (NAM)	2,065	16.6
5	John McNair (D)	7,168	50.9
	Hitner (W)	6,336	45.0
6	William Everhart (W)	7,641	54.2
	Mur (D)	6,464	45.8
7	Samuel A. Bridges (D)	8,339	52.7
	Taylor (W)	7,486	47.3
8	Henry A. Muhlenberg (D)	7,543	68.5
	Beiber (W)	3,476	31.6
9	Isaac E. Heister (W)	8,840	57.8
	Samp (D)	6,456	42.2
10	Ner Middleswarth (W)	7,921	55.8
	Seir (D)	6,278	44.2
11	Christian M. Straub (D)	5,729	51.5
	Krebs (W)	5,388	48.5

	Candidates	Votes	%
12	Hendrick B. Wright (D)	7,523	50.6
	Fuller (W)	7,350	49.4
13	Asa Packer (D)	8,909	74.6
	Foster (W)	3,035	25.4
14	Galusha A. Grow (D)	8,062	94.2
	Horton (W)	495	5.8
15	James Gamble (D)	8,742	59.2
	Irwin (W)	6,026	40.8
16	William H. Kurtz (D)	9,513	56.6
	Biddle (W)	7,306	43.4
17	Samuel L. Russell (W)	9,216	51.0
	Danr (D)	8,845	49.0
18	John McCulloch (W)	7,847	56.2
	Shaffr (D)	6,112	43.8
19	Augustus Drum (D)	7,968	57.2
	Kuhns (W)	5,959	42.8
20	John L. Dawson (D)	9,791	56.8
	Gow (W)	7,460	43.2
21	David Ritchie (W)	4,939	52.2
	Shan (D)	4,532	47.9
22	Thomas M. Howe (W)	4,620	54.8
	Gibn (D)	3,817	45.2
23	Michael C. Trout (D)	5,369	45.6
	Alln (W)	5,340	45.4
	Unidentified Candidate (F SOIL)	1,056	9.0
24	Carlton B. Curtis (D)	8,321	65.5
	Kerr (W)	4,375	34.5
25	John Dick (W)	6,057	54.8
	Cutr (D)	4,049	36.6
	Unidentified Candidate (F SOIL)	951	8.6

VERMONT

	Candidates	Votes	%
1	James Meacham (W)	7,138	56.5
	Pierpoint (F SOIL)	2,801	22.2
	Tucke (D)	2,704	21.4
2	Andrew Tracy (W)	9,319	52.2
	Daniel Kellogg (D)	3,261	18.3
	Isaac Fletcher (F SOIL)	2,928	16.4
	Hugh H. Henry (D)	1,675	9.4
3	Alvah Sabin (W)	5,706	48.3
	Heyward (D)	3,803	32.2
	Kasson (F SOIL)	2,294	19.4

VIRGINIA

Special Election

		Votes	%
15	Sherrard Clemens (D)	✔	

WISCONSIN

	Candidates	Votes	%
1	Daniel Wells Jr (D)	8,342	46.5
	Dur (F SOIL)	5,731	31.9
	Dur (W)	3,870	21.6
2	Ben C. Eastman (D)	10,893	53.9
	Abbott (W)	7,816	38.7
	Enos (F SOIL)	1,506	7.5
3	John B. Macy (D)	14,596	55.6
	Shafter (W)	9,513	36.2
	McKee (F SOIL)	2,168	8.3

1853 House Elections

ALABAMA

	Candidates	Votes	%
1	Philip Phillips (SO RTS D)	4,880	50.5
	E. Lockwood (UN W)	4,777	49.5
2	James Abercrombie (UN W)	7,474	56.1
	D. Clopton (D)	5,838	43.9
3	Sampson W. Harris (SO RTS D)	6,394	79.8
	Moore (UN W)	1,622	20.2
4	William R. Smith (UN D)	3,045	34.7
	Sydenham Moore (SO RTS D)	2,974	33.8
	S. F. Hale (W)	2,769	31.5
5	George S. Houston (D)	4,022	95.0
6	Williamson R. W. Cobb (UN D)	5,221	58.2
	C. C. Clay Jr. (D)	3,744	41.8
7	James F. Dowdell (SO RTS D)	6,098	65.6
	T. G. Garrett (IUN W)	3,200	34.4

CONNECTICUT

		Votes	%
1	James T. Pratt (D)	8,225	52.3
	Charles Chapman (W)	6,963	44.2
2	Colin M. Ingersoll (D)	8,551	53.1
	Austin Baldwin (W)	6,773	42.0
3	Nathan Belcher (D)	6,129	51.8
	Daniel P. Tyler (W)	3,906	33.0
	Albert G. Stark (F SOIL)	1,800	15.2
4	Origen S. Seymour (D)	8,700	54.2
	William W. Welch (W)	7,249	45.2

GEORGIA

		Votes	%
1	James L. Seward (D)	4,429	51.1
	Barton (W)	4,238	48.9
2	Alfred H. Colquitt (D)	6,795	52.1
	Johnson (W)	6,249	47.9
3	David J. Bailey (D)	5,232	50.0
	Robert P. Trippe (W)	5,227	50.0
4	William B. W. Dent (D)	6,701	51.3
	Calhoun (W)	6,368	48.7
5	Elijah W. Chastain (D)	8,118	50.8
	Tumlin (D)	7,866	49.2
6	Junius Hillyer (D)	5,439	64.8
	Wofld (D)	2,954	35.2
7	David A. Reese (W)	4,997	56.3
	Saffold (D)	3,883	43.7
8	Alexander H. Stephens (W)	5,634	69.7
	Jones (D)	2,444	30.3

KENTUCKY

		Votes	%
1	Linn Boyd (D)	7,585	57.6
	Jefferson Brown (ID)	5,590	42.4
2	Ben E. Grey (W)	7,076	52.5
	W. J. Davie (D)	6,408	47.5
3	Presley Ewing (W)	5,318	100.0
4	James S. Crisman (D)	5,657	50.2
	Thomas E. Bramlette (W)	5,622	49.8
5	Clement S. Hill (W)	6,126	50.5
	James W. Stone (D)	5,996	49.5
6	John M. Elliott (D)	6,257	53.8
	Jeremiah S. Pierce (W)	5,376	46.2
7	William Preston (W)	6,609	57.7
	S. S. English (D)	4,847	42.3
8	John C. Breckinridge (D)	6,532	52.1
	Robert P. Letcher (W)	6,006	47.9
9	Leander M. Cox (AM)	6,606	52.5
	James M. Rice (D)	5,974	47.5
10	Richard H. Stanton (D)	7,583	51.8
	George B. Hodge (W)	7,070	48.3

LOUISIANA

		Votes	%
1	William Dunbar (D)	4,550	62.8
	Gayarre (W)	2,691	37.2

	Candidates	Votes	%
2	Theodore G. Hunt (W)	6,558	54.6
	Davis (D)	5,445	45.4
3	John Perkins Jr. (D)	4,965	56.7
	Pond (W)	3,787	43.3
4	Roland Jones (D)	7,494	56.8
	Smith (W)	5,695	43.2

MARYLAND

		Votes	%
1	John R. Franklin (W)	5,815	53.1
	Stevn (I)	5,127	46.9
2	Jacob Shower(I)	7,246	53.4
	Wethered (W)	6,330	46.6
3	Joshua Vansant (ID)	5,876	53.7
	Preston (W)	5,061	46.3
4	Henry May (ID)	6,792	51.3
	Walsh (W)	6,440	48.7
5	William T. Hamilton (ID)	7,545	54.0
	Thomas (W)	6,429	46.0
6	Augustus R. Sollers (W)	3,815	61.0
	Jenr (I)	2,438	39.0

MISSISSIPPI

		Votes	%
1	Daniel B. Wright (D)	8,984	51.6
	Nabers (W)	8,414	48.4
2	William T. S. Barry (D)	7,039	50.7
	Wilcox (W)	6,837	49.3
3	Otho R. Singleton (D)	8,367	55.7
	McLung (W)	6,669	44.4
4	Wiley P. Harris (D)		100.0
AL	William Barksdale (D)	29,702	54.1
	Unidentified Candidate (W)	25,183	45.9

MISSOURI [1]

		Votes	%
3	James J. Lindley (W)	6,828	50.6
	Jackson (A-BEN D)	6,674	49.4
7	Samuel Caruthers (W)	4,447	39.8
	Jackson (BENTON D)	2,542	22.8
	English (A-BEN D)	2,424	21.7
	Rosier (BENTON D)	1,750	15.7

NEW HAMPSHIRE

		Votes	%
1	George W. Kittredge (D)	10,168	53.2
	Amos Tuck (W)	8,962	46.9
2	George W. Morrison (D)	9,050	67.5
	Hughes (W)	4,353	32.5
3	Harry Hibbard (D)	9,635	56.1
	Perkins (W)	7,556	44.0

NORTH CAROLINA

		Votes	%
1	Henry M. Shaw (D)	4,833	50.5
	David Outlaw (W)	4,746	49.6
2	Thomas Ruffin(D)	5,812	68.7
	W. C. Loftin (ID)	2,653	31.3
3	Wliam S. Ashe (D)	5,520	62.2
	Walter F. Leake (LD D)	3,351	37.8
4	Sion H. Rogers (W)	4,201	38.9
	Abraham W. Venable (LD D)	4,133	38.3
	Augustus M. Lewis (A-LD D)	2,454	22.8
5	John Kerr (W)	6,037	86.2
	Abraham Rencher (ID)	963	13.8
6	Richard C. Puryear (W)	6,173	51.6
	George D. Boyd (D)	5,788	48.4
7	F. Burton Craige (D)	5,965	51.4
	James W. Osborne (W)	5,649	48.6
8	Thomas L. Clingman (D)	7,606	59.3
	Burgess S. Gaither (W)	5,214	40.7

RHODE ISLAND

	Candidates	Votes	%
1	Thomas Davis (D)	5,524	50.8
	George G. King (W)	4,942	45.5
2	Benjamin B. Thurston (D)	4,436	90.5
	Elisha M. Aldrich (W)	450	9.2

SOUTH CAROLINA

		Votes	%
1	John McQueen (D)		100.0
2	William Aiken (D)		100.0
3	Laurence M. Keitt (D)		100.0
4	Preston S. Brooks (SSR D)	2,098	32.3
	Sullivan	1,497	23.0
	Francis W. Pickens (NULL D)	1,492	23.0
	Marshall	1,415	21.8
5	James L. Orr (D)		100.0
6	William W. Boyce (SSR D)	2,549	51.0
	Moses	2,270	45.4

TENNESSEE

		Votes	%
1	Brookins Campbell (D)	5,525*	37.1
	Nathaniel G. Taylor (W)	5,387	36.2
	Albert G. Watkins (W)	3,988	26.8
2	William M. Churchwell (D)	6,266	56.6
	Maynard (W)	4,797	43.4
3	Samuel A. Smith (D)	7,703	55.5
	Van Dyke (W)	6,180	44.5
4	William Cullom (W)	5,630	50.2
	Gardner (D)	5,593	49.8
5	Charles Ready (W)	6,143	57.3
	Barry (D)	4,577	42.7
6	George W. Jones (D)		100.0
7	Robert M. Bugg (W)	6,421	52.3
	Pavott (D)	5,865	47.7
8	Felix K. Zollicoffer (W)	5,808	53.0
	Allison (D)	5,157	47.0
9	Emerson Etheridge (W)		100.0
10	Frederick P. Stanton (D)	5,126	50.0
	Yerger (W)	5,120	50.0

TEXAS

		Votes	%
1	George M. Smyth (D)	12,126	98.8
2	Peter H. Bell (D)	5,918	41.4
	William R. Scurry (D)	2,963	20.7
	G. K. Lewis (D)	2,411	16.9
	B. F. Carothers (W)	2,126	14.9
	F. M. Blake (D)	869	6.1

VIRGINIA

		Votes	%
1	Thomas H. Bayly (D)		100.0
2	John S. Millson (D)	3,206	56.7
	Chambliss (W)	2,071	36.6
	Roberts (I)	379	6.7
3	John S. Caskie (D)	4,333	54.9
	Coleman (W)	3,561	45.1
4	William O. Goode (D)		100.0
5	Thomas S. Bocock (D)	4,304	51.7
	Wootton (D)	3,586	43.1
	Arnett (I)	428	5.2
6	Paulus Powell (D)	4,751	54.8
	Mosely (W)	3,912	45.2
7	William Smith (D)	4,223	51.8
	Snowden (W)	3,931	48.2
8	Charles J. Faulkner (D)	6,106	52.3
	Boteler (W)	5,560	47.7
9	John Letcher (D)		100.0
10	Zedekiah Kidwell (D)		100.0
11	John F. Snodgrass (D)	4,707	40.2
	Lewis (W)	4,497	38.4
	Sterrett (W)	2,506	21.4
12	Henry A. Edmonson (D)		100.0
13	Fayette McMullen (D)		100.0

1. Missouri elected two additional House members to raise its total to the seven seats allotted by the 1850 census. The state was redistricted from five seats to seven, with the new districts labeled ''3'' and ''7''. The 3rd congressional district of 1853 is not the same 3rd district that elected a representative in 1852. (See Missouri 1852, p. 751.)

1854 House Elections

ARKANSAS

	Candidates	Votes	%
1	Alfred B. Greenwood (D)	15,374	97.3
2	Albert Rust (D)	8,893	67.0
	E. G. Walker (W)	4,371	32.9

CALIFORNIA

	Candidates	Votes	%
AL	James W. Denver (A-BROD D)	36,819✔	
	Philemon T. Herbert (A-BROD D)	36,542✔	
	G. W. Bowie (W)	34,741	
	Cal Benham (W)	34,411	
	J. Churchman (BROD D)	10,006	
	J. A. Mc Dougal (BROD D)	9,968	
	M. S. Latham (BROD D)	1,843	

DELAWARE

		Votes	%
AL	Elisha D. Cullen (AM)	6,820	51.9
	George Read Riddle (D)	6,334	48.2

FLORIDA

		Votes	%
AL	Augustus Maxwell (D)	5,642	55.2
	Thomas Brown (W)	4,583	44.8

ILLINOIS

		Votes	%
1	Elihu B. Washburne (R)	8,372	69.3
	William M. Jackon (D)	2,776	23.0
	E. P. Ferry (A-NEB D)	927	7.7
2	James H. Woodworth (R)	6,927	53.1
	Robert S. Blackwell (W)	2,591	19.8
	John B. Turner (D)	2,544	19.5
	Edward L. Mayo (A-NEB D)	996	7.6
3	Jesse O. Norton (R)	10,474	62.8
	John A. Drake (D)	6,216	37.2
4	James Knox (R)	10,146	57.0
	Unidentified Candidate (D)	7,588	42.6
5	William A. Richardson (D)	8,935	52.4
	Arch Williams (R)	8,122	47.6
6	Thomas L. Harris (D)	10,090	50.5
	Richard Gates (R)	9,890	49.5
7	James C. Allen (D)	8,452‡	50.0
	William B. Archer (R)	8,451	50.0
8	Lyman Trumbull (R)	7,917*	58.1
	Philip B. Fouke (D)	5,306	38.9
9	Samuel S. Marshall (D)	8,497	64.4
	L. Jay S. Turney (R)	2,911	22.0
	Dewitt C. Barber	1,276	9.7

INDIANA

		Votes	%
1	Smith Miller (NEB D)	9,864	52.2
	Hall (R)	9,051	47.9
2	William H. English (NEB D)	8,931	51.7
	Shanter (R)	8,345	48.3
3	George G. Dunn (R)	9,989	54.5
	Dunm (NEB D)	8,329	45.5
4	William Cumback (R)	9,061	51.9
	Holn (NEB D)	8,391	48.1
5	David P. Holloway (R)	9,419	64.3
	Buckles (NEB D)	5,242	35.8
6	Lucien Barbour (R)	9,824	51.4
	Henkr (NEB D)	9,286	48.6
7	Harvey D. Scott (R)	9,515	52.6
	Davis (NEB D)	8,580	47.4
8	Daniel Mace (R)	10,357	56.9
	Davis (NEB D)	7,838	43.1
9	Schuyler Colfax (R)	9,989	54.9
	Eddy (NEB D)	8,223	45.2
10	Samuel Brenton (R)	7,485	56.0
	Chamln (NEB D)	5,881	44.0

	Candidates	Votes	%
11	John U. Pettit (R)	9,389	56.6
	Slack (NEB D)	7,201	43.4

IOWA

		Votes	%
1	Augustus Hall (D)	11,213	50.3
	R. L. B. Clark (R)	11,042	49.5
2	James Thorington (R)	11,424	53.3
	Stephen Hempstead (D)	9,872	46.1

KENTUCKY

Special Election

		Votes	%
3	Francis M. Bristow (W)	2,533	81.6
	A. J. Harberson (D)	572	18.4

MAINE

		Votes	%
1	John M. Wood (R)	9,227	59.8
	Samuel Wells (D)	6,196	40.2
2	John J. Perry (R)	10,007	57.8
	William Kimball (D)	7,313	42.2
3	Ebenezer Knowlton (R)	5,995	43.9
	J. G. Dickerson (D)	4,072	29.8
	E. W. Farley (W)	3,587	26.3
4	Samuel P. Benson (R)	11,610	77.0
	George Rogers (D)	3,467	23.0
5	Israel Washburn Jr (R)	10,224	63.0
	Samuel H. Blake (D)	6,010	37.0
6	Thomas J. D. Fuller (D)	4,713	42.4
	J. A. Milliken (R)	4,307	38.7
	N. Smith Jr. (W)	2,099	18.9

MASSACHUSETTS

		Votes	%
1	Robert B. Hall (AM)	5,353	63.3
	Thomas D. Eliot (W)	2,238	26.5
	Abraham H. Howland	812	9.6
2	James Buffington (AM)	8,074	68.2
	Samuel L. Crocker (W)	1,914	16.2
	Charles R. Vickery	1,064	9.0
	Gersham B. Weston (F SOIL)	774	6.5
3	William S. Damrell (AM)	8,668	74.4
	Nathaniel F. Safford (W)	1,933	16.6
	Edward Avery	624	5.4
4	Linus B. Comins (AM)	4,972	57.4
	Samuel H. Walley (W)	2,770	32.0
	Samuel R. Spinney	913	10.5
5	Anson Burlingame (AM)	5,967	61.5
	William Appleton (W)	3,109	32.1
	William Parmenter (D)	604	6.2
6	Timothy Davis (AM)	7,428	65.3
	Charles W. Upham (W)	3,231	28.4
	Nathaniel J. Lord	633	5.6
7	Nathaniel P. Banks (AM)	8,928	73.3
	Luther V. Bell (W)	2,481	20.4
	Bowen Bualman	724	5.9
8	Chauncy L. Knapp (AM)	7,004	62.7
	Tappan Wentworth (W)	3,556	31.8
	Daniel Needham	593	5.3
9	Alexander De Witt (AM)	8,797	77.0
	Isaac Davis (D)	1,526	13.4
	Ira M. Barton (W)	851	7.5
10	Henry Morris (AM)	7,723*	64.6
	Edward Dickinson (W)	2,757	23.1
	Stephen C. Bemis	1,338	11.2
11	Mark Trafton (AM)	6,640	50.4
	John L. Goodrich (W)	3,998	30.4
	Whiting Griswold	2,505	19.0

Special Election

		Votes	%
1	Thomas D. Eliot (W)	4,059	51.5
	Abraham Howland	3,741	47.4

MICHIGAN

	Candidates	Votes	%
1	William A. Howard (R)	9,877	53.1
	David Stuart	8,723	46.9
2	Henry Waldron (R)	11,055	57.7
	David A. Noble (D)	8,113	42.3
3	David S. Walbridge (R)	12,865	55.8
	Samuel Clark (D)	10,178	44.1
4	George W. Peck (D)	11,233	53.2
	Moses Wisner (R)	9,863	46.7

MISSOURI

		Votes	%
1	Luther M. Kennett (W)	6,259	52.4
	Benton (BENTON D)	5,298	44.4
2	Gilchrist Porter (W)	8,119	54.1
	Corneck	6,877	45.9
3	James J. Lindley (W)	8,150	52.5
	Fournoy (A-BEN D)	7,386	47.5
4	Mordecai Oliver (W)	6,129	44.1
	Leonard (A-BEN D)	4,998	35.9
	Lowe (BENTON D)	2,787	20.0
5	John G. Miller (W)	6,372*	46.2
	Price (BENTON D)	4,904	35.5
	Hough (A-BEN D)	2,530	18.3
6	John S. Phelps (A-BEN D)	8,342	51.1
	Johnson (BENTON D)	7,982	48.9
7	Samuel Caruthers (W)	8,045	58.9
	Jones (BENTON D)	5,625	41.2

NEW JERSEY

		Votes	%
1	Isaiah D. Clawson (W)	6,269	42.9
	Mulford (NEB)	4,383	30.0
	Hazltn (TEMP)	3,949	27.1
2	George R. Robbins (W)	10,539	57.6
	Rue (NEB)	7,769	42.4
3	James Bishop (W)	9,051	54.4
	Lilly (NEB)	7,603	45.7
4	George Vail (NEB)	7,281	51.7
	Osborn (A-NEB)	6,816	48.4
5	Alexander C. M. Pennington (W)	8,137	54.4
	Darey (NEB)	6,816	45.6

NEW YORK

		Votes	%
1	William W. Valk (SOFTD&AM)	3,753	28.1
	Allen (HARD D)	2,778	20.8
	Vail (W)	2,676	20.1
	Lord (SOFT D)	2,227	16.7
	Disosway (TEMP)	1,902	14.3
2	James S. T. Stranahan (W)	7,927	50.9
	Taylor (HARD D)	7,623	49.0
3	Guy R. Pelton (W & AM)	4,084	52.6
	Clinton (HARD D)	2,559	33.0
	Miner (SOFT D)	1,123	14.5
4	John Kelly (SOFT D)	3,068	36.0
	Walsh (HARD D)	3,047	35.7
	Bryle (W & AM)	1,594	18.7
	Macomber (W)	821	9.6
5	Thomas R. Whitney (W & AM)	3,321	30.9
	Andrews (W)	2,765	25.7
	Hamilton (HARD D)	2,718	25.3
	Berry (SOFT D)	1,954	18.2
6	John Wheeler (HARDD&AM)	5,101	46.3
	Murphy (SOFT D)	2,533	23.0
	Marshal (W)	2,256	20.5
	Mead (I HARD D)	1,128	10.2
7	Thomas Child Jr (W & AM)	6,557*	56.3
	Kennedy (SOFT D)	5,094	43.7
8	Abram Wakeman (W & AM)	4,895	51.2
	Curtis (HARD D)	2,969	31.1
	Fellows (SOFT D)	1,699	17.8
9	Bayard Clarke (W & AM)	7,764	61.1
	Branth (HARD D)	2,540	20.0

NEW YORK

Candidates	Votes	%
Whiting (HARD D)	2,038	16.0
10 Ambrose S. Murray (W)	5,209	44.0
Woodward (HARDD&AM)	4,574	38.6
Strtn (SOFT D)	2,053	17.4
11 Rufus H. King (W)	8,576	63.0
Strong (HARD D)	5,042	37.0
12 Killian Miller (W)	8,376	51.1
McClellan (SOFTD&AM)	5,540	33.8
Wilson (HARD D)	2,486	15.2
13 Russell Sage (W & AM)	6,954	63.2
Clum (SOFT D)	2,075	18.9
Cook (HARD D)	1,971	17.9
14 Samuel Dickson (W)	4,638	32.2
Harct (SOFTD&AM)	4,270	29.6
Pruyn (SOFT D)	3,244	22.5
Hamilton	2,255	15.7
15 Edward Dodd (W)	6,760	37.7
Clark (HARD D)	6,358	35.4
Hughes (SOFT D)	2,428	13.5
Andrews (TEMP)	2,399	13.4
16 George A. Simmons (W)	5,533	48.7
Bailey (SOFTD&AM)	3,062	26.9
Thomas (SOFT D)	1,752	15.4
Flanders (HARD D)	1,025	9.0
17 Francis E. Spinner (SOFT D)	7,618	46.5
Alexander (W)	5,357	32.7
Benton (HARD D)	3,414	20.8
18 Thomas R. Horton (W)	9,431	51.3
Jackson (HARD D)	8,945	48.7
19 Jonas A. Hughson (W)	6,744	43.3
Palmer (SOFT D)	6,444	41.3
Hawes (F SOIL)	1,339	8.6
Sturges	1,066	6.8
20 Orsamus B. Matteson (W)	6,492	38.2
Johnson (SOFT D)	5,172	30.4
Huntington (W)	4,759	28.0
21 Henry Bennett (W)	9,757	56.0
Tompkins (HARD D)	5,579	32.0
Crocker (SOFT D)	2,077	11.9
22 Andrew Z. McCarty (W)	5,535	32.2
Babcock (SOFT D)	4,728	27.5
Case (F SOIL)	3,652	21.2
Lewis (HARD D)	3,281	19.1
23 William A. Gilbert (W)	6,251	46.4
Ives (SOFT D)	5,645	41.9
Brown (HARD D)	1,513	11.2
24 Amos P. Granger (W)	4,803	37.5
Alvord (SOFT D)	4,109	32.1
Noxon (W & AM)	3,409	26.6
25 Edwin B. Morgan (W)	7,684	48.4
Midton (SOFTD&AM)	6,910	43.5
Aldrich (SOFT D)	1,296	8.2
26 Andrew Oliver (SOFTD&AM)	6,880	48.0
Seeley (W)	5,304	37.0
Howell (HARD D)	2,163	15.1
27 John M. Parker (W)	7,915	59.3
McDowell (SOFT D)	3,467	26.0
Cushing (HARD D)	1,964	14.7
28 William H. Kelsey (W & AM)	11,061	70.8
Hastings (SOFT D)	4,450	28.5
29 John Williams (SOFTD&AM)	5,609	47.9
Carpenter (W)	4,227	36.1
Sibley (HARD D)	1,865	15.9
30 Benjamin Pringle (W & AM)	9,510	57.6
Laning (SOFT D)	3,829	23.2
Belden (HARD D)	2,483	15.0
31 Thomas T. Flagler (W & AM)	7,190	76.6
Baker (HARD D)	1,231	13.1
Chase (F SOIL)	962	10.3

Candidates	Votes	%
32 Solomon G. Haven (W & AM)	9,075	62.8
Hatch (SOFT D)	5,388	37.3
33 Francis S. Edwards (W & AM)	8,359	55.6
Fenton (SOFT D)	6,442	42.8

OHIO

	Candidates	Votes	%
1	Timothy C. Day (R)	7,716	63.5
	George H. Pendleton (D)	4,442	36.5
2	John Scott Harrison (R)	7,562	66.0
	Groek (D)	3,891	34.0
3	Lewis D. Campbell (R)	9,058	58.3
	Valm (D)	6,493	41.8
4	Matthias H. Nicholas (R)	10,307	70.2
	Dorsey (D)	4,377	29.8
5	Richard Mott (R)	8,253	61.6
	Commager (D)	5,141	38.4
6	Jonas R. Emrie (R)	9,990	65.0
	Ellison (D)	5,370	35.0
7	Aaron Harlan (R)	9,928	81.1
	Hinkson (D)	2,307	18.9
8	Benjamin Stanton (R)	11,000	76.7
	Dial (D)	3,350	23.3
9	Cooper K. Watson (R)	8,399	59.9
	Plants (D)	5,618	40.1
10	Oscar F. Moore (R)	8,865	65.3
	Davis (D)	4,706	34.7
11	Valentine B. Horton (R)	9,818	58.7
	Smith (D)	6,907	41.3
12	Samuel Galloway (R)	9,698	60.3
	Olds (D)	6,390	39.7
13	John Sherman (R)	8,617	59.8
	Lindy (D)	5,794	40.2
14	Philemon Bliss (R)	8,788	59.3
	Johnson (D)	6,041	40.7
15	William Sapp (R)	9,371	59.0
	Dunbar (D)	6,516	41.0
16	Edward Ball (R)	7,265	58.9
	Galighr (D)	5,072	41.1
17	Charles J. Albright (R)	8,332	58.1
	Wire (D)	6,017	41.9
18	Benjamin F. Leiter (R)	8,738	63.4
	Spalding (D)	5,053	36.6
19	Edward Wade (R)	7,699	71.4
	Wilder (D)	3,079	28.6
20	Joshua R. Giddings (R)	6,972	64.8
	Lee (D)	3,782	35.2
21	John A. Bingham (R)	9,860	65.3
	Unidentified Candidate (D)	5,238	34.7

PENNSYLVANIA

	Candidates	Votes	%
1	Thomas B. Florence (D)	6,439	51.8
	Morris (W)	5,999	48.2
2	Job R. Tyson (W)	5,654	61.8
	Haml (D)	3,500	38.2
3	William Millward (W)	5,888	51.6
	Landy (D)	5,525	48.4
4	Jacob Broom (NAM)	6,747	53.0
	Philps (D)	5,993	47.0
5	John Cadwalader (D)	7,842	50.0
	Jones (W)	7,834	50.0
6	John Hickman (D)	8,733	59.0
	Brooml (W)	6,077	41.0
7	Samuel C. Bradshaw (W)	8,527	51.0
	Samuel A. Bridges (D)	8,182	49.0
8	J. Glancy Jones (D)	8,152	59.8
	Myers (W)	5,486	40.2

	Candidates	Votes	%
9	Anthony E. Roberts (W)	6,561	40.5
	Hiester	5,371	33.2
	Leferre	4,266	26.3
10	John C. Kunkel (W)	8,500	58.4
	Bougtr (D)	6,049	41.6
11	James H. Campbell (W)	5,384	51.5
	Dewart (D)	5,081	48.6
12	Henry M. Fuller (W)	9,115	56.3
	Wright (D)	7,087	43.7
13	Asa Packer (D)	9,136	58.7
	Stewart (W)	6,433	41.3
14	Galusha A. Grow (F SOIL D)		100.0
15	John J. Pierce (W)	9,588	56.0
	White (D)	7,528	44.0
16	Lemuel Todd (W)	10,472	55.7
	Booham (D)	8,319	44.3
17	David F. Robison (W)	9,641	51.7
	Reilly (D)	9,025	48.4
18	John R. Edie (W)	8,423	72.4
	Cresswl (D)	3,218	27.6
19	John Covode (W)	9,342	58.7
	Drum (D)	6,585	41.3
20	Jonathan Knight (W)	9,912	56.8
	Montgomery (D)	7,552	43.2
21	David Ritchie (W)	5,705	60.6
	Shaler (D)	3,714	39.4
22	Samuel A. Purviance (W)	5,926	60.7
	Palmer (D)	3,832	39.3
23	John Allison (W)	7,808	60.2
	Trout (D)	5,172	39.9
24	David Barclay (D)	10,415	74.7
	Arthurs (W)	3,527	25.3
25	John Dick (W)		100.0

Special Election

	Candidates	Votes	%
8	J. Glancy Jones (D)	5,078	60.0
	Keim (W)	3,382	40.0

SOUTH CAROLINA

	Candidates	Votes	%
1	John McQueen (D)	5,154	67.4
	Wilson	2,488	32.6
2	William Aiken (D)		100.0
3	Laurence M. Keitt (D)		100.0
4	Preston S. Brooks (SSR D)	6,118	66.7
	Garlington	3,051	33.3
5	James L. Orr (D)		100.0
6	William W. Boyce (SSR D)		100.0

VERMONT

	Candidates	Votes	%
1	James Meacham (W)	8,626	70.3
	S. W. Jewett (D)	3,464	28.3
2	Justin S. Morrill (W)	8,380	50.2
	J. W. D. Parker (D)	5,848	35.0
	Oscar L. Shafter	2,473	14.8
3	Alvah Sabin (W)	7,862	68.4
	W. Heywood (D)	3,608	31.4

WISCONSIN

	Candidates	Votes	%
1	Daniel Wells Jr (D)	8,458	54.6
	Spooner (R)	7,026	45.4
2	Cadwallader C. Washburn (R)	11,936	60.2
	Hoyt (D)	7,894	39.8
3	Charles Billinghurst (R)	13,359	60.9
	Macy (D)	8,596	39.2

1855 House Elections

ALABAMA

	Candidates	Votes	%
1	Percy Walker (AM)	5,656	52.4
	James A. Stallworth (D)	5,137	47.6
2	Eli S. Shorter (A-KN D)	6,718	55.0
	J. C. Alford (AM)	5,490	45.0
3	James F. Dowdell (D)	6,327	52.2
	T. H. Watts (AM)	5,786	47.8
4	William R. Smith (AM)	4,984	61.1
	Sydenham Moore (D)	3,177	38.9
5	George S. Houston (D)	5,770	100.0
6	Williamson R. W. Cobb (D)	6,260	62.9
	J. M. Adams (A-KN I)	3,697	37.1
7	Sampson W. Harris (D)	6,990	57.3
	W. B. Martin (A-KN ID)	5,220	42.8

CONNECTICUT

	Candidates	Votes	%
1	Ezra Clark Jr (AM)	8,519	52.0
	Pratt (D)	7,852	48.0
2	John Woodruff (AM)	9,876	55.5
	Arld (D)	7,918	44.5
3	Sidney Dean (AM)	8,055	67.5
	White (D)	3,877	32.5
4	William W. Welch (AM)	9,701	55.7
	Noble (D)	7,702	44.3

GEORGIA

	Candidates	Votes	%
1	James L. Seward (D)	6,179	57.6
	Varnadoe (AM)	4,541	42.4
2	Martin J. Crawford (D)	7,746	52.0
	Hawkins (AM)	7,153	48.0
3	Robert P. Trippe (AM)	6,112	54.0
	Smith (D)	5,216	46.1
4	Hiram Warner (D)	6,883	50.3
	Hill (AM)	6,813	49.7
5	John H. Lumpkin (D)	11,290	58.6
	Tumlin (AM)	7,978	41.4
6	Howell Cobb (D)	9,203	63.8
	Franklin (AM)	5,227	36.2
7	Nathaniel G. Foster (AM)	4,792	51.1
	Stephens (D)	4,580	48.9
8	Alexander H. Stephens (D)	5,808	65.4
	Lamar (AM)	3,079	34.7

KENTUCKY

	Candidates	Votes	%
1	Henry C. Burnett (D)	9,323	62.0
	W. G. Hughes (AM)	5,708	38.0
2	John P. Campbell (AM)	7,533	55.3
	Samuel O. Peyton (D)	6,092	44.7
3	Warner L. Underwood (AM)	7,362	56.9
	James P. Bates (D)	5,580	43.1
4	Albert G. Talbott (D)	6,586	50.1
	F. T. Fox (AM)	6,570	49.9
5	Joshua H. Jewett (D)	7,076	51.6
	C. G. Wintersmith (AM)	6,628	48.4
6	John M. Elliott (D)	7,685	54.8
	George W. Dunlap (AM)	6,340	45.2
7	Humphrey Marshall (AM)	6,932	61.3
	William Preston (D)	4,378	38.7
8	Alexander Keith Marshall (AM)	7,039	56.0
	James O. Harrison (D)	5,536	44.0
9	Leander M. Cox (AM)	8,085	55.1
	R. H. Stanton (D)	6,598	44.9
10	Samuel F. Swope (AM)	7,490	51.7
	Henry C. Harris (D)	6,991	48.3

LOUISIANA

	Candidates	Votes	%
1	George Eustis Jr (AM)	2,588	53.4
	Albert Fabre (D)	2,258	46.6
2	Miles Taylor (D)	6,175	51.5
	Hunt (AM)	5,810	48.5
3	Thomas G. Davidson (D)	4,731	50.6
	Pond (AM)	4,616	49.4
4	John M. Sandidge (D)	8,942	58.1
	Lewis (AM)	6,461	42.0

MARYLAND

	Candidates	Votes	%
1	James A. Stewart (D)	6,173	51.3
	Dennis (AM)	5,868	48.7
2	James B. Ricaud (AM)	8,479	56.6
	Jacob Shower (D)	6,506	43.4
3	J. Morrison Harris (AM)	6,538	50.2
	Vansant (D)	6,484	49.8
4	H. Winter Davis (AM)	7,988	51.6
	May (D)	7,493	48.4
5	Henry W. Hoffman (AM)	8,320	52.4
	Hamiln (D)	7,569	47.6
6	Thomas F. Bowie (D)	5,539	53.9
	Watkins (AM)	4,736	46.1

MASSACHUSETTS

Special Election

	Candidates	Votes	%
10	Calvin C. Chaffee (AM)	4,716	36.0
	John W. Foster	4,349	33.2
	Haynes H. Chilson	3,317	25.3
	Edward Dickenson (W)	725	5.5

MISSISSIPPI

	Candidates	Votes	%
1	Daniel B. Wright (D)	6,547	56.4
	J. H. R. Taylor (AM)	5,055	43.6
2	Hendley S. Bennett (D)	4,229	51.9
	L. E. Housten (AM)	3,922	48.1
3	William Barksdale (D)	6,850	55.3
	Joseph B. Cobb (AM)	5,542	44.7
4	William A. Lake (W)	5,196	52.0
	Otho R. Singleton (D)	4,792	48.0
5	John A. Quitman (D)	5,887	58.5
	Giles M. Hillyer (W)	4,178	41.5

NEW HAMPSHIRE

	Candidates	Votes	%
1	James Pike (AM)	12,806	56.9
	Kittredge (D)	9,697	43.1
2	Mason W. Tappan (AM)	12,202	59.3
	Morrison (D)	8,392	40.8
3	Aaron H. Cragin (AM)	11,715	59.1
	Wheeler (D)	8,099	40.9

NORTH CAROLINA

	Candidates	Votes	%
1	Robert T. Paine (AM)	5,228	51.7
	Henry M. Shaw (D)	4,882	48.3
2	Thomas Ruffin (D)	6,739	66.1
	Thomas J. Latham (AM)	3,464	34.0
3	Warren Winslow (D)	5,929	54.9
	David Reid (AM)	4,863	45.1
4	Lawrence O'B. Branch (D)	6,794	61.7
	James B. Shepard (AM)	4,223	38.3
5	Edwin G. Reade (AM)	7,061	65.3
	John Kerr (W)	3,756	34.7

	Candidates	Votes	%
6	Richard C. Puryear (AM)	6,516	51.4
	Alfred M. Scales (D)	6,150	48.6
7	F. Burton Craige (D)	6,745	62.2
	Samuel N. Stowe (AM)	4,104	37.8
8	Thomas L. Clingman (D)	8,079	55.1
	Leander B. Carmichael (AM)	6,584	44.9

RHODE ISLAND

	Candidates	Votes	%
1	Nathaniel B. Durfee (AM)	5,004	72.9
	Thomas Davis (D)	1,576	23.0
2	Benjamin B. Thurston (AM)	4,359	87.9

TENNESSEE

	Candidates	Votes	%
1	Albert G. Watkins (D)	7,781	50.9
	Taylor (AM)	7,511	49.1
2	William H. Sneed (AM)	6,246	54.0
	Cummins (D)	5,327	46.0
3	Samuel A. Smith (D)	7,872	51.8
	Anderson (AM)	7,331	48.2
4	John H. Savage (D)	6,016	52.0
	Cullom (AM)	5,563	48.0
5	Charles Ready (AM)	7,069	91.8
	Keeble (D)	632	8.2
6	George W. Jones (D)	8,476	65.6
	Gordon (AM)	4,445	34.4
7	John V. Wright (D)	7,927	57.2
	Kendrick (AM)	5,922	42.8
8	Felix K. Zollicoffer (AM)	6,958	58.9
	Torbett (D)	4,857	41.1
9	Emerson Etheridge (AM)	7,952	51.8
	Freeman (D)	7,394	48.2
10	Thomas Rivers (AM)	5,860	53.3
	Currin (D)	5,136	46.7

TEXAS

	Candidates	Votes	%
1	Peter H. Bell (D)	10,342	50.1
	Hancock (AM)	10,311	49.9
2	Lemuel D. Evans (AM)	14,379	60.2
	Ward (D)	9,496	39.8

VIRGINIA

	Candidates	Votes	%
1	Thomas H. Bayly (D)		100.0
2	John S. Millson (D)	4,769	53.3
	Watts (AM)	4,180	46.7
3	John S. Caskie (D)	5,951	52.1
	Scott (AM)	5,466	47.9
4	William O. Goode (D)	1,163	63.8
	Tazewell (AM)	661	36.2
5	Thomas S. Bocock (D)	4,566	52.9
	Claiborne (AM)	4,073	47.2
6	Paulus Powell (D)	3,834	56.3
	Ligon (AM)	2,976	43.7
7	William Smith (D)		100.0
8	Charles J. Faulkner (D)	7,158	50.7
	Boteler (AM)	6,959	49.3
9	John Letcher (D)		100.0
10	Zedekiah Kidwell (D)	6,615	56.7
	Pendleton (AM)	5,059	43.3
11	John S. Carlisle (AM)	8,333	51.2
	Lewis (D)	7,942	48.8
12	Henry A. Edmundson (D)	7,492	54.0
	Staples (AM)	6,385	46.0
13	Fayette McMullen (D)	4,289	60.5
	Trigg (AM)	2,803	39.5

1856 House Elections

ARKANSAS

1	Alfred B. Greenwood (D)	15,399	71.4
	Thomason (AM)	6,161	28.6
2	Edward A. Warren (D)	11,835	57.6
	Fowler (AM)	8,701	42.4

CALIFORNIA

AL	Joseph C. McKibbin (D)	50,895✔	
	Charles L. Scott (D)	50,813✔	
	B. C. Whitman (AM)	36,078	
	A. B. Dibble (AM)	35,325	
	L. P. Rankin (R)	21,975	
	J. D. Turner (R)	21,164	

DELAWARE

AL	William G. Whiteley (D)	8,111	56.1
	Elisha D. Cullen (AM)	6,360	44.0

FLORIDA

AL	George S. Hawkins (D)	6,392	53.1
	James M. Baker (AM)	5,650	46.9

ILLINOIS

1	Elihu B. Washburne (R)	18,070	72.6
	Richard S. S. Malony (D)	6,227	25.0
2	John F. Farnsworth (R)	21,518	67.2
	John Van Nortwick (D)	9,814	30.7
3	Owen Lovejoy (R)	19,068	59.4
	Osgood (D)	13,007	40.5
4	William Kellogg (R)	16,175	51.1
	James W. Davison (D)	14,474	45.7
5	Isaac N. Morris (D)	12,059	53.7
	Jackson Grimshaw (R)	10,294	45.8
6	Thomas L. Harris (D)	14,196	54.0
	John Williams (R)	12,077	46.0
7	Aaron Shaw (D)	12,994	56.8
	Henry P. H. Bromwell (R)	9,878	43.2
8	Robert Smith (D)	11,299	60.1
	I. D. Lansing (R)	7,512	39.9
9	Samuel S. Marshall (D)	15,968	81.5
	Benjamin L. Wiley (R)	3,419	17.4

Special Elections

5	Jacob C. Davis (D)	12,212	52.6
	Thomas C. Sharp (R)	8,182	35.2
	James B. Kyle	2,826	12.2
7	James C. Allen (D)	13,081	56.3
	William B. Archer (R)	10,136	43.7
8	I. L. D. Morrison (D)	10,756	55.8
	John Thomas (R)	8,231	42.7

INDIANA

1	James Lockhart (D)	12,747	61.5
	Veach (R)	7,977	38.5
2	William H. English (D)	10,577	57.2
	Wilson (R)	7,927	42.8
3	James Hughes (D)	10,629	53.8
	Hendks (R)	9,113	46.2
4	James B. Foley (D)	10,451	53.7
	Cumback (R)	8,998	46.3
5	David Kilgore (R)	11,132	60.8
	Johnson (D)	7,183	39.2
6	James M. Gregg (D)	11,787	52.1
	Coburn (R)	10,840	47.9
7	John G. Davis (D)	11,137	53.9
	Usher (R)	9,529	46.1

8	James Wilson (R)	11,302	50.5
	Voorhees (D)	11,072	49.5
9	Schuyler Colfax (R)	12,921	52.1
	Stuart (D)	11,890	47.9
10	Samuel Brenton (R)	10,699	51.7
	Lowry (D)	9,989	48.3
11	John U. Pettit (R)	11,235	51.8
	Garver (D)	10,443	48.2

IOWA

1	Samuel R. Curtis (R)	18,065	50.2
	Augustus Hall (D)	17,110	47.5
2	Timothy Davis (R)	21,888	57.9
	Shepherd Leffler (D)	15,868	42.0

MAINE

1	John M. Wood (R)	11,215	53.4
	Little (COALIT)	9,776	46.6
2	Charles J. Gilman (R)	12,953	57.3
	Pillsbury (COALIT)	9,670	42.7
3	Nehemiah Abbott (R)	10,562	56.1
	Ingalls (COALIT)	8,252	43.9
4	Freeman H. Morse (R)	13,750	65.0
	Bronson (COALIT)	7,378	35.0
5	Israel Washburn Jr (R)	12,517	60.1
	Sanborn (COALIT)	8,312	39.9
6	Stephen C. Foster (R)	8,503	52.9
	Wiswell (COALIT)	7,567	47.1

MASSACHUSETTS

1	Robert B. Hall (R)	7,904	69.6
	Moses Bates Jr (D)	1,830	16.1
	Daniel Fisher (AM)	1,601	14.1
2	James Buffington (R)	11,658	72.4
	Charles R. Vickery (D)	3,314	20.6
	Danius Dunbar (AM)	1,132	7.0
3	William L. Damrell (R)	10,433	61.5
	Arthur W. Austin (D)	5,077	29.9
	Alfred B. Ely (AM)	1,435	8.5
4	Linus B. Comins (R)	5,188	45.8
	Charles G. Greene (D)	4,431	39.1
	Benjamin F. Cooke (AM)	1,678	14.8
5	Anson Burlingame (AM)	6,582	50.2
	William Appleton (D & AM)	6,513	49.7
6	Timothy Davis (R)	10,044	69.4
	Ruth J. Lord (D)	3,214	22.2
	Benjamin Parley Poor (AM)	1,121	7.7
7	Nathaniel P. Banks (R)	10,814	61.9
	Isaac H. Wright (D)	4,593	26.3
	Isaac Storey (AM)	2,049	11.7
8	Chauncey L. Knapp (R)	9,616	67.4
	Benjamin F. Butler (D)	3,686	25.9
	Abiel L. Lewis (AM)	864	6.1
9	Eli Thayer (R)	8,920	53.7
	Alex Dewitt (AM)	4,414	26.6
	Nathaniel Wood (D)	2,987	18.0
10	Calvin C. Chaffee (R)	10,845	72.4
	William C. Fowler (D & AM)	4,081	27.2
11	Henry L Dawes (R)	6,709	43.8
	Josiah D. Weston (D)	4,398	28.7
	Mark Trafton (AM)	4,194	27.4

MICHIGAN

1	William A. Howard (R)	13,658	51.6
	George Lathrop (D)	12,791	48.4
2	Henry Waldron (R)	16,467	62.1
	John S. Barry (D)	10,064	37.9
3	David S. Walbridge (R)	23,970	59.6
	Flavius Littlejohn (D)	16,268	40.4
4	De Witt C. Leach (R)	18,715	55.2
	George W. Peck (D)	15,186	44.8

MISSOURI

1	Francis P. Blair Jr (BENTON D)	6,035	43.8
	Kennett (AM)	5,549	40.3
	Reynolds (D)	2,181	15.8
2	Thomas L. Anderson (AM)	8,876	52.1
	Richmond (D)	8,149	47.9
3	James S. Green (D)	10,126*	55.3
	Lindley (AM)	8,172	44.7
4	James Craig (D)	8,742	56.8
	Moss (AM)	6,274	40.8
5	Samuel H. Woodson (AM)	6,006	41.6
	Douglas (D)	4,684	32.4
	Price (BENTON D)	3,755	26.0
6	John S. Phelps (D)	9,718	58.1
	Emerson (AM)	6,911	41.3
7	Samuel Caruthers (D)	8,291	52.7
	Perryman (AM)	4,883	31.0
	Stevson (BENTON D)	2,556	16.3

Special Election

5	Thomas P. Akers (AM)	6,569	55.8
	Jackson (D)	5,211	44.2

NEW JERSEY

1	Isaiah D. Clawson (FUS)	9,673	56.8
	Hineline (D)	7,351	43.2
2	George R. Robbins (FUS)	11,723	52.3
	Wall (D)	10,692	47.7
3	Garnett B. Adrain (D)	10,781	52.5
	Bishop (FUS)	9,768	47.5
4	John Huyler (D)	9,165	52.7
	Osborne (R)	5,876	33.8
	Inglis (AM)	2,355	13.5
5	Jacob R. Wortendyke (D)	9,099	42.9
	Dodd (R)	6,480	30.5
	Betts (AM)	5,638	26.6

NEW YORK

1	John A. Searing (D)	8,960	44.1
	Jennings (AM)	5,892	29.0
	Lord (R)	5,449	26.8
2	George Taylor (D)	8,591	40.8
	Stranhan (R)	5,869	27.9
	Wood (AM)	5,476	26.0
	McCue	1,123	5.3
3	Daniel E. Sickles (D)	5,716	53.2
	Duganne (AM)	2,905	27.0
	Guy R. Pelton (R)	2,126	19.8
4	John Kelly (D)	8,319	72.0
	Gould (AM)	1,735	15.0
	Ryckman (R)	1,497	13.0
5	William B. Maclay (D)	5,863	41.6
	Northp (AM)	3,798	26.9
	Andrews (R)	3,274	23.2
	Hamilton (ID)	1,169	8.3
6	John Cochrane (D)	7,531	49.6
	Stillman (R)	3,991	26.3
	Williams (AM)	3,658	24.1
7	Elijah Ward (D)	6,531	41.0
	Briggs (AM)	4,461	28.0
	Nye (R)	4,100	25.7
	Bulloc	854	5.4
8	Horace F. Clark (D)	7,482	50.2
	Abram Wakeman (R)	3,760	25.3
	Knapp (AM)	3,651	24.5
9	John B. Haskin (D)	7,195	39.5
	Strang (R)	5,935	32.6
	Cobb (AM)	5,084	27.9
10	Ambrose S. Murray (R)	6,156	39.3
	Fowler (D)	5,581	35.6
	Trotter (AM)	3,936	25.1

NEW YORK

Candidates	Votes	%
11 William F. Russell (D)	6,878	38.9
Fream (AM)	5,902	33.4
Brodhd (R)	4,912	27.8
12 John Thompson (R)	9,247	45.5
Chamberlain (D)	7,972	39.2
Teller (AM)	3,116	15.3
13 Abram B. Olin (R)	5,206	37.0
Griswold (D)	4,758	33.8
Fonda (AM)	4,108	29.2
14 Erastus Corning (D)	8,296	46.0
Perry (AM)	5,095	28.3
Van Dyck (R)	4,631	25.7
15 Edward Dodd (R)	11,717	51.6
Cramer (AM)	5,633	24.8
Gray (D)	5,373	23.7
16 George W. Palmer (R)	6,799	44.5
Averill (D)	4,363	28.5
Ross (AM)	4,129	27.0
17 Francis E. Spinner (R)	14,722	70.7
Dodge (AM)	6,115	29.4
18 Clark B. Cochrane (R)	9,719	44.6
Rossiter (D)	6,123	28.1
Smith (AM)	5,936	27.3
19 Oliver A. Morse (R)	10,724	54.7
Gregory (D & AM)	8,881	45.3
20 Orsamus B. Matteson (R)	10,618	56.2
Johnson (D & AM)	8,275	43.8
21 Henry Bennett (R)	13,357	62.0
Hyde (D & AM)	8,192	38.0
22 Henry C. Goodwin (R)	14,380	65.0
Clark (D)	6,080	27.5
Culver (AM)	1,671	7.6
23 Charles B. Hoard (R)	11,149	64.6
Dorwin (D)	6,070	35.2
24 Amos P. Granger (R)	9,748	61.0
Peck (D)	4,525	28.3
Beach (AM)	1,720	10.8
25 Edwin B. Morgan (R)	12,631	63.3
Richmond (D)	3,685	18.5
Fosgt (AM)	3,644	18.3
26 Emory B. Pottle (R)	9,368	53.0
Andrew Oliver (AM)	4,411	25.0
Ogden (D)	3,897	22.1
27 John M. Parker (R)	12,383	56.3
Hathaway (D)	8,377	38.1
Lawr (AM)	1,229	5.6
28 William H. Kelsey (R)	10,509	53.4
Hallett (AM)	4,895	24.9
Angel (D)	4,266	21.7
29 Samuel G. Andrews (R)	7,786	51.0
Paine (D)	4,337	28.4
Clark (AM)	3,156	20.7
30 Judson W. Sherman (R)	13,867	64.0
Richmond (D)	5,032	23.2
Cooly (AM)	2,758	12.7
31 Silas M. Burroughs (R)	6,885	51.7
Hunt (AM)	4,694	35.3
Church (D)	1,731	13.0
32 Israel T. Hatch (D)	7,399	37.2
Spaulding (R)	6,923	34.8
Haven (AM)	5,548	27.9
33 Reuben E. Fenton (R)	12,046	64.3
Allen (D)	3,436	18.3
Edwds (AM)	3,251	17.4

OHIO

Candidates	Votes	%
1 George H. Pendleton (D)	6,133	47.1
Taft (R)	4,256	32.7
Tornce (AM)	2,642	20.3
2 William S. Groesbeck (D)	5,738	43.1
Gurley (R)	4,343	32.6
Harrison (AM)	3,229	24.3
3 Lewis D. Campbell (R)	9,338‡	50.1
Clement I. Vallandigham (D)	9,319	50.0
4 Mathias H. Nichols (R)	9,415	49.7
Dorsey (D)	9,172	48.4
5 Richard Mott (R)	10,018	51.0
Edgerton (D)	9,157	46.6
6 Joseph R. Cockerill (D)	8,603	48.7
Jonas R. Emrie (R)	7,460	42.2
Trimbel (AM)	1,598	9.1
7 Aaron Harlan (R)	9,027	59.7
Ward (D)	5,076	33.6
Elsbury (AM)	1,011	6.7
8 Benjamin Stanton (R)	9,756	56.7
Runkle (D)	6,210	36.1
Glover (AM)	1,239	7.2
9 Lawrence W. Hall (D)	9,561	49.7
Cooper K. Watson (R)	9,382	48.7
10 Joseph Miller (D)	7,403	42.6
Hoffman (D)	5,633	32.4
Oscar F. Moore (AM)	4,326	24.9
11 Valentine B. Horton (R)	10,272	50.9
Medill (D)	9,927	49.2
12 Samuel S. Cox (D)	8,938	48.7
Galloway (R)	8,582	46.7
13 John Sherman (R)	9,926	58.4
Bramback (D)	7,065	41.6
14 Philemon Bliss (R)	10,414	57.8
Firestone (D)	7,617	42.2
15 Joseph Burns (D)	9,194	50.1
Sapp (R)	9,143	49.9
16 Cydnor B. Tompkins (R)	7,248	48.0
Smith (D)	6,462	42.8
Haynes (AM)	1,382	9.2
17 William Lawrence (D)	8,085	47.8
Albright (R)	6,805	40.3
Davenport (AM)	2,013	11.9
18 Benjamin F. Leiter (R)	9,394	58.0
Lahm (D)	6,799	42.0
19 Edward Wade (R)	9,431	67.9
Hilliard (D)	4,467	32.1
20 Joshua R. Giddings (R)	9,567	66.6
Burchard (D)	4,795	33.4
21 John A. Bingham (R)	9,444	57.7
Woods (D)	6,933	42.3

PENNSYLVANIA

Candidates	Votes	%
1 Thomas B. Florence (D)	9,495	56.6
Knight (UN)	7,275	43.4
2 Edward Joy Morris (UN)	6,411	51.6
Marsll (D)	6,018	48.4
3 James Landy (D)	7,933	54.0
William Millward (UN)	6,753	46.0
4 Henry M. Phillips (D)	9,279	50.7
Forst (D)	6,560	35.9
William D. Kelley (R)	2,457	13.4
5 Owen Jones (D)	9,674	54.9
Mulvany (UN)	7,961	45.1
6 John Hickman (D)	8,024	48.9
Bowen (UN)	7,851	47.9
7 Henry Chapman (D)	10,321	54.0
Bradshaw (UN)	8,789	46.0
8 J. Glancy Jones (D)	9,951	71.6
Yoder (UN)	3,947	28.4
9 Anthony E. Roberts (UN)	10,001	54.6
Heister (D)	8,320	45.4
10 John C. Kunkel (UN)	9,227	55.6
Eyer (D)	7,360	44.4
11 William L. Dewart (D)	8,959	58.3
Campbell (UN)	6,418	41.7
12 John G. Montgomery (D)	10,442	57.7
Smith (UN)	7,657	42.3
13 William H. Dimmick (D)	11,235	68.9
E. S. Dimk (UN)	5,065	31.1
14 Galusha A. Grow (R)	13,325	71.3
Sherwd (D)	5,361	28.7
15 Allison White (D)	9,980	51.4
Irwin (UN)	9,450	48.6
16 John A. Ahl (D)	11,191	53.7
Todd (UN)	9,670	46.4
17 Wilson Reilly (D)	10,224	51.3
Pumroy (UN)	9,715	48.7
18 John R. Edie (UN)	8,792	50.8
Pershing (D)	8,508	49.2
19 John Covode (UN)	10,409	54.4
McKinley (D)	8,724	45.6
20 William Montgomery (D)	10,256	52.2
Knight (UN)	9,411	47.9
21 David Ritchie (R)	7,674	54.6
McCans (D)	5,944	42.3
22 Samuel A. Purviance (R)	6,840	57.1
Gibson (D)	4,854	40.5
23 William Stewart (UN)	8,552	61.0
Cunningham (D)	5,467	39.0
24 James L. Gillis (D)	9,785	51.8
Myers (UN)	9,114	48.2
25 John Dick (R)	8,944	68.0
McFadn (D)	4,215	32.0

SOUTH CAROLINA[1]

Candidates	Votes	%
1 John McQueen (D)		100.0
2 W. Porcher Miles (D)	2,323	50.5
James Gadsden	1,684	36.6
John Cunningham	590	12.8
3 Laurence M. Keitt (D)		100.0
4 Preston S. Brooks (SSR D) *		100.0
5 James L. Orr (D)		100.0
6 William W. Boyce (SSR D)		100.0

Special Elections

Candidates	Votes	%
3 Laurence M. Keitt (D)	✓	
4 Preston S. Brooks (SSR D)	7,922	100.0

VERMONT

Candidates	Votes	%
1 Eliakim Persons Walton (R)	10,398	76.2
Needhm (D)	3,242	23.8
2 Justin S. Morrill (R)	13,695	75.9
Chase (D)	4,358	24.1
3 Homer Elihu Royce (R)	9,116	74.4
Bingm (D)	3,134	25.6

WISCONSIN

Candidates	Votes	%
1 John F. Potter (R)	13,111	50.6
Hadley (D)	12,814	49.4
2 Cadwallader C. Washburn (R)	26,004	61.6
Crawford (D)	16,233	38.4
3 Charles Billinghurst (R)	25,808	52.2
Hobart (D)	23,648	47.8

---

1. Preston S. Brooks of South Carolina's 4th district, who was serving in the 34th Congress (1855-57) following his election in 1854, resigned July 14, 1856. He was subsequently re-elected to the 34th Congress in a special election which appears on this page. He took his seat Aug. 1, 1856 and was re-elected in the general election later in 1856 to the 35th Congress (1857-59). He died Jan. 27, 1857, and thus did not serve in that Congress.

Laurence M. Keitt of the 3rd district was also serving in the 34th Congress when he resigned July 16, 1856. Subsequently re-elected to the 34th Congress in the special election shown on this page to fill the vacancy caused by his resignation, he returned to the House Aug. 6, 1856. Later that year he was re-elected to the 35th Congress in the general election.

1857 House Elections

ALABAMA

	Candidates	Votes	%
1	James A. Stallworth (D)	7,058	62.0
	J. McCaskill (AM)	4,330	38.0
2	Eli S. Shorter (D)	7,417	62.5
	B. Peterson (AM)	4,454	37.5
3	James F. Dowdell (D)	6,505	50.3
	T. J. Judge (SR W)	6,419	49.7
4	Sydenham Moore (D)	6,432	56.5
	W. R. Smith (AM)	4,952	43.5
5	George S. Houston (D)	4,853	55.1
	D. Hubbard (SO RTS D)	3,956	44.9
6	Williamson R. W. Cobb (D)	5,975	61.0
	Henry Sanford (D)	3,594	36.7
7	Jabez L. M. Curry (D)	8,311	98.5

CONNECTICUT

	Candidates	Votes	%
1	Ezra Clark Jr (R)	8,410	51.3
	Hubbard (D)	7,973	48.7
2	Samuel Arnold (D)	9,403	51.4
	Woodruff (R)	8,906	48.6
3	Sidney Dean (R)	6,082	54.9
	Hovey (D)	5,006	45.2
4	William D. Bishop (D)	8,403	50.1
	Ferry (R)	8,387	50.0

GEORGIA

	Candidates	Votes	%
1	James L. Seward (D)	5,870	51.2
	Bartow (AM)	5,093	44.4
2	Martin J. Crawford (D)	8,220	56.4
	Elam (AM)	6,365	43.6
3	Robert P. Trippe (AM)	5,803	51.7
	Bailey (D)	5,423	48.3
4	Lucius J. Gartrell (D)	8,008	53.6
	Tidwell (AM)	6,939	46.4
5	Augustus R. Wright (D)	9,669	63.0
	Hooper (AM)	5,690	37.1
6	James Jackson (D)	7,751	56.6
	Simmons (ID)	5,956	43.5
7	Joshua Hill (AM)	4,800	51.5
	L. Stephens (D)	4,525	48.5
8	Alexander H. Stephens (D)	5,151	55.7
	Miller (AM)	4,096	44.3

KENTUCKY

	Candidates	Votes	%
1	Henry C. Burnett (D)	8,989	75.3
	Owen Grimes (AM)	2,945	24.7
2	Samuel O. Peyton (D)	7,212	53.9
	James L. Johnson (AM)	6,173	46.1
3	Warner L. Underwood (AM)	6,359	50.8
	Joseph H. Lewis (D)	6,156	49.2
4	Albert G. Talbott (D)	7,025	50.6
	William C. Anderson (AM)	6,861	49.4
5	Joshua H. Jewett (D)	7,377	59.6
	Bryan R. Young (AM)	4,996	40.4
6	John M. Elliott (D)	7,470	55.7
	John A. Moore (AM)	5,950	44.3
7	Humphrey Marshall (AM)	6,085	55.0
	Thomas H. Holt (D)	4,979	45.0
8	James B. Clay (D)	6,577	50.5
	Roger W. Hanson (AM)	6,451	49.5
9	John C. Mason (D)	8,148	52.0
	Leander M. Cox (AM)	7,534	48.0
10	John W. Stevenson (D)	8,748	67.3
	William Rankin (AM)	4,185	32.2

LOUISIANA

	Candidates	Votes	%
1	George Eustis Jr (AM)	2,336	60.5
	Villiers (D)	1,528	39.5
2	Miles Taylor (D)	4,950	50.3
	Burke (AM)	4,892	49.7
3	Thomas G. Davidson (D)	4,270	54.9
	Watrsn (AM)	3,512	45.1
4	John M. Sandidge (D)	9,060	63.5
	Sparks (AM)	5,205	36.5

MARYLAND

	Candidates	Votes	%
1	James A. Stewart (D)	6,339	50.7
	Townsend (AM)	6,163	49.3
2	James B. Ricaud (AM)	8,701	52.3
	McHenry (D)	7,935	47.7
3	J. Morrison Harris (AM)	8,761	61.6
	William Pinkney Whyte (D)	5,455	38.4
4	H. Winter Davis (AM)	10,515	72.6
	Henry P. Brooks (D)	3,979	27.5
5	Jacob M. Kunkel (D)	8,376	50.5
	Hoffman (AM)	8,208	49.5
6	Thomas F. Bowie (D)	5,735	56.3
	Blackistone (AM)	4,453	43.7

MINNESOTA

(Became a state May 11, 1858)

	Candidates	Votes	%
AL	William W. Phelps (D)	18,218✓	
	James M. Cavanaugh (D)	18,064✓	
	G. L. Becker (D)	18,019	
	C. Aldrich (R)	16,955	
	M. S. Wilkinson (R)	16,938	
	H. A. Swift (R)	16,827	

MISSISSIPPI

	Candidates	Votes	%
1	Lucius Q. C. Lamar (D)	3,705	61.8
	James L. Alcorn (W)	2,288	38.2
2	Reuben Davis (D)	5,026	59.4
	Charles Clark (W)	3,431	40.6
3	William Barksdale (D)	5,129	97.7
4	Otho R. Singleton (D)	5,940	54.3
	William H. Lake (W)	4,997	45.7
5	John A. Quitman (D)	4,017	98.1

NEW HAMPSHIRE

	Candidates	Votes	%
1	James Pike (R)	12,242	52.2
	Kittridge (D)	11,206	47.8
2	Mason W. Tappan (R)	10,685	53.8
	Morrison (D)	9,180	46.2
3	Aaron H. Cragin (R)	10,983	52.7
	Wheeler (D)	9,841	47.3

NORTH CAROLINA

	Candidates	Votes	%
1	Henry M. Shaw (D)	5,293	50.2
	William N. H. Smith (AM)	5,255	49.8
2	Thomas Ruffin (D)	5,940	90.6
3	Warren Winslow (D)	6,337	81.0
	O. P. Meares (AM)	1,488	19.0
4	Lawrence O'B. Branch (D)	7,375	87.0
5	John A. Gilmer (AM)	5,692	54.0
	Stephen W. Williams (D)	4,845	46.0
6	Alfred M. Scales (D)	7,679	52.5
	Richard C. Puryear (AM)	6,950	47.5
7	F. Burton Craige (D)	6,482	92.2
8	Thomas L. Clingman (D)	8,674	69.8

PENNSYLVANIA

Special Election

	Candidates	Votes	%
12	Paul Leidy (D)	9,826	61.0
	Smith Thompson (R)	6,294	39.0

RHODE ISLAND

	Candidates	Votes	%
1	Nathaniel B. Durfee (R)	5,442	73.3
	Ambrose E. Burnside (D)	1,961	26.4
2	William D. Brayton (AM & R)	3,933	54.4
	Charles Jackson (D)	3,209	44.4

SOUTH CAROLINA

Special Election

	Candidates	Votes	%
4	Milledge L. Bonham (SSR D)	3,646	63.5
	C. P. Sullivan	2,093	36.5

TENNESSEE

	Candidates	Votes	%
1	Albert G. Watkins (D)	7,647	50.6
	Taylor (AM)	7,471	49.4
2	Horace Maynard (AM)	5,565	50.9
	Wallace (D)	5,360	49.1
3	Samuel A. Smith (D)	7,662	53.0
	Heiskell (AM)	6,800	47.0
4	John H. Savage (D)	6,435	55.2
	Pickett (AM)	5,232	44.8
5	Charles Ready (AM)	6,151	51.3
	Guild (D)	5,851	48.8
6	George W. Jones (D)	8,516	100.0
7	John V. Wright (D)	8,620	83.8
	McElrath (AM)	1,665	16.2
8	Felix K. Zollicoffer (AM)	6,088	52.2
	James M. Quarles (D)	5,580	47.8
9	John D. C. Atkins (D)	8,603	50.4
	Etheridge (AM)	8,474	49.6
10	William T. Avery (D)	6,006	51.3
	Stevens (AM)	5,707	48.7

TEXAS

	Candidates	Votes	%
1	John H. Reagan (D)	15,799	61.0
	Evans (AM)	10,085	39.0
2	Guy M. Bryan (D)	21,142	80.8
	Howth (AM)	5,013	19.2

VIRGINIA

	Candidates	Votes	%
1	Muscoe R. H. Garnett (D)	1,881	60.5
	Critcher (AM)	1,226	39.5
2	John S. Millson (D)		100.0
3	John S. Caskie (D)	5,148	63.7
	Crane (AM)	2,931	36.3
4	William O. Goode (D)	3,579	76.0
	Collier (AM)	1,132	24.0
5	Thomas S. Bocock (D)		100.0
6	Paulus Powell (D)		100.0
7	William Smith (D)	5,332	57.5
	Snowdon (AM)	3,941	42.5
8	Charles J. Faulkner (D)	6,631	59.5
	Lucas (AM)	4,516	40.5
9	John Letcher (D)		100.0
10	Sherrard Clemens (D)	7,074	71.5
	Dunngton (AM)	2,821	28.5
11	Albert G. Jenkins (D)	7,758	53.8
	Carlisle (AM)	6,653	46.2
12	Henry A. Edmundson (D)		100.0
13	George W. Hopkins (D)	5,318	50.3
	Martin (AM)	5,249	49.7

1858 House Elections

ARKANSAS

	Candidates	Votes	%
1	Thomas C. Hindman (D)	19,146	87.0
	W. M. Crosby (AM)	2,864	13.0
2	Albert Rust (D)	16,302	70.3
	Thomas S. Drew (ID)	3,780	16.3
	James A. Jones (AM)	3,106	13.4

CALIFORNIA [1]

	Candidates	Votes	%
AL	Joseph C. McKibbin (A-LEC DR)	32,102*	
	W. L. Dudley (A-LEC D)	22,782*	
	L. L. Tracy (R)	9,381	

DELAWARE

	Candidates	Votes	%
AL	William G. Whiteley (D)	7,868	51.4
	Morris	7,452	48.6

FLORIDA

	Candidates	Votes	%
AL	George S. Hawkins (D)	6,465	61.4
	Westcott (ID)	4,070	38.6

ILLINOIS

	Candidates	Votes	%
1	Elihu B. Washburne (R)	15,811	69.8
	Hiram Bright (D)	6,457	28.5
2	John F. Farnsworth (R)	21,797	61.1
	Thomas Dyer (D)	13,198	37.0
3	Owen Lovejoy (R)	22,313	57.7
	George W. Armstrong (D)	14,988	38.8
4	William Kellogg (R)	19,487	52.8
	James W. Davidson (D)	16,860	45.7
5	Isaac N. Morris (D)	13,529	52.7
	Jackson Grimshaw (R)	11,648	45.4
6	Thomas L. Harris (D)	16,193*	57.6
	James N. Mathews (R)	11,646	41.4
7	James C. Robinson (D)	13,588	53.5
	Richard J. Oglesby (R)	11,760	46.3
8	Phillip B. Fouke (D)	11,490	57.2
	John Baker (R)	8,410	41.8
9	John A. Logan (D)	15,878	84.2
	David L. Phillips (R)	2,796	14.8

INDIANA

	Candidates	Votes	%
1	William E. Niblack (D)	10,329	53.6
	Hovey (A-LEC D)	8,946	46.4
2	William H. English (D)	9,293	55.6
	Wilson (R)	7,434	44.4
3	William McKee Dunn (R)	9,363	52.8
	Hughes (D)	8,385	47.2
4	William S. Holman (D)	9,425	54.5
	Hackleman (R)	7,856	45.5
5	David Kilgore (R)	9,383	61.3
	Devlin (D)	5,921	38.7
6	Albert G. Porter (R)	10,776	52.6
	Rar (D)	9,716	47.4
7	John G. Davis (A-LEC D)	10,893	59.0
	Sect (D)	7,584	41.1
8	James Wilson (R)	11,028	51.5
	Blake (D)	10,387	48.5
9	Schuyler Colfax (R)	14,541	53.6
	Walker (D)	12,610	46.4
10	Charles Case (R)	10,780	53.4
	Dawson (D)	9,417	46.6
11	John U. Pettit (R)	10,748	51.7
	Coffroth (D)	10,038	48.3

IOWA

	Candidates	Votes	%
1	Samuel R. Curtis (R)	23,529	50.7
	Henry H. Trimble (D)	22,929	49.4
2	William Vandever (R)	25,503	52.8
	William E. Leffingwell (D)	22,764	47.2

MAINE

	Candidates	Votes	%
1	Daniel E. Somes (R)	10,410	50.6
	Drew (D)	9,955	48.4
2	John J. Perry (R)	12,031	54.5
	Hastings (D)	10,032	45.5
3	Ezra B. French (R)	8,994	50.2
	Johnson (D)	8,931	49.8
4	Freeman H. Morse (R)	10,552	60.1
	Gile (D)	6,990	39.8
5	Israel Washburn Jr (R)	10,300	55.7
	Wiley (D)	8,184	44.3
6	Stephen C. Foster (R)	8,297	51.5
	Bradbury (D)	7,804	48.5

MASSACHUSETTS

	Candidates	Votes	%
1	Thomas D. Eliot (R)	4,854	72.6
	Moses Bates Jr. (D)	1,709	25.6
2	James Buffinton (R)	7,385	71.4
	John Wilson (D)	2,941	28.5
3	Charles F. Adams (R)	6,524	54.9
	Authur W. Austin (D)	3,880	32.6
	Moses G. Cobb (AM)	1,462	12.3
4	Alexander H. Rice (R)	4,507	47.7
	Samuel W. Waldron (D)	3,511	37.2
	Newell A. Thompson (AM)	1,396	14.8
5	Anson Burlingame (R)	6,214	51.5
	John F. Heard (D)	5,823	48.2
6	John B. Alley (R)	5,587	52.0
	Otis P. Lord (AM)	3,017	28.1
	George B. Loring (D)	2,116	19.7
7	Daniel W. Gooch (R)	7,129	60.3
	Charles A. Welch (R)	3,868	32.7
	Elihu C. Baker (AM)	810	6.9
8	Charles R. Train (R)	6,196	58.9
	Benjamin F. Butler (D)	3,514	33.4
	Josiah H. Temple (AM)	576	5.5
9	Eli Thayer (R)	7,280	70.9
	Nathaniel Wood (D)	2,962	28.8
10	Charles Delano (R)	6,847	64.1
	Charles Osgood (D)	3,276	30.7
11	Henry L. Dawes (R)	7,631	60.8
	Thomas F. Plunkett (D)	4,911	39.1

Special Election

	Candidates	Votes	%
7	Daniel W. Gooch (R)	4,168	61.5
	George Ashborne	2,162	31.9

MICHIGAN

	Candidates	Votes	%
1	George B. Cooper (D)	13,123‡	50.1
	William A. Howard (R)	13,048	49.8
2	Henry Waldron (R)	14,655	59.1
	Consider A. Stacy (D)	10,138	40.9
3	Francis W. Kellogg (R)	21,952	55.7
	Thomas B. Church (D)	17,438	44.3
4	De Witt C. Leach (R)	16,193	51.7
	Robert W. Davis (D)	15,120	48.3

MISSOURI

	Candidates	Votes	%
1	John R. Barrett (D)	7,057‡	36.5
	Francis P. Blair Jr. (R)	6,631	34.3
	Buck (AM)	5,668	29.3
2	Thomas L. Anderson (ID)	10,902	64.2
	Hendern (D)	6,089	35.8
3	John B. Clark (D)		.0
4	James Craig (D)	12,439	61.4
	Adams	7,824	38.6
5	Samuel H. Woodson (AM)	7,942	53.3
	Reid (D)	6,947	46.7
6	John S. Phelps (D)	13,424	62.5
	Richardson	8,050	37.5
7	John W. Noell (D)	10,404	64.2
	Zeigler	5,808	35.8

NEW JERSEY

	Candidates	Votes	%
1	John T. Nixon (R)	8,393	48.0
	Walker (D)	5,342	30.6
	Jones (AM)	3,739	21.4
2	John L. N. Stratton (R)	11,471	56.7
	Wall (D)	8,767	43.3
3	Garnett B. Adrain (R)	9,713	51.2
	Paterson (D)	9,255	48.8
4	Jetur R. Riggs (A-LEC D)	8,837	52.0
	Huyler (D)	8,154	48.0
5	William Pennington (R)	11,641	53.8
	Wortendyke (D)	9,982	46.2

NEW YORK

	Candidates	Votes	%
1	Luther C. Carter (R AM)	8,122	52.5
	John A. Searing (D)	7,339	47.5
2	James Humphrey (R AM)	6,475	36.8
	Litchfield (ID)	5,581	31.7
	Taylor (D)	4,578	26.0
	Backhouse (AM)	974	5.5
3	Daniel E. Sickles (D)	3,177	35.0
	Amor J. Williamson (R AM)	3,015	33.3
	Walbe (ID)	2,874	31.7
4	Thomas J. Barr (ID)	3,949	39.7
	Stephens (D)	2,671	26.8
	Brennau (R)	2,290	23.0
	Farmer (D)	710	7.1
5	William B. Maclay (D)	5,780	49.8
	Hamilton (R AM)	4,982	42.9
	Dean (AM)	821	7.1
6	John Cochrane (D)	7,336	57.1
	McCurdy (R AM)	5,520	42.9
7	George Briggs (R AM)	8,306	55.8
	Ward (D)	6,591	44.2
8	Horace F. Clark (R AM)	9,035	58.8
	Herrick (D)	6,338	41.2
9	John B. Haskin (R AM)	7,637	48.3
	Kemble (D)	7,624	48.2
10	Charles H. Van Wyck (R)	6,681	48.4
	Niven (D)	5,532	40.1
	Friend (ID)	1,587	11.5
11	William S. Kenyon (R AM)	8,166	50.3
	Strong (D)	8,067	49.7
12	Charles L. Beale (R AM)	10,750	56.2
	McClellan (D)	8,385	43.8
13	Abram B. Olin (R AM)	8,267	61.1
	Seymour (D)	5,254	38.9
14	John H. Reynolds (R AM)	9,571	52
	Erastus Corning (D)	8,371	46
15	James B. McKean (R)	11,428	53.8
	Odell (D)	9,808	46.2
16	George W. Palmer (R)	7,058	47.9
	Waldo (D)	6,079	41.3
	Watson (AM)	1,589	10.8
17	Francis E. Spinner (R)	12,582	68.7
	Goodrich (D)	5,737	31.3
18	Clark B. Cochrane (R AM)	10,581	53.2
	Goodyear (D)	9,320	46.8
19	James H. Graham (R)	9,981	55.1
	Parker (D)	8,142	44.9
20	Roscoe Conkling (R)	11,084	57.3
	Root (D)	8,251	42.7
21	R. Holland Duell (R)	10,951	57.3
	Sands (D)	8,147	42.7
22	M. Lindley Lee (R)	11,450	57.4
	Asher Tyler (D)	7,425	37.2
	Perry (AM)	1,065	5.3

Footnote, see p. 761.

NEW YORK

	Candidates	Votes	%
23	Charles B. Hoard (R)	9,162	56.1
	Lyon (D)	7,177	43.9
24	Charles B. Sedgwick (R)	8,478	55.1
	Taylor (D)	6,267	40.7
25	Martin Butterfield (R)	10,855	60.7
	Griswold (D)	5,389	30.2
	Sisson (AM)	1,631	9.1
26	Emory B. Pottle (R)	8,598	54.5
	Ogden (D)	7,173	45.5
27	Alfred Wells (R)	10,131	49.2
	Arnot (D)	9,788	47.5
28	William Irvine (R)	9,382	53.3
	Bradley (D)	6,568	37.3
	Denston (AM)	1,651	9.4
29	Alfred Ely (R)	7,276	52.8
	Trimmer (D)	5,114	37.1
	Angle (AM)	1,393	10.1
30	Augustus Frank (R)	9,917	56.6
	Skinner (D)	5,355	30.5
	Black (AM)	2,264	12.9
31	Silas M. Burroughs (R)	6,093	52.5
	Trott (D)	3,376	29.1
	White (AM)	2,132	18.4
32	Elbridge G. Spaulding (R AM)	12,427	62.2
	Hatch (D)	7,539	37.8
33	Reuben E. Fenton (R)	10,018	60.3
	Jenks (D)	4,711	28.4
	Johnn (AM)	1,886	11.4

NORTH CAROLINA

Special Election

		Votes	%
8	Zebulon B. Vance (AM)	8,321	57.0
	William W. Avery (D)	6,272	43.0

OHIO

		Votes	%
1	George H. Pendleton (D)	7,131	51.2
	Day (R)	6,785	48.8
2	John A. Gurley (R)	8,054	52.6
	Groesbeck (D)	7,263	47.4
3	Clement L. Vallandigham (D)	9,903	50.5
	Campbell (R)	9,715	49.5
4	William Allen (D)	9,558	50.5
	Nichols (R)	9,371	49.5
5	James M. Ashley (R)	10,532	51.2
	Mungen (D)	9,986	48.5
6	William Howard (D)	7,792	51.6
	Clark (R)	6,922	45.8
7	Thomas Corwin (R)	8,866	63.9
	Blair (D)	5,020	36.2
8	Benjamin Stanton (R)	8,716	59.5
	Hubbard (D)	5,928	40.5
9	John Carey (R)	9,304	50.3
	Hall (D)	9,197	49.7
10	Carey A. Trimble (R)	10,592	55.1
	Joseph Miller (D)	8,643	44.9

	Candidates	Votes	%
11	Charles D. Martin (D)	9,723	50.7
	Nelson H. Van Vorhes (R)	9,446	49.3
12	Samuel S. Cox (D)	9,560	51.8
	Case (R)	8,913	48.3
13	John Sherman (R)	9,426	57.1
	Patrick (D)	7,095	43.0
14	Cyrus Spink (R)	9,438	56.3
	Jeffries (D)	7,318	43.7
15	William Helmick (R)	8,949	50.7
	Burns (D)	8,719	49.4
16	Cydnor B. Tomkins (R)	7,677	52.8
	Money (D)	6,855	47.2
17	Thomas C. Theaker (R)	7,311	50.3
	Spriggs (D)	7,219	49.7
18	Sidney Edgerton (R)	8,184	53.3
	Ranney (D)	7,162	46.7
19	Edward Wade (R)	8,557	65.1
	Gray (D)	4,597	35.0
20	John Hutchins (R)	8,321	62.8
	Tod (D)	4,541	34.3
21	John A. Bingham (R)	8,883	57.5
	Mans (D)	6,577	42.5

OREGON

(Became a state Feb. 14, 1859)

		Votes	%
AL	La Fayette Grover (D)	5,859	57.9
	James K. Kelley (OPP)	4,210	41.6

PENNSYLVANIA

		Votes	%
1	Thomas B. Florence (D)	6,823	43.3
	Ryan (UN)	6,492	41.2
	Nebg (A-LEC D)	2,442	15.5
2	Edward Joy Morris (UN)	5,653	58.4
	Martin (D)	4,030	41.6
3	John P. Verree (UN)	6,977	54.2
	Landy (D)	5,834	45.4
4	William Millward (UN)	9,749	59.3
	Phillips (D)	6,451	39.2
5	John Wood (UN)	9,701	57.4
	Jones (D)	7,209	42.6
6	John Hickman (A-LEC D)	6,786	40.8
	Manley (D)	5,185	31.2
	Broomall (UN)	4,676	28.1
7	Henry C. Longnecker (UN)	8,324	50.8
	Roberts (D)	8,076	49.2
8	John Schwartz (UN)	7,321	50.1
	Jones (D)	7,302	49.9
9	Thaddeus Stevens (U)	9,513	60.0
	Hopkins (D)	6,341	40.0
10	John W. Killinger (UN)	8,897	61.4
	Weidle (D)	5,589	38.6
11	James H. Campbell (UN)	7,153	47.2
	Dewart (D)	4,387	29.0
	Cake (A-LEC D)	3,614	23.9
12	George W. Scranton (UN)	10,023	61.8
	McReynolds (D)	6,186	38.2
13	William H. Dimmick (D)	8,009	55.0
	Shoemaker (UN)	6,566	45.1

	Candidates	Votes	%
14	Galusha A. Grow (UN)	11,165	76.9
	Parkhurst (D)	3,359	23.1
15	James T. Hale (UN)	9,238	55.7
	Allison White (D)	7,349	44.3
16	Benjamin F. Junkin (UN)	8,646	50.1
	Fisher (D)	8,600	49.9
17	Edward McPherson (UN)	9,348	50.7
	Reilly (D)	9,081	49.3
18	Samuel S. Blair (UN)	9,114	57.7
	Pershing (D)	6,679	42.3
19	John Covode (UN)	9,257	53.1
	Foster (D)	8,165	46.9
20	William Montgomery (D)	9,254	61.5
	Knight (UN)	5,798	38.5
21	James K. Moorhead (UN)	6,539	57.3
	Burke (D)	4,879	42.7
22	Robert McKnight (UN)	5,438	55.3
	Williams (A-TAX)	3,903	39.7
	Birmingham (D)	502	5.1
23	William Stewart (UN)	6,721	64.0
	McGuffin (D)	3,777	36.0
24	Chapin Hall (UN)	8,905	52.3
	Gillis (D)	8,111	47.7
25	Elijah Babbitt (UN)	6,360	60.7
	Marshall (D)	4,113	39.3

Special Election

		Votes	%
8	William H. Keim (R)	6,156	52.0
	Wanner (D)	5,687	48.0

SOUTH CAROLINA

		Votes	%
1	John McQueen (D)		100.0
2	William P. Miles (D)		100.0
3	Lawrence M. Keitt (D)		100.0
4	Milledge L. Bonham (SSR D)		100.0
5	John D. Ashmore (D)	7,198	59.4
	Thomas O. P. Vernon	4,926	40.6
6	William W. Boyce (SSR D)		100.0

VERMONT

		Votes	%
1	Eliakim P. Walton (R)	9,615	72.9
	Eastman (D)	3,577	27.1
2	Justin S. Morrill (R)	11,576	70.7
	Chase (D)	4,806	29.3
3	Homer E. Royce (R)	7,418	69.3
	Bingham (D)	3,280	30.7

WISCONSIN

		Votes	%
1	John F. Potter (R)	14,428	56.4
	Brown (D)	11,171	43.6
2	Cadwallader C. Washburn (R)	23,917	54.3
	Dunn (D)	20,167	45.8
3	Charles H. Larrabee (D)	23,910	51.0
	Billinghurst (R)	23,011	49.0

1. *According to the Biographical Directory, Charles L. Scott and John C. Burch represented California in the House of Representatives for the 36th Congress (1859-61). But neither one is listed in the ICPSR returns for the 1858 election as a candidate. Congressional Quarterly was unable to resolve the discrepancy. According to the Biographical Directory, McKibbin was defeated for re-election in 1858 to the 36th Congress.*

1859 House Elections

ALABAMA

	Candidates	Votes	%
1	James A. Stallworth (D)	7,352	63.3
	F. B. Shepard (SEC D)	4,258	36.7
2	James L. Pugh (D)	2,643	81.1
	J. E. Sappington (SO RTS)	615	18.9
3	David Clopton (D)	6,879	50.8
	T. J. Judge (SR W)	6,666	49.2
4	Sydenham Moore (D)	1,648	96.9
5	George S. Houston (D)	5,964	58.1
	W. A. Hewlett (D)	4,298	41.9
6	Williamson R. W. Cobb (D)	5,731	55.0
	Alex Snodgrass (D)	2,112	20.3
	Edwin Wallace	1,885	18.1
	H. R. Beaver	695	6.7
7	Jabez L. M. Curry (SO RTS D)	✔	

CONNECTICUT

		Votes	%
1	Dwight Loomis (R)	9,940	49.6
	Alvan P. Hyde (D)	9,875	49.3
2	John Woodruff (R)	10,669	50.6
	Samuel Arnold (D)	10,347	49.0
3	Alfred A. Burnham (R)	7,586	51.7
	Rufus L. Baker (D)	6,883	47.0
4	Orris S. Ferry (R)	11,536	51.3
	William D. Bishop (D)	10,966	48.7

GEORGIA

		Votes	%
1	Peter E. Love (D)	7,253	65.1
	McIntyre (OPP)	3,881	34.9
2	Martin J. Crawford (D)	8,279	56.3
	Douglas (OPP)	6,437	43.7
3	Thomas Hardman (OPP)	5,636	50.7
	Speer (D)	5,483	49.3
4	Lucius J. Gartrell (D)	8,877	59.5
	Wright (OPP)	6,053	40.5
5	John W. H. Underwood (D)	12,339	85.1
	Shackleford (OPP)	2,162	14.9
6	James Jackson (D)	9,644	74.8
	Lytle (OPP)	3,251	25.2
7	Joshua Hill (OPP)	4,492	50.8
	Harper (D)	4,353	49.2
8	John J. Jones (D)	4,912	52.2
	Wright (OPP)	4,507	47.9

ILLINOIS[1]

Special Elections

		Votes	%
6	Charles D. Hodges (D)	11,014	61.1
	James C. Coukling	6,951	38.6
6	John A. McClernand (D)	14,337	58.9
	John M. Palmer	10,001	41.1

KENTUCKY

		Votes	%
1	Henry C. Burnett (D)	11,540	83.7
	William Morrow	2,248	16.3
2	Samuel O. Peyton (D)	7,939	52.4
	James S. Jackson (UNT)	7,199	47.6
3	Francis M. Bristow (D)	7,164	56.2
	W. W. Sale (D)	5,575	43.8
4	William C. Anderson (AM)	7,204	50.0
	James S. Chrisman (D)	7,201	50.0
5	John Young Brown (D)	6,927	57.8
	J. H. Jewett (ID)	5,066	42.2
6	Green Adams (AM)	8,164	53.0
	T. T. Garrard (D)	7,231	47.0
7	Robert Mallory (UN D)	6,416	53.1
	Thomas Holt (D)	5,675	46.9
8	William E. Simms (D)	6,932	50.2
	John M. Harlan	6,865	49.8

	Candidates	Votes	%
9	Laban T. Moore (N AM)	8,505	50.8
	James W. Moore (D)	8,227	49.2
10	John W. Stevenson (D)	9,295	61.4
	Thomas L. Jones	5,839	38.6

LOUISIANA

		Votes	%
1	John E. Bouligny (OPP)	2,215	55.2
	Lasere (D)	1,796	44.8
2	Miles Taylor (D)	5,908	57.0
	Nichols (OPP)	4,459	43.0
3	Thomas G. Davidson (D)	6,288	89.7
	Cannon (OPP)	726	10.4
4	John M. Landrum (D)	8,823	73.3
	Jones (OPP)	3,220	26.7

MARYLAND

		Votes	%
1	James A. Stewart (D)	6,934	52.1
	Cox (AM)	6,384	47.9
2	Edwin H. Webster (AM)	9,237	52.0
	McHenry (D)	8,518	48.0
3	J. Morrison Harris (AM)	9,612	69.5
	William P. Preston (D)	4,224	30.5
4	H. Winter Davis (AM)	10,068	78.3
	William G. Harrison (I)	2,796	21.7
5	Jacob M. Kunkel (D)	8,852	50.4
	Hoffman (AM)	8,719	49.6
6	George W. Hughes (D)	6,337	54.2
	Hagner (I)	5,353	45.8

MINNESOTA

		Votes	%
AL	Cyrus Aldrich (R)	21,360 ✔	
	William Windom (R)	21,016 ✔	
	James M. Cavanaugh (D)	17,666	
	Graham (D)	17,514	

MISSISSIPPI

		Votes	%
1	L. Q. C. Lamar (D)	4,140	97.8
2	Reuben Davis (D)	7,555	96.3
3	William Barksdale (D)	6,699	100.0
4	Otho R. Singleton (D)	6,686	74.7
	Frank Smith (UN D)	2,262	25.3
5	John L. McRae (D)	4,567	89.8
	G. W. Wilcox	517	10.2

NEW HAMPSHIRE

		Votes	%
1	Gilman Marston (R)	12,839	51.5
	Marcy (D)	12,082	48.5
2	Mason W. Tappan (R)	11,288	52.5
	George (D)	10,228	47.5
3	Thomas M. Edwards (R)	11,717	52.4
	Burns (D)	10,639	47.6

NORTH CAROLINA

		Votes	%
1	William N. H. Smith (OPP D)	6,045	52.2
	Henry M. Shaw (D)	5,531	47.8
2	Thomas Ruffin (D)	4,382	90.2
3	Warren Winslow (D)	4,774	78.8
	Malcom J. McDuffie (D & AM)	1,284	21.2
4	Lawrence O'B. Branch (D)	5,764	70.2
	Linn B. Sanders (OPP D)	2,446	29.8
5	John A. Gilmer (OPP D)	6,361	58.1
	Stephen E. Williams (D)	4,512	41.2
6	James M. Leach (OPP D)	8,566	52.8
	Alfred M. Scales (D)	7,664	47.2
7	F. Burton Craige (D)	5,495	57.4
	Samuel H. Walkup (OPP D)	4,075	42.6
8	Zebulon B. Vance (OPP D)	8,026	55.9
	David Coleman (D)	6,331	44.1

OREGON

	Candidates	Votes	%
AL	Lansing Stout (D)	5,646	50.1
	David Logan (R)	5,630	49.9

RHODE ISLAND[2]

		Votes	%
1	Christopher Robinson (AM & R)	3,797	49.0
	Thomas Davis (R)	2,422	31.2
	Olney Arnold (D)	1,532	19.8
2	William D. Brayton (R)	3,101	63.9
	Alfred Anthony (D)	1,746	36.0

Special Election

		Votes	%
1	Christopher Robinson (AM & R)	3,414	56.0
	Thomas Davis (R)	2,648	43.4

TENNESSEE

		Votes	%
1	Thomas A. R. Nelson (OPP)	7,931	50.3
	Haynes (D)	7,827	49.7
2	Horace Maynard (OPP)	6,476	56.8
	Ramsay (D)	4,930	43.2
3	Reese B. Brabson (OPP)	8,372	50.2
	Smith (D)	8,313	49.8
4	William B. Stokes (OPP)	6,633	51.9
	Savage (D)	6,160	48.2
5	Robert H. Hatton (OPP)	6,719	53.5
	Charles Ready (I & D)	5,844	46.5
6	James H. Thomas (D)	9,023	100.0
7	John V. Wright (D)	9,380	77.6
	Gibbs (OPP)	2,711	22.4
8	James M. Quarles (OPP)	6,994	52.9
	Menees (D)	6,236	47.1
9	Emerson Etheridge (OPP)	9,437	50.0
	Atkins (D)	9,430	50.0
10	William T. Avery (D)	5,954	50.3
	Sneed (OPP)	5,648	47.7

TEXAS

		Votes	%
1	John H. Reagan (D)	20,565	85.3
	Ochiltree	3,541	14.7
2	Andrew J. Hamilton (ID)	16,521	50.7
	Waul (D)	16,079	49.3

VIRGINIA

		Votes	%
1	Muscoe H. R. Garnett (D)		100.0
2	John S. Millson (D)		100.0
3	Daniel C. De Jarnette (ID&OPP)	5,581	50.5
	Caskie (D)	5,481	49.6
4	William O. Goode (D)	3,820	63.6
	Flournoy (ID&OPP)	2,185	36.4
5	Thomas S. Bocock (D)		100.0
6	Shelton F. Leake (ID)	5,003	59.2
	Powell (D)	3,453	40.8
7	William Smith (D)	5,147	49.4
	Thomas (OPP)	4,845	46.5
8	Alexander R. Boteler (OPP)	6,616	50.6
	Faulkner (D)	6,449	49.4
9	John T. Harris (ID)	5,345	52.2
	Skinner (D)	4,900	47.8
10	Sherrard Clemens (D)		100.0
11	Albert G. Jenkins (D)	9,038	55.6
	Laidley (OPP)	7,228	44.4
12	Henry A. Edmundson (D)		100.0
13	Elbert S. Martin (ID)	6,382	53.4
	Floyd (D)	5,579	46.6

Special Election

		Votes	%
4	Roger A. Pryor (D)	✔	

Footnotes, see p. 764.

1860 House Elections

ARKANSAS

(Seceded May 8, 1861)

	Candidates	Votes	%
1	Thomas C. Hindman (D)	20,051*	67.4
	Cypert (I)	9,699	32.6
2	Gantt (I)	16,569*	56.0
	Mitchell (D)	13,007	44.0

DELAWARE

		Votes	%
AL	George P. Fisher (UN)	7,732	48.4
	Briggs (SO D)	7,475	46.8

FLORIDA

(Seceded Jan. 11, 1861)

		Votes	%
AL	R. B. Hilton (D)	7,722*	59.9
	B. F. Allen (KST U)	5,172	40.1

ILLINOIS

		Votes	%
1	Elihu B. Washburne (R)	21,436	70.6
	Theodore A. C. Beard (D)	8,929	29.4
2	Isaac N. Arnold (R)	30,834	64.4
	Augustus M. Herrington (D)	16,950	35.4
3	Owen Lovejoy (R)	29,600	59.9
	Robert N. Murray (D)	18,843	38.2
4	William Kellogg (R)	25,668	54.6
	Robert G. Ingersoll (D)	21,297	45.3
5	William A. Richardson (D)	16,946	53.5
	Bug Prentiss (R)	14,684	46.4
6	John A. McClernand (D)	21,206	56.6
	Henry Case (R)	16,244	43.4
7	James C. Robinson (D)	19,206	54.1
	James T. Cunningham (R)	16,313	45.9
8	Philip B. Fouke (D)	16,592	55.2
	Joseph Gillespie (R)	13,315	44.3
9	John A. Logan (D)	20,863	79.5
	Unidentified Candidate (R)	5,207	19.9

INDIANA

		Votes	%
1	John Law (D)	13,476	55.7
	Debruler (R)	10,731	44.3
2	James A. Cravens (D)	10,811	51.3
	Davis (R)	10,272	48.7
3	William McKee Dunn (R)	11,545	54.5
	Daily (D)	9,622	45.5
4	William S. Holman (D)	10,299	50.7
	Yatar (R)	10,007	49.3
5	George W. Julian (R)	12,237	62.0
	Bickle (D)	7,501	38.0
6	Albert G. Porter (R)	13,029	52.3
	Walpole (D)	11,887	47.7
7	Daniel W. Voorhees (D)	12,535	52.1
	Nelson (R)	11,516	47.9
8	Albert S. White (R)	13,310	53.7
	Wilson (D)	11,489	46.3
9	Schuyler Colfax (R)	16,860	55.6
	Cathcart (D)	13,458	44.4
10	William Mitchell (R)	14,267	55.6
	Kenkle (D)	11,378	44.4
11	John P. C. Shanks (R)	13,885	54.1
	Steele (D)	11,796	45.9

IOWA

		Votes	%
1	Samuel R. Curtis (R)	33,936	52.9
	C. C. Cole (D)	30,240	47.1
2	William Vandever (R)	36,805	57.5
	Ben M. Samuels (D)	27,206	42.5

MAINE

	Candidates	Votes	%
1	John N. Goodwin (R)	12,018	53.0
	Hayes (D)	10,556	46.5
2	Charles W. Walton (R)	12,806	55.6
	Record (D)	10,192	44.3
3	Samuel C. Fessenden (R)	10,065	52.5
	Johnson (D)	9,090	47.4
4	Anson P. Morrill (R)	12,666	61.6
	Fuller (D)	7,262	35.3
5	John H. Rice (R)	12,317	59.8
	Blake (D)	7,965	38.7
6	Frederick A. Pike (R)	9,451	53.9
	Bradbury (D)	7,893	45.1

MASSACHUSETTS

		Votes	%
1	Thomas D. Eliot (R)	7,350	72.5
	Daniel Fisher	1,061	10.5
	Moses Bates	878	8.7
	F. C. Sandford	845	8.3
2	James Buffinton (R)	10,103	68.4
	Aaron Hobart	4,409	29.9
3	Charles F. Adams (R)	10,530	58.4
	Leverett Saltonstall	7,449	41.3
4	Alexander H. Rice (R)	7,292	52.3
	Erastus B. Bigelow	6,645	47.6
5	William Appleton (R)	8,014	50.8
	Anson Burlingame	7,756	49.2
6	John B. Alley (R)	9,644	63.1
	Otis P. Lord	2,471	16.2
	Jefferson Knight	2,200	14.4
7	Daniel W. Gooch (R)	11,373	60.2
	Charles A. Welch	6,730	35.6
8	Charles R. Train (R)	9,272	64.6
	A. R. Brown	2,390	16.6
	Winthrop E. Faulkner	2,239	15.6
9	Goldsmith F. Bailey (R)	9,745	54.6
	Eli Thayer (I)	7,949	44.6
10	Charles Delano (R)	10,021	75.1
	Josiah Allis	2,528	18.9
	B. Leavitt	744	5.6
11	Henry L. Dawes (R)	10,409	67.6
	Norman T. Leonard	4,396	28.5

MICHIGAN

		Votes	%
1	Bradley F. Granger (R)	16,997	52.5
	George V. N. Lathrop (D)	15,216	47.0
2	Fernando C. Beaman (R)	19,162	60.1
	Salathiel C. Coffenberry (D)	12,700	39.8
3	Francis W. Kellogg (R)	28,641	59.0
	Thomas B. Church (D)	19,737	40.6
4	Rowland E. Trowbridge (R)	23,650	55.3
	Edward Thompson (D)	19,099	44.7

MINNESOTA

		Votes	%
AL	Cyrus Aldrich (R)	22,333✔	
	William Windom (R)	22,165✔	
	James George (D)	12,172	
	J. M. Gilman (D)	12,168	
	A. J. Edgerton (SO D)	787	
	J. W. Taylor (SO D)	776	

MISSOURI

		Votes	%
1	Francis P. Blair Jr. (R)	11,453	44.1
	John H. Barret (D)	9,967	38.4
	Todd (AM)	4,542	17.5
2	James S. Rollins (OPP)	11,161	50.6
	Henderson (D)	10,908	49.4
3	John B. Clark (D)	14,822	59.1
	Hawkins (OPP)	10,276	40.9

	Candidates	Votes	%
4	Elijah H. Norton (D)	13,797	62.3
	Scott (OPP)	8,350	37.7
5	John W. Reid (D)	11,689	52.8
	Mitchell (OPP)	10,432	47.2
6	John S. Phelps (D)	11,363	55.0
	Rains (OPP)	9,301	45.0
7	John W. Noell (D)	11,191	73.6
	Perryman (OPP)	4,007	26.4

Special Election

		Votes	%
1	John R. Barret (D)	12,682‡	50.3
	Francis P. Blair Jr (R)	12,538	49.7

NEW JERSEY

		Votes	%
1	John T. Nixon (R)	10,843	52.7
	Leaming (D)	9,737	47.3
2	John L. N. Stratton (R)	13,582	52.8
	Green (D)	12,154	47.2
3	William G. Steele (D)	12,843	55.2
	Berthoud (R)	10,438	44.8
4	George T. Cobb (D)	10,789	52.6
	Edsall (R)	9,711	47.4
5	Nehemiah Perry (D)	16,200	50.6
	Pennington (R)	15,802	49.4

NEW YORK

		Votes	%
1	Edward H. Smith (FUS)	11,882	52.8
	Carter (R)	10,631	47.2
2	Moses F. Odell (FUS)	13,322	55.1
	Humphrey (R)	10,870	44.9
3	Benjamin Wood (D)	5,892	52.8
	Williamson (R)	4,585	41.1
	Savage (ID)	675	6.1
4	James E. Kerrigan (ID)	5,145	41.3
	Tuomy (D)	3,989	32.0
	Commerford (R)	3,324	26.7
5	William Wall (R)	6,877	41.0
	Taylor (D)	6,811	40.6
	Duffy (ID)	3,085	18.4
6	Frederick A. Conkling (R)	6,536	35.1
	Cochran (ID)	6,360	34.2
	Chanler (D)	5,724	30.7
7	Elijah Ward (D)	10,814	56.2
	Dow (R)	8,417	43.8
8	Isaac C. Delaplaine (D)	13,576	59.0
	Abram Wakeman (R)	9,417	41.0
9	Edward Haight (D)	11,389	53.5
	Nelson (R)	9,882	46.5
10	Charles H. Van Wyck (R)	8,311	50.5
	St. John (FUS)	8,163	49.6
11	John B. Steele (D)	9,938	50.4
	Sylvester (R)	9,789	49.6
12	Stephen Baker (R)	11,795	52.0
	Wager (D)	10,514	46.3
13	Abram B. Olin (R)	8,650	51.1
	McConihe (D)	8,268	48.9
14	Erastus Corning (D)	10,814	51.9
	Olcott (R)	10,043	48.2
15	James B. McKean (R)	14,924	58.8
	Davis (D)	10,474	41.2
16	William A. Wheeler (R)	10,571	58.7
	Hand (D)	7,427	41.3
17	Socrates N. Sherman (R)	16,134	68.4
	Foote (D)	7,456	31.6
18	Chauncey Vibbard (D)	12,019	50.9
	Mix (R)	11,602	49.1
19	Richard Franchot (R)	11,310	57.0
	Walworth (D)	8,542	43.0
20	Roscoe Conkling (R)	12,536	58.3
	Grove (D)	8,973	41.7
21	R. Holland Duell (R)	13,960	62.2
	Hitchcock (D)	4,923	21.9
	Nelson (BRECK D)	3,559	15.9

NEW YORK

	Candidates	Votes	%
22	William E. Lansing (R)	15,253	63.7
	Chapman (D)	8,682	36.3
23	Ambrose W. Clark (R)	11,865	59.9
	Starbuck (D)	7,568	38.2
24	Charles B. Sedgwick (R)	11,175	60.4
	Teft (D)	6,088	32.9
	Hay (BRECK D)	1,233	6.7
25	Theodore M. Pomeroy (R)	14,437	64.5
	Beardsley (D)	7,961	35.5
26	Jacob P. Chamberlain (R)	11,581	58.3
	Lewis (D)	8,153	41.0
27	Alexander S. Diven (R)	13,482	57.2
	Dowe (D)	10,088	42.8
28	Robert B. Van Valkenburg (R)	13,167	60.8
	Walker (D)	8,507	39.3
29	Alfred Ely (R)	10,704	59.4
	Reynolds (D)	7,314	40.6
30	Augustus Frank (R)	15,342	67.5
	Robinson (D)	7,389	32.5
31	Burt Van Horn (R)	8,662	58.8
	Ely (D)	5,882	39.9
32	Elbridge G. Spaulding (R)	12,256	52.8
	Haven (D)	10,947	47.2
33	Reuben E. Fenton (R)	14,303	66.8
	Lee (D)	7,111	33.2

Special Election

		Votes	%
31	Edwin R. Reynolds (R)	8,759	59.4
	Peck (D)	5,801	39.4

OHIO

		Votes	%
1	George H. Pendleton (D)	7,485	48.9
	Spencer (R)	6,582	43.0
	Jones	1,250	8.2
2	John A. Gurley (R)	8,469	48.1
	Long (D)	7,586	43.1
	Harrison	1,555	8.8
3	Clement L. Vallandigham (D)	11,052	50.2
	Craighead (R)	10,918	49.6
4	William Allen (D)	11,756	51.7
	Hart (R)	10,968	48.3
5	James M. Ashley (R)	13,756	52.3
	Steedman (D)	12,552	47.7
6	Chilton A. White (D)	10,046	53.2
	Murphy (R)	8,828	46.8
7	Thomas Corwin (R)	10,693	70.0
	Telfair (D)	3,082	20.2
	Stokes	1,512	9.9
8	Samuel Shellabarger (R)	10,931	58.3
	Harrison (D)	7,831	41.7
9	Warren P. Noble (D)	12,650	51.1
	Carey (R)	12,096	48.9
10	Carey A. Trimble (R)	11,593	51.3
	Hutchinson (D)	11,025	48.7
11	Valentine B. Horton (R)	11,965	51.5
	Martin (D)	11,275	48.5

	Candidates	Votes	%
12	Samuel S. Cox (D)	11,014	52.1
	Galloway (R)	10,131	47.9
13	John Sherman (R)	11,428	57.2
	Burns (D)	8,564	42.8
14	Harrison G. O. Blake (R)	12,040	57.1
	Prentiss (D)	9,053	42.9
15	Robert H. Nugen (D)	10,281	52.1
	William Helmick (R)	9,439	47.9
16	William P. Cutler (R)	8,560	50.2
	Jewett (D)	8,496	49.8
17	James R. Morris (D)	9,609	51.0
	Thomas C. Theaker (R)	8,510	45.2
18	Sidney Edgerton (R)	9,720	58.3
	Starkweather (D)	6,956	41.7
19	Albert G. Riddle (R)	11,927	69.1
	Williams (D)	5,343	30.9
20	John Hutchins (R)	10,840	72.0
	Wilson (D)	4,222	28.0
21	John A. Bingham (R)	9,170	61.2
	Wells (D)	5,053	33.7
	Blakeley	768	5.1

OREGON

		Votes	%
AL	George K. Sheil (D)	6,632	50.4
	D. Logan (R)	6,529	49.6

PENNSYLVANIA

		Votes	%
1	John M. Butler (R)	8,581	45.1
	William E. Lehman (D)	8,383	44.1
	King (UN)	2,057	10.8
2	Edward Joy Morris (R)	6,259	46.6
	Brodhead (D)	5,410	40.3
	Fuller (UN)	1,760	13.1
3	John P. Verre (R)	8,931	49.1
	Kline (D)	8,909	49.0
4	William D. Kelley (R)	11,568	49.3
	Morgan (D)	10,195	43.4
	Robinson (UN)	1,715	7.3
5	William Morris Davis (R)	10,020	50.8
	Ingersoll (D)	9,724	49.3
6	John Hickman (R)	10,140	56.8
	Brinton (D)	7,701	43.2
7	Thomas B. Cooper (D)	10,762	50.3
	Longnecker (R)	10,620	49.7
8	Sydenham E. Ancona (D)	9,993	58.4
	Smith (R)	7,111	41.6
9	Thaddeus Stevens (R)	12,964	96.5
10	John W. Killinger (R)	12,246	62.1
	Worrell (D)	7,488	37.9
11	James H. Campbell (R)	9,867	50.9
	Hughes (D)	9,518	49.1
12	George W. Scranton (R)	11,719	51.5
	Randall (D)	11,024	48.5
13	Philip Johnson (D)	12,208	57.3
	Shoemaker (R)	9,096	42.7
14	Galusha A. Grow (R)	14,922	71.4
	Sherwood (D)	5,984	28.6

	Candidates	Votes	%
15	James T. Hale (R)	11,907	53.8
	Fleming (D)	10,243	46.2
16	Joseph Bailey (D)	12,069	50.8
	Junkin (R)	11,712	49.3
17	Edward McPherson (R)	11,945	51.2
	Schell (D)	11,372	48.8
18	Samuel S. Blair (R)	11,185	57.6
	McAllister (D)	8,220	42.4
19	John Covode (R)	11,769	54.7
	Phelps (D)	9,761	45.3
20	Jesse Lazear (D)	10,607	52.9
	Stewart (R)	9,443	47.1
21	James K. Morehead (R)	10,507	61.3
	Kerr (D)	6,631	38.7
22	Robert McKnight (R)	7,978	72.8
	Mitchell (D)	2,979	27.2
23	John W. Wallace (R)	7,636	55.6
	Holstein (D)	6,102	44.4
24	John D. Patton (R)	11,745	52.6
	Kerr (D)	10,582	47.4
25	Elijah Babbitt (R)	10,705	65.9
	Wilson (D)	5,551	34.2

Special Election

		Votes	%
8	Jacob K. McKenty (D)	9,595	56.2
	McKnight (R)	7,482	43.8

SOUTH CAROLINA[1]

(Seceded Dec. 20, 1860)

			%
1	John McQueen (D)		
	C. W. Miller		
2	William P. Miles (D)		100.0
3	George P. Elliott		
	Lewis M. Ayer		
4	Milledge L. Bonham (SSR D)		100.0
5	John D. Ashmore (D)		100.0
6	William W. Boyce (SSR D)		100.0

VERMONT

		Votes	%
1	Eliakim Persons Walton (R)	10,268	75.2
	Wilcox (D)	3,389	24.8
2	Justin S. Morrill (R)	12,555	79.2
	Charles N. Davenport (D)	3,295	20.8
3	Portus Baxter (R)	8,326	76.3
	Chaffee (D)	2,588	23.7

WISCONSIN

		Votes	%
1	John F. Potter (R)	16,197	54.5
	Arnold (D)	13,508	45.5
2	Luther Hanchett (R)	36,223	61.2
	Reynolds (D)	23,008	38.8
3	A. Scott Sloan (R)	34,002	54.0
	Charles H. Larrabee (D)	28,986	46.0

1859 Elections

1. *Rep. Thomas L. Harris died Nov. 24, 1858, following his re-election to the 36th Congress (1859-61). In a special election in January 1859 to fill the remaining few months of Harris' term in the 35th Congress (1857-59), the winner was Charles D. Hodges. John A. McClernand was elected in November 1859 to the unexpired term in the 36th Congress.*

2. *In the 1st district, no candidate received the majority required by state law for election. In a later special election, Christopher Robinson was finally chosen.*

1860 Election

1. *South Carolina's six representatives withdrew from the House before the beginning of the 37th Congress (1861-63), and thus never assumed the seats they were elected to.*

1861 House Elections

ALABAMA

(Seceded Jan. 11, 1861)

CALIFORNIA [1]

	Candidates	Votes	%
AL	Timothy G. Phelps (R)	51,651✔	
	Aaron A. Sargent (R)	50,692✔	
	H. Edgerton (UN D)	35,449	
	J. C. McKibben (UN D)	35,401	
	D. O. Shattuck (SEC D)	31,712	
	H. P. Barber (SEC D)	31,591	
AL	Frederick F. Low	39,059	45.6
	F. Gunahl	24,036	28.1
	J.R. Gitchell	22,550	26.3

CONNECTICUT

	Candidates	Votes	%
1	Dwight Loomis (R)	10,701	50.3
	Hyde (D)	10,563	49.7
2	James E. English (D)	12,490	52.3
	Wdff (R)	11,396	47.7
3	Alfred A. Burnham (R)	8,701	57.3
	Baker (D)	6,496	42.8
4	George C. Woodruff (D)	11,739	50.2
	Ferry (R)	11,668	49.9

GEORGIA

(Seceded Jan. 28, 1861)

ILLINOIS

Special Election

		Votes	%
6	Anthony L. Knapp (D)	8,283	98.0

IOWA

Special Election

	Candidates	Votes	%
1	James F. Wilson (R)	28,133	56.7
	Juirus E. Neal (D)	20,328	40.9

KANSAS

(Became a state Jan. 29, 1861)

AL	Martin F. Conway (R)		✔

KENTUCKY

		Votes	%
1	Henry C. Burnett (SEC D)	8,988	59.1
	Lawrence S. Trimble (UN)	6,225	40.9
2	James S. Jackson (UN)	9,281	73.4
	John T. Bunch (SEC D)	3,364	26.6
3	Henry Grider (UN)	10,392	77.0
	Joseph H. Lewis (SEC D)	3,113	23.1
4	Aaron Harding (UN)	10,339	80.7
	Albert G. Talbott (SEC D)	2,469	19.3
5	Charles A. Wickliffe (UN)	8,217	75.1
	H. E. Read (SEC D)	2,719	24.9
6	George W. Dunlop (UN)	8,101	97.3
7	Robert Mallory (UN)	11,035	79.4
	Horatio W. Bruce (SEC D)	2,862	20.6
8	John J. Crittenden (UN)	8,272	59.2
	William E. Simms (SEC D)	5,706	40.8
9	William H. Wadsworth (UN)	12,130	75.9
	John L. Williams (SEC D)	3,850	24.1
10	John W. Menzies (UN)	8,373	64.9
	Overton P. Hogan (SEC D)	3,774	29.3
	Thomas L. Jones	698	5.4

LOUISIANA

(Seceded Jan. 26, 1861)

MARYLAND

	Candidates	Votes	%
1	John W. Crisfield (UN R)	7,181	57.4
	Hny (PEACE D)	5,331	42.6
2	Edwin H. Webster (UN R)	7,251	98.3
3	Cornelius L. L. Leary (UN R)	6,702	52.0
	Preston (PEACE D)	6,200	48.1
4	Henry May (PEACE D)	8,424	57.6
	Davis (UN R)	6,214	42.5
5	Francis Thomas (UN R)	10,582	97.1
6	Charles B. Calvert (UN R)	4,467	50.9
	Harris (PEACE D)	4,305	49.1

MISSISSIPPI

(Seceded Jan. 9, 1861)

NEW HAMPSHIRE

		Votes	%
1	Gilman Marston (R)	13,055	52.9
	Marcy (D)	11,642	47.1
2	Edward H. Rollins (R)	10,763	52.4
	Bell (D)	9,791	47.6
3	Thomas M. Edwards (R)	11,778	54.2
	Burns (D)	9,940	45.8

NORTH CAROLINA

(Seceded May 21, 1861)

RHODE ISLAND

		Votes	%
1	William P. Sheffield (UN)	6,998	51.2
	Robinson (R)	6,656	48.7
2	George H. Browne (UN)	4,411	53.3
	Brayton (R)	3,856	46.6

TENNESSEE

(Seceded June 8, 1861)

TEXAS

(Seceded Feb. 1, 1861)

VIRGINIA

(Seceded April 17, 1861)

1. California had two seats in the House during the 36th Congress (1859-61), but following the reapportionment after the census of 1860 it would have been entitled to three in the 38th Congress (1863-65). Most states held House elections in even-numbered years, so those which were entitled to larger House representation would have had to wait until after the election of 1862 to claim it. But California held its regular House election in 1861, and tried to fill three seats.

Phelps and Sargent were elected to California's two regular seats. The Biographical Directory says that Frederick F. Low presented credentials and claimed a third seat Dec. 2, 1861, but the House May 6, 1862, declared him not entitled to a seat. Following passage of an act of June 2, 1862, granting California its third seat before it normally would have received it, he was admitted.

The ballot arrangement for California's 1861 House election was ambiguous. The ICPSR returns suggest that Low, Gunahl and Gitchell were probably listed in a separate column on the ballot as candidates in a separate at-large election for the prospective third seat, and Low's claim to the seat would be based on his having finished first among the three.

A second possibility is that all nine candidates for the House ran against each other in one at-large election. Low would have finished with the third highest number of votes in such a contest, and could conceivably have claimed the House seat on that basis.

1862 House Elections

DELAWARE

Candidates	Votes	%
AL William Temple (D)	8,051	50.1
George P. Fisher (UN)	8,014	49.9

ILLINOIS

	Candidates	Votes	%
1	Isaac N. Arnold (R)	10,025	54.5
	Francis C. Sherman (D)	8,387	45.6
2	John F. Farnsworth (R)	12,612	72.5
	Neil Donnelly (D)	4,785	27.5
3	Elihu B. Washburne (R)	10,496	60.7
	Elias B. Stiles (D)	6,785	39.3
4	Charles M. Harris (D)	11,626	57.2
	Charles B. Lawrence (R)	8,711	42.8
5	Owen Lovejoy (R)	11,683	50.1
	Thomas J. Henderson (D)	11,020	47.3
6	Jesse O. Norton (R)	10,604	55.7
	F. Lyle Dickey (D)	8,419	44.3
7	John R. Eden (D)	11,361	53.2
	Elijah McCarty (R)	10,004	46.8
8	John T. Stuart (D)	12,808	52.8
	Leonard Swett (R)	11,443	47.2
9	Lewis W. Ross (D)	13,391	99.1
10	Anthony L. Knapp (D)	14,259	64.8
	Samuel W. Moulton (R)	7,712	35.0
11	James C. Robinson (D)	13,644	71.2
	Stephen G. Hicks (R)	5,521	28.8
12	William R. Morrison (D)	10,999	61.6
	Robert Smith (R)	6,854	38.4
13	William J. Allen (D)	9,497	68.8
	Milton Bartley (R)	4,290	31.1
AL	James C. Allen (D)	136,257	53.2
	Ebon C. Ingersoll (R)	119,819	46.8

Special Election

	Candidates	Votes	%
9	William J. Allen (D)	4,795	35.7
	Irham W. Hayrin	4,053	30.2
	Samuel S. Marshall	3,983	29.6

INDIANA

	Candidates	Votes	%
1	John Law (D)	11,963	53.1
	Johnson (UN R)	10,583	46.9
2	James A. Cravens (D)	10,911	64.7
	May (UN R)	5,951	35.3
3	Henry W. Harrington (D)	11,524	53.4
	William McKee Dunn (UN R)	10,044	46.6
4	William S. Holman (D)	10,926	57.8
	Gavin (UN R)	7,992	42.3
5	George W. Julian (UN R)	9,272	55.6
	Johnson (D)	7,414	44.4
6	Ebenezer Dumont (UN R)	12,525	53.4
	Contt (D)	10,954	46.7
7	Daniel W. Voorhees (D)	12,457	55.5
	Scott (R)	9,976	44.5
8	Godlove S. Orth (UN R)	12,032	51.8
	Pettit (D)	11,181	48.2
9	Schuyler Colfax (UN R)	14,768	50.4
	Turpie (D)	14,546	49.6
10	Joseph K. Edgerton (D)	12,353	50.9
	Mitchell (UN R)	11,917	49.1
11	James F. McDowell (D)	13,142	51.8
	Shanks (UN R)	12,219	48.2

IOWA

	Candidates	Votes	%
1	James F. Wilson (R)	12,705	54.8
	Joseph K. Hornish (D)	10,486	45.2
2	Hiram Price (R)	12,433	58.2
	Edward H. Thayer (D)	8,930	41.8
3	William B. Allison (R)	12,112	58.8
	Dennis A. Mahoney (D)	8,452	41.1
4	Josiah B. Grinnell (R)	12,900	52.8
	Hugh M. Martin (D)	11,529	47.2
5	John A. Kasson (R)	10,306	58.4
	D. O. Finch (D)	7,346	41.6
6	Asahel W. Hubbard (R)	5,386	66.2
	John F. Duncombe (D)	2,755	33.8

KANSAS

	Candidates	Votes	%
AL	A. Carter Wilder (R)	9,671	63.3
	Marcus J. Parrott (UN)	4,666	30.6
	William G. Mathias (D)	930	6.1

KENTUCKY

Special Elections

	Candidates	Votes	%
1	Samuel L. Casey (R)	541	54.1
	L. S. Trimble	442	44.2
2	George H. Yeaman (UN)	2,242	55.7
	Edward R. Weir	1,756	43.6

LOUISIANA[1]

Special Elections

	Candidates	Votes	%
1	Benjamin F. Flanders (UN)	2,330	93.7
	Bolgny (UN)	157	6.3
2	Michael Hahn (UN)	2,581	57.8
	Durell (UN)	1,450	32.5
	Barker (SEC)	436	9.8

MAINE

	Candidates	Votes	%
1	Lorenzo D. M. Sweat (D)	10,452	48.9
	Goodwin (R)	10,205	47.8
2	Sidney Perham (R)	9,976	56.7
	Bates (D)	7,519	42.7
3	James G. Blaine (R)	9,971	54.9
	Gould (D)	7,153	39.4
4	John H. Rice (R)	8,107	60.4
	Boynton (D)	3,806	28.4
5	Frederick A. Pike (R)	8,998	54.3
	White (D)	7,308	44.1

MASSACHUSETTS

	Candidates	Votes	%
1	Thomas D. Eliot (R)	8,399	74.2
	Daniel Fisher (PP)	2,762	24.4
2	Oakes Ames (R)	9,271	61.1
	William D. Swan (PP)	5,907	38.9
3	Alexander H. Rice (R)	5,044	50.1
	John Sleeper (PP)	5,020	49.8
4	Samuel Hooper (R)	5,828	52.1
	Josiah G. Abbott (PP)	5,351	47.8
5	John B. Alley (R)	8,505	61.0
	Benjamin Poole (PP)	5,398	38.7
6	Daniel W. Gooch (R)	8,124	56.9
	Oliver Hazzard Perry (PP)	6,150	43.1
7	George S. Boutwell (R)	7,994	55.2
	Benjamin F. Thomas (PP)	6,496	44.8
8	John D. Baldwin (R)	10,128	66.2
	Paul Whitin (PP)	5,178	33.8
9	William B. Washburne (R)	14,311	99.2
10	Henry L. Dawes (R)	7,449	56.3
	Chester W. Chapin (PP)	5,785	43.7

MICHIGAN

	Candidates	Votes	%
1	Fernando C. Beaman (R)	13,400	50.4
	Ebenezer J. Penniman (D)	13,210	49.6
2	Charles Upson (R)	14,148	55.4
	John W. Turner (D)	11,387	44.6
3	John W. Longyear (R)	12,317	51.7
	Bradley F. Granger (D)	11,488	48.3
4	Francis W. Kellogg (R)	10,013	57.8
	Thomas B. Church (D)	7,308	42.2
5	Augustus C. Baldwin (D)	10,697	50.6
	Rowland E. Trowbridge (R)	10,435	49.4
6	John F. Driggs (R)	8,188	53.7
	John Moore (D)	7,047	46.2

MINNESOTA

	Candidates	Votes	%
1	William Windom (R)	8,663	57.4
	A. G. Chatfield (D)	6,423	42.6
2	Ignatius Donnelly (R)	7,091	58.6
	W. J. Cullen (D)	5,019	41.5

MISSOURI

	Candidates	Votes	%
1	Francis P. Blair Jr (R)	4,743‡	40.0
	Samuel Knox (EMANCIP)	4,590	38.7
	Bogy (D)	2,536	21.4
2	Henry T. Blow (EMANCIP)	7,164	69.6
	Allen (D)	2,984	29.0
3	John W. Noell (EMANCIP)		✔
	John G. Scott (D)		
	Lawson (I)		
4	Sempronius H. Boyd (EMANCIP)		✔
	Phelps (D)		
5	Joseph W. McClurg (EMANCIP)	4,930	53.2
	Thomas L. Price (D)	4,333	46.8
6	Austin A. King (D)	4,243	45.3
	Birch (SEC)	2,857	30.5
	Samuel (ID)	1,626	17.4
	Bouton (EMANCIP)	644	6.9
7	Benjamin F. Loan (EMANCIP)	6,580	48.4
	John P. Bruce (D)	4,554	33.5
	Branch (I)	2,465	18.1
8	William A. Hall (D)	6,244	53.0
	Green (EMANCIP)	5,534	47.0
9	James S. Rollins	7,700	73.4
	Krekel (EMANCIP)	2,797	26.7

NEW JERSEY

	Candidates	Votes	%
1	John F. Starr (UN)	9,491	51.4
	Stratton (D)	8,961	48.6
2	George Middleton (D)	12,182	52.9
	Brown (UN)	10,834	47.1
3	William G. Steele (D)	15,708	63.3
	Brwnsn (UN)	9,093	36.7
4	Andrew J. Rogers (D)	12,791	56.1
	Linn (UN)	10,024	43.9
5	Nehemiah Perry (D)	10,779	58.6
	Bradley (UN)	7,622	41.4

NEW YORK

	Candidates	Votes	%
1	Henry G. Stebbins (D)	9,908	56.1
	McCormick (UN)	7,759	43.9
2	Martin Kalbfleisch (D)	10,586	66.3
	Wall (UN)	5,381	33.7
3	Moses F. Odell (D)	8,915	54.3
	Humphrey (UN)	7,506	45.7
4	Benjamin Wood (D)	7,828	63.3
	Walbridge (UN)	4,535	36.7
5	Fernando Wood (D)	8,176	70.1
	Duffy (UN)	3,488	29.9
6	Elijah Ward (D)	6,942	54.3
	Conkling (UN)	4,839	37.9
	Blunt (I)	996	7.8
7	John W. Chanler (D)	9,326	76.1
	Burr (UN)	2,937	24.0
8	James Brooks (D)	9,625	63.3
	Cowdin (UN)	5,570	36.7

1. Elected from areas under federal control.

NEW YORK

Candidates	Votes	%
9 Anson Herrick (D)	7,323	64.2
Murphy (UN)	4,085	35.8
10 William Radford (D)	8,878	45.8
Haight (UN)	7,921	40.9
Suffn (I)	2,576	13.3
11 Charles H. Winfield (D)	9,326	55.2
Fullerton (UN)	7,572	44.8
12 Homer A. Nelson (D)	10,712	53.0
Beale (UN)	9,512	47.0
13 John B. Steele (D)	10,263	54.9
Cornell (UN)	8,422	45.1
14 Erastus Corning (D)	15,715	59.6
Smith (UN)	10,665	40.4
15 John A. Griswold (D)	12,226	52.8
Dodd (UN)	10,939	47.2
16 Orlando Kellogg (UN)	7,654	52.3
Burhans (D)	6,987	47.7
17 Calvin T. Hulburd (UN)	12,015	67.2
Judson (D)	5,867	32.8
18 James M. Marvin (UN)	13,096	51.0
Blood (D)	12,582	49.0
19 Samuel F. Miller (UN)	14,918	52.5
Parker (D)	13,523	47.6
20 Ambrose W. Clark (UN)	14,826	57.3
Carryl (D)	11,031	42.7
21 Francis Kernan (D)	9,943	50.3
Conkling (UN)	9,845	49.8
22 De Witt C. Littlejohn (UN)	12,667	60.0
Titus (D)	8,453	40.0
23 Thomas T. Davis (UN)	13,032	58.5
Strong (D)	9,257	41.5
24 Theodore M. Pomeroy (UN)	13,834	55.3
Hadley (D)	11,196	44.7
25 Daniel Morris (UN)	11,615	58.7
Lord (D)	8,157	41.3
26 Giles W. Hotchkiss (UN)	13,889	58.7
Day (D)	9,781	41.3
27 Robert B. Van Valkenburg (UN)	14,887	58.0
Hathawy (D)	10,774	42.0
28 Freeman Clarke (UN)	11,193	53.2
Church (D)	9,833	46.8
29 Augustus Frank (UN)	10,470	52.1
Hunt (D)	9,627	47.9
30 John Ganson (D)	12,400	58.0
Spaulding (UN)	8,985	42.0
31 Reuben E. Fenton (UN)	11,950	63.1
Caldwell (D)	6,982	36.9

OHIO

Candidates	Votes	%
1 George H. Pendleton (D)	7,545	54.0
Groesbeck (UN R)	6,418	46.0
2 Alexander Long (D)	7,212	50.5
Gurley (UN R)	7,081	49.5
3 Robert C. Schenck (UN R)	13,027	52.5
Vallandigham (D)	11,770	47.5
4 John F. McKinney (D)	10,218	52.0
West (UN R)	9,435	48.0
5 Francis C. Le Blond (D)	10,561	63.0
Gatch (UN R)	6,202	37.0
6 Joseph W. White (D)	10,087	52.0
Briggs (UN R)	9,320	48.0
7 Samuel S. Cox (D)	10,372	50.7
Shellabarger (UN R)	10,100	49.3
8 William Johnston (D)	9,012	51.1
Godman (UN R)	8,642	49.0
9 Warren P. Noble (D)	11,765	52.8
Worcester (UN R)	10,523	47.2
10 James M. Ashley (UN R)	6,908	38.6
Waite	5,781	32.3
Phlpa	5,232	29.2
11 Wells A. Hutchins (D)	8,605	56.2
Bundy (UN R)	6,702	43.8
12 William E. Finck (D)	13,631	62.8
Trimble (UN R)	8,087	37.2
13 John O'Neill (D)	12,763	56.8
Wright (UN R)	9,699	43.2
14 George Bliss (D)	10,490	50.1
Welker (UN R)	10,454	49.9
15 James R. Morris (D)	10,332	52.9
Cutler (UN R)	9,183	47.1
16 Chilton A. White (D)	12,299	55.2
Bingham (UN R)	9,999	44.8
17 Ephraim R. Eckley (UN R)	10,018	52.4
Belden (D)	9,085	47.6
18 Rufus P. Spalding (UN R)	9,293	68.8
Paige (D)	4,183	31.0
19 James A. Garfield (UN R)	13,288	66.3
Wood (D)	6,763	33.7

OREGON

Candidates	Votes	%
AL John R. McBride (UN R)	6,809	65.2
A. E. Wait (D)	3,632	34.8

PENNSYLVANIA

Candidates	Votes	%
1 Samuel J. Randall (D)	7,720	55.2
Webb (UN)	6,273	44.8
2 Charles O'Neill (UN)	8,614	58.7
Biddle (D)	6,068	41.3
3 Leonard Myers (UN)	8,285	50.1
Kline (D)	8,243	49.9
4 William D. Kelley (UN)	8,946	52.4
Nichn (D)	8,118	47.6
5 M. Russell Thayer (UN)	9,605	50.2
Carrin (D)	9,543	49.8
6 John D. Stiles (D)	11,316	58.3
Krause (UN)	8,092	41.7
7 John M. Broomall (UN)	9,891	60.6
McCall (D)	6,445	39.5
8 Sydenham E. Ancona (D)	10,022	67.2
Wanner (UN)	4,898	32.8
9 Thaddeus Stevens (UN)	11,174	62.7
Steinn (D)	6,650	37.3
10 Myer Strouse (D)	9,239	52.0
Campbell (UN)	8,518	48.0
11 Philip Johnson (D)	11,676	81.8
Rouch (UN)	2,592	18.2
12 Charles Denison (D)	11,408	54.2
Grow (UN)	9,641	45.8
13 Henry W. Tracy (UN)	9,520	55.3
Clark (D)	7,703	44.7
14 William H. Miller (D)	10,630	51.3
Patterson (UN)	10,109	48.7
15 Joseph Baily (UN)	11,965	55.1
Glossbrenner (D)	9,746	44.9
16 Alexander H. Coffroth (D)	10,963	51.3
Edward McPherson (UN)	10,426	48.7
17 Archibald McAllister (D)	8,328	52.4
Blair (UN)	7,556	47.6
18 James T. Hale (UN)	9,272	49.4
Armstrong (UN)	8,855	47.2
19 Glenni W. Scofield (UN)	9,954	51.3
Courtht (D)	9,462	48.7
20 Amos Myers (UN)	12,404	51.7
Church (D)	11,586	48.3
21 John L. Dawson (D)	10,234	50.6
Steward (UN)	10,009	49.4
22 James K. Moorhead (UN)	8,037	58.6
Hamilton (D)	5,678	41.4
23 Thomas Williams (UN)	8,989	54.1
Ziegler (D)	7,635	45.9
24 Jesse Lazear (D)	9,984	51.1
Wallace (UN)	9,547	48.9

WISCONSIN

Candidates	Votes	%
1 James S. Brown (D)	14,291	54.1
Potter (R)	12,106	45.9
2 Ithamar C. Sloan (R)	13,105	54.4
Guppy (D)	10,974	45.6
3 Amasa Cobb (D)	11,365	55.3
Simpson (R)	9,184	44.7
4 Charles A. Eldridge (D)	15,343	61.5
Bragg (R)	9,613	38.5
5 Ezra Wheeler (D)	11,021	52.4
Brown (R)	10,005	47.6
6 Luther Hanchett (R)	9,276*	57.5
Stoddard (D)	6,774	42.0

1863 House Elections

CALIFORNIA

Candidates	Votes	%
AL Corneilus Cole (UN R)	65,085✓	
Thomas B. Shannon (UN R)	64,914✓	
William Higby (UN R)	64,883✓	
J. B. Weller (D)	43,567	
John Bigle (D)	43,520	

CONNECTICUT

	Candidates	Votes	%
1	Henry C. Deming (R)	10,493	50.8
	Hyde (D)	10,158	49.2
2	James E. English (D)	11,450	52.4
	Warner (R)	10,420	47.7
3	Augustus Brandegee (UN R)	8,878	58.2
	Convse (D)	6,381	41.8
4	John H. Hubbard (R)	11,248	50.8
	Woodruff (D)	10,892	49.2

DELAWARE

Special Election

	Candidates	Votes	%
AL	Nathaniel B. Smithers (UN)	8,220	99.8

KENTUCKY

	Candidates	Votes	%
1	Lucien Anderson (UN)	4,323	82.4
	L. S. Trimble (D)	711	13.6
2	George H. Yeaman (UN)	8,311	72.9
	John H. McHenry Jr. (D)	3,087	27.1
3	Henry Grider (UN)	8,654	87.0
	Thomas C. Winfrey (D)	1,293	13.0
4	Aaron Harding (UN)	10,435	80.6
	William J. Heady (D)	2,508	19.4

	Candidates	Votes	%
5	Robert Mallory (UN)	6,257	71.6
	Nathaniel Wolfe (D)	2,477	28.4
6	Green Clay Smith (UN)	6,936	61.9
	J. W. Menzies (D)	2,283	20.4
	J. W. Leathers (D)	1,970	17.6
7	Brutus J. Clay (UN)	4,711	50.4
	J. T. Boyle (D)	2,487	26.6
	R. A. Buckner (D)	2,143	22.9
8	William H. Randall (UN)	8,321	97.2
9	William H. Wadsworth (UN)	6,889	89.0
	Thomas S. Brown (D)	849	11.0

MARYLAND

	Candidates	Votes	%
1	John A. J. Creswell (UN R)	6,743	55.2
	Crisfield (D)	5,482	44.8
2	Edwin H. Webster (UN R)	7,736	100.0
3	Henry Winter Davis (UN R)	6,200	99.7
4	Francis Thomas (UN R)	13,462	100.0
5	Benjamin G. Harris (D)	4,939	46.9
	Holland (UN R)	3,352	31.8
	Calvert (KST U)	2,237	21.3

MISSOURI

Special Election

	Candidates	Votes	%
3	John G. Scott (D)	3,559	50.3
	Lindsay (UN)	3,070	43.4
	Bogy (ID)	444	6.3

NEW HAMPSHIRE

	Candidates	Votes	%
1	Daniel Marcy (D)	12,059	50.2
	Eastman (R)	11,979	49.8

	Candidates	Votes	%
2	Edward H. Rollins (R)	10,365	50.9
	George (D)	9,999	49.1
3	James W. Patterson (R)	10,847	50.6
	Burns (D)	10,571	49.4

RHODE ISLAND

	Candidates	Votes	%
1	Thomas A. Jenckes (R)	6,532	58.2
	Bradley (D)	4,616	41.1
2	Nathan F. Dixon (R)	4,077	56.4
	Browne (D)	3,121	43.2

VERMONT

	Candidates	Votes	%
1	Frederick E. Woodbridge (R)	8,565	70.8
	John A. S. White (D)	3,486	28.8
2	Justin S. Morrill (R)	11,358	70.3
	Charles N. Davenport (D)	4,785	29.6
3	Portus Baxter (R)	7,234	71.0
	Giles Harrington (D)	2,673	26.2

WEST VIRGINIA

(Became a state June 19, 1863)

	Candidates	Votes	%
1	Jacob B. Blair (UN R)	8,066	93.0
	Dehass (UN R)	605	7.0
2	William G. Brown (UN R)	3,576	57.9
	Burdett (UN R)	1,804	29.2
	Zinn (UN R)	800	12.9
3	Kellian V. Whaley (UN R)	2,746	55.7
	Frost (UN R)	2,184	44.3

House Candidates Index

For an index of all House candidates listed in this section (pages 701 to 1061), see pages 1180-1273. Instructions for use of the House Candidates Index appear on page 1180.

1864 House Elections

CALIFORNIA

	Candidates	Votes	%
1	Donald C. McRuer (UN R)	20,370	58.9
	J. B. Crocker (D)	14,191	41.1
2	William Higby (UN R)	23,414	61.6
	J. W. Coffroth (D)	14,581	38.4
3	John Bidwell (UN R)	18,255	56.1
	Jack Temple (D)	14,273	43.9

DELAWARE

		Votes	%
AL	John A. Nicholson (D)	8,762	51.5
	Nathaniel B. Smithers (UN R)	8,253	48.5

ILLINOIS

		Votes	%
1	John Wentworth (UN R)	18,557	56.5
	Cyrus H. McCormick (D)	14,277	43.5
2	John F. Farnsworth (UN R)	18,298	77.8
	M. C. Johnson (D)	5,237	22.3
3	Elihu B. Washburne (UN R)	15,711	67.9
	Elius B. Stiles (D)	7,421	32.1
4	Abner C. Harding (UN R)	13,569	51.6
	Charles M. Harris (D)	12,721	48.4
5	Ebon C. Ingersoll (UN R)	18,152	61.7
	James S. Echels (D)	11,287	38.3
6	Burton C. Cook (UN R)	15,598	61.0
	Samuel K. Casey (D)	9,980	39.0
7	Henry P. H. Bromwell (UN R)	15,373	56.1
	John R. Eden (D)	12,027	43.9
8	Shelby M. Cullom (UN R)	15,812	53.0
	John T. Stuart (D)	14,027	47.0
9	Lewis W. Ross (D)	15,296	55.6
	Hugh Fullerton (UN R)	12,239	44.5
10	Anthony Thornton (UN R)	16,902	58.1
	N. M. Knapp (D)	12,176	41.9
11	Samuel S. Marshall (D)	16,703	61.0
	Ethelbert Callahan (UN R)	10,696	39.0
12	John Baker (UN R)	11,817	50.2
	William R. Morrison (D)	11,741	49.8
13	Andrew J. Kuykendall (UN R)	11,762	52.1
	William J. Allen (D)	10,759	47.7
AL	Samuel W. Moulton (UN R)	190,216	54.5
	J. C. Allen (D)	158,781	45.5

Special Election

		Votes	%
5	Ebon C. Ingersoll (R)	12,986	62.8
	H. M. Wead	7,677	37.1

INDIANA

		Votes	%
1	William E. Niblack (D)	14,718	53.9
	Cyrus M. Allen (UN R)	12,616	46.2
2	Michael C. Kerr (D)	11,407	54.3
	William W. Curry (UN R)	9,614	45.7
3	Ralph Hill (UN R)	12,017	51.8
	Henry W. Harrington (D)	11,173	48.2
4	John H. Farquhar (UN R)	10,015	50.2
	George Berry (D)	9,949	49.8
5	George W. Julian (UN R)	13,529	68.7
	James Brown (D)	6,161	31.3
6	Ebenezer Dumont (UN R)	18,886	63.4
	John Love (D)	10,905	36.6
7	Daniel W. Voorhees (D)	12,880‡	51.2
	Henry D. Washburn (UN R)	12,296	48.8
8	Godlove S. Orth (UN R)	13,536	52.3
	James F. Harney (D)	12,349	47.7
9	Schuyler Colfax (UN R)	16,658	52.7
	David Turpie (D)	14,942	47.3
10	Joseph D. Defrees (UN R)	14,617	51.0
	Joseph K. Edgerton (D)	14,037	49.0
11	Thomas F. Stillwell (UN R)	15,623	53.9
	James F. McDowell (D)	13,383	46.1

IOWA

	Candidates	Votes	%
1	James F. Wilson (UN R)	16,977	65.2
	J. K. Hornish (D)	9,078	34.8
2	Hiram Price (UN R)	16,571	65.3
	George H. Parker (D)	8,822	34.7
3	William B. Allison (UN R)	16,130	60.4
	B. B. Richards (D)	10,578	39.6
4	Josiah B. Grinnell (UN R)	17,169	61.5
	Ira C. Mitchell (D)	10,619	38.1
5	John A. Kasson (UN R)	13,640	65.8
	M. D. McHenry (D)	7,104	34.3
6	Asahel W. Hubbard (UN R)	8,455	72.8
	Seander Chapman (D)	3,162	27.2

KANSAS

		Votes	%
AL	Sidney Clarke (R)	10,820	52.7
	A. L. Lee (R-UNION)	9,708	47.3

MAINE

		Votes	%
1	John Lynch (UN)	15,096	54.6
	Sweat (D)	12,568	45.4
2	Sidney Perham (UN)	13,030	61.0
	Andrews (D)	8,344	39.0
3	James G. Blaine (UN)	14,055	59.3
	Gould (D)	9,647	40.7
4	John H. Rice (UN)	11,002	61.2
	Madigan (D)	6,983	38.8
5	Frederick A. Pike (UN)	12,538	58.2
	White (D)	9,016	41.8

MARYLAND

		Votes	%
1	Hiram McCullough (D)	9,677	60.5
	J. A. J. Cresswell (UN R)	6,307	39.5
2	Edwin H. Webster (UN R)	9,541	69.9
	William Kimmell (D)	4,102	30.1
3	Charles E. Phelps (UN R)	9,313	84.2
	A. Lewis Knott (D)	1,753	15.8
4	Francis Thomas (UN R)	11,898	61.2
	Syester (D)	7,551	38.8
5	Benjamin G. Harris (D)	8,839	72.3
	John C. Holland (UN R)	3,389	27.7

MASSACHUSETTS

		Votes	%
1	Thomas D. Eliot (UNT)	13,687	82.8
	Sylvanus B. Phinney (D)	2,850	17.2
2	Oakes Ames (UNT)	13,591	72.1
	James McGuire (D)	5,266	27.9
3	Alexander H. Rice (UNT)	9,711	62.3
	John S. Sleeper (D)	5,864	37.7
4	Samuel Hooper (UNT)	10,403	65.5
	Josiah B. Abbott (D)	5,485	34.5
5	John B. Alley (UNT)	13,086	75.8
	Joseph B. Morss (D)	4,158	24.1
6	Daniel W. Gooch (UNT)	13,082	71.7
	Thomas J. Greenwood (D)	5,174	28.3
7	George S. Boutwell (UNT)	12,087	69.0
	Theodore H. Sweetser (D)	5,433	31.0
8	John D. Baldwin (UNT)	12,955	74.8
	George Hodges (D)	4,377	25.3
9	William B. Washburn (UNT)	15,721	81.5
	Nathaniel Wood (D)	3,575	18.5
10	Henry L. Dawes (UNT)	11,600	64.7
	Harry Arnold (D)	6,315	35.2

MICHIGAN

		Votes	%
1	Fernando C. Beaman (UN)	17,908	53.4
	David A. Noble (D)	15,602	46.5
2	Charles Upson (UN)	19,151	60.4
	Nathaniel A. Balch (D)	12,538	39.6

	Candidates	Votes	%
3	John W. Longyear (UN)	15,432	54.7
	David Johnson (D)	12,758	45.3
4	Thomas W. Ferry (UN)	13,428	59.2
	Frederick Hall (D)	9,256	40.8
5	Rowland E. Trowbridge (UN)	12,651	51.5
	Augustus C. Baldwin (D)	11,937	48.5
6	John F. Driggs (UN)	12,784	53.4
	William Willard (D)	11,166	46.6

MINNESOTA

		Votes	%
1	William Windom (UN R)	13,965	60.6
	Henry W. Lamberton (D)	9,092	39.4
2	Ignatius Donnelly (UN R)	10,874	57.0
	John M. Gilman (D)	8,211	43.0

MISSOURI

		Votes	%
1	John Hogan (D)	6,026	43.2
	Charles P. Johnson (RAD R)	4,781	34.2
	Samuel Knox (RAD R)	3,157	22.6
2	Henry T. Blow (RAD R)	11,580	90.2
	E. Stafford	1,253	9.8
3	Thomas E. Noell (RAD R)	4,075	61.7
	D. C. Tuttle (D)	1,868	28.3
	W. T. Leeper (I RAD R)	659	10.0
4	John R. Kelso (I RAD R)	3,841	49.3
	Sempronius H. Boyd (RAD R)	3,548	45.6
	M. J. Hubble (D)	400	5.1
5	Joseph W. McClurg (RAD R)	6,976	72.4
	Sample Orr (D)	2,659	27.6
6	Robert T. Van Horn (RAD R)	3,498	47.2
	Elijah H. Norton (D)	3,226	43.5
	Austin A. King (ID)	695	9.4
7	Benjamin F. Loan (RAD R)	10,445	85.9
	H. B. Branch	1,674	13.8
8	John F. Benjamin (RAD R)	8,536	74.1
	John M. Glover (C)	2,978	25.9
9	George W. Anderson (RAD R)	5,329	51.8
	Odon Guitar (D)	4,950	48.2

NEVADA

(Became a state Oct. 31, 1864)

		Votes	%
AL	Henry G. Worthington (UN R)	9,776	59.9
	A. C. Bradford (D)	6,552	40.1

NEW JERSEY

		Votes	%
1	John F. Starr (UN)	12,091	54.4
	Dickinson (D)	10,126	45.6
2	William A. Newell (UN)	13,953	51.6
	Middleton (D)	13,091	48.4
3	Charles Sitgreaves (D)	16,942	58.4
	Scranton (UN)	12,080	41.6
4	Andrew J. Rogers (D)	14,059	53.6
	Little (UN)	12,173	46.4
5	Edwin R. V. Wright (D)	13,390	53.9
	Wakeman (UN)	11,448	46.1

NEW YORK

		Votes	%
1	Stephen Taber (D)	12,232	55.0
	George V. Curtis (UN)	10,023	45.0
2	Teunis G. Bergen (D)	13,630	60.7
	Samuel T. Maddox (UN)	8,829	39.3
3	James Humphrey (UN)	11,752	51.3
	Thomas H. Faron (D)	11,168	48.7
4	Morgan Jones (TAM D)	9,605	57.2
	William Walsh (MOZART D)	5,512	32.8
	Carolan O. Bryant (UN)	1,684	10.0
5	Nelson Taylor (TAM D)	9,272	53.1
	William B. Maclay (MOZART D)	4,286	24.5

NEW YORK

Candidates	Votes	%
Epes P. Ellery (UN)	3,921	22.4
6 Henry J. Raymond (UN)	7,315	42.4
Elijah Ward (TAM D)	6,929	40.2
Eli P. Norton (MOZART D)	1,647	9.6
Rush C. Hawkins (IRR U)	1,347	7.8
7 John Winthrop Chanler (UN)	11,513	67.1
William Boardman (D)	5,638	32.9
8 James Brooks (D)	8,583‡	39.8
William E. Dodge (R)	8,435	39.1
Thomas J. Barr (TAM D)	4,544	21.1
9 William A. Darling (UN)	5,822	38.9
Fernando Wood (MOZART D)	4,749	31.7
Anson Herrick (TAM D)	4,397	29.4
10 William Radford (D)	13,033	56.1
Francis Larkin (UN)	10,218	44.0
11 Charles H. Winfield (D)	9,975	50.6
Ambrose S. Murray (UN)	9,736	49.4
12 John H. Ketcham (UN)	12,229	51.4
Homer A. Nelson (D)	11,559	48.6
13 Edwin N. Hubbell (D)	11,373	53.1
Theodore B. Gates (UN)	10,028	46.9
14 Charles Goodyear (D)	17,497	57.5
John H. Gardiner (UN)	12,942	42.5
15 John A. Griswold (UN)	15,251	54.1
William A. Van Alstyne (D)	12,928	45.9
16 Orlando Kellogg (UN)	8,988	53.9
Thomas S. Gray (D)	7,675	46.1
17 Calvin T. Hulburd (UN)	13,183	70.0
William J. Averill (D)	5,659	30.0
18 James M. Marvin (UN)	14,453	51.6
Alonzo C. Paige (D)	13,572	48.4
19 Demas Hubbard Jr (UN)	17,067	54.8
Hezekiah Sturges (D)	14,078	45.2
20 Addison H. Laflin (UN)	16,441	56.4
Frederick W. Hubbard (D)	12,704	43.6
21 Roscoe Conkling (UN)	11,966	52.5
Francis Kernan (D)	10,816	47.5
22 Sidney T. Holmes (UN)	14,638	60.0
Albertus Perry (D)	9,781	40.1
23 Thomas T. Davis (UN)	14,800	58.6
William C. Ruger (D)	10,464	41.4
24 Theodore M. Pomeroy (UN)	16,027	57.5
George W. Cuyler (D)	11,832	42.5
25 Daniel Morris (UN)	12,763	58.8
Barzillai Slosson (D)	8,962	41.3
26 Giles W. Hotchkiss (UN)	15,543	59.0
John Magee (D)	10,806	41.0
27 Hamilton Ward (UN)	16,945	60.3
Andrew J. McNett (D)	11,176	39.7
28 Roswell Hart (UN)	13,081	52.5
James L. Angle (D)	11,841	47.5
29 Burt Van Horn (UN)	12,671	57.1
James M. Willett (D)	9,533	42.9
30 James M. Humphrey (D)	13,231	50.7
Samuel J. Holley (UN)	12,861	49.3
31 Henry Van Aernam (UN)	13,996	65.5
Jonas K. Button (D)	7,374	34.5

Special Election

1 Dwight Townsend (D)	11,828	55.0
Henry G. Stebbins (UN)	9,697	45.1

OHIO

Candidates	Votes	%
1 Benjamin Eggleston (UN R)	9,893	57.0
George E. Pugh (D)	7,464	43.0
2 Rutherford B. Hays (UN R)	10,425	58.7
J. C. Butler (D)	7,327	41.3
3 Robert C. Schenck (UN R)	14,371	55.3
David A. Houk (D)	11,605	44.7
4 William Lawrence (UN R)	12,242	56.1
John F. McKinney (D)	9,578	43.9
5 Frank C. Le Blond (D)	11,048	55.2
Moses B. Walker (UN R)	8,957	44.8
6 Reader W. Clarke (UN R)	12,615	55.3
Chilton A. White (D)	10,183	44.7
7 Samuel Shellabarger (UN R)	12,756	57.1
Samuel S. Cox (D)	9,587	42.9
8 James R. Hubbell (UN R)	10,903	54.8
William Johnston (D)	8,983	45.2
9 Ralph P. Buckland (UN R)	13,511	53.6
Warren P. Noble (D)	11,717	46.4
10 James M. Ashley (UN R)	11,732	51.8
Americus V. Rice (D)	10,905	48.2
11 Hezekiah S. Bundy (UN R)	11,581	59.8
William A. Hutchins (D)	7,793	40.2
12 William E. Finck (D)	12,965	53.3
Job E. Stevenson (UN R)	11,349	46.7
13 Columbus Delano (UN R)	11,876	50.5
Charles Follet (D)	11,651	49.5
14 Martin Welker (UN R)	12,844	55.5
George Bliss (D)	10,313	44.5
15 Tobias A. Plants (UN R)	12,847	57.3
James M. Morris (D)	9,564	42.7
16 John A. Bingham (UN R)	12,377	52.7
Joseph White (D)	11,119	47.3
17 Ephraim R. Eckley (UN R)	12,758	59.3
J. H. Wallace (D)	8,746	40.7
18 Rufus P. Spalding (UN R)	14,472	68.5
J. H. Wade (D)	6,661	31.5
19 James A. Garfield (UN R)	18,086	74.1
Halsey H. Moses (D)	6,315	25.9

OREGON

AL	James H. D. Henderson (UN R)	8,759	59.4
	James K. Kelly (D)	5,996	40.6

PENNSYLVANIA

1	Samuel J. Randall (D)	9,764	55.8
	John M. Butler (UN R)	7,742	44.2
2	Charles O'Neill (UN R)	11,767	61.8
	William M. Reilly (D)	7,290	38.3
3	Leonard Myers (UN R)	11,467	53.4
	Charles Buckwalter (D)	9,992	46.6
4	William D. Kelley (UN R)	13,088	58.4
	Charles Northrop (D)	9,344	41.7
5	M. Russell Thayer (UN R)	11,007	50.6
	Henry P. Ross (D)	10,729	49.4
6	Benjamin M. Boyer (D)	12,847	57.1
	George Bullock (UN R)	9,661	42.9
7	John M. Broomall (UN R)	10,908	60.1
	John C. Beatty (D)	7,231	39.9
8	Sydenham E. Ancona (D)	12,076	66.9
	William M. Heister (UN R)	5,971	33.1

Candidates	Votes	%
9 Thaddeus Stevens (UN R)	11,804	61.7
Henry M. North (D)	7,344	38.4
10 Myer Strouse (D)	11,154	51.2
Howell Fisher (UN R)	10,629	48.8
11 Philip Johnson (D)	13,007	67.1
James L. Selfridge (UN R)	6,384	32.9
12 Charles Dennison (D)	10,573	51.3
Winthrop W. Ketcham (UN R)	10,058	48.8
13 Ulysses Mercur (UN R)	9,727	52.7
Victor E. Piollet (D)	8,723	47.3
14 George F. Miller (UN R)	11,619	51.2
W. H. Miller (D)	11,092	48.8
15 Adam J. Glossbrenner (D)	13,382	55.9
Joseph Baily (UN R)	10,576	44.1
16 William H. Koontz (UN R)	11,242‡	50.2
Alexander H. Coffroth (D)	11,174	49.9
17 Abraham A. Barker (UN R)	9,225	51.4
Robert L. Johnston (D)	8,716	48.6
18 Stephen F. Wilson (UN R)	11,533	51.9
Theo Wright (D)	10,681	48.1
19 Glenni W. Scofield (UN R)	11,631	54.0
William Bigler (D)	9,914	46.0
20 Charles V. Culver (UN R)	13,350	52.8
William L. Corbett (D)	11,942	47.2
21 John L. Dawson (D)	10,855	50.3
Smith Fuller (UN R)	10,730	49.7
22 James K. Moorhead (UN R)	11,233	61.6
James H. Hopkins (D)	7,013	38.4
23 Thomas Williams (UN R)	11,682	59.0
William J. Kountz (D)	8,122	41.0
24 George V. Lawrence (UN R)	11,727	53.7
Jesse Lazear (D)	10,112	46.3

VERMONT

1	Frederick E. Woodbridge (UN)	9,133	71.5
	Samuel Wells (D)	3,626	28.4
2	Justin S. Morrill (UN	12,409	72.0
	Unidentified Candidate (D)	4,793	27.8
3	Portus Baxter (UN)	9,408	74.1
	Giles Harrington (D)	3,281	25.9

WEST VIRGINIA

1	Chester D. Hubbard (UN R)	7,198	62.5
	Samuel Crane	4,315	37.5
2	George R. Latham (UN R)	5,663	84.4
	William B. Zinn	721	10.8
3	Kellian V. Whaley (UN R)	2,446	66.8
	John M. Phelps	1,216	33.2

WISCONSIN

1	Halbert E. Paine (R)	13,716	50.9
	Cary (D)	13,230	49.1
2	Ithamar C. Sloan (R)	15,148	60.3
	Smith (D)	9,969	39.7
3	Amasa Cobb (R)	14,342	63.2
	Rodolf (D)	8,354	36.8
4	Charles A. Eldridge (D)	15,547	58.9
	Sloan (R)	10,835	41.1
5	Philetus Sawyer (R)	12,576	56.8
	Bouck (D)	9,550	43.2
6	Walter D. McIndoe (R)	12,962	65.5
	Reed (D)	6,836	34.5

1865 House Elections

ALABAMA [1]

	Candidates	Votes	%
1	Charles C. Langdon	2,628*	60.2
	Mathews	918	21.0
	Cleveland	812	18.6
2	George Freeman	6,038*	82.7
	Benjamin Gardner	1,249	17.1
3	Cullen A. Battle	3,914*	44.5
	George Reese	2,031	23.1
	Robert F. Ligon	1,891	21.5
	E. Hamill	671	7.6
4	J. Taylor	5,619*	69.6
	C. W. Lee	2,446	30.3
5	Burwell Pope	3,218	38.9
	James Shield	3,187	38.6
	Morris	1,620	19.6
6	Thomas J. Foster	3,511*	45.1
	Sheats	1,992	25.6
	Skinner	1,471	18.9
	Garth	491	6.3

CONNECTICUT

		Votes	%
1	Henry C. Deming (UN R)	10,619	56.0
	Mitchell (D)	8,033	42.4
2	Samuel L. Warner (UN R)	11,236	54.1
	Russell (D)	9,521	45.9
3	Augustus Brandegee (UNR)	8,566	66.3
	Allen (D)	4,349	33.7
4	John H. Hubbard (UN R)	11,747	56.3
	Taylor (D)	9,112	43.7

KENTUCKY

		Votes	%
1	Lawrence S. Trimble (C)	5,749	61.9
	C. D. Bradley (UN)	3,542	38.1
2	Burwell C. Ritter (C)	6,974	54.7
	George H. Yeaman (UN)	5,786	45.3
3	Henry Grider (C)	6,528	57.3
	J. H. Lowry (UN)	4,871	42.7
4	Aaron Harding (C)	9,437	72.1
	Marion C. Taylor (UN)	3,652	27.9
5	Lovell H. Rousseau (UN)	5,751	54.1
	Robert Mallory (C)	4,704	44.3
6	Green Clay Smith (UN)	7,666	54.4
	A. H. Ward (C)	6,421	45.6
7	George S. Shanklin (C)	7,624	65.9
	Speed S. Fry (UN)	3,943	34.1
8	William H. Randell (UN)	10,634	73.6
	T. T. Garrard (C)	3,824	26.5
9	Samuel McKee (UN)	8,163	56.7
	J. Smith Hurt (C)	6,241	43.3

MARYLAND

Special Election

	Candidates	Votes	%
2	John L. Thomas Jr (UN R)	4,677	83.1
	Kimmel (D)	950	16.9

MASSACHUSETTS

Special Election

		Votes	%
6	Nathaniel P. Banks (UNT)	8,128	80.4
	Thomas Greenwood (D)	1,938	19.2

NEVADA

		Votes	%
AL	Delos R. Ashley (UN)	3,691	62.5
	H. K. Mitchell (D)	2,215	37.5

NEW HAMPSHIRE

		Votes	%
1	Gilman Marston (UN)	12,906	55.9
	Marcy (D)	10,190	44.1
2	Edward H. Rollins (UN)	10,984	55.3
	Clark (D)	8,894	44.7
3	James W. Patterson (UN)	11,687	56.2
	Bingham (D)	9,099	43.8

NEW YORK

Special Election

		Votes	%
16	Robert S. Hale (UN)	7,146	54.5
	Halsey R. Wing (D)	5,979	45.6

NORTH CAROLINA [2]

		Votes	%
1	Jesse R. Stubbs	*	
2	Charles C. Clark (N UNION)	4,479*	93.1
3	Thomas C. Fuller (N UNION)	3,094*	52.8
	Alexander Little (N UNION)	2,292	39.2
	Thomas S. Ashe (N UNION)	469	8.0
4	Josiah Turner Jr (N UNION)	4,179*	54.1
	John P. H. Russ (N UNION)	3,229	41.8
5	Bedford Brown (N UNION)	4,354*	50.6
	Lewis Hawes (N UNION)	4,257	49.4
6	Samuel H. Walkup (N UNION)	3,455*	41.4
	James G. Ramsay (N UNION)	3,397	40.7
	William Sloan (N UNION)	1,503	18.0
7	Alexander H. Jones (N UNION)	*	
	Tod R. Caldwell (N UNION)		
	Burgess S. Gaither (N UNION)		
	J. R. Love (N UNION)		

RHODE ISLAND

	Candidates	Votes	%
1	Thomas A. Jenckes (R)	5,683	99.1
2	Nathan F. Dixon (R)	2,384	64.9
	Bradford (D)	1,286	35.0

TENNESSEE

(Readmitted July 24, 1866)

		Votes	%
1	Nathaniel G. Taylor (UN)	5,056	49.2
	J. R. Miller (C)	3,620	35.2
	Randolph	1,594	15.5
2	Horace Maynard (UN)	5,599	53.0
	J. A. Cooper (C)	2,081	19.7
	Hank	1,650	15.7
	Boyd	1,210	11.5
3	William B. Stokes (UN)	2,599	68.3
	Asa Faulkner (C)	1,024	26.9
	Hood	181	4.8
4	Edmund Cooper (C)	5,318	96.2
5	William B. Campbell (C)	1,311	86.3
	S. J. Carter (UN)	208	13.7
6	Samuel M. Arnell (UN)	1,547	74.8
	Dorsey B. Thomas (C)	521	25.2
7	Isaac R. Hawkins (UN)	2,068	62.7
	Etheridge (C)	704	21.4
	Saunders	525	15.9
8	John W. Leftwich (C)	1,368	44.9
	John Bullock (UN)	597	19.6
	Sands	589	19.3
	Dunlap	493	16.2

VIRGINIA [3]

		Votes	%
1	Curtis	978*	37.8
	Christian	856	33.1
	Doug	756	29.2
2	L. H. Chandler (UN)	1,583*	50.2
	John S. Millson	1,029	32.6
	Kilby	544	17.2
3	B. Johnson Barbour	4,944*	79.4
	Pendleton	906	14.6
	Martin Lipscomb	334	5.4
4	Robert Ridgway	3,369*	76.9
	Alexander Fitzpatrick	1,010	23.1
5	Davis	1,718*	29.3
	Stovall	1,675	28.6
	Mosby	1,187	20.2
	Withers	958	16.3
6	Alexander H. H. Stuart	4,653*	67.3
	John F. Lewis	2,194	31.7
7	Robert Y. Conrad	4,853*	72.1
	Lewis McKenzie	1,722	25.6
8	Hoge	4,897*	64.6
	Miller	1,259	16.6
	Longley	1,118	14.8

1. Alabama held elections for the House but none of the winners was seated. The state was not readmitted until July 13, 1868.
2. North Carolina held elections for the House but none of the winners was seated. The state was not readmitted until July 4, 1868.
3. Virginia held elections for the House but none of the winners was seated. The state was not readmitted until Jan. 26, 1870.

1866 House Elections

ALABAMA[1]
Special Election

Candidates	Votes	%
2 J. M. Wiley		
J. L. Pugh		
Bolling Hall		
J. Clements		

DELAWARE

	Votes	%
AL John A. Nicholson (D)	9,933	53.7
John L. McKim (R)	8,553	46.3

ILLINOIS

	Votes	%
1 Norman B. Judd (R)	15,247	72.9
M. R. M. Wallace (D)	5,667	27.1
2 John F. Farnsworth (R)	16,185	82.9
E. M. Haines (D)	3,346	17.1
3 Elihu B. Washburne (R)	14,657	70.9
Thomas J. Turner (D)	5,897	28.5
4 Abner C. Harding (R)	15,952	54.4
John S. Thompson (D)	13,391	45.6
5 Ebon C. Ingersoll (R)	18,437	65.6
Silas Ramsey (D)	9,665	34.4
6 Burton C. Cook (R)	15,015	66.0
S. H. Harris (D)	7,721	34.0
7 Henry P. H. Bromwell (R)	17,410	56.7
Charles Black (D)	13,272	43.3
8 Shelby M. Cullom (R)	18,623	56.2
Edwin S. Fowler (D)	14,520	43.8
9 Lewis W. Ross (D)	15,496	51.3
Charles E. Lippencott (R)	14,721	48.7
10 Albert G. Burr (D)	17,116	53.7
Henry Case (R)	14,743	46.3
11 Samuel S. Marshall (D)	16,668	53.7
Edward Kitchell (R)	14,378	46.3
12 Jehu Baker (R)	13,032	52.2
William R. Morrison (D)	11,956	47.9
13 Green B. Raum (R)	13,459	51.1
William J. Allen (D)	12,890	48.9
AL John A. Logan (R)	203,045	57.9
T. Lyle Dickey (D)	147,435	42.1

INDIANA

	Votes	%
1 William E. Niblack (D)	17,255	52.0
Debruler (R)	15,905	48.0
2 Michael C. Kerr (D)	13,421	53.5
Gresham (R)	11,678	46.5
3 Morton C. Hunter (R)	13,848	51.3
Harrgtn (D)	13,158	48.7
4 William S. Holman (D)	11,921	51.9
Grover (R)	11,052	48.1
5 George W. Julian (R)	13,416	65.1
Bundy (D)	7,188	34.9
6 John Coburn (R)	16,719	54.0
Lord (D)	14,245	46.0
7 Henry D. Washburn (R)	14,871	50.9
Claypl (D)	14,358	49.1
8 Godlove S. Orth (R)	14,933	50.4
Purdue (D)	14,728	49.7
9 Schuyler Colfax (R)	20,221	52.8
David Turpie (D)	18,073	47.2
10 William Williams (R)	17,414	51.9
Lowry (D)	16,142	48.1
11 John P. C. Shanks (R)	18,145	54.3
Snow (D)	15,268	45.7

IOWA

	Votes	%
1 James F. Wilson (R)	16,388	60.9
Fitz Henry Warren (D)	10,515	39.1
2 Hiram Price (R)	16,257	63.8
John P. Cook (D)	9,220	36.2

Candidates	Votes	%
3 William B. Allison (R)	15,472	58.7
Reuben Noble (D)	10,470	39.7
4 William Loughridge (R)	18,529	59.8
Cyms H. Mackey (D)	12,395	40.0
5 Grenville M. Dodge (R)	14,236	59.0
James M. Tuttle (D)	9,897	41.0
6 Asahel W. Hubbard (R)	9,970	69.9
J. D. Thompson (D)	3,938	27.6

KANSAS

	Votes	%
AL Sidney Clarke (R)	19,200	70.0
C. W. Blair (N UNION)	8,206	29.9

KENTUCKY

Special Elections

	Votes	%
3 Elijah Hise (D)	6,493	74.3
P. B. Hawkins (UN)	2,244	25.7
5 Lovell H. Rousseau (R)	2,494	99.0
6 Andrew H. Ward (D)	8,725	88.4
R. R. Carpenter (UN)	1,068	10.8

MAINE

	Votes	%
1 John Lynch (R)	15,612	57.0
Sweat (D)	11,753	42.9
2 Sidney Perham (R)	13,883	65.3
Morrill	7,363	34.7
3 James G. Blaine (R)	14,909	63.8
Heath (D)	8,338	35.7
4 John A. Peters (R)	11,911	64.4
Weston (D)	6,565	35.5
5 Frederick A. Pike (R)	12,422	61.0
Crosby (D)	7,773	38.1

MARYLAND

	Votes	%
1 Hiram McCullough (D)	11,729	74.2
George Russum (R)	4,052	25.6
2 Stevenson Archer (D)	7,091	58.6
John Thomas (R)	5,014	41.4
3 Charles E. Phelps (D)	5,545	54.8
J. J. Stewart (R)	4,568	45.2
4 Francis Thomas (R)	10,252	52.6
William Omauleby (D)	9,230	47.4
5 Frederick Stone (D)	8,708	81.1
William Albert (R)	2,032	18.9

MASSACHUSETTS

	Votes	%
1 Thomas D. Eliot (R)	8,184	84.1
Mathias Ellias (D)	1,539	15.8
2 Oakes Ames (R)	9,581	79.4
Unidentified Candidate (D)	2,456	20.4
3 Ginery Twichell (R)	6,084	66.5
William Aspinwall (D)	2,601	28.4
P. R. Guiney (WM)	463	5.1
4 Samuel Hooper (R)	7,901	71.2
Joseph Wightman (D)	3,187	28.7
5 Benjamin F. Butler (R)	9,021	75.6
William D. Northend (D)	2,838	23.8
6 Nathaniel P. Banks (R)	10,075	74.7
F. O. Prince (D)	3,366	24.9
7 George S. Boutwell (R)	9,847	77.3
Leverett Saltonstall (D)	2,885	22.7
8 John D. Baldwin (R)	9,039	82.5
William A. Williams (D)	1,901	17.4
9 William B. Washburn (R)	11,895	87.0
Levi Haywood (D)	1,768	12.9
10 Henry L. Dawes (R)	8,125	65.7
Abijah W. Chapin (D)	4,185	33.9

MICHIGAN

Candidates	Votes	%
1 Fernando C. Beaman (R)	17,319	56.3
Chipman (D)	13,443	43.7
2 Charles Upson (R)	19,623	63.6
Severns (D)	11,228	36.4
3 Austin Blair (R)	16,240	56.9
Granger (D)	12,288	43.1
4 Thomas W. Ferry (R)	15,305	65.2
Hutchins (D)	8,154	34.8
5 Rowland E. Trowbridge (R)	14,046	54.6
Bancroft (D)	11,664	45.4
6 John F. Driggs (R)	14,476	57.8
Rose (D)	10,570	42.2

MINNESOTA

	Votes	%
1 William Windom (R)	14,810	64.2
Jones (D)	8,245	35.8
2 Ignatius Donnelly (R)	12,022	60.8
Colvill (D)	7,754	39.2

MISSOURI

	Votes	%
1 William A. Pile (R)	6,728	50.8
John Hogan	6,510	49.2
2 Carman A. Newcomb (R)	9,568	59.1
William V. N. Bay	6,636	41.0
3 Thomas E. Noell (RAD R)	✔	
Albert Jackson		
4 Joseph J. Gravely (R)	✔	
John S. Waddill		
5 Joseph W. McClurg (RAD R)	✔	
Thomas L. Price		
6 Robert T. Van Horn (R)	✔	
James H. Birgh		
L. S. McCoy		
7 Benjamin F. Loan (RAD R)	✔	
George A. Hawley		
8 John F. Benjamin (R)	✔	
John M. Glover		
9 George W. Anderson (RAD R)	✔	
William F. Switzler (D)		

NEBRASKA
(Became a state March 1, 1867)

	Votes	%
AL John Taffe (UN R)	4,621	53.0
A. S. Paddock (D)	4,072	46.7

Special Election

	Votes	%
AL Turner M. Marquette (R)	4,820	54.2
J. R. Brooke (D)	4,072	45.8

NEVADA

	Votes	%
AL Delos R. Ashley (R)	5,047	54.6
H. K. Mitchell (D)	4,196	45.4

NEW JERSEY

	Votes	%
1 William Moore (R)	12,468	57.8
Slape (D)	9,108	42.2
2 Charles Haight (D)	13,825	50.6
Newell (R)	13,476	49.4
3 Charles Sitgreaves (D)	15,768	54.9
Davidson (R)	12,955	45.1
4 John Hill (R)	13,861	50.5
Rogers (D)	13,399	48.8
5 George A. Halsey (R)	12,782	51.9
Gilchrist (D)	11,847	48.1

1. The winner of this election is unknown and was not seated by the House.

NEW YORK

	Candidates	Votes	%
1	Stephen Taber (D)	10,458	52.8
	William H. Gleason (R)	9,362	47.2
2	Demas Barnes (D)	15,614	62.5
	James A. Vanbrunt (R)	8,985	36.0
3	William E. Robinson (D)	12,634	53.9
	Simeon B. Chittenden (R)	10,803	46.1
4	John Fox (D)	14,003	78.9
	Horace Greeley (R)	3,743	21.1
5	John Morrissey (ID)	9,162	51.0
	Nelson Taylor (D)	6,503	36.2
	Eneas Elliott (R)	2,293	12.8
6	Thomas E. Stewart (C)	9,452	55.2
	Charles S. Spencer (R)	6,955	40.6
7	John W. Chanler (D)	11,503	63.0
	George F. Steinbrenner (R)	6,743	37.0
8	James Brooks (D)	13,816	62.7
	Legrand B. Cannon (R)	8,210	37.2
9	Fernando Wood (D)	9,605	54.6
	William A. Darling (R)	7,995	45.4
10	William H. Robertson (R)	12,012	54.7
	William Radford (D)	9,957	45.3
11	Charles H. Van Wyck (R)	10,194	50.7
	Isaac Anderson (D)	9,933	49.4
12	John H. Ketcham (R)	12,535	53.6
	Casper P. Collier (D)	10,840	46.4
13	Thomas Cornell (R)	10,521	50.8
	Joseph H. Tuthill (D)	10,179	49.2
14	John V. L. Pruyn (D)	15,620	51.1
	Joseph H. Ramsey (R)	14,972	48.9
15	John A. Griswold (R)	15,689	60.2
	Nathaniel B. Milliman (D)	10,373	39.8
16	Orange Ferris (R)	9,341	55.8
	George V. Hoyle (D)	7,412	44.2
17	Calvin T. Hulburd (R)	13,449	72.4
	Darius W. Lawrence (D)	5,116	27.6
18	James M. Marvin (R)	15,496	55.7
	Thomas R. Horton (D)	12,342	44.3
19	William C. Fields (R)	17,277	55.9
	Stephen C. Johnson (D)	13,621	44.1
20	Addison H. Laflin (R)	16,498	58.4
	Edward S. Lansing (D)	11,734	41.6
21	Roscoe Conkling (R)	12,470*	53.0
	Palmer V. Kellogg (D)	11,053	47.0
22	John C. Churchill (R)	14,461	62.1
	Albertus Perry (D)	8,827	37.9
23	Dennis McCarthy (R)	15,260	60.5
	William C. Ruger (D)	9,966	39.5
24	Theodore M. Pomeroy (R)	16,189	58.7
	George Humphreys (D)	11,404	41.3
25	William H. Kelsey (R)	12,637	60.3
	Henry O. Chesebro (D)	8,334	39.7
26	William S. Lincoln (R)	16,264	60.0
	Henry McCormick (D)	10,849	40.0
27	Hamilton Ward (R)	17,750	60.8
	John G. Collins (D)	11,435	39.2
28	Lewis Selye (D)	12,791	54.3
	Roswell Hart (R)	10,757	45.7
29	Burt Van Horn (R)	12,204	57.2
	Harlow S. Comstock (D)	9,131	42.8
30	James M. Humphrey (D)	13,402	52.6
	Almon M. Clapp (R)	12,085	47.4
31	Henry Van Aernam (R)	14,405	66.4
	Hanson A. Risley (D)	7,299	33.6

Special Election

3	John W. Hunter (D)	12,774	54.4
	Simeon B. Chittenden (R)	10,715	45.6

OHIO

	Candidates	Votes	%
1	Benjamin Eggleston (UN R)	10,422	52.3
	George H. Pendleton (D)	9,496	47.7
2	Rutherford B. Hayes (UN R)	11,549	56.2
	Theodore Cook (D)	8,991	43.8
3	Robert C. Schenck (UN R)	15,027	51.8
	J. Durbin Ward (D)	13,960	48.2
4	William Lawrence (UN R)	13,313	54.6
	John F. McKinney (D)	11,059	45.4
5	William Mungen (D)	13,524	55.4
	Moses B. Walker (UN R)	10,872	44.6
6	Reader W. Clarke (UN R)	13,846	53.0
	William Howard (D)	12,267	47.0
7	Samuel Shellabarger (UN R)	13,687	54.3
	Thomas Miller (D)	11,516	45.7
8	Cornelius S. Hamilton (UN R)	11,710	54.3
	William P. Reid (D)	9,858	45.7
9	Ralph P. Buckland (UN R)	15,231	52.2
	T. P. Finefrock (D)	13,944	47.8
10	James M. Ashley (UN R)	14,873	53.4
	H. S. Commager (D)	12,956	46.6
11	John T. Wilson (UN R)	12,783	56.2
	Oscar F. Moore (D)	9,945	43.8
12	Philadelph Van Trump (D)	14,546	56.2
	Wells S. Jones (UN R)	11,336	43.8
13	George W. Morgan (D)	13,228‡	50.5
	Columbus Delano (UN R)	12,957	49.5
14	Martin Welker (UN R)	13,494	53.4
	J. B. Young (D)	11,787	46.6
15	Tobias A. Plants (UN R)	12,816	54.4
	M. D. Follett (D)	10,752	45.6
16	John A. Bingham (UN R)	13,369	52.8
	C. H. Mitchner (D)	11,947	47.2
17	Ephraim R. Eckley (UN R)	13,917	60.0
	Louis Schaefer (D)	9,275	40.0
18	Rufus P. Spalding (UN R)	14,479	64.5
	Oliver H. Payne (D)	7,974	35.5
19	James A. Garfield (UN R)	18,362	71.3
	D. C. Coolman (D)	7,376	28.7

OREGON

AL	Rufus Mallory (R)	10,362	51.4
	James D. Fay (D)	9,808	48.6

PENNSYLVANIA

1	Samuel J. Randall (D)	12,192	61.2
	Charles Gibbons (R)	7,728	38.8
2	Charles O'Neill (R)	12,612	57.1
	John Hulme (D)	9,475	42.9
3	Leonard Myers (R)	12,520	52.1
	C. Buckwalter (D)	11,516	47.9
4	William D. Kelley (R)	14,551	54.6
	John Welsh (D)	12,126	45.5
5	Caleb N. Taylor (R)	12,259	51.0
	H. P. Ross (D)	11,800	49.0
6	Benjamin M. Boyer (D)	14,009	55.0
	David Thomas (R)	11,447	45.0
7	John N. Broomall (R)	12,011	58.5
	N. Pratt (D)	8,531	41.5
8	J. Lawrence Getz (D)	13,188	65.3
	D. J. Lincoln (R)	6,999	34.7
9	Thaddeus Stevens (R)	14,298	62.2
	S. H. Reynolds (D)	8,675	37.8

	Candidates	Votes	%
10	Henry L. Cake (R)	13,186	50.4
	C. D. Gloninger (D)	12,971	49.6
11	Daniel M. Van Auken (D)	15,907	63.4
	William Lilly (R)	9,195	36.6
12	Charles Denison (D)	15,280	53.5
	James Archibald (R)	13,274	46.5
13	Ulysses Mercur (R)	11,940	52.9
	William Elwell (D)	10,653	47.2
14	George F. Miller (R)	14,190	52.8
	Bower (D)	12,675	47.2
15	Adam J. Glossbrenner (D)	15,830	55.9
	R. M. Henderson (R)	12,489	44.1
16	William H. Koontz (R)	13,589	51.2
	Sharpe (D)	12,964	48.8
17	Daniel J. Morrell (R)	11,298	52.4
	R. L. Johnston (D)	10,249	47.6
18	Stephen F. Wilson (R)	14,734	53.7
	Theo F. Wright (D)	12,688	46.3
19	Glenni W. Scofield (R)	15,107	54.8
	W. W. L. Scott (D)	12,481	45.2
20	Darwin A. Finney (R)	17,106	52.9
	A. B. McCalmont (D)	15,225	47.1
21	John Covode (R)	13,023	50.7
	Wier (D)	12,669	49.3
22	James K. Moorhead (R)	12,720	56.9
	J. B. Switzer (D)	9,655	43.2
23	Thomas Williams (R)	14,197	58.6
	B. G. Childs (D)	10,012	41.4
24	George V. Lawrence (R)	13,391	53.1
	W. Montgomery (D)	11,853	47.0

VERMONT [1]

1	Frederick E. Woodbridge (R)	10,568	77.5
	Samuel Wells (D)	3,036	22.3
2	Luke P. Poland (R)	10,844	72.2
	Charles M. Chase (D)	3,935	26.2
3	Portus Baxter (R)	7,329*	46.8
	Hogt (D)	4,511	28.8
	Brigham	3,395	21.7

WEST VIRGINIA

1	Chester D. Hubbard (R)	10,001	54.8
	D. D. Johnson (D)	8,239	45.2
2	Bethuel M. Kitchen (R)	8,296	61.5
	E. W. Andrews (D)	5,190	38.5
3	Daniel Polsley (R)	4,927	58.8
	John H. Oley (D)	3,456	41.2

WISCONSIN

1	Halbert E. Paine (R)	14,678	58.8
	Brown (D)	10,298	41.2
2	Benjamin F. Hopkins (R)	14,129	61.5
	Pease (D)	8,833	38.5
3	Amasa Cobb (R)	13,006	63.0
	Virgin (D)	7,655	37.1
4	Charles A. Eldridge (D)	12,839*	56.6
	Hatch (R)	9,855	43.4
5	Philetus Sawyer (R)	14,341	60.5
	Martin (D)	9,347	39.5
6	Cadwallader C. Washburn (R)	13,161	66.4
	Park (D)	6,648	33.6

1. No candidate received a majority of the vote in the 3rd district, which was required for election. Portus Baxter declined to enter a later special election held to determine a winner. Worthington C. Smith (R) was eventually elected; returns are unavailable. (Majority vote requirement, see p. 703.)

1867 House Elections

CALIFORNIA

	Candidates	Votes	%
1	Samuel B. Axtell (D)	18,793	57.3
	Timothy G. Phelps (R)	13,989	42.7
2	William Higby (R)	16,053	52.1
	J. W. Coffroth (D)	14,786	48.0
3	James A. Johnson (D)	14,767	50.6
	C. Hartson (R)	14,394	49.4

CONNECTICUT

		Votes	%
1	Richard D. Hubbard (D)	11,994	51.1
	Henry C. Deming (R)	11,477	48.9
2	Julius Hotchkiss (D)	14,730	53.2
	Cyrus Northrop (R)	12,937	46.8
3	Henry H. Starkweather (R)	9,723	55.4
	Earl Martin (D)	7,827	44.6
4	William H. Barnum (D)	13,083	51.9
	Phineas T. Barnum (R)	12,103	48.0

KENTUCKY

		Votes	%
1	Lawrence S. Trimble (D)	9,787	84.6
	George G. Symes (R)	1,780	15.4
2	John Y. Brown (D)	8,922*	69.2
	Samuel E. Smith (R)	2,816	21.8
	B. C. Ritter (C)	1,155	9.0
3	Elijah Hise (D)	7,740	86.6
	George D. Blakey (R)	1,201	13.4
4	J. Proctor Knott (D)	8,199	74.6
	Marion C. Taylor (R)	2,277	20.7
5	Asa P. Grover (D)	7,118	69.3
	R. J. Jacob (C)	2,417	23.5
	William A. Bullitt (R)	742	7.2
6	Thomas L. Jones (D)	9,488	72.4
	W. L. Rankin (R)	3,587	27.4

	Candidates	Votes	%
7	James B. Beck (D)	9,716	76.1
	William Brown (R)	1,664	13.0
	Charles Hanson (C)	1,388	10.9
8	George M. Adams (D)	7,609	51.2
	Milton L. Rice (R)	7,244	48.8
9	John D. Young (D)	9,042	51.8
	Samuel McKee (R)	7,563✔	43.3

Special Election

		Votes	%
3	Jacob S. Golladay (D)	6,619	76.2
	J. R. Curd (C)	1,175	13.5
	W. T. Jackman (R)	850	9.8

MISSOURI

Special Election

3	James R. McCormick (D)		✔
	James H. Chase (R)		

NEW HAMPSHIRE

		Votes	%
1	Jacob H. Ela (R)	13,243	51.9
	Daniel Marcy (D)	12,247	48.0
2	Aaron F. Stevens (R)	11,260	52.2
	Edward W. Harrington (D)	10,305	47.8
3	Jacob Benton (R)	11,294	52.2
	Harry Bingham (D)	10,246	47.3

OHIO

Special Election

		Votes	%
2	Samuel F. Cary (IR)	10,390	52.1
	Richard Smith (R)	9,431	47.3

PENNSYLVANIA

Special Election

	Candidates	Votes	%
12	George W. Woodward (D)	12,623	51.1
	W. W. Kotcham (R)	12,078	48.9

RHODE ISLAND

		Votes	%
1	Thomas A. Jenckes (R)	4,311	97.7
2	Nathan F. Dixon (R)	2,669	64.2
	Carder (D)	1,480	35.6

TENNESSEE

		Votes	%
1	Roderick R. Butler (R)	12,472✔	
	J. White (C)	1,746	
	Joseph Powell (R)		
2	Horace Maynard (R)	11,994	79.8
	John Williams (C)	3,039	20.2
3	William B. Stokes (R)	8,030	83.3
	Eli G. Fleming (C)	1,614	16.7
4	James Mullins (R)	9,448	74.6
	Edward Cooper (C)	3,221	25.4
5	John Trimble (R)	9,357✔	
	Bailey Peyton (C)	3,163	
	D. H. Mason (IR)		
6	Samuel M. Arnell (R)	7,596	77.8
	Dorsey B. Thomas (C)	2,170	22.2
7	Isaac R. Hawkins (R)	5,000	83.6
	W. P. Coldwell (C)	981	16.4
8	David A. Nunn (R)	9,057	59.4
	J. F. Leftwick (C)	6,189	40.6

1868 House Elections

ALABAMA[1]
(Readmitted July 13, 1868)

Candidates	Votes	%
1 Francis W. Kellogg (R)	16,094	100.0
2 Charles W. Buckley (R)	8,440	100.0
3 Benjamin W. Norris (R)	9,451	99.6
4 Charles W. Pierce (R)	19,593	99.8
5 John B. Callis (R)	3,569	54.0
J. W. Burke	2,458	37.2
Whitley Thomas Ewing	573	8.7
6 Thomas Haughey	2,678	44.1
McCauley	1,440	23.7
Cramer	1,021	16.8
Snelling (R)	825	13.6

ARKANSAS[2]
(Readmitted June 22, 1868)

Candidates	Votes	%
1 Logan H. Roots (R)	7,151	50.6
Charles S. Cameron (D)	6,987	49.4
2 Anthony A. C. Rogers (D)	6,518	55.0
James T. Elliott (R)	5,332	45.0
3 Thomas Boles (R)	9,547	62.9
L. B. Nash (D)	5,630	37.1

CALIFORNIA

Candidates	Votes	%
1 Samuel B. Axtell (D)	23,632	54.1
F. M. Pixley (R)	20,081	45.9
2 Aaron A. Sargent (R)	18,264	54.7
J. W. Coffroth (D)	15,124	45.3
3 James A. Johnson (D)	15,792	50.4
C. Hartson (R)	15,527	49.6

DELAWARE

Candidates	Votes	%
AL Benjamin T. Biggs (D)	10,961	58.9
Torbert (R)	7,636	41.1

FLORIDA[3]
(Readmitted June 25, 1868)

Candidates	Votes	%
AL Charles M. Hamilton (R)	✓	
Friend (D)		
Liberty Billings		

GEORGIA[4]

Candidates	Votes	%
1 Joseph W. Clift (R)	11,990	59.6
Fitch (D)	8,141	40.4
2 Nelson Tift (D)	13,645	53.9
Richard H. Whitely (R)	11,696	46.2
3 William P. Edwards (R)	12,806	52.5
Alexander (D)	11,581	47.5
4 Samuel F. Gove (R)	11,078	50.4
Lochrane (D)	10,917	49.6
5 Charles H. Prince (R)	✓	
Hilliard (D)		
6 John H. Christy (D)	8,340*	51.3
John A. Wimpey (R)	7,929	48.7
7 Pierce M. B. Young (D)	11,160	58.1
James Adkins (R)	8,054	41.9

ILLINOIS

Candidates	Votes	%
1 Norman B. Judd (R)	27,414	58.8
M. R. M. Wallace (D)	19,233	41.2
2 John F. Farnsworth (R)	20,725	76.7
A. M. Herrington (D)	6,307	23.3
3 Elihu B. Washburne (R)	18,584	65.9
W. J. McKim (D)	9,612	34.1
4 John B. Hawley (R)	17,269	52.6
James W. Singleton (D)	15,547	47.4
5 Ebon C. Ingersoll (R)	20,991	60.2
John N. Niglas (D)	13,686	39.2

ILLINOIS

Candidates	Votes	%
6 Burton C. Cook (R)	19,607	62.1
Oliver C. Gray (D)	11,946	37.9
7 Jesse H. Moore (R)	22,321	56.5
Thomas Brewer (D)	17,171	43.5
8 Shelby M. Cullom (R)	22,193	53.5
B. S. Edwards (D)	19,309	46.5
9 Thompson W. McNeely (D)	17,877	53.9
Leonard F. Ross (R)	15,279	46.1
10 Albert G. Burr (D)	21,420	55.2
Iona B. Turner (R)	17,397	44.8
11 Samuel S. Marshall (D)	20,475	55.2
James S. Martin (R)	16,642	44.8
12 John B. Hays (D)	14,980	52.9
William M. Snyder (D)	13,338	47.1
13 John M. Crebs (D)	14,764	50.9
Green B. Raum (R)	14,261	49.1
AL John A. Logan (R)	249,422	55.5
William W. O'Brien (D)	199,861	44.5

INDIANA

Candidates	Votes	%
1 William E. Niblack (D)	18,116	52.1
Veatch (R)	16,631	47.9
2 Michael C. Kerr (D)	18,779	60.3
Gresham (R)	12,343	39.7
3 William S. Holman (D)	15,665	51.3
Lamb (R)	14,903	48.8
4 George W. Julian (R)	13,413	50.2
Reid (D)	13,297	49.8
5 John Coburn (R)	15,715	51.7
Keightly (D)	14,683	48.3
6 Daniel W. Voorhees (D)	16,582	50.2
Carter (R)	16,455	49.8
7 Godlove S. Orth (R)	16,117	50.7
Mahlon D. Manson (D)	15,660	49.3
8 Daniel D. Pratt (R)	17,227*	53.5
Ross (D)	14,946	46.5
9 John P. C. Shanks (R)	15,597	51.6
Lowry (D)	14,656	48.4
10 William Williams (R)	16,551	53.8
Ellison (D)	14,228	46.2
11 Jasper Packard (R)	15,489	52.1
Farrand (D)	14,268	48.0

IOWA

Candidates	Votes	%
1 George W. McCrary (R)	17,718	58.2
T. W. Clagett (D)	12,705	41.8
2 William Smyth (R)	18,753	58.6
William E. Leffingwell (D)	13,227	41.4
3 William B. Allison (R)	20,119	58.5
William Mills (D)	14,120	41.1
4 William Loughridge (R)	24,057	59.3
J. P. Irish (D)	16,531	40.7
5 Francis W. Palmer (R)	20,409	60.4
P. Gad Bryan (D)	13,402	39.6
6 Charles Pomeroy (R)	16,775	72.8
G. A. L. Roszell (D)	6,257	27.2

KANSAS

Candidates	Votes	%
AL Sidney Clarke (R)	29,324	67.7
C. W. Blair (D)	13,969	32.3

KENTUCKY

Candidates	Votes	%
1 Lawrence S. Trimble (D)	13,608	87.0
Charles A. Marshall (R)	1,731	11.1
2 William N. Sweeney (D)	12,786	78.3
Samuel W. Langley (R)	3,538	21.7

KENTUCKY

Candidates	Votes	%
3 Jacob S. Golladay (D)	9,469	80.4
William E. Hobson (R)	2,303	19.6
4 J. Proctor Knott (D)	13,166	87.9
William H. Hays (R)	1,811	12.1
5 Boyd Winchester (D)	15,108	90.9
J. B. English (R)	1,515	9.1
6 Thomas L. Jones (D)	14,082	69.7
O. W. Root (R)	6,137	30.4
7 James B. Beck (D)	13,019	84.6
Charles Eginton (R)	2,373	15.4
8 George M. Adams (D)	10,318	51.1
Sydney M. Barnes (R)	9,861	48.9
9 John M. Rice (D)	10,510	61.2
J. L. Zeigler (R)	6,652	38.8

LOUISIANA[5]
(Readmitted July 9, 1868)

Candidates	Votes	%
1 Louis St.Martin (D)	12,377*	85.1
J. Hale Sypher (R)	2,175	15.0
2 Caleb S. Hunt (D)	14,829	44.8
Lionel A. Sheldon (R)	9,695✓	29.3
J. W. Menard (R)	8,615	26.0
3 Adolphe Bailey (D)	17,513	67.1
Chester B. Darrall (R)	8,593✓	32.9
4 Michael Ryan (D)	13,352	64.4
Joseph P. Newsham (R)	7,395✓	35.6
5 G. W. McCranie (D)	13,716*	67.9
Frank Morey (R)	3,423	16.9
P. J. Kennedy (R)	3,076	15.2

MAINE

Candidates	Votes	%
1 John Lynch (R)	16,818	53.6
Charles A. Shaw (D)	14,579	46.4
2 Samuel P. Morrill (R)	14,281	59.6
Alonzo Garcelon (D)	9,653	40.3
3 James G. Blaine (R)	16,121	57.3
E. Wilder Farley (D)	11,982	42.6
4 John A. Peters (R)	13,338	61.2
George W. Ladd (D)	8,304	38.1
5 Eugene Hale (R)	14,363	55.2
Arno Wiswell (D)	11,680	44.9

MARYLAND

Candidates	Votes	%
1 Samuel Hambleton (D)	12,703	73.4
Henry R. Torbert (R)	4,606	26.6
2 Stevenson Archer (D)	12,671	68.6
John T. Ensor (R)	5,796	31.4
3 Thomas Swann (D)	13,056	69.7
Adam E. King (R)	5,667	30.3
4 Patrick Hamill (D)	12,289	51.3
Daniel E. Weisel (R)	11,653	48.7
5 Frederick Stone (D)	9,924	82.0
William J. Albert (R)	2,176	18.0

MASSACHUSETTS

Candidates	Votes	%
1 James Buffinton (R)	12,975	78.5
Philandor Cobb	3,486	21.1
2 Oakes Ames (R)	14,498	71.8
Edward Arery (D)	5,695	28.2
3 Ginery Twichell (R)	9,074	56.8
Edwin C. Bailey (D)	6,892	43.1
4 Samuel Hooper (R)	11,328	56.9
Peter Harvey (D)	8,592	43.1
5 Benjamin F. Butler (R)	13,109	65.5
Otis P. Lord (D)	5,061	25.3
Richard A. Dana Jr (IR)	1,811	9.1
6 Nathaniel P. Banks (R)	13,933	65.9
Frederick O. Prince (D)	7,187	34.0

Footnotes, see p. 777.

MASSACHUSETTS

	Candidates	Votes	%
7	George S. Boutwell (R)	13,214	65.4
	Leverett Saltonstall (D)	6,995	34.6
8	George F. Hoar (R)	14,317	74.1
	Henry H. Stevens (D)	4,974	25.8
9	William B. Washburn (R)	16,985	82.9
	Levi Heywood (D)	1,814	8.9
	Charles Heywood (D)	1,691	8.3
10	Henry L. Dawes (R)	12,260	62.1
	Abijah W. Chapin (D)	7,490	37.9

MICHIGAN

		Votes	%
1	Fernando C. Beaman (R)	22,197	51.9
	Merrill I. Mills (D)	20,595	48.1
2	William L. Stoughton (R)	25,205	59.2
	Henry Chamberlain (D)	17,401	40.8
3	Austin Blair (R)	19,268	54.2
	Isaac M. Crane (D)	16,268	45.8
4	Thomas W. Ferry (R)	23,043	62.7
	Lyman G. Mason (D)	13,714	37.3
5	Omar D. Conger (R)	16,347	52.8
	Byron G. Stout (D)	14,622	47.2
6	Randolph Strickland (R)	20,118	54.6
	William Newton (D)	16,720	45.4

MINNESOTA

		Votes	%
1	Morton S. Wilkinson (R)	23,764	61.9
	Batchelder (D)	14,646	38.1
2	Eugene M. Wilson (D)	13,506	40.5
	Ignatius Donnelly (OPP R)	11,265	33.8
	Andrews (R)	8,598	25.8

MISSISSIPPI[6]

(Readmitted Feb. 23, 1870)

		Votes	%
1	Townsend (D)	11,029	65.5
	Wofford (R)	5,823	34.6
2	Martin (D)	11,504	65.5
	Railsback (R)	6,068	34.5
3	Turner (D)	11,681	53.4
	Sullivan (R)	10,181	46.6
4	George C. McKee (R)	20,444	56.9
	Potter (D)	15,510	43.1
5	Martin (D)	12,686	51.6
	Pierce (R)	11,886	48.4

MISSOURI

		Votes	%
1	Erastus Wells (D)	9,734	50.5
	William A. Pile (R)	9,553	49.5
2	Gustavus A. Finkelnburg (R)	11,506	58.2
	James J. Lindley (D)	8,279	41.8
3	James R. McCormick (D)	5,153	54.9
	John F. Bush (R)	4,226	45.1
4	Sempronius H. Boyd (R)	8,919	58.5
	Charles B. McAfee (D)	4,949	32.5
	John R. Kelso (R)	1,384	9.1
5	Samuel S. Burdett (R)	11,187	58.5
	John F. Phillips (D)	7,941	41.5
6	Robert T. Van Horn (R)	5,427	54.3
	James Shields (D)	4,560	45.7
7	Joel F. Asper (R)	15,272	65.5
	Mordecai Oliver (D)	8,029	34.5
8	John F. Benjamin (R)	8,954	52.1
	John F. Williams (D)	8,248	48.0
9	David P. Dyer (R)	5,407	52.1
	William F. Switzler (D)	4,981	48.0

Special Election

		Votes	%
5	John H. Stover (R)	11,387	59.5
	Ignatius Hazel (D)	7,757	40.5

NEBRASKA

	Candidates	Votes	%
AL	John Taffe (R)	8,715	58.5
	Andrew J. Poppleton (D)	6,192	41.5

NEVADA

		Votes	%
AL	Thomas Fitch (R)	6,230	53.8
	William F. Anderson (D)	5,349	46.2

NEW JERSEY

		Votes	%
1	William Moore (R)	15,214	56.9
	Samuel J. Bayard (D)	11,539	43.1
2	Charles Haight (D)	16,299	51.3
	James F. Rusling (R)	15,494	48.7
3	John T. Bird (D)	19,580	55.9
	Amos Clark (R)	15,456	44.1
4	John Hill (R)	16,468	50.1
	Philip Rafferty (D)	16,389	49.9
5	Orestes Cleveland (D)	19,110	53.1
	George A. Halsey (R)	16,862	46.9

NEW YORK

		Votes	%
1	Henry A. Reeves (D)	13,338	52.8
	Alfred M. Wood (R)	11,945	47.3
2	John G. Schumacher (D)	24,418	66.2
	Henry S. Bellows (R)	12,492	33.8
3	Henry W. Slocum (D)	16,598	54.7
	Samuel Booth (R)	13,734	45.3
4	John Fox (D)	20,074	83.3
	Charles V. Lewis (R)	4,024	16.7
5	John Morrissey (D)	16,064	69.4
	James M. McCartin (R)	4,494	19.4
	George Francis Train (ID)	2,583	11.2
6	Samuel S. Cox (D)	12,362	56.1
	George Starr (R)	9,682	43.9
7	Hervey C. Calkin (D)	18,485	75.5
	Joseph C. Pinckney (R)	5,987	24.5
8	James Brooks (D)	21,487	68.5
	William Laimbeer (R)	9,866	31.5
9	Fernando Wood (D)	14,648	57.5
	Francis A. Thomas (R)	9,087	35.6
	John Savage (ID)	1,759	6.9
10	Clarkson N. Potter (D)	16,533	56.6
	David O. Bradley (R)	12,700	43.4
11	George W. Greene (D)	11,620‡	50.7
	Charles H. Van Wyck (R)	11,298	49.3
12	John H. Ketcham (R)	13,568	50.8
	Charles Wheaton (D)	13,144	49.2
13	John A. Griswold (D)	12,201	51.1
	Thomas Cornell (R)	11,692	48.9
14	Stephen L. Mayham (D)	18,477	54.0
	Joseph H. Ramsay (R)	15,734	46.0
15	Adolphus H. Tanner (R)	17,054	53.8
	Jason C. Osgood (D)	14,641	46.2
16	Orange Ferriss (R)	10,428	55.9
	Robert W. Livingston (D)	8,218	44.1
17	William A. Wheeler (R)	15,262	70.8
	William H. Wallace (D)	6,284	29.2
18	Stephen Sanford (R)	16,611	53.4
	John H. White (D)	14,508	46.6
19	Charles Knapp (R)	17,949	55.2
	Francis H. Gilbert (D)	14,584	44.8
20	Addison H. Laflin (R)	16,856	55.5
	Andrew Cornwall (D)	13,508	44.5
21	Alexander H. Bailey (R)	12,543	52.7
	J. Thomas Spriggs (D)	11,240	47.3
22	John C. Churchill (R)	15,761	71.9
	Charles Stebbins Jr (D)	6,169	28.1
23	Dennis McCarthy (R)	16,470	59.0
	William Porter (D)	11,455	41.0
24	George W. Cowles (R)	17,234	57.5
	Elmore P. Ross (D)	12,743	42.5
25	William H. Kelsey (R)	13,418	58.3
	Lester B. Faulkner (D)	9,610	41.7

	Candidates	Votes	%
26	Giles W. Hotchkiss (R)	17,398	58.6
	Alvin Devereaux (D)	12,280	41.4
27	Hamilton Ward (R)	18,647	58.6
	Curtiss C. Gardiner (D)	13,180	41.4
28	Noah Davis (R)	15,389	54.8
	John McConville (D)	12,699	45.2
29	John Fisher (R)	13,432	56.6
	James Jackson Jr (D)	10,294	43.4
30	David S. Bennett (R)	16,004	52.8
	Isaac A. Verplanck (D)	14,293	47.2
31	Porter Sheldon (R)	15,416	64.6
	John S. Beggs (D)	8,433	35.4

NORTH CAROLINA[7]

(Readmitted July 4, 1868)

		Votes	%
1	Clinton L. Cobb (R)	15,474	56.5
	David A. Barnes (C)	11,893	43.5
2	David Heaton (R)	14,895	54.8
	Thomas S. Kenan (C)	12,293	45.2
3	Oliver H. Dockery (R)	15,314	53.4
	A. A. McKoy (C)	13,353	46.6
4	John T. Deweese (R)	14,796	52.2
	Sion H. Rogers (C)	13,556	47.8
5	Israel G. Lash (R)	14,525	56.6
	Livingston Brown (C)	11,123	43.4
6	Francis E. Shober (C)	12,192	52.3
	Nathaniel Boyden (R)	11,103	47.7
7	Plato Durham (C)	10,347	50.0
	Alexander H. Jones (R)	10,329✔	50.0

Special Elections

		Votes	%
1	John R. French (R)	14,664	58.5
	Henry A. Gilliam (C)	10,407	41.5
2	David Heaton (R)	14,693	56.8
	Thomas S. Kenan (C)	11,172	43.2
3	Oliver H. Dockery (R)	15,090	56.9
	Thomas C. Fuller (C)	11,444	43.1
4	John T. Deweese (R)	14,436	55.4
	Samuel T. Williams (C)	11,630	44.6
5	Israel G. Lash (R)	13,020	58.7
	David F. Caldwell (C)	9,141	41.2
6	Nathaniel Boyden (R)	11,477	52.8
	Calvin I. Cowles (R)	10,251	47.2
7	Alexander H. Jones (R)	10,049	54.2
	Burgess S. Gaither (C)	8,467	45.7

OHIO

		Votes	%
1	Philip W. Strader (D)	10,483	50.5
	Benjamin Eggleston (R)	10,272	49.5
2	Job E. Stevenson (R)	11,694	51.1
	Samuel F. Cary (D)	11,197	48.9
3	Robert C. Schenck (R)	16,293	50.7
	C. L. Vallandigham (D)	15,818	49.3
4	William Lawrence (R)	13,656	51.2
	John S. Leedom (D)	13,027	48.8
5	William Mungen (D)	15,435	59.3
	Thomas E. Grissell (R)	10,589	40.7
6	John A. Smith (R)	13,463	50.7
	Nelson Barrere (D)	13,120	49.4
7	James J. Winans (R)	13,978	50.2
	John H. Thomas (D)	13,873	49.8
8	John Beatty (R)	12,198	52.0
	J. H. Benson (D)	11,250	48.0
9	Edward F. Dickinson (D)	16,322	52.7
	William H. Gibson (R)	14,677	47.4
10	Truman H. Hoag (D)	15,507	51.5
	James M. Ashley (R)	14,595	48.5
11	John T. Wilson (R)	13,614	54.2
	John Sands (D)	11,503	45.8
12	Philadelph Van Trump (D)	16,287	58.9
	Nelson J. Turney (R)	11,374	41.1
13	George W. Morgan (D)	14,614	53.0
	Charles Cooper (R)	12,980	47.0

Footnotes, see p. 777.

OHIO

	Candidates	Votes	%
14	Martin Welker (R)	13,575	50.9
	L. R. Critchfield (D)	13,113	49.1
15	Eliakim H. Moore (R)	13,773	51.8
	Martin D. Follett (D)	12,817	48.2
16	John A. Bingham (R)	13,757	50.8
	Josiah M. Estep (D)	13,341	49.2
17	Jacob A. Ambler (R)	14,998	56.4
	Daniel T. Lawson (D)	11,602	43.6
18	William H. Upson (R)	18,359	60.5
	Franklin T. Backus (D)	11,980	39.5
19	James A. Garfield (R)	20,187	67.4
	James McEwen	9,759	32.6

Special Election

		Votes	%
8	John Beatty (R)	11,820	51.8
	Burns	10,985	48.2

OREGON

		Votes	%
AL	Joseph S. Smith (D)	11,754	52.7
	David Logan (R)	10,555	47.3

PENNSYLVANIA

		Votes	%
1	Samuel J. Randall (D)	14,745	63.7
	Benjamin L. Berry (R)	8,408	36.3
2	Charles O'Neill (R)	14,533	55.0
	Thomas B. Florence (D)	11,913	45.1
3	John Moffet (D)	13,856‡	50.2
	Leonard Myers (R)	13,729	49.8
4	William D. Kelley (R)	17,107	52.9
	James M. Nicholson (D)	15,248	47.1
5	John R. Reading (D)	13,199‡	50.1
	Caleb N. Taylor (R)	13,158	49.9
6	John D. Stiles (D)	15,247	54.8
	John R. Breitenbach (R)	12,568	45.2
7	Washington Townsend (R)	12,771	57.4
	Robert C. Monaghan (D)	9,481	42.6
8	J. Lawrence Getz (D)	13,738	64.8
	Henry S. Eckert (R)	7,472	35.2
9	Oliver J. Dickey (R)	14,993	63.4
	Hiram B. Swarr (D)	8,674	36.7
10	Henry L. Cake (R)	12,501	50.5
	James J. Conner (D)	12,276	49.6
11	Daniel M. Van Auken (D)	17,930	63.4
	John Torrey (R)	10,367	36.6
12	George W. Woodward (D)	16,687	52.8
	Theodore Strong (R)	14,898	47.2
13	Ulysses Mercur (R)	12,723	50.6
	Victor E. Piolet (D)	12,412	49.4
14	John B. Packer (R)	15,598	54.7
	Joseph F. Knipe (D)	12,902	45.3

	Candidates	Votes	%
15	Richard J. Haldeman (D)	15,818	55.8
	Samuel Small (R)	12,519	44.2
16	John Cessna (R)	13,653	50.3
	Fran M. Kimmell (D)	13,509	49.7
17	Daniel J. Morrell (R)	12,100	52.4
	John P. Linton (D)	11,006	47.6
18	William H. Armstrong (R)	16,760	53.2
	Levi A. Mackey (D)	14,732	46.8
19	Glenni W. Scofield (R)	16,903	54.1
	Rasselas Brown (D)	14,355	45.9
20	Calvin W. Gilfillan (R)	18,079	52.6
	Robert M. Defrance (D)	16,267	47.4
21	Henry D. Foster (D)	13,807	50.1
	John Covode (R)	13,766✔	49.9
22	James S. Negley (R)	15,175	58.7
	Andrew Burt (D)	10,696	41.3
23	Darwin Phelps (R)	16,095	59.3
	Lewis Z. Mitchell (D)	11,046	40.7
24	Joseph B. Donley (R)	13,860	52.1
	David Crawford (D)	12,737	47.9

Special Elections

		Votes	%
9	Oliver J. Dickey (R)	15,000	63.3
	Robert Crane (D)	8,689	36.7
20	S. Newton Pettus (R)	17,906	52.2
	James B. Knox (D)	16,390	47.8

RHODE ISLAND

		Votes	%
1	Thomas A. Jenckes (R)	7,995	66.4
	Arnold (D)	3,980	33.1
2	Nathan F. Dixon (R)	4,133	60.9
	Waterhouse (D)	2,640	38.9

SOUTH CAROLINA[8]

(Readmitted July 9, 1868)

		Votes	%
1	B. Frank Whittemore (R)	17,467	61.3
	H. J. Covington (D)	11,017	38.7
2	Christopher C. Bowen (R)	25,845	75.7
	R. W. Seymour (D)	8,296	24.3
3	J. P. Reed (D)	11,774	57.3
	Solomon L. Hoge (R)	8,766✔	42.7
4	William D. Simpson (D)	14,098	59.0
	Alexander S. Wallace (R)	9,807✔	41.0
AL	J. P. M. Epping	68,477*	50.2
	E. E. Dickson	67,654	49.6

Special Elections

		Votes	%
1	B. Frank Whittemore (R)	17,512	74.2
	J. N. Frierson (D)	6,075	25.8
2	Christopher C. Bowen (R)	18,000	96.0
	W. Brisbane (R)	5,322	28.4
3	M. Simeon Corley (R)	15,681	71.0
	S. McGowan (D)	6,413	29.0

	Candidates	Votes	%
4	James H. Goss (R)	12,016	57.2
	S. McAllilly (D)	8,993	42.8

TENNESSEE

		Votes	%
1	Roderick R. Butler (R)	10,107	98.5
2	Horace Maynard (R)	10,403	79.5
	C. Houk (I)	2,681	20.5
3	William B. Stokes (R)	5,915	74.4
	E. A. Garrett (I)	2,037	25.6
4	C. A. Sheafe (D)	4,476	54.0
	Lewis Tillman (R)	3,810✔	46.0
5	William F. Prosser (R)	5,804	56.5
	Joseph Motley (D)	2,655	25.8
	Samuel C. Mercer (I)	1,817	17.7
6	Samuel M. Arnell (R)	5,143	70.6
	John J. Buck (IR)	2,141	29.4
7	Isaac R. Hawkins (R)	2,825	71.3
	George R. Foote (D)	1,136	28.7
8	John W. Leftwich (D)	6,533	40.6
	William J. Smith (R)	5,543✔	34.4
	David A. Nunn (R)	4,024	25.0

VERMONT

		Votes	%
1	Charles W. Willard (R)	13,999	76.1
	John Cain (D)	4,396	23.9
2	Luke P. Poland (R)	15,407	74.6
	Charles M. Chase (D)	5,252	25.4
3	Worthington C. Smith (R)	11,105	72.4
	Waldo Brigham (D)	4,237	27.6

WEST VIRGINIA

		Votes	%
1	Issac H. Duval (R)	11,569	51.9
	H. S. Walker (D)	10,729	48.1
2	James C. McGrew (R)	9,147	58.4
	William G. Brown (D)	6,517	41.6
3	John S. Witcher (R)	6,215	56.4
	Charles P. J. Moore (D)	4,806	43.6

WISCONSIN

		Votes	%
1	Halbert E. Paine (R)	17,513	50.6
	Mitchell (D)	17,084	49.4
2	Benjamin F. Hopkins (R)	18,333	59.2
	Winans (D)	12,659	40.9
3	Amasa Cobb (R)	17,903	61.6
	Passmore (D)	11,162	38.4
4	Charles A. Eldridge (D)	17,688	57.3
	Frisby (R)	13,205	42.7
5	Philetus Sawyer (R)	19,622	55.8
	Vilas (D)	15,534	44.2
6	Cadwallader C. Washburn (R)	21,236	64.9
	Ellis (D)	11,481	35.1

1. These were six special elections to fill Alabama's House seats for the remainder of the 40th Congress (1867-69).

2. These three elections were for a full two-year term in the 41st Congress (1869-71). Arkansas was readmitted to the Union and had three representatives for part of the 40th Congress (1867-69), but returns for their election were not available.

3. Florida was readmitted during the 40th Congress (1867-69) and Charles M. Hamilton served for the remainder of that Congress. He was then re-elected to a full term in the 41st Congress (1869-71). The Florida candidates shown on page 619 were running for the full term in the 41st Congress.

4. Figures represent returns in seven special elections held April 20, 1868. All winners listed, except John H. Christy in the 6th District, were seated July 25, 1868 to serve for the remainder of the 40th Congress (1867-69), even though Georgia had not been formally re-admitted to the Union.

On the convening of the 41st Congress in 1869, the six incumbent Georgia Representatives claimed their election of April 20, 1868 also entitled them to seats in the 41st Congress. The House rejected the claim and Georgia then elected representatives to the 41st Congress, but these returns are not available. According to Georgia secretary of state archives, William Wiseham Paine (D) served in the House from the 1st

District March 4, 1869, to March 3, 1871; Marion Bethune (R), 3rd District, served Jan. 16, 1871-March 3, 1871; and Stephen Alfestus Corker (D), 5th District, served Jan. 24, 1871-March 3, 1871. No returns on their elections are available. Georgia was readmitted to representation by act of July 15, 1870.

5. Louisiana was readmitted during the 40th Congress (1867-69) and elected several representatives, but these returns are unavailable. The five elections shown here are for a full two-year term in the 41st Congress (1869-71).

6. No representatives from Mississippi were seated from this election. Mississippi was not readmitted until Feb. 23, 1870.

7. The special elections were for unexpired terms in the 40th Congress (1867-69). The general elections were for full two-year terms in the 41st Congress (1869-71).

8. The "Special Elections" were to fill unexpired terms in the 40th Congress (1867-69), while the others were for full terms in the 41st Congress (1869-71). The at-large election in which J. P. M. Epping was the apparent winner was rejected by the House. According to the Biographical Directory, a number of southern states upon readmission claimed that since their slaves were emancipated, they were entitled to larger delegations in the House. Epping's election falls in this category. The claims were rejected by the House.

1869 House Elections

ALABAMA

	Candidates	Votes	%
1	Alfred E. Buck (R)	14,191	54.0
	W. D. Mann (D)	12,080	46.0
2	Charles W. Buckley (R)	14,933	58.1
	A. N. Worthy (D)	10,786	41.9
3	Robert S. Heflin (R)	9,895	50.6
	J. C. Parkinson (D)	9,652	49.4
4	Charles Hays (R)	17,243	71.5
	John B. Reed (D)	4,881	20.2
	C. W. Dunstan (I)	2,010	8.3
5	Peter M. Dox (D)	6,047	55.1
	W. J. Haralson (R)	4,933	44.9
6	William C. Sherrod (D)	4,932	57.7
	J. J. Hinds (R)	2,836	33.2
	Thomas Haughey (I)	775	9.1

CONNECTICUT

	Candidates	Votes	%
1	Julius L. Strong (R)	11,617	51.6
	Dixon (D)	10,881	48.4
2	Stephen W. Kellogg (R)	13,102	50.8
	Babk (D)	12,678	49.2
3	Henry H. Starkweather (R)	9,212	57.5
	Conv (D)	6,813	42.5
4	William H. Barnum (D)	13,075	52.3
	William H. Beard (R)	11,915	47.7

ILLINOIS

Special Election

		Votes	%
3	Horatio C. Burchard (R)	6,213	76.1
	John V. Eustace	1,843	22.6

MASSACHUSETTS

	Candidates	Votes	%
	Special Election		
7	George M. Brooks (R)	8,809	67.3
	Leverett Saltonstall (D)	4,284	32.7

MISSISSIPPI

		Votes	%
1	George E. Harris (R)	10,215	61.5
	Jefferson L. Wafford (C)	6,389	38.5
2	Joseph L. Morphis (R)	9,089	62.9
	William Kellogg (C)	5,353	37.1
3	Henry W. Barry (R)	12,912	62.9
	Schuyler B. Steers (C)	7,630	37.1
4	George C. McKee (R)	25,082	71.9
	Archie C. Fisk (C)	9,811	28.1
5	Legrand W. Perce (R)	14,450	64.1
	Leroy S. Brown (C)	8,080	35.9

NEW HAMPSHIRE

		Votes	%
1	Jacob H. Ela (R)	13,138	53.6
	E. A. Hibbard (D)	11,376	46.4
2	Aaron F. Stevens (R)	11,513	53.9
	Edward W. Harrington (D)	9,866	46.2
3	Jacob Benton (R)	11,254	51.3
	Hosea W. Parker (D)	10,691	48.7

TEXAS

(Readmitted March 30, 1870)

		Votes	%
1	George W. Whitmore (R)	8,456	52.0
	James Armstrong (D)	7,406	45.6

	Candidates	Votes	%
	John C. Conner (D)	6,378	41.9
	B. F. Grafton (R)	4,355	28.6
	J. F. Johnson (ID)	3,540	23.2
	R. H. Taylor (I)	944	6.2
3	William T. Clark (R)	16,582	65.9
	Jacob Elliot (D)	8,564	34.0
4	Edward Degener (R)	9,312	47.7
	J. L. Haynes (D)	9,240	47.3

VIRGINIA [1]

(Readmitted Jan. 26, 1870)

		Votes	%
1	Richard S. Ayer (RAD)	8,023	29.7
	Joseph Segar (I)	7,377	27.3
	Norton (I)	6,523	24.2
	Lewis (C)	5,056	18.7
2	James H. Platt Jr (RAD)	16,781	53.4
	D. J. Godwin (C)	11,255	35.8
	Bayne (I)	2,736	8.7
3	Charles H. Porter (RAD)	17,311	55.0
	J. W. Hunnicut (C)	13,101	41.6
4	George W. Booker (C)	13,101	48.0
	George Tucker (RAD)	9,568	35.0
	Stowell (I)	4,639	17.0
5	Robert Ridgway (C)	16,732	55.2
	G. G. Curtis (RAD)	13,571	44.8
6	William Milnes Jr (C)	12,123	56.8
	John T. Harris (I)	6,815	31.9
	Phelps (RAD)	2,425	11.4
7	Lewis McKenzie (C)	15,878	58.9
	Charles Whittlesey (RAD)	11,073	41.1
8	James King Gibson (C)	14,717	69.6
	G. S. Smith (RAD)	6,244	29.5
AL	Joseph Segar (C)	117,499*	53.9
	A. M. Crane (RAD)	100,424	46.1

1. According to the Biographical Directory Virginia claimed an extra House seat and elected Joseph Segar at-large to fill it. The House rejected the claim.

1870 House Elections

ALABAMA

	Candidates	Votes	%
1	Benjamin S. Turner (R)	18,226	57.5
	S. J. Cumming (D)	13,466	42.5
2	Charles W. Buckley (R)	19,647	55.4
	M. B. Welbourn (D)	15,831	44.6
3	William A. Handley (D)	12,710	57.1
	B. W. Norris (R)	9,568	43.0
4	Charles Hays (R)	18,373	52.6
	J. G. Harris (D)	16,540	47.4
5	Peter M. Dox (D)	10,689	70.3
	L. J. Standifee (R)	4,523	29.7
6	Joseph H. Sloss (D)	9,221	69.4
	B. O. Masterson (R)	4,068	30.6

ARKANSAS

	Candidates	Votes	%
1	James M. Hanks (D)	5,394	61.4
	Logan H. Roots (R)	3,398	38.7
2	Oliver P. Snyder (R)	8,956	59.1
	A. A. C. Rogers (D)	6,211	41.0
3	John Edwards (D)	6,874‡	53.7
	Thomas Boles (R)	5,919	46.3

DELAWARE

	Candidates	Votes	%
AL	Benjamin T. Biggs (D)	11,446	55.6
	Joshua T. Heald (R)	9,150	44.4

FLORIDA

	Candidates	Votes	%
AL	Josiah T. Walls (R)	12,439‡	51.3
	Silas L. Niblack (D)	11,810	48.7

GEORGIA

(Readmitted July 15, 1870)

	Candidates	Votes	%
1	Archibald T. MacIntyre (D)	15,581	56.9
	Virgil Hillyer (R)	9,662	35.3
	A. A. Bradley (IR)	2,142	7.8
2	Nelson Tift (D)	14,969	51.5
	Richard H. Whiteley (R)	14,088	48.5
3	John S. Bigby (R)	14,212	52.9
	William F. Wright (D)	12,649	47.1
4	Thomas J. Speer (R)	11,211	51.1
	Winburn J. Lawton (D)	10,725	48.9
5	Dudley M. DuBose (D)	15,363	62.3
	Isham S. Fannin (R)	9,302	37.7
6	William P. Price (D)	10,358	68.6
	John A. Wimpey (R)	3,911	25.9
	Weir Boyd (ID)	823	5.5
7	Pierce M. B. Young (D)	14,768	73.8
	George P. Burnett (R)	5,257	26.3

ILLINOIS

	Candidates	Votes	%
1	Charles B. Farwell (R)	20,342	57.5
	John Wentworth (D)	15,025	42.4
2	John F. Farnsworth (R)	8,396	48.6
	J. C. Stoughton (P)	6,516	37.8
	Richard Bischop (D)	2,349	13.6
3	Horatio C. Burchard (R)	11,718	65.3
	Charles Betts (D)	6,219	34.6
4	John B. Hawley (R)	12,023	50.1
	P. L. Cable (D)	11,982	49.9
5	Bradford N. Stevens (D)	11,579	51.7
	E. C. Ingersoll (R)	9,963	44.5
6	Burton C. Cook (R)	10,452	56.5
	Julias Avery (D)	7,839	42.4
7	Jesse H. Moore (R)	14,089	51.2
	Andrew J. Hunter (D)	13,418	48.8
8	James C. Robinson (D)	13,702	50.1
	Jonathan Merriam (R)	12,448	45.6
9	Thompson W. McNeely (D)	12,691	55.2
	B. F. Westlake (R)	10,297	44.8

	Candidates	Votes	%
10	Edward Y. Rice (D)	13,963	53.7
	J. W. Kitchell (R)	12,028	46.3
11	Samuel S. Marshall (D)	15,771	57.7
	William H. Robinson (R)	11,546	42.3
12	John B. Hays (R)	10,903	51.8
	William Hartzell (D)	10,126	48.2
13	John M. Crebs (D)	13,947	53.0
	Daniel W. Munn (R)	12,366	47.0
AL	John A. Logan (R)	168,801*	53.2
	William B. Anerson (D)	145,191	45.8

INDIANA

	Candidates	Votes	%
1	William E. Niblack (D)	17,577	53.4
	Hy C. Gooding (R)	15,327	46.6
2	Michael C. Kerr (D)	16,950	60.4
	Carr (R)	11,116	39.6
3	William S. Holman (D)	15,396	54.3
	Pritchard (R)	12,972	45.7
4	Jeremiah M. Wilson (R)	12,561	50.0
	David S. Gooding (D)	12,557	50.0
5	John Coburn (R)	14,123	50.8
	Cottrell (D)	13,707	49.3
6	Daniel W. Voorhees (D)	17,268	52.2
	Dunn (R)	15,843	47.9
7	Mahlon D. Manson (D)	15,539	50.6
	L. Wallace (R)	15,146	49.4
8	James F. Tyner (R)	15,113	53.5
	J. T. Henderson (D)	13,149	46.5
9	John P. C. Shanks (R)	13,790	50.7
	Colerick (D)	13,396	49.3
10	William Williams (R)	14,130	60.8
	M. S. Hascall (IR)	9,112	39.2
11	Jasper Packard (R)	14,459	52.6
	S. I. Anthony (D)	13,052	47.4

IOWA

	Candidates	Votes	%
1	George W. McCrary (R)	13,327	57.2
	Edmund Jaeger (D)	9,961	42.8
2	Aylett R. Cotton (R)	13,586	59.3
	William E. Leffingwell (D)	9,338	40.7
3	William G. Donnan (R)	15,927	59.2
	John T. Stoneman (D)	10,961	40.8
4	Madison M. Walden (R)	19,005	56.0
	William T. Smith (D)	14,883	43.9
5	Frank W. Palmer (R)	19,798	61.2
	B. F. Montgomery (D)	12,516	38.7
6	Jackson Orr (R)	16,993	73.9
	C. C. Smettzer (D)	5,977	26.0

Special Election

	Candidates	Votes	%
2	William P. Wolf (R)	13,858	66.6
	J. M. Preston (D)	4,834	23.2
	R. M. Preston	1,048	5.0

KANSAS

	Candidates	Votes	%
AL	David P. Lowe (R)	40,368	65.8
	R. C. Foster (D)	20,950	34.2

KENTUCKY

	Candidates	Votes	%
1	Edward Crossland (D)	7,930	64.4
	N. R. Black (R)	2,982	24.2
	W. C. Clark (ID)	1,405	11.4
2	Henry D. McHenry (D)	8,214	59.9
	Milton J. Roach (R)	5,490	40.1
3	Joseph H. Lewis (D)	7,314	56.4
	D. R. Carr (R)	5,657	43.6
4	William B. Read (D)	9,314	70.9
	James M. Fidler (R)	3,831	29.1
5	Boyd Winchester (D)	10,599	66.1
	James Speed (R)	5,426	33.9

	Candidates	Votes	%
6	William E. Arthur (D)	9,213	66.7
	Thomas Wrightson (R)	4,578	33.1
7	James B. Beck (D)	14,312	56.7
	William Brown (R)	10,916	43.3
8	George M. Adams (D)	12,226	50.0
	Hugh F. Finley (R)	12,208	50.0
9	John M. Rice (D)	9,823	60.3
	George M. Thomas (R)	6,463	39.7

Special Election

	Candidates	Votes	%
3	Joseph H. Lewis (D)	9,847	65.1
	J. H. Lowry	5,289	34.9

LOUISIANA

	Candidates	Votes	%
1	J. Hale Sypher (R)	13,971	62.0
	A. W. Walker (D)	8,579	38.0
2	Lionel A. Sheldon (R)	17,512	69.6
	John A. Walsh (D)	7,640	30.4
3	Chester B. Darrall (R)	13,202	60.9
	Adolph Bailey (D)	8,483	39.1
4	James McCleery (R)	11,786	62.2
	Michael Ryan (D)	7,171	37.8
5	Frank Morey (R)	9,521	58.7
	J. D. Watkins (D)	6,713	41.4

MAINE

	Candidates	Votes	%
1	John Lynch (R)	12,571	53.2
	Haines (D)	11,075	46.8
2	William P. Frye (R)	10,245	56.3
	Black (D)	7,924	43.6
3	James G. Blaine (R)	11,590	55.0
	Farley (D)	9,279	44.1
4	John A. Peters (R)	9,962	57.6
	Emery (D)	7,322	42.3
5	Eugene Hale (R)	10,086	52.9
	Carlton (D)	8,876	46.5

MARYLAND

	Candidates	Votes	%
1	Samuel Hambleton (D)	17,314	56.5
	Henry R. Torbert (R)	13,348	43.5
2	Stevenson Archer (D)	14,622	64.5
	W. M. Marine (R)	8,062	35.5
3	Thomas Swann (D)	15,137	59.2
	Washington Booth (R)	10,414	40.8
4	John Ritchie (D)	14,304	53.4
	John E. Smith (R)	12,486	46.6
5	William H. Merrick (D)	15,231	53.1
	James A. Gary (R)	13,440	46.9

MASSACHUSETTS

	Candidates	Votes	%
1	James Buffinton (R)	8,281	64.3
	Robert Pitnam (I)	2,667	20.7
	William W. Comstock (D)	1,704	13.2
2	Oakes Ames (R)	9,367	60.0
	Edward Avery (D)	6,013	38.5
3	Ginery Twichell (R)	6,233	50.7
	William Gaiton (D)	5,640	45.9
4	Samuel Hooper (R)	8,025	56.0
	Leopold Morse (D)	5,605	39.1
5	Benjamin F. Butler (R)	8,333	60.4
	William Endicott (D)	4,297	31.1
	Unidentified Candidate (I)	1,076	7.8
6	Nathaniel P. Banks (R)	10,548	64.4
	John K. Tarbox (D)	5,123	31.3
7	George M. Brooks (R)	8,406	57.6
	Seth Adams (D)	4,561	31.3
	J. Chillis Kimball (LAB REF)	1,489	10.2
8	George F. Hoar (R)	8,487	56.2
	Alvin Cook (D)	4,282	28.4
	Moses Johnson (LAB REF)	1,734	11.5

MASSACHUSETTS

	Candidates	Votes	%
9	William B. Washburn (R)	10,903	70.4
	Lysander B. Jaquith (D)	4,185	27.0
10	Henry L. Dawes (R)	8,419	52.9
	Reuben Noble (D)	7,077	44.5

MICHIGAN

		Votes	%
1	Henry Waldron (R)	18,348	50.6
	N. B. Eldridge (D)	17,447	48.2
2	William L. Stoughton (R)	17,502	54.6
	Henry Chamberlain (D)	13,923	43.5
3	Austin Blair (R)	15,236	51.5
	D. D. Hughes (D)	13,768	46.6
4	Thomas W. Ferry (R)	16,854*	60.8
	Myron Rider (D)	10,384	37.4
5	Omar D. Conger (R)	13,782	49.9
	Byron G. Stout (D)	13,593	49.2
6	Jabez G. Sutherland (D)	16,618	52.7
	John F. Driggs (R)	14,879	47.2

MINNESOTA

		Votes	%
1	Mark H. Dunnell (R)	19,606	56.8
	Buck (D)	14,904	43.2
2	John T. Averill (R)	17,133	54.2
	Donnelly (D)	14,491	45.8

MISSISSIPPI

1	George E. Harris (R)		✔
2	Joseph L. Morphis (R)		✔
3	Henry W. Barry (R)		✔
4	George C. McKee (R)		✔
5	Legrand W. Perce (R)		✔

MISSOURI

		Votes	%
1	Erastus Wells (D)	7,629	50.9
	Charles Johnson (LR)	5,444	36.3
	Iron Z. Smith (RAD R)	1,928	12.9
2	Gustavus A. Finkelnburg (LR)	12,708	90.3
	A. Vanwormer (RAD R)	1,359	9.7
3	James R. McCormick (D)	7,572	63.5
	G. J. Vanallen (RAD R)	2,331	19.6
	William M. Nalle (LR)	2,015	16.9
4	Harrison E. Havens (RAD R)	8,830	54.4
	William E. Gilmore (LR)	7,416	45.7
5	Samuel S. Burdett (RAD R)	10,790	47.1
	George R. Smith (LR)	9,066	39.6
	Douglass Dale (D)	3,062	13.4
6	Abraham Comingo (D)	12,511	58.9
	George R. Smith (RAD R)	8,718	41.1
7	Isaac C. Parker (LR)	13,713	56.1
	John H. Ellis (D)	10,723	43.9
8	James G. Blair (LR)	11,710	56.3
	J. T. K. Hayward (RAD R)	9,106	43.8
9	Andrew King (D)	10,393	59.7
	David P. Dyer (LR)	3,803	21.8
	Edward Draper (RAD R)	3,227	18.5

NEBRASKA

		Votes	%
AL	John Taffe (R)	12,375	60.8
	George B. Lake (D)	7,967	39.2

NEVADA

		Votes	%
AL	Charles W. Kendall (D)	6,821	52.5
	Thomas Fitch (R)	6,161	47.5

NEW JERSEY

		Votes	%
1	John W. Hazleton (R)	14,502	53.8
	Benjamin F. Lee (D)	12,469	46.2

	Candidates	Votes	%
2	Samuel C. Forker (D)	15,899	50.7
	William A. Newell (R)	15,452	49.3
3	John T. Bird (D)	18,007	55.7
	Robert Rusling (R)	14,323	44.3
4	John Hill (R)	18,057	54.1
	Philip Rafferty (D)	15,304	45.9
5	George A. Halsey (R)	18,092	54.2
	Orestes Cleveland (D)	14,694	44.0

NEW YORK

		Votes	%
1	Dwight Townsend (D)	12,632	52.4
	Caleb C. Norvell (R)	11,466	47.6
2	Thomas Kinsella (D)	20,704	62.4
	Silas B. Dutcher (R)	12,482	37.6
3	Henry W. Slocum (D)	13,799	53.8
	Erastus D. Webster (R)	8,623	33.6
	R. M. Whiting Jr. (IR)	3,248	12.7
4	Robert B. Roosevelt (D)	10,702	63.0
	M. T. McMahon (R&YD)	5,501	32.4
5	William R. Roberts (D)	14,556	86.0
	James A. Briggs (R)	2,215	13.1
6	Samuel S. Cox (D)	9,228	52.9
	Greeley (R)	8,203	47.1
7	Smith Ely Jr (D)	12,514	73.9
	McAlpin (R)	3,503	20.7
	Willis (R)	929	5.5
8	James Brooks (D)	12,845	52.6
	George Wilkes (R)	7,348	30.1
	J. Wadsworth (YD)	4,243	17.4
9	Fernando Wood (D)	15,630	64.8
	W. S. Hillyer (YD&R)	4,789	19.9
	Morris Ellinger (R)	3,708	15.4
10	Clarkson N. Potter (D)	14,249	57.2
	James Westervelt (R)	10,685	42.9
11	Charles St.John (R)	11,247	51.1
	Sherman (D)	10,747	48.9
12	John H. Ketcham (R)	14,432	55.1
	Philip (D)	11,748	44.9
13	Joseph H. Tuthill (D)	11,559	50.7
	Lindsley (R)	11,257	49.3
14	Eli Perry (D)	17,716	54.6
	Harder (R)	14,726	45.4
15	Joseph M. Warren (D)	17,793	60.4
	J. Thomas Davis (R)	11,659	39.6
16	John Rogers (D)	9,444	50.5
	Andrew Williams (R)	9,272	49.5
17	William A. Wheeler (R)	13,020	69.6
	George Mott (D)	5,699	30.4
18	John M. Carroll (D)	14,828	48.6
	James M. Marvin (R)	13,390	43.9
	Samuel McKean (IR)	2,286	7.5
19	Elizur H. Prindle (R)	16,752	53.8
	Juliand (D)	14,389	46.2
20	Clinton L. Merriam (R)	14,863	53.5
	Andrew Cornwall (D)	12,899	46.5
21	Ellis H. Roberts (R)	12,322	53.7
	Weaver (D)	10,606	46.3
22	William E. Lansing (R)	13,450	56.5
	M. J. Shoecraft (D)	9,780	41.1
23	R. Holland Duell (R)	12,954	55.1
	Dennis McCarthy (IR & D)	10,540	44.9
24	John E. Seeley (R)	15,276	55.7
	Daniels (D)	12,134	44.3
25	William H. Lamport (R)	12,115	56.4
	Harlow L. Comstock (D)	9,367	43.6
26	Milo Goodrich (R)	15,471	56.3
	Apgar (D)	12,029	43.7
27	H. Boardman Smith (R)	16,276	54.9
	Lucius Robinson (D)	13,352	45.1
28	Freeman Clarke (R)	13,844	55.3
	J. H. White (D)	11,187	44.7
29	Seth Wakeman (R)	12,134	57.3
	James G. Shepard (D)	9,039	42.7
30	William Williams (D)	15,018	51.0
	Bass (R)	14,415	49.0
31	Walter L. Sessions (R)	10,170	50.9
	Murray (D)	9,793	49.1

Special Election

28	Charles H. Holmes (R)		✔
	Alex P. Butts		

NORTH CAROLINA

	Candidates	Votes	%
1	Clinton L. Cobb (R)	10,054	60.7
	Timothy Morgan (IR)	6,520	39.3
2	Charles R. Thomas (R)	15,099	55.0
	Lott W. Humphrey (C)	12,352	45.0
3	Alfred M. Waddell (C)	13,828	50.6
	Oliver H. Dockery (R)	13,477	49.4
4	Sion H. Rogers (C)	14,106	51.7
	James Harris (R)	13,201	48.3
5	James M. Leach (C)	12,541	52.6
	William L. Scott (R)	11,302	47.4
6	Francis E. Shober (C)	12,474	60.0
	Frederick H. Sprague (R)	8,324	40.0
7	James C. Harper (C)	10,967	56.7
	Alexander H. Jones (R)	8,373	43.3

Special Elections [1]

		Votes	%
2	Joseph Dixon (R)	14,976	54.7
	C. J. O'Hagan (C)	12,396	45.3
4	Robert B. Gilliam (C)	14,014*	50.8
	Madison Hawkins (R)	13,556	49.2
4	John Manning Jr. (C)	11,797	50.7
	Joseph W. Holden (R)	11,472	49.3

OHIO

		Votes	%
1	Aaron F. Perry (R)	8,039	52.4
	Milton Sayler (D)	7,294	47.6
2	Job E. Stevenson (R)	9,294	54.6
	Samuel F. Cary (D)	7,745	45.5
3	Lewis D. Campbell (D)	14,838	50.1
	Robert C. Schenck (R)	14,785	49.9
4	John F. McKinney (D)	11,966	50.2
	W. B. McClung (R)	11,741	49.3
5	Charles L. Lamison (D)	11,997	57.4
	Clark (R)	8,894	42.6
6	John A. Smith (R)	12,063	49.8
	J. W. Denver (D)	11,827	48.8
7	Samuel Shellabarger (R)	13,488	52.8
	Hugh J. Jewett (D)	12,060	47.2
8	John Beatty (R)	10,610	52.0
	James R. Hubbell (D)	9,450	46.3
9	Charles Foster (R)	13,274	51.2
	Edward F. Dickinson (D)	12,498	48.2
10	Erasmus D. Peck (R)	11,302	52.2
	William F. Lockwood (D)	10,242	47.3
11	John T. Wilson (R)	11,294	52.6
	Ralph Leete (D)	10,189	47.4
12	Philadelph Van Trump (D)	14,123	57.9
	Charles E. Brown (R)	10,265	42.1
13	George W. Morgan (D)	14,196	54.1
	C. W. Potwin (R)	12,047	45.9
14	James Monroe (R)	12,271	51.3
	L. R. Critchfield (D)	11,545	48.3
15	William P. Sprague (R)	11,263	51.3
	John Cartwright (D)	10,547	48.0
16	John A. Bingham (R)	12,435	51.0
	Robert E. Chambers (D)	11,958	49.0
17	Jacob A. Ambler (R)	11,685	55.1
	John Ball (D)	9,514	44.9
18	William H. Upson (R)	11,053	60.7
	J. M. Coffinberry (D)	6,695	36.8
19	James A. Garfield (R)	13,538	65.1
	Howard (D)	7,263	34.9

OREGON

		Votes	%
AL	James H. Slater (D)	11,588	50.8
	Joseph G. Wilson (R)	11,245	49.3

PENNSYLVANIA

		Votes	%
1	Samuel J. Randall (D)	10,853	61.8
	Benjamin Huckell (R)	6,705	38.2
2	John V. Creely (D)	11,059	52.2
	Charles O'Neill (R)	10,134	47.8
3	Leonard Myers (R)	9,778	53.6
	John Moffet (D)	8,453	46.4

1. Rep. John T. Deweese of the 4th district resigned Feb. 28, 1870. In the first special election held to fill the remainder of Deweese's term in the 41st Congress (1869-71),

Robert B. Gilliam was elected, but he never claimed the seat. In a second special election, John Manning Jr. was elected and took his seat Dec. 7, 1870.

PENNSYLVANIA

	Candidates	Votes	%
4	William D. Kelley (R)	14,324	55.2
	William B. Thomas (D)	11,622	44.8
5	Alfred C. Harmer (R)	11,561	50.4
	John R. Reading (D)	11,401	49.7
6	Ephraim L. Acker (D)	12,049	52.1
	John A. Oliver (R)	11,072	47.9
7	Washington Townsend (R)	10,408	55.8
	J. H. Askin (D)	8,231	44.2
8	J. Lawrence Getz (D)	10,411	67.4
	Nicholas Hunter (R)	5,045	32.6
9	Oliver J. Dickey (R)	9,722	56.7
	A. K. Witmer (D)	7,411	43.3
10	John W. Killinger (R)	11,326	51.4
	Cyrus D. Gloninger (D)	10,697	48.6
11	John B. Storm (D)	12,454	70.3
	William Davis (R)	5,269	29.7
12	Lazarus D. Shoemaker (R)	13,279	52.4
	J. B. McCollum (D)	12,059	47.6
13	Ulysses Mercur (R)	11,117	50.3
	Charles B. Brockway (D)	10,993	49.7
14	John B. Packer (R)	13,620	54.7
	E. G. Scott (D)	11,266	45.3
15	Richard J. Haldeman (D)	13,866	57.1
	William B. Rober (R)	10,416	42.9
16	Benjamin F. Meyers (D)	12,859	50.0
	John Cessna (R)	12,844	50.0
17	R. Milton Speer (D)	10,335	50.0
	Daniel J. Morrell (R)	10,324	50.0
18	Henry Sherwood (D)	13,205	50.1
	William H. Armstrong (R)	13,178	50.0
19	Glenni W. Scofield (R)	13,055	51.2
	Selden Marvin (D)	12,451	48.8
20	Samuel Griffith (D)	14,146	51.4
	Calvin W. Gilfillan (R)	13,377	48.6
21	Henry D. Foster (D)	12,399	51.5
	Andrew Stewart (R)	11,669	48.5
22	James S. Negley (R)	11,230	54.5
	James H. Hopkins (D)	8,018	38.9
	Frew (IR)	1,372	6.7
23	Ebenezer McJunkin (R)	12,591	58.6
	William Sirwell (D)	8,891	41.4
24	William McClelland (D)	12,264	51.6
	Joseph B. Donley (R)	11,505	48.4

RHODE ISLAND

	Candidates	Votes	%
1	Benjamin T. Eames (R)	4,952	50.9
	Thomas A. Jenckes (R)	1,977	20.3
	Van Slyck (D)	1,402	14.4
	Davis (R)	1,085	11.1

	Candidates	Votes	%
2	James M. Pendleton (R)	1,457	57.7
	Rodman (D)	941	37.2

SOUTH CAROLINA[1]

	Candidates	Votes	%
1	Joseph H. Rainey (R)	20,221	63.5
	C. W. Dudley (D)	11,628	36.5
2	Robert C. De Large (IR)	16,686‡	49.6
	Christopher C. Bowen (R)	15,700	46.7
3	Robert B. Elliott (R)	20,664	59.6
	John E. Bacon (D)	13,994	40.4
4	Alexander S. Wallace (R)	16,746	55.3
	Isaac G. McKissick (D)	13,442	44.4
AL	J. P. M. Epping (R)	71,803*	50.0
	L. Wimbush (R)	71,742	50.0

Special Election

		Votes	%
1	Joseph H. Rainey (R)	20,385	86.5
	C. W. Dudley (D)	3,192	13.5

TENNESSEE

	Candidates	Votes	%
1	Roderick R. Butler (R)	6,584	47.1
	James White (D)	5,979	42.7
	N. G. Taylor (IR)	1,432	10.2
2	Horace Maynard (R)	8,351	51.7
	A. Blizard (D)	7,819	48.4
3	Abraham E. Garrett (D)	9,602	69.7
	William B. Stokes (R)	4,168	30.3
4	John M. Bright (D)	11,827	86.5
	James Mullins (R)	1,843	13.5
5	Edward J. Golliday (D)	7,991	59.6
	William F. Prosser (R)	5,428	40.5
6	Washington C. Whitthorne (D)	9,057	76.3
	T. J. Cypert (R)	2,816	23.7
7	Robert P. Caldwell (D)	8,227	81.7
	John Norman (R)	1,848	18.3
8	William W. Vaughan (D)	13,990	72.4
	W. J. Smith (R)	5,346	27.7

VERMONT

	Candidates	Votes	%
1	Charles W. Willard (R)	10,476	74.0
	John Cain (D)	3,675	26.0
2	Luke P. Poland (R)	10,479	76.6
	L. S. Partridge (D)	3,206	23.4
3	Worthington C. Smith (R)	9,116	75.0
	Henry Gillett (D)	3,047	25.1

VIRGINIA [2]

	Candidates	Votes	%
1	John Critcher (C)	10,252	46.3
	Walter W. Douglas (RAD)	6,618	29.9
	Daniel M. Norton (RAD)	5,293	23.9
2	James H. Platt Jr (RAD)	15,880	59.2
	Robert B. Bolling (C)	10,902	40.7
3	Charles H. Porter (RAD)	13,555	56.0
	Albert Ordway (C)	10,647	44.0
4	William H. H. Stowell (RAD)	13,205	56.9
	William L. Owen (C)	9,989	43.1
5	Richard T. W. Duke (C)	12,596	52.4
	Alexander Rives (RAD)	11,430	47.6
6	John T. Harris	7,006	49.3
	Corbin M. Reynolds	4,591	32.3
	C. Douglas Gray	2,626	18.5
7	Elliott M. Braxton (C)	12,719	53.1
	Lewis McKenzie (RAD)	11,203	46.8
8	William Terry (C)	9,916	56.9
	Fayette McMullen (I)	4,017	23.0
	Robert W. Hughes (RAD)	3,508	20.1
AL	Raleigh T. Daniel (C)	78,437*	99.6

Special Election

		Votes	%
5	Richard T. W. Duke (C)	12,469	52.3
	Alexander Rives (RAD)	11,378	47.7

WEST VIRGINIA

	Candidates	Votes	%
1	John J. Davis (D)	11,630	52.4
	Nathan Goff Jr (R)	10,569	47.6
2	James C. McGrew (R)	9,011	52.7
	O. P. Downey (D)	8,098	47.3
3	Frank Hereford (D)	8,732	54.9
	Witcher (R)	7,189	45.2

WISCONSIN

	Candidates	Votes	%
1	Alexander Mitchell (D)	16,558	57.5
	Lyon (R)	12,250	42.5
2	Gerry W. Hazelton (R)	11,467	54.5
	Cook (D)	9,568	45.5
3	J. Allen Barber (R)	11,503	58.5
	Strachan (D)	8,157	41.5
4	Charles A. Eldridge (D)	15,019	62.4
	Watrous (R)	9,056	37.6
5	Philetus Sawyer (R)	17,258	59.4
	Stringm (R)	11,822	40.7
6	Jeremiah M. Rusk (R)	15,042	61.3
	Meggett (D)	9,514	38.7

1871 House Elections

CALIFORNIA

	Candidates	Votes	%
1	Sherman O. Houghton (R)	25,971	51.6
	L. Archer (D)	24,374	48.4
2	Aaron A. Sargent (R)	18,065	54.0
	J. W. Coffroth (D)	15,382	46.0
3	John M. Coghlan (R)	18,503	51.7
	George Pearce (D)	17,309	48.3

CONNECTICUT

	Candidates	Votes	%
1	Julius L. Strong (R)	11,983	50.5
	Goodrich (D)	11,736	49.5
2	Stephen W. Kellogg (R)	13,784	50.0
	Kendrick (D)	13,761	50.0
3	Henry H. Starkweather (R)	8,937	54.5
	Stedman (D)	7,472	45.5

	Candidates	Votes	%
4	William H. Barnum (D)	13,653	52.1
	Coffing (R)	12,577	48.0

ILLINOIS

Special Elections

		Votes	%
6	Henry Snapp (R)	9,112	57.2
	Lorenzo Leland (D)	6,809	42.8
AL	John L. Beveridge (R)	136,879	53.9
	L. L. Hayes (D)	116,482	45.9

NEW HAMPSHIRE

	Candidates	Votes	%
1	Ellery A. Hibbard (D)	12,444	50.3
	William B. Small (R)	12,085	48.8

	Candidates	Votes	%
2	Samuel N. Bell (D)	11,484	51.5
	Aaron F. Stevens (R)	10,635	47.7
3	Hosea W. Parker (D)	11,170	49.5
	Simon W. Griffin (R)	11,038	48.9

TEXAS

	Candidates	Votes	%
1	William S. Herndon (D)	16,172	58.3
	G. W. Whitmore (R)	11,572	41.7
2	John C. Connor (D)	18,285	75.5
	A. M. Bryant (R)	5,948	24.6
3	De Witt C. Giddings (D)	23,374‡	53.4
	William T. Clark (R)	20,406	46.6
4	John Hancock (D)	17,010	57.4
	Edward Degener (R)	12,636	42.6

1870 Elections

1. South Carolina claimed an extra seat in the House and J. P. M. Epping was elected at-large to fill it. The House refused to seat him. (See South Carolina 1868, p. 777.)

2. Virginia claimed an extra seat in the House, and Raleigh T. Daniel was elected at-large to fill it. The House refused to seat him. (See Virginia 1869, p. 777.)

1872 House Elections

ALABAMA

	Candidates	Votes	%
1	Frederick G. Bromberg (LR)	15,607	54.2
	Benjamin S. Turner (R)	13,174	45.8
2	James T. Rapier (R)	19,397	54.5
	Oates (LR)	16,221	45.5
3	Charles Pelham (R)	14,957	51.0
	William A. Handley (LR)	14,371	49.0
4	Charles Hays (R)	20,333	57.4
	Smith (LR)	15,121	42.7
5	John H. Caldwell (LR)	10,544	62.6
	Campbell (R)	6,293	37.4
6	Joseph H. Sloss (LR)	9,288	66.9
	Parrish (R)	4,593	33.1
AL	Alexander White (R)	89,480✔	
	Charles C. Sheats (R)	89,195✔	
	Baker (D)	81,311	
	Jolly (D)	81,171	

ARKANSAS

1	Lucien C. Gause (D)	11,591	54.1
	Asa Hodges (R)	9,853✔	46.0
2	Marcus L. Bell (D)	13,758	52.8
	Oliver P. Snyder (R)	12,284✔	47.2
3	Thomas M. Gunter (D)	12,298‡	56.6
	William W. Wilshire (R)	9,431	43.4
AL	William J. Hynes (B-T R)	40,023	50.0
	J. M. Bradley (MR)	39,586	49.4

CALIFORNIA

1	Charles Clayton (R)	11,938	52.2
	William A. Piper (LR)	10,883	47.6
2	Horace Frank Page (R)	13,803	51.5
	Pasz Coggins (LR)	12,816	47.8
3	John K. Luttrell (LR)	14,032	51.7
	J. M. Coghlan (R)	13,110	48.3
4	Sherman O. Houghton (R)	10,396	53.2
	E. J. C. Kewen (LR)	9,030	46.2

CONNECTICUT

Special Election

1	Joseph R. Hawley (R)	13,030	51.2
	William W. Eaton (D)	12,397	48.8

DELAWARE

AL	James R. Lofland (R)	11,377	50.8
	Wright (LR)	11,015	49.2

FLORIDA

AL	William J. Purman (R)	17,537✔	
	Josiah T. Walls (R)	17,503✔	
	Silas L. Niblack (LR)	15,881	
	Charles W. Jones (LR)	15,811	

GEORGIA

1	Morgan Rawls (LR)	8,319‡	54.4
	Andrew Sloan (R)	6,979	45.6
2	Richard H. Whiteley (R)	9,616	50.2
	G. J. Wright (LR)	9,530	49.8
3	Philip Cook (LR)	6,147	57.8
	Brown (R)	4,490	42.2
4	Henry R. Harris (LR)	10,319	54.9
	M. Bethune (R)	8,466	45.1
5	James C. Freeman (R)	10,910	50.7
	Glenn (LR)	10,631	49.4
6	James H. Blount (LR)	9,993	61.7
	Anderson (R)	6,196	38.3

	Candidates	Votes	%
7	Pierce M. B. Young (LR)	8,067	64.5
	Dever (R)	4,443	35.5
8	Ambrose R. Wright (LR)	9,697*	56.3
	Clayton (R)	6,230	36.2
	D. M. Dubose	1,293	7.5
9	Hiram P. Bell (LR)	7,437	63.2
	Darrell (R)	4,325	36.8

Special Election

4	Erasmus Williams Beck (D)	✔ #	

ILLINOIS

1	John B. Rice (R)	12,870	64.0
	Lusien B. Otis (LR)	7,235	36.0
2	Jasper D. Ward (R)	12,182	57.9
	Carter Henry Harrison (LR)	8,873	42.1
3	Charles B. Farwell (R)	9,202	65.0
	John Valcoulon Lemoyne (LR)	4,962	35.0
4	Stephen A. Hurlbut (R)	15,532	75.2
	Seymour G. Bronson (LR)	5,134	24.8
5	Horatio C. Burchard (R)	14,036	65.1
	James Dinsmoor (LR)	7,538	34.9
6	John B. Hawley (R)	13,123	64.5
	Calvin Truesdale (LR)	7,216	35.5
7	Franklin Corwin (R)	12,404	59.9
	G. D. A. Parks (LR)	8,293	40.1
8	Greenbury L. Fort (R)	13,401	61.7
	George O. Barnes (LR)	8,304	38.3
9	Granville Barrere (R)	12,600	53.9
	N. C. Worthington (LR)	10,799	46.2
10	William H. Ray (R)	12,962	52.1
	William H. Neece (LR)	11,897	47.9
11	Robert M. Knapp (LR)	13,818	55.2
	Asa C. Matthews (R)	10,939	43.7
12	James C. Robinson (LR)	13,234	51.8
	M. N. Chamberlin (R)	12,311	48.2
13	John McNulta (R)	13,490	54.7
	Clifton H. Moore (LR)	10,850	44.0
14	Joseph G. Cannon (R)	15,161	57.1
	William Nelson (LR)	11,405	42.9
15	John R. Eden (LR)	14,653	54.4
	George Hunt (R)	12,298	45.6
16	James S. Martin (R)	12,266	50.5
	Silas L. Bryan (LR)	12,016	49.5
17	William R. Morrison (LR)	13,215	53.9
	John H. Hay (R)	11,316	46.1
18	Isaac Clements (R)	12,999	53.1
	George W. Wall (LR)	11,478	46.9
19	Samuel S. Marshall (LR)	13,297	54.1
	Green B. Raum (R)	11,282	45.9

INDIANA

1	William E. Niblack (LR)	19,259	50.2
	Heilman (R)	19,127	49.8
2	Simeon K. Wolfe (LR)	19,336	58.6
	Voyles (R)	13,652	41.4
3	William S. Holman (LR)	16,367	52.1
	Herod (R)	15,039	47.9
4	Jeremiah M. Wilson (R)	14,499	50.7
	Gooding (LR)	14,119	49.3
5	John Coburn (R)	18,794	51.1
	McNutt (LR)	18,001	48.9
6	Morton C. Hunter (R)	18,792	50.9
	Daniel Wolsey Voorhees (LR)	18,135	49.1
7	Thomas J. Cason (R)	17,927	50.3
	Mahlon Dickerson Manson (LR)	17,730	49.7
8	James M. Tyner (R)	19,737	54.0
	Whiteside (LR)	16,798	46.0
9	John E. Neff (LR)	17,082	50.0
	John Peter Cleaver Shanks (R)	17,058✔	50.0
10	Henry B. Sayler (R)	17,334	53.4
	Long (LR)	15,149	46.6
11	Jaspar Packard (R)	16,813	51.5

	Candidates	Votes	%
	Hendricks (LR)	15,828	48.5
AL	William Williams (R)	188,762✔	
	Godlove S. Orth (R)	188,664✔	
	Michael C. Kerr (LR)	188,502	
	John S. Williams (LR)	188,227	

IOWA

1	George W. McCrary (R)	15,149	58.0
	James M. Shelby (D)	10,961	42.0
2	Aylett R. Cotton (R)	12,521	50.4
	William E. Leffingwell (D)	12,346	49.7
3	William G. Donnan (R)	13,654	53.7
	John T. Stoneman (D)	11,774	46.3
4	Henry O. Pratt (R)	15,615	77.0
	A. T. Lusch (D)	4,574	22.6
5	James Wilson (R)	15,531	67.6
	John P. Irish (D)	7,434	32.4
6	William Loughridge (R)	14,638	55.4
	H. H. Trimble (D)	11,703	44.3
7	John A. Kasson (R)	14,909	65.9
	Q. Palmer (D)	7,702	34.1
8	James W. McDill (R)	12,675	64.4
	W. W. Merritt (D)	6,999	35.6
9	Jackson Orr (R)	12,402	66.8
	John F. Duncomb (D)	6,152	33.1

KANSAS

AL	David P. Lowe (R)	67,400✔	
	William A. Phillips (R)	67,114✔	
	Stephen A. Cobb (R)	66,345✔	
	Samuel A. Riggs (D)	34,450	
	R. B. Mitchell (D)	33,985	
	W. R. Laughlin (D)	33,264	

KENTUCKY

1	Edward Crossland (D)	10,276	64.0
	J. H. Trabue (I)	2,510	15.6
	H. H. Houston	1,796	11.2
	John Martin	1,473	9.2
2	John Y. Brown (D)	10,878	95.3
3	Charles W. Milliken (D)	8,796	64.3
	Jacob S. Golladay	4,853	35.5
4	William B. Read (D)	8,221	92.8
	E. H. Hobson	548	6.2
5	Elisha D. Standiford (D)	11,179	68.9
	W. P. Boone	5,053	31.1
6	William E. Arthur (D)	11,424	63.5
	Harvey Myers	6,564	36.5
7	James B. Beck (D)	13,978	68.9
	S. F. J. Trabue	6,322	31.1
8	Milton J. Durham (D)	10,736	51.6
	W. O. Bradley (R)	10,063	48.4
9	George M. Adams (D)	9,683	54.2
	A. T. Woods (R)	8,199	45.9
10	John D. Young (D)	9,075	50.5
	J. M. Burns (R)	8,885	49.5

LOUISIANA

1	J. Hale Sypher (R)	12,300‡	50.2
	Effingham Lawrence (LR)	12,225	49.9
2	Lionel A. Sheldon (R)	17,068	52.5
	Randall L. Gibson (LR)	15,453	47.5
3	Chester Bidwell Darrall (R)	14,396	53.7
	J. B. Price (LR)	7,724	28.8
	Elbert Gantt (LR)	4,701	17.5
4	Samuel Peters (R)	13,787*	64.0
	E. C. Davidson (LR)	7,752	36.0
5	Frank Morey (R)	14,060	62.1
	G. W. McCraney (LR)	8,597	37.9
AL	George Augustus Sheridan (D)	64,975	55.1
	Pinckney B. S. Pinchback (R)	53,011	44.9

LOUISIANA

Special Election

Candidates	Votes	%
4 Harry Lott (R)	13,790	64.0
Alexander Boarman (LR)	7,768	36.0

MAINE

1 John H. Burleigh (R)	15,485	53.8
Clifford (D)	13,216	45.9
2 William P. Frye (R)	13,540	59.1
Alonzo Garcelon (D)	9,362	40.8
3 James G. Blaine (R)	15,084	56.6
Lang (D)	11,566	43.4
4 Samuel Hersey (R)	13,804	61.3
Emery (D)	8,706	38.7
5 Eugene Hale (R)	14,181	55.7
Frederick Augustus Pike (D)	11,300	44.3

MARYLAND

1 Ephraim K. Wilson (LR)	12,464	51.3
Spence (R)	11,826	48.7
2 Stevenson Archer (LR)	10,591	50.7
Hancock (R)	10,303	49.3
3 William J. O'Brien (LR)	9,670	53.7
Turner (R)	8,346	46.3
4 Thomas Swann (LR)	12,148	52.7
Griswold (R)	10,886	47.3
5 William J. Albert (R)	11,405	52.6
Merrick (LR)	10,300	47.5
6 Lloyd Lowndes Jr (R)	14,258	53.2
Ritchie (LR)	12,545	46.8

MASSACHUSETTS

1 James Buffinton (R)	12,448	82.6
Joseph M. Day (LR)	2,609	17.3
2 Benjamin W. Harris (R)	13,752	73.0
Edward Avery (LR)	5,090	27.0
3 William Whiting (R)	8,931	63.4
Samuel C. Cobb (LR)	5,139	36.5
4 Samuel Hooper (R)	8,715	58.1
Leopold Morse (LR)	6,262	41.8
5 Daniel W. Gooch (R)	12,472	60.8
Nathaniel P. Banks (LR)	8,039	39.2
6 Benjamin F. Butler (R)	11,881	67.2
Charles P. Thompson (LR)	5,737	32.5
7 Ebenezer R. Hoar (R)	11,742	64.9
John K. Tarbox (LR)	5,989	33.1
8 John M. S. Williams (R)	11,929	67.2
William W. Warren (LR)	5,829	32.8
9 George F. Hoar (R)	12,696	71.0
George F. Verry (LR)	5,012	28.0
10 Alvah Crocker (R)	14,919	76.4
D. W. Bond (LR)	4,588	23.5
11 Henry L. Dawes (R)	12,260	63.9
John F. Arnold (LR)	6,927	36.1

Special Election

7 Constantine C. Esty (R)	13,583	71.4
George Stevens	5,274	27.7

MICHIGAN

1 Moses W. Field (R)	11,703	53.8
Bagg (D)	9,843	45.3
2 Henry Waldron (R)	17,427	62.4
Mahan (D)	10,522	37.6
3 George Willard (R)	17,822	62.6
Parkhurst (D)	10,275	36.1
4 Julius C. Burrows (R)	16,717	59.3
Potter (D)	11,451	40.6
5 Wilder Foster (R)	17,353	66.5
McReynolds (D)	8,744	33.5
6 Josiah W. Begole (R)	19,486	58.0
Baldwin (D)	13,994	41.6

Candidates	Votes	%
7 Omar D. Conger (R)	12,037	60.5
Richardson (D)	7,790	39.2
8 Nathan B. Bradley (R)	11,333	58.0
Wisner (D)	7,995	40.9
9 Jay A. Hubbell (R)	11,951	68.3
Ely (D)	5,546	31.7

MINNESOTA

1 Mark H. Dunnell (R)	20,806	65.6
M. S. Wilkinson (D)	10,901	34.4
2 Horace B. Strait (R)	15,712	57.4
C. C. Graham (D)	11,668	42.6
3 John T. Averill (R)	19,663	60.7
G. L. Becker (D)	12,712	39.3

MISSISSIPPI

1 Lucius Q. C. Lamar (LR)	9,679	66.2
Flournoy	4,954	33.9
2 Albert R. Howe (R)	14,831	64.4
Alcorn (LR)	8,216	35.7
3 Henry W. Barry (R)	15,047	70.0
Bolding (LR)	6,440	30.0
4 Jason R. Niles (R)	15,795	69.7
5 George C. McKee (R)	14,817	64.7
Shelby (LR)	8,073	35.3
6 John R. Lynch (R)	15,101	64.0
Cassidy (LR)	8,509	36.0

MISSOURI

1 Edwin O. Stanard (R)	5,271	50.7
Grosvenor (LR)	5,129	49.3
2 Erastus Wells (LR)	8,268	58.7
Bryton (R)	5,807	41.3
3 William H. Stone (LR)	5,197	51.7
Hilton (R)	4,859	48.3
4 Robert A. Hatcher (LR)	13,340	74.4
Ward (R)	4,594	25.6
5 Richard P. Bland (LR)	9,974	53.1
Seay (R)	8,820	46.9
6 Harrison E. Havens (R)	13,156	51.1
McAffee (LR)	12,578	48.9
7 Thomas T. Crittenden (LR)	16,341	52.5
Burdett (R)	14,770	47.5
8 Abram Comingo (LR)	13,235	64.4
Twichell (R)	7,317	35.6
9 Isaac C. Parker (R)	12,136	50.2
Pike (LR)	12,053	49.8
10 Ira B. Hyde (R)	13,953	53.1
Mansur (LR)	12,318	46.9
11 John B. Clark Jr. (LR)	17,341	67.7
Demotte (R)	8,280	32.3
12 John M. Glover (LR)	13,006	54.9
Benjamin (R)	10,672	45.1
13 Aylett H. Buckner (LR)	16,249	67.8
Flagg (R)	7,710	32.2

NEBRASKA

AL Lorenzo Crounse (R)	17,124	62.2
Warner (LR)	10,412	37.8

NEVADA

AL Charles W. Kendall (D)	7,847	52.3
C. C. Goodwin	7,146	47.7

NEW JERSEY

1 John W. Hazleton (R)	15,312	63.1
Clute (LR)	8,948	36.9
2 Samuel A. Dobbins (R)	14,192	54.6
Forker (LR)	11,787	45.4

Candidates	Votes	%
3 Amos Clark Jr (R)	14,794	54.0
Patterson (LR)	12,618	46.0
4 Robert Hamilton (LR)	13,458	55.0
Potts (R)	10,994	45.0
5 William W. Phelps (R)	12,701	56.0
Woodruff (LR)	9,986	44.0
6 Marcus L. Ward (R)	16,061	60.7
Randall (LR)	10,403	39.3
7 Isaac W. Scudder (R)	10,377	53.3
Taylor (LR)	9,108	46.7

NEW YORK

1 Henry J. Scudder (R)	13,877	54.1
Covert (LR)	11,797	46.0
2 John G. Schumaker (LR)	13,345	58.7
Perry (R)	8,378	36.8
3 Stewart L. Woodford (R)	15,177	56.9
Goodrich (LR)	11,506	43.1
4 Philip S. Crooke (R)	11,012	51.9
Colahan (LR)	10,202	48.1
5 William R. Roberts (LR)	20,281	79.1
Matthew Stewart (R)	5,356	20.9
6 James Brooks (LR)	16,645	76.9
Adolph G. Dunn (R)	5,005	23.1
7 Thomas J. Creamer (LR)	10,012	54.7
Conrad Geib (R)	8,279	45.3
8 John D. Lawson (R)	13,305	58.6
Charles P. Shaw (LR)	9,395	41.4
9 David B. Mellish (R)	7,841	37.8
John Hardy (APOLLO)	7,068	34.1
Michael Connolly (LR)	5,847	28.2
10 Fernando Wood (LR)	10,526	52.2
William A. Darling (R)	9,641	47.8
11 Clarkson N. Potter (LR)	15,204	51.7
Flagg (R)	14,179	48.3
12 Charles St.John (R)	11,842	51.1
Horton (LR)	11,318	48.9
13 John O. Whitehouse (LR)	14,859	51.6
Ketchim (R)	13,932	48.4
14 David M. De Witt (LR)	12,031	50.0
Maxwell (R)	12,014	50.0
15 Eli Perry (LR)	18,676	51.6
Adams (R)	17,538	48.4
16 James S. Smart (R)	17,835	57.2
Thayer (LR)	13,352	42.8
17 Robert S. Hale (R)	11,025	57.4
Heaton (LR)	8,174	42.6
18 William A. Wheeler (R)	14,725	69.2
Cantwell (LR)	6,565	30.8
19 Henry H. Hathorn (R)	17,762	54.6
Judson (LR)	14,756	45.4
20 David Wilbur (R)	17,368	53.4
Sturges (LR)	15,171	46.6
21 Clinton L. Merriam (R)	17,337	56.7
Brockway (LR)	13,220	43.3
22 Ellis H. Roberts (R)	13,284	55.9
Sherman (LR)	10,481	44.1
23 William E. Lansing (R)	15,410	58.7
Foster (LR)	10,841	41.3
24 R. Holland Duell (R)	15,457	53.8
Hiscock (LR)	13,289	46.2
25 Clinton D. MacDougall (R)	16,486	57.2
Graves (LR)	12,325	42.8
26 William H. Lamport (R)	12,886	57.0
White (LR)	9,730	43.0
27 Thomas C. Platt (R)	16,603	55.3
Goodrich (LR)	13,406	44.7
28 Horace Boardman Smith (R)	18,738	56.8
Hayt (LR)	14,262	43.2
29 Freeman Clarke (R)	16,342	56.7
Gordon (LR)	12,470	43.3
30 George G. Hoskins (R)	13,233	58.0
Southworth (LR)	9,599	42.0
31 Lyman K. Bass (R)	17,929	58.3
Williams (LR)	12,813	41.7
32 Walter L. Sessions (R)	12,922	57.4
Murray (LR)	9,573	42.6
AL Lyman Tremain (R)	438,396	52.2
Samuel S. Cox (LR)	400,797	47.8

NORTH CAROLINA

Candidates	Votes	%
1 Clinton L. Cobb (R)	13,522	52.8
David M. Carter (D)	12,101	47.2
2 Charles R. Thomas (R)	20,072	63.3
William H. Kitchen (D)	11,627	36.7
3 Alfred M. Waddell (D)	14,286	52.7
Neil McKay (R)	12,848	47.4
4 William A. Smith (R)	13,879	51.4
Sion H. Rogers (D)	13,147	48.7
5 James M. Leach (D)	10,755	50.6
Thomas Settle (R)	10,497	49.4
6 Thomas S. Ashe (D)	12,700	54.6
Oliver H. Dockery (R)	10,561	45.4
7 William M. Robbins (D)	10,072	54.4
David M. Furches (R)	8,459	45.7
8 Robert B. Vance (D)	11,038	55.5
William G. Candler (R)	8,853	44.5

OHIO

Candidates	Votes	%
1 Milton Sayler (D)	12,474	58.4
Benjamin Eggleston (R)	8,905	41.7
2 Henry B. Banning (D)	11,034	53.7
Rutherford B. Hayes (R)	9,532	46.4
3 John Q. Smith (R)	14,929	52.1
John W. Sohn (D)	13,700	47.8
4 Lewis B. Gunckel (R)	16,604	52.9
J. J. Winans (D)	14,677	46.8
5 Charles N. Lamison (D)	15,530	60.3
Samuel Lybrand (R)	10,224	39.7
6 Isaac R. Sherwood (R)	13,471	51.9
F. H. Hurd (D)	12,406	47.8
7 Lawrence T. Neal (D)	13,379	52.5
John T. Wilson (R)	12,106	47.5
8 William Lawrence (R)	14,748	57.8
J. J. Musson (D)	10,705	41.9
9 James W. Robinson (R)	13,573	50.4
George W. Morgan (D)	13,146	48.8
10 Charles Foster (R)	14,997	51.0
Rush R. Sloane (D)	14,271	48.6
11 Hezekiah S. Bundy (R)	13,267	56.2
Samuel A. Nash (D)	10,360	43.9
12 Hugh J. Jewett (D)	15,613	58.5
James Taylor (R)	10,936	41.0
13 Milton I. Southard (D)	15,109	54.5
Lucius P. Marsh (R)	12,638	45.6
14 John Berry (D)	13,668	57.8
Thomas E. Douglass (R)	9,925	42.0
15 William P. Sprague (R)	12,987	51.9
Richard R. Hudson (D)	11,996	47.9
16 Lorenzo Danford (R)	14,350	56.3
C. L. Poorman (D)	11,052	43.4
17 Laurin D. Woodworth (R)	15,368	54.0
Richard Brown (D)	13,106	46.0
18 James Monroe (R)	14,662	58.6
N. S. Townshend (D)	10,298	41.2
19 James A. Garfield (R)	19,189	69.4
M. Sutliff (D)	8,254	29.9
20 Richard C. Parsons (R)	13,101	55.4
Selah Chamberlain (D)	10,377	43.9

OREGON

Candidates	Votes	%
AL Joseph G. Wilson (R)	13,168	51.7
John Burnett (D)	12,317	48.3

PENNSYLVANIA

Candidates	Votes	%
1 Samuel J. Randall (LR)	10,133	53.4
Houst (R)	8,845	46.6
2 Charles O'Neill (R)	17,253	63.9
Morris (LR)	9,728	36.1
3 Leonard Meyers (R)	15,429	59.4
Vogelbach (LR)	10,530	40.6
4 William D. Kelley (R)	20,955	61.2
Mitchell (LR)	13,301	38.8
5 Alfred C. Harmer (R)	14,743	55.1
Phillips (LR)	12,040	45.0
6 James S. Biery (R)	13,906	55.0
Witte (LR)	11,400	45.1

Candidates	Votes	%
7 Washington Townsend (R)	14,011	61.4
Taylor (LR)	8,819	38.6
8 Heister Clymer (LR)	13,854	64.0
Millhol (R)	7,783	36.0
9 A. Herr Smith (R)	14,501	63.0
North (LR)	8,526	37.0
10 John W. Killinger (R)	14,419	56.6
Rielly (LR)	11,049	43.4
11 John B. Storm (LR)	16,808	61.4
Howell (R)	10,569	38.6
12 Lazarus D. Shoemaker (R)	17,551	51.1
Woodward (LR)	16,811	48.9
13 James D. Strawbridge (R)	13,079	51.7
Rhodes (LR)	12,243	48.4
14 John B. Packer (R)	17,545	56.5
Rutherford (LR)	13,486	43.5
15 John A. Magee (LR)	15,358	53.2
Sponsler (R)	13,532	46.8
16 John Cessna (R)	14,383	52.4
Meyers (LR)	13,067	47.6
17 R. Milton Speer (LR)	12,011	51.3
Barker (R)	11,422	48.7
18 Sobieski Ross (R)	17,041	53.8
Henry Sherwood (LR)	14,627	46.2
19 Carlton B. Curtis (R)	17,742	52.2
Kane (LR)	16,238	47.8
20 Hiram Richmond (R)	20,704	52.6
Samuel Griffith (LR)	18,627	47.4
21 Alexander W. Taylor (R)	13,980	51.3
Foster (LR)	13,289	48.7
22 James S. Negley (R)	17,248	61.2
King (LR)	10,930	38.8
23 Ebenezer McJunkin (R)	17,431	60.7
Johnston (LR)	11,306	39.3
24 William S. Moore (R)	14,195	51.9
McClelland (LR)	13,169	48.1
AL Glenni W. Scofield (R)	358,013	53.3
E. B. Wright (LR)	314,014	46.7
AL Charles Albright (R)	360,546	53.7
Richard Vaux (LR)	311,036	46.3
AL Lemuel Todd (R)	357,743	53.3
J. H. Hopkins (LR)	313,534	46.7

Special Election

13 Frank Charles Bunnell (R)	6,000✔	#	
Piolett (D)	5,001	#	

SOUTH CAROLINA

Candidates	Votes	%
1 Joseph H. Rainey (R)	19,765	100.0
2 Alonzo J. Ransier (R)	20,061	75.4
William Gurney (D)	6,549	24.6
3 Robert B. Elliott (R)	21,627	92.8
4 Alexander S. Wallace (R)	14,590	53.1
B. F. Perry (D)	12,879	46.9
AL Richard H. Cain (R)	68,825	71.2
L. E. Johnson (ID)	26,394	27.3

TENNESSEE

Candidates	Votes	%
1 Roderick R. Butler (R)	10,289	56.7
Carter (LR)	7,849	43.3
2 Jacob M. Thornburgh (R)	10,015	55.7
Caldwell (LR)	5,403	30.1
Garrett (I)	2,563	14.3
3 William Crutchfield (R)	10,041	52.8
Key (LR)	8,960	47.2
4 John M. Bright (LR)	12,585	69.8
Steele (R)	5,442	30.2
5 Horace H. Harrison (R)	10,033	42.1
Gellad (LR)	8,131	34.1
Brien (I)	5,684	23.8
6 Washington C. Whitthorne (LR)	9,058	53.9
Gibbs (R)	6,849	40.7
Morris (I)	903	5.4
7 John D. C. Atkins (LR)	11,411	55.6
Murray (R)	7,734	37.7
Travis (I)	1,369	6.7
8 David A. Nunn (R)	7,580	37.9
Campbell (LR)	5,967	29.8

Candidates	Votes	%
Caldw (I)	4,476	22.4
Beel (I)	1,979	9.9
9 Barbour Lewis (R)	13,784	56.7
Haynes (LR)	10,541	43.3
AL Horace Maynard (R)	80,825	44.0
Benjamin F. Cheatham (LR)	65,188	35.5
Andrew Johnson (I)	37,900	20.6

TEXAS

Candidates	Votes	%
1 William S. Herndon (D)	13,417	57.1
R. K. Smith	8,780	37.4
William Chambers	1,261	5.4
2 William P. McLean (D)	15,924	73.9
F. W. Minor	5,617	26.1
3 De Witt C. Giddings (D)	20,464	51.5
A. J. Evans	19,287	48.5
4 John Hancock (D)	18,172	61.7
W. O. Hutchinson	11,281	38.3
AL Asa H. Willie (D)	69,085✔	
Roger Q. Mills (D)	68,936✔	
Evans (R)	47,096	
Norton (R)	47,075	

VERMONT

Candidates	Votes	%
1 Charles W. Willard (R)	14,061	79.5
Heaton (LR)	3,618	20.5
2 Luke P. Poland (R)	11,070	65.3
Steele (LR)	2,929	17.3
J. M. Pierce (I)	2,554	15.1
3 George W. Hendee (R)	11,473	78.3
Adams (LR)	3,182	21.7

VIRGINIA

Candidates	Votes	%
1 James B. Sener (R)	10,685	50.9
E. M. Braxton (CD)	10,312	49.1
2 James H. Platt Jr (R)	15,554	59.9
Baker R. Lee (CD)	10,339	39.8
3 J. Ambler Smith (R)	13,082	51.1
George D. Wise (CD)	12,514	48.9
4 William H. H. Stowell (R)	15,393	65.6
P. W. McKinney (CD)	8,068	34.4
5 Alexander M. Davis (R)	9,175‡	50.5
Christopher Y. Thomas (CD)	8,975	49.4
6 Thomas Whitehead (CD)	11,401	51.3
J. Foote Johnson (I)	10,779	48.5
7 John T. Harris (CD)	10,894	61.8
C. T. O. Ferrall (I)	6,738	38.2
8 Eppa Hunton (CD)	11,782	56.2
Edward Daniels (R)	9,178	43.8
9 Rees T. Bowen (CD)	10,352	66.1
Robert W. Hughes (R)	5,304	33.9

WEST VIRGINIA

Candidates	Votes	%
1 Benjamin Wilson (D)	8,054	52.4
John J. Davis (D)	7,317✔	47.6
2 John M. Hagans (R)	3,441	82.3
Alexander R. Boteler (R)	387	9.3
Ward Lamar	255	6.1
3 Frank Hereford (D)	11,417	80.5
J. B. Walker (R)	2,769	19.5

WISCONSIN

Candidates	Votes	%
1 Charles G. Williams (R)	15,666	62.6
Sloan (D)	9,380	37.5
2 Gerry W. Hazelton (R)	13,408	53.2
Smith (D)	11,784	46.8
3 J. Allen Barber (R)	13,745	58.2
Warden (D)	9,880	41.8
4 Alexander Mitchell (D)	13,281	65.1
Winkler (R)	7,120	34.9
5 Charles A. Eldridge (D)	15,587	55.5
Baetz (R)	12,507	44.5

WISCONSIN

Candidates	Votes	%		Candidates	Votes	%		Candidates	Votes	%
6 Philetus Sawyer (R)	15,803	56.1		7 Jeremiah M. Rusk (R)	16,183	65.4		8 Alexander S. McDill (R)	10,711	59.7
Lindsley (D)	12,358	43.9		Marston (D)	8,547	34.6		Carson (D)	7,238	40.3

1873 House Elections

CONNECTICUT

1 Joseph R. Hawley (R)	12,030	52.8
Kendall (D)	10,764	47.2
2 Stephen W. Kellogg (R)	12,761	51.2
English (D)	12,173	48.8
3 Henry H. Starkweather (R)	7,764	56.4
Bill (D)	6,000	43.6
4 William H. Barnum (D)	12,561	53.8
Miner (R)	10,797	46.2

LOUISIANA

4 George Luke Smith (D)	✔ #

MICHIGAN

Special Election

5 William B. Williams (R)	6,598	50.4
Comstock (D)	6,484	49.6

NEW HAMPSHIRE

1 William B. Small (R)	12,103	49.8
Hibbard (D)	11,725	48.2
2 Austin F. Pike (R)	10,780	49.3
Bell (D)	10,773	49.3
3 Hosea W. Parker (D)	10,633	49.9
Griffin (R)	10,295	48.3

OREGON

Special Election

AL James W. Nesmith (D)	8,194	57.2
Smith (R)	6,123	42.8

RHODE ISLAND

1 Benjamin T. Eames (R)	8,977	74.0
Thomas Davis (D)	3,138	25.9
2 James M. Pendleton (R)	4,310	63.2
George H. Browne (D)	2,505	36.8

Explanation of Symbols in House Returns

In the returns for House elections *symbols* are used to denote special circumstances. In cases where no symbol is used, the candidate who received the most votes won the election to the House. The following is a key to the symbols used:

✔ Elected to the House. The symbol is used to identify winning candidates in three types of situations: (1) When candidates ran for two or more at-large seats in states which chose all of their at-large representatives in a single election, or ran in a multi-member district; (2) when the vote total and percentage of one or more of the candidates are unavailable and (3) when a candidate who did not receive the highest vote total was seated by the House. (*Explanation of multi-member districts, see p. 678.*)

‡ The symbol is used when an election dispute resulted in the unseating of a representative *after* he was sworn in. (*For discussion of specific cases, consult the* Biographical Directory of the American Congress 1774-1971, *U.S. Government Printing Office, Washington, D.C. 1971; hereafter referred to as the* Biographical Directory.)

* The symbol is used for three types of situations: (1) When a representative-elect died or declined his seat before the constitutionally set date for the beginning of his term—March 4 until 1935, and Jan. 3 thereafter; (2) when the House refused to seat any candidate claiming election to a seat and (3) when state law required a candidate to obtain a popular vote majority for election to the House, but the candidate receiving the most votes failed to receive a majority. (*For discussion of specific cases, consult the* Biographical Directory; *explanation of majority vote requirement, see p. 703.*)

Information for 1824-1973 returns was obtained from a source other than the Inter-University Consortium for Political and Social Research. (*For a listing of other sources, see p. 1062.*)

Footnotes. Numbered footnotes are used to explain unusual situations, such as a series of elections in the same year in the same House district, anomalies resulting from reapportionment and special procedures for conducting House elections in certain states.

1874 House Elections

ALABAMA

Candidates	Votes	%
1 Jeremiah Haralson (R)	19,545	53.6
Frederick G. Bromberg (D)	16,953	46.5
2 Jeremiah N. Williams (D)	20,180	51.3
James T. Rapier (R)	19,124	48.7
3 Taul Bradford (D)	19,424	58.0
Betts (R)	14,076	42.0
4 Charles Hays (R)	23,900	56.5
Jones (D)	18,378	43.5
5 John H. Caldwell (D)	13,011	59.2
Sheffield (R)	8,969	40.8
6 Goldsmith W. Hewitt (D)	15,048	62.1
Joseph H. Sloss (R)	9,172	37.9
AL Burwell B. Lewis (D)	106,023	54.1
Hristopher C. Sheets (R)	89,909	46.0
AL William H. Forney (D)	106,080	54.0
Alexander White (R)	89,909	46.0

ARKANSAS

Candidates	Votes	%
1 Lucien C. Gause (C)	9,211	64.0
Rogers (R)	5,183	36.0
2 William F. Slemmons (C)	12,166	53.7
Clayton (R)	10,485	46.3
3 William W. Wilshire (C)	11,733	65.0
Hynes (R)	6,328	35.0
4 Thomas M. Gunter (C)	7,828	90.8
Lander (R)	791	9.2

DELAWARE

Candidates	Votes	%
AL James Williams (D)	12,602	53.3
James R. Lofland (R)	11,024	46.7

FLORIDA

Candidates	Votes	%
1 William J. Purman (R)	10,052	51.7
Henderson (D)	9,377	48.3
2 Josiah T. Walls (R)	8,557‡	51.1
Jesse J. Finley (D)	8,178	48.9

GEORGIA

Candidates	Votes	%
1 Julian Hartridge (D)	11,252	59.4
Bryant (R)	6,714	35.5
John Wimberley (IR)	974	5.1
2 William E. Smith (D)	12,098	55.3
Whiteley (R)	9,789	44.7
3 Philip Cook (D)	8,677	67.4
Brown (R)	4,199	32.6
4 Henry R. Harris (D)	9,230	100.0
5 Milton A. Candler (D)	12,450	66.5
Mills (R)	6,273	33.5
6 James H. Blount (D)	10,007	78.4
Gove (R)	2,756	21.6
7 William H. Felton (I)	7,587	49.6
William H. Dabney (D)	7,505	49.1
8 Alexander H. Stephens (D)	6,822	99.8
9 Garnett McMillan (D)	7,885*	77.3
O'Neal (R)	2,318	22.7

ILLINOIS

Candidates	Votes	%
1 Bernard G. Caulfield (D)	10,211	51.0
Sidney Smith (R)	9,803	49.0
2 Carter H. Harrison (D)	9,189	49.2
Jasper D. Ward (R)	9,181	49.1
3 Charles B. Farwell (R)	8,177‡	50.1
John V. Le Moyne (D)	7,991	49.0
4 Stephen A. Hurlbut (R)	9,326	53.3
John F. Farnsworth (D)	8,167	46.7
5 Horatio C. Burchard (R)	9,232	56.8
David J. Pinkney (D)	7,008	43.1

Candidates	Votes	%
6 Thomas J. Henderson (R)	9,390	59.8
Isaac H. Elliott (D)	6,299	40.1
7 Alexander Campbell (D)	10,308	56.6
Franklin Corwin (R)	7,905	43.4
8 Greenbury L. Fort (R)	8,753	53.9
J. G. Bayne (D)	7,463	45.9
9 Richard H. Whiting (R)	9,755	50.7
Leonard F. Ross (D)	9,495	49.3
10 John C. Bagby (D)	9,784	52.6
Henderson Richey (R)	8,824	47.4
11 Scott Wike (D)	11,489	59.2
David Beatty (R)	7,429	38.3
12 William M. Springer (D)	10,623	48.1
Andrew Simpson (R)	9,027	40.9
J. B. Turner (IR)	2,417	11.0
13 Adlai E. Stevenson (D)	11,135	52.6
John McNulta (R)	9,903	46.8
14 Joseph G. Cannon (R)	11,244	51.5
James H. Pickrell (D)	10,603	48.5
15 John R. Eden (D)	12,084	52.8
Jacob W. Wilkin (R)	10,789	47.2
16 William A. J. Sparks (D)	8,723	42.2
James S. Martin (R)	7,932	38.4
Rolla B. Henry (IR)	4,023	19.5
17 William R. Morrison (D)	13,086	60.8
John I. Rinaker (R)	8,438	39.2
18 William Hartzell (D)	10,866	53.9
Isaac Clements (R)	9,280	46.1
19 William B. Anderson (ID)	8,293	38.9
Samuel S. Marshall (D)	7,556	35.4
Green B. Rainn (R)	5,486	25.7

INDIANA

Candidates	Votes	%
1 Benoni S. Fuller (D)	12,864	50.7
Heilman (R)	12,527	49.3
2 James Douglas Williams (D)	17,404	64.6
Ferguson (R)	9,088	33.7
3 Michael C. Kerr (D)	13,891	52.3
Cravens (R)	12,682	47.7
4 Jeptha D. New (D)	13,683	52.5
Robinson (R)	12,378	47.5
5 William S. Holman (D)	13,302	55.1
Claypool (R)	10,835	44.9
6 Milton Stapp Robinson (R)	12,471	44.0
Johnson (D)	12,017	42.4
A. V. Pendleton (I)	3,888	13.7
7 Franklin Landers (D)	16,977	50.9
John Coburn (R)	16,411	49.2
8 Morton C. Hunter (R)	14,005	50.4
Rice (D)	13,798	49.6
9 Thomas J. Cason (R)	13,188	42.3
McClarg (D)	12,754	40.9
C. J. Bowles (I)	5,259	16.9
10 William Summerville Haymond (D)	15,088	51.1
Calkins (R)	14,423	48.9
11 James L. Evans (R)	14,595	52.1
Cox (D)	13,426	47.9
12 Andrew H. Hamilton (D)	14,318	53.2
Taylor (R)	12,623	46.9
13 John H. Baker (R)	13,671	50.1
Kelley (D)	13,613	49.9

IOWA

Candidates	Votes	%
1 George W. McCrary (R)	11,384	54.5
Leroy G. Palmer (A-MONOP)	9,521	45.5
2 John Q. Tufts (R)	10,779	51.6
J. S. Sheean (A-MONOP)	10,122	48.4
3 Lucien Lester Ainsworth (A-MONOP)	11,066	50.1
Charles F. Granger (R)	11,007	49.8
4 Henry O. Pratt (R)	10,725	60.4
John Bowman (A-MONOP)	6,975	39.3

Candidates	Votes	%
5 James Wilson (R)	12,724	63.0
James Wilkinson (A-MONOP)	7,481	37.0
6 Ezekiel Silas Sampson (R)	12,461	56.1
E. N. Gates (A-MONOP)	9,737	43.8
7 John A. Kasson (R)	12,274	55.2
John D. Whitman (A-MONOP)	9,974	44.8
8 James W. McDill (R)	10,808	57.1
Anson Rood (A-MONOP)	8,115	42.8
9 Samuel Addison Oliver (R)	12,657	64.9
C. E. Whiting (A-MONOP)	6,825	35.0

KANSAS

Candidates	Votes	%
1 William A. Phillips (R)	20,087	60.2
M. J. Parrott (D)	11,223	33.6
N. Green (G)	2,074	6.2
2 John R. Goodin (I)	14,965	51.2
S. A. Cobb (R)	14,240	48.7
3 William R. Brown (R)	14,581	59.3
J. K. Hudson (I)	9,932	40.4

KENTUCKY

Candidates	Votes	%
1 Andrew R. Boone (D)	5,882	45.5
Oscar Turner (ID)	5,799	44.8
T. J. Pickett (IR)	1,255	9.7
2 John Y. Brown (D)	7,381	61.3
George Smith (I)	3,864	32.1
E. R. Weir (R)	797	6.6
3 Charles W. Millikin (D)	6,875	72.9
Franklin Gorin (IR)	2,086	22.1
4 J. Proctor Knott (D)	8,182	64.0
Clement S. Hill (I)	4,601	36.0
5 Edward Y. Parsons (D)	4,300	78.6
John T. Gray (I)	859	15.7
L. O. Wood (I)	313	5.7
6 Thomas L. Jones (D)	7,268	48.9
Charles Eginton (R)	4,141	27.9
O. P. Hogan (I)	3,452	23.2
7 Joseph C. S. Blackburn (D)	11,298	69.1
Edward C. Marshall (I)	5,045	30.9
8 Milton J. Durham (D)	8,195	94.8
J. L. McMurtry (R)	438	5.1
9 John D. White (R)	8,774	51.3
Harrison Cockrell (D)	8,145	47.6
10 John B. Clarke (D)	9,324	58.9
John Means (R)	6,326	40.0

LOUISIANA

Candidates	Votes	%
1 Randall L. Gibson (D)	✔	
2 E. John Ellis (D)	✔	
3 Chester B. Darrall (R)	✔	
J. A. Preux (D)		
4 William M. Levy (D)	✔	
5 Frank Morey (R)	†	
William B. Spencer (D)		
6 Charles E. Nash (R)	✔	

MAINE

Candidates	Votes	%
1 John H. Burleigh (R)	12,275	53.2
Bradbury (D)	10,805	46.8
2 William P. Frye (R)	9,088	57.1
Clark (D)	6,673	41.9
3 James G. Blaine (R)	11,494	56.8
E. K. O'Brien (D)	8,693	43.0
4 Samuel F. Hersey (R)	9,648*	58.8
Boynton (D)	6,705	40.9
5 Eugene Hale (R)	10,695	56.9
Spofford (D)	8,116	43.1

MARYLAND

Candidates	Votes	%
1 Philip F. Thomas (D)	12,465	55.1
Golds (R)	10,147	44.9
2 Charles B. Roberts (D)	10,682	56.5
Ensor (R)	8,238	43.5
3 William J. O'Brien (D)	9,237	65.7
Suter (R)	4,834	34.4
4 Thomas Swann (D)	10,244	60.1
Cox (R)	6,810	39.9
5 Eli J. Henkle (D)	11,856	53.2
Hagner (R)	10,452	46.9
6 William Walsh (D)	12,974	50.2
Lloyd Lowndes (R)	12,896	49.9

MASSACHUSETTS

Candidates	Votes	%
1 James Buffinton (R)	9,927	68.8
Louis Laphani (D & L)	4,171	28.9
2 Benjamin W. Harris (R)	9,651	59.0
Edward Avery (D & L)	6,688	40.9
3 Henry L. Pierce (R)	8,011	61.9
Benjamin Dean (D & L)	4,927	38.1
4 Rufus S. Frost (R)	6,721‡	50.6
Josiah G. Abbott (D & L)	6,511	49.0
5 Nathaniel P. Banks (D & L)	13,438	64.8
Daniel W. Gooch (R)	7,263	35.0
6 Charles P. Thompson (D & L)	8,716	52.9
Benjamin F. Butler (R)	7,747	47.1
7 John K. Tarbox (D & L)	8,979	54.8
James C. Ayer (R)	7,415	45.2
8 William Wirt Warren (D & L)	8,585	52.0
John M. S. Williams (R)	7,861	47.6
9 George F. Hoar (R)	9,423	51.2
Eli Thayer (D & L)	8,961	48.7
10 Julius H. Seelye (D & L)	7,773	41.8
Charles A. Stevens (R)	7,353	39.5
Henry C. Hill	3,474	18.7
11 Chester W. Chapin (D & L)	11,964	65.5
Henry Alexander Jr. (R)	6,227	34.1

MICHIGAN

Candidates	Votes	%
1 Alpheus S. Williams (D)	10,848	54.8
Field (R)	8,892	44.9
2 Henry Waldron (R)	14,611	52.8
Robison (D)	13,075	47.2
3 George Willard (R)	13,372	50.5
Livermore (D)	12,174	45.9
4 Allen Potter (I)	13,317	52.0
Burrows (R)	12,278	48.0
5 William B. Williams (R)	13,370	51.5
Wilber (D)	12,212	47.0
6 George H. Durand (D)	17,758	50.9
Begole (R)	16,122	46.2
7 Omar D. Conger (R)	10,185	54.0
Goodrich (D)	8,203	43.5
8 Nathan B. Bradley (R)	10,258	50.7
Lewis (D)	9,979	49.3
9 Jay A. Hubbell (R)	12,877	78.8
Noble (D)	3,460	21.2

MINNESOTA

Candidates	Votes	%
1 Mark H. Dunnell (R)	16,716	54.9
Waite (D)	13,712	45.1
2 Horace B. Strait (R)	13,742	50.4
Cox (D)	13,521	49.6
3 William S. King (R)	18,179	53.4
Wilson (D)	15,861	46.6

MISSOURI

Candidates	Votes	%
1 Edward C. Kehr (D)	5,921	51.0
Stanard (R)	5,693	49.0
2 Erastus Wells (D)	9,040	71.5
Fisher (R)	3,597	28.5

Candidates	Votes	%
3 William H. Stone (D)	7,145	56.7
Wingate (R)	5,466	43.3
4 Robert A. Hatcher (D)	19,087	100.0
5 Richard P. Bland (D)	11,350	56.0
Seay (R)	8,929	44.0
6 Charles H. Morgan (D)	12,869	54.7
Thrasher (R)	10,640	45.3
7 John F. Philips (D)	14,446	88.8
Lay (R)	1,831	11.3
8 Benjamin J. Franklin (D)	11,546	63.9
Alexander (I)	3,595	19.9
Powell (R)	2,926	16.2
9 David Rea (D)	12,953	55.5
Thompson (R)	10,395	44.5
10 Rezin A. De Bolt (D)	11,727	50.5
Hyde (I)	11,510	49.5
11 John B. Clark Jr. (D)	19,344	100.0
12 John M. Glover (D)	12,206	57.9
Lipscomb (I)	8,867	42.1
13 Aylett H. Buckner (D)	17,516	76.1
Krezel (R)	5,491	23.9

NEBRASKA

Candidates	Votes	%
AL Lorenzo Crounse (R)	22,532	62.7
James W. Savage (D)	8,360	23.3
James W. Davis (I)	4,074	11.3

NEVADA

Candidates	Votes	%
AL William Woodburn (R)	9,317	52.1
Ellis (D)	8,567	47.9

NEW JERSEY

Candidates	Votes	%
1 Clement H. Sinnickson (R)	14,209	52.2
Albtson (D)	13,019	47.8
2 Samuel A. Dobbins (R)	13,977	51.8
Smith (D)	13,011	48.2
3 Miles Ross (D)	15,682	53.5
Clark (R)	13,629	46.5
4 Robert Hamilton (D)	14,585	59.5
Place (R)	9,931	40.5
5 Augustus W. Cutler (D)	11,677	50.0
Phelps (R)	11,670	50.0
6 Frederick H. Teese (D)	13,876	50.2
Marcus L. Ward (R)	13,768	49.8
7 Augustus A. Hardenbergh (D)	13,189	61.5
Isaac W. Scudder (R)	8,272	38.5

NEW YORK

Candidates	Votes	%
1 Henry B. Metcalfe (D)	12,184	52.6
French (R)	11,002	47.5
2 John G. Schumaker (D)	15,123	69.5
Wood (R)	6,652	30.6
3 Simeon B. Chittenden (D)	14,539	61.8
Ostrander (R)	8,996	38.2
4 Archibald M. Bliss (D)	12,439	61.3
Bennett (R)	7,862	38.7
5 Edwin R. Meade (D)	9,199	50.5
Hogan (I)	9,024	49.5
6 Samuel S. Cox (D)	13,762	80.1
Campbell (R)	3,428	19.9
7 Smith Ely Jr. (D)	7,689	54.5
Spencer (R)	6,418	45.5
8 Elijah Ward (D)	10,113	52.3
Lawson (R)	9,232	47.7
9 Fernando Wood (D)	8,763	50.6
Hardy (I)	6,428	37.1
Robert S. Newton	2,131	12.3
10 Abram S. Hewitt (D)	9,503	54.0
O'Brien (I)	8,083	46.0
11 Benjamin A. Willis (D)	10,354	56.3
Bailey (I)	8,036	43.7
12 N. Holmes Odell (D)	12,082	58.2
Wight (R)	8,391	40.4

Candidates	Votes	%
13 John O. Whitehouse (D)	16,181	57.2
Beale (R)	11,344	40.1
14 George M. Beebe (D)	14,518	56.4
Everett (R)	11,229	43.6
15 John H. Bagley Jr. (D)	16,205	56.1
Stebbins (R)	12,700	43.9
16 Charles H. Adams (R)	12,626	44.1
Terrance J. Quinn (D)	9,903	34.6
Eli Perry (D)	6,108	21.3
17 Martin I. Townsend (R)	15,445	50.9
Hughes (D)	14,931	49.2
18 Andrew Williams (R)	11,251	57.4
Waldo (D)	8,336	42.6
19 William A. Wheeler (R)	12,323	68.9
Sawyer (D)	5,553	31.1
20 Henry H. Hathorn (R)	15,933	51.2
Sanders (D)	15,183	48.8
21 Samuel F. Miller (R)	15,574	51.9
Allaben (D)	14,431	48.1
22 George A. Bagley (R)	14,391	52.1
Graves (D)	13,255	48.0
23 Scott Lord (D)	11,922	52.2
Roberts (R)	10,496	46.0
24 William H. Baker (R)	12,123	52.2
Warner (D)	11,109	47.8
25 Elias W. Leavenworth (R)	14,949	57.3
Comstock (D)	11,158	42.7
26 Clinton D. MacDougall (R)	13,433	53.1
Wilson (D)	11,857	46.9
27 Elbridge G. Lapham (R)	10,814	49.7
Pierpont (D)	9,770	44.9
S. B. Ayres (TEMP)	1,163	5.4
28 Thomas C. Platt (R)	13,766	49.6
Jones (D)	13,013	46.9
29 Charles C. B. Walker (D)	17,020	54.6
Hakes (R)	14,148	45.4
30 John M. Davy (R)	12,770	49.2
Angle (D)	12,522	48.2
31 George B. Hoskins (R)	11,323	54.7
Buck (D)	9,398	45.4
32 Lyman K. Bass (R)	15,968	51.6
Nicholls (D)	14,970	48.4
33 Augustus F. Allen (D)	12,302*	54.1
Sessions (R)	10,459	46.0

Special Election

Candidates	Votes	%
9 Richard Schell (D)	12,562	67.9
John Hardy (ID)	5,947	32.1

NORTH CAROLINA

Candidates	Votes	%
1 Jesse J. Yeats (D)	14,071	52.8
Clinton L. Cobb (R)	12,590	47.2
2 John A. Hyman (R)	18,176	62.0
George W. Blount (D)	11,144	38.0
3 Alfred M. Waddell (D)	15,572	52.2
Neil McKay (R)	14,285	47.8
4 Joseph J. Davis (D)	14,924	52.9
James H. Headen (R)	13,312	47.2
5 Alfred M. Scales (D)	10,529	54.2
William F. Henderson (R)	8,909	45.8
6 Thomas S. Ashe (D)	13,579	64.5
E. C. Davidson (I)	7,469	35.5
7 William M. Robbins (D)	11,372	61.9
Columbus L. Cook (R)	6,999	38.1
8 Robert B. Vance (D)	11,126	61.8
Plato Durham (IC)	6,887	38.2

OHIO

Candidates	Votes	%
1 Milton Sayler (D)	11,566	61.5
John K. Green (R)	7,250	38.5
2 Henry B. Banning (D)	10,852	53.8
Job E. Stevenson (R)	9,317	46.2
3 John S. Savage (D)	12,972	52.3
John Q. Smith (R)	11,810	47.6
4 John A. McMahon (D)	15,411	51.5
Lewis B. Gunckle (R)	14,312	47.8

OHIO

Candidates	Votes	%
5 Americus V. Rice (D)	13,477	61.9
Reynold K. Lytle (R)	8,279	38.0
6 Frank H. Hurd (D)	13,108	51.9
Albert M. Pratt (R)	11,271	44.6
7 Lawrence T. Neal (D)	11,333	55.4
Thomas W. Gordon (R)	9,108	44.5
8 William Lawrence (R)	10,756	48.6
Joseph E. Pearson (D)	10,378	46.9
9 E. F. Poppleton (D)	11,627	48.7
James W. Robinson (R)	11,199	46.9
10 Charles Foster (R)	13,778	49.8
George E. Seney (D)	13,619	49.2
11 John L. Vance (D)	12,437	53.7
H. S. Bundy (R)	10,496	45.3
12 Ansel T. Walling (D)	13,580	57.5
David Taylor Jr. (R)	9,667	40.9
13 Milton I. Southard (D)	13,602	57.8
John H. Barnhill (R)	9,651	41.0
14 Jacob B. Cowan (D)	12,394	62.0
William W. Armstrong (R)	7,214	36.1
15 Nelson H. Van Vorhes (R)	11,655	51.4
Wiley H. Oldham (D)	10,656	47.0
16 Lorenzo Danford (R)	12,097	52.6
Henry Boyles (D)	10,861	47.2
17 Laurin D. Woodworth (R)	11,113	49.6
David M. Wilson (D)	10,837	48.4
18 James Monroe (R)	12,229	54.5
John K. McBride (D)	10,095	45.0
19 James A. Garfield (R)	12,591	55.6
Daniel B. Woods (D)	6,245	27.6
R. H. Hurlburt (IR)	3,427	15.1
20 Henry B. Payne (D)	13,849	54.2
Richard C. Parsons (R)	11,330	44.3

Special Election

	Votes	%
12 William E. Finck (D)	14,090	59.3
David Taylor Jr. (R)	9,301	39.2

OREGON

	Votes	%
AL George A. La Dow (D)	9,642	38.1
Richard Williams (R)	9,340	36.9
T. W. Davenport (I)	6,350	25.1

PENNSYLVANIA

	Votes	%
1 Chapman Freeman (R)	9,637	48.2
T. B. Florence (D)	7,970	39.9
David Branson (I)	2,370	11.9
2 Charles O'Neill (R)	11,692	54.8
Benjamin Rush (D)	9,660	45.2
3 Samuel J. Randall (D)	9,703	57.8
D. F. Houston (R)	7,060	42.1
4 William D. Kelley (R)	12,436	57.9
W. V. McGrath (D)	9,049	42.1
5 John Robbins (D)	10,228	38.0
A. C. Harmer (R)	9,095	33.8
L. Myers (IR)	7,579	28.2
6 Washington Townsend (R)	9,485	57.8
J. S. Forwood (D)	6,916	42.2
7 Allan Wood (R)	12,630	52.5
E. L. Acker (D)	11,432	47.5
8 Heister Clymer (D)	10,553	66.3
Charles B. McNight (R)	5,358	33.7
9 A. Herr Smith (R)	10,505	62.8
William Patton (D)	6,220	37.2
10 William Mutchler (D)	13,737	67.2
S. V. B. Kachline (I)	6,710	32.8
11 Francis D. Collins (D)	12,986	69.0
A. W. Butler (R)	5,846	31.0
12 Winthrop W. Ketcham (R)	7,932	52.5
H. B. Wright (D)	7,165	47.5
13 James B. Reilly (D)	8,600	51.2
Theodore Garrettson (R)	8,056	48.0

Candidates	Votes	%
14 John B. Packer (R)	12,528	56.4
William M. Breslin (D)	9,673	43.6
15 Joseph Powell (D)	12,183	50.2
B. Laporte (R)	12,082	49.8
16 Sobieski Ross (R)	10,660	53.3
W. W. Early (D)	9,331	46.7
17 John Reilly (D)	11,727	52.6
S. S. Blair (R)	10,580	47.4
18 William S. Stenger (D)	12,804	52.1
Langhorne Wister (R)	11,781	47.9
19 Levi Maish (D)	14,534	58.7
H. G. McNair (R)	7,230	29.2
William McConky (I)	2,984	12.1
20 Levi A. Mackey (D)	12,050	58.1
C. T. Alexander (I)	8,677	41.9
21 Jacob Turney (D)	12,065	57.7
Andrew Stewart (R)	8,854	42.3
22 James H. Hopkins (D)	10,091	55.8
James S. Negley (R)	7,777	43.0
23 Alexander G. Cochran (D)	5,206	40.0
Thomas M. Bayne (R)	4,996	38.4
S. A. Purviance (I)	2,803	21.6
24 John W. Wallace (R)	9,347	52.3
George W. Miller (D)	8,538	47.7
25 George A. Jenks (D)	11,627	51.1
Harry White (R)	11,109	48.9
26 James Sheakley (D)	12,810	50.1
John G. White (R)	12,737	49.9
27 Albert G. Egbert (D)	10,393	50.0
C. B. Curtis (R)	10,381	50.0

RHODE ISLAND

	Votes	%
1 Benjamin T. Eames (R)	2,292	73.3
Beach (D)	824	26.4
2 Latimer W. Ballou (R)	2,362	65.0
Redman (D)	1,235	34.0

SOUTH CAROLINA

	Votes	%
1 Joseph H. Rainey (R)	14,360	51.4
Samuel Lee (I REF D)	13,563	48.6
2 Edmund W. M. Mackey (I REF D)	16,746‡	54.1
Charles W. Buttz (R)	14,204	45.9
3 Solomon L. Hoge (R)	16,431	56.1
Samuel McGowan (D)	12,873	43.9
4 Alexander S. Wallace (R)	16,452	53.2
J. B. Kershaw (D)	14,455	46.8
5 Robert Smalls (R)	17,752	79.4
J. P. M. Epping (I)	4,461	20.0

Special Election

	Votes	%
3 Lewis Cass Carpenter (R)	21,248	99.6

TENNESSEE

	Votes	%
1 William McFarland (D)	8,783	55.7
Butler (R)	6,995	44.3
2 Jacob M. Thornburgh (R)	8,168	52.7
Mabry (D)	7,338	47.3
3 George G. Dibrell (D)	9,559	65.7
Nelson (R)	4,597	31.6
4 John W. Head (D)	10,430*	100.0
5 John M. Bright (D)	10,224	72.7
Wisener (R)	3,831	27.3
6 John F. House (D)	11,992	62.4
Harrison (R)	7,227	37.6
7 Washington C. Whitthorne (D)	9,672	78.2
Gibbs (R)	1,773	14.3
G. W. Blackburn (IR)	928	7.5
8 John D. C. Atkins (D)	9,446	66.4
Muse (D)	4,789	33.6
9 William P. Caldwell (D)	11,128	72.0
Nunn (R)	4,336	28.0
10 H. Casey Young (D)	13,825	60.4
Lewis (R)	9,071	39.6

Candidates	Votes	%

Special Election

	Votes	%
4 Samuel McClary Fite (CD)	✔	

TEXAS

	Votes	%
1 John H. Reagan (D)	5,793	75.6
William Chambers	1,855	24.2
2 David B. Culberson (D)	3,804	99.6
3 James W. Throckmorton (D)	4,392	93.0
J. M. Valentine	262	5.5
4 Roger Q. Mills (D)	9,395	72.2
Pleasant M. Yell (R)	3,615	27.8
5 John Hancock (D)	3,526	97.3
6 Gustave Schleicher (D)	5,082	69.3
Jeremiah Galvan	2,234	30.5

VERMONT

	Votes	%
1 Charles H. Joyce (R)	9,638	69.5
Heaton (D)	2,597	18.7
Charles W. Willard	1,635	11.8
2 Dudley C. Denison (IR)	7,038	44.7
Luke P. Poland (R)	5,756	36.6
C. W. Davenport (D)	1,960	12.5
3 George W. Hendee (R)	9,043	71.3
Edwards (D)	3,646	28.7

VIRGINIA

	Votes	%
1 Beverly B. Douglas (D)	10,783	50.7
James B. Sinen (R)	10,488	49.3
2 John Goode Jr. (D)	13,521	49.4
James H. Platt Jr. (R)	13,390	49.0
3 Gilbert C. Walker (D)	13,325	55.3
Rush Bargess (R)	10,710	44.5
4 William H. H. Stowell (R)	14,583	63.9
W. H. Mann (D)	8,201	35.9
5 George C. Cabell (D)	10,291	57.1
C. Y. Thomas (R)	7,723	42.9
6 John Randolph Tucker (D)	10,708	65.2
J. F. Johnson (R)	5,707	34.8
7 John T. Harris (D)	9,266	73.6
John F. Lewis (R)	3,214	25.5
8 Eppa Hunton (D)	9,809	51.4
James Barbour (R)	9,291	48.6
9 William Terry (D)	8,052	48.4
Fayette McMullen (ID)	6,760	40.6
George W. Henderlite (R)	1,821	11.0

WEST VIRGINIA

	Votes	%
1 Benjamin Wilson (D)	12,796	50.3
Nathan Goff Jr. (R)	12,631	49.7
2 Charles J. Faulkner (D)	11,499	57.5
Alexander R. Boteler (R)	8,064	40.3
3 Frank Hereford (D)	13,524	63.6
John D. Witcher (R)	7,745	36.4

WISCONSIN

	Votes	%
1 Charles G. Williams (R)	12,568	56.9
Fratt (REF)	9,532	43.1
2 Lucien B. Caswell (R)	11,676	50.5
Cook (REF)	11,459	45.9
3 Henry S. Magoon (R)	11,535	52.6
Thompson (REF)	10,400	47.4
4 William P. Lynde (REF)	12,046	55.8
Ludington (R)	9,545	44.2
5 Samuel D. Burchard (REF)	15,784	61.5
Barber (R)	9,889	38.5
6 Alanson M. Kimball (R)	14,733	50.2
Bouck (REF)	14,641	49.8
7 Jeremiah M. Rusk (R)	13,637	57.2
Fulton (REF)	10,196	42.8
8 George W. Cate (REF)	9,546	50.0
McDill (R)	9,544	50.0

1875 House Elections

CALIFORNIA

Candidates	Votes	%
1 William A. Piper (D)	12,417	49.0
Iva P. Rankin (R)	6,791	26.8
John F. Swift (I)	6,103	24.1
2 Horace F. Page (R)	13,624	43.4
Hy Larkin (D)	12,329	39.3
C. R. Tuttle (I)	5,414	17.3
3 John K. Luttrell (D)	18,468	55.1
C. B. Denio (R)	8,284	24.7
Charles F. Reed (I)	6,761	20.2
4 Peter D. Wigginton (D)	15,649	48.7
S. O. Houghton (R)	11,090	34.5
J. S. Thompson (I)	5,413	16.8

CONNECTICUT

	Votes	%
1 George M. Landers (D)	13,434	50.5
Joseph R. Hawley (R)	12,946	48.7
2 James Phelps (D)	15,440	51.6
Stephen Wright Kellogg (R)	13,831	46.3
3 Henry H. Starkweather (R)	9,000	51.1
Foster (D)	8,054	45.7
4 William H. Barnum (D)	14,273	53.8
Hubbard (R)	11,648	43.9

ILLINOIS

Special Election

Candidates	Votes	%
1 Bernard G. Caulfield (D)	3,461	80.7
Henry Vallettee	454	10.6
William H. Eddy	308	7.2

MASSACHUSETTS

Special Elections

	Votes	%
1 William W. Crapo (R)	9,553	65.5
Charles G. Davis	5,017	34.4
10 Charles A. Stevens (R)	2,850	43.7
Henry M. Burleigh	2,369	36.3
Lafayette Mattby	727	11.1
Levi Stockbridge	562	8.6

MISSISSIPPI

	Votes	%
1 Lucius Q. C. Lamar (D)	19,233	100.0
2 G. Wiley Wells (I)	19,250	59.4
Howe (R)	13,149	40.6
3 Hernando D. Money (D)	15,128	68.1
Powers (R)	7,085	31.9
4 Otho R. Singleton (D)	19,890	66.6
Niles (R)	9,987	33.4

Candidates	Votes	%
5 Charles E. Hooker (D)	16,255	59.9
Hill (R)	10,878	40.1
6 John R. Lynch (R)	13,746	50.5
Seal (D)	13,460	49.5

NEW HAMPSHIRE

	Votes	%
1 Frank Jones (D)	13,967	50.0
Withhorn (R)	13,631	48.8
2 Samuel N. Bell (D)	13,084	49.9
Pike (R)	12,930	49.3
3 Henry W. Blair (R)	12,389	50.1
Kent (D)	12,180	49.3

NEW YORK

Special Election

	Votes	%
33 Nelson I. Norton (R)	10,770	53.9
Charles S. Cary	9,139	45.7

OREGON

Special Election

	Votes	%
AL La Fayette Lane (D)	9,373	47.6
H. Warren (R)	9,106	46.3

House Candidates Index

For an index of all House candidates listed in this section (pages 701 to 1061), see pages 1180-1273. Instructions for use of the House Candidates Index appear on page 1180.

1876 House Elections

ALABAMA

	Candidates	Votes	%
1	James T. Jones (D)	10,582	49.3
	Bromberg (ID)	8,771	40.8
	Turner (R)	2,132	9.9
2	Hilary A. Herbert (D)	11,435	54.9
	Hall (R)	9,393	45.1
3	Jeremiah N. Williams (D)	14,089	78.3
	Betts (R)	3,896	21.7
4	Charles M. Shelley (D)	9,655	37.8
	Haralson (R)	8,670	33.9
	James T. Rapier (COLOR R)	7,236	28.3
5	Robert F. Ligon (R)	13,107	64.8
	Booth (D)	7,120	35.2
6	Goldsmith W. Hewitt (D)	13,634	100.0
7	William H. Forney (D)	14,319	100.0
8	William W. Garth (D)	14,529	62.0
	McClellan (ID)	8,910	38.0

ARKANSAS

		Votes	%
1	Lucien C. Gause (D)	15,840	97.5
2	William F. Slemons (D)	15,566	52.4
	Snyder (R)	14,159	47.6
3	Jordan E. Cravens (BOLT D)	8,277	35.9
	McClure (R)	8,016	34.7
	Stuart (D)	5,927	25.7
4	Thomas M. Gunter (D)	12,355	74.7
	Huckleberry (R)	4,176	25.3

CALIFORNIA

		Votes	%
1	Horace Davis (R)	22,134	53.3
	William A. Piper (D)	19,363	46.7
2	Horace F. Page (R)	20,815	56.7
	G. J. Carpenter (D)	15,916	43.3
3	John K. Luttrell (D)	19,846	51.1
	Joseph McKenney (R)	18,990	48.9
4	Romualdo Pacheco (R)	19,104‡	50.0
	Peter D. Wigginton (D)	19,083	49.9

COLORADO[1]

(Became a state Aug. 1, 1876)

		Votes	%
AL	James B. Belford (LR)	13,532‡	51.9
	Thomas M. Patterson (D)	12,541	48.1

Special Election

		Votes	%
AL	James B. Belford (R)	13,302	52.0
	Thomas M. Patterson (D)	12,267	48.0

CONNECTICUT

		Votes	%
1	George M. Landers (D)	15,529	50.0
	Hawley (R)	15,390	49.5
2	James Phelps (D)	19,500	53.4
	Stephen Wright Kellogg (R)	16,777	45.9
3	John T. Wait (R)	11,283	53.8
	Waller (D)	9,535	45.4
4	Levi Warner (D)	17,233	52.5
	Robert Hubbard (R)	15,501	47.2

Special Election

		Votes	%
4	Levi Warner (D)	17,250	52.7
	Robert Hubbard (R)	15,459	47.3

DELAWARE

		Votes	%
AL	James Williams (D)	13,169	55.4
	Bird (R)	10,592	44.6

FLORIDA

	Candidates	Votes	%
1	Robert H. M. Davidson (D)	13,163	51.1
	Purman (R)	12,623	49.0
2	Horatio Bisbee Jr. (R)	11,470‡	50.0
	Jesse J. Finley (D)	11,453	50.0

GEORGIA

		Votes	%
1	Julian Hartridge (D)	11,465	65.9
	Bayant (R)	5,922	34.1
2	William E. Smith (D)	13,627	63.0
	Whitney (R)	8,015	37.0
3	Philip Cook (D)	10,684	71.4
	Pierce (R)	4,280	28.6
4	Henry R. Harris (D)	13,797	70.5
	Hilliard (R)	5,785	29.5
5	Milton A. Candler (D)	18,083	67.5
	Markham (R)	8,714	32.5
6	James H. Blount (D)	12,996	74.0
	Gove (R)	4,578	26.1
7	William H. Felton (ID)	13,269	55.1
	Dabney (R)	10,807	44.9
8	Alexander H. Stephens (D)	14,471	91.9
	Tennelle (R)	1,277	8.1
9	Benjamin H. Hill (D)	14,790*	100.0

ILLINOIS

		Votes	%
1	William Aldrich (R)	16,578	53.2
	John R. Hoxie (D)	14,101	45.2
2	Carter H. Harrison (D)	14,732	50.9
	George R. Davis (R)	14,090	48.7
3	Lorenzo Brentano (R)	11,722	50.6
	John V. Lemoyne (D)	11,435	49.4
4	William Lathrop (R)	13,241	48.4
	John F. Farnsworth (D)	8,149	29.8
	Stephen A. Hurlbut (IR)	5,991	21.9
5	Horatio C. Burchard (R)	15,793	59.8
	Pattison (D)	10,600	40.2
6	Thomas J. Henderson (R)	15,560	60.6
	Charles Dunham (D)	9,821	38.3
7	Philip C. Hayes (R)	14,849	52.7
	Alexander Campbell (D)	13,313	47.3
8	Greenbury L. Fort (R)	15,011	55.1
	George W. Parker (D)	12,211	44.9
9	Thomas A. Boyd (R)	14,548	49.8
	George A. Wilson (D)	14,001	47.9
10	Benjamin F. Marsh (R)	14,252	51.1
	J. H. Hungate (D)	13,496	48.4
11	Robert M. Knapp (D)	17,949	58.7
	Joseph Robbins (R)	12,618	41.2
12	William M. Springer (D)	17,400	55.8
	David L. Phillips (R)	13,754	44.1
13	Thomas F. Tipton (R)	15,229	50.4
	Adlai E. Stevenson (D)	14,977	49.6
14	Joseph G. Cannon (R)	17,796	52.0
	John C. Black (D)	16,404	48.0
15	John R. Eden (D)	18,714	57.5
	George D. Chape (R)	13,765	42.3
16	William A. J. Sparks (D)	14,591	53.3
	Edwin M. Ashcraft (R)	12,763	46.7
17	William R. Morrison (D)	17,036	56.7
	Henry S. Baker (R)	13,029	43.3
18	William Hartzell (D)	14,691	50.0
	Benjamin L. Wiley (R)	14,671	50.0
19	Richard W. Townshend (D)	12,720	44.3
	Edward Bonham (R)	8,558	29.8
	William B. Anderson (G)	7,463	26.0

INDIANA

		Votes	%
1	Benoni S. Fuller (D)	14,727	50.6
	C. A. Debruler (R)	13,158	45.2
2	Thomas R. Cobb (D)	18,918	56.3
	Loveless (R)	13,735	40.9

	Candidates	Votes	%
3	George A. Bicknell (D)	17,225	57.4
	Newsom (R)	11,747	39.2
4	Leonidas Sexton (R)	14,902	49.9
	Woolen (D)	14,570	48.8
5	Thomas M. Browne (R)	15,578	52.5
	Holman (D)	14,069	47.5
6	Milton Stapp Robinson (R)	17,403	49.3
	Chamber (D)	17,118	48.5
7	John Hanna (R)	19,634	49.8
	Franklin Landers (D)	18,236	46.2
8	Morton C. Hunter (R)	14,265	44.4
	McLean (D)	13,155	41.0
	Davis (G)	4,704	14.6
9	Michael D. White (R)	16,990	50.0
	Williams (D)	13,564	39.9
	Leroy Templeton (G)	3,449	10.1
10	William Henry Calkins (R)	17,952	51.8
	William Summerville Haymond (D)	16,693	48.1
11	James L. Evans (R)	18,030	52.2
	Armstrong (D)	16,482	47.8
12	Andrew H. Hamilton (D)	18,842	58.5
	Bonham (R)	12,718	39.5
13	John H. Baker (R)	18,481	52.9
	Kelley (D)	16,273	46.6

Special Elections

		Votes	%
2	Andrew Humphreys (D)	18,724	55.7
	W. F. Spicely (R)	14,919	44.4
3	Nathan Tracy Carr (D)	17,214	59.4
	Ara E. S. Long (R)	11,782	40.6

IOWA

		Votes	%
1	Joseph C. Stone (R)	17,188	53.4
	Wesley C. Hobbs (D)	14,814	46.1
2	Hiram Price (R)	16,439	52.8
	Jeremiah Henry Murphy (D)	14,683	47.2
3	Theodore W. Burdick (R)	17,423	51.5
	Jeffrey M. Griffith (D)	16,100	47.6
4	Nathaniel C. Deering (R)	20,770	68.9
	Cyrus Foreman (D)	9,379	31.1
5	Rush Clark (R)	19,274	60.4
	Nathan Worley (D)	11,154	35.0
6	Ezekiel Silas Sampson (R)	18,768	54.7
	H. B. Hendershott (D)	14,719	42.9
7	Henry J. B. Cummings (R)	19,496	58.3
	Samuel J. Gilpin (D)	11,688	34.9
	Andrew Hastie (G)	2,160	6.5
8	William F. Sapp (R)	19,358	56.0
	L. R. Bolter (D)	15,236	44.0
9	S. Addison Oliver (R)	19,563	63.5
	Samuel Rees (D)	10,583	34.3

KANSAS

		Votes	%
1	William A. Phillips (R)	29,352	64.8
	Thomas Fenlon (D)	15,642	34.5
2	Dudley C. Haskell (R)	22,088	55.7
	J. R. Goodin (IG)	17,518	44.2
3	Thomas Ryan (R)	25,171	68.3
	S. J. Crawford (IG)	11,634	31.6

KENTUCKY

		Votes	%
1	Andrew R. Boone (D)	10,994	45.1
	Oscar Turner (ID)	7,540	30.9
	H. H. Houston (R)	5,835	23.9
2	James A. McKenzie (D)	17,557	65.2
	J. Z. Moore (R)	9,374	34.8
3	John W. Caldwell (D)	13,285	54.0
	E. L. Mottley (R)	10,590	43.1
4	J. Proctor Knott (D)	15,735	68.9
	J. W. Lewis (R)	7,053	30.9

---

1. The special election in Colorado in 1876 was held to elect a representative for the remainder of the 44th Congress (1875-77). The general election House race was for a full two-year term in the 45th Congress (1877-79).

KENTUCKY

Candidates	Votes	%
5 Albert S. Willis (D)	15,046	73.0
Walter Evans (R)	5,567	27.0
6 John G. Carlisle (D)	16,404	66.9
John J. Landrum (R)	8,133	33.1
7 Joseph C. S. Blackburn (D)	18,884	62.5
T. O. Shackelford (R)	11,348	37.5
8 Milton J. Durham (D)	15,484	55.0
W. O. Bradley (R)	12,654	44.9
9 Thomas Turner (D)	13,103	50.8
Robert Boyd (R)	12,710	49.2
10 John B. Clarke (D)	14,409	57.7
O. S. Deming (R)	10,561	42.3

Special Election

5 Henry Watterson (D)	11,567	94.5
William J. Heady	677	5.5

LOUISIANA

1 Randall L. Gibson (D)	14,876	55.4
William M. Burwell (R)	11,978	44.6
2 E. John Ellis (D)	14,145	55.1
Henry C. Dibble (R)	11,515	44.9
3 Chester B. Darrall (R)	15,782‡	51.8
Joseph H. Acklen (D)	14,695	48.2
4 Joseph B. Elam (D)	12,136	51.3
George L. Smith (R)	11,540	48.7
5 John Edwards Leonard (R)	14,423	52.6
William W. Farmer (D)	13,016	47.4
6 Edward W. Robertson (D)	15,520	58.2
Charles E. Nash (R)	11,147	41.8

MAINE

1 Thomas B. Reed (R)	16,248	51.4
John M. Goodwin (D)	15,156	47.9
2 William P. Frye (R)	13,681	55.7
S. Clifford Belcher (D)	10,323	42.0
3 Stephen D. Lindsey (R)	15,741	55.2
E. K. O'Brien (D)	12,788	44.8
4 Llewellyn Powers (R)	12,866	53.8
John P. Donworth (D)	10,069	42.1
5 Eugene Hale (R)	15,089	55.1
William H. McClellan (D)	12,278	44.8

Special Election

3 Edwin Flye (R)	15,611	54.8
Isaac Reed (D)	12,848	45.1

MARYLAND

1 Daniel M. Henry (D)	15,287	56.2
Spence (R)	11,905	43.8
2 Charles B. Roberts (D)	15,033	55.6
Morrison J. Harris (R)	11,984	44.4
3 William Kimmell (D)	14,251	62.4
W. E. Goldsborough (R)	8,592	37.6
4 Thomas Swann (D)	15,259	54.5
James H. Butler (R)	12,728	45.5
5 Eli J. Henkle (D)	14,436	55.2
John Henry Sellman (R)	11,705	44.8
6 William Walsh (D)	15,727	50.0
Louis McComas (R)	15,713	50.0

MASSACHUSETTS

1 William W. Crapo (R)	14,153	69.6
Day (D)	6,179	30.4
2 Benjamin W. Harris (R)	15,550	61.4
Avery (D)	9,757	38.5
3 Walbridge A. Field (R)	9,323‡	50.0
Benjamin Dean (D)	9,315	50.0
4 Leopold Morse (D)	10,249	52.6
Frost (R)	9,215	47.3

Candidates	Votes	%
5 Nathaniel P. Banks (R)	13,325	51.9
Frothingham (D)	12,317	47.9
6 George B. Loring (R)	12,319	52.4
Thompson (D)	11,171	47.5
7 Benjamin F. Butler (R)	12,100	51.6
Tarbox (D)	9,379	40.0
Hoar (IR)	1,955	8.3
8 William C. Claflin (R)	14,245	53.2
Warren (D)	12,497	46.7
9 William W. Rice (R)	13,890	57.5
Verry (D)	10,248	42.4
10 Amasa Norcross (R)	15,779	63.9
Lamb (D)	8,928	36.1
11 George D. Robinson (R)	11,922	54.0
Chapin (D)	9,760	44.2

MICHIGAN

1 Alpheus S. Williams (D)	14,471	50.5
Duffield (R)	12,417	43.3
Ruehle (G)	1,736	6.1
2 Edwin Willits (R)	19,211	52.0
Robison (D)	17,024	46.1
3 Jonas H. McGowan (R)	19,878	51.8
Livermore (D)	17,223	44.9
4 Edwin W. Keightley (R)	18,716	53.4
Chamberlain (D & G)	11,330	46.6
5 John W. Stone (R)	21,908	54.1
Harris (D & G)	18,546	45.8
6 Mark S. Brewer (R)	23,356	51.9
Durand (D)	21,615	48.1
7 Omar D. Conger (R)	15,818	54.1
Chadwick (D)	13,177	45.1
8 Charles C. Ellsworth (R)	16,098	50.5
Potter (D)	15,760	49.5
9 Jay A. Hubbell (R)	18,224	59.0
Kilbourne (D & G)	12,656	41.0

MINNESOTA

1 Mark H. Dunnell (R)	26,010	61.8
Stacy (D)	16,064	38.2
2 Horace B. Strait (R)	19,730	52.5
Wilder (D)	14,990	39.9
Donnelly (G)	2,879	7.7
3 Jacob H. Stewart (R)	22,823	52.4
McNair (D)	20,717	47.6

MISSISSIPPI

1 Henry L. Muldrow (D)	20,597	76.2
Lee (R)	6,420	23.8
2 Vannoy H. Manning (D)	20,328	61.0
Watson (R)	12,589	37.8
3 Hernando D. Money (D)	17,983	71.1
Chisholm (R)	7,320	28.9
4 Otho R. Singleton (D)	19,130	80.8
Hancock (R)	4,547	19.2
5 Charles E. Hooker (D)	19,858	69.7
Shaughnessey (R)	8,646	30.3
6 James R. Chalmers (D)	15,788	56.0
John R. Lynch (R)	12,386	44.0

MISSOURI

1 Anthony Ittner (R)	7,043	50.7
E. C. Kerr (D)	6,834	49.2
2 Nathan Cole (R)	7,316	41.3
E. Wells (D)	7,026	39.7
A. W. Slayback (D)	3,229	18.2
3 Lyne S. Metcalfe (R)	8,099	50.1
Richard G. Frost (D)	8,080	49.9
4 Robert A. Hatcher (D)	21,390	79.0
L. Davis	3,953	14.6
W. Ballentine	1,738	6.4
5 Richard P. Bland (D)	14,599	56.1
J. Q. Thompson (R)	11,414	43.9

Candidates	Votes	%
6 Charles H. Morgan (D)	18,080	49.9
H. E. Havens (R)	17,357	47.9
7 Thomas T. Crittenden (D)	18,700	54.9
J. H. Stover (R)	15,353	45.1
8 Benjamin J. Franklin (D)	15,229	68.0
D. S. Twitchell (R)	7,160	32.0
9 David Rea (D)	15,715	54.1
B. F. Loan (R)	13,343	45.9
10 Henry M. Pollard (R)	16,582	51.0
R. A. Debolt (D)	15,802	48.6
11 John B. Clark Jr. (D)	21,671	68.6
M. L. Demotte (R)	9,915	31.4
12 John M. Glover (D)	16,154	57.1
Hayward (R)	11,646	41.1
13 Aylett H. Buckner (D)	21,573	79.2
T. B. Robinson (R)	4,715	17.3

NEBRASKA

AL Frank Welch (R)	30,900	59.7
Joseph Hollman (D)	17,206	33.2
Marvin Warren (G)	3,589	6.9

NEVADA

AL Thomas Wren (R)	10,241	52.3
Ellis (D)	9,330	47.7

NEW JERSEY

1 Clement H. Sinnickson (R)	17,362	52.9
Simrman (D)	15,472	47.1
2 John H. Pugh (R)	16,015	50.8
Smith (D)	15,485	49.2
3 Miles Ross (D)	18,525	54.7
Atherton (R)	15,359	45.3
4 Alvah A. Clark (D)	17,351	59.3
Veghte (ID)	11,900	40.7
5 Augustus W. Cutler (D)	15,034	53.9
Mills (R)	12,882	46.2
6 Thomas B. Peddie (R)	17,565	51.5
Righter (D)	16,041	47.0
7 Augustus A. Hardenbergh (D)	17,260	60.2
Stiastny (R)	11,391	39.8

NEW YORK

1 James W. Covert (D)	20,145	56.7
King (R)	15,222	42.8
2 William D. Veeder (D)	13,406	60.2
Cavanagh (R)	8,331	37.4
3 Simeon B. Chittenden (R)	18,110	50.2
Dakin (D)	17,858	49.5
4 Archibald M. Bliss (D)	18,506	61.5
Spitzer (R)	11,492	38.2
5 Nicholas Muller (D)	15,259	75.2
Kerrigan (I)	4,755	23.4
6 Samuel S. Cox (D)	17,098	95.0
7 Anthony Eickhoff (D)	13,199	68.1
Groom (R)	6,051	31.2
8 Anson G. McCook (R)	13,221	51.3
Ward (D)	12,408	48.1
9 Fernando Wood (D)	14,280	62.1
Ducunha (R)	8,217	35.8
10 Abram S. Hewitt (D)	17,136	69.6
Babcock (R)	6,805	27.6
11 Benjamin A. Willis (D)	12,519	49.7
Morton (R)	12,092	48.0
12 Clarkson N. Potter (D)	16,078	59.0
Brandreth (R)	11,160	41.0
13 John H. Ketcham (R)	18,225	52.7
Davies (D)	16,113	46.6
14 George M. Beebe (D)	17,732	54.7
Sweet (R)	14,667	45.3
15 Stephen L. Mayham (D)	20,498	55.7
Tremper (R)	16,267	44.2

NEW YORK

	Candidates	Votes	%
16	Terence J. Quinn (D)	17,497	51.3
	Harris (R)	16,596	48.7
17	Martin I. Townsend (R)	19,689	53.0
	Parmenter (D)	17,448	47.0
18	Andrew Williams (R)	13,177	56.3
	Platt (D)	10,246	43.7
19	Amaziah B. James (R)	17,275	66.4
	Magove (D)	8,756	33.6
20	John H. Starin (R)	19,142	51.4
	Decker (D)	18,089	48.6
21	Solomon Bundy (R)	18,825	52.5
	Matteson (D)	17,056	47.5
22	George A. Bagley (R)	18,668	53.6
	Smith (D)	15,995	45.9
23	William J. Bacon (R)	13,779	51.3
	Lord (D)	13,069	48.7
24	William H. Baker (R)	16,555	57.3
	Bond (D & P)	11,798	40.8
25	Frank Hiscock (R)	18,425	57.1
	Pratt (D)	13,834	42.9
26	John H. Camp (R)	19,036	56.1
	Vanauken (D)	14,879	43.9
27	Elbridge G. Lapham (R)	14,726	55.3
	Comstock (D)	11,852	44.5
28	Jeremiah W. Dwight (R)	18,839	54.3
	Jones (D)	15,662	45.1
29	John N. Hungerford (R)	21,087	54.0
	Loveridge (D)	17,973	46.0
30	E. Kirke Hart (D)	17,797	50.7
	Davy (D)	17,138	48.8
31	Charles B. Benedict (D)	12,250	42.3
	Hoskins (R)	11,866	41.0
	Thomas T. Flagler (IR)	4,837	16.7
32	Daniel N. Lockwood (D)	20,125	50.5
	Spaulding (R)	19,716	49.4
33	George W. Patterson (R)	16,910	61.3
	Unidentified Candidate (D)	10,601	38.4

NORTH CAROLINA

1	Jesse J. Yeates (D)	15,151	51.7
	D. McDonald Lindsey (R)	14,154	48.3
2	Curtis H. Brogden (R)	21,060	64.0
	Wharton J. Green (D)	11,874	36.1
3	Alfred M. Waddell (D)	17,515	52.5
	William P. Canaday (R)	15,826	47.5
4	Joseph J. Davis (D)	16,832	52.5
	Isaac J. Young (R)	15,229	47.5
5	Alfred M. Scales (D)	13,264	54.7
	James E. Boyd (R)	11,001	45.3
6	Walter L. Steele (D)	17,256	62.7
	Allen Jordan (R)	10,283	37.3
7	William M. Robbins (D)	13,724	59.2
	Thomas J. Dula (R)	9,467	40.8
8	Robert B. Vance (D)	15,868	67.9
	Erastus P. Hampton (R)	7,493	32.1

OHIO

1	Milton Sayler (D)	14,144	51.2
	Manning F. Force (R)	13,474	48.8
2	Henry B. Banning (D)	14,133	50.1
	Stanley Matthews (R)	14,058	49.9
3	Mills Gardner (R)	16,594	50.8
	John S. Savage (D)	16,098	49.2
4	John A. McMahon (D)	18,557	50.0
	John Howard (R)	18,461	49.7
5	Americus V. Rice (D)	20,643	62.0
	J. L. H. Long (R)	12,645	38.0
6	Jacob D. Cox (R)	17,276	50.0
	Frank H. Hurd (D)	15,361	44.5
	E. B. Hall (P)	1,887	5.5
7	Henry L. Dickey (D)	14,859	52.3
	A. L. Brown (R)	13,518	47.6
8	J. Warren Keifer (R)	17,728	55.5
	George Arthur (D)	14,012	43.9
9	John S. Jones (R)	15,968	50.7
	L. F. Poppleton (D)	15,175	48.2

	Candidates	Votes	%
10	Charles Foster (R)	17,324	50.3
	John H. Hudson (D)	17,053	49.5
11	Henry S. Neal (R)	15,213	50.9
	John L. Vance (D)	14,639	49.0
12	Thomas Ewing (D)	19,628	57.2
	George K. Nash (R)	14,541	42.4
13	Milton I. Southard (D)	17,706	54.7
	John H. Barnhill (R)	14,642	45.2
14	Ebenezer B. Finley (D)	16,654	60.0
	Peter S. Grosscut (R)	11,067	39.9
15	Nelson H. Van Vorhes (R)	14,620	50.5
	William W. Poston (D)	14,113	48.8
16	Lorenzo Danford (R)	16,089	53.7
	William Lawrence (D)	13,837	46.2
17	William McKinley Jr (R)	16,489	50.2
	Levi L. Lanborn (D)	13,185	40.2
	John B. Powell (G)	2,446	7.5
18	James Monroe (R)	16,906	56.9
	John J. Hall (D)	12,772	43.0
19	James A. Garfield (R)	20,012	63.8
	John S. Casement (D)	11,352	36.2
20	Amos Townsend (R)	17,894	55.0
	Henry B. Payne (D)	14,516	44.6

OREGON

AL	Richard Williams (R)	15,347	51.9
	L. F. Lane (D)	14,239	48.1

PENNSYLVANIA

1	Chapman Freeman (R)	15,021	57.2
	J. S. Thackray (D)	11,231	42.8
2	Charles O'Neill (R)	15,198	56.1
	C. H. Gibson (D)	11,881	43.9
3	Samuel J. Randall (D)	11,651	56.3
	Benjamin L. Berry (R)	9,041	43.7
4	William D. Kelley (R)	18,820	60.2
	J. T. School (D)	12,432	39.8
5	Alfred C. Harmer (R)	17,973	55.0
	Jacob Duvall (D)	14,722	45.0
6	William Ward (R)	15,220	61.0
	W. D. Hartman (D)	9,717	39.0
7	I. Newton Evans (R)	15,765	52.5
	Abel Rambo (D)	14,247	47.5
8	Hiester Clymer (D)	15,239	65.6
	H. D. Markley (R)	6,213	26.7
	C. Shearer (G)	1,780	7.7
9	A. Herr Smith (R)	17,419	64.5
	George Nauman (D)	9,574	35.5
10	Samuel A. Bridges (D)	20,113	62.1
	Howard J. Reeder (R)	12,255	37.9
11	Francis D. Collins D)	18,548	64.6
	D. J. Waller (D)	10,172	35.4
12	Hendrick B. Wright (D)	13,557	52.7
	H. B. Payne (D)	12,101	47.0
13	James B. Reilly (D)	10,107	50.2
	J. S. Nutting (R)	10,026	49.8
14	John W. Killinger (R)	16,453	53.6
	W. B. Wilson (D)	13,723	44.7
15	Edward Overton Jr. (R)	16,954	53.1
	Joseph Powell (D)	14,952	46.9
16	John I. Mitchell (R)	13,575	50.3
	Henry White (D)	12,097	44.8
17	Jacob M. Campbell (R)	14,668	50.9
	John Reilly (D)	14,148	49.1
18	William S. Stenger (D)	15,301	50.1
	Thad M. Mahon (R)	15,232	49.9
19	Levi Maish (D)	18,932	57.7
	C. H. Bressler (R)	13,898	42.3
20	Levi A. Mackey (D)	16,229	59.2
	R. V. B. Lincoln (R)	11,193	40.8
21	Jacob Turney (D)	16,962	57.1
	Jacob Rush (R)	12,763	42.9
22	Russell Errett (R)	14,551	53.0
	James H. Hopkins (D)	12,913	47.0
23	Thomas M. Bayne (R)	12.506	59.6
	A. G. Cochrane (D)	8,326	39.7
24	William S. Shallenberger (R)	13,151	55.0

	Candidates	Votes	%
	R. B. McComb (D)	10,648	44.5
25	Harry White (R)	15,156	53.1
	George A. Jenks (D)	13,397	46.9
26	John M. Thompson (R)	18,511	52.7
	James Sheakley (D)	16,486	46.9
27	Lewis F. Watson (R)	15,640	55.9
	W. L. Scott (D)	12,093	43.2

Special Election

12	W. H. Stanton (D)	12,703	50.3
	Edward Jones (R)	12,417	49.1

RHODE ISLAND

1	Benjamin T. Eames (R)	8,516	62.5
	Brunsen (D)	5,063	37.2
2	Latimer W. Ballou (R)	7,179	57.3
	Page (D)	5,295	42.3

SOUTH CAROLINA

1	Joseph H. Rainey (R)	18,180	52.2
	John S. Richardson (D)	16,661	47.8
2	Richard H. Cain (R)	21,385	62.1
	Michael P. O'Connor (D)	13,028	37.9
3	D. Wyatt Aiken (D)	21,479	58.0
	L. Cass Carpenter (R)	15,553	42.0
4	John H. Evins (D)	21,875	57.7
	A. S. Wallace (R)	16,071	42.4
5	Robert Smalls (R)	19,954	51.9
	G. D. Tilman (D)	18,516	48.1

Special Election

2	Charles W. Buttz (R)	21,378	62.1
	Michael P. O'Connor (D)	13,030	37.9

TENNESSEE

1	James H. Randolph (R)	12,349	52.4
	McFarland (D)	11,215	47.6
2	Jacob M. Thornburgh (R)	14,328	59.9
	Cullom (D)	9,603	40.1
3	George G. Dibrell (D)	13,132	61.5
	Drake (R)	8,218	38.5
4	Haywood Y. Riddle (D)	11,957	70.6
	Cox (R)	3,545	20.9
	Patton (R)	1,437	8.5
5	John M. Bright (D)	15,094	74.0
	Galbraith (R)	5,309	26.0
6	John F. House (D)	15,719	63.6
	Presser (R)	8,987	36.4
7	Washington C. Whitthorne (D)	12,257	68.7
	Cliffe (R)	3,757	21.0
	G. W. Blackburn (IR)	1,841	10.3
8	John D. C. Atkins (D)	13,412	61.8
	Hawkins (R)	8,296	38.2
9	William P. Caldwell (D)	14,799	69.5
	Folk (R)	6,509	30.6
10	H. Casey Young (D)	13,014	51.8
	Randolph (R)	12,134	48.3

TEXAS

1	John H. Reagan (D)	13,097	67.0
	L. W. Cooper (R)	6,415	32.8
2	David B. Culberson (D)	17,326	65.5
	S. H. Russell (R)	9,130	34.5
3	James W. Throckmorton (D)	24,138	91.4
	J. C. Bigger (R)	2,281	8.6
4	Roger Q. Mills (D)	20,975	73.2
	J. P. Osterhaut (R)	7,655	26.7
5	De Witt C. Giddings (D)	15,886	54.3
	G. W. Jones (R)	13,277	45.4
6	Gustave Schleicher (D)	12,242	81.2
	James P. Newcomb (R)	2,693	17.9

VERMONT

Candidates	Votes	%
1 Charles H. Joyce (R)	14,496	67.2
Childs (D)	7,057	32.7
2 Dudley C. Denison (R)	13,630	70.0
Dickey (D)	5,739	29.5
3 George W. Hendee (R)	11,974	68.5
Edwards (D)	5,367	30.7

1 Beverly B. Douglas (D)	14,228	56.5
L. C. Boiston (R)	10,940	43.5
2 John Goode Jr. (D)	16,885	53.0
Joseph Secar (R)	14,989	47.0
3 Gilbert C. Walker (D)	15,536	53.6
Charles S. Mills (R)	13,430	46.4
4 Joseph Jorgensen (R)	13,896	51.9
William E. Hunton Jr. (D)	12,492	46.7

Candidates	Votes	%
5 George C. Cabell (D)	15,146	60.6
Daniel S. Lewis (R)	9,842	39.4
6 John R. Tucker (D)	16,425	59.6
George H. Burch (R)	11,127	40.4
7 John T. Harris (D)	17,143	73.1
Evenett W. Early (R)	6,250	26.7
8 Eppa Hunton (D)	16,660	62.1
I. C. O'Neal (R)	10,175	37.9
9 Auburn L. Pridemore (D)	15,127	75.8
George T. Egbert (R)	4,791	24.0

WEST VIRGINIA

1 Benjamin Wilson (D)	17,902	52.7
G. F. Scott (R)	16,067	47.3
2 Benjamin F. Martin (D)	18,156	56.0
Ward H. Lamon (R)	14,283	44.0
3 John E. Kenna (D)	20,292	61.5
Benjamin J. Redmund (R)	12,719	38.5

WISCONSIN

Candidates	Votes	%
1 Charles G. Williams (R)	18,206	59.3
Winslow (D)	12,478	40.6
2 Lucien B. Caswell (R)	15,073	50.5
Orton (D)	14,745	49.4
3 George C. Hazelton (R)	15,582	54.4
Orton (D)	13,034	45.5
4 William P. Lynde (D)	17,653	59.6
Smith (R)	11,952	40.4
5 Edward S. Bragg (D)	19,544	58.1
Carter (R)	14,031	41.7
6 Gabriel Bouck (D)	20,623	53.6
Kimball (R)	17,847	46.4
7 Herman L. Humphrey (R)	20,702	58.4
Gage (D)	13,220	37.3
8 Thaddeus C. Pound (R)	14,838	51.7
Cate (D)	13,860	48.3

1877 House Elections

GEORGIA

Special Election

9 Hiram P. Bell (D)	5,173	49.1
Speer (I)	3,734	35.5
Archer (R)	1,619	15.4

NEW HAMPSHIRE

1 Frank Jones (D)	13,925	49.8
Marston (R)	13,885	49.7
2 James F. Briggs (R)	13,209	52.0
Sulloway (D)	12,111	47.7
3 Henry W. Blair (R)	12,682	51.6
Kent (D)	11,832	48.1

NEW YORK

Special Election

7 David Dudley Field (D)	4,884	77.1
Christian Goetz (R)	1,435	22.7

1878 House Elections

ALABAMA

	Candidates	Votes	%
1	Thomas H. Herndon (D)	6,577	69.1
	Bailey (G)	2,941	30.9
2	Hilary A. Herbert (D)	8,364	56.3
	N. Armstrong (G)	6,505	43.8
3	William J. Samford (D)	6,199	88.4
	Strange (ID)	676	9.6
4	Charles M. Shelley (D)	8,514	55.4
	Haralson (R)	6,545	42.6
5	Thomas Williams (D)	6,537	70.5
	Nunn (G)	2,734	29.5
6	Burwell B. Lewis (D)	7,652	70.5
	Smith (ID)	3,201	29.5
7	William H. Forney (D)	2,653	96.6
8	William M. Lowe (GD)	10,373	55.6
	Garth (D)	8,279	44.4

ARKANSAS

	Candidates	Votes	%
1	Poindexter Dunn (D)	8,863	100.0
2	William F. Slemons (D)	11,226	57.2
	Bradley (G)	8,390	42.8
3	Jordan E. Cravens (D)	7,202	51.2
	Rice (G)	6,868	48.8
4	Thomas M. Gunter (D)	5,361	59.8
	Cunningham (ID)	2,639	29.4
	Smith (G)	969	10.8

COLORADO

	Candidates	Votes	%
AL	James B. Belford (R)	14,294	49.9
	Thomas M. Patterson (D)	12,003	41.9
	Childs (G)	2,329	8.1

CONNECTICUT

	Candidates	Votes	%
1	Joseph R. Hawley (R)	14,187	52.2
	Landers (D)	11,900	43.8
2	James Phelps (D)	16,504	53.2
	Douglas (R)	14,231	45.9
3	John T. Wait (R)	9,236	53.8
	Carter (D)	7,571	44.1
4	Frederick Miles (R)	14,109	48.7
	Bruggerhoff (D)	12,930	44.6
	Taylor (N)	1,848	6.4

DELAWARE

	Candidates	Votes	%
AL	Edward L. Martin (D)	10,576	78.1
	Jackson (NG)	2,966	21.9

FLORIDA

	Candidates	Votes	%
1	Robert H. M. Davidson (D)	11,527	58.1
	Conover (R)	8,302	41.9
2	Noble A. Hull (D)	9,648‡	50.1
	Horatio Bisbee Jr. (R)	9,626	49.9

GEORGIA

	Candidates	Votes	%
1	John C. Nicholls (D)	8,477	62.8
	Corker (G)	5,031	37.2
2	William E. Smith (D)	8,126	69.1
	Wade (R)	3,643	31.0
3	Philip Cook (D)	2,628	99.8
4	Henry Persons (ID)	13,336	56.9
	Harris (D)	10,101	43.1
5	Nathaniel J. Hammond (D)	10,269	55.6
	Arnold (R)	8,196	44.4
6	James H. Blount (D)	3,192	99.4
7	William H. Felton (ID)	14,315	52.5
	Lester (D)	12,971	47.5

	Candidates	Votes	%
8	Alexander H. Stephens (D)	3,673	98.6
9	Emory Speer (ID)	10,897	50.3
	Billups (D)	10,675	49.3

ILLINOIS

	Candidates	Votes	%
1	William Aldrich (R)	12,165	.51.8
	James R. Doolittle (D)	7,136	30.4
	John McAscliff (SOC)	2,322	9.9
	William V. Barr (NG)	1,844	7.9
2	George R. Davis (R)	10,347	49.6
	Miles Kehoe (D)	6,111	29.3
	George A. Schilling (SOC)	2,473	11.9
	James Felch (NG)	1,600	7.7
3	Hiram Barber Jr. (R)	9,574	53.1
	Lambert Tree (D)	5,280	29.3
	Benjamin Sebley (I)	2,306	12.8
4	John C. Sherwin (R)	12,753	61.8
	Jonathan C. Staighton (D)	4,438	21.5
	Augustus Adams (NG)	3,448	16.7
5	Robert M. A. Hawk (R)	11,042	53.4
	Mortimer D. Hathaway (D)	4,823	23.3
	John M. King (NG)	4,804	23.2
6	Thomas J. Henderson (R)	10,964	52.5
	James W. Haney (NG)	6,675	31.9
	Charles Dunham (D)	3,257	15.6
7	Philip C. Hayes (R)	10,712	46.5
	Alexander Campbell (NG)	6,512	28.3
	W. S. Brooks (D)	5,795	25.2
8	Greenbury L. Fort (R)	11,271	49.7
	Chris C. Strawn (NG)	6,575	29.0
	Thomas M. Shaw (D)	4,822	21.3
9	Thomas A. Boyd (R)	10,543	43.8
	George A. Wilson (D)	9,802	40.7
	Aloxr H. Keighan (NG)	3,749	15.6
10	Benjamin F. Marsh (R)	11,814	44.5
	Delos P. Phelps (D)	11,238	42.3
	Alson J. Streeter (NG)	3,496	13.2
11	James W. Singleton (D)	11,961	54.5
	James P. Dimmitt (R)	6,956	31.7
	William H. Pogue (P)	3,034	13.8
12	William M. Springer (D)	12,542	47.7
	John Cook (R)	9,146	34.8
	John Mathers (NG)	4,611	17.5
13	Adlai E. Stevenson (D)	13,870	53.2
	Thomas F. Tipton (R)	12,058	46.3
14	Joseph G. Cannon (R)	13,698	46.2
	Maldon Jones (D)	11,527	38.8
	Jesse Harper (NG)	4,451	15.0
15	Albert P. Forsythe (R)	13,106	50.3
	Hiram B. Decias (D)	12,942	49.7
16	William A. J. Sparks (D)	11,493	48.7
	Basil B. Smith (R)	9,946	42.2
	James Creed (NG)	2,139	9.1
17	William R. Morrison (D)	12,436	50.5
	John Baker (D)	10,605	43.0
	William E. Moberly (NG)	1,598	6.5
18	John R. Thomas (R)	12,686	46.6
	N. J. Allen (D)	12,074	44.4
	S. J. Davis (NG)	2,454	9.0
19	Richard W. Townshend (D)	12,603	53.3
	Robert Bell (D)	8,190	34.6
	Seth F. Crews (NG)	2,847	12.0

INDIANA

	Candidates	Votes	%
1	William Heilman (R)	13,928	48.7
	Thomas E. Garvin (D)	13,099	45.8
	Thomas F. Debruler (NG)	1,595	5.6
2	Thomas R. Cobb (D)	17,317	55.1
	Richard M. Welman (R)	12,032	38.3
	William L. Green (NG)	2,103	6.7
3	George A. Bicknell (D)	15,074	57.9
	Ara E. S. Long (R)	9,369	36.0

	Candidates	Votes	%
	John F. Willy (NG)	1,588	6.1
4	Jeptha D. New (D)	15,146	50.5
	Leonidas Sexton (R)	14,655	48.9
5	Thomas M. Browne (R)	13,776	50.1
	William S. Holman (D)	12,936	47.0
6	William R. Myers (D)	16,167	47.9
	William Grose (R)	15,548	46.1
	Reuben A. Riley (NG)	2,044	6.1
7	Gilbert De La Matyr (A-D-FUS)	18,720	51.2
	John Hanna (R)	17,881	48.9
8	Abraham J. Hostetler (D)	13,164	40.9
	Morton C. Hunter (R)	12,124	37.6
	Henry A. White (NG)	6,929	21.5
9	Godlove S. Orth (R)	15,608	43.7
	James McCabe (D)	15,510	43.5
	Leroy Templeton (NG)	4,571	12.8
10	William H. Calkins (R)	15,365	45.2
	Morgan H. Weir (D)	13,408	39.4
	John N. Skinner (NG)	5,252	15.4
11	Calvin Cowgill (R)	15,547	47.8
	David D. Dykeman (D)	13,102	40.3
	David Moss (NG)	3,866	11.9
12	Walpole G. Colerick (D)	17,067	63.7
	John Studebaker (R & NG)	9,712	36.3
13	John B. Baker (R)	15,184	47.2
	John B. Stoll (D)	13,523	42.0
	William C. Williams (NG)	3,462	10.8

IOWA

	Candidates	Votes	%
1	Moses A. McCoid (R)	12,705	48.6
	Wesley C. Hobbs (D)	7,945	30.4
	A. H. Bereman (G)	5,505	21.0
2	Hiram Price (R)	13,337	49.8
	W. F. Brannan (D)	9,509	35.5
	Jacob Geiger (G)	3,960	14.8
3	Thomas Updegraff (R)	12,723	43.9
	Fred O'Donnall (D)	10,886	37.5
	S. T. Spangler (G)	5,406	18.6
4	Nathaniel C. Deering (R)	17,134	60.8
	L. H. Weller (G)	5,742	20.4
	William V. Allen (D)	5,293	18.8
5	Rush Clark (R)	14,205	52.8
	George Carter (G)	12,011	44.6
6	James Baird Weaver (D & G)	16,366	53.3
	Ezekiel Silas Sampson (R)	14,308	46.6
7	Edward Hooker Gillette (D & G)	16,474	51.4
	Henry Johnson Brodhead Cummings (R)	15,546	48.5
8	William F. Sapp (R)	15,343	50.2
	George C. Hieks (G)	7,760	25.4
	John H. Keatley (R)	7,453	24.4
9	Cyrus C. Carpenter (R)	16,489	54.7
	L. Q. Hoggatt (G & D)	12,338	41.0

KANSAS

	Candidates	Votes	%
1	John A. Anderson (R)	30,457	59.6
	J. R. McClure (D)	14,919	29.2
	E. Gale (G)	5,716	11.2
2	Dudley C. Haskell (R)	19,029	45.0
	C. W. Blair (D)	13,327	31.5
	P. P. Elder (G)	9,962	23.5
3	Thomas Ryan (R)	25,228	56.8
	F. Doster (G)	11,055	24.9
	J. B. Fugate (D)	8,109	18.3

KENTUCKY

	Candidates	Votes	%
1	Oscar Turner (ID)	6,878	42.9
	L. S. Trimble (D)	5,611	35.0
	E. W. Bagby (R)	3,554	22.2

KENTUCKY

	Candidates	Votes	%
2	James A. McKenzie (D)	8,328	61.2
	John W. Feighan (R)	3,189	23.4
	Francis M. English (G)	2,051	15.1
3	John W. Caldwell (D)	9,354	46.3
	W. G. Hunter (R)	8,502	42.1
	George Wright (G)	2,339	11.6
4	J. Proctor Knott (D)	8,969	64.5
	J. D. Belden (R)	4,616	33.2
5	Albert Willis (D)	9,115	40.5
	J. Watts Kearney (D)	7,492	33.3
	Horace Scott (R)	5,508	24.5
6	John G. Carlisle (D)	5,901	75.6
	Joseph H. Hermes (I)	1,877	24.1
7	Joseph C. S. Blackburn (D)	8,632	69.7
	S. T. Drane (R)	3,548	28.7
8	Philip B. Thompson Jr. (D)	12,538	53.8
	George Denny (R)	10,766	46.2
9	Thomas Turner (D)	10,784	55.4
	John Dills	8,392	43.2
10	Elijah C. Phister (D)	7,293	65.2
	B. F. Bennett (R)	2,645	23.7
	James Kilgore (G)	1,224	11.0

LOUISIANA

		Votes	%
1	Randall L. Gibson (D)	12,419	63.6
	H. C. Castellanos (R)	7,108	36.4
2	E. John Ellis (D)	10,263	59.0
	E. N. Cullom (RG)	6,076	34.9
	Michael Hahn (R)	1,065	6.1
3	Joseph Hayes Acklen (D)	10,309	48.8
	R. O. Hebert (R)	7,163	33.9
	W. B. Merchant (ID)	3,666	17.3
4	Joseph B. Elam (D)	14,432	89.2
	J. M. Wells (R)	1,756	10.9
5	J. Floyd King (D)	17,261	77.9
	J. T. Ludling (R)	4,905	22.1
6	Edward W. Robertson (D)	13,977	66.1
	W. L. Larimore (I)	7,155	33.9

MAINE

		Votes	%
1	Thomas B. Reed (R)	13,483	46.2
	Samuel J. Anderson (D)	9,332	32.0
	Edward H. Gove (NG)	6,348	21.8
2	William P. Frye (R)	11,431	49.0
	Solon Chase (NG)	8,472	36.3
	S. Clifford Belcher (D)	3,407	14.6
3	Stephen D. Lindsey (R)	11,384	44.4
	William Philbrick (NG)	8,333	32.5
	Franklin Smith (D)	5,895	23.0
4	George W. Ladd (NG)	12,921	56.1
	Llewellyn Powers (R)	10,095	43.8
5	Thompson H. Murch (NG)	11,371	47.3
	Eugene Hale (R)	10,251	42.7
	Joseph H. Martin (D)	2,255	9.4

MARYLAND

		Votes	%
1	Daniel M. Henry (D)	11,419	52.5
	Graham (R)	10,338	47.5
2	J. Fred. C. Talbott (D)	9,826	66.9
	Milligan (ID)	3,598	24.5
	McCombs (G)	1,268	8.6
3	William Kimmel (D)	11,676	70.4
	Thompson (LAB)	4,908	29.6
4	Robert M. McLane (D)	11,064	59.0
	Holland (R)	6,671	35.6
5	Eli J. Henkle (D)	11,558	54.4
	Crane (R)	9,679	45.6
6	Milton G. Urner (R)	14,148	53.2
	Peter (D)	12,437	46.8

MASSACHUSETTS

		Votes	%
1	William W. Crapo (R)	12,575	62.2
	Ellis (D)	7,383	36.5

	Candidates	Votes	%
2	Benjamin W. Harris (R)	14,579	58.4
	Dean (N)	5,472	21.9
	Avery (D)	4,374	17.5
3	Walbridge A. Field (R)	10,919	50.5
	Dean (D)	10,478	48.5
4	Leopold Morse (D)	11,647	60.0
	Brimmer (R)	7,654	39.4
5	Selwyn Z. Bowman (R)	15,308	58.2
	Clark (D, N)	10,918	41.5
6	George B. Loring (R)	10,339	44.4
	E. Moody Boynton (N)	10,226	43.9
	Carleton (D)	2,658	11.4
7	William A. Russell (R)	13,169	55.2
	Tarbox (D)	7,700	32.3
	Stevens (N)	2,831	11.9
8	William Claflin (R)	14,300	54.3
	Bradford (D)	11,758	44.7
9	William W. Rice (R)	13,295	59.0
	Thayer (D)	8,960	39.8
10	Amasa Norcross (R)	13,051	55.5
	W. F. Whitney (N)	6,839	29.1
	Grinnell	3,609	15.3
11	George D. Robinson (R)	10,927	51.4
	Lathrop (BUT D&N)	7,994	37.6
	Dunham (D)	2,069	9.7

MICHIGAN

		Votes	%
1	John S. Newberry (R)	9,894	40.8
	Williams (D)	8,567	35.3
	Heffron (NG)	5,760	23.7
2	Edwin Willits (R)	14,312	44.5
	Card (D)	9,557	29.7
	Thomas (NG)	7,742	24.1
3	Jonas H. McGowan (R)	14,381	41.7
	Dawson (NG)	12,347	35.8
	Upton (D)	6,341	18.4
4	Julius C. Burrows (R)	14,236	47.1
	Eldred (D)	8,171	27.1
	Sherwood (NG)	7,791	25.8
5	John W. Stone (R)	15,983	45.8
	Comstock (NG)	15,273	43.7
	Hoyt (D)	3,468	9.9
6	Mark S. Brewer (R)	18,459	45.1
	McCurdy (D)	15,549	38.0
	Meade (NG)	6,271	15.3
7	Omar D. Conger (R)	11,939	47.4
	Mitchell (D)	8,940	35.5
	Mallory (NG)	4,316	17.1
8	Roswell G. Horr (R)	11,993	39.7
	Thompson (D)	9,571	31.7
	Hoyt (NG)	8,500	28.2
9	Jay A. Hubbell (R)	15,264	53.1
	Power (D)	7,478	26.0
	Parmelee (NG)	6,014	20.9

MINNESOTA

		Votes	%
1	Mark H. Dunnell (R)	18,613	59.2
	Meighen (D)	12,845	40.8
2	Henry Poehler (D)	14,467	51.3
	Strait (R)	13,743	48.7
3	William D. Washburn (R)	20,954	53.9
	Donnelly (D)	17,938	46.1

MISSISSIPPI

		Votes	%
1	Henry L. Muldrow (D)	9,632	59.3
	Davis (G)	6,533	40.3
2	Vannoy H. Manning (D)	7,339	53.5
	Amacker (N)	5,969	43.5
3	Hernando D. Money (D)	4,028	99.7
4	Otho R. Singleton (D)	4,650	99.6
5	Charles E. Hooker (D)	4,816	87.5
	Deason (R)	686	12.5
6	James R. Chalmers (D)	6,663	82.7
	Castello (R)	1,370	17.0

MISSOURI

	Candidates	Votes	%
1	Martin L. Clardy (D)	9,437	48.3
	H. Ziegenhein (R)	6,498	33.3
	E. Eshbaugh (G)	2,476	12.7
	F. Westermeyer (SOC)	1,110	5.7
2	Erastus Wells (D)	7,669	42.7
	Nathan Cole (R)	7,403	41.2
	John Hogan (G)	2,391	13.3
3	Richard G. Frost (D)	7,237	45.5
	L. S. Metcalf (R)	5,319	33.4
	H. C. Vandillen (G)	2,213	13.9
	Bartholomeus (SOC)	1,140	7.2
4	Lowndes H. Davis (D)	12,052	61.4
	Sol G. Kitchen (R)	6,834	34.8
5	Richard P. Bland (D)	11,291	56.6
	J. J. Ware (G)	8,022	40.2
6	James R. Waddill (D)	17,769	44.0
	C. G. Burton (R)	11,622	28.8
	M. H. Ritchey (G)	11,004	27.2
7	Alfred M. Lay (D)	16,960	51.5
	James Boyd (G)	8,810	26.8
	A. Underwood (R)	7,170	21.8
8	Samuel L. Sawyer (D)	9,727	49.0
	John T. Crisp (D)	8,917	44.9
	L. G. Jeffers (G)	1,227	6.2
9	Nicholas Ford (G)	17,430	51.7
	David Rea (D)	16,257	48.2
10	Gideon F. Rothwell (D)	14,793	47.2
	H. M. Pollard (R)	10,875	34.7
	E. J. Broaddus (G)	5,682	18.1
11	John B. Clark Jr. (D)	16,600	98.9
12	William H. Hatch (D)	12,463	45.1
	John M. London (G)	10,597	38.3
	Dan M. Draper (R)	4,578	16.6
13	Aylett H. Buckner (D)	15,591	59.2
	T. J. C. Fagg (G & R)	8,575	32.6
	T. B. Robinson (R)	2,164	8.2

NEBRASKA

		Votes	%
AL	Edward K. Valentine (R)	28,347	56.4
	J. W. Davis (D & G)	21,722	43.3

Special Election

		Votes	%
AL	Thomas J. Majors (R)	28,211	57.3
	Alex Bear (D)	21,015	42.7

NEVADA

		Votes	%
AL	Rollin M. Daggett (R)	9,727	51.8
	Deal (D)	9,047	48.2

NEW HAMPSHIRE

		Votes	%
1	Joshua G. Hall (R)	13,510	50.3
	Norris (D)	11,026	41.1
	Chesley (G)	2,284	8.5
2	James F. Briggs (R)	12,981	52.1
	A. W. Sulloway (D)	9,860	39.5
	C. A. Sulloway (G)	2,077	8.3
3	Evarts W. Farr (R)	11,708	48.8
	Kent (D)	10,663	44.5
	Johnson (G)	1,496	6.2

NEW JERSEY

		Votes	%
1	George M. Robeson (R)	14,924	48.1
	Grosscup (G)	9,879	31.9
	Stratton (D)	6,215	20.0
2	Hezekiah B. Smith (D & G)	14,610	50.6
	Pugh (R)	13,699	47.4
3	Miles Ross (D)	13,509	44.2
	Clark (R)	13,176	43.1
	Hope (G)	3,843	12.6
4	Alvah A. Clark (D)	11,449	45.1
	Potts (R)	9,852	38.8
	Larrison (G)	4,111	16.2

NEW JERSEY

Candidates	Votes	%
5 Charles H. Voorhis (R)	10,893	44.9
Demarest (D)	10,089	41.6
Potter (G)	3,268	13.5
6 John L. Blake (R)	14,771	49.7
Allbright (D)	12,832	43.2
Bliss (G)	2,106	7.1
7 Lewis A. Brigham (R)	13,199	50.8
Laverty (D)	11,234	43.3
Winant (G)	1,424	5.5

NEW YORK

Candidates	Votes	%
1 James W. Covert (D)	13,809	50.8
Otis (R)	11,798	43.4
Crooks (G)	1,430	5.3
2 Daniel O'Reilly (R & ID)	13,138	54.8
Litchfield (D)	9,881	41.2
3 Simeon B. Chittenden (R)	16,667	58.2
Huntley (D)	10,017	35.0
4 Archibald M. Bliss (D)	13,020	53.8
Lyon (R)	8,742	36.2
5 Nicholas Muller (TAM)	9,466	52.3
Bourke (A-TAM)	8,327	46.0
6 Samuel S. Cox (G & TAM)	10,908	62.4
D'Vries (A-TAM)	6,327	36.2
7 Edwin Einstein (R& A-TAM)	7,617	48.3
Eickhoff (TAM)	7,162	45.4
Jahelka (G)	803	5.1
8 Anson G. McCook (R)	12,854	60.4
Jerome (TAM)	7,512	35.3
9 Fernando Wood (TAM)	7,277	36.7
Hardy (A-TAM)	6,480	32.7
Berryman (R)	5,726	28.9
10 James O'Brien (A-TAM)	11,319	53.3
Potter (TAM)	9,046	42.6
11 Levi P. Morton (R)	14,078	64.7
Willis (TAM)	7,060	32.4
12 Alexander Smith (R)	11,338*	49.5
Cobb (D)	9,083	39.7
N. Smith (G)	2,421	10.6
13 John H. Ketcham (R)	18,240	62.6
Baker (D)	9,700	33.3
14 John W. Ferdon (R)	11,861	44.4
Beebe (D)	11,323	42.4
Voorhis (G)	3,261	12.2
15 William Lounsbery (D)	13,680	47.4
Nichols (R)	11,442	39.7
Erkson (G)	3,524	12.2
16 John M. Bailey (R)	12,199	41.0
Woods (D)	12,004	40.4
Hilton (G)	5,455	18.3
17 Walter A. Wood (R)	16,771	55.3
Patterson (D)	9,655	31.8
Ferguson (G)	3,878	12.8
18 John Hammond (R)	10,650	54.8
Ross (D)	5,765	29.7
McDonald (G)	3,005	15.5
19 Amaziah B. James (R)	12,133	70.5
Hasbrouck (D)	5,056	29.4
20 John H. Starin (R)	17,738	56.7
Thomson (D)	10,880	34.8
Wendell (G)	2,588	8.3
21 David Wilber (R)	15,377	48.1
Scofield (D)	10,180	31.8
Cone (G)	6,017	18.8
22 Warner Miller (R)	14,855	51.4
Brown (D)	11,658	40.3
Lewis (G)	2,102	7.3
23 Cyrus D. Prescott (R)	9,762	42.9
Spriggs (D)	8,730	38.4
Mitchell (G)	3,787	16.6
24 Joseph Mason (R)	12,043	50.6
Sebastian Duffy (G & D)	11,307	47.5
25 Frank Hiscock (R)	14,599	55.9
Wieting (G & D)	11,174	42.8
26 John H. Camp (R)	14,355	53.0
Walley (D)	10,979	40.5
Durston (D)	1,638	6.1
27 Elbridge G. Lapham (R)	12,270	54.4
Pierpont (G & D)	10,232	45.4

Candidates	Votes	%
28 Jeremiah W. Dwight (R)	15,569	53.9
Howe (G)	11,162	38.7
Mudge (D)	1,883	6.5
29 David P. Richardson (R)	14,330	42.8
Babcock (D)	10,960	32.7
Beaumont (G)	8,174	24.4
30 John Van Voorhis (R)	12,008	43.4
Lamberton (D)	10,367	37.5
Brown (G)	2,760	10.0
Alphonso A. Hopkins (P)	2,476	9.0
31 Richard Crowley (R)	12,529	56.7
Davis (D)	8,713	39.5
32 Ray V. Pierce (R)	18,998	52.3
Lockwood (D)	16,105	44.3
33 Henry Van Aernam (R)	11,364	49.8
Morris (D)	6,732	29.5
Vinton (G)	4,689	20.6

Special Election

	Votes	%
16 John M. Bailey (R)	12,062	40.5
Francis H. D. Woods (D)	11,962	40.2
Philip E. Marshall (G)	5,549	18.7

NORTH CAROLINA

	Votes	%
1 Joseph J. Martin (R)	12,135‡	49.2
Jesse J. Yeates (D)	12,084	49.0
2 William H. Kitchin (D)	10,704	42.9
James E. O'Hara (IR)	9,682	38.8
James H. Harris (R)	3,948	15.8
3 Daniel L. Russell (G & R)	11,611	51.9
Alfred M. Waddell (D)	10,730	48.0
4 Joseph J. Davis (D)	11,864	51.1
Josiah Turner (IR)	8,353	36.0
Wiley D. Jones (R)	2,911	12.5
5 Alfred M. Scales (D)	10,326	57.3
Albion W. Tourgee (R)	7,680	42.6
6 Walter L. Steele (D)	4,908	92.1
7 Robert F. Armfield (D)	4,753	55.7
John M. Brower (G & R)	3,650	42.8
8 Robert B. Vance (D)	2,894	96.8

OHIO

	Votes	%
1 Benjamin Butterworth (R)	12,756	50.5
Milton Sayler (D)	12,036	47.7
2 Thomas L. Young (R)	12,914	50.9
Leonard W. Goss (D)	11,940	47.0
3 John A. McMahon (D)	15,437	51.0
Emanuel Schultz (R)	14,352	47.5
4 J. Warren Keifer (R)	15,895	56.6
William V. Marquis (D)	10,805	38.5
5 Benjamin Le Fevre (D)	14,676	48.5
Harrison Wilson (R)	12,843	42.5
Stephen Johnson (G)	2,392	7.9
6 William D. Hill (D)	16,110	52.4
James L. Price (R)	12,072	39.3
William C. Holgate (G)	2,544	8.3
7 Frank H. Hurd (D)	13,182	40.7
James B. Luckey (R)	11,278	34.9
Henry Kahlo (G)	7,893	24.4
8 Ebenezer B. Finley (D)	16,237	50.2
Charles Foster (R)	14,982	46.3
9 George L. Converse (D)	17,786	48.9
Lorenzo English (R)	16,798	46.2
10 Thomas Ewing (D)	12,679	50.4
Valentine B. Horton (R)	12,245	48.7
11 Henry L. Dickey (D)	15,355	50.4
W. W. McKnight (R)	13,986	45.9
12 Henry S. Neal (R)	14,566	52.0
James Emmitt (D)	12,490	44.6
13 Adoniram J. Warner (D)	11,950	46.7
Nelson H. Van Voorhees (R)	11,827	46.2
George E. Geddes (G)	1,487	5.8
14 Gibson Atherton (D)	14,350	49.2
Isaac Morton (R)	12,063	41.7
Thomas J. McGinnis (G)	2,491	8.6
15 George W. Geddes (D)	15,597	54.3
Goshorn A. Jones (R)	11,029	38.4

Candidates	Votes	%
George W. Pepper (G)	1,849	6.4
16 William McKinley Jr. (R)	15,489	49.8
Aquila Wiley (D)	14,255	45.8
17 James Monroe (R)	17,213	54.2
Lewis Miller (D & G)	14,575	45.9
18 Jonathan T. Updegraff (R)	15,320	50.6
Daniel T. Lawson (D)	12,593	41.6
George Smith (G)	2,231	7.4
19 James A. Garfield (R)	17,166	61.4
John C. Hubbard (D)	7,553	27.0
Grandison. N. Tuttle (G)	3,148	11.3
20 Amos Townsend (R)	13,081	47.8
Joseph M. Poe (D)	7,271	26.6
Gilbert O. Shove (P)	4,934	18.0
William H. Doan (G)	2,085	7.6

OREGON

	Votes	%
AL John Whiteaker (D)	16,744	49.9
H. K. Hines (R)	15,593	46.5

PENNSYLVANIA

	Votes	%
1 Henry H. Bingham (R)	13,751	56.5
William McCandless (D)	6,324	26.0
Maxwell Stevenson (G)	4,267	17.5
2 Charles O'Neill (R)	14,063	59.5
Charles H. Gibson (D)	9,177	38.8
3 Samuel J. Randall (D)	10,717	57.4
John Shedden (RG)	7,970	42.7
4 William D. Kelley (RG)	17,786	60.3
Charles H. Barnes (D)	11,697	39.7
5 Alfred C. Harmer (R)	16,784	55.8
David E. Dallam (D)	11,745	39.1
U. S. Stephens (G)	1,539	5.1
6 William Ward (R)	13,041	57.8
Bethel M. Custer (D)	8,285	36.7
7 William Godshalk (R)	15,092	51.3
Oliver P. James (D)	13,754	46.8
8 Hiester Clymer (D)	12,419	58.6
H. Maltzberger (R)	6,428	30.4
Daniel B. Yoder (G)	2,330	11.0
9 A. Herr Smith (R)	15,486	62.8
W. R. Wilson (D)	8,605	34.9
10 Reuben K. Bachman (D)	16,678	58.7
A. Brower Longaker (G)	7,329	25.8
George W. Whittaker (R)	4,429	15.6
11 Robert Klotz (D)	8,211	31.8
Edwin Albright (R)	8,116	31.4
E. E. Orvis (G)	5,193	20.1
C. B. Brockway (D)	4,339	16.8
12 Hendrick B. Wright (D & G)	11,817	55.9
Henry Roberts (R)	9,124	43.2
13 John W. Ryon (D)	7,320	36.3
Charles N. Brumm (G)	7,128	35.4
Howell Fisher (R)	5,698	28.3
14 John W. Killinger (R)	13,660	46.1
M. J. D. Withington (D)	12,033	40.6
D. S. Earley (G)	3,962	13.4
15 Edward Overton Jr (R)	13,160	49.2
D. C. Dewitt (D)	9,320	34.9
William H. Dimmick (D)	3,783	14.1
16 John I. Mitchell (R)	11,133	41.0
J. F. Davis (G)	10,163	37.4
R. B. Smith (D)	5,849	21.6
17 Alexander H. Coffroth (D)	12,472	46.3
Jacob M. Campbell (R)	12,167	45.2
Samuel Adams (G)	2,275	8.5
18 Horatio G. Fisher (R)	14,878	49.1
William S. Stenger (D)	14,671	48.4
19 Frank E. Beltzhoover (D)	17,819	57.5
Thomas E. Cochran (R)	12,321	39.8
20 Seth H. Yocum (G & R)	13,454	50.1
Andrew G. Curtin (D)	13,381	49.9
21 Morgan R. Wise (D)	12,880	49.5
S. M. Bailey (R)	9,330	35.8
A. L. McFarlane (G)	3,819	14.7
22 Russell Errett (R)	9,099	38.0
David Kirk (G)	7,447	31.1
James K. P. Duff (D)	7,260	30.4

PENNSYLVANIA

	Candidates	Votes	%
23	Thomas M. Bayne (R)	9,104	51.2
	C. F. Mckenna (D)	5,621	31.6
	Samuel Watson (G)	2,781	15.6
24	William S. Shallenberger (R)	11,261	48.6
	R. W. Clendennin (D)	10,025	43.2
		1,911	8.2
25	Harry White (R)	10,715	37.6
	James M. Guffey (D)	8,931	31.3
	James Mosgrove (G)	8,874	31.1
26	Samuel B. Dick (R)	14,010	41.7
	William C. Plummer (G)	12,716	37.8
	John T. Bard (D)	6,558	19.5
27	James H. Osmer (R)	11,205	44.5
	George A. Allen (D)	8,551	34.0
	Cyrus C. Camp (G)	5,127	20.4

RHODE ISLAND

	Candidates	Votes	%
1	Nelson W. Aldrich (R)	5,969	74.5
	Thomas Davis (D)	1,332	16.6
	Lycurgus Sayles (G)	625	7.8
2	Latimer W. Ballou (R)	5,431	53.3
	Jerothmul B. Barnaby (D)	4,438	43.6

SOUTH CAROLINA

	Candidates	Votes	%
1	John S. Richardson (D)	22,707	61.7
	J. H. Rainey (R)	14,096	38.3
2	Michael P. O'Connor (D)	20,568	60.9
	E. W. M. Mackey (R)	13,182	39.1
3	D. Wyatt Aiken (D)	24,533	79.1
	J. F. Ensor (R)	6,348	20.5
4	John H. Evins (D)	22,702	96.8
5	George D. Tillman (D)	26,409	71.2
	Robert Smalls (R)	10,664	28.8

TENNESSEE

	Candidates	Votes	%
1	Robert L. Taylor (D)	11,698	51.6
	Pettibone (R)	10,960	48.4
2	Leonidas C. Houk (R)	9,548	57.1
	Watkins (ID)	7,167	42.9
3	George G. Dibrell (D)	9,399	69.1
	Wheeler (R)	4,205	30.9
4	Benton McMillin (D)	7,966	65.0
	Golliday (ID)	4,291	35.0
5	John M. Bright (D)	8,385	65.4
	Lillard (D)	2,594	20.2

Candidates	Votes	%
Warder (R)	965	7.5
Isbell (G)	876	6.8
6 John F. House (D)	9,614	57.2
Akers (G)	4,666	27.8
Prosser (R)	2,403	14.3
7 Washington C. Whitthorne (D)	6,581	43.2
Moore (D)	5,533	36.3
Hughes (G)	3,133	20.6
8 John D. C. Atkins (D)	8,361	61.4
Warren (G)	5,257	38.6
9 Charles B. Simonton (D)	7,998	63.7
Black (G)	4,564	36.3
10 H. Casey Young (D)	5,522	54.8
Randolph (R)	3,199	31.7
Keller (G)	1,357	13.5

TEXAS

	Candidates	Votes	%
1	John H. Reagan (D)	18,038	98.7
2	David B. Culberson (D)	19,721	63.1
	O'Neill (G)	9,617	30.8
3	Olin Wellborn (D)	40,845	80.5
	Daggett (R)	9,718	19.2
4	Roger Q. Mills (D)	30,535	75.7
	Smith (R)	9,039	22.4
5	George W. Jones (G & D)	21,095	51.6
	Hancock (D)	19,721	48.2
6	Gustave Schleicher (D)	19,699*	56.7
	Ireland (ID)	15,050	43.3

VERMONT

	Candidates	Votes	%
1	Charles H. Joyce (R)	12,599	68.1
	Randall (D)	5,894	31.8
2	James M. Tyler (R)	12,281	71.3
	Dickey (D)	4,890	28.4
3	Bradley Barlow (N)	8,367	60.4
	Grout (R)	4,330	31.3
	Waterman (D)	1,095	7.9

VIRGINIA

	Candidates	Votes	%
1	Richard Lee T. Beale (D)	7,266	48.3
	George C. Round (R)	5,474	36.4
	John Critcher (ID)	2,296	15.3
2	John Goode Jr. (D)	11,547	56.7
	John F. Dezendorf (R)	8,808	43.3
3	Joseph E. Johnston (D)	5,787	58.1
	William W. Newman (G)	4,172	41.9

	Candidates	Votes	%
4	Joseph Jorgensen (R)	12,322	60.7
	William E. Hinton (D)	7,976	39.3
5	George C. Cabell (D)	8,545	66.7
	William A. Witcher (ID)	4,267	33.3
6	John Randolph Tucker (D)	7,893	63.4
	Camm Patteson (ID)	4,520	36.3
7	John T. Harris (D)	7,235	56.4
	John Paul (D)	5,580	43.5
8	Eppa Hunton (D)	5,772	77.9
	John R. Carton (ID)	1,119	15.1
	James Cochran (I)	506	6.8
9	James B. Richmond (D)	5,120	33.7
	Fayette McMullens (ID)	4,827	31.7
	Samuel H. Newberry (ID)	4,640	30.5

WEST VIRGINIA

	Candidates	Votes	%
1	Benjamin Wilson (D)	15,857	49.0
	J. R. Hubbard (R)	12,448	38.4
	James Bassell (N)	4,086	12.6
2	Benjamin F. Martin (D)	15,421	56.6
	F. A. Burr (R)	7,587	27.9
	J. H. Thompson (N)	4,231	15.5
3	John E. Kenna (D)	19,040	54.0
	Henry I. Walker (R)	16,213	46.0

WISCONSIN

	Candidates	Votes	%
1	Charles G. Williams (R)	14,629	59.5
	Parker (D)	9,949	40.5
2	Lucien B. Caswell (R)	12,607	51.5
	Davis (D)	9,502	38.8
	Tenney (G)	2,376	9.7
3	George C. Hazelton (R)	11,695	50.2
	King (D)	11,603	49.8
4	Peter V. Deuster (D)	11,157	47.4
	Frisby (R)	11,022	46.8
	Judd (G)	1,351	5.7
5	Edward S. Bragg (D)	12,392	46.2
	Smith (R)	10,285	38.3
	Giddings (G)	4,157	15.5
6	Gabriel Bouck (D)	14,349	45.9
	Jones (R)	11,748	37.6
	Steele (G)	5,144	16.5
7	Herman L. Humphrey (R)	15,256	54.2
	Parker (D)	12,880	45.8
8	Thaddeus C. Pound (R)	12,795	52.8
	Barrows (D)	11,421	47.2

1879 House Elections

CALIFORNIA

Special Elections

	Candidates	Votes	%
1	Horace Davis (R)	20,074	48.4
	Clitus Barbour (WMP/L)	18,448	44.5
	C. R. Sumner (D)	2,940	7.1
2	Horace F. Page (R)	19,386	51.9
	T. J. Clunie (D)	12,847	34.4

		Votes	%
	H. P. Williams (WMP/L)	5,139	13.8
3	Campbell P. Berry (D-WM)	20,019	50.1
	Joseph McKennon (R)	19,800	49.6
4	Romualdo Pacheco (R)	15,391	40.5
	Wallace Leach (D)	12,109	31.8
	J. J. Ayres (WMP/L)	10,527	27.7

NEW YORK

Special Election

	Candidates	Votes	%
12	Waldo Hutchins (D)	13,543	56.9
	N. Smith (R)	10,146	42.7

1880 House Elections

ALABAMA

Candidates	Votes	%
1 Thomas H. Herndon (D)	10,027	53.8
J. Gillett (R)	5,595	30.0
F. H. Threatt (R)	2,303	12.4
2 Hilary A. Herbert (D)	13,271	59.8
Strobach (R)	8,884	40.0
3 William C. Oates (D)	10,614	64.3
A. A. Mabson (R)	5,836	35.3
4 Charles M. Shelley (D)	9,301‡	52.7
James Q. Smith (R)	6,650	37.7
Stevens (R)	1,693	9.6
5 Thomas Williams (D)	11,219	100.0
6 Goldsmith W. Hewitt (D)	10,043	100.0
7 William H. Forney (D)	13,636	71.4
Arthur Bingham (R)	5,468	28.6
8 Joseph Wheeler (D)	12,808‡	50.1
William M. Lowe (GD)	12,765	49.9

Special Election

6 Newton N. Clements	9,973	100.0

ARKANSAS

1 Poindexter Dunn (D)	15,753	60.2
Johnson (R)	10,407	39.8
2 James K. Jones (D)	16,517	47.3
Williams (R)	14,513	41.5
Garland (G)	3,920	11.2
3 Jordan E. Cravens (D)	15,781	57.7
Boles (R)	11,552	42.3
4 Thomas M. Gunter (D)	7,387	42.8
Peel (ID)	5,731	33.2
Murphy (R)	4,125	23.9

CALIFORNIA

1 William S. Rosecrans (D-WM)	21,005	51.0
Horace Davis (R)	19,496	47.3
2 Horace F. Page (R)	22,038	53.5
J. R. Glasscock (D-WM)	18,859	45.8
3 Campbell P. Berry (D)	21,743	51.2
George A. Knight (R)	20,494	48.2
4 Romualdo Pacheco (R)	17,768	45.8
W. A. Leach (D)	17,577	45.3
J. F. Godfrey	3,461	8.9

COLORADO

AL James B. Belford (R)	27,069	50.8
Robert S. Morrison (D)	24,476	46.0

CONNECTICUT

1 John R. Buck (R)	17,048	52.6
Beach (D)	15,114	46.7
2 James Phelps (D)	21,632	51.7
Wallace (R)	20,068	48.0
3 John T. Wait (R)	12,099	56.1
Sawyer (D)	9,125	42.3
4 Frederick Miles (R)	18,168	50.4
Peet (D)	17,634	48.9

DELAWARE

AL Edward L. Martin (D)	14,966	51.1
Houston (R)	14,336	48.9

FLORIDA

1 Robert H. M. Davidson (D)	14,971	57.5
Witherspoon (R)	11,082	42.5

Candidates	Votes	%
2 Jesse J. Finley (D)	13,105‡	52.3
Horatio Bisbee Jr. (R)	11,953	47.7

GEORGIA

1 George R. Black (D)	11,712	58.6
Collins (R)	8,265	41.4
2 Henry G. Turner (D)	11,496	64.2
Brimberry (R)	6,417	35.8
3 Philip Cook (D)	7,122	68.7
Parker (R)	3,245	31.3
4 Hugh Buchanan (D)	9,998	58.1
Pou (ID)	7,224	42.0
5 Nathaniel J. Hammond (D)	11,947	62.6
Clark (R)	7,133	37.4
6 James H. Blount (D)	8,373	100.0
7 Judson C. Clements (D)	11,572	51.9
Felton (ID)	10,727	48.1
8 Alexander H. Stephens (D)	11,341	99.9
9 Emory Speer (ID)	12,653	59.6
Bell (D)	8,590	40.4

ILLINOIS

1 William Aldrich (R)	22,307	53.8
John Mattocks (D)	18,024	43.5
2 George R. Davis (R)	20,603	54.8
V. F. Farnsworth (D)	16,014	42.6
3 Charles B. Farwell (R)	16,627	57.3
Perry H. Smith Jr (D)	11,903	41.0
4 John C. Sherwin (R)	20,381	68.9
Norman C. Warner (D)	8,055	27.2
5 Robert M. A. Hawk (R)	17,061	59.5
Larmon G. Johnson (D)	7,468	26.0
John M. King (D)	4,160	14.5
6 Thomas J. Henderson (R)	16,650	57.6
Bernard N. Trusdell (D)	9,631	33.3
P. L. McKinney (G)	2,637	9.1
7 William Cullen (R)	16,628	53.8
Daniel Evans (D)	12,064	39.0
Royal E. Barber (G)	2,204	7.1
8 Lewis E. Payson (R)	16,704	54.4
Robert R. Wallace (D)	13,972	45.5
9 John H. Lewis (R)	14,658	46.5
John S. Lee (D)	14,294	45.4
William H. Reynolds (G)	2,548	8.1
10 Benjamin F. Marsh (R)	14,798	50.4
Robert Holloway (D)	13,877	47.2
11 James W. Singleton (D)	17,842	55.6
William H. Edgar (R)	12,490	38.9
A. B. Allen (G)	1,765	5.5
12 William M. Springer (D)	17,376	51.6
Isaac L. Morrison (R)	14,761	43.8
13 Dietrich Smith (R)	16,433	50.5
Adlai E. Stevenson (D)	16,115	49.5
14 Joseph G. Cannon (R)	19,710	52.6
James R. Scott (D)	17,734	47.4
15 Samuel W. Moulton (D)	19,364	53.5
Albert P. Forsythe (R)	16,810	46.5
16 William A. J. Sparks (D)	15,392	50.2
P. E. Heasmer (R)	13,921	45.4
17 William H. Morrison (D)	16,950	51.5
John B. Hay (R)	15,986	48.5
18 John R. Thomas (R)	16,873	51.1
William Hartzell (D)	15,146	45.9
19 Richard W. Townsend (D)	18,021	52.9
Charles W. Pavey (R)	14,561	42.8

INDIANA

1 William Heilman (R)	17,719	49.4
John Kleiner (D)	17,420	48.6
2 Thomas R. Cobb (D)	18,443	54.3
Braden (R)	14,676	43.2

Candidates	Votes	%
3 Strother M. Stockslager (D)	18,800	55.2
Charles (R)	14,493	42.6
4 William S. Holman (D)	17,388	52.0
J. O. Cravens (R)	15,641	46.7
5 Courtland C. Matson (D)	17,411	49.5
Treat (R)	16,496	46.9
6 Thomas M. Browne (R)	22,136	62.2
Miller (D)	12,676	35.6
7 Stanton J. Peelle (R)	17,610	48.3
Byfield (D)	16,736	45.9
Delamatyr (NG)	2,135	5.9
8 Robert B. F. Peirce (R)	19,291	49.0
Hanna (D)	16,995	43.1
Copner (NG)	3,120	7.9
9 Godlove S. Orth (R)	18,287	49.6
William Ralph Myers (D)	17,475	47.4
10 Mark L. DeMotte (R)	18,024	51.5
Skinner (D)	17,006	48.5
11 George Washington Steele (R)	20,246	48.1
Slack (D)	19,713	46.8
Studebaker (NG)	2,168	5.2
12 Walpole G. Colerick (D)	17,800	51.1
Taylor (R)	17,030	48.9
13 William Henry Calkins (R)	17,981	49.2
McDonald (D)	16,817	46.0

IOWA

1 Moses A. McCoid (R)	17,117	53.9
W. B. Culbertson (D)	12,119	38.2
D. P. Stubbs (G)	2,497	7.9
2 Sewall S. Farwell (R)	17,465	54.9
Roderick Rose (D)	13,100	41.2
3 Thomas Updegraff (R)	17,359	51.8
William G. Stewart (D)	13,969	41.7
M. H. Moore (G)	2,193	6.5
4 Nathaniel C. Deering (R)	21,940	65.4
Joseph S. Root (D)	8,731	26.0
M. B. Doolittle (G)	2,191	6.5
5 William G. Thompson (R)	20,016	59.8
R. E. Austin (D)	11,315	33.8
A. F. Palmer (G)	2,114	6.3
6 Marsena E. Cutts (R)	18,017‡	50.1
John Calhoun Cook (D & G)	17,911	49.8
7 John A. Kasson (R)	19,932	53.8
Edward Hooker Gillette (D & G)	16,776	45.3
8 William P. Hepburn (R)	24,358	56.3
Robert Percival (D)	12,984	30.0
H. C. Ayres (G)	5,920	13.7
9 Cyrus Clay Carpenter (R)	25,533	63.4
P. M. Guthrie (D)	12,267	30.5
Daniel Campbell (G)	2,363	5.9

KANSAS

1 John A. Anderson (R)	48,599	61.8
C. C. Burnes (D)	22,727	28.9
John Davis (G)	7,318	9.3
2 Dudley C. Haskell (R)	30,758	56.4
Louis F. Green (D)	23,737	43.5
3 Thomas Ryan (R)	41,094	60.9
J. Wade McDonald (D)	16,976	25.2
D. P. Mitchell (G LAB)	9,396	13.9

KENTUCKY

1 Oscar Turner (D)	11,448	53.6
R. B. Ratliff (R)	6,318	29.6
W. W. Tice (D)	3,572	16.7
2 James A. McKenzie (D)	14,694	52.0
John Feland (R)	8,354	29.5
Charles W. Cook (G)	5,233	18.5

KENTUCKY

Candidates	Votes	%
3 John W. Caldwell (D)	13,089	50.7
M. T. Flippin (R)	10,967	42.6
George Wright (G)	1,736	6.7
4 J. Proctor Knott (D)	13,778	59.2
William T. Thurmond (R)	6,603	28.4
L. E. Green (G)	2,820	12.1
5 Albert S. Willis (D)	11,934	48.5
Thomas E. Burns (R)	8,445	34.3
Thomas Hays (D)	3,794	15.4
6 John G. Carlisle (D)	17,291	63.7
Oliver H. Root (R)	9,862	36.3
7 Joseph C. S. Blackburn (D)	16,799	70.6
Lycander Hord (R)	5,692	23.9
W. C. Goodloe (R)	1,207	5.1
8 Philip B. Thompson Jr. (D)	14,249	53.0
Speed S. Fry (R)	12,004	44.6
9 John D. White (R)	15,317	53.5
Thomas Turner (D)	13,326	46.5
10 Elijah C. Phister (D)	13,944	51.8
George M. Thomas (R)	12,955	48.1

LOUISIANA

	Votes	%
1 Randall L. Gibson (D)	10,526	66.6
A. J. Ker (R)	5,291	33.5
2 E. John Ellis (D)	10,032	60.0
Michael Hahn (R)	6,701	40.1
3 Chester B. Darrall (R)	13,371	63.2
J. S. Billiu (D)	7,794	36.8
4 Newton C. Blanchard (D)	12,446	88.4
A. C. Wells (R)	1,638	11.6
5 J. Floyd King (D)	15,305	82.2
R. H. Lanier (R)	3,318	17.8
6 Edward W. Robertson (D)	9,941	64.9
Alexander Smith (R)	5,372	35.1

MAINE

	Votes	%
1 Thomas B. Reed (R)	16,920	49.8
Samuel J. Anderson (D & G)	16,803	49.4
2 William P. Frye (R)	14,417	53.6
Frank M. Fogg (D & G)	12,343	45.9
3 Stephen D. Lindsey (R)	15,131	50.5
William Philbrick (D & G)	14,824	49.5
4 George W. Ladd (D & G)	14,047	51.5
Charles A. Boutelle (R)	13,194	48.4
5 Thompson H. Murch (D & G)	14,942	51.6
Seth L. Milliken (R)	13,977	48.3

MARYLAND

	Votes	%
1 George W. Covington (D)	16,025	54.2
Smith (D)	13,532	45.8
2 J. Fred. C. Talbott (D)	14,988	52.7
Webster (R)	13,472	47.3
3 Fetter S. Hoblitzell (D)	13,629	57.7
Horner (R)	9,975	42.3
4 Robert M. McLane (D)	15,702	53.7
Maund (R)	13,540	46.3
5 Andrew G. Chapman (D)	14,448	53.3
Wilmer (R)	12,665	46.7
6 Milton G. Urner (R)	17,129	50.5
Schley (D)	16,339	48.2

MASSACHUSETTS

	Votes	%
1 William W. Crapo (R)	16,384	69.7
Davis (D)	6,669	28.4
2 Benjamin W. Harris (R)	17,047	62.8
Dean (D)	9,718	35.8
3 Ambrose A. Ranney (R)	13,132	51.9
Dearborn (D)	12,073	47.7
4 Leopold Morse (D)	10,616	49.4
Hayes (R)	10,501	48.9
5 Selwyn Z. Bowman (R)	16,688	55.9
Beebe (D)	11,729	39.3

Candidates	Votes	%
6 Eben F. Stone (R)	14,124	54.2
Boynton (D)	11,900	45.7
7 William A. Russell (R)	14,982	58.8
Aldrich (D)	10,027	39.4
8 John W. Candler (R)	16,644	58.2
Russell (D)	11,542	40.3
9 William W. Rice (R)	14,935	61.5
McCafferty (D)	8,925	36.7
10 Amasa Norcross (R)	15,608	62.8
Ivord (D)	8,627	34.7
11 George D. Robinson (R)	14,235	58.3
Woodworth (D)	10,007	41.0

MICHIGAN

	Votes	%
1 Henry W. Lord (R)	15,962	49.9
Maybury (D)	15,388	48.1
2 Edwin Willits (R)	18,945	50.7
Waldby (D)	16,596	44.4
3 Edward S. Lacey (R)	21,267	52.9
Pringle (D)	9,739	24.2
Hodge (G)	8,959	22.3
4 Julius C. Burrows (R)	19,096	53.4
Powers (D)	12,424	34.8
Yaple (NG)	4,193	11.7
5 George W. Webber (R)	22,824	52.1
Randall (D)	11,435	26.1
Blanchard (G)	9,506	21.7
6 Oliver L. Spaulding (R)	23,551	49.5
Winans (D)	18,235	38.3
Begole (G)	5,690	12.0
7 Omar D. Conger (R)	17,490*	53.5
Black (D)	13,806	42.2
8 Roswell G. Horr (R)	21,224	48.3
Tarsney (D)	18,857	42.9
Smith (G)	3,829	8.7
9 Jay A. Hubbell (R)	23,437	60.1
Pratt (D)	14,642	37.5

MINNESOTA

	Votes	%
1 Mark H. Dunnell (R)	22,392	51.1
Wells (D)	13,768	31.4
Ward (IR)	7,656	17.5
2 Horace B. Strait (R)	24,508	56.7
Poehler (D)	18,707	43.3
3 William D. Washburn (R)	36,428	60.5
Sibley (D)	23,804	39.5

MISSISSIPPI

	Votes	%
1 Henry L. Muldrow (D)	14,456	74.7
Morphis (R)	3,828	19.8
Davidson (G)	1,058	5.5
2 Vannoy H. Manning (D)	15,255	52.9
George M. Buchanan (R)	9,996	34.7
Harris (G)	3,585	12.4
3 Hernando D. Money (D)	11,722	80.7
Gunn (G)	2,790	19.2
4 Otho R. Singleton (D)	13,749	76.7
Drennan (D)	4,177	23.3
5 Charles E. Hooker (D)	11,771	63.5
Deason (IR)	5,618	30.3
6 James R. Chalmers (D)	9,172‡	63.0
John R. Lynch (R)	5,393	37.0

MISSOURI

	Votes	%
1 Martin L. Clardy (D)	11,681	51.6
Fletcher (D)	10,892	48.2
2 Thomas Allen (D)	12,458	55.4
Rosenblatt (R)	10,022	44.6
3 Richard G. Frost (D)	9,487‡	49.8
Gustavus Sessinghaus (R)	9,290	48.8
4 Lowndes H. Davis (D)	19,949	94.1
Simpson (GD)	1,251	5.9
5 Richard P. Bland (D)	12,977	54.5
Palmer (GD)	10,799	45.4

Candidates	Votes	%
6 Ira S. Hazeltine (G & R)	22,787	50.1
Waddill (D)	22,680	49.8
7 Theron M. Rice (G & R)	19,744	50.8
Philips (D)	19,146	49.2
8 Robert T. Van Horn (R)	8,050	33.2
Allen (D)	7,656	31.6
Crisp (D)	7,459	30.8
9 Nicholas Ford (G & R)	20,770	50.0
Craig (D)	20,768	50.0
10 Joseph H. Burrows (G & R)	17,284	50.1
Mansur (D)	17,219	49.9
11 John B. Clark Jr. (D)	17,021	69.7
Heberling (GD)	7,370	30.2
12 William H. Hatch (D)	17,401	53.3
London (G & R)	15,236	46.7
13 Aylett H. Buckner (D)	17,233	69.3
Haley (GD)	7,394	29.7

NEBRASKA

	Votes	%
AL Edward K. Valentine (R)	52,648	62.5
James E. North (D)	23,634	28.1

NEVADA

	Votes	%
AL George W. Cassidy (D)	9,815	53.4
Daggett (R)	8,578	46.6

NEW HAMPSHIRE

	Votes	%
1 Joshua G. Hall (R)	16,310	51.5
Sanborn (D)	15,047	47.5
2 James F. Briggs (R)	14,480	52.4
Sulloway (R)	13,000	47.1
3 Evarts W. Farr (R)	13,861*	51.3
Bingham (D)	12,896	47.7

NEW JERSEY

	Votes	%
1 George M. Robeson (R)	19,807	53.6
Carter (D)	16,350	44.2
2 J. Hart Brewer (R)	18,580	52.4
Smith (D)	16,536	46.6
3 Miles Ross (D)	19,725	53.3
Robbins (R)	16,953	45.8
4 Henry S. Harris (D)	17,043	56.1
Kilpatrick (R)	12,870	42.4
5 John Hill (R)	16,766	52.0
Cutler (D)	15,165	47.0
6 Phineas Jones (R)	20,424	52.5
Balbach Jr (D)	17,888	46.0
7 Augustus A. Hardenbergh (D)	19,462	56.7
Brigham (R)	14,714	42.9

NEW YORK

	Votes	%
1 Perry Belmont (D)	20,805	53.1
J. A. King (R)	18,163	46.3
2 William E. Robinson (D)	20,122	60.7
Daniel O'Reilly (R)	12,166	36.7
3 J. Hyatt Smith (D & G)	22,085	51.3
S. B. Chittenden (R)	20,626	48.0
4 Archibald M. Bliss (D)	20,030	56.9
D. W. Talmage (R)	14,614	41.5
5 Benjamin Wood (D)	11,411	47.6
N. Muller (ID)	9,750	40.6
C. L. Brockmeier (R)	2,714	11.3
6 Samuel S. Cox (D)	17,025	69.7
Victor Heimberger (R)	7,162	29.3
7 Philip Henry Dugro (D)	11,723	49.5
W. W. Astor (R)	11,550	48.8
8 Anson G. McCook (R)	17,392	57.9
John G. Davis (D)	12,468	41.5
9 Fernando Wood (D)	10,842*	38.0
J. L. N. Hunt (R)	9,313	32.6
John Hardy	8,251	28.9

NEW YORK

Candidates	Votes	%
10 Abram S. Hewitt (D)	19,961	65.3
James Talcott (R)	10,098	33.1
11 Levi P. Morton (R)	18,232	54.7
James W. Gerard (D)	14,898	44.7
12 Waldo Hutchins (D)	15,852	51.6
Alex Taylor Jr. (R)	14,803	48.2
13 John H. Ketcham (R)	20,355	56.8
Edward L. Gaul (D)	15,312	42.7
14 Lewis Beach (D)	16,664	49.8
Charles T. Pierson (R)	16,134	48.2
15 Thomas Cornell (R)	18,845	50.7
John S. Pindar (D)	17,991	48.4
16 Michael N. Nolan (D)	19,176	52.7
S. O. Vanderpool (R)	16,974	46.7
17 Walter A. Wood (R)	21,902	80.8
R. H. Ferguson (D)	5,163	19.1
18 John Hammond (R)	14,281	58.6
T. H. Walker (D)	9,360	38.4
19 Abraham X. Parker (R)	17,569	66.7
A. Andrus (D)	8,385	31.8
20 George West (R)	21,693	56.2
N. H. Decker (D)	16,490	42.8
21 Ferris Jacobs Jr. (R)	19,078	51.7
F. R. Gilbert (D)	16,496	44.7
22 Warner Miller (R)	19,792	55.3
Dennis O'Brien (D)	15,906	44.4
23 Cyrus D. Prescott (R)	14,499	52.8
R. E. Sutton (D)	12,532	45.6
24 Joseph Mason (R)	17,101	57.9
Benjamin F. Lewis (D)	11,510	39.0
25 Frank Hiscock (R)	19,828	57.4
William C. Ruger (D)	14,634	42.4
26 John H. Camp (R)	20,259	56.4
P. H. Van Auken (D)	14,555	40.5
27 Elbridge G. Lapham (R)	15,673	55.2
C. W. Bennett (D)	12,263	43.2
28 Jeremiah W. Dwight (R)	19,510	54.7
F. Davis Jr. (D)	15,082	42.3
29 David P. Richardson (R)	21,211	52.4
T. K. Beecher (GD)	19,288	47.6
30 John Van Voorhis (R)	21,481	55.4
A. S. Warner (D)	16,701	43.1
31 Richard Crowley (R)	15,759	54.7
R. S. Stevens (D)	12,871	44.6
32 Jonathan Scoville (D)	22,702	50.0
M. P. Bush (R)	22,329	49.2
33 Henry Van Aernam (R)	17,429	58.5
Van Campen (D)	10,584	35.5

NORTH CAROLINA

Candidates	Votes	%
1 Louis C. Latham (D)	14,796	50.9
Cyrus W. Grandy (R)	14,290	49.1
2 Orlando Hubbs (R)	19,259	57.2
William H. Kitchin (D)	14,305	42.5
3 John W. Shackelford (D)	16,356	51.1
William P. Canaday (R)	15,017	46.9
4 William R. Cox (D)	17,557	52.0
Moses A. Bledsoe (R)	16,241	48.1
5 Alfred M. Scales (D)	13,634	52.8
Thomas B. Keogh (R)	11,623	45.0
6 Clement Dowd (D)	16,401	57.0
William R. Myers (R)	12,366	43.0
7 Robert F. Armfield (D)	13,331	53.9
David M. Furches (R)	11,383	46.1
8 Robert B. Vance (D)	14,099	65.0
Natt Atkinson (I)	6,244	28.8
Samuel L. Love (I)	1,336	6.2

OHIO

Candidates	Votes	%
1 Benjamin Butterworth (R)	16,455	52.0
Samuel F. Hunt (D)	15,157	47.9
2 Thomas L. Young (R)	17,385	51.5
Henry B. Banning (D)	16,381	48.5
3 Henry L. Morey (R)	17,863	49.7
Durbin Ward (D)	17,835	49.6

Candidates	Votes	%
4 Emanuel Schultz (R)	21,572	50.0
John A. McMahon (D)	21,244	49.3
5 Benjamin Le Fevre (D)	23,598	60.1
W. K. Boone (R)	15,488	39.5
6 James M. Ritchie (R)	19,773	49.4
Frank H. Hurd (D)	19,097	47.7
7 John P. Leedom (D)	17,365	52.6
Alphonso Hart (R)	15,663	47.4
8 J. Warren Keifer (R)	21,182	57.3
Frank Chance (D)	15,264	41.3
9 James S. Robinson (R)	18,146	51.0
Caleb H. Norris (D)	17,007	47.8
10 John B. Rice (D)	18,394	50.9
Morgan D. Shaffer (D)	17,026	47.1
11 Henry S. Neal (R)	17,218	52.9
William A. Hutchins (D)	15,080	46.3
12 George L. Converse (D)	21,673	54.4
John Groce (D)	17,484	43.9
13 Gibson Atherton (D)	19,038	53.0
Appleton B. Clarke (R)	16,565	46.1
14 George W. Geddes (D)	18,520	59.3
S. Ellis Fink (R)	12,653	40.5
15 Rufus R. Dawes (R)	16,283	50.1
A. J. Warner (D)	15,781	48.5
16 Jonathan T. Updegraff (R)	17,998	54.2
James F. Charlesworth (D)	15,150	45.7
17 William McKinley Jr. (R)	20,221	53.5
Leroy D. Thoman (D)	16,650	44.1
18 Addison S. McClure (R)	18,570	57.0
David L. Wadsworth (D)	13,474	41.4
19 Ezra B. Taylor (R)	22,794	67.3
Charles D. Adams (D)	10,116	29.9
20 Amos Townsend (R)	20,333	56.0
John C. Hutchins (D)	15,106	41.6

OREGON

Candidates	Votes	%
AL Melvin C. George (R)	19,578	51.4
John Whiteaker (D)	18,181	47.8

PENNSYLVANIA

Candidates	Votes	%
1 Henry H. Bingham (R)	18,914	57.2
George R. Snowden (D)	14,178	42.8
2 Charles O'Neill (R)	18,924	60.9
A. S. Hartranft (D)	12,122	39.0
3 Samuel J. Randall (D)	13,639	57.8
Benjamin L. Berry (R)	9,912	42.0
4 William D. Kelley (R)	25,968	61.2
George Bull (D)	16,487	38.8
5 Alfred C. Harmer (R)	23,468	57.2
John K. Folwell (D)	17,332	42.3
6 William Ward (R)	18,368	60.8
R. J. Monaghan (D)	11,847	39.2
7 William Godshalk (R)	17,944	52.6
John Slingluff (D)	16,080	47.1
8 Daniel Ermentrout (D)	16,049	63.1
J. Howard Jacobs (R)	9,152	36.0
9 A. Herr Smith (R)	19,466	64.3
J. L. Steinmetz (D)	10,655	35.2
10 William Mutchler (D)	21,464	61.3
Hiram H. Fisher (R)	13,326	38.1
11 Robert Klotz (D)	19,812	62.3
W. J. Scott (R)	11,465	36.1
12 Joseph A. Scranton (R)	13,455	47.1
D. W. Connelly (D)	10,948	38.3
Hendk B. Wright (NG)	4,174	14.6
13 Charles N. Brumm (G & R)	12,038	52.2
John W. Ryon (D)	11,007	47.8
14 Samuel F. Barr (R)	18,320	52.7
Grant Weidman (D)	15,771	45.4
15 Cornelius C. Jadwin (R)	18,223	55.2
Robert H. Packer (D)	13,602	41.2
16 Robert J. C. Walker (R)	17,850	50.8
David Kirk (D & G)	17,304	49.2
17 Jacob M. Campbell (R)	17,300	51.6
A. H. Coffroth (D)	15,864	47.3
18 Horatio G. Fisher (R)	16,847	51.1
R. Milton Speer (D)	16,130	48.9

Candidates	Votes	%
19 Frank E. Beltzhoover (D)	20,858	57.5
Charles J. Little (R)	15,351	42.3
20 Andrew G. Curtin (D)	17,461	54.7
Thomas H. Murray (R)	14,472	45.3
21 Morgan C. Wise (D)	18,486	53.7
James E. Sayers (R)	11,879	34.5
George W. K. Minor (NG)	4,083	11.9
22 Russell Errett (R)	18,241	53.3
James H. Hopkins (D)	14,084	41.1
M. J. Sullivan (G)	1,923	5.6
23 Thomas M. Bayne (R)	15,641	63.2
George T. Miller (D)	8,278	33.5
24 William S. Shallenberger (R)	15,567	56.6
J. M. Clark (D)	10,986	39.9
25 James Mosgrove (D & G)	16,044	51.2
Harry White (R)	15,287	48.8
26 Samuel H. Miller (R)	17,630	47.9
James H. Caldwell (D)	14,976	40.7
W. C. Plummer (NG)	3,895	10.6
27 Lewis F. Watson (R)	15,740	52.0
Alf Short (D & G)	14,438	47.7

RHODE ISLAND

Candidates	Votes	%
1 Nelson W. Aldrich (R)	9,641	67.6
Isaac Lawrence (D)	4,446	31.2
2 Jonathan Chace (R)	8,515	58.0
Franklin Treat (D)	6,031	41.1

SOUTH CAROLINA

Candidates	Votes	%
1 John S. Richardson (D)	20,142	63.3
Samuel J. Lee (R)	11,674	36.7
2 Michael P. O'Connor (D)	17,569‡	58.8
Edmund W. M. Mackey (R)	12,297	41.2
3 D. Wyatt Aiken (D)	27,863	74.1
C. J. Stollbrand (R)	9,758	25.9
4 John H. Evins (D)	27,985	69.7
A. Blythe (R)	11,780	29.3
5 George D. Tillman (D)	23,325‡	60.4
Robert Smalls (R)	15,287	39.6

TENNESSEE

Candidates	Votes	%
1 Augustus H. Pettibone (R)	15,117	52.5
Taylor (D)	13,693	47.5
2 Leonidas C. Houk (R)	17,479	65.1
Williams (D)	9,380	34.9
3 George G. Dibrell (D)	12,806	53.6
Case (R)	9,918	41.5
4 Benton McMillin (D)	12,405	65.0
Sanders (R)	6,694	35.1
5 Richard Warner (LOWTAX D)	7,777	36.3
Bright (D)	6,307	29.4
Holman (R)	5,077	23.7
Tillman (G)	2,263	10.6
6 John F. House (D)	15,631	60.6
McClain (R)	9,389	36.4
7 Washington C. Whitthorne (D)	11,118	58.0
Hughes (R)	8,056	42.0
8 John D. C. Atkins (D)	10,999	46.6
Hawkins (R)	9,876	41.9
Travis (D)	2,723	11.5
9 Charles B. Simonton (D)	12,150	52.8
Shackleford (R)	10,865	47.2
10 William R. Moore (R)	11,844	50.7
Young (D)	10,998	47.1

TEXAS

Candidates	Votes	%
1 John H. Reagan (D)	21,227	77.7
S. R. Withers (R)	6,095	22.3
2 David B. Culberson (D)	26,624	68.6
H. F. O'Neal (G)	12,194	31.4
3 Olin Wellborn (D)	48,005	78.7
J. C. Kirby (G)	13,014	21.3

TEXAS

Candidates	Votes	%
4 Roger Q. Mills (D)	30,087	62.6
J. T. Brady (G)	17,977	37.4
5 George W. Jones (G)	22,941	50.3
Seth Shepard (D)	22,708	49.7
6 Christopher C. Upson (D)	27,521	97.3

VERMONT

Candidates	Votes	%
1 Charles H. Joyce (R)	15,645	68.6
Randall (D)	6,771	29.7
2 James M. Tyler (R)	15,960	69.0
Campbell (D)	6,698	29.0
3 William W. Grout (R)	12,253	61.9
Curree (D)	6,191	31.3
Tarbell (G)	1,256	6.4

VIRGINIA

Candidates	Votes	%
1 George T. Garrison (D)	11,595	48.2
John W. Woltz (R)	10,250	42.6
John Critcher (READJ)	2,217	9.2
2 John F. Dezendorf (R)	14,775	52.6

Candidates	Votes	%
John Goode (D)	9,709	34.6
B. W. Lacy (READJ)	3,600	12.8
3 George D. Wise (D)	10,931	55.9
John S. Wise (READJ)	8,566	43.8
4 Joseph Jorgensen (R)	13,825	70.1
Samuel F. Coleman (D)	5,771	29.2
5 George C. Cabell (D)	11,778	51.9
John T. Stovall (READJ)	10,919	48.1
6 John Randolph Tucker (D)	13,646	59.5
James A. Frazier (READJ)	9,265	40.4
7 John Paul (READJ)	10,665	49.3
Henry C. Allen (D)	9,938	45.9
8 John S. Barbour (D)	15,546	56.6
Sampson P. Bagley (R)	9,170	33.4
James H. Williams (READJ)	2,732	10.0
9 Abram Fulkerson (READJ)	8,096	40.7
Connally F. Trigg (D)	7,621	38.3
G. G. Goodell (R)	3,660	18.4

WEST VIRGINIA

Candidates	Votes	%
1 Benjamin Wilson (D)	18,460	46.6
John H. Hutchinson (R)	18,350	46.3
James Bassil (G)	2,515	6.3

Candidates	Votes	%
2 John B. Hogue (D)	17,277	50.5
J. T. Hoke (R)	14,565	42.6
D. Farnsworth (G)	2,356	6.9
3 John E. Kenna (D)	21,407	57.0
H. I. Walker (R)	16,097	42.9

WISCONSIN

Candidates	Votes	%
1 Charles G. Williams (R)	19,014	61.0
Babbitt (D)	11,782	37.8
2 Lucien B. Caswell (R)	16,041	52.0
Gregory (D)	14,390	46.6
3 George C. Hazelton (R)	16,236	55.6
Cothren (D)	12,941	44.3
4 Peter V. Deuster (D)	17,574	53.7
Sanger (R)	15,018	45.9
5 Edward S. Bragg (D)	16,984	51.6
Colman (R)	14,753	44.8
6 Richard W. Guenther (R)	20,168	52.5
Bouck (D)	16,807	43.7
7 Herman L. Humphrey (R)	23,179	64.7
Froeman (D)	10,994	30.7
8 Thaddeus C. Pound (R)	19,256	56.8
Silverthorn (D)	14,590	43.1

1881 House Elections

MAINE

Special Election

Candidates	Votes	%
2 Nelson Dingley Jr. (R)	10,961	65.3
Gilbert (G)	5,519	32.9

MICHIGAN

Special Election

	Votes	%
11 John T. Rich (R)	15,279	55.7
Cyrenius P. Black	10,740	39.2

NEW YORK

Special Elections

	Votes	%
9 John Hardy (D)	13,013	62.4
Murphy (R)	7,705	37.0
11 Roswell P. Flower (D)	13,739	56.0
Astor (R)	10,626	43.3
22 Charles R. Skinner (R)	16,222	54.8
Lansing (D)	13,065	44.1
27 James W. Wadsworth (R)	12,086	54.2
Faulkner (D)	9,600	43.0

RHODE ISLAND

Special Election

	Votes	%
1 Henry J. Spooner (R)	3,623	66.4
Henry O. Sisson (D)	1,103	20.2
C. C. Van Zandt (R)	709	13.0

1882 House Elections

ALABAMA

	Candidates	Votes	%
1	Thomas H. Herndon (D)	9,609	57.4
	Smith (R)	7,130	42.6
2	Hilary A. Herbert (D)	12,823	58.4
	Rice (R)	9,121	41.6
3	William C. Oates (D)	11,238	87.9
	Millen (R)	1,549	12.1
4	Charles M. Shelley (D)	7,119‡	60.8
	George H. Craig (R)	4,435	37.9
5	Thomas Williams (D)	9,629	62.0
	McCoy (ID)	5,880	37.9
6	Goldsmith W. Hewitt (D)	6,402	72.7
	Carpenter (G)	2,406	27.3
7	William H. Forney (D)	7,750	80.7
	Bingham (R)	1,859	19.4
8	Luke Pryor (D)	12,155	51.6
	Shelby (ID)	11,418	48.4

ARKANSAS

		Votes	%
1	Poindexter Dunn (D)	12,685	94.4
	J. B. Miles (R)	719	5.4
2	James K. Jones (D)	14,831	55.5
	J. A. Williams (R)	11,525	43.1
3	John H. Rogers (D)	10,522	57.3
	M. W. Benjamin (R)	7,840	42.7
4	Samuel W. Peel (D)	5,668	80.6
	Truman Niman (R)	1,008	14.3
AL	Clifton R. Breckinridge (D)	43,619	66.6
	C. E. Cunningham (G)	21,422	32.7

CALIFORNIA

		Votes	%
1	William S. Rosecrans (D)	22,733	59.4
	Paul Neumann (R)	14,847	38.8
2	James H. Budd (D)	20,229	50.5
	H. F. Page (R)	19,246	48.1
3	Barclay Henley (D)	21,807	51.3
	J. J. DeHaven (R)	19,470	45.8
4	Pleasant B. Tully (D)	23,105	54.3
	George L. Woods (R)	18,387	43.2
AL	John R. Glascock (D)	87,259✔	
	Charles A. Sumner (D)	87,233✔	
	W. W. Morrow (R)	73,647	
	Henry Edgerton (R)	73,454	
	J. B. Hotchkiss (P)	2,776	
	J. Yarnell (P)	2,722	
	Warren Chase (G)	1,139	
	S. Maybell (G)	1,090	

COLORADO

		Votes	%
AL	James B. Belford (R)	30,847	50.2
	S. S. Wallace (D)	29,380	47.8

CONNECTICUT

		Votes	%
1	William W. Eaton (D)	14,740	50.7
	John R. Buck (R)	14,047	48.3
2	Charles L. Mitchell (D)	19,325	51.7
	Merwin (R)	17,530	46.9
3	John T. Wait (R)	9,882	53.4
	Penrose (D)	8,227	44.5
4	Edward W. Seymour (D)	15,703	51.8
	Coe (R)	14,263	47.0

DELAWARE

		Votes	%
AL	Charles B. Lore (D)	16,563	53.0
	Washington Hastings (R)	14,640	46.9

FLORIDA

	Candidates	Votes	%
1	Robert H. M. Davidson (D)	11,244	51.5
	Skinner (R)	7,017	32.2
	McKinnon	3,553	16.3
2	Horatio Bisbee Jr. (R)	13,122	50.6
	Finley (D)	12,823	49.4

GEORGIA

		Votes	%
1	John C. Nichols (D)	6,055	60.9
	Atkins (R)	3,884	39.1
2	Henry G. Turner (D)	7,794	63.9
	Wessolowsky (R)	4,406	36.1
3	Charles F. Crisp (D)	4,121	92.6
	Harrall (R)	329	7.4
4	Hugh Buchanan (D)	5,583	78.5
	Pou (I)	1,502	21.1
5	Nathaniel J. Hammond (D)	10,788	65.2
	Buck (IR)	5,756	34.8
6	James H. Blount (D)	3,514	99.3
7	Judson C. Clements (D)	12,408	53.6
	Felton (D)	10,746	46.4
8	Seaborn Reese (D)	4,384	96.0
9	Allen D. Candler (D)	14,521	54.9
	Speer (ID)	11,915	45.1
AL	Thomas Hardeman (D)	79,540	76.3
	Forsyth (R)	24,645	23.7

Special Election

		Votes	%
8	Seaborn Reese (D)	4,282	100.0

ILLINOIS

		Votes	%
1	Ransom W. Dunham (R)	11,571	50.9
	John W. Downes (D)	10,534	46.3
2	John F. Finerty (ID)	9,360	56.2
	Henry F. Sheridan (D)	6,939	41.6
3	George R. Davis (R)	12,511	53.2
	William T. Black (A-MON D)	10,274	43.7
4	George E. Adams (R)	11,686	53.3
	Lamberd Tree (D)	9,446	43.1
5	Reuben Ellwood (R)	12,994	70.6
	William Price (D)	5,127	27.9
6	Robert R. Hitt (R)	12,726	57.1
	James S. Ticknor (D)	9,045	40.6
7	Thomas J. Henderson (R)	12,751	61.1
	Larmon G. Johnson (D)	6,369	30.5
	M. B. Loyd (P)	1,673	8.0
8	William Cullen (R)	13,851	46.9
	Patrick C. Haley (D)	13,673	46.3
9	Lewis E. Payson (R)	12,619	52.4
	E. B. Buck (D)	9,243	38.4
	O. W. Barnard (G)	2,138	8.9
10	Nicholas E. Worthington (D)	13,571	48.3
	John H. Lewis (R)	13,180	46.9
11	William W. Neece (D)	14,604	45.3
	Benjamin F. Marsh (R)	13,975	43.3
	Richard Haney (P)	3,671	11.4
12	James M. Riggs (D)	15,316	49.0
	James W. Singleton (ID)	11,782	37.7
	Philip N. Minier (P)	4,130	13.2
13	William M. Springer (D)	18,360	54.4
	Dietrich C. Smith (R)	14,042	41.6
14	Jonathan H. Rowell (R)	15,273	48.8
	Adlai E. Stevenson (D)	14,598	46.7
15	Joseph G. Cannon (R)	15,868	51.1
	Andrew J. Hunter (D)	14,651	47.2
16	Aaron Shaw (D)	14,557	50.7
	E. B. Green (R)	13,689	47.7
17	Samuel W. Moulton (D)	14,495	55.9
	William H. Barlow (R)	10,068	38.8
	B. W. F. Corley (P)	1,386	5.3
18	William R. Morrison (D)	14,906	52.2
	W. C. Keuffner (R)	12,561	44.0

	Candidates	Votes	%
19	Richard W. Townshend (D)	15,606	60.7
	George C. Ross (R)	9,930	38.6
20	John R. Thomas (R)	14,504	49.0
	William K. Murphy (D)	14,113	47.6

Special Election

		Votes	%
5	Robert R. Hitt (R)	12,430	59.9
	Larmon G. Johnson (D)	8,138	39.2

INDIANA

		Votes	%
1	John Kleiner (D)	18,048	51.6
	William Heilman (R)	16,399	46.9
2	Thomas R. Cobb (D)	16,339	55.1
	A. J. Hostetter (R)	13,288	44.8
3	Strother M. Stockslager (D)	17,122	56.2
	Will T. Walker (R)	12,538	41.2
4	William S. Holman (D)	16,640	55.4
	W. J. Johnson (R)	13,146	43.8
5	Courtland C. Matson (D)	16,851	55.9
	Wallingford (R)	13,298	44.1
6	Thomas M. Browne (R)	19,562	60.1
	J. L. Pender (D)	12,249	37.6
7	Stanton J. Peelle (R)	17,451‡	49.4
	William Estin English (D)	17,373	49.1
8	John Edward Lamb (D)	18,110	47.9
	Robert Bruce Frasen Peirce (R)	17,823	47.2
9	Thomas Bayless Ward (D)	17,357	49.7
	Godlove S. Orth (R)	16,481	47.2
10	Thomas J. Wood (D)	17,237	49.5
	Mark Lindsey Demotte (R)	16,223	46.6
11	George Washington Steele (R)	19,863	48.6
	Dailey (D)	19,530	47.8
12	Robert Lowry (D)	16,986	54.4
	Glasgow (R)	13,623	43.6
13	William Henry Calkins (R)	17,478	47.9
	Winterbotham (D)	17,087	46.8
	Shively (NG)	1,942	5.3

Special Election

		Votes	%
9	Charles T. Doxey (R)		✔

IOWA

		Votes	%
1	Moses A. McCoid (R)	13,549	48.1
	Benton J. Hall (D)	13,311	47.3
2	Jeremiah Henry Murphy (D)	15,760	54.6
	Sewell S. Farwell (R)	12,561	43.5
3	David B. Henderson (R)	12,907	50.4
	C. M. Durham (D)	11,604	45.3
4	Luman Hamlin Weller (D)	11,473	51.5
	Thomas Updegraff (R)	10,762	48.3
5	James Wilson (R)	11,791‡	47.5
	Benjamin Todd Frederick (D)	11,768	47.4
	David Platner (G)	1,253	5.1
6	Marsena E. Cutts (R)	11,250	40.4
	James Baird Weaver (G)	8,569	30.8
	C. H. Mackey (D)	8,040	28.9
7	John A. Kasson (R)	13,631	50.8
	T. C. Gilpin (D)	7,068	26.3
	E. H. Gillette (G)	6,131	22.9
8	William P. Hepburn (R)	13,792	51.7
	D. M. Clark (G)	7,344	27.5
	Lewis Bonnett (D)	5,533	20.7
9	William H. M. Pusey (D)	14,186	49.0
	Albert Raney Anderson (G)	11,987	41.4
	J. B. Hatton (G)	2,753	9.5
10	Adoniram J. Holmes (R)	14,250	62.2
	John Cliggitt (D)	6,853	29.9
	Josial Doane (G)	1,799	7.9
11	Isaac S. Struble (R)	15,315	58.0
	John P. Allison (D)	9,867	37.3

KANSAS

Candidates	Votes	%
1 John A. Anderson (R)	41,251	68.3
Charles H. Moody (G LAB)	17,816	29.5
2 Dudley C. Haskell (R)	23,601	48.7
N. F. Acers (D)	19,116	39.5
Alfred Taylor (G LAB)	5,710	11.8
3 Thomas Ryan (R)	36,091	57.1
John C. Cannon (D)	17,729	28.1
D. J. Cole (G LAB)	9,356	14.8
AL Samuel R. Peters (R)	99,866✔	
Edmund N. Morrill (R)	98,649✔	
Bishop W. Perkins (R)	98,338✔	
Lewis Hanback (R)	97,354✔	
Samuel N. Wood (D)	83,433	
O'Flanagan (D)	59,872	
Leland (D)	58,079	
Davis (G LAB)	26,701	
Phillips (G LAB)	25,644	
Williams (G LAB)	22,243	
Bennett (G LAB)	1,417	
Cannon (G LAB)	588	

KENTUCKY

Candidates	Votes	%
1 Oscar Turner (ID)	8,705	39.3
John R. Grace (D)	7,627	34.5
Henry Houston (R)	5,803	26.2
2 James F. Clay (D)	5,747	70.7
W. M. Fuqua (R)	1,979	24.3
3 John E. Halsell (D)	13,546	50.4
W. G. Hunter (R)	13,356	49.7
4 Thomas A. Robertson (D)	5,878	74.8
W. H. Parrish (R)	1,974	25.1
5 Albert S. Willis (D)	6,492	62.5
Silas F. Miller (R)	3,557	34.3
6 John G. Carlisle (D)	4,990	98.2
7 Joseph C. S. Blackburn (D)	11,789	63.8
John W. Asbury (R)	6,692	36.2
8 P. B. Thompson Jr. (D)	11,202	52.0
R. L. Ewell (R)	10,338	48.0
9 William W. Culbertson (R)	11,217	53.0
Z. Smith Hurt (D)	9,948	47.0
10 John D. White (R)	14,240	52.5
G. M. Adams (D)	12,870	47.5
11 Frank L. Wolford (D)	12,007	54.7
D. R. Carr (R)	9,934	45.3

LOUISIANA

	Votes	%
1 Carleton Hunt (D)	8,498	63.7
A. C. Janin (R)	4,852	36.3
2 E. John Ellis (D)	7,701	58.4
Morris Marks (IR)	2,789	21.1
Henry Demas (R)	2,666	20.2
3 William Pitt Kellogg (R)	7,453	45.7
Joseph Hayes Acklen (D)	5,564	34.1
Taylor Beattie (IR)	3,301	20.2
4 Newton C. Blanchard (D)	5,765	99.8
5 J. Floyd King (D)	13,295	76.9
W. L. Mcmillen (R)	3,986	23.1
6 Andrew S. Herron (D)	8,004*	66.9
Louis Trager (R)	3,965	33.1

MAINE

	Votes	%
AL Thomas B. Reed (R)	72,811✔	
Nelson Dingley Jr (R)	72,494✔	
Charles A. Boutelle (R)	72,352✔	
Seth Llewellyn Milliken (R)	72,310✔	
Daniel H. Thing (FUS)	63,321	
Joseph Dane (FUS)	63,304	
George W. Ladd (FUS)	63,192	
Thompson H. Murch (FUS)	62,616	
W. F. Eaton (G)	1,319	
B. D. Averill (G)	1,290	
B. K. Kalloch (G)	1,260	
Eben O. Gerry (G)	1,241	
James M. Stone (IR&P)	583	

Candidates	Votes	%
Henry Tallman (P)	295	
N. G. Axtell (P)	293	
Joseph E. Ladd (P)	291	
Charles E. Nash (IR)	264	
Daniel Stickney (IR)	198	

MARYLAND

	Votes	%
1 George W. Covington (D)	13,170	52.8
Millikin (R)	11,788	47.2
2 J. Fred C. Talbott (D)	12,728	52.2
Blair (R)	11,641	47.8
3 Fetter S. Hoblitzell (D)	13,917	56.8
Lang (R)	9,029	36.8
Kimmel (ID)	1,576	6.4
4 John V. L. Findlay (D)	14,457	53.1
Stockbridge (R)	12,793	47.0
5 Hart B. Holton (R)	13,550	53.0
Chapman (D)	12,011	47.0
6 Louis E. McComas (R)	15,720	51.7
Blair (D)	14,440	47.5

MASSACHUSETTS

	Votes	%
1 Robert T. Davis (R)	11,475	66.0
Nicholas Hathaway (D)	5,581	32.1
2 John D. Long (R)	12,915	53.9
Edgar E. Dean (D)	10,152	42.4
3 Ambrose A. Ranney (R)	11,968	57.8
Horatio E. Swasey (D)	8,540	41.3
4 Patrick A. Collins (D)	12,884	73.1
Charles T. Gallagher (R)	4,546	25.8
5 Leopold Morse (D)	11,301	56.0
Selwyn Z. Bowman (R)	8,791	43.6
6 Henry B. Lovering (D & G)	12,840	51.8
Elisha S. Converse (R)	11,960	48.2
7 Eben F. Stone (R)	10,056	44.3
Charles P. Thompson (D)	8,764	38.6
Eben Moody Boynton (G)	3,825	16.9
8 William A. Russell (R)	11,269	51.0
Charles S. Lilley (D)	10,743	48.6
9 Theodore Lyman (CSR&D)	12,076	54.4
John W. Candler (R)	9,703	43.7
10 William W. Rice (R)	11,846	55.5
John Hopkins (D)	9,404	44.1
11 William Whiting (R)	14,485	64.2
Edward J. Sawyer (D)	7,600	33.7
12 George D. Robinson (R)	11,294	53.3
Reuben Noble (D)	9,889	46.7

MICHIGAN

	Votes	%
1 William C. Maybury (FUS)	16,148	57.4
Henry W. Lord (R)	11,209	39.8
2 Nathaniel B. Eldredge (D)	15,251	48.2
John K. Boies (R)	14,709	46.5
3 Edward S. Lacey (R)	18,023	52.0
Hiram C. Hodge (FUS)	16,329	47.1
4 George L. Yaple (FUS)	16,329	50.4
Julius C. Burrows (R)	16,077	49.6
5 Julius Houseman (FUS)	16,725	49.5
William O. Webster (R)	16,609	49.2
6 Edwin B. Winans (FUS)	18,516	49.8
Oliver L. Spaulding (R)	18,484	49.8
7 Ezra C. Carleton (FUS)	11,540	50.6
John T. Rich (R)	11,252	49.4
8 Roswell G. Horr (R)	14,872	50.7
Charles J. Willet (FUS)	13,918	47.5
9 Byron M. Cutcheon (R)	13,529	55.4
Stephen Bronson (FUS)	10,897	44.6
10 Herschel H. Hatch (R)	11,327	52.6
Andrew C. Maxwell (FUS)	7,749	36.0
Jesse M. Miller	2,434	11.3
11 Edward Breitung (R)	11,428	68.5
Peter White (FUS)	4,840	29.0

MINNESOTA

Candidates	Votes	%
1 Milo White (R)	12,458	49.1
A. Bierman (D)	11,789	46.4
2 James B. Wakefield (R)	17,187	63.6
F. A. Bohrer (D)	6,750	25.0
J. A. Latimer (P)	3,085	11.4
3 Horace B. Strait (R)	16,583	68.2
C. P. Adams (D)	7,047	29.0
4 William D. Washburn (R)	17,380	51.5
A. A. Ames (D)	14,820	43.9
5 Knute Nelson (IR)	16,956	47.8
C. F. Kindred (R)	12,238	34.5
E P. Barnum (D)	6,248	17.6

MISSISSIPPI

	Votes	%
1 Henry L. Muldrow (D)	6,390	81.9
Lyon (R)	1,414	18.1
2 James R. Chalmers (I)	9,729‡	52.3
Vannoy H. Manning (D)	8,749	47.0
3 Elza Jeffords (R)	4,127	69.1
Clarke (D)	1,321	22.1
Waddell	521	8.7
4 Hernando D. Money (D)	6,848	68.8
Griffin (R)	2,644	26.5
5 Otho R. Singleton (D)	6,121	98.9
6 Henry S. Van Eaton (D)	7,615	53.2
Lynch (R)	6,706	46.8
7 Ethelbert Barksdale (D)	10,933	66.6
Hill (R)	5,478	33.4

MISSOURI

	Votes	%
1 William H. Hatch (D)	16,243	57.4
Glover (ID)	11,415	40.3
2 Armstead M. Alexander (D)	19,033	57.7
Dorsey (R)	8,628	26.2
Quayle (GD)	5,302	16.1
3 Alexander M. Dockery (D)	17,261	52.9
Thomas (R)	12,887	39.5
Burrows (G & R)	2,485	7.6
4 James N. Burnes (D)	13,325	51.1
Reed (R)	10,571	40.5
Sisson (GD)	2,185	8.4
5 Alexander Graves (D)	12,695	58.8
Crisp (ID)	8,672	40.1
6 John Cosgrove (D)	17,149	60.2
Alldridge (GD)	11,349	39.8
7 Aylett H. Buckner (D)	14,370	55.2
Daudt (R)	9,857	37.9
McNair (GD)	1,786	6.9
8 John J. O'Neill (D)	6,446	47.7
Sessinghaus (R)	4,795	35.5
Dailey (D)	1,282	9.5
Sullivan (GD)	997	7.4
9 James O. Broadhead (D)	6,860	48.7
McLean (R)	6,758	48.0
10 Martin L. Clardy (D)	13,536	57.2
Manistre (R)	7,455	31.5
Jackson (G & R)	2,667	11.3
11 Richard P. Bland (D)	14,259	54.9
Wallace (R)	10,530	40.5
12 Charles H. Morgan (D)	14,768	53.9
Terrell (R)	9,061	33.1
Spring (G)	3,550	13.0
13 Robert W. Fyan (D)	13,904	42.9
Cloud (R)	12,424	38.3
Haseltine (G)	6,122	18.9
14 Lowndes H. Davis (D)	14,023	58.1
Carroll (R)	7,177	29.8
Kitchen (G)	2,920	12.1

Special Election

	Votes	%
9 James O. Broadhead (D)	6,591	49.4
McLean (R)	6,386	47.9

NEBRASKA

	Candidates	Votes	%
1	Archibald J. Weaver (R)	17,022	50.9
	John I. Reddick (D)	12,690	38.0
	W. S. Gilbert (A-MONOP)	3,707	11.1
2	James Laird (R)	12,983	49.8
	V. S. Moore (A-MONOP)	10,012	38.4
	F. A. Harman (D)	3,070	11.8
3	Edward K. Valentine (R)	11,272	39.5
	W. H. Munger (D)	9,932	34.8
	M. K. Turner (A-MONOP)	7,342	25.7

NEVADA

		Votes	%
AL	George W. Cassidy (D)	7,720	54.4
	Powning (R)	6,462	45.6

NEW HAMPSHIRE

		Votes	%
1	Martin A. Haynes (R)	19,378	54.4
	Chandler (D)	15,920	44.7
2	Ossian Ray (R)	21,294	52.2
	Hosley (D)	19,139	46.9

NEW JERSEY

		Votes	%
1	Thomas M. Ferrell (D)	16,541	50.1
	Robeson (R)	14,825	44.9
2	J. Hart Brewer (R)	15,604	51.3
	Parker Jr. (D)	14,535	47.8
3	John Kean Jr. (R)	15,186	48.2
	Ross (D)	12,891	40.9
	Urner (G)	3,463	11.0
4	Benjamin F. Howey (R)	11,567	49.2
	Harris (D, P)	11,073	47.1
5	William W. Phelps (R)	14,341	50.4
	Ryle (D)	12,703	44.6
6	William H. F. Fiedler (D)	17,200	53.2
	Blake (R)	14,780	45.7
7	William McAdoo (D)	15,147	56.6
	Collins (R)	11,566	43.2

NEW YORK

		Votes	%
1	Perry Belmont (D)	18,688	77.6
	Townsend (ID)	4,957	20.6
2	William E. Robinson (D)	19,004	63.1
	Boody (R & ID)	10,778	35.8
3	Darwin R. James (R)	19,260	52.5
	Hester (D)	16,882	46.0
4	Felix Campbell (D)	18,282	61.5
	Godard (R)	10,732	36.1
5	Nicholas Muller (D)	16,148	86.7
6	Samuel S. Cox (D)	16,624	74.6
	Quinn (R)	5,307	23.8
7	William Dorsheimer (D)	11,401	57.7
	Brodsky (R)	6,787	34.4
	McCabe (L)	1,562	7.9
8	John J. Adams (D)	12,089	51.3
	Russell (R)	10,904	46.3
9	John Hardy (D)	16,191	69.2
	O'Beirne (R)	7,217	30.8
10	Abram S. Hewitt (D)	22,144	90.7
11	Orlando B. Potter (D)	15,049	51.9
	Strong (R)	13,947	48.1
12	Waldo Hutchins (D)	15,663	63.7
	Long (R)	8,938	36.3
13	John H. Ketcham (R)	16,217	90.1
	Dorland (D)	916	5.1
14	Lewis Beach (D)	13,454	49.8
	Low (R)	12,821	47.5
15	John H. Bagley Jr. (D)	16,625	55.7
	Bray (R)	13,168	44.1
16	Thomas J. Van Alstyne (D)	17,797	57.0
	Van Heusen (R)	11,404	36.5
	Lemon Thompson (LAB)	2,010	6.4
17	Henry G. Burleigh (R)	17,685	100.0

	Candidates	Votes	%
18	Frederick A. Johnson (R)	10,667	87.8
	Fassett (D)	1,476	12.2
19	Abraham X. Parker (R)	12,578	63.1
	Smith (D)	7,365	36.9
20	Edward Wemple (D)	17,831	50.0
	West (R)	17,742	49.8
21	George W. Ray (R)	15,188	48.0
	Babcock (D)	14,742	46.6
22	Charles R. Skinner (R)	15,236	52.2
	Davenport (D)	13,967	47.8
23	John T. Spriggs (D)	12,299	51.9
	Fox (R)	10,623	44.8
24	Newton W. Nutting (R)	11,516	52.0
	Rhodes (D)	9,905	44.8
25	Frank Hiscock (R)	14,563	48.7
	Davis (D)	13,831	46.2
26	Sereno E. Payne (R)	13,607	48.8
	Hammond (D)	12,651	45.3
27	James W. Wadsworth (R)	12,013	52.3
	Pierpont (D)	10,931	47.6
28	Stephen C. Millard (R)	15,087	51.8
	Davis Jr. (D)	13,378	45.9
29	John Arnot Jr. (D)	17,769	50.0
	Baxter (R)	14,988	42.1
	Baldwin (P)	2,081	5.9
30	Halbert S. Greenleaf (D)	18,042	56.2
	Vanvoorhis (R)	12,308	38.4
31	Robert S. Stevens (D)	12,009	53.6
	Watson (R)	9,379	41.8
32	William F. Rogers (D)	20,531	49.5
	Moulton (R)	19,804	47.7
33	Francis B. Brewer (R)	12,123	51.4
	Lowry (D)	9,591	40.7
AL	Henry Slocum (D)	503,934	56.1
	Unidentified Candidate (R)	394,232	43.9

NORTH CAROLINA

		Votes	%
1	Walter F. Pool (L)	14,213	51.0
	Louis C. Latham (D)	13,628	48.9
2	James E. O'Hara (R)	18,531	93.8
	Unidentified Candidate (D)	1,226	6.2
3	Wharton J. Green (D)	16,095	50.8
	William P. Canaday (L)	15,595	49.2
4	William R. Cox (D)	16,586	50.6
	Thomas P. Devereux (L)	16,174	49.4
5	Alfred M. Scales (D)	12,533	55.4
	John R. Winston (L)	9,932	43.9
6	Clement Dowd (D)	15,549	57.2
	William Johnston (L)	11,648	42.8
7	Tyre York (L)	11,415	48.6
	William M. Robbins (D)	11,159	47.5
8	Robert B. Vance (D)	13,000	56.4
	William M. Cooke Jr. (L)	10,038	43.6
AL	Risden T. Bennett (D)	111,763	50.1
	Oliver H. Dockery (L)	111,320	49.9

OHIO

		Votes	%
1	John F. Follett (D)	14,540	51.4
	Benjamin Butterworth (R)	13,721	48.5
2	Isaac M. Jordan (D)	15,983	53.0
	Amor Smith (R)	14,166	47.0
3	Robert M. Murray (D)	16,106	49.6
	Emanuel Shultz (R)	15,826	48.8
4	Benjamin Le Fevre (D)	16,596	62.7
	Jacob S. Conklin (R)	9,683	36.6
5	George E. Seney (D)	16,619	59.0
	Lovell B. Harris (R)	11,006	39.1
6	William D. Hill (D)	16,201	49.7
	Joseph H. Brigham (R)	15,480	47.5
7	Henry L. Morey (R)	14,451‡	49.7
	James E. Campbell (D)	14,410	49.6
8	J. Warren Keifer (R)	14,397	50.2
	J. H. Young (D)	13,171	45.9
9	James S. Robinson (R)	15,864	48.8
	Thomas E. Powell (D)	15,458	47.5
10	Frank H. Hurd (D)	14,534	51.2
	Charles A. King (R)	13,430	47.3

	Candidates	Votes	%
11	John W. McCormick (R)	15,228	53.3
	John P. Leedom (D)	13,037	45.6
12	Alphonso Hart (R)	16,898	48.9
	Lawrence T. Neal (D)	16,888	48.9
13	George L. Converse (D)	17,766	54.2
	H. C. Drinkle (R)	14,092	43.0
14	George W. Geddes (D)	14,277	51.2
	Rollin A. Horr (R)	12,604	45.2
15	Adoniram J. Warner (D)	13,739	50.4
	Rufus R. Dawes (R)	13,048	47.9
16	Beriah Wilkins (D)	19,743	57.3
	A. B. Clark (R)	14,422	41.9
17	Jonathan T. Updegraff (R)	14,165*	50.4
	Ross J. Alexander (D)	13,265	47.2
18	William McKinley Jr. (R)	16,906‡	48.2
	Jonathan H. Wallace (D)	16,898	48.2
19	Ezra B. Taylor (R)	15,739	62.7
	David L. Rockwell (D)	7,708	30.7
20	David R. Paige (D)	14,090	47.9
	Addison S. McClure (R)	13,980	47.6
21	Martin A. Foran (D)	15,946	54.3
	Sylvester T. Everett (R)	11,408	38.9
	William H. Doan (P)	1,999	6.8

OREGON

		Votes	%
AL	Melvin C. George (R)	22,517	54.0
	W. D. Fenton (D)	19,152	46.0

PENNSYLVANIA

		Votes	%
1	Henry H. Bingham (R)	15,709	55.7
	John Cadwalader (D)	11,875	42.1
2	Charles O'Neill (R)	14,984	56.7
	W. Wurt Dundas (D)	11,440	43.3
3	Samuel J. Randall (D)	11,688	61.6
	W. M. Maull (R)	7,302	38.5
4	William D. Kelley (R)	21,896	61.3
	C. M. Swaim (D)	13,824	38.7
5	Alfred C. Harmer (R)	19,049	53.2
	T. J. Martin (D&I)	16,776	46.8
6	James B. Everhart (R)	14,615	59.1
	J. Edward Clyde (D)	9,810	39.7
7	I. Newton Evans (R)	15,732	51.0
	W. W. H. Davis (D)	15,102	49.0
8	Daniel Ermentrout (D)	15,623	64.2
	Isaac McHose (R)	8,466	34.8
9	A. Herr Smith (R)	16,425	62.8
	William B. Given (D)	9,740	37.2
10	William Mutchler (D)	19,867	63.1
	James S. Biery (R)	11,644	37.0
11	John B. Storm (D)	17,810	64.5
	H. C. Smith (R)	9,805	35.5
12	Daniel W. Connelly (D)	11,811	47.9
	Joseph A. Scranton (R)	10,822	43.9
	R. J. Flick (G LAB)	2,016	8.2
13	Charles N. Brumm (G LAB R)	10,773	51.5
	J. M. Wetherill (D)	10,149	48.5
14	Samuel F. Barr (R)	14,184	46.3
	Henry McCormick (D)	14,039	45.9
	John McLeery (IR)	1,870	6.1
15	George A. Post (D)	11,555	42.1
	C. C. Jadwin (IR)	9,101	33.1
	Edward Overton (R)	5,675	20.7
16	William W. Brown (R)	12,876	48.8
	H. W. Earley (D)	11,747	44.5
	J. Stickel (G LAB)	1,756	6.7
17	Jacob M. Campbell (R)	14,961	49.2
	Alex F. Coffroth (D)	14,410	47.4
18	Louis E. Atkinson (R)	14,779	50.6
	F. M. Kimmell (D)	14,049	48.1
19	William A. Duncan (D)	16,780	54.8
	William McSherry (ID)	13,603	44.4
20	Andrew G. Curtin (D)	16,515	59.3
	Samuel H. Orwig (R)	11,288	40.5
21	Charles E. Boyle (D)	16,033	55.6
	Charles S. Seaton (G LAB R)	12,709	44.1
22	James H. Hopkins (D)	12,420	47.5
	Russell Errett (R)	11,191	42.8
	James Campbell (G LAB)	2,345	9.0

PENNSYLVANIA

Candidates	Votes	%
23 Thomas M. Bayne (R)	11,734	83.7
S. G. Barnes (G LAB)	1,882	13.4
24 George V. Lawrence (R)	11,674	50.4
J. G. McConahy (D)	10,888	47.0
25 John D. Patton (D)	13,990	51.9
Harry White (R)	12,990	48.2
26 Samuel H. Miller (R)	14,098	47.9
J. H. Caldwell (D)	13,365	45.4
27 Samuel M. Brainerd (R)	11,170	45.8
H. B. Plumer (D)	10,247	42.0
W. T. Everson (G LAB&P)	2,992	12.3
AL Mortimer Elliott (D)	352,855	47.5
Marriott Brosius (R)	323,255	43.5
William McMichael (IR)	40,995	5.5

RHODE ISLAND

	Votes	%
1 Henry J. Spooner (R)	3,515	70.0
Oscar Lapham (D)	1,491	29.7
2 Jonathan Chace (R)	3,349	64.6
Wheeler (D)	1,831	35.3

SOUTH CAROLINA

	Votes	%
1 Samuel Dibble (D)	8,674	56.9
J. B. Campbell (IG&R)	6,565	43.1
2 George D. Tillman (D)	11,388	67.8
E. M. Brayton (R)	5,361	31.9
3 D. Wyatt Aiken (D)	9,245	84.7
T. H. Russell (G & R)	1,677	15.4
4 John H. Evins (D)	11,662	71.8
D. R. Elkins (G)	4,588	28.2
5 John J. Hemphill (D)	9,518	56.0
E. B. C. Cash (IG&R)	7,471	44.0
6 George W. Dargan (D)	10,814	64.7
E. H. Deas (R)	3,628	21.7
A. H. Bowen (G)	2,263	13.6
7 Edmund W. M. Mackey (R)	18,469	64.8
Samuel Lee (IR)	10,017	35.2

TENNESSEE

	Votes	%
1 Augustus H. Pettibone (R)	14,702	53.9
Taylor (D)	12,571	46.1
2 Leonidas C. Houck (R)	14,535	62.2
Rule (IR)	8,821	37.8
3 George G. Dibrell (D)	11,403	53.5
Trewhitt (R)	9,698	45.5
4 Benton McMillin (D)	14,452	77.9
Stokes (R)	4,106	22.1
5 Richard Warner (D)	10,911	54.4
Tillman (STC D)	7,906	39.4
Duggan R)	1,247	6.2
6 Andrew J. Caldwell ()	15,951	61.9
Dillon (R)	8,856	34.4

Candidates	Votes	%
7 John G. Ballentine (D)	12,635	63.0
Perkins (ID)	7,432	37.0
8 John M. Taylor (D)	10,995	51.8
Hawkins (R)	8,175	38.5
Warren (G)	1,479	7.0
9 Rice A. Pierce (D)	12,812	61.1
Lyle (R)	7,885	37.6
10 H. Casey Young (D)	10,696	51.1
Smith (R)	9,837	47.0

TEXAS

	Votes	%
1 Charles Stewart (D)	14,882	62.5
William Chambers (R)	8,850	37.2
2 John H. Reagan (D)	12,035	82.6
3 James H. Jones (D)	14,045	57.9
S. H. Russell (R)	9,492	39.1
4 David B. Culberson (D)	13,487	63.4
E. L. Dehoney (G)	7,785	36.6
5 James W. Throckmorton (D)	16,163	72.0
J. N. Dixon (G)	6,280	28.0
6 Olin Wellborn (D)	17,510	71.6
J. C. Kearby (G)	6,949	28.4
7 Thomas P. Ochiltree (I)	12,457	55.8
George P. Finlay (D)	9,851	44.1
8 James F. Miller (D)	12,297	59.0
R. Zapp (G)	6,528	31.3
Joseph O'Connor (I)	1,774	8.5
9 Roger Q. Mills (D)	14,730	63.9
J. D. Rankin (G)	8,329	36.1
10 John Hancock (D)	16,098	62.2
E. J. Davis (R)	9,783	37.8
11 Samuel W. T. Lanham (D)	10,493	51.0
J. W. Barnett (G)	4,744	23.1
J. H. Davenport (ID)	3,807	18.5
S. C. Buck (ID)	1,532	7.4

VERMONT

	Votes	%
1 John W. Stewart (R)	15,638	69.3
Syman W. Redington (D)	6,009	26.6
2 Luke P. Poland (R)	12,795	51.8
George S. Fletcher (D)	6,363	25.8
Wilpam W. Grout (R)	4,598	18.6

VIRGINIA

	Votes	%
1 Robert M. Mayo (READJ)	10,505‡	49.6
George T. Garrison (D)	10,504	49.6
2 Harry Libbey (READJ)	13,226	49.7
Richard C. Marshall (D)	10,282	38.6
John F. Dezendorf (R)	3,114	11.7
3 George D. Wise (D)	10,736	57.1
John Ambler Smith (READJ)	8,060	42.9

Candidates	Votes	%
4 Benjamin S. Hooper (READJ)	14,764	75.5
W. A. Reese (D)	4,552	23.3
5 George C. Cabell (D)	12,948	53.0
William H. Sims (READJ)	11,489	47.0
6 John Randolph Tucker (D)	12,765	55.0
J. Henry Rives (READJ)	10,362	44.6
7 John Paul (READJ)	12,146‡	50.2
Charles T. O'Ferrall (D)	11,941	49.4
8 John S. Barbour (D)	14,256	60.6
Richard R. Farr (READJ)	9,034	38.4
9 Henry Bowen (READJ)	10,073	57.7
Abram Fulkerson (D)	5,603	32.1
Samuel H. Newberry (I)	1,467	8.4
AL John S. Wise (READJ)	99,992	50.4
John E. Massey (D)	94,184	47.4

WEST VIRGINIA

	Votes	%
1 Nathan Goff Jr. (R)	14,154	52.2
John H. Good (D)	12,335	45.5
2 William L. Wilson (D)	11,406	48.5
John W. Mason (R)	11,396	48.5
3 John E. Kenna (D)	10,279*	58.3
E. S. Buttrick (R)	5,814	33.0
P. B. Reynolds (G)	1,454	8.3
4 Eustace Gibson (D)	11,151	47.9
George Loomis (R)	9,863	42.3
A. R. Barber (G)	2,287	9.8

WISCONSIN

	Votes	%
1 John Winans (D)	12,307	46.6
C. G. Williams (R)	11,853	44.9
C. M. Blackman (P)	2,217	8.4
2 Daniel H. Sumner (D)	10,671	50.4
J. S. Rowell (R)	8,870	41.9
3 Burr W. Jones (D)	13,035	46.0
G. C. Hazelton (R)	7,924	28.0
E. W. Keyes (IR)	3,791	13.4
S. D. Hastings (P)	3,152	11.1
4 Peter V. Deuster (D)	9,688	48.6
F. C. Winckler (R)	8,320	41.7
G. B. Goodwin (LAB)	1,922	9.6
5 Joseph Rankin (D)	12,933	62.7
L. Howland (R)	6,108	29.6
6 Richard Guenther (R)	10,303	44.1
A. Haben (D)	9,265	39.7
T. D. Kanouse (P)	3,275	14.0
7 Gilbert M. Woodward (D)	11,908	48.1
C. M. Butt (R)	10,604	42.8
B. F. Parker (P)	1,887	7.6
8 William T. Price (R)	14,059	55.4
W. F. Bailey (D)	11,315	44.6
9 Isaac Stephenson (R)	12,774	47.4
G. L. Park (D)	12,518	46.4
H. H. Woodmansec (P)	1,460	5.4

1883 House Elections

KANSAS

Special Election

	Votes	%
2 Edward H. Funston (R)	24,116	57.4
S. A. Riggs (D)	17,924	42.6

LOUISIANA

Special Election

	Votes	%
6 Edward T. Lewis (D)	6,366	91.8
Louis Trager (R)	568	8.2

OHIO[1]

Special Election

	Votes	%
16 Joseph D. Taylor (R)	14,179	53.5
Ross J. Alexander (D)	12,313	46.5
16 Joseph D. Taylor (R)	14,159	53.5
Ross J. Alexander (D)	12,322	46.5

1. The first special election in the 16th district was held in January 1883 to fill the remaining two months of the term in the 47th Congress (1881-83). The second special election was held in February 1883, to fill the House seat for a full term in the 48th Congress (1883-85). Both elections were necessitated by the death of Rep. Jonathan T. Updegraff Nov. 30, 1882, following his re-election to the 48th Congress.

1884 House Elections

ALABAMA

	Candidates	Votes	%
1	James T. Jones (D)	8,871	58.1
	Thweatt (R)	6,403	41.9
2	Hilary A. Herbert (D)	11,331	55.8
	Whitehead (R)	8,991	44.2
3	William C. Oates (D)	10,965	71.6
	Mabson (R)	4,349	28.4
4	Alexander C. Davidson (D)	14,225	63.7
	Craig (R)	6,749	30.2
5	Thomas W. Sadler (D)	10,775	98.0
6	John M. Martin (D)	10,132	99.3
7	William H. Forney (D)	14,187	63.3
	Ewing (R)	8,217	36.7
8	Joseph Wheeler (D)	12,912	52.8
	Day (IR)	11,559	47.2

ARKANSAS

		Votes	%
1	Poindexter Dunn (D)	15,002	61.7
	Remmel (R)	9,322	38.3
2	Clifton R. Breckinridge (D)	13,792	53.0
	Rogers (R)	12,229	47.0
3	James K. Jones (D)	16,193*	54.1
	Mitchell (R)	13,722	45.9
4	John H. Rogers (D)	15,174	57.3
	Sarber (R)	11,307	42.7
5	Samuel W. Peel (D)	11,542	69.1
	Keenor (R)	5,158	30.9

CALIFORNIA

		Votes	%
1	Barclay Henley (D)	16,461	49.7
	T. L. Carothers (R)	16,316	49.3
2	James A. Louttit (R)	18,327	49.4
	Charles A. Sumner (D)	18,208	49.1
3	Joseph McKenna (R)	17,435	55.8
	J. A. Glascock (D)	13,197	42.3
4	William W. Morrow (R)	15,083	58.7
	R. P. Hastings (D)	10,422	40.6
5	Charles N. Felton (R)	17,014	51.6
	F. J. Sullivan (D)	15,676	47.6
6	Henry H. Markham (R)	17,397	49.1
	A. F. Devalle (D)	16,988	47.9

COLORADO

		Votes	%
AL	George G. Symes (R)	35,446	53.2
	Charles S. Thomas (D)	28,720	43.1

CONNECTICUT

		Votes	%
1	John R. Buck (R)	16,589	49.7
	William W. Eaton (D)	16,285	48.8
2	Charles L. Mitchell (D)	22,589	50.8
	Allen (R)	20,573	46.3
3	John T. Wait (R)	11,700	54.4
	Johnson (D)	9,258	43.1
4	Edward W. Seymour (D)	18,526	49.0
	Coe (R)	18,373	48.6

DELAWARE

		Votes	%
AL	Charles B. Lore (D)	17,054	56.7
	Anthony Higgins (R)	12,978	43.2

FLORIDA

		Votes	%
1	Robert H. M. Davidson (D)	14,619	55.1
	Locke (R)	11,893	44.9
2	Charles Dougherty (D)	17,248	51.8
	Bisbee (R)	15,857	47.6

GEORGIA

	Candidates	Votes	%
1	Thomas M. Norwood (D)	10,857	64.4
	Pleasant (R)	6,012	35.6
2	Henry G. Turner (R)	7,828	100.0
3	Charles F. Crisp (D)	9,963	69.6
	Bell (R)	4,268	29.8
4	Henry R. Harris (D)	10,608	52.4
	Henry Person (ID)	5,473	27.0
	Milner (R)	4,156	20.5
5	Nathaniel J. Hammond (D)	9,008	63.7
	Martin (R)	5,130	36.3
6	James H. Blount (R)	7,922	100.0
7	Judson C. Clements (D)	10,496	71.1
	Kirkwood (R)	3,417	23.1
8	Seaborn Reese (D)	7,834	70.4
	Martin (R)	3,250	29.2
9	Allen D. Candler (D)	8,137	100.0
10	George T. Barnes (D)	9,166	86.2
	Wright (R)	1,277	12.0

ILLINOIS

		Votes	%
1	Ransom W. Dunham (R)	20,245	56.7
	William M. Tilden (D)	14,655	41.1
2	Francis Lawler (D)	13,954	54.7
	John F. Finnerty (R&A-MONO)	11,552	45.3
3	James H. Ward (D)	15,601	43.5
	William E. Mason (R)	10,806	30.1
	Charles Fitz Simmons (R)	8,928	24.9
4	George E. Adams (R)	18,333	53.8
	John P. Altgeld (D)	15,291	44.9
5	Reuben Ellwood (R & P)	20,500	68.4
	Richard Bishop (D)	9,424	31.5
6	Robert R. Hitt (R)	18,048	61.5
	E. W. Blaisdell (D)	10,891	37.1
7	Thomas J. Henderson (R)	15,498	57.6
	James S. Eckels (D)	10,689	39.7
8	Ralph Plumb (R)	18,707	51.8
	Pat C. Haley (D)	15,953	44.2
9	Lewis E. Payson (R)	16,481	53.4
	James Kirk (D)	13,716	44.5
10	Nicholas E. Worthington (D)	16,758	50.1
	Julius S. Starr (R)	16,582	49.6
11	William H. Neece (A-MON D)	18,291	50.1
	Alexander P. Petrie (R)	17,864	48.9
12	James M. Riggs (D)	22,046	57.7
	Thomas G. Black (R)	15,177	39.7
13	William M. Springer (D)	20,808	53.1
	James M. Taylor (R)	16,971	43.3
14	Jonathan H. Rowell (R)	18,052	51.4
	C. C. Clark (D)	15,673	44.6
15	Joseph G. Cannon (R)	17,852	50.2
	John C. Black (D)	17,360	48.8
16	Silas Z. Landes (D)	17,109	50.2
	James McCartney (R)	16,791	49.2
17	John R. Eden (D)	18,402	55.0
	Howland J. Hamlin (G & R)	14,576	43.5
18	William R. Morrison (D)	17,695	53.2
	Thomas B. Needles (R)	15,136	45.5
19	Richard W. Townshend (D)	18,296	56.7
	Thomas S. Ridgway (R)	13,615	42.2
20	John R. Thomas (R)	17,890	52.1
	Fountain E. Albright (D)	15,788	45.9

INDIANA

		Votes	%
1	John J. Kleiner (D)	19,930	51.5
	William H. Gudgel (R)	18,493	47.8
2	Thomas R. Cobb (D)	18,832	55.5
	George H. Reiley (R)	15,128	44.6
3	Jonas G. Howard (D)	19,550	56.3
	James Keigwin (R)	14,923	43.0
4	William S. Holman (D)	17,233	52.6
	John O. Cravens (R)	15,494	47.2

(IOWA column continued)

	Candidates	Votes	%
5	Courtland C. Matson (D)	17,951	51.3
	George W. Grubbs (R)	16,582	47.4
6	Thomas M. Browne (R)	22,115	61.1
	Nelson G. Smith (D)	13,625	37.7
7	William D. Bynum (D)	20,240	51.0
	Stanton J. Peelle (R)	18,995	47.9
8	James C. Johnston (R)	20,185	50.0
	John Edward Lamb (D)	20,035	49.6
9	Thomas B. Ward (D)	19,241	49.7
	Charles T. Doxey (R)	18,628	48.1
10	William D. Owen (R)	19,262	50.0
	Thomas J. Wood (D)	18,781	48.8
11	George W. Steele (R)	22,679	48.7
	Meredith H. Kidd (D)	22,625	48.6
12	Robert Lowry (D)	19,507	52.5
	T. P. Keator (R)	16,957	45.7
13	George Ford (D)	20,971	52.7
	Henry Thayer (R)	18,792	47.3

Special Election

		Votes	%
13	Benjamin Franklin Shively (N)	20,964	52.8
	John Reynolds (R)	18,736	47.2

IOWA

		Votes	%
1	Benton Jay Hall (D)	16,734	50.0
	John S. Woolson (R)	16,661	49.7
2	Jeremiah Henry Murphy (D)	19,730	56.4
	William T. Shaw (R)	15,241	43.6
3	David B. Henderson (R)	16,431	52.1
	John J. Linehan (D)	15,105	47.9
4	William Elijah Fuller (R)	15,082	50.4
	Luman Hamlin Weller (G & D)	14,852	49.6
5	Benjamin Todd Frederick (D)	16,679	50.2
	Milo P. Smith (R)	16,541	49.7
6	James Baird Weaver (G & D)	16,684	50.1
	Frank T. Campbell (R)	16,617	49.9
7	Edwin H. Conger (R)	19,274	54.8
	W. H. McHenry (D)	15,924	45.2
8	William P. Hepburn (R)	17,671	53.6
	S. R. Davis (D)	15,294	46.4
9	Joseph H. Lyman (R)	19,071	50.7
	William H. M. Pusey (D)	18,509	49.2
10	Adoniram J. Holmes (R)	20,328	62.7
	H. C. McCoy (D)	12,117	37.3
11	Isaac S. Struble (R)	24,063	58.4
	Thomas F. Barbee (D)	17,107	41.6

Special Election

		Votes	%
7	Hiram Ypsilanti Smith (R)	18,905	53.9
	E. H. Kridler (D)	16,151	46.1

KANSAS

		Votes	%
1	Edmund N. Morrill (R)	19,535	55.1
	Thomas P. Fenlon (D)	15,934	44.9
2	Edward H. Funston (R)	22,518	60.4
	W. J. Nicholson (D)	14,703	39.4
3	Bishop W. Perkins (R)	23,854	56.3
	G. W. Gabriel (D)	13,341	31.5
	W. A. Tipton (G LAB)	5,163	12.2
4	Thomas Ryan (R)	26,177	61.9
	S. N. Wood (D)	15,799	37.4
5	John A. Anderson (R)	22,548	64.1
	A. A. Carnahan (D)	10,866	30.9
	M. D. Tenney (G LAB)	1,784	5.1
6	Lewis Hanback (R)	14,776	59.5
	L. C. Uhl (D)	10,068	40.5
7	Samuel R. Peters (R)	25,740	61.0
	H. M. Bickel (D)	15,913	37.7

KENTUCKY

Candidates	Votes	%
1 William J. Stone (D)	10,503	41.8
Oscar Turner (ID)	7,440	29.6
H. H. Houston (R)	7,161	28.5
2 Polk Laffoon (D)	12,472	56.8
T. Z. Moore (R)	9,485	43.2
3 John E. Halsell (D)	12,833	55.3
J. S. Golladay (R)	10,376	44.7
4 Thomas A. Robertson (D)	12,153	100.0
5 Albert S. Willis (D)	12,152	59.0
A. E. Wilson (R)	8,373	40.7
6 John G. Carlisle (D)	15,261	60.6
J. J. Landrum (R)	9,329	37.1
7 William C. P. Breckinridge (D)	16,236	93.2
D. W. Lindsey (R)	1,173	6.7
8 James B. McCreary (D)	14,924	53.9
J. M. Sebastian (R)	12,778	46.1
9 William H. Wadsworth (R)	16,189	50.2
Frank Powers (D)	16,087	49.8
10 William P. Taulbee (D)	14,266	53.7
A. J. Auxier (R)	12,308	46.3
11 Frank L. Wolford (D)	10,748	52.0
W. W. Jones (R)	9,932	48.0

LOUISIANA

Candidates	Votes	%
1 Louis St.Martin (D)	5,685	41.9
Carleton Hunt (ID)	4,458	32.9
J. A. Acklin (R)	3,411	25.2
2 Michael Hahn (R)	7,356	54.7
W. T. Houston (D)	6,103	45.4
3 Edward J. Gay (D)	15,302	51.2
William Pitt Kellogg (R)	14,603	48.8
4 Newton C. Blanchard (D)	12,269	89.9
J. B. Slattery (R)	1,377	10.1
5 J. Floyd King (D)	11,692	59.1
Charles J. Boatner (ID)	5,513	27.9
Frank Morey (R)	2,565	13.0
6 Alfred B. Irion (D)	9,927	61.6
C. C. Swayzie (R)	6,197	38.4

MAINE

Candidates	Votes	%
1 Thomas B. Reed (R)	17,594	51.0
N. Cleaves (D)	16,669	48.3
2 Nelson Dingley Jr. (R)	20,795	55.1
D. R. Hastings (D)	15,006	39.8
3 Seth L. Milliken (R)	20,083	57.9
Daniel H. Thing (D)	13,866	40.0
4 Charles A. Boutelle (R)	19,643	56.1
John F. Lynch (D)	14,165	40.5

MARYLAND

Candidates	Votes	%
1 Charles H. Gibson (D)	16,726	53.3
Russum (R)	14,641	46.7
2 Frank T. Shaw (D)	16,274	53.8
Blair (R)	14,003	46.3
3 William H. Cole (D)	16,032	58.6
Pentz (R)	10,756	39.3
4 John V. L. Findlay (D)	15,726	51.2
Brown (R)	14,324	46.7
5 Barnes Compton (D)	15,612	51.6
Holton (R)	14,641	48.4
6 Louis E. McComas (R)	17,995	52.3
Nelson (D)	16,379	47.6

MASSACHUSETTS

Candidates	Votes	%
1 Robert T. Davis (R)	14,080	66.5
Weston Howland (D)	5,307	25.1
2 John D. Long (R)	15,039	53.0
William Everett (D)	9,734	34.3
Edgar E. Dean (G)	2,630	9.3
3 Ambrose A. Ranney (R)	13,596	53.0
Horatio Swasey (D)	9,248	36.1
Eleazer B. Loring (G)	2,412	9.4

Candidates	Votes	%
4 Patrick A. Collins (D)	13,664	64.8
Joseph H. O'Neill (R)	7,182	34.1
5 Edward D. Hayden (R)	13,290	52.0
Robert Trete Paine Jr. (D)	11,018	43.1
6 Henry B. Lovering (D & G)	15,146	49.6
Henry Cabot Lodge (R)	14,881	48.7
7 Eben F. Stone (R)	12,475	47.8
Richard S. Spofford (D)	9,623	36.9
John Baker (G)	3,948	15.1
8 Charles H. Allen (R)	12,643	53.6
Charles S. Lilley (D)	9,446	40.1
9 Frederick D. Ely (R)	12,265	47.4
Henry E. Fales (D)	6,301	24.4
Theodore Lyman (I)	4,265	16.5
Henry E. Lemon Jr. (G)	2,429	9.4
10 William W. Rice (R)	13,940	58.8
James E. Esterbrook (D)	6,556	27.6
Unidentified Candidate (G)	2,637	11.1
11 William Whiting (R)	15,335	59.9
David Hill (D)	8,693	34.0
12 Francis W. Rockwell (R)	13,012	51.7
Jarvis N. Dunham (D)	10,856	43.1

MICHIGAN

Candidates	Votes	%
1 William C. Maybury (D)	21,673	55.8
John Atkinson (R)	15,549	40.0
2 Nathaniel B. Eldredge (D & G)	17,710	46.9
Edward P. Allen (R)	17,656	46.7
Charles Mosher (P)	2,420	6.4
3 James O'Donnell (R)	20,438	48.5
Henry F. Pennington (D & G)	19,210	45.5
Michael J. Fanning (P)	2,531	6.0
4 Julius C. Burrows (R)	18,564	48.8
George L. Yaple (D & G)	18,212	47.9
5 Charles C. Comstock (D & G)	20,406	47.6
John C. Fitzgerald (R)	20,050	46.7
Wilson C. Edsell (P)	2,449	5.7
6 Edwin B. Winans (D & G)	19,857	48.8
James C. Willson (R)	18,377	45.2
Leander C. Smith (P)	2,445	6.0
7 Ezra C. Carlton (D)	14,535	50.2
Edgar Weeks (R)	12,316	42.5
8 Timothy E. Tarsney (D)	19,446	50.6
Roswell G. Horr (R)	17,824	46.4
9 Byron M. Cutcheon (R)	18,963	51.4
Silas S. Fallas (D & G)	16,207	44.0
10 Spencer O. Fisher (D & G)	15,366	52.4
Charles F. Gibson (R)	13,081	44.6
11 Seth C. Moffatt (R)	16,464	64.7
John Powers (D)	8,992	35.3

MINNESOTA

Candidates	Votes	%
1 Milo White (R)	16,604	53.3
A. Bierman (D)	13,961	44.8
2 James B. Wakefield (R)	20,813	64.0
J. J. Thornton (D)	10,639	32.7
3 Horace B. Strait (R)	16,456	51.3
I. Donnelly (D)	15,038	46.9
4 John B. Gilfillan (R)	28,930	53.2
O. C. Merriman (D)	24,496	45.0
5 Knute Nelson (R)	25,609	66.0
L. L. Baxter (D)	13,176	34.0

MISSISSIPPI

Candidates	Votes	%
1 John M. Allen (D)	11,862	81.7
Chandler (R)	2,657	18.3
2 James B. Morgan (D)	13,963	57.5
Chalmers (R)	10,008	41.2
3 Thomas C. Catchings (D)	9,783	69.5
Pearce (R)	4,297	30.5
4 Frederick G. Barry (D)	13,200	69.8
Frazee (R)	5,723	30.2

Candidates	Votes	%
5 Otho R. Singleton (D)	11,934	76.5
Smith (R)	3,665	23.5
6 Henry S. Van Eaton (D)	10,190	60.8
Lynch (R)	6,570	39.2
7 Ethelbert Barksdale (D)	10,946	66.6
Yellowley (R)	5,485	33.4

MISSOURI

Candidates	Votes	%
1 William H. Hatch (D)	18,932	54.3
Gray (FUS)	15,955	45.7
2 John B. Hale (D)	20,204	56.2
Norville (FUS)	15,749	43.8
3 Alexander M. Dockery (D)	19,129	53.4
Harwood (FUS)	15,854	44.2
4 James N. Burnes (D)	16,397	55.5
Kelly (FUS)	13,141	44.5
5 William Warner (FUS)	16,176	52.5
Graves (D)	14,651	47.5
6 John T. Heard (D)	21,107	56.7
Shirk (FUS)	16,139	43.3
7 John E. Hutton (D)	16,712	52.8
Reynolds (FUS)	14,946	47.2
8 John J. O'Neill (D)	9,657	54.7
Eccles (FUS)	8,006	45.3
9 John M. Glover (D)	9,830	54.7
McLean (FU)	8,133	45.3
10 Martin L. Clardy (D)	15,329	52.8
Morse (FUS)	12,797	44.1
11 Richard P. Bland (D)	16,959	54.3
Dallmyer (FUS)	14,288	45.7
12 William J. Stone (D)	20,091	55.3
Warden (FUS)	16,222	44.7
13 William H. Wade (FUS)	20,101	50.3
Thomas (D)	17,981	45.0
14 William Dawson (D)	17,694	61.6
Cramer (FUS)	11,020	38.4

NEBRASKA

Candidates	Votes	%
1 Archibald J. Weaver (R)	22,644	50.0
Charles H. Brown (D)	21,669	47.8
2 James Laird (R)	21,182	52.9
J. H. Stickel (D)	17,650	44.1
3 George W. E. Dorsey (R)	25,685	54.7
William Neville (D)	20,671	44.1

NEVADA

Candidates	Votes	%
AL William Woodburn (R)	6,797	53.1
George W. Cassidy (D)	6,002	46.9

NEW HAMPSHIRE

Candidates	Votes	%
1 Martin A. Haynes (R)	20,623	51.8
McKinney (D)	18,383	46.2
2 Jacob H. Gallinger (R)	22,801	51.5
George (D)	20,426	46.1

NEW JERSEY

Candidates	Votes	%
1 George Hires (R)	19,745	50.0
Ferrell (D)	18,003	45.6
2 James Buchanan (R)	19,144	51.5
Gauntt (D)	16,853	45.4
3 Robert S. Green (D)	19,604	50.8
John Kean Jr. (R)	17,756	46.0
4 James N. Pidcock (D)	15,225	51.3
Howey (R)	12,972	43.7
5 William W. Phelps (R)	17,367	51.7
Stevenson (D)	15,126	45.0
6 Herman Lehlbach (R)	21,162	49.4
Fiedler (D)	20,818	48.6
7 William McAdoo (D)	21,985	56.7
Brigham (R)	16,654	43.0

NEW YORK

Candidates	Votes	%
1 Perry Belmont (D)	22,050	54.9
Platt (R)	18,104	45.1
2 Felix Campbell (D)	17,503	58.5
Sheridan (R)	11,771	39.4
3 Darwin R. James (R)	20,125	60.5
Smith (D)	13,000	39.1
4 Peter P. Mahoney (D)	18,971	57.8
Mullholland (R)	13,339	40.7
5 Archibald M. Bliss (D)	13,985	50.1
Worth (R)	12,865	46.1
6 Nicholas Muller (D)	13,307	56.9
House (R)	6,796	29.1
Fitzgerald (ID)	2,863	12.2
7 John J. Adams (D)	15,864	65.3
Conkling (R)	8,228	33.9
8 Samuel S. Cox (TAM D)	19,386	80.7
Hall (CO D)	4,483	18.7
9 Joseph Pulitzer (D)	15,518	63.6
Thum (R)	8,497	34.8
10 Abram S. Hewitt (D)	15,254	64.1
Biglin (R)	8,392	35.3
11 Truman A. Merriman (CO D)	19,588	62.4
Hardy (TAM D)	11,563	36.8
12 Abraham Dowdney (D)	18,380	61.3
Perley (R)	11,354	37.8
13 Egbert L. Viele (D)	17,622	60.6
Smith (R)	11,027	37.9
14 William G. Stahlnecker (D)	17,507	51.9
McAlpin (R)	15,745	46.7
15 Lewis Beach (D)	17,728	51.7
Snow (R)	15,794	46.0
16 John H. Ketcham (R)	18,942	54.1
Huntington (D)	15,391	43.9
17 James G. Lindsley (R)	20,557	50.9
Bagley (D)	18,671	46.2
18 Henry G. Burleigh (R)	20,732	88.0
McClellan (P)	2,775	11.8
19 John Swinburne (R)	19,790	53.0
Van Alstyne (D)	17,286	46.3
20 George West (R)	21,174	51.2
Wemple (D)	19,467	47.0
21 Frederick A. Johnson (R)	19,049	58.6
Smith (D)	13,462	41.4
22 Abraham X. Parker (R)	22,541	62.1
Hall (D)	12,920	35.6
23 John T. Spriggs (D)	18,164	49.9
Cookingham (R)	17,327	47.6
24 John S. Pindar (D)	17,884	50.5
Ramsey (R)	16,772	47.4
25 Frank Hiscock (R)	21,148	56.4
W. Porter (D, P)	16,326	43.5
26 Stephen C. Millard (R)	23,773	519
Remick (D)	18,783	42.6
27 Sereno E. Payne (R)	26,446	57.1
Beardsley (D)	17,798	38.4
28 John Arnot Jr. (D-R)	28,000	91.0
Beecher (G)	2,044	6.6
29 Ira Davenport (R)	19,987	52.5
Pierpont (D)	16,377	43.0
30 Charles S. Baker (R)	16,733	50.2
Greenleaf (D)	15,496	46.5
31 John G. Sawyer (R)	17,529	51.4
Stevens (D)	14,474	42.4
Richmond (P)	1,869	5.5
32 John M. Farquhar (R)	17,469	50.0
Lockwood (D)	17,302	49.5
33 John B. Weber (R)	14,545	49.1
Payne (D)	13,957	47.2
34 Walter L. Sessions (R)	24,068	54.7
Smith (D)	15,525	35.3
Sill (P)	2,522	5.7

NORTH CAROLINA

Candidates	Votes	%
1 Thomas G. Skinner (D)	16,381	53.8
John B. Respess (R)	14,093	46.3
2 James E. O'Hara (R)	22,309	58.7
Frederick A. Woodward (D)	15,699	41.3
3 Wharton J. Green (D)	16,785	57.8
Curtis H. Brogden (R)	12,156	41.9

Candidates	Votes	%
4 William R. Cox (D)	18,930	58.5
Josiah Turner (R)	13,448	41.5
5 James W. Reid (D)	15,047	54.6
Leonidas C. Edwards (R)	12,522	45.4
6 Risden T. Bennett (D)	19,344	58.0
Oliver H. Dockery (R)	14,010	42.0
7 John S. Henderson (D)	14,262	56.8
James G. Ramsey (R)	10,851	43.2
8 William H. H. Cowles (D)	11,422	58.7
Leander L. Green (R)	8,036	41.3
9 Thomas D. Johnston (D)	13,024	53.2
Hamilton G. Ewart (R)	11,465	46.8

OHIO

Candidates	Votes	%
1 Benjamin Butterworth (R)	17,929	52.1
John F. Follett (D)	16,320	47.4
2 Charles E. Brown (R)	19,718	52.8
Adam A. Kramer (D)	17,513	46.9
3 James E. Campbell (D)	16,398	50.3
Henry L. Morey (R)	15,986	49.0
4 Charles M. Anderson (D)	21,087	50.0
John F. Sinks (R)	20,786	49.3
5 Benjamin Le Fevre (D)	21,968	56.3
William D. Davis (R)	16,852	43.2
6 William D. Hill (D)	20,684	54.1
Hiram C. Glenn (R)	17,154	44.9
7 George E. Seney (D)	20,615	54.5
Daniel Babst Jr. (R)	16,609	43.9
8 John Little (R)	23,019	58.5
James W. Denver (D)	15,381	39.1
9 William C. Cooper (R)	18,415	51.1
E. F. Poppleton (D)	16,634	46.2
10 Jacob Romeis (R)	17,605	50.0
Frank H. Hurd (D)	17,366	49.4
11 William W. Ellsberry (D)	15,251	50.7
Alphonzo Hart (R)	14,841	49.3
12 Albert C. Thompson (R)	15,782	53.8
Leo Ebert (D)	13,384	45.7
13 Joseph H. Outhwaite (D)	23,475	55.2
Allen Miller (R)	18,607	43.8
14 Charles H. Grosvenor (R)	17,008	56.0
John L. Vance (D)	11,281	37.2
Christopher Evans (G)	1,689	5.6
15 Beriah Wilkins (D)	20,717	54.1
Elijah Little (R)	17,421	45.5
16 George W. Geddes (D)	18,528	50.0
Henry C. Hedges (R)	17,835	48.2
17 Adoniram J. Warner (D)	19,173	49.9
Joseph D. Taylor (R)	18,957	49.3
18 Isaac H. Taylor (R)	22,459	56.3
Jonathan H. Wallace (D)	16,309	40.9
19 Ezra B. Taylor (R)	27,039	65.0
Horace Alvord (D)	13,053	31.4
20 William McKinley Jr. (R)	22,672	51.6
David R. Paige (D)	20,643	47.0
21 Martin A. Foran (D & G)	19,154	51.4
Charles C. Burnett (R)	17,884	48.0

OREGON

Candidates	Votes	%
AL Binger Herman (R)	25,699	52.1
John Myers (D)	23,652	47.9

PENNSYLVANIA

Candidates	Votes	%
1 Henry H. Bingham (R)	20,227	60.2
Tipton (D)	13,403	39.9
2 Charles O'Neill (R)	18,336	60.5
Dotts (D)	11,952	39.5
3 Samuel J. Randall (D)	12,340	57.7
Gumper (R)	9,055	42.3
4 William D. Kelley (R)	27,421	63.3
Fahy (D)	15,817	36.5
5 Alfred C. Harmar (R)	26,618	99.9
6 James B. Everhart (R)	18,593	60.5
Heckel (D)	11,551	37.6

Candidates	Votes	%
7 I. Newton Evans (R)	18,048	52.4
Ross (D)	16,425	47.7
8 Daniel Ermentrout (D)	16,577	63.8
Richards (R)	9,405	36.2
9 John A. Hiestand (R)	19,649	65.6
Haldeman (D)	9,894	33.0
10 William H. Sowden (D)	20,797	59.2
Chidsey (R)	14,349	40.8
11 John B. Storm (D)	19,394	60.4
Walter (R)	12,622	39.3
12 Joseph A. Scranton (R)	17,016	51.3
Connoly (D)	15,179	45.7
13 Charles N. Brumm (R)	12,875	52.4
Reilly (D)	11,677	47.6
14 Franklin Bound (R)	20,767	57.7
Foster (D)	15,256	42.4
15 Frank C. Bunnell (R)	17,006	54.4
Post (D)	12,679	40.6
16 William W. Brown (R)	19,400	53.3
Kennedy (D)	16,440	45.2
17 Jacob M. Campbell (R)	19,579	54.3
Enfield (D)	16,005	44.4
18 Louis E. Atkinson (R)	18,367	54.6
Patterson (D)	15,277	45.4
19 William A. Duncan (D)	20,356*	55.9
Seitz (R)	16,094	44.2
20 Andrew G. Curtin (R)	17,656	51.4
Patton (D)	16,419	47.8
21 Charles E. Boyle (D)	19,506	52.8
Ray (R)	17,006	46.0
22 James S. Negley (R)	20,136	56.7
Hopkins (D)	15,113	42.5
23 Thomas M. Bayne (R)	15,854	64.9
Foster (D)	8,073	33.0
24 Oscar L. Jackson (R)	16,436	57.0
Stockdale (D)	11,538	40.0
25 Alexander C. White (R)	16,714	52.8
Reitz (D)	14,929	47.2
26 George W. Fleeger (R)	17,290	47.0
McKinney (D)	15,674	42.6
Roberts (IR)	2,702	7.4
27 William L. Scott (D)	16,002	49.2
Mackey (R)	15,340	47.1
AL Edwin S. Osborne (R)	478,240	53.2
Davis (D)	401,042	44.6

Special Election

19 John Augustus Swope (D)	✔		#

RHODE ISLAND

Candidates	Votes	%
1 Henry J. Spooner (R)	10,140	60.0
Tiba O. Slocum (D)	5,976	35.4
2 William A. Pirce (R)	7,752‡	50.1
Charles H. Page (D)	5,995	38.7
Alfred B. Chadsey (P)	1,501	9.7

SOUTH CAROLINA

Candidates	Votes	%
1 Samuel Dibble (D)	8,612	73.5
W. N. Taft (R)	3,108	26.5
2 George D. Tillman (D)	11,419	85.6
E. J. Dickersin (R)	1,920	14.4
3 D. Wyatt Aiken (D)	10,855	93.5
John R. Tolbert (R)	752	6.5
4 William H. Perry (D)	13,008	100.0
5 John J. Hemphill (D)	9,861	77.4
C. C. Macey (R)	2,881	22.6
6 George W. Dargan (D)	10,465	76.1
Edmund H. Deas (R)	3,289	23.9
7 Robert Smalls (R)	8,419	64.8
William Elliott (D)	4,584	35.3

Special Election

4 John Bratton (D)	3,339✔	#

TENNESSEE

Candidates	Votes	%
1 Augustus H. Pettibone (R)	15,478	54.4
King (D)	12,981	45.6
2 Leonidas C. Houk (R)	19,357	68.3
Ledgerwood (D)	8,975	31.7

TENNESSEE

	Candidates	Votes	%
3	John R. Neal (D)	14,284	51.2
	Evans (R)	13,624	48.8
4	Benton McMillin (D)	12,956	88.0
	Smith (R)	1,771	12.0
5	James D. Richardson (D)	13,285	58.5
	Warder (R)	7,144	31.4
	Martin (ID)	1,882	8.3
6	Andrew J. Caldwell (D)	16,873	58.2
	Baker (R)	12,124	41.8
7	John G. Ballentine (D)	12,157	55.7
	Cliff (R)	9,682	44.3
8	John M. Taylor (D)	12,783	52.6
	Warren (R)	11,529	47.4
9	Presley T. Glass (D)	13,451	55.0
	Etheridge (R)	11,019	45.0
10	Zachary Taylor (R)	14,271	51.0
	Harris (D)	13,713	49.0

TEXAS

	Candidates	Votes	%
1	Charles Stewart (D)	24,150	99.9
2	John H. Reagan (D)	16,840	67.1
	A. T. Monroe (R)	8,276	33.0
3	James H. Jones (D)	23,504	97.2
4	David B. Culberson (D)	23,165	100.0
5	James W. Throckmorton (D)	29,462	98.9
6	Olin Wellborn (D)	27,804	85.5
	J. C. Bigger (R)	4,721	14.5
7	William H. Crain (D)	15,471	59.2
	R. B. Rentfro (R)	9,586	36.7
8	James F. Miller (D)	17,143	66.9
	W. P. Burns (R)	8,473	33.1
9	Roger Q. Mills (D)	22,333	71.2

	Candidates	Votes	%
	J. P. Osterhout (R)	9,049	28.8
10	Joseph D. Sayers (D)	21,523	63.7
	J. B. Rector (IR)	12,253	36.3
11	Samuel W. T. Lanham (D)	29,738	99.4

VERMONT

	Candidates	Votes	%
1	John W. Stewart (R)	18,899	73.5
	George H. Simmons (D)	6,591	25.6
2	William W. Grout (R)	20,026	69.6
	Martin H. Goddard (D)	8,479	29.5

VIRGINIA

	Candidates	Votes	%
1	Thomas Croxton (D)	14,136	51.0
	R. M. Mayo (R)	13,579	49.0
2	Harry Libby (R)	19,083	58.3
	R. C. Marshall (D)	13,652	41.7
3	George D. Wise (D)	15,741	52.4
	Robert T. Hubard (R)	14,301	47.6
4	James D. Brady (R)	11,408	40.5
	George E. Rives (D)	10,326	36.6
	Joseph P. Evans	6,451	22.9
5	George C. Cabell (D)	13,588	55.0
	J. W. Hartwell (R)	11,100	45.0
6	John W. Daniel (D)	17,177	55.9
	R. P. W. Morris (R)	13,526	44.1
7	Charles T. O'Ferrall (D)	15,791	56.4
	J. B. Webb (R)	12,221	43.6
8	John S. Barbour (D)	15,792	55.6
	Duff Green (R)	12,598	44.4
9	Connally F. Trigg (D)	13,844	52.2
	Daniel F. Bailey (R)	12,660	47.8

	Candidates	Votes	%
10	John R. Tucker (D)	15,059	52.1
	Jacob Yost (R)	13,872	48.0

WEST VIRGINIA

		Votes	%
1	Nathan Goff Jr. (R)	17,462	50.3
	John Brannon (D)	17,258	49.7
2	William L. Wilson (D)	18,266	52.2
	Francis M. Reynolds (R)	16,737	47.8
3	Charles P. Snyder (D)	15,359	53.7
	James W. Davis (R)	13,240	46.3
4	Eustace Gibson (D)	16,598	50.2
	A. R. Barbee (G & R)	16,445	49.8

WISCONSIN

		Votes	%
1	Lucien B. Caswell (R)	19,284	54.6
	Ernst Merton (D)	14,590	41.3
2	Edward S. Bragg (D)	16,865	55.4
	Samuel S. Barney (R)	12,643	41.6
3	Robert M. LaFollette (R)	17,433	48.1
	Burr W. Jones (D)	16,942	46.7
	John M. Olin (P)	1,885	5.2
4	Isaac W. Van Schaick (R)	16,783	49.1
	P. V. Deuster (D)	15,907	46.5
5	Joseph Rankin (D)	17,851	59.3
	Charles Luling (R)	11,610	38.5
6	Richard W. Guenther (R)	16,425	49.9
	A. L. Smith (D)	15,197	46.2
7	Ormsby B. Thomas (R)	18,437	52.6
	G. M. Woodward (D)	15,446	44.1
8	William T. Price (R & P)	24,460	60.2
	L. R. Larson (D)	16,183	39.8
9	Isaac Stephenson (R)	23,414	53.5
	James Meehan (D)	19,885	45.4

1885 House Elections

ILLINOIS

Special Election

5	Albert J. Hopkins (R)	8,977	73.3
	Richard Bishop (D)	3,211	26.2

NORTH CAROLINA

Special Election

5	James W. Reid (D)	4,707	90.5
	Joseph S. Worth (R)	356	6.8

RHODE ISLAND

Special Election

2	Nathan F. Dixon (R)	2,258	69.3
	Philip W. Hawkins (D)	998	30.6

1886 House Elections

ALABAMA

	Candidates	Votes	%
1	James T. Jones (D)	4,220	99.6
2	Hilary A. Herbert (D)	5,659	100.0
3	William C. Oates (D)	4,660	100.0
4	Alexander C. Davidson (D)	14,913	71.2
	McDuffie (R)	3,526	16.8
	Turner (IR)	2,519	12.0
5	James E. Cobb (D)	5,558	87.8
	Edwards (R)	775	12.2
6	John H. Bankhead (D)	7,968	64.6
	Long (R)	4,369	35.4
7	William H. Forney (D)	7,549	62.0
	Hardie (R)	4,608	37.8
8	Joseph Wheeler (D)	11,684	57.5
	Jackson (R)	8,639	42.5

ARKANSAS

	Candidates	Votes	%
1	Poindexter Dunn (D)	6,092	100.0
2	Clifton R. Breckinridge (D)	8,612	54.4
	D. D. Leach (R)	4,380	27.7
	R. B. Carllee (AG WHEEL)	2,846	18.0
3	Thomas C. McRae (D)	8,909	57.8
	J. C. Ray (R)	4,169	27.0
	L. H. Hitt (G)	2,343	15.2
4	John H. Rogers (D)	8,314	62.1
	Isom P. Langley (LAB)	5,077	37.9
5	Samuel W. Peel (D)	4,746	100.0

CALIFORNIA

	Candidates	Votes	%
1	Thomas L. Thompson (D)	16,499	50.0
	C. A. Gartern (R)	15,526	47.1
2	Marion Biggs (D)	17,667	49.8
	J. C. Campbell (R)	16,594	46.8
3	Joseph McKenna (R)	15,801	53.0
	H. C. McPike (D)	13,277	44.5
4	William W. Morrow (R)	11,413	48.4
	F. McCoppin (D)	9,854	41.8
	C. A. Sumner (LAB)	2,184	9.3
5	Charles N. Felton (R)	16,328	48.5
	F. J. Sullivan (D)	16,209	48.2
6	William Vandever (R)	18,259	47.3
	Joe D. Lynch (D)	18,204	47.1
	W. H. Harris (P)	2,159	5.6

COLORADO

	Candidates	Votes	%
AL	George G. Symes (R)	27,732	47.6
	Myron W. Reed (D)	26,929	46.2
	Joseph Murray (P)	3,597	6.2

CONNECTICUT

	Candidates	Votes	%
1	Robert J. Vance (D)	14,898	48.3
	John R. Buck (R)	14,552	47.2
2	Carlos French (D)	18,730	47.9
	Lewis (R)	17,402	44.5
3	Charles A. Russell (R)	9,366	48.9
	Hyde (D)	8,718	45.5
	Rockwell (P)	1,066	5.6
4	Miles T. Granger (D)	16,235	47.8
	Miles (R)	15,914	46.9

DELAWARE

	Candidates	Votes	%
AL	John B. Penington (D)	13,837	62.2
	Cooper (TEMP REF)	8,393	37.8

FLORIDA

	Candidates	Votes	%
1	Robert H. M. Davidson (D)	14,493	66.2
	Pendleton (R)	7,389	33.8
2	Charles Dougherty (D)	18,890	54.1
	Greeley (R)	15,764	45.2

GEORGIA

	Candidates	Votes	%
1	Thomas M. Norwood (D)	2,061	99.2
2	Henry G. Turner (D)	2,411	99.7
3	Charles F. Crisp (D)	1,704	100.0
4	Thomas W. Grimes (D)	2,909	89.8
	Carmical (I)	330	10.2
5	John D. Stewart (D)	2,999	100.0
6	James H. Blount (D)	1,722	99.9
7	Judson C. Clements (D)	5,043	75.5
	Felton (I)	1,537	23.0
8	Henry H. Carlton (D)	2,322	97.7
9	Allen D. Candler (D)	2,355	98.9
10	George T. Barnes (D)	1,944	99.6

ILLINOIS

	Candidates	Votes	%
1	Ransom W. Dunham (R)	12,321	46.9
	Edgar Terhunr (D)	7,258	27.6
	Harvey Sheldon Jr. (UN LAB)	6,358	24.2
2	Frank Lawler (D)	7,369	39.3
	Daniel F. Gluson (UN LAB)	7,353	39.3
	Charles W. Woodman (R)	3,976	21.2
3	William E. Mason (R)	13,721	66.2
	B. W. Goodhur (UN LAB)	6,352	30.7
4	George E. Adams (R)	12,147	48.1
	J. B. Taylor (D)	7,480	29.6
	I. A. Hawkins (UN LAB)	4,997	19.8
5	Albert J. Hopkins (R)	14,224	62.9
	J. F. Glidden (D)	6,258	27.7
	Charles Wheaton (P)	2,121	9.4
6	Robert R. Hitt (R)	13,106	55.5
	James McNamara (D)	8,650	36.6
	Spencer Rising (P)	1,878	8.0
7	Thomas J. Henderson (R)	12,586	58.2
	Sherwood Dixon (D)	7,731	35.8
	David E. Holmes (P)	1,296	6.0
8	Ralph Plumb (R)	16,827	52.1
	Hiram H. Cady (D)	13,893	43.0
9	Lewis E. Payson (R)	13,753	54.2
	Mathews H. Peters (D)	10,633	41.9
10	Philip Sidney Post (R)	15,186	48.7
	Nicholas E. Worthington (D)	15,157	48.6
11	William A. Gest (R)	16,733	48.8
	William H. Neece (D & G)	16,397	47.9
12	George A. Anderson (D & G)	18,718	57.5
	Oruan Pierson (R)	12,755	39.2
13	William M. Springer (D)	17,433	49.5
	James A. Connelly (R)	16,453	46.7
14	Jonathan H. Rowell (R)	15,319	51.0
	William Voorhees (D)	12,917	43.0
	William W. Alder (P)	1,786	6.0
15	Joseph G. Cannon (R)	16,739	50.9
	D. H. Lindsey (D)	15,314	46.6
16	Silas Z. Landes (D)	16,424	50.2
	Charles Churchill (R)	15,564	47.6
17	Edward Lane (D)	14,937	53.9
	Robert McWilliams (R)	11,557	41.7
18	Jehu Baker (R)	15,396	50.8
	William R. Morrison (D)	14,234	46.9
19	Richard W. Townshend (D)	16,316	56.1
	James S. Martin (R)	11,972	41.2
20	John R. Thomas (R)	16,246	50.9
	William Hartzell (D)	15,074	47.3

INDIANA

	Candidates	Votes	%
1	Alvin P. Hovey (R)	18,258	49.0
	J. E. McCullough (D)	16,901	45.4
2	John H. O'Neal (D)	16,075	51.8
	M. S. Ragsdale (R)	14,871	47.9
3	Jonas G. Howard (D)	12,458	46.4
	James K. Marsh (ID)	9,854	36.7
	James Kugwin (D)	3,714	13.8
4	William S. Holman (D)	15,777	50.8
	Thomas J. Lucas (R)	14,989	48.3
5	Courtland Cushing Matson (D)	16,694	49.9
	Ira J. Chase (R)	16,162	48.3
6	Thomas M. Browne (R)	20,397	60.4
	George S. Jones (D)	12,253	36.3
7	William D. Bynum (D)	22,882	51.3
	Addison C. Harris (R)	21,108	47.3
8	James T. Johnston (R)	20,918	50.6
	John Edward Lamb (D)	19,816	47.9
9	Joseph B. Cheadle (R)	22,437	53.0
	Benjamin F. Ham (D)	19,021	44.9
10	William D. Owen (R)	18,114	52.1
	Hiram D. Hattery (D)	16,041	46.1
11	George Washington Steele (R)	19,649	48.9
	James C. Branyan (D)	19,241	47.9
12	James B. White (R)	17,900	51.8
	Robert Lowry (D)	15,416	44.6
13	Benjamin Franklin Shively (D)	19,105	50.5
	Jasper Packard (R)	18,087	47.8

IOWA

	Candidates	Votes	%
1	John Henry Gear (R)	16,115	51.1
	Benton Jay Hall (FUS)	15,078	47.8
2	Walter I. Hayes (FUS)	15,309	48.0
	Thomas J. O'Meara (LAB)	8,602	27.0
	Samuel Jordan Kirkwood (R)	8,009	25.1
3	David B. Henderson (R)	18,201	54.4
	W. H. Chamberlain (FUS)	15,272	45.6
4	William Elijah Fuller (R)	17,062	53.0
	Willard C. Earle (FUS)	15,132	47.0
5	Daniel Kerr (R)	16,696	51.0
	Benjamin Todd Frederick (FUS)	15,963	48.8
6	James Baird Weaver (FUS)	16,572	50.9
	John A. Donnell (R)	15,954	49.0
7	Edwin H. Conger (R)	15,165	51.6
	W. L. Carpenter (FUS)	14,239	48.4
8	Albert Raney Anderson (IR)	17,970	53.2
	William P. Hepburn (R)	15,745	46.7
9	Joseph Lyman (R)	16,953	53.4
	John H. Keatley (FUS)	14,747	46.5
10	Adoniram J. Holmes (R)	16,767	56.6
	George Wilmot (FUS)	12,868	43.4
11	Isaac S. Struble (R)	15,356	58.4
	E. C. Palmer (FUS)	10,919	41.5

KANSAS

	Candidates	Votes	%
1	Edmund N. Morrill (R)	17,347	55.3
	E. Bierer (D)	13,832	44.1
2	Edward H. Funston (R)	18,037	51.9
	Charles Robinson (D)	15,416	44.3
3	Bishop W. Perkins (R)	19,614	53.4
	Frank Bacon (D)	15,875	43.2
4	Thomas Ryan (R)	21,961	56.2
	John Martin (D)	15,706	40.2
5	John A. Anderson (R)	19,240	53.1
	J. G. Lowe (D)	12,751	35.2
	A. S. Wilson (IR)	3,856	10.6
6	Erastus J. Turner (R)	19,624	58.5
	W. S. Gile (D)	11,359	33.9
	C. H. Moody (A-MONOP)	2,098	6.3
7	Samuel R. Peters (R)	34,515	56.2
	Thomas George (D)	25,070	40.8

KENTUCKY

	Candidates	Votes	%
1	William J. Stone (D)	9,730	53.4
	Oscar Turner (ID)	8,476	46.5
2	Polk Laffoon (D)	10,715	58.2
	George W. Jolly (R)	7,695	41.8
3	W. Godfrey Hunter (R)	13,379	51.8
	John S. Rhea (D)	12,372	47.9

KENTUCKY

	Candidates	Votes	%
4	Alexander B. Montgomery (D)	9,892	56.6
	J. D. Belden (R)	7,572	43.4
5	Asher G. Caruth (D)	9,964	50.4
	A. E. Willson (R)	9,824	49.7
6	John G. Carlisle (D)	6,476	53.3
	George H. Thoebe (LAB)	5,651	46.5
7	William C. P. Breckinridge (D)	4,791	99.7
8	James B. McCreary (D)	10,540	59.8
	Thomas Todd (R)	7,077	40.2
9	George M. Thomas (R)	13,693	50.3
	Garrett S. Wall (D)	13,546	49.7
10	William P. Taulbee (D)	11,940	51.6
	William L. Hurst (R)	11,194	48.4
11	Hugh L. Finly (R)	12,824	53.2
	W. H. Botts (D)	11,278	46.8

LOUISIANA

1	Theodore S. Wilkinson (D)	11,350	87.3
	William M. Burwell (R)	1,649	12.7
2	Matthew D. Lagan (D)	7,930	53.7
	A. Hero Jr. (R)	6,537	44.3
3	Edward J. Gay (D)	14,782	55.1
	Chester B. Darrall	11,692	43.6
4	Newton C. Blanchard (D)	5,747	99.8
5	Cherubusco Newton (D)	13,618	95.6
6	Edward W. Robertson (D)	9,676	95.8

Special Election

2	Nathaniel Dick Wallace (D)	✔	#

MAINE

1	Thomas B. Reed (R)	15,486	49.9
	W. H. Clifford (D)	14,298	46.0
2	Nelson Dingley Jr. (R)	18,137	53.3
	Alonzo Garcelon (D)	11,920	35.1
	William T. Eustis (P-LAB)	3,939	11.6
3	Seth Llewellyn Milliken (R)	17,992	56.5
	Joseph E. Ladd (D)	12,781	40.1
4	Charles A. Boutelle (R)	17,372	54.6
	John F. Lynch (D)	13,655	42.9

MARYLAND

1	Charles H. Gibson (D)	12,791	49.3
	Hodson (R)	11,640	44.8
	Melson (P)	1,529	5.9
2	Frank T. Shaw (D)	12,016	55.5
	Marine (R)	8,362	38.6
	Zouck (P)	1,283	5.9
3	Harry W. Rusk (D)	13,634	72.3
	Bosse (LAB-R)	3,300	17.5
	Glass (P)	1,726	9.2
4	Isidor Rayner (D)	14,750	62.6
	Findlay (I)	7,220	30.6
	Weatherby (R)	1,569	6.7
5	Barnes Compton (D)	13,579	54.8
	Tuck (R)	10,850	43.8
6	Louis E. McComas (R)	16,851	49.7
	Baughman (D)	16,438	48.5

MASSACHUSETTS

1	Robert T. Davis (R)	9,416	58.6
	McLaughlin (D)	5,768	35.9
	Hatfield (P)	847	5.3
2	John D. Long (R)	11,317	52.2
	Morse (D)	9,495	43.8
3	Leopold Morse (D)	11,199	53.7
	Ranney (R)	9,438	45.3
4	Patrick A. Collins (D)	11,201	73.4
	Cutler (R)	3,829	25.1
5	Edward D. Hayden (R)	11,364	57.3
	Randall (P)	8,006	40.3
6	Henry Cabot Lodge (R)	13,495	50.5
	Lovering (D)	12,767	47.8
7	William Cogswell (R)	9,863	46.9
	French (D)	8,489	40.4

	Candidates	Votes	%
	Spaulding (G & P)	2,663	12.7
8	Charles H. Allen (R)	10,216	50.2
	Donovan (D)	9,684	47.6
9	Edward Burnett (D)	10,354	48.7
	Ely (R)	10,143	47.7
10	John E. Russell (D)	9,728	49.7
	Rice (R)	8,977	45.8
11	William Whiting (R)	10,861	53.5
	Currier (D)	8,098	39.9
	Watkins (P)	1,320	6.5
12	Francis W. Rockwell (R)	10,181	49.6
	Joyner (D)	9,366	45.6

MICHIGAN

1	John Logan Chipman (D)	17,367	51.0
	Henry A. Robinson (R)	15,801	46.4
2	Edward P. Allen (R)	16,518	47.9
	Lester H. Salsbury (D)	15,486	45.0
	Alfred O. Crozier (P)	2,448	7.1
3	James O'Donnell (R)	20,215	51.4
	Patrick Hankerd (D)	15,499	39.4
	Hiram J. Miller (P)	3,594	9.1
4	Julius C. Burrows (R)	18,257	50.7
	Harvey C. Sherwood (D)	15,744	43.7
	Jesse S. Boyden (P)	1,999	5.6
5	Melbourne H. Ford (D)	18,567	46.7
	George W. McBride (R)	18,120	45.6
	Edward L. Briggs (P)	3,086	7.8
6	Mark S. Brewer (R)	19,034	48.1
	John H. Fedewa (D)	17,148	43.3
	Azariah S. Partridge (P)	3,427	8.7
7	Justin R. Whiting (D)	13,777	48.6
	John P. Sanborn (R)	12,963	45.8
	William F. Clark (P)	1,593	5.6
8	Timothy E. Tarsney (D)	18,301	48.4
	Roswell G. Horr (R)	17,615	46.5
	George W. Abbey (P)	1,930	5.1
9	Byron M. Cutcheon (R)	17,226	50.9
	Lyman G. Mason (D)	14,198	42.0
	Lathrop S. Ellis (P)	2,393	7.1
10	Spencer O. Fisher (D)	15,047	53.3
	Henry M. Loud (R)	12,900	45.7
11	Seth C. Moffatt (R)	14,485	53.6
	John Power (D)	12,242	45.3

MINNESOTA

1	Thomas Wilson (D)	17,491	52.0
	John A. Lovely (R)	14,663	3.6
2	John Lind (R)	22,908	59.8
	A. H. Bullis (D&F ALNC)	13,260	34.6
	George J. Day (P)	2,114	5.5
3	John L. MacDonald (D)	16,788	50.3
	B. B. Herbert (R)	15,583	46.7
4	Edmund Rice (D)	34,034	52.4
	J. B. Gilfillan (R)	28,909	44.5
5	Knute Nelson (R)	43,937	97.3

MISSISSIPPI

1	John M. Allen (D)	3,140	99.2
2	James B. Morgan (D)	7,857	62.1
	Chalmers (R)	4,791	37.9
3	Thomas C. Catchings (D)	4,518	65.5
	Simrall (R)	2,382	34.5
4	Frederick G. Barry (D)	2,964	96.1
5	Chapman L. Anderson (D)	4,289	99.4
6	Thomas R. Stockdale (D)	8,284	68.4
	Lynch (R)	3,825	31.6
7	Charles E. Hooker (D)	4,507	100.0

MISSOURI

1	William H. Hatch (D)	17,323	54.5
	Harrison (R)	14,455	45.5

	Candidates	Votes	%
2	Charles H. Mansur (D)	17,171	49.2
	Hale (ID)	16,441	47.1
3	Alexander M. Dockery (D)	19,689	56.0
	Harwood (R)	15,327	43.6
4	James N. Burnes (D)	14,051	53.2
	Dunn (R)	11,964	45.3
5	William Warner (R)	16,368	50.9
	Phillips (D)	15,583	48.4
6	John T. Heard (D)	21,558	53.6
	Guitar (R)	18,678	46.4
7	John E. Hutton (D)	15,212	53.7
	Martin (R)	13,135	46.3
8	John J. O'Neill (D)	8,166	47.8
	Cumings (R)	6,802	39.8
	Wind (UN LAB)	2,030	11.9
9	John M. Glover (D)	7,202	44.3
	Nathan Frank (R)	7,102	43.7
	Davisson (UN LAB)	1,792	11.0
10	Martin L. Clardy (D)	13,145	45.1
	Ledergerber (R)	12,097	41.5
	Ratchford (UN LAB)	3,927	13.5
11	Richard P. Bland (D)	16,594	54.3
	Parker (R)	13,996	45.8
12	William J. Stone (D)	21,205	53.9
	Kimball (R)	17,540	44.5
13	William H. Wade (R)	14,631	51.8
	Cravens (D)	12,674	44.9
14	James P. Walker (D)	18,400	63.6
	Davidson (FUS)	10,533	36.4

NEBRASKA

1	John A. McShane (D)	23,396	54.9
	Church Howe (R)	16,373	38.4
	George Bigelow (P)	2,867	6.7
2	James Laird (R)	21,373	51.5
	W. A. McKeighan (D)	16,315	39.3
	C. S. Harrison (P)	3,789	9.1
3	George W. E. Dorsey (R)	28,681	55.2
	A. H. Webster (D)	20,933	40.3

NEVADA

AL	William Woodburn (R)	6,700	54.2
	J. H. Macmillan (D)	5,670	45.8

NEW HAMPSHIRE

1	Luther F. McKinney (D)	18,370	49.1
	Martin A. Haynes (R)	18,165	48.5
2	Jacob H. Gallinger (R)	19,715	49.8
	William W. Bailey (D)	18,549	46.9

NEW JERSEY

1	George Hires (R)	18,347	49.0
	Wescott (D)	15,013	40.1
	Nicholson (P)	4,072	10.9
2	James Buchanan (R)	17,767	50.2
	Reed (D)	15,065	42.6
	Brown (P)	2,547	7.2
3	John Kean Jr. (R)	15,567	46.5
	McMahon (D)	14,930	44.6
	Parker (P)	2,980	8.9
4	James N. Pidcock (D)	11,686	44.9
	Vanblarcom (R)	11,563	44.4
	Morrow (P)	2,772	10.7
5	William W. Phelps (R)	15,297	51.8
	Skinner (D)	12,461	42.2
	Church (P)	1,780	6.0
6	Herman Lehlbach (R)	15,492	40.8
	Haynes (D)	13,719	36.1
	Beckmeyer (LAB)	6,331	16.7
	Anderson (P)	2,429	6.4
7	William McAdoo (D)	15,688	49.7
	Hammerschlag (R)	11,435	36.2
	Kerr (ID)	3,668	11.6

NEW YORK

	Candidates	Votes	%
1	Perry Belmont (D)	16,286	50.0
	McCormick (R)	15,360	47.1
2	Felix Campbell (D)	16,679	70.8
	Donovan (R)	5,580	23.7
3	Stephen V. White (R)	12,740	48.6
	Bell (D)	12,568	48.0
4	Peter P. Mahoney (D)	13,879	53.6
	O'Connor (R)	10,251	39.6
5	Archibald M. Bliss (D)	11,583	50.1
	Waters (R)	11,111	48.0
6	Amos J. Cummings (D)	13,799	96.4
7	Lloyd S. Bryce (D)	12,895	64.2
	Lawson (R)	6,972	34.7
8	Timothy J. Campbell (D)	12,179	50.4
	Grady (ID)	11,799	48.8
9	Samuel S. Cox (D)	13,754	62.3
	Wagener (R)	8,259	37.4
10	Francis B. Spinola (D)	10,847	50.7
	Rice (R)	10,320	48.2
11	Truman A. Merriman (D)	24,502	97.8
12	W. Bourke Cockran (D)	15,886	59.3
	Pell (R)	10,680	39.9
13	Ashbel P. Fitch (R)	17,614	55.3
	Viele (D)	13,939	43.8
14	William G. Stahlnecker (D)	15,828	51.2
	Wood (R)	13,392	44.3
15	Henry Bacon (D)	13,488	48.7
	Stivers (R)	13,027	47.0
16	John H. Ketcham (R)	15,585	55.2
	Sackett (D)	11,583	41.0
17	Stephen T. Hopkins (R)	17,805	52.3
	Lounsbery (D)	14,317	42.1
	Howie (P)	1,872	5.5
18	Edward W. Greenman (D)	17,082	49.8
	Burleigh (R)	15,819	46.1
19	Nicholas T. Kane (D)	16,552	47.8
	Swinburne (R)	16,385	47.3
20	George West R)	16,339	54.7
	Wick (D)	10,035	33.6
	French (P)	3,344	11.2
21	John H. Moffitt (R)	15,376	68.4
	Winslow (P)	6,049	26.9
22	Abraham X. Parker (R)	14,450	57.5
	Corbin (D)	9,120	36.3
	Huntington (P)	1,523	6.1
23	James S. Sherman (R)	15,914	49.2
	Spriggs (D)	14,430	44.6
	Hendee (P)	1,966	6.1
24	David Wilber (R)	16,314	50.3
	Smith (D)	14,549	44.9
25	Frank Hiscock (R)	16,087*	58.2
	Angel (D)	11,498	41.6
26	Milton De Lano (R)	19,155	55.3
	Downs (D)	12,362	35.7
	Williams (P)	3,086	8.9
27	Newton W. Nutting (R)	21,465	60.7
	Beardsley (D)	11,679	33.0
28	Thomas S. Flood (R)	14,124	52.3
	McGuire (D)	11,611	43.0
29	Ira Davenport (R)	17,047	82.8
	Ladd (D)	3,009	14.6
30	Charles S. Baker (R)	13,170	53.2
	Bacon (D)	10,509	42.5
31	John G. Sawyer (R)	14,611	54.3
	Wadsworth (D)	10,022	37.2
	Sparrow (P)	2,286	8.5
32	John M. Farquhar (R)	16,785	55.2
	Rogers (D)	13,452	44.2
33	John B. Weber (R)	12,215	49.3
	Spalding (D)	11,082	44.7
	Smith (P)	1,465	5.9
34	William G. Laidlaw (R)	16,966	52.8
	Wood (D)	9,305	28.9
	Huntington (P)	5,505	17.1

NORTH CAROLINA

	Candidates	Votes	%
1	Louis C. Latham (D)	13,390	54.6
	Lycurgus J. Barrett	10,635	43.4
2	Furnifold M. Simmons (D)	15,158	44.8
	James E. O'Hara (R)	13,060	38.6
	Israel B. Abbott (IR)	5,020	14.9
3	Charles W. McClammy (D)	14,538	60.7
	F. D. Koonce (R)	8,164	34.1
4	John Nichols (I)	15,861	52.4
	John W. Graham (D)	14,423	47.6
5	John M. Brower (R)	13,282	49.7
	James W. Reid (D)	11,702	43.8
6	Alfred Rowland (D)	14,261	62.5
	Charles R. Jones (ID)	7,659	33.6
7	John S. Henderson (D)	10,565	78.6
	Joseph A. Blair	1,473	11.0
	James E. Walker (P)	1,401	10.4
8	William H. H. Cowles (D)	9,997	65.2
	Leander L. Green (R)	5,325	34.7
9	Thomas D. Johnston (D)	11,754	54.2
	William H. Malone (ID)	7,014	32.3
	Alexander H. Jones (R)	2,934	13.5

OHIO

	Candidates	Votes	%
1	Benjamin Butterworth (R)	15,522	53.4
	Samuel A. Miller (D)	13,166	45.3
2	Charles E. Brown (R)	17,009	52.3
	Hugh Shiels (D)	15,210	46.8
3	Elihu S. Williams (R)	17,235	47.1
	Robert M. Murray (D)	16,102	44.0
	Jacob W. Nigh (LAB)	2,132	5.8
4	Samuel S. Yoder (D)	16,959	59.2
	Theodore W. Brotherton (R)	10,753	37.5
5	George E. Seney (D)	16,996	70.8
	David Harpster (R)	5,023	20.9
	Rudolph Rock (P)	1,629	6.8
6	Melvin M. Boothman (R)	19,476	50.0
	William D. Hill (D)	18,099	46.5
7	James E. Campbell (D)	15,303	48.4
	John Little (R)	15,301	48.4
8	Robert P. Kennedy (R)	18,080	49.6
	Thomas R. McMillen (D)	16,692	45.8
9	William C. Cooper (R)	17,659	49.8
	John C. Levering (D)	15,790	44.6
	William H. Elsom (P)	1,900	5.4
10	Jacob Romeis (R)	17,180	51.7
	Frank H. Hurd (D)	15,592	46.9
11	Albert C. Thompson (R)	17,550	55.3
	Irvin Dungan (D)	13,202	41.6
12	Jacob J. Pugsley (R)	18,283	49.6
	James W. Denver (D)	17,025	46.2
13	Joseph H. Outhwaite (D)	20,310	51.7
	William Shepard (R)	17,730	45.1
14	Charles P. Wickham (R)	13,835	49.1
	Thomas G. Bristor (D)	12,764	45.3
	Corydon L. Tambling (P)	1,576	5.6
15	Charles H. Grosvenor (R)	15,794	51.0
	Adoniram J. Warner (D)	14,324	46.3
16	Beriah Wilkins (D)	20,258	53.3
	Caleb B. Downs (R)	16,284	42.8
17	Joseph D. Taylor (R)	17,623	52.4
	David C. Kennon (D)	14,010	41.7
	James M. Monroe (P)	1,948	5.8
18	William McKinley Jr (R)	18,776	49.1
	Wallace H. Phelps (D)	16,217	42.4
19	Ezra B. Taylor (R)	17,707	63.2
	Thaddeus E. Hoyt (D)	7,831	28.0
	Charles E. Holt (P)	2,291	8.2
20	George W. Crouse (R)	15,777	48.5
	William Dorsey (D)	14,890	45.8
	John J. Ashenhurst (P)	1,805	5.6
21	Martin A. Foran (D)	14,899	51.2
	Amos Townsend (R)	13,466	46.3

OREGON

	Candidates	Votes	%
AL	Binger Hermann (R)	26,918	49.0
	N. L. Butler (D)	25,221	46.0
	G. M. Miller (P)	2,753	5.0

PENNSYLVANIA

	Candidates	Votes	%
1	Henry H. Bingham (R)	18,225	60.0
	Ryan (D)	11,826	38.9
2	Charles O'Neill (R)	15,480	59.9
	Beasley (D)	9,847	38.1
3	Samuel J. Randall (D)	11,320	98.4
4	William D. Kelley (R)	25,391	62.7
	Laverty (D)	13,882	34.3
5	Alfred C. Harmer (R)	23,464	57.4
	Smith (D)	12,276	30.1
	Herwig (LAB)	4,159	10.2
6	Smedley Darlington (R)	11,841	41.4
	Dickinson (D)	10,529	36.8
	Everhart (IR)	4,966	17.4
7	Robert M. Yardley (R)	17,079	52.0
	Satterthwaite (D)	14,944	45.5
8	Daniel Ermentrout (D)	13,978	59.6
	Stitzel (R)	9,163	39.0
9	John A. Hiestand (R)	18,683	65.7
	McGovern (D)	9,049	31.8
10	William H. Sowden (D)	21,370	96.8
11	Charles R. Buckalew (D)	18,337	95.9
12	John Lynch (D)	14,176	48.3
	Joseph A. Scranton (R)	13,526	46.1
	Knapp (P)	1,663	5.7
13	Charles N. Brumm (R)	11,293	50.2
	Shepherd (D)	10,519	46.8
14	Franklin Bound (R)	17,116	51.9
	McDevitt (D)	14,485	43.9
15	Frank C. Bunnell (R)	16,113	56.3
	Piollet (D)	10,453	36.5
	Dodson (P)	2,041	7.1
16	Henry C. McCormick (R)	17,393	55.3
	Keenan (D)	12,567	40.0
17	Edward Scull (R)	16,548	49.7
	Tate (D)	15,649	47.0
18	Louis E. Atkinson (R)	17,020	54.2
	Jacobs (D)	13,773	43.9
19	Levi Maish (D)	18,174	54.3
	Seitz (R)	14,228	42.5
20	John Patton (R)	16,566	48.8
	Hall (D)	16,413	48.4
21	Welty McCullogh (R)	15,381	45.2
	Donnelly (D)	15,126	44.4
	Rafferty (D)	2,581	7.6
22	John Dalzell (R)	16,631	54.3
	Parkinson (D)	12,626	41.2
23	Thomas M. Bayne (R)	12,133	58.9
	Alcorn (D)	7,094	34.4
	Rabe (P)	1,385	6.7
24	Oscar L. Jackson (R)	14,787	55.3
	Baird (D)	10,347	38.7
	Irish (P)	1,465	5.5
25	James T. Maffett (R)	14,322	51.3
	St.Clair (D)	12,700	45.5
26	Norman Hall (D)	14,565	46.3
	Roberts (R)	14,034	44.6
	Cunningham (P)	2,288	7.3
27	William L. Scott (D)	14,787	48.5
	Mackey (R)	13,574	44.5
	Andrews (P)	2,140	7.0
AL	Edwin S. Osborne (R)	415,166	50.8
	Maxwell Stevenson (D)	367,551	45.0

RHODE ISLAND [1]

	Candidates	Votes	%
1	Henry J. Spooner (R)	3,457	52.9
	Oscar Lapham (D)	2,337	35.7
	Howard (P)	746	11.4
2	Charles S. Bradley (D)	5,426*	48.2
	Nathan F. Dixon (R)	4,849	43.1
	Chace (P)	852	7.6

SOUTH CAROLINA

	Candidates	Votes	%
1	Samuel Dibble (D)	3,315	100.0
2	George D. Tillman (D)	5,232	99.6
3	James C. Cothran (D)	4,402	99.8

1. No candidate in the 2nd district secured the majority needed to win in the general election. (Majority vote requirement, see p. 703.)

SOUTH CAROLINA

Candidates	Votes	%
4 William H. Perry (D)	4,470	100.0
5 John J. Hemphill (D)	4,696	99.9
6 George W. Dargan (D)	4,361	98.7
7 William Elliott (D)	6,493	52.1
Robert Smalls (R)	5,961	47.9

TENNESSEE

Candidates	Votes	%
	16,393	60.0
James White (D)	10,953	40.1
2 Leonidas C. Houk (R)	15,837	67.0
S. G. Heiskell (D)	7,780	32.9
3 John R. Neal (D)	14,115	50.6
John T. Wilder (R)	13,768	49.4
4 Benton McMillin (D)	12,441	61.5
J. J. Turner (R)	7,792	38.5
5 James D. Richardson (D)	13,756	68.9
S. D. Mathew (R)	6,210	31.1
6 Joseph E. Washington (D)	14,919	61.8
John H. Nye (R)	9,218	38.2
7 Washington C. Whitthorne (D)	12,083	58.8
G. W. Blackburn (R)	8,459	41.2
8 Benjamin A. Enloe (D)	13,059	53.5
S. W. Hawkins (R)	11,362	46.5
9 Presley T. Glass (D)	14,272	59.0
D. A. Nunn (R)	9,934	41.0
10 James Phelan (D)	11,979	60.0
Zack Taylor (R)	7,983	40.0

TEXAS

Candidates	Votes	%
1 Charles Stewart (D)	16,844	61.9
H. D. Johnson (R)	10,344	38.0
2 John H. Reagan (D)	16,413*	95.7
Constantine B. Kilgore (D)	16,695	69.3
W. E. Farmer (I)	7,359	30.6
4 David B. Culberson (D)	17,234	78.5
James T. Fleming (I)	4,701	21.4
5 Silas Hare (D)	11,774	41.8
G. B. Pickett (ID)	8,315	29.5
H. C. Mack (I)	8,065	28.6

Candidates	Votes	%
6 Jo Abbott (D)	19,185	59.9
J. C. Kearby (I)	11,756	36.7
7 William H. Crain (D)	18,511	89.1
J. L. Haynes (R)	1,293	6.2
8 Littleton W. Moore (D)	22,908	92.1
W. O. Hutchinson (R)	1,912	7.7
9 Roger Q. Mills (D)	17,168	60.2
J. D. Rankin (P-LAB)	11,337	39.8
10 Joseph D. Sayers (D)	26,809	78.1
J. P. Newcomb (R)	7,492	21.8
11 Samuel W. T. Lanham (D)	21,980	74.0
Unidentified Candidate (I)	7,744	26.1

VERMONT

Candidates	Votes	%
1 John W. Stewart (R)	15,632	72.5
Waldo Brigham (D)	5,655	26.2
2 William W. Grout (R)	18,685	69.4
Harley E. Folsom (D)	8,176	30.4

VIRGINIA

Candidates	Votes	%
1 Thomas H. B. Browne (R)	12,591	54.1
Thomas Croxton (D)	10,696	45.9
2 George E. Bowden (R)	15,449	60.7
Marshall Parks (D)	9,993	39.3
3 George D. Wise (D)	14,001	52.7
Edmond Waddell Jr. (R)	12,549	47.2
4 William E. Gaines (R)	14,708	70.2
Mann Page (D)	6,233	29.8
5 John R. Brown (R)	12,773	57.1
George C. Cabell (D)	9,614	42.9
6 Samuel I. Hopkins (LAB)	9,470	50.9
Samuel Griffin (D)	9,020	48.4
7 Charles T. O'Ferrall (D)	11,580	51.7
John E. Roller (ID)	10,816	48.3
8 William H. F. Lee (D)	9,836	57.5
W. C. Elam (R)	7,274	42.5
9 Henry Bowen (R)	13,826	57.6
R. R. Henry (D)	10,196	42.4

Candidates	Votes	%
10 Jacob Yost (R)	12,975	53.4
James Bumgardner Jr. (D)	11,321	46.6

WEST VIRGINIA

Candidates	Votes	%
1 Nathan Goff Jr. (R)	17,559	50.8
John Bannon (D)	16,732	48.4
2 William L. Wilson (D)	17,112	49.9
W. H. H. Flick (R)	17,022	49.6
3 Charles P. Snyder (D)	14,906	50.6
James H. Brown (R)	14,011	47.6
4 Charles E. Hogg (D)	16,434	50.3
John H. Hutchinson (R)	15,687	48.0

WISCONSIN

Candidates	Votes	%
1 Lucien B. Caswell (R)	13,739	46.9
James R. Doolittle (D)	13,166	44.9
Edward G. Durand (P)	2,404	8.2
2 Richard Guenther (R)	15,366	55.7
A. K. Delaney (D)	11,138	40.4
3 Robert M. LaFollette (R)	16,711	50.3
Hugh J. Gallagher (D)	13,201	39.8
T. C. Richmond (P)	3,258	9.8
4 Henry Smith (LAB)	13,355	42.5
Thomas H. Brown (R)	9,645	30.7
John Black (D)	8,233	26.2
5 Thomas R. Hudd (D)	15,716	60.6
G. Keusterman (R)	10,168	39.2
6 Charles B. Clark (R)	15,983	54.6
Andrew Haben (D)	11,526	39.4
E. D. Kanouse (P)	1,761	6.0
7 Ormsby B. Thomas (R)	16,720	54.2
S. N. Dickenson (D)	11,917	38.7
S. B. Loomis (P)	2,175	7.1
8 William T. Price (R)	23,857*	66.7
James Bracklin (D)	11,850	33.2
9 Isaac Stephenson (R)	22,518	55.8
John Ringle (D)	17,763	44.0
Special Election		
5 Thomas R. Hudd (D)	9,633	62.2
Charles Luling (R)	5,852	37.8

1887 House Elections

LOUISIANA

Special Election

Candidates	Votes	%
6 Samuel M. Robertson (D)	6,706	72.5
John Yoist (R)	2,550	27.6

MICHIGAN

Special Election

	Votes	%
11 Henry W. Seymour (R)	11,014	49.7
Bartley Breen (FUS)	10,612	47.8

NEW YORK

Special Elections

	Votes	%
19 Charles Tracey (D)	17,796	49.9
Bailey (R)	16,187	45.4
25 James J. Belden (R)	20,144	60.0
Davis (D)	11,608	34.6
Sinclair (P)	1,798	5.4

RHODE ISLAND[1]

Special Elections

	Votes	%
2 Charles H. Page (D)	5,790	49.3
William A. Pirce (R)	5,495	46.7

Candidates	Votes	%
2 Warren O. Arnold (R)	8,086	51.8
Charles S. Bradley (D)	7,248	46.4

WISCONSIN

Special Elections

	Votes	%
8 Hugh H. Price (R)	12,238	69.9
James Bardon (D)	5,209	29.8
8 Nils P. Haugen (R)	8,159	46.3
Samuel C. Johnson (D)	6,803	38.6
Peter Truax (P)	2,620	14.9

1. The first special election, won by Charles H. Page, was to fill a vacancy in the 49th Congress (1885-87). A majority of the total vote was apparently not required to win this election. (Majority vote requirement, see p. 703.)

The second special, won by Warren O. Arnold, was for a full term in the 50th Congress (1887-89). The seat had been left unfilled in the regular 1886 general election because no candidate had the requisite majority. (See Rhode Island 1886, p. 812.)

House Candidates Index

For an index of all House candidates listed in this section (pages 701 to 1061), see pages 1180-1273. Instructions for use of the House Candidates Index appear on page 1180.

1888 House Elections

ALABAMA

Candidates	Votes	%
1 Richard H. Clarke (D)	11,594	62.0
Frank H. Threet (R)	7,105	38.0
2 Hilary A. Herbert (D)	14,041	66.1
Buckley (R)	7,204	33.9
3 William C. Oates (D)	13,287	82.3
Harvey (R)	2,868	17.8
4 Louis W. Turpin (D)	18,778‡	77.0
John V. McDuffie (R)	5,625	23.1
5 James E. Cobb (D)	12,597	64.7
Bingham (R)	6,861	35.3
6 John H. Bankhead (D)	16,491	67.8
Hanlan (R)	7,849	32.3
7 William H. Forney (D)	17,706	65.7
Hardy (R)	8,265	30.7
8 Joseph Wheeler (D)	14,091	61.6
McClellan (R)	8,770	38.4

ARKANSAS

Candidates	Votes	%
1 William H. Cate (D)	15,576‡	51.9
Lewis P. Featherston (IR)	14,228	47.4
2 Clifton R. Breckinridge (D)	17,857‡	51.2
John M. Clayton (R)	17,011	48.8
3 Thomas C. McRae (D)	20,046	59.7
J. A. Ansley (I)	13,553	40.3
4 John H. Rogers (D)	20,448	57.7
I. McCracken (I)	14,933	42.2
5 Samuel W. Peel (D)	15,649	68.9
E. P. Watson (I)	5,000	22.0
John Gates (R)	2,075	9.1

CALIFORNIA

Candidates	Votes	%
1 John J. De Haven (R)	19,345	49.9
T. L. Thompson (D)	19,019	49.0
2 Marion Biggs (D)	19,064	50.7
John A. Eagon (R)	17,541	46.6
3 Joseph McKenna (R)	19,912	56.0
Ben Morgan (D)	14,633	41.2
4 William W. Morrow (R)	14,217	50.6
Robert Ferral (D)	13,624	48.5
5 Thomas J. Clunie (D)	20,276	48.9
L. G. Phelps (R)	20,225	48.8
6 William Vandever (R)	35,406	52.4
R. B. Terry (D)	29,453	43.5

COLORADO

Candidates	Votes	%
AL Hosea Townsend (R)	50,620	55.0
Thomas Macon (D)	37,725	41.0

CONNECTICUT

Candidates	Votes	%
1 William E. Simonds (R)	18,255	49.7
Vance (D)	17,442	47.5
2 Washington F. Wilcox (D)	24,959	49.6
Lines (R)	24,161	48.0
3 Charles A. Russell (R)	11,710	49.8
Hall (D)	10,962	46.6
4 Frederick Miles (R)	21,003	48.7
Seymour (D)	20,977	48.7

DELAWARE

Candidates	Votes	%
AL John B. Penington (D)	16,396	55.2
Charles H. Treat (R)	12,935	43.5

FLORIDA

Candidates	Votes	%
1 Robert H. M. Davidson (D)	19,822	67.1
Benjamin (R)	9,727	32.9

Candidates	Votes	%
2 Robert Bullock (D)	19,512	52.8
Goodrich (R)	17,417	47.2

GEORGIA

Candidates	Votes	%
1 Rufus E. Lester (D)	11,736	69.6
Floyd Snelson (R)	5,116	30.4
2 Henry G. Turner (D)	11,000	100.0
3 Charles F. Crisp (D)	9,254	72.7
Peter O. Gibson (R)	3,130	24.6
4 Thomas W. Grimes (D)	9,798	70.4
Marion Bethune (R)	4,122	29.6
5 John D. Stewart (D)	10,971	68.6
George S. Thomas (R)	5,032	31.4
6 James H. Blount (D)	8,931	100.0
7 Judson C. Clements (D)	9,051	74.8
Z. B. Hargraves (R)	3,054	25.2
8 Henry H. Carlton (D)	7,348	76.7
E. T. Fleming (R)	2,227	23.3
9 Allen D. Candler (D)	11,260	53.0
Thaddeus Pickett (I)	9,975	47.0
10 George T. Barnes (D)	6,474	89.0
Judson W. Lyon (R)	797	11.0

ILLINOIS

Candidates	Votes	%
1 Abner Taylor (R)	26,553	52.7
James F. Todd (D)	22,697	45.1
2 Frank Lawler (D)	19,051	59.2
Daniel F. Gleason (R)	12,969	40.3
3 William E. Mason (R)	23,671	50.8
Milton R. Freshwater (D)	21,295	45.7
4 George E. Adams (R)	22,273	51.3
Jonathan B. Taylor (D)	19,755	45.5
5 Albert J. Hopkins (R)	20,077	63.0
James Herrington (D)	10,018	31.4
John M. Strong (P)	1,765	5.5
6 Robert R. Hitt (R)	18,139	57.2
Rufus M. Cook (D)	11,903	37.6
George Richardson (P)	1,659	5.2
7 Thomas J. Henderson (R)	16,380	56.7
Owen G. Lovejoy (D)	11,341	39.2
8 Charles A. Hill (R)	20,596	51.4
Lafayette W. Brewer (D)	17,454	43.6
9 Lewis E. Payson (R)	16,871	51.5
Herman W. Snow (D)	14,490	44.2
10 Philip S. Post (R)	18,824	52.6
Nicholas E. Worthington (D)	16,166	45.2
11 William H. Gest (R)	19,657	51.3
William Prentiss (D)	17,580	45.8
12 Scott Wike (D)	21,938	54.1
William H. Collins (R)	16,628	41.0
13 William M. Springer (D)	21,364	51.4
Charles Kerr (R)	18,450	44.4
14 Jonathan H. Rowell (R)	18,570	50.1
Ethelbert Stewart (D)	16,740	45.2
15 Joseph G. Cannon (R)	19,897	51.8
Robert L. McKinlay (D)	17,204	44.8
16 George W. Fithian (D)	17,742	49.6
Edwin Harlan (R)	17,037	47.6
17 Edward Lane (D)	19,385	54.8
John J. Brown (R)	14,775	41.7
18 William S. Forman (D)	16,167	47.7
Jehu Baker (R)	16,151	47.7
19 Richard W. Townshend (D)	18,086	53.0
W. L. Crim (R)	15,615	45.8
20 George W. Smith (R)	19,005	51.6
Thomas T. Robinson (D)	17,186	46.6

INDIANA

Candidates	Votes	%
1 William F. Parrett (D)	20,647	49.3
Frank B. Posey (R)	20,627	49.3
2 John H. O'Neall (D)	18,537	52.3
Thomas N. Braxton (R)	16,653	47.0

Candidates	Votes	%
3 Jason B. Brown (D)	18,274	54.0
Stephen D. Sayles (R)	15,198	44.9
4 William S. Holman (D)	16,905	50.7
Manly D. Wilson (R)	16,176	48.5
5 George W. Cooper (D)	18,206	49.6
Henry C. Duncan (R)	17,506	47.7
6 Thomas M. Browne (R)	23,424	60.3
Douglas Morris (D)	14,302	36.8
7 William D. Bynum (D)	27,227	50.9
Thomas E. Chandler (R)	25,500	47.6
8 Elijah V. Brookshire (D)	23,153	49.0
James F. Johnston (R)	23,084	48.8
9 Joseph B. Cheadle (R)	24,717	53.1
James McCabe (D)	20,267	43.5
10 William D. Owen (R)	19,546	50.4
Valentine Zimmerman (D)	18,390	47.5
11 Augustus N. Martin (D)	22,375	48.9
George W. Steele (R)	21,900	47.8
12 Charles A. O. McClellan (D)	20,139	50.4
James B. White (R)	18,828	47.1
13 Benjamin F. Shively (D & LAB)	21,561	49.4
William Hoynes (R)	21,206	48.6

IOWA

Candidates	Votes	%
1 John H. Gear (R)	18,130	51.0
John J. Seerley (D)	17,256	48.5
2 Walter I. Hayes (D)	20,874	56.8
Parker W. McManus (R&LAB)	15,842	43.1
3 David B. Henderson (R)	21,457	56.0
B. B. Richards (D)	16,872	44.0
4 Joseph H. Sweney (R)	18,852	52.4
L. S. Reque (D)	16,630	46.2
5 Daniel Kerr (R)	19,453	52.5
J. H. Preston (D)	16,937	45.7
6 John F. Lacey (R)	18,009	51.0
James B. Weaver (D & LAB)	17,181	48.6
7 Edwin H. Conger (R)	18,424	55.8
A. E. Morrison (D)	13,027	39.5
8 James P. Flick (R)	19,207	50.9
A. R. Anderson (D & LAB)	18,212	48.2
9 Joseph R. Reed (R)	20,380	52.6
D. M. Harris (D)	16,686	43.0
10 Jonathan P. Dolliver (R)	20,864	56.8
J. A. Yeoman (D)	15,496	42.2
11 Isaac S. Struble (R)	21,472	57.1
M. A. Kilso (D)	15,213	40.4

KANSAS

Candidates	Votes	%
1 Edmund N. Morrill (R)	20,879	56.3
E. K. Townsend (D)	14,536	39.2
2 Edward H. Funston (R)	24,632	54.6
J.T. Burris (D)	14,969	33.2
Delos Walker (UN LAB)	5,517	12.2
3 Bishop W. Perkins (R)	23,315	50.4
W. H. Utley (UN LAB)	11,775	25.5
J. A. Eaton (D)	10,556	22.8
4 Thomas Ryan (R)	29,338	59.8
D. Overmeyer (D)	14,323	29.2
John Heaton (UN LAB)	4,350	8.9
5 John A. Anderson (R)	22,848	59.6
N. D. Toby (D)	14,347	37.4
6 Erastus J. Turner (R)	23,428	57.4
S. W. McElroy (D)	12,282	30.1
H. A. Hart (UN LAB)	4,550	11.2
7 Samuel R. Peters (R)	37,935	53.2
C. S. Ebey (D)	22,616	31.7
S. H. Snyder (UN LAB)	9,489	13.3

KENTUCKY

Candidates	Votes	%
1 William J. Stone (D)	14,195	60.2
Edwin Earley (R)	8,850	37.6

KENTUCKY

Candidates	Votes	%
2 William T. Ellis (D)	16,459	54.8
George W. Jolly (R)	13,006	43.3
3 Isaac H. Goodnight (D)	17,365	52.4
W. Godfrey Hunter (R)	15,630	47.1
4 Alexander B. Montgomery (D)	15,477	57.9
C. M. Pendleton (R)	11,019	41.3
5 Asher G. Caruth (D)	16,588	54.9
Augustus E. Willson (R)	13,561	44.9
6 John G. Carlisle (D)	18,907	58.7
Robert Hamilton (R)	12,887	40.0
7 William C. P. Breckinridge (D)	18,920	57.5
Armstead M. Swope (R)	13,265	40.3
8 James B. McCreary (D)	16,209	51.5
R. L. Ewell (R)	14,660	46.6
9 Thomas H. Paynter (D)	18,664	49.9
Drury J. Burchett (R)	18,285	48.9
10 John H. Wilson (R)	15,725	50.6
B. F. Day (D)	15,247	49.1
11 Hugh F. Finley (R)	15,822	52.4
F. L. Wolford (D)	14,006	46.4

LOUISIANA

Candidates	Votes	%
1 Theodore S. Wilkinson (D)	8,979	64.5
Charles B. Wilson (R)	4,927	35.4
2 H. Dudley Coleman (R)	9,121	50.5
Benjamin C. Elliott (D)	8,947	49.5
3 Edward J. Gay (D)	18,854	74.8
James R. Jolley (R)	6,341	25.2
4 Newton C. Blanchard (D)	16,302	94.4
W. E. Maples (R)	963	5.6
5 Charles J. Boatner (D)	21,275	93.9
Frank Morey (R)	1,151	5.1
6 Samuel M. Robertson (D)	12,078	73.7
W. H. Harrison (R)	4,314	26.3

MAINE

Candidates	Votes	%
1 Thomas B. Reed (R)	18,288	52.3
William Emery (D)	15,849	45.3
2 Nelson Dingley Jr. (R)	21,075	55.2
Charles E. Allen (D)	15,614	40.9
3 Seth L. Milliken (R)	20,558	58.0
S. S. Brown (D)	14,026	39.5
4 Charles A. Boutelle (R)	19,823	54.6
T. J. Stewart (D)	15,481	42.7

MARYLAND

Candidates	Votes	%
1 Charles H. Gibson (D)	15,627	48.3
Hodson (R)	15,145	46.8
2 Herman Stump (D)	18,470	51.2
Lang (R)	16,588	46.0
3 Harry W. Rusk (D)	19,578	57.2
Brinton (R)	14,289	41.7
4 Henry Stockbridge Jr. (R)	19,078	49.5
Rayner (D)	18,998	49.3
5 Barnes Compton (D)	16,000‡	49.8
Sydney E. Mudd (R)	15,819	49.2
6 Louis E. McComas (R)	19,056	51.6
Douglas (D)	17,422	47.2

MASSACHUSETTS

Candidates	Votes	%
1 Charles S. Randall (R)	14,588	60.8
Cummings (D)	5,103	21.3
Delano (D)	3,468	14.5
2 Elijah A. Morse (R)	17,072	54.2
Quincy (D)	13,388	42.5
3 John F. Andrew (D)	16,338	52.0
Beard (R)	14,780	47.0
4 Joseph H. O'Neil (D)	14,749	68.0
Morrison (R)	6,718	31.0
5 Nathaniel P. Banks (R)	14,929	51.8
Higginson (D)	13,465	46.7

Candidates	Votes	%
6 Henry Cabot Lodge (R)	19,598	56.3
Usher (D)	14,304	41.1
7 William Cogswell (R)	16,796	56.8
Roads (D)	12,224	41.3
8 Frederic T. Greenhalge (R)	14,493	55.3
Donovan (D)	11,273	43.0
9 John W. Candler (R)	15,714	52.2
Burnett (D)	13,678	45.4
10 Joseph H. Walker (R)	13,965	52.0
Sayles (D)	12,050	44.9
11 Rodney Wallace (R)	16,335	56.4
Skinner (D)	11,519	39.7
12 Francis W. Rockwell (R)	14,853	52.1
Ely (D)	12,826	45.0

MICHIGAN

Candidates	Votes	%
1 J. Logan Chipman (D)	25,179	52.4
Hibbard Baker (R)	22,076	45.9
2 Edward P. Allen (R)	19,660	49.3
Willard Stearns (D & G)	18,096	45.3
Charles M. Fellows (P)	2,010	5.0
3 James O'Donnell (R)	24,097	53.5
Eugene Pringle (D)	17,495	38.9
Almon G. Bruce (P)	2,609	5.8
4 Julius C. Burrows (R)	21,649	52.9
Charles S. Maynard (D)	17,464	42.7
5 Charles E. Belknap (R)	26,309	50.4
Melbourne H. Ford (D)	23,642	45.3
6 Mark S. Brewer (R)	21,271	47.6
Orlando F. Barnes (D)	20,904	46.8
William W. Root (P)	2,251	5.0
7 Justin R. Whiting (D)	16,894	47.7
William Hartsuff (R)	16,488	46.6
8 Aaron T. Bliss (R)	23,028	50.4
Timothy E. Tarsney (D)	20,943	45.9
9 Byron M. Cutcheon (R)	23,025	52.2
Hiram B. Hudson (D)	18,651	42.2
Lathrop S. Ellis (P)	2,476	5.6
10 Frank W. Wheeler (R)	18,959	48.3
Spencer O. Fisher (D)	18,844	48.0
11 Samuel M. Stephenson (R)	20,336	52.8
John Power (D)	16,978	44.1

MINNESOTA

Candidates	Votes	%
1 Mark H. Dunnell (R)	18,829	50.4
Thomas Wilson (D)	16,985	45.4
2 John Lind (R)	25,699	57.0
M. S. Wilkinson (D)	16,480	36.5
D. W. Edwards (P)	2,924	6.5
3 Darwin S. Hall (R)	19,259	51.4
J. L. Macdonald (D)	16,391	43.7
4 Samuel P. Snider (R)	44,329	53.8
E. Rice (D)	34,323	41.7
5 Solomon G. Comstock (R)	31,350	52.7
Charles Canning (D)	23,833	40.1
Z.D. Scott (P)	4,254	7.2

MISSISSIPPI

Candidates	Votes	%
1 John M. Allen (D)	11,353	86.8
Joseph M. Bynum (R)	1,732	13.2
2 John B. Morgan (D)	13,978	70.6
James R. Chalmers (R)	5,817	29.4
3 Thomas C. Catchings (D)	11,624	71.6
James Hill (R)	4,614	28.4
4 Clarke Lewis (D)	12,855	84.3
Matthew K. Mister (R)	2,396	15.7
5 Chapman L. Anderson (D)	16,247	80.3
F. M. B. Cook (R)	3,993	19.7
6 Thomas R. Stockdale (D)	10,580	70.3
Leon C. Duchesne (R)	4,464	29.7
7 Charles E. Hooker (D)	11,977	77.0
Henry Kernaghan (R)	3,587	23.1

MISSOURI

Candidates	Votes	%
1 William H. Hatch (D)	20,049	52.9
Brock (R)	17,349	45.8

Candidates	Votes	%
2 Charles H. Mansur (D)	21,608	53.8
Eubanks (R)	16,949	42.2
3 Alexander M. Dockery (D)	20,414	53.4
Love (R)	16,743	43.8
4 James N. Burnes (D)	16,866*	52.5
Hartwig (R)	13,729	42.7
5 John C. Tarsney (D)	22,635	52.5
Bullene (R)	20,499	47.5
6 John T. Heard (D)	25,129	52.0
Upton (R)	21,249	44.0
7 Richard H. Norton (D)	18,275	52.8
Edwards (R)	16,312	47.2
8 Frederick G. Niedringhaus (R)	14,210	52.2
O'Neill (D)	12,394	45.5
9 Nathan Frank (R)	13,762	54.7
Castleman (D)	11,312	45.0
10 William M. Kinsey (R)	18,980	50.8
Clardy (D)	16,886	45.2
11 Richard P. Bland (D)	18,095	50.4
Musick (R)	15,836	44.1
Needham (UN LAB)	1,954	5.5
12 William J. Stone (D)	24,054	49.4
Hannah (R)	19,431	39.9
Page (UN LAB)	4,613	9.5
13 William H. Wade (R)	16,480	48.4
Matlock (D)	13,601	40.0
Alter (UN LAB)	3,792	11.1
14 James P. Walker (D)	19,878	58.4
Whybark (R)	14,139	41.6

Special Election

	Votes	%
4 Charles F. Booher (D)	12,750	52.3
R. Posegate (R)	11,632	47.7

NEBRASKA

Candidates	Votes	%
1 William J. Connell (R)	32,926	49.8
J. Sterling Morton (D)	29,519	44.7
2 James Laird (R)	30,959	53.4
W. G. Hastings (D)	21,201	36.6
George Scott (P)	4,114	7.1
3 George W. E. Dorsey (R)	42,188	54.2
E. P. Weatherby (D)	31,118	40.0

NEVADA

Candidates	Votes	%
AL Horace F. Bartine (R)	6,921	54.9
G. W. Cassidy (D)	5,682	45.1

NEW HAMPSHIRE

Candidates	Votes	%
1 Alonzo Nute (R)	21,754	49.6
McKinney (D)	21,395	48.8
2 Orren C. Moore (R)	23,517	50.2
Mann (D)	22,540	48.1

NEW JERSEY

Candidates	Votes	%
1 Christopher A. Bergen (R)	24,906	53.6
Brindle (D)	19,440	41.9
2 James Buchanan (R)	22,407	52.4
Beasley (D)	19,104	44.6
3 Jacob A. Geissenhainer (D)	22,961	51.7
Kean (R)	20,368	45.8
4 Samuel Fowler (D)	12,190	39.4
Voorhees (R)	12,117	39.2
Roe (ID)	5,079	16.4
5 Charles D. Beckwith (R)	20,277	50.2
Hoagland (D)	19,205	47.6
6 Herman Lehlbach (R)	25,536	49.9
Haynes (D)	24,762	48.4
7 William McAdoo (D)	26,498	56.1
Collins (R)	20,424	43.3

NEW YORK

Candidates	Votes	%
1 James W. Covert (D)	24,374	50.8
Cromwell (R)	22,711	47.3
2 Felix Campbell (D)	23,497	56.3
T. Seward (R)	17,625	42.2
3 William C. Wallace (R)	21,281	52.9
Combs (D)	18,410	45.7
4 John M. Clancy (D)	20,987	59.1
Robinson (R)	14,060	39.6
5 Thomas F. Magner (D)	18,613	52.2
Hesse (R)	16,469	46.2
6 Frank T. Fitzgerald (TAM D&UL)	13,079	55.8
Cavanagh (R)	9,833	42.0
7 Edward J. Dunphy (TAM D)	10,257	40.6
Taintor (R)	8,343	33.0
Lloyd S. Bryce (CIT&CO D)	6,482	25.7
8 John H. McCarthy (TAM D)	14,827	52.3
Campbell (CIT&CO D)	9,778	34.5
Schwartz (R)	3,456	12.2
9 Samuel S. Cox (UN LAB&D)	18,267	68.3
McMackin (R)	7,320	27.4
10 Francis B. Spinola (UN LAB&D)	13,749	52.1
Boyhan (R & UL)	12,016	45.5
11 John Quinn (UN LAB&D)	20,073	55.3
Winch (R & UL)	15,619	43.0
12 Roswell P. Flower (D&UN LAB)	25,546	65.8
Hildreth (R)	12,273	31.6
13 Ashbel P. Fitch (D)	28,580	58.9
Hoyt (R)	19,412	40.0
14 William G. Stahlnecker (UN LAB&D)	22,485	53.7
Wood (R)	18,356	43.9
15 Moses D. Stivers (R)	18,358	48.8
Bacon (UN LAB&D)	18,284	48.6
16 John H. Ketcham (R)	18,912	74.6
Downing (P)	6,370	25.1
17 Charles J. Knapp (R)	21,826	50.2
Gilbert (D)	20,217	46.5
18 John A. Quackenbush (R)	23,639	53.4
Sanford (D)	19,717	44.6
19 Charles Tracey (D)	21,294	52.3
Dodge (R)	18,988	46.6
20 John Sanford (R)	23,966	52.2
Westbrook (D)	20,665	45.0
21 John H. Moffitt (R)	21,361	95.2
22 Frederick Lansing (R)	24,309	62.0
Sawyer (D)	13,582	34.7
23 James S. Sherman (R)	20,119	50.8
McMahon (D)	18,387	46.4
24 David Wilber (R)	18,502	50.2
John S. Pindar (D)	17,273	46.9
25 James J. Belden (R)	24,672	78.0
Vanderbilt (D)	6,691	21.2
26 Milton De Lano (R)	26,267	55.4
Maloney (D)	18,955	40.0
27 Newton W. Nutting (R)	28,803	58.6
Titus (D)	18,327	37.3
28 Thomas S. Flood (R)	16,822	50.3
Tuttle (D)	15,564	46.5
29 John Raines (R)	21,794	53.6
Dininny (D)	16,969	41.7
30 Charles S. Baker (R)	21,810	55.4
Nash (D)	16,106	40.9
31 John G. Sawyer (R)	19,506	54.4
Stevens (D)	14,082	39.3
Barnum (P)	2,284	6.4
32 John M. Farquhar (R)	22,468	51.6
Mackey (D)	20,859	47.9
33 John McC. Wiley (D)	15,705	48.8
Crowley (R)	15,141	47.0
34 William G. Laidlaw (R)	27,453	58.9
Howe (D)	15,523	33.3
Corey (P)	3,170	6.8

NORTH CAROLINA

Candidates	Votes	%
1 Thomas G. Skinner (D)	16,615	51.4
Elihu A. White (R)	15,457	47.8

Candidates	Votes	%
2 Henry P. Cheatham (R)	16,704	51.0
Furnifold M. Simmons (D)	16,051	49.0
3 Charles W. McClammy (D)	16,809	56.7
William Robinson (R)	12,825	43.3
4 Benjamin H. Bunn (D)	19,926	53.4
John Nichols (R)	17,368	46.6
5 John M. Brower (R)	15,940	50.4
James T. Morehead (D)	15,265	48.2
6 Alfred Rowland (D)	20,502	58.1
Caleb P. Lockey (R)	14,797	41.9
7 John S. Henderson (D)	15,122	54.3
William J. Ellis (R)	12,125	43.5
8 William H. H. Cowles (D)	13,139	56.7
Edward W. Ward (R)	10,031	43.3
9 Hamilton G. Ewart (R)	15,433	50.9
Thomas D. Johnston (D)	14,915	49.2

OHIO

Candidates	Votes	%
1 Benjamin Butterworth (R)	19,336	51.9
Otway J. Cosgrave (D)	17,437	46.8
2 John A. Caldwell (R)	21,627	51.0
Clinton W. Gerard (D)	20,031	47.2
3 Elihu S. Williams (R)	20,912	49.2
George W. Houk (D)	20,497	48.2
4 Samuel S. Yoder (D)	22,296	58.9
Robert L. Mattingly (R)	14,500	38.3
5 George E. Seney (D)	22,075	56.1
Wilson Vance (R)	16,081	40.9
6 Melvin M. Boothman (R)	22,434	48.4
Gaylard M. Saltzgaber (D)	22,339	48.2
7 Henry L. Morey (R)	17,600	49.9
John M. Pattison (D)	16,742	47.5
8 Robert P. Kennedy (R)	20,898	51.8
Andrew R. Bolin (D)	17,628	43.7
9 William C. Cooper (R)	19,491	50.7
John S. Braddock (D)	17,267	44.9
10 William E. Haynes (D)	19,637	50.7
Jacob Romeis (R)	18,496	47.8
11 Albert C. Thompson (R)	20,802	55.6
Joseph W. Shinn (D)	15,817	42.3
12 Jacob J. Pugsley (R)	20,133	49.6
Lawrence T. Neal (D)	19,453	47.9
13 Joseph H. Outhwaite (D)	24,869	51.4
John B. Neil (R)	22,298	46.1
14 Charles P. Wickham (R)	16,211	49.5
David L. Wadsworth (D)	15,254	46.6
15 Charles H. Grosvenor (R)	17,591	51.9
John P. Spriggs (D)	15,284	45.1
16 James W. Owens (D)	24,444	53.8
Edwin L. Lybarger (R)	19,819	43.6
17 Joseph D. Taylor (R)	20,584	54.4
William Lawrence Jr. (D)	15,580	41.2
18 William McKinley Jr. (R)	25,249	52.3
George P. Ikert (D)	21,160	43.8
19 Ezra B. Taylor (R)	22,991	63.5
Henry Apthorp (D)	11,091	30.6
William H. Dana (P)	2,004	5.5
20 Martin L. Smyser (R)	19,381	50.6
Calvin P. Humphrey (D)	17,283	45.1
21 Theodore E. Burton (R)	20,086	49.8
Tom L. Johnson (D)	19,470	48.3

OREGON

Candidates	Votes	%
AL Binger Hermann (R)	32,820	54.5
John M. Gearin (D)	25,413	42.2

PENNSYLVANIA

Candidates	Votes	%
1 Henry H. Bingham (R)	22,523	57.1
Flanigan (D)	16,838	42.7
2 Charles O'Neill (R)	16,776	57.2
Dougherty (D)	12,368	42.2
3 Samuel J. Randall (D)	17,642	99.4
4 William D. Kelley (R)	32,841	58.1
Ayers (D)	23,202	41.1

Candidates	Votes	%
5 Alfred C. Harmer (R)	29,466	56.2
Herwig (D)	22,781	43.4
6 Smedley Darlington (R)	19,299	58.1
Greenwood (D)	12,799	38.5
7 Robert M. Yardley (R)	22,226	50.7
Ross (D)	21,215	48.4
8 William Mutchler (D)	18,071	59.8
Reeder (R)	11,731	38.8
9 David B. Brunner (D)	27,032	60.3
Biery (R)	17,373	38.8
10 Marriott Brosius (R)	21,796	66.4
Haldeman (D)	10,622	32.4
11 Joseph A. Scranton (R)	10,844	51.1
Collins (D)	9,158	43.2
Lathrope (P)	1,212	5.7
12 Edwin S. Osborne (R)	16,117	51.3
Lynch (D)	14,618	46.5
13 James B. Reilly (D)	13,258	51.0
Brumm (RG)	12,570	48.4
14 John W. Rife (R)	20,206	58.3
Bower (D)	13,944	40.3
15 Myron B. Wright (R)	18,833	56.8
Ham (D)	12,494	37.7
Brown (P)	1,810	5.5
16 Henry C. McCormick (R)	19,204	54.2
Steck (D & LAB)	15,550	43.9
17 Charles R. Buckalew (D)	14,012	54.5
Robinson (R)	11,356	44.2
18 Louis E. Atkinson (R)	20,583	56.2
McWilliams (D)	15,867	43.3
19 Levi Maish (D)	21,480	55.1
Young (R)	16,901	43.4
20 Edward Scull (R)	21,739	54.3
Greevy (D)	17,458	43.6
21 Samuel A. Craig (R)	24,151	54.0
Donnelly (D)	18,930	42.3
22 John Dalzell (R)	21,970	62.0
Parkinson (D)	13,065	36.9
23 Thomas M. Bayne (R)	13,999	66.8
Langfitt (D)	6,711	32.0
24 Joseph W. Ray (R)	26,246	53.2
Wampler (D)	21,908	44.4
25 Charles C. Townsend (R)	21,636	56.5
Griffith (D)	14,481	37.8
26 William C. Culbertson (R)	16,924	52.5
Burns (D)	13,852	43.0
27 Lewis F. Watson (R)	13,582	53.2
Rankin (D)	9,370	36.7
Miller (P)	1,670	6.5
28 James Kerr (D)	17,588	53.5
Rynder (R)	14,899	45.3

RHODE ISLAND

Candidates	Votes	%
1 Henry J. Spooner (R)	11,092	53.3
Oscar Lapham (D)	9,002	43.3
2 Warren O. Arnold (R)	10,940	55.9
Baker (D)	8,049	41.1

SOUTH CAROLINA

Candidates	Votes	%
1 Samuel Dibble (D)	8,540	86.7
S. W. McKinlay (R)	1,296	13.2
2 George D. Tillman (D)	10,704	86.8
Seymour E. Smith (R)	1,405	11.4
3 James S. Cothran (D)	8,758	99.8
4 William H. Perry (D)	11,410	100.0
5 John J. Hemphill (D)	9,559	99.7
6 George W. Dargan (D)	8,586	95.7
7 William Elliott (D)	8,358‡	54.2
Thomas E. Miller (R)	7,003	45.4

TENNESSEE

Candidates	Votes	%
1 Alfred A. Taylor (R)	19,465	59.9
Wilcox (D)	12,324	38.0
2 Leonidas C. Houk (R)	23,368	68.8
Heiskell (D)	9,844	29.0

TENNESSEE

	Candidates	Votes	%
3	H. Clay Evans (R)	18,641	50.0
	Bates (D)	18,353	49.2
4	Benton McMillin (D)	16,162	61.6
	Wooten (R)	10,068	38.4
5	James D. Richardson (D)	17,754	67.8
	Shoffner (R)	8,426	32.2
6	Joseph E. Washington (D)	18,956	57.2
	Young (R)	12,677	38.3
7	Washington C. Whitthorne (D)	14,362	57.8
	Hagard (R)	10,507	42.3
8	Benjamin A. Enloe (D)	14,385	54.7
	Smith (R)	11,905	45.3
9	Rice A. Pierce (D)	17,217	63.0
	Brown (R)	10,127	37.0
10	James Phelan (D)	20,149	63.2
	Eaton (R)	11,730	36.8

TEXAS

	Candidates	Votes	%
1	Charles Stewart (D)	16,242	49.8
	Lock McDaniel (R)	12,003	36.8
	Jack Davis (I)	4,271	13.1
2	William H. Martin (D)	16,210	70.9
	R. M. Humphries (UN LAB)	6,656	29.1
3	Constantine B. Kilgore (D)	20,579	68.0
	W. E. Farmer (LAB-R)	9,697	32.0
4	David B. Culberson (D)	26,060	99.9
5	Silas Hare (D)	26,946	85.0
	J. W. Thomas (R)	4,468	14.1
6	Jo O. Abbott (D)	26,815	68.9
	Sam Evans (LAB)	12,126	31.1
7	William H. Crain (D)	15,610	56.4
	Calvin J. Brewster (R)	12,070	43.6
8	Littleton W. Moore (D)	21,022	69.3
	T. C. Cook (R)	8,460	27.9

	Candidates	Votes	%
9	Roger Q. Mills (D)	20,701	57.5
	E. A. Jones (ID R&P)	15,316	42.5
10	Joseph D. Sayers (D)	24,094	66.3
	A. Belknap (R)	12,251	33.7
11	Samuel W. T. Lanham (D)	28,535	85.9
	D. M. Rumph (R)	3,403	10.2

VERMONT

	Candidates	Votes	%
1	John W. Stewart (R)	23,892	70.2
	Ozro Meacham (D)	9,746	28.6
2	William W. Grout (R)	24,219	70.8
	George W. Smith (D)	9,605	28.1

VIRGINIA

	Candidates	Votes	%
1	Thomas H. B. Browne (R)	14,731	50.7
	G. S. Kendall (D)	14,317	49.3
2	George E. Bowden (R)	19,821	58.7
	R. C. Marshall (D)	13,726	40.6
3	George D. Wise (D)	15,608‡	50.4
	Edmond Waddill Jr (R)	15,347	49.6
4	Edward C. Venable (D)	13,298‡	45.6
	John M. Langston (R)	12,657	43.4
	R. W. Arnold	3,207	11.0
5	Posey G. Lester (D)	14,417	52.5
	J. D. Blackwell (R)	13,044	47.5
6	Paul C. Edmunds (D)	17,559	55.6
	P. H. M. Caull (R)	13,822	43.8
7	Charles T. O'Ferrall (D)	16,443	54.3
	J. E. Roller (R)	13,623	45.0
8	William H. F. Lee (D)	15,414	51.8
	Park Agnew (R)	14,291	48.0
9	John A. Buchanan (D)	16,520	50.7
	Henry Bowen (R)	16,042	49.3
10	Henry St.George Tucker (D)	14,587	51.0
	Jacob Yost (R)	13,994	49.0

WEST VIRGINIA

	Candidates	Votes	%
1	John O. Pendleton (D)	19,264‡	49.5
	George W. Atkinson (R)	19,242	49.5
2	William L. Wilson (D)	20,468	50.1
	W. H. H. Flick (R)	20,091	49.2
3	John D. Alderson (D)	15,474	50.8
	James H. McGinnis (R)	14,681	48.2
4	James M. Jackson (D)	19,837‡	49.7
	Charles B. Smith (R)	19,834	49.6

WISCONSIN

	Candidates	Votes	%
1	Lucien B. Caswell (R)	19,311	53.4
	Joseph B. Doe Jr (D)	14,997	41.5
	Stephen Faville (P)	1,809	5.0
2	Charles Barwig (D)	16,813	53.2
	E. C. McFetridge (R)	13,859	43.8
3	Robert M. LaFollette (R)	19,052	50.0
	John B. Parkinson (D)	16,123	42.3
	T. C. Richmond (P)	2,654	7.0
4	Isaac W. Van Schaick (R)	22,212	50.8
	Henry Smith (D & LAB)	20,685	47.3
5	George H. Brickner (D)	17,051	55.2
	Gustav Kustermann (R)	12,825	41.5
6	Charles B. Clark (R)	17,977	52.5
	Charles W. Felger (D)	14,213	41.5
7	Ormsby B. Thomas (R)	19,918	53.5
	Frank P. Coburn (D)	15,433	41.5
	J. H. Mosely (P)	1,871	5.0
8	Nils P. Haugen (R)	26,909	57.0
	S. C. Johnson (D & LAB)	16,476	34.9
	Charles Alexander (P)	3,687	7.8
9	Myron H. McCord (R)	27,538	50.5
	H. W. Early (D)	24,775	45.4

1889 House Elections

ILLINOIS

Special Election

	Candidates	Votes	%
19	James R. Williams (D)	14,858	54.6
	Thomas S. Ridgway (R)	10,462	38.4
	John P. Stelle (F ALNC)	1,645	6.0

KANSAS

Special Election

	Candidates	Votes	%
4	Harrison Kelley (R)	10,506	85.3
	John Heaston (D)	1,530	12.4

LOUISIANA

Special Election

	Candidates	Votes	%
3	Edward J. Gay (D)	18,856	74.8
	Jolley (R)	6,351	25.2

MISSOURI

Special Election

	Candidates	Votes	%
4	Robert P. C. Wilson (D)	12,496	51.4
	R. Posegate (R)	11,812	48.6

MONTANA

(Became a State Nov. 8, 1889)

		Votes	%
AL	Thomas H. Carter (R)	19,915	51.9
	Martin Maginnis (D)	18,435	48.1

NEBRASKA

Special Election

		Votes	%
2	Gilbert L. Laws (R)	27,775	54.8
	C. D. Casper (D)	21,123	41.7

NEW YORK

Special Elections

		Votes	%
6	Charles H. Turner (D)	6,811	82.3
	Collier (R)	1,149	13.9
9	Amos J. Cummings (D)	15,508	99.7

	Candidates	Votes	%
27	Sereno E. Payne (R)	20,794	60.1
	Hopkins (D)	13,249	38.3

NORTH DAKOTA

(Became a State Nov. 2, 1889)

		Votes	%
AL	Henry C. Hansbrough (R)	26,077	68.5
	Maratta (D)	12,006	31.5

SOUTH DAKOTA

(Became a State Nov. 2, 1889)

		Votes	%
AL	Oscar S. Gifford (R)	54,983✔	
	John A. Pickler (R)	54,105✔	
	Linneus Q. Jeffries (D)	23,229	
	S. M. Booth (D)	22,541	

WASHINGTON

(Became a State Nov. 11, 1889)

		Votes	%
AL	John L. Wilson (R)	34,039	58.1
	Thomas C. Griffiths (D)	24,492	41.8

1890 House Elections

ALABAMA

	Candidates	Votes	%
1	Richard Henry Clarke (D)	10,071	69.9
	Frank H. Threatt (R)	2,448	17.0
	A. J. Warner	1,890	13.1
2	Hilary A. Herbert (D)	10,611	79.8
	S. A. Pilley	2,681	20.2
3	William C. Oates (D)	10,268	91.7
	Treadwell	930	8.3
4	Louis W. Turpin (D)	9,595	52.1
	John V. McDuffie (R)	4,931	26.8
	G. McCall	3,899	21.2
5	James E. Cobb (D)	5,548	99.8
6	John H. Bankhead (D)	9,182	95.1
7	William H. Forney (D)	10,054	59.2
	Butler	6,060	35.7
	Logan	862	5.1
8	Joseph Wheeler (D)	16,821	58.2
	R. W. Austin	12,076	41.8

ARKANSAS

		Votes	%
1	William H. Cate (D	15,437	51.0
	L. P. Featherston (POP)	14,834	49.0
2	Clifton R. Breckinridge (D)	20,816	51.1
	I. P. Langley (POP)	19,941	48.9
3	Thomas C. McRae (D)	13,111	96.6
4	William L. Terry (D)	12,670	62.9
	E. M. Harrison (R)	7,488	37.1
5	Samuel W. Peel (D)	7,734	97.4

Special Election

		Votes	%
2	Clifton R. Breckinridge (D)	20,828	51.0
	Isom P. Langley (POP)	20,017	49.0

CALIFORNIA

		Votes	%
1	Thomas J. Geary (D)	19,334	49.3
	J.A. Barham (R)	19,117	48.7
2	Anthony Caminetti (D)	18,644	49.0
	G. G. Blanchard (R)	18,485	48.6
3	Joseph McKenna (R)	20,834	55.0
	J. P. Irish (D)	15,997	42.2
4	John P. Cutting (R)	13,196	49.2
	Robert Ferral (D)	12,091	45.1
	Thomas V. Cator (REF D)	1,492	5.6
5	Eugene F. Loud (R)	22,871	52.7
	T. J. Clunie (D)	19,899	45.8
6	William W. Bowers (R)	33,522	50.4
	W. J. Curtis (D)	28,904	43.5

Special Election

		Votes	%
1	Thomas J. Geary (D)	15,750	49.6
	J. A. Barham (R)	15,397	48.5

COLORADO

		Votes	%
AL	Hosea Townsend (R)	43,118	51.3
	T. J. O'Donnell (D)	34,736	41.3
	J. D. Burr (I)	5,207	12.0

CONNECTICUT

		Votes	%
1	Lewis Sperry (D)	16,195	49.8
	Simonds (R)	15,503	47.7
2	Washington F. Wilcox (D)	23,367	52.9
	Hubbard (R)	19,836	44.9
3	Charles A. Russell (R)	10,541	50.7
	Wells (D)	9,549	45.9
4	Robert E. De Forest (D)	18,777	50.2
	Miles (R)	17,821	47.7

DELAWARE

	Candidates	Votes	%
AL	John W. Causey (D)	17,848	50.6
	Henry P. Carmon (R)	17,150	48.7

FLORIDA

		Votes	%
1	Stephen R. Mallory (D)	11,731	77.7
	Reed (R)	3,362	22.3
2	Robert Bullock (D)	16,735	58.7
	Shipling (R)	11,786	41.3

GEORGIA

		Votes	%
1	Rufus G. Lester (D)	10,905	77.7
	Michael G. Doyle (R)	3,127	22.3
2	Henry G. Turner (D)	7,361	88.6
	C. B. Matteson (R)	948	11.4
3	Charles F. Crisp (D)	8,038	86.6
	Peter O. Gibson (R)	1,248	13.4
4	Charles L. Moses (D)	9,609	73.7
	Walter L. Johnson (R)	3,438	26.4
5	Leonidas F. Livingston (D)	8,688	70.7
	Will Haight (R)	3,608	29.3
6	James H. Blount (D)	2,860	100.0
7	R. W. Everett (D)	11,031	54.8
	W. H. Felton (D)	8,460	42.0
8	Thomas G. Lawson (D)	3,405	100.0
9	Thomas E. Winn (D)	10,315	58.8
	T. Pickett (I)	4,087	23.3
	S. A. Darnell (R)	3,133	17.9
10	Thomas G. Watson (D)	5,456	90.1
	Anthony E. Williams (R)	597	9.9

IDAHO

(Became a state July 3, 1890)

		Votes	%
AL	Willis Sweet (R)	10,171	56.0
	Alex E. Mayhew (D)	7,985	44.0

Special Election

		Votes	%
AL	Willis Sweet (R)	10,130	55.8
	Alex E. Mayhew (D)	8,026	44.2

ILLINOIS

		Votes	%
1	Abner Taylor (R)	22,235	50.0
	William G. Ewing (D)	21,796	49.0
2	Lawrence E. McGann (D)	17,383	60.4
	John G. Schaar (R)	10,633	36.9
3	Allan C. Durborow Jr. (D)	21,069	53.7
	William E. Mason (R)	17,943	45.7
4	Walter C. Newberry (D)	19,835	50.1
	George E. Adams (R)	19,173	48.4
5	Albert J. Hopkins (R)	15,845	59.1
	Jacob Haish (D)	9,664	36.4
6	Robert R. Hitt (R)	14,028	50.9
	Andrew Ashton (D)	13,517	49.1
7	Thomas J. Henderson (R)	12,946	53.8
	John W. Blee (D)	10,374	43.1
8	Lewis Steward (D)	17,496	49.4
	Charles A. Hill (R)	16,794	47.4
9	Herman W. Snow (D)	15,427	50.1
	Lewis E. Payson (R)	14,480	47.0
10	Philip S. Post (R)	16,194	50.1
	George A. Wilson (D)	15,576	48.2
11	Benjamin T. Cable (D)	19,334	51.2
	William H. Gest (R)	17,461	46.3
12	Scott Wike (D)	20,805	58.1
	Milton McClure (R)	13,336	37.2
13	William M. Springer (D)	20,951	54.3
	Jesse Hanon (R)	15,946	41.4
14	Owen Scott (D)	16,670	49.5
	Jonathan H. Rowell (R)	15,448	45.9

	Candidates	Votes	%
15	Samuel T. Busey (D)	19,010	49.7
	Joseph G. Cannon (R)	18,428	48.2
16	George W. Fithian (D)	16,473	50.3
	John D. Reeder (R)	15,957	48.7
17	Edward Lane (D)	16,700	51.7
	Fletcher H. Chapman (R)	9,761	30.2
	Edward Roessler (F ALNC)	4,845	15.0
18	William S. Forman (D)	16,279	51.7
	Cicero J. Lindley (R)	14,529	46.2
19	James R. Williams (D)	17,410	56.4
	George W. Pillow (R)	12,613	40.9
20	George H. Smith (D)	17,580	49.5
	William S. Morris (D)	16,273	45.9

INDIANA

		Votes	%
1	William F. Parrett (D)	17,730	50.4
	James S. Wright (R)	16,875	48.0
2	John L. Bretz (D)	14,697	43.6
	William N. Darnell (R)	11,996	35.6
	Sampson Cox (PP)	6,649	19.7
3	Jason B. Brown (D)	16,369	56.2
	William J. Durham (R)	12,430	42.7
4	William S. Holman (D)	15,639	52.4
	John T. Rankin (R)	13,867	46.4
5	George W. Cooper (D)	17,070	51.5
	John G. Dunbar (R)	15,355	46.3
6	Henry U. Johnson (R)	18,786	57.3
	David S. Trowbridge (D)	12,807	39.1
7	William D. Bynum (D)	27,401	54.2
	John J. W. Billingsly (R)	22,086	43.7
8	Elijah V. Brookshire (D)	21,389	52.8
	James A. Mount (R)	18,333	45.2
9	Daniel Waugh (R)	20,752	50.2
	Leroy Templeton (D)	19,453	47.1
10	David H. Patton (D)	17,262	50.3
	William D. Owen (R)	16,100	46.9
11	Augustus N. Martin (D)	20,813	51.5
	Cyrus R. Bryant (R)	18,000	44.5
12	Charles A. O. McClellan (D)	17,970	54.7
	Jaques N. Babcock (R)	13,920	42.4
13	Benjamin F. Shively (D)	20,311	52.2
	H. B. Wilson (R)	17,614	45.2

IOWA

		Votes	%
1	John J. Seerley (D)	17,459	51.4
	John H. Gier (R)	16,388	48.2
2	Walter I. Hayes (D)	20,748	63.8
	Bruce T. Seaman (R)	11,740	36.1
3	David B. Henderson (R)	19,689	50.2
	C. F. Couch (D)	19,491	49.7
4	Walter H. Butler (D)	17,972	52.7
	J. H. Swaney (R)	16,023	47.0
5	John T. Hamilton (D)	18,153	50.1
	George R. Struble (R)	17,860	49.2
6	Frederick E. White (D)	17,092	49.0
	John F. Lacey (R)	16,572	47.5
7	John A. T. Hull (R)	16,821	53.9
	H. C. Hargis (D)	14,276	45.8
8	James P. Flick (R)	19,003	49.6
	Allen R. Anderson (D)	18,887	49.3
9	Thomas Bowman (D)	18,685	50.1
	Joseph R. Reed (R)	17,322	46.4
10	Jonathan P. Dolliver (R)	18,395	51.7
	I. L. Woode (D)	17,084	48.0
11	George D. Perkins (R)	15,972	44.6
	John Pallison (D)	15,065	42.1
	A. J. Westfall (PP)	4,658	13.0

Special Election

		Votes	%
7	Edward R. Hayes (R)	16,702	54.1
	J. H. Barnett	14,142	45.8

KANSAS

Candidates	Votes	%
1 Case Broderick (R)	14,630	41.7
Thomas Moonlight (D)	13,250	37.7
L. C. Clark (ALNC D)	7,176	20.4
2 Edward H. Funston (R)	17,713	43.9
A. F. Allen (ALNC D)	12,273	30.4
J. B. Chapman (D)	10,130	25.1
3 Benjamin H. Clover (ALNC D)	23,492	55.2
Bishop W. Perkins (R)	19,061	44.8
4 John G. Otis (ALNC D)	24,993	55.6
Harrison Kelley (R)	19,984	44.4
5 John Davis (ALNC D)	19,482	52.9
William A. Phillips (R)	13,998	38.0
Park S. Warren (D)	3,337	9.1
6 William Baker (ALNC D)	20,749	62.6
Webb McNall (R)	12,105	36.5
7 Jerry Simpson (ALNC D)	32,603	56.4
James R. Hallowell (R)	25,181	43.6

KENTUCKY

	Votes	%
1 William J. Stone (D)	9,749	66.9
E. F. Franks (R)	3,743	25.7
William Curd (P)	1,086	7.5
2 William T. Ellis (D)	13,983	56.9
H. R. Bourland (R&F ALNC)	10,592	43.1
3 Isaac H. Goodnight (D)	11,649	61.1
Addison D. James (R)	7,426	38.9
4 Alexander B. Montgomery (D)	11,036	61.2
G. W. Long (R)	6,990	38.8
5 Asher G. Caruth (D)	14,395	60.8
St. John Boyle (R)	9,291	39.2
6 William W. Dickerson (D)	11,310	62.3
Weden O'Neal (R)	6,801	37.4
7 William C. P. Breckinridge (D)	7,146	92.9
Hiram Ford (P)	442	5.7
8 James B. McCreary (D)	7,430	94.8
J. C. Gilliam (R)	394	5.0
9 Thomas H. Paynter (D)	15,276	60.0
Alexander Bruce (R)	10,053	39.5
10 John W. Kendall (D)	10,746	53.8
R. C. Hill (R)	9,218	46.1
11 John H. Wilson (R)	9,612	60.5
E. J. Howard (D)	5,964	37.5

Special Election

	Votes	%
6 William W. Dickerson (D)	8,412	63.7
Wesley M. Rardin (R)	4,742	35.9

LOUISIANA

	Votes	%
1 Adolph Meyer (D)	10,824	63.2
H. C. Warmoth (R)	6,155	36.0
2 Matthew D. Lagan (D)	10,948	61.6
H. D. Coleman (R)	6,412	36.1
3 Andrew Price (D)	11,318	99.4
4 Newton C. Blanchard (D)	8,307	96.3
5 Charles J. Boatner (D)	11,793	92.7
6 Samuel M. Robertson (D)	6,611	99.9

MAINE

	Votes	%
1 Thomas B. Reed (R)	16,797	57.2
M. P. Frank (D)	11,971	40.7
2 Nelson Dingley Jr. (R)	16,499	58.0
E. Allen (D)	11,187	39.3
3 Seth L. Milliken (R)	14,477	54.5
Charles Baker (D)	11,011	41.5
4 Charles A. Boutelle (R)	15,713	56.2
Josiah Crosby (D)	11,144	39.9

MARYLAND

	Votes	%
1 Henry Page (D)	14,817	52.4
George M. Russum (R)	12,437	44.0

Candidates	Votes	%
2 Herman Stump (D)	17,740	57.1
John E. Wilson (R)	12,130	39.0
3 Harry Wells Rusk (D)	16,914	59.1
Royal H. Pullman (R)	11,273	39.4
4 Isidor Rayner (D)	18,740	59.7
Henry H. Goldsborough (R)	12,106	38.6
5 Barnes Compton (D)	14,697	54.0
Sidney E. Mudd (R)	12,479	45.8
6 William M. McKaig (D)	16,940	49.3
Louis E. McComas (R)	16,775	48.8

MASSACHUSETTS

	Votes	%
1 Charles S. Randall (R)	8,728	53.8
Charles R. Codman (D)	6,518	40.2
John D. Flint (P)	984	6.1
2 Elijah A. Morse (R)	12,339	52.3
Bushrod Morse (D)	10,489	44.4
3 John F. Andrew (D)	14,992	56.2
Edward L. Pierce (R)	11,184	41.9
4 Joseph H. O'Neil (D)	11,780	72.4
Thomas Copeland (R)	4,170	25.6
5 Sherman Hoar (D)	13,081	53.0
James A. Fox (R)	10,807	43.8
6 Henry Cabot Lodge (R)	14,579	50.0
William Everett (D)	13,539	46.4
7 William Cogswell (R)	12,496	51.5
Jonas H. French (D)	10,910	45.0
8 Moses T. Stevens (D)	11,726	49.9
Frederic T. Greenhalge (R)	11,272	47.9
9 George Fred Williams (D)	12,207	48.5
John W. Candler (R)	12,076	48.0
10 Joseph H. Walker (R)	11,130	49.4
Charles B. Pratt (D)	10,431	46.3
11 Frederick S. Coolidge (D)	9,304	40.0
Timothy G. Spaulding (R)	9,145	39.3
Myron P. Walker (IR)	3,533	15.2
Henry C. Smith (P)	1,260	5.4
12 John C. Crosby (D)	12,106	49.0
Francis W. Rockwell (R)	11,724	47.5

MICHIGAN

	Votes	%
1 J. Logan Chipman (D)	21,791	56.5
Hibbard Baker (R)	15,861	41.1
2 James S. Gorman (D)	16,471	49.1
Edward P. Allen (R)	14,568	43.4
Thomas F. Moore (P)	2,522	7.5
3 James O'Donnell (R)	16,679	44.5
John W. Fletcher (D)	14,216	37.9
Robert Fraser (P)	3,423	9.1
Samuel Dickie (INDUST)	3,187	8.5
4 Julius C. Burrows (R)	16,067	45.3
George L. Yaple (D)	15,673	44.1
George F. Cunningham (P)	2,843	8.0
5 Melbourne Ford (D)	22,451	49.6
Charles W. Watkins (R)	20,153	44.5
Edward L. Briggs (P)	2,587	5.7
6 Byron G. Stout (D)	17,140	44.5
William Ball (R)	16,457	42.7
Jay Sessions (P)	3,004	7.8
George W. Caswell (INDUST)	1,940	5.0
7 Justin R. Whiting (D)	14,553	50.7
James S. Ayres (R)	12,566	43.8
8 Henry M. Youmans (D)	17,230	47.2
Aaron T. Bliss (R)	17,154	47.0
William M. Smith (P)	2,106	5.8
9 Harrison H. Wheeler (D)	15,854	45.7
Byron M. Cutcheon (R)	15,794	45.6
Oscar M. Brownson (P)	2,778	8.0
10 Thomas A. E. Weadock (D)	16,721	50.6
Watts S. Humphrey (R)	15,055	45.6
11 Samuel M. Stephenson (R)	16,667	50.4
John Semer (D)	14,549	44.0
William H. Simmons (P)	1,759	5.3

MINNESOTA

Candidates	Votes	%
1 William H. Harries (D)	17,198	53.6
Dunnell (R)	14,875	46.4
2 John Lind (R)	20,789	49.2
Baker (ALNC D)	20,306	48.1
3 Osee M. Hall (D)	17,639	50.5
D. S. Hall (R)	13,106	37.5
Gamble (ALNC D)	3,054	8.8
4 James N. Castle (D)	35,903	51.8
R. Snider (R)	30,175	43.5
5 Kittel Halvorson (ALNC D)	21,514	37.7
Comstock (R)	19,372	33.9
Whiteman (D)	16,203	28.4

MISSISSIPPI

	Votes	%
1 John M. Allen (D)	3,501	100.0
2 John C. Kyle (D)	8,282	70.5
G. M. Buchanan (R)	3,468	29.5
3 Thomas C. Catchings (D)	8,689	76.2
James Hill (R)	2,717	23.8
4 Clarke Lewis (D)	6,753	81.1
W. D. Frazer (R)	1,572	18.9
5 Joseph H. Beeman (D)	6,305	100.0
6 Thomas R. Stockdale (D)	9,340	71.3
H. C. Griffin (R)	3,768	28.8
7 Charles E. Hooker (D)	6,284	75.6
J. M. Matthews (R)	2,028	24.4

MISSOURI

	Votes	%
1 William H. Hatch (D)	20,234	56.7
Harrington (R)	15,080	42.3
2 Charles H. Mansur (D)	20,527	57.2
Pettyjohn (R)	13,147	36.7
Donovan (UN LAB)	2,188	6.1
3 Alexander M. Dockery (D)	20,594	55.0
Kinney (R)	13,139	35.1
Hillis (UN LAB)	3,681	9.8
4 Robert P. C. Wilson (D)	15,753	51.4
Ford (R)	12,444	40.6
Whipple (UN LAB)	2,191	7.2
5 John C. Tarsney (D)	19,387	57.7
Twitchell (R)	13,505	40.2
6 John T. Heard (D)	24,027	54.6
Redman (R)	16,365	37.2
Alldredge (UN LAB)	3,625	8.2
7 Richard H. Norton (D)	17,926	58.1
Barnett (R)	12,946	41.9
8 John J. O'Neill (D)	11,621	54.9
Joy (R)	9,563	45.1
9 Seth W. Cobb (D)	10,576	58.8
Prosser (R)	6,962	38.7
10 Samuel Byrns (D)	16,744	52.5
Kinsey (R)	15,095	47.3
11 Richard P. Bland (D)	18,991	56.1
Erwin (R)	14,885	43.9
12 David A. De Armond (D)	21,556	48.2
Lewis (R)	14,441	32.3
Wykoff (UN LAB)	8,537	19.1
13 Robert W. Fyan (D)	16,488	49.9
Wade (R)	13,728	41.6
Vertrees (UN LAB)	2,803	8.5
14 Marshall Arnold (D)	19,312	59.7
Rogers (R)	13,037	40.3

Special Election

	Votes	%
14 Robert H. Whitelaw (D)	19,329	60.8
Farnsworth (R)	12,481	39.2

MONTANA

	Votes	%
AL William W. Dixon (D)	15,411	49.6
Thomas H. Carter (R)	15,128	48.7

NEBRASKA

	Candidates	Votes	%
1	William Jennings Bryan (D)	32,376	44.5
	W. J. Connell (R)	25,663	35.3
	Allen Root (I)	13,066	18.0
2	William A. McKeighan (I & D)	36,104	61.1
	N. V. Harlan (R)	21,776	36.9
3	Omer M. Kem (I)	31,731	39.4
	George W. E. Dorsey (R)	25,440	31.6
	W. H. Thompson (D)	22,353	27.8

NEVADA

	Candidates	Votes	%
AL	Horace F. Bartine (R)	6,610	53.4
	George W. Cassidy (D)	5,736	46.3

NEW HAMPSHIRE

	Candidates	Votes	%
1	Luther F. McKinney (D)	21,432	50.7
	David A. Taggart (R)	20,296	48.0
2	Warren F. Daniell (D)	21,438	49.7
	Orren C. Moore (R)	21,079	48.8

NEW JERSEY

	Candidates	Votes	%
1	Christopher A. Bergen (R)	19,082	50.9
	Newell (D)	16,372	43.7
	Nicholson (P)	2,007	5.4
2	James Buchanan (R)	17,515	50.0
	Haven (D)	16,352	46.6
3	Jacob A. Geissenhainer (D)	20,266	54.6
	Clark Jr (R)	15,748	42.4
4	Samuel Fowler (D)	13,459	56.5
	Goodman (R)	8,775	36.8
	Schenk (P)	1,583	6.7
5	Cornelius A. Cadmus (D)	16,815	50.4
	Beckwith (R)	15,459	46.4
6	Thomas D. English (D)	23,278	50.9
	Condit (R)	21,468	46.9
7	Edward F. McDonald (D)	21,875	56.0
	McEwan Jr. (R)	16,761	42.9

NEW YORK

	Candidates	Votes	%
1	James W. Covert (D)	18,999	56.0
	John Lewis Childs (R)	14,085	41.5
2	David A. Boody (D)	21,609	57.7
	James Gresham (R)	15,028	40.1
3	William J. Coombs (D)	15,670	48.9
	William . Wallace (R)	15,652	48.8
4	John M. Clancy (D)	18,216	67.6
	Andrew J. Perry (R)	8,454	31.4
5	Thomas F. Magner (D)	16,470	58.4
	John R. Smith (R)	10,814	38.4
6	John R. Fellows (D)	10,170	57.2
	Cornelius Donovan (R)	5,574	31.3
	Edwin L. Abbett (CO D)	1,928	10.8
7	Edward J. Dunphy (D)	10,855	60.0
	William Morgan (R)	4,351	24.1
	William T. Croasdale (CO D)	2,787	15.4
8	Timothy J. Campbell (D)	15,958	77.9
	Samuel Rinaldo (R)	3,840	18.7
9	Amos J. Cummings (D)	14,252	71.8
	John Weiss (R)	4,462	22.5
	Christian Ensminger (CO D)	1,072	5.4
10	Francis B. Spinola (D)	13,884	70.5
	Cortlandt S. Van Rensselaer (R)	5,288	26.9
11	John De Witt Warner (D)	17,033	64.2
	Charles A. Flammer (R)	8,850	33.3
12	Roswell P. Flower (D)	19,160	69.4
	Charles H. Blair (R)	7,187	26.0
13	Ashbel P. Fitch (D)	28,268	68.9
	Percy D. Adams (R)	11,820	28.8
14	William G. Stahlnecker (D)	18,391	53.4
	J. Thomas Stearns (R)	12,211	35.5
	Alexander Taylor Jr.	2,561	7.4
15	Henry Bacon (D)	14,640	50.9
	Clarence Lexow (R)	13,061	45.4

	Candidates	Votes	%
16	John H. Ketcham (R)	13,474	75.3
	William W. Smith (P)	4,428	24.7
17	Isaac N. Cox (D)	15,439	53.5
	Theodore C. Teale (R)	13,429	46.5
18	John A. Quackenbush (R)	17,185	50.2
	Michael F. Collins (D)	15,939	46.6
19	Charles Tracey (D)	18,021	56.9
	Angus McDuffie Shoemaker (R)	12,942	40.9
20	John Sanford (R)	18,369	50.4
	Alexander B. Baucus (D)	16,788	46.1
21	John M. Wever (R)	13,314	55.6
	Anthony J.B. Ross (D)	9,820	41.0
22	Leslie W. Russell (R)	13,893	56.3
	Smith T. Woolworth (D)	9,116	36.9
	Henry P. Forbes (P)	1,679	6.8
23	Henry W. Bentley (D)	15,449	50.4
	James S. Sherman (R)	14,933	48.7
24	George Van Horn (D)	14,127	48.3
	Frank B. Arnold (R)	13,929	47.6
25	James J. Belden (R)	17,283	57.1
	William Stitt (D)	11,455	37.8
	Andrew N. Vanderbilt (P)	1,547	5.1
26	George W. Ray (R)	17,804	51.7
	Thomas H. Beal (D)	14,402	41.9
	Mott C. Dixon (P)	2,208	6.4
27	Sereno E. Payne (R)	17,970	50.6
	Edwin K. Burnham (D)	15,978	45.0
28	Hosea H. Rockwell (D)	12,440	47.9
	Henry T. Noyes (R)	12,351	47.6
29	John Raines (R)	14,722	49.7
	Demerville Page (D)	13,369	45.1
	Daniel J. Chittenden (P)	1,540	5.2
30	Halbert S. Greenleaf (D)	15,047	48.5
	John Van Voorhis (R)	14,796	47.7
31	James W. Wadsworth (R)	13,716	82.2
	Alva Carpenter (D)	2,275	13.6
32	Daniel N. Lockwood (D)	21,213	55.7
	Benjamin H. Williams (R)	16,240	42.6
33	Thomas L. Bunting (D)	12,585	51.6
	George A. Davis (R)	10,793	44.2
34	Warren B. Hooker (R)	15,843	54.7
	Hiram Smith (D)	10,117	35.0
	Jesse D. Rogers (P)	2,981	10.3

Special Election

	Candidates	Votes	%
24	John S. Pindar (D)	14,030	48.1
	Frank B. Arnold (R)	13,916	47.7

NORTH CAROLINA

	Candidates	Votes	%
1	William A. B. Branch (D)	16,436	56.3
	Claude M. Bernard (R)	12,683	43.4
2	Henry P. Cheatham (R)	16,942	51.7
	James M. Mewborne (D)	15,713	47.9
3	Benjamin F. Grady (D)	17,348	67.0
	George C. Scurlock (R)	8,541	33.0
4	Benjamin H. Bunn (D)	18,995	59.8
	Alexander McIver (R&F ALNC)	12,417	39.1
5	Archibald H. A. Williams (D)	16,143	52.6
	John M. Brower (R)	14,204	46.2
6	Sydenham B. Alexander (D)	16,820	66.6
	Richard M. Norment (R)	8,424	33.4
7	John S. Henderson (D)	13,246	57.4
	Pleasant C. Thomas (R)	9,280	40.2
8	William H. H. Cowles (D)	8,586	53.7
	Edward W. Faucette (R)	7,256	45.4
9	William T. Crawford (D)	15,979	51.8
	Hamilton G. Ewart (R)	14,851	48.2

NORTH DAKOTA

	Candidates	Votes	%
AL	Martin N. Johnson (R)	21,365	59.0
	Benton (D)	14,830	41.0

OHIO

	Candidates	Votes	%
1	Bellamy Storer (R)	16,661	53.3
	O. J. Cosgrave (D)	14,373	46.0

	Candidates	Votes	%
2	John A. Caldwell (R)	22,021	59.9
	Oliver Brown (D)	14,291	38.9
3	George W. Houk (D)	21,270	51.5
	H. L. Morey (R)	18,639	45.1
4	Martin K. Gantz (D)	20,705	49.5
	William P. Orr (R)	19,295	46.2
5	Fernando C. Layton (D)	20,179	52.7
	L. K. Stroup (R)	15,973	41.7
6	Dennis D. Donovan (D)	18,741	51.0
	J. H. Brigham (R)	17,029	46.3
7	William E. Haynes (D)	18,126	52.4
	J. M. Ashley (R)	16,070	46.4
8	Darius D. Hare (D)	17,414	48.3
	Charles Foster (R)	17,220	47.7
9	Joseph H. Outhwaite (D)	18,550	51.8
	T. B. Wilson (R)	16,418	45.8
10	Robert E. Doan (R)	19,353	52.5
	J. Q. Smith (D)	15,569	42.2
	R. Rathburn (P)	1,954	5.3
11	John M. Pattison (D)	16,110	51.9
	D. W. C. Loudon (R)	13,157	42.4
12	W. H. Enochs (R)	16,851	61.1
	Ezra V. Dean (D)	9,814	35.6
13	Irvine Dungan (D)	16,225	50.7
	William T. Lewis (R)	14,759	46.1
14	James W. Owens (D)	19,193	53.2
	Samuel Slade (R)	15,773	43.8
15	Michael D. Harter (D)	19,832	52.5
	G. L. Sackett (R)	16,084	42.6
16	John G. Warwick (D)	20,059	49.3
	William McKinley Jr. (R)	19,757	48.6
17	Albert J. Pearson (D)	14,928	49.8
	C. L. Poorman (R)	14,224	47.5
18	Joseph D. Taylor (R)	16,993	56.0
	H. H. McFadden (D)	11,783	38.8
	S. W. Wilkins (P)	1,568	5.2
19	Ezra B. Taylor (R)	19,419	58.5
	T. E. Hoyt (D)	11,972	36.1
	Richard Brown (P)	1,753	5.3
20	Vincent A. Taylor (R)	22,672	58.1
	H. L. Stewart (D)	14,748	37.8
21	Tom L. Johnson (D)	17,646	54.6
	T. E. Burton (R)	14,256	44.1

OREGON

	Candidates	Votes	%
AL	Binger Herman (R)	40,176	54.8
	Robert A. Miller (D)	30,263	41.3

PENNSYLVANIA

	Candidates	Votes	%
1	Henry H. Bingham (R)	22,166	60.3
	Edwin G. Flanagan (D)	14,497	39.5
2	Charles O'Neill (R)	16,324	62.2
	Edwin F. Lott (D)	9,785	37.3
3	William McAleer (D)	13,121	56.6
	Richard Vaux (ID)	10,037	43.3
4	John E. Reyburn (R)	33,253	60.9
	William M. Ayres (D)	20,988	38.4
5	Alfred C. Harmer (R)	30,616	61.2
	J. Henry Taylor (D)	19,213	38.4
6	John B. Robinson (R)	17,447	55.0
	Thomas W. Pierce (D)	13,342	42.1
7	Edwin Hallowell (D)	20,810	49.5
	Irving P. Wauger (R)	20,623	49.1
8	William Mutchler (D)	17,424	62.3
	George M. Davies (R)	10,549	37.7
9	David B. Brunner (D)	26,627	62.8
	Daniel H. Wingerd (R)	15,434	36.4
10	Marriott Brosius (R)	19,126	66.4
	D. F. Magee (D)	9,358	32.5
11	Lemuel Amerman (D)	9,336	48.6
	Joseph A. Scranton (R)	9,033	47.0
12	George W. Shonk (R)	14,558	51.3
	John B. Reynolds (D)	13,074	46.0
13	James B. Reilly (D)	13,308	52.9
	John T. Shoener (R)	11,828	47.1
14	John W. Rife (R)	17,795	54.8
	William L. Gorgas (D)	14,308	44.0

PENNSYLVANIA

Candidates	Votes	%
15 Myron B. Wright (R)	16,076	51.8
Clar W. Canfield (D)	13,854	44.7
16 Albert C. Hopkins (R)	15,824	48.5
Mortimer F. Elliott (D)	15,773	48.3
17 Simon P. Wolverton (D)	15,178	60.2
W. C. Farnsworth (R)	9,234	36.6
18 Louis E. Atkinson (R)	17,443	50.9
George W. Skinner (D)	16,834	49.1
19 Frank E. Beltzhoover (D)	21,969	58.7
D. K. Trimmer (R)	14,860	39.7
20 Edward Scull (R)	17,434	49.5
Thomas H. Greevy (D)	16,908	48.0
21 George F. Huff (R)	21,212	51.8
Jacob Creps (D)	19,714	48.2
22 John Dalzell (R)	21,464	60.9
William J. Brennan (D)	13,559	38.4
23 William A. Stone (R)	13,904	66.8
Morrison Foster (D)	6,788	32.6
24 Andrew J. Stewart (R)	21,708‡	49.0
Alexander K. Craig (D)	21,585	48.7
25 Eugene P. Gillespie (D)	13,797	38.3
Thomas W. Phillips (R)	10,636	29.5
Alex McDowell (R)	10,531	29.2
26 Matthew Griswold (R)	13,779	49.8
A. L. Tilden (D)	12,891	46.6
27 Charles W. Stone (R)	12,718	54.5
Robert W. Dunn (D)	9,405	40.3
D. H. Boulton (P)	1,212	5.2
28 George F. Kribbs (D)	17,636	56.4
Daniel C. Oyster (R)	12,944	41.4

Special Elections

3	Richard Vaux (D)	7,977	92.1
4	John E. Reyburn (R)	25,152	59.9
	William M. Ayres (D)	16,573	39.5
27	Charles W. Stone (R)	11,825	72.0
	Robert W. Dunn (D)	4,499	27.4

RHODE ISLAND [1]

1	Oscar Lapham (D)	10,382	52.6
	Henry J. Spooner (R)	8,616	43.6
2	Charles H. Page (D)	8,341*	47.8
	Warren O. Arnold (R)	8,325	47.7

SOUTH CAROLINA

1	William H. Brawley (D)	7,249	84.2
	William D. Crum (R)	1,349	15.7
2	George D. Tillman (D)	9,996	85.6
	S. E. Smith (R)	1,671	14.3
3	George Johnstone (D)	8,942	91.4
	John R. Tolbert (R)	803	8.2
4	George W. Shell (D)	10,372	81.9
	J. F. Ensor (R)	2,258	17.8
5	John J. Hemphill (D)	9,432	87.1
	G. G. Alexander (R)	1,321	12.2
6	Eli T. Stackhouse (D)	9,022	78.8
	Edmund H. Deas (R)	2,352	20.5
7	William Elliott (D)	3,792	44.4
	Thomas E. Miller (R)	3,315	38.8
	E. W. Brayton (IR)	1,410	16.5

SOUTH DAKOTA

AL	John A. Pickler (R)	34,856✔	
	John R. Gamble (R)	34,553✔	
	F. A. Leavitt (I)	24,907	

Candidates	Votes	%
Fred Zipp (I)	24,808	
F. A. Clark (D)	17,527	
W. Y. Quigley (D)	17,267	

TENNESSEE

1	Alfred A. Taylor (R)	11,466	49.0
	R. R. Butler (IR)	10,717	45.8
2	Leonidas C. Houk (R)	12,765	60.1
	J. C. J. Williams (D)	7,378	34.8
3	Henry C. Snodgrass (D)	13,773	50.3
	H. Clay Evans (R)	13,250	48.4
4	Benton McMillin (D)	14,514	64.0
	C. W. Garratt (R)	7,630	33.7
5	James D. Richardson (D)	12,890	68.4
	P. C. Smithson (R)	4,340	23.0
	H. R. Moore (P)	1,474	7.8
6	Joseph E. Washington (D)	11,656	74.4
	L. M. Watson (R)	2,708	17.3
	W. D. Turnley (P)	1,302	8.3
7	Nicholas N. Cox (D)	10,362	60.7
	A. M. Hughes Jr. (R)	5,364	31.4
	John Graham (P)	1,289	7.6
8	Benjamin A. Enloe (D)	12,444	62.7
	J. R. McKinney (R)	4,469	22.5
	George T. McCall (R)	1,339	6.7
	John T. Warren (P)	1,070	5.4
9	Rice A. Pierce (D)	12,191	70.6
	W. F. Poston (R)	3,959	22.9
	J. B. Cummings (P)	1,109	6.4
10	Josiah Patterson (D)	9,108	74.5
	L. B. Eaton (R)	3,033	24.8

TEXAS

1	Charles Stewart (D)	19,356	63.1
	E.L. Angier (R)	11,292	36.8
2	John B. Long (D)	12,973	99.6
3	Constantine B. Kilgore (D)	19,038	71.3
	L. B. Fish (R)	7,340	27.5
4	David B. Culberson (D)	17,290	74.8
	J. C. Gibbons (R)	5,279	22.8
5	Joseph W. Bailey (D)	26,791	81.9
	A. W. Achison (R)	4,252	13.0
	W. R. Lamb (I)	1,683	5.1
6	Jo Abbott (D)	29,982	85.7
	Darter Isaac (R)	4,430	12.7
7	William H. Crain (D)	18,550	67.2
	J. V. Spohn (R)	9,069	32.8
8	Littleton W. Moore (D)	20,739	71.2
	William Greene (R)	8,368	28.8
9	Roger Q. Mills (D)	21,847	79.6
	D. W. Roberts (R)	5,600	20.4
10	Joseph D. Sayers (D)	32,479	92.4
	W. G. Robinson (R)	2,537	7.2
11	Samuel W. T. Lanham (D)	38,348	97.8

VERMONT

1	H. Henry Powers (R)	17,136	66.5
	Thomas W. Moloney (D)	8,605	33.4
2	William W. Grout (R)	18,092	66.8
	Stephen C. Shurtleff (D)	8,960	33.1

VIRGINIA

1	William A. Jones (D)	14,613	54.3
	I.H. Bayly Browne (R)	12,150	45.2

Candidates	Votes	%
2 John W. Lawson (D)	13,484	50.7
George E. Bowden (R)	12,317	46.3
3 George D. Wise (D)	13,937	99.9
4 James F. Epes (D)	13,325	57.1
J. M. Langston (R)	9,991	42.8
5 Posey G. Lester (D)	10,569	82.0
S. C. Adams (I)	1,360	10.6
J. Ring (I)	959	7.4
6 Paul C. Edmunds (D)	11,615	92.6
William J. Shelburne (P)	901	7.2
7 Charles T. O'Ferrall (D)	10,167	89.0
I. M. Underwood (P)	1,225	10.7
8 William H. F. Lee (D)	13,499	57.0
Frank Hume (ID)	10,181	43.0
9 John A. Buchanan (D)	15,324	56.1
George T. Mills (R)	11,977	43.9
10 Henry St.George Tucker (D)	9,721	94.6
A. J. Taylor (I)	531	5.2

WASHINGTON

AL	John L. Wilson (R)	29,133	56.0
	Carroll (D)	22,861	44.0

WEST VIRGINIA

1	John O. Pendleton (D)	18,470	50.2
	William P. Hubbard (R)	17,831	48.5
2	William L. Wilson (D)	20,439	52.5
	George Hourian (R)	18,374	47.2
3	John D. Alderson (D)	20,433	56.1
	Theophilus Gaines (R)	15,778	43.3
4	Jones Capehart (D)	19,576	52.3
	C.B. Smith (R)	17,648	47.2

WISCONSIN

1	Clinton Babbitt (D)	14,532	48.3
	Cooper (R)	14,209	47.3
2	Charles Barwig (D)	17,826	65.8
	D. C. Van Brunt (R)	9,266	34.2
3	Allen R. Bushnell (D)	16,432	49.2
	Robert M. LaFollette (R)	15,430	46.2
4	John L. Mitchell (D)	24,679	56.1
	R.C. Spencer (R)	17,605	40.0
5	George H. Brickner (D)	17,708	67.2
	Blackstock (R)	8,093	30.7
6	Lucas M. Miller (D)	15,573	51.7
	Clark (R)	13,409	44.5
7	Frank P. Coburn (D)	15,399	50.8
	Thomas (R)	13,397	44.2
8	Nils P. Haugen (R)	17,609	49.2
	Bailey (D)	15,261	42.7
	Jones (P)	2,911	8.1
9	Thomas Lynch (D)	24,491	54.4
	Myron H. McCord (R)	19,161	42.6

WYOMING

(Became a state July 10, 1890)

AL	Clarence D. Clark (R)	9,087	58.2
	George T. Beck (D)	6,520	41.8

1. *No candidate in the 2nd district received the majority of the vote required for election.*
(Majority vote requirement, p. 703.)

1891 House Elections

MICHIGAN

Special Election

Candidates	Votes	%
5 Charles E. Belknap (R)	14,652	44.5
John S. Lawrence (D)	13,150	40.0
Edward Hutchins (PP)	3,687	11.2

NEW YORK

Special Elections

2	Alfred C. Chapin (D)	24,018	52.7
	Bristow (R)	21,522	47.3
10	W. Bourke Cockran (TAM&NY D)	13,234	63.5
	Townsend (R)	7,160	34.4
12	Joseph J. Little (TAM&NY D)	19,306	58.1
	McMichael (R)	11,465	34.5
22	Newton M. Curtis (R)	19,096	54.8
	Porter (D)	14,423	41.4

RHODE ISLAND [1]

Special Election

Candidates	Votes	%
2 Charles H. Page (D)	6,899	85.4
Warren O. Arnold (R)	721	8.9
Tripp (P)	461	5.7

SOUTH DAKOTA

Special Election

AL	John L. Jolley (R)	17,614	44.5
	Henry W. Smith (I)	14,687	37.1
	James M. Wood (D)	7,299	18.4

TENNESSEE

Special Election

Candidates	Votes	%
2 John C. Houk (R)	14,095	63.7
J. C. J. Williams (D)	7,829	35.4

VIRGINIA

Special Election

8 Elisha E. Meredith (R)	8,891	67.8
John Ambler Brooks	4,218	32.2

1. *Since no candidate running for the House in Rhode Island's 2nd District in 1890 received the majority needed for election (see Rhode Island 1890, p. 821), a special election in 1891 was ordered by the legislature. According to the Biographical Directory, incumbent Warren O. Arnold, who had run for re-election in 1890, but failed to win a majority, refused to participate actively in the special election. Without serious opposition, Charles H. Page won easily.*

1892 House Elections

ALABAMA

	Candidates	Votes	%
1	Richard H. Clarke (D)	12,514	60.5
	William Mason (K POP)	7,156	34.6
2	Jesse F. Stallings (D)	16,781	58.6
	Frank Baltzell (K POP)	10,331	36.1
	John D. Bibb (R)	1,506	5.3
3	William Oates (D)	16,885	62.4
	J. F. Tate (K POP)	9,931	36.7
4	Gaston A. Robbins (D)	16,159	60.7
	Adolphus P. Longshore (K POP)	8,534	32.1
	George H. Craig (R)	1,848	6.9
5	James E. Cobb (D)	13,456	49.4
	M. W. Whatley (K POP)	11,468	42.1
	John McDuffie (R)	2,306	8.5
6	John Bankhead (D)	14,342	62.8
	T. M. Barbour (K POP)	6,453	28.2
	Ignatius Green (I)	2,054	9.0
7	William H. Denson (D)	10,911	54.3
	William Wood (K POP)	9,091	45.2
8	Joseph Wheeler (D)	15,607	52.4
	R. W. Austin (POP)	11,868	39.9
	R. T. Blackwell (R)	2,279	7.7
9	L. W. Turpin (D)	19,848	67.4
	Joseph H. Parsons (POP)	8,954	30.4

ARKANSAS

		Votes	%
1	Philip D. McCulloch Jr. (D)	16,680	63.6
	Jacob Trieber (R)	9,541	36.4
2	Clifton R. Breckinridge (D)	16,508	70.8
	W. B. W. Heartsill (PP)	6,808	29.2
3	Thomas C. McRae (D)	17,493	68.1
	J. O. A. Bush (PP)	8,197	31.9
4	William L. Terry (D)	13,630	69.7
	T. M. C. Birmingham (PP)	5,910	30.2
5	Hugh A. Dinsmore (D)	13,698	57.2
	J. E. Bryan (PP)	10,267	42.8
6	Robert Neill (D)	16,594	87.6
	George Martin (I)	1,926	10.2

CALIFORNIA

		Votes	%
1	Thomas J. Geary (D)	19,308	56.8
	Edw. W. Davis (R)	13,123	38.6
2	Anthony Caminetti (D)	20,741	53.2
	John F. Davis (R)	16,781	43.1
3	Samuel G. Hilborn (R)	13,163‡	43.2
	Warren B. English (D)	13,138	43.1
	J. L. Lyon (PP)	3,495	11.5
4	James G. Maguire (D)	14,997	49.2
	C. O. Alexander (R)	13,226	43.4
	E. P. Burman (PP)	1,980	6.5
5	Eugene F. Loud (R)	14,660	46.4
	J. W. Ryland (D)	13,694	43.3
	J. J. Morrison (PP)	2,484	7.9
6	Marion Cannon (D, PP)	20,680	56.3
	Hervey Lindley (R)	14,271	38.8
7	William W. Bowers (R)	15,856	41.6
	Olin Welborn (D)	14,869	39.0
	Hiram Hamilton (PP)	5,578	14.6

Special Election

		Votes	%
3	Samuel G. Hilborn (R)	16,911	47.3
	Warren B. English (D)	14,493	40.5
	J. L. Lyon (PP)	4,326	12.1

COLORADO

		Votes	%
1	Lafayette Pence (D & POP)	20,004	49.1
	Earl B. Coe (R)	17,609	43.2
	John G. Taylor (D)	2,240	5.5
2	John C. Bell (D & POP)	31,587	61.0
	Henderson H. Eddy (R)	19,572	37.8

CONNECTICUT

	Candidates	Votes	%
1	Lewis Sperry (D)	19,068	49.0
	Henry (R)	18,506	47.5
2	James P. Pigott (D)	27,624	50.9
	Kellogg (R)	24,772	45.7
3	Charles A. Russell (R)	11,928	49.5
	Thayer (D)	11,277	46.8
4	Robert E. DeForest (D)	24,035	51.3
	Frederick Miles (R)	21,825	46.6

DELAWARE

		Votes	%
AL	John W. Causey (D)	18,554	49.9
	Jonathan S. Willis (R)	18,080	48.6

FLORIDA

		Votes	%
1	Stephen R. Mallory (PP & D)	16,114	99.2
2	Charles M. Cooper (D)	14,668	75.8
	Austin S. Mann (PP)	4,636	24.0

GEORGIA

		Votes	%
1	Rufus E. Lester (D)	12,337	62.6
	Louis M. Pleasant (R)	4,414	22.4
	W. R. Kemp (PP)	2,944	15.0
2	Benjamin E. Russell (D)	11,517	65.2
	I. H. Hand (PP)	6,060	34.3
3	Charles F. Crisp (D)	11,574	69.9
	F. D. Wimberly (PP & R)	4,982	30.1
4	Charles L. Moses (D)	12,779	64.1
	J. H. Turner (PP & R)	7,145	35.9
5	Leonidas F. Livingston (D)	9,732	60.2
	Samuel Small (PP & R)	6,447	39.9
6	Thomas B. Cabaniss (D)	11,628	64.6
	C. F. Turner (PP & R)	6,387	35.5
7	John W. Maddox (D)	13,572	65.9
	John A. Sibley (PP & R)	7,037	34.2
8	Thomas G. Lawson (D)	11,133	66.7
	James B. Robins (PP & R)	5,550	33.3
9	Farish T. Tate (D)	13,952	59.5
	Thaddeus K. Pickett (PP & R)	9,481	40.5
10	James C. C. Black (D)	17,772	59.0
	Thomas E. Watson (PP & R)	12,330	41.0
11	Henry G. Turner (D)	11,091	65.3
	Lucius C. Mattox (PP & R)	5,882	34.7

IDAHO

		Votes	%
AL	Willis Sweet (R)	8,549	44.1
	Edward B. True (D)	6,029	31.1
	James Gunn (PP)	4,567	23.6

ILLINOIS

		Votes	%
1	J. Frank Aldrich (R)	39,726	49.7
	Edwin B. Smith (D)	37,904	47.4
2	Lawrence E. McGann (D)	32,609	68.9
	Edward D. Connor (R)	14,168	29.9
3	Allan C. Durborow Jr. (D)	38,652	57.4
	Thomas C. Macmillan (R)	27,392	40.7
4	Julius Goldzier (D)	34,454	52.2
	William Vocke (R)	29,851	45.2
5	Albert J. Hopkins (R)	19,864	58.1
	Samuel Alschuler (D)	12,486	36.5
	Henry Wood (P)	1,861	5.4
6	Robert R. Hitt (R)	18,307	54.9
	Henry D. Dennis (D)	12,794	38.4
7	Thomas J. Henderson (R)	15,849	52.1
	James E. McPherran (D)	11,350	37.3
	Horace M. Gilbert (PP)	1,965	6.5
8	Robert A. Childs (R)	20,852	48.2
	Lewis Steward (D)	20,835	48.2

	Candidates	Votes	%
9	Hamilton K. Wheeler (R)	16,921	48.2
	Herman W. Snow (D)	16,403	46.7
10	Philip Sidney Post (R)	19,215	49.7
	James W. Hunter (D)	17,246	44.6
11	Benjamin F. Marsh (R)	19,652	48.0
	Truman Plantz (D)	18,594	45.4
12	John J. McDannold (D)	22,207	53.1
	T. M. Rogers (R)	15,940	38.1
	William Hess (PP)	2,489	6.0
13	William M. Springer (D)	22,954	52.1
	Charles P. Kane (R)	18,238	41.4
14	Benjamin F. Funk (R)	18,578	48.0
	Owen Scott (D)	18,264	47.2
15	Joseph G. Cannon (R)	20,596	49.6
	Samuel T. Busey (D)	19,098	46.0
16	George W. Fithian (D)	17,320	46.0
	J. O. Burton (R)	16,540	43.9
	Thomas Ratcliff (PP)	2,794	7.4
17	Edward Lane (D)	19,107	51.9
	John N. Gwin (R)	13,710	37.2
	Presley G. Donaldson (PP)	2,554	6.9
18	William S. Forman (D)	17,696	49.2
	W. A. Northcott (R)	16,552	46.0
19	James R. Williams (D)	18,411	49.8
	Norman H. Moss (R)	14,972	40.5
	Joseph H. Crasno (PP)	2,599	7.0
20	George W. Smith (R)	19,944	51.7
	Benjamin W. Pope (D)	17,446	45.2
AL	John C. Black (D)	425,336✓	
	Andrew J. Hunter (D)	423,868✓	
	Richard Yates (R)	399,321	
	George S. Willits (R)	399,096	
	Frances E. Andrews (P)	25,596	
	James S. Felter (P)	25,428	
	Jesse Harper (PP)	21,707	
	Michael McDonough (PP)	21,541	

INDIANA

		Votes	%
1	Arthur H. Taylor (D)	19,720	47.4
	A. P. Twineham (R)	19,266	46.3
	Moses Smith (PP)	2,110	5.1
2	John L. Bretz (D)	17,700	47.9
	Ben L. Willoughby (R)	15,731	42.6
	Merrick W. Ackerty (PP)	3,010	8.2
3	Jason B. Brown (D)	20,928	51.6
	William W. Borden (R)	17,957	44.3
4	William S. Holman (D)	19,008	52.5
	Samuel M. Jones (R)	15,927	44.0
5	George W. Cooper (D)	17,698	48.3
	John Worrell (R)	16,640	45.4
6	Henry U. Johnson (R)	20,444	56.7
	Luther M. Mering (D)	11,820	32.8
	Nathan T. Butts (PP)	2,581	7.2
7	William D. Bynum (D)	28,267	49.5
	Charles L. Henry (R)	26,951	47.2
8	Elijah V. Brookshire (D)	22,949	48.4
	Winfield S. Carpenter (R)	21,327	45.0
9	Daniel Waugh (R)	23,416	50.1
	Eli W. Brown (D)	19,291	41.3
	George W. Swan (PP)	2,517	5.4
10	Thomas Hammond (D)	18,298	46.1
	William Johnston (R)	18,256	46.0
11	Augustus N. Martin (D)	21,893	45.9
	William T. Daley (R)	21,060	44.1
	Joshua Strange (PP)	3,026	6.3
12	William F. McNagny (D)	19,991	50.0
	Adolph J. You (R)	16,926	42.3
	Calvin Husselman (PP)	2,027	5.1
13	Charles G. Conn (D)	21,627	50.4
	James S. Dodge (R)	19,687	45.9

IOWA

		Votes	%
1	John H. Gear (R)	18,416	49.4
	John J. Surley (D)	17,787	47.7

IOWA

	Candidates	Votes	%
2	Walter I. Hayes (D)	23,129	58.9
	John H. Munroe (R)	15,357	39.1
3	David B. Henderson (R)	22,045	51.3
	James H. Shields (D)	20,586	47.9
4	Thomas Updegraff (R)	19,681	51.5
	W. H. Butler (D)	18,091	47.4
5	Roberts G. Cousins (R)	20,033	49.9
	John T. Hamilton (D)	18,935	47.2
6	John F. Lacey (R)	17,747	47.1
	F. E. White (D)	16,572	44.0
	E. S. Owens (PP)	2,889	7.7
7	John A. T. Hull (R)	19,963	54.0
	Joseph A. Dyer (D)	13,883	37.5
	Ed A. Ott (PP)	2,562	6.9
8	William P. Hepburn (R)	20,299	49.8
	Thomas L. Maxwell (D)	15,968	39.2
	Walter S. Scott (PP)	3,687	9.0
9	Alva L. Hager (R)	20,287	49.3
	John E. F. McGee (D)	17,809	43.3
	F. W. Myers (PP)	2,610	6.4
10	Jonathan P. Dolliver (R)	23,402	53.7
	J. J. Ryan (D)	18,458	42.4
11	George D. Perkins (R)	21,984	50.6
	Daniel Campbell (D-PP)	20,707	47.6

KANSAS

1	Case Broderick (R)	19,401	54.5
	Fred J. Close (PP)	15,782	44.3
2	Edward H. Funston (R)	22,900‡	49.4
	Horace L. Moore (D-PP)	22,817	49.2
3	Thomas J. Hudson (D-PP)	23,998	52.2
	L. U. Humphrey (R)	21,594	47.0
4	Charles Curtis (R)	25,327	52.0
	E. V. Wharton (D-PP)	22,603	46.4
5	John Davis (PP)	20,162	50.3
	Joseph R. Burton (R)	18,842	47.0
6	William Baker (PP)	19,398	49.9
	H. L. Pestana (R)	17,887	46.0
7	Jeremiah Simpson (D-PP)	33,812	50.8
	Chester I. Long (R)	32,053	48.2
AL	William A. Harris (PP & D)	164,624	50.7
	George T. Anthony (R)	155,791	48.0

KENTUCKY

1	William J. Stone (D)	15,295	53.0
	W. J. Deboe (R)	8,438	29.2
	B. C. Key (POP)	4,686	16.2
2	William T. Ellis (D)	15,053	47.4
	J. T. Kimbly (R)	9,781	30.8
	Thomas S. Pettit (POP)	6,903	21.8
3	Isaac H. Goodnight (D)	14,986	47.2
	W. G. Hunter (R)	14,056	44.2
	C. W. Biggers (POP)	2,742	8.6
4	Alexander B. Montgomery (D)	16,043	48.1
	C. M. Barnett (R)	11,385	34.1
	M. R. Gardner (POP)	5,954	17.8
5	Asher G. Caruth (D)	20,445	58.7
	Augustus E. Willson (R)	13,767	39.6
6	Albert S. Berry (D)	18,564	60.7
	Weden O'Neal (R)	10,731	35.1
7	William C. P. Breckinridge (D)	16,588	62.0
	T. J. Hardin (R)	9,433	35.3
8	James B. McCreary (D)	14,092	100.0
9	Thomas H. Paynter (D)	18,295	53.3
	John P. McCartney (R)	15,339	44.7
10	Marcus C. Lisle (D)	14,515	54.9
	Charles W. Russell (R)	11,943	45.1
11	Silas R. Adams (R)	17,087	59.5
	James R. Hindman (D)	10,483	36.5

Special Election

10	Joseph M. Kendall (D)	5,846	91.2
	C. F. Ward	544	8.5

LOUISIANA

	Candidates	Votes	%
1	Adolph Meyer (D)	10,878	69.2
	James Wilkinson (ID)	4,787	30.5
2	Robert C. Davey (D)	12,588	67.4
	Morris Marks (POP & R)	6,102	32.7
3	Andrew Price (D)	14,033	81.8
	I. J. Willis (POP & R)	3,123	18.2
4	Newton C. Blanchard (D)	16,432	76.1
	T. J. Guice (POP & R)	5,167	23.9
5	Charles J. Boatner (D)	19,371	72.3
	R. P. Welch (POP & R)	4,301	16.0
	A. A. Gundy (ID)	3,119	11.6
6	Samuel M. Robertson (D)	11,758	85.2
	J. Kleinpeter (POP & R)	2,043	14.8

MAINE

1	Thomas B. Reed (R)	16,312	51.5
	D. H. Ingraham (D)	14,635	46.2
2	Nelson Dingley Jr. (R)	17,194	52.4
	D. J. McGillicuddy (D)	13,546	41.3
3	Seth L. Milliken (R)	15,582	50.3
	W. P. Thompson (D)	13,700	44.2
4	Charles A. Boutelle (R)	16,549	51.3
	D. A. H. Powers (D)	12,261	38.0
	S. D. Leavitt (ID)	1,616	5.0

MARYLAND

1	Robert F. Brattan (D)	15,608	49.7
	George M. Russum (R)	13,714	43.6
	D. Miles (P)	1,778	5.7
2	J. Fred C. Talbott (D)	22,772	54.0
	George Baker (R)	17,926	42.5
3	Harry Wells Rusk (D)	19,806	58.4
	Charles Herzog (R)	13,679	40.3
4	Isidor Rayner (D)	21,455	58.4
	Alburtus Spates (R)	14,646	39.8
5	Barnes Compton (D)	15,391	52.3
	Thomas Parrau (R)	13,505	45.9
6	William M. McKaig (D)	18,899	49.8
	George Willington (R)	18,292	48.2

Special Election

1	John Brown (D)	15,502	52.3
	George M. Russum (R)	13,787	46.5

MASSACHUSETTS

1	Ashley B. Wright (R)	14,198	48.8
	John C. Crosby (D)	13,995	48.1
2	Frederick H. Gillett (R)	15,131	52.4
	Edward Howard (D)	12,718	44.1
3	Joseph H. Walker (R)	14,139	50.1
	John R. Thayer (D)	13,262	47.0
4	Lewis D. Apsley (R)	16,209	53.7
	Frederic S. Coolidge (D)	13,058	43.3
5	Moses T. Stevens (D)	14,423	52.3
	William S. Knox (R)	12,645	45.8
6	William Cogswell (R)	16,385	58.4
	Henry B. Little (D)	10,228	36.5
7	Henry Cabot Lodge (R)	17,002*	52.7
	William Everett (D)	14,391	44.6
8	Samuel W. McCall (R)	15,671	51.6
	John F. Andrew (D)	14,679	48.4
9	Joseph H. O'Neil (D)	14,354	61.1
	Benjamin C. Lane (R)	8,622	36.7
10	Michael J. McEttrick (D & CIT)	9,507	33.4
	Harrison H. Atwood (R)	8,822	31.0
	William S. McNary (D)	7,591	26.7
	Richard C. Humphreys (I)	2,235	7.9
11	William F. Draper (R)	16,961	53.1
	George Fred Williams (D)	14,404	45.1
12	Elijah A. Morse (R)	17,316	56.0
	Elbridge Cushman (D)	12,673	41.0
13	Charles S. Randall (R)	13,945	60.7
	Henry C. Thacher (D)	9,006	39.2

MICHIGAN

	Candidates	Votes	%
1	John Logan Chipman (D)	20,239	52.4
	Frank J. Hecker (R)	17,533	45.4
2	James S. Gorman (D)	22,007	47.0
	James O'Donnell (R)	21,443	45.8
3	Julius C. Burrows (R)	21,287	50.1
	Daniel Strange (D)	15,802	37.2
	Leroy E. Lockwood (POP)	2,898	6.8
	Paul T. Butler (P)	2,510	5.9
4	Henry F. Thomas (R)	21,352	49.1
	George L. Yaple (D & POP)	20,246	46.5
5	Charles E. Belknap (R)	20,139	47.8
	George F. Richardson (D & POP)	20,120✓	47.8
6	David D. Aitken (R)	21,046	46.5
	Byron G. Stout (D)	19,669	43.5
	Arthur E. Cole (POP)	2,289	5.1
7	Justin R. Whiting (D)	16,125	46.3
	Philip L. Wixson (R)	15,602	44.8
	Alfred Pagett (POP)	1,837	5.3
8	William S. Linton (R)	17,411	49.2
	Henry H. Youmins (D & POP)	15,886	44.9
9	John W. Moon (R)	13,969	47.0
	Harrison H. Wheeler (D)	13,053	43.9
	Charles A. Sessions (P)	1,673	5.6
10	Thomas A. E. Weadock (D)	14,858	47.7
	James Van Kleeck (R)	14,599	46.9
11	John Avery (R)	18,359	50.6
	Woodbridge N. Ferris (D & POP)	16,038	44.2
	George R. Catton (P)	1,886	5.2
12	Samuel M. Stephenson (R)	20,097	50.7
	J. Maurice Finn (D & POP)	16,674	42.1

MINNESOTA

1	James A. Tawney (R)	18,146	49.0
	William H. Harries (D)	14,995	40.5
	James I. Vermilya (PP)	2,342	6.3
2	James T. McCleary (R)	18,207	48.4
	Winfield S. Hammond (D)	11,298	30.0
	S. C. Long (PP)	6,268	16.7
3	Osee M. Hall (D)	15,890	44.8
	Joel P. Heatwole (R)	14,727	41.5
	Ferdinand Borchert (PP)	3,464	9.8
4	Andrew R. Kiefer (R)	16,624	48.6
	James N. Castle (D)	13,435	39.2
	James G. Dougherty (PP)	2,213	6.5
	David Morgan (P)	1,963	5.7
5	Loren Fletcher (R)	18,463	46.1
	James W. Lawrence (D)	15,960	39.9
	Thomas H. Lucas (PP)	3,151	7.9
	J. T. Caton (P)	2,458	6.1
6	Melvin R. Baldwin (D)	17,317	43.4
	Dolson B. Searle (R)	16,941	42.4
	A. C. Parsons (PP)	3,973	10.0
7	Haldor E. Boen (PP)	12,614	35.6
	Henry Feig (R)	12,529	35.4
	W. F. Kelso (D)	7,526	21.3
	L. F. Hampson (P)	2,731	7.7

MISSISSIPPI

1	John M. Allen (D)	5,605	79.8
	James Burkitt (PP)	1,272	18.1
2	John C. Kyle (D)	6,113	77.8
	J. H. Simpson (PP)	1,740	22.2
3	Thomas C. Catchings (D)	2,750	93.4
	George W. Gayles (R)	194	6.6
4	Hernando D. Money (D)	6,223	61.4
	Frank Burkitt (PP)	3,905	38.6
5	John S. Williams (D)	7,541	71.4
	W. P. Ratliff (PP)	3,028	28.7
6	Thomas R. Stockdale (D)	4,984	82.5
	T. N. Jackson (PP)	1,054	17.5
7	Charles E. Hooker (D)	4,984	72.4
	S. W. Robinson (PP)	1,695	24.6

MISSOURI

Candidates	Votes	%
1 William H. Hatch (D)	19,263	50.0
Cramer (R)	15,919	41.3
Bronson (PP)	3,316	8.6
2 Uriel S. Hall (D)	21,928	53.7
Burkholder (R)	16,626	40.7
Jackson (PP)	2,317	5.7
3 Alexander M. Dockery (D)	18,749	48.8
Birch (R)	15,288	39.8
Reece (PP)	4,365	11.4
4 Daniel D. Burnes (D)	15,859	46.7
Crowther (R)	14,600	43.0
Wilcox (PP)	3,221	9.5
5 John C. Tarsney (D)	19,407	55.0
Davis (R)	14,240	40.4
6 David A. De Armond (D)	16,545	46.3
Cundiff (R)	13,151	36.8
Donnohue (PP)	5,587	15.6
7 John T. Heard (D)	21,549	48.7
Hastain (R)	17,843	40.3
Pinkham (PP)	4,847	11.0
8 Richard P. Bland (D)	18,927	53.3
Murphy (R)	16,453	46.4
9 James Beauchamp Clark (D)	17,536	53.0
Morsey (R)	14,944	45.2
10 Richard Bartholdt (R)	15,628	54.6
Kehr (D)	12,465	43.5
11 Charles F. Joy (R)	14,969‡	49.5
John J. O'Neill (D)	14,902	49.3
12 Seth W. Cobb (D)	12,813	52.0
Rodgers (R)	11,481	46.6
13 Robert W. Fyan (D)	19,993	57.1
Whitledge (R)	15,006	42.8
14 Marshall Arnold (D)	19,440	49.8
Clarke (R)	15,737	40.3
Taber (PP)	3,864	9.9
15 Charles H. Morgan (D)	17,489	44.2
Purdy (R)	15,767	39.8
Withers (PP)	5,815	14.7

MONTANA

Candidates	Votes	%
AL Charles S. Hartman (R)	17,934	41.4
William W. Dixon (D)	17,762	41.0
Caldwell Edwards (PP)	7,027	16.2

NEBRASKA

Candidates	Votes	%
1 William Jennings Bryan (D)	13,784	44.9
Allen W. Field (R)	13,644	44.4
Jerome Shamp (POP)	2,409	7.9
2 David H. Mercer (R)	11,488	45.3
George W. Doane (D)	10,388	40.9
Robert L. Wheeler (POP)	3,152	12.4
3 George Meiklejohn (R)	13,635	39.2
George F. Keiper (D)	10,630	30.6
W. A. Poynter (POP)	9,636	27.7
4 Eugene J. Hainer (R)	15,648	41.8
William H. Dech (POP)	11,486	30.7
Victor Vifquain (D)	8,988	24.0
5 William A. McKeighan (D & POP)	17,490	53.7
W. E. Andrews (R)	14,230	43.7
6 Omer M. Kem (POP)	16,328	46.1
James Whitehead (R)	14,197	40.1
A. T. Gatewood (D)	4,202	11.9

NEVADA

Candidates	Votes	%
AL Francis G. Newlands (POP SIL)	7,171	72.5
William Woodburn (R)	2,295	23.2

NEW HAMPSHIRE

Candidates	Votes	%
1 Henry W. Blair (R)	21,031	49.9
Charles F. Stone (D)	20,412	48.4
2 Henry M. Baker (R)	21,425	49.3
Hosea W. Parker (D)	20,996	48.3

NEW JERSEY

Candidates	Votes	%
1 Henry C. Loudenslager (R)	25,099	50.7
Porch (D)	22,511	45.4
2 John J. Gardner (R)	22,716	50.7
Wetherill (D)	20,592	45.9
3 Jacob A. Geissenhainer (D)	20,407	53.0
Hoffman (R)	17,080	44.4
4 Johnston Cornish (D)	21,765	48.0
Howey (R)	20,726	45.7
Johnston (P)	2,307	5.1
5 Cornelius A. Cadmus (D)	20,693	50.7
Doherty (R)	19,231	47.1
6 Thomas D. English (D)	21,651	51.0
Richard W. Parker (R)	20,284	47.8
7 George B. Fielder (D)	22,416	49.9
Cole (R)	19,585	43.6
Edward F. McDonald (D)	2,368	5.3
8 John T. Dunn (D)	14,393	50.4
Chamberlin (R)	13,470	47.1

NEW YORK

Candidates	Votes	%
1 James W. Covert (D)	21,550	52.1
John Lewis Childs (R)	18,749	45.3
2 John M. Clancy (D)	20,697	59.1
William H. Grace (R)	13,593	38.8
3 Joseph C. Hendrix (D)	21,607	55.9
Michael J. Dady (R)	15,907	41.1
4 William J. Coombs (D)	22,818	58.5
Charles B. Hobbs (R)	14,885	38.1
5 John H. Graham (D)	16,675	50.8
Charles G. Bennett (R)	14,488	44.2
6 Thomas F. Magner (D)	17,151	56.1
John Greaney (R)	12,131	39.7
7 Franklin Bartlett (D)	14,905	66.3
Samuel A. Brown (R)	7,122	31.7
8 Edward J. Dunphy (D)	15,287	66.3
Austin E. Ford (R)	7,132	30.9
9 Timothy J. Campbell (D)	16,897	66.2
John Phelan (R)	7,175	28.1
10 Daniel E. Sickles (D)	18,452	58.0
Charles E. Coon (R)	12,224	38.5
11 Amos J. Cummings (D)	16,780	63.0
Abraham H. Sarasohn (R)	8,355	31.4
12 William Bourke Cockran (D)	16,575	65.6
Daniel Butterfield (R)	7,766	30.7
13 J. De Witt Warner (D)	18,979	60.8
James J. Flick (R)	11,181	35.8
14 John R. Fellows (D)	26,267	57.8
H. Charles Ullman (R)	17,442	38.4
15 Ashbel P. Fitch (D)	27,741	61.2
Henry C. Robinson (R)	15,872	35.0
16 William Ryan (D)	25,795	55.0
George A. Brandreth (R)	19,312	41.2
17 Francis Marvin (R)	17,806	48.5
Henry Bacon (D)	17,659	48.1
18 Jacob Le Fever (R)	21,034	49.3
Isaac N. Cox (D)	20,114	47.1
19 Charles D. Haines (D)	20,757	50.7
John A. Quackenbush (R)	19,104	46.6
20 Charles Tracey (D)	19,509	50.3
John G. Ward (R)	17,883	46.1
21 Simon J. Schermerhorn (D)	24,508	49.5
Erastus F. Beadle (R)	23,181	46.8
22 Newton Martin Curtis (R)	26,207	57.4
Warren Curtis (D)	16,707	36.6
23 John M. Wever (R)	25,690	57.7
George S. Weed (D)	16,947	38.1
24 Charles A. Chickering (R)	23,858	55.8
William A. Kelley (D)	17,283	40.4
25 James S. Sherman (R)	20,443	49.7
Henry W. Bentley (D)	19,299	46.9
26 George W. Ray (R)	28,979	85.9
George F. Hand (P)	3,871	11.5
27 James . Belden (R)	25,737	55.5
Riley V. Miller (D)	18,412	39.7
28 Sereno E. Payne (R)	28,723	55.3
Hull Greenfield (D)	20,601	39.7
29 Charles W. Gillet (R)	21,443	50.4
Franz S. Wolf (D)	17,646	41.5
Albert C. Hill (P)	2,242	5.3
30 James W. Wadsworth (R)	24,205	51.2
John F. McDonald (D)	19,679	41.6
Albert J. Rumsey (P)	2,494	5.3
31 John Van Voorhis (R)	19,762	47.8
Donald McNaughton (D)	19,255	46.6
32 Daniel N. Lockwood (D)	16,440	52.9
Rowland B. Mahany (R)	12,966	41.8
33 Charles Daniels (R)	19,701	53.0
John S. Hertel (D)	15,548	41.8
34 Warren B. Hooker (R)	24,951	55.0
Andrew J. McNett (D)	15,098	33.3
Benjamin W. Taylor (P)	2,905	6.4
F. Eugene Hammond (POP)	2,395	5.3

NORTH CAROLINA

Candidates	Votes	%
1 William A. B. Branch (D)	14,263	55.1
Reddick Gatling (PP)	11,579	44.7
2 Frederick A. Woodard (D)	13,925	44.4
Henry P. Cheatham (R)	11,896	37.9
Edward A. Thorne (PP)	5,457	17.4
3 Benjamin F. Grady (D)	12,457	45.0
Frank D. Koonce (PP)	9,869	35.6
Asoph M. Clark (R)	5,271	19.0
4 Benjamin H. Bunn (D)	14,630	48.4
William F. Strowd (PP)	13,125	43.4
John H. Williamson (R)	2,106	7.0
5 Thomas Settle (R)	14,148	43.3
Archibald H. A. Williams (D)	13,746	42.1
William R. Lindsay (PP)	4,358	13.3
6 Sydenham B. Alexander (D)	16,624	57.8
Atlas A. Maynard (PP)	12,127	42.1
7 John S. Henderson (D)	14,303	49.2
Alfred E. Holton (R)	9,136	31.4
Alonzo C. Shuford (PP)	5,399	18.6
8 William H. Bower (D)	16,886	50.1
Joseph B. Wilcox (R)	13,215	39.2
Robert L. Patton (PP)	3,564	10.6
9 William T. Crawford (D)	16,010	50.9
Jeter C. Pritchard (R)	14,560	46.3

NORTH DAKOTA

Candidates	Votes	%
AL Martin N. Johnson (R)	17,715	49.0
O'Brien (D)	11,021	30.5
Foss (I)	7,439	20.6

OHIO

Candidates	Votes	%
1 Bellamy Storer (R)	19,269	50.6
Robert B. Bowler (D)	18,014	47.3
2 John A. Caldwell (R)	22,240	51.5
Charles T. Greve (D)	20,074	46.5
3 George W. Houk (D)	24,686	53.0
Charles C. Donley (R)	20,370	43.7
4 Fernando C. Layton (D)	20,417	56.7
C. S. Mauk (R)	12,823	35.6
5 Dennis D. Donovan (D)	19,873	53.4
George L. Griffeth (R)	15,269	41.0
6 George W. Hulick (R)	21,341	51.4
John M. Pattison (D)	18,091	43.6
7 George W. Wilson (R)	19,434	49.6
Martin K. Gantz (D)	17,608	45.0
8 Luther M. Strong (R)	21,742	51.7
Fremont Arford (D)	18,384	43.7
9 Byron F. Ritchie (D)	20,041	48.0
James M. Ashley (D)	20,027	48.0
10 William H. Enochs (R)	19,847	55.2
Irvine Dungan (D)	15,486	43.0
11 Charles H. Grosvenor (R)	19,905	51.4
Charles E. Peoples (D)	17,254	44.6

OHIO

	Candidates	Votes	%
12	Joseph H. Outhwaite (D)	20,298	52.6
	Edward N. Huggins (R)	17,045	44.2
13	Darius D. Hare (D)	24,186	54.8
	Lewis W. Hull (R)	17,937	40.7
14	Michael D. Harter (D)	22,285	49.8
	Elizur G. Johnson (R)	20,396	45.6
15	Henry C. Van Voorhis (R)	18,718	49.4
	Milton Turner (D)	17,550	46.4
16	Albert J. Pearson (D)	17,314	47.5
	Christian L. Poorman (R)	17,273	47.3
17	James A. D. Richards (D)	23,077	55.8
	Arthur H. Walkey (R)	16,723	40.5
18	George B. Ikirt (D)	22,600	48.2
	Thomas R. Morgan Sr. (R)	21,389	45.6
19	Stephen A. Northway (R)	23,870	55.2
	A. H. Tidball (D)	16,069	37.2
	Bailey S. Dean (P)	2,185	5.1
20	William White (R)	17,417	49.1
	John S. Ellen (D)	16,460	46.4
21	Tom L. Johnson (D)	17,389	53.4
	Orlando J. Hodge (R)	14,165	43.5

Special Election

16	Lewis P. Ohliger (D)	20,220	52.5
	George Adams (R)	16,958	44.0

OREGON

1	Binger Hermann (R)	18,929	46.5
	R. M. Veatch (D)	13,019	32.0
	M. V. Rork (POP)	7,518	18.5
2	William R. Ellis (R)	15,657	44.9
	James H. Slater (D)	12,120	34.7
	John C. Luce (POP)	5,940	17.0

PENNSYLVANIA

1	Henry H. Bingham (R)	22,908	62.6
	Edwin G. Flanigen (D)	13,693	37.4
2	Charles O'Neill (R)	16,107	64.0
	John J. Malony (D)	9,056	36.0
3	William McAleer (ID)	15,516	73.8
	William W. Ker (R)	5,500	26.2
4	John E. Reyburn (R)	37,200	61.4
	Elbridge E. Nock (D)	22,950	37.9
5	Alfred C. Harmer (R)	32,638	60.4
	Frederick A. Herwig (D)	21,426	39.6
6	John B. Robinson (R)	19,129	55.3
	Garrett C. Smedley (D)	13,938	40.3
7	Irving P. Wanger (R)	21,985	49.5
	Edwin Hallowell (D)	21,805	49.0
8	William Mutchler (D)	17,837	60.6
	Thomas C. Walton (R)	11,593	39.4
9	Constantine J. Erdman (D)	28,175	62.1
	H. A. Muhlenberg (R)	17,217	37.9
10	Marriott Brosius (R)	20,052	64.7
	John E. Malone (D)	10,266	33.1
11	Joseph A. Scranton (R)	10,814	49.0
	Lemuel Amerman (D)	10,225	46.3
12	William H. Hines (D)	15,554	50.1
	Charles D. Foster (R)	14,092	45.4
13	James B. Reilly (D)	13,440	53.2
	Charles W. Brumm (R)	11,539	45.7
14	Ephraim M. Woomer (R)	19,058	56.0
	William M. Breslin (D)	13,993	41.1
15	Myron B. Wright (R)	17,241	55.1
	Roger S. Searle (D)	12,655	40.4
16	Albert C. Hopkins (R)	17,966	52.6
	Frederick K. Wright (D)	14,724	43.1
17	Simon P. Wolverton (D)	15,333	58.4
	Chandlee Eves (R)	10,030	38.2
18	Thaddeus M. Mahon (R)	19,247	54.1
	William W. Trout (D)	15,631	44.0
19	Frank E. Beltzhoover (D)	21,963	56.6
	Nesbit S. Ross (R)	16,198	41.7
20	Josiah D. Hicks (R)	22,601	56.0
	Lucian D. Woodruff (D)	17,420	43.2

	Candidates	Votes	%
21	Daniel B. Heiner (R)	23,942	52.6
	John B. Keenan (D)	20,245	44.5
22	John Dalzell (R)	22,674	58.3
	James W. Breen (D)	15,939	41.0
23	William A. Stone (R)	14,628	63.6
	Frank C. Osburn (D)	8,177	35.6
24	William A. Sipe (D)	25,224	48.2
	Ernest F. Acheson (R)	23,971	45.8
25	Thomas W. Phillips (R)	19,658	51.8
	Eugene P. Gillespie (D)	15,559	41.0
	Judson W. Vandeventer (P)	1,930	5.1
26	Joseph C. Sibley (D)	17,887	54.9
	Theodore L. Flood (R)	14,500	44.5
27	Charles W. Stone (R)	12,479	51.9
	James D. Hancock (D)	9,523	39.6
	Charles Lott (P)	1,486	6.2
28	George F. Kribbs (D)	17,285	54.3
	Charles E. Andrews (R)	13,284	41.7
AL	William Lilly (R)	512,557✔	
	Alexander McDowell (R)	511,433✔	
	George A. Allen (R)	448,714	
	Thomas Polk Merritt (D)	447,456	
	Simeon B. Chase (P)	23,677	
	James T. McCrory (P)	22,930	
	S. P. Chase (P)	7,466	
	G. W. Dawson (PP)	7,313	
	J. Mahlon Barnes (SOC LAB)	674	
	Thomas Grundy (SOC LAB)	625	

Special Election

24	William A. Sipe (D)	25,181	49.1
	Andrew Stewart (R)	24,635	48.1

RHODE ISLAND[1]

1	Melville Bull (R)	13,645*	49.3
	Oscar Lapham (D)	13,051	47.2
2	Adin B. Capron (R)	11,523*	49.5
	Charles H. Page (D)	10,591	45.5

SOUTH CAROLINA

1	William H. Brawley (D)	6,318	99.8
2	W. Jasper Talbert (D)	8,001	99.6
3	Asbury C. Latimer (D)	8,330	89.7
	John R. Tolbert (R)	787	8.5
4	George W. Shell (D)	10,401	85.7
	Joshua A. T. Ensor (R)	1,730	14.3
5	Thomas J. Strait (D)	8,791	80.7
	E. Brooks Sligh (R)	2,099	19.3
6	John L. McLaurin (D)	10,133	84.6
	E. J. Sawyer (R)	1,832	15.3
7	George W. Murray (R)	4,995	50.0
	E. M. Moise (D)	4,955	49.6

Special Election

6	John L. McLaurin (D)	8,572	90.2
	Sawyer (R)	934	9.8

SOUTH DAKOTA

AL	John A. Pickler (R)	33,769✔	
	William V. Lucas (R)	33,350✔	
	J. E. Kelley (PP)	25,444	
	William Lardner (PP)	24,539	
	L. E. Whitcher (D)	14,218	
	Chauncey L. Wood (D)	736	

TENNESSEE

1	Alfred A. Taylor (R)	17,890	56.2
	W. J. McSween (D)	13,207	41.5
2	John C. Houk (R)	18,952	67.2
	W. L. Welcker (D)	7,815	27.7
3	Henry C. Snodgrass (D)	15,984	47.5
	H. Clay Evans (R)	15,035	44.6

	Candidates	Votes	%
	Frank P. Dickey (POP)	2,171	6.5
4	Benton McMillin (D)	14,010	55.5
	W. D. Gold (R & ID)	11,225	44.5
5	James D. Richardson (D)	13,709	61.1
	Thomas J. Ogilivie (R)	8,062	36.0
6	Joseph E. Washington (D)	15,645	62.0
	John B. Allen (R)	9,002	35.7
7	Nicholas N. Cox (D)	12,113	57.5
	W. A. Witherspoon (POP)	8,480	40.3
8	Benjamin A. Enloe (D)	13,038	50.2
	P. H. Threasher (R)	12,920	49.7
9	James C. McDearmon (D)	14,334	56.1
	Rice A. Pearce (ID)	10,883	42.6
10	Josiah Patterson (D)	12,164	71.8
	T. V. Neal (R)	4,785	28.2

TEXAS

1	Joseph C. Hutcheson (D)	14,489	59.7
	J. B. Stephenson (PP)	6,081	25.1
	Daniel Taylor (R)	3,703	15.3
2	Samuel B. Cooper (D)	19,894	61.4
	T. A. Wilson (PP)	10,275	31.7
3	Constantine B. Kilgore (D)	16,335	57.3
	J. M. Perdue (PP)	12,177	42.7
4	David B. Culberson (D)	16,521	52.3
	Pat B. Clark (PP)	10,371	32.8
	J. A. Hurley (R)	4,709	14.9
5	Joseph W. Bailey (D)	24,983	66.2
	R. B. Bell (LW R)	8,170	21.7
	John Grant (R)	4,563	12.1
6	Jo Abbott (D)	24,913	59.3
	J. C. Kearby (PP & R)	17,078	40.6
7	George C. Pendleton (D)	19,937	56.1
	I. N. Barber (PP)	15,587	43.8
8	Charles K. Bell (D)	17,997	54.5
	Evan Jones (PP)	12,937	39.2
	C. C. Drake (R)	2,009	6.1
9	Joseph D. Sayers (D)	19,763	61.5
	J. M. Horner (PP & R)	12,384	38.5
10	Walter Gresham (D)	13,017	48.6
	A. J. Rosenthal (R)	9,452	35.3
	E. O. Meitzn (PP)	4,297	16.1
11	William H. Crain (D)	15,257	52.4
	C. G. Brewster (R)	8,075	27.7
	Ben Terrell (PP)	5,770	19.8
12	Thomas M. Paschal (D)	13,930	50.1
	Henry Terrell (R)	7,290	26.2
	T. J. McMinn (PP)	6,574	23.6
13	Jeremiah V. Cockrell (D)	21,922	65.5
	W. J. Maltby (PP)	9,825	29.4

Special Election

9	Edwin LeRoy Antony (D)	✔	#

VERMONT

1	H. Henry Powers (R)	19,427	65.9
	Felix W. McGettrick (D)	9,396	31.9
2	William W. Grout (R)	18,568	66.7
	George W. Smith (D)	8,649	31.1

VIRGINIA

1	William A. Jones (D)	15,004	56.2
	Orres A. Browne (R)	11,543	43.2
2	D. Gardiner Tyler (D)	17,432	55.6
	P. C. Garrigan (IR)	8,594	27.4
	John F. Deyendorf (R)	3,870	12.3
3	George D. Wise (D)	18,595	63.9
	Walter E. Grant (R)	10,489	36.1
4	James F. Epes (D)	10,330	52.1
	J. Thomas Goode (POP)	9,462	47.8
5	Claude A. Swanson (D)	14,112	53.9
	Benjamin T. Jones (POP)	12,066	46.1
6	Paul C. Edmunds (D)	18,265	58.6
	Thomas E. Cobbs (POP)	12,924	41.4
7	Charles T. O'Ferrall (D)	18,558	64.0
	J. R. C. Lewis (POP)	10,441	36.0

1. In both congressional districts, no candidate received the majority of the votes necessary to win in the 1892 general election. (See Rhode Island 1893, p. 671.)

VIRGINIA

Candidates	Votes	%
8 Elisha E. Meredith (D)	17,124	63.0
B. B. Turner (POP)	10,066	37.0
9 James W. Marshall (D)	18,431	55.9
Henry C. Wood (R)	12,699	38.5
George R. Cowan (POP)	1,709	5.2
10 Henry St. George Tucker (D)	17,779	57.7
D. Mott Robertson (POP)	13,027	42.3

WASHINGTON

	Votes	%
AL William H. Doolittle (R)	35,434 ✔	
John L. Wilson (R)	35,407 ✔	
Thomas Carroll (D)	30,659	
James A. Munday (D)	27,014	
M. F. Knox (PP)	20,083	
J. C. Van Patton (PP)	19,891	
D. E. Newberry (P)	2,412	
A. C. Dickinson (P)	2,357	

WEST VIRGINIA

Candidates	Votes	%
1 John O. Pendleton (D)	19,314	47.6
B. B. Dovener (R)	19,108	47.1
2 William L. Wilson (D)	21,807	50.2
J. Nelson Wisner (R)	20,702	47.7
3 John D. Alderson (D)	22,696	51.3
Edgar P. Rucker (R)	20,750	46.9
4 James Capehart (D)	22,006	52.4
Charles T. Caldwell (R)	19,924	47.4

WISCONSIN

Candidates	Votes	%
1 Henry Allen Cooper (R)	20,222	52.3
Babbitt (D)	16,449	42.5
Murdock (P)	2,021	5.2
2 Charles Barwig (D)	21,303	55.9
L. B. Caswell (R)	15,003	39.4
3 Joseph W. Babcock (R)	19,506	50.4
A. H. Krauskop (D)	16,419	42.4
4 John L. Mitchell (D)	19,616*	50.2
Theobald Otjen (R)	18,294	46.8

Candidates	Votes	%
5 George H. Brickner (D)	17,929	51.7
Julius Wechselberg (R)	15,960	46.0
6 Owen A. Wells (D)	20,212	51.1
Emil Baensch (R)	17,847	45.1
7 George B. Shaw (R)	15,344	48.5
Frank P. Coburn (D)	13,074	41.3
Ole B. Oleson (P)	1,635	5.2
8 Lyman E. Barnes (D)	18,187	52.9
H. A. Frambach (R)	15,173	44.1
9 Thomas Lynch (D)	19,608	52.2
Myron H. McCord (R)	16,519	44.0
10 Nils P. Haugen (R)	17,674	50.6
Daniel Bachanan Jr. (D)	13,044	37.4
Peter L. Scritsmier (PP)	4,186	12.0

WYOMING

	Votes	%
AL Henry A. Coffeen (D)	8,855	51.3
Clarence D. Clark (R)	8,394	48.6

1893 House Elections

MASSACHUSETTS

Special Election

	Votes	%
7 William Everett (D)	9,733	46.3
William E. Barrett (R)	9,699	46.1

MICHIGAN

Special Election

	Votes	%
1 Levi T. Griffin (D)	18,854	50.3
James H. Stone (R)	17,587	46.9

OHIO

Special Election

10 Hezekiah S. Bundy (R)	✔	

PENNSYLVANIA

Special Elections

	Votes	%
2 Robert Adams Jr (R)	10,487	97.0
8 Howard Mutchler (D)	10,143	64.0
Frank Reeder (R)	5,663	35.8

RHODE ISLAND[1]

Special Elections

	Votes	%
1 Oscar Lapham (D)	11,298	47.7
Melville Bull (R)	10,816	45.7
2 Charles H. Page (D)	10,670	47.6
Adin B. Capron (R)	10,021	44.7
Lewis (P)	1,571	7.0

WISCONSIN

Special Election

	Votes	%
4 Peter J. Somers (D)	13,567	51.3
Theobald Otgen (R)	12,125	45.8

1. No candidate in either congressional district had received a majority of the vote in the November 1892 general election for the House, so a special election was necessary in April 1893. Under the usual practice, the state kept holding elections until a majority was received, but in 1893 it was agreed that whoever received the most votes in the special election would be considered as elected, regardless of whether a majority was achieved. So Lapham and Page were elected and took their seats in the 53rd Congress (1893-95) even though neither won a majority and would not have qualified under the usual practices of Rhode Island law. The majority requirement — which caused problems in elections for other offices as well as the House — was repealed in a referendum in November 1893. (Majority vote requirement, see p. 703.)

1894 House Elections

ALABAMA

	Candidates	Votes	%
1	Richard H. Clarke (D)	6,314	76.9
	Sibley (POP)	1,898	23.1
2	Jesse F. Stallings (D)	9,728	64.6
	Gardner (POP)	5,324	35.4
3	George P. Harrison (D)	10,719	65.2
	Robinson (POP)	5,713	34.8
4	Gaston A. Robbins (D)	10,494‡	58.6
	William F. Aldrich (R)	7,406	41.4
5	James E. Cobb (D)	10,651‡	51.8
	Albert T. Goodwyn (POP)	9,903	48.2
6	John H. Bankhead (D)	5,721	55.8
	Sanford (POP)	2,622	25.6
	Long (R)	1,914	18.7
7	Milford W. Howard (POP)	6,838	66.5
	William H. Denson (D)	3,452	33.6
8	Joseph Wheeler (D)	8,901	57.9
	Crandall (POP)	6,474	42.1
9	Oscar W. Underwood (D)	7,319‡	54.3
	Truman H. Aldrich (R)	6,153	45.7

Special Election

		Votes	%
3	George P. Harrison (D)	10,822	65.3
	W. C. Robinson (POP)	5,743	34.7

ARKANSAS

		Votes	%
1	Philip D. McCulloch Jr. (D)	6,025	81.8
	Russ Coffman (POP)	1,299	17.6
2	John S. Little (D)	5,097	94.5
3	Thomas C. McRae (D)	6,193	97.1
4	William L. Terry (D)	6,299	62.2
	P. Raleigh (D)	2,260	22.3
	J. H. Cherry (POP)	1,557	15.4
5	Hugh A. Dinsmore (D)	7,531	56.8
	T. J. Hunt (R)	4,976	37.5
	W. M. Peel (POP)	759	5.7
6	Robert Neill (D)	6,439	65.0
	H. H. Myers (R)	3,153	31.8

CALIFORNIA

		Votes	%
1	John A. Barham (R)	15,101	41.1
	Thomas J. Geary (D)	13,570	37.0
	Robert F. Grigsby (PP)	7,246	19.7
2	Grove L. Johnson (R)	19,302	43.0
	Anthony Caminetti (D)	15,732	35.1
	Burdett Cornell (PP)	8,946	20.0
3	Samuel G. Hilborn (R)	15,795	45.5
	Warren B. English (D)	13,103	37.8
	W. A. Vann (PP)	5,162	14.9
4	James G. Maguire (D)	14,748	48.3
	Thomas B. Shannon (R)	9,785	32.0
	B. K. Collier (PP)	5,627	18.4
5	Eugene F. Loud (R)	13,379	35.9
	Joseph P. Kelly (D)	8,384	22.5
	James T. Rogers (PP)	7,820	21.0
	James Denman (I DEMOC)	6,811	18.3
6	James McLachlan (R)	18,746	44.3
	George S. Patton (D)	11,693	27.6
	W. C. Bowman (PP)	9,769	23.1
	J. E. McComas (P)	2,120	5.0
7	William W. Bowers (R)	18,434	42.9
	W. H. Alford (D)	12,111	28.2
	J. L. Gilbert (PP)	10,719	25.0

COLORADO

		Votes	%
1	John F. Shafroth (R)	47,710	55.3
	La Fayette Pence (POP)	34,223	39.7
2	John C. Bell (POP & D)	47,703	51.7
	T. M. Bowen (R)	42,369	45.9

CONNECTICUT

	Candidates	Votes	%
1	E. Stevens Henry (R)	20,322	55.4
	Lewis Sperry (D)	15,115	41.2
2	Nehemiah D. Sperry (R)	28,749	54.9
	Pigott (D)	21,821	41.7
3	Charles A. Russell (R)	12,095	55.5
	Beckwith (D)	9,047	41.6
4	Ebenezer J. Hill (R)	24,012	55.2
	Deforest (D)	18,559	42.7

DELAWARE

		Votes	%
AL	Jonathan S. Willis (R)	19,699	50.7
	S. H. Bancroft Jr. (D)	18,492	47.6

FLORIDA

		Votes	%
1	Stephen M. Sparkman (D)	12,397	85.1
	D. L. McKinnon (POP)	2,135	14.7
2	Charles M. Cooper (D)	9,229	79.6
	M. Atkinson (POP)	2,334	20.1

GEORGIA

		Votes	%
1	Rufus E. Lester (D)	14,024	72.0
	J. F. Brown (PP)	5,453	28.0
2	Benjamin E. Russell (D)	10,073	62.4
	William E. Smith (PP)	6,064	37.6
3	Charles F. Crisp (D)	9,037	74.7
	Andrew White (PP)	3,062	25.3
4	Charles L. Moses (D)	10,293	57.4
	Carey Thornton (PP)	7,637	42.6
5	Leonidas F. Livingston (D)	7,781	59.7
	Robert Todd (PP)	5,264	40.4
6	Charles L. Bartlett (D)	11,671	65.5
	W. T. Whitaker (PP)	6,147	34.5
7	John W. Maddox (D)	11,500	54.4
	William H. Felton (PP)	9,646	45.6
8	Thomas G. Lawson (D)	11,066	59.5
	W. T. Carter (PP)	7,527	40.5
9	Farish C. Tate (D)	13,059	56.1
	J. N. Twitty (PP)	10,201	43.9
10	James C. C. Black (D)	20,942	60.8
	Thomas E. Watson (PP)	13,498	39.2
11	Henry G. Turner (PP)	9,085	60.2
	W. S. Johnson (PP)	6,015	39.8

IDAHO

		Votes	%
AL	Edgar Wilson (R)	10,383	43.4
	James Gunn (PP)	7,547	31.5
	James M. Ballentine (D)	5,834	24.4

ILLINOIS

		Votes	%
1	J. Frank Aldrich (R)	33,902	63.2
	Max Dembufsky (D)	12,854	23.9
	Howard S. Taylor (POP)	5,996	11.2
2	William Lorimer (R)	21,194	45.6
	John J. Hanahan (D)	16,852	36.2
	John Z. White (POP)	8,484	18.2
3	Lawrence E. McGann (D)	15,356‡	44.4
	Hugh R. Belknap (R)	15,325	44.3
	John B. Clarke (POP)	3,945	11.4
4	Charles W. Woodman (R)	14,017	38.2
	Frank Lawler (I)	10,638	29.0
	T. E. Ryan (D)	8,801	24.0
	Patrick J. Miniter (POP)	2,812	7.7
5	George E. White (R)	18,732	49.5
	Edward T. Noonan (D)	14,875	39.3
	Charles G. Dixon (POP)	4,143	10.9
6	Edward D. Cooke (R)	17,602	47.3
	Julius Goldzier (D)	15,433	41.5

	Candidates	Votes	%
	Louis W. Rogers (POP)	4,159	11.2
7	George Edmund Foss (R)	25,546	59.3
	Philip Jackson (D)	11,450	26.6
	Henry D. Lloyd (POP)	6,109	14.2
8	Albert J. Hopkins (R)	22,631	66.0
	Lewis Steward (D)	9,104	26.6
9	Robert R. Hitt (R)	24,177	63.9
	David F. Thompson (D)	11,301	29.9
10	Philip S. Post (R)	22,949*	63.7
	Jonas W. Olson (D)	9,770	27.1
	William W. Mathews (POP)	2,143	6.0
11	Walter Reeves (R)	19,372	52.3
	Robert R. Gibbons (D)	14,390	38.8
	William M. Hirschy (POP)	2,216	6.0
12	Joseph G. Cannon (R)	21,122	59.4
	Thomas F. Donovan (D)	11,925	33.5
13	Vespasian Warner (R)	20,896	57.8
	A. J. Barr (D)	12,725	35.2
14	Joseph R. Graff (R)	20,579	51.2
	George O. Barnes (D)	17,224	42.8
15	Benjamin F. Marsh (R)	20,550	48.4
	Truman Plantz (D)	19,115	45.0
16	Finis E. Downing (D)	17,816‡	46.5
	John I. Rinaker (R)	17,776	46.4
	Peter D. Stout (POP)	1,929	5.0
17	James A. Connolly (R)	20,441	50.3
	William M. Springer (D)	17,503	43.0
18	Frederick Remann (R)	16,669	49.4
	Edward Lane (D)	14,069	41.7
	Joseph S. Barnes (POP)	2,020	6.0
19	Benson Wood (R)	20,028	48.2
	George W. Fithian (D)	18,758	45.1
20	Orlando Burrell (R)	17,429	47.6
	James R. Williams (D)	15,775	43.1
	Harvey G. Jones (POP)	2,769	7.6
21	Everett J. Murphy (R)	18,958	48.0
	John J. Higgins (D)	17,159	43.4
	Henry C. McDill (POP)	2,764	7.0
22	George W. Smith (R)	18,180	57.4
	Francis M. Youngblood (D)	10,585	33.4
	John J. Hall (POP)	2,509	7.9

INDIANA

		Votes	%
1	James A. Hemenway (R)	20,535	47.8
	Arthur H. Taylor (D)	18,245	42.5
	James A. Boyce (POP)	3,820	8.9
2	Alexander M. Hardy (R)	17,624	47.6
	John L. Bretz (D)	15,896	42.9
	Elisha A. Riggins (POP)	3,217	8.7
3	Robert J. Tracewell (R)	19,709	49.0
	Strother M. Stockslager (D)	19,153	47.6
4	James E. Watson (R)	17,905	48.9
	William S. Holman (D)	17,471	47.7
5	Jesse Overstreet (R)	18,286	49.5
	George W. Cooper (D)	16,416	44.4
6	Henry U. Johnson (R)	22,724	63.1
	Nimrod R. Elliott (D)	10,707	29.7
7	Charles L. Henry (R)	29,900	51.1
	William D. Bynum (D)	25,557	43.7
8	George W. Faris (R)	23,238	48.0
	Elijah V. Brookshire (D)	20,669	42.7
	Morton C. Rankin (POP)	3,658	7.6
9	J. Frank Hanly (R)	25,479	54.1
	A. G. Burkhart (D)	20,237	43.0
10	Jethro A. Hatch (R)	20,858	51.0
	Valentine Zimmerman (D)	16,923	41.4
	Samuel M. Hathorn (POP)	2,296	5.6
11	George W. Steele (R)	25,008	50.1
	Augustus N. Martin (D)	21,079	42.2
12	Jacob D. Leighty (R)	19,658	49.9
	William F. McNagny (D)	17,145	43.5
	Freeman Kelly (POP)	2,195	5.6
13	Lemuel W. Royse (R)	23,523	52.3
	Lewellyn Wanner (D)	19,376	43.1

IOWA

	Candidates	Votes	%
1	Samuel M. Clark (R)	17,583	51.9
	W. A. Buckworth (D)	13,747	40.6
	J. O. Bube (PP)	2,065	6.1
2	George M. Curtis (R)	18,710	48.4
	Walter I. Hayes (D)	18,274	47.2
3	David B. Henderson (R)	22,892	57.1
	Stephen H. Bashor (D-PP)	17,200	42.9
4	Thomas Updegraff (R)	20,457	57.4
	James F. Babcock (D)	13,267	37.2
5	Robert G. Cousins (R)	21,261	55.2
	William P. Daniels (D)	15,487	40.2
6	John F. Lacey (R)	18,418	50.9
	W. H. Taylor (D)	11,587	32.0
	Allen Clark (PP)	5,663	15.7
7	John A. T. Hull (R)	20,167	60.9
	J. R. Barcoft (D-PP)	12,942	39.1
8	William P. Hepburn (R)	21,672	55.3
	Frank G. Stuart (D-PP)	17,538	44.7
9	Alva L. Hager (R)	21,874	53.3
	James B. Weaver (D-PP)	18,817	45.8
10	Jonathan P. Dolliver (R)	25,262	59.9
	J. C. Baker (D-PP)	16,905	40.1
11	George D. Perkins (R)	22,406	54.7
	Bernard Graiser (D)	12,425	30.3
	J. L. Bartholomew (PP)	5,265	12.8

KANSAS

	Candidates	Votes	%
1	Case Broderick (R)	19,202	54.2
	H. C. Solomon (FUS)	15,844	44.7
2	Orrin L. Miller (R)	22,763	53.9
	F. A. Willard (PP)	13,811	32.7
	H. L. Moore (D)	4,780	11.3
3	Snyder S. Kirkpatrick (R)	20,631	49.3
	Jeremiah D. Botkin (PP)	18,505	44.2
	William F. Sapp (D)	2,695	6.4
4	Charles Curtis (R)	25,154	53.3
	S. M. Scott (PP)	18,790	39.8
	Thomas J. O'Neil (D)	2,546	5.4
5	William A. Calderhead (R)	18,428	49.1
	John Davis (PP)	15,831	42.1
	C. W. Brandenburg (D)	2,788	7.4
6	William Baker (PP)	16,585	45.7
	Abram H. Ellis (R)	16,391	45.1
	Roscoe G. Heard (D)	2,934	8.1
7	Chester I. Long (R)	27,444	50.9
	Jerry Simpson (D-PP)	25,459	47.2
AL	Richard W. Blue (R)	147,858	50.4
	W. A. Harris (PP)	114,429	39.0
	Joseph G. Lowe (D)	26,093	8.9

KENTUCKY

	Candidates	Votes	%
1	John K. Hendrick (D)	13,912	49.8
	Ben C. Keys (POP)	10,794	38.7
	W. J. Chitwood (R)	2,701	9.7
2	John D. Clardy (D)	13,363	46.8
	Elijah G. Sebree Jr. (R)	10,381	36.3
	Henry Turner (POP)	4,385	15.3
3	W. Godfrey Hunter (R)	16,545	49.7
	C. McElroy (D)	15,644	47.0
4	John W. Lewis (R)	16,826	51.0
	Alexander B. Montgomery (D)	15,636	47.4
5	Walter Evans (R)	20,592	55.6
	E. J. McDermott (D)	16,442	44.4
6	Albert S. Berry (D)	14,008	52.1
	Thomas B. Mathews (R)	11,968	44.5
7	William C. Owens (D)	13,677	48.7
	George Denny Jr. (R)	13,576	48.4
8	James B. McCreary (D)	13,532	50.6
	Phil Roberts (R)	12,155	45.4
9	Samuel J. Pugh (R)	19,058	50.2
	Rawleigh K. Hart (D)	18,396	48.4
10	Joseph M. Kendall (D)	14,845‡	50.4
	Nathan T. Hopkins (R)	14,592	49.6
11	David G. Colson (R)	14,628	47.7
	George E. Stone (D)	10,932	35.6
	Silas Adams (IR)	4,975	16.2

Special Election

	Candidates	Votes	%
10	William M. Beckner (D)	14,231	52.3
	John L. Bosley (R)	12,970	47.7

LOUISIANA

	Candidates	Votes	%
1	Adolph Meyer (D)	13,405	65.5
	H. P. Kernochan (R)	6,676	32.6
2	Charles F. Buck (D)	14,864	66.8
	H. D. Coleman (R)	7,211	32.4
3	Andrew Price (D)	14,388	60.8
	Taylor Beattle (R)	8,620	36.5
4	Henry W. Ogden (D)	12,257	67.4
	B. W. Bailey (POP)	5,932	32.6
5	Charles J. Boatner (D)	14,755‡	76.4
	Alexis Benoit (POP)	4,549	23.6
6	Samuel M. Robertson (D)	7,981	78.2
	M. R. Wilson (POP)	2,230	21.8

Special Election

	Candidates	Votes	%
4	Henry W. Ogden (D)	8,261	71.2
	C. D. Hicks (POP & R)	3,333	28.7

MAINE

	Candidates	Votes	%
1	Thomas B. Reed (R)	17,086	63.5
	J. W. Deering (D)	8,901	33.1
2	Nelson Dingley Jr. (R)	18,097	63.7
	D. J. McGillicuddy (D)	8,059	28.4
	Elb Y. Turner (PP)	1,693	6.0
3	Seth L. Milliken (R)	16,891	64.7
	M. R. Leighton (D)	6,663	25.5
	G. C. Sheldon (PP)	1,986	7.6
4	Charles A. Boutelle (R)	17,383	65.5
	A. L. Simpson (D)	6,879	25.9

MARYLAND

	Candidates	Votes	%
1	Joshua W. Miles (D)	13,953	43.2
	A. L. Dryden (R)	12,914	40.0
	B. P. Miles (P)	2,728	8.4
	B. Morris (PP)	2,728	8.4
2	William B. Baker (R)	19,291	48.0
	J. F. Talbott (D)	19,100	47.5
3	Harry W. Rusk (D)	16,228	49.8
	William Booze (R)	15,709	48.2
4	John K. Cowen (D)	17,184	50.5
	Robert Smith (R)	16,178	47.5
5	Charles E. Coffin (R)	15,443	52.0
	John Rogers (D)	13,421	45.2
6	George L. Wellington (R)	19,709	52.1
	Frederick Williams (D)	16,742	44.2

Special Elections

	Candidates	Votes	%
1	W. L. Henry (D)	13,858	46.3
	Joseph Mallalieu (R)	12,955	43.2
	James Anthony (P)	2,763	9.2
5	Charles E. Coffin (R)	15,492	52.0
	George Welles (D)	13,495	45.3

MASSACHUSETTS

	Candidates	Votes	%
1	Ashley B. Wright (R)	14,018	55.2
	Addison L. Green (D)	9,961	39.2
2	Frederick H. Gillett (R)	15,480	61.4
	Edward A. Hall (D)	7,924	31.4
3	Joseph H. Walker (R)	13,788	59.4
	Charles Haggerty (D)	8,251	35.6
4	Lewis D. Apsley (R)	16,992	64.8
	John J. Desmond (D)	8,432	32.2
5	William S. Knox (R)	14,372	51.7
	George W. Fifield (D)	12,341	44.4
6	William Cogswell (R)	16,206	68.3
	Henry B. Little (D)	5,747	24.2
	Joseph K. Harris (PP)	1,772	7.5

	Candidates	Votes	%
7	William E. Barrett (R)	16,453	57.7
	Samuel K. Hamilton (D)	9,601	33.7
8	Samuel W. McCall (R)	15,188	61.5
	Charles A. Conant (R)	8,747	35.4
9	John F. Fitzgerald (D)	11,459	53.3
	Jesse M. Gove (R)	9,545	44.4
10	Harrison H. Atwood (R)	9,833	35.9
	Michael J. McEttrick (D & CIT)	8,868	32.4
	William S. McNary (D)	7,113	26.0
11	William F. Draper (R)	16,905	62.0
	Bentley Wirt Warren (D)	9,456	34.7
12	Elijah A. Morse (R)	15,865	65.3
	William H. Jordan (D)	6,359	26.2
	Elbridge Gerry Brown (PP)	2,065	8.5
13	John Simpkins (R)	13,497	61.1
	Robert Howard (D)	8,548	38.7

MICHIGAN

	Candidates	Votes	%
1	John B. Corliss (R)	18,605	55.0
	Levi T. Griffin (D)	13,441	39.7
2	George Spalding (R)	23,708	54.7
	Thomas E. Barkworth (PP & D)	17,596	40.6
3	Julius Burrows (R)	20,115*	58.7
	Nathaniel H. Stewart (D)	8,075	23.6
	Frederick Lackore (PP)	3,888	11.3
	Lucian W. Underwood (P)	2,217	6.5
4	Henry F. Thomas (R)	21,722	58.8
	Leroy F. Weaver (D)	9,874	26.7
	Sullivan Cook (PP)	3,744	10.1
5	William Alden Smith (R)	19,973	58.5
	Gideon L. Rutherford (D)	10,405	30.5
	Josiah Tibbitts (PP)	2,168	6.4
6	David D. Aitken (R)	22,894	57.3
	Elliott R. Wilcox (D)	13,831	34.6
	Thomas C. Williams (P)	2,394	6.0
7	Horace G. Snover (R)	18,172	54.6
	Ezra C. Carleton (D)	12,334	37.1
8	William S. Linton (R)	16,565	54.1
	Rowland Connor (D)	10,118	33.0
	Emery L. Brewer (P)	1,572	5.1
	Poe R. Crosby (PP)	1,778	5.8
9	Roswell P. Bishop (R)	15,761	58.4
	William T. Evans (D)	7,142	26.5
	Norman B. Farnsworth (PP)	2,768	10.3
10	Rousseau O. Crump (R)	16,304	52.6
	Worthy L. Churchill (D)	12,456	40.2
	Alexander Forsyth (PP)	2,130	6.9
11	John Avery (R)	19,575	62.2
	Hiram B. Hudson (D)	6,503	20.7
	William T. Pitt (PP)	3,660	11.6
	Austin Barber (P)	1,728	5.5
12	Samuel M. Stephenson (R)	20,935	64.0
	Rush Culver (D)	8,714	27.0
	Andrew E. Anderson (PP)	3,053	9.3

MINNESOTA

	Candidates	Votes	%
1	James A. Tawney (R)	22,651	58.0
	John Moonan (D)	10,479	26.8
	Thomas G. Meighen (PP)	4,675	12.0
2	James T. McCleary (R)	23,136	53.9
	L. C. Long (PP)	10,362	24.2
	James H. Baker (D)	7,912	18.5
3	Joel P. Heatwole (R)	19,461	49.2
	Osee M. Hall (D)	14,193	35.9
	J. M. Bowler (PP)	4,988	12.6
4	Andrew R. Keifer (R)	20,573	56.5
	Edw. J. Darragh (D)	10,168	28.0
	Francis H. Clark (PP)	5,055	13.9
5	Loren Fletcher (R)	20,465	51.1
	Oliver T. Erickson (D)	11,506	28.7
	Ernest F. Clark (PP)	7,043	17.6
6	Charles A. Towne (R)	25,487	53.3
	M. R. Baldwin (D)	15,846	33.2
	Kittl Halvorsen (PP)	6,475	13.5
7	Frank M. Eddy (R)	18,200	43.5
	Haldor E. Boen (PP)	17,408	41.6

MINNESOTA

Candidates	Votes	%
Thomas N. McLean (D)	3,486	8.3
Ole Kron (P)	2,726	6.5

MISSISSIPPI

Candidates	Votes	%
1 John M. Allen (D)	3,177	76.3
J. A. Brown (PP)	985	23.7
2 John C. Kyle (D)	3,845	75.3
R. J. Lyle (PP)	1,067	20.9
3 Thomas C. Catchings (D)	1,696	87.1
Thomas Monuh (P)	207	10.6
4 Hernando D. Money (D)	5,213	57.9
J. H. Jamison (PP)	3,751	41.7
5 John Sharp Williams (D)	5,319	69.1
W. P. Ratiff (POP)	2,380	30.9
6 Walter McK. Denny (D)	3,889	64.6
A. C. Hathorn (POP)	2,127	35.4
7 James G. Spencer (D)	3,597	70.5
A. M. Newman (PP)	1,329	26.1

MISSOURI

Candidates	Votes	%
1 Charles N. Clark (R)	15,786	44.3
Hatch (D)	15,367	43.1
London (PP)	4,270	12.0
2 Uriel S. Hall (D)	18,039	48.8
Loomis (R)	16,178	43.8
Goodson (PP)	2,761	7.5
3 Alexander M. Dockery (D)	16,230	44.5
Orton (R)	15,890	43.6
Penny (PP)	4,053	11.1
4 George C. Crowther (R)	15,695	47.8
Ellison (D)	14,034	42.7
Missemer (PP)	2,910	8.9
5 John C. Tarsney (D)	16,538‡	47.3
Robert T. Van Horn (R)	5,798	45.2
Crosby (PP)	2,541	7.3
6 David A. De Armond (D)	13,735	40.7
Lewis (R)	13,643	40.4
Francisco (PP)	6,391	18.9
7 John P. Tracey (R)	17,775	45.5
Heard (D)	17,490	44.7
Tippin (PP)	3,567	9.1
8 Joel D. Hubbard (R)	16,885	45.4
Richard P. Bland (D)	16,815	45.2
Alldredge (PP)	3,528	9.5
9 William M. Treloar (R)	15,082	49.2
Clark (D)	14,950	48.8
10 Richard Bartholdt (R)	16,654	62.2
Coppinger (D)	8,887	33.2
11 Charles F. Joy (R)	15,175	52.5
Espenschled (D)	12,893	44.6
12 Seth W. Cobb (D)	10,095	53.4
Sterrett (R)	7,469	39.5
Nelson (I)	1,094	5.8
13 John H. Raney (R)	16,849	51.3
Fox (D)	16,021	48.7
14 Norman A. Mozley (R)	16,184	43.9
Arnold (D)	15,097	40.9
Livingston (PP)	5,591	15.2
15 Charles G. Burton (R)	16,630	45.2
Morgan (D)	14,036	38.2
Bigbee (PP)	5,741	15.6

MONTANA

Candidates	Votes	%
AL Charles S. Hartman (R)	23,140	47.0
Robert B. Smith (PP)	15,240	30.9
Hal S. Corbett (D)	10,369	21.1

NEBRASKA

Candidates	Votes	%
1 Jesse B. Strode (R)	18,185	56.8
Austin H. Weir (D-POP I)	12,730	39.8
2 David Mercer (R)	12,946	50.8
James E. Boyd (D)	8,165	32.0
D. Clem Deaver (POP I)	4,007	15.7

Candidates	Votes	%
3 George D. Meiklejohn (R)	16,531	45.2
John M. Devine (POP)	11,138	30.5
W. A. Hensley (D)	8,018	21.9
4 Eugene J. Hainer (R)	19,493	50.4
William L. Stark (D-POP I)	15,542	40.2
Shannon S. Alley (D)	2,763	7.1
5 William E. Andrews (R)	16,270	48.9
W. A. McKeighan (D-POP I)	15,460	46.5
6 O. M. Kem (D-POP I)	17,077	52.3
Matt A. Daugherty (R)	14,676	45.0

NEVADA

Candidates	Votes	%
AL Francis G. Newlands (D SIL)	4,581	44.4
Bartine (R)	2,774	26.9
J. C. Doughty (POP)	2,751	26.7

NEW HAMPSHIRE

Candidates	Votes	%
1 Cyrus A. Sulloway (R)	22,730	56.3
John B. Nash (D)	16,507	40.9
2 Henry M. Baker (R)	23,416	56.3
Charles McDaniel (D)	17,122	41.2

NEW JERSEY

Candidates	Votes	%
1 Henry C. Loudenslager (R)	24,462	61.0
Ferrell (D)	12,082	30.1
2 John J. Gardner (R)	22,641	60.5
Haines (D)	12,900	34.5
3 Benjamin F. Howell (R)	18,403	53.7
Geisenhainer (D)	14,427	42.1
4 Mahlon Pitney (R)	16,116	49.0
Cornish (D)	14,709	44.7
5 James F. Stewart (R)	16,441	54.9
Demarest (D)	10,469	34.9
Ball (SOC LAB)	2,511	8.4
6 Richard W. Parker (R)	23,219	57.9
English (D)	14,746	36.8
7 Thomas McEwan Jr. (R)	23,500	48.8
Stevens (D)	2,207	48.2
8 Charles N. Fowler (R)	19,041	57.4
Dunn (D)	12,805	38.6

NEW YORK

Candidates	Votes	%
1 Richard C. McCormick (R)	20,864	56.9
Joseph Fitch (D)	14,961	40.8
2 Denis M. Hurley (R)	14,507	45.1
James O. Cleveland (D)	13,194	41.0
Daniel Bradley (D-REF)	3,924	12.2
3 Francis H. Willis (R)	18,568	49.8
James A. Murtha Jr. (D)	14,215	38.2
Stephen Perry Sturges (D-REF)	3,741	10.0
4 Israel T. Fischer (R)	19,802	51.5
William J. Coombs (D)	17,514	45.6
5 Charles G. Bennett (R)	19,372	58.8
Anton Vigelius (D)	11,885	36.1
6 James R. Howe (R)	14,427	51.5
Arthur Somers (D)	12,525	44.7
7 Franklin Bartlett (D)	9,138	47.0
Austin E. Ford (R)	7,676	39.5
John Murphy (STATE D)	2,159	11.1
8 James J. Walsh (D)	9,466‡	50.3
John M. Mitchell (R)	9,099	48.3
9 Henry C. Miner (D)	8,038	35.1
Timothy J. Campbell (SOCIAL D)	7,084	31.0
John Simpson (R)	5,214	22.8
Daniel Deleon (SOC LAB)	2,358	10.3
10 Andrew J. Campbell (R)	13,845*	46.5
Daniel E. Sickles (D)	12,982	43.6
George Karsch (STATE D)	2,331	7.8
11 William Sulzer (D)	11,208	47.9
Ferdinand Eidmann (R)	10,524	45.0
Francis H. Koenig (SOC WB)	1,448	6.2

Candidates	Votes	%
12 George B. McClellan (D)	10,933	47.4
Robert A. Chesebrough (R)	9,592	41.6
George Walton Green (STATE D)	2,042	8.9
13 Richard C. Shannon (R)	13,555	46.3
Amos J. Cummings (D)	13,089	44.7
Edward C. Baker (STATE D)	1,943	6.6
14 Lemuel E. Quigg (R)	24,332	55.4
John Connelly (D)	18,355	41.8
15 Philip B. Low (R)	21,562	48.0
Jacob A. Cantor (D)	17,028	37.9
Robert G. Monroe (STATE D)	4,827	10.7
16 Benjamin L. Fairchild (R)	24,853	54.1
William Ryan (D)	19,294	42.0
17 Benjamin B. Odell Jr. (R)	19,327	57.5
Eugene S. Ives (D)	13,520	40.2
18 Jacob Le Fever (R)	22,169	55.8
William M. Ketcham (D)	16,640	41.9
19 Frank S. Black (R)	20,954	53.4
Charles D. Haines (D)	17,514	44.6
20 George N. Southwick (R)	19,199	51.1
Charles Tracey (D)	17,549	46.7
21 David Forrest Wilber (R)	24,472	53.1
George Vanhorn (D)	20,395	44.2
22 Newton M. Curtis (R)	22,383	61.0
Thomas R. Hossie (D)	12,785	34.8
23 Wallace T. Foote Jr. (R)	25,526	69.p
Winslow C. Watson (D)	11,143	30.1
24 Charles A. Chickering (R)	23,320	61.3
Washington T. Henderson (D)	13,473	35.4
25 James S. Sherman (R)	22,371	56.2
John D. Henderson (D)	16,130	40.5
26 George W. Ray (R)	29,149	63.8
Sherrill E. Smith (D)	15,877	34.8
27 Theodore L. Poole (R)	24,647	57.3
Walter E. Northrup (D)	16,307	37.9
28 Sereno E. Payne (R)	29,528	61.4
Eli McConnell (D)	15,926	33.1
29 Charles W. Gillet (R)	22,051	54.1
George Henry Roberts (D)	16,510	40.5
30 James S. Wadsworth (R)	24,541	59.8
Francis Murphy (D)	13,950	34.0
31 Henry C. Brewster (R)	21,488	55.6
John D. Lynn (D)	15,530	40.2
32 Rowland B. Mahany (R)	15,548	51.3
J. Cavin (D)	13,893	44.3
33 Charles Daniels (R)	23,595	65.5
J. Morgenstein (D)	11,095	30.8
34 Warren B. Hooker (R)	25,964	64.2
Staley N. Wood (D)	10,674	26.4
Andrew Yates Freeman (P)	2,181	5.4

Special Elections

Candidates	Votes	%
14 Lemuel E. Quigg (R)	13,535	50.1
Brown (D)	12,586	46.6
15 Isidor Straus (D)	15,364	55.5
Sigrist (R)	10,653	38.5

NORTH CAROLINA

Candidates	Votes	%
1 Harry Skinner (PP)	16,510	54.9
William A. B. Branch (D)	13,546	45.1
2 Frederick A. Woodard (D)	14,721	50.0
Henry P. Cheatham (R)	9,413	31.9
Howard F. Freeman	5,314	18.0
3 John G. Shaw (D)	10,699	39.1
Cyrus Thompson (PP)	9,705	35.5
Oscar J. Spear (R)	6,966	25.5
4 William F. Strowd (PP & R)	18,667	56.5
Charles M. Cooke (D)	14,335	43.4
5 Thomas Settle (R)	16,934	50.8
Augustus W. Graham (D)	14,046	42.2
William Merritt	2,104	6.3
6 James H. Lockhart (D)	13,996‡	50.8
Charles H. Martin (PP)	13,505	49.0
7 Alonzo C. Shuford (PP)	15,383	53.9
John S. Henderson (D)	13,124	46.0
8 Romulus Z. Linney (PP & R)	18,775	54.6
William H. Bower (D)	15,491	45.1

NORTH CAROLINA

Candidates	Votes	%
9 Richmond Pearson (R)	16,869	50.2
William T. Crawford (D)	16,734	49.8

NORTH DAKOTA

AL Martin N. Johnson (R)	21,615	57.3
Muir (POP)	15,660	41.5

OHIO

1	Charles P. Taft (R)	19,315	61.0
	Hiram D. Peck (D)	10,378	32.8
	Thomas John Donnelly (PP)	1,679	5.3
2	Jacob H. Bromwell (R)	22,221	62.5
	James B. Matson (D)	10,667	30.0
	Robert H. H. Wheeler (PP)	2,456	6.9
3	Paul J. Sorg (D)	22,529	48.0
	Andrew L. Harris (R)	22,327	47.6
4	Fernando C. Layton (D)	15,388	47.2
	William D. Davies (R)	13,910	42.6
	Joseph White (PP)	2,323	7.1
5	Francis B. De Witt (R)	16,546	49.4
	John S. Snook (D)	14,899	44.5
	Henry L. Goll (PP)	2,015	6.0
6	George W. Hulick (R)	20,283	57.3
	Joseph L. Stephens (D)	12,505	35.3
7	George W. Wilson (R)	18,021	54.9
	Charles E. Gain (D)	11,731	35.8
8	Luther M. Strong (R)	21,730	58.5
	Elijah T. Dunn (D)	11,740	31.6
	George Riddle (PP)	2,045	5.5
9	James Harding Southard (R)	20,715	54.8
	Byron F. Ritchie (D)	14,109	37.3
	George Candee (PP, P)	2,964	7.8
10	Lucien J. Fenton (R)	19,768	62.5
	John O. Yates (D)	9,465	30.0
11	Charles H. Grosvenor (R)	20,731	56.9
	Eli Reynolds Lash (D)	11,601	31.8
	William H. Crawford (PP)	3,115	8.6
12	David K. Watson (R)	18,953	49.4
	Joseph H. Outhwaite (D)	17,362	45.3
	George F. Ebner (PP)	2,015	5.3
13	Stephen R. Harris (R)	19,131	46.0
	Boston G. Young (D)	18,453	44.4
	Amos Kellar (PP)	2,983	7.2
14	Winfield S. Kerr (R)	21,302	54.6
	James C. Laser (D)	14,262	36.6
15	Henry C. Van Voorhis (R)	19,291	56.7
	Charles Richardson (D)	12,010	35.3
16	Lorenzo Danford (R)	17,481	55.9
	Albert O. Barnes (D)	10,300	33.0
	James Brettelle (PP)	1,977	6.3
17	Addison S. McClure (R)	19,061	48.8
	James A. D. Richards (D)	17,403	44.5
	William F. Loyd (PP)	2,268	5.8
18	Robert W. Tayler (R)	20,803	49.0
	Edward S. Raff (D)	11,051	26.0
	Jacob S. Coxey (PP)	8,912	21.0
19	Stephen A. Northway (R)	22,361	62.9
	Henry Apthorp (D)	7,164	20.2
	George A. Wise (PP)	4,492	12.6
20	Clifton B. Beach (R)	17,327	59.1
	H. B. Harrington (D)	8,351	28.5
	Luther S. Copper (PP)	2,456	8.4
21	Theodore E. Burton (R)	17,968	53.4
	Tom L. Johnson (D)	13,260	39.4
	George A. Groot (PP)	1,805	5.4

Special Election

2	Jacob H. Bromwell (R)	22,247	62.4
	James B. Matson (D)	10,709	30.1
	William R. Fox (PP)	2,448	6.9

OREGON

1	Binger Hermann (R)	22,264	47.6
	Charles Miller (POP)	12,620	27.0

Candidates	Votes	%
J. K. Weatherford (D)	10,790	23.1
2 William R. Ellis (R)	18,875	47.9
Joseph Waldrop (POP)	10,749	27.3
James H. Raley (D)	9,013	22.9

PENNSYLVANIA

1	Henry H. Bingham (R)	26,957	70.7
	Denis J. Callaghan (D)	10,995	28.8
2	Robert Adams Jr. (R)	17,550	75.7
	Max Herzberg (D)	5,488	23.7
3	Frederick Halterman (R)	13,443	65.8
	Joseph P. McCullen (D)	6,980	34.2
4	John E. Reyburn (R)	42,461	71.8
	Gustav A. Muller (D)	16,056	27.2
5	Alfred C. Harmer (R)	38,986	74.8
	David Moffet (D)	12,530	24.1
6	John B. Robinson (R)	20,717	64.7
	Thomas E. Parke (D)	9,803	30.6
7	Irving P. Wanger (R)	22,913	54.8
	John Todd (D)	18,087	43.3
8	Joseph J. Hart (R)	14,762	49.2
	William S. Kirkpatrick (R)	14,565	48.5
9	Constantine J. Erdman (D)	21,273	51.7
	Jeremiah S. Trexler (R)	19,325	47.0
10	Marriott Brosius (R)	19,266	70.9
	John A. Coyle (D)	7,181	26.4
11	Joseph A. Scranton (R)	14,104	51.1
	Edward Merrifield (D)	12,027	43.5
12	John Leisenring (R)	18,114	56.1
	William H. Hines (D)	12,644	39.2
13	Charles N. Brumm (R)	13,947	54.3
	James B. Reilly (D)	11,718	45.7
14	Ephraim M. Woomer (R)	19,139	64.1
	William H. Minick (D)	9,177	30.7
15	Myron B. Wright (R)	15,651*	64.3
	Rhamanthus M. Stocker (D)	7,501	30.8
16	Fred C. Leonard (R)	16,791	53.8
	James B. Benson (D)	11,687	37.5
	Andrew Sherwood (P)	1,676	5.4
17	Monroe H. Kulp (R)	12,677	49.3
	Charles R. Buckalew (D)	11,783	45.8
18	Thaddeus M. Mahon (R)	19,597	61.1
	D. G. Smith (D)	12,456	38.9
19	James A. Stable (R)	21,138	52.1
	Peter H. Strubinger (D)	18,754	46.2
20	Josiah D. Hicks (R)	23,969	62.9
	Thomas J. Burke (D)	12,592	33.1
21	Daniel B. Heiner (R)	24,754	56.7
	William M. Fairman (D)	14,107	32.3
22	John Dalzell (R)	29,136	76.6
	James A. Wakefield (D)	7,430	19.5
23	William A. Stone (R)	13,731	77.6
	James Semple (D)	3,420	19.3
24	Ernest F. Acheson (R)	27,538	57.2
	William A. Sipe (D)	17,304	35.9
25	Thomas W. Phillips (R)	22,156	61.6
	Joseph C. Vanderlin (D)	10,435	29.0
	William J. Kirker (PP)	1,919	5.3
26	Matthew Griswold (R)	15,729	52.9
	Joseph C. Sibley (D)	13,265	44.6
27	Charles W. Stone (R)	11,717	61.1
	John F. Parsons (D)	4,845	25.2
	S. P. McCalmont (P)	1,724	9.0
28	William C. Arnold (R)	16,994	50.6
	Aaron Williams (D)	15,197	45.2
AL	Galusha A. Grow (R, IR)	571,124✔	
	George F. Huff (R, IR)	566,290✔	
	Henry Meyer (D)	328,677	
	Thomas Collins (D)	324,623	
	Elisha Kent Kane (P)	23,481	
	Lewis G. Jordan (P)	22,980	
	Victor A. Lotier (PP)	17,820	
	B. F. Greenman (PP)	17,299	
	Ernest Kreft (SOC LAB)	1,524	
	Gottfried Metzler (SOC LAB)	1,466	

Special Election

AL	Galusha A. Grow (R)	485,804	60.4
	James Denton Hancock (D)	297,966	37.0

RHODE ISLAND

Candidates	Votes	%
1 Melville Bull (R)	11,422	57.2
Oscar Lapham (D)	7,311	36.6
2 Warren O. Arnold (R)	11,259	59.8
Garvin (D)	6,555	34.8

SOUTH CAROLINA

1	William Elliott (D)	5,650‡	59.1
	George W. Murray (R)	3,913	40.9
2	W. Jasper Talbert (D)	5,942	99.5
3	Asbury C. Latimer (D)	5,778	81.3
	Robert Moorman (R)	985	13.9
4	Stanyarne Wilson (D)	8,425	75.1
	L. D. Metton (R)	2,771	24.7
5	Thomas J. Straight (D)	6,141	67.6
	G. G. Alexander (R)	1,545	17.0
	W. R. Davie (ID)	1,163	12.8
6	John L. McLaurin (D)	8,171	76.9
	J. E. Wilson (R)	2,452	23.1
7	J. William Stokes (D)	7,358‡	73.0
	James B. Johnston (R)	2,656	26.3

SOUTH DAKOTA

AL	Robert J. Gamble (R)	40,683✔	
	John A. Pickler (R)	40,623✔	
	John E. Kelley (I)	27,379	
	Freeman Knowles (I)	27,348	
	William A. Lynch (D)	8,102	
	Roger F. Connor (D)	8,041	
	George A. Ragan (P)	872	
	A. Jamieson (P)	833	

TENNESSEE

1	William C. Anderson (R)	18,017	61.7
	Thad A. Cox (D)	8,542	29.2
	R. S. Cheves (P)	2,662	9.1
2	Henry R. Gibson (R)	16,215	53.2
	John C. Hauk (R-D)	13,191	43.3
3	Foster V. Brown (R)	17,019	52.2
	H. C. Snadgrass (D)	13,947	42.7
	F. B. Dickey (POP)	1,669	5.1
4	Benton McMillin (D)	11,958	54.2
	J. A. Denton (R)	10,115	45.8
5	James D. Richardson (D)	11,440	53.7
	W. W. Enloe (POP)	9,543	44.8
6	James E. Washington (D)	11,234	54.0
	Tip Gamble (R)	4,798	23.1
	T. N. Lewis (POP)	4,783	23.0
7	Nicholas N. Cox (D)	9,098	52.6
	H. F. Farris (R)	6,366	36.8
	J. K. P. Blackburn (POP)	1,844	10.7
8	John E. McCall (R)	13,064	51.6
	B. A. Enloe (D)	12,243	48.4
9	James C. McDearmon (D)	10,634	57.1
	Atwood Pierson (POP)	7,983	42.9
10	Josiah Patterson (D)	6,654	66.1
	J. N. Brown (R)	1,955	19.4
	R. J. Rawlings (POP)	1,454	14.5

TEXAS

1	Joseph C. Hutcheson (D)	14,920	55.0
	J. J. Burroughs (POP)	10,037	37.0
	L. E. Dunn (R)	2,164	8.0
2	Samuel B. Cooper (D)	23,323	59.3
	B. A. Calhoun (POP)	16,025	40.7
3	Charles H. Yoakum (D)	15,461	55.5
	J. M. Perdue (POP)	12,411	44.5
4	David B. Culberson (D)	15,872	49.2
	J. H. Davis (POP)	14,604	45.3
	H. S. Sanderson (R)	1,728	5.4
5	Joseph W. Bailey (D)	19,722	56.7
	N. M. Browder (POP)	13,540	38.9
6	Jo Abbott (D)	19,965	49.2
	J. C. Kearby (POP)	19,621	48.4

TEXAS

Candidates	Votes	%
7 George C. Pendleton (D)	18,822	52.4
I. N. Barber (POP)	17,092	47.6
8 Charles K. Bell (D)	16,480	50.6
C. H. Jenkins (POP)	16,104	49.4
9 Joseph D. Sayers (D)	18,460	52.7
W. O. Hutchison (POP)	16,591	47.3
10 Miles Crowley (D)	12,177	39.4
A. J. Rosenthal (R)	10,874	35.2
J. C. McBride (POP)	7,847	25.4
11 William H. Crain (D)	17,946	52.7
V. Weldon (POP)	16,089	47.3
12 George H. Noonan (R)	11,958	43.4
A. W. Houston (D)	11,045	40.1
A. V. Gates (POP)	4,545	16.5
13 Jeremiah V. Cockrell (D)	13,687	39.8
D. B. Gilliland (POP)	13,321	38.8
J. M. Dean (ID)	5,780	16.8

VERMONT

	Votes	%
1 H. Henry Powers (R)	21,546	75.5
Vernon A. Rutlard (D)	6,987	24.5
2 William W. Grout (R)	20,337	75.2
George S. Fletcher (D)	6,658	24.6

VIRGINIA

	Votes	%
1 William A. Jones (D)	11,598	60.1
James J. McDonald (R)	6,944	36.0
2 D. Gardiner Tyler (D)	12,375	56.3
T. R. Borland (R)	8,868	40.3
3 Tazewell Ellett (D)	11,745	63.3
J. W. Southward (R)	4,653	25.1
James M. Gregory (POP)	1,788	9.6
4 William R. McKenney (D)	8,773‡	48.1
Robert T. Thorp (R)	7,909	43.3
J. Haskins Hobson (POP)	1,107	6.1
5 Claude A. Swanson (D)	10,750	52.3
George W. Cornett (R)	8,417	41.0
G. W. B. Hale (POP)	1,121	5.5

Candidates	Votes	%
6 Peter J. Otey (D)	10,602	47.1
John Hampton Hoge (R)	8,288	36.9
O. C. Rucker (POP)	3,550	15.8
7 Smith S. Turner (D)	11,041	52.1
Robert J. Walker (R)	9,500	44.9
8 Elisha E. Meredith (D)	10,801	54.3
P. H. McCaull (R)	8,450	42.5
9 James Alexander Walker (R)	14,287	51.2
H. S. K. Morison (D)	13,332	47.8
10 Henry St. George Tucker (D)	12,422	50.3
J. Yost (R)	11,530	46.7

Special Election

	Votes	%
7 Smith S. Turner (D)	7,882	65.0
E. D. Root	4,189	34.5

WASHINGTON

	Votes	%
AL William H. Doolittle (R)	35,981✔	
Samuel C. Hyde (R)	35,075✔	
W. P. C. Adams (PP, SPP)	26,285	
J. C. Van Patten (PP, SPP)	25,643	
B. F. Heuston (D)	14,602	
N. T. Caton (D)	14,503	
W. W. Van Dusen (P)	210	
B. F. Brown (P)	203	
W. P. C. Adams (SPP)	157	
Lawrence E. Doyle (I)	110	

WEST VIRGINIA

	Votes	%
1 Blackburn B. Dovener (R)	21,821	53.4
John A. Howard (D)	17,375	42.5
2 Alston G. Dayton (R)	23,444	51.8
William S. Wilson (D)	21,397	47.3
3 James H. Huling (R)	23,457	53.5
John D. Alderson (D)	19,538	44.5
4 Warren Miller (R)	20,795	52.0
Thomas H. Harvey (D)	17,767	44.4

WISCONSIN

Candidates	Votes	%
1 Henry Allen Cooper (R)	21,972	56.7
Andrew Kull (D)	12,334	31.8
Hamilton Utley (PP)	2,828	7.3
2 Edward Sauerhering (R)	18,197	47.9
Charles Barwig (D)	17,932	47.2
3 Joseph W. Babcock (R)	22,262	58.2
Cyrus M. Butt (D & POP)	14,608	38.2
4 Theobald Otjen (R)	17,719	47.9
David S. Rose (D)	12,214	33.0
Henry Smith (PP)	7,092	19.2
5 Samuel S. Barney (R)	18,681	52.6
Henry Blank (D)	13,057	36.7
Fred C. Runge (PP)	3,794	10.7
6 Samuel A. Cook (R)	21,718	55.8
Owen A. Wells (D)	14,919	38.3
7 Michael Griffin (R)	17,489	57.4
George W. Levis (D)	9,996	32.8
Clements H. Van Worner (PP)	1,626	5.3
8 Edward S. Minor (R)	19,902	54.2
Lyman E. Barnes (D)	15,522	42.3
9 Alexander Stewart (R)	22,741	56.0
Thomas Lynch (D)	14,910	36.7
John F. Miles (PP)	2,187	5.4
10 John J. Jenkins (R)	19,836	57.9
E. C. Kennedy (D)	9,054	26.4
William Munro (PP)	3,855	11.3

Special Election

	Votes	%
7 Michael Griffin (R)	17,766	57.8
George W. Levis (D)	9,992	32.5
Clement H. Van Worner (PP)	1,619	5.3

WYOMING

	Votes	%
AL Frank W. Mondell (R)	10,068	52.6
Henry A. Coffeen (D)	6,152	32.2
Shakespeare E. Sealey (POP)	2,906	15.2

1895 House Elections

Special Elections

	Votes	%
10 George W. Prince (R)	21,829	66.0
Fred K. Bastian (D)	8,392	25.4
E. K. Kempster	2,877	8.7
18 William F. L. Hadley (R)	15,291	51.8
Edward Lane (D)	12,040	40.8

MASSACHUSETTS

Special Election

	Votes	%
6 William H. Moody (R)	15,064	66.3
Harvey N. Shepard (D)	5,819	25.6
Wilbert Ormand Dwinell (PP)	1,299	5.7

MICHIGAN

Special Election

	Votes	%
3 Alfred Milnes (R)	16,167	51.7
Albert M. Todd (DPOP PFS)	14,851	47.5

NEW YORK

Special Election

	Votes	%
10 Amos J. Cummin (TAM)	15,295	56.4
R. A. Greacen (R)	10,223	37.7

PENNSYLVANIA[1]

Special Elections

	Votes	%
15 Edwin J. Jorden (R)	13,445	64.1
Rhamanthus M. Stocker (D)	6,690	31.9
15 James H. Codding (R)	14,356	66.0
Rhamanthus M. Stocker (D)	6,575	30.2

1. Edwin J. Jorden was elected to fill an unexpired term in the 53rd Congress (1893-95) following the death of incumbent Myron B. Wright. Wright had previously been re-elected to the 54th Congress (1895-97). James H. Codding was elected to a full two-year term to replace Wright. (See Pennsylvania's 15th district for 1892 and 1894, pp. 826, 831.)

1896 House Elections

ALABAMA

	Candidates	Votes	%
1	George W. Taylor (D SIL)	11,890	70.5
	Frank H. Threatt (R)	4,281	25.4
2	Jesse Stallings (D SIL)	11,703	55.9
	Thomas H. Clarke (D SM)	5,361	25.6
	John C. Fonville (POP)	3,856	18.4
3	Henry Clayton (D SIL)	11,671	52.6
	George L. Comer (D SM)	5,754	25.9
	Emmett C. Jackson (POP)	759	21.5
4	Thomas S. Plowman (D SIL)	10,312‡	56.3
	William F. Aldrich (POP & R)	7,345	40.1
5	Willis Brewer (D SIL)	13,587	60.9
	A. T. Goodwyn (POP & R)	8,742	39.2
6	John H. Bankhead (D)	10,148	55.1
	A. S. Van de Graaf (D SM)	4,985	27.1
	George S. Youngblood (POP)	3,295	17.9
7	Milford W. Howard (POP)	6,168	35.8
	William I. Bullock (D SIL)	5,628	32.7
	Curtis (R)	4,982	28.9
8	Joseph Wheeler (D)	15,640	56.7
	Oscar R. Hundley (R)	11,630	42.1
9	Oscar Underwood (D SIL)	13,499	63.0
	Grattan B. Crowe (POP)	5,618	26.2
	Lawson (D SM)	2,316	10.8

ARKANSAS

		Votes	%
1	Philip D. McCulloch Jr. (D)	20,419	76.8
	F. W. Tucker (R)	6,178	23.2
2	John S. Little (D)	19,099	74.7
	C. D. Greaves (R)	6,483	25.3
3	Thomas C. McRae (D)	19,321	70.0
	J. B. Freidheim (R)	8,273	30.0
4	William L. Terry (D)	16,133	70.6
	C. C. Waters (R)	6,714	29.4
5	Hugh A. Dinsmore (D)	17,566	65.9
	W. H. Neal (R)	9,087	34.1
6	Stephen Brundidge Jr. (D)	17,106	77.4
	B. F. Bodenhammer (R)	5,010	22.7

CALIFORNIA

		Votes	%
1	John A. Barham (R)	17,826	49.7
	Fletcher A. Cutler (D)	16,328	45.5
2	Marion De Vries (D&I POP)	24,434	55.5
	Grove L. Johnson (R)	18,613	42.3
3	Samuel G. Hilborn (R)	19,778	54.0
	Warren B. English (D-PP)	16,119	44.0
4	James G. Maguire (D-PP)	19,074	61.0
	Thomas B. O'Brien (R)	10,940	35.0
5	Eugene F. Loud (R)	19,351	48.6
	Joseph P. Kelly (D)	10,494	26.4
	A. B. Kinne (PP)	8,825	22.2
6	Charles A. Barlow (D-PP)	24,157	48.9
	James McLachlan (R)	23,494	47.6
7	Curtis H. Castle (D-PP)	19,183	46.7
	William W. Bowers (R)	18,939	46.1
	William H. Carlson (I)	2,139	5.2

COLORADO

		Votes	%
1	John F. Shafroth (FUS)	67,821	84.9
	T. E. McClelland (R)	9,625	12.1
2	John C. Bell (FUS)	84,018	84.5
	T. F. Hoffmire (R)	14,385	14.5

CONNECTICUT

		Votes	%
1	E. Stevens Henry (R)	27,623	66.7
	Tuttle (D)	10,859	26.2
	Hyde (ND)	2,114	5.1
2	Nehemiah D. Sperry (R)	35,944	59.3
	Fuller (D)	22,317	36.8

	Candidates	Votes	%
3	Charles A. Russell (R)	15,269	64.0
	Fanning (D)	7,665	32.1
4	Ebenezer J. Hill (R)	30,658	63.3
	Houlihan (D)	15,723	32.5

DELAWARE

		Votes	%
AL	Levin Irving Handy (D)	15,407	44.0
	Jonathan S. Willis (AK R)	11,159	31.8
	Robert G. Houston (HIG R)	7,123	20.3

FLORIDA

		Votes	%
1	Stephen M. Sparkman (D)	14,822	77.5
	E. K. Nichols (R)	2,797	14.6
	J. Asakiah Williams (POP)	1,308	6.8
2	Robert W. Davis (D)	14,375	61.9
	Joseph N. Stripling (R)	6,633	28.6

GEORGIA

		Votes	%
1	Rufus E. Lester (D)	8,063	53.8
	Joseph F. Doyle (R)	4,095	27.3
	George H. Miller (POP)	2,826	18.9
2	James M. Griggs (D)	7,104	53.2
	J. E. Peterson (R)	3,780	28.3
	John A. Sibley (POP)	2,483	18.6
3	Elijah B. Lewis (D)	7,459	70.7
	Seaborn S. Montgomery (POP)	3,096	29.3
4	William C. Adamson (D)	8,519	65.2
	A. H. Freeman (R)	4,304	32.9
5	Leonidas F. Livingston (D)	9,258	58.0
	J. C. Hendrix (R)	6,715	42.0
6	Charles L. Bartlett (D)	8,236	63.7
	A. A. Murphy (POP)	4,696	36.3
7	John W. Maddox (D)	10,719	53.4
	W. L. Massey (R)	5,087	25.4
	J. W. McGarrity (POP)	4,256	21.2
8	William M. Howard (D)	9,088	61.6
	G. L. Anderson (POP)	2,962	20.1
	W. Patrick Henry (R)	2,701	18.3
9	Farish C. Tate (D)	11,037	54.2
	H. P. Farrow (R)	5,421	26.6
	Thomas C. Winn (POP)	3,926	19.3
10	William H. Fleming (D)	10,119	58.8
	John T. West (POP)	7,105	41.3
11	William G. Brantley (D)	9,141	60.3
	Benjamin Milliken (POP)	6,019	39.7

IDAHO

		Votes	%
AL	James T. Gunn (POP & D)	13,187	46.6
	William E. Borah (SIL R)	9,034	32.0
	John T. Morrison (R)	6,054	21.4

ILLINOIS

		Votes	%
1	James R. Mann (R)	51,582	67.6
	James H. Teller (D)	23,123	30.3
2	William Lorimer (R)	35,045	54.3
	John Z. White (D & POP)	28,309	43.9
3	Hugh R. Belknap (R)	22,075	50.0
	Clarence S. Darrow (D&SILVER)	21,485	48.7
4	Daniel W. Mills (R)	22,364	50.9
	James McAndrews (D&SILVER)	20,454	46.5
5	George E. White (R)	23,053	50.9
	Edward T. Noonan (D & POP)	19,975	44.1
6	Edward D. Cooke (R)	25,723	56.3
	Joseph L. Martin (D & POP)	19,144	41.9
7	George Edmund Foss (R)	41,510	65.1
	Olaf E. Ray (D & POP)	21,213	33.3

	Candidates	Votes	%
8	Albert J. Hopkins (R)	32,073	70.1
	Simeon N. Hoover (D)	12,861	28.1
9	Robert R. Hitt (R)	32,949	67.2
	Charles O. Knudson (D)	15,241	31.1
10	George W. Prince (R)	31,459	64.0
	William R. Moore (D)	15,741	32.0
11	Walter Reeves (R)	24,765	56.5
	Charles M. Golden (D)	18,514	42.2
12	Joseph G. Cannon (R)	28,566	59.9
	George L. Vance (D & POP)	18,613	39.1
13	Vespasian Warner (R)	27,324	58.2
	Frank M. Palmer (D & POP)	18,811	40.1
14	Joseph V. Graff (R)	25,144	50.9
	Nicholas E. Worthington (D)	23,413	47.4
15	Benjamin F. Marsh (R)	24,605	49.7
	William H. Neece (D)	24,296	49.1
16	William H. Hinrichsen (D & POP)	26,615	56.0
	John I. Rinaker (R)	20,472	43.1
17	James A. Connolly (R)	23,813	49.4
	Benjamin F. Caldwell (D)	23,714	49.2
18	Thomas M. Jett (D)	22,358	51.5
	William F. L. Hadley (R)	20,599	47.4
19	Andrew J. Hunter (D & POP)	23,960	50.0
	Benson Wood (R)	22,793	47.6
20	James R. Campbell (D & POP)	22,359	53.3
	Orlando Burrel (R)	19,508	46.5
21	Jehu Baker (D)	23,581	50.4
	Everett J. Murphy (R)	23,119	49.6
22	George W. Smith (R)	22,066	55.3
	John J. Hale (D & POP)	17,811	44.7

INDIANA

		Votes	%
1	James A. Hemenway (R)	21,807	49.6
	Thomas Duncan (D)	20,856	47.4
2	Robert W. Miers (D)	21,757	48.2
	Alexander M. Hardy (R)	20,759	46.0
	Newel J. Motsinger (POP)	2,625	5.8
3	William J. Zenor (D)	22,418	52.6
	Robert J. Tracewell (R)	19,984	46.9
4	William S. Holman (D)	23,594	50.8
	Marcus R. Sulzer (R)	22,769	49.0
5	George W. Faris (R)	25,290	50.4
	John Clark Ridpath (D & POP)	24,925	49.6
6	Henry U. Johnson (R)	24,083	52.4
	Charles A. Robinson (D & POP)	21,867	47.6
7	Jesse Overstreet (R)	29,075	53.8
	Charles M. Cooper (D & POP)	24,187	44.8
8	Charles L. Henry (R)	30,045	52.3
	John R. Brunt (D & POP)	27,413	47.7
9	Charles B. Landis (R)	23,616	50.3
	Joseph B. Cheadle (D & POP)	23,367	49.7
10	Edgar D. Crumpacker (R)	28,259	55.0
	Martin L. Kruger (D & POP)	23,120	45.0
11	George W. Steele (R)	27,853	53.5
	Joseph H. Larimer (D)	23,584	45.3
12	James N. Robinson (D & POP)	22,752	50.6
	Jacob D. Leighty (R)	22,196	49.4
13	Lemuel W. Royse (R)	25,514	51.6
	Charles Kellison (D & POP)	23,928	48.4

IOWA

		Votes	%
1	Samuel M. Clark (R)	21,944	53.7
	Sabut M. Casey (D-PP)	18,649	45.6
2	George M. Curtis (R)	23,202	52.8
	Alfred Hurst (D)	19,882	45.2
3	David B. Henderson (R)	29,654	60.7
	George Stachl (D)	19,231	39.3
4	Thomas Updegraff (R)	26,659	59.6
	F. D. Bayless (D-PP)	17,791	39.8
5	Robert G. Cousins (R)	26,133	57.7
	John R. Caldwell (D-PP)	18,765	41.5

IOWA

	Candidates	Votes	%
6	John F. Lacey (R)	21,970	51.1
	F. E. White (D-PP)	20,769	48.3
7	John A. T. Hull (R)	25,578	56.9
	Frank W. Evans (D-PP)	19,352	43.1
8	William P. Hepburn (R)	24,783	50.9
	W. H. Robb (D-PP)	23,956	49.2
	Alva L. Hager (R)	24,904	52.4
	L. T. Genning (D-PP)	22,522	47.4
9	Jonathan P. Dolliver (R)	33,523	59.4
10	John B. Romans (D-PP)	22,555	40.0
11	George D. Perkins (R)	29,601	56.1
	H. Vanwagener (D-PP)	22,773	43.2

KANSAS

		Votes	%
1	Case Broderick (R)	22,115	53.1
	H. E. Ballou (D-PP)	19,513	46.9
2	Mason S. Peters (D-PP)	26,307	50.4
	John P. Harris (R)	25,919	49.6
3	Edwin R. Ridgely (D-PP)	27,034	54.2
	S. S. Kirkpatrick (R)	22,849	45.8
4	Charles Curtis (R)	26,643	50.7
	John Madden (D-PP)	25,889	49.3
5	William D. Vincent (D-PP)	19,735	50.8
	W. A. Calderhead (R)	19,101	49.2
6	Nelson B. McCormick (PP)	18,257	50.8
	A. H. Ellis (R)	16,106	44.9
7	Jeremiah Simpson (D-PP)	29,789	52.5
	Chester I. Long (R)	26,966	47.5
AL	Jeremiah D. Botkin (PP & D)	168,420	51.3
	R. W. Blue (R)	158,147	48.2

KENTUCKY

		Votes	%
1	Charles K. Wheeler (D)	14,808	37.4
	G. P. Thomas (R)	12,842	32.4
	B. F. Keys (POP)	11,991	30.3
2	John D. Clardy (D)	23,535	57.0
	E. T. Franks (R)	17,276	41.8
3	John S. Rhea (D)	19,670	49.6
	W. G. Hunter (R)	19,324	48.7
4	David H. Smith (D)	21,655	49.1
	John W. Lewis (R)	20,222	45.8
5	Walter Evans (R)	27,780	59.7
	John Y. Brown (D)	17,150	36.8
6	Albert S. Berry (D)	16,660	58.9
	Richard P. Ernst (R)	11,638	41.1
7	Evan E. Settle (D)	18,826	52.5
	W. C. P. Breckinridge (R-GOLD D)	17,019	47.5
8	George M. Davison (R)	18,110	53.7
	John B. Thompson (D)	15,629	46.3
9	Samuel J. Pugh (R)	22,014	50.5
	W. Larue Thomas (D)	21,591	49.5
10	Thomas Y. Fitzpatrick (D)	17,453	51.9
	John W. Langley (R)	16,196	48.1
11	David G. Colson (R)	22,391	56.2
	James D. Black (D)	12,878	32.3
	J. D. White (I)	4,547	11.4

LOUISIANA

		Votes	%
1	Adolph Meyer (D)	10,776	70.5
	Armand Romain (IR)	3,982	26.1
2	Robert C. Davey (D)	10,269	60.8
	James Legendre (NR)	5,235	31.0
	Fred N. Wicker (R)	1,344	8.0
3	Robert F. Broussard (D)	9,323	57.7
	Taylor Beattle (NR)	6,490	40.2
4	Henry W. Ogden (D)	10,775	66.7
	B. W. Bailey (POP)	4,726	29.3
5	Samuel T. Baird (D)	11,494	70.2
	Alexis Benoit (POP)	4,870	29.8
6	Samuel M. Robertson (D)	11,872	72.0
	C. C. Duson (NR)	3,686	22.4
	William M. Thompson (POP)	924	5.6

MAINE

	Candidates	Votes	%
1	Thomas B. Reed (R)	19,329	66.9
	E. W. Staples (D)	8,790	30.4
2	Nelson Dingley Jr. (R)	22,418	69.2
	A. Levensaler (D)	8,424	26.0
3	Seth L. Milliken (R)	20,900	68.2
	M. S. Holway (D)	8,024	26.2
4	Charles A. Boutelle (R)	21,300	65.9
	A. J. Chase (D)	9,166	28.4

MARYLAND

		Votes	%
1	Isaac A. Barber (R)	17,969	48.5
	John Miles (D SIL)	17,389	46.9
2	William B. Baker (R)	28,530	53.6
	George Jewett (D SIL)	23,163	43.5
3	William S. Booze (R)	22,671	57.2
	Thomas Weeks (D)	15,977	40.3
4	William W. McIntire (R)	24,899	59.3
	William Ogden (D)	16,424	39.1
5	Sydney E. Mudd (R)	18,954	54.3
	Robert Mass (D)	15,442	44.3
6	John McDonald (R)	22,400	53.3
	Blair Lee (D)	18,837	44.8

MASSACHUSETTS

		Votes	%
1	Ashley B. Wright (R)	18,075	65.4
	Patrick H. Sheehan (D)	8,579	31.0
2	Frederick H. Gillett (R)	19,793	71.8
	Thomas A. Fitzgibbon (D)	7,778	28.2
3	Joseph H. Walker (R)	18,993	72.5
	John O'Gara (D)	7,185	27.4
4	George W. Weymouth (R)	20,062	69.3
	I. Porter Morse (D)	8,847	30.6
5	William S. Knox (R)	17,835	60.7
	John H. Harrington (D)	11,531	39.3
6	William H. Moody (R)	19,947	72.8
	Eben Moody Boynton (D)	7,460	27.2
7	William E. Barrett (R)	22,759	68.2
	Philip J. Doherty (D)	10,609	31.8
8	Samuel W. McCall (R)	22,054	74.4
	Frederick H. Jackson (D)	7,590	25.6
9	John F. Fitzgerald (D)	13,979	54.7
	Walter Lincoln Sears (R)	7,819	30.6
	John A. Ryan (D SIL)	3,238	12.7
10	Samuel J. Barrows (R)	17,147	50.4
	Bordman Hall (D)	14,259	41.9
	William L. Chase (R CIT)	2,612	7.7
11	Charles F. Sprague (R)	22,993	69.3
	William H. Baker (D)	10,154	30.6
12	William C. Lovering (R)	21,107	76.8
	Elbridge Gerry Brown (PPL DR S)	6,354	23.1
13	John Simpkins (R)	17,685	74.7
	James Francis Morris (D)	5,993	25.3

MICHIGAN

		Votes	%
1	John B. Corliss (R)	24,021	55.5
	Edwin Henderson (DPUS)	19,291	44.5
2	George Spalding (R)	26,557	50.5
	Thomas E. Barkworth (DPUS)	25,061	47.7
3	Albert M. Todd (DPUS)	24,466	49.4
	Alfred Milnes (R)	24,041	48.5
4	Edward L. Hamilton (R)	26,518	53.6
	Roman I. Jarvis (DPUS)	22,994	46.4
5	William Alden Smith (R)	26,819	54.8
	George P. Hummer (DPUS)	22,155	45.2
6	Samuel W. Smith (R)	26,889	53.4
	Quincy A. Smith (DPUS)	23,474	46.6
7	Horace G. Snover (R)	22,761	55.5
	O'Brien J. Atkinson (DPUS)	18,267	44.5
8	Ferdinand Brucker (DPUS)	20,992	51.0
	William S. Linton (R)	20,158	49.0
9	Roswell P. Bishop (R)	20,418	58.3
	Armond F. Tibbitts (DPUS)	14,243	40.6

MICHIGAN (continued)

	Candidates	Votes	%
10	Rousseau O. Crump (R)	19,535	52.7
	Charles S. Hampton (DPUS)	17,536	47.3
11	William S. Mesick (R)	24,368	54.9
	Jonathan G. Ramsdell (DPUS)	19,605	44.1
12	Carlos D. Shelden (R)	29,612	70.4
	Henry W. Seymour (DPUS)	12,479	29.7

MINNESOTA

		Votes	%
1	James A. Tawney (R)	27,920	60.7
	P. Fitzpatrick (PP &)	17,219	37.4
2	James T. McCleary (R)	29,481	57.1
	Frank A. Day (PP & D)	21,142	40.9
3	Joel P. Heatwole (R)	24,483	55.9
	H. J. Peck (PP & D)	18,532	42.3
4	Frederick C. Stevens (R)	24,854	62.2
	Francis H. Clark (PP & D)	14,640	36.7
5	Loren Fletcher (R)	24,508	53.2
	S. M. Owen (PP & D)	21,521	46.8
6	R. Page W. Morris (R)	30,317	50.6
	Charles A. Towne (PP & D)	29,598	49.4
7	Frank M. Eddy (R)	26,003	50.9
	Edwin E. Lommen (PP & D)	23,932	46.8

MISSISSIPPI

		Votes	%
1	John M. Allen (D)	7,221	86.9
	A. W. Kearley (POP)	752	9.1
2	William V. Sullivan (D)	6,941	70.2
	F. E. Ray (POP)	1,472	14.9
	W. D. Miller (GOLD D)	779	7.9
	M. A. Montgomery (R)	692	7.0
3	Thomas C. Catchings (D)	3,069	75.8
	J. R. Chalmers (F SIL R)	532	13.1
	C. J. Jones (R)	369	9.1
4	Andrew F. Fox (D)	8,343	70.0
	R. K. Prewitt (POP)	3,086	25.9
5	John Sharp Williams (D)	10,475	80.1
	W. H. Stinson (POP)	2,248	17.2
6	William F. Love (D)	6,718	64.3
	N. C. Hathorn (POP)	2,683	25.7
	H. C. Griffin (R)	1,055	10.1
7	Patrick Henry (D)	7,327	84.7
	G. M. Cain (POP)	897	10.4

MISSOURI

		Votes	%
1	Richard P. Giles (D)	24,044*	53.3
	Clark (R)	19,320	42.8
2	Robert N. Bodine (D)	25,862	55.7
	Loomis (R)	19,367	41.7
3	Alexander M. Dockery (D)	23,952	53.5
	Orton (R)	18,634	41.6
4	Charles F. Cochran (D)	21,512	54.7
	Crowther (R)	17,683	45.0
5	William S. Cowherd (D)	25,966	54.9
	Neff (R)	21,306	45.1
6	David A. De Armond (D)	22,524	53.5
	Hamilton (R)	16,722	39.7
	Linton (PP)	2,606	6.2
7	James Cooney (D)	27,846	53.5
	Tracy (R)	21,772	41.8
8	Richard P. Bland (D)	24,605	53.7
	Hubbard (R)	19,754	43.1
9	James Beauchamp Clark (D)	19,970	53.0
	Treloar (R)	17,475	46.4
10	Richard Bartholdt (R)	25,513	73.2
	Lemp (D)	9,060	26.0
11	Charles F. Joy (R)	28,341	53.3
	Hunt (D-PP)	24,676	46.4
12	Charles E. Pearce (R)	21,483	54.9
	Kern (D)	17,568	44.9
13	Edward Robb (D)	22,310	51.9
	Steel (R)	19,062	44.4
14	Willard D. Vandiver (D)	25,089	49.6
	Snider (R)	20,659	40.8
	Livingston (PP)	4,860	9.6

MISSOURI

Candidates	Votes	%
15 Maecenas E. Benton (D)	24,155	55.7
Burton (R)	17,010	39.2

MONTANA

AL Charles S. Hartman (SIL R)	33,932	78.1
O. F. Goddard (R)	9,492	21.9

NEBRASKA

1 Jesse B. Strode (R)	17,356	49.4
Jefferson H. Broady (D-POP I)	17,137	48.8
2 David H. Mercer (R)	14,861	52.3
Edward R. Duffie (D-POP I)	13,286	46.8
3 Samuel Maxwell (D-POP I)	23,487	54.8
R. L. Hammond (R)	18,633	43.4
4 William L. Stark (D-POP I)	20,515	50.5
E. J. Hainer (R)	18,844	46.4
5 Roderick D. Sutherland (D-POP I)	18,332	52.8
William E. Andrews (R)	15,541	44.8
6 William L. Greene (D-POP I)	19,378	55.7
Addison E. Cady (R)	14,841	42.7

NEVADA

AL Francis G. Newlands (D SIL)	6,429	66.3
James C. Doughty (PP)	1,948	20.1
M. J. Davis (R)	1,319	13.6

NEW HAMPSHIRE

1 Cyrus A. Sulloway (R)	25,661	63.0
John B. Nash (D)	13,928	34.2
2 Frank G. Clarke (R)	26,689	64.3
Daniel M. White (D)	13,877	33.4

NEW JERSEY

1 Henry C. Loudenslager (R)	33,659	64.2
John T. Wright (D & N S)	17,118	32.6
2 John J. Gardner (R)	31,418	66.0
Abraham E. Conrow (D & N S)	13,969	29.3
3 Benjamin F. Howell (R)	24,308	57.8
John A. Wells (D)	16,087	38.3
4 Mahlon Pitney (R & ND)	20,494	52.5
Augustus W. Cutler (D)	17,517	44.8
5 James F. Stewart (R)	23,845	59.9
Addison Ely (D)	13,667	34.3
6 Richard Wayne Parker (R)	31,059	64.2
Joseph A. Beecher (D)	15,393	31.8
7 Thomas McEwan Jr. (R)	30,557	51.8
Alexander C. Young (D)	26,080	44.2
8 Charles N. Fowler (R)	25,131	61.7
Freeman O. Willey (D)	13,487	33.1

NEW YORK

1 Joseph M. Belford (R)	27,191	59.4
William D. Marvel (D)	15,923	34.8
2 Denis M. Hurley (R)	18,268	50.8
John M. Clancy (D)	15,901	44.2
3 Francis H. Wilson (R)	23,813	56.3
Charles F. Brandt (D)	16,260	38.5
4 Israel F. Fischer (R)	25,810	56.2
Thomas F. Larkin (D)	18,381	40.0
5 Charles G. Bennett (R)	22,605	57.4
Thomas S. Delaney (D)	14,186	36.1
6 James R. Howe (R)	15,314	49.1
William Fickermann (D)	14,287	45.8
7 John H. G. Vehslage (D)	11,032	51.9
Franklin Bartlett (R & ND)	9,848	46.4
8 John Murray Mitchell (R & ND)	10,488	52.6
James J. Walsh (D)	9,219	46.3

Candidates	Votes	%
9 Thomas J. Bradley (D)	11,002	46.3
Timothy J. Campbell (R & ND)	8,379	35.2
Daniel Deleon (SOC LAB)	4,371	18.4
10 Amos J. Cummings (D)	17,446	53.3
Clarence W. Meade (R)	14,245	43.5
11 William Sulzer (D)	12,195	48.8
Ferdinand Eldmann (R)	10,435	41.8
Herman Miller (SOC LAB)	2,011	8.1
12 George B. McClellan (D)	12,815	50.9
Charles A. Hess (R)	11,038	43.9
13 Richard C. Shannon (R)	15,413	48.0
Thomas Smith (D)	14,067	43.8
14 Lemuel E. Quigg (R)	27,875	55.5
John Quincy Adams (D)	18,553	37.0
15 Philip B. Low (R & ND)	29,602	54.5
William H. Burke (D)	22,520	41.5
16 William L. Ward (R)	30,709	52.6
Eugene B. Travis (D)	23,456	40.2
17 Benjamin B. Odell Jr. (R)	22,622	58.5
David A. Morrison (D)	15,500	40.1
18 John H. Ketcham (R)	25,531	60.9
Richard E. Connell (D)	15,956	38.0
19 Aaron V. S. Cochrane (R)	23,509	55.7
George G. Miller (D)	17,735	42.0
20 George N. Southwick (R)	22,342	54.7
Thomas F. Wilkinson (D)	17,637	43.2
21 David Forrest Wilber (R)	28,567	55.7
John H. Bagley (D)	22,267	43.4
22 Lucius N. Littauer (R)	32,269	93.3
23 Wallace T. Foote Jr. (R)	30,475	97.0
24 Charles A. Chickering (R)	27,242	61.4
Oscar M. Wood (D)	16,248	36.6
25 James S. Sherman (R)	26,996	60.8
Cornelius Haley (D)	16,512	37.2
26 George W. Ray (R)	34,686	60.8
Alexander D. Wales (D)	20,383	35.7
27 James J. Belden (R)	27,427	53.2
Theodore L. Poole (D)	22,657	44.0
28 Sereno E. Payne (R)	33,628	62.4
Robert L. Drummond (D)	19,822	36.8
29 Charles W. Gillet (R)	27,192	59.7
Henry W. Bowes (D)	17,994	39.5
30 James W. Wadsworth (R)	28,478	57.3
Frank P. Hulette (D)	19,066	38.4
31 Henry C. Brewster (R)	25,399	56.9
William E. Ryan (D)	17,109	38.3
32 Rowland B. Mahany (R)	18,623	54.7
Charles Rung (D)	14,765	43.4
33 De Alva S. Alexander (R)	27,573	63.0
Harvey W. Richardson (D)	14,636	33.4
34 Warren B. Hooker (R)	30,696	86.0
David F. Allen (POP & R)	3,298	9.2

NORTH CAROLINA

1 Harry Skinner (POP & R)	20,724	58.3
Wilson H. Lucas (D)	14,849	41.7
2 George H. White (R)	19,332	51.6
Frederick A. Woodard (D)	15,378	41.1
D. S. Moss (POP)	2,738	7.3
3 John E. Fowler (POP & R)	17,989	58.9
Frank Thompson (D)	12,536	41.1
4 William F. Strowd (POP)	20,977	55.6
Edward W. Pou (D)	16,405	43.5
5 William W. Kitchin (D)	19,082	49.9
Thomas Settle (R)	18,639	48.8
6 Charles H. Martin (POP & R)	22,051	56.1
James A. Lockhart (D)	17,235	43.9
7 Alonzo C. Shuford (POP & R)	17,669	55.3
Samuel J. Pemberton (D)	14,289	44.7
8 Romulus Z. Linney (POP & R)	19,419	51.8
Rufus A. Doughton (D)	18,007	48.0
9 Richmond Pearson (POP & R)	20,495	51.6
Joseph S. Adams (D)	19,189	48.3

NORTH DAKOTA

AL Martin N. Johnson (R)	25,233	54.0
Burke (FUS)	21,172	45.3

OHIO

Candidates	Votes	%
1 William B. Shattuc (R)	27,093	60.8
Thomas J. Donnelly (D)	17,466	39.2
2 Jacob H. Bromwell (R)	30,075	59.0
David S. Oliver (D)	20,878	41.0
3 John L. Brenner (D)	27,435	49.7
Robert M. Nevin (R)	27,334	49.5
4 George A. Marshall (D)	25,688	59.5
John P. MacLean (R)	16,671	38.6
5 David Meekison (D)	24,383	56.1
Francis B. DeWitt (R)	18,478	42.5
6 Seth W. Brown (R)	25,360	53.9
Harry W. Paxton (D)	21,358	45.4
7 Walter L. Weaver (R)	22,745	51.4
Francis M. Hunt (D)	21,171	47.8
8 Archibald Lybrand (R)	26,211	53.8
McEldin Dun (D)	22,519	46.2
9 James H. Southard (R)	29,603	53.5
Stephen Brophy (D)	25,698	46.5
10 Lucien J. Fenton (R)	24,809	57.9
T. S. Hogan (D)	18,029	42.1
11 Charles H. Grosvenor (R)	24,333	54.8
William E. Finck Jr. (D)	19,850	44.7
12 John J. Lentz (D)	23,673	49.7
David K. Watson (R)	23,624	49.6
13 James A. Norton (D)	28,878	54.4
Stephen R. Harris (R)	23,506	44.3
14 Winfield S. Kerr (R)	26,850	52.0
John B. Coffinberry (D)	24,574	47.6
15 Henry Clay Van Voorhis (R)	22,560	52.6
James B. Tannehill (D)	19,837	46.2
16 Lorenzo Danford (R)	21,690	53.8
Henry H. McFadden (D)	18,635	46.2
17 John A. McDowell (D)	26,109	54.7
Addison S. McClure (R)	21,169	44.3
18 Robert W. Tayler (R)	29,814	54.2
Isaac R. Sherwood (D)	24,770	45.0
19 Stephen A. Northway (R)	31,789	60.3
William T. Sawyer (D)	20,626	39.1
20 Clifton B. Beach (R)	24,531	52.8
A. T. Vantassel (D)	21,384	46.0
21 Theodore E. Burton (R)	25,527	55.2
L. A. Russell (D)	20,025	43.3

OREGON

1 Thomas H. Tongue (R)	19,355	40.4
W. S. Vanderburg (POP)	19,292	40.3
Jefferson Myers (D)	7,914	16.5
2 William R. Ellis (R)	12,617	30.4
Martin Quinn (POP)	12,239	29.5
H. H. Northup (SM D)	8,807	21.2
A. S. Bennett (D)	7,099	17.1

PENNSYLVANIA

1 Henry H. Bingham (R)	32,466	69.7
Horace E. James (D)	13,962	30.0
2 Robert Adams Jr (R)	22,205	78.0
Fenton P. F. Mullins (D)	6,100	21.4
3 William McAleer (D)	11,655	49.7
Frederick Halterman (R)	9,556	40.7
Samuel E. Hudson (F SIL)	2,064	8.8
4 James Rankin Young (R)	59,147	77.6
Mark D. Cunningham (D)	16,536	21.7
5 Alfred C. Harmer (R)	47,953	76.1
Frank D. Wright (D)	14,484	23.0
6 Thomas S. Butler (BUT R)	15,016	39.4
John B. Robinson (ROB R)	13,369	35.1
William H. Berry (DN&FS)	9,288	24.4
7 Irving P. Wanger (R)	26,725	60.7
Charles S. Van de Grift (D)	16,740	38.1
8 William S. Kirkpatrick (R)	17,072	50.5
Laird H. Barber (D)	16,743	49.5
9 Daniel Ermentrout (D)	26,123	51.1
Oliver Williams (R)	23,022	45.0
10 Marriott Brosius (R)	24,122	73.3
Edward D. Reilly (D)	8,252	25.1

PENNSYLVANIA

	Candidates	Votes	%
11	William Connell (R)	18,598	61.6
	Edward Merrifield (D)	10,741	35.6
12	Morgan B. Williams (R)	20,920	52.4
	John M. Garman (D)	17,976	45.0
13	Charles N. Brumm (R)	16,613	53.0
	Watson F. Shepherd (D)	14,512	46.3
14	Marlin E. Olmsted (R)	25,014	87.6
	Abraham Mattis (PP)	1,948	6.8
15	James H. Codding (R)	20,210	61.6
	Charles Percival Shaw (D)	11,444	34.9
16	Horace B. Packer (R)	21,543	56.2
	Luther B. Seibert (D)	15,152	39.5
17	Monroe H. Kulp (R)	15,195	50.1
	Alphonsus Walsh (D)	14,073	46.4
18	Thaddeus M. Mahon (R)	22,455	61.2
	Willis F. Kearns (D)	14,222	38.8
19	George J. Benner (D)	22,160	49.7
	Frank E. Hollar (R)	21,382	48.0
20	Josiah D. Hicks (MCK SM)	19,974	43.8
	Robert C. McNamara (D)	17,297	37.9
	Joseph E. Thropp (PT)	7,468	16.4
21	Edward E. Robbins (R)	32,149	59.9
	Samuel S. Blyholder (D)	19,464	36.3
22	John Dalzell (R)	28,860	69.0
	John F. Miller (D)	12,788	30.6
23	William A. Stone (R)	21,379	77.2
	Morrison Foster (D)	6,191	22.3
24	Ernest F. Acheson (R)	36,554	57.1
	John Purman (D)	26,538	41.5
25	James J. Davidson (R)	26,529*	59.5
	John G. McConahy (D)	17,050	38.2
26	John C. Sturtevant (R)	18,840	50.4
	Joseph C. Sibley (D)	18,114	48.5
27	Charles W. Stone (R)	15,777	58.3
	William J. Breene (D)	10,058	37.2
28	William C. Arnold (R)	19,295	50.2
	Jackson L. Spangler (D)	18,090	47.1
AL	Galusha A. Grow (R, MCK CIT)	711,346✔	
	Samuel A. Davenport (R, MCK CIT)	708,633✔	
	Jerome T. Ailman (D, PP)	418,218	
	DeWitt C. DeWitt (D, F SIL)	413,802	
	Abraham A. Barker (P)	18,336	
	George Alcorn (P)	18,091	
	John P. Correll (PP)	7,482	
	Hay Walker Jr. (JEFFS)	7,255	
	Benjamin C. Potts (JEFFS)	7,237	
	Emil Guwang (SOC LAB)	1,455	
	Fred W. Long (SOC LAB)	1,432	
	Henry S. Kent (N)	671	
	Isaac G. Pollard (N)	663	

RHODE ISLAND

	Candidates	Votes	%
1	Melville Bull (R)	17,378	63.7
	Brown (D)	8,542	31.3
2	Adin B. Capron (R)	16,612	63.5
	Garvin (D)	8,088	30.9

SOUTH CAROLINA

	Candidates	Votes	%
1	William Elliott (D)	4,648	63.7
	George W. Murray (LW R)	2,478	34.0
2	W. Jasper Talbert (D)	7,999	92.4
	B. P. Chatfield (R)	635	7.3
3	Asbury C. Latimer (D)	9,746	92.0
	A. C. Merrick (B&T R)	659	6.2
4	Stanyarne Wilson (D)	11,230	92.2
	John F. Jones (R)	838	9.0
5	Thomas J. Strait (D)	8,511	91.0
	John F. Jones (R)	838	9.0
6	John L. McLaurin (D)	9,731	87.7
	J. E. Wilson (B&T R)	878	7.9
7	J. William Stokes (D)	8,065	85.5
	T. B. Johnson (B&T R)	1,342	14.2

Special Election

	Candidates	Votes	%
7	J. William Stokes (D)	8,223	88.3
	T. B. Johnson (B&T R)	1,068	11.5

SOUTH DAKOTA

	Candidates	Votes	%
AL	Freeman Knowles (PP)	41,216✔	
	John E. Kelley (PP)	41,122✔	
	Robert J. Gamble (R)	40,943	
	Coe I. Crawford (R)	40,575	
	K. Lewis (P)	723	
	M. H. Alexander (P)	683	

TENNESSEE

	Candidates	Votes	%
1	Walter P. Brownlow (R)	25,075	62.4
	L. L. Lawrence (D)	13,956	34.7
2	Henry R. Gibson (R)	28,112	74.3
	W. L. Ledgerwood (D)	9,448	25.0
3	John A. Moon (D)	19,498	51.9
	W. J. Clift (R)	17,716	47.2
4	Benton McMillin (D)	18,070	59.6
	C. H. Whitney (R)	12,269	40.4
5	James D. Richardson (D)	16,089	58.6
	Syd Houston (R)	9,000	32.8
	W. W. Erwin (POP)	2,384	8.7
6	John W. Gaines (D SIL)	17,646	57.5
	J. C. McReynold (GOLD D)	12,135	39.5
7	Nicholas N. Cox (D)	15,434	55.2
	A. M. Hughes Jr. (R)	10,744	38.4
	J. K. P. Blackburn (POP)	1,794	6.4
8	Thetus W. Sims (D)	16,568	53.4
	J. E. McCall (R)	13,219	42.6
9	Rice A. Pierce (D SIL)	19,138	64.1
	J. H. McDowell (POP)	10,714	35.9
10	Edward W. Carmack (D SIL)	10,924	48.8
	Josiah Patterson (GOLD D)	10,556	47.1

TEXAS

	Candidates	Votes	%
1	Thomas H. Ball (D)	19,161	55.5
	Joe H. Eagle (POP & R)	15,189	44.0
2	Samuel B. Cooper (D)	25,158	57.0
	B. A. Calhoun (POP)	12,822	29.0
	J. M. Claiborne (R)	6,188	14.0
3	Reese C. De Graffenreid (D)	21,208	56.5
	W. E. Farmer (POP)	16,351	43.5
4	John W. Cranford (D)	20,187	54.0
	J. H. Davis (POP)	13,703	36.7
	M. W. Johnson (R)	3,468	9.3
5	Joseph W. Bailey (D)	28,416	61.2
	W. D. Gordon (R)	13,242	28.5
	R. C. Foster (POP)	4,747	10.2
6	Robert E. Burke (D)	33,144	56.8
	Barnett Gibbs (POP)	25,230	43.2
7	Robert L. Henry (D)	26,151	55.2
	T. A. Pope (R)	11,632	24.5
	W. F. Douthitt (POP)	9,634	20.3
8	Samuel W. T. Lanham (D)	20,935	53.4
	C. H. Jenkins (POP)	17,510	44.7
9	Joseph D. Sayers (D)	20,381	51.4
	W. K. Makemson (R)	11,495	29.0
	Reddin Andrews (POP)	6,787	17.1
10	Robert B. Hawley (R)	17,936	45.7
	J. H. Shelburne (D)	15,757	40.2
	Noah Allen (POP)	5,476	14.0
11	Rudolph Kleburg (D)	19,059	45.6
	H. Gras (R)	18,449	44.1
	J. M. Smith (POP)	4,074	9.8
12	James L. Slayden (D)	14,744	46.0
	G. H. Noonan (R)	13,558	42.3
	Taylor McRae (POP)	3,730	11.6
13	John H. Stephens (D)	22,988	61.0
	H. L. Bentley (R)	14,219	37.8

UTAH

(Became a state Jan. 4, 1896)

	Candidates	Votes	%
AL	William H. King (D)	47,456	61.2
	Holbrook (SIL R)	27,813	35.9

Special Election

	Candidates	Votes	%
AL	C. E. Allen (R)	20,563	49.7
	B. H. Roberts (D)	19,666	47.5

VERMONT

	Candidates	Votes	%
1	H. Henry Powers (R)	26,145	76.4
	Peter F. McManus (D)	7,693	22.5
2	William W. Grout (R)	26,319	80.4
	Henry E. Fitzgerald (D)	6,202	18.9

VIRGINIA

	Candidates	Votes	%
1	William A. Jones (D)	15,525	58.4
	Walter B. Tyler (R)	10,752	40.5
2	William A. Young (D)	15,789‡	50.5
	Richard A. Wise (R)	13,390	42.8
	W. M. Whaley (SM D)	1,895	6.1
3	John Lamb (D)	16,634	55.5
	L. L. Lewis (R)	12,716	42.5
4	Sydney P. Epes (D)	12,894‡	54.4
	Robert T. Thorp (R)	10,273	43.4
5	Claude A. Swanson (D)	14,333	51.0
	John R. Brown (R)	13,782	49.0
6	Peter J. Otey (D)	17,187	57.0
	Duval Radford (SM D)	11,682	38.7
7	James Hay (D)	17,447	55.8
	Robert J. Walker (R)	13,250	42.4
8	John F. Rixey (D)	17,030	56.1
	Patrick H. McCaull (R)	13,114	43.2
9	James Alexander Walker (R)	20,024	52.7
	Samuel Walker Williams (D)	17,944	47.3
10	Jacob Yost (R)	16,095	49.8
	Henry D. Flood (D)	16,047	49.6

WASHINGTON

	Candidates	Votes	%
AL	James Hamilton Lewis (PP)	51,554✔	
	William C. Jones (PP)	51,158✔	
	W. H. Doolittle (R)	38,196	
	S. C. Hyde (R)	37,939	
	C. A. Salyer (P)	1,011	
	Martin Olsen (P)	887	
	C. E. Mix (N)	154	

WEST VIRGINIA

	Candidates	Votes	%
1	Blackburn B. Dovener (R)	25,232	53.5
	W. W. Arnett (D)	21,687	46.0
2	Alston G. Dayton (R)	25,500	52.3
	William G. Brown (D)	23,249	47.7
3	Charles P. Dorr (R)	29,277	52.9
	E. W. Wilson (D)	26,029	47.1
4	Warren Miller (R)	24,942	51.2
	Walter Pendleton (D)	23,774	48.8

WISCONSIN

	Candidates	Votes	%
1	Henry Allen Cooper (R)	28,235	64.1
	Jeremiah L. Mahoney (D)	14,723	33.4
2	Edward Sauerherring (R)	24,011	56.5
	William H. Rogers (D)	17,480	41.1
3	Joseph W. Babcock (R)	26,691	63.8
	Alfred J. Davis (D)	15,168	36.2
4	Theobald Otjen (R)	25,896	54.2
	Robert Schilling (D)	21,429	44.9
5	Samuel S. Barney (R)	26,613	61.0
	George W. Winans (D)	16,492	37.8
6	James H. Davidson (R)	26,649	57.7
	William F. Gruenewald (D)	18,944	41.0
7	Michael Griffin (R)	24,073	65.8
	Caleb M. Hilliard (D)	11,718	32.0
8	Edward S. Minor (R)	26,471	60.3
	George W. Cate (D)	16,845	38.4
9	Alexander Stewart (R)	30,438	63.2
	William W. O'Keefe (D)	17,705	36.8
10	John J. Jenkins (R)	28,149	65.5
	Frederick H. Remington (D)	14,823	34.5

WYOMING

	Candidates	Votes	%
AL	John E. Osborne (D)	10,310	49.1
	F. W. Mondell (R)	10,044	47.9

1897 House Elections

ILLINOIS

Special Election

Candidates	Votes	%
6 Henry Sherman Boutell (R)	10,211	51.4
Vincent H. Perkins (D)	9,349	47.0

MAINE

Special Election

3 E. C. Burleigh (R)	9,699	73.9
Frederick W. Plaisted (D)	3,128	23.8

MASSACHUSETTS

Special Election

Candidates	Votes	%
1 George P. Lawrence (R)	11,889	58.6
Roger P. Donoghue (D)	7,573	37.3

MISSOURI

Special Election

1 James T. Lloyd (D)	18,809	56.9
Clark (R)	13,158	39.8

NEW YORK

Special Election

Candidates	Votes	%
3 Edmund H. Driggs (D)	16,753	47.6
William A. Prendergast (R)	14,557	41.4
Horatio C. King (ND)	3,390	9.6

PENNSYLVANIA

Special Election

25 Joseph B. Showalter (R)	12,221	66.2
Salem Heilman (D)	6,222	33.7

House Candidates Index

For an index of all House candidates listed in this section (pages 701 to 1061), see pages 1180-1273. Instructions for use of the House Candidates Index appear on page 1180.

1898 House Elections

ALABAMA

	Candidates	Votes	%
1	George W. Taylor (D)	5,886	84.7
	Johnson (COLOR R)	1,061	15.3
2	Jesse Stallings (D)	9,145	83.3
	Simmons (R)	1,620	14.8
3	Henry Clayton (D)	8,287	96.6
4	Gaston A. Robbins (D)	6,915‡	54.9
	William F. Aldrich (R)	5,685	45.1
5	Willis Brewer (D)	8,842	77.8
	Smith (R)	2,504	22.0
6	John H. Bankhead (D)	7,009	69.8
	Daniel N. Cooper (R)	2,942	29.3
7	John L. Burnett (D)	6,949	44.4
	Oliver Day Street (R)	5,032	32.2
	Lathrop (R)	3,592	23.0
8	Joseph Wheeler (D)	6,368	99.9
9	Oscar W. Underwood (D)	7,155	83.0
	McEniry (R)	1,051	12.2

ARKANSAS

		Votes	%
1	Philip D. McCulloch (D)	4,103	99.3
2	John S. Little (D)	3,615	99.8
3	Thomas C. McRae (D)	4,066	100.0
4	William T. Terry (D)	3,665	99.0
5	Hugh A. Dinsmore (D)	6,633	71.0
	J. T. Hopper (R)	2,706	29.0
6	Stephen Brundidge Jr. (D)	2,732	99.9

CALIFORNIA

		Votes	%
1	John A. Barham (R)	19,598	51.8
	Emmet Seawell (D & POP)	18,244	48.2
2	Marion De Vries (D & POP)	25,196	55.2
	Frank D. Ryan (R)	20,400	44.7
3	Victor H. Metcalf (R)	20,592	57.3
	John Aubrey Jones (D & POP)	14,051	39.1
4	Julius Kahn (R)	13,695	50.0
	James H. Barry (D & POP)	12,084	44.1
5	Eugene F. Loud (R)	20,254	51.8
	William Craig (D & POP)	17,352	44.3
6	Russell J. Waters (R)	24,050	52.6
	Charles A. Barlow (D & POP)	20,499	44.9
7	James C. Needham (R)	20,793	50.1
	Curtis H. Castle (D & POP)	20,680	49.8

COLORADO

		Votes	%
1	John F. Shafroth (FUS)	43,111	67.6
	Charles Hartsell (R)	18,580	29.1
2	John C. Bell (FUS)	52,372	64.9
	B. Clark Wheeler (R)	27,583	34.2

CONNECTICUT

		Votes	%
1	E. Stevens Henry (R)	18,818	55.5
	Vance (D)	13,520	39.9
2	Nehemiah D. Sperry (R)	27,004	51.9
	Webb (D)	23,556	45.2
3	Charles A. Russell (R)	12,218	58.1
	Thayer (D)	8,507	40.4
4	Ebenezer J. Hill (R)	23,707	56.1
	Lyman (D)	17,754	42.0

DELAWARE

		Votes	%
AL	John H. Hoffecker (R)	17,566	53.1
	L. Irving Handy (D)	15,053	45.5

FLORIDA

	Candidates	Votes	%
1	Robert W. Davis (D)	12,150	71.8
	H. L. Anderson (R)	4,773	28.2
2	Stephen M. Sparkman (D)	13,506	84.1
	E. R. Gunby (R)	2,543	15.8

GEORGIA

		Votes	%
1	Rufus E. Lester (D)	5,344	86.0
	John E. Myrick (R)	873	14.0
2	James M. Griggs (D)	8,298	80.0
	J. H. Smith (R)	2,071	20.0
3	Elijah B. Lewis (D)	3,539	96.2
4	William C. Adamson (D)	3,218	99.1
5	Leonidas F. Livingston (D)	3,027	97.6
6	Charles L. Bartlett (D)	3,008	99.9
7	John W. Maddox (D)	5,296	80.7
	A. B. Austin (POP)	1,252	19.1
8	William M. Howard (D)	4,379	83.5
	John A. Neese (POP)	861	16.4
9	Farish C. Tate (D)	9,277	72.3
	J. P. Brooke (POP)	3,557	27.7
10	William H. Fleming (D)	2,290	97.6
11	William G. Brantley (D)	9,256	69.2
	J. M. Wilkinson (R)	4,112	30.8

IDAHO

		Votes	%
AL	Edgar Wilson (SIL-R-D)	17,694	45.3
	Weldon B. Heyburn (R)	13,056	33.4
	James Gunn (PP)	7,428	19.0

ILLINOIS

		Votes	%
1	James R. Mann (R)	37,506	63.2
	Rollin B. Organ (D)	20,424	34.4
2	William Lorimer (R)	27,151	52.1
	C. Porter Johnson)D)	23,354	44.8
3	George P. Foster (D)	18,463	53.3
	Hugh R. Belknap (R)	15,659	45.2
4	Thomas Cusack (D)	18,876	52.6
	Daniel W. Mills (R)	16,656	46.4
5	Edward T. Noonan (D)	19,186	53.3
	George E. White (R)	16,018	44.5
6	Henry Sherman Boutell (R)	18,283	50.7
	Emil Hoechster (D)	17,167	47.6
7	George Edmund Foss (R)	30,903	60.8
	Frank O. Rogers (D)	18,572	36.5
8	Albert J. Hopkins (R)	19,592	68.2
	John W. Leonard (D)	8,000	27.8
9	Robert R. Hitt (R)	22,165	64.9
	William H. Wagner (D)	11,020	32.3
10	George W. Prince (R)	24,469	66.1
	Francis E. Andrews (D)	12,042	32.5
11	Walter Reeves (R)	20,060	53.5
	Maurice T. Moloney (D)	16,564	44.1
12	Joseph G. Cannon (R)	21,484	59.1
	John M. Thompson (D)	14,178	39.0
13	Vespasian Warner (R)	20,635	56.6
	Jerome G. Quisenbery (D)	14,977	41.1
14	Joseph V. Graff (R)	21,417	51.6
	Sam N. Barnes (D)	19,431	46.8
15	Benjamin F. Marsh (R)	21,143	49.1
	Joseph A. Roy (D)	20,901	48.6
16	William Elza Williams (D)	21,682	54.6
	James H. Danskin (R)	17,021	42.9
17	Ben F. Caldwell (D)	23,293	51.9
	Isaac R. Mills (R)	21,053	46.9
18	Thomas M. Jett (D)	18,829	49.5
	Benjamin F. Johnston (R)	18,109	47.6
19	Joseph B. Crowley (D)	21,520	50.5
	William W. Jacobs (R)	20,006	47.0
20	James R. Williams (D)	18,321	51.5
	Theodore G. Risley (R)	16,307	45.9

	Candidates	Votes	%
21	William A. Rodenberg (R)	20,461	49.1
	Frederick J. Kern (D)	19,956	47.9
22	George W. Smith (R)	17,200	54.5
	A. B. Garrett (D)	14,131	44.8

INDIANA

		Votes	%
1	James A. Hemenway (R)	20,383	50.7
	Thomas Duncan (D)	19,337	48.1
2	Robert W. Miers (D)	20,245	50.3
	William R. Gardiner (R)	18,656	46.4
3	William T. Zenor (D)	21,111	55.2
	Isaac F. Whiteside (R)	16,791	43.9
4	Francis M. Griffith (D)	21,751	52.2
	Charles W. Lee (R)	19,733	47.3
5	George W. Faris (R)	22,557	49.4
	Samuel R. Hamill (D)	22,305	48.8
6	James E. Watson (R)	21,048	52.6
	Charles A. Robinson (D)	18,844	47.1
7	Jesse Overstreet (R)	25,868	51.8
	Leon O. Bailey (D)	23,269	46.6
8	George W. Cromer (R)	25,388	50.1
	Orlando J. Lotz (D)	24,021	47.4
9	Charles B. Landis (R)	22,447	50.2
	Joseph B. Cheadle (D)	21,357	47.7
10	Edgar D. Crumpacker (R)	24,656	55.0
	John Ross (D)	20,206	45.0
11	George W. Steele (R)	24,367	52.7
	George W. Michael (D)	20,281	43.9
12	James M. Robinson (D)	19,484	51.3
	Christian B. Stevens (R)	18,044	47.5
13	Abraham L. Brick (R)	23,368	51.4
	Medary M. Hathaway (D)	20,886	46.0

IOWA

		Votes	%
1	Thomas Hedge (R)	17,817	54.3
	D. J. O'Connell (D)	14,568	44.4
2	Joseph R. Lane (R)	18,790	50.6
	John J. Ney (D)	17,508	47.1
3	David B. Henderson (R)	22,512	59.1
	John H. Howell (D)	15,493	40.7
4	Gilbert N. Haugen (R)	21,468	59.8
	T. T. Blaise (D)	13,849	38.6
5	Robert G. Cousins (R)	21,335	55.9
	L. J. Rowell (D)	15,970	41.9
6	John F. Lacey (R)	19,738	50.9
	James B. Weaver (D)	18,267	47.1
7	John A. T. Hull (R)	19,913	59.3
	Charles O. Holly (D)	12,261	36.5
8	William P. Hepburn (R)	22,327	53.1
	George L. Finn (D)	18,503	44.0
9	Smith McPherson (R)	21,976	54.8
	J. A. Lyons (D)	17,484	43.6
10	Jonathan P. Dolliver (R)	25,180	57.6
	Edwin Anderson (D)	17,777	40.7
11	Lot Thomas (R)	22,400	56.6
	Arthur S. Garretson (D)	16,117	40.7

KANSAS

		Votes	%
1	Charles Curtis (R)	23,899	59.6
	W. W. Price (D-PP)	16,187	40.4
2	Justin D. Bowersock (R)	21,029	52.5
	M. S. Peters (D-PP)	19,024	47.5
3	Edwin R. Ridgely (D-PP)	21,739	51.4
	S. S. Kirkpatrick (R)	20,589	48.6
4	James M. Miller (R)	20,312	53.9
	Henderson S. Martin (D-PP)	17,410	46.2
5	William A. Calderhead (R)	18,991	53.5
	W. D. Vincent (D-PP)	16,508	46.5
6	William A. Reeder (R)	16,833	49.7
	N. B. McCormick (PP)	14,732	43.5
	William G. Hoffer (D)	2,334	6.9

KANSAS

	Candidates	Votes	%
7	Chester I. Long (R)	26,622	51.7
	Jerry Simpson (D-PP)	24,834	48.3
AL	Willis J. Bailey (R)	147,691	52.5
	J. D. Botkin (D-PP)	130,801	46.5

KENTUCKY

		Votes	%
1	Charles K. Wheeler (D)	10,580	67.7
	G. W. Reeves (R)	5,036	32.2
2	Henry D. Allen (D)	8,939	57.3
	W. T. Fowler (R)	4,463	28.6
	G. W. Jolly (I)	1,641	10.5
3	John S. Rhea (D)	14,771	54.9
	M. P. Creel (R)	11,748	43.7
4	David H. Smith (D)	16,696	55.3
	Charles Biford (R)	12,826	42.5
5	Oscar Turner (D)	14,770	49.6
	Walter Evans (R)	14,202	47.7
6	Albert S. Berry (D)	13,130	59.4
	W. M. Donson (R)	8,962	40.6
7	Evan E. Settle (D)	12,904	67.7
	T. J. Hardin (R)	6,168	32.3
8	George G. Gilbert (D)	13,047	50.8
	G. M. Davson (R)	12,206	47.5
9	Samuel J. Pugh (R)	✓	
	Mordecal Williams (D)		
10	Thomas Y. Fitzpatrick (D)	13,456	54.1
	W. J. Seitz (R)	11,402	45.9
11	Vincent Boreing (R)	15,706	51.5
	J. D. White (IR)	11,324	37.2
	H. H. Tye (D)	3,319	10.9

LOUISIANA

		Votes	%
1	Adolph Meyer (D)	5,422	85.8
	C. W. Keeting (R)	896	14.2
2	Robert C. Davey (D)	6,802	86.6
	Frank N. Wicker (R)	1,054	13.4
3	Robert F. Broussard (D)	4,928	84.9
	Charles Fontelleu (R)	874	15.1
4	Phanor Breazeale (D)	4,524	75.3
	Hardy L. Brian (POP)	1,476	24.6
5	Samuel T. Baird (D)	3,558	74.0
	J. G. Taliaferro (R)	1,096	22.8
6	Samuel M. Robertson (D)	2,494	99.6

MAINE

		Votes	%
1	Thomas B. Reed (R)	14,598	59.8
	L. F. McKinney (D)	9,072	37.2
2	Nelson Dingley Jr. (R)	15,149*	63.7
	John Scott (D)	8,126	34.2
3	Edwin C. Burleigh (R)	12,854	64.3
	F. W. Plaisted (D)	6,634	33.2
4	Charles A. Boutelle (R)	12,380	66.5
	A. J. Chase (D)	5,534	29.7

Special Election

		Votes	%
1	Amos L. Allen (R)	12,337	61.6
	L. F. McKinney (D)	7,705	38.4

MARYLAND

		Votes	%
1	John W. Smith (D)	16,748	47.9
	W. F. Jackson (R)	15,823	45.3
	J. Swann (P)	1,823	5.2
2	William B. Baker (R)	20,806	48.4
	Richard Tippett (D)	20,436	47.5
3	Frank C. Wachter (R)	17,508	49.1
	J. Schwatka (D)	17,386	48.8
4	James W. Denny (D)	17,260	48.8
	William McIntire (R)	16,664	47.1
5	Sydney E. Mudd (R)	17,248	52.1
	J. S. Cummings (D)	14,672	44.3
6	George Alexander Parre (R)	18,878	54.8
	T. A. Poffenberger (D)	14,372	41.8

MASSACHUSETTS

	Candidates	Votes	%
1	George P. Lawrence (R)	14,315	58.0
	Charles P. Davis (D)	8,760	35.5
	Edward A. Buckland (SOC LAB)	1,602	6.5
2	Frederick H. Gillett (R)	13,327	60.3
	Robert E. Bisbee (D)	8,054	36.5
3	John R. Thayer (D)	11,167	50.4
	Joseph H. Walker (R)	11,008	49.6
4	George W. Weymouth (R)	14,411	62.9
	I. Porter Morse (D)	8,485	37.1
5	William S. Knox (R)	14,737	51.8
	Joseph J. Flynn (D)	13,716	48.2
6	William H. Moody (R)	13,494	64.5
	E. Moody Boynton (D)	6,035	28.9
	Albert L. Gillen (D SOCIAL)	1,390	6.6
7	Ernest W. Roberts (R)	16,559	55.8
	Walter L. Ramsdell (D)	12,338	41.6
8	Samuel W. McCall (R)	14,935	69.9
	George A. Perkins (D)	5,846	27.4
9	John F. Fitzgerald (D)	10,303	48.7
	Franz H. Krebs (R)	5,450	25.8
	James A. Gallvan (DI)	5,000	23.6
10	Henry F. Naphen (D)	17,149	55.2
	Samuel J. Barrows (R)	13,909	44.8
11	Charles F. Sprague (R)	17,001	61.3
	William H. Baker (D)	10,709	38.6
12	William C. Lovering (R)	13,653	65.9
	Philip E. Brady (D)	6,210	30.0
13	William S. Greene (R)	13,463	68.6
	Charles T. Luce (D)	4,868	24.8
	Thomas Stevenson (SOC LAB)	1,287	6.6

MICHIGAN

		Votes	%
1	John B. Corliss (R)	16,659	51.2
	James H. Pound (DPUS)	15,401	47.3
2	Henry C. Smith (R)	21,912	51.2
	Orrin R. Pierce (DPUS)	19,999	46.7
3	Washington Gardner (R)	21,182	51.6
	Albert M. Todd (DPUS)	19,864	48.4
4	Edward L. Hamilton (R)	21,740	54.8
	Roman I. Jarvis (DPUS)	17,146	43.2
5	William Alden Smith (R)	22,021	56.8
	George R. Perry (DPUS)	16,064	41.4
6	Samuel W. Smith (R)	22,981	55.8
	Charles Fishbeck (DPUS)	17,171	41.7
7	Edgar Weeks (R)	18,623	58.6
	Fred E. Burton (DPUS)	12,888	40.5
8	Joseph W. Fordney (R)	16,798	52.7
	Ferdinand Brucker (DPUS)	15,089	47.3
9	Roswell P. Bishop (R)	15,687	61.3
	Chauncey J. Chaddock (DPUS)	9,291	36.3
10	Rousseau O. Crump (R)	16,482	55.3
	Robert J. Kelly (DPUS)	13,230	44.4
11	William S. Mesick (R)	18,545	59.9
	Alva W. Nichols (DPUS)	11,799	38.1
12	Carlos D. Shelden (R)	19,895	66.9
	Solomon S. Curry (DPUS)	8,921	30.0

MINNESOTA

		Votes	%
1	James A. Tawney (R)	18,939	59.3
	White (PP & D)	11,931	37.3
2	James T. McCleary (R)	21,296	57.0
	Evans (D)	14,784	39.6
3	Joel P. Heatwole (R)	19,271	56.9
	Hinds (D)	13,183	38.9
4	Frederick C. Stevens (R)	15,952	54.1
	Willis (D)	11,602	39.3
5	Loren Fletcher (R)	18,736	55.4
	Caton (PP & D)	2,896	38.1
6	R. Page W. Morris (R)	22,194	50.1
	Towne (PP & D)	21,731	49.0
7	Frank M. Eddy (R)	20,409	52.6
	Ringdal (PP & D)	16,715	43.1

MISSISSIPPI

	Candidates	Votes	%
1	John M. Allen (D)	2,469	100.0
2	Thomas Spight (D)	2,949	92.9
	C. M. Haynie (POP)	167	5.3
3	Thomas C. Catchings (D)	2,068	85.1
	C. T. Jones (COLOR R)	363	14.9
4	Andrew F. Fox (D)	3,431	77.1
	Raleigh Brewer (POP)	1,020	22.9
5	John Sharp Williams (D)	4,941	97.0
6	Frank A. McLain (D)	3,276	53.7
	M. M. Evans (ID)	1,390	22.8
	N. C. Hathorn (POP)	998	16.4
	H. C. Turley (R)	427	7.0
7	Patrick Henry (D)	3,278	91.0

Special Election

		Votes	%
2	Thomas Spight (D)	2,722	46.6
	Z. M. Stephens	2,461	42.2
	L. L. Pearson	653	11.2

MISSOURI

		Votes	%
1	James T. Lloyd (D)	20,068	55.3
	Seaber (R)	15,460	42.6
2	William W. Rucker (D)	20,768	56.3
	Irwin (R)	15,627	42.4
3	John Dougherty (D)	19,560	53.1
	Goodrich (R)	16,440	44.6
4	Charles F. Cochran (D)	18,294	52.9
	Brewster (R)	16,261	47.1
5	William S. Cowherd (D)	20,487	53.6
	Welborn (R)	17,144	44.8
6	David A. De Armond (D)	16,645	52.0
	Jurden (R)	13,595	42.4
7	James Cooney (D)	22,586	55.2
	Robertson (R)	17,642	43.1
8	Richard P. Bland (D)	21,674	53.1
	Vosholl (R)	18,831	46.2
9	James Beauchamp Clark (D)	17,463	4.4
	Shackelford (R)	14,449	45.0
10	Richard Bartholdt (R)	19,850	59.3
	Gill (D)	13,254	39.6
11	Charles F. Joy (R)	21,315	52.3
	Noonan (D)	18,657	45.7
12	Charles E. Pearce (R)	15,300	52.6
	Kern (D)	12,989	44.7
13	Edward Robb (D)	20,601	52.0
	Reppy (R)	18,314	46.2
14	Willard D. Vandiver (D)	21,771	51.3
	Miley (R)	18,650	43.9
15	Maecenas E. Benton (D)	20,202	54.3
	Williams (R)	16,918	45.5

MONTANA

		Votes	%
AL	Albert J. Campbell (D)	23,351	46.9
	Thomas C. Marshall (R)	14,829	29.8
	Thomas S. Hogan (PP&SIL R)	11,607	23.3

NEBRASKA

		Votes	%
1	Elmer J. Burkett (R)	16,960	53.9
	James Manahan (D & POP)	14,466	46.0
2	David H. Mercer (R)	11,951	52.0
	G. M. Hitchcock (D & POP)	11,023	48.0
3	John S. Robinson (D & POP)	18,722	51.9
	W. F. Norris (R)	17,333	48.1
4	William L. Stark (D & POP)	18,904	50.7
	E. H. Hinshaw (R)	18,377	49.3
5	Roderick D. Sutherland (D & POP)	16,354	51.4
	C. E. Adams (R)	15,487	48.6
6	William L. Greene (D & POP)	15,415	53.5
	Norris Brown (R)	13,401	46.5

NEVADA

Candidates	Votes	%
AL Francis G. Newlands (D SIL)	5,766	65.0
Thomas Wren (PP)	3,111	35.1

NEW HAMPSHIRE

Candidates	Votes	%
1 Cyrus A. Sulloway (R)	21,373	52.2
Edgar J. Knowlton (D)	18,518	45.2
2 Frank G. Clarke (R)	22,395	55.5
Warren F. Daniell (D)	17,266	42.8

NEW JERSEY

Candidates	Votes	%
1 Henry C. Loudenslager (R)	23,864	54.3
Samuel Iredell (D)	18,102	41.2
2 John J. Gardner (R)	24,035	56.1
John F. Hall (D)	17,367	40.5
3 Benjamin F. Howell (R)	19,412	49.8
Patrick Convery (D)	18,683	48.0
4 Joshua S. Salmon (D)	17,866	51.5
John I. Blair Reiley (R)	15,207	43.8
5 James F. Stewart (R)	18,367	50.6
Francis J. Marley (D)	16,342	45.0
6 Richard Wayne Parker (R)	23,843	52.5
Henry G. Atwater (D)	20,150	44.4
7 William D. Daly (D)	30,270	57.8
Zebina K. Pangborn (R)	20,162	38.5
8 Charles N. Fowler (R)	20,230	54.1
Edward H. Snyder (D)	15,878	42.4

NEW YORK

Candidates	Votes	%
1 Townsend Scudder (D)	22,893	49.8
Joseph M. Belford (R)	22,483	48.9
2 John J. Fitzgerald (D)	18,431	55.6
Denis M. Hurley (R)	14,323	43.2
3 Edmund H. Driggs (D)	20,995	50.7
William A. Prendergast (R)	19,872	48.0
4 Bertram T. Clayton (D)	24,581	52.8
Israel T. Fischer (R)	20,893	44.9
5 Frank E. Wilson (D)	19,579	51.4
Charles E. Bennett (R)	16,669	43.8
6 Mitchell May (D)	16,215	55.4
Henry C. Fischer (R)	11,899	40.6
7 Nicholas Muller (D)	14,122	66.5
Charles Wilmot Townsend (R)	6,639	31.3
8 Daniel J. Riordan (D)	10,716	58.6
John Murray Mitchell (R)	7,347	40.2
9 Thomas J. Bradley (D)	11,694	56.8
John Stiebling (R)	6,447	31.3
Lucien Sanial (SOC LAB)	2,396	11.7
10 Amos J. Cummings (D)	18,859	62.8
Elijah M. Fisher (R)	10,620	35.4
11 William Sulzer (D)	14,364	62.8
William Volkel (R)	6,178	27.0
Howard Balkam (SOC LAB)	2,310	10.1
12 George B. McClellan (D)	15,108	64.5
Howard Conkling (R)	7,710	32.9
13 Jefferson M. Levy (D)	17,985	59.8
James W. Perry (R)	11,393	37.9
14 William Astor Chanler (D)	31,604	54.3
Lemuel E. Quigg (R)	25,209	43.3
15 Jacob Ruppert Jr. (D)	31,292	57.8
Philip B. Low (R)	20,848	38.5
16 John Q. Underhill (D)	32,578	54.6
James Irving Burns (R)	26,130	43.8
17 Arthur S. Tompkins (R)	19,195	54.2
Samuel D. Roberson (D)	15,564	43.9
18 John H. Ketcham (R)	23,276	55.1
Thomas E. Benedict (D)	18,348	43.4
19 Aaron V. S. Cochrane (R)	19,553	49.1
John Henry Livingston (D)	19,565	49.1
20 Martin H. Glynn (D)	20,026	50.1
George N. Southwick (R)	19,475	48.7
21 John K. Stewart (R)	25,561	50.9
Stephen L. Mayham (D)	23,347	46.5
22 Lucius N. Littauer (R)	27,083	61.3
Dennis B. Lucy (D)	15,448	35.0

Candidates	Votes	%
23 Louis W. Emerson (R)	25,662	96.3
24 Charles A. Chickering (R)	23,991	58.9
Eber T. Strickland (D)	15,724	38.6
25 James S. Sherman (R)	22,368	52.8
Walter Ballou (D)	19,160	45.2
26 George W. Ray (R)	30,007	58.6
Edward E. Pease (D)	19,199	37.5
27 Michael E. Driscoll (R)	26,025	56.5
George H. Gilbert (D)	14,207	30.9
Thomas Crimmins	2,434	5.3
John McCarthy	2,433	5.3
28 Sereno E. Payne (R)	29,536	59.4
John H. Young (D)	18,831	37.9
29 Charles W. Gillet (R)	22,348	52.7
Albert L. Childs (D)	18,311	43.2
30 James W. Wadsworth (R)	25,799	55.8
James T. Gordon (D)	18,911	40.9
31 James M. E. O'Grady (R)	20,717	51.8
John R. Fanning (D)	17,227	43.1
32 William H. Ryan (D)	15,546	49.5
Rowland B. Mahany (R)	14,858	47.4
33 De Alva S. Alexander (R)	22,924	55.8
Harvey W. Richardson (D)	17,233	41.9
34 Warren B. Hooker (R)	25,856*	62.8
William J. Sanbury (D)	13,666	33.2

NORTH CAROLINA

Candidates	Votes	%
1 John H. Small (D)	19,732	51.8
Harry Skinner (POP & R)	18,263	47.9
2 George H. White (R)	17,560	49.5
William E. Fountain (D)	14,947	42.1
James B. Lloyd (POP)	2,447	6.9
3 Charles R. Thomas (D)	16,008	50.3
John E. Fowler (POP & R)	15,819	49.7
4 John M. Atwater (POP & D)	19,416	51.1
Joseph J. Jenkins (POP & R)	18,577	48.9
5 William W. Kitchin (D)	20,869	52.9
Spencer B. Adams (POP & R)	18,607	47.1
6 John D. Bellamy (D)	23,213	57.2
Oliver H. Dockery (POP & R)	17,359	42.8
7 Theodore F. Kluttz (D)	20,733	58.5
Morrison H. Caldwell (POP)	14,651	41.3
8 Romulus Z. Linney (POP & R)	17,414	51.7
Edward F. Lovell (D)	16,137	47.9
9 William T. Crawford (D)	19,606‡	50.2
Richmond Pearson (POP)	19,368	49.6

NORTH DAKOTA

Candidates	Votes	%
AL Burleigh F. Spalding (R)	27,776	60.9
Creel (FUS)	17,844	39.1

OHIO

Candidates	Votes	%
1 William B. Shattuc (R)	20,132	58.5
John F. Follett (D)	13,980	40.6
2 Jacob H. Bromwell (R)	22,506	58.0
Charles L. Swain (D)	15,998	41.3
3 John L. Brenner (D)	21,449	50.1
William J. White (R)	21,327	49.9
4 Robert B. Gordon (D)	18,020	57.7
Philip Sheets (R)	12,276	39.3
5 David Meekison (D)	19,264	54.1
Alfred N. Wilcox (R)	15,612	43.9
6 Seth W. Brown (R)	19,896	54.0
Lewis H. Whiteman (D)	16,206	44.0
7 Walter L. Weaver (R)	17,565	49.5
John L. Zimmerman (D)	17,159	48.4
8 Archibald Lybrand (R)	21,560	51.6
Harvey Walter Doty (D)	19,156	45.8
9 James H. Southard (R)	21,913	54.8
Samuel E. Niece (D)	18,081	45.2
10 Stephen Morgan (R)	19,297	58.4
Alva Crabtree (D)	13,769	41.6
11 Charles H. Grosvenor (R)	19,806	54.6
Charles E. Peoples (D)	16,434	45.3

Candidates	Votes	%
12 John J. Lentz (D)	21,232	50.2
Edward N. Huggins (R)	20,530	48.6
13 James A. Norton (D)	21,410	54.1
Henry L. Wenner (R)	17,606	44.5
14 Winfield Kerr (R)	22,464	54.0
Thomas A. Gruber (D)	19,134	46.0
15 Henry Clay Van Voorhis (R)	19,404	54.0
Henry R. Stanbery (D)	16,509	46.0
16 Lorenzo Danford (R)	16,263	54.9
Elliott D. Moore (D)	13,377	45.1
17 John A. McDowell (D)	19,989	55.5
George E. Broome (R)	16,016	44.5
18 Robert W. Tayler (R)	22,635	51.8
Charles C. Weybrecht (D)	19,575	44.8
19 Charles Dick (R)	23,358	64.9
Isaac H. Phelps (D)	12,612	35.1
20 Fremont O. Phillips (R)	16,894	56.5
William J. Hart (D)	11,992	40.1
21 Theodore E. Burton (R)	17,599	59.2
Lemuel A. Russell (D)	10,823	36.4

Special Election

	Votes	%
19 Charles Dick (R)	23,359	65.0
Unidentified Candidate (D)	12,574	35.0

OREGON

Candidates	Votes	%
1 Thomas H. Tongue (R)	21,324	49.0
R. M. Veatch (FUS)	19,287	44.3
2 Malcolm A. Moody (R)	21,291	54.2
C. M. Donaldson (FUS)	14,634	37.2
H. E. Courtney (POP)	2,273	5.8

PENNSYLVANIA

Candidates	Votes	%
1 Henry H. Bingham (R)	25,665	72.1
Michael Francis Doyle (D)	8,213	23.1
2 Robert Adams Jr. (R)	19,547	83.5
Herman V. Hetzel (D)	3,850	16.5
3 William McAleer (R, D)	18,321	98.3
4 James Rankin Young (R)	41,627	72.7
Gideon Sibley (D)	12,250	21.4
Clinton C. Hancock (P)	3,372	5.9
5 Alfred C. Harmer (R)	39,239	79.8
Frank D. Wright (D)	9,942	20.2
6 Thomas S. Butler (BC)	15,169	53.7
John B. Robinson (ROBINSON, HG)	6,537	23.6
William H. Berry (D, L)	6,514	23.1
7 Irving P. Wanger (R)	21,567	53.1
Clinton Rorer (D)	17,782	44.0
8 Laird H. Barber (D)	16,400	54.8
William S. Kirkpatrick (R)	13,516	45.2
9 Daniel Ermentrout (D)	24,137	57.3
Jeremiah S. Parvin (R)	16,613	39.4
10 Marriott Brosius (R)	17,482	67.9
A. J. Steinman (D)	7,083	27.5
11 William Connell (R)	11,404	46.1
M. F. Sando (D)	9,861	39.8
Freeman Leach (P, HG)	3,164	12.8
12 Stanley W. Davenport (D)	17,220	49.9
Morgan B. Williams (R)	15,772	45.7
13 James W. Ryan (D)	15,042	54.2
Charles N. Brumm (R)	12,542	45.2
14 Marlin E. Olmsted (R)	19,352	60.8
Wilson W. Gray (D)	9,926	31.2
Lee L. Grumbine (P)	2,564	8.1
15 Charles Frederick Wright (R)	14,541	55.3
Archibald B. Gammell (D)	9,331	35.5
Chauncey S. Russell (P)	2,416	9.2
16 Horace B. Packer (R)	15,839	49.4
Jonathan F. Strieby (D)	12,858	40.1
Lewis P. Thurston (P)	3,378	10.5
17 Rufus K. Polk (D)	14,792	51.8
William Hartman Woodin (R)	12,487	43.8
18 Thaddeus M. Mahon (R)	17,722	57.8
Robert McMeen (D)	12,921	42.2

PENNSYLVANIA

Candidates	Votes	%
19 Edward D. Ziegler (D)	20,126	51.4
Robert J. Lewis (R)	19,016	48.6
20 Joseph E. Thropp (R)	19,358	48.9
James M. Walters (D)	17,858	45.2
John J. Irwin (P)	2,091	5.3
21 Summers M. Jack (R)	23,277	55.7
Jacob R. Spiegel (D)	16,191	38.7
Thomas J. Baldridge (P)	2,360	5.6
22 John Dalzell (R)	25,693	66.6
George W. Acklin (D)	11,049	28.6
23 William H. Graham (R)	14,008	68.1
John H. Stevenson (D)	5,608	27.3
24 Ernest F. Acheson (R)	25,524	54.5
Mark M. Cochran (D)	21,290	45.5
25 Joseph B. Showalter (R)	18,220	51.3
M. L. Lockwood (D)	15,271	43.0
John A. Bailey (P)	2,006	5.7
26 Athelston Gaston (D)	13,516	47.8
George H. Higgins (R)	13,482	47.6
27 Joseph C. Sibley (D)	14,138	52.1
Charles W. Stone (R)	11,757	43.3
28 James K. P. Hall (D)	17,550	52.1
William C. Arnold (R)	14,209	42.2
George W. Rheem (P)	1,898	5.6
AL Galusha A. Grow (R)	532,890✔	
Samuel A. Davenport (R)	520,774✔	
Jerry N. Weiler (D, PP)	357,500	
Franklin P. Iams (D)	350,214	
George H. Garber (P)	48,600	
Pennock E. Sharpless (P)	47,543	
John R. Root (SOC LAB)	4,495	
Donald L. Munro (SOC LAB)	4,300	
Dennis E. Johnston (PP)	3,995	
J. Acker Guss (L)	839	
Charles P. Shaw (L)	837	

RHODE ISLAND

	Votes	%
1 Melville Bull (R)	12,081	60.4
Hogan (D)	6,392	31.9
Theinert (SOC LAB)	1,081	5.4
2 Adin B. Capron (R)	9,095	52.0
Garvin (D)	6,435	36.8
Dana (SOC LAB)	1,473	8.4

SOUTH CAROLINA

	Votes	%
1 William Elliott (D)	3,030	66.5
G. W. Murray (R)	1,529	33.5
2 W. Jasper Talbert (D)	4,013	97.0
3 Asbury C. Latimer (D)	4,029	92.1
R. R. Tolbert (R)	332	7.6
4 Stanyarne Wilson (D)	4,467	96.4
5 David L. Finley (D)	4,230	100.0
6 James Norton (D)	4,765	96.9
7 J. William Stokes (D)	4,433	89.8
James Weston (R)	505	10.2

SOUTH DAKOTA

	Votes	%
AL Robert J. Gamble (R)	38,780✔	
Charles H. Burke (R)	36,295✔	
J. E. Kelley (FUS)	32,314	
F. Knowles (FUS)	32,240	
A. Jamieson (P)	882	
M. D. Alexander (P)	849	

TENNESSEE

	Votes	%
1 Walter P. Brownlow (R)	14,616	55.0
Gouchenaur (D)	11,732	44.1
2 Henry R. Gibson (R)	13,848	66.3
Davis (D)	6,904	33.1

Candidates	Votes	%
3 John A. Moon (D)	13,347	58.9
Cate (R)	9,209	40.6
4 Charles E. Snodgrass (D)	13,413	62.3
Morgan (R)	8,122	37.7
5 James D. Richardson (D)	11,087	69.8
Elliott (R)	4,800	30.2
6 John W. Gaines (D)	11,539	78.8
Napier (R)	2,088	14.3
Gill (P)	1,021	7.0
7 Nicholas N. Cox (D)	9,590	70.3
Cunningham (R)	4,055	29.7
8 Thetus W. Sims (D)	10,747	60.3
Hinkle (R)	6,549	36.8
9 Rice A. Pierce (D)	9,860	76.8
Reville (R)	2,728	21.3
10 Edward W. Carmack (D)	8,419	81.8
Vernon (R)	1,873	18.2

TEXAS

	Votes	%
1 Thomas H. Ball (D)	18,544	67.2
O. A. Blackwell (R)	5,276	19.1
Joe Eagle (POP)	3,764	13.6
2 Samuel B. Cooper (D)	22,086	68.9
T. J. Russell (POP)	7,853	24.5
J. A. McAyeal (R)	2,021	6.3
3 Reese C. De Graffenreid (D)	17,996	66.3
H. D. Wood (POP)	9,169	33.8
4 John L. Sheppard (D)	18,190	63.6
J. L. Whittle (POP)	10,409	36.4
5 Joseph W. Bailey (D)	16,978	74.1
W. S. Holt (POP)	4,345	19.0
A. W. Acheson (R)	1,487	6.5
6 Robert E. Burke (D)	25,116	65.8
T. B. Goren (POP)	9,677	25.4
A. J. Houston (R)	3,375	8.8
7 Robert L. Henry (D)	22,203	68.7
A. W. Cunningham (POP)	7,927	24.5
Russell Kingsbury (R)	2,197	6.8
8 Samuel W. T. Lanham (D)	18,580	58.1
W. J. Shands (POP)	11,138	34.9
Arthur Springer (R)	2,239	7.0
9 Albert S. Burleson (D)	20,378	61.7
G. W. Jones (POP)	12,628	38.3
10 Robert B. Hawley (R)	17,759	48.0
W. S. Robson (D)	16,462	44.5
J. W. Baird (POP)	2,604	7.0
11 Rudolph Kleberg (D)	18,319	55.5
B. L. Crouch (R)	14,687	44.5
12 James L. Slayden (D)	16,363	56.1
G. H. Nooran (R)	10,472	35.9
A. B. Surber	2,114	7.3
13 John H. Stephens (D)	25,000	73.5
J. J. Eager (POP)	8,995	26.5

UTAH

	Votes	%
AL Brigham H. Roberts (D)	35,646*	54.6
Eldridge (R)	29,603	45.4

VERMONT

	Votes	%
1 H. Henry Powers (R)	20,350	71.7
Herbert F. Brigham (D)	8,026	28.3
2 William W. Grout (R)	17,728	74.6
C. A. G. Jackson (D)	5,967	25.1

VIRGINIA

	Votes	%
1 William A. Jones (D)	8,934	66.5
Joseph A. Bristow (R)	4,270	31.8
2 William A. Young (D)	12,183‡	55.8
Richard A. Wise (R)	6,204	28.4

Candidates	Votes	%
William S. Holland (IR)	3,445	15.8
3 John Lamb (D)	7,058	69.1
Otis H. Russell (R)	1,914	18.8
Benjamin B. Weisiger (R)	1,138	11.1
4 Sydney P. Epes (D)	8,633	57.5
R. T. Thorp (R)	5,889	39.2
5 Claude A. Swanson (D)	13,459	57.0
E. Parr (R)	9,858	41.8
6 Peter J. Otey (D)	10,759	66.9
Daniel Butler (R)	2,535	15.8
Charles A. Heermans (R)	2,310	14.4
7 James Hay (D)	9,841	77.1
D. C. O'Flaherty (D SIL)	2,931	23.0
8 John F. Rixey (D)	6,469	88.6
Edward Hughes (I)	616	8.4
9 William F. Rhea (D)	17,344	51.0
James A. Walker (R)	16,595	48.8
10 Julian M. Quarles (D)	10,784	56.1
Robert T. Hubard (R)	8,377	43.6

WASHINGTON

	Votes	%
AL Wesley L. Jones (R)	39,809✔	
Francis W. Cushman (R)	38,983✔	
James Hamilton Lewis (PP)	36,385	
William C. Jones (PP)	32,903	
A. C. Dickenson (P)	1,169	
C. L. Haggard (P)	1,037	
M. A. Hamilton (SOC LAB)	929	
Walter Walker (SOC LAB)	897	

WEST VIRGINIA

	Votes	%
1 Blackburn B. Dovener (R)	20,891	51.9
J. V. Blair (R)	19,031	47.3
2 Alston G. Dayton (R)	23,364	50.3
John T. McGraw (D)	22,720	49.0
3 David Johnston (D)	22,802	50.6
William S. Edwards (R)	22,037	48.9
4 Romeo H. Freer (R)	21,727	50.8
George I. Neal (D)	20,896	48.8

WISCONSIN

	Votes	%
1 Henry Allen Cooper (R)	19,887	61.5
Clinton Babbitt (D)	11,447	35.4
2 Herman B. Dahle (R)	16,892	50.4
James E. Jones (D)	15,768	47.0
3 Joseph W. Babcock (R)	19,195	59.5
Thomas L. Cleary (D)	12,037	37.3
4 Theobald Otjen (R)	15,903	47.3
Joseph G. Donnelly (D)	14,022	41.7
Robert Schilling (PP)	2,227	6.6
5 Samuel S. Barney (R)	17,056	51.8
Charles E. Armin (D)	13,233	40.2
6 James H. Davidson (R)	20,107	53.6
Frank C. Stewart (D)	1,680	44.5
7 John J. Esch (R)	16,136	64.7
John F. Doherty (D)	8,128	32.6
8 Edward S. Minor (R)	16,910	54.2
Philip Sheridan (D)	13,668	43.8
9 Alexander Stewart (R)	20,825	58.1
Wells M. Ruggles (D)	14,373	401
10 John J. Jenkins (R)	17,601	63.2
John R. Mathews (D)	8,435	30.3

WYOMING

	Votes	%
AL Frank W. Mondell (R)	10,762	54.7
Constantine P. Arnold (D)	8,466	43.0

1899 House Elections

MAINE

Special Election

Candidates	Votes	%
2 Charles E. Littlefield (R)	11,624	81.0
John Scott (D)	2,736	19.1

MISSOURI

Special Election

	Votes	%
8 Dorsey W. Shackleford (D)	19,331	53.6
W. J. Vosholl (R)	15,858	44.0

NEBRASKA

Special Election

Candidates	Votes	%
6 William Neville (FUS)	18,759	53.4
Moses P. Kinkaid (R)	16,399	46.6

NEW YORK

Special Election

	Votes	%
34 Edward B. Vreeland (R)	21,773	63.7
S. E. Lewis (D)	12,406	36.3

OHIO

Special Election

Candidates	Votes	%
16 Joseph J. Gill (R)	19,368	55.5
Lavosier Spence (D)	15,302	43.8

PENNSYLVANIA

Special Election

	Votes	%
9 Henry D. Green (D)	17,736	59.9
Jeremiah S. Parvin	11,878	40.1

1900 House Elections

ALABAMA

	Candidates	Votes	%
1	George Taylor (D)	9,804	82.7
	John W. Schell (R)	2,046	17.3
2	Ariosto A. Wiley (D)	12,496	98.3
3	Henry Clayton (D)	13,420	80.2
	W. O. Mulkey (POP & R)	3,179	19.0
4	Sidney J. Bowie (D)	10,733	97.3
5	Charles W. Thompson (D)	15,767	66.9
	Andrew J. Milstead (R)	7,782	33.0
6	John Bankhead (D)	8,073	65.7
	Thomas B. Morton (R)	4,218	34.3
7	John L. Burnett (D)	10,549	51.8
	N. B. Spears (R)	9,802	48.2
8	William Richardson (D)	13,193	59.7
	A. N. Holland (R)	8,900	40.3
9	Oscar Underwood (D)	10,591	99.9

Special Election

		Votes	%
8	William Richardson (D)	14,632	84.8
	Cutler Smith (R)	2,631	15.2

ARKANSAS

		Votes	%
1	Philip D. McCulloch (D)	17,066	72.4
	T. O. Fitzpatrick (R)	6,496	27.6
2	John S. Little (D)	13,792	67.9
	E. H. Vance Jr. (R)	6,522	32.1
3	Thomas C. McRae (D)	14,945	63.3
	B. M. Foreman (R)	8,664	36.7
4	Charles C. Reid (D)	12,336	65.3
	Sam Davis (R)	6,556	34.7
5	Hugh A. Dinsmore (D)	13,924	61.1
	U. S. Bratton (R)	8,885	39.0
6	Stephen Brundidge Jr. (D)	12,256	68.9
	C. F. Cole (R)	5,527	31.1

CALIFORNIA

		Votes	%
1	Frank L. Coombs (R)	21,227	55.3
	James F. Farraher (D)	16,270	42.4
2	Samuel D. Woods (R)	23,019	50.4
	J. D. Sproul (D)	21,851	47.9
3	Victor H. Metcalf (R)	22,109	58.3
	Frank Freeman (D)	14,408	38.0
4	Julius Kahn (R)	18,904	56.8
	R. Porter Ashe (D)	12,336	37.1
5	Eugene F. Loud (R)	21,651	54.4
	J. H. Henry (D)	16,781	42.1
6	James McLachlan (R)	27,081	51.8
	William Graves (D)	19,793	37.9
	Unidentified Candidate (SOC LAB)	3,674	7.0
7	James Carson Needham (R)	23,450	52.4
	W. D. Crichton (D)	18,981	42.4

Special Election

		Votes	%
2	Samuel D. Woods (R)	22,799	51.0
	J. D. Sproul (D)	21,917	49.0

COLORADO

		Votes	%
1	John F. Shafroth (FUS)	54,591	55.3
	Robert W. Bonynge (R)	41,518	42.1
2	John C. Bell (FUS)	66,361	56.0
	Herschel M. Hogg (R)	51,287	43.3

CONNECTICUT

		Votes	%
1	E. Stevens Henry (R)	25,048	58.2
	Tuttle (D)	16,836	39.1
2	Nehemiah D. Sperry (R)	33,205	52.9
	Gildersleeve (D)	28,349	45.2

	Candidates	Votes	%
3	Charles A. Russell (R)	14,727	60.4
	Potter (D)	9,284	38.1
4	Ebenezer J. Hill (R)	29,579	58.2
	Lyman (D)	20,520	40.3

DELAWARE

		Votes	%
AL	Lewis Heisler Ball (R)	22,353	53.1
	Alexander M. Daly (D)	19,157	45.5

Special Election

		Votes	%
AL	Walter O. Hoffecker (R)	22,389	53.5
	Edward Fowler (D)	19,012	45.4

FLORIDA

		Votes	%
1	Stephen M. Sparkman (D)	13,440	87.0
	G. Brown Patterson (R)	2,005	13.0
2	Robert W. Davis (D)	13,011	80.0
	John M. Cheney (R)	3,259	20.0

GEORGIA

		Votes	%
1	Rufus E. Lester (D)	7,272	64.0
	W. R. Leaken (R)	4,098	36.0
2	James M. Griggs (D)	7,299	99.7
3	Elijah B. Lewis (D)	6,119	99.9
4	William C. Adamson (D)	7,234	76.0
	A. H. Freeman (R)	2,238	23.5
5	Leonidas F. Livingston (D)	8,828	76.6
	Charles I. Brannan (I)	2,685	23.3
6	Charles L. Bartlett (D)	7,375	94.1
	J. T. Dickey (POP)	449	5.7
7	John W. Maddox (D)	9,113	62.0
	S. J. McKnight (POP)	4,574	31.1
	J. J. Hamilton (R)	1,006	6.9
8	William H. Howard (D)	6,952	92.0
	S. P. Bond (POP)	597	7.9
9	Farish C. Tate (D)	9,140	83.6
	H. L. Peeples (POP)	1,690	15.5
10	William H. Fleming (D)	5,585	92.2
11	W. G. Brantley (D)	8,587	66.8
	W. H. Marston (R)	4,263	33.2

IDAHO

		Votes	%
AL	Thomas L. Glenn (POP & D)	28,079	51.1
	J. T. Morrison (R)	26,860	48.9

ILLINOIS

		Votes	%
1	James R. Mann (R)	52,775	63.0
	Leon Hornstein (D)	28,858	34.5
2	John J. Feely (D)	34,946	50.1
	William Lorimer (R)	32,921	47.2
3	George P. Foster (D)	23,142	55.4
	William E. O'Neill (R)	17,920	42.9
4	James McAndrews (D)	24,435	54.4
	Daniel W. Mills (R)	19,346	43.1
5	William F. Mahoney (D)	23,648	53.8
	Charles C. Carnahan (R)	19,254	43.8
6	Henry Sherman Boutell (R)	22,655	49.5
	Emil Hoechster (D)	22,125	48.3
7	George Edmund Foss (R)	41,841	57.5
	William Peacock (D)	28,581	39.3
8	Albert J. Hopkins (R)	32,452	68.5
	John W. Leonard (D)	13,683	28.9
9	Robert R. Hitt (R)	32,616	65.7
	Hiram A. Brooks (D)	15,692	31.6
10	George W. Prince (R)	33,454	65.2
	Lavergne B. DeForest (D)	16,699	32.6

	Candidates	Votes	%
11	Walter Reeves (R)	25,367	56.1
	Edgar P. Holley (D)	18,835	41.6
12	Joseph G. Cannon (R)	30,633	60.2
	C. M. Briggs (D)	19,226	37.8
13	Vespasian Warner (R)	26,865	56.2
	John Eddy (D)	19,397	40.6
14	Joseph V. Graff (R)	25,169	49.5
	Jesse Black Jr (D)	24,775	48.7
15	J. Ross Mickey (D)	24,491	49.5
	Benjamin F. Marsh (R)	24,175	48.8
16	Thomas J. Selby (D)	25,795	55.7
	Thomas Worthington (R)	19,618	42.3
17	Ben F. Caldwell (D)	25,673	51.2
	David Ross (R)	23,648	47.2
18	Thomas M. Jett (D)	22,847	50.8
	John Jacob Brenholt (R)	21,245	47.2
19	Joseph B. Crowley (D)	24,536	50.7
	Horace S. Clark (R)	23,057	47.6
20	James R. Williams (D)	21,976	51.8
	Alexander M. Funkhouser (R)	19,716	46.4
21	Frederick J. Kern (D)	25,299	49.8
	William A. Rodenberg (R)	24,810	48.8
22	George W. Smith (R)	22,349	55.5
	Lindorf O. Whitnel (D)	17,528	43.6

INDIANA

		Votes	%
1	James H. Hemenway (R)	22,262	49.7
	Alfred Dale Owen (D)	22,060	49.3
2	Robert W. Miers (D)	24,420	51.8
	Peter R. Wadsworth (R)	21,799	46.3
3	William T. Zenor (D)	24,049	54.9
	Hugh T. O'Conner (R)	19,440	44.4
4	Francis M. Griffith (D)	24,249	51.2
	Nathan Powell (R)	22,641	47.8
5	Elias S. Holliday (R)	25,932	50.6
	Frank A. Horner (D)	24,244	47.3
6	James E. Watson (R)	24,203	52.0
	David W. McKee (D)	21,320	45.8
7	Jesse Overstreet (R)	31,021	52.4
	Frank B. Burke (D)	27,012	45.7
8	George W. Cromer (R)	31,949	51.7
	Joseph T. Day (D)	28,180	45.6
9	Charles B. Landis (R)	24,138	50.3
	David F. Allen (D)	22,621	47.1
10	Edgar D. Crumpacker (R)	29,537	55.5
	John Ross (D)	23,045	43.3
11	George W. Steele (R)	29,177	53.3
	William J. Houck (D)	23,688	43.2
12	James M. Robinson (D)	22,750	49.7
	Robert B. Hanna (R)	22,122	48.4
13	Abraham L. Brick (R)	26,592	51.1
	Charles C. Bower (D)	24,376	46.8

IOWA

		Votes	%
1	Thomas Hedge (R)	21,419	53.1
	D. J. O'Connell (D)	18,051	44.8
2	John N. W. Rumple (R)	23,202	50.4
	Henry Vollmer (D)	21,737	47.2
3	David B. Henderson (R)	30,181	61.4
	Willis N. Birdsall (D)	18,856	38.3
4	Gilbert N. Haugen (R)	27,659	61.2
	John Foley (D)	16,796	37.1
5	Robert G. Cousins (R)	27,124	59.5
	Daniel Kerr (D)	18,266	40.1
6	John F. Lacey (R)	22,956	53.2
	A. C. Steck (D)	19,812	45.9
7	John A. T. Hull (R)	28,508	61.6
	George C. Crozier (D)	16,365	35.4
8	William P. Hepburn (R)	26,798	54.7
	V. R. McGinnis (D)	21,347	43.6
9	Walter I. Smith (R)	27,155	56.8
	S. B. Wadsworth (D)	20,207	42.3

IOWA

	Candidates	Votes	%
10	James P. Conner (R)	36,584	62.9
	Robert F. Dale (D)	20,648	35.5
11	Lot Thomas (R)	32,716	60.2
	William Muloaney (D)	20,564	37.8

Special Elections

9	Walter I. Smith (R)	27,154	57.3
	S. B. Wadsworth (D)	20,229	42.7
10	James P. Conner (R)	35,009	63.8
	Robert F. Dale (D)	19,830	36.2

KANSAS

1	Charles Curtis (R)	28,733	59.1
	George W. Glick (D-PP)	19,915	40.9
2	Justin D. Bowersock (R)	28,083	52.3
	M. S. Peters (D-PP)	25,623	47.7
3	Alfred M. Jackson (D-PP)	26,760	50.0
	George W. Wheatley (R)	26,492	49.5
4	James M. Miller (R)	24,106	53.8
	Thomas H. Grisham (D-PP)	20,670	46.2
5	William A. Calderhead (R)	22,436	53.9
	W. D. Vincent (D-PP)	19,211	46.1
6	William A. Reeder (R)	19,660	48.9
	John B. Dykes (PP)	15,083	37.6
	Tully Scott (D)	5,430	13.5
7	Chester I. Long (R)	31,479	51.2
	Claud Duval (D-PP)	29,960	48.8
AL	Charles F. Scott (R)	180,162	52.3
	J. D. Botkin (D-PP)	160,980	46.7

KENTUCKY

1	Charles K. Wheeler (D)	25,264	59.6
	Keys (R)	16,809	39.7
2	Henry D. Allen (D)	23,410	53.9
	Lynch (R)	19,788	45.6
3	John S. Rhea (D)	19,505‡	50.0
	J. McKenzie Moss (R)	19,344	49.6
4	David H. Smith (D)	24,920	53.2
	Jolly (R)	21,944	46.8
5	Harvey S. Irwin (R)	25,085	53.7
	Gregory (D)	21,374	45.8
6	Daniel L. Gooch (D)	22,572	56.7
	Shaw (R)	16,857	42.3
7	South Trimble (D)	20,325	54.7
	Stoll (R)	16,810	45.3
8	George G. Gilbert (D)	17,646	51.2
	Willms (R)	16,602	48.1
9	James N. Kehoe (D)	23,197	50.3
	Pugh (R)	22,961	49.7
10	James B. White (R)	19,443	51.8
	Hopkins (D)	18,070	48.2
11	Vincent Boreing (R)	34,406	69.2
	Smith (D)	15,281	30.8

LOUISIANA

1	Adolph Meyer (D)	9,727	81.0
	William Brophy (R)	2,274	18.9
2	Robert C. Davey (D)	11,420	77.8
	Samuel C. Heaslip (R)	3,234	22.0
3	Robert F. Broussard (D)	9,382	62.3
	Frank B. Williams (R)	5,673	37.7
4	Phanor Breazeale (D)	8,592	86.9
	F. M. Welch (R)	1,290	13.1
5	Joseph E. Ransdell (D)	6,172	90.8
	Henry E. Hardtner (R)	628	9.2
6	Samuel M. Robertson (D)	7,432	83.6
	James H. Ducote (R)	1,455	16.4

MAINE

1	Amos L. Allen (R)	17,803	60.3
	John J. Lynch (D)	10,040	34.0
	D. P. Parker (P)	1,533	5.2

	Candidates	Votes	%
2	Charles E. Littlefield (R)	19,215	61.0
	H. H. Monroe (D)	11,439	36.3
3	Edwin C. Burleigh (R)	17,057	60.7
	A. F. Gerald (D)	10,241	36.4
4	Charles A. Boutelle (R)	18,826*	66.3
	Thomas White (D)	8,765	30.9

MARYLAND

1	William H. Jackson (R)	19,714	50.2
	John P. Moore (D)	18,173	46.3
2	Albert A. Blakeney (R)	27,710	48.7
	J. F. C. Talbott (D)	27,420	48.2
3	Frank C. Wachter (R)	21,641	51.8
	Robert Fulton Leach Jr. (D)	19,570	46.8
4	Charles R. Schirm (R)	21,932	51.4
	James W. Denny (D)	20,149	47.2
5	Sydney E. Mudd (R)	20,936	54.2
	Benjamin H. Camalier (D)	17,305	44.8
6	George A. Pearre (R)	23,541	53.0
	Charles A. Little (D)	20,161	45.4

Special Election

1	Josiah L. Kerr (R)	19,320	50.9
	Edwin H. Brown (D)	18,650	49.1

MASSACHUSETTS

1	George P. Lawrence (R)	16,520	58.0
	James H. Bryan (D)	10,924	38.4
2	Frederick H. Gillett (R)	17,604	60.6
	Thomas W. Kenefick (D)	10,766	37.1
3	John R. Thayer (D)	16,039	50.2
	Charles G. Washburn (R)	15,909	49.8
4	Charles Q. Tirrell (R)	19,718	65.3
	Charles D. Lewis (D)	10,493	34.7
5	William S. Knox (R)	15,887	49.4
	Joseph J. Flynn (D)	15,466	48.1
6	William H. Moody (R)	18,328	64.6
	Daniel N. Crowley (D)	6,534	23.0
	Albert L. Gillen (D SOCIAL)	2,725	9.6
7	Ernest W. Roberts (R)	19,595	60.3
	Henry Winn (D)	10,815	33.3
8	Samuel W. McCall (R)	19,901	69.4
	Philip T. Nickerson (D)	7,970	27.8
9	Joseph A. Conry (D)	14,701	66.7
	Charles T. Witt (R)	6,633	30.1
10	Henry F. Naphen (D)	23,507	59.0
	George B. Pierce (R)	16,318	41.0
11	Samuel L. Powers (R)	21,761	60.0
	William H. Baker (D)	10,885	30.0
	Moorfield Storey (I)	2,858	7.9
12	William C. Lovering (R)	17,788	61.4
	Charles F. King (D)	7,434	25.7
	Charles E. Lowell (D SOCIAL)	2,404	8.3
13	William S. Greene (R)	16,337	69.1
	Charles T. Luce (D)	5,954	25.2

MICHIGAN

1	John B. Corliss (R)	24,785	54.0
	Rufus W. Jacklin (D)	20,295	44.2
2	Henry C. Smith (R)	26,945	52.4
	Martin A. Loennecker (D)	23,368	45.5
3	Washington Gardner (R)	25,998	53.3
	Stephen D. Williams (D)	21,306	43.6
4	Edward L. Hamilton (R)	26,883	55.6
	Roman I. Jarvis (D)	20,498	42.4
5	William Alden Smith (R)	27,898	55.6
	William F. McKnight (D)	21,497	42.8
6	Samuel W. Smith (R)	27,941	53.9
	Everett L. Bray (D)	22,532	43.4
7	Edgar Weeks (R)	22,924	57.7
	Justin R. Whiting (D)	15,938	40.1

	Candidates	Votes	%
8	Joseph W. Fordney (R)	21,522	53.5
	Wellington R. Burt (D)	17,212	42.8
9	Roswell P. Bishop (R)	21,408	62.4
	Frank L. Fowler (D)	12,197	35.5
10	Rousseau O. Crump (R)	23,308	59.3
	Lee E. Joslyn (D)	15,241	38.8
11	Archibald B. Darragh (R)	29,540	66.1
	George Killeen (D)	15,064	33.7
12	Carlos D. Shelden (R)	33,759	72.7
	Edward F. Legendre (D)	11,516	24.8

MINNESOTA

1	James A. Tawney (R)	23,112	56.0
	Brown (PP & D)	18,130	44.0
2	James T. McCleary (R)	30,558	59.8
	Mathews (PP & D)	18,933	37.1
3	Joel P. Heatwole (R)	23,110	57.7
	Schaller (PP & D)	16,498	41.2
4	Frederick C. Stevens (R)	21,322	57.7
	Stone (PP & D)	14,886	40.3
5	Loren Fletcher (R)	24,724	59.4
	Stockwell (D)	14,269	34.3
6	R. Page W. Morris (R)	31,792	55.5
	Truelson (PP & D)	24,219	42.3
7	Frank M. Eddy (R)	25,738	51.8
	Daly (PP & D)	21,012	42.3
	Aaker (P)	2,483	5.0

MISSISSIPPI

1	Ezekiel S. Candler Jr. (D)	6,749	95.4
2	Thomas Speight (D)	7,548	93.8
	John S. Burton (R)	500	6.2
3	Patrick Henry (D)	3,202	100.0
4	Andrew F. Fox (D)	8,211	86.0
	W. D. Frazee (R)	688	7.2
	Raleigh Brewer (POP)	653	6.8
5	John Sharp Williams (D)	9,385	99.9
6	Frank A. McLain (D)	7,032	87.0
	H. C. Turley (R)	1,048	13.0
7	Charles E. Hooker (D)	5,722	92.6
	N. M. Hollingsmith (MID ROAD)	457	7.4

MISSOURI

1	James T. Lloyd (D)	23,920	55.4
	Pickler (R)	19,189	44.5
2	William W. Rucker (D)	25,046	57.4
	Irwin (R)	18,485	42.4
3	John Dougherty (D)	22,993	54.5
	Leeper (R)	19,131	45.3
4	Charles F. Cochran (D)	22,211	53.1
	Kennish (R)	19,595	46.9
5	William S. Cowherd (D)	27,644	52.7
	Brown (R)	24,367	46.4
6	David A. De Armond (D)	20,017	53.9
	Jurden (R)	16,366	44.0
7	James Cooney (D)	26,834	55.4
	Parsons (R)	21,601	44.6
8	Dorsey W. Shackleford (D)	23,718	53.4
	Moore (R)	20,634	46.5
9	James Beauchamp Clark (D)	19,202	53.9
	Flagg (R)	16,451	46.1
10	Richard Bartholdt (R)	24,252	55.2
	Bolte (D)	17,848	40.7
11	Charles F. Joy (R)	28,375	51.7
	O'Malley (D)	25,607	46.6
12	James J. Butler (D)	22,104‡	53.2
	William M. Horton (R)	18,551	44.7
13	Edward Robb (D)	23,798	53.7
	Reppy (R)	20,524	46.3
14	Willard D. Vandiver (D)	26,434	53.0
	Mozley (R)	23,364	46.8
15	Maecenas E. Benton (D)	26,804	53.5
	Holmes (R)	22,678	45.3

MONTANA

	Candidates	Votes	%
AL	Caldwell Edwards (D)	28,130	45.8
	Samuel G. Murray (R)	23,207	37.8
	Cornielius F. Kelley (ID)	9,443	15.4

NEBRASKA

	Candidates	Votes	%
1	Elmer J. Burkett (R)	19,449	53.1
	George W. Berge (FUS)	16,548	45.2
2	David H. Mercer (R)	16,277	51.8
	Edgar Howard (FUS)	14,807	47.1
3	John S. Robinson (FUS)	22,425	49.4
	John R. Hays (R)	22,250	49.0
4	William L. Stark (FUS)	21,032	49.9
	John D. Pope (R)	20,435	48.5
5	Ashton C. Shallenberger (FUS)	17,688	49.4
	Webster L. Morlan (R)	17,279	48.2
6	William Neville (FUS)	17,699	48.7
	M. P. Kinkaid (R)	17,501	48.2

NEVADA

	Candidates	Votes	%
AL	Francis G. Newlands (D & SILVER)	5,975	58.8
	E. S. Farrington (R)	4,190	41.2

NEW HAMPSHIRE

	Candidates	Votes	%
1	Cyrus A. Sulloway (R)	26,072	58.6
	Timothy J. Howard (D)	17,401	39.1
2	Frank D. Currier (R)	27,440	60.0
	Henry F. Hollis (D)	17,517	38.3

NEW JERSEY

	Candidates	Votes	%
1	Henry C. Loudenslager (R)	31,942	59.7
	George Pfeiffer Jr. (D)	19,169	35.8
2	John J. Gardner (R)	31,359	62.0
	Thomas J. Prickett (D)	17,351	34.3
3	Benjamin F. Howell (R)	24,286	55.0
	James J. Bergen (D)	18,781	42.6
4	Joshua S. Salmon (D)	19,661	50.1
	H. Burdett Herr (R)	18,017	45.9
5	James F. Stewart (R)	24,323	53.6
	John Johnson (D)	19,708	43.4
6	Richard Wayne Parker (R)	32,830	60.7
	George H. Lambert (D)	19,477	36.0
7	Allan L. McDermott (D)	33,713	50.8
	Marshall Vanwinkle (R)	30,472	46.0
8	Charles N. Fowler (R)	27,121	58.8
	Edward A. S. Man (D)	17,510	38.0

Special Election

		Votes	%
7	Allan L. McDermott (D)	33,898	52.6
	Marshall Vanwinkle (R)	30,472	47.3

NEW YORK

	Candidates	Votes	%
1	Frederick Storm (R)	28,046	51.2
	Rowland Miles (D)	25,715	46.9
2	John J. Fitzgerald (D)	18,387	50.1
	Henry B. Ketcham (R)	18,066	49.2
3	Henry Bristow (R)	24,660	51.4
	Edmund H. Driggs (D)	22,904	47.7
4	Harry A. Hanbury (R)	28,596	50.8
	Bertram T. Clayton (D)	26,955	47.9
5	Frank E. Wilson (D)	22,041	49.1
	Jacob Worth (R)	21,164	47.1
6	George H. Lindsay (D)	18,073	54.7
	Bert Reiss (R)	14,460	43.8
7	Nicholas Muller (D)	13,654	58.5
	James R. O'Beirne (R)	9,323	39.9
8	Thomas J. Creamer (D)	10,330	50.1
	Richard Vancott (R)	10,157	49.3
9	Henry M. Goldfogle (D)	13,570	57.6
	Theodore Cox (R)	7,438	31.6
	Rudolph Katz (SOC LAB)	1,261	5.4
	Alexander Jones (SOCIAL D)	1,190	5.1
10	Amos J. Cummings (D)	20,585	60.9
	John Glass Jr. (R)	12,886	38.1
11	William Sulzer (D)	14,055	55.7
	Charles Schwick (R)	8,976	35.6
12	George B. McClellan (D)	15,177	57.9
	Herbert Parsons (R)	10,736	41.0
13	Oliver H. P. Belmont (D)	18,021	53.7
	William R. Wilcox (R)	14,781	44.0
14	William H. Douglas (R)	36,904	52.1
	John Sprunt Hill (D)	32,167	45.5
15	Jacob Ruppert Jr. (D)	31,592	49.6
	Elias Goodman (R)	29,837	46.8
16	Cornelius A. Pugsley (D)	37,665	48.8
	Norton P. Otis (R)	36,954	47.9
17	Arthur S. Tompkins (R)	22,663	54.9
	John D. Blauvelt (D)	17,953	43.5
18	John H. Ketcham (R)	25,618	96.4
19	William H. Draper (R)	24,104	56.3
	Edward F. McCormick (D)	17,936	41.9
20	George N. Southwick (R)	22,360	52.3
	Martin H. Glynn (D)	19,904	46.5
21	John K. Stewart (R)	30,027	53.2
	Joseph B. Handy (D)	24,965	44.3
22	Lucius N. Littauer (R)	32,436	64.5
	William L. Pert (D)	16,085	32.0
23	Louis W. Emerson (R)	30,604	65.7
	Charles A. Burke (D)	14,977	32.1
24	Albert D. Shaw (R)	27,272*	60.8
	James S. Boyer (D)	16,385	36.5
25	James S. Sherman (R)	26,782	57.5
	Henry Martin (D)	18,831	40.5
26	George W. Ray (R)	34,184	58.0
	Myron B. Ferris (D)	22,542	38.2
27	Michael E. Driscoll (R)	31,409	62.2
	Luke McHenry (D)	17,993	35.6
28	Sereno E. Payne (R)	33,998	59.2
	Robert L. Drummond (D)	21,789	37.9
29	Charles W. Gillet (R)	25,330	52.4
	Frank J. Nelson (D)	21,358	44.2
30	James W. Wadsworth (R)	29,368	56.1
	Charles Ward (D)	21,196	40.5
31	James Breck Perkins (R)	26,187	53.6
	Martin S. Mindnich (D)	20,064	41.1
32	William H. Ryan (D)	18,088	49.6
	Rowland B. Mahany (R)	17,772	48.7
33	De Alva S. Alexander (R)	29,120	59.5
	Harvey W. Richardson (D)	19,529	39.9
34	Edward B. Vreeland (R)	32,357	63.7
	Stillman E. Lewis (D)	16,547	32.6

NORTH CAROLINA

	Candidates	Votes	%
1	John H. Small (D)	18,709	57.4
	Abner Alexander (R)	9,493	29.1
	Isaac M. Meekins (IR)	4,355	13.4
2	Claude Kitchin (D)	22,901	64.6
	Joseph J. Martin (R)	12,521	35.3
3	Charles R. Thomas (D)	13,541	53.8
	John E. Fowler (POP)	11,632	46.2
4	Edward W. Pou (D)	18,929	57.1
	Jesse A. Giles (R)	13,057	39.4
5	William W. Kitchin (D)	18,538	52.5
	John R. Joyce (R)	16,687	47.3
6	John D. Bellamy (D)	18,902	72.5
	Oliver H. Dockery (R)	7,146	27.4
7	Theodore F. Kluttz (D)	15,712	52.3
	John Q. Holton (R)	13,380	44.5
8	Spencer Blackburn (R)	19,629	52.3
	John C. Buxton (D)	17,778	47.4
9	James M. Moody (R)	19,334	52.8
	William T. Crawford (D)	17,250	47.1

NORTH DAKOTA

	Candidates	Votes	%
AL	Thomas F. Marshall (R)	34,887	61.0
	Hildreth (D&I)	21,175	37.0

OHIO

	Candidates	Votes	%
1	William B. Shattuc (R)	26,434	58.2
	John B. Peaslee (D)	18,430	40.6
2	Jacob H. Bromwell (R)	28,029	54.3
	Henry Ketter (D)	22,859	44.3
3	Robert M. Nevin (R)	28,882	49.5
	Ulysses F. Bickley (D)	28,728	49.2
4	Robert B. Gordon (D)	25,870	59.9
	Edwin C. Wright (R)	17,327	40.1
5	John S. Snook (D)	22,884	54.4
	Frederick L. Hay (R)	19,176	45.6
6	Charles Q. Hildebrant (R)	24,610	54.2
	Adam Bridge (D)	20,407	45.0
7	Thomas B. Kyle (R)	24,818	54.7
	Stewart L. Tatum (D)	20,326	44.8
8	William R. Warnock (R)	26,287	54.4
	William J. Frey (D)	21,748	45.0
9	James H. Southard (R)	29,544	51.6
	Negley D. Cochran (D)	26,697	46.6
10	Stephen Morgan (R)	26,244	60.2
	James K. McClung (D)	17,369	39.8
11	Charles H. Grosvenor (R)	25,154	57.8
	Thomas H. Craig (D)	18,174	41.7
12	Emmett Tompkins (R)	25,705	49.5
	John J. Lentz (D)	25,687	49.5
13	James A. Norton (D)	29,672	56.1
	Daniel W. Locke (R)	23,062	43.6
14	William Woodburn Skiles (R)	28,021	52.6
	William G. Sharp (D)	25,247	47.4
15	Henry C. Van Voorhis (R)	22,623	51.3
	L. W. Ellenwood (D)	21,458	48.6
16	Joseph J. Gill (R)	22,838	56.0
	Marion Huffman (D)	17,926	44.0
17	John W. Cassingham (D)	26,275	55.0
	George Adams (R)	21,283	44.5
18	Robert W. Tayler (R)	31,479	54.6
	John H. Morris (D)	25,026	43.4
19	Charles Dick (R)	34,129	62.4
	Charles E. Chadman (D)	20,351	37.2
20	Jacob A. Beidler (R)	22,776	45.8
	H. B. Harrington (D)	22,087	44.4
	Fremont O. Phillips (I.R.)	3,973	8.0
21	Theodore E. Burton (R)	28,605	55.1
	Sylvester V. McMahon (D)	21,947	42.3

OREGON

	Candidates	Votes	%
1	Thomas H. Tongue (R)	21,212	49.5
	Bernard Daly (FUS-D-PO)	18,193	42.4
2	Malcolm Moody (R)	22,088	55.1
	William Smith (FUS-D-PO)	12,708	31.7
	J. E. Simmons (MID ROAD)	3,384	8.4

PENNSYLVANIA

	Candidates	Votes	%
1	Henry H. Bingham (R)	29,973	71.5
	Michael Francis Doyle (D)	11,765	28.1
2	Robert Adams Jr (R)	19,657	79.7
	William E. Hooper (D)	4,998	20.3
3	Henry Burk (R)	11,095	52.7
	William McAleer (D, MLP)	9,839	46.7
4	James Rankin Young (R)	55,648	75.5
	Peter J. Hughes (D)	17,330	23.5
5	Edward de V. Morrell (R)	45,089	75.7
	Samuel R. Carter (D)	13,898	23.3
6	Thomas S. Butler (R)	26,379	70.2
	Nathaniel M. Ellis (D)	10,098	26.9
7	Irving P. Wanger (R)	25,422	57.1
	Christopher Vanartsdalen (D)	18,542	41.7
8	Howard Mutchler (D)	18,448	51.3
	Russel C. Stewart (R)	16,753	46.6
9	Henry D. Green (D)	29,160	55.9
	William Kerper Stevens (R)	22,758	43.6
10	Marriott Brosius (R)	23,143	71.8
	Louis N. Spencer (D)	8,502	26.4

PENNSYLVANIA

	Candidates	Votes	%
11	William Connell (R)	15,536	49.5
	Michael F. Conry (D)	13,598	43.3
12	Henry W. Palmer (R)	18,931	54.3
	S. W. Davenport (A-TRUST)	13,698	39.3
13	George R. Patterson (R)	15,519	52.4
	James W. Ryan (D)	13,895	46.9
14	Marlin E. Olmsted (R)	23,726	89.5
	Edwin H. Molly (P)	1,451	5.5
	Benjamin L. Forster (D)	1,335	5.0
15	Charles F. Wright (R)	18,261	56.7
	William B. Packard (D)	12,396	38.5
16	Elias Deemer (R)	19,844	52.6
	Otto G. Kaupp (D)	16,509	43.8
17	Rufus K. Polk (D)	16,615	54.3
	Clarence F. Huth (R)	13,071	42.7
18	Thaddeus M. Mahon (R)	20,756	58.9
	James G. Heading (D)	14,464	41.1
19	Robert J. Lewis (R)	22,266	50.3
	Harry N. Gitt (D)	21,280	48.1
20	Alvin Evans (R)	30,777	62.5
	James M. Walters (D)	17,450	35.4
21	Summers M. Jack (R)	32,909	61.6
	Curtis H. Gregg (D)	19,156	35.9
22	John Dalzell (R)	36,409	69.7
	John F. Miller (D)	14,343	27.5
23	William H. Graham (R)	19,957	74.6
	John Huckenstine (D)	6,142	23.0
24	Ernest F. Acheson (R)	35,939	58.7
	Wooda N. Carr (D)	23,568	38.5
25	Joseph B. Showalter (R)	24,472	55.5
	M. L. Lockwood (D)	19,641	44.5
26	Arthur L. Bates (R)	18,723	53.6
	Athelston Gaston (D)	14,918	42.7
27	Joseph C. Sibley (R)	15,804	50.8
	Lewis Emery Jr. (D, LIN)	13,906	44.7
28	J. K. P. Hall (D)	19,132	49.5
	A. A. Clearwater (R)	18,511	47.9
AL	Galusha A. Grow (R)	683,941	
	Robert H. Foerderer (R)	675,099	
	Harry E. Grim (D)	411,552	
	Nicholas M. Edwards (D)	409,918	
	William W. Hague (P)	24,531	
	Lee L. Grumbine (P)	24,412	
	John W. Slayton (SOC)	4,026	
	Edward Kuppinger (SOC)	3,995	
	John R. Root (SOC LAB)	2,660	
	Donald L. Monro (SOC LAB)	2,657	
	Robert Bringham (PP)	795	
	George Main (PP)	775	
	Benjamin A. Bubbett	278	

Special Election

		Votes	%
5	Edward de V. Morrell (R)	34,789	100.0

RHODE ISLAND

		Votes	%
1	Melville Bull (R)	16,591	59.5
	Gorman (D)	9,498	34.0
2	Adin B. Capron (R)	13,975	57.8
	Garvin (D)	8,870	36.7

SOUTH CAROLINA

		Votes	%
1	William Elliott (D)	3,666	72.7
	W. W. Beckett (R)	1,378	27.3
2	William J. Talbert (D)	6,713	97.7
3	Asbury C. Latimer (D)	7,834	97.5
4	Joseph T. Johnston (D)	8,189	97.1
5	David E. Finley (D)	5,634	96.8
6	Robert B. Scarborough (D)	7,608	94.2
	R. A. Stuart (R)	473	5.9
7	J. William Stokes (D)	7,285	93.2
	Alexander D. Dantzler (R)	534	6.8

SOUTH DAKOTA

		Votes	%
AL	Charles H. Burke (R)	53,583	
	Eben W. Martin (R)	53,549	

	Candidates	Votes	%
	Andrew E. Lee (FUS)	40,560	
	Joseph B. Moore (FUS)	40,151	
	O. A. Harpel (P)	1,323	
	M. Rogers (P)	1,188	
	Edm. F. English (POP)	305	
	John M. Pease (POP)	304	

TENNESSEE

		Votes	%
1	Walter P. Brownlow (R)	22,374	62.8
	Reaves (D)	13,107	36.8
2	Henry R. Gibson (R)	22,062	68.7
	Park (D)	9,913	30.9
3	John A. Moon (D)	18,363	52.1
	Sharp (R)	16,591	47.1
4	Charles E. Snodgrass (D)	15,659	59.8
	Gore (R)	10,515	40.1
5	James D. Richardson (D)	14,653	68.0
	McClain (R)	6,895	32.0
6	John W. Gaines (D)	17,192	71.9
	Brock (R)	6,256	26.2
7	Lemuel P. Padgett (D)	12,636	54.4
	Fuzzell (I)	10,610	45.6
8	Thetus W. Sims (D)	14,509	53.1
	Hawkins (R)	12,258	44.8
9	Rice A. Pierce (D)	16,680	71.8
	Austin (R)	6,050	26.0
10	Malcolm R. Patterson (D)	10,218	62.1
	Taylor (R)	6,247	37.9

TEXAS

		Votes	%
1	Thomas H. Ball (D)	11,887	65.7
	S. E. Tracy (R)	5,391	29.8
2	Samuel B. Cooper (D)	31,774	98.5
3	Reese C. De Graffenreid (D)	19,091	61.0
	C. G. White (R)	12,230	39.1
4	John L. Sheppard (D)	17,647	57.6
	J. C. Gibbons (R)	9,818	32.1
	J. L. Darwin (POP)	3,154	10.3
5	Choice B. Randell (D)	28,074	90.4
	J. W. Thomas (R)	1,790	5.8
6	Robert E. Burke (D)	33,220	77.7
	S. H. Lumpkin (POP)	7,432	17.4
7	Robert L. Henry (D)	27,243	92.1
8	Samuel W. T. Lanham (D)	24,093	68.2
	J. S. Daley (POP)	6,465	18.3
	N. A. Dodge (R)	4,760	13.5
9	Albert S. Burleson (D)	25,494	91.3
	Nat Q. Henderson (R)	2,419	8.7
10	George F. Burgess (D)	18,203	59.5
	Walter C. Jones (R)	12,255	40.1
11	Rudolph Kleberg (D)	21,329	59.2
	B. L. Crouch (R)	14,706	40.8
12	James L. Slayden (D)	18,421	60.8
	C. C. Drake (R)	11,530	38.1
13	John H. Stephens (D)	30,726	85.1
	C. W. Johnson (R)	5,354	14.8

UTAH

		Votes	%
AL	George Sutherland (R)	46,180	50.1
	W. H. King (D)	45,939	49.9

VERMONT

		Votes	%
1	David J. Foster (R)	22,845	68.5
	Ozro Meacham (D)	9,441	28.3
2	Kittredge Haskins (R)	23,273	75.5
	George T. Swasey (D)	7,291	23.7

VIRGINIA

		Votes	%
1	William A. Jones (D)	16,076	64.1
	James Monroe Stubbs (R)	8,737	34.9

	Candidates	Votes	%
2	Harry L. Maynard (D)	20,113	62.2
	R. A. Wise (R)	10,203	31.6
3	John Lamb (D)	15,274	65.6
	Edgar Allan (R)	7,793	33.5
4	Francis R. Lassiter (D)	12,796	61.4
	C. E. Wilson (R)	8,058	38.6
5	Claude A. Swanson (D)	14,293	58.1
	John R. Whitehead (R)	10,292	41.9
6	Peter J. Otey (D)	15,948	77.5
	J. B. Stovall (R)	2,467	12.0
	A. E. Fairweather (I)	2,152	10.5
7	James Hay (D)	17,276	63.4
	C. M. Gibbens (R)	9,995	36.7
8	John F. Rixey (D)	17,071	63.2
	William J. Rogers (R)	9,858	36.5
9	William F. Rhea (D)	20,164	52.3
	James A. Walker (R)	18,412	47.7
10	Henry D. Flood (D)	16,064	54.3
	Robert T. Hubard (R)	12,913	43.7

Special Election

		Votes	%
4	Francis R. Lassiter (D)	3,217	98.7

WASHINGTON

		Votes	%
AL	Wesley L. Jones (R)	55,393	
	Francis W. Cushman (R)	55,268	
	J. T. Ronald (D)	45,448	
	F. C. Robertson (D)	44,882	
	Guy Posson (P)	2,239	
	J. A. Adams (P)	2,059	
	William Hogan (SOCIAL D)	1,954	
	Herman F. Titus (SOCIAL D)	1,916	
	Walter Walker (SOC LAB)	922	
	Christian F. Larsen (SOC LAB)	878	

WEST VIRGINIA

		Votes	%
1	Blackburn B. Dovener (R)	27,767	54.2
	William E. Haymond (D)	22,778	44.5
2	Alston G. Dayton (R)	27,735	51.9
	Thomas B. Davis (D)	25,347	47.4
3	Joseph Holt Gaines (R)	34,243	55.1
	David E. Johnson (D)	27,667	44.5
4	James H. Hughes (R)	28,476	53.2
	Creed Collins (D)	24,748	46.2

WISCONSIN

		Votes	%
1	Henry A. Cooper (R)	28,256	64.1
	Gilbert T. Hodges (D)	14,556	33.0
2	Herman B. Dahle (R)	22,175	52.8
	John A. Aylward (D)	18,819	44.8
3	Joseph W. Babcock (R)	26,593	63.5
	Edward L. Luckow (D)	14,017	33.5
4	Theobold Otjen (R)	24,637	49.5
	George W. Peck (D)	21,691	43.5
	Robert Meister (SOCIAL D)	2,991	6.0
5	Samuel S. Barney (R)	23,089	52.4
	Charles H. Weisse (D)	18,066	41.0
	Henry C. Berger (SOC LAB)	2,284	5.2
6	James H. Davidson (R)	26,326	55.8
	James W. Watson (D)	19,758	41.9
7	John J. Esch (R)	22,715	65.2
	John P. Rice (D)	11,254	32.3
8	Edward S. Minor (R)	25,263	60.2
	Nathan F. Morgan (D)	16,740	39.9
9	Webster E. Brown (R)	33,329	64.7
	Ernest Schweppe (D)	16,988	33.0
10	John J. Jenkins (R)	29,144	68.7
	Frank A. Partlow (D)	11,930	28.1

WYOMING

		Votes	%
AL	Frank W. Mondell (R)	14,539	59.2
	John Charles Thompson (D)	10,017	40.8

1901 House Elections

PENNSYLVANIA				TEXAS		
Special Election				**Special Election**		
Candidates	Votes	%		Candidates	Votes	%
10 Henry B. Cassel (R)	12,465	73.9		6 Dudley G. Wooten (D)	11,174	84.1
Daniel R. McCormick (D)	4,410	26.1		Philip Lindsey	2,063	15.5

Explanation of Symbols in House Returns

In the returns for House elections *symbols* are used to denote special circumstances. In cases where no symbol is used, the candidate who received the most votes won the election to the House. The following is a key to the symbols used:

✔ Elected to the House. The symbol is used to identify winning candidates in three types of situations: (1) When candidates ran for two or more at-large seats in states which chose all of their at-large representatives in a single election, or ran in a multi-member district; (2) when the vote total and percentage of one or more of the candidates are unavailable and (3) when a candidate who did not receive the highest vote total was seated by the House. *(Explanation of multi-member districts, see p. 678.)*

‡ The symbol is used when an election dispute resulted in the unseating of a representative *after* he was sworn in. *(For discussion of specific cases, consult the* Biographical Directory of the American Congress 1774-1971, *U.S. Government Printing Office, Washington, D.C. 1971; hereafter referred to as the* Biographical Directory.)

* The symbol is used for three types of situations: (1) When a representative-elect died or declined his seat before the constitutionally set date for the beginning of his term—March 4 until 1935, and Jan. 3 thereafter; (2) when the House refused to seat any candidate claiming election to a seat and (3) when state law required a candidate to obtain a popular vote majority for election to the House, but the candidate receiving the most votes failed to receive a majority. *(For discussion of specific cases, consult the* Biographical Directory; *explanation of majority vote requirement, see p. 703.)*

Information for 1824-1973 returns was obtained from a source other than the Inter-University Consortium for Political and Social Research. *(For a listing of other sources, see p. 1062.)*

Footnotes. Numbered footnotes are used to explain unusual situations, such as a series of elections in the same year in the same House district, anomalies resulting from reapportionment and special procedures for conducting House elections in certain states.

1902 House Elections

ALABAMA

	Candidates	Votes	%
1	George W. Taylor (D)	5,364	89.8
	E. B. Hubbard (R)	545	9.1
2	Ariosto A. Wiley (D)	7,696	89.9
	Julius Sternfeld (R)	861	10.1
3	Henry D. Clayton (D)	7,595	84.1
	M. W. Carden (R)	905	10.0
	J. P. Pelham (R)	535	5.9
4	Sydney J. Bowie (D)	6,880	69.3
	J. A. Edwards (R)	3,048	30.7
5	Charles W. Thompson (D)	9,043	78.4
	R. S. Nolen (R)	2,495	21.6
6	John H. Bankhead (D)	7,481	72.8
	William B. Ford (R)	2,798	27.2
7	John L. Burnett (D)	9,298	52.9
	O. D. Street (R)	8,044	45.8
8	William Richardson (D)	7,935	80.8
	James Jackson (R)	1,889	19.2
9	Oscar W. Underwood (D)	6,782	77.3
	J. Clyde Miller (R)	1,793	20.4

ARKANSAS

	Candidates	Votes	%
1	Robert B. Macon (D)	4,796	99.8
2	Stephen Brundidge Jr. (D)	4,549	84.1
	R. S. Coffman (R)	858	15.9
3	Hugh A. Dinsmore (D)	4,808	72.4
	W. L. McPherson (R)	1,833	27.6
4	John S. Little (D)	4,213	78.7
	F. A. Youmans (R)	1,142	21.3
5	Charles C. Reid (D)	4,530	79.6
	Henry M. Sugg (R)	1,161	20.4
6	Joseph T. Robinson (D)	5,195	89.3
	W. H. Carpenter (R)	622	10.7
7	Robert Minor Wallace (D)	4,730	83.0
	R. L. Floyd (R)	971	17.0

CALIFORNIA

	Candidates	Votes	%
1	James N. Gillett (R)	21,268	50.5
	Thomas S. Ford (D)	19,696	46.7
2	Theodore A. Bell (D)	21,536	49.2
	Frank L. Coombs (R)	21,181	48.3
3	Victor H. Metcalf (R)	20,532	66.2
	Calvin B. White (D)	8,574	27.7
	M. W. Wilkins (SOC)	1,556	5.0
4	Edward J. Livernash (D & UN LAB)	16,146	49.2
	Julius Kahn (R)	16,005	48.7
5	William J. Wynn (D&UN LAB)	22,712	56.5
	E. F. Loud (R)	16,577	41.2
6	James C. Needham (R)	17,268	53.5
	Gaston M. Ashe (D)	13,732	42.6
7	James McLachlan (R)	19,407	64.8
	Carl A. Johnson (D)	8,075	27.0
8	Milton J. Daniels (R)	20,135	51.9
	William E. Smythe (D)	15,819	40.8
	N. A. Richardson (SOC)	2,091	5.4

COLORADO

	Candidates	Votes	%
1	John F. Shafroth (D)	41,440‡	49.0
	Robert W. Bonynge (R)	38,648	45.7
2	Herschel M. Hogg (R)	47,546	47.6
	John C. Bell (FUS)	45,234	45.3
AL	Franklin E. Brooks (R)	85,217	46.1
	Alva Adams (D)	84,367	45.6

CONNECTICUT

	Candidates	Votes	%
1	E. Stevens Henry (R)	20,289	52.4
	O'Neil (D)	17,211	44.4
2	Nehemiah D. Sperry (R)	29,658	54.7
	Morse (D)	22,283	41.1
3	Frank B. Brandegee (R)	12,547	58.7
	Potter (D)	8,364	39.1
4	Ebenezer J. Hill (R)	24,333	54.0
	Bishop (D)	19,888	44.2
AL	George L. Lilley (R)	83,666	52.6
	Cummings (D)	70,590	44.3

Special Election

	Candidates	Votes	%
3	Frank B. Brandegee (R)	5,208	94.2

DELAWARE

	Candidates	Votes	%
AL	Henry A. Houston (D)	16,396	42.9
	William Michael Byrne (UN R)	12,998	34.0
	Lewis Heisler Ball (R)	8,028	21.0

FLORIDA

	Candidates	Votes	%
1	Stephen M. Sparkman (D)	5,597	100.0
2	Robert W. Davis (D)	6,488	100.0
3	William B. Lamar (D)	4,249	100.0

GEORGIA

	Candidates	Votes	%
1	Rufus E. Lester (D)	4,349	100.0
2	James M. Griggs (D)	3,797	100.0
3	Elijah B. Lewis (D)	2,957	100.0
4	William C. Adamson (D)	2,883	100.0
5	Leonidas F. Livingston (D)	2,485	100.0
6	Charles L. Bartlett (D)	4,522	100.0
7	John W. Maddox (D)	5,305	93.2
	S. J. McKnight (POP)	389	6.8
8	William M. Howard (D)	3,139	100.0
9	F. Carter Tate (D)	4,749	99.6
10	Thomas W. Hardwick (D)	2,675	100.0
11	William G. Brantley (D)	3,606	100.0

IDAHO

	Candidates	Votes	%
AL	Burton L. French (R)	32,384	54.3
	Joseph Henry Hutchinson (D)	24,878	41.7

ILLINOIS

	Candidates	Votes	%
1	Martin Emerich (D)	16,591	51.3
	Martin B. (R)	15,339	47.4
2	James R. Mann (R)	18,697	60.1
	Frank Brust (D)	9,532	30.6
	Bernard Berlyn (SOC)	2,332	7.5
3	William Warfield Wilson (R)	13,977	53.5
	Dan Morgan Smith Jr. (D)	10,517	40.3
4	George P. Foster (D)	14,698	92.6
	F. Finsterbach (SOC)	850	5.4
5	James McAndrews (D)	12,346	88.7
	Jacob Winnen (SOC)	1,263	9.1
6	William Lorimer (R)	16,540	49.7
	Allan C. Durborow (D)	15,555	46.7
7	Phillip Knopf (R)	18,167	51.1
	John M. Hess (D)	13,443	37.8
	James H. Bard (SOC)	3,471	9.8
8	William F. Mahoney (D)	19,688	90.6
	George D. Evans (SOC)	1,546	7.1
9	Henry Sherman Boutell (R)	15,857	50.8
	Lockwood Honore (D)	13,774	44.1
10	George Edmund Foss (R)	15,318	57.5
	John J. Philbin (D)	9,733	36.6
11	Howard M. Snapp (R)	20,549	64.1
	James O. Monroe (D)	9,968	31.1
12	Charles E. Fuller (R)	19,812	62.5
	Julian R. Steward (D)	9,356	29.5
	Frank S. Regan (P)	2,558	8.1
13	Robert R. Hitt (R)	19,229	65.5
	Louis Dickes (D)	9,401	32.0
14	Benjamin F. Marsh (R)	19,404	55.9
	John W. Lusk (D)	13,195	38.0
15	George W. Prince (R)	21,899	55.5
	Jonas W. Olson (D)	16,045	40.7
16	Joseph V. Graff (R)	19,360	54.5
	John M. Niehaus (D)	15,623	43.9
17	John A. Sterling (R)	18,331	54.4
	Z. F. Yost (D)	14,040	41.6
18	Joseph G. Cannon (R)	22,941	58.3
	Henry C. Bell (D)	15,254	38.8
19	Vespasian Warner (R)	24,155	53.3
	W. B. Hinds (D)	19,895	43.9
20	Henry T. Rainey (D)	20,165	56.5
	James H. Danskin (R)	14,889	41.7
21	Ben F. Caldwell (D)	20,774	54.0
	Leroy Anderson (R)	16,998	44.2
22	William A. Rodenberg (R)	21,101	52.6
	Fred J. Kern (D)	18,747	46.7
23	Joseph B. Crowley (D)	20,735	52.4
	Hiram Gilmore Vansandt (R)	17,557	44.4
24	James R. Williams (D)	17,971	49.5
	Pleasant T. Chapman (R)	17,719	48.8
25	George W. Smith (R)	18,743	51.9
	James Lingle (D)	16,444	45.5

INDIANA

	Candidates	Votes	%
1	James A. Hemenway (R)	21,524	52.0
	John W. Spencer (D)	17,833	43.1
2	Robert W. Miers (D)	21,162	49.5
	John C. Chaney (R)	20,423	47.7
3	William T. Zenor (D)	20,740	54.6
	Edmund A. Maginness (R)	16,784	44.2
4	Francis M. Griffith (D)	21,751	52.0
	Joshua M. Spencer (R)	18,894	45.2
5	Elias S. Holliday (R)	23,795	50.3
	John A. Wiltermood (D)	21,562	45.6
6	James E. Watson (R)	23,641	52.9
	James T. Arbuckle (D)	19,535	43.7
7	Jesse Overstreet (R)	25,191	52.0
	Jacob P. Dunn (D)	20,933	43.2
8	George W. Cromer (R)	25,842	52.0
	James Edward Truesdale (D)	21,474	43.2
9	Charles B. Landis (R)	25,824	51.0
	Lex J. Kirkpatrick (D)	23,317	46.0
10	Edgar D. Crumpacker (R)	26,016	56.4
	William Guthrie (D)	19,428	42.1
11	Frederick K. Landis (R)	24,390	52.6
	John C. Nelson (D)	19,596	42.3
	Bennet L. Shugart (P)	2,344	5.1
12	James M. Robinson (D)	19,320	48.1
	Clarence C. Gilhams (R)	19,035	47.4
13	Abraham L. Brick (R)	24,206	50.3
	Frank E. Hering (D)	22,289	46.3

IOWA

	Candidates	Votes	%
1	Thomas Hedge (R)	15,266	51.7
	John E. Craig (D)	13,343	45.2
2	Martin J. Wade (D)	19,825	49.6
	William Hoffman (R)	18,667	46.7
3	Benjamin P. Birdsall (R)	22,300	54.5
	Horace Boise (D)	16,761	40.9
4	Gilbert N. Haugen (R)	19,303	56.1
	A. L. Sortor Jr. (D)	14,280	41.5

IOWA

Candidates	Votes	%
5 Robert G. Cousins (R)	19,516	56.5
Anthony P. Daly (D)	13,733	39.8
6 John F. Lacey (R)	18,828	51.2
John P. Reese (D)	17,015	46.2
7 John A. T. Hull (R)	19,037	61.6
Parley Sheldon (D)	9,914	32.1
8 William P. Hepburn (R)	21,657	59.4
F. M. Stuart (D)	14,796	40.6
9 Walter I. Smith (R)	20,997	59.6
George W. Cullison (D)	13,639	38.7
10 James P. Connor (R)	25,596	64.1
Kasper Faltison (D)	12,822	32.1
11 Lot Thomas (R)	21,854	62.4
James M. Parsons (D)	12,721	36.3

KANSAS

Candidates	Votes	%
1 Charles Curtis (R)	23,954	62.8
John E. Wagner (D)	13,774	36.1
2 Justin D. Bowersock (R)	23,608	54.2
Noah Bowman (D)	19,250	44.2
3 Philip P. Campbell (R)	22,753	53.7
Alfred M. Jackson (D)	18,690	44.1
4 James M. Miller (R)	20,799	58.7
Thomas H. Grisham (D)	14,361	40.5
5 William A. Calderhead (R)	18,921	56.5
Andrew Sherer (D)	13,930	41.6
6 William A. Reeder (R)	18,307	53.2
C. M. Cole (D)	15,832	46.0
7 Chester I. Long (R)	30,123*	56.8
Vernon J. Rose (D)	22,300	42.1
AL Charles F. Scott (R)	158,307	56.1
J. D. Botkin (D)	115,342	40.9

KENTUCKY

Candidates	Votes	%
1 Ollie M. James (D)	12,731	66.4
C. H. Linn (R)	5,469	28.5
2 Augustus O. Stanley (D)	15,522	52.3
R. W. Slack (R)	13,675	46.1
3 John S. Rhea (D)	16,820	50.7
J. McKenzie Moss (R)	16,056	48.4
4 David H. Smith (D)	14,054	93.1
J. A. Barret (P)	881	5.8
5 J. Swagar Sherley (D)	17,896	50.0
Harvey S. Irwin (R)	15,892	44.4
6 Daniel Linn Gooch (D)	12,978	50.8
Applegate (R)	10,370	40.6
Breill (SOC)	1,683	6.6
7 South Trimble (D)	12,093	59.9
W. L. Cannon (R)	7,639	37.8
8 George G. Gilbert (D)	13,531	53.2
Lawson Sumrall (R)	11,458	45.1
9 James N. Kehoe (D)	20,823	52.4
W. H. Castner (R)	18,493	46.6
10 Frank A. Hopkins (D)	15,947	55.7
John G. White (R)	12,458	43.5
11 Vincent Boreing (R)	13,443	69.2
J. P. Harrison (D)	5,076	26.1

LOUISIANA

Candidates	Votes	%
1 Adolph Meyer (D)	3,910	81.9
Oliver S. Livaudais (R)	866	18.1
2 Robert C. Davey (D)	5,014	85.2
Robert E. Lee (R)	868	14.8
3 Robert F. Broussard (D)	2,725	79.4
William E. Howell (R)	707	20.6
4 Phanor Breazeale (D)	2,567	94.3
S. M. Thomas (R)	156	5.7
5 Joseph E. Ransdell (D)	2,645	91.9
Henry B. Taliaferro (R)	232	8.1
6 Samuel M. Robertson (D)	2,124	75.9
Clarence S. Hebert (R)	673	24.1
7 Arsene P. Pujo (D)	3,233	85.6
Gilbert L. Dupre (R)	545	14.4

MAINE

Candidates	Votes	%
1 Amos L. Allen (R)	16,232	58.2
Seth C. Gordon (D)	11,097	39.8
2 Charles E. Littlefield (R)	17,297	58.1
Horatio G. Foss (D)	11,739	39.5
3 Edwin C. Burleigh (R)	15,613	64.3
E. N. Benson (D)	8,032	33.1
4 Llewellyn Powers (R)	16,349	64.6
Thomas White (D)	7,763	30.7

MARYLAND

	Votes	%
1 William H. Jackson (R)	17,968	50.6
James E. Ellegood (D)	16,179	45.5
2 J. Fred. C. Talbott (D)	16,971	50.8
William T. Page (R)	15,422	46.2
3 Frank C. Wachter (R)	15,214	48.8
Lee S. Meyer (D)	15,031	48.2
4 James W. Denny (D)	16,105	50.0
Charles R. Schirm (R)	15,519	48.1
5 Sydney E. Mudd (R)	17,621	56.9
B. H. Camalier (D)	12,781	41.3
6 George A. Pearre (R)	18,310	54.1
C. F. Kenneweg (D)	14,479	42.8

MASSACHUSETTS

	Votes	%
1 George P. Lawrence (R)	14,093	54.0
Henry M. Fern (D)	9,949	38.1
2 Frederick H. Gillett (R)	14,067	58.1
Arthur F. Nutting (D)	6,998	28.9
George H. Wrenn (SOC)	2,779	11.5
3 John R. Thayer (D)	14,382	49.1
Rufus B. Dodge (R)	13,602	46.4
4 Charles Q. Tirrell (R)	15,660	53.4
Marcus A. Coolidge (D)	10,564	36.0
John F. Mullen (SOC)	2,739	9.3
5 Butler Ames (R)	13,648	48.4
John T. Sparks (D)	12,765	45.3
6 Augustus P. Gardner (R)	16,164	51.4
Samuel Roads Jr. (D)	12,246	39.0
George E. Littlefield (SOC)	2,679	8.5
7 Ernest W. Roberts (R)	15,728	54.3
Arthur Lyman (D)	9,034	31.2
William B. Turner (SOC)	2,811	9.7
8 Samuel W. McCall (R)	15,077	57.6
Grenville S. MacFarland (D)	8,872	33.9
Charles W. White (SOC)	1,634	6.2
9 John A. Keliher (D CIT)	10,352	38.1
Joseph A. Conry (DN)	10,099	37.2
Charles T. Witt (R)	5,108	18.8
James J. McVey (SOC)	1,581	5.8
10 William S. McNary (D)	17,569	54.1
William W. Towle (R)	11,374	35.1
John Weaver Sherman (SOC)	3,506	10.8
11 John A. Sullivan (D)	16,333	49.4
Eugene N. Foss (R)	14,467	43.8
George G. Cutting (SOC)	2,230	6.8
12 Samuel L. Powers (R)	14,807	52.6
Frederic J. Stimson (D)	10,303	36.6
J. Frank Hayward (SOC)	2,683	9.5
13 William S. Greene (R)	13,565	67.9
Charles T. Luce (D)	5,241	26.2
Elijah Humphries (P)	1,178	5.9
14 William C. Lovering (R)	14,410	57.3
Charles A. Gilday (D)	5,447	21.7
Isaac W. Skinner (SOC)	4,300	17.1

Special Election

	Votes	%
6 Augustus P. Gardner (R)	15,561	52.1
Samuel Roads Jr. (D)	11,348	38.0
George E. Littlefield (SOC)	2,606	8.7

MICHIGAN

Candidates	Votes	%
1 Alfred Lucking (D)	20,009	53.6
John B. Corliss (R)	16,743	44.9
2 Charles E. Townsend (R)	22,198	53.3
Frederick B. Wood (D)	18,390	44.2
3 Washington Gardner (R)	19,741	56.7
Warner J. Sampson (D)	13,900	40.0
4 Edward L. Hamilton (R)	20,617	57.1
Thomas O'Hara (D)	15,368	42.5
5 William Alden Smith (R)	19,040	60.2
Myron H. Walker (D)	11,525	36.5
6 Samuel W. Smith (R)	23,869	56.3
William H. S. Wood (D)	18,300	43.2
7 Henry McMorran (R)	17,830	57.3
Martin Crocker (D)	12,481	40.1
8 Joseph W. Fordney (R)	17,392	56.7
Henry M. Youmans (D)	11,389	37.1
9 Roswell P. Bishop (R)	14,502	66.0
Daniel W. Goodenough (D)	6,166	28.1
10 George A. Loud (R)	17,069	57.9
Michael O'Brien (D)	11,846	40.2
11 Archibald B. Darragh (R)	18,174	69.7
David J. Erwin (D)	7,891	30.3
12 H. Olin Young (R)	21,224	71.5
John Power (D)	8,467	28.5

MINNESOTA

	Votes	%
1 James A. Tawney (R)	19,561	60.9
McGovern (D)	12,545	39.1
2 James T. McCleary (R)	16,100	63.4
Andrews (D)	9,316	36.7
3 Charles R. Davis (R)	16,700	58.9
Kolars (D)	10,996	38.8
4 Frederick C. Stevens (R)	17,404	60.4
Gieske (D)	11,412	39.6
5 John Lind (D)	19,863	51.3
Fletcher (R)	17,809	46.0
6 Clarence B. Buckman (R)	17,894	56.6
Dubois (D)	13,705	43.4
7 Andrew J. Volstead (R)	20,826	78.6
Forsberg (PP)	5,397	20.4
8 J. Adam Bede (R)	14,613	60.8
Fay (D)	8,882	37.0
9 Halvor Steenerson (R)	18,055	61.4
Moen (PP)	6,784	23.1
McKinnon (D)	4,572	15.6

MISSISSIPPI

	Votes	%
1 Ezekiel S. Candler Jr. (D)	3,245	100.0
2 Thomas Speight (D)	2,523	100.0
3 Benjamin G. Humphreys (D)	1,146	100.0
4 Wilson S. Hill (D)	2,834	100.0
5 Adam M. Byrd (D)	3,081	100.0
6 Eaton J. Bowers (D)	1,774	100.0
7 Frank A. McLain (D)	2,022	100.0
8 John Sharp Williams (D)	1,433	100.0

MISSOURI

	Votes	%
1 James T. Lloyd (D)	16,972	56.2
Robison (R)	13,179	43.6
2 William W. Rucker (D)	18,045	57.6
Schmitz (R)	13,293	42.4
3 John Dougherty (D)	17,270	54.2
Ward (R)	14,618	45.8
4 Charles F. Cochran (D)	18,392	55.9
Gilmer (R)	14,510	44.1
5 William S. Cowherd (D)	20,628	58.1
Vanhorn (R)	14,393	40.6
6 David A. De Armond (D)	15,639	54.3
Shafer (R)	13,124	45.6
7 Courtney W. Hamlin (D)	19,277	52.7
Peale (R)	17,250	47.2
8 Dorsey W. Shackleford (D)	14,465	52.4
Enloe (R)	13,133	47.6

MISSOURI

	Candidates	Votes	%
9	James Beauchamp Clark (D)	18,591	55.7
	Tubbs (R)	14,770	44.3
10	Richard Bartholdt (R)	21,516	55.1
	Blow (D)	15,262	39.1
11	John T. Hunt (D)	14,913	57.5
	Charles F. Joy (R)	10,077	38.9
12	James J. Butler (D)	15,316	62.5
	Reynolds (R)	8,698	35.5
13	Edward Robb (D)	15,442	52.8
	Raney (R)	13,793	47.2
14	Willard D. Vandiver (D)	19,868	54.1
	Kinsalving (R)	16,788	45.7
15	Maecenas E. Benton (D)	20,038	51.0
	Lacaff (R)	18,511	47.1
16	J. Robert Lamar (D)	14,102	52.0
	Russell (R)	12,996	47.9

MONTANA

		Votes	%
AL	Joseph M. Dixon (R)	24,626	46.2
	John M. Evans (D)	19,560	36.7
	Martin Dee (LAB&POP)	6,005	11.3
	George B. Sproule (SOC)	3,131	5.9

NEBRASKA

		Votes	%
1	Elmer J. Burkett (R)	16,534	56.9
	Howard H. Hanks (FUS)	11,603	39.9
2	Gilbert M. Hitchcock (FUS)	13,509	50.9
	David H. Mercer (R)	11,669	43.9
	Bernard McCaffery (SOC)	1,379	5.2
3	John J. McCarthy (R)	19,201	50.0
	John S. Robinson (FUS)	18,541	48.3
4	Edmund H. Hinshaw (R)	19,337	52.4
	William L. Stark (FUS)	16,838	45.6
5	George W. Norris (R)	14,927	49.5
	A. C. Shallenberger (FUS)	14,746	48.9
6	Moses P. Kinkaid (R)	16,699	52.5
	Patrick H. Barry (FUS)	13,997	44.0

NEVADA

		Votes	%
AL	Clarence D. Van Duzer (D SIL)	5,848	53.6
	E. S. Farrington (R)	5,073	46.5

NEW HAMPSHIRE

		Votes	%
1	Cyrus A. Sulloway (R)	22,491	58.0
	Albert S. Langley (D)	15,218	39.2
2	Frank D. Currier (R)	22,138	58.0
	George E. Bales (D)	14,986	39.2

NEW JERSEY

		Votes	%
1	Henry C. Loudenslager (R)	20,371	55.4
	Richard T. Miller (D)	15,279	41.6
2	John J. Gardner (R)	19,966	62.5
	Thomas A. Gash (D)	9,465	29.6
	Marion R. Owen (P)	2,323	7.3
3	Benjamin F. Howell (R)	20,014	51.4
	Jacob A. Geisenhainer (D)	18,345	47.2
4	William M. Lanning (R)	18,972	51.4
	Lewis Perrine (D)	16,966	46.0
5	Charles N. Fowler (R)	21,030	49.6
	Dewitt C. Flanagan (D)	19,881	46.8
6	William Hughes (D)	24,084	52.4
	William Barbour (R)	20,236	44.0
7	Richard Wayne Parker (R)	19,878	56.6
	George A. Miller (D)	14,371	40.9
8	William H. Wiley (R)	18,814	59.3
	Henry G. Atwater (D)	12,005	37.8
9	Allan Benny (D)	14,492	49.1
	Robert Carey (R)	13,700	46.4
10	Allan L. McDermott (D)	19,311	61.6
	James D. Manning (R)	10,595	33.8

NEW YORK

	Candidates	Votes	%
1	Townsend Scudder (D)	17,788	49.8
	Frederic Storm (R)	17,681	49.5
2	George H. Lindsay (D)	18,728	61.9
	James R. Howe (R)	9,593	31.7
3	Charles T. Dunwell (R)	17,457	48.3
	Hugh E. Rogers (D)	17,043	47.2
4	Frank E. Wilson (D)	16,415	50.9
	William Schnitzpan (R)	13,695	42.5
5	Edward M. Bassett (D)	16,149	48.8
	Harry A. Hanbury (R)	15,216	46.0
6	Robert Baker (D)	17,886	49.5
	Henry Bristow (R)	17,420	48.2
7	John J. Fitzgerald (D)	23,112	67.5
	James T. Williamson (R)	10,432	30.5
8	Timothy D. Sullivan (D)	26,107	69.4
	Montague Lessler (R)	10,386	27.6
9	Henry M. Goldfogle (D)	7,739	55.6
	Charles S. Adler (R)	4,235	30.5
	Alexander Jonas (SOCIAL D)	1,355	9.7
10	William Sulzer (D)	15,451	62.2
	William Blau (R)	6,088	24.5
	H. G. Wilshire (SOCIAL D)	1,873	7.5
	James T. Hunter (SOC LAB)	1,391	5.6
11	William Randolph Hearst (D)	26,953	69.1
	Henry Birrell (R)	10,841	27.8
12	George B. McClellan (D)	21,275	71.1
	Charles Thongood (R)	7,039	23.5
13	Francis Burton Harrison (D)	15,524	51.7
	James W. Perry (R)	13,987	46.5
14	Ira Edgar Rider (D)	20,402	63.7
	Andrew J. Anderson (R)	8,492	26.5
	William Ehret (SOCIAL D)	2,348	7.3
15	William H. Douglass (R)	12,575	49.8
	Henry B. Martin (D)	12,161	48.2
16	Jacob Ruppert Jr (D)	15,657	62.5
	William R. Spooner (R)	7,485	29.9
17	Frank E. Shober (D)	19,248	50.6
	Harvey T. Andrews (R)	17,731	46.6
18	Joseph A. Goulden (D)	28,411	61.8
	Frank C. Schaeffler (R)	14,844	32.3
19	Norton P. Otis (R)	17,878	48.7
	Cornelius A. Pugsley (D)	17,338	47.2
20	Thomas W. Bradley (R)	19,747	55.5
	Theodore H. Babcock (D)	14,874	41.8
21	John H. Ketcham (R)	22,363	57.3
	Curtis F. Hoag (D)	15,777	40.4
22	William H. Draper (R)	21,689	57.5
	John H. Morrison (D)	15,698	41.6
23	George N. Southwick (R)	28,858	55.2
	B. Cleveland Sloan (D)	22,459	42.9
24	George J. Smith (R)	26,842	55.8
	Clifford Champion (D)	20,045	41.7
25	Lucius N. Littauer (R)	23,018	55.1
	Frank Beebe (D)	18,132	43.4
26	William H. Flack (R)	27,816	70.8
	Henry Holland (D)	10,392	26.4
27	James S. Sherman (R)	21,743	52.4
	Edward Lewis (D)	18,497	44.5
28	Charles L. Knapp (R)	23,196	58.9
	C. Frank Smith (D)	14,883	37.8
29	Michael E. Driscoll (R)	27,023	60.1
	Martin F. Dillon (D)	16,330	36.3
30	John W. Dwight (R)	28,211	62.2
	Charles D. Pratt (D)	17,176	37.8
31	Sereno E. Payne (R)	24,130	60.1
	Harry B. Harpending (D)	14,833	37.0
32	James Breck Perkins (R)	22,119	52.5
	William Degraff (D)	15,933	37.8
	Charles R. Bach (SOCIAL D)	2,249	5.3
33	Charles W. Gillet (R)	21,587	54.5
	Frank P. Frost (D)	16,494	41.7
34	James W. Wadsworth (R)	26,007	56.2
	Dean F. Currie (D)	18,787	40.6
35	William H. Ryan (D)	19,884	55.3
	John M. Farquhar (R)	14,715	40.9

	Candidates	Votes	%
36	De Alva S. Alexander (R)	21,525	55.9
	Ole L. Snyder (D)	16,016	41.6
37	Edward B. Vreeland (R)	27,579	67.8
	George J. Ball (D)	11,470	28.2

NORTH CAROLINA

		Votes	%
1	John H. Small (D)	14,086	88.5
	H. E. Hodges (R)	1,834	11.5
2	Claude Kitchin (D)	12,705	99.0
3	Charles R. Thomas (D)	11,198	71.0
	G. E. Butler (R)	4,567	29.0
4	Edward W. Pou (D)	13,799	82.7
	John W. Atwater	2,105	12.6
5	William W. Kitchin (D)	17,900	65.3
	J. L. Patterson (R)	9,511	34.7
6	Gilbert B. Patterson (D)	9,901	69.1
	Albert H. Slocumb (R)	4,430	30.9
7	Robert N. Page (D)	13,269	83.5
	E. H. Morris (R)	2,482	15.6
8	Theodore F. Kluttz (D)	15,632	52.4
	E. S. Blackburn (R)	14,158	47.4
9	Edwin Y. Webb (D)	14,087	61.6
	G. B. Hiss (R)	8,778	38.4
10	James M. Gudger Jr. (D)	12,700	50.4
	James M. Moody (R)	12,517	49.6

NORTH DAKOTA

		Votes	%
AL	Thomas F. Marshall (R)	32,976✔	
	Burleigh F. Spalding (R)	32,854✔	
	Ueland	14,775	
	Lovell (D)	14,392	
	King (SOC)	1,195	

OHIO

		Votes	%
1	Nicholas Longworth (R)	24,082	67.9
	Thomas Bentham (D)	9,471	26.7
2	Herman P. Goebel (R)	24,274	61.8
	Harry C. Busch (D)	12,095	30.8
	William R. Fox (SOC)	2,681	6.8
3	Robert M. Nevin (R)	25,406	52.8
	Thomas A. Selz (D)	19,551	40.6
4	Harvey C. Garber (D)	18,342	54.5
	Lewis H. Rogers (R)	14,879	44.2
5	John S. Snook (D)	19,086	53.6
	George Russell (R)	16,548	46.4
6	Charles Q. Hildebrant (R)	19,609	55.1
	William G. Thompson (D)	15,188	42.6
7	Thomas B. Kyle (R)	18,381	55.0
	Chester Bryan (D)	13,994	41.9
8	William R. Warnock (R)	22,177	55.9
	William H. Niven (R)	16,643	42.0
9	James H. Southard (R)	23,815	56.6
	Charles I. York (D)	15,873	37.7
10	Stephen Morgan (R)	21,593	59.6
	C. E. Belcher (D)	14,118	39.0
11	Charles H. Grosvenor (R)	23,124	53.7
	Edward I. Lawrence (D)	19,487	45.3
12	De Witt C. Badger (D)	18,569	50.4
	Cyrus Huling (R)	17,793	48.3
13	Amos H. Jackson (R)	22,496	49.4
	James A. Norton (D)	22,169	48.7
14	William W. Skiles (R)	22,365	54.9
	George B. Neal (D)	17,615	43.2
15	Henry C. Van Voorhis (R)	17,462	49.3
	Ernest B. Schneider (D)	16,850	47.6
16	Joseph J. Gill (R)	16,129	56.9
	Joseph V. Lawler (D)	11,501	40.6
17	John W. Cassingham (D)	19,753	52.9
	W. B. Stevens (R)	17,563	47.1
18	James Kennedy (R)	22,461	53.8
	William J. Foley (D)	10,502	25.1
	Thomas J. Duffy (LAB)	7,923	19.0
19	Charles Dick (R)	24,732	62.0
	Oliver D. Everhard (D)	13,261	33.3
20	Jacob A. Beidler (R)	20,523	52.4
	Charles A. Kohl (D)	16,885	43.1

OHIO

	Candidates	Votes	%
21	Theodore E. Burton (R)	24,353	57.0
	Edmund G. Vail (D)	16,805	39.3

OREGON

	Candidates	Votes	%
1	Thomas H. Tongue (R)	23,585*	52.9
	J. K. Weatherford (D)	16,213	36.4
	B. F. Ramp (SOC)	2,576	5.8
2	John N. Williamson (R)	23,397	53.5
	W. F. Butcher (D)	15,598	35.7
	Diedrich T. Gerdes (SOC)	2,753	6.3

PENNSYLVANIA

	Candidates	Votes	%
1	Henry H. Bingham (R, UN)	32,119	100.0
2	Robert Adams Jr. (R, UN)	35,274	99.4
3	Henry Burk (R, UN)	36,911	98.8
4	Robert H. Foerderer (R, UN)	21,094	98.3
5	Edward de V. Morrell (R, UN)	25,358	98.9
6	George D. McCreary (R, BALLOT)	30,626	98.4
7	Thomas S. Butler (R)	20,062	65.4
	Frank B. Rhodes (D)	9,751	31.8
8	Irving P. Wanger (R, BALLOT)	22,689	52.0
	Charles E. Ingersoll (D)	20,080	46.1
9	Henry B. Cassel (R)	18,287	69.7
	James F. McCoy (D)	7,036	26.8
10	George Howell (A-MACH)	13,600‡	48.4
	William Connell (R, BALLOT)	13,139	46.8
11	Henry W. Palmer (R, P)	16,787	48.3
	T. R. Martin (D, WMP/L)	14,091	40.5
	C. F. Quinn (SOC)	3,911	11.2
12	George R. Patterson (R)	14,151	49.2
	James W. Ryan (D)	12,402	43.1
	Thomas J. Lannon (SOC)	1,928	6.7
13	Marcus C. L. Kline (D)	24,771	54.1
	William H. Sowden (D)	19,772	43.2
14	Charles F. Wright (R)	14,401	54.9
	James West (D)	10,727	40.9
15	Elias Deemer (R)	17,518	52.4
	James Mansel (D, P)	15,012	44.9
16	Charles H. Dickerman (D)	14,019	50.3
	Fred A. Godcharles (R)	13,171	47.2
17	Thaddeus M. Mahon (R)	21,197	55.9
	Harry I. Huber (D)	16,740	44.1
18	Marlin E. Olmsted (R)	22,193	59.7
	Benjamin L. Forster (D)	13,715	36.9
19	Alvin Evans (R)	20,814	56.8
	Robert E. Creswell (D)	15,690	42.8
20	Daniel F. Lafean (R)	15,553	50.5
	William McClean (D)	14,962	48.5
21	Solomon R. Dresser (R)	16,722	53.5
	Delos Eugene Hibner (D)	13,243	42.4
22	George F. Huff (R)	18,827	57.7
	Charles M. Heineman (D)	13,014	39.9
23	Allen F. Cooper (R)	15,546	51.1
	Orram W. Kennedy (D)	13,791	45.3
24	E. F. Acheson (REG)	15,147	55.1
	Charles R. Eckert (D)	9,974	36.3
25	A. L. Bates (R)	15,538	52.4
	A. B. Osborne (D)	11,311	38.1
	Faye B. Ocamb (SOC)	1,639	5.5
26	Joseph H. Shull (D)	15,765	53.3
	Fred Nesbit (R)	11,599	39.2
	James Hughes (SOC)	1,671	5.7
27	William O. Smith (R)	16,018	57.9
	Alfred W. Smiley (D)	10,618	38.4
28	Joseph C. Sibley (R)	17,616	52.5
	James B. Watson (D)	12,889	38.4
	Richard A. Buzza (P)	3,042	9.1
29	George Shiras III (D & CIT)	14,553	49.4
	William H. Graham (R)	14,535	49.4
30	John Dalzell (R)	19,085	95.1

	Candidates	Votes	%
31	H. Kirke Porter (D & CIT)	16,241	52.6
	James F. Burke (R)	14,532	47.1
32	James W. Brown (D & CIT)	14,517	50.8
	A. J. Barchfeld (R)	13,471	47.1

Special Election

		Votes	%
17	Alexander Billmeyer (D)	14,658	54.7
	William K. Lord (R)	12,143	45.3

RHODE ISLAND

	Candidates	Votes	%
1	Daniel L. D. Granger (D)	15,198	49.0
	Melville Bull (R)	14,535	46.9
2	Adin B. Capron (R)	13,680	50.2
	Unidentified Candidate (D)	12,657	46.5

SOUTH CAROLINA

	Candidates	Votes	%
1	George S. Legare (D)	3,749	95.5
2	George W. Croft (D)	5,134	95.3
3	Wyatt Aiken (D)	5,082	98.9
4	Joseph T. Johnson (D)	4,642	98.7
5	David E. Finley (D)	4,535	99.3
6	Robert B. Scarborough (D)	3,981	100.0
7	Asbury F. Lever (D)	4,220	96.2

SOUTH DAKOTA

	Candidates	Votes	%
AL	Eben W. Martin (R)	48,454✓	
	Charles H. Burke (R)	48,310✓	
	Wilson (D)	21,113	
	Robinson (D)	20,814	
	Knowles (SOC)	2,738	
	Price (SOC)	2,578	
	Kelley (P)	2,319	
	Smith (P)	2,252	

TENNESSEE

	Candidates	Votes	%
1	Walter P. Brownlow (R)	15,373	61.2
	Lyle (D)	9,751	38.8
2	Henry R. Gibson (R)	11,993	55.5
	Hannah (D)	9,636	44.6
3	John A. Moon (D)	14,152	97.6
4	Morgan C. Fitzpatrick (D)	11,509	64.9
	West (R)	6,228	35.1
5	James D. Richardson (D)	10,314	76.8
	Parker (R)	3,113	23.2
6	John W. Gaines (D)	9,422	82.3
	Tillman (D)	2,025	17.7
7	Lemuel P. Padgett (D)	9,470	75.3
	Gregory (R)	3,106	24.7
8	Thetus W. Sims (D)	9,293	52.8
	Davis (R)	8,317	47.2
9	Rice A. Pierce (D)	7,371	82.5
	Kellar (R)	1,567	17.5
10	Malcolm R. Patterson (D)	7,869	83.2
	Phelan (R)	1,500	15.9

TEXAS

	Candidates	Votes	%
1	Morris Sheppard (D)	19,214	83.2
	John Hurley (R)	3,875	16.8
2	Samuel B. Cooper (D)	17,165	86.7
	Warren McDaniel (R)	2,632	13.3
3	Gordon J. Russell (D)	16,628	95.0
4	Choice B. Randell (D)	17,464	85.1
	C. A. Gray (R)	3,063	14.9
5	Jack Beall (D)	16,310	88.4
	S. H. Lumpkin (R)	1,633	8.9
6	Scott Field (D)	16,753	100.0
7	Alexander W. Gregg (D)	13,162	100.0
8	Thomas H. Ball (D)	14,301	68.0
	Lock McDaniel (R)	6,431	30.6
9	George F. Burgess (D)	18,316	61.3
	B. R. Burow (R)	11,574	38.7

	Candidates	Votes	%
10	Albert S. Burleson (D)	20,539	87.2
	Charles Schenken (R)	2,990	12.7
11	Robert L. Henry (D)	14,548	94.2
12	Oscar W. Gillespie (D)	16,220	82.6
	S. A. Greenwell (R)	3,424	17.4
13	John A. Stephens (D)	24,027	91.8
	R. O. Rector (R)	2,034	7.8
14	James L. Slayden (D)	19,889	78.4
	D. H. Meek (R)	4,915	19.4
15	John N. Garner (D)	16,542	60.6
	John C. Scott (R)	10,707	39.2
16	William R. Smith (D)	22,118	88.0
	D. G. Hunt (R)	2,911	11.6

Special Elections

		Votes	%
4	Morris Sheppard (D)	8,972	86.1
	Frank Lee	1,426	13.7
14	Gordon Russell (D)	13,710	100.0

UTAH

	Candidates	Votes	%
AL	Joseph Howell (R)	43,710	51.5
	William H. King (D)	38,196	45.0

VERMONT

	Candidates	Votes	%
1	David J. Foster (R)	16,007	75.2
	J. Walter Lyons (D)	4,394	20.6
2	Kittredge Haskins (R)	17,532	76.8
	Harris Miller (D)	4,150	18.2

VIRGINIA

	Candidates	Votes	%
1	William A. Jones (D)	7,381	72.8
	Malcolm A. Coles (R)	2,762	27.2
2	Harry L. Maynard (D)	9,746	75.9
	Robert M. Hughes (R)	2,917	22.7
3	John Lamb (D)	5,300	81.1
	B. W. Edwards (R)	969	14.8
4	Robert G. Southall (D)	5,717	90.0
	R. T. Vaughan	507	8.0
5	Claude A. Swanson (D)	10,363	60.8
	Beverly A. Davis (R)	6,414	37.6
6	Carter Glass (D)	6,345	79.4
	Aaron Graham (P)	1,418	17.8
7	James Hay (D)	8,461	64.7
	S. J. Hoffman (R)	4,620	35.3
8	John F. Rixey (D)	6,618	76.7
	W. K. Skinker (R)	2,011	23.3
9	Campbell Slemp (R)	13,694	50.4
	William F. Rhea (D)	13,476	49.6
10	Henry D. Flood (D)	9,119	68.3
	James Lyons	4,235	31.7

Special Election

		Votes	%
6	Carter Glass (D)	6,556	95.4

WASHINGTON

	Candidates	Votes	%
AL	Francis W. Cushman (R)	58,453✓	
	Wesley L. Jones (R)	58,193✓	
	William E. Humphrey (R)	57,435✓	
	George F. Cotterill (D)	33,435	
	Frank B. Cole (D)	32,406	
	O. R. Holcomb (D)	31,497	
	George W. Scott (SOC)	4,612	
	D. Burgess (SOC)	4,585	
	J. H. C. Scurlock (SOC)	4,546	
	O. L. Fowler (P)	1,732	
	W. J. McKean (P)	1,725	
	A. H. Sherwood (P)	1,708	
	William McCormick (SOC LAB)	817	
	Jense C. Martin (SOC LAB)	808	
	Hans P. Jorgensen (SOC LAB)	801	

WEST VIRGINIA

Candidates	Votes	%
1 Blackburn B. Dovener (R)	19,962	52.1
Owen S. McKinney (D)	16,922	44.1
2 Alston G. Dayton (R)	20,968	50.9
John T. McGraw (D)	19,628	47.6
3 Joseph Holt Gaines (R)	19,014	51.7
James H. Miller (D)	17,215	46.8
4 Harry C. Woodyard (R)	19,158	52.0
W. N. Chancellor (D)	16,968	46.1
5 James A. Hughes (R)	20,164	53.3
David E. Johnson (D)	17,617	46.6

WISCONSIN

Candidates	Votes	%
1 Henry Allen Cooper (R)	20,437	60.7
Lewis C. Baker (D)	12,122	36.0
2 Henry C. Adams (R)	17,519	52.8
John J. Wood Jr (D)	14,483	43.6
3 Joseph W. Babcock (R)	19,405	60.8
Jackson Silbaugh (D)	11,155	35.0
4 Theobald Otjen (R)	15,101	44.1
John F. Donovan (D)	13,468	39.3
Herman W. Bisborins (SOCIAL D)	5,167	15.1
5 William H. Stafford (R)	14,971	45.8
Henry Smith (D)	10,971	33.6
H. C. Berger (SOCIAL D)	6,060	18.6
6 Charles H. Weisse (D)	17,991	52.2
William H. Froehlich (R)	14,575	42.3
7 John J. Esch (R)	18,694	64.6
William Cernahan (D)	9,343	32.3
8 James H. Davidson (R)	19,553	57.8
T. H. Patterson (D)	12,651	37.4
9 Edward S. Minor (R)	15,958	57.1
Edward Decker (D)	11,479	41.1
10 Webster E. Brown (R)	19,554	55.6
Burt Williams (D)	14,935	42.5
11 John J. Jenkins (R)	19,329	67.4
Joseph A. Rene (D)	8,261	28.8

WYOMING

Candidates	Votes	%
AL Frank W. Mondell (R)	15,808	64.0
Charles P. Clemmons (D)	8,892	36.0

1904 House Elections

ALABAMA

Candidates	Votes	%
1 George W. Taylor (D)	7,686	100.0
2 Ariosto A. Wiley (D)	10,177	100.0
3 Henry D. Clayton (D)	9,566	98.3
4 Sydney J. Bowie (D)	7,087	76.3
J. W. Kitchens (R)	2,201	23.7
5 J. Thomas Heflin (D)	10,105	76.3
B. W. Walker (R)	3,095	23.4
6 John H. Bankhead (D)	8,873	76.6
S. R. Crumpton (R)	2,718	23.5
7 John L. Burnett (D)	9,819	55.9
T. W. Powell (R)	7,756	44.1
8 William Richardson (D)	9,898	84.3
J. W. Roberts (R)	1,846	15.7
9 Oscar W. Underwood (D)	9,615	81.7
J. T. Blakemore (R)	1,775	15.1

Special Election

5 J. Thomas Heflin (D)	4,065	99.7

ARKANSAS

1 Robert B. Macon (D)	14,391	99.3
2 Stephen Brundidge Jr. (D)	9,065	62.7
F. W. Tucker (R)	5,388	37.3
3 John C. Floyd (D)	9,719	56.3
J. F. Mayes (R)	7,547	43.7
4 John S. Little (D)	9,308	59.4
James Brizzolara (R)	6,352	40.6
5 Charles C. Reid (D)	11,371	60.9
A. S. Fowler (R)	7,288	39.1
6 Joseph T. Robinson (D)	9,459	62.0
R. C. Thompson (R)	5,810	38.1
7 Robert Minor Wallace (D)	14,147	99.1

CALIFORNIA

1 James N. Gillett (R)	21,602	54.1
A. Caminetti (D)	15,706	39.3
A. J. Gaylord (SOC)	2,197	5.5
2 Duncan E. McKinlay (R)	22,873	49.2
Theodore A. Bell (D)	21,640	46.6
3 Joseph R. Knowland (R)	24,637	68.6
Henry C. McPike (D)	7,210	20.1
M. Lesser (SOC)	3,617	10.1
4 Julius Kahn (R)	20,012	56.8
Edward J. Livernash (D&UN LAB)	12,812	36.4
William Costley (SOC)	2,267	6.4
5 E. A. Hayes (R)	23,701	52.3
William J. Wynn (D)	18,025	39.8
6 James C. Needham (R)	18,828	55.1
William M. Conley (D)	13,074	38.3
7 James McLachlan (R)	31,091	64.2
W. O. Morton (D)	11,259	23.3
F. I. Wheat (SOC)	3,594	7.4
John Sobieski (P)	2,467	5.1
8 S. C. Smith (R)	23,683	55.6
William T. Lucas (D)	12,861	30.2
N. A. Richardson (SOC)	4,636	10.9

Special Election

3 Joseph R. Knowland (R)	24,564	77.5
Henry C. McPike (D)	7,123	22.5

COLORADO

1 Robert W. Bonynge (R)	55,940	51.0
Clay B. Whitford (D)	50,022	45.6
2 Herschel M. Hogg (R)	68,101	52.0
Joseph H. Maupin (D)	58,554	44.7
AL Franklin E. Brooks (R)	121,236	50.2
John F. Shafroth (D)	112,373	46.5

CONNECTICUT

Candidates	Votes	%
1 E. Stevens Henry (R)	26,363	56.9
Morse (D)	18,218	39.3
2 Nehemiah D. Sperry (R)	36,832	56.9
Fisk (D)	24,679	38.1
3 Frank B. Brandegee (R)	15,541	60.2
Tanner (D)	9,718	37.7
4 Ebenezer J. Hill (R)	31,822	59.1
Hallen (D)	20,760	38.6
AL George L. Lilley (R)	108,918	57.1
Kennedy (D)	75,212	39.4

DELAWARE

AL Hiram R. Burton (R)	23,512	53.7
Edward D. Hearne (D)	19,552	44.6

FLORIDA

1 Stephen M. Sparkman (D)	8,418	75.1
E. R. Gunby (R)	2,257	20.1
2 Frank Clark (D)	10,711	77.2
J. M. Cheney (R)	2,767	19.9
3 William B. Lamar (D)	6,463	84.3
L. M. Ware (R)	986	12.9

GEORGIA

1 Rufus E. Lester (D)	7,246	94.9
2 James M. Griggs (D)	8,034	99.9
3 Elijah B. Lewis (D)	6,908	99.0
4 William C. Adamson (D)	7,850	91.6
J. F. Jones (R)	722	8.4
5 Leonidas F. Livingston (D)	9,387	71.4
C. P. Goree (R)	3,760	28.6
6 Charles L. Bartlett (D)	7,197	96.4
7 Gordon Lee (D)	10,350	69.2
T. Pickett (R)	4,606	30.8
8 William M. Howard (D)	7,616	88.9
W. M. Hairston (POP)	877	10.2
9 Thomas M. Bell (D)	12,813	68.1
James Finley (R)	6,000	31.9
10 Thomas W. Hardwick (D)	8,606	91.6
H. M. Porter (POP)	788	8.4
11 William G. Brantley (D)	9,970	77.3
A. B. Finley (D)	2,921	22.7

IDAHO

AL Burton L. French (R)	44,813	63.7
Benjamin F. Clay (D)	20,146	28.6
John H. Morrison (SOC)	4,209	6.0

ILLINOIS

1 Martin B. Madden (R)	24,097	58.0
John S. Oehmen (D)	9,166	22.1
David S. Geer (R)	5,175	12.5
Edward Loewenthal (SOC)	2,334	5.6
2 James R. Mann (R)	29,010	66.3
Charles B. Stafford (D)	9,221	21.1
H. Van Middlesworth (SOC)	4,817	11.0
3 William W. Wilson (R)	22,709	61.7
Willis C. Stone (D)	8,749	23.8
Edward Dierkes (SOC)	4,476	12.2
4 Charles S. Wharton (R)	13,481	45.2
George P. Foster (D)	9,947	33.4
James W. Johnson (SOC)	5,944	20.0
5 Anthony Michalek (R)	12,904	44.9
Charles J. Vopicka (D)	12,019	41.9
Robert W. Schoening (SOC)	3,480	12.1

Candidates	Votes	%
6 William Lorimer (R)	21,824	50.8
George P. Gubbins (D)	12,309	28.7
Arthur Gourley (P)	6,112	14.2
A. S. Edwards (SOC)	2,690	6.3
7 Philip Knopf (R)	29,100	59.4
George S. Foster (D)	12,490	25.5
George Koop (SOC)	6,540	13.4
8 Charles McGavin (R)	20,107	51.7
William Preston Harrison (D)	13,025	33.5
Marcus H. Taft (SOC)	4,223	10.9
9 Henry S. Boutell (R)	22,442	57.2
Quin O'Brien (D)	13,525	34.5
Adolph Harrick (SOC)	2,801	7.1
10 George Edmund Foss (R)	27,096	66.2
James L. Turnock (D)	10,243	25.0
Robert Knox (SOC)	2,917	7.1
11 Howard M. Snapp (R)	31,019	70.7
James O. Monroe (D)	9,324	21.2
12 Charles E. Fuller (R)	33,898	70.2
Alex Vaughey (D)	9,718	20.1
David A. Syme (P)	2,481	5.1
13 Robert R. Hitt (R)	26,454	67.7
John Erwin (D)	10,049	25.7
14 Benjamin F. Marsh (R)	24,004	58.4
David W. Matthews (D)	12,256	29.8
John Higgins (SOC)	2,852	6.9
15 George W. Prince (R)	29,792	60.7
Meredith Walker (D)	15,159	30.9
16 Joseph V. Graff (R)	25,803	60.5
Thomas Cooper (D)	13,780	32.3
17 John A. Sterling (R)	23,414	58.8
Z. F. Yost (D)	12,978	32.6
William W. Houser (P)	2,285	5.7
18 Joseph G. Cannon (R)	30,520	62.0
Coulson V. McClenathan (D)	15,168	30.8
19 William B. McKinley (R)	30,574	56.9
Adolph Sumerlin (D)	19,931	37.1
20 Henry T. Rainey (D)	19,881	48.9
Cornelius J. Doyle (R)	18,329	45.1
21 Zeno J. Rives (R)	21,330	47.7
Ben F. Caldwell (D)	20,238	45.2
22 William A. Rodenberg (R)	25,770	53.5
J. Nick Perrin (D)	19,494	40.5
23 Frank L. Dickson (R)	21,931	47.7
M. D. Foster (D)	21,123	45.9
William P. Habberton (P)	2,404	5.2
24 Pleasant T. Chapman (R)	20,556	50.7
J. R. Williams (D)	18,664	46.1
25 George W. Smith (R)	22,527	55.6
Charles L. Otrich (D)	14,668	36.2
Charles F. Kiest (P)	2,306	5.7

INDIANA

1 James A. Hemenway (R)	23,158*	51.1
Albert G. Holcomb (D)	19,399	42.8
2 John C. Chaney (R)	25,143	49.7
Robert W. Miers (D)	23,670	46.8
3 William T. Zenor (D)	22,708	53.1
John E. Dillon (R)	19,119	44.7
4 Lincoln Dixon (D)	23,451	50.8
Anderson Percifield (R)	21,516	46.6
5 Elias S. Holliday (R)	28,192	52.0
Claude G. Bowers (D)	23,101	42.6
6 James E. Watson (R)	29,089	56.3
Uriah S. Jackson (D)	22,046	42.7
7 Jesse Overstreet (R)	34,178	57.1
Levi P. Harlan (D)	23,334	39.0
8 George W. Cromer (R)	29,462	52.2
Edward C. Dehority (D)	22,097	39.1
Aaron Worth (P)	3,675	6.5
9 Charles B. Landis (R)	29,492	52.9
Clyde H. Jones (D)	23,267	41.8
10 Edgar D. Crumpacker (R)	31,583	58.5
Worth W. Pepple (D)	21,451	39.7

INDIANA

	Candidates	Votes	%
11	Frederick Landis (R)	29,591	53.6
	Clement M. Holderman (D)	21,406	38.8
	Edward H. Kennedy (P)	3,364	6.1
12	Newton W. Gilbert (R)	23,203	50.5
	James M. Robinson (D)	21,322	46.4
13	Abraham L. Brick (R)	29,361	55.1
	Frank E. Hering (D)	21,454	40.3

IOWA

	Candidates	Votes	%
1	Thomas Hedge (R)	19,929	54.7
	John E. Craig (D)	14,886	40.9
2	Albert F. Dawson (R)	22,116	48.1
	Martin J. Wade (D)	21,930	47.7
3	Benjamin P. Birdsall (R)	29,297	65.3
	J. W. Mallon (D)	14,200	31.6
4	Gilbert N. Haugen (R)	26,399	64.5
	W. O. Holman (D)	13,403	32.8
5	Robert G. Cousins (R)	25,313	59.7
	John A. Green (D)	15,019	35.4
6	John F. Lacey (R)	23,213	58.4
	S. A. Brewster (D)	13,840	34.9
7	John A. T. Hull (R)	27,637	64.3
	John T. Mulvaney (D)	12,046	28.0
8	William P. Hepburn (R)	26,603	63.0
	John V. Bennett (D)	14,518	34.4
9	Walter I. Smith (R)	27,214	63.9
	H. Wilcox (D)	13,907	32.7
10	James P. Conner (R)	34,977	67.3
	W. J. Branagan (D)	14,531	28.0
11	Elbert H. Hubbard (R)	32,560	69.1
	P. D. Vanoosterhaut (D)	13,521	28.7

KANSAS

	Candidates	Votes	%
1	Charles Curtis (R)	25,376	57.8
	A. M. Harvey (D)	17,808	40.6
2	Justin D. Bowersock (R)	26,443	54.8
	C. F. Hutchings (D)	20,308	42.1
3	Philip P. Campbell (R)	29,998	59.5
	William H. Ryan (D)	15,762	31.2
	T. C. Davis (SOC)	4,696	9.3
4	James M. Miller (R)	24,185	62.8
	Frank B. Lowrance (D-PP)	14,326	37.2
5	William A. Calderhead (R)	22,076	65.1
	John A. Flack (D-PP)	11,825	34.9
6	William A. Reeder (R)	21,808	60.5
	H. O. Caster (D)	13,274	36.8
7	Victor Murdock (R)	35,598	60.4
	M. Belisle (D)	19,548	33.2
AL	Charles F. Scott (R)	187,983	60.3
	Francis M. Brady (D)	105,479	33.9

KENTUCKY

	Candidates	Votes	%
1	Ollie M. James (D)	25,558	62.3
	J. C. Spaight (R)	13,755	33.5
2	Augustus O. Stanley (D)	20,732	55.7
	W. A. Overby (R)	16,517	44.3
3	James M. Richardson (D)	18,432	50.1
	W. H. Jones (R)	18,332	49.9
4	David H. Smith (D)	21,979	53.1
	Ben L. Bruner (R)	19,419	46.9
5	J. Swagar Sherley (D)	23,712	51.0
	William C. Owens (R)	22,229	47.8
6	Joseph L. Rhinock (D)	18,854	50.7
	Leslie T. Applegate (R)	16,089	43.3
7	South Trimble (D)	20,356	60.0
	Joseph W. Calvert (R)	13,187	38.9
8	George G. Gilbert (D)	16,481	52.4
	N. D. Miles (R)	14,536	46.2
9	Joseph B. Bennett (R)	21,335	50.1
	James N. Kehoe (D)	21,291	50.0
10	Frank A. Hopkins (D)	19,154	51.9
	Theodore D. Blakey (R)	17,736	48.1
11	Don C. Edwards (R)	31,349	70.3
	George E. Stone (D)	13,200	29.6

LOUISIANA

	Candidates	Votes	%
1	Adolph Meyer (D)	9,157	89.8
	Hugh S. Suthon (R)	791	7.8
2	Robert C. Davey (D)	9,786	91.0
	George H. Vennard (R)	798	7.4
3	Robert F. Broussard (D)	5,649	84.5
	Henry N. Pharr (R)	1,038	15.5
4	John T. Watkins (D)	6,266	99.1
5	Joseph E. Ransdell (D)	5,747	95.4
6	Samuel M. Robertson (D)	5,351	88.1
	L. E. Bentley (R)	721	11.9
7	Arsene P. Pujo (D)	5,432	84.2
	Joseph Lassalle (R)	1,007	15.6

MAINE

	Candidates	Votes	%
1	Amos L. Allen (R)	18,301	57.2
	L. R. Moore (D)	13,320	41.6
2	Charles E. Littlefield (R)	19,176	57.2
	Horatio G. Foss (D)	13,785	41.2
3	Edwin C. Burleigh (R)	18,541	60.3
	E. N. Benson (D)	11,678	38.0
4	Llewellyn Powers (R)	20,501	62.4
	William R. Pattangall (D)	11,600	35.3

MARYLAND

	Candidates	Votes	%
1	Thomas A. Smith (D)	17,582	49.4
	William H. Jackson (R)	17,072	48.0
2	J. Fred. C. Talbott (D)	18,922	52.2
	Robert Garrett (R)	16,734	46.2
3	Frank C. Wachter (R)	17,405	51.8
	Lee S. Meyer (D)	15,373	45.8
4	John Gill Jr. (D)	18,464	51.8
	William C. Smith (R)	16,754	47.0
5	Sydney E. Mudd (R)	16,896	53.6
	Richard S. Hill (D)	13,762	43.6
6	George A. Pearre (R)	19,131	53.9
	Walter A. Johnston (D)	15,077	42.5

MASSACHUSETTS

	Candidates	Votes	%
1	George P. Lawrence (R)	17,217	58.0
	Charles Giddings (D)	11,117	37.4
2	Frederick H. Gillett (R)	17,611	63.5
	George W. Wheelwright (D)	7,992	28.8
	George H. Wrenn (SOC)	1,744	6.3
3	Rockwood Hoar (R)	17,796	61.1
	John B. Ratigan (D)	10,617	36.4
4	Charles Q. Tirrell (R)	18,982	61.4
	Marcus A. Coolidge (D)	10,478	33.9
5	Butler Ames (R)	16,287	54.6
	Alexander B. Bruce (D)	12,657	42.5
6	Augustus P. Gardner (R)	18,157	61.0
	Daniel N. Crowley (D)	8,880	29.8
	James F. Carey (SOC)	2,716	9.1
7	Ernest W. Roberts (R)	20,821	62.9
	William A. Kelley (D)	10,165	30.7
8	Samuel W. McCall (R)	21,511	89.1
	Thomas A. Scott (SOC)	2,623	10.9
9	John A. Keliher (D)	17,003	67.7
	Walter L. Sears (R)	6,895	27.5
10	William S. McNary (D)	19,211	57.3
	Jay B. Crawford (R)	12,740	38.0
11	John A. Sullivan (D)	18,045	51.6
	Eugene N. Foss (R)	15,990	45.7
12	John W. Weeks (R)	19,312	61.3
	Augustus Hemenway (D)	10,813	34.3
13	William S. Greene (R)	13,631	62.8
	Francis M. Kennedy (D)	8,064	37.2
14	William C. Lovering (R)	18,415	60.4
	Thomas H. Buttimer (D)	7,100	23.3
	Charles H. Coulter (SOC)	4,279	14.0

MICHIGAN

	Candidates	Votes	%
1	Edwin Denby (R)	28,874	58.0
	Alfred Lucking (D)	20,490	41.2
2	Charles E. Townsend (R)	28,797	59.2
	John P. Kirk (D)	18,874	38.8
3	Washington Gardner (R)	28,089	63.4
	Lloyd C. Feighner (D)	13,535	30.6
4	Edward L. Hamilton (R)	28,066	66.5
	Theodore G. Beaver (D)	14,143	33.5
5	William Alden Smith (R)	30,869	70.3
	Vernon H. Smith (D)	12,253	27.9
6	Samuel W. Smith (R)	31,403	61.4
	Charles A. Durand (D)	18,224	35.6
7	Henry McMorran (R)	25,562	66.4
	Charles Wellman (D)	12,619	32.8
8	Joseph W. Fordney (R)	24,417	65.2
	Henry J. Patterson (D)	11,898	31.8
9	Roswell P. Bishop (R)	22,463	71.7
	George S. Stanley (D)	7,076	22.6
10	George A. Loud (R)	27,187	70.4
	Stephen P. Flynn (D)	10,527	27.3
11	Archibald B. Darragh (R)	31,661	73.0
	William A. Bahlke (D)	10,639	24.5
12	H. Olin Young (R)	36,655	80.3
	John W. Black (D)	7,915	17.3

MINNESOTA

	Candidates	Votes	%
1	James A. Tawney (R)	23,188	64.5
	Nelson (D)	12,770	35.5
2	James T. McCleary (R)	19,246	64.1
	Jones (D)	10,784	35.9
3	Charles R. Davis (R)	20,116	66.0
	Craven (D)	10,386	34.1
4	Frederick C. Stevens (R)	25,631	100.0
5	Loren Fletcher (R)	21,933	51.3
	Kohler (D)	15,923	37.2
	Hirshfield (LAB)	3,184	7.4
6	Clarence B. Buckman (R)	19,309	54.0
	Vandyke (D)	16,430	46.0
7	Andrew J. Volstead (R)	27,060	100.0
8	J. Adam Bede (R)	22,095	76.9
	Hughes (D)	6,626	23.1
9	Halvor Steenerson (R)	27,061	100.0

MISSISSIPPI

	Candidates	Votes	%
1	Ezekiel S. Candler Jr. (D)	8,049	100.0
2	Thomas Spight (D)	7,279	100.0
3	Benjamin G. Humphreys (D)	3,744	100.0
4	Wilson S. Hill (D)	7,135	100.0
5	Adam Byrd (D)	9,362	99.0
6	Eaton J. Bowers (D)	6,563	93.6
	C. W. Banks (SOC)	449	6.4
7	Frank McLain (D)	5,730	100.0
8	John S. Williams (D)	4,934	100.0

MISSOURI

	Candidates	Votes	%
1	James T. Lloyd (D)	20,216	51.4
	Higbee (R)	19,131	48.6
2	William W. Rucker (D)	21,639	53.8
	Hudson (R)	18,596	46.2
3	Frank B. Klepper (R)	19,088	50.4
	D. Sullinger (D)	18,791	49.6
4	Frank B. Fulkerson (R)	19,831	51.7
	Wilson (D)	18,531	48.3
5	Edgar C. Ellis (R)	23,874	49.2
	Cowherd (D)	22,912	47.2
6	David A. De Armond (D)	17,678	51.5
	Rhodes (R)	16,637	48.5
7	John Welborn (R)	23,682	51.6
	Hamlin (D)	22,204	48.4
8	Dorsey W. Shackleford (D)	16,059	51.6
	Chalfant (R)	15,091	48.5
9	James Beauchamp Clark (D)	21,508	51.9
	Garber (R)	19,937	48.1
10	Richard Bartholdt (R)	34,254	58.5
	Tichacek (D)	21,271	36.3
11	John T. Hunt (R)	17,018	49.1
	Caulfield (R)	16,326	47.1

MISSOURI

Candidates	Votes	%
12 Ernest E. Wood (D)	15,134‡	50.3
Harry M. Coudrey (R)	14,177	47.1
13 Marion E. Rhodes (R)	16,166	50.6
Edward Robb (D)	15,788	49.4
14 William T. Tyndall (R)	23,401	52.8
Russell (D)	20,873	47.1
15 Cassius M. Shartel (R)	21,654	49.0
Benton (D)	19,646	44.4
16 Arthur P. Murphy (R)	15,159	50.1
J. Robert Lamar (D)	15,123	49.9

MONTANA

Candidates	Votes	%
AL Joseph M. Dixon (R)	32,957	51.7
Austin C. Gormley (D-LAB-PP)	26,729	42.0
John H. Walsh (SOC)	4,025	6.3

NEBRASKA

Candidates	Votes	%
1 Elmer J. Burkett (R)	19,786*	59.7
Hugh Lamaster (FUS)	11,863	35.8
2 John L. Kennedy (R)	14,417	46.8
Gilbert M. Hitchcock (FUS)	13,628	44.2
Clark W. Adair (SOC)	2,534	8.2
3 John J. McCarthy (R)	24,151	51.9
Patrick E. McKillip (FUS)	21,210	45.6
4 Edmond H. Hinshaw (R)	23,407	57.9
Charles F. Gilbert (FUS)	15,702	38.8
5 George W. Norris (R)	19,645	56.1
Harry H. Mauck (FUS)	13,831	39.5
6 Moses P. Kinkaid (R)	22,580	58.8
Walter B. McNeel (FUS)	13,725	35.8

NEVADA

Candidates	Votes	%
AL Clarence D. Van Duzer (D & SILVER)	5,525	48.5
J. A. Yerington (R)	5,301	46.5
Reinhold Sadler (STAL SIL)	572	5.0

NEW HAMPSHIRE

Candidates	Votes	%
1 Cyrus A. Sulloway (R)	25,364	58.9
Napoleon J. Dyer (D)	16,866	39.1
2 Frank D. Currier (R)	26,748	60.7
Harry W. Daniell (D)	16,462	37.4

NEW JERSEY

Candidates	Votes	%
1 Henry C. Loudenslager (R)	26,169	60.3
Swackhamer (D)	15,365	35.4
2 John J. Gardner (R)	26,296	63.7
Perry (D)	13,035	31.6
3 Benjamin F. Howell (R)	24,565	56.1
Otis (D)	17,862	40.8
4 Ira W. Wood (R)	22,579	54.7
Stevens (D)	16,953	41.1
5 Charles N. Fowler (R)	24,488	52.3
Martine (D)	19,254	41.1
6 Henry C. Allen (R)	26,612	47.8
William Hughes (D)	26,102	46.9
7 Richard W. Parker (R)	25,578	61.4
Jackson (D)	14,347	34.5
8 William H. Wiley (R)	24,148	63.2
Seymour (D)	11,607	30.4
9 Marshall Van Winkle (R)	19,824	50.7
Benny (D)	17,399	44.5
10 Allan L. McDermott (D)	21,293	53.8
Walker (R)	15,959	40.3

NEW YORK

Candidates	Votes	%
1 William W. Cocks (R)	25,481	55.7
William Willett Jr. (D)	19,362	42.3

Candidates	Votes	%
2 George H. Lindsay (D)	18,506	55.8
Herbert J. Knapp (R)	12,899	38.9
3 Charles T. Dunwell (R)	21,208	52.6
Ephraim Byk (D)	17,571	43.5
4 Charles P. Law (R)	19,418	49.4
Frank E. Wilson (D)	17,684	45.0
5 George E. Waldo (R)	21,299	51.8
John J. Roach (D)	18,889	45.9
6 William M. Calder (R)	22,109	52.4
Robert Baker (D)	19,430	46.0
7 John J. Fitzgerald (D)	23,463	62.6
Robert H. Haskell (R)	13,282	35.4
8 Timothy D. Sullivan (D)	24,532	61.5
Frank L. Frugone (R)	14,262	35.7
9 Henry M. Goldfogle (D)	5,982	39.7
Joseph Levenson (R)	5,667	37.7
Joseph Barondess (SOCIAL D)	3,167	21.0
10 William Sulzer (D)	13,381	51.0
William Byrnes (R)	9,383	35.8
Isidor Phillips (SOCIAL D)	2,789	10.6
11 William Randolph Hearst (D)	26,255	59.3
Henry Clay Piercy (R)	16,594	37.5
12 William Bourke Cochran (D)	20,972	63.1
Henry Carey (R)	10,500	31.6
13 Herbert Parsons (R)	18,700	52.9
Edward Swann (D)	16,038	45.4
14 Charles A. Towne (D)	21,627	57.1
Lucian Knapp (R)	12,664	33.4
William F. Ehret (SOCIAL D)	2,973	7.8
15 Jacob Van Vechten Olcott (R)	16,924	51.7
M. Francis Loughman (D)	15,199	46.4
16 Jacob Ruppert Jr. (D)	15,049	52.7
Theodore Prince (R)	11,212	39.3
Adolph Groelinger (SOCIAL D)	1,882	6.6
17 William S. Bennett (R)	25,655	51.3
Franklin Leonard Jr (D)	23,029	46.0
18 Joseph A. Goulden (D)	32,266	57.2
William W. Niles (R)	20,606	36.5
19 John E. Andrus (R)	24,199	54.1
J. Harvey Bell (D)	19,079	42.7
20 Thomas W. Bradley (R)	23,224	55.5
Charles C. Dill (D)	17,562	42.0
21 John H. Ketcham (R)	24,791	95.9
22 William H. Draper (R)	25,755	59.4
Isaac C. Blandy (D)	16,261	37.5
23 George N. Southwick (R)	33,763	55.7
Daniel C. McElwain (D)	25,618	42.3
24 Frank J. Lefevre (R)	30,980	95.5
25 Lucius N. Littauer (R)	27,290	54.8
Joseph A. Kellogg (D)	20,491	41.1
26 William H. Flack (R)	33,564	67.5
Henry Holland (D)	14,801	29.8
27 James S. Sherman (R)	26,657	54.5
William H. Squires (D)	20,892	42.7
28 Charles L. Knapp (R)	27,357	60.2
Henry Purcell (D)	15,808	34.8
29 Michael E. Driscoll (R)	33,738	62.6
Harrison W. Coley (D)	18,324	34.0
30 John W. Dwight (R)	32,272	59.8
George L. Church (D)	19,846	36.8
31 Sereno E. Payne (R)	29,760	61.5
D. J. Vanauken (D)	17,576	36.4
32 James Breck Perkins (R)	30,091	58.9
Henry Selden Bacon (D)	17,382	34.1
33 Jacob Sloat Fassett (R)	26,276	57.5
Frank P. Frost (D)	18,055	39.5
34 James W. Wadsworth (R)	32,364	60.5
James E. Crisfield (D)	19,328	36.2
35 William H. Ryan (D)	20,840	49.4
Warren P. Bender (R)	19,943	47.2
36 De Alva S. Alexander (R)	27,958	59.8
Edwin Gaw Flanigen (D)	17,569	37.6
37 Edward B. Vreeland (R)	33,573	67.7
S. B. McClure (D)	13,229	26.7

NORTH CAROLINA

Candidates	Votes	%
1 John H. Small (D)	13,065	80.5
D. O. Newberry (R)	3,167	19.5
2 Claude Kitchin (D)	12,064	86.3
P. C. Jenkins (R)	1,919	13.7
3 Charles R. Thomas (D)	10,645	66.0
W. S. Robinson (R)	5,496	34.1
4 Edward W. Pou (D)	12,658	70.9
Claude Pearson (R)	5,197	29.1
5 William W. Kitchin (D)	16,497	58.7
C. A. Reynolds (R)	11,546	41.1
6 Gilbert B. Patterson (D)	9,770	70.0
O. J. Spears (R)	4,193	30.0
7 Robert N. Page (D)	12,642	58.5
L. D. Mendenhall (R)	8,986	41.6
8 E. Spencer Blackburn (R)	15,566	50.3
W. C. Newland (D)	15,321	49.5
9 Edwin Y. Webb (D)	13,822	58.1
J. F. Newell (R)	9,957	41.9
10 James M. Gudger Jr. (D)	13,554	51.7
H. G. Ewart (R)	12,666	48.3

NORTH DAKOTA

Candidates	Votes	%
AL Thomas F. Marshall (R)	49,111✔	
Asle J. Gronna (R)	47,648✔	
N. P. Rasmussen (D)	15,622	
A. G. Burr (D)	15,398	
L. F. Dow (SOC)	1,734	
E. D. Herring (SOC)	1,697	
B. H. Tibbets (P)	971	
N. A. Colby (P)	967	

OHIO

Candidates	Votes	%
1 Nicholas Longworth (R)	32,105	68.7
Braxton W. Campbell (D)	11,631	24.9
Bishop W. Mason (SOC)	2,737	5.9
2 Herman P. Goebel (R)	31,873	62.8
Charles A. Miller (D)	14,215	28.0
John F. Ditchen (SOC)	4,487	8.8
3 Robert M. Nevin (R)	31,626	53.0
Charles Conley (D)	25,594	42.9
4 Harvey C. Garber (D)	20,653	50.8
R. D. Kahle (R)	18,858	46.4
5 William W. Campbell (R)	19,707	49.4
Timothy T. Ansberry (D)	19,383	48.6
6 Thomas E. Scroggy (R)	21,485	51.4
James Runyan (D)	19,148	45.8
7 J. Warren Keifer (R)	25,245	60.0
P. E. Montanus (D)	15,966	37.9
8 Ralph D. Cole (R)	27,523	60.5
Henry F. MacCracken (D)	16,257	35.8
9 James H. Southard (R)	35,128	63.7
William H. Althof (D)	16,488	29.9
10 Henry Bannon (R)	25,097	62.6
Matthew S. Merriman (D)	13,316	33.2
11 Charles H. Grosvenor (R)	29,415	58.9
John T. Bridwell (D)	19,501	39.1
12 Edward L. Taylor Jr. (R)	25,178	56.6
Dewitt C. Badger (D)	17,999	40.5
13 Grant E. Mouser (R)	25,054	49.5
D. R. Crissinger (D)	24,004	47.4
14 Amos R. Webber (R)	29,187	57.4
Benjamin F. Long (D)	19,318	38.0
15 Beman G. Dawes (R)	20,763	48.4
Ernest B. Schneider (D)	20,231	47.2
16 Capell L. Weems (R)	23,265	59.1
H. W. Hermann (D)	13,676	34.8
17 Martin L. Smyser (R)	23,847	50.7
J. E. Hurst (D)	21,571	45.8
18 James Kennedy (R)	36,939	63.9
W. J. Foley (D)	16,472	28.5
19 W. Aubrey Thomas (R)	35,676	68.9
Charles J. McCormick (D)	11,942	23.1
F. N. Prevey (SOC)	2,927	5.7
20 Jacob A. Beidler (R)	29,475	59.8
Charles W. Lapp (D)	17,106	34.7
21 Theodore E. Burton (R)	33,930	86.6
Max S. Hayes (SOC)	4,144	10.6

OHIO
Special Elections

	Candidates	Votes	%
14	Amos R. Webber (R)	29,148	57.3
	Benjamin F. Long (D)	19,350	38.0
19	W. Aubrey Thomas (R)	35,802	83.5
	Charles J. McCormick (D)	5,467	12.8

OREGON

		Votes	%
1	Binger Hermann (R)	23,970	51.2
	R. M. Veatch (D)	17,157	36.7
	H. Gould (P)	2,867	6.1
	B. F. Ramp (SOC)	2,800	6.0
2	John N. Williamson (R)	27,126	57.6
	J. E. Simmons (D)	12,773	27.1
	George R. Cook (SOC)	3,678	7.8
	H. W. Stone (P)	3,535	7.5

PENNSYLVANIA

		Votes	%
1	Henry H. Bingham (R)	42,228	84.7
	Joseph L. Galen (D)	7,623	15.3
2	Robert Adams Jr. (R)	41,637	84.9
	John Cadwalader Jr. (D)	7,010	14.3
3	George A. Castor (R)	39,982	83.3
	John H. Fow (D, I)	7,873	16.4
4	Reuben O. Moon (R)	25,610	81.1
	Charles F. Stilz (D)	5,253	16.6
5	Edward de V. Morrell (R)	28,146	78.8
	David Moffet (D)	6,524	18.3
6	George D. McCreary (R)	34,984	76.7
	William A. Carr (D)	8,709	19.1
7	Thomas S. Butler (R)	26,145	77.5
	Archibald M. Holding (D)	6,470	19.2
8	Irving P. Wanger (R)	26,099	60.9
	Joseph J. Broadhurst (D)	15,847	37.0
9	Henry B. Cassel (R)	17,685	54.7
	Milton J. Brecht (CI/IC)	11,526	35.6
	Hugh M. North Jr (D)	2,894	8.9
10	Thomas H. Dale (R)	15,003	53.2
	George Howell (D)	12,683	44.9
11	Henry W. Palmer (R)	23,324	60.8
	William L. Raeder (D)	14,224	37.1
12	George R. Patterson (R)	17,419	57.4
	Harry O. Haag (D)	12,005	39.6
13	Marcus C. L. Kline (D)	25,711	50.1
	William H. Sowden (R)	23,781	46.4
14	Mial E. Lilly (R)	15,568	58.4
	John Kuhbach (D)	8,696	32.6
	William S. H. Heermans (P)	2,393	9.0
15	Elias Deemer (R)	19,807	58.3
	George B. McMetzger (D)	11,959	35.2
16	E. W. Samuel (R)	14,969	51.6
	Henry E. Davis (D)	13,191	45.5
17	Thaddeus M. Mahon (R)	22,860	61.4
	O. C. Bowers (D)	13,337	35.8
18	Marlin E. Olmsted (R)	26,996	67.6
	John L. Saylor (D)	11,663	29.2
19	John M. Reynolds (R)	23,164	54.9
	Joseph E. Thropp (D, P)	19,066	45.1
20	Daniel F. Lafean (R)	19,088	55.8
	William McSherry (D)	14,782	43.2
21	Solomon R. Dresser (R)	18,281	59.6
	Charles W. Shaffer (D)	9,559	31.2
	Samuel C. Watts (P)	2,407	7.9
22	George F. Huff (R)	21,547	65.5
	Charles M. Heineman (D)	9,824	29.9
23	Allen F. Cooper (R)	18,206	58.7
	Charles F. Uhl Jr. (D)	10,597	34.2
	George H. Hocking (P)	2,226	7.2
24	Ernest F. Acheson (R)	23,131	69.4
	William J. Mellon (D)	8,420	25.3
	John J. Ashenhurst (P)	1,798	5.4
25	Arthur L. Bates (R)	17,271	61.9
	E. W. McArthur (D)	8,082	28.9
	R. C. Loupe (P)	1,644	5.9
26	G. A. Schneebeli (R)	14,763	45.3
	J. Davis Brodhead (D, CIT)	12,895	39.6

	Candidates	Votes	%
	Joseph H. Shull (PURE POL)	3,759	11.5
27	William O. Smith (R)	18,697	71.8
	A. C. Smith (D)	7,353	28.2
28	Joseph C. Sibley (R)	19,861	55.2
	Salem Heilman (D)	10,651	29.6
	John E. Gill (P)	4,640	12.9
29	William H. Graham (R)	18,400	80.1
	W. H. S. Thomson (D)	3,437	15.0
30	John Dalzell (R)	17,322	79.0
	M. L. Thompson (D)	3,330	15.2
31	James Francis Burke (R)	18,403	75.2
	John F. McGrath (D)	5,289	21.6
32	A. J. Barchfeld (R)	19,383	75.9
	John Pierce (D)	4,690	18.4

RHODE ISLAND

		Votes	%
1	Daniel L. D. Granger (D)	15,583	49.5
	Stiness (R)	15,450	49.0
2	Adin B. Capron (R)	18,212	56.8
	Owen (D)	13,278	41.4

SOUTH CAROLINA

		Votes	%
1	George S. Legare (D)	6,068	91.3
	J. A. Noland (R)	346	5.2
2	James O'H. Patterson (D)	7,421	94.6
	Isaac Myers (R)	423	5.4
3	Wyatt Aiken (D)	7,659	98.1
4	Joseph T. Johnson (D)	8,516	97.5
5	David E. Finley (D)	7,928	97.9
6	J. Edwin Ellerbe (D)	8,348	95.7
7	Asbury F. Lever (D)	8,726	93.8
	Charles C. Jocobs (R)	563	6.1

SOUTH DAKOTA

		Votes	%
AL	Eben W. Martin (R)	70,002✔	
	Charles H. Burke (R)	69,936✔	
	Wesley A. Stuart (D)	22,692	
	W. A. Lynch (D)	22,640	
	H. W. Smith (SOC)	3,115	
	S. A. Cochrane (SOC)	3,064	
	A. Jamison (P)	3,012	
	C. K. Thompson (P)	2,961	
	A. J. McCain (POP)	1,216	
	G. W. Lattin (POP)	1,175	

TENNESSEE

		Votes	%
1	Walter P. Brownlow (R)	19,657	68.9
	R. E. Styll (D)	8,879	31.1
2	Nathan W. Hale (R)	14,963	70.9
	Staples (D)	6,013	28.5
3	John A. Moon (D)	16,541	53.2
	Sharp (R)	14,285	46.0
4	Mounce G. Butler (D)	13,359	53.3
	Pickering (R)	11,596	46.2
5	William C. Houston (D)	13,581	68.7
	Brown (R)	6,192	31.3
6	John W. Gaines (D)	13,777	79.0
	Maxwell (R)	3,517	20.2
7	Lemuel P. Padgett (D)	13,090	61.9
	Hughes (R)	8,027	38.0
8	Thetus W. Sims (D)	13,395	53.9
	Davis (R)	11,452	46.1
9	Finis J. Garrett (D)	16,222	74.9
	Walker (R)	5,443	25.1
10	Malcolm R. Patterson (D)	13,595	75.9
	Matthews (R)	4,307	24.1

TEXAS

		Votes	%
1	Morris Sheppard (D)	12,473	72.1
	J. A. Armistead (R)	4,838	28.0
2	Moses L. Broocks (D)	13,119	76.2
	A. J. Houston (R)	4,099	23.8

	Candidates	Votes	%
3	Gordon J. Russell (D)	12,473	73.7
	C. T. White (R)	4,441	26.3
4	Choice B. Randell (D)	14,435	90.4
	R. E. Martin (R)	1,537	9.6
5	Jack Beall (D)	14,292	86.0
	J. J. Cypert (R)	2,327	14.0
6	Scott Field (D)	9,438	100.0
7	Alexander W. Gregg (D)	8,040	100.0
8	John M. Pinckney (D)	9,804	69.1
	H. F. McGregor (R)	4,384	30.9
9	George F. Burgess (D)	14,316	72.3
	B. L. Osgood (D)	5,484	27.7
10	Albert S. Burleson (D)	11,761	100.0
11	Robert L. Henry (D)	10,305	84.4
	Joe E. Williams (R)	1,912	15.7
12	Oscar W. Gillespie (D)	12,480	74.4
	Frank B. Stanley	2,357	14.1
	J. M. Mallett (R)	1,933	11.5
13	John H. Stephens (D)	18,604	89.6
	James M. Kindred (R)	2,157	10.4
14	James L. Slayden (D)	15,097	98.3
15	John N. Garner (D)	10,647	64.9
	J. S. Morin (R)	5,767	35.1
16	William R. Smith (D)	17,488	83.1
	Logan McPherson (R)	3,562	16.9

UTAH

		Votes	%
AL	Joseph Howell (R)	52,675	51.8
	Orlando W. Powers (D)	37,445	36.8
	Ogden Hiles (AM)	6,796	6.7

VERMONT

		Votes	%
1	David J. Foster (R)	23,208	70.4
	Frank L. Graves (D)	8,868	26.9
2	Kittredge Haskins (R)	23,781	74.8
	Harland B. Howe (D)	7,066	22.2

VIRGINIA

		Votes	%
1	William A. Jones (D)	7,826	77.1
	Trader (R)	2,331	23.0
2	Harry L. Maynard (D)	10,762	78.3
	Robert M. Hughes (R)	2,800	20.4
3	John Lamb (D)	7,121	78.0
	Edgar Allan Jr. (R)	1,020	11.2
	George A. Harrison (IR)	773	8.5
4	Robert G. Southall (D)	6,031	82.8
	Charles Alexander (R)	1,248	17.1
5	Claude A. Swanson (D)	8,893	65.0
	J. B. Stovall (R)	4,793	35.0
6	Carter Glass (D)	7,798	69.1
	Samuel H. Hoge (R)	3,429	30.4
7	James Hay (D)	9,051	64.7
	Charles M. Kelzel (R)	4,949	35.4
8	John F. Rixey (D)	7,986	76.6
	Ernest Linoln Howard (R)	2,443	23.4
9	Campbell Slemp (R)	15,627	57.2
	J. C. Wysor (D)	11,710	42.8
10	Henry D. Flood (D)	9,183	61.3
	George A. Revercomb (R)	5,460	36.5

WASHINGTON

		Votes	%
AL	Francis W. Cushman (R)	93,328✔	
	Wesley L. Jones (R)	92,743✔	
	William E. Humphrey (R)	92,436✔	
	James J. Anderson (D)	35,698	
	Howard Hathaway (D)	35,636	
	W. T. Beck (D)	35,193	
	T. C. Wiswell (SOC)	9,005	
	George Croston (SOC)	8,940	
	H. D. Jory (SOC)	8,940	
	Ferdinand B. Hawes (P)	3,059	
	Henry Brown (P)	3,052	
	William Bonstein (SOC LAB)	1,320	
	R. McDonald (SOC LAB)	1,308	
	G. Norling (SOC LAB)	1,306	

WEST VIRGINIA

	Candidates	Votes	%
1	Blackburn B. Dovener (R)	27,459	54.3
	J. W. Barnes (D)	21,100	41.7
2	Alston G. Dayton (R)	24,225	51.6
	Stuart W. Walker (D)	21,888	46.6
3	Joseph Holt Gaines (R)	26,236	52.8
	H. B. Davenport (D)	22,125	44.5
4	Harry C. Woodyard (D)	22,942	53.6
	Allen C. Murdock (R)	18,912	44.2
5	James A. Hughes (R)	27,593	55.8
	S. S. Altezer (D)	21,276	43.0

WISCONSIN

	Candidates	Votes	%
1	Henry Allen Cooper (R)	25,125	59.5
	Calvin Stewart (D)	13,379	31.7

	Candidates	Votes	%
	J. W. Born (SOCIAL D)	2,461	5.8
2	Henry C. Adams (R)	22,773	57.7
	John J. Wood (D)	15,265	38.7
3	Joseph W. Babcock (R)	19,047	48.8
	Herman Grotophorst (D)	18,662	47.8
4	Theobald Otjen (R)	17,582	43.8
	Peter J. Sommers (D)	12,385	30.8
	W. R. Gaylord (SOCIAL D)	9,625	24.0
5	William H. Stafford (R)	17,231	44.8
	Victor L. Berger (SOCIAL D)	10,626	27.6
	Arthur Dopp (D)	9,978	26.0
6	Charles H. Weisse (D)	20,665	53.4
	Roy L. Morse (R)	17,687	45.7
7	John J. Esch (R)	25,505	66.8
	N. C. Basheller (D)	11,271	29.5

	Candidates	Votes	%
8	James H. Davidson (R)	25,233	63.1
	C. F. Crane (D)	12,889	32.2
9	Edward S. Minor (R)	19,764	58.1
	R. J. McGrehan (D)	13,124	38.6
10	Webster E. Brown (R)	29,392	65.4
	Wells M. Ruggles (D)	14,121	31.4
11	John J. Jenkins (R)	31,270	74.8
	George C. Cooper (D)	8,637	20.7

WYOMING

	Candidates	Votes	%
AL	Frank W. Mondell (R)	19,862	64.6
	T. S. Taliaferro Jr (D)	9,903	32.2

1905 House Election

ILLINOIS

Special Election

		Votes	%
14	James McKinney (R)	12,356	57.2
	James Howard Pattee	7,316	33.9
	Homer L. Darby	1,176	5.4

House Candidates Index

For an index of all House candidates listed in this section (pages 701 to 1061), see pages 1180-1273. Instructions for use of the House Candidates Index appear on page 1180.

1906 House Elections

ALABAMA

	Candidates	Votes	%
1	George W. Taylor (D)	3,592	100.0
2	Ariosto A. Wiley (D)	6,001	88.9
	J. C. Fonville (R)	751	11.1
3	Henry D. Clayton (D)	6,922	100.0
4	William B. Craig (D)	5,783	100.0
5	J. Thomas Heflin (D)	6,940	100.0
6	Richmond P. Hobson (D)	8,308	100.0
7	John L. Burnett (D)	8,265	62.7
	C. B. Kennamer (R)	4,914	37.3
8	William Richardson (D)	5,873	94.9
	John T. Masterson (R)	317	5.1
9	Oscar W. Underwood (D)	7,864	100.0

ARKANSAS

	Candidates	Votes	%
1	Robert B. Macon (D)	5,635	82.2
	D. F. Taylor (R)	1,223	17.8
2	Stephen Brundidge Jr (D)	5,137	80.9
	E. J. Mason (R)	1,216	19.1
3	John C. Floyd (D)	5,715	63.8
	W. N. Ivie (R)	3,246	36.2
4	William Ben Cravens (D)	7,290	65.5
	George Tilles (R)	3,840	34.5
5	Charles C. Reid (D)	5,967	75.1
	Alonzo Hedges (R)	1,976	24.9
6	Joseph T. Robinson (D)	5,473	84.4
	R. C. Thompson (R)	1,010	15.6
7	Robert M. Wallace (D)	3,255	99.1

CALIFORNIA

	Candidates	Votes	%
1	William F. Englebright (R)	18,954	54.1
	F. W. Taft (D)	13,984	39.9
2	Duncan E. McKinlay (R)	23,411	51.8
	W. A. Beard (D)	20,262	44.8
3	Joseph R. Knowland (R)	21,510	60.0
	Hugh W. Brunk (D)	7,716	21.5
	Charles C. Boynton (I LEAGUE)	3,614	10.1
	William McDevitt (SOC)	2,514	7.0
4	Julius Kahn (R)	5,678	62.4
	David S. Hirshberg (D)	3,016	33.2
5	Everis A. Hayes (R)	22,530	52.6
	Hiram G. Davis (D)	17,925	41.9
	Joseph Lawrence (SOC)	2,343	5.5
6	James C. Needham (R)	18,928	55.6
	Harry A. Greene (D)	12,868	37.8
7	James McLachlan (R)	22,338	56.7
	Robert G. Laucks (D)	11,197	28.4
	Claude Riddle (SOC)	3,641	9.3
	Levi D. Johnson (P)	2,189	5.6
8	Sylvester C. Smith (R)	22,548	55.6
	C. A. Barlow (D)	13,992	34.5
	N. A. Richardson (SOC)	4,001	9.9

Special Election

	Candidates	Votes	%
1	William F. Englebright (R)	18,125	95.2

COLORADO

	Candidates	Votes	%
1	Robert William Bonynge (R)	47,549	55.5
	Charles F. Tew (D)	31,133	36.3
	Luella Twining (SOC)	4,989	5.8
2	Warren A. Haggott (R)	54,869	49.3
	William W. Rowan (D)	46,783	42.1
	Flavius E. Ashburn (SOC)	7,666	6.9
AL	George W. Cook (R)	102,426	52.2
	Samuel W. Belford (D)	76,792	39.1
	Guy E. Miller (SOC)	12,668	6.5

CONNECTICUT

	Candidates	Votes	%
1	E. Stevens Henry (R)	21,605	56.8
	Holden (D)	15,039	39.6
2	Nehemiah D. Sperry (R)	29,058	53.1
	Wallace (D)	23,757	43.4
3	Edwin W. Higgins (R)	12,391	57.3
	Larue (D)	8,833	40.8
4	Ebenezer J. Hill (R)	26,484	56.9
	Beers (D)	18,969	40.8
AL	George L. Lilley (R)	88,115	54.8
	Donahue (D)	67,747	42.1

DELAWARE

	Candidates	Votes	%
AL	Hiram R. Burton (R)	20,210	52.8
	David T. Marvel (D)	17,118	44.8

FLORIDA

	Candidates	Votes	%
1	Stephen M. Sparkman (D)	6,212	86.5
	C. C. Allen (SOC)	967	13.5
2	Frank Clark (D)	8,792	88.1
	J. F. McClelland (SOC)	1,179	11.8
3	William B. Lamar (D)	5,415	93.4
	T. B. Meeker (SOC)	384	6.6

GEORGIA

	Candidates	Votes	%
1	Charles G. Edwards (D)	4,964	92.1
	D. B. Rigdon (R)	429	8.0
2	James M. Griggs (D)	3,425	100.0
3	Elijah B. Lewis (D)	2,386	100.0
4	William C. Adamson (D)	2,705	100.0
5	Leonidas F. Livingston (D)	3,030	100.0
6	Charles L. Bartlett (D)	3,374	100.0
7	Gordon Lee (D)	3,132	100.0
8	William M. Howard (D)	2,246	100.0
9	Thomas M. Bell (D)	3,159	100.0
10	Thomas W. Hardwick (D)	1,743	99.8
11	William G. Brantley (D)	2,748	100.0

IDAHO

	Candidates	Votes	%
AL	Burton L. French (R)	42,134	58.6
	Murray R. Hattabaugh (D)	23,818	33.1
	Edward L. Rigg (SOC)	4,834	6.7

ILLINOIS

	Candidates	Votes	%
1	Martin B. Madden (R)	17,015	59.3
	Martin Emerich (D)	10,015	34.9
2	James R. Mann (R)	20,660	63.4
	Herbert J. Friedman (D)	8,565	26.3
	Bernard Berlyn (SOC)	3,032	9.3
3	William W. Wilson (R)	14,130	49.7
	Paul A. Dratz (D)	6,569	23.1
	Willis C. Stone (I LG)	4,775	16.8
	James A. Prout (SOC)	2,457	8.6
4	James T. McDermott (D)	9,997	46.7
	Charles S. Wharton (R)	8,377	39.1
	James McCarthy (SOC)	2,859	13.3
5	Adolph J. Sabath (D)	9,545	46.1
	Anthony Michalek (R)	8,634	41.7
	Joseph Kral (SOC)	2,373	11.5
6	William Lorimer (R)	18,153	55.4
	Edmund J. Stack (D)	10,734	32.8
	Walter F. Huggins (SOC)	2,082	6.4
	Edward E. Blake (P)	1,794	5.5
7	Philip Knopf (R)	18,595	51.3
	Frank Buchanan (D)	11,383	31.4
	George Koop (SOC)	5,587	15.4

	Candidates	Votes	%
8	Charles McGavin (R)	11,421	40.0
	Stanley H. Kunz (D)	11,336	39.7
	Abraham Priess (I LG)	3,128	11.0
	James B. Smiley (SOC)	2,664	9.3
9	Henry S. Boutell (R)	15,316	50.6
	Arthur J. Donoghue (D)	8,504	28.1
	John M. Vail (I LG)	3,607	11.9
	Charles L. Breckon (SOC)	2,592	8.6
10	George Edmund Foss (R)	18,886	62.7
	Charles L. Young (D)	7,598	25.2
	Lewis W. Hardy (SOC)	2,777	9.2
11	Howard M. Snapp (R)	18,569	60.7
	Benjamin P. Alschuler (D)	9,104	29.8
	George McGinnis (P)	2,201	7.2
12	Charles E. Fuller (R)	19,463	86.9
	Victor Irving Clark (P)	1,712	7.6
	A. A. Patterson (SOC)	1,224	5.5
13	Frank O. Lowden (R)	16,590	51.2
	James P. Wilson (D)	14,747	45.5
14	James McKinney (R)	18,583	54.7
	David W. Matthews (D)	12,978	38.2
15	George W. Prince (R)	19,975	54.2
	Hiram N. Wheeler (D)	14,191	38.5
16	Joseph V. Graff (R)	16,983	50.3
	Louis F. Meek (D)	13,876	41.1
	C. E. Stebbins (P)	1,966	5.8
17	John A. Sterling (R)	16,804	55.8
	L. W. MacNeil (D)	11,377	37.8
	James H. Burrows (P)	1,927	6.4
18	Joseph G. Cannon (R)	22,804	58.4
	Charles G. Taylor (D)	12,777	32.7
19	William B. McKinley (R)	23,662	52.7
	John W. Yantis (D)	19,247	42.9
20	Henry T. Rainey (D)	19,578	54.9
	Jacob G. Pope (R)	14,645	41.1
21	Benjamin F. Caldwell (D)	22,429	53.5
	Zeno J. Rives (R)	17,396	41.5
22	William A. Rodenberg (R)	23,138	56.2
	James J. McInerney (D)	15,371	37.3
23	Martin D. Foster (D)	21,680	49.5
	Frank S. Dickson (R)	20,361	46.5
24	Pleasant T. Chapman (R)	17,990	51.1
	James R. Williams (D)	16,241	46.2
25	George W. Smith (R)	17,835	52.6
	James M. Joplin (D)	14,240	42.0

Special Election

	Candidates	Votes	%
13	Frank O. Lowden (R)	17,003	96.9

INDIANA

	Candidates	Votes	%
1	John H. Foster (R)	20,278	50.0
	Gustavus V. Menzies (D)	18,959	46.7
2	John C. Chaney (R)	22,299	48.7
	Cyrus E. Davis (D)	21,889	47.8
3	William E. Cox (D)	18,606	49.3
	George H. Hester (R)	18,151	48.1
4	Lincoln Dixon (D)	20,049	51.0
	John H. Kamman (R)	18,181	46.2
5	Elias S. Holliday (R)	22,532	48.8
	Claud G. Bowers (D)	21,579	46.8
6	James E. Watson (R)	22,135	49.5
	Thomas H. Kuhn (D)	20,629	46.2
7	Jesse Overstreet (R)	28,020	52.8
	Frank E. Gavin (D)	23,234	43.8
8	John A. M. Adair (D)	24,027	51.4
	George W. Cromer (R)	19,783	42.3
9	Charles B. Landis (R)	23,865	49.5
	Marion E. Clodfelter (D)	21,633	44.9
10	Edgar D. Crumpacker (R)	24,695	54.0
	William Darroch (D)	20,072	43.9
11	George W. Rauch (D)	22,988	50.2
	Frederick Landis (R)	19,833	43.3
	Levi T. Pennington (P)	2,367	5.2

INDIANA

Candidates	Votes	%
12 Clarence C. Gilhams (R)	19,695	48.6
John W. Morr (D)	19,345	47.7
13 Abraham L. Brick (R)	23,360	48.0
Benjamin F. Shively (D)	23,153	47.5

Special Election

	Votes	%
12 Clarence C. Gilhams (R)	19,249	50.5
John W. Morr (D)	18,870	49.5

IOWA

Candidates	Votes	%
1 Charles A. Kennedy (R)	16,145	49.1
George S. Tracy (D)	15,875	48.3
2 Albert F. Dawson (R)	20,112	50.2
George W. Ball (D)	18,520	46.2
3 Benjamin P. Birdsall (R)	22,315	57.7
J. C. Murtagh (D)	15,113	39.0
4 Gilbert N. Haugen (R)	20,731	60.6
M. J. Carter (D)	12,739	37.2
5 Robert G. Cousins (R)	19,076	54.3
Robert C. Stinton (D)	14,612	41.6
6 Daniel W. Hamilton (D)	18,987	51.8
John F. Lacey (R)	16,713	45.6
7 John A. T. Hull (R)	19,617	59.2
John Nathan Smith (D)	11,464	34.6
8 William Peter Hepburn (R)	19,516	53.0
Joel S. Estes (D)	16,074	43.7
9 Walter I. Smith (R)	21,863	60.7
William C. Campbell (D)	13,250	36.8
10 James Perry Conner (R)	26,017	60.9
John B. Butler (D)	15,317	35.9
11 Elbert H. Hubbard (R)	22,236	55.9
Charles A. Dickson (D)	16,893	42.5

KANSAS

Candidates	Votes	%
1 Charles Curtis (R)	22,790*	57.5
W. D. Webb (D)	16,215	40.9
2 Charles F. Scott (R)	23,521	53.1
Mason S. Peters (D)	19,653	44.4
3 Philip P. Campbell (R)	25,669	52.5
Francis M. Brady (D)	19,807	40.5
Fred D. Warren (SOC)	2,908	5.9
4 James Monroe Miller (R)	17,393	53.5
J. W. Moore (D)	14,313	44.0
5 William A. Calderhead (R)	18,183	54.1
Hugh Alexander (D)	14,561	43.3
6 William A. Reeder (R)	21,212	51.9
John B. Rea (D)	17,116	41.9
7 Edmond H. Madison (R)	21,580	55.0
O. H. Truman (D)	15,623	39.8
8 Victor Murdock (R)	14,862	56.5
F. B. Lawrance (D)	10,427	39.6

KENTUCKY

Candidates	Votes	%
1 Ollie M. James (D)	12,870	85.9
J. D. Smith (P)	2,118	14.1
2 Augustus O. Stanley (D)	13,282	61.9
Paul M. Moore (R)	7,406	34.5
3 Addison D. James (R)	14,987	50.2
James M. Richardson (D)	14,288	47.8
4 Ben Johnson (D)	15,128	59.1
M. L. Heavrin (R)	9,819	38.4
5 J. Swagar Sherley (D)	15,698	54.8
William C. Owens (R)	12,210	42.6
6 Joseph L. Rhinock (D)	13,358	48.3
William F. Schuerman (R)	12,973	46.9
7 William P. Kimball (D)	15,658	74.0
Joseph W. Calvert (R)	5,066	23.9
8 Harvey Helm (D)	13,182	55.1
L. W. Bethurum (R)	10,164	42.4
9 Joseph B. Bennett (R)	18,430	51.4
James N. Kehoe (D)	17,314	48.2
10 John W. Langley (R)	17,254	50.7
Frank A. Hopkins (D)	16,343	48.0
11 Don C. Edwards (R)	15,645	61.9
Ancil Gatliff (D)	8,714	34.5

LOUISIANA

Candidates	Votes	%
1 Adolph Meyer (D)	8,667	90.0
Henry Seiner (R)	681	7.1
2 Robert C. Davey (D)	6,349	91.9
A. L. Redden (R)	409	5.9
3 Robert F. Broussard (D)	4,267	85.0
S. P. Watts (R)	753	15.0
4 John T. Watkins (D)	3,210	97.3
5 Joseph E. Ransdell (D)	3,177	100.0
6 George K. Favrot (D)	3,270	92.4
John Deblieux (R)	269	7.6
7 Arsene P. Pujo (D)	3,761	66.1
C. C. Duson (R)	1,762	31.0

MAINE

Candidates	Votes	%
1 Amos L. Allen (R)	16,903	51.9
James C. Hamlen (D)	15,254	46.8
2 Charles E. Littlefield (R)	18,708	50.9
Daniel J. McGillicuddy (D)	17,346	47.2
3 Edwin C. Burleigh (R)	16,682	51.7
E. J. Lawrence (D)	14,891	46.2
4 Llewellyn Powers (R)	17,279	54.9
George M. Hanson (D)	13,705	43.6

MARYLAND

Candidates	Votes	%
1 William H. Jackson (R)	18,567	51.5
Thomas A. Smith (D)	16,124	44.8
2 J. Fred C. Talbott (D)	17,870	50.3
Robert Garrett (R)	16,618	46.7
3 Harry B. Wolf (D)	15,725	49.8
William W. Johnson (R)	14,841	47.0
4 John Gill Jr. (D)	18,010	50.7
John V. L. Findlay Jr. (R)	16,306	45.9
5 Sydney E. Mudd (R)	16,798	53.7
George M. Smith (D)	13,405	42.8
6 George A. Pearre (R)	16,136	55.3
Harvey R. Spessard (D)	11,232	38.5

MASSACHUSETTS

Candidates	Votes	%
1 George P. Lawrence (R)	15,622	59.7
Frank J. Lawler (D)	9,528	36.4
2 Frederick H. Gillett (R)	15,873	61.3
Edward A. Hall (D)	8,412	32.5
George H. Wrenn (SOC)	1,622	6.3
3 Charles G. Washburn (R)	15,686	58.6
William I. McLoughlin (D)	10,415	38.9
4 Charles Q. Tirrell (R)	20,750	79.0
Timothy Richardson (SOC)	5,501	20.9
5 Butler Ames (R)	15,778	54.2
Joseph J. Flynn (D)	12,881	44.2
6 Augustus P. Gardner (R)	18,390	54.8
George A. Schofield (D)	14,055	41.9
7 Ernest W. Roberts (R)	21,752	66.4
John A. O'Keefe (D)	9,816	30.0
8 Samuel W. McCall (R)	17,952	59.4
Frederick S. Deitrick (D)	11,690	38.7
9 John A. Keliher (D)	15,997	68.1
Edward C. Webb (R)	6,256	26.6
George W. Galvin (SOC)	1,242	5.3
10 Joseph F. O'Connell (D)	18,979	54.9
Edward B. Callender (R)	14,621	42.3
11 Andrew J. Peters (D)	18,099	53.9
Daniel W. Lane (R)	14,670	43.7
12 John W. Weeks (R)	18,948	61.5
David W. Murray (D)	10,591	34.4
13 William S. Greene (R)	14,236	68.3
Francis M. Kennedy (D)	6,603	31.7
14 William C. Lovering (R)	18,002	61.8
Thomas F. Loorem (D)	6,815	23.4
Daniel A. White (SOC)	4,301	14.8

MICHIGAN

Candidates	Votes	%
1 Edwin Denby (R)	23,741	57.5
Frederick F. Ingram (D)	16,975	41.1
2 Charles E. Townsend (R)	23,397	96.2
3 Washington Gardner (R)	16,821	58.4
John B. Shipman (D)	10,388	36.1
4 Edward L. Hamilton (R)	18,553	60.6
George R. Herkimer (D)	11,561	37.8
5 William Alden Smith (R)	18,487*	88.9
John E. Nicles (SOC)	1,302	6.3
6 Samuel W. Smith (R)	24,001	60.4
Peter B. Delisle (D)	14,360	36.1
7 Henry McMorran (R)	17,100	59.6
William Springer (D)	11,028	38.4
8 Joseph W. Fordney (R)	16,849	92.4
9 James C. McLaughlin (R)	14,374	69.8
Charles G. Wing (D)	5,288	25.7
10 George A. Loud (R)	18,958	97.2
11 Archibald B. Darragh (R)	18,110	70.7
Arthur J. Lacy (D)	7,517	29.3
12 H. Olin Young (R)	22,271	75.6
John F. Ryan (D)	6,315	21.4

MINNESOTA

Candidates	Votes	%
1 James A. Tawney (R)	17,352	57.8
French (D)	12,676	42.2
2 Winfield S. Hammond (D)	13,526	50.5
McCleary (R)	12,466	46.5
3 Charles R. Davis (R)	19,461	100.0
4 Frederick C. Stevens (R)	19,300	64.3
Scholle (D)	9,179	30.6
Lando (PUB OWN)	1,544	5.1
5 Frank M. Nye (R)	23,742	55.6
Larrabee (D)	16,448	38.5
6 Charles A. Lindbergh (R)	16,752	56.1
Tift (D)	13,115	43.9
7 Andrew G. Volstead (R)	21,491	100.0
8 J. Adam Bede (R)	18,640	75.6
Peterson (PUB OWN)	6,025	24.4
9 Halvor Steenerson (R)	22,145	80.1
Boen (PUB OWN)	5,490	19.9

MISSISSIPPI

Candidates	Votes	%
1 Ezekiel S. Candler Jr. (D)	2,566	100.0
2 Thomas Spight (D)	2,567	100.0
3 Benjamin G. Humphreys (D)	1,540	100.0
4 Wilson S. Hill (D)	2,536	100.0
5 Adam Byrd (D)	2,782	100.0
6 F. A. McLain (D)	1,933	100.0
7 Eaton J. Bowers (D)	4,077	95.9
8 John S. Williams (D)	2,091	100.0

MISSOURI

Candidates	Votes	%
1 James T. Lloyd (D)	19,796	54.3
Clements (R)	16,655	45.7
2 William W. Rucker (D)	20,732	56.7
Beazell (R)	15,814	43.2
3 Joshua W. Alexander (D)	18,669	52.9
Unidentified Candidate (R)	16,616	47.1
4 Charles F. Booher (D)	18,631	51.3
Fulkerson (R)	17,458	48.1
5 Edgar C. Ellis (R)	21,496	52.2
Wallace (D)	19,710	47.8
6 David A. De Armond (D)	17,574	53.0
Atkeson (R)	15,579	47.0
7 Courtney W. Hamlin (D)	22,248	51.3
Welborn (R)	20,497	47.3
8 Dorsey W. Shackleford (D)	16,245	53.4
Quigley (R)	14,186	46.6
9 James Beauchamp Clark (D)	21,364	54.3
Garber (R)	17,972	45.7
10 Richard Bartholdt (R)	31,639	61.9
Coale (D)	16,336	32.0
Hoehn (SOC)	3,102	6.1

MISSOURI

Candidates	Votes	%
11 Henry S. Caulfield (R)	13,171	47.8
Neville (D)	13,133	47.6
12 Harry M. Coudrey (R)	11,281	50.1
Selph (D)	10,451	46.4
13 Madison R. Smith (D)	16,056	50.7
Rhodes (R)	15,628	49.3
14 Joseph J. Russell (D)	24,288	51.4
Tyndall (R)	22,799	48.3
15 Thomas Hackney (D)	20,677	48.3
Caulkins (R)	20,402	47.6
16 J. Robert Lamar (D)	15,366	50.7
Murphy (R)	14,939	49.3

MONTANA

Candidates	Votes	%
AL Charles N. Pray (R&A-T R)	28,368	50.5
Thomas J. Walsh (D & LAB)	22,894	40.8
John Hudson (SOC)	4,638	8.3

NEBRASKA

Candidates	Votes	%
1 Ernest M. Pollard (R)	14,771	52.8
T. J. Doyle (D & PPI)	11,870	42.4
2 Gilbert M. Hitchcock (D)	11,644	51.0
John L. Kennedy (R)	11,136	48.8
3 John F. Boyd (R)	18,837	49.0
Guy T. Graves (D & PPI)	18,546	48.2
4 Edmund H. Hinshaw (R)	19,032	55.0
J. J. Thomas (D & PPI)	15,211	44.0
5 George W. Norris (R)	16,450	53.1
Roderick D. Sutherland (D & PPI)	14,031	45.3
6 Moses P. Kinkaid (R)	18,677	57.1
G. L. Shumway (D & PPI)	13,147	40.2

NEVADA

Candidates	Votes	%
AL George A. Bartlett (D&SILVER)	7,320	51.4
Oscar J. Smith (R)	5,665	39.8
H. T. Jardine (SOC)	1,251	8.8

NEW HAMPSHIRE

Candidates	Votes	%
1 Cyrus A. Sulloway (R)	22,701	57.8
Charles A. Morse (D)	15,601	39.7
2 Frank D. Currier (R)	23,073	58.0
Henri T. Ledoux (D)	15,669	39.4

NEW JERSEY

Candidates	Votes	%
1 Henry C. Loudenslager (R)	20,674	65.8
Summerill (D)	9,308	29.6
2 John J. Gardner (R)	19,637	63.0
Perry (D)	8,921	28.6
3 Benjamin F. Howell (R)	20,472	54.3
Harvey (D)	16,638	44.1
4 Ira W. Wood (R)	17,497	52.9
Southwick (D)	13,989	42.3
5 Charles N. Fowler (R)	19,760	48.8
Martine (D & ID)	19,208	47.5
6 William Hughes (D)	25,438	50.2
Burke (R)	23,335	46.1
7 Richard W. Parker (R)	16,493	49.5
Kaemer (D)	15,983	48.0
8 Le Gage Pratt (D)	18,334	56.9
Gottlob (R)	12,460	38.7
9 Eugene W. Leake (D)	18,367	55.4
Pickett (R)	12,628	38.1
10 James A. Hamill (D)	22,882	65.2
Cruse (R)	9,305	26.5

NEW YORK

Candidates	Votes	%
1 William W. Cocks (R)	22,569	60.3
Monson Morris (D)	14,418	38.5
2 George H. Lindsay (D)	11,420	39.2
John J. McManus (I LEAGUE)	9,069	31.2
Ernest C. Wagner (R)	7,591	26.1
3 Charles T. Dunwell (R)	16,546	45.5
Walter B. Raymond (D)	10,707	29.5
Henry Clay Peters (I LEAGUE)	8,089	22.3
4 Charles B. Law (R)	17,079	41.3
Herman H. Torborg (D)	12,114	29.3
Edson Lawrence (I LEAGUE)	10,590	25.6
5 George E. Waldo (R)	19,832	46.1
John J. Roach (D)	11,995	27.9
Michael A. Fitzgerald (I LEAGUE)	10,575	24.6
6 William M. Calder (R)	21,195	54.9
Robert Baker (D & IL)	17,102	44.3
7 John J. Fitzgerald (D)	15,055	47.1
Charles R. Banks (R)	8,433	26.4
John T. Moran (I LEAGUE)	8,220	25.7
8 Daniel J. Riordan (D)	21,340	65.6
Frank L. Frugone (R)	10,632	32.7
9 Henry M. Goldfogle (D)	7,276	53.3
Morris Hillquit (SOC)	3,586	26.3
Charles S. Adler (R)	2,734	20.0
10 William Sulzer (D & IL)	15,962	71.3
Frederick J. Etzel (R)	4,843	21.6
Alexander Jonas (SOC)	1,560	7.0
11 Charles V. Fornes (D & IL)	26,511	70.3
Charles W. Lefler (R)	10,640	28.2
12 William Bourke Cockran (D & IL)	20,481	71.4
Henry Carey (R)	7,410	25.8
13 Herbert Parsons (R)	16,381	55.0
William H. Jackson (D)	9,881	33.2
Frank Hendrick (I LEAGUE)	3,172	10.7
14 William Willett Jr. (D)	17,675	46.3
Frank E. Losee (R)	10,006	26.2
Charles E. Shober (I LEAGUE)	8,110	21.3
Richard Morton (SOC)	2,328	6.1
15 Jacob Van Vechten Olcott (R)	16,210	54.8
John J. Halligan (D & IL)	13,123	44.4
16 Francis Burton Harrison (D & IL)	16,954	66.3
Jacob R. Schiff (R)	7,062	27.6
17 William S. Bennet (R)	27,159	53.1
Francis E. Shober (D & IL)	23,284	45.5
18 Joseph A. Goulden (D)	28,339	46.9
James L. Wells (R)	17,943	29.7
James T. Farrelly (I LEAGUE)	12,109	20.1
19 John E. Andrus (R)	23,356	53.8
Timothy Healy (D)	19,218	44.3
20 Thomas W. Bradley (R)	21,191	55.9
Victor A. Wilder (D, I LEAGUE)	16,111	42.5
21 Samuel McMillan (R)	20,717	51.0
Percy W. Decker (D, I LEAGUE)	19,745	48.6
22 William H. Draper (R)	22,344	55.3
Thomas A. Paterson (D, I LEAGUE)	17,188	42.5
23 George N. Southwick (R)	29,099	50.7
George C. Hisgen (D, I LEAGUE)	27,344	47.7
24 George W. Fairchild (R)	24,474	51.3
Walter Scott (D, I LEAGUE)	23,215	48.7
25 Cyrus Durey (R)	25,041	54.4
Frank Beebe (D)	18,385	40.7
26 George R. Malby (R)	26,209	70.2
Andrew B. Cooney (D)	10,931	29.3
27 James S. Sherman (R)	24,027	53.3
James K. O'Connor (D, U LAB)	19,757	43.8
28 Charles L. Knapp (R)	23,451	60.7
Jay C. Bardo (D)	12,573	32.5
Frank H. Lewis (P)	2,197	5.7
29 Michael E. Driscoll (R)	30,350	61.4
William W. Vanbrocklin (D)	17,385	35.2
30 John W. Dwight (R)	27,069	59.9
Amasa G. Genung (D)	16,269	36.0
31 Sereno E. Payne (R)	25,475	62.6
Dudley M. Warner (D)	14,150	34.8
32 James Breck Perkins (R)	25,343	52.4
William L. Manning (D)	21,393	44.2
33 Jacob Sloat Fassett (R)	21,235	55.0
Frank P. Frost (D)	15,883	41.1
34 Peter A. Porter (D, IND CONG)	25,837	55.6
James W. Wadsworth (D)	19,935	42.9
35 William H. Ryan (D)	22,140	56.5
Frank X. Bernhardt (R)	16,494	42.1
36 De Alva S. Alexander (R)	24,457	58.0
John W. Williams (D)	16,209	38.5
37 Edward B. Vreeland (R)	25,468	65.2
Mark Graves (D)	11,562	29.6

NORTH CAROLINA

Candidates	Votes	%
1 John H. Small (D)	11,401	75.8
J. Q. A. Wood (R)	3,610	24.0
2 Claude Kitchin (D)	10,057	84.6
J. R. Gaskill (R)	1,816	15.3
3 Charles R. Thomas (D)	10,382	66.3
W. R. Dixon (R)	5,280	33.7
4 Edward W. Pou (D)	12,161	69.8
Berry Godwin (R)	5,270	30.2
5 William W. Kitchin (D)	16,503	59.6
C. A. Reynolds (R)	11,089	40.0
6 Hannibal L. Godwin (D)	9,729	67.7
James B. Schulken (R)	4,645	32.3
7 Robert N. Page (D)	11,780	56.7
G. D. B. Reynolds (R)	9,008	43.3
8 Richard N. Hackett (D)	16,907	51.6
E. S. Blackburn (R)	15,841	48.4
9 Edwin Y. Webb (D)	12,727	58.6
F. Roberts (R)	8,988	41.4
10 William T. Crawford (D)	13,049	51.6
James J. Britt (R)	12,200	48.2

NORTH DAKOTA

Candidates	Votes	%
AL Thomas F. Marshall (R)	38,923✔	
Asle J. Gronna (R)	36,772✔	
A. G. Burr (D)	21,350	
John D. Benton (D)	21,050	
H. Halvorson (SOC)	1,151	
W. J. Bailey (SOC)	1,129	

OHIO

Candidates	Votes	%
1 Nicholas Longworth (R)	25,161	56.9
Thomas H. Bentham (D)	18,004	40.7
2 Herman P. Goebel (R)	23,219	59.1
John H. Meyer (D)	12,258	31.2
Harry R. Probasco (I)	2,259	5.8
3 J. Eugene Harding (R)	24,567	49.5
James E. Campbell (D)	22,837	46.0
4 William E. Tou Velle (D)	17,582	55.6
J. C. Rosser (R)	12,934	40.9
5 Timothy T. Ansberry (D)	17,256	50.7
William M. Campbell (R)	16,241	47.7
6 Matthew R. Denver (D)	17,471	50.6
Charles Q. Hildebrant (R)	16,291	47.2
7 J. Warren Keifer (R)	15,975	53.8
William B. Rodgers (D)	12,387	41.8
8 Ralph D. Cole (R)	21,524	54.9
Homer Southard (D)	16,396	41.9
9 Isaac R. Sherwood (D, I)	18,411	47.8
E. G. McClelland (R)	18,370	47.7
10 Henry Bannon (R)	17,979	53.3
Thomas H. B. Jones (D)	14,686	43.5
11 Albert Douglas (R)	21,247	50.4
Oliver W. H. Wright (D)	19,914	47.2
12 Edward L. Taylor Jr. (R)	19,629	56.9
William A. Taylor (D)	13,351	38.7
13 Grant E. Mouser (R)	20,736	49.2
Daniel R. Crissinger (D)	20,463	48.5

OHIO

	Candidates	Votes	%
14	J. Ford Laning (R)	20,962	51.7
	William H. Budd (D)	18,443	45.5
15	Beman G. Dawes (R)	18,364	49.6
	George White (D)	16,945	45.8
16	Capell L. Weems (R)	14,712	53.9
	Frank A. Summers (D)	11,347	41.6
17	William A. Ashbrook (D)	19,982	49.3
	Martin L. Suyser (R)	19,497	48.1
18	James Kennedy (R)	19,684	49.5
	John C. Welty (D)	17,840	44.9
19	W. Aubrey Thomas (R)	20,341	61.3
	Thaddeus E. Hoyt (D)	10,926	32.9
20	Paul Howland (R)	19,439	51.8
	Charles W. Lapp (D)	16,966	45.3
21	Theodore E. Burton (R)	20,826	92.9
	Robert Bandlow (SOC)	1,376	6.1

OREGON

		Votes	%
1	Willis C. Hawley (R)	23,120	49.1
	Charles V. Galloway (D)	19,340	41.1
	W. W. Myers (SOC)	2,794	5.9
2	William R. Ellis (R)	28,315	61.0
	James Harvey Graham (D)	12,151	26.2
	A. M. Paul (SOC)	3,532	7.6
	H. W. Stone (P)	2,408	5.2

PENNSYLVANIA

		Votes	%
1	Henry H. Bingham (R, JEFF)	24,280	63.7
	E. Spencer Miller (LINCOLN)	8,718	22.9
	Joseph L. Galen (D)	4,738	12.4
2	John E. Reyburn (R, LINCOLN)	28,140	85.7
	G. Frank Stephens (D)	4,262	13.0
3	J. Hampton Moore (R, JEFF)	20,337	63.6
	William J. O'Brien (LINCOLN, D)	11,240	35.1
4	Reuben O. Moon (R, LINCOLN)	26,289	85.6
	Horace S. Fogel (D)	3,993	13.0
5	William W. Foulkrod (R, LINCOLN)	29,390	86.1
	Thomas P. Dolan (D)	3,987	11.7
6	George D. McCreary (R, LINCOLN)	38,269	84.6
	Francis X. Ward (D)	6,425	14.2
7	Thomas S. Butler (R, BC)	19,676	70.0
	John J. Buckley (D, P)	8,249	29.3
8	Irving P. Wanger (R, CP)	22,416	54.6
	Walter F. Leedom (D, LINCOLN)	18,231	44.4
9	Henry B. Cassel (R)	18,903	67.7
	J. Harold Wickersham (LINCOLN)	9,007	32.3
10	T. D. Nichols (D)	18,037	60.3
	Thomas H. Dale (R, LINCOLN)	11,796	39.4
11	John T. Lenahan (D)	16,176	50.6
	Bennett J. Cobleigh (RO SOC D)	9,627	30.1
	William H. Dettry (SOC)	5,197	16.3
12	Charles N. Brumm (R)	15,652	58.5
	Watson F. Shepperd (D)	10,247	38.3
13	John H. Rothermel (D)	21,885	54.2
	J. Wilmer Fisher (R)	16,488	40.8
	Morris E. Gibson (SOC)	2,044	5.1
14	George W. Kipp (D)	12,091	49.2
	Mial E. Lilly (R)	11,288	46.0
15	William B. Wilson (D)	14,582	48.2
	Elias Deemer (R)	14,201	47.0
16	John G. McHenry (D)	14,707	53.8
	Edmund W. Samuel (R, P)	12,131	44.4
17	Benjamin K. Focht (R)	17,130	52.2
	William Alexander (D)	14,036	42.8
18	Marlin E. Olmsted (R)	22,447	58.9
	John Lindner (D)	14,457	37.9

	Candidates	Votes	%
19	John M. Reynolds (R)	17,521	50.6
	Joseph E. Thropp (D, LINCOLN)	13,649	39.4
	Warren W. Bailey (BRYAN)	2,140	6.2
20	Daniel F. Lafean (R)	15,653	50.7
	Horace Keesey (D)	15,204	49.3
21	Charles F. Barclay (R, P)	15,210	57.5
	Hugh S. Taylor (D)	10,572	40.0
22	George F. Huff (R)	15,924	59.0
	Silas A. Kline (D, LINCOLN)	10,490	38.9
23	Allen F. Cooper (R)	15,008	54.7
	Ernest O. Kooser (D, LINCOLN)	10,309	37.6
	John O. Stoner (P)	1,789	6.5
24	Ernest F. Acheson (R)	15,490	49.2
	Robert K. Aiken (D, LINCOLN)	14,163	45.0
25	Arthur L. Bates (R)	13,564	60.6
	Andrew J. Palm (D, P)	8,109	36.2
26	J. Davis Brodhead (D, LINCOLN)	15,371	54.3
	Gustav A. Schneebeli (R)	12,427	43.9
27	Joseph G. Beale (R)	14,646	58.3
	S. C. Hepler (D)	9,101	36.2
	Enoch McGary (P)	1,392	5.5
28	Nelson P. Wheeler (R)	16,550	52.7
	Earl H. Beshlin (D)	10,433	33.2
	H. E. Horne (P)	3,750	11.9
29	William H. Graham (R, CIT)	17,688	91.8
30	John Dalzell (R, CIT)	13,984	65.1
	Robert J. Black (D, UN LAB)	6,452	30.0
31	James Francis Burke (R, CIT)	13,364	67.5
	Frank Lackner (D)	5,740	29.0
32	A. J. Barchfeld (R)	14,525	68.1
	M. C. O'Donovan (D)	4,811	22.6

RHODE ISLAND

		Votes	%
1	Daniel L. D. Granger (D)	16,846	50.4
	Dyer (R)	16,030	48.0
2	Adin B. Capron (R)	16,979	53.0
	Garvin (D)	14,593	45.5

SOUTH CAROLINA

		Votes	%
1	George S. Legare (D)	3,965	99.3
2	James O'H. Patterson (D)	4,588	95.3
3	Wyatt Aiken (D)	2,938	100.0
4	Joseph T. Johnson (D)	5,124	98.7
5	David E. Finley (D)	3,585	100.0
6	J. Edwin Ellerbe (D)	3,483	100.0
7	Asbury F. Lever (D)	5,191	97.5

SOUTH DAKOTA

		Votes	%
AL	Philo Hall (R)	48,096✔	
	William H. Parker (R)	48,010✔	
	William S. Elder (D)	19,976	
	Samuel A. Ramsey (D)	19,791	
	C. V. Templeton (P)	3,392	
	R. J. Day (P)	3,313	
	James Kirwan (SOC)	2,439	
	Henry A. Berge (SOC)	2,322	

TENNESSEE

		Votes	%
1	Walter P. Brownlow (R)	17,249	52.1
	John H. Coldwell (D)	9,145	27.6
	A. A. Taylor (IR)	6,700	20.2
2	Nathan W. Hale (R)	13,817	71.5
	E. L. Foster (D)	5,125	26.5
3	John A. Moon (D)	15,388	56.9
	T. W. Peace (R)	11,409	42.2
4	Cordell Hull (D)	11,951	53.6
	John E. Oliver (R)	10,312	46.3
5	William C. Houston (D)	11,450	71.5
	T. W. Wade (R)	4,446	27.8

	Candidates	Votes	%
6	John W. Gaines (D)	12,546	79.8
	J. W. Johnson (R)	2,981	19.0
7	Lemuel P. Padgett (D)	12,750	68.7
	Joe P. Kidd (R)	5,818	31.3
8	Thetus W. Sims (D)	11,209	50.7
	J. C. R. McCall (R)	10,874	49.2
9	Finis J. Garrett (D)	11,538	76.9
	Yandell Hann (R)	3,437	22.9
10	George W. Gordon (D)	10,378	95.4

TEXAS

		Votes	%
1	Morris Sheppard (D)	9,479	90.6
	Phil E. Baer (R)	886	8.5
2	Samuel B. Cooper (D)	9,593	93.0
	J. H. Kurth (R)	622	6.0
3	Gordon J. Russell (D)	8,522	89.3
	G. W. L. Smith (R)	753	7.9
4	Choice B. Randell (D)	11,508	87.3
	W. G. McGinnis (R)	1,678	12.7
5	Jack Beall (D)	9,060	91.9
	A. M. Cochran (R)	525	5.3
6	Rufus Hardy (D)	5,536	92.1
7	Alexander W. Gregg (D)	6,590	100.0
8	John M. Moore (D)	8,536	84.3
	W. A. Matthai (R)	1,593	15.7
9	George F. Burgess (D)	10,257	75.6
	A. M. Waugh (R)	3,043	22.4
10	Albert S. Burleson (D)	8,103	88.6
	Carl Beck (R)	1,041	11.4
11	Robert L. Henry (D)	7,183	100.0
12	Oscar W. Gillespie (D)	9,790	95.6
13	John H. Stephens (D)	14,120	90.0
	E. E. Diggs (R)	1,295	8.3
14	James L. Slayden (D)	10,811	80.1
	D. Doole (R)	2,692	19.9
15	John N. Garner (D)	9,284	63.7
	T. W. Moore (R)	5,281	36.3
16	William R. Smith (D)	13,030	92.0
	Ben Vantuys (R)	744	5.3

UTAH

		Votes	%
AL	Joseph Howell (R)	42,620	50.1
	Orlando W. Powers (D)	28,031	33.0
	Thomas Weir (AM)	11,411	13.4

VERMONT

		Votes	%
1	David J. Foster (R)	20,660	69.0
	Edwin B. Clift (D)	8,957	29.9
2	Kittredge Haskins (R)	20,738	70.1
	John H. Fenter (D)	8,157	27.6

VIRGINIA

		Votes	%
1	William A. Jones (D)	5,773	81.7
	Bristow (R)	1,294	18.3
2	Harry L. Maynard (D)	4,358	74.5
	Hughes (R)	1,489	25.5
3	John Lamb (D)	3,908	82.2
	Hanson (R)	639	13.4
4	Francis R. Lassiter (D)	2,615	100.0
5	Edward W. Saunders (D)	6,194	50.9
	Simmons (R)	5,972	49.1
6	Carter Glass (D)	4,060	74.8
	Heermans (R)	1,336	24.6
7	James Hay (D)	5,573	70.1
	Beecher (R)	2,372	29.9
8	John F. Rixey (D)	5,059*	84.0
	Henderson (R)	962	16.0
9	Campbell Slemp (R)	13,798	54.0
	Bruce (D)	11,757	46.0
10	Henry D. Flood (D)	5,962	68.9
	Gregory (R)	2,696	31.1

WASHINGTON

		Votes	%
AL	Francis W. Cushman (R)	71,921✔	
	Wesley L. Jones (R)	71,656✔	

WASHINGTON

Candidates	Votes	%
William E. Humphrey (R)	71,353✔	
William Blackman (D)	31,811	
Patrick S. Byrne (D)	30,689	
Dudley Eshleman (D)	30,369	
Emil Herman (SOC)	8,431	
J. H. Barkley (SOC)	8,420	
A. Wagenknecht (SOC)	8,367	
J. M. Wilkin (P)	2,584	
A. S. Caton (P)	2,582	
William Everett (P)	2,571	

WEST VIRGINIA

	Votes	%
1 William P. Hubbard (R)	19,362	52.5
T. S. Riley (D)	15,315	41.5
2 George C. Sturgiss (R)	20,384	53.7
M. H. Dent (D)	16,712	44.0
3 Joseph Holt Gaines (R)	19,888	52.8
George Byrne (D)	15,482	41.1

Candidates	Votes	%
4 Harry C. Woodyard (R)	16,310	52.3
George W. Hardman (D)	13,637	43.8
5 James A. Hughes (R)	22,395	57.4
Joseph S. Miller (D)	15,971	40.9

WISCONSIN

	Votes	%
1 Henry Allen Cooper (R)	16,226	61.1
John J. Cunningham (D)	8,818	33.2
Moses Hull (SOCIAL D)	1,504	5.7
2 John M. Nelson (R)	14,806	51.5
George W. Levis (D)	12,881	44.8
3 James W. Murphy (D)	14,701	50.1
Joseph W. Babcock (R)	13,690	46.6
4 William J. Cary (R)	12,231	41.3
Edmund T. Melms (SOCIAL D)	8,759	29.6
Thomas J. Fleming (D)	8,656	29.2
5 William H. Stafford (R)	13,948	44.3
Albert J. Welch (SOCIAL D)	8,870	28.1
Joseph G. Donnelly (D)	8,192	26.0

Candidates	Votes	%
6 Charles H. Weisse (D)	19,446	63.3
Alvin Dreger (R)	10,512	34.2
7 John J. Esch (R)	18,042	72.7
Charles F. Hulle (D)	6,779	27.3
8 James H. Davidson (R)	16,966	59.7
John E. McMuller (D)	9,594	33.8
9 Gustav Kustermann (R)	14,180	60.5
Phillip A. Badour (D)	8,689	37.1
10 Elmer A. Morse (R)	20,225	63.6
Dennis D. Conway (D)	10,669	33.5
11 John J. Jenkins (R)	19,002	74.9
Francis J. Maguire (D)	5,147	20.3

Special Election

	Votes	%
2 John M. Nelson (R)	10,098	71.2
Grant Thomas (PRI R)	3,703	26.1

WYOMING

	Votes	%
AL Frank W. Mondell (R)	16,813	62.2
John C. Hamm (D)	8,944	33.1

1907 House Elections

MICHIGAN

Special Election

Candidates	Votes	%
5 Gerrit John Diekema (R)	11,898	51.8
George P. Hummer (D)	10,508	45.7

OKLAHOMA

(Became a state Nov. 16, 1907)

	Votes	%
1 Bird S. McGuire (R)	22,362	50.3
William L. Eagleton (D)	21,003	47.3
2 Elmer L. Fulton (D)	26,006	51.0
Thompson B. Ferguson (R)	25,028	49.0

	Votes	%
3 James S. Davenport (D)	26,370	52.8
Henry D. Hubbard (R)	23,623	47.3
4 Charles D. Carter (D)	29,782	62.6
Frank C. Disney (R)	15,752	33.1
5 Scott Ferris (D)	32,935	66.2
Loren G. McKnight (R)	14,883	29.9

1908 House Elections

ALABAMA

	Candidates	Votes	%
1	George W. Taylor (D)	7,457	100.0
2	S. Hubert Dent Jr. (D)	10,754	100.0
3	Henry D. Clayton (D)	9,993	100.0
4	William B. Craig (D)	6,239	65.1
	J. Osmond Middleton (R)	3,341	34.9
5	J. Thomas Heflin (D)	8,024	83.9
	W. W. Wadsworth	1,543	16.1
6	Richmond P. Hobson (D)	9,211	78.0
	Henry T. Nations	2,593	22.0
7	John L. Burnett (D)	8,972	56.0
	N. H. Freeman (R)	7,046	44.0
8	William Richardson (D)	9,691	82.7
	Jeremiah Murphy (R)	2,028	17.3
9	Oscar W. Underwood (D)	11,288	79.4
	J. B. Sloan	2,567	18.1

Special Election

2	Oliver C. Wiley (D)	7,710	100.0

ARKANSAS

1	Robert B. Macon (D)	12,957	66.5
	C. T. Bloodworth (R)	6,534	33.5
2	William A. Oldfield (D)	13,056	63.8
	H. H. Myers (R)	7,421	36.2
3	John C. Floyd (D)	13,710	59.9
	W. T. Mills (R)	9,186	40.1
4	William B. Cravens (D)	13,064	59.8
	Edwin Mechem (R)	8,779	40.2
5	Charles C. Reid (D)	15,331	66.1
	Guy W. Caron (R)	7,849	33.9
6	Joseph T. Robinson (D)	24,389	100.0
7	Robert M. Wallace (D)	12,354	59.8
	S. R. Young (R)	8,312	40.2

CALIFORNIA

1	William F. Englebright (R)	20,624	54.1
	E. W. Holland (D)	14,031	36.8
	D. N. Cunningham (SOC)	2,898	7.6
2	Duncan E. McKinlay (R)	28,627	57.4
	W. K. Hays (D)	19,193	38.5
3	Joseph R. Knowland (R)	27,857	64.1
	George W. Peckham (D)	9,889	22.8
	O. H. Philbrick (SOC)	4,052	9.3
4	Julius Kahn (R)	9,202	52.7
	James G. Maguire (D)	7,497	42.9
5	Everis A. Hayes (R)	28,127	49.1
	George A. Tracy (D)	24,531	42.8
	E. H. Misner (SOC)	3,640	6.4
6	James C. Needham (R)	21,323	52.0
	Fred P. Feliz (D)	15,868	38.7
	W. M. Pattison (SOC)	2,288	5.6
7	James McLachlan (R)	37,244	51.9
	Jud R. Rush (D)	25,445	35.4
	A. R. Holston (SOC)	4,432	6.2
	M. W. Atwood (P)	3,899	5.4
8	Sylvester C. Smith (R)	29,305	55.7
	W. E. Shepherd (D)	18,245	34.7
	N. A. Richardson (SOC)	5,025	9.6

COLORADO

1	Atterson W. Rucker (D)	60,643	49.9
	Robert William Bonynge (R)	57,597	47.4
2	John A. Martin (D)	65,814	48.7
	Warren A. Haggott (R)	64,553	47.8
AL	Edward T. Taylor (D)	126,934	48.4
	James C. Burger (R)	121,265	46.2

CONNECTICUT

	Candidates	Votes	%
1	E. Stevens Henry (R)	26,829	59.5
	Gerth (D)	15,595	34.6
2	Nehemiah D. Sperry (R)	36,083	55.0
	Reilly (D)	26,832	40.9
3	Edwin W. Higgins (R)	14,935	60.3
	Hunter (D)	9,190	37.1
4	Ebenezer J. Hill (R)	32,843	60.7
	Wilson (D)	19,423	35.9
AL	John Q. Tilson (R)	111,557	58.6
	Avery (D)	70,029	36.8

DELAWARE

AL	William H. Heald (R)	24,314	50.7
	Levin Irving Handy (D)	22,515	46.9

FLORIDA

1	Stephen M. Sparkman (D)	9,971	75.2
	George W. Allen (R)	1,990	15.0
	C. C. Allen (SOC)	1,297	9.8
2	Frank Clark (D)	10,726	75.9
	William R. O'Neal (R)	2,552	18.1
	A. N. Jackson (SOC)	862	6.1
3	Dannitte H. Mays (D)	9,314	80.2
	William H. Northup (R)	1,712	14.7

GEORGIA

1	Charles G. Edwards (D)	9,845	95.7
2	James M. Griggs (D)	9,273	100.0
3	Dudley M. Hughes (D)	7,627	99.7
4	William C. Adamson (D)	7,242	100.0
5	Leonidas F. Livingston (D)	8,909	100.0
6	Charles L. Bartlett (D)	6,575	100.0
7	Gordon Lee (D)	11,396	100.0
8	William M. Howard (D)	7,112	100.0
9	Thomas M. Bell (D)	11,653	100.0
10	Thomas W. Hardwick (D)	6,853	100.0
11	William G. Brantley (D)	9,741	100.0

IDAHO

AL	Thomas R. Hamer (R)	49,983	52.0
	James L. McClear (D)	37,605	39.2
	Halbert Barton (SOC)	6,248	6.5

ILLINOIS

1	Martin B. Madden (R)	23,370	60.9
	Matthew L. Mandable (D)	13,692	35.7
2	James R. Mann (R)	32,024	64.8
	John T. Donahoe (D)	14,351	29.0
3	William Warfield Wilson (R)	24,979	56.0
	Fred J. Crowley (D)	15,995	35.8
4	James T. McDermott (D)	16,606	54.7
	Charles S. Wharton (R)	12,196	40.2
5	Adolph J. Sabath (D)	12,997	53.3
	Anthony Michalek (R)	9,876	40.5
	Morris Siskind (SOC)	1,285	5.3
6	William Lorimer (R)	32,540	61.1
	Frank C. Wood (D)	17,093	32.1
7	Fred Lundin (R)	31,513	54.1
	Frank Buchanan (D)	20,088	34.5
	George Koop (SOC)	4,183	7.2
8	Thomas Gallagher (D)	15,963	49.2
	Philip M. Ksycki (R)	14,660	45.2
9	Henry Sherman Boutell (R)	21,110	56.2
	Charles C. Stilwell (D)	13,544	36.1

	Candidates	Votes	%
10	George Edmund Foss (R)	31,130	62.0
	Western Starr (D)	14,840	29.6
11	Howard M. Snapp (R)	29,821	61.2
	Coll McNaughton (D)	15,875	32.6
12	Charles E. Fuller (R)	33,340	65.4
	M. N. Armstrong (D)	13,795	27.1
13	Frank O. Lowden (R)	24,797	61.4
	William C. Green (D)	13,273	32.9
14	James McKinney (R)	23,394	54.3
	Matt J. McEniry (D)	16,745	38.9
15	George W. Prince (R)	26,770	50.9
	W. Emery Lancaster (D)	22,410	42.6
16	Joseph V. Graff (R)	23,880	53.2
	James W. Hill (D)	18,557	41.3
17	John A. Sterling (R)	22,014	53.2
	C. S. Schneider (D)	16,737	40.5
	William P. Allin (P)	2,228	5.4
18	Joseph G. Cannon (R)	29,170	54.9
	Henry C. Bell (D)	21,795	41.0
19	William B. McKinley (R)	30,588	52.9
	Fred B. Hamill (D)	24,913	43.1
20	Henry T. Rainey (D)	24,023	55.3
	James H. Danskin (R)	17,726	40.8
21	James M. Graham (D)	23,433	47.9
	H. Clay Wilson (R)	21,716	44.4
22	William A. Rodenberg (R)	27,858	50.2
	Charles A. Karch (D)	24,341	43.9
23	Martin D. Foster (D)	28,181	53.6
	Frank S. Dickson (R)	23,772	45.2
24	Pleasant T. Chapman (R)	21,833	52.4
	John Q. A. Ledbetter (D)	18,333	44.0
25	Napoleon B. Thistlewood (R)	24,319	51.6
	I. R. Spilman (D)	20,537	43.6

Special Election

25	Napoleon B. Thistlewood (R)	12,263	47.2
	William H. Warder (D)	8,620	33.2
	Sam T. Brush	3,987	15.3

INDIANA

1	John W. Boehne (D)	23,054	48.3
	John H. Foster (R)	22,965	48.1
2	William A. Cullop (D)	27,172	50.0
	John C. Chaney (R)	24,609	45.3
3	William E. Cox (D)	24,139	54.9
	John W. Lewis (R)	18,966	43.1
4	Lincoln Dixon (D)	25,231	53.6
	James A. Cox (R)	20,726	44.0
5	Ralph W. Moss (D)	28,844	48.9
	Howard Maxwell (R)	27,361	46.4
6	William O. Barnard (R)	27,053	49.2
	Thomas H. Kuhn (D)	25,905	47.2
7	Charles A. Korbly (D)	34,686	49.2
	Jesse Overstreet (R)	34,003	48.2
8	John A. M. Adair (D)	29,259	52.5
	Nathan B. Hawkins (R)	23,890	42.9
9	Martin A. Morrison (D)	27,540	48.9
	Charles B. Landis (R)	26,449	47.0
10	Edgar D. Crumpacker (R)	32,954	54.4
	William Darroch (D)	26,742	44.1
11	George W. Rauch (D)	25,526	48.3
	Charles H. Good (R)	24,313	46.0
12	Cyrus Cline (D)	25,051	50.6
	Clarence L. Gilhams (R)	22,706	45.8
13	Henry A. Barnhart (D)	28,509	48.2
	Charles W. Miller (R)	28,229	47.7

Special Election

13	Henry A. Barnhart (D)	28,131	48.4
	Charles W. Miller (R)	27,708	47.7

IOWA

Candidates	Votes	%
1 Charles A. Kennedy (R)	18,318	51.2
George S. Tracy (D)	16,695	46.7
2 Albert F. Dawson (R)	22,915	51.0
Mark A. Walsh (D)	21,050	46.9
3 Charles E. Pickett (R)	25,530	57.6
Charles Elliott (D)	17,362	39.2
4 Gilbert N. Haugen (R)	20,929	55.3
M. E. Geiser (D)	16,296	43.1
5 James W. Good (R)	22,773	57.3
Samuel K. Tracy (D)	15,994	40.2
6 Nathan E. Kendall (R)	18,900	48.3
Daniel W. Hamilton (D)	18,628	47.6
7 John A. T. Hull (R)	24,931	55.7
Charles O. Holley (D)	17,620	39.4
8 William D. Jamieson (D)	20,436	49.2
William P. Hepburn (R)	20,126	48.4
9 Walter I. Smith (R)	23,215	55.8
R. C. Spencer (D)	17,661	42.4
10 Frank P. Woods (R)	29,608	61.4
Montague Hakes (D)	17,256	35.8
11 Elbert H. Hubbard (R)	26,572	57.1
W. G. Sears (D)	19,033	40.9

KANSAS

Candidates	Votes	%
1 Daniel R. Anthony Jr. (R)	27,792	57.6
F. M. Pearl (D)	19,842	41.1
2 Charles F. Scott (R)	28,499	50.5
B. J. Sheridan (D)	26,242	46.5
3 Philip P. Campbell (R)	29,207	49.8
T. J. Hudson (D)	23,377	39.8
Ben F. Wilson (SOC)	5,776	9.8
4 James M. Miller (R)	20,978	55.3
Thomas M. Grisham (D)	16,024	42.2
5 William A. Calderhead (R)	21,093	51.6
R. A. Lovitt (D)	18,555	45.4
6 William A. Reeder (R)	22,200	48.6
John R. Connelly (D)	21,923	48.0
7 Edmond H. Madison (R)	26,315	52.5
Samuel I. Hale (D)	21,460	42.9
8 Victor Murdock (R)	19,029	56.4
Frank B. Lawrence (D)	13,477	39.9

KENTUCKY

Candidates	Votes	%
1 Ollie M. James (D)	27,435	64.1
Porter (R)	15,163	35.4
2 Augustus O. Stanley (D)	23,320	54.3
Worsham (R)	19,302	45.0
3 Robert Y. Thomas Jr. (D)	20,079	49.8
James (R)	19,583	48.6
4 Ben Johnson (D)	24,344	53.2
Gaddle (R)	21,246	46.4
5 J. Swagar Sherley (D)	27,953	51.7
Kinkead (R)	25,513	47.1
6 Joseph L. Rhinock (D)	23,945	55.4
Ingils (R)	18,057	41.8
7 James C. Cantrill (D)	21,157	59.0
Bristow (R)	14,697	41.0
8 Harvey Helm (D)	17,725	51.8
Benthrum (R)	16,049	46.9
9 Joseph B. Bennett (R)	22,832	50.0
Kehoe (D)	22,107	48.4
10 John W. Langley (R)	20,092	52.0
Davis (D)	18,570	48.0
11 Don C. Edwards (R)	36,073	69.8
Patterson (D)	14,729	28.5

LOUISIANA

Candidates	Votes	%
1 Albert Estopinal (D)	13,923	87.9
Henry C. Warmoth (R)	1,916	12.1
2 Robert C. Davey (D)	14,447*	95.7
3 Robert F. Broussard (D)	5,845	75.9
Carlton R. Beattie (R)	1,696	22.0
4 John T. Watkins (D)	7,188	88.2
W. S. Emmons (SOC)	513	6.3

Candidates	Votes	%
John F. Slattery (R)	449	5.5
5 Joseph E. Ransdell (D)	7,110	96.5
6 Robert C. Wickliffe (D)	7,108	91.8
George J. Reiley (R)	632	8.2
7 Arsene P. Pujo (D)	8,270	93.4
Alex Hymes (SOC)	585	6.6

MAINE

Candidates	Votes	%
1 Amos L. Allen (R)	18,887	53.5
John C. Scates (D)	15,615	44.2
2 John P. Swasey (R)	18,479	50.7
Daniel J. McGillicuddy (D)	17,115	46.9
3 Edwin C. Burleigh (R)	18,282	53.1
Samuel W. Gould (D)	15,611	45.3
4 Frank E. Guernsey (R)	19,659	54.1
George M. Hanson (D)	16,152	44.4

MARYLAND

Candidates	Votes	%
1 James Harry Covington (D)	19,381	52.7
William H. Jackson (R)	16,547	45.0
2 J. Fred C. Talbott (D)	21,526	52.2
Robert Garrett (R)	19,040	46.1
3 John Kronmiller (R)	14,772	49.1
Harry B. Wolf (D)	14,510	48.2
4 John Gill Jr. (D)	18,562	52.1
John P. Hill (R)	16,626	46.7
5 Sydney E. Mudd (D)	15,057	49.2
George M. Smith (D)	14,740	48.2
6 George A. Pearre (R)	18,619	49.1
David J. Lewis (D)	18,073	47.6

MASSACHUSETTS

Candidates	Votes	%
1 George P. Lawrence (R)	17,990	60.2
David T. Clark (D)	10,765	36.0
2 Frederick H. Gillett (R)	17,515	62.0
John L. Rice (D)	7,839	27.8
George W. Curtis (I LEAGUE)	1,623	5.8
3 Charles G. Washburn (R)	18,265	62.2
William I. McLoughlin (D)	9,654	32.9
4 Charles Q. Tirrell (R)	18,842	55.0
John J. Mitchell (D)	15,431	45.0
5 Butler Ames (R)	16,251	56.0
Joseph J. Flynn (DI)	11,910	41.1
6 Augustus P. Gardner (R)	22,093	69.4
Arthur Withington (D)	7,334	23.0
Franklin H. Wentworth (SOC)	2,418	7.6
7 Ernest W. Roberts (R)	22,179	68.9
George Brickett (D)	7,958	24.7
Clarence L. McIver (I LEAGUE)	2,078	6.5
8 Samuel W. McCall (R)	19,147	63.6
Frederick S. Deitrick (D)	9,638	32.0
9 John A. Keliher (D)	14,060	62.3
John A. Campbell (R)	6,002	26.6
Junius T. Auerbach (I LEAGUE)	2,492	11.1
10 Joseph F. O'Connell (D)	16,553	46.4
J. Mitchell Galvin (R)	16,549	46.4
11 Andrew J. Peters (D)	15,881	48.7
Daniel W. Lane (R)	15,447	47.4
12 John W. Weeks (R)	21,097	66.0
Jesse C. Ivy (D)	9,069	28.4
Albert E. George (I LEAGUE)	1,779	5.6
13 William S. Greene (R)	16,870	72.5
John F. McGuinness (D)	4,977	21.4
Charles W. Copeland (I LEAGUE)	1,436	6.2
14 William C. Lovering (R)	20,959	66.8
Eliot L. Packard (D)	6,709	21.4
Charles B. Drew (I LEAGUE)	1,855	5.9
George J. Alcott (SOC)	1,851	5.9

MICHIGAN

Candidates	Votes	%
1 Edwin Denby (R)	30,696	56.4
William D. Mahon (D)	21,695	39.9
2 Charles E. Townsend (R)	28,442	58.0
James C. Henderson (D)	19,306	39.4
3 Washington Gardner (R)	24,078	53.7
Hiram C. Blackman (D)	18,907	42.1
4 Edward L. Hamilton (R)	27,074	59.4
Charles H. Kimmerle (D)	16,731	36.7
5 Gerrit J. Diekema (R)	25,030	54.1
Edwin F. Sweet (D)	19,437	42.0
6 Samuel W. Smith (R)	32,043	56.8
Frank L. Dodge (D)	21,304	37.8
7 Henry McMorran (R)	22,879	59.4
William Springer (D)	13,843	36.0
8 Joseph W. Fordney (R)	21,210	59.7
Jenner E. Morse (D)	13,948	39.3
9 James C. McLaughlin (R)	22,459	72.1
Cornelius Gerber (D)	8,688	27.9
10 George A. Loud (R)	24,780	64.6
Lewis P. Coumans (D)	12,677	33.1
11 Francis H. Dodds (R)	29,402	70.5
Leavitt S. Griswold (D)	12,315	29.5
12 H. Olin Young (R)	35,310	72.2
Patrick H. Obrien (D)	13,586	27.8

MINNESOTA

Candidates	Votes	%
1 James A. Tawney (R)	20,464	53.6
French (D)	17,708	46.4
2 Winfield S. Hammond (D)	17,716	55.7
McCleary (R)	14,091	44.3
3 Charles R. Davis (R)	19,896	59.7
4 Frederick C. Stevens (R)	21,818	60.8
Peebles (D)	12,395	34.5
5 Frank M. Nye (R)	24,542	61.7
Thomas P. Dwyer (D)	13,429	33.8
6 Charles A. Lindbergh (R)	22,574	63.2
Gilkinson (D)	13,174	36.9
7 Andrew J. Volstead (R)	26,597	100.0
8 Clarence B. Miller (R)	27,873	81.6
Halliday (PUB OWN)	6,298	18.4
9 Halvor Steenerson (R)	17,957	50.0
Sageng (D)	15,010	41.8
Braaten (PUB OWN)	2,985	8.3

MISSISSIPPI

Candidates	Votes	%
1 Ezekiel S. Candler Jr. (D)	8,043	100.0
2 Thomas Spight (D)	7,511	100.0
3 Benjamin G. Humphreys (D)	4,808	100.0
4 Thomas U. Sisson (D)	8,039	100.0
5 Adam M. Byrd (D)	9,750	100.0
6 Eaton J. Bowers (D)	8,702	100.0
7 William A. Dickson (D)	6,807	94.7
H. C. Turley (R)	384	5.3
8 James W. Collier (D)	5,657	100.0

MISSOURI

Candidates	Votes	%
1 James T. Lloyd (D)	22,133	52.4
Chamberlain (R)	19,122	45.2
2 William W. Rucker (D)	23,263	55.6
Haley (R)	18,266	43.6
3 Joshua W. Alexander (D)	20,387	52.6
Eads (R)	18,341	47.3
4 Charles F. Booher (D)	21,671	53.1
Reed (R)	18,908	46.4
5 William P. Borland (D)	31,635	52.7
Ellis (R)	27,289	45.5
6 David A. De Armond (D)	18,532	52.7
Atkeson (R)	16,372	46.6
7 Courtney W. Hamlin (D)	24,731	49.8
Whitaker (R)	23,927	48.2
8 Dorsey W. Shackleford (D)	17,230	52.3
Irwin (R)	15,691	47.7
9 James Beauchamp Clark (D)	23,090	51.5
Roy (R)	21,702	48.4

MISSOURI

	Candidates	Votes	%
10	Richard Bartholdt (R)	49,127	60.4
	Thompson (D)	28,634	35.2
11	Patrick F. Gill (D)	21,001	50.9
	Findly (R)	19,195	46.5
12	Harry M. Coudrey (R)	16,471	49.7
	Selph (D)	15,930	48.1
13	Politte Elvins (R)	17,125	50.3
	Smith (D)	16,918	49.7
14	Charles A. Crow (R)	25,951	48.3
	Russell (D)	25,187	46.8
15	Charles H. Morgan (R)	23,040	47.9
	Hackney (D)	22,410	46.6
16	Arthur P. Murphy (R)	16,835	50.8
	J. Robert Lamar (D)	16,295	49.2

MONTANA

		Votes	%
AL	Charles N. Pray (R)	32,819	48.9
	Thomas D. Long (D)	29,032	43.2
	Lewis J. Duncan (SOC)	5,318	7.9

NEBRASKA

		Votes	%
1	John A. Maguire (D & PPI)	19,651	51.2
	E. M. Pollard (R)	18,716	48.8
2	Gilbert M. Hitchcock (D)	18,781	52.6
	A. W. Jefferies (R)	16,206	45.4
3	James P. Latta (D & PPI)	26,832	51.6
	J. F. Boyd (R)	24,865	47.8
4	Edmund H. Hinshaw (R)	22,674	50.0
	C. F. Gilbert (D & PPI)	21,819	48.1
5	George W. Norris (R)	20,649#	49.4
	F. W. Ashton (D & PPI)	20,627	49.4
6	Moses P. Kinkaid (R)	25,786	50.7
	W. H. Westover (D & PPI)	23,317	45.8

NEVADA

		Votes	%
AL	George A. Bartlett (D)	11,253	47.3
	H. B. Maxson (R)	7,552	31.7
	A. L. Fitzgerald (INDEP)	3,031	12.7
	J. Critchfield (SOC)	1,965	8.3

NEW HAMPSHIRE

		Votes	%
1	Cyrus A. Sulloway (R)	24,413	56.9
	Michael J. White (D)	17,400	40.5
2	Frank D. Currier (R)	26,007	59.3
	Frederick M. Colby (D)	16,666	38.0

NEW JERSEY

		Votes	%
1	Henry C. Loudenslager (R)	27,443	58.4
	Grosscup (D)	17,640	37.5
2	John J. Gardner (R)	23,906	52.2
	Grubb (D)	20,506	44.8
3	Benjamin F. Howell (R)	26,302	56.6
	Clark (D)	19,766	42.5
4	Ira W. Wood (R)	23,919	56.5
	Steele (D)	17,210	40.7
5	Charles N. Fowler (R)	27,948	55.5
	Barber (D)	20,485	40.7
6	William Hughes (D)	29,516	49.5
	Foxhall (R)	27,989	46.9
7	Richard W. Parker (R)	24,863	56.6
	Townsend (D)	18,104	41.2
8	William H. Wiley (R)	24,536	57.9
	Le Gage Pratt (D)	16,276	38.4
9	Eugene F. Kinkead (D)	23,485	54.5
	Critchfield (D)	18,608	43.2
10	James A. Hamill (D)	23,820	57.7
	Dwyer (R)	16,105	39.0

NEW YORK

		Votes	%
1	William W. Cocks (R)	29,459	56.6
	Monson Morris (D)	19,519	37.5

	Candidates	Votes	%
2	George H. Lindsay (D)	15,455	53.9
	William Liebermann (R)	9,999	34.9
	Edward Walsh (I LEAGUE)	1,886	6.6
3	Otto Godfrey Foelker (R)	18,614	50.3
	James P. Maher (D)	15,395	41.6
4	Charles B. Law (R)	23,944	49.7
	Edward R. Gilman (D)	18,910	39.2
	Otto Wegener (SOC)	2,707	5.6
	Arthur S. Colborne (I LEAGUE)	2,542	5.3
5	Richard Young (R)	28,075	54.2
	J. Harry Snook (D)	19,897	38.4
6	William M. Calder (R)	22,050	55.4
7	John J. Fitzgerald (D)	17,773	58.5
	William R. A. Koehl (R)	10,296	33.9
	William T. Smith (I LEAGUE)	1,841	6.1
8	Daniel J. Riordan (D)	22,329	62.5
	James E. Winterbottom (R)	11,484	32.2
9	Henry M. Goldfogle (D)	6,194	53.8
	Morris Hillquit (SOC)	2,483	21.6
	Louis I. Cherey (R)	2,312	20.1
10	William Sulzer (D)	10,602	54.4
	Gustave Hartman (R)	6,511	33.4
	Morris Brown (SOC)	1,754	9.0
11	Charles V. Fornes (D)	20,637	58.9
	Laurence L. Driggs (R)	11,700	33.4
	Alexander Porter (I LEAGUE)	1,853	5.3
12	Michael F. Conroy (D)	16,757	60.9
	Victor H. Duras (R)	8,090	29.4
	James D. Bush (I LEAGUE)	1,482	5.4
13	Herbert Parsons (R)	15,108	51.4
	Gerald Hull Gray (D)	12,380	42.2
14	William Willett Jr. (D)	21,643	52.2
	Emanuel Castka (R)	14,189	34.2
	Philip H. Schmitt (SOC)	3,055	7.4
	Herbert Wade (I LEAGUE)	2,485	6.0
15	Jacob Van Vechten Olcott (R)	16,921	56.5
	Rhinelander Waldo (D)	12,531	41.8
16	Francis Burton Harrison (D)	12,555	50.8
	Francis A. Adams (R)	8,822	35.7
	John Parr (SOC)	1,966	8.0
	Edwin D. Ackerman (I LEAGUE)	1,334	5.4
17	William S. Bennet (R)	32,764	53.5
	William Madoo (D)	24,736	40.4
18	Joseph A. Goulden (D)	35,569	51.5
	Joel Elias Spingarn (R)	25,590	37.1
	Frank McGarry (I LEAGUE)	4,144	6.0
	George B. Staring (SOC)	3,649	5.3
19	John E. Andrus (R)	27,966	55.6
	William H. Lynn (D)	19,851	39.4
20	Thomas W. Bradley (R)	23,927	55.9
	Richard E. King (D)	17,979	42.0
21	Hamilton Fish (R)	22,832	52.0
	Andrew C. Zabriskie (D)	19,725	44.9
22	William H. Draper (R)	22,980	52.7
	Winfield A. Huppuch (D)	19,074	43.7
23	George N. Southwick (R)	30,593	48.5
	William H. Keeler (D)	30,008	47.6
24	George W. Fairchild (R)	28,496	53.8
	G. Hyde Clark (D)	23,059	43.5
25	Cyrus Durey (R)	27,152	54.4
	Joseph D. Baucus (D)	19,927	39.9
26	George R. Malby (R)	30,615	66.4
	Ellis Woodworth (D)	14,914	32.3
27	Charles S. Millington (R)	26,962	54.0
	Curtis F. Alliaume (D)	21,365	42.8
28	Charles L. Knapp (R)	25,948	57.9
	Andrew C. Cornwall (D)	15,756	35.1
	Sylvanus V. Barker (P)	2,372	5.3
29	Michael E. Driscoll (R)	33,664	59.1
	Alphonso E. Fitch (D)	20,527	36.0
30	John W. Dwight (R)	30,622	57.4
	Alexander D. Wales (D)	19,818	37.2
31	Sereno E. Payne (R)	28,990	59.7
	John A. Curtis (D)	17,891	36.8
32	James B. Perkins (R)	33,025	56.4
	Herman S. Searle (D)	22,858	39.0

	Candidates	Votes	%
33	Jacob Sloat Fassett (R)	24,580	52.2
	James A. Parsons (R)	20,319	43.1
34	James S. Simmons (R)	30,298	54.7
	Frank W. Brown (D)	23,298	42.1
35	Daniel A. Driscoll (D)	25,866	55.2
	L. Bradley Dorr (R)	20,093	42.9
36	De Alva S. Alexander (R)	30,621	58.2
	William H. Follette (D)	20,790	39.5
37	Edward Butterfield Vreeland (R)	32,327	62.4
	Sanford H. Thorne (D)	15,718	30.4

NORTH CAROLINA

		Votes	%
1	John H. Small (D)	13,119	71.1
	I. M. Meekins (R)	5,342	28.9
2	Claude Kitchin (D)	12,275	78.2
	M. Ferguson (R)	3,361	21.4
3	Charles R. Thomas (D)	11,544	59.4
	Eli W. Hill (R)	7,896	40.6
4	Edward W. Pou (D)	13,463	60.0
	Willis G. Briggs (R)	8,966	40.0
5	John M. Morehead (R)	19,288	50.1
	A. L. Brooks (D)	18,938	49.2
6	Hannibal L. Godwin (D)	12,542	66.3
	Albert H. Slocumb (R)	6,385	33.7
7	Robert N. Page (D)	15,057	56.2
	Z. V. Walser (R)	11,732	43.8
8	Charles H. Cowles (R)	16,863	52.1
	R. N. Hackett (D)	15,488	47.8
9	Edwin Y. Webb (D)	16,530	55.0
	John A. Smith (R)	13,514	45.0
10	John G. Grant (R)	15,245	50.5
	William T. Crawford (D)	14,884	49.3

NORTH DAKOTA

		Votes	%
AL	Asle J. Gronna (R)	57,357✔	
	Louis B. Hanna (R)	55,610✔	
	T. D. Casey (D)	29,426	
	O. G. Major (D)	28,448	
	Francis Cooper (I)	591	
	E. D. Herring (I)	533	

OHIO

		Votes	%
1	Nicholas Longworth (R)	30,444	55.2
	Thomas P. Hart (D)	23,224	42.1
2	Herman P. Goebel (R)	28,008	48.6
	Charles N. Danenhower (D)	27,904	48.4
3	James M. Cox (D)	32,524	48.1
	John Eugene Harding (I)	19,306	28.5
	William G. Frizell (R)	12,593	18.6
4	William E. Tou Velle (D)	26,896	58.2
	Thomas J. Mulligan (R)	18,305	39.6
5	Timothy T. Ansberry (D)	23,712	57.7
	William W. Campbell (R)	16,745	40.7
6	Matthew R. Denver (D)	23,192	51.6
	Jesse Taylor (R)	21,592	48.0
7	J. Warren Keifer (R)	24,323	51.2
	O. E. Duff (D)	21,503	45.2
8	Ralph D. Cole (R)	24,476	50.0
	William R. Niven (D)	23,271	47.5
9	Isaac R. Sherwood (D)	29,171	47.8
	James H. Southard (R)	27,523	45.1
	Charles H. Miller (SOC)	3,285	5.4
10	Adna R. Johnson (R)	23,687	53.8
	Thomas H. B. Jones (D)	18,918	43.0
11	Albert Douglas (R)	27,796	49.9
	L. A. Sears (D)	26,650	47.8
12	Edward L. Taylor Jr. (R)	29,483	54.5
	Benjamin F. Gayman (D)	22,813	42.2
13	Carl C. Anderson (D)	29,736	53.2
	Grant E. Mouser (R)	25,019	44.7
14	William G. Sharp (D)	28,525	50.0
	Frank V. Owen (R)	26,799	47.0
15	James Joyce (R)	22,186	48.8
	George White (D)	22,129	48.7
16	David A. Hollingsworth (R)	23,318	51.7

OHIO

Candidates	Votes	%
N. A. McCombs (D)	19,914	44.2
17 William A. Ashbrook (D)	28,712	55.3
John F. Harrison (R)	21,341	41.1
18 James Kennedy (R)	32,287	48.3
John J. Whitacre (D)	29,040	43.4
19 W. Aubrey Thomas (R)	32,182	55.3
Stephen A. Robinson (D)	22,529	38.7
20 Paul Howland (R)	32,839	55.9
Charles Lapp (D)	23,592	40.1
21 Theodore E. Burton (R)	31,968*	59.3
James E. Wertman (D)	19,451	36.1

OKLAHOMA

Candidates	Votes	%
1 Bird S. McGuire (R)	23,312	50.6
Henry S. Johnston (D)	20,501	44.5
2 Dick T. Morgan (R)	26,273	46.9
Elmer L. Fulton (D)	25,349	45.2
Charles P. Randall (SOC)	4,443	7.9
3 Charles E. Creager (R)	24,952	48.3
James S. Davenport (D)	23,881	46.2
Winston T. Banks (SOC)	2,827	5.5
4 Charles D. Carter (D)	22,047	50.6
Benjamin F. Hackett (R)	15,727	36.1
M. C. Carter (SOC)	5,769	13.3
5 Scott Ferris (D)	31,026	55.7
Thompson (R)	19,149	34.4
Davis (SOC)	5,478	9.8

OREGON

Candidates	Votes	%
1 Willis C. Hawley (R)	31,889	58.8
J. J. Whitney (D)	14,841	27.4
W. S. Richards (SOC)	4,349	8.0
Daniel Staver (P)	3,189	5.9
2 William R. Ellis (R)	35,579	63.6
John A. Jeffrey (D)	13,865	24.8
G. E. Sanders (SOC)	3,855	6.9

PENNSYLVANIA

Candidates	Votes	%
1 Henry H. Bingham (R, CITY)	27,507	76.2
Michael J. Geraghty (D)	7,773	21.5
2 Joel Cook (R, CITY)	24,579	77.4
William Schlipf Jr. (D)	6,381	20.1
3 J. Hampton Moore (R, CITY)	23,877	76.6
William Beerli (D)	6,608	21.2
4 Reuben O. Moon (R)	17,518	66.2
Haines D. Albright (D, CITY)	7,613	28.8
5 William W. Foulkrod (R, CITY)	21,756	66.7
Michael Donohue (D)	8,488	26.0
6 George D. McCreary (R, CITY)	31,129	72.5
Frederick J. Bailey (D)	10,205	23.8
7 Thomas S. Butler (R)	26,684	69.3
D. P. Hibberd (D)	10,364	26.9
8 Irving P. Wanger (R)	26,384	59.9
Wynne James (D)	17,684	40.1
9 William W. Griest (R)	22,022	74.8
George B. Willson (D)	7,428	25.2
10 Thomas D. Nichols (D)	16,855	51.1
John R. Farr (R)	16,138	48.9
11 Henry W. Palmer (R, P)	21,033	51.9
John H. Bigelow (D)	18,569	45.8
12 Alfred B. Garner (R)	17,446	51.9
Robert E. Lee (D)	15,339	45.6
13 John H. Rothermel (D)	27,655	53.3
Alex N. Ulrich (R)	21,416	41.3
14 Charles C. Pratt (R)	15,024	51.2
George W. Kipp (D)	12,980	44.3
15 William B. Wilson (D)	18,592	50.4
Elias Deemer (R)	16,577	44.9
16 John G. McHenry (D)	18,412	57.1
Edmund W. Samuel (R)	12,866	39.9

Candidates	Votes	%
17 Benjamin K. Focht (R, P)	23,761	62.8
George C. Bentz (D)	14,044	37.2
18 Marlin E. Olmsted (R)	27,717	62.8
John L. Whisler (D)	13,876	31.5
19 John M. Reynolds (R)	26,157	62.2
Humphrey D. Tate (D)	15,906	37.8
20 Daniel F. Lafean (R)	19,176	52.0
Edward D. Ziegler (D)	16,928	45.9
21 Charles F. Barclay (R)	15,631	50.3
W. Harrison Walker (D)	12,848	41.4
B. W. McCoy (P)	1,888	6.1
22 George F. Huff (R)	19,339	51.0
Silas W. Kline (D)	16,234	42.8
R. A. Dornon (P)	2,338	6.2
23 Allen F. Cooper (R)	16,769	50.7
Milton R. Travis (D)	12,125	36.7
William M. Likins (P)	3,366	10.2
24 John K. Tener (R)	20,538	52.2
Charles H. Akens (D)	10,985	27.9
Frank Fish (P)	5,982	15.2
25 Arthur L. Bates (R)	16,457	52.6
John B. Brooks (D)	11,995	38.4
N. J. MacIntyre (P)	1,849	5.9
26 A. Mitchell Palmer (D)	18,865	52.8
Gustav A. Schneebeli (R)	15,123	42.3
27 Jonathan N. Langham (R)	19,010	59.7
John Smith Shirley (D)	10,088	31.7
J. T. Pender (P)	2,739	8.6
28 Nelson P. Wheeler (R)	18,728	55.1
Till Reiss (D)	11,256	33.1
J. M. Brown (P)	4,018	11.8
29 William H. Graham (R)	15,616	65.5
John G. Schirmer (D)	5,401	22.6
J. W. Slayton (SOC)	1,500	6.3
John A. McConnell (P)	1,337	5.6
30 John Dalzell (R)	15,574	58.2
Edward F. Duffy (D)	7,512	28.1
William Adams (SOC)	2,001	7.5
Joseph Fidler (P)	1,674	6.3
31 James Francis Burke (R)	13,380	66.6
Thomas B. Alcorn (D)	5,320	26.5
32 Andrew J. Barchfeld (R, UN LAB)	17,015	58.1
John Murphy (D)	8,769	29.9
Thomas F. Kennedy (SOC)	1,871	6.4
H. S. Gleiss (P)	1,648	5.6

RHODE ISLAND

Candidates	Votes	%
1 William P. Sheffield (R)	18,222	48.6
Granger (D)	18,141	48.4
2 Adin B. Capron (R)	21,374	60.9
Cooney (D)	12,634	36.0

SOUTH CAROLINA

Candidates	Votes	%
1 George S. Legare (D)	5,759	90.1
A. R. Prioleau (R)	631	9.9
2 James O'H. Patterson (D)	8,440	99.3
3 Wyatt Aiken (D)	10,274	100.0
4 Joseph T. Johnston (D)	10,806	100.0
5 David E. Finley (D)	9,468	100.0
6 J. Edwin Ellebert (D)	9,035	100.0
7 Asbury F. Lever (D)	9,950	90.9
R. H. Richardson (R)	998	9.1

SOUTH DAKOTA

Candidates	Votes	%
AL Eben W. Martin (R)	67,582✔	
Charles H. Burke (R)	67,400✔	
Robert E. Dowdell (D)	38,758	
Andrew H. Olson (D)	38,624	
E. S. Chappell (P)	3,785	
L. R. Erskine (P)	3,733	
T. G. Deffebach (SOC)	2,676	
S. H. Goodfellow (SOC)	2,660	
L. V. Schneider (SOJ)	55	
W. S. Bray (SOJ)	55	

Special Election

Candidates	Votes	%
AL Eben W. Martin (R)	65,962	62.3
W. W. Soule (D)	39,865	37.7

TENNESSEE

Candidates	Votes	%
1 Walter P. Brownlow (R)	21,998	79.5
J. T. Fugate (D)	5,686	20.5
2 Richard W. Austin (R)	15,337	50.9
N. W. Hale (D)	14,528	48.2
3 John A. Moon (D)	18,403	60.2
John T. Raulston (R)	12,174	39.8
4 Cordell Hull (D)	15,193	54.9
R. Q. Lillard (R)	12,419	44.9
5 William C. Houston (D)	13,123	69.7
Z. T. Cason (R)	5,697	30.2
6 Joseph W. Byrns (D)	18,192	97.3
7 Lemuel P. Padgett (D)	14,499	64.2
J. S. Beasley (R)	8,087	35.8
8 Thetus W. Sims (D)	12,874	57.5
R. H. Thrasher (R)	9,446	42.2
9 Finis J. Garrett (D)	14,312	73.3
W. L. Terrell (R)	5,205	26.7
10 George W. Gordon (D)	13,672	96.1

TEXAS

Candidates	Votes	%
1 Morris Sheppard (D)	14,775	84.7
H. L. McQuiston (R)	2,304	13.2
2 Martin Dies (D)	14,559	81.9
C. E. Smith (R)	2,719	15.3
3 Gordon J. Russell (D)	11,651	74.3
J. A. Harper (R)	3,289	21.0
4 Choice B. Randell (D)	16,017	80.6
R. H. Crabb (R)	3,205	16.1
5 Jack Beall (D)	17,840	84.4
Marion T. Connor (R)	3,177	15.0
6 Rufus Hardy (D)	10,350	84.4
C. L. McCoy (R)	1,919	15.6
7 Alexander W. Gregg (D)	8,625	97.6
8 John M. Moore (D)	12,285	77.6
T. M. Kennerly (R)	3,482	22.0
9 George F. Burgess (D)	13,191	67.6
O. S. York (R)	5,897	30.2
10 Albert S. Burleson (D)	13,314	80.7
Joseph W. Burke (R)	3,185	19.3
11 Robert L. Henry (D)	10,114	100.0
12 Oscar W. Gillespie (D)	17,778	81.6
W. A. Dodge (R)	3,095	14.2
13 John H. Stephens (D)	24,705	84.3
Jasper W. Haney (R)	3,715	12.7
14 James L. Slayden (D)	16,801	99.5
15 John N. Garner (D)	11,682	61.7
W. T. Moore (R)	7,179	37.9
16 William R. Smith (D)	22,159	88.7
G. W. Boynton (R)	2,544	10.2

UTAH

Candidates	Votes	%
AL Joseph Howell (R)	57,544	51.6
L. R. Martineau (D)	35,981	32.3
Charles I. Douglas (AM)	13,484	12.1

VERMONT

Candidates	Votes	%
1 David J. Foster (R)	22,190	71.8
Emile Blais (D)	8,028	26.0
2 Frank Plumley (R)	22,868	75.0
Andrew J. Sibley (D)	6,914	22.7

VIRGINIA

Candidates	Votes	%
1 William A. Jones (D)	9,733	74.2
George N. Wise (R)	3,287	25.1
2 Harry L. Maynard (D)	7,358	70.7
D. L. Groner (R)	3,026	29.1
3 John Lamb (D)	8,105	77.2
J. G. Luce (R)	2,339	22.3

VIRGINIA

Candidates	Votes	%
4 Francis R. Lassiter (D)	7,200	99.9
5 Edward W. Saunders (D)	7,079	50.3
J. M. Parsons (R)	6,988	49.6
6 Carter Glass (D)	8,807	65.9
M. Hartman (R)	3,421	25.6
J. M. Parsons	994	7.4
7 James Hay (D)	9,560	62.9
L. Pritchard (R)	5,652	37.2
8 Charles C. Carlin (D)	10,182	79.7
J. W. Gregg (R)	2,597	20.3
9 C. Bascom Slemp (R)	15,693	56.3
J. C. Byars (D)	12,192	43.7
10 Henry D. Flood (D)	10,140	65.8
W. C. Franklin (R)	5,281	34.3

WASHINGTON

Candidates	Votes	%
1 William E. Humphrey (R)	39,643	63.7
Charles H. Miller (D)	21,089	33.9
2 Francis W. Cushman (R)	29,850	69.8
Browder D. Brown (D)	12,006	28.1
3 Miles Pointdexter (R)	38,369	61.0
William Goodyear (D)	23,227	36.9

WEST VIRGINIA

Candidates	Votes	%
1 William P. Hubbard (R)	27,351	51.3
E. L. Robinson (D)	23,580	44.2
2 George C. Sturgiss (R)	25,322	51.1
B. H. Hines (D)	22,771	45.9
3 Joseph Holt Gaines (R)	29,266	53.2
Andrew Price (D)	23,355	42.5
4 Harry C. Woodyard (R)	21,777	51.9
W. O. Parsons (D)	19,095	45.5
5 James A. Hughes (R)	31,958	55.6
L. H. Clarke (D)	24,778	43.1

WISCONSIN

Candidates	Votes	%
1 Henry Allen Cooper (R)	26,728	60.6
H. A. Moehlenpah (D)	14,018	31.8
2 John M. Nelson (R)	20,925	53.6
J. E. Jones (D)	17,748	45.5
3 Arthur W. Kopp (R)	21,409	55.8
J. W. Murphy (D)	16,010	41.7
4 William J. Cary (R)	15,509	39.1
William J. Kershaw (D)	14,370	36.2

Candidates	Votes	%
Ed T. Melms (SOCIAL D)	9,788	24.7
5 William H. Stafford (R)	16,394	40.4
G. Holmes Daubner (D)	12,871	31.8
Albert J. Welch (SOCIAL D)	11,279	27.8
6 Charles H. Weisse (D)	23,317	57.8
George Spratt (R)	16,184	40.1
7 John J. Esch (R)	25,202	68.0
B. F. Keeler (D)	11,466	31.0
8 James H. Davidson (R)	23,097	57.3
Lyman J. Nash (D)	14,984	37.2
9 Gustav Kustermann (R)	18,562	53.6
L. Lindauer (D)	15,249	44.1
10 Elmer A. Morse (R)	26,081	60.9
Wells M. Ruggles (D)	16,777	39.1
11 Irvine L. Lenroot (R)	30,104	71.7
J. S. Konkel (D)	10,467	24.9

WYOMING

Candidates	Votes	%
AL Frank W. Mondell (R)	21,431	57.1
Hayden M. White (D)	13,643	36.3
James Morgan (SOC)	2,486	6.6

1909 House Elections

ILLINOIS

Special Election

Candidates	Votes	%
6 William J. Moxley (R)	14,623	48.4
Carl L. Barnes	8,342	27.6
Frank S. Ryan	6,435	21.3

LOUISIANA

Special Election

Candidates	Votes	%
2 Samuel L. Gilmore (D)	5,535	100.0

1910 House Elections

ALABAMA

	Candidates	Votes	%
1	George W. Taylor (D)	7,071	97.0
2	S. Hubert Dent Jr. (D)	9,593	100.0
3	Henry D. Clayton (D)	9,573	100.0
4	Fred L. Blackmon (D)	8,286	69.9
	J. M. Atkins (R)	3,572	30.1
5	J. Thomas Heflin (D)	10,058	100.0
6	Richmond P. Hobson (D)	9,296	81.5
	Andrew D. Mitchell (R)	2,114	18.5
7	John L. Burnett (D)	9,496	51.4
	M. W. Howard (R)	8,977	48.6
8	William Richardson (D)	8,785	98.1
9	Oscar W. Underwood (D)	10,114	100.0

ARKANSAS

	Candidates	Votes	%
1	Robert B. Macon (D)	2,803	100.0
2	William A. Oldfield (D)	5,053	81.7
	J. T. Hall (R)	1,131	18.3
3	John C. Floyd (D)	5,131	55.6
	B. S. Granger (R)	4,197	45.5
4	William B. Cravens (D)	3,369	100.0
5	Henderson M. Janeway (D)	5,505	76.4
	A. C. Remmel (R)	1,702	23.6
6	Joseph T. Robinson (D)	4,701	81.6
	B. C. Thompson (R)	1,062	18.4
7	William S. Goodwin (D)	5,266	82.2
	A. L. Wilson (R)	1,143	17.8

CALIFORNIA

	Candidates	Votes	%
1	John E. Raker (D)	16,704	45.4
	William F. Englebright (R)	16,570	45.1
	W. M. Morgan (SOC)	3,231	8.8
2	William Kent (R)	25,346	50.1
	I. G. Zumwalt (D)	22,229	44.0
	W. H. Ferber (SOC)	2,647	5.2
3	Joseph R. Knowland (R-D)	34,291	81.9
	S. Miller (SOC)	6,653	15.9
4	Julius Kahn (R)	10,188	56.2
	Walter Macarthur (D)	6,636	36.6
	Austin Lewis (SOC)	1,178	6.5
5	Everis Anson Hayes (R)	33,265	59.4
	Thomas E. Hayden (D)	15,345	27.4
	E. L. Reguin (SOC)	7,052	12.6
6	James C. Needham (R)	19,717	47.3
	A. L. Cowell (D)	18,408	44.1
	Richard Kirk (SOC)	2,568	6.2
7	William D. Stephens (R)	36,435	58.7
	Lorin A. Handley (D)	13,340	21.5
	T. W. Williams (SOC)	10,305	16.6
8	Sylvester C. Smith (R)	28,202	50.5
	William G. Irving (D)	18,958	34.0
	George A. Garrett (SOC)	7,302	13.1

COLORADO

	Candidates	Votes	%
1	Atterson W. Rucker (D)	40,458	40.8
	James C. Burger (R)	37,966	38.3
	George J. Kindel (P)	17,144	17.3
2	John A. Martin (D)	60,201	48.6
	James A. Orr (R)	57,006	46.0
AL	Edward T. Taylor (D)	105,700	47.9
	Isaac H. Stevens (R)	101,722	46.1

CONNECTICUT

	Candidates	Votes	%
1	E. Stevens Henry (R)	19,367	48.1
	Augustine Lonergan (D)	18,132	45.0
2	Thomas L. Reilly (D)	27,492	48.7
	Shepard (R)	24,480	43.3
	Paecht (SOC)	3,708	6.6

	Candidates	Votes	%
3	Edwin W. Higgins (R)	10,011	47.8
	Raymond J. Jodoin (D)	9,933	47.4
4	Ebenezer J. Hill (R)	23,479	48.4
	Wilson (D)	20,636	42.5
	Peach (SOC)	3,606	7.4
AL	John Q. Tilson (R)	79,585	47.9
	Ingersoll (D)	73,221	44.1
	Beardsley (SOC)	10,304	6.2

DELAWARE

	Candidates	Votes	%
AL	William H. Heald (R)	22,410	50.9
	Robert C. White (D)	20,281	46.1

FLORIDA

	Candidates	Votes	%
1	Stephen M. Sparkman (D)	10,525	81.8
	C. C. Allen (SOC)	2,346	18.2
2	Frank Clark (D)	11,626	78.5
	Thomas W. Cox (SOC)	1,804	12.2
	Thomas C. Buddington (R)	1,372	9.3
3	Dannitte H. Mays (D)	8,844	89.6
	Eric Vonaxelson (SOC)	1,032	10.5

GEORGIA

	Candidates	Votes	%
1	Charles Edwards (D)	2,019	100.0
2	Seaborn A. Roddenberry (D)	3,179	100.0
3	Dudley Hughes (D)	2,855	100.0
4	William C. Adamson (D)	2,815	100.0
5	William S. Howard (D)	4,091	100.0
6	Charles L. Bartlett (D)	3,351	100.0
7	Gordon Lee (D)	7,146	75.8
	Walter Akerman (R)	2,285	24.2
8	Samuel J. Tribble (ID)	8,635	58.1
	William Howard (D)	6,222	41.9
9	Thomas M. Bell (D)	4,285	100.0
10	Thomas Hardwick (D)	4,331	75.3
	C. E. McGregor (ID)	1,418	24.7
11	William Brantley (D)	3,160	100.0

IDAHO

	Candidates	Votes	%
AL	Burton L. French (R)	46,401	55.4
	A. M. Bowen (D)	31,832	38.0
	Rolla Myer (SOC)	5,463	6.5

ILLINOIS

	Candidates	Votes	%
1	Martin B. Madden (R)	14,920	50.0
	Michael E. Maher (D)	13,466	45.1
2	James R. Mann (R)	20,128	48.4
	John Charles Vaughan (D)	18,717	45.0
	J. O. Bentall (SOC)	2,711	6.5
3	William Warfield Wilson (R)	16,661	44.9
	Fred J. Crowley (D)	16,604	44.8
	J. Clifford Cox (SOC)	2,920	7.9
4	James T. McDermott (D)	15,764	62.9
	Michael G. Walsh (R)	7,028	28.1
	Peter Bulthouse (SOC)	1,994	8.0
5	Adolph J. Sabath (D)	13,936	71.7
	Louis H. Clusmann (R)	3,533	18.2
	Joseph J. Kral (SOC)	1,775	9.1
6	Edmund J. Stack (D)	22,951	51.1
	William J. Moxley (R)	17,178	38.2
	George Chant (SOC)	3,551	7.9
7	Frank Buchanan (D)	22,520	43.6
	Frederick Lundin (R)	21,096	40.8
	John Collins (SOC)	7,016	13.6
8	Thomas Gallagher (D)	14,281	58.7
	Daniel D. Coffey (R)	7,975	32.8
	John Drexler (SOC)	1,903	7.8

	Candidates	Votes	%
9	Lynden Evans (D)	13,501	45.7
	Frederick H. Gansbergen (R)	12,991	44.0
	Frank Shiflersmith (SOC)	2,650	9.0
10	George Edmund Foss (R)	20,130	47.7
	Richard J. Finnegan (D)	17,541	41.5
	Robert C. Magisen (SOC)	3,370	8.0
11	Ira C. Copley (R)	17,899	57.1
	Frank O. Hawley (D)	11,276	36.0
12	Charles E. Fuller (R)	20,665	62.3
	J. W. Rausch (D)	9,185	27.7
	Thomas Johnson (SOC)	2,277	6.9
13	John C. McKenzie (R)	17,249	61.3
	O. H. Wright (D)	9,752	34.7
14	James McKinney (R)	17,004	52.3
	Clyde H. Tavenner (D)	12,980	40.0
	Milton L. Morrill (SOC)	1,658	5.1
15	George W. Prince (R)	16,753	47.0
	Albert E. Bergland (D)	16,487	46.3
16	Claudius U. Stone (D)	17,633	51.2
	Joseph V. Graff (R)	15,024	43.6
17	John A. Sterling (R)	16,601	52.0
	Louis Fitzhenry (D)	14,215	44.5
18	Joseph G. Cannon (R)	20,943	53.0
	William L. Cundiff (D)	16,186	41.0
19	William B. McKinley (R)	23,107	52.6
	I. J. Martin (D)	19,259	43.9
20	Henry T. Rainey (D)	20,194	59.3
	James H. Danskin (R)	12,961	38.0
21	James M. Graham (D)	19,886	50.1
	H. Clay Wilson (R)	17,318	43.6
22	William A. Rodenberg (R)	23,024	49.7
	Bruce A. Campbell (D)	18,787	40.6
	Henry Groeteka (SOC)	3,826	8.3
23	Martin D. Foster (D)	23,535	53.7
	J. H. Loy (R)	18,230	41.6
24	H. Robert Fowler (D)	17,235	48.8
	Pleasant T. Chapman (R)	16,918	47.9
25	Napoleon B. Thistlewood (R)	18,233	49.1
	William D. Lyerle (D)	16,442	44.2

INDIANA

	Candidates	Votes	%
1	John W. Boehne (D)	22,420	52.3
	Francis B. Posey (R)	18,606	43.4
2	William A. Cullop (D)	22,960	48.4
	Oscar E. Bland (R)	21,419	45.2
3	William E. Cox (D)	21,670	58.4
	Harry C. Poindexter (R)	14,969	40.3
4	Lincoln Dixon (D)	22,001	53.8
	John H. Kemman (R)	17,921	43.8
5	Ralph W. Moss (D)	25,917	51.6
	Frank Tilley (R)	21,267	42.4
6	Finley P. Gray (D)	23,740	49.0
	William O. Barnard (R)	22,242	45.9
7	Charles A. Korbly (D)	30,330	50.3
	Linton A. Cox (R)	26,968	44.7
8	John A. M. Adair (D)	25,454	51.8
	Rollin Warner (R)	19,309	39.3
	Orville G. Overcarsh (SOC)	2,910	5.9
9	Martin A. Morrison (D)	24,434	48.0
	Everett E. Neal (R)	23,841	46.8
10	Edgar D. Crumpacker (R)	27,722	50.3
	John B. Peterson (D)	25,692	46.6
11	George W. Rauch (D)	22,528	47.8
	John L. Thompson (R)	21,282	45.2
12	Cyrus Cline (D)	19,754	49.9
	Owen N. Heaton (R)	17,937	45.3
13	Henry A. Barnhart (D)	25,253	48.2
	John L. Moorman (R)	24,153	46.1

IOWA

	Candidates	Votes	%
1	Charles A. Kennedy (R)	15,602	51.9
	J. A. S. Pollard (D)	13,427	44.7

IOWA

	Candidates	Votes	%
2	Irvin S. Pepper (D)	19,815	51.5
	Charles Grilk (R)	16,971	44.1
3	Charles E. Pickett (R)	19,324	54.3
	John D. Denison Jr (D)	15,572	43.7
4	Gilbert N. Haugen (R)	16,928	49.9
	Daniel D. Murphy (D)	16,708	49.3
5	James W. Good (R)	16,953	51.8
	S. C. Huber (D)	14,676	44.8
6	Nathan E. Kendall (R)	16,335	48.2
	Daniel W. Hamilton (D)	15,914	47.0
7	Solomon F. Prouty (R)	17,722	53.1
	Clint L. Price (D)	14,534	43.5
8	Horace M. Towner (R)	19,548	54.9
	Frank Q. Stewart (D)	15,565	43.7
9	Walter I. Smith (R)	18,763	52.0
	W. F. Cleeland (D)	16,916	46.9
10	Frank P. Woods (R)	26,927	97.0
11	Elbert H. Hubbard (R)	22,199	59.9
	M. M. White (D)	14,377	38.8

KANSAS

		Votes	%
1	Daniel R. Anthony Jr. (R)	21,852	72.3
	J. B. Chapman (D)	7,486	24.8
2	Alexander C. Mitchell (R)	23,282	50.9
	John Caldwell (D)	19,852	43.4
3	Phillip P. Campbell (R)	20,771	44.5
	Jeremiah D. Botkin (D)	19,943	42.7
	C. S. Bendure (SOC)	5,748	12.3
4	Fred S. Jackson (R)	17,111	54.9
	Henderson S. Martin (D)	14,051	45.1
5	Rollin R. Rees (R)	17,680	51.3
	G. T. Helvering (D)	15,775	45.8
6	Isaac D. Young (R)	21,020	50.9
	Frank S. Rockefeller (D)	18,985	46.0
7	Edmond H. Madison (R)	24,925	53.1
	George A. Neeley (D)	20,133	42.9
8	Victor Murdock (R)	16,239	87.3
	George Burnett (SOC)	2,354	12.7

KENTUCKY

		Votes	%
1	Ollie M. James (D)	11,574	89.3
	C. L. Harney (SOC)	1,389	10.7
2	Augustus O. Stanley (D)	12,040	62.2
	R. J. Salmon (R)	6,902	35.7
3	Robert Y. Thomas Jr. (D)	16,063	51.3
	W. H. Jones (R)	14,850	47.5
4	Ben Johnson (D)	18,263	59.2
	D. W. Gaddie (R)	11,952	38.8
5	J. Swagar Sherley (D)	21,437	53.2
	J. Wheeler McGee (R)	17,376	43.1
6	Arthur B. Rouse (D)	15,454	55.6
	Charles W. Nagel (R)	11,007	39.6
7	James C. Cantrill (D)	13,858	56.0
	M. C. Rankin (R)	10,877	44.0
8	Harvey Helm (D)	12,412	56.9
	Hugh Miller (R)	9,385	43.1
9	William J. Fields (D)	19,350	50.8
	Joseph B. Bennett (R)	18,737	49.2
10	John W. Langley (R)	20,664	52.4
	A. Floyd Byrd (D)	18,766	47.6
11	Caleb Powers (R)	25,622	60.5
	Elza Bertrand (D)	16,357	38.6

LOUISIANA

		Votes	%
1	Albert Estopinal (D)	11,932	89.5
	John A. Wogan (R)	1,408	10.6
2	H. Garland Dupre (D)	10,218	83.2
	Victor Loisel (R)	2,071	16.9
3	Robert F. Broussard (D)	4,011	91.0
	Jules Dreyfus (R)	395	9.0
4	John T. Watkins (D)	4,244	95.9
5	Joseph E. Ransdell (D)	4,469	99.0
6	Robert C. Wickliffe (D)	4,016	100.0
7	Arsene P. Pujo (D)	7,393	91.3
	J. R. Jones (SOC)	706	8.7

Special Election

	Candidates	Votes	%
2	H. Garland Dupre (D)	10,333	82.7
	Victor Loisel (R)	2,160	17.3

MAINE

		Votes	%
1	Asher C. Hinds (R)	17,521	49.8
	W. M. Pennell (D)	16,901	48.0
2	Daniel J. McGillicuddy (D)	18,938	52.6
	John P. Swasey (R)	16,227	45.1
3	Samuel W. Gould (D)	17,187	51.1
	Edwin C. Burleigh (R)	15,798	46.9
4	Frank E. Guernsey (R)	18,017	50.3
	George M. Hanson (D)	17,516	48.9

MARYLAND

		Votes	%
1	James Harry Covington (D)	18,341	51.6
	A. Lincoln Dryden (R)	16,066	45.2
2	Joshua Frederick C. Talbott (D)	19,352	51.8
	William B. Baker (R)	17,124	45.8
3	George Konig (D)	15,028	48.4
	Charles W. Main (R)	14,740	47.5
4	John Charles Linthicum (D)	17,478	50.8
	Addison E. Mullikin (R)	15,698	45.7
5	Thomas Parran (R)	15,706	49.5
	J. Enos Ray Jr. (D)	14,879	46.9
6	David J. Lewis (D)	16,585	48.1
	Brainard Henry Warner Jr. (R)	15,896	46.1

MASSACHUSETTS

		Votes	%
1	George P. Lawrence (R)	14,109	48.9
	Edward Morgan (D)	13,244	45.9
	Louis B. Clark (SOC)	1,476	5.1
2	Frederick H. Gillett (R)	14,242	48.8
	William G. McKechnie (D)	13,774	47.2
3	John A. Thayer (D)	15,243	51.2
	Charles G. Washburn (R)	14,544	48.8
4	William H. Wilder (R)	16,965	49.1
	John J. Mitchell (D)	16,835	48.7
5	Butler Ames (R)	13,760	51.1
	James H. Carmichael (D)	13,163	48.9
6	Augustus P. Gardner (R)	17,272	54.0
	William H. O'Brien (D)	12,038	37.6
	James F. Carey (SOC)	2,667	8.3
7	Ernest W. Roberts (R)	16,624	50.7
	Walter H. Creamer (D)	14,337	43.7
	W. Lathrop Meaker (DPPC)	1,837	5.6
8	Samuel W. McCall (R)	15,854	53.4
	Frederick S. Deitrick (D)	13,842	46.6
9	William F. Murray (D)	11,652	49.0
	John A. Keliher (DI)	10,037	42.2
	William H. Oakes (R)	2,081	8.8
10	James M. Curley (D)	20,345	56.3
	J. Mitchel Galvin (R)	15,783	43.7
11	Andrew J. Peters (D)	18,933	59.2
	William Dudley (R)	13,033	40.8
12	John W. Weeks (R)	19,037	56.4
	Daniel J. Daley (D)	14,696	43.6
13	William S. Greene (R)	14,079	58.9
	James F. Morris (D)	9,831	41.1
14	Robert O. Harris (R)	15,753	47.9
	Thomas C. Thacher (D)	15,686	47.6

Special Election

		Votes	%
4	John J. Mitchell (D)	16,688	50.0
	William H. Wilder (R)	16,664	50.0

MICHIGAN

		Votes	%
1	Frank E. Doremus (D)	20,843	52.0
	Edwin Denby (R)	17,676	44.1

	Candidates	Votes	%
2	William W. Wedemeyer (R)	21,485	57.0
	John V. Sheehan (D)	15,125	40.1
3	John M. C. Smith (R)	18,606	57.7
	Nathaniel H. Stewart (D)	11,935	37.0
4	Edward L. Hamilton (R)	17,282	56.2
	John E. Barnes (D)	12,185	39.6
5	Edwin F. Sweet (D)	15,219	48.4
	Gerrit J. Diekema (R)	14,589	46.4
6	Samuel W. Smith (R)	23,321	52.9
	Alva M. Cummins (D)	18,403	41.7
7	Henry McMorran (R)	15,897	55.6
	Thomas Wellman (D)	11,595	40.5
8	Joseph W. Fordney (R)	14,878	56.5
	James P. Devereaux (D)	10,571	40.2
9	James C. McLaughlin (R)	13,029	65.7
	Emery D. Weimer (D)	6,171	31.1
10	George A. Loud (R)	15,060	59.8
	Albert Miller (D)	8,746	34.7
11	Francis H. Dodds (R)	16,179	64.8
	Hubbard Head (D)	7,157	28.7
12	H. Olin Young (R)	24,661	73.6
	Gideon T. Werline (D)	8,751	26.1

MINNESOTA

		Votes	%
1	Sydney Anderson (R)	18,315	55.3
	Buck (D)	14,816	44.7
2	Winfield S. Hammond (D)	14,745	53.2
	Ellsworth (R)	12,426	44.8
3	Charles R. Davis (R)	21,863	100.0
4	Frederick C. Stevens (R)	18,830	56.6
	Gieske (D)	12,495	37.6
	Stratton (PUB OWN)	1,953	5.9
5	Frank M. Nye (R)	17,433	50.0
	Dyer (D)	15,113	43.3
	Lindsay (PUB OWN)	2,323	6.7
6	Charles A. Lindbergh (R)	25,272	100.0
7	Andrew J. Volstead (R)	24,395	100.0
8	Clarence B. Miller (R)	17,018	53.7
	Jaques (D)	10,305	32.5
	Watkins (PUB OWN)	4,354	13.7
9	Halvor Steenerson (R)	24,572	74.5
	Sanders (PUB OWN)	8,421	25.5

MISSISSIPPI

		Votes	%
1	Ezekiel S. Candler Jr. (D)	2,904	100.0
2	Hubert D. Stephens (D)	3,304	100.0
3	Benjamin G. Humphreys (D)	1,799	100.0
4	Thomas U. Sisson (D)	3,719	100.0
5	Samuel A. Witherspoon (D)	3,921	100.0
6	Pat Harrison (D)	4,011	99.4
7	William A. Dickson (D)	2,468	100.0
8	James W. Collier (D)	1,739	100.0

MISSOURI

		Votes	%
1	James T. Lloyd (D)	19,953	54.2
	Higbee (R)	15,572	42.3
2	William W. Rucker (D)	21,090	55.6
	Haley (R)	16,122	42.5
3	Joshua W. Alexander (D)	19,213	56.3
	Davisson (R)	14,900	43.7
4	Charles F. Booher (D)	20,231	55.1
	Amick (R)	15,825	43.1
5	William P. Borland (D)	31,026	54.6
	Lea (R)	23,982	42.2
6	Clement C. Dickinson (D)	17,504	53.2
	Devol (R)	14,374	43.7
7	Courtney W. Hamlin (D)	22,433	49.1
	Hall (R)	21,951	48.0
8	Dorsey W. Shackleford (D)	16,642	53.3
	Norfleet (R)	14,349	45.9
9	James Beauchamp Clark (D)	23,124	54.5
	Roy (R)	19,105	45.0
10	Richard Bartholdt (R)	53,298	60.8
	Charles J. Maurer (D)	28,054	32.0
	Hoehn (SOC)	5,865	6.7

MISSOURI

Candidates	Votes	%
11 Theron E. Catlin (R)	20,089‡	49.7
Patrick F. Gill (D)	18,695	46.3
12 Leonidas Dyer (R)	15,965	53.1
Thomas E. Kinney (D)	13,121	43.7
13 Walter L. Hensley (D)	16,020	49.3
Elvins (R)	15,386	47.4
14 Joseph J. Russell (D)	23,612	47.8
Crow (R)	22,463	45.5
Hafner (SOC)	2,973	6.0
15 James A. Daugherty (D)	21,259	47.4
Morgan (R)	20,443	45.6
16 Thomas L. Rubey (D)	16,239	52.1
Murphy (R)	14,763	47.4

MONTANA

AL Charles N. Pray (R)	32,519	49.4
Charles S. Hartman (D)	28,071	42.7
J. Frank Mabie (SOC)	5,184	7.9

NEBRASKA

1 John A. Maguire (D & PPI)	16,501	50.4
William Hayward (R)	15,763	48.2
2 C. O. Lobeck (D)	15,912	48.9
Abraham L. Sutton (R)	15,673	48.1
3 James P. Latta (D & PPI)	25,945	57.7
J. F. Boyd (R)	18,566	41.3
4 Charles H. Sloan (R)	20,807	50.8
Benjamin F. Good (D & PPI)	19,540	47.8
5 George W. Norris (R)	19,929	53.7
Roderick D. Sutherland (D & PPI)	15,925	42.9
6 Moses P. Kinkaid (R)	24,327	52.8
William J. Taylor (D & PPI)	19,682	42.7

NEVADA

AL Edwin E. Roberts (R)	10,066	49.9
Charles S. Sprague (D)	7,688	38.1
Ashley Grant Miller (SOC)	2,409	12.0

NEW HAMPSHIRE

1 Cyrus A. Sulloway (R)	20,941	50.5
Eugene E. Reed (D)	20,093	48.5
2 Frank D. Currier (R)	21,639	55.1
Henry H. Metcalf (D)	16,913	43.0

NEW JERSEY

1 Henry C. Loudenslager (R)	21,394	48.6
Nowrey (D)	20,554	46.7
2 John J. Gardner (R)	22,861	51.6
Hampton (D)	16,915	38.2
Riddle (I)	3,508	7.9
3 Thomas J. Scully (D)	24,657	54.8
Howell (R)	20,160	44.8
4 Ira W. Wood (R)	19,354	49.1
Libbey (D)	19,089	48.4
5 William E. Tuttle Jr. (D)	23,768	51.0
Runyon (R)	20,675	44.4
6 William Hughes (D)	29,458	51.6
McClave (R)	25,301	44.3
7 Edward W. Townsend (D)	21,962	54.0
Parker (R)	17,756	43.7
8 Walter I. McCoy (D)	19,364	51.2
William H. Wiley (R)	16,847	44.6
9 Eugene F. Kinkead (D)	23,784	62.3
Record (R)	13,390	35.1
10 James A. Hamill (D)	26,266	70.2
Seibel (R)	10,104	27.0

NEW YORK

Candidates	Votes	%
1 Martin W. Littleton (D & IL)	26,974	54.0
William W. Cocks (R)	21,826	43.7
2 George H. Lindsay (D)	14,248	59.2
Ladislaus W. Schwenk (R & IL)	8,304	34.5
Paul Muller Jr. (SOC)	1,428	5.9
3 James P. Maher (D)	15,432	48.3
Alfred T. Hobley (R & IL)	14,570	45.6
John J. Jennings (SOC)	1,806	5.7
4 Frank E. Wilson (D & IL)	20,676	46.6
Charles B. Law (R)	20,295	45.8
Barnet Wolff (SOC)	3,257	7.4
5 William C. Redfield (D & IL)	26,220	51.7
Warren I. Lee (R)	22,576	44.5
6 William M. Calder (R)	17,249	48.6
Michael E. Butler (D)	16,805	47.3
7 John J. Fitzgerald (D)	16,847	67.3
William R. A. Koehl (R & IL)	7,748	31.0
8 Daniel J. Riordan (D)	20,683	66.2
George S. Husch (R)	8,311	26.6
9 Henry M. Goldfogle (D)	4,606	46.8
Meyer London (SOC)	3,322	33.8
Jacob W. Block (R & IL)	1,850	18.8
10 William Sulzer (D & IL)	9,850	60.2
Anthony M. McCabe (R)	4,807	29.4
John Mullen (SOC)	1,694	10.4
11 Charles V. Fornes (D)	17,384	61.2
Henry H. Curran (R & IL)	10,171	35.8
12 Michael Conry (D)	14,376	62.7
Peter R. Gatens (R & IL)	7,467	32.6
13 Jefferson M. Levy (D)	11,539	50.4
Herbert Parsons (R)	9,951	43.5
14 John Joseph Kindred (D)	20,875	54.3
Victor Hugo Duras (R & IL)	14,018	36.5
William F. Ehret (SOC)	3,481	9.1
15 Thomas G. Patten (D & IL)	13,838	54.4
William M. Bennett (R)	11,152	43.8
16 Francis Burton Harrison (D)	10,450	55.0
Samuel Bell Thomas (CIV A)	6,518	34.3
George F. Miner (SOC)	2,012	10.6
17 Henry George Jr. (D & IL)	28,306	50.7
William S. Bennet (R)	26,010	46.6
18 Steven B. Ayres (D)	33,660	51.2
Gottlieb Haneke (R & IL)	27,607	42.0
Joshua Wauhope (SOC)	4,354	6.6
19 John E. Andrus (R)	23,140	49.7
Cornelius A. Pugsley (D)	22,247	47.7
20 Thomas W. Bradley (R)	19,363	51.6
John Bigelow Jr. (D)	17,307	46.2
21 Richard E. Connell (D)	18,832	49.8
Hamilton Fish (R)	18,315	48.4
22 William H. Draper (R)	20,424	51.8
Elisha C. Tower (D)	17,277	43.8
23 Henry S. De Forest (R)	28,218	48.1
Curtis N. Douglas (D)	26,228	44.7
Harvey A. Simmons (SOC)	2,978	5.1
24 George W. Fairchild (R)	23,636	49.9
George M. Palmer (D)	22,416	47.3
25 Theron Akin (D, I LEAGUE)	21,754	48.9
Cyrus Durey (R)	21,442	48.2
26 George R. Malby (R)	21,980	55.7
Thomas Cantwell (D)	15,584	39.5
27 Charles A. Talcott (D & IL)	22,458	50.8
Charles S. Millington (R)	20,242	45.8
28 Luther W. Mott (R, I LEAGUE)	18,844	50.1
George W. Reeves (D)	15,629	41.5
Charles F. Simpson (P)	2,514	6.7
29 Michael E. Driscoll (R)	26,589	52.5
Henry E. Wilson (D & IL)	20,281	40.0
30 John W. Dwight (R)	21,789	49.2
Ira A. Hix (D, I LEAGUE)	18,346	41.4
Frank Dewitt Reese (P)	3,521	8.0
31 Sereno E. Payne (R)	21,121	51.8
John Colmey (D)	17,728	43.5
32 Henry G. Danforth (R)	26,375	52.7
George P. Decker (D)	21,176	42.3
33 Edwin S. Underhill (D)	19,517	49.5
Jacob Sloat Fassett (R)	17,556	44.5
34 James S. Simmons (R)	25,051	54.0

Candidates	Votes	%
	Elliot W. Horton (D)	19,307	41.6
35 Daniel A. Driscoll (D & IL)	21,727	56.9
Patrick J. Keeler (R)	14,605	38.3
36 Charles Bennett Smith (D & IL)	20,685	48.9
De Alva S. Alexander (R)	20,684	48.8
37 Edward Butterfield Vreeland (R)	20,530	53.1
J. William Sanbury (D, I LEAGUE)	14,314	37.0
Arthur A. Amidon (P)	2,099	5.4

NORTH CAROLINA

1 John H. Small (D)	11,544	75.3
Henry T. King (R)	3,721	24.3
2 Claude Kitchin (D)	10,749	85.1
R. H. Norfleet (R)	1,867	14.8
3 John M. Faison (D)	10,428	58.1
George E. Butler (R)	7,505	41.8
4 Edward W. Pou (D)	13,728	65.8
R. A. P. Cooley (R)	7,110	34.1
5 Charles M. Stedman (D)	20,392	54.2
David H. Blair (R)	17,060	45.3
6 Hannibal L. Godwin (D)	10,806	71.7
Iredell Meares (R)	4,257	28.3
7 Robert N. Page (D)	14,367	56.5
John J. Parker (R)	11,006	43.3
8 Robert L. Doughton (D)	16,560	51.1
Charles H. Cowles (R)	15,801	48.8
9 Edwin Y. Webb (D)	16,574	59.3
S. S. McNinch (R)	11,332	40.6
10 James M. Gudger Jr. (D)	15,901	51.8
John G. Grant (R)	14,771	48.1

NORTH DAKOTA

AL Louis B. Hanna (R)	51,556✔	
Henry T. Helgesen (R)	50,600✔	
Tobias D. Casey (D)	25,880	
M. A. Hildreth (D)	25,322	
Arthur Hagendorf (SOC)	3,225	
N. H. Bjornstead (SOC)	3,179	

OHIO

1 Nicholas Longworth (R)	24,453	51.1
Thomas P. Hart (D)	21,497	44.9
2 Alfred G. Allen (D)	24,323	47.9
Herman P. Goebel (D)	23,834	47.0
3 James M. Cox (D)	31,539	55.5
George R. Young (R)	18,730	33.0
Harmon Evans (SOC)	6,275	11.0
4 J. Henry Goeke (D)	20,865	58.4
C. E. Johnston (R)	13,482	37.7
5 Timothy T. Ansberry (D)	21,201	60.1
C. S. Roe (R)	13,309	37.7
6 Matthew R. Denver (D)	20,056	54.0
Jesse Taylor (R)	17,105	46.0
7 James D. Post (D)	20,776	52.8
J. Warren Keifer (R)	17,569	44.6
8 Frank B. Willis (R)	21,030	50.0
Thomas C. Mahon (D)	19,519	46.4
9 Isaac R. Sherwood (D)	21,908	48.0
J. Kent Hamilton (R)	19,593	43.0
W. F. Ries (SOC)	3,917	8.6
10 Robert M. Switzer (R)	18,548	51.3
Edmond H. Willis (D)	16,250	45.0
11 Horatio C. Claypool (D)	22,894	49.9
Albert Douglas (R)	20,168	44.0
Austin B. Shinn (SOC)	2,397	5.2
12 Edward L. Taylor Jr. (R)	17,696	39.9
Frank S. Monnett (D)	15,151	34.2
Jacob C. Bachman (SOC)	11,142	25.1
13 Carl C. Anderson (D)	30,196	63.7
Miles H. McLaughlin (R)	15,486	32.7
14 William G. Sharp (D)	25,287	54.6
George H. Chamberlain (R)	18,459	39.8

OHIO

	Candidates	Votes	%
15	George White (D)	19,723	49.3
	James Joyce (R)	17,674	44.2
	Frank Martin (SOC)	2,218	5.6
16	William B. Francis (D)	15,731	46.6
	David A. Hollingsworth (R)	15,323	45.4
	Robert J. Murray (SOC)	2,325	6.9
17	William A. Ashbrook (D)	25,875	59.3
	A. B. Critchfield (R)	14,964	34.3
	Edward Schmidt (SOC)	2,508	5.8
18	John J. Whitacre (D)	23,568	46.6
	James Kennedy (R)	20,617	40.8
	Thomas Williams (SOC)	4,907	9.7
19	Ellsworth R. Bathrick (D)	19,255	46.0
	W. Aubrey Thomas (R)	18,290	43.7
	Paul G. Miller (SOC)	3,720	8.9
20	Paul Howland (R)	20,699	46.8
	William Gordon (D)	20,519	46.4
	John G. Willert (SOC)	2,847	6.4
21	Robert J. Bulkley (D)	18,091	48.1
	James H. Cassidy (R)	16,716	44.5
	Karl A. Cheyney (SOC)	2,649	7.1

OKLAHOMA

	Candidates	Votes	%
1	Bird S. McGuire (R)	20,301	49.2
	Neil E. McNeill (D)	18,415	44.7
	W. L. Reynolds (SOC)	2,522	6.1
2	Dick T. Morgan (R)	25,134	46.1
	Elmer L. Fulton (D)	24,062	44.1
	H. I. Bryant (SOC)	5,382	9.9
3	James S. Davenport (D)	25,312	50.0
	Charles E. Creager (R)	22,367	44.2
	G. M. Snyder (SOC)	2,923	5.8
4	Charles D. Carter (D)	21,959	55.6
	Charles M. Campbell (R)	11,979	30.4
	J. N. Gilmore (SOC)	5,534	14.0
5	Scott Ferris (D)	28,600	58.9
	J. H. Franklin (R)	13,425	27.6
	H. H. Stallard (SOC)	6,539	13.5

OREGON

	Candidates	Votes	%
1	Willis C. Hawley (R)	26,256	48.6
	R. G. Smith (D)	18,232	33.7
	C. W. Sherman (SOC)	4,971	9.2
	W. P. Elmore (P)	4,585	8.5
2	Abraham W. Lafferty (R)	30,642	51.8
	John Manning (D)	19,477	32.9
	William A. Crawford (SOC)	5,583	9.4
	George B. Pratt (P)	3,464	5.9

PENNSYLVANIA

	Candidates	Votes	%
1	Henry H. Bingham (R, P)	28,054	69.9
	Henry V. Garrett (KEY, WM PENN)	8,827	22.0
	Michael J. Geraghty (D)	2,657	6.6
2	Joel Cook (R, WMP/L)	24,888*	69.4
	Daniel W. Simpkins (KEY, WM PENN)	7,665	21.4
	Edward B. Seiberlich (D)	2,542	7.1
3	J. Hampton Moore (R, WMP/L)	23,994	69.2
	James G. Ramsdell (KEY)	7,030	20.3
	William A. Hayes (D)	2,712	7.8
4	Reuben O. Moon (R, WMP/L)	16,309	72.6
	William C. Mitchell (D)	2,459	10.9
	Albert W. Sanson (WM PENN, CITY)	2,526	11.2
5	Michael Donohoe (KEY, D)	19,209	48.4
	William W. Foulkrod (R, WMP/L)	18,016	45.4
	Martin McCue (SOC)	2,328	5.9
6	George D. McCreary (R, WMP/L)	25,747	46.2
	Frank H. Hawkins (KEY, WM PENN)	23,672	42.5

	Candidates	Votes	%
	William A. Carr (D)	4,319	7.8
7	Thomas S. Butler (R)	16,490	51.7
	Eugene C. Bonniwell (KEY, D)	14,498	45.5
8	Robert E. Difenderfer (D, KEY)	19,683	49.6
	Irving P. Wanger (R)	19,016	48.1
9	William W. Griest (R)	14,718	79.1
	James G. McSparran (D)	3,120	16.8
10	John R. Farr (R)	13,457	50.4
	P. F. Calpin (D)	11,240	42.1
11	Charles C. Bowman (R, P)	14,384‡	47.5
	George R. McLean (D)	13,834	45.7
	Charles F. Quinn (SOC, FEDR LAB)	2,079	6.9
12	Robert E. Lee (D)	9,492	40.1
	Robert D. Heaton (R)	9,441	39.9
	C. F. Foley (SOC)	4,739	20.0
13	John H. Rothermel (D)	19,680	49.8
	John K. Hahn (R)	12,939	32.7
	Caleb Harrison (SOC)	6,209	15.7
14	George W. Kipp (KEY, D)	10,276	49.0
	Charles C. Pratt (R)	9,481	45.2
15	William B. Wilson (D)	13,624	49.74
	Clarence L. Peaslee (R)	10,588	38.6
	Clarence C. Ricker (SOC)	2,004	7.3
16	John G. McHenry (D, R)	12,578	53.0
	Theodore C. Harter (KEY)	6,366	26.8
	Jacob W. Renn (SOC)	3,818	16.1
17	Benjamin K. Focht (R)	14,473	50.8
	J. Murray Africa (D)	11,681	41.0
18	Marlin E. Olmsted (R)	21,221	59.7
	W. Jonathan Kiefer (D)	11,686	32.9
19	Jesse L. Hartman (R)	18,133	60.4
	Isaiah Scheenline (D)	7,669	25.5
	Stewart C. Cowan (P)	2,173	7.2
	Anslem B. Kirsch (SOC)	2,048	6.8
20	Daniel F. Lafean (R)	15,713	50.9
	Andrew R. Brodbeck (D)	13,786	44.7
21	Charles E. Patton (R)	10,493	49.6
	William C. Heinle (D)	6,903	32.6
	George W. Fox (SOC)	2,389	11.3
	Charles E. Patton (P)	1,363	6.4
22	Curtis H. Gregg (D, KEY)	12,988	42.3
	J. David McJunkin (R)	12,490	40.7
	Robert Dudley (SOC)	3,242	10.6
	E. S. Littell (P)	1,981	6.5
23	S. Crago Thomas (R)	13,665	52.9
	Jesse H. Wise (D, KEY)	8,894	34.4
	Washington Herd (SOC)	2,036	7.9
24	Charles Matthews (R)	15,177	44.1
	Henry H. Wilson (KEY, D)	14,372	41.8
	Charles A. Collins (SOC)	3,332	9.7
25	Arthur L. Bates (R)	10,668	46.4
	John B. Brooks (D, KEY)	9,632	41.9
	George B. Allen (SOC)	1,377	6.0
	Richard A. Buzza (P)	1,313	5.7
26	A. Mitchell Palmer (D)	16,284	61.3
	Robert Brown (R)	8,867	33.4
27	J. N. Langham (R)	13,073	58.8
	John Smith Shirler (D)	5,451	24.5
	John Houk (P)	2,479	11.1
	M. A. Vanhorn (SOC)	1,245	5.6
28	Peter M. Speer (R)	10,932	41.7
	William J. Breene (D)	9,492	36.2
	John E. Gill (P)	3,047	11.6
	John R. McKeown (SOC)	2,163	8.3
29	Stephen G. Porter (R)	14,785	74.2
	George T. McConnell (SOC)	2,468	12.4
	Fleming Jamieson (D)	2,110	10.6
30	John Dalzell (R)	13,261	46.5
	Robert J. Black (P, UN LAB)	7,807	27.4
	W. J. Wright (SOC)	2,942	10.3
	James A. Wakefield (KEY, D)	4,208	14.8
31	James Francis Burke (R)	12,996	64.5
	John J. Thorpe (KEY, D)	5,798	28.8
	John Connor (SOC)	1,164	5.8
32	A. J. Barchfeld (R)	13,483	49.7
	Hermann L. Hegner (KEY, D)	9,933	36.6
	Valentine Remmel (SOC)	3,152	11.6

RHODE ISLAND

	Candidates	Votes	%
1	George F. O'Shaunessy (D)	17,532	51.3
	William P. Sheffield (R)	15,681	45.9
2	George H. Utter (R)	18,983	57.2
	Cooney (D)	13,704	41.3

SOUTH CAROLINA

		Votes	%
1	George S. Legare (D)	3,432	97.4
2	James F. Byrnes (D)	4,392	100.0
3	Wyatt Aiken (D)	3,381	99.9
4	Joseph T. Johnston (D)	7,616	98.9
5	David E. Finley (D)	3,470	100.0
6	J. Edwin Ellerbe (D)	3,734	100.0
7	Asbury F. Lever (D)	4,762	95.6

SOUTH DAKOTA

		Votes	%
AL	Charles H. Burke (R)	64,777✔	
	Eben W. Martin (R)	64,495✔	
	W. W. Soule (D)	32,655	
	J. E. Kelley (D)	32,329	
	Knute Lewis (P)	4,139	
	W. J. Edgar (P)	4,124	
	Isaac M. Burnside (I)	1,641	

TENNESSEE

		Votes	%
1	Sam R. Sells (R)	20,955	74.0
	Cy H. Lyle (D)	7,380	26.1
2	Richard W. Austin (R)	15,761	57.3
	N. W. Hale (R)	11,755	42.7
3	John A. Moon (D)	17,654	56.9
	Charles R. Evans (R)	12,953	41.7
4	Cordell Hull (D)	19,298	78.9
	J. T. Odum (ID)	5,169	21.1
5	William C. Houston (D)	16,697	98.9
6	Joseph W. Byrns (D)	16,764	87.0
	W. H. Jackson (SOC)	2,502	13.0
7	Lemuel P. Padgett (D)	21,299	96.8
8	Thetus W. Sims (D)	13,764	57.9
	S. E. Murrey (R)	9,860	41.5
9	Finis J. Garrett (D)	15,000	85.8
	J. W. Brown (R)	1,416	8.1
	W. R. Landrum (IR)	940	5.4
10	George W. Gordon (D)	14,862	94.8
	T. H. Haines (SOC)	824	5.3

Special Election

		Votes	%
1	Zachary D. Massey (R)	19,181	77.4
	Cy H. Lyle (D)	5,618	22.7

TEXAS

		Votes	%
1	Morris Sheppard (D)	10,707	87.4
	Velmar Antle (R)	1,148	9.4
2	Martin Dies (D)	10,898	94.4
3	James Young (D)	9,450	98.9
4	Choice B. Randell (D)	9,719	88.9
	C. A. Gray (R)	1,208	11.1
5	Jack Beall (D)	10,939	95.0
6	Rufus Hardy (D)	7,826	97.9
7	Alexander W. Gregg (D)	6,566	88.2
	Willis Kendall (R)	843	11.3
8	John M. Moore (D)	11,654	90.4
	A. M. Lawson (R)	1,112	8.6
9	George F. Burgess (D)	10,244	78.0
	E. C. Webster (R)	2,108	16.1
10	Albert S. Burleson (D)	10,118	100.0
11	Robert L. Henry (D)	7,384	98.6
12	Oscar Callaway (D)	10,525	82.0
	Robert G. Martin (SOC)	1,270	9.9
	C. C. Littleton (R)	836	6.5
13	John H. Stephens (D)	19,543	83.4
	T. S. Bugbee (R)	2,039	8.7
	John I. Green (SOC)	1,488	6.4
14	James L. Slayden (D)	14,251	94.8

TEXAS

Candidates	Votes	%
15 John N. Garner (D)	14,300	71.7
Noah Allen (R)	5,287	26.5
16 William R. Smith (D)	18,258	85.4
W. H. Harvey (SOC)	1,749	8.2
Robert A. Webb (R)	1,384	6.5

UTAH

Candidates	Votes	%
AL Joseph Howell (R)	50,614	49.5
Ferdinand Erickson (D)	32,730	32.0
Allen T. Sanford (AM)	14,042	13.7

VERMONT

Candidates	Votes	%
1 David J. Foster (R)	18,951	68.6
P. M. Meldon (D)	8,215	29.7
2 Frank Plumley (R)	18,185	73.4
Alexander Cochran (D)	6,226	25.1

VIRGINIA

Candidates	Votes	%
1 William A. Jones (D)	5,908	80.5
George N. Wise (R)	1,431	19.5
2 Edward E. Holland (D)	6,649	79.6
H. H. Rumble (R)	1,703	20.4
3 John Lamb (D)	5,408	86.9
W. R. Vawter (R)	813	13.1
4 Robert Turnbull (D)	3,769	100.0
5 Edward W. Saunders (D)	7,537	50.5
John M. Parsons (R)	7,382	49.5
6 Carter Glass (D)	5,203	87.6
W. Allison (R)	734	12.4
7 James Hay (D)	5,818	58.0
John Paul (R)	2,589	25.8
S. Lupton (I)	1,631	16.3

Candidates	Votes	%
8 Charles C. Carlin (D)	4,669	100.0
9 Campbell Bascom Slemp (R)	16,958	50.3
Henry C. Stuart (D)	16,731	49.7
10 Henry D. Flood (D)	5,878	100.0

WASHINGTON

Candidates	Votes	%
1 William E. Humphrey (R)	27,717	51.2
W. W. Black (D)	20,116	37.2
W. W. Smith (SOC)	5,088	9.4
2 Stanton Warburton (R)	20,448	57.5
Maurice Langhorne (D)	10,288	28.9
Leslie E. Aller (SOC)	3,978	11.2
3 William L. LaFollette (R)	30,126	62.1
Harry D. Merritt (D)	14,423	29.7
David C. Coates (SOC)	3,998	8.2

WEST VIRGINIA

Candidates	Votes	%
1 John W. Davis (D)	20,370	48.9
Charles E. Carrigan (R)	16,962	40.7
A. L. Bauer (SOC)	3,243	7.8
2 William G. Brown Jr. (D)	21,276	53.3
George C. Sturgiss (R)	16,791	42.1
3 Adam H. Littlepage (D)	21,311	47.3
Joseph H. Gaines (R)	20,105	44.6
L. C. Rogers (SOC)	2,799	6.2
4 John M. Hamilton (D)	17,822	51.9
Harry C. Woodyard (R)	15,592	45.4
5 James A. Hughes (R)	25,007	51.8
Rankin Wiley (D)	22,154	45.9

WISCONSIN

Candidates	Votes	%
1 Henry Allen Cooper (R)	15,096	57.2
Calvin Stewart (D)	8.606	32.6

Candidates	Votes	%
Michael Yabs (SOCIAL D)	1,869	7.1
2 John M. Nelson (R)	14,009	51.5
Albert C. Schmedeman (D)	12,090	44.4
3 Arthur W. Kopp (R)	13,360	56.0
William Coffland (D)	9,042	37.9
4 William J. Cary (R)	12,261	38.0
William R. Gaylord (SOCIAL D)	11,814	36.7
William J. Kershaw (D)	8,081	25.1
5 Victor L. Berger (SOCIAL D)	13,497	38.3
Henry F. Cochems (R)	13,147	37.3
Joseph P. Carney (D)	8,433	23.9
6 Michael E. Burke (D)	15,749	51.0
William H. Froelich (R)	13,278	43.0
John C. Boll (SOCIAL D)	1,705	5.5
7 John J. Esch (R)	15,365	63.1
Paul W. Mahoney (D)	7,365	30.2
8 James H. Davidson (R)	15,934	55.2
Fred B. Rawson (D)	10,654	36.9
Richard W. Burke (SOCIAL D)	2,005	7.0
9 Thomas F. Konop (D)	12,140	45.6
Gustav Kustermann (R)	12,135	45.6
Thomas J. Oliver (SOCIAL D)	1,777	6.7
10 Elmer A. Morse (R)	17,360	54.2
John F. Lamont (D)	11,798	36.8
Lynn Thompson (SOCIAL D)	2,882	9.0
11 Irvine L. Lenroot (R)	19,224	88.5
Henry M. Parks (SOCIAL D)	2,473	11.4

WYOMING

Candidates	Votes	%
AL Frank W. Mondell (R)	20,312	54.7
W. B. Ross (D)	14,659	39.5
J. B. Morgan (SOC)	2,155	5.8

1911 House Elections

ARIZONA
(Became a state Feb. 14, 1912)

Candidates	Votes	%
AL Carl Hayden (D)	11,556	54.1
John S. Williams (R)	8,485	39.7
John Halberg (SOC)	1,252	5.9

NEW MEXICO
(Became a state Jan. 6, 1912)

Candidates	Votes	%
AL George Curry (R)✔	30,162	
Harvey B. Fergusson (D)✔	29,999	

Candidates	Votes	%
Elfego Baca (R)	28,836	
Paz Valverde (D)	28,353	
J. W. Hansen (SOC)	1,845	
C. Cutting (SOC)	1,745	

PENNSYLVANIA
Special Elections

Candidates	Votes	%
2 William Stuart Reyburn (R)	15,470	76.3
Henry Baur (D)	4,373	21.6

Candidates	Votes	%
14 W. D. B. Ainey (R)	13,860	55.6
Oscar H. Rockwell (D, KEY)	11,062	44.4

TENNESSEE
Special Election

Candidates	Votes	%
10 Kenneth D. McKellar (D)	11,573	85.0
W. A. Weatherall (SOC)	2,040	15.0

1912 House Elections

ALABAMA

	Candidates	Votes	%
1	George W. Taylor (D)	7,414	97.2
2	S. Hubert Dent Jr. (D)	11,197	100.0
3	Henry D. Clayton (D)	11,225	100.0
4	Fred L. Blackmon (D)	7,740	67.4
	A. P. Longshore (PROG)	3,060	26.6
	W. H. Sturdivant (R)	693	6.0
5	J. Thomas Heflin (D)	10,210	100.0
6	Richmond P. Hobson (D)	10,065	82.0
	Charles P. Lunsford (R)	2,210	18.0
7	John L. Burnett (D)	9,770	54.5
	Sumter Cogswell (PROG)	5,462	30.4
	John J. Stephens (R)	2,711	15.1
8	William Richardson (D)	10,753	88.4
	William E. Hotchkiss (R)	1,160	9.5
9	Oscar W. Underwood (D)	12,584	88.7
	Frederick B. Parker (R)	1,598	11.3
AL	John W. Abercrombie (D)	87,519	87.8
	Asa E. Stratton (R)	9,589	9.6

ARIZONA

		Votes	%
AL	Carl Hayden (D)	11,389	48.4
	Robert S. Fisher (PROG)	5,819	24.7
	Thomas E. Campbell (R)	3,110	13.2
	A. Charles Smith (SOC)	3,034	12.9

ARKANSAS

		Votes	%
1	Thaddeus H. Caraway (D)	15,036	100.0
2	William A. Oldfield (D)	11,880	73.0
	G. W. Wells (R)	4,394	27.0
3	John C. Floyd (D)	10,849	64.6
	J. F. Carlton (R)	5,954	35.4
4	Otis T. Wingo (D)	11,680	67.6
	J. O. Livesay (R)	5,601	32.4
5	Henderson M. Jacoway (D)	13,438	70.3
	A. C. Remmel (R)	5,680	29.7
6	Samuel M. Taylor (D)	15,879	100.0
7	William S. Goodwin (D)	10,956	69.4
	Pat McNalley (R)	4,824	30.6

CALIFORNIA

		Votes	%
1	William Kent (PROG)	20,341	37.3
	I. G. Zumwalt (D)	18,756	34.4
	Edward H. Hart (R)	10,585	19.4
	Joseph Bredsteen (SOC)	4,892	9.0
2	John E. Raker (D)	23,467	62.6
	Frank M. Rutherford (R)	10,178	27.2
	J. C. Williams (SOC)	3,818	10.2
3	Charles F. Curry (R)	31,060	58.8
	Gilbert McMillan Ross (D)	15,197	28.8
	William L. Wilson (SOC)	6,522	12.4
4	Julius Kahn (R)	25,515	56.1
	Bert Schlesinger (D)	14,884	32.7
	Norman W. Pendleton (SOC)	5,090	11.2
5	John I. Nolan (R)	27,902	52.3
	Stephen V. Costello (D)	18,516	34.7
	E. L. Reguin (SOC)	6,962	13.0
6	Joseph R. Knowland (R)	35,219	53.7
	J. Stitt Wilson (SOC)	26,234	40.0
	Hiram A. Luttrell (D)	4,135	6.3
7	Denver S. Church (D)	23,752	44.1
	James C. Needham (R)	22,994	42.6
	J. S. Cato (SOC)	7,171	13.3
8	Everis A. Hayes (R)	29,861	50.9
	James B. Holohan (D)	20,620	35.2
	Robert Whitaker (SOC)	8,125	13.9
9	Charles W. Bell (R)	28,845	47.2
	Thomas H. Kirk (D)	14,571	23.8
	Ralph L. Criswell (SOC)	11,123	18.2
	George S. Yarnall (P)	6,510	10.7
10	William D. Stephens (R)	43,637	53.4

	Candidates	Votes	%
	George Ringo (D)	17,890	21.9
	Fred C. Wheeler (SOC)	17,126	21.0
11	William Kettner (D)	24,822	42.7
	Samuel C. Evans (R)	21,426	36.9
	Noble Asa Richardson (SOC)	7,059	12.1
	Helen M. Stoddard (P)	4,842	8.3

COLORADO

		Votes	%
1	George J. Kindel (D)	54,504	45.8
	W. J. L. Crank (PROG-BMR)	30,121	25.3
	Rice W. Means (R)	24,887	20.9
	J. W. Martin (SOC)	6,755	5.7
2	Harry H. Seldomridge (D)	63,271	44.5
	Charles A. Ballreich (R)	40,990	28.8
	Neil N. McLean (RO PROG)	27,975	19.7
	S. A. Van Buskirk (SOC)	9,993	7.0
AL	Edward T. Taylor (D)	115,143✔	
	Edward Keating (D)	110,516✔	
	Clarence P. Dodge (PROG-BMR)	64,835	
	Samuel H. Kinsley (R)	63,714	
	Jesse J. Laton (R)	62,085	
	Charles E. Fisher (PROG-BMR)	58,764	
	Robert Knight (SOC)	16,108	
	F. W. Brainard (SOC)	15,808	
	Samuel S. Stutzman (P)	5,853	

CONNECTICUT

		Votes	%
1	Augustine Lonergan (D)	17,256	40.0
	Bissell (R)	16,726	38.7
	Alsop (PROG)	6,445	14.9
2	Bryan F. Mahan (D)	14,936	41.8
	King (R)	14,421	40.3
	Davis (PROG)	4,742	13.3
3	Thomas L. Reilly (D)	16,267	42.7
	Tilson (R)	12,989	34.1
	Henderson (PROG)	5,480	14.4
	Applegate (SOC)	2,658	7.0
4	Jeremiah Donovan (D)	15,616	37.6
	Hill (R)	14,188	34.1
	Vincent (PROG)	8,263	19.9
	Hunter (SOC)	2,849	6.9
5	William Kennedy (D)	12,073	39.2
	Bradstreet (R)	11,724	38.0
	Hoadley (PROG)	4,807	15.6
	Hull (SOC)	1,923	6.2

DELAWARE

		Votes	%
AL	Franklin Brockson (D)	22,485	46.2
	George H. Hall (R)	16,740	34.4
	Hiram R. Burton (N PROG)	5,497	11.3
	Louis A. Drexler (PROG)	2,825	5.8

FLORIDA

		Votes	%
1	Stephen M. Sparkman (D)	12,400	78.5
	C. C. Allen (SOC)	1,901	12.0
2	Frank Clark (D)	14,035	80.5
	J. J. Collins (SOC)	1,318	7.6
	John W. Howell (R)	1,210	6.9
	C. E. Speir (PROG)	875	5.0
3	Emmett Wilson (D)	9,057	86.4
	W. N. Lamberry (SOC)	659	6.3
AL	Claude L'Engle (D)	34,324	77.4
	A. N. Jackson (SOC)	3,636	8.2
	George W. Allen (R)	2,942	6.6
	E. R. Gunby (PROG)	2,680	6.0

GEORGIA

	Candidates	Votes	%
1	Charles G. Edwards (D)	7,944	95.7
2	Seaborn A. Roddenberry (D)	7,957	100.0
3	Charles R. Crisp (D)	7,321	100.0
4	William C. Adamson (D)	8,904	100.0
5	William Schley Howard (D)	12,000	100.0
6	Charles L. Bartlett (D)	13,171	100.0
7	Gordon Lee (D)	14,099	100.0
8	Samuel J. Tribble (D)	10,013	100.0
9	Thomas M. Bell (D)	12,496	100.0
10	Thomas W. Hardwick (D)	6,474	100.0
11	John R. Walker (D)	7,922	100.0
12	Dudley M. Hughes (D)	7,791	100.0

IDAHO

		Votes	%
AL	Burton L. French (R)	53,542✔	
	Addison T. Smith (R)	43,571✔	
	Perry W. Mitchell (D)	30,172	
	Edward M. Pugmire (D)	30,053	
	P. Monroe Smock (PROG)	12,066	
	G. W. Belloit (SOC)	11,393	
	E. L. Riggs (SOC)	11,389	
	John Tucker (P)	1,176	
	Johathan G. Carrick (P)	1,169	

ILLINOIS

		Votes	%
1	Martin B. Madden (R)	13,608	52.2
	Andrew Donovan (D)	9,967	38.2
	William F. Barnard (SOC)	2,217	8.5
2	James R. Mann (R)	21,374	37.4
	John Charles Vaughan (D)	15,827	27.7
	Thomas D. Knight (PROG)	15,042	26.3
	John C. Flora (SOC)	4,637	8.1
3	George E. Gorman (D)	16,285	33.2
	William W. Wilson (R)	14,133	28.8
	Franklin P. Simons (PROG)	13,039	26.6
	George H. Gibson (SOC)	5,123	10.4
4	James T. McDermott (D)	14,225	57.3
	Charles J. Tomkiewicz (R)	6,097	24.6
	Carl F. Gauger (SOC)	4,503	18.1
5	Adolph J. Sabath (D)	11,150	51.8
	Jacob Gartenstein (R)	4,192	19.5
	Charles Toepper (SOC)	3,359	15.6
	L. H. Clusman (PROG)	2,825	13.1
6	James McAndrews (D)	22,520	45.3
	Arthur W. Fulton (R)	18,974	38.2
	John Will (SOC)	7,776	15.6
7	Frank Buchanan (D)	19,452	28.2
	Elton C. Armitage (PROG)	18,816	27.3
	Niels Juul (R)	15,265	22.1
	Otto C. Christensen (SOC)	15,043	21.8
8	Thomas Gallagher (D)	10,922	52.4
	William G. Herrmann (R)	6,030	29.0
	N. F. Holm (SOC)	3,674	17.6
9	Fred A. Britten (R)	11,650	34.6
	Lynden Evans (D)	10,210	30.3
	C. O. Ludlow (PROG)	7,566	22.5
	Frank Schiflersmith (SOC)	3,964	11.8
10	Charles M. Thomson (PROG)	21,028	35.2
	George Edmund Foss (R)	17,325	29.0
	Frank L. Fowler (D)	15,515	26.0
	Charles A. Larson (SOC)	5,311	8.9
11	Ira C. Copley (R)	25,750	61.1
	Thomas H. Riley (D)	14,330	34.0
12	William H. Hinebaugh (PROG)	18,334	36.4
	Charles E. Fuller (R)	16,905	33.6
	J. W. Rausch (D)	12,234	24.3
13	John C. McKenzie (R)	14,398	36.5
	I. F. Edwards (PROG)	11,875	30.1
	Ray Rariden (D)	11,704	29.7
14	Clyde H. Tavenner (D)	17,024	47.3

ILLINOIS

Candidates	Votes	%
Charles J. Searle (R)	15,816	44.0
Charles Block (SOC)	2,466	6.9
15 Stephen A. Hoxworth (D)	17,156	35.8
Charles F. Kincheloe (PROG)	15,173	31.7
George W. Prince (R)	12,008	25.1
John C. Sjodin (SOC)	2,642	5.5
16 Claudius U. Stone (D)	20,956	45.7
William E. Cadmus (PROG)	12,659	27.6
Frederick H. Smith (R)	9,295	20.3
Rudolf Pfeiffer (SOC)	2,474	5.4
17 Louis Fitz Henry (D)	14,966	38.0
John A. Sterling (R)	13,572	34.5
George E. Stump (PROG)	9,266	23.6
18 Frank T. O'Hair (D)	19,485	38.9
Joseph G. Cannon (R)	18,707	37.3
E. F. Royse (PROG)	9,511	19.0
19 Charles M. Borchers (D)	22,166	40.2
William B. McKinley (R)	20,643	37.4
John H. Chadwick (PROG)	10,755	19.5
20 Henry T. Rainey (D)	21,203	54.1
E. E. Brass (R)	9,478	24.2
B. O. Aylesworth (PROG)	7,007	17.9
21 James M. Graham (D)	21,361	46.8
H. Clay Wilson (R)	13,556	29.7
Robert Johns (PROG)	7,286	16.0
Herman Rahm (SOC)	2,554	5.6
22 William N. Baltz (D)	23,112	43.5
William A. Rodenberg (R)	19,438	36.6
Utten S. Nixon (PROG)	5,608	10.6
William C. Pierce (SOC)	4,276	8.1
23 Martin D. Foster (D)	26,938	52.4
Robert B. Clark (R)	12,837	25.0
George W. Jones (PROG)	9,116	17.7
24 H. Robert Fowler (D)	19,811	47.7
James B. Blackman (R)	15,004	36.1
A. J. Gibbons (PROG)	5,129	12.3
25 Robert P. Hill (D)	19,992	43.3
Napoleon B. Thistlewood (R)	16,706	36.2
Robert T. Cook (PROG)	6,545	14.2
AL Lawrence B. Stringer (D)	415,386	
William Elza Williams (D)	401,497	
William E. Mason (R)	313,608	
Lawrence P. Boyle (PROG)	311,311	
B. M. Maxey (PROG)	304,072	
Burnett M. Chiperfield (R)	299,940	
Walter Huggins (SOC)	84,352	
D. L. Thomas (SOC)	84,027	
Walter H. Harris (P)	15,721	
James H. Shaw (P)	15,590	
George Martin (SOC LAB)	4,118	
Joseph Fenyves (SOC LAB)	4,012	

INDIANA

Candidates	Votes	%
1 Charles Lieb (D)	20,014	45.7
D. H. Ortmeyer (R)	13,158	30.0
Humphrey C. Heldt (PROG)	6,022	13.7
William H. Rainey (SOC)	3,737	8.5
2 William A. Cullop (D)	22,082	45.3
Oscar E. Bland (R)	15,858	32.6
John N. Dyer (PROG)	6,001	12.3
John L. B. Shepherd (SOC)	3,888	8.0
3 William E. Cox (D)	23,150	51.5
William D. Barnes (R)	10,049	22.4
S. G. Wilkinson (PROG)	10,005	22.3
4 Lincoln Dixon (D)	24,250	52.4
Rollin A. Turner (R)	12,436	26.9
Charles Zoller Jr. (PROG)	7,540	16.3
5 Ralph W. Moss (D)	20,634	45.2
F. W. Blankenlaker (R)	11,995	26.3
Joseph W. Amis (SOC)	8,268	18.1
William Houston (PROG)	3,351	7.3
6 Finly H. Gray (D)	19,987	43.9
William L. Risk (R)	11,242	24.7
Gierluf Jansen (PROG)	10,797	23.7
7 Charles A. Korbly (D)	28,901	42.8
Joseph V. Zartman (PROG)	18,402	27.3
Thomas H. Shipp (R)	13,320	19.7
Frank J. Hays (SOC)	5,501	8.2

Candidates	Votes	%
8 John A. M. Adair (D)	23,530	46.5
E. C. Toner (PROG)	13,157	26.0
I. P. Watts (R)	8,298	16.4
Hunter McDonald (SOC)	3,611	7.1
9 Martin A. Morrison (D)	23,574	45.1
William Robinson (R)	15,901	30.4
John F. Neil (PROG)	9,205	17.6
10 John B. Peterson (D)	18,401	38.8
E. D. Crumpacker (R)	17,294	36.5
John O. Bowers (PROG)	9,793	20.6
11 George W. Rauch (D)	21,894	43.8
John W. G. Stewart (R)	12,213	24.4
Edgar M. Baldwin (PROG)	10,830	21.7
Ernest Malott (SOC)	2,813	5.6
12 Cyrus Cline (D)	19,903	48.3
Charles R. Lane (R)	11,147	27.1
Louis N. Littman (PROG)	8,114	19.7
13 Henry A. Barnhart (D)	24,968	43.9
R. Clarence Stephens (PROG)	13,822	24.3
Charles A. Carlisle (R)	13,787	24.3
Ervin H. Cady (SOC)	2,937	5.2

IOWA

Candidates	Votes	%
1 Charles A. Kennedy (R)	14,167	42.1
Joshua F. Elder (D)	12,114	36.0
Joe S. Crail (PROG)	6,457	19.2
2 Irvin S. Pepper (D)	24,769	85.7
Michael T. Kennedy (SOC)	3,176	11.0
3 Maurice Connolly (D)	19,445	42.3
Charles E. Picket (R)	18,166	39.6
Robert E. Leach (PROG)	6,640	14.5
4 Gilbert N. Haugen (R)	19,829	52.6
G. A. Meyer (D)	16,764	44.5
5 James W. Good (R)	19,030	47.7
S. C. Huber (D)	17,631	44.2
6 Sanford Kirkpatrick (D)	14,915	42.5
M. A. McCord (R)	13,796	39.3
John H. Patton (PROG)	4,350	12.4
Andrew Engle (SOC)	2,060	5.9
7 Solomon F. Prouty (R)	17,465	43.2
Clint L. Price (D)	14,075	34.8
George C. White (PROG)	5,944	14.7
8 Horace M. Towner (R)	18,462	49.2
V. R. McGinnis (D)	15,477	41.3
L. W. Laughlin (PROG)	2,704	7.2
9 William R. Green (R)	20,030	53.3
Orris Mosher (D)	16,369	43.5
10 Frank P. Woods (R)	25,263	53.9
Nelson L. Rood (D)	15,242	32.5
S. B. Philpot (PROG)	5,251	11.2
11 George C. Scott (R)	18,568	40.1
A. Vanwagenen (D)	16,168	34.9
J. W. Hallam (PROG)	10,405	22.5

Special Election

Candidates	Votes	%
11 George C. Scott (R)	18,041	41.1
A. Vanwagenen (D)	15,910	36.2
J. W. Hallam (PROG)	10,003	22.8

KANSAS

Candidates	Votes	%
1 Daniel R. Anthony Jr. (R)	22,978	51.8
J. B. Chapman (D)	20,646	46.5
2 Joseph Taggart (D)	25,830	50.1
J. L. Brady (R)	21,995	42.7
Unidentified Candidate (SOC)	3,705	7.2
3 Philip P. Campbell (R)	20,973	39.0
Francis M. Brady (D)	20,142	37.4
George D. Brewer (SOC)	12,732	23.6
4 Dudley Doolittle (D)	16,997	48.6
Fred S. Jackson (R)	16,479	47.1
5 Guy T. Helvering (D)	19,618	49.8
Rollin R. Rees (R)	18,098	45.9

Candidates	Votes	%
6 John R. Connelly (D)	20,065	48.0
I. D. Young (R)	19,077	45.6
Daniel W. Stoner (SOC)	2,102	5.0
7 George A. Neeley (D)	26,140	51.3
Gordon L. Finley (R)	21,690	42.5
M. L. Amos (SOC)	2,828	5.6
8 Victor Murdock (R)	17,958	53.4
John I. Saunders (D)	14,488	43.1

KENTUCKY

Candidates	Votes	%
1 Alben W. Barkley (D)	22,591	64.5
Charles Furgeson (R)	10,664	30.4
I. O. Ford (SOC)	1,787	5.1
2 Augustus O. Stanley (D)	19,739	71.3
L. R. Fox (PROG)	6,500	23.5
Carr Hawkins (SOC)	1,462	5.3
3 Robert Y. Thomas Jr. (D)	18,220	47.9
T. B. Dixon (R)	11,181	29.4
J. D. Duncan (PROG)	7,456	19.6
4 Ben Johnson (D)	22,168	53.2
E. R. Bassett (PROG)	11,907	28.6
John C. Thompson (R)	6,713	16.1
5 J. Swagar Sherley (D)	24,795	46.2
Henry I. Fox (PROG)	23,115	43.0
E. J. Ashcraft (R)	3,823	7.1
6 Arthur B. Rouse (D)	20,690	57.3
D. B. Wallace (R)	7,255	20.1
J. G. Blackburn (PROG)	5,701	15.8
M. A. Brinkman (SOC)	2,489	6.9
7 James C. Cantrill (D)	24,617	80.8
J. E. Jones (PROG)	5,841	19.2
8 Harvey Helm (D)	18,690	71.0
J. W. Dinsmore (PROG)	7,631	29.0
9 William J. Fields (D)	27,415	50.7
Harry Bailey (R)	16,608	30.7
E. S. Hutchins (PROG)	8,903	16.5
10 John W. Langley (R)	12,200	69.8
W. T. Stafford (PROG)	5,286	30.2
11 Caleb Powers (R)	18,531	46.4
Ben V. Smith (D)	11,760	29.5
H. H. Seavey (PROG)	9,044	22.7

LOUISIANA

Candidates	Votes	%
1 Albert Estopinal (D)	14,770	100.0
2 H. Garland Dupre (D)	14,406	100.0
3 Robert F. Broussard (D)	5,035	100.0
4 John T. Watkins (D)	5,693	93.5
Lee Norris (SOC)	394	6.5
5 Walter Elder (D)	5,795	100.0
6 Lewis L. Morgan (D)	6,101	100.0
7 Ladislas Lazaro (D)	4,943	87.4
Otis Putnam (SOC)	713	12.6
8 James B. Aswell (D)	6,033	77.7
J. R. Jones (SOC)	1,734	22.3

MAINE

Candidates	Votes	%
1 Asher C. Hinds (R)	17,635	51.7
M. T. O'Brien (D)	15,580	45.7
2 Daniel J. McGillicuddy (D)	18,077	50.4
W. B. Skelton (R)	16,796	46.8
3 Forrest Goodwin (R)	17,221	49.9
Samuel W. Gould (D)	16,512	47.8
4 Frank E. Guernsey (R)	20,198	54.4
C. N. Mullen (D)	16,725	45.0

MARYLAND

Candidates	Votes	%
1 James Harry Covington (D)	17,606	85.2
Robert D. Grier (PROG)	2,303	11.2
2 Joshua Frederick C. Talbott (D)	22,087	59.9
Labin Sparks (R)	13,732	37.2
3 George Konig (D)	15,189	54.7
Albert M. Sproesser (R)	11,078	39.9
4 J. Charles Linthicum (D)	19,075	60.9
Jacob F. Murback (R)	11,257	35.9

MARYLAND

	Candidates	Votes	%
5	Frank O. Smith (D)	13,085	49.0
	Thomas Parran (R)	12,168	45.5
6	David J. Lewis (D)	20,434	56.0
	Charles D. Wagaman (R)	14,147	38.8

MASSACHUSETTS

		Votes	%
1	Allen T. Treadway (R)	12,920	42.8
	Richard J. Morrissey (D)	12,075	40.0
	Samuel P. Blagden (PROG)	3,883	12.9
2	Frederick H. Gillett (R)	12,301	42.8
	William G. McKechnie (D)	10,940	38.1
	Thomas L. Hisgen (PROG)	5,442	18.9
3	William Henry Wilder (R)	12,945	45.0
	M. Fred O'Connell (D)	9,742	33.8
	Stephen M. Marshall (PROG)	5,287	18.4
4	Samuel E. Winslow (R)	15,153	49.6
	John A. Thayer (D)	11,216	36.7
	Burton W. Potter (PROG)	3,626	11.9
5	John Jacob Rogers (R)	12,827	44.8
	Humphrey O'Sullivan (D)	11,037	38.5
	William N. Osgood (PROG)	4,200	14.7
6	Augustus P. Gardner (R)	16,918	49.8
	George A. Schofield (D)	9,704	28.6
	Arthur L. Nason (PROG)	7,326	21.6
7	Michael F. Phelan (D)	12,964	45.9
	Frank P. Bennett Jr. (R)	8,952	31.7
	Lynn M. Ranger (PROG)	5,086	18.0
8	Frederick S. Deitrick (D)	12,484	40.5
	Frederick W. Dallinger (R)	11,209	36.4
	Henry C. Long (PROG)	6,665	21.6
9	Ernest W. Roberts (R)	14,021	45.1
	Henry C. Rowland (D)	8,732	28.1
	John Herbert (PROG)	7,364	23.7
10	William F. Murray (D)	12,031	64.0
	Daniel T. Callahan (PROG)	3,711	19.7
	Loyal L. Jenkins (R)	2,418	12.9
11	Andrew J. Peters (D)	17,875	64.0
	Sherwin L. Cook (R)	8,786	31.5
12	James M. Curley (D)	14,875	48.8
	James B. Connolly (PROG)	9,001	29.5
	Charles H. S. Robinson (R)	5,812	19.1
13	John W. Weeks (R)	15,934*	45.1
	John J. Mitchell (D)	13,583	38.4
	George A. Fiel (PROG)	5,853	16.6
14	Edward Gilmore (D)	11,939	33.9
	Henry L. Kincaide (PROG)	11,341	32.2
	Robert O. Harris (R)	9,968	28.3
	John McCarty (SOC)	2,005	5.7
15	William S. Greene (R)	11,207	45.1
	John W. Coughlin (D)	8,975	36.1
	Alvin G. Weeks (PROG)	4,172	16.8
16	Thomas C. Thacher (D)	10,461	40.2
	William J. Bullock (R)	8,186	31.5
	Thomas Thompson (PROG)	6,540	25.1

MICHIGAN

		Votes	%
1	Frank E. Doremus (D)	22,573	38.3
	James H. Pound (N PROG)	16,801	28.5
	Ezra P. Beechler (R)	16,687	28.3
2	Samuel W. Beakes (D)	16,761	35.0
	William W. Wedemeyer (R)	16,650	34.8
	Hubert F. Probert (N PROG)	13,660	28.5
3	John M. C. Smith (R)	14,609	32.7
	Claude S. Carney (D)	14,482	32.4
	Edward N. Dingley (N PROG)	12,907	28.9
	Levant L. Rogers (SOC)	2,746	6.1
4	Edward L. Hamilton (R)	14,788	34.2
	Albert E. Beebe (D)	14,382	33.2
	George M. Valentine (N PROG)	12,712	29.4
5	Carl E. Mapes (R)	16,749	35.3
	Edwin F. Sweet (D)	16,148	34.0
	Suel A. Sheldon (N PROG)	11,747	24.7

	Candidates	Votes	%
6	Samuel W. Smith (R)	21,686	36.9
	Alva M. Cummins (D)	18,412	31.3
	William S. Kellogg (N PROG)	18,157	30.9
7	Louis C. Cramton (R)	15,089	37.0
	Loren A. Sherman (N PROG)	12,588	30.8
	John J. Bell (D)	11,998	29.4
8	Joseph W. Fordney (R)	13,215	34.4
	Albert L. Chandler (N PROG)	11,593	30.1
	Miles J. Purcell (D)	11,527	30.0
9	James C. McLaughlin (R)	11,966	39.1
	William H. Sears (N PROG)	10,619	34.7
	Herman R. O'Connor (D)	8,020	26.2
10	Roy O. Woodruff (N PROG)	12,882	35.1
	George A. Loud (R)	12,141	33.1
	Lewis P. Coumans (D)	10,129	27.6
11	Francis O. Lindquist (R)	19,303	48.2
	Archie McCall (D)	9,361	23.4
	John W. Patchin (N PROG)	9,231	23.1
12	William J. MacDonald (N PROG)	18,433‡	38.4
	H. Olin Young (R)	18,190	37.9
	John Power (D)	10,322	21.5
AL	Patrick H. Kelley (R)	185,657	34.3
	William H. Hill (N PROG)	174,451	32.2
	Edward Frensdorf (D)	152,188	28.1

MINNESOTA

		Votes	%
1	Sydney Anderson (R)	24,681	69.6
	Clinton Robinson (D)	10,786	30.4
2	Winfield S. Hammond (D)	14,718	50.3
	Franklin F. Ellsworth (R)	13,093	44.7
	John R. Hollister (PUB OWN)	1,479	5.1
3	Charles R. Davis (R)	18,536	61.3
	Frank L. Glotzbach (D)	9,763	32.3
	Frank F. Marzahn (P)	1,919	6.4
4	Frederick C. Stevens (R)	15,479	36.8
	James J. Regan (D)	11,333	27.0
	H. T. Halbert (PROG)	9,220	21.9
	Albert Rosenquist (PUB OWN)	6,021	14.3
5	George R. Smith (R)	17,861	44.3
	Thomas D. Schall (PROG)	8,574	21.3
	Thomas P. Dwyer (D)	6,987	17.3
	Thomas E. Latimer (PUB OWN)	6,929	17.2
6	Charles A. Lindbergh (R)	21,286	62.5
	Andrew J. Gilkinson (D)	9,920	29.1
	A. W. Uhl (PUB OWN)	2,839	8.3
7	A. J. Volstead (R)	25,053	100.0
8	Clarence G. Miller (R)	20,523	50.8
	John Jenswold Jr. (D)	12,494	30.9
	Morris Kaplan (PUB OWN)	7,398	18.3
9	Halvor Steenerson (R)	22,481	66.8
	M. A. Brattland (PUB OWN)	11,190	33.2
AL	James Manahan (R)	154,308	55.1
	Carl Johnson Buell (D)	69,652	24.9
	J. S. Ingalls (PUB OWN)	30,042	10.7
	William G. Calderwood (P)	25,863	9.2

MISSISSIPPI

		Votes	%
1	Ezekiel S. Candler Jr. (D)	7,951	100.0
2	Hubert D. Stephens (D)	5,801	100.0
3	Benjamin G. Humphreys (D)	3,154	100.0
4	Thomas U. Sisson (D)	7,402	100.0
5	Samuel A. Witherspoon (D)	7,996	100.0
6	Pat Harrison (D)	7,347	96.1
7	Percy E. Quin (D)	4,486	100.0
8	James W. Collier (D)	4,660	100.0

MISSOURI

		Votes	%
1	James T. Lloyd (D)	20,874	53.9
	Bonfoey (R)	12,144	31.4
	Warner (PROG)	5,686	14.7

	Candidates	Votes	%
2	William W. Rucker (D)	22,786	57.3
	Haley (R)	10,132	25.5
	Williams (PROG)	6,776	17.1
3	Joshua W. Alexander (D)	20,179	52.8
	Morroway (R)	11,192	29.3
	Wightman (PROG)	6,812	17.8
4	Charles F. Booher (D)	20,232	53.8
	Hickman (R)	11,284	30.0
	Robinson (PROG)	5,347	14.2
5	William P. Borland (D)	33,397	52.9
	Sumner (PROG)	21,863	34.6
	Kimbrell (R)	5,759	9.1
6	Clement C. Dickinson (D)	17,858	52.2
	Dunaway (R)	9,093	26.6
	Theilmann (PROG)	6,788	19.9
7	Courtney W. Hamlin (D)	23,178	48.9
	Owen (R)	15,685	33.1
	Blain (PROG)	7,305	15.4
8	Dorsey W. Shackleford (D)	16,219	53.0
	Peters (R)	11,965	39.1
	Pemberton (PROG)	2,391	7.8
9	James Beauchamp Clark (D)	21,782	56.5
	Cole (R)	16,283	42.2
10	Richard Bartholdt (R)	33,242	37.6
	O'Connor (D)	31,227	35.3
	Siebert (PROG)	16,417	18.6
	Hoehn (SOC)	7,154	8.1
11	William L. Igoe (D)	19,653	50.4
	Catlin (R)	12,448	31.9
	Ward (PROG)	4,812	12.3
12	Leonidas C. Dyer (R)	11,981‡	43.6
	Michael J. Gill (D)	11,249	41.0
	Cotton (PROG)	3,041	11.1
13	Walter L. Hensley (D)	16,079	52.1
	Nipper (R)	13,406	43.4
14	Joseph J. Russell (D)	26,081	46.5
	Curry (R & PROG)	25,066	44.7
	Bumpas (SOC)	4,957	8.8
15	Perl D. Decker (D)	21,000	46.0
	McPherson (R)	12,850	28.2
	Gregg (PROG)	7,797	17.1
	Bedingfield (SOC)	3,203	7.0
16	Thomas L. Rubey (D)	15,908	52.3
	O'Bannon (R)	10,811	35.6
	Bradford (PROG)	3,678	12.1

MONTANA

		Votes	%
AL	Thomas Stout (D)	25,891✔	
	John M. Evans (D)	24,492✔	
	Charles N. Pray (R)	23,505	
	William R. Allen (R)	19,633	
	Thomas M. Everett (PROG)	16,644	
	George A. Horkan (PROG)	15,336	
	Henri Labeau (SOC)	10,271	
	J. Frank Mabie (SOC)	10,056	

NEBRASKA

		Votes	%
1	John A. Maguire (D & PPI)	17,410	50.5
	Paul F. Clark (R & PROG)	15,706	45.6
2	Charles O. Lobeck (D & PPI)	16,075	47.4
	Howard H. Baldridge (R & PROG)	15,662	46.2
	J. N. Carter (SOC)	2,146	6.3
3	Daniel V. Stephens (D)	26,229	53.1
	Joseph C. Cook (R & PROG)	21,677	43.9
4	Charles H. Sloan (R & PROG)	22,293	53.0
	Charles M. Skiles (D & PPI)	18,279	43.4
5	Silas R. Barton (R & PROG)	18,818	49.0
	Roderick D. Sutherland (D & PPI)	17,522	45.7
6	Moses P. Kinkaid (R)	24,766	47.5
	W. J. Taylor (D & PPI)	18,529	35.5
	Florence Armstrong (P)	4,997	9.6
	Fred J. Warren (SOC)	3,758	7.2

NEVADA

Candidates	Votes	%
AL Edwin E. Roberts (R)	7,380	37.3
Clay Tallman (D)	7,311	37.0
John E. Worden (SOC)	3,011	15.2
George Springmeyer (PROG)	2,072	10.5

NEW HAMPSHIRE

Candidates	Votes	%
1 Eugene E. Reed (D)	18,888	45.4
Cyrus A. Sulloway (R)	17,363	41.7
Samuel O. Titus (PROG)	4,307	10.4
2 Raymond B. Stevens (D)	21,794	53.6
Frank D. Currier (R)	17,961	44.2

NEW JERSEY

Candidates	Votes	%
1 William J. Browning (R)	14,512	39.3
Craven (D)	13,170	35.6
Jess (RO PROG)	5,891	15.9
2 J. Thompson Baker (D)	16,130	43.1
Gardner (R)	12,330	33.0
Potter (PROG)	7,384	19.7
3 Thomas J. Scully (D)	20,596	56.9
Brown (R)	14,363	39.7
4 Allan B. Walsh (D)	13,222	45.0
Blackman (R)	8,607	29.3
Gill (PROG)	6,685	22.7
5 William E. Tuttle Jr. (D)	13,920	41.0
Runyon (R)	10,085	29.7
Ennis (PROG)	7,393	21.8
Matthews (SOC)	2,066	6.1
6 Lewis J. Martin (D)	15,216	46.5
McClave (R)	8,373	25.6
Sage (PROG)	7,007	21.4
7 Robert G. Bremner (D)	9,990	42.2
Smith (R)	6,666	28.2
Marelli (PROG)	4,746	20.0
Luthringer (SOC)	1,649	7.0
8 Eugene F. Kinkead (D)	14,058	52.3
Bouton (R & PROG)	9,527	35.4
Tew (TAFT)	2,269	8.4
9 Walter I. McCoy (D)	10,196	42.4
Walker (PROG)	6,403	26.6
Parker (R)	5,818	24.2
Bohm	1,454	6.1
10 Edward W. Townsend (D)	10,854	39.6
Morgan (PROG)	7,847	28.6
Adams (R)	7,111	25.9
Cairns	1,514	5.5
11 John J. Eagan (D)	14,208	62.3
Besson (R)	7,018	30.8
Reilly	1,429	6.3
12 James A. Hamill (D)	17,980	67.5
Record (R & PROG)	8,089	30.4

Special Election

Candidates	Votes	%
6 Archibald C. Hart (D)	17,197	38.8
Smith (R)	15,325	34.6
Shay (PROG)	11,287	25.5
David J. Haney (D)	3,369	7.6

NEW MEXICO

Candidates	Votes	%
AL Harvey B. Fergusson (D)	22,139	45.6
Nathan Jaffa (R)	17,892	36.9
Andrew Eggum (SOC)	5,882	12.1
Marcos C. DeBaca (PROG)	2,644	5.5

NEW YORK

Candidates	Votes	%
1 Lathrop Brown (D)	16,505	40.7
Frederick C. Hicks (R)	11,753	29.0
W. Bourke Cockran (N PROG)	11,306	27.9
2 Denis O'Leary (D)	23,090	57.0
Felix Fritsche (N PROG)	7,175	17.7
Frank E. Hopkins (R)	6,941	17.1
William Danmar (SOC)	2,918	7.2
3 Frank E. Wilson (D)	12,658	48.0
Frank F. Schulz (R)	6,633	25.1
Westervelt Prentice (N PROG)	4,918	18.6
John H. Jennings (SOC)	1,801	6.8
4 Harry Howard Dale (D)	9,059	47.1
Samuel Greenblatt (N PROG)	5,139	26.7
William Liebermann (R & IL)	3,574	18.6
Robert J. Nolan (SOC)	1,441	7.5
5 James P. Maher (D)	12,504	46.0
John S. Gaynor (R)	7,677	28.2
Charles J. Ryan (N PROG)	5,794	21.3
6 William M. Calder (R)	21,691	47.9
Robert H. Roy (D)	13,290	29.4
Jesse Fuller Jr. (IL & NPR)	9,310	20.6
7 John J. Fitzgerald (D)	16,082	59.1
Michael A. Fitzgerald (I LEAGUE)	5,513	20.3
John E. Brady (R)	5,021	18.5
8 Daniel J. Griffin (D)	17,403	52.0
Albert H. T. Banzhaf (IL & NPR)	8,867	26.5
Ernest P. Seelman (R)	6,027	18.0
9 James H. O'Brien (D)	15,903	41.0
John F. Kennedy (N PROG)	10,362	26.7
Oscar W. Swift (R)	10,122	26.1
William Koenig (SOC)	2,027	5.2
10 Herman A. Metz (D)	7,459	36.6
Jacob L. Holtzmann (N PROG)	5,889	28.9
Reuben L. Haskell (R & IL)	5,174	25.4
Barnet Wolff (SOC)	1,785	8.8
11 Daniel J. Riordan (D)	15,417	60.1
William Wirt Mills (IL & NPR)	5,570	21.7
William G. Rose (R)	4,078	15.9
12 Henry M. Goldfogle (D & IL)	4,592	39.3
Meyer London (SOC)	3,646	31.2
Henry Moskowitz (N PROG)	2,602	22.3
Alexander Wolf (R)	839	7.2
13 Timothy D. Sullivan (D)	5,697	50.6
Sigmund S. Rotter (N PROG)	3,615	32.1
John B. G. Rinehart (R & IL)	1,151	10.2
Joshua Wauhope (SOC)	790	7.0
14 Jefferson M. Levy (D)	8,950	49.4
Abraham H. Goodman (N PROG)	4,457	24.6
E. Crosby Kindleberger (R)	3,468	19.1
Marie Macdonald (SOC)	958	5.3
15 Michael F. Conry (D)	16,791	61.7
James H. Hickey (N PROG)	4,791	17.6
Francis A. O'Neill (R)	4,721	17.4
16 Peter J. Dooling (D)	15,036	56.3
Francis C. Dale (R & IL)	5,929	22.2
Timothy Healy (N PROG)	5,019	18.8
17 John F. Carew (D)	12,350	51.8
Lindon Bates Jr. (IL & NPR)	5,516	23.1
Ogden L. Mills (R)	4,891	20.5
18 Thomas G. Patten (D)	13,704	50.0
Amos R. E. Pinchot (N PROG)	6,644	24.3
S. Walter Kaufman (R & IL)	4,943	18.0
Algernon Lee (SOC)	2,085	7.6
19 Walter M. Chandler (IL & NPR)	13,987	39.2
Franklin Leonard Jr. (D)	13,684	38.3
Alexander Brough (R)	7,104	19.9
20 Francis Burton Harrison (D)	5,221	41.7
Julius H. Reiter (N PROG)	4,694	37.5
Abram Goodman (R & IL)	1,596	12.8
Nicholas Aleinikoff (SOC)	996	8.0
21 Henry George Jr. (D & IL)	13,189	47.0
Jerome F. Reilly (N PROG)	8,384	29.9
Martin C. Ansorge (R)	5,265	18.8
22 Henry Bruckner (D)	15,886	47.7
Irving M. Crane (N PROG)	9,462	28.4
Rufus P. Johnston (R)	6,098	18.3
Charles Gall (SOC)	1,835	5.5
23 Joseph A. Goulden (D)	19,320	44.3
Edward J. L. Raldiris (N PROG)	13,150	30.1
Peter Wynne (R & IL)	8,779	20.1
Fred Paulitsch (SOC)	2,351	5.4
24 Woodson R. Oglesby (D, I LEAGUE)	17,804	44.1
Alfred E. Smith (N PROG)	12,496	30.9
Barton E. Kingman (R)	8,219	20.3
25 Benjamin Irving Taylor (D, I LEAGUE)	16,168	42.2
James W. Husted (R)	12,522	32.7
John C. Bucher (N PROG)	8,559	22.3
26 Edmund Platt (R)	20,618	44.5
John K. Sague (D)	20,191	43.6
Augustus B. Gray (N PROG)	4,418	9.5
27 George McClellan (D)	23,743	48.3
Charles B. Ward (R)	19,125	38.9
Horatio Seymour Manning (N PROG)	4,779	9.7
28 Peter G. Ten Eyck (D)	23,193	44.1
Daniel H. Prior (R)	23,076	43.9
Joseph F. McLaughlin (N PROG)	4,918	9.4
29 James S. Parker (R)	22,348	44.0
Milton K. Huppuch (D)	18,180	35.8
Frederick E. Draper Jr. (N PROG)	8,163	16.1
30 Samuel Wallin (R)	14,194	33.1
R. E. Lee Reynolds (D)	13,881	32.4
George R. Lunn (SOC)	9,468	22.1
Edward Everett Hale (N PROG)	4,721	11.0
31 Edwin A. Merritt Jr. (R)	18,458	46.8
Dennis B. Lucey (D)	12,995	33.0
John B. Burnham (N PROG)	7,971	20.2
32 Luther W. Mott (R, P)	21,607	45.6
Robert E. Gregg (D)	15,848	33.4
William W. Kelley (N PROG)	8,926	18.8
33 Charles A. Talcott (D)	17,855	38.0
Homer P. Snyder (R)	16,703	35.6
Benjamin Thorne Gilbert (N PROG)	9,914	21.1
34 George W. Fairchild (R)	22,072	43.8
James J. Byard Jr (D, I LEAGUE)	20,322	40.3
Jared C. Estelow (N PROG)	5,572	11.1
35 John R. Clancy (D)	18,009	35.4
Michael E. Driscoll (R)	17,874	35.1
Giles H. Stilwell (N PROG)	11,626	22.8
36 Sereno E. Payne (R)	20,604	42.2
Richard C. S. Drummond (D)	17,900	36.7
Wilson M. Gould (N PROG)	8,151	16.7
37 Edwin S. Underhill (D)	19,526	39.9
Thomas F. Fennell (R)	18,335	37.5
Wiley W. Capron (N PROG)	7,891	16.1
38 Thomas B. Dunn (R)	15,776	35.4
George P. Decker (D)	14,440	32.4
A. Emerson Babcock (N PROG)	11,202	25.2
Kendrick P. Shedd (SOC)	2,657	6.0
39 Henry G. Danforth (R)	17,881	39.1
Charles Ward (D)	15,529	33.9
Silas L. Strivings (N PROG)	10,413	22.8
40 Robert H. Gittins (D)	16,065	37.5
James S. Simmons (R)	14,450	33.7
Frank C. Ferguson (N PROG)	9,889	23.1
41 Charles B. Smith (D)	14,866	40.5
George A. Davis (R)	9,578	26.1

NEW YORK

Candidates	Votes	%
Henry Kobler (N PROG)	9,471	25.8
Edward Simon Jr. (SOC)	2,528	6.9
42 Daniel A. Driscoll (D)	14,851	45.7
Willard H. Ticknor (R)	8,613	26.5
L. Bradley Dorr (N PROG)	7,161	22.0
43 Charles M. Hamilton (R)	17,346	37.9
Manton M. Wyvell (D)	12,479	27.3
Samuel A. Carlson (N PROG)	11,709	25.6

Special Elections

Candidates	Votes	%
13 George W. Loft (D & IL)	5,945	51.2
Samuel M. Hyman (R)	2,409	20.7
Victor Tozzi (N PROG)	2,132	18.4
Joshua Wanhope (SOC)	828	7.1
20 Jacob A. Cantor (D & IL)	5,337	41.9
Isaac A. Hourwich (N PROG)	3,206	25.2
Louis H. Guterman (R)	2,991	23.5
Edward F. Cassidy (SOC)	1,210	9.5

NORTH CAROLINA

Candidates	Votes	%
1 John H. Small (D)	12,537	98.4
2 Claude Kitchin (D)	11,091	91.9
Thomas B. Brown (R)	982	8.1
3 John M. Faison (D)	11,624	65.8
James T. Kennedy (R)	6,042	34.2
4 Edward W. Pou (D)	13,906	79.5
John F. Mitchell (R)	3,586	20.5
5 Charles M. Stedman (D)	21,075	56.1
C. W. Curry (R)	15,995	42.6
6 Hannibal L. Godwin (D)	13,028	98.6
7 Robert N. Page (D)	17,873	58.9
R. Don Laws (R)	12,449	41.1
8 Robert L. Doughton (D)	15,180	55.6
George D. B. Reynolds (R)	12,078	44.2
9 Edwin Y. Webb (D)	17,072	62.7
J. A. Smith (PROG)	7,869	28.9
D. B. Paul (R)	2,228	8.2
10 James M. Gudger Jr. (D)	16,183	53.1
R. Hilliard Staton (R)	14,237	46.7

NORTH DAKOTA

Candidates	Votes	%
1 Henry T. Helgesen (R)	17,156	61.1
V. R. Lovell (D)	9,609	34.2
2 George M. Young (R)	16,912	64.3
J. A. Minckler (D)	7,426	28.2
John A. Yoder (SOC)	1,922	7.3
3 Patrick D. Norton (R)	12,935	50.7
Hal Halvorsen (D)	7,306	28.7
Arthur Leseuer (SOC)	5,254	20.6

OHIO

Candidates	Votes	%
1 Stanley E. Bowdle (D)	22,330	42.0
Nicholas Longworth (R)	22,229	41.8
Millard F. Andrew (PROG)	5,771	10.9
Lawrence A. Zitt (SOC)	2,853	5.4
2 Alfred G. Allen (D)	26,066	46.6
Otto J. Renner (R)	21,113	37.7
William B. Hay (PROG)	4,940	8.8
R. S. Moore (SOC)	3,820	6.8
3 Warren Gard (D)	26,711	42.9
Bert B. Buckley (R)	15,339	24.7
Frederick Guy Strickland (SOC)	12,774	20.5
Edward G. Pease (PROG)	6,976	11.2
4 J. Henry Goeke (D)	21,512	53.8
John L. Cable (R)	10,267	25.7
William E. Rudy (PROG)	4,993	12.5
Scott Wilkins (SOC)	2,132	5.3
5 Timothy T. Ansberry (D)	20,091	64.0
Edward Staley (R)	10,177	32.4
6 Simeon D. Fess (R)	18,090	49.2
D. K. Hempstead (D)	17,300	47.0

Candidates	Votes	%
7 James D. Post (D)	19,301	46.7
R. M. Hughey (R)	18,595	45.0
Winfield S. Tibbetts (SOC)	3,002	7.3
8 Frank B. Willis (R)	19,379	43.8
W. W. Durbin (D)	17,965	40.6
Lemuel G. Herbert (PROG)	5,429	12.3
9 Isaac R. Sherwood (D)	26,528	53.3
Holland C. Webster (PROG)	17,490	35.1
Thomas C. Devine (SOC)	5,769	11.6
10 Robert M. Switzer (R)	13,606	37.1
Charles M. Caldwell (D)	13,424	36.6
William E. Pricer (PROG)	7,091	19.3
William Miller (SOC)	2,581	7.0
11 Horatio C. Claypool (D)	21,469	49.1
Albert Douglas (R)	18,729	42.8
Albert Smith (SOC)	3,519	8.1
12 Clement L. Brumbaugh (D)	24,340	52.3
Edward L. Taylor Jr. (R)	14,682	31.5
Jacob L. Bachman (SOC)	7,095	15.2
13 John A. Key (D)	26,395	53.4
Miles H. McLaughlin (R)	13,021	26.3
Benjamin F. Sheidler (PROG)	6,779	13.7
George P. Maxwell (SOC)	3,272	6.6
14 William G. Sharp (D)	25,523	59.0
W. S. Kerr (R)	14,142	32.7
George A. Storck (SOC)	3,569	8.3
15 George White (D)	18,169	43.9
James Joyce (R)	14,678	35.5
Howard E. Buker (PROG)	4,968	12.0
F. L. Martin (SOC)	3,033	7.3
16 William B. Francis (D)	16,568	45.6
David A. Hollingsworth (R)	15,781	43.5
Robert Carson (SOC)	3,953	10.9
17 William A. Ashbrook (D)	25,453	72.1
Albert R. Milner (PROG)	5,895	16.7
Dan McCarton (SOC)	3,958	11.2
18 John J. Whitacre (D)	23,936	43.6
Roscoe C. McCullough (R)	23,350	42.5
George F. Lelansky (SOC)	7,617	13.9
19 Ellsworth R. Bathrick (D)	20,251	35.9
W. S. Harris (PROG)	16,035	28.4
Hiram E. Starkey (R)	11,574	20.5
C. E. Sheplin (SOC)	7,805	13.8
20 William Gordon (D)	24,385	40.3
Frank W. Woods (PROG)	18,194	30.1
Paul Howland (R)	12,733	21.0
John G. Willert (SOC)	5,240	8.7
21 Robert J. Bulkley (D)	20,742	42.9
Augustus R. Hatton (PROG)	13,760	28.5
Frederick L. Taft (R)	8,811	18.2
Fred C. Ruppel (SOC)	5,059	10.5
AL Robert M. Crosser (D)	423,301	41.6
Lawrence K. Langdon (R)	297,355	29.3
Randolph W. Walton (PROG)	192,809	19.0
Harry D. Thomas (SOC)	91,201	9.0

OKLAHOMA

Candidates	Votes	%
1 Bird S. McGuire (R)	19,035	45.0
John J. Davis (D)	18,456	43.7
A. W. Renshaw (SOC)	4,447	10.5
2 Dick T. Morgan (R)	24,349	43.8
J. J. Carney (D)	23,773	42.8
P. D. McKenzie (SOC)	7,486	13.5
3 James S. Davenport (D)	27,184	49.5
R. T. Daniel (R)	20,884	38.0
Lewis B. Irvin (SOC)	6,429	11.7
4 Charles D. Carter (D)	23,987	51.3
F. W. Holt (SOC)	11,513	24.6
E. N. Wright (R)	11,239	24.1
5 Scott Ferris (D)	29,574	56.2
C. O. Clark (R)	11,987	22.8
H. H. Stallard (SOC)	11,033	21.0
AL William H. Murray (D)	121,411✓	
Claude Weaver (D)	120,753✓	
Joseph B. Thompson (D)	120,371✓	
Alvin D. Allen (R)	87,468	

Candidates	Votes	%
James L. Brown (R)	87,262	
Emory D. Brownlee (R)	86,883	
Oscar T. Ameringer (SOC)	41,235	
J. T. Cumbie (SOC)	41,073	
J. Luther Langston (SOC)	41,022	

OREGON

Candidates	Votes	%
1 Willis C. Hawley (R)	26,925	43.1
R. G. Smith (D)	15,410	24.6
John W. Campbell (PROG)	8,679	13.9
W. S. Richards (SOC)	7,181	11.5
O. A. Stillman (P)	4,335	6.9
2 Nicholas J. Sinnott (R)	15,121	53.5
James H. Graham (D)	8,322	29.4
C. H. Abercrombie (SOC)	3,037	10.7
George L. Cleaver (P)	1,800	6.4
3 Abraham W. Lafferty (R & PROG)	16,783	42.9
M. G. Munly (D)	11,553	29.6
Thomas McCusker (I)	6,280	16.1
Lee Campbell (SOC)	3,065	7.8

PENNSYLVANIA

Candidates	Votes	%
1 William S. Vare (R, WASH)	25,205	68.7
John H. Hall (D, KEY)	10,492	28.6
2 George S. Graham (R, LINCOLN)	14,803	50.7
William Schlipf Jr (D, KEY)	7,604	26.0
Harry W. Lambirth (WASH)	5,796	19.9
3 J. Hampton Moore (R, LINCOLN)	15,492	54.1
John H. Fow (D)	6,212	21.7
Harry E. Walter (WASH, KEY)	5,920	20.7
4 George W. Edmonds (WASH, R)	21,728	68.5
Thomas T. Nelson (D)	8,482	26.7
5 Michael Donohoe (D, WASH)	22,001	55.2
Henry S. Borneman (R, LINCOLN)	15,181	38.1
John Whitehead (SOC)	2,604	6.5
6 J. Washington Logue (D, KEY)	22,091	43.5
Frederick S. Drake (WASH)	19,642	31.0
Harry A. Mackey (R, RO PROG)	19,291	30.5
7 Thomas S. Butler (RO PROG)	18,276	46.7
Robert E. Difenderfer (D & KEY)	12,225	31.2
Frederick A. Howard (WASH)	7,647	19.5
8 Robert E. Difenderfer (D & KEY)	18,230	38.2
Oscar O. Bean (R)	15,840	33.2
Thomas K. Ober Jr. (WASH)	12,205	25.6
9 William W. Griest (R K & WASH)	14,112	42.7
John N. Hetrick (B MOOSE)	9,947	30.1
Richard M. Reilly (D)	8,043	24.3
10 John R. Farr (R & WASH)	14,939	49.6
Michael A. McGinley (D & KEY)	12,777	42.5
11 John J. Casey (D & KEY)	15,343	40.5
Clarence D. Coughlin (WASH)	10,597	27.9
Charles C. Bowman (R P & PROG)	9,864	26.0
C. F. Quinn (SOC)	2,119	5.6
12 Robert E. Lee (D K & PROG)	14,902	50.4
Alfred B. Garner (R & WASH)	10,463	35.4
Cornelius F. Foley (SOC)	3,464	11.7
13 John H. Rothermel (D)	26,369	50.6
Claude T. Reno (R & WASH)	20,403	39.2
Clarence T. Wixson (SOC)	4,938	9.5
14 William D. B. Ainey (R K & WASH)	14,747	61.1

PENNSYLVANIA

	Candidates	Votes	%
	Joel G. Hill (D)	8,384	34.7
15	Edgar R. Kiess (R & WASH)	14,211	45.9
	William B. Wilson (D & KEY)	13,643	44.1
	Aaron Noll (SOC)	2,282	7.4
16	John V. Lesher (D)	14,209	47.1
	I. Clinton Kline (R & WASH)	12,783	42.4
	George W. Dornbach (SOC)	2,737	9.1
17	Frank L. Dershem (D & KEY)	14,073	38.9
	Benjamin K. Focht (R & PROG)	10,978	30.3
	Frank B. Clayton (WASH)	9,442	26.1
18	Aaron S. Kreider (R BM & PR)	14,485	32.3
	David L. Kaufman (D & KEY)	14,082	31.4
	Henry C. Demming (WASH)	13,504	30.1
19	Warren Worth Bailey (D)	13,626	31.8
	Lynn A. Brua (WASH)	12,688	29.6
	Jesse L. Hartman (R & PROG)	12,633	29.5
	D. W. B. Murphy (SOC)	2,879	6.7
20	Andrew R. Brodbeck (D)	16,514	46.0
	Daniel F. Lafean (R & BM)	14,283	39.8
	Robert C. Bair (WASH)	3,186	8.9
21	Charles E. Patton (R K & WASH)	13,732	50.3
	James A. Gleason (D)	10,588	38.8
	George Fox (SOC)	2,041	7.5
22	Abraham L. Keister (R & WASH)	15,560	41.6
	Curtis H. Gregg (D & PROG)	14,943	39.9
	Charles Cunningham (SOC)	4,735	12.7
	Daniel K. Albright (P)	2,206	5.9
23	Wooda N. Carr (D)	12,211	38.8
	Thomas S. Crago (R)	7,836	24.9
	Harvey L. Berkeley (WASH)	7,588	24.1
	Charles L. Gans (SOC)	2,928	9.3
24	Henry W. Temple (WASH)	11,495	30.8
	Charles Matthews (R)	10,797	28.9
	S. A. Lacock (D)	8,585	23.0
	George C. Frethy (SOC)	5,082	13.6
25	Milton W. Shreve (R & WASH)	13,078	47.6
	Turner W. Shacklett (D)	10,446	38.0
	Sidney A. Schwartz (SOC)	2,727	9.9
26	A. Mitchell Palmer (D)	18,201	53.4
	Francis A. March Jr. (R & WASH)	14,451	42.4
27	J. N. Langham (R & WASH)	17,138	56.7
	Foster M. Mohney (D)	9,472	31.4
	Thomas Jackson Fredericks (SOC)	1,858	6.2
	John Houk (P)	1,743	5.8
28	Willis J. Hulings (WASH)	10,363	31.4
	John P. Hines (D)	9,741	29.5
	Peter M. Speer (R)	7,136	21.6
	John R. McKeown (SOC)	4,097	12.4
	J. W. Neilly (P)	1,692	5.1
29	Stephen G. Porter (R & WASH)	15,925	61.3
	Joseph Gallagher (D)	5,509	21.2
	George T. McConnell (SOC)	3,899	15.0
30	M. Clyde Kelly (RKW & ROPR)	17,230	54.5
	Fred H. Merrick (SOC)	7,570	24.0
	Delmont K. Ferree (D & PROG)	6,708	21.2
31	James Francis Burke (R & WASH)	10,679	51.1
	William A. Prosser (SOC)	5,101	24.4
	Joseph F. Joyce (D)	4,894	23.4
32	Andrew J. Barchfeld (R & WASH)	12,265	40.8
	Herman L. Hegner (D & PROG)	7,987	26.5
	Thomas F. Kennedy (SOC)	5,672	18.9
	William McClintock Shrodes (KEY)	4,169	13.9

	Candidates	Votes	%
AL	John M. Morin (WASH, R)	618,537✔	
	Anderson H. Walters (WASH, R)	608,709✔	
	Frederick E. Lewis (WASH, R)	607,702✔	
	Arthur R. Rupley (WASH, R)	606,709✔	
	George Benton Shaw (D)	357,562	
	George R. McLean (D)	352,396	
	Joseph Howley (D)	346,814	
	E. E. Greenawalt (D)	343,163	
	John W. Slayton (SOC)	81,785	
	William Parker (SOC)	81,125	
	Charles W. Erwin (SOC)	80,808	
	E. S. Musser (SOC)	80.247	
	Howard R. Sheppard (KEY)	21,553	
	E. L. McKee (P)	21,074	
	Henry S. Gill (P)	20,465	
	Howard J. Force (P)	20,284	
	Thomas H. Hamilton (P)	20,213	
	Albin Garrett (KEY)	20,088	
	Charles A. Hawkins (KEY)	19,701	
	Daniel W. Simkins (KEY)	18,961	
	William H. Thomas (INDL)	1,081	

Special Election

	Candidates	Votes	%
1	William S. Vare (R)	20,461	87.8
	Henry V. Garrett (KEY)	2,762	11.9

RHODE ISLAND

	Candidates	Votes	%
1	George F. O'Shaunessy (D)	13,057	50.3
	Sheffield (R)	9,663	37.2
	Bolan (PROG)	3,044	11.7
2	Peter G. Gerry (D)	10,728	42.9
	Bliss (R)	10,335	41.4
	Ball (PROG)	3,642	14.6
3	Ambrose Kennedy (R)	11,718	49.0
	Rattey (D)	9,841	41.2
	Tuttle (PROG)	2,158	9.0

SOUTH CAROLINA

	Candidates	Votes	%
1	George S. Legare (D)	4,550*	97.2
2	James F. Byrnes (D)	6,133	100.0
3	Wyatt Aiken (D)	7,458	100.0
4	Joseph T. Johnson (D)	10,144	100.0
5	David E. Finley (D)	7,901	100.0
6	J. Willard Ragsdale (D)	6,446	100.0
7	Asbury F. Lever (D)	6,660	98.5

SOUTH DAKOTA

	Candidates	Votes	%
1	Charles H. Dillon (R)	25,498	55.9
	Robert E. Dowdell (D)	18,050	39.6
2	Charles H. Burke (R)	23,170	57.1
	C. Boyd Barrett Sr. (D)	14,283	35.2
3	Eben W. Martin (R)	15,141	52.5
	Harry L. Gandy (D)	12,154	42.1
	J. E. Ballinger (SOC)	1,564	5.4

TENNESSEE

	Candidates	Votes	%
1	Sam R. Sells (R)	16,660	50.9
	Z. D. Massey (PROG R)	16,053	49.0
2	Richard W. Austin (R)	12,712	47.6
	W. H. Buttram (PROG R)	7,025	26.3
	J. C. J. Williams (R)	6,681	25.0
3	John A. Moon (D)	18,240	67.4
	C. S. Stewart (R)	6,380	23.6
	J. W. Eastman (PROG)	2,168	8.0
4	Cordell Hull (D)	17,077	64.9
	I. J. Human (R)	9,166	34.8
5	William C. Houston (D)	12,055	54.3
	J. C. Beasley (D)	8,437	38.0
	Doak Aydelott (D)	1,685	7.6
6	Joseph W. Byrns (D)	15,341	82.0
	J. A. Althauser (R)	2,862	15.3
7	Lemuel P. Padgett (D)	12,751	55.1
	C. W. Turner (D)	10,380	44.8

	Candidates	Votes	%
8	Thetus W. Sims (D)	12,451	54.2
	J. W. Ross (R)	8,368	36.4
	C. Grissam (PROG)	2,017	8.8
9	Finis J. Garrett (D)	13,392	79.0
	B. C. Cochran (R)	3,500	20.7
10	Kenneth D. McKellar (D)	12,910	94.3
	George Pardue (SOC)	777	5.7

TEXAS

	Candidates	Votes	%
1	Horace W. Vaughan (D)	13,288	85.9
	S. L. Willyard	1,646	10.6
2	Martin Dies (D)	14,116	80.3
	J. A. Freeland	2,415	13.7
3	James Young (D)	12,158	96.6
4	Sam Rayburn (D)	13,900	89.6
	C. E. Obsuchain	1,340	8.6
5	Jack Beall (D)	16,915	96.6
6	Rufus Hardy (D)	9,743	96.0
7	Alexander W. Gregg (D)	9,132	100.0
8	Joe H. Eagle (D)	13,762	83.3
	Jeff N. Miller (R)	1,658	10.0
	J. E. Curd	1,111	6.7
9	George F. Burgess (D)	13,738	99.7
10	Albert S. Burleson (D)	12,383	100.0
11	Robert L. Henry (D)	11,429	98.1
12	Oscar Calloway (D)	17,283	97.6
13	John H. Stephens (D)	25,630	89.0
	L. B. Lindsey	1,656	5.8
	H. H. Cooper (R)	1,465	5.1
14	James L. Slayden (D)	17,675	97.5
15	John N. Garner (D)	17,231	99.9
16	William R. Smith (D)	23,763	99.9
AL	Daniel E. Garrett (D)	235,065✔	
	Hatton W. Sumners (D)	234,591✔	
	D. D. Richardson (SOC)	24,466	
	J. M. Haggard (SOC)	24,398	
	R. B. Harrison (R)	22,795	
	J. E. Elgin (R)	22,656	
	Z. T. White (PROG)	16,422	
	F. M. Etheridge (PROG)	16,408	
	E. H. Coniber (P)	1,195	

UTAH

	Candidates	Votes	%
AL	Joseph Howell (R)	43,133✔	
	Jacob Johnson (R)	42,047✔	
	Mathonihah Thomas (D)	37,192	
	T. D. Johnson (D)	36,640	
	Stephen H. Love (PROG)	22,358	
	Lewis Larson (PROG)	21,934	
	Murray E. King (SOC)	8,971	
	William M. Knerr (SOC)	8,953	
	Elias Anderson (SOC LAB)	505	
	Harry S. Joseph (NON PART)	187	

VERMONT

	Candidates	Votes	%
1	Frank L. Greene (R)	15,469	59.8
	Patrick M. Meldon (D)	9,154	35.4
2	Frank Plumley (R)	13,316	58.0
	O. C. Sawyer (D)	8,268	36.0

VIRGINIA

	Candidates	Votes	%
1	William A. Jones (D)	10,361	91.0
	T. E. Coleman (SOC)	753	6.6
2	Edward E. Holland (D)	10,061	89.1
	Nathaniel T. Green (PROG)	1,121	9.9
3	Andrew Jackson Montague (D)	10,541	97.6
4	Walter A. Watson (D)	7,847	96.4
5	Edward W. Saunders (D)	9,479	62.1
	A. B. Hamner (D)	5,449	35.7
6	Carter Glass (D)	8,194	72.8
	James S. Browning (PROG)	2,312	20.6
7	James Hay (D)	10,015	71.5
	George N. Earman (R)	3,539	25.3

VIRGINIA

	Candidates	Votes	%
8	Charles C. Carlin (D)	9,083	90.7
	F. T. Evans (SOC)	628	6.3
9	C. Bascom Slemp (R)	14,868	50.0
	R. A. Ayers (D)	13,857	46.6
10	Henry D. Flood (D)	9,615	74.5
	E. J. McCulloch (PROG)	2,458	19.0
	Nathan Parkins (SOC)	842	6.5

WASHINGTON

	Candidates	Votes	%
1	William E. Humphrey (R)	35,252	31.0
	Daniel Landon (PROG)	34,562	30.4
	Charles G. Heifner (D)	26,973	23.7
	Joseph Gilbert (SOC)	16,987	14.9
2	Albert Johnson (R)	25,497	32.5
	Stanton Warburton (PROG)	24,214	30.9
	James A. Munday (D)	16,790	21.4
	Leslie E. Aller (SOC)	11,999	15.3
3	William L. LaFollette (R)	35,049	33.1
	Roscoe M. Drumheller (D)	31,148	29.4
	F. M. Goodwin (PROG)	29,666	28.0
	Robert Burnes Martin (SOC)	10,138	9.6
AL	Jacob A. Falconer (PROG)	95,049✔	
	James W. Bryan (PROG)	90,348✔	
	Henry B. Dewey (R)	87,613	
	J. E. Frost (R)	86,300	
	E. O. Connor (D)	73,133	
	Henry M. White (D)	72,184	

	Candidates	Votes	%
	M. E. Giles (SOC)	39,772	
	Alfred Wagenknecht (SOC)	39,134	
	N. A. Thompson (P)	8,185	

WEST VIRGINIA

	Candidates	Votes	%
1	John W. Davis (D)	24,777	45.0
	G. A. Laughlin (R)	24,613	44.7
	D. M. S. Holt (SOC)	4,230	7.7
2	William G. Brown Jr (D)	23,669	47.5
	W. C. Conley (R)	23,455	47.0
3	Samuel B. Avis (R)	26,041	46.1
	A. B. Littlepage (D)	24,573	43.5
	L. C. Rogers (SOC)	5,213	9.2
4	Hunter H. Moss Jr (R)	20,445	50.2
	J. M. Hamilton (D)	19,346	47.5
5	James A. Hughes (R)	33,128	51.9
	J. F. Beaver (D)	27,697	43.4
AL	Howard Sutherland (R)	128,467	49.2
	Ben H. Hiner (D)	114,485	43.9
	William A. Peter (SOC)	13,944	5.3

WISCONSIN

	Candidates	Votes	%
1	Henry Allen Cooper (R)	18,914	53.2
	Calvin Stewart (D)	13,816	38.8
2	Michael E. Burke (D)	20,665	55.2
	Henry J. Grell (R)	14,698	39.3

	Candidates	Votes	%
3	John M. Nelson (R)	22,388	52.9
	Albert Long (D)	18,219	43.1
4	William J. Cary (D)	14,906	44.9
	Winfield R. Gaylord (SOCIAL D)	10,840	32.6
	John M. Beffel (R)	6,945	20.9
5	William H. Stafford (D)	15,933	41.3
	Victor L. Berger (SOCIAL D)	14,025	36.3
	James F. Trottman (R)	8,251	21.4
6	Michael K. Reily (D)	16,742	48.7
	James H. Davidson (R)	15,505	45.1
7	John J. Esch (R)	20,065	61.0
	William N. Coffland (D)	10,795	32.8
8	Edward E. Browne (R)	17,099	54.6
	Arthur J. Plowman (D)	12,266	39.2
9	Thomas F. Konop (D)	16,843	48.5
	Elmer A. Morse (R)	16,139	46.4
10	James A. Frear (R)	19,915	65.1
	Charles Donohue (D)	8,794	28.7
11	Irvine L. Lenroot (R)	17,466	59.6
	Henry A. Johnson (D)	7,998	27.3
	Ellis B. Harris (SOCIAL D)	3,122	10.7

WYOMING

	Candidates	Votes	%
AL	Frank W. Mondell (R)	19,130	46.4
	Thomas P. Fahey (D)	14,720	35.7
	Charles E. Winter (PROG)	4,828	11.7
	Anthony Carlson (SOC)	2,230	5.4

1914 House Elections

ALABAMA

	Candidates	Votes	%
1	Oscar L. Gray (D)	4,609	98.5
2	S. Hubert Dent Jr. (D)	7,470	100.0
3	Henry B. Steagall (D)	8,220	100.0
4	Fred L. Blackmon (D)	5,441	99.9
5	J. Thomas Heflin (D)	8,100	100.0
6	William B. Oliver (D)	8,539	79.7
	Samuel L. Studdard (R)	2,178	20.3
7	John L. Burnett (D)	8,905	53.1
	Thomas H. Stephens (R)	6,922	41.3
8	Edward B. Almon (D)	6,101	96.6
9	George Huddleston (D)	6,756	83.7
	Robert Fullenweider (R)	1,316	16.3
AL	John W. Abercrombie (D)	62,830	78.0
	James F. Abercrombie (R)	12,832	15.9

Special Election

		Votes	%
3	William O. Mulkey (D)	6,225	53.7
	J. J. Speight	5,367	46.3

ARIZONA

		Votes	%
Al	Carl Hayden (D)	33,306	74.6
	Henry L. Eads (R)	7,586	17.0
	Ulrich Grill (SOC)	3,773	8.5

ARKANSAS

		Votes	%
1	Thaddeus H. Caraway (D)	4,806	100.0
2	William A. Oldfield (D)	5,253	100.0
3	John N. Tillman (D)	7,588	61.8
	W. N. Ivie (R)	4,087	33.3
4	Otis T. Wingo (D)	5,166	82.0
	L. C. Packard (PROG)	1,135	18.0
5	Henderson M. Jacoway (D)	5,586	100.0
6	Samuel K. Taylor (D)	4,110	100.0
7	William S. Goodwin (D)	4,757	100.0

CALIFORNIA

		Votes	%
1	William Kent (I-PR-SOC)	35,403	47.6
	Edward H. Hart (R)	28,166	37.8
	O. F. Meldon (P)	7,987	10.7
2	John E. Raker (D SOC)	32,575	64.6
	James T. Matlock (R & PROG)	15,716	31.2
3	Charles F. Curry (R-D-PROG)	66,034	85.0
	David T. Ross (SOC)	6,752	8.7
	Edwin F. Vanvlear (P)	4,911	6.3
4	Julius Kahn (R & PROG)	41,044	69.1
	Henry Colombat (D)	13,550	22.8
	A. K. Gifford (SOC)	3,928	6.6
5	John I. Nolan (R-D-PROG)	53,875	83.3
	Mads P. Christensen (SOC)	7,366	11.4
	Frederick Head (P)	3,410	5.3
6	John A. Elston (PROG)	36,164	44.4
	George H. Derrick (R)	30,704	37.7
	Howard H. Caldwell (SOC)	11,355	13.9
7	Denver S. Church (D)	39,389	49.9
	A. M. Drew (R)	25,106	31.8
	Harry M. McKee (SOC)	7,797	9.9
	Don A. Allen (P)	6,573	8.3
8	Everis A. Hayes (R)	36,499	49.1
	L. D. Bohnett (PROG D)	33,706	45.3
	Joseph Merritt Horton (P)	4,157	5.6
9	Charles H. Randall (P & D)	28,097	30.9
	Charles W. Bell (PROG)	27,560	30.3
	Frank C. Roberts (R)	25,176	27.7
	Henry A. Hart (SOC)	10,084	11.1

	Candidates	Votes	%
10	William D. Stephens (PROG)	44,141	38.4
	H. Z. Osborne (R)	33,172	28.9
	Nathan Newby (R)	17,810	15.5
	Ralph L. Criswell (SOC)	14,900	13.0
11	William Kettner (D & PROG)	47,165	52.7
	James Carson Needham (R)	25,001	27.9
	James S. Edwards (P)	11,278	12.6
	Kaspar Bauer (SOC)	6,033	6.7

COLORADO

		Votes	%
1	Benjamin C. Hilliard (D)	26,169	44.7
	Horace Phelps (R)	21,569	36.9
	A. W. Rucker (WILSON I)	5,445	9.3
2	Charles R. Timberlake (R)	30,749	45.7
	Harry H. Seldomridge (D)	28,290	42.0
	Charles E. Fisher (PROG)	8,256	12.3
3	Edward Keating (D)	37,191	53.3
	Neil N. McLean (R & PROG)	32,567	46.7
4	Edward T. Taylor (D)	26,562	57.8
	H. J. Baird (R & PROG)	15,015	32.7
	George Kunkle (SOC)	4,353	9.5

CONNECTICUT

		Votes	%
1	P. Davis Oakey (R)	19,899	46.7
	Augustine Lonergan (D)	19,043	44.7
2	Richard P. Freeman (R)	18,255	52.5
	Mahan (D)	14,270	41.0
3	John Q. Tilson (R)	16,072	46.5
	Reilly (D)	15,310	44.3
4	Ebenezer J. Hill (R)	20,231	51.0
	Jeremiah Donovan (D)	16,610	41.8
5	James P. Glynn (R)	14,543	48.9
	Kennedy (D)	12,877	43.3

DELAWARE

		Votes	%
AL	Thomas W. Miller (R)	22,922	50.1
	Franklin Brockson (D)	20,681	45.2

FLORIDA

		Votes	%
1	Stephen M. Sparkman (D)	5,956	99.2
2	Frank Clark (D)	4,577	100.0
3	Emmett Wilson (D)	5,484	98.8
4	William J. Sears (D)	7,934	99.8

GEORGIA

		Votes	%
1	Charles G. Edwards (D)	5,600	100.0
2	Frank Park (D)	5,633	100.0
3	Charles R. Crisp (D)	4,357	100.0
4	William C. Adamson (D)	4,754	100.0
5	William S. Howard (D)	4,780	88.2
	Dewar (PROG)	640	11.8
6	James W. Wise (D)	7,100	100.0
7	Gordon Lee (D)	10,364	100.0
8	Samuel J. Tribble (D)	7,673	100.0
9	Thomas M. Bell (D)	12,943	100.0
10	Carl Vinson (D)	5,833	100.0
11	John R. Walker (D)	4,959	100.0
12	Dudley M. Hughes (D)	6,836	100.0

IDAHO

		Votes	%
AL	Addison T. Smith (R)	45,365 ✓	
	Robert M. McCracken (R)	43,918 ✓	
	James H. Forney (D)	39,736	
	Bert H. Miller (D)	37,000	
	Charles W. Luck (EP)	8,295	

	Candidates	Votes	%
	A. B. Clark (SOC)	8,093	
	G. W. Beloit (SOC)	8,061	
	E. H. Rettig (EP)	7,399	
	R. P. Logan (P)	1,329	
	J. J. Pugh (P)	1,276	

ILLINOIS

		Votes	%
1	Martin B. Madden (R)	13,063	53.2
	James M. Quinlan (D)	9,060	36.9
	Henry M. Ashton (PROG)	1,758	7.2
2	James R. Mann (R)	21,612	48.5
	Mark B. O'Leary (D)	11,940	26.8
	John C. Vaughan (PROG)	8,506	19.1
	Thomas P. Costello (SOC)	2,532	5.7
3	William W. Wilson (R)	18,511	44.9
	Joseph E. Pendergast (D)	16,614	40.3
	William C. Lewis (PROG)	4,001	9.7
	George W. Stone (SOC)	2,093	5.1
4	James T. McDermott (D)	13,313	58.2
	William W. Wilcox (R)	7,019	30.7
	Harry P. Turner (SOC)	1,422	6.2
5	Adolph J. Sabath (D)	9,921	54.2
	Abram J. Harris (R)	4,390	24.0
	E. F. Napieralski (PROG)	2,623	14.3
	Jacob Danhoff (SOC)	1,364	7.5
6	James McAndrews (D)	23,103	45.5
	Frederick E. Coyne (R)	17,328	34.1
	Robert F. Kolb (PROG)	6,161	12.1
	Frank L. Wood (SOC)	4,162	8.2
7	Frank Buchanan (D)	22,377	39.3
	Niels Juul (R)	20,143	35.4
	Carl D. Thompson (SOC)	7,663	13.5
	Charles S. Stewart (PROG)	6,724	11.8
8	Thomas Gallagher (D)	12,524	69.5
	Edward I. Williams (R)	3,558	19.7
	Henry Anielewski (SOC)	1,159	6.4
9	Fred A. Britten (R)	11,358	43.2
	Oscar F. Nelson (D)	8,242	31.4
	R. T. Crane (PROG)	5,365	20.4
	Frank Schiflersmith (SOC)	1,315	5.0
10	George Edmund Foss (R)	18,038	38.8
	John F. Waters (D)	13,096	28.2
	Charles M. Thomson (PROG)	13,039	28.0
	John M. Work (SOC)	2,343	5.0
11	Ira C. Copley (PROG)	18,371	40.5
	Frank W. Shepherd (R)	17,197	37.9
	John A. Logan (D)	9,098	20.1
12	Charles E. Fuller (R)	20,811	50.8
	William H. Hinebaugh (PROG)	9,700	23.7
	George V. B. Weeks (D)	8,726	21.3
13	John C. McKenzie (R)	18,143	57.9
	Frank H. Goodwin (D)	8,735	27.9
	Isaac N. Evans (PROG)	4,054	12.9
14	Clyde H. Tavenner (D)	17,221	44.1
	Frank E. Abbey (R)	16,132	41.3
	Henry E. Burgess (PROG)	4,272	10.9
15	Edward J. King (R)	16,217	41.3
	Edward P. Allen (D)	14,537	37.0
	Julius Kespohl (PROG)	7,122	18.1
16	Claude U. Stone (D)	18,399	48.8
	George A. Zeller (R)	16,462	43.7
17	John A. Sterling (R)	16,720	48.1
	Louis Fitzhenry (D)	14,842	42.7
	George E. Stump (PROG)	2,757	7.9
18	Joseph G. Cannon (R)	22,035	47.1
	Frank T. O'Hair (D)	20,005	42.8
	Wendell P. Kay (PROG)	4,112	8.8
19	William B. McKinley (R)	25,576	51.0
	Charles M. Borchers (D)	19,931	39.7
	Frank B. Thomas (PROG)	4,083	8.1
20	Henry T. Rainey (D)	20,340	58.0
	Jarvis E. Dubois (R)	12,885	36.8
21	Loren E. Wheeler (R)	20,800	47.8
	James M. Graham (D)	18,361	42.2
	Porter Paddock (PROG)	2,417	5.6

ILLINOIS

	Candidates	Votes	%
22	William A. Rodenberg (R)	23,362	46.5
	William N. Baltz (D)	21,364	42.5
	Charles F. Stelzel (PROG)	2,799	5.6
	M. E. Kirkpatrick (SOC)	2,772	5.5
23	Martin D. Foster (D)	24,414	53.1
	John J. Bundy (R)	18,036	39.3
	Logan B. Skipper (PROG)	2,659	5.8
24	Thomas S. Williams (R)	18,311	49.9
	H. Robert Fowler (D)	17,369	47.3
25	Edward E. Dennison (R)	20,271	48.5
	Robert P. Hill (D)	17,922	42.8
	George W. Dowell (PROG)	2,468	5.9
AL	Burnett M. Chiperfield (R)	388,896✔	
	William Elza Williams (D)	375,465✔	
	J. McLean Davis (R)	373,682	
	Thomas P. Sullivan (D)	356,678	
	Harry L. Heer (PROG)	113,510	
	George N. Kreider (PROG)	105,088	
	Dan R. Thomas (SOC)	42,841	
	Carl Strover (SOC)	41,949	
	Frank E. Herrick (P)	7,644	
	John A. Shields (P)	7,275	
	Harry (SOC LAB)	2,060	

INDIANA

	Candidates	Votes	%
1	Charles Lieb (D)	20,488	46.6
	S. Wallace Cook (R)	17,661	40.1
	U. H. Seider (PROG)	3,519	8.0
2	William A. Cullop (D)	21,451	44.3
	O. E. Bland (R)	19,145	39.5
	J. B. Wilson (PROG)	5,087	10.5
3	William E. Cox (D)	23,679	56.4
	Edgar D. Bush (R)	12,260	29.2
	Lawson Mace (PROG)	5,344	12.7
4	Lincoln Dixon (D)	22,795	50.3
	M. D. Wilson (R)	16,856	37.2
	Roy W. Ewing (PROG)	4,609	10.2
5	Ralph W. Moss (D)	21,785	45.9
	R. L. Shattuck (R)	17,552	37.0
	Otis E. Gulley (PROG)	5,254	11.1
6	Finly H. Gray (D)	18,371	41.4
	P. J. Lynch (R)	14,880	33.6
	Elbert Russell (PROG)	9,449	21.3
7	Merrill Moores (R)	26,451	42.0
	Charles S. Korbly (D)	21,343	33.9
	Paxton Hibben (PROG)	10,530	16.7
	W. H. Henry (SOC)	4,002	6.4
8	John A. M. Adair (D)	21,840	44.5
	A. H. Vestal (R)	13,160	26.8
	H. L. Kitselman (PROG)	10,785	22.0
9	Martin A. Morrison (D)	21,992	42.8
	F. S. Purnell (R)	21,035	40.9
	C. A. Ford (PROG)	6,198	12.1
10	William R. Wood (R)	22,318	45.4
	John B. Peterson (D)	17,735	36.0
	William H. Ade (PROG)	8,637	17.6
11	George W. Rauch (D)	20,666	41.6
	S. L. Strickler (R)	16,999	34.3
	B. B. Shively (PROG)	8,106	16.3
12	Cyrus Cline (D)	18,612	46.9
	Charles R. Lane (R)	15,052	37.9
	H. M. Widney (P)	3,976	10.0
13	Henry A. Barnhart (D)	25,134	44.4
	A. J. Hickney (R)	19,771	34.9
	R. S. Stephens (PROG)	8,542	15.1

IOWA

	Candidates	Votes	%
1	Charles A. Kennedy (R)	14,866	49.2
	F. B. Whittaker (D)	12,381	41.0
	Daniel B. Heller (PROG)	1,600	5.3
2	Harry E. Hull (R)	20,145	50.8
	W. J. McDonald (D)	16,940	42.8
3	Burton E. Sweet (R)	22,386	56.5
	James C. Murtagh (D)	15,427	39.0
4	Gilbert N. Haugen (R)	20,001	56.6
	G. A. Meyer (D)	13,653	38.6
5	James W. Good (R)	20,752	56.2
	Joseph Mekota (D)	14,497	39.2
6	C. William Ramseyer (R)	16,616	48.1
	W. H. Hamilton (D)	14,552	42.1
7	Cassius C. Dowell (R)	17,225	53.8
	John T. Mulvaney (D)	10,871	33.9
	John E. Holmes (PROG)	2,193	6.9
8	Horace M. Towner (R)	19,817	54.1
	H. E. Valentine (D)	14,324	39.1
9	William R. Green (R)	19,265	53.9
	H. S. Mosher (D)	14,677	41.1
10	Frank P. Woods (R)	24,192	54.5
	D. M. Kelleher (D)	14,401	32.5
	William B. Quarton (PROG)	4,656	10.5
11	Thomas J. Steele (D)	21,259	48.9
	George C. Scott (R)	17,600	40.5
	Edward H. Crane (PROG)	3,724	8.6

Special Election

	Candidates	Votes	%
2	Henry Vollmer (D)	12,625	44.5
	Harry E. Hull (R)	10,809	38.1
	Charles P. Hanley (PROG)	3,709	13.1

KANSAS

	Candidates	Votes	%
1	Daniel R. Anthony Jr. (R)	31,539	51.6
	J. B. Chapman (D)	20,279	33.2
	Sheffield Ingalls (PROG)	9,259	15.2
2	Joseph Taggart (D)	28,412	41.7
	John H. Crider (R)	24,732	36.3
	J. L. Brady (PROG)	12,271	18.0
3	Philip P. Campbell (R)	30,644	41.2
	P. J. McGinley (D)	21,492	28.9
	L. F. Fuller (SOC)	11,370	15.3
	G. E. Bertch (PROG)	7,871	10.6
4	Dudley Doolittle (D)	23,894	47.0
	Howard F. Martindale (R)	19,331	38.0
	N. D. Welty (PROG)	6,626	13.0
5	Guy T. Helvering (D)	25,142	45.7
	W. A. Calderhead (R)	22,756	41.4
	Loring Trott (PROG)	7,083	12.9
6	John R. Connelly (D)	27,359	47.0
	John B. Dykes (R)	21,353	36.7
	Eva Morley Murphy (PROG)	6,847	11.8
7	Jouett Shouse (D)	27,740	39.7
	John S. Simmons (R)	26,181	37.5
	O. W. Dawson (PROG)	12,537	18.0
8	William A. Ayres (R)	21,512	46.6
	Charles L. Davidson (PROG)	11,907	25.8
	Ezra Branine (R)	11,520	24.9

KENTUCKY

	Candidates	Votes	%
1	Alben W. Barkley (D)	18,407	65.9
	Edwin Farley (R)	8,522	30.5
2	David H. Kincheloe (D)	15,019	57.0
	Alvin H. Clark (R)	10,593	40.2
3	Robert Y. Thomas Jr. (D)	16,020	49.7
	J. F. Taylor (R)	14,414	44.7
4	Ben Johnson (D)	17,218	56.9
	W. Sherman Ball (R)	11,496	38.0
5	J. Swagar Sherley (D)	23,765	60.6
	Charles T. Gardiner (PROG)	8,106	20.7
	Roy Wilhoit (R)	6,611	16.9
6	Arthur B. Rouse (D)	18,018	87.9
	Emmett Orr (PROG)	1,689	8.2
7	James Campbell Cantrill (D)	20,040	61.2
	Louis L. Bristow (R)	12,295	37.5
8	Harvey Helm (D)	14,393	55.0
	James P. Spilman (R)	10,460	40.0
9	William J. Fields (D)	22,739	53.0
	H. Glenn Ireland (R)	19,291	45.0
10	John W. Langley (R)	13,150	61.5
	F. Tom Hatcher (D)	7,755	36.3

	Candidates	Votes	%
11	Caleb Powers (R)	16,686	70.8
	John H. Wilson (I)	6,893	29.2

LOUISIANA

	Candidates	Votes	%
1	Albert Estopinal (D)	9,657	91.4
	Louis Henry Burns (PROG)	903	8.6
2	H. Garland Dupre (D)	8,641	81.7
	Louis Lebourgeois (PROG)	1,939	18.3
3	Whitmell P. Martin (PROG)	6,030	56.6
	Henri Gueydan (D)	4,604	43.2
4	John Thomas Watkins (D)	3,330	96.4
5	Riley J. Wilson (D)	2,865	95.1
6	Lewis L. Morgan (D)	3,190	99.4
7	Ladislas Lazaro (D)	3,792	86.0
	Walter F. Dietz (SOC)	615	14.0
8	James B. Aswell (D)	4,466	85.9
	J. R. Jones (SOC)	729	14.0

MAINE

	Candidates	Votes	%
1	Asher C. Hinds (R)	16,622	47.0
	John C. Scates (D)	16,035	45.4
	W. C. Emerson (PROG)	2,276	6.4
2	Daniel J. McGillicuddy (D)	16,508	46.9
	H. M. Sewall (R)	11,335	32.2
	A. C. Wheeler (PROG)	6,539	18.6
3	John A. Peters (R)	19,600	46.5
	W.R. Pattangall (D)	18,085	42.9
	E. M. Thompson (PROG)	3,697	8.8
4	Frank E. Guernsey (R)	12,707	45.0
	C. W. Mullen (D)	10,021	35.5
	Del Merrill (PROG)	5,371	19.0

MARYLAND

	Candidates	Votes	%
1	Jesse D. Price (D)	17,543	49.0
	Robert F. Duer (R)	17,146	47.9
2	Joshua Frederick C. Talbott (D)	23,124	53.5
	William J. Heaps (R)	17,956	41.5
3	Charles P. Coady (D)	16,279	52.9
	John A. Janetzke (R)	12,901	41.9
4	J. Charles Linthicum (D)	19,791	58.2
	Thomas T. Hammond (R)	12,595	37.0
5	Sydney E. Mudd (R)	16,236	48.6
	Richard A. Johnson (D)	15,179	45.5
6	David J. Lewis (D)	19,494	49.1
	Frederick N. Zihlman (R)	18,752	47.2

Special Election

	Candidates	Votes	%
1	Jesse D. Price (D)	17,858	74.7
	Thomas S. Hodson (PROG)	6,053	25.3

MASSACHUSETTS

	Candidates	Votes	%
1	Allen T. Treadway (R)	15,556	55.0
	Morton H. Burdick (D)	10,695	37.8
2	Frederick H. Gillett (R)	15,635	56.3
	Edward M. Lewis (D & PROG)	11,252	40.5
3	Calvin D. Paige (R)	15,838	56.0
	Owen A. Hoban (D)	10,539	37.2
	Jonas Bemis (PROG)	1,925	6.8
4	Samuel E. Winslow (R)	16,972	57.8
	Hugh O'Rourke (D)	12,373	42.2
5	John Jacob Rogers (R)	17,249	62.1
	J. Joseph O'Connor (D)	9,136	32.9
	William N. Osgood (PROG)	1,404	5.1
6	Augustus P. Gardner (R)	19,960	69.2
	George A. Schofield (D)	7,692	26.7
7	Michael F. Phelan (D)	13,962	50.4
	Charles Cabot Johnson (R)	11,530	41.6
8	Frederick W. Dallinger (R & PROG)	15,227	49.7
	Frederick S. Deitrick (D)	14,359	46.9

MASSACHUSETTS

	Candidates	Votes	%
9	Ernest W. Roberts (R)	16,087	54.8
	Peter W. Collins (D)	9,773	33.3
	H. Huestis Newton (PROG)	3,482	11.9
10	Peter F. Tague (D)	12,409	73.7
	James A. Cochran (R)	3,018	17.9
	Daniel T. Callahan (PROG)	1,407	8.4
11	George Holden Tinkham (R)	13,510	49.8
	Francis J. Horgan (D)	11,863	43.7
	Henry Clay Peters (PROG)	1,765	6.5
12	James A. Gallivan (D)	18,315	66.2
	Charles H. S. Robinson (R)	7,673	27.7
	Chester R. Lawrence (PROG)	1,678	6.1
13	William H. Carter (R)	17,988	50.5
	John J. Mitchell (D)	15,935	44.7
14	Richard Olney (D)	13,246	36.5
	Harry C. Howard (R)	12,556	34.6
	Henry L. Kincaide (PROG)	9,147	25.2
15	William S. Greene (R)	12,729	57.9
	James F. Morris (D)	7,495	34.1
	Alvin G. Weeks (PROG)	1,746	8.0
16	Joseph Walsh (R)	11,322	46.9
	Thomas C. Thacher (D)	10,153	42.0
	Thomas Thompson (PROG)	2,669	11.1

MICHIGAN

	Candidates	Votes	%
1	Frank E. Doremus (D)	19,197	62.5
	Charles E. McCarty (R)	9,483	30.9
2	Samuel W. Beakes (D)	18,085	45.2
	Mark R. Bacon (R)	17,876	44.7
	Hubert F. Probert (N PROG)	3,345	8.4
3	John M. C. Smith (R)	15,644	45.6
	Orville J. Cornell (D)	13,245	38.6
	Edward N. Dingley (N PROG)	3,846	11.2
4	Edward L. Hamilton (R)	18,577	53.2
	Albert E. Beebe (D)	13,452	38.5
	J. Mark Harvey (N PROG)	1,826	5.2
5	Carl E. Mapes (R)	17,223	58.7
	Thaddeus B. Taylor (D)	9,031	30.8
	Alvin E. Ewing (N PROG)	1,823	6.2
6	Patrick H. Kelley (R)	19,154	49.3
	Frank L. Dodge (D)	15,013	38.7
	William S. Kellogg (N PROG)	3,696	9.5
7	Louis C. Cramton (R)	20,294	60.0
	John F. Murphy (D)	9,488	28.0
	Jefferson G. Brown (N PROG)	3,342	9.9
8	Joseph W. Fordney (R)	20,249	52.7
	Laurence W. Smith (D)	15,729	40.9
9	James C. McLaughlin (R)	16,148	55.3
	Amos O. White (D)	6,602	22.6
	William H. Sears (N PROG)	4,913	16.8
10	George A. Loud (R)	13,854	45.5
	Roy O. Woodruff (N PROG)	8,167	26.8
	Charles W. Hitchcock (D)	7,564	24.8
11	Frank D. Scott (R)	18,290	55.5
	Francis T. McDonald (D)	9,977	30.3
	Herbert F. Baker (N PROG)	3,246	9.9
12	W. Frank James (R)	14,562	49.3
	William J. Macdonald (N PROG)	9,205	31.1
	Frederic J. Bawden (D)	4,962	16.8
13	Charles A. Nichols (R)	17,091	62.6
	Antonio Entenza (D)	7,417	27.2
	Ralph Hall Ferris (N PROG)	2,001	7.3

MINNESOTA

	Candidates	Votes	%
1	Sydney Anderson (R)	23,939	65.6
	Witherstine (D)	12,540	34.4
2	Franklin F. Ellsworth (R)	18,888	55.3
	Flittie (D)	10,760	31.5
	Dehual (PROG)	3,206	9.4

	Candidates	Votes	%
3	Charles R. Davis (R)	21,151	57.4
	Avery (D)	13,791	37.4
	Mackintosh (PROG)	1,899	5.2
4	Carl C. Van Dyke (D)	16,988	55.2
	Stevens (R)	11,058	35.9
	Mahoney (SOC)	2,221	7.2
5	George R. Smith (R)	12,576	40.7
	Van Lear (SOC)	10,312	33.3
	Long (D)	4,423	14.3
	Powers (PROG)	3,618	11.7
6	Charles A. Lindbergh (R)	15,364	47.5
	Dubois (D)	11,409	35.2
	Thomason (SOC)	3,769	11.6
	Sharkey (PROG)	1,836	5.7
7	Andrew J. Volstead (R)	28,815	100.0
8	Clarence B. Miller (R)	14,135	50.4
	Nelson (D)	8,872	31.6
	Towne (SOC)	4,179	14.9
9	Halvor Steenerson (R)	24,173	76.4
	Brattland (PUB OWN)	7,489	23.7
10	Thomas D. Schall (PROG)	12,786	39.1
	Jepson (D)	11,383	34.8
	Swenson (D)	8,522	26.1

MISSISSIPPI

	Candidates	Votes	%
1	Ezekiel S. Candler Jr. (D)	5,251	100.0
2	Hubert D. Stephens (D)	5,159	100.0
3	Benjamin G. Humphreys (D)	2,125	98.0
4	Thomas U. Sisson (D)	4,684	95.6
5	Samuel A. Witherspoon (D)	6,451	92.8
	C. W. Smith (SOC)	500	7.2
6	Pat Harrison (D)	6,225	95.5
7	Percy E. Quin (D)	3,702	100.0
8	James W. Collier (D)	2,233	96.9

MISSOURI

	Candidates	Votes	%
1	James T. Lloyd (D)	18,712	56.2
	Brown (R)	12,783	38.4
2	William W. Rucker (D)	22,243	98.7
3	Joshua W. Alexander (D)	18,072	55.6
	Morroway (R)	11,933	36.7
	Courtney (PROG)	2,045	6.3
4	Charles F. Booher (D)	17,293	53.5
	Otis (R)	13,907	43.1
5	William P. Borland (D)	36,966	70.5
	Brown (PROG)	9,309	17.8
	Orr (R)	5,387	10.3
6	Clement C. Dickinson (D)	15,402	56.4
	Young (R)	9,474	34.7
	Theilmann (PROG)	1,989	7.3
7	Courtney W. Hamlin (D)	21,953	52.0
	Lovan (R)	18,025	42.7
8	Dorsey W. Shackleford (D)	15,546	52.2
	Gentry (R)	13,918	46.8
9	James Beauchamp Clark (D)	20,058	55.8
	Brown (R)	14,733	41.0
10	Jacob E. Meeker (R)	44,912	54.2
	Curlee (D)	30,153	36.4
	Brandt (SOC)	5,162	6.2
11	William L. Igoe (D)	17,163	51.1
	Hamilton (R)	15,152	45.1
12	Leonidas C. Dyer (R)	12,047	53.2
	Collins (D)	9,768	43.1
13	Walter L. Hensley (D)	15,796	50.2
	Reppy (R)	14,832	47.1
14	Joseph J. Russell (D)	23,295	47.0
	Brown (R)	22,266	44.9
	Knecht (SOC)	3,150	6.4
15	Perl D. Decker (D)	19,827	48.1
	Manlove (R)	18,471	44.8
16	Thomas L. Rubey (D)	16,340	53.0
	Diffenderffer (R)	13,057	42.4

MONTANA

	Candidates	Votes	%
AL	John M. Evans (D)	37,011 ✔	
	Thomas Stout (D)	35,156 ✔	

	Candidates	Votes	%
	Wash J. McCormick (R)	26,161	
	Fletcher Maddox (R)	26,046	
	Lewis J. Duncan (SOC)	12,282	
	W. E. Kent (SOC)	9,424	
	Wellington D. Rankin (PROG)	6,654	
	James M. Brinson (PROG)	6,166	

NEBRASKA

	Candidates	Votes	%
1	C. F. Reavis (R)	15,462	48.1
	John A. Maguire (D & PPI)	15,138	47.1
2	Charles O. Lobeck (D)	16,773	58.1
	Thomas W. Blackburn (R)	8,979	31.1
	Nathan Merriam (PROG)	1,616	5.6
3	Daniel V. Stephens (D & PPI)	26,488	57.7
	O. S. Spillman (R & PROG)	18,007	39.2
4	Charles H. Sloan (R & PROG)	22,948	54.8
	Walter H. Rhodes (D & PPI)	18,177	43.4
5	Ashton C. Shallenberger (D & PPI)	16,387	48.7
	Silas R. Barton (R & PROG)	16,217	48.2
6	Moses P. Kinkaid (R & PROG)	29,226	57.1
	Frank J. Taylor (D & PPI)	19,346	37.8

NEVADA

	Candidates	Votes	%
AL	Edwin E. Roberts (R)	8,915	42.0
	Leonard B. Fowler (D)	8,031	37.8
	Martin J. Scanlan (SOC)	4,294	20.2

NEW HAMPSHIRE

	Candidates	Votes	%
1	Cyrus A. Sulloway (R)	20,657	50.0
	Eugene E. Reed (D)	19,140	46.3
2	Edward H. Wason (R)	21,793	54.8
	Charles J. French (D)	16,101	40.5

NEW JERSEY

	Candidates	Votes	%
1	William J. Browning (R)	24,142	58.5
	Nowrey (D)	13,271	32.1
2	Isaac Bacharach (R)	21,448	54.3
	Baker (D)	14,352	36.3
	Bright (RO PROG)	2,276	5.8
3	Thomas J. Scully (D)	21,338	50.7
	Havens (R)	19,303	45.8
4	Elijah C. Hutchinson (R)	17,078	50.9
	Walsh (D)	13,766	41.0
	Thorn (RO PROG)	1,711	5.1
5	John H. Capstick (R)	16,951	45.7
	William E. Tuttle Jr. (D)	15,718	42.4
	May (RO PROG)	2,218	6.0
	Seeholzor (SOC)	1,854	5.0
6	Archibald C. Hart (D)	16,286	45.4
	Prince (R)	15,880	44.3
7	Dow H. Drukker (R)	12,664	54.7
	Cabell (D)	6,944	30.0
	Demarest (SOC)	3,370	14.6
8	Edward W. Gray (R)	13,438	44.9
	McDonald (D)	11,678	39.1
	Archibald (PROG R)	2,232	7.5
9	Richard W. Parker (R)	9,482	37.3
	Gregory (R)	8,069	31.7
	Seymour (D)	5,672	22.3
	Bohn (SOC)	1,342	5.3
10	Frederick R. Lehlbach (R)	13,765	47.5
	Edward W. Townsend (D)	12,278	42.4
11	John J. Eagan (D)	17,551	64.9
	Straus (R)	8,400	31.1
12	James A. Hamill (D)	16,260	62.6
	Higginbotham Jr. (R)	7,379	28.4
	Anderson (PROG R)	1,313	5.1

NEW JERSEY

Special Elections

Candidates	Votes	%
7 Dow H. Drukker (R)	10,613	49.0
O'Byrne (D)	5,240	24.2
Demarest (SOC)	5,064	23.4
9 Richard W. Parker (R)	4,675	50.1
Seymour (D)	4,178	44.8
Bohn (SOC)	475	5.1

NEW MEXICO

AL	Benigno C. Hernandez (R)	23,812	51.3
	H. B. Fergusson (D)	19,805	42.7

NEW YORK

	Candidates	Votes	%
1	Frederick C. Hicks (R)	17,726	47.6
	Lathrop Brown (D)	17,722	47.5
2	Charles Pope Caldwell (D)	21,330	54.5
	Frank E. Hopkins (R)	10,552	27.0
	Lawrence T. Gresser (I)	3,672	9.4
	Benjamin Katz (SOC)	2,352	6.0
3	Joseph V. Flynn (D)	11,298	50.1
	George B. Serenbetz (R)	8,368	37.1
	Joseph E. Kleinn (SOC)	1,559	6.9
4	Harry Howard Dale (D)	7,860	47.0
	John Kissel (R & IL)	5,496	32.9
	J. Chante Lipes (SOC)	1,870	11.2
	Max Schaffer (PROG)	1,404	8.4
5	James P. Maher (D)	11,754	49.5
	Alfred T. Hobley (R)	8,327	35.1
	John S. Gaynor (PROG&IL)	2,512	10.6
6	Frederick W. Rowe (R & IL)	22,262	53.8
	Leroy W. Ross (D)	16,180	39.1
7	John J. Fitzgerald (D & IL)	15,065	65.9
	C. G. Finney Wilcox (R)	6,659	29.1
8	Daniel J. Griffin (D & IL)	20,213	62.0
	Thomas E. Clark (R)	9,935	30.5
9	Oscar W. Swift (R & IL)	18,547	48.7
	James H. O'Brien (D)	15,224	40.0
	Anna C. Wright (SOC)	2,371	6.2
10	Reuben L. Haskell (R PR IL)	8,213	40.5
	Phillip A. Riley (D)	6,240	30.8
	Alex S. Drescher (A-BOSS)	2,884	14.2
	Harry D. Smith (SOC)	2,732	13.5
11	Daniel J. Riordan (D)	13,200	59.0
	George S. Schofield (R)	7,680	34.3
12	Meyer London (SOC)	5,969	49.5
	Henry M. Goldfogle (D AM IL)	4,947	41.1
	Benjamin Borowsky (R & PROG)	1,133	9.4
13	George W. Loft (D AM IL)	5,934	58.2
	James E. March (R & PROG)	3,081	30.2
	Bouck White (SOC)	1,177	11.6
14	Michael F. Farley (D & IL)	7,310	46.5
	Fiorello H. LaGuardia (R)	5,331	33.9
	Henry L. Slobodin (SOC)	1,534	9.8
	John B. Golden (PROG)	1,456	9.3
15	Michael F. Conry (D & IL)	13,846	65.1
	Oscar W. Ehrhorn (R & PROG)	6,698	31.5
16	Peter J. Dooling (D & IL)	12,874	62.5
	Harry B. Stowell (R)	6,012	29.2
	William J. Moran (PROG)	1,156	5.6
17	John F. Carew (D)	10,243	53.7
	Lindon Bates Jr. (R PR IL)	7,851	41.2
18	Thomas G. Patten (D & IL)	12,434	53.2
	George B. Francis (R & PROG)	8,804	37.7
	Ernest Ramn (SOC)	2,047	8.8
19	Walter M. Chandler (PROG&IL)	10,682	34.1
	Joseph L. Buttenweiser (D)	10,150	32.4

	Candidates	Votes	%
	Albert Ottinger (R)	9,588	30.6
20	Isaac Siegel (R PR IL)	4,923	44.1
	Jacob A. Cantor (D)	4,843	43.3
	Ludwig Schmidt (SOC)	1,356	12.1
21	Murray Hulbert (D & IL)	11,575	51.2
	Martin Ansorge (R AM&PR)	9,826	43.5
22	Henry Buckner (D)	17,886	62.4
	Francis J. Kuerzi (R IL PR)	8,900	31.0
	Maxie McDonald (SOC)	1,770	6.2
23	Joseph A. Goulden (D)	18,822	44.1
	Robert L. Niles (R & IL)	12,060	28.3
	Steven B. Ayres (PROG&BUS)	8,228	19.3
	M. Rubinow (SOC)	3,378	7.9
24	Woodson R. Oglesby (D)	17,605	43.8
	William Foster (R)	16,554	41.2
	Alfred E. Smith (PROG)	3,143	7.8
	Allen L. Benson (SOC)	2,238	5.6
25	James W. Husted (R)	17,888	51.7
	Benjamin Irving Taylor (D)	14,369	41.5
26	Edmund Platt (R)	21,634	58.0
	Alonzo F. Albott (D)	14,412	38.6
27	Charles B. Ward (R)	22,505	53.0
	George McClellan (D)	18,074	42.6
28	Rollin B. Sanford (R)	27,158	51.9
	Peter G. Ten Eyck (D PR&IL)	24,405	46.6
29	James S. Parker (R)	29,454	63.7
	James Farrell (D & PROG)	15,171	32.8
30	William B. Charles (R)	16,521	42.4
	William C. D. Willson (D)	9,950	25.5
	Philip H. Callery (SOC)	5,705	14.6
	Theron Akin (PROG)	5,105	13.1
31	Edwin A. Merritt Jr. (R)	17,720*	54.6
	Andrew J. Cooney (D)	7,850	24.2
	Howard D. Hadley (PROG)	5,351	16.5
32	Luther W. Mott (R & PROG)	24,684	63.6
	John Fitzgibbons (D)	11,544	29.7
33	Homer P. Snyder (R)	21,144	52.6
	Charles A. Talcott (D)	15,035	37.4
	George H. Spitzli (PROG)	2,582	6.4
34	George W. Fairchild (R)	22,786	56.2
	George J. West (D)	12,564	31.0
	Albert S. Barnes (PROG, P)	4,610	11.4
35	Walter W. Magee (R)	23,075	52.8
	John R. Clancy (D)	15,131	34.6
	Hugh M. Tilroe (PROG)	3,211	7.3
36	Sereno E. Payne (R)	22,523*	58.9
	Herman L. Kelly (D)	10,970	28.7
	Amasa J. Parker (PROG)	2,278	6.0
	Wallace E. Brown (P)	1,995	5.2
37	Harry H. Pratt (R)	16,081	38.9
	John Seeley (D)	14,056	34.0
	Milo Shanks (P)	8,438	20.4
	Jonas S. Vanduzer (PROG)	2,075	5.0
38	Thomas B. Dunn (R)	21,250	57.7
	George P. Decker (D)	8,832	24.0
	Oscar M. Arnold (SOC)	5,324	14.5
39	Henry G. Danforth (R)	23,694	63.8
	M. A. Bowen (D)	9,776	26.3
	Daniel M. Anthony (PROG)	2,027	5.5
40	S. Wallace Dempsey (R)	22,324	57.4
	Robert H. Gittins (D)	12,857	33.1
	Frank C. Ferguson (PROG)	2,395	6.2
41	Charles B. Smith (D)	11,915	38.0
	Frank J. Eberle (R)	11,324	36.1
	Conrad J. Meyer (PROG)	6,488	20.7
42	Daniel A. Driscoll (D)	13,081	46.9
	Willard H. Ticknor (R)	12,633	45.3
43	Charles M. Hamilton (R)	20,726	60.6
	Manton M. Wyvell (D)	7,619	22.3
	Ernest H. Woodruff (P)	2,159	6.3
	Walter N. Renwick (PROG)	2,119	6.2

NORTH CAROLINA

1	John H. Small (D)	8,940	99.8
2	Claude Kitchin (D)	6,964	88.6

	Candidates	Votes	%
	W. O. Dixon (R)	879	11.2
3	George E. Hood (D)	8,620	57.7
	Buck H. Crumpler (R)	6,305	42.2
4	Edward W. Pou (D)	11,141	99.9
5	Charles M. Stedman (D)	18,592	55.9
	John T. Benbow (R)	13,990	42.0
6	Hannibal L. Godwin (D)	8,392	65.0
	Robert W. Davis (R)	4,521	35.0
7	Robert N. Page (D)	14,789	53.5
	Theo E. McCrary (R)	12,863	46.5
8	Robert L. Doughton (D)	14,976	53.2
	Frank A. Linney (R)	13,160	46.8
9	Edwin Y. Webb (D)	15,136	54.2
	Jacob F. Newell (R)	12,777	45.8
10	James J. Britt (R)	15,347	51.3
	James M. Gudger Jr. (D)	14,579	48.7

NORTH DAKOTA

1	Henry T. Helgesen (R)	16,565	56.0
	F. Bartholomew (D)	12,217	41.3
2	George M. Young (R)	18,680	68.4
	James J. Weeks (D)	7,073	25.9
	N. H. Bjornstad (SOC)	1,553	5.7
3	Patrick D. Norton (R)	15,547	57.1
	Halvor Halvorson (D)	7,394	27.2
	S. Griffith (SOC)	3,791	13.9

OHIO

1	Nicholas Longworth (R)	29,822	52.9
	Stanley E. Bowdle (D)	24,054	42.7
2	Alfred G. Allen (D)	27,811	48.6
	Stanley Struble (R)	26,656	46.6
3	Warren Gard (D)	29,707	45.9
	Frank I. Brown (R)	23,535	36.3
	Fred Guy Strickland (SOC)	8,859	13.7
4	J. E. Russell (R)	25,096	47.9
	N. W. Cunningham (D)	24,114	46.1
5	Nelson E. Matthews (R)	19,859	47.8
	T. T. Ansberry (D)	19,281	46.4
	Curtis A. Baxter (PROG)	2,409	5.8
6	Charles C. Kearns (R)	19,456	50.6
	William A. Inman (D)	17,766	46.2
7	Simeon D. Fess (R)	37,847	58.7
	Charles E. Buroker (D)	22,544	35.0
8	John A. Key (R)	22,490	51.0
	John H. Clark (D)	20,453	46.4
9	Isaac R. Sherwood (D)	29,399	53.8
	William E. Cordill (R)	16,152	29.5
	Herbert P. Whitney (PROG)	5,949	10.9
	Edward Hoskins (SOC)	3,200	5.9
10	Robert M. Switzer (R)	18,001	54.0
	C. L. Martzolff (D)	12,375	37.1
	Edgar Ervin (PROG)	2,981	8.9
11	Edwin D. Ricketts (R)	17,708	47.0
	Horatio C. Claypool (D)	17,598	46.7
12	Clement L. Brumbaugh (D)	25,608	46.9
	Ralph E. Westfall (R)	22,489	41.2
	Frank E. Hayden (PROG)	3,278	6.0
	Fred P. Zimpfer (SOC)	3,178	5.8
13	Arthur W. Overmeyer (D)	22,085	46.8
	Charles S. Hatfield (R)	22,011	46.7
14	Seward H. Williams (R)	21,717	41.6
	E. R. Bathrick (D)	20,339	39.0
	Henry M. Hagelbarger (PROG)	5,602	10.7
	C. E. Sheplin (SOC)	4,079	7.8
15	William C. Mooney (R)	21,145	45.8
	George White (D)	21,046	45.5
16	Roscoe C. McCulloch (R)	28,609	52.5
	Ed J. Meyer (D)	20,658	37.9
	G. A. Kohr (SOC)	3,933	7.2
17	William A. Ashbrook (D)	29,504	56.3
	Walter A. Irvine (R)	21,375	40.8
18	David A. Hollingsworth (R)	23,650	45.9
	William B. Francis (D)	22,476	43.7
	Fred White (SOC)	2,936	5.7
19	John G. Cooper (R)	24,471	52.4
	William S. King (D)	16,897	36.2

OHIO

Candidates	Votes	%
G. L. Arner (SOC)	2,971	6.4
W. S. Harris (PROG)	2,363	5.1
20 William Gordon (D)	23,541	55.7
James E. Mathews (R)	14,215	33.6
C. E. Ruthenberg (SOC)	2,418	5.7
Frank G. Carpenter (PROG)	2,127	5.0
21 Robert Crosser (D)	18,962	61.1
Harry L. Vail (R)	9,039	29.1
Tom Clifford (SOC)	1,979	6.4
22 Henry I. Emerson (R)	17,166	39.1
Roy A. Tuttle (D)	16,093	36.7
J.R. McQuigg (PROG)	9,023	20.6

OKLAHOMA

Candidates	Votes	%
1 James S. Davenport (D)	15,489	46.4
Gill (R)	14,251	42.7
Lafayette (SOC)	3,318	9.9
2 William W. Hastings (D)	12,719	49.1
Cook (R)	8,569	33.1
Crain (SOC)	4,420	17.1
3 Charles D. Carter (D)	17,474	50.3
Norman (SOC)	10,588	30.5
Elting (R)	6,479	18.7
4 William H. Murray (D)	13,758	42.2
Flynn (R)	9,395	28.8
Hughes (SOC)	9,198	28.2
5 Joseph B. Thompson (D)	14,040	47.6
Pope (R)	9,286	31.5
Lurry (SOC)	5,391	18.3
6 Scott Ferris (D)	14,578	48.1
Campbell (R)	8,291	27.4
J. T. Cumbie (SOC)	6,671	22.0
7 James V. McClintic (D)	11,861	43.3
Stallard (SOC)	9,021	32.9
Mills (R)	6,179	22.6
8 Dick T. Morgan (R)	13,294	41.7
Johnston (D)	12,529	39.3
Green (SOC)	4,231	13.3
Alexander (PROG)	1,645	5.2

OREGON

Candidates	Votes	%
1 Willis C. Hawley (R)	51,295	46.4
Frederick Holister (D)	32,639	29.5
Curtis P. Coe (P)	16,465	14.9
W. S. Richards (SOC)	7,415	6.7
2 Nicholas J. Sinnott (R & PROG)	24,176	47.5
George L. Cleaver (P)	15,685	30.8
Sam Evans (D)	11,013	21.7
3 Clifton N. McArthur (R)	26,636	35.6
A. F. Flegel (D)	23,697	31.6
A. W. Lafferty (I-PO)	16,649	22.2
Arthur L. Moulton (PROG-P)	5,770	7.7

PENNSYLVANIA

Candidates	Votes	%
1 William S. Vare (R, RO PROG)	31,800	77.6
Lawrence E. McCrossin (D)	4,220	10.3
John Burt (WASH, P)	4,491	11.0
2 George S. Graham (R, KEY)	24,371	77.4
Patrick P. Conway (D, WASH)	6,582	20.9
3 J. Hampton Moore (R, KEY)	24,468	79.2
John H. Fow (D)	3,303	10.7
Abraham L. Weinstock (WASH, RO PROG)	2,642	8.6
4 George W. Edmonds (R, WASH)	28,460	83.2
Patrick H. Lynch (D)	4,853	14.2
5 Peter E. Costello (R)	26,352	60.8
Michael Donohoe (D, WASH)	15,113	34.9
6 George P. Darrow (R, B MOOSE)	38,068	56.1
Frederick S. Drake (WASH)	13,884	20.4

Candidates	Votes	%
J. Washington Logue (D, KEY)	14,656	21.6
7 Thomas S. Butler (R)	23,239	63.6
Norris B. Slack (D)	8,340	22.8
Arthur H. Tomlinson (WASH)	4,096	11.2
8 Henry W. Watson (R)	22,691	50.9
Harry E. Grim (D)	15,706	35.2
Harold G. Knight (WASH)	4,941	11.1
9 William W. Griest (R)	17,410	61.0
John N. Hetrick (D, WASH)	10,439	36.6
10 John R. Farr (R, WASH)	16,474	54.7
John J. Loftus (D, KEY)	12,044	40.0
11 John J. Casey (D, B MOOSE)	22,762	57.1
Lewis P. Kniffen (R, WASH)	16,011	40.2
12 Robert D. Heaton (R)	17,213	53.7
Robert E. Lee (D)	12,416	38.7
William W. Thorn (WASH)	1,619	5.1
13 Arthur Granville Dewalt (D)	19,887	45.5
John K. Stauffer (R)	14,850	33.9
John L. Stewart (WASH)	4,516	10.3
L. Birch Wilson Jr. (SOC)	4,138	9.5
14 Louis T. McFadden (R)	9,153	40.3
Fred W. Dean (D)	6,219	27.4
Dana R. Stephens (WASH)	6,196	27.3
15 Edgar R. Kiess (R)	11,525	41.8
John J. Reardon (D)	8,118	29.5
Montfort T. Stokes (WASH, P)	6,447	23.4
Peter J. Homler (SOC)	1,472	5.3
16 John V. Lesher (D)	12,982	44.3
Charles H. Robbins (R)	9,129	31.2
W. W. Heffner (WASH)	4,719	16.1
17 Benjamin K. Focht (R)	14,176	41.4
Frank L. Dershem (D)	12,597	36.8
Charles L. Johnson (WASH)	5,894	17.2
18 Aaron S. Kreider (R)	23,789	52.3
David L. Kaufman (D)	13,159	28.9
John H. Kreider (WASH)	6,378	14.0
19 Warren Worth Bailey (D, UN)	14,993	35.8
Jesse L. Hartman (R)	14,503	34.6
Lynn A. Brua (WASH, P)	10,246	24.5
20 C. William Beales (R)	14,225	45.3
Andrew R. Brodbeck (D)	13,483	43.0
Robert C. Bair (WASH)	2,419	7.7
21 Charles H. Rowland (R)	10,403	39.3
William E. Tobias (D)	9,339	35.3
Guy B. Mayo (WASH)	4,574	17.3
22 Abraham L. Keister (R, PERS LIB)	15,214	43.7
James B. Hammond (D, WASH)	14,802	42.5
Joseph B. Slack (SOC)	2,867	8.2
A. P. Hutchison (P)	1,961	5.6
23 Robert F. Hopwood (R)	14,308	44.7
Wooda N. Carr (D)	11,801	36.9
Charles F. Hood (WASH)	3,565	11.1
24 William M. Brown (R)	14,694*	41.0
Henry W. Temple (WASH)	10,771	30.1
Samuel A. Barnum (D)	7,051	19.7
H. R. Norman (SOC)	2,370	6.6
25 Michael Liebel Jr. (D)	10,025	36.6
Milton W. Shreve (R)	9,222	33.6
Frank C. Lockwood (WASH, P)	6,449	23.5
F. J. Weaver (SOC)	1,735	6.3
26 Henry J. Steele (D, PERS LIB)	15,118	51.3
John D. Hoffman (R)	8,306	28.2
Edward Hart (WASH)	4,671	15.8
27 S. Taylor North (R)	10,560	36.5
R. M. Matson (D)	8,822	30.5
Charles P. Wolfe (WASH)	6,744	23.3
Samuel Dible (P)	1,673	5.8
28 S. H. Miller (R)	9,379	30.8
William McIntyre (D)	8,043	26.4
Willis J. Hulings (WASH)	6,825	22.4

Candidates	Votes	%
William P. F. Ferguson (P)	4,420	14.5
William McKay (SOC)	1,806	5.9
29 Stephen Geyer Porter (R, WASH)	20,543	76.1
John M. Henry (D)	3,972	14.7
Henry Peter (SOC)	1,879	7.0
30 William H. Coleman (R, PERS LIB)	16,620	48.6
M. Clyde Kelly (WASH, D)	15,268	44.9
Andrew Hunter (SOC)	2,232	6.5
31 John M. Morin (R, D)	17,659	78.2
William A. Prosser (SOC, P)	4,333	19.2
32 Andrew J. Barchfeld (R, PERS LIB)	15,109	47.0
W. McClintock (WASH, RO PROG)	7,938	24.7
Guy E. Campbell (D)	6,626	20.6
John W. Slayton (SOC)	2,464	7.7
AL Thomas S. Crago (R, PERS LIB)	514,270✓	
John R. K. Scott (R, PERS LIB)	513,676✓	
Mahlon M. Garland (R, PERS LIB)	507,626✓	
Daniel F. Lafean (R, PERS LIB)	501,804✓	
Robert S. Bright (D)	281,154	
Arthur B. Clark (D)	272,829	
Martin Jennings Caton (D)	265,474	
Charles N. Crosby (D)	263,280	
Lex N. Mitchell (WASH, B MOOSE)	193,106	
Arthur R. Rupley (WASH, B MOOSE)	185,553	
Anderson H. Walters (WASH, B MOOSE)	185,028	
Harry Watson (WASH, B MOOSE)	180,744	
Edward W. Hayden (SOC)	43,932	
W. S. Greely King (SOC)	43,188	
Dennis O'Brien Coughlin (SOC)	43,148	
Charles Sehl (SOC)	42,048	
George Hart (P)	27,561	
James J. Patton (P)	27,038	
S. Harper Smith (P)	26,075	
B. R. Pike (P)	24,709	
Joseph B. Holtz (KEY)	1,462	
Howard S. Welker (KEY)	1,387	
Albert W. Binz (KEY)	1,343	
A. M. Fisher (INDL)	1,124	
John Lipsett (KEY)	1,080	
James Erwin (INDL)	759	
H. G. Meinel (INDL)	558	

RHODE ISLAND

Candidates	Votes	%
1 George F. O'Shaunessy (D)	12,983	49.8
Burchard (R)	12,080	46.3
2 Walter R. Stiness (R)	13,072	49.0
Gerry (D)	12,097	45.4
3 Ambrose Kennedy (R)	13,849	55.3
Haven (D)	10,110	40.4

SOUTH CAROLINA

Candidates	Votes	%
1 Richard S. Whaley (D)	3,018	98.5
2 James F. Byrnes (D)	4,688	100.0
3 Wyatt Aiken (D)	4,521	100.0
4 Joseph T. Johnson (D)	6,175	99.5
5 David E. Finley (D)	5,180	100.0
6 J. Willard Ragsdale (D)	4,263	100.0
7 Asbury F. Lever (D)	5,231	95.2

SOUTH DAKOTA

Candidates	Votes	%
1 Charles H. Dillon (R)	22,058	57.9
Theodore Bailey (D)	13,678	35.9

SOUTH DAKOTA

	Candidates	Votes	%
2	Royal C. Johnson (R)	20,054	57.9
	John M. King (D)	11,810	34.1
3	Harry L. Gandy (D)	12,454	51.8
	William G. Rice (R)	10,732	44.6

TENNESSEE

		Votes	%
1	Sam R. Sells (R)	15,959	61.3
	James B. Cox (PROG)	7,753	29.8
	Cy H. Lyle (D)	2,337	9.0
2	Richard W. Austin (R)	14,870	67.0
	H. H. Hannah (D)	6,949	31.3
3	John A. Moon (D)	19,407	90.2
	G. W. James (R)	2,111	9.8
4	Cordell Hull (D)	19,152	98.2
5	William C. Houston (D)	14,694	71.7
	H. C. Watts (ID)	5,810	28.3
6	Joseph W. Byrns (D)	19,319	94.4
7	Lemuel P. Padgett (D)	18,227	97.3
8	Thetus W. Sims (D)	14,421	54.4
	J. E. Deford (R)	11,930	45.0
9	Finis J. Garrett (D)	15,582	83.2
	R. C. Cochran (R)	3,062	16.4
10	Kenneth D. McKellar (D)	19,160	93.0
	J. O. Davison (SOC)	1,447	7.0

TEXAS

		Votes	%
1	Eugene Black (D)	10,711	87.7
	J. C. Thompson (SOC)	1,498	12.3
2	Martin Dies (D)	11,425	84.0
	A. Lingan (SOC)	2,132	15.7
3	James Young (D)	11,584	75.2
	E. T. Bryant (SOC)	3,818	24.8
4	Sam Rayburn (D)	9,762	85.0
	C. E. Obenchain (SOC)	1,449	12.6
5	Hatton W. Sumners (D)	10,430	94.9
6	Rufus Hardy (D)	7,772	86.4
	W. H. Wilson (R)	1,229	13.7
7	Alexander W. Gregg (D)	7,001	100.0
8	Joe H. Eagle (D)	10,078	84.7
	E. B. Miller (SOC)	1,090	9.2
	S. L. Hain (R)	725	6.1
9	George F. Burgess (D)	11,083	88.5
	B. F. Wright (SOC)	1,169	9.3
10	James P. Buchanan (D)	8,351	100.0
11	Robert L. Henry (D)	6,677	92.9
	Duncan Carrick (R)	484	6.7
12	Oscar Calloway (D)	11,997	85.4
	S. J. Browson (R)	2,043	14.5
13	John H. Stephens (D)	15,680	87.0
	C. T. Griffin (R)	2,335	13.0
14	James L. Slayden (D)	13,896	90.7
	John A. Currie (SOC)	921	6.0
15	John N. Garner (D)	15,678	100.0
16	William R. Smith (D)	15,181	99.9
AL	James H. Davis (D)	173,803✔	
	Atkins Jeff. McLemore (D)	173,177✔	
	Nat B. Hunt (SOC)	24,557	
	Reddin Andrews (SOC)	24,276	

Candidates	Votes	%
Charles A. Warnken (R)	10,538	
E. E. Diggs (R)	10,489	
J. E. Williams (PROG)	1,542	
H. L. McCuiston (PROG)	1,541	

UTAH

		Votes	%
1	Joseph Howell (R)	29,481	49.4
	Larson (D & PROG)	27,440	45.9
2	James H. Mays (D & PROG)	25,617	47.5
	Leatherwood (R)	25,459	47.2
	Kempton (SOC)	2,861	5.3

VERMONT

		Votes	%
1	Frank L. Greene (R)	19,237	62.9
	Daniel E. O'Sullivan (D)	6,817	22.3
	Raymond McFarland (PROG, P)	4,064	13.3
2	Porter H. Dale (R, P)	17,743	57.5
	John Reardon (D)	6,868	22.2
	Fraser Metzger (PROG)	5,481	17.8

VIRGINIA

		Votes	%
1	William A. Jones (D)	4,742	94.3
2	Edward E. Holland (D)	4,039	87.9
	E. B. Everton (SOC)	406	8.8
3	Andrew J. Montague (D)	5,054	95.8
4	Walter A. Watson (D)	2,887	96.2
5	Edward W. Saunders (D)	6,534	65.5
	Charles A. Hermans (R)	2,771	27.8
6	Carter Glass (D)	3,823	90.7
	B. F. Ginther (SOC)	391	9.3
7	James Hay (D)	4,569	87.0
	E. C. Garrison (R)	685	13.0
8	Charles C. Carlin (D)	5,864	75.4
	Joseph L. Crupper (R)	1,753	22.5
9	C. Bascom Slemp (R)	15,321	51.4
	R. Tate Irvine (D)	14,153	47.5
10	Henry D. Flood (D)	7,105	68.4
	George A. Revercomb (R)	3,124	30.1

WASHINGTON

		Votes	%
1	William E. Humphrey (R)	25,320	36.9
	William Hickman Moore (D)	18,336	26.7
	Austin E. Griffith (PROG)	18,134	26.4
	Glenn E. Hoover (SOC)	5,827	8.5
2	Lindley H. Hadley (R)	23,551	35.8
	Earl W. Husted (D)	15,032	22.9
	J. E. Campbell (PROG)	14,394	21.9
	George E. Boomer (SOC)	10,099	15.4
3	Albert Johnson (R)	33,556	42.6
	Charles Drury (D)	21,978	27.9
	S. Warburton (PROG)	11,677	14.8
	Leslie E. Aller (SOC)	8,775	11.1
4	William L. LaFollette (R)	25,541	46.2
	Roscoe M. Drumheller (D)	16,896	30.6

Candidates	Votes	%
M. A. Peacock (PROG)	6,952	12.6
John Storland (SOC)	3,309	6.0
5 Clarence C. Dill (D)	24,410	36.6
Harry Rosenhaupt (R)	20,033	30.0
Thomas Corkery (PROG)	15,509	23.2
J. C. Harkness (SOC)	4,502	6.8

WEST VIRGINIA

		Votes	%
1	Matthew M. Neely (D)	21,115	44.4
	George E. White (R)	20,654	43.5
	M. S. Holt (SOC)	3,054	6.4
2	William G. Brown Jr. (D)	20,666	47.5
	George M. Bowers (R)	19,305	44.4
3	Adam B. Littlepage (D)	21,890	43.4
	S. B. Avis (R)	21,457	42.5
	H. F. Link (SOC)	4,769	9.5
4	Hunter H. Moss Jr. (R)	18,356	48.9
	J. M. Hamilton (D)	17,532	46.7
5	Edward Cooper (R)	27,975	49.4
	George S. Neal (D)	24,839	43.9
AL	Howard Sutherland (R)	110,520	47.0
	Hodges (D)	102,223	43.4
	Kintzer (SOC)	11,944	5.1

WISCONSIN

		Votes	%
1	Henry Allen Cooper (R)	16,547	58.2
	Calvin Stewart (D)	9,911	34.9
2	Michael E. Burke (D)	16,809	52.2
	Edward Voigt (R)	14,071	43.7
3	John M. Nelson (R)	17,511	54.8
	W. F. Pierstorff (D)	13,216	41.4
4	William G. Cary (R)	9,911	36.5
	Winfield Gaylord (SOCIAL D)	9,546	35.1
	Francis A. Cannon (D)	7,490	27.6
5	William H. Stafford (R)	15,620	46.7
	Victor L. Berger (SOCIAL D)	11,674	34.9
	Lawrence McGreal (D)	5,988	17.9
6	Michael K. Reilly (D)	15,115	49.5
	James H. Davidson (R)	13,998	45.9
7	John J. Esch (R)	15,113	63.5
	Virgil W. Cady (D)	7,558	31.8
8	Edward E. Browne (R)	13,863	55.5
	Albert C. Schmidt (D)	9,880	39.6
9	Thomas F. Konop (D)	15,462	51.3
	John W. Reynolds (D)	13,525	44.9
10	James A. Frear (R)	13,377	60.9
	Andrew Sutherland (D)	7,326	33.4
11	Irvine L. Lenroot (R)	15,834	65.3
	John L. Molone (D)	6,746	27.8
	Otto F. Eick (SOCIAL D)	1,580	6.5

WYOMING

		Votes	%
AL	Frank W. Mondell (R)	21,362	51.3
	Douglas A. Preston (D)	17,246	41.5

1915 House Elections

PENNSYLVANIA

Special Election

	Candidates	Votes	%
24	Henry W. Temple (R)	27,307	65.6
	Carl E. Gibson (D)	9,295	22.3
	W. K. Ramsey (SOC)	3,362	8.1

1916 House Elections

ALABAMA

	Candidates	Votes	%
1	Oscar L. Gray (D)	8,538	100.0
2	S. Hubert Dent Jr. (D)	12,524	97.6
3	Henry B. Steagall (D)	11,761	100.0
4	Fred L. Blackmon (D)	8,443	67.6
	J. B. Atkinson (R)	4,055	32.5
5	J. Thomas Heflin (D)	8,908	81.4
	W. D. Harwell (R)	2,039	18.6
6	William B. Oliver (D)	6,620	100.0
7	John L. Burnett (D)	10,894	60.1
	T. H. Davidson (R)	7,231	39.9
8	Edward B. Almon (D)	11,862	85.2
	W. R. Hutchens (R)	1,812	13.0
9	George Huddleston (D)	11,139	86.1
	Francis Latady (R)	1,565	12.1
10	William B. Bankhead (D)	8,091	54.3
	Newman H. Freeman (R)	6,813	45.7

ARIZONA

	Candidates	Votes	%
AL	Carl Hayden (D)	34,377	65.7
	Henry L. Eads (R)	14,907	28.5
	J. R. Barnette (SOC)	3,060	5.9

ARKANSAS

	Candidates	Votes	%
1	Thaddeus H. Caraway (D)	21,440	100.0
2	William A. Oldfield (D)	17,256	73.6
	G. W. Wells (R)	6,205	26.5
3	John N. Tillman (D)	16,438	62.4
	A. J. Russell (R)	9,918	37.6
4	Otis T. Wingo (D)	25,457	100.0
5	Henderson M. Jacoway (D)	19,973	74.2
	G. A. McConnell (R)	6,930	25.8
6	Samuel M. Taylor (D)	25,901	100.0
7	William S. Goodwin (D)	16,823	71.9
	J. G. Brown (R)	6,573	28.1

CALIFORNIA

	Candidates	Votes	%
1	Clarence F. Lea (D)	32,797	48.8
	Edward H. Hart (R)	28,769	42.8
	Mary M. Morgan (SOC)	3,730	5.6
2	John E. Raker (D SOC)	30,042	71.0
	James T. Matlock (R)	12,282	29.0
3	Charles F. Curry (R)	48,193	66.7
	O. W. Kennedy (D)	16,900	23.4
	Ben Cooper (SOC)	4,455	6.2
4	Julius Kahn (R)	51,968	77.2
	J. M. Fernald (D)	10,579	15.7
	A. K. Gifford (SOC)	3,775	5.6
5	John I. Nolan (R-D)	59,333	84.6
	Charles A. Preston (SOC)	6,708	9.6
	Frederick Head (P)	4,046	5.8
6	John A. Elston (R & PROG)	56,520	64.6
	H. Avery Whitney (D)	19,787	22.6
	Luella Twining (SOC)	7,588	8.7
7	Denver S. Church (D)	38,787	51.0
	W. W. Phillips (R)	27,676	36.4
	Harry M. McKee (SOC)	5,492	7.2
	J. F. Butler (P)	4,042	5.3
8	Everis A. Hayes (R-D)	50,659	68.6
	George S. Walker (PROG-P)	17,576	23.8
	Cora Pattleton Wilson (SOC)	5,564	7.5
9	Charles H. Randall (P D-R&PR)	58,826	57.8
	Charles W. Bell (I)	33,270	32.7
	Ralph L. Criswell (SOC)	9,661	9.5
10	Henry Z. Osborne (R)	63,913	49.3
	Rufus V. Bowden (D)	33,225	25.6
	Henry Stanley Benedict (PROG)	14,305	11.0

Candidates	Votes	%
James H. Ryckman (SOC)	9,000	6.9
Henry Clay Needham (P)	8,781	6.8

		Votes	%
11	William Kettner (D)	42,051	44.5
	Robert C. Harbison (R)	33,765	35.7
	James S. Edwards (P)	14,759	15.6

Special Election

		Votes	%
10	Henry Stanley Benedict (PROG)	19,032	56.4
	Joy Clark	7,147	21.2

COLORADO

		Votes	%
1	Benjamin C. Hilliard (D)	30,146	48.5
	William N. Vaile (R)	26,121	42.1
	George J. Kindel (L)	3,306	5.3
2	Charles B. Timberlake (R)	42,665	55.9
	R. E. Jones (D)	29,334	38.4
	J. Edward Johnson (SOC)	3,884	5.1
3	Edward Keating (D)	40,183	53.8
	George E. McClelland (R)	31,137	41.7
4	Edward T. Taylor (D)	30,926	65.8
	Henry J. Baird (R)	13,397	28.5
	Emery D. Cox (SOC)	2,695	5.7

CONNECTICUT

		Votes	%
1	Augustine Lonergan (D)	24,565	49.6
	Oakey (R)	22,876	46.2
2	Richard P. Freeman (R)	20,406	52.7
	Dunn (R)	17,233	44.5
3	John Q. Tilson (R)	20,859	48.5
	Reilly (D)	20,272	47.2
4	Ebenezer J. Hill (R)	25,917	53.8
	Donovan (D)	20,700	43.0
5	James P. Glynn (R)	16,872	49.8
	Kennedy (D)	15,882	46.9

DELAWARE

		Votes	%
AL	Albert F. Polk (D)	24,395	47.6
	Thomas W. Miller (R)	24,202	47.3

FLORIDA

		Votes	%
1	Herbert J. Drane (D)	15,353	82.2
	H. W. Bishop (R)	2,164	11.6
	Frank L. Sullivan (SOC)	1,158	6.2
2	Frank Clark (D)	10,047	79.9
	W. H. Gober (R)	1,367	10.9
	F. P. Coffin (P)	1,156	9.2
3	Walter Kehoe (D)	12,241	83.7
	Peter H. Miller (R)	2,393	16.4
4	William J. Sears (D)	14,748	68.9
	D. T. Gerow (R)	5,071	23.7
	A. N. Jackson (SOC)	1,592	7.4

GEORGIA

		Votes	%
1	James W. Overstreet (D)	9,203	99.9
2	Frank Park (D)	9,462	100.0
3	Charles R. Crisp (D)	8,040	100.0
4	William C. Adamson (D)	9,871	100.0
5	William S. Howard (D)	13,174	88.8
	Moore	1,656	11.2
6	James W. Wise (D)	7,370	100.0
7	Gordon Lee (D)	12,831	77.9
	Walter Akerman	3,382	20.5
8	Samuel J. Tribble (D)	13,891*	99.9
9	Thomas M. Bell (D)	15,369	88.9
	Adams	1,926	11.1
10	Carl Vinson (D)	5,702	100.0
11	John R. Walker (D)	11,826	100.0
12	William W. Larsen (D)	9,816	95.8

IDAHO

	Candidates	Votes	%
AL	Burton L. French (R)	64,648✔	
	Addison T. Smith (R)	63,790✔	
	Marion J. Kerr (D)	55,807	
	John V. Stanley (D)	54,339	
	Albert B. Clark (SOC)	8,079	
	Sam G. Gilleland (SOC)	8,033	

ILLINOIS

		Votes	%
1	Martin B. Madden (R)	20,380	59.1
	William J. Hennessey (D)	13,380	38.8
2	James R. Mann (R)	44,159	63.0
	Philip H. Treacy (D)	22,722	32.4
3	William W. Wilson (R)	35,885	55.7
	Bernard McMahon (D)	25,954	40.3
4	Charles Martin (D)	18,722	58.5
	John Golombiewski (R)	11,793	36.8
5	Adolph J. Sabath (D)	12,884	60.7
	David T. Alexander (R)	6,850	32.3
	Charles Toepper (SOC)	1,500	7.1
6	James McAndrews (D)	39,749	48.5
	Arthur W. Fulton (R)	37,347	45.6
	Charles H. Hair (SOC)	4,586	5.6
7	Niels Juul (R)	47,514	50.9
	Frank Buchanan (D)	37,460	40.1
	Carl D. Thompson (SOC)	8,372	9.0
8	Thomas Gallagher (D)	14,970	63.4
	Frank Sullivan (R)	8,636	36.6
9	Fred A. Britten (R)	20,609	59.2
	Eugene L. McGarry (D)	12,295	35.3
	Andrew Lafin (SOC)	1,891	5.4
10	George Edmund Foss (R)	44,749	59.3
	Samuel C. Herren (D)	22,398	29.7
	Carl Hjalmar Lundquist (I)	4,622	6.1
11	Ira C. Copley (R)	38,418	69.0
	William C. Mooney (D)	15,715	28.2
12	Charles E. Fuller (R)	35,741	66.0
	Walter Panneck (D)	16,033	29.6
13	John C. McKenzie (R)	28,123	68.1
	F. P. Dudley (D)	12,436	30.1
14	William J. Graham (R)	23,099	48.5
	Clyde H. Tavenner (D)	22,591	47.4
15	Edward J. King (R)	28,143	54.5
	Edward P. Allen (D)	21,604	41.9
16	Clifford Ireland (R)	25,091	49.9
	Claude U. Stone (D)	24,073	47.9
17	John A. Sterling (R)	23,956	56.6
	S. A. Rathbun	17,571	41.5
18	Joseph G. Cannon (R)	29,318	54.2
	Armand E. Smith (D)	23,668	43.7
19	William B. McKinley (R)	33,162	52.7
	F. R. Dove (D)	28,870	45.8
20	Henry T. Rainey (D)	24,364	55.6
	Walter B. Sayler (R)	19,019	43.4
21	Loren E. Wheeler (R)	26,367	50.0
	Thomas Rees (D)	23,936	45.4
22	William A. Rodenberg (R)	31,958	50.4
	D. H. Mudge (D)	29,451	46.5
23	Martin D. Foster (D)	28,805	52.9
	Harry C. Ferriman (R)	24,328	44.7
24	Thomas S. Williams (R)	23,768	55.0
	Louis W. Goetzman (D)	18,540	42.9
25	Edward E. Denison (R)	27,905	52.2
	Andrew J. Rendleman (D)	24,034	44.9
AL	Medill McCormick (R)	707,958✔	
	William E. Mason (R)	687,198✔	
	William Elza Williams (D)	546,471	
	Joseph O. Kosture (D)	538,756	
	J. Louis Engdahl (SOC)	49,842	
	Walter Huggins (SOC)	48,842	
	Charles W. Williams (P)	9,569	
	Unidentified Candidate (P)	9,366	
	Frank Hosking (SOC LAB)	1,790	
	John Kowatzrk (SOC LAB)	1,739	

INDIANA

	Candidates	Votes	%
1	George F. Denton (D)	23,278	48.1
	S. Wallace Cook (R)	22,955	47.4
2	Oscar E. Bland (R)	24,764	47.3
	William A. Cullop (D)	23,759	45.4
	Z. M. Garten (SOC)	2,860	5.5
3	William E. Cox (D)	24,738	52.1
	John H. Edwards (R)	21,831	46.0
4	Lincoln Dixon (D)	24,925	51.5
	Mauley D. Wilson (R)	22,730	47.0
5	Everett Sanders (R)	20,977	40.6
	Ralph W. Moss (D)	20,270	39.3
	E. V. Debs (SOC)	8,866	17.2
6	Daniel W. Comstock (R)	23,831	48.6
	Finley H. Gray (D)	22,853	46.6
7	Merrill Moores (R)	40,862	51.8
	Chalmer Schlosser (D)	34,732	44.1
8	Albert H. Vestal (R)	26,135	48.0
	Jacob F. Denny (D)	23,854	43.8
9	Fred S. Purnell (R)	27,712	50.4
	David F. Maish (D)	24,547	44.6
10	William R. Wood (R)	31,895	56.9
	George E. Hershman (D)	23,077	41.1
11	Milton Kraus (R)	25,005	46.3
	George W. Rauch (D)	24,578	45.5
12	Louis William Fairfield (R)	23,863	51.2
	Cyrus Cline (D)	20,603	44.2
13	Harry A. Barnhart (D)	30,537	47.7
	Andrew J. Hickey (R)	30,246	47.2

IOWA

	Candidates	Votes	%
1	Charles A. Kennedy (R)	20,421	58.6
	F. B. Whitaker (D)	14,276	41.0
2	Harry E. Hull (R)	25,548	55.3
	M. F. Cronin (D)	18,591	40.3
3	Burton E. Sweet (R)	31,567	67.0
	James C. Murtagh (D)	14,825	31.4
4	Gilbert N. Haugen (R)	23,416	57.9
	Earl Evans (D)	16,490	40.8
5	James W. Good (R)	27,438	64.1
	Robert Melvin Peet (D)	14,654	34.2
6	C. William Ramseyer (R)	21,757	57.3
	S. Kirkpatrick (D)	14,927	39.3
7	Cassius C. Dowell (R)	25,993	61.7
	H. C. Evans (D)	14,677	34.8
8	Horace M. Towner (R)	24,195	59.0
	H. B. Bracewell (D)	15,940	38.9
9	William R. Green (R)	23,446	55.4
	John C. Pryor (D)	18,743	44.3
10	Frank P. Woods (R)	32,332	63.6
	J. R. Files (D)	17,300	34.1
11	George C. Scott (R)	26,066	49.6
	Thomas J. Steele (D)	25,935	49.4

KANSAS

	Candidates	Votes	%
1	Daniel R. Anthony Jr. (R)	37,705	55.8
	Herbert J. Corwine (D)	23,272	34.4
	Eva Harding (I)	5,144	7.6
2	Edward C. Little (R)	42,780	50.4
	Joseph Taggart (D)	38,815	45.7
3	Phillip P. Campbell (R)	40,272	47.8
	William S. Hyatt (D)	32,837	39.0
	T. P. Laughlin (SOC)	9,177	10.9
4	Dudley Doolittle (D)	29,370	51.5
	Clyde W. Miller (R)	26,831	47.0
5	Guy T. Helvering (D)	32,198	50.4
	Charles M. Harger (R)	29,861	46.8
6	John R. Connelly (D)	40,005	56.4
	Otis L. Benton (R)	28,332	40.0
7	Jouett Shouse (D)	38,099	43.9
	J. S. Simmons (R)	31,621	36.4
	Howard E. Kershner (P)	13,566	15.6
8	William A. Ayres (D)	26,993	51.0
	Thomas C. Wilson (R)	24,220	45.8

KENTUCKY

	Candidates	Votes	%
1	Alben W. Barkley (D)	30,029	63.7
	Thomas (R)	16,128	34.2
2	David H. Kincheloe (D)	24,138	54.2
	Fowler (R)	19,953	44.8
3	Robert Y. Thomas Jr. (D)	22,194	49.6
	Taylor (R)	22,180	49.6
4	Ben Johnson (D)	25,012	52.7
	Haswell (R)	21,958	46.3
5	J. Swagar Sherley (D)	29,204	50.1
	Owens (R)	27,861	47.8
6	Arthur B. Rouse (D)	27,001	62.5
	Sheppard (R)	14,959	34.7
7	James C. Cantrill (D)	28,734	59.8
	Manby (R)	19,304	40.2
8	Harvey Helm (D)	21,187	53.7
	Neat (R)	18,036	45.7
9	William J. Fields (D)	32,957	54.3
	Pennington (R)	27,119	44.7
10	John W. Langley (R)	19,113	60.9
	Stanton (D)	11,981	38.2
11	Caleb Powers (R)	33,867	70.0
	Dishman (D)	14,280	29.5

LOUISIANA

	Candidates	Votes	%
1	Albert Estopinal (D)	17,939	100.0
2	H. Garland Dupre (D)	16,328	100.0
3	Whitmell P. Martin (PROG)	6,481	49.0
	Wade O. Martin (D)	6,382	48.3
4	John T. Watkins (D)	8,306	100.0
5	Riley J. Wilson (D)	7,650	97.6
6	Jared Y. Sanders (D)	7,377	100.0
7	Ladislas Lazaro (D)	7,307	94.9
	M. McManus (SOC)	394	5.1
8	James B. Aswell (D)	7,318	94.2
	H. O. Bower (SOC)	449	5.8

MAINE

	Candidates	Votes	%
1	Louis B. Goodall (R)	20,357	54.2
	Stevens (D)	16,807	44.8
2	Wallace H. White Jr. (R)	19,338	50.1
	McGillicuddy (D)	18,791	48.7
3	John A. Peters (R)	23,656	53.5
	Bunker (D)	20,002	45.3
4	Ira G. Hersey (R)	17,647	57.4
	Pierce (D)	12,969	42.2

MARYLAND

	Candidates	Votes	%
1	Jesse D. Price (D)	17,047	48.6
	Robert F. Duer (R)	16,981	48.4
2	Joshua Frederick C. Talbott (D)	24,648	50.3
	William H. Lawrence (R)	20,420	41.7
	John S. Green (P)	3,513	7.2
3	Charles P. Coady (D)	16,546	52.5
	Charles W. Main (R)	13,857	44.0
4	J. Charles Linthicum (D)	19,774	52.5
	J. Frank Fox (R)	17,030	45.2
5	Sydney E. Mudd (R)	17,407	53.9
	Jackson H. Ralston (D)	13,909	43.0
6	Frederick N. Zihlman (R)	19,932	51.1
	Henry Dorsey Etchison (D)	17,214	44.1

MASSACHUSETTS

	Candidates	Votes	%
1	Allen T. Treadway (R)	19,667	60.2
	Timothy C. Collins (D)	11,795	36.1
2	Frederick H. Gillett (R)	20,064	60.3
	Theobald M. Connor (D)	11,895	35.7
3	Calvin D. Paige (R)	19,371	66.2
	Michael A. Scanlon (D)	9,905	33.8
4	Samuel E. Winslow (R)	17,647	55.6
	John H. Hunt (D)	13,315	41.9

	Candidates	Votes	%
5	John Jacob Rogers (R)	20,345	64.7
	Roger Sherman Hoar (D)	11,097	35.3
6	Augustus P. Gardner (R)	21,916	67.3
	Arthur Howard (D)	8,578	26.4
	Charles W. Fitzgerald (SOC)	2,049	6.3
7	Michael F. Phelan (D)	16,597	51.2
	Charles Neal Barney (R)	14,350	44.3
8	Frederick W. Dallinger (R)	21,178	59.7
	Frederick S. Deitrick (D)	14,308	40.3
9	Alvan T. Fuller (I)	17,079	50.5
	Ernest W. Roberts (R)	16,765	49.5
10	Peter F. Tague (D)	13,646	78.7
	James L. Hourihan (R)	3,684	21.3
11	George Holden Tinkham (R)	18,424	60.1
	Francis J. Horgan (D)	12,244	39.9
12	James A. Gallivan (D)	22,105	67.6
	Charles H. S. Robinson (R)	10,613	32.4
13	William H. Carter (R)	25,527	66.3
	William H. Murphy (D)	12,985	33.7
14	Richard Olney (D)	21,707	53.2
	Henry L. Kincaide (R)	17,702	43.4
15	William S. Greene (R)	15,788	63.2
	Arthur J. B. Cartier (D)	9,203	36.8
16	Joseph Walsh (R)	18,505	68.8
	Ralph W. Crosby (D)	8,392	31.2

MICHIGAN

	Candidates	Votes	%
1	Frank E. Doremus (D)	29,571	51.2
	Hugh Shepherd (R)	26,679	46.2
2	Mark R. Bacon (R)	27,182‡	49.0
	Samuel W. Beakes (D)	27,133	48.9
3	John M. C. Smith (R)	24,897	49.4
	James W. Marsh (D)	23,117	45.8
4	Edward L. Hamilton (R)	26,764	55.5
	Roy J. Wade (D)	20,445	42.4
5	Carl E. Mapes (R)	24,258	51.1
	Peter J. Danhof (D)	21,639	45.6
6	Patrick H. Kelley (R)	38,110	54.0
	William S. Kellogg (D)	30,664	43.5
7	Louis C. Cramton (R)	30,101	66.9
	Varnum J. Bowers (D)	14,020	31.1
8	Joseph W. Fordney (R)	28,288	53.6
	William A. Seegmiller (D)	23,692	44.9
9	James C. McLaughlin (R)	24,624	58.3
	Curtis D. Alway (D)	15,726	37.3
10	Gilbert A. Currie (R)	24,240	58.1
	Henry C. Haller (D)	16,056	38.5
11	Frank D. Scott (R)	24,840	60.6
	John J. Reycraft (D)	14,499	35.4
12	W. Frank James (R)	22,998	64.1
	William J. Macdonald (D & PROG)	12,882	35.9
13	Charles A. Nichols (R)	32,317	59.3
	Eugene P. Berry (D)	20,921	38.4

MINNESOTA

	Candidates	Votes	%
1	Sydney Anderson (R)	25,278	65.5
	Lamberton (D)	13,290	34.5
2	Franklin F. Ellsworth (R)	29,392	100.0
3	Charles R. Davis (R)	25,527	71.1
	Kelly Jr. (D)	10,354	28.9
4	Carl C. Van Dyke (D)	23,516	61.2
	Reese (R)	11,737	30.6
5	Ernest Lundeen (R)	19,131	42.4
	Bowler (D)	11,849	26.3
	Latimer (SOC)	7,526	16.7
	Markve (P)	6,599	14.6
6	Harold Knutson (R)	20,889	56.8
	Donohue (D)	13,107	35.7
	Knutsen (P)	2,766	7.5
7	Andrew J. Volstead (R)	21,300	53.6
	Lobeck (P)	11,961	30.1
	Townsend (D)	6,518	16.4

887

MINNESOTA

Candidates	Votes	%
8 Clarence B. Miller (R)	17,758	51.6
Anderson (SOC)	9,034	26.3
Wheeler (P)	7,621	22.2
9 Halvor Steenerson (R)	25,429	66.8
Swanson (D)	8,313	21.8
Thompson (SOC)	4,347	11.4
10 Thomas D. Schall (PROG)	19,696	45.0
Jepson (R)	13,170	30.1
Cronin (D)	7,148	16.3
Soltis (SOC)	3,782	8.6

MISSISSIPPI

Candidates	Votes	%
1 Ezekiel S. Candler Jr. (D)	✔	
2 Hubert D. Stephens (D)	✔	
3 Benjamin G. Humphreys (D)	✔	
4 Thomas U. Sisson (D)	✔	
5 William A. Venable (D)	✔	
6 Pat Harrison (D)	✔	
7 Percy E. Quin (D)	✔	
8 James W. Collier (D)	✔	

MISSOURI

Candidates	Votes	%
1 Milton A. Romjue (D)	22,840	54.4
Brown (R)	18,566	44.2
2 William W. Rucker (D)	24,964	57.7
Pickett (R)	17,936	41.5
3 Joshua W. Alexander (D)	21,658	54.2
Moulton (R)	17,769	44.5
4 Charles F. Booher (D)	22,155	53.6
Geiger (R)	18,632	45.1
5 William P. Borland (D)	46,065	58.7
Kimbrell (R)	31,292	39.9
6 Clement C. Dickinson (D)	18,869	54.2
Crawford (R)	15,948	45.8
7 Courtney W. Hamlin (D)	26,766	50.5
Houston (R)	25,953	48.9
8 Dorsey W. Shackleford (D)	17,599	52.0
Gentry (R)	16,255	48.0
9 James Beauchamp Clark (D)	23,755	51.9
Cole (R)	21,704	47.5
10 Jacob E. Meeker (R)	63,663	57.7
Brennan (D)	43,271	39.3
11 William L. Igoe (D)	23,928	56.8
Barto (R)	17,434	41.4
12 Leonidas C. Dyer (R)	16,345	55.9
Gill (D)	12,465	42.6
13 Walter L. Hensley (D)	17,850	49.7
Rhodes (R)	17,537	48.8
14 Joseph J. Russell (D)	30,889	49.3
Hill (R)	29,727	47.4
15 Perl D. Decker (D)	26,240	49.8
Manlove (R)	24,013	45.6
16 Thomas L. Rubey (D)	17,303	51.0
Harrison (R)	16,058	47.3

MONTANA

Candidates	Votes	%
AL John M. Evans (D)	84,499 ✔	
Jeanette Rankin (R)	76,932 ✔	
Harry B. Mitchell (D)	70,578	
George W. Farr (R)	66,974	
John H. McGuffey (SOC)	9,002	
Albert F. Meissener (SOC)	8,479	

NEBRASKA

Candidates	Votes	%
1 C. Frank Reavis (R & PROG)	21,021	54.5
John A. Maguire (D & PPI)	16,894	43.8
2 Charles O. Lobeck (D & PPI)	25,617	55.6
Benjamin S. Baker (R)	17,578	38.1
G. C. Porter (SOC)	2,922	6.3

Candidates	Votes	%
3 Daniel V. Stephens (D & PPI)	28,055	51.6
William P. Warner (R & PROG)	25,541	47.0
4 Charles H. Sloan (R & PROG)	24,054	55.3
William L. Stark (D & PPI)	18,798	43.2
5 Ashton C. Shallenberger (D PPI&PR)	22,686	54.0
Silas R. Barton (R)	18,293	43.5
6 Moses P. Kinkaid (R & PROG)	33,559	57.4
Ed B. McDermott (D & PPI)	22,317	38.1

NEVADA

Candidates	Votes	%
AL Edwin E. Roberts (R)	14,106	43.6
Edwin E. Caine (D)	13,100	40.5
M. J. Scanlan (SOC)	5,125	15.9

NEW HAMPSHIRE

Candidates	Votes	%
1 Cyrus A. Sulloway (R)	21,826	51.5
Woodbury (D)	19,806	46.8
2 Edward H. Wason (R)	22,296	51.7
Stevens (D)	20,145	46.7

NEW JERSEY

Candidates	Votes	%
1 William J. Browning (R)	26,589	58.8
Cattell (D)	15,329	33.9
2 Isaac Bacharach (R)	24,865	59.7
Myers (D)	14,220	34.2
3 Thomas J. Scully (D)	21,896	48.6
Carson (R)	21,694	48.1
4 Elijah C. Hutchinson (R)	18,131	50.0
Beekman (D)	16,926	46.6
5 John H. Capstick (R)	20,951	51.8
Tuttle Jr. (D)	17,176	42.5
6 John R. Ramsey (R)	21,464	50.8
Heath (D)	18,770	44.4
7 Dow H. Drukker (R)	15,931	53.0
Beardmore (D)	7,980	26.6
Kershot (SOC)	3,326	11.1
Schweikert (NP)	2,617	8.7
8 Edward W. Gray (R)	18,663	52.7
Kinkead (D)	15,395	43.5
9 Richard W. Parker (R)	14,641	47.9
Matthews (D)	13,625	44.6
Wherett (SOC)	1,923	6.3
10 Frederick R. Lehlbach (R)	21,822	60.7
Flanagan (D)	12,341	34.3
11 John J. Eagan (D)	15,769	59.2
Brennan (R)	9,049	34.0
12 James A. Hamill (D)	17,365	57.0
Dear (R)	12,058	39.6

NEW MEXICO

Candidates	Votes	%
AL William B. Walton (D)	32,731	49.0
B. C. Hernandez (R)	32,056	48.0

NEW YORK

Candidates	Votes	%
1 Frederick C. Hicks (R IL&NPR)	29,041	63.2
Lathrop Brown (D & AM)	16,302	35.5
2 Charles Pope Caldwell (D IL)	24,110	51.8
Theron H. Burden (R AM)	19,504	41.9
Benjamin Katz (SOC)	2,611	5.6
3 Joseph V. Flynn (D & IL)	11,670	49.3
Jared J. Chambers (R NPR AM)	10,381	43.9
William A. Ross (SOC)	1,552	6.6

Candidates	Votes	%
4 Harry Howard Dale (D & IL)	8,861	48.2
Michael Stein (R NPR AM)	7,044	38.3
Richard Haffner (SOC)	2,451	13.3
5 James P. Maher (D & IL)	12,658	49.9
Charles W. Philipbar (R NPR AM)	11,264	44.4
Hans A. Hansen (SOC)	1,357	5.4
6 Frederick W. Rowe (R NPR)	29,107	60.7
Charles I. Stengle (D & IL)	17,436	36.4
7 John J. Fitzgerald (D IL NPR)	15,454	63.5
Ralph Waldo Bowman (R)	8,330	34.2
8 Daniel J. Griffin (D IL NPR)	22,850	60.7
Wilmot L. Morehouse (R)	13,387	35.6
9 Oscar W. Swift (R & P)	25,701	57.0
Herman H. Torborg (DIL A NP)	16,575	36.8
Ludwig Lore (SOC)	2,815	6.2
10 Reuben L. Haskell (R IL&NPR)	11,057	45.0
Frank Wasserman (D & AM)	8,853	36.1
William M. Feigenbaum (SOC)	4,567	18.6
11 Daniel J. Riordan (D IL)	13,047	56.2
Montague Lessler (R NPR)	9,535	41.1
12 Meyer London (SOC)	6,103	47.4
Leon Sanders (D IL)	5,763	44.8
Louis M. Block (R)	968	7.5
13 Christopher D. Sullivan (D & IL)	5,114	48.0
Frank Dostal (R NPR AM)	3,886	36.5
Hilda G. Claessens (SOC)	1,644	15.4
14 Fiorello H. LaGuardia (R NPR AM)	7,272	43.3
Michael F. Farley (D & IL)	6,915	41.2
William I. Sockheim (SOC)	2,536	15.1
15 Michael F. Conry (D & IL)	13,362*	59.9
William Henkel Jr. (R)	7,996	35.8
16 Peter J. Dooling (D & IL)	12,115	51.6
Walbridge S. Taft (R NPR)	10,761	45.9
17 John F. Carew (D & IL)	11,213	51.2
Lindell T. Bates (R NPR)	9,764	44.6
18 George B. Francis (R IL&NPR)	12,196	46.1
Thomas G. Patten (D)	11,826	44.7
Irving Ottenberg (SOC)	2,407	9.1
19 Walter M. Chandler (R IL&NPR)	19,922	54.8
Michael Schaap (D)	14,817	40.8
20 Isaac Siegel (R IL&NPR)	4,542	36.0
Morris Hillquit (SOC)	4,129	32.7
Bernard R. Rosenblatt (D)	3,907	31.0
21 Murray Hulbert (D & IL)	14,107	53.1
Martin Ansorge (R NPR)	10,953	41.3
Alexander Braunstein (SOC)	1,434	5.4
22 Henry Bruckner (D IL NPR)	21,284	63.5
James A. Francis (R)	9,878	29.5
Max B. Gollin (SOC)	2,244	6.7
23 Daniel C. Oliver (D)	25,535	46.9
William S. Bennett (RIL A NP)	22,856	42.0
J. George Gobsevage (SOC)	5,810	10.7
24 Benjamin L. Fairchild (RIL P NP)	25,713	53.7
Woodson R. Oglesby (D & AM)	18,439	38.5
Mary G. Schonberg (SOC)	3,710	7.8
25 James W. Husted (R)	23,363	59.5
Chester D. Pugsley (D IL NPR)	14,816	37.7
26 Edmund Platt (R IL&NPR)	23,314	54.2
Rosslyn M. Cox (D)	18,825	43.8
27 Charles B. Ward (RIL A NP)	24,634	56.4
James O. Woodward (D)	17,674	40.5
28 Rollin B. Sanford (R NPR)	27,722	55.5
Michael F. Collins (D IL)	21,436	42.9

NEW YORK

Candidates	Votes	%
29 James S. Parker (R NPR)	31,888	89.2
Charles E. Robbins (P)	2,134	6.0
30 George R. Lunn (DIL ANPI)	19,818	47.1
Henry S. Deforest (R)	19,199	45.6
Herbert M. Merrill (SOC)	2,126	5.1
31 Bertrand H. Snell (R)	24,938	67.2
Louis F. Roberts (D)	10,934	29.5
32 Luther W. Mott (R IL&NPR)	28,744	62.7
Otto Pfaff (D)	14,323	31.2
33 Homer P. Snyder (R NPR AM)	25,299	55.6
Charles A. Talcott (D)	18,944	41.6
34 George W. Fairchild (R IL&NPR)	27,075	58.7
Cortland A. Wilber (D)	15,895	34.5
Levi Hoag (P)	2,537	5.5
35 Walter W. Magee (R IL&NPR)	31,429	60.9
Arlington H. Mallery (D)	16,059	31.1
36 Norman J. Gould (R NPR)	28,325	62.3
Hiram G. Hotchkiss (D)	15,293	33.6
37 Harry H. Pratt (R IL&NPR)	23,029	49.9
Frederick W. Palmer (D & AM)	20,291	44.0
38 Thomas B. Dunn (R)	29,894	65.1
Jacob Gerling (D)	13,867	30.2
39 Archie D. Sanders (R)	28,393	65.1
David A. White (D)	13,424	30.8
40 S. Wallace Dempsey (R)	27,652	61.9
Andrew B. Gilfillan (D NPR)	15,011	33.6
41 Charles B. Smith (D & AM)	21,265	56.2
William H. Crosby (R P NPR)	15,508	41.0
42 William F. Waldow (R NPR)	16,623	51.0
Daniel A. Driscoll (D)	15,411	47.3
43 Charles M. Hamilton (R NPR)	27,186	64.7
A. F. French (D)	11,414	27.2

NORTH CAROLINA

Candidates	Votes	%
1 John H. Small (D)	13,211	72.2
Leslie E. Jones (R)	5,098	27.8
2 Claude Kitchin (D)	13,255	86.9
W. O. Dixon (R)	1,999	13.1
3 George E. Hood (D)	12,269	58.0
George E. Butler (R)	8,889	42.0
4 Edward W. Pou (D)	15,305	64.3
Joseph J. Jenkins (R)	8,483	35.7
5 Charles M. Stedman (D)	23,932	52.5
Gilliam Grissom (R)	21,429	47.0
6 Hannibal L. Godwin (D)	13,337	63.9
Alex L. McCaskill (R)	7,521	36.1
7 Leonidas D. Robinson (D)	20,518	54.7
Presley E. Brown (R)	17,021	45.3
8 Robert L. Doughton (D)	17,249	52.8
H. Sinclair Williams (R)	15,411	47.2
9 Edwin Y. Webb (D)	18,855	53.5
Charles E. Greene (R)	16,381	46.5
10 Zebulon Weaver (D)	18,023‡	50.0
James J. Britt (R)	18,014	50.0

NORTH DAKOTA

Candidates	Votes	%
1 Henry T. Helgesen (R)	20,709	59.9
George A. Bangs (D)	13,236	38.3
2 George M. Young (R)	22,227	71.7
Hugh McDonald (D)	7,638	24.6
3 Patrick D. Norton (R)	20,393	65.2
Charles Simon (D)	8,293	26.5
Anton Klemmens (SOC)	2,586	8.3

OHIO

Candidates	Votes	%
1 Nicholas Longworth (R)	33,903	56.7
Edward H. Brink (D)	24,290	40.6
2 Victor Heintz (R)	29,612	49.4
Stanley E. Bowdle (D)	28,156	47.0
3 Warren Gard (D)	37,982	53.3
Charles W. Dustin (R)	28,571	40.1
Jeremiah F. Mincker (SOC)	4,699	6.6
4 Benjamin F. Welty (D)	29,486	53.7
J. E. Russell (R)	25,378	46.3
5 John S. Snook (D)	22,852	52.8
Nelson E. Matthews (R)	20,424	47.2
6 Charles C. Kearns (R)	21,315	49.6
A. G. Turnipseed (D)	20,811	48.5
7 Simeon D. Fess (R)	39,975	94.8
8 John A. Key (D)	25,164	53.9
John H. Clark (R)	21,525	46.1
9 Isaac R. Sherwood (D)	31,921	58.2
Frank L. Mulholland (R)	19,882	36.2
Thomas C. Devine (SOC)	3,091	5.6
10 Robert M. Switzer (R)	21,185	58.0
Charles W. Haslett (D)	15,375	42.1
11 Horatio C. Claypool (D)	20,144	50.5
Edwin D. Ricketts (R)	19,022	47.7
12 Clement L. Brumbaugh (D)	31,362	52.8
Hugh Huntington (R)	26,415	44.5
13 Arthur W. Overmeyer (D)	26,882	54.4
Franklin P. Riegle (R)	21,523	43.6
14 Ellsworth R. Bathrick (D)	32,301	53.4
S. H. Williams (R)	26,010	43.0
15 George White (D)	23,221	48.8
W. C. Mooney (R)	22,934	48.2
16 Roscoe C. McCulloch (R)	31,945	56.2
John J. Whitacre (D)	24,948	43.9
17 William A. Ashbrook (D)	31,749	56.2
E. Lee Porterfield (R)	23,705	42.0
18 David A. Hollingsworth (R)	26,991	49.8
William B. Francis (D)	24,538	45.3
19 John G. Cooper (R)	26,983	55.3
William S. King (D)	21,828	44.7
20 William Gordon (D)	26,950	58.2
Eugene Quigley (R)	17,235	37.2
21 Robert Crosser (D)	22,263	65.0
R. S. Taylor (R)	10,138	29.6
Moses Benjamin (SOC)	1,845	5.4
22 Henry I. Emerson (R)	29,270	55.4
Stephen M. Young (D)	23,611	44.7

OKLAHOMA

Candidates	Votes	%
1 Thomas A. Chandler (R)	18,218	45.6
James S. Davenport (D)	17,949	44.9
Reese (SOC)	3,671	9.2
2 William W. Hastings (D)	15,158	52.5
Henry Ward (R)	10,224	35.4
J.A.Lewis (SOC)	3,511	12.2
3 Charles D. Carter (D)	21,182	55.1
Gratton C. McVay (R)	10,386	27.0
H.M.Shelton (SOC)	6,862	17.9
4 Thomas D. McKeown (D)	19,076	48.3
James E. Gresham (R)	12,399	31.4
Allen C. Adams (SOC)	8,026	20.3
5 Joseph B. Thompson (D)	17,828	49.5
George H. Dodson (R)	12,716	35.3
Robert L. Allen (SOC)	5,294	14.7
6 Scott Ferris (D)	18,212	50.8
H.H.Hinkle (R)	10,930	30.5
O.M.Morris (SOC)	6,727	18.8
7 James V. McClintic (D)	17,810	53.8
H.H. Stallard (SOC)	8,140	24.6
T.W. Jones Jr. (R)	7,030	21.2
8 Dick T. Morgan (R)	16,691	45.1
Z.A. Harris (D)	14,816	40.0
Joseph Otii (SOC)	5,158	13.9

OREGON

Candidates	Votes	%
1 Willis C. Hawley (R & PROG)	60,530	56.6
Mark V. Weatherford (D & P)	39,101	36.6
W. S. Richards (SOC)	7,243	6.8
2 Nicholas J. Sinnott (R-D-PROG)	36,059	84.6
James Hickman Barkley (SOC)	6,028	14.1
3 Clifton N. McArthur (R)	35,832	47.6
A. W. Lafferty (I PROG)	27,649	36.7
John A. Jeffrey (D)	9,824	13.0

PENNSYLVANIA

Candidates	Votes	%
1 William S. Vare (R)	33,330	71.7
Lawrence E. McCrossin (D)	12,243	26.3
2 George S. Graham (R, WASH)	23,921	76.0
Thomas E. Shea (D)	7,117	22.6
3 J. Hampton Moore (R, KEY)	23,753	73.6
Joseph Hagerty (D)	7,611	23.6
4 George W. Edmonds (R, WASH)	26,122	68.2
Patrick H. Lynch (D)	11,101	29.0
5 Peter E. Costello (R, PERS LIB)	29,689	59.3
Michael Donohoe (D, KEY)	17,074	34.1
6 George P. Darrow (R, WASH)	56,207	67.6
J. Washington Logue (D, KEY)	25,665	30.9
7 Thomas S. Butler (R)	27,879	63.0
Edward B. Cassatt (D, WASH)	15,102	34.1
8 Henry Winfield Watson (R)	28,852	57.0
Joseph Heacock (D)	20,232	40.0
9 William W. Griest (R)	20,058	64.2
Henry F. Myers (D)	9,506	30.4
10 John R. Farr (R, B MOOSE)	17,823	53.1
Victor Burschel (D)	14,694	43.7
11 T. W. Templeton (R)	24,123	53.2
John J. Casey (D, KEY)	19,185	42.3
12 Robert D. Heaton (R, WASH)	19,172	61.1
Robert E. Lee (D)	11,340	36.1
13 Arthur G. Dewalt (D)	28,296	49.9
Horace W. Schantz (R, WASH)	23,412	41.3
Elwood W. Leffier (SOC)	4,507	7.9
14 Louis T. McFadden (R)	13,638	55.6
John D. Brennan (D)	8,881	36.2
William S. H. Heermans (P)	1,279	5.2
15 Edgar R. Kiess (R, P)	18,478	59.5
Chester H. Ashton (D)	10,766	34.7
P. A. McGowan (SOC)	1,789	5.8
16 John V. Lesher (D)	16,490	51.8
I. Clinton Kline (R, P)	14,154	44.5
17 Benjamin K. Focht (R, P)	18,673	50.4
George A. Harris (D)	17,420	47.0
18 Aaron S. Kreider (R)	24,630	51.6
Harry B. Saussaman (D)	20,343	42.7
19 John M. Rose (R)	22,652	50.4
Warren Worth Bailey (D, UN)	21,007	46.8
20 Andrew R. Brodbeck (D)	18,490	50.2
Samuel K. McCall (R, WASH)	16,327	44.3
21 Charles H. Rowland (R)	14,150	47.6
William E. Tobias (D, P)	13,938	46.9
George Fox (SOC)	1,605	5.4
22 Edward E. Robbins (R, WASH)	19,978	48.4
Silas A. Kline (D)	16,165	39.2
Charles Cunningham (SOC)	2,945	7.1
R. S. Irwin (P)	2,153	5.2
23 Bruce F. Sterling (D)	17,348	48.2
Robert F. Hopwood (R, WASH)	16,453	45.7
24 Henry W. Temple (R, WASH)	22,839	54.3
William J. Mellon (D)	14,679	34.9
W. K. Ramsey (SOC)	2,839	6.8
25 Henry A. Clark (R)	13,441	43.1
Charles N. Crosby (D)	13,068	41.9

PENNSYLVANIA

Candidates	Votes	%
William W. Kincaid (P, WASH)	3,038	9.7
Ralph W. Tillotson (SOC)	1,612	5.2
26 Henry J. Steele (D, SOC)	18,374	53.5
Winfred D. Lewis (R, WASH)	14,857	43.2
27 Nathan L. Strong (R, WASH)	17,702	55.9
Harry C. Golden (D)	10,751	34.0
John B. Desantis (P)	1,793	5.7
28 Orrin D. Bleakley (R)	16,514	47.9
E. H. Beshlin (D)	12,406	36.0
A. R. Rich (P)	3,470	10.1
William E. Ashe (SOC)	2,102	6.1
29 Stephen Geyer Porter (R, WASH)	21,123	67.8
A. M. Thompson (D)	7,518	24.1
Karl C. Jursek (SOC)	1,869	6.0
30 M. Clyde Kelly (D, P)	18,637	47.6
William H. Coleman (R, B MOOSE)	18,386	46.9
William Adams (SOC)	2,147	5.5
31 John M. Morin (R, D)	20,497	87.2
F. C. Brittain (P)	1,504	6.4
James Devlin (SOC)	1,504	6.4
32 Guy E. Campbell (D, B MOOSE)	17,134	45.8
Andrew J. Barcheld (R)	17,088	45.7
William W. Nooning (SOC)	2,422	6.5
AL Thomas S. Crago (R, RO PROG)	668,581✓	
John R. K. Scott (R, RO PROG)	661,930✓	
Mahlon M. Garland (R, PERS LIB)	654,945✓	
Joseph McLaughlin (R)	605,657✓	
Thomas Ross (D)	471,308	
John J. Moore (D)	439,881	
Joseph T. Kinsley (D)	439,846	
Jacob B. Waidelich (D)	427,923	
William A. Prosser (SOC)	46,896	
Elizabeth N. Baer (SOC)	45,441	
John W. Slayton (SOC)	45,330	
Fred Willard Whiteside (SOC)	43,314	
Fred Groff (P)	29,937	
Frank L. Morton (P)	26,483	
B. C. McGrew (P)	26,116	
J. C. Rummel (P)	24,952	
Robert C. Bair (WASH)	24,529	
Arthur G. Graham (WASH)	24,219	
J. C. Buchanan (KEY)	3,703	
Michael Donohoe (KEY)	3,517	
M. J. Lewis (KEY)	3,382	
Robert C. Bair (B MOOSE)	3,356	
Arthur G. Graham (B MOOSE)	3,245	
Oliver Knight (SINGLE T)	931	
Royd E. Morrison (SINGLE T)	833	
Jerome C. Reis (SINGLE T)	769	
Alfred Guerrero (SINGLE T)	729	
Richard Love (INDL)	616	
B. H. Brenner (INDL)	591	
H. G. Meinel (INDL)	458	
G. W. Ohls (INDL)	455	

RHODE ISLAND

	Votes	%
1 George F. O'Shaunessy (D)	15,996	53.9
Dixon (R)	13,099	44.2
2 Walter R. Stiness (R)	15,784	54.9
Mowry (D)	12,207	42.5
3 Ambrose Kennedy (R)	14,376	50.4
McDonald (D)	13,427	47.1

SOUTH CAROLINA

	Votes	%
1 Richard S. Whaley (D)	4,999	95.4
2 James F. Byrnes (D)	7,681	98.5

Candidates	Votes	%
3 Fred H. Dominick (D)	9,447	100.0
4 Samuel J. Nichols (D)	11,312	99.4
5 David E. Finley (D)	8,846*	100.0
6 J. Willard Ragsdale (D)	9,767	99.1
7 Asbury F. Lever (D)	9,817	93.5
I. S. Leevy (R)	683	6.5

SOUTH DAKOTA

	Votes	%
1 Charles H. Dillon (R)	28,674	58.1
Anderson (D)	19,846	40.2
2 Royal C. Johnson (R)	28,366	60.2
Batterton (D)	16,342	34.7
3 Harry L. Gandy (D)	16,581	55.6
Bartine (R)	12,203	41.0

TENNESSEE

	Votes	%
1 Sam R. Sells (R)	23,651	96.9
2 Richard W. Austin (R)	19,835	90.0
Fitsgerald (D)	1,195	5.4
3 John A. Moon (D)	19,018	53.9
Jessie M. Littleton (R)	16,004	45.3
4 Cordell Hull (D)	17,170	60.2
J. F. Benson (R)	11,287	39.6
5 William C. Houston (D)	14,656	86.5
Sid Houston (R)	2,287	13.5
6 Joseph W. Byrns (D)	17,190	83.7
C. E. Tippens (R)	2,919	14.2
7 Lemuel P. Padgett (D)	15,313	63.0
G. A. Yost (R)	8,955	36.8
8 Thetus W. Sims (D)	13,474	50.3
L. M. Rhodes (R)	13,255	49.5
9 Finis J. Garrett (D)	17,826	75.4
W. N. Beasley (R)	5,817	24.6
10 Hubert F. Fisher (D)	14,926	72.8
W. Wilkerson (COLORED)	2,677	13.1
John W. Farley (R)	2,089	10.2

TEXAS

	Votes	%
1 Eugene Black (D)	16,525	83.3
David H. Morris (R)	2,182	11.0
J. C. Thompson (SOC)	1,122	5.7
2 Martin Dies (D)	16,956	86.1
J. B. Truitt (SOC)	1,462	7.4
A. E. Sweatland (R)	1,266	6.4
3 James Young (D)	15,168	88.3
J. L. Scoggin (SOC)	2,014	11.7
4 Sam Rayburn (D)	17,785	83.5
G. J. Barlow (R)	2,043	9.6
W. J. Lennon (SOC)	1,460	6.9
5 Hatton W. Sumners (D)	24,949	88.2
B. F. Crews (R)	2,879	10.2
6 Rufus Hardy (D)	12,046	95.3
7 Alexander W. Gregg (D)	10,921	79.5
Theo F. Heiger (R)	1,541	11.2
8 J. H. Eagle (D)	18,980	82.2
Ira P. Jones (R)	3,276	14.2
9 Joseph J. Mansfield (D)	16,453	76.2
C. M. Hughes (R)	4,149	19.2
10 James P. Buchanan (D)	15,634	86.7
Robert A. Brooks (R)	2,405	13.3
11 Tom Connally (D)	14,695	87.7
John L. Vaughn (R)	1,443	8.6
12 James C. Wilson (D)	20,175	85.7
Henry Zweifel (R)	1,843	7.8
Leland G. Baker (SOC)	1,517	6.5
13 Marion Jones (D)	33,942	85.8
J. L. Vannatto (R)	3,125	7.9
J. A. Pressly (SOC)	2,489	6.3
14 James L. Slayden (D)	22,435	79.4
D. F. Johnson (R)	5,815	20.6
15 John N. Garner (D)	16,906	73.4
H. M. Wingback (R)	5,551	24.1
16 Thomas L. Blanton (D)	30,650	85.2
T. B. Holiday (SOC)	2,826	7.9
C. O. Harris (R)	2,503	7.0

Candidates	Votes	%
AL Atkins Jeff. McLemore (D)	300,302✓	
Daniel E. Garrett (D)	298,966✓	
Charles A. Warnken (R)	46,914	
M. A. Taylor (R)	46,467	
Arch Lingan (SOC)	18,583	
W. D. Simpson (SOC)	18,192	
I. E. Teague (P)	1,525	
E. G. Cook (P)	1,457	

UTAH

	Votes	%
1 Milton H. Welling (D, PROG)	40,035	55.5
Timothy C. Hoyt (R)	29,902	41.5
2 James H. Mays (D, PROG)	39,847	56.9
Charles R. Mabey (R)	27,778	39.7

VERMONT

	Votes	%
1 Frank L. Greene (R)	22,030	71.1
Emmett B. Daley (D)	7,972	25.7
2 Porter H. Dale (R, P)	22,692	72.2
G. Herbert Pape (D)	7,983	25.4

VIRGINIA

	Votes	%
1 William A. Jones (D)	9,772	76.5
William W. Butzner (R)	2,823	22.1
2 Edward E. Holland (D)	10,123	82.4
Luther B. Way (R)	1,939	15.8
3 Andrew Jackson Montague (D)	10,967	93.6
F. E. Maxey (SOC)	751	6.4
4 Walter A. Watson (D)	8,119	90.8
5 Edward W. Saunders (D)	10,614	57.8
Beverly A. Davis (R)	7,601	41.4
6 Carter Glass (D)	9,119	73.6
George W. Wilson (R)	2,920	23.6
7 Thomas W. Harrison (D)	10,052	61.8
John Paul (R)	6,064	37.3
8 Charles C. Carlin (D)	9,168	71.8
Joseph L. Crupper (R)	3,450	27.0
9 C. Bascom Slemp (R)	17,848	51.9
E. Lee Trinkle (D)	16,430	47.8
10 Henry D. Flood (D)	11,282	69.9
C. P. Nair (R)	4,583	28.4

Special Election

	Votes	%
7 Thomas W. Harrison (D)	9,918	61.3
John Paul (R)	6,110	37.8

WASHINGTON

	Votes	%
1 John F. Miller (R)	38,769	50.3
George F. Cotterill (D)	35,718	46.3
2 Lindley H. Hadley (R)	31,655	47.1
Frances C. Axtell (D)	28,075	41.7
R. J. Olinger (SOC)	7,537	11.2
3 Albert Johnson (R)	47,415	57.1
George P. Fishburne (D)	29,949	36.1
W. F. Ferguson (SOC)	5,662	6.8
4 William L. LaFollette (R)	33,980	58.8
Charles W. Masterson (D)	21,189	36.7
5 Clarence C. Dill (D)	37,479	51.5
Tom Corkery (R)	32,298	44.4

WEST VIRGINIA

	Votes	%
1 Matthew M. Neely (D)	22,138	50.7
T. W. Fleming (R)	21,574	49.4
2 George M. Bowers (R)	24,055	50.9
Samuel V. Woods (D)	23,194	49.1
3 Stuart F. Reed (R)	23,442	50.7
Fleming N. Alderson (D)	22,762	49.3
4 Harry C. Woodyard (R)	23,139	50.3
T. A. Null (D)	22,855	49.7

WEST VIRGINIA

Candidates	Votes	%
5 Edward Cooper (R)	25,563	51.7
G. R. C. Wiles (D)	23,857	48.3
6 Adam B. Littlepage (D)	25,963	51.5
M. V. Godbey (R)	24,415	48.5

WISCONSIN

Candidates	Votes	%
1 Henry Allen Cooper (R)	24,851	61.6
Jay W. Page (D)	12,587	31.2
2 Edward Voigt (R)	20,718	51.3
Michael E. Burke (D)	18,546	45.9
3 John M. Nelson (R)	26,785	61.8
M. J. Briggs (D)	15,198	35.1

Candidates	Votes	%
4 William J. Cary (R)	12,361	35.5
Winfield R. Gaylord (SOCIAL D)	11,380	32.7
Anthony Szczerbinski (D)	10,757	30.9
5 William H. Stafford (R)	19,585	45.4
Victor L. Berger (SOCIAL D)	15,936	36.9
Lyman H. Browne (D)	7,420	17.2
6 James H. Davidson (R)	20,317	52.3
Michael K. Reilly (D)	17,080	44.0
7 John Jacob Esch (R)	24,157	68.2
Herman Grotophorst (D)	9,549	27.0
8 Edward E. Browne (R)	23,089	67.5
John Kalmes (D)	10,083	29.5

Candidates	Votes	%
9 David G. Classon (R)	20,614	52.5
Thomas F. Konop (D)	18,078	46.0
10 James A. Frear (R)	23,320	69.6
Andrew J. Sutherland (D)	9,367	28.0
11 Irvine L. Lenroot (R)	22,740	67.4
George C. Cooper (D)	8,726	25.9
Henry M. Parks (SOCIAL D)	2,252	6.7

WYOMING

	Votes	%
AL Frank W. Mondell (R)	24,693	49.0
John D. Clark (D)	24,156	48.0

1917 House Election

PENNSYLVANIA

Special Election

	Votes	%
28 Earl H. Beshlin (D, P)	12,878	47.6
U. G. Lyons (R)	11,100	41.0
Willis J. Hulings (WASH)	1,622	6.0
Richard Crawshaw (SOC)	1,452	5.4

House Candidates Index

For an index of all House candidates listed in this section (pages 701 to 1061), see pages 1180-1273. Instructions for use of the House Candidates Index appear on page 1180.

1918 House Elections

ALABAMA

	Candidates	Votes	%
1	John McDuffie (D)	3,721	100.0
2	S. Hubert Dent Jr. (D)	5,717	100.0
3	Henry B. Steagall (D)	5,868	100.0
4	Fred L. Blackmon (D)	4,266	66.2
	J. A. Bingham (R)	2,183	33.9
5	J. Thomas Heflin (D)	6,254	100.0
6	William B. Oliver (D)	2,741	100.0
7	John L. Burnett (D)	7,221	56.2
	O. D. Street (R)	5,622	43.8
8	Edward B. Almon (D)	5,598	100.0
9	George Huddleston (D)	6,338	85.8
	J. O. Thompson (R)	1,051	14.2
10	William B. Bankhead (D)	5,765	100.0

ARIZONA

		Votes	%
AL	Carl Hayden (D)	26,805	60.4
	Thomas Maddock (R)	16,822	37.9

ARKANSAS

		Votes	%
1	Thaddeus H. Caraway (D)	10,343	100.0
2	William A. Oldfield (D)	10,775	100.0
3	John N. Tillman (D)	14,995	100.0
4	Otis Wingo (D)	12,279	100.0
5	Henderson M. Jacoway (D)	11,045	100.0
6	Samuel M. Taylor (D)	10,444	100.0
7	William S. Goodwin (D)	8,692	100.0

CALIFORNIA

		Votes	%
1	Clarence F. Lea (DR)	42,063	99.7
2	John E. Raker (DR SOC P)	28,249	99.9
3	Charles F. Curry (R-D)	51,690	91.6
	A. K. Gifford (SOC)	4,746	8.4
4	Julius Kahn (R-D-PROG)	38,278	86.6
	William Short (SOC)	5,913	13.4
5	John I. Nolan (R-D)	40,375	87.0
	Thomas F. Feeley (SOC)	6,032	13.0
6	John A. Elston (R-D)	59,082	88.4
	Luella Twining (SOC)	7,721	11.6
7	Henry E. Barbour (R)	33,476	52.1
	Henry Hawson (D)	30,745	47.9
8	Hugh S. Hersman (D)	31,167	53.0
	Everis A. Hayes (R)	27,641	47.0
9	Charles H. Randall (P & D)	38,782	53.0
	Montaville Flowers (R)	31,689	43.3
10	Henry Z. Osborne (R-D-P)	72,773	88.0
	James H. Ryckman (SOC)	9,725	11.8
11	William Kettner (D R&SOC)	45,915	72.2
	Stella B. Irvine (P)	17,642	27.8

COLORADO

		Votes	%
1	William N. Vaile (R)	27,815	54.2
	Stack (D)	16,364	31.9
	Hilliard (I)	6,112	11.9
2	Charles B. Timberlake (R)	41,562	61.5
	Jones (D)	26,044	38.5
3	Guy U. Hardy (R)	31,715	51.0
	Keating (D)	29,075	46.7
4	Edward T. Taylor (D)	22,423	65.7
	Logan (R)	11,695	34.3

CONNECTICUT

		Votes	%
1	Augustine Lonergan (D)	21,169	53.5
	Quigley (R)	16,868	42.6
2	Richard P. Freeman (R)	16,251	53.1
	Fenton (D)	13,467	44.0

	Candidates	Votes	%
3	John Q. Tilson (R)	17,401	50.5
	O'Keefe (D)	15,711	45.6
4	Schuyler Merritt (R)	19,008	53.6
	Peck (D)	15,386	43.4
5	James P. Glynn (R)	13,455	50.1
	Seery (D)	12,640	47.1

DELAWARE

		Votes	%
AL	Caleb R. Layton (R)	21,226	51.4
	Albert F. Polk (D)	19,652	47.6

FLORIDA

		Votes	%
1	Herbert J. Drane (D)	8,446	100.0
2	Frank Clark (D)	6,322	100.0
3	John H. Smithwick (D)	6,644	100.0
4	William J. Sears (D)	10,401	100.0

GEORGIA

		Votes	%
1	James W. Overstreet (D)	4,253	100.0
2	Frank Park (D)	3,953	100.0
3	Charles R. Crisp (D)	3,244	100.0
4	William C. Wright (D)	4,991	100.0
5	William D. Upshaw (D)	5,251	100.0
6	James W. Wise (D)	4,707	100.0
7	Gordon Lee (D)	5,960	82.5
	T. R. Glenn (R)	1,261	17.5
8	Charles H. Brand (D)	5,797	100.0
9	Thomas M. Bell (D)	6,911	81.5
	John M. Johnson (R)	1,570	18.5
10	Carl Vinson (D)	3,440	100.0
11	William C. Lankford (D)	4,959	100.0
12	William W. Larsen (D)	3,808	100.0

IDAHO

		Votes	%
1	Burton L. French (R)	27,084	63.4
	L. I. Purcell (D)	15,672	36.7
2	Addison T. Smith (R)	32,274	63.2
	C. R. Jeppesen (D)	18,827	36.8

ILLINOIS

		Votes	%
1	Martin B. Madden (R)	12,580	55.3
	George Mayer (D)	9,776	43.0
2	James R. Mann (R)	29,099	59.5
	Leo S. Lebosky (D)	17,895	36.6
3	William W. Wilson (R)	24,011	52.9
	Fred J. Crowley (D)	19,372	42.7
4	John W. Rainey (D)	15,514	94.6
	Carl G. Hoffman (SOC)	886	5.4
5	Adolph J. Sabath (D)	10,517	69.1
	Louis C. Mau (R)	3,789	24.9
	Emil Jaeger (SOC)	919	6.0
6	James McAndrews (D)	32,638	55.9
	Hervey C. Foster (R)	22,692	38.8
	William F. Kruse (SOC)	3,101	5.3
7	Niels Juul (R)	35,428	51.3
	Frank M. Padden (D)	26,261	38.0
	J. Louis Engdahl (SOC)	7,387	10.7
8	Thomas Gallagher (D)	11,472	78.2
	Dan Parrillo (R)	3,201	21.8
9	Fred A. Britten (R)	12,654	53.0
	James H. Poage (D)	10,074	42.2
10	Carl R. Chindblom (R)	33,097	62.1
	Philip J. Finnegan (D)	16,933	31.8
	Irving St. John Tucker (SOC)	3,284	6.2
11	Ira C. Copley (R)	25,744	92.9
	Carl F. Schutz (SOC)	1,954	7.1
12	Charles E. Fuller (R)	25,623	93.1
	Oscar Ogren (SOC)	1,895	6.9
13	John C. McKenzie (R)	20,861	96.2

	Candidates	Votes	%
14	William J. Graham (R)	20,635	90.6
	Edmond B. Passmore (SOC)	1,791	7.9
15	Edward J. King (R)	21,334	60.2
	Edward P. Allen (D)	13,148	37.1
16	Clifford Ireland (R)	20,617	57.3
	Leander O. Eagleton (D)	14,759	41.0
17	Frank L. Smith (R)	19,123	69.7
	C. S. Schneider (D)	8,321	30.3
18	Joseph G. Cannon (R)	22,427	60.3
	Frank M. Crangle (D)	14,402	38.7
19	William B. McKinley (R)	26,259	60.8
	Thomas B. Jack (D)	16,474	38.1
20	Henry T. Rainey (D)	17,355	55.0
	Frank E. Blane (R)	14,184	45.0
21	Loren E. Wheeler (R)	20,380	50.4
	James M. Graham (D)	19,064	47.2
22	William A. Rodenberg (R)	21,925	51.3
	J. Nick Perrin (D)	18,592	43.5
	Marshal E. Kirkpatrick (SOC)	2,240	5.2
23	Edwin B. Brooks (R)	20,619	49.9
	Martin D. Foster (D)	19,397	46.9
24	Thomas S. Williams (R)	18,689	59.4
	James R. Campbell (D)	12,412	39.4
25	Edward E. Denison (R)	22,886	60.4
	D. T. Woodard (D)	15,000	39.6
AL	Richard Yates (R)	501,974✓	
	William E. Mason (R)	479,533✓	
	William Elza Williams (D)	361,505	
	Michael H. Cleary (D)	356,168	
	Clarence C. Brooks (SOC)	33,835	
	Frank Watts (SOC)	32,065	
	Edward E. Blake (P)	3,189	
	Charles P. Corson (P)	3,110	
	William Hartness (SOC LAB)	2,956	
	Joseph Hamrle (SOC LAB)	2,790	

Special Election

		Votes	%
4	John W. Rainey (D)	13,094	65.5
	O. W. Christopher (R)	4,366	21.8
	Kasimer P. Gugis (SOC)	2,530	12.7

INDIANA

		Votes	%
1	Oscar R. Luhring (R)	20,440	52.0
	George K. Denton (D)	18,837	48.0
2	Oscar E. Bland (R)	23,943	53.6
	Fred F. Bays (D)	19,731	44.2
3	James W. Dunbar (R)	20,556	50.3
	William E. Cox (D)	19,989	48.9
4	John S. Benham (R)	20,745	50.4
	Lincoln Dixon (D)	20,428	49.6
5	Everett Sanders (R)	20,271	50.5
	Ralph W. Moss (D)	19,213	47.9
6	Richard N. Elliott (R)	21,266	54.2
	Harry G. Strickland (D)	17,755	45.3
7	Merrill Moores (R)	29,714	58.3
	Chalmer Schlosser (D)	20,284	39.8
8	Albert H. Vestal (R)	24,124	53.5
	William H. Eichorn (D)	19,421	43.1
9	Fred S. Purnell (R)	25,486	55.9
	Charles F. Howard (D)	18,948	41.6
10	William R. Wood (R)	26,384	61.4
	George P. Kirschman (D)	16,064	37.4
11	Milton W. Krauss (R)	24,358	54.0
	George W. Rauch (D)	19,849	44.0
12	Louis W. Fairfield (R)	22,251	54.7
	Harry H. Hilgeman (D)	17,538	43.1
13	Andrew J. Hickey (R)	27,269	52.8
	Henry A. Barnhart (D)	23,274	45.1

IOWA

		Votes	%
1	Charles A. Kennedy (R)	15,921	60.6
	Edward L. Hirsch (D)	10,358	39.4

IOWA

Candidates	Votes	%
2 Harry E. Hull (R)	19,958	54.7
Nathan D. Ely (D)	14,395	39.5
William E. McIntosh (SOC)	2,140	5.9
3 Burton E. Sweet (R)	22,997	64.7
Harry B. Clark (D)	12,527	35.3
4 Gilbert N. Haugen (R)	20,643	64.7
Joseph C. Campbell (D)	11,283	35.3
5 James W. Good (R)	20,655	65.1
Sherman W. Dewolf (D)	11,078	34.9
6 C. William Ramseyer (R)	17,082	56.1
Buell McCash (D)	12,988	42.6
7 Cassius C. Dowell (R)	18,182	66.8
H. C. Evans (D)	8,493	31.2
8 Horace M. Towner (R)	20,409	64.5
D. Fulton Rice (D)	11,258	35.6
9 William R. Green (R)	22,234	99.8
10 Lester J. Dickinson (R)	23,635	64.3
J. R. Files (D)	13,153	35.8
11 William D. Boies (R)	21,665	56.4
Thomas J. Steele (D)	16,461	42.8

KANSAS

Candidates	Votes	%
1 Daniel R. Anthony Jr. (R)	33,720	65.0
Frank E. Whitney (D)	17,100	33.0
2 Edward C. Little (R)	32,653	57.2
Henderson S. Martin (D)	23,262	40.8
3 Phillip P. Campbell (R)	32,837	54.8
C. E. Pile (D)	22,849	38.1
4 Homer Hoch (R)	26,880	58.8
Dudley Doolittle (D)	17,787	38.9
5 James G. Strong (R)	29,703	60.8
Guy T. Helvering (D)	18,112	37.1
6 Hays B. White (R)	30,427	55.4
John R. Connelly (D)	22,898	41.7
7 Jasper N. Tincher (R)	37,875	56.2
Jouett Shouse (D)	27,722	41.1
8 William A. Ayres (D)	22,167	51.2
Charles C. Mack (R)	20,279	46.9

KENTUCKY

Candidates	Votes	%
1 Alben W. Barkley (D)	19,998	66.8
W. G. Howard (R)	9,947	33.2
2 David H. Kincheloe (D)	18,749	57.7
Ben T. Robinson (R)	13,740	42.3
3 Robert Y. Thomas Jr. (D)	18,032	52.3
Bishop S. Huntsman (R)	16,443	47.7
4 Ben Johnson (D)	18,834	52.5
John P. Haswell Jr. (R)	17,075	47.6
5 Charles F. Ogden (R)	21,788	51.3
J. Swager Sherley (D)	20,703	48.7
6 Arthur B. Rouse (D)	19,039	68.3
Virgil Weaver (R)	8,842	31.7
7 James C. Cantrill (D)	19,612	60.9
A. B. Hammond (R)	12,590	39.1
8 Harvey Helm (D)	15,270*	52.8
Robert L. Davidson (R)	13,673	47.2
9 William J. Fields (D)	21,810	54.6
Trumbo Sindegas (R)	18,106	45.4
10 John W. Langley (R)	13,284	67.1
David Hays (D)	6,511	32.9
11 John M. Robison (R)	24,730	76.4
Nat W. Elliott (D)	7,656	23.6

LOUISIANA

Candidates	Votes	%
1 Albert Estopinal (D)	11,060	100.0
2 H. Garland Dupre (D)	10,391	100.0
3 Whitmell P. Martin (D)	2,888	100.0
4 John T. Watkins (D)	5,299	100.0
5 Riley J. Wilson (D)	3,831	100.0
6 Jared Y. Sanders (D)	3,659	100.0
7 Ladislas Lazaro (D)	3,584	100.0
8 James B. Aswell (D)	4,082	100.0

MAINE

Candidates	Votes	%
1 Louis B. Goodall (R)	15,565	53.8
L. B. Swett (D)	13,388	46.2
2 Wallace H. White Jr. (R)	17,928	54.2
D. J. McGillicuddy (D)	15,144	45.8
3 John A. Peters (R)	20,293	57.6
Chase (D)	14,930	42.4
4 Ira G. Hersey (R)	14,275	58.1
L. G. C. Brown (D)	10,313	41.9

MARYLAND

Candidates	Votes	%
1 William N. Andrews (R)	14,199	50.5
Jesse D. Price (D)	13,913	49.5
2 Carville D. Benson (D)	17,985	54.3
Charles J. Hull (R)	14,758	44.6
3 Charles P. Coady (D)	12,422	58.4
Charles A. Jording (R)	8,244	38.8
4 J. Charles Linthicum (D)	14,689	57.0
Walter E. Knickman (R)	10,718	41.6
5 Sydney E. Mudd (R)	13,266	53.7
Frank M. Duvall (D)	10,987	44.5
6 Frederick H. Zihlman (R)	14,872	54.9
Henry Dorsey Etchison (D)	11,489	42.4

Special Election

	Votes	%
2 Carville D. Benson (D)	17,748	54.7
Herbert R. Wooden (R)	14,674	45.3

MASSACHUSETTS

Candidates	Votes	%
1 Allen T. Treadway (R)	15,933	58.3
Thomas F. Cassidy (D)	11,394	41.7
2 Frederick H. Gillett (R)	20,277	99.9
3 Calvin D. Paige (R)	15,267	60.5
Eaton D. Sargent (D)	9,982	39.5
4 Samuel E. Winslow (R)	14,141	52.5
John F. McGrath (D)	12,792	47.5
5 John Jacob Rogers (R)	20,496	99.2
6 Willfred W. Lufkin (R)	21,147	88.9
Estus E. Eames (SOC)	2,648	11.1
7 Michael F. Phelan (D)	14,437	57.3
Charles Cabot Johnson (R)	10,754	42.7
8 Frederick W. Dallinger (R)	16,858	60.3
James F. Aylward (D)	11,093	39.7
9 Alvan T. Fuller (R)	17,597	68.7
Henry C. Rowland (D)	8,022	31.3
10 John F. Fitzgerald (D)	7,241‡	47.3
Peter F. Tague (I)	7,003	45.7
Hammond T. Fletcher (R)	1,071	7.0
11 George Holden Tinkham (R)	13,644	56.4
Francis J. Horgan (D)	10,529	43.6
12 James A. Gallivan (D)	18,349	70.4
Harrison H. Atwood (R)	7,709	29.6
13 Robert Luce (R)	18,257	59.3
Aloysius J. Doon (D)	12,538	40.7
14 Richard Olney (D)	18,009	56.6
Louis F. R. Langelier (R)	13,832	43.4
15 William S. Greene (R)	12,952	61.7
Arthur J. B. Cartier (D)	8,031	38.3
16 Joseph Walsh (R)	13,874	62.4
Frederic Tudor (D)	8,357	37.6

MICHIGAN

Candidates	Votes	%
1 Frank E. Doremus (D)	22,549	60.4
James W. Hanley (R)	14,063	37.6
2 Earl C. Michener (R)	20,831	55.7
Samuel W. Beakes (D)	16,276	43.5
3 John M. C. Smith (R)	20,385	61.8
Howard W. Cavanagh (D)	12,119	36.8
4 Edward L. Hamilton (R)	20,904	65.9
James O'Hara (D)	10,842	34.2
5 Carl E. Mapes (R)	22,917	66.8
Peter J. Danhof (D)	10,783	31.5
6 Patrick H. Kelley (R)	29,183	97.3

Candidates	Votes	%
7 Louis C. Cramton (R)	20,573	73.3
John W. Scully (D)	7,155	25.5
8 Joseph W. Fordney (R)	22,240	62.8
Miles J. Purcell (D)	13,153	37.2
9 James C. McLaughlin (R)	17,624	66.4
Charles M. Black (D)	8,317	31.3
10 Gilbert A. Currie (R)	18,409	68.0
Henry C. Haller (D)	8,312	30.7
11 Frank D. Scott (R)	16,365	66.7
Michael J. Doyle (D)	8,183	33.3
12 W. Frank James (R)	17,315	69.8
Albert S. Ley (D)	6,681	26.9
13 Charles A. Nichols (R)	24,525	66.9
Louis W. McClear (D)	11,617	31.7

MINNESOTA

	Votes	%
1 Sydney Anderson (R)	29,337	100.0
2 Franklin F. Ellsworth (R)	24,888	69.0
Simon (D)	11,161	31.0
3 Charles R. Davis (R)	20,092	53.4
Farrell (D)	17,530	46.6
4 Carl C. Van Dyke (D)	18,736	62.0
Mallory (D)	11,498	38.0
5 Walter H. Newton (R)	21,607	57.6
Robertson (D)	15,912	42.4
6 Harold Knutson (R)	22,633	72.3
Russell (D)	8,660	27.7
7 Andrew J. Volstead (R)	21,406	56.3
Lobeck (N)	16,587	43.7
8 William L. Carss (UN LAB)	17,266	57.1
Miller (D)	12,964	42.9
9 Halvor Steenerson (R)	26,303	100.0
10 Thomas D. Schall (R)	25,866	71.1
Finlayson (D)	10,534	28.9

MISSISSIPPI

	Votes	%
1 Ezekiel S. Candler Jr. (D)	4,240	100.0
2 Hubert D. Stephens (D)	4,270	100.0
3 Benjamin G. Humphreys (D)	2,339	100.0
4 Thomas U. Sisson (D)	4,135	96.3
5 William W. Venable (D)	6,174	100.0
6 Paul B. Johnson (D)	4,972	94.3
F. T. Maxwell (SOC)	303	5.7
7 Percy E. Quin (D)	3,093	93.4
J. B. Sternberger (SOC)	220	6.6
8 James W. Collier (D)	2,376	98.8

MISSOURI

	Votes	%
1 Milton A. Romjue (D)	17,184	54.2
Frank C. Millspaugh (R)	14,255	45.0
2 William W. Rucker (D)	19,769	98.7
3 Joshua W. Alexander (D)	15,910	52.9
Frost (R)	14,117	46.9
4 Charles F. Booher (D)	15,707	51.7
McNeeley (R)	14,597	48.0
5 William T. Bland (D)	31,561	62.7
Reeves (R)	18,540	36.8
6 Clement C. Dickinson (D)	14,898	52.7
Atkeson (R)	13,188	46.7
7 Samuel C. Major (D)	20,300	49.8
Salts (R)	20,222	49.6
8 William L. Nelson (D)	13,326	50.4
Gentry (R)	13,133	49.6
9 James Beauchamp Clark (D)	18,248	51.7
Dyer (R)	16,719	47.4
10 Cleveland A. Newton (R)	50,390	60.2
Read (D)	30,080	35.9
11 William L. Igoe (D)	16,229	96.8
12 Leonidas C. Dyer (R)	12,612	58.9
Rosenfeld (D)	8,538	39.9
13 Marion E. Rhodes (R)	14,776	51.4
Brewster (D)	13,773	47.9
14 Edward D. Hayes (D)	21,472	50.5
Russell (D)	21,001	49.4
15 Isaac V. McPherson (R)	19,133	51.0

MISSOURI

Candidates	Votes	%
Decker (D)	17,826	47.5
16 Thomas L. Rubey (D)	13,490	49.9
Shelton (R)	13,320	49.2

Special Election

10 Frederick Essen (R)	49,416	59.6
Read (D)	30,536	36.8

MONTANA

1 John M. Evans (D)	25,530	47.9
Frank B. Linderman (R)	22,398	42.1
Tom Kane (N)	5,335	10.0
2 Carl W. Riddick (R)	24,960	49.4
Harry B. Mitchell (D)	22,826	45.1
Joseph Pope (N)	2,786	5.5

NEBRASKA

1 C. Frank Reavis (R)	18,097	62.3
Frank A. Peterson (D)	10,945	37.7
2 Albert W. Jefferis (R)	13,302	50.9
Charles Lobeck (D)	12,839	49.1
3 Robert E. Evans (R)	22,654	52.0
Daniel V. Stephens (D)	20,903	48.0
4 Melvin O. McLaughlin (R)	21,041	58.1
W. H. Smith (D)	14,763	40.8
5 William E. Andrews (R)	17,819	50.8
A. C. Shallenberger (D)	17,268	49.2
6 Moses P. Kinkaid (R)	28,563	60.8
Charles W. Pool (D)	17,820	37.9

NEVADA

AL Charles R. Evans (D)	12,670	51.3
Sylvester S. Downer (R)	10,660	43.2
H. H. Cordill (SOC)	1,377	5.6

NEW HAMPSHIRE

1 Sherman E. Burroughs (R)	18,658	52.2
William N. Rogers (D)	17,122	47.9
2 Edward H. Wason (R)	19,343	56.5
Harry F. Lake (D)	14,923	43.6

NEW JERSEY

1 William J. Browning (R)	23,785	63.8
Dickerson (D)	10,627	28.5
2 Isaac Bacharach (R)	20,744	67.9
French (D)	8,610	28.2
3 Thomas J. Scully (D)	19,965	53.1
Carson (R)	17,068	45.4
4 Elijah C. Hutchinson (R)	17,875	55.1
Vanderbilt (D)	14,556	44.9
5 Ernest R. Ackerman (R)	17,510	52.7
Clement (D)	13,545	40.7
Furber (SOC)	1,755	5.3
6 John R. Ramsey (R)	18,663	53.3
Sibbald (D)	15,542	44.4
7 Amos H. Radcliffe (R)	12,515	53.6
Delaney (D)	8,581	36.8
Derrick (SOC)	1,657	7.1
8 Cornelius A. McGlennon (D)	12,436	48.7
Ross (R)	12,137	47.6
9 Daniel F. Minahan (D)	10,996	50.4
Parker (R)	9,338	42.8
Bircher (SOC)	1,303	6.0
10 Frederick R. Lehlbach (R)	12,566	48.3
Flannagan (D)	11,979	46.1
Poole (SOC)	1,450	5.6
11 John J. Eagan (D)	14,281	67.5
Brennan (R)	4,979	23.5
Reilly (SOC)	1,894	9.0

Candidates	Votes	%
12 James A. Hamill (D)	17,781	70.8
Bierch (R)	6,048	24.1
Bausch (SOC)	1,277	5.1

Special Election

5 William F. Birch (R)	17,481	53.0
Clement (D)	13,771	41.7
Furber (SOC)	1,760	5.3

NEW MEXICO

AL Bendigno C. Hernandez (R)	23,862	50.7
G. A. Richardson (D)	22,627	48.1

NEW YORK

1 Frederick C. Hicks (R-D-P)	53,579	96.6
2 Charles Pope Caldwell (R, D)	54,394	85.9
William Burkle (SOC)	8,946	14.1
3 John MacCrate (R, D)	14,720	48.9
Michael Fogarty (BUSINESS)	10,249	34.1
Joseph A. Whitehorn (SOC)	5,107	17.0
4 Thomas H. Cullen (D)	23,146	75.2
Ralph Waldo Bowman (R & P)	6,599	21.4
5 John B. Johnston (D)	32,090	55.8
George A. Green (R)	23,844	41.5
6 Frederick W. Rowe (R & P)	26,806	46.6
Franklin Taylor (D)	26,476	46.0
Bernard J. Riley (SOC)	4,287	7.5
7 James P. Maher (D)	19,834	58.9
John Hill Morgan (R & P)	9,309	27.7
James O'Neal (SOC)	4,513	13.4
8 William E. Cleary (D)	24,069	54.5
Allison L. Adams (R)	14,778	33.5
Abraham H. Shulman (SOC)	5,114	11.6
9 David J. O'Connell (D)	28,882	45.8
Oscar W. Swift (R & P)	27,393	43.5
Wilhemus B. Robinson (SOC)	6,751	10.7
10 Reuben L. Haskell (R)	17,441	40.2
George W. Martin (D)	15,911	36.7
Abraham I. Shiplacoff (SOC)	9,987	23.0
11 Daniel J. Riordan (D)	21,525	71.2
William H. Michales (R)	7,080	23.4
12 Henry M. Goldfogle (R, D)	7,452	52.9
Meyer London (SOC)	6,625	47.0
13 Christopher D. Sullivan (R, D)	6,962	66.4
Algernon Lee (SOC)	3,502	33.4
14 Fiorello H. LaGuardia (R, D)	14,523	69.7
Scott Nearing (SOC)	6,214	29.8
15 Peter J. Dooling (D)	23,492	78.4
Jacob I. Wiener (R)	5,373	17.9
16 Thomas F. Smith (D)	21,289	71.9
Thomas Rock (R)	6,188	20.9
Samuel E. Beardsley (SOC)	2,057	6.9
17 Herbert C. Pell Jr. (D)	19,593	50.2
Frederick C. Tanner (R)	17,839	45.7
18 John F. Carew (D)	23,806	71.2
Julius M. Leder (R)	4,797	14.4
Pauline Newman (SOC)	4,741	14.2
19 Joseph Rowan (D)	24,961	48.3
Walter M. Chandler (R)	23,125	44.8
Theresa Malkiel (SOC)	3,319	6.4
20 Isaac Siegel (R-D)	9,417	60.9
Morris Hillquit (SOC)	6,005	38.9
21 Jerome F. Donovan (D)	33,233	53.4
John A. Bolles (R)	25,677	41.2
George Fraser Miller (SOC)	3,156	5.1
22 Anthony J. Griffin (D)	22,713	69.9
Sadie Kost (R)	5,269	16.2
Patrick J. Murphy (SOC)	4,323	13.3

Candidates	Votes	%
23 Richard F. McKiniry (D)	39,573	55.2
Owen A. Haley (R)	17,975	25.1
Max Geisler (SOC)	14,146	19.7
24 James V. Ganly (D)	28,636	44.3
Benjamin L. Fairchild (R & P)	27,037	41.8
Irvin E. Klein (SOC)	8,968	13.9
25 James W. Husted (R)	22,562	56.2
Arthur O. Sherman (D)	16,248	40.5
26 Edmund Platt (R)	30,010	57.1
George A. Coleman (D)	20,727	39.4
27 Charles B. Ward (R)	30,839	53.9
John K. Evans (D & P)	25,620	44.7
28 Rollin B. Sanford (R & P)	41,981	54.5
Joseph A. Lawson (D)	33,712	43.8
29 James S. Parker (R)	42,035	62.3
Gustavus A. Rogers (D)	23,139	34.3
30 Frank Crowther (R)	24,443	47.9
George R. Lunn (D & P)	23,820	46.7
Herbert M. Merrill (SOC)	2,786	5.5
31 Bertrand H. Snell (R)	30,701	71.6
Elizabeth Arthur (D)	10,459	24.4
32 Luther W. Mott (R)	37,068	63.2
Charles A. Hitchcock (D)	17,742	30.2
Stephen R. Lockwood (P)	3,263	5.6
33 Homer P. Snyder (R)	31,120	54.0
Clarence E. Williams (D)	23,340	40.5
34 William H. Hill (R)	38,597	57.4
Lavern P. Butts (D)	21,748	32.4
Julius E. Rogers (P)	6,373	9.5
35 Walter W. Magee (R)	42,769	59.3
Ben Wiles (D)	23,378	32.4
36 Norman J. Gould (R & P)	40,991	70.9
Everett E. Calman (D)	16,857	29.1
37 Alanson B. Houghton (R & P)	38,310	62.9
Frederick W. Palmer (D)	21,800	35.8
38 Thomas B. Dunn (R)	37,029	62.1
Jacob Gerling (D)	16,563	27.8
John W. Dennis (SOC)	4,098	6.9
39 Archie B. Sanders (R & P)	35,481	68.9
Clara B. Mann (D)	14,816	28.8
40 S. Wallace Dempsey (R)	35,710	63.0
Matthew P. Young (D)	17,962	31.7
Lee P. Smith (SOC)	3,045	5.4
41 Clarence MacGregor (R)	16,492	41.2
Charles B. Smith (D & P)	16,458	41.2
Franklin P. Brill (SOC)	7,038	17.6
42 James M. Mead (D)	16,453	46.2
William F. Waldow (R)	15,390	43.2
Hattie Kreuger (SOC)	3,099	8.7
43 Daniel A. Reed (R & P)	35,693	73.4
Frank H. Mott (D)	11,351	23.3

NORTH CAROLINA

1 John H. Small (D)	10,427	75.4
C. R. Pugh (R)	3,401	24.6
2 Claude Kitchin (D)	9,986	100.0
3 Samuel L. Brinson (D)	10,205	59.3
Claude R. Wheatley (R)	7,000	40.7
4 Edward W. Pou (D)	12,853	68.1
Robert H. Dixon (R)	6,028	31.9
5 Charles M. Stedman (D)	21,076	55.9
John W. Kurfees (R)	16,635	44.1
6 Hannibal L. Godwin (D)	9,575	72.1
Alexander L. McCaskill (R)	3,702	27.9
7 Leonidas D. Robinson (D)	18,275	59.3
James D. Gregg (R)	12,552	40.7
8 Robert L. Doughton (D)	16,105	53.8
Frank A. Linney (R)	13,826	46.2
9 Edwin Y. Webb (D)	16,982	57.0
Charles A. Jonas (R)	12,830	43.0
10 Zebulon Weaver (D)	16,323	51.7
James J. Britt (R)	15,271	48.3

NORTH DAKOTA

1 John M. Baer (R)	16,428	55.1
Fred Bartholomew (D)	13,416	45.0

NORTH DAKOTA

Candidates	Votes	%
2 George M. Young (R)	20,516	74.5
L. N. Torson (D)	7,038	25.5
3 James H. Sinclair (R)	17,564	66.2
Halvor Halvorson (D)	8,951	33.8

OHIO

	Votes	%
1 Nicholas Longworth (R)	27,030	56.5
Sidney G. Stricker (D)	20,826	43.5
2 Ambrose E. B. Stephens (R)	25,406	52.1
Richard A. Powell (D)	21,867	44.8
3 Warren Gard (D)	29,653	49.2
Charles W. Dustin (R)	26,625	44.2
John M. Cahalane (SOC)	3,978	6.6
4 Benjamin F. Welty (D)	22,580	50.5
J. E. Russell (R)	22,136	49.5
5 Charles J. Thompson (R)	19,071	52.6
John S. Snook (D)	17,162	47.4
6 Charles C. Kearns (R)	18,592	52.8
A. G. Turnipseed (D)	16,591	47.2
7 Simeon D. Fess (R)	34,554	61.6
George H. Thorne (D)	21,043	37.5
8 R. Clint Cole (R)	20,688	52.9
John A. Key (D)	18,441	47.1
9 Isaac R. Sherwood (D)	25,122	55.1
James M. Ashley (R)	18,398	40.3
10 Israel M. Foster (R)	18,438	100.0
11 Edwin D. Ricketts (R)	17,608	53.5
H. C. Claypool (D)	15,287	46.5
12 Clement L. Brumbaugh (D)	23,444	50.5
John C. Speaks (R)	22,216	47.8
13 James T. Begg (R)	21,552	53.0
Arthur W. Overmeyer (D)	18,775	46.1
14 Martin L. Davey (D)	25,932	50.3
Charles Dick (R)	24,170	46.9
15 C. Ellis Moore (R)	20,063	52.5
George White (D)	18,169	47.5
16 Roscoe C. McCulloch (R)	29,893	61.3
Joseph C. Breitenstein (D)	17,694	36.3
17 William A. Ashbrook (D)	24,436	52.1
William M. Morgan (R)	22,499	47.9
18 Frank Murphy (R)	22,899	53.0
William B. Francis (D)	20,272	47.0
19 John G. Cooper (R)	26,857	95.6
20 Charles A. Mooney (D)	19,776	55.0
Jerry R. Zmunt (R)	13,759	38.3
C. E. Ruthenberg (SOC)	2,429	6.8
21 John J. Babka (D)	15,511	55.9
Harry L. Vail (R)	10,417	37.5
Tom Clifford (SOC)	1,829	6.6
22 Henry I. Emerson (R)	32,745	100.0

OKLAHOMA

	Votes	%
1 Everette B. Howard (D)	15,394	50.6
T.A. Chandler (R)	14,506	47.6
2 William W. Hastings (D)	11,601	58.9
Gus H. Tinch (R)	7,670	39.0
3 Charles D. Carter (D)	15,635	66.8
H.J. Fowler (R)	6,982	29.8
4 Thomas D. McKeown (D)	13,861	57.0
E.R. Waite (R)	9,706	39.9
5 Joseph B. Thompson (D)	13,303	57.4
B.A. McAleer (R)	9,180	39.6
6 Scott Ferris (D)	12,085	54.8
L.A. Holmes (R)	8,925	40.5
7 James V. McClintic (D)	11,190	59.7
C.B. Leedy (R)	6,014	32.1
Orville E. Enfield (SOC)	1,526	8.2
8 Dick T. Morgan (R)	15,261	56.3
C.H. Hyde (D)	10,633	39.2

OREGON

	Votes	%
1 Willis C. Hawley (R-D-P)	57,245	89.6
Harlin Talbert (SOC)	6,624	10.4
Candidates	Votes	%
2 Nicholas J. Sinnott (R)	18,312	61.3
James Harvey Graham (D)	10,461	35.0
3 Clinton N. McArthur (R)	23,277	48.4
John S. Smith (D)	15,728	32.7
A. W. Lafferty (I-N)	7,661	15.9

PENNSYLVANIA

	Votes	%
1 William S. Vare (R, WASH)	26,120	76.4
Paul B. Cassidy (D)	7,146	20.9
2 George S. Graham (R, WASH)	20,578	81.5
John H. Berkley (D)	4,295	17.0
3 J. Hampton Moore (R, P)	20,099	78.8
William A. Hayes (D)	5,046	19.8
4 George W. Edmonds (R, WASH)	19,187	68.8
Joseph E. Fabian (D)	7,874	28.2
5 Peter E. Costello (R, SOC)	25,169	69.6
Emanuel R. Clinton (D)	10,987	30.4
6 George P. Darrow (R, P)	42,376	72.1
John K. Laughlin (D)	15,722	26.8
7 Thomas S. Butler (R)	23,882	76.1
James G. Milbourn (D)	6,702	21.3
8 Henry Winfield Watson (R)	23,127	63.4
Harry E. Grim (D, F PLAY)	12,213	33.5
9 William W. Griest (R)	17,398	77.1
Austin E. McCullough (D)	4,537	20.1
10 Patrick McLane (D, F PLAY)	11,765‡	50.0
John R. Farr (R, P)	11,564	49.1
11 John J. Casey (D, SOC)	16,547	50.1
Edmund N. Carpenter (R, P)	16,505	49.9
12 John Reber (R)	13,500	57.3
James J. Moran (D, F PLAY)	9,712	41.2
13 Arthur G. Dewalt (D, F PLAY)	19,776	51.9
J. Wilmer Fisher (R, WASH)	15,608	40.9
L. Birch Wilson Jr (SOC)	2,397	6.3
14 Louis T. McFadden (R)	11,267	66.0
A. M. Cornell (D)	4,873	28.6
15 Edgar R. Kiess (R, P)	14,153	63.8
Charles E. Spotts (D)	7,372	33.2
16 John V. Lesher (D)	11,782	48.7
Albert W. Duy (R)	11,509	47.6
17 Benjamin K. Focht (R)	16,762	59.0
Scott S. Leiby (D, P)	11,348	39.9
18 Aaron S. Kreider (R)	24,981	86.2
John A. Sprenkle (P)	2,905	10.0
19 John M. Rose (R, P)	20,036	61.4
Bernard J. Clark (D)	11,857	36.4
20 Edward S. Brooks (R, WASH)	15,362	52.5
Andrew R. Brodbeck (D, P)	13,525	46.2
21 Evan J. Jones (R, SOC)	12,673	56.5
William E. Tobias (D)	8,958	39.9
22 Edward E. Robbins (R, P)	17,160*	61.1
George H. McWherter (D, F PLAY)	9,904	35.3
23 Samuel A. Kendall (R)	14,550	50.1
Bruce F. Sterling (D, P)	14,029	48.3
24 Henry W. Temple (R, P)	18,851	69.1
William M. Hartman (D)	7,398	27.1
25 Milton W. Shreve (R, WASH)	11,164	51.0
Charles N. Crosby (D)	8,766	40.0
26 Henry J. Steele (D, F PLAY)	11,872	49.4
Francis A. March Jr. (R, WASH)	9,781	40.7
Delbert Strader Bachman (P, I PROG)	2,035	8.5
27 Nathan L. Strong (R, P)	14,804	70.7
Don C. Corbett (D)	5,686	27.2
28 Willis J. Hulings (R, WASH)	13,751	55.5
Earl H. Beshlin (D, P)	10,367	41.9

Candidates	Votes	%
29 Stephen G. Porter (R, D)	19,045	89.0
C. G. Porter (P)	1,222	5.7
Henry Peter (SOC)	1,138	5.3
30 M. Clyde Kelly (R, D)	21,559	90.5
H. J. Lohr (SOC)	2,262	9.5
31 John M. Morin (R, D)	14,081	91.4
William A. Prosser (SOC)	773	5.0
32 Guy E. Campbell (R, D)	20,567	87.2
John W. Slayton (SOC)	1,553	6.6
William C. Wallace (P)	1,458	6.2
AL William J. Burke (R)	546,373✔	
Mahlon M. Garland (R)	529,510✔	
Thomas S. Crago (R, WASH)	527,961✔	
Anderson H. Walters (R, WASH)	525,615✔	
Joseph F. Gorman (D)	276,836	
J. Calvin Strayer (D, F PLAY)	268,533	
Samuel R. Tarner (D, F PLAY)	264,971	
Fred Ikeler (D, F PLAY)	264,065	
O. D. Brubaker (P)	29,309	
Elisha Kent Kane (P)	26,473	
Albert Gaddis (P)	25,347	
E. L. McKee (P)	23,793	
Cora M. Bixler (SOC)	23,273	
Henry W. Schlegel (SOC)	21,831	
John C. Euler (SOC)	21,477	
Harry T. Vaughn (SOC)	21,143	
John W. Dix (SINGLE T)	2,211	
Lewis Ryan (SINGLE T)	2,129	
Oliver McKnight (SINGLE T)	2,006	
Calvin B. Power (SINGLE T)	1,631	

RHODE ISLAND

	Votes	%
1 Clark Burdick (R)	14,478	54.3
Green (D)	11,556	43.4
2 Walter R. Stiness (R)	14,710	56.0
Casey (D)	10,914	41.6
3 Ambrose Kennedy (R)	14,037	52.6
Troy (D)	12,176	45.6

SOUTH CAROLINA

	Votes	%
1 Richard S. Whaley (D)	2,328	100.0
2 James F. Byrnes (D)	3,155	100.0
3 Fred H. Dominick (D)	3,701	100.0
4 Samuel J. Nichols (D)	4,069	100.0
5 William F. Stevenson (D)	3,640	100.0
6 J. Willard Ragsdale (D)	3,626	100.0
7 Asbury F. Lever (D)	4,761	96.4

SOUTH DAKOTA

	Votes	%
1 Charles A. Christopherson (R)	19,443	54.1
Dowdell (D)	14,899	41.5
2 Royal C. Johnson (R)	21,657	72.1
McArthur (D)	8,401	28.0
3 Harry L. Gandy (D)	10,865	50.7
Atwater (R)	7,805	36.4
Ayers (I)	2,526	11.8

TENNESSEE

	Votes	%
1 Sam R. Sells (R)	13,752	100.0
2 J. Will Taylor (R)	13,868	73.3
Sam Johnson (D)	4,879	25.8
3 John A. Moon (D)	12,566	100.0
4 Cordell Hull (D)	11,646	100.0
5 Ewen L. Davis (D)	11,089	100.0
6 Joseph W. Byrns (D)	10,794	100.0
7 Lemuel P. Padgett (D)	10,178	100.0
8 Thetus W. Sims (D)	9,010	100.0
9 Finis J. Garrett (D)	11,122	100.0
10 Hubert F. Fisher (D)	11,606	100.0

TEXAS

	Candidates	Votes	%
1	Eugene Black (D)	9,640	100.0
2	John C. Box (D)	10,474	100.0
3	James Young (D)	10,183	100.0
4	Sam Rayburn (D)	9,755	100.0
5	Hatton W. Sumners (D)	6,946	100.0
6	Rufus Hardy (D)	10,496	86.9
	Charles W. Beck (R)	1,577	13.1
7	Clay S. Briggs (D)	6,671	100.0
8	Joe H. Eagle (D)	7,554	96.1
9	Joseph J. Mansfield (D)	7,672	100.0
10	James P. Buchanan (D)	8,576	100.0
11	Tom T. Connally (D)	9,304	100.0
12	James C. Wilson (D)	9,307	100.0
13	Lucian W. Parrish (D)	9,700	100.0
14	Carlos Bee (D)	8,038	68.4
	John D. Hartman (R)	3,717	31.6
15	John N. Garner (D)	6,814	100.0
16	Claude Hudspeth (D)	6,211	100.0
17	Thomas L. Blanton (D)	11,194	100.0
18	Marvin Jones (D)	10,497	95.3

UTAH

		Votes	%
1	Milton H. Welling (D)	25,327	54.9
	William H. Wattis (R)	20,478	44.4
2	James H. Mays (D & PROG)	23,931	58.7
	William Spry (R)	16,134	39.6

VERMONT

		Votes	%
1	Frank L. Greene (R)	16,301	75.9
	John Higgins (D)	5,179	24.1
2	Porter H. Dale (R, P)	16,145	74.5
	John B. Reardon (D)	5,518	25.5

VIRGINIA

	Candidates	Votes	%
1	S. Otis Bland (D)	4,835	99.9
2	Edward E. Holland (D)	3,420	100.0
3	Andrew Jackson Montague (D)	3,074	100.0
4	Walter A. Watson (D)	2,506	99.9
5	Edward W. Saunders (D)	3,880	100.0
6	Carter Glass (D)	2,705*	99.6
7	Thomas W. Harrison (D)	3,767	88.8
	John Paul (R)	466	11.0
8	Charles C. Carlin (D)	4,501*	100.0
9	C. Bascom Slemp (R)	8,089	93.9
	D. B. Dale (D)	515	6.0
10	Henry D. Flood (D)	4,699	99.7

WASHINGTON

		Votes	%
1	John F. Miller (R)	23,326	50.6
	J. M. Hawthorne (D)	20,488	44.4
	Hulet M. Wells (SOC)	2,333	5.1
2	Lindley H. Hadley (R)	19,797	53.7
	Joseph A. Sloan (D)	15,059	40.8
	James M. Salter (SOC)	2,045	5.5
3	Albert Johnson (R)	29,178	66.6
	Theodore Hoss (D)	12,407	28.3
	O. T. Clark (SOC)	2,243	5.1
4	John W. Summers (R)	17,439	55.3
	William E. McCroskey (D)	13,335	42.3
5	J. Stanley Webster (R)	22,426	52.2
	C. C. Dill (D)	20,061	46.7

WEST VIRGINIA

		Votes	%
1	Matthew M. Neely (D)	17,428	52.8
	Charles J. Schuck (R)	15,330	46.4
2	George M. Bowers (R)	18,444	52.7
	B. H. Hiner (D)	16,084	46.0
3	Stuart F. Reed (R)	19,414	53.9
	Ernest Randolph (D)	16,254	45.1

	Candidates	Votes	%
4	Harry C. Woodyard (R)	19,679	55.2
	Stuart H. Bowman (D)	15,799	44.3
5	Wells Goodykoontz (R)	19,304	54.2
	W. W. McNeal (D)	16,332	45.8
6	Leonard S. Echols (R)	19,851	51.5
	Adam B. Littlepage (D)	18,020	46.8

WISCONSIN

		Votes	%
1	Clifford E. Randall (R)	13,177	42.3
	Cooper (I)	9,018	28.9
	Stewart (D)	7,718	24.8
2	Edward Voigt (R)	15,289	44.0
	Clifford (D)	12,532	36.1
	Ameringer (SOC)	6,936	20.0
3	James G. Monahan (R)	18,398	73.4
	Warner (I)	4,397	17.5
	Reynolds (I)	2,232	8.9
4	John C. Kleczka (R)	16,524	58.1
	Melms (SOC)	11,890	41.8
5	Victor L. Berger (SOC)	17,920*	43.7
	Joseph P. Carney (D)	12,450	30.3
	Stafford (R)	10,678	26.0
6	Florian Lampert (R)	12,728	41.5
	Husting (D)	10,856	35.4
	Thompson (SOC)	6,737	22.0
7	John J. Esch (R)	16,140	70.9
	Bentley (D)	6,109	26.8
8	Edward E. Browne (R)	13,755	51.8
	Brown (D)	6,862	25.9
	Krzycki (SOC)	5,904	22.3
9	David G. Classon (R)	16,352	60.4
	McDonald (D)	10,702	39.6
10	James A. Frear (R)	16,900	90.2
	Frawley (I)	1,814	9.7
11	Adolphus P. Nelson (R)	16,413	84.3
	Jensen (SOC)	2,976	15.3

WYOMING

		Votes	%
AL	Frank W. Mondell (R)	26,244	64.2
	Hayden M. White (D)	14,639	35.8

1919 House Elections

OKLAHOMA

Special Election

		Votes	%
5	J. W. Harreld (R)	11,782	51.3
	Claude Weaver (D)	11,076	48.2

PENNSYLVANIA

Special Election

		Votes	%
22	John H. Wilson (D)	10,148	51.1
	John M. Jamison (R)	9,721	48.9

1920 House Elections

ALABAMA

	Candidates	Votes	%
1	John McDuffie (D)	12,978	98.7
2	John R. Tyson (D)	18,469	99.6
3	Henry B. Steagall (D)	11,959	82.5
	Dallas B. Smith (R)	2,532	17.5
4	Fred L. Blackmon (D)	12,236*	59.6
	A. P. Longshore (R)	8,305	40.4
5	William B. Bolling (D)	13,290	73.5
	W. M. Russell (R)	4,793	26.5
6	William B. Oliver (D)	8,721	100.0
7	Lilius B. Rainey (D)	23,709	50.5
	Charles B. Kennamer (R)	22,970	49.0
8	Edward B. Almon (D)	17,640	76.4
	W. E. Hotchkiss (R)	5,306	23.0
9	George Huddleston (D)	26,776	85.4
	Alex Birch (R)	4,452	14.2
10	William B. Bankhead (D)	15,465	52.6
	W. L. Chenault (R)	13,737	46.7

ARIZONA

	Candidates	Votes	%
AL	Carl Hayden (D)	35,397	57.8
	James A. Dunseath (R)	25,841	42.2

ARKANSAS

	Candidates	Votes	%
1	William J. Driver (D)	19,843	73.6
	T. H. Mayes (R)	7,110	26.4
2	William A. Oldfield (D)	16,080	66.4
	Thad Rowden (R)	8,137	33.6
3	John N. Tillman (D)	14,341	53.3
	John I. Worthington (R)	12,587	46.7
4	Otis Wingo (D)	19,722	64.1
	W. H. Dunblazier (R)	11,031	35.9
5	Henderson M. Jacoway (D)	21,948	73.2
	G. A. McConnell (R)	8,039	26.8
6	Samuel M. Taylor (D)	18,028	69.4
	W. R. Day (R)	7,956	30.6
7	Tilman B. Parks (D)	18,303	72.2
	J. C. Russell (R)	7,064	27.9

CALIFORNIA

	Candidates	Votes	%
1	Clarence F. Lea (D-R)	34,427	61.7
	Charles A. Bodwell Jr. (I)	18,569	33.3
2	John E. Raker (D R&SOC)	26,172	99.9
3	Charles F. Curry (R)	54,984	74.7
	J. W. Struckenbruck (D)	14,964	20.3
4	Julius Kahn (R-D)	50,841	84.6
	Milton Harlan (SOC)	9,289	15.5
5	John I. Nolan (R-D)	50,274	82.1
	Thomas Conway (SOC)	10,952	17.9
6	John A. Elston (R)	75,610	83.3
	Maynard Shipley (SOC)	15,151	16.7
7	Henry E. Barbour (R-D)	57,647	87.2
	Harry M. McKee (SOC)	8,449	12.8
8	Arthur M. Free (R)	46,823	64.0
	Hugh S. Hersman (D SOC)	26,311	36.0
9	Charles F. Van de Water (R)	62,952*	59.7
	Charles H. Randall (P & D)	36,675	34.8
	Mary E. Garbutt (SOC)	5,819	5.5
10	Henry Z. Osborne (R-D-P)	97,469	82.6
	Upton Sinclair (SOC)	20,439	17.3
11	Philip D. Swing (D)	59,425	72.8
	Hugh L. Dickson (D)	22,144	27.1

COLORADO

	Candidates	Votes	%
1	William N. Vaile (R)	45,658	66.9
	Benjamin C. Hilliard (D)	22,557	33.1
2	Charles B. Timberlake (R)	57,512	66.4
	A. F. Browns (D)	29,158	33.6
3	Guy U. Hardy (R)	43,426	57.7
	Samuel J. Burris (D)	31,896	42.4
4	Edward T. Taylor (D)	25,994	55.3
	Merle D. Vincent (R)	20,991	44.7

CONNECTICUT

	Candidates	Votes	%
1	E. Hart Fenn (R)	53,461	60.5
	Joseph F. Dutton (D)	30,757	34.8
2	Richard P. Freeman (R)	39,432	63.7
	Thomas R. Murray (D)	20,868	33.7
3	John Q. Tilson (R)	45,406	63.7
	William F. Alcorn (D)	22,357	31.4
4	Schuyler Merritt (R)	54,715	66.3
	Harry J. Platt (D)	25,087	30.4
5	James P. Glynn (R)	34,621	58.7
	Michael L. Caine (D)	22,950	38.9

DELAWARE

	Candidates	Votes	%
AL	Caleb R. Layton (R)	52,145	55.7
	James R. Clements (D)	40,206	43.0

FLORIDA

	Candidates	Votes	%
1	Herbert J. Drane (D)	26,385	78.1
	H. B. Jeffries (R)	4,729	14.0
2	Frank Clark (D)	15,143	84.9
	Fred Cubberly (R)	2,383	13.4
3	J. H. Smithwick (D)	17,199	86.2
	Millard M. Owens (R)	2,753	13.8
4	William J. Sears (D)	38,355	74.4
	C. D. Bowen (R)	11,159	21.7

GEORGIA

	Candidates	Votes	%
1	James W. Overstreet (D)	10,156	82.5
	E. S. Fuller (R)	2,161	17.5
2	Frank Park (D)	2,217	100.0
3	Charles R. Crisp (D)	7,001	92.6
	H. E. Locket (R)	563	7.4
4	William C. Wright (D)	10,040	100.0
5	William D. Upshaw (D)	10,649	70.1
	John W. Martin (D)	4,544	29.9
6	James W. Wise (D)	9,325	97.7
7	Gordon Lee (D)	18,385	99.6
8	Charles H. Brand (D)	11,708	100.0
9	Thomas M. Bell (D)	13,265	62.2
	O. L. Barnwell (R)	8,053	37.8
10	Carl Vinson (D)	8,685	100.0
11	William C. Lankford (D)	9,012	100.0
12	William W. Larsen (D)	8,461	100.0

IDAHO

	Candidates	Votes	%
1	Burton L. French (R)	34,654	59.3
	Nell K. Irion (D)	15,218	26.0
	Riley Rice (I)	8,605	14.7
2	Addison T. Smith (R)	49,642	63.0
	William P. Whitaker (D)	29,130	37.0

ILLINOIS

	Candidates	Votes	%
1	Martin B. Madden (R)	41,907	75.9
	James A. Gorman (D)	12,398	22.5
2	James R. Mann (R)	92,217	72.9
	James J. Leddy (D)	29,754	23.5
3	Elliott W. Sproul (R)	73,547	67.4
	Thomas M. Crane (D)	30,631	28.1
4	John W. Rainey (D)	23,230	48.9
	John Golombiewski (R)	21,546	45.3
	Charles Beranek (SOC)	2,750	5.8
5	Adolph J. Sabath (D)	14,374	45.3
	Jacob Gartenstein (R)	14,076	44.4
	William Neumann (SOC)	3,290	10.4
6	John J. Gorman (R)	88,975	63.8
	James McAndrews (D)	40,576	29.1
	William F. Kruse (SOC)	9,937	7.1
7	M. A. Michaelson (R)	110,758	70.0
	William J. Cullerton (D)	34,202	21.6
	Samuel Holland (SOC)	12,097	7.7
8	Stanley Henry Kunz (D)	15,432	49.2
	Dan Parrillo (R)	14,627	46.6
9	Fred A. Britten (R)	40,548	72.5
	Eugene L. McGarry (D)	13,257	23.7
10	Carl R. Chindblom (R)	101,361	74.4
	John Haderlin (D)	30,924	22.7
11	Ira C. Copley (R)	68,691	80.4
	Anton Nemanich Jr. (D)	14,885	17.4
12	Charles E. Fuller (R)	67,391	95.8
13	John C. McKenzie (R)	48,453	80.5
	J. L. Dickson (D)	10,821	18.0
14	William J. Graham (R)	49,329	67.1
	Andrew Olson (D)	21,822	29.7
15	Edward J. King (R)	49,852	69.0
	William F. Gilroy (D)	20,771	28.7
16	Clifford Ireland (R)	47,936	67.4
	Jefferson Earle Houston (D)	21,438	30.1
17	Frank H. Funk (R)	42,790	70.5
	Frank Gillespie (D)	17,912	29.5
18	Joseph G. Cannon (R)	53,772	64.1
	Armand E. Smith (D)	27,295	32.5
19	Allen F. Moore (R)	63,124	63.7
	Edward F. Poorman (D)	35,210	35.5
20	Guy L. Shaw (R)	33,375	53.1
	Henry T. Rainey (D)	29,466	46.9
21	Loren E. Wheeler (R)	43,223	52.0
	J. Earl Major (D)	29,054	34.9
	Duncan McDonald (F-LAB)	8,970	10.8
22	William A. Rodenberg (R)	49,802	54.8
	Guy R. McCasland (D)	26,866	29.6
	Cornelius J. Hayes (F-LAB)	11,929	13.1
23	Edwin B. Brooks (R)	44,950	54.4
	Albert H. Gravenhorst (D)	34,740	42.1
24	Thomas S. Williams (R)	38,472	60.9
	Asher R. Cox (D)	22,019	34.9
25	Edward E. Denison (R)	49,145	58.2
	J. Herman Clayton (D)	28,444	33.7
	John H. Reed (F-LAB)	5,690	6.7
AL	Richard Yates (R)	1,369,673✔	
	William E. Mason (R)	1,355,392✔	
	William Murphy (D)	579,799	
	C. S. Schneider (D)	565,792	
	Frank H. Hall (SOC)	66,385	
	John Hubert (SOC)	65,150	
	Gifford Ernest (F-LAB)	49,432	
	Robert Weber (F-LAB)	49,191	
	Margaret Wintringer (P)	19,123	
	W. W. Jones (P)	9,136	
	Henry Schilling (SOC LAB)	3,429	
	Frank K. Kuchenbecker (SOC LAB)	2,985	
	Henry Neil (I)	627	

INDIANA

	Candidates	Votes	%
1	Oscar R. Luhring (R)	44,694	51.7
	William E. Wilson (D)	36,834	42.6
2	Oscar E. Bland (R)	47,896	52.1
	William A. Cullop (D)	39,349	42.8
3	James W. Dunbar (R)	44,743	51.0
	John W. Ewing (D)	42,569	48.5
4	John S. Benham (R)	46,360	53.0
	Harry C. Canfield (D)	41,163	47.0
5	Everett Sanders (R)	46,464	52.1
	Charles S. Batt (D)	36,403	40.8

INDIANA

	Candidates	Votes	%
6	Richard N. Elliott (R)	48,752	55.3
	William A. Yarling (D)	38,721	43.9
7	Merrill Moores (R)	79,782	54.9
	Henry N. Spaan (D)	61,893	42.6
8	Albert H. Vestal (R)	54,416	56.8
	Charles A. Paddock (D)	38,725	40.4
9	Fred S. Purnell (R)	56,465	55.9
	Ben M. Scifres (D)	42,766	42.4
10	William R. Wood (R)	62,438	65.5
	Fred Barnett (D)	26,139	27.4
	James H. McGill (F-LAB)	5,086	5.3
11	Milton Kraus (R)	51,106	54.7
	Samuel E. Cook (D)	40,088	42.9
12	Louis W. Fairfield (R)	49,709	58.6
	Joseph R. Harrison (D)	31,182	36.8
13	Andrew J. Hickey (R)	62,206	59.8
	George Y. Hepler (D)	39,253	37.7

IOWA

		Votes	%
1	William F. Kopp (R)	38,100	64.5
	E. W. McManus (D)	20,977	35.5
2	Harry E. Hull (R)	50,160	89.0
	F. B. Althouse (F-LAB)	6,058	10.8
3	Burton E. Sweet (R)	67,859	97.1
4	Gilbert N. Haugen (R)	53,083	74.6
	Carl Evans (D)	18,104	25.4
5	James W. Good (R)	58,197	99.9
6	C. William Ramseyer (R)	41,644	65.9
	O. P. Meyers (D)	21,538	34.1
7	Cassius C. Dowell (R)	66,367	98.1
8	Horace M. Towner (R)	49,522	99.6
9	William R. Green (R)	48,558	82.1
	Hattie T. Harl (I)	10,607	17.9
10	Lester J. Dickinson (R)	67,700	96.0
11	William D. Boies (R)	64,342	69.7
	E. H. Birmingham (D)	27,953	30.3

KANSAS

		Votes	%
1	Daniel R. Anthony Jr. (R)	42,471	67.2
	J. B. Billard (D)	20,730	32.8
2	Edward C. Little (R)	48,307	58.9
	C. A. Bowman (D)	31,862	38.9
3	Philip P. Campbell (R)	47,220	60.4
	J. D. Turkington (D)	30,932	39.6
4	Homer Hoch (R)	32,619	67.0
	Walter W. Austin (D)	14,944	30.7
5	James G. Strong (R)	38,992	68.6
	Thomas F. Johnson (D)	16,303	28.7
6	Hays B. White (R)	36,400	61.9
	J. C. Ruppenthal (D)	20,600	35.0
7	Jasper N. Tincher (R)	49,601	62.9
	J. R. Beeching (D)	26,992	34.2
8	Richard E. Bird (R)	30,076	49.4
	W. A. Ayres (D)	29,899	49.1

KENTUCKY

		Votes	%
1	Alben W. Barkley (D)	50,635	64.3
	Miller Hughes (R)	28,070	35.7
2	David H. Kincheloe (D)	45,741	55.8
	Erskine B. Bassett (R)	36,280	44.2
3	Robert Y. Thomas (D)	36,430	50.4
	John H. Gilliam (R)	35,873	49.6
4	Ben Johnson (D)	41,620	52.5
	John P. Haswell (R)	37,702	47.5
5	Charles F. Ogden (R)	67,436	53.7
	James H. Richmond (D)	55,037	43.9
6	Arthur B. Rouse (D)	39,833	53.7
	Rodney G. Bryson (R)	26,099	35.2
	Harry V. Dill (I)	8,231	11.1
7	James C. Cantrill (D)	52,780	100.0
8	Ralph Gilbert (D)	37,381	52.0
	King Swope (R)	34,525	48.0
9	William J. Fields (D)	51,530	52.9
	W. G. Blair (R)	45,897	47.1
10	John W. Langley (R)	33,035	100.0

	Candidates	Votes	%
11	John M. Robsion (R)	64,248	75.4
	J. E. Sampson (D)	20,926	24.6

LOUISIANA

		Votes	%
1	James O'Connor (D)	19,716	99.9
2	H. Garland Dupre (D)	19,777	100.0
3	Whitmell P. Martin (D)	4,201	100.0
4	John N. Sandlin (D)	10,507	100.0
5	Riley J. Wilson (D)	9,502	100.0
6	George K. Favrot (D)	9,426	100.0
7	Ladislas Lazaro (D)	8,551	100.0
8	James B. Aswell (D)	10,357	100.0

MAINE

		Votes	%
1	Carroll L. Beedy (R)	30,810	66.6
	F. H. Haskell (D)	15,456	33.4
2	Wallace H. White Jr. (R)	35,015	62.5
	W. N. Price (D)	20,978	37.5
3	John A. Peters (R)	38,533	66.7
	A. C. Towle (D)	19,276	33.3
4	Ira G. Hersey (R)	30,872	72.3
	L. G. C. Brown (D)	11,805	27.7

MARYLAND

		Votes	%
1	Thomas Alan Goldsborough (D)	29,969	52.5
	William N. Andrews (R)	27,090	47.5
2	Albert A. Blakeney (R)	41,608	49.7
	Carville D. Benson (D)	34,151	40.8
	Samuel C. Appleby (I)	5,679	6.8
3	John Philip Hill (R)	24,617	49.4
	Charles P. Coady (D)	23,104	46.4
4	J. Charles Linthicum (D)	32,135	42.4
	William O. Atwood (R)	30,891	40.8
	Walter E. Knickman (I)	8,417	11.1
5	Sydney E. Mudd (R)	29,867	58.9
	Thomas S. Klinger (D)	18,569	36.6
6	Frederick N. Zihlman (R)	35,864	56.3
	Frank W. Mish (D)	25,992	40.8

MASSACHUSETTS

		Votes	%
1	Allen T. Treadway (R)	36,105	61.5
	Thomas F. Cassidy (D)	22,577	38.5
2	Frederick H. Gillett (R)	47,658	99.9
3	Calvin D. Paige (R)	38,313	71.5
	Nixon Campbell (D)	15,311	28.6
4	Samuel E. Winslow (R)	37,323	56.8
	John F. McGrath (D)	28,438	43.2
5	John Jacob Rogers (R)	41,861	70.1
	Jackson Palmer (D)	17,861	29.9
6	Willfred W. Lufkin (R)	47,231	75.3
	John P. O'Connell (L-LAB D)	15,523	24.7
7	Robert S. Maloney (R)	28,009	47.6
	Michael F. Phelan (D)	25,691	43.7
	George F. Hogan (P)	5,121	8.7
8	Frederick W. Dallinger (R)	54,246	72.9
	Whitfield L. Tuck (D)	12,754	17.1
	John D. Lynch (I)	7,407	10.0
9	Charles L. Underhill (R)	43,111	71.1
	Maurice F. Ahearn (D)	17,542	28.9
10	Peter F. Tague (D)	14,535	51.0
	James E. Maguire (R)	13,995	49.1
11	George Holden Tinkham (R)	40,278	68.5
	Alfred J. Moore (D)	18,553	31.5
12	James A. Gallivan (D)	32,622	58.6
	Harrison A. Atwood (R)	18,259	32.8
	William H. O'Brien (PP CAND)	4,813	8.6
13	Robert Luce (R)	56,451	70.9
	Charles F. McCarthy (D)	23,122	29.1
14	Louis A. Frothingham (R)	46,894	60.4
	Richard Olney (D)	28,596	36.8

	Candidates	Votes	%
15	William S. Greene (R)	28,095	60.2
	Arthur J. B. Cartier (D)	18,615	39.9
16	Joseph Walsh (R)	40,303	84.8
	George Richards (LAB)	7,239	15.2

MICHIGAN

		Votes	%
1	George P. Codd (R)	89,171	80.3
	Frank Murphy (D)	19,803	17.8
2	Earl C. Michener (R)	61,857	70.9
	William H. Moore (D)	25,281	29.0
3	William H. Frankhauser (R)	50,778	71.4
	Gordon L. Stewart (D)	19,652	27.6
4	John C. Ketcham (R)	47,671	75.1
	Roman I. Jarvis Sr. (D)	15,199	23.9
5	Carl E. Mapes (R)	53,379	75.0
	Frank C. Jarvis (D)	15,963	22.4
6	Patrick H. Kelley (R)	102,627	72.7
	Frank L. Dodge (D)	33,319	23.6
7	Louis C. Cramton (R)	53,416	80.1
	John Hooker (D)	12,755	19.1
8	Joseph W. Fordney (R)	54,337	72.2
	Austin M. Brown (D)	20,766	27.6
9	James C. McLaughlin (R)	42,992	76.3
	Michael B. Danaher (D)	12,095	21.5
10	Roy O. Woodruff (R)	43,678	75.5
	David J. Lynch (D)	13,935	24.1
11	Frank D. Scott (R)	41,529	100.0
12	W. Frank James (R)	41,783	80.4
	Edward C. Anthony (D)	8,446	16.3
13	Vincent M. Brennan (R)	78,116	68.1
	James H. Lee (D)	31,369	27.3

Special Election

		Votes	%
13	Clarence J. McLeod (R)	77,975	72.8
	James H. Lee (D)	29,110	27.2

MINNESOTA

		Votes	%
1	Sydney Anderson (R)	50,387	70.4
	Julius I. Reiter (F-LAB)	21,158	29.6
2	Frank Clague (R)	49,181	65.2
	H. A. Fuller (I)	19,274	25.6
	Frank Simon (D)	6,934	9.2
3	Charles R. Davis (R)	41,678	58.8
	James M. Millett (D)	15,146	21.4
	R. A. Pomadt (I)	14,034	19.8
4	Oscar E. Keller (R)	38,792	58.7
	Thomas J. Brady (D)	22,610	34.2
	Carl W. Cummins (I)	4,702	7.1
5	Walter H. Newton (R)	54,962	57.6
	Lynn Thompson (F-LAB)	22,584	23.7
	Ernest Lundeen (I)	9,573	10.0
	T. O. Dahl (D)	8,357	8.8
6	Harold Knutson (R)	47,954	69.0
	Charles A. Lindbergh (I)	21,587	31.0
7	Andrew J. Volstead (R)	36,822	47.5
	Ole J. Kvale (I)	35,370	45.6
	James C. Mitchell (D)	5,358	6.9
8	Oscar J. Larson (R)	33,428	50.8
	William L. Carss (D)	32,395	49.2
9	Halvor Steenerson (R)	39,122	52.7
	N. E. Thormodson (I)	28,443	38.3
	Frank Jeffers (D)	6,741	9.1
10	Thomas D. Schall (R)	54,971	68.3
	John G. Soltis (F-LAB)	18,590	23.1
	H. A. Finlayson (D)	6,917	8.6

MISSISSIPPI

		Votes	%
1	John E. Rankin (D)	10,400	100.0
2	Bill G. Lowrey (D)	6,960	100.0
3	Benjamin G. Humphreys (D)	6,338	100.0
4	Thomas U. Sisson (D)	8,979	93.8
	J. A. Washington (SOC)	598	6.2
5	Ross A. Collins (D)	11,507	94.1
6	Paul B. Johnson (D)	9,483	86.2
	L. B. Collins (R)	906	8.2

MISSISSIPPI

Candidates	Votes	%
T. J. Lyon (SOC)	610	5.6
7 Percy E. Quin (D)	6,695	92.7
8 James W. Collier (D)	5,944	95.4

MISSOURI

Candidates	Votes	%
1 Frank C. Millspaugh (R)	34,259	50.5
Milton A. Romjue (D)	32,952	48.6
2 William W. Rucker (D)	38,771	52.7
B. F. Beazell (R)	34,645	47.1
3 Henry F. Lawrence (R)	33,949	51.9
Jacob L. Milligan (D)	31,475	48.1
4 Charles L. Faust (R)	38,047	54.1
L. C. Gabbert (D)	32,098	45.7
5 Edgar C. Ellis (R)	79,075	50.1
William T. Bland (D)	77,793	49.3
6 William O. Atkeson (R)	29,802	52.2
Clement C. Dickinson (D)	26,995	47.3
7 Roscoe C. Patterson (R)	50,213	54.9
Sam C. Major (D)	40,541	44.3
8 Sidney C. Roach (R)	30,158	53.8
William L. Nelson (D)	25,733	45.9
9 Theodore W. Hukriede (R)	39,213	52.2
Champ Clark (D)	35,626	47.5
10 Cleveland A. Newton (R)	122,100	61.1
Hughes (D)	65,472	32.8
11 Harry B. Hawes (D)	35,726	49.8
Bernard P. Bogy (R)	33,592	46.8
12 Leonidas C. Dyer (R)	28,400	60.6
Samuel Rosenfeld (D)	16,901	36.1
13 Marion E. Rhodes (R)	30,610	55.2
A. T. Brewster (D)	24,394	44.0
14 Edward D. Hays (R)	56,525	56.8
Robert L. Ward (D)	41,547	41.8
15 Isaac V. McPherson (R)	44,176	55.7
E. M. Roseberry (D)	33,844	42.7
16 Samuel A. Shelton (R)	28,500	54.5
Thomas L. Rubey (D)	23,510	45.0

MONTANA

Candidates	Votes	%
1 Washington J. McCormick (R)	39,729	57.2
Burton Watson (D)	29,688	42.8
2 Carl W. Riddick (R)	68,486	64.9
M. McCusker (D)	37,104	35.1

NEBRASKA

Candidates	Votes	%
1 C. Frank Reavis (R)	35,293	67.6
Frank A. Peterson (D)	16,880	32.4
2 Albert W. Jefferis (R)	33,196	64.4
James O'Hara (D)	18,346	35.6
3 Robert E. Evans (R)	38,370	54.0
Webb Rice (D)	17,171	24.2
Marie Weekes (I)	15,516	21.8
4 Melvin O. McLaughlin (R)	34,384	62.5
Albert P. Sprague (D)	20,662	37.5
5 William E. Andrews (R)	31,695	58.3
Harry S. Dungan (D)	22,663	41.7
6 Moses P. Kinkaid (R)	49,122	64.5
Thomas C. Grimes (D)	20,790	27.3
Lucien Stebbins (I)	6,222	8.2

NEVADA

Candidates	Votes	%
AL Samuel S. Arentz (R)	13,149	48.9
Charles R. Evans (D)	9,167	34.1
Paul Jones (I)	3,349	12.5

NEW HAMPSHIRE

Candidates	Votes	%
1 Sherman E. Burroughs (R)	46,606	59.3
Rosecrans W. Pillsbury (D)	31,354	39.9
2 Edward H. Wason (R)	46,720	61.4
Charles J. French (D)	29,376	38.6

NEW JERSEY

Candidates	Votes	%
1 Francis F. Patterson Jr. (R)	55,885	65.3
W. P. Kramer (D)	23,711	27.7
2 Isaac Bacharach (R)	51,006	70.0
William E. Jonah (D)	21,511	29.5
3 T. Frank Appleby (R)	55,098	64.4
W. E. Ramsay (D)	29,796	34.8
4 Elijah C. Hutchinson (R)	39,582	55.0
Charles Browne (D)	31,695	44.0
5 Ernest R. Ackerman (R)	53,681	68.8
R. E. Clement (D)	21,949	28.1
6 Randolph Perkins (R)	54,334	66.4
Thomas A. Shields (D)	25,764	31.5
7 Amos H. Radcliff (R)	33,844	64.5
Nicholas Hughes (D)	15,291	29.2
Frank Hubschmitt (SOC)	2,939	5.6
8 Herbert W. Taylor (R)	41,898	59.3
C. A. McGlennon (D)	27,822	39.4
9 Richard W. Parker (R)	32,240	59.3
Daniel F. Minahan (D)	20,244	37.3
10 Frederick R. Lehlbach (R)	40,965	63.6
Dallas Flannagan (D)	19,548	30.4
11 Archibald E. Olpp (R)	30,046	55.2
John J. Eagan (D)	23,402	43.0
12 Charles F. X. O'Brien (D)	34,527	53.1
Walter Williams (R)	29,080	44.8

Special Election

Candidates	Votes	%
1 Francis F. Patterson Jr. (R)	54,971	67.2
W. P. Kramer (D)	23,279	28.5

NEW MEXICO

Candidates	Votes	%
AL Nestor Montoya (R)	54,672	51.9
Antonio Lucero (D)	49,426	46.9

NEW YORK

Candidates	Votes	%
1 Frederick C. Hicks (R & P)	61,502	69.5
Alfred J. Kennedy (D)	24,868	28.1
2 John J. Kindred (D)	42,530	47.7
Rudolph Hantusch (R)	40,201	45.1
William Burkle Sr. (SOC)	5,872	6.6
3 John Kissel (R)	16,576	44.6
Christian J. McWilliams (D)	15,224	40.9
Harry W. Laidler (SOC)	5,257	14.1
4 Thomas H. Cullen (D)	21,070	56.2
James J. Astorita (R)	14,686	39.2
5 Ardolph L. Kline (R)	42,129	58.2
Edward Cassin (D)	27,650	38.2
6 Warren I. Lee (R)	44,527	59.4
William F. X. Geoghan (D)	22,476	30.0
W. W. Passage (SOC)	6,867	9.2
7 Michael J. Hogan (R)	20,489	46.5
James P. Maher (D)	16,554	37.6
Jean Jacques Coronel (SOC)	6,561	14.9
8 Charles G. Bond (R)	30,916	49.1
William E. Cleary (D)	22,586	35.8
Victor H. Lawn (SOC)	9,124	14.5
9 Andrew N. Petersen (R)	41,399	52.1
David J. O'Connell (D)	30,212	38.1
Wilhemus B. Robinson (SOC)	7,420	9.3
10 Lester D. Volk (R)	25,808	50.0
Gilbert H. Rhoades (D)	14,071	27.3
James O'Neal (SOC)	11,529	22.4
11 Daniel J. Riordan (D)	19,097	50.7
Wilbur F. Wakeman (R)	17,358	46.1
12 Meyer London (SOC)	10,212	54.1
Henry M. Goldfogle (D, R)	8,654	45.9
13 Christopher D. Sullivan (D, R)	8,979	64.6
Charles W. Irwin (SOC)	4,925	35.4
14 Nathan S. Perlman (R, D)	18,042	67.9
Algernon Lee (SOC)	8,515	32.1
15 Thomas J. Ryan (R)	18,936	51.6
Peter J. Dooling (D)	14,971	40.8
16 W. Bourke Cockran (D)	19,275	53.0
Warren S. Fisher (R & P)	14,336	39.4
Bertha H. Mailly (SOC)	2,748	7.6
17 Ogden L. Mills (R)	33,659	62.0
Herbert C. Pell Jr. (D)	18,345	33.8
18 John F. Carew (D)	12,169	31.2
Henry J. O'Connor (R)	11,148	28.6
Jeremiah A. O'Leary (F-LAB)	9,998	25.7
Marie MacDonald (SOC)	5,668	14.5
19 Walter M. Chandler (R)	41,832	59.2
William Kennelly (D)	23,126	32.7
Esther Friedman (SOC)	5,667	8.0
20 Isaac Siegel (R, D)	12,605	57.2
Morris Hillquit (SOC)	9,442	42.8
21 Martin C. Ansorge (R)	48,959	58.7
Jerome F. Donovan (D)	28,535	34.2
22 Anthony J. Griffin (D)	20,389	45.7
Wilbur J. Murphy (R)	17,657	39.6
Patrick J. Murphy (SOC)	6,580	14.7
23 Albert B. Rossdale (R)	38,915	39.4
Richard F. McKiniry (D)	36,835	37.3
Abraham Josephson (SOC)	22,949	23.3
24 Benjamin L. Fairchild (R)	50,409	53.7
James V. Ganly (D)	28,006	29.8
George Orr (SOC)	15,550	16.6
25 James W. Husted (R & P)	49,829	67.4
A. Outram Sherman (D)	20,632	27.9
26 Hamilton Fish Jr. (R & P)	43,916	63.7
Rosslyn M. Cox (D)	22,772	33.0
27 Charles B. Ward (R)	42,504	60.8
John R. Green (D)	23,115	33.1
28 Peter G. Ten Eyck (D)	51,210	53.8
Edward J. Halter (R)	42,214	44.4
29 James S. Parker (R & P)	54,313	67.9
J. Ward Russell (D)	23,663	29.6
30 Frank Crowther (R & P)	41,413	61.9
John E. Kelly (D)	18,687	27.9
Harry Christian (SOC)	6,242	9.3
31 Bertrand H. Snell (R & P)	45,059	74.7
John C. Russell (D)	14,772	24.5
32 Luther W. Mott (R & P)	53,249	72.6
Newton S. Beebe (D)	20,085	27.4
33 Homer P. Snyder (R)	47,251	64.6
Roger W. Huntington (D)	21,732	29.7
34 John Davenport Clarke (R)	52,809	69.8
Charles R. Seymour (D)	21,496	28.4
35 Walter W. Magee (R)	60,018	65.0
John F. Nash (D)	25,699	27.8
36 Norman J. Gould (R & P)	49,160	67.6
George K. Shuler (D)	23,534	32.4
37 Alanson B. Houghton (R & P)	51,512	68.0
Charles L. Durham (D)	21,762	28.7
38 Thomas B. Dunn (R & P)	56,796	66.0
Hiram R. Wood (D)	20,281	23.6
Charles Messinger (SOC)	8,369	9.7
39 Archie D. Sanders (R & P)	53,079	71.1
David A. White (D)	17,602	23.6
George Weber (SOC)	3,943	5.3
40 S. Wallace Dempsey (R & P)	56,129	69.5
Frank S. Nicholson (D)	19,253	23.8
Augustus Meas (SOC)	5,389	6.7
41 Clarence MacGregor (R & P)	30,560	54.5
Al J. Egloff (D)	20,692	36.9
Martin B. Heisler (SOC)	4,836	8.6
42 James M. Mead (D)	22,869	48.3
C. Hamilton Cook (R & P)	21,224	44.9
John H. Gibbons (SOC)	3,218	6.8
43 Daniel A. Reed (R & P)	52,343	74.4
Fred H. Sylvester (D)	13,720	19.5
Gust C. Peterson (SOC)	4,273	6.1

NORTH CAROLINA

Candidates	Votes	%
1 Hallett S. Ward (D)	21,414	74.1
Wheeler Martin (R)	7,495	25.9

NORTH CAROLINA

	Candidates	Votes	%
2	Claude Kitchin (D)	20,890	86.1
	W. O. Dixon (R)	3,367	13.9
3	Samuel L. Brinson (D)	21,547	56.9
	Richard L. Herring (R)	16,347	43.1
4	Edward W. Pou (D)	26,470	65.3
	James D. Parker (R)	14,084	34.7
5	Charles M. Stedman (D)	45,301	54.1
	William D. Merritt (R)	38,484	45.9
6	Homer L. Lyon (D)	24,174	68.7
	R. S. White (R)	11,040	31.4
7	William C. Hammer (D)	37,071	53.1
	William H. Cox (R)	32,784	46.9
8	Robert L. Doughton (D)	32,934	51.2
	J. Ike Campbell (R)	31,456	48.9
9	Alfred L. Bulwinkle (D)	40,195	53.0
	Jake F. Newell (R)	35,686	47.0
10	Zebulon Weaver (D)	36,923	51.6
	L. L. Jenkins (R)	34,625	48.4

NORTH DAKOTA

	Candidates	Votes	%
1	Olger B. Burtness (R)	43,530	57.6
	John M. Baer (I N-PART)	32,072	42.4
2	George M. Young (R)	34,849	51.7
	Ole H. Olson (I N-PART)	32,618	48.4
3	James H. Sinclair (R &	41,409	62.9
	R. H. Johnson (D&I)	24,460	37.1

OHIO

	Candidates	Votes	%
1	Nicholas Longworth (R)	57,328	57.6
	John H. Allen (D)	40,195	40.4
2	Ambrose E. B. Stephens (R)	47,797	52.6
	Thomas H. Morrow (D)	41,781	46.0
3	Roy G. Fitzgerald (R)	66,259	50.2
	William G. Pickrel (D)	59,214	44.9
4	John S. Cable (R)	50,478	52.6
	B. F. Welty (D)	45,489	47.4
5	Charles J. Thompson (R)	40,384	61.4
	Newt Bronson (D)	25,395	38.6
6	Charles C. Kearns (R)	38,044	55.2
	Cleona Searles (D)	30,903	44.8
7	Simeon D. Fess (R)	73,794	61.0
	Paul F. Dye (D)	47,196	39.0
8	R. Clint Cole (R)	43,473	54.3
	Fred E. Guthery (D)	36,665	45.8
9	William W. Chalmers (R)	49,732	56.5
	Isaac R. Sherwood (D)	38,292	43.5
10	Israel M. Foster (R)	38,436	64.2
	Benjamin F. Reynolds (D)	21,429	35.8
11	Edwin D. Ricketts (R)	33,524	51.7
	Mell G. Underwood (D)	31,359	48.3
12	John C. Speaks (R)	62,247	57.9
	Arthur P. Lamneck (D)	43,845	40.8
13	James T. Begg (R)	48,416	64.5
	Alfred Waggoner (D)	26,646	35.5
14	Charles L. Knight (R)	63,010	52.6
	Martin L. Davey (D)	56,507	47.2
15	C. Ellis Moore (R)	42,419	58.3
	John Sherman Talbott (D)	30,326	41.7
16	Joseph H. Himes (R)	56,584	56.9
	John McSweeney Jr. (D)	42,799	43.1
17	William M. Morgan (R)	46,968	50.2
	William A. Ashbrook (D)	46,675	49.8
18	Frank Murphy (R)	52,862	61.7
	Albert O. Barnes (D)	32,802	38.3
19	John G. Cooper (R)	60,147	70.4
	James Kennedy (D)	25,250	29.6
20	Miner G. Norton (R)	35,483	56.0
	Charles A. Mooney (D)	27,223	42.9
21	Harry C. Gahn (R)	27,127	59.1
	John J. Babka (D)	18,252	39.7
22	Theodore E. Burton (R)	91,062	74.3
	Mathew B. Excell (D)	30,738	25.1

OKLAHOMA

	Candidates	Votes	%
1	Thomas A. Chandler (R)	42,782	53.3
	E. B. Howard (D)	35,201	43.8
2	Alice M. Robertson (R)	24,188	48.8
	W. W. Hastings (D)	23,979	48.4
3	Charles D. Carter (D)	33,347	51.3
	James L. Shinaberger (R)	27,465	42.2
	Robert L. Allen (SOC)	4,227	6.5
4	Joseph C. Pringey (R)	31,458	48.6
	Tom D. McKeown (D)	29,832	46.1
	J. E. Bartos (SOC)	3,438	5.3
5	Fletcher B. Swank (D)	35,067	50.6
	B. T. Hainer (R)	31,304	45.2
6	Lorraine M. Gensman (R)	26,076	47.7
	Elmer Thomas (D)	25,304	46.3
	J. V. Kolachny (SOC)	3,202	5.9
7	James V. McClintic (D)	21,422	49.4
	D. Montgomery (R)	17,664	40.8
	O. E. Enfield (SOC)	4,251	9.8
8	Manuel Herrick (R)	31,265	53.9
	Zack A. Harris (D)	23,405	40.4
	H. C. Geist (SOC)	3,304	5.7

Special Election

	Candidates	Votes	%
8	Charles Swindall (R)	32,420	55.3
	Zach A. Harris (D)	22,389	38.2
	H. C. Geist (SOC)	3,835	6.5

OREGON

	Candidates	Votes	%
1	Willis C. Hawley (R-D-P)	75,597	90.2
	Harlin Talbert (SOC)	8,258	9.9
2	Nicholas J. Sinnott (R)	29,655	69.4
	James Harvey Graham (D)	13,049	30.6
3	Clifton N. McArthur (R)	37,884	51.9
	Esther Lovejoy (P)	31,853	43.6

PENNSYLVANIA

	Candidates	Votes	%
1	William S. Vare (R)	43,108	73.9
	Lawrence E. McCrossin (D)	11,682	20.0
	H. J. Nelson (SOC)	3,509	6.0
2	George S. Graham (R)	34,848	78.7
	Herman Becker (D)	7,877	17.8
3	Harry C. Ransley (R, LAB)	29,075	77.2
	Joseph Hagerty (D)	6,991	18.6
4	George W. Edmonds (R)	41,102	72.3
	Harry J. Ruesscamp (D)	12,003	21.1
	L. L. Klein (SOC)	2,969	5.2
5	James J. Connolly (R)	48,455	69.1
	Henry J. Burns (D)	15,671	22.4
6	George P. Darrow (R, P)	104,576	73.5
	Harry S. Jeffery (D)	33,363	23.5
7	Thomas S. Butler (R, P)	52,863	75.6
	Freeland S. Brown (D)	15,942	22.8
8	Henry W. Watson (R)	44,032	67.5
	Harvey S. Plummer (D)	18,605	28.5
9	William W. Griest (R)	29,252	74.2
	David F. Magee (D)	9,504	24.1
10	Charles R. Connell (R)	35,181	52.1
	Patrick McLane (D)	30,411	45.0
11	Clarence D. Coughlin (R, P)	45,092	59.7
	John J. Casey (D, SOC)	30,412	40.3
12	John Reber (R)	26,816	55.2
	Thomas J. Butler (D)	21,787	44.8
13	Fred B. Gernerd (R)	38,026	50.6
	Harry J. Dunn (D, LAB)	29,922	39.8
	Charles E. Yeager (SOC)	6,245	8.3
14	Louis T. McFadden (R, P)	27,782	76.0
	Thomas A. Doherty (D)	8,248	22.6
15	Edgar R. Kiess (R, P)	30,182	71.6
	C. Edmund Gilmore (D)	10,802	25.6
16	I. Clinton Kline (R, P)	25,980	52.1
	John V. Lesher (D)	22,417	45.0
17	Benjamin K. Focht (R, P)	29,874	62.6
	John C. Dunkle (D)	17,234	36.1
18	Aaron S. Kreider (R, P)	42,745	64.1
	Milton H. Plank (D)	18,951	28.4
	George A. Herring (LAB)	4,110	6.2
19	John M. Rose (R)	35,068	53.5
	Warren Worth Bailey (D)	18,865	28.8

	Candidates	Votes	%
	William T. Welsh (LAB, SOC)	9,842	15.0
20	Edward S. Brooks (R)	22,989	51.7
	Charles A. Hawkins (D, P)	20,701	46.5
21	Evan J. Jones (R, P)	27,780	63.4
	J. D. Connelly (D, LAB)	15,000	34.2
22	Adam M. Wyant (R)	30,540	51.6
	John H. Wilson (D)	22,533	38.1
	S. E. Miller (SOC)	3,234	5.5
23	Samuel A. Kendall (R, P)	36,152	59.0
	Bruce F. Sterling (D)	23,517	38.4
24	Henry W. Temple (R, P)	42,402	73.3
	Samuel Amspoker (D)	15,405	26.7
25	Milton W. Shreve (P, I)	19,706	43.0
	Robert J. Firman (R)	18,785	41.0
	Max B. Haibach (D)	5,442	11.9
26	William H. Kirkpatrick (R)	25,446	56.0
	George W. Geiser Jr. (D)	19,219	42.3
27	Nathan L. Strong (R, P)	31,209	71.4
	Lafayette F. Sutter (D, P)	10,814	24.7
28	Harris J. Bixler (R, D)	28,718	56.4
	Willis J. Hulings (P, CIT)	20,676	40.6
29	Stephen G. Porter (R, P)	32,766	69.5
	George J. Shaffer (D)	10,749	22.8
	James J. Marshall (SOC)	3,604	7.7
30	M. Clyde Kelly (R, D)	51,850	91.5
	Charles A. Fike (SOC)	4,847	8.6
31	John M. Morin (R, D)	29,399	89.8
	Albert R. Jerling (SOC)	2,280	7.0
32	Guy E. Campbell (R, D)	44,307	83.9
	Earl O. Gunther (SOC)	4,552	8.6
	George E. Briggs (P)	3,953	7.5
AL	Anderson H. Walters (R)	1,140,836✓	
	William J. Burke (R)	1,134,013✓	
	Mahlon M. Garland (R)	1,126,406*	
	Joseph McLaughlin (R)	1,108,538✓	
	John P. Bracken (D)	466,564	
	M. J. Hanlan (D)	463,866	
	Charles M. Bowman (D)	459,552	
	John B. McDonough (D)	444,306	
	Flora J. Diefenderfer (P)	89,683	
	George Hart (P)	85,771	
	Luther S. Kauffman (P)	85,375	
	Charles J. Bauer (SOC)	67,596	
	A. M. Buckwalter (SOC)	66,628	
	Edward W. Hayden (SOC)	65,928	
	Henry W. Schlegel (SOC)	65,058	
	F. E. Whittlesey (P)	60,278	
	Frieda S. Miller (LAB)	25,265	
	Howard Cessna (LAB)	24,062	
	William A. Hagan (SINGLE T)	1,795	
	William R. Kline (SINGLE T)	1,790	
	Thomas A. Kavanagh (SINGLE T)	1,766	
	Joseph E. Robinson (SINGLE T)	1,727	
	Joseph P. Smith (INDL)	1,197	
	Frank Kalcec (INDL)	977	
	Herman Spittal (INDL)	810	
	Joseph Rack (INDL)	794	

Special Election

	Candidates	Votes	%
3	Harry C. Ransley (R, LAB)	29,097	76.6
	Joseph Hagerty (D)	7,041	18.6

RHODE ISLAND

	Candidates	Votes	%
1	Clark Burdick (R)	37,116	67.9
	Patrick J. Boyle (D)	17,537	32.1
2	Walter R. Stiness (R)	33,801	62.5
	Luigi De Pasquale (D)	19,004	35.1
3	Ambrose Kennedy (R)	34,775	59.7
	Herve J. Legace (D)	22,386	38.4

SOUTH CAROLINA

	Candidates	Votes	%
1	W. Turner Logan (D)	6,301	92.6
	Saspartas (R)	502	7.4
2	James F. Byrnes (D)	6,685	100.0
3	Fred H. Dominick (D)	9,699	100.0
4	John J. McSwain (D)	13,436	100.0
5	William F. Stevenson (D)	10,186	100.0
6	Philip H. Stoll (D)	8,681	100.0
7	Hampton P. Fulmer (D)	9,412	91.9
	Hawkins (R)	834	8.1

SOUTH DAKOTA

		Votes	%
1	Charles A. Christopherson (R)	39,231	56.2
	Engebret J. Holter (NON PART)	15,810	22.6
	Ralph E. Johnson (D)	14,815	21.2
2	Royal C. Johnson (R)	44,759	62.3
	Frank Wahlen (NON PART)	18,357	25.5
	Lewis W. Bicknell (D)	8,770	12.2
3	William Williamson (R)	19,335	48.0
	Harry L. Gandy (D)	16,214	40.2
	O. E. Farnam (NON PART)	4,765	11.8

TENNESSEE

		Votes	%
1	B. Carroll Reece (R)	46,010	98.3
2	J. Will Taylor (R)	37,722	74.8
	Curtis Gentry (D)	12,436	24.7
3	Joseph Brown (R)	29,366	51.6
	John A. Moon (D)	27,144	47.7
4	Wynne F. Clouse (R)	22,440	50.3
	Cordell Hull (D)	22,109	49.5
5	Ewin L. Davis (D)	14,845	61.9
	Jesse Davenport (R)	9,102	38.0
6	Joseph W. Byrns (D)	24,422	82.9
	W. T. Perry (R)	4,679	15.9
7	Lemuel P. Padgett (D)	17,517	55.7
	A. M. Hughes (R)	13,813	43.9
8	Lon A. Scott (R)	22,938	50.6
	Gordon Browning (D)	22,279	49.1
9	Finis J. Garrett (D)	25,409	68.3
	John R. Walker Jr (R)	11,671	31.4
10	Hubert F. Fisher (D)	23,987	80.8
	Wayman Wilkerson (I, R)	4,927	16.6

TEXAS

		Votes	%
1	Eugene Black (D)	17,814	92.3
	G. T. Bartlett (R)	1,497	7.8
2	John C. Box (D)	21,692	92.8
	G. E. H. Meyer (AM)	1,671	7.2
3	Morgan G. Sanders (D)	15,575	83.2
	J. A. Butler (R)	3,149	16.8
4	Sam Rayburn (D)	17,795	77.6
	A. W. Acheson (R)	5,124	22.4
5	Hatton W. Sumners (D)	19,785	80.2
	J. O. Burleson (R)	4,883	19.8
6	Rufus Hardy (D)	17,555	72.5
	Clyde Essex (AM)	3,668	15.2
	D. H. Merrill (R)	2,512	10.4

	Candidates	Votes	%
7	Clay Stone Briggs (D)	12,656	96.6
8	Daniel E. Garrett (D)	18,474	55.7
	E. B. Barden (R)	7,001	21.1
	M. H. Broyles (B&T R)	5,750	17.4
	J. M. Gibson (AM)	1,918	5.8
9	Joseph J. Mansfield (D)	12,311	58.7
	James W. Rugeley (R)	8,667	41.3
10	James P. Buchanan (D)	14,411	65.5
	B. G. Neighbors (AM)	7,597	34.5
11	Tom T. Connally (D)	15,621	79.1
	W. D. Lewis (AM)	4,124	20.9
12	Fritz G. Lanham (D)	20,925	80.5
	Sam Davidson (R)	4,203	16.2
13	Lucian W. Parish (D)	18,951	88.4
	C. W. Johnson (R)	2,483	11.6
14	Harry M. Wurzbach (R)	17,265	55.6
	Carlos Bee (D)	13,771	44.4
15	John N. Garner (D)	10,265	99.9
16	Claude B. Hudspeth (D)	15,658	69.7
	William S. Easterling (R)	6,796	30.3
17	Thomas L. Blanton (D)	22,311	83.8
	W. D. Cowan (AM)	4,298	16.2
18	Marvin Jones (D)	25,996	97.0

UTAH

		Votes	%
1	Don B. Colton (R)	41,749	57.3
	James W. Funk (D)	27,974	38.4
2	Elmer O. Leatherwood (R)	39,235	54.8
	Mathonihah Thomas (D)	28,201	39.4

VERMONT

		Votes	%
1	Frank L. Greene (R)	33,670	74.7
	Jeremiah C. Duriok (D)	11,398	25.3
2	Porter H. Dale (R, P)	34,221	78.7
	Harry W. Witters (D)	9,189	21.1

VIRGINIA

		Votes	%
1	Schuyler Otis Bland (D)	14,646	79.8
	S. P. Powell (R)	3,562	19.4
2	Joseph T. Deal (D)	15,318	73.6
	Menalcus Lankford (R)	5,389	25.9
3	Andrew J. Montague (D)	20,069	72.5
	Walker G. Decourcy (R)	4,146	15.0
	H. H. Price	2,682	9.7
4	Patrick Henry Drewry (D)	11,427	92.6
	F. L. Mason (R)	909	7.4
5	Rorer A. James (D)	15,567	58.4
	S. Floyd Landreth (R)	11,109	41.6
6	James P. Woods (D)	13,101	59.0
	W. M. Doah (R)	9,114	41.0
7	Thomas W. Harrison (D)	13,221‡	50.9
	John Paul (R)	12,773	49.1
8	R. Walton Moore (D)	13,142	71.7
	F. M. Brooks (R)	5,200	28.4
9	C. Bascom Slemp (R)	28,057	54.8
	Bolling H. Handy (D)	23,100	45.2
10	Henry D. Flood (D)	14,811	64.8
	James H. C. Grasty (R)	8,027	35.1

WASHINGTON

	Candidates	Votes	%
1	John F. Miller (R)	51,459	56.7
	James A. Duncan (F-LAB)	28,154	31.0
	Hugh C. Todd (D)	11,184	12.3
2	Lindley H. Hadley (R)	39,315	59.8
	William Bouck (F-LAB)	26,398	40.2
3	Albert Johnson (R)	50,667	55.7
	Homer T. Bone (F-LAB)	27,824	30.6
	George P. Fishburne (D)	12,553	13.8
4	John W. Summers (R)	37,986	63.2
	Fred Miller (D)	11,353	18.9
	Knute Hill (F-LAB)	10,735	17.9
5	J. Stanley Webster (R)	39,228	58.1
	Charles A. Fleming (D)	28,300	41.9

WEST VIRGINIA

		Votes	%
1	Benjamin L. Rosenbloom (R)	40,818	50.3
	Matthew M. Neely (D)	40,393	49.7
2	George M. Bowers (R)	43,238	56.8
	Forrest W. Brown (D)	32,896	43.2
3	Stuart F. Reed (R)	45,146	57.7
	Robert F. Kidd (D)	33,056	42.3
4	Harry C. Woodyard (R)	47,146	55.4
	John L. Conner (D)	37,951	44.6
5	Wells Goodykoontz (R)	45,193	54.1
	W. W. McNeal (D)	38,394	45.9
6	Leonard Sidney Echols (R)	51,747	54.4
	William Edwin Wilson (D)	43,327	45.6

WISCONSIN

		Votes	%
1	Henry Allen Cooper (R)	51,144	75.9
	Andrew F. Stahl (D)	13,661	20.3
2	Edward Voigt (R)	39,563	67.3
	Harry W. Bolens (D)	14,291	24.3
	Jacob F. Miller (SOC)	4,969	8.5
3	John M. Nelson (R)	44,359	69.1
	James W. Murphy (D)	19,794	30.8
4	John C. Kleczka (R)	28,854	50.2
	Robert Buech (SOC)	22,137	38.6
	Gerald P. Hayes (D)	6,436	11.2
5	William H. Stafford (R)	40,777	54.5
	Victor L. Berger (SOC)	34,004	45.5
6	Florian Lampert (R)	38,034	68.7
	Leo P. Fox (D)	11,606	21.0
	Edward C. Damrow (SOC)	5,714	10.3
7	Joseph D. Beck (R)	37,137	78.4
	Robert H. Clarke (D)	8,929	18.8
8	Edward E. Browne (R)	34,215	61.8
	George W. Lippert (SOC)	14,661	26.5
	Leo P. Pasternacki (D)	6,425	11.6
9	David G. Classon (R)	32,027	59.2
	Andrew R. McDonald (D)	20,108	37.2
10	James A. Frear (R)	44,658	99.4
11	Adolphus P. Nelson (R)	38,057	85.3
	John P. Jensen (D)	6,524	14.6

WYOMING

		Votes	%
AL	Frank W. Mondell (R)	34,689	61.5
	Wade H. Fowler (D)	14,952	26.5
	James Morgan (F-LAB)	6,021	10.7

1921 House Election

PENNSYLVANIA

Special Election

		Votes	%
AL	Thomas S. Crago (R)	705,876	68.2
	John P. Bracken (D)	225,268	21.8
	B. E. P. Prugh (P)	74,837	7.2

1922 House Elections

ALABAMA

	Candidates	Votes	%
1	John McDuffie (D)	13,960	100.0
2	John R. Tyson (D)	9,255	100.0
3	Henry B. Steagall (D)	9,141	90.3
	Charles E. Roberts	987	9.8
4	Lamar Jeffers (D)	9,976	81.5
	J. C. Harper	2,265	18.5
5	William B. Bowling (D)	10,411	80.4
	W. M. Russell	2,539	19.6
6	William B. Oliver (D)	4,864	100.0
7	Miles C. Allgood (D)	18,597	62.6
	B. L. Noogin	11,130	37.4
8	Edward B. Almon (D)	12,303	96.3
9	George Huddleston (D)	11,300	94.7
	G. L. Lemon	630	5.3
10	William B. Bankhead (D)	14,803	63.2
	W. A. McMurray	8,631	36.8

ARIZONA

	Candidates	Votes	%
AL	Carl Hayden (D)	37,262	71.9
	Emma M. Guild (R)	14,601	28.2

ARKANSAS

	Candidates	Votes	%
1	William J. Driver (D)	1,454	100.0
2	William A. Oldfield (D)	5,220	86.7
	J. N. Hout	798	13.3
3	John N. Tillman (D)	5,327	98.2
4	Otis Wingo (D)	7,330	79.5
	George Tillis	1,896	20.6
5	Heartsill Ragon (D)	5,944	79.7
	John W. White	1,513	20.3
6	Lewis E. Sawyer (D)	3,232	100.0
7	Tilman B. Parks (D)	2,167	100.0

CALIFORNIA

	Candidates	Votes	%
1	Clarence F. Lea (DR)	53,129	100.0
2	John E. Raker (DR)	32,981	100.0
3	Charles F. Curry (R-D)	71,316	91.5
	Marcus H. Steely (SOC)	6,561	8.4
4	Julius Kahn (R-D)	46,527	82.9
	Hugo Ernst (SOC)	9,547	17.0
5	John I. Nolan (R-D)	49,414*	99.8
6	James H. MacLafferty (R)	59,858	66.4
	Hugh W. Brunk (D)	22,711	25.2
	Elvina S. Beals (SOC)	7,616	8.4
7	Henry E. Barbour (R-D)	67,000	99.9
8	Arthur Monroe Free (R-D)	57,926	99.8
9	Walter F. Lineberger (R)	66,265	59.1
	Charles H. Randall (P & D)	45,794	40.9
10	Henry Z. Osborne (R-D-P)	98,739*	99.9
11	Philip D. Swing (R-D)	79,039	91.3
	George Bauer (SOC)	7,466	8.6

Special Election

		Votes	%
6	James H. MacLafferty (I)	53,285	68.4
	Hugh W. Brunk (I)	24,626	31.6

COLORADO

	Candidates	Votes	%
1	William N. Vaile (R)	32,939	55.5
	Benjamin C. Hilliard (D)	25,477	42.9
2	Charles B. Timberlake (R)	43,601	57.3
	Charles M. Worth (D)	32,443	42.7
3	Guy U. Hardy (R)	43,508	52.4
	Chester B. Horn (D)	39,500	47.6
4	Edward T. Taylor (D)	30,331	64.3
	Merle D. Vincent (R)	16,878	35.8

CONNECTICUT

	Candidates	Votes	%
1	E. Hart Fenn (R)	40,124	52.2
	Joseph F. Dutton (D)	35,003	45.6
2	Richard P. Freeman (R)	31,484	55.4
	Raymond J. Jodoin (D)	24,732	43.5
3	John Q. Tilson (R)	36,247	52.3
	Stephen Whitney (D)	31,674	45.7
4	Schuyler Merritt (R)	35,274	53.9
	Archibald McNeil (D)	28,992	44.3
5	Patrick B. O'Sullivan (D)	27,359	49.7
	James P. Glynn (R)	27,065	49.1

DELAWARE

	Candidates	Votes	%
AL	William H. Boyce (D)	39,126	53.9
	Caleb R. Layton (R)	32,577	44.9

FLORIDA

	Candidates	Votes	%
1	Herbert J. Drane (D)	14,371	82.9
	William M. Gober (R)	2,961	17.1
2	Frank Clark (D)	6,931	100.0
3	John H. Smithwick (D)	7,564	100.0
4	William J. Sears (D)	15,678	82.3
	Howard W. McCay (R)	3,362	17.6

GEORGIA

	Candidates	Votes	%
1	R. Lee Moore (D)	5,579	90.0
	D. H. Clarke (R)	426	6.9
2	Frank Park (D)	5,449	100.0
3	Charles R. Crisp (D)	7,298	100.0
4	William C. Wright (D)	4,777	100.0
5	William D. Upshaw (D)	4,646	93.1
	Max H. Wilensky	347	7.0
6	James W. Wise (D)	6,961	100.0
7	Gordon Lee (D)	7,278	100.0
8	Charles H. Brand (D)	5,148	100.0
9	Thomas M. Bell (D)	11,088	94.6
10	Carl Vinson (D)	4,639	100.0
11	William C. Lankford (D)	6,879	100.0
12	William W. Larsen (D)	5,020	100.0

IDAHO

	Candidates	Votes	%
1	Burton L. French (R)	24,167	46.8
	George Waters (D)	13,772	26.7
	W. W. Deal (PROG)	13,673	26.5
2	Addison T. Smith (R)	33,206	47.8
	W. P. Whitaker (D)	19,875	28.6
	Dow Dunning (PROG)	16,450	23.7

ILLINOIS

	Candidates	Votes	%
1	Martin B. Madden (R)	23,895	59.1
	George Mayer (D)	15,999	39.6
2	James R. Mann (R)	58,694*	58.2
	Adam F. Bloch (D)	38,487	38.2
3	Elliott W. Sproul (R)	48,486	48.8
	Thomas M. Crane (D)	47,335	47.7
4	John W. Rainey (D)	32,403	69.2
	Henry G. Dobler (R)	13,328	28.5
5	Adolph J. Sabath (D)	20,377	66.5
	Jacob Gartenstein (R)	9,007	29.4
6	James R. Buckley (D)	58,928	48.2
	John J. Gorman (R)	58,886	48.2
7	M. Alfred Michaelson (R)	69,367	49.8
	Frank M. Padden (D)	61,035	43.8
	John M. Collins (SOC)	7,276	5.2
8	Stanley Henry Kunz (D)	18,749	65.3
	Fred S. DeCola (R)	9,311	32.5
9	Fred A. Britten (R)	26,143	60.0
	James A. Prendergast (D)	16,223	37.3

	Candidates	Votes	%
10	Carl R. Chindblom (R)	62,324	61.6
	Bernard Moulton Wiedinger (D)	35,535	35.1
11	Frank R. Reid (R)	43,581	68.8
	Edward J. O'Beirne (D)	18,816	29.7
12	Charles E. Fuller (R)	46,893	77.6
	John A. Dowdall (D)	11,733	19.4
13	John C. McKenzie (R)	30,064	70.0
	William G. Curtiss (D)	12,319	28.7
14	William J. Graham (R)	34,946	59.9
	L. S. Mayer (D)	21,541	36.9
15	Edward J. King (R)	36,547	60.1
	Charles C. Craig (D)	23,298	38.3
16	William E. Hull (R)	39,372	55.2
	Jesse Black Jr. (D)	30,395	42.6
17	Frank H. Funk (R)	28,466	55.7
	Frank Gillespie (D)	22,233	43.5
18	William P. Holaday (R)	35,880	52.8
	Andrew B. Dennis (D)	30,123	44.4
19	Allen F. Moore (R)	39,636	54.4
	Raymond D. Meeker (D)	32,529	44.6
20	Henry T. Rainey (D)	31,430	54.2
	Guy L. Shaw (R)	26,541	45.8
21	J. Earl Major (D)	37,661	49.3
	Loren E. Wheeler (R)	33,086	43.3
	Duncan McDonald (F-LAB)	4,438	5.8
22	Edward E. Miller (R)	34,224	47.6
	Edward E. Campbell (D)	31,539	43.9
	Daniel L. Thomas (F-LAB)	4,980	7.0
23	William W. Arnold (D)	38,908	52.5
	Edwin B. Brooks (R)	34,610	46.7
24	Thomas S. Williams (R)	29,141	50.8
	Dempsey T. Woodard (D)	28,252	49.2
25	Edward E. Denison (R)	37,907	54.4
	A. S. Caldwell (D)	28,697	41.2
AL	Richard Yates (R)	943,684✔	
	Henry R. Rathborne (R)	911,599✔	
	Simon J. Gorman (D)	666,583	
	William Murphy (D)	662,059	
	Fred W. Wenschoff (SOC)	36,311	
	Andrew Lafin (SOC)	35,655	
	Edward Ellis Carr (F-LAB)	32,595	
	Henry W. Olinger (F-LAB)	30,756	

Special Election

		Votes	%
AL	Winnifred Mason Huck (R)	865,971	52.6
	Allen D. Albert (D)	710,716	43.2

INDIANA

	Candidates	Votes	%
1	William E. Wilson (D)	42,797	53.6
	Oscar R. Luhring (R)	35,835	44.9
2	Arthur H. Greenwood (D)	43,632	49.5
	Oscar E. Bland (R)	42,752	48.5
3	Frank Gardner (D)	43,344	53.5
	Samuel A. Lambdin (R)	37,202	46.0
4	Harry C. Canfield (D)	43,749	51.1
	John S. Benham (R)	41,825	48.9
5	Everett Sanders (R)	38,759	49.5
	Charles H. Bidaman (D)	37,748	48.2
6	Richard N. Elliott (R)	39,281	51.6
	James A. Clifton (D)	36,818	48.4
7	Merrill Moores (R)	49,629	53.9
	Joseph P. Turk (D)	41,118	44.6
8	Albert H. Vestal (R)	43,470	52.2
	John W. Tyndall (D)	39,169	47.0
9	Fred S. Purnell (R)	46,919	51.5
	George Lee Moffett (D)	42,074	46.2
10	William R. Wood (R)	45,590	59.2
	William F. Spencer (D)	30,835	40.0
11	Samuel E. Cook (D)	45,389	52.8
	Milton Kraus (R)	39,285	45.7
12	Louis W. Fairfield (R)	36,045	51.1
	Charles W. Branstrator (D)	34,457	48.9

INDIANA

	Candidates	Votes	%
13	Andrew J. Hickey (R)	50,003	53.7
	Esther Kathleen O'Keefe (D)	43,053	46.3

IOWA

	Candidates	Votes	%
1	William F. Kopp (R)	26,651	65.0
	John M. Lindley (D)	14,056	34.3
2	Harry E. Hull (R)	27,450	51.4
	Wayne G. Cook (D)	25,620	47.9
3	Thomas J. B. Robinson (R)	34,518	57.6
	Fred P. Hageman (D)	24,304	40.6
4	Gilbert N. Haugen (R)	32,586	57.1
	A. M. Schanke (D)	24,532	43.0
5	Cyrenus Cole (R)	33,607	68.0
	G. A. Smith (D)	15,825	32.0
6	C. William Ramseyer (R)	28,702	61.9
	James E. Craven (D)	17,489	37.7
7	Cassius C. Dowell (R)	34,012	62.3
	Winfred E. Robb (D)	19,987	36.6
8	Horace M. Towner (R)	30,551	56.6
	J. P. Daughton (D)	23,478	43.5
9	William R. Greene (R)	31,757	61.7
	Paul W. Richards (D)	19,722	38.3
10	Lester J. Dickinson (R)	41,290	71.1
	Mrs. Jett W. Douglas (D)	16,781	28.9
11	William D. Boies (R)	36,050	60.0
	Guy M. Gillette (D)	24,027	40.0

KANSAS

	Candidates	Votes	%
1	Daniel R. Anthony Jr. (R)	39,463	63.7
	Frank Gragg (D)	22,480	36.3
2	Edward C. Little (R)	41,482	54.4
	William H. Thompson (D)	34,816	45.6
3	William H. Sproul (R)	38,321	49.0
	Charles Stephens (D)	37,829	48.4
4	Homer Hoch (R)	29,657	62.0
	Walter W. Austin (D)	17,294	36.2
5	James G. Strong (R)	32,064	56.3
	Clarence E. Hatfield (D)	24,881	43.7
6	Hays B. White (R)	33,464	54.1
	F. W. Boyd (D)	26,666	43.1
7	Jasper N. Tincher (R)	47,515	58.3
	A. S. Allphin (D)	32,159	39.5
8	William A. Ayres (D)	37,581	62.3
	Richard E. Bird (R)	22,721	37.7

KENTUCKY

	Candidates	Votes	%
1	Alben W. Barkley (D)	9,492	70.0
	F. M. McClain (R)	4,075	30.0
2	David H. Kincheloe (D)	14,837	63.5
	George W. Jolly (R)	8,541	36.5
3	Robert Y. Thomas Jr. (D)	21,189	60.9
	W. O. Moats (R)	13,613	39.1
4	Ben Johnson (D)	19,142	93.1
	P. N. Woodruff (F-LAB)	1,429	7.0
5	Maurice H. Thatcher (R)	38,806	49.1
	Kendrick R. Lewis (D)	35,124	44.4
	Herman F. Young (F-LAB)	5,154	6.5
6	Arthur B. Rouse (D)	18,131	63.9
	Leo E. Keller (NON PL)	9,197	32.4
7	James C. Cantrill (D)	9,389	100.0
8	Ralph Gilbert (D)	21,296	57.4
	D. H. Kincaid (R)	15,802	42.6
9	William J. Fields (D)	22,816	65.1
	J. H. Stricklin (R)	12,249	34.9
10	John N. Langley (R)	17,067	55.5
	F. T. Hatcher (D)	13,668	44.5
11	John M. Robsion (R)	28,086	66.6
	C. J. Sipple (D)	11,396	27.0
	H. H. Seavy (F-LAB)	2,670	6.3

LOUISIANA

	Candidates	Votes	%
1	James O'Connor (D)	14,760	100.0
2	H. Garland Dupre (D)	12,287	100.0

	Candidates	Votes	%
3	Whitmel P. Martin (D)	1,954	99.7
4	John N. Sandlin (D)	3,618	100.0
5	Riley J. Wilson (D)	2,345	100.0
6	George K. Favrot (D)	3,317	99.5
7	Ladislas Lazaro (D)	3,069	99.5
8	James B. Aswell (D)	2,987	100.0

MAINE

	Candidates	Votes	%
1	Carroll L. Beedy (R)	26,050	58.7
	Louis A. Donahue (D)	18,312	41.3
2	Wallace H. White Jr. (R)	25,719	53.7
	B. G. McIntire (D)	22,150	46.3
3	John E. Nelson (R)	30,654	58.4
	Leon O. Tebbetts (D)	21,828	41.6
4	Ira G. Hersey (R)	18,641	60.8
	James W. Sewall (D)	11,997	39.2

MARYLAND

	Candidates	Votes	%
1	T. Alan Goldsborough (D)	27,117	55.8
	Charles J. Butler (R)	21,524	44.3
2	Millard E. Tydings (D)	36,565	52.8
	Albert Alex Blakeney (R)	31,053	44.8
3	John Philip Hill (R)	27,740	67.3
	Antony Dimarco (D)	12,454	30.2
4	J. Charles Linthicum (D)	33,322	61.7
	L. Edward Wolf (R)	18,972	35.1
5	Sydney E. Mudd (R)	23,764	50.8
	Clarence M. Roberts (D)	21,112	45.1
6	Frederick N. Zihlman (R)	22,261	50.7
	Frank W. Mish (D)	20,838	47.5

MASSACHUSETTS

	Candidates	Votes	%
1	Allen T. Treadway (R)	26,229	50.7
	Thomas F. Cassidy (D)	25,529	49.3
2	Frederick H. Gillett (R)	28,639	59.6
	Joseph E. Kerigan (D)	19,376	40.4
3	Calvin D. Paige (R)	26,944	56.4
	M. Fred O'Connell (D)	19,311	40.4
4	Samuel E. Winslow (R)	32,942	52.8
	William H. Dyer (D)	29,399	47.2
5	John Jacob Rogers (R)	33,673	64.0
	Andrew E. Barrett (D)	18,936	36.0
6	A. Piatt Andrew (R)	36,426	77.0
	Charles I. Pettingell (D)	10,895	23.0
7	William P. Connery Jr. (D)	30,493	56.0
	Frederick Butler (R)	23,978	44.0
8	Frederick W. Dallinger (R)	42,248	65.9
	John F. Daly (D)	21,893	34.1
9	Charles L. Underhill (R)	31,229	57.7
	Arthur D. Healey (D)	22,867	42.3
10	Peter F. Tague (D)	21,029	79.5
	Loyal L. Jenkins (R)	5,422	20.5
11	George Holden Tinkham (R)	33,396	60.3
	David J. Brickley (D)	21,999	39.7
12	James A. Gallivan (D)	42,779	75.9
	Alexander H. Rice (R)	13,575	24.1
13	Robert Luce (R)	50,710	100.0
14	Louis A. Frothingham (R)	41,490	63.3
	David W. Murray (D)	24,014	36.7
15	William S. Greene (R)	25,179	57.4
	Arthur J. B. Cartier (D)	18,662	42.6
16	Charles L. Gifford (R)	23,862	54.4
	James P. Doran (D)	20,021	45.6

MICHIGAN

	Candidates	Votes	%
1	Robert H. Clancy (D)	22,996	55.4
	Hugh Shepherd (R)	17,722	42.7
2	Earl C. Michener (R)	31,509	57.4
	James W. Helme (D)	23,393	42.6
3	John M. C. Smith (R)	23,869	61.1
	George Burr Smith (D)	15,226	39.0
4	John C. Ketcham (R)	26,050	65.4
	Homer S. Carr (D)	13,772	34.6

	Candidates	Votes	%
5	Carl E. Mapes (R)	25,853	71.1
	Claude O. Taylor (D)	10,501	28.9
6	Grant M. Hudson (R)	46,791	61.4
	Charles R. Adair (D)	29,241	38.3
7	Louis C. Cramton (R)	35,328	72.3
	Patrick H. Kane (D)	13,431	27.5
8	Bird J. Vincent (R)	33,864	63.4
	De Witt Vought (D)	19,538	36.6
9	James C. McLaughlin (R)	21,703	95.6
10	Roy O. Woodruff (R)	23,792	100.0
11	Frank D. Scott (R)	24,390	69.3
	Robert H. Rayburn (D)	10,823	30.7
12	W. Frank James (R)	26,228	79.4
	Frederick Kappler (D)	6,784	20.6
13	Clarence J. McLeod (R)	28,871	69.8
	Ferris H. Fitch (D)	11,948	28.9

MINNESOTA

	Candidates	Votes	%
1	Sydney Anderson (R)	36,698	57.3
	J. F. Lynn (D)	27,316	42.7
2	Frank Clague (R)	47,591	100.0
3	Charles R. Davis (R)	42,708	69.8
	Lillien Cox Gault (D)	18,462	30.2
4	Oscar E. Keller (R)	33,259	58.7
	Paul E. Doty (D)	20,187	35.6
	O. J. McCartney (I)	3,243	5.7
5	Walter H. Newton (R)	45,221	53.9
	John R. Coan (D)	38,760	46.2
6	Harold Knutson (R)	37,201	60.9
	Peter J. Seberger (F-LAB)	19,365	31.7
	John Knutsen (I)	4,550	7.4
7	Ole J. Kvale (F-LAB)	42,832	59.7
	Andrew J. Volstead (R)	28,918	40.3
8	Oscar J. Larson (R)	32,420	53.0
	William L. Carss (D)	28,757	47.0
9	Knud Wefald (F-LAB)	35,551	56.3
	Halvor Steenerson (R)	27,590	43.7
10	Thomas D. Schall (R)	53,424	80.6
	Henry B. Rutledge (D)	12,843	19.4

MISSISSIPPI

	Candidates	Votes	%
1	John E. Rankin (D)	9,407	99.8
2	Bill G. Lowrey (D)	7,985	94.7
	William McDonough (R)	450	5.3
3	Benjamin G. Humphreys (D)	4,403	97.0
4	T. Jeff Busby (D)	9,260	98.2
5	Ross A. Collins (D)	11,336	96.3
6	T. Webber Wilson (D)	12,640	98.2
7	Percy E. Quin (D)	5,842	97.4
8	James W. Collier (D)	5,609	99.0

MISSOURI

	Candidates	Votes	%
1	Milton A. Romjue (D)	30,102	55.8
	Frank C. Millspaugh (R)	23,577	43.7
2	Ralph F. Lozier (D)	34,041	61.7
	E. Y. Keiter (R)	21,016	38.1
3	Jacob L. Milligan (D)	25,997	52.1
	Henry F. Lawrence (R)	23,919	47.9
4	Charles L. Faust (R)	28,110	51.5
	William E. Spratt (D)	26,394	48.4
5	Henry L. Jost (D)	62,702	53.0
	Edgar C. Ellis (R)	55,262	46.7
6	Clement C. Dickinson (D)	27,038	53.3
	William O. Atkeson (R)	23,492	46.3
7	Samuel C. Major (D)	36,950	50.7
	Roscoe C. Patterson (R)	35,627	48.9
8	Sidney C. Roach (R)	25,927	54.6
	Mrs. St.Clair Moss (D)	21,559	45.4
9	Clarence Cannon (D)	30,063	56.6
	Theodore W. Hukriede (R)	23,058	43.4
10	Cleveland A. Newton (R)	71,827	59.4
	A. A. Alexander (D)	46,704	38.7
11	Harry B. Hawes (D)	24,839	58.4
	Bernard P. Bogy (R)	17,188	40.4
12	Leonidas C. Dyer (R)	15,667	56.7
	David D. Israel (D)	11,679	42.3

MISSOURI

	Candidates	Votes	%
13	J. Scott Wolff (D)	23,622	51.6
	Marion E. Rhodes (R)	21,870	47.8
14	James F. Fullbright (D)	37,896	52.0
	Edward D. Hays (R)	34,573	47.4
15	Joe J. Manlove (R)	32,843	52.8
	Frank H. Lee (D)	28,801	46.3
16	Thomas L. Rubey (D)	25,989	53.7
	Phil A. Bennett (R)	22,153	45.8

MONTANA

1	John M. Evans (D)	36,589	57.0
	Washington J. McCormick (R)	26,684	41.6
2	Scott Leavitt (R)	46,499	54.3
	Preston B. Moss (D)	39,147	45.7

NEBRASKA

1	John H. Morehead (D)	25,079	49.2
	Walter L. Anderson (R)	23,075	45.3
2	Willis G. Sears (R)	26,308	48.2
	James H. Hanley (D)	25,251	46.2
	Roy M. Harrop (PROG)	3,048	5.6
3	Edgar Howard (D)	34,843	48.4
	Robert E. Evans (R)	32,930	45.7
	John Havekost (PROG)	4,252	5.9
4	Melvin O. McLaughlin (R)	29,743	51.0
	H. B. Cummins (D)	25,504	43.8
	John O. Schmidt (PROG)	3,034	5.2
5	Ashton C. Shallenberger (D)	26,923	45.9
	William E. Andrews (R)	25,456	43.4
	S. J. Franklin (PROG)	6,250	10.7
6	Robert G. Simmons (R)	41,558	51.3
	Charles W. Beal (D)	35,784	44.2

NEVADA

AL	Charles L. Richards (D)	15,991	57.0
	A. Grant Miller (R)	12,084	43.0

NEW HAMPSHIRE

1	William N. Rogers (D)	36,793	54.5
	John Scammon (R)	30,694	45.5
2	Edward H. Wason (R)	31,570	53.0
	William H. Barry (D)	27,980	47.0

NEW JERSEY

1	Francis F. Patterson Jr. (R)	46,505	60.5
	Ethan P. Wescott (D)	29,381	38.2
2	Isaac Bacharach (R)	50,925	69.8
	Charles S. Stevens (D)	22,001	30.2
3	Elmer H. Geran (D)	44,337	50.3
	T. Frank Appleby (R)	43,809	49.7
4	Charles Browne (D)	32,422	52.8
	Elijah C. Hutchinson (R)	28,934	47.2
5	Ernest R. Ackerman (R)	43,460	56.7
	Monell Sayre (D)	32,039	41.8
6	Randolph Perkins (R)	41,564	52.5
	Thomas A. Shields (D)	37,561	47.5
7	George N. Seger (R)	26,613	54.6
	Wilmer A. Cadmus (D)	21,190	43.5
8	Frank J. McNulty (D)	40,379#	58.5
	Warren P. Coon (R)	27,936	40.5
9	Daniel F. Minahan (D)	21,276	52.6
	Richard W. Parker (R)	19,182	47.4
10	Frederick R. Lehlbach (R)	28,570	57.4
	John F. Cahill (D)	21,211	42.6
11	John J. Eagan (D)	39,957	66.8
	Archibald E. Olpp (R)	18,399	30.8
12	Charles F. X. O'Brien (D)	51,596	74.3
	William A. O'Brien (R)	17,372	25.0

NEW MEXICO

	Candidates	Votes	%
AL	John Morrow (D)	59,254	54.0
	Adelina Otero-Warren (R)	49,698	45.3

NEW YORK

1	Robert L. Bacon (R)	47,191	57.6
	S. A. Warner Baltazzi (DFL)	32,224	39.3
2	John J. Kindred (D)	60,306	72.1
	Frank E. Hopkins (R)	19,560	23.4
3	George W. Lindsay (D)	21,513	65.4
	John Kissel (R)	8,587	26.1
	William W. Passage (SOC &F-L)	2,716	8.3
4	Thomas H. Cullen (D)	27,100	76.5
	Dominic E. Picone (R)	7,104	20.1
5	Loring M. Black Jr. (D)	33,840	54.9
	Ardolph L. Kline (R)	25,917	42.1
6	Charles I. Stengle (D)	31,363	48.3
	Warren I. Lee (R)	28,240	43.5
	Mina Eskenazi (SOC &F-L)	4,713	7.3
7	John F. Quayle (D)	21,688	53.4
	Michael J. Hogan (R)	14,772	36.4
	Henry Fruchter (SOC &F-L)	3,807	9.4
8	William E. Cleary (D)	34,622	56.4
	Charles G. Bond (R)	19,745	32.1
	David P. Berenberg (SOC &F-L)	6,804	11.1
9	David J. O'Connell (D)	38,833	58.1
	Andrew N. Petersen (R)	23,251	34.8
	Wilhelmus B. Robinson (SOC &F-L)	4,528	6.8
10	Emanuel Celler (D)	20,210	45.6
	Lester D. Volk (R)	17,099	38.6
	Jerome T. Dehunt (SOC &F-L)	6,522	14.7
11	Daniel J. Riordan (D)	29,134	67.6
	Joseph B. Handy (R)	12,889	29.9
12	Samuel Dickstein (D)	11,027	60.9
	Meyer London (SOC &F-L)	5,900	32.6
	Louis Zeltner (R)	1,183	6.5
13	Christopher D. Sullivan (D)	11,424	66.7
	Murray D. Firstman (R)	3,041	17.8
	Abraham Lefkowitz (SOC &F-L)	2,659	15.5
14	Nathan D. Perlman (R)	8,782	37.4
	David H. Knott (D)	8,173	34.8
	Jacob Panken (SOC &F-L)	6,459	27.5
15	John J. Boylan (D)	20,382	60.8
	Thomas Jefferson Ryan (R)	12,205	36.4
16	W. Bourke Cockran (D)	23,370*	70.0
	John C. O'Connor (R)	8,277	24.8
17	Ogden L. Mills (R)	21,274	50.5
	Herman A. Metz (D)	19,355	46.0
18	John F. Carew (D)	24,248	66.8
	Albert E. Schwartz (R)	8,398	23.1
	Ben Howe (SOC &F-L)	3,535	9.7
19	Samuel Marx (D)	29,798*	50.3
	Walter M. Chandler (R)	26,172	44.2
20	Fiorello H. LaGuardia (P)	8,492	38.3
	Henry Frank (D)	8,324	37.5
	William Karlin (SOC &F-L)	5,260	23.7
21	Royal H. Weller (D)	32,393	48.2
	Martin C. Ansorge (R)	32,053	47.6
22	Anthony J. Griffin (D)	29,544	72.8
	Charles Francis Connolly (R)	7,188	17.7
	Ernest Bohm (SOC &F-L)	3,752	9.2
23	Frank Oliver (D)	50,382	56.5
	Albert B. Rossdale (R)	25,154	28.2
	Salvatore Ninfo (SOC &F-L)	12,411	13.9
24	James V. Ganly (D)	40,058	47.4
	Benjamin L. Fairchild (R)	35,656	42.2
	Philip Umstadter (SOC &F-L)	8,873	10.5
25	J. Mayhew Wainwright (R & P)	33,674	53.3

	Candidates	Votes	%
	Robert A. Osborn (D)	27,412	43.4
26	Hamilton Fish Jr. (R F-L-P)	34,633	61.1
	Thomas Pendell (D)	20,831	36.7
27	Charles B. Ward (R)	30,154	46.5
	John J. Burns (DFL)	27,937	43.1
	H. Westlake Coons (P)	5,830	9.0
28	Parker Corning (D)	54,570	55.3
	Charles M. Winchester (R)	42,531	43.1
29	James S. Parker (R & P)	45,895	60.5
	William H. Faxon (D)	28,726	37.9
30	Frank Crowther (R & P)	32,225	53.3
	George H. Derry (D)	25,261	41.8
31	Bertrand H. Snell (R F-L-P)	38,205	68.3
	J. Franklin Sharp (D)	17,257	30.9
32	Luther W. Mott (R)	44,091	65.1
	M. J. Daley (D)	22,279	32.9
33	Homer P. Snyder (R)	31,978	49.6
	Fred J. Sisson (D)	30,118	46.7
34	John D. Clarke (R & P)	40,902	62.7
	Clayton L. Wheeler (D)	23,323	35.8
35	Walter W. Magee (R)	47,119	54.1
	Frederick W. Thomson (D)	37,785	43.4
36	John Taber (R & P)	43,633	65.5
	David J. Sims (D)	22,980	34.5
37	Gale H. Stalker (R & P)	42,144	59.2
	Charles P. Smith (DFL)	28,290	39.7
38	Meyer Jacobstein (D)	35,319	47.5
	Frederick T. Pierson (R)	33,690	45.5
	Joel Moses (SOC)	5,101	6.9
39	Archie D. Sanders (R)	37,852	60.5
	David A. White (DFL)	22,585	36.1
40	S. Wallace Dempsey (R-F-LAB)	41,754	63.4
	Philip Clancy (D)	21,590	32.8
41	Clarence MacGregor (R)	25,342	55.4
	William P. Greiner (D)	16,301	35.7
	Frank Ehrenfried (SOC)	4,067	8.9
42	James M. Mead (DFL)	25,070	61.9
	Louis J. Schwendler (R)	12,494	30.9
	Jacob F. Griesinger (SOC)	2,913	7.2
43	Daniel A. Reed (R & P)	40,374	70.5
	Frederick Garfield (D)	15,261	26.7

NORTH CAROLINA

1	Hallett S. Ward (D)	10,201	80.8
	C. E. Kramer (R)	2,421	19.2
2	Claude Kitchin (D)	8,533	100.0
3	Charles L. Abernethy (D)	14,101	67.1
	Thomas J. Hood (R)	6,924	32.9
4	Edward W. Pou (D)	17,205	68.0
	F. Eugene Hester (R)	8,086	32.0
5	Charles M. Stedman (D)	33,694	62.3
	Lucy B. Patterson (R)	20,380	37.7
6	Homer L. Lyon (D)	14,996	74.0
	William J. McDonald (R)	5,266	26.0
7	William C. Hammer (D)	30,629	56.5
	W. B. Love (R)	23,592	43.5
8	Robert L. Doughton (D)	31,340	56.1
	J. Ike Campbell (R)	24,493	43.9
9	Alfred L. Bulwinkle (D)	28,596	59.9
	R. H. Shuford (R)	19,168	40.1
10	Zebulon Weaver (D)	37,626	57.2
	Ralph A. Fisher (R)	28,192	42.8

NORTH DAKOTA

1	Olger B. Burtness (R)	45,959	100.0
2	George M. Young (R)	36,528	69.8
	J. W. Deemey (PROG)	15,834	30.2
3	James H. Sinclair (R)	33,499	64.2
	E. J. Hughes (IR)	18,672	35.8

OHIO

1	Nicholas Longworth (R)	45,253	57.1
	Sidney G. Stricker (D)	30,945	39.0

OHIO

Candidates	Votes	%
2 Ambrose E. B. Stephens (R)	39,898	54.0
John R. Quane (D)	30,051	40.6
Charles A. Herbst (F-LAB)	4,001	5.4
3 Roy G. Fitzgerald (R)	52,111	51.8
Warren Gard (D)	46,127	45.9
4 John C. Cable (R)	43,251	54.6
J. Henry Goeke (D)	35,916	45.4
5 Charles J. Thompson (R)	31,700	53.0
Frank C. Kniffin (D)	28,067	47.0
6 Charles C. Kearns (R)	32,416	51.2
William N. Gableman (D)	30,939	48.8
7 Charles Brand (R)	54,180	58.5
Charles B. Zimmerman (D)	38,522	41.6
8 R. Clint Cole (R)	37,065	52.1
H. H. Hartman (D)	34,105	47.9
9 Isaac R. Sherwood (D)	45,059	51.3
William W. Chalmers (R)	42,712	48.7
10 Israel M. Foster (R)	30,341	63.0
James Sharp (D)	17,811	37.0
11 Mell G. Underwood (D)	29,058	51.7
Edwin D. Ricketts (R)	27,162	48.3
12 John C. Speaks (R)	47,265	55.1
H. Sage Valentine (D)	37,875	44.2
13 James T. Begg (R)	38,994	56.4
Arthur W. Overmeyer (D)	30,199	43.6
14 Martin L. Davey (D)	49,935	52.0
Frank E. Whittemore (R)	46,087	48.0
15 C. Ellis Moore (R)	32,894	51.4
James R. Alexander (D)	30,120	47.1
16 John McSweeney Jr. (D)	43,590	51.8
J. H. Himes (R)	39,881	47.3
17 William M. Morgan (R)	42,331	50.4
William A. Ashbrook (D)	41,745	49.7
18 Frank Murphy (R)	41,572	57.0
Marion Huffman (D)	25,449	34.9
Jacob S. Carey Sr. (I)	5,907	8.1
19 John G. Cooper (R)	40,492	59.3
W. B. Kilpatrick (D)	27,836	40.7
20 Charles A. Mooney (D)	23,469	54.4
Minor G. Morton (D)	17,968	41.7
21 Robert Crosser (D)	18,645	55.1
Harry C. Gahn (R)	14,024	41.4
22 Theodore E. Burton (R)	57,781	73.4
William J. Zoul (D)	20,511	26.1

OKLAHOMA

Candidates	Votes	%
1 Everette B. Howard (D)	39,135	54.7
T. A. Chandler (R)	32,478	45.4
2 William W. Hastings (D)	30,418	57.7
Alice M. Robertson (R)	21,973	41.7
3 Charles D. Carter (D)	39,464	71.6
Philas S. Jones (R)	15,022	27.3
4 Thomas D. McKeown (D)	39,247	65.2
Joseph C. Pringey (R)	20,568	34.2
5 Fletcher B. Swank (D)	46,120	62.7
U. S. Stone (R)	26,893	36.6
6 Elmer Thomas (D)	30,532	56.6
L. M. Gensman (R)	22,757	42.2
7 James V. McClintic (D)	28,956	70.2
W. G. Roe (R)	11,444	27.8
8 Milton C. Garber (R)	29,068	52.0
Zach A. Harris (D)	26,111	46.7

OREGON

Candidates	Votes	%
1 Willis C. Hawley (R)	64,567	100.0
2 Nicholas J. Sinnott (R)	22,861	59.2
James Harvey Graham (D)	15,789	40.9
3 Elton Watkins (D)	36,690	47.6
Clifton N. McArthur (R)	35,696	46.3

PENNSYLVANIA

Candidates	Votes	%
1 William S. Vare (R)	46,946	83.6
Stephen Flanagan (D)	8,227	14.7
2 George S. Graham (R, P)	31,470	85.4
Ellen Duane Davis (D)	4,739	12.9
3 Harry C. Ransley (R)	33,058	84.4
Edward P. Carroll (D)	5,507	14.1
4 George W. Edmonds (R, P)	28,757	74.1
Joseph K. Willing (D)	8,954	23.1
5 James J. Connolly (R, WELFARE)	31,357	76.6
James J. Sweeney (D)	7,717	18.9
6 George A. Welsh (R)	44,159	73.4
Robert J. Sterrett (D)	13,629	22.7
7 George P. Darrow (R, P)	31,580	74.2
John W. Graham (D, VL)	9,694	22.8
8 Thomas S. Butler (R)	30,349	61.1
William T. Ellis (D, INDL)	18,306	36.9
9 Henry Winfield Watson (R)	32,052	61.8
C. William Freed (D)	18,083	34.9
10 William W. Griest (R)	33,545	52.8
Frank C. Musser (D, LANCAST)	30,017	47.2
11 Laurence H. Watres (R, P)	23,266	50.1
Patrick McLane (D)	22,540	48.5
12 John J. Casey (D, SOC)	35,953	54.1
Clarence D. Coughlin (R, P)	30,532	45.9
13 George Franklin Brumm (R, P)	23,218	52.9
Charles F. Ditchey (D)	19,305	44.0
14 William M. Croll (D)	31,592	48.2
Fred B. Gernerd (R)	29,617	45.2
George W. Snyder (SOC)	4,294	6.6
15 Louis T. McFadden (R, P)	20,399	64.0
T. Francis Carroll (D)	11,498	36.1
16 Edgar R. Kiess (R, P)	17,499	57.2
James M. Rook (D)	12,014	39.2
17 Herbert W. Cummings (D, SOC)	22,588	57.4
I. Clinton Kline (R, P)	16,796	42.6
18 Edward M. Beers (R, P)	24,675	54.6
King Alexander (D)	20,069	44.4
19 Frank C. Sites (D)	33,570	53.6
Aaron S. Kreider (R, P)	28,115	44.9
20 George M. Wertz (R, P)	12,276	41.9
Warren Worth Bailey (D, SOC)	11,969	40.9
Robert M. Palmer (RO)	2,671	9.1
Faber V. McCloskey (LAB)	2,337	8.0
21 J. Banks Kurtz (R, P)	13,106	47.5
Daniel S. Brumbaugh (D)	11,425	41.4
Earl W. Rothrock (LAB, SOC)	3,050	11.1
22 Samuel F. Glatfelter (D)	22,181	53.0
Mahlon N. Haines (R, P)	17,694	42.3
23 William Irvin Swoope (R, SOC)	16,928	48.0
J. Frank Snyder (D)	14,292	40.5
Elisha Kent Kane (P)	4,041	11.5
24 Samuel A. Kendall (R, P)	18,261	54.0
Harrison N. Boyd (D)	12,937	38.3
Herman G. Lepley (SOC)	1,985	5.9
25 Henry W. Temple (R, SOC)	14,098	53.5
Charles I. Faddis (D)	12,242	46.5
26 Thomas W. Phillips Jr (R)	17,730	51.5
John G. Cobler (D, P)	15,533	45.1
27 Nathan L. Strong (R)	18,682	53.6
Jane E. Leonard (D)	12,927	37.1
28 Harry J. Bixler (R, P)	22,631	64.4
Charles E. Bordwell (D)	11,604	33.0
29 Milton W. Shreve (R, P)	19,043	58.9
Charles N. Crosby (D)	11,917	36.9
30 Everett Kent (D)	25,644	58.2
William H. Kirkpatrick (R)	17,844	40.5
31 Adam M. Wyant (R, P)	17,421	53.4
James M. Cramer (D)	13,081	40.1
Harry Eckard (SOC)	2,146	6.6
32 Stephen Geyer Porter (R)	19,942	70.0
P. M. O'Donnell (D)	5,938	20.9
33 M. Clyde Kelly (R, D)	21,899	87.4
William Adams (SOC)	3,106	12.4

Candidates	Votes	%
34 John M. Morin (R)	15,499	72.7
William N. McNair (D, P)	5,134	24.1
35 James M. Magee (R)	16,227	53.9
Louis K. Manley (D, P)	12,838	42.6
36 Guy E. Campbell (R, D)	20,783	91.7
William W. Nooning (SOC)	1,880	8.3

RHODE ISLAND

Candidates	Votes	%
1 Clark Burdick (R)	25,860	54.1
George F. O'Shaunessy (D)	21,935	45.9
2 Richard S. Aldrich (R)	26,247	52.6
Percy J. Cantwell (D)	23,680	47.4
3 Jeremiah E. O'Connell (D)	36,147	62.6
Isaac Gill (R)	21,581	37.4

SOUTH CAROLINA

Candidates	Votes	%
1 W. Turner Logan (D)	5,992	94.0
S. L. Blomgren (R)	383	6.0
2 James F. Byrnes (D)	4,163	100.0
3 Fred H. Dominick (D)	3,822	100.0
4 John J. McSwain (D)	8,346	97.3
5 William F. Stevenson (D)	4,015	100.0
6 Allard H. Gasque (D)	3,642	100.0
7 Hampton C. Fulmer (D)	4,411	98.5

SOUTH DAKOTA

Candidates	Votes	%
1 Charles A. Christopherson (R)	31,250	48.9
John Stredronsky (D)	16,372	25.6
G. L. Hasvold (NON PART)	16,230	25.4
2 Royal C. Johnson (R)	37,208	64.5
Andrew Francis Lockhart (NON PART)	18,968	32.9
3 William Williamson (R)	18,819	49.2
George Philip (D)	14,857	38.8
George H. Smith (NON PART)	4,581	12.0

TENNESSEE

Candidates	Votes	%
1 B. Carroll Reece (R)	17,050	77.0
J. T. Fugate (D)	5,085	23.0
2 J. Will Taylor (R)	14,988	64.3
J. Rupert Reynolds (D)	8,330	35.7
3 Sam D. McReynolds (D)	20,603	61.3
R. L. Burnett (R)	13,027	38.7
4 Cordull Hull (D)	20,323	62.6
W. F. Clouse (R)	12,125	37.4
5 Ewin L. Davis (D)	11,634	100.0
6 Joseph W. Byrns (D)	19,596	100.0
7 William C. Salmon (D)	13,662	78.2
S. A. Vest (R)	3,818	21.8
8 Gordon Browning (D)	16,571	57.3
Lon A. Scott (R)	12,328	42.7
9 Finis J. Garrett (D)	15,822	84.8
Homer T. Tatum (R)	2,846	15.3
10 Hubert F. Fisher (D)	10,407	89.1
Thomas C. Phelen (I)	1,279	10.9

Special Election

	Votes	%
7 Clarence W. Turner (D)	12,914	86.3
S. W. Williams (R)	2,053	13.7

TEXAS

Candidates	Votes	%
1 Eugene Black (D)	15,697	93.5
G. T. Bartlett (R)	1,087	6.5
2 John C. Box (D)	21,216	94.8
C. A. Lord (R)	1,171	5.2
3 Morgan G. Sanders (D)	16,323	91.7
L. B. Crawford (R)	1,478	8.3
4 Sam Rayburn (D)	21,327	91.1
C. A. Gray (R)	2,079	8.9

TEXAS

Candidates	Votes	%
5 Hatton W. Sumners (D)	23,051	88.3
Heber Page (R)	3,046	11.7
6 Luther A. Johnson (D)	18,938	94.0
D. H. Merrill (R)	1,208	6.0
7 Clay Stone Briggs (D)	12,171	93.3
Frank Sneed Camper (R)	880	6.7
8 Daniel E. Garrett (D)	20,058	85.3
E. B. Barden (R)	3,454	14.7
9 Joseph J. Mansfield (D)	17,479	64.7
Willett Wilson (R)	9,554	35.3
10 James P. Buchanan (D)	18,590	81.0
W. J. Kveton (R)	4,374	19.1
11 Tom T. Connally (D)	16,092	90.8
R. A. Hanrick (R)	1,630	9.2
12 Fritz G. Lanham (D)	20,014	91.9
Joe Kingsberry Jr. (R)	1,772	8.1
13 Guinn Williams (D)	21,187	93.2
J. B. Schmitz (R)	1,538	6.8
14 Harry M. Wurzbach (R)	19,083	54.8
Harry Hertzberg (D)	15,760	45.2
15 John N. Garner (D)	14,319	100.0
16 Claude B. Hudspeth (D)	18,164	81.0
J. A. Simpson (R)	4,257	19.0
17 Thomas L. Blanton (D)	24,576	91.6
W. D. Girand (R)	2,266	8.4
18 Marvin Jones (D)	24,515	93.7
H. O. Ward (R)	1,649	6.3

UTAH

	Votes	%
1 Don B. Colton (R)	33,188	52.7
Milton H. Welling (D)	27,801	44.2
2 Elmer O. Leatherwood (R)	28,591	50.5
David C. Dunbar (D)	26,145	46.1

VERMONT

	Votes	%
1 Frederick G. Fleetwood (R, P)	19,359	52.1
James E. Kennedy (D)	17,821	47.9
2 Porter H. Dale (R, P)	25,981	78.4
John J. Wilson (D)	7,170	21.6

VIRGINIA

Candidates	Votes	%
1 Schuyler Otis Bland (D)	8,639	83.5
George N. Wise (R)	1,492	14.4
2 Joseph T. Deal (D)	7,367	86.5
Percy S. Stephenson (R)	1,045	12.3
3 Andrew Jackson Montague (D)	7,746	90.1
Channing M. Ward (R)	847	9.9
4 Patrick Henry Drewry (D)	5,737	86.2
Herbert Rogers (R)	822	12.4
5 James M. Hooker (D)	11,458	70.9
Charles P. Smith (R)	4,699	29.1
6 Clifton A. Woodrum (D)	9,505	77.9
J. W. McWane (R)	2,688	22.0
7 Thomas W. Harrison (D)	12,954	62.3
John Paul (R)	7,841	37.7
8 R. Walton Moore (D)	8,702	83.3
John Sidney Wiley (R)	1,741	16.7
9 George C. Peery (D)	32,163	52.4
John H. Hassinger (R)	29,227	47.6
10 Henry St.George Tucker (D)	8,635	77.4
John Martin (R)	2,521	22.6

WASHINGTON

	Votes	%
1 John F. Miller (R)	29,579	57.4
Edgar C. Snyder (D)	13,127	25.5
Fred N. Nelson (F-LAB)	8,862	17.2
2 Lindley H. Hadley (R)	29,906	59.0
Fred A. Clise (D)	10,608	20.9
P. B. Tyler (F-LAB)	10,150	20.0
3 Albert Johnson (R)	45,482	76.3
J. M. Phillips (F-LAB)	14,158	23.7
4 John W. Summers (R)	29,697	68.5
Charles R. Hill (D)	10,337	23.9
Elihu Bowles (F-LAB)	3,292	7.6
5 J. Stanley Webster (R)	26,982	49.2
Sam B. Hill (D)	24,810	45.2
Harry J. Vaughan (F-LAB)	3,095	5.6

WEST VIRGINIA

Candidates	Votes	%
1 Benjamin L. Rosenbloom (R)	28,644	52.6
Raymond Kenny (D)	25,794	47.3
2 Robert E. L. Allen (D)	27,320	51.5
George M. Bowers (R)	24,764	46.6
3 Stuart F. Reed (R)	32,066	50.5
Eskridge H. Morton (D)	31,382	49.5
4 George W. Johnson (D)	32,355	50.7
Harry C. Woodyard (R)	31,448	49.3
5 Thomas J. Lilly (D)	35,354	51.5
Wells Goodykoontz (R)	33,267	48.5
6 J. Alfred Taylor (D)	42,320	54.2
Leonard S. Echols (R)	34,901	44.7

WISCONSIN

	Votes	%
1 Henry Allen Cooper (R)	37,958	94.4
Niels P. Nielsen (SOC)	2,179	5.4
2 Edward Voight (R)	32,494	80.9
William F. Schanen (D)	7,667	19.1
3 John M. Nelson (R)	33,002	79.7
Martha Riley (ID)	8,379	20.2
4 John C. Schafer (R)	19,179	46.0
Edmund T. Melms (SOC)	18,548	44.5
Joseph F. Drezdzon (D)	3,918	9.4
5 Victor L. Berger (SOC)	30,045	53.3
William H. Stafford (R)	26,274	46.6
6 Florian Lampert (R)	34,365	86.0
William E. Cavanaugh (ID)	5,572	14.0
7 Joseph D. Beck (R)	27,371	87.4
Bert A. Jolivette (ID)	3,923	12.5
8 Edward E. Browne (R)	33,860	91.8
Herman A. Marth (I SOC)	2,946	8.0
9 George J. Schneider (R)	35,117	61.5
Henry Graass (IR)	22,015	38.5
10 James A. Frear (R)	29,781	98.3
11 Hubert H. Peavey (R)	36,635	99.0

WYOMING

	Votes	%
AL Charles E. Winter (R)	30,885	53.3
Robert R. Rose (D)	27,017	46.7

1923 House Elections

ALABAMA

Special Election

2 Lister Hill D)	4,483	100.0

ARKANSAS

Special Election

6 James B. Reed (D)	1,793	100.0

ILLINOIS

Special Elections

2 Morton D. Hull (R)	56,355	53.9
Barratt O'Hara (D)	42,427	40.6
Seymorse Stedman (SOC)	5,759	5.5
4 Thomas A. Doyle (D)	17,624	95.0

IOWA

Special Election

8 Hiram K. Evans (R)	14,334	52.6
J. P. Daughton (D)	12,901	47.4

NEW YORK

Special Elections

11 Anning S. Prall (D)	28,215	72.9
Guy O. Walser (R)	9,972	25.8
16 John J. O'Connor (D, R)	27,746	96.7
19 Sol Bloom (D)	17,909	49.8
Walter M. Chandler (R)	17,718	49.3
24 Benjamin L. Fairchild (R)	43,475	49.0
Edward R. Koch (D)	38,435	43.3
Alexander Braunstein (SOC)	6,913	7.8
32 Thaddeus C. Sweet (R)	41,775	65.1
Daniel C. Burke (D)	21,391	33.4

1924 House Elections

ALABAMA

	Candidates	Votes	%
1	John McDuffie (D)	9,932	86.1
	Frank J. Thompson (R)	1,604	13.9
2	Lister Hill (D)	15,066	100.0
3	Henry B. Steagall (D)	10,425	87.7
	Carlos E. Roberts (R)	1,457	12.3
4	Lamar Jeffers (D)	9,945	75.6
	J. O. Middleton (R)	3,208	24.4
5	William B. Bowling (D)	8,492	78.3
	John C. Walker (R)	2,355	21.7
6	William B. Oliver (D)	6,672	100.0
7	Miles C. Allgood (D)	15,984	57.1
	B. S. Cooley (R)	11,987	42.9
8	Edward B. Almon (D)	13,353	81.5
	G. M. Huckaba (R)	3,040	18.5
9	George Huddleston (D)	18,958	99.9
10	William B. Bankhead (D)	11,394	59.7
	W. A. McMurray (R)	7,706	40.4

ARIZONA

	Candidates	Votes	%
AL	Carl Hayden (D)	40,329	82.4
	W. J. Galbraith (R)	8,628	17.6

ARKANSAS

	Candidates	Votes	%
1	William J. Driver (D)	15,514	77.2
	Virgil Greene (R)	4,580	22.8
2	William A. Oldfield (D)	11,412	73.8
	M. D. Bowers (R)	4,057	26.2
3	John N. Tilman (D)	13,202	60.0
	J. S. Thompson (R)	8,789	40.0
4	Otis T. Wingo (D)	15,935	72.5
	Charles A. Darling (R)	6,060	27.6
5	Heartsill Ragon (D)	16,287	76.8
	Powell Clayton (R)	4,922	23.2
6	James B. Reed (D)	13,101	75.6
	Martin A. Eisele (R)	4,219	24.4
7	Tilman B. Parks (D)	13,975	76.5
	J. K. Prescott (R)	4,302	23.5

CALIFORNIA

	Candidates	Votes	%
1	Clarence F. Lea (D-R)	47,250	99.9
2	John E. Raker (D-R)	30,590	100.0
3	Charles F. Curry (R-D)	61,512	80.7
	James H. Barkley (SOC)	14,665	19.3
4	Julius Kahn (R-D)	44,048*	81.0
	William McDevitt (SOC)	10,360	19.0
5	Lawrence J. Flaherty (R-D)	38,893	76.2
	Isabel C. King (SOC)	12,175	23.8
6	Albert E. Carter (R)	68,547	57.5
	John L. Davie (I)	42,873	35.9
	Herbert L. Coggins (SOC)	7,858	6.6
7	Henry E. Barbour (R-D)	65,740	99.9
8	Arthur Monroe Free (R-D)	55,713	97.9
9	Walter F. Lineberger (R)	119,993	63.9
	Charles H. Randall (P D SOC)	67,735	36.1
10	John D. Fredericks (R)	133,780	62.3
	Robert W. Richardson (D)	80,870	37.7
11	Philip D. Swing (DR SOC P)	93,811	100.0

COLORADO

	Candidates	Votes	%
1	William N. Vaile (R)	47,155	54.2
	James G. Edgeworth (D)	36,519	42.0
2	Charles B. Timberlake (R)	51,028	56.9
	James M. Taylor (D)	31,378	35.0
	James A. Ownbey (LAF)	6,630	7.4
3	Guy U. Hardy (R)	53,877	58.7
	Charles B. Hughes (D)	37,976	41.3

	Candidates	Votes	%
4	Edward T. Taylor (D)	33,262	65.5
	Webster S. Whinnery (R)	17,486	34.5

CONNECTICUT

	Candidates	Votes	%
1	E. Hart Fenn (R)	61,451	66.8
	Johnstone Vance (D)	29,381	31.9
2	Richard P. Freeman (R)	42,161	65.0
	Fenton (D)	22,258	34.3
3	John Q. Tilson (R)	48,963	67.9
	William T. Hoyt (D)	21,858	30.3
4	Schuyler Merritt (R)	57,966	71.1
	Walling (D)	22,031	27.0
5	James P. Glynn (R)	34,548	55.0
	Patrick B. O'Sullivan (D, PROG)	28,248	45.0

DELAWARE

	Candidates	Votes	%
AL	Robert G. Houston (R)	51,536	58.6
	William H. Boyce (D)	35,943	40.9

FLORIDA

	Candidates	Votes	%
1	Herbert J. Drane (D)	23,244	80.0
	A. W. Gage (R)	5,816	20.0
2	Robert A. Green (D)	11,021	90.7
	H. O. Brown (R)	1,137	9.4
3	John H. Smithwick (D)	12,660	84.1
	J. H. Drummond (R)	2,389	15.9
4	William J. Sears (D)	25,318	62.5
	G. W. Bingham (R)	12,183	30.1
	Billy Parker (AM)	2,993	7.4

GEORGIA

	Candidates	Votes	%
1	Charles G. Edwards (D)	14,694	93.2
2	E. E. Cox (D)	10,667	100.0
3	Charles R. Crisp (D)	8,138	100.0
4	William C. Wright (D)	10,420	100.0
5	William D. Upshaw (D)	16,608	100.0
6	Samuel Rutherford (D)	12,488	100.0
7	Gordon Lee (D)	20,008	99.9
8	Charles H. Brand (D)	12,261	100.0
9	Thomas M. Bell (D)	17,007	87.5
	J. M. Johnson (R)	2,425#	12.5
10	Carl Vinson (D)	9,280	100.0
11	William C. Lankford (D)	11,590	100.0
12	William W. Larsen (D)	11,754	100.0

IDAHO

	Candidates	Votes	%
1	Burton L. French (R)	33,347	61.8
	Perry Mitchell (D)	20,234	37.5
2	Addison T. Smith (R)	44,365	54.6
	William A. Shuldberg (PROG)	23,257	28.6
	Asher B. Wilson (D)	13,470	16.6

ILLINOIS

	Candidates	Votes	%
1	Martin B. Madden (R)	43,661	73.1
	James F. Doyle (D)	13,623	22.8
2	Morton D. Hull (R)	113,349	74.5
	Frank A. Wright (D)	37,482	24.6
3	Elliott W. Sproul (R)	87,563	67.0
	Joseph F. Timmis (D)	42,278	32.3
4	Thomas A. Doyle (D)	30,955	56.0
	Stanley Jankowski (R)	23,947	43.3
5	Adolph J. Sabath (D)	20,588	57.8
	Bernard A. Weaver (R)	14,730	41.4
6	John J. Gorman (R)	116,066	67.8
	James R. Buckley (D)	53,463	31.2

	Candidates	Votes	%
7	M. Alfred Michaelson (R)	133,563	67.7
	Hynek M. Howell (D)	46,253	23.5
	Edward A. Russell	13,040	6.6
8	Stanley Henry Kunz (D)	17,799	53.1
	Ernest D. Potts (R)	13,853	41.3
	Gerard Kasmarek	1,675	5.0
9	Fred A. Britten (R)	42,829	76.6
	Urban A. Lavery (D)	12,541	22.4
10	Carl R. Chindblom (R)	126,383	80.0
	John P. Reed (D)	30,474	19.3
11	Frank R. Reid (R)	83,696	84.2
	Charles L. Schwartz (D)	15,246	15.3
12	Charles E. Fuller (R)	68,696	84.5
	Marvin C. Parsons (PROG)	12,105	14.9
13	William R. Johnson (R)	49,717	77.8
	William G. Curtiss (D)	13,887	21.7
14	John C. Allen (R)	48,920	64.7
	William A. Schaeffer (D)	26,680	35.3
15	Edward J. King (R)	53,123	69.2
	Henry E. Schmiedeskamp (D)	23,051	30.0
16	William E. Hull (R)	43,098	55.4
	Charles C. Hatcher (D)	34,185	44.0
17	Frank H. Funk (R)	40,226	60.1
	Frank Gillespie (D)	26,497	39.6
18	William P. Holaday (R)	52,992	64.4
	Andrew B. Dennis (D)	29,034	35.3
19	Charles Adkins (R)	55,605	56.5
	Edward F. Poorman (D)	42,490	43.1
20	Henry T. Rainey (D)	36,669	53.0
	Guy L. Shaw (R)	32,569	47.0
21	Loren E. Wheeler (R)	45,588	50.0
	J. Earl Major (D)	44,414	48.7
22	Edward M. Irwin (R)	56,525	57.7
	Edward E. Campbell (D)	40,604	41.5
23	William W. Arnold (D)	45,644	53.9
	Charles J. Metzger (R)	38,670	45.7
24	Thomas S. Williams (R)	35,356	54.1
	H. Robert Fowler (D)	29,954	45.9
25	Edward E. Denison (R)	47,080	58.1
	Philip N. Lewis (D)	33,638	41.5
AL	Richard Yates (R)	1,519,021✔	
	Henry R. Rathbone (R)	1,513,708✔	
	Mary Ward Hart (D)	669,555	
	Allen D. Albert (D)	658,265	
	Gus C. Sandberg (SOC)	17,580	
	John C. Flora (SOC)	17,438	
	J. E. Procium (SOC LAB)	2,437	
	C. E. Clouse (SOC LAB)	2,368	
	Robert Minor (WP AM)	2,235	
	E. B. Hewlett (WP AM)	2,160	
	Patrick H. Morrissey (IR)	752	
	Dora Welty (CLP)	396	
	James W. Hill (CLP)	363	

INDIANA

	Candidates	Votes	%
1	Harry E. Rowbottom (R)	48,203	52.1
	William E. Wilson (D)	44,335	47.9
2	Arthur H. Greenwood (D)	43,690	49.8
	John E. Sedwick (R)	43,073	49.1
3	Frank Gardner (D)	44,376	52.8
	Lindley M. Barlow (R)	39,446	46.9
4	Harry C. Canfield (D)	48,803	58.2
	James W. Hill (R)	35,007	41.8
5	Noble J. Johnson (R)	46,264	55.5
	J. R. Shannon (D)	28,573	34.3
	Jesse Rice Burks (P)	7,476	9.0
6	Richard N. Elliott (R)	46,094	55.3
	Lawrence A. Handley (D)	37,309	44.7
7	Ralph E. Updike (R)	94,751	60.0
	Joseph P. Turk (D)	62,279	39.4
8	Albert H. Vestal (R)	51,864	55.8
	John A. M. Adair (D)	41,119	44.2
9	Fred S. Purnell (R)	51,280	54.5
	James P. Davis (D)	41,973	44.6

INDIANA

Candidates	Votes	%
10 William R. Wood (R)	67,143	66.8
Harry O. Rhodes (D)	33,344	33.2
11 Albert R. Hall (R)	47,978	54.0
Samuel E. Cook (D)	39,998	45.0
12 David Hogg (R)	49,921	58.4
Charles W. Branstrator (D)	35,565	41.6
13 Andrew J. Hickey (R)	69,042	61.7
James L. Harmon (D)	42,895	38.3

IOWA

Candidates	Votes	%
1 William F. Kopp (R)	42,711	71.4
James M. Bell (D)	17,100	28.6
2 F. Dickinson Letts (R)	49,416	60.1
W. Thompson (D)	32,842	39.9
3 Thomas J. B. Robinson (R)	54,921	68.5
Willis N. Birdsall (D)	25,213	31.5
4 Gilbert N. Haugen (R)	50,811	71.1
J. M. Berry (D)	20,646	28.9
5 Cyrenus Cole (R)	52,180	70.2
W. N. Townsend (D)	22,175	29.8
6 C. William Ramseyer (R)	42,848	69.3
James V. Curran (D)	18,976	30.7
7 Cassius C. Dowell (R)	66,550	78.3
William M. Wade (D)	18,454	21.7
8 Lloyd Thurston (R)	42,222	62.5
Le Roy Munyon (D)	25,321	37.5
9 William R. Green (R)	49,153	68.4
Charles F. Paschel (D)	22,741	31.6
10 Lester J. Dickinson (R)	59,954	75.4
R. F. Mitchell (D)	19,571	24.6
11 William D. Boies (R)	56,152	61.5
A. Sykes (D)	35,086	38.5

KANSAS

Candidates	Votes	%
1 Daniel R. Anthony Jr. (R)	49,676	70.8
Lee Eppinger (D)	20,474	29.2
2 Chauncey B. Little (D)	43,285	48.8
Russell Dyer (R)	39,523	44.6
Arthur L. McKenney (I)	5,895	6.7
3 William H. Sproul (R)	49,482	57.3
Charles Stephens (D)	36,876	42.7
4 Homer Hoch (R)	34,731	65.0
R. W. Woodside (D)	18,728	35.0
5 James G. Strong (R)	38,754	60.0
C. E. Hatfield (D)	25,842	40.0
6 Hays B. White (R)	35,690	52.5
John R. Connelly (D)	32,285	47.5
7 Jasper N. Tincher (R)	48,826	54.6
Nellie Cline (D)	40,583	45.4
8 William A. Ayres (D)	44,312	60.6
Chester I. Long (R)	28,868	39.5

Special Election

Candidates	Votes	%
2 U. S. Guyer (R)	55,765	62.0
Mrs. James A. Cable (D)	34,170	38.0

KENTUCKY

Candidates	Votes	%
1 Alben W. Barkley (D)	41,861	67.0
R. L. Myre (R)	20,669	33.1
2 David H. Kincheloe (D)	35,717	100.0
3 Robert Y. Thomas Jr (D)	33,084	52.7
George Baker (R)	29,753	47.4
4 Ben Johnson (D)	34,954	53.5
Z. T. Proctor (R)	29,865	45.7
5 Maurice Thatcher (R)	60,403	54.5
Sam H. McMeekin (D)	50,508	45.5
6 Arthur B. Rouse (D)	36,400	49.5
B. S. Landram (R)	21,951	29.8
William H. Bornhorst (PROG)	15,219	20.7
7 Virgil Chapman (D)	40,654	100.0
8 Ralph Gilbert (D)	29,888	100.0

Candidates	Votes	%
9 Fred M. Vinson (D)	45,899	54.5
George Osborne (D)	38,295	45.5
10 John W. Langley (R)	31,057	59.7
Alex L. Ratliff (D)	20,577	39.6
11 John M. Robsion (R)	57,130	74.4
Nat B. Sewell (D)	19,626	25.6

Special Election

Candidates	Votes	%
9 Fred M. Vinson (D)	15,681	72.9
W. S. Yazell (R)	5,822	27.1

LOUISIANA

Candidates	Votes	%
1 James O'Connor (D)	20,027	100.0
2 J. Zach Spearing (D)	19,503	100.0
3 Whitmell P. Martin (D)	6,209	100.0
4 John N. Sandlin (D)	9,893	100.0
5 Riley J. Wilson (D)	8,523	100.0
6 Bolivar E. Kemp (D)	10,216	100.0
7 Ladislas Lazaro (D)	10,054	100.0
8 James B. Aswell (D)	8,886	100.0

MAINE

Candidates	Votes	%
1 Carroll L. Beedy (R)	39,269	59.2
William M. Ingraham (D)	27,058	40.8
2 Wallace H. White Jr. (R)	34,335	57.8
Bertrand G. McIntire (D)	25,086	42.2
3 John E. Nelson (R)	40,730	62.1
Leon O. Tebbetts (D)	24,860	37.9
4 Ira G. Hersey (R)	34,011	62.0
Clinton C. Stevens (D)	20,851	38.0

MARYLAND

Candidates	Votes	%
1 Thomas Alan Goldsborough (D)	27,963	57.0
Harry T. Phoebus (R)	21,060	43.0
2 Millard E. Tydings (D)	35,051	53.2
Edward Ridgely Simpson (R)	29,421	44.7
3 John Philip Hill (R)	23,760	61.5
George Heller (D)	14,217	36.8
4 J. Charles Linthicum (D)	28,054	59.9
John R. M. Staum (R)	17,773	38.0
5 Stephen W. Gambrill (D)	24,971	51.6
Thomas B. R. Mudd (R)	23,412	48.4
6 Frederick N. Zihlman (R)	33,800	53.8
David C. Winebrenner (D)	28,016	44.6

Special Election

Candidates	Votes	%
5 Stephen W. Gambrill (D)	23,474	50.3
Thomas B. R. Mudd (R)	23,204	49.7

MASSACHUSETTS

Candidates	Votes	%
1 Allen T. Treadway (R)	38,359	58.5
Thomas F. Cassidy (D)	27,246	41.5
2 George B. Churchill (R)	41,126	57.3
Joseph E. Kerigan (D)	30,703	42.7
3 Frank H. Foss (R)	38,626	64.4
Wilfrid J. Lamoureux (D)	21,368	35.6
4 George R. Stobbs (R)	43,221	57.3
William H. Dyer (D)	31,022	41.2
5 John Jacob Rogers (R)	46,841	67.4
Humphrey O'Sullivan (D)	22,691	32.6
6 A. Piatt Andrew (R)	55,023	100.0
7 William P. Connery Jr (D)	34,710	55.7
Charles A. Littlefield (R)	27,600	44.3
8 Harry I. Thayer (R)	52,051	62.0
Daniel P. Leahy (D)	31,844	38.0
9 Charles L. Underhill (R)	42,212	59.0
Arthur D. Healey (D)	29,398	41.1
10 John J. Douglass (D)	19,558	58.9
Peter F. Tague (D)	8,694	26.2
James E. Maguire (R)	4,168	12.6

Candidates	Votes	%
11 George Holden Tinkham (R)	46,865	66.0
Timothy J. Driscoll (D)	24,111	34.0
12 James A. Gallivan (D)	51,108	73.4
Howard A. Morton (R)	18,573	26.7
13 Robert Luce (R)	61,851	69.3
Edwin F. Tuttle (D)	27,450	30.7
14 Louis A. Frothingham (R)	59,746	69.1
David W. Murray (D)	26,686	30.9
15 Joseph W. Martin Jr. (R)	33,360	58.4
Arthur J. B. Cartier (D)	23,764	41.6
16 Charles L. Gifford (R)	37,913	69.5
John H. Backus Jr. (D)	14,051	25.8

MICHIGAN

Candidates	Votes	%
1 John B. Sosnowski (R)	76,566	67.5
Robert H. Clancy (D)	36,516	32.2
2 Earl C. Michener (R)	69,680	73.8
James W. Helme (D)	24,742	26.2
3 Arthur B. Williams (R)	50,375	65.1
Claude S. Carney (D)	27,044	34.9
4 John C. Ketcham (R)	49,060	70.3
Fremont Evans (D)	20,631	29.6
5 Carl E. Mapes (R)	58,682	81.3
Harry C. White (D)	13,497	18.7
6 Grant M. Hudson (R)	173,705	85.6
Willis M. Brewer (D)	29,191	14.4
7 Louis C. Cramton (R)	60,404	80.8
Varnum J. Bowers (D)	14,291	19.1
8 Bird J. Vincent (R)	64,749	77.5
William A. Seegmiller (D)	18,795	22.5
9 James C. McLaughlin (R)	47,386	84.1
Charles M. Black (D)	8,781	15.6
10 Roy O. Woodruff (R)	47,555	81.3
Judson E. Richardson (D)	10,944	18.7
11 Frank D. Scott (R)	41,686	73.3
Prentiss M. Brown (D)	15,222	26.8
12 W. Frank James (R)	47,114	100.0
13 Clarence J. McLeod (R)	95,747	88.4
Joel R. Moore (D)	12,526	11.6

MINNESOTA

Candidates	Votes	%
1 Allen J. Furlow (R)	41,484	53.4
Julius J. Reiter (F-LAB)	28,558	36.8
L. B. Hanna (D)	7,659	9.9
2 Frank Clague (R)	45,730	60.5
O. F. Swanjord (F-LAB)	29,901	39.5
3 August H. Andresen (R)	40,398	57.3
A. C. Welch (F-LAB)	30,093	42.7
4 Oscar E. Keller (R)	39,217	47.8
Dan W. Lawler (D)	30,277	36.9
Julius F. Emme (F-LAB)	12,629	15.4
5 Walter H. Newton (R)	68,333	58.9
A. G. Bastis (F-LAB)	36,804	31.7
John S. Crosby (D)	10,967	9.5
6 Harold Knutson (R)	39,800	54.1
S. C. Shipstead (F-LAB)	33,831	46.0
7 Ole J. Kvale (F-LAB)	43,555	58.5
Gunnar B. Bjornson (R)	30,871	41.5
8 William L. Carss (F-LAB)	46,926	54.3
Victor L. Power (R)	39,505	45.7
9 Knud Wefald (F-LAB)	38,248	56.8
F. H. Peterson (R)	29,095	43.2
10 Godfrey G. Goodwin (R)	47,749	53.8
George D. Brewer (F-LAB)	36,490	41.1
Frank Hicks (D)	4,485	5.1

MISSISSIPPI

Candidates	Votes	%
1 John E. Rankin (D)	13,971	100.0
2 Bill G. Lowery (D)	10,534	100.0
3 William M. Whittington (D)	9,282	100.0
4 T. Jeff Busby (D)	12,861	95.7
5 Ross A. Collins (D)	14,738	100.0
6 T. Webber Wilson (D)	17,337	100.0
7 Percy E. Quin (D)	9,547	100.0
8 James W. Collier (D)	10,278	100.0

MISSOURI

	Candidates	Votes	%
1	Milton A. Romjue (D)	37,831	57.3
	Frank Millspaugh (R)	28,175	42.7
2	Ralph F. Lozier (D)	41,643	62.8
	Sweeney (R)	24,195	36.5
3	Jacob L. Milligan (D)	33,285	52.8
	Henry F. Lawrence (R)	29,773	47.2
4	Charles L. Faust (R)	35,752	51.3
	John McDaniel (D)	33,948	48.7
5	Edgar C. Ellis (R)	87,124	49.8
	George H. Combs Jr. (D)	85,581	48.9
6	Clement C. Dickinson (D)	28,911	53.8
	William O. Atkeson (R)	24,815	46.2
7	Samuel C. Major (D)	46,264	52.0
	O. B. Whitaker (R)	42,686	48.0
8	William L. Nelson (D)	28,895	50.8
	Sidney C. Roach (R)	27,955	49.2
9	Clarence Cannon (D)	38,228	56.1
	George E. Hackmann (R)	29,509	43.3
10	Cleveland A. Newton (R)	123,199	61.2
	Henry J. Schleper (D)	70,976	35.3
11	Harry B. Hawes (D)	31,940	50.6
	Michael J. Hart (R)	29,972	47.5
12	Leonidas C. Dyer (R)	25,749	63.2
	Jerome F. Duggan (D)	14,022	34.4
13	Charles E. Kiefner (R)	27,743	53.0
	J. Scott Wolff (D)	24,598	47.0
14	Ralph E. Bailey (R)	46,541	50.3
	James F. Fulbright (D)	46,020	49.7
15	Joe J. Manlove (R)	39,148	56.4
	William G. Warner (D)	30,051	43.3
16	Thomas L. Rubey (D)	28,353	55.8
	William P. Elmer (R)	22,426	44.2

MONTANA

1	John M. Evans (D)	44,139	63.9
	John O. Davies (R)	24,012	34.8
2	Scott Leavitt (R)	55,190	61.4
	Joseph Kirschwing (D)	28,708	32.0
	Charles E. Taylor (F-LAB)	5,938	6.6

NEBRASKA

1	John H. Morehead (D & PROG)	33,584	51.8
	Roy H. Thorpe (R)	29,755	45.9
2	Willis G. Sears (R)	38,382	55.5
	William V. Jamieson (D)	24,756	35.8
	Roy M. Harrop (PROG)	6,059	8.8
3	Edgar Howard (D & PROG)	46,631	57.5
	E. C. Houston (R)	34,541	42.6
4	Melvin O. McLaughlin (R)	32,235	49.0
	E. E. Placek (D)	28,962	44.0
	John O. Schmidt (PROG)	4,563	6.9
5	Ashton C. Shallenberger (D & PROG)	34,766	53.8
	William E. Andrews (R)	29,871	46.2
6	Robert G. Simmons (R)	54,686	59.2
	Charles W. Beal (D)	32,275	34.9
	Jesse Gandy (P)	5,467	5.9

NEVADA

AL	Samuel S. Arentz (R)	13,107	50.4
	Charles L. Richards (D)	12,880	49.6

NEW HAMPSHIRE

1	Fletcher Hale (R)	44,758	55.2
	William N. Rogers (D)	36,306	44.8
2	Edward H. Wason (R)	47,588	61.4
	William H. Barry (D)	29,880	38.6

NEW JERSEY

1	Francis F. Patterson Jr. (R)	64,592	69.1
	Robert A. Irving (D)	25,232	27.0

	Candidates	Votes	%
2	Isaac Bacharach (R)	67,668	76.2
	Charles S. Stevens (D)	21,185	23.8
3	T. Frank Appleby (R)	67,445*	60.3
	Elmer H. Geran (D)	44,361	39.7
4	Charles A. Eaton (R)	41,734	53.8
	Charles Browne (D)	35,840	46.2
5	Ernest R. Ackerman (R)	69,423	72.3
	Monell Sayre (D)	26,662	27.8
6	Randolph Perkins (R)	66,555	66.3
	Alfred T. Holley (D)	30,954	30.8
7	George N. Seger (R)	44,932	73.0
	Andrew J. Callahan (D)	13,441	21.8
8	Herbert W. Taylor (R)	45,744	57.0
	Frank J. McNulty (D)	34,463	43.0
9	Franklin W. Fort (R)	32,916	59.3
	Daniel F. Minahan (D)	20,356	36.7
10	Frederick R. Lehlbach (R)	50,890	70.1
	Moses Greenwood (D)	18,578	25.6
11	Oscar L. Auf der Heide (D)	37,813	60.5
	John F. Gardner (R)	22,085	35.3
12	Mary T. Norton (D)	44,815	61.7
	Douglas D. T. Story (R)	26,368	36.3

NEW MEXICO

AL	John Morrow (D)	57.802	51.2
	J. Felipe Hubbell (R)	53,960	47.8

NEW YORK

1	Robert L. Bacon (R)	87,370	67.1
	Ira L. Terry (D)	39,765	30.5
2	John J. Kindred (D)	73,757	62.6
	Frank E. Hopkins (R)	40,507	34.4
3	George W. Lindsay (D)	22,621	64.8
	Herman E. Sprigade (R)	9,804	28.1
	Joseph A. Weil (SOC)	2,488	7.1
4	Thomas H. Cullen (D)	27,008	73.9
	Joseph Rosenbaum (R)	8,780	24.0
5	Loring M. Black Jr. (D)	37,200	51.1
	William T. Simpson (R)	33,938	46.6
6	Andrew L. Somers (D)	42,894	47.8
	Warren I. Lee (R)	41,110	45.8
	W. W. Passage (SOC)	5,779	6.4
7	John F. Quayle (D)	24,048	56.7
	Otis S. Carroll (R)	14,650	34.5
	Jacob Axelrad (SOC)	3,730	8.8
8	William E. Cleary (D)	49,479	51.3
	Max Perlman (R)	38,638	40.1
	William M. Feigenbaum (SOC)	8,333	8.6
9	David J. O'Connell (D)	43,655	50.2
	Andrew N. Petersen (R)	38,708	44.5
	Wilhelmus B. Robinson (SOC)	4,620	5.3
10	Emanuel Celler (D)	25,251	50.0
	James N. Little (R)	19,444	38.5
	Joseph A. Whitehorn (SOC)	5,449	10.8
11	Anning S. Prall (D)	34,265	68.7
	Frederick W. Lahr (R)	14,990	30.0
12	Samuel Dickstein (D)	14,994	75.8
	Harry Schlissel (R)	2,464	12.5
	Israel Feinberg (SOC)	2,164	10.9
13	Christopher D. Sullivan (D)	13,708	71.1
	Murray D. Firstman (R)	3,960	20.6
	Julius Hochman (SOC)	1,600	8.3
14	Nathan D. Perlman (R)	12,046	44.1
	William Irving Sirovich (D)	11,920	43.6
	William Karlin (SOC)	3,165	11.6
15	John J. Boylan (D)	28,132	77.0
	Warren Bigelow (R)	7,732	21.2
16	John J. O'Connor (D)	27,585	72.3
	L. Wilfred Eidt (R)	9,329	24.4
17	Ogden L. Mills (R)	31,553	57.0
	Charles E. Gehring (D)	22,526	40.7
18	John F. Carew (D)	25,975	66.1
	Charles W. Ferry (R)	10,777	27.4
	Samuel E. Beardsley (SOC)	2,519	6.4

	Candidates	Votes	%
19	Sol Bloom (D)	39,760	54.5
	Walter M. Chandler (R)	31,008	42.5
20	Fiorello H. LaGuardia (SOC)	10,756	42.7
	Henry Frank (D)	7,141	28.4
	Isaac Siegel (R)	7,099	28.2
21	Royal H. Weller (D)	43,793	52.5
	Charles H. Roberts (R)	35,881	43.1
22	Anthony J. Griffin (D)	30,469	69.7
	William E. Devlin (R)	10,169	23.3
	Joseph B. Hagerty (SOC)	3,081	7.1
23	Frank Oliver (D)	67,650	56.3
	Albert B. Rossdale (R)	35,721	29.7
	August Claessens (SOC)	15,771	13.1
24	Benjamin L. Fairchild (R)	50,745	45.5
	John J. Kinney (D)	49,948	44.7
	Philip Umstadter (SOC&PROG)	10,937	9.8
25	J. Mayhew Wainwright (R)	57,539	64.8
	A. Outram Sherman (D)	26,909	30.3
26	Hamilton Fish Jr. (R)	55,386	69.7
	Rosslyn M. Cox (D)	21,621	27.2
27	Harcourt J. Pratt (R)	45,764	58.6
	William C. DeWitt (D)	30,805	39.4
28	Parker Corning (D)	57,194	52.7
	Charles H. Johnson (R)	50,108	46.2
29	James S. Parker (R)	60,730	67.2
	James E. Dwyer (D)	28,079	31.1
30	Frank Crowther (R)	47,073	62.9
	James P. Boyle (D & PROG)	24,840	33.2
31	Bertrand H. Snell (R)	45,372	70.5
	John M. Cantwell (D)	19,018	29.5
32	Thaddeus C. Sweet (R)	52,506	68.9
	Charles R. Lee (D)	23,715	31.1
33	Frederick M. Davenport (R)	48,591	58.1
	Albert R. Kessinger (D)	33,068	39.5
34	Harold S. Tolley (R)	61,547	69.7
	Charles R. Seymour (D)	24,800	28.1
35	Walter W. Magee (R)	70,268	64.7
	John J. Kesel (D)	35,008	32.2
36	John Taber (R)	57,865	71.7
	Michael J. Maney (D)	22,890	28.3
37	Gale H. Stalker (R)	59,498	66.9
	Charles L. Durham (D)	27,763	31.2
38	Meyer Jacobstein (D&SOC)	63,997	65.4
	John J. McInerney (R)	33,895	34.6
39	Archie D. Sanders (R)	58,165	67.9
	Michael L. Coleman (D)	23,689	27.7
40	S. Wallace Dempsey (R)	66,939	67.8
	Thurman W. Stoner (D)	26,382	26.7
	Eustace Reynolds (SOC)	5,478	5.5
41	Clarence MacGregor (R)	40,449	68.1
	Edward C. Dethloff (D)	13,754	23.1
	Frank Ehrenfried (SOC)	5,237	8.8
42	James M. Mead (D)	28,152	50.1
	Richard S. Persons (R)	25,256	45.0
43	Daniel A. Reed (R & SOC)	61,769	91.0
	J. Samuel Fowler (PROG)	6,141	9.0

NORTH CAROLINA

1	Lindsay C. Warren (D)	16,387	78.5
	Peter D. Burgess (R)	4,478	21.5
2	John H. Kerr (D)	16,312	93.3
	M. R. Vick (R)	1,169	6.7
3	Charles L. Abernethy (D)	17,685	67.7
	William H. Fisher (R)	8,431	32.3
4	Edward W. Pou (D)	24,057	69.6
	Young Z. Parker (R)	10,505	30.4
5	Charles M. Stedman (D)	44,048	59.3
	Thomas C. Carter (R)	30,255	40.7
6	Homer L. Lyon (D)	21,682	72.7
	William J. McDonald (R)	8,153	27.3
7	William C. Hammer (D)	36,491	55.2
	S. Carter Williams (R)	29,652	44.8
8	Robert L. Doughton (D)	34,692	56.5
	James D. Dorsett (R)	26,666	43.5
9	Alfred L. Bulwinkle (D)	37,370	57.7
	John A. Hendricks (R)	27,427	42.3

NORTH CAROLINA

	Candidates	Votes	%
10	Zebulon Weaver (D)	41,030	55.5
	Lewis P. Hamlin (R)	32,871	44.5

NORTH DAKOTA

	Candidates	Votes	%
1	Olger B. Burtness (R)	44,573	75.4
	Walter Welford (D)	14,511	24.6
2	Thomas Hall (R)	31,212	52.1
	Gerald P. Nye (PROG)	28,193	47.0
3	James H. Sinclair (R)	37,925	73.4
	R. A. Johnson (D)	13,730	26.6

Special Election

	Candidates	Votes	%
2	Thomas Hall (R)	33,460	51.0
	Gerald P. Nye (PROG)	32,205	49.0

OHIO

	Candidates	Votes	%
1	Nicholas Longworth (R)	58,185	61.7
	Thomas B. Paxton (D)	36,065	38.3
2	Ambrose E. B. Stephens (R)	47,331	58.1
	Robert J. O'Donnell (D)	34,118	41.9
3	Roy Fitzgerald (R)	73,513	62.3
	John P. Rogers (D)	43,426	36.8
4	W. T. Fitzgerald (R)	43,984	50.8
	Hugh T. Mathers (D)	42,652	49.2
5	Charles J. Thompson (R)	31,046	51.5
	Frank C. Kniffin (D)	29,245	48.5
6	Charles C. Kearns (R)	33,064	53.0
	Ed. N. Kennedy (D)	29,283	47.0
7	Charles Brand (R)	61,557	63.9
	C. K. Wolf (D)	34,709	36.1
8	Brooks Fletcher (D)	38,439	53.2
	R. Clint Cole (R)	33,258	46.0
9	William W. Chalmers (R)	54,792	51.6
	Isaac R. Sherwood (D)	48,442	45.6
10	Thomas A. Jenkins (R)	32,617	64.5
	W. F. Rutherford (D)	17,923	35.5
11	Mell G. Underwood (D)	35,696	59.5
	Edwin D. Ricketts (R)	24,272	40.5
12	John C. Speaks (R)	58,705	58.7
	Lowry F. Sater (D)	41,291	41.3
13	James T. Begg (R)	45,307	62.1
	John Dreitzler (D)	27,623	37.9
14	Martin L. Davey (D)	62,314	50.8
	Arthur W. Doyle (R)	60,251	49.2
15	C. Ellis Moore (R)	39,155	56.1
	James R. Alexander (D)	30,608	43.9
16	John McSweeney (D)	51,491	51.5
	Thomas C. Hunsicker (R)	45,559	45.6
17	William M. Morgan (R)	50,226	57.9
	J. Freer Bittinger (D)	36,532	42.1
18	Frank Murphy (R)	56,206	66.3
	James M. Barton (D)	26,656	31.4
19	John G. Cooper (R)	67,581	75.5
	Phebe T. Sutliff (D)	21,926	24.5
20	Charles A. Mooney (D)	34,173	59.7
	Harvey Drucker (R)	22,507	39.3
21	Robert Crosser (D)	24,889	53.2
	Harry C. Gahn (R)	21,629	46.2
22	Theodore E. Burton (R)	95,174#	61.8
	Samuel B. Fitzsimmons (D)	32,970#	21.4
	Alfred F. Coyle (I)	25,489#	16.6

OKLAHOMA

	Candidates	Votes	%
1	Samuel J. Montgomery (R)	45,949	49.3
	Wayne W. Bayless (D)	45,806	49.2
2	William W. Hastings (D)	30,352	54.9
	P. E. Reed (R)	24,413	44.2
3	Charles D. Carter (D)	38,674	68.1
	Don Welch (R)	15,433	27.2
4	Thomas D. McKeown (D)	36,437	58.8
	Charles E. Wells (R)	23,313	37.6
5	Fletcher B. Swank (D)	44,683	59.4
	John Golobie (R)	28,510	37.9

	Candidates	Votes	%
6	Elmer Thomas (D)	31,188	56.4
	Lorraine M. Gensman (R)	21,915	39.6
7	James V. McClintic (D)	26,582	66.6
	Walter S. Mills (R)	10,316	25.8
	M. Shadid (F-LAB)	3,041	7.6
8	Milton C. Garber (R)	34,020	51.0
	V. P. Crowe (D)	29,710	44.5

OREGON

	Candidates	Votes	%
1	Willis C. Hawley (R)	72,910	63.5
	Harvey L. Clark (D)	25,293	22.0
	W. J. Butler (I)	13,494	11.8
2	Nicholas J. Sinnott (R)	29,937	61.6
	James H. Graham (D)	18,652	38.4
3	Maurice E. Crumpacker (R)	50,834	54.7
	Elton Watkins (D & PROG)	39,731	42.7

PENNSYLVANIA

	Candidates	Votes	%
1	William S. Vare (R)	59,287	84.4
	Joseph A. Robbins (D, PROG)	7,631	10.9
2	George S. Graham (R)	37,645	82.7
	Jessie L. Collet (D, LAB)	6,355	14.0
3	Harry C. Ransley (R)	39,171	83.9
	Edward P. Carroll (D)	4,092	8.8
	Jennie Dorriblum (SOC, LAB)	3,301	7.1
4	Benjamin M. Golder (R)	40,783	77.8
	Adolph Class (D)	8,365	16.0
	Henry P. Thomas (SOC)	3,237	6.2
5	James J. Connolly (R)	47,033	81.0
	Daniel J. C. O'Donnell (D)	7,525	13.0
	Harry Calse (SOC)	3,118	5.4
6	George A. Welsh (R)	66,340	74.6
	Francis I. J. Coyle (D, LAB)	17,457	19.6
7	George P. Darrow (R, P)	55,990	80.7
	Thomas A. O'Hara (D)	9,999	14.4
8	Thomas S. Butler (R)	63,480	80.7
	Gordon H. Cilley (D, PROG)	12,816	16.3
9	Henry W. Watson (R)	60,316	72.5
	C. William Freed (D)	18,843	22.7
10	William W. Griest (R)	35,257	60.4
	Frank C. Musser (D, INDL)	22,503	38.6
11	Laurence H. Watres (R)	35,461	56.7
	David Fowler (D, LAB)	25,471	40.7
12	Edmund N. Carpenter (R, P)	44,483	55.6
	John J. Casey (D, SOC)	35,562	44.4
13	George Franklin Brumm (R, P)	35,737	69.5
	Thomas J. Butler (D)	14,637	28.5
14	Charles J. Esterly (R)	43,335	50.5
	William M. Croll (D)	36,582	42.6
	Raymond S. Hofses (SOC)	5,884	6.9
15	Louis T. McFadden (R, P)	27,565	68.8
	Charles M. Driggs (D, LAB)	11,854	29.6
16	Edgar R. Kiess (R, P)	26,865	55.5
	Thomas Wood (D)	18,246	37.7
	P. A. McGowan (LAB, SOC)	3,317	6.8
17	Frederick W. Magrady (R, P)	27,969	53.5
	Herbert W. Cummings (D, LAB)	24,321	46.5
18	Edward M. Beers (R, P)	35,743	66.4
	Meredith Meyers (D, LAB)	18,048	33.6
19	Joshua W. Swartz (R)	39,465	53.9
	Frank C. Sites (D, P)	33,038	45.1
20	Anderson H. Walters (R, P)	23,519	50.1
	Warren Worth Bailey (D, LAB)	23,456	49.9
21	J. Banks Kurtz (R, SOC)	27,335	69.4
	Harry K. Filler (D)	7,290	18.5
	J. E. Miller (LAB)	4,748	12.1

	Candidates	Votes	%
22	Franklin Menges (R)	26,924	53.4
	Samuel F. Glatfelter (D, P)	22,784	45.2
23	William Irvin Swoope (R, P)	31,205	64.7
	Edward R. Benson (D, LAB)	17,008	35.3
24	Samuel A. Kendall (R, P)	31,443	68.5
	Harrison N. Boyd (D)	11,810	25.7
25	Henry W. Temple (R, SOC)	27,192	62.5
	Grant Furlong (D)	15,641	36.0
26	Thomas W. Phillips Jr. (R)	38,723	68.8
	John G. Cobler (D, P)	15,307	27.2
27	Nathan L. Strong (R)	33,267	58.9
	John H. Murray (P)	11,208	19.8
	Harry W. Fee (D)	10,119	17.9
28	Harris J. Bixler (R, P)	43,247	79.1
	William G. Barker (D)	11,409	20.9
29	Milton W. Shreve (R)	27,502	57.7
	Edward M. Murphy (D)	10,304	21.6
	Elizabeth R. Culbertson (P, LAB)	8,261	17.3
30	William R. Coyle (R)	31,036	50.9
	Everett Kent (D, LAB)	28,723	47.1
31	Adam M. Wyant (R, SOC)	36,314	60.4
	Chester D. Sensenich (D, LAB)	23,790	39.6
32	Stephen Geyer Porter (R, P)	31,102	79.5
	P. M. O'Donnell (D)	5,055	12.9
33	M. Clyde Kelly (R, P)	37,314	81.1
	Gilbert F. Myer (D)	6,017	13.1
34	John M. Morin (R, LAB)	22,669	82.5
	William N. McNair (D)	3,289	12.0
35	James M. Magee (R, PROG)	28,381	59.9
	John W. Slayton (LAB, SOC)	9,039	19.1
	John Murphy (D)	5,755	12.1
	Thomas P. Moran (INDL)	2,544	5.4
36	Guy E. Campbell (R, D)	34,266	87.2
	William H. Bright (P)	5,048	12.8

RHODE ISLAND

	Candidates	Votes	%
1	Clark Burdick (R)	44,952	65.2
	Alfred H. Jones (D)	23,958	34.8
2	Richard S. Aldrich (R)	44,870	63.9
	Charles M. Hall (D)	25,361	36.1
3	Jeremiah E. O'Connell (D)	35,224	51.7
	Louis Monast (R)	32,953	48.3

SOUTH CAROLINA

	Candidates	Votes	%
1	Thomas S. McMillan (D)	5,278	95.4
2	Butler B. Hare (D)	6,695	100.0
3	Fred H. Dominick (D)	8,331	100.0
4	John J. McSwain (D)	7,718	100.0
5	William F. Stevenson (D)	7,689	100.0
6	Allard H. Gasque (D)	6,278	100.0
7	Hampton P. Fulmer (D)	7,249	100.0

SOUTH DAKOTA

	Candidates	Votes	%
1	Charles A. Christopherson (R)	39,138	53.5
	Warren E. Beck (D)	19,904	27.2
	William Bartling (I)	7,206	9.9
	William T. Jones (F-LAB)	6,901	9.4
2	Royal C. Johnson (R)	44,869	60.3
	Walter P. Wohlheter (F-LAB)	11,468	15.4
	Fred H. Hildebrandt (I)	10,067	13.5
	Jack P. Reinhard (D)	8,043	10.8
3	William Williamson (R)	28,150	58.3
	John R. Russell (D)	10,026	20.8
	Arthur W. Atwood (F-LAB)	6,950	14.4

TENNESSEE

	Candidates	Votes	%
1	B. Carroll Reece (R)	23,445	62.6
	R. M. Barry (D)	11,362	30.3
	F. P. Robinson	1,970	5.3
2	J. Will Taylor (R)	28,975	96.3
3	Sam D. McReynolds (D)	22,857	56.9
	May Giles Howard (R)	17,341	43.1
4	Cordell Hull (D)	16,908	100.0
5	Ewin L. Davis (D)	11,373	81.7
	A. L. Davidson (R)	2,551	18.3
6	Joseph W. Byrns (D)	19,756	100.0
7	Edward E. Eslick (D)	13,547	100.0
8	Gordon Browning (D)	12,940	100.0
9	Finis J. Garrett (D)	18,367	100.0
10	Hubert F. Fisher (D)	16,306	74.0
	George H. Poole	2,923	13.3
	Harry Speers (R)	2,801	12.7

TEXAS

		Votes	%
1	Eugene Black (D)	28,218	90.9
	R. B. Johnson (R)	2,826	9.1
2	John C. Box (D)	41,188	89.9
	A. E. Sweatland (R)	4,625	10.1
3	Morgan G. Sanders (D)	30,618	100.0
4	Sam Rayburn (D)	31,825	91.1
	C. A. Gray (R)	3,111	8.9
5	Hatton W. Sumners (D)	43,781	87.6
	George G. Atkinson (R)	6,193	12.4
6	Luther A. Johnson (D)	33,169	93.2
	Tyler Haswell (R)	2,440	6.9
7	Clay Stone Briggs (D)	23,947	89.1
	John T. Wheeler (R)	2,941	10.9
8	Daniel E. Garrett (D)	35,189	86.0
	Clarence A. Miller (R)	5,712	14.0
9	Joseph J. Mansfield (D)	31,444	82.3
	Ed. Franz (R)	6,742	17.7
10	James P. Buchanan (D)	36,681	90.5
	Otto Stolley (R)	3,850	9.5
11	Tom T. Connally (D)	29,247	88.2
	C. C. Baker (R)	3,918	11.8
12	Fritz G. Lanham (D)	33,186	100.0
13	Guinn Williams (D)	32,721	88.6
	C. W. Johnson Jr. (R)	4,197	11.4
14	Harry M. Wurzbach (R)	31,784	62.4
	D. S. Davenport (D)	19,165	37.6
15	John N. Garner (D)	22,776	99.9
16	Claude B. Hudspeth (D)	27,506	82.6
	Vernon L. Sullivan (R)	5,800	17.4
17	Thomas L. Blanton (D)	44,377	100.0
18	Marvin Jones (D)	42,399	89.7
	A. B. Spencer (R)	4,887	10.3

UTAH

	Candidates	Votes	%
1	Don B. Colton (R)	40,883	54.9
	Frank Francis (D)	33,644	45.1
2	Elmer O. Leatherwood (R)	41,888	56.7
	James H. Waters (D)	32,045	43.3

VERMONT

1	Elbert S. Brigham (R, P)	36,278	76.0
	Allan T. Calhoun (D)	11,457	24.0
2	Ernest Willard Gibson (R, P)	41,099	82.8
	Harry C. Shurtleff (D)	8,479	17.1

VIRGINIA

1	Schuyler Otis Bland (D)	16,958	99.9
2	Joseph T. Deal (D)	11,795	65.8
	Menalcus Lankford (R)	6,145	34.3
3	Andrew Jackson Montague (D)	20,864	100.0
4	Patrick Henry Drewry (D)	12,106	100.0
5	Joseph Whitehead (D)	16,371	76.0
	G. A. De Hart (R)	5,181	24.0
6	Clifton A. Woodrum (D)	13,917	69.0
	F. W. McWane (R)	6,251	31.0
7	Thomas W. Harrison (D)	13,013	59.2
	J. H. Ruebush (R)	7,294	33.2
	Dabney C. Harrison (I)	1,692	7.7
8	R. Walton Moore (D)	14,113	79.9
	John G. Dudley (R)	3,551	20.1
9	George C. Peery (D)	31,407	52.6
	C. Henry Harman (R)	28,341	47.4
10	Henry St.George Tucker (D)	14,472	69.7
	Henry S. Reid (R)	6,288	30.3

WASHINGTON

1	John F. Miller (R)	53,152	78.8
	David J. Williams (D)	13,922	20.6
2	Lindley H. Hadley (R)	37,636	57.4
	Lloyd L. Black (D)	27,154	41.4
3	Albert Johnson (R)	60,272	70.5
	O. M. Nelson (PROG)	25,146	29.4
4	John W. Summers (R)	36,918	65.3
	H. C. Bohlke (D)	12,254	21.7
	Knute Hill (F-LAB)	7,380	13.1
5	Sam B. Hill (D)	36,844	50.7
	J. Edward Ferguson (R)	35,815	49.3

WEST VIRGINIA

	Candidates	Votes	%
1	Carl G. Bachmann (R)	47,318	55.2
	George W. Oldham (D)	38,417	44,8
2	Frank L. Bowman (R)	41,825	50.1
	Robert E. Lee Allen (D)	40,474	48.5
3	John M. Wolverton (R)	45,995	51.9
	Robert H. Kidd (D)	42,626	48.1
4	Harry C. Woodyard (R)	47,136	51.2
	George W. Johnson (D)	44,877	48.8
5	James French Strother (R)	50,629	51.5
	Thomas Jefferson Lilly (D)	47,719	48.5
6	J. Alfred Taylor (D)	56,570	49.8
	Leonard S. Echols (R)	55,089	48.5

WISCONSIN

1	Henry Allen Cooper (R)	60,770	72.0
	Calvin Stewart (D)	23,612	28.0
2	Edward Voigt (R)	44,617	70.5
	Ernst C. Wrucke (D)	18,696	29.5
3	John M. Nelson (R)	56,868	77.0
	William Victora (D)	16,968	23.0
4	John C. Schafer (R)	30,837	49.6
	Leo Krzycki (SOC)	19,770	31.8
	Thomas H. Dorr (D)	11,524	18.6
5	Victor L. Berger (SOC)	32,211	41.6
	Ernst A. Braun (R)	31,702	41.0
	Raymond Moore (D)	13,441	17.4
6	Florian Lampert (R)	45,982	70.6
	Michael K. Reilly (D)	19,128	29.4
7	Joseph D. Beck (R)	47,075	80.0
	W. D. Martin (D)	10,228	17.4
8	Edward E. Browne (R)	47,423	99.9
9	George J. Schneider (R)	45,159	71.0
	T. J. Reinert (D)	18,449	29.0
10	James A. Frear (R)	46,563	78.7
	Thomas A. Ryan (D)	10,481	17.7
11	Hubert H. Peavey (R)	48,234	78.1
	John Cadigan (D)	13,455	21.8

WYOMING

AL	Charles E. Winter (R)	43,026	60.1
	Theodore Wanerus (D)	28,537	39.9

1925 House Election

NEW JERSEY

Special Election

3	Stewart H. Appleby (R)	53,925	53.3
	J. Lyle Kinmonth (D)	47,271	46.7

1926 House Elections

ALABAMA

Candidates	Votes	%
1 John McDuffie (D)	8,297	84.0
Aubrey Boyles (R)	1,578	16.0
2 Lister Hill (D)	10,170	100.0
3 Henry B. Steagall (D)	7,619	94.6
C. E. Roberts (R)	437	5.4
4 Lamar Jeffers (D)	8,392	68.1
Omar H. Reynolds (R)	3,933	31.9
5 William B. Bowling (D)	9,012	88.4
John A. Alexander (R)	1,183	11.6
6 William B. Oliver (D)	3,984	99.0
7 Miles C. Allgood (D)	14,937	64.7
John J. Stephens (R)	8,162	35.3
8 Edward B. Almon (D)	8,800	90.1
Robert M. Sims (R)	964	9.9
9 George Huddleston (D)	7,260	94.4
Frank H. Lathrop (R)	430	5.6
10 William B. Bankhead (D)	11,895	100.0

ARIZONA

	Votes	%
AL Lewis W. Douglas (D)	43,725	64.1
Otis J. Baughn (R)	24,502	35.9

ARKANSAS

	Votes	%
1 William J. Driver (D)	3,680	100.0
2 William A. Oldfield (D)	4,013	78.8
J. L. McKamey (R)	1,081	21.2
3 John N. Tillman (D)	5,696	64.4
Hardy Kuykendall (R)	3,146	35.6
4 Otis T. Wingo (D)	4,729	100.0
5 Heartsill Ragon (D)	4,282	88.2
Harry M. Williams (R)	574	11.8
6 James B. Reed (D)	3,013	100.0
7 Tillman B. Parks (D)	3,498	100.0

CALIFORNIA

	Votes	%
1 Clarence.F. Lea (D-R)	60,207	100.0
2 Harry L. Englebright (R)	32,264	99.8
3 Charles F. Curry (R-D)	72,912	100.0
4 Florence P. Kahn (R)	37,353	63.8
Chauncey F. Tramutolo (D)	18,210	31.1
William McDevitt (SOC)	2,960	5.1
5 Richard J. Welch (R-D)	47,694	100.0
6 Albert E. Carter (R)	91,995	100.0
7 Henry E. Barbour (R-D)	73,271	100.0
8 Arthur Monroe Free (R)	60,384	67.7
Philip G. Sheehy (D)	28,836	32.3
9 William E. Evans (R)	102,270	59.5
Charles H. Randall (P & D)	61,719	35.9
10 Joe Crail (R-D-P)	144,677	86.8
N. Jackson Wright (SOC)	21,997	13.2
11 Philip D. Swing (R-D)	89,726	100.0

COLORADO

	Votes	%
1 William N. Vaile (R)	39,909	54.9
Benjamin C. Hilliard (D)	30,337	41.7
2 Charles B. Timberlake (R)	55,581	66.6
William B. Washburn (D)	27,939	33.5
3 Guy U. Hardy (R)	46,916	54.0
Edmond I. Crockett (D)	40,009	46.0
4 Edward T. Taylor (D)	32,092	66.7
Webster S. Whinnery (R)	15,990	33.3

CONNECTICUT

	Votes	%
1 E. Hart Fenn (R)	45,054	63.0
Henry J. Calnen (D)	25,777	36.0
2 Richard P. Freeman (R)	33,809	61.7
Hermon J. Gibbs (D)	20,538	37.5
3 John Q. Tilson (R)	40,055	65.6
John E. Doughan (D)	20,281	33.2
4 Schuyler Merritt (R)	44,477	68.4
John Held Jr. (D)	19,623	30.2
5 James P. Glynn (R)	28,687	58.5
Arthur F. O'Leary (D)	20,352	41.5

DELAWARE

	Votes	%
AL Robert G. Houston (R)	38,909	56.9
Merrill H. Tilghman (D)	29,424	43.1

FLORIDA

	Votes	%
1 Herbert J. Drane (D)	16,034	72.8
Ora E. Chapin (RP & DC)	6,007	27.3
2 Robert A. Green (D)	6,727	86.2
A. F. Knotts (R)	1,080	13.8
3 Tom A. Yon (D)	7,156	86.8
J. H. Drummond (R)	1,084	13.2
4 William J. Sears (D)	19,578	73.6
W. C. Lawson (RDC)	4,235	15.9
E. D. Housholder (R)	2,783	10.5

GEORGIA

	Votes	%
1 Charles G. Edwards (D)	7,641	100.0
2 E. E. Cox (D)	2,384	100.0
3 Charles R. Crisp (D)	3,422	100.0
4 William C. Wright (D)	2,583	100.0
5 Leslie J. Steele (D)	2,919	99.9
6 Samuel Rutherford (D)	2,365	100.0
7 Malcolm C. Tarver (D)	5,902	94.1
George A. Coffee	373	5.9
8 Charles H. Brand (D)	3,124	100.0
9 Thomas M. Bell (D)	7,788	100.0
10 Carl Vinson (D)	3,015	100.0
11 William C. Lankford (D)	3,461	100.0
12 William W. Larsen (D)	2,388	100.0

IDAHO

	Votes	%
1 Burton L. French (R)	31,250	66.3
L. L. Burtenshaw (D, PROG)	15,903	33.7
2 Addison T. Smith (R)	40,960	60.6
H. F. Fait (PROG)	15,368	22.7
Mary George Gray (D)	11,259	16.7

ILLINOIS

	Votes	%
1 Martin B. Madden (R)	26,559	68.2
James F. Doyle (D)	12,283	31.5
2 Morton D. Hull (R)	71,750	65.5
Michael C. Walsh (D)	37,518	34.3
3 Elliott W. Sproul (R)	57,692	52.7
Edward J. Glackin (D)	51,590	47.1
4 Thomas A. Doyle (D)	30,817	62.9
John J. Dever (R)	18,184	37.1
5 Adolph J. Sabath (D)	18,027	58.8
Matt J. Vogel (R)	12,643	41.2
6 James T. Igoe (D)	74,817	52.6
John J. Gorman (R)	67,419	47.4
7 M. Alfred Michaelson (R)	86,405	57.8
John S. Hall (D)	62,469	41.8
8 Stanley Henry Kunz (D)	15,321	55.3
Wencil F. Hetman (R)	12,388	44.7
9 Fred A. Britten (R)	26,530	97.8
10 Carl R. Chindblom (R)	68,137	66.0
William X. Meyer (D)	35,123	34.0
11 Frank R. Reid (R)	44,574	69.5
Edward J. O'Beirne (D)	19,600	30.5
12 John T. Buckbee (R)	36,597	57.8
John A. Logan Warren (D)	26,727	42.2
13 William R. Johnson (R)	30,197	74.8
John Ascher (D)	10,190	25.2
14 John C. Allen (R)	33,089	68.0
John W. Casto (D)	15,572	32.0
15 Edward J. King (R)	35,396	62.6
F. William Heckenkamp Jr. (D)	21,157	37.4
16 William E. Hull (R)	37,110	63.3
Carl M. Behrman (D)	21,530	36.7
17 Homer W. Hall (R)	31,874	64.9
Frank Gillespie (D)	17,220	35.1
18 William P. Holaday (R)	44,111	65.2
Wilbur Hickman (D)	23,569	34.8
19 Charles Adkins (R)	40,456	62.3
Joel T. Davis (D)	24,507	37.7
20 Henry T. Rainey (D)	29,935	57.8
Horace H. Bancroft (R)	21,875	42.2
21 J. Earl Major (D)	39,365	52.8
Loren E. Wheeler (R)	35,191	47.2
22 Edward M. Irwin (R)	38,714	58.5
William N. Baltz (D)	27,428	41.5
23 William W. Arnold (D)	38,575	55.9
Erastus D. Telford (R)	29,896	43.3
24 Thomas S. Williams (R)	26,295	56.1
John Marshall Karns (D)	20,612	43.9
25 Edward E. Denison (R)	36,644	59.6
A. F. Gourley (D)	24,849	40.4
AL Henry R. Rathbone (R)	987,968 ✓	
Richard Yates (R)	986,090 ✓	
Frank J. Wise (D)	631,708	
Charles A. Karch (D)	616,713	
Mrs. P. J. Carlson (PROG)	5,413	
Charles Pogoreles (SOC)	2,662	
George Koop (SOC)	2,476	
James S. O'Rourke (SOC LAB)	1,977	
A. H. Otto Beneze (SOC LAB)	1,746	
Charles D. Harrison (HL)	451	
Andrew A. Gour (CLP)	431	
Mary C. Connor (CLP)	428	

INDIANA

	Votes	%
1 Harry E. Rowbottom (R)	37,503	52.4
William E. Wilson (D)	34,061	47.6
2 Arthur H. Greenwood (D)	44,690	55.4
John E. Sedwick (R)	35,964	44.6
3 Frank Gardner (D)	42,422	54.6
W. Clyde Martin (R)	35,229	45.4
4 Harry C. Canfield (D)	42,882	53.9
John W. Holcomb (R)	36,655	46.1
5 Noble J. Johnson (R)	43,458	57.8
Henry W. Moore (D)	31,693	42.2
6 Richard N. Elliott (R)	38,347	55.2
William H. Myers (D)	31,107	44.8
7 Ralph E. Updike (R)	48,313	52.1
William D. Headrick (D)	44,142	47.6
8 Albert H. Vestal (R)	40,963	53.8
Claude H. Ball (D)	35,205	46.2
9 Fred S. Purnell (R)	43,891	52.6
Roy W. Adney (D)	39,597	47.4
10 William R. Wood (R)	52,286	68.2
Harry O. Rhodes (D)	24,349	31.8
11 Albert R. Hall (R)	42,519	54.2
Samuel E. Cook (D)	35,870	45.8
12 David Hogg (R)	38,936	55.3
Waldemar E. Eickhoff (D)	31,442	44.7
13 Andrew J. Hickey (R)	52,541	54.9
Charles Weidler (D)	43,119	45.1

IOWA

	Candidates	Votes	%
1	William F. Kopp (R)	27,358	70.6
	James M. Bell (D)	11,408	29.4
2	F. Dickinson Letts (R)	29,200	59.1
	J. P. Gallagher (D)	19,612	39.7
3	Thomas J. B. Robinson (R)	32,180	70.2
	Ellis E. Wilson (D)	13,696	29.9
4	Gilbert N. Haugen (R)	30,611	60.4
	Frank E. Howard (D)	20,076	39.6
5	Cyrenus Cole (R)	31,253	71.8
	C. E. Watters (D)	12,263	28.2
6	C. William Ramseyer (R)	27,967	66.3
	W. L. Etter (D)	14,193	33.7
7	Cassius C. Dowell (R)	34,159	76.9
	William M. Wade (D)	10,255	23.1
8	Lloyd Thurston (R)	30,568	61.9
	W. S. Bradley (D)	18,743	37.9
9	William R. Greene (R)	30,373	67.2
	Charles F. Paschel (D)	14,837	32.8
10	Lester J. Dickinson (R)	39,677	97.7
11	William D. Boies (R)	35,381	64.4
	R. J. Koehler (D)	19,542	35.6

KANSAS

		Votes	%
1	Daniel R. Anthony Jr. (R)	46,232	100.0
2	Ulysses S. Guyer (R)	37,465	51.6
	Chauncey B. Little (D)	35,108	48.3
3	William H. Sproul (R)	35,510	50.5
	Thurman Hill (D)	34,765	49.5
4	Homer Hoch (R)	29,285	65.2
	Edwin F. Hammond (D)	15,643	34.8
5	James G. Strong (R)	33,817	62.8
	Rex Montgomery (D)	20,033	37.2
6	Hays B. White (R)	31,159	50.1
	W. H. Clark (D)	31,065	49.9
7	Clifford R. Hope (R)	49,072	64.1
	Harry F. Brown (D)	27,374	35.8
8	William A. Ayres (D)	32,096	60.1
	Fred L. Bell (R)	21,350	40.0

KENTUCKY

		Votes	%
1	William V. Gregory (D)	28,306	67.8
	Mrs. William H. Mason (R)	13,460	32.2
2	David H. Kincheloe (D)	23,445	56.2
	Ernest Rowe (R)	18,279	43.8
3	John W. Moore (D)	24,303	56.2
	Charles E. Whittle (R)	18,941	43.8
4	Henry D. Moorman (D)	24,348	55.3
	Pal Garner (R)	19,658	44.7
5	Maurice H. Thatcher (R)	51,328	54.8
	S. M. Russell (D)	42,339	45.2
6	Orie S. Ware (D)	26,063	57.2
	E. H. Daugherty (R)	19,487	42.8
7	Virgil Chapman (D)	26,924	100.0
8	Ralph Gilbert (D)	21,938	54.5
	E. W. Draffen (R)	18,321	45.5
9	Fred M. Vinson (D)	31,063	59.1
	Trumbo Snedegar (R)	21,498	40.9
10	Katherine Langley (R)	20,463	58.4
	Doug Hays (D)	14,578	41.6
11	John M. Robsion (R)	38,474	100.0

Special Elections

		Votes	%
3	John W. Moore (D)	27,640	52.9
	Thurman B. Dixon (R)	24,580	47.1
10	Andrew J. Kirk (R)	10,540	60.7
	J. C. Cantrell (D)	6,838	39.4

LOUISIANA

		Votes	%
1	James O'Connor (D)	14,486	94.3
	Gus Oertling (R)	869	5.7
2	J. Zach Spearing (D)	15,110	100.0
3	Whitmell P. Martin (D)	3,488	100.0
4	John N. Sandlin (D)	5,490	100.0

	Candidates	Votes	%
5	Riley J. Wilson (D)	2,778	100.0
6	Bolivar E. Kemp (D)	4,055	100.0
7	Ladislas Lazaro (D)	3,721	100.0
8	James B. Aswell (D)	4,192	100.0

MAINE

		Votes	%
1	Carroll L. Beedy (R)	27,040	62.8
	Richard E. Hersom (D)	16,032	37.2
2	Wallace H. White Jr. (R)	26,593	56.6
	Charles M. Starbird (D)	20,422	43.4
3	John E. Nelson (R)	30,216	64.8
	Edward Chase (D)	16,421	35.2
4	Ira G. Hersey (R)	22,858	62.9
	Frank A. Peabody (D)	13,457	37.1

MARYLAND

		Votes	%
1	T. Alan Goldsborough (D)	30,845	59.1
	Lawrence B. Towers (R)	21,359	40.9
2	William P. Cole Jr. (D)	50,305	58.9
	Linwood L. Clark (R)	34,327	40.2
3	Vincent L. Palmisano (D)	21,466	58.7
	John J. McGinity (D)	14,284	39.1
4	J. Charles Linthicum (D)	32,620	62.0
	Julius F. Diehl (R)	19,531	37.1
5	Stephen W. Gambrill (D)	26,905	55.1
	Thomas Brackett Reed Mudd (R)	21,911	44.9
6	Frederick N. Zihlman (R)	35,247	58.3
	Frank W. Mish (D)	24,749	40.9

MASSACHUSETTS

		Votes	%
1	Allen T. Treadway (R)	37,878	58.8
	Eugene A. Lynch (D)	26,592	41.3
2	Henry L. Bowles (R)	36,333	64.0
	John Hall (D)	20,450	36.0
3	Frank H. Foss (R)	35,887	62.8
	Joseph E. Casey (D)	21,257	37.2
4	George R. Stobbs (R)	37,744	57.7
	Peter F. Sullivan (D)	27,706	42.3
5	Edith Nourse Rogers (R)	46,464	71.1
	James M. Hurley (D)	18,846	28.9
6	A. Piatt Andrew (R)	39,918	76.9
	James McPherson (D)	11,975	23.1
7	William P. Connery Jr. (D)	32,130	64.0
	George F. Hogan (R)	18,045	36.0
8	Frederick W. Dallinger (R)	46,642	63.7
	John P. Brennan (D)	26,601	36.3
9	Charles L. Underhill (R)	34,468	57.8
	Francis X. Tyrrell (D)	25,211	42.2
10	John J. Douglass (D)	29,443	100.0
11	George Holden Tinkham (R, D)	48,948	100.0
12	James A. Gallivan (D)	49,865	100.0
13	Robert Luce (R)	50,463	64.0
	John P. Tierney (D)	28,346	36.0
14	Louis A. Frothingham (R)	51,920	66.2
	Frank A. Manning (D)	26,469	33.8
15	Joseph W. Martin Jr. (R)	33,687	65.2
	Minerva D. Kepple (D)	17,963	34.8
16	Charles L. Gifford (R)	35,235	68.0
	George Fox Tucker (D)	16,570	32.0

Special Election

		Votes	%
8	Frederick W. Dallinger (R)	44,761#	64.3
	John P. Brennan (D)	24,800#	35.7

MICHIGAN

		Votes	%
1	Robert H. Clancy (R)	27,004	74.1
	William M. Donnelly (D)	9,119	25.0
2	Earl C. Michener (R)	38,182	66.7
	Boyez Dansard (D)	19,034	33.3

	Candidates	Votes	%
3	Joseph L. Hooper (R)	30,704	70.2
	Frank L. Willison (D)	13,034	29.8
4	John C. Ketcham (R)	31,881	72.3
	Earl B. Sill (D)	12,223	27.7
5	Carl E. Mapes (R)	29,653	80.2
	Frank C. Jarvis (D)	7,339	19.8
6	Grant M. Hudson (R)	67,796	68.0
	Frank L. Dodge (D)	31,945	32.0
7	Louis C. Cramton (R)	35,967	78.1
	Frank W. Merrick (D)	10,081	21.9
8	Bird J. Vincent (R)	39,541	100.0
9	James C. McLaughlin (R)	24,927	99.3
10	Roy O. Woodruff (R)	23,875	100.0
11	Frank P. Bohn (R)	25,816	77.6
	Robert H. Wright (D)	7,468	22.4
12	W. Frank James (R)	37,117	100.0
13	Clarence J. McLeod (R)	26,190	68.0
	Henry A. Behrendt (D)	12,152	31.6

MINNESOTA

		Votes	%
1	Allen J. Furlow (R)	46,956	74.5
	L. B. Hanna (D)	16,070	25.5
2	Frank Clague (R)	56,679	100.0
3	August H. Andresen (R)	40,484	63.3
	August M. Gagen (F-LAB)	13,636	21.3
	Charles C. Kolars (D)	9,825	15.4
4	Melvin J. Maas (R)	22,976#	54.3
	Thomas V. Sullivan (F-LAB)	17,355#	41.0
5	Walter H. Newton (R)	47,162	64.8
	Albert G. Bastis (F-LAB)	19,647	27.0
	Fred Jensen (D)	5,942	8.2
6	Harold Knutson (R)	39,570	59.4
	Joseph B. Himsel (F-LAB)	27,076	40.6
7	Ole J. Kvale (F-LAB)	41,151	59.0
	E. E. Howard (R)	28,641	41.0
8	William L. Carss (F-LAB)	41,766	55.4
	Oscar J. Larson (R)	33,606	44.6
9	Conrad G. Selvig (R)	33,477	50.7
	Knud Wefald (F-LAB)	32,505	49.3
10	Godfrey G. Goodwin (R)	36,897	59.1
	Ernest Lundeen (F-LAB)	21,552	34.5
	Henry A. Finlayson (D)	4,013	6.4

MISSISSIPPI

		Votes	%
1	John E. Rankin (D)	3,423	100.0
2	Bill G. Lowrey (D)	3,167	100.0
3	William M. Whittington (D)	2,949	100.0
4	T. Jeff Busby (D)	3,945	100.0
5	Ross A. Collins (D)	4,832	100.0
6	T. Webber Wilson (D)	4,792	100.0
7	Percy E. Quin (D)	1,781	100.0
8	James W. Collier (D)	2,028	100.0

MISSOURI

		Votes	%
1	Milton A. Romjue (D)	29,629	60.4
	J. Frank Culler (R)	19,384	39.5
2	Ralph F. Lozier (D)	31,999	62.4
	Sam A. Clark (R)	19,243	37.5
3	Jacob L. Milligan (D)	26,596	56.3
	Charles T. McLaughlin (R)	20,611	43.7
4	Charles L. Faust (R)	30,320	56.3
	J. C. Whitsell (D)	23,573	43.7
5	George H. Combs Jr. (D)	78,700	56.2
	Edgar C. Ellis (R)	61,189	43.7
6	Clement C. Dickinson (D)	24,161	55.2
	Millard E. Lane (R)	19,524	44.6
7	Samuel C. Major (D)	37,392	52.1
	Harold T. Lincoln (R)	34,339	47.8
8	William L. Nelson (D)	26,156	56.2
	C. W. Thomas (R)	20,422	43.8
9	Clarence Cannon (D)	28,720	61.2
	Osmund Haenssler (R)	18,163	38.7
10	Henry F. Niedringhaus (R)	91,419	66.1
	Irvin Sale (D)	46,880	33.9

MISSOURI

	Candidates	Votes	%
11	John J. Cochran (D)	22,854	52.6
	Henri Chouteau (R)	20,554	47.3
12	Leonidas C. Dyer (R)	14,494	61.3
	David D. Israel (D)	9,120	38.6
13	Clyde Williams (D)	23,338	50.6
	Charles E. Kiefner (R)	22,764	49.3
14	James F. Fullbright (D)	40,871	51.5
	James F. Adams (R)	38,501	48.5
15	Joe J. Manlove (R)	36,995	59.7
	Robert W. Moore (D)	24,786	40.0
16	Thomas L. Rubey (D)	25,032	56.5
	Anna Covert (R)	19,251	43.5

Special Election

	Candidates	Votes	%
11	John J. Cochran (D)	22,971	52.8
	Henri Chouteau (R)	20,521	47.2

MONTANA

	Candidates	Votes	%
1	John M. Evans (D)	38,527	59.4
	Ronald Higgins (R)	25,898	39.9
2	Scott Leavitt (R)	48,617	54.9
	Harry B. Mitchell (D)	37,306	42.1

NEBRASKA

	Candidates	Votes	%
1	John H. Morehead (D)	30,840	55.3
	George W. Marsh (R)	24,169	43.4
2	Willis G. Sears (R)	33,211	59.5
	Grenville P. North (D)	22,641	40.5
3	Edgar Howard (D)	43,915	60.7
	John F. Nesbit (R)	21,075	29.1
	Willis E. Reed (LAF I)	7,383	10.2
4	John N. Norton (D)	31,107	50.6
	Melvin O. McLaughlin (R)	30,397	49.4
5	Ashton C. Shallenberger (D-LAF I)	36,058	60.3
	W. E. Andrews (R)	23,781	39.7
6	Robert G. Simmons (R)	55,330	65.8
	Thomas C. Osborne (D)	28,746	34.2

NEVADA

	Candidates	Votes	%
AL	Samuel S. Arentz (R)	17,598	57.7
	Maurice J. Sullivan (D)	12,910	42.3

NEW HAMPSHIRE

	Candidates	Votes	%
1	Fletcher Hale (R)	40,566	61.4
	F. Clyde Keefe (D)	25,555	38.7
2	Edward H. Wason (R)	36,598	63.2
	George H. Duncan (D)	21,312	36.8

NEW JERSEY

	Candidates	Votes	%
1	Charles A. Wolverton (R)	57,522	69.7
	Edward J. Kelleher (D)	24,990	30.3
2	Isaac Bacharach (R)	53,147	80.6
	Frank Melville (D)	12,775	19.4
3	Harold Hoffman (R)	61,484	60.7
	Fred W. DeVoe (D)	39,074	38.6
4	Charles A. Eaton (R)	35,948	62.0
	William M. Williams (D)	22,059	38.0
5	Ernest R. Ackerman (R)	50,209	63.7
	Frank K. Sauer (D)	28,644	36.3
6	Randolph Perkins (R)	58,244	62.9
	Francis C. Koehler (D)	33,132	35.8
7	George N. Seger (R)	29,383	70.6
	Susan A. McNair (D)	11,083	26.6
8	Paul J. Moore (D)	39,436	58.1
	Herbert W. Taylor (R)	28,273	41.6
9	Franklin W. Fort (R)	19,751	60.2
	James J. Whalen (D)	13,058	39.8
10	Frederick R. Lehlbach (R)	28,960	64.8
	Edward W. Townsend (D)	15,727	35.2
11	Oscar L. Auf der Heide (D)	45,877	76.1
	George M. Eichler (R)	14,083	23.4
12	Mary T. Norton (D)	54,082	83.1
	Philip W. Grece (R)	11,034	17.0

NEW MEXICO

	Candidates	Votes	%
AL	John Morrow (D)	55,433	51.4
	Juan A. A. Sedillo (R)	52,075	48.3

NEW YORK

	Candidates	Votes	%
1	Robert L. Bacon (R)	82,090	63.4
	W. Irving Vanderpoel (D)	45,699	35.3
2	John J. Kindred (D)	89,062	69.4
	Louis C. Gosdorfer (R)	37,163	29.0
3	George W. Lindsay (D)	21,713	75.1
	Walter H. Kreiner (R)	5,984	20.7
4	Thomas H. Cullen (D)	24,734	78.1
	George H. Teommey Sr. (R)	6,624	20.9
5	Loring M. Black Jr. (D)	34,488	56.0
	Robert C. Lee (R)	26,295	42.7
6	Andrew L. Somers (D)	47,407	57.0
	William F. Heissenbuttel (R)	30,906	37.2
	William W. Passage (SOC)	4,799	5.8
7	John F. Quayle (D)	22,551	65.0
	Harland B. Tibbetts (R)	9,747	28.1
	Mendel Bromberg (SOC)	2,394	6.9
8	Patrick J. Carley (D)	62,091	61.4
	George W. Criss (R)	30,548	30.2
	W. M. Feigenbaum (SOC)	8,526	8.4
9	David J. O'Connell (D)	45,191	57.1
	Edward W. Patterson (R)	31,131	39.3
10	Emanuel Celler (D)	24,102	58.3
	Samuel Rubin (R)	13,428	32.5
	Abraham I. Shiplacoff (SOC)	3,576	8.6
11	Anning S. Prall (D)	34,584	72.2
	Esli L. Sutton (R)	12,929	27.0
12	Samuel Dickstein (D)	13,135	79.7
	Joseph D. Tarlowe (R)	2,142	13.0
	Harry Rogoff (SOC)	1,201	7.3
13	Christopher D. Sullivan (D)	12,307	75.7
	John Fanelle (R)	3,067	18.9
	Algernon Lee (SOC)	846	5.2
14	William Irving Sirovich (D)	11,809	49.4
	Nathan D. Perlman (R)	10,688	44.8
	Samuel E. Beardsley (SOC)	1,277	5.4
15	John J. Boylan (D)	24,083	80.8
	John J. Curry (R)	5,312	17.8
16	John J. O'Connor (D)	24,476	76.7
	Fred W. Meyer (R)	6,918	21.7
17	William W. Cohen (D)	22,401	50.4
	Louis W. Stotesbury (R)	21,251	47.8
18	John F. Carew (D)	25,832	77.7
	Bernard Katzen (R)	6,076	18.3
19	Sol Bloom (D)	36,274	64.6
	Harold Korn (R)	18,810	33.5
20	Fiorello H. LaGuardia (R & PROG)	9,122	47.1
	H. Warren Hubbard (D)	9,067	46.8
	George Dobsevage (SOC)	1,058	5.5
21	Royal H. Weller (D)	38,111	55.4
	Emanuel Hertz (R)	29,359	42.7
22	Anthony J. Griffin (D)	26,372	73.2
	R. Fred Talento (R)	8,037	22.3
23	Frank Oliver (D)	78,582	65.7
	Morris S. Schector (R)	29,247	24.5
	Samuel Orr (SOC)	10,689	8.9
24	James M. Fitzpatrick (D)	54,153	50.6
	Benjamin L. Fairchild (R)	47,439	44.3
	Patrick J. Murphy (SOC)	5,509	5.1
25	J. Mayhew Wainwright (R)	50,080	62.3
	David L. Frank (D)	28,853	35.9
26	Hamilton Fish Jr. (R)	43,173	63.1
	Walter G. Russell (D)	23,232	34.0
27	Harcourt J. Pratt (R)	44,557	61.3
	Ransom H. Gillett (D)	28,112	38.7
28	Parker Corning (D)	63,919	58.6
	George W. Greene (R)	43,342	39.7
29	James S. Parker (R, D)	81,798	97.9
30	Frank Crowther (R)	38,043	57.3
	E. Watson Gardiner (D)	26,510	39.9
31	Bertrand H. Snell (R)	40,474	70.1
	Abner D. Whitney (D)	17,237	29.9
32	Thaddeus C. Sweet (R)	46,232	67.9
	John M. Reynolds (D)	21,007	30.8
33	Frederick M. Davenport (R)	40,845	56.2
	Isaac C. Flint (D)	30,265	41.6
34	John D. Clarke (R)	52,363	71.6
	Bernard J. McGuire (D)	20,792	28.4
35	Walter W. Magee (R)	62,889	62.0
	Wilber M. Jones (D)	38,581	38.0
36	John Taber (R)	48,783	70.0
	J. Seldon Brandt (D)	20,886	30.0
37	Gale H. Stalker (R)	46,757	58.2
	Edwin S. Underhill (D)	32,618	40.6
38	Meyer Jacobstein (D)	42,803	48.9
	James E. Cuff (R)	41,191	47.1
39	Archie D. Sanders (R)	48,623	67.7
	David A. White (D)	20,449	28.5
40	S. Wallace Dempsey (R)	60,310	65.7
	William F. Sheehan (D)	27,751	30.3
41	Clarence MacGregor (R)	35,739	65.1
	Robert M. Smyth (D)	16,913	30.8
42	James M. Mead (D)	28,873	58.1
	John Buno McGrath (R)	19,362	38.9
43	Daniel A. Reed (R & SOC)	44,073	73.9
	John B. Leach (D)	15,555	26.1

NORTH CAROLINA

	Candidates	Votes	%
1	Lindsay C. Warren (D)	9,501	100.0
2	John H. Kerr (D)	7,484	100.0
3	Charles L. Abernethy (D)	14,520	72.5
	Roscoe Butler (R)	5,498	27.5
4	Edward W. Pou (D)	18,000	69.6
	Hobart Brantley (R)	7,881	30.5
5	Charles M. Stedman (D)	32,727	59.8
	O. C. Durland (R)	22,016	40.2
6	Homer L. Lyon (D)	12,888	62.3
	Leaman Baggett (R)	7,810	37.7
7	William C. Hammer (D)	31,332	55.9
	S. Carter Williams (R)	24,769	44.2
8	Robert L. Doughton (D)	30,520	58.6
	O. F. Pool (R)	21,543	41.4
9	Alfred L. Bulwinkle (D)	26,354	56.8
	Garrett D. Bailey (R)	20,045	43.2
10	Zebulon Weaver (D)	36,829	55.8
	R. Kenneth Smathers (R)	29,200	44.2

NORTH DAKOTA

	Candidates	Votes	%
1	Olger B. Burtness (R)	37,326	79.9
	R. E. Smith (D)	6,136	13.1
	Donald McDonald (F-LAB)	3,246	7.0
2	Thomas Hall (R)	33,607	66.3
	J. L. Page (D)	13,735	27.1
	C. W. Reichert (F-LAB)	3,350	6.6
3	James H. Sinclair (R)	42,923	87.8
	Reuben H. Leavitt (R)	5,960	12.2

OHIO

	Candidates	Votes	%
1	Nicholas Longworth (R)	45,317	62.9
	John C. Rogers (D)	26,511	36.8
2	Ambrose E. B. Stephens (R)	36,608*	58.2
	R. J. O'Donnell (D)	26,322	41.8
3	Roy Fitzgerald (R)	50,639	60.4
	T. A. McCann (D)	33,253	39.6
4	W. T. Fitzgerald (R)	32,236	50.7
	B. F. Welty (D)	31,293	49.3

OHIO

	Candidates	Votes	%
5	Charles J. Thompson (R)	23,638	50.7
	Frank Kniffin (D)	23,022	49.3
6	Charles Kearns (R)	27,688	52.9
	B. F. Kennedy (D)	24,630	47.1
7	Charles Brand (R)	45,699	67.2
	H. E. Rice (D)	22,314	32.8
8	Thomas Brooks Fletcher (D)	30,167	56.5
	James R. Hopley (R)	23,247	43.5
9	William W. Chalmers (R)	47,331	64.5
	C. W. Davis (D)	23,947	32.6
10	Thomas A. Jenkins (R)	25,571	63.9
	Guy Stevenson (D)	14,460	36.1
11	Mell Underwood (D)	29,950	62.1
	Walter S. Barrett (R)	18,300	37.9
12	John C. Speaks (R)	41,119	56.5
	H. S. Atkinson (D)	31,724	43.6
13	James T. Begg (R)	36,444	65.1
	G. C. Steineman (D)	19,571	34.9
14	Martin L. Davey (D)	53,659	65.4
	Arthur Sweeney (R)	28,446	34.7
15	C. Ellis Moore (R)	28,519	54.6
	E. B. Schneider (D)	23,703	45.4
16	John McSweeney (D)	40,283	59.8
	C. D. McClintock (R)	27,116	40.2
17	William M. Morgan (R)	36,249	55.0
	J. F. Bittinger (D)	29,674	45.0
18	Frank Murphy (R)	36,599	65.4
	John F. Nolan (D)	19,341	34.6
19	John G. Cooper (R)	45,788	72.3
	James Kennedy (D)	17,513	27.7
20	Charles Mooney (D)	22,050	100.0
21	Robert Crosser (D)	17,819	62.4
	Harry C. Gahn (R)	10,733	37.6
22	Theodore E. Burton (R)	55,589	100.0

OKLAHOMA

		Votes	%
1	Everette B. Howard (D)	33,475	50.6
	Samuel J. Montgomery (R)	32,692	49.4
2	William W. Hastings (D)	24,024	56.9
	H. L. Wineland (R)	18,220	43.1
3	Wiburn Cartwright (D)	28,883	67.1
	George W. Strawn (R)	13,964	32.5
4	Thomas D. McKeown (D)	29,208	59.4
	Charles E. Wells (R)	19,997	40.6
5	Fletcher B. Swank (D)	29,988	60.6
	Barritt Galloway (R)	19,491	39.4
6	Jed Johnson (D)	21,838	54.2
	Fred W. Lankard (R)	18,188	45.1
7	James V. McClintic (D)	17,962	70.4
	Walter S. Mills (R)	7,416	29.1
8	Milton C. Garber (R)	27,377	58.8
	C. H. Hyde (D)	18,957	40.7

OREGON

		Votes	%
1	Willis C. Hawley (R)	67,020	71.1
	Newton W. Borden (D)	27,273	28.9
2	Nicholas J. Sinnott (R)	29,357	70.4
	John S. Hodgin (D)	12,348	29.6
3	Maurice E. Crumpacker (R)	51,889	71.8
	Joseph K. Carson Jr. (D & PROG)	20,372	28.2

PENNSYLVANIA

		Votes	%
1	James M. Hazlett (R)	64,781	92.8
	William L. Rooney (D)	4,799	6.9
2	George S. Graham (R)	37,470	91.3
	John Joseph Shanahan (D)	3,223	7.9
3	Harry C. Ransley (R)	42,661	93.2
	Frank J. McDonnell (D)	2,827	6.2
4	Benjamin M. Golder (R)	34,904	82.9
	David Louis Ullman (D)	5,977	14.2
5	James J. Connolly (R, P)	46,997	85.9
	Daniel J. C. O'Donnell (D)	6,507	11.9

	Candidates	Votes	%
6	George A. Welsh (R)	51,844	79.4
	Thomas A. Logue (D)	10,344	15.8
7	George P. Darrow (R)	44,411	80.5
	Harry J. Conway (D)	9,440	17.1
8	Thomas S. Butler (R, SOC)	44,664	82.2
	Frank B. Rhodes (D)	8,802	16.2
9	Henry W. Watson (R)	38,350	71.3
	Richard J. Hamilton (D, LAB)	14,337	26.7
10	William W. Griest (R, LAB)	28,664	66.8
	W. W. Heidelbaugh (D, I)	14,272	33.2
11	Laurence H. Watres (R, P)	32,091	70.1
	Joseph J. Walsh (D)	13,662	29.9
12	John J. Casey (R, D)	49,467	76.5
	Edmund N. Carpenter (P)	15,166	23.5
13	Cyrus M. Palmer (R)	22,850	54.3
	Neal J. Ferry (D)	18,480	43.9
14	Robert Grey Bushong (R)	30,240	50.2
	Arthur G. Dewalt (D)	26,930	44.7
	Raymond S. Hofses (SOC, LAB)	3,050	5.1
15	Louis T. McFadden (R, P)	19,864	69.4
	C. M. Driggs (D)	8,763	30.6
16	Edgar R. Kiess (R, D)	26,047	99.9
17	Frederick W. Magrady (R, P)	19,717	52.7
	Herbert W. Cummings (D, SOC)	17,695	47.3
18	Edward M. Beers (R, P)	26,067	67.8
	Frederick A. Rupp (D)	12,349	32.1
19	Isaac H. Doutrich (R, LAB)	32,833	60.1
	Frank C. Sites (D)	21,563	39.5
20	J. Russell Leech (R)	16,254	54.8
	Warren Worth Bailey (D, LAB)	11,182	37.7
	Harry Crichton (P)	2,217	7.5
21	J. Banks Kurtz (R, P)	18,094	74.7
	Harry K. Filler (D)	4,799	19.8
	Charles Kutz (LAB)	1,215	5.0
22	Franklin Menges (R, P)	20,485	57.0
	Samuel F. Glatfelter (D)	15,268	42.5
23	J. Mitchell Chase (R, P)	22,337	69.8
	Clarence R. Kramer (D)	9,664	30.2
24	Samuel Austin Kendall (R, SOC)	20,097	75.7
	Clark W. Martin (D)	6,464	24.3
25	Henry W. Temple (R, P)	17,004	58.8
	James S. Pates (D, LAB)	11,890	41.2
26	J. Howard Swick (R, LAB)	22,062	62.0
	James P. Leaf (D, P)	13,516	38.0
27	Nathan L. Strong (R, LAB)	27,757	74.5
	D. A. Dorn (D)	9,038	24.3
28	Thomas C. Cochran (R, D)	30,520	99.7
29	Milton W. Shreve (R)	17,870	82.6
	William H. Kerschner (P)	3,758	17.4
30	Everett Kent (D, LAB)	24,392	50.9
	William R. Coyle (R)	22,981	47.9
31	Adam M. Wyant (R)	24,911	65.7
	Albert H. Bell (D, P)	12,175	32.1
32	Stephen G. Porter (R, LAB)	28,290	82.3
	Walter P. Berner (D)	4,680	13.6
33	M. Clyde Kelly (R, D)	31,886	96.1
34	John M. Morin (R, D)	28,783	98.8
35	Harry A. Estep (R)	23,881	77.5
	John Murphy (D)	4,242	13.8
	James M. Magee (LAB, P)	2,191	7.1
36	Guy C. Campbell (R, D)	25,474	84.2
	Ellsworth C. Trott (P)	3,264	10.8

RHODE ISLAND

		Votes	%
1	Clark Burdick (R)	32,459	63.0
	Arthur L. Conaty (D)	19,066	37.0
2	Richard S. Aldrich (R)	33,542	61.8
	Clarence E. Palmer (D)	20,738	38.2
3	Louis Monast (R)	29,366	50.4
	Jeremiah E. O'Connell (D)	28,909	49.6

SOUTH CAROLINA

	Candidates	Votes	%
1	Thomas S. McMillan (D)	2,244	100.0
2	Butler B. Hare (D)	1,766	100.0
3	Fred H. Dominick (D)	2,374	100.0
4	John J. McSwain (D)	2,057	100.0
5	William F. Stevenson (D)	2,416	100.0
6	Allard H. Gasque (D)	1,532	100.0
7	Hampton P. Fulmer (D)	1,933	100.0

SOUTH DAKOTA

		Votes	%
1	Charles A. Christopherson (R)	37,185	56.3
	J. E. House (D)	26,103	39.5
2	Royal C. Johnson (R)	38,928	64.3
	Fred H. Hildebrandt (D)	21,585	35.7
3	William Williamson (R)	22,932	52.3
	Arthur W. Watwood (D)	20,902	47.7

TENNESSEE

		Votes	%
1	B. Carroll Reece (R)	10,553	88.0
	W. L. Giles (D)	1,439	12.0
2	J. Will Taylor (R)	11,789	99.8
3	Sam D. McReynolds (D)	13,012	75.6
	L. D. Copeland (R)	4,194	24.4
4	Cordell Hull (D)	10,726	71.4
	Mrs. Wilson Thompson (R)	4,292	28.6
5	Ewin L. Davis (D)	5,481	100.0
6	Joseph W. Byrns (D)	10,271	100.0
7	Edward E. Eslick (D)	8,049	100.0
8	Gordon Browning (D)	9,456	100.0
9	Finis J. Garrett (D)	9,180	100.0
10	Hubert F. Fisher (D)	4,217	100.0

TEXAS

		Votes	%
1	Eugene Black (D)	9,828	94.4
	D. F. Wimmer (R)	579	5.6
2	John C. Box (D)	11,955	95.6
3	Morgan G. Sanders (D)	11,336	91.2
	Enoch G. Fletcher (R)	1,098	8.8
4	Sam Rayburn (D)	13,499	89.9
	Henry C. Barlow (R)	1,524	10.1
5	Hatton W. Sumners (D)	29,687	96.5
6	Luther A. Johnson (D)	10,162	96.1
7	Clay Stone Briggs (D)	7,678	94.1
	S. R. Halstead (R)	478	5.9
8	Daniel E. Garrett (D)	8,459	91.0
	J. M. Gibson (R)	842	9.1
9	Joseph J. Mansfield (D)	10,577	82.6
	E. F. Glaze (R)	2,228	17.4
10	James P. Buchanan (D)	12,051	93.2
	W. H. Matthaei (R)	886	6.9
11	Tom T. Connally (D)	8,481	94.2
	W. H. Black (R)	526	5.8
12	Fritz G. Lanham (D)	10,466	94.4
	David Sutton (R)	620	5.6
13	Guinn Williams (D)	12,406	94.0
	Mel E. Peters (R)	797	6.0
14	Harry M. Wurzbach (R)	14,224	57.2
	A. D. Rogers (D)	10,633	42.8
15	John N. Garner (D)	13,551	82.8
	Hardie H. Jeffries (R)	2,825	17.3
16	Claude B. Hudspeth (D)	15,732	86.1
	A. W. Norcop (R)	2,542	13.9
17	Thomas L. Blanton (D)	15,935	93.7
	H. B. Tanner (R)	1,065	6.3
18	Marvin Jones (D)	18,027	93.6
	S. E. Fish (R)	1,237	6.4

UTAH

		Votes	%
1	Don B. Colton (R)	44,007	61.4
	Ephraim Bergeson (D)	27,198	38.0
2	Elmer O. Leatherwood (R)	42,073	60.2
	William R. Wallace Jr. (D)	27,006	38.6

VERMONT

	Candidates	Votes	%
1	Elbert S. Brigham (R)	27,419	72.3
	Allan T. Calhoun (D)	10,529	27.7
2	Ernest Willard Gibson (R)	27,711	80.4
	George F. Root (D)	6,753	19.6

VIRGINIA

		Votes	%
1	Schuyler Otis Bland (D)	3,847	99.9
2	Joseph T. Deal (D)	7,741	65.4
	L. S. Parsons (R)	4,093	34.6
3	Andrew Jackson Montague (D)	3,738	99.8
4	Patrick Henry Drewry (D)	2,694	99.3
5	Joseph Whitehead (D)	6,491	100.0
6	Clifton A. Woodrum (D)	2,936	99.8
7	Thomas W. Harrison (D)	8,302	64.9
	Walter R. Talbot (R)	3,758	29.4
	Dabney C. Harrison (I)	727	5.7
8	R. Walton Moore (D)	5,655	95.4
9	George C. Peery (D)	28,304	53.4
	S. R. Hurley (R)	24,685	46.6
10	Henry St. George Tucker (D)	4,657	99.8

WASHINGTON

	Candidates	Votes	%
1	John F. Miller (R)	35,944	51.1
	Stephen F. Chadwick (D)	34,401	48.9
2	Lindley H. Hadley (R)	35,510	68.5
	Frances C. Axtell (D)	15,876	30.6
3	Albert Johnson (R)	58,361	100.0
4	John W. Summers (R)	34,199	99.8
5	Sam B. Hill (D)	29,157	52.1
	Jack T. Fancher (R)	26,783	47.9

WEST VIRGINIA

		Votes	%
1	Carl G. Bachmann (R)	31,839	52.2
	George W. Oldham (D)	29,117	47.8
2	Frank L. Bowman (R)	32,803	54.0
	Robert E. Lee Allen (D)	27,744	45.7
3	William S. O'Brien (D)	31,954	51.7
	John M. Wolverton (R)	29,819	48.3
4	James A. Hughes (R)	36,394	52.4
	John D. Sweeney (D)	33,065	47.6
5	James F. Strother (R)	44,263	53.3
	Emmet F. Scaggs (D)	38,723	46.7
6	Edward T. England (R)	45,898	50.1
	J. Alfred Taylor (D)	45,681	49.9

WISCONSIN

	Candidates	Votes	%
1	Henry Allen Cooper (R)	50,531	100.0
2	Charles A. Kading (R)	29,785	69.5
	Ernest C. Wrucke (D)	8,285	19.3
	John H. Kaiser (I-PROG-R)	4,817	11.2
3	John Mandt Nelson (R)	41,666	99.9
4	John C. Schafer (R)	20,324	48.0
	Edmund T. Melms (SOC)	14,911	35.2
	William J. Kershaw (D)	7,099	16.8
5	Victor L. Berger (SOC)	26,377	48.8
	William H. Stafford (R)	24,297	44.9
	Rose Horwitz (D)	3,394	6.3
6	Florian Lampert (R)	34,445	75.9
	B. F. Sheridan (D)	10,895	24.0
7	Joseph D. Beck (R)	32,479	86.1
	A. H. Schubert (ID)	3,628	9.6
8	Edward E. Browne (R)	35,472	91.8
	R. J. Walsh (ID)	3,130	8.1
9	George J. Schneider (R)	41,498	99.9
10	James A. Frear (R)	40,888	97.4
11	Hubert H. Peavey (R)	31,105	70.1
	Theodore M. Thomas (I-PROG-R)	11,860	26.7

WYOMING

		Votes	%
AL	Charles E. Winter (R)	39,392	60.8
	Thomas M. Fagan (D)	25,082	38.7

1927 House Elections

LOUISIANA

Special Election

7	Rene L. DeRouen (D)	3,699	98.5

NEW YORK

Special Election

35	Clarence E. Hancock (R)	68,502	69.0
	Henry B. Brewster (D)	29,302	29.5

Explanation of Symbols in House Returns

In the returns for House elections *symbols* are used to denote special circumstances. In cases where no symbol is used, the candidate who received the most votes won the election to the House. The following is a key to the symbols used:

✔ Elected to the House. The symbol is used to identify winning candidates in three types of situations: (1) When candidates ran for two or more at-large seats in states which chose all of their at-large representatives in a single election, or ran in a multi-member district; (2) when the vote total and percentage of one or more of the candidates are unavailable and (3) when a candidate who did not receive the highest vote total was seated by the House. (*Explanation of multi-member districts, see p. 678.*)

‡ The symbol is used when an election dispute resulted in the unseating of a representative *after* he was sworn in. (*For discussion of specific cases, consult the* Biographical Directory of the American Congress 1774-1971, *U.S. Government Printing Office, Washington, D.C. 1971; hereafter referred to as the* Biographical Directory.)

* The symbol is used for three types of situations: (1) When a representative-elect died or declined his seat before the constitutionally set date for the beginning of his term—March 4 until 1935, and Jan. 3 thereafter; (2) when the House refused to seat any candidate claiming election to a seat and (3) when state law required a candidate to obtain a popular vote majority for election to the House, but the candidate receiving the most votes failed to receive a majority. (*For discussion of specific cases, consult the* Biographical Directory; *explanation of majority vote requirement, see p. 703.*)

Information for 1824-1973 returns was obtained from a source other than the Inter-University Consortium for Political and Social Research. (*For a listing of other sources, see p. 1062.*)

Footnotes. Numbered footnotes are used to explain unusual situations, such as a series of elections in the same year in the same House district, anomalies resulting from reapportionment and special procedures for conducting House elections in certain states.

1928 House Elections

ALABAMA

	Candidates	Votes	%
1	John McDuffie (D)	16,712	100.0
2	Lister Hill (D)	20,945	100.0
3	Henry B. Steagall (D)	14,611	100.0
4	Lamar Jeffers (D)	13,271	63.1
	A. B. Baxley (R)	7,768	36.9
5	Lafayette L. Patterson (D)	13,067	100.0
6	William B. Oliver (D)	9,539	100.0
7	Miles C. Allgood (D)	18,186	51.7
	Wallace M. Sloan (R)	16,983	48.3
8	Edward B. Almon (D)	20,006	100.0
9	George Huddleston (D)	23,553	100.0
10	William B. Bankhead (D)	15,133	58.2
	John A. Posey (R)	10,862	41.8

Special Election

5	Lafayette L. Patterson (D)	7,683	99.9

ARIZONA

AL	Lewis W. Douglas (D)	50,231	61.6
	Guy Axline (R)	31,382	38.5

ARKANSAS

1	William J. Driver (D)	24,844	83.9
	S. E. Simonson (R)	4,770	16.1
2	William A. Oldfield (D)	18,772*	77.4
	J. L. McKamey (R)	5,471	22.6
3	Claude A. Fuller (D)	18,160	57.7
	Sam B. Cecil (R)	13,129	41.7
4	Otis Wingo (D)	21,494	71.9
	G. W. Johnston (R)	8,397	28.1
5	Heartsill Ragon (D)	25,583	78.2
	Alonzo A. Ross (R)	7,144	21.8
6	David D. Glover (D)	28,101	100.0
7	Tilman B. Parks (D)	20,954	81.5
	Pat McNally (R)	4,759	18.5

CALIFORNIA

1	Clarence F. Lea (D-R)	56,381	100.0
2	Harry L. Englebright (R-D)	32,455	100.0
3	Charles F. Curry (R-D)	77,750	100.0
4	Florence P. Kahn (R)	50,206	74.9
	Harry W. Hutton (I)	16,838	25.1
5	Richard J. Welch (R-D)	51,708	100.0
6	Albert E. Carter (R-D)	113,579	99.9
7	Henry E. Barbour (R-D)	71,195	99.9
8	Arthur Monroe Free (R)	80,613	68.0
	Cecelia C. Casserly (D)	37,947	32.0
9	William E. Evans (R)	222,261	77.0
	James B. Ogg (D)	58,263	20.2
10	Joe Crail (R-D)	301,028	93.5
	Harry Sherr (SOC)	19,659	6.1
11	Philip D. Swing (R-D)	127,115	100.0

COLORADO

1	William R. Eaton (R)	63,258	58.1
	S. Harrison White (D)	44,713	41.1
2	Charles B. Timberlake (R)	62,375	66.5
	Earl E. House (D)	31,480	33.5
3	Guy U. Hardy (R)	64,116	64.9
	Harry A. McIntyre (D)	34,670	35.1
4	Edward T. Taylor (D)	30,142	58.8
	William P. Dale (R)	21,089	41.2

CONNECTICUT

	Candidates	Votes	%
1	E. Hart Fenn (R)	75,743	53.1
	Herman P. Kopplemann (D)	65,922	46.2
2	Richard P. Freeman (R)	48,590	56.0
	William M. Citron (D)	37,786	43.5
3	John Q. Tilson (R)	58,337	52.3
	Nicholas Moseley (D)	52,358	46.9
4	Schuyler Merritt (R)	71,649	56.1
	Anthony Sunderland (D)	55,106	43.2
5	James P. Glynn (R)	43,332	52.4
	Edward Mascolo (D)	39,354	47.6

DELAWARE

AL	Robert G. Houston (R)	66,361	63.6
	John M. Richardson (D)	38,045	36.4

FLORIDA

1	Herbert J. Drane (D)	42,003	58.4
	Abner B. Brown (R)	29,871	41.6
2	Robert A. Green (D)	17,228	83.9
	Thomas Peter Chaires (R)	3,310	16.1
3	Tom A. Yon (D)	22,167	100.0
4	Ruth Bryan Owen (D)	67,130	64.9
	William C. Lawson (R)	36,288	35.1

GEORGIA

1	Charles G. Edwards (D)	16,438	100.0
2	E. E. Cox (D)	15,235	100.0
3	Charles R. Crisp (D)	11,183	100.0
4	William C. Wright (D)	16,037	100.0
5	Leslie J. Steele (D)	19,328	100.0
6	Samuel Rutherford (D)	15,310	100.0
7	Malcolm C. Tarver (D)	23,251	100.0
8	Charles H. Brand (D)	15,940	100.0
9	Thomas M. Bell (D)	22,916	100.0
10	Carl Vinson (D)	12,644	100.0
11	William C. Lankford (D)	18,044	100.0
12	William W. Larsen (D)	13,862	100.0

IDAHO

1	Burton L. French (R)	43,770	68.9
	Joe Tyler (D)	19,064	30.0
2	Addison T. Smith (R)	53,236	64.1
	Ralph W. Harding (D)	29,422	35.4

ILLINOIS

1	Oscar De Priest (R)	24,479	47.8
	Harry Baker (D)	20,664	40.3
	William Harrison	5,861	11.4
2	Morton D. Hull (R)	126,005	62.1
	Michael C. Walsh (D)	76,909	37.9
3	Elliott W. Sproul (R)	101,384	51.4
	Henry P. Bergen (D)	95,999	48.6
4	Thomas A. Doyle (D)	40,940	64.3
	Frank George Zelezinski (R)	22,741	35.7
5	Adolph J. Sabath (D)	25,225	69.8
	Edward J. Gates (R)	10,799	29.9
6	James T. Igoe (D)	143,989	60.3
	Samuel L. Golan (R)	94,941	39.7
7	M. Alfred Michaelson (R)	164,447	57.8
	Emil Selten (D)	119,933	42.2
8	Stanley Henry Kunz (D)	24,517	70.8
	Edward Walz (R)	10,110	29.2
9	Fred A. Britten (R)	43,394	62.0
	James T. McDermott (D)	26,450	37.8

	Candidates	Votes	%
10	Carl R. Chindblom (R)	138,386	62.6
	Joseph A. Weber (D)	82,598	37.4
11	Frank R. Reid (R)	97,938	68.9
	Edwin L. Wilson (D)	44,306	31.2
12	John T. Buckbee (R)	82,938	73.8
	Jules Vallatt (D)	29,385	26.2
13	William R. Johnson (R)	53,985	73.7
	William G. Curtis (D)	19,209	26.2
14	John C. Allen (R)	53,680	64.3
	William H. Hartzell (D)	29,768	35.7
15	Edward J. King (R)	57,284*	64.2
	James H. Andrews (D)	31,944	35.8
16	William E. Hull (R)	59,190	61.1
	George H. Rinkenberger (D)	37,662	38.9
17	Homer W. Hall (R)	47,266	65.0
	Frank Gillespie (D)	25,480	35.0
18	William P. Holaday (R)	57,373	62.0
	James H. Elliott (D)	35,213	38.0
19	Charles Adkins (R)	73,243	66.2
	W. W. Reeves (D)	37,358	33.8
20	Henry T. Rainey (D)	38,409	56.0
	E. T. Hunter (R)	30,100	43.9
21	Frank M. Ramey (R)	52,320	50.1
	J. Earl Major (D)	52,183	49.9
22	Edward M. Irwin (R)	72,448	56.0
	Eugene W. Kreitner (D)	56,825	44.0
23	William W. Arnold (D)	49,378	53.9
	C. T. Wade (R)	42,263	46.1
24	Thomas S. Williams (R)	36,239	58.4
	Val B. Campbell (D)	25,773	41.6
25	Edward E. Denison (R)	51,025	54.4
	A. F. Gourley (D)	42,799	45.6
AL	Ruth Hanna McCormick (R)	1,711,651✔	
	Richard Yates (R)	1,673,962✔	
	Charles F. Brown (D)	1,171,520	
	C. D. Joplin (D)	1,111,253	
	Florence Kirkpatrick (SOC)	11,958	
	John E. Mahoney (SOC)	11,538	
	Elizabeth G. Doty (WCP AM)	2,887	
	Frank Gushes (WCP AM)	2,802	
	James S. O'Rourke (SOC LAB)	1,384	
	Thomas Buckley (SOC LAB)	1,340	

INDIANA

1	Harry E. Rowbottom (R)	49,013	50.8
	John W. Boehne Jr. (D)	47,404	49.2
2	Arthur H. Greenwood (D)	45,901	50.2
	Orville T. Stout (R)	44,941	49.1
3	James W. Dunbar (R)	47,768	51.1
	Frank Gardner (D)	45,718	48.9
4	Harry C. Canfield (D)	44,671	52.5
	Charles S. Hisey (R)	40,345	47.5
5	Noble J. Johnson (R)	51,138	56.1
	Henry W. Moore (D)	39,538	43.3
6	Richard N. Elliott (R)	50,795	57.0
	William H. Larrabee (D)	38,326	43.0
7	Louis Ludlow (D)	94,643	51.5
	Ralph E. Updike (R)	88,263	48.0
8	Albert H. Vestal (R)	59,704	58.3
	Don C. Ward (D)	42,645	41.7
9	Fred S. Purnell (R)	53,998	57.2
	George L. Mackintosh (D)	40,357	42.8
10	William R. Wood (R)	87,972	62.0
	John W. Sobraske (D)	53,874	38.0
11	Albert R. Hall (R)	49,326	54.1
	M. Clifford Townsend (D)	41,836	45.9
12	David Hogg (R)	56,436	55.3
	Samuel D. Jackson (D)	45,592	44.7
13	Andrew J. Hickey (R)	90,618	59.8
	Chester A. Perkins (D)	60,993	40.2

IOWA

Candidates	Votes	%
1 William F. Kopp (R)	45,806	100.0
2 F. Dickinson Letts (R)	49,691	57.0
Frank C. Titzell (D)	37,442	43.0
3 Thomas J. B. Robinson (R)	60,025	60.9
Leo F. Tierney (D)	38,469	39.1
4 Gilbert N. Haugen (R)	50,938	61.4
Erwin Larson (D)	31,968	38.6
5 Cyrenus Cole (R)	54,603	66.3
Maurice Cahill (D)	27,793	33.7
6 C. William Ramseyer (R)	43,259	65.2
C. Ver Ploeg (D)	23,065	34.8
7 Cassius C. Dowell (R)	72,404	100.0
8 Lloyd Thurston (R)	43,050	60.0
James Pearson (D)	28,686	40.0
9 Charles E. Swanson (R)	47,632	63.2
W. J. Burke (D)	27,760	36.8
10 Lester J. Dickinson (R)	59,374	100.0
11 Ed H. Campbell (R)	49,279	70.9
George Finch (D)	20,244	29.1

KANSAS

1 William P. Lambertson (R)	48,543	68.3
Maurice P. O'Keefe (D)	22,492	31.7
2 Ulysses S. Guyer (R)	66,044	70.2
Lee R. Hettick (D)	28,106	29.9
3 William H. Sproul (R)	45,121	53.4
Joe E. Gaitskill (D)	39,323	46.6
4 Homer Hoch (R)	38,664	74.2
C. T. Neihart (D)	13,450	25.8
5 James G. Strong (R)	45,053	69.9
John F. Corder (D)	19,425	30.1
6 Charles I. Sparks (R)	41,272	63.4
William H. Clark (D)	23,836	36.6
7 Clifford R. Hope (R)	58,001	69.5
W. C. Dickey (D)	25,433	30.5
8 William A. Ayres (D)	46,117	58.4
Richard E. Bird (R)	32,802	41.6

KENTUCKY

1 William V. Gregory (D)	36,325	56.8
Miller Hughes (R)	27,581	43.2
2 David H. Kincheloe (D)	38,093	52.7
Clark M. Donald (R)	34,194	47.3
3 Charles W. Roark (R)	37,216	52.8
John W. Moore (D)	33,210	47.2
4 John D. Craddock (R)	39,244	53.1
Henry D. Moorman (D)	34,639	46.9
5 Maurice H. Thatcher (R)	96,926	60.2
Arthur Yager (D)	64,201	39.8
6 J. Lincoln Newhall (R)	48,009	53.1
Brent Spence (D)	42,309	46.8
7 Robert E. Lee Blackburn (R)	43,604	53.5
Virgil Chapman (D)	37,936	46.5
8 Lewis L. Walker (R)	33,931	52.7
Ralph Gilbert (D)	30,424	47.3
9 Elva R. Kendall (R)	51,019	52.9
Fred M. Vinson (D)	45,426	47.1
10 Katherine Langley (R)	39,541	56.1
A. J. May (D)	30,919	43.9
11 John M. Robsion (R)	74,929	79.8
H. F. Reed (D)	18,939	20.2

LOUISIANA

1 James O'Connor (D)	28,066	100.0
2 J. Zach Spearing (D)	33,176	69.4
Peter I. J. Fletchinger (R)	14,661	30.7
3 Whitmell P. Martin (D)	15,219	100.0
4 John N. Sandlin (D)	14,949	100.0
5 Riley J. Wilson (D)	11,827	100.0
6 Bolivar E. Kemp (D)	18,379	100.0
7 Rene L. DeRouen (D)	16,582	100.0
8 James B. Aswell (D)	14,618	100.0

MAINE

Candidates	Votes	%
1 Carroll L. Beedy (R)	40,255	67.7
Elvington P. Spinney (D)	19,219	32.3
2 Wallace H. White Jr. (R)	36,791	65.5
Albert Beliveau (D)	19,420	34.6
3 John E. Nelson (R)	36,686	74.6
S. Curtis C. Ward (D)	12,498	25.4
4 Donald F. Snow (R)	32,223	75.0
Clinton C. Stevens (D)	10,753	25.0

MARYLAND

1 T. Alan Goldsborough (D)	28,795	50.7
A. Stengle Marine (R)	28,059	49.4
2 Linwood L. Clark (R)	69,267	53.3
William P. Cole Jr. (D)	59,912	46.1
3 Vincent L. Palmisano (D)	27,377	49.8
John Philip Hill (R)	27,047	49.2
4 J. Charles Linthicum (D)	41,432	54.5
John P. Brandau (R)	34,112	44.8
5 Stephen W. Gambrill (D)	31,403	51.9
Oliver Metzerott (R)	28,574	47.2
6 Frederick N. Zihlman (R)	47,789	56.2
David J. Lewis (D)	37,197	43.8

MASSACHUSETTS

1 Allen T. Treadway (R)	51,791	55.7
Daniel A. Martin (D)	41,216	44.3
2 William Kirk Kaynor (R)	52,344	54.4
John D. O'Connor (D)	43,856	45.6
3 Frank H. Foss (R)	46,204	57.1
Joseph E. Casey (D)	34,776	42.9
4 George R. Stobbs (R)	51,145	54.8
Freeman M. Saltus (D)	42,115	45.2
5 Edith Nourse Rogers (R)	56,004	61.1
Cornelius F. Cronin (D)	35,713	38.9
6 A. Piatt Andrew (R)	58,293	68.2
George J. Ferguson (D)	27,130	31.8
7 William P. Connery Jr. (R-D)	61,697	100.0
8 Frederick W. Dallinger (R)	71,850	57.2
James P. Brennan (D)	53,721	42.8
9 Charles L. Underhill (R)	48,947	50.3
Arthur D. Healey (D)	48,290	49.7
10 John J. Douglass (D)	42,594	85.0
Edward L. Donnelly (R)	7,498	15.0
11 George Holden Tinkham (R)	52,576	58.4
Maurice J. Tobin (D)	37,514	41.6
12 John W. McCormack (D)	64,351	76.4
Herbert W. Burr (R)	19,937	23.7
13 Robert Luce (R)	74,097	58.2
Thomas D. Lavelle (D)	53,266	41.8
14 Richard B. Wigglesworth (R)	73,598	61.3
Christopher M. Clifford (D)	46,498	38.7
15 Joseph W. Martin Jr. (R)	39,905	56.8
John F. Trainor (D)	30,373	43.2
16 Charles L. Gifford (R)	49,202	63.1
Willard E. Boyden (D)	23,590	30.3
Frank J. Manning (SOC)	5,115	6.6

MICHIGAN

1 Robert H. Clancy (R)	64,606	61.5
William M. Donnelly (D)	39,870	38.0
2 Earl C. Michener (R)	86,804	73.6
Grover L. Morden (D)	31,223	26.5
3 Joseph Hooper (R)	71,650	79.5
William Fitzgerald (D)	18,535	20.6
4 John C. Ketcham (R)	60,334	75.4
Roman I. Jarvis Sr. (D)	19,708	24.6
5 Carl E. Mapes (R)	73,241	78.8
Frank C. Jarvis (D)	19,627	21.1
6 Grant M. Hudson (R)	238,223	72.5
A. Bruce Atwell (D)	89,085	27.1

[MICHIGAN continued]

Candidates	Votes	%
7 Louis C. Cramton (R)	61,439	73.9
Varnum J. Bowers (D)	21,659	26.1
8 Bird J. Vincent (R)	65,600	75.4
Burnett J. Abbott (D)	21,387	24.6
9 James C. McLaughlin (R)	51,246	99.8
10 Roy O. Woodruff (R)	43,800	73.7
Judson E. Richardson (D)	15,598	26.3
11 Frank P. Bohn (R)	44,546	67.2
Carl R. Henry (D)	21,760	32.8
12 W. Frank James (R)	47,069	69.1
L. A. Barry (D)	21,039	30.9
13 Clarence J. McLeod (R)	70,513	64.9
John S. Hall (D)	37,574	34.6

MINNESOTA

1 Victor Christgau (R)	59,628	64.8
James F. Lynn (D)	32,398	35.2
2 Frank Clague (R)	60,259	69.4
J. A. Cashel (D)	26,606	30.6
3 August H. Andresen (R)	52,526	58.8
Charles C. Kolars (D)	19,844	22.2
Henry Arens (F-LAB)	15,749	17.6
4 Melvin Joseph Maas (R)	39,648	36.0
John P. J. Dolan (D)	31,521	28.6
Howard Y. Williams (F-LAB)	23,068	21.0
Fred A. Snyder (I)	15,365	14.0
5 Walter H. Newton (R)	80,856	58.6
James Robertson (D)	31,528	22.9
Ferdinand Johnson (F-LAB)	24,869	18.0
6 Harold Knutson (R)	55,663	66.3
John Knutsen (F-LAB)	28,276	33.7
7 Ole J. Kvale (F-LAB)	56,029	66.9
Lawrence M. Carlson (R)	27,735	33.1
8 William A. Pittenger (R)	43,777	44.2
William L. Carss (F-LAB)	42,508	42.9
Dana C. Reed (D)	9,784	9.9
9 Conrad G. Selvig (R)	45,319	55.2
Knud Wefald (F-LAB)	36,853	44.9
10 Godfrey G. Goodwin (R)	60,100	56.4
C. R. Hedlund (F-LAB)	23,774	22.3
Ernest W. Erickson (D)	22,702	21.3

MISSISSIPPI

1 John E. Rankin (D)	13,816	100.0
2 Wall Doxey (D)	12,276	100.0
3 William M. Whittington (D)	13,039	100.0
4 T. Jeff Busby (D)	13,456	100.0
5 Ross A. Collins (D)	17,967	100.0
6 Robert S. Hall (D)	18,212	100.0
7 Percy E. Quin (D)	12,338	100.0
8 James W. Collier (D)	11,442	100.0

MISSOURI

1 Milton A. Romjue (D)	35,702	52.9
J. Frank Culler (R)	31,751	47.1
2 Ralph Lozier (D)	37,829	53.2
Lloyd V. Harmon (R)	33,273	46.8
3 Jacob L. Milligan (D)	32,665	50.0
H. F. Lawrence (R)	32,626	50.0
4 Charles L. Faust (R)	43,733*	57.1
Richard M. Duncan (D)	32,892	42.9
5 Edgar C. Ellis (R)	113,043	50.5
Floyd E. Jacobs (D)	110,529	49.4
6 Thomas J. Halsey (R)	30,557	53.2
C. C. Dickinson (D)	26,838	46.8
7 John W. Palmer (R)	52,317	53.3
Samuel C. Major (D)	45,832	46.7
8 William L. Nelson (D)	32,877	55.3
David W. Peters (R)	26,619	44.7
9 Clarence Cannon (D)	41,036	54.5
A. H. Steinbeck (R)	34,248	45.5
10 Henry F. Niedringhaus (R)	164,083	55.0
John R. Green (D)	134,324	45.0

MISSOURI

	Candidates	Votes	%
11	John J. Cochran (D)	44,130	57.4
	William Gray (R)	32,706	42.6
12	Leonidas C. Dyer (R)	24,701	58.4
	Joseph L. McLemore (D)	17,609	41.6
13	Charles E. Kiefner (R)	30,535	50.6
	Clyde Williams (D)	29,842	49.4
14	Dewey Short (R)	57,880	53.9
	James F. Fulbright (D)	49,495	46.1
15	Joe J. Manlove (R)	52,142	64.6
	George B. Lang (D)	28,551	35.4
16	Rowland L. Johnston (R)	29,848	53.5
	S. A. Cunningham (D)	25,899	46.5

MONTANA

1	John M. Evans (D)	44,618	57.3
	Mark D. Fitzgerrald (R)	32,796	42.1
2	Scott Leavitt (R)	70,682	67.9
	B. A. Taylor (D)	33,033	31.7

NEBRASKA

1	John H. Morehead (D)	39,202	50.4
	Elmer J. Burkett (R)	38,583	49.6
2	Willis G. Sears (R)	52,801	56.0
	Harry B. Fleharty (D)	41,424	44.0
3	Edgar Howard (D)	50,974	54.9
	James Nichols (R)	41,967	45.2
4	Charles H. Sloan (R)	37,114	50.2
	J. N. Norton (D)	36,896	49.9
5	Fred G. Johnson (R)	37,853	51.0
	Ashton C. Shallenberger (D)	36,383	49.0
6	Robert G. Simmons (R)	81,581	74.3
	John McCoy (D)	28,215	25.7

NEVADA

AL	Samuel S. Arentz (R)	18,815	58.6
	Charles Lee Horsey (D)	13,287	41.4

NEW HAMPSHIRE

1	Fletcher Hale (R)	53,642	57.5
	Francis C. Keefe (D)	39,568	42.4
2	Edward H. Wason (R)	54,642	60.0
	Alfred W. Levensaler (D)	36,275	39.9

NEW JERSEY

1	Charles A. Wolverton (R)	109,510	74.9
	Alfred R. White (D)	36,778	25.1
2	Isaac Bacharach (R)	99,109	76.3
	George R. Greis (D)	30,856	23.7
3	Harold G. Hoffman (R)	95,669	63.0
	John R. Phillips Jr. (D)	56,290	37.0
4	Charles A. Eaton (R)	65,149	63.6
	Orren Jack Turner (D)	37,341	36.4
5	Ernest R. Ackerman (R)	95,458	67.4
	Roswell S. Nichols (D)	46,211	32.6
6	Randolph Perkins (R)	98,859	61.7
	Frank L. Sample (D)	60,988	38.1
7	George N. Seger (R)	54,896	57.0
	Abram Klenert (D)	41,012	42.6
8	Fred A. Hartley Jr. (R)	64,915#	50.1
	Paul J. Moore (D)	64,594#	49.9
9	Franklin W. Fort (R)	46,685	56.5
	Francis X. Purcell (D)	35,730	43.3
10	Frederick R. Lehlbach (R)	74,154	62.1
	Eugene J. O'Mara (D)	45,287	37.9
11	Oscar L. Auf der Heide (D)	51,982	62.1
	George M. Eichler (R)	31,728	37.9
12	Mary T. Norton (D)	56,748	62.0
	Philip W. Grece (R)	34,817	38.0

NEW MEXICO

	Candidates	Votes	%
AL	Albert Gallatin Simms (R)	61,208	52.2
	John Morrow (D)	56,045	47.8

NEW YORK

1	Robert L. Bacon (R)	143,230	62.0
	Thomas J. Cuff (D)	83,535	36.2
2	William F. Brunner (D)	137,214	62.4
	Jacob A. Visel (R)	78,536	35.7
3	George W. Lindsay (D)	26,626	72.2
	Francis J. Nicosia (R)	9,139	24.8
4	Thomas H. Cullen (D)	34,496	75.0
	Charles O. Winnie (R)	10,696	23.2
5	Loring M. Black Jr. (D)	50,158	56.7
	Robert C. Lee (R)	35,935	40.6
6	Andrew L. Somers (D)	70,953	53.9
	John L. Lotsch (R)	53,700	40.8
	Bernard J. Riley (SOC)	7,026	5.3
7	John F. Quayle (D)	30,897	67.2
	Peter S. Gehris (R)	13,211	28.7
8	Patrick J. Carley (D)	108,028	58.5
	William A. Blank (R)	66,180	35.8
	William M. Feigenbaum (SOC)	10,551	5.7
9	David J. O'Connell (D)	60,097	51.1
	Ernest C. Wagner (R)	53,552	45.5
10	Emanuel Celler (D)	31,152	58.0
	William G. Bushell (R)	18,411	34.3
	Abraham I. Shiplacoff (SOC)	3,645	6.8
11	Anning S. Prall (D)	44,820	66.4
	James A. Simonson (R)	22,099	32.7
12	Samuel Dickstein (D)	15,093	78.7
	Samuel K. Beier (R)	3,321	17.3
13	Christopher D. Sullivan (D)	16,062	77.3
	Jacob Rosenberg (R)	4,076	19.6
14	William I. Sirovich (D)	16,602	54.4
	Sol Ullman (R)	11,974	39.2
	August Claessens (SOC)	1,648	5.4
15	John J. Boylan (D)	30,849	77.6
	Gabriel L. Kaplan (R)	8,294	20.9
16	John J. O'Connor (D)	29,351	68.7
	Michael G. Panzer (R)	12,600	29.5
17	Ruth Baker Pratt (R)	36,655	51.8
	Philip Berolzheimer (D)	32,466	45.9
18	John F. Carew (D)	30,030	74.0
	Bernard Katzen (R)	9,562	23.6
19	Sol Bloom (D)	48,054	59.4
	David Steinhardt (R)	30,617	37.8
20	Fiorello H. LaGuardia (R)	11,956	50.1
	Saul J. Dickheiser (D)	10,856	45.5
21	Royal H. Weller (D)	56,992*	53.3
	Edward A. Johnson (R)	45,610	42.7
22	Anthony J. Griffin (D)	35,711	71.5
	Thomas J. Burke (R)	12,868	25.7
23	Frank Oliver (D)	128,372	66.6
	Henry H. Spitz (R)	52,588	27.3
24	James M. Fitzpatrick (D)	96,556	54.2
	Benjamin L. Fairchild (R)	72,408	40.6
	Louis Painken (SOC)	9,347	5.2
25	J. Mayhew Wainwright (R)	79,228	59.9
	Herbert McKennis (D)	50,589	38.3
26	Hamilton Fish Jr. (R)	69,445	63.6
	George C. Rogers (D)	36,591	33.5
27	Harcourt J. Pratt (R)	59,183	62.8
	Robert R. Livingston (D)	34,993	37.2
28	Parker Corning (D)	77,365	58.2
	Franklin D. Sargent (R)	53,383	40.1
29	James S. Parker (R)	71,326	62.8
	Theodore A. Knapp (D)	40,541	35.7
30	Frank Crowther (R)	58,022	59.8
	E. Watson Gardiner (D)	36,956	38.1
31	Bertrand H. Snell (R)	52,702	63.3
	John C. Howard (D)	30,602	36.7
32	Francis D. Culkin (D)	65,009	67.5
	Frank Bowman (D)	30,201	31.3
33	Frederick M. Davenport (R)	62,746	56.5

	Candidates	Votes	%
34	John D. Clarke (R)	80,531	71.0
	William W. Lampman (D)	32,925	29.0
35	Clarence E. Hancock (R)	90,370	61.8
	Augustus C. Stevens (D)	52,926	36.2
36	John Taber (R)	68,095	69.1
	Joseph P. Craugh (D)	30,503	30.9
37	Gale H. Stalker (R & SOC)	78,789	70.4
	Paul Smith (D)	33,212	29.7
38	James L. Whitley (R)	47,298	36.0
	Charles Stanton (D)	43,009	32.7
	William MacFarlane (I)	38,324	29.2
39	Archie D. Sanders (R)	69,615	65.0
	Frank L. Morris (D)	34,175	31.9
40	S. Wallace Dempsey (R)	99,896	65.4
	John M. Powers (D)	46,860	30.7
41	Edmund F. Cooke (R)	44,641	52.7
	Fred C. Fornes (D)	37,057	43.7
42	James M. Mead (D)	44,373	56.1
	C. Hamilton Cook (R)	31,785	40.2
43	Daniel A. Reed (R)	73,571	76.0
	Arthur E. Towne (D)	23,176	24.0

NORTH CAROLINA

1	Lindsay C. Warren (D)	23,140	76.3
	Marion B. Prescott (R)	7,209	23.8
2	John H. Kerr (D)	24,129	88.9
	J. L. Johnston (R)	3,005	11.1
3	Charles L. Abernethy (D)	21,740	55.7
	William G. Mebane (R)	17,307	44.3
4	Edward W. Pou (D)	31,288	65.6
	Lossing L. Wrenn (R)	16,434	34.4
5	Charles M. Stedman (D)	54,980	50.1
	Junius H. Harden (R)	54,813	49.9
6	J. Bayard Clark (D)	26,061	61.4
	W. C. Downing (R)	16,364	38.6
7	William C. Hammer (D)	41,124	51.3
	A. I. Ferree (R)	39,106	48.7
8	Robert L. Doughton (D)	37,535	50.9
	W. S. Bogle (R)	36,251	49.1
9	Charles A. Jonas (R)	49,799	51.6
	Alfred L. Bulwinkle (D)	46,756	48.4
10	George M. Pritchard (R)	49,045	50.2
	Zebulon Weaver (D)	48,607	49.8

NORTH DAKOTA

1	Olger B. Burtness (R)	53,941	77.5
	W. S. Hooper (D)	15,646	22.5
2	Thomas Hall (R)	42,844	61.7
	J. L. Page (D)	26,566	38.3
3	James H. Sinclair (R)	52,220	84.8
	Reuben H. Leavitt (D)	9,335	15.2

OHIO

1	Nicholas Longworth (R)	80,812	61.8
	Arthur Espy (D)	49,880	38.2
2	William E. Hess (R)	63,605	53.9
	James H. Cleveland (D)	54,332	46.1
3	Roy Fitzgerald (R)	101,050	64.4
	Frank L. Humphrey (D)	55,767	35.6
4	John L. Cable (R)	56,291	57.5
	William Klinger (D)	41,677	42.5
5	Charles J. Thompson (R)	36,096	53.5
	Frank C. Kniffin (D)	31,385	46.5
6	Charles C. Kearns (R)	43,519	56.9
	George D. Nye (D)	33,020	43.1
7	Charles Brand (R)	75,753	68.8
	Harry E. Rice (D)	34,323	31.2
8	Grant E. Mouser Jr. (R)	42,199	52.2
	Brooks Fletcher (D)	38,651	47.8
9	William W. Chalmers (R)	82,560	61.9
	William P. Clarke (D)	50,601	38.0
10	Thomas A. Jenkins (R)	38,347	69.9
	Charles E. Poston (D)	16,551	30.2
11	Mell G. Underwood (D)	34,257	52.8
	Edwin D. Ricketts (R)	30,574	47.2

OHIO

Candidates	Votes	%
12 John C. Speaks (R)	82,574	62.2
Carl H. Valentine (D)	50,216	37.8
13 Joe E. Baird (R)	54,174	61.4
William C. Martin (D)	34,015	38.6
14 Francis Seiberling (R)	106,253	64.4
A. F. O'Neil (D)	58,848	35.6
15 C. Ellis Moore (R)	50,941	65.8
Frank H. Ward (D)	26,441	34.2
16 C. B. McClintock (R)	73,966	56.4
John McSweeney (D)	55,778	42.5
17 William M. Morgan (R)	56,823	58.2
Charles West (D)	40,846	41.8
18 B. Frank Murphy (R)	71,378	69.2
John J. Whitacre (D)	31,422	30.5
19 John G. Cooper (R)	89,731	68.7
Locke Miller (D)	40,948	31.3
20 Charles A. Mooney (D)	47,313	62.3
Oscar V. Hensley (R)	28,381	37.4
21 Robert Crosser (D)	39,090	59.8
Joseph F. Lange (R)	26,267	40.2
22 Chester C. Bolton (R)	151,565	69.8
Simon B. Fitzsimmons (D)	65,742	30.3

OKLAHOMA

Candidates	Votes	%
1 Charles O'Connor (R)	63,641	52.2
Everette B. Howard (D)	58,148	47.7
2 William W. Hastings (D)	31,287	51.9
E. L. Kirby (R)	28,959	48.0
3 Wilburn Cartwright (D)	39,467	64.1
Robert N. Allen (R)	21,804	35.4
4 Thomas D. McKeown (D)	37,191	50.5
Fred L. Patrick (R)	36,151	49.1
5 Ulysses S. Stone (R)	44,814	50.9
Fletcher B. Swank (D)	42,856	48.7
6 Jed Johnson (D)	32,820	53.4
Walter C. Stephens (R)	28,304	46.0
7 James V. McClintic (D)	27,670	55.6
Walter S. Mills (R)	21,758	43.7
8 Milton C. Garber (R)	48,445	63.8
J. P. Battenberg (D)	27,135	35.7

OREGON

Candidates	Votes	%
1 Willis C. Hawley (R)	91,839	70.9
Harvey G. Starkweather (D)	33,772	26.1
2 Robert R. Butler (R)	28,865	55.7
Walter M. Pierce (D)	22,108	42.6
3 Franklin F. Korell (R)	75,835	67.6
William C. Culbertson (D)	29,673#	26.5

PENNSYLVANIA

Candidates	Votes	%
1 James M. Beck (R)	45,070	49.8
William L. Rooney (D)	44,956	49.7
2 George S. Graham (R)	34,432	64.6
John J. Shanahan (D)	18,697	35.1
3 Harry C. Ransley (R)	30,458	57.4
James J. Hayes (D)	22,559	42.5
4 Benjamin M. Golder (R)	49,877	61.2
Thomas J. Carroll (D, LAB)	31,082	38.1
5 James J. Connolly (R, D)	110,648	99.4
6 George A. Welsh (R)	89,362	59.8
Bruce A. Metzger (D)	59,410	39.7
7 George P. Darrow (R)	91,305	68.0
Thomas A. O'Hara (D)	42,217	31.5
8 James Wolfenden (R)	116,266	76.2
Henry W. Davis (D)	34,607	22.7
9 Henry W. Watson (R)	102,019	76.3
Richard Vaux (D)	31,389	23.5
10 William W. Griest (R, LAB)	55,623	82.5
John A. McSparran (D)	11,395	16.9
11 Laurence H. Watres (R, P)	48,626	50.3
Frank M. Walsh (D)	48,017	49.7

Candidates	Votes	%
12 John J. Casey (D, LAB)	70,943	51.6
Henry W. Merritt (R, P)	66,661	48.4
13 George Franklin Brumm (R)	46,486	55.5
Bernard V. O'Hare (D)	37,243	44.5
14 Charles J. Esterly (R)	76,670	61.9
Abraham B. Rothermel (D)	36,176	29.2
Howard McDonough (SOC, LAB)	10,950	8.8
15 Louis T. McFadden (R, D)	50,770	93.8
Cornelia Bryce Pinchot (P)	3,348	6.2
16 Edgar R. Kiess (R, P)	48,041	74.0
Thomas Wood (D)	16,693	25.7
17 Frederick W. Magrady (R)	45,437	60.0
Samuel M. Shipman (D, P)	30,290	40.0
18 Edward E. Beers (R, LAB)	55,736	81.0
Frederick A. Rupp (D)	13,070	19.0
19 Isaac H. Doutrich (R, LAB)	80,291	80.3
John E. Blair (D)	19,032	19.1
20 J. Russell Leech (R)	29,383	53.3
George E. Wolfe (D, LAB)	25,737	46.7
21 J. Banks Kurtz (R, LAB)	42,965	76.2
Harry K. Filler (D)	13,420	23.8
22 Franklin Menges (R, P)	44,198	63.3
John H. Myers (D)	25,622	36.7
23 J. Mitchel Chase (R, LAB)	43,294	74.0
T. E. Costello (D)	15,219	26.0
24 Samuel A. Kendall (R, P)	42,118	64.3
J. Calvin Core (D)	23,176	35.4
25 Henry W. Temple (R, P)	34,806	59.6
James S. Pates (D)	23,260	39.9
26 J. Howard Swick (R, P)	64,160	72.2
C. Hale Sipe (D)	24,352	27.4
27 Nathan L. Strong (R, P)	52,868	75.2
Harry W. Fee (D)	17,433	24.8
28 Thomas C. Cochran (R, P)	59,143	74.3
Harry B. Mitchell (D)	20,443	25.7
29 Milton W. Shreve (R, P)	42,747	60.4
Albert L. Thomas (D)	28,004	39.6
30 William R. Coyle (R)	48,421	56.9
Everett Kent (D, LAB)	36,612	43.1
31 Adam M. Wyant (R, P)	50,981	95.8
32 Stephen G. Porter (R)	48,837	64.6
Edward S. Michalowski (D)	26,145	34.6
33 M. Clyde Kelly (R, D)	81,328	99.0
34 Patrick J. Sullivan (R, D)	48,638	97.4
35 Harry A. Estep (R)	42,450	57.3
John J. Murray (D)	30,619	41.4
36 Guy E. Campbell (R, P)	48,190	60.3
William E. Madden Jr. (D)	31,151	39.0

Special Election

	Votes	%
8 James Wolfenden (R)	116,504	97.8

RHODE ISLAND

Candidates	Votes	%
1 Clark Burdick (R)	42,366	55.6
John J. Cooney (D)	33,902	44.5
2 Richard S. Aldrich (R)	43,772	55.6
Sumner Mowry (D)	34,947	44.4
3 Jeremiah E. O'Connell (D)	45,605	57.1
Louis Monast (R)	34,223	42.9

SOUTH CAROLINA

Candidates	Votes	%
1 Thomas S. McMillan (D)	8,469	100.0
2 Butler B. Hare (D)	7,648	100.0
3 Fred H. Dominick (D)	10,917	100.0
4 John J. McSwain (D)	8,873	100.0
5 William F. Stevenson (D)	8,911	100.0
6 Allard H. Gasque (D)	7,757	100.0
7 Hampton P. Fulmer (D)	8,772	100.0

SOUTH DAKOTA

Candidates	Votes	%
1 Charles A. Christopherson (R)	54,573	58.4
A. O. Steensland (D)	38,055	40.7

Candidates	Votes	%
2 Royal C. Johnson (R)	54,846	57.2
Fred Hildebrandt (D)	39,970	41.7
3 William Williamson (R)	33,245	55.7
Arthur W. Watwood (D)	26,412	44.3

TENNESSEE

Candidates	Votes	%
1 B. Carroll Reece (R)	28,142	78.6
W. I. Giles (D)	7,646	21.4
2 J. Will Taylor (R)	30,917	68.9
Leon Jourolmon (D)	13,968	31.1
3 Sam D. McReynolds (D)	25,667	53.4
Silas Williams (R)	22,405	46.6
4 Cordell Hull (D)	17,141	68.2
S. H. Justice (R)	7,999	31.8
5 Ewin L. Davis (D)	12,847	80.4
John F. Aplinger	3,126#	19.6
6 Joseph W. Byrns (D)	24,738	79.9
E. L. Bradbury (R)	6,220	20.1
7 Edward E. Eslick (D)	16,893	93.0
S. E. Stephens (R)	1,268	7.0
8 Gordon Browning (D)	17,868	66.1
Harvey E. Cantrell (R)	9,184	34.0
9 Jere Cooper (D)	20,184	90.1
Carmack Murchison (R)	2,222	9.9
10 Hubert F. Fisher (D)	21,524	81.3
R. L. Harper (R)	4,964	18.7

TEXAS

Candidates	Votes	%
1 Wright Patman (D)	24,267	87.9
Richard E. Stephens (R)	3,349	12.1
2 John C. Box (D)	38,901	100.0
3 Morgan G. Sanders (D)	22,221	100.0
4 Sam Rayburn (D)	23,847	84.2
Floyd Harry (R)	4,488	15.8
5 Hatton W. Sumners (D)	42,482	100.0
6 Luther A. Johnson (D)	26,412	90.7
H. Lee Monroe (R)	2,714	9.3
7 Clay Stone Briggs (D)	21,461	88.4
A. J. Long (R)	2,827	11.6
8 Daniel E. Garrett (D)	43,891	81.8
George E. Kepple (R)	9,739	18.2
9 Joseph J. Mansfield (D)	24,742	86.9
Louis B. Allen (R)	3,718	13.1
10 James P. Buchanan (D)	27,890	91.9
David H. Morris (R)	2,457	8.1
11 Oliver H. Crass (D)	21,484	90.9
R. C. Bush (R)	2,141	9.1
12 Fritz G. Lanham (D)	30,905	79.6
David Sutter (R)	7,921	20.4
13 Guinn Williams (D)	30,926	88.5
Mrs. P. A. Welty (R)	4,026	11.5
14 Augustus McCloskey (D)	29,085‡	50.3
Harry M. Wurzbach (R)	28,766	49.7
15 John N. Garner (D)	28,417	100.0
16 Claude B. Hudspeth (D)	31,132	100.0
17 Robert Q. Lee (D)	41,727	100.0
18 Marvin Jones (D)	58,667	86.5
V. C. Nelson (R)	9,137	13.5

UTAH

Candidates	Votes	%
1 Don B. Colton (R)	50,274	60.9
Knox Patterson (D)	31,889	38.6
2 Elmer O. Leatherwood (R)	46,866	50.2
Joshua H. Paul (D)	46,025	49.3

VERMONT

Candidates	Votes	%
1 Elbert S. Brigham (R)	44,082	63.0
Jeremiah C. Durick (D)	25,095	35.9
2 Ernest Willard Gibson (R)	47,141	79.3
Harry W. Witters (D)	11,356	19.1

VIRGINIA

Candidates	Votes	%
1 Schuyler Otis Bland (D)	23,912	99.7
2 Menalcus Lankford (R)	18,614	55.9
Joseph T. Deal (D)	14,668	44.1
3 Andrew J. Montague (D)	23,350	75.9
J. D. Peake (I)	5,854	19.0
James E. Maynard (I)	1,561	5.1
4 Patrick Henry Drewry (D)	16,904	99.7
5 Joseph Whitehead (D)	16,672	54.3
Taylor G. Vaughan (R)	14,049	45.7
6 Clifton A. Woodrum (D)	25,091	99.7
7 Jacob A. Garber (R)	15,243	50.4
Thomas W. Harrison (D)	15,009	49.6
8 R. Walton Moore (D)	24,368	99.1
9 Joseph C. Shaffer (R)	32,696	50.8
William H. Rouse (D)	31,722	49.2
10 Henry St.George Tucker (D)	14,817	56.9
M. J. Putnam (R)	11,230	43.1

WASHINGTON

Candidates	Votes	%
1 John F. Miller (R)	70,703	65.5
Hugh Todd (D)	36,858	34.1
2 Lindley H. Hadley (R)	59,534	99.3
3 Albert Johnson (R)	77,314	70.0
O. M. Nelson (D)	33,217	30.1

Candidates	Votes	%
4 John W. Summers (R)	48,766	77.1
H. C. Bohlke (D)	14,512	22.9
5 Sam B. Hill (D)	50,323	58.5
Thomas Corkery (R)	35,660	41.5

WEST VIRGINIA

Candidates	Votes	%
1 Carl G. Bachmann (R)	62,646	60.6
Paul R. Wellman (D)	40,666	39.4
2 Frank L. Bowman (R)	52,424	55.7
Ben H. Hiner (D)	41,640	44.2
3 John M. Wolverton (R)	45,167	50.4
William S. O'Brien (D)	44,477	49.6
4 James A. Hughes (R)	55,672	57.0
Harry H. Darnall (D)	42,057	43.0
5 Hugh Ike Shott (R)	63,559	53.4
John Kee (D)	55,376	46.6
6 Joe L. Smith (D)	67,845	50.1
Edward T. England (R)	67,617	49.9

WISCONSIN

Candidates	Votes	%
1 Henry Allen Cooper (R)	83,069	80.2
William C. Kiernan (D)	20,534	19.8
2 Charles A. Kading (R)	53,530	69.9
Eugene A. Clifford (D)	23,101	30.1

Candidates	Votes	%
3 John Mandt Nelson (R)	62,938	74.7
William Victora (D)	20,262	24.1
4 John C. Schafer (R)	37,685	44.1
William J. Kershaw (D)	28,956	33.9
Walter Polakowski (SOC)	18,885	22.1
5 William H. Stafford (R)	41,265	38.9
Victor L. Berger (SOC)	40,536	38.2
Thomas O'Malley (D)	24,037	22.7
6 Florian Lampert (R)	53,952	69.2
Morley G. Kelly (D)	24,009	30.8
7 Merlin Hull (R)	49,590	72.4
A. H. Schubert (D)	18,530	27.0
8 Edward E. Browne (R)	47,848	74.0
R. J. Walsh (D)	16,316	25.2
9 George J. Schneider (R)	52,300	60.4
James H. McGillan (D)	33,302	38.5
10 James A. Frear (R)	59,314	81.4
Miles H. McNally (D)	13,590	18.6
11 Hubert H. Peavey (R)	56,586	80.8
Frank P. Kennedy (D)	11,962	17.1

WYOMING

	Votes	%
AL Vincent M. Carter (R)	38,935	51.8
W. S. Kimball (D)	35,972	47.8

1929 House Elections

KENTUCKY

Special Election

	Votes	%
3 John W. Moore (D)	19,669	51.3
Homer Beliles (R)	18,644	48.7

LOUISIANA
Special Election

	Votes	%
3 Numa F. Montet (D)	11,460	57.7
M. E. Norman (R)	8,399	42.3

MISSOURI
Special Election

	Votes	%
4 David Hopkins (R)	23,898	53.0
Louis V. Stigall (D)	21,179	47.0

NEW YORK

Special Election

	Votes	%
21 Joseph A. Gavagan (D)	39,893	56.7
Hubert T. Delany (R&SQDEAL)	26,666	37.9
Frank Crosswaith (SOC)	3,561	5.1

House Candidates Index

For an index of all House candidates listed in this section (pages 701 to 1061), see pages 1180-1273. Instructions for use of the House Candidates Index appear on page 1180.

1930 House Elections

ALABAMA

	Candidates	Votes	%
1	John McDuffie (D)	16,839	100.0
2	Lister Hill (D)	22,630	100.0
3	Henry B. Steagall (D)	13,398	100.0
4	Lamar Jeffers (D)	13,502	65.2
	E. D. Banks (I)	7,209	34.8
5	Lafayette L. Patterson (D)	13,221	100.0
6	William B. Oliver (D)	9,439	100.0
7	Miles C. Allgood (D)	18,932	61.1
	John B. Isbell (R)	12,062	38.9
8	Edward B. Almon (D)	18,570	100.0
9	George Huddleston (D)	24,484	81.0
	Hollis B. Parris (I)	5,750	19.0
10	William B. Bankhead (D)	14,388	64.2
	Charles P. G. Lunsford (R)	8,009	35.8

ARIZONA

		Votes	%
AL	Lewis W. Douglas (D)	52,342	100.0

ARKANSAS

		Votes	%
1	William J. Driver (D)	19,103	100.0
2	John E. Miller (D)	18,623	100.0
3	Claude A. Fuller (D)	28,809	100.0
4	Effiegene Wingo (D)	21,753	100.0
5	Heartsill Ragon (D)	21,896	100.0
6	David D. Glover (D)	18,127	100.0
7	Tilman B. Parks (D)	15,860	100.0

CALIFORNIA

		Votes	%
1	Clarence F. Lea (D-R)	66,703	100.0
2	Harry L. Englebright (R-D)	35,941	99.9
3	Charles F. Curry (WRITE IN)	43,336	53.4
	J. M. Inman (R)	26,785#	33.0
	Frank H. Buck (D)	9,172#	11.3
4	Florence P. Kahn (R-D)	47,397	100.0
5	Richard J. Welch (R-D)	59,853	100.0
6	Albert E. Carter (R-D)	110,190	100.0
7	Henry E. Barbour (R-D)	79,041	100.0
8	Arthur Monroe Free (R-D)	93,377	99.9
9	William E. Evans (R)	182,176	99.9
10	Joe Crail (R)	162,502	75.0
	John F. Dockweiler (D)	54,231	25.0
11	Philip D. Swing (R-D)	124,092	100.0

COLORADO

		Votes	%
1	William R. Eaton (R)	39,907	50.3
	Lawrence Lewis (D)	38,152	48.1
2	Charles B. Timberlake (R)	55,099	59.3
	O. E. Webb (D)	37,760	40.7
3	Guy U. Hardy (R)	55,170	60.7
	Guy M. Weybright (D)	35,744	39.3
4	Edward T. Taylor (D)	34,536	67.0
	Webster S. Whinnery (R)	17,051	33.1

CONNECTICUT

		Votes	%
1	Augustine Lonergan (D)	51,551	50.3
	Clarence W. Seymour (R)	50,877	49.7
2	Richard P. Freeman (R)	37,801	53.1
	William C. Fox (D)	33,329	46.9
3	John Q. Tilson (R)	45,329	52.1
	James A. Shanley (D)	40,269	46.3
4	William L. Tierney (D)	50,769	49.7
	Schuyler Merritt (R)	49,209	48.2
5	Edward W. Goss (R)	33,302	50.5
	Martin E. Gormley (D)	32,584	49.5

Special Election

	Candidates	Votes	%
5	Edward W. Goss (R)	33,284	50.6
	Martin E. Gormley (D)	32,479	49.4

DELAWARE

		Votes	%
AL	Robert G. Houston (R)	48,493	55.4
	John P. Le Fevre (D)	38,891	44.4

FLORIDA

		Votes	%
1	Herbert J. Drane (D)	24,792	67.7
	L. E. Womack (R)	11,819	32.3
2	Robert A. Green (D)	7,060	100.0
3	Tom A. Yon (D)	11,796	99.8
4	Ruth Bryan Owen (D)	40,422	99.9

GEORGIA

		Votes	%
1	Charles G. Edwards (D)	2,465	100.0
2	E. E. Cox (D)	2,518	100.0
3	Charles R. Crisp (D)	2,440	100.0
4	William C. Wright (D)	2,721	100.0
5	Robert Ramspeck (D)	10,752	100.0
6	Samuel Rutherford (D)	4,333	100.0
7	Malcolm C. Tarver (D)	5,590	100.0
8	Charles H. Brand (D)	5,058	93.2
	W. N. Phillips (I)	369#	6.8
9	John S. Wood (D)	7,089	100.0
10	Carl Vinson (D)	2,691	100.0
11	William C. Lankford (D)	6,462	80.9
	H. J. Carswell (R)	1,526#	19.1
12	William W. Larsen (D)	2,444	100.0

IDAHO

		Votes	%
1	Burton L. French (R)	34,527	64.9
	Compton I. White (D)	18,657	35.1
2	Addison T. Smith (R)	46,342	63.2
	W. F. Alworth (D)	27,002	36.8

ILLINOIS

		Votes	%
1	Oscar De Priest (R)	23,719	58.4
	Harry Baker (D)	16,747	41.2
2	Morton D. Hull (R)	76,665	54.4
	Michael C. Walsh (D)	63,341	44.9
3	Edward A. Kelly (D)	83,028	58.1
	Elliott W. Sproul (R)	59,644	41.8
4	Harry P. Beam (D)	36,736	69.3
	Frank George Zelezinski (R)	16,192	30.5
5	Adolph J. Sabath (D)	21,460	66.2
	Frank V. Kara (R)	10,816	33.3
6	James T. Igoe (D)	120,408	66.7
	Henry R. Lundblad (R)	59,052	32.7
7	Leonard W. Schuetz (D)	111,525	55.0
	James C. Moreland (R)	90,844	44.8
8	Peter C. Granata (R)	16,565	51.8
	Stanley H. Kunz (D)	15,394	48.1
9	Fred A. Britten (R)	24,028	99.4
10	Carl R. Chindblom (R)	72,938	50.8
	John E. Hesse (D)	70,621	49.2
11	Frank R. Reid (R)	56,957	63.1
	Elmer P. Schaefer (D)	33,169	36.8
12	John T. Buckbee (R)	55,754	76.1
	Richard J. O'Halloran (D)	17,497	23.9
13	William R. Johnson (R)	28,113	70.2
	John A. Ascher (D)	11,937	29.8
14	John C. Allen (R)	36,370	56.9
	William H. Hartzell (D)	27,592	43.1
15	Burnett M. Chiperfield (R)	35,114	56.5
	J. Hays Paxton (D)	27,031	43.5

	Candidates	Votes	%
16	William E. Hull (R)	36,572	52.8
	Edwin S. Carr (D)	32,692	47.2
17	Homer W. Hall (R)	27,696	58.4
	C. S. Schneider (D)	19,711	41.6
18	William P. Holaday (R)	38,102	56.8
	Charles R. Hill (D)	29,012	43.2
19	Charles Adkins (R)	43,794	55.4
	Charles M. Borchers (D)	35,310	44.6
20	Henry T. Rainey (D)	37,537	64.9
	William J. Thornton (R)	20,262	35.1
21	J. Earl Major (D)	46,058	57.1
	Roger E. Chapin (R)	34,521	42.8
22	Charles A. Karch (D)	48,281	50.3
	Ed. M. Irwin (R)	47,715	49.7
23	William W. Arnold (D)	49,111	62.6
	Joe Frank Allen (R)	29,291	37.4
24	Claude V. Parsons (D)	27,325	50.0
	James V. Heidinger (R)	27,296	50.0
25	Kent E. Keller (D)	38,796	52.6
	Edward E. Denison (R)	34,927	47.4
AL	William H. Dieterich (D)	1,062,606✔	
	Richard Yates (R)	991,083✔	
	Walter Nesbit (D)	975,422	
	Frank L. Smith (R)	890,327	
	Emil Z. Levitin (SOC)	9,526	
	Morris A. Gold (SOC)	9,207	
	William S. Feinberg (AM NAT)	1,337	
	John W. McLain (AM NAT)	1,228	
	I. J. Brown (LIB)	884	
	Charles A. Reinhart (LIB)	824	

Special Elections

		Votes	%
15	Burnett M. Chiperfield (R)	34,063	56.2
	J. Hays Paxton (D)	26,467	43.7
24	Claude V. Parsons (D)	26,929	50.2
	James V. Heidinger (R)	26,732	49.8

INDIANA

		Votes	%
1	John W. Boehne Jr. (D)	46,836	53.9
	Harry E. Rowbottom (R)	40,015	46.1
2	Arthur H. Greenwood (D)	52,452	59.5
	Ray S. Sisson (R)	35,689	40.5
3	Eugene B. Crowe (D)	45,070	50.2
	James W. Dunbar (R)	44,808	49.9
4	Harry C. Canfield (D)	46,396	57.1
	Scott Thompson (R)	34,856	42.9
5	Courtland C. Gillen (D)	43,355	51.5
	Noble J. Johnson (R)	40,919	48.6
6	William H. Larrabee (D)	40,803	51.8
	Richard N. Elliott (R)	37,969	48.2
7	Louis Ludlow (D)	87,777	61.6
	Archibald M. Hall (R)	53,822	37.8
8	Albert H. Vestal (R)	44,203	50.0
	Claude E. Ball (D)	44,194	50.0
9	Fred S. Purnell (R)	43,681	50.2
	Harry L. Matlock (D)	43,346	49.8
10	William R. Wood (R)	53,702	53.3
	Charles J. Murphy (D)	47,057	46.7
11	Glenn Griswold (D)	41,823	51.3
	Albert R. Hall (R)	39,771	48.7
12	David R. Hogg (R)	43,286	52.3
	Thomas P. Riddle (D)	39,488	47.7
13	Samuel B. Pettengill (D)	62,609	51.3
	Andrew J. Hickey (R)	59,361	48.7

IOWA

		Votes	%
1	William F. Kopp (R)	27,053	63.3
	Max A. Conrad (D)	15,538	36.4
2	Bernhard M. Jacobsen (D)	30,006	55.4
	F. D. Letts (R)	24,113	44.6

IOWA

	Candidates	Votes	%
3	Thomas J. B. Robinson (R)	27,098	63.0
	W. L. Beecher (D)	15,908	37.0
4	Gilbert N. Haugen (R)	29,224	59.1
	Wilbur L. Peck (D)	20,236	40.9
5	Cyrenus Cole (R)	23,221	53.8
	H. M. Cooper (D)	19,931	46.2
6	C. William Ramseyer (R)	25,875	60.6
	S. F. McConnell (D)	16,811	39.4
7	Cassius C. Dowell (R)	36,715	76.5
	Carl Evans (D)	11,272	23.5
8	Lloyd Thurston (R)	27,960	51.5
	James Pearson (D)	26,373	48.5
9	Charles E. Swanson (R)	27,873	57.1
	June M. Fickel (D)	20,587	42.2
10	Fred C. Gilchrist (R)	34,915	66.1
	Paul Anderson (D)	17,540	33.2
11	Ed H. Campbell (R)	37,659	73.8
	Fordyce W. Bisbee (D)	13,382	26.2

KANSAS

	Candidates	Votes	%
1	William P. Lambertson (R)	53,799	100.0
2	Ulysses S. Guyer (R)	49,844	56.8
	Chauncey B. Little (D)	37,991	43.3
3	Harold McGugin (R)	42,106	52.7
	Earl Knight (D)	37,807	47.3
4	Homer Hoch (R)	30,840	58.4
	James E. Hilkey (D)	21,933	41.6
5	James G. Strong (R)	33,871	53.9
	Clyde Short (D)	28,971	46.1
6	Charles I. Sparks (R)	40,132	61.6
	Robert Good (D)	24,975	38.4
7	Clifford R. Hope (R)	52,858	61.1
	A. S. Allphin (D)	33,627	38.9
8	William A. Ayres (D)	57,173	74.7
	Stella B. Haines (R)	19,325	25.3

KENTUCKY

	Candidates	Votes	%
1	William V. Gregory (D)	24,622	100.0
2	Glover H. Cary (D)	21,685	100.0
3	John W. Moore (D)	25,981	99.7
4	Cap R. Carden (D)	30,910	52.3
	John Craddock (R)	28,220	47.7
5	Maurice H. Thatcher (R)	61,832	97.9
6	Brent Spence (D)	31,520	56.9
	J. Lincoln Newhall (R)	18,891	34.1
	Blaine McLaughlin (I)	4,746	8.6
7	Virgil Chapman (D)	33,402	57.8
	Robert Blackburn (R)	24,380	42.2
8	Ralph Gilbert (D)	25,688	57.5
	Patrick H. Taylor (R)	19,023	42.6
9	Fred M. Vinson (D)	42,671	59.7
	Elva R. Kendall (R)	28,850	40.3
10	Andrew J. May (D)	27,159	52.9
	Katherine Langley (R)	24,172	47.1
11	Charles Finley (R)	48,535	66.3
	Will Ward Duffield (D)	24,716	33.7

Special Elections

		Votes	%
2	John L. Dorsey Jr. (D)	21,406#	100.0
11	Charles Finley (R)	14,148	76.0
	M. B. Sewell (D)	4,471	24.0

LOUISIANA

	Candidates	Votes	%
1	Joachim O. Fernandez (D)	30,629	95.8
2	Paul H. Maloney (D)	30,739	97.2
3	Numa F. Montet (D)	8,517	100.0
4	John N. Sandlin (D)	11,833	100.0
5	Riley J. Wilson (D)	11,168	100.0
6	Bolivar E. Kemp (D)	15,524	100.0
7	Rene L. DeRouen (D)	9,293	100.0
8	James B. Aswell (D)	12,383	100.0

MAINE

	Candidates	Votes	%
1	Carroll L. Beedy (R)	23,434	61.4
	Thomas F. Locke (D)	14,741	38.6
2	Donald B. Partridge (R)	24,338	56.2
	Albert Beliveau (D)	18,943	43.8
3	John E. Nelson (R)	25,099	64.3
	Leo D. Lamond (D)	13,948	35.7
4	Donald F. Snow (R)	15,199	66.0
	Clinton C. Stevens (D)	7,839	34.0

MARYLAND

	Candidates	Votes	%
1	T. Alan Goldsborough (D)	34,553	57.3
	A. Stengle Marine (R)	25,792	42.7
2	William F. Cole Jr. (D)	79,963	59.3
	Linwood L. Clark (R)	54,914	40.7
3	Vincent L. Palmisano (D)	28,633	53.4
	John Philip Hill (R)	24,170	45.1
4	J. Charles Linthicum (D)	49,471	65.0
	W. O. Atwood (R)	26,661	35.0
5	Stephen Warfield Gambrill (D)	40,315	65.3
	A. Kingsley Love (R)	21,463	34.7
6	David J. Lewis (D)	42,526	53.6
	Frederick N. Zihlman (R)	36,815	46.4

MASSACHUSETTS

	Candidates	Votes	%
1	Allen T. Treadway (R)	41,334	54.9
	Hugh McLean (D)	33,934	45.1
2	William J. Granfield (D)	46,432	55.5
	Joshua L. Brooks (R)	37,247	44.5
3	Frank H. Foss (R)	36,620	57.1
	Frank W. Barr (D)	27,568	43.0
4	Pehr G. Holmes (R)	42,996	54.7
	David Goldstein (D)	35,661	45.3
5	Edith Nourse Rogers (R)	50,541	66.3
	Joseph M. Halloran (D)	25,742	33.8
6	A. Piatt Andrew (R)	50,814	76.4
	Charles D. Smith (D)	15,683	23.6
7	William P. Connery Jr. (D)	45,521	67.6
	Charles W. Lovett (R)	21,821	32.4
8	Frederick W. Dallinger (R)	57,428	56.6
	John P. Brennan (D)	44,041	43.4
9	Charles L. Underhill (R)	41,040	50.7
	Joseph J. Borgatti (D)	39,948	49.3
10	John J. Douglass (D)	33,218	87.3
	Edward I. Donnelly (R)	4,815	12.7
11	George Holden Tinkham (R)	40,417	63.0
	John Joseph Kelleher (D)	23,739	37.0
12	John W. McCormack (D)	50,894	76.7
	Samuel Abrams (R)	15,422	23.3
13	Robert Luce (R)	55,470	55.9
	Donald M. Hill (D)	43,800	44.1
14	Richard B. Wigglesworth (R)	56,803	57.3
	Edward G. Morris (D)	42,307	42.7
15	Joseph W. Martin Jr. (R)	37,100	64.1
	William J. Murphy (D)	20,780	35.9
16	Charles L. Gifford (R)	39,953	69.6
	John D. W. Bodfish (I)	17,467	30.4

MICHIGAN

	Candidates	Votes	%
1	Robert H. Clancy (R)	44,021	82.2
	William M. Donnelly (D)	8,758	16.4
2	Earl C. Michener (R)	41,478	58.0
	Edward Frensdorf (D)	29,979	41.9
3	Joseph L. Hooper (R)	36,190	71.1
	Rosslyn L. Sowers (D)	14,737	28.9
4	John C. Ketcham (R)	34,980	66.1
	Roman I. Jarvis Sr. (D)	17,953	33.9
5	Carl E. Mapes (R)	31,297	98.7
6	Seymour H. Person (R)	124,797	70.2
	Patrick H. O'Brien (D)	50,221	28.2
7	Jesse P. Wolcott (R)	42,256	94.3
	Emerald B. Dixon (D)	2,534	5.7
8	Bird J. Vincent (R)	38,891	67.4
	Michael J. Hart (D)	18,838	32.6
9	James C. McLaughlin (R)	31,318	75.0
	Loren N. O'Brien (D)	10,462	25.0
10	Roy O. Woodruff (R)	31,033	78.8
	Henry C. Haller (D)	8,345	21.2
11	Frank P. Bohn (R)	34,971	100.0
12	W. Frank James (R)	36,909	98.1
13	Clarence J. McLeod (R)	39,064	78.8
	Walter I. McKenzie (D)	9,575	19.3

MINNESOTA

	Candidates	Votes	%
1	Victor Christgau (R)	45,330	65.1
	Matt Fitzpatrick (F-LAB)	24,357	35.0
2	Frank Clague (R)	38,431	53.7
	L. A. Fritsche (F-LAB)	33,092	46.3
3	August H. Andresen (R)	35,704	48.1
	Francis H. Shoemaker (F-LAB)	21,118	28.4
	Joseph J. Moriarity (D)	17,485	23.5
4	Melvin J. Maas (R)	48,633	66.5
	Claus V. Hammerstrom (F-LAB)	16,180	22.1
	Frank Munger Sr. (D)	6,593	9.0
5	W. I. Nolan (R)	55,502	61.3
	Silas M. Bryan (D)	32,215	35.6
6	Harold Knutson (R)	44,058	60.6
	John Knutsen (F-LAB)	19,461	26.8
	P. J. Russell (D)	9,197	12.7
7	Paul John Kvale (F-LAB)	58,334	81.2
	Frank Hopkins (R)	13,506	18.8
8	William A. Pittenger (R)	55,802	63.3
	William L. Carss (F-LAB)	29,001	32.9
9	Conrad G. Selvig (R)	37,531	53.3
	Knud Wefald (F-LAB)	32,874	46.7
10	Godfrey G. Goodwin (R)	38,391	49.5
	Erling Swenson (F-LAB)	37,182	48.0

MISSISSIPPI

	Candidates	Votes	%
1	John E. Rankin (D)	5,378	100.0
2	Wall Doxey (D)	4,202	100.0
3	William M. Whittington (D)	4,282	100.0
4	Jeff Busby (D)	4,017	100.0
5	Ross A. Collins (D)	5,107	100.0
6	Robert S. Hall (D)	5,995	100.0
7	Percy E. Quinn (D)	3,356	100.0
8	James W. Collier (D)	2,560	100.0

MISSOURI

	Candidates	Votes	%
1	Milton A. Romjue (D)	28,974	61.8
	J. F. Culler (R)	17,898	38.2
2	Ralph F. Lozier (D)	30,020	62.8
	Pearl Gehrig (R)	17,746	37.1
3	Jacob L. Milligan (D)	25,853	58.9
	H. F. Lawrence (R)	18,074	41.2
4	David Hopkins (R)	33,284	50.8
	Romulus E. Culver (D)	32,208	49.2
5	Joseph B. Shannon (D)	102,569	64.3
	Edgar C. Ellis (R)	56,918	35.7
6	Clement C. Dickinson (D)	24,713	54.9
	Thomas J. Halsey (R)	20,249	45.0
7	Samuel C. Major (D)	36,543	51.8
	John W. Palmer (R)	33,964	48.2
8	William L. Nelson (D)	27,321	57.9
	E. J. Melton (R)	19,850	42.1
9	Clarence Cannon (D)	25,796	62.4
	Frank H. Hollmann (R)	15,472	37.5
10	Henry F. Niedringhaus (R)	93,433	99.8
11	John J. Cochran (D)	17,726	99.9
12	Leonidas C. Dyer (R)	14,195	99.8
13	Clyde Williams (D)	27,633	53.1
	Charles E. Kiefner (R)	24,378	46.9
14	James F. Fulbright (D)	45,332	51.6
	Dewey Short (R)	42,579	48.4

MISSOURI

	Candidates	Votes	%
15	Joe J. Manlove (R)	37,788	57.8
	Frank H. Lee (D)	27,387	41.9
16	William E. Barton (D)	25,392	52.4
	Rowland L. Johnston (R)	23,025	47.6

MONTANA

1	John M. Evans (D)	39,166	56.1
	Mark D. Fitzgarrald (R)	29,793	42.7
2	Scott Leavitt (R)	52,943	52.8
	Tom Stout (D)	45,438	45.3

NEBRASKA

1	John H. Morehead (D)	34,662	63.9
	Ralph S. Moseley (R)	19,589	36.1
2	Malcolm Baldridge (R)	34,114	50.6
	Edward R. Burke (D)	33,276	49.4
3	Edgar Howard (D)	53,221	69.3
	H. Halderson (R)	23,599	30.7
4	John N. Norton (D)	35,812	56.0
	Charles H. Sloan (R)	28,196	44.1
5	Ashton C. Shallenberger (D)	34,915	55.6
	Fred G. Johnson (R)	27,932	44.4
6	Robert G. Simmons (R)	65,766	72.8
	John McCoy (D)	24,519	27.2

NEVADA

AL	Samuel S. Arentz (R)	18,279	54.4
	Maurice J. Sullivan (D)	15,343	45.6

NEW HAMPSHIRE

1	Fletcher Hale (R)	37,570	56.3
	Napoleon J. Dyer (D)	29,166	43.7
2	Edward H. Wason (R)	34,253	59.7
	Eaton D. Sargent (D)	23,157	40.3

NEW JERSEY

1	Charles A. Wolverton (R)	78,019	79.1
	Francis G. Homan (D)	19,486	19.8
2	Isaac Bacharach (R)	67,729	79.7
	Hans Froehlicher Jr. (D)	17,125	20.1
3	William H. Sutphin (D)	57,911	51.1
	Thomas M. Gopsill (R)	54,889	48.5
4	Charles A. Eaton (R)	39,019	57.6
	Charles Browne (D)	28,330	41.9
5	Ernest R. Ackerman (R)	65,178	65.3
	Warren N. Gaffney (D)	33,851	33.9
6	Randolph Perkins (R)	72,868	56.5
	Archibald C. Hart (D)	55,283	42.8
7	George N. Seger (R)	35,636	53.7
	Harry Joelson (D)	29,879	45.0
8	Fred A. Hartley Jr. (R)	44,038	50.4
	Paul J. Moore (D)	43,195	49.4
9	Peter A. Cavicchia (R)	24,312	53.8
	Daniel F. Minahan (D)	20,497	45.4
10	Frederick R. Lehlbach (R)	44,435	66.6
	Edward W. Simms (D)	21,539	32.3
11	Oscar L. Auf der Heide (D)	44,691	73.0
	Irving W. Taft (R)	16,087	26.3
12	Mary T. Norton (D)	53,565	75.9
	Douglas D. T. Story (R)	16,715	23.7

NEW MEXICO

AL	Dennis Chavez (D)	65,228	57.5
	Albert G. Simms (R)	47,955	42.3

NEW YORK

	Candidates	Votes	%
1	Robert L. Bacon (R)	96,390	58.4
	James S. Shevlin (D)	64,172	38.9
2	William F. Brunner (D)	110,081	67.5
	James C. MacDevitt (R)	45,651	28.0
3	George W. Lindsay (D)	20,525	75.1
	James A. Campbell (R)	5,159	18.9
	Joseph A. Weil (SOC)	1,443	5.3
4	Thomas H. Cullen (D)	25,935	79.8
	Charles A. Walter (R)	5,713	17.6
5	Loring M. Black Jr. (D)	35,580	63.4
	Henry C. Reiners (R)	18,150	32.3
6	Andrew L. Somers (D)	46,681	47.0
	Joseph G. Myerson (R)	29,862	30.1
	Norman Thomas (SOC)	21,938	22.1
7	John F. Quayle (D)	22,387*	65.0
	Louis W. Arnold Jr. (R)	8,884	25.8
	Benjamin Jackson (SOC)	2,749	8.0
8	Patrick J. Carley (D)	80,119	57.2
	Benjamin Ammerman (R)	36,421	26.0
	Baruch C. Vladeck (SOC)	23,662	16.9
9	David J. O'Connell (D)	48,065*	58.9
	William Koch (R)	27,698	34.0
	Wilhelmus B. Robinson (SOC)	5,783	7.1
10	Emanuel Celler (D)	23,711	58.0
	George J. Beldock (R)	11,532	28.2
	Abraham I. Shiplacoff (SOC)	5,050	12.4
11	Anning S. Prall (D)	37,148	71.1
	Wilbur F. Wakeman (R)	13,856	26.5
12	Samuel Dickstein (D)	14,327	79.1
	Gustave J. Landau (R)	2,663	14.7
	Marx Lewis (SOC)	941	5.2
13	Christopher D. Sullivan (D)	13,034	76.6
	Michael R. Matteo (R)	3,192	18.8
14	William I. Sirovich (D)	12,431	47.3
	Jacob Panken (SOC)	6,793	25.9
	Edward E. Spafford (R)	6,658	25.4
15	John J. Boylan (D)	21,758	81.3
	Alexander Todd (R)	4,377	16.4
16	John J. O'Connor (D)	20,707	72.1
	Irwin Ira Rackoff (R)	7,081	24.7
17	Ruth Baker Pratt (R)	19,913	43.3
	Louis B. Brodsky (D)	19,218	41.8
	Heywood Broun (SOC)	6,841	14.9
18	Martin J. Kennedy (D)	22,131	77.0
	Patrick S. Hickey (R)	5,288	18.4
19	Sol Bloom (D)	35,322	66.9
	Julius D. Tobias (R)	14,919	28.3
20	Fiorello H. LaGuardia (R)	10,606	52.1
	Vincent H. Auleta (D)	8,709	42.8
21	Joseph A. Gavagan (D)	42,468	60.2
	Mortimer Kraus (R)	24,202	34.3
	Frank R. Crosswaith (SOC)	3,699	5.2
22	Anthony J. Griffin (D)	25,198	73.9
	William E. Devlin (R)	7,060	20.7
	Andrew A. MacLean (SOC)	1,832	5.4
23	Frank Oliver (D)	93,426	67.1
	George M. Fayles (R)	27,456	19.7
	Samuel Orr (SOC)	16,539	11.9
24	James M. Fitzpatrick (D)	79,917	57.0
	Benjamin L. Fairchild (R)	48,154	34.3
	Louis Weil (SOC)	12,224	8.7
25	Charles D. Millard (R)	51,332	50.3
	Thomas George Barnes (D)	34,940	34.2
	John M. Holzworth (REPEAL L)	14,086	13.8
26	Hamilton Fish Jr. (R)	46,082	61.1
	John K. Sague (D)	26,545	35.2
27	Harcourt J. Pratt (R)	41,423	52.9
	Guernsey T. Cross (D)	35,574	45.4
28	Parker Corning (D)	74,386	63.5
	Laura B. Treadwell (R)	40,628	34.7
29	James S. Parker (R)	51,341	58.5
	Theodore A. Knapp (D)	35,316	40.2
30	Frank Crowther (R)	36,190	52.1
	Izetta Jewel Miller (D)	31,567	45.4
31	Bertrand H. Snell (R)	36,308	61.8
	Rufus A. Prescott (D)	21,811	37.1

	Candidates	Votes	%
32	Francis D. Culkin (R)	43,625	66.6
	Walter W. Wilcox (D)	20,905	31.9
33	Frederick M. Davenport (R)	39,810	50.3
	James J. Loftis (D&SOC)	39,340	49.7
34	John D. Clarke (R)	51,460	68.2
	James F. Byrne (D)	23,968	31.8
35	Clarence E. Hancock (R)	63,955	57.6
	Frederick B. Northrup (D)	44,336	40.0
36	John Taber (R)	43,132	63.3
	Joseph P. Craugh (D)	23,763	34.9
37	Gale N. Stalker (R)	44,374	59.4
	Julian P. Bretz (D)	28,723	38.4
38	James L. Whitley (R)	50,083	55.3
	Nelson E. Spencer (D)	37,500	41.4
39	Archie D. Sanders (R)	40,069	55.8
	James M. Dwyer (D)	29,610	41.2
40	Walter Gresham Andrews (R)	61,333	63.1
	Roland Crangle (D)	27,268	28.0
	Frank C. Perkins (I CIT AL)	5,126	5.3
41	Edmund F. Cooke (R)	26,995	48.9
	Henry F. Jerge (D)	25,861	46.9
42	James M. Mead (D)	33,195	65.6
	Frank A. Dorn (R)	16,072	31.8
43	Daniel A. Reed (R)	38,913	70.6
	Mattie C. Dellone (D)	14,755	26.8

Special Election

18	Martin J. Kennedy (D)	8,716	80.5
	Bernard Katzen (R)	1,898	17.5

NORTH CAROLINA

1	Lindsay C. Warren (D)	17,985	100.0
2	John H. Kerr (D)	15,987	93.4
	E. Dana Dickens (R)	1,124	6.6
3	Charles L. Abernethy (D)	20,197	66.4
	W. G. Mebane (R)	10,215	33.6
4	Edward W. Pou (D)	25,724	73.4
	John C. Matthews (R)	9,339	26.6
5	Franklin W. Hancock Jr. (D)	54,277	61.3
	John F. Reynolds (R)	34,259	38.7
6	J. Bayard Clark (D)	20,786	71.4
	C. Ed Taylor (R)	8,348	28.7
7	J. Walter Lambeth (D)	38,229	59.0
	Colin G. Spencer (R)	26,583	41.0
8	Robert L. Doughton (D)	44,068	60.1
	E. F. Wakefield (R)	29,307	39.9
9	Alfred L. Bulwinkle (D)	44,699	54.1
	Charles A. Jonas (R)	37,911	45.9
10	Zebulon Weaver (D)	52,964	56.2
	Brownlow Jackson (R)	41,224	43.8

NORTH DAKOTA

1	Olger B. Burtness (R)	42,598	75.0
	J. E. Garvey (D)	14,208	25.0
2	Thomas Hall (R)	33,863	55.6
	P. W. Lanier (D)	25,780	42.3
3	James H. Sinclair (R)	50,917	77.8
	R. H. Leavitt (D)	12,296	18.8

OHIO

1	Nicholas Longworth (R)	50,481	51.8
	John W. Pattison (D)	46,974	48.2
2	William E. Hess (R)	46,347	50.3
	Charles Sawyer (D)	45,761	49.7
3	Byron B. Harlan (D)	62,107	50.8
	Roy G. Fitzgerald (R)	60,249	49.2
4	John L. Cable (R)	43,104	53.4
	Gainor Jennings (D)	37,673	46.6
5	Frank C. Kniffin (D)	29,117	51.4
	Charles J. Thompson (R)	27,497	48.6

OHIO

Candidates	Votes	%
6 James G. Polk (D)	37,158	52.7
Charles C. Kearns (R)	33,300	47.3
7 Charles Brand (R)	50,595	56.4
John L. Zimmerman Jr. (D)	39,142	43.6
8 Grant E. Mouser Jr. (R)	35,663	51.3
Carl W. Smith (D)	33,906	48.7
9 Wilbur M. White (R)	49,498	57.6
Scott Stahl (D)	36,375	42.4
10 Thomas A. Jenkins (R)	31,836	62.4
H. L. Crary (D)	19,157	37.6
11 Mell G. Underwood (D)	37,887	64.0
Ned Thacher (R)	21,339	36.0
12 Arthur P. Lamneck (D)	59,330	57.5
John C. Speaks (R)	43,840	42.5
13 William L. Fiesinger (D)	38,067	52.0
Joe E. Baird (R)	35,199	48.0
14 Francis Seiberling (R)	61,628	50.3
Dow W. Harter (D)	60,951	49.7
15 C. Ellis Moore (R)	35,611	51.2
H. R. McClintock (D)	33,968	48.8
16 C. B. McClintock (R)	51,113	52.0
William R. Thom (D)	47,237	48.0
17 Charles West (D)	45,633	51.4
William M. Morgan (R)	43,197	48.6
18 B. Frank Murphy (R)	47,096	60.5
Emerson Campbell (D)	30,815	39.6
19 John G. Cooper (R)	53,966	56.9
W. B. Kilpatrick (D)	40,960	43.2
20 Charles A. Mooney (D)	42,123	75.3
Max D. Gustin (R)	13,824	24.7
21 Robert Crosser (D)	30,722	51.3
George H. Bender (R)	29,081	48.6
22 Chester C. Bolton (R)	91,222	56.9
Edw. F. Carran (D)	55,868	34.8
Helen Green (I)	13,372	8.3

OKLAHOMA

1 Wesley E. Disney (D)	41,902	50.2
Charles O'Connor (R)	41,642	49.8
2 William W. Hastings (D)	31,093	61.5
E. L. Kirby (R)	19,464	38.5
3 Wilburn Cartwright (D)	39,943	80.4
Palestine Brice (R)	9,721	19.6
4 Thomas D. McKeown (D)	42,885	69.7
M. L. Matson (R)	18,616	30.3
5 Fletcher B. Swank (D)	38,215	58.7
U. S. Stone (R)	26,943	41.4
6 Jed Johnson (D)	35,969	71.7
Ann W. Dillard (R)	14,233	28.4
7 James V. McClintic (D)	29,829	78.2
R. C. Holt (R)	8,298	21.8
8 Milton C. Garber (R)	35,027	60.4
H. B. King (D)	22,784	39.3

OREGON

1 Willis C. Hawley (R)	55,855	55.5
William A. Delzell (D)	44,810	44.5
2 Robert R. Butler (R)	25,304	66.0
Robert E. Bradford (D)	13,061	34.0
3 Charles H. Martin (D)	49,316	55.1
F. F. Korell (R)	35,483	39.7
Peter Streiff Jr. (I SOC)	4,690	5.2

PENNSYLVANIA

1 James M. Beck (R)	57,382	78.9
John P. Mulrenan (D)	14,918	20.5
2 George S. Graham (R)	34,387	84.6
Charles S. Hill (D)	6,084	15.0
3 Harry C. Ransley (R)	38,346	84.4
Edward P. Carroll (D)	6,921	15.2
4 Benjamin M. Golder (R)	41,549	78.0
Thomas J. Carroll (D)	11,084	20.8
5 James J. Connolly (R)	57,501	76.6
Frank W. Dougherty (D)	17,182	22.9

Candidates	Votes	%
6 George A. Welsh (R)	66,799	76.1
John P. Boylan (D)	21,004	23.9
7 George P. Darrow (R)	61,573	77.5
Robert V. Bolger (D)	17,860	22.5
8 James Wolfenden (R)	84,521	80.5
Harry D. Wescott (D)	20,443	19.5
9 Henry W. Watson (R)	63,286	73.0
John F. Headly (D)	23,375	27.0
10 J. Roland Kinzer (R)	32,455	77.3
William A. Brinkman (D)	9,547	22.7
11 Patrick J. Boland (D, R)	62,994	100.0
12 C. Murray Turpin (R)	53,336	57.8
John T. Kmetz (D, LAB)	38,938	42.2
13 George Franklin Brumm (R, D)	47,344	92.3
William Wilhelm (U)	3,968	7.7
14 Norton L. Lichtenwalner (D)	44,546	52.4
Robert Grey Bushong (R)	29,164	34.3
Andrew P. Bower (SOC)	11,309	13.3
15 Louis T. McFadden (R, P)	29,150	72.6
Frank J. Price (D)	10,998	27.4
16 Robert F. Rich (R)	32,964	75.5
J. Drew Fague (D)	10,719	24.5
17 Frederick W. Magrady (R)	31,247	60.5
Samuel M. Shipman (D, L)	20,413	39.5
18 Edward M. Beers (R)	39,116	68.0
T. Z. Minehart (D)	18,389	32.0
19 Isaac H. Doutrich (R)	64,345	79.4
Harold V. McNair (D)	16,685	20.6
20 J. Russell Leech (R, P)	20,361	54.9
George E. Wolfe (D, LAB)	16,740	45.1
21 J. Banks Kurtz (R)	25,619	71.8
Bernard J. Clark (D)	10,045	28.2
22 Harry L. Haines (D)	27,943	54.4
Franklin Menges (R)	22,716	44.2
23 J. Mitchell Chase (R)	28,916	70.8
Maxwell J. Moore (D)	11,954	29.3
24 Samuel A. Kendall (R)	28,279	67.6
Milton M. Brooke (D)	13,581	32.4
25 Henry W. Temple (R, LAB)	27,561	69.8
James S. Pates (D)	11,910	30.2
26 J. Howard Swick (R, D)	50,858	100.0
27 Nathan L. Strong (R)	42,569	79.2
D. R. Tomb (D)	11,200	20.8
28 Thomas C. Cochran (R)	36,367	70.9
Guy Thorne (D)	14,953	29.1
29 Milton W. Shreve (R)	24,511	54.5
Charles N. Crosby (D)	20,470	45.5
30 William R. Coyle (R)	28,503	50.8
Everett Kent (D)	27,621	49.2
31 Adam M. Wyant (R, P)	38,999	70.5
James M. Cramer (D)	15,022	27.2
32 Edmund F. Erk (R)	36,355	82.6
Edward S. Michalowski (D)	7,294	16.6
33 M. Clyde Kelly (R, D)	47,187	96.4
34 Patrick J. Sullivan (R, D)	29,074	97.6
35 Harry A. Estep (R)	31,172	81.6
John Murphy (D)	7,005	18.3
36 Guy E. Campbell (R, D)	46,172	99.9

Special Elections

16 Robert F. Rich (R)	32,393	99.5
32 Edmund F. Erk (R)	35,176	99.9

RHODE ISLAND

1 Clark Burdick (R)	39,712	57.5
Samuel W. Smith Jr. (D)	29,341	42.5
2 Richard S. Aldrich (R)	40,037	54.7
Arthur L. Conaty (D)	33,164	45.3
3 Francis B. Condon (D)	43,463	56.4
William R. Fortin (R)	33,605	43.6

Special Election

3 Francis Condon (D)	43,429	56.5
William R. Fortin (R)	33,387	43.5

SOUTH CAROLINA

Candidates	Votes	%
1 Thomas S. McMillan (D)	2,536	100.0
2 Butler B. Hare (D)	2,149	100.0
3 Fred H. Dominick (D)	2,221	100.0
4 John J. McSwain (D)	3,685	100.0
5 William F. Stevenson (D)	2,319	100.0
6 Allard H. Gasque (D)	1,881	100.0
7 Hampton P. Fulmer (D)	1,372	100.0

SOUTH DAKOTA

1 Charles A. Christopherson (R)	41,151	84.7
Henry Borman (I)	7,451	15.3
2 Royal C. Johnson (R)	38,195	52.4
Fred H. Hildebrandt (D)	34,245	47.0
3 William Williamson (R)	27,083	55.8
Theodore B. Werner (D)	21,473	44.2

TENNESSEE

1 Oscar B. Lovette (IR)	20,893	53.4
B. Carroll Reece (R)	18,241	46.6
2 J. Will Taylor (R)	17,831	55.5
E. E. Patton (IR)	13,355	41.6
3 Sam D. McReynolds (D)	21,401	100.0
4 John R. Mitchell (D)	15,269	100.0
5 Ewin L. Davis (D)	11,792	92.0
George Motlow (R)	1,032	8.1
6 Joseph W. Byrns (D)	13,879	93.3
E. L. Bradbury (I)	990	6.7
7 Edward E. Eslick (D)	13,927	100.0
8 Gordon Browning (D)	14,024	100.0
9 Jere Cooper (D)	17,979	100.0
10 Edward H. Crump (D)	23,746	93.7

TEXAS

1 Wright Patman (D)	9,160	94.7
Thomas A. Clark (R)	515	5.3
2 Martin Dies (D)	14,236	100.0
3 Morgan G. Sanders (D)	8,162	100.0
4 Sam Rayburn (D)	9,385	88.8
Floyd Harry (R)	1,189	11.2
5 Hatton W. Sumners (D)	9,924	88.1
Clinton S. Bailey (R)	1,344	11.9
6 Luther A. Johnson (D)	12,396	100.0
7 Clay Stone Briggs (D)	9,357	100.0
8 Daniel E. Garrett (D)	12,877	100.0
9 Joseph J. Mansfield (D)	14,855	86.9
George Seydler Sr. (R)	2,239	13.1
10 James P. Buchanan (D)	12,780	100.0
11 Oliver H. Cross (D)	10,381	100.0
12 Fritz G. Lanham (D)	9,846	100.0
13 Guinn Williams (D)	12,840	91.1
W. C. Witcher (R)	1,257	8.9
14 Harry M. Wurzbach (R)	27,206	59.3
Henry B. Dielmann (D)	18,707	40.7
15 John N. Garner (D)	20,733	77.5
Carlos G. Watson (R)	6,016	22.5
16 R. Ewing Thomason (D)	18,915	84.1
Mitchell Waldrop (R)	3,581	15.9
17 Thomas L. Blanton (D)	17,199	100.0
18 Marvin Jones (D)	26,697	93.3
S. E. Fish (R)	1,934	6.8

Special Election

17 Thomas L. Blanton (D)	10,225	56.1
Mrs. R. Q. Lee	8,012	43.9

UTAH

1 Don B. Colton (R)	45,875	60.8
Joseph Ririe (D)	29,210	38.7
2 Frederick C. Loofbourow (R)	35,106	44.3
Joshua H. Paul (D)	33,618	42.4
George N. Lawrence (LIB)	10,303	13.0

UTAH

Special Election

2	Frederick C. Loofbourow (R)	35,349	44.1
	Joshua H. Paul (D)	33,915	42.3
	George N. Lawrence (LIB)	10,591	13.2

VERMONT

1	John E. Weeks (R)	25,170	58.0
	Joseph A. McNamara (D)	18,205	42.0
2	Ernest W. Gibson (R)	23,904	81.2
	James Cosgrove (D)	5,536	18.8

VIRGINIA

1	Schuyler Otis Bland (D)	7,324	91.0
	W. A. Rowe	705	8.8
2	Menalcus Lankford (R)	14,678	54.4
	Joseph T. Deal (D)	12,297	45.6
3	Andrew Jackson Montague (D)	6,134	87.4
	R. Houston Brett (IR)	853	12.2
4	Patrick Henry Drewry (D)	4,296	99.9
5	Thomas G. Burch (D)	7,095	99.9
6	Clifton A. Woodrum (D)	5,979	99.7
7	John W. Fishburne (D)	13,951	58.4
	Jacob A. Garber (R)	9,934	41.6
8	Howard W. Smith (D)	11,201	79.3
	F. M. Brooks (R)	2,742	19.4
9	John W. Flannagan Jr. (D)	32,802	55.6
	Joseph C. Shaffer (R)	26,244	44.5

Candidates		Votes	%
10	Henry St.George Tucker (D)	7,229	85.9
	Carney Kelly Rosser (IR)	620	7.4
	M. J. Putman (R)	563	6.7

WASHINGTON

1	Ralph A. Horr (R)	43,998	55.8
	Charles G. Heifner (D)	32,365	41.0
2	Lindley H. Hadley (R)	47,679	89.7
	William M. Bouck (F-LAB)	3,428	6.5
3	Albert Johnson (R)	63,451	100.0
4	John W. Summers (R)	35,917	100.0
5	Sam B. Hill (D)	43,059	74.3
	T. W. Symons Jr. (R)	14,892	25.7

WEST VIRGINIA

1	Carl G. Bachmann (R)	43,919	56.1
	Robert L. Ramsey (D)	34,368	43.9
2	Frank L. Bowman (R)	36,079	50.8
	Jennings Randolph (D)	34,968	49.2
3	Lynn S. Hornor (D)	37,970	51.4
	John M. Wolverton (R)	35,853	48.6
4	Robert L. Hogg (R)	43,152	50.3
	Mary M. Johnson (D)	42,677	49.7
5	Hugh Ike Shott (R)	44,978	52.2
	T. J. Lilly (D)	41,162	47.8
6	Joe L. Smith (D)	80,648	56.6
	Fred O. Blue (R)	61,876	43.4

Special

4	Robert L. Hogg (R)	41,455	53.8
	Mary M. Johnson (D)	35,649	46.2

WISCONSIN

Candidates		Votes	%
1	Henry Allen Cooper (R)	46,272*	95.7
2	Charles A. Kading (R)	37,071	71.5
	A. A. Nowak (D)	14,780	28.5
3	John M. Nelson (R)	43,184	95.1
4	John C. Schafer (R)	26,763	46.6
	William F. Quick Sr. (SOC)	20,789	36.2
	William J. Kershaw (D)	8,871	15.5
5	William H. Stafford (R)	27,533	42.2
	James P. Sheehan (SOC)	26,357#	40.4
	Thomas O'Malley (D)	10,947	16.8
6	Michael K. Reilly (D)	25,605	50.2
	Philip Lehner (R)	24,986	49.0
7	Gardner R. Withrow (R)	31,530	82.3
	Merlin Hull (R)	5,606	14.6
8	Gerald J. Boileau (R)	30,045	79.1
	William F. Collins (R)	7,927	20.9
9	George J. Schneider (R)	43,080	100.0
10	James A. Frear (R)	36,804	97.5
11	Hubert H. Peavey (R)	43,004	100.0

Special Election

6	Michael K. Reilly (D)	25,400	50.6
	Philip Lehner (R)	24,825	49.4

WYOMING

AL	Vincent M. Carter (R)	44,890	65.6
	John P. Rusk (D)	23,519	34.4

1931 House Elections

LOUISIANA

Special Elections

8	John H. Overton (D)	4,674	99.9

NEW YORK [1]

Special Elections

7	Matthew V. O'Malley (D)	9,969	70.0
	Leonard Greenstone (R)	4,014	28.2
7	John J. Delaney (D)	24,587	69.3
	William L. Padgett (R)	7,840	22.1
	Abraham Zucker (SOC)	2,724	7.7

9	Stephen A. Rudd (D)	15,342	71.5
	William Koch (R)	5,605	26.1

TEXAS

Special Election

14	Richard M. Kleberg (D)	19,038	46.9
	C. W. Johnson	13,945	34.4
	C. W. Anderson	5,759	14.2

WISCONSIN

Special Election

1	Thomas R. Amlie (R)	14,447	54.4
	O. J. Bouma (SOC)	7,282	27.4
	G. H. Herzog (ID)	3,440	13.0

1. *Rep. John F. Quayle died Nov. 27, 1930, following his re-election to the 72nd Congress (1931-33). According to the Biographical Directory, Matthew V. O'Malley was elected Feb. 17, 1931 to fill Quayle's seat for the term beginning March 4, 1931. O'Malley died May 26, 1931. In a second special election, John J. Delaney was elected to fill the seat for the remainder of the term.*

1932 House Elections

ALABAMA

	Candidates	Votes	%
1	John D. McDuffie (D)	20,675	100.0
2	Lister Hill (D)	28,250	95.7
3	Henry B. Steagall (D)	20,959	100.0
4	Lamar Jeffers (D)	20,960	83.9
	Hogan D. Stewart (R)	4,016	16.1
5	Miles C. Allgood (D)	24,783	80.2
	Joe Brown (R)	6,135	19.8
6	William B. Oliver (D)	15,296	100.0
7	William B. Bankhead (D)	21,322	73.5
	James B. Sloan (R)	7,699	26.5
8	Edward B. Almon (D)	23,705	100.0
9	George Huddleston (D)	31,539	86.2
	Paul G. Parsons (R)	3,701	10.1

ARIZONA

	Candidates	Votes	%
AL	Lewis W. Douglas (D)	75,469*	70.8
	H. B. Wilkinson (R)	29,710	27.9

ARKANSAS

	Candidates	Votes	%
1	William J. Driver (D)	35,975	100.0
2	John E. Miller (D)	23,351	92.1
	Ira J. Mock (R)	1,995	7.9
3	Claude A. Fuller (D)	30,337	100.0
4	William B. Cravens (D)	30,443	100.0
5	Heartsill Ragon (D)	29,240	90.7
	A. L. Barber (R)	3,001	9.3
6	David D. Glover (D)	33,503	100.0
7	Tilman B. Parks (D)	30,340	100.0

CALIFORNIA

	Candidates	Votes	%
1	Clarence F. Lea (D-R)	73,400	99.9
2	Harry L. Englebright (R-D)	43,146	100.0
3	Frank H. Buck (D)	61,694	56.8
	Charles F. Curry (R)	46,887	43.1
4	Florence P. Kahn (R-D)	67,425	85.3
	Milen C. Dempster (SOC)	11,603	14.7
5	Richard J. Welch (R-D)	67,349	100.0
6	Albert E. Carter (R-D)	75,528	99.9
7	Ralph R. Eltse (R)	45,944	45.5
	Frank V. Cornish (D)	32,365	32.0
	J. Stitt Wilson (SOC)	22,767	22.5
8	John J. McGrath (D)	65,455	56.9
	Arthur M. Free (R)	49,487	43.1
9	Denver S. Church (D)	50,125	61.6
	Henry E. Barbour (R)	31,209	38.4
10	Henry E. Stubbs (D)	50,390	55.3
	Arthur S. Crites (R)	40,794	44.7
11	William E. Evans (R)	57,739	51.8
	Albert D. Hadley (D)	38,240	34.3
	Marshall V. Hartranft (LIB)	15,520	13.9
12	John H. Hoeppel (D)	43,122	45.8
	Frederick F. Houser (R)	40,674	43.2
	Richard M. Cannon (P)	10,308	11.0
13	Charles Kramer (D)	65,261	52.6
	Charles H. Randall (R)	53,449	43.1
14	Thomas F. Ford (D)	47,368	57.1
	William D. Campbell (R)	35,598	42.9
15	William L. Traeger (R)	67,390	52.8
	John M. Costello (D)	57,518	45.1
16	John F. Dockweiler (D)	70,333	54.9
	Clyde Woodworth (R)	57,718	45.1
17	Charles J. Colden (D)	50,720	62.2
	A. E. Henning (R)	26,868	32.9
18	John H. Burke (D)	48,179	53.2
	Robert Henderson (R)	33,817	37.4
	William E. Hinshaw (I)	8,399	9.3

	Candidates	Votes	%
19	Sam L. Collins (R)	56,889	51.0
	B. Z. McKinney (D)	51,796	46.4
20	George Burnham (R)	43,757	50.3
	Claude Chandler (D)	43,304	49.7

COLORADO

	Candidates	Votes	%
1	Lawrence Lewis (D)	70,826	54.4
	William R. Eaton (R)	56,601	43.5
2	Fred Cummings (D)	63,399	52.9
	George H. Bradfield (R)	56,516	47.1
3	John A. Martin (D)	59,882	50.9
	Guy U. Hardy (R)	57,793	49.1
4	Edward T. Taylor (D)	40,736	66.0
	Richard C. Callen (R)	20,993	34.0

CONNECTICUT

	Candidates	Votes	%
1	Herman P. Kopplemann (D)	72,807	48.8
	Clarence W. Seymour (R)	70,920	47.5
2	William L. Higgins (R)	45,232	49.4
	William C. Fox (D)	45,011	49.2
3	Francis T. Maloney (D)	57,881	48.4
	T. A. D. Jones (R)	55,254	46.2
4	Schuyler Merritt (R)	71,670	49.7
	William M. Tierney (D)	64,268	44.5
	Arnold E. Freese (SOC)	7,237	5.0
5	Edward W. Goss (R)	42,132	49.3
	Martin E. Gormley (D)	42,054	49.2
AL	Charles M. Bakewell (R)	284,438	48.5
	William M. Citron (D)	282,557	48.2

DELAWARE

	Candidates	Votes	%
AL	Wilbur L. Adams (D)	51,698	46.1
	Reuben Satterthwaite Jr (R)	48,841	43.6
	Francis Burgette Short (P)	10,560	9.4

FLORIDA

	Candidates	Votes	%
1	J. Hardin Peterson (D)	61,381	76.4
	Arthur R. Thompson (R)	19,010	23.7
2	Robert A. Green (D)	22,213	100.0
3	Millard F. Caldwell (D)	28,208	100.0
4	J. Mark Wilcox (D)	86,101	99.6
AL	William J. Sears (D)	186,284	75.2
	Glenn B. Skipper (R)	61,300	24.8

GEORGIA

	Candidates	Votes	%
1	Homer C. Parker (D)	24,429	93.4
	E. K. Overstreet Jr. (R)	1,726	6.6
2	E. E. Cox (D)	22,446	100.0
3	B. T. Castellow (D)	22,691	100.0
4	Emmett M. Owen (D)	24,783	99.9
5	Robert Ramspeck (D)	26,657	100.0
6	Carl Vinson (D)	19,615	99.9
7	M. C. Tarver (D)	24,689	85.2
	Regina Rambo Benson (I)	4,295	14.8
8	Braswell Deen (D)	20,021	95.6
9	John S. Wood (D)	24,673	80.6
	J. M. Johnson (R)	5,898	19.3
10	Charles H. Brand (D)	23,911	100.0

IDAHO

	Candidates	Votes	%
1	Compton I. White (D)	42,784	54.9
	Burton L. French (R)	32,545	41.8
2	Thomas C. Coffin (D)	58,138	55.0
	Addison T. Smith (R)	46,293	43.8

ILLINOIS

	Candidates	Votes	%
1	Oscar De Priest (R)	33,672	54.8
	Harry Baker (D)	26,959	43.9
2	P. H. Moynihan (R)	113,447	50.8
	Victor L. Schlaeger (D)	102,099	45.7
3	Edward A. Kelly (D)	120,093	55.8
	Elliott W. Sproul (R)	95,282	44.2
4	Harry P. Beam (D)	53,722	74.2
	Casimir T. Janowski (R)	18,659	25.8
5	Adolph J. Sabath (D)	30,747	70.9
	Samuel S. Epstein (R)	12,254	28.3
6	Thomas J. O'Brien (D)	164,187	63.2
	Alfred F. Rueben (R)	95,637	36.8
7	Leonard W. Schuetz (D)	190,446	58.1
	M. A. Michaelson (R)	134,801	41.1
8	Leo Kocialkowski (D)	30,147	72.2
	Peter C. Granata (R)	11,625	27.8
9	Fred A. Britten (R)	40,253	52.0
	James McAndrews (D)	36,596	47.3
10	James Simpson Jr. (R)	101,671	41.1
	Charles H. Weber (D)	100,449	40.6
	Ralph E. Church (I)	45,067	18.2
11	Frank R. Reid (R)	82,195	50.4
	James A. Howell (D)	80,862	49.6
12	John T. Buckbee (R)	65,122	53.1
	Charles H. Linscott (D)	57,578	46.9
13	Leo E. Allen (R)	44,655	56.1
	Orestes H. Wright (D)	34,917	43.9
14	Chester Thompson (D)	50,277	53.9
	John C. Allen (R)	43,082	46.2
15	J. Leroy Adair (D)	55,739	56.9
	Burnett M. Chiperfield (R)	42,255	43.1
16	Everett M. Dirksen (R)	67,949	60.3
	Edwin S. Carr (D)	44,802	39.7
17	Frank Gillespie (D)	43,198	53.5
	Homer W. Hall (R)	37,594	46.5
18	James A. Meeks (D)	58,483	56.6
	William P. Holaday (R)	44,787	43.4
19	D. C. Dobbins (D)	72,366	57.7
	Charles Adkins (R)	53,151	42.4
20	Henry T. Rainey (D)	48,612	63.8
	William J. Thornton (R)	27,540	36.2
21	J. Earl Major (D)	66,213	59.8
	Roy M. Seeley (R)	44,430	40.1
22	Edwin M. Schaefer (D)	88,151	63.8
	Stewart Campbell (R)	49,965	36.2
23	William W. Arnold (D)	64,551	64.3
	T. Edward Austin (R)	35,885	35.7
24	Claude V. Parsons (D)	43,107	58.8
	Arthur A. Miles (R)	30,175	41.2
25	Kent E. Keller (D)	64,286	59.6
	Edward E. Denison (R)	43,580	40.4
AL	Martin A. Brennan (D)	1,676,274✓	
	Walter Nesbit (D)	1,655,147✓	
	Richard Yates (R)	1,421,221	
	Julius Klein (R)	1,406,771	
	Hyman Schneid (SOC)	38,486	
	George Koop (SOC)	36,324	
	Anthony Pszczolkowski (COM)	11,243	
	Leslie Raymond Hurt (COM)	11,019	
	W. F. Alexander (SOC LAB)	2,837	
	Clifton Crawford (SOC LAB)	2,684	
	Pasquale Iovino (I)	1,067	

INDIANA

	Candidates	Votes	%
1	William T. Schulte (D)	45,473	50.0
	Oscar A. Ahlgren (R)	42,575	46.8
2	George R. Durgan (D)	73,357	54.0
	William R. Wood (R)	61,897	45.6
3	Samuel B. Pettengill (D)	67,686	55.1
	Andrew J. Hickey (R)	52,965	43.2

INDIANA

Candidates	Votes	%
4 James I. Farley (D)	73,258	56.1
David Hogg (R)	56,602	43.3
5 Glenn Griswold (D)	70,698	53.5
J. Raymond Schutz (R)	59,904	45.3
6 Virginia E. Jenckes (D)	74,827	53.6
Fred S. Purnell (R)	64,081	45.9
7 Arthur H. Greenwood (D)	78,356	56.7
George W. Henley (R)	59,949	43.4
8 John W. Boehne Jr. (D)	83,396	63.5
French Clements (R)	48,031	36.6
9 Eugene B. Crowe (D)	76,157	57.5
Chester A. Davis (R)	55,868	42.2
10 Finly H. Gray (D)	68,974	52.0
Ephriam F. Bowen (R)	63,398	47.8
11 William H. Larrabee (D)	67,871	54.2
Dale B. Spencer (R)	57,006	45.5
12 Louis Ludlow (D)	70,128	52.1
William H. Harrison (R)	61,241	45.5

IOWA

Candidates	Votes	%
1 Edward C. Eicher (D)	55,378	54.2
W. F. Kopp (R)	46,738	45.8
2 Bernhard M. Jacobsen (D)	71,914	58.7
Frank Elliott (R)	50,636	41.3
3 Albert C. Willford (D)	48,939	50.6
T. J. B. Robinson (R)	47,776	49.4
4 Fred Biermann (D)	62,598	59.7
Gilbert N. Haugen (R)	42,217	40.3
5 Lloyd Thurston (R)	51,909	50.1
Lloyd Ellis (D)	51,732	49.9
6 Cassius C. Dowell (R)	56,962	56.5
Charles S. Cooter (D)	43,891	43.5
7 Otha D. Wearin (D)	57,803	56.3
Charles E. Swanson (R)	44,925	43.7
8 Fred C. Gilchrist (R)	47,834	53.4
William T. Branagan (D)	41,772	46.6
9 Guy M. Gillette (D)	61,755	54.9
Ed. H. Campbell (R)	50,796	45.1

KANSAS

Candidates	Votes	%
1 William P. Lambertson (R)	59,241	57.8
M. R. Howard (D)	34,244	33.4
George C. Hall (I)	9,019	8.8
2 Ulysses S. Guyer (R)	60,902	51.7
B. J. Sheridan (D)	56,805	48.3
3 Harold McGugin (R)	52,881	52.9
E. W. Patterson (D)	44,910	44.9
4 William Randolph Carpenter (D)	45,246	50.2
Homer Hoch (R)	44,621	49.5
5 William A. Ayres (D)	65,713	73.9
W. L. Farquharson (R)	23,176	26.1
6 Kathryn E. O'Loughlin (D)	62,818	55.6
Charles I. Sparks (R)	50,242	44.4
7 Clifford R. Hope (R)	59,269	55.6
Aaron Coleman (D)	47,418	44.5

KENTUCKY

Candidates	Votes	%
AL Fred M. Vinson (D)	575,289✔	
John Young Brown (D)	574,278✔	
Brent Spence (D)	574,035✔	
Andrew J. May (D)	573,966✔	
Virgil Chapman (D)	573,719✔	
Glover H. Cary (D)	573,504✔	
William V. Gregory (D)	573,233✔	
Cap R. Carden (D)	573,219✔	
Finley Hamilton (D)	573,061✔	
Hillard H. Smith (R)	391,878	
Robert Blackburn (R)	391,673	
William Lewis (R)	390,977	
George P. Ellison (R)	390,839	
D. E. McClure (R)	390,474	
J. C. Speight (R)	390,370	
Hugh H. Asher (R)	390,148	
B. T. Rountree (R)	390,141	

Candidates	Votes	%
Frank B. Russell (R)	389,950	
J. T. Scopes (SOC)	3,273	
W. G. Haag (SOC)	3,261	
C. E. Trimble (SOC)	3,260	
E. L. Nance (SOC)	3,256	
E. C. Schulz (SOC)	3,256	
J. J. Thobe (SOC)	3,246	
J. M. Woodward (SOC)	3,237	
H. L. Harwood (SOC)	3,236	
D. S. Bennett (SOC)	3,234	
Frank Reynolds (COM)	241	
George N. Conway (COM)	236	

LOUISIANA

Candidates	Votes	%
1 Joachim O. Fernandez (D)	48,784	100.0
2 Paul H. Maloney (D)	50,327	100.0
3 Numa F. Montet (D)	18,340	100.0
4 John N. Sandlin (D)	26,262	100.0
5 Riley J. Wilson (D)	25,853	100.0
6 Bolivar E. Kemp (D)	25,238	100.0
7 Rene L. DeRouen (D)	24,233	100.0
8 Cleveland Dear (D)	25,644	100.0

MAINE

Candidates	Votes	%
1 Carroll L. Beedy (R)	41,034	51.0
Joseph E. F. Connolly (D)	39,381	49.0
2 Edward C. Moran (D)	44,490	51.8
John E. Nelson (R)	40,703	47.4
3 John G. Utterback (D)	34,520	50.1
Ralph O. Brewster (R)	34,226	49.6

MARYLAND

Candidates	Votes	%
1 T. Alan Goldsborough (D)	39,471	64.9
Harry T. Phoebus (R)	21,387	35.1
2 William P. Cole Jr. (D)	87,841	67.3
David L. Elliott (R)	42,740	32.7
3 Vincent L. Palmisano (D)	34,724	72.8
R. Palmer Ingram (R)	11,370	23.8
4 Ambrose J. Kennedy (D)	46,463	66.0
Claude B. Sweezey (R)	22,231	31.6
5 Stephen W. Gambrill (D)	42,329	70.4
A. Kingsley Love (R)	17,835	29.6
6 David J. Lewis (D)	49,126	58.4
Harold C. Smith (R)	34,989	41.6

Special Election

Candidates	Votes	%
4 Ambrose J. Kennedy (D)	46,781	100.0

MASSACHUSETTS

Candidates	Votes	%
1 Allen T. Treadway (R)	56,767	54.7
Thomas F. Cassidy (D)	44,211	42.6
2 William J. Granfield (D)	52,346	49.9
Joshua L. Brooks (R)	47,920	45.7
3 Frank H. Foss (R)	50,617	51.5
M. Fred O'Connell (D)	47,632	48.5
4 Pehr G. Holmes (R)	56,408	55.0
John Walsh (D)	46,081	45.0
5 Edith Nourse Rogers (R)	74,459	59.9
James J. Bruin (D)	49,788	40.1
6 A. Piatt Andrew (R)	65,728	67.7
James D. Burns (D)	31,416	32.3
7 William P. Connery Jr. (D)	61,591	56.6
Charles W. Lovett (R)	44,331	40.7
8 Arthur D. Healey (D)	50,266	51.1
George H. Norton (R)	48,070	48.9
9 Robert Luce (R)	61,178	51.4
Frederick S. Deitrick (D)	56,425	47.4
10 George Holden Tinkham (R)	60,926	60.3
John Crehan (D)	40,099	39.7
11 John J. Douglass (D)	45,343	85.7
William F. McDonald (R)	7,583	14.3
12 John W. McCormack (D)	69,994	72.9
Bernard Ginsburg (R)	25,995	27.1

Candidates	Votes	%
13 Richard B. Wigglesworth (R)	64,589	58.4
Edward G. Morris (D)	45,964	41.6
14 Joseph William Martin Jr. (R)	51,680	56.8
Andrew J. McGraw (D)	39,259	43.2
15 Charles L. Gifford (R)	53,066	57.5
Thomas H. Buckley (D)	36,556	39.6

MICHIGAN

Candidates	Votes	%
1 George G. Sadowski (D)	51,620	68.1
Charles H. Mahoney (R)	21,764	28.7
2 John C. Lehr (D)	51,592	50.6
Earl C. Michener (R)	49,257	48.3
3 Joseph L. Hooper (R)	49,383	50.2
Charles E. Gauss (D)	46,093	46.9
4 George Foulkes (D)	46,927	51.6
John C. Ketcham (R)	42,922	47.2
5 Carl E. Mapes (R)	52,870	51.3
Winfield H. Caslow (D)	48,686	47.3
6 Claude E. Cady (D)	55,478	47.8
Seymour H. Person (R)	45,818	39.5
Grant M. Hudson (R)	14,541	12.5
7 Jesse P. Wolcott (R)	51,974	56.1
James G. Tucker (D)	38,738	41.8
8 Michael J. Hart (D)	53,959	53.5
William M. Smith (R)	45,263	44.9
9 Harry W. Musselwhite (D)	40,200	52.2
James C. McLaughlin (R)	36,434	47.3
10 Roy O. Woodruff (R)	38,937	54.0
William J. Kelly (D)	32,376	44.9
11 Prentiss M. Brown (D)	39,261	50.1
Frank P. Bohn (R)	37,311	47.6
12 W. Frank James (R)	48,014	62.5
Levi S. Rice (D)	26,925	35.0
13 Clarence J. McLeod (R)	50,437	52.4
Clarence E. Seebaldt (D)	43,374	45.1
14 Carl M. Weideman (D)	53,789	50.4
Robert H. Clancy (R)	50,491	47.3
15 John D. Dingell (D)	52,376	48.3
Charles Bowles (R)	49,801	46.0
16 John Lesinski (D)	43,369	53.0
Frank P. Darin (R)	36,174	44.2
17 George A. Dondero (R)	51,918	52.6
Harry Mitchell (D)	44,325	44.9

MINNESOTA

Candidates	Votes	%
AL Magnus Johnson (F-LAB)	388,616✔	
Paul John Kvale (F-LAB)	380,444✔	
Henry Arens (F-LAB)	361,724✔	
Ernest Lundeen (F-LAB)	350,455✔	
Theodore Christianson (R)	337,110✔	
Einar Hoidale (D)	321,949✔	
Ray P. Chase (R)	321,102✔	
Francis H. Shoemaker (F-LAB)	317,109✔	
Harold Knutson (R)	313,221✔	
August H. Andresen (R)	312,198	
W. I. Nolan (R)	306,266	
Conrad G. Selvig (R)	304,846	
J. A. A. Burnquist (R)	302,356	
J. L. Peterson (F-LAB)	298,331	
Henry G. Teigan (F-LAB)	291,837	
C. F. Gaarenstroom (F-LAB)	291,687	
William A. Pittenger (R)	291,478	
N. J. Holmberg (R)	287,381	
A. C. Townley (F-LAB)	261,120	
Robert C. Bell (D)	237,881	
John P. Coughlin (D)	214,462	
Silas M. Bryan (D)	207,419	
Emil E. Holmes (D)	205,673	
James R. Bennett (D)	198,421	
Donald A. Chapman (D)	190,530	
Hugh T. Kennedy (D)	186,466	
John Bowe (D)	184,587	
Victor Christgau (STICKER)	82,826	

MINNESOTA

Candidates	Votes	%
J. W. Anderson (COM)	16,299	
M. Karson (COM)	9,573	
Fred Lequier (COM)	8,927	
Melvin Maas (STICKER)	784	

MISSISSIPPI

		Votes	%
1	John E. Rankin (D)	19,549	97.0
2	Wall Doxey (D)	15,092	98.5
3	Will M. Whittington (D)	13,562	95.8
4	Jeff Busby (D)	14,072	97.8
5	Ross A. Collins (D)	19,123	97.1
6	William M. Colmer (D)	22,831	94.5
7	Russell Ellzey (D)	25,725	95.6

MISSOURI

		Votes	%
AL	John J. Cochran (D)	1,013,824✔	
	James R. Claiborne (D)	1,004,170✔	
	Joseph B. Shannon (D)	1,002,545✔	
	Clyde Williams (D)	1,000,218✔	
	Clarence Cannon (D)	997,642✔	
	Frank H. Lee (D)	997,148✔	
	James E. Ruffin (D)	996,969✔	
	Ralph F. Lozier (D)	995,676✔	
	Jacob L. Milligan (D)	995,002✔	
	Reuben T. Wood (D)	994,487✔	
	Milton A. Romjue (D)	994,123✔	
	Richard M. Duncan (D)	988,200✔	
	Clement C. Dickinson (D)	981,847✔	
	Leonidas C. Dyer (R)	609,268	
	Henry F. Niedringhaus (R)	603,345	
	James Stewart (R)	589,615	
	John M. Hadley (R)	589,205	
	Carl Otto (R)	588,647	
	Louis E. Miller (R)	588,246	
	Phil A. Bennett (R)	586,272	
	Sam A. Clark (R)	586,215	
	Joe J. Manlove (R)	585,840	
	Rowland L. Johnston (R)	584,256	
	David Hopkins (R)	582,662	
	John W. Palmer (R)	582,324	
	Manvel H. Davis (R)	578,995	
	Phillips (SOC)	11,658	
	Morrison (SOC)	11,637	
	Langley (SOC)	11,625	
	Becker (SOC)	11,606	
	Elliff (SOC)	11,598	
	Anderson (SOC)	11,573	
	Henschel (SOC)	11,571	
	Davidson (SOC)	11,543	
	Turner (SOC)	11,493	
	Hill (SOC)	11,459	
	Harrison (SOC)	11,417	
	Shumaker (SOC)	11,356	
	Thayer (SOC)	11,324	
	Benz (COM)	627	

MONTANA

		Votes	%
1	Joseph P. Monaghan (D)	51,159	59.0
	Mark D. Fitzgarrald (R)	33,333	38.4
2	Roy E. Ayers (D)	64,103	52.5
	Scott Leavitt (R)	53,890	44.1

NEBRASKA

		Votes	%
1	John H. Morehead (D)	63,022	58.0
	Marcus L. Poteet (R)	43,653	40.2
2	Edward R. Burke (D)	51,728	51.3
	Malcolm Baldridge (R)	44,209	43.8
3	Edgar Howard (D)	74,207	66.0
	H. Halderson (R)	32,954	29.3
4	Ashton C. Shallenberger (D)	53,713	44.8
	Fred G. Johnson (R)	38,938	32.5
	Charles G. Binderup	21,100	17.6

	Candidates	Votes	%
5	Terry Carpenter (D)	53,586	51.3
	Robert G. Simmons (R)	49,200	47.1

NEVADA

		Votes	%
AL	James G. Scrugham (D)	24,979	60.8
	Samuel S. Arentz (R)	16,133	39.2

NEW HAMPSHIRE

		Votes	%
1	William N. Rogers (D)	50,306	51.3
	William P. Straw (R)	47,646	48.6
2	Charles W. Tobey (R)	50,156	52.8
	Jeremiah J. Doyle (D)	44,459	46.8

NEW JERSEY

		Votes	%
1	Charles A. Wolverton (R)	89,816	60.2
	Samuel T. French (D)	54,701	36.7
2	Isaac Bacharach (R)	60,963	62.9
	Harry R. Coulomb (D)	35,257	36.4
3	William H. Sutphin (D)	61,253	50.9
	Stanley Washburn (R)	58,217	48.4
4	D. Lane Powers (R)	51,794	55.0
	Monell Sayre (D)	40,705	43.2
5	Charles A. Eaton (R)	60,713	53.2
	Frederick M. P. Pearse (D)	51,964	45.6
6	Donald H. McLean (R)	65,653	57.4
	Fred C. Hyer (D)	47,938	41.9
7	Randolph Perkins (R)	52,003	51.6
	Hamilton Cross (D)	47,688	47.3
8	George N. Seger (R)	50,997	49.2
	Harry Joelson (D)	50,759	48.9
9	Edward A. Kenney (D)	53,822	47.6
	Joseph W. Marini (R)	52,968	46.8
10	Fred A. Hartley Jr. (R)	53,316	55.2
	William W. Harrison (D)	41,901	43.4
11	Peter A. Cavicchia (R)	47,495	49.8
	John J. McCloskey (D)	46,540	48.8
12	Frederick R. Lehlbach (R)	54,783	56.1
	Joseph M. Degnan (D)	40,746	41.7
13	Mary T. Norton (D)	73,779	72.1
	Mortimer Neuman (R)	27,964	27.3
14	Oscar L. Auf der Heide (D)	77,519	75.1
	Vincent P. McGann (R)	24,448	23.7

NEW MEXICO

		Votes	%
AL	Dennis Chavez (D)	95,363	63.5
	Jose E. Armijo (R)	52,905	35.2

NEW YORK

		Votes	%
1	Robert L. Bacon (R)	153,435	54.0
	Cornelius V. Whitney (D)	121,909	42.9
2	William F. Brunner (D)	172,512	68.6
	Horace A. Demarest (R)	68,525	27.3
3	George W. Lindsay (D)	33,750	80.8
	Edgar H. Hazelwood (R)	5,799	13.9
4	Thomas H. Cullen (D)	39,562	82.1
	Conrad F. Printzlien (R)	7,429	15.4
5	Loring M. Black Jr. (D)	51,932	64.8
	Irving C. Maltz (R)	24,814	31.0
6	Andrew L. Somers (D)	81,011	57.0
	Joseph P. Byrne (R)	42,221	29.7
	Harry W. Laidler (SOC)	15,568	11.0
7	John J. Delaney (D)	36,088	72.5
	Richard W. Thomas (R)	9,696	19.5
	David M. Cory (SOC)	3,181	6.4
8	Patrick J. Carley (D)	140,853	62.1
	Daniel Adelman (R)	49,471	21.8
	Baruch C. Vladeck (SOC)	31,930	14.1
9	Stephen A. Rudd (D)	69,634	59.9
	James Virdone (R)	38,047	32.7
	Abraham I. Shiplacoff (SOC)	7,496	6.5

		Votes	%
10	Emanuel Celler (D)	36,460	63.9
	William A. Ronalds (R)	14,167	24.8
	Louis Sadoff (SOC)	5,334	9.3
11	Anning S. Prall (D)	50,418	69.2
	Frank Homer Fay (R)	20,323	27.9
12	Samuel Dickstein (D)	21,248	86.5
	Henry Steinberg (R)	2,068	8.4
13	Christopher D. Sullivan (D)	21,939	86.5
	John Rosenberg (R)	2,513	9.9
14	William I. Sirovich (D)	20,668	60.7
	Henry A. Lowenberg (R)	9,651	28.3
	August Claessens (SOC)	2,735	8.0
15	John J. Boylan (D)	30,112	80.9
	Charles Coudert Nast (R)	5,987	16.1
16	John J. O'Connor (D)	29,485	67.1
	Eugene S. Taliaferro (R)	12,449	28.3
17	Theodore A. Peyser (D)	36,397	52.9
	Ruth Pratt (R)	29,776	43.3
18	Martin J. Kennedy (D)	30,245	75.1
	Patrick S. Hickey (R)	7,997	19.9
19	Sol Bloom (D)	57,400	69.0
	William L. Carns (R)	21,758	26.2
20	James J. Lanzetta (D)	16,447	50.7
	Fiorello H. LaGuardia (R)	15,227	47.0
21	Joseph A. Gavagan (D)	67,583	64.6
	Oscar J. Smith (R)	28,955	27.7
	Frank R. Crosswaith (SOC)	7,390	7.1
22	Anthony J. Griffin (D)	38,172	76.7
	Wilbur J. Murphy (R)	8,768	17.6
23	Frank Oliver (D)	131,852	69.5
	Samuel L. Krinn (R)	31,753	16.7
	Samuel Orr (SOC)	21,349	11.3
24	James M. Fitzpatrick (D)	128,881	60.1
	Benjamin L. Fairchild (R & LP)	65,189	30.4
	Esther Friedman (SOC)	15,389	7.2
25	Charles D. Millard (R)	80,909	54.3
	Jesse B. Perlman (D)	63,345	42.5
26	Hamilton Fish Jr. (R)	61,687	58.3
	Roslyn M. Cox (D)	43,174	40.8
27	Philip A. Goodwin (R & LP)	52,099	52.5
	Clifford L. Miller (D)	46,154	46.5
28	Parker Corning (D)	89,096	64.7
	Isaac G. Braman (R)	47,706	34.7
29	James S. Parker (R & LP)	65,359	57.8
	John J. Nyhoff (D)	46,935	41.5
30	Frank Crowther (R & LP)	55,981	55.5
	George D. Lamberton (D)	42,632	42.3
31	Bertrand H. Snell (R)	47,937	57.5
	Kenneth Gardner (D)	35,153	42.1
32	Francis D. Culkin (R & LP)	56,654	61.9
	John C. Purcell (D)	34,199	37.3
33	Fred J. Sisson (D)	53,427	50.0
	Frederick M. Davenport (R & LP)	52,398	49.0
34	John D. Clarke (R)	58,735	53.3
	Charles R. Seymour (D)	44,174	40.1
	Leon Ray Steenburg (LAW PRES)	6,676	6.1
35	Clarence E. Hancock (R)	79,345	55.6
	Edmund L. Weston (D)	60,376	42.3
36	John Taber (R & LP)	58,484	60.9
	Lithgow Osborne (D)	36,648	38.2
37	Gale H. Stalker (R & LP)	55,305	52.5
	Julian P. Bretz (D)	48,048	45.6
38	James L. Whitley (R)	64,003	46.2
	Charles Stanton (D)	58,775	42.4
	Arthur Rathjen (LAW PRES)	12,097	8.7
39	James W. Wadsworth (R)	50,855	47.1
	David A. White (D)	35,367	32.8
	Ernest R. Clark (LAW PRES)	20,209	18.7
40	Walter Gresham Andrews (R)	92,929	61.8
	Ralph W. Nolan (D)	54,363	36.1
41	Alfred F. Beiter (D)	45,120	50.1
	Edmund F. Cooke (R)	42,743	47.4
42	James M. Mead (D)	51,516	62.0
	Henry Adsit Bull (R)	30,230	36.4

NEW YORK

	Candidates	Votes	%
43	Daniel A. Reed (R & LP)	55,988	60.1
	Gerald A. Herrick (D)	34,561	37.1
AL	Elmer E. Studley (D)	2,363,627✓	
	John Fitzgibbons (D)	2,333,787✓	
	Nicholas Howard Pinto (R)	1,756,343	
	Sherman J. Lowell (R)	1,740,325	
	G. August Gerber (SOC)	166,781	
	Fred Sander (SOC)	163,648	
	Elizabeth Smart (LAW PRES)	74,436	
	J. Elmer Cates (LAW PRES)	68,622	
	Jacob Berlin (SOC LAB)	12,546	
	O. Martin Olson (SOC LAB)	11,623	

NORTH CAROLINA

	Candidates	Votes	%
1	Lindsay C. Warren (D)	32,790	90.8
	John B. Respass (R)	3,313	9.2
2	John H. Kerr (D)	34,325	96.0
3	Charles L. Abernethy (D)	30,395	73.2
	H. B. Ivey (R)	11,146	26.8
4	Edward W. Pou (D)	51,103	76.0
	L. P. Dixon (R)	16,129	24.0
5	Franklin W. Hancock Jr. (D)	40,825	70.2
	L. L. Wall (R)	17,326	29.8
6	William B. Umstead (D)	38,074	67.8
	William I. Ward (R)	18,093	32.2
7	J. Bayard Clark (D)	35,416	80.4
	J. M. Byrd (R)	8,657	19.6
8	J. Walter Lambeth (D)	49,584	65.4
	A. H. Ragan (R)	26,260	34.6
9	Robert L. Doughton (D)	51,145	63.5
	P. P. Dulin (R)	29,421	36.5
10	Alfred L. Bulwinkle (D)	63,776	59.7
	Charles A. Jonas (R)	43,067	40.3
11	Zebulon Weaver (D)	64,667	62.3
	Crawford F. James (R)	39,180	37.7

NORTH DAKOTA

	Candidates	Votes	%
AL	James H. Sinclair (R)	144,339✓	
	William Lemke (R)	135,339✓	
	W. D. Lynch (D)	72,659	
	R. B. Murphy (D)	71,695	
	Pat J. Barrett (I)	690	
	Ella Reeve Bloor (I)	678	

OHIO

	Candidates	Votes	%
1	John B. Hollister (R)	66,018	54.4
	Edward H. Brink (D)	55,416	45.6
2	William E. Hess (R)	58,971	50.7
	Ed. F. Alexander (D)	57,258	49.3
3	Byron B. Harlan (D)	85,069	54.8
	Edith McClure Patterson (R)	66,107	42.6
4	Frank L. Kloeb (D)	59,003	54.6
	John L. Cable (R)	49,100	45.4
5	Frank C. Kniffin (D)	44,433	60.0
	William L. Manahan (R)	29,605	40.0
6	James G. Polk (D)	50,913	56.2
	Mack Sauer (R)	39,668	43.8
7	L. T. Marshall (R)	65,064	53.0
	Aaron J. Halloran (D)	57,715	47.0
8	Brooks Fletcher (D)	45,930	52.7
	Grant E. Mouser Jr. (R)	41,234	47.3
9	Warren J. Duffey (D)	56,755	47.7
	Wilbur M. White (R)	54,078	45.4
10	Thomas A. Jenkins (R)	41,654	58.9
	Charles M. Hogan (D)	29,027	41.1
11	Mell G. Underwood (D)	44,380	63.0
	David J. Lewis (R)	26,075	37.0
12	Arthur P. Lamneck (D)	63,135	50.2
	John C. Speaks (R)	62,704	49.8
13	William L. Fiesinger (D)	56,070	58.9
	Walter E. Kruger (R)	39,122	41.1
14	Dow W. Harter (D)	93,057	53.9
	Francis Seiberling (R)	78,852	45.7

Candidates	Votes	%
15 Robert T. Secrest (D)	50,313	56.6
C. Ellis Moore (R)	38,113	42.9
16 William R. Thom (D)	67,670	51.6
C. B. McClintock (R)	63,609	48.5
17 Charles West (D)	55,396	51.8
William M. Morgan (R)	51,611	48.2
18 Lawrence E. Imhoff (D)	56,576	50.3
Frank Murphy (R)	56,013	49.8
19 John G. Cooper (R)	74,534	53.3
D. F. Dunlavy (D)	65,024	46.5
20 Martin L. Sweeney (D)	52,933	98.8
21 Robert Crosser (D)	49,436	65.2
Gerard Pilliod (R)	25,527	33.7
22 Chester C. Bolton (R)	141,296	58.7
Florence E. Allen (D)	98,427	40.9
AL Charles V. Truax (D)	1,206,631✓	
Stephen M. Young (D)	1,200,946✓	
George H. Bender (R)	1,109,562	
L. T. Palmer (R)	1,102,567	
Edward R. Stafford (P)	24,625	
Alfred H. Stratton (P)	18,844	
John Rehms (COM)	7,053	
William Hughey (COM)	6,010	

OKLAHOMA

Candidates	Votes	%
1 Wesley E. Disney (D)	81,080	63.3
Frank Frantz (R)	46,472	36.3
2 William W. Hastings (D)	46,710	70.5
William F. Head (R)	19,567	29.5
3 Wilburn Cartwright (D)	59,090	85.3
Walter Colbert (R)	10,225	14.8
4 Thomas D. McKeown (D)	61,867	75.5
E. W. Kemp (R)	20,069	24.5
5 Fletcher B. Swank (D)	64,303	64.3
Paul Huston (R)	35,785	35.8
6 Jed Johnson (D)	53,869	79.3
George E. Young (R)	14,048	20.7
7 James V. McClintic (D)	43,809	77.9
W. G. Roe (R)	8,756	15.6
T. H. McLemore (I)	3,651	6.5
8 E. W. Marland (D)	51,404	61.3
M. C. Garber (R)	31,677	37.8
AL Will Rogers (D)	467,644	72.8
R. A. Howard (R)	171,415	26.7

OREGON

Candidates	Votes	%
1 James W. Mott (R)	82,443	51.2
Harvey G. Starkweather (D)	60,066	37.3
W. J. Butler (I)	12,417	7.7
2 Walter M. Pierce (D)	30,219	48.2
Robert R. Butler (R)	25,169	40.1
Hugh E. Brady (I)	5,133	8.2
3 Charles H. Martin (D)	74,397	59.0
Homer D. Angell (R)	40,650	32.2

PENNSYLVANIA

Candidates	Votes	%
1 Harry C. Ransley (R, D)	65,508	91.5
Harry T. Glenn (F PLAY)	4,933	6.9
2 James M. Beck (R, R&P)	42,233	59.2
John J. Shanahan (D, LAB)	27,571	38.7
3 Alfred M. Waldron (R, R&P)	53,044	57.4
Frank M. O'Brien (D)	37,487	40.6
4 George W. Edmonds (R)	43,086	52.9
William J. O'Rourke (D)	36,198	44.4
5 James J. Connolly (R, L)	49,516	55.3
Carroll J. Agnew (D, A-CB)	36,240	40.5
6 Edward Lowber Stokes (R, L)	44,884	51.0
Harry V. Dougherty (D, R&P)	40,440	45.9
7 George P. Darrow (R)	62,031	62.2
James C. Crumlish (D)	35,096	35.2
8 James Wolfenden (R, L)	70,177	65.8
Matthew Randall (D)	32,139	30.1

Candidates	Votes	%
9 Henry W. Watson (R)	40,726	50.3
Norton L. Lichtenwalner (D)	37,490	46.3
10 J. Roland Kinzer (R, P)	62,682	61.5
Richard P. McGrann (D, REPEAL)	36,841	36.2
11 Patrick J. Boland (D, R)	69,684	95.9
12 C. Murray Turpin (R)	57,377	50.8
John J. Casey (D, SOC)	55,650	49.2
13 George Franklin Brumm (R, D)	97,120	90.8
14 William E. Richardson (D)	29,386	41.0
Thomas L. Rhodes (R)	22,898	31.9
Raymond S. Hofses (SOC)	19,319	27.0
15 Louis T. McFadden (R, D)	71,345	95.9
16 Robert F. Rich (R, P)	46,044	63.5
Paul A. Rothfuss (D)	24,671	34.0
17 J. William Ditter (R, L)	59,693	59.9
Phillip Childs Pendleton (D, R&P)	32,706	32.8
18 Benjamin K. Focht (R)	28,749	48.3
J. G. Harry Rippman (D)	19,230	32.3
Omer B. Poulson (CIT)	11,568	19.4
19 Isaac H. Doutrich (R)	59,120	58.1
Carl K. Deen (D)	37,752	37.1
20 Thomas C. Cochran (R, P)	44,754	53.6
D. J. Driscoll (D)	38,798	46.4
21 Francis E. Walter (D)	39,996	52.7
William R. Coyle (R)	34,189	45.1
22 Harry L. Haines (D, P)	51,894	57.2
Leighton C. Taylor (R)	37,434	41.3
23 J. Banks Kurtz (R, P)	35,342	49.2
Frederick B. Kerr (D)	33,948	47.2
24 J. Buell Snyder (D)	33,633	53.0
Samuel A. Kendall (R, P)	28,498	44.9
25 Charles I. Faddis (D)	36,781	56.1
Henry W. Temple (R, P)	27,351	41.7
26 J. Howard Swick (R, P)	45,029	54.0
Sam B. Wilson (D)	38,402	46.0
27 Nathan L. Strong (R, P)	52,884	50.7
D. A. Dorn (D)	42,763	41.0
28 William M. Berlin (D, JOBLESS)	43,619	55.2
Adam M. Wyant (R, P)	32,177	40.8
29 Charles N. Crosby (D, I)	30,106	50.1
Milton W. Shreve (R, P)	27,949	46.5
30 Twing Brooks (D)	35,186	47.2
Edward F. Erk (R, I)	35,045	47.0
31 Clyde Kelly (R, D)	68,944	85.5
Leo O. Guthrie (REPEAL)	6,031	7.5
William B. Kane (SOC)	5,620	7.0
32 Michael J. Muldowney (R, JOBLESS)	24,785	53.3
Anne E. Felix (D)	18,986	40.9
33 Henry Ellenbogen (D, JOBLESS)	35,612	52.0
Harry A. Estep (R)	30,076	43.9
34 Matthew A. Dunn (D, JOBLESS)	40,651	49.9
Guy E. Campbell (R, L)	36,101	44.3

Special Elections

Candidates	Votes	%
6 Robert L. Davis (R)	63,929	54.1
Leo J. Horton (D)	54,178	45.9
18 Joseph F. Biddle (R)	38,584	59.3
Meredith Meyers (D)	26,370	40.6

RHODE ISLAND

Candidates	Votes	%
1 Francis B. Condon (D)	70,566	55.6
Clark Burdick (R)	56,153	44.2
2 John M. O'Connell (D)	73,086	54.7
Thomas P. Hazard (R)	60,153	45.0

SOUTH CAROLINA

Candidates	Votes	%
1 Thomas S. McMillan (D)	14,415	95.9
2 Hampton P. Fulmer (D)	18,699	97.9
3 John C. Taylor (D)	19,286	99.2

SOUTH CAROLINA

Candidates	Votes	%
4 John J. McSwain (D)	23,041	98.4
5 James P. Richards (D)	15,046	98.5
6 Allard H. Gasque (D)	14,159	98.7

SOUTH DAKOTA

1 Fred H. Hildebrandt (D)	110,047	53.1
C. A. Christopherson (R)	92,062	44.4
2 Theodore B. Werner (D)	36,839	55.7
William Williamson (R)	29,066	43.9

TENNESSEE

1 B. Carroll Reece (R)	30,336	45.7
O. B. Lovette (I)	27,888	42.0
Albert C. Tipton (D)	7,950	12.0
2 J. Will Taylor (R)	32,460	57.7
Hamilton S. Burnett (D)	22,818	40.5
3 Sam D. McReynolds (D)	28,758	91.6
4 Ridley Mitchell (D)	30,580	82.6
W. H. Crowell (R)	5,882	15.9
5 Joseph W. Byrns (D)	33,833	87.6
J. Y. Freeman (R)	4,066	10.5
6 Clarence W. Turner (D)	15,779	79.1
G. C. Stephenson (R)	3,915	19.6
7 Gordon Browning (D)	20,315	77.8
Willoughy Stewart (R)	5,485	21.0
8 Jere Cooper (D)	19,871	88.2
Mary Burnett (R)	2,307	10.2
9 Edward H. Crump (D)	38,001	90.1
S. A. Godsey (R)	2,953	7.0

TEXAS

1 Wright Patman (D)	30,854	98.0
2 Martin Dies (D)	51,999	95.4
3 M. G. Sanders (D)	36,507	100.0
4 Sam Rayburn (D)	23,404	95.2
5 Hatton W. Sumners (D)	52,598	92.1
G. J. McManus (R)	4,539	7.9
6 Luther A. Johnson (D)	32,966	100.0
7 Clay S. Briggs (D)	28,490	95.3
8 Daniel E. Garrett (D)	57,882*	92.0
W. E. Long (R)	5,015	8.0
9 J. J. Mansfield (D)	33,366	97.5
10 J. P. Buchanan (D)	33,232	100.0
11 O. H. Cross (D)	35,186	96.6
12 Fritz G. Lanham (D)	41,151	93.3
George Calvert (R)	2,968	6.7
13 W. D. McFarlane (D)	33,023	100.0
14 Richard M. Kleberg (D)	69,471	91.5
Frank B. Vaughn (R)	6,456	8.5
15 John N. Garner (D)	44,300*	88.4
C. G. Watson (R)	5,785	11.6
16 R. E. Thomason (D)	49,068	99.7
17 Thomas L. Blanton (D)	43,959	100.0
18 Marvin Jones (D)	76,918	96.1

Candidates	Votes	%
AL George B. Terrell (D)	794,521	✔
Sterling P. Strong (D)	794,333	✔
Joseph W. Bailey Jr. (D)	790,024	✔
Enoch J. Fletcher (R)	62,957	
F. A. Blankenbeckler (R)	60,360	
J. A. Simpson (R)	59,390	
H. M. Shelton (SOC)	2,534	
P. L. Petersen (SOC)	2,530	
Ben O. Miller (SOC)	2,424	
P. A. Spain (LIB)	188	
H. G. Eastridge (LIB)	172	

UTAH

1 Abe Murdock (D)	47,776	50.7
Don B. Colton (R)	44,827	47.6
2 J. W. Robinson (D)	62,400	56.0
Frederick C. Loofbourow (R)	46,919	42.1

VERMONT

AL Ernest Willard Gibson (R)	86,194	64.4
Joseph A. McNamara (D)	47,591	35.6

VIRGINIA

AL Clifton A. Woodrum (D)	206,631 ✔	
Andrew J. Montague (D)	205,133 ✔	
Schuyler Otis Bland (D)	204,372 ✔	
Thomas G. Burch (D)	204,069 ✔	
A. Willis Robertson (D)	203,727 ✔	
Howard W. Smith (D)	203,023 ✔	
Patrick Henry Drewry (D)	202,800 ✔	
Colgate W. Darden Jr. (D)	202,759 ✔	
John W. Flannagan Jr. (D)	201,474 ✔	
Menalcus Lankford (R)	92,586	
J. A. Garber (R)	84,464	
Fred W. McWane (R)	82,480	
Roland E. Chase (R)	81,909	
George Cole Scott (R)	81,025	
Henry A. Wise (R)	78,622	
W. M. Brown (I)	43,936	
C. C. Berkeley (I)	43,202	
R. Lindsay Gordon Jr. (I)	16,504	
A. J. Dunning Jr. (P)	16,392	
Albon James Royal (SOC)	4,782	
Winston F. Dawson (SOC)	4,629	
Herman R. Ansell (SOC)	4,603	
David G. George (SOC)	4,165	
Angie M. Norris (SOC)	3,956	
J. F. Spaulding (SOC)	3,601	
Frank Lyon	207	

Special Election

10 Joel W. Flood (D)	23,129	99.9

WASHINGTON

Candidates	Votes	%
1 Marion A. Zioncheck (D)	80,665	55.6
John F. Miller (R)	62,283	42.9
2 Monrad C. Wallgren (D)	49,002	56.1
Lindley H. Hadley (R)	30,780	35.2
Floyd Hatfield (LIB)	6,687	7.7
3 Martin F. Smith (D)	38,713	46.9
Albert Johnson (R)	28,388	34.4
J. T. Sullivan (LIB)	15,427	18.7
4 Knute Hill (D)	41,708	56.3
John W. Summers (R)	32,360	43.7
5 Sam B. Hill (D)	73,041	96.8
6 Wesley Lloyd (D)	44,573	50.1
John T. McCutcheon (R)	32,760	36.8
Tom Martin (LIB)	11,554	13.0

WEST VIRGINIA

1 Robert L. Ramsay (D)	58,060	50.9
Carl G. Bachmann (R)	55,023	48.3
2 Jennings Randolph (D)	55,556	53.4
Frank L. Bowman (R)	48,055	46.2
3 Lynn S. Hornor (D)	52,287	53.6
John M. Wolverton (R)	45,274	46.4
4 George W. Johnson (D)	62,848	52.3
Robert L. Hogg (R)	56,993	47.4
5 John Kee (D)	61,277	52.1
Hugh Ike Shott (R)	56,355	47.9
6 Joe L. Smith (D)	102,896	56.4
James O. Lakin (R)	79,470	43.6

WISCONSIN

1 George W. Blanchard (R)	50,874	48.5
William D. Thompson (D)	48,093	45.8
2 Charles W. Henney (D)	63,091	56.2
John B. Gay (R)	47,193	42.0
3 Gardner R. Withrow (R)	59,535	61.1
John J. Boyle (D)	37,846	38.9
4 Raymond J. Cannon (D)	61,058	51.0
John C. Schafer (R)	33,609	28.1
Walter Polakowski (SOC)	24,377	20.4
5 Thomas O'Malley (D)	57,294	43.8
Joseph A. Padway (R)	32,559	24.9
Herman O. Kent (SOC)	30,534	23.3
6 Michael K. Reilly (D)	59,055	59.1
Louis J. Fellenz (R)	38,708	38.7
7 Gerald J. Boileau (R)	49,322	51.4
Frank D. Chapman (D)	46,737	48.7
8 James Hughes (D)	53,414	50.7
George J. Schneider (R)	51,932	49.3
9 James A. Frear (R)	52,680	56.9
Miles H. McNally (D)	39,874	43.1
10 Hubert H. Peavey (R)	49,764	59.2
Peter B. Cadigan (D)	33,448	39.8

WYOMING

AL Vincent M. Carter (R)	44,816	49.7
Paul R. Greever (D)	43,056	47.7

1933 House Elections

ARIZONA

Special Election

AL Isabella S. Greenway (D)	24,163	73.6
D. E. Sumpter (SOC)	5,556	16.9
H. B. Wilkinson (R)	3,123	9.5

LOUISIANA

Special Election

6 Mrs. Bolivar E. Kemp (D)	5,029*	99.8

NEW YORK

Special Election

34 Marian W. Clarke (R)	16,806	59.3
John J. Burns (D)	11,559	40.8

1934 House Elections

ALABAMA

	Candidates	Votes	%
1	John McDuffie (D)	13,076	99.7
2	Lister Hill (D)	18,592	100.0
3	Henry B. Steagall (D)	13,191	100.0
4	Sam Hobbs (D)	14,728	87.6
	Charles R. Robinson (R)	2,086	12.4
5	Joe Starnes (D)	22,040	75.2
	J. C. Swann (R)	7,282	24.8
6	William B. Oliver (D)	12,342	100.0
7	William B. Bankhead (D)	22,001	80.4
	J. W. Dodd (I)	5,361	19.6
8	Archibald H. Carmichael (D)	13,817	100.0
9	George Huddleston (D)	19,317	95.0

ARIZONA

	Candidates	Votes	%
AL	Isabella S. Greenway (D)	65,914	68.6
	H. A. Smith (R)	28,283	29.5

ARKANSAS

	Candidates	Votes	%
1	William J. Driver (D)	20,136	100.0
2	John E. Miller (D)	18,629	100.0
3	Claude A. Fuller (D)	17,363	66.3
	Pat W. Murphy (R)	8,823	33.7
4	William B. Cravens (D)	21,157	100.0
5	David D. Terry (D)	20,209	100.0
6	John L. McClellan (D)	19,078	100.0
7	Tilman B. Parks (D)	13,887	95.8

CALIFORNIA

	Candidates	Votes	%
1	Clarence F. Lea (D-R)	98,661	93.6
	Allen K. Gifford (SOC)	6,698	6.4
2	Harry L. Englebright (R-D-PROG)	66,370	100.0
3	Frank H. Buck (D)	65,566	53.3
	J. M. Inman (R & PROG)	56,222	45.7
4	Florence P. Kahn (R)	50,491	48.0
	Chauncey Tramutolo (D)	46,871	44.5
5	Richard J. Welch (R-D-PROG)	89,751	93.8
	Alexander Noral (COM)	5,933	6.2
6	Albert E. Carter (R-D-PROG)	48,180	99.8
7	John H. Tolan (D)	51,962	52.3
	Ralph R. Eltse (R)	47,414	47.7
8	John J. McGrath (R-D-PROG)	107,325	99.9
9	B. W. Gearhart (R-D)	77,650	100.0
10	Henry E. Stubbs (D)	68,475	64.4
	George R. Bliss (R)	37,860	35.6
11	John Steven McGroarty (D)	66,999	53.5
	William E. Evans (R)	56,350	45.0
12	John Henry Hoeppel (D)	52,595	50.6
	Frederick F. Houser (R)	51,216	49.3
13	Charles Kramer (D)	83,384	62.4
	Thomas K. Case (R)	27,993	21.0
	Charles H. Randall (PROG)	18,760	14.0
14	Thomas F. Ford (D)	52,761	57.7
	William D. Campbell (R)	33,945	37.1
15	John M. Costello (D)	67,247	50.5
	William I. Traeger (R)	65,858	49.5
16	John F. Dockweiler (D-R)	119,332	98.8
17	Charles J. Colden (D)	60,045	70.3
	C. P. Wright (R)	20,508	24.0
	Richard Pomeroy (SOC)	4,721	5.5
18	Byron N. Scott (D)	52,377	56.3
	William Brayton (R)	40,179	43.2
19	Sam L. Collins (R-D)	97,119	88.6
	A. B. Hillabold	12,301	11.2
20	George Burnham (R)	51,682	52.4
	Ed V. Izac (D & PROG)	46,957	47.6

COLORADO

	Candidates	Votes	%
1	Lawrence Lewis (D)	59,744	56.0
	William R. Eaton (R)	34,073	32.0
	Charles W. Varnum (OLD AGE)	9,511	8.9
2	Fred Cummings (D)	64,719	55.9
	George H. Bradfield (R)	49,142	42.4
3	John A. Martin (D)	73,281	64.2
	W. O. Peterson (R)	39,753	34.8
4	Edward T. Taylor (D)	39,747	67.3
	Harry McDevitt (R)	17,234	29.2

CONNECTICUT

	Candidates	Votes	%
1	Herman P. Kopplemann (D)	74,533	54.3
	Anson T. McCook (R)	59,240	43.2
2	William L. Higgins (R)	44,899	49.6
	John M. Dowe (D)	43,816	48.4
3	James A. Shanley (D)	55,894	48.8
	Joseph F. Morrissey (R)	52,832	46.1
4	Schuyler Merritt (R)	54,178	44.1
	Edward T. Buckingham (D)	45,835	37.3
	Arnold E. Freese (SOC)	21,021	17.1
5	J. Joseph Smith (D)	42,594	51.4
	Edward W. Goss (R)	38,547	46.5
AL	William M. Citron (D)	263,794	51.4
	Charles M. Bakewell (R)	249,146	48.6

DELAWARE

	Candidates	Votes	%
AL	John George Stewart (R)	52,468	53.1
	John C. Hazzard (D)	45,927	46.5

FLORIDA

	Candidates	Votes	%
1	J. Hardin Peterson (D)	42,051	100.0
2	Robert A. Green (D)	13,740	100.0
3	Millard F. Caldwell (D)	16,740	100.0
4	J. Mark Wilcox (D)	59,286	100.0
AL	William J. Sears (D)	125,263	100.0

GEORGIA

	Candidates	Votes	%
1	Hugh Peterson Jr. (D)	5,392	100.0
2	E. E. Cox (D)	3,369	100.0
3	Bryant T. Castellow (D)	4,078	100.0
4	E. M. Owen (D)	5,131	95.5
5	Robert Ramspeck (D)	5,206	100.0
6	Carl Vinson (D)	3,067	100.0
7	Malcolm C. Tarver (D)	5,179	100.0
8	Braswell Deen (D)	4,501	100.0
9	B. Frank Whelchel (D)	8,391	100.0
10	Paul Brown (D)	8,129	100.0

IDAHO

	Candidates	Votes	%
1	Compton I. White (D)	42,223	61.9
	Burton L. French (R)	25,969	38.1
2	D. Worth Clark (D)	57,547	60.5
	Heber Q. Hale (R)	37,200	39.1

ILLINOIS

	Candidates	Votes	%
1	Arthur W. Mitchell (D)	27,963	53.0
	Oscar De Priest (R)	24,829	47.0
2	Raymond S. McKeough (D)	104,479	56.3
	P. H. Moynihan (R)	81,034	43.7
3	Edward A. Kelly (D)	122,109	63.5
	Frank M. Fulton (R)	70,329	36.6
4	Harry P. Beam (D)	53,448	78.8
	Frank George Zelezinski (R)	14,401	21.2
5	Adolph J. Sabath (D)	29,107	72.5
	John A. Stanek (R)	10,923	27.2
6	Thomas J. O'Brien (D)	148,645	65.7
	Arnold L. Lund (R)	77,462	34.3
7	Leonard W. Schuetz (D)	185,658	64.0
	Raymond J. Peacock (R)	104,079	35.9
8	Leo Kocialkowski (D)	27,682	74.1
	Edward Richard Piszatowski (R)	9,671	25.9
9	James McAndrews (D)	36,949	56.3
	Fred A. Britten (R)	28,663	43.7
10	Ralph E. Church (R)	100,161	51.3
	David B. Maloney (D)	94,993	48.7
11	Chauncey W. Reed (R)	69,469	50.3
	James A. Howell (D)	68,748	49.7
12	John T. Buckbee (R)	57,126	55.3
	C. H. Smith (D)	46,111	44.7
13	Leo S. Allen (R)	40,423	60.5
	Edward S. Nicholas (D)	26,427	39.5
14	Chester Thompson (D)	44,965	53.3
	John C. Allen (R)	39,330	46.7
15	J. Leroy Adair (D)	48,682	54.9
	Burnett M. Chiperfield (R)	40,035	45.1
16	Everett M. Dirksen (R)	58,716	65.4
	Rayburn L. Russell (D)	31,044	34.6
17	Leslie C. Arends (R)	36,552	52.1
	Frank Gillespie (D)	33,621	47.9
18	James A. Meeks (D)	48,791	52.0
	Elmer A. Taylor (R)	44,617	47.6
19	Donald C. Dobbins (D)	59,179	53.9
	Charles H. Fletcher (R)	50,571	46.1
20	Scott W. Lucas (D)	39,761	56.9
	Warren W. Wright (R)	30,085	43.1
21	Harry H. Mason (D)	49,825	51.0
	Frank M. Ramey (R)	47,330	48.4
22	Edwin M. Schaefer (D)	62,161	56.3
	Jesse R. Brown (R)	48,285	43.7
23	William W. Arnold (D)	51,712	55.5
	Ben O. Sumner (R)	41,520	44.5
24	Claude V. Parsons (D)	39,442	51.7
	James V. Heidinger (R)	36,891	48.3
25	Kent E. Keller (D)	55,824	54.8
	J. Lester Buford (R)	45,955	45.2
AL	Michael L. Igoe (D)	1,507,714✔	
	Martin A. Brennan (D)	1,459,890✔	
	C. Wayland Brooks (R)	1,201,373	
	Milton E. Jones (R)	1,112,802	
	Walter Nesbit (N PROG)	19,329	
	Arthur McDowell (SOC)	13,586	
	Harold O. Hatcher (SOC)	13,580	
	Martin Powroznik (N PROG)	7,778	
	Frank Earl Herrick (P)	4,863	
	Clay F. Gaumer (P)	4,659	
	John L. Lindsey (SOC LAB)	3,396	
	Frank Schnur (SOC LAB)	3,195	

INDIANA

	Candidates	Votes	%
1	William T. Schulte (D)	44,983	53.5
	E. Miles Norton (R)	38,531	45.9
2	Frederick Landis (R)	72,552*	53.9
	George R. Durgan (D)	61,610	45.8
3	Samuel B. Pettengill (D)	55,283	50.7
	Andrew J. Hickey (R)	52,410	48.1
4	James I. Farley (D)	58,625	51.7
	David Hogg (R)	54,510	48.1
5	Glenn Griswold (D)	68,079	54.1
	Albert R. Hall (R)	56,420	44.8
6	Virginia E. Jenckes (D)	67,521	49.8
	Fred S. Purnell (R)	67,138	49.6
7	Arthur H. Greenwood (D)	73,324	51.5
	Gerald W. Landis (R)	67,987	47.7
8	John W. Boehne Jr. (D)	75,268	56.9
	Charles F. Werner (R)	56,470	42.7
9	Eugene B. Crowe (D)	68,329	52.1
	Chester A. Davis (R)	62,403	47.6

INDIANA

Candidates	Votes	%
10 Finly H. Gray (D)	64,939	51.5
Robert F. Murray (R)	60,693	48.1
11 William H. Larrabee (D)	61,476	54.4
Ralph A. Scott (R)	50,350	44.5
12 Louis Ludlow (D)	60,358	55.6
Delbert O. Wilmeth (R)	47,134	43.4

IOWA

1 Edward C. Eicher (D)	48,544	55.4
E. R. Hicklin (R)	39,047	44.6
2 Bernhard M. Jacobsen (D)	60,654	64.0
M. B. Andelfinger (R)	34,153	36.0
3 John W. Gwynne (R)	42,063	54.5
Albert C. Willford (D)	35,159	45.5
4 Fred Biermann (D)	49,504	53.1
C. A. Benson (R)	43,794	46.9
5 Lloyd Thurston (R)	54,699	53.0
Ernest H. Fabritz (D)	48,449	47.0
6 Hubert Utterback (D)	50,828	52.5
Cassius C. Dowell (R)	46,084	47.6
7 Otha D. Wearin (D)	51,395	52.0
Charles E. Swanson (R)	47,508	48.0
8 Fred C. Gilchrist (R)	45,875	53.2
Joseph J. Meyers (D)	40,434	46.9
9 Guy M. Gillette (D)	58,598	64.2
Thomas H. McBride (R)	32,639	35.8

KANSAS

1 William P. Lambertson (R)	66,293	60.5
John H. Arnett (D)	43,205	39.5
2 Ulysses S. Guyer (R)	60,401	49.7
Howard E. Payne (D)	59,698	49.1
3 Edward W. Patterson (D)	51,793	50.0
Harold McGugin (R)	49,710	48.0
4 William Randolph Carpenter (D)	50,309	52.6
Hal E. Harlan (R)	45,346	47.4
5 John M. Houston (D)	49,610	57.0
Ira C. Watson (R)	31,511	36.2
C. F. Whitson	4,661	5.4
6 Frank Carlson (R)	62,824	51.1
Kathryn O'Loughlin McCarthy (D)	60,028	48.8
7 Clifford R. Hope (R)	63,952	54.6
L. E. Webb (D)	53,104	45.4

KENTUCKY

1 William V. Gregory (D)	18,868	61.1
John W. Taylor (R)	12,008	38.9
2 Glover H. Cary (D)	18,410	75.1
William M. Likins (P)	5,188	21.2
3 Emmet O'Neal (D)	48,664	56.2
Frank M. Drake (R)	36,922	42.6
4 Cap R. Carden (D)	25,669	52.1
James Tudor (R)	23,644	48.0
5 Brent Spence (D)	24,666	65.1
J. L. Newhall (R)	11,576	30.6
6 Virgil Chapman (D)	34,641	60.0
W. D. Rogers (R)	23,070	40.0
7 Andrew J. May (D)	35,642	52.9
Harry H. Ramey (R)	31,799	47.2
8 Fred M. Vinson (D)	35,288	59.2
George R. Ellison (R)	24,358	40.8
9 John M. Robsion (R)	42,741	77.0
L. L. Terrell (D)	12,736	23.0

LOUISIANA

1 Joachim O. Fernandez (D)	45,678	99.9
2 Paul H. Maloney (D)	45,793	100.0
3 Numa F. Montet (D)	12,636	100.0
4 John N. Sandlin (D)	14,680	100.0
5 Riley J. Wilson (D)	14,158	100.0
6 Jared Y. Sanders Jr. (D)	19,377	100.0

Candidates	Votes	%
7 Rene L. DeRouen (D)	16,528	100.0
8 Cleveland Dear (D)	17,213	100.0

Special Election

6 Jared Y. Sanders Jr. (D)	9,649	99.6

MAINE

1 Simon M. Hamlin (D)	48,235	50.8
Carroll L. Beedy (R)	46,635	49.2
2 Edward C. Moran Jr. (D)	52,491	53.2
Zelma M. Dwinal (R)	46,200	46.8
3 Ralph O. Brewster (R)	44,024	51.4
J. G. Utterback (D)	41,710	48.7

MARYLAND

1 T. Alan Goldsborough (D)	41,627	64.0
H. Burdett Messenger (R)	23,378	36.0
2 William P. Cole (D)	75,244	57.7
Theodore F. Brown (R)	51,303	39.3
3 Vincent L. Palmisano (D)	27,988	66.4
F. Stanley Porter (R)	13,042	30.9
4 Ambrose J. Kennedy (D)	37,006	59.1
William J. Stocksdale (R)	24,162	38.6
5 Stephen W. Gambrill (D)	39,734	61.4
Joseph Allison Wilmer (R)	24,364	37.7
6 David J. Lewis (D)	45,605	50.3
Frederick N. Zihlman (R)	44,244	48.8

MASSACHUSETTS

1 Allen T. Treadway (R)	51,046	57.6
George E. Haggerty (D)	35,061	39.6
2 William J. Granfield (D)	47,894	51.2
Charles R. Clason (R)	42,495	45.5
3 Joseph E. Casey (D)	46,830	50.1
Frank H. Foss (R)	46,572	49.9
4 Pehr G. Holmes (R)	54,601	57.5
James H. Ferguson (D)	38,984	41.0
5 Edith Nourse Rogers (R)	75,754	62.2
Jeremiah J. O'Sullivan (D)	46,124	37.8
6 A. Piatt Andrew (R)	64,610	100.0
7 William P. Connery Jr. (D)	62,666	59.1
C. F. Nelson Pratt (R)	40,988	38.6
8 Arthur D. Healey (D)	53,581	58.6
William S. Howe (R)	37,873	41.4
9 Richard M. Russell (D)	60,141	52.6
Robert Luce (R)	54,198	47.4
10 George Holden Tinkham (R, D)	84,244	100.0
11 John P. Higgins (D)	46,383	100.0
12 John W. McCormack (D)	78,783	82.8
Francis A. Pentoney (R)	16,370	17.2
13 Richard B. Wigglesworth (R)	58,653	54.9
Francis H. Foy (D)	48,241	45.1
14 Joseph W. Martin Jr. (R)	46,411	54.8
Arthur E. Seagrave (D)	38,325	45.2
15 Charles L. Gifford (R)	46,446	53.4
John D. W. Bodfish (D)	38,336	44.0

MICHIGAN

1 George G. Sadowski (D)	40,054	65.8
Charles A. Roxborough (R)	19,194	31.5
2 Earl C. Michener (R)	40,119	50.2
John C. Lehr (D)	38,972	48.7
3 Henry M. Kimball (R)	41,587	55.0
Paul H. Todd (D)	32,928	43.6
4 Clare E. Hoffman (R)	45,224	58.2
George Foulkes (D)	31,646	40.7
5 Carl E. Mapes (R)	39,682	50.5
Thomas F. McAllister (D)	37,847	48.2
6 William W. Blackney (R)	42,424	50.6
Claude E. Cady (D)	41,100	49.0

Candidates	Votes	%
7 Jesse P. Wolcott (R)	42,857	59.9
Frank J. Wiegand (D)	27,690	38.7
8 Fred L. Crawford (R)	40,333	51.5
Michael J. Hart (D)	35,945	45.9
9 Albert J. Engel (R)	33,222	52.0
Harry W. Musselwhite (D)	30,513	47.7
10 Roy O. Woodruff (R)	36,719	59.5
Hubert J. Gaffney (D)	24,526	39.8
11 Prentiss M. Brown (D)	39,293	54.8
John J. O'Hara (R)	32,460	45.2
12 Frank E. Hook (D)	37,298	52.1
W. Frank James (R)	34,281	47.9
13 Clarence J. McLeod (R)	35,879	56.7
John H. Slevin (D)	25,869	40.9
14 Louis C. Rabaut (D)	45,301	62.2
John H. McPherson (R)	26,006	35.7
15 John D. Dingell (D)	40,119	54.4
Charles Bowles (R)	32,011	43.4
16 John Lesinski (D)	32,269	52.7
Clyde M. Ford (R)	27,487	44.9
17 George A. Dondero (R)	35,562	53.8
Charles P. Webster (D)	29,250	44.2

MINNESOTA

1 August H. Andresen (R)	51,099	46.6
John W. Feller (D)	29,581	27.0
Otto Baudler (F-LAB)	29,038	26.5
2 Elmer J. Ryan (D)	43,677	37.2
Henry Arens (F-LAB)	37,663	32.1
L. P. Johnson (R)	35,968	30.7
3 Ernest Lundeen (F-LAB)	59,097	53.3
Josiah H. Chase (R)	28,637	25.8
John W. Schmidt (D)	22,556	20.3
4 Melvin J. Maas (R)	37,933	36.8
A. E. Smith (F-LAB)	30,354	29.5
John J. McDonough (D)	24,122	23.4
Charles J. Andre (I)	10,180	9.9
5 Theodore Christianson (R)	45,875	39.3
Dewey W. Johnson (F-LAB)	42,322	36.2
Sidney Benson (D)	27,814	23.8
6 Harold Knutson (R)	56,642	46.2
Magnus Johnson (F-LAB)	46,346	37.8
Frank R. Weber (D)	19,572	16.0
7 Paul John Kvale (F-LAB)	65,261	59.3
Richard T. Daly (D)	44,762	40.7
8 William A. Pittenger (R)	39,513	35.7
F. H. Shoemaker (I)	25,386	23.0
A. L. Winterquist (F-LAB)	25,024	22.6
Jerry A. Harri (D)	18,707	16.9
9 Richard T. Buckler (F-LAB)	41,822	44.2
Ole O. Sageng (R)	27,522	29.1
Martin Oscar Brandon (D)	25,210	26.7

MISSISSIPPI

1 John E. Rankin (D)	6,825	100.0
2 Wall Doxey (D)	5,721	100.0
3 William M. Whittington (D)	3,586	100.0
4 Aaron Lane Ford (D)	8,051	100.0
5 Aubert C. Dunn (D)	9,412	100.0
6 William M. Colmer (D)	9,002	100.0
7 Dan R. McGehee (D)	14,730	100.0

MISSOURI

1 Milton A. Romjue (D)	52,273	54.8
J. Grover Morgan (R)	42,513	44.5
2 William L. Nelson (D)	59,557	58.6
Logan (R)	41,916	41.2
3 Richard M. Duncan (D)	61,548	60.6
William A. Black (R)	39,953	39.3
4 C. Jasper Bell (D)	82,995	81.7
Horace Guffin (R)	18,368	18.1
5 Joseph B. Shannon (D)	96,798	84.3
Claude E. Sowers (R)	17,889	15.6
6 Reuben T. Wood (D)	58,902	55.1
Oliver J. Page (R)	47,769	44.7

MISSOURI

	Candidates	Votes	%
7	Dewey Short (R)	65,211	52.9
	Frank H. Lee (D)	57,446	46.6
8	Clyde Williams (D)	54,006	54.4
	Breuer (R)	45,354	45.7
9	Clarence Cannon (D)	41,514	62.4
	Voelkerding (R)	24,380	36.7
10	Orville Zimmerman (D)	42,865	58.2
	McAnally (R)	29,949	40.7
11	Thomas C. Hennings (D)	59,119	56.4
	Leonidas C. Dyer (R)	44,693	42.6
12	James R. Claiborne (D)	70,754	51.0
	Cleveland A. Newton (R)	66,108	47.7
13	John J. Cochran (D)	60,198	65.5
	George W. Strodtman (R)	31,165	33.9

MONTANA

	Candidates	Votes	%
1	Joseph P. Monaghan (D)	55,877	67.8
	D. D. Evans (R)	25,567	31.0
2	Roy E. Ayers (D)	79,856	69.8
	Stanley E. Felt (R)	33,703	29.5

NEBRASKA

	Candidates	Votes	%
1	Henry C. Luckey (D)	55,897	52.8
	Marcus L. Poteet (R)	45,258	42.8
2	Charles F. McLaughlin (D)	46,790	54.2
	Herbert Rhoades (R)	36,743	42.5
3	Karl Stefan (R)	69,363	57.8
	Edgar Howard (D)	50,707	42.2
4	C. G. Binderup (D)	69,275	58.4
	James W. Hammond (R)	49,357	41.6
5	Harry B. Coffee (D)	55,709	52.1
	Albert N. Mathers (R)	49,161	45.9

NEVADA

	Candidates	Votes	%
AL	James G. Scrugham (D)	29,691	71.2
	George B. Russell (R)	11,992	28.8

NEW HAMPSHIRE

	Candidates	Votes	%
1	William N. Rogers (D)	48,568	53.9
	Arthur B. Jenks (R)	41,425	46.0
2	Charles W. Tobey (R)	42,706	53.3
	Harry B. Metcalf (D)	37,122	46.3

NEW JERSEY

	Candidates	Votes	%
1	Charles A. Wolverton (R)	81,634	61.2
	Willis Tullis Porch (D)	48,770	36.6
2	Isaac Bacharach (R)	49,824	50.4
	Charles W. Ackley (D)	48,743	49.3
3	William H. Sutphin (D)	58,670	52.2
	Oliver F. Van Camp (R)	53,170	47.3
4	D. Lane Powers (R)	48,760	56.7
	Walter Lincoln Whittlesey (D)	36,326	42.2
5	Charles A. Eaton (R)	54,938	51.7
	Charles S. MacKenzie (D)	50,395	47.4
6	Donald H. McLean (R)	51,528	52.5
	Richard U. Strong (D)	45,581	46.4
7	Randolph Perkins (R)	47,083	51.4
	Hamilton Cross (D)	43,771	47.7
8	George N. Seger (R)	45,123	53.6
	Frank J. Van Noort (D)	37,119	44.1
9	Edward A. Kenney (D)	54,941	54.6
	John Pollock (R)	44,704	44.4
10	Fred A. Hartley Jr. (R)	40,205	52.9
	William Herda Smith (D)	35,261	46.4
11	Peter A. Cavicchia (R)	34,110	50.0
	Edward L. O'Neill (D)	33,531	49.1
12	Frederick R. Lehlbach (R)	39,817	54.3
	Charles P. McCann (D)	32,546	44.4
13	Mary T. Norton (D)	73,342	73.2
	Anthony L. Montelli (R)	26,447	26.4
14	Edward J. Hart (D)	77,020	77.7
	Fred G. Tauber (R)	21,081	21.3

NEW MEXICO

	Candidates	Votes	%
AL	John J. Dempsey (D)	76,833	51.8
	M. F. Miera (R)	70,659	47.7

NEW YORK

	Candidates	Votes	%
1	Robert L. Bacon (RCF & LP)	127,082	56.0
	Gerald Morrell (D)	93,794	41.4
2	William F. Brunner (D)	140,520	69.6
	Thomas J. Styles (R & VIC)	48,306	23.9
3	Joseph L. Pfeifer (D)	26,738	72.8
	Alex Pisciotta (R CF&REC)	8,179	22.3
4	Thomas H. Cullen (D & REC)	29,858	74.5
	Charles E. Miller (R VIC&CF)	8,935	22.3
5	Marcellus H. Evans (D & REC)	41,154	64.7
	Frank E. Davis (RCF & LP)	19,010	29.9
6	Andrew L. Somers (D & LP)	70,164	60.9
	Donald C. Strachan (R & CF)	30,671	26.6
	Jacob Axelrad (SOC)	10,327	9.0
7	John J. Delaney (D)	28,945	67.9
	Joseph M. Aimee (RCF & LP)	9,897	23.2
	Alexander Kahn (SOC & LP)	2,503	5.9
8	Richard J. Tonry (D & REC)	111,247	59.2
	Sigurd J. Arnesen (R & CF)	44,423	23.6
	Baruch C. Vladeck (SOC)	22,149	11.8
9	Stephen A. Rudd (D)	56,617	60.6
	Murray Rosof (R & CF)	30,462	32.6
	Theodore Shapiro (SOC)	4,738	5.1
10	Emanuel Celler (D LP & L)	31,193	60.9
	Michael C. Antonelli (R CF&REC)	14,770	28.8
	Samuel H. Friedman (SOC)	3,470	6.8
11	James A. O'Leary (D)	36,393	59.9
	Arthur L. Willshaw (R)	15,595	25.7
	Vernon B. Hampton (RC I)	6,666	11.0
12	Samuel Dickstein (D)	14,895	76.8
	Solomon Siss (R & CF)	3,029	15.6
13	Christopher D. Sullivan (D)	13,090	72.3
	John Rosenberg (R)	3,828	21.1
14	William I. Sirovich (D)	15,437	52.8
	Frederick J. Groehl (R)	9,744	33.4
	Rachel Panken (SOC)	2,259	7.7
	Peter E. Cacchione (COM)	1,612	5.5
15	John J. Boylan (D)	23,482	80.2
	Frank J. McCoy (R)	4,726	16.1
16	John J. O'Connor (D)	22,528	66.3
	J. Homer Cudmore (R)	9,735	28.6
17	Theodore A. Peyser (D)	29,338	53.9
	George A. Spiegelberg (R CST&CF)	22,688	41.7
18	Martin J. Kennedy (D)	23,480	69.0
	Charles W. Ferry (R)	8,832	26.0
19	Sol Bloom (D & LP)	42,614	65.3
	Harold Goldman (R & CF)	18,612	28.5
20	Vito Marcantonio (R & CF)	13,083	46.6
	James J. Lanzetta (LAW PRES)	12,836	45.8
21	Joseph A. Gavagan (D)	62,042	68.2
	Kenneth Cameron (R & CF)	23,534	25.9
22	Anthony J. Griffin (D)	28,535	69.3
	John J. Sochurek (R & IV)	9,162	22.3
23	Charles A. Buckley (D)	109,319	64.2
	Isaac F. Becker (R)	31,028	18.2
	Samuel Orr (SOC)	14,333	8.4
24	James M. Fitzpatrick (D)	104,652	60.1
	John H. Nichols (R)	51,535	29.6
	Solomon Perrin (SOC)	11,256	6.5
25	Charles D. Millard (R)	63,782	54.8
	Homer A. Stebbins (D)	49,469	42.5
26	Hamilton Fish Jr. (R SOC&LP)	50,849	61.9
	Thomas Pendell (D)	31,292	38.1
27	Philip A. Goodwin (R & SOC)	46,924	55.7
	Willis G. Nash (D & LP)	37,295	44.3
28	Parker Corning (D)	89,511	70.1
	Frank R. Lanagan (R)	36,117	28.3
29	William D. Thomas (R & LP)	56,401	58.4
	Buell G. Brayton (D)	38,054	39.4
30	Frank Crowther (R & LP)	42,740	50.8
	Carroll A. Gardner (D)	39,048	46.4
31	Bertrand H. Snell (R)	43,942	62.0
	Kenneth Gardner (D)	26,308	37.1
32	Francis D. Culkin (R & LP)	49,055	67.0
	Annie D. Mills (D)	22,959	31.3
33	Fred J. Sisson (D)	45,831	49.1
	Frederick M. Davenport (R)	45,579	48.9
34	Bert Lord (R)	50,528	60.2
	Charles C. Flaesch (D)	32,075	38.2
35	Clarence E. Hancock (R)	65,732	54.7
	Richard P. Byrne (D)	50,599	42.1
36	John Taber (R)	45,431	61.0
	Dennis F. Sullivan (D)	27,129	36.4
37	W. Sterling Cole (R)	48,964	59.8
	Julian P. Bretz (D)	28,979	35.4
38	James P. B. Duffy (D)	64,434	54.2
	James L. Whitley (R & LP)	50,066	42.1
39	James W. Wadsworth Jr. (R & LP)	49,915	56.2
	David A. White (D)	36,658	41.3
40	Walter G. Andrews (R)	69,353	55.7
	Frank S. Anderson (D)	50,532	40.6
41	Alfred F. Beiter (D)	45,830	55.7
	Carlton A. Fisher (R)	33,793	41.1
42	James M. Mead (D)	49,251	63.8
	Walter J. Lohr (R & LP)	26,036	33.7
43	Daniel A. Reed (R & LP)	42,513	63.3
	Peter B. Hogan (D)	21,856	32.6
AL	Caroline O'Day (D)	1,978,670✓	
	Matthew J. Merritt (D)	1,952,039✓	
	Natalie F. Couch (R)	1,417,271	
	William B. Groat Jr (R)	1,387,460	
	Charles W. Noonan (SOC)	141,799	
	August Claessens (SOC)	138,778	
	Henry Sheppard (COM)	48,851	
	Emanuel Levin (COM)	47,812	
	Dorothy Frooks (LAW PRES)	19,853	
	William E. Barron (LAW PRES)	16,770	
	Jeremiah D. Crowley (SOC LAB)	7,529	
	Jacob Berlin (SOC LAB)	6,701	

Special Election

	Candidates	Votes	%
29	William D. Thomas (R)	25,048	60.1
	John J. Nyhoff (D)	16,030	38.5

NORTH CAROLINA

	Candidates	Votes	%
1	Lindsay C. Warren (D)	11,786	87.8
	R. C. Dozier (R)	1,637	12.2
2	John H. Kerr (D)	11,329	100.0
3	Graham A. Barden (D)	20,218	67.1
	W. B. Rouse (R)	9,922	32.9
4	Harold D. Cooley (D)	29,431	68.5
	Hobart Brantley (R)	13,507	31.5
5	Franklin W. Hancock Jr. (D)	28,221	100.0
6	William B. Umstead (D)	21,241	69.0
	B. C. Campbell (R)	9,543	31.0
7	J. Bayard Clark (D)	17,774	78.9
	Louis Goodman (R)	4,747	21.1

NORTH CAROLINA

	Candidates	Votes	%
8	J. Walter Lambeth (D)	35,794	58.0
	Avalon E. Hall (R)	25,974	42.1
9	Robert L. Doughton (D)	44,780	58.2
	J. M. Prevette (R)	32,171	41.8
10	Alfred L. Bulwinkle (D)	43,483	53.5
	Calvin R. Edney (R)	37,820	46.5
11	Zebulon Weaver (D)	56,199	59.6
	Halsey B. Leavitt (R)	38,126	40.4

Special Election

4	Harold D. Cooley (D)	16,881	93.8
	Hobart Brantley (R)	1,110	6.2

NORTH DAKOTA

AL	William Lemke (R)	144,705✓	
	Usher L. Burdick (R)	114,841✓	
	William D. Lynch (D)	85,771	
	G. F. Lamb (D)	79,338	
	J. H. Sinclair (I)	46,304	
	Jasper Haaland (I)	1,299	
	Effie Kjorstad (I)	1,090	

OHIO

1	John B. Hollister (R)	53,985	55.8
	Edwin G. Becker (D)	42,723	44.2
2	William E. Hess (R)	51,171	55.1
	Charles E. Miller (D)	41,701	44.9
3	Byron B. Harlan (D)	67,695	53.6
	Howard F. Heald (R)	56,480	44.8
4	Frank L. Kloeb (D)	48,613	53.9
	Guy D. Hawley (R)	41,504	46.1
5	Frank C. Kniffin (D)	34,249	55.5
	Davis B. Johnson (R)	27,423	44.5
6	James G. Polk (D)	42,340	52.2
	Albert L. Daniels (R)	38,538	47.5
7	Leroy T. Marshall (R)	56,453	56.6
	C. W. Rich (D)	43,226	43.4
8	Brooks Fletcher (D)	39,466	52.2
	Gertrude Jones (R)	36,112	47.8
9	Warren J. Duffey (D)	61,037	62.3
	Frank L. Mulholland (R)	35,732	36.5
10	Thomas A. Jenkins (R)	36,824	58.4
	W. F. Marting (D)	26,278	41.6
11	Mell G. Underwood (D)	36,020	57.4
	Renick W. Dunlap (R)	26,723	42.6
12	Arthur P. Lamneck (D)	63,396	55.7
	John C. Speaks (R)	50,386	44.3
13	William L. Fiesinger (D)	43,617	54.3
	Walter E. Kruger (R)	35,889	44.7
14	Dow W. Harter (D)	65,152	49.1
	Carl D. Sheppard (R)	63,274	47.7
15	Robert T. Secrest (D)	42,722	55.7
	Kenneth C. Ray (R)	33,950	44.3
16	William R. Thom (D)	59,354	56.7
	C. B. McClintock (R)	45,390	43.3
17	William A. Ashbrook (D)	49,211	54.0
	James A. Glenn (R)	41,954	46.0
18	Lawrence E. Imhoff (D)	49,160	55.4
	Frank Murphy (R)	39,642	44.6
19	John G. Cooper (R)	56,200	51.2
	Locke Miller (D)	52,023	47.4
20	Martin L. Sweeney (D)	50,611	67.9
	Joseph E. Cassidy (R)	21,952	29.4
21	Robert W. Crosser (D)	47,540	63.8
	Frank W. Sotak (R)	25,253	33.9
22	Chester C. Bolton (R)	99,535	52.1
	William C. Dixon (D)	88,551	46.3
AL	Charles V. Truax (D)	1,061,857✓	
	Stephen M. Young (D)	1,050,089✓	
	George H. Bender (R)	905,233	
	L. L. Marshall (R)	871,432	
	Ben Atkins (COM)	13,972	
	John Marshall (COM)	13,808	

OKLAHOMA

	Candidates	Votes	%
1	Wesley E. Disney (D)	61,470	60.1
	Robert W. Kellough (R)	39,085	38.2
2	Jack Nichols (D)	40,210	62.2
	C. E. Creager (R)	24,001	37.1
3	Wilburn Cartwright (D)	50,435	76.9
	John D. Morrison (R)	14,202	21.7
4	P. L. Gassaway (D)	47,140	67.5
	James S. Davidson (R)	19,875	28.5
5	Josh Lee (D)	58,322	74.6
	Paul Huston (R)	18,640	23.9
6	Jed Johnson (D)	37,567	67.2
	George E. Young (R)	15,567	27.8
7	Sam C. Massingale (D)	35,210	76.0
	Fred Langley (R)	8,214	17.7
	Orville E. Enfield (SOC)	2,891	6.2
8	Phil Ferguson (D)	40,248	56.8
	T. J. Sargent (R)	30,019	42.4
AL	Will Rogers (D)	354,542	66.9
	U. S. Stone (R)	162,991	30.7

OREGON

1	James W. Mott (R)	67,286	49.9
	R. R. Turner (D)	51,443	38.1
	Emmett W. Gulley (I)	12,963	9.6
2	Walter M. Pierce (D)	29,221	56.7
	Jay H. Upton (R)	21,255	41.3
3	William A. Ekwall (R)	43,900	41.1
	Walter B. Gleason (D)	41,152	38.5
	Andrew C. Smith (I)	9,968	9.3

PENNSYLVANIA

1	Harry C. Ransley (R)	46,039	52.1
	Joseph Marinelli (D)	41,733	47.2
2	William H. Wilson (R)	44,478	54.7
	James P. McGranery (D)	36,212	44.6
3	Clare Gerald Fenerty (R)	53,512	52.0
	Michael Joseph Bradley (D)	48,141	46.8
4	J. Burrwood Daly (D)	45,901	49.7
	George W. Edmonds (R)	45,526	49.2
5	Frank J. G. Dorsey (D)	50,650	52.2
	James J. Connolly (R)	45,287	46.7
6	Michael J. Stack (D)	50,977	50.8
	Robert L. Davis (R)	48,308	48.2
7	George P. Darrow (R)	56,990	52.7
	James C. Crumlich (D)	50,207	46.4
8	James Wolfenden (R)	60,139	57.2
	John E. McDonough (D)	43,426	41.3
9	Oliver W. Frey (D)	40,494	50.2
	Theodore R. Gardner (R)	38,427	47.6
10	J. Roland Kinzer (R, P)	58,773	57.6
	Charles T. Carpenter (D)	42,540	41.7
11	Patrick J. Boland (R, D)	76,568	98.1
12	C. Murray Turpin (R)	60,608	51.4
	John J. Casey (D, SOC)	56,554	48.0
13	James H. Gildea (D)	54,309	50.1
	David W. Bechtel (R)	49,584	45.7
14	William E. Richardson (D, R)	39,134	63.3
	Raymond S. Hofses (SOC)	19,871	32.2
15	C. Elmer Dietrich (D)	39,566	50.1
	Louis T. McFadden (R, P)	38,905	49.3
16	Robert F. Rich (R, P)	38,761	53.0
	Paul A. Rothfuss (D, SOC)	32,436	44.4
17	J. William Ditter (R)	50,149	56.2
	Howard J. Dager (D)	37,541	42.1
18	Benjamin K. Focht (R, P)	37,992	55.6
	B. Stiles Duncan (D)	30,320	44.4
19	Isaac H. Doutrich (R)	62,576	55.1
	Forrest Mercer (D)	48,743	42.9
20	D. J. Driscoll (D)	48,245	52.7
	Leon H. Gavin (R)	40,050	43.7
21	Francis E. Walter (D, P)	41,789	58.6
	T. Fred Woodley (R)	28,520	40.0
22	Harry L. Haines (D)	49,629	54.6
	Emanuel C. Beck (R)	39,719	43.7

	Candidates	Votes	%
23	Don Gingery (D)	41,088	52.4
	J. Banks Kurtz (R, P)	34,631	44.2
24	J. Buell Snyder (D)	43,530	57.3
	Paul H. Griffith (R, P)	31,904	42.0
25	Charles I. Faddis (D, SOC)	39,122	59.4
	Albert S. Sickman (R)	25,435	38.6
26	Charles R. Eckert (D)	52,243	59.1
	J. Howard Swick (R, P)	35,302	40.0
27	Joseph Gray (D)	59,891	54.4
	Nathan L. Strong (R, P)	49,005	44.5
28	William M. Berlin (D, R)	63,262	92.5
29	Charles N. Crosby (D)	32,530	52.5
	Will Rose (R)	28,292	45.6
30	J. Twing Brooks (D)	40,864	53.4
	Edmund F. Erk (R, RO)	34,412	45.0
31	James E. Quinn (D)	44,711	52.3
	Clyde Kelly (R, P)	38,984	45.6
32	Theodore L. Moritz (D)	24,275	43.3
	Michael J. Muldowney (R)	19,134	34.1
	Alexander H. Schullman (I)	8,441	15.0
	Anne E. Felix (HE)	2,865	5.1
33	Henry Ellenbogen (D, R)	72,584	95.2
34	Matthew A. Dunn (D, R)	72,215	89.2
	Guy E. Campbell (LFD)	5,474	6.8

RHODE ISLAND

1	Francis Bernard Condon (D)	70,516	59.0
	John C. Cosseboom (R)	49,087	41.0
2	John Matthew O'Connell (D)	69,765	55.8
	George C. Clark (R)	55,191	44.2

SOUTH CAROLINA

1	Thomas S. McMillan (D)	4,264	97.7
2	Hampton P. Fulmer (D)	3,518	99.2
3	John C. Taylor (D)	3,830	99.4
4	John J. McSwain (D)	4,681	99.4
5	James P. Richards (D)	2,645	98.7
6	Allard H. Gasque (D)	2,983	99.3

SOUTH DAKOTA

1	Fred H. Hildebrandt (D)	122,932	58.5
	C. A. Christopherson (R)	84,830	40.4
2	Theodore B. Werner (D)	35,467	52.5
	Francis H. Case (R)	32,105	47.5

TENNESSEE

1	B. Carroll Reece (R)	22,156	56.8
	W. A. S. Furlow (D)	13,708	35.2
2	J. Will Taylor (R)	25,729	58.7
	T. C. Drinnon (D)	9,740	22.2
	E. E. Patton (I)	7,081	16.2
3	Sam D. McReynolds (D)	21,559	60.0
	Pat H. Thach (R)	14,387	40.0
4	J. Ridley Mitchell (D)	26,064	78.4
	H. E. McLean (R)	7,182	21.6
5	Joseph W. Byrns (D)	26,856	100.0
6	Clarence W. Turner (D)	16,102	100.0
7	Herron Pearson (D)	15,808	100.0
8	Jere Cooper (D)	18,112	100.0
9	Walter Chandler (D)	46,363	100.0

TEXAS

1	Wright Patman (D)	18,608	98.5
2	Martin Dies (D)	16,628	100.0
3	Morgan G. Sanders (D)	14,790	100.0
4	Sam Rayburn (D)	16,684	96.8
5	Hatton Sumners (D)	27,302	96.9
6	Luther Johnson (D)	16,294	100.0
7	Nat Patton (D)	18,063	99.1
8	Joe H. Eagle (D)	40,400	99.5
9	Joseph J. Mansfield (D)	23,257	100.0
10	James P. Buchanan (D)	19,306	100.0
11	Oliver H. Cross (D)	20,383	100.0

TEXAS

	Candidates	Votes	%
12	Fritz G. Lanham (D)	24,984	98.4
13	W. D. McFarlane (D)	21,005	100.0
14	Richard M. Kleberg (D)	26,276	100.0
15	Milton H. West (D)	20,102	88.0
	G. C. Mann (R)	2,739	12.0
16	R. Ewing Thomason (D)	11,063	100.0
17	Thomas L. Blanton (D)	17,266	100.0
18	Marvin Jones (D)	23,202	96.9
19	George Mahon (D)	20,169	100.0
20	Maury Maverick (D)	17,810	98.6
21	Charles L. South (D)	26,093	100.0

UTAH

		Votes	%
1	Abe Murdock (D)	55,800	64.4
	Arthur Woolley (R)	29,878	34.5
2	J. Will Robinson (D)	58,175	62.3
	Frederick Loofbourow (R)	34,007	36.4

VERMONT

		Votes	%
AL	Charles A. Plumley (R)	73,809	56.9
	Carroll E. Jenkins (D)	54,967	42.4

VIRGINIA

		Votes	%
1	Schuyler Otis Bland (D)	7,637	91.4
2	Colgate W. Darden Jr. (D)	11,102	76.1
	Gerould M. Rumble (R)	3,321	22.8
3	Andrew Jackson Montague (D)	9,738	80.5
	Roy C. Parks (R)	2,129	17.6
4	Patrick Henry Drewry (D)	7,850	93.4
5	Thomas G. Burch (D)	11,964	88.2
	Henry P. Wilder	1,168	8.6
6	Clifton A. Woodrum (D)	10,738	67.1
	Thomas J. Wilson Jr. (R)	5,060	31.6

	Candidates	Votes	%
7	A. Willis Robertson (D)	14,903	68.3
	J. Everett Will (R)	6,562	30.1
8	Howard W. Smith (D)	14,191	78.8
	John Locke Green (R)	3,583	19.9
9	John W. Flannagan Jr. (D)	20,532	58.1
	Fred C. Parks (R)	12,355	35.0
	Bruce Crawford (I)	2,402	6.8

WASHINGTON

		Votes	%
1	Marion A. Zioncheck (D)	68,395	57.7
	Bert C. Ross (R)	38,350	32.4
	Cecil R. Fuller (CNM)	8,500	7.2
2	Mon C. Wallgren (D)	50,486	67.0
	Payson Peterson (R)	23,638	31.4
3	Martin F. Smith (D)	48,887	69.2
	Russell V. Mack (R)	21,750	30.8
4	Knute Hill (D)	35,702	56.4
	John W. Summers (R)	27,637	43.6
5	Sam B. Hill (D)	58,901	76.2
	Mansfield E. Mack (R)	18,397	23.8
6	Wesley Lloyd (D)	52,314	70.5
	Emery Asbury (R)	21,883	29.5

WEST VIRGINIA

		Votes	%
1	Robert L. Ramsay (D)	52,714	53.3
	Carl G. Bachmann (R)	45,442	45.9
2	Jennings Randolph (D)	54,531	57.6
	Herbert E. Hannis (R)	39,832	42.1
3	Andrew Edmiston (D)	54,885	53.6
	James A. Rusmisell (R)	46,978	45.9
4	George W. Johnson (D)	60,684	50.4
	Robert B. McDougle (R)	59,013	49.1
5	John Kee (D)	54,659	58.5
	C. M. (Casey) Jones (R)	38,599	41.3
6	Joe L. Smith (D)	67,671	61.4
	Frank C. Burdette (R)	42,147	38.3

WISCONSIN

	Candidates	Votes	%
1	Thomas R. Amlie (PROG)	32,397	37.4
	Judson W. Staplekamp (R)	28,459	32.9
	Ralph V. Brown (D)	23,532	27.2
2	Harry Sauthoff (PROG)	41,458	41.8
	Charles W. Henney (D)	33,347	33.6
	John B. Gay (R)	22,995	23.2
3	Gardner R. Withrow (PROG)	47,311	52.1
	Levi H. Bancroft (R)	25,851	28.5
	Bart E. McGonigle (D)	17,222	19.0
4	Raymond J. Cannon (D)	33,886	38.6
	John C. Schafer (R)	19,840	22.6
	Marvin V. Baxter (SOC)	18,166	20.7
	Laurence C. Gram (PROG)	15,364	17.5
5	Thomas O'Malley (D)	32,931	34.7
	Otto Hauser (SOC)	23,334	24.6
	Arthur T. Spence (R)	21,533	22.7
	Carl J. Ludwig (PROG)	16,693	17.6
6	Michael K. Reilly (D)	34,664	42.3
	Walter D. Corrigan (PROG)	28,477	34.7
	William J. Campbell (R)	18,825	23.0
7	Gerald J. Boileau (PROG)	41,321	48.5
	Frank D. Chapman (D)	24,871	29.2
	Caspar Wallrich (R)	17,461	20.5
8	George J. Schneider (PROG)	39,505	43.8
	Gerald F. Clifford (D)	34,397	38.2
	L. Herman Waite (R)	15,748	17.5
9	Merlin Hull (PROG)	42,422	49.6
	Willis E. Donley (D)	20,828	24.3
	Knute Anderson (R)	20,043	23.4
10	Bernard J. Gehrmann (PROG)	29,397	35.4
	Hubert H. Peavey (R)	24,850	29.9
	Charles P. Cadigan (D)	24,689	29.7

WYOMING

		Votes	%
AL	Paul R. Greever (D)	53,288	58.3
	Charles E. Winter (R)	37,492	41.0

1935 House Election

INDIANA

Special Election

2	Charles A. Halleck (R)	50,324	52.7
	George R. Durgan (D)	45,089	47.3

1936 House Elections

ALABAMA

	Candidates	Votes	%
1	Frank W. Boykin (D)	23,421	100.0
2	Lister Hill (D)	32,452	99.1
3	Henry B. Steagall (D)	22,535	100.0
4	Sam Hobbs (D)	22,615	86.4
	Charles R. Robinson (R)	3,556	13.6
5	Joe Starnes (D)	29,891	100.0
6	Pete Jarman (D)	18,325	100.0
7	William B. Bankhead (D)	25,126	73.0
	J. B. Weaver (R)	9,311	27.0
8	John J. Sparkman (D)	27,788	99.7
9	Luther Patrick (D)	36,405	91.8
	J. G. Bass (R)	3,177	8.0

ARIZONA

		Votes	%
AL	John R. Murdock (D)	84,403	77.6
	G. L. Burgess (R)	20,383	18.7

ARKANSAS

		Votes	%
1	William J. Driver (D)	32,066	100.0
2	John E. Miller (D)	19,146	85.6
	J. N. Hout Jr. (R)	3,224	14.4
3	Claude A. Fuller (D)	18,417	65.3
	J. S. Thompson (R)	9,796	34.7
4	William B. Cravens (D)	25,902	100.0
5	David D. Terry (D)	26,102	100.0
6	John L. McClellan (D)	25,411	100.0
7	Wade Kitchens (D)	20,117	95.4

CALIFORNIA

		Votes	%
1	Clarence F. Lea (D)	58,073	53.8
	Nelson B. Van Matre (R)	48,647	45.1
2	Harry L. Englebright (R-D-PROG)	51,416	100.0
3	Frank H. Buck (D-R)	93,110	90.4
	Walter Schaefer	5,310	5.2
4	Franck R. Havenner (D & PROG)	64,063	58.5
	Florence P. Kahn (R)	43,805	40.0
5	Richard J. Welch (R-D-PROG)	82,910	94.8
	Lawrence Ross (COM)	4,545	5.2
6	Albert E. Carter (R-D)	103,712	91.0
	Clarence E. Rust (SOC)	8,247	7.2
7	John H. Tolan (D)	69,463	59.8
	Charles W. Fisher (R)	46,647	40.2
8	John Joseph McGrath (D & PROG)	78,557	57.6
	Alonzo L. Baker (R)	57,808	42.4
9	Bertrand W. Gearhart (R-D)	82,360	97.0
10	Henry E. Stubbs (D)	72,367	69.5
	George R. Bliss (R)	31,700	30.4
11	John Steven McGroarty (D)	69,679	50.5
	Carl Hinshaw (R)	54,914	39.8
	Robert S. Funk (PROG)	12,340	8.9
12	H. Jerry Voorhis (D)	62,034	53.7
	Frederick F. Houser (R)	53,445	46.3
13	Charles Kramer (D-R)	119,251	89.4
	Floyd Seaman	6,946	5.2
14	Thomas F. Ford (D)	63,365	61.0
	William D. Campbell (R)	25,497	24.6
	Albert L. Johnson (PROG)	12,874	12.4
15	John M. Costello (D & PROG)	99,107	69.0
	Ernest Walker Sawyer (R)	44,559	31.0
16	John F. Dockweiler (D)	90,986	57.7
	Raymond V. Darby (R)	66,583	42.2
17	Charles J. Colden (D)	68,189	71.9
	Leonard Roach (R)	24,981	26.3
18	Byron N. Scott (D)	61,415	58.9
	James F. Collins (R)	42,748	41.0

	Candidates	Votes	%
19	Harry R. Sheppard (D)	70,339	53.8
	Sam L. Collins (R)	59,071	45.2
20	Edouard V. M. Izac (D)	59,208	56.4
	Ed P. Sample (R)	44,925	42.8

COLORADO

		Votes	%
1	Lawrence Lewis (D)	100,704	69.0
	Harry Zimmerhackel (R)	41,574	28.5
2	Fred Cummings (D)	66,420	53.3
	George H. Bradfield (R)	57,145	45.8
3	John A. Martin (D)	74,013	60.2
	J. Arthur Phelps (R)	48,871	39.8
4	Edward T. Taylor (D)	42,010	65.5
	John S. Woody (R)	22,175	34.6

CONNECTICUT

		Votes	%
1	Herman P. Kopplemann (D)	101,766	57.9
	Walter E. Batterson (R)	66,005	37.6
2	William J. Fitzgerald (D)	55,369	50.9
	William L. Higgins (R)	50,369	46.3
3	James A. Shanley (D)	77,295	54.6
	John F. Lynch (R)	57,243	40.4
4	Alfred N. Phillips Jr. (D)	80,875	50.0
	Schuyler Merritt (R)	67,768	41.9
5	J. Joseph Smith (D)	55,897	58.6
	J. Warren Upson (R)	39,230	41.1
AL	William N. Citron (D)	371,572	53.9
	Francis Pallotti (R)	282,618	41.0

DELAWARE

		Votes	%
AL	William F. Allen (D)	65,485	51.7
	John George Stewart (R)	55,664	44.0

FLORIDA

		Votes	%
1	J. Hardin Peterson (D)	61,855	74.5
	B. L. Hamner (R)	21,215	25.5
2	R. A. Green (D)	47,520	100.0
3	Millard Caldwell (D)	34,239	100.0
4	J. Mark Wilcox (D)	46,854	70.6
	Thomas E. Swanson (R)	19,515	29.4
5	Joe Hendricks (D)	42,937	79.9
	C. F. Batchelder (R)	10,802	20.1

GEORGIA

		Votes	%
1	Hugh Peterson Jr. (D)	25,846	100.0
2	E. E. Cox (D)	21,405	100.0
3	Stephen Pace (D)	25,613	100.0
4	E. M. Owen (D)	24,643	100.0
5	Robert Ramspeck (D)	35,540	89.4
	H. H. Alexander (R)	4,213	10.6
6	Carl Vinson (D)	20,595	100.0
7	Malcolm C. Tarver (D)	31,343	92.6
	L. Mitchell Johnson (R)	2,493	7.4
8	Braswell Deen (D)	24,695	94.9
	Ben J. Ford (R)	1,320	5.1
9	B. Frank Whelchel (D)	23,682	75.4
	John M. Johnson (R)	7,739	24.6
10	Paul Brown (D)	27,147	100.0

IDAHO

		Votes	%
1	Compton I. White (D)	58,941	70.3
	John S. Heckathorn (R)	24,959	29.8
2	D. Worth Clark (D)	67,238	60.5
	Henry C. Dworshak (R)	43,834	39.5

ILLINOIS

	Candidates	Votes	%
1	Arthur W. Mitchell (D)	35,376	55.1
	Oscar De Priest (R)	28,640	44.6
2	Raymond S. McKeough (D)	163,198	55.6
	P. H. Moynihan (R)	130,197	44.4
3	Edward A. Kelly (D)	156,425	59.3
	Frank M. Fulton (R)	106,300	40.3
4	Harry P. Beam (D)	69,931	80.8
	Irene A. Tomas (R)	16,591	19.2
5	Adolph J. Sabath (D)	35,019	77.4
	Max Price (R)	10,252	22.6
6	Thomas J. O'Brien (D)	204,548	65.5
	Frederick A. Virkus (R)	107,649	34.5
7	Leonard W. Schuetz (D)	248,835	59.2
	James C. Moreland (R)	158,755	37.7
8	Leo Kocialkowski (D)	34,452	78.6
	Edw. Richard Piszatowski (R)	8,945	20.4
9	James McAndrews (D)	60,307	59.2
	Bertha Baur (R)	41,587	40.8
10	Ralph E. Church (R)	158,497	51.4
	Charles J. Wightman (D)	140,225	45.5
11	Chauncey W. Reed (R)	99,027	56.0
	John R. Barber (D)	77,938	44.0
12	Noah M. Mason (R)	69,721	51.6
	D. O. Thompson (D)	58,263	43.1
	D. S. Gishwiller (TOWN OAP)	7,203	5.3
13	Leo E. Allen (R)	52,495	58.4
	David L. Trunck (D)	37,346	41.6
14	Chester Thompson (D)	58,809	54.4
	Clinton Searle (R)	49,250	45.6
15	Lewis L. Boyer (D)	54,703	49.4
	Joe E. Anderson (R)	53,531	48.3
16	Everett M. Dirksen (R)	68,964	53.2
	Charles C. Dickman (D)	60,559	46.8
17	Leslie C. Arends (R)	46,646	52.6
	Frank Gillespie (D)	42,071	47.4
18	James A. Meeks (D)	61,286	53.8
	Hugh M. Luckey (R)	52,730	46.3
19	Hugh M. Rigney (D)	77,446	55.7
	William H. Wheat (R)	61,535	44.3
20	Scott W. Lucas (D)	48,128	56.7
	Harry C. Montgomery (R)	36,732	43.3
21	Frank W. Fries (D)	62,769	51.7
	Frank M. Ramey (R)	58,573	48.2
22	Edwin M. Schaefer (D)	96,589	59.1
	Jesse R. Brown (R)	66,960	40.9
23	Laurence F. Arnold (D)	62,044	55.2
	Ben O. Sumner (R)	50,354	44.8
24	Claude V. Parsons (D)	45,740	51.7
	W. A. Spence (R)	42,764	48.3
25	Kent E. Keller (D)	68,995	53.9
	J. Lester Buford (R)	59,101	46.1
AL	Lewis J. Long (D)	2,062,886✔	
	Edwin V. Champion (D)	2,032,432✔	
	Rodney H. Brandon (R)	1,568,552	
	John T. Dempsey (R)	1,564,889	
	Severin H. Hanson (UN PROG)	83,886	
	Rad Burnett (UN PROG)	81,551	
	Ina M. White (SOC)	7,817	
	Nate Egnor (SOC)	7,651	
	Mary Morgan Williams (P)	3,269	
	Frank Earl Herrick (P)	3,262	
	Edward K. Schooley (SOC LAB)	2,374	
	Mathilda M. Deavers (SOC LAB)	2,235	

INDIANA

		Votes	%
1	William T. Schulte (D)	68,210	66.4
	Fred F. Schultz (R)	34,259	33.3
2	Charles A. Halleck (R)	73,072	51.5
	Hugh A. Barnhart (D)	68,318	48.2

INDIANA

	Candidates	Votes	%
3	Samuel B. Pettingill (D)	71,315	56.2
	Andrew J. Hickey (R)	52,462	41.4
4	James I. Farley (D)	72,210	55.2
	David Hogg (R)	58,519	44.8
5	Glenn Griswold (D)	70,854	52.6
	Benjamin J. Brown (R)	63,517	47.2
6	Virginia A. Jenckes (D)	82,096	54.9
	Noble J. Johnson (R)	66,942	44.8
7	Arthur Greenwood (D)	81,901	53.8
	Gerald W. Landis (R)	69,928	45.9
8	John W. Boehne Jr. (D)	89,548	62.6
	Charles F. Werner (R)	50,590	35.4
9	Eugene B. Crowe (D)	74,486	54.2
	Chester A. Davis (R)	62,714	45.7
10	Finly H. Gray (D)	73,547	52.6
	Clarence M. Brown (R)	66,299	47.4
11	William H. Larrabee (D)	80,856	59.4
	Don Roberts (R)	53,801	39.5
12	Louis Ludlow (D)	77,510	57.7
	Homer Elliott (R)	54,885	40.9

IOWA

	Candidates	Votes	%
1	Edward C. Eicher (D)	55,721	51.0
	John N. Calhoun (R)	53,474	49.0
2	William S. Jacobsen (D)	70,923	54.6
	Charles Penningroth (R)	55,255	42.5
3	John W. Gwynne (R)	53,928	53.2
	A. C. Willford (D)	47,391	46.8
4	Fred Biermann (D)	56,308	50.6
	Henry O. Talle (R)	51,805	46.6
5	Lloyd Thurston (R)	63,802	51.5
	Kenneth F. Baldridge (D)	58,971	47.6
6	Cassius C. Dowell (R)	63,026	52.4
	Harry B. Dunlap (D)	55,975	46.5
7	Otha D. Wearin (D)	61,398	50.4
	Henry K. Peterson (R)	59,834	49.2
8	Fred C. Gilchrist (R)	56,076	52.5
	Ray Murray (D)	48,403	45.3
9	Vincent F. Harrington (D)	63,995	53.5
	Fred B. Wolf (R)	53,675	44.9

KANSAS

	Candidates	Votes	%
1	William P. Lambertson (R)	66,158	58.3
	Howard S. Miller (D)	47,303	41.7
2	Ulysses S. Guyer (R)	72,038	53.3
	David C. Doten (D)	60,049	44.5
3	Edward W. Patterson (D)	55,541	48.4
	Harold McGugin (R)	52,235	45.5
	L. P. Beard (I)	6,921	6.0
4	Edward H. Rees (R)	51,732	54.5
	C. D. Hill (D)	42,818	45.1
5	John M. Houston (D)	62,501	60.0
	J. B. Patterson (R)	41,656	40.0
6	Frank Carlson (R)	61,669	52.0
	Arthur Connelly (D)	56,850	48.0
7	Clifford R. Hope (R)	66,553	56.0
	Thomas A. Ralston (D)	52,370	44.0

KENTUCKY

	Candidates	Votes	%
1	Noble J. Gregory (D)	58,265	71.9
	R. N. Brumfield (R)	22,757	28.1
2	Glover H. Cary (D)	70,949*	64.0
	Claude E. Smith (R)	39,887	36.0
3	Emmet O'Neal (D)	85,034	60.3
	W. A. Armstrong (R)	52,600	37.3
4	Edward W. Creal (D)	54,616	59.0
	Stanley Jaggers (R)	37,979	41.0
5	Brent Spence (D)	57,842	66.7
	Ervin L. Bramlage (R)	25,011	28.8
6	Virgil Chapman (D)	70,094	57.9
	A. R. Anderson (R)	48,771	40.3
7	Andrew J. May (D)	40,366	55.9
	John B. Mollette (R)	31,865	44.1
8	Fred M. Vinson (D)	60,474	58.7
	W. Hoffman Wood (R)	42,507	41.3

	Candidates	Votes	%
9	John M. Robsion (R)	67,199	61.6
	George L. Tye (D)	41,958	38.4

LOUISIANA

		Votes	%
1	Joachim O. Fernandez (D)	61,142	100.0
2	Paul H. Maloney (D)	65,345	100.0
3	Robert L. Mouton (D)	20,605	100.0
4	Overton Brooks (D)	26,152	99.9
5	Newton V. Mills (D)	29,144	100.0
6	John K. Griffith (D)	34,908	100.0
7	Rene L. DeRouen (D)	27,563	100.0
8	A. Leonard Allen (D)	27,071	100.0

MAINE

		Votes	%
1	James C. Oliver (R)	60,565	57.9
	Simon M. Hamlin (D)	44,106	42.1
2	Clyde H. Smith (R)	53,822	51.6
	Ernest L. McLean (D)	38,986	37.4
	J. C. Leckemby (IR)	8,197	7.9
3	Ralph O. Brewster (R)	56,044	60.8
	Wallace F. Mabee (D)	36,103	39.2

MARYLAND

		Votes	%
1	T. Alan Goldsborough (D)	38,705	60.0
	O. Straughn Lloyd (R)	25,780	40.0
2	William P. Cole Jr. (D)	98,515	61.7
	Henry C. Whiteford (R)	60,003	37.6
3	Vincent L. Palmisano (D)	37,446	60.5
	John Philip Hill (R)	23,941	38.7
4	Ambrose J. Kennedy (D)	46,132	51.5
	Daniel Ellison (R)	39,653	44.3
5	Stephen Warfield Gambrill (D)	47,145	64.7
	Roscoe C. Rowe (R)	25,036	34.4
6	David J. Lewis (D)	53,504	56.4
	Harry W. Le Gore (R)	40,823	43.0

MASSACHUSETTS

		Votes	%
1	Allen T. Treadway (R)	60,043	50.5
	Owen Johnson (D)	52,342	44.0
2	Charles R. Clason (R)	57,618	49.0
	Agnes C. Reavey (D)	52,197	44.3
3	Joseph E. Casey (D)	64,960	54.1
	Bernard W. Doyle (R)	54,154	45.1
4	Pehr G. Holmes (R)	61,624	51.5
	Edward A. Ryan (D)	56,770	47.4
5	Edith Nourse Rogers (R)	90,845	62.8
	Daniel J. Coughlin (D)	48,701	33.7
6	George J. Bates (R)	79,145	68.6
	John E. Taffe (TOWN-SJD)	36,171	31.4
7	William P. Connery Jr. (D)	76,521	59.1
	C. F. Nelson Pratt (R)	51,009	39.4
8	Arthur D. Healey (D)	60,211	52.6
	William S. Howe (R)	46,446	40.5
	Nelson F. Wright (UN)	6,010	5.3
9	Robert Luce (R)	70,852	50.6
	Richard M. Russell (D)	61,582	44.0
10	George Holden Tinkham (R)	74,251	59.5
	William F. Madden (D)	39,112	31.4
	John McLaren (TOWN-C-L)	11,349	9.1
11	John P. Higgins (D)	53,129	81.3
	Joseph M. De Napoli (R)	8,523	13.1
12	John W. McCormack (D)	78,711	68.7
	Albert P. McCulloch (FACP R)	35,827	31.3
13	Richard B. Wigglesworth (R)	76,793	58.5
	Harry J. Dowd (D)	54,576	41.5
14	Joseph W. Martin Jr. (R)	58,758	53.3
	Arthur E. Seagrave (D)	38,609	35.0
	Lawrence O. Witter (UN)	12,872	11.7
15	Charles L. Gifford (R)	58,355	50.1
	John D. W. Bodfish (D)	42,538	36.5

Candidates	Votes	%
John Henry McNeece (TOWN SJ)	12,419	10.7

MICHIGAN

		Votes	%
1	George G. Sadowski (D)	72,713	80.4
	Charles A. Roxborough (R)	17,265	19.1
2	Earl C. Michener (R)	53,845	51.7
	Charles E. Downing (D)	50,238	48.3
3	Paul W. Shafer (R)	54,767	51.8
	Rosslyn L. Sowers (D)	50,956	48.2
4	Clare E. Hoffman (R)	49,641	50.5
	Guy M. Tyler (D)	44,365	45.1
5	Carl E. Mapes (R)	49,860	48.2
	Thomas F. McAllister (D)	48,998	47.4
6	Andrew J. Transue (D)	72,556	57.7
	William W. Blackney (R)	53,140	42.3
7	Jesse P. Wolcott (R)	54,693	59.9
	Albert A. Wagner (D)	36,462	39.9
8	Fred L. Crawford (R)	45,379	46.8
	Michael J. Hart (D)	44,309	45.7
	Clarence J. Brainerd (UN)	7,249	7.5
9	Albert J. Engel (R)	40,675	50.2
	Jack Eliasohn (D)	40,095	49.5
10	Roy O. Woodruff (R)	41,997	57.6
	William J. Kelly (D)	30,784	42.3
11	John Luecke (D)	44,528	52.8
	Herbert J. Rushton (R)	39,602	46.9
12	Frank E. Hook (D)	46,284	54.7
	W. Frank James (R)	37,714	44.6
13	George D. O'Brien (D)	63,479	55.1
	Clarence J. McLeod (R)	49,910	43.3
14	Louis C. Rabaut (D)	66,791	55.9
	Frederick M. Alger Jr. (R)	41,130	34.4
	Edgar J. Auclair (THIRD)	10,660	8.9
15	John D. Dingell (D)	68,264	57.5
	Nathaniel H. Goldstick (R)	49,443	41.6
16	John Lesinski (D)	56,589	58.3
	Clyde M. Ford (R)	35,223	36.3
17	George A. Dondero (R)	51,603	47.7
	Draper Allen (D)	50,463	46.6
	Maynard Seibert (UN)	5,593	5.2

MINNESOTA

		Votes	%
1	August H. Andresen (R)	60,980	50.7
	Chester Watson (F-LAB)	27,753	23.1
	Richard W. Morin (D)	26,058	21.7
2	Elmer J. Ryan (D)	47,567	39.2
	Henry Arens (F-LAB)	39,489	32.6
	Christian J. Laurisch (D)	34,268	28.3
3	Henry G. Teigan (F-LAB)	58,023	46.3
	Milton Lindbloom (R)	40,775	32.5
	Martin A. Hogan (D)	15,170	12.1
	Mrs. Frank McConville (I)	11,476	9.2
4	Melvin J. Maas (R)	48,399	38.3
	Howard Y. Williams (F-LAB)	48,039	38.0
	A. B. C. Doherty (D)	28,957	22.9
5	Dewey W. Johnson (F-LAB)	67,349	47.8
	Walter H. Newton (R)	58,110	41.3
	M. J. Dillon (D)	15,337	10.9
6	Harold Knutson (R)	55,504	46.1
	C. A. Ryan (F-LAB)	47,707	39.6
	Joseph H. Kowalkowski (D)	17,235	14.3
7	Paul John Kvale (F-LAB)	56,310	49.7
	H. Carl Andersen (R)	37,190	32.8
	C. L. Cole (D)	19,878	17.5
8	John T. Bernard (F-LAB)	69,788	56.4
	William A. Pittenger (R)	53,914	43.6
9	Richard Thompson Buckler (F-LAB)	48,256	48.5
	Elmer A. Haugen (R)	31,181	31.3
	Martin O. Brandon (D)	20,165	20.3

MISSISSIPPI

		Votes	%
1	John E. Rankin (D)	19,208	98.0
2	Wall Doxey (D)	13,632	98.9

MISSISSIPPI

Candidates	Votes	%
3 William M. Whittington (D)	15,688	97.5
4 A. L. Ford (D)	14,444	100.0
5 Ross A. Collins (D)	26,150	99.4
6 William M. Colmer (D)	25,385	100.0
7 Daniel R. McGehee (D)	32,004	97.5

MISSOURI

Candidates	Votes	%
1 Milton A. Romjue (D)	68,447	55.4
James G. Morgan (R)	55,032	44.5
2 William L. Nelson (D)	81,293	58.1
O. B. Whitaker (R)	58,610	41.9
3 Richard M. Duncan (D)	86,199	58.8
Miles Elliott (R)	60,411	41.2
4 C. Jasper Bell (D)	103,492	74.6
Paul R. Byrum (R)	35,081	25.3
5 Joseph B. Shannon (D)	113,946	73.7
Lowell R. Johnson (R)	40,546	26.2
6 Reuben T. Wood (D)	74,202	53.0
Thomas H. Douglas (R)	65,679	46.9
7 Dewey Short (R)	73,861	52.5
Gene Frost (D)	66,695	47.4
8 Clyde Williams (D)	65,780	56.6
C. M. Becker (R)	50,216	43.2
9 Clarence Cannon (D)	62,623	61.8
Herschel Schooley (R)	38,706	38.2
10 Orville Zimmerman (D)	65,168	61.4
Linder Deimund (R)	40,860	38.5
11 Thomas C. Hennings (D)	94,330	61.1
L. C. Dyer (R)	59,536	38.6
12 C. Arthur Anderson (D)	125,333	56.2
Harry P. Rosecan (R)	97,151	43.5
13 John J. Cochran (D)	85,630	68.2
Harry E. Wiehe (R)	39,714	31.6

MONTANA

Candidates	Votes	%
1 Jerry J. O'Connell (D)	54,816	63.4
H. L. Hart (R)	31,231	36.1
2 James F. O'Connor (D)	79,190	64.9
T. S. Stockdal (R)	42,454	34.8

NEBRASKA

Candidates	Votes	%
1 Henry C. Luckey (D)	61,104	53.3
Ernest B. Perry (R)	52,137	45.5
2 Charles F. McLaughlin (D)	66,833	62.0
Jackson B. Chase (R)	38,511	35.7
3 Karl Stefan (R)	83,587	70.5
John Havekost (D)	31,967	27.0
4 Charles Binderup (D)	66,763	55.3
Arthur J. Denney (R)	51,524	42.7
5 Harry B. Coffee (D)	62,714	58.3
Cullen N. Wright (R)	36,396	33.8
Frank Brown (UN)	7,912	7.4

NEVADA

Candidates	Votes	%
AL James G. Scrugham (D)	25,575	58.4
Ed C. Peterson (R)	11,785	26.9
Harry H. Austin (I)	6,444	14.7

NEW HAMPSHIRE

Candidates	Votes	%
1 Arthur B. Jenks (R)	51,920‡	50.0
Alphonse Roy (D)	51,370	49.5
2 Charles W. Tobey (R)	53,706	53.7
Daniel J. Hagerty (D)	45,437	45.4

NEW JERSEY

Candidates	Votes	%
1 Charles A. Wolverton (R)	84,980	51.8
Guy Lee Jr. (D)	75,631	46.1
2 Elmer H. Wene (D)	55,580	50.0
Isaac Bacharach (R)	50,958	45.8
3 William H. Sutphin (D)	68,189	50.6
Albert B. Hermann (R)	64,237	47.7
4 D. Lane Powers (R)	58,258	52.3
Joseph A. Daly (D)	52,735	47.4
5 Charles A. Eaton (R)	65,459	50.9
Charles S. Mackenzie (D)	62,904	48.9
6 Donald H. McLean (R)	62,525	50.2
Frank Moore (D)	61,351	49.3
7 J. Parnell Thomas (R)	58,021	51.6
H. P. J. Hoffmann (D)	54,163	48.2
8 George N. Seger (R)	57,778	50.8
Leo V. Becker (D)	52,430	46.1
9 Edward A. Kenney (D)	67,874	53.9
Lawrence A. Cavinato (R)	57,547	45.7
10 Fred A. Hartley Jr. (R)	52,197	50.2
Lindsay H. Rudd (D)	51,532	49.6
11 Edward L. O'Neill (D)	54,402	52.6
Peter A. Cavicchia (R)	48,672	47.1
12 Frank W. Towey Jr. (D)	54,688	49.9
Frederick R. Lehlbach (R)	54,363	49.6
13 Mary T. Norton (D)	93,702	75.8
John J. Grossi (R)	27,615	22.3
14 Edward J. Hart (D)	96,053	79.3
Fred G. Tauber (R)	23,985	19.8

NEW MEXICO

Candidates	Votes	%
AL John J. Dempsey (D)	106,951	63.1
M. Ralph Brown (R)	62,375	36.8

NEW YORK

Candidates	Votes	%
1 Robert L. Bacon (R)	185,891	55.2
Gerald Morrell (D, UN)	144,562	42.9
2 William B. Barry (D)	222,217	69.2
Allen E. R. Craig (R)	90,437	28.2
3 Joseph L. Pfeifer (D)	40,640	80.3
Jerome E. Licari (R)	8,680	17.2
4 Thomas H. Cullen (D)	43,917	77.7
William G. Nolan (R)	11,594	20.5
5 Marcellus H. Evans (D)	63,661	64.9
Frank A. Dalton (R)	30,995	31.6
6 Andrew L. Somers (D)	126,094	69.1
Donald C. Strachan (R)	43,862	24.1
7 John J. Delaney (D)	46,154	75.5
Joseph M. Aimee (R)	12,085	19.8
8 Donald L. O'Toole (D)	217,568	72.2
Nathan Greenbaum (R)	64,002	21.2
9 Eugene J. Keogh (D)	91,803	65.6
Robert E. Hower (R)	42,456	30.4
10 Emanuel Celler (D)	47,872	68.8
Mortimer H. Michaels (R)	17,643	25.4
11 James A. O'Leary (D)	56,307	66.7
Archibald Cooper (R)	25,553	30.3
12 Samuel Dickstein (D)	19,280	86.5
Joseph Levine (R)	2,136	9.6
13 Christopher D. Sullivan (D)	20,456	79.7
Vincent A. Marsicano (R)	4,254	16.6
14 William I. Sirovich (D)	25,528	61.5
Emanuel A. Manginelli (R)	13,059	31.4
15 John J. Boylan (D)	32,435	77.5
Arthur Wyler (R)	7,953	19.0
16 John J. O'Connor (D)	33,082	60.0
J. Homer Cudmore (R)	17,832	32.3
17 Theodore A. Peyser (D)	48,611	52.1
Frederick F. Greenman (R)	41,430	44.4
18 Martin J. Kennedy (D)	36,317	72.9
William I. Cohen (R)	11,851	23.8
19 Sol Bloom (D)	74,160	69.5
William S. Bennet (R)	24,835	23.3
20 James J. Lanzetta (D)	18,772	51.2
Vito Marcantonio (R, ALL PP)	17,212	46.9
21 Joseph A. Gavagan (D)	114,626	73.7
Melinda Alexander (R)	31,504	20.3
22 Edwin W. Curley (D)	49,495	77.6
Victor Santini (R)	12,220	19.2
23 Charles A. Buckley (D)	202,730	74.3
Isaac F. Becker (R)	51,623	18.9
24 James M. Fitzpatrick (D)	183,823	65.2
Oliver C. Carpenter (R)	82,759	29.4
25 Charles D. Millard (R)	97,953	56.3
Homer A. Stebbins (D)	73,132	42.0
26 Hamilton Fish (R)	72,302	58.5
Alpha R. Whiton (D, AM LAB)	49,137	39.7
27 Philip A. Goodwin (R)	61,748	57.2
D. Roy Shafer (D)	44,220	40.9
28 William T. Byrne (D)	85,004	58.4
Colin D. Macrae (R)	52,498	36.1
29 E. Harold Cluett (D)	74,644	61.3
John J. Nyhoff (R)	44,567	36.6
30 Frank Crowther (R)	57,482	51.6
Earl E. Cummins (D, AM LAB)	51,590	46.3
31 Bertrand H. Snell (R)	54,160	58.8
George C. Owens (D)	31,752	34.5
Jesse W. Williams (TOWN)	6,185	6.7
32 Francis D. Culkin (R)	65,761	66.1
Paul J. Woodard (D)	32,318	32.5
33 Fred J. Douglas (R)	63,281	53.1
Fred J. Sisson (D, AM LAB)	45,969	38.6
William D. Arquint	8,479	7.1
34 Bert Lord (R)	75,580	60.6
John T. Buckley (D)	47,857	38.4
35 Clarence E. Hancock (R)	85,702	54.3
Arthur H. Perrin (D)	59,540	37.8
Robert H. Anderson (YP)	9,798	6.2
36 John Taber (R)	61,271	59.2
William A. Aiken (D)	32,318	31.2
John E. DuBois (TOWN)	8,003	7.7
37 W. Sterling Cole (R)	73,018	64.5
Paul Smith (D)	38,560	34.1
38 George B. Kelly (D)	82,708	51.6
Joseph Fritsch Jr (R)	72,910	45.5
39 James W. Wadsworth (R)	66,869	58.5
Donald J. Corbett (D)	41,699	36.5
40 Walter Gresham Andrews (R)	94,682	52.5
John L. Beyer (D)	68,241	37.8
Melvin L. Payne (UN&SQD)	13,593	7.5
41 Alfred F. Beiter (D, AM LAB)	55,508	50.4
Fred Kohler (R)	45,113	41.0
42 James M. Mead (D, AM LAB)	57,132	56.4
Eugene D. Crooker (R)	32,395	32.0
Anthony Fitzgibbons (UN)	6,840	6.8
43 Daniel A. Reed (R)	56,129	54.9
Clare Barnes (D)	44,585	43.6
AL Matthew J. Merritt (D)	3,013,931✔	
Caroline O'Day (D)	2,992,057✔	
Natalie F. Couch (R)	2,078,803	
Anthony J. Contiguglia (R)	2,028,865	
Edna Mitchell Blue (SOC)	102,133	
Frank R. Crosswaith (SOC)	101,184	
Roy Hudson (COM)	69,336	
Simon W. Gerson (COM)	68,868	

NORTH CAROLINA

Candidates	Votes	%
1 Lindsay C. Warren (D)	35,333	90.2
John Wilkinson (R)	3,833	9.8
2 John H. Kerr (D)	37,771	95.2
3 Graham A. Barden (D)	34,524	74.3
Julian T. Gaskill (R)	11,967	25.7
4 Harold D. Cooley (D)	56,703	76.8
A. I. Ferree (R)	17,179	23.3
5 Frank W. Hancock Jr. (D)	48,500	73.3
Edward F. Butler (R)	17,671	26.7
6 William B. Umstead (D)	46,329	69.8
Willis H. Slane (R)	20,092	30.3
7 J. Bayard Clark (D)	41,549	83.2
W. C. Downing (R)	8,396	16.8
8 J. Walter Lambeth (D)	54,846	64.1
Kyle Hayes (R)	30,699	35.9
9 Robert L. Doughton (D)	60,223	64.8
Watt Gragg (R)	32,659	35.2

NORTH CAROLINA

	Candidates	Votes	%
10	Alfred L. Bulwinkle (D)	79,059	65.0
	Calvin R. Edney (R)	42,650	35.0
11	Zebulon Weaver (D)	73,645	63.0
	Clyde H. Jarrett (R)	43,346	37.1

NORTH DAKOTA

		Votes	
AL	William Lemke (R)	131,117	
	Usher L. Burdick (R)	115,913	
	Henry Holt (D)	100,609	
	J. J. Nygaard (D)	89,713	
	I. J. Moe (I)	3,310	
	P. H. Miller (I)	3,273	
	E. A. Johansson (I)	2,697	
	Jasper Haaland (I)	540	
	W. D. Webster (I)	461	

OHIO

		Votes	%
1	Joseph A. Dixon (D)	71,935	52.1
	John B. Hollister (R)	66,082	47.9
2	Herbert S. Bigelow (D)	67,213	51.8
	William E. Hess (R)	62,546	48.2
3	Byron B. Harlan (D)	101,115	55.9
	Robert N. Brumbaugh (R)	70,023	38.7
	Leonidas E. Speer (I)	9,886	5.5
4	Frank L. Kloeb (D)	61,927	53.7
	Robert W. Turner (R)	53,352	46.3
5	Frank C. Kniffin (D)	41,693	53.1
	Stephen S. Beard (R)	33,212	42.3
6	James G. Polk (D)	54,904	54.6
	Emory F. Smith (R)	45,733	45.4
7	Arthur W. Aleshire (D)	68,456	50.4
	L. T. Marshall (R)	67,454	49.6
8	Brooks Fletcher (D)	49,668	53.9
	Grant E. Mouser Jr. (R)	42,565	46.2
9	John F. Hunter (D)	75,737	56.3
	Raymond E. Hilderbrand (R)	55,043	40.9
10	Thomas A. Jenkins (R)	46,965	57.7
	O. J. Kleffner (D)	34,477	42.3
11	Harold K. Claypool (D)	41,773	53.4
	L. P. Mooney (R)	33,249	42.5
12	Arthur P. Lamneck (D)	88,222	57.7
	Grant P. Ward (R)	64,766	42.3
13	Dudley A. White (R)	46,623	47.3
	Forrest R. Black (D)	39,042	39.6
	Merrell E. Martin (I)	12,959	13.1
14	Dow W. Harter (D)	118,659	58.1
	Carl D. Sheppard (R)	77,039	37.7
15	Robert T. Secrest (D)	53,263	55.7
	Kenneth C. Ray (R)	42,053	44.0
16	William R. Thom (D)	89,911	59.2
	H. Ross Ake (R)	54,979	36.2
17	William A. Ashbrook (D)	69,446	57.7
	James A. Glenn (R)	48,270	40.1
18	Lawrence E. Imhoff (D)	83,052	60.6
	Earl R. Lewis (R)	54,119	39.5
19	Michael J. Kirwan (D)	93,636	58.4
	John G. Cooper (R)	65,926	41.1
20	Martin L. Sweeney (D)	54,295	54.4
	Blase A. Buonpane (R)	23,367	23.4
	John L. Mihelich (I)	22,158	22.2
21	Robert Crosser (D)	70,596	74.8
	Harry C. Gahn (R)	23,811	25.2
22	Anthony A. Fleger (D)	131,250	51.3
	Chester C. Bolton (R)	124,446	48.7
AL	John McSweeney (D)	1,553,059	
	Harold G. Mosier (D)	1,493,053	
	George H. Bender (R)	1,226,247	
	L. L. Marshall (R)	1,121,370	
	William C. Sandberg (COM)	8,945	

Special Elections

		Votes	%
11	Peter F. Hammond (D)	41,310	56.5
	John L. Moriarty (R)	31,864	43.6
AL	Daniel S. Earhart (D)	1,479,284	58.3
	Benson Ogier (R)	1,057,473	41.7

OKLAHOMA

	Candidates	Votes	%
1	Wesley E. Disney (D)	81,286	57.7
	Jo O. Ferguson (R)	58,983	41.9
2	Jack Nichols (D)	45,724	63.5
	V. S. Cannon (R)	26,310	36.5
3	Wilburn Cartwright (D)	58,261	79.9
	John D. Morrison (R)	14,672	20.1
4	Lyle H. Boren (D)	63,306	72.7
	Fred L. Patrick (R)	23,615	27.1
5	Robert P. Hill (D)	78,873	70.2
	John William Mee (R)	33,071	29.4
6	Jed Johnson (D)	52,373	72.8
	L. M. Gensman (R)	19,495	27.1
7	Sam C. Massingale (D)	46,940	83.3
	Clyde J. Matherly (R)	9,396	16.7
8	Phil Ferguson (D)	47,497	58.9
	T. J. Sargent (R)	32,858	40.7
AL	Will Rogers (D)	475,567	70.7
	John C. Burns (R)	193,487	28.8

OREGON

		Votes	%
1	James W. Mott (R)	114,073	65.6
	E. W. Kirkpatrick (D)	59,788	34.4
2	Walter M. Pierce (D)	46,412	68.0
	Roy W. Ritner (R)	21,813	32.0
3	Nan Wood Honeyman (D)	78,624	53.2
	William A. Ekwall (R)	45,872	31.0
	John A. Jeffrey (I)	21,848	14.8

PENNSYLVANIA

		Votes	%
1	Leon Sacks (D, D-OP)	67,276	64.6
	Harry C. Ransley (R, R-OP)	34,813	33.4
2	James P. McGranery (D, D-OP)	65,779	59.8
	William H. Wilson (R, R-OP)	41,267	37.5
3	Michael J. Bradley (D)	75,445	60.8
	Clare Gerald Fenerty (R, R-OP)	48,035	38.7
4	J. Burrwood Daly (D, D-OP)	77,406	62.8
	Boies Penrose Jr. (R, R-OP)	41,545	33.7
5	Frank J. G. Dorsey (D, D-OP)	72,210	56.6
	James J. Connolly (R, R-OP)	46,238	36.2
6	Michael J. Stack (D, D-OP)	84,487	61.1
	George F. Holmes (R, R-OP)	51,892	37.5
7	Ira Walton Drew (D, D-OP)	77,949	51.8
	George P. Darrow (R)	71,794	47.7
8	James Wolfenden (R)	73,335	52.2
	Howard Kirk (D, D-OP)	66,119	47.1
9	Oliver W. Frey (D)	56,108	51.0
	Theodore R. Gardner (R)	50,361	45.8
10	J. Roland Kinzer (R)	72,181	52.7
	H. Clay Burkholder (D)	62,768	45.8
11	Patrick J. Boland (D)	75,905	57.5
	John J. Owens (R)	50,123	38.0
12	J. Harold Flannery (D)	99,161	53.7
	C. Murray Turpin (R)	84,902	46.0
13	James H. Gildea (D, D-OP)	83,662	54.6
	James H. Kirchner (R)	68,772	44.9
14	Guy L. Moser (D, D-OP)	46,192	53.2
	Charles E. Roth (R)	28,001	32.3
15	Albert G. Rutherford (R)	55,268	54.3
	C. Elmer Dietrich (D)	45,808	45.0
16	Robert F. Rich (R)	54,040	51.8
	Paul A. Rothfuss (D, D-OP)	49,249	47.2
17	J. William Ditter (R)	67,850	53.9
	George H. Bartholomew (D)	55,083	43.8
18	Benjamin K. Focht (R)	49,243	54.0
	John M. Keichline (D)	41,881	46.0

	Candidates	Votes	%
19	Guy J. Swope (D)	73,374	51.4
	Isaac H. Doutrich (R, R-OP)	67,884	47.5
20	Benjamin Jarrett (R)	58,738	48.4
	D. J. Driscoll (D)	56,941	46.9
21	Francis E. Walter (D)	56,566	56.8
	William R. Coyle (R)	39,537	39.7
22	Harry L. Haines (D)	66,306	54.7
	Frank S. Magill (R, R-OP)	49,273	40.6
23	Don Gingery (D)	53,629	48.9
	Benjamin C. Jones (R)	46,726	42.6
24	J. Buell Snyder (D)	62,009	60.5
	Davis W. Henderson (R)	40,067	39.1
25	Charles I. Faddis (D)	61,988	65.5
	John C. Judson (R)	30,208	31.9
26	Charles R. Eckert (D)	71,332	56.0
	Orville Brown (R)	52,925	41.5
27	Joseph Gray (D)	83,908	54.1
	Walter E. Morris (R)	67,809	43.7
28	Robert G. Allen (D)	67,169	60.2
	James B. Weaver (R, R-OP)	42,259	37.9
29	Charles N. Crosby (D, D-OP)	48,993	53.7
	Will Rose (R)	40,687	44.6
30	Peter J. Demuth (D, D-OP)	65,465	59.4
	James A. Geltz (R, R-OP)	43,878	39.8
31	James L. Quinn (D, D-OP)	81,544	63.0
	James H. McClure (R)	45,742	35.3
32	Herman P. Eberharter (D, D-OP)	49,722	66.2
	Jacob E. Kalson (R, R-OP)	21,067	28.0
33	Henry Ellenbogen (D, D-OP)	70,601	64.5
	Edward O. Tabor (R)	38,383	35.1
34	Matthew A. Dunn (D, D-OP)	80,194	64.4
	Elmer A. Barchfeld (R, R-OP)	43,827	35.2

RHODE ISLAND

		Votes	%
1	Aime J. Forand (D)	74,058	50.5
	Charles F. Risk (R)	62,199	42.4
	Dunn (UN)	9,973	6.8
2	John M. O'Connell (D)	75,899	47.8
	Harry Sandager (R)	71,981	45.3
	Dougherty (UN)	10,689	6.7

SOUTH CAROLINA

		Votes	%
1	Thomas S. McMillan (D)	15,772	96.9
2	H. P. Fulmer (D)	21,653	98.3
3	John C. Taylor (D)	18,983	99.0
4	G. Heyward Mahon Jr. (D)	25,468	98.9
5	James P. Richards (D)	15,748	99.2
6	Allard H. Gasque (D)	16,027	99.3

Special Election

		Votes	%
4	G. Heyward Mahon Jr. (D)	24,715	100.0

SOUTH DAKOTA

		Votes	%
1	Fred H. Hildebrandt (D)	110,829	50.6
	Karl Mundt (R)	108,259	49.4
2	Francis H. Case (R)	34,812	51.7
	Theodore B. Werner (D)	32,549	48.3

TENNESSEE

		Votes	%
1	B. Carroll Reece (R)	33,501	60.4
	William M. Crawford (D)	17,289	31.2
	Charles W. Clark	4,684	8.4
2	J. Will Taylor (R)	40,595	50.8
	John T. O'Connor (D)	38,991	48.8
3	Sam D. McReynolds (D)	32,065	68.0
	William Hillery (R)	15,096	32.0
4	J. Ridley Mitchell (D)	33,154	81.8
	H. E. McLean (R)	7,382	18.2

Candidates	Votes	%
2 Jennings Randolph (D)	78,856	59.9
C. S. Musser (R)	52,847	40.1
3 Andrew Edmiston (D)	82,059	59.3
John M. Wolverton (R)	56,251	40.7
4 George W. Johnson (D)	80,856	53.5
Raymond V. Humphreys (R)	70,304	46.5
5 John Kee (D)	79,855	64.5
C. M. Jones (R)	44,010	35.5
6 Joe L. Smith (D)	98,148	63.9
M. F. Matheny (R)	55,536	36.1

TENNESSEE

Candidates	Votes	%
5 Richard M. Atkinson (D)	34,277	94.1
E. L. Bradbury (R)	2,163	5.9
6 Clarence W. Turner (D)	20,390	80.9
M. C. Ridings (R)	4,819	19.1
7 Herron Pearson (D)	20,432	100.0
8 Jere Cooper (D)	27,032	93.8
Allen J. Strawbridge (R)	1,780	6.2
9 Walter Chandler (D)	58,034	99.2

TEXAS

	Votes	%
1 Wright Patman (D)	29,351	97.6
2 Martin Dies (D)	39,484	100.0
3 Morgan G. Sanders (D)	29,482	96.3
4 Sam Rayburn (D)	33,355	97.5
5 Hatton W. Sumners (D)	43,954	88.5
D. C. Humphrey (R)	5,579	11.2
6 Luther A. Johnson (D)	29,574	97.3
7 Nat Patton (D)	29,011	97.6
8 Albert Thomas (D)	61,616	91.8
R. B. Nichols (R)	5,456	8.1
9 Joseph J. Mansfield (D)	36,968	93.2
F. W. Dusek (R)	2,700	6.8
10 James P. Buchanan (D)	33,631	99.5
11 W. R. Poage (D)	31,227	100.0
12 Fritz Lanham (D)	39,708	93.3
Arnold Davis (R)	2,845	6.7
13 William D. McFarlane (D)	40,935	95.2
14 Richard M. Kleberg (D)	39,576	92.1
Howell Ward (R)	3,408	7.9
15 Milton H. West (D)	29,598	82.6
J. A. Simpson (R)	6,244	17.4
16 R. Ewing Thomason (D)	26,353	100.0
17 Clyde L. Garrett (D)	35,386	100.0
18 Marvin Jones (D)	44,652	94.1
S. E. Fish (R)	2,526	5.3
19 George H. Mahon (D)	39,059	100.0
20 Maury Maverick (D)	34,478	71.6
E. W. Clements (R)	12,056	25.0
21 Charles L. South (D)	37,964	88.6
M. J. Bierschwale (R)	4,891	11.4

UTAH

	Votes	%
1 Abe Murdock (D)	68,877	69.2
Charles W. Dunn (R)	30,415	30.6
2 J. Will Robinson (D)	81,119	69.8
A. V. Watkins (R)	34,855	30.0

VERMONT

Candidates	Votes	%
AL Charles A. Plumley (R)	83,091	59.2
John B. Candon (D)	56,334	40.1

VIRGINIA

	Votes	%
1 S. Otis Bland (D)	20,012	80.9
William A. Dickinson (R)	4,592	18.6
2 Norman R. Hamilton (D)	29,269	88.7
G. M. Rumble (R)	3,287	10.0
3 Andrew Jackson Montague (D)	28,803	84.4
Charles G. Wilson (R)	4,936	14.5
4 Patrick Henry Drewry (D)	19,539	90.4
John Martin (R)	1,832	8.5
5 Thomas G. Burch (D)	25,752	64.9
Taylor G. Vaughan (R)	13,890	35.0
6 Clifton A. Woodrum (D)	25,327	60.7
T. X. Parsons (R)	16,404	39.3
7 A. Willis Robertson (D)	24,790	63.9
J. Everett Will (R)	13,814	35.6
8 Howard W. Smith (D)	28,052	75.4
John Locke Green (R)	8,685	23.3
9 John W. Flannagan Jr. (D)	31,918	62.2
Luther E. Fuller (R)	19,400	37.8

WASHINGTON

	Votes	%
1 Warren G. Magnuson (D)	103,967	63.7
Frederick J. Wettrick (R)	58,794	36.0
2 Mon C. Wallgren (D)	64,214	63.6
Payson Peterson (R)	36,508	36.2
3 Martin F. Smith (D)	67,159	72.0
Herbert H. Sieler (R)	25,717	27.6
4 Knute Hill (D)	48,264	57.9
John W. Summers (R)	35,063	42.0
5 Charles H. Leavy (D)	76,048	70.8
Warren O. Dow (R)	31,218	29.1
6 John M. Coffee (D)	66,333	67.3
Paul A. Preus (R)	31,724	32.2

WEST VIRGINIA

	Votes	%
1 Robert L. Ramsay (D)	75,859	59.9
Charles J. Shuck (R)	50,885	40.2

WISCONSIN

	Votes	%
1 Thomas R. Amlie (PROG)	49,402	43.1
Paul E. Jorgensen (R)	44,687	39.0
Wolf (D)	20,597	18.0
2 Harry Sauthoff (PROG)	57,874	47.9
Frank R. Bentley (R)	34,565	28.6
Dempsey (D)	28,326	23.5
3 Gardner R. Withrow (PROG)	56,141	51.2
J. Charles Pile (R)	38,698	35.3
McGonigle (D)	14,920	13.6
4 Raymond J. Cannon (D)	63,565	47.3
Paul Gauer (PROG)	42,029	31.2
Schafer (R)	28,930	21.5
5 Thomas O'Malley (D)	60,716	41.5
Carl P. Dietz (PROG)	50,466	34.5
Spence (R)	35,121	24.0
6 Michael K. Reilly (D)	41,688	39.3
Frank B. Keefe (R)	38,904	36.7
Poltl (PROG)	25,395	24.0
7 Gerald J. Boileau (PROG)	48,637	47.0
Arthur W. Prehn (R)	30,555	29.5
Coleman (D)	24,315	23.5
8 George J. Schneider (PROG)	38,721	33.5
John E. Cashman (D)	38,138	33.0
Farrell (R)	33,459	28.9
9 Merlin Hull (PROG)	61,593	80.7
Edwin J. Larkin (D)	14,702	19.3
10 Bernard J. Gehrmann (PROG)	49,005	51.5
Philip E. Nelson (R)	30,121	31.7
Bostrom (D)	15,956	16.8

WYOMING

	Votes	%
AL Paul R. Greever (D)	56,204	57.2
Frank A. Barrett (R)	41,362	42.1

1937 House Elections

NEW YORK

Special Election

	Votes	%
17 Bruce Barton (R)	35,314#	47.6
Stanley Osserman (D)	21,599#	29.1
George Backer (AM LAB)	9,325#	12.6

OKLAHOMA

Special Election

	Votes	%
5 Gomer Smith (D)	21,131	74.5
Harlan Deupree (R)	7,132	25.2

PENNSYLVANIA

Special Election

	Votes	%
18 Richard M. Simpson (R)	34,104	58.0
Lowell H. Alexander (D)	24,735	42.0

TEXAS

Special Election

	Votes	%
10 Lyndon B. Johnson (D)	8,280	27.7
Morton Harris	5,111	17.1
Polk Shelton	4,420	14.8
Sam V. Stone	4,048	13.5
C. N. Avery	3,951	13.2
Houghton Brownell	3,019	10.1

1938 House Elections

ALABAMA

Candidates	Votes	%
1 Frank W. Boykin (D)	9,853	100.0
2 George Grant (D)	15,569	100.0
3 Henry B. Steagall (D)	10,089	100.0
4 Sam Hobbs (D)	11,113	88.2
C. W. McKay (R)	1,488	11.8
5 Joe Starnes (D)	16,587	99.7
6 Pete Jarman (D)	10,246	100.0
7 William B. Bankhead (D)	17,903	71.3
E. M. Reed (R)	7,207	28.7
8 John J. Sparkman (D)	10,266	100.0
9 Luther Patrick (D)	12,627	93.5
J. G. Bass (R)	878	6.5

ARIZONA

	Votes	%
AL John R. Murdock (D)	83,556	80.3
M. E. Cassidy (R)	20,502	19.7

ARKANSAS

	Votes	%
1 Ezekiel C. Gathings (D)	23,274	100.0
2 Wilbur D. Mills (D)	18,913	100.0
3 Clyde T. Ellis (D)	22,141	100.0
4 William B. Cravens (D)	22,272	100.0
5 David D. Terry (D)	23,949	100.0
6 William F. Norrell (D)	17,662	100.0
7 Wade Kitchens (D)	16,145	100.0

CALIFORNIA

	Votes	%
1 Clarence F. Lea (D-R)	73,636	62.9
Ernest S. Mitchell (TOWN)	43,320	37.0
2 Harry L. Englebright (R D P T)	71,496	99.9
3 Frank H. Buck (D-R)	119,236	92.7
Nora Conklin (COM)	8,271	6.4
4 Franck R. Havenner (D & PROG)	64,452	61.2
Kennett B. Dawson (R)	40,842	38.8
5 Richard J. Welch (R-D-PROG)	91,868	100.0
6 Albert E. Carter (R D P T)	118,632	94.1
Dave L. Saunders (COM)	7,015	5.6
7 John H. Tolan (D)	62,599	55.3
Charles Wade Snook (R)	50,504	44.6
8 John Z. Anderson (R)	84,084	55.0
John J. McGrath (D)	68,681	45.0
9 Bertrand W. Gearhart (R-D)	91,128	96.2
10 Alfred J. Elliott (D)	84,791	67.2
F. Fred Hoelscher (R)	41,194	32.7
11 Carl Hinshaw (R)	68,712	47.0
Carl Stuart Hamblen (D)	59,993	41.0
Ralph D. Horton (TOWN)	12,713	8.7
12 H. Jerry Voorhis (D)	75,003	60.7
Eugene W. Nixon (R)	40,457	32.8
Russell R. Hand (TOWN)	7,903	6.4
13 Charles Kramer (D & PROG)	96,258	65.6
K. L. Stockton (R T)	44,808	30.6
14 Thomas F. Ford (D)	67,588	67.8
William D. Campbell (R)	31,375	31.5
15 John M. Costello (D)	83,086	60.2
O. D. Thomas (R)	51,483	37.3
16 Leland M. Ford (R-D)	97,407	62.8
John F. Dockweiler (D)	32,863	21.2
Ted E. Felt (TOWN)	16,045	10.3
17 Lee E. Geyer (D)	56,513	58.6
Clifton A. Hix (R)	26,891	27.9
Fred C. Wagner (TOWN)	8,870	9.2
18 Thomas M. Eaton (R)	52,216	48.5
Byron N. Scott (D)	51,874	48.2

Candidates	Votes	%
19 Harry R. Sheppard (D)	75,819	53.3
C. T. Johnson (R T)	66,402	46.7
20 Edouard V. M. Izac (D)	65,243	60.4
John L. Bacon (R)	42,710	39.5

COLORADO

	Votes	%
1 Lawrence Lewis (D)	83,517	65.3
William I. Reilly (R)	42,758	33.4
2 Fred Cummings (D)	65,448	51.7
William S. Hill (R)	60,259	47.6
3 John A. Martin (D)	72,736	57.4
Henry Leonard (R)	54,007	42.6
4 Edward T. Taylor (D)	43,596	63.7
John S. Woody (R)	24,805	36.3

CONNECTICUT

	Votes	%
1 William J. Miller (R)	68,229	43.2
Herman P. Kopplemann (D)	64,483	40.8
Edward C. Roffler (SOC)	24,718	15.7
2 Thomas R. Ball (R)	48,180	48.3
William J. Fitzgerald (D)	45,056	45.2
Thomas E. Bowman (SOC)	6,333	6.4
3 James A. Shanley (D)	55,893	43.4
Ranulf Compton (R)	55,501	43.1
Harry Watstein (SOC)	17,111	13.3
4 Albert E. Austin (R)	61,161	43.1
Alfred N. Phillips Jr. (D)	44,626	31.4
Charles H. McLevy (SOC)	35,328	24.9
5 J. Joseph Smith (D)	39,824	42.0
Roy E. Rice (R)	39,652	41.8
John W. Ring (SOC)	15,369	16.2
AL Boleslaus J. Monkiewicz (R)	271,329	43.1
William M. Citron (D)	250,013	39.7
Arthur F. King (SOC)	99,717	15.8

DELAWARE

	Votes	%
AL George S. Williams (R)	60,661	55.9
William F. Allen (D)	46,989	43.3

FLORIDA

	Votes	%
1 J. Hardin Peterson (D)	43,837	100.0
2 Robert A. Green (D)	24,830	100.0
3 Millard Caldwell (D)	20,174	100.0
4 Arthur P. Cannon (D)	29,621	81.5
J. S. G. Gallagher (R)	6,705	18.5
5 Joe Hendricks (D)	27,894	100.0

GEORGIA

	Votes	%
1 Hugh Peterson (D)	10,920	99.3
2 E. E. Cox (D)	5,137	100.0
3 Stephen Pace (D)	5,987	100.0
4 E. M. Owen (D)	5,413	100.0
5 Robert Ramspeck (D)	6,906	97.2
6 Carl Vinson (D)	4,360	100.0
7 Malcoln Tarver (D)	5,622	100.0
8 W. Benjamin Gibbs (D)	4,929	100.0
9 B. Frank Whelchel (D)	8,934	100.0
10 Paul Brown (D)	9,044	94.4

IDAHO

	Votes	%
1 Compton I. White (D)	48,318	62.8
Rex T. Henson (R)	28,640	37.2
2 Henry C. Dworshak (R)	54,527	53.6
Bert H. Miller (D)	47,199	46.4

ILLINOIS

Candidates	Votes	%
1 Arthur W. Mitchell (D)	30,207	53.4
William L. Dawson (R)	26,396	46.6
2 Raymond S. McKeough (D)	129,620	54.4
Noble W. Lee (R)	108,483	45.6
3 Edward A. Kelly (D)	127,597	56.0
Goodwin L. Dosland (R)	100,357	44.0
4 Harry P. Beam (D)	61,504	76.4
Dominic M. Janec Jr. (R)	18,962	23.6
5 Adolph J. Sabath (D)	32,104	74.8
Max Price (R)	10,842	25.3
6 A. F. Maciejewski (D)	154,818	58.7
Robert Isham Randolph (R)	109,031	41.3
7 Leonard W. Schuetz (D)	192,750	54.3
James C. Moreland (R)	162,069	45.7
8 Leo Kocialkowski (D)	31,823	75.3
Rena E. Pikiel (R)	10,440	24.7
9 James McAndrews (D)	44,064	52.7
Charles S. Dewey (R)	39,512	47.3
10 Ralph E. Church (R)	141,685	58.1
Joseph F. Elward (D)	102,234	41.9
11 Chauncey W. Reed (R)	94,565	65.9
William J. Bossingham (D)	48,876	34.1
12 Noah M. Mason (R)	67,326	60.7
Edward C. Hunter (D)	43,631	39.3
13 Leo E. Allen (R)	45,177	65.6
Theodore A. Secker (D)	23,708	34.4
14 Anton J. Johnson (R)	44,243	51.5
Chester Thompson (D)	41,682	48.5
15 Robert B. Chiperfield (R)	47,703	54.5
Lewis L. Boyer (D)	39,779	45.5
16 Everett M. Dirksen (R)	61,012	63.5
James C. Dillon (D)	35,081	36.5
17 Leslie C. Arends (R)	45,235	60.9
Thomas V. Watson (D)	29,023	39.1
18 Jessie Sumner (R)	56,587	55.3
James A. Meeks (D)	45,691	44.7
19 William H. Wheat (R)	59,446	51.5
Hugh M. Rigney (D)	55,956	48.5
20 James M. Barnes (D)	37,184	55.4
Stuart E. Pierson (R)	29,907	44.6
21 Frank W. Fries (D)	52,173	50.3
Frank M. Ramey (R)	51,651	49.8
22 Edwin A. Schaefer (D)	66,743	52.5
Jesse R. Brown (R)	60,518	47.6
23 Laurence F. Arnold (D)	49,537	53.8
O. A. James (R)	42,572	46.2
24 Claude V. Parsons (D)	40,633	51.1
R. R. Randolph (R)	38,889	48.9
25 Kent E. Keller (D)	59,203	52.3
R. G. Crisenberry (R)	53,999	47.7
AL Thomas V. Smith (D)	1,572,870✔	
John C. Martin (D)	1,560,283✔	
Stephen A. Day (R)	1,472,638	
Simon E. Lantz (R)	1,456,535	
Harmon W. Reed (P)	9,337	
A. G. Carnine (P)	8,808	

INDIANA

	Votes	%
1 William T. Schulte (D)	56,630	54.9
M. Elliott Belshaw (R)	46,370	45.0
2 Charles A. Halleck (R)	79,304	57.8
Homer Stonebraker (D)	57,860	42.2
3 Robert A. Grant (R)	61,836	51.0
George N. Beamer (D)	59,359	49.0
4 George W. Gillie (R)	72,567	58.1
James I. Farley (D)	52,293	41.9
5 Forest A. Harness (R)	73,102	54.7
Glenn Griswold (D)	60,643	45.3
6 Noble J. Johnson (R)	71,883	50.6
Virginia E. Jenckes (D)	70,128	49.4
7 Gerald W. Landis (R)	78,870	51.6
Arthur H. Greenwood (D)	74,001	48.4
8 John W. Boehne Jr. (D)	76,780	56.4
Charles F. Werner (R)	59,254	43.6

INDIANA

Candidates	Votes	%
9 Eugene B. Crowe (D)	70,237	52.1
Clifford H. Long (R)	64,541	47.9
10 Raymond S. Springer (R)	73,782	53.5
Finly H. Gray (D)	64,176	46.5
11 William H. Larrabee (D)	65,646	51.6
William O. Nelson (R)	61,627	48.4
12 Louis Ludlow (D)	65,368	53.7
Charles Jewett (R)	56,319	46.3

IOWA

Candidates	Votes	%
1 Thomas E. Martin (R)	46,636	57.7
James P. Gaffney (D)	33,765	41.8
2 William S. Jacobsen (D)	48,155	50.3
Alfred C. Mueller (R)	47,535	49.7
3 John W. Gwynne (R)	45,541	59.7
W. F. Hayes (D)	30,158	39.5
4 Henry O. Talle (R)	48,640	51.9
Fred Biermann (D)	44,601	47.6
5 Karl M. LeCompte (R)	50,860	53.9
Ruth F. Hollingshead (D)	43,452	46.1
6 Cassius C. Dowell (R)	53,505	58.5
Hubert Utterback (D)	37,056	40.5
7 Ben F. Jensen (R)	54,922	59.0
Roger F. Warin (D)	37,992	40.8
8 Fred C. Gilchrist (R)	51,934	62.5
H. Lloyd Marshall (D)	30,632	36.9
9 Vincent F. Harrington (D)	46,705	49.7
Albert F. Swanson (R)	46,366	49.3

KANSAS

Candidates	Votes	%
1 William P. Lambertson (R)	65,945	60.3
H. N. Hensley (D)	43,374	39.7
2 Ulysses S. Guyer (R)	70,605	56.4
W. F. Jackson (D)	54,582	43.6
3 Thomas D. Winter (R)	56,361	53.4
Edward W. Patterson (D)	49,117	46.6
4 Edward H. Rees (R)	55,419	63.1
J. Donald Coffin (D)	32,443	36.9
5 John M. Houston (D)	43,990	50.3
Stanley Taylor (R)	43,480	49.7
6 Frank Carlson (R)	69,989	63.4
Roy L. Hamilton (D)	40,466	36.6
7 Clifford R. Hope (R)	72,893	65.5
Claude E. Main (D)	38,357	34.5

KENTUCKY

Candidates	Votes	%
1 Noble J. Gregory (D)	35,332	76.0
Alvin Schutz (R)	11,153	24.0
2 Beverly M. Vincent (D)	36,170	63.8
Richard Slack (R)	20,566	36.3
3 Emmet O'Neal (D)	57,227	61.2
Frank A. Ropke (R)	36,361	38.9
4 Edward W. Creal (D)	32,179	59.2
Harry H. Wilson (R)	22,139	40.8
5 Brent Spence (D)	28,383	68.4
Joseph A. Kreke (R)	13,095	31.6
6 Virgil Chapman (D)	38,148	64.9
Chester D. Silvers (R)	20,471	34.8
7 Andrew J. May (D)	27,655	53.2
Hillard H. Smith (R)	24,337	46.8
8 Joe B. Bates (D)	39,006	58.8
H. Clell Hayes (R)	27,308	41.2
9 John M. Robsion (R)	42,901	66.8
Bert Rowland (D)	21,327	33.2

Special Election

8 Joe B. Bates (D)	21,318	52.9
James C. Sparks (R)	18,972	47.1

LOUISIANA

1 Joachim O. Fernandez (D)	50,453	100.0
2 Paul H. Maloney (D)	47,746	100.0

Candidates	Votes	%
3 Robert L. Mouton (D)	5,236	100.0
4 Overton Brooks (D)	10,661	99.6
5 Newt V. Mills (D)	11,644	100.0
6 John K. Griffith (D)	12,225	100.0
7 Rene L. DeRouen (D)	5,313	100.0
8 A. Leonard Allen (D)	9,088	100.0

MAINE

1 James C. Oliver (R)	57,642	59.0
H. B. Emery (D)	40,103	41.0
2 Clyde H. Smith (R)	55,718	48.9
F. H. Dubord (D)	46,900	41.1
J. C. Leckemby (R)	8,197	7.2
3 Ralph O. Brewster (R)	51,485	63.4
Melvin P. Roberts (D)	29,771	36.6

MARYLAND

1 T. Alan Goldsborough (D)	38,926	62.8
Charles H. Gibson (R)	23,096	37.2
2 William P. Cole Jr. (D)	91,231	66.3
Irving H. Mezger (R)	44,699	32.5
3 Thomas D'Alesandro Jr. (D)	29,891	56.6
John A. Janetzke Jr. (R)	22,909	43.4
4 Ambrose J. Kennedy (D)	37,416	50.2
Daniel Ellison (R)	37,126	49.8
5 Stephen W. Gambrill (D)	46,678*	68.0
A. Kingsley Love (R)	19,604	28.6
6 William D. Byron (D)	46,200	50.8
A. Charles Stewart (R)	44,734	49.2

MASSACHUSETTS

1 Allen T. Treadway (R)	64,886	58.8
Owen Johnson (D)	45,397	41.2
2 Charles R. Clason (R)	68,106	61.9
James F. Egan (D)	41,935	38.1
3 Joseph E. Casey (D)	58,600	51.8
J. Walton Tuttle (R)	54,557	48.2
4 Pehr G. Holmes (R)	62,874	54.1
Edward A. Ryan (D)	53,266	45.9
5 Edith Nourse Rogers (R)	104,912	74.8
Francis J. Roane (D)	35,323	25.2
6 George J. Bates (R)	82,434	74.7
James D. Burns (D)	27,967	25.3
7 Lawrence J. Connery (D)	83,618	63.7
George W. Eastman (R)	47,533	36.2
8 Arthur D. Healey (D)	62,152	55.1
Rufus H. Bond (R)	50,711	44.9
9 Robert Luce (R)	70,059	50.7
Thomas H. Eliot (D)	68,258	49.4
10 George Holden Tinkham (R)	78,052	64.4
Martin J. Kelly (D)	43,093	35.6
11 Thomas A. Flaherty (D)	56,939	100.0
12 John W. McCormack (D)	86,618	77.1
Henry J. Allen (R)	25,678	22.9
13 Richard B. Wigglesworth (R)	86,389	68.4
Andrew T. Clancy (D)	39,939	31.6
14 Joseph W. Martin Jr. (R)	63,608	58.7
Lawrence J. Bresnahan (D)	43,876	40.5
15 Charles L. Gifford (R)	66,054	59.0
John D. W. Bodfish (D)	45,867	41.0

MICHIGAN

1 Rudolph G. Tenerowicz (D)	71,533	80.4
Charles A. Roxborough (R)	16,752	18.8
2 Earl C. Michener (R)	58,921	64.4
Walter C. Averill Jr. (D)	32,468	35.5
3 Paul W. Shafer (R)	58,128	66.1
Gordon L. Stewart (D)	29,832	33.9
4 Clare E. Hoffman (R)	49,279	59.2
Felix A. Racette (D)	33,912	40.8
5 Carl E. Mapes (R)	50,473	59.1
Tunis Johnson (D)	34,991	40.9

Candidates	Votes	%
6 William W. Blackney (R)	66,612	55.0
Andrew J. Transue (D)	54,491	45.0
7 Jesse P. Wolcott (R)	62,910	69.0
Charles F. Mann (D)	28,259	31.0
8 Fred L. Crawford (R)	52,250	58.7
Louis C. Schwinger (D)	36,758	41.3
9 Albert J. Engel (R)	40,849	58.2
Noel P. Fox (D)	29,397	41.9
10 Roy O. Woodruff (R)	44,818	66.4
Harold C. Bellows (D)	22,615	33.5
11 Fred Bradley (R)	40,904	51.4
John Luecke (D)	38,707	48.6
12 Frank E. Hook (D)	43,453	51.7
John B. Bennett (R)	40,587	48.3
13 Clarence J. McLeod (R)	50,123	50.6
George D. O'Brien (D)	48,443	48.9
14 Louis C. Rabaut (D)	62,872	57.6
O. Z. Ide (R)	45,967	42.1
15 John D. Dingell (D)	57,401	54.0
Archie C. Fraser (R)	48,429	45.6
16 John Lesinski (D)	49,101	55.1
John L. Carey (R)	39,623	44.5
17 George A. Dondero (R)	63,769	61.4
Samuel G. Backus (D)	39,784	38.3

MINNESOTA

1 August H. Andresen (R)	74,493	64.9
Ray G. Moonan (D)	40,340	35.1
2 Elmer J. Ryan (D)	53,258	43.6
Joseph P. O'Hara (R)	43,919	35.9
C. F. Gaarenstroom (F-LAB)	25,060	20.5
3 John G. Alexander (R)	53,442	45.3
Henry G. Teigan (F-LAB)	50,505	42.8
Martin A. Hogan (D)	14,073	11.9
4 Melvin J. Maas (R)	60,252	53.1
Howard Y. Williams (F-LAB)	40,558	35.8
A. B. C. Doherty (D)	12,619	11.1
5 Oscar Youngdahl (R)	67,722	54.7
Dewey W. Johnson (F-LAB)	45,568	36.8
John L. Gleason (D)	10,598	8.6
6 Harold Knutson (R)	79,900	63.2
Harry W. Christenson (F-LAB)	36,023	28.5
Harold F. Deering (D)	10,448	8.3
7 H. Carl Andersen (R)	49,394	42.6
Paul John Kvale (F-LAB)	42,572	36.7
J. L. O'Connor (D)	19,330	16.7
8 William A. Pittenger (R)	67,960	51.8
John T. Bernard (F-LAB)	54,381	41.4
Merle J. McKeon (D)	8,945	6.8
9 Richard Thompson Buckler (F-LAB)	44,017	42.0
Ole O. Sageng (R)	40,383	38.5
Martin O. Brandon (D)	20,425	19.5

MISSISSIPPI

1 John E. Rankin (D)	4,384	100.0
2 Wall Doxey (D)	4,134	100.0
3 William M. Whittington (D)	2,172	100.0
4 Aaron Lane Ford (D)	3,502	100.0
5 Ross A. Collins (D)	11,540	100.0
6 William M. Colmer (D)	4,873	100.0
7 Dan R. McGehee (D)	4,834	100.0

MISSOURI

1 Milton A. Romjue (D)	43,607	54.7
J. G. Morgan (R)	36,064	45.2
2 William L. Nelson (D)	51,451	57.9
Mrs. George B. Simmons (R)	37,294	42.0
3 Richard M. Duncan (D)	50,501	55.3
Fred Maughmer (R)	40,801	44.7

MISSOURI

	Candidates	Votes	%
4	C. Jasper Bell (D)	71,940	80.4
	George E. Kimball (R)	17,560	19.6
5	Joseph B. Shannon (D)	75,810	81.0
	Leslie J. Lyons (R)	17,809	19.0
6	Reuben T. Wood (D)	52,774	50.3
	Phil A. Bennett (R)	52,159	49.7
7	Dewey Short (R)	63,758	56.3
	Frank H. Lee (D)	49,396	43.6
8	Clyde Williams (D)	56,489	55.3
	Homer S. Cotton (R)	45,673	44.7
9	Clarence Cannon (D)	40,686	60.5
	F. B. Meyer (R)	26,510	39.4
10	Orville Zimmerman (D)	44,182	58.9
	Ralph Hutchison (R)	30,804	41.1
11	Thomas C. Hennings (D)	63,332	61.8
	William E. Buder (R)	38,866	37.9
12	C. Arthur Anderson (D)	78,481	52.0
	Russell J. Horsefield (R)	71,831	47.6
13	John J. Cochran (D)	59,202	69.0
	William Gray (R)	26,476	30.9

MONTANA

1	Jacob Thorkelson (R)	49,253	54.4
	Jerry J. O'Connell (D)	41,319	45.6
2	James F. O'Connor (D)	63,506	53.8
	W. C. Husband (R)	54,632	46.2

NEBRASKA

1	George H. Heinke (R)	45,527	47.0
	Henry C. Luckey (D)	45,178	46.6
	Catherine F. McGerr	6,153	6.4
2	Charles F. McLaughlin (D)	46,927	57.3
	M. F. Mulvaney (R)	32,685	39.9
3	Karl Stefan (R)	78,765	75.3
	Edgar Howard (D)	25,862	24.7
4	Carl T. Curtis (R)	59,794	58.2
	Charles G. Binderup (D)	42,957	41.8
5	Harry B. Coffee (D)	57,192	62.4
	William E. Shuman (R)	31,225	34.1

NEVADA

AL	James G. Scrugham (D)	30,156	66.4
	Harry E. Stewart (R)	15,285	33.6

NEW HAMPSHIRE

1	Arthur B. Jenks (R)	52,444	54.0
	Alphonse Roy (D)	44,681	46.0
2	Foster Stearns (R)	49,696	59.1
	Alvin A. Lucier (D)	34,452	40.9

NEW JERSEY

1	Charles A. Wolverton (R)	96,518	62.0
	Thomas M. Madden (D)	58,450	37.5
2	Walter Sooy Jeffries (R)	57,090	50.6
	Elmer H. Wene (D)	55,344	49.1
3	Walter H. Sutphin (D)	64,621	50.5
	James K. Allardice (R)	63,345	49.5
4	D. Lane Powers (R)	62,123	61.3
	Richard J. Hughes (D)	38,921	38.4
5	Charles A. Eaton (R)	71,661	56.7
	Franklin W. Rice (D)	54,690	43.2
6	Donald H. McLean (R)	63,583	61.4
	Richard F. Green (D)	38,667	37.4
7	J. Parnell Thomas (R)	64,147	64.0
	Edward W. Wildrick (D)	35,628	35.6
8	George N. Seger (R)	61,988	59.2
	Fred Hoelscher (D)	42,030	40.2
9	Frank C. Osmers Jr. (R)	64,903	59.3
	Vincent Clausen (D)	43,641	39.9
10	Fred A. Hartley Jr. (R)	51,025	55.6
	Lindsay H. Rudd (D)	36,273	39.5

	Candidates	Votes	%
11	Albert L. Vreeland (R)	43,747	50.4
	Edward L. O'Neill (D)	38,885	44.8
12	Robert W. Kean (R)	48,854	55.0
	Frank W. Towey Jr (D)	36,736	41.3
13	Mary T. Norton (D)	89,287	79.8
	T. Burton Coyle (R)	22,459	20.1
14	Edward J. Hart (D)	86,128	78.6
	Henry T. Stuhr (R)	23,166	21.1

NEW MEXICO

AL	John J. Dempsey (D)	90,608	58.4
	Pearce Rodey (R)	64,281	41.4

NEW YORK

1	Leonard W. Hall (R)	184,539	63.0
	John F. Kiernan (D)	99,521	34.0
2	William B. Barry (D, AM LAB)	175,009	67.6
	George Archinal (R, C)	81,534	31.5
3	Joseph L. Pfeifer (D)	28,317	64.8
	Philip Tirone (R)	10,174	23.3
	Bernard Kleban (AM LAB)	4,898	11.2
4	Thomas H. Cullen (D, AM LAB)	31,881	74.5
	Edwin R. Kaprat (R)	10,620	24.8
5	Marcellus H. Evans (D)	45,387	58.3
	Francis H. Warland (R, CITY FUS)	23,410	30.1
	Joseph Dermody (AM LAB)	8,352	10.7
6	Andrew L. Somers (D, PROG)	78,530	52.0
	Gustav Drews (R, AM LAB)	69,793	46.2
7	John J. Delaney (D)	29,823	59.6
	John J. Blust (R)	9,930	19.8
	Bernard Reswick (AM LAB)	9,734	19.5
8	Donald L. O'Toole (D)	134,461	54.1
	Dorothy J. Bellanca (AM LAB, R)	111,252	44.7
9	Eugene J. Keogh (D, CITY FUS)	60,164	54.1
	Nelson S. Kirk II (R)	37,740	34.0
	Spencer K. Binyon (AM LAB)	12,199	11.0
10	Emanuel Celler (D, AM LAB)	43,881	73.5
	Arthur H. J. MacMullen (R)	14,852	24.9
11	James A. O'Leary (D)	40,407	58.9
	Percy C. Ryder (R)	23,220	33.9
	John V. Murphy (AM LAB)	4,527	6.6
12	Samuel Dickstein (D, AM LAB)	17,295	89.0
	Hyman Hecht (R)	1,865	9.6
13	Christopher D. Sullivan (D)	13,313	63.8
	John Rosenberg (R)	3,809	18.3
	Eugene P. Connolly (AM LAB)	3,541	17.0
14	William I. Sirovich (D, AM LAB)	23,722	68.4
	Maurice Wahl (R)	10,392	30.0
15	Michael J. Kennedy (D)	22,237	67.3
	John Kane Jr. (R)	7,477	22.6
	Daniel L. McDonough (AM LAB)	3,103	9.4
16	James H. Fay (D, AM LAB)	24,500	52.1
	John J. O'Connor (R, AJAC)	22,037	46.9
17	Bruce Barton (R, I PROG)	40,421	55.0
	Walter H. Liebman (D)	26,581	36.2
	George Backer (AM LAB)	6,120	8.3
18	Martin J. Kennedy (D)	25,817	60.8
	Raymond S. Fanning (R)	12,952	30.5
	Martin C. Kyne (AM LAB)	3,440	8.1
19	Sol Bloom (D)	43,134	53.3
	Robert P. Levis (R, I PROG)	22,741	28.1
	Joseph Schlossberg (AM LAB, SOC)	15,033	18.6

	Candidates	Votes	%
20	Vito Marcantonio (R, AM LAB)	18,960	59.7
	James J. Lanzetta (D)	12,376	39.0
21	Joseph A. Gavagan (D, AM LAB)	84,629	69.5
	Lorenzo H. King (R)	36,034	29.6
22	Edward W. Curley (D, CITY FUS)	34,094	64.5
	Arthur D. Fisher (R)	12,177	23.0
	Thomas C. O'Leary (AM LAB)	6,141	11.6
23	Charles A. Buckley (D, L)	120,474	50.8
	Isidore Nagler (AM LAB, SOC)	67,273	28.4
	Robert H. Brennen (R, I PROG)	49,235	20.8
24	James M. Fitzpatrick (D, CITY FUS)	116,733	48.7
	Louis Goldrich (R)	79,537	33.2
	Bartholomew F. Murphy (AM LAB)	40,931	17.1
25	Ralph A. Gamble (R)	94,865	64.9
	Homer A. Stebbins (D)	46,730	32.0
26	Hamilton Fish (R)	67,837	64.3
	Ben Martin (D, AM LAB)	36,937	35.0
27	Lewis K. Rockefeller (R, SOC)	58,565	61.0
	George W. Markey (D, AM LAB)	37,452	39.0
28	William T. Byrne (D)	88,037	60.5
	William B. Cornell (R)	54,610	37.5
29	E. Harold Cluett (R)	74,888	65.0
	Harry M. Brooks (D, AM LAB)	40,004	34.7
30	Frank Crowther (R)	58,691	60.1
	C. Dorothea Greene (D)	38,535	39.4
31	Wallace E. Pierce (R)	49,240	64.1
	George C. Owens (D)	19,784	25.7
	Jesse W. Williams (TOWN)	7,638	9.9
32	Francis D. Culkin (R)	60,947	75.5
	Virginia A. Spencer (D)	19,631	24.3
33	Fred J. Douglas (R)	63,857	61.2
	Ralph A. Peters (D)	37,195	35.7
34	Bert Lord (R)	67,330	65.3
	John V. Johnson (D, AM LAB)	35,456	34.4
35	Clarence E. Hancock (R)	90,078	64.1
	Caleb Candee Brown Jr. (D, AM LAB)	50,083	35.6
36	John Taber (R)	48,344	54.7
	George F. Davie (D)	20,636	23.3
	Charles P. Russell (AM LAB, TOWN)	19,020	21.5
37	W. Sterling Cole (R)	57,648	60.5
	David Moses (D, AM LAB)	37,216	39.1
38	Joseph J. O'Brien (R)	80,963	55.8
	George B. Kelly (D, AM LAB)	63,325	43.7
39	James W. Wadsworth (R)	65,489	65.8
	J. Frank Gilligan (D)	28,292	28.4
	Edward J. Wagner (AM LAB)	5,460	5.5
40	Walter G. Andrews (R)	92,271	62.6
	John L. Beyer (D)	50,705	34.4
41	J. Francis Harter (R)	46,784	50.5
	Alfred F. Beiter (D, AM LAB)	45,516	49.1
42	Pius L. Schwert (D, AM LAB)	39,287	45.8
	John C. Butler (R)	36,326	42.3
	John A. Ulinski (OB)	9,537	11.1
43	Daniel A. Reed (R)	53,261	65.3
	Samuel A. Carlson (D, AM LAB)	28,289	34.7
AL	Caroline O'Day (D, AM LAB)	2,363,463✓	
	Matthew J. Merritt (D, AM LAB)	2,352,159✓	
	Helen Z. M. Rodgers (R, I PROG)	2,011,507	
	Richard B. Scandrett Jr. (R, I PROG)	1,990,455	

NEW YORK

Candidates	Votes	%
Israel Amter (COM)	105,681	
Edna Mitchell Blue (SOC)	25,214	
Brendan Sexton (SOC)	24,990	
Jeremiah D. Crowley (IND GOVT)	5,080	
William Herlet (IND GOVT)	4,291	

NORTH CAROLINA

	Candidates	Votes	%
1	Lindsay C. Warren (D)	12,083	100.0
2	John H. Kerr (D)	9,955	100.0
3	Graham A. Barden (D)	17,507	100.0
4	Harold D. Cooley (D)	26,932	63.9
	Willis G. Briggs (R)	15,209	36.1
5	Alonzo D. Folger (D)	25,472	69.7
	John W. Kurfees Jr. (R)	11,087	30.3
6	Carl T. Durham (D)	15,730	75.2
	Oscar G. Barker (D)	5,188	24.8
7	J. Bayard Clark (D)	17,175	75.7
	Edgar C. Geddie (R)	5,501	24.3
8	William O. Burgin (D)	34,757	55.2
	John R. Jones (R)	28,187	44.8
9	Robert L. Doughton (D)	43,912	60.9
	Monroe Adams (R)	28,202	39.1
10	Alfred L. Bulwinkle (D)	48,590	56.5
	Frank A. Patton (R)	37,360	43.5
11	Zebulon Weaver (D)	61,508	63.8
	Vonno L. Gudger (R)	34,912	36.2

NORTH DAKOTA

	Candidates	Votes	%
AL	William Lemke (R)	153,288✔	
	Usher L. Burdick (R)	149,047✔	
	Howard I. Henry (D)	55,125	
	Alfred S. Dale (D)	44,691	
	J. B. Field (I)	8,109	

OHIO

	Candidates	Votes	%
1	Charles H. Elston (R)	63,285	58.2
	Joseph A. Dixon (D)	45,536	41.8
2	William E. Hess (R)	61,480	59.0
	Herbert S. Bigelow (D)	42,773	41.0
3	Harry N. Routzohn (R)	73,534	55.9
	Byron B. Harlan (D)	58,139	44.2
4	Robert F. Jones (R)	56,399	59.8
	William B. Swonger (D)	33,284	35.3
5	Cliff Clevenger (R)	37,027	56.9
	Frank C. Kniffin (D)	28,109	43.2
6	James G. Polk (D)	43,646	50.5
	Emory F. Smith (R)	42,847	49.5
7	Clarence J. Brown (R)	68,185	57.6
	Arthur W. Aleshire (D)	50,163	42.4
8	Frederick C. Smith (R)	40,772	54.6
	Brooks Fletcher (D)	33,972	45.5
9	John F. Hunter (D)	56,306	50.4
	Homer A. Ramey (R)	55,441	49.6
10	Thomas A. Jenkins (R)	47,036	66.0
	Elsie Stanton (D)	24,198	34.0
11	Harold K. Claypool (D)	33,764	52.1
	Tom P. White (R)	31,004	47.9
12	John M. Vorys (R)	64,409	50.9
	Arthur P. Lamneck (D)	62,026	49.1
13	Dudley A. White (R)	56,204	69.4
	William L. Fiesinger (D)	24,749	30.6
14	Dow W. Harter (D)	87,303	53.4
	Edward S. Sheck (R)	76,346	46.7
15	Robert T. Secrest (D)	42,573	52.3
	P. W. Griffiths (R)	38,903	47.8
16	Jim Seccombe (R)	62,176	50.7
	William R. Thom (D)	60,382	49.3
17	William A. Ashbrook (D)	51,305	52.6
	Walter B. Woodward (R)	46,300	47.4
18	Earl R. Lewis (R)	56,468	50.3
	Lawrence E. Imhoff (D)	55,809	49.7
19	Michael J. Kirwan (D)	76,268	52.4
	William P. Barnum (R)	69,214	47.6

	Candidates	Votes	%
20	Martin L. Sweeney (D)	54,185	70.4
	Thomas F. McCafferty (R)	22,775	29.6
21	Robert Crosser (D)	53,180	68.7
	J. E. Chizek (R)	24,240	31.3
22	Chester C. Bolton (R)	109,494	55.5
	Anthony A. Fleger (D)	87,635	44.5
AL	George H. Bender (R)	1,177,982✔	
	Lycurgus L. Marshall (R)	1,101,194✔	
	John McSweeney (D)	1,068,916	
	Stephen M. Young (D)	1,015,035	

Special Election

		Votes	%
4	Walter H. Albaugh (R)	47,631	54.9
	Roy E. Layton (D)	39,112	45.1

OKLAHOMA

	Candidates	Votes	%
1	Wesley E. Disney (D)	55,253	63.2
	A. M. Armstrong (R)	31,755	36.3
2	Jack Nichols (D)	38,058	71.3
	Bruce L. Keenan (R)	15,335	28.7
3	Wilburn Cartwright (D)	42,616	85.4
	Frank D. McSherry (R)	7,286	14.6
4	Lyle H. Boren (D)	44,233	71.7
	Ed Ball (R)	17,506	28.4
5	A. S. Mike Monroney (D)	47,692	71.9
	Harlan Deupree (R)	18,271	27.6
6	Jed Johnson (D)	33,808	69.5
	James F. Rowell (R)	14,617	30.1
7	Sam C. Massingale (D)	24,986	76.1
	A. L. Smith (R)	7,862	23.9
8	Phil Ferguson (D)	34,113	50.2
	Charles E. Knox (R)	33,438	49.2
AL	Will Rogers (D)	306,241	68.7
	R. R. Wilson (R)	137,733	30.9

OREGON

	Candidates	Votes	%
1	James W. Mott (R)	119,965	70.7
	Andrew C. Burk (D)	49,666	29.3
2	Walter M. Pierce (D)	35,200	57.9
	U. S. Balentine (R)	25,557	42.1
3	Homer D. Angell (R)	69,049	50.9
	Nan Wood Honeyman (D)	66,498	49.1

PENNSYLVANIA

	Candidates	Votes	%
1	Leon Sachs (D, D-OP)	54,819	53.5
	John Alessandroni (R)	47,692	46.5
2	James P. McGranery (D)	51,565	52.4
	Edward W. Henry (R)	46,248	47.0
3	Michael J. Bradley (D)	61,686	52.0
	William T. Connor (R, R-OP)	56,958	48.0
4	J. Burrwood Daly (D)	60,514	53.8
	Edward F. Roberts (R)	51,343	45.7
5	Fred C. Gartner (R)	63,877	52.5
	Frank J. G. Dorsey (D)	56,492	46.5
6	Francis J. Myers (D)	62,524	49.9
	J. Howard Berry Jr. (R)	59,548	47.5
7	George P. Darrow (R)	84,077	59.3
	Ira W. Drew (D)	57,046	40.2
8	James Wolfenden (R)	84,103	67.6
	C. Fenno Hoffman (D)	40,324	32.4
9	Charles L. Gerlach (R)	56,589	56.7
	Oliver W. Frey (D)	43,055	43.1
10	J. Roland Kinzer (R)	78,986	64.1
	Thomas Jefferson McClelland (D)	43,928	35.7
11	Patrick J. Boland (D)	66,626	52.5
	William F. Hallstead (R, R-OP)	60,307	47.5
12	J. Harold Flannery (D)	98,715	51.2
	Michael A. Yeosock (R)	94,108	48.8
13	Ivor D. Fenton (R, R-OP)	79,468	53.2
	James H. Gildea (D)	69,817	46.8
14	Guy L. Moser (D)	34,678	52.7
	John C. Evans (R)	31,068	47.3

	Candidates	Votes	%
15	Albert G. Rutherford (R)	58,571	61.6
	Harry M. Turrell (D, D-OP)	36,096	37.9
16	Robert F. Rich (R, R-OP)	63,241	61.5
	Paul A. Rothfuss (D)	38,908	37.8
17	J. William Ditter (R)	72,225	68.5
	Carroll L. Rutter (D)	32,921	31.2
18	Richard M. Simpson (R)	53,067	60.5
	Richard L. Schroyer (D)	34,578	39.5
19	John C. Kunkel (R, R-OP)	77,354	55.0
	Guy J. Swope (D)	63,180	45.0
20	Benjamin Jarrett (R)	65,547	61.8
	Earl H. Beshlin (D, D-OP)	40,511	38.2
21	Francis E. Walter (D)	43,276	50.2
	Alonzo L. Reinhard (R)	41,665	48.4
22	Chester H. Gross (R)	55,565	50.3
	Harry L. Haines (D, D-OP)	54,880	49.7
23	James E. Van Zandt (R)	61,372	57.1
	Don Gingery (D, D-OP)	45,694	42.5
24	J. Buell Snyder (D)	47,045	51.2
	J. C. Glassburn (R)	44,604	48.5
25	Charles I. Faddis (D, D-OP)	43,604	53.1
	Warren S. Burchinal (R)	38,549	46.9
26	Louis E. Graham (R)	59,754	52.4
	Charles R. Eckert (D, D-OP)	53,434	46.8
27	Harve Tibbott (R, R-OP)	81,690	55.8
	Joseph H. Gray (D, D-OP)	63,790	43.5
28	Robert G. Allen (D, D-OP)	52,034	53.9
	Roy C. McKenna (R)	44,196	45.8
29	Robert L. Rodgers (R)	46,856	53.8
	Norbert James Fitzgerald (D)	39,762	45.6
30	Robert J. Corbett (R)	53,541	51.2
	Peter J. DeMuth (D, D-OP)	51,028	48.8
31	John McDowell (R, R-OP)	57,392	50.7
	James J. Quinn (D)	55,211	48.8
32	Herman P. Eberharter (D)	48,025	63.3
	Jacob E. Kalson (R)	27,440	36.2
33	Joseph A. McArdle (D, D-OP)	54,888	51.6
	James I. Marsh (R)	51,427	48.4
34	Matthew A. Dunn (D, D-OP)	55,502	50.0
	Robert B. McKinley (R)	55,055	49.6

RHODE ISLAND

	Candidates	Votes	%
1	Charles F. Risk (R)	73,394	50.3
	Aime J. Forand (D)	72,484	49.7
2	Harry Sandager (R, GOOD GOV)	87,932	57.0
	Edward J. Fenelon Jr. (D)	66,408	43.0

SOUTH CAROLINA

	Candidates	Votes	%
1	Thomas S. McMillan (D)	7,649	98.2
2	Hampton P. Fulmer (D)	7,236	98.8
3	Butler B. Hare (D)	10,028	99.6
4	Joseph R. Bryson (D)	8,995	99.4
5	James P. Richards (D)	6,191	99.8
6	John L. McMillan (D)	5,707	99.2

SOUTH DAKOTA

	Candidates	Votes	%
1	Karl E. Mundt (R)	111,805	54.0
	Emil Loriks (D)	95,353	46.0
2	Francis H. Case (R)	41,335	61.5
	Theodore B. Werner (D)	25,932	38.6

TENNESSEE

	Candidates	Votes	%
1	B. Carroll Reece (R)	23,251	58.0
	John A. Armstrong (D)	10,609	26.5
	James P. Kinett	4,382	10.9
2	J. Will Taylor (R)	32,312	64.1
	Judd Acuff (I)	16,079	31.9

945

TENNESSEE

Candidates	Votes	%
3 Sam D. McReynolds (D)	21,804	73.9
Joe F. Benson (R)	7,708	26.1
4 Albert Gore (D)	25,220	100.0
5 Joseph Byrns (D)	16,819	90.6
William I. Love (I)	1,749	9.4
6 Clarence W. Turner (D)	14,318	82.2
John U. McDonough (I)	1,957	11.2
Maurice C. Riding	1,146	6.6
7 Herron Pearson (D)	19,554	100.0
8 Jere Cooper (D)	18,173	95.4
9 Walter Chandler (D)	43,976	98.4

TEXAS

Candidates	Votes	%
1 Wright Patman (D)	14,833	98.8
2 Martin Dies (D)	12,816	100.0
3 Lindley Beckworth (D)	17,115	100.0
4 Sam Rayburn (D)	16,523	97.9
5 Hatton W. Sumners (D)	10,344	95.3
6 Luther A. Johnson (D)	15,619	100.0
7 Nat Patton (D)	16,467	100.0
8 Albert Thomas (D)	36,989	98.3
9 Joseph J. Mansfield (D)	16,680	100.0
10 Lyndon B. Johnson (D)	14,476	100.0
11 W. R. Poage (D)	14,664	100.0
12 Fritz G. Lanham (D)	12,972	100.0
13 Ed Gossett (D)	20,620	100.0
14 Richard M. Kleberg (D)	23,438	100.0
15 Milton H. West (D)	18,995	100.0
16 R. Ewing Thomason (D)	9,237	100.0
17 Clyde L. Garrett (D)	17,107	100.0
18 Marvin Jones (D)	18,048	100.0
19 George H. Mahon (D)	16,372	100.0
20 Paul J. Kilday (D)	16,703	100.0
21 Charles L. South (D)	21,671	93.0
M. J. Bierschwale (R)	1,621	7.0

UTAH

Candidates	Votes	%
1 Abe Murdock (D)	52,927	59.7
LeRoy B. Young (R)	35,790	40.3
2 J. W. Robinson (D)	58,456	62.3
Dean F. Brayton (R)	35,359	37.7

VERMONT

Candidates	Votes	%
AL Charles A. Plumley (R)	71,901	64.0
James P. Leamy (D)	40,483	36.0

VIRGINIA

Candidates	Votes	%
1 Schuyler Otis Bland (D)	7,191	99.7
2 Colgate W. Darden Jr. (D)	15,276	87.2
Carl P. Spaeth	2,142	12.2
3 David E. Satterfield Jr. (D)	5,560	99.7
4 Patrick Henry Drewry (D)	5,805	99.9
5 Thomas G. Burch (D)	5,761	99.6
6 Clifton A. Woodrum (D)	11,509	55.9
Fred W. McWane (R)	9,083	44.1
7 A. Willis Robertson (D)	11,398	63.9
Charles C. Leap (R)	6,449	36.1
8 Howard W. Smith (D)	13,796	99.6
9 John W. Flannagan Jr. (D)	21,235	66.7
L. E. Gulliford (R)	10,612	33.3

WASHINGTON

Candidates	Votes	%
1 Warren G. Magnuson (D)	90,768	61.7
Matthew W. Hill (R)	56,293	38.3
2 Mon C. Wallgren (D)	58,313	61.5
Charles A. Sather (R)	36,442	38.5
3 Martin F. Smith (D)	52,305	60.3
Walter S. Talbott (R)	34,394	39.7
4 Knute Hill (D)	38,647	50.4
Frank Miller (R)	37,969	49.6
5 Charles H. Leavy (D)	52,782	57.1
Norman A. Ericson (R)	38,858	42.0
6 John M. Coffee (D)	64,871	73.0
Willard V. Young (R)	24,002	27.0

WEST VIRGINIA

Candidates	Votes	%
1 Andrew C. Schiffler (R)	57,043	54.8
Robert L. Ramsey (D)	47,051	45.2
2 Jennings Randolph (D)	53,277	54.6
Melvin C. Snyder (R)	44,334	45.4
3 Andrew Edmiston (D)	53,722	55.3
H. Roy Waugh (R)	43,407	44.7

Candidates	Votes	%
4 George W. Johnson (D)	65,965	52.9
Raymond V. Humphreys (R)	58,749	47.1
5 John Kee (D)	55,501	61.3
Hartley Sanders (R)	34,989	38.7
6 Joe L. Smith (D)	67,818	62.3
R. E. O'Connor (R)	40,965	37.7

WISCONSIN

Candidates	Votes	%
1 Stephen Bolles (R)	45,247	49.1
Francis H. Wendt (PROG)	29,478	32.0
Calvin Stewart (D)	14,573	15.8
2 Charles Hawks Jr. (R)	42,154	44.9
Harry Sauthoff (PROG)	40,656	43.3
Reinhold A. Gerth (D)	11,185	11.9
3 Harry W. Griswold (R)	43,495	50.1
Gardner R. Withrow (PROG)	36,509	42.0
Bart E. McGonigle (D)	6,887	7.9
4 John C. Schafer (R)	34,196	32.0
Thaddeus F. B. Wasielewski (D)	33,559	31.4
Paul Gauer (PROG)	30,817	28.8
Raymond J. Cannon (I)	7,498	7.0
5 Lewis D. Thill (R)	47,032	43.1
Thomas O'Malley (D)	31,154	28.6
Alfred Benson (PROG)	29,874	27.4
6 Frank B. Keefe (R)	46,082	53.6
Michael K. Reilly (D)	25,842	30.1
Adam F. Poltl (PROG)	13,258	15.4
7 Reid F. Murray (R)	41,662	48.9
Gerald J. Boileau (PROG)	32,442	38.0
James J. Cavanaugh (D)	9,727	11.4
8 Joshua L. Johns (R)	33,354	36.2
George J. Schneider (PROG)	29,035	31.5
John E. Cashman (D)	28,221	30.6
9 Merlin Hull (PROG)	42,880	53.4
Hugh M. Jones (R)	32,375	40.3
William F. Crane (D)	5,066	6.3
10 Bernard J. Gehrmann (PROG)	45,874	57.5
James H. Carroll (R)	33,854	42.5

WYOMING

Candidates	Votes	%
AL Frank O. Horton (R)	49,975	52.9
Paul R. Greever (D)	44,525	47.1

1939 House Election

PENNSYLVANIA

Special Election

	Votes	%
4 John Edward Sheridan (D)	52,250	51.8
Boies Penrose (R)	48,648	48.2

1940 House Elections

ALABAMA

	Candidates	Votes	%
1	Frank W. Boykin (D)	25,993	100.0
2	George Grant (D)	33,433	100.0
3	Henry B. Steagall (D)	22,906	100.0
4	Sam Hobbs (D)	24,870	87.9
	Thomas G. McNaron (R)	3,428	12.1
5	Joe Starnes (D)	31,966	100.0
6	Pete Jarman (D)	18,881	100.0
7	Walter Will Bankhead (D)	27,696	70.9
	A. W. Hargett (R)	11,368	29.1
8	John J. Sparkman (D)	29,020	100.0
9	Luther Patrick (D)	39,660	99.2

ARIZONA

	Candidates	Votes	%
AL	John R. Murdock (D)	99,424	71.1
	K. T. Palmer (R)	40,360	28.9

ARKANSAS

	Candidates	Votes	%
1	Ezekiel C. Gathings (D)	33,127	100.0
2	Wilbur D. Mills (D)	25,718	100.0
3	Clyde E. Ellis (D)	21,060	71.1
	Clyde M. Williams (R)	8,566	28.9
4	Fadjo Cravens (D)	28,999	100.0
5	David D. Terry (D)	36,067	100.0
6	William F. Norrell (D)	27,972	100.0
7	Oren Harris (D)	26,994	100.0

CALIFORNIA

	Candidates	Votes	%
1	Clarence F. Lea (D-R)	103,547	93.0
	Albert J. Lima (COM)	5,647	5.1
2	Harry L. Englebright (R D P T)	71,033	100.0
3	Frank H. Buck (D-R)	135,461	91.0
	C. H. Farman (P)	10,539	7.1
4	Thomas Rolph (R)	75,369	54.6
	Franck R. Havenner (D & PROG)	61,341	44.4
5	Richard J. Welch (R-D)	119,122	95.8
6	Albert E. Carter (R D P T)	131,584	96.0
7	John H. Tolan (D)	72,838	55.5
	Ralph M. Eltse (R)	56,808	43.3
8	John Z. Anderson (R-D)	148,180	96.5
9	Bertrand W. Gearhart (R-D)	99,708	99.9
10	Alfred J. Elliott (D-R)	125,845	96.8
11	Carl Hinshaw (R-D-PROG)	170,504	96.2
12	H. Jerry Voorhis (D)	99,494	64.0
	Irwin W. Minger (R)	54,731	35.2
13	Charles Kramer (D-R)	127,167	75.6
	Charles H. Randall (PROG-P)	36,406	21.7
14	Thomas F. Ford (D)	73,137	64.2
	Herbert L. Herberts (R)	37,939	33.3
15	John M. Costello (D)	94,435	56.2
	Norris J. Nelson (R & PROG)	71,667	42.6
16	Leland Merritt Ford (R-D)	188,004	96.2
17	Lee E. Geyer (D)	75,109	65.5
	Clifton A. Hix (R)	32,862	28.6
18	Ward Johnson (R)	73,932	54.3
	Byron N. Scott (D)	60,764	44.6
19	Harry R. Sheppard (D)	84,931	52.9
	Lotus H. Loudon (R)	75,495	47.0
20	Edouard V. M. Izac (D)	69,874	51.1
	Ed Fletcher (R)	66,132	48.3

COLORADO

	Candidates	Votes	%
1	Lawrence Lewis (D)	110,078	64.6
	James D. Parriott (R)	59,427	34.9
2	William S. Hill (R)	76,859	53.3
	Fred Cummings (D)	66,662	46.2
3	J. Edgar Chenoweth (R)	70,842	52.1
	Byron G. Rogers (D)	65,269	48.0
4	Edward T. Taylor (D)	44,095	59.4
	Paul W. Crawford (R)	30,126	40.6

Special Election

		Votes	%
3	William E. Burney (D)	68,225	51.0
	Henry Leonard (R)	65,675	49.1

CONNECTICUT

	Candidates	Votes	%
1	Herman P. Kopplemann (D)	109,880	54.2
	William J. Miller (R, SOC)	92,980	45.8
2	William J. Fitzgerald (D)	63,021	52.4
	Thomas R. Ball (R)	56,825	47.3
3	James A. Shanley (D)	84,439	53.6
	Ranulf Compton (R, UN)	73,078	46.4
4	Le Roy D. Downs (D)	90,942	49.0
	Albert E. Austin (R)	90,239	48.6
5	J. Joseph Smith (D)	62,783	54.9
	Frank T. Johnson (R)	51,049	44.7
AL	Lucien J. Maciora (D)	407,868	52.1
	Boleslaus J. Monkiewicz (R)	365,851	46.8

DELAWARE

	Candidates	Votes	%
AL	Philip A. Traynor (D)	68,205	50.6
	George S. Williams (R)	64,384	47.8

FLORIDA

	Candidates	Votes	%
1	J. Hardin Peterson (D)	88,158	100.0
2	Robert A. Green (D)	68,797	89.1
	Francis McHale (R)	8,382	10.9
3	Robert L. F. Sikes (D)	36,573	100.0
4	Arthur P. Cannon (D)	84,594	75.3
	Bert L. Acker (R)	27,815	24.7
5	Joe Hendricks (D)	49,715	75.4
	Emory Akerman (R)	16,214	24.6

GEORGIA

	Candidates	Votes	%
1	Hugh Peterson (D)	28,601	99.5
2	E. E. Cox (D)	19,443	96.8
3	Stephen Pace (D)	22,882	100.0
4	A. Sidney Camp (D)	25.609	100.0
5	Robert Ramspeck (D, I)	41,677	99.9
6	Carl Vinson (D)	21,966	99.9
7	Malcolm C. Tarver (D)	32,280	86.4
	Lewis H. Crawford (R)	5,062	13.6
8	John S. Gibson (D, R)	24,454	100.0
9	B. Frank Whelchel (D)	25,461	84.4
	William C. Horton (R)	4,025	13.3
10	Paul Brown (D)	18,291	98.7

IDAHO

	Candidates	Votes	%
1	Compton I. White (D)	62,107	62.0
	Edward Gaffney (R)	37,999	38.0
2	Henry C. Dworshak (R)	69,804	53.1
	Ira H. Masters (D)	61,726	46.9

ILLINOIS

	Candidates	Votes	%
1	Arthur W. Mitchell (D)	34,641	53.0
	William E. King (R)	30,698	47.0
2	Raymond S. McKeough (D)	155,698	51.5
	P. H. Moynihan (R)	146,927	48.6
3	Edward A. Kelly (D)	148,382	51.1
	Waldemar J. Roehler (R)	141,768	48.9
4	Harry P. Beam (D)	74,977	77.4
	Henry F. Schmudde (R)	21,858	22.6
5	Adolph J. Sabath (D)	35,637	71.0
	Martin Dykema (R)	14,540	29.0
6	A. F. Maciejewski (D)	187,393	56.2
	Joseph Wagner (R)	146,852	43.8
7	Leonard W. Schuetz (D)	229,161	50.9
	James C. Moreland (R)	220,793	49.1
8	Leo Kocialkowski (D)	40,074	78.1
	Anthony V. Champagne (R)	11,232	21.9
9	Charles S. Dewey (R)	56,806	53.3
	James McAndrews (D)	49,816	46.7
10	George A. Paddock (R)	199,418	61.3
	John Haderlein (D)	125,827	38.7
11	Chauncey W. Reed (R)	128,645	64.6
	Edgar O. Eakin (D)	70,581	35.4
12	Noah M. Mason (R)	90,744	60.6
	August C. Engh (D)	58,945	39.4
13	Leo E. Allen (R)	65,698	67.6
	John B. Hayes (D)	31,502	32.4
14	Anton J. Johnson (R)	60,909	52.4
	Forest Dizotell (D)	55,451	47.7
15	Robert B. Chiperfield (R)	65,639	56.4
	Russell M. Gunn (D)	50,820	43.6
16	Everett M. Dirksen (R)	79,780	58.1
	M. R. Clark (D)	57,567	41.9
17	Leslie C. Arends (R)	56,712	61.1
	J. Joseph Pitts (D)	36,102	38.9
18	Jessie Sumner (R)	64,409	53.2
	James A. Meeks (D)	56,744	46.8
19	William H. Wheat (R)	75,933	50.6
	Alfred D. Huston (D)	74,091	49.4
20	James M. Barnes (D)	44,824	51.7
	Hardin E. Hanks (R)	41,806	48.3
21	Evan Howell (R)	67,896	51.6
	Frank W. Fries (D)	63,740	48.4
22	Edwin M. Schaefer (D)	98,162	53.8
	Calvin D. Johnson (R)	84,381	46.2
23	Laurence F. Arnold (D)	65,062	51.4
	Ben O. Sumner (R)	61,521	48.6
24	James V. Heidinger (R)	49,731	53.6
	Claude V. Parsons (D)	43,050	46.4
25	Cecil W. Bishop (R)	69,165	50.5
	Kent E. Keller (D)	67,891	49.5
AL	William G. Stratton (R)	2,050,493✔	
	Stephen A. Day (R)	2,020,008✔	
	Thomas V. Smith (D)	1,968,143	
	Walter J. Orlikoski (D)	1,913,950	
	Harry Fleischman (SOC)	7,377	
	Lee S. Gregory (SOC)	7,191	
	Willis Ray Wilson (P)	6,786	
	Lena Duell Vincent (P)	6,621	

INDIANA

	Candidates	Votes	%
1	William T. Schulte (D)	71,606	60.8
	Elliot Belshaw (R)	45,947	39.0
2	Charles A. Halleck (R)	87,652	58.1
	James O. Cox (D)	63,290	41.9
3	Robert A. Grant (R)	73,914	51.3
	George Sands (D)	70,208	48.7
4	George W. Gillie (R)	80,259	58.0
	Frank E. Corbett (D)	58,157	42.0
5	Forest A. Harness (R)	78,691	54.7
	George W. Wolf (D)	65,200	45.3
6	Noble J. Johnson (R)	80,595	52.3
	Lenhardt E. Bauer (D)	73,449	47.7
7	Gerald W. Landis (R)	81,632	52.2
	Charles H. Bedwell (D)	74,746	47.8
8	John W. Boehne Jr. (D)	87,141	55.5
	Charles F. Werner (R)	69,761	44.5
9	Earl Wilson (R)	71,624	50.9
	Eugene B. Crowe (D)	69,227	49.2
10	Raymond S. Springer (R)	80,725	53.0
	Don C. Ward (D)	71,478	47.0
11	William H. Larrabee (D)	79,070	51.7
	Maurice G. Robinson (R)	73,867	48.3

INDIANA

Candidates	Votes	%
12 Louis Ludlow (D)	80,954	52.9
James A. Collins (R)	72,174	47.1

IOWA

Candidates	Votes	%
1 Thomas E. Martin (R)	70,120	60.4
Zoe S. Nabers (D)	46,040	39.6
2 William S. Jacobsen (D)	75,774	52.2
W. A. McCullough (R)	69,298	47.8
3 John W. Gwynne (R)	65,425	60.0
Ernest J. Seemann (D)	43,709	40.1
4 Henry O. Taile (R)	66,691	56.4
Morgan J. McEnaney (D)	51,558	43.6
5 Karl M. LeCompte (R)	66,940	53.3
Roy E. Stevens (D)	58,718	46.7
6 Paul Cunningham (R)	70,707	52.3
E. Frank Fox (D)	64,314	47.6
7 Ben F. Jensen (R)	71,633	58.6
Ernest M. Miller (D)	50,644	41.4
8 Fred C. Gilchrist (R)	64,687	58.1
Frank J. Lund (D)	46,597	41.9
9 Vincent F. Harrington (D)	67,017	50.8
Albert F. Swanson (R)	64,877	49.2

KANSAS

Candidates	Votes	%
1 William P. Lambertson (R)	64,766	61.0
Clive R. Lane (D)	41,375	39.0
2 Ulysses S. Guyer (R)	73,659	54.0
Harold H. Harding (D)	62,787	46.0
3 Thomas D. Winter (R)	60,381	55.2
W. E. Ledbetter (D)	48,971	44.8
4 Edward H. Rees (R)	58,183	62.5
Dudley Doolittle (D)	34,957	37.5
5 John M. Houston (D)	58,486	52.5
Stanley Taylor (R)	52,901	47.5
6 Frank Carlson (R)	69,627	60.9
Max Jones (D)	44,702	39.1
7 Clifford R. Hope (R)	75,349	63.9
Claude E. Main (D)	42,518	36.1

KENTUCKY

Candidates	Votes	%
1 Noble J. Gregory (D)	60,777	100.0
2 Beverly M. Vincent (D)	69,905	100.0
3 Emmet O'Neal (D)	96,253	60.0
Ben J. Brumleve (R)	64,053	40.0
4 Edward W. Creal (D)	55,561	58.5
Lewis H. Mather (R)	39,447	41.5
5 Brent Spence (D)	51,954	61.2
Henry J. Cook (R)	32,981	38.8
6 Virgil Chapman (D)	74,463	60.5
William D. Rogers (R)	48,700	39.5
7 Andrew J. May (D)	44,185	56.8
James W. Turner (R)	33,574	43.2
8 Joe B. Bates (D)	61,881	58.0
H. Clell Hayes (R)	44,736	42.0
9 John M. Robsion (R)	71,750	62.5
Bert Rowland (D)	43,013	37.5

LOUISIANA

Candidates	Votes	%
1 F. Edward Hebert (D)	58,234	100.0
2 Hale Boggs (D)	56,026	100.0
3 James Domengeaux (D)	27,081	66.0
David W. Pipes Jr. (R)	13,933	34.0
4 Overton Brooks (D)	33,704	100.0
5 Newt V. Mills (D)	33,462	100.0
6 Jared Y. Sanders Jr. (D)	41,173	100.0
7 Vance Plauche (D)	28,518	100.0
8 A. Leonard Allen (D)	28,904	100.0

MAINE

Candidates	Votes	%
1 James C. Oliver (R)	55,503	63.4
Peter M. McDonald (D)	32,018	36.6

Candidates	Votes	%
2 Margaret Chase Smith (R)	57,152	64.6
Edward J. Beauchamp (D)	31,334	35.4
3 Frank Fellows (R)	46,732	66.1
Thomas N. Curran (D)	23,934	33.9

MARYLAND

Candidates	Votes	%
1 David J. Ward (D)	36,057	53.9
Robert F. Duer (R)	30,810	46.1
2 William P. Cole Jr. (D)	113,495	65.7
Theodore F. Brown (R)	59,223	34.3
3 Thomas D'Alesandro Jr. (D)	38,540	61.5
John A. Janetzke (R)	24,153	38.5
4 John A. Meyer (D)	50,120	56.6
Daniel Ellison (R)	38,444	43.4
5 Lansdale Sasscer (D)	58,418	71.0
John N. Torvestad (R)	23,857	29.0
6 William D. Byron (D)	60,037	53.5
Walter P. Johnson (R)	52,258	46.5

MASSACHUSETTS

Candidates	Votes	%
1 Allen T. Treadway (R)	72,750	57.1
Clifford J. Akey (D)	54,634	42.9
2 Charles R. Clason (R)	76,373	58.4
Patrick A. Doyle (D)	54,428	41.6
3 Joseph E. Casey (D)	72,839	54.6
Edward T. Simoneau (R)	60,676	45.4
4 Pehr G. Holmes (R)	70,542	53.2
Frank J. McGrail (D)	60,988	46.0
5 Edith Nourse Rogers (R)	120,435	76.2
Francis J. Roane (D)	37,593	23.8
6 George J. Bates (R)	88,834	71.6
James D. Burns (D)	35,214	28.4
7 Lawrence J. Connery (D)	89,966	62.1
William Henry Haskell (R)	52,701	36.4
8 Arthur D. Healey (D)	71,127	55.4
John J. Irwin (R)	57,217	44.6
9 Thomas H. Eliot (D)	81,523	52.1
Robert Luce (R)	74,922	47.9
10 George Holden Tinkham (R)	78,029	59.1
David M. Owens (D)	54,093	40.9
11 Thomas A. Flaherty (D)	58,041	81.5
Benjamin J. Green (R)	13,176	18.5
12 John W. McCormack (D)	97,588	78.1
Henry J. Allen (R)	27,302	21.9
13 Richard B. Wigglesworth (R)	92,651	65.0
Francis G. O'Neill (D)	48,606	34.1
14 Joseph W. Martin Jr. (R)	65,780	54.4
Harold E. Cole (R)	55,241	45.7
15 Charles L. Gifford (R)	73,358	57.8
George F. Backus (D)	53,581	42.2

MICHIGAN

Candidates	Votes	%
1 Rudolph G. Tenerowicz (D)	87,451	79.9
Donald J. Marshall (R)	21,399	19.5
2 Earl C. Michener (R)	72,235	62.3
Redmond M. Burr (D)	43,733	37.7
3 Paul W. Shafer (R)	74,614	62.1
Charles T. McSherry (D)	45,138	37.6
4 Clare E. Hoffman (R)	65,666	61.8
Harvey Hope Jarvis (D)	40,443	38.1
5 Bartel J. Jonkman (R)	65,240	53.7
Garrett Heyns (D)	56,172	46.3
6 William W. Blackney (R)	77,340	51.1
Charles R. Adair (D)	73,629	48.6
7 Jesse P. Wolcott (R)	73,926	65.2
Albert A. Wagner (D)	39,416	34.8
8 Fred L. Crawford (R)	68,265	61.2
Louis C. Schwinger (D)	43,297	38.8
9 Albert J. Engel (R)	52,343	56.9
Noel P. Fox (D)	39,667	43.1
10 Roy O. Woodruff (R)	52,685	61.9
William J. Kelly (D)	32,289	37.9
11 Fred Bradley (R)	48,087	51.1
Wendell L. Lund (D)	45,826	48.7

Candidates	Votes	%
12 Frank E. Hook (D)	47,429	51.3
John B. Bennett (R)	44,733	48.4
13 George D. O'Brien (D)	66,985	54.6
Clarence J. McLeod (R)	55,115	44.9
14 Louis C. Rabaut (D)	80,463	59.0
George B. Shaeffer (R)	55,910	41.0
15 John D. Dingell (D)	85,239	61.9
Archie C. Fraser (R)	52,131	37.9
16 John Lesinski (D)	73,956	58.8
Robert Ford (R)	51,276	40.8
17 George A. Dondero (R)	82,809	54.7
Draper Allen (D)	68,195	45.1

MINNESOTA

Candidates	Votes	%
1 August H. Andresen (R)	88,814	64.6
Francis L. Murphy (D)	27,479	20.1
Endre B. Anderson (F-LAB)	20,700	15.1
2 Joseph P. O'Hara (R)	66,610	49.0
Elmer J. Ryan (D)	57,673	42.5
C. E. McNaught (F-LAB)	11,534	8.5
3 Richard P. Gale (R)	63,854	43.5
Henry G. Teigan (F-LAB)	50,222	34.2
Martin A. Hogan (D)	28,321	19.3
4 Melvin J. Maas (R)	68,525	58.8
George L. Siegel (F-LAB)	32,898	28.3
Willard J. Moran (D)	15,050	12.9
5 Oscar Youngdahl (R)	79,491	52.1
Dewey W. Johnson (F-LAB)	52,289	34.3
Lamoine Montgomery Dowling (D)	20,720	13.6
6 Harold Knutson (R)	84,023	61.5
E. Thomas O'Brien (D)	52,504	38.5
7 H. Carl Andersen (R)	65,958	50.7
Harold L. Peterson (F-LAB)	42,356	32.6
J. L. O'Connor (D)	21,796	16.8
8 William A. Pittenger (R)	74,521	54.2
John T. Bernard (F-LAB)	39,252	28.5
M. W. Raihala (D)	23,845	17.3
9 Richard Thompson Buckler (F-LAB)	48,999	43.4
Colvin G. Butler (R)	48,324	42.8
Frank H. Timm (D)	15,507	13.7

MISSISSIPPI

Candidates	Votes	%
1 John E. Rankin (D)	19,390	100.0
2 Wall Doxey (D)	16,939	100.0
3 William M. Whittington (D)	16,597	100.0
4 Aaron Lane Ford (D)	15,329	100.0
5 Ross A. Collins (D)	24,079	100.0
6 William M. Colmer (D)	26,679	100.0
7 Dan R. McGehee (D)	29,799	100.0

MISSOURI

Candidates	Votes	%
1 Milton A. Romjue (D)	62,461	50.5
Henry S. Beardsley (R)	61,123	49.5
2 William L. Nelson (D)	77,922	53.8
Roy O. Miller (R)	66,794	46.2
3 Richard M. Duncan (D)	77,424	53.3
Fred Maughmer (R)	67,757	46.7
4 C. Jasper Bell (D)	72,331	60.0
John W. Mitchell (R)	48,181	40.0
5 Joseph B. Shannon (D)	63,202	54.2
Forest W. Hanna (R)	53,390	45.8
6 Philip A. Bennett (R)	78,746	53.7
Reuben T. Wood (D)	67,902	46.3
7 Dewey Short (R)	86,541	59.3
Vernon Sigars (D)	59,344	40.7
8 Clyde Williams (D)	64,263	51.1
Parke M. Banta (R)	61,567	48.9
9 Clarence Cannon (D)	60,204	55.3
F. B. Meyer (R)	48,704	44.7
10 Orville Zimmerman (D)	69,859	57.4
C. E. Davenport (R)	51,755	42.6

MISSOURI

Candidates	Votes	%
11 John B. Sullivan (D)	85,722	55.7
Charles J. Riley (R)	68,088	44.3
12 Walter C. Ploeser (R)	127,005	53.9
C. Arthur Anderson (D)	108,605	46.1
13 John J. Cochran (D)	82,417	64.5
W. S. Sanford (R)	45,262	35.5

MONTANA

	Votes	%
1 Jeanette Rankin (R)	56,616	54.5
Jerry J. O'Connell (D)	47,352	45.5
2 James F. O'Connor (D)	83,101	62.0
Melvin N. Hoiness (R)	49,710	37.1

NEBRASKA

	Votes	%
1 Oren S. Copeland (R)	64,431	55.6
Henry C. Luckey (D)	51,524	44.4
2 Charles F. McLaughlin (D)	68,760	56.6
Theodore W. Metcalfe (R)	52,669	43.4
3 Karl Stefan (R)	90,561	80.0
Victor J. McGonigle (D)	19,253	17.0
4 Carl T. Curtis (R)	66,966	57.7
R. O. Canaday (D)	29,311	25.3
Charles G. Binderup	19,807	17.1
5 Harry B. Coffee (D)	63,025	58.1
Bert Howard (R)	45,548	42.0

NEVADA

	Votes	%
AL James G. Scrugham (D)	32,714	64.5
Ralph W. Lattin (R)	18,032	35.5

NEW HAMPSHIRE

	Votes	%
1 Arthur B. Jenks (R)	57,982	51.1
Alphonse Roy (D)	55,434	48.9
2 Foster Stearns (R)	55,530	53.0
Daniel J. Moriarty (D)	49,260	47.0

NEW JERSEY

	Votes	%
1 Charles A. Wolverton (R)	97,547	55.5
Harry Roye (D)	77,931	44.3
2 Elmer H. Wene (D)	60,392	52.2
Walter Sooy Jeffries (R)	55,382	47.8
3 William H. Sutphin (D)	76,048	51.7
Joseph C. Irwin (R)	70,890	48.2
4 D. Lane Powers (R)	69,834	55.9
Thomas S. Dignan (D)	54,909	44.0
5 Charles A. Eaton (R)	82,840	55.9
Charles R. M. Tuttle (D)	65,200	44.0
6 Donald H. McLean (R)	78,361	54.9
James E. Downes (D)	62,888	44.1
7 J. Parnell Thomas (R)	82,287	64.6
Mort L. O'Connell (D)	44,527	35.0
8 Gordon Canfield (R)	72,197	58.6
Addison P. Rosenkrans (D)	50,622	41.1
9 Frank C. Osmers Jr. (R)	91,352	62.7
Abram A. Lebson (D)	54,254	37.2
10 Fred A. Hartley Jr. (R)	64,699	56.8
William E. Holmwood (D)	46,934	41.2
11 Albert L. Vreeland (R)	61,606	55.8
Mary C. Duffy (D)	46,130	41.8
12 Robert Winthrop Kean (R)	67,996	53.7
Thomas J. Halleran (D)	53,677	42.4
13 Mary T. Norton (D)	92,356	70.2
Raymond J. Cuddy (R)	39,274	29.8
14 Edward J. Hart (D)	84,538	65.3
Otto Trankler (R)	44,893	34.7

NEW MEXICO

	Votes	%
AL Clinton P. Anderson (D)	106,972	58.8
Herman R. Crile (R)	75,085	41.2

NEW YORK

Candidates	Votes	%
1 Leonard W. Hall (R)	267,873	63.7
Frederic S. Farah (D)	141,774	33.7
2 William B. Barry (D)	216,309	52.8
Thomas J. Styles (R)	170,004	41.5
Matthew Napear (AM LAB)	20,827	5.1
3 Joseph L. Pfeifer (D, AM LAB)	42,884	70.6
Samuel Rosenthal (R)	17,839	29.4
4 Thomas H. Cullen (D)	36,995	56.2
Alfred A. Larossa (R)	25,207	38.3
Michael Giaratano (AM LAB)	3,636	5.5
5 James J. Heffernan (D, AM LAB)	63,295	55.2
Marcellus H. Evans (R)	51,428	44.8
6 Andrew L. Somers (D)	130,391	57.7
Alfred E. Buck (R)	58,507	25.9
Irving B. Altman (AM LAB)	31,945	14.1
7 John J. Delaney (D, AM LAB)	50,189	72.8
Julius Reinlieb (R)	18,765	27.2
8 Donald L. O'Toole (D)	217,599	56.8
Jacob M. Offenhender (R)	103,753	27.1
Benjamin Brenner (AM LAB)	52,972	13.8
9 Eugene J. Keogh (D, AM LAB)	92,559	57.7
William J. McGahie (R)	67,901	42.3
10 Emanuel Celler (D, AM LAB)	57,286	71.4
Edward H. Wilson (R)	21,358	26.6
11 James A. O'Leary (D)	46,616	49.4
Thomas Garrett (R)	42,631	45.1
Wellington Roe (AM LAB)	5,193	5.5
12 Samuel Dickstein (D)	17,176	72.1
Bernard Harkavy (AM LAB)	3,664	15.4
Joseph Levine (R)	2,976	12.5
13 Louis J. Capozzoli (D)	18,334	62.7
John Rosenberg (R)	8,367	28.6
Gino Bardi (AM LAB)	2,534	8.7
14 M. Michael Edelstein (D)	26,455	56.9
Peter J. Bakanatch (R)	13,940	30.0
Samuel Burt (AM LAB)	6,103	13.1
15 Michael J. Kennedy (D)	26,314	59.7
Arthur A. Wyler (R)	13,158	29.8
Joseph Curran (AM LAB)	4,623	10.5
16 William T. Pheiffer (R)	31,020	48.7
James H. Fay (D)	28,837	45.3
Thomas Darcy (AM LAB)	3,874	6.1
17 Kenneth F. Simpson (R)	54,636	50.8
Samuel Kramer (D)	47,155	43.8
Morris Watson (AM LAB)	5,845	5.4
18 Martin J. Kennedy (D)	31,151	52.7
James B. Walker Jr. (R)	24,312	41.2
Shaemas O'Sheal (AM LAB)	3,612	6.1
19 Sol Bloom (D)	71,018	62.8
Daniel J. Riesner (R)	32,821	29.0
Benjamin M. Zelman (AM LAB)	9,209	8.2
20 Vito Marcantonio (R, AM LAB)	25,254	62.5
James J. Lanzetta (D)	15,160	37.5
21 Joseph A. Gavagan (D)	108,139	63.2
Charles H. Roberts (R)	46,324	27.1
Alfred K. Stern (AM LAB)	16,529	9.7
22 Walter A. Lynch (D)	44,296	60.1
F. Shepard Cornell (R)	23,532	31.9
Frank R. Crosswaith (AM LAB)	5,931	8.0
23 Charles A. Buckley (D)	190,396	56.5
Lowell H. Brown (R)	88,083	26.1
Jack Altman (AM LAB)	50,293	14.9
24 James M. Fitzpatrick (D)	161,577	47.7
Ralph W. Gwinn (R)	136,835	40.4
George Thomas (AM LAB)	35,233	10.4
25 Ralph A. Gamble (R)	125,412	64.0
Homer A. Stebbins (D)	64,889	33.1
26 Hamilton Fish (R)	68,715	51.9
Hardy Steeholm (D)	59,739	45.1

Candidates	Votes	%
27 Lewis K. Rockefeller (R)	65,618	58.0
George J. Mutari (D, AM LAB)	47,610	42.1
28 William T. Byrne (D)	89,592	57.8
William V. A. Waterman (R)	59,344	38.3
29 E. Harold Cluett (R)	82,328	63.7
Salvatore J. Leombruno (D)	43,588	33.7
30 Frank Crowther (R)	66,159	54.8
Burlin G. McKillip (D)	51,270	42.5
31 Clarence E. Kilburn (R)	58,727	62.5
Horatio W. Thomas (D, AM LAB)	35,307	37.5
32 Francis D. Culkin (R)	71,782	68.8
Frank M. McCormack (D)	30,105	28.8
33 Fred J. Douglas (R)	72,412	56.5
Samuel H. Miller (D)	52,469	40.9
34 Edwin Arthur Hall (R)	93,990	68.3
Donald W. Kramer (D)	41,027	29.8
35 Clarence E. Hancock (R)	97,688	56.8
Flora D. Johnson (D)	69,730	40.6
36 John Taber (R)	64,507	59.6
John W. Kennelly (D)	40,929	37.8
37 W. Sterling Cole (R)	76,630	64.9
David Moses (D)	38,878	32.9
38 Joseph J. O'Brien (R)	92,866	51.9
George B. Kelly (D, AM LAB)	86,197	48.1
39 James W. Wadsworth (R)	73,316	60.4
J. Frederick Colson (D, AM LAB)	48,133	39.6
40 Walter Gresham Andrews (R)	119,972	61.1
Robert A. Hoffman (D, AM LAB)	76,468	38.9
41 Alfred F. Beiter (D, AM LAB)	62,843	52.3
J. Francis Harter (R)	57,335	47.7
42 Pius L. Schwert (D, AM LAB)	64,250	58.8
Edward F. Moss (R)	44,866	41.0
43 Daniel A. Reed (R)	67,520	62.2
Milton A. Bissell (D, AM LAB)	40,980	37.8
AL Caroline O'Day (D, AM LAB)	3,199,019✔	
Matthew J. Merritt (D, AM LAB)	3,182,936✔	
Mary Donlon (R)	2,830,517	
Messmore Kendall (R)	2,812,066	
Helen G. H. Estella (P)	5,679	
Neil Dow Cranmer (P)	5,212	

NORTH CAROLINA

	Votes	%
1 Herbert C. Bonner (D)	36,722	92.8
John A. Wilkinson (R)	2,851	7.2
2 John H. Kerr (D)	41,217	100.0
3 Graham A. Barden (D)	33,760	75.0
Julian T. Gaskill (R)	11,248	25.0
4 Harold D. Cooley (D)	57,610	79.4
Ezra Parker (R)	14,926	20.6
5 Alonzo D. Folger (D)	53,778	77.2
Ottis James Reynolds (R)	15,872	22.8
6 Carl T. Durham (D)	55,549	78.5
Gilliam Grissom (R)	15,259	21.6
7 J. Bayard Clark (D)	41,663	85.3
Fred R. Keith (R)	7,168	14.7
8 William O. Burgin (D)	57,879	67.2
F. D. B. Harding (R)	28,232	32.8
9 Robert L. Doughton (D)	60,875	68.3
Monroe Adams (R)	28,287	31.7
10 Alfred L. Bulwinkle (D)	87,156	69.8
Ernest M. Morgan (R)	37,736	30.2
11 Zebulon Weaver (D)	75,763	69.0
Robert Frank Jarrett (R)	34,104	31.0

NORTH DAKOTA

Candidates	Votes	%
AL Usher L. Burdick (R)	148,227✔	
Charles R. Robertson (R)	111,125✔	
R. J. Downey (D)	63,662	
Adolph Michelson (D)	63,028	
Thomas Hall (I)	23,399	
John Omdahl (I)	20,845	

OHIO

	Candidates	Votes	%
1	Charles H. Elston (R)	84,622	58.0
	Joseph A. Dixon (D)	61,382	42.0
2	William E. Hess (R)	77,769	56.3
	James E. O'Connell (D)	60,410	43.7
3	Greg Holbrock (D)	103,291	52.6
	Harry N. Routzohn (R)	93,002	47.4
4	Robert F. Jones (R)	65,603	57.8
	Clarence C. Miller (D)	47,820	42.2
5	Cliff Clevenger (R)	48,040	60.7
	C. H. Armbruster (D)	31,063	39.3
6	Jacob E. Davis (D)	52,769	52.2
	Chester P. Fitch (R)	48,257	47.8
7	Clarence J. Brown (R)	83,415	58.3
	J. Fuller Trump (D)	59,667	41.7
8	Frederick C. Smith (R)	49,218	52.5
	Kenneth M. Petri (D)	44,605	47.5
9	John F. Hunter (D)	86,956	54.7
	Wilbur M. White (R)	71,927	45.3
10	Thomas A. Jenkins (R)	48,217	58.9
	John P. Kelso (D)	33,698	41.1
11	Harold K. Claypool (D)	43,548	53.8
	Ray W. Davis (R)	37,398	46.2
12	John M. Vorys (R)	91,767	51.3
	A. P. Lammeck (D)	87,115	48.7
13	A. D. Baumhart Jr. (R)	62,442	60.8
	Werner S. Haslinger (D)	40,274	39.2
14	Dow W. Harter (D)	121,037	52.3
	Walter B. Wanamaker (R)	108,016	46.6
15	Robert T. Secrest (D)	57,359	58.8
	Clair A. Young (R)	40,233	41.2
16	William R. Thom (D)	92,469	56.4
	Jim Seccombe (R)	71,629	43.7
17	J. Harry McGregor (R)	69,102	55.1
	Ralph C. Lutz (D)	56,343	44.9
18	Lawrence E. Imhoff (D)	79,718	54.5
	Earl R. Lewis (R)	66,666	45.5
19	Michael J. Kirwan (D)	122,075	61.9
	Charles H. Anderson (R)	75,016	38.1
20	Martin L. Sweeney (D)	72,385	67.7
	George Pillersdorf (R)	34,609	32.4
21	Robert Crosser (D)	79,602	77.1
	J. E. Chizek (R)	23,658	22.9
22	Frances P. Bolton (R)	165,322	56.7
	Anthony A. Fleger (D)	126,273	43.3
AL	George H. Bender (R)	1,519,628✔	
	Stephen M. Young (D)	1,483,934✔	
	L. L. Marshall (R)	1,386,696	
	Francis W. Durbin (D)	1,384,800	

OKLAHOMA

	Candidates	Votes	%
1	Wesley E. Disney (D)	93,366	62.2
	W. R. Boyd (R)	56,112	37.4
2	Jack Nichols (D)	50,351	62.2
	E. O. Clark (R)	30,630	37.8
3	Wilburn Cartwright (D)	68,344	79.0
	Frank D. McSherry (R)	18,145	21.0
4	Lyle H. Boren (D)	69,040	71.1
	Clyde T. Patrick (R)	28,046	28.9
5	A. S. Mike Monroney (D)	93,457	72.4
	U. S. Stone (R)	34,942	27.1
6	Jed Johnson (D)	52,338	70.1
	Walter Hubbell (R)	22,343	29.9
7	Sam C. Massingale (D)	39,884	70.0
	Place Montgomery (R)	16,246	28.5
8	Ross Rizley (R)	48,737	53.8
	Phil Ferguson (D)	41,417	45.7
AL	Will Rogers (D)	479,433	65.7
	John W. Harreld (R)	245,384	33.6

OREGON

	Candidates	Votes	%
1	James W. Mott (R)	145,675	68.4
	Charles A. Robertson (D)	63,940	30.0
2	Walter M. Pierce (D)	44,832	56.3
	Rex Ellis (R)	33,529	42.1
3	Homer D. Angell (R)	84,275	49.9
	Nan Wood Honeyman (D)	80,930	47.9

PENNSYLVANIA

	Candidates	Votes	%
1	Leon Sacks (D)	64,599	61.7
	Emanuel W. Beloff (R)	39,770	38.0
2	James P. McGranery (D)	62,844	60.9
	Augustus Trask Ashton (R)	39,489	38.3
3	Michael J. Bradley (D)	77,436	63.1
	Frank J. Kownacki (R)	44,757	36.5
4	John Edward Sheridan (D)	74,458	63.0
	Benjamin M. Golder (R)	42,578	36.1
5	Francis R. Smith (D)	76,724	55.8
	Fred C. Gartner (R)	60,109	43.7
6	Francis J. Myers (D)	82,550	61.1
	Frank F. Truscott (R)	51,313	38.0
7	Hugh Scott (R)	79,416	50.9
	Gilbert Cassidy (D)	76,054	48.8
8	James Wolfenden (R)	69,649	59.6
	E. Adele Scott Saul (D)	46,960	40.2
9	Charles L. Gerlach (R)	55,919	52.4
	Henry V. Scheirer (D)	50,632	47.4
10	J. Roland Kinzer (R)	72,843	57.7
	George M. May (D)	53,333	42.2
11	Patrick J. Boland (D)	65,368	52.6
	Joseph F. Gunster (R)	58,831	47.4
12	J. Harold Flannery (D)	101,854	57.8
	J. Henry Pool (R)	74,305	42.2
13	Ivor D. Fenton (R)	70,647	50.5
	James H. Gildea (D)	68,501	48.9
14	Guy L. Moser (D)	48,140	56.0
	Joseph C. Evans (R)	31,839	37.1
	Raymond S. Hofses (SOC)	4,980	5.8
15	Albert G. Rutherford (R)	46,740	59.3
	F. R. Clark (D)	31,675	40.2
16	Robert F. Rich (R)	61,167	60.5
	Hugh Gilmore (D)	39,988	39.5
17	J. William Ditter (R)	75,006	62.2
	Victor Eppstein (D)	45,616	37.8
18	Richard M. Simpson (R)	46,595	57.6
	John W. Keichline (D)	34,328	42.4
19	John C. Kunkel (R)	74,420	54.4
	John A. Smith (D)	62,298	45.6
20	Benjamin Jarrett (R)	64,189	58.2
	John R. Boland Jr. (D)	44,919	40.8
21	Francis E. Walter (D)	52,530	56.2
	T. Fred Woodley (R)	40,863	43.7
22	Harry L. Haines (D)	60,848	54.8
	Chester H. Gross (R)	49,532	44.6
23	James E. Van Zandt (R)	57,027	56.3
	William M. Aukerman (D)	44,263	43.7
24	J. Buell Snyder (D)	54,631	56.6
	J. Clark Glassburn (R)	41,641	43.2
25	Charles I. Faddis (D)	58,442	61.0
	Lucius McK. Crumrine (R)	37,357	39.0
26	Louis E. Graham (R)	64,669	50.9
	Peter P. Reising (D)	62,273	49.1
27	Harve Tibbott (R)	75,243	51.6
	Joseph Gray (D)	69,736	47.9
28	Augustine B. Kelley (D)	58,772	55.5
	James M. Underwood (R)	44,528	42.0
29	Robert L. Rodgers (R)	50,147	54.3
	James F. Lavery (D)	41,924	45.4
30	Thomas E. Scanlon (D)	62,450	50.1
	Robert J. Corbett (R)	62,097	49.9
31	Samuel A. Weiss (D)	76,819	55.7
	John McDowell (R)	59,960	43.5
32	Herman P. Eberharter (D)	62,121	68.6
	Samuel M. Jackson (R)	28,196	31.1
33	Joseph A. McArdle (D)	70,824	55.0
	James I. Marsh (R)	57,737	44.9
34	James A. Wright (D)	75,004	53.8
	Robert B. McKinley (R)	64,336	46.2

RHODE ISLAND

	Candidates	Votes	%
1	Aime J. Forand (D)	87,530	57.6
	Charles F. Risk (R)	64,539	42.4
2	John E. Fogarty (D)	87,332	53.8
	Harry Sandager (R)	74,987	46.2

SOUTH CAROLINA

		Votes	%
1	L. Mendel Rivers (D)	16,626	98.4
2	Hampton P. Fulmer (D)	14,920	98.6
3	Butler B. Hare (D)	15,977	98.9
4	Joseph R. Bryson (D)	23,825	97.3
5	James P. Richards (D)	14,754	99.2
6	John L. McMillan (D)	12,074	99.0

SOUTH DAKOTA

		Votes	%
1	Karl E. Mundt (R)	135,406	59.6
	Oscar Fosheim (D)	91,967	40.5
2	Francis H. Case (R)	47,051	66.1
	Arthur W. Watwood (D)	24,177	33.9

TENNESSEE

		Votes	%
1	B. Carroll Reece (R)	39,577	68.7
	R. E. Walker (D)	18,051	31.3
2	John Jennings Jr. (R)	41,274	56.6
	Clay Jones (D)	31,663	43.4
3	Estes Kefauver (D)	35,332	68.7
	Jerome Taylor (R)	16,099	31.3
4	Albert Gore (D)	38,278	88.9
	H. E. McLean (R)	4,777	11.1
5	J. Percy Priest (I)	24,565	50.2
	Joseph W. Byrns Jr. (D)	20,933	42.8
	Julian H. Campbell (R)	3,459	7.1
6	Wirt Courtney (D)	24,536	100.0
7	Herron Pearson (D)	25,590	100.0
8	Jere Cooper (D)	32,002	92.1
	Julian Palmer	2,760	7.9
9	Clifford Davis (D)	55,952	96.0

TEXAS

		Votes	%
1	Wright Patman (D)	27,030	100.0
2	Martin Dies (D)	43,597	100.0
3	Lindley Beckworth (D)	47,292	100.0
4	Sam Rayburn (D)	46,333	100.0
5	Hatton W. Sumners (D)	57,789	87.5
	Floyd E. Royer (R)	8,273	12.5
6	Luther A. Johnson (D)	33,546	100.0
7	Nat Patton (D)	30,384	98.2
8	Albert Thomas (D)	89,796	95.2
9	Joseph J. Mansfield (D)	52,754	100.0
10	Lyndon B. Johnson (D)	48,442	100.0
11	W. R. Poage (D)	41,432	99.9
12	Fritz G. Lanham (D)	54,108	100.0
13	Ed Gossett (D)	50,076	96.5
14	Richard M. Kleberg (D)	59,016	100.0
15	Milton H. West (D)	32,300	92.5
	J. A. Simpson (R)	2,628	7.5
16	R. Ewing Thomason (D)	34,515	99.9
17	Sam Russell (D)	45,456	100.0
18	Eugene Worley (D)	51,660	96.5
19	George H. Mahon (D)	56,343	100.0
20	Paul J. Kilday (D)	47,075	83.4
	Harry Hotchkin (R)	9,296	16.5
21	Charles L. South (D)	49,468	92.8
	Ray Ridenhower (R)	3,832	7.2

UTAH

		Votes	%
1	Walter K. Granger (D)	62,654	57.1
	LeRoy B. Young (R)	47,021	42.9
2	J. W. Robinson (D)	84,874	62.8
	A. Sherman Christensen (R)	50,332	37.2

VERMONT

Candidates	Votes	%
AL Charles A. Plumley (R)	89,637	63.8
Michael J. Rock (D)	50,804	36.2

VIRGINIA

	Candidates	Votes	%
1	Schuyler Otis Bland (D)	22,493	99.9
2	Colgate W. Darden Jr. (D)	29,788	100.0
3	Dave E. Satterfield Jr. (D)	34,885	96.8
4	Patrick Henry Drewry (D)	19,043	96.0
5	Thomas G. Burch (D)	25,631	100.0
6	Clifton A. Woodrum (D)	30,046	68.1
	Fred W. McWane (R)	13,864	31.4
7	A. Willis Robertson (D)	26,233	65.1
	J. A. Garber (R)	13,964	34.7
8	Howard W. Smith (D)	33,031	79.0
	Henry B. Goodloe (R)	8,794	21.0
9	John W. Flannagan Jr. (D)	32,412	57.3
	Fred C. Parks (R)	24,109	42.7

WASHINGTON

	Candidates	Votes	%
1	Warren G. Magnuson (D)	113,988	61.6
	Fred J. Wettrick (R)	71,110	38.4
2	Henry M. Jackson (D)	66,314	57.4
	Payson Peterson (R)	49,209	42.6
3	Martin F. Smith (D)	60,529	55.3
	Russell V. Mack (R)	48,700	44.5

	Candidates	Votes	%
4	Knute Hill (D)	50,493	51.3
	Frank Miller (R)	48,003	48.7
5	Charles H. Leavy (D)	67,582	55.5
	Walt Horan (R)	54,258	44.5
6	John M. Coffee (D)	71,536	62.8
	Paul A. Preus (R)	42,334	37.2

WEST VIRGINIA

	Candidates	Votes	%
1	Robert L. Ramsay (D)	72,717	53.2
	A. C. Schiffler (R)	63,906	46.8
2	Jennings Randolph (D)	77,045	57.5
	Summers H. Sharp (R)	56,911	42.5
3	Andrew Edmiston (D)	79,441	56.6
	H. Roy Waugh (R)	60,810	43.4
4	George W. Johnson (D)	82,979	52.7
	Harry O. Hiteshew (R)	74,491	47.3
5	John Kee (D)	81,903	62.9
	Hartley Sanders (R)	48,223	37.1
6	Joe L. Smith (D)	105,927	61.7
	R. E. O'Connor (R)	65,762	38.3

WISCONSIN

	Candidates	Votes	%
1	Stephen Bolles (R)	69,276	55.8
	Stanley W. Slagg (PROG)	28,308	22.8
	Jacob M. Weisman (D)	26,520	21.4
2	Harry Sauthoff (PROG)	60,481	44.2
	Charles Hawks Jr. (R)	58,121	42.5
	Thomas R. Brooks (D)	18,237	13.3

	Candidates	Votes	%
3	William H. Stevenson (R)	54,457	46.0
	Gardner R. Withrow (PROG)	52,131	44.0
	George T. Doherty (R)	11,806	10.0
4	Thaddeus F.B. Wasielewski (D)	57,381	35.6
	Leonard C. Fons (PROG)	52,907	32.8
	John C. Schafer (R)	50,796	31.5
5	Lewis D. Thill (R)	73,728	44.4
	James M. Pasch (PROG)	54,501	32.8
	Francis T. Murphy (D)	37,872	22.8
6	Frank B. Keefe (R)	66,821	57.4
	Jacob A. Fessler (D)	30,162	25.9
	Walter D. Corrigan (PROG)	19,387	16.7
7	Reid F. Murray (R)	58,696	51.6
	Gerald J. Boileau (PROG)	40,558	35.7
	Wallace A. Bloedorn (D)	14,495	12.7
8	Joshua L. Johns (R)	61,987	55.9
	Michael F. Kresky (PROG)	49,005	44.2
9	Merlin Hull (PROG)	61,009	52.8
	John R. Nygaard (R)	47,825	41.4
	James E. Hughes (D)	6,763	5.9
10	Bernard J. Gehrmann (PROG)	50,776	48.0
	Peter Van Nostrand (R)	37,819	35.7
	John G. Green (D)	17,284	16.3

WYOMING

	Candidates	Votes	%
AL	John J. McIntyre (D)	57,030	53.4
	Frank O. Horton (R)	49,701	46.5

1941 House Elections

MISSISSIPPI

Special Election

	Candidates	Votes	%
2	Jamie L. Whitten (D)	8,703	69.3
	L. A. Plye	3,865	30.8

NEW YORK

Special Elections

	Candidates	Votes	%
14	Arthur G. Klein (D, LIB)	8,615	68.0
	George A. Hastings (R)	3,337	26.3

	Candidates	Votes	%
	Leonard H. Wacker (AM LAB)	714	5.6
17	Joseph Clark Baldwin (R)	23,254	52.9
	Dean Alfange (D)	16,690	38.0
	Eugene P. Connolly (AM LAB)	3,985	9.1
42	John C. Butler (R)	15,065	40.6
	Hattie E. Schwert (D, AM LAB)	13,554	36.5
	Edmund P. Radwan (NEW DEAL)	7,787	21.0

OKLAHOMA

Special Election

	Candidates	Votes	%
7	Victor Wickersham (D)	19,884	82.5
	George Davidson (R)	4,004	16.6

WISCONSIN

Special Election

	Candidates	Votes	%
1	Lawrence H. Smith (R)	29,638	63.6
	Thomas R. Amlie (D)	16,949	36.4

House Candidates Index

For an index of all House candidates listed in this section (pages 701 to 1061), see pages 1180-1273. Instructions for use of the House Candidates Index appear on page 1180.

1942 House Elections

ALABAMA

Candidates	Votes	%
1 Frank W. Boykin (D)	5,600	100.0
2 George Grant (D)	6,672	100.0
3 Henry B. Steagall (D)	5,043	100.0
4 Sam Hobbs (D)	7,468	100.0
5 Joe Starnes (D)	11,841	100.0
6 Pete Jarman (D)	7,556	100.0
7 Carter Manasco (D)	9,788	100.0
8 John J. Sparkman (D)	5,954	100.0
9 John P. Newsome (D)	8,802	95.6

ARIZONA

Candidates	Votes	%
AL Richard F. Harless (D)	56,357✔	
John R. Murdock (D)	55,825✔	
George R. Darnell (R)	23,015	
Joseph S. Jenckes Jr. (R)	18,205	
Morris Graham (COM)	375	

ARKANSAS

Candidates	Votes	%
1 Ezekiel C. Gathings (D)	13,998	100.0
2 Wilbur D. Mills (D)	11,380	100.0
3 J. William Fulbright (D)	16,111	100.0
4 Fadjo Cravens (D)	14,733	100.0
5 Brooks Hays (D)	16,850	100.0
6 William F. Norrell (D)	13,166	100.0
7 Oren Harris (D)	12,108	100.0

CALIFORNIA

Candidates	Votes	%
1 Clarence F. Lea (D-R)	78,281	93.2
Albert Jason Lima (COM)	5,703	6.8
2 Harry L. Englebright (R D T)	50,094	99.8
3 J. Leroy Johnson (R)	63,982	54.5
Joseph B. O'Neil (D)	53,521	45.6
4 Thomas Rolph (R-D)	62,735	98.2
5 Richard J. Welch (R-D)	85,747	92.7
Walter Raymond Lambert (COM)	6,749	7.3
6 Albert E. Carter (R-D)	108,585	92.4
Clarence Paton (COM)	8,532	7.3
7 John H. Tolan (D-R)	77,292	99.4
8 John Z. Anderson (R-D)	91,536	99.6
9 Bertrand W. Gearhart (R-D)	65,791	99.9
10 Alfred J. Elliott (D-R)	43,864	99.8
11 George E. Outland (D)	31,611	50.7
A. J. Dingeman (R)	30,781	49.3
12 H. Jerry Voorhis (D)	53,705	56.8
Robert P. Shuler (R & P)	40,780	43.2
13 Norris Poulson (R)	38,577	49.2
Charles Kramer (D)	33,060	42.2
Calvert S. Wilson (TOWN)	6,306	8.0
14 Thomas F. Ford (D)	49,326	66.9
Herbert L. Herberts (R)	24,349	33.0
15 John M. Costello (D-R)	88,798	86.1
B. Tarkington Dowden (PRC TOWN)	10,185	9.9
16 Will Rogers Jr. (D)	61,437	53.7
Leland Merritt Ford (R)	52,023	45.4
17 Cecil R. King (D-R)	92,260	99.8
18 Ward Johnson (R)	53,136	56.8
Francis H. Gentry (D)	40,339	43.1
19 Chet Holifield (D)	34,918	63.1
Carlton H. Casjens (R)	20,446	36.9
20 Carl Hinshaw (R)	62,628	48.4
Joseph O. Donovan (D)	55,479	42.9
Virgil G. Hinshaw (P)	6,864	5.3
21 Harry R. Sheppard (D-R)	38,419	96.4
22 John Phillips (R)	42,765	57.6
N. E. West (D)	31,440	42.4
23 Edouard V. M. Izac (D)	42,864	50.5
James B. Abbey (R)	42,087	49.5

COLORADO

Candidates	Votes	%
1 Lawrence Lewis (D)	58,143	53.4
Olaf H. Jacobson (R)	50,083	46.0
2 William S. Hill (R)	64,984	67.7
Julian E. Hall (D)	30,485	31.7
3 J. Edgar Chenoweth (R)	55,838	62.7
J. C. Jarrett (D)	33,154	37.3
4 Robert F. Rockwell (R)	28,460	58.8
Elizabeth E. Pellet (D)	19,979	41.3

CONNECTICUT

Candidates	Votes	%
1 William J. Miller (R)	72,306	51.4
Herman P. Kopplemann (D)	68,435	48.6
2 John D. McWilliams (R)	46,426	51.3
William J. Fitzgerald (D)	43,934	48.6
3 Ranulf Compton (R)	57,612	51.7
James J. Shanley (D)	53,825	48.3
4 Clare Boothe Luce (R)	63,719	46.5
LeRoy D. Downs (D)	56,861	41.5
David Mansell (SOC)	15,573	11.4
5 Joseph E. Talbot (R)	42,602	53.6
William A. Patten (D)	36,327	45.7
AL Boleslaus J. Monkiewicz (R)	283,280	49.8
Lucien J. Maciora (D)	257,941	45.3

DELAWARE

Candidates	Votes	%
AL Earle D. Willey (R)	45,376	53.6
Philip A. Traynor (D)	38,791	45.8

FLORIDA

Candidates	Votes	%
1 J. Hardin Peterson (D)	25,037	100.0
2 Emory H. Price (D)	15,777	100.0
3 Robert L. F. Sikes (D)	11,739	100.0
4 Arthur P. Cannon (D)	25,056	81.4
Bert Leigh Acker (R)	5,725	18.6
5 Joe Hendricks (D)	16,850	70.9
Emory Akerman (R)	6,906	29.1
AL Robert A. Green (D)	91,120	100.0

GEORGIA

Candidates	Votes	%
1 Hugh Peterson (D)	6,980	98.2
2 E. E. Cox (D)	3,793	100.0
3 Stephen Pace (D)	4,818	100.0
4 A. Sidney Camp (D)	5,106	100.0
5 Robert Ramspeck (D)	9,176	96.0
6 Carl Vinson (D)	5,725	100.0
7 Malcolm Tarver (D)	5,172	100.0
8 John Gibson (D)	4,785	100.0
9 B. Frank Whelchel (D)	7,404	71.1
Roscoe Pickett (I)	3,013	28.9
10 Paul Brown (D)	5,393	100.0

IDAHO

Candidates	Votes	%
1 Compton I. White (D)	30,105	54.1
H. C. Baldridge (R)	25,562	45.9
2 Henry C. Dworshak (R)	45,805	54.8
Ira H. Masters (D)	37,815	45.2

ILLINOIS

Candidates	Votes	%
1 William L. Dawson (D)	26,280	52.8
William E. King (R)	23,537	47.3
2 William A. Rowan (D)	110,069	50.8
Thomas J. Downs (R)	106,552	49.2
3 Fred E. Busbey (R)	115,390	51.3
Edward A. Kelly (D)	109,409	48.7
4 Martin Gorski (D)	60,623	78.7
Arthur Joseph Rutshaw (R)	16,396	21.3
5 Adolph J. Sabath (D)	29,167	72.2
Clem Graver (R)	11,255	27.8
6 Thomas J. O'Brien (D)	149,342	57.4
Raymond E. Trafelet (R)	110,823	42.6
7 Leonard W. Schuetz (D)	179,906	50.3
James C. Moreland (R)	177,931	49.7
8 Thomas S. Gordon (D)	33,425	78.8
Rena E. Pikiel (R)	8,995	21.2
9 Charles S. Dewey (R)	40,803	51.3
Irwin N. Walker (D)	38,679	48.7
10 Ralph E. Church (R)	150,558	63.0
Jack Bairstow (D)	88,266	37.0
11 Chauncey W. Reed (R)	97,316	71.0
Joseph S. Perry (D)	39,829	29.0
12 Noah M. Mason (R)	68,426	71.4
Tony R. Berrettini (D)	27,405	28.6
13 Leo E. Allen (R)	48,500	79.4
Michael M. Kinney (D)	12,596	20.6
14 Anton J. Johnson (R)	47,294	59.3
Robert M. Harper (D)	32,450	40.7
15 Robert B. Chiperfield (R)	48,677	62.1
Montgomery B. Carrott (D)	29,741	37.9
16 Everett M. Dirksen (R)	55,135	68.8
James D. Carrigan (D)	24,969	31.2
17 Leslie C. Arends (R)	44,563	72.4
Frank Gillespie (D)	17,023	27.6
18 Jessie Sumner (R)	51,281	62.4
Fred E. Butcher (D)	30,852	37.6
19 William H. Wheat (R)	56,657	57.3
Alfred D. Huston (D)	42,171	42.7
20 Sid Simpson (R)	31,360	51.0
James M. Barnes (D)	30,131	49.0
21 Evan Howell (R)	54,585	58.1
William P. Roberts (D)	39,318	41.9
22 Calvin D. Johnson (R)	67,313	55.7
Harry C. Odum (D)	53,470	44.3
23 Charles W. Vursell (R)	47,526	52.7
Laurence F. Arnold (D)	42,736	47.4
24 James V. Heidinger (R)	37,008	58.4
Leroy Barham (D)	26,377	41.6
25 C. W. Bishop (R)	49,965	55.1
Kent E. Keller (D)	40,762	44.9
AL Stephen A. Day (R)	1,481,419	51.3
Benjamin S. Adamowski (D)	1,395,053	48.3

INDIANA

Candidates	Votes	%
1 Ray J. Madden (D)	44,334	53.6
Samuel W. Cullison (R)	38,450	46.5
2 Charles A. Halleck (R)	63,120	61.2
Emmett Ferguson (D)	39,943	38.8
3 Robert A. Grant (R)	66,434	55.2
Lewis J. Murphy (D)	53,992	44.8
4 George W. Gillie (R)	61,032	61.0
Samuel C. Cleland (D)	39,032	39.0
5 Forest A. Harness (R)	80,464	55.7
Edward C. Hays (D)	63,994	44.3
6 Noble J. Johnson (R)	65,764	58.1
Floyd I. McMurray (D)	47,363	41.9
7 Gerald W. Landis (R)	69,044	56.9
O. A. Noland (D)	52,386	43.1
8 Charles M. LaFollette (R)	67,237	53.7
John W. Boehne Jr. (D)	57,868	46.3
9 Earl Wilson (R)	55,949	55.9
Roy Huckleberry (D)	44,096	44.1
10 Raymond S. Springer (R)	67,201	57.4
William H. Larrabee (D)	49,963	42.6
11 Louis Ludlow (D)	79,932	50.3
Howard M. Meyer (R)	79,136	49.8

IOWA

Candidates	Votes	%
1 Thomas E. Martin (R)	55,139	61.5
Vern W. Nall (D)	32,893	36.7

IOWA

Candidates	Votes	%
2 Henry O. Talle (R)	62,290	57.4
William S. Jacobsen (D)	46,310	42.6
3 John W. Gwynne (R)	54,124	60.7
William D. Kearney (D)	35,065	39.3
4 Karl M. LeCompte (R)	52,258	64.5
Thomas L. Curran (D)	28,745	35.5
5 Paul Cunningham (R)	48,578	63.2
E. Frank Fox (D)	28,287	36.8
6 Fred C. Gilchrist (R)	46,843	60.3
Edward Breen (D)	30,802	39.7
7 Ben F. Jensen (R)	49,086	64.2
Jess Alton (D)	27,409	35.8
8 Charles B. Hoeven (R)	42,154	64.6
Walter T. Mahoney (D)	23,059	35.4

KANSAS

Candidates	Votes	%
1 William P. Lambertson (R)	49,962	59.2
John E. Barrett (D)	34,404	40.8
2 Ulysses S. Guyer (R)	48,594	59.1
Herbert L. Drake (D)	33,625	40.9
3 Thomas D. Winter (R)	40,789	59.9
William E. Murphy (D)	27,364	40.2
4 Edward H. Rees (R)	55,612	55.7
John M. Houston (D)	44,313	44.4
5 Clifford R. Hope (R)	54,655	66.6
S. S. Alexander (D)	27,381	33.4
6 Frank Carlson (R)	49,403	64.2
Lud W. Strnad (D)	27,590	35.8

KENTUCKY

Candidates	Votes	%
1 Noble J. Gregory (D)	17,027	67.5
Walter L. Prince (R)	8,195	32.5
2 Beverly M. Vincent (D)	21,866	100.0
3 Emmet O'Neal (D)	39,866	55.2
J. R. Todd (R)	32,404	44.8
4 Edward W. Creal (D)	23,871	55.7
Don Victor Drye (R)	19,015	44.3
5 Brent Spence (D)	18,510	53.5
Lewis R. Kimberly (R)	12,073	34.9
Ed Wimmer (I)	3,806	11.0
6 Virgil Chapman (D)	27,382	100.0
7 Andrew J. May (D)	22,160	50.6
Elmer E. Gabbard (R)	21,620	49.4
8 Joe B. Bates (D)	22,499	56.0
F. A. Easterling (R)	17,644	44.0
9 John M. Robsion (R)	34,440	100.0

LOUISIANA

Candidates	Votes	%
1 F. Edward Hebert (D)	20,973	100.0
2 Paul H. Maloney (D)	19,007	100.0
3 James Domengeaux (D)	6,260	100.0
4 Overton Brooks (D)	7,184	100.0
5 Charles E. McKenzie (D)	7,949	100.0
6 James H. Morrison (D)	9,313	100.0
7 Henry D. Larcade Jr. (D)	6,201	100.0
8 A. Leonard Allen (D)	8,100	100.0

MAINE

Candidates	Votes	%
1 Robert Hale (R)	38,128	57.0
Louis J. Brann (D)	28,759	43.0
2 Margaret Chase Smith (R)	42,062	67.6
Bradford C. Redonnett (D)	20,164	32.4
3 Frank Fellows (R)	31,728	100.0

MARYLAND

Candidates	Votes	%
1 David Jenkins Ward (D)	25,270	55.9
William H. Lloyd (R)	19,938	44.1
2 Harry Streett Baldwin (D)	57,865	62.2
George R. Norris (R)	35,228	37.8
3 Thomas D'Alesandro Jr. (D)	20,450	73.3
Edward S. Panetti (R)	7,469	26.8
4 Daniel Ellison (R)	22,673	50.9
John M. Wyatt (D)	21,845	49.1
5 Lansdale G. Sasscer (D)	33,191	66.7
John Torvestad (R)	16,596	33.3
6 J. Glenn Beall (R)	45,724	59.5
E. Brooke Lee (D)	31,187	40.6

MASSACHUSETTS

Candidates	Votes	%
1 Allen T. Treadway (R)	50,302	56.7
Frank Hurley (D)	36,257	40.9
2 Charles R. Clason (R)	58,781	61.6
John J. Granfield (D)	36,675	.38.4
3 Philip J. Philbin (D)	46,412	50.4
Alfred Woollacott (R)	45,689	49.6
4 Pehr G. Holmes (R)	57,323	57.2
John S. Sullivan (D)	42,895	42.8
5 Edith Nourse Rogers (R)	95,231	100.0
6 George J. Bates (R)	68,739	75.3
James D. Burns (D)	22,523	24.7
7 Thomas J. Lane (D)	68,073	100.0
8 Angier L. Goodwin (R)	57,016	56.2
Frederick McDermott (D)	44,401	43.8
9 Charles L. Gifford (R)	50,902	58.8
George F. Backus (D)	35,633	41.2
10 Christian A. Herter (R)	64,247	51.2
William A. Carey (D)	61,359	48.9
11 James M. Curley (D)	60,850	69.3
Vincent Mottola (R)	27,008	30.7
12 John W. McCormack (D)	76,043	78.7
Francis P. O'Neill (R)	20,600	21.3
13 Richard B. Wigglesworth (R)	62,608	59.3
Francis H. Foy (D)	42,995	40.7
14 Joseph W. Martin Jr. (R)	54,977	59.4
Terrance J. Lomax Jr. (D)	37,598	40.6

MICHIGAN

Candidates	Votes	%
1 George G. Sadowski (D)	48,620	78.0
John B. Sosnowski (R)	13,691	22.0
2 Earl C. Michener (R)	40,439	63.1
Redmond M. Burr (D)	23,277	36.3
3 Paul Shafer (R)	41,002	65.7
Harold E. Steinbacher (D)	20,334	32.6
4 Clare E. Hoffman (R)	42,653	68.6
Dean Morley (D)	19,065	30.7
5 Bartel J. Jonkman (R)	37,020	54.0
Herman J. Wierenga (D)	30,840	45.0
6 William W. Blackney (R)	48,364	57.6
David M. Martin (D)	34,893	41.6
7 Jesse P. Wolcott (R)	46,946	67.3
Leroy S. Wilson (D)	22,775	32.7
8 Fred L. Crawford (R)	45,182	66.9
Michael J. Hart (D)	21,689	32.1
9 Albert J. Engel (R)	34,548	65.4
Arnold B. Coxhill (D)	17,954	34.0
10 Roy O. Woodruff (R)	31,895	60.1
John E. Morrison (D)	20,852	39.3
11 Fred Bradley (R)	32,579	58.0
Paul L. Adams (D)	23,555	42.0
12 John B. Bennett (R)	31,643	51.5
Frank E. Hook (D)	27,983	45.6
13 George D. O'Brien (D)	33,807	51.1
Clarence J. McLeod (R)	32,298	48.9
14 Louis C. Rabaut (D)	50,707	58.7
Claude G. McDonald (R)	35,638	41.3
15 John D. Dingell (D)	52,384	64.6
Ivan L. Bowman (R)	28,694	35.4
16 John Lesinski (D)	42,911	58.5
Robert W. Ford (R)	30,480	41.5
17 George A. Dondero (R)	56,607	56.8
Dorothy K. Roosevelt (D)	43,036	43.2

MINNESOTA

Candidates	Votes	%
1 August H. Andresen (R)	58,387	66.2
Harold R. Atwood (D)	29,771	33.8
2 Joseph P. O'Hara (R)	60,028	70.0
R. J. Neunsinger (D)	13,866	16.2
Charles D. Peterson (F-LAB)	11,819	13.8
3 Richard P. Gale (R)	44,662	49.0
Charles Munn (F-LAB)	29,936	32.9
William J. Gallagher (D)	16,505	18.1
4 Melvin J. Maas (R)	45,903	65.1
William Mahoney (F-LAB)	17,071	24.2
Edward K. Delaney (D)	6,938	9.8
5 Walter H. Judd (R)	60,883	63.8
Joseph Gilbert (F-LAB)	18,566	19.5
Thomas P. Ryan (D)	15,976	16.7
6 Harold Knutson (R)	49,295	57.1
E. Thomas O'Brien (D)	37,070	43.0
7 H. Carl Andersen (R)	46,570	54.8
Theodor S. Slen (D)	21,192	24.9
Francis H. Shoemaker (F-LAB)	17,241	20.3
8 William A. Pittenger (R)	51,803	58.2
Rudolph Rautio (F-LAB)	21,786	24.5
E. J. Larsen (D)	10,284	11.6
S. B. Ruohoniemi (D)	5,148	5.8
9 Harold C. Hagen (F-LAB)	35,265	50.4
John W. Padden (R)	34,661	49.6

MISSISSIPPI

Candidates	Votes	%
1 John E. Rankin (D)	7,079	100.0
2 Jamie L. Whitten (D)	5,698	100.0
3 William M. Whittington (D)	5,552	100.0
4 Thomas G. Abernethy (D)	5,660	100.0
5 W. Arthur Winstead (D)	10,548	100.0
6 William M. Colmer (D)	7,462	100.0
7 Dan R. McGehee (D)	9,699	100.0

MISSOURI

Candidates	Votes	%
1 Samuel W. Arnold (R)	41,809	55.5
Milton A. Romjue (D)	33,465	44.5
2 Max Schwabe (R)	37,635	50.4
William L. Nelson (D)	37,069	49.6
3 William C. Cole (R)	40,227	56.4
Richard M. Duncan (D)	31,108	43.6
4 C. Jasper Bell (D)	30,227	60.5
John W. Mitchell (R)	19,709	39.5
5 Roger C. Slaughter (D)	27,243	50.9
Ralph B. Innis (R)	26,163	48.9
6 Philip A. Bennett (R)	46,735*	54.6
Sam M. Wear (D)	38,946	45.5
7 Dewey Short (R)	49,595	63.5
Ralph C. Max (D)	28,542	36.5
8 William P. Elmer (R)	39,422	51.5
Clyde Williams (D)	37,072	48.5
9 Clarence Cannon (D)	30,082	54.6
Carl E. Starkloff (R)	24,912	45.2
10 Orville Zimmerman (D)	29,514	56.7
Merrill Spitler (R)	22,555	43.3
11 Louis E. Miller (R)	36,133	50.4
John B. Sullivan (D)	35,510	49.6
12 Walter C. Ploeser (R)	68,329	57.0
Martin L. Neaf (D)	51,646	43.1
13 John J. Cochran (D)	37,651	61.3
D. E. Horn (R)	23,770	38.7

MONTANA

Candidates	Votes	%
1 Mike Mansfield (D)	42,754	59.0
H. K. Hazelbaker (R)	28,603	39.5
2 James F. O'Connor (D)	50,489	52.0
F. F. Haynes (R)	45,051	46.4

NEBRASKA

Candidates	Votes	%
1 Carl T. Curtis (R)	69,651	66.6
Ralph G. Brooks (D)	31,422	30.0
2 Howard Buffett (R)	40,646	53.2
Charles F. McLaughlin (D)	35,743	46.8
3 Karl Stefan (R)	61,813	66.3
George Hally (D)	27,708	29.7

NEBRASKA

	Candidates	Votes	%
4	Arthur L. Miller (R)	55,914	67.1
	Tom Lanigan (D)	27,406	32.9

NEVADA

	Candidates	Votes	%
AL	Maurice J. Sullivan (D)	21,100	53.6
	Ernest Brooks (R)	18,289	46.4

NEW HAMPSHIRE

	Candidates	Votes	%
1	Chester E. Merrow (R)	43,281	52.1
	Thomas A. Murray (D)	39,743	47.9
2	Foster Stearns (R)	42,718	58.4
	Henry J. Proulx (D)	30,473	41.6

NEW JERSEY

	Candidates	Votes	%
1	Charles A. Wolverton (R)	74,867	61.4
	Ralph W. Wescott (D)	46,445	38.1
2	Elmer H. Wene (D)	40,478	53.0
	Benjamin D. Foulois (D)	35,930	47.0
3	James C. Auchincloss (R)	51,573	53.4
	William H. Sutphin (D)	45,037	46.6
4	D. Lane Powers (R)	51,498	63.8
	William H. Thompson Jr. (D)	29,088	36.0
5	Charles A. Eaton (R)	61,896	64.7
	J. Ellis Kirkham (D)	32,999	34.5
6	Donald H. McLean (R)	52,211	57.8
	George R. Walsh (D)	36,425	40.4
7	J. Parnell Thomas (R)	55,424	68.8
	Emil M. Wulster (D)	25,171	31.2
8	Gordon Canfield (R)	56,582	66.6
	Irving Abramson (D)	28,060	33.0
9	Harry L. Towe (R)	51,692	61.8
	Frank H. Hennessy (D)	32,021	38.3
10	Fred A. Hartley Jr. (R)	37,189	53.0
	Frederic Bigelow (D)	31,504	44.9
11	Frank L. Sundstrom (R)	36,500	58.9
	William Freiday (D)	23,630	38.2
12	Robert W. Kean (R)	43,942	60.8
	Joseph Siegler (D)	26,188	36.3
13	Mary T. Norton (D)	73,766	79.6
	Raymond J. Cuddy (R)	18,894	20.4
14	Edward J. Hart (D)	75,322	78.9
	Otto A. Trankler (R)	20,161	21.1

NEW MEXICO

	Candidates	Votes	%
AL	Clinton P. Anderson (D)	62,320✔	
	Antonio M. Fernandez (D)	57,474✔	
	William A. Sutherland (R)	43,627	
	Reese P. Fullerton (R)	43,071	

NEW YORK

	Candidates	Votes	%
1	Leonard W. Hall (R)	197,473	68.1
	Rene A. Carreau (D)	83,453	28.8
	William F. Brunner (AM LAB)	28,224	11.4
2	William B. Barry (D)	125,090	50.3
	William D. Rawlins (R)	95,240	38.3
3	Joseph L. Pfeifer (D)	18,700	59.6
	Samuel Rosenthal (R)	8,979	28.6
	Joseph A. Weil (AM LAB)	3,693	11.8
4	Thomas H. Cullen (D)	21,456	63.3
	Frederick H. Gutkes (R)	10,070	29.7
	Matthew P. Coleman (AM LAB)	2,370	7.0
5	James J. Heffernan (D, AM LAB)	44,522	65.7
	Charles G. Jochum (R)	23,285	34.3
6	Andrew L. Somers (D, AM LAB)	96,990	72.2
	Theodore R. Studwell (R)	37,427	27.8
7	John J. Delaney (D, AM LAB)	27,688	72.8
	Harry Boyarsky (R)	10,353	27.2
8	Donald L. O'Toole (D, AM LAB)	158,685	72.8
	George F. Picken (R)	59,408	27.2
9	Eugene J. Keogh (D)	44,064	45.7
	William J. Drake (R)	41,491	43.0
	Albert Slade (AM LAB)	10,957	11.4
10	Emanuel Celler (D, AM LAB)	32,026	68.5
	Jerome Lewis (R)	14,693	31.5
11	James A. O'Leary (D, AM LAB)	31,723	57.9
	Robert S. Woodward (R)	23,029	42.1
12	Samuel Dickstein (D, AM LAB)	13,584	87.0
	Hyman Hecht (R)	2,031	13.0
13	Louis J. Capozzoli (D, AM LAB)	11,245	74.0
	John Rosenberg (R)	3,947	26.0
14	Arthur G. Klein (D, AM LAB)	17,652	63.7
	Stuart Scheftel (R)	10,037	36.3
15	Thomas F. Burchill (D)	14,746	58.7
	Walter A. Lockwood (R)	7,566	30.1
	John Rogan (AM LAB)	2,798	11.1
16	James H. Fay (D, AM LAB)	18,710	50.1
	William T. Pheiffer (R)	18,630	49.9
17	Joseph Clark Baldwin (R, AM LAB)	38,079	61.0
	Carl Sherman (D)	24,365	39.0
18	Martin J. Kennedy (D)	18,636	52.8
	Garrow T. Geer Jr. (R, AM LAB)	16,665	47.2
19	Sol Bloom (D, AM LAB)	41,566	67.5
	Clarence McMillan (R)	20,000	32.5
20	Vito Marcantonio (R, D)	18,924	100.0
21	Joseph A. Gavagan (D, AM LAB)	60,588	66.3
	Herbert Malkin (R)	30,796	33.7
22	Walter A. Lynch (D, AM LAB)	25,933	67.1
	Richard C. Califano (R)	12,714	32.9
23	Charles A. Buckley (D, AM LAB)	142,395	74.0
	William J. Waterman (R)	50,063	26.0
24	James M. Fitzpatrick (D, AM LAB)	117,198	57.5
	Ralph W. Gwinn (R)	86,506	42.5
25	Ralph A. Gamble (R)	85,024	69.7
	James J. Butterly (D)	33,040	27.1
26	Hamilton Fish (R)	48,793	52.2
	Ferdinand A. Hoyt (D, AM LAB)	44,751	47.8
27	Jay LeFevre (R)	53,626	63.1
	Sharon J. Mauhs (D, AM LAB)	31,426	36.9
28	William T. Byrne (D, AM LAB)	86,767	62.9
	Ernest B. Morris (R)	51,190	37.1
29	Dean P. Taylor (R, AM LAB)	69,794	68.8
	John T. Degnan (D)	31,616	31.2
30	Bernard W. Kearney (R)	53,147	62.6
	Burlin G. McKillip (D)	29,414	34.6
31	Clarence E. Kilburn (R)	43,197	69.0
	Thomas Q. Ryan (D, AM LAB)	19,448	31.0
32	Francis D. Culkin (R)	50,970	73.2
	Vanche F. Milligan (D)	17,631	25.3
33	Fred J. Douglas (R)	53,030	60.3
	Stanard Dow Butler (D, AM LAB)	34,965	39.7
34	Edwin Arthur Hall (R)	53,762	60.8
	Arthur J. Ruland (D)	33,276	37.6
35	Clarence E. Hancock (R)	82,021	64.5
	Arthur B. McGuire (D)	42,270	33.2
36	John Taber (R)	47,620	62.6
	Charles Osborne (D, AM LAB)	28,502	37.4
37	W. Sterling Cole (R)	54,700	70.9
	Daniel Crowley (D, AM LAB)	22,452	29.1
38	Joseph J. O'Brien (R)	77,970	59.1
	Walden Moore (D, AM LAB)	53,889	40.9
39	James W. Wadsworth (R, D)	83,195	100.0
40	Walter Gresham Andrews (R)	91,222	68.8
	Julian Park (D, AM LAB)	41,459	31.2
41	Joseph Mruk (R)	49,239	57.4
	Alfred F. Beiter (D, AM LAB)	36,589	42.6
42	John C. Butler (R)	39,650	53.7
	Frank J. Caffery (D, AM LAB)	34,248	46.3
43	Daniel Reed (R)	43,730	64.3
	Clare Barnes (D)	20,867	30.7
	Nelson M. Fuller (AM LAB)	3,466	5.1
AL	Winifred C. Stanley (R)	1,965,794✔	
	Matthew J. Merritt (D, AM LAB)	1,909,706✔	
	Charles Muzzicato (R)	1,887,688	
	Flora D. Johnson (D, AM LAB)	1,872,321	
	Benjamin J. Davis Jr. (COM)	52,002	
	Elizabeth Gurley Flynn (COM)	50,305	
	Layle Lane (SOC)	22,361	
	Amicus Most (SOC)	19,249	

NORTH CAROLINA

	Candidates	Votes	%
1	Herbert C. Bonner (D)	8,444	92.6
	J. C. Meekins Jr. (R)	671	7.4
2	John H. Kerr (D)	7,124	100.0
3	Graham A. Barden (D)	9,596	100.0
4	Harold D. Cooley (D)	20,703	65.2
	Wiley L. Ward (R)	11,064	34.8
5	John Hamlin Folger (D)	20,601	67.5
	S. Evan Hall (R)	9,899	32.5
6	Carl T. Durham (D)	16,548	74.5
	Hobart M. Patterson (R)	5,660	25.5
7	J. Bayard Clark (D)	12,112	100.0
8	William O. Burgin (D)	27,146	56.5
	A. D. Barber (R)	20,868	43.5
9	Robert L. Doughton (D)	29,213	100.0
10	Cameron Morrison (D)	26,785	55.4
	Charles A. Jonas (R)	21,535	44.6
11	Alfred L. Bulwinkle (D)	20,270	100.0
12	Zebulon Weaver (D)	30,438	65.3
	Gola P. Ferguson (R)	16,150	34.7

NORTH DAKOTA

	Candidates	Votes	%
AL	Usher L. Burdick (R)	85,936✔	
	William Lemke (R)	65,905✔	
	Charles R. Robertson (IR)	48,472	
	Halvor L. Halvorson (D)	47,972	
	E. A. Johanson (D)	31,547	

OHIO

	Candidates	Votes	%
1	Charles H. Elston (R)	54,120	61.5
	William H. Hessler (D)	33,884	38.5
2	William E. Hess (R)	53,083	64.0
	Nicholas Bauer (D)	29,823	36.0
3	Harry P. Jeffrey (R)	51,477	51.6
	Greg Holbrock (D)	48,338	48.4
4	Robert F. Jones (R)	39,275	63.5
	Clarence C. Miller (D)	22,567	36.5
5	Cliff Clevenger (R)	30,667	63.7
	Ferdinand E. Warren (D)	17,514	36.4
6	Edward O. McCowen (R)	33,171	51.1
	Jacob E. Davis (D)	31,793	48.9
7	Clarence J. Brown (R)	52,270	69.1
	George H. Smith (D)	23,384	30.9
8	Frederick C. Smith (R)	33,797	59.8
	Brooks Fletcher (D)	22,753	40.2
9	Homer A. Ramey (R)	47,377	51.8
	John F. Hunter (D)	44,027	48.2

OHIO

Candidates	Votes	%
10 Thomas A. Jenkins (R)	29,691	64.2
Oral Daugherty (D)	16,582	35.8
11 Walter E. Brehm (R)	31,385	61.3
Harold K. Claypool (D)	19,817	38.7
12 John M. Vorys (R)	56,558	58.4
A. P. Lamneck (D)	40,290	41.6
13 Alvin Weichel (R)	37,923	61.6
E. C. Alexander (D)	23,618	38.4
14 Ed Rowe (R)	60,868	51.3
Dow W. Harter (D)	57,759	48.7
15 P. W. Griffiths (R)	35,137	60.2
Charles W. Lynch (D)	23,213	39.8
16 Henderson H. Carson (R)	50,657	52.7
William R. Thom (D)	45,531	47.3
17 J. Harry McGregor (R)	47,565	62.8
Samuel A. Anderson (D)	28,235	37.3
18 Earl R. Lewis (R)	43,279	53.3
Lawrence E. Imhoff (D)	37,951	46.7
19 Michael J. Kirwan (D)	60,248	56.4
James T. Begg (R)	46,567	43.6
20 Michael A. Feighan (D)	34,462	61.8
Harry T. Marshall (R)	14,001	25.1
Marie R. Sweeney (I)	7,289	13.1
21 Robert Crosser (D)	35,109	63.9
William J. Rogers (R)	19,137	34.8
22 Frances P. Bolton (R)	92,644	57.1
James Metzenbaum (D)	69,601	42.9
AL George H. Bender (R)	945,995	56.9
Stephen M. Young (D)	717,692	43.1

OKLAHOMA

1 Wesley E. Disney (D)	42,907	54.2
W. R. Boyd (R)	35,174	44.4
2 Jack Nichols (D)	21,651	50.5
E. O. Clark (R)	21,266	49.6
3 Paul Stewart (D)	23,317	78.6
Frank D. McSherry (R)	6,346	21.4
4 Lyle H. Boren (D)	23,921	56.8
Charles E. Wells (R)	18,177	43.2
5 A. S. Mike Monroney (D)	36,736	69.7
George Wesley Colvert (R)	15,738	29.9
6 Jed Johnson (D)	19,945	57.9
J. L. Hart Jr. (R)	14,532	42.2
7 Victor Wickersham (D)	14,042	70.0
Roscoe C. Holt (R)	6,009	30.0
8 Ross Rizley (R)	30,522	60.3
Julius W. Cox (D)	19,765	39.1

OREGON

1 James W. Mott (R)	49,021	64.3
Earl A. Nott (D)	27,208	35.7
2 Lowell Stockman (R)	26,723	61.4
Walter M. Pierce (D)	16,809	38.6
3 Homer D. Angell (R)	55,775	51.8
Thomas R. Mahoney (D)	51,870	48.2
4 Harris Ellsworth (R)	29,385	60.0
Edward C. Kelly (D)	19,632	40.0

PENNSYLVANIA

1 James Gallagher (R)	44,519	53.5
Leon Sacks (D)	38,768	46.6
2 James P. McGranery (D)	36,258	50.5
Augustus Trask Ashton (R)	35,545	49.5
3 Michael J. Bradley (D)	47,515	51.4
John R. K. Scott (R)	45,014	48.7
4 John Edward Sheridan (D)	43,284	53.2
Howard T. Scott (R)	36,689	45.1
5 C. Frederick Pracht (R)	48,781	51.1
Francis R. Smith (D)	46,691	48.9
6 Francis J. Myers (D)	53,284	55.3
William H. Sylk (R)	42,995	44.7
7 Hugh Scott (R)	60,836	55.7
Thomas Z. Minehart (D)	48,373	44.3

Candidates	Votes	%
8 James Wolfenden (R)	48,210	58.5
Vernon A. O'Rourke (D)	34,164	41.5
9 Charles L. Gerlach (R)	41,282	62.0
Francis L. Collum (D)	25,284	38.0
10 J. Roland Kinzer (R)	52,380	68.8
Daniel J. C. O'Donnell (D)	23,784	31.2
11 John W. Murphy (D)	43,585	55.8
James K. Peck (R)	34,527	44.2
12 Thomas Byron Miller (R)	55,679	54.5
Daniel J. Flood (D)	46,550	45.5
13 Ivor D. Fenton (R)	50,721	58.2
J. Noble Hirsch (D)	36,466	41.8
14 Daniel K. Hoch (D)	23,247	51.0
John C. Griesemer (R)	19,498	42.8
Raymond Hofses (SOC)	2,783	6.1
15 Wilson D. Gillette (R)	63,077	65.7
Michael E. Yurkovsky (D)	32,953	34.3
16 Thomas E. Scanlon (D)	47,920	51.3
Robert Van Der Voort (R)	45,472	48.7
17 J. William Ditter (R)	52,661	69.2
Charles W. Moyer (D)	23,492	30.9
18 Richard M. Simpson (R)	33,147	62.0
John W. Mann (D, I)	20,340	38.0
19 John C. Kunkel (R)	62,119	66.0
A. S. Beshore (D)	31,969	34.0
20 Leon H. Gavin (R)	37,738	64.5
John C. Brecht (D)	20,171	34.5
21 Francis E. Walter (D)	32,498	53.5
William Radford Coyle (R)	28,272	46.5
22 Chester H. Gross (R)	34,202	50.0
Harry L. Haines (D)	34,131	49.9
23 James E. Van Zandt (R)	38,235	61.0
Harry E. Diehl (D)	24,432	39.0
24 J. Buell Snyder (D)	33,480	51.1
Carl H. Hoffman (R)	32,014	48.9
25 Grant Furlong (D)	38,316	50.3
M. B. Armstrong (R)	37,903	49.7
26 Louis E. Graham (R)	41,730	58.5
Peter P. Reising (D)	29,652	41.5
27 Harve Tibbott (R)	50,153	55.6
Eddie McCloskey (D)	40,096	44.4
28 Augustine B. Kelley (D)	32,886	53.5
Edward R. Stirling (R)	28,543	46.5
29 Robert L. Rodgers (R)	40,243	59.3
James F. Lavery (D)	27,573	40.7
30 Samuel A. Weiss (D)	43,482	56.4
John McDowell (R)	33,568	43.6
31 Herman P. Eberharter (D)	50,316	58.1
Robert Garland (R)	36,239	41.9
32 James A. Wright (D)	41,798	51.6
James Grove Fulton (R)	39,262	48.4
AL William I. Troutman (R)	1,360,664	54.7
Inez B. Peel (D)	1,105,992	44.4

RHODE ISLAND

1 Aime J. Forand (D)	68,242	59.0
Charles H. Eden (R)	47,480	41.0
2 John E. Fogarty (D)	69,411	57.4
Harry Sandager (R)	51,471	42.6

SOUTH CAROLINA

1 L. Mendel Rivers (D)	5,452	100.0
2 Hampton P. Fulmer (D)	4,448	100.0
3 Butler B. Hare (D)	3,201	100.0
4 Joseph R. Bryson (D)	4,228	100.0
5 James P. Richards (D)	3,122	100.0
6 John L. McMillan (D)	2,905	100.0

SOUTH DAKOTA

1 Karl E. Mundt (R)	81,373	59.9
Fred Hildebrandt (D)	54,457	40.1
2 Francis H. Case (R)	30,389	71.9
George M. Bailey (D)	11,892	28.1

TENNESSEE

Candidates	Votes	%
1 B. Carroll Reece (R)	19,777	96.1
2 John Jennings Jr. (R)	18,613	53.6
John T. O'Connor (D)	16,132	46.4
3 Estes Kefauver (D)	14,704	75.7
Walter M. Higgins (R)	3,831	19.7
4 Albert Gore (D)	7,667	68.9
H. E. McLean (R)	3,463	31.1
5 Jim Nance McCord (D)	9,841	100.0
6 J. Percy Priest (D)	4,945	100.0
7 Wirt Courtney (D)	8,689	100.0
8 Thomas J. Murray (D)	9,151	61.2
P. W. Maddox (D)	5,801	38.8
9 Jere Cooper (D)	7,354	89.3
S. Homer Tatum (R)	882	10.7
10 Clifford Davis (D)	23,660	100.0

TEXAS

1 Wright Patman (D)	9,502	100.0
2 Martin Dies (D)	10,128	100.0
3 Lindley Beckworth (D)	10,929	100.0
4 Sam Rayburn (D)	11,768	100.0
5 Hatton W. Sumners (D)	10,568	100.0
6 Luther A. Johnson (D)	10,726	100.0
7 Nat Patton (D)	11,043	99.1
8 Albert Thomas (D)	31,038	96.9
9 Joseph J. Mansfield (D)	13,852	100.0
10 Lyndon B. Johnson (D)	12,799	100.0
11 W. R. Poage (D)	7,554	100.0
12 Fritz Lanham (D)	25,894	100.0
13 Ed Gossett (D)	12,677	98.1
14 Richard M. Kleberg (D)	16,212	100.0
15 Milton H. West (D)	12,169	100.0
16 R. Ewing Thomason (D)	6,612	100.0
17 Sam Russell (D)	13,261	100.0
18 Eugene Worley (D)	10,739	100.0
19 George Mahon (D)	12,216	100.0
20 Paul J. Kilday (D)	8,860	81.7
W. H. Turner (R)	1,980	18.3
21 O. Clark Fisher (D)	16,554	100.0

UTAH

1 Walter K. Granger (D)	36,297	50.2
J. Bracken Lee (R)	36,028	49.8
2 J. W. Robinson (D)	43,582	55.8
Reed E. Vetterli (R)	34,586	44.3

VERMONT

AL Charles A. Plumley (R)	40,751	70.2
John B. Candon (D)	17,304	29.8

VIRGINIA

1 Schuyler Otis Bland (D)	5,207	100.0
2 Winder R. Harris (D)	5,369	100.0
3 David E. Satterfield Jr. (D)	5,822	99.9
4 Patrick Henry Drewry (D)	4,457	99.8
5 Thomas G. Burch (D)	8,166	93.1
Howard H. Carwile (SOC)	601	6.9
6 Clifton A. Woodrum (D)	10,510	93.4
Stephen A. Moore (SOC)	724	6.4
7 A. Willis Robertson (D)	7,521	99.7
8 Howard W. Smith (D)	13,380	86.6
Harrie Byrd Conlin (R)	1,757	11.4
9 John W. Flannagan Jr. (D)	16,655	63.6
Cary Ingram Crockett (R)	9,534	36.4

WASHINGTON

1 Warren G. Magnuson (D)	69,010	65.5
Harold H. Stewart (R)	35,910	34.1
2 Henry M. Jackson (D)	39,628	59.9
Payson Peterson (R)	26,573	40.1

WASHINGTON

	Candidates	Votes	%
3	Fred Norman (R)	34,462	57.1
	Martin F. Smith (D)	25,894	42.9
4	Hal Holmes (R)	34,495	63.6
	Knute Hill (D)	19,751	36.4
5	Walt Horan (R)	47,242	62.7
	C. C. Dill (D)	28,076	37.3
6	John M. Coffee (D)	42,666	64.0
	Ralph Woods (R)	23,650	35.5

WEST VIRGINIA

	Candidates	Votes	%
1	Andrew C. Schiffier (R)	42,787	54.7
	Robert L. Ramsey (D)	35,498	45.3
2	Jennings Randolph (D)	32,935	50.2
	Charles G. Baker (R)	32,676	49.8
3	Edward G. Rohrbough (R)	37,135	53.2
	Andrew Edmiston (D)	32,682	46.8
4	Hubert S. Ellis (R)	48,697	52.2
	George W. Johnson (D)	44,528	47.8

	Candidates	Votes	%
5	John Kee (D)	36,625	57.2
	B. F. Howard (R)	27,400	42.8
6	Joe L. Smith (D)	46,281	51.8
	Houston G. Young (R)	43,043	48.2

WISCONSIN

	Candidates	Votes	%
1	Lawrence H. Smith (R)	46,453	71.9
	Bernard F. Magruder (D)	16,848	26.1
2	Harry Sauthoff (PROG)	43,412	50.2
	Charles Hawks Jr. (R)	34,272	39.6
	Thomas R. Brooks (D)	8,315	9.6
3	William H. Stevenson (R)	34,177	46.9
	Gardner R. Withrow (PROG)	31,092	42.6
	William D. Carroll (D)	7,385	10.1
4	Thaddeus F. B. Wasielewski (D)	46,819	48.8
	John C. Schafer (R)	29,104	30.3
	John C. Brophy (PROG)	17,468	18.2
5	Howard J. McMurray (D)	44,337	43.2
	Lewis D. Thill (R)	38,345	37.4

	Candidates	Votes	%
	Roy A. Roush (PROG)	16,409	16.0
6	Frank B. Keefe (R)	41,385	62.2
	Eugene Schallern (D)	13,364	20.1
	Adam F. Poltl (PROG)	10,645	16.0
7	Reid F. Murray (R)	40,520	71.9
	John A. Kennedy (D)	15,821	28.1
8	LaVern R. Dilweg (D)	40,002	54.5
	Joshua H. Johns (R)	33,441	45.5
9	Merlin Hull (PROG)	37,919	61.8
	George H. Hipke (R)	19,972	32.6
	Jack E. Joyce (D)	3,448	5.6
10	Alvin E. O'Konski (R)	33,143	48.4
	Bernard J. Gehrmann (PROG)	28,169	41.1
	John G. Green (D)	7,198	10.5

WYOMING

	Candidates	Votes	%
AL	Frank A. Barrett (R)	37,965	50.7
	John J. McIntyre (D)	36,892	49.3

1943 House Elections

KANSAS

Special Election

	Candidates	Votes	%
2	Errett P. Scrivner (R)	19,798	69.1
	Herbert L. Drake (D)	8,859	30.9

KENTUCKY

Special Election

	Candidates	Votes	%
4	Chester O. Carrier (R)	29,855	63.4
	J. Dan Talbott (D)	17,218	36.6

MISSOURI

Special Election

	Candidates	Votes	%
6	Marion T. Bennett (R)	36,448	62.9
	Sam M. Wear (D)	21,496	37.1

1944 House Elections

ALABAMA

Candidates	Votes	%
1 Frank W. Boykin (D)	19,082	100.0
2 George M. Grant (D)	24,180	100.0
3 George W. Andrews (D)	20,470	100.0
4 Sam Hobbs (D)	19,391	84.5
O. D. Beard (R)	3,554	15.5
5 Albert Rains (D)	25,317	100.0
6 Pete Jarman (D)	14,561	100.0
7 Carter Manasco (D)	21,671	34.1
I. B. Burdick (R)	11,202	34.1
8 John J. Sparkman (D)	24,023	100.0
9 Luther Patrick (D)	31,767	81.7
H. H. Grooms (R)	7,120	18.3

ARIZONA

Candidates	Votes	%
AL John R. Murdock (D)	88,532✔	
Richard F. Harless (D)	86,691✔	
Margaret Adams Rockwell (R)	39,035	
A. M. Ward (R)	36,352	
A. Walter Gehres (P)	469	

ARKANSAS

Candidates	Votes	%
1 Ezekiel C. Gathings (D)	32,501	100.0
2 Wilbur D. Mills (D)	24,977	100.0
3 James W. Trimble (D)	20,061	63.3
Lonzo A. Ross (R)	11,613	36.7
4 Fadjo Cravens (D)	30,310	100.0
5 Brooks Hays (D)	33,215	87.1
Ross (R)	4,902	12.9
6 William F. Norrell (D)	31,785	100.0
7 Oren Harris (D)	27,851	100.0

CALIFORNIA

Candidates	Votes	%
1 Clarence F. Lea (D-R)	92,706	99.9
2 Clair Engle (D)	48,201	63.8
Jesse M. Mayo (R)	27,312	36.2
3 J. Leroy Johnson (R-D)	131,705	99.9
4 Franck R. Havenner (D)	73,582	50.1
Thomas Rolph (R)	73,367	49.9
5 Richard J. Welch (R-D)	112,151	100.0
6 George P. Miller (D)	104,441	52.0
Albert E. Carter (R)	96,395	48.0
7 John H. Tolan (D-R)	81,762	57.9
Chesley M. Walter (R)	59,360	42.0
8 John Z. Anderson (R)	94,218	56.5
Arthur L. Johnson (D)	72,420	43.5
9 Bertrand W. Gearhart (R-D)	66,845	99.5
10 Alfred J. Elliott (D-R)	60,001	99.9
11 George E. Outland (D)	52,218	56.0
Fred J. Hart (R)	41,005	44.0
12 H. Jerry Voorhis (D)	77,385	55.3
Roy P. McLaughlin (R)	62,524	44.7
13 Ned R. Healy (D)	66,854	54.9
Norris Poulson (R)	54,792	45.0
14 Helen Gahagan Douglas (D)	65,729	51.5
William D. Campbell (R)	61,767	48.4
15 Gordon L. McDonough (R)	100,305	56.6
Hal Styles (D)	73,655	41.6
16 Ellis E. Patterson (D)	105,835	54.1
Jesse Randolph Kellems (R)	89,700	45.9
17 Cecil R. King (D-R)	147,217	99.8
18 Clyde G. Doyle (D)	95,090	55.6
Ward Johnson (R)	75,749	44.3
19 Chet Holifield (D)	65,758	71.7
Carlton H. Casjens (R)	25,852	28.2
20 Carl Hinshaw (R)	112,663	51.8
Archibald B. Young (D)	101,090	46.5

Candidates	Votes	%
21 Harry R. Sheppard (D)	48,539	58.5
Earl S. Webb (R)	34,409	41.5
22 John Phillips (R-D)	88,537	99.8
23 Edouard V. M. Izac (D)	86,707	55.1
James B. Abbey (R)	70,787	45.0

COLORADO

	Votes	%
1 Dean M. Gillespie (R)	90,151	51.8
Charles A. Graham (D)	83,253	47.8
2 William S. Hill (R)	83,264	62.3
David J. Miller (D)	49,079	36.8
3 J. Edgar Chenoweth (R)	69,492	56.3
Arthur M. Wimmell (D)	53,904	43.7
4 Robert F. Rockwell (R)	38,671	61.7
John L. Heuschkel (D)	24,039	38.3

CONNECTICUT

	Votes	%
1 Herman P. Kopplemann (D)	120,100	54.0
William J. Miller (R)	102,257	46.0
2 Chase Going Woodhouse (D)	63,013	51.2
John D. McWilliams (R)	59,973	48.8
3 James P. Geelan (D)	82,472	51.5
Ranulf Compton (R)	77,753	48.5
4 Clare Boothe Luce (R)	102,043	49.9
Margaret Connor (D)	100,035	48.9
5 Joseph E. Talbot (R)	60,137	52.2
Peter M. Higgins (D)	54,885	47.7
AL Joseph F. Ryter (D)	424,146	51.2
Boleslaus J. Monkiewicz (R)	397,725	48.1

DELAWARE

	Votes	%
AL Philip A. Traynor (D)	63,649	50.3
Earle D. Willey (R)	62,378	49.3

FLORIDA

	Votes	%
1 J. Hardin Peterson (D)	84,280	100.0
2 Emory H. Price (D)	66,604	100.0
3 Robert L. F. Sikes (D)	51,693	100.0
4 Pat Cannon (D)	65,900	72.0
Edith Shaffer Stearn (R)	25,643	28.0
5 Joe Hendricks (D)	48,602	67.5
Emory Akerman (R)	23,406	32.5
6 Dwight L. Rogers (D)	32,491	69.7
Edward W. Greb (R)	14,134	30.3

GEORGIA

	Votes	%
1 Hugh Peterson (D)	24,468	100.0
2 E. E. Cox (D)	21,791	100.0
3 Stephen Pace (D)	25,276	100.0
4 A. Sidney Camp (D)	27,375	100.0
5 Robert Ramspeck (D)	50,257	94.5
H. A. Alexander (I)	2,929	5.5
6 Carl Vinson (D)	18,989	100.0
7 Malcolm Tarver (D)	31,400	100.0
8 John S. Gibson (D)	21,916	100.0
9 John S. Wood (D)	25,880	100.0
10 Paul Brown (D)	25,102	100.0

IDAHO

	Votes	%
1 Compton I. White (D)	49,581	56.6
Robert L. Brainard (R)	37,998	43.4
2 Henry C. Dworshak (R)	61,751	52.3
Phil J. Evans (D)	56,249	47.7

ILLINOIS

Candidates	Votes	%
1 William L. Dawson (D)	42,713	62.0
William E. King (R)	26,204	38.0
2 William A. Rowan (D)	186,089	57.3
Thomas J. Downs (R)	138,579	42.7
3 Edward A. Kelly (D)	158,944	52.0
Fred E. Busbey (R)	146,961	48.0
4 Martin Gorski (D)	79,243	80.4
Leo J. Kozicki (R)	19,346	19.6
5 Adolph J. Sabath (D)	38,370	76.3
Max Price (R)	11,929	23.7
6 Thomas J. O'Brien (D)	211,056	59.9
Charles J. Anderson Jr. (R)	140,069	39.7
7 William W. Link (D)	261,473	54.6
Charles H. Garland (R)	217,207	45.4
8 Thomas S. Gordon (D)	39,866	79.2
John F. Uczciwek (R)	10,474	20.8
9 Alexander J. Resa (D)	61,168	52.8
Charles S. Dewey (R)	54,698	47.2
10 Ralph E. Church (R)	193,948	55.8
Curtis D. MacDougall (D)	153,644	44.2
11 Chauncey W. Reed (R)	128,064	66.2
Otto Joseph Hruby Jr. (D)	65,296	33.8
12 Noah M. Mason (R)	86,228	61.0
Herbert J. Max (D)	55,236	39.1
13 Leo E. Allen (R)	59,372	70.0
Garret J. Schutt (D)	25,482	30.0
14 Anton J. Johnson (R)	55,812	54.4
Carl M. Seaberg (D)	46,759	45.6
15 Robert B. Chiperfield (R)	58,358	59.3
Ray Simpkins (D)	40,093	40.7
16 Everett M. Dirksen (R)	70,301	59.0
M. R. Clark (D)	48,779	41.0
17 Leslie C. Arends (R)	52,706	66.4
Ruth G. Fillingham (D)	26,732	33.7
18 Jessie Sumner (R)	58,617	56.9
Carl B. Jewell (D)	44,340	43.1
19 Rolla C. McMillen (R)	70,942	55.8
George M. Brown (D)	56,247	44.2
20 Sid Simpson (R)	38,922	55.6
Don Irving (D)	31,092	44.4
21 Evan Howell (R)	62,879	55.7
Thomas L. Jarrett (D)	50,050	44.3
22 Melvin Price (D)	83,311	50.8
Calvin D. Johnson (R)	80,616	49.2
23 Charles W. Vursell (R)	56,712	54.7
J. E. McMackin (D)	46,957	45.3
24 James V. Heidinger (R)	42,927	58.2
Early C. Phelps (D)	30,808	41.8
25 C. W. Bishop (R)	57,672	53.5
Kent E. Keller (D)	50,140	46.5
AL Emily Taft Douglas (D)	2,030,755	52.3
Stephen A. Day (R)	1,839,518	47.4

Special Election

	Votes	%
19 Rolla McMillen (R)	4,722	98.7

INDIANA

	Votes	%
1 Ray J. Madden (D)	75,635	61.3
Otto G. Fifield (R)	46,969	38.1
2 Charles A. Halleck (R)	78,061	61.6
James O. Cox (D)	48,103	37.9
3 Robert A. Grant (R)	85,362	51.8
Marshall A. Kizer (D)	78,621	47.7
4 George W. Gillie (R)	81,110	59.9
Robert W. Bushee (D)	53,636	39.6
5 Forest A. Harness (R)	94,274	53.1
Bennett H. Rockey (D)	80,208	45.1
6 Noble J. Johnson (R)	75,517	55.2
Otis G. Jamison (D)	60,758	44.5
7 Gerald W. Landis (R)	73,417	53.9
Arthur H. Greenwood (D)	62,136	45.6

INDIANA

Candidates	Votes	%
8 Charles M. LaFollette (R)	84,095	52.0
Charles J. Eichel (D)	76,905	47.6
9 Earl Wilson (R)	62,831	55.6
George W. Elliott (D)	49,380	43.7
10 Raymond S. Springer (R)	82,582	54.3
Sidney E. Baker (D)	67,724	44.5
11 Louis Ludlow (D)	114,051	51.1
Judson L. Stark (R)	108,503	48.6

IOWA

1 Thomas E. Martin (R)	78,729	56.7
Clair A. Williams (D)	60,048	43.3
2 Henry O. Talle (R)	86,903	55.9
George C. Classen (D)	68,489	44.1
3 John W. Gwynne (R)	74,901	56.8
William D. Kearney (D)	56,985	43.2
4 Karl M. LeCompte (R)	59,658	54.9
Harold J. Fleck (D)	49,098	45.2
5 Paul Cunningham (R)	66,260	54.1
Ralph N. Lynch (D)	56,138	45.8
6 James I. Dolliver (R)	60,153	58.8
Charles Hanna (D)	42,098	41.1
7 Ben F. Jensen (R)	66,905	61.5
Albert McGinn (D)	41,802	38.4
8 Charles B. Hoeven (R)	58,537	56.2
Lester S. Gillette (D)	45,682	43.8

KANSAS

1 Albert M. Cole (R)	71,565	67.3
Ralph Ulm (D)	34,731	32.7
2 Errett P. Scrivner (R)	68,815	59.1
Albert Baker (D)	47,676	40.9
3 Thomas D. Winter (R)	52,361	60.2
Herman L. Gees (D)	34,645	39.8
4 Edward H. Rees (R)	90,186	58.6
William J. Kropp (D)	63,843	41.5
5 Clifford R. Hope (R)	72,370	69.0
A. E. Hawes (D)	32,557	31.0
6 Frank Carlson (R)	63,035	66.0
Dan M. McCarthy (D)	32,408	34.0

KENTUCKY

1 Noble J. Gregory (D)	51,369	69.3
A. R. Anderson (R)	22,196	29.9
2 Earle C. Clements (D)	57,948	57.3
Otis White (R)	42,802	42.4
3 Emmet O'Neal (D)	79,922	57.3
Garland R. Hubbard (R)	59,190	42.5
4 Frank L. Chelf (D)	48,671	54.5
Chester O. Carrier (R)	40,317	45.2
5 Brent Spence (D)	45,228	58.0
Olin W. Davis (R)	32,606	41.8
6 Virgil Chapman (D)	63,404	58.8
George W. Boner (R)	44,214	41.0
7 Andrew J. May (D)	33,406	52.5
Elmer Gabbard (R)	30,165	47.4
8 Joe B. Bates (D)	48,969	54.3
Thomas S. Yates (R)	41,154	45.6
9 John M. Robsion (R)	68,908	68.8
H. F. Reed (D)	31,019	31.0

LOUISIANA

1 F. Edward Hebert (D)	55,887	100.0
2 Paul H. Maloney (D)	56,636	100.0
3 James Domengeaux (D)	28,123	100.0
4 Overton Brooks (D)	27,886	100.0
5 Charles E. McKenzie (D)	25,462	100.0
6 James H. Morrison (D)	38,561	100.0
7 Henry D. Larcade Jr. (D)	26,931	100.0
8 A. Leonard Allen (D)	23,083	100.0

Special Election

3 James Domengaux (D)	26,093	100.0

MAINE

Candidates	Votes	%
1 Robert Hale (R)	47,721	68.8
Andrew A. Pettis (D)	21,620	31.2
2 Margaret Chase Smith (R)	46,545	67.8
David H. Staples (D)	22,139	32.2
3 Frank Fellows (R)	35,644	77.9
Ralph E. Graham (D)	10,102	22.1

MARYLAND

1 Dudley G. Roe (D)	30,257	50.8
Wilmer F. Davis (R)	29,298	49.2
2 H. S. Baldwin (R)	97,239	57.0
Wilfred T. McQuaid (R)	73,469	43.0
3 Thomas D'Alesandro Jr. (D)	39,032	73.5
John W. Benson (R)	14,046	26.5
4 George Fallon (D)	47,088	59.2
Daniel Ellison (R)	32,416	40.8
5 Lansdale Sasscer (D)	51,318	64.9
C. Maurice Weidemeyer (R)	27,821	35.2
6 J. Glenn Beall (R)	63,079	57.9
Daniel F. McMullen (D)	45,877	42.1

MASSACHUSETTS

1 John W. Heselton (R)	63,693	50.5
James P. McAndrews (D)	62,525	49.5
2 Charles R. Clason (R)	75,571	55.7
Michael W. Albano (D)	60,195	44.3
3 Philip J. Philbin (D)	78,848	61.5
Wilfred P. Bazinet (R)	49,300	38.5
4 Pehr G. Holmes (R)	76,097	55.5
Frank J. McGrail (D)	60,967	44.5
5 Edith Nourse Rogers (R)	109,242	73.2
Milton A. Wesson (D)	39,911	26.8
6 George J. Bates (R)	87,211	67.0
John M. Bresnahan (D)	42,937	33.0
7 Thomas J. Lane (D)	78,008	67.9
Ernest Bentley (R)	36,877	32.1
8 Angier L. Goodwin (R)	79,912	57.5
Frederick J. McDermott (D)	59,058	42.5
9 Charles L. Gifford (R)	75,803	58.5
William McAuliffe (D)	53,820	41.5
10 Christian A. Herter (R)	100,334	55.8
William A. Carey (D)	79,380	44.2
11 James M. Curley (D)	75,469	65.6
Lester W. Bowen (R)	39,523	34.4
12 John W. McCormack (D)	97,469	75.8
Henry J. Allen (R)	31,178	24.2
13 Richard B. Wigglesworth (R)	97,013	65.8
Andrew T. Clancy (D)	50,377	34.2
14 Joseph W. Martin Jr. (R)	79,928	62.0
Edmond P. Talbot (D)	48,993	38.0

MICHIGAN

1 George G. Sadowski (D)	103,782	80.6
John B. Sosnowski (R)	24,542	19.1
2 Earl C. Michener (R)	80,054	64.8
Redmond M. Burr (D)	43,536	35.0
3 Paul W. Shafer (R)	73,134	62.5
Charles V. Hampton (D)	42,902	36.7
4 Clare E. Hoffman (R)	68,233	64.1
Bernard T. Foley (D)	37,754	35.5
5 Bartel J. Jonkman (R)	73,034	57.8
J. Neal Lamoreaux (D)	53,437	42.3
6 William W. Blackney (R)	87,105	55.2
Robert B. McLaughlin (D)	70,104	44.5
7 Jesse P. Wolcott (R)	79,455	65.9
Charles F. Mann (D)	40,298	33.4
8 Fred L. Crawford (R)	75,700	67.5
William A. Hemmer (D)	35,982	32.1
9 Albert J. Engel (R)	56,308	62.6
Arnold B. Coxhill (D)	33,705	37.4
10 Roy O. Woodruff (R)	54,066	64.8
William J. Kelly (D)	29,108	34.9

Candidates	Votes	%
11 Fred Bradley (R)	46,985	59.0
Cecil W. Bailey (D)	32,400	40.7
12 Frank E. Hook (D)	41,481	50.6
John B. Bennett (R)	40,573	49.5
13 George D. O'Brien (D)	80,565	57.9
Clarence J. McLeod (R)	58,101	41.8
14 Louis C. Rabaut (D)	98,988	56.4
Claude G. McDonald (R)	76,358	43.5
15 John D. Dingell (D)	100,879	63.7
Harry Henderson (R)	57,070	36.1
16 John Lesinski (D)	95,483	61.4
Albert A. Riddering (R)	59,456	38.2
17 George A. Dondero (R)	116,242	56.4
John W. L. Hicks (D)	87,767	42.6

MINNESOTA

1 August H. Andresen (R)	77,798	61.7
Andrew Meldahl (DFL)	48,301	38.3
2 Joseph P. O'Hara (R)	91,867	75.7
L. J. Kilbride (DFL)	29,548	24.3
3 William J. Gallagher (DFL)	71,856	50.9
Richard P. Gale (R)	69,277	49.1
4 Frank T. Starkey (DFL)	64,434	51.8
Melvin J. Maas (R)	59,994	48.2
5 Walter H. Judd (R)	81,798	56.6
Edgar T. Buckley (DFL)	62,761	43.4
6 Harold Knutson (R)	76,421	64.6
Harry M. O'Brien (DFL)	38,947	32.9
7 H. Carl Andersen (R)	75,315	65.9
Arthur F. Nellermoe (DFL)	38,949	34.1
8 William A. Pittinger (R)	62,600	51.9
William McKinnon (DFL)	58,131	48.2
9 Harold C. Hagen (R)	58,080	59.2
Halvor Langslet (DFL)	40,018	40.8

MISSISSIPPI

1 John E. Rankin (D)	17,793	96.9
2 Jamie L. Whitten (D)	16,251	98.7
3 William M. Whittington (D)	16,222	96.4
4 Thomas G. Abernethy (D)	13,343	100.0
5 W. Arthur Winstead (D)	22,924	100.0
6 William M. Colmer (D)	31,742	95.7
7 Dan R. McGehee (D)	29,594	92.8
L. R. Collins (R)	2,313	7.3

MISSOURI

1 Samuel W. Arnold (R)	52,561	50.8
Edward M. Jayne (D)	50,910	49.2
2 Max Schwabe (R)	60,857	50.1
Lue C. Lozier (D)	60,587	49.9
3 William C. Cole (R)	61,720	50.6
Maurice Hoffman (D)	60,273	49.4
4 C. Jasper Bell (D)	60,594	57.2
John W. Mitchell (R)	45,381	42.8
5 Roger C. Slaughter (D)	53,320	52.6
Ralph B. Innis (R)	48,127	47.4
6 Marion T. Bennett (R)	71,705	57.0
George A. Clason (D)	54,095	43.0
7 Dewey Short (R)	76,180	64.0
A. L. McCawley (D)	42,929	36.0
8 Albert S. J. Carnahan (D)	54,010	50.5
William P. Elmer (R)	52,924	49.5
9 Clarence Cannon (D)	50,594	53.2
William Barton (R)	44,476	46.8
10 Orville Zimmerman (D)	55,243	56.7
Ralph Hutchison (R)	42,129	43.3
11 John B. Sullivan (D)	69,351	58.9
Louis E. Miller (R)	48,435	41.1
12 Walter C. Ploeser (R)	118,394	51.8
Phelim O'Toole (D)	110,060	48.2
13 John J. Cochran (D)	76,408	100.0

MONTANA

Candidates	Votes	%
1 Mike Mansfield (D)	57,008	67.9
M. S. Galasso (R)	26,141	31.1
2 James F. O'Connor (D)	61,123	54.0
F. F. Haynes (R)	51,372	45.4

NEBRASKA

1 Carl T. Curtis (R)	100,816	69.9
Charles A. Chappell (D)	43,341	30.1
2 Howard Buffett (R)	78,686	59.5
Mabel Gillespie (D)	53,637	40.5
3 Karl Stefan (R)	84,251	68.4
George Hally (D)	34,317	27.8
4 Arthur L. Miller (R)	72,647	63.1
Tom Lanigan (D)	34,394	29.9
Willis B. Furman	8,102	7.0

NEVADA

AL Berkeley L. Bunker (D)	32,648	63.1
Rex Bell (R)	19,096	36.9

NEW HAMPSHIRE

1 Chester E. Merrow (R)	57,537	50.9
Fortunat E. Normandin (D)	55,492	49.1
2 Sherman Adams (R)	55,911	54.4
Harry Carlson (D)	46,872	45.6

NEW JERSEY

1 Charles A. Wolverton (R)	87,950	50.4
John F. Gorman (D)	86,178	49.4
2 T. Millet Hand (R)	51,194	54.4
Edison Hedges (D)	42,862	45.6
3 James C. Auchincloss (R)	80,438	57.0
Arnold E. Ascherfeld (D)	60,769	43.0
4 D. Lane Powers (R)	68,647	55.6
Don Guinness (D)	54,680	44.3
5 Charles A. Eaton (R)	87,129	58.4
Andrew D. Desmond (D)	61,153	41.0
6 Clifford P. Case (R)	84,143	55.5
Walter H. Van Hoesen (D)	65,344	43.1
7 J. Parnell Thomas (R)	86,759	66.0
James J. Cannon (D)	44,423	33.8
8 Gordon Canfield (R)	75,479	58.5
Harry Smith (D)	53,136	41.2
9 Harry L. Towe (R)	93,687	63.5
Elmer I. Zabriskie (D)	53,847	36.5
10 Fred A. Hartley Jr. (R)	62,004	53.0
Luke A. Kiernan Jr. (D)	53,577	45.8
11 Frank L. Sundstrom (R)	58,586	51.7
John J. Francis (D)	52,376	46.3
12 Robert W. Kean (R)	67,680	50.6
John W. Suling (D)	63,087	47.2
13 Mary T. Norton (D)	89,736	69.9
Frank J. V. Gimino (R)	38,336	29.9
14 Edward J. Hart (D)	79,158	63.2
Otto Trankler (R)	46,076	36.8

NEW MEXICO

AL Clinton P. Anderson (D)	85,244✔	
Antonio M. Fernandez (D)	80,752✔	
Manuel Lujan (R)	66,644	
Ben F. Meyer (R)	66,309	

NEW YORK

1 Edgar A. Sharp (R)	92,044	69.6
Edward Hudson (D, AM LAB)	40,294	30.4
2 Leonard W. Hall (R)	131,906	67.9
John S. Thorp (D, AM LAB)	62,242	32.1
3 Henry J. Latham (R)	108,118	60.6
George H. Bruns (D, AM LAB)	70,163	39.4
4 William B. Barry (D, AM LAB)	73,098	52.8
Alfred J. Phillips (R)	65,390	47.2
5 James A. Roe (D, AM LAB)	90,338	54.3
Raymond S. Richmond (R)	76,014	45.7
6 James J. Delaney (D, AM LAB)	81,228	55.2
Otto Schuler (R)	65,821	44.8
7 John J. Delaney (D, AM LAB)	73,868	63.4
Roy M. D. Richardson (R)	42,716	36.6
8 Joseph L. Pfeifer (D, AM LAB)	55,565	59.5
Frank W. Porcaro (R)	37,816	40.5
9 Eugene J. Keogh (D, L)	63,040	55.4
Harry Chiert (R)	34,517	30.2
Jacob A. Salzman (AM LAB)	16,521	14.4
10 Andrew L. Somers (D, AM LAB)	78,753	57.8
Philip Kahaner (R)	36,854	27.0
Louis P. Goldberg (L)	20,719	15.2
11 James J. Heffernan (D, AM LAB)	95,213	65.8
John Patrick Devery (R)	49,442	34.2
12 John J. Rooney (D, AM LAB)	51,411	55.0
William G. Nolan (R)	42,007	45.0
13 Donald L. O'Toole (D, AM LAB)	81,640	60.3
Clarence W. Archibald (R)	53,854	39.8
14 Leo F. Rayfiel (D, L)	85,534	58.3
Bernard P. Levy (R)	32,393	22.1
James V. King (AM LAB)	28,766	19.6
15 Emanuel Celler (D, AM LAB)	105,943	81.1
Nathan J. Paulson (R)	24,650	18.9
16 Ellsworth B. Buck (R)	55,647	53.5
Rae L. Egbert (D, AM LAB)	48,411	46.5
17 Joseph Clark Baldwin (R)	77,196	52.4
Max Waterman (D)	57,769	39.2
Seon Felshin (AM LAB)	12,278	8.3
18 Vito Marcantonio (D, R)	82,316	100.0
19 Samuel Dickstein (D, AM LAB)	69,973	73.3
William I. Lehrfeld (R)	25,494	26.7
20 Sol Bloom (D, AM LAB)	87,724	70.8
Lawrence S. Mayers (R)	36,197	29.2
21 James H. Torrens (D, AM LAB)	91,747	69.3
Herbert Malkin (R)	40,718	30.7
22 Adam C. Powell Jr. (D, R)	83,140	100.0
23 Walter A. Lynch (D, AM LAB)	126,245	79.5
William J. Waterman (R)	32,594	20.5
24 Benjamin J. Rabin (D, AM LAB)	102,684	84.8
Morris Schaeffer (R)	18,461	15.2
25 Charles A. Buckley (D, AM LAB)	114,248	62.1
Roderick Stephens (R)	50,274	27.3
John A. Devany Jr (CST)	19,561	10.6
26 Peter A. Quinn (D, AM LAB)	91,665	56.4
Samuel T. Shay (R)	70,746	43.6
27 Ralph W. Gwinn (R)	90,699	61.9
Joseph E. Venuti (D, AM LAB)	55,756	38.1
28 Ralph A. Gamble (R)	90,623	65.5
John H. Jackson (D, AM LAB)	47,646	34.5
29 Augustus W. Bennet (D, AM LAB)	70,630	53.0
Hamilton Fish (R, JEFF)	62,583	47.0
30 Jay LeFevre (R)	88,067	63.0
Sharon J. Mauhs (D, AM LAB)	51,725	37.0
31 Bernard W. Kearney (R)	85,178	60.0
Alexander Grasso (D, AM LAB)	56,706	40.0
32 William T. Byrne (D, AM LAB)	85,147	57.2
Miles A. McGrane Jr. (R)	63,603	42.8
33 Dean P. Taylor (R)	95,299	62.6
Thomas P. McLoughlin (D)	52,354	34.4
34 Clarence E. Kilburn (R)	75,532	62.9
John D. Van Kennen (D)	44,557	37.1
35 Hadwen C. Fuller (R)	65,857	52.3
Samuel L. Miller Jr. (D, AM LAB)	60,025	47.7
36 Clarence E. Hancock (R)	79,535	53.2
George M. Haight (D, AM LAB)	70,012	46.8
37 Edwin Arthur Hall (R)	75,246	69.2
James S. Byrne (D, AM LAB)	33,465	30.8
38 John Taber (R)	75,432	65.6
Frank J. Erwin (D)	36,327	31.6
39 W. Sterling Cole (R)	75,740	68.1
Charlotte D. Curren (D)	31,152	28.0
40 George F. Rogers (D, AM LAB)	90,369	50.4
Joseph J. O'Brien (R)	88,782	49.6
41 James W. Wadsworth (R)	71,988	63.2
Jean Walrath (D, AM LAB)	41,991	36.8
42 Walter Gresham Andrews (R)	83,781	57.2
William Haeseler Jr. (D, AM LAB)	62,590	42.8
43 Edward J. Elsaesser (R)	74,366	51.1
Raymond J. Barnes (D, AM LAB)	71,216	48.9
44 John C. Butler (R)	72,402	50.1
Leon A. Dombrowski (D, AM LAB)	72,164	49.9
45 Daniel A. Reed (R)	64,456	64.1
Orrin H. Parker (D, AM LAB)	36,050	35.9

NORTH CAROLINA

1 Herbert C. Bonner (D)	30,149	90.6
R. Clarence Dozier (R)	3,139	9.4
2 John H. Kerr (D)	34,949	95.9
3 Graham A. Barden (D)	30,447	71.6
H. B. Kornegay (R)	12,055	28.4
4 Harold D. Cooley (D)	53,340	74.7
J. Ira Lee (R)	18,046	25.3
5 John H. Folger (D)	42,982	66.5
John J. Ingle (R)	21,669	33.5
6 Carl T. Durham (D)	50,003	73.3
Worth Henderson (R)	18,195	26.7
7 J. Bayard Clark (D)	39,342	79.3
Josiah A. Maultsby (R)	10,260	20.7
8 William O. Burgin (D)	48,244	59.8
B. C. Brock (R)	32,450	40.2
9 Robert L. Doughton (D)	50,595	58.8
Emory C. McCall (R)	35,506	41.2
10 Joe W. Ervin (D)	50,605	65.4
Loomis F. Klutz (R)	26,757	34.6
11 Alfred L. Bulwinkle (D)	41,576	65.6
C. V. Moss (R)	21,829	34.4
12 Zebulon Weaver (D)	52,042	64.2
Lewis P. Hamlin (R)	28,965	35.8

NORTH DAKOTA

AL William Lemke (R)	101,007✔	
Charles R. Robertson (R)	91,419✔	
Halvor L. Halvorson (D)	56,699	
J. R. Kennedy (D)	44,708	
Usher L. Burdick (IR)	39,888	
George McClellan	3,135	
A. C. Townley	2,307	

OHIO

1 Charles H. Elston (R)	82,373	56.8
Frank J. Richter (D)	62,617	43.2
2 William E. Hess (R)	78,185	56.0
J. Harry Moore (D)	61,473	44.0

OHIO

	Candidates	Votes	%
3	Edward J. Gardner (D)	104,247	52.6
	Harry P. Jeffrey (R)	94,064	47.4
4	Robert F. Jones (R)	67,829	61.2
	Earl Ludwig (D)	42,983	38.8
5	Cliff Clevenger (R)	48,490	68.1
	T. Walter Williams (D)	22,740	31.9
6	Edward O. McCowen (R)	45,284	51.8
	John W. Bush (D)	42,167	48.2
7	Clarence J. Brown (R)	84,770	61.7
	John L. Cashin (D)	52,403	38.1
8	Frederick C. Smith (R)	51,253	59.8
	Roy Warren Roof (D)	34,494	40.2
9	Homer A. Ramey (R)	82,735	51.6
	John F. Hunter (D)	77,693	48.4
10	Thomas A. Jenkins (R)	43,388	64.4
	Elsie Stanton (D)	23,986	35.6
11	Walter E. Brehm (R)	38,263	53.6
	Mell G. Underwood Jr. (D)	33,098	46.4
12	John M. Vorys (R)	97,856	54.3
	Forrest F. Smith (D)	82,503	45.7
13	Alvin F. Weichel (R)	67,298	100.0
14	Walter B. Huber (D)	117,770	50.6
	Ed Rowe (R)	115,145	49.4
15	P. W. Griffiths (R)	47,710	60.0
	Olney R. Gillogly (D)	31,756	40.0
16	William E. Thom (D)	85,755	52.7
	Henderson H. Carson (R)	75,948	46.6
17	J. Harry McGregor (R)	73,206	62.9
	Thomas A. Wilson (D)	43,271	37.2
18	Earl R. Lewis (R)	65,847	51.1
	Ross Michener (D)	63,098	48.9
19	Michael J. Kirwan (D)	120,191	63.4
	Herschel Hunt (R)	69,403	36.6
20	Michael A. Feighan (D)	75,218	75.9
	A. R. McNamara (R)	23,945	24.2
21	Robert Crosser (D)	77,525	77.7
	Harry C. Gahn (R)	22,288	22.3
22	Frances P. Bolton (R)	185,187	57.4
	Don O. Cameron (D)	137,546	42.6
AL	George H. Bender (R)	1,542,422	53.1
	William Glass (D)	1,362,843	46.9

OKLAHOMA

	Candidates	Votes	%
1	George B. Schwabe (R)	71,545	51.1
	Dennis Bushyhead (D)	68,561	48.9
2	William G. Stigler (D)	39,052	58.0
	E. O. Clark (R)	28,282	42.0
3	Paul Stewart (D)	51,135	76.2
	Russell Overstreet (R)	16,016	23.9
4	Lyle H. Boren (D)	47,733	61.7
	Ralph R. Kirchner (R)	29,582	38.3
5	A. S. Mike Monroney (D)	85,132	62.7
	Howard B. Hopps (R)	50,207	37.0
6	Jed Johnson (D)	41,987	60.0
	Ted R. Fisher (R)	27,979	40.0
7	Victor Wickersham (D)	35,895	70.8
	J. Warren White (R)	14,790	29.2
8	Ross Rizley (R)	43,878	57.6
	Philip C. Ferguson (D)	31,737	41.6

Special Election

		Votes	%
2	William G. Stigler (D)	22,036	54.4
	Ralph R. Kirchner (R)	18,502	45.6

OREGON

		Votes	%
1	James W. Mott (R)	80,106	66.7
	O. Henry Oleen (D)	39,928	33.3
2	Lowell Stockman (R)	43,145	65.7
	C. J. Shorb (D)	22,498	34.3
3	Homer D. Angell (R)	95,605	55.1
	Lester Sheeley (D)	77,814	44.9
4	Harris Ellsworth (R)	53,356	64.0
	Floyd K. Dover (D)	30,024	36.0

PENNSYLVANIA

		Votes	%
1	William A. Barrett (D)	73,289	58.4
	James Gallagher (R)	52,159	41.6

	Candidates	Votes	%
2	William T. Granahan (D)	97,351	62.7
	Charles M. Mosser (R)	57,849	37.3
3	Michael J. Bradley (D)	80,920	58.3
	Joseph M. Pratt (R)	57,856	41.7
4	John Edward Sheridan (D)	80,367	66.2
	Franklin J. Maloney (R)	41,018	33.8
5	William J. Green Jr. (D)	74,744	54.2
	C. Frederick Pracht (R)	63,085	45.8
6	Herbert J. McGlinchey (D)	78,123	50.7
	Hugh Scott (R)	75,794	49.2
7	James Wolfenden (R)	72,289	51.5
	Vernon A. O'Rourke (D)	68,161	48.5
8	Charles J. Gerlach (R)	59,497	58.0
	Marie M. Bickert (D)	43,073	42.0
9	J. Roland Kinzer (R)	71,129	61.3
	H. Clay Burkholder (D)	44,952	38.7
10	John W. Murphy (D)	59,047	56.4
	Walter W. Kohler (R)	45,593	43.6
11	Daniel J. Flood (D)	71,843	52.2
	Thomas Byron Miller (R)	65,922	47.9
12	Ivor D. Fenton (R)	65,960	56.8
	Charles E. Klinger (D)	50,153	43.2
13	Daniel K. Hoch (D)	43,233	54.1
	Randolph Stauffer (R)	33,240	41.6
14	Wilson D. Gillette (R)	51,333	65.0
	Clement J. Reap (D)	27,653	35.0
15	Robert F. Rich (R)	52,826	61.0
	Richard F. Hartzell (D)	33,750	39.0
16	Samuel K. McConnell Jr. (R)	79,555	63.7
	Marvin B. Brunner (D)	45,392	36.3
17	Richard M. Simpson (R)	45,198	64.5
	John W. Mann (D, I)	24,875	35.5
18	John C. Kunkel (R)	81,814	62.5
	Howard K. Beard (D)	49,080	37.5
19	Leon H. Gavin (R)	49,670	63.3
	John C. Brecht (D)	27,655	35.2
20	Francis E. Walter (D)	51,594	57.3
	Charles A. P. Bartlett (R)	38,460	42.7
21	Chester H. Gross (R)	55,984	52.6
	Josiah W. Gitt (D)	50,548	47.5
22	D. Emmert Brumbaugh (R)	50,000	57.8
	Bernard J. D. Clark (D)	36,476	42.2
23	J. Buell Snyder (D)	44,585	54.6
	Carl H. Hoffman (R)	37,062	45.4
24	Thomas E. Morgan (D)	52,500	62.2
	Gilbert E. Koedel (R)	31,940	37.8
25	Louis E. Graham (R)	61,544	50.4
	Samuel G. Neff (D)	60,473	49.6
26	Harve Tibbott (R)	58,743	52.6
	Eddie McCloskey (D)	52,994	47.4
27	Augustine B. Kelley (D)	61,263	59.7
	Edward J. Howard (R)	41,289	40.3
28	Robert L. Rodgers (R)	68,675	54.6
	James F. Lavery (D)	57,044	45.4
29	Howard E. Campbell (R)	63,086	50.2
	John F. Lowers (D)	62,592	49.8
30	Robert J. Corbett (R)	60,391	51.7
	Thomas E. Scanlon (D)	56,423	48.3
31	James G. Fulton (R)	71,222	53.8
	James A. Wright (D)	61,104	46.2
32	Herman P. Eberharter (D)	83,724	71.6
	Gregory Zatkovich (R)	33,221	28.4
33	Samuel A. Weiss (D)	75,796	69.3
	Ray A. Liddle (R)	33,651	30.8

RHODE ISLAND

		Votes	%
1	Aime J. Forand (D)	88,179	61.9
	Charles A. Curran (R)	54,233	38.1
2	John E. Fogarty (D)	87,189	57.8
	Charles T. Algren (R)	63,778	42.3

SOUTH CAROLINA

		Votes	%
1	L. Mendel Rivers (D)	15,326	92.8
	O. H. Wilcox (R)	1,190	7.2
2	John J. Riley (D)	19,342	98.0
3	Butler B. Hare (D)	13,105	97.0
4	Joseph R. Bryson (D)	20,988	95.7

	Candidates	Votes	%
5	James P. Richards (D)	14,435	98.1
6	John L. McMillan (D)	14,164	98.0

SOUTH DAKOTA

		Votes	%
1	Karl E. Mundt (R)	113,769	64.0
	Grover Lothrop (D)	63,981	36.0
2	Francis H. Case (R)	33,119	69.0
	H. W. Clarkson (D)	14,869	31.0

TENNESSEE

		Votes	%
1	B. Carroll Reece (R)	45,498	100.0
2	John Jennings Jr. (R)	45,416	55.5
	Lowell Blanchard (D)	36,441	44.5
3	Estes Kefauver (D)	32,497	67.8
	Foster Johnson (R)	11,541	24.1
	Ernest W. Forstner (I)	3,894	8.1
4	Albert Gore (D)	20,684	65.1
	E. M. Shelley (R)	9,642	30.4
5	Harold H. Earthman (D)	27,087	85.5
	W. H. Crowell (R)	4,598	14.5
6	J. Percy Priest (D)	28,752	97.0
7	Wirt Courtney (D)	22,592	100.0
8	Thomas J. Murray (D)	19,822	63.3
	A. Bradley Frazier (R)	11,509	36.7
9	Jere Cooper (D)	25,250	87.8
	Homer Tatum (R)	3,510	12.2
10	Clifford Davis (D)	47,569	100.0

TEXAS

		Votes	%
1	Wright Patman (D)	39,404	100.0
2	Jesse M. Combs (D)	54,258	94.0
	Lanar Cecil (R)	3,442	6.0
3	Lindley Beckworth (D)	36,954	93.3
	O. P. Stephens (R)	2,668	6.7
4	Sam Rayburn (D)	40,039	100.0
5	Hatton W. Sumners (D)	62,459	71.4
	C. D. Turner (R)	25,027	28.6
6	Luther A. Johnson (D)	36,884	100.0
7	Tom Pickett (D)	32,850	96.1
8	Albert Thomas (D)	90,963	92.3
	L. B. Robinson (R)	7,555	7.7
9	Joseph J. Mansfield (D)	56,194	93.4
	Lewis Allen (R)	3,967	6.6
10	Lyndon B. Johnson (D)	44,602	92.9
	A. H. Bartelt (R)	3,423	7.1
11	W. R. Poage (D)	39,866	95.3
12	Fritz Lanham (D)	59,119	100.0
13	Ed Gossett (D)	53,503	95.4
14	John E. Lyle (D)	53,756	100.0
15	Milton H. West (D)	35,862	100.0
16	R. Ewing Thomason (D)	31,658	100.0
17	Sam Russell (D)	43,785	96.8
18	Eugene Worley (D)	47,588	93.3
	M. C. P. Bybee (R)	3,435	6.7
19	George H. Mahon (D)	53,326	100.0
20	Paul J. Kilday (D)	39,394	100.0
21	O. Clark Fisher (D)	47,796	88.1
	M. J. Lehman (R)	6,474	11.9

UTAH

		Votes	%
1	Walter K. Granger (D)	59,755	57.8
	B. H. Stringham (R)	43,642	42.2
2	J. Will Robinson (D)	89,844	62.3
	Quayle Cannon Jr. (R)	54,440	37.7

VERMONT

		Votes	%
AL	Charles A. Plumley (R)	76,800	62.4
	Robert W. Ready (D)	46,230	37.6

VIRGINIA

		Votes	%
1	S. Otis Bland (D)	23,284	81.2
	Walter Johnson (R)	5,391	18.8

VIRGINIA

Candidates	Votes	%
2 Ralph H. Daughton (D)	21,268	57.7
Thomas L. Woodward (R)	9,304	25.2
W. B. Shafer Jr. (I)	6,302	17.1
3 David E. Satterfield Jr. (D)	32,918	100.0
4 Patrick Henry Drewry (D)	15,724	100.0
5 Thomas G. Burch (D)	24,781	84.6
Howard H. Carwile (I)	4,509	15.4
6 Clifton A. Woodrum (D)	30,844	68.7
John Strickler (R)	13,798	30.8
7 A. Willis Robertson (D)	24,967	59.9
D. Wampler Earman (R)	16,738	40.1
8 Howard W. Smith (D)	31,618	60.1
Elizabeth Chilton Murray (ID)	11,019	21.0
Lawrence Michael (IR)	9,019	17.2
9 John W. Flannagan Jr. (D)	33,943	56.3
Ralph L. Lincoln (R)	26,373	43.7

WASHINGTON

Candidates	Votes	%
1 Hugh De Lacy (D)	118,354	53.1
Robert H. Harlin (R)	103,099	46.2
2 Henry M. Jackson (D)	74,676	60.4
Payson Peterson (R)	48,974	39.6
3 Charles Savage (D)	57,942	52.0
Fred Norman (R)	53,503	48.0

Candidates	Votes	%
4 Hal Holmes (R)	56,211	60.2
Al McCoy (D)	37,150	39.8
5 Walt Horan (R)	62,648	52.3
Edward J. Reilly (D)	57,235	47.7
6 John M. Coffee (D)	80,679	61.2
Thor C. Tollefson (R)	51,119	38.8

WEST VIRGINIA

Candidates	Votes	%
1 Matthew M. Neely (D)	58,313	50.4
A. C. Schiffler (R)	57,363	49.6
2 Jennings Randolph (D)	58,695	54.1
Melvin C. Muntzing (R)	49,722	45.9
3 Cleveland M. Bailey (D)	57,912	52.5
Edward G. Rohrbough (R)	52,457	47.5
4 Hubert S. Ellis (R)	68,204	51.2
E. B. Pennybacker (D)	64,986	48.8
5 John Kee (D)	65,463	61.7
Hartley Sanders (R)	40,568	38.3
6 E. H. Hedrick (D)	84,369	58.3
J. W. Maxwell (R)	60,457	41.7

WISCONSIN

Candidates	Votes	%
1 Lawrence H. Smith (R)	74,223	74.8
John K. Kyle (PROG)	24,013	24.2

Candidates	Votes	%
2 Robert K. Henry (R)	74,937	56.8
John W. Nash (D)	34,145	25.9
Herbert C. Schenk (PROG)	22,095	16.7
3 William H. Stevenson (R)	74,092	69.9
William D. Carroll (D)	26,978	25.4
4 Thaddeus F.B. Wasielewski (D)	103,583	63.5
Robert Blackwood (R)	55,375	34.0
5 Andrew J. Biemiller (D)	88,606	50.8
Lewis D. Thill (R)	78,834	45.2
6 Frank B. Keefe (R)	74,487	66.5
Henry Danes (D)	36,180	32.3
7 Reid F. Murray (R)	73,531	69.3
William H. Ludwig (D)	31,991	30.1
8 John W. Byrnes (R)	64,623#	51.1
La Vern R. Dilweg (R)	57,458#	45.5
9 Merlin Hull (PROG)	48,064	98.5
10 Alvin E. O'Konski (R)	54,731	57.8
Elizabeth Hawkes (D)	29,773	31.4
Harry P. Van Guilder (PROG)	9,567	10.1

WYOMING

Candidates	Votes	%
AL Frank A. Barrett (R)	53,533	55.7
Charles E. Norris (D)	42,569	44.3

1945 House Elections

ILLINOIS

Special Election

Candidates	Votes	%
24 Roy Clippinger (R)	5,617	98.9

MONTANA

Special Election

	Votes	%
2 Wesley A. D'Ewart (R)	26,158	50.4
Leo C. Graybill (D)	22,126	42.6
Robert Yellowtail (I)	3,417	6.6

1946 House Elections

ALABAMA

	Candidates	Votes	%
1	Frank W. Boykin (D)	12,448	100.0
2	George M. Grant (D)	17,711	100.0
3	George W. Andrews (D)	13,397	100.0
4	Sam Hobbs (D)	16,299	88.1
	Roger S. Bingham (R)	2,207	11.9
5	Albert Rains (D)	21,560	100.0
6	Pete Jarman (D)	13,551	100.0
7	Carter Manasco (D)	22,853	72.7
	M. H. Woodward (R)	8,565	27.3
8	John J. Sparkman (D)	17,624*	92.4
	Arthur South (R)	1,453	7.6
9	Laurie C. Battle (D)	29,940	94.1
	J. G. Bass (R)	1,880	5.9

ARIZONA

	Candidates	Votes	%
AL	John R. Murdock (D)	74,948✔	
	Richard F. Harless (D)	71,836✔	
	Denver C. Henson (R)	37,033	
	John H. Curnutte (R)	36,185	
	Karl M. Wilson (COM)	831	

ARKANSAS

	Candidates	Votes	%
1	Ezekiel C. Gathings (D)	20,250	100.0
2	Wilbur D. Mills (D)	22,955	100.0
3	James W. Trimble (D)	24,950	100.0
4	Fadjo Cravens (D)	13,844	100.0
5	Brooks Hays (D)	21,777	85.2
	James R. Harris (R)	2,881	11.3
6	William F. Norrell (D)	23,892	84.7
	M. O. Evans (I)	4,305	15.3
7	Oren Harris (D)	15,584	100.0

CALIFORNIA

	Candidates	Votes	%
1	Clarence F. Lea (D-R)	77,653	99.8
2	Clair Engle (D-R)	57,895	100.0
3	Leroy Johnson (R-D)	116,792	100.0
4	Franck R. Havenner (D)	60,655	52.9
	Truman R. Young (R)	54,113	47.2
5	Richard J. Welch (R-D)	94,293	100.0
6	George P. Miller (D-R)	118,548	99.9
7	John J. Allen Jr. (R)	61,508	56.2
	Patrick W. McDonough (D)	47,988	43.8
8	John Z. Anderson (R-D)	113,325	99.9
9	Bertrand W. Gearhart (R)	50,171	53.7
	Hubert Phillips (D)	43,244	46.3
10	Alfred J. Elliott (D-R)	51,843	99.8
11	Ernest K. Bramblett (R)	41,902	53.1
	George E. Outland (D)	36,996	46.9
12	Richard M. Nixon (R)	65,586	56.0
	H. Jerry Voorhis (D)	49,994	42.7
13	Norris Poulson (R)	48,071	51.8̅
	Ned R. Healy (D)	44,712	48.2
14	Helen Gahagan Douglas (D)	53,536	54.3
	Frederick M. Roberts (R)	44,914	45.6
15	Gordon L. McDonough (R-D)	106,020	99.4
16	Donald L. Jackson (R)	78,264	53.9
	Harold Harby (R)	45,951	31.6
	Ellis E. Patterson	20,945	14.4
17	Cecil R. King (D-R)	110,654	99.4
18	Willis W. Bradley (R)	67,363	52.8
	Clyde Doyle (D)	60,218	47.2
19	Chet Holifield (D-R)	50,666	97.2
20	Carl Hinshaw (R)	98,283	59.3
	Everett G. Burkhalter (D)	67,317	40.6
21	Harry R. Sheppard (D)	37,229	52.7
	Lowell E. Lathrop (R)	33,395	47.3
22	John Phillips (R)	59,935	62.1
	Ray Adkinson (D)	36,649	37.9
23	Charles K. Fletcher (R)	69,411	56.3
	Ed V. Izac (D)	53,898	43.7

COLORADO

	Candidates	Votes	%
1	John A. Carroll (D)	60,513	51.8
	Dean M. Gillespie (R)	55,724	47.7
2	William S. Hill (R)	54,768	65.7
	Frank A. Safranek (D)	27,393	32.9
3	J. Edgar Chenoweth (R)	45,043	54.6
	Walter W. Johnson (D)	37,496	45.4
4	Robert F. Rockwell (R)	28,894	58.8
	Thomas Matthews (D)	20,290	41.3

CONNECTICUT

	Candidates	Votes	%
1	William J. Miller (R)	93,006	53.1
	Herman P. Kopplemann (D)	82,231	46.9
2	Horace Seely-Brown Jr. (R)	59,828	55.3
	Chase Going Woodhouse (D)	48,376	44.7
3	Ellsworth B. Foote (R)	76,408	58.9
	James P. Geelan (D)	53,404	41.1
4	John Davis Lodge (R)	93,513	57.1
	Henry A. Mucci (D)	57,913	35.4
	Stanley W. Mayhew (SOC)	9,427	5.8
5	James T. Patterson (R)	51,790	53.1
	Thomas Radzevich (D)	39,785	40.8
	John C. Cluney (SOC, CLUNEY)	5,984	6.1
AL	Antoni N. Sadlak (R)	377,972	55.6
	Joseph F. Ryter (D)	277,872	40.9

DELAWARE

	Candidates	Votes	%
AL	J. Caleb Boggs (R)	63,516	56.4
	Philip A. Traynor (D)	49,105	43.6

FLORIDA

	Candidates	Votes	%
1	J. Hardin Peterson (D)	31,145	100.0
2	Emory H. Price (D)	26,093	100.0
3	Robert L. F. Sikes (D)	18,455	100.0
4	George A. Smathers (D)	37,002	71.9
	Norman N. Curtis (R)	14,458	28.1
5	Joe Hendricks (D)	24,695	61.3
	M. J. Moss Jr. (R)	15,591	38.7
6	Dwight L. Rogers (D)	13,733	71.1
	Joseph P. Moe (R)	5,591	28.9

GEORGIA

	Candidates	Votes	%
1	Prince H. Preston (D)	20,937	99.8
2	E. E. Cox (D)	10,805	100.0
3	Stephen Pace (D)	8,961	100.0
4	A. Sidney Camp (D)	8,476	100.0
5	James C. Davis (D)	31,444	61.6
	Helen Douglas Mankin (I)	19,527#	38.3
6	Carl Vinson (D)	13,566	100.0
7	Henderson Lanham (D)	7,573	100.0
8	W. M. Wheeler (D)	8,986	100.0
9	John Wood (D)	14,815	100.0
10	Paul Brown (D)	16,398	100.0

Special Election

	Candidates	Votes	%
5	Helen Douglas Mankin (D)	11,067	36.5
	Thomas L. Camp	10,275	33.9
	Ben T. Huiet	2,724	9.0
	J. E. B. Stewart	2,363	7.8

IDAHO

	Candidates	Votes	%
1	Abe McGregor Goff (R)	37,326	50.6
	Compton I. White (D)	36,509	49.5
2	John Sanborn (R)	63,692	60.7
	Pete Leguineche (D)	41,231	39.3

ILLINOIS

	Candidates	Votes	%
1	William L. Dawson (D)	38,040	56.8
	William E. King (R)	28,945	43.2
2	Richard B. Vail (R)	156,697	51.3
	William A. Rowan (D)	148,995	48.7
3	Fred E. Busbey (R)	169,543	57.2
	Edward A. Kelly (D)	126,638	42.8
4	Martin Gorski (D)	68,113	70.7
	John T. Parsons (R)	28,251	29.3
5	Adolph J. Sabath (D)	34,904	71.6
	Michael A. Francisco (R)	13,859	28.4
6	Thomas J. O'Brien (D)	171,778	52.0
	Harold C. Woodward (R)	158,702	48.0
7	Thomas L. Owens (R)	252,981	55.0
	William W. Link (D)	206,963	45.0
8	Thomas S. Gordon (D)	38,317	77.3
	Scott John Vitell (R)	11,266	22.7
9	Robert J. Twyman (R)	54,615	51.3
	Alexander J. Resa (D)	51,788	48.7
10	Ralph E. Church (R)	201,010	64.7
	Harold H. Kolbe (D)	109,712	35.3
11	Chauncey W. Reed (R)	120,640	74.9
	Louis William Oswald (D)	40,355	25.1
12	Noah M. Mason (R)	73,431	69.1
	Richard G. Myrland (D)	32,816	30.9
13	Leo E. Allen (R)	48,238	77.8
	Michael M. Kinney (D)	13,767	22.2
14	Anton J. Johnson (R)	45,723	62.1
	Carl E. Wright Jr. (D)	27,877	37.9
15	Robert B. Chiperfield (R)	49,895	64.3
	Henry D. Sullivan (D)	27,667	35.7
16	Everett M. Dirksen (R)	64,534	67.5
	Hans A. Spading (D)	31,091	32.5
17	Leslie C. Arends (R)	45,969	71.2
	Carl Vrooman (D)	18,617	28.8
18	Edward H. Jenison (R)	56,537	65.1
	C. E. Spang (D)	30,305	34.9
19	Rolla C. McMillen (R)	64,063	62.5
	Olive Remington Goldman (D)	38,485	37.5
20	Sidney E. Simpson (R)	34,923	58.8
	Don Irving (D)	24,508	41.2
21	Evan Howell (R)	55,609	55.1
	Roscoe Bonjean (D)	45,293	44.9
22	Melvin Price (D)	69,669	50.7
	Calvin D. Johnson (R)	67,665	49.3
23	Charles W. Vursell (R)	51,440	54.9
	Homer Kasserman (D)	42,237	45.1
24	Roy Clippinger (R)	37,909	58.9
	Edward Hines (D)	26,483	41.1
25	C. W. Bishop (R)	53,831	59.8
	Sherman S. Carr (D)	36,217	40.2
AL	William G. Stratton (R)	1,906,717	55.1
	Emily Taft Douglas (D)	1,539,248	44.5

INDIANA

	Candidates	Votes	%
1	Ray J. Madden (D)	51,809	51.9
	Charles W. Gannon (R)	46,677	46.8
2	Charles A. Halleck (R)	66,423	61.3
	Margaret A. Afflis (D)	40,847	37.7
3	Robert A. Grant (R)	73,239	55.6
	John S. Gonas (D)	57,425	43.6
4	George W. Gillie (R)	59,790	59.4
	Walter E. Frederick (D)	39,766	39.5
5	Forest A. Harness (R)	79,752	55.0
	William W. Welsh (D)	61,364	42.3
6	Noble J. Johnson (R)	65,926	57.4
	Thomas A. Sigler (D)	47,972	41.7
7	Gerald W. Landis (R)	63,667	50.7
	James E. Noland (D)	59,908	47.7
8	Edward A. Mitchell (R)	66,050	51.8
	Winfield K. Denton (D)	60,385	47.3
9	Earl Wilson (R)	58,384	55.8
	Oliver O. Dixon (D)	45,316	43.3

INDIANA

Candidates	Votes	%
10 Raymond S. Springer (R)	70,969	59.3
Frank C. Unger (D)	44,807	37.4
11 Louis Ludlow (D)	79,040	51.1
Albert J. Beveridge (R)	74,745	48.3

IOWA

1 Thomas E. Martin (R)	52,488	61.5
Clair A. Williams (D)	32,849	38.5
2 Henry O. Talle (R)	60,111	59.1
Richard V. Bernhart (D)	41,544	40.9
3 John W. Gwynne (R)	48,346	62.0
Dan J. P. Ryan (D)	29,661	38.0
4 Karl M. LeCompte (R)	43,753	58.4
A. E. Augustine (D)	31,203	41.6
5 Paul Cunningham (R)	41,679	59.4
Vince L. Browner (D)	28,490	40.6
6 James I. Dolliver (R)	40,595	63.4
Oscar E. Johnson (D)	23,422	36.6
7 Ben F. Jensen (R)	40,152	63.0
Philip A. Allen (D)	23,567	37.0
8 Charles B. Hoeven (R)	37,868	68.6
George A. Heikens (D)	17,303	31.4

KANSAS

1 Albert M. Cole (R)	63,076	64.3
James W. Lowry (D)	35,045	35.7
2 Errett P. Scrivner (R)	56,363	58.8
Murray H. Hodges (D)	39,484	41.2
3 Herbert A. Meyer (R)	41,624	55.4
Jo E. Gaitskill (D)	33,578	44.7
4 Edward H. Rees (R)	68,658	56.2
William P. Warren (D)	53,617	43.9
5 Clifford R. Hope (R)	54,578	62.7
Arthur L. Sparks (D)	32,538	37.4
6 Wint Smith (R)	44,343	58.1
G. E. Bengtson (D)	28,911	37.9

KENTUCKY

1 Noble J. Gregory (D)	32,121	66.2
William E. Porter (R)	16,064	33.1
2 Earle C. Clements (D)	38,020	56.6
Thomas W. Hines (R)	29,124	43.4
3 Thruston B. Morton (R)	61,899	58.1
Emmet O'Neal (D)	44,599	41.9
4 Frank L. Chelf (D)	33,116	53.1
Don Victor Drye Sr. (R)	29,304	47.0
5 Brent Spence (D)	26,444	51.2
Marion W. Moore (R)	25,240	48.8
6 Virgil Chapman (D)	43,176	55.0
W. D. Rogers (R)	35,368	45.0
7 W. Howes Meade (R)	30,070	59.4
A. J. May (D)	20,596	40.7
8 Joe B. Bates (D)	33,408	52.6
Ray Schmauch (R)	30,127	47.4
9 John M. Robsion (R)	54,306	100.0

LOUISIANA

1 F. Edward Hebert (D)	29,329	91.8
Dennison Suarez (R)	2,614	8.2
2 Hale Boggs (D)	29,457	90.7
Harold M. Herbst (R)	3,037	9.4
3 James Domengeaux (D)	4,595	100.0
4 Overton Brooks (D)	8,499	100.0
5 Otto E. Passman (D)	6,049	100.0
6 James H. Morrison (D)	8,781	100.0
7 Henry D. Larcade Jr. (D)	5,907	100.0
8 A. Leonard Allen (D)	7,740	100.0

MAINE

1 Robert Hale (R)	38,975	59.6
John C. Fitzgerald (D)	26,378	40.4

Candidates	Votes	%
2 Margaret Chase Smith (R)	39,791	60.7
Edward J. Beauchamp (D)	25,739	39.3
3 Frank Fellows (R)	31,622	72.9
John M. Coghill (D)	11,743	27.1

MARYLAND

1 Edward T. Miller (R)	27,364	50.9
Dudley George Roe (D)	26,360	49.1
2 Hugh A. Meade (D)	69,211	52.4
David G. Harry (R)	62,760	47.6
3 Thomas D'Alesandro Jr. (D)	24,347	63.9
Edward N. Kowzan (R)	13,761	36.1
4 George H. Fallon (D)	31,453	57.2
Paul Robertson (R)	23,499	42.8
5 Lansdale G. Sasscer (D)	40,929	58.2
Edwin A. Glenn (R)	29,406	41.8
6 J. Glenn Beall (R)	55,667	58.1
Arch McDonald (D)	40,198	41.9

MASSACHUSETTS

1 John W. Heselton (R)	59,222	58.0
John J. Falvey (D)	40,549	39.7
2 Charles R. Clason (R)	59,754	51.4
Foster Furcolo (D)	56,459	48.6
3 Philip J. Philbin (D)	69,038	62.2
Carroll H. Balcom (R)	42,033	37.8
4 Harold D. Donohue (D)	59,847	49.5
Pehr G. Holmes (R)	58,663	48.5
5 Edith Nourse Rogers (R)	98,488	71.6
Oliver S. Allen (D)	38,575	28.0
6 George J. Bates (R)	79,790	70.2
Richard B. O'Keefe (D)	33,823	29.8
7 Thomas J. Lane (D)	59,871	60.8
Ernest Bentley (R)	37,250	37.8
8 Angier L. Goodwin (R)	76,305	63.5
Anthony M. Roche (D)	43,827	36.5
9 Charles L. Gifford (R)	69,831	60.8
William McAuliffe (D)	43,367	37.8
10 Christian A. Herter (R)	96,607	64.0
Paul J. McCarty (D)	54,421	36.0
11 John F. Kennedy (D)	69,093	71.9
Lester W. Bowen (R)	26,007	27.1
12 John W. McCormack (D)	92,622	100.0
13 Richard B. Wigglesworth (R)	87,839	67.5
James J. Goode Jr. (D)	42,274	32.5
14 Joseph W. Martin Jr. (R)	71,566	63.6
Martha Sharp (D)	40,999	36.4

MICHIGAN

1 George G. Sadowski (D)	57,753	65.9
John B. Sosnowski (R)	29,293	33.4
2 Earl C. Michener (R)	66,486	71.2
William R. Kelley (D)	26,141	28.0
3 Paul W. Shafer (R)	59,823	68.9
Herschel W. Carney (D)	25,914	29.9
4 Clare E. Hoffman (R)	58,798	72.5
Harvey Hope Jarvis (D)	21,514	26.5
5 Bartel J. Jonkman (R)	63,093	71.6
Earle W. Reynolds (D)	25,022	28.4
6 William W. Blackney (R)	69,203	57.3
Arthur Elliott (D)	50,684	42.0
7 Jesse P. Wolcott (R)	64,404	74.2
Earl J. Tallman (D)	21,708	25.0
8 Fred L. Crawford (R)	58,725	72.6
J. Charles Mottashed (D)	21,375	26.4
9 Albert J. Engel (R)	49,017	71.8
J. Willard Krause (D)	18,828	27.6
10 Roy O. Woodruff (R)	44,853	71.1
Herman N. Butler (D)	17,737	28.1
11 Fred Bradley (R)	41,436	65.9
Cecil W. Bailey (D)	21,340	33.9
12 John B. Bennett (R)	40,717	54.4
Frank E. Hook (D)	33,799	45.2

Candidates	Votes	%
13 Howard A. Coffin (R)	50,539	52.8
George D. O'Brien (D)	44,883	46.9
14 Harold F. Youngblood (R)	69,968	53.3
Louis C. Rabaut (D)	60,808	46.3
15 John D. Dingell (D)	59,111	51.9
Harry Henderson (R)	54,296	47.7
16 John Lesinski (D)	57,773	51.9
Albert A. Riddering (R)	52,376	47.1
17 George A. Dondero (R)	102,336	64.7
John W. L. Hicks (D)	54,928	34.7

MINNESOTA

1 August H. Andresen (R)	65,906	68.4
Karl F. Rolvaag (DFL)	30,439	31.6
2 Joseph P. O'Hara (R)	69,487	76.0
L. J. Kilbride (DFL)	21,947	24.0
3 George MacKinnon (R)	57,397	51.5
Roy W. Wier (DFL)	52,797	47.3
4 Edward J. Devitt (R)	45,667	51.5
Frank T. Starkey (DFL)	41,897	47.2
5 Walter H. Judd (R)	66,837	58.3
Douglas Hall (DFL)	47,777	41.7
6 Harold Knutson (R)	55,401	57.4
J. Edward Anderson (DFL)	41,147	42.6
7 H. Carl Andersen (R)	57,869	65.4
Donald M. Lawson (DFL)	30,667	34.6
8 John A. Blatnik (DFL)	62,876	57.7
William A. Pittenger (R)	46,189	42.4
9 Harold C. Hagen (R)	50,031	63.9
Verner Nelson (DFL)	28,211	36.1

MISSISSIPPI

1 John E. Rankin (D)	5,429	100.0
2 Jamie L. Whitten (D)	6,411	100.0
3 William M. Whittington (D)	4,265	100.0
4 Thomas G. Abernethy (D)	10,017	100.0
5 W. Arthur Winstead (D)	7,122	100.0
6 William M. Colmer (D)	6,448	100.0
7 John Bell Williams (D)	10,345	100.0

MISSOURI

1 Samuel W. Arnold (R)	37,584	50.3
Walter G. Stillwell (D)	37,105	49.7
2 Max Schwabe (R)	44,292	51.1
Will N. Nelson Jr. (D)	42,437	48.9
3 William C. Cole (R)	38,828	52.8
William Orr Sawyers (D)	34,730	47.2
4 C. Jasper Bell (D)	41,843	55.1
Vernon D. Fulcrut (R)	34,066	44.9
5 Albert L. Reeves Jr. (R)	42,065	53.7
Enos A. Axtell (D)	36,324	46.3
6 Marion T. Bennett (R)	54,034	58.6
Tom B. Hembree (D)	38,113	41.4
7 Dewey Short (R)	50,588	65.4
Don Ervin (D)	26,712	34.6
8 Parke M. Banta (R)	42,076	51.1
A. S. J. Carnahan (D)	40,241	48.9
9 Clarence Cannon (D)	35,253	53.9
William Barton (R)	30,199	46.1
10 Orville Zimmerman (D)	37,236	60.6
Walter K. Dillon (R)	24,164	39.4
11 Claude I. Bakewell (R)	41,202	50.8
John B. Sullivan (D)	39,879	49.2
12 Walter C. Ploeser (R)	93,136	58.2
Henry W. Simpson (D)	66,884	41.8
13 Frank M. Karsten (D)	41,229	54.8
Alfred L. Grattendick (R)	34,062	45.2

MONTANA

1 Mike Mansfield (D)	47,418	57.6
W. R. Rankin (R)	34,958	42.4
2 Wesley A. D'Ewart (R)	58,307	54.1
John J. Holmes (D)	48,564	45.1

NEBRASKA

Candidates	Votes	%
1 Carl T. Curtis (R)	73,602	66.4
William H. Meier (D)	37,280	33.6
2 Howard Buffett (R)	53,398	58.3
Frank A. Jelen (D)	38,125	41.7
3 Karl Stefan (R)	64,016	72.2
Hans O. Jensen (D)	20,161	22.7
Paul Burke (I)	4,516#	5.1
4 Arthur L. Miller (R)	57,708	71.3
Stanley D. Long (D)	23,234	28.7

NEVADA

Candidates	Votes	%
AL Charles H. Russell (R)	28,859	58.8
Malcolm McEachin (D)	20,187	41.2

NEW HAMPSHIRE

Candidates	Votes	%
1 Chester E. Merrow (R)	53,909	59.8
Josaphet T. Benoit (D)	36,316	40.3
2 Norris Cotton (R)	45,963	64.9
Patrick J. Hinchey (D)	24,904	35.1

NEW JERSEY

Candidates	Votes	%
1 Charles A. Wolverton (R)	82,919	63.5
George F. Neutze (D)	47,631	36.5
2 T. Millet Hand (R)	54,511	67.1
Edward T. Keeley (D)	26,740	32.9
3 James C. Auchincloss (R)	70,302	64.9
John W. Zimmermann (D)	36,177	33.4
4 Frank A. Mathews Jr. (R)	50,221	52.6
Charles R. Howell (D)	45,225	47.4
5 Charles A. Eaton (R)	69,338	61.3
John J. George (D)	43,593	38.6
6 Clifford P. Case (R)	69,395	64.7
Walter H. Van Hoesen (D)	35,378	33.0
7 J. Parnell Thomas (R)	65,426	69.0
Robert B. Meyner (D)	29,418	31.0
8 Gordon Canfield (R)	57,616	70.5
John V. Breslin (D)	23,007	28.2
9 Harry L. Towe (R)	74,870	69.1
John M. Mehler (D)	33,553	31.0
10 Fred A. Hartley Jr. (R)	44,619	52.5
Peter W. Rodino Jr. (D)	38,889	45.7
11 Frank L. Sundstrom (R)	46,034	60.4
Robert F. J. McGarry (D)	28,545	37.5
12 Robert W. Kean (R)	55,732	63.6
Raymond C. Connell (D)	30,389	34.7
13 Mary T. Norton (D)	69,440	64.4
John A. Jones (R)	36,270	33.7
14 Edward J. Hart (D)	65,979	63.2
Edward P. Nicolay (R)	38,008	36.4

NEW MEXICO

Candidates	Votes	%
AL Georgia L. Lusk (D)	66,420✔	
Antonio M. Fernandez (D)	65,242✔	
Earl Douglas (R)	60,519	
Herman G. Baca (R)	58,937	

NEW YORK

Candidates	Votes	%
1 W. Kingsland Macy (R)	83,877	77.3
Eugene T. O'Neill (D)	22,855	21.1
2 Leonard W. Hall (R)	123,873	78.4
Josephine U. Mayes (D, AM LAB)	34,217	21.6
3 Henry J. Latham (R)	98,722	69.7
Aloysius J. Maickel (D)	32,002	22.6
4 Gregory McMahon (R)	57,176	53.3
Emily B. Barry (D)	38,227	35.6
George H. Rooney (AM LAB)	7,439	6.9
5 Robert Tripp Ross (R)	66,754	53.0
James A. Phillips (D, AM LAB)	59,092	47.0
6 Robert J. Nodar Jr. (R)	59,438	53.9

Candidates	Votes	%
James J. Delaney (D, AM LAB)	50,944	46.1
7 John J. Delaney (D, AM LAB)	49,449	57.5
Roy M. D. Richardson (R)	36,510	42.5
8 Joseph L. Pfeifer (D, AM LAB)	34,876	53.9
Paul W. Williams (R)	29,851	46.1
9 Eugene J. Keogh (D, L)	41,304	48.6
Samuel R. Scialabba (R)	27,289	32.1
Anthony Scimeca (AM LAB)	16,359	19.3
10 Andrew L. Somers (D, AM LAB)	57,658	57.9
Victor Wichum (R)	33,642	33.8
August Claessens (L)	8,314	8.4
11 James J. Heffernan (D, AM LAB)	69,089	60.4
Alfred C. McKenzie (R)	45,279	39.6
12 John J. Rooney (D)	36,399	54.0
Vincent J. Longhi (R, AM LAB)	31,052	46.0
13 Donald L. O'Toole (D, AM LAB)	51,406	53.5
Charles H. Weadon (R)	44,674	46.5
14 Leo F. Rayfiel (D, AM LAB)	79,336	75.0
Robert H. Thayer (R)	26,450	25.0
15 Emanuel Celler (D, AM LAB)	78,543	78.7
Lauri T. Laisi (R)	21,094	21.1
16 Ellsworth B. Buck (R, VETS V)	49,758	61.2
John Burry (D, AM LAB)	31,583	38.8
17 Frederic R. Coudert Jr. (R)	66,063	57.5
Myron Sulzberger (D)	39,216	34.2
Joseph Clark Baldwin (AM LAB)	9,527	8.3
18 Vito Marcantonio (D, AM LAB)	42,229	54.2
Frederick V. P. Bryan (R)	35,693	45.8
19 Arthur G. Klein (D, AM LAB)	48,437	71.4
William I. Lehrfeld (R)	19,410	28.6
20 Sol Bloom (D, AM LAB)	57,208	61.1
Jules J. Justin (R)	36,450	38.9
21 Jacob K. Javits (R, L)	46,897	46.0
Daniel Flynn (D)	40,652	39.9
Eugene P. Connolly (AM LAB)	14,359	14.1
22 Adam Clayton Powell Jr. (D, AM LAB)	32,573	62.5
Grant Reynolds (R)	19,514	37.5
23 Walter A. Lynch (D)	52,616	43.4
Peter Wynne (R)	30,534	25.2
David A. Schlossberg (AM LAB)	25,229	20.8
William Wacks (L)	12,803	10.6
24 Benjamin J. Rabin (D)	39,316	44.2
Roy Soden (AM LAB)	24,249	27.3
David Scher (R)	16,931	19.0
Bernice Benedick (L)	8,504	9.6
25 Charles A. Buckley (D)	47,142	32.5
Charles Garside (R)	46,853	32.3
Edward V. Morand (AM LAB)	25,353	17.5
Ira J. Palestine (L)	15,814	10.9
John A. Devany (VETS V)	9,791	6.8
26 David Potts (R)	58,061	44.1
Peter A. Quinn (D)	49,067	37.3
Gerald O'Reilly (AM LAB)	17,379	13.2
Augustus Batten (L)	7,140	5.4
27 Ralph W. Gwinn (R)	84,882	68.6
Francis X. Nulty (D, AM LAB)	38,950	31.5
28 Ralph A. Gamble (R)	83,533	75.4
Morris Karnes (D, AM LAB)	27,236	24.6
29 Katharine St. George (R)	60,769	58.2
James K. Welsh (D, VETS F)	40,174	38.4
30 Jay LeFevre (R)	80,469	69.5
John F. Killgrew (D, AM LAB)	35,240	30.5

Candidates	Votes	%
31 Bernard W. Kearney (R)	66,395	59.2
Carroll A. Gardner (D, AM LAB)	45,777	40.8
32 William T. Byrne (D, AM LAB)	79,042	55.1
William K. Sanford (R)	64,325	44.9
33 Dean P. Taylor (R)	89,778	69.9
David J. Fitzgerald (D, AM LAB)	38,666	30.1
34 Clarence E. Kilburn (R)	64,217	73.0
William G. Houk (D)	22,368	25.4
35 Hadwen C. Fuller (R)	58,040	54.3
Frank A. Emma (D, AM LAB)	48,854	45.7
36 R. Walter Riehlman (R)	76,372	63.3
Lawson Barnes (D, AM LAB)	44,371	36.7
37 Edwin Arthur Hall (R)	59,920	71.7
Charles R. Wilson (D, AM LAB)	23,687	28.3
38 John Taber (R)	63,382	72.1
George T. Franklin (D)	24,576	27.9
39 W. Sterling Cole (R)	61,330	72.6
William Heidt Jr. (D, AM LAB)	23,205	27.4
40 Kenneth B. Keating (R)	84,852	60.5
George F. Rogers (D, AM LAB)	55,321	39.5
41 James W. Wadsworth (R)	65,975	71.5
Charles J. Reap (D, AM LAB)	26,332	28.5
42 Walter Gresham Andrews (R)	71,862	62.6
William R. Lupton (D, AM LAB)	43,028	37.4
43 Edward J. Elsaesser (R)	71,758	62.6
Charles P. McCabe (D)	38,108	33.2
44 John C. Butler (R)	67,495	57.5
James B. Downey (D, AM LAB)	49,798	42.5
45 Daniel A. Reed (R)	53,327	70.4
Joseph E. Proudman (D, AM LAB)	20,205	26.7

Special Election

Candidates	Votes	%
19 Arthur G. Klein (D)	17,360	49.5
Johannes Stell (AM LAB)	13,415	38.2
William S. Shea (R)	4,314	12.3

NORTH CAROLINA

Candidates	Votes	%
1 Herbert C. Bonner (D)	9,993	89.2
Zeno O. Ratcliff (R)	1,208	10.8
2 John H. Kerr (D)	9,426	100.0
3 Graham A. Barden (D)	14,798	66.7
H. B. Kornegay (R)	7,385	33.3
4 Harold D. Cooley (D)	22,977	65.7
Ben L. Spence (R)	12,005	34.3
5 John H. Folger (D)	26,316	62.9
S. Evan Hall (R)	15,521	37.1
6 Carl T. Durham (D)	18,564	63.4
A. A. McDonald (R)	10,721	36.6
7 J. Bayard Clark (D)	15,428	73.9
H. Edmund Rodgers (R)	5,445	26.1
8 Charles B. Deane (D)	29,920	54.2
Joseph H. Whicker Sr. (R)	25,305	45.8
9 Robert L. Doughton (D)	36,007	54.9
Clyde R. Greene (R)	29,585	45.1
10 Hamilton C. Jones (D)	24,614	53.9
P. C. Burkholder (R)	21,096	46.2
11 Alfred L. Bulwinkle (D)	25,544	58.5
C. Y. Nanney Jr. (R)	18,143	41.5
12 Monroe M. Redden (D)	43,690	60.5
Guy Weaver (R)	28,531	39.5

Special Elections

Candidates	Votes	%
8 Jane Pratt (D)	31,058	79.5
H. Frank Hulin (R)	8,017	20.5
10 Sam J. Ervin Jr. (D)	2,303	99.7

NORTH DAKOTA

Candidates	Votes	%
AL William Lemke (R)	103,205✓	
Charles R. Robertson (R)	102,087✓	
James M. Hanley (D)	41,189	
Edwin Cooper (D)	29,865	

OHIO

	Candidates	Votes	%
1	Charles H. Elston (R)	72,909	64.2
	G. Andrews Espy (D)	40,594	35.8
2	William E. Hess (R)	67,067	63.2
	Francis G. Davis (D)	39,112	36.8
3	Raymond H. Burke (R)	71,171	52.0
	Edward J. Gardner (D)	65,749	48.0
4	Robert F. Jones (R)	46,718	59.2
	Merl J. Bragg (D)	32,160	40.8
5	Cliff Clevenger (R)	30,623	60.3
	Willard Thomas (D)	20,163	39.7
6	Edward O. McCowen (R)	39,992	54.8
	Franklin E. Smith (D)	33,013	45.2
7	Clarence J. Brown (R)	63,390	68.0
	Carl H. Ehl (D)	29,824	32.0
8	Frederick C. Smith (R)	40,755	64.0
	John T. Siemon (D)	22,945	36.0
9	Homer A. Ramey (R)	59,394	50.1
	Michael V. DiSalle (D)	59,057	49.9
10	Thomas A. Jenkins (R)	35,406	66.7
	H. A. McCown (D)	17,719	33.4
11	Walter E. Brehm (R)	31,576	60.6
	Lester S. Reid (D)	20,543	39.4
12	John M. Vorys (R)	74,691	62.0
	Arthur P. Lamneck (D)	45,779	38.0
13	Alvin F. Weichel (R)	49,725	72.1
	Frank W. Thomas (D)	19,237	27.9
14	Walter B. Huber (D)	88,178	52.6
	Fred W. Danner (R)	77,674	46.4
15	Percy W. Griffiths (R)	36,564	53.2
	Robert T. Secrest (D)	32,159	46.8
16	Henderson H. Carson (R)	65,639	55.8
	William R. Thom (D)	51,931	44.2
17	J. Harry McGregor (R)	57,167	65.3
	Wesley W. Purdy (D)	30,406	34.7
18	Earl R. Lewis (R)	55,140	58.8
	Eugene A. Blum (D)	38,606	41.2
19	Michael J. Kirwan (D)	88,872	59.9
	Norman W. Adams (R)	59,607	40.2
20	Michael A. Feighan (D)	49,670	67.0
	Walter E. Obert (R)	24,476	33.0
21	Robert Crosser (D)	49,111	64.0
	James S. Hudec (R)	27,657	36.0
22	Frances P. Bolton (R)	174,823	69.1
	Earl Heffley (D)	69,050	27.3
AL	George H. Bender (R)	1,281,864	59.5
	William M. Boyd (D)	871,660	40.5

OKLAHOMA

	Candidates	Votes	%
1	George B. Schwabe (R)	61,205	54.5
	Oras A. Shaw (D)	51,041	45.5
2	William G. Stigler (D)	32,559	63.1
	Ferd P. Snider (R)	19,029	36.9
3	Carl Albert (D)	38,699	85.0
	Eleanor L. Watson (R)	6,835	15.0
4	Glen D. Johnson (D)	36,559	64.4
	Pliney S. Frye (R)	20,230	35.6
5	A. S. Mike Monroney (D)	47,173	52.0
	Carmon C. Harris (R)	43,508	48.0
6	Toby Morris (D)	30,408	65.7
	Joe Hart Jr. (R)	15,912	34.4
7	Preston E. Peden (D)	26,585	78.7
	J. Warren White (R)	7,204	21.3
8	Ross Rizley (R)	30,240	54.8
	Tom Hieronymus (D)	24,954	45.2

OREGON

	Candidates	Votes	%
1	Walter Norblad (R)	67,535	72.0
	Lyman Ross (D)	26,278	28.0

	Candidates	Votes	%
2	Lowell Stockman (R)	32,541	67.4
	Lamar Townsend (D)	15,744	32.6
3	Homer D. Angell (R)	74,061	56.7
	Lew Wallace (D)	56,525	43.3
4	Harris Ellsworth (R)	42,868	69.2
	Louis A. Wood (D)	19,118	30.8

PENNSYLVANIA

	Candidates	Votes	%
1	James Gallagher (R)	70,680	57.3
	William Barrett (D)	52,593	42.7
2	Robert N. McGarvey (R)	70,474	51.4
	William T. Granahan (D)	66,674	48.6
3	Hardie Scott (R)	83,618	62.1
	Albert S. Townsend (D)	50,962	37.9
4	Franklin J. Maloney (R)	55,239	50.2
	John Edward Sheridan (D)	49,025	44.6
	John K. Rice (U CIT)	5,688	5.2
5	George W. Sarbacher Jr. (R)	73,946	56.9
	William J. Green Jr. (D)	56,086	43.1
6	Hugh Scott (R)	82,671	58.5
	Herbert J. McGlinchey (D)	58,557	41.5
7	E. Wallace Chadwick (R)	76,021	66.5
	Vernon A. O'Rourke (D)	38,253	33.5
8	Charles L. Gerlach (R)	49,196	59.0
	Henry Chapin (D)	34,260	41.1
9	Paul B. Dague (R)	64,311	72.7
	Edgar Campbell (D)	24,175	27.3
10	James P. Scoblick (R)	47,704	51.0
	Frank X. Murray (D)	45,843	49.0
11	Mitchell Jenkins (R)	58,413	50.8
	Daniel J. Flood (D)	56,570	49.2
12	Ivor D. Fenton (R)	62,151	62.7
	Ralph M. Bashore (D)	36,954	37.3
13	Frederick A. Muhlenberg (R)	33,409	54.6
	Daniel K. Hoch (D)	25,073	41.0
14	Wilson D. Gillette (R)	43,142	67.4
	James S. Fields (D)	20,842	32.6
15	Robert F. Rich (R)	44,264	68.5
	Richard F. Hartzell (D)	20,376	31.5
16	Samuel K. McConnell Jr. (R)	76,314	74.4
	William L. Batt Jr. (D)	26,305	25.6
17	Richard M. Simpson (R)	37,194	66.2
	Lowell H. Alexander (D)	18,972	33.8
18	John C. Kunkel (R)	77,349	69.0
	William B. Freeland (D)	34,708	31.0
19	Leon H. Gavin (R)	41,500	68.0
	Lloyd N. Huth (D)	18,199	29.8
20	Francis E. Walter (D)	39,751	52.5
	Norman A. Peil (R)	36,008	47.5
21	Chester H. Gross (R)	45,559	52.0
	John W. Brehm (D)	42,118	48.0
22	James E. Van Zandt (R)	42,217	65.9
	John A. Shartle (D)	21,853	34.1
23	William J. Crow (R)	34,194	52.9
	John W. Rankin (D)	30,493	47.1
24	Thomas E. Morgan (D)	39,749	56.8
	Roy A. Purviance (R)	30,231	43.2
25	Louis E. Graham (R)	53,932	58.8
	Samuel G. Neff (D)	37,723	41.2
26	Harve Tibbott (R)	49,573	54.6
	Thomas A. Owens (D)	41,224	45.4
27	Augustine B. Kelley (D)	46,137	52.9
	Roy C. McKenna (R)	41,030	47.1
28	Carroll D. Kearns (R)	56,835	63.9
	Charles W. Webb (D)	32,166	36.1
29	John McDowell (R)	55,329	53.5
	Harry J. Davenport (D)	48,091	46.5
30	Robert J. Corbett (R)	57,827	60.1
	James W. Knox (D)	38,362	39.9
31	James G. Fulton (R)	70,419	63.8
	Edward A. Schultz (D)	40,010	36.2
32	Herman P. Eberharter (D)	62,963	62.8
	Ignatius J. Pillart (R)	37,247	37.2
33	Frank Buchanan (D)	51,656	57.9
	John Robert Brown Jr. (R)	37,555	42.1

RHODE ISLAND

	Candidates	Votes	%
1	Aime J. Forand (D)	74,324	56.7
	Raymond A. Mailloux (R)	55,900	42.6
2	John E. Fogarty (D)	74,349	52.6
	John J. Kelly Jr. (R)	66,987	47.4

SOUTH CAROLINA

		Votes	%
1	L. Mendel Rivers (D)	5,354	99.5
2	John J. Riley (D)	4,795	98.6
3	W. J. Bryan Dorn (D)	3,527	99.9
4	Joseph R. Bryson (D)	3,363	99.6
5	James P. Richards (D)	3,357	100.0
6	John L. McMillan (D)	5,671	96.9

SOUTH DAKOTA

		Votes	%
1	Karl E. Mundt (R)	76,720	61.5
	Merton B. Tice (D)	48,065	38.5
2	Francis H. Case (R)	28,011	73.7
	John B. Reinhard (D)	10,008	26.3

TENNESSEE

		Votes	%
1	Dayton E. Phillips (R)	24,144	100.0
2	John Jennings Jr. (R)	28,752	84.0
	James Douglas Wyrick (I)	5,485	16.0
3	Estes Kefauver (D)	26,779	90.8
	George Bagwell (I)	2,725	9.2
4	Albert A. Gore (D)	7,624	67.5
	H. E. McLean (R)	3,673	32.5
5	Joe L. Evins (D)	11,646	100.0
6	J. Percy Priest (D)	7,178	77.1
	Will T. Perry (R)	2,135	22.9
7	Wirt Courtney (D)	11,658	100.0
8	Thomas J. Murray (D)	11,891	100.0
9	Jere Cooper (D)	12,685	100.0
10	Clifford Davis (D)	37,069	100.0

TEXAS

		Votes	%
1	Wright Patman (D)	11,929	100.0
2	Jesse M. Combs (D)	19,909	96.2
3	Lindley Beckworth (D)	10,686	100.0
4	Sam Rayburn (D)	11,957	93.7
	Floyd Harry (R)	800	6.3
5	J. Frank Wilson (D)	12,267	75.8
	L. W. Stayart (R)	3,921	24.2
6	Olin E. Teague (D)	11,421	100.0
7	Tom Pickett (D)	14,810	100.0
8	Albert Thomas (D)	42,163	90.8
	R. F. Burns (R)	4,253	9.2
9	Joseph J. Mansfield (D)	16,712	100.0
10	Lyndon B. Johnson (D)	16,947	100.0
11	W. R. Poage (D)	9,178	100.0
12	Wingate H. Lucas (D)	15,266	87.7
	E. M. Hyder (R)	2,146	12.3
13	Ed Gossett (D)	17,714	100.0
14	John E. Lyle (D)	30,064	100.0
15	Milton H. West (D)	16,674	100.0
16	R. Ewing Thomason (D)	8,114	100.0
17	Omar Burleson (D)	14,874	100.0
18	Eugene Worley (D)	12,475	74.1
	F. T. O'Brien (R)	4,357	25.9
19	George H. Mahon (D)	15,791	94.6
	M. D. Temple (R)	905	5.4
20	Paul J. Kilday (D)	10,543	100.0
21	O. Clark Fisher (D)	15,943	100.0

UTAH

		Votes	%
1	Walter K. Granger (D)	44,888	50.1
	David J. Wilson (R)	44,784	49.9
2	William A. Dawson (R)	56,402	52.7
	J. Will Robinson (D)	50,598	47.3

VERMONT

	Candidates	Votes	%
AL	Charles A. Plumley (R)	46,985	64.3
	Matthew J. Caldbeck (D)	26,056	35.7

VIRGINIA

	Candidates	Votes	%
1	S. Otis Bland (D)	13,863	75.0
	Walter Johnson (R)	4,628	25.0
2	Porter Hardy Jr. (D)	19,267	65.7
	Sidney H. Kelsey (R)	10,078	34.3
3	J. Vaughan Gary (D)	21,947	73.3
	Earle Lutz (R)	7,974	26.7
4	Patrick Henry Drewry (D)	13,636	87.1
	Andrew S. Condrey (P)	2,012	12.9
5	Thomas B. Stanley (D)	17,741	73.5
	William L. Creasy (R)	6,390	26.5
6	J. Lindsay Almond Jr. (D)	20,068	64.8
	Frank R. Angell (R)	10,641	34.4
7	Burr P. Harrison (D)	19,535	62.3
	Karl Jenkins (R)	11,813	37.7
8	Howard Worth Smith (D)	21,252	62.1
	Lawrence Michael (R)	12,950	37.9
9	John W. Flannagan Jr. (D)	20,610	51.8
	S. H. Sutherland (R)	17,152	43.1
	John Albert Goodpasture Jr. (I)	2,026	5.1

Special Elections

		Votes	%
5	Thomas B. Stanley (D)	17,862	75.4
	William L. Creasy (R)	5,829	24.6

	Candidates	Votes	%
7	Burr P. Harrison (D)	19,711	62.5
	Karl Jenkins (R)	11,809	37.5

WASHINGTON

	Candidates	Votes	%
1	Homer R. Jones (R)	113,289	63.8
	Hugh De Lacy (D)	64,155	36.2
2	Henry M. Jackson (D)	54,089	53.1
	Payson Peterson (R)	47,838	46.9
3	Fred Norman (R)	47,875	53.9
	Charles R. Savage (D)	40,980	46.1
4	Hal Holmes (R)	51,476	67.6
	Earl S. Coe (D)	24,662	32.4
5	Walt Horan (R)	58,535	61.3
	John T. Little (D)	34,870	36.5
6	Thor C. Tollefson (R)	56,702	53.9
	John M. Coffee (D)	48,431	46.1

WEST VIRGINIA

		Votes	%
1	Francis J. Love (R)	45,691	53.1
	Matthew M. Neely (D)	40,370	46.9
2	Melvin C. Snyder (R)	41,224	51.4
	Jennings Randolph (D)	39,041	48.6
3	Edward G. Rohrbough (R)	42,386	51.5
	Cleveland M. Bailey (D)	39,872	48.5
4	Hubert S. Ellis (R)	54,932	52.7
	M. G. Burnside (D)	49,408	47.4

	Candidates	Votes	%
5	John Kee (D)	43,154	56.9
	Hartley Sanders (R)	32,754	43.2
6	Erland H. Hedrick (D)	57,461	53.0
	Harold H. Neff (R)	51,064	47.1

WISCONSIN

		Votes	%
1	Lawrence H. Smith (R)	58,344	56.5
	John R. Redstrom (D)	44,188	42.8
2	Robert K. Henry (R)	68,794*	62.9
	William G. Rice (D)	39,657	36.3
3	William H. Stevenson (R)	65,177	96.1
4	John C. Brophy (R)	49,144	36.5
	Edmund V. Bobrowicz (D)	44,398	33.0
	Thaddeus F. B. Wasielewski (I)	38,502	28.6
5	Charles J. Kersten (R)	76,364	54.1
	Andrew J. Biemiller (D)	59,764	42.3
6	Frank B. Keefe (R)	58,444	64.2
	Edwin W. Webster (D)	31,550	34.7
7	Reid F. Murray (R)	60,390	71.6
	Elmer E. Fraley (D)	23,481	27.8
8	John W. Byrnes (R)	67,840	64.7
	Martin J. Young (D)	37,013	35.3
9	Merlin Hull (R)	70,527	99.0
10	Alvin E. O'Konski (R)	40,263	53.0
	Henry J. Berquist (D)	32,238	42.4

WYOMING

		Votes	%
AL	Frank A. Barrett (R)	44,512	56.0
	John J. McIntyre (D)	34,946	44.0

1947 House Elections

NEW YORK

Special Election

		Votes	%
14	Abraham J. Multer (D, L)	47,849	58.2
	Victor J. Rabinowitz (AM LAB)	20,800	25.3
	Jacob P. Fefkowitz (R)	13,597	16.5

WISCONSIN

Special Election

		Votes	%
2	Glenn R. Davis (R)	24,023	50.6
	Thompson (D)	23,181	48.8

1948 House Elections

ALABAMA

	Candidates	Votes	%
1	Frank W. Boykin (D)	19,778	100.0
2	George M. Grant (D)	21,271	100.0
3	George W. Andrews (D)	16,279	100.0
4	Sam Hobbs (D)	17,282	85.0
	B. Hogan Stewart (R)	3,054	15.0
5	Albert Rains (D)	20,548	100.0
6	Edward deGraffenried (D)	13,968	82.4
	W. P. Ivey (R)	2,994	17.7
7	Carl A. Elliott (D)	21,552	100.0
8	Robert E. Jones Jr. (D)	19,060	88.4
	Harry J. Frahn (R)	2,510	11.6
9	Laurie C. Battle (D)	33,781	87.1
	Hiram Dodd (R)	5,006	12.9

ARIZONA

1	John R. Murdock (D)	42,565	58.4
	John H. Udall (R)	29,864	41.0
2	Harold A. Patten (D)	54,066	62.8
	Albert R. Buehman (R)	30,140	35.0

ARKANSAS

1	Ezekiel C. Gathings (D)	34,676	100.0
2	Wilbur D. Mills (D)	29,922	100.0
3	James W. Trimble (D)	27,278	68.6
	Dalton Dotson (R)	12,462	31.4
4	Boyd Tackett (D)	29,338	87.8
	C. R. Starbird (R)	4,094	12.3
5	Brooks Hays (D)	36,440	87.0
	Thad Tisdale (R)	5,471	13.1
6	William F. Norrell (D)	40,291	100.0
7	Oren Harris (D)	32,982	100.0

CALIFORNIA

1	Hubert B. Scudder (R)	82,947	54.5
	Sterling J. Norgard (D-IP)	68,951	45.3
2	Clair Engle (D-R)	78,555	100.0
3	Leroy Johnson (R-D)	166,571	84.4
	James B. Willard (I PROG)	30,878	15.6
4	Franck R. Havenner (D)	73,704	51.0
	William S. Mailliard (R)	68,875	47.7
5	Richard J. Welch (R-D)	116,347	100.0
6	George P. Miller (D-R)	194,985	99.9
7	John J. Allen Jr. (R)	78,534	51.4
	Buel G. Gallagher (D-IP)	74,318	48.6
8	Jack Z. Anderson (R-D)	161,743	79.9
	Paul Taylor (I PROG)	40,670	20.1
9	Cecil F. White (D)	72,826	51.3
	Bertrand W. Gearhart (R)	66,563	46.9
10	Thomas H. Werdel (R-D)	67,448	71.3
	Sam James Miller (I PROG)	27,168	28.7
11	Ernest K. Bramblett (R-D)	87,143	80.7
	Cole Weston (I PROG)	14,582	13.5
	George E. Outland	6,157	5.7
12	Richard M. Nixon (R-D)	141,509	86.9
	Una W. Rice (I PROG)	19,631	12.1
13	Norris Poulson (R)	62,951	52.6
	Ned R. Healy (D-IP)	56,624	47.3
14	Helen Gahagan Douglas (D)	89,581	65.3
	W. Wallace Braden (R)	44,611	32.5
15	Gordon L. McDonough (R-D)	131,933	83.0
	Maynard J. Omerberg (I PROG)	27,007	17.0
16	Donald L. Jackson (R)	121,198	57.0
	Ellis E. Patterson (D-IP)	91,268	42.9
17	Cecil R. King (D-R)	194,782	99.9
18	Clyde Doyle (D)	105,687	51.1
	Willis W. Bradley (R)	92,721	44.9
19	Chet Holifield (D)	72,900	69.7
	Joseph Francis Quigley (R)	28,698	27.5

	Candidates	Votes	%
20	Carl Hinshaw (R-D)	204,710	81.5
	William B. Esterman (I PROG)	46,232	18.4
21	Harry R. Sheppard (D)	61,383	55.2
	Lowell E. Lathrop (R)	47,411	42.6
22	John Phillips (R-D)	115,697	99.9
23	Clinton D. McKinnon (D)	112,534	55.8
	Charles K. Fletcher (R)	87,138	43.2

COLORADO

1	John A. Carroll (D)	106,096	64.8
	Christopher F. Cusack (R)	57,541	35.2
2	William S. Hill (R)	71,868	51.9
	George L. Bickel (D)	66,579	48.1
3	John H. Marsalis (D)	65,114	50.7
	J. Edgar Chenoweth (R)	63,312	49.3
4	Wayne N. Aspinall (D)	34,695	51.9
	Robert F. Rockwell (R)	32,206	48.1

CONNECTICUT

1	Abraham A. Ribicoff (D)	127,802	54.7
	William J. Miller (R)	103,294	44.2
2	Chase Going Woodhouse (D)	69,339	51.7
	Horace Seely-Brown Jr. (R)	64,916	48.4
3	John A. McGuire (D)	84,449	49.7
	Ellsworth B. Foote (R)	83,310	49.0
4	John Davis Lodge (R)	117,727	55.2
	William Gaston (D)	92,618	43.4
5	James T. Patterson (R)	62,804	51.1
	Vincent P. Kiernan (D)	58,300	47.4
AL	Antoni N. Sadlak (R)	433,311	49.3
	Fred Trotta (D)	429,348	48.8

DELAWARE

AL	J. Caleb Boggs (R)	71,127	50.6
	J. Carl McGuigan (D)	68,909	49.0

FLORIDA

1	J. Hardin Peterson (D)	66,348	100.0
2	Charles E. Bennett (D)	55,715	91.1
	Camille Geneau (R)	5,413	8.9
3	Robert L. F. Sikes (D)	30,730	100.0
4	George A. Smathers (D)	63,665	81.0
	J. L. Wambaugh (R)	14,912	19.0
5	A. S. Herlong Jr. (D)	46,939	70.7
	M. J. Moss Jr. (R)	19,501	29.4
6	Dwight L. Rogers (D)	31,933	66.7
	Rolf Kaltenborn (R)	15,977	33.4

GEORGIA

1	Prince H. Preston (D)	42,677	100.0
2	E. E. Cox (D)	26,815	100.0
3	Stephen Pace (D)	32,098	100.0
4	A. Sidney Camp (D)	33,522	100.0
5	James C. Davis (D)	54,637	99.6
6	Carl Vinson (D)	29,446	100.0
7	Henderson Lanham (D)	45,195	100.0
8	W. M. Wheeler (D)	35,608	100.0
9	John S. Wood (D)	29,699	100.0
10	Paul Brown (D)	35,479	100.0

IDAHO

1	Compton I. White (D)	46,846	51.8
	Abe McGregor Goff (R)	41,404	45.7
2	John C. Sanborn (R)	61,690	50.7
	Asael Lyman (D)	59,006	48.5

ILLINOIS

	Candidates	Votes	%
1	William L. Dawson (D)	98,690	67.0
	William E. King (R)	43,034	29.2
2	Barratt O'Hara (D)	91,648	50.5
	Richard B. Vail (R)	85,119	46.9
3	Neil J. Linehan (D)	91,204	52.9
	Fred E. Busbey (R)	81,175	47.1
4	James V. Buckley (D)	89,557	52.1
	Leslie E. Salter (R)	82,310	47.9
5	Martin Gorski (D)	114,660	72.5
	John L. Waner (R)	43,610	27.6
6	Thomas J. O'Brien (D)	127,918	68.4
	John M. Coan (R)	53,548	28.6
7	Adolph J. Sabath (D)	133,199	73.7
	Francis C. Sperry (R)	47,602	26.3
8	Thomas S. Gordon (D)	101,098	65.1
	Herbert F. Geisler (R)	54,316	35.0
9	Sidney R. Yates (D)	91,271	54.5
	Robert J. Twyman (R)	73,301	43.8
10	Richard W. Hoffman (R)	109,031	58.1
	Marvin J. Peters (D)	78,533	41.9
11	Chester A. Chesney (D)	80,750	50.8
	James C. Moreland (R)	78,269	49.2
12	Edgar A. Jonas (R)	98,956	51.4
	Blair L. Varnes (D)	88,795	46.1
13	Ralph E. Church (R)	123,978	68.0
	Willard C. Walters (D)	58,340	32.0
14	Chauncey W. Reed (R)	94,962	68.3
	Richard Plum (D)	44,050	31.7
15	Noah M. Mason (R)	74,213	56.4
	G. M. Wells (D)	57,296	43.6
16	Leo E. Allen (R)	76,840	58.5
	Albert H. Manus Jr. (D)	54,481	41.5
17	Leslie C. Arends (R)	71,220	62.8
	Carl Vrooman (D)	42,226	37.2
18	Harold H. Velde (R)	61,652	52.1
	Dale E. Sutton (D)	56,688	47.9
19	Robert B. Chiperfield (R)	69,733	54.0
	Fred J. Brown (D)	59,397	46.0
20	Sid Simpson (R)	59,067	53.1
	Henry D. Sullivan (D)	52,235	46.9
21	Peter F. Mack Jr. (D)	69,619	53.1
	Joseph L. Moore (R)	61,452	46.9
22	Rolla C. McMillen (R)	64,625	53.2
	Olive Remington Goldman (D)	56,893	46.8
23	Edward H. Jenison (R)	57,800	51.8
	Wayne R. Cook (D)	53,885	48.3
24	Charles W. Vursell (R)	57,732	50.6
	John David Upchurch (D)	56,262	49.4
25	Melvin Price (D)	101,927	69.5
	Russell H. Classen (R)	44,728	30.5
26	C. W. Bishop (R)	54,993	51.9
	Kent E. Keller (D)	51,028	48.1

INDIANA

1	Ray J. Madden (D)	78,898	60.7
	Theodore L. Sendak (R)	50,194	38.6
2	Charles A. Halleck (R)	71,907	55.2
	Theodore J. Smith (D)	57,245	44.0
3	Thurman C. Crook (D)	86,382	51.9
	Robert A. Grant (R)	78,935	47.5
4	Edward H. Kruse Jr. (D)	66,689	50.8
	George W. Gillie (R)	63,403	48.3
5	John R. Walsh (D)	91,861	51.9
	Forest A. Harness (R)	82,730	46.8
6	Cecil M. Harden (R)	66,414	49.9
	Jack J. O'Grady (D)	65,931	49.5
7	James E. Noland (D)	74,396	53.7
	Gerald W. Landis (R)	62,855	45.4
8	Winfield K. Denton (D)	89,990	55.4
	Edward A. Mitchell (R)	71,634	44.1
9	Earl Wilson (R)	59,787	51.6
	Christopher D. Moritz (D)	55,333	47.7

INDIANA

	Candidates	Votes	%
10	Ralph Harvey (R)	76,036	52.5
	Robert C. Oliver (D)	67,081	46.3
11	Andrew Jacobs Sr. (D)	103,046	50.6
	George L. Denny (R)	98,451	48.4

IOWA

	Candidates	Votes	%
1	Thomas E. Martin (R)	70,959	53.6
	James D. France (D)	60,860	45.9
2	Henry O. Talle (R)	82,139	53.6
	T. W. Mullaney (D)	70,272	45.9
3	H. R. Gross (R)	78,838	58.3
	Dan J. P. Ryan (D)	56,002	41.4
4	Karl LeCompte (R)	53,384	51.5
	Steven V. Carter (D)	49,894	48.2
5	Paul Cunningham (R)	60,103	50.8
	Vincent L. Browner (D)	57,370	48.5
6	James I. Dolliver (R)	55,641	55.8
	James E. Irwin (D)	43,997	44.2
7	Ben F. Jensen (R)	59,173	56.9
	W. A. Byers (D)	44,857	43.1
8	Charles B. Hoeven (R)	56,970	55.2
	L. J. McGivern (D)	45,796	44.4

KANSAS

	Candidates	Votes	%
1	Albert M. Cole (R)	68,395	60.5
	James L. Quinn (D)	44,711	39.5
2	Errett P. Scrivner (R)	68,324	51.9
	Philip A. Dergance (D)	63,431	48.1
3	Herbert A. Meyer (R)	46,935	55.0
	Marcus C. Black (D)	38,391	45.0
4	Edward H. Rees (R)	88,605	55.6
	William J. Kropp (D)	70,778	44.4
5	Clifford R. Hope (R)	77,160	65.0
	Henry D. Parkinson (D)	41,614	35.0
6	Wint Smith (R)	55,013	57.6
	Leslie E. Davis (D)	40,553	42.4

KENTUCKY

	Candidates	Votes	%
1	Noble J. Gregory (D)	50,720	100.0
2	John Whitaker (D)	54,586	63.4
	Mallam Lake (R)	31,527	36.6
3	Thruston B. Morton (R)	74,168	53.0
	Ralph H. Logan (D)	64,877	46.3
4	Frank L. Chelf (D)	45,538	59.5
	Stanley Jaggers (R)	31,062	40.6
5	Brent Spence (D)	47,518	66.2
	George T. Smith (R)	24,240	33.8
6	Thomas R. Underwood (D)	60,659	60.7
	John N. Menefee (R)	39,251	39.3
7	Carl D. Perkins (D)	39,788	60.5
	W. Howes Meade (R)	26,007	39.5
8	Joe B. Bates (D)	52,328	58.6
	Hubert Counts (R)	34,127	38.2
9	James S. Golden (R)	60,309	100.0

LOUISIANA

	Candidates	Votes	%
1	F. Edward Hebert (D)	36,748	100.0
2	Hale Boggs (D)	61,316	100.0
3	Edwin E. Willis (D)	26,587	66.4
	J. Paulin Duhe (R)	13,437	33.6
4	Overton Brooks (D)	32,045	100.0
5	Otto E. Passman (D)	34,362	100.0
6	James H. Morrison (D)	47,515	100.0
7	Henry D. Larcade Jr. (D)	36,053	100.0
8	A. Leonard Allen (D)	33,613	100.0

MAINE

	Candidates	Votes	%
1	Robert Hale (R)	52,536	62.5
	James A. McVicar (D)	31,528	37.5
2	Charles P. Nelson (R)	50,552	67.2
	Benjamin J. Arena (D)	24,698	32.8

	Candidates	Votes	%
3	Frank Fellows (R)	38,692	70.9
	F. Davis Clark (D)	15,888	29.1

MARYLAND

	Candidates	Votes	%
1	Edward T. Miller (R)	29,700	52.4
	S. Scott Beck Jr. (D)	27,024	47.6
2	William P. Bolton (D)	99,157	55.2
	A. Earl Shipley (R)	76,235	42.5
3	Edward A. Garmatz (D)	32,138	68.8
	John A. Janetzke Jr. (R)	13,131	28.1
4	George H. Fallon (D)	38,486	58.2
	James W. Miller (R)	21,084	31.9
	John E. T. Camper (PROG)	6,552	9.9
5	Lansdale G. Sasscer (D)	45,902	59.7
	C. Maurice Weidemeyer (R)	30,997	40.3
6	J. Glenn Beall (R)	59,856	55.3
	F. Byrne Austin (D)	48,304	44.7

MASSACHUSETTS

	Candidates	Votes	%
1	John W. Heselton (R)	75,582	57.2
	Patrick J. O'Malley (D)	56,604	42.8
2	Foster Furcolo (D)	81,775	54.9
	Charles R. Clason (R)	67,267	45.1
3	Philip J. Philbin (D)	104,601	73.9
	Carroll H. Balcom (R)	36,855	26.1
4	Harold D. Donohue (D)	89,064	59.2
	John J. Maginnis (R)	61,448	40.8
5	Edith Nourse Rogers (R)	139,288	100.0
6	George J. Bates (R)	108,179	100.0
7	Thomas J. Lane (D)	100,333	79.2
	A. Prescott Barker (R)	26,339	20.8
8	Angier L. Goodwin (R)	75,844	51.0
	Anthony M. Roche (D)	72,767	49.0
9	Donald W. Nicholson (R)	82,750	56.7
	Jacinto F. Diniz (D)	63,275	43.3
10	Christian A. Herter (R)	118,741	69.5
	Walter A. O'Brien Jr. (D)	52,022	30.5
11	John F. Kennedy (D)	106,366	100.0
12	John W. McCormack (D)	125,015	100.0
13	Richard B. Wigglesworth (R)	89,913	56.6
	David J. Concannon (D)	69,050	43.4
14	Joseph W. Martin Jr. (R)	87,973	61.4
	Joseph M. Mendonca (D)	55,369	38.6

MICHIGAN

	Candidates	Votes	%
1	George G. Sadowski (D)	101,954	83.5
	Rudolph G. Tenerowicz (R)	19,609	16.1
2	Earl C. Michener (R)	65,006	55.8
	Preston W. Slosson (D)	50,148	43.0
3	Paul W. Shafer (R)	64,637	59.4
	Leeman J. McCarty (D)	42,146	38.7
4	Clare E. Hoffman (R)	61,059	64.9
	Tom Surprise (D)	31,429	33.4
5	Gerald R. Ford Jr. (R)	74,191	60.5
	Fred J. Barr Jr. (D)	46,972	38.3
6	William W. Blackney (R)	73,465	49.8
	George D. Stevens (D)	72,681	49.3
7	Jesse P. Wolcott (R)	68,903	59.0
	Harvey C. Whetzel (D)	47,040	40.3
8	Fred L. Crawford (R)	61,394	61.3
	Louis C. Schwinger (D)	37,125	37.1
9	Albert J. Engel (R)	51,771	58.5
	John George Hosko (D)	35,805	40.5
10	Roy O. Woodruff (R)	49,206	63.3
	Edward J. Daugherty (D)	27,742	35.7
11	Charles E. Potter (R)	48,633	63.6
	Violet L. Patterson (D)	27,265	35.6
12	John B. Bennett (R)	42,955	56.6
	Gene A. Saari (D)	32,485	42.8
13	George D. O'Brien (D)	76,947	62.5
	Howard A. Coffin (R)	45,761	37.1
14	Louis C. Rabaut (D)	99,227	57.0
	Harold F. Youngblood (R)	74,474	42.7
15	John D. Dingell (D)	92,579	65.0
	Charles G. Burns (R)	49,286	34.6

	Candidates	Votes	%
16	John Lesinski (D)	97,826	62.5
	Kirby L. Wilson Jr. (R)	57,730	36.9
17	George A. Dondero (R)	116,427	52.7
	John J. Brown (D)	103,390	46.8

MINNESOTA

	Candidates	Votes	%
1	August H. Andresen (R)	80,345	61.4
	Karl F. Rolvaag (DFL)	50,533	38.6
2	Joseph P. O'Hara (R)	82,886	63.9
	Milton F. Maxwell (DFL)	46,894	36.1
3	Roy W. Wier (DFL)	87,171	54.6
	George MacKinnon (R)	72,402	45.4
4	Eugene J. McCarthy (DFL)	78,476	59.4
	Edward J. Devitt (R)	53,574	40.6
5	Walter H. Judd (R)	76,313	54.0
	Marcella F. Killen (DFL)	65,113	46.0
6	Fred Marshall (DFL)	66,601	51.7
	Harold Knutson (R)	62,194	48.3
7	H. Carl Andersen (R)	63,879	52.5
	James M. Youngdale (DFL)	57,863	47.5
8	John A. Blatnik (DFL)	88,501	66.6
	William A. Berlin (R)	44,306	33.4
9	Harold C. Hagen (R)	57,189	54.6
	Oscar A. Johnson (DFL)	47,476	45.4

MISSISSIPPI

	Candidates	Votes	%
1	John E. Rankin (D)	16,800	100.0
2	Jamie L. Whitten (D)	13,771	100.0
3	William M. Whittington (D)	17,369	100.0
4	Thomas G. Abernethy (D)	15,290	98.4
5	W. Arthur Winstead (D)	22,641	100.0
6	William M. Colmer (D)	29,751	100.0
7	John Bell Williams (D)	36,663	100.0

MISSOURI

	Candidates	Votes	%
1	Clare Magee (D)	56,226	57.6
	Wat Arnold (R)	41,365	42.4
2	Morgan M. Moulder (D)	66,062	56.7
	Max Schwabe (R)	50,372	43.2
3	Philip J. Welch (D)	69,599	57.1
	William C. Cole (R)	52,290	42.9
4	Theodore Leonard Irving (D)	74,752	64.1
	Richard A. Erickson (R)	41,576	35.7
5	Richard W. Bolling (D)	59,961	55.9
	Albert L. Reeves Jr. (R)	47,371	44.1
6	George H. Christopher (D)	63,390	51.4
	Marion T. Bennett (R)	59,959	48.6
7	Dewey Short (R)	61,242	54.0
	Thomas A. Johnson (D)	52,255	46.0
8	Albert S. J. Carnahan (D)	60,081	57.2
	Parke M. Banta (R)	44,887	42.8
9	Clarence Cannon (D)	56,669	61.7
	Robert V. Niedner (R)	35,232	38.3
10	Paul C. Jones (D)	67,564	71.6
	W. K. Dillon (R)	26,760	28.4
11	John B. Sullivan (D)	78,162	64.7
	Claude I. Bakewell (R)	40,719	33.7
12	Raymond W. Karst (D)	132,920	55.0
	Walter C. Ploeser (R)	107,861	44.6
13	Frank M. Karsten (D)	77,245	70.6
	Charles P. McBride (R)	32,217	29.4

MONTANA

	Candidates	Votes	%
1	Mike Mansfield (D)	64,276	67.9
	Albert H. Angstman (R)	29,937	31.6
2	Wesley A. D'Ewart (R)	61,124	51.0
	Willard E. Fraser (D)	58,711	49.0

NEBRASKA

	Candidates	Votes	%
1	Carl T. Curtis (R)	76,359	57.2
	Frank B. Morrison (D)	57,031	42.8

NEBRASKA

Candidates	Votes	%
2 Eugene D. O'Sullivan (D)	58,443	51.4
Howard Buffett (R)	55,199	48.6
3 Karl Stefan (R)	71,513	64.8
Duane K. Peterson (D)	38,846	35.2
4 Arthur L. Miller (R)	65,549	63.6
C. Edgar Leafdale (D)	37,511	36.4

NEVADA

	Votes	%
AL Walter S. Baring (D)	29,733	50.7
Charles H. Russell (R)	28,972	49.4

NEW HAMPSHIRE

	Votes	%
1 Chester E. Merrow (R)	64,794	55.5
Peter R. Poirier (D)	51,262	43.9
2 Norris Cotton (R)	59,505	57.4
Richard W. Leonard (D)	43,289	41.8

NEW JERSEY

	Votes	%
1 Charles A. Wolverton (R)	89,211	53.0
John W. Donges (D)	77,012	45.8
2 T. Millet Hand (R)	62,804	61.7
William E. Stringer (D)	38,194	37.5
3 James C. Auchincloss (R)	87,538	58.5
Charles F. Sullivan (D)	59,810	40.0
4 Charles R. Howell (D)	77,018	61.5
Albert C. Jones (R)	48,204	38.5
5 Charles A. Eaton (R)	92,286	57.4
George C. Miller (D)	66,387	41.3
6 Clifford P. Case (R)	83,285	55.3
H. Frank Pettit (D)	61,465	40.8
7 J. Parnell Thomas (R)	72,873	56.2
John J. Carlin (D)	56,095	43.2
8 Gordon Canfield (R)	59,191	47.5
Charles S. Joelson (D)	59,043	47.4
9 Harry L. Towe (R)	90,153	62.3
James S. Brown (D)	54,682	37.8
10 Peter W. Rodino Jr. (D)	58,668	50.7
Anthony Guiliano (R)	52,898	45.7
11 Hugh J. Addonizio (D)	52,644	47.7
Frank L. Sundstrom (R)	50,920	46.2
12 Robert W. Kean (R)	63,232	48.6
Harry Dudkin (D)	58,495	44.9
13 Mary T. Norton (D)	84,487	68.1
Leon Banach (R)	39,661	32.0
14 Edward J. Hart (D)	76,881	62.8
Michael Bongiovanni (R)	45,564	37.2

NEW MEXICO

	Votes	%
AL John E. Miles (D)	108,529✔	
Antonio M. Fernandez (D)	105,300✔	
Ben F. Meyer (R)	76,695	
Herman G. Baca (R)	73,661	
Clinton E. Jencks (PROG)	805	

NEW YORK

	Votes	%
1 W. Kingsland Macy (R)	101,924	66.0
Harold W. Worzel (D)	48,816	31.6
2 Leonard W. Hall (R)	144,052	68.1
Richard T. Mayes (D, L)	62,142	29.4
3 Henry J. Latham (R)	104,476	56.5
George J. Gross (D)	65,247	35.3
4 L. Gary Clemente (D)	62,190	46.9
Gregory McMahon (R)	58,192	43.8
Thomas J. McCabe (AM LAB)	7,681	5.8
5 T. Vincent Quinn (D, L)	83,213	49.8
Robert Tripp Ross (R)	72,012	43.1
Morris Pottish (AM LAB)	11,994	7.2
6 James J. Delaney (D, L)	76,828	54.2
Robert Nodar Jr. (R)	55,844	39.4
Irma Lindheim (AM LAB)	9,092	6.4
7 John J. Delaney (D, AM LAB)	65,162*	60.0

Candidates	Votes	%
Francis E. Dorn (R, L)	43,483	40.0
8 Joseph L. Pfeifer (D, AM LAB)	61,037	67.7
Benjamin F. Westervelt Jr (R)	25,773	28.6
9 Eugene J. Keogh (D, L)	59,711	56.2
Philip Hodes (R)	26,700	25.1
Murray Rosof (AM LAB)	19,803	18.6
10 Andrew L. Somers (D, L)	69,502	56.1
Arthur S. Hirsch (R)	32,290	26.1
Ada B. Jackson (AM LAB)	22,067	17.8
11 James J. Heffernan (D, L)	74,974	54.9
Alfred C. McKenzie (R)	41,289	30.2
Frank Serri (AM LAB)	20,340	14.9
12 John J. Rooney (D, L)	55,021	60.4
John J. Miller (R)	29,061	31.9
Vincent J. Longhi (AM LAB)	6,968	7.7
13 Donald L. O'Toole (D, L)	66,111	52.8
Charles A. Fisher (R)	44,718	35.7
James Griesi (AM LAB)	14,440	11.5
14 Abraham J. Multer (D, R)	103,676	77.8
Lee Pressman (AM LAB)	29,502	22.2
15 Emanuel Celler (D, AM LAB)	94,828	81.4
Henry D. Dorfman (R)	21,703	18.6
16 James J. Murphy (D, L)	51,185	49.3
Frank A. Pavis (R)	45,623	44.0
Frank Cremonesi (AM LAB)	6,991	6.7
17 Frederic R. Coudert Jr. (R)	74,581	53.2
Arthur T. Sawyer (D, L)	52,101	37.2
Alvin Udell (AM LAB)	13,401	9.6
18 Vito Marcantonio (AM LAB)	36,278	36.9
John P. Morrissey (D)	31,211	31.7
John Ellis (R, L)	30,899	31.4
19 Arthur G. Klein (D, AM LAB)	77,426	74.4
Herbert Lasky (R)	20,697	19.9
Stephen C. Vladeck (L)	5,886	5.7
20 Sol Bloom (D, L)	73,866	59.4
Jules J. Justin (R)	34,819	28.0
Eugene P. Connolly (AM LAB)	15,727	12.6
21 Jacob K. Javits (R, L)	66,527	50.7
Paul O'Dwyer (D, AM LAB)	64,654	49.3
22 Adam Clayton Powell Jr. (D, AM LAB)	63,523	76.4
Harold C. Burton (R)	14,012	16.9
Edna D. Moseley (L)	5,583	6.7
23 Walter A. Lynch (D, R)	121,523	83.0
Leon Straus (AM LAB)	24,903	17.0
24 Isidore Dollinger (D, R)	74,971	63.1
Leo Isacson (AM LAB)	43,933	37.0
25 Charles A. Buckley (D, R)	138,706	82.2
Albert E. Kahn (AM LAB)	30,112	17.8
26 Christopher C. McGrath (D, L)	91,456	54.8
David M. Potts (R)	57,061	34.2
Nicholas Carnes (AM LAB)	18,379	11.0
27 Ralph W. Gwinn (R)	81,144	52.1
Richard W. McSpedon (D, L)	67,541	43.4
28 Ralph A. Gamble (R)	88,822	62.7
Charles J. Nager (D, L)	46,335	32.7
29 Katharine St.George (R)	79,229	60.1
William G. Pendergast (D, L)	48,063	36.5
30 Jay LeFevre (R)	91,649	64.8
Robert R. Decormier (D, AM LAB)	49,691	35.2
31 Bernard W. Kearney (R)	77,725	55.3
William M. Murphy (D, L)	58,215	41.4
32 William T. Byrne (D, L)	88,476	55.6
Lawrence J. Collins (R)	65,341	41.1
33 Dean P. Taylor (R)	98,618	63.7
Joseph T. Hammer (D, L)	52,059	33.6
34 Clarence E. Kilburn (R)	70,715	60.7
Francis K. Purcell (D)	43,777	37.6
35 John C. Davies (D, L)	62,855	48.9
Hadwen C. Fuller (R)	62,717	48.8
36 R. Walter Riehlman (R)	78,409	50.5
Richard T. Mosher (D, L)	71,847	46.3

Candidates	Votes	%
37 Edwin Arthur Hall (R)	65,848	63.4
Myron C. Sloat (D)	35,503	34.2
38 John Taber (R)	66,695	58.0
Francis J. Souhan (D)	48,222	42.0
39 W. Sterling Cole (R)	70,659	64.3
Donald J. O'Connor (D, L)	37,272	33.9
40 Kenneth B. Keating (R)	90,305	51.4
George F. Rogers (D, AM LAB)	85,505	48.6
41 James W. Wadsworth Jr. (R)	67,882	59.1
Bernard E. Hart (D)	45,155	39.3
42 William L. Pfeiffer (R)	75,842	51.1
Mary Louise Nice (D, L)	69,290	46.6
43 Anthony F. Tauriello (D, L)	72,388	50.8
Edward J. Elsaesser (R)	66,729	46.9
44 Chester C. Gorski (D, L)	79,795	51.8
John C. Butler (R)	71,275	46.2
45 Daniel A. Reed (R)	58,340	60.1
Hubert D. Bliss (D)	35,406	36.5

Special Election

	Votes	%
24 Leo Isacson (AM LAB)	22,697	55.9
Karl Propper (D)	12,598	31.0
Dean Alfange (L)	3,843	9.5

NORTH CAROLINA

	Votes	%
1 Herbert C. Bonner (D)	31,850	92.7
Zeno O. Ratcliff (R)	2,507	7.3
2 John H. Kerr (D)	36,227	96.0
3 Graham A. Barden (D)	34,997	78.8
Perry G. Crumpler (R)	9,407	21.2
4 Harold D. Cooley (D)	57,658	78.1
Joel A. Johnson (R)	15,866	21.5
5 Richard Thurmond Chatham (D)	47,575	72.7
John Tucker Day (R)	17,041	26.1
6 Carl T. Durham (D)	50,659	72.1
Ralph O. Smith (R)	17,906	25.5
7 F. Ertel Carlyle (D)	43,292	84.3
J. O. West (R)	7,839	15.3
8 Charles B. Deane (D)	46,941	62.7
Lafayette Williams (R)	27,924	37.3
9 Robert L. Doughton (D)	51,586	59.6
Clyde R. Greene (R)	35,008	40.4
10 Hamilton C. Jones (D)	48,043	59.6
Roy A. Harmon (R)	32,321	40.1
11 Alfred L. Bulwinkle (D)	40,009	64.9
Calvin R. Edney (R)	21,614	35.1
12 Monroe M. Redden (D)	52,036	63.1
W. W. Candler (R)	30,456	36.9

NORTH DAKOTA

	Votes	%
AL William Lemke (R)	132,343✔	
Usher L. Burdick (R)	128,454✔	
Alfred Dale (D)	56,702	
John M. Weiler	1,758	

OHIO

	Votes	%
1 Charles H. Elston (R)	73,952	51.7
Morse Johnson (D)	69,240	48.4
2 Earl T. Wagner (D)	75,062	52.9
William E. Hess (R)	66,968	47.2
3 Edward Breen (D)	110,204	58.2
Raymond H. Burke (R)	79,162	41.8
4 William M. McCulloch (R)	57,321	55.7
Earl Ludwig (D)	45,534	44.3
5 Cliff Clevenger (R)	34,950	52.1
Dan Batt (D)	32,076	47.9
6 James G. Polk (D)	46,944	53.1
Edward O. McCowen (R)	41,492	46.9
7 Clarence J. Brown (R)	71,737	100.0
8 Frederick C. Smith (R)	43,929	54.5
Andrew T. Durbin (D)	36,685	45.5

OHIO

	Candidates	Votes	%
9	Thomas H. Burke (D)	85,409	53.8
	Homer A. Ramey (R)	73,394	46.2
10	Thomas A. Jenkins (R)	38,330	57.9
	Delmar A. Canaday (D)	27,913	42.1
11	Walter E. Brehm (R)	33,796	50.9
	Joseph C. Allen (D)	32,667	49.2
12	John M. Vorys (R)	95,575	52.1
	Robert M. Draper (D)	87,770	47.9
13	Alvin F. Weichel (R)	55,408	59.2
	Dwight A. Blackmore (D)	38,264	40.9
14	Walter B. Huber (D)	125,346	57.2
	Ed Rowe (R)	92,535	42.2
15	Robert T. Secrest (D)	45,575	56.4
	P. W. Griffiths (R)	35,294	43.6
16	John McSweeney (D)	79,859	52.6
	Henderson H. Carson (R)	71,871	47.4
17	J. Harry McGregor (R)	60,234	52.9
	Robert W. Levering (D)	53,651	47.1
18	Wayne L. Hays (D)	65,475	54.1
	Earl R. Lewis (R)	55,455	45.9
19	Michael J. Kirwan (D)	134,448	68.1
	William Bacon (R)	63,079	31.9
20	Michael A. Feighan (D)	64,241	100.0
21	Robert Crosser (D)	72,417	76.0
	Harry W. Mitchell (R)	22,932	24.1
22	Frances P. Bolton (R)	170,085	54.7
	Jack G. Day (D)	141,018	45.3
AL	Stephen M. Young (D)	1,455,972	52.0
	George H. Bender (R)	1,342,409	48.0

OKLAHOMA

	Candidates	Votes	%
1	William Franklin Gilmer (D)	77,949	53.3
	George B. Schwabe (R)	68,423	46.8
2	William G. Stigler (D)	43,801	70.6
	George T. Balch (R)	18,236	29.4
3	Carl Albert (D)	57,300	83.9
	Russell Overstreet (R)	11,007	16.1
4	Tom Steed (D)	53,419	72.1
	Clyde T. Patrick (R)	20,716	27.9
5	A. S. Mike Monroney (D)	95,248	67.4
	Carmon C. Harris (R)	45,985	32.6
6	Toby Morris (D)	47,857	73.7
	George E. Young (R)	17,100	26.3
7	Victor E. Wickersham (D)	39,380	79.4
	J. Warren White (R)	10,236	20.6
8	George H. Wilson (D)	42,417	58.0
	Martin Garber (R)	30,687	42.0

OREGON

	Candidates	Votes	%
1	Walter Norblad (R)	88,587	63.3
	Edward E. Gideon (D)	45,904	32.8
2	Lowell Stockman (R)	42,730	58.2
	C. J. Shorb (D)	30,743	41.8
3	Homer D. Angell (R)	99,464	55.5
	Roland C. Bartlett (D)	66,436	37.1
	Peggy T. Carlson (PROG)	13,171	7.4
4	Harris Ellsworth (R)	65,606	66.6
	William F. Tanton (D & PROG)	32,931	33.4

PENNSYLVANIA

	Candidates	Votes	%
1	William A. Barrett (D)	70,165	53.4
	John De Nero (R)	61,165	46.6
2	William T. Granahan (D)	82,863	54.4
	Robert N. McGarvey (R)	69,604	45.7
3	Hardie Scott (R)	76,009	52.0
	Maurice S. Osser (D)	70,075	48.0
4	Earl Chudoff (D)	70,129	55.7
	Franklin J. Maloney (R)	50,236	39.9
5	William J. Green Jr. (D)	77,221	50.7
	George W. Sarbacher Jr. (R)	75,007	49.3
6	Hugh Scott (R)	86,755	57.0
	Herbert J. McGlinchey (D)	65,535	43.0

	Candidates	Votes	%
7	Benjamin F. James (R)	91,394	61.3
	Arnold M. Snyder (D)	56,263	37.8
8	Franklin H. Lichtenwalter (R)	62,229	59.2
	Wynne James Jr. (D)	42,878	40.8
9	Paul B. Dague (R)	74,726	67.1
	W. Roger Simpson (D)	36,677	32.9
10	Harry P. O'Neill (D)	64,289	58.5
	Nelson Nichols (R)	45,587	41.5
11	Daniel J. Flood (D)	68,628	51.8
	Robert H. Stroh (R)	63,797	48.2
12	Ivor D. Fenton (R)	68,089	60.6
	John Oshinskie (D)	44,345	39.4
13	George M. Rhodes (D)	40,415	50.3
	Frederick A. Muhlenberg (R)	37,261	46.4
14	Wilson D. Gillette (R)	47,715	65.2
	David Burchell (D)	25,484	34.8
15	Robert F. Rich (R, P)	48,760	61.6
	Patrick A. McGowan (D)	30,457	38.5
16	Samuel K. McConnell Jr. (R)	84,997	66.9
	Harry Hellar Kelly (D)	42,118	33.1
17	Richard M. Simpson (R)	38,735	64.5
	Ira Garman (D)	21,339	35.5
18	John C. Kunkel (R)	81,704	63.7
	Theodore C. Frederick Jr. (D)	46,586	36.3
19	Leon H. Gavin (R)	43,520	63.7
	Francis J. Manno (D)	24,800	36.3
20	Francis E. Walter (D)	54,041	58.8
	Roy E. James (R)	37,904	41.2
21	James F. Lind (D)	54,152	53.7
	Chester H. Gross (R)	46,701	46.3
22	James E. Van Zandt (R)	46,451	60.4
	Julia Luigia Maietta (D)	30,454	39.6
23	Anthony Cavalcante (D)	42,084	54.3
	William J. Crow (R)	35,384	45.7
24	Thomas E. Morgan (D)	56,282	65.4
	Roy A. Purviance (R)	29,768	34.6
25	Louis E. Graham (R)	56,966	52.6
	Andrew G. Katcher (D)	51,391	47.4
26	Robert L. Coffey Jr. (D)	62,061	55.4
	Harve Tibbott (R)	50,005	44.6
27	Augustine B. Kelley (D)	64,943	62.2
	W. Urban Gillespie (R)	39,517	37.8
28	Carroll D. Kearns (R)	65,276	54.5
	James A. Kennedy (D)	54,402	44.5
29	Harry J. Davenport (D)	63,454	54.2
	John McDowell (R)	53,609	45.8
30	Robert J. Corbett (R)	56,932	50.3
	J. R. Montgomery (D)	56,233	49.7
31	James G. Fulton (R)	75,147	56.4
	John J. Kane Jr. (D)	58,113	43.6
32	Herman P. Eberharter (D)	80,600	72.7
	Albert J. Weilersbacher (R)	30,328	27.3
33	Frank Buchanan (D)	74,508	69.2
	Albert G. Brown (R)	33,107	30.8

RHODE ISLAND

	Candidates	Votes	%
1	Aime J. Forand (D)	95,045	62.0
	Oscar J. V. Hurteau (R)	58,209	38.0
2	John E. Fogarty (D)	98,586	59.7
	Thomas J. Paolino (R)	66,672	40.3

SOUTH CAROLINA

	Candidates	Votes	%
1	L. Mendel Rivers (D)	24,529	89.1
	W. T. Baggott (D)	2,989	10.9
2	Hugo S. Sims Jr. (D)	27,677	96.5
3	James B. Hare (D)	19,181	97.8
4	Joseph R. Bryson (D)	26,098	94.9
	James B. Gaston (R)	1,410	5.1
5	James P. Richards (D)	14,544	97.1
6	John L. McMillan (D)	21,703	97.1

SOUTH DAKOTA

	Candidates	Votes	%
1	Harold O. Lovre (R)	99,062	53.5
	Merton B. Tice (D)	85,957	46.5

	Candidates	Votes	%
2	Francis H. Case (R)	36,713	65.9
	Jessie E. Sanders (D)	18,988	34.1

TENNESSEE

	Candidates	Votes	%
1	Dayton E. Phillips (R)	54,439	84.7
	Arthur W. Bright (D)	9,806	15.3
2	John Jennings Jr. (R)	43,849	58.0
	Thomas P. Fowler (IR)	31,743	42.0
3	James B. Frazier Jr. (D)	44,683	67.3
	W. E. Michael (R)	20,740	31.3
4	Albert Gore (D)	21,445	64.3
	Tom T. Tucker Jr. (R)	11,910	35.7
5	Joe L. Evins (D)	27,777	100.0
6	J. Percy Priest (D)	28,951	81.4
	Jesse L. Perry (R)	6,056	17.0
7	James P. Sutton (D)	28,058	100.0
8	Thomas J. Murray (D)	25,170	69.2
	J. Sam Johnson Jr. (R)	11,229	30.9
9	Jere Cooper (D)	26,033	91.1
	S. Homer Tatum (R)	2,555	8.9
10	Clifford Davis (D)	49,371	93.1
	Dwight V. Kyle (R)	3,670	6.9

TEXAS

	Candidates	Votes	%
1	Wright Patman (D)	40,162	100.0
2	Jesse M. Combs (D)	55,072	93.3
	Don Parker (R)	3,978	6.7
3	Lindley Beckworth (D)	36,361	88.7
	R. E. Kennedy (R)	4,642	11.3
4	Sam Rayburn (D)	38,211	100.0
5	J. Frank Wilson (D)	66,484	98.4
6	Olin E. Teague (D)	18,731	99.8
7	Tom Pickett (D)	27,945	100.0
8	Albert Thomas (D)	100,721	85.5
	Joe Ingraham (R)	17,124	14.5
9	Clark W. Thompson (D)	55,606	100.0
10	Homer Thornberry (D)	45,007	100.0
11	W. R. Poage (D)	39,795	96.2
12	Wingate H. Lucas (D)	61,206	89.1
	Elton M. Hyder (R)	7,480	10.9
13	Ed Gossett (D)	44,274	100.0
14	John E. Lyle Jr. (D)	59,163	88.9
	J. M. Swafford (R)	7,202	10.8
15	Lloyd M. Bentsen Jr. (D)	27,402	100.0
16	Ken Regan (D)	37,173	99.5
17	Omar Burleson (D)	34,078	100.0
18	Eugene Worley (D)	48,985	88.7
	J. Evetts Haley (R)	6,266	11.3
19	George Mahon (D)	58,585	95.6
20	Paul J. Kilday (D)	43,709	75.3
	J. P. Ledvina (R)	14,376	24.8
21	O. Clark Fisher (D)	45,274	100.0

UTAH

	Candidates	Votes	%
1	Walter K. Granger (D)	66,641	59.0
	David J. Wilson (R)	46,229	41.0
2	Reva Beck Bosone (D)	92,770	57.5
	William A. Dawson (R)	68,693	42.5

VERMONT

	Candidates	Votes	%
AL	Charles A. Plumley (R)	74,076	60.7
	Robert W. Ready (D)	47,767	39.2

VIRGINIA

	Candidates	Votes	%
1	S. Otis Bland (D)	24,746	80.0
	Stanley G. Adams (R)	5,753	18.6
2	Porter Hardy Jr. (D)	28,071	61.2
	Walter E. Hoffman (R)	15,800	34.4
3	J. Vaughan Gary (D)	33,950	72.9
	Richard C. Poage (R)	11,291	24.3
4	Watkins M. Abbitt (D)	22,029	100.0

VIRGINIA

	Candidates	Votes	%
5	Thomas B. Stanley (D)	23,879	99.5
6	Clarence G. Burton (D)	29,589	64.7
	John Strickler (R)	15,854	34.7
7	Burr P. Harrison (D)	25,799	60.4
	Stephen D. Timberlake (R)	16,890	39.6
8	Howard W. Smith (D)	33,563	54.8
	Tyrrell Krum (R)	25,420	41.5
9	Thomas B. Fugate (D)	33,550	52.4
	T. Eugene Worrell (R)	30,466	47.6

Special Election

		Votes	%
6	Clarence G. Burton (D)	30,841	65.2
	John Strickler (R)	16,435	34.8

WASHINGTON

		Votes	%
1	Hugh B. Mitchell (D)	100,030	50.8
	Homer R. Jones (R)	92,215	46.8
2	Henry M. Jackson (D)	83,824	61.6
	Payson Peterson (R)	48,413	35.6
3	Russell V. Mack (R)	61,856	52.1
	Charles R. Savage (D)	56,947	47.9

	Candidates	Votes	%
4	Hal Holmes (R)	58,105	53.2
	John F. Eubank (D)	51,195	46.8
5	Walt Horan (R)	67,757	54.6
	John F. McKay (D)	56,343	45.4
6	Thor C. Tollefson (R)	72,988	55.1
	Jack E. Knudsen (D)	54,166	40.9

WEST VIRGINIA

		Votes	%
1	Robert L. Ramsay (D)	68,829	57.3
	Francis J. Love (R)	51,381	42.7
2	Harley O. Staggers (D)	61,786	54.7
	Melvin C. Snyder (R)	51,226	45.3
3	Cleveland M. Bailey (D)	68,055	57.1
	Edward G. Rohrbough (R)	51,123	42.9
4	Maurice G. Burnside (D)	72,378	53.1
	Hubert S. Ellis (R)	64,001	46.9
5	John Kee (D)	71,664	65.1
	Hartley Sanders (R)	38,446	34.9
6	Erland H. Hedrick (D)	99,842	62.5
	D. L. Salisbury (R)	59,900	37.5

WISCONSIN

	Candidates	Votes	%
1	Lawrence H. Smith (R)	67,387	51.9
	Jack Harvey (D)	61,791	47.6
2	Glenn R. Davis (R)	74,306	53.9
	Horace W. Wilkie (D)	62,953	45.6
3	Gardner R. Withrow (R)	69,727	69.2
	Frank J. Antoine (D)	30,650	30.4
4	Clement J. Zablocki (D)	89,391	55.9
	John C. Brophy (R)	63,161	39.5
5	Andrew J. Biemiller (D)	91,072	53.1
	Charles J. Kersten (R)	76,782	44.8
6	Frank B. Keefe (R)	60,675	55.5
	Kenneth Kunde (D)	47,844	43.8
7	Reid F. Murray (R)	64,531	62.5
	Ralph E. Kronenwetter (D)	37,307	36.1
8	John W. Byrnes (R)	70,905	56.7
	Martin J. Young (D)	53,287	42.6
9	Merlin Hull (R)	76,903	98.1
10	Alvin E. O'Konski (R)	52,124	54.8
	Daniel W. Hoan (D)	39,523	41.6

WYOMING

		Votes	%
AL	Frank A. Barrett (R)	50,218	51.5
	L. G. Flannery (D)	47,246	48.5

1949 House Elections

NEW YORK

Special Election

	Candidates	Votes	%
7	Louis B. Heller (D, L)	22,939	54.8
	Francis E. Dorn (R)	16,179	38.7
	Minneola Ingersoll (AM LAB)	2,712	6.5
10	Edna F. Kelly (D)	48,945	55.1
	Jules Cohen (L)	24,419	27.5
	George H. Fankuchen (R)	15,514	17.5
20	Franklin D. Roosevelt Jr (L, FF)	40,822	50.7
	Benjamin Shalleck (D)	24,352	30.2
	William H. McIntyre (R)	10,026	12.5
	Annette T. Rubinstein (AM LAB)	5,348	6.6

House Candidates Index

For an index of all House candidates listed in this section (pages 701 to 1061), see pages 1180-1273. Instructions for use of the House Candidates Index appear on page 1180.

1950 House Elections

ALABAMA

	Candidates	Votes	%
1	Frank W. Boykin (D)	14,206	100.0
2	George M. Grant (D)	17,441	100.0
3	George W. Andrews (D)	10,914	100.0
4	Kenneth A. Roberts (D)	14,608	93.7
	J. P. Carter (R)	980	6.3
5	Albert Rains (D)	17,269	100.0
6	Edward deGraffenried (D)	11,709	100.0
7	Carl A. Elliott (D)	20,580	100.0
8	Robert E. Jones Jr. (D)	13,742	100.0
9	Laurie C. Battle (D)	30,743	100.0

ARIZONA

		Votes	%
1	John R. Murdock (D)	51,526	60.6
	Carl W. Divelbiss (R)	33,528	39.4
2	Harold A. Patten (D)	63,991	69.1
	John H. Curnutte (R)	28,622	30.9

ARKANSAS

		Votes	%
1	Ezekiel C. Gathings (D)	47,238	100.0
2	Wilbur D. Mills (D)	31,048	100.0
3	James W. Trimble (D)	34,434	100.0
4	Boyd Tackett (D)	43,156	100.0
5	Brooks Hays (D)	54,338	100.0
6	William F. Norrell (D)	46,467	100.0
7	Oren Harris (D)	39,121	100.0

CALIFORNIA

		Votes	%
1	Hubert B. Scudder (R)	85,122	54.0
	Roger Kent (D)	72,584	46.0
2	Clair Engle (D-R)	85,103	100.0
3	Leroy Johnson (R-D)	177,269	100.0
4	Franck R. Havenner (D)	83,078	67.2
	Raymond D. Smith (R)	40,569	32.8
5	John F. Shelley (D-R)	117,888	100.0
6	George P. Miller (D-R)	192,342	100.0
7	John J. Allen Jr. (R)	74,069	55.3
	Lyle E. Cook (D)	59,976	44.7
8	Jack Z. Anderson (R-D)	168,510	83.1
	John A. Peterson (I PROG)	34,176	16.9
9	Allan Oakley Hunter (R)	76,015	52.0
	Cecil F. White (D)	70,201	48.0
10	Thomas H. Werdel (R)	59,313	53.6
	Ardis M. Walker (D)	51,409	46.4
11	Ernest K. Bramblett (R)	59,780	52.1
	Marion R. Walker (D)	55,020	47.9
12	Patrick J. Hillings (R)	107,933	60.1
	Steve Zetterberg (D)	71,682	39.9
13	Norris Poulson (R-D)	83,296	84.8
	Ellen P. Davidson (I PROG)	14,789	15.1
14	Samuel William Yorty (D)	47,653	49.4
	Jack W. Hardy (R)	35,543	36.8
	Charlotta A. Bass (I PROG)	13,364	13.8
15	Gordon L. McDonough (R-D)	112,704	87.1
	Jeanne Cole (I PROG)	16,559	12.8
16	Donald L. Jackson (R)	115,970	59.2
	Esther Murray (D)	79,744	40.7
17	Cecil R. King (D-R)	166,334	99.9
18	Clyde Doyle (D)	97,177	50.5
	Craig Hosmer (R)	95,308	49.5
19	Chet Holifield (D-R)	73,317	90.9
	Myra Tanner Weiss (I)	7,329	9.1
20	Carl Hinshaw (R-D)	211,012	85.1
	William B. Esterman (I PROG)	26,508	10.7
21	Harry R. Sheppard (D)	62,994	57.4
	R. E. Reynolds (R)	46,693	42.6
22	John Phillips (R-D)	114,497	99.9
23	Clinton D. McKinnon (D)	94,137	51.0
	Leslie E. Gehres (R)	90,398	49.0

COLORADO

	Candidates	Votes	%
1	Byron Rogers (D)	70,165	50.3
	Richard Luxford (R)	67,436	48.4
2	William S. Hill (R)	73,045	57.5
	George L. Bickel (D)	53,313	42.0
3	J. Edgar Chenoweth (R)	58,831	51.6
	John H. Marsalis (D)	55,110	48.4
4	Wayne N. Aspinall (D)	35,797	57.3
	Jack Evans (R)	26,674	42.7

CONNECTICUT

		Votes	%
1	Abraham A. Ribicoff (D)	134,258	58.1
	Harry Schwolsky (R)	96,251	41.7
2	Horace Seely-Brown Jr. (R)	68,747	50.8
	Chase Going Woodhouse (D)	66,523	49.2
3	John A. McGuire (D)	89,391	51.9
	Ellsworth B. Foote (R)	82,304	47.8
4	Albert P. Morano (R)	111,939	53.1
	Dennis M. Carroll (D)	88,682	42.1
5	James T. Patterson (R)	65,915	53.0
	J. Gregory Lynch (D)	56,752	45.7
AL	Antoni N. Sadlak (R)	433,912	49.4
	Joseph W. Bogdanski (D)	426,485	48.6

DELAWARE

		Votes	%
AL	J. Caleb Boggs (R)	73,313	56.7
	Henry M. Winchester (D)	56,091	43.4

FLORIDA

		Votes	%
1	Chester B. McMullen (D)	40,466	100.0
2	Charles E. Bennett (D)	34,334	100.0
3	Robert L. F. Sikes (D)	24,548	100.0
4	Bill Lantaff (D)	65,758	82.1
	Joseph Edward Worton (R)	14,305	17.9
5	A. S. Herlong Jr. (D)	32,475	76.5
	Carl K. Landes (R)	9,958	23.5
6	Dwight L. Rogers (D)	31,205	100.0

GEORGIA

		Votes	%
1	Prince H. Preston (D)	29,716	100.0
2	E. E. Cox (D)	18,920	100.0
3	E. L. Forrester (D)	24,221	100.0
4	A. Sidney Camp (D)	21,900	100.0
5	James C. Davis (D)	49,317	100.0
6	Carl Vinson (D)	22,402	100.0
7	Henderson Lanham (D)	23,595	100.0
8	W. M. Wheeler (D)	21,573	100.0
9	John S. Wood (D)	20,943	100.0
10	Paul Brown (D)	27,568	100.0

IDAHO

		Votes	%
1	John T. Wood (R)	41,823	50.5
	Gracie Pfost (D)	41,040	49.5
2	Hamer Budge (R)	66,966	57.1
	James H. Hawley Jr. (D)	50,255	42.9

ILLINOIS

		Votes	%
1	William L. Dawson (D)	69,056	61.6
	Archibald James Carey Jr. (R)	41,944	37.4
2	Richard B. Vail (R)	83,023	53.6
	Barratt O'Hara (D)	71,945	46.4
3	Fred E. Busbey (R)	87,241	54.5
	Neil J. Linehan (D)	72,676	45.4
4	William E. McVey (R)	73,542	55.8
	James V. Buckley (D)	58,190	44.2
5	John C. Kluczynski (D)	91,589	65.6
	Edward M. Gaynor (R)	48,052	34.4
6	Thomas J. O'Brien (D)	106,701	64.5
	John M. Fay (R)	58,534	35.4
7	Adolph J. Sabath (D)	109,841	71.8
	Henry E. Hayes (R)	43,211	28.2
8	Thomas S. Gordon (D)	77,736	59.3
	Philip Grontkowski (R)	53,305	40.7
9	Sidney R. Yates (D)	74,699	51.8
	Maxwell A. Goodwin (R)	69,552	48.2
10	Richard W. Hoffman (R)	117,498	66.5
	Charles J. Michal (D)	59,127	33.5
11	Timothy P. Sheehan (R)	81,358	56.7
	Chester A. Chesney (D)	62,050	43.3
12	Edgar A. Jonas (R)	96,489	56.2
	Charles J. Komaiko (D)	75,226	43.8
13	Marguerite Stitt Church (R)	140,750	74.1
	Thomas F. Dolan (D)	49,187	25.9
14	Chauncey W. Reed (R)	103,312	74.2
	Homer R. McElroy (D)	35,856	25.8
15	Noah M. Mason (R)	82,155	63.3
	Wayne F. Caskey (D)	47,633	36.7
16	Leo E. Allen (R)	82,190	67.3
	Russell J. Goldman (D)	39,944	32.7
17	Leslie C. Arends (R)	74,643	66.8
	Joe W. Russell (D)	37,096	33.2
18	Harold H. Velde (R)	72,499	61.6
	Walter Durley Boyle (D)	45,214	38.4
19	Robert B. Chiperfield (R)	69,379	59.0
	John Michael Kerwin Jr. (D)	48,286	41.0
20	Sid Simpson (R)	62,138	59.3
	Howard Manning (D)	42,647	40.7
21	Peter F. Mack Jr. (D)	67,704	52.8
	Benjamin S. Deboice (R)	60,530	47.2
22	William L. Springer (R)	67,668	60.7
	Robert B. Borchers (D)	43,795	39.3
23	Edward H. Jenison (R)	63,669	55.9
	Laurence F. Arnold (D)	50,143	44.1
24	Charles W. Vursell (R)	62,692	55.3
	John David Upchurch (D)	50,638	44.7
25	Melvin Price (D)	78,812	64.9
	Rogers D. Jones (R)	42,696	35.1
26	C. W. Bishop (R)	53,207	51.2
	Kent E. Keller (D)	50,759	48.8

INDIANA

		Votes	%
1	Ray J. Madden (D)	62,666	52.6
	Paul Cyr (R)	56,063	47.0
2	Charles A. Halleck (R)	74,872	57.2
	Dale E. Beck (D)	55,153	42.2
3	Shepard J. Crumpacker Jr. (R)	83,816	52.8
	Thurman C. Crook (D)	73,646	46.4
4	E. Ross Adair (R)	69,741	56.2
	Edward H. Kruse Jr. (D)	53,550	43.1
5	John V. Beamer (R)	91,929	54.1
	John R. Walsh (D)	76,878	45.3
6	Cecil M. Harden (R)	69,789	52.4
	Jack H. Mankin (D)	62,915	47.2
7	William G. Bray (R)	68,885	50.0
	James E. Noland (D)	67,992	49.3
8	Winfield K. Denton (D)	78,750	51.1
	Herman L. McCray (R)	74,573	48.3
9	Earl Wilson (R)	63,229	54.9
	Charles W. Long (D)	51,350	44.6
10	Ralph Harvey (R)	81,392	58.7
	Vernon J. Dwyer (D)	56,149	40.5
11	Charles B. Brownson (R)	116,068	56.5
	Andrew Jacobs Sr. (D)	88,418	43.0

IOWA

		Votes	%
1	Thomas E. Martin (R)	70,058	61.7
	James D. France (D)	43,140	38.0

IOWA

	Candidates	Votes	%
2	Henry O. Talle (R)	79,066	58.8
	Eugene J. Kean (D)	55,359	41.2
3	Harold R. Gross (R)	73,490	64.0
	James O. Babcock (D)	40,786	35.5
4	Karl M. LeCompte (R)	51,168	56.7
	Steven V. Carter (D)	38,649	42.8
5	Paul Cunningham (R)	57,429	56.9
	Gibson C. Holliday (D)	43,105	42.7
6	James I. Dolliver (R)	56,982	64.6
	Maurice O'Reilly (D)	30,877	35.0
7	Ben F. Jensen (R)	55,291	62.1
	James A. Hart (D)	33,617	37.7
8	Charles B. Hoeven (R)	56,942	64.1
	L. J. McGivern (D)	31,689	35.7

KANSAS

1	Albert M. Cole (R)	66,607	66.5
	Ewell Steward (D)	33,562	33.5
2	Errett P. Scrivner (R)	56,862	52.2
	Milton Sullivant (D)	52,015	47.8
3	Myron V. George (R)	42,263	54.7
	Barnes Griffith (D)	35,028	45.3
4	Edward H. Rees (R)	77,856	58.9
	Louis A. Donnell (D)	54,438	41.2
5	Clifford R. Hope (R)	60,608	61.0
	Robert L. Bock (D)	38,767	39.0
6	Wint Smith (R)	51,653	59.6
	F. F. Wasinger (D)	35,087	40.5

Special Election

3	Myron V. George (R)	41,676	54.5
	Barnes Griffith (D)	34,845	45.5

KENTUCKY

1	Noble J. Gregory (D)	34,970	100.0
2	John A. Whitaker (D)	41,226	100.0
3	Thruston B. Morton (R)	62,363	55.5
	Alex P. Humphrey (D)	49,935	44.5
4	Frank L. Chelf (D)	35,529	100.0
5	Brent Spence (D)	33,920	63.3
	Thomas W. Hardesty (R)	19,670	36.7
6	Thomas R. Underwood (D)	39,762	100.0
7	Carl D. Perkins (D)	34,767	56.1
	O. W. Thompson (R)	27,190	43.9
8	Joe B. Bates (D)	37,727	60.5
	Elmer C. Roberts (R)	24,627	39.5
9	James S. Golden (R)	46,928	100.0

LOUISIANA

1	F. Edward Hebert (D)	35,456	100.0
2	Hale Boggs (D)	39,232	100.0
3	Edwin E. Willis (D)	21,591	100.0
4	Overton Brooks (D)	25,529	100.0
5	Otto E. Passman (D)	22,478	100.0
6	James H. Morrison (D)	34,718	100.0
7	Henry D. Larcade Jr. (D)	22,931	100.0
8	A. Leonard Allen (D)	25,140	100.0

MAINE

1	Robert Hale (R)	48,869	54.0
	Lucia M. Cormier (D)	41,620	46.0
2	Charles P. Nelson (R)	49,743	57.7
	John J. Maloney Jr. (D)	36,506	42.3
3	Frank Fellows (R)	38,289	62.9
	John V. Keenan (D)	22,605	37.1

MARYLAND

1	Edward T. Miller (R)	36,005	57.0
	Thomas F. Johnson (D)	27,122	43.0
2	James P. S. Devereux (R)	99,497	50.2
	William P. Bolton (D)	96,498	48.7

	Candidates	Votes	%
3	Edward A. Garmatz (D)	27,646	65.7
	Louis R. Milio (R)	14,430	34.3
4	George H. Fallon (D)	34,769	56.8
	James W. Miller (R)	25,287	41.3
5	Lansdale G. Sasscer (D)	54,152	57.5
	Thomas S. Carr (R)	40,031	42.5
6	J. Glenn Beall (R)	70,707	61.9
	Russell Peter Hartle (D)	43,540	38.1

MASSACHUSETTS

1	John W. Heselton (R)	88,018	68.9
	Anna Sullivan (D)	39,717	31.1
2	Foster Furcolo (D)	76,497	54.6
	Chester T. Skibinski (R)	63,493	45.4
3	Philip J. Philbin (D)	93,591	71.5
	John F. Fuller (R)	37,258	28.5
4	Harold D. Donohue (D)	76,881	56.9
	John Winslow (R)	57,483	42.6
5	Edith Nourse Rogers (R)	116,474	76.1
	Clement Gregory McDonough (D)	36,530	23.9
6	William H. Bates (R)	94,162	73.7
	Richard M. Russell (D)	33,578	26.3
7	Thomas J. Lane (D)	91,854	78.5
	Laurence A. Doyle (R)	24,307	20.8
8	Angier L. Goodwin (R)	71,938	53.9
	John B. Carr (D)	61,559	46.1
9	Donald W. Nicholson (R)	78,655	58.1
	August J. Cormier (D)	55,949	41.3
10	Christian A. Herter (R)	88,549	57.8
	Francis X. Hurley (D)	63,618	41.5
11	John F. Kennedy (D)	87,699	82.3
	Vincent J. Celeste (R)	18,302	17.2
12	John W. McCormack (D)	102,940	84.0
	John J. Biggins (R)	16,746	13.7
13	Richard B. Wigglesworth (R)	90,387	62.2
	David J. Concannon (D)	54,243	37.3
14	Joseph W. Martin Jr. (R)	84,508	64.3
	Edward P. Grace (D)	46,332	35.3

MICHIGAN

1	Thaddeus M. Machrowicz (D)	75,478	82.2
	Rudolph G. Tenerowicz (R)	14,619	15.9
2	George Meader (R)	61,574	60.4
	John P. Dawson (D)	39,771	39.0
3	Paul W. Shafer (R)	58,489	61.4
	Thomas B. Woodworth (D)	35,877	37.6
4	Clare E. Hoffman (R)	58,625	68.6
	Forest A. Schoonard (D)	26,301	30.8
5	Gerald R. Ford Jr. (R)	72,829	66.7
	James H. McLaughlin (D)	35,927	32.9
6	William W. Blackney (R)	70,100	52.8
	Herbert W. Devine (D)	61,435	46.3
7	Jesse P. Wolcott (R)	66,951	63.0
	Roy E. Visnaw (D)	38,953	36.6
8	Fred L. Crawford (R)	55,001	60.5
	Leland S. Jennings (D)	35,164	38.7
9	Ruth Thompson (R)	43,910	54.5
	Noel P. Fox (D)	36,222	45.0
10	Roy O. Woodruff (R)	47,489	66.2
	William J. Kelly (D)	24,198	33.8
11	Charles E. Potter (R)	50,523	66.5
	Fred L. Hanscom (D)	25,254	33.2
12	John B. Bennett (R)	43,010	61.7
	John Sabol (D)	26,667	38.3
13	George D. O'Brien (D)	56,388	61.4
	Clarence J. McLeod (R)	35,178	38.3
14	Louis C. Rabaut (D)	76,938	51.5
	Richard Durant (R)	72,137	48.3
15	John D. Dingell (D)	73,238	64.1
	Robert L. Berry (R)	40,865	35.7
16	John Lesinski Jr. (D)	80,229	60.7
	Kirby L. Wilson Jr. (R)	50,873	38.5
17	George A. Dondero (R)	114,274	55.6
	Eugene G. Donohoe (D)	90,712	44.1

MINNESOTA

	Candidates	Votes	%
1	August H. Andresen (R)	75,016	67.1
	Burton Chambers (DFL)	36,839	32.9
2	Joseph P. O'Hara (R)	69,304	59.9
	Harry Sieben (DFL)	46,452	40.1
3	Roy W. Wier (DFL)	73,786	51.7
	Alfred D. Lindley (R)	68,947	48.3
4	Eugene J. McCarthy (DFL)	59,930	60.4
	Ward Fleming (R)	39,307	39.6
5	Walter H. Judd (R)	71,243	58.7
	Marcella F. Killen (DFL)	48,759	40.2
6	Fred Marshall (DFL)	63,911	56.2
	Robert F. Lee (R)	49,879	43.8
7	H. Carl Andersen (R)	65,644	61.7
	Carl J. Eastvold (DFL)	40,785	38.3
8	John A. Blatnik (DFL)	72,440	62.9
	William A. Pittenger (R)	42,705	37.1
9	Harold C. Hagen (R)	56,928	61.9
	Curtiss Olson (DFL)	30,808	33.5

MISSISSIPPI

1	John E. Rankin (D)	8,994	92.5
	Glenn Haynes (R)	730	7.5
2	Jamie L. Whitten (D)	5,891	100.0
3	Frank E. Smith (D)	6,529	92.5
	Nelson E. Taylor (R)	529	7.5
4	Thomas G. Abernethy (D)	12,602	95.8
5	W. Arthur Winstead (D)	13,395	97.6
6	William M. Colmer (D)	15,964	87.9
	Frank H. Harper (I)	2,199	12.1
7	John Bell Williams (D)	19,321	96.4

MISSOURI

1	Clare Magee (D)	43,384	54.4
	Wat Arnold (R)	36,403	45.6
2	Morgan M. Moulder (D)	49,408	53.0
	Max Schwabe (R)	43,816	47.0
3	Philip J. Welch (D)	48,244	51.1
	William C. Cole (R)	46,154	48.9
4	Theodore Leonard Irving (D)	53,424	61.6
	Vernon D. Fulcrut (R)	33,367	38.5
5	Richard W. Bolling (D)	45,762	54.5
	Richard C. Jensen (R)	38,276	45.6
6	Orland K. Armstrong (R)	55,176	50.7
	George H. Christopher (D)	53,593	49.3
7	Dewey Short (R)	60,557	58.7
	Daniel J. Leary (D)	42,629	41.3
8	Albert S. J. Carnahan (D)	49,894	54.7
	Parke M. Banta (R)	41,406	45.4
9	Clarence Cannon (D)	43,950	61.5
	John H. Fahien (R)	27,573	38.6
10	Paul C. Jones (D)	44,469	100.0
11	John B. Sullivan (D)	57,225	64.5
	Sidney J. Redman (R)	31,163	35.2
12	Thomas B. Curtis (R)	110,757	50.9
	Raymond W. Karst (D)	106,728	49.0
13	Frank M. Karsten (D)	58,832	68.2
	Hal A. Hamilton (R)	27,366	31.7

MONTANA

1	Mike Mansfield (D)	54,394	60.3
	Ralph Y. McGinnis (R)	34,945	38.7
2	Wesley A. D'Ewart (R)	65,003	54.1
	John J. Holmes (D)	53,854	44.8

NEBRASKA

1	Carl T. Curtis (R)	67,164	54.5
	Clarence G. Miles (D)	55,972	45.5
2	Howard Buffett (R)	71,126	63.5
	Eugene D. O'Sullivan (D)	40,939	36.5
3	Karl Stefan (R)	68,889	66.9
	Duane K. Peterson (D)	34,017	33.1
4	Arthur L. Miller (R)	64,661	65.8
	Hans J. Holtorf Jr. (R)	33,562	34.2

NEVADA

Candidates	Votes	%
AL Walter S. Baring (D)	31,843	52.8
A. E. MacKenzie (R)	28,485	47.2

NEW HAMPSHIRE

	Candidates	Votes	%
1	Chester E. Merrow (R)	57,371	57.5
	Frank L. Sullivan (D)	42,371	42.5
2	Norris Cotton (R)	55.116	64.5
	George Brummer (D)	30,389	35.5

NEW JERSEY

	Candidates	Votes	%
1	Charles A. Wolverton (R)	85,100	56.8
	John J. Crean (D)	64,868	43.3
2	T. Millet Hand (R)	54,897	54.3
	Elmer H. Wene (D)	46,121	45.7
3	James C. Auchincloss (R)	79,374	62.4
	John C. Applegate (D)	47,055	37.0
4	Charles R. Howell (D)	60,364	52.2
	Gill Robb Wilson (R)	55,364	47.8
5	Charles A. Eaton (R)	80,678	61.6
	Thomas Chabrak (D)	50,220	38.4
6	Clifford P. Case (R)	74,739	62.2
	Harry Mopsick (D)	45,376	37.8
7	William B. Widnall (R)	79,421	69.7
	Emil M. Wulster (D)	34,578	30.3
8	Gordon Canfield (R)	60,420	63.6
	Charles H. Roemer (D)	34,194	36.0
9	Harry L. Towe (R)	67,712	57.8
	Karl D. Van Wagner (D)	38,421	32.8
	Carl E. Ring (I)	10,932	9.3
10	Peter W. Rodino Jr. (D)	60,432	61.0
	William H. Rawson (R)	38,613	39.0
11	Hugh J. Addonizio (D)	46,242	51.6
	Albert L. Vreeland (R)	42,581	47.5
12	Robert Winthrop Kean (R)	54,123	53.1
	Harry Dudkin (D)	45,525	44.7
13	Alfred D. Sieminski (D)	55,008	51.9
	Edward S. Binkowski (R)	43,851	41.4
	Michael A. Fiore (IPP CH)	7,072	6.7
14	Edward J. Hart (D)	61,410	59.2
	Michael Bongiovanni (R)	42,272	40.8

NEW MEXICO

	Candidates	Votes	%
AL	John J. Dempsey (D)	97,187✔	
	Antonio M. Fernandez (D)	96,291✔	
	Steiner Mason (R)	75,447	
	Jose E. Armijo (R)	68,762	

NEW YORK

	Candidates	Votes	%
1	Ernest Greenwood (D, L)	76,375	49.2
	W. Kingsland Macy (R)	76,240	49.1
2	Leonard W. Hall (R)	129,291	67.1
	Lawrence W. McKeown (D, L)	60,152	31.2
3	Henry J. Latham (R)	92,466	56.3
	James Pasta (D)	55,285	33.6
	Mark Starr (L)	11,122	6.8
4	L. Gary Clemente (D, L)	55,793	54.2
	Gregory McMahon (R)	43,055	41.8
5	T. Vincent Quinn (D)	63,620	48.4
	Robert Tripp Ross (R)	54,061	41.1
	Bernard Brown (L)	7,857	6.0
6	James J. Delaney (D, L)	60,725	56.8
	Herbert Suppan (R)	41,615	38.9
7	Louis B. Heller (D, L)	47,466	57.0
	Francis E. Dorn (R)	30,379	36.5
	Lester Zirin (AM LAB)	5,454	6.6
8	Victor L. Anfuso (D)	42,305	61.9
	Joseph R. Fontanetta (R)	18,551	27.2
	Antonio Iandiorio (AM LAB)	4,119	6.0
9	Eugene J. Keogh (D, R)	73,280	91.0
	Helen Wishnofsky (AM LAB)	7,267	9.0

	Candidates	Votes	%
10	Edna F. Kelly (D, L)	66,847	67.1
	David L. Samuels (R)	25,485	25.6
	Gerald Root (AM LAB)	7,327	7.4
11	James J. Heffernan (D, L)	67,560	62.9
	Alfred C. McKenzie (R)	31,558	29.4
	Blanche Katz (AM LAB)	8,270	7.7
12	John J. Rooney (D, L)	42,396	61.6
	Joseph J. Petito (R)	22,796	33.1
	Vincent J. Longhi (AM LAB)	3,628	5.3
13	Donald L. O'Toole (D, L)	54,919	59.6
	James F. O'Hara (R)	35,418	36.7
	Ralph Shapiro (AM LAB)	6,247	6.5
14	Abraham J. Multer (D, L)	75,020	70.6
	P. Vincent Landi (R)	21,350	20.1
	Helen Phillips (AM LAB)	9,859	9.3
15	Emanuel Celler (D, L)	72,396	72.8
	Louis H. Heiger (R)	17,144	17.2
	William Podell (AM LAB)	9,916	10.0
16	James J. Murphy (D, L)	42,516	50.5
	Edward J. McCormick (R)	37,363	44.4
	Frank Cremonesi (AM LAB)	4,340	5.2
17	Frederic R. Coudert Jr. (R)	57,247	53.4
	Irving M. Engel (D, L)	44,502	41.5
	Robert T. Leicester (AM LAB)	5,492	5.1
18	James G. Donovan (D, R)	49,448	57.8
	Vito Marcantonio (AM LAB)	36,095	42.2
19	Arthur G. Klein (D, L)	58,616	66.4
	Edward I. Goldberg (R)	21,034	23.8
	Bernard Harkavy (AM LAB)	8,597	9.7
20	Franklin D. Roosevelt Jr. (D, L)	57,432	62.1
	Henry V. Poor (R)	29,305	31.7
	John W. Darr Jr. (AM LAB)	5,717	6.2
21	Jacob K. Javits (R)	62,604	61.7
	Bennett I. Schlessel (D)	33,349	32.9
	William M. Mandel (AM LAB)	5,419	5.4
22	Adam Clayton Powell Jr. (D)	35,233	63.5
	Elmer A. Carter (R, L)	15,208	27.4
	John Quillian (AM LAB)	5,050	9.1
23	Sidney A. Fine (D)	64,270	56.3
	William J. Waterman (R)	22,103	19.4
	Harold Bauman (L)	17,882	15.7
	Robert Diamond (AM LAB)	9,847	8.6
24	Isidore Dollinger (D)	54,628	62.5
	Barnett Levy (R)	11,303	12.9
	Herman Woskow (L)	10,774	12.3
	Stephen J. White (AM LAB)	10,755	12.3
25	Charles A. Buckley (D)	64,353	46.8
	Solon S. Kane (R)	40,552	29.5
	Max Bloom (L)	20,929	15.2
	Charles J. Hendley (AM LAB)	11,707	8.5
26	Christopher C. McGrath (D)	69,152	51.4
	Fred E. Schiemann (R)	44,598	33.1
	Ernest Doerfler (L)	11,518	8.6
	August Buhr (AM LAB)	9,333	6.9
27	Ralph W. Gwinn (R)	78,221	55.9
	George A. Brenner (D, L)	59,759	42.7
28	Ralph A. Gamble (R)	79,490	67.5
	Morris E. Lasker (D)	35,059	29.8
29	Katharine St. George (R)	72,721	61.8
	Harry O. Prince (D, L)	43,315	36.8
30	James Ernest Wharton (R)	86,053	65.8
	James R. Bourne (D)	41,833	32.0
31	Bernard W. Kearney (R)	79,007	64.1
	John H. Peterson (D)	41,680	33.8
32	William T. Byrne (D)	90,420	58.8
	John T. Casey (R)	60,087	39.1
33	Dean P. Taylor (R)	100,425	69.0
	Joseph T. Hammer (D)	42,680	29.3
34	Clarence E. Kilburn (R)	67,739	66.4
	Mildred McGill (D)	32,446	31.8
35	William R. Williams (R)	60,657	51.6
	John C. Davies (D, L)	54,284	46.2
36	R. Walter Riehlman (R)	81,508	61.9
	Alfred W. Haight (D, L)	50,107	38.9

	Candidates	Votes	%
37	Edwin Arthur Hall (R)	60,278	64.6
	John J. Burns (D, L)	33,018	35.4
38	John Taber (R)	68,474	68.8
	Robert G. Gordon (D, L)	31,115	31.2
39	W. Sterling Cole (R)	64,377	66.3
	Donald J. O'Connor (D, L)	31,639	32.6
40	Kenneth B. Keating (R)	103,710	65.8
	A. Roger Clarke (D, L)	52,363	33.2
41	Harold C. Ostertag (R)	64,801	64.1
	Bernard E. Hart (D, L)	35,370	35.0
42	William E. Miller (R)	75,377	58.6
	Mary Louise Nice (D, L)	53,310	41.4
43	Edmund P. Radwan (R)	61,781	50.8
	Anthony F. Tauriello (D, L)	58,327	48.0
44	John C. Butler (R)	69,260	50.3
	Chester C. Gorski (D, L)	66,541	48.3
45	Daniel A. Reed (R)	54,490	66.0
	Frederick S. Buck (D)	27,317	33.1

NORTH CAROLINA

	Candidates	Votes	%
1	Herbert C. Bonner (D)	14,698	92.8
	Zeno O. Ratcliff (R)	1,147	7.2
2	John H. Kerr (D)	15,602	100.0
3	Graham A. Barden (D)	21,287	100.0
4	Harold D. Cooley (D)	34,580	72.8
	Ray F. Swain (R)	12,945	27.2
5	Richard Thurmond Chatham (D)	29,598	100.0
6	Carl T. Durham (D)	27,751	75.4
	A. A. McDonald (R)	9,075	24.6
7	F. Ertel Carlyle (D)	21,911	84.0
	Irvin B. Tucker Jr. (R)	4,171	16.0
8	Charles B. Deane (D)	40,834	59.6
	T. E. Story (R)	27,688	40.4
9	Robert L. Doughton (D)	47,183	61.2
	Fate J. Beal (R)	29,982	38.9
10	Hamilton C. Jones (D)	33,591	52.3
	Louis G. Rogers (R)	30,591	47.7
11	Woodrow W. Jones (D)	31,712	68.9
	A. W. Whitehurst (R)	14,293	31.1
12	Monroe M. Redden (D)	46,851	63.7
	John A. Wagner (R)	26,710	36.3

Special Election

	Candidates	Votes	%
11	Woodrow W. Jones (D)	31,460	67.3
	A. W. Whitehurst (R)	15,295	32.7

NORTH DAKOTA

	Candidates	Votes	%
AL	Fred G. Aandahl (R)	119,047✔	
	Usher L. Burdick (R)	110,534✔	
	Ervin Schumacher (D)	62,322	
	E. A. Johansson (D)	32,946	

OHIO

	Candidates	Votes	%
1	Charles H. Elston (R)	77,507	59.1
	Rollin H. Everett (D)	53,760	41.0
2	William E. Hess (R)	69,543	52.7
	Earl T. Wagner (D)	62,542	47.4
3	Edward Breen (D)	92,840	54.5
	Paul F. Schenck (R)	77,634	45.5
4	William M. McCulloch (R)	65,640	66.8
	Carleton Carl Reiser (D)	32,686	33.2
5	Cliff Clevenger (R)	36,096	57.5
	Dan Batt (D)	26,689	42.5
6	James G. Polk (D)	40,335	50.8
	Edward O. McCowen (R)	38,996	49.2
7	Clarence J. Brown (R)	77,660	68.4
	Ben J. Goldman (D)	35,818	31.6
8	Jackson E. Betts (R)	47,761	62.7
	W. Dexter Hazen (D)	28,379	37.3
9	Frazier Reams (I)	51,024	36.6
	Thomas H. Burke (D)	45,268	32.4
	Homer A. Ramey (R)	43,301	31.0

OHIO

Candidates	Votes	%
10 Thomas A. Jenkins (R)	39,584	65.2
William J. Curry (D)	21,117	34.8
11 Walter E. Brehm (R)	33,648	53.1
Mell G. Underwood Jr. (D)	29,687	46.9
12 John M. Vorys (R)	117,396	64.1
John W. Guy (D)	65,860	35.9
13 Alvin F. Weichel (R)	58,484	70.9
Dwight A. Blackmore (D)	24,042	29.1
14 William H. Ayres (R)	102,868	48.7
Walter B. Huber (D)	100,947	47.8
15 Robert T. Secrest (D)	47,448	61.6
Holland M. Gary (R)	29,573	38.4
16 Frank T. Bow (R)	77,306	50.7
John McSweeney (D)	75,255	49.3
17 J. Harry McGregor (R)	71,382	64.3
Robert W. Levering (D)	39,726	35.8
18 Wayne L. Hays (D)	58,295	50.8
Robert L. Quinn (R)	56,508	49.2
19 Michael J. Kirwan (D)	119,245	63.8
Henry P. Kosling (R)	67,661	36.2
20 Michael A. Feighan (D)	60,565	74.2
Paul W. Cassidy (R)	21,044	25.8
21 Robert Crosser (D)	66,341	75.5
William Hodge (R)	21,588	24.6
22 Frances P. Bolton (R)	219,788	62.7
Chat Paterson (D)	130,623	37.3
AL George H. Bender (R)	1,447,154	53.9
Stephen M. Young (D)	1,237,409	46.1

OKLAHOMA

Candidates	Votes	%
1 George B. Schwabe (R)	72,367	52.9
Dixie Gilmer (D)	64,481	47.1
2 William G. Stigler (D)	36,552	66.2
Cleo Crain (R)	18,687	33.8
3 Carl Albert (D)	46,404	82.8
Charles Powell (R)	9,639	17.2
4 Tom Steed (D)	43,838	68.1
Glenn O. Young (R)	20,527	31.9
5 John Jarman (D)	72,877	58.8
C. E. Barnes (R)	51,008	41.2
6 Toby Morris (D)	38,166	67.1
George Campbell (R)	18,743	32.9
7 Victor Wickersham (D)	28,733	67.1
K. B. Cornell (R)	14,078	32.9
8 Page H. Belcher (R)	38,285	54.2
George H. Wilson (D)	32,401	45.8

OREGON

Candidates	Votes	%
1 Walter Norblad (R)	93,547	66.5
Roy R. Hewitt (D)	47,155	33.5
2 Lowell Stockman (R)	41,365	55.4
Vernon Bull (D)	33,282	44.6
3 Homer D. Angell (R)	90,232	50.7
Carl C. Donaugh (D)	77,606	43.6
4 Harris Ellsworth (R)	63,211	59.5
David C. Shaw (D)	43,053	40.5

PENNSYLVANIA

Candidates	Votes	%
1 William A. Barrett (D)	69,300	53.8
Robert M. Sebastian (R)	59,593	46.2
2 William T. Granahan (D)	83,344	57.0
Max Slepin (R)	62,970	43.0
3 Hardie Scott (R)	68,217	50.3
Maurice S. Osser (D)	67,286	49.7
4 Earl Chudoff (D)	65,255	57.5
Theodore O. Spaulding (R)	48,280	42.5
5 William J. Green Jr. (D)	84,177	55.5
George W. Sarbacher Jr. (R)	67,525	44.5
6 Hugh Scott (R)	74,316	50.0
Ethan Allen Doty (D)	73,913	49.7
7 Benjamin F. James (R)	91,387	62.7
Hubert P. Earle (D)	54,425	37.3
8 Albert C. Vaughn (R)	56,300	58.2
George F. Kane (D)	40,502	41.8
9 Paul B. Dague (R)	70,368	67.2
Philip Ragan (D)	34,317	32.8
10 Harry P. O'Neill (D)	56,158	51.5
Fraser P. Donlan (R)	52,859	48.5
11 Daniel J. Flood (D)	77,466	54.4
Elwood H. Jones (R)	65,015	45.6
12 Ivor D. Fenton (R)	67,135	56.8
James H. Gildea (D)	51,028	43.2
13 George M. Rhodes (D)	36,335	49.8
James W. Bertolet (R)	34,640	47.5
14 Wilson D. Gillette (R)	45,986	60.9
John E. Snedeker (D)	29,538	39.1
15 Alvin R. Bush (R)	47,697	60.7
Paul A. Rothfuss (D)	28,759	36.6
16 Samuel K. McConnell Jr. (R)	81,366	66.2
Leon C. MacMullen (D)	41,642	33.9
17 Richard M. Simpson (R)	40,029	62.8
James L. Gatins (D)	23,762	37.3
18 Walter M. Mumma (R)	78,577	63.7
James M. Quigley (D)	44,871	36.4
19 Leon H. Gavin (R)	42,719	62.8
Fred C. Barr (D)	25,348	37.2
20 Francis E. Walter (D)	49,660	58.3
George M. Berg (R)	35,487	41.7
21 James F. Lind (D)	48,550	52.2
Francis Worley (R)	44,465	47.8
22 James E. Van Zandt (R)	42,701	59.5
Arthur H. Reede (D)	29,080	40.5
23 Edward L. Sittler Jr. (R)	39,431	51.8
Anthony Cavalcante (D)	36,740	48.2
24 Thomas E. Morgan (D)	46,875	59.1
John J. Cairns Jr. (R)	32,470	40.9
25 Louis E. Graham (R)	55,866	52.4
Samuel Gunnett Neff (D)	50,686	47.6
26 John P. Saylor (R)	63,445	52.5
Lewis E. Evans (D)	57,396	47.5
27 Augustine B. Kelley (D)	53,229	57.1
George E. Berry Jr. (R)	40,037	42.9
28 Carroll D. Kearns (R)	67,604	57.0
Steve Filipkowski (D)	51,060	43.0
29 Harmar D. Denny Jr. (R)	54,076	52.6
Harry J. Davenport (D)	48,198	46.9
30 Robert J. Corbett (R)	58,096	56.5
J. R. Montgomery (D)	44,778	43.5
31 James G. Fulton (R)	82,525	67.5
Wilber I. Newstetter Jr. (D)	39,776	32.5
32 Herman P. Eberharter (D)	66,077	68.7
James E. Dougherty (R)	30,088	31.3
33 Frank Buchanan (D)	63,257	65.8
Cornelius McLaughlin Sr. (R)	32,858	34.2

RHODE ISLAND

Candidates	Votes	%
1 Aime J. Forand (D)	90,065	63.2
Francis R. Foley (R)	52,553	36.9
2 John E. Fogarty (D)	93,039	60.8
Wilford S. Budlong (R)	60,036	39.2

SOUTH CAROLINA

Candidates	Votes	%
1 L. Mendel Rivers (D)	6,753	100.0
2 John J. Riley (D)	9,747	100.0
3 W. J. Bryan Dorn (D)	8,126	100.0
4 Joseph R. Bryson (D)	7,976	99.9
5 James P. Richards (D)	10,648	100.0
6 John L. McMillan (D)	7,131	100.0

SOUTH DAKOTA

Candidates	Votes	%
1 Harold O. Lovre (R)	116,173	60.8
Merton B. Tice (D)	74,983	39.2
2 E. Y. Berry (R)	34,533	60.3
Sam H. Bober (D)	22,737	39.7

TENNESSEE

Candidates	Votes	%
1 B. Carroll Reece (R)	33,308	46.5
Dayton Phillips (IR)	20,121	28.1
Kyle K. King (D)	18,260	25.5
2 Howard H. Baker (R)	38,585	52.2
Frank W. Wilson (D)	35,349	47.8
3 James B. Frazier Jr. (D)	23,807	100.0
4 Albert Gore (D)	11,112	100.0
5 Joe L. Evins (D)	15,283	100.0
6 J. Percy Priest (D)	10,047	65.9
James W. Perkins (I)	5,189	34.1
7 James P. Sutton (D)	13,520	100.0
8 Thomas J. Murray (D)	13,623	100.0
9 Jere Cooper (D)	9,276	100.0
10 Clifford Davis (D)	15,128	100.0

TEXAS

Candidates	Votes	%
1 Wright Patman (D)	12,444	100.0
2 Jesse M. Combs (D)	16,900	100.0
3 Lindley Beckworth (D)	11,784	91.1
R. E. Kennedy (R)	1,145	8.9
4 Sam Rayburn (D)	11,546	100.0
5 J. Frank Wilson (D)	23,568	100.0
6 Olin Teague (D)	8,118	98.1
7 Tom Pickett (D)	12,557	100.0
8 Albert Thomas (D)	19,068	77.8
B. F. Hanna (R)	5,427	22.2
9 Clark W. Thompson (D)	20,200	100.0
10 Homer Thornberry (D)	13,703	100.0
11 W. R. Poage (D)	10,576	100.0
12 Wingate H. Lucas (D)	13,179	80.7
H. G. Neely (R)	3,162	19.4
13 Ed Gossett (D)	14,761	100.0
14 John E. Lyle Jr. (D)	31,201	100.0
15 Lloyd M. Bentsen Jr. (D)	18,524	100.0
16 Ken Regan (D)	8,928	100.0
17 Omar Burleson (D)	10,228	100.0
18 Walter Rogers (D)	25,666	52.5
B. H. Guill (R)	23,259	47.5
19 George Mahon (D)	17,828	93.9
M. D. Temple (R)	1,162	6.1
20 Paul J. Kilday (D)	9,138	100.0
21 O. Clark Fisher (D)	16,334	100.0

Special Election

Candidates	Votes	%
18 Ben H. Guill (R)	✔	#

UTAH

Candidates	Votes	%
1 Walter K. Granger (D)	54,161	51.1
Preston L. Jones (R)	51,868	48.9
2 Reva B. Bosone (D)	84,283	53.4
Ivy B. Priest (R)	73,535	46.6

VERMONT

Candidates	Votes	%
AL Winston L. Prouty (R)	65,248	73.4
Herbert B. Comings (D)	22,709	25.6

VIRGINIA

Candidates	Votes	%
1 Edward J. Robeson Jr. (D)	18,741	81.0
Nile Straughan (R)	2,518	10.9
Stanley S. Garner (I)	1,878	8.1
2 Porter Hardy Jr. (D)	14,846	99.9
3 J. Vaughan Gary (D)	15,300	89.6
Phronia A. McNeill (PROG)	1,095	6.4
4 Watkins M. Abbitt (D)	8,325	99.9
5 Thomas B. Stanley (D)	9,433	99.9
6 Clarence G. Burton (D)	12,287	99.3
7 Burr P. Harrison (D)	19,932	69.4
J. A. Garber (R)	8,786	30.6
8 Howard W. Smith (D)	29,730	57.2
Tyrrell Krum (R)	21,071	40.6
9 Thomas B. Fugate (D)	26,802	58.4
George C. Sutherland (R)	19,118	41.6

Special Election

Candidates	Votes	%
1 Edward J. Robeson Jr (D)	10,988	42.5
William A. Wright	7,667	29.6
Blake T. Newton	5,425	21.0
Nile Straughan (R)	1,792	6.9

WASHINGTON

Candidates	Votes	%
1 Hugh B. Mitchell (D)	90,053	51.4
F. F. Powell (R)	84,024	47.9
2 Henry M. Jackson (D)	73,296	61.2
Herb Wilson (R)	45,737	38.2
3 Russell V. Mack (R)	55,056	52.9
Gordon M. Quarnstrom (D)	48,623	46.8
4 Hal Holmes (R)	61,544	64.3
Ted Little (D)	34,174	35.7
5 Walt Horan (R)	60,273	54.8
Robert Dellwo (D)	49,767	45.2
6 Thor C. Tollefson (R)	71,785	60.5
John M. Coffee (D)	46,249	39.0

WEST VIRGINIA

Candidates	Votes	%
1 Robert L. Ramsay (D)	53,584	51.7
Francis J. Love (R)	49,987	48.3

Candidates	Votes	%
2 Harley O. Staggers (D)	53,485	54.4
Melvin C. Snyder (R)	44,925	45.7
3 Cleveland M. Bailey (D)	56,794	54.4
Rush D. Holt (R)	47,589	45.6
4 Maurice G. Burnside (D)	64,265	51.7
Hubert S. Ellis (R)	60,171	48.4
5 John Kee (D)	61,000	65.8
Arnold G. Porterfield (R)	31,777	34.3
6 Erland H. Hedrick (D)	85,793	61.6
Latelle M. LaFollette Jr. (R)	53,466	38.4

WISCONSIN

Candidates	Votes	%
1 Lawrence H. Smith (R)	70,883	57.2
Jack Harvey (D)	53,071	42.8
2 Glenn R. Davis (R)	75,281	57.6
Horace W. Wilkie (D)	55,117	42.2
3 Gardner R. Withrow (R)	54,783	58.8
Patrick J. Lucey (D)	38,265	41.0

Candidates	Votes	%
4 Clement J. Zablocki (D)	83,564	60.9
John C. Brophy (R)	53,702	39.1
5 Charles J. Kersten (R)	75,955	51.6
Andrew J. Biemiller (D)	71,203	48.4
6 William K. Van Pelt (R)	66,289	65.1
Kenneth Kunde (D)	35,618	35.0
7 Reid F. Murray (R)	63,433	68.3
Edward G. Gilbertson (D)	29,408	31.7
8 John W. Byrnes (R)	71,908	62.1
John W. Reynolds Jr. (D)	43,877	37.9
9 Merlin Hull (R)	60,337	70.8
Arthur L. Henning (D)	24,871	29.2
10 Alvin E. O'Konski (R)	46,722	57.0
Rodney J. Edwards (D)	35,281	43.0

WYOMING

Candidates	Votes	%
AL William Henry Harrison (R)	50,865	54.5
John B. Clark (D)	42,483	45.5

1951 House Elections

KENTUCKY

Special Election

	Votes	%
6 John C. Watts (D)	28,599	55.3
Otis C. Thomas (R)	23,108	44.7

MISSOURI

Special Election

	Votes	%
11 Claude I. Bakewell (R)	25,849#	57.3
Harry Schendel (D)	19,275#	42.7

NEW YORK

Special Election

	Votes	%
5 Robert Tripp Ross (R)	17,300	53.1
Hugh Quinn (D)	11,438	35.1
George Cranmore (L)	2,641	8.1

TEXAS

Special Election

		Votes	%
13	Frank Ikard (D)	8,970	31.0
	Jenkins	5,363	18.5
	Jackson	5,101	17.6
	Wagonseller	4,225	14.6
	McFarland	2,786	9.6
	Crouch	2,423	8.4

1952 House Elections

ALABAMA

Candidates	Votes	%
1 Frank W. Boykin (D)	30,758	100.0
2 George Grant (D)	38,421	100.0
3 George W. Andrews (D)	29,321	100.0
4 Kenneth A. Roberts (D)	31,389	100.0
5 Albert Rains (D)	43,843	100.0
6 Armistead I. Selden Jr. (D)	24,058	100.0
7 Carl Elliott (D)	33,533	72.6
Cyrus Kitchens (R)	12,689	27.5
8 Robert E. Jones Jr. (D)	41,293	87.3
H. G. Williams (R)	5,984	12.7
9 Laurie C. Battle (D)	51,537	100.0

ARIZONA

1 John J. Rhodes (R)	66,512	54.0
John R. Murdock (D)	56,622	46.0
2 Harold A. Patten (D)	71,245	56.9
William C. Frey (R)	54,021	43.1

ARKANSAS

1 Ezekiel C. Gathings (D)	42,494	100.0
2 Wilbur D. Mills (D)	36,252	100.0
3 James W. Trimble (D)	49,284	56.0
Jack Joyce (R)	38,784	44.0
4 Oren Harris (D)	65,374	100.0
5 Brooks Hays (D)	53,056	78.8
Alonzo A. Ross (R)	13,105	19.5
6 William F. Norrell (D)	62,378	100.0

CALIFORNIA

1 Hubert B. Scudder (R-D)	137,801	86.3
Carl Sullivan (I PROG)	21,734	13.6
2 Clair Engle (D)	124,179	100.0
3 John E. Moss Jr. (D)	87,335	50.8
Leslie E. Wood (R)	82,133	47.8
4 William S. Mailliard (R)	102,359	55.0
Franck R. Havenner (D)	83,748	45.0
5 John F. Shelley (D-R)	107,542	100.0
6 Robert L. Condon (D)	87,768	50.6
John F. Baldwin Jr. (R)	85,756	49.4
7 John J. Allen Jr. (R-D)	120,666	84.2
John Allen Johnson (I PROG)	22,408	15.6
8 George P. Miller (D-R)	156,445	99.9
9 J. Arthur Younger (R)	71,426	53.1
Harold F. Taggart (D)	61,028	45.3
10 Charles S. Gubser (R)	106,375	59.2
Arthur L. Johnson (D)	70,271	39.1
11 Leroy Johnson (R-D)	101,052	87.1
Leslie B. Schlingheyde (I PROG)	14,999	12.9
12 A. Oakley Hunter (R-D)	103,587	99.3
13 Ernest K. Bramblett (R)	79,496	51.0
Will Hayes (D)	76,516	49.0
14 Harlan Hagen (D)	70,809	51.0
Thomas H. Werdel (R)	68,011	49.0
15 Gordon L. McDonough (R-D)	142,545	99.7
16 Donald L. Jackson (R)	79,127	59.7
Jerry K. Harter (D)	53,337	40.2
17 Cecil R. King (D)	114,650	54.6
Robert H. Finch (R)	92,587	44.1
18 Craig Hosmer (R)	90,438	55.5
Joseph M. Kennick (D)	72,457	44.5
19 Chet Holifield (D-R)	126,606	87.0
Ida Alvarez (I PROG)	13,724	9.4
20 Carl Hinshaw (R-D)	109,509	99.7
21 Edgar W. Hiestand (R)	112,100	53.6
Everett G. Burkhalter (D)	97,007	46.4
22 Joseph F. Holt (R)	85,039	60.5
Dean E. McHenry (D)	55,534	39.5

Candidates	Votes	%
23 Clyde Doyle (D-R)	138,356	87.3
Olive T. Thompson (I PROG)	17,501	11.1
24 Norris Poulson (R-D)	119,799	87.2
Bertram L. Sharp (I PROG)	17,307	12.6
25 Patrick J. Hillings (R)	135,465	64.3
Woodrow Wilson Sayre (D)	75,125	35.7
26 Samuel William Yorty (D-R)	157,973	88.0
Horace V. Alexander (I PROG)	21,465	12.0
27 Harry R. Sheppard (D)	68,773	55.0
Carl B. Hilliard (R)	56,202	45.0
28 James B. Utt (R)	106,972	63.0
Lionel Van Deerlin (D)	62,779	37.0
29 John Phillips (R-D)	73,144	99.7
30 Bob Wilson (R)	121,332	59.6
Degraff Austin (D)	82,311	40.4

COLORADO

1 Byron G. Rogers (D)	101,864	50.8
Mason Knuckles (R)	97,442	48.6
2 William S. Hill (R)	113,566	63.1
Ralph L. Williams (D)	66,300	36.9
3 J. Edgar Chenoweth (R)	84,739	57.7
John H. Marsalis (D)	62,025	42.3
4 Wayne N. Aspinall (D)	39,676	50.0
Howard M. Shults (R)	39,647	50.0

CONNECTICUT

1 Thomas J. Dodd (D)	160,080	54.0
John Ashmead (R)	136,540	46.0
2 Horace Seely-Brown Jr. (R)	90,827	55.5
William M. Citron (D)	72,868	44.5
3 Albert W. Cretella (R)	111,018	52.8
John A. McGuire (D)	99,408	47.2
4 Albert P. Morano (R)	164,689	60.1
Joseph P. Lyford (D)	107,881	39.4
5 James T. Patterson (R)	83,848	56.7
John A. Speziale (D)	64,020	43.3
AL Antoni N. Sadlak (R)	601,238	55.0
Stanley J. Pribyson (D)	489,645	44.8

DELAWARE

AL Herbert B. Warburton (R)	88,285	51.9
Joseph J. Scannel (D)	81,730	48.1

FLORIDA

1 Courtney Campbell (D)	69,149	50.7
William C. Cramer (R)	67,286	49.3
2 Charles E. Bennett (D)	64,080	100.0
3 Robert L. F. Sikes (D)	74,909	100.0
4 Bill Lantaff (D)	115,611	66.0
Dorothea M. B. Vermorel (R)	59,458	34.0
5 A. S. Herlong Jr. (D)	89,943	100.0
6 Dwight L. Rogers (D)	55,901	60.8
Janet H. Fitzgerald (R)	36,113	39.3
7 James A. Haley (D)	36,973	56.3
Kent S. McKinley (R)	28,725	43.7
8 D. R. Matthews (D)	43,447	100.0

GEORGIA

1 Prince H. Preston (D)	57,088	100.0
2 E. E. Cox (D)	42,226*	100.0
3 E. L. Forrester (D)	53,161	100.0
4 A. Sidney Camp (D)	52,327	100.0
5 James C. Davis (D)	83,920	100.0

Candidates	Votes	%
6 Carl Vinson (D)	49,635	100.0
7 Henderson Lanham (D)	65,416	99.9
8 W. M. Wheeler (D)	51,349	99.9
9 Phil M. Landrum (D)	47,327	100.0
10 Paul Brown (D)	44,646	100.0

IDAHO

1 Gracie Pfost (D)	54,725	50.3
John T. Wood (R)	54,134	49.7
2 Hamer H. Budge (R)	103,047	66.2
W. H. Jensen (D)	52,692	33.8

ILLINOIS

1 William L. Dawson (D)	95,899	73.5
Edgar G. Brown (R)	34,571	26.5
2 Barratt O'Hara (D)	94,253	51.4
Richard B. Vail (R)	89,080	48.6
3 Fred E. Busbey (R)	102,328	54.5
Neil J. Linehan (D)	85,539	45.5
4 William E. McVey (R)	131,215	56.6
Arthur E. Dillner (D)	100,809	43.5
5 John C. Kluczynski (D)	104,960	64.5
Ernest L. Kaysen (R)	57,775	35.5
6 Thomas J. O'Brien (D)	112,121	63.1
John L. Roach (R)	65,537	36.9
7 Adolph J. Sabath (D)	111,960*	70.0
Louis F. Capuzi (R)	48,000	30.0
8 Thomas S. Gordon (D)	87,871	59.0
William F. Cooper (R)	61,048	41.0
9 Sidney R. Yates (D)	87,285	52.4
Robert R. Siegrist (R)	79,429	47.6
10 Richard W. Hoffman (R)	138,560	65.0
John Schaffenegger (D)	74,467	35.0
11 Timothy P. Sheehan (R)	103,265	59.4
Stanley W. Morten (D)	70,691	40.6
12 Edgar A. Jonas (R)	113,762	55.7
Philip A. Fleischman (D)	90,444	44.3
13 Marguerite Stitt Church (R)	184,696	70.6
Lawrence J. Hayes (D)	77,068	29.4
14 Chauncey W. Reed (R)	137,881	71.5
William E. Hartnett (D)	54,953	28.5
15 Noah M. Mason (R)	103,398	63.7
Stanley Hubbs (D)	59,050	36.4
16 Leo E. Allen (R)	110,182	66.5
John P. Barton (D)	55,399	33.5
17 Leslie C. Arends (R)	105,042	63.6
John A. Kinneman (D)	60,112	36.4
18 Harold H. Velde (R)	83,706	55.2
John T. McNaughton (D)	67,905	44.8
19 Robert B. Chiperfield (R)	94,141	60.8
Ray Simkins (D)	60,619	39.2
20 Sidney E. Simpson (R)	84,994	61.8
John R. Roy (D)	52,586	38.2
21 Peter F. Mack Jr. (D)	94,026	52.5
Edward H. Jenison (R)	85,248	47.6
22 William L. Springer (R)	92,851	63.0
David W. Beggs Jr. (D)	54,576	37.0
23 Charles Vursell (R)	89,428	57.7
W. Carl Johnston (D)	65,442	42.3
24 Melvin Price (D)	117,408	64.8
Phyllis Stewart Schlafly (R)	63,778	35.2
25 C. W. Bishop (R)	88,810	56.2
C. Edwin Hair (D)	69,245	43.8

INDIANA

1 Ray J. Madden (D)	93,187	56.4
Elliott Belshaw (R)	71,617	43.3
2 Charles A. Halleck (R)	94,795	63.3
L. Dewey Burham (D)	54,025	36.1
3 Shepard J. Crumpacker Jr. (R)	107,839	54.5
Charles C. Price (D)	88,776	44.9

INDIANA

Candidates	Votes	%
4 E. Ross Adair (R)	95,613	63.7
Howard L. Morrison (D)	53,154	35.4
5 John V. Beamer (R)	114,081	56.9
Philip C. Dermond (D)	84,825	42.3
6 Cecil M. Harden (R)	86,899	55.7
Jack H. Mankin (D)	68,709	44.0
7 William G. Bray (R)	85,601	56.1
Thomas J. Courtney (D)	66,218	43.4
8 D. Bailey Merrill (R)	98,226	52.6
Winfield K. Denton (D)	87,770	47.0
9 Earl Wilson (R)	74,052	56.4
Edward Lewis (D)	56,759	43.2
10 Ralph Harvey (R)	103,937	59.9
Fred V. Culp (D)	67,932	39.1
11 Charles B. Brownson (R)	160,929	59.4
John C. Carvey (D)	109,403	40.4

IOWA

Candidates	Votes	%
1 Thomas E. Martin (R)	105,526	62.9
Clair A. Williams (D)	62,011	36.9
2 Henry O. Talle (R)	114,553	62.2
T. W. Mullaney (D)	69,421	37.7
3 H. R. Gross (R)	109,992	65.8
George R. Laub (D)	56,871	34.0
4 Karl M. LeCompte (R)	73,317	61.9
Earl E. Glassburner (D)	44,900	37.9
5 Paul Cunningham (R)	95,057	58.8
Alvin P. Meyer (D)	66,303	41.0
6 James I. Dolliver (R)	86,842	68.7
Francis G. Cutler (D)	39,245	31.1
7 Ben F. Jensen (R)	82,462	67.3
Thomas J. Keleher (D)	39,999	32.6
8 Charles B. Hoeven (R)	94,561	99.7

KANSAS

Candidates	Votes	%
1 Howard S. Miller (D)	68,909	51.5
Albert M. Cole (R)	64,963	48.5
2 Errett P. Scrivner (R)	91,676	57.3
Claude L. Rice (D)	68,396	42.7
3 Myron V. George (R)	57,126	59.5
Fred L. Hedges (D)	38,960	40.6
4 Edward H. Rees (R)	118,206	59.4
Bill Porter (D)	80,697	40.6
5 Clifford R. Hope (R)	90,967	70.9
Art McAnarney (D)	37,361	29.1
6 Wint Smith (R)	66,723	62.6
Horace A. Santry (D)	39,955	37.5

KENTUCKY

Candidates	Votes	%
1 Noble J. Gregory (D)	66,106	65.8
W. Mallam Lake (R)	34,360	34.2
2 Garrett L. Withers (D)	57,518	54.4
David C. Brodie (R)	48,191	45.6
3 John M. Robsion Jr. (R)	95,041	54.0
B. L. Shamburger (D)	80,347	45.7
4 Frank L. Chelf (D)	55,670	55.9
R. H. Hutchison Jr. (R)	43,981	44.1
5 Brent Spence (D)	78,431	55.4
William D. Cochran (R)	63,058	44.6
6 John C. Watts (D)	68,554	56.3
Leslie A. Henderson (R)	53,297	43.7
7 Carl D. Perkins (D)	53,238	58.2
Curtis Clark (R)	38,290	41.8
8 James S. Golden (R)	78,584	68.9
W. D. Scalf (D)	35,556	31.2

LOUISIANA

Candidates	Votes	%
1 F. Edward Hebert (D)	71,448	66.4
George W. Reese Jr. (R)	36,161	33.6
2 Hale Boggs (D)	68,112	100.0
3 Edwin E. Willis (D)	33,184	100.0
4 Overton Brooks (D)	40,724	100.0
5 Otto E. Passman (D)	32,743	100.0

Candidates	Votes	%
6 James H. Morrison (D)	61,744	100.0
7 T. A. Thompson (D)	40,811	100.0
8 George S. Long (D)	31,476	100.0

MAINE

Candidates	Votes	%
1 Robert Hale (R)	56,239	61.6
James A. McVicar (D)	35,078	38.4
2 Charles P. Nelson (R)	55,393	66.8
Leland B. Currier (D)	27,527	33.2
3 Clifford G. McIntire (R)	45,095	76.2
Philip R. Sharpe (D)	14,103	23.8

MARYLAND

Candidates	Votes	%
1 Edward T. Miller (R)	47,164	61.0
Dudley George Roe (D)	30,162	39.0
2 James P. S. Devereux (R)	95,811	61.4
A. Gordon Boone (D)	60,121	38.6
3 Edward A. Garmatz (D)	60,659	70.9
Jerry Toula (R)	24,879	29.1
4 George H. Fallon (D)	54,215	54.7
Samuel Hopkins (R)	44,974	45.3
5 Frank Small Jr. (R)	68,405	50.4
Richard E. Lankford (D)	67,366	49.6
6 DeWitt S. Hyde (R)	94,603	57.8
Stella B. Werner (D)	69,050	42.2
7 Samuel N. Friedel (D)	63,652	51.4
William F. Laukaitis (R)	60,277	48.6

MASSACHUSETTS

Candidates	Votes	%
1 John W. Heselton (R)	101,512	67.1
William H. Burns (D)	49,379	32.7
2 Edward P. Boland (D)	88,424	51.8
Troy T. Murray (R)	81,847	48.0
3 Philip J. Philbin (D)	108,743	67.3
Frank D. Walker (R)	52,348	32.4
4 Harold D. Donohue (D)	93,530	54.4
Carl A. Sheridan (R)	77,536	45.1
5 Edith Nourse Rogers (R)	146,269	75.9
Helen M. Fitzgerald (D)	45,650	23.7
6 William H. Bates (R)	139,657	95.1
7 Thomas J. Lane (D)	105,662	74.7
John L. Southwick Jr. (R)	34,663	24.5
8 Angier L. Goodwin (R)	85,918	50.9
John C. Carr Jr. (D)	82,114	48.7
9 Donald W. Nicholson (R)	103,708	59.2
James F. O'Neill (D)	71,129	40.6
10 Laurence Curtis (R)	101,221	54.3
Frederick C. Hailer Jr. (D)	84,021	45.1
11 Thomas P. O'Neill (D)	86,532	69.3
Jesse A. Rogers (R)	37,816	30.3
12 John W. McCormack (D)	111,986	82.2
James S. Tremblay (R)	24,271	17.8
13 Richard B. Wigglesworth (R)	114,761	60.6
David J. Crowley (D)	74,730	39.4
14 Joseph W. Martin Jr. (R)	108,215	63.2
Edward F. Doolan (D)	62,554	36.5

MICHIGAN

Candidates	Votes	%
1 Thaddeus M. Machrowicz (D)	118,695	84.2
Rudolph G. Tenerowicz (R)	21,442	15.2
2 George Meader (R)	101,341	63.4
John P. Dawson (D)	58,024	36.3
3 Paul W. Shafer (R)	95,061	62.0
Kenneth G. Brown (D)	57,666	37.6
4 Clare E. Hoffman (R)	87,703	66.6
Murle E. Gorton (D)	43,450	33.0
5 Gerald R. Ford Jr. (R)	109,807	66.3
Vincent E. O'Neill (D)	55,147	33.3
6 Kit Clardy (R)	108,263	52.6
Donald Hayworth (D)	96,682	47.0
7 Jesse P. Wolcott (R)	101,936	60.3
Ira D. McCoy (D)	66,699	39.5

Candidates	Votes	%
8 Alvin M. Bentley (R)	91,731	66.6
Clarence V. Smazel (D)	45,431	33.0
9 Ruth Thompson (R)	70,456	59.5
John H. Piercey (D)	47,456	40.1
10 Elford A. Cederberg (R)	69,727	67.5
William J. Kelly (D)	33,602	32.5
11 Victor A. Knox (R)	54,883	59.3
Prentiss M. Brown Jr. (D)	37,701	40.7
12 John B. Bennett (R)	47,160	58.2
E. Burr Sherwood (D)	33,892	41.8
13 George D. O'Brien (D)	88,473	64.8
Clarence J. McLeod (R)	47,881	35.1
14 Louis C. Rabaut (D)	117,027	53.1
Richard Durant (R)	103,366	46.9
15 John D. Dingell (D)	109,109	66.7
Gregory M. Pillon (R)	54,236	33.2
16 John Lesinski Jr. (D)	139,011	60.6
Harold J. Smith (R)	89,159	38.9
17 Charles G. Oakman (R)	94,517	52.9
Martha W. Griffiths (D)	84,001	47.0
18 George A. Dondero (R)	108,673	56.2
Arthur J. Law (D)	84,308	43.6

MINNESOTA

Candidates	Votes	%
1 August H. Andresen (R)	103,218	69.4
George Alfson (DFL)	45,496	30.6
2 Joseph P. O'Hara (R)	101,641	67.7
Richard T. Malone (DFL)	48,404	32.3
3 Roy W. Wier (DFL)	115,008	52.2
Ed Willow (R)	105,320	47.8
4 Eugene J. McCarthy (DFL)	98,015	61.7
Roger G. Kennedy (R)	60,827	38.3
5 Walter H. Judd (R)	99,027	59.2
Karl F. Rolvaag (DFL)	68,326	40.8
6 Fred Marshall (DFL)	74,041	52.6
J. Arthur Bensen (R)	66,764	47.4
7 H. Carl Andersen (R)	87,460	62.7
James M. Youngdale (DFL)	52,144	37.4
8 John A. Blatnik (DFL)	91,465	62.6
Ernest R. Orchard (R)	54,756	37.5
9 Harold C. Hagen (R)	70,402	60.6
Curtiss T. Olson (DFL)	45,874	39.5

MISSISSIPPI

Candidates	Votes	%
1 Thomas G. Abernethy (D)	40,333	100.0
2 Jamie L. Whitten (D)	29,025	100.0
3 Frank E. Smith (D)	23,906	87.2
Paul Clark (R)	3,523	12.8
4 John Bell Williams (D)	50,318	100.0
5 Arthur Winstead (D)	39,919	94.1
Henry J. Maddox (R)	2,501	5.9
6 William M. Colmer (D)	51,227	100.0

MISSOURI

Candidates	Votes	%
1 Frank M. Karsten (D)	126,583	64.2
Eugene A. Miller (R)	70,479	35.8
2 Thomas B. Curtis (R)	125,625	56.9
Donald McClanahan (D)	95,208	43.1
3 Leonor K. Sullivan (D)	107,428	64.8
Claude I. Bakewell (R)	58,413	35.2
4 Jeffrey P. Hillelson (R)	96,988	53.3
Leonard Irving (D)	84,899	46.7
5 Richard Bolling (D)	90,357	56.0
Frank C. Rayburn (R)	70,898	44.0
6 William C. Cole (R)	89,428	52.4
Robert O. Richardson (D)	81,237	47.6
7 Dewey Short (R)	115,842	61.7
John Hosmer (D)	71,936	38.3
8 A. S. J. Carnahan (D)	69,068	52.9
Francis E. Howard (R)	61,621	47.2
9 Clarence Cannon (D)	98,965	54.8
S. W. (Wat) Arnold (R)	81,806	45.3
10 Paul C. Jones (D)	71,156	60.7
Andrew Sandegren (R)	46,033	39.3
11 Morgan M. Moulder (D)	74,362	50.4
Max Schwabe (R)	73,104	49.6

MONTANA

	Candidates	Votes	%
1	Lee Metcalf (D)	55,679	50.3
	Wellington D. Rankin (R)	54,086	48.9
2	Wesley A. D'Ewart (R)	90,210	62.0
	Willard E. Fraser (D)	55,203	38.0

NEBRASKA

1	Carl T. Curtis (R)	117,336	72.1
	Samuel Freeman (D)	45,523	28.0
2	Roman L. Hruska (R)	81,185	56.1
	James A. Hart (D)	63,485	43.9
3	Robert D. Harrison (R)	89,879	71.9
	Alan A. Dusatko (D)	35,213	28.2
4	Arthur L. Miller (R)	98,032	73.3
	Francis D. Lee (D)	35,628	26.7

NEVADA

AL	Clifton Young (R)	40,683	50.5
	Walter S. Baring (D)	39,912	49.5

NEW HAMPSHIRE

1	Chester E. Merrow (R)	82,689	60.2
	Peter R. Poirier (D)	54,746	39.8
2	Norris Cotton (R)	80,061	66.5
	John Guay (D)	40,373	33.5

NEW JERSEY

1	Charles A. Wolverton (R)	118,367	55.0
	Alfred R. Pierce (D)	96,162	44.7
2	T. Millet Hand (R)	79,955	63.4
	Charles Edward Rupp (D)	46,174	36.6
3	James C. Auchincloss (R)	124,292	64.4
	John W. Zimmermann (D)	67,642	35.0
4	Charles R. Howell (D)	84,733	54.7
	John J. Inglesby (R)	70,076	45.3
5	Peter H. B. Frelinghuysen Jr. (R)	133,276	62.2
	Aldona L. Appleton (D)	80,922	37.8
6	Clifford P. Case (R)	121,252	63.9
	H. Frank Pettit (D)	67,159	35.4
7	William B. Widnall (R)	130,603	68.3
	Vito A. Concilio (D)	60,553	31.7
8	Gordon Canfield (R)	97,338	62.6
	John J. Winberry (D)	54,367	35.0
9	Frank C. Osmers Jr. (R)	125,402	66.2
	William H. McNulty (D)	63,175	33.4
10	Peter W. Rodino Jr. (D)	78,612	56.9
	Alexander J. Matturri (R)	57,740	41.8
11	Hugh J. Addonizio (D)	68,273	52.2
	William O. Barnes Jr. (R)	60,461	46.3
12	Robert Winthrop Kean (R)	84,949	54.8
	Martin S. Fox (D)	70,046	45.2
13	Alfred D. Sieminski (D)	72,987	55.2
	Julius D. Canter (R)	54,581	41.2
14	Edward J. Hart (D)	67,109	51.5
	William J. Bozzuffi (R)	59,112	45.4

NEW MEXICO

AL	John J. Dempsey (D)	121,477✔	
	Antonio M. Fernandez (D)	119,925✔	
	Homer J. Berkshire (R)	112,297	
	Ed Guthmann (R)	109,595	

NEW YORK

1	Stuyvesant Wainwright (R)	114,135	60.4
	Ernest Greenwood (D, L)	74,174	39.3
2	Steven B. Derounian (R)	132,512	68.8
	Joseph Liff (D)	54,725	28.4
3	Frank J. Becker (R)	128,007	65.4
	Richard A. O'Leary (D)	60,800	31.0
4	Henry J. Latham (R)	123,132	62.6
	Joseph J. Perrini (D, L)	70,755	36.0
5	Albert H. Bosch (R)	86,168	53.5
	L. Gary Clemente (D, L)	73,083	45.3
6	Lester Holtzman (D, L)	105,261	49.2
	Robert Tripp Ross (R)	104,720	48.9
7	James J. Delaney (D, L)	87,204	51.0
	William Adam Schulz (R)	80,896	47.3
8	Louis B. Heller (D, L)	75,772	65.3
	Benjamin F. Westervelt Jr. (R)	37,884	32.6
9	Eugene J. Keogh (D, L)	83,841	61.1
	Joseph M. Soviero (R)	48,998	35.7
10	Edna F. Kelly (D, L)	105,302	71.2
	George W. Thomas (R)	42,498	28.8
11	Emanuel Celler (D, L)	127,091	73.8
	Henry D. Dorfman (R)	37,244	21.6
12	Francis E. Dorn (R)	75,895	52.7
	Donald L. O'Toole (D, L)	65,650	45.6
13	Abraham J. Multer (D, L)	112,152	68.3
	P. Vincent Landi (R)	45,664	27.8
14	John J. Rooney (D, L)	86,952	64.2
	Jacob P. Lefkowitz (R)	45,004	33.2
15	John H. Ray (R)	97,023	57.9
	James J. Murphy (D, L)	69,538	41.5
16	Adam Clayton Powell Jr. (D)	72,562	73.9
	Richard L. Baltimore Jr. (R)	15,937	16.2
	Clarence Francis (L)	7,125	7.3
17	Frederic R. Coudert Jr. (R)	84,821	57.0
	Harry Grossman (D, L)	60,624	40.7
18	James G. Donovan (D, R)	88,629	92.6
	Vito Magli (AM LAB)	7,047	7.4
19	Arthur G. Klein (D, L)	77,267	66.0
	Edward I. Goldberg (R)	34,795	29.7
20	Franklin D. Roosevelt Jr. (D, L)	81,591	60.2
	Clarence C. Vambell (R)	49,905	36.8
21	Jacob K. Javits (R, L)	89,866	63.4
	John C. Hart (D)	47,637	33.6
22	Sidney A. Fine (D)	90,474	58.0
	Martin Greene (R)	38,681	24.8
	David Wells (L)	21,606	13.9
23	Isidore Dollinger (D)	78,350	63.8
	Sidney S. Flaum (R)	23,238	18.9
	Harry Kavesh (L)	14,393	11.7
	Howard Fast (AM LAB)	6,834	5.6
24	Charles A. Buckley (D)	82,343	46.5
	Solon S. Kane (R)	58,096	32.8
	Herman Woskow (L)	29,425	16.6
25	Paul A. Fino (R)	85,308	50.1
	Bernard J. O'Connell (D)	68,862	40.4
	Louis Schifrin (L)	13,325	7.8
26	Ralph A. Gamble (R)	116,091	67.3
	Flora Chudson (D, L)	55,184	32.0
27	Ralph W. Gwinn (R)	108,575	58.5
	George A. Brenner (D, L)	75,781	40.9
28	Katharine St. George (R)	102,476	65.6
	Marion K. Sanders (D, L)	52,994	33.9
29	J. Ernest Wharton (R)	115,502	69.8
	Walter Donnaruma (D)	46,727	28.2
30	Leo W. O'Brien (D, L)	101,178	53.7
	John F. Forner Jr. (R)	86,651	46.0
31	Dean P. Taylor (R)	114,656	70.6
	Helen Nolan Neil (D)	44,367	27.3
32	Bernard W. Kearney (R)	111,025	67.4
33	Clarence E. Kilburn (R)	98,653	69.0
	Maurice N. McGrath (D)	41,803	29.2
34	William R. Williams (R)	97,488	58.8
	Charles Ray Wilson (D)	65,080	39.3
35	R. Walter Riehlman (R)	113,778	63.2
	Arthur B. McGuire (D, L)	65,763	36.5
36	John Taber (R)	110,304	69.9
	Donald J. O'Connor (D, L)	47,189	29.9
37	W. Sterling Cole (R)	131,172	69.4
	Jean Ivory (D, L)	57,474	30.4
38	Kenneth B. Keating (R)	128,566	69.3
	Victor Kruppenbacher (D, L)	56,177	30.3
39	Harold C. Ostertag (R)	107,501	65.8
	O. Richard Judson (D, L)	55,483	34.0
40	William E. Miller (R)	102,565	59.6
	E. Dent Lackey (D, L)	69,087	40.2
41	Edmund P. Radwan (R)	95,755	55.9
	Anthony F. Tauriello (D, L)	75,552	44.1
42	John R. Pillion (R)	100,434	55.2
	Chester C. Gorski (D, L)	81,201	44.6
43	Daniel A. Reed (R)	91,534	66.2
	Harry D. Johnson (D)	44,276	32.0

Special Election

32	Leo W. O'Brien (D, L)	66,849	70.8
	John F. Forner Jr. (R)	27,276	28.9

NORTH CAROLINA

1	Herbert C. Bonner (D)	43,104	100.0
2	L. H. Fountain (D)	51,213	94.8
	W. B. White (R)	2,822	5.2
3	Graham A. Barden (D)	45,458	76.2
	Everette L. Peterson (R)	14,239	23.9
4	Harold D. Cooley (D)	79,520	75.3
	Paul C. West (R)	26,039	24.7
5	Thurmond Chatham (D)	74,884	98.2
6	Carl T. Durham (D)	84,203	69.5
	Louis F. Ferree (R)	36,912	30.5
7	F. Ertel Carlyle (D)	62,884	98.5
8	Charles B. Deane (D)	67,764	59.9
	Walter B. Love (R)	45,451	40.2
9	Hugh Q. Alexander (D)	68,624	51.5
	Walter P. Johnson (R)	64,662	48.5
10	Charles Raper Jonas (R)	82,428	57.4
	Hamilton C. Jones (D)	61,149	42.6
11	Woodrow W. Jones (D)	61,540	63.0
	George M. Pritchard (R)	36,157	37.0
12	George A. Shuford (D)	63,045	56.9
	Hugh Montieth (R)	47,752	43.1

NORTH DAKOTA

AL	Usher L. Burdick (R)	181,218✔	
	Otto Krueger (R)	156,829✔	
	Edward Nesemeier (D)	49,829	

OHIO

1	Gordon H. Scherer (R)	96,385	61.6
	Walter A. Kelly (D)	60,015	38.4
2	William E. Hess (R)	90,417	56.6
	Earl T. Wagner (D)	69,341	43.4
3	Paul F. Schenck (R)	112,325	51.1
	Thomas B. Talbot (D)	107,551	48.9
4	William M. McCulloch (R)	93,442	68.3
	Carleton Carl Reiser (D)	43,426	31.7
5	Cliff Clevenger (R)	72,168	63.2
	Dan Batt (D)	42,104	36.9
6	James G. Polk (D)	67,220	50.1
	Leo Blackburn (R)	66,896	49.9
7	Clarence J. Brown (R)	98,354	100.0
8	Jackson E. Betts (R)	75,768	68.7
	Henry P. Drake (D)	34,474	31.3
9	Frazier Reams (I)	74,821	40.9
	Thomas H. Burke (D)	61,047	33.4
	Gilmore Flues (R)	46,989	25.7
10	Thomas A. Jenkins (R)	63,339	64.0
	Delmar A. Canaday (D)	35,666	36.0
11	Oliver P. Bolton (R)	91,204	58.8
	Robert J. Kilpatrick (D)	63,930	41.2
12	John M. Vorys (R)	134,693	62.3
	George T. Tarbutton (D)	81,665	37.8
13	Alvin F. Weichel (R)	63,344	58.8
	George C. Steinemann (D)	44,467	41.3
14	William H. Ayres (R)	117,745	58.5
	Walter B. Huber (D)	83,463	41.5
15	Robert T. Secrest (D)	62,913	64.3
	P. W. Griffiths (R)	34,966	35.7
16	Frank T. Bow (R)	98,447	54.4
	John McSweeney (D)	82,522	45.6

OHIO

Candidates	Votes	%
17 J. Harry McGregor (R)	94,624	68.2
James J. Mayer (D)	44,117	31.8
18 Wayne L. Hays (D)	78,277	55.8
Clarence L. Wetzel (R)	62,081	44.2
19 Michael J. Kirwan (D)	91,074	66.3
Allen Russell (R)	46,202	33.7
20 Michael A. Feighan (D)	109,211	65.2
John H. Ferguson (R)	58,271	34.8
21 Robert Crosser (D)	100,340	68.6
Lawrence O. Payne (R)	45,896	31.4
22 Frances P. Bolton (R)	87,316	58.8
Chat Paterson (D)	61,197	41.2
23 George H. Bender (R)	85,752	64.6
Michael P. O'Brien (D)	47,090	35.5

OKLAHOMA

Candidates	Votes	%
1 Page Belcher (R)	121,442	58.6
H. G. Dickey (D)	85,647	41.4
2 Ed Edmondson (D)	92,407	59.2
Edward E. Easton (R)	60,550	38.8
3 Carl Albert (D)	73,185	77.9
Frank D. McSherry (R)	20,735	22.1
4 Tom Steed (D)	67,024	58.7
John L. Goode (R)	46,446	40.7
5 John Jarman (D)	128,627	62.4
Edwin Whitney Burch (R)	77,425	37.6
6 Victor E. Wickersham (D)	98,823	63.3
K. B. Cornell (R)	57,261	36.7

OREGON

Candidates	Votes	%
1 Walter Norblad (R)	124,720	68.0
Robert B. Jones (D)	58,796	32.0
2 Sam Coon (R)	57,155	58.5
John G. Jones (D)	40,550	41.5
3 Homer D. Angell (R)	125,504	54.0
Alfred H. Corbett (D)	107,099	46.0
4 Harris Ellsworth (R)	100,970	66.3
Walter A. Swanson (D)	51,298	33.7

PENNSYLVANIA

Candidates	Votes	%
1 William A. Barrett (D)	89,879	68.2
James Iannucci (R)	41,948	31.8
2 William T. Granahan (D)	105,553	61.8
Daniel J. McCauley Jr. (R)	65,159	38.2
3 James A. Byrne (D)	81,837	58.4
Morton Witkin (R)	58,191	41.6
4 Earl Chudoff (D)	90,077	69.9
Joseph R. Burns (R)	38,228	29.7
5 William J. Green Jr (D)	104,112	54.2
Philip Richman (R)	88,040	45.8
6 Hugh Scott (R)	93,368	51.7
Harrington Herr (D)	87,124	48.2
7 Benjamin F. James (R)	127,918	61.7
Murray P. Zealor (D)	79,423	38.3
8 Karl C. King (R)	83,966	59.3
Wilson H. Stephenson (D)	57,723	40.7
9 Paul B. Dague (R)	100,578	66.2
Philip E. Ragan (D)	51,268	33.8
10 Joseph L. Carrigg (R)	89,820	53.6
Harry P. O'Neill (D)	77,758	46.4
11 Edward J. Bonin (R)	80,310	50.2
Daniel J. Flood (D)	79,722	49.8
12 Ivor D. Fenton (R)	79,859	60.7
Peter Krehel (D)	51,736	39.3
13 Samuel K. McConnell Jr. (R)	114,672	66.4
Frank A. Keegan (D)	57,974	33.6
14 George M. Rhodes (D)	48,427	49.7
James W. Bertolet (R)	48,019	49.2
15 Francis E. Walter (D)	61,566	54.8
John Russell Craig (R)	50,871	45.2
16 Walter M. Mumma (R)	83,493	61.7
David V. Randall (D)	51,825	38.3
17 Alvin R. Bush (R)	82,058	64.2
Patrick A. McGowan (D)	44,376	34.7

Candidates	Votes	%
18 Richard M. Simpson (R)	75,723	63.5
Philip R. Shoemaker (D)	43,555	36.5
19 S. Walter Stauffer (R)	72,466	52.3
James F. Lind (D)	66,165	47.7
20 James E. Van Zandt (R)	62,804	62.8
Joseph A. Moran (D)	37,152	37.2
21 Augustine B. Kelley (D)	73,223	52.9
J. Cleveland McKenna (R)	65,252	47.1
22 John P. Saylor (R)	77,391	52.4
William D. Shettig (D)	70,218	47.6
23 Leon H. Gavin (R)	73,001	67.8
Fred C. Barr (D)	34,633	32.2
24 Carroll D. Kearns (R)	90,276	57.1
Clinton J. Bebell (D)	67,790	42.9
25 Louis E. Graham (R)	77,577	50.4
Frank M. Clark (D)	76,214	49.6
26 Thomas E. Morgan (D)	105,581	59.1
Edward J. Sittler Jr. (R)	72,981	40.9
27 James C. Fulton (R)	118,915	62.6
Thomas J. O'Toole (D)	71,039	37.4
28 Herman P. Eberharter (D)	98,432	58.7
Harmar D. Denny (R)	69,288	41.3
29 Robert J. Corbett (R)	115,069	61.7
Lee T. Sellars (D)	71,573	38.4
30 Vera Buchanan (D)	115,292	63.6
Peter F. Bender (R)	65,926	36.4

RHODE ISLAND

Candidates	Votes	%
1 Aime J. Forand (D)	105,404	54.9
Berthelot Leclaire (R)	86,523	45.1
2 John E. Fogarty (D)	115,057	53.4
James O. Watts (R)	100,305	46.6

SOUTH CAROLINA

Candidates	Votes	%
1 L. Mendel Rivers (D)	30,483	100.0
2 John J. Riley (D)	42,201	100.0
3 W. J. Bryan Dorn (D)	44,237	93.8
David Dows (R)	2,849	6.0
4 Joseph R. Bryson (D)	77,850	100.0
5 James P. Richards (D)	42,081	93.9
Herbert L. Crosland (R)	2,722	6.1
6 John L. McMillan (D)	41,328	100.0

SOUTH DAKOTA

Candidates	Votes	%
1 Harold O. Lovre (R)	151,449	68.5
Goldie Wells (D)	69,777	31.5
2 E. Y. Berry (R)	45,688	69.0
George A. Bangs (D)	20,561	31.0

TENNESSEE

Candidates	Votes	%
1 B. Carroll Reece (R)	70,556	65.9
Arthur W. Bright (D)	36,477	34.1
2 Howard H. Baker (R)	84,977	69.0
Boyd W. Cox (D)	38,268	31.1
3 James B. Frazier Jr. (D)	56,473	70.0
Joseph M. Parker (R)	24,177	30.0
4 Joe L. Evins (D)	65,787	100.0
5 J. Percy Priest (D)	49,925	67.5
Homer P. Wall (R)	24,056	32.5
6 Pat Sutton (D)	56,878	100.0
7 Tom Murray (D)	39,529	100.0
8 Jere Cooper (D)	34,877	100.0
9 Clifford Davis (D)	101,427	85.7
William P. Chenault (I)	16,972	14.3

TEXAS

Candidates	Votes	%
1 Wright Patman (D)	56,491	100.0
2 Jack Brooks (D)	83,267	79.0
R. C. Reed (R)	22,108	21.0
3 Brady Gentry (D)	57,033	100.0
4 Sam Rayburn (D)	47,888	100.0
5 J. Frank Wilson (D)	172,539	100.0
6 Olin E. Teague (D)	49,461	100.0

Candidates	Votes	%
7 John Dowdy (D)	52,420	100.0
8 Albert Thomas (D)	200,608	100.0
9 Clark W. Thompson (D)	96,214	100.0
10 Homer Thornberry (D)	65,924	100.0
11 W. R. Poage (D)	59,088	100.0
12 Wingate Lucas (D)	101,964	100.0
13 Frank Ikard (D)	72,373	100.0
14 John E. Lyle Jr. (D)	94,866	100.0
15 Lloyd M. Bentsen Jr. (D)	63,753	99.9
16 Ken Regan (D)	67,782	100.0
17 Omar Burleson (D)	59,386	100.0
18 Walter Rogers (D)	77,661	100.0
19 George Mahon (D)	87,894	100.0
20 Paul J. Kilday (D)	64,841	100.0
21 O. C. Fisher (D)	65,762	100.0
AL Martin Dies (D, R)	1,979,811	100.0

UTAH

Candidates	Votes	%
1 Douglas R. Stringfellow (R)	76,545	60.5
Ernest R. McKay (D)	49,898	39.5
2 William A. Dawson (R)	105,296	52.6
Reva Beck Bosone (D)	95,084	47.5

VERMONT

Candidates	Votes	%
AL Winston L. Prouty (R)	109,871	71.8
Herbert B. Comings (D)	43,187	28.2

VIRGINIA

Candidates	Votes	%
1 Edward J. Robeson Jr. (D)	24,836	99.6
2 Porter Hardy Jr. (D)	28,948	99.9
3 J. Vaughan Gary (D)	36,085	57.5
Walter R. Gambill (R)	26,488	42.2
4 Watkins M. Abbitt (D)	23,806	99.8
5 Thomas B. Stanley (D)	19,971	99.9
6 Richard H. Poff (R)	34,041	51.5
Clarence G. Burton (D)	31,997	48.4
7 Burr P. Harrison (D)	37,360	79.1
Glenn W. Ruebush (R)	9,876	20.9
8 Howard W. Smith (D)	29,670	75.7
Homer G. Richey (I)	9,495	24.2
9 William C. Wampler (R)	35,047	51.7
M. M. Long (D)	32,735	48.3
10 Joel T. Broyhill (R)	33,152	50.2
Edmund D. Campbell (D)	32,830	49.7

WASHINGTON

Candidates	Votes	%
1 Thomas M. Pelly (R)	121,926	51.4
Stimson Bullitt (D)	114,617	48.3
2 Jack Westland (R)	91,853	54.2
Harry F. Henson (D)	77,179	45.6
3 Russell V. Mack (R)	75,165	53.3
Gordon M. Quarnstrom (D)	65,715	46.6
4 Hal Holmes (R)	92,551	67.6
William Bryan (D)	44,464	32.5
5 Walter F. Horan (R)	82,530	56.0
Robert D. Dellwo (D)	64,820	44.0
6 Thor C. Tollefson (R)	110,169	59.8
John J. O'Connell (D)	74,143	40.2
AL Don Magnuson (D)	515,213	50.5
Al Canwell (R)	504,783	49.5

WEST VIRGINIA

Candidates	Votes	%
1 Robert H. Mollohan (D)	72,218	52.9
Francis J. Love (R)	64,216	47.1
2 Harley O. Staggers (D)	67,172	51.5
Kermit R. Mason (R)	63,320	48.5
3 Cleveland M. Bailey (D)	71,926	53.4
Frank Love (R)	62,839	46.6
4 Will E. Neal (R)	82,104	53.3
M. G. Burnside (D)	71,819	46.7

WEST VIRGINIA

Candidates	Votes	%
5 Elizabeth Kee (D)	83,653	63.8
Cyrus H. Gadd (R)	47,519	36.2
6 Robert C. Byrd (D)	104,387	55.6
Latelle M. LaFollette (R)	83,429	44.4

WISCONSIN

Candidates	Votes	%
1 Lawrence H. Smith (R)	99,742	59.4
Arnie W. Agnew (D)	68,269	40.6
2 Glenn R. Davis (R)	116,542	62.9
Horace W. Wilkie (D)	68,665	37.1

Candidates	Votes	%
3 Gardner R. Withrow (R)	96,908	75.1
Edna Bowen (D)	32,165	24.9
4 Clement J. Zablocki (D)	131,098	64.3
John C. Schafer (R)	72,869	35.7
5 Charles J. Kersten (R)	112,048	51.6
Andrew J. Biemiller (D)	105,013	48.4
6 William K. Van Pelt (R)	103,464	71.7
Ralph A. Norem (D)	40,910	28.3
7 Melvin R. Laird (R)	95,049	72.3
Ernest Kluck (D)	36,387	27.7
8 John W. Byrnes (R)	114,183	73.6
Robert C. Schultz (D)	40,980	26.4

Candidates	Votes	%
9 Merlin Hull (R)	81,258	65.2
Kent L. Pillsbury (D)	43,437	34.8
10 Alvin E. O'Konski (R)	73,527	67.4
Roland Kannenberg (D)	35,597	32.6

WYOMING

Candidates	Votes	%
AL William Henry Harrison (R)	76,161	60.1
Robert R. Ross Jr. (D)	50,559	39.9

1953 House Elections

GEORGIA

Special Election

Candidates	Votes	%
2 J. L. Pilcher (D)	10,936	35.5
H. Grady Rawls	9,764	31.7
H. L. Wingate Jr.	6,073	19.7
John E. Sheffield Jr.	3,130	10.2

ILLINOIS

Special Election

Candidates	Votes	%
7 James B. Bowler (D)	31,600	83.5
Philip J. Boffa (R)	6,239	16.5

NEW JERSEY

Special Election

	Votes	%
6 Harrison A. Williams Jr. (D)	68,871	50.8
George F. Hetfield (R)	66,796	49.2

VIRGINIA

Special Election

Candidates	Votes	%
5 William M. Tuck (D)	16,693	57.8
Lorne R. Campbell	12,182	42.2

WISCONSIN

Special Election

	Votes	%
9 Lester R. Johnson (D)	27,852	56.9
Arthur L. Padrutt (R)	21,127	43.1

1954 House Elections

ALABAMA

	Candidates	Votes	%
1	Frank W. Boykin (D)	27,462	100.0
2	George Grant (D)	30,661	100.0
3	George Andrews (D)	22,371	100.0
4	Kenneth A. Roberts (D)	28,660	100.0
5	Albert Rains (D)	38,257	100.0
6	Armistead I. Selden Jr. (D)	18,753	100.0
7	Carl Elliott (D)	31,988	78.9
	W. B. Engle (R)	8,547	21.1
8	Robert E. Jones Jr. (D)	29,414	91.6
	Adin Batson (R)	2,689	8.4
9	George Huddleston Jr. (D)	40,986	100.0

ARIZONA

		Votes	%
1	John J. Rhodes (R)	60,423	53.1
	L. S. Adams (D)	53,307	46.9
2	Stewart L. Udall (D)	68,085	62.1
	Henry Zipf (R)	41,587	37.9

ARKANSAS

		Votes	%
1	Ezekiel C. Gathings (D)	38,951	100.0
2	Wilbur D. Mills (D)	33,038	100.0
3	James W. Trimble (D)	60,035	100.0
4	Oren Harris (D)	51,579	100.0
5	Brooks Hays (D)	51,828	100.0
6	William F. Norrell (D)	44,833	100.0

CALIFORNIA

		Votes	%
1	Hubert B. Scudder (R)	83,762	59.1
	Max Kortum (D)	58,004	40.9
2	Clair Engle (D-R)	113,104	100.0
3	John E. Moss Jr. (D)	96,238	65.3
	James H. Phillips (R)	51,111	34.7
4	William S. Mailliard (R)	88,439	61.2
	Philip A. O'Rourke (D)	52,980	36.7
5	John F. Shelley (D-R)	86,428	100.0
6	John F. Baldwin Jr. (R)	72,336	50.9
	Robert L. Condon (D)	69,776	49.1
7	John J. Allen Jr. (R)	64,083	53.0
	Stanley K. Crook (D)	56,807	47.0
8	George P. Miller (D)	101,803	65.4
	Jess M. Ritchie (R)	53,869	34.6
9	J. Arthur Younger (R)	60,648	54.5
	Harold F. Taggart (D)	50,619	45.5
10	Charles S. Gubser (R)	94,418	61.2
	Paul V. Birmingham (D)	59,843	38.8
11	Leroy Johnson (R)	54,716	52.6
	Carl Sugar (D)	49,388	47.4
12	B. F. Sisk (D)	63,911	53.8
	Oakley Hunter (R)	54,903	46.2
13	Charles M. Teague (R)	69,287	52.5
	Timothy I. O'Reilly (D)	62,786	47.5
14	Harlan Hagen (D)	75,194	65.1
	Al Blain (R)	40,270	34.9
15	Gordon L. McDonough (R)	77,651	56.9
	Frank P. O'Sullivan (D)	58,785	43.1
16	Donald L. Jackson (R)	63,124	60.8
	S. Mark Hogue (D)	40,659	39.2
17	Cecil R. King (D)	97,828	60.1
	Robert H. Finch (R)	64,967	39.9
18	Craig Hosmer (R)	71,213	55.0
	Joseph M. Kennick (D)	58,647	45.0
19	Chet Holifield (D)	90,269	74.8
	Raymond R. Pritchard (R)	30,404	25.2
20	Carl Hinshaw (R)	71,213	71.2
	Eugene Radding (D)	28,838	28.8
21	Edgar W. Hiestand (R)	100,258	58.7
	William E. Roskam (D)	70,486	41.3
22	Joe Holt (R)	65,165	58.2
	William M. Costley (D)	46,875	41.8
23	Clyde Doyle (D)	90,729	70.9
	Frank G. Bussing (R)	34,911	27.3
24	Glenard P. Lipscomb (R)	65,431	56.9
	George Arnold (D)	49,592	43.1
25	Patrick J. Hillings (R)	113,027	65.2
	John G. Sobieski (D)	60,370	34.8
26	James Roosevelt (D)	94,261	60.1
	Theodore R. Owings (R)	62,585	39.9
27	Harry R. Sheppard (D)	65,389	64.8
	Martin K. Barrett (R)	35,594	35.3
28	James B. Utt (R)	95,680	66.2
	Harriet Enderle (D)	48,785	33.8
29	John Phillips (R)	42,420	57.9
	Bruce Shangle (D)	30,781	42.1
30	Bob Wilson (R)	94,623	60.4
	Ross T. McIntire (D)	61,994	39.6

COLORADO

		Votes	%
1	Byron G. Rogers (D)	84,745	55.6
	Ellen G. Harris (R)	67,210	44.1
2	William S. Hill (R)	80,162	55.3
	Lacy L. Wilkinson (D)	64,776	44.7
3	J. Edgar Chenoweth (R)	62,884	53.0
	Alva B. Adams (D)	55,750	47.0
4	Wayne N. Aspinall (D)	34,294	53.5
	Charles E. Wilson (R)	29,818	46.5

CONNECTICUT

		Votes	%
1	Thomas J. Dodd (D)	148,935	57.0
	Wallace Barnes (R)	112,526	43.0
2	Horace Seely-Brown Jr. (R)	72,833	50.7
	Henry H. Pierce Jr. (D)	70,853	49.3
3	Albert W. Cretella (R)	94,977	52.7
	James F. Gartland (D)	85,369	47.3
4	Albert P. Morano (R)	123,890	56.2
	Edward R. Fay Jr. (D)	91,184	41.4
5	James T. Patterson (R)	68,451	52.8
	David Brady (D)	61,313	47.3
AL	Antoni N. Sadlak (R)	474,585	51.0
	Joseph P. Lyford (D)	455,887	49.0

DELAWARE

		Votes	%
AL	Harris B. McDowell Jr. (D)	79,201	54.9
	Lillian I. Martin (R)	65,035	45.1

FLORIDA

		Votes	%
1	William C. Cramer (R)	52,287	50.8
	Courtney Campbell (D)	50,744	49.3
2	Charles E. Bennett (D)	14,376	100.0
3	Robert L. F. Sikes (D)	27,013	100.0
4	Dante B. Fascell (D)	47,697	100.0
5	A. S. Herlong Jr. (D)	35,971	100.0
6	Dwight L. Rogers (D)	39,148	100.0
7	James A. Haley (D)	23,469	55.5
	E. B. Sutton (D)	18,850	44.5
8	D. R. Matthews (D)	16,732	100.0

GEORGIA

		Votes	%
1	Prince H. Preston (D)	26,205	83.7
	Frank Downing	5,100	16.3
2	J. L. Pilcher (D)	26,705	99.9
3	E. L. Forrester (D)	34,973	100.0
4	John J. Flynt Jr. (D)	32,400	100.0
5	James C. Davis (D)	54,069	64.4
	Charles A. Moye Jr. (R)	29,911	35.6
6	Carl Vinson (D)	26,250	100.0
7	Henderson L. Lanham (D)	35,147	100.0
8	Iris Faircloth Blitch (D)	27,037	100.0
9	Phil M. Landrum (D)	26,849	100.0
10	Paul Brown (D)	28,068	100.0

IDAHO

		Votes	%
1	Gracie B. Pfost (D)	50,214	54.9
	Erwin H. Schwiebert (R)	41,293	45.1
2	Hamer H. Budge (R)	81,824	60.8
	William P. Whitaker (D)	52,681	39.2

ILLINOIS

		Votes	%
1	William L. Dawson (D)	71,472	75.3
	Genoa S. Washington (R)	23,470	24.7
2	Barratt O'Hara (D)	80,016	61.6
	Richard B. Vail (R)	49,970	38.4
3	James C. Murray (D)	77,675	53.8
	Fred E. Busbey (R)	66,767	46.2
4	William E. McVey (R)	94,125	52.2
	William A. Rowan (D)	86,372	47.9
5	John C. Kluczynski (D)	92,780	73.2
	S. Charles Bubacz (R)	33,987	26.8
6	Thomas J. O'Brien (D)	99,590	71.7
	Orville F. Corbin (R)	39,289	28.3
7	James B. Bowler (D)	97,398	78.4
	Charles M. Barrett (R)	26,763	21.6
8	Thomas S. Gordon (D)	74,837	68.4
	James L. Doherty (R)	34,535	31.6
9	Sidney R. Yates (D)	73,187	60.3
	Ralph Lee Goodman (R)	48,130	39.7
10	Richard W. Hoffman (R)	90,961	57.3
	Helen J. Kelleher (D)	67,903	42.7
11	Timothy P. Sheehan (R)	67,141	50.9
	Harry H. Semrow (D)	64,788	49.1
12	Charles A. Boyle (D)	82,518	54.1
	Edgar A. Jonas (R)	69,999	45.9
13	Marguerite Stitt Church (R)	146,184	69.6
	Richard A. Griffin (D)	63,852	30.4
14	Chauncey W. Reed (R)	100,024	72.4
	Richard Plum (D)	38,161	27.6
15	Noah M. Mason (R)	72,576	62.8
	Richard A. Mohan (D)	42,934	37.2
16	Leo E. Allen (R)	77,557	100.0
17	Leslie C. Arends (R)	79,044	65.0
	Branson Wright (D)	42,600	35.0
18	Harold H. Velde (R)	59,963	57.5
	Howard S. Beeney (D)	44,408	42.6
19	Robert B. Chiperfield (R)	64,772	56.5
	John M. Kerwin Jr. (D)	49,876	43.5
20	Sidney E. Simpson (R)	68,104	62.9
	James A. Barry (D)	40,165	37.1
21	Peter F. Mack Jr. (D)	83,501	54.8
	Edward H. Jenison (R)	68,924	45.2
22	William L. Springer (R)	66,797	62.0
	Robert W. Martin (D)	40,873	38.0
23	Charles W. Vursell (R)	69,179	52.9
	Albert R. Imle (D)	61,493	47.1
24	Melvin Price (D)	90,482	69.2
	John T. Thomas (R)	40,358	30.9
25	Kenneth J. Gray (D)	69,562	52.6
	C. W. Bishop (R)	62,659	47.4

INDIANA

		Votes	%
1	Ray J. Madden (D)	81,217	61.4
	Robert H. Moore (R)	50,439	38.2
2	Charles A. Halleck (R)	73,717	59.6
	James H. Berg (D)	49,996	40.4
3	Shepard J. Crumpacker Jr. (R)	85,884	50.4
	John Brademas (D)	83,851	49.2
4	E. Ross Adair (R)	71,436	59.8
	Fred W. Greene (D)	47,384	39.7

INDIANA

Candidates	Votes	%
5 John V. Beamer (R)	88,428	53.1
John R. Walsh (D)	76,972	46.2
6 Cecil M. Harden (R)	67,371	52.5
John W. King (D)	60,896	47.5
7 William G. Bray (R)	75,608	55.4
George D. Gettinger (D)	60,594	44.4
8 Winfield K. Denton (D)	82,264	52.1
D. Bailey Merrill (R)	74,960	47.5
9 Earl Wilson (R)	61,285	51.7
Wilfred J. Ullrich (D)	57,350	48.3
10 Ralph Harvey (R)	76,132	55.9
Inez M. Scholl (D)	59,103	43.4
11 Charles B. Brownson (R)	108,044	54.9
Charles H. Boswell (D)	88,173	44.8

IOWA

	Votes	%
1 Fred Schwengel (R)	67,128	57.0
John O'Connor (D)	50,577	43.0
2 Henry O. Talle (R)	72,231	55.4
Ruben V. Austin (D)	58,092	44.6
3 H. R. Gross (R)	68,307	62.1
George R. Laub (D)	41,622	37.9
4 Karl M. LeCompte (R)	49,608	55.6
Herschel C. Loveless (D)	39,652	44.4
5 Paul Cunningham (R)	61,355	55.6
James A. McLaughlin (D)	49,063	44.4
6 James I. Dolliver (R)	53,457	60.3
Lumund F. Wilcox (D)	35,137	39.7
7 Ben F. Jensen (R)	51,022	60.4
Elmer G. Carlson (D)	33,492	39.6
8 Charles B. Hoeven (R)	55,214	63.8
Roy B. Holland (D)	31,296	36.2

KANSAS

	Votes	%
1 William H. Avery (R)	56,079	54.3
Howard S. Miller (D)	47,165	45.7
2 Errett P. Scrivner (R)	64,263	54.7
Newell A. George (D)	53,302	45.3
3 Myron V. George (R)	41,342	55.4
William W. Monypeny (D)	33,307	44.6
4 Ed H. Rees (R)	77,920	56.2
Robert M. Green (D)	60,697	43.8
5 Clifford R. Hope (R)	64,023	64.9
Robert L. Bock (D)	34,691	35.1
6 Wint Smith (R)	43,831	53.3
Elmo J. Mahoney (D)	38,369	46.7

KENTUCKY

	Votes	%
1 Noble J. Gregory (D)	62,210	100.0
2 William H. Natcher (D)	49,231	100.0
3 John M. Robsion Jr. (R)	72,073	50.2
Harrison M. Robertson (D)	71,500	49.8
4 Frank Chelf (D)	49,496	100.0
5 Brent Spence (D)	63,640	61.0
M. J. See (R)	40,679	39.0
6 John C. Watts (D)	59,434	60.9
Robert L. Milby (R)	38,145	39.1
7 Carl D. Perkins (D)	44,353	60.4
Curtis Clark (R)	29,115	39.6
8 Eugene T. Siler (R)	56,182	63.4
Mitchel S. Fannin (D)	32,128	36.3

LOUISIANA

	Votes	%
1 F. Edward Hebert (D)	38,213	82.3
George W. Reese Jr. (R)	8,212	17.7
2 Hale Boggs (D)	37,583	100.0
3 Edwin E. Willis (D)	15,808	100.0
4 Overton Brooks (D)	24,587	100.0
5 Otto E. Passman (D)	21,831	100.0
6 James H. Morrison (D)	30,082	100.0
7 T. Ashton Thompson (D)	21,525	100.0
8 George S. Long (D)	18,482	100.0

MAINE

Candidates	Votes	%
1 Robert Hale (R)	47,327	52.1
James C. Oliver (D)	43,561	47.9
2 Charles P. Nelson (R)	45,819	54.0
Thomas E. Delahanty (D)	39,075	46.0
3 Clifford G. McIntire (R)	39,749	60.5
Kenneth B. Colbath (D)	25,912	39.5

MARYLAND

1 Edward T. Miller (R)	35,221	55.6
Edward Turner (D)	28,184	44.5
2 James P. S. Devereux (R)	67,179	56.1
William P. Bolton (D)	52,540	43.9
3 Edward A. Garmatz (D)	45,531	97.2
4 George H. Fallon (D)	40,029	57.2
Arthur W. Sherwood (R)	29,921	42.8
5 Richard E. Lankford (D)	60,850	53.7
Frank Small Jr. (R)	52,420	46.3
6 DeWitt S. Hyde (R)	69,658	51.4
Edward J. Ryan (D)	65,760	48.6
7 Samuel N. Friedel (D)	49,221	54.5
Edward C. Dukehart (R)	41,027	45.5

MASSACHUSETTS

1 John W. Heselton (R)	68,420	55.6
John J. Dwyer (D)	54,675	44.4
2 Edward P. Boland (D)	77,899	59.6
Vernon E. Bradley (R)	52,725	40.4
3 Philip J. Philbin (D)	110,013	100.0
4 Harold D. Donohue (D)	83,053	57.1
Andrew B. Holmstrom (R)	62,318	42.9
5 Edith Nourse Rogers (R)	139,989	100.0
6 William H. Bates (R)	91,916	71.2
Andrew J. Gillis (D)	37,216	28.8
7 Thomas J. Lane (D, R)	102,659	100.0
8 Torbert H. Macdonald (D)	74,568	53.2
Angier L. Goodwin (R)	65,614	46.8
9 Donald W. Nicholson (R)	81,378	56.6
James F. O'Neill (D)	62,445	43.4
10 Laurence Curtis (R)	72,502	50.7
Jackson J. Holtz (D)	70,608	49.3
11 Thomas P. O'Neill Jr. (D)	75,613	78.2
Charles S. Bolster (R)	21,039	21.8
12 John W. McCormack (D)	79,073	100.0
13 Richard B. Wigglesworth (R)	90,924	58.0
James F. Gardner (D)	65,854	42.0
14 Joseph W. Martin Jr. (R)	87,840	62.0
Edward F. Doolan (D)	53,818	38.0

MICHIGAN

1 Thaddeus M. Machrowicz (D)	91,435	88.3
Rudolph G. Tenerowicz (R)	11,731	11.3
2 George Meader (R)	69,825	59.8
J. Henry Owens (D)	46,817	40.1
3 August E. Johansen (R)	65,942	59.4
Charles C. Wickett (D)	44,574	40.2
4 Clare E. Hoffman (R)	62,025	62.3
Gordon A. Elferdink (D)	37,500	37.7
5 Gerald R. Ford Jr. (R)	81,702	63.3
Robert S. McAllister (D)	47,453	36.7
6 Don Hayworth (D)	80,325	51.1
Kit Clardy (R)	76,335	48.6
7 Jesse P. Wolcott (R)	71,651	52.8
Ira D. McCoy (D)	63,797	47.0
8 Alvin M. Bentley (R)	65,813	62.7
Clarence V. Smazel (D)	38,828	37.0
9 Ruth Thompson (R)	50,659	55.7
Theodore E. A. Engstrom (D)	39,966	44.0
10 Elford A. Cederberg (R)	50,570	61.4
William J. Kelly (D)	31,794	38.6
11 Victor A. Knox (R)	41,665	54.9
Harold Beaton (D)	34,204	45.1

	Votes	%
12 John B. Bennett (R)	39,531	55.9
Frank E. Hook (D)	31,187	44.1
13 Charles C. Diggs Jr. (D)	64,716	65.8
Landon Knight (R)	33,127	33.7
14 Louis C. Rabaut (D)	97,297	58.2
Joseph A. Moynihan Jr. (R)	69,503	41.6
15 John D. Dingell (D)	85,100	72.7
Gregory M. Pillon (R)	31,815	27.2
16 John Lesinski (D)	121,557	67.9
Stanley A. Grendel (R)	56,815	31.7
17 Martha W. Griffiths (D)	75,258	52.2
Charles G. Oakman (R)	68,613	47.6
18 George A. Dondero (R)	80,771	53.9
Paul Sutton (D)	69,131	46.1

MINNESOTA

1 August H. Andresen (R)	72,686	60.9
Robert C. Olson (DFL)	46,678	39.1
2 Joseph P. O'Hara (R)	71,592	57.9
Harry Sieben (DFL)	52,089	42.1
3 Roy W. Wier (DFL)	98,467	54.4
Edward Willow (R)	82,389	45.6
4 Eugene J. McCarthy (DFL)	81,651	63.0
Richard C. Hansen (R)	47,933	37.0
5 Walter H. Judd (R)	69,901	55.8
Anders Thompson (DFL)	55,452	44.2
6 Fred Marshall (DFL)	72,922	61.9
Oscar J. Jerde (R)	44,850	38.1
7 H. Carl Andersen (R)	60,120	52.6
Douglas P. Hunt (DFL)	54,140	47.4
8 John A. Blatnik (DFL)	89,778	71.8
Ernie Orchard (R)	35,241	28.2
9 Coya Knutson (DFL)	48,999	51.2
Harold C. Hagen (R)	46,664	48.8

MISSISSIPPI

1 Thomas G. Abernethy (D)	15,944	100.0
2 Jamie L. Whitten (D)	13,516	100.0
3 Frank E. Smith (D)	13,468	100.0
4 John Bell Williams (D)	19,164	100.0
5 Arthur Winstead (D)	17,400	100.0
6 William M. Colmer (D)	21,806	100.0

MISSOURI

1 Frank M. Karsten (D)	89,649	66.3
Bill Bangert (R)	45,653	33.7
2 Thomas B. Curtis (R)	83,861	54.7
Eugene H. Buder (D)	69,450	45.3
3 Leonor K. Sullivan (D)	67,715	71.0
George W. Curran (R)	27,598	29.0
4 George H. Christopher (D)	62,012	51.6
Jeffrey P. Hillelson (R)	58,152	48.4
5 Richard Bolling (D)	50,874	58.9
Samuel Lee Chaney (R)	35,477	41.1
6 W. R. Hull Jr. (D)	60,380	53.6
William C. Cole (R)	52,203	46.4
7 Dewey Short (R)	67,918	53.6
J. M. Lowry (D)	58,729	46.4
8 A. S. J. Carnahan (D)	52,658	57.3
Dorman L. Steelman (R)	39,326	42.8
9 Clarence Cannon (D)	65,862	59.0
Noel Carpenter (R)	45,765	41.0
10 Paul C. Jones (D)	34,009	63.9
Clyde Whaley (R)	19,179	36.1
11 Morgan M. Moulder (D)	54,384	55.3
L. C. Davis (R)	43,959	44.7

MONTANA

1 Lee Metcalf (D)	52,614	56.0
Winfield E. Page (R)	41,375	44.0
2 Orvin B. Fjare (R)	66,103	50.6
LeRoy H. Anderson (D)	64,495	49.4

NEBRASKA

Candidates	Votes	%
1 Phil Weaver (R)	68,563	58.6
Frank B. Morrison (D)	48,457	41.4
2 Jackson B. Chase (R)	52,471	53.0
James A. Hart (D)	46,629	47.1
3 Robert D. Harrison (R)	61,124	65.2
Ernest M. Luther (D)	32,562	34.8
4 Arthur L. Miller (R)	68,189	70.4
Carlton W. Laird (D)	28,695	29.6

NEVADA

	Votes	%
AL Clifton Young (R)	42,321	54.5
Walter S. Baring (D)	35,318	45.5

NEW HAMPSHIRE

	Votes	%
1 Chester E. Merrow (R)	54,052	50.2
Thomas J. McIntyre (D)	53,584	49.8
2 Perkins Bass (R)	51,010	60.4
George F. Brown (D)	33,415	39.6

NEW JERSEY

	Votes	%
1 Charles A. Wolverton (R)	92,070	54.4
J. Frank Crawford (D)	77,100	45.5
2 T. Millet Hand (R)	65,551	63.6
Clayton E. Burdick (D)	37,541	36.4
3 James C. Auchincloss (R)	89,085	57.6
Charles F. Sullivan (D)	65,685	42.4
4 Frank Thompson Jr. (D)	72,884	58.4
William G. Freeman (R)	51,998	41.6
5 Peter H. B. Frelinghuysen (R)	99,946	59.3
Luther H. Martin (D)	68,702	40.7
6 Harrison A. Williams Jr. (D)	85,784	56.1
Fred E. Shepard (R)	64,164	41.9
7 William B. Widnall (R)	99,977	63.2
Eugene E. Demarest (D)	58,211	36.8
8 Gordon Canfield (R)	65,359	54.8
Charles S. Joelson (D)	53,844	45.1
9 Frank C. Osmers Jr. (R)	87,008	60.2
Walter J. O'Connell (D)	57,445	39.8
10 Peter W. Rodino Jr. (D)	62,384	63.4
William E. McGlynn (R)	36,056	36.6
11 Hugh J. Addonizio (D)	52,311	56.3
Philip Insabella (R)	38,351	41.2
12 Robert Winthrop Kean (R)	59,151	53.1
Martin S. Fox (D)	52,314	46.9
13 Alfred D. Sieminski (D)	60,108	60.8
Norman Roth (R)	26,638	26.9
Jeremiah J. O'Callaghan (I)	12,174	12.3
14 T. James Tumulty (D)	58,069	62.4
Vincent J. Dellay (R)	32,485	34.9

NEW MEXICO

	Votes	%
AL John J. Dempsey (D)	111,713✔	
Antonio M. Fernandez (D)	109,837✔	
Thomas H. Childers (R)	77,151	
Warren R. Cobean (R)	76,528	

NEW YORK

	Votes	%
1 Stuyvesant Wainwright (R)	108,130	63.1
Ernest Greenwood (D, L)	62,853	36.7
2 Steven B. Derounian (R)	98,610	63.7
William R. Brennan Jr. (D, L)	55,477	35.8
3 Frank J. Becker (R)	93,396	58.3
John T. Cogley (D, L)	66,703	41.7
4 Henry J. Latham (R)	74,621	54.2
Thomas A. Dent (D)	55,479	40.3
Robert A. Rose (L)	7,526	5.5
5 Albert H. Bosch (R)	50,778	51.7
William Kerwick (D)	43,086	43.9
6 Lester Holtzman (D, L)	81,033	54.4
Seymour Halpern (R)	67,681	45.5
7 James J. Delaney (D, L)	62,541	59.0
Joseph Stockinger (R)	43,525	41.0
8 Victor L. Anfuso (D, L)	51,993	77.7
Eugene J. Renne (R)	14,948	22.3
9 Eugene J. Keogh (D, L)	59,392	71.1
Harry Keller (R)	22,808	27.3
10 Edna F. Kelly (D, L)	80,541	76.8
Abraham Sher (R)	22,479	21.4
11 Emanuel Celler (D, L)	103,788	83.5
Henry D. Dorfman (R)	20,452	16.5
12 Francis E. Dorn (R)	49,449	51.3
Donald L. O'Toole (D, L)	46,926	48.7
13 Abraham J. Multer (D, L)	89,907	78.8
Joseph Moriber (R)	21,881	19.2
14 John J. Rooney (D, L)	61,879	73.1
Alfred A. Manti (R)	21,598	25.5
15 John H. Ray (R)	56,020	51.6
Vincent R. Fitzpatrick (D, L)	52,292	48.1
16 Adam Clayton Powell Jr. (D)	43,545	77.6
Harold C. Burton (R)	8,904	15.9
Formington Taylor (L)	3,701	6.6
17 Frederic R. Coudert Jr. (R)	48,999	50.2
Anthony B. Akers (D, L)	48,685	49.8
18 James G. Donovan (D, R)	49,850	86.8
Amos Basel (L)	6,219	10.8
19 Arthur G. Klein (D, L)	56,634	74.6
Henry E. Delrosso (R)	19,310	25.4
20 Irwin D. Davidson (D, L)	58,030	67.2
Warren L. Schnur (R)	26,462	30.7
21 Herbert Zelenko (D, L)	63,284	67.8
Floyd Cramer (R)	29,995	32.2
22 Sidney A. Fine (D, L)	72,091	67.9
Henry Rose (R)	18,952	17.8
Louis Schifrin (L)	13,249	12.5
23 Isidore Dollinger (D)	58,490	75.6
Philip Myer (R)	9,976	12.9
Bernice Benedick (L)	8,869	11.5
24 Charles A. Buckley (D)	69,552	58.3
Charles V. Scanlan (R)	31,670	26.6
Elias Rosenblatt (L)	18,067	15.2
25 Paul A. Fino (R)	59,409	50.4
Salvatore J. Milano (D)	50,818	43.1
Ernest Doerfler (L)	7,624	6.5
26 Ralph A. Gamble (R)	81,608	64.0
Julia L. Crews (D, L)	45,892	36.0
27 Ralph W. Gwinn (R)	83,866	57.2
John R. Harold (D, L)	62,797	42.8
28 Katharine St. George (R)	79,587	64.9
Paul G. Reilly (D)	40,109	32.7
29 J. Ernest Wharton (R)	88,227	66.5
Robert D. Byron (D)	42,084	31.7
30 Leo W. O'Brien (D, L)	104,585	61.2
James W. Smith (R)	66,319	38.8
31 Dean P. Taylor (R)	86,768	66.3
Joseph R. MacLaren (D, L)	44,212	33.8
32 Bernard W. Kearney (R)	77,891	61.5
David C. Prince (D, L)	48,808	38.5
33 Clarence E. Kilburn (R)	70,708	68.1
Harold Blake (D)	31,279	30.1
34 William R. Williams (R)	77,659	59.3
Vernon E. Olin (D, L)	53,112	40.6
35 R. Walter Riehlman (R)	90,002	63.5
James H. O'Connor (D, L)	51,358	36.3
36 John Taber (R)	79,850	68.4
Daniel J. Carey (D, L)	36,910	31.6
37 W. Sterling Cole (R)	94,840	71.7
John E. Bloomer (D, L)	37,525	28.3
38 Kenneth B. Keating (R)	103,293	71.9
Rubin Brodsky (D, L)	40,400	28.1
39 Harold C. Ostertag (R)	82,769	64.8
George W. Cooke (D, L)	45,000	35.2
40 William E. Miller (R)	77,016	60.9
Mariano A. Lucca (D)	46,956	37.1
41 Edmund P. Radwan (R)	77,259	63.1
Bernard J. Wojtkowiak (D, L)	45,144	36.9
42 John R. Pillion (R)	82,707	57.6
John J. Zablotny (D, L)	60,880	42.4
43 Daniel A. Reed (R)	66,852	64.8
James F. Crowley (D)	34,590	33.5

NORTH CAROLINA

	Votes	%
1 Herbert C. Bonner (D)	20,650	92.5
W. T. Love (R)	1,685	7.5
2 L. H. Fountain (D)	14,471	100.0
3 Graham A. Barden (D)	24,837	77.3
Christine P. Odom (R)	7,301	22.7
4 Harold D. Cooley (D)	34,406	100.0
5 Thurmond Chatham (D)	31,781	66.2
Joe New (R)	16,194	33.8
6 Carl T. Durham (D)	30,118	74.3
Rufus K. Haworth Jr. (R)	10,446	25.8
7 F. Ertel Carlyle (D)	21,669	81.3
J. O. West (R)	5,001	18.8
8 Charles B. Deane (D)	39,028	59.1
Harold W. Gavin (R)	26,966	40.9
9 Hugh Q. Alexander (D)	54,103	52.2
William E. Stevens Jr. (R)	49,555	47.8
10 Charles Raper Jonas (R)	51,492	57.5
J. C. Sedberry (D)	38,080	42.5
11 Woodrow W. Jones (D)	36,766	67.5
R. R. Ramsey (R)	17,721	32.5
12 George A. Shuford (D)	44,258	61.6
Charles Cunningham (R)	27,651	38.5

NORTH DAKOTA

	Votes	%
AL Usher L. Burdick (R)	124,845✔	
Otto Krueger (R)	106,341✔	
P. W. Lanier (D)	64,089	
Raymond G. Vendsel (D)	49,183	

OHIO

	Votes	%
1 Gordon H. Scherer (R)	71,042	64.3
Mrs. Warwick B. Hobart (D)	39,421	35.7
2 William E. Hess (R)	69,695	58.4
Earl T. Wagner (D)	49,690	41.6
3 Paul F. Schenck (R)	82,701	52.6
Thomas B. Talbot (D)	74,585	47.4
4 William M. McCulloch (R)	67,762	67.6
Forrest L. Blankenship (D)	32,474	32.4
5 Cliff Clevenger (R)	49,265	59.5
Martin W. Feigert (D)	33,483	40.5
6 James G. Polk (D)	54,044	52.2
Leo Blackburn (R)	49,531	47.8
7 Clarence J. Brown (R)	62,821	63.9
G. Louie Wren (D)	35,504	36.1
8 Jackson E. Betts (R)	52,196	63.1
Thomas M. Dowd (D)	30,592	37.0
9 Thomas L. Ashley (D)	48,471	36.4
Frazier Reams (I)	44,656	33.6
Irving C. Reynolds (R)	39,933	30.0
10 Thomas A. Jenkins (R)	45,277	61.7
Truman A. Morris (D)	28,150	38.3
11 Oliver P. Bolton (R)	74,065	65.3
Edward C. Kaley (D)	39,404	34.7
12 John M. Vorys (R)	94,585	61.5
Jacob F. Myers (D)	59,210	38.5
13 A. D. Baumhart Jr. (R)	46,524	59.1
George C. Steinemann (D)	32,177	40.9
14 William H. Ayres (R)	82,086	54.6
John L. Smith (D)	68,204	45.4
15 John E. Henderson (R)	38,524	54.0
Max Lewis Underwood (D)	32,795	46.0
16 Frank T. Bow (R)	79,371	58.3
Thomas H. Nichols (D)	56,787	41.7
17 J. Harry McGregor (R)	63,301	64.6
Robert W. Levering (D)	34,638	35.4
18 Wayne L. Hays (D)	59,165	57.3
Walter L. Hunston (R)	44,143	42.7
19 Michael J. Kirwan (D)	69,324	67.5
David S. Edwards (R)	33,352	32.5

OHIO

District	Candidates	Votes	%
20	Michael A. Feighan (D)	81,304	67.7
	John H. Ferguson (R)	38,865	32.3
21	Charles A. Vanik (D)	76,201	76.0
	Francis E. Young (R)	24,076	24.0
22	Frances P. Bolton (R)	61,738	58.4
	Chat Paterson (D)	44,072	41.7
23	William E. Minshall Jr. (R)	69,994	67.5
	Bernice S. Pyke (D)	33,639	32.5

OKLAHOMA

District	Candidates	Votes	%
1	Page Belcher (R)	79,151	58.8
	Ben Crowley (D)	55,391	41.2
2	Ed Edmondson (D)	67,872	64.7
	Percy Butler (R)	37,030	35.3
3	Carl Albert (D)	52,662	83.3
	Jasper N. Butler (R)	10,554	16.7
4	Tom Steed (D)	43,915	100.0
5	John Jarman (D)	72,380	66.0
	George E. Young (R)	37,223	34.0
6	Victor E. Wickersham (D)	62,119	69.3
	Reece L. Russell (R)	27,492	30.7

OREGON

District	Candidates	Votes	%
1	Walter Norblad (R)	98,592	63.0
	Donnell Mitchell (D)	57,882	37.0
2	Sam Coon (R)	43,731	52.6
	Al Ullman (D)	39,475	47.4
3	Edith Green (D)	103,976	52.4
	Tom McCall (R)	94,368	47.6
4	Harris Ellsworth (R)	70,695	55.9
	Charles O. Porter (D)	55,775	44.1

PENNSYLVANIA

District	Candidates	Votes	%
1	William A. Barrett (D)	68,531	61.5
	Joseph A. Graham Jr. (R)	42,893	38.5
2	William T. Granahan (D)	80,377	61.3
	Albert A. Ciardi (R)	50,857	38.8
3	James A. Byrne (D)	61,639	55.4
	Charles H. Sporkin (R)	49,702	44.6
4	Earl Chudoff (D)	60,564	65.7
	W. Beverly Carter Jr. (R)	31,551	34.2
5	William J. Green Jr. (D)	87,435	55.0
	Francis P. McCusker (R)	71,462	45.0
6	Hugh Scott (R)	74,328	50.6
	Alexander Hemphill (D)	72,587	49.4
7	Benjamin F. James (R)	101,282	60.9
	O. Arthur Cappiello (D)	65,086	39.1
8	Karl C. King (R)	62,897	51.2
	John P. Fullam (D)	59,848	48.8
9	Paul B. Dague (R)	76,163	62.7
	Edward G. Wilson (D)	45,402	37.4
10	Joseph L. Carrigg (R)	74,515	50.5
	Robert H. Jones (D)	73,046	49.5
11	Daniel J. Flood (D)	70,254	50.9
	Edward J. Bonin (R)	67,682	49.1
12	Ivor D. Fenton (R)	62,779	55.5
	Charles E. Lotz (D)	50,373	44.5
13	Samuel K. McConnell Jr. (R)	91,639	64.3
	Joseph C. Mansfield (D)	50,796	35.7
14	George M. Rhodes (D)	50,765	62.0
	Donald F. Spang (R)	31,136	38.0
15	Francis E. Walter (D)	56,871	61.6
	LeRoy Mikels (R)	35,464	38.4
16	Walter M. Mumma (R)	69,240	59.8
	Richard A. Swank (D)	46,619	40.2
17	Alvin R. Bush (R)	57,928	56.5
	William T. Longe (D)	44,543	43.5
18	Richard M. Simpson (R)	58,959	55.9
	Robert M. Meyers (D)	46,463	44.1
19	James M. Quigley (D)	62,108	51.0
	S. Walter Stauffer (R)	59,594	49.0
20	James E. Van Zandt (R)	48,561	56.3
	John R. Stewart (D)	37,725	43.7
21	Augustine B. Kelley (D)	70,224	61.1
	Herbert O. Morrison (R)	44,789	38.9
22	John P. Saylor (R)	66,270	51.9
	Robert S. Glass (D)	61,474	48.1
23	Leon H. Gavin (R)	53,616	61.9
	Fred C. Barr (D)	33,044	38.1
24	Carroll D. Kearns (R)	66,005	52.0
	Edmund T. Rogers (D)	60,842	48.0
25	Frank M. Clark (D)	66,223	53.5
	Louis E. Graham (R)	57,657	46.5
26	Thomas E. Morgan (D)	95,531	65.3
	Branko Stupar (R)	50,768	34.7
27	James G. Fulton (R)	92,533	62.8
	Charles J. Chamberlin (D)	54,876	37.2
28	Herman P. Eberharter (D)	85,550	65.1
	Guy C. Read (R)	45,913	34.9
29	Robert J. Corbett (R)	83,846	60.6
	William G. Foley (D)	54,511	39.4
30	Vera D. Buchanan (D)	98,318	69.0
	David J. Smith (R)	44,157	31.0

RHODE ISLAND

District	Candidates	Votes	%
1	Aime J. Forand (D)	89,678	59.1
	Arthur Carrelas (R)	61,990	40.9
2	John E. Fogarty (D)	105,522	60.5
	James O. Watts (R)	68,869	39.5

SOUTH CAROLINA

District	Candidates	Votes	%
1	L. Mendel Rivers (D)	33,402	97.8
2	John J. Riley (D)	44,484	97.7
3	W. J. Bryan Dorn (D)	30,790	99.3
4	Robert T. Ashmore (D)	43,857	99.2
5	James P. Richards (D)	26,950	100.0
6	John L. McMillan (D)	31,141	98.9

SOUTH DAKOTA

District	Candidates	Votes	%
1	Harold O. Lovre (R)	102,797	58.0
	Francis G. Dunn (D)	74,450	42.0
2	E. Y. Berry (R)	34,476	63.9
	Ray Satterlee (D)	19,444	36.1

TENNESSEE

District	Candidates	Votes	%
1	B. Carroll Reece (R)	32,991	62.5
	Arthur Bright (D)	19,828	37.5
2	Howard H. Baker (R)	47,989	58.0
	C. Howard Bozeman (D)	34,688	42.0
3	James B. Frazier Jr. (D)	30,558	59.2
	O. M. Spence (R)	21,081	40.8
4	Joe L. Evins (D)	27,613	100.0
5	J. Percy Priest (D)	20,849	90.8
	Robert M. Donihi (R)	2,123	9.2
6	Ross Bass (D)	26,081	99.4
7	Tom Murray (D)	17,708	100.0
8	Jere Cooper (D)	15,078	100.0
9	Clifford Davis (D)	40,121	83.5
	W. A. Danielson (R)	7,926	16.5

TEXAS

District	Candidates	Votes	%
1	Wright Patman (D)	18,104	100.0
2	Jack Brooks (D)	25,008	100.0
3	Brady Gentry (D)	20,767	100.0
4	Sam Rayburn (D)	15,177	100.0
5	Bruce Alger (R)	27,982	52.9
	Wallace Savage (D)	24,904	47.1
6	Olin E. Teague (D)	15,161	100.0
7	John Dowdy (D)	18,361	100.0
8	Albert Thomas (D)	60,374	62.1
	W. B. Butler (R)	36,405	37.4
9	Clark W. Thompson (D)	29,972	100.0
10	Homer Thornberry (D)	23,752	100.0
11	W. R. Poage (D)	17,739	100.0
12	Jim Wright (D)	35,611	98.8
13	Frank Ikard (D)	25,085	100.0
14	John J. Bell (D)	36,284	93.8
	D. C. DeWitt (R)	2,384	6.2
15	Joe M. Kilgore (D)	29,113	100.0
16	J. T. Rutherford (D)	25,122	100.0
17	Omar Burleson (D)	18,484	100.0
18	Walter Rogers (D)	25,430	64.9
	Leroy LaMaster (R)	13,756	35.1
19	George Mahon (D)	26,829	100.0
20	Paul J. Kilday (D)	23,533	100.0
21	O. C. Fisher (D)	25,381	100.0
AL	Martin Dies (D)	555,446	88.0
	Tom Nolan (R)	75,472	12.0

UTAH

District	Candidates	Votes	%
1	Henry Aldous Dixon (R)	55,542	53.4
	Walter K. Granger (D)	48,535	46.6
2	William A. Dawson (R)	90,864	57.2
	Reva Beck Bosone (D)	68,090	42.8

VERMONT

District	Candidates	Votes	%
AL	Winston L. Prouty (R)	70,143	61.4
	John J. Boylan Jr. (D)	44,141	38.6

VIRGINIA

District	Candidates	Votes	%
1	Edward J. Robeson Jr. (D)	16,029	99.8
2	Porter Hardy Jr. (D)	18,190	74.4
	George V. Credle Jr. (R)	6,243	25.6
3	J. Vaughan Gary (D)	19,466	58.0
	J. Calvitt Clarke Jr. (R)	14,088	42.0
4	Watkins M. Abbitt (D)	14,728	99.9
5	William M. Tuck (D)	13,042	99.9
6	Richard H. Poff (R)	32,855	62.3
	Ernest Robertson (D)	19,727	37.4
7	Burr P. Harrison (D)	22,025	74.2
	John Paul Ruddick (R)	7,669	25.8
8	Howard W. Smith (D)	17,321	66.6
	C. S. Lenhart (I)	8,679	33.4
9	W. Pat Jennings (D)	39,238	50.5
	William C. Wampler (R)	38,239	49.2
10	Joel T. Broyhill (R)	29,221	53.8
	John C. Webb (D)	24,667	45.4

WASHINGTON

District	Candidates	Votes	%
1	Thomas M. Pelly (R)	101,913	52.6
	Hugh B. Mitchell (D)	91,721	47.4
2	Jack Westland (R)	73,264	52.2
	Harry F. Henson (D)	67,232	47.9
3	Russell V. Mack (R)	70,844	64.9
	Clyde V. Tisdale (D)	38,344	35.1
4	Hal Holmes (R)	67,171	61.0
	Fred Yoder (D)	42,911	39.0
5	Walt Horan (R)	68,628	58.6
	Art Garton (D)	48,542	41.4
6	Thor C. Tollefson (R)	80,241	55.2
	John T. McCutcheon (D)	65,011	44.8
AL	Don Magnuson (D)	464,045	57.3
	Al Canwell (R)	342,089	42.2

WEST VIRGINIA

District	Candidates	Votes	%
1	Robert H. Mollohan (D)	52,609	52.7
	Arch A. Moore Jr. (R)	47,199	47.3
2	Harley O. Staggers (D)	50,283	55.0
	Albert M. Morgan (R)	41,171	45.0
3	Cleveland M. Bailey (D)	54,684	58.9
	Joseph B. Lightburn (R)	38,218	41.1
4	M. G. Burnside (D)	56,498	50.2
	Will E. Neal (R)	55,994	49.8
5	Elizabeth Kee (D)	52,349	67.5
	Fred O. Blue (R)	25,267	32.6
6	Robert C. Byrd (D)	73,535	62.7
	Pat B. Withrow Jr. (R)	43,685	37.3

WISCONSIN

Candidates	Votes	%
1 Lawrence H. Smith (R)	65,562	54.4
Edward A. Krenzke (D)	54,864	45.6
2 Glenn R. Davis (R)	74,460	54.0
Gaylord A. Nelson (D)	63,449	46.0
3 Gardner R. Withrow (R)	56,228	62.1
Joseph A. Seep (D)	34,375	37.9

Candidates	Votes	%
4 Clement J. Zablocki (D)	100,120	71.1
John C. Schafer (R)	40,723	28.9
5 Henry S. Reuss (D)	77,208	52.3
Charles J. Kersten (R)	70,565	47.8
6 William K. Van Pelt (R)	68,653	62.5
Russell S. Johnson (D)	41,191	37.5
7 Melvin R. Laird (R)	57,581	59.1
Kenneth E. Anderson (D)	39,828	40.9
8 John W. Byrnes (R)	73,588	62.0
Jerome J. Reinke (D)	45,037	38.0

Candidates	Votes	%
9 Lester R. Johnson (D)	52,485	55.4
William E. Owen (R)	42,234	44.6
10 Alvin E. O'Konski (R)	49,325	59.8
Basil G. Kennedy (D)	33,219	40.2

WYOMING

Candidates	Votes	%
AL E. Keith Thomson (R)	61,111	56.2
Sam Tully (D)	47,660	43.8

1956 House Elections

ALABAMA

Candidates	Votes	%
1 Frank W. Boykin (D)	31,469	100.0
2 George Grant (D)	36,613	100.0
3 George W. Andrews (D)	29,547	100.0
4 Kenneth A. Roberts (D)	33,591	73.4
Roy Banks (R)	12,166	26.6
5 Albert Rains (D)	45,281	100.0
6 Armistead I. Selden Jr. (D)	22,513	100.0
7 Carl Elliott (D)	31,988	100.0
8 Robert E. Jones Jr. (D)	46,730	80.1
Mrs. James G. Fortney (R)	11,634	19.9
9 George Huddleston Jr. (D)	56,414	65.9
W. L. Longshore Jr. (R)	29,222	34.1

ARIZONA

Candidates	Votes	%
1 John J. Rhodes (R)	78,998	54.9
William P. Mahoney Jr. (D)	64,805	45.1
2 Stewart L. Udall (D)	82,110	60.1
John G. Speiden (R)	54,596	39.9

ARKANSAS

Candidates	Votes	%
1 Ezekiel C. Gathings (D)	25,622	100.0
2 Wilbur D. Mills (D)	19,540	100.0
3 James W. Trimble (D)	54,481	61.4
William S. Spicer (R)	34,318	38.7
4 Oren Harris (D)	37,284	100.0
5 Brooks Hays (D)	56,271	100.0
6 William F. Norrell (D)	42,447	100.0

CALIFORNIA

Candidates	Votes	%
1 Hubert B. Scudder (R)	102,604	53.6
Clement W. Miller (D)	88,962	46.4
2 Clair Engle (D-R)	136,544	100.0
3 John E. Moss Jr. (D)	132,930	68.6
Noel C. Stevenson (R)	60,889	31.4
4 William S. Mailliard (R)	109,188	61.9
James L. Quigley (D)	67,132	38.1
5 John F. Shelley (D-R)	104,358	100.0
6 John F. Baldwin Jr. (R)	98,683	53.7
H. Roberts Quinney (D)	84,965	46.3
7 John J. Allen Jr. (R)	75,932	52.8
Laurence L. Cross (D)	67,931	47.2
8 George P. Miller (D)	136,720	65.6
Robert Lee Watkins (R)	71,700	34.4
9 J. Arthur Younger (R)	96,388	60.3
James T. McKay (D)	63,504	39.7
10 Charles S. Gubser (R)	128,891	60.7
William H. Vatcher Jr. (D)	83,586	39.3
11 John J. McFall (D)	70,630	53.1
Leroy Johnson (R)	62,448	46.9
12 B. F. Sisk (D)	109,920	73.0
Robert B. Moore (R)	40,663	27.0
13 Charles M. Teague (R)	104,009	59.6
William Kirk Stewart (D)	70,567	40.4
14 Harlan Hagen (D)	94,461	63.0
Myron D. Tisdel (R)	55,509	37.0
15 Gordon L. McDonough (R)	97,182	57.9
Emery S. Petty (D)	70,681	42.1
16 Donald L. Jackson (R)	83,050	60.8
G. Robert Fleming (D)	53,624	39.2
17 Cecil R. King (D)	157,270	64.9
Charles A. Franklin (R)	84,900	35.1
18 Craig Hosmer (R)	103,108	59.3
Raymond C. Simpson (D)	70,911	40.8
19 Chet Holifield (D)	116,287	73.8
Roy E. Reynolds (R)	41,269	26.2
20 H. Allen Smith (R)	85,459	70.8
Eugene Radding (D)	35,249	29.2

Candidates	Votes	%
21 Edgar W. Hiestand (R)	153,679	62.6
W. C. Stethem (D)	91,683	37.4
22 Joe Holt (R)	97,317	59.8
Irving Glasband (D)	65,314	40.2
23 Clyde Doyle (D & P)	120,109	70.9
E. Elgie Calvin (R)	49,198	29.1
24 Glenard P. Lipscomb (R)	84,120	61.9
Fay Porter (D)	51,692	38.1
25 Patrick J. Hillings (R)	166,305	63.8
John G. Sobieski (D)	94,180	36.2
26 James Roosevelt (D)	133,036	68.8
Edward H. Gibbons (R)	60,230	31.2
27 Harry R. Sheppard (D-R)	124,662	99.8
28 James B. Utt (R)	159,456	64.5
Gordon T. Shepard (D)	87,691	35.5
29 Dalip S. Saund (D)	54,989	51.5
Jacqueline Cochran Odlum (R)	51,690	48.4
30 Bob Wilson (R)	142,753	66.8
George A. Cheney (D)	71,112	33.3

COLORADO

Candidates	Votes	%
1 Byron G. Rogers (D)	116,487	57.8
Robert S. McCollum (R)	85,127	42.2
2 William S. Hill (R)	107,153	53.4
Byron L. Johnson (D)	93,572	46.6
3 J. Edgar Chenoweth (R)	74,196	50.2
Alva B. Adams (D)	73,503	49.8
4 Wayne N. Aspinall (D)	48,489	61.8
Hugh L. Caldwell (R)	30,026	38.2

CONNECTICUT

Candidates	Votes	%
1 Edwin H. May Jr. (R)	161,360	53.5
Patrick J. Ward (D)	139,147	46.1
2 Horace Seely-Brown Jr. (R)	99,274	59.1
Douglas J. Bennet (D)	68,847	41.0
3 Albert W. Cretella (R)	126,850	60.0
Robert N. Giaimo (D)	84,568	40.0
4 Albert P. Morano (R)	194,333	68.4
Jack Stock (D)	88,487	31.1
5 James T. Patterson (R)	91,690	61.9
Luke F. Martin (D)	56,375	38.1
AL Antoni N. Sadlak (R)	683,387	61.5
Matthew P. Kuta (D)	428,709	38.6

DELAWARE

Candidates	Votes	%
AL Harry G. Haskell Jr. (R)	91,538	52.0
Harris B. Mcdowell Jr. (D)	84,644	48.0

FLORIDA

Candidates	Votes	%
1 William C. Cramer (R)	105,958	56.4
Winton H. King (D)	82,075	43.7
2 Charles E. Bennett (D)	66,614	100.0
3 Robert L. F. Sikes (D)	86,272	89.6
Arthur Barker Sr. (R)	10,042	10.4
4 Dante B. Fascell (D)	120,509	60.9
Leland Hyzer (R)	77,301	39.1
5 A. S. Herlong Jr. (D)	73,498	51.4
Arnold L. Lund (R)	69,378	48.6
6 Paul G. Rogers (D)	73,259	54.7
Dorothy A. Smith (R)	60,570	45.3
7 James A. Haley (D)	47,985	62.4
G. M. Nelson (R)	28,900	37.6
8 Donald R. Matthews (D)	39,362	100.0

GEORGIA

Candidates	Votes	%
1 Prince H. Preston (D)	40,360	78.3
Harry P. Anestos (I)	10,931	21.2
2 J. L. Pilcher (D)	41,270	100.0
3 E. L. Forrester (D)	51,703	100.0

Candidates	Votes	%
4 John J. Flynt Jr. (D)	51,568	100.0
5 James C. Davis (D)	85,292	59.2
Randolph W. Thrower (R)	58,777	40.8
6 Carl Vinson (D)	42,766	100.0
7 Henderson Lanham (D)	69,873	99.5
8 Iris Faircloth Blitch (D)	50,068	100.0
9 Phil M. Landrum (D)	47,360	100.0
10 Paul Brown (D)	41,812	99.8

IDAHO

Candidates	Votes	%
1 Gracie B. Pfost (D)	60,170	55.1
Louise Shadduck (R)	48,974	44.9
2 Hamer H. Budge (R)	90,738	60.0
J. W. Reynolds (D)	60,552	40.0

ILLINOIS

Candidates	Votes	%
1 William L. Dawson (D)	66,704	64.4
George W. Lawrence (R)	36,847	35.6
2 Barratt O'Hara (D)	86,386	55.3
George B. McKibbin (R)	69,892	44.7
3 Emmet F. Byrne (R)	92,907	51.5
James C. Murray (D)	87,677	48.6
4 William E. McVey (R)	155,441	60.0
Michael Hinko (D)	103,494	40.0
5 John C. Kluczynski (D)	96,399	61.8
Lawrence Welnowski (R)	59,608	38.2
6 Thomas J. O'Brien (D)	94,281	62.0
John J. Dillon (R)	57,750	38.0
7 James B. Bowler (D)	93,732	71.7
Gabriel L. Grimaldi (R)	37,068	28.3
8 Thomas S. Gordon (D)	73,628	59.5
Victor O. Wright (R)	50,055	40.5
9 Sidney R. Yates (D)	75,511	54.0
Johann S. Ackerman (R)	64,237	46.0
10 Harold R. Collier (R)	132,928	64.5
Marvin E. Lore (D)	73,331	35.6
11 Timothy P. Sheehan (R)	95,140	55.5
Roman C. Pucinski (D)	76,400	44.5
12 Charles A. Boyle (D)	100,273	53.2
Edgar A. Jonas (R)	88,315	46.8
13 Marguerite Stitt Church (R)	229,358	71.6
Helen Benson Leys (D)	91,059	28.4
14 Russell W. Keeney (R)	151,236	70.6
Harold J. Spelman (D)	63,067	29.4
15 Noah M. Mason (R)	103,557	64.6
Stanley Hubbs (D)	56,802	35.4
16 Leo E. Allen (R)	106,734	63.7
Glen F. Kunkle (D)	60,748	36.3
17 Leslie C. Arends (R)	106,463	64.9
C. E. Spang (D)	57,467	35.1
18 Robert H. Michel (R)	87,187	58.8
Fred Allen (D)	61,099	41.2
19 Robert B. Chiperfield (R)	85,497	55.8
Martin P. Sutor (D)	67,691	44.2
20 Sidney E. Simpson (R)	79,641	59.7
Henry W. Pollock (D)	53,882	40.4
21 Peter F. Mack Jr. (D)	94,565	53.5
Frederic S. O'Hara (R)	82,251	46.5
22 William L. Springer (R)	93,399	62.3
E. H. Winegarner (D)	56,612	37.7
23 Charles W. Vursell (R)	79,862	52.6
Albert R. Imle (D)	72,070	47.4
24 Melvin Price (D)	121,381	68.2
Waldo E. Schellenger (R)	56,568	31.8
25 Kenneth J. Gray (D)	82,845	53.8
Samuel J. Scott (R)	71,048	46.2

INDIANA

Candidates	Votes	%
1 Ray J. Madden (D)	93,658	52.6
Donald K. Stimson Jr. (R)	84,125	47.2
2 Charles A. Halleck (R)	94,852	62.2
Thurman C. Crook (D)	57,049	37.4

INDIANA

Candidates	Votes	%
3 F. Jay Nimtz (R)	109,907	53.1
John Brademas (D)	97,196	46.9
4 E. Ross Adair (R)	96,531	63.5
F. Dean Bechtol (D)	55,284	36.3
5 John V. Beamer (R)	113,586	56.4
William C. Whitehead (D)	86,797	43.1
6 Cecil M. Harden (R)	86,020	55.0
John W. King (D)	70,035	44.8
7 William G. Bray (R)	87,635	57.2
Vernon R. Hill (D)	65,482	42.8
8 Winfield K. Denton (D)	95,699	50.1
D. Bailey Merrill (R)	95,003	49.7
9 Earl Wilson (R)	70,926	53.4
Wilfrid J. Ullrich (D)	61,465	46.3
10 Ralph Harvey (R)	98,301	56.3
Gerald C. Carmony (D)	75,665	43.3
11 Charles B. Brownson (R)	155,541	59.4
John C. Carvey (D)	106,021	40.5

IOWA

Candidates	Votes	%
1 Fred D. Schwengel (R)	94,223	58.0
Ronald O. Bramhall (D)	68,287	42.0
2 Henry O. Talle (R)	95,999	51.4
Leonard G. Wolf (D)	90,843	48.6
3 H. R. Gross (R)	97,590	58.6
Michael Micich (D)	69,076	41.5
4 Karl M. LeCompte (R)	58,024	50.7
Steven V. Carter (D)	56,406	49.3
5 Paul Cunningham (R)	85,178	51.1
William F. Denman (D)	81,418	48.9
6 Merwin Coad (D)	64,625	50.1
James I. Dolliver (R)	64,427	49.9
7 Ben F. Jensen (R)	64,967	55.4
John L. Jensen (D)	52,389	44.6
8 Charles B. Hoeven (R)	76,165	60.1
Robert J. Salem (D)	50,597	39.9

KANSAS

Candidates	Votes	%
1 William H. Avery (R)	69,841	53.1
Howard S. Miller (D)	60,313	45.8
2 Errett P. Scrivner (R)	93,609	54.9
Newell A. George (D)	77,049	45.2
3 Myron V. George (R)	48,246	55.0
Denver D. Hargis (D)	39,407	45.0
4 Edward H. Rees (R)	111,970	53.8
John D. Montgomery (D)	96,002	46.2
5 J. Floyd Breeding (D)	64,392	50.5
John W. Crutcher (R)	63,057	49.5
6 Wint Smith (R)	52,145	51.1
Elmo J. Mahoney (D)	49,933	48.9

KENTUCKY

Candidates	Votes	%
1 Noble J. Gregory (D)	75,726	100.0
2 William H. Natcher (D)	55,103	52.3
R. B. Blankenship (R)	50,266	47.7
3 John M. Robsion Jr. (R)	111,598	56.8
Philip Ardery (D)	84,912	43.2
4 Frank Chelf (D)	51,675	56.3
John B. Preston (R)	40,129	43.7
5 Brent Spence (D)	59,402	55.9
Jule Appel (R)	46,821	44.1
6 John C. Watts (D)	69,468	52.7
Wallace Jones (R)	62,313	47.3
7 Carl D. Perkins (D)	77,564	52.4
Scott Craft (R)	70,450	47.6
8 Eugene Siler (R)	80,067	71.7
W. D. Scalf (D)	31,632	28.3

LOUISIANA

Candidates	Votes	%
1 F. Edward Hebert (D)	69,500	100.0
2 Hale Boggs (D)	69,715	64.5
George R. Blue (R)	38,344	35.5
3 Edwin E. Willis (D)	19,075	100.0
4 Overton Brooks (D)	40,583	68.1
Calhoun Allen Jr. (R)	19,041	31.9
5 Otto E. Passman (D)	18,210	100.0
6 James H. Morrison (D)	58,414	100.0
7 T. A. Thompson (D)	36,432	100.0
8 George S. Long (D)	18,341	100.0

MAINE

Candidates	Votes	%
1 Robert Hale (R)	58,028	50.0
James C. Oliver (D)	57,999	50.0
2 Frank M. Coffin (D)	55,430	53.4
James L. Reid (R)	48,292	46.6
3 Clifford G. McIntire (R)	44,095	60.7
Kenneth B. Colbath (D)	28,612	39.4

MARYLAND

Candidates	Votes	%
1 Edward T. Miller (R)	42,731	55.7
Hamilton P. Fox (D)	33,961	44.3
2 James P. S. Devereux (R)	103,103	58.1
A. Gordon Boone (D)	74,224	41.9
3 Edward A. Garmatz (D)	48,397	69.8
Harry Kemper (R)	20,990	30.3
4 George H. Fallon (D)	44,260	53.8
George Denys Hubbard (R)	37,957	46.2
5 Richard E. Lankford (D)	88,227	56.8
William B. Prendergast (R)	67,072	43.2
6 Dewitt S. Hyde (R)	100,580	54.3
John R. Foley (D)	84,837	45.8
7 Samuel N. Friedel (D)	70,512	59.0
David A. Halley (R)	48,949	41.0

MASSACHUSETTS

Candidates	Votes	%
1 John W. Heselton (R)	92,269	63.6
Howard W. Shea (D)	52,213	36.0
2 Edward P. Boland (D)	103,563	61.2
Foster W. Doty (R)	65,598	38.8
3 Philip J. Philbin (D)	114,848	70.9
Robert A. Parker (R)	47,041	29.1
4 Harold D. Donohue (D)	104,653	59.4
Mary R. Wheeler (R)	71,437	40.6
5 Edith Nourse Rogers (R)	150,957	73.3
Lawrence E. Corcoran (D)	55,038	26.7
6 William H. Bates (R)	131,310	100.0
7 Thomas J. Lane (D)	87,415	64.5
Robert T. Breed (R)	48,173	35.5
8 Torbert H. Macdonald (D)	92,463	54.8
C. Eugene Farnam (R)	76,312	45.2
9 Donald W. Nicholson (R)	111,860	61.1
William McAuliffe (D)	71,245	38.9
10 Laurence Curtis (R)	93,327	53.0
Jackson J. Holtz (D)	82,882	47.0
11 Thomas P. O'Neill Jr. (D)	83,532	75.3
Rudolph E. Mottola (R)	27,384	24.7
12 John W. McCormack (D)	89,943	82.5
James S. Tremblay (R)	19,099	17.5
13 Richard B. Wigglesworth (R)	109,950	55.6
Richard E. McCormack (D)	87,719	44.4
14 Joseph W. Martin Jr. (R)	111,420	62.4
Edward F. Doolan (D)	67,183	37.6

MICHIGAN

Candidates	Votes	%
1 Thaddeus M. Machrowicz (D)	112,290	86.1
Walter Czarnecki (R)	18,137	13.9
2 George Meader (R)	105,940	63.1
Franklin J. Shepherd (D)	61,456	36.6
3 August E. Johansen (R)	100,056	63.8
Truman Barkhuff (D)	56,119	35.8
4 Clare E. Hoffman (R)	83,876	62.0
Samuel I. Clark (D)	51,491	38.0
5 Gerald R. Ford Jr. (R)	120,349	67.1
George E. Clay (D)	58,899	32.9
6 Charles E. Chamberlain (R)	116,570	50.8
Don Hayworth (D)	112,603	49.0
7 Robert J. McIntosh (R)	114,674	53.7
Ira D. McCoy (D)	98,928	46.3
8 Alvin M. Bentley (R)	93,357	64.1
William R. Hart (D)	51,897	35.6
9 Robert P. Griffin (R)	68,166	56.0
William E. Baker (D)	53,609	44.0
10 Elford A. Cederberg (R)	72,781	65.6
William J. Kelly (D)	38,166	34.4
11 Victor A. Knox (R)	53,117	56.1
Prentiss M. Brown Jr. (D)	41,600	43.9
12 John B. Bennett (R)	45,721	56.3
Joseph S. Mack (D)	35,434	43.7
13 Charles C. Diggs Jr. (D)	87,353	69.8
Willis F. Ward (R)	37,860	30.2
14 Louis C. Rabaut (D)	122,070	56.8
Harold F. Youngblood (R)	92,933	43.2
15 John D. Dingell (D)	111,827	74.1
Larry Middleton (R)	38,973	25.8
16 John Lesinski (D)	176,663	64.1
Arthur Kurtz (R)	98,172	35.6
17 Martha W. Griffiths (D)	112,811	53.3
George E. Smith (R)	98,432	46.5
18 William S. Broomfield (R)	141,058	56.7
Paul Sutton (D)	107,609	43.3

MINNESOTA

Candidates	Votes	%
1 August H. Andresen (R)	92,092	61.5
Arnold L. Fredriksen (DFL)	57,747	38.5
2 Joseph P. O'Hara (R)	97,520	63.8
Harold Zupp (DFL)	55,336	36.2
3 Roy W. Wier (DFL)	127,356	52.0
George Mikan (R)	117,716	48.0
4 Eugene J. McCarthy (DFL)	103,320	64.1
Edward C. Slettedahl (R)	57,947	35.9
5 Walter H. Judd (R)	82,258	56.0
Joseph Robbie (DFL)	64,602	44.0
6 Fred Marshall (DFL)	76,396	56.2
Joseph L. Kaczmarek (D)	59,568	43.8
7 H. Carl Andersen (R)	76,271	55.9
Clint Haroldson (DFL)	60,168	44.1
8 John A. Blatnik (DFL)	108,565	73.2
Alfred J. Weinberg (R)	39,795	26.8
9 Coya Knutson (DFL)	58,916	52.7
Harold C. Hagen (R)	52,937	47.3

MISSISSIPPI

Candidates	Votes	%
1 Thomas G. Abernethy (D)	38,021	100.0
2 Jamie L. Whitten (D)	23,513	100.0
3 Frank E. Smith (D)	19,369	100.0
4 John Bell Williams (D)	42,085	100.0
5 Arthur Winstead (D)	35,461	100.0
6 William M. Colmer (D)	47,083	100.0

MISSOURI

Candidates	Votes	%
1 Frank M. Karsten (D)	136,873	66.3
Bill Bangert (R)	69,661	33.7
2 Thomas B. Curtis (R)	123,596	51.8
James L. Sullivan (D)	114,837	48.2
3 Leonor K. Sullivan (D)	96,416	69.7
Sidney R. Redmond (R)	42,023	30.4
4 George H. Christopher (D)	98,106	51.8
Jeffrey P. Hillelson (R)	91,392	48.2
5 Richard Bolling (D)	77,287	57.2
Lemot Jones Jr. (R)	57,778	42.8
6 W. R. Hull Jr. (D)	85,021	52.0
Stanley I. Dale (R)	78,637	48.1
7 Charles H. Brown (D)	90,986	50.3
Dewey Short (R)	89,926	49.7
8 A. S. J. Carnahan (D)	69,336	54.3
Frank W. May (R)	58,425	45.7
9 Clarence Cannon (D)	100,065	100.0
10 Paul C. Jones (D)	69,536	100.0

MISSOURI

Candidates	Votes	%
11 Morgan M. Moulder (D)	72,594	50.8
George H. Miller (R)	70,286	49.2

MONTANA

	Votes	%
1 Lee Metcalf (D)	69,644	62.1
W. D. McDonald (R)	42,591	38.0
2 Leroy H. Anderson (D)	76,805	50.9
Orvin B. Fjare (R)	74,164	49.1

NEBRASKA

	Votes	%
1 Phil Weaver (R)	102,012	67.0
Samuel Freeman (D)	50,351	33.1
2 Glenn Cunningham (R)	77,253	53.4
Joseph V. Benesch (D)	65,039	45.0
3 Robert D. Harrison (R)	62,645	50.1
Lawrence Brock (D)	62,399	49.9
4 Arthur L. Miller (R)	81,731	65.8
Carlton W. Laird (D)	42,583	34.3

NEVADA

	Votes	%
AL Walter S. Baring (D)	51,100	54.2
Richard W. Horton (R)	43,154	45.8

NEW HAMPSHIRE

	Votes	%
1 Chester E. Merrow (R)	78,296	57.4
James B. Sullivan (D)	58,104	42.6
2 Perkins Bass (R)	77,019	66.0
George F. Brown (D)	39,726	34.0

NEW JERSEY

	Votes	%
1 Charles A. Wolverton (R)	133,153	58.3
J. Frank Crawford (D)	94,758	41.5
2 T. Millet Hand (R)	83,433*	67.9
Thomas C. Stewart (D)	39,383	32.0
3 James C. Auchincloss (R)	136,780	65.3
Sidney Shiff (D)	72,617	34.7
4 Frank Thompson Jr. (D)	89,646	54.5
William H. Wells (R)	74,737	45.5
5 Peter H. B. Frelinghuysen Jr. (R)	153,829	64.5
Francis C. Foley (D)	84,374	35.4
6 Florence P. Dwyer (R)	106,414	50.6
Harrison A. Williams Jr. (D)	102,015	48.5
7 William B. Widnall (R)	151,573	70.7
Daniel Amster (D)	62,924	29.3
8 Gordon Canfield (R)	96,494	60.8
Walter H. Gardner (D)	61,464	38.7
9 Frank C. Osmers Jr. (R)	135,498	67.8
Robert D. Gruen (D)	63,728	31.9
10 Peter W. Rodino Jr. (D)	71,311	56.1
G. George Addonizio (R)	55,761	43.9
11 Hugh J. Addonizio (D)	63,482	51.7
Chester K. Ligham (R)	57,447	46.8
12 Robert Winthrop Kean (R)	90,032	59.7
Irving L. Hodes (D)	58,364	38.7
13 Alfred D. Sieminski (D)	54,841	45.0
Norman H. Roth (R)	54,784	44.9
14 Vincent J. Dellay (R)	61,600	52.3
T. James Tumulty (D)	53,713	45.6

NEW MEXICO

	Votes	%
AL John J. Dempsey (D)	129,625✔	
Antonio M. Fernandez (D)	128,330*	
Dudley Cornell (R)	114,719	
Forrest Atchley (R)	112,531	

NEW YORK

	Votes	%
1 Stuyvesant Wainwright (R)	191,356	65.8
T. Bronson O'Reilly (D, L)	99,304	34.2

Candidates	Votes	%
2 Steven B. Derounian (R)	148,098	67.5
Julius J. Damato (D, L)	71,422	32.5
3 Frank J. Becker (R)	143,559	61.9
Francis X. Hardiman (D, L)	88,245	38.1
4 Henry J. Latham (R)	116,470	55.8
Joseph J. Perrini (D, L)	92,217	44.2
5 Albert H. Bosch (R)	87,154	58.6
John J. Quinn (D, L)	61,678	41.4
6 Lester Holtzman (D, L)	128,545	56.9
Albert H. Buschmann (R)	97,558	43.2
7 James J. Delaney (D, L)	78,030	50.0
Joseph Stockinger (R)	77,928	50.0
8 Victor L. Anfuso (D, L)	59,998	65.6
Julius Reinlieb (R)	31,399	34.4
9 Eugene J. Keogh (D, L)	75,814	62.8
Benjamin W. Feldman (R)	44,916	37.2
10 Edna F. Kelly (D, L)	100,808	73.2
Abraham Sher (R)	36,878	26.8
11 Emanuel Celler (D, L)	131,508	77.7
Henry D. Dorfman (R)	37,651	22.3
12 Francis E. Dorn (R)	76,137	57.6
Donald L. O'Toole (D, L)	56,035	42.4
13 Abraham J. Multer (D, L)	110,469	71.2
Joseph Moriber (R)	44,771	28.8
14 John J. Rooney (D, L)	77,706	64.2
Jacob P. Lefkowitz (R)	43,343	35.8
15 John H. Ray (R)	98,093	61.4
Ralph Di Iorio (D, L)	60,989	38.2
16 Adam Clayton Powell Jr. (D)	59,339	69.7
Joseph A. Bailey (R)	16,960	19.9
Formington Taylor (L)	8,801	10.3
17 Frederic R. Coudert Jr. (R)	68,874	50.9
Anthony B. Akers (D, L)	66,396	49.1
18 Alfred E. Santangelo (D, L)	47,953	58.0
James G. Donovan (R)	34,748	42.0
19 Leonard Farbstein (D, L)	68,411	68.4
Maurice G. Henry Jr. (R)	31,546	31.6
20 Ludwig Teller (D, L)	70,726	63.8
Milton H. Adler (R)	40,191	36.2
21 Herbert Zelenko (D, L)	81,464	66.5
Dalton J. Shapo (R)	41,070	33.5
22 James C. Healey (D)	88,441	64.1
Henry Rose (R)	34,084	24.7
David I. Wells (L)	15,524	11.3
23 Isidore Dollinger (D)	70,238	68.5
Philip Myer (R)	22,414	21.9
Hyman Fromowitz (L)	9,880	9.6
24 Charles A. Buckley (D)	90,076	54.7
Harold Grosberg (R)	53,172	32.3
Elias Rosenblatt (L)	21,444	13.0
25 Paul A. Fino (R)	104,771	59.4
Edward A. Cunningham (D)	62,729	35.5
Bernard Tobacman (L)	8,989	5.1
26 Edwin B. Dooley (R)	123,996	67.5
Julia L. Crews (D, L)	59,842	32.6
27 Ralph W. Gwinn (R)	117,100	58.1
William D. Carlebach (D, L)	84,568	41.9
28 Katharine St. George (R)	103,114	62.2
William H. Mauldin (D, L)	62,770	37.8
29 J. Ernest Wharton (R)	124,211	71.4
Vincent di Gennaro (D, L)	49,725	28.6
30 Leo W. O'Brien (D, L)	104,022	55.8
Robert E. Gray (R)	82,429	44.2
31 Dean P. Taylor (R)	116,682	71.8
Theodore A. Knapp (D, L)	45,767	28.2
32 Bernard W. Kearney (R)	107,959	67.5
R. Joseph Giblin (D, L)	52,064	32.5
33 Clarence E. Kilburn (R)	103,419	72.7
Louis C. Britton (D, L)	38,793	27.3
34 William R. Williams (R)	95,681	57.5
Edwin L. Slusarczyk (D, L)	70,837	42.5
35 R. Walter Riehlman (R)	124,108	67.1
Thomas J. Lowery (D)	59,534	32.2
36 John Taber (R)	109,101	69.6
Lewis S. Bell (D, L)	47,764	30.4
37 Sterling Cole (R)	136,044	71.7
Francis P. Hogan (D, L)	53,830	28.4

Candidates	Votes	%
38 Kenneth B. Keating (R)	135,572	71.7
Reed Harding (D, L)	53,477	28.3
39 Harold C. Ostertag (R)	116,043	70.5
William H. Mostyn (D, L)	48,634	29.5
40 William E. Miller (R)	117,051	64.3
A. Thorne Hills (D, L)	64,872	35.7
41 Edmund P. Radwan (R)	99,151	64.4
Edward P. Jehle (D, L)	54,776	35.6
42 John R. Pillion (R)	117,178	58.7
James Kane Jr. (D)	80,568	40.3
43 Daniel A. Reed (R)	93,079	68.7
T. Joseph Lynch (D, L)	42,476	31.3

Special Election

	Votes	%
22 James C. Healey (D)	9,473	72.3
Sidney Burnstein (L)	1,943	14.8
Barnett Davis (R)	1,691	12.9

NORTH CAROLINA

	Votes	%
1 Herbert C. Bonner (D)	44,271	88.6
Zeno O. Ratcliff (R)	5,693	11.4
2 L. H. Fountain (D)	49,812	100.0
3 Graham A. Barden (D)	47,251	78.8
Joe Reynolds (R)	12,698	21.2
4 Harold D. Cooley (D)	76,560	100.0
5 Ralph J. Scott (D)	58,552	59.7
Joe New (R)	39,561	40.3
6 Carl T. Durham (D)	73,111	100.0
7 Alton Lennon (D)	65,424	84.0
C. Dana Malpass (R)	12,477	16.0
8 A. Paul Kitchin (D)	64,220	59.5
Fred Myers (R)	43,732	40.5
9 Hugh Q. Alexander (D)	68,181	53.9
A. M. Miller (R)	58,407	46.1
10 Charles Raper Jonas (R)	89,743	62.6
Ben E. Douglas (D)	53,475	37.3
11 Basil L. Whitener (D)	59,417	100.0
12 George A. Shuford (D)	55,927	54.5
Richard C. Clarke Jr. (R)	46,760	45.5

NORTH DAKOTA

	Votes	%
AL Usher L. Burdick (R)	143,514✔	
Otto Krueger (R)	136,003✔	
Agnes Geelan (D)	85,743	
S. B. Hocking (D)	83,284	

OHIO

	Votes	%
1 Gordon H. Scherer (R)	91,181	64.7
Leonard D. Slutz (D)	49,701	35.3
2 William E. Hess (R)	109,099	65.5
James T. Dewan (D)	57,554	34.5
3 Paul F. Schenck (R)	135,152	59.0
R. William Patterson (D)	93,782	41.0
4 William M. McCulloch (R)	93,607	68.8
Ortha O. Barr Jr. (D)	42,416	31.2
5 Cliff Clevenger (R)	69,774	62.3
George E. Rafferty (D)	42,181	37.7
6 James G. Polk (D)	72,229	54.5
Albert L. Daniels (R)	60,300	45.5
7 Clarence J. Brown (R)	91,439	66.0
Joseph A. Sullivan (D)	47,220	34.1
8 Jackson E. Betts (R)	70,690	63.5
Robert M. Corry (D)	40,716	36.6
9 Thomas L. Ashley (D)	100,696	55.3
Harvey G. Straub (R)	81,562	44.8
10 Thomas A. Jenkins (R)	71,295	100.0
11 David S. Dennison Jr. (R)	96,707	58.4
James P. Bennett (D)	68,831	41.6
12 John M. Vorys (R)	128,682	61.8
Walter J. Shapter Jr. (D)	79,597	38.2
13 A. D. Baumhart Jr. (R)	79,324	70.7
J. P. Henderson (D)	32,900	29.3
14 William H. Ayres (R)	123,105	58.9
Bernard Rosen (D)	85,946	41.1
15 John E. Henderson (R)	55,126	60.5
Herbert U. Smith (D)	35,954	39.5

OHIO

Candidates	Votes	%
16 Frank T. Bow (R)	101,324	55.2
John McSweeney (D)	82,206	44.8
17 J. Harry McGregor (R)	88,931	66.5
Robert W. Levering (D)	44,806	33.5
18 Wayne L. Hays (D)	78,962	59.6
Joseph Miller (R)	53,627	40.5
19 Michael J. Kirwan (D)	92,924	68.7
Ralph E. Turner (R)	42,293	31.3
20 Michael A. Feighan (D)	105,562	65.3
John H. Ferguson (R)	56,209	34.8
21 Charles A. Vanik (D)	96,106	71.6
Charles H. Loeb (R)	38,060	28.4
22 Frances P. Bolton (R)	96,468	66.7
Harry A. Blachman (D)	48,169	33.3
23 William E. Minshall Jr. (R)	102,707	69.0
George A. Hurley (D)	46,247	31.1

OKLAHOMA

Candidates	Votes	%
1 Page Belcher (R)	114,896	57.2
Harry B. Moreland (D)	86,123	42.8
2 Ed Edmondson (D)	83,976	60.2
Percy Butler (R)	55,416	39.8
3 Carl Albert (D)	60,620	76.5
Chapin Wallace (R)	18,182	23.0
4 Tom Steed (D)	57,416	61.1
Harold H. Potter (R)	36,534	38.9
5 John Jarman (D)	110,416	63.7
Hobart H. Hobbs (R)	62,812	36.3
6 Toby Morris (D)	86,770	68.9
Fred L. Coogan (R)	39,153	31.1

OREGON

Candidates	Votes	%
1 Walter Norblad (R)	109,360	54.7
Jason Lee (D)	90,567	45.3
2 Al Ullman (D)	53,219	50.7
Sam Coon (R)	51,844	49.4
3 Edith Green (D)	146,250	61.6
Phil J. Roth (R)	91,239	38.4
4 Charles O. Porter (D)	90,355	51.3
Harris Ellsworth (R)	85,860	48.7

PENNSYLVANIA

Candidates	Votes	%
1 William A. Barrett (D)	74,511	62.7
A. J. Cammarota (R)	44,333	37.3
2 Kathryn E. Granahan (D)	95,567	62.3
Robert F. Frankenfield (R)	57,773	37.7
3 James A. Byrne (D)	71,161	59.9
Charles H. Sporkin (R)	47,550	40.1
4 Earl Chudoff (D)	75,374	69.1
Horace C. Scott (R)	33,672	30.9
5 William J. Green Jr. (D)	107,021	53.3
James J. Schissler (R)	93,612	46.7
6 Hugh Scott (R)	90,966	51.5
Herbert J. McGlinchey (D)	85,541	48.5
7 Benjamin F. James (R)	137,764	61.9
William A. Welsh (D)	84,764	38.1
8 Willard S. Curtin (R)	98,023	55.9
John P. Fullam (D)	77,229	44.1
9 Paul B. Dague (R)	110,230	68.4
Edward G. Wilson (D)	50,947	31.6
10 Joseph L. Carrigg (R)	91,103	55.8
Jerome P. Casey (D)	72,178	44.2
11 Daniel J. Flood (D)	83,178	53.1
Enoch H. Thomas Jr. (R)	73,606	47.0
12 Ivor D. Fenton (R)	72,125	56.5
George G. Lindsay (D)	55,642	43.6
13 Samuel K. McConnell Jr. (R)	127,627	66.7
Alfred M. Klein (D)	63,610	33.3
14 George M. Rhodes (D)	51,088	51.3
Thomas K. Leinbach (R)	48,129	48.4
15 Francis E. Walter (D)	63,204	55.6
George M. Berg (R)	50,491	44.4

Candidates	Votes	%
16 Walter M. Mumma (R)	84,617	60.5
Guy J. Swope (D)	55,260	39.5
17 Alvin R. Bush (R)	74,748	58.6
Dean R. Fisher (D)	52,900	41.4
18 Richard M. Simpson (R)	77,833	59.9
Ross E. Hershberger (D)	52,180	40.1
19 S. Walter Stauffer (R)	79,448	53.8
James M. Quigley (D)	68,171	46.2
20 James E. Van Zandt (R)	65,457	63.0
John R. Stewart (D)	38,483	37.0
21 Augustine B. Kelley (D)	78,744	56.8
Herbert O. Morrison (R)	59,786	43.2
22 John P. Saylor (R)	85,540	56.9
Joseph C. Dolan (D)	64,689	43.1
23 Leon H. Gavin (R)	72,365	66.1
Grace M. Sloan (D)	37,122	33.9
24 Carroll D. Kearns (R)	93,824	57.8
William D. Thomas (D)	68,625	42.2
25 Frank M. Clark (D)	81,339	51.3
Sidney L. Lockley (R)	77,150	48.7
26 Thomas E. Morgan (D)	104,049	61.9
I. Willits McCaskey (R)	64,129	38.1
27 James G. Fulton (R)	126,247	66.0
Kenneth L. Stilley (D)	64,917	34.0
28 Herman P. Eberharter (D)	88,725	57.8
Richard C. Witt (R)	64,905	42.3
29 Robert J. Corbett (R)	114,109	64.7
Joseph A. Guerrier (D)	62,225	35.3
30 Elmer J. Holland (D)	103,389	59.8
Ross V. Walker (R)	69,495	40.2

RHODE ISLAND

Candidates	Votes	%
1 Aime J. Forand (D)	96,732	55.8
Samuel H. Ramsay (R)	76,714	44.2
2 John E. Fogarty (D)	105,496	52.2
Thomas H. Needham (R)	96,568	47.8

SOUTH CAROLINA

Candidates	Votes	%
1 L. Mendel Rivers (D)	31,112	100.0
2 John J. Riley (D)	49,284	100.0
3 W. J. Bryan Dorn (D)	39,270	92.9
Mrs. Maka Knox (R)	2,885	6.8
4 Robert T. Ashmore (D)	53,722	85.1
Dan H. Wallace Jr (R)	9,393	14.9
5 Robert Hemphill (D)	36,454	100.0
6 John L. McMillan (D)	39,749	100.0

SOUTH DAKOTA

Candidates	Votes	%
1 George McGovern (D)	116,516	52.4
Harold O. Lovre (R)	105,835	47.6
2 E. Y. Berry (R)	36,681	55.9
Tom Eastman Jr. (D)	28,984	44.1

TENNESSEE

Candidates	Votes	%
1 B. Carroll Reece (R)	86,531	72.1
Arthur Bright (D)	33,403	27.9
2 Howard H. Baker (R)	90,127	100.0
3 James B. Frazier Jr. (D)	55,715	53.7
P. H. Wood (R)	47,954	46.3
4 Joe L. Evins (D)	56,191	98.4
5 J. Carlton Loser (D)	54,318	74.5
George S. Spence (R)	18,585	25.5
6 Ross Bass (D)	47,098	100.0
7 Tom Murray (D)	36,301	100.0
8 Jere Cooper (D)	27,485	100.0
9 Clifford Davis (D)	90,874	71.8
Herbert Harper (R)	35,783	28.3

TEXAS

Candidates	Votes	%
1 Wright Patman (D)	54,837	100.0
2 Jack Brooks (D)	81,343	100.0
3 Lindley Beckworth (D)	47,570	83.5
R. E. Kennedy (R)	9,402	16.5

Candidates	Votes	%
4 Sam Rayburn (D)	41,867	100.0
5 Bruce Alger (R)	102,380	55.6
Henry Wade (D)	81,705	44.4
6 Olin Teague (D)	42,383	100.0
7 John Dowdy (D)	44,456	100.0
8 Albert Thomas (D)	137,950	60.5
C. A. Friloux Jr. (R)	86,640	38.0
9 Clark W. Thompson (D)	88,487	100.0
10 Homer Thornberry (D)	68,697	100.0
11 W. R. Poage (D)	56,990	100.0
12 Jim Wright (D)	110,196	100.0
13 Frank Ikard (D)	66,108	100.0
14 John Young (D)	85,922	87.3
Olive B. Stichter (R)	12,517	12.7
15 Joe M. Kilgore (D)	64,011	100.0
16 J. T. Rutherford (D)	50,704	64.6
Charles H. Gibson (R)	27,821	35.4
17 Omar Burleson (D)	53,003	100.0
18 Walter Rogers (D)	75,243	100.0
19 George Mahon (D)	85,566	100.0
20 Paul J. Kilday (D)	67,707	100.0
21 O. C. Fisher (D)	60,344	100.0
AL Martin Dies (D)	1,436,831	98.5

UTAH

Candidates	Votes	%
1 Henry Aldous Dixon (R)	74,107	60.9
Carlyle F. Gronning (D)	47,533	39.1
2 William A. Dawson (R)	119,683	57.6
Oscar W. McConkie Jr. (D)	87,970	42.4

VERMONT

Candidates	Votes	%
AL Winston L. Prouty (R)	103,736	67.1
Camille E. St. Amour (D)	50,797	32.9

VIRGINIA

Candidates	Votes	%
1 Edward J. Robeson Jr. (D)	31,839	50.8
Horace E. Henderson (R)	30,799	49.2
2 Porter Hardy Jr. (D)	46,958	76.4
William R. Burns (R)	14,483	23.6
3 J. Vaughan Gary (D)	46,109	59.1
Roy E. Cabell Jr. (R)	31,947	40.9
4 Watkins M. Abbitt (D)	51,434	99.9
5 William M. Tuck (D)	39,771	67.4
Jackson L. Kiser (R)	19,263	32.6
6 Richard H. Poff (R)	51,279	62.1
John L. Whitehead (D)	31,043	37.6
7 Burr P. Harrison (D)	40,069	69.0
A. R. Dunning (R)	17,970	31.0
8 Howard W. Smith (D)	38,648	67.3
Horace B. Clay (R)	18,813	32.7
9 W. Pat Jennings (D)	49,448	54.1
William C. Wampler (R)	41,957	45.9
10 Joel T. Broyhill (R)	53,149	56.2
Warren D. Quenstedt (D)	40,553	42.9

WASHINGTON

Candidates	Votes	%
1 Thomas M. Pelly (R)	129,768	58.1
James B. Wilson (D)	93,492	41.9
2 Jack Westland (R)	105,975	56.0
Payson Peterson (D)	83,195	44.0
3 Russell V. Mack (R)	80,520	56.5
Al McCoy (D)	61,962	43.5
4 Hal Holmes (R)	76,769	50.4
Frank LeRoux (D)	75,519	49.6
5 Walt Horan (R)	83,230	53.8
Tom Delaney (D)	71,571	46.2
6 Thor C. Tollefson (R)	108,014	54.0
John T. McCutcheon (D)	91,878	46.0
AL Don Magnuson (D)	621,118	58.5
Philip Evans (R)	439,896	41.5

WEST VIRGINIA

Candidates	Votes	%
1 Arch A. Moore Jr. (R)	65,096	50.3
C. Lee Spillers (D)	64,334	49.7
2 Harley O. Staggers (D)	63,327	52.4
Mary Elkins (R)	57,597	47.6
3 Cleveland M. Bailey (D)	62,240	51.5
Daniel L. Louchery (R)	58,623	48.5
4 Will E. Neal (R)	78,225	52.8
M. G. Burnside (D)	69,871	47.2
5 Elizabeth Kee (D)	68,638	60.7
William H. Sanders (R)	44,479	39.3
6 Robert C. Byrd (D)	99,854	57.4
Cleo S. Jones (R)	74,110	42.6

WISCONSIN

Candidates	Votes	%
1 Lawrence H. Smith (R)	94,882	57.1
Gerald T. Flynn (D)	71,379	42.9
2 Donald E. Tewes (R)	101,444	55.3
Robert W. Kastenmeier (D)	81,922	44.7
3 Gardner R. Withrow (R)	74,000	61.2
Norman M. Clapp (D)	46,911	38.8
4 Clement J. Zablocki (D)	128,213	65.7
William J. Burke (R)	67,063	34.3
5 Henry S. Reuss (D)	118,603	57.8
Russell Wirth Jr. (R)	86,764	42.3
6 William K. Van Pelt (R)	96,783	67.2
Rudolph J. Ploetz (D)	47,277	32.8

Candidates	Votes	%
7 Melvin R. Laird (R)	80,143	61.9
Margaret Anderson (D)	49,442	38.2
8 John W. Byrnes (R)	97,952	64.7
Milo Singler (D)	53,567	35.4
9 Lester R. Johnson (D)	62,476	51.4
Arthur L. Peterson (R)	59,024	48.6
10 Alvin E. O'Konski (R)	67,250	64.5
Carl E. Lauri (D)	36,941	35.5

WYOMING

	Votes	%
AL Keith Thomson (R)	69,903	58.2
Jerry A. O'Callaghan (D)	50,225	41.8

1957 House Elections

ILLINOIS

Special Election

	Votes	%
7 Roland V. Libonati (D)	32,221	88.1
Anthony C. Catena (R)	4,353	11.9

NEW JERSEY

Special Election

	Votes	%
2 Milton W. Glenn (R)	58,129	54.8
Joseph G. Hancock (D)	47,647	44.9

House Candidates Index

For an index of all House candidates listed in this section (pages 701 to 1061), see pages 1180-1273. Instructions for use of the House Candidates Index appear on page 1180.

1958 House Elections

ALABAMA

	Candidates	Votes	%
1	Frank W. Boykin (D)	19,499	100.0
2	George Grant (D)	27,972	100.0
3	George W. Andrews (D)	17,389	100.0
4	Kenneth A. Roberts (D)	25,133	100.0
5	Albert Rains (D)	31,687	100.0
6	Armistead I. Selden Jr. (D)	18,557	100.0
7	Carl Elliott (D)	29,936	100.0
8	Robert E. Jones (D)	22,710	100.0
9	George Huddleston Jr. (D)	38,229	86.3
	Frank L. Mason (R)	6,050	13.7

ALASKA

(Became a state Jan. 3, 1959)

		Votes	%
AL	Ralph J. Rivers (D)	27,945	57.5
	Henry A. Benson (R)	20,699	42.6

ARIZONA

		Votes	%
1	John J. Rhodes (R)	86,959	59.3
	Joe Haldiman Jr. (D)	59,816	40.8
2	Stewart L. Udall (D)	79,651	60.9
	John G. Speiden (R)	51,140	39.1

ARKANSAS

		Votes	%
1	Ezekiel C. Gathings (D)		100.0
2	Wilbur D. Mills (D)		100.0
3	James W. Trimble (D)		100.0
4	Oren Harris (D)		100.0
5	Dale Alford (WRITE IN)	30,739	51.0
	Brooks Hays (D)	29,483	49.0
6	William F. Norrell (D)		100.0

CALIFORNIA

		Votes	%
1	Clem W. Miller (D)	102,096	54.9
	Frederick G. Dupuis (R)	83,807	45.1
2	Harold T. Johnson (D)	90,850	61.0
	Curtis W. Tarr (R)	58,199	39.1
3	John E. Moss Jr. (D-R)	169,727	100.0
4	William S. Mailliard (R)	98,574	60.0
	George D. Collins Jr. (D)	65,798	40.0
5	John F. Shelley (D-R)	99,171	100.0
6	John F. Baldwin Jr. (R)	92,669	51.0
	Howard H. Jewel (D)	89,192	49.0
7	Jeffery Cohelan (D)	65,699	50.9
	John J. Allen Jr. (R)	63,270	49.1
8	George P. Miller (D-R)	181,437	100.0
9	J. Arthur Younger (R)	90,735	58.8
	Elma D. Oddstad (D)	63,597	41.2
10	Charles S. Gubser (R)	118,715	54.6
	Russell B. Bryan (D)	98,894	45.4
11	John J. McFall (D)	86,924	69.3
	Fredrick S. Van Dyke (R)	38,427	30.7
12	B. F. Sisk (D)	112,702	81.1
	Daniel K. Halpin (R)	26,228	18.9
13	Charles M. Teague (R)	98,381	57.0
	William Kirk Stewart (D)	74,160	43.0
14	Harlan Hagen (D-R)	120,347	99.9
15	Gordon L. McDonough (R)	77,267	52.0
	Emery S. Petty (D)	71,192	48.0
16	Donald L. Jackson (R)	70,724	57.8
	Melvin Lennard (D)	51,616	42.2
17	Cecil R. King (D)	182,965	75.3
	Leonard Di Miceli (R)	59,973	24.7
18	Craig Hosmer (R)	95,682	60.0
	Harry S. May (D)	63,684	40.0
19	Chet Holifield (D)	131,421	83.4
	Harry Vincent Leppek (R)	26,092	16.6
20	H. Allen Smith (R)	72,311	66.0
	Raymond Robert Farrell (D)	37,331	34.1

	Candidates	Votes	%
21	Edgar W. Hiestand (R)	127,238	51.9
	Mrs. Rudd Brown (D)	118,141	48.1
22	Joe Holt (R)	87,785	55.4
	Irving Glasband (D)	70,777	44.6
23	Clyde Doyle (D-R)	140,817	100.0
24	Glenard P. Lipscomb (R)	68,184	56.4
	William H. Ware Jr. (D)	52,804	43.6
25	George A. Kasem (D)	135,009	50.1
	Prescott O. Lieberg (R)	134,406	49.9
26	James Roosevelt (D)	125,495	72.2
	Crispus Wright (R)	48,248	27.8
27	Harry R. Sheppard (D)	105,062	72.3
	Robert M. Castle (R)	40,317	27.7
28	James B. Utt (R)	152,855	58.2
	T. R. Boyett (D)	109,794	41.8
29	Dalip S. Saund (D)	64,518	62.4
	John Babbage (R)	38,899	37.6
30	Bob Wilson (R)	112,290	55.3
	Lionel Van Deerlin (D)	90,641	44.7

COLORADO

		Votes	%
1	Byron G. Rogers (D)	107,567	66.7
	John L. Harpel (R)	53,801	33.3
2	Byron L. Johnson (D)	95,409	53.9
	John G. Mackie (R)	80,467	45.5
3	J. Edgar Chenoweth (R)	63,655	50.2
	Fred M. Betz (D)	63,112	49.8
4	Wayne N. Aspinall (D)	43,785	63.6
	J. R. (Dick) Wells (R)	25,048	36.4

CONNECTICUT

		Votes	%
1	Emilio Q. Daddario (D)	146,115	54.3
	Edwin H. May Jr. (R)	122,770	45.7
2	Chester Bowles (D)	79,672	53.3
	Horace Seely-Brown Jr. (R)	69,837	46.7
3	Robert N. Giaimo (D)	101,028	56.2
	Albert W. Cretella (R)	78,665	43.8
4	Donald J. Irwin (D)	119,766	50.9
	Albert P. Morano (R)	115,505	49.1
5	John S. Monagan (D)	72,604	53.8
	James T. Patterson (R)	62,353	46.2
AL	Frank Kowalski (D)	542,315	56.0
	Antoni N. Sadlak (R)	425,452	44.0

DELAWARE

		Votes	%
AL	Harris B. McDowell Jr. (D)	76,797	50.2
	Harry G. Haskell Jr. (R)	76,099	49.8

FLORIDA

		Votes	%
1	William C. Cramer (R)	79,876	58.8
	Winton H. King (D)	56,005	41.2
2	Charles E. Bennett (D)	32,975	100.0
3	Robert L. F. Sikes (D)	27,855	100.0
4	Dante B. Fascell (D)	56,051	100.0
5	A. Sydney Herlong Jr. (D)	63,245	67.0
	William C. Coleman (R)	31,188	33.0
6	Paul G. Rogers (D)	71,189	71.5
	Charles P. Ware (R)	28,355	28.5
7	James A. Haley (D)	28,953	100.0
8	D. R. Matthews (D)	18,669	100.0

GEORGIA

		Votes	%
1	Prince H. Preston (D)	13,488	100.0
2	John L. Pilcher (D)	8,712	100.0
3	E. L. Forrester (D)	16,703	100.0
4	John J. Flynt Jr. (D)	17,054	100.0
5	James C. Davis (D)	32,135	100.0

	Candidates	Votes	%
6	Carl Vinson (D)	15,569	100.0
7	Harlan Erwin Mitchell (D)	13,913	100.0
8	Iris Faircloth Blitch (D)	12,940	100.0
9	Phil M. Landrum (D)	14,019	100.0
10	Paul Brown (D)	14,103	100.0

Special Election

		Votes	%
7	Harlan Erwin Mitchell (D)	16,426	95.5

IDAHO

		Votes	%
1	Gracie B. Pfost (D)	60,083	62.4
	A. B. Curtis (R)	36,178	37.6
2	Hamer H. Budge (R)	78,553	55.0
	Tim Brennan (D)	64,214	45.0

ILLINOIS

		Votes	%
1	William L. Dawson (D)	60,778	72.2
	Theodore R. M. Howard (R)	23,384	27.8
2	Barratt O'Hara (D)	75,691	68.3
	Harold E. Marks (R)	34,203	30.9
3	William T. Murphy (D)	79,886	56.5
	Emmet F. Byrne (R)	55,513	39.2
4	Edward J. Derwinski (R)	106,691	52.0
	Leland H. Rayson (D)	98,657	48.0
5	John C. Kluczynski (D)	96,591	76.1
	Theodore Wozniak (R)	30,374	23.9
6	Thomas J. O'Brien (D)	90,796	73.1
	Frank S. Estes (R)	33,392	26.9
7	Roland V. Libonati (D)	90,974	83.0
	Anthony C. Catena (R)	18,595	17.0
8	Daniel D. Rostenkowski (D)	73,413	74.6
	William F. H. Schmidt (R)	25,011	25.4
9	Sidney R. Yates (D)	70,989	67.0
	Homer P. Hargraves Jr. (R)	34,909	33.0
10	Harold R. Collier (R)	84,045	54.3
	William J. McGah Jr. (D)	70,621	45.7
11	Roman C. Pucinski (D)	79,167	56.7
	Timothy P. Sheehan (R)	60,347	43.3
12	Charles A. Boyle (D)	85,129	60.8
	Allen A. Freeman (R)	54,967	39.2
13	Marguerite Stitt Church (R)	165,910	67.1
	Laurence A. Kusek (D)	81,326	32.9
14	Elmer J. Hoffman (R)	96,381	64.3
	Peter J. Fiefer (D)	53,449	35.7
15	Noah M. Mason (R)	58,829	52.5
	Dorothy G. O'Brien (D)	53,196	47.5
16	Leo E. Allen (R)	71,049	61.4
	Milton A. Lundstrom (D)	44,723	38.6
17	Leslie C. Arends (R)	70,125	61.0
	William T. Larkin (D)	44,821	39.0
18	Robert H. Michel (R)	57,929	59.5
	James W. McGee (D)	39,464	40.5
19	Robert B. Chiperfield (R)	52,049	50.5
	John C. Watson (D)	51,104	49.5
20	Edna Simpson (R)	57,412	55.5
	Henry W. Pollock (D)	46,076	44.4
21	Peter F. Mack Jr. (D)	87,134	58.8
	Norma Eaton (R)	61,137	41.2
22	William L. Springer (R)	65,080	60.5
	Carlton H. Myers (D)	42,533	39.5
23	George E. Shipley (D)	65,114	50.1
	Charles W. Vursell (R)	64,927	49.9
24	Melvin Price (D)	94,231	76.1
	Alex Chouinard (R)	29,670	24.0
25	Kenneth J. Gray (D)	78,385	58.2
	Carl D. Sneed (R)	56,257	41.8

INDIANA

		Votes	%
1	Ray J. Madden (D)	95,801	66.4
	Edward P. Keck (R)	47,588	33.0
2	Charles A. Halleck (R)	71,933	52.2
	George H. Bowers (D)	65,792	47.8

INDIANA

	Candidates	Votes	%
3	John Brademas (D)	101,802	56.9
	F. Jay Nimtz (R)	77,014	43.1
4	E. Ross Adair (R)	69,745	50.1
	W. Robert Fleming (D)	69,478	49.9
5	J. Edward Roush (D)	97,184	53.7
	John V. Beamer (R)	83,852	46.3
6	Fred Wampler (D)	71,669	51.5
	Cecil M. Harden (R)	67,549	48.5
7	William G. Bray (R)	77,045	53.8
	Thomas L. Lemon (D)	66,217	46.2
8	Winfield K. Denton (D)	100,611	61.5
	Franklin E. Katterjohn (R)	63,005	38.5
9	Earl Hogan (D)	62,810	50.3
	Earl Wilson (R)	62,064	49.7
10	Randall S. Harmon (D)	76,757	50.8
	Ralph Harvey (R)	74,500	49.3
11	Joseph W. Barr (D)	113,674	52.1
	Charles B. Brownson (R)	104,555	47.9

IOWA

		Votes	%
1	Fred Schwengel (R)	59,577	53.4
	Thomas J. Dailey (D)	51,996	46.6
2	Leonard G. Wolf (D)	67,022	51.1
	Henry O. Talle (R)	64,073	48.9
3	H. R. Gross (R)	61,920	53.7
	Michael Micich (D)	53,467	46.3
4	Steven V. Carter (D)	42,479	52.0
	John Kyl (R)	39,233	48.0
5	Neal Smith (D)	61,693	52.3
	Paul Cunningham (R)	56,320	47.7
6	Merwin Coad (D)	57,491	58.3
	Robert E. Waggoner (R)	41,204	41.8
7	Ben F. Jensen (R)	41,053	51.5
	Ellsworth O. Hays (D)	38,660	48.5
8	Charles B. Hoeven (R)	49,418	52.7
	Donald E. O'Brien (D)	44,310	47.3

KANSAS

		Votes	%
1	William H. Avery (R)	60,198	51.2
	Robert W. Domme (D)	55,749	47.4
2	Newell A. George (D)	69,954	50.8
	Errett P. Scrivner (R)	67,882	49.3
3	Denver D. Hargis (D)	42,718	51.7
	Myron V. George (R)	39,872	48.3
4	Edward H. Rees (R)	89,611	50.7
	Warner Moore (D)	87,244	49.3
5	J. Floyd Breeding (D)	60,549	53.1
	Clifford R. Hope Jr. (R)	53,387	46.9
6	Wint Smith (R)	43,782	49.2
	Elmo J. Mahoney (D)	43,549	49.0

KENTUCKY

		Votes	%
1	Frank Stubblefield (D)	41,214	85.0
	James G. Bondy (R)	7,263	15.0
2	William H. Natcher (D)	38,941	76.1
	Wayland Render (R)	12,239	23.9
3	Frank W. Burke (D)	73,121	52.2
	John M. Robsion Jr. (R)	67,059	47.8
4	Frank Chelf (D)	19,310	100.0
5	Brent Spence (D)	34,919	71.9
	Jule Appel (R)	13,631	28.1
6	John C. Watts (D)	29,199	94.7
	Wallace Jones	1,622	5.3
7	Carl D. Perkins (D)	56,756	65.8
	E. L. Raybourn (R)	29,505	34.2
8	Eugene Siler (R)	34,728	68.0
	W. D. Scalf (D)	16,311	32.0

LOUISIANA

		Votes	%
1	F. Edward Hebert (D)	41,861	100.0
2	Hale Boggs (D)	46,614	91.8
	John Patrick Conway (R)	4,160	8.2
3	Edwin E. Willis (D)	8,692	100.0
4	Overton Brooks (D)	23,844	100.0
5	Otto E. Passman (D)	14,900	100.0
6	James H. Morrison (D)	20,599	100.0
7	T. A. Thompson (D)	10,328	100.0
8	Harold B. McSween (D)	11,125	100.0

MAINE

		Votes	%
1	James C. Oliver (D)	55,686	52.1
	Robert Hale (R)	51,231	47.9
2	Frank M. Coffin (D)	59,054	61.3
	Neil Bishop (R)	37,219	38.7
3	Clifford G. McIntire (R)	40,156	56.0
	Gerald J. Grady (D)	31,616	44.1

MARYLAND

		Votes	%
1	Thomas F. Johnson (D)	32,328	50.6
	Edward T. Miller (R)	31,610	49.4
2	Daniel B. Brewster (D)	87,667	61.0
	Fife Symington (R)	56,165	39.1
3	Edward A. Garmatz (D)	49,649	84.0
	Harry Kemper (R)	9,470	16.0
4	George H. Fallon (D)	45,646	71.6
	Louis W. Collier (R)	18,094	28.4
5	Richard E. Lankford (D)	96,919	75.1
	Robert E. Ennis (R)	32,072	24.9
6	John R. Foley (D)	78,987	51.4
	DeWitt S. Hyde (R)	74,683	48.6
7	Samuel N. Friedel (D)	72,692	73.6
	Elizabeth P. Brown (R)	26,144	26.5

MASSACHUSETTS

		Votes	%
1	Silvio O. Conte (R)	66,067	55.3
	James M. Burns (D)	52,853	44.2
2	Edward P. Boland (D)	103,079	100.0
3	Phillip J. Philbin (D)	114,483	100.0
4	Harold D. Donohue (D)	93,993	63.8
	Charles D. Briggs Jr. (R)	53,359	36.2
5	Edith Nourse Rogers (R)	116,072	66.0
	William H. Sullivan (D)	59,746	34.0
6	William H. Bates (R)	106,807	100.0
7	Thomas J. Lane (D)	84,243	75.6
	Robert T. Breed (R)	27,215	24.4
8	Torbert H. Macdonald (D)	91,263	66.4
	Gordon F. Hughes (R)	46,274	33.6
9	Hastings Keith (R)	82,659	54.7
	John Almeida Jr. (D)	68,486	45.3
10	Laurence Curtis (R)	71,100	52.2
	John L. Saltonstall Jr. (D)	65,159	47.8
11	Thomas P. O'Neill Jr. (D)	68,353	80.4
	Elliott H. Stone (R)	16,669	19.6
12	John W. McCormack (D)	72,523	100.0
13	James A. Burke (D)	89,073	53.5
	William W. Jenness (R)	77,400	46.5
14	Joseph W. Martin Jr. (R)	90,751	61.0
	Edward F. Doolan (D)	57,920	39.0

MICHIGAN

		Votes	%
1	Thaddeus M. Machrowicz (D)	82,288	90.4
	Walter Czarnecki (R)	8,502	9.3
2	George Meader (R)	73,954	58.8
	Robert G. Hall (D)	51,323	40.8
3	August E. Johansen (R)	68,144	60.4
	John R. O'Meara (D)	44,189	39.2
4	Clare E. Hoffman (R)	59,780	59.9
	Gordon A. Elferdink (D)	39,765	39.8
5	Gerald R. Ford Jr. (R)	88,156	63.6
	Richard F. Vander Veen (D)	50,203	36.2
6	Charles E. Chamberlain (R)	92,313	52.1
	Don Hayworth (D)	84,418	47.7
7	James G. O'Hara (D)	87,299	50.7
	Robert J. McIntosh (R)	84,531	49.1
8	Alvin M. Bentley (R)	69,858	62.2
	James O. Pino (D)	42,467	37.8
9	Robert P. Griffin (R)	56,780	56.7
	Jan B. Vanderploeg (D)	43,196	43.1
10	Elford A. Cederberg (R)	54,316	61.1
	Daniel E. Reed (R)	34,390	38.7
11	Victor A. Knox (R)	41,689	52.3
	Prentiss M. Brown Jr. (D)	37,995	47.6
12	John B. Bennett (R)	39,239	57.0
	Joseph S. Mack (D)	29,506	42.9
13	Charles C. Diggs Jr. (D)	57,354	72.7
	Charles P. White (R)	21,280	27.0
14	Louis C. Rabaut (D)	97,236	64.2
	Lois V. Nair (R)	53,987	35.7
15	John D. Dingell (D)	79,216	78.5
	Austin W. Curtis Jr. (R)	21,414	21.2
16	John Lesinski (D)	145,665	71.8
	Ralph B. Guy (R)	56,488	27.8
17	Martha W. Griffiths (D)	96,660	60.3
	Lucas S. Miel (R)	63,323	39.5
18	William S. Broomfield (R)	101,100	52.6
	Leslie H. Hudson (D)	90,526	47.1

MINNESOTA

		Votes	%
1	Albert H. Quie (R)	73,345	57.0
	Eugene P. Foley (DFL)	55,445	43.1
2	Ancher Nelsen (R)	71,623	57.1
	Conrad H. Hammar (DFL)	53,869	42.9
3	Roy W. Wier (DFL)	98,449	51.6
	Leonard E. Lindquist (R)	92,190	48.4
4	Joseph E. Karth (DFL)	72,952	56.4
	Frank S. Farrell (R)	56,484	43.6
5	Walter H. Judd (R)	59,739	57.3
	Joseph Robbie (DFL)	44,453	42.7
6	Fred Marshall (DFL)	73,881	64.3
	Hugo Holmstrom (R)	41,018	35.7
7	H. Carl Andersen (R)	61,265	53.3
	A. I. Johnson (DFL)	53,689	46.7
8	John A. Blatnik (DFL)	97,046	75.6
	Roy W. Ranum (R)	31,343	24.4
9	Odin Langen (R)	47,863	50.7
	Coya Knutson (DFL)	46,473	49.3

Special Election

		Votes	%
1	Albert H. Quie (R)	44,276	50.3
	Eugene P. Foley (DFL)	43,674	49.7

MISSISSIPPI

		Votes	%
1	Thomas G. Abernethy (D)	12,413	100.0
2	Jamie L. Whitten (D)	7,982	100.0
3	Frank E. Smith (D)	4,644	100.0
4	John Bell Williams (D)	8,665	100.0
5	Arthur Winstead (D)	14,517	100.0
6	William M. Colmer (D)	13,243	100.0

MISSOURI

		Votes	%
1	Frank M. Karsten (D)	99,368	75.8
	Paul E. Corning Jr. (R)	31,804	24.3
2	Thomas B. Curtis (R)	88,321	51.9
	James L. Sullivan (D)	81,811	48.1
3	Leonor K. Sullivan (D)	63,679	79.2
	Josiah C. Thomas (R)	16,753	20.8
4	George H. Christopher (D)	72,792	64.0
	James A. Rahm (R)	40,912	36.0
5	Richard Bolling (D)	53,622	70.0
	Richard W. Byrne (R)	22,953	30.0
6	W. R. Hull Jr. (D)	64,277	64.9
	Clyde M. Kirk (R)	34,758	35.1
7	Charles H. Brown (D)	76,239	53.7
	Noel Cox (R)	65,666	46.3
8	A. S. J. Carnahan (D)	58,628	64.3
	Francis Howard (R)	32,543	35.7
9	Clarence Cannon (D)	67,555	64.8
	Anthony Schroeder (R)	36,758	35.2

MISSOURI

	Candidates	Votes	%
10	Paul C. Jones	44,892	70.7
	Gilbert Degenhardt (R)	18,633	29.3
11	Morgan M. Moulder (D)	54,014	56.9
	Don W. Owensby (R)	40,839	43.1

MONTANA

		Votes	%
	Lee Metcalf (D)	68,586	69.5
	Jean Walterskirschen (R)	30,111	30.5
2	LeRoy H. Anderson (D)	79,140	61.0
	Ashton Jones (R)	50,633	39.0

NEBRASKA

		Votes	%
1	Phil Weaver (R)	62,770	53.4
	Clair A. Callan (D)	54,705	46.6
2	Glenn Cunningham (R)	67,660	64.8
	Francis M. Casey (D)	36,842	35.3
3	Lawrence Brock (D)	53,033	55.1
	Robert D. Harrison (R)	43,236	44.9
4	Donald F. McGinley (D)	50,870	52.3
	Arthur L. Miller (R)	46,474	47.7

NEVADA

		Votes	%
AL	Walter S. Baring (D)	55,053	66.9
	Robert C. Horton (R)	27,275	33.1

NEW HAMPSHIRE

		Votes	%
1	Chester E. Merrow (R)	62,734	58.5
	Alphonse Roy (D)	44,051	41.0
2	Perkins Bass (R)	52,636	58.4
	Stuart V. Nims (D)	37,212	41.3

NEW JERSEY

		Votes	%
1	William T. Cahill (R)	96,619	50.3
	Alexander Feinberg (D)	94,790	49.3
2	Milton W. Glenn (R)	58,621	53.4
	Joseph G. Hancock (D)	50,558	46.1
3	James C. Auchincloss (R)	98,826	56.1
	Thomas F. Guthrie Jr. (D)	77,423	43.9
4	Frank Thompson Jr. (D)	83,388	63.0
	A. Jerome Moore (R)	48,990	37.0
5	Peter H. B. Frelinghuysen Jr. (R)	111,250	55.7
	David S. North (D)	87,966	44.0
6	Florence P. Dwyer (R)	88,084	51.1
	Jack B. Dunn (D)	80,779	46.9
7	William B. Widnall (R)	103,169	59.6
	J. Emmet Cassidy (D)	69,250	40.0
8	Gordon Canfield (R)	68,385	58.1
	Joseph R. Brumale (D)	48,481	41.2
9	Frank C. Osmers Jr. (R)	92,513	57.4
	Daniel W. Allen (D)	67,633	42.0
10	Peter W. Rodino Jr. (D)	60,482	63.9
	G. George Addonizio (R)	32,946	34.8
11	Hugh J. Addonizio (D)	50,821	59.3
	John P. Langan (R)	34,821	40.7
12	George M. Wallhauser (R)	57,510	52.7
	Thomas J. Holleran (D)	49,463	45.3
13	Cornelius E. Gallagher (D)	61,094	66.1
	Samuel F. Kanis (R)	23,001	24.9
14	Dominick V. Daniels (D)	56,475	62.9
	Frank A. Musto (R)	29,614	33.0

NEW MEXICO

		Votes	%
AL	Joseph M. Montoya (D)	124,924✔	
	Thomas G. Morris (D)	115,928✔	
	William A. Thompson (R)	72,922	
	George W. McKim (R)	70,925	

NEW YORK

	Candidates	Votes	%
1	Stuyvesant Wainwright (R)	155,387	57.5
	Otis G. Pike (D, L)	115,019	42.5
2	Steven B. Derounian (R)	113,820	60.5
	Walter A. Lynch Jr. (D, L)	74,194	39.5
3	Frank J. Becker (R)	109,245	54.4
	A. William Larson (D, L)	91,514	45.6
4	Seymour Halpern (R)	78,054	52.6
	Joseph J. Perrini (D, L)	70,437	47.4
5	Albert A. Bosch (R)	56,839	52.1
	William Kerwick (D)	47,661	43.7
6	Lester Holtzman (D, L)	106,762	63.6
	George T. Reilly (R)	61,204	36.4
7	James J. Delaney (D, L)	71,007	61.1
	Edward V. Lisoski (R)	45,135	38.9
8	Victor L. Anfuso (D, L)	43,656	71.7
	Leon F. Nadrowski (R)	17,271	28.4
9	Eugene J. Keogh (D, L)	61,816	72.1
	Anton Eyring (R)	23,957	27.9
10	Edna F. Kelly (D, L)	77,351	76.1
	Jerome P. Schneider (R)	24,286	23.9
11	Emanuel Celler (D, L)	105,011	81.4
	Jesse M. Browser (R)	24,034	18.6
12	Francis E. Dorn (R)	51,861	52.7
	Thomas J. Cuite (D)	39,275	39.9
	Leroy Bowman (L)	7,322	7.4
13	Abraham J. Multer (D, L)	88,406	76.1
	Hyman D. Siegel (R)	27,701	23.9
14	John J. Rooney (D, L)	60,703	70.6
	Anthony D'Allessandro (R)	25,319	29.4
15	John H. Ray (R, U TAX)	65,318	52.8
	Vincent R. Fitzpatrick (D, L)	58,351	47.2
16	Adam Clayton Powell Jr. (D, R)	56,383	90.8
	Earl Brown (L)	5,705	9.2
17	John V. Lindsay (R)	54,459	53.9
	Anthony B. Akers (D, L)	46,570	46.1
18	Alfred E. Santangelo (D)	36,601	59.4
	George A. Eyer Jr. (R)	20,848	33.8
	Manuel Velazquez (L)	4,201	6.8
19	Leonard Farbstein (D, L)	55,069	73.1
	Gonzales Suarez (R)	20,232	26.9
20	Ludwig Teller (D, L)	50,735	67.0
	Milton H. Adler (R)	24,933	33.0
21	Herbert Zelenko (D, L)	67,743	72.5
	Carl Medonick (R)	25,699	27.5
22	James C. Healey (D)	65,996	65.2
	Alex J. Soled (R)	20,777	20.5
	David I. Wells (L)	14,391	14.2
23	Isidore Dollinger (D)	49,452	71.5
	Simon M. Koenig (R)	12,278	17.7
	Hector Mathew (L)	7,469	10.8
24	Charles A. Buckley (D)	71,616	56.2
	Charles V. Scanlan (R)	35,993	28.3
	Murray Koenig (L)	19,759	15.5
25	Paul A. Fino (R)	79,857	57.8
	Neal P. Bottiglieri (D, L)	58,396	42.2
26	Edwin B. Dooley (R)	98,677	63.2
	Phil E. Gilbert Jr. (D, L)	57,465	36.8
27	Robert R. Barry (R)	104,240	58.2
	Richard W. McSpedon (D, L)	74,883	41.8
28	Katharine St.George (R)	84,536	59.7
	David Sive (D)	53,981	38.1
29	J. Ernest Wharton (R)	93,647	63.4
	Christopher D. Morris (D, L)	54,153	36.6
30	Leo W. O'Brien (D, L)	109,744	64.7
	George H. Witbeck Jr. (R)	59,958	35.3
31	Dean P. Taylor (R)	87,704	63.8
	John R. Cummins (D, L)	49,777	36.2
32	Samuel S. Stratton (D, L)	73,384	54.0
	Walter C. Shaw (R)	62,443	46.0
33	Clarence E. Kilburn (R)	73,698	64.8
	Robert P. McDonald (D, L)	40,010	35.2
34	Alexander Pirnie (R)	70,482	50.8
	Edwin L. Slusarczyk (D, L)	68,271	49.2
35	R. Walter Riehlman (R)	90,285	53.8
	Caryl M. Kline (D, L)	77,449	46.2
36	John Taber (R)	84,019	64.7
	Frank B. Lent (D, L)	45,822	35.3
37	Howard W. Robison (R)	101,279	65.8
	Francis P. Hogan (D, L)	52,636	34.2
38	Jessica McC Weis (R)	92,944	58.2
	Alphonse L. Cassetti (D, L)	66,806	41.8
39	Harold C. Ostertag (R)	90,004	65.2
	Harold L. Rakov (D, L)	48,144	34.8
40	William E. Miller (R)	90,066	60.8
	Mariano A. Lucca (D)	54,728	36.9
41	Thaddeus J. Dulski (D, L)	60,360	50.3
	James O. Moore Jr. (R)	59,634	49.7
42	John R. Pillion (R)	99,799	58.9
	Joseph R. Stiglmeier (D, L)	69,747	41.1
43	Daniel A. Reed (R)	68,896	63.8
	T. Joseph Lynch (D)	36,799	34.1

Special Election

		Votes	%
37	Howard W. Robison (R)	45,920	59.8
	Francis P. Hogan (D, L)	30,891	40.2

NORTH CAROLINA

		Votes	%
1	Herbert C. Bonner (D)	12,743	100.0
2	L. H. Fountain (D)	17,061	100.0
3	Graham A. Barden (D)	22,426	79.1
	Joe A. Dunn (R)	5,927	20.9
4	Harold D. Cooley (D)	30,505	75.6
	L. T. Dark Jr. (R)	9,863	24.4
5	Ralph J. Scott (D)	40,544	71.6
	William E. Morrow (R)	16,048	28.4
6	Carl T. Durham (D)	35,715	100.0
7	Alton Lennon (D)	27,902	89.0
	C. Dana Malpass (R)	3,461	11.0
8	A. Paul Kitchin (D)	43,793	63.4
	F. D. B. Harding (R)	25,276	36.6
9	Hugh Q. Alexander (D)	57,672	66.5
	William White (R)	29,065	33.5
10	Charles Raper Jonas (R)	56,487	51.9
	David Clark (D)	52,306	48.1
11	Basil L. Whitener (D)	37,926	100.0
12	David M. Hall (D)	52,609	62.5
	W. Harold Sams (R)	31,524	37.5

NORTH DAKOTA

		Votes	%
AL	Quentin N. Burdick (D)	99,562✔	
	Don L. Short (R)	97,862✔	
	Orris G. Nordhougen (R)	92,124	
	S. B. Hocking (D)	78,889	

OHIO

		Votes	%
1	Gordon H. Scherer (R)	70,686	56.6
	W. Ted Osborne (D)	54,119	43.4
2	William E. Hess (R)	86,656	54.7
	James O. Bradley (D)	71,674	45.3
3	Paul F. Schenck (R)	102,806	52.4
	Thomas B. Talbot (D)	93,401	47.6
4	William M. McCulloch (R)	73,448	61.0
	Marjorie Conrad Struna (D)	46,933	39.0
5	Delbert L. Latta (R)	52,612	53.9
	George Rafferty (D)	44,971	46.1
6	James G. Polk (D)	76,566	62.0
	Elmer S. Barrett (R)	46,924	38.0
7	Clarence J. Brown (R)	75,085	60.5
	Joseph A. Sullivan (D)	48,994	39.5
8	Jackson E. Betts (R)	62,232	61.3
	Virgil M. Gase (D)	39,343	38.7
9	Thomas L. Ashley (D)	102,115	61.6
	William K. Gernheuser (R)	63,660	38.4
10	Walter H. Moeller (D)	47,939	52.9
	Homer E. Abele (R)	42,607	47.1

OHIO

Candidates	Votes	%
11 Robert E. Cook (D)	79,468	50.3
David Dennison Jr. (R)	78,501	49.7
12 Samuel L. Devine (R)	100,684	54.4
Walter J. Shapter Jr. (D)	84,470	45.6
13 Albert D. Baumhart Jr. (R)	65,169	58.9
J. William McCray (D)	45,390	41.1
14 William H. Ayres (R)	114,827	60.1
Jack B. Arnold (D)	76,138	39.9
15 John E. Henderson (R)	48,316	57.3
Herbert U. Smith (D)	36,062	42.7
16 Frank T. Bow (R)	100,678	57.4
John G. Freedom (D)	74,660	42.6
17 Robert W. Levering (D)	63,650	51.7
Lawrence Burns (R)	59,490	48.3
18 Wayne L. Hays (D)	88,813	71.6
Francis Wallace (R)	35,322	28.5
19 Michael J. Kirwan (D)	93,660	75.0
Loren E. Van Brocklin (R)	31,192	25.0
20 Michael A. Feighan (D)	113,200	79.4
Malvern E. Schultz (R)	29,308	20.6
21 Charles A. Vanik (D)	93,987	80.4
Ermer L. Watson (R)	22,956	19.6
22 Frances P. Bolton (R)	71,139	55.3
Chat Paterson (D)	57,508	44.7
23 William E. Minshall Jr. (R)	95,267	66.5
Daniel Winston (D)	47,953	33.5

OKLAHOMA

Candidates	Votes	%
1 Page H. Belcher (R)	74,853	50.8
Herbert William Wright Jr. (D)	71,190	48.3
2 Ed Edmondson (D)	75,492	79.1
Milo Ritter (R)	19,996	20.9
3 Carl Albert (D)	43,868	90.9
Chapin Wallace (R)	4,398	9.1
4 Tom Steed (D)	43,837	74.1
Rolla C. Calkins (R)	15,359	26.0
5 John Jarman (D)	79,917	82.3
Hobart H. Hobbs (R)	17,137	17.7
6 Toby Morris (D)	54,967	66.7
Fred L. Coogan (R)	27,425	33.3

OREGON

Candidates	Votes	%
1 Walter Norblad (R)	95,420	54.9
Robert Y. Thornton (D)	78,362	45.1
2 Al Ullman (D)	50,166	61.1
Marion T. Weatherford (R)	31,987	38.9
3 Edith Green (D)	131,164	65.8
John Johnston (R)	68,235	34.2
4 Charles O. Porter (D)	79,166	56.3
Paul Geddes (R)	61,386	43.7

PENNSYLVANIA

Candidates	Votes	%
1 William A. Barrett (D)	67,531	64.7
Gerard Iannelli (R)	36,854	35.3
2 Kathryn E. Granahan (D)	84,058	66.3
Maurice M. Green (R)	42,759	33.7
3 James A. Byrne (D)	65,201	63.5
James Thomas McDermott (R)	37,420	36.5
4 Robert N. C. Nix (D)	63,031	72.6
Cecil B. Moore (R)	23,845	27.5
5 William J. Green Jr. (D)	100,680	55.3
D. Donald Jamieson (R)	81,530	44.8
6 Herman Toll (D)	83,491	55.4
Fred C. Gartner (R)	67,205	44.6
7 William H. Milliken Jr. (R)	114,275	59.2
Hubert P. Earle (D)	78,747	40.8
8 Willard S. Curtin (R)	85,010	54.3
Harold Lefcourt (D)	71,583	45.7
9 Paul B. Dague (R)	88,193	61.9
James C. N. Paul (D)	54,220	38.1
10 Stanley A. Prokop (D)	74,890	50.4
Joseph L. Carrigg (R)	73,601	49.6

Candidates	Votes	%
11 Daniel J. Flood (D)	89,167	61.7
Herman C. Kersteen (R)	55,349	38.3
12 Ivor D. Fenton (R)	64,960	54.9
Charles E. Lotz (D)	53,402	45.1
13 John A. Lafore Jr. (R)	104,156	62.9
John T. Synnestvedt (D)	61,475	37.1
14 George M. Rhodes (D)	51,281	58.3
Thomas C. Anthony Jr. (R)	36,170	41.1
15 Francis E. Walter (D)	60,742	61.1
Luther H. Ackerman (R)	38,726	38.9
16 Walter M. Mumma (R)	70,810	56.6
John H. Bream (D)	54,245	43.4
17 Alvin Bush (R)	65,071	56.0
C. Max Hess (D)	51,053	44.0
18 Richard M. Simpson (R)	67,719	56.3
Ross E. Hershberger (D)	52,514	43.7
19 James M. Quigley (D)	67,603	51.5
S. Walter Stauffer (R)	63,749	48.5
20 James E. Van Zandt (R)	61,010	64.9
Julia L. Maietta (D)	33,060	35.1
21 John H. Dent (D)	70,828	59.2
Edward S. Stiteler (R)	48,925	40.9
22 John P. Saylor (R)	77,407	57.0
Robert S. Glass (D)	58,434	43.0
23 Leon H. Gavin (R)	60,080	61.1
Thomas P. Kennedy (D)	38,179	38.9
24 Carroll D. Kearns (R)	76,870	53.8
James P. O'Brien (D)	65,937	46.2
25 Frank M. Clark (D)	80,704	58.9
Thomas W. King Jr. (R)	56,375	41.1
26 Thomas E. Morgan (D)	92,755	64.8
Harry T. Zimmer Jr. (R)	50,403	35.2
27 James G. Fulton (R)	105,990	64.1
Emery F. Bacon (D)	59,283	35.9
28 William S. Moorhead (D)	82,081	67.3
Harry L. Verbofsky (R)	39,900	32.7
29 Robert J. Corbett (R)	97,203	63.6
Lee T. Sellars (D)	55,575	36.4
30 Elmer J. Holland (D)	98,244	66.7
Harold E. Morgan (R)	49,093	33.3

RHODE ISLAND

	Votes	%
1 Aime J. Forand (D)	97,425	62.9
Francis E. Martineau (R)	57,581	37.2
2 John E. Fogarty (D)	117,506	63.3
Robert L. Gammell (R)	67,942	36.6

SOUTH CAROLINA

	Votes	%
1 L. Mendel Rivers (D)	13,538	100.0
2 John J. Riley (D)	13,677	100.0
3 W. J. Bryan Dorn (D)	9,528	99.9
4 Robert T. Ashmore (D)	17,247	100.0
5 Robert W. Hemphill (D)	9,780	100.0
6 John L. McMillan (D)	12,862	100.0

SOUTH DAKOTA

	Votes	%
1 George McGovern (D)	107,202	53.4
Joe Foss (R)	93,388	46.6
2 E. Y. Berry (R)	31,908	55.6
J. T. McCullen (D)	25,491	44.4

TENNESSEE

	Votes	%
1 B. Carroll Reece (R)	42,615	58.7
Mayne W. Miller (D)	29,999	41.3
2 Howard H. Baker (R)	49,420	67.7
John Grady O'Hara Sr. (D)	23,470	32.2
3 James B. Frazier Jr. (D)	31,267	100.0
4 Joe L. Evins (D)	38,062	100.0
5 J. Carlton Loser (D)	30,879	94.4
Porter Freeman (R)	1,824#	5.6
6 Ross Bass (D)	33,445	97.2
7 Tom Murray (D)	24,053	100.0
8 Robert A. Everett (D)	19,145	100.0
9 Clifford Davis (D)	46,550	100.0

TEXAS

Candidates	Votes	%
1 Wright Patman (D)	19,203	100.0
2 Jack Brooks (D)	47,092	100.0
3 Lindley Beckworth (D)	22,751	100.0
4 Sam Rayburn (D)	15,942	100.0
5 Bruce Alger (R)	62,722	52.6
Barefoot Sanders (D)	56,566	47.4
6 Olin Teague (D)	25,827	100.0
7 John Dowdy (D)	22,733	96.7
8 Albert Thomas (D)	33,393	88.2
R. E. Nesmith (R)	4,477	11.8
9 Clark W. Thompson (D)	36,012	100.0
10 Homer Thornberry (D)	28,990	100.0
11 W. R. Poage (D)	21,900	100.0
12 Jim Wright (D)	38,180	100.0
13 Frank Ikard (D)	27,671	100.0
14 John Young (D)	37,861	100.0
15 Joe M. Kilgore (D)	28,404	100.0
16 J. T. Rutherford (D)	28,744	100.0
17 Omar Burleson (D)	25,123	100.0
18 Walter Rogers (D)	34,617	100.0
19 George Mahon (D)	29,068	100.0
20 Paul J. Kilday (D)	23,539	100.0
21 O. C. Fisher (D)	26,497	100.0
22 Bob Casey (D)	43,660	61.7
T. Everton Kennerly (R)	23,317	33.0
Jack Gardner	3,789	5.4

UTAH

	Votes	%
1 Henry Aldous Dixon (R)	58,141	53.9
M. Blaine Peterson (D)	49,735	46.1
2 David S. King (D)	91,213	51.1
William A. Dawson (R)	87,234	48.9

VERMONT

	Votes	%
AL William H. Meyer (D)	63,131	51.5
Harold J. Arthur (R)	59,536	48.5

VIRGINIA

	Votes	%
1 Thomas N. Downing (D)	31,765	99.9
2 Porter Hardy Jr. (D)	32,758	100.0
3 J. Vaughan Gary (D)	34,040	76.1
Richard R. Ryder (R)	10,668	23.9
4 Watkins M. Abbitt (D)	37,679	87.1
Frank M. McCann (I)	5,556	12.9
5 William M. Tuck (D)	26,322	100.0
6 Richard H. Poff (R)	37,779	56.7
Richard F. Pence (D)	28,530	42.9
7 Burr P. Harrison (D)	30,486	76.6
Henry A. Oder Jr. (I)	9,294	23.4
8 Howard W. Smith (D)	28,815	99.7
9 W. Pat Jennings (D)	34,685	76.6
T. L. Maness (I)	10,615	23.4
10 Joel T. Broyhill (R)	37,764	52.3
Joseph H. Freehill (D)	33,553	46.5

WASHINGTON

	Votes	%
1 Thomas M. Pelly (R)	98,897	70.1
Robert Odman (D)	42,128	29.9
2 Jack Westland (R)	62,152	53.6
Hugh B. Mitchell (D)	53,436	46.1
3 Russell V. Mack (R)	69,745	60.9
Victor A. Meyers (D)	44,515	38.9
4 Catherine May (R)	66,544	54.0
Frank LeRoux (D)	56,308	45.7
5 Walt Horan (R)	67,072	53.2
Tom Delaney (D)	58,431	46.3
6 Thor C. Tollefson (R)	63,560	53.5
John M. Coffee (D)	54,536	45.9
7 Don Magnuson (D)	96,841	70.9
Bob Jones (R)	39,708	29.1

WEST VIRGINIA

Candidates	Votes	%
1 Arch A. Moore Jr. (R)	55,613	54.6
Robert H. Mollohan (D)	46,262	45.4
2 Harley O. Staggers (D)	57,761	62.7
Ward W. Keesecker (R)	34,436	37.4
3 Cleveland M. Bailey (D)	59,084	59.9
Rex Keith Bumgardner (R)	39,507	40.1
4 Ken Hechler (D)	60,794	51.5
Will E. Neal (R)	57,291	48.5
5 Elizabeth Kee (D)	63,873	99.8
6 John M. Slack Jr. (D)	93,209	66.1
F. O'Dair Duff (R)	47,852	33.9

WISCONSIN

Candidates	Votes	%
1 Gerald T. Flynn (D)	63,065	50.6
Eleanor J. Smith (R)	61,615	49.4
2 Robert W. Kastenmeier (D)	78,009	52.1
Donald E. Tewes (R)	71,748	47.9
3 Gardner R. Withrow (R)	47,858	51.2
Norman M. Clapp (D)	45,608	48.8
4 Clement J. Zablocki (D)	112,226	74.1
James J. Arnold (R)	39,167	25.9
5 Henry S. Reuss (D)	104,374	69.5
Otto R. Werkmeister (R)	45,901	30.5
6 William K. Van Pelt (R)	61,490	52.8
James Megellas (D)	55,031	47.2

Candidates	Votes	%
7 Melvin R. Laird (R)	59,186	60.5
Kenneth Traeger (D)	38,702	39.5
8 John W. Byrnes (R)	69,682	57.3
Milo Singler (D)	51,887	42.7
9 Lester R. Johnson (D)	55,420	63.1
Charles A. Hornbeck (R)	32,425	36.9
10 Alvin E. O'Konski (R)	58,801	67.1
Basil G. Kennedy (D)	28,830	32.9

WYOMING

Candidates	Votes	%
AL Keith Thomson (R)	59,894	53.6
Ray Whitaker (D)	51,886	46.4

1959 House Elections

HAWAII

(Became a state Aug. 21, 1959)

Candidates	Votes	%
AL Daniel K. Inouye (D)	111,727	68.2
Charles H. Silva (R)	51,058	31.2

IOWA

Special Election

	Votes	%
4 John Henry Kyl (R)#	28,326	52.3
C. Edwin Gilmour (D)	25,809	47.7

NEW YORK

Special Election

	Votes	%
43 Charles E. Goodell (R)	27,454	65.0
Robert E. McCaffery (D)	14,250	33.8

Explanation of Symbols in House Returns

In the returns for House elections *symbols* are used to denote special circumstances. In cases where no symbol is used, the candidate who received the most votes won the election to the House. The following is a key to the symbols used:

✔ Elected to the House. The symbol is used to identify winning candidates in three types of situations: (1) When candidates ran for two or more at-large seats in states which chose all of their at-large representatives in a single election, or ran in a multi-member district; (2) when the vote total and percentage of one or more of the candidates are unavailable and (3) when a candidate who did not receive the highest vote total was seated by the House. *(Explanation of multi-member districts, see p. 678.)*

‡ The symbol is used when an election dispute resulted in the unseating of a representative *after* he was sworn in. *(For discussion of specific cases, consult the* Biographical Directory of the American Congress 1774-1971, *U.S. Government Printing Office, Washington, D.C. 1971; hereafter referred to as* the Biographical Directory.)

* The symbol is used for three types of situations: (1) When a representative-elect died or declined his seat before the constitutionally set date for the beginning of his term—March 4 until 1935, and Jan. 3 thereafter; (2) when the House refused to seat any candidate claiming election to a seat and (3) when state law required a candidate to obtain a popular vote majority for election to the House, but the candidate receiving the most votes failed to receive a majority. *(For discussion of specific cases, consult the* Biographical Directory; *explanation of majority vote requirement, see p. 703.)*

Information for 1824-1973 returns was obtained from a source other than the Inter-University Consortium for Political and Social Research. *(For a listing of other sources, see p. 1062.)*

Footnotes. Numbered footnotes are used to explain unusual situations, such as a series of elections in the same year in the same House district, anomalies resulting from reapportionment and special procedures for conducting House elections in certain states.

1960 House Elections

ALABAMA

Candidates	Votes	%
1 Frank W. Boykin (D)	45,225	100.0
2 George Grant (D)	44,487	100.0
3 George Andrews (D)	33,881	100.0
4 Kenneth A. Roberts (D)	34,855	99.9
5 Albert Rains (D)	48,772	100.0
6 Armistead I. Selden Jr. (D)	23,245	100.0
7 Carl Elliott (D)	36,124	100.0
8 Robert E. Jones (D)	52,411	79.2
H. G. Williams (R)	13,800	20.8
9 George Huddleston Jr. (D)	70,567	67.3
William P. Ivey (R)	34,317	32.7

ALASKA

Candidates	Votes	%
AL Ralph J. Rivers (D)	33,546	56.8
R. L. (Ron) Rettig (R)	25,517	43.2

ARIZONA

Candidates	Votes	%
1 John J. Rhodes (R)	121,563	59.2
Richard F. Harless (D)	83,676	40.8
2 Stewart L. Udall (D)	95,512	55.8
Mac C. Matheson (R)	75,811	44.3

ARKANSAS

Candidates	Votes	%
1 Ezekiel C. Gathings (D)		100.0
2 Wilbur D. Mills (D)		100.0
3 James W. Trimble (D)		100.0
4 Oren Harris (D)		100.0
5 Dale Alford (D)	57,617	82.7
L. J. Churchill (R)	12,054	17.3
6 William F. Norrell (D)		100.0

CALIFORNIA

Candidates	Votes	%
1 Clem Miller (D)	115,829	51.6
Fred G. Dupuis (R)	108,505	48.4
2 Harold T. Johnson (D)	109,565	62.7
Fredric H. Nagel Jr. (R)	65,198	37.3
3 John E. Moss Jr. (D)	200,439	100.0
4 William S. Mailliard (R)	118,249	65.3
Phillips S. Davies (D)	62,814	34.7
5 John F. Shelley (D)	104,507	83.7
Nick Verreos (R)	20,305	16.3
6 John F. Baldwin (R)	128,418	58.7
Douglas R. Page (D)	90,260	41.3
7 Jeffery Cohelan (D)	79,776	57.0
Lewis F. Sherman (R)	60,065	43.0
8 George P. Miller (D)	152,476	62.0
Robert E. Hannon (R)	93,403	38.0
9 J. Arthur Younger (R)	116,589	59.2
John D. Kaster (D)	80,227	40.8
10 Charles S. Gubser (R)	170,063	58.9
Russell B. Bryan (D)	118,520	41.1
11 John J. McFall (D)	97,368	65.4
Clifford B. Bull (R)	51,473	34.6
12 B. F. Sisk (D-R)	141,974	99.9
13 Charles M. Teague (R)	146,072	65.0
L. Boyd Finch (D)	78,597	35.0
14 Harlen Hagen (D)	97,026	56.5
G. Ray Arnett (R)	74,800	43.5
15 Gordon L. McDonough (R)	89,234	51.3
Norman H. Martell (D)	84,650	48.6
16 Alphonzo Bell (R)	83,601	55.4
Jerry Pacht (D)	67,318	44.6
17 Cecil R. King (D)	206,620	67.7
Tom Coffee (R)	98,510	32.3
18 Craig Hosmer (R)	129,851	70.0
D. Patrick Ahern (D)	55,735	30.0
19 Chet Holifield (D)	145,479	78.2
Gordon S. McWilliams (R)	40,491	21.8

Candidates	Votes	%
20 H. Allen Smith (R)	90,214	70.1
Gareth W. Sadler (D)	38,497	29.9
21 Edgar W. Hiestand (R)	179,376	58.4
Mrs. Rudd Brown (D)	127,591	41.6
22 James C. Corman (D)	104,919	51.1
Lemoine Blanchard (R)	100,321	48.9
23 Clyde Doyle (D)	148,415	74.2
Emmett A. Schwartz (R)	51,548	25.8
24 Glenard P. Lipscomb (R)	82,497	59.7
Norman Hass (D)	55,613	40.3
25 John H. Rousselot (R)	182,545	53.6
George A. Kasem (D)	158,289	46.4
26 James Roosevelt (D)	150,318	73.4
William E. McIntyre (R)	54,540	26.6
27 Harry R. Sheppard (D)	123,645	66.8
Robert M. Castle (R)	61,484	33.2
28 James B. Utt (R)	241,765	60.9
Max E. Woods (D)	155,221	39.1
29 D. S. Saund (D)	76,139	57.1
Charles H. Jameson (R)	57,319	43.0
30 Bob Wilson (R)	158,679	59.3
Walter Wencke (D)	108,882	40.7

COLORADO

Candidates	Votes	%
1 Byron G. Rogers (D)	121,610	60.0
Robert D. Rolander (R)	81,042	40.0
2 Peter H. Dominick (R)	150,964	57.6
Byron L. Johnson (D)	111,077	42.4
3 J. Edgar Chenoweth (R)	85,825	52.1
Franklin R. Stewart (D)	79,069	48.0
4 Wayne N. Aspinall (D)	58,731	68.5
Charles P. Casteel (R)	26,961	31.5

CONNECTICUT

Candidates	Votes	%
1 Emilio Q. Daddario (D)	193,330	58.5
Thomas F. Brennan (R)	137,386	41.5
2 Horace Seely-Brown Jr. (R)	93,971	50.1
William L. St. Onge (D)	93,515	49.9
3 Robert N. Giaimo (D)	124,547	54.9
Albert W. Cretella (R)	102,271	45.1
4 Abner W. Sibal (R)	160,654	51.3
Donald J. Irwin (D)	150,205	48.0
5 John S. Monagan (D)	88,310	55.1
James T. Patterson (R)	71,964	44.9
AL Frank Kowalski (D)	657,680	54.0
Antoni N. Sadlak (R)	560,803	46.0

DELAWARE

Candidates	Votes	%
AL Harris B. McDowell Jr. (D)	98,227	50.5
James T. McKinstry (R)	96,337	49.5

FLORIDA

Candidates	Votes	%
1 William C. Cramer (R)	159,515	58.4
James M. McEwen (D)	113,504	41.6
2 Charles E. Bennett (D)	94,570	82.5
J. Edward Musser (R)	20,090	17.5
3 Robert L. F. Sikes (D)	95,062	100.0
4 Dante B. Fascell (D)	194,023	70.5
Hugh M. Tartaglia (R)	81,209	29.5
5 A. Sydney Herlong Jr. (D)	113,938	100.0
6 Paul G. Rogers (D)	138,226	62.0
John D. Kruse (R)	84,776	38.0
7 James A. Haley (D)	65,144	61.4
Henry S. Bartholomew (R)	40,923	38.6
8 D. R. Matthews (D)	46,794	100.0

GEORGIA

Candidates	Votes	%
1 G. Elliott Hagan (D)	53,749	100.0
2 J. L. Pilcher (D)	43,596	100.0

Candidates	Votes	%
3 E. L. Forrester (D)	55,005	99.7
4 John J. Flynt Jr. (D)	53,394	100.0
5 James C. Davis (D)	80,023	99.7
6 Carl Vinson (D)	44,237	100.0
7 John W. Davis (D)	69,717	74.2
E. Ralph Ivey (R)	24,285	25.8
8 Iris Faircloth Blitch (D)	50,456	99.8
9 Phil M. Landrum (D)	57,549	100.0
10 Robert G. Stephens Jr. (D)	41,679	99.9

HAWAII

Candidates	Votes	%
AL Daniel K. Inouye (D)	135,827	74.4
Fred Titcomb (R)	46,812	25.6

IDAHO

Candidates	Votes	%
1 Gracie B. Pfost (D)	68,863	60.4
Thomas A. Leupp (R)	45,166	39.6
2 Ralph R. Harding (D)	90,161	51.2
Hamer H. Budge (R)	86,100	49.9

ILLINOIS

Candidates	Votes	%
1 William L. Dawson (D)	75,938	77.8
Genoa S. Washington (R)	21,660	22.2
2 Barratt O'Hara (D)	103,535	66.6
Bernard E. Epton (R)	52,028	33.4
3 William T. Murphy (D)	114,523	59.1
Emmet F. Byrne (R)	79,307	40.9
4 Edward J. Derwinski (R)	179,480	55.7
Frank G. Sulewski (D)	142,772	44.3
5 John C. Kluczynski (D)	121,240	71.2
Edward J. Tomek (R)	49,030	28.8
6 Thomas J. O'Brien (D)	107,474	71.7
Frank Estes (R)	42,361	28.3
7 Roland Victor Libonati (D)	28,494	54.5
Lawrence J. Blasi (R)	23,840	45.6
8 Dan Rostenkowski (D)	81,092	67.2
Henry Klinger Jr. (R)	39,651	32.8
9 Sidney R. Yates (D)	80,681	60.1
Chester E. Emanuelson (R)	53,686	40.0
10 Harold R. Collier (R)	126,671	57.1
Edward V. Hanrahan (D)	95,214	42.9
11 Roman C. Pucinski (D)	101,224	54.0
Timothy P. Sheehan (R)	86,305	46.0
12 Edward R. Finnegan (D)	94,907	50.8
Theodore P. Fields (R)	91,978	49.2
13 Marguerite Stitt Church (R)	268,647	66.0
Tyler Thompson (D)	138,348	34.0
14 Elmer J. Hoffman (R)	167,128	63.8
Hayes Beall (D)	94,945	36.2
15 Noah M. Mason (R)	93,986	50.5
Dorothy G. O'Brien (D)	92,301	49.6
16 John B. Anderson (R)	115,693	62.3
Edwin M. Nelson (D)	69,944	37.7
17 Leslie C. Arends (R)	107,896	61.3
William T. Larkin (D)	68,020	38.7
18 Robert H. Michel (R)	94,388	59.3
Richard A. Estep (D)	64,885	40.7
19 Robert B. Chiperfield (R)	82,622	50.6
John C. Watson (D)	80,700	49.4
20 Paul Findley (R)	77,286	55.6
Montgomery B. Carrott (D)	61,790	44.4
21 Peter F. Mack Jr. (D)	102,154	54.7
J. Waldo Ackerman Jr. (R)	84,471	45.3
22 William L. Springer (R)	98,438	61.4
James T. Nally (D)	61,837	38.6
23 George E. Shipley (D)	80,718	51.6
Frank H. Walker (R)	75,809	48.4
24 Melvin Price (D)	144,560	72.2
Phyllis Schlafly (R)	55,620	27.8
25 Kenneth J. Gray (D)	92,227	57.9
Gordon E. Kerr (R)	67,067	42.1

INDIANA

Candidates	Votes	%
1 Ray J. Madden (D)	136,443	64.7
Philip P. Parker (R)	73,984	35.1
2 Charles A. Halleck (R)	95,920	57.5
George H. Bowers (D)	70,464	42.2
3 John Brademas (D)	115,070	52.4
F. Jay Nimtz (R)	104,430	47.6
4 E. Ross Adair (R)	100,419	58.2
Byron McCammon (D)	72,251	41.8
5 J. Edward Roush (D)	107,357#	50.0
George O. Chambers (R)	107,258#	50.0
6 Richard L. Roudebush (R)	84,662	52.0
Fred Wampler (D)	78,247	48.0
7 William G. Bray (R)	95,998	60.1
Thomas C. Cravens (D)	63,646	39.9
8 Winfield K. Denton (D)	108,058	53.2
Alvan V. Burch (R)	94,694	46.6
9 Earl Wilson (R)	71,402	50.6
Earl Hogan (D)	69,761	49.4
10 Ralph Harvey (R)	104,885	57.1
Randall S. Harmon (D)	78,716	42.9
11 Donald Cogley Bruce (R)	154,676	53.7
Joseph W. Barr (D)	133,153	46.2

IOWA

Candidates	Votes	%
1 Fred Schwengel (R)	104,737	60.9
Walter J. Guenther (D)	67,287	39.1
2 James E. Bromwell (R)	108,137	52.6
Leonard G. Wolf (D)	97,608	47.4
3 H. R. Gross (R)	99,046	56.3
Edward J. Gallagher Jr. (D)	76,837	43.7
4 John Kyl (R)	65,016	56.6
C. Edwin Gilmour (D)	49,918	43.4
5 Neal Smith (D)	91,808	53.0
Floyd M. Burgeson (R)	81,474	47.0
6 Merwin Coad (D)	70,353	53.6
Curtis G. Riehm (R)	60,834	46.4
7 Ben F. Jensen (R)	66,037	55.8
Duane Orton (D)	52,214	44.2
8 Charles B. Hoeven (R)	77,583	57.5
Donald E. O'Brien (D)	57,333	42.5

KANSAS

Candidates	Votes	%
1 William H. Avery (R)	84,816	63.1
Marshall G. Gardiner (D)	49,598	36.9
2 Robert F. Ellsworth (R)	95,346	52.3
Newell A. George (D)	86,905	47.7
3 Walter L. McVey (R)	49,429	51.2
Denver D. Hargis (D)	47,127	48.8
4 Garner E. Shriver (R)	119,275	55.2
William I. Robinson (D)	96,706	44.8
5 J. Floyd Breeding (D)	75,687	55.5
Joe W. Hunter (R)	60,794	44.5
6 Bob Dole (R)	62,335	59.3
William A. Davis (D)	42,869	40.8

KENTUCKY

Candidates	Votes	%
1 Frank A. Stubblefield (D)	66,248	100.0
2 William H. Natcher (D)	55,877	100.0
3 Frank W. Burke (D)	115,421	50.3
Henry R. Heyburn (R)	114,263	49.8
4 Frank Chelf (D)	48,743	100.0
5 Brent Spence (D)	63,555	55.4
Jule Appel (R)	51,125	44.6
6 John C. Watts (D)	74,500	54.7
Howard A. Dickey (R)	61,795	45.3
7 Carl D. Perkins (D)	82,746	56.1
Herbert Rowland (R)	64,687	43.9
8 Eugene Siler (R)	81,903	71.8
Donald R. Shepherd (D)	32,163	28.2

LOUISIANA

Candidates	Votes	%
1 F. Edward Hebert (D)	70,465	82.2
Norman W. Prendergast (R)	15,314	17.9
2 Hale Boggs (D)	81,034	78.0
Elliot Ross Buckley (R)	22,818	22.0
3 Edwin E. Willis (D)	52,428	83.6
Floyd J. Duplantis (R)	10,286	16.4
4 Overton Brooks (D)	48,286	74.2
Fred C. McClanahan (R)	16,827	25.8
5 Otto E. Passman (D)	22,181	100.0
6 James H. Morrison (D)	78,640	85.6
Charles H. Dillemuth (R)	13,233	14.4
7 T. A. Thompson (D)	60,007	100.0
8 Harold B. McSween (D)	28,492	100.0

MAINE

Candidates	Votes	%
1 Peter Garland (R)	85,821	53.8
James C. Oliver (D)	73,826	46.2
2 Stanley R. Tupper (R)	71,271	53.2
John C. Donovan (D)	62,309	46.5
3 Clifford G. McIntire (R)	73,742	64.1
David G. Roberts (D)	41,307	35.9

MARYLAND

Candidates	Votes	%
1 Thomas F. Johnson (D)	42,219	53.6
Edward T. Miller (R)	36,508	46.4
2 Daniel B. Brewster (D)	126,452	58.6
Fife Symington (R)	89,262	41.4
3 Edward A. Garmatz (D)	57,154	80.3
Robert J. Gerstung (R)	14,026	19.7
4 George H. Fallon (D)	48,145	65.5
Melvin R. Kenney (R)	25,394	34.5
5 Richard E. Lankford (D)	120,773	62.2
Carlyle J. Lancaster (R)	73,433	37.8
6 Charles McC. Mathias Jr. (R)	115,088	52.0
John R. Foley (D)	106,098	48.0
7 Samuel N. Friedel (D)	81,474	64.5
David M. Blum (R)	44,779	35.5

MASSACHUSETTS

Candidates	Votes	%
1 Silvio O. Conte (R)	102,921	68.5
William H. Burns (D)	46,863	31.2
2 Edward P. Boland (D)	135,815	100.0
3 Philip J. Philbin (D)	145,237	100.0
4 Harold D. Donohue (D)	122,364	64.5
Robert N. Scola (R)	67,270	35.5
5 F. Bradford Morse (R)	123,161	54.5
William C. Madden (D)	102,765	45.5
6 William H. Bates (R)	112,835	65.9
Mary Kennedy (D)	58,312	34.1
7 Thomas J. Lane (D)	117,237	100.0
8 Torbert H. Macdonald (D)	114,333	65.8
Ward Collins Cramer (R)	59,550	34.3
9 Hastings Keith (R)	110,955	55.7
Edward F. Harrington (D)	88,222	44.3
10 Laurence Curtis (R)	98,257	58.2
Joseph J. Mulhern (D)	70,510	41.8
11 Thomas P. O'Neill Jr. (D)	87,866	100.0
12 John W. McCormack (D)	86,057	100.0
13 James A. Burke (D)	126,936	58.5
Charles J. Gabriel (R)	89,921	41.5
14 Joseph W. Martin Jr. (R)	115,209	60.3
Edward F. Doolan (D)	75,815	39.7

MICHIGAN

Candidates	Votes	%
1 Thaddeus M. Machrowicz (D)	102,948	88.4
Walter Czarnecki (R)	13,157	11.3
2 George Meader (R)	110,124	59.6
Thomas P. Payne (D)	74,276	40.2
3 August E. Johansen (R)	100,918	60.6
Samuel I. Clark (D)	65,402	39.2
4 Clare E. Hoffman (R)	90,831	62.3
Edward Burns (D)	54,655	37.5
5 Gerald R. Ford Jr. (R)	131,461	66.8
William S. Reamon (D)	65,064	33.1
6 Charles E. Chamberlain (R)	138,355	56.6
Jerome F. O'Rourke (D)	105,864	43.3
7 James G. O'Hara (D)	142,795	53.3
Robert J. McIntosh (R)	124,750	46.6
8 James Harvey (R)	94,405	62.2
Mary M. Harden (D)	57,126	37.6
9 Robert P. Griffin (R)	77,541	59.6
Donald G. Jennings (D)	52,375	40.3
10 Elford A. Cederberg (R)	75,846	62.1
Daniel E. Reed (D)	46,140	37.8
11 Victor A. Knox (R)	54,300	54.9
Prentiss M. Brown Jr. (D)	44,650	45.1
12 John B. Bennett (R)	48,422	60.8
Robert C. McCarthy (D)	31,137	39.1
13 Charles C. Diggs Jr. (D)	76,812	71.4
Robert B. Blackwell (R)	30,369	28.2
14 Louis C. Rabaut (D)	132,602	62.7
Lois V. Nair (R)	78,548	37.1
15 John D. Dingell (D)	111,671	79.4
Robert J. Robbins (R)	28,532	20.3
16 John Lesinski (D)	211,733	66.0
Lee H. Clark (R)	108,332	33.8
17 Martha W. Griffiths (D)	134,660	57.6
Richard E. Morell (R)	98,721	42.2
18 William S. Broomfield (R)	163,233	55.9
James Kellis (D)	128,678	44.0

MINNESOTA

Candidates	Votes	%
1 Albert H. Quie (R)	100,381	60.5
George Shepherd (DFL)	65,422	39.5
2 Ancher Nelsen (R)	96,471	57.2
Russel Schwandt (DFL)	72,239	42.8
3 Clark MacGregor (R)	154,847	51.6
Roy W. Wier (DFL)	139,908	46.6
4 Joseph E. Karth (DFL)	108,738	61.0
Joseph J. Mitchell (R)	69,635	39.0
5 Walter H. Judd (R)	86,223	60.9
George W. Matthews (DFL)	55,377	39.1
6 Fred Marshall (DFL)	87,332	59.6
Frank L. King (R)	59,305	40.4
7 H. Carl Andersen (R)	73,487	52.5
Gordon E. Duenow (DFL)	66,609	47.6
8 John A. Blatnik (DFL)	107,154	69.5
Jerry H. Ketola (R)	47,099	30.5
9 Odin Langen (R)	62,332	52.2
Coya Knutson (DFL)	57,114	47.8

MISSISSIPPI

Candidates	Votes	%
1 Thomas G. Abernethy (D)	44,381	93.6
Edward W. Scott (R)	3,018	6.4
2 Jamie L. Whitten (D)	23,942	100.0
3 Frank E. Smith (D)	25,592	92.7
W. A. Clark (R)	2,018	7.3
4 John Bell Williams (D)	58,974	100.0
5 Arthur Winstead (D)	40,480	100.0
6 William M. Colmer (D)	59,372	100.0

MISSOURI

Candidates	Votes	%
1 Frank M. Karsten (D)	161,394	70.8
Sam J. Kallaos (R)	66,640	29.2
2 Thomas B. Curtis (R)	150,327	56.7
Richard L. Carp (D)	114,803	43.3
3 Leonor K. Sullivan (D)	87,637	73.3
Morton L. Schwartz (R)	31,902	26.7
4 William J. Randall (D)	111,557	54.0
Kenneth K. Lowe (R)	95,070	46.0
5 Richard Bolling (D)	74,834	61.0
Clinton H. Gates (R)	47,810	39.0
6 W. R. Hull Jr. (D)	93,285	54.6
Ethan H. Campbell (R)	77,638	45.4
7 Durward G. Hall (R)	107,208	54.9
Charles H. Brown (D)	88,162	45.1
8 Richard Ichord (D)	79,020	58.0
Curtis J. Tindel (R)	57,234	42.0
9 Clarence Cannon (D)	107,384	59.8
Anthony C. Schroeder (R)	72,098	40.2
10 Paul C. Jones (D)	69,997	100.0
11 Morgan M. Moulder (D)	74,866	50.1
Robert A. Bartel (R)	74,505	49.9

MONTANA

	Candidates	Votes	%
1	Arnold Olsen (D)	63,081	53.3
	George P. Sarsfield (R)	55,347	46.7
2	James F. Battin (R)	78,277	50.9
	Leo Graybill Jr. (D)	75,507	49.1

NEBRASKA

1	Phil Weaver (R)	89,016	55.8
	Gerald T. Whelan (D)	70,626	44.2
2	Glenn Cunningham (R)	101,347	66.6
	Joseph V. Benesch (D)	50,768	33.4
3	Ralph F. Beermann (R)	67,129	51.3
	Lawrence Brock (D)	63,838	48.7
4	Dave Martin (R)	69,754	51.1
	Donald F. McGinley (D)	66,699	48.9

NEVADA

AL	Walter S. Baring (D)	59,616	57.5
	George W. Malone (R)	43,986	42.5

NEW HAMPSHIRE

1	Chester E. Merrow (R)	88,118	56.6
	Romeo J. Champagne (D)	67,717	43.5
2	Perkins Bass (R)	77,701	60.3.
	Stuart V. Nims (D)	51,145	39.7

NEW JERSEY

1	William T. Cahill (R)	153,817	57.6
	John A. Healey (D)	112,802	42.2
2	Milton W. Glenn (R)	77,894	56.6
	John A. Miller (D)	59,520	43.2
3	James C. Auchincloss (R)	139,590	53.1
	Katharine E. White (D)	123,280	46.9
4	Frank Thompson Jr. (D)	115,761	60.2
	A. Jerome Moore (R)	76,067	39.6
5	Peter H. B. Frelinghuysen Jr. (R)	170,859	58.6
	Jerome H. Taub (D)	120,302	41.3
6	Florence P. Dwyer (R)	136,723	57.7
	Jack B. Dunn (D)	98,043	41.4
7	William B. Widnall (R)	156,758	63.7
	James Dobbins (D)	88,649	36.0
8	Charles S. Joelson (D)	88,100	52.0
	Walter P. Kennedy (R)	74,165	43.8
9	Frank C. Osmers Jr. (R)	127,088	58.1
	Vincent T. McKenna (D)	91,065	41.6
10	Peter W. Rodino Jr. (D)	84,859	65.3
	Alphonse A. Miele (R)	43,238	33.3
11	Hugh J. Addonizio (D)	75,533	61.4
	Frank A. Palmieri (R)	44,580	36.2
12	George M. Wallhauser (R)	76,945	50.2
	Robert R. Peacock (D)	73,119	47.7
13	Cornelius E. Gallagher (D)	80,490	68.3
	Samuel F. Kanis (R)	37,350	31.7
14	Dominick V. Daniels (D)	64,359	57.4
	Frank A. Musto (R)	46,770	41.7

NEW MEXICO

AL	Thomas C. Morris (D)	172,577	58.0
	John D. Robb (R)	124,101	41.7
AL	Joseph M. Montoya (D)	176,514	58.6
	Edward W. Balcomb (R)	123,683	41.1

NEW YORK

1	Otis G. Pike (D, L)	187,286	50.4
	Stuyvesant Wainwright (R)	184,549	49.6
2	Steven B. Derounian (R)	139,423	61.0
	John J. Drury (D, L)	89,176	39.0
3	Frank J. Becker (R)	133,416	54.1
	Julius J. Rosen (D, L)	113,143	45.9

	Candidates	Votes	%
4	Seymour Halpern (R)	115,736	55.1
	Bernard A. Helfat (D)	94,390	44.9
5	Joseph P. Addabbo (D, L)	60,453	54.2
	George Archinal (R)	51,129	45.8
6	Lester Holtzman (D, L)	155,904	65.6
	Vincent L. Pitaro (R)	81,694	34.4
7	James J. Delaney (D, L)	92,424	60.7
	Edward V. Lisoski (R)	59,882	39.3
8	Victor L. Anfuso (D, L)	60,030	72.9
	Leon F. Nadrowski (R)	22,318	27.1
9	Eugene J. Keogh (D, L)	84,941	72.3
	Herman Sanders (R)	32,538	27.7
10	Edna F. Kelly (D, L)	98,938	76.6
	Jerome P. Schneider (R)	30,243	23.4
11	Emanuel Celler (D, L)	139,397	81.6
	Seymour Besunder (R)	31,378	18.4
12	Hugh L. Carey (D, L)	65,996	50.4
	Francis E. Dorn (R)	64,899	49.6
13	Abraham J. Multer (D, L)	117,087	75.4
	Joseph A. DeMarco (R)	38,189	24.6
14	John J. Rooney (D, L)	80,972	70.6
	Carlo G. Colavito (R)	33,769	29.4
15	John H. Ray (R)	80,218	48.7
	John M. Murphy (D)	77,812	47.2
16	Adam Clayton Powell Jr. (D)	59,957	71.6
	Joseph A. Bailey (R)	14,706	17.6
	Arthur O. Boyer (L)	9,093	10.9
17	John V. Lindsay (R)	81,006	60.2
	William J. Vanden Heuvel (D, L)	53,574	39.8
18	Alfred E. Santangelo (D)	47,749	58.3
	Charles Muzzicato (R)	27,419	33.5
	Faustino Louis Garcia (L)	6,680	8.2
19	Leonard Farbstein (D, L)	68,445	72.4
	Thomas P. O'Callaghan (R)	26,054	27.6
20	William F. Ryan (D)	55,272	55.7
	Morris Aarons (R)	30,046	30.3
	Ludwig Teller (L)	13,884	14.0
21	Herbert Zelenko (D, L)	87,775	74.6
	Thomas H. Bartzos (R)	29,835	25.4
22	James C. Healey (D)	78,717	65.0
	Dominick A. Fusco (R)	24,958	20.6
	David I. Wells (L)	17,438	14.4
23	Jacob H. Gilbert (D)	61,474	70.6
	Benjamin Thornley (R)	15,208	17.5
	Nicholas B. Gyory (L)	10,420	12.0
24	Charles A. Buckley (D)	89,140	56.6
	Michael R. Cappelli (R)	43,110	27.4
	Murray Koenig (L)	25,283	16.1
25	Paul A. Fino (R)	112,187	59.8
	Eugene L. Sugarman (D)	66,539	35.5
26	Edwin B. Dooley (R)	98,506	52.6
	Phil E. Gilbert Jr. (D, L)	88,879	47.4
27	Robert R. Barry (R)	121,533	56.3
	John R. Harold (D)	86,997	40.3
28	Katharine St. George (R)	107,179	58.7
	James E. Truex (D, L)	75,448	41.3
29	J. Ernest Wharton (R)	103,966	56.7
	Gore Vidal (D, L)	79,252	43.3
30	Leo W. O'Brien (D, L)	117,692	62.9
	Irving I. Waxman (R)	69,549	37.1
31	Carleton J. King (R)	99,604	60.4
	Louis E. Wolfe (D, L)	65,305	39.6
32	Samuel S. Stratton (D, L)	98,990	62.3
	W. Clyde Wright (R)	59,890	37.7
33	Clarence E. Kilburn (R)	91,710	61.9
	Edward J. Gosier (D)	53,130	35.9
34	Alexander Pirnie (R)	98,063	55.3
	Edwin L. Slusarczyk (D, L)	79,153	44.7
35	R. Walter Riehlman (R)	105,241	53.8
	Jerome M. Wilson (D)	87,347	44.6
36	John Taber (R)	84,441	52.6
	Francis J. Souhan (D, L)	76,120	47.4
37	William R. Robison (R)	123,782	63.4
	Joseph V. Julian (D, L)	71,354	36.6
38	Jessica McC. Weis (R)	114,871	57.6
	Arthur B. Curran Jr. (D, L)	84,716	42.4
39	Harold C. Ostertag (R)	103,162	59.7
	Henry R. Dutcher Jr. (D, L)	69,704	40.3

	Candidates	Votes	%
40	William E. Miller (R)	104,752	53.6
	Mariano A. Lucca (D)	85,005	43.5
41	Thaddeus J. Dulski (D, L)	82,114	56.2
	Ralph J. Radwan (R)	63,889	43.8
42	John R. Pillion (R)	122,073	55.4
	Charles J. McCabe (D)	93,492	42.4
43	Charles E. Goodell (R)	87,585	62.8
	T. Joseph Lynch (D)	48,423	34.7

Special Election

23	Jacob H. Gilbert (D)	4,594	82.3
	Simon M. Koenig (R)	574	10.3
	Hector Mathew (L)	411	7.4

NORTH CAROLINA

1	Herbert C. Bonner (D)	48,809	86.6
	Zeno O. Ratcliff (R)	7,587	13.5
2	L. H. Fountain (D)	51,156	87.8
	L. Paul Gooding (R)	7,135	12.2
3	David N. Henderson (D)	51,193	71.2
	Jack D. Brinson (R)	20,674	28.8
4	Harold D. Cooley (D)	75,464	66.6
	Elam Reamuel Temple Jr. (R)	37,821	33.4
5	Ralph J. Scott (D)	66,079	57.6
	Russell F. Biggam (R)	48,572	42.4
6	Horace R. Kornegay (D)	79,809	59.6
	Holland L. Robb (R)	54,028	40.4
7	Alton Lennon (D)	71,726	76.5
	Joel C. Clifton (R)	21,997	23.5
8	A. Paul Kitchin (D)	71,429	56.3
	A. M. Snipes (R)	55,372	43.7
9	Hugh Q. Alexander (D)	75,909	53.1
	W. S. Bogle (R)	67,033	46.9
10	Charles Raper Jonas (R)	97,138	58.6
	David Clark (D)	68,761	41.5
11	Basil L. Whitener (D)	65,478	61.1
	Kelly Dixon (R)	41,763	38.9
12	Roy A. Taylor (D)	61,170	52.0
	Heinz Rollman (R)	56,368	48.0

Special Election

12	Roy A. Taylor (D)	28,744	98.6

NORTH DAKOTA

AL	Don L. Short (R)	135,579✔	
	Hjalmar Nygaard (R)	127,118✔	
	Raymond Vendsel (D)	120,773	
	Anson J. Anderson (D)	109,207	

OHIO

1	Gordon H. Scherer (R)	88,899	58.9
	W. Ted Osborne (D)	62,043	41.1
2	Donald D. Clancy (R)	118,046	57.4
	H. A. Sand (D)	87,531	42.6
3	Paul F. Schenck (R)	167,117	62.0
	R. William Patterson (D)	102,237	38.0
4	William M. McCulloch (R)	99,683	65.4
	Joseph J. Murphy (D)	52,797	34.6
5	Delbert L. Latta (R)	85,175	67.3
	Tom P. McRitchie (D)	41,375	32.7
6	William H. Harsha Jr. (R)	80,124	55.2
	Franklin E. Smith (D)	65,045	44.8
7	Clarence J. Brown (R)	105,026	65.5
	Joseph A. Sullivan (D)	55,451	34.6
8	Jackson E. Betts (R)	81,373	67.7
	Virgil M. Gase (D)	38,871	32.3
9	Thomas Ludlow Ashley (D)	108,688	56.9
	Howard C. Cook (R)	82,433	43.1
10	Walter H. Moeller (D)	58,085	52.5
	Oakley C. Collins (R)	52,479	47.5
11	Robert E. Cook (D)	104,183	51.0
	David S. Dennison Jr. (R)	99,991	49.0
12	Samuel L. Devine (R)	140,236	60.7
	Richard E. Liming (D)	90,894	39.3

OHIO

Candidates	Votes	%
13 Charles A. Mosher (R)	73,110	51.4
J. William McCray (D)	69,033	48.6
14 William H. Ayres (R)	145,526	61.5
John H. Mihaly (D)	91,103	38.5
15 Tom V. Moorehead (R)	49,742	51.2
Herbert U. Smith (D)	47,366	48.8
16 Frank T. Bow (R)	130,542	62.5
John G. Freedom (D)	78,257	37.5
17 John M. Ashbrook (R)	79,609	53.0
Robert W. Levering (D)	70,470	47.0
18 Wayne L. Hays (D)	96,474	65.6
Walter Jay Hunston (R)	50,698	34.5
19 Michael J. Kirwan (D)	102,874	68.9
Paul E. Stevens (R)	46,537	31.2
20 Michael A. Feighan (D)	113,302	67.8
Leonard G. Richter (R)	53,845	32.2
21 Charles A. Vanik (D)	103,460	73.0
William O. Walker (R)	38,326	27.0
22 Frances P. Bolton (R)	88,389	56.9
Chat Paterson (D)	66,930	43.1
23 William E. Minshall (R)	123,364	67.3
Daniel Winston (D)	59,893	32.7

Special Election

	Votes	%
6 Ward M. Miller (R)	76,520	55.4
Gladys E. Davis (D)	61,713	44.6

OKLAHOMA

	Votes	%
1 Page Belcher (R)	133,964	63.8
Yates Land (D)	75,934	36.2
2 Ed Edmondson (D)	79,732	57.0
Bill Sharp (R)	60,253	43.0
3 Carl Albert (D)	56,138	74.9
George B. Sherritt (R)	18,799	25.1
4 Tom Steed (D)	54,181	60.7
Don H. Crall (R)	35,028	39.3
5 John Jarman (D)	125,286	66.6
Hobart H. Hobbs (R)	62,971	33.5
6 Victor Wickersham (D)	68,192	50.4
Clyde Wheeler Jr. (R)	67,116	49.6

OREGON

	Votes	%
1 Walter Norblad (R)	144,743	65.1
Marv Owens (D)	77,689	34.9
2 Al Ullman (D)	62,690	59.6
Ronald E. Phair (R)	42,516	40.4
3 Edith Green (D)	157,243	63.9
Wallace L. Lee (R)	88,906	36.1
4 Edwin R. Durno (R)	96,022	51.1
Charles O. Porter (D)	91,947	48.9

PENNSYLVANIA

	Votes	%
1 William A. Barrett (D)	88,805	77.0
Michael Grasso Jr. (R)	26,601	23.1
2 Kathryn E. Granahan (D)	109,452	72.3
Joseph C. Bruno (R)	42,019	27.7
3 James A. Byrne (D)	80,258	69.7
Joseph Patrick Gorham (R)	34,956	30.3
4 Robert N. C. Nix (D)	84,053	78.4
Clarence M. Smith (R)	23,146	21.6
5 William J. Green Jr. (D)	140,658	61.0
James W. Gilmour (R)	90,087	39.0
6 Herman Toll (D)	109,275	59.6
David O. Maxwell (R)	74,132	40.4
7 William H. Milliken Jr. (R)	136,021	53.0
Henry Gouley (D)	120,839	47.0
8 Willard S. Curtin (R)	121,564	56.1
Donald V. Hock (D)	95,140	43.9
9 Paul B. Dague (R)	128,917	66.6
Howard H. Halsey (D)	64,659	33.4
10 William W. Scranton (R)	97,012	54.8
Stanley A. Prokop (D)	80,097	45.2
11 Daniel J. Flood (D)	115,042	67.1
Donald B. Ayers (R)	56,428	32.9

Candidates	Votes	%
12 Ivor D. Fenton (R)	72,061	52.4
William H. Deitman (D)	65,585	47.7
13 Richard S. Schweiker (R)	142,966	61.8
Warren H. Ballard (D)	88,486	38.2
14 George M. Rhodes (D)	60,211	53.8
James H. Mantis (R)	51,746	46.2
15 Francis E. Walter (D)	67,830	55.2
Woodrow A. Horn (R)	55,125	44.8
16 Walter M. Mumma (R)	93,831	62.5
Miles Albright (D)	56,267	37.5
17 Herman T. Schneebeli (R)	82,040	56.7
Dean R. Fisher (D)	62,695	43.3
18 J. Irving Whalley	88,397	62.3
Robert M. Meyers (D)	53,453	37.7
19 George A. Goodling (R)	88,776	53.2
James M. Quigley (D)	78,043	46.8
20 James E. Van Zandt (R)	77,776	67.8
Robert H. Hendershot (D)	36,997	32.2
21 John H. Dent (D)	85,853	56.0
William L. Batten (R)	65,551	42.8
22 John P. Saylor (R)	89,261	57.4
William D. Patton (D)	66,383	42.7
23 Leon H. Gavin (R)	74,542	62.4
John H. Cartwright (D)	43,927	36.8
24 Carroll D. Kearns (R)	95,149	51.0
Chester C. Hampton (D)	91,498	49.0
25 Frank M. Clark (D)	102,750	58.1
Fred A. Obley (R)	74,217	41.9
26 Thomas E. Morgan (D)	111,362	63.6
Bartley P. Osborne (R)	63,702	36.4
27 James G. Fulton (R)	127,995	59.1
Margaret Lee Walgren (D)	88,660	40.9
28 William S. Moorhead (D)	99,491	67.8
Arthur O. Sharron (R)	47,232	32.2
29 Robert J. Corbett (R)	117,009	59.2
Russell M. Douthett (D)	80,497	40.8
30 Elmer J. Holland (D)	126,619	68.6
Jerome H. Meyers (R)	58,063	31.4

Special Election

	Votes	%
18 J. Irving Whalley (R)	86,527	62.3
Robert M. Meyers (D)	52,324	37.7

RHODE ISLAND

	Votes	%
1 Fernard J. St.Germain (D)	117,162	66.2
Theophile Martin (R)	59,737	33.8
2 John E. Fogarty (D)	151,544	70.4
Robert L. Gammell (R)	63,795	29.6

SOUTH CAROLINA

	Votes	%
1 L. Mendel Rivers (D)	47,153	100.0
2 John J. Riley (D)	63,207	100.0
3 William J. Bryan Dorn (D)	52,398	100.0
4 Robert T. Ashmore (D)	68,973	100.0
5 Robert W. Hemphill (D)	46,815	99.8
6 John L. McMillan (D)	49,780	100.0

SOUTH DAKOTA

	Votes	%
1 Ben Reifel (R)	126,033	54.9
Ray Fitzgerald (D)	103,755	45.2
2 E. Y. Berry (R)	42,550	59.8
W. H. Raff (D)	28,666	40.3

TENNESSEE

	Votes	%
1 B. Carroll Reece (R)	103,872	75.4
Arthur Bright (D)	33,873	24.6
2 Howard H. Baker (R)	98,839	100.0
3 James B. Frazier Jr. (D)	62,827	100.0
4 Joe L. Evins (D)	60,730	100.0
5 J. Carlton Loser (R)	42,524	100.0
6 Ross Bass (D)	55,736	100.0
7 Tom Murray (D)	34,130	100.0
8 Robert A. Everett (D)	30,124	100.0
9 Clifford Davis (D)	120,159	100.0

TEXAS

Candidates	Votes	%
1 Wright Patman (D)	58,674	100.0
2 Jack Brooks (D)	75,657	69.7
F. S. Newmann (R)	32,473	29.9
3 Lindley Beckworth (D)	59,386	100.0
4 Sam Rayburn (D)	44,902	100.0
5 Bruce Alger (R)	129,886	57.3
Joe Pool (D)	96,709	42.7
6 Olin Teague (D)	56,603	100.0
7 John Dowdy (D)	61,586	100.0
8 Albert Thomas (D)	76,767	68.6
Anthony J. P. Farris (R)	24,486	21.9
Robert Nesmith (CST)	10,684	9.5
9 Clark Thompson (D)	98,586	94.3
P. D. Rogers (CST)	5,981	5.7
10 Homer Thornberry (D)	75,165	98.1
11 W. R. Poage (D)	64,351	100.0
12 Jim Wright (D)	115,797	100.0
13 Frank Ikard (D)	75,972	100.0
14 John Young (D)	105,792	100.0
15 Joe Kilgore (D)	76,421	100.0
16 J. T. Rutherford (D)	63,634	58.9
Dorothy Wynell (CST)	24,996	23.1
Ford Chapman (R)	19,491	18.0
17 Omar Burleson (D)	60,401	77.6
Max Mossholder (CST)	17,400	22.4
18 Walter Rogers (D)	79,675	100.0
19 George Mahon (D)	77,415	85.7
J. R. Anderson (CST)	12,953	14.3
20 Paul J. Kilday (D)	84,487	100.0
21 O. C. Fisher (D)	63,277	100.0
22 Bob Casey (D)	109,418	58.3
J. C. Noonan (R)	73,503	39.2

UTAH

	Votes	%
1 M. Blaine Peterson (D)	65,939	50.0
A. Walter Stevenson (R)	65,871	50.0
2 David S. King (D)	120,771	50.8
Sherman P. Lloyd (R)	116,881	49.2

VERMONT

	Votes	%
AL Robert T. Stafford (R)	94,905	57.2
William H. Meyer (D)	71,111	42.8

VIRGINIA

	Votes	%
1 Thomas N. Downing (D)	53,768	82.4
Richard A. May (R)	11,429	17.5
2 Porter Hardy Jr. (D)	49,750	75.8
Louis B. Fine (R)	15,758	24.0
3 J. Vaughan Gary (D)	52,908	77.8
T. Coleman Andrews	14,907	21.9
4 Watkins M. Abbitt (D)	39,408	99.5
5 William M. Tuck (D)	30,154	98.9
6 Richard H. Poff (R)	60,371	82.4
J. B. Brayman (SOCIAL D)	12,700	17.3
7 Burr P. Harrison (D)	42,199	99.6
8 Howard W. Smith (D)	42,890	75.7
Lawrence M. Traylor (R)	13,410	23.7
9 W. Pat Jennings (D)	47,372	58.0
E. Summers Sheffey (R)	34,280	42.0
10 Joel T. Broyhill (R)	64,408	55.0
Ralph Kaul (D)	52,647	45.0

WASHINGTON

	Votes	%
1 Thomas M. Pelly (R)	124,721	70.2
Carl Viking Holman (D)	53,009	29.8
2 Jack Westland (R)	87,802	60.2
Payson Peterson (D)	58,154	39.8
3 Julia Butler Hansen (D)	76,930	53.4
Dale M. Nordquist (R)	67,060	46.6
4 Catherine May (R)	94,210	58.8
Roy Mundy (D)	65,964	41.2
5 Walt Horan (R)	94,042	59.4
Bernard J. Gallagher (D)	64,321	40.6

WASHINGTON

Candidates	Votes	%
6 Thor C. Tollefson (R)	83,158	56.5
John G. McCutcheon (D)	64,167	43.6
7 Don Magnuson (D)	95,663	50.0
John Stender (R)	95,524	50.0

Special Election

3 Julia Butler Hansen (D)	71,416	53.1
Dale M. Nordquist (R)	63,058	46.9

WEST VIRGINIA

1 Arch A. Moore Jr. (R)	81,018	60.3
Steven D. Narick (D)	53,318	39.7
2 Harley O. Staggers (D)	74,184	60.3
Charles J. Whiston (R)	48,903	39.7

Candidates	Votes	%
3 Cleveland M. Bailey (D)	71,718	59.8
James M. Knowles Jr. (R)	48,258	40.2
4 Ken Hechler (D)	82,931	53.2
Clyde Pinson (R)	73,052	46.8
5 Elizabeth Kee (D)	77,524	69.5
L. M. LaFollette (R)	34,052	30.5
6 John M. Slack Jr. (D)	108,452	61.8
George W. King (R)	67,070	38.2

WISCONSIN

1 Henry C. Schadeberg (R)	97,662	52.7
Gerald T. Flynn (D)	87,646	47.3
2 Robert W. Kastenmeier (D)	119,885	53.4
Donald E. Tewes (R)	104,744	46.6
3 Vernon W. Thomson (R)	71,677	54.6
Norman M. Clapp (D)	59,527	45.4

Candidates	Votes	%
4 Clement J. Zablocki (D)	155,789	71.7
Samuel P. Murray (R)	61,468	28.3
5 Henry S. Reuss (D)	126,314	57.7
Kirby Hendee (R)	92,526	42.3
6 William K. Van Pelt (R)	91,450	55.8
James Megellas (D)	72,442	44.2
7 Melvin R. Laird (R)	95,152	67.1
Kenneth Traeger (D)	46,606	32.9
8 John W. Byrnes (R)	101,132	58.8
Milo Singler (D)	70,740	41.2
9 Lester R. Johnson (D)	74,268	56.6
Perry M. Hull (R)	57,069	43.5
10 Alvin E. O'Konski (R)	73,114	95.0

WYOMING

AL William Henry Harrison (R)	70,241	52.3
Hepburn T. Armstrong (D)	64,090	47.7

1961 House Elections

ARIZONA

Special Election

2 Morris K. Udall (D)	51,304#	51.0
Mac C. Matheson (R)	49,297#	49.0

ARKANSAS

Special Election

6 Catherine D. Norrell (D)	10,209#	43.1
John Harris Jones (D)	5,955#	25.1
M. C. Lewis Jr. (D)	5,499#	23.2
James F. Cross (D)	1,727#	7.3

LOUISIANA

Special Election

4 Joe D. Waggonner Jr. (D)	33,892	54.5
Charlton H. Lyons (R)	28,250	45.5

MICHIGAN

Special Election

1 Lucien N. Nedzi (D)	33,690#	85.5
Walter Czarnecki (R)	5,729#	14.5

PENNSYLVANIA

Special Election

16 John C. Kunkel (R)	43,220	65.6
Kathryn Z. Vanderslice (D)	22,698	34.4

TENNESSEE

Special Election

1 Louise G. Reece (R)	29,819#	62.9
William W. Faw (D)	15,718#	33.2

TEXAS [1]

Special Elections

4 Ray Roberts (D)	8,154	36.9
R. C. Slagle (D)	5,945	26.9
David Brown (D)	2,393	10.8
Conner Harrington (R)	2,353	10.6
Jack Finney (D)	2,211	10.0
13 Graham B. Purcell Jr. (D)	8,960	33.6
Joe Meissner (R)	6,740	25.3
Jack Hightower (D)	6,157	23.1
Vernon Stewart (D)	2,706	10.2
Jimmy P. Horany (D)	2,076	7.8
20 Henry B. Gonzalez (D)	52,696	54.6
John Goode	42,511	44.0

1. In Texas special elections for the House held prior to 1961, all candidates ran against each other in one election regardless of party; the candidate receiving the most votes was the winner. Thus Lyndon B. Johnson won a 1937 special election with 27.7 per cent of the vote (see p. 941).

The Texas law was changed in 1961 to require that in a special election, if no candidate received a majority, a special election runoff would be held between the top two candidates.

Thus, in the three House special elections held in Texas in 1961, only the election in the 20th district produced a majority vote winner. In the 4th and 13th districts, no candidate received a majority. Runoff special elections between the top two candidates in each district were held in 1962; see page 1005.

1962 House Elections

ALABAMA

Candidates	Votes	%
AL George Huddleston Jr. (D)	304,210✔	
Armistead I. Selden Jr. (D)	295,882✔	
George Andrews (D)	293,182✔	
George Grant (D)	288,074✔	
Albert Rains (D)	271,075✔	
Kenneth A. Roberts (D)	269,410✔	
Robert E. Jones (D)	258,674✔	
Carl Elliott (D)	257,299✔	
John H. Buchanan Jr. (R)	141,202	
Tom Abernethy (R)	138,963	
Evan Foreman Jr. (R)	136,339	
J. Chester Robinson (N SR)	32,446	

ALASKA

Candidates	Votes	%
AL Ralph J. Rivers (D)	31,953	54.5
Lowell Thomas Jr. (R)	26,638	45.5

ARIZONA

Candidates	Votes	%
1 John J. Rhodes (R)	113,240	58.7
Howard V. Peterson (D)	79,763	41.3
2 Morris K. Udall (D)	64,510	58.3
Richard K. Burke (R)	46,219	41.7
3 George F. Senner Jr. (D)	25,359	56.0
John P. Clark (R)	19,933	44.0

ARKANSAS

Candidates	Votes	%
1 Ezekiel C. Gathings (D)		100.0
2 Wilbur D. Mills (D)		100.0
3 James W. Trimble (D)	58,786	69.4
Cy Carney Jr. (R)	25,987	30.7
4 Oren Harris (D)	74,972	77.4
Warren Lieblong (R)	21,818	22.5

CALIFORNIA

Candidates	Votes	%
1 Clem Miller (D)	100,962*	50.8
Don H. Clausen (R)	97,949	49.2
2 Harold T. Johnson (D)	106,239	64.6
Fredric H. Nagel Jr. (R)	58,150	35.4
3 John E. Moss Jr (D)	138,257	74.8
George W. G. Smith (R)	46,510	25.2
4 Robert L. Leggett (D)	55,563	56.5
L. V. Honsinger (R)	42,762	43.5
5 John F. Shelley (D)	64,493	80.4
Roland S. Charles (R)	15,670	19.5
6 William S. Mailliard (R)	105,762	58.7
John A. O'Connell (D)	74,429	41.3
7 Jeffery Cohelan (D)	86,215	64.5
Leonard L. Cantando (R)	47,409	35.5
8 George P. Miller (D)	97,014	72.5
Harold Petersen (R)	36,810	27.5
9 Don Edwards (D)	79,616	65.9
Joseph Francis Donovan (R)	41,104	34.0
10 Charles S. Gubser (R)	106,419	60.7
James P. Thurber Jr. (D)	68,885	39.3
11 J. Arthur Younger (R)	101,963	62.3
William J. Keller (R)	61,623	37.7
12 Burt L. Talcott (R)	75,424	61.3
William K. Stewart (D)	47,576	38.7
13 Charles M. Teague (R)	84,743	64.9
George J. Holgate (D)	45,746	35.1
14 John F. Baldwin (R)	99,040	62.9
Charles R. Weidner (D)	58,369	37.1
15 John J. McFall (D)	97,322	70.0
Arthur L. Young (R)	41,726	30.0
16 B. F. Sisk (D)	108,339	71.9
Arthur L. Selland (R)	42,401	28.1

Candidates	Votes	%
17 Cecil R. King (D)	74,964	67.2
Ted Bruinsma (R)	36,663	32.8
18 Harlan Hagen (D)	91,684	58.9
Ray Arnett (R)	64,037	41.1
19 Chet Holifield (D)	78,436	61.6
Robert T. Ramsay (R)	48,976	38.4
20 H. Allen Smith (R)	119,938	70.6
Leon Mayer (D)	49,850	29.4
21 Augustus F. Hawkins (D)	73,465	84.5
Herman Smith (R)	13,371	15.4
22 James C. Corman (D)	75,294	53.6
Charles S. Foote (R)	65,087	46.4
23 Clyde Doyle (D)	83,269	64.2
Del Clawson (R)	46,488	35.8
24 Glenard P. Lipscomb (R)	120,884	70.3
Knox Mellon (D)	50,970	29.7
25 Ronald Brooks Cameron (D)	62,371	53.1
John H. Rousselot (R)	53,961	45.9
26 James Roosevelt (D)	112,162	68.3
Daniel Beltz (R)	52,063	31.7
27 Everett G. Burkhalter (D)	66,979	52.1
Edgar W. Hiestand (R)	61,538	47.9
28 Alphonzo Bell (R)	162,233	64.0
Robert J. Felixson (D)	91,305	36.0
29 George E. Brown Jr. (D)	73,740	55.6
H. L. Richardson (R)	58,760	44.3
30 Edward R. Roybal (D)	69,008	56.5
Gordon L. McDonough (R)	53,104	43.5
31 Charles H. Wilson (D)	76,631	52.2
Gordon Hahn (R)	70,154	47.8
32 Craig Hosmer (R)	115,915	70.7
J. J. Johovich (D)	47,917	29.2
33 Harry R. Sheppard (D)	96,192	59.0
William R. Thomas (R)	66,764	41.0
34 Richard T. Hanna (D)	90,758	55.9
Robert A. Geier (R)	71,478	44.1
35 James B. Utt (R)	133,737	68.5
Burton Shamsky (D)	61,395	31.5
36 Bob Wilson (R)	91,626	61.8
William C. Godfrey (D)	56,637	38.2
37 Lionel Van Deerlin (D)	63,821	51.3
Dick Wilson (R)	60,460	48.6
38 Patrick Minor Martin (R)	68,583	55.9
Dalip S. Saund (D)	54,022	44.1

COLORADO

Candidates	Votes	%
1 Byron G. Rogers (D)	94,680	56.0
William B. Chenoweth (R)	74,392	44.0
2 Donald G. Brotzman (R)	134,939	61.9
Conrad L. McBride (D)	83,235	38.2
3 J. Edgar Chenoweth (R)	74,848	54.7
Albert J. Tomsic (D)	62,097	45.3
4 Wayne N. Aspinall (D)	42,462	58.7
Leo R. Sommerville (R)	29,943	41.4

CONNECTICUT

Candidates	Votes	%
1 Emilio Q. Daddario (D)	162,844	57.5
James F. Collins (R)	118,767	41.9
2 William L. St.Onge (D)	83,652	50.8
Moses A. Savin (R)	81,010	49.2
3 Robert Giaimo (D)	104,728	56.0
Daniel Reinhardsen Jr. (R)	82,215	44.0
4 Abner W. Sibal (R)	132,595	52.0
Francis X. Lennon Jr. (D)	122,362	48.0
5 John S. Monagan (D)	83,321	58.5
John A. Rand (R)	59,072	41.5
AL Bernard F. Grabowski (D)	543,424	52.7
John M. Lupton (R)	487,575	47.3

DELAWARE

Candidates	Votes	%
AL Harris B. McDowell Jr. (D)	81,166	52.9
Wilmer F. Williams (R)	71,934	46.9

FLORIDA

Candidates	Votes	%
1 Robert L. F. Sikes (D)	35,781	81.9
M. M. Woolley (R)	7,902	18.1
2 Charles E. Bennett (D)	41,378	99.7
3 Claude Pepper (D)	59,985	57.6
Bob Peterson (R)	44,164	42.4
4 Dante B. Fascell (D)	67,136	64.5
J. C. McGlon Jr. (R)	36,981	35.5
5 A. Sydney Herlong Jr. (D)	54,383	65.2
Hubert H. Hevey Jr. (R)	29,008	34.8
6 Paul G. Rogers (D)	102,396	64.2
Frederick A. Kibbe (R)	57,112	35.8
7 James A. Haley (D)	52,417	66.8
F. Onell Rogells (R)	26,042	33.2
8 D. R. Matthews (D)	23,387	100.0
9 Don Fuqua (D)	23,651	75.3
Wilfred C. Varn (R)	7,735	24.6
10 Sam M. Gibbons (D)	41,426	70.6
Victor A. Rule (R)	17,214	29.4
11 Edward J. Gurney (R)	46,814	51.9
John A. Sutton (D)	43,348	48.1
12 William C. Cramer (R)	78,982	64.5
Grover C. Criswell Jr. (D)	43,431	35.5

GEORGIA

Candidates	Votes	%
1 G. Elliott Hagan (D)	25,229	97.6
2 John L. Pilcher (D)	18,967	96.3
3 E. L. Forrester (D)	25,001	100.0
4 John J. Flynt Jr. (D)	21,214	100.0
5 Charles L. Weltner (D)	60,583	55.6
L. J. O'Callaghan (R)	48,466	44.4
6 Carl Vinson (D)	19,701	100.0
7 John W. Davis (D)	28,994	72.4
Ralph Ivey (R)	11,048	27.6
8 J. Russell Tuten (D)	19,694	100.0
9 Phil M. Landrum (D)	25,942	100.0
10 Robert G. Stephens Jr. (D)	27,169	100.0

HAWAII

Candidates	Votes	%
AL Thomas P. Gill (D)	123,649✔	
Spark M. Matsunaga (D)	123,599✔	
Albert W. Evensen (R)	70,880	
Richard Ike Sutton (R)	46,292	

IDAHO

Candidates	Votes	%
1 Compton I. White Jr. (D)	51,422	53.0
Erwin H. Schwiebert (R)	45,552	47.0
2 Ralph R. Harding (D)	83,152	52.8
Orval Hansen (R)	74,203	47.2

ILLINOIS

Candidates	Votes	%
1 William L. Dawson (D)	98,305	74.1
Benjamin C. Duster (R)	34,379	25.9
2 Barratt O'Hara (D)	78,119	62.3
Philip G. Bixler (R)	47,336	37.7
3 William T. Murphy (D)	82,866	51.6
Ernest E. Michaels (R)	77,814	48.4
4 Edward J. Derwinski (R)	114,954	64.9
Richard E. Friedman (D)	62,189	35.1
5 John C. Kluczynski (D)	84,455	63.4
Joseph Potempa (R)	48,825	36.6
6 Thomas J. O'Brien (D)	72,183	77.7
Adolph Herda (R)	20,690	22.3
7 Roland Victor Libonati (D)	86,677	78.8
Joseph D. Day (R)	23,285	21.2
8 Dan Rostenkowski (D)	112,778	60.8
Irvin R. Tchon (R)	72,726	39.2

ILLINOIS

	Candidates	Votes	%
9	Edward R. Finnegan (D)	80,378	54.8
	Thomas E. Ward (R)	66,196	45.2
10	Harold R. Collier (R)	149,761	66.6
	Joseph A. Salerno (D)	74,986	33.4
11	Roman C. Pucinski (D)	103,677	52.7
	Henry J. Hyde (R)	92,910	47.3
12	Robert McClory (R)	76,335	63.9
	John Clark Kimball (D)	43,200	36.1
13	Donald Rumsfeld (R)	139,230	63.5
	John A. Kennedy (D)	79,419	36.2
14	Elmer J. Hoffman (R)	107,285	59.7
	Jerome M. Ziegler (D)	72,390	40.3
15	Charlotte T. Reid (R)	77,718	60.3
	Stanley H. Cowan (D)	49,444	38.3
16	John B. Anderson (R)	78,594	66.9
	Walter S. Busky (D)	38,853	33.1
17	Leslie C. Arends (R)	87,612	62.5
	Donald M. Laughlin (D)	52,592	37.5
18	Robert H. Michel (R)	75,957	61.2
	Francis D. Nash (D)	48,177	38.8
19	Robert T. McLoskey (R)	66,547	55.9
	David Dedoncker (D)	52,482	44.1
20	Paul Findley (R)	100,558	52.9
	Peter F. Mack Jr. (D)	89,522	47.1
21	Kenneth J. Gray (D)	96,971	60.0
	Frank H. Walker (R)	64,687	40.0
22	William L. Springer (R)	70,870	59.8
	Bob Wilson (D)	47,745	40.3
23	George E. Shipley (D)	99,133	51.7
	Edward J. Jenison (R)	92,562	48.3
24	Melvin Price (D)	95,522	73.8
	Kurt Glaser (R)	33,993	26.3

INDIANA

		Votes	%
1	Ray J. Madden (D)	104,212	60.5
	Harold Moody (R)	67,230	39.0
2	Charles A. Halleck (R)	82,971	57.6
	John J. Murray (D)	61,076	42.4
3	John Brademas (D)	92,609	51.9
	Charles W. Ainlay (R)	85,845	48.1
4	E. Ross Adair (R)	80,693	55.6
	Ronald R. Ross (D)	64,553	44.4
5	J. Edward Roush (D)	92,264	51.6
	George O. Chambers (R)	86,403	48.4
6	Richard L. Roudebush (R)	76,506	52.7
	Fred Wampler (D)	68,777	47.3
7	William G. Bray (R)	82,160	57.8
	Elden C. Tipton (D)	59,953	42.2
8	Winfield K. Denton (D)	95,126	55.7
	Earl J. Heseman (R)	75,731	44.3
9	Earl Wilson (R)	65,287	52.1
	John Pritchard (D)	59,985	47.9
10	Ralph Harvey (R)	81,007	52.9
	John E. Mitchell (D)	72,009	47.1
11	Donald Cogley Bruce (R)	127,763	54.3
	Andrew Jacobs Jr. (D)	107,747	45.8

IOWA

		Votes	%
1	Fred Schwengel (R)	65,975	61.1
	Harold Stephens (D)	42,000	38.9
2	James E. Bromwell (R)	67,475	52.8
	Frank W. Less (D)	60,296	47.2
3	H. R. Gross (R)	66,337	56.7
	Neel F. Hill (D)	50,580	43.3
4	John Kyl (R)	65,538	55.9
	Gene W. Glenn (D)	51,810	44.2
5	Neal Smith (D)	73,963	62.8
	Sonja C. Egenes (R)	43,877	37.2
6	Charles B. Hoeven (R)	66,940	58.5
	Donald W. Murray (D)	47,542	41.5
7	Ben F. Jensen (R)	56,341	56.1
	Edward J. Peters (D)	44,171	44.0

KANSAS

		Votes	%
1	Bob Dole (R)	102,499	55.8
	J. Floyd Breeding (D)	81,092	44.2

	Candidates	Votes	%
2	William H. Avery (R)	72,945	65.2
	Harry F. Kehoe (D)	38,923	34.8
3	Robert F. Ellsworth (R)	60,865	63.4
	Bill Sparks (D)	35,166	36.6
4	Garner E. Shriver (R)	72,712	66.9
	Lawrence J. Wetzel (D)	35,922	33.1
5	Joe Skubitz (R)	66,705	53.3
	Wade A. Myers (D)	58,453	46.7

KENTUCKY

		Votes	%
1	Frank A. Stubblefield (D)	53,240	100.0
2	William H. Natcher (D)	45,999	100.0
3	M. G. (Gene) Snyder (R)	94,579	50.8
	Frank W. Burke (D)	91,544	49.2
4	Frank Chelf (D)	57,956	52.9
	Clyde Middleton (R)	51,637	47.1
5	Eugene Siler (R)	59,326	100.0
6	John C. Watts (D)	53,454	100.0
7	Carl D. Perkins (D)	70,195	56.8
	C. Alex Parker Jr. (R)	52,640	42.6

LOUISIANA

		Votes	%
1	F. Edward Hebert (D)	57,326	100.0
2	Hale Boggs (D)	57,395	67.2
	David C. Treen (R)	27,971	32.8
3	Edwin E. Willis (D)	26,170	100.0
4	Joe D. Waggonner Jr. (D)	29,754	100.0
5	Otto E. Passman (D)	24,609	100.0
6	James H. Morrison (D)	48,894	100.0
7	T. Ashton Thompson (D)	33,983	100.0
8	Gillis W. Long (D)	25,682	64.0
	John W. Lewis Jr. (R)	14,448	36.0

MAINE

		Votes	%
1	Stanley R. Tupper (R)	85,864	59.6
	Ronald Kellam (D)	58,129	40.4
2	Clifford G. McIntire (R)	72,349	51.1
	William D. Hathaway (D)	69,159	48.9

MARYLAND

		Votes	%
1	Rogers C. B. Morton (R)	33,674	53.2
	Thomas F. Johnson (D)	29,653	46.8
2	Clarence D. Long (D)	85,383	51.9
	Fife Symington (R)	79,075	48.1
3	Edward A. Garmatz (D)	41,446	100.0
4	George H. Fallon (D)	35,077	72.3
	John E. Brondau (R)	13,425	27.7
5	Richard E. Lankford (D)	85,612	59.5
	Joseph M. Baker Jr. (R)	58,332	40.5
6	Charles McC. Mathias Jr. (R)	106,212	60.9
	John Foley (D)	68,116	39.1
7	Samuel N. Friedel (D)	57,958	70.0
	Caroline R. Ramsay (R)	24,825	30.0
AL	Carlton R. Sickles (D)	388,107	55.7
	Newton Steers (R)	308,792	44.3

MASSACHUSETTS

		Votes	%
1	Silvio O. Conte (R)	106,498	74.4
	William K. Hefner (D)	36,711	25.6
2	Edward P. Boland (D)	92,340	67.8
	Samuel S. Rodman (R)	43,873	32.2
3	Philip J. Philbin (D)	129,326	72.4
	Frank Anthony (R)	49,418	27.7
4	Harold D. Donohue (D)	145,166	90.4
	Stanley Shogren (P)	15,310	9.5
5	F. Bradford Morse (R)	112,455	57.4
	Thomas J. Lane (D)	83,504	42.6
6	William H. Bates (R)	113,104	56.2
	George J. O'Shea (D)	88,187	43.8
7	Torbert H. Macdonald (D)	119,117	71.6
	Gordon F. Hughes (R)	47,289	28.4
8	Thomas P. O'Neill Jr. (D)	100,814	73.0
	Howard Greyber (R)	37,374	27.1

	Candidates	Votes	%
9	John W. McCormack (D)	105,565	100.0
10	Joseph W. Martin Jr. (R)	124,091	65.5
	Edward F. Doolan (D)	65,443	34.5
11	James A. Burke (D)	121,030	64.3
	Harry F. Stimpson (R)	67,138	35.7
12	Hastings Keith (R)	107,000	64.2
	Alexander Byron (D)	59,681	35.8

MICHIGAN

		Votes	%
1	Lucien N. Nedzi (D)	82,321	89.3
	Walter Czarnecki (R)	9,916	10.8
2	George Meader (R)	88,427	58.4
	Thomas P. Payne (D)	63,036	41.6
3	August E. Johansen (R)	77,316	59.5
	Paul H. Todd Jr. (D)	52,667	40.5
4	Edward Hutchinson (R)	73,308	63.8
	Leland D. Mitchell (D)	41,620	36.2
5	Gerald R. Ford Jr. (R)	110,043	67.0
	William G. Reamon (D)	54,112	33.0
6	Charles E. Chamberlain (R)	112,861	54.5
	Don Hayworth (D)	94,157	45.5
7	James G. O'Hara (D)	127,067	56.3
	H. Charles Knill (R)	98,742	43.7
8	James Harvey (R)	77,022	60.5
	Jerome T. Hart (D)	50,376	39.5
9	Robert P. Griffin (R)	66,645	59.4
	Donald G. Jennings (D)	45,536	40.6
10	Elford A. Cederberg (R)	63,452	61.5
	Hubert C. Evans (D)	39,771	38.5
11	Victor A. Knox (R)	48,244	56.7
	Warren P. Cleary (D)	36,886	43.3
12	John B. Bennett (R)	41,784	63.3
	William J. Bolognesi (D)	24,240	36.7
13	Charles C. Diggs Jr. (D)	59,688	71.2
	Robert B. Blackwell (R)	24,134	28.8
14	Harold M. Ryan (D)	108,025	61.8
	Lois V. Nair (R)	66,889	38.2
15	John D. Dingell (D)	94,197	83.0
	Ernest Richards (R)	19,258	17.0
16	John Lesinski Jr. (D)	180,626	67.9
	Laverne D. Elliott (R)	85,485	32.1
17	Martha W. Griffiths (D)	122,021	59.3
	James F. O'Neil (R)	83,870	40.7
18	William S. Broomfield (R)	149,863	59.6
	George J. Fulkerson (D)	101,468	40.4
AL	Neil Staebler (D)	1,392,221	52.0
	Alvin M. Bentley (R)	1,282,082	47.9

Special Election

		Votes	%
14	Harold M. Ryan (D)	30,367#	50.5
	Robert E. Waldron (R)	29,600#	49.2

MINNESOTA

		Votes	%
1	Albert H. Quie (R)	90,632	57.5
	David L. Graven (DFL)	66,956	42.5
2	Ancher Nelsen (R)	81,557	62.2
	Conrad H. Hammar (DFL)	49,543	37.8
3	Clark MacGregor (R)	87,730	60.2
	Irving R. Keldsen (DFL)	58,066	39.8
4	Joseph E. Karth (DFL)	93,519	59.5
	Harry Strong (R)	63,766	40.5
5	Donald M. Fraser (DFL)	87,002	51.8
	Walter H. Judd (R)	80,865	48.2
6	Alec G. Olson (DFL)	77,310	50.1
	Robert J. Odegard (R)	76,962	49.9
7	Odin Langen (R)	70,546	52.0
	Harding C. Noblitt (DFL)	65,161	48.0
8	John A. Blatnik (DFL)	101,567	65.7
	Jerry H. Ketola (R)	52,996	34.3

MISSISSIPPI

		Votes	%
1	Thomas G. Abernathy (D)	26,251	100.0
2	Jamie L. Whitten (D)	31,344	100.0
3	John Bell Williams (D)	38,093	100.0

MISSISSIPPI		
Candidates	**Votes**	**%**
4 Arthur Winstead (D)	21,730	83.0
Sterling P. Davis (I)	4,461	17.0
5 William M. Colmer (D)	39,735	100.0

MISSOURI		
1 Frank M. Karsten (D)	82,216	70.7
Charles F. Cherry (R)	34,089	29.3
2 Thomas B. Curtis (R)	102,861	56.3
Philip V. Maher (D)	79,732	43.7
3 Leonor K. Sullivan (D)	81,346	70.5
J. Marvin Krause (R)	34,031	29.5
4 William J. Randall (D)	59,599	53.9
John D. Fox (R)	50,945	46.1
5 Richard Bolling (D)	54,166	58.9
Walter McCarty (R)	37,835	41.1
6 W. R. Hull Jr. (D)	62,366	55.3
Ethan H. Campbell (R)	50,339	44.7
7 Durward G. Hall (R)	84,631	57.7
Jim Thomas (D)	62,082	42.3
8 Richard Ichord (D)	77,535	59.0
David W. Bernhardt (R)	53,862	41.0
9 Clarence Cannon (D)	74,254	61.2
Anthony C. Schroeder (R)	47,026	38.8
10 Paul C. Jones (D)	50,581	60.6
Truman Farrow (R)	32,828	39.4

MONTANA		
1 Arnold Olsen (D)	55,611	52.8
Wayne Montgomery (R)	49,760	47.2
2 James F. Battin (R)	79,315	55.4
Leo Graybill Jr. (D)	63,755	44.6

NEBRASKA		
1 Ralph F. Beermann (R)	85,559	50.9
Clair A. Callan (D)	73,768	43.9
George C. Menkens	8,794	5.2
2 Glenn Cunningham (R)	83,139	69.5
Thomas N. Bonner (D)	36,577	30.6
3 Dave Martin (R)	103,079	65.6
John A. Hoffman (D)	54,058	34.4

NEVADA		
AL Walter S. Baring (D)	66,866	71.7
J. Carlton Adair (R)	26,458	28.4

NEW HAMPSHIRE		
1 Louis C. Wyman (R)	65,651	53.1
J. Oliva Huot (D)	57,910	46.9
2 James C. Cleveland (R)	56,152	57.5
Eugene S. Daniell (D)	41,539	42.5

NEW JERSEY		
1 William T. Cahill (R)	119,633	58.8
Neil F. Deighan Jr. (D)	83,405	41.0
2 Milton W. Glenn (R)	61,285	52.7
Paul R. Porreca (D)	54,317	46.7
3 James C. Auchincloss (R)	82,220	56.9
Peter J. Gannon (D)	62,258	43.1
4 Frank Thompson Jr. (D)	88,668	63.8
Ephraim Tomlinson (R)	49,952	35.9
5 Peter H. B. Frelinghuysen Jr. (R)	86,133	66.0
Eugene M. Friedman (D)	43,347	33.2
6 Florence P. Dwyer (R)	110,143	59.6
Lillian Walsh Egolf (D)	73,436	39.8
7 William B. Widnall (R)	110,926	61.4
J. Emmet Cassidy (D)	68,330	37.8
8 Charles S. Joelson (D)	75,820	65.0
Walter W. Porter Jr. (R)	39,903	34.2

Candidates	**Votes**	**%**
9 Frank C. Osmers Jr. (R)	89,345	56.9
Donald R. Sorkow (D)	66,140	42.2
10 Peter W. Rodino Jr. (D)	62,616	72.8
Charles Allan Baretski (R)	22,819	26.5
11 Joseph G. Minish (D)	48,102	59.5
Frank A. Palmieri (R)	30,244	37.4
12 George M. Wallhauser (R)	57,169	52.5
Robert R. Peacock (D)	50,783	46.6
13 Cornelius E. Gallagher (D)	62,636	77.1
Eugene P. Kenny (R)	17,063	21.0
14 Dominick V. Daniels (D)	54,000	70.6
Michael J. Bell (R)	21,303	27.9
15 Edward J. Patten (D)	86,651	56.7
Bernard F. Rodgers (R)	66,142	43.3

NEW MEXICO		
AL Thomas G. Morris (D)	152,684	64.4
Junio Lopez (R)	84,457	35.6
AL Joseph M. Montoya (D)	128,651	52.5
Jack C. Redman (R)	116,262	47.5

NEW YORK		
1 Otis G. Pike (D, L)	85,619	61.7
Walter M. Ormsby (R)	53,133	38.3
2 James R. Grover Jr. (R)	70,352	55.7
Robert J. Flynn (D, L)	55,963	44.3
3 Steven B. Derounian (R)	86,430	59.2
George Soll (D, L)	59,635	40.8
4 John W. Wydler (R)	74,508	56.4
Joseph A. Daley (D, L)	56,438	42.7
5 Frank J. Becker (R)	89,964	57.5
Franklin Bear (D, L)	66,502	42.5
6 Seymour Halpern (R)	96,475	63.3
Leonard L. Finz (D, L)	55,883	36.7
7 Joseph P. Addabbo (D, L)	80,983	59.3
George Archinal (R)	55,654	40.7
8 Benjamin S. Rosenthal (D, L)	104,895	66.4
Arthur McCrossen (R)	53,122	33.6
9 James J. Delaney (D)	85,987	58.8
Charles H. Cohen (R)	51,325	35.1
Mark Starr (L)	9,051	6.2
10 Emanuel Celler (D, L)	90,216	80.0
Seymour Besunder (R)	21,210	19.0
11 Eugene J. Keogh (D, L)	60,082	71.6
Abraham L. Banner (R)	23,844	28.4
12 Edna F. Kelly (D, L)	106,375	70.0
Louis London Goldberg (R)	45,492	30.0
13 Abraham J. Multer (D, L)	116,753	74.6
Melvyn M. Rothman (R)	39,765	25.4
14 John J. Rooney (D, L)	54,298	70.9
Leon F. Nadrowski (R)	22,287	29.1
15 Hugh L. Carey (D, L)	55,602	50.2
Francis E. Dorn (R)	55,219	49.8
16 John M. Murphy (D)	57,666	47.5
Robert T. Connor (R)	55,821	45.9
George B. Murphy (L)	8,043	6.6
17 John V. Lindsay (R)	98,024	68.7
Martin B. Dworkis (D, L)	44,728	31.3
18 Adam Clayton Powell Jr. (D)	59,125	69.6
Ramon A. Martinez (R)	18,313	21.6
Mae P. Watts (L)	7,457	8.8
19 Leonard Farbstein (D)	59,880	58.5
Richard S. Aldrich (R, OP)	31,244	30.5
Bentley Kassal (L)	11,233	11.0
20 William F. Ryan (D, L)	94,425	72.6
Gilbert A. Robinson (R)	35,664	27.4
21 James C. Healey (D)	65,242	67.4
Stanley L. Slater (R)	20,354	21.0
Lillian Gulker (L)	11,187	11.6
22 Jacob H. Gilbert (D)	51,241	70.4
Oscar Gonzalez-Suarez (R)	14,901	20.5
David Grand (L)	6,629	9.1

23 Charles A. Buckley (D)	69,836	54.4
John J. Parker (R)	39,692	30.9
John P. Hagan (L)	18,749	14.6
24 Paul A. Fino (R)	77,785	60.1
Alfred E. Santangelo (D)	46,455	35.9
25 Robert R. Barry (R)	109,989	61.5
A. Frank Reel (D, L)	68,859	38.5
26 Ogden R. Reid (R)	93,064	60.9
Stanley W. Church (D, L)	59,725	39.1
27 Katharine St.George (R)	86,958	57.9
William F. Ward Jr. (D, L)	63,306	42.1
28 J. Ernest Wharton (R)	94,531	64.1
Morton E. Gilday (D, L)	52,994	35.9
29 Leo W. O'Brien (D, L)	126,313	60.1
Wolfgang J. Riemer (R)	83,719	39.9
30 Carleton J. King (R)	108,860	63.8
William W. Egan (D)	57,822	33.9
31 Clarence E. Kilburn (R)	66,283	60.0
Francis J. Healey (D, L)	44,171	40.0
32 Alexander Pirnie (R)	77,875	57.6
Virgil C. Crisafulli (D, L)	57,414	42.4
33 Howard W. Robison (R)	92,460	66.8
Theodore W. Maurer (D)	41,412	29.9
34 R. Walter Riehlman (R)	84,780	54.8
Lee Alexander (D)	67,149	43.4
35 Samuel S. Stratton (D, L)	78,560	54.5
Janet Hill Gordon (R)	65,697	45.5
36 Frank J. Horton (R)	96,581	59.3
Robert R. Bickal (D, L)	66,371	40.7
37 Harold C. Ostertag (R)	101,821	64.3
Norman C. Katner (D, L)	56,428	35.7
38 Charles E. Goodell (R)	83,361	68.4
T. Joseph Lynch (D)	36,992	30.3
39 John R. Pillion (R)	99,527	62.6
Angelo S. Deloia (D, L)	55,774	35.1
40 William E. Miller (R)	72,706	52.0
E. Dent Lackey (D, L)	67,004	48.0
41 Thaddeus J. Dulski (D, L)	93,982	71.5
Daniel J. Kij (R)	37,544	28.5

Special Election		
6 Benjamin S. Rosenthal (D, L)	16,115#	44.5
Thomas F. Galvin (R)	15,851#	43.8
Emil Levin (I)	4,245#	11.7

NORTH CAROLINA		
1 Herbert C. Bonner (D)	17,898	100.0
2 L. H. Fountain (D)	21,050	100.0
3 David N. Henderson (D)	34,056	100.0
4 Harold D. Cooley (D)	45,249	58.1
George E. Ward (R)	32,593	41.9
5 Ralph J. Scott (D)	47,009	59.2
A. M. Snipes (R)	32,427	40.8
6 Horace R. Kornegay (D)	43,021	59.9
Blackwell P. Robinson (R)	28,827	40.1
7 Alton Lennon (D)	33,173	77.0
James E. Walsh Jr. (R)	9,895	23.0
8 Charles R. Jonas (R)	64,703	56.0
A. Paul Kitchin (D)	50,926	44.0
9 James T. Broyhill (R)	67,608	50.5
Hugh Q. Alexander (D)	66,332	49.5
10 Basil L. Whitener (D)	52,641	55.1
Carrol M. Barringer (R)	42,908	44.9
11 Roy A. Taylor (D)	70,791	55.2
Robert Brown (R)	57,422	44.8

NORTH DAKOTA		
1 Hjalmar C. Nygaard (R)	61,330	54.6
Scott Anderson (D)	50,924	45.4
2 Don L. Short (R)	56,203	54.0
Robert Vogel (D)	47,825	46.0

OHIO

	Candidates	Votes	%
1	Carl W. Rich (R)	74,320	62.7
	Monica Nolan (D)	44,264	37.3
2	Donald D. Clancy (R)	105,750	62.8
	H. A. Sand (D)	62,733	37.2
3	Paul F. Schenck (R)	113,584	57.0
	Martin A. Evers (D)	85,573	43.0
4	William M. McCulloch (R)	77,790	70.3
	Marjorie Conrad Struna (D)	32,866	29.7
5	Delbert L. Latta (R)	69,272	70.4
	William T. Hunt (D)	29,114	29.6
6	William H. Harsha (R)	72,743	60.4
	Jerry C. Rasor (D)	47,737	39.6
7	Clarence J. Brown (R)	83,680	67.7
	Robert A. Riley (D)	39,908	32.3
8	Jackson E. Betts (R)	66,458	70.1
	Morris Laderman (D)	28,400	29.9
9	Thomas L. Ashley (D)	86,443	57.4
	Martin A. Janis (R)	64,279	42.7
10	Homer E. Abele (R)	46,158	52.3
	Walter H. Moeller (D)	42,131	47.7
11	Oliver P. Bolton (R)	74,573	50.6
	Robert E. Cook (D)	72,936	49.5
12	Samuel L. Devine (R)	130,316	68.3
	Paul D. Cassidy (D)	60,563	31.7
13	Charles A. Mosher (R)	63,858	55.1
	J. Grant Keys (D)	52,030	44.9
14	William H. Ayres (R)	100,909	53.7
	Oliver Ocasek (D)	86,947	46.3
15	Robert T. Secrest (D)	41,856	52.4
	Tom V. Moorehead (R)	38,095	47.7
16	Frank T. Bow (R)	96,512	60.1
	Ed Witmer (D)	64,213	40.0
17	John M. Ashbrook (R)	69,976	58.6
	Robert W. Levering (D)	49,415	41.4
18	Wayne L. Hays (D)	66,327	61.0
	John J. Carrigg (R)	42,336	39.0
19	Michael J. Kirwan (D)	75,967	62.2
	William Vincent Williams (R)	46,200	37.8
20	Michael A. Feighan (D)	91,544	71.0
	Leonard G. Richter (R)	37,325	29.0
21	Charles A. Vanik (D)	79,514	79.9
	Leodis Harris (R)	20,027	20.1
22	Frances P. Bolton (R)	74,603	64.6
	Edward Corrigan (D)	35,353	30.6
23	William E. Minshall (R)	107,510	71.5
	Emil C. Weber (D)	42,907	28.5
AL	Robert Taft Jr. (R)	1,786,018	60.5
	Richard D. Kennedy (D)	1,164,776	39.5

OKLAHOMA

		Votes	%
1	Page Belcher (R)	102,585	68.6
	Herbert W. Wright Jr. (D)	46,949	31.4
2	Ed Edmondson (D)	65,968	56.7
	Bill Sharp (R)	50,481	43.4
3	Carl Albert (D)	56,010	100.0
4	Tom Steed (D)	66,000	100.0
5	John Jarman (D)	90,392	68.9
	William P. Pointon Jr. (R)	40,825	31.1
6	Victor Wickersham (D)	56,508	53.6
	Glenn L. Gibson (R)	48,985	46.4

OREGON

		Votes	%
1	Walter Norblad (R)	119,263	61.8
	R. Blaine Whipple (D)	73,641	38.2
2	Al Ullman (D)	53,335	64.0
	Robert W. Chandler (R)	29,995	36.0
3	Edith Green (D)	131,573	66.0
	Stanley E. Hartman (R)	67,830	34.0
4	Robert B. Duncan (D)	83,660	53.9
	Carl Fisher (R)	71,483	46.1

PENNSYLVANIA

		Votes	%
1	William A. Barrett (D)	102,722	63.5
	Winifred H. Malinowsky (R)	58,953	36.5

	Candidates	Votes	%
2	Robert N. C. Nix (D)	86,812	67.1
	Arthur C. Thomas (R)	42,607	32.9
3	James A. Byrne (D)	81,405	59.3
	Joseph R. Burns (R)	55,827	40.7
4	Herman Toll (D)	104,300	56.0
	Frank J. Barbera (R)	82,014	44.0
5	William J. Green Jr. (D)	94,501	55.9
	Michael J. Bednarek (R)	74,557	44.1
6	George M. Rhodes (D)	112,959	51.2
	Ivor D. Fenton (R)	107,724	48.8
7	William H. Milliken (R)	136,955	60.8
	John A. Reilly (D)	88,482	39.3
8	Willard S. Curtin (R)	101,853	54.8
	James A. Michener (D)	84,043	45.2
9	Paul B. Dague (R)	113,880	67.2
	Richard C. Keller (D)	55,565	32.8
10	Joseph M. McDade (R)	95,754	52.5
	William D. Combar (D)	86,680	47.5
11	Daniel J. Flood (D)	101,754	66.5
	Donald B. Ayers (R)	51,263	33.5
12	J. Irving Whalley (R)	98,190	60.5
	A. Reed Hayes (D)	64,227	39.5
13	Richard S. Schweiker (R)	135,847	66.6
	Lee F. Driscoll Jr. (D)	68,234	33.4
14	William S. Moorhead (D)	93,130	65.7
	Joseph M. Beatty (R)	48,726	34.4
15	Francis E. Walter (D)	63,574	57.5
	Woodrow A. Horn (R)	46,928	42.5
16	John C. Kunkel (R)	90,113	66.7
	John A. Walter (D)	44,932	33.3
17	Herman T. Schneebeli (R)	96,088	62.9
	William W. Litke (D)	56,692	37.1
18	Robert J. Corbett (R)	108,433	64.3
	Edward F. Cook (D)	60,260	35.7
19	George A. Goodling (R)	82,924	56.8
	Earl D. Warner (D)	62,995	43.2
20	Elmer J. Holland (D)	106,971	67.4
	Budd Edward Sheppard (R)	51,688	32.6
21	John H. Dent (D)	80,410	59.6
	Charles E. Scalf (R)	54,543	40.4
22	John P. Saylor (R)	82,584	57.5
	Donald J. Perry (D)	61,054	42.5
23	Leon H. Gavin (R)	79,158	58.6
	Frank M. O'Neil (D)	54,798	40.6
24	James D. Weaver (R)	82,213	51.4
	Peter J. Joyce (D)	77,749	48.6
25	Frank M. Clark (D)	87,552	56.4
	Harvey R. Robinson (R)	67,630	43.6
26	Thomas E. Morgan (D)	94,932	61.7
	Jerome Hahn (R)	58,945	38.3
27	James G. Fulton (R)	112,034	65.5
	Margaret Lee Walgren (D)	58,984	34.5

RHODE ISLAND

		Votes	%
1	Fernard J. St.Germain (D)	80,333	56.8
	R. Gordon Butler (R)	61,186	43.2
2	John E. Fogarty (D)	127,184	71.8
	John F. Kennedy (R)	49,955	28.2

SOUTH CAROLINA

		Votes	%
1	L. Mendel Rivers (D)	39,176	100.0
2	Albert W. Watson (D)	39,149	52.8
	Floyd D. Spence (R)	34,947	47.2
3	W. J. Bryan Dorn (D)	34,545	100.0
4	Robert T. Ashmore (D)	47,044	100.0
5	Robert W. Hemphill (D)	28,989	93.9
	Robert M. Doster (R)	1,861	6.0
6	John L. McMillan (D)	36,811	100.0

Special Election

		Votes	%
2	Corinne B. Riley (D)	3,626#	100.0

SOUTH DAKOTA

		Votes	%
1	Ben Reifel (R)	113,975	59.2
	Ralph A. Nauman (D)	78,421	40.8

	Candidates	Votes	%
2	E. Y. Berry (R)	37,092	61.5
	M. W. Morrie Clarkson (D)	23,243	38.5

TENNESSEE [1]

		Votes	%
1	James Quillen (R)	49,320	53.9
	Herbert Silvers (D)	40,113	43.8
2	Howard H. Baker (R)	61,306	70.6
	Tally R. Livingston (D)	25,579	29.4
3	Bill Brock (R)	47,604	51.1
	Wilkes T. Thrasher Jr. (D)	45,597	48.9
4	Joe L. Evins (D)	46,005	87.9
	Arch M. Eaton Sr. (I)	6,310	12.1
5	Richard Fulton	47,756	60.4
	J. Carleton Loser	30,182	38.2
6	Ross Bass (D)	36,404	81.8
	J. J. Underwood Jr. (I)	8,120	18.2
7	Tom Murray (D)	24,746	100.0
8	Robert A. Everett (D)	23,521	97.3
9	Clifford Davis (D)	55,345	50.6
	Robert B. James (R)	54,132	49.5

TEXAS

		Votes	%
1	Wright Patman (D)	26,669	67.3
	James Timberlake (R)	12,938	32.7
2	Jack Brooks (D)	47,137	68.8
	Roy James Jr. (R)	21,385	31.2
3	Lindley Beckworth (D)	26,915	52.0
	William Steger (R)	24,803	48.0
4	Ray Roberts (D)	23,573	72.0
	Conner Harrington (R)	9,165	28.0
5	Bruce Alger (R)	89,938	56.3
	Bill Jones (D)	69,813	43.7
6	Olin E. Teague (D)	33,617	100.0
7	John Dowdy (D)	37,756	88.2
	Raymond Ramage (R)	5,045	11.8
8	Albert Thomas (D)	51,285	71.5
	Anthony Farris (R)	20,475	28.5
9	Clark W. Thompson (D)	56,179	66.3
	Dave Oaks (R)	28,594	33.7
10	Homer Thornberry (D)	43,396	63.3
	Jim Dobbs (R)	25,165	36.7
11	W. R. Poage (D)	41,698	100.0
12	Jim Wright (D)	53,705	60.6
	Del Barron (R)	34,879	39.4
13	Graham B. Purcell (D)	37,941	67.1
	Joe Meissner (R)	18,578	32.9
14	John Young (D)	60,803	70.4
	Lawrence E. Hoover (R)	25,623	29.7
15	Joe Kilgore (D)	53,552	100.0
16	Ed Foreman (R)	44,095	53.8
	J. T. Rutherford (D)	37,821	46.2
17	Omar Burleson (D)	46,895	100.0
18	Walter Rogers (D)	43,389	58.8
	Jack Seale (R)	30,393	41.2
19	George Mahon (D)	46,925	67.1
	Dennis Taylor (R)	23,022	32.9
20	Henry B. Gonzalez (D)	62,776	100.0
21	O. C. Fisher (D)	39,261	76.1
	E. S. Mayer Jr. (R)	12,310	23.9
22	Bob Casey (D)	73,141	53.6
	Ross Baker (R)	63,452	46.5
AL	Joe Pool (D)	870,860	56.1
	Desmond A. Barry (R)	680,569	43.9

Special Runoff Elections [2]

		Votes	%
4	Ray Roberts (D)	16,109	54.3
	R. C. Slagle Jr. (D)	13,572	45.7
13	Graham B. Purcell Jr. (D)	23,905	62.9
	Joe Meissner (R)	14,098	37.1

UTAH

		Votes	%
1	Laurence J. Burton (R)	59,032	50.9
	Morris Blaine Peterson (D)	56,989	49.1

Footnotes, see p. 1006.

UTAH

	Candidates	Votes	%
2	Sherman P. Lloyd (R)	108,355	53.9
	Bruce S. Jenkins (D)	92,631	46.1

VERMONT

		Votes	%
AL	Robert T. Stafford (R)	68,822	56.7
	Harold Raynolds (D)	52,535	43.3

VIRGINIA

		Votes	%
1	Thomas N. Downing (D)	21,664	99.7
2	Porter Hardy Jr. (D)	30,306	75.0
	Louis B. Fine (R)	10,121	25.0
3	J. Vaughan Gary (D)	28,914	49.8
	Louis H. Williams (R)	28,566	49.2
4	Watkins M. Abbitt (D)	30,642	99.5
5	William M. Tuck (D)	13,827	99.8
6	Richard H. Poff (R)	44,060	65.2
	John P. Wheeler (D)	23,280	34.5
7	John O. Marsh Jr. (D)	26,302	50.6
	J. Kenneth Robinson (R)	25,704	49.4
8	Howard W. Smith (D)	20,931	98.7
9	W. Pat Jennings (D)	32,893	61.2
	Leon Owens (R)	20,851	38.8
10	Joel T. Broyhill (R)	49,611	55.4
	Augustus C. Johnson (D)	39,940	44.6

WASHINGTON

	Candidates	Votes	%
1	Thomas M. Pelly (R)	108,561	73.7
	Alice Franklin Bryant (D)	38,669	26.3
2	Jack Westland (R)	70,498	59.8
	Milo Moore (D)	47,333	40.2
3	Julia Butler Hansen (D)	69,045	65.3
	Edwin J. Alexander (R)	36,629	34.7
4	Catherine May (R)	83,182	67.0
	David A. Gallant (D)	40,887	33.0
5	Walt Horan (R)	78,504	64.4
	Bernard J. Gallagher (D)	43,333	35.6
6	Thor C. Tollefson (R)	79,838	71.1
	Dawn Olson (D)	32,513	28.9
7	K. W. Stinson (R)	86,106	56.6
	Don Magnuson (D)	66,052	43.4

WEST VIRGINIA

		Votes	%
1	Arch A. Moore Jr. (R)	97,556	59.9
	Cleveland M. Bailey (D)	65,328	40.1
2	Harley O. Staggers (D)	62,291	58.7
	Cooper P. Benedict (R)	43,769	41.3
3	John M. Slack Jr. (D)	74,743	61.7
	M. G. Guthrie (R)	46,344	38.3
4	Ken Hechler (D)	83,507	57.8
	Clyde B. Pinson (R)	60,931	42.2
5	Elizabeth Kee (D)	57,405	73.1
	James Strother Crockett (R)	21,144	26.9

WISCONSIN

	Candidates	Votes	%
1	Henry C. Schadeberg (R)	71,657	53.3
	Gerald T. Flynn (D)	62,800	46.7
2	Robert W. Kastenmeier (D)	89,740	52.5
	Ivan H. Kindschi (R)	81,274	47.5
3	Vernon W. Thomson (R)	54,237	61.3
	Walter P. Thoresen (D)	34,240	38.7
4	Clement J. Zablocki (D)	117,029	72.5
	David F. Tillotson (R)	44,368	27.5
5	Henry S. Reuss (D)	103,705	63.6
	Thomas F. Nelson (R)	59,441	36.4
6	William K. Van Pelt (R)	71,298	59.2
	John A. Race (D)	49,238	40.9
7	Melvin R. Laird (R)	68,418	66.1
	John E. Evans (D)	35,151	33.9
8	John W. Byrnes (R)	80,808	62.8
	Owen F. Monfils (D)	47,833	37.2
9	Lester R. Johnson (D)	50,025	55.6
	Dennis B. Danielson (R)	39,955	44.4
10	Alvin E. O'Konski (R)	52,451	63.2
	J. Louis Hanson (D)	30,556	36.8

WYOMING

		Votes	%
AL	William Henry Harrison (R)	71,489	61.4
	Louis A. Mankus (D)	44,985	38.6

1963 House Elections

CALIFORNIA

Special Elections

		Votes	%
1	Don Clausen (R)	79,292	54.2
	William F. Grader (D)	65,339	44.7
23	Del Clawson (R)	33,042	53.2
	Carley V. Porter (D)	21,969	35.4

NORTH DAKOTA

Special Election

		Votes	%
1	Mark Andrews (R)	47,062#	49.1
	John Hove (D)	42,470#	44.3
	John W. Scott (CR)	5,995#	6.3

PENNSYLVANIA

Special Elections

		Votes	%
15	Fred B. Rooney (D)	48,846#	53.5
	Robert G. Bartlett (R)	42,374#	46.5
23	Albert W. Johnson (R)	64,137#	58.4
	William T. Hagerty (D)	45,677#	41.6

TEXAS [1]

Special Election

		Votes	%
10	J. J. Pickle (D)	14,389#	35.0
	Jim Dobbs (R)	13,702#	33.3
	Jack Ritter (D)	13,027#	31.7

Special Runoff Election

		Votes	%
10	J. J. Pickle (D)	27,228#	62.9
	Jim Dobbs (R)	16,052#	37.1

1962 Elections

1. The race in Tennessee's 5th district was held without party affiliation. It was an outgrowth of a disputed Democratic primary between Fulton and Loser. Neither was given the Democratic nomination and the general election was conducted on a non-partisan basis.

2. These elections were runoffs between the two candidates who finished with the most votes in special primaries held in 1961, but failed to win a majority. (See Texas 1961, p. 1001.)

1963 Elections

1. Under Texas's special election law, a majority was required to win the House seat. Since no candidate had a majority in the initial special election, a runoff special election was held between the top two finishers. (See Texas 1961 for explanation of Texas special election law, p. 1001.)

1964 House Elections

ALABAMA

	Candidates	Votes	%
1	Jack Edwards (R)	54,522	59.9
	John Tyson (D)	36,482	40.1
2	William L. Dickinson (R)	49,936	61.7
	George M. Grant (D)	29,628	36.6
3	George Andrews (D)	27,939	100.0
4	Glenn Andrews (R)	40,143	58.6
	Kenneth A. Roberts (D)	27,800	40.6
5	Armistead I. Selden Jr. (D)	42,784	53.0
	Robert French (R)	37,960	47.0
6	John Buchanan (R)	69,246	60.6
	George Huddleston Jr. (D)	45,090	39.4
7	James D. Martin (R)	65,353	59.6
	George C. Hawkins (D)	44,386	40.5
8	Robert E. Jones (D)	43,842	100.0

ALASKA

		Votes	%
AL	Ralph J. Rivers (D)	34,605	51.5
	Lowell Thomas Jr. (R)	32,566	48.5

ARIZONA

		Votes	%
1	John J. Rhodes (R)	140,507	55.3
	John Ahearn (D)	113,669	44.7
2	Morris K. Udall (D)	86,499	58.7
	William E. Kimble (R)	60,782	41.3
3	George F. Senner Jr. (D)	30,565	51.5
	Sam Steiger (R)	28,802	48.5

ARKANSAS

		Votes	%
1	E. C. Gathings (D)		100.0
2	Wilbur D. Mills (D)		100.0
3	James W. Trimble (D)	71,228	54.7
	J. E. Hinshaw (R)	58,884	45.3
4	Oren Harris (D)		100.0

CALIFORNIA

		Votes	%
1	Don H. Clausen (R)	141,018	59.1
	George McCabe (D)	97,651	40.9
2	Harold T. Johnson (D)	125,774	64.6
	Chester C. Merriam (R)	68,835	35.4
3	John E. Moss (D)	166,688	74.3
	Einar B. Gjelsteen (R)	57,630	25.7
4	Robert L. Leggett (D)	84,949	71.9
	Ivan Norris (R)	33,160	28.1
5	Phillip Burton (D)	71,638	100.0
6	William S. Mailliard (R)	125,869	63.7
	Thomas P. O'Toole (D)	71,894	36.4
7	Jeffery Cohelan (D)	100,901	66.1
	Lawrence E. McNutt (R)	51,675	33.9
8	George P. Miller (D)	108,771	70.3
	Donald E. McKay (R)	46,063	29.8
9	Don Edwards (D)	115,954	69.8
	William P. Hyde (R)	50,261	30.2
10	Charles S. Gubser (R)	151,027	63.1
	E. Day Carman (D)	88,240	36.9
11	J. Arthur Younger (R)	116,022	54.8
	W. Mark Sullivan (D)	95,747	45.2
12	Burt L. Talcott (R)	93,112	61.9
	Sanford Bolz (D)	57,243	38.1
13	Charles M. Teague (R)	104,744	57.4
	George E. Taylor (D)	77,763	42.6
14	John F. Baldwin (R)	117,272	64.9
	Russell M. Koch (D)	63,469	35.1
15	John J. McFall (D)	109,560	70.9
	Kenneth B. Gibson (R)	44,977	29.1
16	B. F. Sisk (D)	117,727	66.8
	David T. Harris (R)	58,604	33.2
17	Cecil R. King (D)	95,640	67.7
	Robert Muncaster (R)	45,688	32.3
18	Harlan Hagen (D)	121,304	66.7
	James E. Williams Jr. (R)	60,523	33.3

	Candidates	Votes	%
19	Chet Holifield (D)	97,934	65.4
	C. Everett Hunt (R)	51,747	34.6
20	H. Allen Smith (R)	132,402	67.9
	C. Bernard Kaufman (D)	62,645	32.1
21	Augustus F. Hawkins (D)	106,231	90.3
	Rayfield Lundy (R)	11,374	9.7
22	James C. Corman (D)	94,141	50.5
	Robert C. Cline (R)	92,133	49.5
23	Del Clawson (R)	90,721	55.4
	H. O. Van Petten (D)	72,903	44.5
24	Glenard P. Lipscomb (R)	139,784	67.9
	Bryan W. Stevens (D)	65,967	32.1
25	Ronald Brooks Cameron (D)	81,320	55.4
	Frank J. Walton (R)	65,344	44.6
26	James Roosevelt (D)	136,025	70.4
	Gil Seton (R)	57,209	29.6
27	Ed Reinecke (R)	83,141	51.7
	Tom Bane (D)	77,587	48.3
28	Alphonzo Bell (R)	205,473	65.6
	Gerald H. Gottlieb (D)	107,852	34.4
29	George E. Brown Jr. (D)	90,208	58.6
	Charles J. Farrington Jr. (R)	63,836	41.4
30	Edward R. Roybal (D)	90,329	66.3
	Alfred J. Feder (R)	45,912	33.7
31	Charles H. Wilson (D)	114,246	64.0
	Norman G. Shanahan (R)	64,256	36.0
32	Craig Hosmer (R)	132,603	68.9
	Michael Cullen (D)	59,765	31.1
33	Kenneth W. Dyal (D)	109,047	51.7
	Jerry L. Pettis (R)	101,742	48.3
34	Richard T. Hanna (D)	137,588	58.3
	Robert A. Geier (R)	98,606	41.8
35	James B. Utt (R)	167,791	65.0
	Paul B. Carpenter (D)	90,295	35.0
36	Bob Wilson (R)	105,346	59.1
	Quinton Whelan (D)	73,034	40.9
37	Lionel Van Deerlin (D)	85,624	58.2
	Dick Wilson (R)	61,373	41.8
38	John V. Tunney (D)	85,661	52.8
	Patrick Minor Martin (R)	76,525	47.2

Special Election

		Votes	%
5	Phillip Burton (D)	26,698	53.6
	Nick A. Verreos (R)	12,777	25.7
	Tom Flowers (D)	3,841	7.7
	Joe Bortin (D)	3,327	6.7

COLORADO

		Votes	%
1	Byron G. Rogers (D)	138,475	67.5
	Glenn R. Jones (R)	65,423	31.9
2	Roy H. McVicker (D)	109,526	50.6
	Donald G. Brotzman (R)	106,738	49.4
3	Frank E. Evans (D)	85,404	51.2
	J. Edgar Chenoweth (R)	81,544	48.8
4	Wayne N. Aspinall (D)	106,685	63.0
	Edwin S. Lamm (R)	62,617	37.0

CONNECTICUT

		Votes	%
1	Emilio Q. Daddario (D)	141,310	70.0
	James F. Collins (R)	60,654	30.0
2	William L. St.Onge (D)	119,530	63.3
	Belton A. Copp (R)	69,403	36.7
3	Robert N. Giaimo (D)	126,353	63.9
	Bernard J. Burns (R)	71,393	36.1
4	Donald J. Irwin (D)	117,220	51.8
	Abner W. Sibal (R)	109,027	48.2
5	John S. Monagan (D)	133,072	67.3
	Charles W. Terrell Jr. (R)	64,651	32.7
6	Bernard F. Grabowski (D)	115,498	58.7
	Thomas J. Meskill Jr. (R)	81,105	41.2

DELAWARE

	Candidates	Votes	%
AL	Harris B. McDowell Jr. (D)	112,361	56.6
	James H. Snowden (R)	86,254	43.4

FLORIDA

		Votes	%
1	Robert L. F. Sikes (D)	74,615	98.0
2	Charles E. Bennett (D)	99,191	72.7
	William T. Stockton Jr. (R)	37,283	27.3
3	Claude Pepper (D)	101,162	65.7
	Paul J. O'Neil (R)	52,758	34.3
4	Dante B. Fascell (D)	94,726	63.9
	Jay McGlon (R)	53,468	36.1
5	A. Sydney Herlong Jr. (D)	85,851	100.0
6	Paul G. Rogers (D)	168,573	66.1
	John D. Steele (R)	86,657	34.0
7	James A. Haley (D)	79,504	100.0
8	D. R. Matthews (D)	49,374	99.9
9	Don Fuqua (D)	44,917	98.8
10	Sam M. Gibbons (D)	69,860	99.6
11	Edward J. Gurney (R)	91,731	60.6
	Thomas S. Kenney (D)	59,746	39.4
12	William C. Cramer (R)	98,959	60.6
	F. Marion Harrelson (D)	64,378	39.4

GEORGIA

		Votes	%
1	G. Elliott Hagan (D)	65,146	72.3
	J. Milton Lent (I)	25,006	27.7
2	Maston O'Neal (D)	37,634	99.9
3	Howard H. Callaway (R)	45,545	57.4
	Garland T. Byrd (D)	33,733	42.5
4	James A. Mackay (D)	66,488	56.9
	Roscoe Pickett (R)	50,326	43.1
5	Charles L. Weltner (D)	65,803	54.0
	L. J. O'Callaghan (R)	55,983	46.0
6	John J. Flynt Jr. (D)	69,712	100.0
7	John W. Davis (D)	69,575	54.7
	Ed Chapin (R)	57,562	45.3
8	J. Russell Tuten (D)	49,727	100.0
9	Phil M. Landrum (D)	59,186	60.5
	Jack Prince (D)	38,608	39.5
10	Robert G. Stephens Jr. (D)	45,418	100.0

HAWAII

		Votes	%
AL	Spark M. Matsunaga (D)	140,224✔	
	Patsy Takemoto Mink (D)	106,909✔	
	John E. Milligan (R)	89,425	
	Richard Ike Sutton (R)	56,147	

IDAHO

		Votes	%
1	Compton I. White Jr. (D)	56,203	51.7
	John N. Mattmiller (R)	52,468	48.3
2	George V. Hansen (R)	91,838	52.2
	Ralph R. Harding (D)	84,022	47.8

ILLINOIS

		Votes	%
1	William L. Dawson (D)	150,953	84.9
	Wilbur N. Daniel (R)	26,823	15.1
2	Barratt O'Hara (D)	107,795	67.3
	William F. Scannell (R)	52,416	32.7
3	William T. Murphy (D)	120,711	59.1
	Emmet F. Byrne (R)	83,404	40.9
4	Edward J. Derwinski (R)	144,762	58.9
	Ray J. Rybacki (D)	100,895	41.1
5	John C. Kluczynski (D)	101,626	63.7
	Robert V. Kotowski (R)	57,871	36.3

ILLINOIS

	Candidates	Votes	%
6	Daniel J. Ronan (D)	89,850	83.4
	Joseph W. Halac (R)	17,918	16.6
7	Frank Annunzio (D)	106,708	85.9
	Ray Wolfram (R)	17,471	14.1
8	Dan Rostenkowski (D)	137,715	66.1
	Eugene L. Ebrom (R)	70,624	33.9
9	Sidney R. Yates (D)	113,851	63.9
	Robert S. Decker (R)	64,428	36.1
10	Harold R. Collier (R)	172,499	60.8
	Thomas E. Gause (D)	111,029	39.2
11	Roman C. Pucinski (D)	129,337	56.9
	Chester T. Podgorski (R)	98,132	43.1
12	Robert McClory (R)	97,003	58.6
	John Clark Kimball (D)	68,555	41.4
13	Donald Rumsfeld (R)	165,129	57.8
	Lynn A. Williams (D)	120,449	42.2
14	John N. Erlenborn (R)	145,830	59.0
	Jerome M. Ziegler (D)	101,432	41.0
15	Charlotte T. Reid (R)	103,709	58.4
	Poppy X. Mitchell (D)	73,741	41.6
16	John B. Anderson (R)	93,051	56.4
	Robert E. Brinkmeier (D)	71,992	43.6
17	Leslie C. Arends (R)	96,209	56.4
	Bernard J. Hughes (D)	74,261	43.6
18	Robert H. Michel (R)	91,173	54.0
	Edward P. Kohlbacher (D)	77,711	46.0
19	Gale Schisler (D)	81,800	52.4
	Robert T. McLoskey (R)	74,290	47.6
20	Paul Findley (R)	119,184	54.8
	Lester E. Collins (D)	98,256	45.2
21	Kenneth J. Gray (D)	117,701	65.0
	Mrs. Stillman J. Stanard (R)	63,431	35.0
22	William L. Springer (R)	80,895	53.0
	John J. Desmond (D)	71,875	47.1
23	George E. Shipley (D)	119,447	54.6
	Wayne S. Jones (R)	99,496	45.4
24	Melvin Price (D)	144,743	75.7
	G. S. Mirza (R)	46,419	24.3

INDIANA

		Votes	%
1	Ray J. Madden (D)	133,089	63.7
	Arthur F. Endres (R)	75,226	36.0
2	Charles A. Halleck (R)	88,204	52.9
	John C. Raber (D)	78,566	47.1
3	John Brademas (D)	121,209	60.7
	Robert Lowell Miller (R)	78,642	39.4
4	E. Ross Adair (R)	89,437	52.1
	Max E. Hobbs (D)	82,284	47.9
5	J. Edward Roush (D)	114,252	55.2
	John R. Feighner (R)	92,802	44.8
6	Richard L. Roudebush (R)	86,168	54.1
	Karl O'Lessker (D)	73,002	45.9
7	William G. Bray (R)	84,427	54.2
	Elden C. Tipton (D)	71,461	45.8
8	Winfield K. Denton (D)	109,134	56.5
	Roger H. Zion (R)	84,135	43.5
9	Lee H. Hamilton (D)	74,939	54.4
	Earl Wilson (R)	62,780	45.6
10	Ralph Harvey (R)	89,303	50.5
	Russell E. Davis (D)	87,721	49.6
11	Andrew Jacobs Jr. (D)	149,342	50.5
	Don A. Tabbert (R)	146,424	49.5

IOWA

		Votes	%
1	John R. Schmidhauser (D)	84,042	51.0
	Fred Schwengel (R)	80,697	48.9
2	John C. Culver (D)	97,470	52.2
	James E. Bromwell (R)	89,299	47.8
3	H. R. Gross (R)	83,455	50.1
	Stephen M. Peterson (D)	83,036	49.9
4	Bert Bandstra (D)	85,518	53.6
	John Kyl (R)	73,898	46.4
5	Neal Smith (D)	108,212	69.6
	Benjamin J. Gibson Jr. (R)	46,160	29.7
6	Stanley L. Greigg (D)	86,323	53.2
	Howard N. Sokol (R)	75,478	46.5

	Candidates	Votes	%
7	John R. Hansen (D)	78,243	53.5
	Ben F. Jensen (R)	67,942	46.5

KANSAS

		Votes	%
1	Bob Dole (R)	113,212	51.2
	Bill Bork (D)	108,086	48.8
2	Chester L. Mize (R)	80,806	51.1
	John Montgomery (D)	77,189	48.9
3	Robert F. Ellsworth (R)	89,588	62.2
	A. Clayton Dial (D)	54,522	37.8
4	Garner Shriver (R)	84,800	59.4
	Jack Glaves (D)	58,057	40.6
5	Joe Skubitz (R)	83,120	56.4
	Reb Russell (D)	64,308	43.6

KENTUCKY

		Votes	%
1	Frank Stubblefield (D)	84,574	100.0
2	William H. Natcher (D)	79,519	68.4
	Rhodes Bratcher (R)	36,664	31.6
3	Charles P. Farnsley (D)	117,892	53.8
	M. G. (Gene) Snyder (R)	101,168	46.2
4	Frank Chelf (D)	88,337	61.7
	Clyde Middleton (R)	54,937	38.3
5	Tim Lee Carter (R)	61,137	53.1
	Francis Jones Mills (D)	53,916	46.9
6	John C. Watts (D)	93,322	70.6
	John W. Swope (R)	38,869	29.4
7	Carl D. Perkins (D)	100,929	69.7
	Walter Clay Van Hoose (R)	43,921	30.3

LOUISIANA

		Votes	%
1	F. Edward Hebert (D)	76,455	100.0
2	Hale Boggs (D)	77,009	55.1
	David C. Treen (R)	62,881	45.0
3	Edwin E. Willis (D)	52,532	62.3
	Robert J. Angers Jr. (R)	31,806	37.7
4	Joe D. Waggonner Jr. (D)	44,599	100.0
5	Otto E. Passman (D)	24,544	100.0
6	James H. Morrison (D)	82,686	62.9
	Floyd O. Crawford (R)	48,715	37.1
7	T. A. Thompson (D)	38,492	100.0
8	Speedy O. Long (D)	33,250	54.5
	William S. Walker (R)	27,735	45.5

MAINE

		Votes	%
1	Stanley R. Tupper (R)	95,398	50.1
	Kenneth M. Curtis (D)	95,195	50.0
2	William D. Hathaway (D)	110,931	62.0
	Kenneth P. MacLeod (R)	67,978	38.0

MARYLAND

		Votes	%
1	Rogers C. B. Morton (R)	40,762	53.1
	Harry R. Hughes (D)	36,013	46.9
2	Clarence D. Long (D)	143,132	65.9
	George A. Price (R)	74,067	34.1
3	Edward A. Garmatz (D)	56,295	100.0
4	George H. Fallon (D)	57,229	77.8
	Charles O'D. Evans (R)	16,372	22.2
5	Hervey G. Machen (D)	131,712	61.0
	Edward A. Potts (R)	84,318	39.0
6	Charles McC. Mathias Jr. (R)	134,521	54.5
	Royce Hanson (D)	112,410	45.5
7	Samuel N. Friedel (D)	99,654	79.5
	Thomas C. Hofstetter (R)	25,706	20.5
AL	Carlton R. Sickles (D)	683,143	69.4
	David Scull (R)	301,250	30.6

MASSACHUSETTS

		Votes	%
1	Silvio O. Conte (R)	139,503	100.0
2	Edward P. Boland (D)	125,894	100.0

	Candidates	Votes	%
3	Philip J. Philbin (D)	177,917	100.0
4	Harold D. Donohue (D)	142,339	71.8
	Dudley B. Dumaine (R)	56,034	28.3
5	F. Bradford Morse (R)	137,735	65.0
	George W. Arvanitis (D)	74,133	35.0
6	William H. Bates (R)	141,733	64.6
	James G. Zafris Jr. (D)	77,646	35.4
7	Torbert H. Macdonald (D)	139,095	77.0
	Gordon F. Hughes (R)	41,671	23.1
8	Thomas P. O'Neill Jr. (D)	122,050	100.0
9	John W. McCormack (D)	118,385	80.3
	Jack E. Molesworth (R)	21,557	14.6
	Noel A. Day (I)	7,440	5.1
10	Joseph W. Martin Jr. (R)	133,403	63.0
	Edward F. Doolan (D)	78,415	37.0
11	James A. Burke (D)	179,261	100.0
12	Hastings Keith (R)	115,656	59.6
	Alexander Byron (D)	78,313	40.4

MICHIGAN

		Votes	%
1	John Conyers Jr. (D)	138,589	83.6
	Robert B. Blackwell (R)	25,735	15.5
2	Weston E. Vivian (D)	77,806	50.4
	George Meader (R)	76,280	49.4
3	Paul H. Todd (D)	85,001	52.7
	August E. Johansen (R)	76,350	47.3
4	Edward Hutchinson (R)	83,391	54.3
	Russell H. Holcomb (D)	70,212	45.7
5	Gerald R. Ford (R)	101,810	61.2
	William G. Reamon (D)	64,488	38.8
6	Charles E. Chamberlain (R)	88,882	56.6
	Boyd K. Benedict (D)	68,265	43.4
7	John C. Mackie (D)	104,115	65.7
	Claude E. Sadler (R)	54,307	34.3
8	James Harvey (R)	84,588	54.7
	Sanford A. Brown (D)	69,931	45.3
9	Robert P. Griffin (R)	95,376	57.4
	Daniel Griffen (D)	70,693	42.6
10	Elford A. Cederberg (R)	87,232	56.6
	Hubert C. Evans (D)	66,835	43.4
11	Raymond F. Clevenger (D)	86,557	53.3
	Victor A. Knox (R)	75,955	46.7
12	James G. O'Hara (D)	126,769	74.8
	Robert G. Powell (R)	42,615	25.2
13	Charles C. Diggs Jr. (D)	102,413	85.8
	Bruce Watson (R)	16,585	13.9
14	Lucien N. Nedzi (D)	120,308	66.9
	George Bashara (R)	59,487	33.1
15	William D. Ford (D)	103,724	71.0
	John F. Fellrath Jr. (R)	42,464	29.1
16	John D. Dingell (D)	112,763	73.4
	Raymond B. Leonard (R)	40,673	26.5
17	Martha W. Griffiths (D)	136,230	72.8
	William P. Harrington (R)	50,580	27.0
18	William S. Broomfield (R)	109,777	59.5
	Frank J. Sierawski (D)	74,576	40.4
19	Billie S. Farnum (D)	88,441	53.4
	Richard D. Kuhn (R)	77,204	46.6

MINNESOTA

		Votes	%
1	Albert H. Quie (R)	108,639	55.3
	George Daley (DFL)	87,789	44.7
2	Ancher Nelsen (R)	97,804	58.4
	Charles V. Simpson (DFL)	69,801	41.7
3	Clark MacGregor (R)	125,464	57.0
	Richard J. Parish (DFL)	94,682	43.0
4	Joseph E. Karth (DFL)	144,801	73.0
	John M. Drexler (R)	52,221	26.3
5	Donald M. Fraser (DFL)	127,963	61.9
	John W. Johnson (R)	78,767	38.1
6	Alec G. Olson (DFL)	95,848	51.8
	Robert J. Odegard (R)	89,228	48.2
7	Odin Langen (R)	84,304	50.8
	Ben M. Wichterman (DFL)	81,718	49.2
8	John A. Blatnik (DFL)	124,277	69.4
	David W. Glossbrenner (R)	54,691	30.6

MISSISSIPPI

Candidates	Votes	%
1 Thomas G. Abernethy (D)	60,052	100.0
2 Jamie L. Whitten (D)	70,218	100.0
3 John Bell Williams (D)	84,503	100.0
4 Prentiss Walker (R)	35,277	55.7
Arthur Winstead (D)	28,057	44.3
5 William M. Colmer (D)	83,120	100.0

MISSOURI

Candidates	Votes	%
1 Frank M. Karsten (D)	140,848	76.9
Theodore J. Fischer (R)	42,351	23.1
2 Thomas B. Curtis (R)	130,894	53.1
Sidney B. McClanahan (D)	115,446	46.9
3 Leonor K. Sullivan (D)	123,193	71.7
Howard C. Ohlendorf (R)	48,709	28.3
4 William J. Randall (D)	109,375	63.9
James M. Taylor (R)	61,854	36.1
5 Richard Bolling (D)	91,721	67.9
Robert B. Langworthy (R)	43,314	32.1
6 W. R. Hull Jr. (D)	110,532	64.7
Henry E. Wurst (R)	60,356	35.3
7 Durward G. Hall (R)	102,926	51.7
Jim Thomas (D)	96,120	48.3
8 Richard Ichord (D)	117,672	65.2
Ben A. Rogers (R)	62,823	34.8
9 William L. Hungate (D)	112,907	62.3
Anthony C. Schroeder (R)	68,032	37.6
10 Paul C. Jones (D)	89,698	67.4
Carl F. Painter (R)	43,304	32.6

Special Election

	Votes	%
9 William L. Hungate (D)	102,422	62.5
Anthony C. Schroeder (R)	61,439	37.5

MONTANA

	Votes	%
1 Arnold Olsen (D)	64,847	53.6
Wayne Montgomery (R)	55,417	45.8
2 James F. Battin (R)	84,241	54.1
Jack C. Toole (D)	71,461	45.9

NEBRASKA

	Votes	%
1 Clair A. Callan (D)	107,683	51.3
Ralph F. Beermann (R)	102,113	48.7
2 Glenn Cunningham (R)	81,660	53.1
John Richard Swenson (D)	72,003	46.9
3 Dave Martin (R)	104,380	52.8
William E. Colwell (D)	93,236	47.2

NEVADA

	Votes	%
AL Walter S. Baring (D)	82,748	63.3
George Von Tobel (R)	47,989	36.7

NEW HAMPSHIRE

	Votes	%
1 J. Oliva Huot (D)	79,097	51.4
Louis C. Wyman (R)	74,939	48.7
2 James C. Cleveland (R)	62,680	50.1
Charles B. Officer (D)	62,382	49.9

NEW JERSEY

	Votes	%
1 William T. Cahill (R)	150,805	56.2
William J. Procacci (D)	117,227	43.7
2 Thomas C. McGrath Jr. (D)	73,264	50.8
Milton W. Glenn (R)	70,997	49.2
3 James J. Howard (D)	105,803	50.4
Marcus Daly (R)	104,063	49.6
4 Frank Thompson Jr. (D)	134,747	67.5
Ephraim Tomlinson (R)	64,447	32.3
5 Peter H. B. Frelinghuysen (R)	122,168	63.6
Eugene M. Friedman (D)	70,001	36.4

Candidates	Votes	%
6 Florence P. Dwyer (R)	140,999	59.7
Richard J. Traynor (D)	95,021	40.3
7 William B. Widnall (R)	144,585	56.5
Edward H. Ihnen (D)	110,328	43.1
8 Charles S. Joelson (D)	112,483	67.5
J. Palmer Murphy (R)	53,732	32.3
9 Henry Helstoski (D)	111,741	50.1
Frank C. Osmers Jr. (R)	109,313	49.0
10 Peter W. Rodino (D)	92,488	74.0
Raymond W. Schroeder (R)	31,306	25.1
11 Joseph G. Minish (D)	82,457	69.6
William L. Stubbs (R)	35,956	30.4
12 Paul J. Krebs (D)	82,726	52.4
David H. Wiener (R)	72,601	46.0
13 Cornelius E. Gallagher (D)	89,360	77.1
Cresenzi W. Castaldo (R)	24,874	21.5
14 Dominick V. Daniels (D)	73,635	74.6
Cecil T. Woolsey (R)	25,068	25.4
15 Edward J. Patten (D)	131,393	63.2
Bernard F. Rodgers (R)	76,686	36.9

NEW MEXICO

	Votes	%
AL Thomas G. Morris (D)	194,407	61.8
Mike Sims (R)	120,349	38.2
AL E. S. Johnny Walker (D)	164,863	51.6
Jack C. Redman (R)	154,780	48.4

NEW YORK

	Votes	%
1 Otis G. Pike (D, L)	126,529	64.9
John J. Hart Jr. (R)	68,362	35.1
2 James R. Grover Jr. (R)	88,390	51.7
Edwyn Silberling (D, L)	82,757	48.4
3 Lester L. Wolff (D, L)	96,503	50.7
Steven B. Derounian (R)	93,883	49.3
4 John W. Wydler (R)	89,971	53.2
Joseph L. Marino (D)	73,148	43.2
5 Herbert Tenzer (D, L)	112,899	55.8
Ralph J. Edsell Jr. (R)	89,455	44.2
6 Seymour Halpern (R)	100,069	57.1
Emil Levin (D)	75,327	43.0
7 Joseph P. Addabbo (D, L)	121,091	69.8
Robert L. Nelson (R)	49,151	28.3
8 Benjamin S. Rosenthal (D, L)	148,696	75.0
Vincent P. Brevetti (R)	44,398	22.4
9 James J. Delaney (D)	109,973	65.9
Charles H. Cohen (R)	48,878	29.3
10 Emanuel Celler (D, L)	118,941	87.5
Samuel W. Held (R)	16,941	12.5
11 Eugene J. Keogh (D, L)	75,073	78.8
Herman Sanders (R)	17,732	18.6
12 Edna F. Kelly (D, L)	141,570	81.7
Carlo G. Colavito (R)	31,737	18.3
13 Abraham J. Multer (D)	129,414	69.1
Gerald S. Held (R)	34,809	18.6
Gerard M. Weisberg (L)	23,148	12.4
14 John J. Rooney (D, L)	68,165	77.4
Victor J. Tirabasso Jr. (R)	19,861	22.6
15 Hugh L. Carey (D, L)	66,567	53.6
Luigi R. Marano (R, C)	57,626	46.4
16 John M. Murphy (D, L)	89,438	61.4
David D. Smith (R, C)	56,238	38.6
17 John V. Lindsay (R)	135,807	71.5
Eleanor C. French (D, L)	44,533	23.5
Kieran O'Doherty (C)	9,491	5.0
18 Adam Clayton Powell Jr. (D)	94,222	84.6
Joseph A. Bailey (R)	11,621	10.4
19 Leonard Farbstein (D)	84,781	68.9
Henry E. Delrosso (R)	24,829	20.2
Edward A. Morrison (L)	12,129	9.9
20 William F. Ryan (D)	124,128	82.5
Ronald N. Gottlieb (R)	23,409	15.6
21 James H. Scheuer (D, L)	91,898	84.3
Henry Rose (R)	15,380	14.1
22 Jacob H. Gilbert (D)	70,147	81.6
Manuel R. Roque (R)	10,134	11.8

Candidates	Votes	%
Joseph A. Mazar (L)	5,026	5.8
23 Jonathan B. Bingham (D)	108,205	71.3
Patrick J. Foley (R)	30,476	20.1
John P. Hagan (L)	10,602	7.0
24 Paul A. Fino (R)	89,814	61.2
Robert J. Malang (D)	51,740	35.3
25 Richard Ottinger (D, L)	122,260	56.2
Robert R. Barry (R)	95,214	43.8
26 Ogden R. Reid (R)	102,064	54.9
Frank Conniff (D, L)	78,546	42.2
27 John G. Dow (D, L)	97,337	51.6
Katherine St. George (R)	91,172	48.4
28 Joseph Y. Resnick (D)	95,820	51.7
J. Ernest Wharton (R, C)	84,008	45.3
29 Leo W. O'Brien (D, L)	158,797	69.2
John D. Meader (R, C)	70,518	30.8
30 Carleton J. King (R)	100,950	50.3
Joseph J. Martin (D, L)	99,841	49.7
31 Robert C. McEwen (R, C)	74,380	54.6
Raymond E. Bishop (D, L)	61,726	45.4
32 Alexander Pirnie (R)	86,717	53.4
Robert Castle (D)	75,660	46.6
33 Howard W. Robison (R)	97,213	58.4
John L. Joy (D, L)	69,277	41.6
34 James M. Hanley (D, L)	96,219	51.2
R. Walter Riehlman (R, C)	91,697	48.8
35 Samuel S. Stratton (D, L)	110,948	64.0
Robert M. Quigley (R, C)	62,463	36.0
36 Frank J. Horton (R)	107,406	56.0
John C. Williams (D)	81,509	42.5
37 Barber B. Conable Jr. (R)	98,923	54.2
Neil F. Bubel (D)	80,411	44.0
38 Charles E. Goodell (R)	90,201	58.4
Robert V. Kelley (D, L)	64,179	41.6
39 Richard D. McCarthy (D, L)	108,235	52.8
John R. Pillion (R)	96,934	47.3
40 Henry P. Smith III (R)	90,745	51.5
Wesley J. Hilts (D)	81,531	46.3
41 Thaddeus J. Dulski (D, L)	130,961	82.1
Joseph A. Klawon (R)	28,578	17.9

NORTH CAROLINA

	Votes	%
1 Herbert C. Bonner (D)	52,567	82.6
Zeno O. Ratcliff (R)	11,108	17.4
2 L. H. Fountain (D)	62,406	100.0
3 David N. Henderson (D)	63,235	67.4
Sherman T. Rock (R)	30,557	32.6
4 Harold D. Cooley (D)	73,470	51.8
James C. Gardner (R)	68,387	48.2
5 Ralph J. Scott (D)	72,254	51.6
W. A. Armfield (R)	67,781	48.4
6 Horace R. Kornegay (D)	84,151	61.4
Walter G. Green (R)	52,964	38.6
7 Alton Lennon (D)	71,357	100.0
8 Charles R. Jonas (R)	85,866	54.3
W. D. James (D)	72,269	45.7
9 James T. Broyhill (R)	88,195	55.2
Robert M. Davis (D)	71,629	44.8
10 Basil L. Whitener (D)	78,684	58.7
W. Hall Young (R)	55,483	41.4
11 Roy A. Taylor (D)	85,880	60.5
Clyde M. Roberts (R)	55,996	39.5

NORTH DAKOTA

	Votes	%
1 Mark Andrews (R)	69,575	52.1
George A. Sinner (D)	63,208	47.4
2 Rolland Redlin (D)	60,751	52.5
Don L. Short (R)	54,878	47.5

OHIO

	Votes	%
1 John J. Gilligan (D)	74,525	51.9
Carl W. Rich (R)	69,114	48.1
2 Donald D. Clancy (R)	122,487	60.5
H. A. Sand (D)	79,824	39.5
3 Rodney M. Love (D)	129,469	52.0
Paul F. Schenck (R)	119,400	48.0

OHIO

	Candidates	Votes	%
4	William M. McCulloch (R)	81,204	55.7
	Robert H. Mihlbaugh (D)	64,667	44.3
5	Delbert L. Latta (R)	80,394	65.9
	Milford Landis (D)	41,621	34.1
6	William H. Harsha (R)	86,015	60.1
	Frank E. Smith (D)	57,223	40.0
7	Clarence J. Brown (R)	93,022	56.8
	Jerry R. Graham (D)	70,857	43.2
8	Jackson E. Betts (R)	73,395	61.8
	Frank Bennett (D)	45,445	38.2
9	Thomas L. Ashley (D)	109,167	62.9
	John O. Celusta (R)	64,401	37.1
10	Walter H. Moeller (D)	54,729	52.4
	Homer E. Abele (R)	49,744	47.6
11	J. William Stanton (R)	102,619	55.4
	C. D. Lambros (D)	82,728	44.6
12	Samuel L. Devine (R)	146,971	55.4
	Robert L. Van Heyde (D)	118,299	44.6
13	Charles A. Mosher (R)	75,945	54.7
	Louis G. Frey (D)	62,780	45.3
14	William H. Ayres (R)	126,088	54.7
	Frances McGovern (D)	104,547	45.3
15	Robert T. Secrest (D)	62,438	66.1
	Randall Metcalf (R)	31,983	33.9
16	Frank T. Bow (R)	101,802	52.2
	Robert B. Freeman (D)	93,255	47.8
17	John M. Ashbrook (R)	75,674	51.5
	Robert W. Levering (D)	71,291	48.5
18	Wayne L. Hays (D)	94,768	68.8
	Allen J. Dalrymple (R)	42,960	31.2
19	Michael J. Kirwan (D)	111,682	76.3
	Albert H. James (R)	34,654	23.7
20	Michael A. Feighan (D)	115,675	74.4
	Joseph A. Cipollone (R)	39,747	25.6
21	Charles A. Vanik (D)	113,157	90.1
	Eugene E. Smith (R)	12,416	9.9
22	Frances P. Bolton (R)	84,183	56.6
	Chat Paterson (D)	64,454	43.4
23	William E. Minshall (R)	131,554	67.2
	Norbert G. Dennerll Jr. (D)	64,162	32.8
AL	Robert E. Sweeney (D)	1,872,351	52.2
	Oliver P. Bolton (R)	1,716,480	47.8

OKLAHOMA

1	Page Belcher (R)	125,377	63.5
	Doug Martin (D)	71,998	36.5
2	Ed Edmondson (D)	90,466	61.4
	George L. Lange (R)	56,843	38.6
3	Carl Albert (D)	62,952	79.0
	Frank D. McSherry (R)	16,706	21.0
4	Tom Steed (D)	98,419	100.0
5	John Jarman (D)	130,014	70.8
	Homer Cowan (R)	53,596	29.2
6	Jed Johnson Jr. (D)	75,879	56.7
	Bayard C. Auchincloss (R)	58,041	43.3

OREGON

1	Wendell Wyatt (R)	122,010	53.1
	R. Blaine Whipple (D)	107,920	46.9
2	Al Ullman (D)	70,136	68.1
	Everett J. Thoren (R)	32,916	31.9
3	Edith Green (D)	157,882	65.6
	Lyle Dean (R)	82,468	34.3
4	Robert B. Duncan (D)	125,752	64.8
	Paul Jaffarian (R)	68,288	35.2

Special Election

1	Wendell Wyatt (R)	125,473	52.8
	R. Blaine Whipple (D)	112,112	47.2

PENNSYLVANIA

1	William A. Barrett (D)	129,471	71.8
	Alvin J. Bello (R)	50,780	28.2
2	Robert N. C. Nix (D)	125,100	80.2
	Melvin C. Howell (R)	30,801	19.8
3	James A. Byrne (D)	111,885	72.0
	John J. Poserina Jr. (R)	43,471	28.0
4	Herman Toll (D)	135,681	64.1
	James R. Cavanaugh (R)	75,901	35.9
5	William J. Green III (D)	117,049	65.2
	Edward H. Rovner (R)	62,446	34.8
6	George M. Rhodes (D)	144,697#	62.1
	James B. Bamford (R)	88,495#	37.9
7	G. Robert Watkins (R)	129,572	51.2
	Leonard Bachman (D)	123,750	48.9
8	Willard S. Curtin (R)	112,472	51.1
	Ralph O. Samuel (D)	107,670	48.9
9	Paul B. Dague (R)	111,545	57.7
	John A. O'Brien (D)	81,823	42.3
10	Joseph M. McDade (R)	90,903	50.8
	James J. Haggerty (D)	88,082	49.2
11	Daniel J. Flood (D)	116,875	77.4
	Charles R. Thomas (R)	34,057	22.6
12	J. Irving Whalley (R)	97,114	58.6
	Paul A. Stephens (D)	68,703	41.4
13	Richard S. Schweiker (R)	139,871	59.1
	William D. Searle (R)	96,849	40.9
14	William S. Moorhead (D)	117,525	74.8
	Alvin D. Capozzi (R)	39,513	25.2
15	Fred B. Rooney (D)	81,062	66.1
	Leo W. McCormick (R)	41,656	33.9
16	John C. Kunkel (R)	90,331	64.1
	William F. Stefanic (R)	50,509	35.9
17	Herman T. Schneebeli (R)	91,504	58.0
	William F. Plankenhorn (D)	66,266	42.0
18	Robert J. Corbett (R)	119,938	62.6
	Frank J. Reed (D)	71,621	37.4
19	N. Neiman Craley Jr. (D)	82,498	50.8
	George A. Goodling (R)	79,809	49.2
20	Elmer J. Holland (D)	126,846	74.4
	Ronald Bryan (R)	43,591	25.6
21	John H. Dent (D)	97,379	65.8
	Thomas M. Schooley Jr. (R)	50,513	34.2
22	John P. Saylor (R)	81,400	57.0
	James E. McCaffery (D)	61,482	43.0
23	Albert W. Johnson (R)	76,575	54.9
	John Still (D)	62,932	45.1
24	Joseph P. Vigorito (D)	92,612	50.8
	James D. Weaver (R)	89,828	49.2
25	Frank M. Clark (D)	121,140	70.3
	John Loth (R)	51,071	29.7
26	Thomas E. Morgan (D)	109,532	68.1
	Paul B. Riggle (R)	51,219	31.9
27	James G. Fulton (R)	120,395	62.7
	John A. Young (D)	71,519	37.3

Special Election

5	William J. Green III (D)	30,904#	58.6
	Edward H. Rovner (R)	21,832#	41.4

RHODE ISLAND

1	Fernard J. St.Germain (D)	110,056	66.3
	Roland H. Blanchette (R)	56,056	33.8
2	John E. Fogarty (D)	168,374	81.4
	Guy J. Wells (R)	38,601	18.7

SOUTH CAROLINA

1	L. Mendel Rivers (D)	64,804	99.6
2	Albert W. Watson (D)	88,682	97.6
3	W. J. Bryan Dorn (D)	65,920	99.9
4	Robert T. Ashmore (D)	81,727	100.0
5	Tom S. Gettys (D)	44,859	66.7
	Robert M. Doster (R)	22,384	33.3
6	John L. McMillan (D)	49,398	65.0
	E. R. Kirkland (R)	26,586	35.0

Special Election

5	Tom S. Gettys (D)	44,241	66.8
	Robert M. Doster (R)	22,031	33.2

SOUTH DAKOTA

	Candidates	Votes	%
1	Ben Reifel (R)	124,791	57.6
	George May (D)	92,057	42.5
2	E. Y. Berry (R)	39,657	56.0
	Byron T. Brown (D)	31,208	44.0

TENNESSEE

1	James H. Quillen (R)	94,535	71.7
	Arthur Bright (D)	37,252	28.3
2	John J. Duncan (R)	84,868	53.8
	Willard V. Yarbrough (D)	70,119	44.5
3	Bill Brock (R)	71,005	54.6
	Robert M. Summitt (D)	59,027	45.4
4	Joe L. Evins (D)	85,286	100.0
5	Richard Fulton (D)	74,597	59.8
	William R. Wills (R)	50,210	40.2
6	William R. Anderson (D)	66,817	78.2
	Cecil R. Hill (R)	18,595	21.8
7	Tom Murray (D)	35,612	53.6
	Julius Hurst (IR)	24,496	36.8
	Earl Maclin (I)	6,382	9.6
8	Robert A. Everett (D)	43,876	93.9
	Sarah Flannary (I)	2,865	6.1
9	George W. Grider (D)	108,425	52.5
	Robert James (R)	97,537	47.2

Special Election

2	Irene Baker (R)	40,708#	55.5
	Willard V. Yarbrough (D)	31,763#	43.3

TEXAS

1	Wright Patman (D)	52,698	74.6
	Mrs. William E. Jones (R)	17,967	25.4
2	Jack Brooks (D)	75,226	62.7
	John Greco (R)	44,772	37.3
3	Lindley Beckworth (D)	53,331	59.3
	James Warren (R)	36,566	40.7
4	Ray Roberts (D)	46,782	81.4
	Fred Banfield (R)	10,707	18.6
5	Earle Cabell (D)	172,287	57.5
	Bruce Alger (R)	127,568	42.5
6	Olin Teague (D)	55,155	82.2
	William Van Winkle (R)	11,967	17.8
7	John Dowdy (D)	64,456	83.6
	James W. Orr (R)	12,606	16.4
8	Albert Thomas (D)	103,595	76.8
	Bob Gilbert (R)	31,351	23.2
9	Clark Thompson (D)	105,631	75.3
	Dave Oakes (R)	34,692	24.7
10	Jake Pickle (D)	80,045	75.8
	Billie Pratt (R)	25,594	24.2
11	W. R. Poage (D)	62,175	81.5
	Charles M. Isenhower (R)	14,094	18.5
12	Jim Wright (D)	107,896	68.5
	Fred Dielman (R)	49,633	31.5
13	Graham Purcell (D)	67,947	75.2
	George Corse (R)	22,429	24.8
14	John Young (D)	105,352	77.5
	Billy Patton (R)	30,522	22.5
15	Eligio de la Garza (D)	66,897	69.4
	Joe Coulter (R)	29,551	30.6
16	Richard C. White (D)	70,262	55.7
	Ed Foreman (R)	55,951	44.3
17	Omar Burleson (D)	59,769	76.4
	Phil M. Bridges (R)	18,440	23.6
18	Walter Rogers (D)	58,701	55.0
	Robert Price (R)	48,054	45.0
19	George Mahon (D)	87,555	77.6
	Joe B. Phillips (R)	25,234	22.4
20	Henry B. Gonzalez (D)	103,464	64.6
	John M. O'Connell (R)	56,601	35.4
21	O. C. Fisher (D)	61,785	78.1
	Harry Claypool (R)	17,295	21.9
22	Bob Casey (D)	136,289	58.1
	Desmond Barry (R)	98,287	41.9
AL	Joe Pool (D)	1,690,674	66.9
	Bill Hayes (R)	826,991	32.7

UTAH

Candidates	Votes	%
1 Laurence J. Burton (R)	75,986	56.0
William G. Bruhn (D)	59,768	44.0
2 David S. King (D)	149,754	57.5
Thomas G. Judd (R)	110,512	42.5

VERMONT

Candidates	Votes	%
AL Robert T. Stafford (R, I)	92,252	56.4
Bernard G. O'Shea (D)	71,193	43.6

VIRGINIA

Candidates	Votes	%
1 Thomas N. Downing (D)	72,819	78.7
Wayne C. Thiessen (R)	19,698	21.3
2 Porter Hardy Jr. (D)	54,315	68.7
Wayne Lustig (R)	17,082	21.6
H. W. Grady Speers Jr. (I)	7,635	9.7
3 David E. Satterfield III (D)	43,880	34.5
Richard D. Obenshain (R)	43,226	34.0
Edward E. Haddock (I)	39,223	30.8
4 Watkins M. Abbitt (D)	53,857	69.5
S. W. Tucker (R)	23,682	30.5
5 William M. Tuck (D)	39,867	63.5
Robert L. Gilliam (R)	22,946	36.5
6 Richard H. Poff (R)	57,987	56.2
William B. Hopkins (D)	45,113	43.8
7 John O. Marsh Jr. (D)	47,888	69.6
Roy Erickson (R)	20,911	30.4

Candidates	Votes	%
8 Howard W. Smith (D)	49,440	69.4
Floyd Caldwell Bagley (I)	21,813	30.6
9 W. Pat Jennings (D)	51,106	58.2
Glen M. Williams (R)	36,668	41.8
10 Joel T. Broyhill (R)	80,370	50.7
Augustus C. Johnson (D)	78,242	49.3

WASHINGTON

Candidates	Votes	%
1 Thomas M. Pelly (R)	117,851	59.9
Edward Palmason (D)	78,876	40.1
2 Lloyd Meeds (D)	88,551	54.9
Jack Westland (R)	72,830	45.1
3 Julia Butler Hansen (D)	102,080	70.2
Harold L. Anderson (R)	43,415	29.8
4 Catherine May (R)	102,964	65.3
Stephen H. Huza (D)	54,819	34.7
5 Thomas S. Foley (D)	84,830	53.5
Walt Horan (R)	73,884	46.6
6 Floyd V. Hicks (D)	79,042	52.1
Thor C. Tollefson (R)	72,702	47.9
7 Brock Adams (D)	125,222	55.5
William Stinson (R)	100,119	44.4

WEST VIRGINIA

Candidates	Votes	%
1 Arch A. Moore Jr. (R)	115,799	61.4
John L. Bailey (D)	72,714	38.6
2 Harley O. Staggers (D)	87,928	65.0
Stanley R. Cox Jr. (R)	47,457	35.1
3 John M. Slack Jr. (D)	103,117	65.4
Jim Comstock (R)	54,566	34.6

Candidates	Votes	%
4 Ken Hechler (D)	109,287	61.2
Jack L. Miller (R)	69,253	38.8
5 James Kee (D)	77,156	70.0
Wade Hampton Ballard III (R)	33,108	30.0

WISCONSIN

Candidates	Votes	%
1 Lynn E. Stalbaum (D)	90,450	51.5
Henry C. Schadeberg (R)	85,117	48.5
2 Robert W. Kastenmeier (D)	108,148	63.6
Carl V. Kolata (R)	61,865	36.4
3 Vernon W. Thomson (R)	91,092	60.6
Harold C. Ristow (D)	59,173	39.4
4 Clement J. Zablocki (D)	125,683	74.2
Edward E. Estkowski (R)	43,773	25.8
5 Henry S. Reuss (D)	107,610	75.9
Robert Taylor (R)	34,059	24.0
6 John A. Race (D)	84,690	50.8
William K. Van Pelt (R)	82,103	49.2
7 Melvin R. Laird (R)	98,110	61.8
Thomas E. Martin (D)	60,758	38.2
8 John W. Byrnes (R)	96,160	59.6
Cletus J. Johnson (D)	65,292	40.4
9 Glenn R. Davis (R)	105,332	55.3
James P. Buckley (D)	85,071	44.7
10 Alvin E. O'Konski (R)	92,198	56.2
Edmund A. Nix (D)	71,983	43.8

WYOMING

Candidates	Votes	%
AL Teno Roncalio (D)	70,693	50.8
William Henry Harrison (R)	68,482	49.2

1965 House Elections

CALIFORNIA

Special Election

		Votes	%
26	Thomas M. Rees (D)	40,430	59.4
	Edward M. Marshall (R)	27,579	40.5

LOUISIANA

Special Election

7	Edwin W. Edwards (D)	✔

OHIO

Special Election

		Votes	%
7	Clarence J. Brown Jr. (R)	70,573	59.6
	James A. Berry (D)	47,830	40.4

SOUTH CAROLINA

Special Election

		Votes	%
2	Albert W. Watson (R)	55,977#	69.3
	Preston H. Callison (D)	24,761#	30.7

House Candidates Index

For an index of all House candidates listed in this section (pages 701 to 1061), see pages 1180-1273. Instructions for use of the House Candidates Index appear on page 1180.

1966 House Elections

ALABAMA

Candidates	Votes	%
1 Jack Edwards (R)	58,515	65.8
Warren L. Finch (D)	30,474	34.2
2 William L. Dickinson (R)	49,203	54.7
Robert F. Whaley (D)	40,832	45.4
3 George Andrews (D)	61,015	100.0
4 Bill Nichols (D)	54,515	58.7
Glenn Andrews (R)	38,402	41.3
5 Armistead I. Selden Jr. (D)	68,486	100.0
6 John Buchanan (R)	64,435	63.4
Walter Emmett Perry (D)	37,131	36.6
7 Tom Bevill (D)	73,987	64.4
Wayman Sherrer (R)	40,972	35.6
8 Robert E. Jones (D)	65,982	71.3
Don Mayhall (R)	26,561	28.7

ALASKA

Candidates	Votes	%
AL Howard W. Pollock (R)	34,040	51.7
Ralph J. Rivers (D)	31,867	48.4

ARIZONA

Candidates	Votes	%
1 John J. Rhodes (R)	102,007	67.2
L. Alton Riggs (D)	49,913	32.9
2 Morris K. Udall (D)	66,813	59.6
G. Alfred McGinnis (R)	45,326	40.4
3 Sam Steiger (R)	57,145	56.9
George F. Senner Jr. (D)	43,219	43.1

ARKANSAS

Candidates	Votes	%
1 E. C. Gathings (D)		100.0
2 Wilbur Mills (D)		100.0
3 John P. Hammerschmidt (R)	83,938	53.1
James W. Trimble (D)	74,009	46.9
4 David Pryor (D)	86,887	65.0
Lynn Lowe (R)	46,804	35.0

Special Election

Candidates	Votes	%
4 David Pryor (D)	85,125	64.5
Lynn Lowe (R)	46,764	35.0

CALIFORNIA

Candidates	Votes	%
1 Don H. Clausen (R)	143,755	64.9
Thomas T. Storer (D)	77,000	34.7
2 Harold T. Johnson (D)	131,145	70.9
William H. Romack (R)	53,753	29.1
3 John E. Moss Jr. (D)	143,177	67.5
Terry G. Feil (R)	69,057	32.5
4 Robert L. Leggett (D)	67,942	59.5
Tom McHatton (R)	46,337	40.5
5 Phillip Burton (D)	56,476	71.3
Terry R. Macken (R)	22,778	28.7
6 William S. Mailliard (R)	132,506	76.6
Lerue Grim (D)	40,514	23.4
7 Jeffery Cohelan (D)	84,644	63.9
Malcolm M. Champlin (R)	46,763	35.3
8 George P. Miller (D)	92,263	65.4
Raymond P. Britton (R)	48,727	34.6
9 Don Edwards (D)	97,311	63.1
Wilbur G. Durkee (R)	56,784	36.9
10 Charles S. Gubser (R)	156,549	69.1
George Leppert (D)	70,013	30.9
11 J. Arthur Younger (R)	113,679	59.4
Mark Sullivan (D)	77,605	40.6
12 Burt L. Talcott (R)	108,070	77.2
Gerald V. Barron (D)	31,787	22.7
13 Charles M. Teague (R)	116,701	67.5
Charles A. Storke (D)	56,240	32.5

Candidates	Votes	%
14 Jerome R. Waldie (D)	108,668	56.4
Frank J. Newman (R)	83,878	43.5
15 John J. McFall (D)	81,733	57.0
Sam Van Dyken (R)	61,550	43.0
16 B. F. Sisk (D)	118,063	71.3
Cecil F. White (R)	47,329	28.6
17 Cecil R. King (D)	76,962	60.8
Don Cortum (R)	49,615	39.2
18 Robert B. Mathias (R)	96,699	55.9
Harlan Hagen (D)	76,346	44.1
19 Chet Holifield (D)	82,592	62.2
William R. Sutton (R)	50,068	37.7
20 H. Allen Smith (R)	128,896	73.4
Raymond Freschi (D)	46,730	26.6
21 Augustus F. Hawkins (D)	74,216	84.8
Norman A. Hodges (R)	13,294	15.2
22 James C. Corman (D)	94,420	53.5
Robert C. Cline (R)	82,207	46.5
23 Del Clawson (R)	93,320	67.4
Ed O'Connor (D)	45,141	32.6
24 Glenard P. Lipscomb (R)	148,190	76.2
Earl G. McNall (D)	46,115	23.7
25 Charles E. Wiggins (R)	70,154	52.6
Ronald Brooks Cameron (D)	63,345	47.5
26 Thomas M. Rees (D)	103,289	62.3
Irving Teichner (R)	62,441	37.7
27 Ed Reinecke (R)	93,890	65.3
John A. Howard (D)	49,785	34.6
28 Alphonzo Bell (R)	211,404	72.3
Lawrence Sherman (D)	81,007	27.7
29 George E. Brown Jr. (D)	69,115	51.1
Bill Orozco (R)	66,079	48.9
30 Edward R. Roybal (D)	72,173	66.4
Henri O'Bryant Jr. (R)	36,506	33.6
31 Charles H. Wilson (D)	92,875	63.4
Theodore Smith (R)	53,708	36.6
32 Craig Hosmer (R)	139,328	80.1
Tracy Odell (D)	34,609	19.9
33 Jerry L. Pettis (R)	102,401	53.5
Kenneth W. Dyal (D)	89,071	46.5
34 Richard T. Hanna (D)	127,976	55.8
Frank La Magna (R)	101,410	44.2
35 James B. Utt (R)	189,582	73.1
Thomas B. Lenhart (D)	69,873	26.9
36 Bob Wilson (R)	119,274	72.7
William C. Godfrey (D)	44,365	27.1
37 Lionel Van Deerlin (D)	80,060	61.1
Samuel S. Vener (R)	50,817	38.8
38 John V. Tunney (D)	83,216	54.5
Robert R. Barry (R)	69,444	45.5

Special Election

Candidates	Votes	%
14 Jerome R. Waldie (D)	71,501#	51.2
Frank J. Newman (R)	43,539#	31.2
John A. Richardson (R)	14,693#	10.5

COLORADO

Candidates	Votes	%
1 Byron G. Rogers (D)	92,688	56.0
Greg Pearson (R)	72,732	44.0
2 Donald G. Brotzman (R)	95,123	51.7
Roy H. McVicker (D)	86,685	47.1
3 Frank E. Evans (D)	76,270	51.7
David W. Enoch (R)	71,213	48.3
4 Wayne N. Aspinall (D)	84,107	58.6
James P. Johnson (R)	59,404	41.4

CONNECTICUT

Candidates	Votes	%
1 Emilio Q. Daddario (D)	100,447	58.0
John L. Bonee (R)	71,353	41.2
2 William L. St.Onge (D)	90,298	56.2
Joseph H. Goldberg (R)	69,402	43.2
3 Robert Giaimo (D)	86,029	53.1
Stelio Salmona (R)	67,226	41.5

Candidates	Votes	%
Robert M. Cook (AM I)	8,730	5.4
4 Donald J. Irwin (D)	89,709	50.9
Abner W. Sibal (R)	86,337	49.0
5 John S. Monagan (D)	96,801	59.1
Romeo G. Petroni (R)	67,094	40.9
6 Thomas J. Meskill Jr. (R)	81,907	48.9
Bernard F. Grabowski (D)	79,865	47.7

DELAWARE

Candidates	Votes	%
AL William V. Roth (R)	90,961	55.8
Harris B. McDowell Jr. (D)	72,132	44.2

FLORIDA

Candidates	Votes	%
1 Robert L. F. Sikes (D)	55,547	95.1
2 Don Fuqua (D)	71,565	76.3
Harold Hill (R)	22,281	23.7
3 Charles E. Bennett (D)	72,038	99.9
4 A. Sydney Herlong Jr. (D)	70,155	100.0
5 Edward J. Gurney (R)	75,875	99.7
6 Sam M. Gibbons (D)	50,772	99.8
7 James A. Haley (D)	64,498	63.2
Joe Z. Lovingood (R)	37,586	36.8
8 William C. Cramer (R)	105,019	70.8
Roy L. Reynolds (D)	43,275	29.2
9 Paul G. Rogers (D)	76,328	100.0
10 J. Herbert Burke (R)	80,989	60.6
Joe Varon (D)	51,636	38.7
11 Claude Pepper (D)	62,195	99.9
12 Dante B. Fascell (D)	62,457	56.9
Mike Thompson (R)	47,226	43.1

GEORGIA

Candidates	Votes	%
1 G. Elliott Hagan (D)	53,413	58.0
Porter W. Carswell (R)	38,619	41.9
2 Maston O'Neal (D)	54,487	100.0
3 Jack Brinkley (D)	42,424	61.2
Billy Mixon (R)	26,255	37.9
4 Ben B. Blackburn (R)	55,249	50.2
James A. Mackay (D)	54,889	49.8
5 Fletcher Thompson (R)	55,423	60.1
Archie Lindsey (D)	36,751	39.9
6 John J. Flynt Jr. (D)	74,175	67.9
G. Paul Jones Jr. (R)	35,048	32.1
7 John W. Davis (D)	65,614	65.0
E. Y. Chapin III (R)	35,383	35.0
8 W. S. Stuckey Jr. (D)	60,059	77.0
Mack F. Mattingly (R)	17,926	23.0
9 Phil M. Landrum (D)	61,930	100.0
10 Robert G. Stephens Jr. (D)	54,141	65.7
Leroy H. Simkins Jr. (R)	28,247	34.3

HAWAII

Candidates	Votes	%
AL Patsy T. Mink (D)	140,880✔	
Spark M. Matsunaga (D)	140,110✔	
John S. Carroll (R)	67,281	
James K. Kealoha (R)	62,473	

IDAHO

Candidates	Votes	%
1 James A. McClure (R)	70,410	51.8
Compton I. White Jr. (D)	65,446	48.2
2 George V. Hansen (R)	79,024	70.3
A. W. Brunt (D)	33,348	29.7

ILLINOIS

Candidates	Votes	%
1 William L. Dawson (D)	91,119	72.6
David R. Reed (R)	34,421	27.4

ILLINOIS

Candidates	Votes	%
2 Barratt O'Hara (D)	83,471	59.2
Philip G. Bixler (R)	57,629	40.8
3 William T. Murphy (D)	83,857	52.0
Albert F. Manion (R)	77,442	48.0
4 Edward J. Derwinski (R)	125,365	72.0
Ray J. Rybacki (D)	48,673	28.0
5 John C. Kluczynski (D)	85,770	56.2
Walter K. Kiltz (R)	66,735	43.8
6 Daniel J. Ronan (D)	84,126	57.0
Samuel A. Decaro (R)	63,374	43.0
7 Frank Annunzio (D)	82,962	80.9
Joseph D. Day (R)	19,650	19.2
8 Daniel D. Rostenkowski (D)	94,631	59.9
John H. Leszynski (R)	63,377	40.1
9 Sydney R. Yates (D)	96,746	59.9
Richard C. Storey Jr. (R)	64,875	40.1
10 Harold R. Collier (R)	132,650	69.4
Frank J. Jirka Jr. (D)	58,376	30.6
11 Roman C. Pucinski (D)	105,996	50.9
John J. Hoellen (R)	102,244	49.1
12 Robert McClory (R)	90,483	69.1
Herbert L. Stern (D)	40,502	30.9
13 Donald Rumsfeld (R)	158,769	76.0
James L. McCabe (D)	50,107	24.0
14 John N. Erlenborn (R)	130,442	71.7
Kenneth McCleary (D)	51,385	28.3
15 Charlotte T. Reid (R)	102,018	72.3
Selwyn L. Boyer (D)	39,123	27.7
16 John B. Anderson (R)	89,990	73.0
Robert M. Whiteford (D)	33,274	27.0
17 Leslie C. Arends (R)	104,240	67.4
Bernard J. Hughes (D)	50,350	32.6
18 Robert H. Michel (R)	80,293	58.4
Thomas V. Cassidy (D)	57,100	41.6
19 Tom Railsback (R)	77,895	52.3
Gale Schisler (D)	71,050	47.7
20 Paul Findley (R)	102,609	62.2
Richard R. Wolfe (D)	62,343	37.8
21 Kenneth J. Gray (D)	103,128	56.2
Bob Beckmeyer (R)	80,382	43.8
22 William L. Springer (R)	96,453	63.3
Cameron B. Satterthwaite (D)	55,818	36.7
23 George E. Shipley (D)	95,156	56.4
Leslie N. Jones (R)	73,463	43.6
24 Melvin Price (D)	82,513	71.5
John S. Guthrie (R)	32,915	28.5

INDIANA

Candidates	Votes	%
1 Ray J. Madden (D)	71,040	58.3
Albert F. Harrigan (R)	50,804	41.7
2 Charles A. Halleck (R)	97,161	57.5
Ralph G. McFadden (D)	71,825	42.5
3 John Brademas (D)	75,321	55.8
Robert A. Ehlers (R)	59,731	44.2
4 E. Ross Adair (R)	94,457	63.5
J. Byron Hayes (D)	54,331	36.5
5 J. Edward Roush (D)	76,176	51.1
Kenneth Bowman (R)	72,873	48.9
6 William G. Bray (R)	124,087	65.7
James M. Nicholson (D)	63,342	33.6
7 John T. Myers (R)	79,864	54.3
Elden C. Tipton (D)	67,135	45.7
8 Roger H. Zion (R)	94,924	51.1
Winfield K. Denton (D)	90,887	48.9
9 Lee H. Hamilton (D)	89,392	53.8
John W. Lewis (R)	76,661	46.2
10 Richard L. Roudebush (R)	94,428	63.4
Robert H. Staton (D)	54,515	36.6
11 Andrew Jacobs Jr. (D)	65,624	55.8
Paul R. Oakes (R)	52,096	44.3

IOWA

Candidates	Votes	%
1 Fred Schwengel (R)	64,795	51.3
John R. Schmidhauser (D)	60,534	47.9
2 John C. Culver (D)	76,281	54.0
Robert M. L. Johnson (R)	65,079	46.0
3 H. R. Gross (R)	79,343	62.1
L. A. Touchae (D)	48,530	38.0
4 John Kyl (R)	65,259	51.7
Bert Bandstra (D)	61,074	48.3
5 Neal Smith (D)	72,875	60.4
Don Mahon (R)	46,981	39.0
6 Wiley Mayne (R)	73,274	57.4
Stanley L. Greigg (D)	53,917	42.3
7 William J. Scherle (R)	64,217	59.0
John R. Hansen (D)	44,529	40.9

KANSAS

Candidates	Votes	%
1 Bob Dole (R)	97,487	68.6
Berniece Henkle (D)	44,569	31.4
2 Chester L. Mize (R)	85,128	62.8
Harry Wiles (D)	50,336	37.2
3 Larry Winn Jr. (R)	60,107	52.9
Marvin E. Rainey (D)	51,108	45.0
4 Garner E. Shriver (R)	86,944	68.7
Paul H. Gerling (D)	39,625	31.3
5 Joe Skubitz (R)	86,944	60.9
Delno E. Bass (D)	55,933	39.2

KENTUCKY

Candidates	Votes	%
1 Frank A. Stubblefield (D)	57,736	70.6
Richard Nicholson (R)	24,085	29.4
2 William H. Natcher (D)	51,311	58.9
R. Douglas Ford (R)	35,770	41.1
3 William O. Cowger (R)	66,577	59.0
Norbert Blume (D)	46,240	41.0
4 M. G. (Gene) Snyder (R)	66,801	53.9
Frank Chelf (D)	56,902	46.0
5 Tim Lee Carter (R)	65,596	75.4
Eugene C. Harter (D)	21,452	24.6
6 John C. Watts (D)	58,182	65.1
William McKinley Hendren (R)	31,266	35.0
7 Carl D. Perkins (D)	65,522	68.9
C. F. See (R)	29,541	31.1

LOUISIANA

Candidates	Votes	%
1 F. Edward Hebert (D)	68,523	100.0
2 Hale Boggs (D)	90,149	68.6
Leonard L. Limes (R)	41,209	31.4
3 Edwin E. Willis (D)	46,533	59.7
Hall M. Lyons (R)	31,444	40.3
4 Joe D. Waggonner Jr. (D)	48,345	100.0
5 Otto E. Passman (D)	38,660	100.0
6 John R. Rarick (D)	86,958	76.6
Crayton G. Hall (R)	26,599	23.4
7 Edwin W. Edwards (D)	34,655	100.0
8 Speedy O. Long (D)	33,183	100.0

MAINE

Candidates	Votes	%
1 Peter N. Kyros (D)	81,302	50.4
Peter A. Garland (R)	72,984	45.2
2 William D. Hathaway (D)	85,956	56.8
Howard M. Foley (R)	65,476	43.2

MARYLAND

Candidates	Votes	%
1 Rogers C. B. Morton (R)	69,940	71.4
H. C. Byrd (D)	28,025	28.6
2 Clarence D. Long (D)	79,963	69.3
Paul T. McHenry Jr. (R)	35,476	30.7
3 Edward A. Garmatz (D)	56,980	100.0
4 George H. Fallon (D)	57,572	74.3
G. Neilson Sigler (R)	19,930	25.7
5 Hervey G. Machen (D)	55,676	53.9
Lawrence J. Hogan (R)	47,703	46.1
6 Charles McC. Mathias Jr. (R)	72,360	70.9
Walter G. Finch (D)	29,637	29.1
7 Samuel N. Friedel (D)	61,959	76.0
Stephen L. Rosenstein (R)	19,584	24.0
8 Gilbert Gude (R)	71,050	54.4
Royce Hanson (D)	59,568	45.6

MASSACHUSETTS

Candidates	Votes	%
1 Silvio O. Conte (R)	109,370	100.0
2 Edward P. Boland (D)	95,985	100.0
3 Philip J. Philbin (D)	126,664	71.0
Howard A. Miller (R)	51,646	29.0
4 Harold D. Donohue (D)	137,681	100.0
5 F. Bradford Morse (R)	140,702	74.8
Charles N. Tsapatsaris (D)	47,377	25.2
6 William H. Bates (R)	127,744	65.7
Daniel L. Parent (D)	66,675	34.3
7 Torbert H. Macdonald (D)	119,543	74.5
Gordon F. Hughes (R)	40,930	25.5
8 Thomas P. O'Neill Jr. (D)	102,104	100.0
9 John W. McCormack (D)	87,879	100.0
10 Margaret M. Heckler (R)	96,675	51.1
Patrick H. Harrington Jr. (D)	92,516	48.9
11 James A. Burke (D)	141,465	74.8
James L. Hofford (R)	47,705	25.2
12 Hastings Keith (R)	98,372	55.0
Edward F. Harrington (D)	80,473	45.0

MICHIGAN

Candidates	Votes	%
1 John Conyers (D)	89,908	84.2
Rhecha R. Ross (R)	16,853	15.8
2 Marvin L. Esch (R)	65,205	51.0
Weston E. Vivian (D)	62,536	49.0
3 Garry Brown (R)	68,912	52.3
Paul H. Todd Jr. (D)	62,984	47.8
4 Edward Hutchinson (R)	78,190	67.8
John V. Martin (D)	37,177	32.2
5 Gerald R. Ford (R)	88,108	68.5
James Mathew Catchick (D)	40,435	31.5
6 Charles E. Chamberlain (R)	85,669	67.3
Lee H. Wenke (D)	41,695	32.7
7 Donald W. Riegle Jr. (R)	71,166	54.1
John C. Mackie (D)	60,408	45.9
8 James Harvey (R)	85,657	69.9
Wager F. Clunis (D)	36,967	30.2
9 Guy Vander Jagt (R)	92,710	66.7
Henry J. Dongvillo (D)	46,266	33.3
10 Elford A. Cederberg (R)	85,754	67.4
Hubert C. Evans (D)	41,410	32.6
11 Phillip E. Ruppe (R)	70,820	51.8
Raymond F. Clevenger (D)	65,875	48.2
12 James G. O'Hara (D)	84,379	65.1
Patrick J. Driscoll (R)	45,199	34.9
13 Charles C. Diggs Jr. (D)	60,660	83.0
Frank Daniels (R)	12,393	17.0
14 Lucien N. Nedzi (D)	77,851	59.7
William J. Kennedy (R)	52,490	40.3
15 William D. Ford (D)	72,987	67.8
Arpo Yemen (R)	34,619	32.2
16 John D. Dingell Jr. (D)	71,787	62.7
John T. Dempsey (R)	42,738	37.3
17 Martha W. Griffiths (D)	90,541	69.2
William P. Harrington (R)	40,334	30.8
18 William S. Broomfield (R)	102,501	67.8
William H. Merrill (D)	48,627	32.2
19 Jack H. McDonald (R)	76,884	57.0
Billie S. Farnum (D)	57,907	43.0

Special Election

Candidates	Votes	%
9 Guy Vander Jagt (R)	91,056	66.6
Henry J. Dongvillo (D)	45,699	33.4

MINNESOTA

Candidates	Votes	%
1 Albert H. Quie (R)	109,312	65.9
George Daley (DFL)	56,547	34.1
2 Ancher Nelson (R)	93,855	66.2
Charles M. Christensen (DFL)	47,899	33.8

MINNESOTA

Candidates	Votes	%
3 Clark MacGregor (R)	122,775	65.4
Elva D. Walker (DFL)	64,861	34.6
4 Joseph Karth (DFL)	91,271	53.4
Stephan Maxwell (R)	79,667	46.6
5 Donald M. Fraser (DFL)	86,953	59.7
William Hathaway (R)	58,816	40.4
6 John M. Zwach (R)	80,710	51.4
Alec G. Olson (DFL)	76,439	48.6
7 Odin Langen (R)	84,914	63.2
Keith C. Davison (DFL)	49,388	36.8
8 John A. Blatnik (DFL)	116,969	100.0

MISSISSIPPI

Candidates	Votes	%
1 Thomas G. Abernethy (D)	47,359	68.8
W. B. Alexander (I)	14,700	21.4
Dock Drummond (I)	6,805	9.9
2 Jamie L. Whitten (D)	53,620	83.5
S. B. Wise (R)	10,622	16.5
3 John Bell Williams (D)	71,377	82.4
Emma Sanders (I)	15,218	17.6
4 G. V. (Sonny) Montgomery (D)	52,138	65.3
L. L. McAllister Jr. (R)	26,027	32.6
5 William M. Colmer (D)	58,080	70.0
James M. Moye (R)	24,865	30.0

MISSOURI

Candidates	Votes	%
1 Frank M. Karsten (D)	62,143	63.9
Robert L. Sharp (R)	35,053	36.1
2 Thomas B. Curtis (R)	102,985	66.2
William B. Milius (D)	52,527	33.8
3 Leonor K. Sullivan (D)	59,014	71.1
Homer McCracken (R)	23,953	28.9
4 William J. Randall (D)	54,330	60.9
Forest Nave Jr. (R)	34,952	39.2
5 Richard Bolling (D)	46,674	61.2
Willis Earl Salyers (R)	29,641	38.8
6 W. R. Hull Jr. (D)	55,418	58.0
John L. Leims (R)	40,185	42.0
7 Durward G. Hall (R)	86,626	62.3
Arch M. Skelton (D)	52,421	37.7
8 Richard Ichord (D)	61,128	58.1
Ben Rogers (R)	44,035	41.9
9 William L. Hungate (D)	68,472	55.3
Anthony C. Schroeder (R)	55,405	44.7
10 Paul C. Jones (D)	48,985	61.0
William Bruckerhoff (R)	31,263	39.0

MONTANA

Candidates	Votes	%
1 Arnold Olsen (D)	67,123	50.8
Richard Smiley (R)	64,925	49.2
2 James F. Battin (R)	76,015	60.2
John Melcher (D)	50,308	39.8

NEBRASKA

Candidates	Votes	%
1 Robert V. Denney (R)	93,628	51.2
Clair A. Callan (D)	89,363	48.8
2 Glenn Cunningham (R)	83,082	64.3
Richard Fellman (D)	46,235	35.8
3 David Martin (R)	115,893	73.0
John Homan (D)	42,920	27.0

NEVADA

Candidates	Votes	%
AL Walter S. Baring (D)	86,467	67.6
Ralph L. Kraemer (R)	41,383	32.4

NEW HAMPSHIRE

Candidates	Votes	%
1 Louis C. Wyman (R)	72,909	56.2
J. Oliva Huot (D)	56,750	43.8
2 James C. Cleveland (R)	66,176	66.7
William H. Barry Jr. (D)	32,838	33.1

NEW JERSEY

Candidates	Votes	%
1 John E. Hunt (R)	68,248	51.4
Michael J. Piarulli (D)	61,469	46.3
2 Charles W. Sandman Jr. (R)	72,014	51.5
Thomas C. McGrath Jr. (D)	65,494	46.9
3 James J. Howard (D)	81,382	52.7
James M. Coleman (R)	72,043	46.6
4 Frank Thompson Jr. (D)	82,271	56.2
Ralph Clark Chandler (R)	63,730	43.5
5 Peter H. B. Frelinghuysen (R)	108,375	70.8
Carter Jefferson (D)	41,476	27.1
6 William T. Cahill (R)	106,406	66.9
Walter Dubrow (D)	48,738	30.7
7 William B. Widnall (R)	101,253	66.4
Robert E. Hamer (D)	51,204	33.6
8 Charles S. Joelson (D)	80,725	59.6
Richard M. DeMarco (R)	51,784	38.2
9 Henry Helstoski (D)	74,320	50.9
Frank C. Osmers Jr. (R)	71,756	49.1
10 Peter W. Rodino Jr. (D)	71,699	64.3
Earl Harris (R)	36,508	32.7
11 Joseph G. Minish (D)	64,023	58.3
Leonard J. Felzenberg (R)	44,803	40.8
12 Florence P. Dwyer (R)	116,701	73.9
Robert F. Allen (D)	37,790	23.9
13 Cornelius E. Gallagher (D)	90,488	71.8
Ruth Swayze (R)	35,486	28.2
14 Dominick V. Daniels (D)	87,741	68.0
Thomas R. McSherry (R)	36,828	28.5
15 Edward J. Patten (D)	81,959	57.0
C. John Stroumtsos (R)	59,706	41.5

NEW MEXICO

Candidates	Votes	%
AL Thomas G. Morris (D)	140,057	55.9
Schuble C. Cook (R)	110,441	44.1
AL E. S. Johnny Walker (D)	126,984	50.5
Robert C. Davidson (R)	124,536	49.5

NEW YORK

Candidates	Votes	%
1 Otis G. Pike (D, L)	101,963	58.9
James M. Catterson Jr. (R)	58,296	33.7
Domenico Crachi Jr. (C)	12,731	7.4
2 James R. Grover Jr. (R)	79,649	54.7
Frank M. Corso (D, L)	49,743	34.1
Edward Campbell (C)	14,820	10.2
3 Lester L. Wolff (D, L)	81,959	50.3
Steven B. Derounian (R)	81,122	49.7
4 John W. Wydler (R)	86,677	59.7
Martin J. Steadman (D, L)	46,555	32.0
Donald H. Serrell (C)	10,035	6.9
5 Herbert Tenzer (D, L)	88,602	49.9
Thomas M. Brennan (R, C)	86,356	48.6
6 Seymour Halpern (R, L)	91,526	59.0
Gilbert T. Redleaf (D)	45,621	29.4
Ronald E. Weiss (C)	17,863	11.5
7 Joseph P. Addabbo (D, L)	93,758	64.9
Louis R. Mercogliano (R)	34,644	24.0
Raymond G. Carpenter (C)	16,070	11.1
8 Benjamin S. Rosenthal (D, L)	115,310	69.6
Thomas C. Gowlan (R)	36,573	22.1
Cyrus S. Julien (C)	13,726	8.3
9 James J. Delaney (D)	75,915	53.5
John F. Haggerty (R, C)	56,754	40.0
David Green (L)	9,182	6.5
10 Emanuel Celler (D, L)	76,439	82.1
Irwin A. Rosenberg (R)	16,702	17.9
11 Frank J. Brasco (D)	39,386	70.6
Benjamin W. Feldman (R)	12,200	21.9
Edward L. Johnson (L)	4,174	7.5
12 Edna F. Kelley (D, L)	87,651	72.7
Alfred Grant Walton (R)	29,390	24.4
13 Abraham J. Multer (D)	95,511	61.9
Mary Gravina (R)	28,750	18.6
Herschell Chanin (L)	20,557	13.3
Michael J. Spadaro (C)	9,463	6.1
14 John J. Rooney (D)	43,142	76.2
Leon F. Nadrowski (R)	13,482	23.8
15 Hugh L. Carey (D, U TAX)	52,919	56.8
Herbert F. Ryan (R, C)	40,181	43.2
16 John M. Murphy (D, L)	71,889	57.4
Frank J. Biondolillo (R, C)	53,346	42.6
17 Theodore R. Kupferman (R)	69,492	47.7
Jerome L. Wilson (D, L)	67,334	46.2
Richard J. Callahan (C)	8,818	6.1
18 Adam C. Powell (D)	45,308*	74.1
Lassen L. Walsh (R)	10,711	17.5
Richard Prideaux (L)	3,954	6.5
19 Leonard Farbstein (D)	53,581	57.8
Henry E. Del Rosso (R, C)	24,340	26.2
Elaine M. Morrison (L)	11,349	12.2
20 William F. Ryan (D, L)	74,215	74.8
Norman C. Harlowe (R)	20,560	20.7
21 James H. Scheuer (D, L)	63,173	83.6
Burton Siegel (R)	12,414	16.4
22 Jacob H. Gilbert (D)	40,787	74.2
Pedro Luis Rodriguez (R, ALL PP)	10,603	19.3
Carlos Rosario (L)	3,552	6.5
23 Jonathan B. Bingham (D, L)	84,540	73.4
Harold Grosberg (R)	21,735	18.9
Walter A. Quinn Jr. (C)	8,949	7.8
24 Paul A. Fino (R, C)	80,882	63.9
Aileen B. Ryan (D)	42,291	33.4
25 Richard L. Ottinger (D, L)	106,952	54.6
Frederick J. Martin Jr. (R)	88,769	45.4
26 Ogden R. Reid (R)	107,031	69.3
Joseph L. Hutner (D)	39,203	25.4
Albert M. Gants (C)	8,159	5.3
27 John G. Dow (D, L)	79,424	47.2
Louis V. Mills (R)	74,816	44.5
Frederick P. Roland (C)	13,946	8.3
28 Joseph Y. Resnick (D, L)	84,940	50.3
Hamilton Fish Jr. (R)	78,258	46.3
29 Daniel E. Button (R, L)	107,671	53.3
Richard J. Conners (D)	91,174	45.1
30 Carleton J. King (R)	113,759	65.0
John S. Hall (D, L)	61,216	35.0
31 Robert C. McEwen (R)	75,680	67.6
Raymond E. Bishop (D, L)	36,273	32.4
32 Alexander Pirnie (R, L)	94,331	72.3
Robert Castle (R)	36,195	27.7
33 Howard W. Robison (R)	88,378	65.7
Blair G. Ewing (D, L)	45,761	34.0
34 James M. Hanley (D)	90,044	55.1
Stewart F. Hancock Jr. (R)	62,559	38.3
35 Samuel S. Stratton (D, L)	93,746	65.8
Frederick D. Dugan (R)	48,668	34.2
36 Frank J. Horton (R)	110,514	67.3
Milo Thomas (D)	37,129	22.6
Robert H. Detig (C)	10,493	6.4
37 Barber B. Conable Jr (R)	104,342	67.7
Kenneth Hed (D)	46,201	30.0
38 Charles E. Goodell (R)	82,137	67.2
Edison Leroy Jr (D)	35,785	29.3
39 Richard D. McCarthy (D, L)	95,671	52.3
John R. Pillion (R, C)	87,230	47.7
40 Henry P. Smith III (R)	85,801	61.2
William Levitt (D, L)	54,303	38.8
41 Thaddeus J. Dulski (D, L)	92,222	76.4
Frank X. Schwab (R, C)	28,491	23.6

Special Election

Candidates	Votes	%
17 Theodore R. Kupferman (R)	44,125	46.4
Orin Lehman (D)	43,206	45.4
Jeffrey St. John (C)	7,796	8.2

NORTH CAROLINA

Candidates	Votes	%
1 Walter B. Jones (D)	43,539	61.4
John P. East (R)	27,434	38.7
2 L. H. Fountain (D)	36,849	65.0
Reece B. Gardiner (R)	19,888	35.1
3 David N. Henderson (D)	33,809	100.0
4 James C. Gardner (D)	60,686	56.5
Harold D. Cooley (D)	46,673	43.5
5 Nick Galifianakis (D)	46,035	53.1
G. Fred Steele Jr. (R)	40,729	46.9
6 Horace R. Kornegay (D)	42,677	51.6
Richard B. Barnwell (R)	40,000	48.4
7 Alton Lennon (D)	40,512	100.0
8 Charles Raper Jonas (R)	56,382	71.5
John G. Plumides (D)	22,465	28.5
9 James T. Broyhill (R)	80,989	63.3
Robert Bingham (D)	46,882	36.7
10 Basil L. Whitener (D)	52,117	56.1
W. Hall Young (R)	40,741	43.9
11 Roy A. Taylor (D)	72,855	52.8
W. Scott Harvey (R)	65,187	47.2

Special Election

1 Walter B. Jones (D)	21,773	60.3
John P. East (R)	14,308	39.7

NORTH DAKOTA

1 Mark Andrews (R)	66,011	66.2
S. F. (Buckshot) Hoffner (D)	33,694	33.8
2 Thomas S. Kleppe (R)	50,801	52.0
Rolland Redlin (D)	46,993	48.1

OHIO

1 Robert Taft Jr. (R)	70,366	52.9
John J. Gilligan (D)	62,580	47.1
2 Donald D. Clancy (R)	102,313	70.7
Thomas E. Anderson (D)	42,367	29.3
3 Charles W. Whalen Jr. (R)	62,471	53.8
Rodney M. Love (D)	53,658	46.2
4 William M. McCulloch (R)	66,142	63.6
Robert H. Mihlbaugh (D)	37,855	36.4
5 Delbert L. Latta (R)	80,906	75.3
John H. Shock (D)	26,503	24.7
6 William H. Harsha (R)	74,847	67.9
Ottie W. Reno (D)	35,345	32.1
7 Clarence J. Brown Jr. (R)	81,225	100.0
8 Jackson E. Betts (R)	78,933	67.1
Frank B. Bennett (D)	38,787	33.0
9 Thomas L. Ashley (D)	83,261	60.8
Jane M. Kuebbeler (R)	53,777	39.2
10 Clarence E. Miller (R)	56,659	52.0
Walter H. Moeller (D)	52,258	48.0
11 J. William Stanton (R)	86,273	69.3
James F. Henderson (D)	38,206	30.7
12 Samuel L. Devine (R)	70,102	64.2
Robert N. Shamansky (D)	39,140	35.8
13 Charles A. Mosher (R)	69,862	65.5
Thomas E. Wolfe (D)	36,751	34.5
14 William H. Ayres (R)	77,819	59.7
Charles F. Madden Jr. (D)	52,646	40.4
15 Chalmers P. Wylie (R)	57,993	59.9
Robert L. Van Heyde (D)	38,805	40.1
16 Frank T. Bow (R)	87,597	61.1
Robert D. Freeman (D)	55,775	38.9
17 John M. Ashbrook (R)	73,132	55.3
Robert T. Secrest (D)	59,031	44.7
18 Wayne L. Hays (D)	73,657	64.2
William H. Weir (R)	41,165	35.9
19 Michael J. Kirwan (D)	86,975	71.9
Donald J. Lewis (R)	34,037	28.1
20 Michael A. Feighan (D)	63,629	76.1
Clarence E. McLeod (R)	20,034	24.0
21 Charles A. Vanik (D)	81,210	81.7
Frederick M. Coleman (R)	18,205	18.3

Candidates	Votes	%
22 Frances P. Bolton (R)	71,927	55.9
Anthony O. Calabrese Jr. (D)	56,803	44.1
23 William E. Minshall (R)	102,513	73.2
Sheldon D. Clark (D)	37,489	26.8
24 Donald E. Lukens (R)	61,194	58.5
James H. Pelley (D)	43,418	41.5

OKLAHOMA

1 Page Belcher (R)	106,259	69.7
Ed Cadenhead (D)	46,286	30.3
2 Ed Edmondson (D)	62,324	53.6
Denzil D. Garrison (R)	53,919	46.4
3 Carl Albert (D)	43,049	77.2
Whit Pate (R)	12,697	22.8
4 Tom Steed (D)	36,719	50.3
Truman T. Branscum (R)	36,355	49.8
5 John Jarman (D)	96,464	69.6
Melvin H. Gragg (R)	42,088	30.4
6 James V. Smith (R)	51,474	51.4
Jed Johnson Jr. (D)	48,755	48.6

OREGON

1 Wendell Wyatt (R)	144,361	74.3
Malcolm H. Cross (D)	49,841	25.7
2 Al Ullman (D)	94,346	63.3
Everett J. Thoren (R)	54,789	36.7
3 Edith Green (D)	114,687	66.9
Lyle Dean (R)	56,598	33.0
4 John R. Dellenback (R)	94,154	62.7
Charles O. Porter (D)	56,007	37.3

PENNSYLVANIA

1 William A. Barrett (D)	90,100	66.1
Beatrice K. Chernock (R)	46,280	33.9
2 Robert N. C. Nix (D)	76,372	59.9
Herbert R. Cain Jr. (R)	51,079	40.1
3 James A. Byrne (D)	64,575	56.6
Walter T. Darmopray (R)	49,434	43.4
4 Joshua Eilberg (D)	98,793	51.9
Robert Baer Cohen (R)	91,620	48.1
5 William J. Green III (D)	86,128	59.1
Michael J. Bednarek (R)	59,515	40.9
6 George M. Rhodes (D)	91,538	56.1
Daniel B. Boyer (R)	71,508	43.9
7 Lawrence G. Williams (R)	101,042	63.2
John J. Logue (D)	58,766	36.8
8 Edward G. Biester Jr. (R)	70,435	59.6
Walter S. Farley Jr. (D)	47,845	40.5
9 G. Robert Watkins (R)	81,516	62.6
Louis F. Waldmann (D)	48,656	37.4
10 Joseph M. McDade (R)	115,765	66.8
Neil Trama (D)	57,615	33.2
11 Daniel J. Flood (D)	110,877	67.2
Gerald C. Broadt (R)	54,032	32.8
12 J. Irving Whalley (R)	107,374	66.9
J. Robert Rohm (D)	53,044	33.1
13 Richard S. Schweiker (R)	134,414	72.5
William D. Searle (D)	51,024	27.5
14 William S. Moorhead (D)	83,967	68.3
Richard L. Thornburgh (R)	39,024	31.7
15 Fred B. Rooney (D)	80,407	52.3
George J. Joseph (R)	73,404	47.7
16 Edwin D. Eshleman (R)	82,527	69.2
Richard F. Charles (D)	36,721	30.8
17 Herman T. Schneebeli (R)	109,169	66.2
William Conrad Reuter (D)	55,761	33.8
18 Robert J. Corbett (R)	107,677	67.1
John R. Wohlfarth (D)	52,714	32.9
19 George A. Goodling (R)	70,445	51.7
N. Neiman Craley Jr. (D)	65,907	48.3
20 Elmer J. Holland (D)	93,068	65.9
Joseph Sabol Jr. (R)	48,229	34.1
21 John H. Dent (D)	80,472	64.2
Edward B. Byrne (R)	44,800	35.8

Candidates	Votes	%
22 John P. Saylor (R)	103,808	67.5
Frank H. Buck (D)	50,017	32.5
23 Albert W. Johnson (R)	81,658	62.8
Robert W. Mitchell (D)	48,373	37.2
24 Joseph P. Vigorito (D)	85,193	55.3
James D. Weaver (R)	68,955	44.7
25 Frank M. Clark (D)	92,073	64.5
John F. Heath (R)	50,639	35.5
26 Thomas E. Morgan (D)	83,687	64.1
Paul P. Riggle (R)	46,957	35.9
27 James G. Fulton (R)	108,731	67.7
Stephen J. Arnold (D)	51,928	32.3

RHODE ISLAND

1 Fernand J. St.Germain (D)	79,046	56.6
Raymond W. Houghton (R)	60,093	43.0
2 John E. Fogarty (D)	117,911	64.7
Everett C. Sammartino (R)	64,438	35.3

SOUTH CAROLINA

1 L. Mendel Rivers (D)	59,055	100.0
2 Albert W. Watson (R)	48,742	64.3
Fred Leclercq (D)	27,013	35.7
3 William J. Bryan Dorn (D)	42,834	57.8
John Grisso (R)	31,331	42.2
4 Robert T. Ashmore (D)	43,611	100.0
5 Thomas S. Gettys (D)	41,550	99.2
6 John L. McMillan (D)	43,090	61.7
Archie C. Odom (R)	26,702	38.3

SOUTH DAKOTA

1 Ben Reifel (R)	80,592	66.7
Francis C. Richter (D)	40,236	33.3
2 E. Y. Berry (R)	63,063	60.5
Jack Allmon (D)	41,155	39.5

TENNESSEE

1 James A. Quillen (R)	86,421	87.1
Temus Bright (I)	12,819	12.9
2 John J. Duncan (R)	87,771	78.9
Jake Armstrong (D)	23,538	21.2
3 Bill Brock (R)	67,705	64.2
Franklin Haney (D)	37,720	35.8
4 Joe L. Evins (D)	72,621	90.0
William Bean (I)	8,061	10.0
5 Richard H. Fulton (D)	55,685	63.0
George Kelly (R)	32,706	37.0
6 William R. Anderson (D)	50,758	79.6
Cecil Hill (I)	12,987	20.4
7 Ray Blanton (D)	45,083	50.6
Julius Hurst (R)	43,118	48.4
8 Robert A. Everett (D)	53,338	75.2
Jim Boyd (R)	17,608	24.8
9 Dan H. Kuykendall (R)	47,489	52.2
George W. Grider (D)	43,553	47.8

TEXAS

1 Wright Patman (D)	50,072	100.0
2 John Dowdy (D)	55,134	99.9
3 Joe Pool (D)	35,081	53.4
James M. Collins (R)	30,588	46.6
4 Ray Roberts (D)	51,895	100.0
5 Earle Cabell (D)	39,977	61.0
Duke Burgess (R)	25,563	39.0
6 Olin Teague (D)	42,017	100.0
7 George Bush (R)	53,756	57.1
Frank Briscoe (D)	39,958	42.4
8 Bob Eckhardt (D)	38,497	92.3
W. D. Spayne (CONST)	3,207	7.7
9 Jack Brooks (D)	47,604	100.0
10 J. J. Pickle (D)	55,424	74.3
Jane Sumner (R)	18,343	24.6

TEXAS

Candidates	Votes	%
11 W. R. Poage (D)	39,140	94.9
Laurel N. Dunn (C)	2,102	5.1
12 Jim Wright (D)	27,070	100.0
13 Graham Purcell (D)	43,820	57.1
D. C. Norwood (R)	32,960	42.9
14 John Young (D)	52,861	100.0
15 Eligio de la Garza (D)	33,129	100.0
16 Richard C. White (D)	33,179	100.0
17 Omar Burleson (D)	52,169	100.0
18 Bob Price (R)	45,209	59.5
Dee D. Miller (D)	30,822	40.5
19 George Mahon (D)	56,792	100.0
20 Henry Gonzalez (D)	41,067	87.1
Robert C. Moore (C)	3,671	7.8
Bert Ellis (CONST)	2,390	5.1
21 O. C. Fisher (D)	60,497	100.0
22 Bob Casey (D)	60,817	100.0
23 Abraham Kazen (D)	50,322	96.4

Special Election

	Votes	%
8 Lera M. Thomas (D)	6,120#	74.0
Louis Leman (R)	2,147#	26.0

UTAH

	Votes	%
1 Laurence J. Burton (R)	99,750	66.5
J. Keith Melville (D)	50,260	33.5
2 Sherman P. Lloyd (R)	96,426	61.3
David S. King (D)	61,001	38.8

VERMONT

	Votes	%
AL Robert T. Stafford (R)	89,097	65.6
William J. Ryan (D)	46,643	34.4

VIRGINIA

Candidates	Votes	%
1 Thomas N. Downing (D)	51,016	99.8
2 Porter Hardy Jr. (D)	33,761	100.0
3 David E. Satterfield III (D)	51,576	99.6
4 Watkins M. Abbitt (D)	45,226	66.6
Edward J. Silverman (C)	14,827	21.8
5 William M. Tuck (D)	32,312	56.2
Robert L. Gilliam (R)	25,203	43.8
6 Richard H. Poff (R)	55,342	80.8
Murray A. Stoller (D)	13,113	19.2
7 John O. Marsh Jr. (D)	42,532	59.2
Edward O. McCue (R)	29,249	40.7
8 William Lloyd Scott (R)	50,782	57.2
George C. Rawlings Jr (D)	37,929	42.8
9 William C. Wampler (R)	49,413	53.7
W. Pat Jennings (D)	42,571	46.3
10 Joel T. Broyhill (R)	58,105	58.3
Clive L. Duval II (D)	41,502	41.7

WASHINGTON

	Votes	%
1 Thomas M. Pelly (R)	120,747	80.3
Alice Franklin Bryant (D)	29,686	19.7
2 Lloyd Meeds (D)	75,357	60.7
Eugene M. Smith (R)	44,727	36.0
3 Julia Butler Hansen (D)	78,601	65.8
Keith Kisor (R)	40,946	34.3
4 Catherine May (R)	77,929	62.1
Gustav Bansmer (D)	38,029	30.3
Floyd Paxton (C)	9,585	7.6
5 Thomas S. Foley (D)	74,571	56.5
Dorothy R. Powers (R)	57,310	43.5
6 Floyd V. Hicks (D)	73,164	60.4
George Mahler (R)	48,041	39.6
7 Brock Adams (D)	104,613	62.8
James Munn (R)	60,065	36.0

WEST VIRGINIA

Candidates	Votes	%
1 Arch A. Moore Jr. (R)	88,364	70.9
William M. Kidd (D)	36,242	29.1
2 Harley O. Staggers (D)	51,235	60.3
George L. Strader (R)	33,676	39.7
3 John M. Slack (D)	60,073	61.6
Mal Guthrie (R)	37,416	38.4
4 Ken Hechler (D)	71,751	59.7
Harry D. Humphreys (R)	48,396	40.3
5 James Kee (D)	42,722	63.6
Elizabeth Ann Bowen (R)	24,470	36.4

WISCONSIN

	Votes	%
1 Henry C. Schadeberg (R)	65,041	51.0
Lynn E. Stalbaum (D)	62,398	49.0
2 Robert W. Kastenmeier (D)	70,311	58.0
William B. Smith (R)	50,850	42.0
3 Vernon W. Thomson (R)	72,586	68.8
John D. Rice (D)	32,849	31.2
4 Clement J. Zablocki (D)	77,690	74.3
James E. Laessig (R)	26,863	25.7
5 Henry S. Reuss (D)	52,332	70.0
Curtis T. Pechtel (R)	22,167	29.7
6 William A. Steiger (R)	67,941	52.4
John A. Race (D)	61,761	47.6
7 Melvin R. Laird (R)	74,942	65.2
Norman L. Myhra (D)	40,093	34.9
8 John W. Byrnes (R)	75,817	61.3
Marvin S. Kagen (D)	47,926	38.7
9 Glenn R. Davis (R)	85,297	64.1
James P. Buckley (D)	47,674	35.9
10 Alvin E. O'Konski (R)	79,282	66.5
Carl E. Lauri (D)	39,863	33.5

WYOMING

	Votes	%
AL William Henry Harrison (R)	62,984	52.3
Al Christian (D)	57,442	47.7

1967 House Elections

CALIFORNIA

Special Primary Election [1]

	Votes	%
11 Paul N. McCloskey Jr. (R)	52,882	34.3
Shirley Temple Black (R)	34,521	22.4
William H. Draper III (R)	19,566	12.7
Roy Archibald (D)	15,069	9.8
Earl B. Whitmore (R)	12,823	8.3
Edward M. Keating (D)	8,813	5.7

Special Election

	Votes	%
11 Paul N. McCloskey Jr. (R)	66,385#	57.8
Roy Archibald (D)	44,319#	38.6

NEW YORK

Special Election [2]

	Votes	%
18 Adam C. Powell (D)	27,963#	86.3
Lucille P. Williams (R)	3,999#	12.3

RHODE ISLAND

Special Election

	Votes	%
2 Robert O. Tiernan (D)	56,051#	48.8
James DiPrete (R)	55,748#	48.5

1. Under California's special election law, a majority of the total vote cast was required for election. If no candidate achieved it, another election would be held with the top candidates from each party competing. In the 11th District, McCloskey had more votes than any other Republican, but not a majority of the total vote, so he became the Republican nominee against Archibald, the top Democrat, in the special election.

2. Following his re-election to the 90th Congress (1967-69) in 1966, Powell was not allowed to take the oath of office in January 1967 and was subsequently excluded by vote of the House March 1, 1967. A special election was held April 11, 1967, to fill the vacancy. Powell was again a candidate and won easily, but he never attempted to claim the seat and it remained vacant for the remainder of the Congress.

1968 House Elections

ALABAMA

	Candidates	Votes	%
1	Jack Edwards (R)	60,318	57.1
	Arnold Debrow (D)	40,593	38.4
	Richard Boone (NDPA)	11,446	10.4
2	William L. Dickinson (R)	60,743	55.4
	Robert Whaley (D)	37,533	34.2
3	George Andrews (D)	86,796	90.8
	Wilbur Johnston (NDPA)	8,031	8.4
4	Bill Nichols (D)	94,726	81.4
	Robert Kerr (R)	12,427	10.7
	T. Clemons (NDPA)	9,248	7.9
5	Walter Flowers (D)	69,110	56.2
	William McKinley Branch (NDPA)	28,040	22.8
	Frank Donaldson (R)	14,582	11.9
	Mike Simpson (I)	9,429	7.7
6	John Buchanan (R)	69,445	59.3
	Quinton Bowers (D)	34,608	29.6
	Thomas Wrenn (NDPA)	12,976	11.1
7	Tom Bevill (D)	106,132	76.1
	Jodie Connell (R)	29,923	21.5
8	Robert E. Jones (D)	85,528	76.1
	Ken Hearn (C)	16,900	15.0
	Charlie Burgess (NDPA)	7,140	6.4

ALASKA

	Candidates	Votes	%
AL	Howard W. Pollock (R)	43,577	54.2
	Nick Begich (D)	36,785	45.8

ARIZONA

	Candidates	Votes	%
1	John J. Rhodes (R)	137,761	71.6
	Robert E. Miller (D)	54,594	28.4
2	Morris K. Udall (D)	102,301	70.3
	G. Alfred McGinnis (R)	43,235	29.7
3	Sam Steiger (R)	79,667	63.4
	Ralph Watkins Jr. (D)	46,072	36.6

ARKANSAS

	Candidates	Votes	%
1	Bill Alexander (D)	80,293	68.9
	Guy Newcomb (R)	36,284	31.1
2	Wilbur D. Mills (D)		100.0
3	John Paul Hammerschmidt (R)	121,771	67.1
	Hardy Croxton (D)	59,642	32.9
4	David Pryor (D)		100.0

CALIFORNIA

	Candidates	Votes	%
1	Don H. Clausen (R)	133,597	75.2
	Donald W. Graham (D)	37,756	21.3
2	Harold T. Johnson (D)	127,744	60.7
	Osmer E. Dunaway (R)	78,986	37.6
3	John E. Moss (D)	107,446	56.0
	Elmore J. Duffy (R)	80,193	41.8
4	Robert L. Leggett (D)	90,126	55.6
	James M. Shumway (R)	67,225	41.5
5	Phillip Burton (D)	95,630	72.8
	Waldo Velasquez (R)	31,157	23.7
6	William S. Mailliard (R)	151,336	73.4
	Phillip Drath (D)	54,928	26.6
7	Jeffery Cohelan (D)	102,689	62.9
	Barney E. Hilburn (R)	48,397	29.6
	Huey P. Newton (PFP)	12,279	7.5
8	George P. Miller (D)	104,768	64.0
	Raymond P. Britton (R)	58,887	36.0
9	Don Edwards (D)	101,329	56.6
	Larry Fargher (R)	77,847	43.5
10	Charles S. Gubser (R)	160,563	67.3
	Grayson S. Taketa (D)	73,720	30.9
11	Paul N. McCloskey Jr. (R)	166,252	79.4
	Urban G. Whitaker (D)	40,957	19.6

	Candidates	Votes	%
12	Burt L. Talcott (R)	143,222	92.6
13	Charles M. Teague (R)	151,608	65.9
	Stanley K. Sheinbaum (D)	78,628	34.2
14	Jerome R. Waldie (D)	152,847	71.6
	David W. Schuh (R)	56,730	26.6
15	John J. McFall (D)	86,386	53.8
	Sam Van Dyken (R)	74,058	46.2
16	B. F. Sisk (D)	97,476	62.5
	Dave Harris (R)	55,188	35.4
17	Glenn M. Anderson (D)	77,250	50.7
	Joe Blatchford (R)	73,351	48.1
18	Robert B. Mathias (R)	100,115	65.2
	Harlan Hagen (D)	51,373	33.5
19	Chet Holifield (D)	99,069	63.1
	Bill Jones (R)	53,842	34.3
20	H. Allen Smith (R)	136,238	69.4
	Don White (D)	57,064	29.1
21	Augustus F. Hawkins (D)	89,536	91.6
	Rayfield Lundy (R)	8,244	8.4
22	James C. Corman (D)	103,695	56.9
	Joe Holt (R)	75,457	41.4
23	Del Clawson (R)	97,232	65.1
	Jim Sperrazzo (D)	52,202	34.9
24	Glenard P. Lipscomb (R)	155,443	72.8
	Fred W. Neal (D)	57,972	27.2
25	Charles E. Wiggins (R)	145,245	68.7
	Keith F. Shirey (D)	66,263	31.3
26	Thomas M. Rees (D)	134,642	65.4
	Irving Teichner (R)	64,505	31.4
27	Ed Reinecke (R)	162,854	72.2
	John T. Butchko (D)	62,824	27.8
28	Alphonzo Bell (R)	173,680	71.3
	John M. Pratt (D)	65,233	26.8
29	George E. Brown Jr. (D)	76,091	52.3
	Bill Orozco (R)	69,485	47.7
30	Edward R. Roybal (D)	76,967	67.4
	Samuel M. Cavnar (R)	37,234	32.6
31	Charles H. Wilson (D)	97,855	58.9
	James R. Dunn (R)	65,004	39.1
32	Craig Hosmer (R)	142,401	73.9
	Arthur J. Gottlieb (D)	46,404	24.1
33	Jerry L. Pettis (R)	123,507	66.3
	Al C. Ballard (D)	59,649	32.0
34	Richard T. Hanna (D)	107,113	50.9
	William J. Teague (R)	103,470	49.1
35	James B. Utt (R)	216,093	72.5
	Thomas B. Lenhart (D)	74,798	25.1
36	Bob Wilson (R)	148,854	71.6
	Don Lindgren (D)	59,011	28.4
37	Lionel Van Deerlin (D)	96,130	64.7
	Mike Schaefer (R)	52,547	35.3
38	John V. Tunney (D)	121,749	62.7
	Robert O. Hunter (R)	68,887	35.5

COLORADO

	Candidates	Votes	%
1	Byron G. Rogers (D)	91,199	45.7
	Frank A. Kemp (R)	82,677	41.5
	Gordon G. Barnewall (DENVER I)	25,499	12.8
2	Donald G. Brotzman (R)	152,153	62.9
	Roy H. McVicker (D)	89,917	37.2
3	Frank E. Evans (D)	88,368	52.1
	Paul Bradley (R)	81,173	47.9
4	Wayne N. Aspinall (D)	92,680	54.7
	Fred E. Anderson (R)	76,776	45.3

CONNECTICUT

	Candidates	Votes	%
1	Emilio Q. Daddario (D)	124,966	62.4
	Roger B. Ladd (R)	74,615	37.3
2	William L. St.Onge (D)	106,203	54.1
	Peter P. Mariani (R)	89,098	45.4
3	Robert Giaimo (D)	102,636	54.0
	Stelio Salmona (R)	80,696	42.5

	Candidates	Votes	%
4	Lowell P. Weicker Jr. (R)	113,749	51.4
	Donald J. Irwin (D)	104,723	47.3
5	John S. Monagan (D)	110,337	56.3
	Gaetano A. Russo Jr. (R)	85,591	43.7
6	Thomas J. Meskill (R)	126,208	62.3
	Robert M. Sharaf (D)	76,413	37.7

DELAWARE

	Candidates	Votes	%
AL	William V. Roth (R)	117,827	58.7
	Harris B. McDowell Jr. (D)	82,993	41.3

FLORIDA

	Candidates	Votes	%
1	Robert L. F. Sikes (D)	116,215	84.7
	John Drzazga (R)	21,063	15.3
2	Don Fuqua (D)	87,313	100.0
3	Charles E. Bennett (D)	103,540	78.9
	Bill Parsons (R)	27,696	21.1
4	Bill Chappell Jr. (D)	86,251	52.8
	William F. Herlong Jr. (R)	76,974	47.2
5	Louis Frey (R)	108,620	61.7
	James C. Robinson (D)	67,505	38.3
6	Sam M. Gibbons (D)	84,193	62.0
	Paul A. Saad (R)	51,637	38.0
7	James A. Haley (D)	91,539	55.0
	Joe Z. Lovingood (R)	74,896	45.0
8	William C. Cramer (R)	117,741	100.0
9	Paul G. Rogers (D)	111,539	56.2
	Robert W. Rust (R)	87,074	43.8
10	J. Herbert Burke (R)	99,844	54.9
	Elton J. Gissendanner (D)	82,138	45.1
11	Claude Pepper (D)	99,154	76.6
	Ronald I. Strauss (R)	30,324	23.4
12	Dante B. Fascell (D)	82,362	57.0
	Mike Thompson (R)	62,032	43.0

GEORGIA

	Candidates	Votes	%
1	G. Elliott Hagan (D)	77,403	68.2
	Joseph J. Tribble (R)	36,118	31.8
2	Maston O'Neal (D)	72,830	100.0
3	Jack Brinkley (D)	55,759	100.0
4	Ben B. Blackburn (R)	78,753	57.5
	James A. Mackay (D)	58,154	42.5
5	Fletcher Thompson (R)	79,258	55.6
	Charles L. Weltner (D)	63,183	44.4
6	John J. Flynt Jr. (D)	97,289	100.0
7	John W. Davis (D)	96,505	99.8
8	W. S. Stuckey Jr. (D)	64,912	100.0
9	Phil M. Landrum (D)	83,829	100.0
10	Robert G. Stephens (D)	80,674	100.0

HAWAII

	Candidates	Votes	%
AL	Spark M. Matsunaga (D)	161,954✔	
	Patsy T. Mink (D)	149,207✔	
	Neal S. Blaisdell (R)	78,733	
	George Dubois (R)	39,233	
	Jon D. Olsen (PFP)	2,432	
	Peter O. Lombardi (PFP)	2,026	

IDAHO

	Candidates	Votes	%
1	James A. McClure (R)	90,870	59.4
	Compton I. White (D)	62,002	40.6
2	Orval Hansen (R)	65,029	52.6
	Darrell Manning (D)	54,256	43.9

ILLINOIS

Candidates	Votes	%
1 William L. Dawson (D)	119,207	84.6
Janet Roberts Jenning (R)	21,758	15.4
2 Abner J. Mikva (D)	106,642	65.4
Thomas R. Ireland (R)	56,513	34.6
3 William T. Murphy (D)	101,729	54.0
Robert A. Podesta (R)	86,535	46.0
4 Edward J. Derwinski (R)	151,216	68.3
Robert E. Creighton (D)	70,145	31.7
5 John C. Kluczynski (D)	96,584	55.4
Joseph J. Krasowski (R)	77,887	44.6
6 Daniel J. Ronan (D)	94,779	59.7
Gerald Dolezal (R)	63,999	40.3
7 Frank Annunzio (D)	86,769	83.1
Thomas J. Lento (R)	17,594	16.9
8 Daniel Rostenkowski (D)	105,003	62.8
Henry S. Kaplinski (R)	62,254	37.2
9 Sidney R. Yates (D)	119,032	64.4
Edward V. Notz (R)	65,687	35.6
10 Harold R. Collier (R)	148,398	66.8
Seymour C. Axelrood (D)	73,766	33.2
11 Roman C. Pucinski (D)	128,152	55.8
John J. Hoellen (R)	101,665	44.2
12 Robert McClory (R)	120,370	70.4
Albert S. Salvi (D)	50,525	29.6
13 Donald Rumsfeld (R)	186,714	72.7
David C. Baylor (D)	69,987	27.3
14 John N. Erlenborn (R)	163,332	71.1
Marc Karson (D)	66,293	28.9
15 Charlotte T. Reid (R)	121,432	68.7
Benjamin P. Alschuler (D)	55,291	31.3
16 John B. Anderson (R)	111,037	67.4
Stan Major (D)	53,838	32.7
17 Leslie C. Arends (R)	122,513	65.3
Lester A. Hawthorne (D)	65,192	34.7
18 Robert H. Michel (R)	106,122	60.9
James G. Hatcher (D)	68,173	39.1
19 Tom Railsback (R)	114,948	63.5
Craig Lovitt (D)	66,135	36.5
20 Paul Findley (R)	124,121	66.2
Donald L. Schilson (D)	63,412	33.8
21 Kenneth J. Gray (D)	111,425	54.2
Val Oshel (R)	94,363	45.9
22 William L. Springer (R)	115,258	64.3
Carl F. Firley (D)	63,957	35.7
23 George E. Shipley (D)	104,349	54.0
Bert Hopper (R)	88,945	46.0
24 Melvin Price (D)	113,507	71.3
John S. Guthrie (R)	45,649	28.7

INDIANA

	Votes	%
1 Ray J. Madden (D)	90,055	56.7
Donald E. Taylor (R)	68,318	43.0
2 Earl F. Landgrebe (R)	104,238	55.1
Edward F. Kelly (D)	85,084	44.9
3 John Brademas (D)	94,452	52.2
William W. Erwin (R)	86,354	47.8
4 E. Ross Adair (R)	98,977	51.4
J. Edward Roush (D)	93,515	48.6
5 Richard L. Roudebush (R)	114,531	63.0
Robert C. Ford (R)	67,370	37.0
6 William G. Bray (R)	142,207	64.9
Phillip L. Bayt (D)	76,940	35.1
7 John T. Myers (R)	115,921	59.8
Elden C. Tipton (D)	78,045	40.2
8 Roger H. Zion (R)	109,585	54.5
K. Wayne Kent (D)	91,642	45.5
9 Lee H. Hamilton (D)	102,707	54.4
Robert D. Garton (R)	86,012	45.6
10 David W. Dennis (R)	98,090	53.9
William J. Norton (D)	83,981	46.1
11 Andrew Jacobs Jr. (D)	80,015	53.1
W. W. Hill Jr. (R)	70,725	46.9

IOWA

	Votes	%
1 Fred Schwengel (R)	91,419	53.0
John R. Schmidhauser (D)	81,049	47.0

Candidates	Votes	%
2 John C. Culver (D)	103,651	55.1
Tom Riley (R)	84,634	45.0
3 H. R. Gross (R)	101,839	64.1
John E. Van Eschen (D)	57,164	36.0
4 John Kyl (R)	83,259	53.9
Bert Bandstra (D)	71,134	46.1
5 Neal Smith (D)	99,586	62.1
Don Mahon (R)	60,710	37.9
6 Wiley Mayne (R)	100,802	65.0
Jerry O'Sullivan (D)	54,171	35.0
7 William Scherle (R)	86,212	64.8
Richard Oshlo (D)	46,774	35.2

KANSAS

	Votes	%
1 Keith G. Sebelius (R)	87,012	51.5
George W. Meeker (D)	82,102	48.6
2 Chester L. Mize (R)	110,768	67.6
Robert A. Swan (D)	53,151	32.4
3 Larry Winn (R)	100,877	62.8
Newell A. George (D)	59,672	37.2
4 Garner E. Shriver (R)	101,991	64.7
Patrick F. Kelly (D)	55,621	35.3
5 Joe Skubitz (R)	107,085	64.5
A. F. Bramble (D)	59,005	35.5

KENTUCKY

	Votes	%
1 Frank A. Stubblefield (D)	72,072	100.0
2 William H. Natcher (D)	65,860	56.4
Robert D. Simmons (R)	50,904	43.6
3 William O. Cowger (R)	70,318	56.0
Tom Ray (D)	55,366	44.1
4 M. G. (Gene) Snyder (R)	103,793	65.0
Gus Sheehan (D)	55,971	35.0
5 Tim Lee Carter (R)	86,391	72.8
Thomas J. Roberts (D)	30,575	25.8
6 John C. Watts (D)	78,536	56.5
Russell G. Mobley (R)	58,905	42.4
7 Carl D. Perkins (D)	82,594	62.0
James D. Nickell (R)	50,699	38.0

LOUISIANA

	Votes	%
1 F. Edward Hebert (D)	70,658	100.0
2 Hale Boggs (D)	81,537	51.2
David C. Treen (R)	77,633	48.8
3 Patrick T. Caffery (D)	39,215	100.0
4 Joe D. Waggonner Jr. (D)	63,788	100.0
5 Otto E. Passman (D)	34,901	100.0
6 John R. Rarick (D)	100,461	79.5
Loyd J. Rockhold (R)	25,867	20.5
7 Edwin W. Edwards (D)	79,709	85.0
Vance W. Plauche (R)	14,126	15.1
8 Speedy O. Long (D)	41,086	100.0

MAINE

	Votes	%
1 Peter N. Kyros (D)	113,501	56.6
Horace A. Hildreth Jr. (R)	86,949	43.4
2 William D. Hathaway (D)	102,369	55.7
Elden H. Shute (R)	81,398	44.3

MARYLAND

	Votes	%
1 Rogers C. B. Morton (R)	87,078	73.6
E. Homer White Jr. (D)	31,250	26.4
2 Clarence D. Long (D)	86,025	59.1
John E. Mudd (R)	59,635	40.9
3 Edward A. Garmatz (D)	63,269	81.3
James E. Chew (R)	14,604	18.8
4 George H. Fallon (D)	60,651	65.6
Thomas Paul Raimondi (R)	31,813	34.4
5 Lawrence J. Hogan (R)	89,073	52.7
Hervey G. Machen (D)	79,870	47.3
6 J. Glenn Beall Jr. (R)	71,714	53.0
Goodloe E. Byron (D)	63,597	47.0

Candidates	Votes	%
7 Samuel N. Friedel (D)	81,048	79.6
Arthur W. Downs (R)	20,745	20.4
8 Gilbert Gude (R)	109,167	60.7
Margaret C. Schweinhaut (D)	70,109	39.1

MASSACHUSETTS

	Votes	%
1 Silvio O. Conte (R)	140,419	99.8
2 Edward P. Boland (D)	126,485	73.7
Frederick M. Whitney Jr. (R)	45,262	26.4
3 Philip J. Philbin (D)	91,587	47.8
Chandler Harrison Stevens (I)	53,047	27.7
Laurence Curtis (R)	46,860	24.5
4 Harold D. Donohue (D)	121,211	61.0
Howard A. Miller Jr. (R)	77,658	39.1
5 F. Bradford Morse (R)	124,930	60.4
Robert C. Maguire (D)	81,875	39.6
6 William H. Bates (R)	136,951	66.1
Deirdre Henderson (D)	70,304	33.9
7 Torbert H. Macdonald (D)	119,562	62.5
William S. Abbot (R)	71,689	34.8
8 Thomas P. O'Neill Jr. (D)	107,645	100.0
9 John W. McCormack (D)	77,347	89.2
Allan C. Freeman (R)	15,906	17.1
10 Margaret M. Heckler (R)	138,220	67.4
Edmund Dinis (D)	66,949	32.6
11 James A. Burke (D)	169,766	100.0
12 Hastings Keith (R)	173,295	99.9

MICHIGAN

	Votes	%
1 John Conyers Jr. (D)	127,847	100.0
2 Marvin L. Esch (R)	90,804	54.4
Weston E. Vivian (D)	75,009	44.9
3 Garry Brown (R)	109,754	65.2
Thomas L. Keenan (D)	58,692	34.8
4 Edward Hutchinson (R)	100,128	65.6
John V. Martin (D)	52,441	34.4
5 Gerald R. Ford (R)	105,085	62.8
Laurence E. Howard (D)	62,219	37.2
6 Charles E. Chamberlain (R)	103,423	64.1
James A. Harrison (D)	57,839	35.9
7 Donald W. Riegle Jr. (R)	104,502	60.7
William R. Blue (D)	67,779	39.3
8 James Harvey (R)	105,238	68.8
Richard E. Davies (D)	47,639	31.2
9 Guy Vander Jagt (R)	111,774	67.5
Jay A. Wabeke (D)	53,886	32.5
10 Elford A. Cederberg (R)	104,791	65.9
Wayne Miller (D)	54,152	34.1
11 Philip E. Ruppe (R)	94,513	58.8
Raymond F. Clevenger (D)	66,251	41.2
12 James G. O'Hara (D)	131,517	70.3
Max B. Harris Jr. (R)	54,760	29.3
13 Charles C. Diggs Jr. (D)	81,951	86.4
Eugene Beauregard (R)	12,873	13.6
14 Lucien N. Nedzi (D)	101,961	63.1
Peter O'Rourke (R)	59,757	37.0
15 William D. Ford (D)	106,960	71.1
John F. Boyle (R)	43,582	29.0
16 John D. Dingell Jr. (D)	105,690	73.9
Monte R. Bona (R)	37,000	25.9
17 Martha W. Griffiths (D)	123,376	74.8
John M. Siviter (R)	40,906	24.8
18 William S. Broomfield (R)	124,025	59.9
Allen Zemmol (D)	82,234	39.7
19 Jack McDonald (R)	104,057	58.0
Garry F. Frink (D)	75,250	42.0

MINNESOTA

	Votes	%
1 Albert H. Quie (R)	138,400	68.8
George Daley (DFL)	62,916	31.3
2 Ancher Nelsen (R)	100,623	59.5
Jon Wefald (DFL)	68,528	40.5

MINNESOTA

Candidates	Votes	%
3 Clark MacGregor (R)	158,989	64.8
Eugene E. Stokowski (DFL)	86,434	35.2
4 Joseph E. Karth (DFL)	129,082	61.3
Emery Barrette (R)	81,392	38.7
5 Donald M. Fraser (DFL)	108,588	57.5
Harmon T. Ogdahl (R)	78,819	41.8
6 John M. Zwach (R)	104,664	56.2
J. Buford Johnson (DFL)	81,578	43.8
7 Odin Langen (R)	83,113	51.3
Bob Bergland (DFL)	79,067	48.8
8 John A. Blatnik (DFL)	115,343	67.6
James A. Hennen (R)	55,209	32.4

MISSISSIPPI

Candidates	Votes	%
1 Thomas G. Abernethy (D)	73,800	100.0
2 Jamie L. Whitten (D)	71,260	100.0
3 Charles H. Griffin (D)	82,896	100.0
4 G. V. (Sonny) Montgomery (D)	78,768	70.1
Prentiss Walker (R)	33,683	30.0
5 William M. Colmer (D)	108,297	100.0

Special Runoff Election[1]

Candidates	Votes	%
3 Charles H. Griffin (D)	87,713#	66.9
Charles Evers (D)	43,303#	33.1

MISSOURI

Candidates	Votes	%
1 William Clay (D)	79,295	64.2
Curtis C. Crawford (R)	44,316	35.9
2 James W. Symington (D)	115,476	53.2
Hugh Scott (R)	101,500	46.8
3 Leonor K. Sullivan (D)	106,150	73.4
Homer McCracken (R)	38,439	26.6
4 William B. Randall (D)	104,056	57.9
Leslie O. Olson (R)	75,790	42.1
5 Richard Bolling (D)	86,681	65.4
Harold Masters (R)	45,951	34.7
6 W. R. Hull Jr. (D)	102,315	54.6
James E. Austin (R)	85,237	45.5
7 Durward G. Hall (R)	123,958	63.8
Edward J. Bonitt (D)	70,455	36.2
8 Richard Ichord (D)	108,416	57.5
Eugene E. Northern (R)	79,179	42.0
9 William L. Hungate (D)	108,184	52.2
Christopher S. Bond (R)	98,923	47.8
10 Bill D. Burlison (D)	78,326	54.0
Vernon H. Landgraf (R)	66,830	46.0

MONTANA

Candidates	Votes	%
1 Arnold Olsen (D)	74,974	53.6
Richard Smiley (R)	64,862	46.4
2 James F. Battin (R)	83,888	67.9
Robert L. Kelleher (D)	39,752	32.2

NEBRASKA

Candidates	Votes	%
1 Robert V. Denney (R)	97,697	54.1
Clair A. Callan (D)	78,374	43.4
2 Glenn Cunningham (R)	87,683	55.2
Mrs. Frank B. Morrison (D)	71,254	44.8
3 Dave Martin (R)	123,838	67.8
J. B. Dean (D)	58,728	32.2

NEVADA

Candidates	Votes	%
AL Walter S. Baring (D)	104,136	72.1
James Michael Slattery (R)	40,209	27.9

NEW HAMPSHIRE

Candidates	Votes	%
1 Louis C. Wyman (R)	100,269	63.4
James T. Keefe (D)	57,959	36.6
2 James C. Cleveland (R)	88,609	71.1
David C. Hoeh (D)	35,942	28.9

NEW JERSEY

Candidates	Votes	%
1 John E. Hunt (R)	105,856	58.0
Thomas S. Higgins (D)	74,703	41.0
2 Charles W. Sandman Jr. (R)	91,218	55.3
David Dichter (D)	73,361	44.4
3 James J. Howard (D)	113,587	57.8
Richard R. Stout (R)	82,441	41.9
4 Frank Thompson Jr. (R)	106,504	53.4
Sydney S. Souter (R)	92,710	46.4
5 Peter H. B. Frelinghuysen Jr. (R)	143,963	68.2
Robert F. Allen (D)	63,208	29.9
6 William T. Cahill (R)	138,060	65.7
Robert A. Gasser (D)	71,338	34.0
7 William B. Widnall (R)	120,523	62.2
Charles S. Gregg (D)	71,123	36.7
8 Charles S. Joelson (D)	100,653	61.4
Richard M. DeMarco (R)	62,661	38.2
9 Henry Helstoski (D)	97,599	49.8
Peter Moraites (R)	95,267	48.7
10 Peter W. Rodino Jr. (D)	89,109	63.8
Celestino Clemente (R)	47,989	34.4
11 Joseph G. Minish (D)	91,496	65.5
George M. Wallhauser Jr. (R)	46,426	33.2
12 Florence P. Dwyer (R)	146,264	71.6
John B. Duff (D)	58,112	28.4
13 Cornelius E. Gallagher (D)	83,151	55.5
Marion D. Dwyer (R)	52,159	34.8
Jeremiah J. O'Callaghan (VI)	9,399	6.3
14 Dominick V. Daniels (D)	87,187	58.5
Joseph Bartletta (R)	50,829	34.1
Mervin Murray (C)	7,634	5.1
15 Edward J. Patten (D)	107,316	54.6
George W. Luke (R)	88,043	44.8

NEW MEXICO

Candidates	Votes	%
1 Manuel Lujan Jr. (R)	88,517	52.9
Thomas G. Morris (D)	78,117	46.6
2 Ed Foreman (R)	71,857	50.5
E. S. Johnny Walker (D)	69,858	49.1

NEW YORK

Candidates	Votes	%
1 Otis G. Pike (D)	118,913	53.9
James M. Catterson Jr. (R)	79,208	35.9
Harold Haar (C)	19,470	8.8
2 James R. Grover Jr. (R, C)	129,731	69.0
Charles A. Heeg (D)	53,552	28.5
3 Lester L. Wolff (D, L)	98,226	52.1
Abe Seldin (R)	75,910	40.2
Daniel L. Rice (C)	14,556	7.7
4 John W. Wydler (R, C)	116,190	70.1
Michael J. Delguidice (D)	45,130	27.2
5 Allard K. Lowenstein (D, L)	99,193	50.7
Mason L. Hampton Jr. (R, C)	96,427	49.3
6 Seymour Halpern (R, L)	95,016	57.5
Franklin Miller (D)	49,676	30.1
Thomas J. Adams (C)	20,511	12.4
7 Joseph P. Addabbo (D, L)	90,204#	66.3
Louis R. Mercogliano (R, C)	45,813#	33.7
8 Benjamin S. Rosenthal (D, L)	120,257	69.8
Jack M. Weinstein (R)	37,314	21.7
Charles Witteck Jr. (C)	14,714	8.5
9 James J. Delaney (D)	69,462	49.7
John F. Haggerty (R, C)	59,690	42.7
Rose L. Rubin (L)	8,935	6.4
10 Emanuel Celler (D, L)	106,622	70.5
Frank L. Martano (R, C)	44,551	29.5
11 Frank J. Brasco (D)	40,460	69.7
Robert J. Hower (R)	10,708	18.4
Basil E. Reynolds (C)	3,807	6.6
Edward L. Johnson (L)	3,101	5.3
12 Shirley Chisholm (D)	34,885	66.5
James Farmer (R, L)	13,777	26.3
Ralph J. Carrano (C)	3,771	7.2
13 Bertram L. Podell (D)	107,960	68.2
Jack Sterngass (R)	25,499	16.1
Kenneth Haber (L)	15,392	9.7
Robert C. Laborde (C)	9,504	6.0
14 John J. Rooney (D, L)	42,149	63.9
Victor J. Tirabasso (R)	18,396	27.9
Alice A. Capatosto (C)	5,422	8.2
15 Hugh L. Carey (D)	59,707	57.6
Frank C. Spinner (R)	31,802	30.7
Stephen P. Marion (C)	7,920	7.6
16 John M. Murphy (D)	73,253	48.8
Frank J. Biondolillo (R, C)	69,126	46.0
Joseph Kottler (L)	7,883	5.3
17 Edward I. Koch (D, L)	84,627	51.7
Whitney North Seymour Jr. (R)	70,086	42.8
Richard J. Callahan (C)	9,030	5.5
18 Adam Clayton Powell Jr. (D)	37,146	80.8
Henry L. Hall (R)	7,215	15.7
19 Leonard Farbstein (D)	44,843	53.3
Donald E. Weeden (R)	27,959	33.2
20 William F. Ryan (D, L)	66,192	78.8
John G. Proudfit (R)	13,968	16.6
21 James H. Scheuer (D, L)	55,129	82.6
Stanley I. Shapiro (R)	8,778	13.2
22 Jacob H. Gilbert (D)	45,144	76.2
James N. Harris (R)	7,087	12.0
Sergio S. Pena (L)	4,402	7.4
23 Jonathan B. Bingham (D, L)	94,108	71.9
Alexander Sacks (R, C)	36,823	28.1
24 Mario Biaggi (D, C)	83,234	60.5
Andrew Mantovani (R)	46,510	33.8
John Patrick Hagan (L)	7,758	5.6
25 Richard L. Ottinger (D, L)	125,415	58.6
Samuel Nakasian (R)	74,275	34.7
Anthony J. DeVito (C)	14,463	6.8
26 Ogden R. Reid (R, L)	130,229	68.1
Paul Davidoff (D)	44,084	23.1
A. Lining Burnet (C)	16,877	8.8
27 Martin B. McKneally (R)	94,689	47.9
John G. Dow (D, L)	88,894	44.9
Frederick P. Roland (C)	14,239	7.2
28 Hamilton Fish Jr. (R)	91,590	48.2
John S. Dyson (D)	86,827	45.6
29 Daniel E. Button (R, CIT)	119,039	56.9
Jacob H. Herzog (D, C)	87,896	42.0
30 Carleton J. King (R, C)	124,995	66.5
Orlando B. Potter (D, L)	62,897	33.5
31 Robert C. McEwen (R, C)	88,562	58.4
K. Daniel Haley (D)	61,947	40.9
32 Alexander Pirnie (R, L)	95,793	64.1
Anthony J. Montoya (D)	43,254	28.9
Albert J. Bushong (C)	10,393	7.0
33 Howard W. Robison (R)	110,080	68.5
Benjamin Nichols (D, L)	50,549	31.5
34 James M. Hanley (D)	96,520	51.3
David V. O'Brien (R)	82,333	43.8
35 Samuel S. Stratton (D)	112,640	69.4
George R. Metcalf (R)	47,849	29.5
36 Frank J. Horton (R)	138,400	70.4
Augustine J. Marvin (D)	46,008	23.4
Leo J. Kesselring (C)	9,916	5.0
37 Barber B. Conable Jr (R)	129,697	71.1
Norman M. Gerhard (D)	50,930	27.9
38 James F. Hastings (R)	90,281	63.4
Wilbur White Jr (D)	47,093	33.1
39 Richard D. McCarthy (D)	120,509	54.6
Daniel E. Weber (R, L)	92,589	42.0

Footnote, see p. 1021.

NEW YORK

Candidates	Votes	%
40 Henry P. Smith III (R, C)	106,984	64.8
Eugene O'Connor (D)	56,201	34.0
41 Thaddeus J. Dulski (D, L)	96,703	77.6
Edward P. Matter (R)	27,920	22.4

Special Election

	Votes	%
13 Bertram L. Podell (D)	36,093#	49.7
Melvin Dubin (NEW LEAD)	27,856#	38.4
Gerald S. Held (R)	4,848#	6.7
Michael V. Ajello (C)	3,806#	5.2

NORTH CAROLINA

	Votes	%
1 Walter B. Jones (D)	75,796	66.2
Reece B. Gardner (R)	38,660	33.8
2 L. H. Fountain (D)	92,542	100.0
3 David N. Henderson (D)	57,244	54.0
Herbert H. Howell (R)	48,815	46.0
4 Nick Galifianakis (D)	77,871	51.5
G. Fred Steele Jr. (R)	73,471	48.6
5 Wilmer Mizell (R)	84,905	52.4
Smith Bagley (D)	77,112	47.6
6 Richardson Preyer (D)	76,028	53.6
William L. Osteen (R)	65,703	46.4
7 Alton A. Lennon (D)	77,419	100.0
8 Earl B. Ruth (R)	70,480	51.2
Voit Gilmore (D)	67,281	48.8
9 Charles Raper Jonas (R)	94,510	100.0
10 James T. Broyhill (R)	87,811	54.9
Basil L. Whitener (D)	72,295	45.2
11 Roy A. Taylor (D)	91,477	56.3
W. Scott Harvey (R)	71,041	43.7

NORTH DAKOTA

	Votes	%
1 Mark Andrews (R)	84,114	66.8
Bruce Hagen (D)	39,692	31.5
2 Thomas S. Kleppe (R)	55,962	49.9
Rolland Redlin (D)	54,655	48.7

OHIO

	Votes	%
1 Robert Taft Jr. (R)	102,219	67.2
Karl F. Heiser (D)	49,830	32.8
2 Donald D. Clancy (R)	108,157	67.4
Don Driehaus (D)	52,327	32.6
3 Charles W. Whalen Jr. (R)	114,549	78.2
Paul Tipps (D)	32,012	21.8
4 William M. McCulloch (R)	129,435	99.9
5 Delbert L. Latta (R)	113,381	71.2
Louis Richard Batzler (D)	45,884	28.8
6 William H. Harsha (R)	107,289	72.4
Kenneth L. Kirby (D)	40,964	27.6
7 Clarence J. Brown Jr. (R)	97,581	63.8
Robert E. Cecile (D)	55,386	36.2
8 Jackson E. Betts (R)	101,974	71.4
Marie Baker (D)	40,898	28.6
9 Thomas L. Ashley (D)	85,280	57.4
Ben Marsh (D)	63,290	42.6
10 Clarence E. Miller (R)	102,890	69.3
Harry B. Crewson (D)	45,686	30.8
11 J. William Stanton (R)	116,323	75.4
Alan D. Wright (D)	38,063	24.7
12 Samuel L. Devine (R)	106,664	67.6
Herbert J. Pfeifer (D)	51,202	32.4
13 Charles A. Mosher (R)	97,158	61.9
Adrian F. Betleski (D)	59,864	38.1
14 William H. Ayres (R)	84,561	55.1
Oliver Ocasek (D)	68,889	44.9
15 Chalmers P. Wylie (R)	98,499	73.1
Russell H. Volkema (D)	35,861	26.6
16 Frank T. Bow (R)	101,495	59.6
Virgil L. Musser (D)	68,916	40.4
17 John M. Ashbrook (R)	100,148	64.9
Robert W. Levering (D)	54,127	35.1
18 Wayne L. Hays (D)	96,711	60.3
James F. Sutherland (R)	63,747	39.7

Candidates	Votes	%
19 Michael J. Kirwan (D)	101,813	69.7
Donald J. Lewis (R)	44,363	30.4
20 Michael A. Feighan (D)	72,918	72.4
J. William Petro (R)	27,827	27.6
21 Louis Stokes (D)	85,509	74.7
Charles P. Lucas (R)	28,931	25.3
22 Charles A. Vanik (D)	102,656	54.7
Frances P. Bolton (R)	84,975	45.3
23 William E. Minshall (R)	106,852	52.0
James V. Stanton (D)	98,825	48.1
24 Donald E. Lukens (R)	105,350	70.4
Lloyd D. Miller (D)	44,400	29.7

OKLAHOMA

	Votes	%
1 Page Belcher (R)	92,513	59.3
John B. Jarboe (D)	63,451	40.7
2 Ed Edmondson (D)	77,192	54.9
Robert G. Smith (R)	63,437	45.1
3 Carl Albert (D)	85,981	68.4
Gerald L. Beasley Jr. (R)	39,740	31.6
4 Tom Steed (D)	67,352	53.6
James W. Smith (R)	58,253	46.4
5 John Jarman (D)	86,420	73.6
Bob Leeper (R)	30,931	26.4
6 John N. Happy Camp (R)	79,992	55.3
John W. Goodwin (D)	64,599	44.7

OREGON

	Votes	%
1 Wendell Wyatt (R)	189,023	80.6
Thomas M. Baggs (D)	45,479	19.4
2 Al Ullman (D)	114,232	63.9
Marv Root (R)	64,478	36.1
3 Edith Green (D)	137,746	69.8
Douglas S. Warren (R)	59,447	30.1
4 John Dellenback (R)	104,159	58.9
Edward N. Fadely (D)	72,579	41.1

PENNSYLVANIA

	Votes	%
1 William A. Barrett (D)	113,696	74.7
Leslie J. Carson Jr. (R)	38,432	25.3
2 Robert N. C. Nix (D)	102,869	70.0
Herbert R. McMaster (R)	44,041	30.0
3 James A. Byrne (D)	75,728	61.3
Richard R. Block (R)	47,813	38.7
4 Joshua Eilberg (D)	131,810	59.3
Alexander Kaptik Jr. (R)	88,229	39.7
5 William J. Green III (D)	108,243	69.1
Gregory J. Meade (R)	48,455	30.9
6 Gus Yatron (D)	94,247	51.4
Peter Yonavick (R)	87,090	47.5
7 Lawrence G. Williams (R)	105,699	56.5
Edward J. O'Halloran (D)	79,782	42.7
8 Edward G. Biester Jr. (R)	94,254	58.0
Richard M. Hepburn (D)	60,324	37.1
9 G. Robert Watkins (R)	100,399	62.9
Philip L. Harding (D)	56,532	35.4
10 Joseph M. McDade (R)	125,916	66.6
Robert J. Landy (D)	61,960	32.8
11 Daniel J. Flood (D)	128,794	70.0
Stanley Bunn (R)	52,475	28.5
12 J. Irving Whalley (R)	119,522	67.5
H. Richard Hostetler (D)	55,838	31.5
13 R. Lawrence Coughlin (R)	141,764	62.0
Robert D. Gates (D)	84,137	36.8
14 William S. Moorhead (D)	96,117	69.4
Algia Gary (R)	39,671	28.7
15 Fred B. Rooney (D)	106,877	58.8
Paul E. Henderson (R)	70,333	38.7
16 Edwin D. Eshleman (R)	98,877	68.9
Robert M. Going (D)	39,507	27.5
17 Herman T. Schneebeli (R, YOUNGMAN)	119,003	66.2
Donald J. Rippon (D)	57,093	31.7
18 Robert J. Corbett (R)	121,664	62.7
William T. Sherman (D)	68,434	35.3

Candidates	Votes	%
19 George A. Goodling (R)	93,352	57.7
Robert L. Myers (D)	65,903	40.8
20 Joseph M. Gaydos (D)	109,236	70.2
Joseph Sabol Jr. (R)	44,037	28.3
21 John H. Dent (D)	93,033	62.8
Thomas H. Young (R, CONST)	55,099	37.2
22 John P. Saylor (R)	98,576	58.0
John P. Murtha (D)	71,297	42.0
23 Albert W. Johnson (R)	87,968	61.5
Alan R. Cleeton (D)	54,453	38.0
24 Joseph P. Vigorito (D)	106,869	61.1
John V. Edwards (R)	66,429	38.0
25 Frank M. Clark (D)	105,048	63.1
Richard L. Doolittle (R)	59,576	35.8
26 Thomas E. Morgan (D)	95,898	63.6
Paul P. Riggle (R)	50,594	33.6
27 James G. Fulton (R)	130,784	66.7
Joseph L. Cosetti (D)	62,638	31.9

RHODE ISLAND

	Votes	%
1 Fernand J. St.Germain (D)	97,945	60.4
Lincoln C. Almond (R)	62,394	38.5
2 Robert O. Tiernan (D)	124,044	61.2
Howard E. Russell Jr. (R)	78,502	38.8

SOUTH CAROLINA

	Votes	%
1 L. Mendel Rivers (D)	95,428	100.0
2 Albert W. Watson (R)	63,877	57.6
Frank K. Sloan (D)	47,053	42.4
3 William J. Bryan Dorn (D)	74,104	66.1
John K. Grisso (R)	35,463	31.7
4 James R. Mann (D)	68,437	61.2
Charles Bradshaw (R)	43,440	38.8
5 Thomas S. Gettys (D)	72,805	74.7
Hugh J. Boyd (R)	21,246	21.8
6 John L. McMillan (D)	58,304	58.3
Ray Harris (R)	39,876	39.9

SOUTH DAKOTA

	Votes	%
1 Ben Reifel (R)	85,232	58.0
Frank E. Denholm (D)	61,738	42.0
2 E. Y. Berry (R)	73,987	59.4
David Garner (D)	50,683	40.7

TENNESSEE

	Votes	%
1 James H. Quillen (R)	100,712	85.2
Arthur Bright (D)	17,441	14.8
2 John J. Duncan (R)	97,832	82.4
Jake Armstrong (D)	17,547	14.8
3 Bill Brock (R)	76,390	57.0
J. William Pope Jr. (D)	57,565	43.0
4 Joe L. Evins (D)	74,041	75.9
J. D. Boles (R)	23,553	24.1
5 Richard Fulton (D)	61,045	48.7
George Kelley (R)	52,836	42.2
William F. Burton Jr. (I)	11,412	9.1
6 William Anderson (D)	61,223	59.4
Ronnie Page (R)	41,923	40.6
7 Ray Blanton (D)	80,893	66.1
John T. Williams (R)	41,457	33.9
8 Robert A. Everett (D)	70,644	100.0
9 Dan Kuykendall (R)	73,293	59.4
James E. Irwin (D)	45,434	36.8

TEXAS

	Votes	%
1 Wright Patman (D)	87,038	100.0
2 John Dowdy (D)	87,565	100.0
3 James M. Collins (R)	81,696	59.4
Robert H. Hughes (D)	55,939	46.0
4 Ray Roberts (D)	95,413	100.0
5 Earle Cabell (D)	79,317	61.4
Roy Wagoner (R)	49,821	38.6

TEXAS

Candidates	Votes	%
6 Olin E. Teague (D)	90,889	100.0
7 George Bush (R)	110,455	100.0
8 Bob Eckhardt (D)	63,256	70.6
Joe Stevens (R)	26,402	29.5
9 Jack Brooks (D)	71,937	60.6
Henry Pressler (R)	46,829	39.4
10 J. J. (Jake) Pickle (D)	85,037	62.1
Ray Gabler (R)	51,933	37.9
11 W. R. Poage (D)	78,127	96.5
12 Jim Wright (D)	86,069	100.0
13 Graham Purcell (D)	83,839	55.8
Frank Crowley (R)	66,477	44.2
14 John Young (D)	89,868	100.0
15 Eligio de la Garza (D)	57,618	100.0
16 Richard C. White (D)	62,491	73.5
Donald Slaughter (R)	22,510	26.5
17 Omar Burleson (D)	90,856	100.0
18 Bob Price (R)	81,715	65.2
J. R. Brown (D)	43,568	34.8
19 George Mahon (D)	79,161	100.0
20 Henry B. Gonzalez (D)	64,112	81.5
Robert Schneider (R)	14,569	18.5
21 O. C. Fisher (D)	91,784	60.8
W. J. Alexander (R)	59,082	39.2
22 Bob Casey (D)	101,498	62.4
Walter Blaney (R)	61,278	37.7
23 Abraham Kazen Jr. (D)	75,026	100.0

Special Election

3 James M. Collins (R)	13,828#	60.0
Mrs. Joe Pool (D)	9,209#	40.0

UTAH

1 Laurence J. Burton (R)	139,456	68.1
Richard J. Maughan (D)	65,265	31.9
2 Sherman P. Lloyd (R)	130,127	61.7
Galen J. Ross (D)	80,948	38.4

VERMONT

AL Robert T. Stafford (R, D)	156,956	99.9

VIRGINIA

Candidates	Votes	%
1 Thomas N. Downing (D)	96,265	72.9
J. Cornelius Fauntleroy Jr. (I)	19,229	14.6
James S. Stafford (R)	16,456	12.5
2 G. William Whitehurst (R)	51,184	54.2
Frederick T. Stant Jr. (D)	43,229	45.8
3 David E. Satterfield III (D)	94,118	60.3
John S. Hansen (R)	62,082	39.7
4 Watkins M. Abbitt (D)	81,723	71.5
S. W. Tucker (R)	32,548	28.5
5 W. C. (Dan) Daniel (D)	70,681	54.6
Weldon W. Tuck (R)	34,608	26.7
Ruth L. Harvey (I)	24,196	18.7
6 Richard H. Poff (R)	91,549	92.2
Tom Hufford (D)	7,221	7.3
7 John O. Marsh Jr. (D)	64,717	54.4
A. R. (Pete) Giesen Jr. (R)	51,349	43.2
8 William L. Scott (R)	92,121	64.9
Andrew H. McCutcheon (D)	49,731	35.1
9 William C. Wampler (R)	71,531	59.9
Joseph P. Johnson Jr. (D)	47,906	40.1
10 Joel T. Broyhill (R)	97,465	59.8
David Kinney (D)	65,474	40.2

WASHINGTON

1 Thomas M. Pelly (R)	124,513	61.4
Don Cole (D)	76,456	37.7
2 Lloyd Meeds (D)	102,522	56.2
Wally Turner (R)	79,800	43.8
3 Julia Butler Hansen (D)	89,777	56.8
Wayne N. Adams (R)	68,387	43.2
4 Catherine May (R)	99,840	66.8
Lee Lukson (D)	49,601	33.2
5 Thomas S. Foley (D)	88,446	56.8
Richard M. Bond (R)	67,304	43.2
6 Floyd V. Hicks (D)	93,399	55.8
Anthony Chase (R)	72,177	43.1
7 Brock Adams (D)	123,429	65.6
Robert Eberle (R)	64,051	34.0

WEST VIRGINIA

Candidates	Votes	%
1 Robert H. Mollohan (D)	85,436	53.9
Tom Sweeney (R)	73,176	46.1
2 Harley O. Staggers (D)	91,022	61.5
George L. Strader (R)	56,911	38.5
3 John Slack (D)	82,911	60.5
Neal A. Kinsolving (R)	54,164	39.5
4 Ken Hechler (D)	94,507	64.2
Ralph Lewis Shannon (R)	52,636	35.8
5 James Kee (D)	80,204	66.2
J. Donald Clark (R)	41,038	33.9

WISCONSIN

1 Henry C. Schadeberg (R)	89,182	50.9
Lynn E. Stalbaum (D)	86,067	49.1
2 Robert W. Kastenmeier (D)	107,804	59.9
Richard D. Murray (R)	72,229	40.1
3 Vernon W. Thomson (R)	95,606	63.7
Gunnar A. Gundersen (D)	54,517	36.3
4 Clement J. Zablocki (D)	118,203	72.6
Walter McCullough (R)	44,558	27.4
5 Henry S. Reuss (D)	76,607	67.8
Robert J. Dwyer (R)	35,536	31.4
6 William A. Steiger (R)	111,934	64.0
John A. Race (D)	60,059	34.3
7 Melvin R. Laird (R)	101,808	64.1
Lawrence Dahl (D)	56,964	35.9
8 John W. Byrnes (R)	111,859	68.0
John E. Nixon (D)	52,660	32.0
9 Glenn R. Davis (R)	126,392	63.1
Carol E. Baumann (D)	73,891	36.9
10 Alvin E. O'Konski (R)	106,266	65.9
Timothy J. Hirsch (D)	54,889	34.1

WYOMING

AL John Wold (R)	77,363	62.7
Velma Linford (D)	45,950	37.3

1969 House Elections

CALIFORNIA[1]

Special Primary

27 Barry Goldwater Jr. (R)	39,580#	31.3
John K. Van de Kamp (D)	17,356#	13.7
James B. Potter Jr. (R)	16,908#	13.4
Jack B. Lindsey (R)	13,818#	10.9
Gary Schlessinger (D)	12,278#	9.7
Patrick D. McGee (R)	8,532#	6.7

Special Election

27 Barry M. Goldwater Jr. (R)	64,734	56.9
John K. Van de Kamp (D)	48,983	43.1

ILLINOIS

Special Election

13 Philip M. Crane (R)	68,418	58.4
Edward A. Warman (D)	48,759	41.6

MASSACHUSETTS

Special Election

6 Michael J. Harrington (D)	72,092#	52.4
William Saltonstall (R)	65,452#	47.6

MONTANA

Special Election

2 John Melcher (D)	45,473#	50.8
W. S. Mather (R)	43,441#	48.6

NEW JERSEY

Special Election

8 Robert A. Roe (D)	67,188	49.2
Eugene Boyle Jr. (R)	66,228	48.5

TENNESSEE

Special Election

8 Ed Jones (D)	33,028#	47.6
W. J. Davis (AM)	16,375#	23.6
Leonard Dunavant (R)	15,773#	22.7

WISCONSIN

Special Election

7 David R. Obey (D)	63,567	51.6
Walter J. Chilsen (R)	59,512	48.4

1968 Elections

1. The election returns shown from Mississippi's 3rd District were from a special runoff between Griffin and Evers, who had finished with the highest number of votes in an earlier special election. Both elections were held under a provision of Mississippi law requiring that all candidates in a special election for the House run against each other, regardless of party affiliations, with a majority required for election. Since neither Evers nor Griffin had a majority, the runoff was required.

The returns from the first special election were as follows: Charles Evers (D), 33,706, 29.3%; Charles H. Griffin (D), 28,927, 25.2; Ellis Bodron (D), 22,842, 19.9; Troy Watkins (D), 10,476, 9.1; Joe Pigott (D), 8,314, 7.2; Hagan Thompson (R), 7,978, 6.9. Source: Mississippi Secretary of State.

1969 Elections

1. No candidate received a majority of the vote, which was required to win in the first special election. Under California's special election law, the highest vote recipients from the first election from each party then faced each other in another election. In this case, Goldwater became the Republican nominee against Van de Kamp, the Democratic nominee.

1970 House Elections

ALABAMA

	Candidates	Votes	%
1	Jack Edwards (R)	63,457	60.6
	John Tyson (D)	27,457	26.2
	Noble Beasley (NDPA)	13,798	13.2
2	William L. Dickinson (R)	62,316	61.4
	Jack Winfield (D)	25,966	25.6
	Percy Smith Jr. (NDPA)	13,281	13.1
3	George Andrews (D)	70,015	89.1
	Detroit Lee (NDPA)	8,537	10.9
4	Bill Nichols (D)	77,701	83.7
	Glenn Andrews (R)	13,217	14.2
5	Walter Flowers (D)	78,368	75.9
	T. Y. Rogers (NDPA)	24,863	24.1
6	John Buchanan (R)	50,060	60.1
	John C. Schmarkey (D)	31,378	37.7
7	Tom Bevill (D)	87,797	100.0
8	Robert E. Jones (D)	76,413	84.9
	Ken Hearn (C)	7,599	8.4
	Thornton Stanley (NDPA)	4,846	5.4

ALASKA

	Candidates	Votes	%
AL	Nick Begich (D)	44,137	55.1
	Frank H. Murkowski (R)	35,947	44.9

ARIZONA

	Candidates	Votes	%
1	John J. Rhodes (R)	99,706	68.5
	Gerald A. Pollock (D)	45,870	31.5
2	Morris K. Udall (D)	86,760	69.0
	Morris Herring (R)	37,561	29.9
3	Sam Steiger (R)	81,239	62.1
	Orren Beaty (D)	49,626	37.9

ARKANSAS

	Candidates	Votes	%
1	Bill Alexander (D)		100.0
2	Wilbur D. Mills (D)		100.0
3	John Paul Hammerschmidt (R)	115,532	66.7
	Donald Poe (D)	57,679	33.3
4	David Pryor (D)		100.0

CALIFORNIA

	Candidates	Votes	%
1	Don H. Clausen (R)	108,358	63.4
	William M. Kortum (D)	62,688	36.7
2	Harold T. Johnson (D)	151,070	77.9
	Lloyd E. Gilbert (R)	37,223	19.2
3	John E. Moss (D)	117,496	61.6
	Elmore J. Duffy (R)	69,811	36.6
4	Robert L. Leggett (D)	103,485	68.0
	Andrew Gyorke (R)	48,783	32.0
5	Phillip Burton (D)	76,567	70.8
	John E. Parks (R)	31,570	29.2
6	William S. Mailliard (R)	96,393	53.4
	Russell R. Miller (D)	84,255	46.6
7	Ronald V. Dellums (D)	89,784	57.3
	John E. Healy (R)	64,691	41.3
8	George P. Miller (D)	104,311	69.0
	Michael A. Crane (R)	46,872	31.0
9	Don Edwards (D)	120,041	69.2
	Mark Guerra (R)	49,556	28.6
10	Charles S. Gubser (R)	135,864	62.0
	Stuart D. McLean (D)	80,530	36.8
11	Paul N. McCloskey Jr. (R)	144,500	77.5
	Robert E. Gomperts (D)	39,188	21.0
12	Burt L. Talcott (R)	95,549	63.6
	O'Brien Riordan (D)	50,942	33.9
13	Charles M. Teague (R)	127,507	59.1
	Gary K. Hart (D)	87,980	40.8
14	Jerome R. Waldie (D)	148,655	74.6
	Byron D. Athan (R)	50,750	25.5

	Candidates	Votes	%
15	John J. McFall (D)	98,442	63.1
	Sam Van Dyken (R)	55,546	35.6
16	B. F. Sisk (D)	95,118	66.4
	Phillip V. Sanchez (R)	43,843	30.6
17	Glenn M. Anderson (D)	83,739	62.2
	Michael C. Donaldson (R)	47,778	35.5
18	Robert B. Mathias (R)	86,071	63.2
	Milton S. Miller (D)	48,415	35.6
19	Chet Holifield (D)	98,578	70.4
	Bill Jones (R)	41,462	29.6
20	H. Allen Smith (R)	116,437	69.1
	Michael M. Stolzberg (D)	50,033	29.7
21	Augustus F. Hawkins (D)	75,127	94.5
	Southey M. Johnson (R)	4,349	5.5
22	James C. Corman (D)	95,256	59.4
	Tom Hayden (R)	63,297	39.5
23	Del Clawson (R)	77,346	63.3
	G. L. Chapman (D)	44,767	36.7
24	John H. Rousselot (R)	124,071	65.1
	Myrlie B. Evers (D)	61,777	32.4
25	Charles E. Wiggins (R)	116,169	63.3
	Leslie W. Craven (D)	64,386	35.1
26	Thomas M. Rees (D)	130,499	71.3
	Nathaniel Jay Friedman (R)	47,260	25.8
27	Barry M. Goldwater Jr. (R)	139,326	66.7
	N. (Toni) Kimmel (D)	63,652	30.5
28	Alphonzo Bell (R)	154,691	69.3
	Don McLaughlin (D)	57,882	25.9
29	George E. Danielson (D)	71,308	62.6
	Tom McMann (R)	42,620	37.4
30	Edward R. Roybal (D)	63,903	68.3
	Samuel M. Cavnar (R)	28,038	30.0
31	Charles H. Wilson (D)	102,071	73.2
	Fred L. Casmir (R)	37,416	26.8
32	Craig Hosmer (R)	119,340	71.5
	Walter L. Mallonee (D)	44,278	26.5
33	Jerry L. Pettis (R)	116,093	72.2
	Chester M. Wright (D)	44,764	27.8
34	Richard T. Hanna (D)	101,664	54.5
	William J. Teague (R)	82,167	44.0
35	John G. Schmitz (R)	192,765	67.0
	Thomas B. Lenhart (D)	87,019	30.3
36	Bob Wilson (R)	132,446	71.5
	Daniel K. Hostetter (D)	44,841	24.2
37	Lionel Van Deerlin (D)	93,952	72.1
	James B. Kuhn (R)	31,968	24.5
38	Victor V. Veysey (R)	87,479	49.8
	David A. Tunno (D)	85,684	48.8

Special Elections [1]

		Votes	%
24	John H. Rousselot (R)	62,749	68.2
	Myrlie B. Evers (D)	29,248	31.8
35	John G. Schmitz (R)	67,209	72.4
	David N. Hartman (D)	25,655	27.6

COLORADO

	Candidates	Votes	%
1	James D. McKevitt (R)	84,843	51.6
	Craig S. Barnes (D)	74,444	45.3
2	Donald G. Brotzman (R)	125,274	63.4
	Richard G. Gebhardt (D)	72,339	36.6
3	Frank E. Evans (D)	87,090	63.7
	John C. Mitchell Jr. (R)	45,610	33.4
4	Wayne N. Aspinall (D)	76,244	55.1
	Bill Gossard (R)	62,169	44.9

CONNECTICUT

	Candidates	Votes	%
1	William R. Cotter (D)	88,374	48.7
	Antonina P. Uccello (R)	87,209	48.1
2	Robert H. Steele (R)	92,846	53.3
	John F. Pickett (D)	81,492	46.7

	Candidates	Votes	%
3	Robert Giaimo (D)	89,042	52.9
	Robert J. Dunn (R)	69,084	41.1
4	Stewart B. McKinney (R)	104,494	56.6
	T. F. Gilroy Daly (D)	78,699	42.6
5	John S. Monagan (D)	96,947	54.8
	James T. Patterson (R)	78,414	44.3
6	Ella T. Grasso (D)	96,969	51.1
	Richard C. Kilbourne (R)	92,906	48.9

Special Election

		Votes	%
2	Robert H. Steele (R)	92,816	53.3
	John F. Pickett (D)	81,333	46.7

DELAWARE

		Votes	%
AL	Pierre S. duPont IV (R)	86,125	53.7
	John Daniello (D)	71,429	44.6

FLORIDA

	Candidates	Votes	%
1	Robert L. F. Sikes (D)	88,744	80.2
	H. D. Shuemake (R)	21,951	19.8
2	Don Fuqua (D)		100.0
3	Charles E. Bennett (D)		100.0
4	Bill Chappell (D)	75,673	57.8
	Leonard V. Wood (R)	55,311	42.2
5	Louis Frey Jr. (R)	110,841	75.8
	Roy Girod (D)	35,398	24.2
6	Sam M. Gibbons (D)	78,832	72.3
	Robert A. Carter (R)	30,252	27.7
7	James A. Haley (D)	78,535	53.4
	Joe Z. Lovingood (R)	68,646	46.6
8	C. W. Bill Young (R)	120,466	67.2
	Ted A. Bailey (D)	58,904	32.8
9	Paul G. Rogers (D)	120,565	70.6
	Emil F. Danciu (R)	50,146	29.4
10	J. Herbert Burke (R)	81,170	54.1
	James J. Ward Jr. (D)	68,847	45.9
11	Claude Pepper (D)		100.0
12	Dante B. Fascell (D)	75,895	71.7
	Robert A. Zinzell (R)	29,935	28.3

GEORGIA

	Candidates	Votes	%
1	G. Elliot Hagan (D)	70,856	100.0
2	Dawson Mathis (D)	59,994	91.8
	Thomas Ragsdale (R)	5,376	8.2
3	Jack Brinkley (D)	54,588	99.5
4	Ben B. Blackburn (R)	85,848	65.2
	Franklin Shumake (D)	45,908	34.8
5	Fletcher Thompson (R)	78,540	57.4
	Andrew Young (D)	58,394	42.6
6	John J. Flynt Jr. (D)	92,500	100.0
7	John W. Davis (D)	80,149	72.5
	Dick Fullerton (R)	30,392	27.5
8	W. S. Stuckey Jr. (D)	52,446	100.0
9	Phil M. Landrum (D)	64,603	71.7
	Bob Cooper (R)	25,476	28.3
10	Robert G. Stephens Jr. (D)	74,075	100.0

HAWAII

	Candidates	Votes	%
1	Spark M. Matsunaga (D)	85,411	72.9
	Richard K. Cockey (R)	31,764	27.1
2	Patsy T. Mink (D)	91,038	100.0

IDAHO

	Candidates	Votes	%
1	James A. McClure (R)	77,515	58.2
	William J. Brauner (D)	55,743	41.8
2	Orval Hansen (R)	66,428	65.7
	Marden E. Wells (D)	31,872	31.5

Footnote, see p. 1026.

ILLINOIS

	Candidates	Votes	%
1	Ralph H. Metcalfe (D)	93,272	91.0
	Janet Roberts Jennings (R)	9,267	9.0
2	Abner J. Mikva (D)	88,252	74.7
	Harold E. Marks (R)	29,853	25.3
3	Morgan F. Murphy (D)	97,693	68.9
	Robert P. Rowan (R)	44,013	31.1
4	Edward J. Derwinski (R)	117,590	68.0
	Melvin W. Morgan (D)	55,328	32.0
5	John C. Kluczynski (D)	97,278	68.8
	Edmund W. Ochenkowski (R)	44,049	31.2
6	George W. Collins (D)	68,182	56.2
	Alex J. Zabrosky (R)	53,240	43.9
7	Frank Annunzio (D)	70,112	87.3
	Thomas J. Lento (R)	10,235	12.7
8	Dan Rostenkowski (D)	98,453	73.9
	Henry S. Kaplinski (R)	34,841	26.1
9	Sidney R. Yates (D)	111,955	75.8
	Edward Wolbank (R)	35,795	24.2
10	Harold R. Collier (R)	107,416	62.2
	R. G. Logan (D)	65,170	37.8
11	Roman C. Pucinski (D)	137,090	71.9
	James R. Mason (R)	53,461	28.1
12	Robert McClory (R)	84,356	62.1
	James J. Cone (D)	51,499	37.9
13	Philip M. Crane (R)	124,649	58.0
	Edward A. Warman (D)	90,364	42.0
14	John N. Erlenborn (R)	122,115	65.5
	William J. Adelman (D)	64,231	34.5
15	Charlotte T. Reid (R)	95,222	68.9
	James E. Todd (D)	43,014	31.1
16	John B. Anderson (R)	83,296	66.8
	John E. Devine Jr. (D)	41,459	33.2
17	Leslie C. Arends (R)	92,917	62.3
	Lester A. Hawthorne (D)	56,340	37.8
18	Robert H. Michel (R)	84,864	66.1
	Rosa Lee Fox (D)	43,601	33.9
19	Tom Railsback (R)	92,247	68.2
	James L. Shaw (D)	43,094	31.8
20	Paul Findley (R)	103,485	67.5
	Billie M. Cox (D)	49,727	32.5
21	Kenneth J. Gray (D)	110,374	62.5
	Fred Evans (R)	66,273	37.5
22	William L. Springer (R)	83,131	59.0
	Robert C. Miller (D)	57,781	41.0
23	George E. Shipley (D)	91,158	54.0
	Phyllis Schlafly (R)	77,762	46.0
24	Melvin Price (D)	88,637	74.2
	Scott R. Randolph (R)	30,784	25.8

Special Election

6	George W. Collins (D)	68,949	55.7
	Alex J. Zabrosky (R)	54,746	44.3

INDIANA

1	Ray J. Madden (D)	73,145	65.6
	Eugene M. Kirtland (R)	38,294	34.4
2	Earl F. Landgrebe (R)	79,163	50.4
	Philip A. Sprague (D)	77,959	49.6
3	John Brademas (D)	87,064	57.5
	Don M. Newman (R)	64,249	42.5
4	J. Edward Roush (D)	86,582	51.9
	E. Ross Adair (R)	80,326	48.1
5	Elwood H. Hillis (R)	86,199	56.0
	Kathleen Z. Williams (D)	67,740	44.0
6	William G. Bray (R)	115,113	60.7
	Terrence D. Straub (D)	74,599	39.3
7	John T. Myers (R)	97,152	57.1
	William D. Roach (D)	73,042	42.9
8	Roger H. Zion (R)	93,088	52.6
	J. David Huber (D)	83,911	47.4
9	Lee H. Hamilton (D)	104,599	62.5
	Richard B. Wathen (R)	62,772	37.5
10	David W. Dennis (R)	81,439	50.8
	Philip R. Sharp (D)	78,871	49.2
11	Andrew Jacobs Jr. (D)	71,329	58.3
	Danny L. Burton (R)	50,990	41.7

IOWA

	Candidates	Votes	%
1	Fred Schwengel (R)	60,270	49.8
	Edward Mezvinsky (D)	59,505	49.2
2	John C. Culver (D)	84,049	60.5
	Cole McMartin (R)	54,932	39.5
3	H. R. Gross (R)	66,087	59.0
	Lyle D. Taylor (D)	45,958	41.0
4	John Kyl (R)	59,396	54.6
	Roger Blobaum (D)	49,369	45.4
5	Neal Smith (D)	73,820	64.9
	Don Mahon (R)	37,374	32.9
6	Wiley Mayne (R)	57,285	57.0
	Fred H. Moore (D)	43,257	43.0
7	William J. Scherle (R)	53,084	62.7
	Lou Galetich (D)	31,552	37.3

KANSAS

1	Keith G. Sebelius (R)	83,923	56.8
	Billy D. Jellison (D)	63,791	43.2
2	William R. Roy (D)	80,161	52.3
	Chester L. Mize (R)	68,843	45.0
3	Larry Winn Jr. (R)	74,603	53.0
	James H. DeCoursey Jr. (D)	64,344	45.7
4	Garner E. Shriver (R)	85,058	63.2
	James C. Junhke (D)	47,004	34.9
5	Joe Skubitz (R)	94,837	66.1
	T. D. Saar Jr. (D)	48,688	33.9

KENTUCKY

1	Frank A. Stubblefield (D)	27,829	100.0
2	William H. Natcher (D)	21,024	100.0
3	Romano L. Mazzoli (D)	50,102	48.5
	William O. Cowger (R)	49,891	48.3
4	M. G. (Gene) Snyder (R)	83,037	66.6
	Charles W. Webster (D)	41,659	33.4
5	Tim Lee Carter (R)	49,266	80.4
	Lyle Leonard Willis (D)	11,977	19.6
6	John C. Watts (D)	44,322	64.9
	Gerald G. Gregory (R)	23,971	35.1
7	Carl D. Perkins (D)	50,672	75.3
	Herbert E. Myers (R)	16,648	24.7

LOUISIANA

1	F. Edward Hebert (D)	66,284	87.4
	Luke J. Fontana (I)	9,602	12.7
2	Hale Boggs (D)	51,812	69.3
	Robert E. Lee (R)	19,703	26.3
3	Patrick T. Caffery (D)	48,677	100.0
4	Joe D. Waggonner Jr. (D)	44,848	100.0
5	Otto E. Passman (D)	31,087	100.0
6	John R. Rarick (D)	36,632	100.0
7	Edwin W. Edwards (D)	24,517	100.0
8	Speedy O. Long (D)	26,607	100.0

MAINE

1	Peter N. Kyros (D)	99,483	59.2
	Ronald T. Speers (R)	68,671	40.8
2	William D. Hathaway (D)	96,235	64.2
	Maynard G. Conners (R)	53,642	35.8

MARYLAND

1	Rogers C. B. Morton (R)	79,594	75.6
	David S. Aland (D)	24,923	23.7
2	Clarence D. Long (D)	87,224	68.5
	Ross Z. Pierpont (R)	40,177	31.5
3	Edward A. Garmatz (D)	52,374	100.0
4	Paul S. Sarbanes (D)	54,936	70.1
	David Fentress (R)	23,491	30.0
5	Lawrence J. Hogan (R)	84,314	61.4
	Royal Hart (D)	52,979	38.6

	Candidates	Votes	%
6	Goodloe E. Byron (D)	59,267	50.8
	George R. Hughes Jr. (R)	55,511	47.6
7	Parren J. Mitchell (D)	60,390	58.7
	Peter Parker (R)	42,566	41.3
8	Gilbert Gude (R)	104,647	63.4
	Thomas Hale Boggs Jr. (D)	60,453	36.6

MASSACHUSETTS

1	Silvio O. Conte (R)	117,045	100.0
2	Edward P. Boland (D)	111,430	100.0
3	Robert F. Drinan (D)	63,942	37.7
	John McGlennon (R)	60,575	35.7
	Philip J. Philbin (WRITE IN)	45,278	26.7
4	Harold D. Donohue (D)	95,016	54.3
	Howard A. Miller Jr. (R)	79,870	45.7
5	F. Bradford Morse (R)	116,666	63.3
	Richard Williams (D)	67,646	36.7
6	Michael J. Harrington (D)	114,276	61.7
	Howard Phillips (R)	70,955	38.3
7	Torbert H. Macdonald (D)	115,597	72.2
	Gordon F. Hughes (R)	44,463	27.8
8	Thomas P. O'Neill Jr. (D)	89,875	100.0
9	Louise Day Hicks (D)	50,269	59.2
	Daniel J. Houton (I)	17,395	20.5
	Laurence Curtis (R)	17,324	20.4
10	Margaret M. Heckler (R)	102,895	57.0
	Bertram A. Yaffe (D)	77,497	43.0
11	James A. Burke (D)	143,026	100.0
12	Hastings Keith (R)	100,432	50.4
	Gerry E. Studds (D)	98,910	49.6

MICHIGAN

1	John Conyers Jr. (D)	93,075	88.2
	Howard L. Johnson (R)	11,876	11.3
2	Marvin L. Esch (R)	88,071	62.5
	R. Michael Stillwagon (D)	52,782	37.5
3	Garry Brown (R)	80,447	56.3
	Richard A. Enslen (D)	62,530	43.7
4	Edward Hutchinson (R)	74,471	61.9
	David R. McCormack (D)	45,838	38.1
5	Gerald R. Ford Jr (R)	88,208	61.4
	Jean McKee (D)	55,337	38.5
6	Charles E. Chamberlain (R)	84,276	60.3
	John A. Cihon (D)	55,591	39.8
7	Donald W. Riegle Jr. (R)	97,683	69.2
	Richard J. Ruhala (D)	41,235	29.2
8	James Harvey (R)	85,634	65.9
	Richard E. Davies (D)	44,400	34.1
9	Guy A. Vander Jagt (R)	94,027	64.4
	Charles Arthur Rogers (D)	51,223	35.1
10	Elford A. Cederberg (R)	82,528	59.1
	Gerald J. Parent (D)	57,031	40.9
11	Philip E. Ruppe (R)	85,323	61.6
	Nino Green (D)	53,146	38.4
12	James G. O'Hara (D)	129,287	76.1
	Patrick Driscoll (R)	38,946	22.9
13	Charles C. Diggs Jr. (D)	56,872	86.2
	Fred Engel (R)	9,141	13.9
14	Lucien N. Nedzi (D)	91,111	70.1
	John L. Owen (R)	38,956	30.0
15	William D. Ford (D)	101,018	80.0
	Ernest C. Fackler (R)	25,340	20.1
16	John D. Dingell (D)	90,540	79.1
	William E. Rostron (R)	23,867	20.9
17	Martha W. Griffiths (D)	108,176	79.7
	Thomas E. Klunzinger (R)	27,608	20.3
18	William S. Broomfield (R)	113,309	64.6
	August Scholle (D)	62,081	35.4
19	Jack McDonald (R)	91,763	58.9
	Fred L. Harris (D)	63,175	40.5

MINNESOTA

1	Albert H. Quie (R)	121,802	69.3
	B. A. Lundeen (DFL)	53,995	30.7
2	Ancher Nelsen (R)	94,080	63.3
	Clifford R. Adams (DFL)	54,498	36.7

MINNESOTA

	Candidates	Votes	%
3	Bill Frenzel (R)	110,921	50.6
	George Rice (DFL)	108,141	49.4
4	Joseph E. Karth (DFL)	131,263	74.2
	Frank L. Loss (R)	45,680	25.8
5	Donald M. Fraser (DFL)	83,207	57.1
	Dick Enroth (R)	61,682	42.3
6	John M. Zwach (R)	88,753	51.8
	Terry Montgomery (DFL)	81,004	47.3
7	Bob Bergland (DFL)	79,378	54.1
	Odin Langen (R)	67,296	45.9
8	John A. Blatnik (DFL)	118,149	78.0
	Paul Reed (R)	38,369	25.3

MISSISSIPPI

	Candidates	Votes	%
1	Thomas G. Abernethy (D)	42,367	100.0
2	Jamie L. Whitten (D)	51,689	86.5
	Eugene Carter (I)	8,092	13.5
3	Charles H. Griffin (D)	50,527	63.7
	Ray Lee (R)	28,847	36.3
4	G. V. (Sonny) Montgomery (D)	66,064	100.0
5	William M. Colmer (D)	58,546	90.4
	Earnest J. Creel (I)	6,225	9.6

MISSOURI

	Candidates	Votes	%
1	William Clay (D)	58,082	90.5
	Gerald G. Frischer (AM MO)	6,078	9.5
2	James W. Symington (D)	93,294	57.6
	Philip R. Hoffman (R)	66,503	41.1
3	Leonor K. Sullivan (D)	73,021	74.8
	Dale F. Troske (R)	24,651	25.2
4	William J. Randall (D)	80,153	60.1
	Leslie O. Olsen (R)	53,204	39.9
5	Richard Bolling (D)	51,668	61.3
	Randall Vanet (R)	31,806	37.8
6	W. R. Hull Jr. (D)	74,496	53.6
	Hugh A. Sprague (R)	63,789	45.9
7	Durward G. Hall (R)	92,965	100.0
8	Richard Ichord (D)	97,560	64.4
	John L. Caskanett (R)	53,181	35.1
9	William L. Hungate (D)	100,988	63.0
	Anthony C. Schroeder (R)	58,103	36.3
10	Bill D. Burlison (D)	62,764	56.0
	Gary Rust (R)	49,355	44.0

MONTANA

	Candidates	Votes	%
1	Richard G. Shoup (R)	64,388	50.5
	Arnold Olsen (D)	63,175	49.5
2	John Melcher (D)	78,082	64.1
	Jack Rehberg (R)	43,752	35.9

NEBRASKA

	Candidates	Votes	%
1	Charles Thone (R)	79,131	50.6
	Clair A. Callan (I)	40,919	26.2
	George Burrows (D)	36,240	23.2
2	John Y. McCollister (R)	69,671	51.8
	John Hlavacek (D)	64,520	48.0
3	Dave Martin (R)	93,705	59.5
	Donald Searcy (D)	63,698	40.5

NEVADA

	Candidates	Votes	%
AL	Walter S. Baring (D)	113,496	82.5
	J. Robert Charles (R)	24,147	17.5

NEW HAMPSHIRE

	Candidates	Votes	%
1	Louis C. Wyman (R)	72,170	67.4
	Chester E. Merrow (D)	34,882	32.6
2	James C. Cleveland (R)	74,219	69.6
	Eugene S. Daniell Jr. (D)	32,374	30.4

NEW JERSEY

	Candidates	Votes	%
1	John E. Hunt (R)	83,726	61.2
	Salvatore T. Mansi (D)	52,567	38.4
2	Charles W. Sandman Jr. (R)	69,392	51.7
	William J. Hughes (D)	64,882	48.3
3	James J. Howard (D)	87,973	55.2
	William F. Dowd (R)	68,675	43.1
4	Frank Thompson Jr. (D)	91,670	58.4
	Edward A. Costigan (R)	65,030	41.4
5	Peter H. B. Frelinghuysen (R)	111,553	66.4
	Ronald C. Eisele (D)	53,436	31.8
6	Edwin B. Forsythe (R)	88,051	53.6
	Charles B. Yates (D)	72,347	44.1
7	William B. Widnall (R)	90,410	58.6
	Arthur J. Lesemann (D)	63,928	41.4
8	Robert A. Roe (D)	75,056	61.0
	Alfred E. Fontanella (R)	48,011	39.0
9	Henry Helstoski (D)	91,589	56.6
	Henry L. Hoebel (R)	68,974	42.6
10	Peter W. Rodino Jr. (D)	71,003	70.0
	Griffith H. Jones (R)	30,460	30.0
11	Joseph G. Minish (D)	68,075	68.5
	James W. Shue (R)	31,369	31.5
12	Florence P. Dwyer (R)	109,537	66.2
	Daniel F. Lundy (D)	55,930	33.8
13	Cornelius E. Gallagher (D)	77,789	71.1
	Raul E. L. Comesanas (R)	27,929	25.5
14	Dominick V. Daniels (D)	77,771	69.7
	Carlo N. DeGennaro (R)	31,161	27.9
15	Edward J. Patten (D)	94,772	61.1
	Peter P. Garibaldi (R)	60,450	38.9

Special Election

	Candidates	Votes	%
6	Edwin B. Forsythe (R)	89,565	54.8
	Charles B. Yates (D)	73,821	45.2

NEW MEXICO

	Candidates	Votes	%
1	Manuel Lujan Jr. (R)	91,187	57.6
	Fabian Chavez Jr. (D)	64,598	40.8
2	Harold Runnels (D)	64,518	50.8
	Ed Foreman (R)	61,074	48.1

NEW YORK

	Candidates	Votes	%
1	Otis G. Pike (D, L)	108,746	52.2
	Malcolm E. Smith Jr. (R, C)	99,503	47.8
2	James R. Grover Jr. (R, C)	107,443	66.1
	Harvey W. Sherman (D, L)	54,996	33.9
3	Lester L. Wolff (D, L)	94,414	54.4
	Raymond J. Rice (R, ENVIRON)	66,196	38.1
	Lola Camardi (C)	12,925	7.5
4	John W. Wydler (R)	91,787	57.1
	Karen S. Burstein (D, L)	56,411	35.1
	Donald A. Derham (C)	12,701	7.9
5	Norman F. Lent (R, C)	93,824	51.0
	Allard K. Lowenstein (D, L)	84,738	46.1
6	Seymour Halpern (R, L)	89,250	77.3
	John J. Flynn (C)	26,244	22.7
7	Joseph P. Addabbo (D, R)	112,983	90.8
	Christopher T. Acer (C)	11,515	9.3
8	Benjamin S. Rosenthal (D, L)	93,666	62.8
	Cosmo J. DiTucci (R, C)	55,406	37.2
9	James J. Delaney (D, R)	102,205	91.9
	Rose L. Rubin (L)	9,025	8.1
10	Emanuel Celler (D, L)	78,324	73.0
	Frank J. Occhiogrosso (R, C)	29,012	27.0
11	Frank J. Brasco (D)	60,919	78.6
	William Sampol (C)	9,462	12.2
	Paul Myrowitz (L)	7,156	9.2

	Candidates	Votes	%
12	Shirley Chisholm (D, L)	31,500	81.8
	John Coleman (R)	5,816	15.1
13	Bertram L. Podell (D)	102,247	77.0
	George W. McKenzie (R)	20,550	15.5
	Herbert Dicker (L)	9,925	7.5
14	John J. Rooney (D)	31,586	55.2
	John F. Jacobs (R, C)	15,222	26.6
	Peter E. Eikenberry (L)	10,452	18.3
15	Hugh L. Carey (D)	50,767	64.7
	Frank C. Spinner (R)	17,931	22.8
	Stephen P. Marion (C)	5,307	6.8
	Carl Saks (L)	4,506	5.7
16	John M. Murphy (D, CSI)	71,553	51.6
	David D. Smith (R, C)	62,597	45.2
17	Edward I. Koch (D, L)	98,300	62.0
	Peter J. Sprague (R)	50,647	32.0
	Richard J. Callahan (C)	9,586	6.1
18	Charles B. Rangel (D, R)	52,651	86.8
	Charles Taylor (L)	6,385	10.5
19	Bella S. Abzug (D)	46,947	52.3
	Barry Farber (R, L)	38,460	42.8
20	William F. Ryan (D, L)	73,509	78.7
	William Goldstein (R)	13,527	14.5
	Francis C. Saunders (C)	6,315	6.8
21	Herman Badillo (D, L)	38,866	83.7
	George B. Smaragdas (C)	7,561	16.3
22	James H. Scheuer (D, L)	50,372	71.6
	Robert M. Schneck (R, C)	19,994	28.4
23	Jonathan B. Bingham (D, L)	78,723	76.2
	George E. Sweeney (R)	16,172	15.7
	Nora M. Kardian (C)	8,456	8.2
24	Mario Biaggi (D, C)	106,942	69.9
	Joseph F. Periconi (R, SILENT)	38,173	24.9
	John Patrick Hagan (L)	7,970	5.2
25	Peter A. Peyser (R)	76,611	42.5
	William Dretzin (D)	66,688	37.0
	Anthony J. DeVito (C)	31,250	17.3
26	Ogden R. Reid (R, L)	109,783	66.4
	Michael A. Coffey (C)	29,702	18.0
	G. Russell James (D)	25,909	15.7
27	John G. Dow (D, L)	89,787	52.2
	Martin B. McKneally (R, C)	82,191	47.8
28	Hamilton Fish Jr. (R)	119,954	70.8
	John J. Greaney (D)	41,908	24.7
29	Samuel S. Stratton (D)	128,017	66.2
	Daniel E. Button (R, L)	65,339	33.8
30	Carleton J. King (R, C)	95,470	57.1
	Edward W. Pattison (D, L)	71,832	42.9
31	Robert C. McEwen (R, C)	90,585	72.4
	Erwin L. Bornstein (D)	34,568	27.6
32	Alexander Pirnie (R, L)	90,884	65.8
	Joseph Simmons (D)	47,306	34.2
33	Howard W. Robison (R)	90,196	66.5
	David Bernstein (D, L)	45,373	33.5
34	John H. Terry (R, C)	88,786	59.5
	Neal P. McCurn (D)	60,452	40.5
35	James M. Hanley (D)	82,425	51.9
	John F. O'Connor (R, C)	76,381	48.1
36	Frank J. Horton (R)	123,209	70.5
	Jordan E. Pappas (D)	38,898	22.3
	David F. Hampson (C)	10,442	6.0
37	Barber B. Conable Jr. (R)	107,677	65.9
	Richard N. Anderson (D, L)	48,061	29.4
38	James F. Hastings (R, C)	94,906	71.4
	James G. Cretekos (D)	37,961	28.6
39	Jack F. Kemp (R, C)	96,989	51.6
	Thomas P. Flaherty (D, L)	90,949	48.4
40	Henry P. Smith III (R, C)	87,183	63.4
	Edward Cuddy (D, L)	50,418	36.6
41	Thaddeus J. Dulski (D, L)	79,151	79.7
	William M. Johns (R, C)	20,108	20.3

NORTH CAROLINA

	Candidates	Votes	%
1	Walter B. Jones (D)	41,674	70.2
	R. Frank Everett (R)	16,217	27.3

NORTH CAROLINA

Candidates	Votes	%
2 L. H. Fountain (D)	38,891	100.0
3 David N. Henderson (D)	41,065	60.1
Herbert H. Howell (R)	27,224	39.9
4 Nick Galifianakis (D)	49,866	52.4
R. Jack Hawke (R)	45,386	47.7
5 Wilmer D. Mizell (R)	68,937	58.1
James G. White (D)	49,663	41.9
6 Richardson Preyer (D)	47,693	66.0
Clifton B. Barham Jr. (R)	20,739	28.7
Lynwood Bullock (AM)	3,849	5.3
7 Alton A. Lennon (D)	37,377	72.0
Frederick R. Weber (R)	14,529	28.0
8 Earl B. Ruth (R)	51,873	56.1
H. Clifton Blue (D)	40,563	43.9
9 Charles Raper Jonas (R)	57,525	66.6
Cy N. Bahakel (D)	28,801	33.4
10 James T. Broyhill (R)	63,936	57.1
Basil L. Whitener (D)	48,113	42.9
11 Roy A. Taylor (D)	90,199	67.0
Luke Atkinson (R)	44,376	33.0

NORTH DAKOTA

	Votes	%
1 Mark Andrews (R)	72,168	65.7
James E. Brooks (D)	37,688	34.3
2 Arthur A. Link (D)	50,416	50.3
Robert P. McCarney (R)	49,888	49.7

OHIO

	Votes	%
1 William J. Keating (R)	89,169	69.1
Bailey W. Turner (D)	39,820	30.9
2 Donald D. Clancy (R)	77,071	55.9
Gerald N. Springer (D)	60,860	44.1
3 Charles W. Whalen Jr. (R)	86,973	74.2
Dempsey A. Kerr (D)	26,735	22.8
4 William M. McCulloch (R)	82,521	64.4
Donald B. Laws (D)	45,619	35.6
5 Delbert L. Latta (R)	92,577	71.2
Carl G. Sherer (D)	37,545	28.9
6 William H. Harsha (R)	82,772	67.8
Raymond H. Stevens (D)	39,265	32.2
7 Clarence J. Brown Jr. (R)	84,448	69.4
Joseph D. Lewis (D)	37,294	30.6
8 Jackson E. Betts (R)	90,916	100.0
9 Thomas L. Ashley (D)	82,777	70.9
Allen H. Shapiro (R)	33,947	29.1
10 Clarence E. Miller (R)	80,838	66.5
Doug Arnett (D)	40,669	33.5
11 William Stanton (R)	91,437	68.3
Ralph Rudd (D)	42,542	31.8
12 Samuel L. Devine (R)	82,486	57.7
James W. Goodrich (D)	60,538	42.3
13 Charles A. Mosher (R)	85,858	61.7
Joseph J. Bartolomeo (D)	53,271	38.3
14 John F. Seiberling Jr. (D)	71,282	56.4
William H. Ayres (R)	55,038	43.6
15 Chalmers P. Wylie (R)	81,536	70.6
Manley L. McGee (D)	34,018	29.4
16 Frank T. Bow (R)	81,208	56.2
Virgil L. Musser (D)	63,187	43.8
17 John M. Ashbrook (R)	79,472	62.2
James C. Hood (D)	44,066	34.5
18 Wayne L. Hays (D)	82,071	68.3
Robert Stewart (R)	38,104	31.7
19 Charles J. Carney (D)	73,222	58.5
Margaret Dennison (R)	52,057	41.6
20 James V. Stanton (D)	70,140	81.3
J. William Petro (R)	16,118	18.7
21 Louis Stokes (D)	74,340	77.6
Bill Mack (R)	21,440	22.4
22 Charles A. Vanik (D)	114,790	71.5
Adrian Fink (R)	45,657	28.5
23 William E. Minshall (R)	111,218	60.0
Ronald M. Mottl (D)	73,765	39.8
24 Walter E. Powell (R)	63,344	51.5
James D. Ruppert (D)	55,455	45.1

Special Election

Candidates	Votes	%
19 Charles J. Carney (D)	70,161	58.4
Margaret Dennison (R)	50,005	41.6

OKLAHOMA

	Votes	%
1 Page Belcher (R)	67,386	55.7
James R. Jones (D)	53,598	44.3
2 Ed Edmondson (D)	87,131	70.8
Gene Humphries (R)	35,989	29.2
3 Carl Albert (D)	112,458	100.0
4 Tom Steed (D)	67,743	63.7
Jay G. Wilkinson (R)	37,081	34.9
5 John Jarman (D)	62,034	73.1
Terry L. Campbell (R)	22,801	26.9
6 John N. Happy Camp (R)	81,959	64.2
R. O. Cassity Jr. (D)	45,742	35.8

OREGON

	Votes	%
1 Wendell Wyatt (R)	147,239	71.8
Vern Cook (D)	57,837	28.2
2 Al Ullman (D)	100,943	71.2
Everett Thoren (R)	40,620	28.7
3 Edith Green (D)	118,919	73.7
Robert E. Dugdale (R)	42,391	26.3
4 John Dellenback (R)	84,474	58.3
James Weaver (D)	60,299	41.7

PENNSYLVANIA

	Votes	%
1 William A. Barrett (D)	79,425	69.2
Joseph S. Ziccardi (R)	34,649	30.2
2 Robert N. C. Nix (D)	70,530	68.2
Edward L. Taylor (R)	32,858	31.8
3 James A. Byrne (D)	54,755	56.4
Gustine J. Pelagatti (R)	42,393	43.6
4 Joshua Eilberg (D)	113,920	59.4
Charles F. Dougherty (R)	77,817	40.6
5 William J. Green III (D)	80,142	66.9
James H. Ring (R)	38,955	32.5
6 Gus Yatron (D)	96,453	65.0
Michael Kitsock (R)	48,397	32.6
7 Lawrence G. Williams (R)	91,042	59.2
Joseph R. Breslin (D)	62,722	40.8
8 Edward G. Biester Jr. (R)	73,041	56.4
Arthur Leo Hennessy Jr. (D)	51,464	39.7
9 John H. Ware III (R)	76,535	59.2
Louis F. Waldman (D)	52,852	40.9
10 Joseph M. McDade (R)	102,716	65.4
Edward J. Smith (D)	51,506	32.8
11 Daniel J. Flood (D)	146,789	96.6
12 J. Irving Whalley (R)	93,385	64.0
Victor J. Karycki Jr. (D)	48,738	33.4
13 R. Lawrence Coughlin (R)	101,953	58.3
Frank R. Romano (D)	68,743	39.3
14 William S. Moorhead (D)	72,509	76.5
Barry Levine (R)	21,572	22.8
15 Fred B. Rooney (D)	93,169	66.9
Charles H. Roberts (R)	44,103	31.7
16 Edwin D. Eshleman (R)	74,006	66.5
John E. Pflum (D)	33,986	30.5
17 Herman T. Schneebeli (R)	88,173	57.9
William P. Zurick (D)	60,714	39.9
18 Robert J. Corbett (R)	87,246	60.2
Ronald E. Leslie (D)	54,639	37.7
19 George A. Goodling (R)	71,497	53.9
Arthur L. Berger (D)	58,399	44.0
20 Joseph M. Gaydos (D)	84,911	77.0
Joseph Honeygosky (R)	22,553	20.5
21 John H. Dent (D)	76,915	68.5
Glenn G. Anderson (R)	33,396	29.7
22 John P. Saylor (R)	81,675	57.7
Joseph F. O'Kicki (D)	58,720	41.5
23 Albert W. Johnson (R)	70,074	57.9
Cecil R. Harrington (D)	50,908	42.1
24 Joseph P. Vigorito (D)	94,029	66.8
Wayne R. Merrick (R)	44,395	31.5

Candidates	Votes	%
25 Frank M. Clark (D)	92,638	69.7
John Loth (R)	37,355	28.1
26 Thomas E. Morgan (D)	80,734	68.4
Domenick A. Cupelli (R)	35,083	29.7
27 James G. Fulton (R)	86,932	60.5
Douglas Walgren (D)	55,050	38.3

Special Election

	Votes	%
9 John H. Ware III (R)	44,077	57.0
Louis F. Waldman (D)	31,353	40.5

RHODE ISLAND

	Votes	%
1 Fernand J. St.Germain (D)	86,283	61.0
Walter J. Miska (R)	52,962	37.4
2 Robert O. Tiernan (D)	121,704	67.2
William A. Dimitri Jr. (R)	61,819	34.2

SOUTH CAROLINA

	Votes	%
1 L. Mendel Rivers (D)	63,891*	100.0
2 Floyd Spence (R)	48,093	53.1
Heyward McDonald (D)	42,005	46.4
3 William Jennings Bryan Dorn (D)	60,708	75.2
H. Grady Ballard (R)	19,981	24.8
4 James R. Mann (D)	52,175	100.0
5 Thomas S. Gettys (D)	43,742	65.9
B. Leonard Phillips (R)	21,911	33.0
6 John L. McMillan (D)	46,966	64.1
Edward B. Baskin (R)	25,546	34.9

SOUTH DAKOTA

	Votes	%
1 Frank E. Denholm (D)	71,636	56.0
Dexter H. Gunderson (R)	56,330	44.0
2 James Abourezk (D)	55,925	52.3
Fred D. Brady (R)	51,092	47.7

TENNESSEE

	Votes	%
1 James H. Quillen (R)	78,896	67.9
David Bruce Shine (D)	37,348	32.1
2 John J. Duncan (R)	85,849	73.3
Roger Cowan (D)	30,146	25.7
3 LaMar Baker (R)	61,527	51.3
Richard Winningham (D)	54,662	45.6
4 Joe L. Evins (D)	86,437	82.6
J. Durelle Boles (R)	18,180	17.4
5 Richard Fulton (D)	89,900	70.6
George Kelly (R)	37,522	29.5
6 William R. Anderson (D)	87,517	81.7
Elmer Davies Jr. (R)	19,622	18.3
7 Ray Blanton (D)	83,904	74.2
W. G. Doss (R)	29,139	25.8
8 Ed Jones (D)	66,590	100.0
9 Dan Kuykendall (R)	72,498	62.6
Michael Osborn (D)	43,279	37.4

TEXAS

	Votes	%
1 Wright Patman (D)	67,883	78.9
James Hogan (R)	18,614	21.6
2 John Dowdy (D)	52,634	73.6
Eugene Hoyt (WRITE IN)	11,987#	17.2
Joe Runnels (WRITE IN)	4,693#	6.8
3 James M. Collins (R)	63,690	60.6
John Mead (D)	41,425	39.4
4 Ray Roberts (D)	70,103	100.0
5 Earle Cabell (D)	57,058	59.7
Frank Crowley (R)	38,481	40.3
6 Olin E. Teague (D)	74,038	100.0
7 Bill Archer (R)	93,457	64.8
Jim Greenwood (D)	50,750	35.2
8 Bob Eckhardt (D)	26,294	100.0

TEXAS

	Candidates	Votes	%
9	Jack Brooks (D)	57,180	64.5
	Henry Pressler (R)	31,483	35.5
10	J. J. Pickle (D)	78,872	100.0
11	W. R. Poage (D)	59,641	99.9
12	Jim Wright (D)	62,057	100.0
13	Graham B. Purcell (D)	80,070	64.9
	Joe Staley (R)	43,319	35.1
14	John Young (D)	62,560	100.0
15	Eligio de la Garza (D)	54,498	76.2
	Ben A. Martinez (R)	17,049	23.8
16	Richard C. White (D)	54,617	82.7
	J. R. Provencio (R)	11,420	17.3
17	Omar Burleson (D)	70,040	100.0
18	Bob Price (R)	52,845	99.9
19	George Mahon (D)	59,996	100.0
20	Henry B. Gonzalez (D)	48,710	100.0
21	O. C. Fisher (D)	76,004	61.4
	Richardson B. Gill (R)	47,868	38.6
22	Bob Casey (D)	73,514	55.7
	A. W. Busch (R)	58,598	44.4
23	Abraham Kazen Jr. (D)	61,068	100.0

UTAH

		Votes	%
1	K. Gunn McKay (D)	95,499	51.3
	Richard Richards (R)	89,269	47.9
2	Sherman P. Lloyd (R)	97,549	52.3
	A. H. (Bob) Nance (D)	87,000	46.6

VERMONT

		Votes	%
AL	Robert T. Stafford (R)	103,806	68.0
	Bernard O'Shea (D)	44,415	29.1

VIRGINIA

	Candidates	Votes	%
1	Thomas N. Downing (D)	71,465	100.0
2	G. William Whitehurst (R)	44,108	61.7
	Joseph T. Fitzpatrick (D)	27,367	38.3
3	David E. Satterfield III (D)	73,123	65.2
	J. Harvie Wilkinson III (R)	35,258	31.5
4	Watkins M. Abbitt (D)	55,246	61.0
	Ben Ragsdale (I)	25,403	28.1
	James M. Helms (R)	9,883	10.9
5	W. C. (Dan) Daniel (D)	54,274	73.0
	Allen T. St.Clair Jr. (R)	20,039	27.0
6	Richard H. Poff (R)	62,350	74.6
	Roy R. White (D)	21,241	25.4
7	J. Kenneth Robinson (R)	52,716	61.8
	Murat Williams (D)	32,642	38.2
8	William L. Scott (R)	68,311	63.7
	Darrel H. Stearns (D)	38,848	36.3
9	William C. Wampler (R)	53,960	60.9
	Tate C. Buchanan (D)	34,609	39.1
10	Joel T. Broyhill (R)	67,650	54.5
	Harold O. Miller (D)	56,603	45.6

WASHINGTON

		Votes	%
1	Thomas M. Pelly (R)	107,072	64.4
	David A. Hughes (D)	53,156	32.0
2	Lloyd Meeds (D)	117,562	72.7
	Edward A. McBride (R)	44,049	27.3
3	Julia Butler Hansen (D)	81,892	59.2
	R. C. (Skip) McConkey (R)	56,566	40.9
4	Mike McCormack (D)	70,119	52.6
	Catherine May (R)	63,244	47.4
5	Thomas S. Foley (D)	88,189	67.0
	George Gamble (R)	43,376	33.0
6	Floyd V. Hicks (D)	98,282	69.4
	John Jarstad (R)	42,213	29.8
7	Brock Adams (D)	99,308	66.6
	Brian Lewis (R)	47,426	31.8

WEST VIRGINIA

	Candidates	Votes	%
1	Robert H. Mollohan (D)	61,296	61.5
	Ken Doll (R)	38,327	38.5
2	Harvey O. Staggers (D)	56,263	62.7
	Richard M. Reddecliff (R)	33,509	37.3
3	John Slack (D)	57,630	65.4
	Neal A. Kinsolving (R)	30,525	34.6
4	Ken Hechler (D)	62,531	67.4
	Ralph Shannon (R)	30,255	32.6
5	James Kee (D)	48,286	70.4
	Marian McQuade (R)	20,261	29.6

WISCONSIN

		Votes	%
1	Les Aspin (D)	87,428	60.9
	Henry C. Schadeberg (R)	56,067	39.1
2	Robert W. Kastenmeier (D)	102,879	68.5
	Norman Anderson (R)	46,620	31.0
3	Vernon W. Thomson (R)	64,891	55.5
	Ray Short (D)	52,085	44.5
4	Clement J. Zablocki (D)	102,464	81.6
	Phillip D. Mrozinski (R)	23,081	18.4
5	Henry S. Reuss (D)	60,630	75.9
	Robert J. Dwyer (R)	18,360	23.0
6	William A. Steiger (R)	98,587	67.7
	Franklin R. Utech (D)	44,794	30.8
7	David R. Obey (D)	88,746	67.6
	Andre E. Le Tendre (R)	41,330	31.5
8	John W. Byrnes (R)	76,893	55.5
	Robert J. Cornell (D)	60,345	43.6
9	Glenn R. Davis (R)	84,732	52.0
	Fred N. Tabak (D)	78,123	48.0
10	Alvin E. O'Konski (R)	66,014	50.9
	Walter Thoresen (D)	62,991	48.6

WYOMING

		Votes	%
AL	Teno Roncalio (D)	58,456	50.3
	Harry Roberts (R)	57,848	49.7

1971 House Elections

KENTUCKY

Special Election

	Candidates	Votes	%
6	William P. Curlin (D)	29,778#	52.6
	Raymond Nutter (R)	21,584#	38.1
	Edgar A. Wallace	4,070#	7.2

MARYLAND

Special Election

	Candidates	Votes	%
1	William O. Mills (R)	31,165	53.4
	Elroy G. Boyer (D)	27,234	46.6

PENNSYLVANIA

Special Election

		Votes	%
18	H. John Heinz III (R)	103,543	66.6
	John E. Connelly (D)	49,269	31.7

SOUTH CAROLINA

Special Election

	Candidates	Votes	%
1	Mendel J. Davis (D)	38,012	48.6
	James B. Edwards (R)	32,227	41.2
	Victoria DeLee (I)	7,965	10.2

1970 Elections

¹ *These two California special elections were held to fill unexpired terms in the 91st Congress (1969-71).*

The returns for special House elections in the 24th and 35th Districts are from elections held after no candidate received a majority of the vote in the initial special primary elections. (California special primary law, see p. 1016)

Special Primary Election returns, 24th District: John H. Rousselot (R), 37,348, 29.0; Bill McColl (R), 35,682, 27.7; Myrlie B. Evers (D), 23,688, 18.4; Patrick J. Hillings (R), 22,394, 17.4; Jack Alex (R), 8,230, 6.4. Rousselot, the top Republican, and Evers, the top Democrat, thus qualified to meet in the special election. Source: California Secretary of State.

Special Primary Election returns, 35th District: Congressional Quarterly was unable to obtain complete official returns. Seven candidates competed for the seat, five Republicans and two Democrats. Schmitz, the Republican receiving the highest number of votes, and Hartman, the top Democrat, qualified to meet in the special election.

1972 House Elections

ALABAMA

	Candidates	Votes	%
1	Jack Edwards (R)	104,606	76.5
	O. W. McCrory (D)	24,357	17.8
	Thomas McAboy Jr. (NDPA)	7,747	5.7
2	William L. Dickinson (R)	80,362	54.9
	Ben C. Reeves (D)	60,769	41.5
3	Bill Nichols (D)	100,045	75.6
	Robert M. Kerr (R)	27,253	20.6
4	Tom Bevill (D)	108,039	69.6
	Ed Nelson (R)	46,551	30.0
5	Robert E. Jones (D)	101,303	74.2
	Digter J. Schrader (R)	33,352	24.4
6	John H. Buchanan Jr. (R)	91,499	59.8
	Ben Erdreich (D)	54,497	35.6
7	Walter Flowers (D)	95,060	84.8
	Lewis Black (NDPA)	15,703	14.0

Special Election

3	Elizabeth Andrews (D)	✔	

ALASKA

		Votes	%
AL	Nick Begich (D)	53,651*	56.2
	Don Young (R)	41,750	43.8

ARIZONA

		Votes	%
1	John J. Rhodes (R)	80,453	57.3
	Gerald A. Pollock (D)	59,900	42.7
2	Morris K. Udall (D)	97,616	63.5
	Gene Savoie (R)	56,188	36.5
3	Sam Steiger (R)	90,710	63.0
	Ted Wyckoff (D)	53,220	37.0
4	John B. Conlan (R)	82,511	53.0
	Jack E. Brown (D)	73,309	47.1

ARKANSAS

		Votes	%
1	Bill Alexander (D)	✔	
2	Wilbur D. Mills (D)	✔	
3	John Paul Hammerschmidt (R)	144,571	77.3
	Guy W. Hatfield (D)	42,481	22.7
4	Ray Thornton (D)	✔	

CALIFORNIA

		Votes	%
1	Don H. Clausen (R)	141,226	62.3
	William A. Nighswonger (D)	77,610	34.2
2	Harold T. Johnson (D)	149,590	68.4
	Frances X. Callahan (R)	62,727	28.7
3	John E. Moss (D)	151,706	69.9
	John Rakus (R)	65,298	30.1
4	Robert L. Leggett (D)	115,038	67.4
	Benjamin Chang (R)	55,540	32.6
5	Phillip Burton (D)	124,164	81.8
	Edlo E. Powell (R)	27,474	18.1
6	William S. Mailliard (R)	119,704	52.1
	Roger Boas (D)	110,144	47.9
7	Ronald V. Dellums (D)	126,913	55.9
	Peter Hannaford (R)	86,587	38.1
	Frank V. Cortese (AM I)	13,550	6.0
8	Fortney H. (Pete) Stark Jr. (R)	102,153	52.9
	Lew M. Warden Jr. (R)	90,970	47.1
9	Don Edwards (D)	123,994	72.3
	Herb Smith (R)	43,140	25.2
10	Charles S. Gubser (R)	140,342	64.6
	B. Frank Gillette (D)	76,839	35.4
11	Leo J. Ryan (D)	114,134	60.5
	Charles E. Chase (R)	69,632	36.9
12	Burt L. Talcott (R)	105,556	51.4
	Julian Camacho (D)	84,174	41.0

	Candidates	Votes	%
13	Charles M. Teague (R)	153,877	73.9
	Lester D. Cleveland (D)	54,299	26.1
14	Jerome R. Waldie (D)	159,335	77.6
	Floyd E. Sims (R)	46,082	22.4
15	John J. McFall (D)	146,358	100.0
16	B. F. Sisk (D)	134,132	79.1
	Carol O. Harner (R)	35,385	20.9
17	Paul N. McCloskey Jr. (R)	110,988	54.5
	James Stewart (D)	73,123	35.9
	James Gordon Knapp (WRITE IN)	19,377	9.5
18	Bob Mathias (R)	110,153	66.4
	Vincent J. Lavery (D)	55,829	33.6
19	Chet Holifield (D)	105,699	67.2
	Kenneth M. Fisher (R)	43,792	27.9
20	Carlos J. Moorhead (R)	122,309	57.4
	John Binkley (D)	90,842	42.6
21	Augustus F. Hawkins (D)	95,050	82.9
	Rayfield Lundy (R)	19,569	17.1
22	James C. Corman (D)	123,863	67.6
	Bruce P. Wolfe (R)	53,603	29.3
23	Del Clawson (R)	120,313	61.4
	Conrad G. Tuohey (D)	75,546	38.6
24	John H. Rousselot (R)	144,057	70.1
	Luther Mandell (D)	61,326	29.9
25	Charles E. Wiggins (R)	118,631	65.0
	Leslie W. Craven (D)	58,323	31.9
26	Thomas M. Rees (D)	164,351	68.7
	Philip Robert Rutta (R)	66,731	27.9
27	Barry Goldwater Jr. (R)	119,475	57.4
	Mark S. Novak (D)	88,548	42.6
28	Alphonzo Bell (R)	144,815	60.7
	Michael Shapiro (D)	89,517	37.5
29	George E. Danielson (D)	92,856	62.7
	Richard E. Ferraro (R)	49,590	33.5
30	Edward R. Roybal (D)	78,193	68.4
	Bill Brophy (R)	32,717	28.6
31	Charles H. Wilson (D)	87,975	52.3
	Ben Valentine (R)	71,395	42.5
	Roberta Lynn Wood (PFP)	8,788	5.2
32	Craig Hosmer (R)	149,514	65.9
	Dennis Murray (D)	72,481	32.0
33	Jerry L. Pettis (R)	140,868	75.0
	Ken Thompson (D)	46,911	25.0
34	Richard T. Hanna (D)	115,880	67.1
	John D. Ratterree (R)	49,971	29.0
35	Glenn M. Anderson (D)	105,667	74.8
	Vernon E. Brown (R)	35,614	25.2
36	William M. Ketchum (R)	88,071	52.7
	Timothy Lemucchi (D)	72,623	43.5
37	Yvonne Brathwaite Burke (D)	123,468	60.2
	Gregg Tria (R)	41,562	20.3
38	George E. Brown Jr. (D)	77,922	55.9
	Howard J. Snider (R)	60,459	43.4
39	Andrew J. Hinshaw (R)	149,081	65.7
	John W. Black (D)	77,817	34.3
40	Bob Wilson (R)	155,269	67.8
	Frank Caprio (D)	69,377	30.3
41	Lionel Van Deerlin (D)	116,980	74.1
	D. Richard Kau (R)	40,997	26.0
42	Clair W. Burgener (R)	158,475	67.5
	Bob Lowe (D)	68,381	29.1
43	Victor V. Veysey (R)	118,536	62.7
	Ernest Z. Robles (D)	70,455	37.3

COLORADO

		Votes	%
1	Patricia Schroeder (D)	101,832	52.0
	James D. McKevitt (R)	93,733	47.9
2	Donald G. Brotzman (R)	132,562	66.3
	Francis W. Brush (D)	66,817	33.4
3	Frank E. Evans (D)	107,511	66.3
	Chuck Brady (R)	54,556	33.7
4	James P. Johnson (R)	94,994	51.0
	Alan Merson (D)	91,151	49.0
5	William L. Armstrong (R)	104,214	62.3
	Byron L. Johnson (D)	60,948	36.5

CONNECTICUT

	Candidates	Votes	%
1	William R. Cotter (D)	130,701	56.9
	Richard M. Rittenband (R)	96,188	41.9
2	Robert H. Steele (R)	142,094	65.9
	Roger Hilsman (D)	73,400	34.1
3	Robert N. Giaimo (D)	121,217	53.3
	Henry A. Povinelli (R)	106,313	46.7
4	Stewart B. McKinney (R)	135,883	63.1
	James P. McLoughlin (D)	79,515	36.9
5	Ronald A. Sarasin (R)	117,578	51.2
	John S. Monagan (D)	112,142	48.8
6	Ella T. Grasso (D)	140,290	60.2
	John F. Walsh (R)	92,783	39.8

DELAWARE

		Votes	%
AL	Pierre S. duPont IV (R)	141,237	62.5
	Norma Handloff (D)	83,230	36.9

FLORIDA

		Votes	%
1	Robert L. F. Sikes (D)	✔	
2	Don Fuqua (D)	✔	
3	Charles E. Bennett (D)	101,441	82.0
	John F. Bowen (R)	22,219	18.0
4	Bill Chappell (D)	92,541	55.9
	P. T. Fleuchaus (R)	72,960	44.1
5	William D. Gunter Jr. (D)	97,902	55.5
	Jack P. Insco (R)	78,463	44.5
6	C. W. Bill Young (R)	156,150	76.0
	Michael O. Plunkett (D)	49,399	24.0
7	Sam Gibbons (D)	91,931	68.0
	Robert A. Carter (R)	43,343	32.0
8	James A. Haley (D)	89,068	57.8
	Roy Thompson Jr. (R)	64,920	42.2
9	Louis Frey Jr. (R)	✔	
10	L. A. (Skip) Bafalis (R)	113,461	62.0
	Bill Sikes (D)	69,502	38.0
11	Paul G. Rogers (D)	116,157	60.2
	Joel Karl Gustafson (R)	76,739	39.8
12	J. Herbert Burke (R)	110,750	62.8
	James T. Stephanis (D)	65,526	37.2
13	William Lehman (D)	92,258	61.6
	Paul D. Bethel (R)	57,418	38.4
14	Claude Pepper (D)	75,131	67.7
	Evelio S. Estrella (R)	35,935	32.4
15	Dante B. Fascell (D)	89,961	56.8
	Ellis S. Rubin (R)	68,320	43.2

GEORGIA

		Votes	%
1	Ronald B. (Bo) Ginn (D)	55,256	100.0
2	Dawson Mathis (D)	65,997	100.0
3	Jack Brinkley (D)	71,756	100.0
4	Ben B. Blackburn (R)	103,155	75.9
	F. Odell Welborn (D)	32,731	24.1
5	Andrew Young (D)	72,289	52.8
	Rodney M. Cook (R)	64,495	47.1
6	John J. Flynt Jr. (D)	70,586	100.0
7	John W. Davis (D)	59,031	58.3
	Charles B. Sherrill (R)	42,265	41.7
8	W. S. Stuckey Jr. (D)	71,283	62.4
	Ronnie Thompson (R)	42,986	37.6
9	Phil M. Landrum (D)	71,801	100.0
10	Robert G. Stephens Jr. (D)	68,096	100.0

HAWAII

		Votes	%
1	Spark M. Matsunaga (D)	73,826	54.7
	Fred W. Rohlfing (R)	61,138	45.3
2	Patsy T. Mink (D)	79,856	57.1
	Diana Hansen (R)	60,043	42.9

IDAHO

	Candidates	Votes	%
1	Steven D. Symms (R)	85,270	55.6
	Edward Williams (D)	68,106	44.4
2	Orval Hansen (R)	102,537	69.2
	Willis H. Ludlow (D)	40,081	27.1

ILLINOIS

	Candidates	Votes	%
1	Ralph H. Metcalfe (D)	136,755	91.4
	Louis H. Coggs (R)	12,877	8.6
2	Morgan F. Murphy (D)	115,306	75.0
	James E. Doyle (R)	38,391	25.0
3	Robert P. Hanrahan (R)	128,329	62.3
	Daniel P. Coman (D)	77,814	37.8
4	Edward J. Derwinski (R)	141,402	70.5
	C. F. Dore (D)	59,057	29.5
5	John C. Kluczynski (D)	121,278	72.8
	Leonard A. Jarzab (R)	45,264	27.2
6	Harold R. Collier (R)	124,486	61.2
	Michael R. Galasso (D)	79,002	38.8
7	George W. Collins (D)	95,018*	82.8
	Thomas J. Lento (R)	19,758	17.2
8	Daniel D. Rostenkowski (D)	110,457	74.0
	Edward L. Stepnowski (R)	38,758	26.0
9	Sidney R. Yates (D)	131,777	68.3
	Clark W. Fetridge (R)	61,083	31.7
10	Samuel H. Young (R)	120,681	51.6
	Abner J. Mikva (D)	113,222	48.4
11	Frank Annunzio (D)	118,637	53.3
	John J. Hoellen (R)	103,773	46.7
12	Philip M. Crane (R)	152,938	74.2
	E. L. Frank (D)	53,055	25.8
13	Robert McClory (R)	98,201	61.5
	Stanley W. Beetham (D)	61,537	38.5
14	John N. Erlenborn (R)	154,794	72.8
	James M. Wall (D)	57,874	27.2
15	Leslie C. Arends (R)	111,022	57.2
	Tim L. Hall (D)	82,925	42.8
16	John B. Anderson (R)	129,640	71.9
	John E. Devine Jr. (D)	50,649	28.1
17	George M. O'Brien (R)	100,175	55.7
	John J. Houlihan (D)	79,840	44.4
18	Robert H. Michel (R)	124,407	64.8
	Stephen L. Nordvall (D)	67,514	35.2
19	Thomas F. Railsback (R)	138,123	100.0
20	Paul Findley (R)	148,419	68.8
	Robert S. O'Shea (D)	67,445	31.2
21	Edward R. Madigan (R)	99,966	54.8
	Lawrence E. Johnson (D)	82,523	45.2
22	George E. Shipley (D)	124,589	56.5
	Robert B. Lamkin (R)	90,390	41.0
23	Melvin Price (D)	121,682	75.1
	Robert Mays (R)	40,428	24.9
24	Kenneth J. Gray (D)	138,867	93.7
	Hugh Muldoon (I)	9,398	6.3

Special Election

		Votes	%
15	Cliffard D. Carlson (R)	31,543	54.8
	Tim L. Hall (D)	26,030	45.2

INDIANA

		Votes	%
1	Ray J. Madden (D)	95,873	56.9
	Bruce R. Haller (R)	72,662	43.1
2	Earl F. Landgrebe (R)	110,406	54.7
	Floyd Fithian (D)	91,533	45.3
3	John Brademas (D)	103,949	55.2
	Don M. Newman (R)	81,369	43.2
4	J. Edward Roush (D)	100,327	51.5
	Allan Bloom (R)	94,492	48.5
5	Elwood Hillis (R)	124,692	64.1
	Kathleen Z. Williams (D)	69,746	35.9
6	William G. Bray (R)	112,525	64.8
	David W. Evans (D)	61,070	35.2
7	John T. Myers (R)	128,688	61.6
	Warren Henegar (D)	80,145	38.4

	Candidates	Votes	%
8	Roger H. Zion (R)	133,850	63.3
	Richard L. Deen (D)	77,371	36.6
9	Lee Hamilton (D)	122,698	62.9
	William A. Johnson (R)	72,325	37.1
10	David W. Dennis (R)	106,798	57.3
	Philip R. Sharp (D)	79,756	42.8
11	William H. Hudnut III (R)	95,839	51.2
	Andrew Jacobs Jr. (D)	91,238	48.8

IOWA

		Votes	%
1	Edward Mezvinsky (D)	107,099	53.4
	Fred Schwengel (R)	91,609	45.7
2	John C. Culver (D)	115,489	59.2
	Theodore R. Ellsworth (R)	79,667	40.8
3	H. R. Gross (R)	109,113	55.7
	Lyle Taylor (D)	86,848	44.3
4	Neal Smith (D)	125,431	59.6
	John Kyl (R)	85,156	40.4
5	William J. Scherle (R)	108,596	55.3
	Tom Harkin (D)	87,937	44.7
6	Wiley Mayne (R)	103,284	52.5
	Berkley Bedell (D)	93,574	47.5

KANSAS

		Votes	%
1	Keith G. Sebelius (R)	145,712	77.2
	Morris Coover (D)	40,678	21.6
2	William R. Roy (D)	106,276	60.6
	Charles D. McAtee (R)	65,071	37.1
3	Larry Winn Jr. (R)	122,358	71.0
	Charles Barsotti (D)	43,777	25.4
4	Garner E. Shriver (R)	120,120	73.2
	John S. Stevens (D)	40,753	24.8
5	Joe Skubitz (R)	128,639	72.3
	Lloyd L. Kitch (D)	49,169	27.7

KENTUCKY

		Votes	%
1	Frank A. Stubblefield (D)	81,456	64.8
	Charles T. Banken (R)	42,286	33.7
2	William H. Natcher (D)	75,871	61.5
	J. C. Carter (R)	47,436	38.5
3	Romano L. Mazzoli (D)	86,810	62.2
	Phil Kaelin Jr. (R)	51,634	37.0
4	M. G. (Gene) Snyder (R)	110,902	73.8
	James W. Rogers (D)	39,332	26.2
5	Tim Lee Carter (R)	109,264	73.6
	Lyle L. Willis (D)	39,301	26.5
6	John Breckinridge (D)	76,185	52.4
	Laban P. Jackson (R)	68,012	46.8
7	Carl D. Perkins (D)	94,840	61.9
	Robert Holcomb (R)	58,286	38.1

LOUISIANA

		Votes	%
1	F. Edward Hebert (D)	78,156	100.0
2	Hale Boggs (D)	68,093*	100.0
3	David C. Treen (R)	71,090	54.0
	J. Louis Watkins Jr. (D)	60,521	46.0
4	Joe D. Waggonner Jr. (D)	74,397	100.0
5	Otto E. Passman (D)	64,027	100.0
6	John R. Rarick (D)	84,275	100.0
7	John B. Breaux (D)	71,901	100.0
8	Gillis W. Long (D)	72,607	68.5
	R. S. Abramson (AM)	17,844	16.8
	Roy C. Strickland (D)	15,517	14.6

Special Election

7	John B. Breaux (D)	✓	

MAINE

		Votes	%
1	Peter N. Kyros (D)	129,408	59.4
	L. Robert Porteous Jr. (R)	88,588	40.6
2	William S. Cohen (R)	106,280	54.4
	Elmer H. Violette (D)	89,135	45.6

MARYLAND

	Candidates	Votes	%
1	William O. Mills (R)	86,326	70.5
	John R. Hargreaves (D)	36,139	29.5
2	Clarence D. Long (D)	123,346	65.8
	John J. Bishop Jr. (R)	64,119	34.2
3	Paul S. Sarbanes (D)	93,093	69.7
	Robert D. Morrow (R)	40,442	30.3
4	Marjorie S. Holt (R)	87,534	59.4
	Werner Fornos (D)	59,877	40.6
5	Lawrence J. Hogan (R)	90,016	62.9
	Edward T. Conroy (D)	53,049	37.1
6	Goodloe E. Byron (D)	107,283	64.8
	Edward J. Mason (R)	58,259	35.2
7	Parren J. Mitchell (D)	83,749	80.1
	Verdell Adair (R)	20,876	20.0
8	Gilbert Gude (R)	137,287	63.9
	Joseph G. Anastasi (D)	77,551	36.1

MASSACHUSETTS

		Votes	%
1	Silvio O. Conte (R)	159,282	99.9
2	Edward P. Boland (D)	137,616	100.0
3	Harold D. Donohue (D)	156,703	99.9
4	Robert F. Drinan (D)	101,714	49.5
	Martin A. Linsky (R)	92,250	44.9
	John T. Collins (IC)	11,141	5.4
5	Paul W. Cronin (R)	110,970	53.5
	John F. Kerry (D)	92,847	44.7
6	Michael J. Harrington (D)	139,667	64.1
	James Brady Moseley (R)	78,381	35.9
7	Torbert H. Macdonald (D)	135,193	67.7
	Joan M. Aliberti (R)	64,357	32.3
8	Thomas P. O'Neill Jr. (D)	142,470	88.7
	John E. Powers Jr. (SOC WORK)	18,169	11.3
9	John Joseph Moakley (I)	70,571	43.2
	Louise Day Hicks (D)	67,143	41.1
	Howard M. Miller (R)	23,177	14.2
10	Margaret M. Heckler (R)	161,708	100.0
11	James A. Burke (D)	154,397	100.0
12	Gerry E. Studds (D)	117,710	50.2
	William D. Weeks (R)	116,592	49.8

MICHIGAN

		Votes	%
1	John Conyers Jr. (D)	131,353	88.4
	Walter F. Girardot (R)	16,096	10.8
2	Marvin L. Esch (R)	103,321	56.0
	Marvin R. Stempien (D)	79,762	43.3
3	Garry Brown (R)	110,082	59.2
	James T. Brignall (D)	74,114	39.9
4	Edward Hutchinson (R)	111,185	67.3
	Charles W. Jameson (D)	54,141	32.8
5	Gerald Ford (R)	118,027	61.1
	Jean McKee (D)	72,782	37.7
6	Charles E. Chamberlain (R)	97,666	50.6
	Bob Carr (D)	95,209	49.4
7	Donald W. Riegle Jr. (R)	114,656	71.4
	Eugene L. Mattison (D)	48,883	30.5
8	James Harvey (R)	100,597	59.3
	Jerome Hart (D)	66,873	39.4
9	Guy A. Vander Jagt (R)	132,268	69.4
	Larry H. Olson (D)	56,236	29.5
10	Elford A. Cederberg (R)	121,368	66.7
	Bennie D. Graves (D)	56,149	30.9
11	Philip E. Ruppe (R)	135,786	69.4
	James Edward McNamara (D)	58,334	29.8
12	James G. O'Hara (D)	83,351	50.7
	David M. Serotkin (R)	80,667	49.0
13	Charles C. Diggs Jr. (D)	97,562	85.6
	Leonard T. Edwards (R)	15,180	13.3
14	Lucien N. Nedzi (D)	93,923	54.9
	Robert V. McGrath (R)	77,273	45.1
15	William D. Ford (D)	97,054	65.8
	Ernest C. Fackler (R)	48,504	32.9
16	John D. Dingell Jr. (D)	110,715	68.1
	William E. Rostron (R)	48,414	29.8
17	Martha W. Griffiths (D)	123,331	66.4
	Ralph E. Judd (R)	60,337	32.5

MICHIGAN

Candidates	Votes	%
18 Robert J. Huber (R)	95,053	52.6
Daniel S. Cooper (D)	85,580	47.4
19 William S. Broomfield (R)	123,697	70.4
George F. Montgomery (D)	50,355	28.6

MINNESOTA

	Candidates	Votes	%
1	Albert H. Quie (R)	142,698	70.7
	Charles S. Thompson (DFL)	59,106	29.3
2	Ancher Nelsen (R)	124,350	57.1
	Charles V. Turnbull (DFL)	93,433	42.9
3	Bill Frenzel (R)	132,638	62.9
	Jim Bell (DFL)	66,070	31.3
	Donald Wright (MINN TAX)	12,234	5.8
4	Joseph E. Karth (DFL)	138,292	72.4
	Steve Thompson (R)	52,786	27.6
5	Donald M. Fraser (DFL)	135,108	65.8
	Allan Davisson (R)	50,014	24.4
	Norm Selby (MINN TAX)	15,845	7.7
6	John M. Zwach (R)	114,537	51.0
	Richard M. Nolan (DFL)	109,955	49.0
7	Bob Bergland (DFL)	133,067	59.1
	Jon O. Haaven (R)	92,283	41.0
8	John A. Blatnik (DFL)	161,823	75.9
	Edward Johnson (R)	51,314	24.1

MISSISSIPPI

	Candidates	Votes	%
1	Jamie L. Whitten (D)	87,526	100.0
2	David R. Bowen (D)	69,892	61.9
	Carl Butler (R)	39,117	34.7
3	G. V. (Sonny) Montgomery (D)	105,722	100.0
4	Thad Cochran (R)	67,655	47.9
	Ellis B. Bodron (D)	62,148	44.0
	Eddie L. McBride (I)	11,571	8.2
5	Trent Lott (R)	77,826	55.4
	Ben Stone (D)	62,101	44.2

MISSOURI

	Candidates	Votes	%
1	William Clay (D)	95,098	64.0
	Richard O. Funsch (R)	53,596	36.0
2	James W. Symington (D)	134,332	63.5
	John W. Cooper Jr. (R)	77,192	36.5
3	Leonor K. Sullivan (D)	124,365	69.3
	Albert Holst (R)	54,523	30.4
4	William J. Randall (D)	108,131	57.4
	Raymond E. Barrows (R)	80,228	42.6
5	Richard Bolling (D)	93,812	62.8
	Vernon E. Rice (R)	53,257	35.6
6	Jerry Litton (D)	110,047	52.2
	Russell Sloan (R)	91,610	43.5
7	Gene Taylor (R)	132,780	63.7
	William Thomas (D)	75,613	36.3
8	Richard Ichord (D)	112,556	62.1
	David R. Countie (R)	68,580	37.9
9	William L. Hungate (D)	132,150	66.5
	Robert L. Prange (R)	66,528	33.5
10	Bill D. Burlison (D)	106,301	64.3
	M. Francis Svendrowski (R)	59,083	35.7

MONTANA

	Candidates	Votes	%
1	Richard G. Shoup (R)	88,373	53.7
	Arnold Olsen (D)	76,073	46.3
2	John Melcher (D)	114,524	76.1
	Richard L. Forester (R)	36,063	24.0

NEBRASKA

	Candidates	Votes	%
1	Charles Thone (R)	126,789	64.2
	Darrel E. Berg (D)	70,570	35.8
2	John Y. McCollister (R)	114,669	63.9
	Patrick L. Cooney (D)	64,696	36.1
3	Dave Martin (R)	133,607	69.6
	Warren Fitzgerald (D)	58,378	30.4

NEVADA

	Candidates	Votes	%
AL	David Towell (R)	94,113	52.2
	James H. Bilbray (D)	86,349	47.9

NEW HAMPSHIRE

		Votes	%
1	Louis C. Wyman (R)	115,732	72.9
	Chester E. Merrow (D)	42,996	27.1
2	James C. Cleveland (R)	107,021	67.6
	Charles B. Officer (D)	51,259	32.4

NEW JERSEY

		Votes	%
1	John E. Hunt (R)	97,650	52.5
	James J. Florio (D)	87,492	47.0
2	Charles W. Sandman Jr. (R)	133,096	65.7
	John D. Rose (D)	69,374	34.3
3	James J. Howard (D)	103,893	53.0
	William F. Dowd (R)	92,285	47.0
4	Frank Thompson Jr (D)	98,206	58.0
	Peter P. Garibaldi (R)	71,030	42.0
5	Peter H. B. Frelinghuysen Jr. (R)	127,310	62.0
	Frederick M. Bohen (D)	78,076	38.0
6	Edwin B. Forsythe (R)	123,610	62.8
	Francis P. Brennen (D)	71,113	36.1
7	William B. Widnall (R)	124,365	57.9
	Arthur J. Lesemann (D)	85,712	39.9
8	Robert A. Roe (D)	104,381	63.1
	Walter E. Johnson (R)	61,073	36.9
9	Henry Helstoski (D)	119,543	55.8
	Alfred D. Schiaffo (R)	94,747	44.2
10	Peter W. Rodino Jr. (D)	94,308	79.8
	Kenneth C. Miller (R)	23,949	20.3
11	Joseph G. Minish (D)	120,227	57.5
	Milton A. Waldor (R)	82,957	39.7
12	Matthew J. Rinaldo (R)	127,690	63.5
	Jerry Fitzgerald English (D)	72,758	36.2
13	Joseph J. Maraziti (R)	109,640	55.7
	Helen S. Meyner (D)	84,492	42.9
14	Dominick V. Daniels (D)	103,089	61.2
	Richard T. Bozzone (R)	57,683	34.3
15	Edward J. Patten (D)	98,155	52.3
	Fuller H. Brooks (R)	89,400	47.7

NEW MEXICO

		Votes	%
1	Manuel Lujan Jr. (R)	118,403	55.7
	Eugene Gallegos (D)	94,239	44.3
2	Harold Runnels (D)	116,152	72.2
	George E. Presson (R)	44,784	27.8

NEW YORK

		Votes	%
1	Otis G. Pike (D)	102,628	52.5
	Joseph H. Boyd (R)	72,133	36.9
	Robert D. L. Gardiner (C)	18,627	9.5
2	James R. Grover Jr. (R)	99,348	65.8
	Fern Coste Dennison (D)	49,454	32.8
3	Angelo D. Roncallo (R)	103,620	57.0
	Carter F. Bales (D)	73,429	40.4
	Lawrence P. Russo (C)	14,768	8.1
4	Norman F. Lent (R)	125,422	62.4
	Elaine B. Horowitz (D)	72,280	36.0
5	John W. Wydler (R)	133,332	62.4
	Ferne M. Steckler (D)	67,709	31.7
6	Lester L. Wolff (D, L)	109,620	51.5
	John T. Gallagher (R, C)	103,038	48.5
7	Joseph P. Addabbo (D, L)	103,110	75.0
	John E. Hall (R)	28,296	20.6
8	Benjamin S. Rosenthal (D, L)	110,293	64.7
	Frank A. La Pina (R, C)	60,166	35.3
9	James J. Delaney (D, R)	141,323	93.4
	Loretta E. Gressey (L)	9,965	6.6
10	Mario Biaggi (D, R)	130,200	93.9
	Michael S. Bank (L)	8,397	6.1

	Candidates	Votes	%
11	Frank J. Brasco (D)	87,869	63.9
	Melvin Solomon (R, C)	43,105	31.3
12	Shirley Chisholm (D, L)	57,821	87.9
	John M. Coleman (R)	6,373	9.7
13	Bertram L. Podell (D)	113,294	65.2
	Joseph F. Marcucci (R)	44,293	25.5
	Leonard M. Simon (L)	9,173	5.3
14	John J. Rooney (D, C)	45,515	53.9
	Allard K. Lowenstein (L)	23,732	28.1
	Francis J. Voyticky (R)	14,813	17.5
15	Hugh L. Carey (D)	77,019	52.2
	John F. Gangemi (R)	63,446	43.0
16	Elizabeth Holtzman (D)	96,984	65.6
	Nicholas R. Macchio (R)	33,828	22.9
	Emanuel Celler (L)	10,337	7.0
17	John N. Murphy (D)	92,252	60.3
	Mario D. Belardino (R, C)	60,812	39.7
18	Edward I. Koch (D, L)	125,117	69.9
	Jane P. Langley (R, C)	52,379	29.3
19	Charles Rangel (D, R)	104,427	96.0
20	Bella S. Abzug (D)	85,558	55.7
	Priscilla M. Ryan (L)	43,045	28.0
	Annette Flatto Levy (R)	18,024	11.7
21	Herman Badillo (D, L)	48,441	86.9
	Manuel A. Ramos (R)	6,366	11.4
22	Jonathan B. Bingham (D, L)	107,448	76.5
	Charles A. Avarello (R, C)	33,045	23.5
23	Peter A. Peyser (R, C)	99,737	50.4
	Richard L. Ottinger (D, L)	98,335	49.6
24	Ogden R. Reid (D, L)	107,979	52.2
	Carl A. Vergari (R, C)	98,818	47.8
25	Hamilton Fish Jr. (R, C)	144,386	71.6
	John M. Burns III (D)	54,271	26.9
26	Benjamin A. Gilman (R)	90,922	47.8
	John G. Dow (D)	74,906	39.3
	Yale Rapkin (C, NEW I)	24,569	12.9
27	Howard W. Robison (R)	114,902	62.2
	David B. Blazer (D)	55,076	29.8
	Patrick M. O'Neil (C)	9,521	5.2
28	Samuel S. Stratton (D)	182,395	80.0
	John F. Ryan Jr. (R, C)	45,623	20.0
29	Carleton J. King (R, C)	148,170	69.9
	Harold B. Gordon (D, L)	63,920	30.1
30	Robert C. McEwen (R, C)	114,193	66.0
	Ernest J. Labaff (D, L)	58,788	34.0
31	Donald J. Mitchell (R, C)	98,454	51.0
	Robert Castle (R)	75,513	39.1
	Franklin Nichols (AP)	12,075	6.3
32	James M. Hanley (D)	111,481	57.2
	Leonard C. Koldin (R, C)	83,451	42.8
33	William F. Walsh (R, C)	132,139	71.4
	Clarence Kadys (D)	53,039	28.6
34	Frank Horton (R)	142,803	72.1
	Jack Rubens (D)	46,509	23.5
35	Barber B. Conable (R)	127,298	67.9
	Terence J. Spencer (D)	53,321	28.4
36	Henry P. Smith III (R, C)	110,238	57.3
	Richard D. (Max) McCarthy (D, L)	82,095	42.7
37	Thaddeus J. Dulski (D, L)	114,603	72.2
	William F. McLaughlin (R, C)	44,103	27.8
38	Jack F. Kemp (R, C)	156,967	73.2
	Anthony P. Lo Russo (D, L)	57,585	26.8
39	James F. Hastings (R, C)	126,147	71.9
	Wilbur White Jr (D)	49,253	28.1

NORTH CAROLINA

		Votes	%
1	Walter, B. Jones (D)	77,438	68.8
	J. Jordan Bonner (R)	35,063	31.2
2	L. H. Fountain (D)	88,798	71.6
	Erick P. Little (R)	35,193	28.4
3	David N. Henderson (D)	56,968	100.0

NORTH CAROLINA

	Candidates	Votes	%
4	Ike F. Andrews (D)	72,972	50.3
	R. Jack Hawke (R)	71,972	49.7
5	Wilmer D. Mizell (R)	101,375	64.8
	Brooks Hays (D)	54,986	35.2
6	L. Richardson Preyer (D)	82,158	93.9
	Lynwood Bullock (AM)	5,331	6.1
7	Charles Rose (D)	57,348	60.4
	Jerry C. Scott (R)	36,726	38.7
8	Earl B. Ruth (R)	82,060	60.2
	Richard Clark (D)	54,198	39.8
9	James G. Martin (R)	80,356	58.9
	James Beatty (D)	56,171	41.1
10	James T. Broyhill (R)	103,119	72.6
	Paul L. Beck (D)	39,025	27.5
11	Roy A. Taylor (D)	94,465	59.6
	Jesse I. Ledbetter (R)	64,062	40.4

NORTH DAKOTA

		Votes	%
AL	Mark Andrews (R)	195,360	72.7
	Richard Ista (D)	72,850	27.1

OHIO

		Votes	%
1	William J. Keating (R)	119,469	70.3
	Karl F. Heiser (D)	50,575	29.7
2	Donald D. Clancy (R)	109,961	62.8
	Penny Manes (D)	65,237	37.2
3	Charles W. Whalen Jr. (R)	111,253	76.2
	John W. Lelack Jr. (D)	34,819	23.8
4	Tennyson Guyer (R)	109,612	62.7
	Dimitri Nicholas (D)	65,216	37.3
5	Delbert L. Latta (R)	132,032	72.8
	Bruce Edwards (D)	49,465	27.3
6	William H. Harsha (R)	128,394	100.0
7	Clarence J. Brown (R)	112,350	73.3
	Dorothy Franke (I)	40,945	26.7
8	Walter E. Powell (R)	80,050	52.2
	James D. Ruppert (D)	73,344	47.8
9	Thomas L. Ashley (D)	110,450	69.1
	Joseph C. Richards (R)	49,388	30.9
10	Clarence E. Miller (R)	129,683	73.2
	Robert H. Wheatley (D)	47,456	26.8
11	J. William Stanton (R)	106,841	68.2
	Dennis M. Callahan (D)	49,891	31.8
12	Samuel L. Devine (R)	103,655	56.1
	James W. Goodrich (D)	81,074	43.9
13	Charles A. Mosher (R)	111,242	68.2
	John Michael Ryan (D)	51,991	31.9
14	John F. Seiberling (D)	135,068	74.4
	Norman W. Holt (R)	46,490	25.6
15	Chalmers P. Wylie (R)	115,779	65.8
	M. L. McGee (D)	55,314	31.4
16	Ralph S. Regula (R)	102,013	57.3
	Virgil L. Musser (D)	75,929	42.7
17	John M. Ashbrook (R)	92,666	57.4
	Raymond C. Beck (D)	62,512	38.7
18	Wayne L. Hays (D)	128,663	70.2
	Robert Stewart (R)	54,572	29.8
19	Charles J. Carney (D)	109,979	64.0
	Norman M. Parr (R)	61,934	36.0
20	James V. Stanton (D)	117,302	84.3
	Thomas E. Vilt (R)	16,624	11.9
21	Louis Stokes (D)	99,190	81.1
	James D. Johnson (R)	13,861	11.3
22	Charles A. Vanik (D)	126,462	63.9
	Donald W. Gropp (R)	64,577	32.6
23	William E. Minshall (R)	98,594	49.4
	Dennis J. Kucinich (D)	94,366	47.3

OKLAHOMA

		Votes	%
1	James R. Jones (D)	91,684	54.4
	J. M. Hewgley (R)	73,786	43.8
2	Clem Rogers McSpadden (D)	105,110	71.1
	Emery H. Toliver (R)	42,632	28.9
3	Carl Albert (D)	101,732	93.4
	Harold J. Marshall (I)	7,242	6.7

	Candidates	Votes	%
4	Tom Steed (D)	85,578	71.3
	William E. Crozier (R)	34,484	28.7
5	John Jarman (D)	69,710	60.4
	Llewllyn L. Keller (R)	45,711	39.6
6	John N. Happy Camp (R)	113,567	72.7
	William Patrick Schmitt (D)	42,663	27.3

OREGON

		Votes	%
1	Wendell Wyatt (R)	166,476	68.6
	Ralph E. Bunch (D)	76,307	31.4
2	Al Ullman (D)	178,537	99.9
3	Edith Green (D)	141,086	62.4
	Mike Walsh (R)	84,697	37.5
4	John Dellenback (R)	138,965	62.0
	Charles O. Porter (D)	83,134	37.1

PENNSYLVANIA

		Votes	%
1	William A. Barrett (D)	118,953	66.1
	Gus A. Pedicone (R)	59,807	33.2
2	Robert N. C. Nix (D)	107,509	70.2
	Frederick D. Bryant (R)	45,753	29.9
3	William J. Green III (D)	101,144	63.3
	Alfred Marroletti (R)	57,787	36.2
4	Joshua Eilberg (D)	129,105	55.9
	William Pfender (R)	102,013	44.1
5	John H. Ware III (R)	121,346	64.7
	Brower B. Yerger (D)	66,329	35.3
6	Gus Yatron (D)	119,557	64.5
	Eugene W. Hubler (R)	64,076	34.6
7	Lawrence G. Williams (R)	122,622	60.6
	Stuart S. Bowie (D)	79,578	39.4
8	Edward G. Biester (R)	115,799	64.4
	Alan Williams (D)	64,069	35.6
9	E. G. Shuster (R)	95,913	61.7
	Earl D. Collins (D)	59,386	38.2
10	Joseph M. McDade (R)	143,670	73.6
	Stanley P. Coveleskie (D)	51,550	26.4
11	Daniel J. Flood (D)	124,336	68.3
	Donald B. Ayers (R)	57,809	31.7
12	John P. Saylor (R)	122,628	68.2
	Joseph Murphy (D)	57,314	31.9
13	R. Lawrence Coughlin (R)	139,085	66.6
	Katherine L. Camp (D)	69,728	33.4
14	William S. Moorhead (D)	106,158	59.3
	Roland S. Catarinella (R)	72,275	40.4
15	Fred B. Rooney (D)	99,937	60.8
	Wardell F. Steigerwalt (R)	64,560	39.3
16	Edwin D. Eshleman (R)	112,292	73.5
	Shirley S. Garrett (D)	40,534	26.5
17	Herman T. Schneebeli (R)	120,214	72.2
	Donald J. Rippon (D)	44,202	26.6
18	H. John Heinz III (R)	144,521	72.8
	Douglas Walgren (D)	53,929	27.2
19	George A. Goodling (R)	93,536	57.5
	Richard P. Noll (D)	67,018	41.2
20	Joseph M. Gaydos (D)	117,933	61.5
	William H. Hunt (R)	73,817	38.5
21	John H. Dent (D)	104,203	62.0
	Thomas H. Young (R)	63,812	38.0
22	Thomas E. Morgan (D)	100,918	60.8
	James R. Montgomery (R)	65,005	39.2
23	Albert W. Johnson (R)	90,615	56.5
	Ernest A. Kassab (D)	69,813	43.5
24	Joseph P. Vigorito (D)	122,092	68.8
	Alvin W. Levenhagen (R)	55,406	31.2
25	Frank M. Clark (D)	97,549	55.8
	Gary A. Myers (R)	77,123	44.2

Special Election[1]

		Votes	%
27	William S. Conover (R)	28,647#	51.1
	Douglas Walgren (D)	25,956#	46.3

RHODE ISLAND

	Candidates	Votes	%
1	Fernand J. St.Germain (D)	120,705	62.4
	John M. Feeley (R)	67,125	34.7
2	Robert O. Tiernan (D)	122,739	63.1
	Donald P. Ryan (R)	77,661	40.0

SOUTH CAROLINA

		Votes	%
1	Mendel J. Davis (D)	61,625	54.5
	J. Sidi Limehouse (R)	51,469	45.5
2	Floyd Spence (R)	83,543	99.9
3	William Jennings Bryan Dorn (D)	82,579	75.2
	Roy Ethridge (R)	27,173	24.8
4	James R. Mann (D)	64,989	66.1
	Wayne N. Whatley (R)	33,363	33.9
5	Tom S. Gettys (D)	66,343	60.9
	B. Leonard Phillips (R)	42,620	39.1
6	Edward L. Young (R)	63,527	54.4
	John W. Jenrette Jr (D)	53,324	45.6

SOUTH DAKOTA

		Votes	%
1	Frank E. Denholm (D)	94,442	60.5
	John Vickerman (R)	61,589	39.5
2	James Abdnor (R)	79,546	54.9
	Pat McKeever (D)	65,415	45.1

TENNESSEE

		Votes	%
1	James H. Quillen (R)	110,868	79.4
	Bernard Cantor (D)	28,736	20.6
2	John J. Duncan (R)	109,925	100.0
3	LaMar Baker (R)	82,561	55.3
	Howard Sompayrac (D)	62,536	41.9
4	Joe L. Evins (D)	93,042	81.1
	Billy Joe Finney (R)	21,689	18.9
5	Richard Fulton (D)	93,555	62.6
	Alfred Adams (R)	55,067	36.8
6	Robin L. Beard (R)	77,263	55.3
	William R. Anderson (D)	60,254	43.1
7	Ed Jones (D)	92,419	70.5
	Stockton Adkins (R)	38,726	29.5
8	Dan Kuykendall (R)	93,173	55.4
	J. O. Patterson Jr. (D)	74,240	44.1

TEXAS

		Votes	%
1	Wright Patman (D)	93,891	100.0
2	Charles Wilson (D)	100,345	73.8
	Charles O. Brightwell (R)	35,600	26.2
3	James Collins (R)	122,984	73.3
	George A. Hughes (D)	44,708	26.7
4	Ray Roberts (D)	95,674	70.2
	James Russell (R)	40,548	29.8
5	Alan Steelman (R)	74,932	55.7
	Earle Cabell (D)	59,601	44.3
6	Olin E. Teague (D)	100,917	72.6
	Carl Nigliazzo (R)	38,086	27.4
7	Bill Archer (R)	171,127	82.3
	Jim Brady (D)	36,899	17.7
8	Bob Eckhardt (D)	73,909	64.6
	Lewis Emerich (R)	39,686	34.7
9	Jack Brooks (D)	89,113	66.2
	Randolph Reed (R)	45,462	33.8
10	J. J. Pickle (D)	130,973	91.2
	Melissa Singler (SOC WORK)	12,682	8.8
11	W. R. Poage (D)	88,861	100.0
12	Jim Wright (D)	84,356	100.0
13	Bob Price (R)	87,084	54.8
	Graham Purcell (D)	71,730	45.2
14	John Young (D)	89,725	100.0
15	Eligio de la Garza (D)	73,994	100.0
16	Richard C. White (D)	81,347	100.0
17	Omar Burleson (D)	95,122	100.0

1. Pennsylvania lost two House seats between the 1970 and 1972 general elections due to redistricting. The special election in the 27th District, held April 25, 1972, was for a partial term expiring Jan. 3, 1973, after which the district ceased to exist.

TEXAS

Candidates	votes	%
18 Barbara C. Jordan (D)	85,672	80.6
Paul Merritt (R)	19,355	18.2
19 George Mahon (D)	97,084	100.0
20 Henry B. Gonzalez (D)	81,443	96.9
21 O. C. Fisher (D)	91,180	56.8
Douglas S. Harlan (R)	69,374	43.2
22 Bob Casey (D)	101,786	70.2
James Griffin (R)	42,094	29.0
23 Abraham Kazen (D)	72,799	100.0
24 Dale Milford (D)	91,054	65.1
Courtney Roberts (R)	48,853	34.9

UTAH

1 K. Gunn McKay (D)	127,027	55.4
Robert K. Wolthuis (R)	96,296	42.0
2 Wayne Owens (D)	132,832	54.5
Sherman P. Lloyd (R)	107,185	44.0

VERMONT

AL Richard W. Mallary (R)	120,924	65.0
William H. Meyer (D)	65,062	35.0

Special Election

AL Richard W. Mallary (R)	39,903#	55.8
J. William O'Brien (D)	26,889#	37.6

VIRGINIA

1 Thomas N. Downing (D)	100,901	78.1
Kenneth D. Wells (R)	28,310	21.9
2 G. William Whitehurst (R)	79,672	73.4
L. Charles Burlage (D)	28,803	26.6
3 David E. Satterfield III (D)	102,523	99.9

Candidates	Votes	%
4 Robert W. Daniel Jr. (R)	57,520	47.1
Robert E. Gibson (D)	45,776	37.5
Robert R. Hardy (I)	8,668	7.1
William E. Ward	6,172	5.1
5 W. C. (Dan) Daniel (D)	83,772	99.9
6 M. Caldwell Butler (R)	75,189	54.6
Willis N. Anderson (D)	53,928	39.2
Roy R. White (I)	8,531	6.2
7 J. Kenneth Robinson (R)	89,120	66.2
Murat Wills Williams (D)	45,513	33.8
8 Stanford E. Parris (R)	60,446	44.4
Robert F. Horan (D)	51,444	37.8
William R. Durland (I)	18,654	13.7
9 William C. Wampler (R)	98,178	71.9
Zane Dale Christian (D)	36,000	26.4
10 Joel T. Broyhill (R)	101,138	56.3
Harold O. Miller (D)	78,638	43.7

Special Election

6 M. Caldwell Butler (R)	61,898	51.8
Willis M. Anderson (D)	47,588	39.8
Roy R. White (I)	10,098	8.4

WASHINGTON

1 Joel Pritchard (R)	107,581	50.9
John Hempelmann (D)	104,959	49.7
2 Lloyd Meeds (D)	114,900	60.5
Bill Reams (R)	75,181	39.6
3 Julia Butler Hansen (D)	122,933	66.3
R. C. (Skip) McConkey (R)	62,564	33.7
4 Mike McCormack (D)	97,593	52.1
Stewart Bledsoe (R)	89,812	47.9
5 Thomas Foley (D)	150,580	81.3
Clarice L. R. Privette (R)	34,742	18.8
6 Floyd V. Hicks (D)	126,349	72.1
Thomas C. Lowry (R)	48,914	27.9

Candidates	Votes	%
7 Brock Adams (D)	140,307	85.4
J. J. (Tiny) Freeman (R)	19,889	12.1

WEST VIRGINIA

1 Robert H. Mollohan (D)	130,062	69.4
George E. Kapnicky (R)	57,724	30.8
2 Harley O. Staggers (D)	128,286	70.0
David Dix (R)	54,949	30.0
3 John M. Slack (D)	118,346	63.7
T. David Higgins (R)	67,441	36.3
4 Ken Hechler (D)	100,600	61.0
Joe Neal (R)	64,242	39.0

WISCONSIN

1 Les Aspin (D)	122,973	64.4
Merrill E. Stalbaum (R)	66,665	34.9
2 Robert W. Kastenmeier (D)	148,136	68.2
J. Michael Kelly (R)	68,167	31.4
3 Vernon W. Thomson (R)	112,905	54.7
Walter Thoresen (D)	91,953	44.6
4 Clement J. Zablocki (D)	149,078	75.7
Phillip D. Mrozinski (R)	45,003	22.8
5 Henry S. Reuss (D)	127,273	77.3
Frederick Van Hecke (R)	33,627	20.4
6 William A. Steiger (R)	130,701	65.8
James A. Adams (D)	63,643	32.0
7 David R. Obey (D)	135,385	62.8
Alvin E. O'Konski (R)	80,207	37.2
8 Harold V. Froehlich (R)	101,634	50.4
Robert J. Cornell (D)	97,795	48.5
9 Glenn R. Davis (R)	128,230	61.4
Ralph A. Fine (D)	76,585	36.7

WYOMING

AL Teno Roncalio (D)	75,632	51.7
Bill Kidd (R)	70,667	48.3

1973 House Elections

ALASKA

Special Election

Candidates	Votes	%
AL Don Young (R)	35,044	51.4
Emil Notti (D)	33,123	48.6

ILLINOIS

Special Election

Candidates	Votes	%
7 Cardiss Collins (D)	33,875#	92.5

LOUISIANA

Special Election

2 Corinne (Lindy) Boggs (D)	42,583	80.4
Robert E. Lee (R)	10,352	19.6

MARYLAND

Special Election

Candidates	Votes	%
1 Robert E. Bauman (R)	27,248	51.2
Frederick C. Malkus (D)	26,001	48.8

1974 House Elections

ALABAMA

	Candidates	Votes	%
1	Jack Edwards (R)	60,710	59.5
	Augusta E. Wilson (D)	37,718	37.0
2	William L. Dickinson (R)	54,089	66.1
	Clair Chisler (D)	27,729	33.9
3	Bill Nichols (D)	63,582	95.9
4	Tom Bevill (D)	77,925	99.8
5	Robert E. Jones (D)	56,375	100.0
6	John Buchanan (R)	54,505	56.6
	Nina Miglionico (D)	39,444	41.0
7	Walter Flowers (D)	73,203	91.0
	Frank P. Walls (C)	5,175	6.4

ALASKA

		Votes	%
AL	Donald E. Young (R)	51,641	53.8
	William L. Hensley (D)	44,280	46.2

ARIZONA[1]

		Votes	%
1	John J. Rhodes (R)	63,847	51.1
	Patricia M. Fullinwider (D)	52,897	42.3
	J. M. Sanders (LLJ)	8,199	6.6
2	Morris K. Udall (D)	84,491	62.0
	Keith Dolgaard (R)	51,886	38.0
3	Sam Steiger (R)	71,497	51.1
	Pat Bosch (D)	68,424	48.9
4	John B. Conlan (R)	78,887	55.3
	Byron T. Brown (D)	63,677	44.7

ARKANSAS

		Votes	%
1	Bill Alexander (D)	104,247	90.6
	James Lawrence Dauer (R)	10,821	9.4
2	Wilbur D. Mills (D)	80,296	58.9
	Judy Petty (R)	56,038	41.1
3	John Paul Hammerschmidt (R)	89,324	51.8
	Bill Clinton (D)	83,030	48.2
4	Ray Thornton (D)		100.0

CALIFORNIA

		Votes	%
1	Harold T. Johnson (D)	138,082	85.8
	Dorothy D. Paradis (AIP)	22,881	14.2
2	Don H. Clausen (R)	95,929	53.0
	Oscar H. Klee (D)	77,232	42.7
3	John E. Moss (D)	122,134	72.3
	Ivaldo Lenci (R)	46,712	27.7
4	Robert L. Leggett (D)	101,152	100.0
5	John L. Burton (D)	88,909	59.6
	Thomas Caylor (R)	56,274	37.7
6	Phillip Burton (D)	85,712	71.3
	Tom Spinosa (R)	26,260	21.8
7	George Miller (D)	83,054	55.6
	Gary Fernandez (R)	66,325	44.4
8	Ronald V. Dellums (D)	95,041	56.6
	Jack Redden (R)	66,386	39.6
9	Fortney H. (Pete) Stark Jr. (D)	92,436	70.6
	Edson Adams (R)	38,521	29.4
10	Don Edwards (D)	87,978	77.0
	John M. Enright (R)	26,288	23.0
11	Leo J. Ryan (D)	106,429	75.8
	Brainard G. Merdinger (R)	29,861	21.3
12	Paul N. McCloskey Jr. (R)	103,692	69.1
	Gary G. Gillmor (D)	46,383	30.9
13	Norman Y. Mineta (D)	78,858	52.6
	George W. Milias (R)	63,573	42.4
14	John J. McFall (D)	102,180	70.9
	Charles M. Gibson (R)	34,775	24.1
15	B. F. Sisk (D)	80,897	72.0
	Carol O. Harner (R)	31,439	28.0
16	Burt L. Talcott (R)	76,356	49.2
	Julian Camacho (D)	74,168	47.8

	Candidates	Votes	%
17	John Krebs (D)	66,675	51.9
	Robert B. Mathias (R)	61,812	48.1
18	William M. Ketchum (R)	67,650	52.7
	George A. Seielstad (D)	60,733	47.3
19	Robert J. Lagomarsino (R)	84,249	56.3
	James D. Loebl (D)	65,469	43.7
20	Barry M. Goldwater Jr. (R)	98,410	61.2
	Arline Mathews (D)	62,326	38.8
21	James C. Corman (D)	88,915	73.5
	Mel Nadell (R)	32,038	26.5
22	Carlos J. Moorhead (R)	81,641	55.8
	Richard Hallin (D)	64,691	44.2
23	Thomas M. Rees (D)	122,076	71.4
	Jack E. Roberts (R)	48,826	28.6
24	Henry A. Waxman (D)	87,521	64.0
	Elliott Stone Graham (R)	45,128	33.0
25	Edward R. Roybal (D)	45,059	100.0
26	John H. Rousselot (R)	82,735	58.9
	Paul A. Conforti (D)	57,685	41.1
27	Alphonzo Bell (R)	102,663	63.9
	John Dalessio (D)	52,236	32.5
28	Yvonne Burke (D)	88,655	80.1
	Tom Neddy (R)	21,957	19.9
29	Augustus F. Hawkins (D)	47,204	100.0
30	George E. Danielson (D)	67,328	74.2
	John J. Perez (R)	23,383	25.8
31	Charles H. Wilson (D)	61,322	70.4
	Norman A. Hodges (R)	23,359	26.8
32	Glenn M. Anderson (D)	84,428	87.7
	Virgil V. Badalich (AIP)	8,874	9.2
33	Del Clawson (R)	72,471	53.4
	Robert E. White (D)	58,492	43.1
34	Mark W. Hannaford (D)	81,151	49.8
	Bill Bond (R)	75,426	46.3
35	Jim Lloyd (D)	61,903	50.3
	Victor V. Veysey (R)	61,168	49.7
36	George E. Brown Jr. (D)	69,766	62.6
	Jim Osgood (R)	35,938	32.3
	William E. Pasley (AIP)	5,711	5.1
37	Jerry L. Pettis (R)	89,849	63.2
	Bobby Ray Vincent (D)	46,783	32.9
38	Jerry M. Patterson (D)	68,335	54.0
	David Rehmann (R)	52,207	41.3
39	Charles E. Wiggins (R)	89,220	55.3
	William E. Farris (D)	65,170	40.4
40	Andrew J. Hinshaw (R)	116,449	63.4
	Roderick J. Wilson (D)	56,850	30.9
	Grayson L. Watkins (AIP)	10,498	5.7
41	Bob Wilson (R)	94,709	54.5
	Colleen M. O'Connor (D)	74,823	43.0
42	Lionel Van Deerlin (D)	70,579	69.9
	Wes Marden (R)	30,435	30.1
43	Clair W. Burgener (R)	115,275	60.4
	Bill Bandes (D)	75,629	39.6

Special Elections [2]

		Votes	%
6	John L. Burton (D)	73,114	50.0
	Thomas Caylor (R)	30,908	21.2
	Terence McGuire (D)	12,777	8.7
	Jean Wall (R)	8,501	5.8
	Sean McCarthy (R)	7,783	5.3
13	Robert J. Lagomarsino (R)	52,140	53.6
	James D. Loebl (D)	18,223	18.8
	James A. Browning (D)	7,536	7.8
	Roger I. Ikola (D)	6,155	6.3
	E.T. Jolicoeur (D)	5,786	6.0

COLORADO

		Votes	%
1	Patricia Schroeder (D)	94,583	58.5
	Frank K. Southworth (R)	66,046	40.8
2	Timothy W. Wirth (D)	93,728	51.9
	Donald G. Brotzman (R)	86,720	48.0
3	Frank E. Evans (D)	91,783	67.9
	E. Keith Records (R)	43,298	32.1

	Candidates	Votes	%
4	James P. Johnson (R)	82,982	52.0
	John S. Carroll (D)	76,452	48.0
5	William L. Armstrong (R)	85,326	57.7
	Ben Galloway (D)	56,888	38.5

CONNECTICUT

		Votes	%
1	William R. Cotter (D)	117,038	62.7
	F. Mac Buckley (R)	67,080	35.9
2	Christopher J. Dodd (D)	104,436	59.0
	Samuel B. Hellier (R)	69,380	39.2
3	Robert N. Giaimo (D)	114,316	65.1
	James F. Altham Jr. (R)	55,177	31.4
4	Stewart B. McKinney (R)	83,630	53.2
	James G. Kellis (D)	71,047	45.2
5	Ronald A. Sarasin (R)	94,998	50.4
	William R. Ratchford (D)	90,407	48.0
6	Anthony J. Moffett (D)	122,785	63.4
	Patsy J. Piscopo (R)	69,942	36.1

DELAWARE

		Votes	%
AL	Pierre S. duPont IV (R)	93,826	58.5
	James R. Soles (D)	63,490	39.6

FLORIDA

		Votes	%
1	Robert L. F. Sikes (D)		100.0
2	Don Fuqua (D)		100.0
3	Charles E. Bennett (D)		100.0
4	Bill Chappell Jr. (D)	74,720	68.2
	Warren A. Hauser (R)	34,867	31.8
5	Richard Kelly (R)	74,954	52.8
	JoAnn Saunders (D)	63,610	44.8
6	C. W. Bill Young (R)	109,302	75.8
	Herbert M. Monrose (D)	34,886	24.2
7	Sam Gibbons (D)		100.0
8	James A. Haley (D)	63,283	56.7
	Joe Z. Lovingood (R)	48,240	43.3
9	Louis Frey Jr. (R)	86,226	76.7
	William D. Rowland (D)	26,255	23.3
10	L. A. (Skip) Bafalis (R)	117,368	73.7
	Evelyn Tucker (D)	41,925	26.3
11	Paul G. Rogers (D)		100.0
12	J. Herbert Burke (R)	61,191	51.0
	Charles Friedman (D)	58,899	49.0
13	William Lehman (D)		100.0
14	Claude Pepper (D)	45,479	69.1
	Michael A. Carricarte (R)	20,383	30.9
15	Dante B. Fascell (D)	68,064	70.5
	S. Peter Capua (R)	28,444	29.5

GEORGIA

		Votes	%
1	Ronald B. (Bo) Ginn (D)	64,958	86.1
	Bill Gowan (R)	10,485	13.9
2	Dawson Mathis (D)	59,514	100.0
3	Jack Brinkley (D)	67,438	87.7
	Carl Savage (R)	9,453	12.3
4	Elliott H. Levitas (D)	61,211	55.1
	Ben B. Blackburn (R)	49,922	44.9
5	Andrew Young (D)	69,221	71.6
	Wyman C. Lowe (R)	27,397	28.3
6	John J. Flynt Jr. (D)	49,082	51.5
	Newt Gingrich (R)	46,308	48.5
7	Lawrence P. McDonald (D)	47,993	50.3
	Quincy Collins (R)	47,450	49.7
8	W. S. (Bill) Stuckey Jr. (D)	59,182	100.0
9	Phil M. Landrum (D)	64,096	74.8
	Ronald D. Reeves (R)	21,540	25.2
10	Robert G. Stephens Jr. (D)	45,843	68.4
	Gary Pleger (R)	21,214	31.6

Footnotes, see p. 1036.

HAWAII

Candidates	Votes	%
1 Spark M. Matsunaga (D)	71,552	59.3
William B. Paul (R)	49,065	40.7
2 Patsy T. Mink (D)	86,916	62.6
Carla W. Coray (R)	51,894	37.4

IDAHO

Candidates	Votes	%
1 Steven D. Symms (R)	75,414	58.3
J. Ray Cox (D)	54,001	41.7
2 George V. Hansen (R)	67,274	55.7
Max Hanson (D)	53,599	44.3

ILLINOIS

Candidates	Votes	%
1 Ralph H. Metcalfe (D)	75,206	93.7
Oscar H. Haynes (R)	4,399	5.5
2 Morgan F. Murphy (D)	65,812	87.5
James Ginderske (R)	9,386	12.5
3 Martin A. Russo (D)	65,336	52.6
Robert P. Hanrahan (R)	58,891	47.4
4 Edward J. Derwinski (R)	68,428	59.2
Ronald A. Rodger (D)	47,096	40.8
5 John C. Kluczynski (D)	93,069	86.0
William H. G. Toms (R)	15,108	14.0
6 Henry J. Hyde (R)	66,027	53.4
Edward V. Hanrahan (D)	57,654	46.6
7 Cardiss Collins (D)	63,962	87.9
Donald L. Metzger (R)	8,800	12.1
8 Dan Rostenkowski (D)	75,011	86.5
Salvatore E. Oddo (R)	11,664	13.5
9 Sidney R. Yates (D)	93,864	100.0
10 Abner J. Mikva (D)	83,457	50.9
Samuel H. Young (R)	80,597	49.1
11 Frank Annunzio (D)	102,541	72.4
Mitchell G. Zadrozny (R)	39,182	27.6
12 Philip M. Crane (R)	70,731	61.1
Betty C. Spence (D)	45,049	38.9
13 Robert McClory (R)	51,405	54.5
Stanley W. Beetham (D)	42,903	45.5
14 John N. Erlenborn (R)	77,718	66.6
Robert H. Renshaw (D)	38,981	33.4
15 Tim L. Hall (D)	61,912	52.0
Cliffard D. Carlson (R)	54,278	45.6
16 John B. Anderson (R)	65,175	55.5
Marshall Hungness (D)	33,724	28.7
W. John Schade Jr. (IND)	18,580	15.8
17 George M. O'Brien (R)	59,984	51.5
John J. Houlihan (D)	56,541	48.5
18 Robert H. Michel (R)	71,681	54.8
Stephen L. Nordvall (D)	59,225	45.2
19 Tom Railsback (R)	84,049	65.3
Jim Gende (D)	44,677	34.7
20 Paul Findley (R)	84,426	54.8
Peter F. Mack (D)	69,551	45.2
21 Edward R. Madigan (R)	78,640	65.8
Richard N. Small (D)	40,896	34.2
22 George E. Shipley (D)	97,921	59.8
William A. Young (R)	65,731	40.2
23 Melvin Price (D)	78,347	80.5
Scott R. Randolph (R)	18,987	19.5
24 Paul Simon (D)	108,417	59.6
Val Oshel (R)	73,634	40.4

INDIANA

Candidates	Votes	%
1 Ray J. Madden (D)	71,759	68.6
Joseph D. Harkin (R)	32,793	31.4
2 Floyd J. Fithian (D)	101,856	61.1
Earl F. Landgrebe (R)	64,950	38.9
3 John Brademas (D)	89,306	64.1
Virginia R. Black (R)	50,116	35.9
4 J. Edward Roush (D)	83,604	51.9
Walter P. Helmke (R)	75,031	46.5
5 Elwood Hillis (R)	95,331	56.6
William T. Sebree (D)	73,239	43.4
6 David W. Evans (D)	78,414	52.4
William G. Bray (R)	71,134	47.6

Candidates	Votes	%
7 John T. Myers (R)	100,128	57.1
Elden C. Tipton (D)	73,802	42.1
8 Philip H. Hayes (D)	100,121	53.4
Roger H. Zion (R)	87,296	46.6
9 Lee H. Hamilton (D)	117,648	71.1
Delson Cox Jr. (R)	47,881	28.9
10 Philip R. Sharp (D)	85,418	54.4
David W. Dennis (R)	71,701	45.6
11 Andrew Jacobs Jr. (D)	81,508	52.5
William H. Hudnut III (R)	73,793	47.5

IOWA

Candidates	Votes	%
1 Edward Mezvinsky (D)	75,687	54.4
James A. S. Leach (R)	63,540	45.6
2 Michael T. Blouin (D)	73,416	51.1
Tom Riley (R)	69,088	48.1
3 Charles E. Grassley (R)	77,468	50.8
Stephen J. Rapp (D)	74,895	49.2
4 Neal Smith (D)	96,755	63.9
Chuck Dick (R)	53,756	35.5
5 Tom Harkin (D)	81,186	51.1
William J. Scherle (R)	77,683	48.9
6 Berkley Bedell (D)	86,315	54.6
Wiley Mayne (R)	71,695	45.4

KANSAS

Candidates	Votes	%
1 Keith G. Sebelius (R)	101,565	58.4
Donald C. Smith (D)	57,326	33.0
Thelma Morgan (A)	13,009	7.5
2 Martha E. Keys (D)	84,864	55.0
John C. Peterson (R)	67,650	43.9
3 Larry Winn Jr. (R)	89,694	62.9
Samuel J. Wells (D)	49,976	35.0
4 Garner E. Shriver (R)	70,401	48.8
Bert Chaney (D)	61,210	42.5
John S. Stevens (A)	12,520	8.7
5 Joe Skubitz (R)	88,646	55.2
Franklin D. Gaines (D)	72,024	44.8

KENTUCKY

Candidates	Votes	%
1 Carroll Hubbard Jr. (D)	70,723	78.2
Charles T. Banken Jr. (R)	16,937	18.7
2 William H. Natcher (D)	56,502	73.0
Art Eddleman (R)	18,312	23.7
3 Romano L. Mazzoli (D)	75,571	69.7
Vincent N. Barclay (R)	28,813	26.6
4 M. G. (Gene) Snyder (R)	63,845	51.7
Kyle Hubbard (D)	59,539	48.3
5 Tim Lee Carter (R)	66,709	68.2
Lyle L. Willis (D)	28,706	29.3
6 John B. Breckinridge (D)	63,010	72.1
Thomas F. Rogers III (R)	21,039	24.1
7 Carl D. Perkins (D)	71,221	75.6
Granville Thomas (R)	22,982	24.4

LOUISIANA [3]

Candidates	Votes	%
1 F. Edward Hebert (D)	48,452	100.0
2 Corinne C. Boggs (D)	58,802	81.8
Diane Morphos (R)	9,632	14.6
3 David C. Treen (R)	55,574	58.5
Charles Grisbaum Jr. (D)	39,412	41.5
4 Joe D. Waggonner Jr. (D)	47,371	100.0
5 Otto E. Passman (D)	43,068	100.0
6 W. Henson Moore (R)		
Jeff LaCaze (D)		
7 John B. Breaux (D)	59,406	89.3
Jeremy J. Millett (IND)	7,131	10.7
8 Gillis W. Long (D)	41,704	100.0

MAINE [4]

Candidates	Votes	%
1 David F. Emery (R)	94,203	50.2
Peter N. Kyros (D)	93,524	49.8

Candidates	Votes	%
2 William S. Cohen (R)	118,154	71.4
Markham L. Gartley (D)	47,399	28.6

MARYLAND

Candidates	Votes	%
1 Robert E. Bauman (R)	59,570	53.0
Thomas J. Hatem (D)	52,853	47.0
2 Clarence D. Long (D)	103,222	77.1
John M. Seney (R)	30,639	22.9
3 Paul S. Sarbanes (D)	93,218	83.8
William H. Mathews (R)	17,967	16.2
4 Marjorie S. Holt (R)	61,208	58.1
Fred L. Wineland (D)	44,059	41.9
5 Gladys N. Spellman (D)	45,211	52.6
John B. Burcham Jr. (R)	40,805	47.4
6 Goodloe E. Byron (D)	90,882	73.7
Elton R. Wampler (R)	32,416	26.3
7 Parren J. Mitchell (D)	43,252	100.0
8 Gilbert Gude (R)	104,675	65.9
Sidney Kramer (D)	54,112	34.1

MASSACHUSETTS

Candidates	Votes	%
1 Silvio O. Conte (R)	107,285	71.1
Thomas R. Manning (D)	43,524	28.9
2 Edward P. Boland (D)	105,763	100.0
3 Joseph D. Early (D)	78,244	49.5
David J. Lionett (R)	60,717	38.4
Douglas J. Rowe (IND)	19,018	12.0
4 Robert F. Drinan (D)	77,286	50.8
Jon Rotenberg (IND)	52,786	34.7
Alvin Mandell (R)	21,922	14.4
5 Paul E. Tsongas (D)	99,518	60.6
Paul W. Cronin (R)	64,596	39.4
6 Michael J. Harrington (D)	119,278	100.0
7 Torbert H. Macdonald (D)	122,165	79.8
James J. Murphy (IND)	30,959	20.2
8 Thomas P. O'Neill Jr. (D)	107,042	87.9
James Kiggin (USLP)	8,363	6.9
Laura Ross (COM)	6,421	5.3
9 John Joseph Moakley (D)	94,804	89.3
L. R. Sherman (USLP)	11,344	10.7
10 Margaret M. Heckler (R)	99,993	64.2
Barry F. Monahan (D)	55,871	35.8
11 James A. Burke (D)	125,978	100.0
12 Gerry E. Studds (D)	138,779	74.8
J. Alan MacKay (R)	46,787	25.2

MICHIGAN

Candidates	Votes	%
1 John Conyers Jr. (D)	97,620	90.7
Walter F. Girardot (R)	9,358	8.7
2 Marvin L. Esch (R)	72,245	52.3
John S. Reuther (D)	62,755	45.4
3 Garry Brown (R)	70,157	51.2
Paul H. Todd Jr. (D)	65,212	47.6
4 Edward Hutchinson (R)	64,731	53.1
Richard E. Daugherty (D)	55,469	45.5
5 Richard F. Vander Veen (D)	80,778	52.6
Paul G. Goebel Jr. (R)	66,659	43.4
6 Bob Carr (D)	73,956	49.3
Clifford W. Taylor (R)	73,309	48.9
7 Donald W. Riegle Jr. (D)	81,014	64.7
Robert E. Eastman (R)	41,603	33.2
8 Bob Traxler (D)	77,795	54.8
James M. Sparling Jr. (R)	61,578	43.4
9 Guy A. Vander Jagt (R)	87,551	56.6
Norman C. Halbower (D)	65,235	42.1
10 Elford A. Cederberg (R)	78,897	53.7
Samuel D. Marble (D)	67,467	45.9
11 Philip E. Ruppe (R)	83,293	50.9
Francis D. Brouillette (D)	79,793	48.8
12 James G. O'Hara (D)	89,822	72.2
Eugene J. Tyza (R)	34,292	27.6
13 Charles C. Diggs Jr. (D)	63,246	87.4
George E. McCall (R)	8,036	11.1
14 Lucien N. Nedzi (D)	93,973	71.2
Herbert O. Steiger (R)	35,723	27.1
15 William D. Ford (D)	86,601	78.1
Jack A. Underwood (R)	23,028	20.8

Footnotes, see p. 1036.

MICHIGAN

	Candidates	Votes	%
16	John D. Dingell (D)	95,834	77.7
	Wallace D. English (R)	25,248	20.5
17	William M. Brodhead (D)	94,242	69.5
	Kenneth C. Gallagher (R)	39,856	29.4
18	James J. Blanchard (D)	83,523	58.7
	Robert J. Huber (R)	57,133	40.2
19	William S. Broomfield (R)	86,846	62.9
	George F. Montgomery (D)	50,924	36.9

Special Elections

		Votes	%
5	Richard F. Vander Veen (D)	53,083	50.9
	Robert Vander Laan (R)	46,160	44.3
8	Bob Traxler (D)	59,993	51.5
	James M. Sparling Jr. (R)	56,548	48.5

MINNESOTA

		Votes	%
1	Albert H. Quie (R)	95,138	62.6
	Uric Scott (D)	56,868	37.4
2	Tom Hagedorn (R)	88,071	53.1
	Steve Babcock (D)	77,780	46.9
3	Bill Frenzel (R)	83,325	60.4
	Bob Riggs (D)	54,630	39.6
4	Joseph E. Karth (D)	95,437	76.0
	Joseph A. Rheinberger (R)	30,083	24.0
5	Donald M. Fraser (D)	90,012	73.8
	Phil Ratte (R)	30,146	24.7
6	Richard Nolan (D)	96,465	55.4
	Jon Grunseth (R)	77,797	44.6
7	Bob Bergland (D)	129,207	75.0
	Dan Reber (R)	43,045	25.0
8	James L. Oberstar (D)	104,740	62.0
	Jerome Arnold (R)	44,298	26.2
	William R. Ojala (EJ)	16,932	10.0

MISSISSIPPI

		Votes	%
1	Jamie L. Whitten (D)	39,158	88.2
	Jack Benney (IND)	5,250	11.8
2	David R. Bowen (D)	37,909	66.1
	Ben F. Hilbun Jr. (R)	15,876	27.7
	H. B. Wells (IND)	3,573	6.2
3	G. V. (Sonny) Montgomery (D)	43,020	100.0
4	Thad Cochran (R)	62,634	70.2
	Kenneth L. Dean (D)	25,699	28.8
5	Trent Lott (R)	52,489	73.0
	Walter W. Murphey (D)	10,333	14.4
	Claudia Mertz (IND)	6,404	8.9

MISSOURI

		Votes	%
1	William (Bill) Clay (D)	61,933	68.3
	Arthur O. Martin (R)	28,707	31.7
2	James W. Symington (D)	85,977	61.0
	Howard C. Ohlendorf (R)	55,026	39.0
3	Leonor K. Sullivan (D)	96,201	74.3
	Jo Ann P. Raisch (R)	31,489	24.3
4	William J. Randall (D)	82,447	67.9
	Claude Patterson (R)	39,055	32.1
5	Richard Bolling (D)	57,081	69.1
	John J. McDonough (R)	24,669	29.9
6	Jerry Litton (D)	101,609	78.9
	Grover H. Speers (R)	27,147	21.1
7	Gene Taylor (R)	79,787	52.3
	Richard L. Franks (D)	72,653	47.7
8	Richard H. Ichord (D)	86,595	69.9
	James A. Noland Jr. (R)	37,369	30.1
9	William L. Hungate (D)	87,546	66.4
	Milton Bischof Jr. (R)	44,318	33.6
10	Bill D. Burlison (D)	77,677	72.8
	Truman Farrow (R)	29,050	27.2

MONTANA

	Candidates	Votes	%
1	Max S. Baucus (D)	74,304	54.8
	Richard G. Shoup (R)	61,309	45.2
2	John Melcher (D)	74,680	63.0
	John K. McDonald (R)	43,853	37.0

NEBRASKA

		Votes	%
1	Charles Thone (R)	82,353	53.3
	Hess Dyas (D)	72,099	46.7
2	John Y. McCollister (R)	72,731	55.2
	Daniel C. Lynch (D)	59,142	44.8
3	Virginia Smith (R)	80,992	50.2
	Wayne W. Ziebarth (D)	80,255	49.8

NEVADA

		Votes	%
AL	James Santini (D)	93,665	55.8
	David Towell (R)	61,182	36.4
	Joel F. Hansen (IA)	13,119	7.8

NEW HAMPSHIRE

		Votes	%
1	Norman E. D'Amours (D)	58,388	52.1
	David A. Banks (R)	53,610	47.9
2	James C. Cleveland (R)	69,068	64.2
	Helen L. Bliss (D)	38,463	35.8

NEW JERSEY

		Votes	%
1	James J. Florio (D)	80,768	57.5
	John E. Hunt (R)	54,069	38.5
2	William J. Hughes (D)	109,763	57.3
	Charles W. Sandman Jr. (R)	79,064	41.3
3	James J. Howard (D)	105,799	68.9
	Kenneth W. Clark (R)	45,932	29.8
4	Frank Thompson Jr. (D)	82,195	66.8
	Henry J. Keller (R)	40,797	33.2
5	Millicent Fenwick (R)	81,498	53.4
	Frederick M. Bohen (D)	66,380	43.5
6	Edwin B. Forsythe (R)	81,190	52.5
	Charles B. Yates (D)	70,353	45.5
7	Andrew Maguire (D)	79,808	49.7
	William B. Widnall (R)	71,377	44.4
	Milton Gralla (IND)	9,520	5.9
8	Robert A. Roe (D)	83,724	73.9
	Herman Schmidt (R)	27,839	24.6
9	Henry Helstoski (D)	99,592	64.5
	Harold A. Pareti (R)	50,859	32.9
10	Peter W. Rodino Jr. (D)	53,094	81.0
	John R. Taliaferro (R)	9,936	15.2
11	Joseph G. Minish (D)	98,957	69.2
	William B. Grant (R)	42,036	29.4
12	Matthew J. Rinaldo (R)	92,829	65.0
	Adam K. Levin (D)	46,246	32.4
13	Helen S. Meyner (D)	86,043	57.3
	Joseph J. Maraziti (R)	64,166	42.7
14	Dominick V. Daniels (D)	85,438	79.9
	Claire J. Sheridan (R)	17,231	16.1
15	Edward J. Patten (D)	92,593	71.0
	E. J. Hammesfahr (R)	35,875	27.5

NEW MEXICO

		Votes	%
1	Manuel Lujan Jr. (R)	106,268	58.6
	Robert A. Mondragon (D)	71,968	39.7
2	Harold Runnels (D)	90,127	66.7
	Donald W. Trubey (R)	43,045	31.9

NEW YORK

		Votes	%
1	Otis G. Pike (D-L)	101,130	65.0
	Donald R. Sallah (R)	44,513	28.6
	Seth C. Morgan (C)	10,038	6.4
2	Thomas J. Downey (D)	58,289	48.8
	James R. Grover Jr. (R)	53,344	44.7
	Neil Greene (C)	7,818	6.5

	Candidates	Votes	%
3	Jerome A. Ambro Jr. (D)	76,383	51.8
	Angelo D. Roncalio (R-C)	67,986	46.1
4	Norman F. Lent (R-C)	85,382	53.6
	Franklin Ornstein (D-L)	73,822	46.4
5	John W. Wydler (R-C)	91,677	54.2
	Allard K. Lowenstein (D-L)	77,356	45.8
6	Lester L. Wolff (D-L)	101,237	66.7
	Edythe Layne (R-C)	50,528	33.3
7	Joseph P. Addabbo (D-R-L)	83,972	100.0
8	Benjamin S. Rosenthal (D-L)	90,200	79.0
	Albert Lemishow (R-C)	23,980	21.0
9	James J. Delaney (D-R-C)	92,231	93.0
	Theodore E. Garrison (L)	6,924	7.0
10	Mario Biaggi (D-R)	75,375	82.4
	Francis L. McHugh (C)	10,250	11.2
	John P. Hagan (L)	5,797	6.3
11	James H. Scheuer (D)	62,388	72.2
	E. G. Desborough (R)	12,297	14.2
	Christopher Acer (C)	7,181	8.3
	Tibby Blum (L)	4,485	5.2
12	Shirley Chisholm (D-L)	26,468	80.2
	Francis J. Voyticky (R)	4,577	13.9
13	Stephen J. Solarz (D-L)	91,008	81.8
	Jack N. Dobosh (R)	20,229	18.2
14	Frederick W. Richmond (D)	33,195	71.3
	Michael Carbajal Jr. (R)	5,360	11.5
	Donald H. Elliott (L)	6,186	13.3
15	Leo C. Zeferetti (D-C)	53,733	58.4
	Austen D. Canade (R)	34,814	37.9
16	Elizabeth Holtzman (D-L)	74,010	78.9
	Joseph L. Gentili (R-C)	19,806	21.1
17	John M. Murphy (D)	63,805	57.7
	Frank J. Biondolillo (R)	28,269	25.6
	Jerome Kretchmer (L)	10,622	9.6
	Michael Ajello (C)	7,808	7.1
18	Edward I. Koch (D-L)	91,985	76.7
	John Boogaerts Jr. (R)	22,560	18.8
19	Charles B. Rangel (D-R-L)	63,146	96.9
20	Bella S. Abzug (D-L)	76,074	78.7
	Stephen Posner (R)	15,053	15.6
21	Herman Badillo (D-L)	28,025	96.7
22	Jonathan B. Bingham (D-L)	77,157	85.1
	Robert Black (R)	8,142	9.0
	John DiGiovanni (C)	5,333	5.9
23	Peter A. Peyser (R-C)	80,361	57.6
	W. S. Greenawalt (D-L)	59,108	42.4
24	Richard L. Ottinger (D)	82,542	57.8
	Charles J. Stephens (R-C)	60,180	42.2
25	Hamilton Fish Jr. (R-C)	103,799	65.3
	Nicholas B. Angell (D)	53,357	33.6
26	Benjamin A. Gilman (R)	81,562	54.0
	John G. Dow (D-L)	58,161	38.5
	Thomas Moore (C)	11,345	7.5
27	Matthew F. McHugh (D-L)	83,562	52.8
	Alfred J. Libous (R)	68,273	43.1
28	Samuel S. Stratton (D)	156,439	80.6
	Wayne E. Wagner (R)	33,493	17.3
29	Edward W. Pattison (D-L)	100,324	54.5
	Carleton J. King (R-C)	83,768	45.5
30	Robert C. McEwen (R-C)	78,117	55.0
	Roger W. Tubby (D-L)	63,893	44.0
31	Donald J. Mitchell (R-C)	94,319	59.6
	Donald J. Reile (D)	59,639	37.7
32	James M. Hanley (D)	88,660	59.1
	William E. Bush (R-C)	61,379	40.9
33	William F. Walsh (R)	97,380	65.3
	Robert H. Bockman (D)	45,043	30.2
34	Frank Horton (R)	105,585	67.5
	Irene Gossin (D)	45,408	29.0
35	Barber B. Conable Jr. (R)	90,269	56.8
	Margaret Costanza (D)	63,012	39.6
36	John J. LaFalce (D-L)	90,498	59.6
	Russell A. Rourke (R-C)	61,442	40.4
37	Henry J. Nowak (D-L)	84,064	75.0
	Joseph R. Bala (R-C)	27,531	24.6
38	Jack F. Kemp (R-C)	126,687	72.1
	Barbara C. Wicks (D-L)	48,929	27.9
39	James F. Hastings (R)	87,321	60.2
	W. L. Parment (D-L)	53,866	37.1

NORTH CAROLINA

Candidates	Votes	%
1 Walter B. Jones (D)	55,323	77.5
Harry McMullan (R)	16,097	22.5
2 L. H. Fountain (D)	52,786	100.0
3 David N. Henderson (D)	50,931	100.0
4 Ike F. Andrews (D)	62,600	64.7
Ward Purrington (R)	33,521	34.6
5 Stephen L. Neal (D)	64,634	52.0
Wilmer Mizell (R)	59,182	47.6
6 Richardson Preyer (D)	56,507	63.7
R. S. Ritchie (R)	31,906	35.9
7 Charles G. Rose III (D)	49,780	100.0
8 W. G. (Bill) Hefner (D)	61,591	57.0
Earl B. Ruth (R)	46,500	43.0
9 James G. Martin (R)	51,032	54.4
Milton Short (D)	41,387	44.1
10 James T. Broyhill (R)	63,382	54.4
Jack L. Rhyne (D)	53,131	45.6
11 Roy A. Taylor (D)	89,163	66.0
Albert F. Gilman (R)	45,983	34.0

NORTH DAKOTA

	Votes	%
AL Mark Andrews (R)	130,184	55.7
Byron Dorgan (D)	103,504	44.3

OHIO

Candidates	Votes	%
1 Willis D. Gradison Jr. (R)	70,284	50.9
Thomas A. Luken (D)	67,685	49.1
2 Donald D. Clancy (R)	71,512	53.4
Edward W. Wolterman (D)	62,530	46.6
3 Charles W. Whalen Jr. (R)	82,159	100.0
4 Tennyson Guyer (R)	81,674	61.5
James L. Gehrlich (D)	51,065	38.5
5 Delbert L. Latta (R)	89,161	62.5
Bruce Edwards (D)	53,391	37.5
7 William H. Harsha (R)	93,400	68.2
Lloyd Allen Wood (D)	42,316	31.2
7 Clarence J. Brown (R)	73,503	60.5
Patrick L. Nelson (D)	34,828	28.7
Dorothy Franke (IND)	13,088	10.8
8 Thomas N. Kindness (R)	51,097	42.4
T. Edward Strinko (D)	45,701	38.0
Don Gingerich (IND)	23,616	19.6
9 Thomas L. Ashley (D)	64,831	52.8
C. S. Finkbeiner Jr. (R)	57,892	47.2
10 Clarence E. Miller (R)	100,521	70.4
H. Kent Bumpass (D)	42,333	29.6
11 J. William Stanton (R)	79,756	60.5
Michael D. Coffey (D)	52,017	39.5
12 Samuel L. Devine (R)	73,303	50.9
Fran Ryan (D)	70,818	49.1
13 Charles A. Mosher (R)	72,881	57.5
Fred M. Ritenauer (D)	53,766	42.5
14 John F. Seiberling (D)	93,931	75.4
Mark Figetakis (R)	30,603	24.6
15 Chalmers P. Wylie (R)	79,376	61.5
Mike McGee (D)	49,683	38.5
16 Ralph S. Regula (R)	92,986	65.6
John G. Freedom (D)	48,754	34.4
17 John M. Ashbrook (R)	70,708	52.7
David D. Noble (D)	63,342	47.3
18 Wayne L. Hays (D)	90,447	65.6
Ralph H. Romig (R)	47,385	34.4
19 Charles J. Carney (D)	97,709	72.7
James L. Ripple (R)	36,649	27.3
20 James V. Stanton (D)	86,405	86.9
Robert A. Frantz (R)	12,991	13.1
21 Louis Stokes (D)	58,969	82.0
Bill Mack (R)	12,986	18.0
22 Charles A. Vanik (D)	112,671	78.7
William J. Franz (R)	30,585	21.3
23 Ronald M. Mottl (D)	53,338	34.8
George E. Mastics (R)	46,810	30.5
Dennis J. Kucinich (IND)	45,186	29.4

Candidates	Votes	%
1 Thomas A. Luken (D)	55,134	51.9
Willis D. Gradison Jr. (R)	51,063	48.1

OKLAHOMA

	Votes	%
1 James R. Jones (D)	88,159	67.9
George Alfred Mizer Jr. (R)	41,697	32.1
2 Theodore Risenhoover (D)	78,046	59.1
Ralph F. Keen (R)	54,110	40.9
3 Carl Albert (D)		100.0
4 Tom Steed (D)		100.0
5 John Jarman (D)	52,107	51.7
M. H. Edwards (R)	48,705	48.3
6 Glenn English (D)	76,392	53.2
John N. Happy Camp (R)	63,731	44.4

OREGON

	Votes	%
1 Les AuCoin (D)	114,629	56.0
Diarmuid O'Scannlain (R)	89,848	43.9
2 Al Ullman (D)	140,963	78.1
Kenneth Brown (R)	39,441	21.9
3 Robert Duncan (D)	129,290	70.4
John Piacentini (R)	54,080	29.5
4 James Weaver (D)	97,580	52.9
John Dellenback (R)	86,950	47.1

PENNSYLVANIA

	Votes	%
1 William A. Barrett (D)	96,988	75.8
Russell M. Nigro (R)	29,772	23.3
2 Robert N. C. Nix (D)	75,033	74.0
Jesse W. Woods Jr. (R)	26,353	26.0
3 William J. Green III (D)	84,675	75.4
Richard P. Colbert (R)	27,692	24.6
4 Joshua Eilberg (D)	123,952	71.0
Isadore Einhorn (R)	50,688	29.0
5 Richard T. Schulze (R)	83,526	59.6
Leo D. McDermott (D)	56,626	40.4
6 Gus Yatron (D)	111,127	74.6
Stephen Postupack (R)	35,805	24.0
7 Robert W. Edgar (D)	89,680	55.3
Stephen J. McEwen Jr. (R)	70,894	43.7
8 Edward G. Biester Jr. (R)	75,313	56.3
William B. Moyer (D)	54,815	40.9
9 E. G. Shuster (R)	73,881	56.5
Robert D. Ford (D)	56,844	43.5
10 Joseph M. McDade (R)	100,793	64.9
Thomas J. Hanlon (D)	54,401	35.1
11 Daniel J. Flood (D)	111,572	74.5
Richard A. Muzyka (R)	38,106	25.5
12 John P. Murtha (D)	89,193	58.1
Harry M. Fox (R)	64,416	41.9
13 R. Lawrence Coughlin (R)	98,985	62.5
Lawrence H. Curry (D)	59,433	37.5
14 William S. Moorhead (D)	93,169	77.4
Zachary Taylor Davis (R)	27,116	22.5
15 Fred B. Rooney (D)	85,905	100.0
16 Edwin D. Eshleman (R)	73,130	63.5
Michael J. Minney (D)	40,273	35.0
17 Herman T. Schneebeli (R)	70,274	52.1
Peter C. Wambach (D)	64,576	47.9
18 H. John Heinz III (R)	107,723	72.1
Francis J. McArdle (D)	41,706	27.9
19 William F. Goodling (R)	66,417	51.4
Arthur L. Berger (D)	61,414	47.6
20 Joseph M. Gaydos (D)	112,237	81.7
Joseph J. Anderko (R)	25,129	18.3
21 John H. Dent (D)	88,701	69.9
C. L. Sconing (R)	38,111	30.1
22 Thomas E. Morgan (D)	83,654	63.6
J. R. Montgomery (R)	41,706	31.7
23 Albert W. Johnson (R)	67,192	52.7
Yates Mast (D)	60,211	47.3
24 Joseph P. Vigorito (D)	76,920	58.6
Clement R. Scalzitti (R)	54,277	41.4
25 Gary A. Myers (R)	74,645	53.8
Frank M. Clark (D)	64,049	46.2

Candidates	Votes	%
12 John P. Murtha (D)	60,538	49.9
Harry M. Fox (R)	60,416	49.8

RHODE ISLAND

	Votes	%
1 Fernand J. St Germain (D)	105,288	72.9
Ernest Barone (R)	39,096	27.1
2 Edward P. Beard (D)	124,759	78.2
Vincent J. Rotondo (R)	34,728	21.8

SOUTH CAROLINA

	Votes	%
1 Mendel J. Davis (D)	63,111	72.7
George B. Rast (R)	22,450	25.9
2 Floyd Spence (R)	58,936	56.1
Matthew J. Perry (D)	45,205	43.0
3 Butler C. Derrick Jr. (D)	55,120	61.8
Marshall J. Parker (R)	34,046	38.2
4 James R. Mann (D)	45,070	63.3
Robert L. Watkins (R)	26,185	36.7
5 Kenneth L. Holland (D)	47,614	61.4
Len Phillips (R)	29,294	37.8
6 John W. Jenrette Jr. (D)	45,396	52.0
Edward L. Young (R)	41,982	48.0

SOUTH DAKOTA

	Votes	%
1 Larry Pressler (R)	78,266	55.3
Frank E. Denholm (D)	63,339	44.7
2 James Abdnor (R)	88,746	67.8
Jack M. Weiland (D)	42,119	32.2

TENNESSEE

	Votes	%
1 James H. Quillen (R)	76,394	64.2
Lloyd Blevins (D)	42,523	35.8
2 John J. Duncan (R)	87,419	70.9
Jesse James Brown (D)	35,920	29.1
3 Marilyn Lloyd (D)	61,926	51.1
LaMar Baker (R)	55,580	45.9
4 Joe L. Evins (D)	94,847	99.9
5 Richard Fulton (D)	88,206	99.8
6 Robin L. Beard Jr. (R)	76,928	56.7
Tim Schaeffer (D)	58,824	43.3
7 Ed Jones (D)	83,231	100.0
8 Harold E. Ford (D)	67,925	49.9
Dan Kuykendall (R)	67,181	49.4

TEXAS

	Votes	%
1 Wright Patman (D)	49,426	68.6
James W. Farris (R)	22,619	31.4
2 Charles Wilson (D)	57,096	100.0
3 James M. Collins (R)	63,489	64.7
Harold Collum (D)	34,623	35.3
4 Ray Roberts (D)	48,209	74.9
Dick LeTourneau (R)	16,113	25.1
5 Alan Steelman (R)	28,446	52.1
Mike McKool (D)	26,190	47.9
6 Olin E. Teague (D)	53,345	83.0
Carl A. Nigliazzo (R)	10,908	17.0
7 Bill Archer (R)	70,363	79.2
Jim Brady (D)	18,524	20.8
8 Bob Eckhardt (D)	30,158	72.2
Donald D. Whitefield (R)	11,605	27.8
9 Jack Brooks (D)	37,275	61.9
Coleman R. Ferguson (R)	22,935	38.1
10 J. J. Pickle (D)	76,240	80.4
Paul A. Weiss (R)	18,560	19.6
11 W. R. Poage (D)	46,828	81.6
Don Clements (R)	9,883	17.2
12 Jim Wright (D)	42,632	78.7
James S. Garvey (R)	11,543	21.3

Candidates	Votes	%
13 Jack Hightower (D)	53,094	*57.6*
Robert Price (R)	39,087	*42.4*
14 John Young (D)	41,066	*100.0*
15 Eligio de la Garza (D)	42,567	*100.0*
16 Richard C. White (D)	42,880	*100.0*
17 Omar Burleson (D)	64,595	*100.0*
18 Barbara C. Jordan (D)	36,597	*84.8*
Robbins Mitchell (R)	6,053	*14.0*
19 George Mahon (D)	49,610	*100.0*
20 Henry B. Gonzalez (D)	39,358	*100.0*
21 Robert Krueger (D)	53,543	*52.6*
Douglas S. Harlan (R)	45,959	*45.2*
22 Bob Casey (D)	47,783	*69.5*
Ron Paul (R)	19,483	*28.4*
23 Abraham Kazen Jr. (D)	47,249	*100.0*
24 Dale Milford (D)	36,085	*76.1*
Joseph Beaman Jr. (R)	9,698	*20.4*

UTAH

	Votes	%
1 K. Gunn McKay (D)	124,793	*62.6*
Ronald W. Inkley (R)	62,807	*31.5*
L. S. Brown (A)	11,664	*5.9*
2 Allan T. Howe (D)	105,739	*49.5*
Stephen M. Harmsen (R)	100,259	*46.9*

VERMONT

	Votes	%
AL James M. Jeffords (R)	74,561	*52.9*
Francis J. Cain (D I VT)	56,342	*40.0*
Michael Parenti (LU)	9,961	*7.1*

VIRGINIA

Candidates	Votes	%
1 Thomas N. Downing (D)	58,338	*99.8*
2 G. William Whitehurst (R)	49,369	*60.0*
Robert R. Richards (D)	32,923	*40.0*
3 David E. Satterfield III (D)	64,627	*88.5*
A. R. Ogden (IND)	7,574	*10.4*
4 Robert W. Daniel Jr. (R)	48,032	*47.2*
Lester E. Schlitz (D)	36,489	*35.9*
Curtis W. Harris (IND)	17,224	*16.9*
5 W. C. (Dan) Daniel (D)	52,459	*99.4*
6 M. Caldwell Butler (R)	45,805	*45.1*
Paul J. Puckett (D)	27,350	*27.0*
Warren D. Saunders (IND)	26,466	*26.1*
7 J. Kenneth Robinson (R)	54,267	*52.6*
George H. Gilliam (D)	48,611	*47.1*
8 Herbert E. Harris (D)	53,074	*57.6*
Stanford E. Parris (R)	38,997	*42.4*
9 William C. Wampler (R)	68,183	*50.9*
Charles J. Horne (D)	65,783	*49.1*
10 Joseph L. Fisher (D)	67,184	*53.6*
Joel T. Broyhill (R)	56,649	*45.2*

WASHINGTON

	Votes	%
1 Joel Pritchard (R)	108,391	*69.5*
W. R. Knedlik (D)	44,655	*28.6*
2 Lloyd Meeds (D)	81,565	*59.7*
Ronald C. Reed (R)	53,157	*38.9*
3 Don Bonker (D)	93,980	*60.9*
A. Ludlow Kramer (R)	58,774	*38.1*
4 Mike McCormack (D)	84,949	*58.9*
Floyd Paxton (R)	59,249	*41.1*
5 Thomas S. Foley (D)	87,959	*64.3*
Gary G. Gage (R)	48,739	*35.7*
6 Floyd V. Hicks (D)	95,354	*71.8*
George M. Nalley (R)	37,400	*28.2*
7 Brock Adams (D)	85,593	*71.1*
Raymond Pritchard (R)	34,847	*28.9*

WEST VIRGINIA

Candidates	Votes	%
1 Robert H. Mollohan (D)	72,457	*59.7*
Joe Laurita Jr. (R)	48,966	*40.3*
2 Harley O. Staggers (D)	73,683	*64.4*
William H. Loy (R)	40,779	*35.6*
3 John M. Slack (D)	77,586	*68.5*
William L. Larcamp (R)	35,623	*31.5*
4 Ken Hechler (D)	66,420	*100.0*

WISCONSIN

	Votes	%
1 Les Aspin (D)	81,902	*70.5*
Leonard W. Smith (R)	34,288	*29.5*
2 Robert W. Kastenmeier (D)	93,561	*64.8*
Elizabeth T. Miller (R)	50,890	*35.2*
3 Alvin J. Baldus (D)	76,668	*51.1*
Vernon W. Thomson (R)	71,171	*47.4*
4 Clement J. Zablocki (D)	84,768	*72.5*
Lewis H. Collison (R)	27,818	*23.8*
5 Henry S. Reuss (D)	65,060	*80.0*
Mildred A. Morries (R)	16,293	*20.0*
6 William A. Steiger (R)	86,652	*59.5*
Nancy J. Simenz (D)	51,571	*35.4*
Harvey C. LeRoy (A)	7,432	*5.1*
7 David R. Obey (D)	104,468	*70.5*
Josef Burger (R)	43,558	*29.4*
8 Robert J. Cornell (D)	79,923	*54.4*
Howard V. Froehlich (R)	66,889	*45.6*
9 Robert W. Kasten Jr. (R)	77,733	*52.9*
Lynn S. Adelman (D)	66,071	*45.0*

WYOMING

	Votes	%
AL Teno Roncalio (D)	69,434	*54.7*
Tom Stroock (R)	57,499	*45.3*

1975 House Elections

CALIFORNIA

Special Election

Candidates	Votes	%
37 Shirley N. Pettis (R)	53,165	*60.5*
Ron Pettis (D)	12,940	*14.7*
James L. Mayfield (D)	11,140	*12.7*
Frank M. Bogert (R)	4,773	*5.4*

ILLINOIS

Special Election

	Votes	%
5 John G. Fary (D)	55,036	*71.9*
Francis X. Lawlor (R)	21,491	*28.1*

LOUISIANA

Special Election [1]

	Votes	%
6 W. Henson Moore (R)	74,802	*54.1*
Jeff LaCaze (D)	63,366	*45.9*

TENNESSEE

Special Election

	Votes	%
5 Clifford Allen (D)	46,593	*64.6*
Bob Olsen (R)	24,901	*34.5*

1974 Election

1. LLJ, the party affiliation of the 1st District candidate, J. M. Sanders, stands for "Life, Liberty, Justice."

2. In the 6th District special election, 146,147 votes were were cast. To win outright without a second election, a candidate needed 73,074 votes. John L. Burton received 73,114 votes, 40 more than needed.

California was redistricted in 1974 for the November general election, changing the numbers of many of the districts. Burton was re-elected to the 94th Congress (1975-77) from the 5th District and Robert J. Lagomarsino from the 19th.

3. There are no reliable final returns for the House race in the 6th District. Post-election results showed Moore leading LaCaze by a handful of votes, but the outcome could not be determined because one voting machine had malfunctioned and did not record votes for LaCaze.

The case went to the Louisiana courts for resolution. LaCaze asked that persons who voted on the malfunctioning machine be polled again in court under oath and their votes added to the total, but the Louisiana Supreme Court rejected this plan and ordered a new election. Moore won easily. (See Louisiana 1975.)

4. The returns from the 1st District House race are not final. Kyros challenged Emery's election before the House Administration Committee, which conducted a partial recount of the returns until Kyros conceded defeat. The recount changed the total votes received by each candidate, but not the result.

1975 Election

1. This election, Jan. 7, 1975, was a court-ordered rerun held after it was found impossible to determine who won the November 1974 House race between the same two candidates. (See Louisiana 1974.)

1976 House Elections

ALABAMA

Candidates	Votes	%
1 Jack Edwards (R)	98,257	62.5
Bill Davenport (D)	58,906	37.5
2 William L. Dickinson (R)	90,069	57.6
J. Carole Keahey (D)	66,288	42.4
3 Bill Nichols (D)	106,935	99.0
4 Tom Bevill (D)	141,490	80.4
Leonard Wilson (R)	34,531	19.6
5 Ronnie G. Flippo (D)	113,553	100.0
6 John Buchanan (R)	92,113	56.7
Mel Bailey (D)	69,384	42.7
7 Walter Flowers (D)	110,496	100.0

ALASKA

Candidates	Votes	%
AL Donald E. Young (R)	83,722	70.8
Eben Hopson (D)	34,194	28.9

ARIZONA

Candidates	Votes	%
1 John J. Rhodes (R)	96,397	57.3
Patricia Fullinwider (D)	68,404	40.7
2 Morris K. Udall (D)	106,054	58.2
Laird Guttersen (R)	71,765	39.4
3 Bob Stump (R)	88,854	47.5
Fred Koory Jr. (R)	79,162	42.3
Bill McCune (NON PART I)	19,149	10.2
4 Eldon Rudd (R)	93,154	48.6
Tony Mason (D)	92,435	48.2

ARKANSAS

Candidates	Votes	%
1 Bill Alexander (D)	116,217	68.9
Harlan (Bo) Holleman (R)	52,565	31.1
2 Jim Guy Tucker (D)	144,780	86.4
James J. Kelly (R)	22,819	13.6
3 John Paul Hammerschmidt (R) [1]		100.0
4 Ray Thornton (D) [1]		100.0

CALIFORNIA

Candidates	Votes	%
1 Harold T. (Bizz) Johnson (D)	160,477	73.9
James E. Taylor (R)	56,539	26.1
2 Don H. Clausen (R)	121,290	56.0
Oscar H. Klee (D)	88,829	41.0
3 John E. Moss (D)	139,779	72.9
George R. Marsh Jr. (R)	52,075	27.1
4 Robert L. Leggett (D)	75,844	46.7
Albert Dehr (R)	75,193	46.3
Joseph E. (Ted) Sheedy (WRITE IN)	11,279	6.9
5 John L. Burton (D)	103,746	61.8
Branwell Fanning (R)	64,008	38.2
6 Phillip Burton (D)	86,493	66.1
Tom Spinosa (R)	35,359	27.0
Emily Siegel (PFP)	6,570	5.0
7 George Miller (D)	147,064	74.7
Robert L. Vickers (R)	45,863	23.3
8 Ronald V. Dellums (D)	122,342	62.1
Philip S. Breck Jr. (R)	68,374	34.7
9 Fortney H. Stark Jr. (D)	116,398	70.8
James K. Mills (R)	44,607	27.1
10 Don Edwards (D)	111,992	72.0
Herb Smith (R)	38,088	24.5
11 Leo J. Ryan (D)	107,618	61.1
Bob Jones (R)	62,435	35.4
12 Paul N. McCloskey Jr. (R)	130,332	66.2
David Harris (D)	61,526	31.3
13 Norman Y. Mineta (D)	135,291	66.8
Ernest L. Konnyu (R)	63,130	31.2
14 John J. McFall (D)	123,285	72.5
Roger A. Blain (R)	46,674	27.5
15 B. F. Sisk (D)	92,735	72.2
Carol O. Harner (R)	35,700	27.8

Candidates	Votes	%
16 Leon E. Panetta (D)	104,545	53.4
Burt L. Talcott (R)	91,160	46.6
17 John Krebs (D)	103,898	65.7
Henry J. Andreas (R)	54,270	34.3
18 William M. Ketchum (R)	101,658	64.2
Dean Close (D)	56,683	35.8
19 Robert J. Lagomarsino (R)	124,201	64.4
Dan Sisson (D)	68,722	35.6
20 Barry M. Goldwater Jr. (R)	146,158	67.2
Patti Lear Corman (D)	71,193	32.8
21 James C. Corman (D)	101,837	66.5
Erwin G. (Ed) Hogan (R)	44,094	28.8
22 Carlos J. Moorhead (R)	114,769	62.6
Robert L. Salley (D)	68,543	37.4
32 Anthony C. (Tony) Beilenson (D)	130,619	60.2
Thomas F. Bartman (R)	86,434	39.8
24 Henry A. Waxman (D)	108,296	67.8
David I. Simmons (R)	51,478	32.2
25 Edward R. Roybal (D)	57,966	71.9
Jim Madrid (R)	17,737	22.0
Marilyn Seals (PFP)	4,922	6.1
26 John H. Rousselot (R)	112,619	65.6
Bruce Latta (D)	59,093	34.4
27 Robert K. Dornan (R)	114,623	54.7
Gary Familian (D)	94,988	45.3
28 Yvonne Brathwaite Burke (D)	114,612	80.2
Edward S. Skinner (R)	28,303	19.8
29 Augustus F. Hawkins (D)	82,515	85.4
Michael D. Germonprez (R)	10,852	11.2
30 George E. Danielson (D)	82,767	74.4
Harry Couch (R)	28,503	25.6
31 Charles H. Wilson (D)	83,155	100.0
32 Glenn M. Anderson (D)	92,034	72.2
Clifford O. Young (R)	35,394	27.8
33 Del Clawson (R)	95,398	55.1
Ted Snyder (D)	77,807	44.9
34 Mark W. Hannaford (D)	100,988	50.7
Daniel E. Lungren (R)	98,147	49.3
35 Jim Lloyd (D)	87,472	53.3
Louis Brutocao (R)	76,765	46.7
36 George E. Brown Jr. (D)	90,830	61.6
Grant C. Carner (R)	49,368	33.5
William E. Pasley (AMI)	7,358	5.0
37 Shirley N. Pettis (R)	133,634	71.1
Douglas C. Nilson Jr. (D)	49,021	26.1
38 Jerry M. Patterson (D)	103,317	63.6
James Combs (R)	59,092	36.4
39 Charles E. Wiggins (R)	122,657	58.6
William E. Farris (D)	86,745	41.4
40 Robert E. Badham (R)	148,512	59.3
Vivian Hall (D)	102,132	40.7
41 Bob Wilson (R)	128,784	57.7
King Golden Jr. (D)	94,590	42.3
42 Lionel Van Deerlin (D)	103,062	76.0
Wes Marden (R)	32,565	24.0
43 Clair W. Burgener (R)	173,576	65.0
Pat Kelly (D)	93,475	35.0

COLORADO

Candidates	Votes	%
1 Patricia Schroeder (D)	103,037	53.2
Don Friedman (R)	89,384	46.2
2 Timothy E. Wirth (D)	121,336	50.5
Ed Scott (R)	118,936	49.5
3 Frank E. Evans (D)	89,308	51.0
Melvin H. Takaki (R)	82,269	47.0
4 James P. Johnson (R)	119,408	53.7
Dan Ogden (D)	78,355	35.2
Dick Davis (I)	20,398	9.2
5 William L. Armstrong (R)	126,784	66.4
Dorothy Hores (D)	64,067	33.6

CONNECTICUT

Candidates	Votes	%
1 William R. Cotter (D)	128,479	57.1
Lucien P. DiFazio Jr. (R)	94,106	41.8

Candidates	Votes	%
2 Christopher J. Dodd (D)	142,684	65.1
Richard M. Jackson (R)	74,743	34.1
3 Robert N. Giaimo (D)	121,623	54.6
John G. Pucciano (R)	96,714	43.4
4 Stewart B. McKinney (R)	126,314	61.0
Geoffrey G. Peterson (R)	76,722	37.1
5 Ronald A. Sarasin (R)	157,009	66.5
Michael J. Adanti (D)	77,308	32.7
6 Anthony J. Moffett (D)	134,914	56.6
Thomas F. Upson (R)	102,364	43.0

DELAWARE

Candidates	Votes	%
AL Thomas B. Evans Jr. (R)	110,677	51.5
Samuel L. Shipley (D)	102,431	47.7

FLORIDA

Candidates	Votes	%
1 Robert L. F. Sikes (D) [1]		100.0
2 Don Fuqua (D) [1]		100.0
3 Charles E. Bennett (D) [1]		100.0
4 Bill Chappell Jr. (D) [1]		100.0
5 Richard Kelly (R)	138,371	59.0
Jo Ann Saunders (D)	96,260	41.0
6 C. W. Bill Young (R)	151,371	65.2
Gabriel Cazares (D)	80,821	34.8
7 Sam M. Gibbons (D)	102,739	65.7
Dusty Owens (R)	53,599	34.3
8 Andy Ireland (D)	103,360	58.0
Robert Johnson (R)	74,794	42.0
9 Louis Frey Jr. (R)	130,509	78.1
Joseph A. Rosier (D)	36,630	21.9
10 L. A. (Skip) Bafalis (R)	164,273	66.3
Bill Sikes (D)	83,413	33.7
11 Paul G. Rogers (D)	199,031	91.1
Clyde Adams (AM)	19,406	8.9
12 J. Herbert Burke (R)	107,268	53.9
Charles Friedman (D)	91,749	46.1
13 William Lehman (D)	127,822	78.3
Lee Arnold Spiegelman (R)	35,357	21.7
14 Claude Pepper (D)	82,665	72.9
Evelio S. Estrella (R)	30,774	27.1
15 Dante B. Fascell (D)	121,292	70.4
Paul R. Cobb (R)	50,941	29.6

GEORGIA

Candidates	Votes	%
1 Ronald B. Ginn (D)	73,826	99.9
2 Dawson Mathis (D)	95,807	99.8
3 Jack Brinkley (D)	93,174	88.7
Steve Dugan (R)	11,829	11.3
4 Elliott H. Levitas (D)	110,261	68.3
George Warren (R)	51,140	31.7
5 Andrew Young (D)	96,056	66.7
Ed Gadrix (R)	47,998	33.3
6 John J. Flynt Jr. (D)	77,532	51.7
Newt Gingrich (R)	72,400	48.3
7 Lawrence P. McDonald (D)	84,587	55.1
Quincy Collins (R)	68,947	44.9
8 Billy Lee Evans (D)	91,351	69.7
Billy Adams (R)	39,623	30.3
9 Ed Jenkins (D)	113,245	79.0
Louise Wofford (R)	29,954	20.9
10 Doug Barnard (D)	94,782	99.9

HAWAII

Candidates	Votes	%
1 Cecil (Cec) Heftel (D)	60,050	43.6
Fred W. Rohlfing (R)	53,745	39.1
Kathy Hoshijo (I GOD GOV)	23,807	17.3
2 Daniel K. Akaka (D)	124,116	79.5
Hank Inouye (R)	23,917	15.3

IDAHO

Candidates	Votes	%
1 Steven D. Symms (R)	95,833	54.6
Ken Pursley (D)	79,662	45.4

Candidates	Votes	%
2 George V. Hansen (R)	84,175	50.6
Stan Kress (D)	82,237	49.4

ILLINOIS

Candidates	Votes	%
1 Ralph H. Metcalfe (D)	126,632	92.3
A. A. Rayner (R)	10,147	7.4
2 Morgan F. Murphy (D)	127,297	84.7
Spencer Leak (R)	23,037	15.3
3 Martin A. Russo (D)	115,591	58.9
Ronald Buikema (R)	79,434	40.5
4 Edward J. Derwinski (R)	124,847	65.8
Ronald A. Rodger (D)	64,924	34.2
5 John G. Fary (D)	119,336	76.9
Vincent Krok (R)	35,756	23.1
6 Henry J. Hyde (R)	106,667	60.6
Marilyn D. Clancy (D)	69,359	39.4
7 Cardiss Collins (D)	88,239	84.8
Newell Ward (R)	15,854	15.2
8 Dan Rostenkowski (D)	105,595	80.5
John F. Urbaszewski (R)	25,512	19.5
9 Sidney R. Yates (D)	121,915	72.1
Thomas J. Wajerski (R)	47,054	27.8
10 Abner J. Mikva (D)	106,804	50.0
Samuel H. Young (R)	106,603	50.0
11 Frank Annunzio (D)	135,755	67.4
Daniel C. Reber (R)	65,680	32.6
12 Philip M. Crane (R)	151,899	72.8
E. L. Frank (D)	56,644	27.2
13 Robert McClory (R)	109,726	66.8
James J. Cummings (D)	49,777	30.3
14 John N. Erlenborn (R)	176,076	74.4
Marie Agnes Fese (D)	60,505	25.6
15 Tom Corcoran (R)	102,555	53.9
Tim L. Hall (D)	87,676	46.1
16 John B. Anderson (R)	114,324	67.9
Stephen Eytalis (D)	54,002	32.1
17 George M. O'Brien (R)	113,145	58.2
Merlin E. Karlock (D)	81,220	41.8
18 Robert H. Michel (R)	108,028	57.7
Matthew Ryan (D)	79,102	42.3
19 Thomas F. Railsback (R)	132,571	68.5
John Craver (D)	60,967	31.5
20 Paul Findley (R)	137,223	63.6
Peter F. Mack Jr. (D)	78,634	36.4
21 Edward R. Madigan (R)	137,037	74.5
Anna Wall Scott (D)	46,996	25.5
22 George E. Shipley (D)	129,187	61.4
Ralph Y. McGinnis (R)	81,102	38.6
23 Melvin Price (D)	128,113	78.6
Sam P. Drenovac (R)	34,825	21.4
24 Paul Simon (D)	152,344	67.4
Peter G. Prineas (R)	73,766	32.6

INDIANA

Candidates	Votes	%
1 Adam Benjamin Jr. (D)	121,155	71.3
Robert J. Billings (R)	48,756	28.7
2 Floyd Fithian (D)	117,617	54.8
William W. Erwin (R)	95,505	44.5
3 John Brademas (D)	101,777	56.9
Thomas L. Thorson (R)	77,094	43.1
4 Dan Quayle (R)	107,762	54.4
J. Edward Roush (D)	88,361	44.6
5 Elwood H. Hillis (R)	127,194	61.7
William C. Stout (D)	78,807	38.3
6 David W. Evans (D)	105,773	54.9
David G. Crane (R)	86,854	45.1
7 John T. Myers (R)	130,005	62.7
John Elden Tipton (D)	77,355	37.3
8 David L. Cornwell (D)	109,013	50.5
Belden Bell (R)	107,013	49.5
9 Lee H. Hamilton (D)	136,056	100.0
10 Philip R. Sharp (D)	114,559	59.8
William G. Frazier (R)	76,890	40.2
11 Andrew Jacobs Jr. (D)	115,895	60.4
Lawrence L. Buell (R)	74,829	39.0

IOWA

Candidates	Votes	%
1 James A. S. Leach (R)	109,694	51.9
Edward Mezvinsky (D)	101,024	47.8
2 Michael T. Blouin (D)	102,980	50.3
Tom Riley (R)	100,344	49.1
3 Charles E. Grassley (R)	117,957	56.5
Stephen J. Rapp (D)	90,981	43.5
4 Neal Smith (D)	145,343	69.1
Charles E. Minor (R)	65,013	30.9
5 Tom Harkin (D)	135,600	64.9
Kenneth R. Fulk (R)	71,377	34.1
6 Berkley Bedell (D)	133,507	67.4
Joanne D. Soper (R)	62,292	31.5

KANSAS

Candidates	Votes	%
1 Keith G. Sebelius (R)	142,311	73.1
Randy D. Yowell (D)	52,459	26.9
2 Martha E. Keys (D)	88,645	50.7
Ross R. Freeman (R)	82,946	47.4
3 Larry Winn Jr. (R)	123,578	68.7
Philip S. Rhoads (D)	52,110	29.0
4 Dan Glickman (D)	90,067	50.3
Garner E. Shriver (R)	86,832	48.5
5 Joe Skubitz (R)	109,573	60.7
Virgil L. Olson (D)	65,340	36.2

KENTUCKY

Candidates	Votes	%
1 Carroll Hubbard Jr. (D)	118,886	82.0
Bob Bersky (R)	26,089	18.0
2 William H. Natcher (D)	79,016	60.4
Walter B. Baker (R)	51,900	39.6
3 Romano L. Mazzoli (D)	80,496	57.2
Denzil J. Ramsey (R)	58,019	41.2
4 M. G. (Gene) Snyder (R)	97,493	55.9
Edward J. Winterberg (D)	77,009	44.1
5 Tim Lee Carter (R)	100,204	66.6
Charles C. Smith (D)	49,128	32.6
6 John Breckinridge (D)	90,695	94.0
Anthony A. McCord (AM)	5,795	6.0
7 Carl D. Perkins (D)	110,450	73.2
Granville Thomas (R)	40,381	26.8

LOUISIANA

Candidates	Votes	%
1 Richard A. Tonry (D)	61,652	47.2
Bob Livingston (R)	56,679	43.4
John R. Rarick (I)	12,227	9.4
2 Corinne (Lindy) (Mrs. Hale) Boggs (D)	85,923	92.6
Jules W. Hillery (I)	6,904	7.4
3 David C. Treen (R)	109,135	73.3
David H. Scheuermann Sr. (D)	39,728	26.7
4 Joe D. Waggonner Jr. (D)	76,406	100.0
5 Jerry Huckaby (D)	83,696	52.5
Frank Spooner (R)	75,574	47.5
6 W. Henson Moore III (R)	99,780	65.2
J. D. DeBlieux (D)	53,212	34.8
7 John B. Breaux (D)	117,196	83.3
Charles F. Huff (R)	23,414	16.7
8 Gillis W. Long (D)	106,285	94.2
Kent Courtney (I)	6,526	5.8

MAINE

Candidates	Votes	%
1 David F. Emery (R)	145,523	57.4
Frederick D. Barton (D)	108,105	42.6
2 William S. Cohen (R)	169,292	77.1
Leighton Cooney (D)	43,150	19.7

MARYLAND

Candidates	Votes	%
1 Robert E. Bauman (R)	85,919	54.1
Roy Dyson (D)	72,993	45.9
2 Clarence D. Long (D)	139,196	70.9
John M. Seney (R)	35,258	18.0
Ronald A. Meroney (I)	21,849	11.1
3 Barbara Mikulski (D)	107,014	74.6
Samuel A. Culotta (R)	36,447	25.4
4 Marjorie S. Holt (R)	95,158	57.7
Werner Fornos (D)	69,855	42.3
5 Gladys N. Spellman (D)	77,836	57.7
John B. Burcham Jr. (R)	57,057	42.3
6 Goodloe E. Bryon (D)	126,801	70.8
Arthur T. Bond (R)	52,203	29.2
7 Parren J. Mitchell (D)	94,991	94.4
William Salisbury (I)	5,642	5.6
8 Newton Steers (R)	111,274	46.8
Lanny Davis (D)	100,343	42.2
Robin Ficker (I)	26,035	11.0

MASSACHUSETTS

Candidates	Votes	%
1 Silvio O. Conte (R)	137,652	63.8
Edward A. McColgan (D)	78,181	36.2
2 Edward P. Boland (D)	134,408	72.4
Thomas P. Swank (R)	41,563	22.4
John D. McCarthy (USLP)	9,776	5.3
3 Joseph D. Early (D)	168,520	100.0
4 Robert F. Drinan (D)	109,268	52.1
Arthur D. Mason (R)	100,562	47.9
5 Paul E. Tsongas (D)	144,217	67.3
Roger P. Durkin (R)	70,036	32.7
6 Michael J. Harrington (D)	121,562	54.8
William E. Bronson (R)	91,655	41.3
7 Edward J. Markey (D)	162,126	76.9
Richard W. Daly (R)	37,063	17.6
8 Thomas P. O'Neill Jr. (D)	133,131	74.4
William A. Barnstead (R)	33,437	18.7
9 John Joseph Moakley (D)	103,901	69.6
Robert G. Cunningham (R)	34,547	23.1
Joseph M. O'Loughlin (I)	7,862	5.3
10 Margaret M. Heckler (R)	176,604	100.0
11 James A. Burke (D)	131,789	69.0
Danielle DeBenedictis (I)	59,240	31.0
12 Gerry E. Studds (D)	222,418	100.0

MICHIGAN

Candidates	Votes	%
1 John Conyers Jr. (D)	126,161	92.4
Isaac Hood (R)	8,927	6.5
2 Carl D. Pursell (R)	95,397	49.8
Edward C. Pierce (D)	95,053	49.6
3 Garry Brown (R)	99,231	50.6
Howard Wolpe (D)	95,261	48.6
4 Dave Stockman (R)	107,881	60.0
Richard E. Daugherty (D)	69,655	38.8
5 Harold S. Sawyer (R)	109,589	53.3
Richard F. Vander Veen (D)	94,973	46.2
6 Bob Carr (D)	108,909	52.7
Clifford W. Taylor (R)	96,008	46.5
7 Dale E. Kildee (D)	124,260	70.0
Robin Widgery (R)	50,301	28.3
8 Bob Traxler (D)	110,127	59.0
E. Brady Denton (R)	75,323	40.4
9 Guy A. Vander Jagt (R)	146,712	70.0
Stephen Fawley (D)	61,641	29.4
10 Elford A. Cederberg (R)	118,726	56.5
Donald J. Albosta (D)	89,980	42.8
11 Philip E. Ruppe (R)	118,871	54.7
Francis D. Brouillette (D)	97,325	44.8
12 David E. Bonior (D)	94,815	52.4
David M. Serotkin (R)	85,326	47.2
13 Charles C. Diggs Jr. (D)	83,387	89.0
Richard A. Golden (R)	9,002	9.6
14 Lucien N. Nedzi (D)	107,563	66.5
John Edward Getz (R)	52,995	32.8
15 William D. Ford (D)	117,313	74.0
James D. Walaskay (R)	39,177	24.7
16 John D. Dingell Jr. (D)	121,682	75.9
William E. Rostron (R)	36,378	22.7
17 William M. Brodhead (D)	112,746	64.3
James W. Burdick (R)	60,476	34.5
18 James J. Blanchard (D)	123,113	66.1
John E. Olsen (R)	60,995	32.8
19 William S. Broomfield (R)	131,799	66.7
Dorothea Becker (D)	64,337	32.6

MINNESOTA

Candidates	Votes	%
1 Albert H. Quie (I-R)	158,177	68.2
Robert C. Olson Jr. (DFL)	70,630	30.5

Candidates	Votes	%
2 Tom Hagedorn (I-R)	148,322	60.3
Gloria Griffin (DFL)	97,488	39.7
3 Bill Frenzel (I-R)	149,013	66.1
Jerome W. Coughlin (DFL)	72,044	32.0
4 Bruce F. Vento (DFL)	133,282	66.4
Andrew Engebretson (I-R)	59,767	29.8
5 Donald M. Fraser (DFL)	138,213	70.7
Richard M. Erdall (I-R)	50,764	26.0
6 Richard M. Nolan (DFL)	147,507	59.8
James Anderson (I-R)	99,201	40.2
7 Bob Bergland (DFL)	174,080	72.0
Bob Leiseth (I-R)	64,333	26.6
8 James L. Oberstar (DFL)	206,755	100.0

MISSISSIPPI

1 Jamie L. Whitten (D)	93,687	100.0
2 David R. Bowen (D)	75,092	63.0
Roland Byrd (R)	42,601	35.7
3 G. V. (Sonny) Montgomery (D)	129,088	93.9
Dorothy Colby Cleveland (R)	8,321	6.1
4 Thad Cochran (R)	101,132	76.0
Sterling P. Davis (D)	28,737	21.6
5 Trent Lott (R)	104,554	68.2
Gerald Blessey (D)	48,724	31.8

MISSOURI

1 William Clay (D)	87,310	65.5
Robert L. Witherspoon (R)	45,874	34.4
2 Robert A. Young (D)	111,568	51.1
Robert O. Snyder (R)	106,811	48.9
3 Richard A. Gephardt (D)	115,109	63.7
Joseph L. Badaracco (R)	65,623	36.3
4 Ike Skelton (D)	115,955	55.9
Richard A. King (R)	91,605	44.1
5 Richard Bolling (D)	100,876	68.0
Joanne M. Collins (R)	41,681	28.1
6 E. Thomas Coleman (R)	120,969	58.5
Morgan Maxfield (D)	83,755	40.5
7 Gene Taylor (R)	133,656	62.0
Dolan G. Hawkins (D)	81,848	38.0
8 Richard Ichord (D)	132,386	67.3
Charles R. Leick (R)	60,179	30.6
9 Harold L. Volkmer (D)	120,325	55.9
J. H. Frappier (R)	94,816	44.1
10 Bill D. Burlison (D)	131,675	72.1
Joe Carron (R)	51,024	27.9

MONTANA

1 Max S. Baucus (D)	111,487	66.4
W. D. (Bill) Diehl (R)	56,297	33.6
2 Ron Marlenee (R)	84,149	55.0
Thomas E. Towe (D)	68,972	45.0

NEBRASKA

1 Charles Thone (R)	146,558	73.2
Pauline F. Anderson (D)	53,703	26.8
2 John J. Cavanaugh (D)	106,296	54.6
Lee Terry (R)	88,352	45.4
3 Virginia Smith (R)	150,720	72.9
James T. Hansen (D)	51,012	24.7

NEVADA

AL James Santini (D)	153,996	77.1
Walden Charles Earhart (R)	24,124	12.1
Janine M. Hansen (IA)	12,038	6.0

NEW HAMPSHIRE

1 Norman E. D'Amours (D)	107,806	68.0
John Adams (R)	48,087	30.3
2 James C. Cleveland (R)	100,911	60.5
J. Joseph Grandmaison (D)	65,792	39.5

NEW JERSEY

Candidates	Votes	%
1 James J. Florio (D)	136,624	70.1
Joseph I. McCullough Jr. (R)	56,363	28.9
2 William J. Hughes (D)	141,753	61.7
James R. Hurley (R)	87,915	38.3
3 James J. Howard (D)	127,164	62.1
Ralph A. Siciliano (R)	75,934	37.1
4 Frank Thompson Jr. (D)	113,281	66.3
Joseph S. Indyk (R)	54,789	32.1
5 Millicent Fenwick (R)	137,803	66.9
Frank R. Nero (D)	64,598	31.3
6 Edwin B. Forsythe (R)	125,920	58.8
Catherine A. Costa (D)	85,053	39.7
7 Andrew Maguire (D)	120,526	56.5
James J. Sheehan (R)	92,624	43.5
8 Robert A. Roe (D)	108,841	70.6
Bessie Doty (R)	44,775	29.0
9 Harold C. Hollenbeck (R)	107,454	53.1
Henry Helstoski (D)	89,723	44.3
10 Peter W. Rodino Jr. (D)	88,245	82.6
Tony Grandison (R)	17,129	16.0
11 Joseph G. Minish (D)	129,026	67.6
Charles A. Poekel Jr. (R)	59,397	31.1
12 Matthew J. Rinaldo (R)	136,973	73.1
Richard A. Buggelli (D)	49,189	26.3
13 Helen S. Meyner (D)	105,291	50.4
William E. Schluter (R)	100,050	47.9
14 Joseph A. LeFante (D)	73,174	49.9
Anthony L. Campenni (R)	66,319	45.2
15 Edward J. Patten (D)	106,170	59.0
Charles W. Wiley (R)	54,487	30.3
Dennis Adams Sr. (I)	14,543	8.1

NEW MEXICO

1 Manuel Lujan Jr. (R)	162,587	72.1
Raymond Garcia (D)	61,800	27.4
2 Harold Runnels (D)	123,563	70.3
Donald W. Trubey (R)	52,131	29.7

NEW YORK

1 Otis G. Pike (D,L)	135,528	65.3
Salvatore Nicosia (R)	61,671	29.7
2 Thomas J. Downey (D,I)	91,241	57.1
Peter Cohalan (R,C)	67,755	42.4
3 Jerome A. Ambro Jr. (D)	94,265	52.0
Howard T. Hogan Jr. (R,C)	84,824	46.8
4 Norman F. Lent (R,C)	106,058	55.8
Gerald P. Halpern (D,L)	83,971	44.2
5 John W. Wydler (R,C)	110,366	55.7
Allard K. Lowenstein (D,L)	87,868	44.3
6 Lester L. Wolff (D,L)	112,422	61.8
Vincent R. Balletta Jr. (R)	60,567	33.3
7 Joseph P. Addabbo (D,R,L)	107,312	94.7
8 Benjamin S. Rosenthal (D,L)	107,295	77.8
Albert Lemishow (R)	30,191	21.9
9 James J. Delaney (D,R,C)	109,552	95.1
10 Mario Biaggi (D,R)	106,222	91.6
Joanne S. Fuchs (C)	5,868	5.1
11 James H. Scheuer (D)	84,770	74.1
Arthur Cuccia (R)	19,203	16.8
Bryan F. Levinson (C)	6,316	5.5
12 Shirley Chisholm (D,L)	43,203	87.0
Horace Morancie (R)	5,336	10.8
13 Stephen J. Solarz (D,L)	110,624	83.7
Jack N. Dobosh (R,C)	21,600	16.3
14 Frederick W. Richmond (D,L)	55,723	85.0
Frank X. Gargiulo (R,C)	8,977	13.7
15 Leo C. Zeferetti (D,C)	69,242	63.2
Ronald J. D'Angelo (R)	33,641	30.7
Arthur J. Paone (L)	6,604	6.0
16 Elizabeth Holtzman (D,L)	93,995	82.9
Gladys Pemberton (R,C)	19,423	17.1
17 John M. Murphy (D)	89,126	65.6
Kenneth J. Grossberger (R)	27,734	20.4
John M. Peters (C)	10,399	7.7
Ned Schneir (L)	8,656	6.4
18 Edward I. Koch (D,L)	112,187	75.1
Sonia Landau (R)	29,728	19.9

Candidates	Votes	%
19 Charles B. Rangel (D,R,L)	91,672	97.0
20 Theodore S. Weiss (D,L)	91,977	83.2
Denise Weiseman (R)	14,114	12.8
21 Herman Badillo (D,R,L)	41,285	98.6
22 Jonathan B. Bingham (D,L)	92,044	86.4
Paul Slotkin (R)	11,130	10.4
23 Bruce F. Caputo (R,C)	93,006	53.6
J. Edward Meyer (D,L)	80,424	46.4
24 Richard L. Ottinger (D)	99,761	54.5
David V. Hicks (R,C)	81,111	44.3
25 Hamilton Fish Jr. (R,C)	139,434	70.5
Minna Post Peyser (D)	58,216	29.5
26 Benjamin A. Gilman (R)	120,049	65.3
John R. Maloney (D)	60,511	32.9
27 Matthew F. McHugh (D,L)	127,048	66.6
William H. Harter (R,C)	63,626	33.4
28 Samuel S. Stratton (D)	170,034	79.0
Mary A. Bradt (R,C)	44,053	20.5
29 Edward W. Pattison (D,L)	100,663	47.0
Joseph A. Martino (R)	96,476	45.0
James E. DeYoung (C)	15,337	7.2
30 Robert C. McEwen (R,C)	95,564	55.7
Norma A. Bartle (D)	75,951	44.3
31 Donald J. Mitchell (R,C)	123,143	66.5
Anita Maxwell (D)	62,032	33.5
32 James M. Hanley (D)	101,419	54.8
George C. Wortley (R,C)	81,597	44.1
33 William F. Walsh (R)	125,163	68.5
Charles R. Welch (D)	48,855	26.7
34 Frank J. Horton (R)	126,566	65.9
William C. Larsen (D)	58,247	30.3
35 Barber B. Conable Jr. (R)	120,738	64.3
Michael Macaluso (D,C)	67,177	35.7
36 John J. LaFalce (D,L)	123,246	66.6
Ralph J. Argen (R,C)	61,701	33.4
37 Henry J. Nowak (D,L)	100,042	78.2
Calvin Kimbrough (R)	23,660	18.5
38 Jack F. Kemp (R,C)	165,702	78.2
Peter J. Geraci (D,L)	46,307	21.8
39 Stanley N. Lundine (D)	109,986	61.8
Richard A. Snowden (R,C)	68,018	38.2

Special Election		
39 Stanley N. Lundine (D)	55,402	61.2
John T. Calkins (R)	35,107	38.8

NORTH CAROLINA

1 Walter B. Jones (D)	98,611	75.9
Joseph M. Ward (R)	29,295	22.5
2 L. H. Fountain (D)	113,368	99.8
3 Charlie Whitley (D)	77,193	68.7
Willard J. Blanchard (R)	35,089	31.2
4 Ike F. Andrews (D)	92,165	60.6
Johnnie L. Gallemore Jr. (R)	59,917	39.4
5 Stephen L. Neal (D)	98,789	54.2
Wilmer D. Mizell (R)	83,129	45.6
6 Richardson Preyer (D)	103,851	96.3
7 Charles Rose (D)	95,463	81.3
M.H. (Mike) Vaughan (R)	21,955	18.7
8 W. G. (Bill) Hefner (D)	99,296	65.7
Carl Eagle (R)	49,094	32.5
9 James G. Martin (R)	82,297	53.5
Arthur Goodman Jr. (D)	70,847	46.1
10 James T. Broyhill (R)	99,882	59.8
John J. Hunt (D)	67,190	40.2
11 Lamar Gudger (D)	93,857	50.9
Bruce B. Briggs (R)	88,752	48.1

NORTH DAKOTA

AL Mark Andrews (R)	181,018	62.4
Lloyd Omdahl (D)	104,263	36.0

OHIO

1 Willis D. Gradison Jr. (R)	109,789	64.8
William F. Bowen (D)	56,995	33.6
2 Thomas A. Luken (D)	88,178	51.4
Donald D. Clancy (R)	83,459	48.6

Candidates	Votes	%
3 Charles W. Whalen Jr. (R)	100,871	69.4
Leonard Stubbs (D)	33,873	23.3
4 Tennyson Guyer (R)	121,173	70.1
Clinton G. Dorsey (D)	51,784	29.9
5 Delbert L. Latta (R)	124,910	67.4
Bruce Edwards (D)	60,304	32.6
6 William H. Harsha (R)	107,064	61.5
Ted Strickland (D)	67,067	38.5
7 Clarence J. Brown Jr. (R)	101,027	64.9
Dorothy Franke (D)	54,755	35.1
8 Thomas N. Kindness (R)	110,775	68.7
John W. Griffin (D)	46,424	28.8
9 Thomas L. Ashley (D)	91,040	54.2
C. S. Finkbeiner (R)	73,919	44.0
10 Clarence E. Miller (R)	127,147	68.8
James A. Plummer (D)	57,757	31.2
11 J. William Stanton (R)	120,716	71.7
Thomas R. West Jr. (D)	47,548	28.3
12 Samuel L. Devine (R)	90,987	46.5
Fran Ryan (D)	89,424	45.7
William R. Moss (I)	15,429	7.9
13 Don J. Pease (D)	108,061	66.0
Woodrow W. Mathna (R)	49,828	30.4
14 John F. Seiberling Jr. (D)	121,652	74.1
James E. Houston (R)	39,917	24.3
15 Chalmers P. Wylie (R)	109,630	65.5
Mike McGee (D)	57,741	34.5
16 Ralph S. Regula (R)	116,374	66.8
John G. Freedom (D)	55,671	32.0
17 John M. Ashbrook (R)	94,874	56.8
John C. McDonald (D)	72,168	43.2
18 Douglas Applegate (D)	116,901	62.9
Ralph R. McCoy (R)	45,735	24.6
William Crabbe (I)	21,537	11.6
19 Charles J. Carney (D)	90,386	50.2
Jack C. Hunter (R)	86,162	47.9
20 Mary Rose Oakar (D)	98,785	81.0
Raymond J. Grabow (I)	20,553	16.9
21 Louis Stokes (D)	91,903	83.8
Barbara Sparks (R)	12,434	11.3
22 Charles A. Vanik (D)	128,535	72.7
Harry A. Hanna (R)	42,727	24.2
32 Ronald M. Mottl (D)	130,576	73.2
Michael T. Scanlon (R)	47,804	26.8

OKLAHOMA

Candidates	Votes	%
1 James R. Jones (D)	100,945	54.0
James M. Inhofe (R)	84,374	45.1
2 Theodore Risenhoover (D)	102,402	54.0
E. L. (Bud) Stewart (R)	87,341	46.0
3 Wes Watkins (D)	151,271	82.0
Gerald L. Beasley Jr. (R)	31,732	17.2
4 Tom Steed (D)	116,425	74.9
M. C. Stanley (R)	34,170	22.0
5 M. H. Edwards (R)	78,651	49.9
Tom Dunlap (D)	74,752	47.4
6 Glenn English (D)	137,498	71.1
Carol McCurley (R)	55,953	28.9

OREGON

Candidates	Votes	%
1 Les AuCoin (D)	154,844	58.7
Philip N. Bladine (R)	109,140	41.3
2 Al Ullman (D)	173,313	72.0
Thomas H. Mercer (R)	67,431	28.0
3 Robert Duncan (D)	148,503	83.9
Martin Simon (I)	28,245	16.0
4 James Weaver (D)	122,475	50.0
Jerry Lausmann (R)	85,943	35.1
Jim Howard (I)	22,104	9.0
Theodora Nathan (I)	14,307	5.8

PENNSYLVANIA

Candidates	Votes	%
1 Michael (Ozzie) Myers (D)	117,087	73.5
Samuel N. Fanelli (R)	40,191	25.2
2 Robert N. C. Nix (D)	109,855	73.5
Jesse W. Woods Jr. (R)	37,907	25.4

Candidates	Votes	%
3 Raymond F. Lederer (D)	98,627	73.2
Terrence J. Schade (R)	35,491	26.3
4 Joshua Eilberg (D)	144,890	67.5
James E. Mugford (R)	69,700	32.5
5 Richard T. Schulze (R)	119,682	59.5
Anthony Campolo (D)	81,299	40.5
6 Gus Yatron (D)	133,624	73.8
Stephen Postupack (R)	46,103	25.5
7 Robert W. Edgar (D)	109,436	54.1
John N. Kenney (R)	92,788	45.9
8 Peter H. Kostmayer (D)	93,855	49.5
John S. Renninger (R)	92,543	48.8
9 E. G. Shuster (R,D)	154,359	100.0
10 Joseph M. McDade (R)	125,218	62.6
Edward Mitchell (D)	74,925	37.4
11 Daniel J. Flood (D)	130,175	70.8
Howard G. Williams (R)	53,621	29.2
12 John P. Murtha (D)	122,504	67.7
Ted Humes (R)	58,489	32.3
13 R. Lawrence Coughlin (R)	130,765	63.4
Gertrude Strick (D)	75,435	36.6
14 William S. Moorhead (D)	114,472	71.7
John F. Bradley (R)	43,308	27.1
15 Fred B. Rooney (D)	108,844	65.2
Alice Sivulich (R)	57,616	34.5
16 Robert S. Walker (R)	97,527	62.3
Michael J. Minney (D)	57,836	37.0
17 Allen E. Ertel (D)	86,158	50.7
H. Joseph Hepford (R)	82,370	48.5
18 Douglas Walgren (D)	113,787	59.5
Robert J. Casey (R)	77,594	40.5
19 William F. Goodling (R)	124,098	70.6
Richard P. Noll (D)	51,686	29.4
20 Joseph M. Gaydos (D)	134,961	75.0
John P. Kostelac (R)	44,432	24.7
21 John H. Dent (D)	99,160	59.4
Robert H. Miller (R)	67,763	40.6
22 Austin J. Murphy (D)	97,036	55.3
Roger Fischer (R)	77,030	43.9
23 Joseph S. Ammerman (D)	95,821	56.5
Albert W. Johnson (R)	73,641	43.5
24 Marc L. Marks (R)	101,048	55.4
Joseph P. Vigorito (D)	79,937	43.8
25 Gary A. Myers (R)	103,632	56.8
Eugene V. Atkinson (D)	78,857	43.2

RHODE ISLAND

Candidates	Votes	%
1 Fernand J. St Germain (D)	116,674	62.4
John J. Slocum Jr. (R)	68,080	36.4
2 Edward P. Beard (D)	154,453	76.5
Thomas V. Iannitti (R)	45,438	22.5

SOUTH CAROLINA

Candidates	Votes	%
1 Mendel J. Davis (D)	89,891	68.9
Lonnie Rowell (R)	40,598	31.1
2 Floyd D. Spence (R)	83,426	57.5
Clyde B. Livingston (D)	60,602	41.8
3 Butler C. Derrick (D)	117,740	99.9
4 James R. Mann (D)	91,721	73.5
Robert L. Watkins (R)	32,983	26.4
5 Kenneth L. Holland (D)	66,073	51.4
Bobby Richardson (R)	62,095	48.3
6 John W. Jenrette Jr. (D)	75,916	55.5
Edward L. Young (R)	60,288	44.0

SOUTH DAKOTA

Candidates	Votes	%
1 Larry Pressler (R)	121,587	79.8
James V. Guffey (D)	29,533	19.4
2 James Abdnor (R)	99,601	69.9
Grace Mickelson (D)	42,968	30.1

TENNESSEE

Candidates	Votes	%
1 James H. (Jimmy) Quillen (R)	97,781	57.9
Lloyd Blevins (D)	69,507	41.2

Candidates	Votes	%
2 John J. Duncan (R)	117,256	62.8
Mike Rowland (D)	69,449	37.2
3 Marilyn Lloyd (D)	123,872	67.5
LaMar Baker (R)	57,116	31.1
4 Albert Gore Jr. (D)	115,392	94.0
William H. McGlamery (I)	7,320	6.0
5 Clifford R. Allen (D)	125,830	92.4
Roger E. Bissell (I)	10,292	7.6
6 Robin L. Beard (R)	116,905	64.5
Ross Bass (D)	64,462	35.5
7 Ed Jones (D)	105,832	100.0
8 Harold E. Ford (D)	100,683	60.7
A. D. Alissandratos (R)	63,819	38.5

TEXAS

Candidates	Votes	%
1 Sam B. Hall Jr. (D)	135,384	83.7
James Hogan (R)	26,334	16.3
2 Charles Wilson (D)	133,910	95.0
James William Doyle III (AM)	6,992	5.0
3 James M. Collins (R)	171,343	74.0
Les E. Shackelford Jr. (D)	60,070	26.0
4 Ray Roberts (D)	105,394	62.7
Frank S. Glenn (R)	62,641	37.3
5 Jim Mattox (D)	67,871	54.0
Nancy Judy (R)	56,056	44.6
6 Olin E. Teague (D)	119,025	65.9
Wes Mowery (R)	60,316	33.4
7 Bill Archer (R)	193,127	100.0
8 Bob Eckhardt (D)	84,404	60.7
Nick Gearhart (R)	54,566	39.2
9 Jack Brooks (D)	112,945	99.9
10 J. J. (Jake) Pickle (D)	160,683	76.8
Paul McClure (R)	48,482	23.2
11 W. R. Poage (D)	92,142	57.4
Jack Burgess (R)	68,373	42.6
12 Jim Wright (D)	101,814	75.8
W. R. Durham (R)	31,941	23.8
13 Jack Hightower (D)	101,798	59.3
Bob Price (R)	69,328	40.4
14 John Young (D)	93,589	61.4
L. Dean Holford (R)	58,788	38.6
15 Eligio de la Garza (D)	102,837	74.4
R. L. (Lendy) McDonald (R)	35,446	25.6
16 Richard C. White (D)	71,876	57.8
Vic Shackelford (R)	52,499	42.2
17 Omar Burleson (D)	127,613	99.9
18 Barbara C. Jordan (D)	93,953	85.5
Sam H. Wright (R)	15,381	14.0
19 George Mahon (D)	87,908	54.6
Jim Reese (R)	72,991	45.4
20 Henry B. Gonzalez (D)	90,173	100.0
21 Robert Krueger (D)	149,395	71.0
Bobby A. Locke (R)	56,211	26.7
22 Bob Gammage (D)	96,535	50.1
Ron Paul (R)	96,267	49.9
23 Abraham Kazen Jr. (D)	96,481	100.0
24 Dale Milford (D)	82,743	63.4
Leo Berman (R)	47,075	36.1

Special Elections [2]

Candidates	Votes	%
1 Sam B. Hall Jr. (D)	20,556	72.0
Glen Jones (D)	6,327	22.2
22 Bob Gammage (D)	15,287	42.1
Ron Paul (R)	14,386	39.6
John S. Brunson (D)	3,670	10.1

Special Runoff Election

Candidates	Votes	%
22 Ron Paul (R)	39,041	56.2
Bob Gammage (D)	30,483	43.8

UTAH

Candidates	Votes	%
1 K. Gunn McKay (D)	155,631	58.2
Joe H. Ferguson (R)	106,542	39.8
2 Dan Marriott (R)	144,861	52.4
Allan T. Howe (D)	110,931	40.1
D. J. McCarty (WRITE IN)	20,508	7.4

VERMONT

Candidates	Votes	%
AL James M. Jeffords (R)	124,458	67.4
John A. Burgess (D,I VT)	60,202	32.6

VIRGINIA

Candidates	Votes	%
1 Paul S. Trible Jr. (R)	71,789	48.6
Robert E. Quinn (D)	70,159	47.5
2 G. William Whitehurst (R)	79,381	65.7
Robert E. Washington (D)	41,464	34.3
3 David E. Satterfield III (D)	129,066	87.9
A. R. Ogden (I)	17,503	11.9
4 Robert W. Daniel Jr. (R)	74,495	53.0
J. W. (Billy) O'Brien (D)	65,982	47.0
5 W. C. (Dan) Daniel (D)	101,038	100.0
6 M. Caldwell Butler (R)	90,830	62.2
Warren D. Saunders (I)	55.115	37.8
7 J. Kenneth Robinson (R)	115,508	81.6
James B. Hutt Jr. (I)	25,731	18.2
8 Herbert E. Harris (D)	83,245	51.6
James R. Tate (R)	68,729	42.6
Michael D. Cannon (I)	9,292	5.8
9 William C. Wampler (R)	96,052	57.3
Charles J. Horne (D)	71,439	42.6
10 Joseph L. Fisher (D)	103,689	54.7
Vincent F. Callahan Jr. (R)	73,616	38.8
E. Stanley Rittenhouse (I)	12,124	6.4

WASHINGTON

Candidates	Votes	%
1 Joel Pritchard (R)	161,354	71.9
Dave Wood (D)	58,006	25.8
2 Lloyd Meeds (D)	107,328	49.3
John Nance Garner (R)	106,786	49.0
3 Don Bonker (D)	145,198	70.8
Chuck Elhart (R)	57,517	28.0
4 Mike McCormack (D)	115,364	57.8
Dick Granger (R)	81,813	41.0
5 Thomas S. Foley (D)	120,415	58.0
Duane Alton (R)	84,262	40.6
6 Norman D. Dicks (D)	137,964	73.5
Robert M. Reynolds (R)	47,539	25.3
7 Brock Adams (D)	133,673	73.0
Raymond Pritchard (R)	46,448	25.4

WEST VIRGINIA

Candidates	Votes	%
1 Robert H. Mollohan (D)	108,103	58.0
John F. McCuskey (R)	78,159	42.0
2 Harley O. Staggers (D)	136,749	73.2
Jim Sloan (R)	50,079	26.8
3 John M. Slack (D)	128,086	99.7
4 Nick J. Rahall (D)	73,626	45.6
Ken Hechler (WRITE IN)	59,067	36.6
E. S. (Steve) Goodman (R)	28,825	17.8

WISCONSIN

Candidates	Votes	%
1 Les Aspin (D)	136,162	64.9
William W. Petrie (R)	71,427	34.0
2 Robert W. Kastenmeier (D)	155,158	65.6
Elizabeth T. Miller (R)	81,350	34.4
3 Alvin J. Baldus (D)	139,083	58.1
Adolf L. Gundersen (R)	100,218	41.9
4 Clement J. Zablocki (D)	172,166	100.0
5 Henry S. Reuss (D)	134,935	77.8
Robert L. Hicks (R)	36,413	21.0
6 William A. Steiger (R)	139,541	63.3
Joseph C. Smith (D)	80,715	36.6
7 David R. Obey (D)	171,366	73.3
Frank A. Savino (R)	60,952	26.1
8 Robert J. Cornell (D)	115,996	50.9
Harold V. Froehlich (R)	107,048	46.9
9 Robert W. Kasten Jr. (R)	163,791	65.9
Lynn M. McDonald (D)	84,706	34.1

WYOMING

Candidates	Votes	%
AL Teno Roncalio (D)	85,721	56.4
Larry Joe Hart (R)	66,147	43.6

1976 Election

1. Arkansas and Florida did not record the votes for unopposed candidates.
2. Texas election law required all candidates in special elections to run against each other, regardless of party. If no candidate received a majority, a special election runoff was held between the two candidates receiving the most votes in the special election.

1977 House Elections

GEORGIA

Special Election [1]

Candidates	Votes	%
5 Wyche Fowler Jr. (D)	29,898	39.6
John Lewis (D)	21,531	28.6
Paul D. Coverdell (R)	16,509	21.9

Special Runoff Election

	Votes	%
5 Wyche Fowler Jr. (D)	54,378	62.4
John Lewis (D)	32,732	37.6

LOUISIANA

Special Election

Candidates	Votes	%
1 Robert L. Livingston (R)	56,121	51.2
Ron Faucheux (D)	40,802	37.2
Sanford Krasnoff (I)	12,665	11.6

MINNESOTA

Special Election

	Votes	%
7 Arlan Stangeland (I-R)	71,340	57.6
Michael J. Sullivan (DFL)	45,490	36.7

WASHINGTON

Special Election

Candidates	Votes	%
7 John E. Cunningham (R)	42,650	54.0
Marvin Durning (D)	35,525	45.0

1977 Election

1. Georgia election law required all candidates in special elections to run against each other, regardless of party. If no candidate received a majority, a special election runoff was held between the two candidates receiving the most votes in the special election.

1978 House Elections

ALABAMA

Candidates	Votes	%
1 Jack Edwards (R)	71,711	63.9
L. W. (Red) Noonan (D)	40,450	36.1
2 William L. Dickinson (R)	57,924	54.0
Wendell Mitchell (D)	49,341	46.0
3 Bill Nichols (D)	74,895	100.0
4 Tom Bevill (D)	87,380	100.0
5 Ronnie G. Flippo (D)	68,985	96.8
6 John Buchanan (R)	65,700	61.7
Don Hawkins (D)	40,771	38.3
7 Richard C. Shelby (D)	77,742	93.8

ALASKA

Candidates	Votes	%
AL Don Young (R)	68,811	55.4
Patrick Rodey (D)	55,176	44.4

ARIZONA

Candidates	Votes	%
1 John J. Rhodes (R)	81,108	71.0
Ken Graves (D)	33,178	29.0
2 Morris K. Udall (D)	67,878	52.5
Tom Richey (D)	58,697	45.4
3 Bob Stump (D)	111,850	85.0
Kathleen Cooke (LIBERT)	19,813	15.0
4 Eldon Rudd (R)	90,768	63.1
Michael L. McCormick (D)	48,661	33.8

ARKANSAS

Candidates	Votes	%
1 Bill Alexander (D)		100.0
2 Ed Bethune (R)	65,285	51.2
Doug Brandon (D)	62,140	48.8
3 John Paul Hammerschmidt (R)	130,086	78.4
William C. Mears (D)	35,748	21.6
4 Beryl F. Anthony Jr. (D)		100.0

CALIFORNIA

Candidates	Votes	%
1 Harold T. Johnson (D)	125,122	59.4
James E. Taylor (R)	85,690	40.6
2 Don H. Clausen (R)	114,451	52.0
Norma Bork (D)	99,712	45.3
3 Robert T. Matsui (D)	105,537	53.4
Sandy Smoley (R)	91,966	46.6
4 Vic Fazio (D)	87,764	55.4
Rex Hime (R)	70,733	44.6
5 John L. Burton (D)	106,046	66.8
Dolores Skore (R)	52,603	33.2
6 Phillip Burton (D)	81,801	68.3
Tom Spinosa (R)	33,515	27.9
7 George Miller (D)	109,676	63.4
Paula Gordon (R)	58,332	33.7
8 Ronald V. Dellums (D)	94,824	57.4
Charles V. Hughes (R)	70,481	42.6
9 Fortney H. (Pete) Stark (D)	88,179	65.4
Robert S. Allen (R)	41,138	30.5
10 Don Edwards (D)	84,488	67.1
Rudy Hansen (R)	41,374	32.9
11 Leo J. Ryan (D)	92,882	60.5
David Welch (R)	54,621	35.6
12 Paul N. McCloskey Jr. (R)	116,982	73.1
Kirsten Olsen (R)	34,472	21.5
13 Norman Y. Mineta (D)	100,809	57.5
Dan O'Keefe (R)	69,306	39.5
14 Norman D. Shumway (R)	95,962	53.4
John J. McFall (D)	76,602	42.6
15 Tony Coelho (D)	75,212	60.1
Chris Patterakis (R)	49,914	39.9
16 Leon E. Panetta (D)	104,550	61.4
Eric Seastrand (R)	65,808	38.6
17 Charles (Chip) Pashayan Jr. (R)	81,296	54.5
John Krebs (D)	67,885	45.5
18 William Thomas (R)	85,663	59.2
Bob Sogge (D)	58,900	40.7

Candidates	Votes	%
19 Robert J. Lagomarsino (R)	123,192	71.7
Jerome Zamos (D)	41,672	24.3
20 Barry M. Goldwater Jr. (R)	129,714	66.4
Pat Lear (D)	65,695	33.6
21 James C. Corman (D)	73,869	59.5
G. (Rod) Walsh (R)	44,519	35.9
22 Carlos J. Moorehead (R)	99,502	64.6
Robert S. Henry (D)	54,442	35.4
23 Anthony C. (Tony) Beilenson (D)	117,498	65.6
Joseph Barbara (R)	61,496	34.4
24 Henry A. Waxman (D)	85,075	62.7
Howard G. Schaefer (R)	44,243	32.6
25 Edward R. Roybal (D)	45,881	67.4
Robert K. Watson (R)	22,205	32.6
26 John H. Rousselot (R)	113,059	100.0
27 Robert K. Dornan (R)	89,392	51.0
Carey Peck (D)	85,880	49.0
28 Julian C. Dixon (D)	97,592	100.0
29 Augustus F. Hawkins (D)	65,214	85.0
Uriah J. Fields (R)	11,512	15.0
30 George E. Danielson (D)	66,241	71.4
Henry Ares (R)	26,511	28.6
31 Charles H. Wilson (D)	55,667	67.7
Don Grimshaw (R)	26,490	32.2
32 Glenn M. Anderson (D)	74,004	71.4
Sonya (Sonny) Mathison (R)	23,242	22.4
Ida Bader (AM I)	6,363	6.1
33 Wayne Grisham (R)	79,533	56.0
Dennis S. Kazarian (D)	62,540	44.0
34 Daniel E. Lungren (R)	90,554	53.7
Mark W. Hannaford (D)	73,608	43.7
35 Jim Lloyd (D)	80,388	54.0
David Dreier (R)	68,442	46.0
36 George E. Brown Jr. (D)	80,448	62.9
Dana Warren Carmody (R)	47,417	37.1
37 Jerry Lewis (R)	106,581	61.4
Dan Corcoran (D)	60,463	34.8
38 Jerry M. Patterson (D)	75,471	58.6
Don Goedeke (R)	53,298	41.4
39 William E. Dannemeyer (R)	112,160	63.7
William E. Farris (D)	63,891	36.3
40 Robert E. Badham (R)	147,882	65.9
Jim McGuy (D)	76,358	34.1
41 Bob Wilson (R)	107,685	58.1
King Golden Jr. (R)	77,540	41.9
42 Lionel Van Deerlin (D)	85,126	73.7
Lawrence C. Mattera (R)	30,319	26.3
43 Clair W. Burgener (R)	167,150	68.7
Ruben B. Brooks (D)	76,308	31.3

COLORADO

Candidates	Votes	%
1 Patricia Schroeder (D)	82,742	61.5
Gene Hutcheson (R)	49,845	37.0
2 Timothy E. Wirth (D)	98,889	52.9
Ed Scott (R)	88,072	47.1
3 Ray Kogovsek (D)	69,669	49.3
Harold L. McCormick (R)	69,303	49.0
4 James P. (Jim) Johnson (R)	103,121	61.2
Morgan Smith (D)	65,241	38.8
5 Ken Kramer (R)	91,933	59.8
Gerry Frank (D)	52,914	34.4
L. W. Dan Bridges (I)	8,933	5.8

CONNECTICUT

Candidates	Votes	%
1 William R. Cotter (D)	102,749	59.5
Ben F. Andrews Jr. (R)	67,828	39.3
2 Christopher J. Dodd (D)	116,624	69.9
Thomas H. Connell (R)	50,167	30.1
3 Robert N. Giaimo (D)	96,830	58.1
John G. Pucciano (R)	66,663	40.0
4 Stewart B. McKinney (R)	83,990	58.4
Michael G. Morgan (D)	59,918	41.6
5 William R. Ratchford (D)	96,738	52.3
George C. Guidera (R)	88,162	47.7

Candidates	Votes	%
6 Toby Moffett (D)	119,537	64.2
Daniel F. MacKinnon (R)	66,664	35.8

DELAWARE

Candidates	Votes	%
AL Thomas B. Evans Jr. (R)	91,689	58.2
Gary E. Hindes (D)	64,863	41.2

FLORIDA

Candidates	Votes	%
1 Earl D. Hutto (D)	85,608	63.3
Warren Briggs (R)	49,715	36.7
2 Don Fuqua (D)	112,649	81.7
Peter L. W. Brathwaite (R)	25,148	18.3
3 Charles E. Bennett (D)		100.0
4 Bill Chappell Jr. (D)	113,302	73.1
Tom Boney (R)	41,647	26.9
5 Richard Kelly (R)	106,319	51.1
David R. Best (D)	101,867	48.9
6 C. W. Bill Young (R)	150,694	78.8
James A. Christison (D)	40,654	21.2
7 Sam Gibbons (D)		100.0
8 Andy Ireland (D)		100.0
9 Bill Nelson (D)	89,543	61.5
Edward J. Gurney (R)	56,074	38.5
10 L. A. (Skip) Bafalis (R)		100.0
11 Dan Mica (D)	123,346	55.3
Bill James (R)	99,757	44.7
12 Edward J. Stack (D)	107,037	61.6
J. Herbert Burke (R)	66,610	38.4
13 William Lehman (D)		100.0
14 Claude Pepper (D)	65,202	63.1
Al Cardenas (R)	38,081	36.9
15 Dante B. Fascell (D)	108,837	74.2
Herbert J. Hoodwin (R)	37,897	25.8

GEORGIA

Candidates	Votes	%
1 Bo Ginn (D)	36,961	100.0
2 Dawson Mathis (D)	42,234	100.0
3 Jack Brinkley (D)	54,881	100.0
4 Elliott H. Levitas (D)	60,284	80.9
Homer Cheung (R)	14,221	19.1
5 Wyche Fowler Jr. (D)	52,739	75.5
Thomas P. Bowles Jr. (R)	17,132	24.5
6 Newt Gingrich (R)	47,078	54.4
Virginia Shapard (D)	39,451	45.6
7 Larry P. McDonald (D)	47,090	66.5
Ernie Norsworthy (R)	23,698	33.5
8 Billy Lee Evans (D)	41,184	100.0
9 Ed Jenkins (D)	47,264	76.9
David G. Ashworth (R)	14,172	23.1
10 Doug Barnard (D)	50,122	100.0

HAWAII

Candidates	Votes	%
1 Cecil (Cec) Heftel (D)	84,552	73.3
William D. Spillane (R)	24,470	21.2
2 Daniel K. Akaka (D)	118,272	85.7
Charles Isaak (R)	15,697	11.4

IDAHO

Candidates	Votes	%
1 Steven D. Symms (R)	86,680	59.9
Roy Truby (D)	57,972	40.1
2 George Hansen (R)	80,591	57.3
Stan Kress (D)	60,040	42.7

ILLINOIS

Candidates	Votes	%
1 Bennett Stewart (D)	47,581	58.5
A. A. Rayner (R)	33,540	41.3
2 Morgan F. Murphy (D)	80,906	86.0
James Wognum (R)	11,104	11.8

Candidates	Votes	%
3 Marty Russo (D)	95,701	65.2
Robert L. Dunne (R)	51,098	34.8
4 Edward J. Derwinski (R)	94,435	66.9
Andrew D. Thomas (D)	46,788	33.1
5 John G. Fary (D)	98,702	84.0
Joseph A. Barracca (R)	18,802	16.0
6 Henry J. Hyde (R)	87,193	66.2
Jeanne P. Quinn (D)	44,543	33.8
7 Cardiss Collins (D)	64,716	86.3
James C. Holt (R)	10,273	13.7
8 Dan Rostenkowski (D)	81,457	86.0
Carl C. LoDico (R)	13,302	14.0
9 Sidney R. Yates (D)	87,543	75.3
John M. Collins (R)	28,673	24.7
10 Abner J. Mikva (R)	89,479	50.2
John E. Porter (R)	88,829	49.8
11 Frank Annunzio (D)	112,365	73.7
John Hoeger (R)	40,044	26.3
12 Philip M. Crane (R)	110,503	79.5
Gilbert Bogen (D)	28,424	20.5
13 Robert McClory (R)	64,060	61.2
Frederick J. Steffen (D)	40,675	38.8
14 John N. Erlenborn (R)	118,741	75.1
James A. Romanyak (D)	39,438	24.9
15 Tom Corcoran (R)	80,856	62.4
Tim L. Hall (D)	48,756	37.6
16 John B. Anderson (R)	76,752	65.4
Ernest W. Dahlin (D)	40,471	34.5
17 George M. O'Brien (R)	94,375	70.6
Clifford J. Sinclair (D)	39,260	29.4
18 Robert H. Michel (R)	85,973	65.9
Virgil R. Grunkemeyer (D)	44,527	34.1
19 Tom Railsback (R)	89,770	100.0
20 Paul Findley (R)	111,054	69.6
Victor W. Roberts (D)	48,426	30.4
21 Edward R. Madigan (R)	97,473	78.3
Kenneth E. Baughman (D)	27,054	21.7
22 Daniel B. Crane (R)	86,051	54.0
Terry L. Bruce (D)	73,331	46.0
23 Melvin Price (D)	74,247	74.2
Daniel J. Stack (R)	25,858	25.8
24 Paul Simon (D)	110,298	65.6
John T. Anderson (R)	57,763	34.4

INDIANA

Candidates	Votes	%
1 Adam Benjamin Jr. (D)	72,367	80.3
Owen W. Crumpacker (R)	17,419	19.3
2 Floyd Fithian (D)	82,402	56.5
J. Philip Oppenheim (R)	52,842	36.2
William Costas (I)	9,368	6.4
3 John Brademas (D)	64,336	55.5
Thomas L. Thorson (R)	50,145	43.3
4 Dan Quayle (R)	80,527	64.4
John D. Walda (D)	42,238	33.8
5 Elwood Hillis (R)	94,950	67.6
Max E. Heiss (D)	45,479	32.4
6 David W. Evans (D)	66,421	52.2
David G. Crane (R)	60,630	47.6
7 John T. Myers (R)	86,955	56.3
Charlotte Zietlow (D)	67,469	43.7
8 H. Joel Deckard (R)	83,019	52.0
David L. Cornwell (D)	76,654	48.0
9 Lee H. Hamilton Jr. (D)	99,727	65.6
Frank I. Hamilton Jr. (R)	52,218	34.4
10 Phil Sharp (D)	73,343	56.1
William G. Frazier (R)	55,999	42.8
11 Andy Jacobs Jr. (D)	61,504	57.2
Charles F. Bosma (R)	45,809	42.6

IOWA

Candidates	Votes	%
1 Jim Leach (R)	79,940	63.5
Dick Myers (D)	45,037	35.8
2 Tom Tauke (R)	72,644	52.3
Michael T. Blouin (D)	65,450	47.1
3 Charles E. Grassley (R)	103,659	74.8
John Knudson (D)	34,880	25.2
4 Neal Smith (D)	88,526	64.7
Charles E. Minor (R)	48,308	35.3

Candidates	Votes	%
5 Tom Harkin (D)	82,333	58.9
Julian B. Garrett (R)	57,377	41.1
6 Berkley Bedell (D)	87,139	66.3
Willis E. Junker (R)	44,320	33.7

KANSAS

Candidates	Votes	%
1 Keith G. Sebelius (R)	131,037	100.0
2 Jim Jeffries (R)	76,419	52.0
Martha Keys (D)	70,460	48.0
3 Larry Winn Jr. (R)	103,265	100.0
4 Dan Glickman (D)	100,139	69.5
James P. Litsey (R)	43,854	30.5
5 Robert Whittaker (R)	86,011	57.0
Donald L. Allegrucci (D)	62,402	41.4

KENTUCKY

Candidates	Votes	%
1 Carroll Hubbard Jr. (D)	44,090	100.0
2 William H. Natcher (D)	36,441	100.0
3 Romano L. Mazzoli (D)	37,346	65.7
Norbert D. Leveronne (R)	17,785	31.3
4 Gene Snyder (R)	62,087	65.8
George C. Martin (D)	32,212	34.2
5 Tim Lee Carter (R)	59,743	79.2
Jesse M. Ramey (D)	15,714	20.8
6 Larry J. Hopkins (R)	52,092	50.6
Tom Easterly (D)	47,436	46.1
7 Carl D. Perkins (D)	51,559	76.5
Granville Thomas (R)	15,861	23.5

LOUISIANA [1]

Candidates	Votes	%
1 Robert L. Livingston (R)		100.0
2 Lindy Boggs (D)		100.0
3 David C. Treen (R)		100.0
4 Claude (Buddy) Leach (D)	65,583	50.1
Jimmy Wilson (R)	65,317	49.9
5 Jerry Huckaby (D)		100.0
6 W. Henson Moore (R)		100.0
7 John B. Breaux (D)		100.0
8 Gillis W. Long (D)		100.0

MAINE

Candidates	Votes	%
1 David F. Emery (R)	120,791	61.5
John Quinn (D)	70,348	35.8
2 Olympia J. Snowe (R)	87,939	50.8
Markham L. Gartley (D)	70,691	40.8

MARYLAND

Candidates	Votes	%
1 Robert E. Bauman (R)	80,202	63.5
Joseph D. Quinn (D)	46,093	36.5
2 Clarence D. Long (D)	98,601	66.4
Malcolm M. McKnight (R)	49,886	33.6
3 Barbara A. Mikulski (D)	91,189	100.0
4 Marjorie S. Holt (R)	71,374	62.0
Sue F. Ward (D)	43,663	38.0
5 Gladys Noon Spellman (D)	64,868	77.2
Saul J. Harris (R)	19,160	22.8
6 Beverly Byron (D)	126,196	89.7
Melvin Perkins (R)	14,545	10.3
7 Parren J. Mitchell (D)	51,996	88.7
Debra Hanania Freeman (I)	6,626	11.3
8 Michael D. Barnes (D)	81,851	51.3
Newton I. Steers Jr. (R)	77,807	48.7

MASSACHUSETTS

Candidates	Votes	%
1 Silvio O. Conte (R)	131,773	100.0
2 Edward P. Boland (D)	101,570	72.8
Thomas J. Swank (R)	37,881	27.2
3 Joseph D. Early (D)	119,337	75.2
Charles Kevin MacLeod (R)	39,259	24.7
4 Robert F. Drinan (D)	111,353	100.0
5 James M. Shannon (D)	90,156	52.2

Candidates	Votes	%
John J. Buckley (R)	48,685	28.2
James J. Gaffney III (I)	33,835	19.6
6 Nicholas Mavroules (D)	97,099	53.8
William E. Bronson (R)	83,511	46.2
7 Edward J. Markey (D)	145,615	84.8
James J. Murphy (I)	26,017	15.2
8 Thomas P. O'Neill Jr. (D)	102,160	74.6
William A. Barnstead (R)	28,566	20.9
9 Joe Moakley (D)	106,805	91.8
Brenda Lee Franklin (SOC WORK)	6,794	5.8
10 Margaret M. Heckler (R)	102,080	61.1
John J. Marino (D)	64,868	38.9
11 Brian J. Donnelly (D)	133,644	91.7
H. Graham Lowry (USLP)	12,044	8.3
12 Gerry E. Studds (D)	176,704	99.9

MICHIGAN

Candidates	Votes	%
1 John Conyers Jr. (D)	89,646	92.9
Robert S. Arnold (R)	6,878	7.1
2 Carl D. Pursell (R)	97,503	67.6
Earl Greene (R)	45,631	31.6
3 Howard Wolpe (D)	83,932	51.3
Garry Brown (R)	79,572	48.7
4 Dave Stockman (R)	95,440	70.6
Morgan L. Hager Jr. (D)	38,204	28.3
5 Harold S. Sawyer (R)	81,794	49.4
Dale R. Sprik (D)	80,622	48.7
6 Bob Carr (D)	97,971	56.7
Mike Conlin (R)	74,718	43.3
7 Dale E. Kildee (D)	105,402	76.6
Gale M. Cronk (R)	29,958	21.8
8 Bob Traxler (D)	103,346	66.6
Norman R. Hughes (R)	51,900	33.4
9 Guy Vander Jagt (R)	122,363	69.6
Howard M. Leroux (D)	53,450	30.4
10 Donald J. Albosta (D)	94,913	51.5
Elford A. Cederberg (R)	89,451	48.5
11 Robert W. Davis (R)	96,351	54.9
Keith McLeod (D)	79,081	45.1
12 David E. Bonior (D)	82,892	54.9
Kirby Holmes (R)	68,063	45.1
13 Charles C. Diggs Jr. (D)	44,771	79.2
Dovie T. Pickett (R)	11,749	20.8
14 Lucien N. Nedzi (D)	84,032	67.4
John Edward Getz (R)	40,716	32.6
15 William D. Ford (D)	95,137	79.6
Edgar Nieten (R)	23,177	19.4
16 John D. Dingell (D)	93,387	76.5
Melvin E. Heuer (R)	26,827	22.0
17 William M. Brodhead (D)	106,303	95.2
18 James J. Blanchard (D)	113,037	74.5
Robert J. Salloum (R)	36,913	24.3
19 William S. Broomfield (R)	117,122	71.3
Betty F. Collier (D)	47,165	28.7

MINNESOTA

Candidates	Votes	%
1 Arlen Erdahl (I-R)	110,090	56.2
Gerry Sikorski (DFL)	83,271	42.5
2 Tom Hagedorn (I-R)	145,415	70.4
John F. Considine (DFL)	61,173	29.6
3 Bill Frenzel (I-R)	128,759	65.7
Michael O. Freeman (DFL)	67,120	34.3
4 Bruce F. Vento (DFL)	95,989	58.0
John R. Berg (I-R)	69,396	42.0
5 Martin Olav Sabo (DFL)	91,673	62.3
Michael Till (I-R)	55,412	37.7
6 Richard Nolan (DFL)	115,880	55.3
Russ Bjorhus (I-R)	93,742	44.7
7 Arlan Stangeland (I-R)	109,456	52.4
Gene R. Wenstrom (DFL)	93,055	44.5
8 James L. Oberstar (DFL)	171,125	87.2
John W. Hull (AM)	25,015	12.7

MISSISSIPPI

Candidates	Votes	%
1 Jamie L. Whitten (D)	57,358	66.6
T. K. Moffett (R)	26,734	31.0

Candidates	Votes	%
2 David R. Bowen (D)	57,678	61.7
Roland Byrd (R)	35,730	38.2
3 G. V. (Sonny) Montgomery (D)	101,685	92.3
Dorothy Cleveland (R)	8,408	7.6
4 Jon C. Hinson (R)	68,225	51.6
John Hampton Stennis (D)	34,837	26.4
Evan Doss (I)	25,134	19.0
5 Trent Lott (R)	97,177	100.0

MISSOURI

Candidates	Votes	%
1 William (Bill) Clay (D)	65,950	66.6
William E. White (R)	30,995	31.3
2 Robert A. Young (D)	102,911	56.4
Robert C. Chase (R)	79,495	43.6
3 Richard A. Gephardt (D)	121,565	81.9
Lee Buchschacher (R)	26,881	18.1
4 Ike Skelton (D)	120,748	72.8
William D. Baker (R)	45,116	27.2
5 Richard Bolling (D)	82,140	72.0
Steven L. Walter (R)	30,360	26.6
6 E. Thomas Coleman (R)	96,574	55.9
Phil Snowden (D)	76,061	44.1
7 Gene Taylor (R)	104,566	61.2
Jim Thomas (D)	66,351	38.8
8 Richard H. Ichord (D)	96,509	60.5
Donald D. Meyer (R)	63,109	39.5
9 Harold L. Volkmer (D)	135,170	74.7
Jerry A. Dent (R)	45,795	25.3
10 Bill D. Burlison (D)	99,148	65.3
James A. Weir (R)	52,687	34.7

MONTANA

Candidates	Votes	%
1 Pat Williams (D)	86,016	57.3
Jim Waltermire (R)	64,093	42.7
2 Ron Marlenee (R)	75,766	56.9
Thomas G. Monahan (D)	57,480	43.1

NEBRASKA

Candidates	Votes	%
1 Douglas K. Bereuter (R)	99,013	58.1
Hess Dyas (D)	71,311	41.9
2 John J. Cavanaugh (D)	77,135	52.3
Harold J. Daub Jr. (R)	70,309	47.7
3 Virginia Smith (R)	141,597	80.0
Marilyn Fowler (D)	35,371	20.0

NEVADA

Candidates	Votes	%
AL Jim Santini (D)	132,513	69.5
Bill O'Mara (R)	44,425	23.3

NEW HAMPSHIRE

Candidates	Votes	%
1 Norman E. D'Amours (D)	82,697	61.6
Daniel M. Hughes (R)	49,131	36.6
2 James C. Cleveland (R)	84,535	68.1
Edgar J. Helms (D)	39,546	31.9

NEW JERSEY

Candidates	Votes	%
1 James J. Florio (D)	106,096	79.4
Robert M. Deitch (R)	26,853	20.1
2 William J. Hughes (D)	112,768	66.4
James H. Biggs (R)	56,997	33.6
3 James J. Howard (D)	83,349	56.0
Bruce G. Coe (R)	64,730	43.5
4 Frank Thompson Jr. (D)	69,259	61.1
Christopher H. Smith (R)	41,833	36.9
5 Millicent Fenwick (R)	100,739	72.6
John T. Fahy (D)	38,108	27.4
6 Edwin B. Forsythe (R)	89,446	60.4
W. Thomas McGann (D)	56,874	38.4
7 Andrew Maguire (D)	78,358	52.5
Margaret S. Roukema (R)	69,543	46.6

Candidates	Votes	%
8 Robert A. Roe (D)	69,496	74.5
Thomas Melani (R)	23,842	25.5
9 Harold C. Hollenback (R)	73,478	48.9
Nicholas S. Mastorelli (D)	56,888	37.9
Henry Helstoski (I)	19,126	12.7
10 Peter W. Rodino Jr. (D)	55,074	86.4
John L. Pelt (R)	8,066	12.6
11 Joseph G. Minish (D)	88,294	70.5
Julius George Feld (R)	35,642	28.5
12 Matthew J. Rinaldo (R)	94,850	73.4
Richard McCormack (D)	34,423	26.6
13 James A. Courter (R)	77,301	51.8
Helen Meyner (D)	71,808	48.2
14 Frank J. Guarini (D)	67,008	63.6
Henry J. Hill (R)	21,355	20.3
Thomas E. McDonough (I)	15,015	14.3
15 Edward J. Patten (D)	55,944	48.3
Charles W. Wiley (R)	53,108	45.8

NEW MEXICO

Candidates	Votes	%
1 Manuel Lujan Jr. (R)	118,075	62.5
Robert Hawk (D)	70,761	37.5
2 Harold Runnels (D)	95,710	100.0

NEW YORK

Candidates	Votes	%
1 William Carney (R, C)	90,115	56.3
John F. Randolph (D)	67,180	41.9
2 Thomas J. Downey (D)	64,807	54.9
Harold J. Withers Jr. (R, C)	53,322	45.1
3 Jerome A. Ambro (D)	70,526	50.9
Gregory W. Carman (R, C)	66,458	47.9
4 Norman F. Lent (R, C)	94,711	66.1
Everett A. Rosenblum (D)	46,508	32.5
5 John W. Wydler (R, C)	84,864	58.4
John W. Matthews (D, L)	60,519	41.6
6 Lester L. Wolff (D, L)	80,799	60.0
Stuart L. Ain (R)	44,304	32.9
Howard Horowitz (C)	9,503	7.1
7 Joseph P. Addabbo (D, R, L)	73,066	94.9
Mark Elliott Scott (C)	3,935	5.1
8 Benjamin S. Rosenthal (D, L)	74,872	78.6
Albert Lemishow (R)	15,165	15.9
Paul C. Ruebenacker (C)	5,165	5.4
9 Geraldine A. Ferraro (D)	51,350	54.2
Alfred A. DelliBovi (R, C)	42,108	44.4
10 Mario Biaggi (D, R, L)	77,979	95.0
Carmen Ricciardi (C)	4,082	5.0
11 James H. Scheuer (D, L)	58,997	78.5
Kenneth Huhn (R, C)	16,206	21.5
12 Shirley Chisholm (D, L)	25,697	87.8
Charles Gibb (R)	3,580	12.2
13 Stephen J. Solarz (D, L)	68,837	81.1
Max Carasso (R, C)	16,002	18.9
14 Frederick Richmond (D. L)	31,339	76.9
Arthur Bramwell (R)	7,516	18.4
15 Leo C. Zeferetti (D, C)	49,272	68.1
Robert P. Whelan (R)	20,508	28.4
16 Elizabeth Holtzman (D, L)	59,703	81.9
Larry Penner (R, UT)	9,405	12.9
John H. Fox (C)	3,782	5.2
17 John M. Murphy (D)	54,228	54.2
John Michael Peters (R, C)	33,071	33.1
Thomas H. Stokes (L)	12,662	12.7
18 S. William Green (R)	60,867	53.3
Carter Burden (D, L)	53,434	46.7
19 Charles B. Rangel (D, R, L)	59,731	96.4
20 Ted Weiss (D. L)	64,275	84.6
Harry Torczyner (R)	11,661	15.4
21 Robert Garcia (D, R, L)	23,950	98.0
22 Jonathan B. Bingham (D, L)	58,727	84.1
Anthony J. Geidel Jr. (R, C)	11,110	15.9
23 Peter A. Peyser (D)	66,354	51.6
Angelo R. Martinelli (R, C)	59,455	46.2
24 Richard L. Ottinger (D)	75,397	56.1
Michael R. Edelman (R, C)	57,451	42.7
25 Hamilton Fish Jr. (R)	114,641	78.2
Gunars M. Ozols (D)	31,213	21.3
26 Benjamin A. Gilman (R)	87,059	62.3

Candidates	Votes	%
Charles E. Holbrook (D, L)	41,870	30.(
William R. Schaeffer Jr. (C)	10,708	7.
27 Matthew F. McHugh (D)	83,413	55.(
Neil Tyler Wallace (R, C)	66,177	44.
28 Samuel S. Stratton (D)	139,575	76.
Paul H. Tocker (R, C)	36,017	19.
29 Gerald B. Solomon (R, C)	99,518	54.(
Edward W. Pattison (D, L)	84,705	46.
30 Robert C. McEwen (R. C)	85,478	60.(
Norma A. Bartle (D, L)	55,785	39.
31 Donald J. Mitchell (R, C)	107,791	100.(
32 James M. Hanley (D)	76,251	52.
Peter J. Del Giorno (R, C)	67,071	46.
33 Gary A. Lee (R)	82,501	56.(
Roy A. Bernardi (D)	58,286	39.
34 Frank Horton (R, D)	122,785	87.
Leo J. Kesselring (C)	18,127	12.
35 Barber B. Conable Jr. (R)	96,119	69.(
Francis C. Repicci (D)	36,428	26.
36 John J. LaFalce (D, L)	99,497	74.
Francina J. Cartonia (R)	31,527	23.
37 Henry J. Nowak (D, L)	70,911	78.(
Charles Roth III (R)	17,585	19.
38 Jack F. Kemp (R, C)	113,928	94.(
James A. Peck (L)	6,204	5.2
39 Stanley N. Lundine (D)	79,385	58.
Crispin M. Maguire (R, C)	56,431	41.

Special Elections

Candidates	Votes	%
18 S. William Green (R)	30,332	50.
Bella S. Abzug (D, L)	29,189	48.
21 Robert Garcia (R, L)	7,959	55.
Louis Nine (D, C)	3,514	24.
Ramon S. Valez (I)	2,280	15.

NORTH CAROLINA

Candidates	Votes	%
1 Walter B. Jones (D)	67,716	80.1
James Newcomb (R)	16,814	19.9
2 L. H. Fountain (D)	61,851	78.2
Barry L. Gardner (R)	15,988	20.2
3 Charlie Whitley (D)	54,452	71.1
Willard J. Blanchard (R)	22,150	28.9
4 Ike F. Andrews (D)	74,249	94.4
Naudeen Beek (LIBERT)	4,436	5.6
5 Stephen L. Neal (D)	68,778	54.2
Hamilton C. Horton Jr. (R)	58,161	45.8
6 Richardson Preyer (D)	58,193	68.4
George Bemus (R)	26,882	31.6
7 Charlie Rose (D)	53,696	69.9
Raymond C. Schrump (R)	23,146	30.1
8 W. G. (Bill) Hefner (D)	63,168	59.0
Roger Austin (R)	43,942	41.0
9 James G. Martin (R)	66,157	68.3
Charles Maxwell (D)	29,761	30.7
10 James T. Broyhill (R)	67,004	100.0
11 Lamar Gudger (D)	75,460	53.4
R. Curtis Ratcliff (R)	65,832	46.6

NORTH DAKOTA

Candidates	Votes	%
AL Mark Andrews (R)	147,746	67.1
Bruce Hagen (D)	68,016	30.9

OHIO

Candidates	Votes	%
1 Bill Gradison (R)	73,593	64.5
Timothy M. Burke (D)	38,669	33.9
2 Thomas A. Luken (D)	64,522	52.4
Stanley J. Aronoff (R)	58,716	47.6
3 Tony P. Hall (D)	62,849	53.8
Dudley P. Kircher (R)	51,833	44.4
4 Tennyson Guyer (R)	85,575	68.5
John W. Griffin (D)	39,360	31.5
5 Delbert L. Latta (R)	85,547	62.6
James R. Sherck (D)	51,071	37.4
6 William H. Harsha (R)	85,592	64.9
Ted Strickland (D)	46,318	35.1

Candidates	Votes	%
7 Clarence J. Brown (R)	92,507	100.0
8 Thomas N. Kindness (R)	81,156	71.4
Lou Schroeder (D)	32,493	28.6
9 Thomas L. Ashley (D)	71,709	63.4
John C. Hoyt (R)	34,326	30.3
10 Clarence E. Miller (R)	99,329	73.9
James A. Plummer (D)	35,039	26.1
11 J. William Stanton (R)	89,327	68.1
Patrick J. Donlin (D)	37,131	28.3
12 Samuel L. Devine (R)	81,573	56.9
James L. Baumann (D)	61,698	43.1
13 Don J. Pease (D)	80,875	65.1
Mark W. Whitfield (R)	43,269	34.9
14 John F. Seiberling (D)	82,356	72.5
Walter J. Vogel (R)	31,311	27.5
15 Chalmers P. Wylie (R)	91,023	71.1
Henry W. Eckhart (D)	37,000	28.9
16 Ralph S. Regula (R)	105,152	78.0
Owen S. Hand Jr. (D)	29,640	22.0
17 John M. Ashbrook (R)	87,010	67.4
Kenneth R. Grier (D)	42,117	32.6
18 Douglas Applegate (D)	71,894	59.5
Bill Ress (R)	48,931	40.5
19 Lyle Williams (R)	71,890	50.7
Charles J. Carney (D)	69,977	49.3
20 Mary Rose Oakar (D)	76,973	100.0
21 Louis Stokes (D)	58,934	86.1
Bill Mack (R)	9,533	13.9
22 Charles A. Vanik (D)	87,551	66.0
Richard W. Sander (R)	30,935	23.3
James F. Sexton (I)	7,126	5.4
Robert E. Lehman (I)	6,960	5.2
23 Ronald M. Mottl (D)	99,975	74.8
Homes S. Taft (R)	33,732	25.2

OKLAHOMA

1 James R. Jones (D)	73,886	59.9
Paula Unruh (R)	49,404	40.1
2 Mike Synar (D)	72,583	54.8
Gary L. Richardson (R)	59,853	45.2
3 Wes Watkins (D)		100.0
4 Tom Steed (D)	62,993	60.3
Scotty Robb (R)	41,421	39.7
5 Mickey Edwards (R)	71,451	79.9
Jesse D. Knipp (D)	17,978	20.1
6 Glenn English (D)	103,512	74.2
Harold Hunter (R)	36,031	25.8

OREGON

1 Les AuCoin (D)	158,706	62.9
Nick Bunick (R)	93,640	37.1
2 Al Ullman (D)	152,099	69.1
Terry L. Hicks (R)	67,547	30.7
3 Robert Duncan (D)	151,895	84.6
Martin Simon (USLP)	27,120	15.1
4 James Weaver (D)	124,745	56.3
Jerry L. Lausmann (R)	96,953	43.7

PENNSYLVANIA

1 Michael (Ozzie) Myers (D)	104,412	71.9
Samuel N. Fanelli (R)	37,913	26.1
2 William H. Gray III (D)	132,594	82.0
Roland J. Atkins (R)	25,785	15.9
3 Raymond F. Lederer (D)	86,915	71.8
Raymond S. Kauffman (R)	33,750	28.2
4 Charles F. Dougherty (R)	119,445	55.8
Joshua Eilberg (D)	87,555	44.2
5 Richard T. Schulze (R)	119,565	75.1
Murray P. Zealor (D)	36,704	24.9
6 Gus Yatron (D)	196,432	73.8
Stephen Mazur (R)	37,746	26.2
7 Robert W. Edgar (D)	79,771	50.3
Eugene D. Kane (R)	78,403	49.4
8 Peter H. Kostmayer (D)	89,276	61.1
G. Roger Bowers (R)	56,776	38.9
9 Bud Shuster (R)	101,151	74.9
Blaine L. Havice Jr. (D)	33,882	25.1

Candidates	Votes	%
10 Joseph M. McDade (R)	116,003	76.5
Gene Basalyga (D)	35,721	23.5
11 Daniel J. Flood (D)	61,433	57.5
Robert P. Hudock (R)	45,335	42.5
12 John P. Murtha (D)	194,216	68.7
Luther V. Elkins (R)	47,442	31.3
13 Lawrence Coughlin (R)	112,711	70.5
Alan B. Rubenstein (D)	47,151	29.5
14 William S. Moorhead (D)	68,004	57.0
Stan Thomas (R)	49,992	41.9
15 Donald L. Ritter (R)	65,986	53.2
Fred B. Rooney (D)	58,077	46.8
16 Robert S. Walker (R)	91,910	77.0
Charles W. Boohar (D)	27,386	23.0
17 Allen E. Ertel (D)	79,234	59.6
Thomas R. Rippon (R)	53,614	40.4
18 Doug Walgren (D)	88,299	57.1
Ted Jacob (R)	65,088	42.1
19 Bill Goodling (R)	105,424	78.7
Rajeshwar Kumar (D)	28,577	21.3
20 Joseph M. Gaydos (D)	97,745	72.1
Kathleen M. Meyer (R)	37,745	27.9
21 Don Bailey (D)	73,712	52.9
Robert H. Miller (R)	65,622	47.1
22 Austin J. Murphy (D)	99,559	71.6
Marilyn C. Ecoff (R)	39,518	28.4
23 William F. Clinger Jr. (R)	73,194	54.3
Joseph S. Ammerman (D)	61,657	45.7
24 Marc L. Marks (R)	87,041	64.0
Joseph F. Vigorito (D)	48,894	36.0
25 Eugene V. Atkinson (D)	68,293	46.5
Tim Shaffer (R)	62,160	42.3
Robert Morris (I)	10,588	7.2

RHODE ISLAND

1 Fernand J. St Germain (D)	86,768	61.2
John J. Slocum Jr. (R)	54,912	38.8
2 Edward P. Beard (D)	87,397	52.6
Claudine Schneider (R)	78,725	47.4

SOUTH CAROLINA

1 Mendel J. Davis (D)	65,835	60.6
C. C. Wannamaker (R)	42,811	39.4
2 Floyd Spence (R)	71,208	57.3
Jack Bass (D)	53,021	42.7
3 Butler Derrick (D)	81,638	82.0
Anthony Panuccio (R)	17,973	18.0
4 Carroll A. Campbell Jr. (R)	51,377	52.1
Max M. Heller (D)	45,484	46.2
5 Ken Holland (D)	63,538	82.7
Harold Hough (I)	13,251	17.3
6 John W. Jenrette Jr. (D)	69,372	100.0

SOUTH DAKOTA

1 Thomas A. Daschle (D)	64,683	50.1
Leo K. Thorsness (R)	64,544	49.9
2 James Abdnor (R)	70,780	56.0
Bob Samuelson (D)	55,516	44.0

TENNESSEE

1 James H. (Jimmy) Quillen (R)	92,143	64.5
Gordon Ball (D)	50,694	35.5
2 John J. Duncan (R)	125,082	81.8
Margaret Francis (D)	27,745	18.2
3 Marilyn Lloyd (D)	108,282	88.9
Dan East (I)	13,535	11.1
4 Albert Gore Jr. (D)	108,695	100.0
5 Bill Boner (D)	68,608	51.4
Bill Goodwin (R)	47,288	35.4
Henry Haile (I)	17,674	13.2
6 Robin L. Beard Jr. (R)	114,630	74.6
Ron Arline (D)	38,954	25.4
7 Ed Jones (D)	96,863	72.9
Ross Cook (R)	36,003	27.1
8 Harold E. Ford (D)	80,776	69.7
Duncan Ragsdale (R)	33,679	29.1

TEXAS

Candidates	Votes	%
1 Sam B. Hall Jr. (D)	73,708	78.1
Fred Hudson (R)	20,700	21.9
2 Charles Wilson (D)	66,986	70.1
Jim (Matt) Dillon (R)	28,584	29.9
3 James M. Collins (R)	96,406	100.0
4 Ray Roberts (D)	58,336	61.5
Frank S. Glenn (R)	36,582	38.5
5 Jim Mattox (D)	35,524	50.3
Tom Pauken (R)	34,672	49.1
6 Phil Gramm (D)	66,025	65.1
Wesley H. Mowrey (R)	35,393	34.9
7 Bill Archer (R)	128,214	85.1
Robert L. Hutchings (D)	22,415	14.9
8 Bob Eckhardt (D)	39,429	61.5
Nick Gearhart (R)	24,673	38.5
9 Jack Brooks (D)	50,792	63.3
Randy Evans (R)	29,473	36.7
10 J. J. Pickle (D)	94,529	76.3
Emmett L. Hudspeth (R)	29,328	23.7
11 J. Marvin Leath (D)	53,354	51.6
Jack Burgess (R)	49,965	48.4
12 Jim Wright (D)	46,456	68.5
Claude K. Brown (R)	21,364	31.5
13 Jack Hightower (D)	75,271	74.9
Clifford A. Jones (D)	25,275	25.1
14 Joe Wyatt (D)	63,953	72.4
Joy Yates (R)	24,325	27.6
15 E. (Kika) de la Garza (D)	54,560	66.2
Robert L. McDonald (R)	27,853	33.8
16 Richard C. White (D)	53,090	70.0
Michael Giere (R)	22,743	30.0
17 Charles W. Stenholm (D)	69,030	68.1
Billy Lee Fisher (R)	32,302	31.9
18 Mickey Leland (D)	36,783	96.8
19 Kent Hance (D)	54,729	53.2
George W. Bush (R)	48,070	46.8
20 Henry B. Gonzalez (D)	51,584	100.0
21 Tom Loeffler (R)	84,336	57.0
Nelson W. Wolff (R)	63,501	43.0
22 Ron Paul (R)	54,643	50.6
Bob Gammage (D)	53,443	49.4
23 Abraham Kazen Jr. (D)	62,649	89.7
Augustin Mata (LRU)	7,185	10.3
24 Martin Frost (D)	39,201	54.1
Leo Berman (R)	33,314	45.9

UTAH

1 Gunn McKay (D)	93,892	51.0
Jed J. Richardson (R)	85,028	46.2
2 Dan Marriott (R)	121,492	62.3
Edwin B. Firmage (D)	68,899	35.3

VERMONT

AL James M. Jeffords (R)	90,688	75.3
S. Marie Dietz (D)	23,228	19.3
Peter Diamondstone (LU)	6,505	5.4

VIRGINIA

1 Paul S. Trible Jr. (R)	89,158	72.1
Lew Puller (D)	34,578	27.9
2 G. William Whitehurst (R)	63,512	100.0
3 David E. Satterfield III (D)	104,550	87.7
Alan R. Ogden (I)	14,453	12.1
4 Robert W. Daniel Jr. (R)	77,827	99.9
5 Dan Daniel (D)	83,575	99.9
6 M. Caldwell Butler (R)	88,647	99.8
7 J. Kenneth Robinson (R)	84,517	64.3
Lewis Fickett (D)	46,950	35.7
8 Herbert E. Harris II (D)	56,137	50.5
John F. Herrity (R)	52,396	47.1
9 William C. Wampler (R)	76,877	61.9
Champ Clark (D)	47,367	38.1
10 Joseph L. Fisher (D)	70,892	53.3
Frank Wolf (R)	61,981	46.6

WASHINGTON

Candidates	Votes	%
1 Joel Pritchard (R)	99,942	64.0
Janice Niemi (D)	52,706	33.7
2 Al Swift (D)	70,620	51.4
John Nance Garner (R)	66,793	48.6
3 Don Bonker (D)	82,616	58.6
Rick Bennett (R)	58,270	41.4
4 Mike McCormack (D)	85,602	61.1
Susan Roylance (R)	54,389	38.9
5 Thomas S. Foley (D)	77,201	48.0
Duane Alton (R)	68,761	42.7
Mel Tonasket (I)	14,887	9.3
6 Norman D. Dicks (D)	71,057	60.9
James E. Beaver (R)	43,640	37.4
7 Mike Lowry (D)	67,450	53.3
John E. Cunningham (R)	59,052	46.7

WEST VIRGINIA

Candidates	Votes	%
1 Robert H. Mollohan (D)	76,372	63.4
Gene A. Haynes (R)	44,062	36.6

Candidates	Votes	%
2 Harley O. Staggers (D)	69,683	55.3
Cleveland K. Benedict (R)	56,272	44.7
3 John M. Slack (D)	74,837	59.2
David M. Staton (R)	51,584	40.8
4 Nick J. Rahall (D)	70,035	100.0

WISCONSIN

Candidates	Votes	%
1 Les Aspin (D)	77,146	54.5
William W. Petrie (R)	64,437	45.5
2 Robert W. Kastenmeier (D)	99,631	57.7
James A. Wright (R)	71,412	41.3
3 Alvin Baldus (D)	96,326	62.8
Michael S. Ellis (R)	57.060	37.2
4 Clement J. Zablocki (D)	101,575	66.1
Elroy G. Honadel (R)	52,125	33.9
5 Henry S. Reuss (D)	85,067	73.1
James R. Medina (R)	30,185	25.9

Candidates	Votes	%
6 William A. Steiger (R)	114,742	69.6
Robert J. Steffes (D)	48,785	29.6
7 David R. Obey (D)	110,874	62.2
Vinton A. Vesta (R)	65,750	36.9
8 Tobias A. Roth (R)	101,856	57.9
Robert J. Cornell (D)	73,925	42.1
9 F. James Sansenbrenner Jr. (R)	118,386	61.1
Matthew J. Flynn (D)	75,207	38.8

WYOMING

Candidates	Votes	%
AL Richard Cheney (R)	75,855	58.6
Bill Bagley (D)	53,522	41.4

1. For the 1978 House elections in Louisiana, an open primary was held with candidates from all parties running on the same ballot. Any candidate who received a majority was elected unopposed without any further appearance on the general election ballot. Where no candidate received 50 percent, there was a general election runoff between the top two finishers regardless of party. This condition prevailed only in Congressional District 4.

1979 House Elections

CALIFORNIA

Special Election

Candidates	Votes	%
11 Bill Royer (R)	52,585	57.3
G. W. Holsinger (D)	37,685	41.1

WISCONSIN

Special Election

	Votes	%
6 Thomas E. Petri (R)	71,715	50.0
Gary R. Goyke (D)	70,492	49.5

1980 House Elections

ALABAMA

Candidates	Votes	%
1 Jack Edwards (R)	111,089	94.8
Steve Smith (LIBERT)	6,130	5.2
2 William L. Dickinson (R)	104,796	60.6
Cecil Wyatt (D)	63,447	36.7
3 Bill Nichols (D)	107,654	100.0
4 Tom Bevill (D)	129,365	97.9
5 Ronnie G. Flippo (D)	117,626	94.1
Betty T. Benson (LIBERT)	7,341	5.9
6 Albert Lee Smith Jr. (R)	95,019	50.5
W.B. (Pete) Clifford (D)	87,536	46.6
7 Richard C. Shelby (D)	122,505	72.6
James E. Bacon (R)	43,320	25.7

ALASKA

	Votes	%
AL Don Young (R)	114,089	73.8
Kevin (Pat) Parnell (D)	39,922	25.8

ARIZONA

	Votes	%
1 John J. Rhodes (R)	136,961	73.3
Steve Jancek (D)	40,045	21.4
2 Morris K. Udall (D)	127,736	58.1
Richard H. Huff (R)	88,653	40.4
3 Bob Stump (D)	141,448	64.3
Bob Croft (R)	65,845	30.0
Sharon Hayse (LIBERT)	12,529	5.7
4 Eldon Rudd (R)	142,565	62.6
Les Miller (D)	85,046	37.4

ARKANSAS

	Votes	%
1 Bill Alexander (D)		100.0
2 Ed Bethune (R)	159,148	78.9
James G. Reid (D)	42,278	21.0
3 John Paul Hammerschmidt (R)		100.0
4 Beryl Anthony Jr. (D)		100.0

CALIFORNIA

	Votes	%
1 Eugene A. Chappie (R)	145,585	53.7
Harold T. Johnson (D)	107,993	39.8
Jim McClarin (LIBERT)	17,497	6.5
2 Don H. Clausen (R)	141,698	54.2
Norma K. Bork (D)	109,789	42.0
3 Robert T. Matsui (D)	170,670	70.6
Joseph Murphy (R)	64,215	26.5
4 Vic Fazio (D)	133,853	65.1
Albert Dehr (R)	60,935	29.6
Robert J. Burnside (LIBERT)	10,267	5.0
5 John L. Burton (D)	101,105	51.1
Dennis McQuaid (R)	89,624	45.3
6 Phillip Burton (D)	93,400	69.4
Tom Spinosa (R)	34,500	25.6
Roy Childs (LIBERT)	6,750	5.0
7 George Miller (D)	142,044	63.3
Giles St. Clair (R)	70,479	31.4
8 Ronald V. Dellums (D)	108,380	55.5
Charles V. Hughes (R)	76,580	39.2
Tom Mikuriya (LIBERT)	10,465	5.3
9 Fortney H. (Pete) Stark (D)	90,504	55.3
William J. Kennedy (R)	67,265	41.1
10 Don Edwards (D)	102,231	62.1
John M. Lutton (R)	45,987	27.9
Joseph Fuhrig (LIBERT)	11,904	7.2
11 Tom Lantos (D)	85,823	46.4
Bill Royer (R)	80,100	43.3
Wilson Branch (PFP)	13,723	7.4
12 Paul N. McCloskey Jr. (R)	143,817	72.2
Kirsten Olsen (D)	37,009	18.6
Bill Evers (LIBERT)	15,073	7.6
13 Norman Y. Mineta (D)	132,246	58.9
W.E. (Ted) Gagne (R)	79,766	35.5
14 Norman D. Shumway (R)	133,979	60.7
Ann Cerney (D)	79,883	36.2

Candidates	Votes	%
15 Tony Coelho (D)	108,072	71.8
Ron Schwartz (R)	37,895	25.2
16 Leon E. Panetta (D)	158,360	71.0
W.A. (Jack) Roth (R)	54,675	24.5
17 Charles Pashayan Jr. (R)	129,159	70.6
Willard H. Johnson (D)	53,780	29.4
18 William M. Thomas (R)	126,046	71.0
Mary (Pat) Timmermans (D)	51,415	29.0
19 Robert J. Lagomarsino (R)	162,854	77.7
Carmen Lodise (D)	36,990	17.6
20 Barry Goldwater Jr. (R)	199,681	78.8
Matt Miller (D)	43,025	17.0
21 Bobbi Fiedler (R)	74,843	48.7
James C. Corman (D)	74,091	48.2
22 Carlos J. Moorhead (R)	115,241	63.9
Pierce O'Donnell (D)	57,477	31.9
23 Anthony C. Beilenson (D)	126,020	63.2
Robert Winckler (R)	62,742	31.5
Jeffrey P. Lieb (LIBERT)	10,623	5.3
24 Henry A. Waxman (D)	93,569	63.8
Roland Cayard (R)	39,744	27.1
25 Edward R. Roybal (D)	49,080	66.0
Richard L. Ferraro Jr. (R)	21,116	28.4
William D. Mitchell (LIBERT)	4,169	5.6
26 Joseph L. Lisoni (D)	40,099	24.4
John H. Rousselot (R)	116,715	70.9
27 Robert K. Dornan (R)	109,807	51.0
Carey Peck (D)	100,061	46.5
28 Julian C. Dixon (D)	108,725	79.2
Robert Reid (R)	23,179	16.9
29 Augustus F. Hawkins (D)	80,095	86.1
Michael A. Hirt (R)	10,282	11.1
30 George E. Danielson (D)	74,119	72.1
J. Arthur Platten (R)	24,136	23.5
31 Mervyn M. Dymally (D)	69,146	64.4
Don Grimshaw (R)	38,203	35.6
32 Glenn M. Anderson (D)	84,057	65.9
John R. Adler (R)	39,260	30.8
33 Wayne Grisham (R)	122,439	70.9
Fred L. Anderson (D)	50,365	29.1
34 Dan Lungren (R)	138,024	71.8
Simone (D)	46,351	24.1
35 David Dreier (R)	100,743	51.8
Jim Lloyd (D)	88,279	45.4
36 George E. Brown Jr. (D)	88,634	52.5
John Paul Stark (R)	73,252	43.4
37 Jerry Lewis (R)	166,640	71.6
Donald M. Rusk (D)	58,462	25.1
38 Jerry M. Patterson (D)	91,880	55.5
Art Jacobson (R)	66,256	40.0
39 William Dannemeyer (R)	175,228	76.3
Leonard L. Lahtinen (D)	54,504	23.7
40 Robert E. Badham (R)	213,999	70.2
Michael F. Dow (D)	66,512	21.8
Dan Mahaffey (LIBERT)	24,486	8.0
41 Bill Lowery (R)	123,187	52.7
Bob Wilson (D)	101,101	43.2
42 Duncan L. Hunter (R)	79,713	53.3
Lionel Van Deerlin (D)	69,936	46.7
43 Clair W. Burgener (R)	299,037	86.5
Tom Metzger (D)	46,383	13.4

COLORADO

	Votes	%
1 Patricia Schroeder (D)	107,364	59.8
Naomi Bradford (R)	67,804	37.7
2 Timothy E. Wirth (D)	153,618	56.4
John McElderry (R)	111,825	41.1
3 Ray Kogovsek (D)	105,820	54.9
Harold McCormick (R)	84,292	43.7
4 Hank Brown (R)	178,221	68.4
Polly Baca Barragan (D)	76,849	29.5
5 Ken Kramer (R)	177,319	72.4
Ed Schreiber (D)	62,003	25.3

CONNECTICUT

	Votes	%
1 William R. Cotter (D)	137,849	63.0

Candidates	Votes	%
Marjorie D. Anderson (R)	80,816	37.0
2 Samuel Gejdenson (D)	119,176	53.4
Tony Guglielmo (R)	104,107	46.6
3 Lawrence J. DeNardis (R)	117,024	52.3
Joseph I. Lieberman (D)	103,903	46.5
4 Stewart B. McKinney (R)	124,285	62.6
John A. Phillips (D)	74,326	37.4
5 William R. Ratchford (D)	117,316	50.4
Edward M. Donahue (R)	115,614	49.6
6 Toby Moffett (D)	142,685	59.0
Nicholas Schaus (R)	98,331	40.6

DELAWARE

	Votes	%
AL Thomas B. Evans Jr. (R)	133,842	61.8
Robert L. Maxwell (D)	81,227	37.5

FLORIDA

	Votes	%
1 Earl Hutto (D)	119,829	61.2
Warren Briggs (R)	75,939	38.8
2 Don Fuqua (D)	138,252	70.6
John R. LaCapra (R)	57,588	29.4
3 Charles E. Bennett (D)	104,672	77.0
Harry Radcliffe (R)	31,208	23.0
4 Bill Chappell Jr. (D)	147,775	65.8
Barney E. Dillard Jr. (R)	76,924	34.2
5 Bill McCollum (R)	177,603	55.8
David Best (D)	140,903	44.2
6 C.W. Bill Young (R)		100.0
7 Sam Gibbons (D)	132,529	71.8
Charles P. Jones (R)	52,138	28.2
8 Andy Ireland (D)	151,613	69.3
Scott Nicholson (R)	61,820	28.2
9 Bill Nelson (D)	139,468	70.4
Stan Dowiat (R)	58,734	29.6
10 L.A. (Skip) Bafalis (R)	272,393	78.9
Richard D. Sparkman (D)	72,646	21.1
11 Dan Mica (D)	201,713	59.5
Al Coogler (R)	137,520	40.5
12 Clay Shaw (R)	128,561	54.5
Alan S. Becker (D)	107,164	45.5
13 William Lehman (D)	127,828	74.9
Alvin E. Entin (R)	42,830	25.1
14 Claude Pepper (D)	95,820	74.9
Evelio S. Estrella (R)	32,027	25.1
15 Dante B. Fascell (D)	132,952	65.4
Herbert J. Hoodwin (R)	70,433	34.6

GEORGIA

	Votes	%
1 Bo Ginn (D)	82,145	100.0
2 Charles F. Hatcher (D)	92,264	73.6
Jack E. Harrell Jr. (R)	33,107	26.4
3 Jack Brinkley (D)	89,040	100.0
4 Elliott H. Levitas (D)	117,091	69.4
Barry E. Billington (R)	51,546	30.6
5 Wyche Fowler Jr. (D)	101,646	74.0
F. William Dowda (R)	35,640	26.0
6 Newt Gingrich (R)	96,071	59.1
Dock H. Davis (D)	66,606	40.9
7 Larry P. McDonald (D)	115,892	68.1
Richard L. Castellucis (R)	54,242	31.9
8 Billy Lee Evans (D)	91,103	74.6
Darwin Carter (R)	31,033	25.4
9 Ed Jenkins (D)	115,576	68.0
David G. Ashworth (R)	54,341	32.0
10 Doug Barnard (D)	102,177	80.2
Bruce J. Neubauer (R)	25,194	19.8

HAWAII

	Votes	%
1 Cecil Heftel (D)	98,256	79.8
Aloma Keen Noble (R)	19,819	16.1
2 Daniel K. Akaka (D)	141,477	89.9
Don G. Smith (LIBERT)	15,903	10.1

IDAHO

Candidates	Votes	%
1 Larry Craig (R)	116,845	53.7
Glenn W. Nichols (D)	100,697	46.3
2 George Hansen (R)	116,196	58.8
Diane Bilyeu (D)	81,364	41.2

ILLINOIS

Candidates	Votes	%
1 Harold Washington (D)	119,562	95.5
2 Gus Savage (D)	129,771	88.1
Marsha A. Harris (R)	17,428	11.8
3 Marty Russo (D)	137,283	68.9
Lawrence C. Sarsoun (R)	61,955	31.1
4 Edward J. Derwinski (R)	152,377	68.0
Richard S. Jalovec (D)	71,814	32.0
5 John G. Fary (D)	106,142	79.6
Robert V. Kotowski (R)	27,136	20.4
6 Henry J. Hyde (R)	123,593	67.0
Mario Raymond Reda (D)	60,951	33.0
7 Cardiss Collins (D)	80,056	85.1
Ruth R. Hooper (R)	14,041	14.9
8 Dan Rostenkowski (D)	98,524	84.7
Walter F. Zilke (R)	17,845	15.3
9 Sidney R. Yates (D)	106,543	73.1
John D. Andrica (R)	39,244	26.9
10 John E. Porter (R)	137,707	60.7
Robert A. Weinberger (D)	89,008	39.3
11 Frank Annunzio (D)	121,166	69.8
Michael R. Zanillo (R)	52,417	30.2
12 Philip M. Crane (R)	185,080	74.1
David McCartney (D)	64,729	25.9
13 Robert McClory (R)	131,448	71.7
Michael Reese (D)	52,000	28.3
14 John N. Erlenborn (R)	202,583	76.8
LeRoy E. Kennel (D)	61,224	23.2
15 Tom Corcoran (R)	150,898	76.7
John P. Quillin (D)	45,721	23.3
16 Lynn M. Martin (R)	132,905	67.4
Douglas R. Aurand (D)	64,224	32.6
17 George M. O'Brien (R)	125,806	65.8
Michael A. Murer (D)	65,305	34.2
18 Robert H. Michel (R)	125,561	62.1
John L. Knuppel (D)	76,471	37.9
19 Tom Railsback (R)	142,616	73.4
Thomas J. Hand (D)	51,753	26.6
20 Paul Findley (R)	123,427	56.0
David L. Robinson (D)	96,950	44.0
21 Edward R. Madigan (R)	132,186	67.6
Penny L. Severns (D)	63,476	32.4
22 Daniel B. Crane (R)	146,014	68.8
Peter M. Voelz (D)	66,065	31.2
23 Melvin Price (D)	107,786	64.4
Ronald L. Davinroy (R)	59,644	35.6
24 Paul Simon (D)	112,134	49.1
John T. Anderson (R)	110,176	48.3

Special Election

	Votes	%
10 John E. Porter (R)	36,981	54.0
Robert Weinberger (D)	30,929	46.0

INDIANA

Candidates	Votes	%
1 Adam Benjamin Jr. (D)	112,016	72.0
Joseph D. Harkin (R)	43,537	28.0
2 Floyd Fithian (D)	122,326	54.1
Ernest Niemeyer (R)	103,957	45.9
3 John P. Hiler (R)	103,972	55.0
John Brademas (D)	85,136	45.0
4 Daniel R. Coats (R)	120,055	60.5
John D. Walda (D)	77,542	39.1
5 Elwood Hillis (R)	129,474	61.7
Nels J. Ackerson (D)	80,378	38.3
6 David W. Evans (D)	98,482	50.2
David G. Crane (R)	97,582	49.8
7 John T. Myers (R)	137,604	66.1
Patrick D. Carroll (D)	69,051	33.2
8 H. Joel Deckard (R)	119,415	55.2
Kenneth C. Snider (D)	97,059	44.8
9 Lee H. Hamilton (D)	136,574	64.4
George Meyers Jr. (R)	75,601	35.6
10 Phil Sharp (D)	103,083	53.4

Candidates	Votes	%
William G. Frazier (R)	90,051	46.6
11 Andy Jacobs Jr. (D)	105,468	57.3
Sheila Suess (R)	78,743	42.7

IOWA

Candidates	Votes	%
1 Jim Leach (R)	133,349	64.1
Jim Larew (D)	72,602	34.9
2 Tom Tauke (R)	111,587	54.0
Steve Sovern (D)	93,175	45.1
3 Cooper Evans (R)	107,869	51.4
Lynn G. Cutler (D)	101,735	48.4
4 Neal Smith (D)	117,896	53.9
Donald C. Young (R)	100,335	45.9
5 Tom Harkin (D)	127,895	60.2
Cal Hultman (R)	84,472	39.8
6 Berkley Bedell (D)	129,460	64.3
Clarence S. Carney (R)	71,866	35.7

KANSAS

Candidates	Votes	%
1 Pat Roberts (R)	121,545	62.3
Phil Martin (D)	73,586	37.7
2 Jim Jeffries (R)	92,107	53.9
Sam Keys (D)	78,859	46.1
3 Larry Winn Jr. (R)	109,294	55.5
Dan Watkins (D)	82,414	41.8
4 Dan Glickman (D)	124,014	68.9
Clay Hunter (R)	55,899	31.1
5 Bob Whittaker (R)	141,029	74.2
David L. Miller (D)	45,676	24.0

KENTUCKY

Candidates	Votes	%
1 Carroll Hubbard Jr. (D)	118,565	100.0
2 William H. Natcher (D)	99,670	65.7
Mark T. Watson (R)	52,110	34.3
3 Romano L. Mazzoli (D)	85,873	63.7
Richard Cesler (R)	46,681	34.6
4 Gene Snyder (R)	126,049	67.0
Phil M. McGary (D)	62,138	33.0
5 Harold Rogers (R)	112,093	67.5
Ted R. Marcum (D)	54,027	32.5
6 Larry J. Hopkins (R)	105,376	58.9
Tom Easterly (D)	72,473	40.5
7 Carl D. Perkins (D)	117,665	100.0

LOUISIANA[1]

Candidates	Votes	%
1 Robert L. Livingston (R)		100.0
2 Lindy Boggs (D)		100.0
3 W. J. (Billy) Tauzin (D)		100.0
4 Buddy Roemer (D)	103,625	63.8
Claude (Buddy) Leach (D)	58,705	36.2
5 Jerry Huckaby (D)		100.0
6 W. Henson Moore (R)		100.0
7 John B. Breaux (D)		100.0
8 Gillis W. Long (D)		100.0

Special Election

	Votes	%
3. W. J. (Billy) Tauzin (D)	62,108	53.0
James Donelon (R)	54,815	47.0

MAINE

Candidates	Votes	%
1 David F. Emery (R)	188,667	68.5
Harold C. Pachios (D)	86,819	31.5
2 Olympia J. Snowe (R)	186,406	78.5
Harold L. Silverman (D)	51,026	21.5

MARYLAND

Candidates	Votes	%
1 Roy Dyson (D)	97,743	51.7
Robert E. Bauman (R)	91,143	48.3
2 Clarence D. Long (D)	121,017	57.4
Helen D. Bentley (R)	89,961	42.6
3 Barbara A. Mikulski (D)	102,293	76.1
Russell T. Schaffer (R)	32,074	23.9
4 Marjorie S. Holt (R)	120,985	71.9
James J. Riley (D)	47,375	28.1
5 Gladys Noon Spellman (D)	106,035	80.5

Candidates	Votes	%
Kevin R. Igoe (R)	25,693	19.
6 Beverly B. Byron (D)	146,101	69.
Raymond E. Beck (R)	62,913	30.
7 Parren J. Mitchell (D)	97,104	88.
Victor Clark Jr. (R)	12,650	11.
8 Michael D. Barnes (D)	148,301	59.
Newton I. Steers Jr. (R)	101,659	40.

MASSACHUSETTS

Candidates	Votes	%
1 Silvio O. Conte (R)	156,415	74.
Helen Poppy Doyle (D)	52,457	25.
2 Edward P. Boland (D)	120,711	67.2
Thomas P. Swank (R)	38,672	21.4
John B. Aubuchon (I)	20,247	11.
3 Joseph D. Early (D)	141,560	72.1
David G. Skehan (R)	54,123	27.
4 Barney Frank (D)	103,466	51.1
Richard A. Jones (R)	95,898	48.
5 James M. Shannon (D)	136,758	66.0
William C. Sawyer (R)	70,547	34.
6 Nicholas Mavroules (D)	111,393	50.1
Thomas H. Trimarco (R)	103,192	47.
7 Edward J. Markey (D)	155,759	100.
8 Thomas P. O'Neill Jr. (D)	128,689	78.4
William A. Barnstead (R)	35,477	21.
9 Joe Moakley (D)	104,010	100.0
10 Margaret M. Heckler (R)	131,794	60.
Robert E. McCarthy (D)	85,629	39.4
11 Brian J. Donnelly (D)	137,066	100.0
12 Gerry E. Studds (D)	195,791	73.2
Paul V. Doane (R)	71,620	26.8

MICHIGAN

Candidates	Votes	%
1 John Conyers Jr. (D)	123,286	94.7
2 Carl D. Pursell (R)	115,562	57.3
Kathleen F. O'Reilly (D)	83,550	41.4
3 Howard Wolpe (D)	113,080	52.0
James S. Gilmore (R)	102,591	47.2
4 Dave Stockman (R)	148,950	74.7
Lyndon G. Furst (D)	47,777	24.0
5 Harold S. Sawyer (R)	118,061	53.1
Dale R. Sprik (D)	101,737	45.8
6 Jim Dunn (R)	111,272	50.6
Bob Carr (D)	108,548	49.4
7 Dale E. Kildee (D)	147,280	92.7
Dennis L. Berry (LIBERT)	11,507	7.2
8 Bob Traxler (D)	124,155	60.7
Norman R. Hughes (R)	77,009	37.1
9 Guy Vander Jagt (R)	168,713	96.3
10 Don Albosta (D)	126,962	52.4
Richard J. Allen (R)	111,496	46.0
11 Robert W. Davis (R)	146,205	65.5
Dan Dorrity (D)	75,515	33.8
12 David E. Bonior (D)	112,698	55.3
Kirk Walsh (R)	90,931	44.1
13 George W. Crockett Jr. (D)	79,719	91.8
M. Michael Hurd (R)	6,473	7.4
14 Dennis M. Hertel (D)	90,362	53.3
Vic Caputo (R)	78,395	46.2
15 William D. Ford (D)	113,492	67.6
Gerald R. Carlson (R)	53,046	31.6
16 John D. Dingell (D)	105,844	69.9
Pamella A. Seay (R)	42,735	28.2
17 William M. Brodhead (D)	127,525	73.1
Alfred L. Patterson (R)	44,313	25.4
18 James J. Blanchard (D)	135,705	65.3
Betty J. Suida (R)	68,575	33.0
19 William S. Broomfield (R)	168,530	72.1
Wayne E. Daniels (D)	60,100	25.9

MINNESOTA[2]

Candidates	Votes	%
1 Arlen Erdahl (I-R)	171,099	71.6
Russell V. Smith (DFL)	67,279	28.2
2 Tom Hagedorn (I-R)	158,082	60.6
Harold J. Bergquist (DFL)	102,586	39.4
3 Bill Frenzel (I-R)	179,393	75.6
Joel Alexander Saliterman (DFL)	57,868	24.4
4 Bruce F. Vento (DFL)	119,182	58.5

Footnotes, see p. 1051.

Candidates	Votes	%
John Berg (I-R)	82,537	40.5
5 Martin Olav Sabo (DFL)	126,451	70.1
John Doherty (I-R)	48,200	26.7
6 Vin Weber (I-R)	140,402	52.7
Archie Baumann (DFL)	126,173	47.3
7 Arlan Stangeland (I-R)	135,084	52.1
Gene Wenstrom (DFL)	124,026	47.9
8 James L. Oberstar (DFL)	182,228	70.4
Edward Fiore (I-R)	72,350	28.0

MISSISSIPPI

1 Jamie L. Whitten (D)	104,269	63.0
T.K. Moffett (R)	61,292	37.0
2 David R. Bowen (D)	96,750	69.6
Frank Drake (R)	42,300	30.4
3 G.V. Montgomery (D)	128,035	100.0
4 Jon C. Hinson (R)	69,321	39.0
Leslie Burl McLemore (I)	52,959	29.8
Britt R. Singletary (D)	52,303	29.4
5 Trent Lott (R)	131,559	73.9
Jimmy McVeay (D)	46,416	26.1

MISSOURI

1 William Clay (D)	91,272	70.2
Bill White (R)	38,667	29.8
2 Robert A. Young (D)	148,227	64.4
John O. Shields (R)	81,762	35.6
3 Richard A. Gephardt (D)	143,132	77.6
Robert A. Cedarburg (R)	41,277	22.4
4 Ike Skelton (D)	151,459	67.8
Bill Baker (R)	71,869	32.2
5 Richard Bolling (D)	110,957	70.1
Vincent E. Baker (R)	47,309	29.9
6 E. Thomas Coleman (R)	149,281	70.6
Vernon King (D)	62,048	29.4
7 Gene Taylor (R)	161,668	67.8
Ken Young (D)	76,844	32.2
8 Wendell Bailey (R)	127,675	57.1
Steve Gardner (D)	95,751	42.9
9 Harold L. Volkmer (D)	135,905	56.5
John W. Turner (R)	104,835	43.5
10 Bill Emerson (R)	116,167	55.2
Bill D. Burlison (D)	94,465	44.8

MONTANA

1 Pat Williams (D)	112,866	61.4
John K. McDonald (R)	70,874	38.6
2 Ron Marlenee (R)	91,431	59.1
Tom Monahan (D)	63,370	40.9

NEBRASKA

1 Douglas K. Bereuter (R)	160,705	78.6
Rex S. Story (D)	43,605	21.3
2 Hal Daub (R)	107,736	53.1
Richard M. Fellman (D)	88,843	43.8
3 Virginia Smith (R)	182,887	83.9
Stan Ditus (D)	34,967	16.0

NEVADA

AL Jim Santini (D)	165,107	67.5
Vince Saunders (R)	63,163	25.8

NEW HAMPSHIRE

1 Norman E. D'Amours (D)	114,061	60.8
Marshall W. Cobleigh (R)	73,565	39.2
2 Judd Gregg (R)	113,304	64.1
Maurice L. Arel (D)	63,350	35.9

NEW JERSEY

1 James J. Florio (D)	147,352	76.7
Scott L. Sibert (R)	42,154	21.9
2 William J. Hughes (D)	135,437	57.5
Beech N. Fox (R)	97,072	41.2
3 James J. Howard (D)	106,269	49.9
Marie Sheehan Muhler (R)	104,184	49.0

Candidates	Votes	%
4 Christopher H. Smith (R)	95,447	56.6
Frank Thompson Jr. (D)	68,480	40.6
5 Millicent Fenwick (R)	156,016	77.5
Kieran E. Pillion Jr. (D)	41,269	20.5
6 Edwin B. Forsythe (R)	125,792	56.3
Lewis M. Weinstein (D)	92,227	41.3
7 Marge Roukema (R)	108,760	50.7
Andrew Maguire (D)	99,737	46.5
8 Robert A. Roe (D)	95,493	67.2
William R. Cleveland (R)	44,625	31.4
9 Harold C. Hollenbeck (R)	116,128	59.1
Gabriel Ambrosio (D)	75,321	38.3
10 Peter W. Rodino Jr. (D)	76,154	85.3
Everett J. Jennings (R)	11,778	13.2
11 Joseph G. Minish (D)	106,155	63.0
Robert A. Davis (R)	57,772	34.3
12 Matthew J. Rinaldo (R)	134,973	77.1
Rose Zeidwerg Monyek (D)	36,577	20.9
13 Jim Courter (R)	152,862	71.6
Dave Stickle (D)	56,251	26.4
14 Frank J. Guarini (D)	86,921	64.2
Dennis E. Teti (R)	45,606	33.7
15 Bernard J. Dwyer (D)	92,457	53.4
William O'Sullivan Jr. (R)	75,812	43.8

NEW MEXICO

1 Manuel Lujan Jr. (R)	125,910	51.0
Bill Richardson (D)	120,903	49.0
2 Joe Skeen (WRITE IN)	61,564	38.0
David King (D)	55,085	34.0
Dorothy Runnels (WRITE IN)	45,343	28.0

NEW YORK

1 William Carney (R,C,RTL)	115,213	56.3
Thomas A. Twomey (D)	85,629	41.9
2 Thomas J. Downey (D)	84,035	56.3
Louis J. Modica (R,RTL)	65,106	43.7
3 Gregory W. Carman (R,C)	87,952	50.1
Jerome A. Ambro (D,RTL)	83,389	47.5
4 Norman F. Lent (R,C,RTL)	117,455	66.8
Charles F. Brennan (D,L)	58,270	33.2
5 Raymond McGrath (R,C,RTL)	105,140	57.7
Karen S. Burstein (D,L)	77,228	42.3
6 John LeBoutillier (R,C,RTL)	89,762	52.8
Lester L. Wolff (D,L)	80,209	47.2
7 Joseph Addabbo (D,R,L)	96,137	95.3
8 Benjamin Rosenthal (D,L)	84,273	75.6
Albert Lemishow (R,C,RTL)	27,156	24.4
9 Geraldine A. Ferraro (D)	63,796	58.3
Vito P. Battista (R,C,RTL)	44,473	40.7
10 Mario Biaggi (D,R,L)	95,322	94.5
11 James H. Scheuer (D,L)	72,798	74.1
Andrew E. Carlan (R,C,RTL)	25,424	25.9
12 Shirley Chisholm (D,L)	35,446	87.1
Charles Gibbs (R)	3,372	8.3
13 Stephen J. Solarz (D,L)	81,954	79.4
Harry DeMell (R,C)	19,536	18.9
14 Fred Richmond (D,L)	45,029	76.1
Christopher Lovell (R,C)	8,257	14.0
Moses S. Harris (I)	4,151	7.0
15 Leo C. Zeferetti (D)	49,684	50.2
Paul M. Atanasio (R,C,RTL)	46,467	46.9
16 Charles E. Schumer (D,L)	67,343	77.5
Theodore Silverman (R,C)	17,050	19.6
17 Guy V. Molinari (R)	69,573	47.8
John M. Murphy (D,RTL)	50,954	35.0
Mary T. Codd (L)	25,118	17.2
18 S. William Green (R)	91,341	56.7
Mark J. Green (D,L)	68,786	42.7
19 Charles B. Rangel (D,R,L)	84,062	96.2
20 Ted Weiss (D,L)	86,454	82.4
James E. Greene (R)	15,350	14.6
21 Robert Garcia (D,R,L)	32,173	98.2
22 Jonathan B. Bingham (D,L)	66,301	83.9
Robert S. Black (R)	9,943	12.6
23 Peter A. Peyser (D)	85,749	56.2
Andrew Albanese (R,C)	66,771	43.8
24 Richard L. Ottinger (D)	100,182	59.4

Candidates	Votes	%
Joseph Christiana (R,C,RTL)	66,689	39.6
25 Hamilton Fish Jr. (R,C)	158,936	81.0
Gunars Ozols (D)	37,369	19.0
26 Benjamin A. Gilman (R)	137,159	74.3
Eugene Victor (D,L)	37,475	20.3
27 Matthew F. McHugh (D)	103,863	55.0
Neil T. Wallace (R,C)	83,096	44.0
28 Samuel S. Stratton (D)	164,088	77.9
Frank Wicks (R)	37,504	17.8
29 Gerald Solomon (R,C,RTL)	141,631	66.7
Rodger L. Hurley (D,L)	70,697	33.3
30 David O'B. Martin (R,C)	111,008	63.8
Mary Anne Krupsak (D,L)	54,896	31.6
31 Donald J. Mitchell (R,RTL)	135,976	77.5
Irving A. Schwartz (D)	39,589	22.5
32 George Wortley (R,C)	108,128	60.4
Jeffery S. Brooks (D, L)	56,535	31.6
Peter J. Del Giorno (RTL)	11,978	6.7
33 Gary A. Lee (R,C)	132,831	75.8
Dolores M. Reed (D,L)	39,542	22.6
34 Frank Horton (R)	133,278	72.9
James Toole (D)	37,883	20.7
35 Barber B. Conable Jr. (R)	127,623	72.2
John M. Owens (D,C)	44,754	25.3
36 John J. LaFalce (D,L)	122,929	71.7
H. William Feder (R,C,RTL)	48,428	28.3
37 Henry J. Nowak (D,L)	94,890	83.0
Roger Heymanowski (R,C)	16,560	14.5
38 Jack F. Kemp (R,C,RTL)	167,434	81.6
Gale A. Denn (D,L)	37,875	18.4
39 Stanley N. Lundine (D)	93,839	54.7
James Abdella (R,C)	75,039	43.8

NORTH CAROLINA

1 Walter B. Jones (D)	108,738	100.0
2 L. H. Fountain (D)	99,297	73.4
Barry L. Gardner (R)	35,946	26.6
3 Charles Whitley (D)	84,862	68.3
Larry J. Parker (R)	39,393	31.7
4 Ike F. Andrews (D)	97,167	52.6
Thurman Hogan (R)	84,631	45.8
5 Stephen L. Neal (D)	99,117	51.0
Anne Bagnal (R)	94,894	48.8
6 Eugene Johnston (R)	80,275	51.1
Richardson Preyer (D)	76,957	48.9
7 Charlie Rose (D)	88,564	68.7
Vivian S. Wright (R)	40,270	31.3
8 W.G. (Bill) Hefner (D)	95,013	58.5
L.E. (Larry) Harris (R)	67,317	41.5
9 James G. Martin (R)	101,156	58.6
Randall R. Kincaid (D)	71,504	41.4
10 James T. Broyhill (R)	120,777	69.7
James O. Icenhour (D)	52,485	30.3
11 William M. Hendon (R)	104,485	53.5
Lamar Gudger (D)	90,789	46.5

NORTH DAKOTA

AL Byron L. Dorgan (D)	166,437	56.8
Jim Smykowski (R)	124,707	42.6

OHIO

1 Bill Gradison (R)	124,080	74.7
Donald J. Zwick (D)	38,529	23.2
2 Thomas A. Luken (D)	103,423	58.7
Tom Atkins (R)	72,693	41.3
3 Tony P. Hall (D)	95,558	57.3
Albert H. Sealy (R)	66,698	40.0
4 Tennyson Guyer (R)	133,795	72.3
Geraldine Tebben (D)	51,150	27.7
5 Delbert L. Latta (R)	137,003	70.4
James R. Sherck (D)	57,704	29.6
6 Bob McEwen (R)	101,288	54.6
Ted Strickland (D)	84,235	45.4
7 Clarence J. Brown (R)	124,137	76.1
Donald Hollister (D)	38,952	23.9
8 Thomas N. Kindness (R)	139,590	76.0
John W. Griffin (D)	44,162	24.0

Candidates	Votes	%
9 Ed Weber (R)	96,927	56.2
Thomas L. Ashley (D)	68,728	39.9
10 Clarence E. Miller (R)	143,403	74.4
Jack E. Stecher (D)	49,433	25.6
11 J. William Stanton (R)	128,507	69.3
Patrick J. Donlin (D)	51,224	27.6
12 Robert N. Shamansky (D)	108,690	52.6
Samuel L. Devine (R)	98,110	47.4
13 Don J. Pease (D)	113,439	63.8
David E. Armstrong (R)	64,296	36.2
14 John F. Seiberling (D)	103,336	64.9
Louis A. Mangels (R)	55,962	35.1
15 Chalmers P. Wylie (R)	129,025	72.6
Terry Freeman (D)	48,708	27.4
16 Ralph S. Regula (R)	149,960	79.3
Larry V. Slagle (D)	39,219	20.7
17 John M. Ashbrook (R)	128,870	72.9
Donald E. Yunker (D)	47,900	27.1
18 Douglas Applegate (D)	134,835	76.1
Gary L. Hammersley (R)	42,354	23.9
19 Lyle Williams (R)	107,032	58.1
Harry Meshel (D)	77,272	41.9
20 Mary Rose Oakar (D)	96,217	100.0
21 Louis Stokes (D)	83,188	88.2
Robert L. Woodall (R)	11,103	11.8
22 Dennis E. Eckart (D)	108,137	55.2
Joseph J. Nahra (R)	80,836	41.3
23 Ronald M. Mottl (D)	144,317	100.0

OKLAHOMA

Candidates	Votes	%
1 James R. Jones (D)	115,381	58.4
Richard C. Freeman (R)	82,293	41.6
2 Mike Synar (D)	101,516	54.0
Gary Richardson (R)	86,544	46.0
3 Wes Watkins (D)		100.0
4 Dave McCurdy (D)	74,245	51.0
Howard Rutledge (R)	71,339	49.0
5 Mickey Edwards (R)	90,053	68.4
David C. Hood (D)	36,815	28.0
6 Glenn English (D)	111,694	64.7
Carol McCurley (R)	60,980	35.3

OREGON

Candidates	Votes	%
1 Les AuCoin (D)	203,532	65.9
Lynn Engdahl (R)	105,083	34.0
2 Denny Smith (R)	141,854	48.8
Al Ullman (D)	138,089	47.5
3 Ron Wyden (D)	156,371	71.9
Darrell R. Conger (R)	60,940	28.0
4 James Weaver (D)	158,745	54.8
Michael Fitzgerald (R)	130,861	45.2

PENNSYLVANIA

Candidates	Votes	%
1 Thomas M. Foglietta (I)	58,737	37.8
Michael (Ozzie) Myers (D)	52,956	34.1
Robert R. Burke (R)	37,893	24.4
2 William H. Gray III (D)	127,106	96.4
3 Raymond F. Lederer (D)	67,942	54.5
William J. Phillips (R)	40,866	32.8
Max Weiner (CONSU)	11,849	9.5
4 Charles F. Dougherty (R)	127,475	63.3
Thomas J. Magrann (D)	73,895	36.7
5 Richard T. Schulze (R)	148,898	75.1
Grady G. Brickhouse (D)	47,092	23.8
6 Gus Yatron (D)	117,965	67.1
George Hulshart (R)	57,844	32.9
7 Robert W. Edgar (D)	99,381	53.1
Dennis J. Rochford (R)	87,643	46.9
8 James K. Coyne (R)	103,585	50.7
Peter H. Kostmayer (D)	99,593	48.7
9 Bud Shuster (R,D)	157,241	100.0
10 Joseph M. McDade (R)	145,703	76.6
Gene Basalyga (D)	43,152	22.7
11 James L. Nelligan (R)	93,621	51.9
Raphael Musto (D)	86,703	48.1
12 John P. Murtha (D)	106,750	59.4
Charles A. Getty (R)	72,999	40.6
13 Lawrence Coughlin (R)	138,212	70.0
Pete Slawek (D)	57,745	29.2

Candidates	Votes	%
14 William J. Coyne (D)	102,545	68.5
Stan Thomas (R)	44,071	29.5
15 Don Ritter (R)	99,874	59.6
Jeanette Reibman (D)	66,626	39.7
16 James A. Woodcock (D)	38,891	23.1
Robert S. Walker (R)	129,765	76.9
17 Allen E. Ertel (D)	97,995	60.6
Daniel S. Seiverling (R)	63,790	39.4
18 Doug Walgren (D)	127,641	68.5
Steven R. Snyder (R)	58,821	31.5
19 Bill Goodling (R)	136,873	76.0
Richard P. Noll (D)	41,584	23.1
20 Joseph M. Gaydos (D)	122,100	72.5
Kathleen M. Meyer (R)	46,313	27.5
21 Don Bailey (D)	112,427	68.4
Dirk Matson (R)	51,821	31.6
22 Austin J. Murphy (D)	118,084	69.5
Marilyn C. Ecoff (R)	50,020	29.5
23 William F. Clinger Jr. (R)	122,855	73.5
Peter Atigan (D)	41,033	24.6
24 Marc L. Marks (R)	86,687	49.7
David C. DiCarlo (D)	86,567	49.6
25 Eugene V. Atkinson (D)	119,817	67.1
Robert H. Morris (R)	58,768	32.9

Special Election

Candidates	Votes	%
11 Raphael Musto (D)	32,073	27.3
James Nelligan (R)	27,496	23.4
Frank Harrison (I)	20,475	17.4
Paul Kanjorski (I)	18,241	15.5
Ted Mitchell (I)	12,009	10.2

RHODE ISLAND

Candidates	Votes	%
1 Fernand J. St Germain (D)	120,756	67.6
William P. Montgomery (R)	57,844	32.4
2 Claudine Schneider (R)	115,057	55.3
Edward P. Beard (D)	92,970	44.7

SOUTH CAROLINA

Candidates	Votes	%
1 Thomas F. Hartnett (R)	81,988	51.6
Charles D. Ravenel (D)	76,743	48.3
2 Floyd Spence (R)	92,306	55.7
Tom Turnipseed (D)	73,353	44.3
3 Butler Derrick (D)	87,680	59.8
Marshall Parker (R)	57,840	39.4
4 Carroll Campbell Jr. (R)	90,941	92.6
Thomas Waldenfels (LIBERT)	6,984	7.1
5 Ken Holland (D)	99,773	87.5
Thomas Campbell (LIBERT)	14,252	12.5
6 John L. Napier (R)	75,964	51.7
John W. Jenrette Jr. (D)	70,747	48.2

SOUTH DAKOTA

Candidates	Votes	%
1 Thomas A. Daschle (D)	109,910	65.8
Bart Kull (R)	57,155	34.2
2 Clint Roberts (R)	88,991	58.4
Kenneth D. Stofferahn (D)	63,447	41.6

TENNESSEE

Candidates	Votes	%
1 James H. Quillen (R)	130,296	86.2
John Curtis (I)	20,816	13.8
2 John J. Duncan (R)	147,947	76.1
Dave Dunaway (D)	46,578	23.9
3 Marilyn Lloyd Bouquard (D)	117,355	61.1
Glen M. Byers (R)	74,761	38.9
4 Albert Gore Jr. (D)	137,612	79.3
James Beau Seigneur (R)	35,954	20.7
5 Bill Boner (D)	118,506	65.4
Mike Adams (R)	62,746	34.6
6 Robin L. Beard Jr. (R)	127,945	99.6
7 Ed Jones (D)	133,606	77.3
Daniel Campbell (R)	39,227	22.7
8 Harold E. Ford (D)	110,139	99.9

TEXAS

Candidates	Votes	%
1 Sam B. Hall Jr. (D)	137,665	100.0
2 Charles Wilson (D)	142,496	69.
F. H. Pannill Sr. (R)	60,742	29.
3 James M. Collins (R)	218,228	79.
Earle S. Porter (D)	49,667	18.
4 Ralph M. Hall (D)	102,787	52.
John H. Wright (R)	93,915	47.
5 Jim Mattox (D)	70,892	51.
Tom Pauken (R)	67,848	48.
6 Phil Gramm (D)	144,816	70.
Dave (Buster) Haskins (R)	59,503	29.
7 Bill Archer (R)	242,810	82.
Robert L. Hutchings (D)	48,594	16.
8 Jack Fields (R)	72,856	51.
Bob Eckhardt (D)	67,921	48.
9 Jack Brooks (D)	103,225	99.
10 J. J. Pickle (D)	135,618	59.
John Biggar (R)	88,940	38.
11 Marvin Leath (D)	128,520	100.0
12 Jim Wright (D)	99,104	59.
Jim Bradshaw (R)	65,005	39.
13 Jack Hightower (D)	98,779	55.
Ron Slover (R)	80,819	45.
14 William N. Patman (D)	93,884	56.
Charles L. Concklin (R)	71,495	43.
15 E. (Kika) de la Garza (D)	105,325	70.0
Lendy McDonald (R)	45,090	30.0
16 Richard C. White (D)	104,734	84.6
Catherine McDivitt (LIBERT)	19,010	15.4
17 Charles W. Stenholm (D)	130,465	100.0
18 Mickey Leland (D)	71,985	79.9
C. L. Kennedy (R)	16,128	17.9
19 Kent Hance (D)	126,632	93.5
J. D. Webster (LIBERT)	8,792	6.5
20 Henry B. Gonzalez (D)	84,113	81.9
Merle W. Nash (R)	17,725	17.3
21 Tom Loeffler (R)	196,424	76.5
Joe Sullivan (D)	58,425	22.8
22 Ron Paul (R)	106,797	51.0
Mike Andrews (D)	101,094	48.3
23 Abraham Kazen Jr. (D)	104,595	69.8
Bobby Locke (R)	45,139	30.1
24 Martin Frost (D)	93,690	61.3
Clay Smothers (R)	59,172	38.7

UTAH

Candidates	Votes	%
1 James V. Hansen (R)	157,111	52.1
Gunn McKay (D)	144,459	47.9
2 Dan Marriott (R)	194,885	67.0
Arthur L. Monson (D)	87,967	30.3

VERMONT

Candidates	Votes	%
AL James M. Jeffords (R)	154,274	79.2
Robin Lloyd (CIT)	24,758	12.7
Peter Diamondstone (LU)	15,218	7.8

VIRGINIA

Candidates	Votes	%
1 Paul S. Trible Jr. (R)	130,130	90.5
Sharon D. Grant (I)	13,688	9.5
2 G. William Whitehurst (R)	97,319	89.8
Kenneth Morrison (LIBERT)	11,003	10.2
3 Thomas J. Bliley Jr. (R)	96,524	51.6
John A. Mapp (D)	60,962	32.6
Howard H. Carwile (I)	19,549	10.5
James B. Turney (LIBERT)	9,852	5.3
4 Robert W. Daniel Jr. (R)	92,557	60.7
Cecil Y. Jenkins (D)	59,930	39.3
5 Dan Daniel (D)	112,143	99.9
6 M. Caldwell Butler (R)	123,125	99.2
7 J. Kenneth Robinson (R)	139,957	99.7
8 Stanford E. Parris (R)	95,624	48.8
Herbert E. Harris II (D)	94,530	48.3
9 William C. Wampler (R)	119,196	69.4
Roosevelt Ferguson (D)	52,636	30.6
10 Frank R. Wolf (R)	110,840	51.1
Joseph L. Fisher (D)	105,883	48.9

WASHINGTON

Candidates	Votes	%
1 Joel Pritchard (R)	180,475	78.3
Robin Drake (D)	41,830	18.1

Candidates	Votes	%
2 Al Swift (D)	162,002	*63.9*
Neal Snider (R)	82,639	*32.6*
3 Don Bonker (D)	155,906	*62.7*
Rod Culp (R)	92,872	*37.3*
4 Sid Morrison (R)	134,691	*57.4*
Mike McCormack (D)	100,114	*42.6*
5 Thomas S. Foley (D)	120,530	*51.9*
John Sonneland (R)	111,705	*48.1*
6 Norman D. Dicks (D)	122,903	*53.6*
Jim Beaver (R)	106,236	*46.4*
7 Mike Lowry (D)	112,848	*57.3*
Ron Dunlap (R)	84,218	*42.7*

WEST VIRGINIA

Candidates	Votes	%
1 Robert H. Mollohan (D)	107,471	*63.6*
Joe Bartlett (R)	61,438	*36.4*
2 Cleve Benedict (R)	102,805	*55.9*

Candidates	Votes	%
Pat R. Hamilton (D)	80,940	*44.1*
3 Mick Staton (R)	94,583	*52.7*
John G. Hutchinson (D)	84,980	*47.3*
4 Nick J. Rahall (D)	117,595	*76.6*
Winton G. Covey Jr. (R)	36,020	*23.4*

Special Election

	Votes	%
3 John G. Hutchinson (D)	51,169	*53.8*
David Staton (R)	43,950	*46.2*

WISCONSIN

Candidates	Votes	%
1 Les Aspin (D)	126,222	*56.2*
Kathryn H. Canary (R)	96,047	*42.8*
2 Robert W. Kastenmeier (D)	142,037	*54.0*
James A. Wright (R)	119,514	*45.4*
3 Steven Gunderson (R)	132,001	*51.0*

Candidates	Votes	%
Alvin Baldus (D)	126,859	*49.0*
4 Clement J. Zablocki (D)	146,437	*70.0*
Elroy C. Honadel (R)	61,027	*29.2*
5 Henry S. Reuss (D)	129,574	*77.0*
David Bathke (R)	37,267	*22.2*
6 Thomas E. Petri (R)	143,980	*59.3*
Gary R. Goyke (D)	98,628	*40.7*
7 David R. Obey (D)	164,340	*64.7*
Vinton A. Vesta (R)	89,745	*35.3*
8 Toby Roth (R)	169,664	*67.7*
Michael R. Monfils (D)	81,043	*32.3*
9 F. James Sensenbrenner (R)	206,227	*78.4*
Gary C. Benedict (D)	56,838	*21.6*

WYOMING

Candidates	Votes	%
AL Richard B. Cheney (R)	116,361	*68.6*
Jim Rogers (D)	53,338	*31.4*
David G. Glancy (D)	24,390	*42.8*

1981 House Elections

MARYLAND

Special Election

Candidates	Votes	%
5 Steny H. Hoyer (D)	42,573	*55.2*
Audrey Scott (R)	33,708	*43.5*

MICHIGAN

Special Election

Candidates	Votes	%
4 Mark Siljander (R)	36,046	*72.6*
Johnie Rodebush (D)	12,461	*25.1*

MISSISSIPPI

Special Election

	Votes	%
4 Wayne Dowdy (D)	55,656	*50.4*
Liles Williams (R)	54,744	*49.6*

OHIO

Special Election

Candidates	Votes	%
4 Michael Oxley (R)	41,987	*50.2*
Dale Locker (D)	41,646	*49.8*

PENNSYLVANIA

Special Election

	Votes	%
3 Joseph F. Smith (R, I)	29,907	*52.5*
David G. Glancy (D)	24,390	*42.8*

1980 Elections

1. For the 1980 House elections in Louisiana, an open primary election was held with candidates from all parties running on the same ballot. Any candidate who received a majority was elected unopposed, with no further appearance on the general election ballot. If no candidate received 50 percent, a runoff was held between the two top finishers.

2. In Minnesota the Democratic Party is known as the Democratic-Farmer-Labor Party and the Republican Party as the Independent-Republican Party; candidates appear on the ballot with these designations.

1982 House Elections

ALABAMA

Candidates	Votes	%
1 Jack Edwards (R)	87,901	61.0
Steve Gudac (D)	54,315	37.7
2 William L. Dickinson (R)	83,290	50.4
Billy Joe Camp (D)	81,904	49.6
3 Bill Nichols (D)	100,864	96.3
4 Tom Bevill (D)	118,595	100.0
5 Ronnie G. Flippo (D)	108,807	80.7
Leopold Yambrek (R)	24,593	18.2
6 Ben Erdreich (D)	88,029	53.2
Albert Lee Smith Jr. (R)	76,726	46.4
7 Richard C. Shelby (D)	124,070	96.8

ALASKA

	Votes	%
AL Don Young (R)	128,274	70.8
Dave Carlson (D)	52,001	28.7

ARIZONA

	Votes	%
1 John McCain (R)	89,116	65.9
William E. Hegarty (D)	41,261	30.5
2 Morris K. Udall (D)	73,468	70.9
Roy B. Laos (R)	28,407	27.4
3 Bob Stump (R)	101,198	63.3
Pat Bosch (D)	58,644	36.7
4 Eldon Rudd (R)	95,620	65.7
Wayne O. Earley (D)	44,182	30.4
5 Jim McNulty (D)	82,938	49.7
Jim Kolbe (R)	80,531	48.3

ARKANSAS

	Votes	%
1 Bill Alexander (D)	124,208	64.8
Chuck Banks (R)	67,427	35.2
2 Ed Bethune (D)	96,775	53.9
Charles L. George (D)	82,913	46.1
3 John Paul Hammerschmidt (R)	133,909	66.0
Jim McDougal (D)	69,089	34.0
4 Beryl Anthony Jr. (D)	121,256	65.6
Bob Leslie (R)	63,661	34.4

CALIFORNIA

	Votes	%
1 Douglas H. Bosco (D)	107,749	49.8
Don H. Clausen (R)	102,043	47.2
2 Gene Chappie (R)	116,172	57.9
John A. Newmeyer (D)	81,314	40.5
3 Robert T. Matsui (D)	194,680	89.6
Bruce A. Daniel (LIBERT)	16,222	7.5
4 Vic Fazio (D)	118,476	63.9
Roger B. Canfield (R)	67,047	36.1
5 Phillip Burton (D)	103,268	57.9
Milton Marks (R)	72,139	40.5
6 Barbara Boxer (D)	96,379	52.4
Dennis McQuaid (R)	82,128	44.6
7 George Miller (D)	126,952	67.2
Paul E. Vallely (R)	56,960	30.2
8 Ronald V. Dellums (D)	121,537	55.9
Claude B. Hutchison Jr. (R)	95,694	44.0
9 Fortney H. (Pete) Stark (D)	104,393	60.7
Bill J. Kennedy (R)	67,702	39.3
10 Don Edwards (D)	77,263	62.7
Bob Herriott (R)	41,506	33.7
11 Tom Lantos (D)	109,812	57.1
Bill Royer (R)	76,462	39.7
12 Ed Zschau (R)	115,365	62.9
Emmett Lynch (D)	61,372	33.5
13 Norman Y. Mineta (D)	110,805	65.9
Tom Kelly (R)	52,806	31.4
14 Norman D. Shumway (R)	134,225	63.4
Baron Reed (D)	77,400	36.6
15 Tony Coelho (D)	86,022	63.7

Candidates	Votes	%
Ed Bates (R)	45,948	34.0
16 Leon E. Panetta (D)	142,630	83.5
G. Richard Arnold (R)	24,448	14.3
17 Charles Pashayan Jr. (R)	80,271	54.0
Gene Tackett (D)	68,364	46.0
18 Richard Lehman (D)	92,762	59.5
Adrian C. Fondse (R)	59,664	38.3
19 Robert J. Lagomarsino (R)	112,486	61.1
Frank Frost (D)	66,042	35.8
20 William M. Thomas (R)	123,312	68.1
Robert J. Bethea (D)	57,769	31.9
21 Bobbi Fiedler (R)	138,474	71.8
George Henry Margolis (D)	46,412	24.1
22 Carlos J. Moorhead (R)	145,831	73.6
Harvey L. Goldhammer (D)	46,521	23.5
23 Anthony C. Beilenson (D)	120,788	59.6
David Armor (R)	82,031	40.4
24 Henry A. Waxman (D)	88,516	65.1
Jerry Zerg (R)	42,133	31.0
25 Edward R. Roybal (D)	71,106	85.5
Daniel John Gorham (LIBERT)	12,060	14.5
26 Howard L. Berman (D)	97,383	59.6
Hal Phillips (R)	66,072	40.4
27 Mel Levine (D)	108,347	59.5
Bart W. Christensen (R)	67,479	37.0
28 Julian C. Dixon (D)	103,469	78.9
David Goerz (R)	24,473	18.7
29 Augustus F. Hawkins (D)	97,028	79.8
Milton R. MacKaig (R)	24,568	20.2
30 Matthew G. (Marty) Martinez (D)	60,905	53.9
John H. Rousselot (R)	52,177	46.1
31 Mervyn M. Dymally (D)	86,718	72.4
Henry C. Minturn (R)	33,043	27.6
32 Glenn M. Anderson (D)	84,663	58.0
Brian Lungren (R)	57,863	39.6
33 David Dreier (R)	112,362	65.2
Paul Servelle (D)	55,514	32.2
34 Esteban Torres (D)	68,316	57.2
Paul R. Jackson (R)	51,026	42.8
35 Jerry Lewis (R)	112,786	68.3
Robert E. Erwin (D)	52,349	31.7
36 George E. Brown Jr. (D)	76,546	54.3
John Paul Stark (R)	64,361	45.7
37 Al McCandless (R)	105,065	59.1
Curtis P. (Sam) Cross (D)	68,510	38.5
38 Jerry M. Patterson (D)	73,914	52.4
William F. Dohr (R)	61,279	43.4
39 William E. Dannemeyer (R)	129,539	72.2
Frank G. Verges (D)	46,681	26.0
40 Robert E. Badham (R)	144,228	71.5
Paul Haseman (D)	52,546	26.1
41 Bill Lowery (R)	140,130	68.9
Tony Brandenburg (D)	58,677	28.8
42 Dan Lungren (R)	142,845	69.0
James P. Spellman (D)	58,690	28.3
43 Ron Packard (R WRITE-IN)	66,444	36.8
Roy (Pat) Archer (D)	57,995	32.1
Johnnie R. Crean (R)	56,297	31.1
44 Jim Bates (D)	78,474	64.9
Shirley M. Gissendanner (R)	38,447	31.8
45 Duncan L. Hunter (R)	117,771	68.6
Richard Hill (D)	50,148	29.2

Special Election

	Votes	%
30 Matthew G. (Marty) Martinez (D)	22,572	32.0
Dennis S. Kazarian (D)	20,313	29.0
Ralph Ramirez (R)	11,033	16.0

Special Runoff Election

	Votes	%
30 Matthew G. (Marty) Martinez (D)	14,593	51.0
Ralph Ramirez (R)	14,043	49.0

COLORADO

Candidates	Votes	%
1 Patricia Schroeder (D)	94,969	60.3
Arch Decker (R)	59,009	37.4
2 Timothy E. Wirth (D)	101,202	61.8
John C. Buechner (R)	59,590	36.4
3 Ray Kogovsek (D)	92,384	53.4
Tom Wiens (R)	77,410	44.8
4 Hank Brown (R)	105,550	69.8
Charles L. (Bud) Bishopp (D)	45,750	30.2
5 Ken Kramer (R)	84,479	59.5
Tom Cronin (D)	57,392	40.5
6 Jack Swigert (R)	98,909	62.2
Steve Hogan (D)	56,598	35.6

CONNECTICUT

	Votes	%
1 Barbara B. Kennelly (D)	126,798	68.1
Herschel A. Klein (R)	58,075	31.2
2 Sam Gejdenson (D)	95,254	55.8
Tony Guglielmo (R)	74,294	43.5
3 Bruce A. Morrison (D)	90,638	49.9
Lawrence J. DeNardis (R)	88,951	49.0
4 Stewart B. McKinney (R)	93,660	56.5
John A. Phillips (D)	71,110	42.9
5 William R. Ratchford (D)	101,362	58.5
Neal B. Hanlon (R)	70,808	40.8
6 Nancy L. Johnson (R)	99,703	51.7
William E. Curry Jr. (D)	92,178	47.8

Special Election

	Votes	%
1 Barbara B. Kennelly (D)	51,431	58.8
Ann P. Uccello (R)	36,085	41.2

DELAWARE

	Votes	%
AL Thomas R. Carper (D)	98,533	52.4
Thomas B. Evans Jr. (R)	87,153	46.3

FLORIDA

	Votes	%
1 Earl Hutto (D)	82,569	74.4
J. Terry Bechtol (R)	28,373	25.6
2 Don Fuqua (D)	79,143	61.7
Ron McNeil (R)	49,101	38.3
3 Charles E. Bennett (D)	73,802	84.1
George Grimsley (R)	13,972	15.9
4 Bill Chappell Jr. (D)	83,895	66.9
Larry Gaudet (R)	41,457	33.1
5 Bill McCollum (R)	69,993	58.8
Dick Batchelor (D)	49,070	41.2
6 Kenneth H. (Buddy) MacKay (D)	85,825	61.3
Ed Havill (R)	54,059	38.6
7 Sam Gibbons (D)	85,331	74.2
Ken Ayers (R)	29,632	25.8
8 C. W. Bill Young (R)		100.0
9 Michael Bilirakis (R)	95,009	51.2
George H. Sheldon (D)	90,697	48.8
10 Andy Ireland (D)		100.0
11 Bill Nelson (D)	101,746	70.6
Joel Robinson (R)	42,422	29.4
12 Tom Lewis (R)	81,893	52.6
Brad Culverhouse (D)	73,913	47.4
13 Connie Mack III (R)	132,951	65.1
Dana N. Stevens (D)	71,239	34.9
14 Daniel A. Mica (D)	128,646	73.0
Steve Mitchell (R)	47,560	27.0
15 E. Clay Shaw Jr. (R)	89,158	57.1
Edward J. Stack (D)	67,083	42.9
16 Larry Smith (D)	91,888	67.9
Maurice Berkowitz (R)	43,458	32.1
17 William Lehman (D)		100.0
18 Claude Pepper (D)	72,183	71.2
Ricardo Nunez (R)	29,196	28.8

Candidates	Votes	%
19 Dante B. Fascell (D)	74,312	58.8
Glenn Rinker (R)	51,969	41.2

GEORGIA

Candidates	Votes	%
1 Lindsay Thomas (D)	65,625	64.1
Herb Jones (R)	36,799	35.9
2 Charles Hatcher (D)	73,897	100.0
3 Richard Ray (D)	74,626	71.0
Tyron Elliott (R)	30,537	29.0
4 Elliott H. Levitas (D)	38,758	65.5
Dick Winder (R)	20,418	34.5
5 Wyche Fowler Jr. (D)	53,264	80.8
J. E. (Billy) McKinney (I)	9,049	13.7
Paul Jones (R)	3,633	5.5
6 Newt Gingrich (R)	62,352	55.3
Jim Wood (D)	50,459	44.7
7 Larry P. McDonald (D)	71,647	61.1
Dave Sellers (R)	45,569	38.9
8 J. Roy Rowland (D)	75,009	100.0
9 Ed Jenkins (D)	86,514	77.0
Charles Sherwood (R)	25,907	23.0
10 Doug Barnard Jr. (D)	80,311	100.0

HAWAII

Candidates	Votes	%
1 Cecil Heftel (D)	134,779	89.9
Rockne H. Johnson (LIBERT)	15,128	10.1
2 Daniel K. Akaka (D)	132,072	89.2
Gregory B. Mills (NP)	9,080	6.2

IDAHO

Candidates	Votes	%
1 Larry E. Craig (R)	86,277	53.7
Larry LaRocco (D)	74,388	46.3
2 George Hansen (R)	83,873	52.3
Richard Stallings (D)	76,608	47.7

ILLINOIS

Candidates	Votes	%
1 Harold Washington (D)	172,641	97.3
2 Gus Savage (D)	140,827	87.0
Kevin Walker Sparks (R)	20,670	12.8
3 Marty Russo (D)	137,391	74.0
Richard D. Murphy (R)	48,268	26.0
4 George M. O'Brien (R)	79,842	54.6
Michael A. Murer (D)	66,323	45.4
5 William O. Lipinski (D)	110,351	75.4
Daniel J. Partyka (R)	35,970	24.6
6 Henry J. Hyde (R)	97,918	68.4
Leroy E. Kennel (D)	45,237	31.6
7 Cardiss Collins (D)	133,978	86.5
Dansby Cheeks (R)	20,994	13.5
8 Dan Rostenkowski (D)	124,318	83.4
Bonnie Hickey (R)	24,666	16.6
9 Sidney R. Yates (D)	114,083	66.5
Catherine Bertini (R)	54,851	32.0
10 John Edward Porter (R)	90,750	59.0
Eugenia S. Chapman (D)	63,115	41.0
11 Frank Annunzio (D)	134,755	72.6
James F. Moynihan (R)	50,967	27.4
12 Philip M. Crane (R)	86,487	66.2
Daniel G. DeFosse (D)	40,108	30.7
13 John N. Erlenborn (R)	113,423	69.8
Robert Bily (D)	49,105	30.2
14 Tom Corcoran (R)	98,262	64.6
Dan McGrath (D)	53,914	35.4
15 Edward R. Madigan (R)	105,038	66.3
Tim L. Hall (D)	53,303	33.7
16 Lynn Martin (R)	89,405	57.2
Carl R. Schwerdtfeger (D)	66,877	42.8
17 Lane Evans (D)	94,483	52.8
Kenneth G. McMillan (R)	84,347	47.2
18 Robert H. Michel (R)	97,406	51.6
G. Douglas Stephens (D)	91,281	48.4
19 Daniel B. Crane (R)	94,483	52.1
John Gwinn (D)	87,231	47.9
20 Richard J. Durbin (D)	100,758	50.4
Paul Findley (R)	99,348	49.6

Candidates	Votes	%
21 Melvin Price (D)	89,500	63.7
Robert H. Gaffner (R)	46,764	33.3
22 Paul Simon (D)	123,693	66.2
Peter G. Prineas (R)	63,279	33.8

INDIANA

Candidates	Votes	%
1 Katie Hall (D)	87,369	56.3
Thomas H. Krieger (R)	66,921	43.1
2 Philip R. Sharp (D)	107,298	56.2
Ralph W. Van Natta (R)	83,593	43.8
3 John Hiler (R)	86,958	51.2
Richard C. Bodine (D)	83,046	48.8
4 Dan Coats (R)	110,155	64.3
Roger M. Miller (D)	60,054	35.1
5 Elwood Hillis (R)	105,469	61.1
Allen B. Maxwell (D)	67,238	38.9
6 Dan Burton (R)	131,100	64.9
George E. Grabianowski (D)	70,764	35.1
7 John T. Myers (R)	115,884	62.3
Stephen S. Bonney (D)	70,249	37.7
8 Francis X. McCloskey (D)	100,592	51.4
Joel Deckard (R)	94,127	48.1
9 Lee H. Hamilton (D)	121,094	67.1
Floyd E. Coates (R)	58,532	32.4
10 Andrew Jacobs Jr. (D)	114,674	66.7
Michael A. Carroll (R)	56,992	33.2

IOWA

Candidates	Votes	%
1 Jim Leach (R)	89,585	59.2
William E. Gluba (D)	61,734	40.8
2 Tom Tauke (R)	99,478	58.8
Brent Appel (D)	69,539	41.1
3 Cooper Evans (R)	104,072	55.5
Lynn G. Cutler (D)	83,581	44.5
4 Neal Smith (D)	118,849	66.0
Dave Readinger (R)	60,534	33.6
5 Tom Harkin (D)	93,333	58.9
Arlyn E. Danker (R)	65,200	41.1
6 Berkley Bedell (D)	101,690	64.3
Al Bremer (R)	56,487	35.7

KANSAS

Candidates	Votes	%
1 Pat Roberts (R)	115,749	68.4
Kent Roth (D)	51,079	30.2
2 Jim Slattery (D)	86,286	57.4
Morris Kay (R)	63,942	42.6
3 Larry Winn Jr. (R)	82,117	59.2
William L. Kostar (D)	53,140	38.3
4 Dan Glickman (D)	107,326	73.9
Gerald Caywood (R)	35,478	24.4
5 Bob Whittaker (R)	103,551	67.6
Lee Rowe (D)	47,676	31.1

KENTUCKY

Candidates	Votes	%
1 Carroll Hubbard Jr. (D)	48,342	100.0
2 William H. Natcher (D)	49,571	73.8
Mark T. Watson (R)	17,561	26.2
3 Romano L. Mazzoli (D)	92,849	65.1
Carl Brown (R)	45,900	32.2
4 Gene Snyder (R)	74,109	54.2
Terry L. Mann (D)	61,937	45.3
5 Harold Rogers (R)	52,928	65.2
Doye Davenport (D)	28,285	34.8
6 Larry J. Hopkins (R)	68,418	56.8
Don Mills (D)	49,839	41.4
7 Carl D. Perkins (D)	82,463	79.4
Tom Hamby (R)	21,436	20.6

LOUISIANA

Candidates	Votes	%
1 Bob Livingston (R)		100.0
2 Lindy (Mrs. Hale) Boggs (D)		100.0
3 W. J. (Billy) Tauzin (D)		100.0
4 Buddy Roemer (D)		100.0

Candidates	Votes	%
5 Jerry Huckaby (D)		100.0
6 Henson Moore (R)		100.0
7 John B. Breaux (D)		100.0
8 Gillis W. Long (D)		100.0

MAINE

Candidates	Votes	%
1 John R. McKernan Jr. (R)	124,850	50.3
John M. Kerry (D)	118,884	47.9
2 Olympia J. Snowe (R)	136,075	66.6
James Patrick Dunleavy (D)	68,086	33.3

MARYLAND

Candidates	Votes	%
1 Roy Dyson (D)	89,503	69.3
C. A. Porter Hopkins (R)	39,656	30.7
2 Clarence D. Long (D)	83,318	52.6
Helen Delich Bentley (R)	75,062	47.4
3 Barbara A. Mikulski (D)	110,042	74.2
H. Robert Scherr (R)	38,259	25.8
4 Marjorie S. Holt (R)	75,617	61.2
Patricia O'Brien Aiken (R)	47,947	38.8
5 Steny H. Hoyer (D)	83,937	79.6
William P. Guthrie (R)	21,533	20.4
6 Beverly B. Byron (D)	102,596	74.4
Roscoe Bartlett (R)	35,321	25.6
7 Parren J. Mitchell (D)	103,496	87.9
M. Leonora Jones (R)	14,203	12.1
8 Michael D. Barnes (D)	121,761	71.3
Elizabeth W. Spencer (R)	48,910	28.7

MASSACHUSETTS

Candidates	Votes	%
1 Silvio O. Conte (R, D)	145,417	100.0
2 Edward P. Boland (D)	118,215	72.6
Thomas P. Swank (R)	44,544	27.4
3 Joseph D. Early (D)	142,611	100.0
4 Barney Frank (D)	121,802	59.5
Margaret M. Heckler (R)	82,804	40.5
5 James M. Shannon (D)	140,177	84.6
Angelo Laudani (LIBERT)	25,224	15.2
6 Nicholas Mavroules (D)	117,723	57.8
Thomas H. Trimarco (R)	85,849	42.2
7 Edward J. Markey (D)	151,305	77.8
David Basile (R)	43,063	22.2
8 Thomas P. O'Neill Jr. (D)	123,296	74.9
Frank Luke McNamara Jr. (R)	41,370	25.1
9 Joe Moakley (D)	102,665	64.1
Deborah R. Cochran (R)	55,030	34.3
10 Gerry E. Studds (D)	138,418	68.7
John E. Conway (R)	63,014	31.3
11 Brian J. Donnelly (D)	144,132	100.0

MICHIGAN

Candidates	Votes	%
1 John Conyers Jr. (D)	125,517	96.7
2 Carl D. Pursell (R)	106,960	65.5
George Wahr Sallade (D)	53,040	32.5
3 Howard Wolpe (D)	96,842	56.3
Richard L. Milliman (R)	73,315	42.6
4 Mark Siljander (R)	87,489	59.7
David A. Masiokas (D)	56,877	38.8
5 Harold S. Sawyer (R)	98,650	53.1
Stephen V. Monsma (D)	87,229	46.9
6 Bob Carr (D)	84,778	51.4
Jim Dunn (R)	78,388	47.5
7 Dale E. Kildee (D)	118,538	75.4
George R. Darrah (R)	36,303	23.1
8 Bob Traxler (D)	113,515	91.0
Sheila M. Hart (LIBERT)	11,219	9.0
9 Guy Vander Jagt (R)	112,504	64.9
Gerald D. Warner (D)	60,932	35.1
10 Don Albosta (D)	102,048	60.1
Lawrence W. Reed (R)	66,080	38.9
11 Robert W. Davis (R)	106,039	60.5
Kent Bourland (D)	69,181	39.5
12 David E. Bonior (D)	103,851	65.9
Ray Contesti (R)	52,312	33.2

Candidates	Votes	%
13 George W. Crockett Jr. (D)	108,351	88.0
Letty Gupta (R)	13,732	11.1
14 Dennis M. Hertel (D)	116,421	94.9
Harold H. Dunn (LIBERT)	6,175	5.0
15 William D. Ford (D)	94,950	72.8
Mitchell Moran (R)	33,904	26.0
16 John D. Dingell (D)	114,006	73.7
David K. Haskins (R)	39,227	25.3
17 Sander Levin (D)	116,901	66.6
Gerald E. Rosen (R)	55,620	31.7
18 Allen J. Sipher (D)	46,545	25.7
William S. Broomfield (R)	132,902	73.3

MINNESOTA

Candidates	Votes	%
1 Timothy J. Penny (DFL)	109,257	51.2
Tom Hagedorn (I-R)	102,298	47.9
2 Vin Weber (I-R)	123,508	54.5
James W. Nichols (DFL)	103,243	45.5
3 Bill Frenzel (I-R)	166,891	72.2
Joel Saliterman (DFL)	60,993	26.4
4 Bruce F. Vento (DFL)	153,494	73.2
Bill James (I-R)	56,248	26.8
5 Martin Olav Sabo (DFL)	136,634	65.5
Keith W. Johnson (I-R)	61,184	29.4
6 Gerry Sikorski (DFL)	109,246	50.8
Arlen Erdahl (I-R)	105,734	49.2
7 Arlan Stangeland (I-R)	108,254	50.3
Gene Wenstrom (DFL)	107,062	49.7
8 James L. Oberstar (DFL)	176,392	76.7
Marjory L. Luce (I-R)	53,467	23.3

MISSISSIPPI

Candidates	Votes	%
1 Jamie L. Whitten (D)	79,726	70.9
Fran Fawcett (R)	32,750	29.1
2 Webb Franklin (R)	74,450	50.3
Robert G. Clark (D)	71,536	48.4
3 G. V. (Sonny) Montgomery (D)	114,530	93.1
James Bradshaw (I)	8,519	6.9
4 Wayne Dowdy (D)	79,977	52.5
Liles Williams (R)	69,469	45.6
5 Trent Lott (R)	82,884	78.5
Arlon (Blackie) Coate (D)	22,634	21.5

MISSOURI

Candidates	Votes	%
1 William Clay (D)	102,656	66.1
William E. White (R)	52,599	33.9
2 Robert A. Young (D)	100,770	56.5
Harold L. Dielmann (R)	77,433	43.5
3 Richard A. Gephardt (D)	131,566	77.9
Richard Foristel (R)	37,388	22.1
4 Ike Skelton (D)	96,388	54.8
Wendell Bailey (R)	79,565	45.2
5 Alan Wheat (D)	96,059	57.9
John A. Sharp (R)	66,664	40.2
6 E. Thomas Coleman (R)	97,993	55.3
Jim Russell (D)	79,053	44.7
7 Gene Taylor (R)	91,391	50.5
David A. Geisler (D)	89,549	49.5
8 Bill Emerson (R)	86,493	53.1
Jerry Ford (D)	76,413	46.9
9 Harold L. Volkmer (D)	99,228	60.8
Larry E. Mead (R)	63,942	39.2

MONTANA

Candidates	Votes	%
1 Pat Williams (D)	100,087	59.7
Bob Davies (R)	62,402	37.2
2 Howard Lyman (D)	65,815	44.2
Ron Marlenee (R)	79,968	53.7

NEBRASKA

Candidates	Votes	%
1 Douglas K. Bereuter (R)	137,675	75.1
Curt Donaldson (D)	45,676	24.9

Candidates	Votes	%
2 Hal Daub (R)	92,639	56.7
Richard M. Fellman (D)	70,431	43.1
3 Virginia Smith (R)	171,853	100.0

NEVADA

Candidates	Votes	%
1 Harry Reid (D)	61,901	57.5
Peggy Cavnar (R)	45,675	42.5
2 Barbara Vucanovich (R)	70,188	55.5
Mary Gojack (D)	52,265	41.3

NEW HAMPSHIRE

Candidates	Votes	%
1 Norman E. D'Amours (D)	76,281	54.9
Robert C. Smith (R)	61,876	44.5
2 Judd Gregg (R)	92,098	70.8
Robert L. Dupay (D)	37,906	29.2

NEW JERSEY

Candidates	Votes	%
1 James J. Florio (D)	110,570	73.3
John A. Dramesi (R)	39,501	26.2
2 William J. Hughes (D)	102,826	68.0
John A. Mahoney (R)	47,069	31.1
3 James J. Howard (D)	104,055	62.3
Marie Sheehan Muhler (R)	60,515	36.2
4 Christopher H. Smith (R)	85,660	52.7
Joseph P. Merlino (D)	75,658	46.5
5 Marge Roukema (R)	104,695	65.3
Fritz Cammerzell (D)	53,659	33.5
6 Bernard J. Dwyer (D)	100,419	68.1
Bertram L. Baker (R)	46,095	31.3
7 Matthew J. Rinaldo (R)	91,837	56.0
Adam K. Levin (D)	70,978	43.3
8 Robert A. Roe (D)	89,980	70.7
Norm Robertson (R)	36,317	28.5
9 Robert G. Torricelli (D)	99,090	53.0
Harold C. Hollenbeck (R)	86,022	46.0
10 Peter W. Rodino Jr. (D)	76,684	82.6
Timothy Lee Jr. (R)	14,551	15.7
11 Joseph G. Minish (D)	105,607	64.3
Rey Redington (R)	57,099	34.8
12 Jim Courter (R)	117,793	66.8
Jeff Connor (D)	57,049	32.3
13 Edwin B. Forsythe (R)	100,061	59.5
George Callas (D)	65,820	39.1
14 Frank J. Guarini (D)	94,021	74.3
Charles J. Catrillo (R)	28,257	22.3

NEW MEXICO

Candidates	Votes	%
1 Manuel Lujan Jr. (R)	74,459	52.4
Jan Alan Hartke (D)	67,534	47.6
2 Joe Skeen (R)	71,021	58.4
Caleb Chandler (D)	50,599	41.6
3 Bill Richardson (D)	84,669	64.5
Marjorie Bell Chambers (R)	46,466	35.4

NEW YORK

Candidates	Votes	%
1 William Carney (R, C, RTL)	88,234	63.9
Ethan C. Eldon (D)	49,787	36.1
2 Thomas J. Downey (D)	80,951	63.9
Paul G. Costello (R, C)	42,790	33.8
3 Robert J. Mrazek (D)	93,846	51.8
John LeBoutillier (R, C)	83,238	46.0
4 Norman F. Lent (R, C)	105,241	60.4
Robert P. Zimmerman (D, L)	63,390	36.4
5 Raymond J. McGrath (R, C)	100,485	58.1
Arnold M. Miller (D, L)	67,002	38.8
6 Joseph P. Addabbo (D, R, L)	95,483	95.9
7 Benjamin S. Rosenthal (D, L)	84,013	77.2
Albert Lemishow (R, C, RTL)	24,832	22.8
8 James H. Scheuer (D, L)	91,830	89.5
John T. Blume (C)	10,741	10.5
9 Geraldine A. Ferraro (D)	75,286	73.2
John J. Weigandt (R)	20,352	19.8

Candidates	Votes	%
Ralph G. Groves (C, RTL)	6,011	5.9
10 Charles E. Schumer (D, L)	89,852	79.2
Stephen Marks (R, C)	21,726	19.2
11 Edolphus Towns (D)	39,357	83.7
James W. Smith (R)	4,449	9.5
12 Major R. Owens (D, L)	44,586	90.5
David Katan Sr. (R)	3,215	6.5
13 Stephen J. Solarz (D, L)	68,549	80.5
Leon F. Nadrowski (R, RTL)	14,257	16.7
14 Guy V. Molinari (R, C, RTL)	67,626	56.1
Leo C. Zeferetti (D)	51,728	42.9
15 Bill Green (R)	66,262	53.6
Betty G. Lall (D, L)	55,483	44.9
16 Charles B. Rangel (D, R, L)	76,626	97.5
17 Ted Weiss (D, L)	113,172	85.0
Louis S. Antonelli (R, C, RTL)	19,928	15.0
18 Robert Garcia (D, R, L)	57,009	98.9
19 Mario Biaggi (D, R, L, RTL)	118,803	93.7
Michael J. McSherry (C)	7,438	5.9
20 Richard L. Ottinger (D)	98,425	56.5
Jon S. Fossel (R, C)	72,005	41.3
21 Hamilton Fish Jr. (R, C)	117,460	75.2
J. Morgan Strong (D)	38,664	24.8
22 Benjamin A. Gilman (R)	92,266	52.9
Peter A. Peyser (D)	73,124	42.0
23 Samuel S. Stratton (D)	164,427	76.1
Frank Wicks (R, NF)	41,386	19.2
24 Gerald B. H. Solomon (R, C, RTL)	140,296	73.9
Roy Esiason (D)	49,441	26.1
25 Sherwood L. Boehlert (R)	93,071	55.8
Anita Maxwell (D)	70,793	42.4
26 David O'B. Martin (R, C)	108,962	71.6
David P. Landy (D)	43,208	28.4
27 George C. Wortley (R)	95,290	53.2
Elaine Lytel (D, L)	79,209	44.2
28 Matthew F. McHugh (D, L)	100,665	56.3
David F. Crowley (R, C)	75,991	42.5
29 Frank Horton (R)	104,412	66.4
William C. Larsen (D)	47,463	30.2
30 Barber B. Conable Jr. (R)	119,105	68.2
Bill Benet (D)	48,764	27.9
31 Jack F. Kemp (R, C)	133,462	75.3
James A. Martin (D, L)	43,843	24.7
32 John J. LaFalce (D, L)	116,386	91.4
Raymond R. Walker (R, C)	8,638	6.8
33 Henry J. Nowak (D)	126,091	84.1
Walter J. Pillich (R, C)	19,791	13.2
34 Stanley N. Lundine (D)	99,502	60.2
James J. Snyder (R, C)	63,972	38.7

NORTH CAROLINA

Candidates	Votes	%
1 Walter B. Jones (D)	79,954	81.3
James F. McIntyre III (R)	17,478	17.8
2 I. T. (Tim) Valentine Jr. (D)	59,617	53.6
John W. Marin (R)	34,293	30.8
H. M. Michaux Jr. (WRITE IN)	15,990	14.4
3 Charles Whitley (D)	68,936	63.6
Eugene (Red) McDaniel (R)	39,046	36.0
4 Ike Andrews (D)	70,369	51.3
William Cobey Jr. (R)	64,955	47.4
5 Stephen L. Neal (D)	87,819	60.3
Anne Bagnal (R)	57,083	39.2
6 Charles Robin Britt (D)	68,696	53.8
Eugene Johnston (R)	58,244	45.6
7 Charlie Rose (D)	68,529	71.0
Edward Johnson (R)	27,015	28.0
8 W. G. (Bill) Hefner (D)	71,691	57.4
Harris D. Blake (R)	52,417	42.0
9 James G. Martin (R)	64,297	57.0
Preston Cornelius (D)	47,258	41.9
10 James T. Broyhill (R)	80,904	92.7
Jhon Rankin (LIBERT)	6,360	7.3
11 James McClure Clarke (D)	85,410	49.9
Bill Hendon (R)	84,085	49.2

NORTH DAKOTA

Candidates	Votes	%
AL Byron L. Dorgan (D)	186,534	71.6
Kent H. Jones (R)	72,241	27.7

OHIO

Candidates	Votes	%
1 Thomas A. Luken (D)	99,143	63.5
John (Jake) Held (R)	52,658	33.7
2 Bill Gradison (R)	97,434	62.7
William J. Luttmer (D)	53,169	34.2
3 Tony P. Hall (D)	119,926	87.7
Kathryn E. Brown (LIBERT)	16,828	12.3
4 Michael G. Oxley (R)	105,087	64.6
Robert W. Moon (D)	57,564	35.4
5 Delbert L. Latta (R)	86,450	55.2
James R. Sherck (D)	70,120	44.8
6 Bob McEwen (R)	92,135	59.2
Lynn Alan Grimshaw (D)	63,435	40.8
7 Michael Dewine (R)	87,842	56.3
Roger D. Tackett (D)	65,543	42.0
8 Thomas N. Kindness (R)	98,527	66.4
John W. Griffin (D)	49,877	33.6
9 Marcy Kaptur (D)	95,162	57.9
Ed Weber (R)	64,459	39.3
10 Clarence E. Miller (R)	100,044	63.3
John M. Buchanan (D)	57,983	36.7
11 Dennis E. Eckart (D)	93,302	60.9
Glen W. Warner (R)	56,616	36.9
12 John R. Kasich (R)	88,335	50.5
Bob Shamansky (D)	82,753	47.3
13 Don J. Pease (D)	92,296	61.2
Timothy Paul Martin (R)	53,376	35.4
14 John F. Seiberling (D)	115,629	70.5
Louis A. Mangels (R)	48,421	29.5
15 Chalmers P. Wylie (R)	104,678	66.3
Greg Kostelac (D)	47,070	29.8
16 Ralph Regula (R)	110,485	65.8
Jeffrey R. Orenstein (D)	57,386	34.2
17 Lyle Williams (R)	98,476	55.1
George D. Tablack (D)	80,375	44.9
18 Douglas Applegate (D)	128,665	100.0
19 Edward F. Feighan (D)	111,760	58.8
Richard G. Anter II (R)	72,682	38.3
20 Mary Rose Oakar (D)	133,603	85.6
Paris T. LeJeune (R)	17,675	11.3
21 Louis Stokes (D)	132,544	86.1
Alan G. Shatteen (R)	21,332	13.9

Special Election

17 Jean Ashbrook (R)	18,106	73.4
Jack Koelbe (D)	6,385	25.9

OKLAHOMA

1 James R. Jones (D)	76,379	54.1
Richard C. Freeman (R)	64,704	45.9
2 Mike Synar (D)	111,895	72.6
Lou Striegel (R)	42,298	27.4
3 Wes Watkins (D)	121,670	82.2
Patrick K. Miller (R)	26,335	17.8
4 Dave McCurdy (D)	84,205	65.0
Howard Rutledge (R)	44,351	34.2
5 Mickey Edwards (R)	98,979	67.2
Dan Lane (D)	42,453	28.8
6 Glenn English (D)	102,811	75.4
Ed Moore (R)	33,519	24.6

OREGON

1 Les AuCoin (D)	118,638	53.8
Bill Moshofsky (R)	101,720	46.2
2 Bob Smith (R)	106,912	55.6
Larryann Willis (D)	85,495	44.4
3 Ron Wyden (D)	159,416	78.3
Thomas H. Phelan (R)	44,162	21.7
4 James Weaver (D)	115,448	59.0
Ross Anthony (R)	80,054	40.9
5 Denny Smith (R)	103,906	51.2
J. Ruth McFarland (D)	98,952	48.8

PENNSYLVANIA

1 Thomas M. Foglietta (D)	103,626	72.3
Michael Marino (R)	38,155	26.6

Candidates	Votes	%
2 William H. Gray III (D)	120,744	76.1
Milton Street (I)	35,205	22.2
3 Robert A. Borski (D)	97,161	50.1
Charles F. Dougherty (R)	94,497	48.7
4 Joseph P. Kolter (D)	100,481	60.1
Eugene V. Atkinson (R)	64,539	38.6
5 Richard T. Schulze (R)	90,648	67.2
Bob Burger (D)	44,170	32.8
6 Gus Yatron (D)	108,230	72.0
Harry B. Martin (R)	42,155	28.0
7 Robert W. Edgar (D)	105,775	55.4
Steve Joachim (R)	85,023	44.6
8 Peter H. Kostmayer (D)	83,242	50.3
Jim Coyne (R)	80,928	48.9
9 Bud Shuster (R)	92,322	65.1
Eugene J. Duncan (D)	49,583	34.9
10 Joseph M. McDade (R)	103,617	67.5
Robert J. Rafalko (D)	49,868	32.5
11 Frank Harrison (D)	90,371	53.5
James L. Nelligan (R)	78,485	46.5
12 John P. Murtha (D)	96,369	61.1
William N. Tuscano (R)	54,212	34.4
13 Lawrence Coughlin (R)	109,198	64.3
Martin J. Cunningham Jr. (D)	59,709	35.2
14 William J. Coyne (D)	120,980	74.9
John R. Clark (R)	32,780	20.3
15 Don Ritter (R)	79,455	57.8
Richard J. Orloski (D)	58,002	42.2
16 Robert S. Walker (R)	93,034	71.3
Jean D. Mowery (D)	37,364	28.7
17 George W. Gekas (R)	84,291	57.6
Larry J. Hochendoner (D)	61,974	42.4
18 Doug Walgren (D)	101,807	54.2
Ted Jacob (R)	84,428	45.0
19 Bill Goodling (R)	101,163	70.8
Larry Becker (D)	41,787	29.2
20 Joseph M. Gaydos (D)	127,281	76.0
Terry T. Ray (R)	38,212	22.8
21 Thomas J. Ridge (R)	80,180	50.2
Anthony (Buzz) Andrezeski (D)	79,451	49.8
22 Austin J. Murphy (D)	123,716	78.7
Frank J. Paterra (R)	32,176	20.5
23 William F. Clinger Jr. (R)	92,424	65.2
Joseph J. Calla Jr. (D)	49,297	34.8

RHODE ISLAND

1 Fernand J. St Germain (D)	97,254	60.7
Burton Stallwood (R)	61,253	38.3
2 Claudine Schneider (R)	96,282	55.6
James V. Aukerman (D)	76,769	44.4

SOUTH CAROLINA

1 Thomas F. Hartnett (R)	63,945	54.3
W. Mullins McLeod (D)	52,916	44.9
2 Floyd Spence (R)	71,569	58.5
Ken Mosely (D)	50,749	41.5
3 Butler Derrick (D)	77,125	90.4
Gordon T. Davis (LIBERT)	8,214	9.6
4 Carroll A. Campbell Jr. (R)	69,802	63.3
Marion E. Tyus (D)	40,394	36.7
5 John Spratt (D)	69,345	67.6
John S. Wilkerson (R)	33,191	32.4
6 Robert M. Tallon Jr. (D)	62,582	52.5
John L. Napier (R)	56,653	47.5

SOUTH DAKOTA

AL Thomas A. Daschle (D)	142,122	51.6
Clint Roberts (R)	133,530	48.4

TENNESSEE

1 James H. Quillen (R)	89,497	74.1
Jessie J. Cable (D)	27,580	22.8
2 John J. Duncan (R)	109,045	100.0
3 Marilyn Lloyd Bouquard (D)	84,967	61.8

Candidates	Votes	%
Glen Byers (R)	49,885	36.3
4 Jim Cooper (D)	93,453	66.1
Cissy Baker (R)	47,865	33.9
5 Bill Boner (D)	109,282	80.1
Laural Steinhice (R)	27,061	19.8
6 Albert Gore Jr. (D)	104,094	100.0
7 Don Sundquist (R)	73,835	50.5
Bob Clement (D)	72,359	49.5
8 Ed Jones (D)	93,945	74.9
Bruce Benson (R)	31,527	25.1
9 Harold E. Ford (D)	112,143	72.4
Joe Crawford (R)	40,812	26.4

TEXAS

1 Sam B. Hall Jr. (D)	100,685	97.5
2 Charles Wilson (D)	91,762	94.3
Ed Richbourg (LIBERT)	5,584	5.7
3 Steve Bartlett (R)	99,852	77.1
James L. McNees Jr. (D)	28,223	21.8
4 Ralph M. Hall (D)	94,134	73.8
Peter J. Collumb (R)	32,221	25.3
5 John Bryant (D)	52,214	64.8
Joe Devaney (R)	27,121	33.7
6 Phil Gramm (R)	91,546	94.5
Ron Hard (LIBERT)	5,288	5.5
7 Bill Archer (R)	108,718	85.0
Dennis Scoggins (D)	17,866	14.0
8 Jack Fields (R)	50,630	56.7
Henry E. Allee (D)	38,041	42.6
9 Jack Brooks (D)	78,965	67.6
John W. Lewis (R)	35,422	30.3
10 J. J. Pickle (D)	121,030	90.1
William G. Kelsey (LIBERT)	8,735	6.5
11 Marvin Leath (D)	83,236	96.3
12 Jim Wright (D)	78,913	68.9
Jim Ryan (R)	34,879	30.5
13 Jack Hightower (D)	86,376	63.6
Ron Slover (R)	47,877	35.3
14 Bill Patman (D)	76,851	60.7
Joe Wyatt Jr. (R)	48,942	38.6
15 E. (Kika) de la Garza (D)	76,544	95.7
16 Ronald Coleman (D)	44,024	53.9
Pat B. Haggerty (R)	36,064	44.2
17 Charles W. Stenholm (D)	109,359	97.1
18 Mickey Leland (D)	68,014	82.6
C. Leon Pickett (R)	12,104	14.7
19 Kent Hance (D)	89,702	81.6
E. L. Hicks (R)	19,062	17.3
20 Henry B. Gonzalez (D)	68,544	91.5
Roger V. Gary (LIBERT)	4,163	5.6
21 Tom Loeffler (R)	106,515	74.6
Charles S. Stough (D)	35,112	24.6
22 Ron Paul (R)	66,536	100.0
23 Abraham Kazen Jr. (D)	51,690	55.3
Jeff Wentworth (R)	41,363	44.2
24 Martin Frost (D)	63,857	72.9
Lucy P. Patterson (R)	22,798	26.0
25 Mike Andrews (D)	63,974	60.4
Mike Faubion (R)	40,112	37.9
26 Tom Vandergriff (D)	69,782	50.1
Jim Bradshaw (R)	69,438	49.9
27 Solomon P. Ortiz (D)	66,604	64.0
Jason Luby (R)	35,209	33.8

UTAH

1 James V. Hansen (R)	111,416	62.8
A. Stephen Dirks (D)	66,006	37.2
2 Dan Marriott (R)	92,109	53.8
Frances Farley (D)	78,981	46.2
3 Howard C. Nielson (R)	108,478	76.9
Henry A. Huish (I)	32,661	23.1

VERMONT

AL James M. Jeffords (R)	114,191	69.2
Mark A. Kaplan (D)	38,296	23.2

VIRGINIA

Candidates	Votes	%
1 Herbert H. Bateman (R)	76,926	53.9
John J. McGlennon (D)	62,379	43.7
2 G. William Whitehurst (R)	78,108	99.9
3 Thomas J. Bliley Jr. (R)	92,928	59.2
John A. Waldrop Jr. (D)	63,946	40.8
4 Norman Sisisky (D)	80,695	54.4
Robert W. Daniel Jr. (R)	67,708	45.6
5 Dan Daniel (D)	88,293	100.0
6 James R. Olin (D)	68,192	49.7
Kevin G. Miller (R)	66,537	48.5
7 J. Kenneth Robinson (R)	76,752	59.9
Lindsay G. Dorrier Jr. (D)	46,514	36.3
8 Stan Parris (R)	69,620	49.7
Herbert E. Harris II (D)	68,071	48.6
9 Frederick C. Boucher (D)	76,205	50.4
William C. Wampler (R)	75,082	49.6
10 Frank R. Wolf (R)	86,506	52.7
Ira M. Lechner (D)	75,361	45.9

WASHINGTON

	Votes	%
1 Joel Pritchard (R)	123,956	67.6
Brian Long (D)	59,444	32.4

Candidates	Votes	%
2 Al Swift (D)	101,383	59.6
Joan Houchen (R)	68,622	40.4
3 Don Bonker (D)	97,323	60.1
J. T. Quigg (R)	59,686	36.8
4 Sid Morrison (R)	112,148	69.8
Charles D. Kilbury (D)	45,990	28.6
5 Thomas S. Foley (D)	109,549	64.3
John Sonneland (R)	60,816	35.7
6 Norman D. Dicks (D)	89,985	62.5
Ted Haley (R)	47,720	33.2
7 Mike Lowry (D)	126,313	70.9
Bob Dorse (R)	51,759	29.1
8 Rodney Chandler (R)	79,209	57.0
Beth Bland (D)	59,824	43.0

WEST VIRGINIA

	Votes	%
1 Alan B. Mollohan (D)	79,529	53.2
John F. McCuskey (R)	70,069	46.8
2 Harley O. Staggers Jr. (D)	87,904	64.0
J. D. Hinkle Jr. (R)	49,413	36.0
3 Bob Wise (D)	84,619	57.9
David Michael Staton (R)	60,844	41.6
4 Nick J. Rahall II (D)	91,184	80.5
Homer L. Harris (R)	22,054	19.5

WISCONSIN

Candidates	Votes	%
1 Les Aspin (D)	95,055	61.0
Peter N. Jannson (R)	59,309	38.1
2 Robert W. Kastenmeier (D)	112,677	60.6
Jim Johnson (R)	71,989	38.7
3 Steve Gunderson (R)	99,304	56.6
Paul Offner (D)	75,132	42.8
4 Clement J. Zablocki (D)	129,557	94.6
5 Jim Moody (D)	99,713	63.5
Rod K. Johnston (R)	54,826	34.9
6 Thomas E. Petri (R)	111,348	65.0
Gordon E. Loehr (D)	59,922	35.0
7 David R. Obey (D)	122,124	68.0
Bernard A. Zimmerman (R)	57,535	32.0
8 Toby Roth (R)	101,379	57.2
Ruth C. Clusen (D)	74,436	42.0
9 F. James Sensenbrenner Jr. (R)	111,503	100.0

WYOMING

	Votes	%
AL Dick Cheney (R)	113,236	71.1
Ted Hommel (D)	46,041	28.9

1983 House Elections

CALIFORNIA

Candidates	Votes	%
Special Election		
5 Sala Burton (D)	44,790	56.9
Dunan Howard (R)	18,305	23.3
Richard Doyle (D)	6,582	8.4

COLORADO

	Votes	%
Special Election		
6 Daniel S. Schaefer (R)	49,816	63.3
Steve Hogan (D)	27,779	35.3

GEORGIA

Special Election (Non-partisan)

Candidates	Votes	%
7 Kathryn McDonald	25,468	30.6
George W. (Buddy) Darden	22,894	27.6
George A. Sellers	20,970	25.2
George Pullen	4,578	5.5
Dan H. Fincher	4,278	5.1

Special Runoff Election (Non-partisan)

	Votes	%
7 George W. (Buddy) Darden	56,267	59.1
Kathryn McDonald	38,949	40.9

ILLINOIS

Special Election

	Votes	%
1 Charles A. Hayes (D)	39,623	93.7
Diane Preacely (R)	2,272	5.4

NEW YORK

Candidates	Votes	%
Special Election		
7 Gary L. Ackerman (D, L)	18,388	48.7
Albert Lemishow (R, C)	8,331	22.1
Douglas F. Schoen (NEIGH)	5,997	15.9
Sheldon Loeffler (I)	4,318	11.4

TEXAS

Special Election

	Votes	%
6 Phil Gramm (R)	46,371	55.3
Dan Kubiak (D)	33,201	39.6

1984 House Elections

ALABAMA

Candidates	Votes	%
1 Sonny Callahan (R)	102,479	51.0
Frank McRight (D)	98,455	49.0
2 William L. Dickinson (R)	118,153	60.3
Larry Lee (D)	75,506	38.6
3 Bill Nichols (D)	120,357	96.2
4 Tom Bevill (D)	120,106	100.0
5 Ronnie G. Flippo (D)	140,542	95.9
6 Ben Erdreich (D)	130,973	59.6
J. T. (Jabo) Waggoner (R)	87,550	39.8
7 Richard C. Shelby (D)	135,834	96.8

ALASKA

	Votes	%
AL Don Young (R)	113,582	55.0
Pegge Begich (D)	86,052	41.7

ARIZONA

	Votes	%
1 John McCain (R)	162,418	78.1
Harry W. Braun III (D)	45,609	21.9
2 Morris K. Udall (D)	106,332	87.7
Lorenzo Torrez (I)	14,869	12.3
3 Bob Stump (R)	156,686	71.8
Bob Schuster (D)	57,748	26.4
4 Eldon Rudd (R)	167,558	100.0
5 Jim Kolbe (R)	116,075	50.9
James F. McNulty Jr. (D)	109,871	48.2

ARKANSAS

	Votes	%
1 Bill Alexander (D)	121,047	97.2
2 Tommy F. Robinson (D)	103,165	47.1
Judy Petty (R)	90,841	41.5
Jim Taylor (I)	25,073	11.4
3 John Paul Hammerschmidt (R)		100.0
4 Beryl Anthony Jr. (D)	117,123	97.9

CALIFORNIA

	Votes	%
1 Douglas H. Bosco (D)	157,037	62.3
David Redick (R)	95,186	37.7
2 Gene Chappie (R)	158,679	69.5
Harry Cozad (D)	69,793	30.5
3 Robert T. Matsui (D)	131,369	100.0
4 Vic Fazio (D)	130,109	61.4
Roger Canfield (R)	77,773	36.7
5 Sala Burton (D)	139,692	72.3
Tom Spinosa (R)	45,930	23.8
6 Barbara Boxer (D)	162,511	68.0
Douglas Binderup (R)	71,011	29.7
7 George Miller (D)	158,306	66.7
Rosemary Thakar (R)	78,985	33.3
8 Ronald V. Dellums (D)	144,316	60.3
Charles Connor (R)	94,907	39.7
9 Fortney H. (Pete) Stark (D)	136,511	69.9
J. T. Eager Beaver (R)	51,399	26.3
10 Don Edwards (D)	102,469	62.4
Robert P. Herriott (R)	56,256	34.3
11 Tom Lantos (D)	147,607	69.9
John J. Hickey (R)	59,625	28.3
12 Ed Zschau (R)	155,795	61.7
Martin Carnoy (D)	91,026	36.0
13 Norman Y. Mineta (D)	139,851	65.2
John D. Williams (R)	70,666	33.0
14 Norman D. Shumway (R)	179,238	73.3
Ruth (Paula) Carlson (D)	58,384	23.9
15 Tony Coelho (D)	109,590	65.5
Carol Harner (R)	54,730	32.7
16 Leon E. Panetta (D)	153,377	70.8
Patricia Smith Ramsey (R)	60,065	27.7
17 Charles Pashayan Jr. (R)	128,802	72.5
Simon Lakritz (D)	48,888	27.5
18 Richard H. Lehman (D)	128,186	67.3

Candidates	Votes	%
Dale L. Ewen (R)	62,339	32.7
19 Robert J. Lagomarsino (R)	153,187	67.3
James C. Carey Jr. (D)	70,278	30.9
20 William M. Thomas (R)	151,732	70.9
Mike LeSage (D)	62,307	29.1
21 Bobbi Fiedler (R)	173,504	72.3
Charles Davis (D)	62,085	25.9
22 Carlos J. Moorhead (R)	184,981	85.2
Michael B. Yauch (LIBERT)	32,036	14.8
23 Anthony C. Beilenson (D)	140,461	61.6
Claude Parrish (R)	84,093	36.9
24 Henry A. Waxman (D)	97,340	63.4
Jerry Zerg (R)	51,010	33.2
25 Edward R. Roybal (D)	74,261	71.7
Roy D. (Bill) Bloxom (R)	24,968	24.1
26 Howard L. Berman (D)	117,080	62.8
Miriam Ojeda (R)	69,372	37.2
27 Mel Levine (D)	116,933	54.9
Robert B. Scribner (R)	88,896	41.8
28 Julian C. Dixon (D)	113,076	75.6
Beatrice M. Jett (R)	33,511	22.4
29 Augustus F. Hawkins (D)	108,777	86.6
Echo Y. Goto (R)	16,781	13.4
30 Matthew G. Martinez (D)	64,378	51.8
Richard Gomez (R)	53,900	43.3
31 Mervyn M. Dymally (D)	100,658	70.7
Henry C. Minturn (R)	41,691	29.3
32 Glenn M. Anderson (D)	102,961	60.7
Roger E. Fiola (R)	62,176	36.6
33 David Dreier (R)	147,363	70.6
Claire K. McDonald (D)	54,147	26.0
34 Esteban Edward Torres (D)	87,060	59.8
Paul R. Jackson (R)	58,467	40.2
35 Jerry Lewis (R)	176,477	85.5
Kevin Akin (PFP)	29,990	14.5
36 George E. Brown Jr. (D)	104,438	56.6
John Paul Stark (R)	80,212	43.4
37 Al McCandless (R)	149,955	63.6
David E. Skinner (D)	85,908	36.4
38 Bob Dornan (R)	86,545	53.2
Jerry M. Patterson (D)	73,231	45.0
39 William E. Dannemeyer (R)	175,788	76.2
Robert E. Ward (D)	54,889	23.8
40 Robert E. Badham (R)	164,257	64.4
Carol Ann Bradford (D)	86,748	34.0
41 Bill Lowery (R)	161,068	63.4
Robert L. Simmons (D)	85,475	33.7
42 Dan Lungren (R)	177,783	73.0
Mary Lou Brophy (D)	60,025	24.6
43 Ron Packard (R)	165,643	74.1
Lois E. Humphreys (D)	50,996	22.8
44 Jim Bates (D)	99,378	69.7
Neill Campbell (R)	39,977	28.0
45 Duncan L. Hunter (R)	149,011	75.1
David W. Guthrie (D)	45,325	22.9

COLORADO

	Votes	%
1 Patricia Schroeder (D)	126,348	62.0
Mary Downs (R)	73,993	36.3
2 Timothy E. Wirth (D)	118,580	53.2
Michael J. Norton (R)	101,488	45.5
3 Mike Strang (R)	122,669	57.1
W. Mitchell (D)	90,063	41.9
4 Hank Brown (R)	146,469	71.1
Mary Fagan Bates (D)	56,462	27.4
5 Ken Kramer (R)	163,654	78.6
William Geffen (D)	44,588	21.4
6 Dan L. Schaefer (R)	171,427	89.4
John Heckman (I)	20,333	10.6

CONNECTICUT

	Votes	%
1 Barbara B. Kennelly (D)	147,748	61.7
Herschel A. Klein (R)	90,823	37.9
2 Sam Gejdenson (D)	124,110	54.4
Roberta F. Koontz (R)	103,119	45.2

Candidates	Votes	%
3 Bruce A. Morrison (D)	129,230	52.6
Lawrence J. DeNardis (R)	115,939	47.2
4 Stewart B. McKinney (R)	165,644	70.4
John M. Ormon (D)	69,666	29.6
5 John G. Rowland (R)	130,700	54.3
William R. Ratchford (D)	109,425	45.5
6 Nancy L. Johnson (R)	155,422	64.0
Arthur H. House (D)	87,489	36.0

DELAWARE

	Votes	%
AL Thomas R. Carper (D)	142,070	58.5
Elise R. W. du Pont (R)	100,650	41.4

FLORIDA

	Votes	%
1 Earl Hutto (D)		100.0
2 Don Fuqua (D)		100.0
3 Charles E. Bennett (D)		100.0
4 Bill Chappell Jr. (D)	134,694	64.8
Alton H. (Bill) Starling (R)	73,218	35.2
5 Bill McCollum (R)		100.0
6 Buddy MacKay (D)	167,409	99.3
7 Sam Gibbons (D)	100,430	58.8
Michael N. Kavouklis (R)	70,280	41.2
8 C. W. Bill Young (R)	184,553	80.3
Robert Kent (D)	45,393	19.7
9 Michael Bilirakis (R)	191,343	78.6
Jack Wilson (D)	52,150	21.4
10 Andy Ireland (R)	126,206	61.9
Patricia M. Glass (D)	77,635	38.1
11 Bill Nelson (D)	145,764	60.5
Rob Quartel (R)	95,115	39.5
12 Tom Lewis (R)		100.0
13 Connie Mack (R)		100.0
14 Daniel A. Mica (D)	153,935	55.4
Don Ross (R)	123,926	44.6
15 E. Clay Shaw Jr. (R)	128,097	65.7
Bill Humphrey (D)	66,833	34.3
16 Larry Smith (D)	108,410	56.4
Tom Bush (R)	83,903	43.6
17 William Lehman (D)		100.0
18 Claude Pepper (D)	76,404	60.5
Ricardo Nunez (R)	49,818	39.5
19 Dante B. Fascell (D)	115,631	64.3
Bill Flanagan (R)	64,317	35.7

GEORGIA

	Votes	%
1 Robert Lindsay Thomas (D)	126,082	81.6
Erie Lee Downing (R)	28,460	18.4
2 Charles Hatcher (D)	110,561	100.0
3 Richard Ray (D)	111,061	81.4
Mitchell Cantu (R)	25,410	18.6
4 Pat Swindall (R)	120,456	53.1
Elliott H. Levitas (D)	106,376	46.9
5 Wyche Fowler Jr. (D)	151,233	100.0
6 Newt Gingrich (R)	116,655	69.1
Gerald Johnson (D)	52,061	30.9
7 George (Buddy) Darden (D)	106,586	55.2
William E. Bronson (R)	86,431	44.8
8 J. Roy Rowland (D)	100,936	100.0
9 Ed Jenkins (D)	109,422	67.5
Frank H. Cofer Jr. (R)	52,731	32.5
10 Doug Barnard Jr. (D)	116,364	100.0

HAWAII

	Votes	%
1 Cecil Heftel (D)	114,844	82.7
William F. Beard (R)	20,608	14.8
2 Daniel K. Akaka (D)	112,377	82.2
A. D. Shipley (R)	20,000	14.6

IDAHO

	Votes	%
1 Larry E. Craig (R)	139,085	68.6
Bill Hellar (D)	63,591	31.4

Candidates	Votes	%
2 Richard H. Stallings (D)	101,287	50.0
George Hansen (R)	101,117	50.0

ILLINOIS

Candidates	Votes	%
1 Charles A. Hayes (D)	177,438	95.6
2 Gus Savage (D)	155,349	83.0
Dale F. Harman (R)	31,865	17.0
3 Marty Russo (D)	143,363	64.4
Richard D. Murphy (R)	79,218	35.6
4 George M. O'Brien (R)	121,744	64.0
Dennis E. Marlow (D)	68,547	36.0
5 William O. Lipinski (D)	106,597	63.6
John M. Paczkowski (R)	61,109	36.4
6 Henry J. Hyde (R)	157,370	75.1
Robert H. Renshaw (D)	52,189	24.9
7 Cardiss Collins (D)	135,493	78.4
James L. Bevel (R)	37,411	21.6
8 Dan Rostenkowski (D)	114,385	71.3
Spiro F. Georgeson (R)	46,030	28.7
9 Sidney R. Yates (D)	144,879	67.5
Herbert Sohn (R)	69,613	32.5
10 John Edward Porter (R)	153,330	72.6
Ruth C. Braver (D)	57,809	27.4
11 Frank Annunzio (D)	138,171	62.6
Charles J. Theusch (R)	82,518	37.4
12 Philip M. Crane (R)	159,582	77.8
Edward J. LaFlamme (D)	45,537	22.2
13 Harris W. Fawell (R)	157,603	67.0
Michael J. Donohue (D)	77,623	33.0
14 John E. Grotberg (R)	135,967	62.2
Dan McGrath (D)	82,756	37.8
15 Edward R. Madigan (R)	149,096	73.2
John M. Hoffman (D)	54,516	26.8
16 Lynn Martin (R)	127,684	58.4
Carl R. Schwerdtfeger (D)	90,850	41.6
17 Lane Evans (D)	128,273	56.7
Kenneth G. McMillan (R)	98,069	43.3
18 Robert H. Michel (R)	136,183	61.0
Gerald A. Bradley (D)	86,884	38.9
19 Terry L. Bruce (D)	117,634	52.3
Daniel B. Crane (R)	107,463	47.7
20 Richard J. Durbin (D)	145,092	61.3
Richard G. Austin (R)	91,728	38.7
21 Melvin Price (D)	127,046	60.2
Robert H. Gaffner (R)	84,148	39.8
22 Kenneth J. Gray (D)	116,952	50.3
Randy Patchett (R)	115,775	49.7

INDIANA

Candidates	Votes	%
1 Peter J. Visclosky (D)	147,035	70.7
Joseph B. Grenchik (R)	59,986	28.8
2 Philip R. Sharp (D)	118,965	53.4
Ken MacKenzie (R)	103,061	46.3
3 John Hiler (R)	115,139	52.4
Michael P. Barnes (D)	103,961	47.3
4 Dan Coats (R)	129,674	60.8
Michael H. Barnard (D)	82,053	38.5
5 Elwood Hillis (R)	143,560	67.9
Allen B. Maxwell (D)	66,631	31.5
6 Dan Burton (R)	178,814	72.7
Howard O. Campbell (D)	65,772	26.8
7 John T. Myers (R)	147,787	67.3
Arthur E. Smith (D)	69,097	31.5
8[1] Richard D. McIntyre (R)	114,278	49.9
Frank McCloskey (D)	113,860	49.8
9 Lee H. Hamilton (D)	137,018	65.1
Floyd E. Coates (R)	72,652	34.5
10 Andrew Jacobs Jr. (D)	115,274	59.0
Joseph P. Watkins (R)	79,342	40.6

IOWA

Candidates	Votes	%
1 Jim Leach (R)	131,182	66.8
Kevin Ready (D)	65,293	33.2
2 Tom Tauke (R)	136,893	63.9
Joe Welsh (D)	77,335	36.1
3 Cooper Evans (R)	133,737	60.7
Joe Johnston (D)	86,574	39.3
4 Neal Smith (D)	136,922	60.7
Robert R. Lockard (R)	88,717	39.3
5 Jim Lightfoot (R)	104,632	50.8
Jerome D. Fitzgerald (D)	101,435	49.2
6 Berkley Bedell (D)	127,706	62.0
Darrel Rensink (R)	78,182	38.0

KANSAS

Candidates	Votes	%
1 Pat Roberts (R)	159,931	76.0
Darrell Ringer (D)	49,015	23.3
2 Jim Slattery (D)	112,263	60.0
Jim Van Slyke (R)	73,045	39.1
3 Jan Meyers (R)	117,159	54.8
John E. Reardon (D)	85,441	39.9
John S. Ralph Jr. (I)	11,302	5.3
4 Dan Glickman (D)	138,917	74.4
William V. Krause (R)	47,776	25.6
5 Bob Whittaker (R)	144,075	73.5
John A. Barnes (D)	49,435	25.2

KENTUCKY

Candidates	Votes	%
1 Carroll Hubbard Jr. (D)	112,180	100.0
2 William H. Natcher (D)	93,042	62.1
Timothy A. Morrison (R)	56,700	37.9
3 Romano L. Mazzoli (D)	145,680	67.7
Suzanne M. Warner (R)	68,185	31.7
4 Gene Snyder (R)	108,398	53.7
William P. Mulloy II (D)	93,640	46.3
5 Harold Rogers (R)	125,164	75.9
Sherman W. McIntosh (D)	39,783	24.1
6 Larry J. Hopkins (R)	126,525	71.4
Jerry Hammond (D)	49,657	28.0
7[2] Carl C. (Chris) Perkins (D)	122,679	73.7
Aubrey Russell (R)	43,890	26.3

LOUISIANA[3]

Candidates	Votes	%
1 Bob Livingston (R)		100.0
2 Lindy (Mrs. Hale) Boggs (D)		100.0
3 W. J. (Billy) Tauzin (D)		100.0
4 Buddy Roemer (D)		100.0
5 Jerry Huckaby (D)		100.0
6 W. Henson Moore (R)		100.0
7 John B. Breaux (D)		100.0
8 Gillis W. Long (D)		100.0

MAINE

Candidates	Votes	%
1 John R. McKernan Jr. (R)	182,785	63.5
Barry J. Hobbins (D)	104,972	36.5
2 Olympia J. Snowe (R)	192,166	75.7
Chipman C. Bull (D)	57,347	22.6

MARYLAND

Candidates	Votes	%
1 Roy Dyson (D)	96,673	58.4
Harlan C. Williams (R)	68,865	41.6
2 Helen Delich Bentley (R)	111,517	51.4
Clarence D. Long (D)	105,571	48.6
3 Barbara A. Mikulski (D)	133,189	68.2
Ross Z. Pierpont (R)	59,493	30.5
4 Marjorie S. Holt (R)	114,430	66.2
Howard M. Greenebaum (D)	58,312	33.8
5 Steny H. Hoyer (D)	116,310	72.2
John E. Ritchie (R)	44,839	27.8
6 Beverly B. Byron (D)	123,383	65.1
Robin Ficker (R)	66,056	34.9
7 Parren J. Mitchell (D)	139,488	100.0
8 Michael D. Barnes (D)	181,947	71.5
Albert Ceccone (R)	70,715	27.8

MASSACHUSETTS

Candidates	Votes	%
1 Silvio O. Conte (R)	162,646	72.9
Mary L. Wentworth (D)	60,372	27.1
2 Edward P. Boland (D)	132,693	68.7
Thomas P. Swank (R)	60,463	31.3
3 Joseph D. Early (D)	148,461	67.4
Kenneth J. Redding (R)	71,765	32.6
4 Barney Frank (D)	172,903	74.2
Jim Forte (R)	60,121	25.8
5 Chester G. Atkins (D)	120,008	53.4
Gregory S. Hyatt (R)	104,912	46.6
6 Nicholas Mavroules (D)	168,662	70.4
Frederick S. Leber (R)	63,363	26.4
7 Edward J. Markey (D)	167,211	71.4
S. Lester Ralph (R)	66,930	28.6
8 Thomas P. O'Neill Jr. (D)	179,617	91.8
Laura Ross (COM)	15,810	8.1
9 Joe Moakley (D)	153,132	99.9
10 Gerry E. Studds (D)	143,062	55.7
Lewis Crampton (R)	113,745	44.3
11 Brian J. Donnelly (D)	172,010	100.0

MICHIGAN

Candidates	Votes	%
1 John Conyers Jr. (D)	152,432	89.4
Edward J. Mack (R)	17,393	10.2
2 Carl D. Pursell (R)	140,688	68.6
Mike McCauley (D)	62,374	30.4
3 Howard Wolpe (D)	106,505	52.9
Jackie McGregor (R)	94,714	47.1
4 Mark D. Siljander (R)	127,907	66.9
Charles S. Rodebaugh (D)	63,159	33.1
5 Paul B. Henry (R)	140,131	61.8
Gary J. McInerney (D)	85,232	37.6
6 Bob Carr (D)	106,705	52.4
Tom Ritter (R)	95,113	46.7
7 Dale E. Kildee (D)	145,070	93.1
Samuel Johnston (I)	10,663	6.8
8 Bob Traxler (D)	126,161	64.4
John Heussner (R)	69,683	35.6
9 Guy Vander Jagt (R)	150,885	70.9
John M. Senger (D)	61,233	28.8
10 Bill Schuette (R)	104,950	50.1
Donald J. Albosta (D)	103,636	49.4
11 Robert W. Davis (R)	126,992	58.6
Tom Stewart (D)	89,640	41.4
12 David E. Bonior (D)	113,772	58.3
Eugene J. Tyza (R)	79,824	40.9
13 George W. Crockett Jr. (D)	132,222	86.6
Robert Murphy (R)	20,416	13.4
14 Dennis M. Hertel (D)	113,610	59.1
John Lauve (R)	77,427	40.3
15 William D. Ford (D)	98,973	59.9
Gerald R. Carlson (R)	66,172	40.1
16 John D. Dingell (D)	121,463	63.7
Frank Grzywacki (R)	68,116	35.7
17 Sander M. Levin (D)	133,064	100.0
18 William S. Broomfield (R)	186,505	79.4
Vivian H. Smargon (D)	46,191	19.7

MINNESOTA[4]

Candidates	Votes	%
1 Timothy J. Penny (DFL)	140,095	57.0
Keith Spicer (I-R)	105,723	43.0
2 Vin Weber (I-R)	153,308	63.1
Todd Lundquist (DFL)	89,770	36.9
3 Bill Frenzel (I-R)	207,819	73.2
Dave Peterson (DFL)	76,132	26.8
4 Bruce F. Vento (DFL)	167,678	73.5
Mary Jane Rachner (I-R)	57,450	25.2
5 Martin Olav Sabo (DFL)	165,075	70.1
Richard D. Wieblen (I-R)	62,642	26.6
6 Gerry Sikorski (DFL)	154,603	60.5
Patrick Trueman (I-R)	101,058	39.5
7 Arlan Stangeland (I-R)	135,087	57.0
Collin C. Peterson (DFL)	101,720	42.9
8 James L. Oberstar (DFL)	165,727	67.2
Dave Rued (I-R)	79,181	32.1

MISSISSIPPI

Candidates	Votes	%
1 Jamie L. Whitten (D)	136,530	88.4
John Hargett (I)	17,991	11.6

Footnotes, see p. 1061.

Candidates	Votes	%
2 Webb Franklin (R)	92,392	50.6
Robert G. Clark (D)	89,154	48.9
3 G. V. (Sonny) Montgomery (D)	158,002	100.0
4 Wayne Dowdy (D)	113,635	55.3
David Armstrong (R)	91,797	45.6
5 Trent Lott (R)	142,637	84.7
Arlon (Blackie) Coate (D)	25,840	15.3

MISSOURI

1 William L. Clay (D)	147,436	68.3
Eric Rathbone (R)	68,538	31.7
2 Robert A. Young (D)	139,123	51.8
John Buechner (R)	127,710	47.5
3 Richard A. Gephardt (D)	193,537	100.0
4 Ike Skelton (D)	150,624	66.9
Carl D. Russell (R)	74,434	33.1
5 Alan Wheat (D)	150,675	66.0
Jim Kenworthy (R)	72,477	31.8
6 E. Thomas Coleman (R)	150,996	64.8
Kenneth C. Hensley (D)	81,917	35.2
7 Gene Taylor (R)	164,586	69.6
Ken Young (D)	71,867	30.4
8 Bill Emerson (R)	134,186	65.4
Bill Blue (D)	70,922	34.6
9 Harold L. Volkmer (D)	123,588	52.9
Carrie Francke (R)	110,100	47.1

MONTANA

1 Pat Williams (D)	126,998	65.6
Gary K. Carlson (R)	61,794	31.9
2 Ron Marlenee (R)	116,932	65.9
Chet Blaylock (D)	60,445	34.1

NEBRASKA

1 Doug Bereuter (R)	158,836	74.1
Monica Bauer (D)	55,508	25.9
2 Hal Daub (R)	139,384	64.9
Thomas F. Cavanaugh (D)	75,210	35.0
3 Virginia Smith (R)	183,901	83.3
Tom Vickers (D)	36,899	16.7

NEVADA

1 Harry Reid (D)	73,242	56.1
Peggy Cavnar (R)	55,391	42.4
2 Barbara F. Vucanovich (R)	99,775	71.2
Andrew Barbano (D)	36,130	25.8

NEW HAMPSHIRE

1 Robert C. Smith (R)	111,627	58.6
Dudley Dudley (D)	76,854	40.3
2 Judd Gregg (R)	138,975	76.2
Larry Converse (D)	42,257	23.2

NEW JERSEY

1 James J. Florio (D)	152,125	71.9
Frederick A. Busch Jr. (R)	58,800	27.8
2 William J. Hughes (D)	132,841	63.2
Raymond G. Massie (R)	77,231	36.7
3 James J. Howard (D)	122,291	53.3
Brian T. Kennedy (R)	105,028	45.8
4 Christopher H. Smith (R)	139,295	61.3
James C. Hedden (D)	87,908	38.7
5 Marge Roukema (R)	171,979	71.2
Rose Brunetto (D)	69,666	28.8
6 Bernard J. Dwyer (D)	118,532	55.9
Dennis Adams (R)	90,862	42.8
7 Matthew J. Rinaldo (R)	165,685	74.2
John F. Feeley (D)	56,798	25.4
8 Robert A. Roe (D)	118,793	62.7
Marguerite A. Page (R)	69,973	36.9

Candidates	Votes	%
9 Robert G. Torricelli (D)	149,493	62.6
Neil Romano (R)	89,166	37.4
10 Peter W. Rodino Jr. (D)	111,244	83.7
Howard E. Berkeley (R)	21,712	16.3
11 Dean A. Gallo (R)	133,662	55.8
Joseph G. Minish (D)	106,038	44.2
12 Jim Courter (R)	148,042	65.0
Peter Bearse (D)	78,167	34.3
13⁵ H. James Saxton (R)	141,136	60.7
James B. Smith (D)	89,307	38.4
14 Frank J. Guarini (D)	115,117	65.7
Edward T. Magee (R)	58,265	33.3

NEW MEXICO

1 Manuel Lujan Jr. (R)	115,808	64.9
Charles Ted Asbury (D)	60,598	34.0
2 Joe Skeen (R)	116,006	74.3
Peter R. York (D)	40,063	25.7
3 Bill Richardson (D)	100,470	60.8
Louis H. Gallegos (R)	62,351	37.7

NEW YORK

1 William Carney (R, C, RTL)	107,029	53.1
George J. Hochbrueckner (D, RP)	94,551	46.9
2 Thomas J. Downey (D, IP)	97,648	54.7
Paul Aniboli (R, C, RTL)	80,855	45.3
3 Robert J. Mrazek (D)	120,191	51.0
Robert P. Quinn (R, C)	112,909	47.9
4 Norman F. Lent (R, C)	154,875	68.9
Sheldon Engelhard (D, L)	65,678	29.2
5 Raymond J. McGrath (R, C)	138,560	62.4
Michael d'Innocenzo (D, IV)	78,429	35.3
6 Joseph P. Addabbo (D, L)	120,098	82.7
Philip J. Veltre (R, C, RTL)	25,040	17.3
7 Gary L. Ackerman (D, L)	97,674	69.3
Gustave A. Reifenkugel (R, C)	43,370	30.7
8 James H. Scheuer (D, L)	104,558	62.8
Robert L. Brandofino (R, C)	62,015	37.2
9 Thomas J. Manton (D)	71,420	52.8
Serphin R. Maltese (R, C, RTL)	63,910	47.2
10 Charles E. Schumer (D, L)	115,867	72.4
John H. Fox (R, C)	42,009	26.3
11 Edolphus Towns (D, L)	81,002	85.2
Nathaniel Hendricks (R)	12,494	13.1
12 Major R. Owens (D, L)	82,047	90.5
Joseph N. O. Caesar (R, C, RTL)	8,609	9.5
13 Stephen J. Solarz (D, L)	82,610	65.9
Lew Y. Levin (R, C, RTL)	42,737	34.1
14 Guy V. Molinari (R, C, RTL)	117,041	70.2
Kevin L. Sheehy (D)	49,776	29.8
15 Bill Green (R, I)	107,644	56.1
Andrew J. Stein (D, L)	84,404	43.9
16 Charles B. Rangel (D, R)	117,759	97.0
17 Ted Weiss (D, L)	162,489	81.5
Kenneth Katzman (R)	33,316	16.7
18 Robert Garcia (D, L)	85,960	89.2
Curtis Johnson (R)	8,970	9.3
19 Mario Biaggi (D, R, L, RTL)	155,067	94.8
Alice Farrell (C)	8,472	5.2
20 Joseph J. DioGuardi (R, C)	106,958	50.1
Oren J. Teicher (D)	102,842	48.2
21 Hamilton Fish Jr. (R, C, RTL)	160,053	78.3
Lawrence W. Grunberger (D)	44,274	21.7
22 Benjamin A. Gilman (R)	144,278	68.5
Bruce M. Levine (D, L)	57,934	27.5
23 Samuel S. Stratton (D)	188,144	77.8
Frank Wicks (R, NF)	53,060	21.9
24 Gerald B. H. Solomon (R, C, RTL)	164,019	73.2
Edward J. Bloch (D)	60,188	26.8
25 Sherwood Boehlert (R)	140,256	72.8
James J. Ball (D)	52,434	27.2
26 David O'B. Martin (R, C)	131,257	70.6
Bernard J. Lammers (D)	54,663	29.4

Candidates	Votes	%
27 George C. Wortley (R, C)	122,215	56.6
Thomas C. Buckel Jr. (D, L)	93,601	43.4
28 Matthew F. McHugh (D)	123,334	56.6
Constance E. Cook (R)	90,324	41.4
29 Frank Horton (R)	138,362	69.6
James R. Toole (D)	48,301	24.3
30 Fred J. Eckert (R, C, RTL)	119,844	54.4
W. Douglas Call (D)	100,066	45.4
31 Jack F. Kemp (R, C, RTL)	168,332	75.0
Peter J. Martinelli (D, L)	56,156	25.0
32 John J. LaFalce (D, L)	139,979	69.4
Anthony J. Murty (R, C, RTL)	61,797	30.6
33 Henry J. Nowak (D, L)	155,198	77.6
David S. Lewandowski (R, C, RTL)	44,880	22.4
34 Stan Lundine (D)	110,902	54.2
Jill Houghton Emery (R, C)	91,016	44.5

NORTH CAROLINA

1 Walter B. Jones (D)	122,815	67.1
Herbert W. Lee (R)	60,153	32.9
2 Tim Valentine (D)	122,292	67.7
Frank H. Hill (R)	58,312	32.3
3 Charles Whitley (D)	100,185	64.1
Danny G. Moody (R)	56,096	35.9
4 Bill Cobey (R)	117,436	50.6
Ike Andrews (D)	114,462	49.4
5 Stephen L. Neal (D)	109,831	50.7
Stuart Epperson (R)	106,599	49.3
6 Howard Coble (R)	102,925	50.6
Robin Britt (D)	100,263	49.3
7 Charlie Rose (D)	92,157	59.2
S. Thomas Rhodes (R)	63,625	40.8
8 W. G. (Bill) Hefner (D)	99,731	50.9
Harris D. Blake (R)	96,354	49.1
9 J. Alex McMillan (R)	109,420	50.1
D. G. Martin (D)	109,099	49.9
10 James T. Broyhill (R)	142,863	73.4
Ted A. Poovey (D)	51,860	26.6
11 Bill Hendon (R)	112,598	51.0
James McClure Clarke (D)	108,284	49.0

NORTH DAKOTA

AL Byron L. Dorgan (D)	242,968	78.7
Lois Ivers Altenburg (R)	65,761	21.3

OHIO

1 Thomas A. Luken (D)	121,577	55.1
Norman A. Murdock (R)	88,859	40.3
2 Bill Gradison (R)	149,856	68.6
Thomas D. Porter (D)	68,597	31.4
3 Tony P. Hall (D)	151,398	100.0
4 Michael G. Oxley (R)	162,199	77.5
William O. Sutton (D)	47,018	22.5
5 Delbert L. Latta (R)	132,582	62.7
James R. Sherck (D)	78,809	37.3
6 Bob McEwen (R)	150,101	74.0
Bob Smith (D)	52,727	26.0
7 Michael DeWine (R)	147,885	76.7
Donald E. Scott (D)	40,621	21.1
8 Thomas N. Kindness (R)	155,200	76.9
John T. Francis (D)	46,673	23.1
9 Marcy Kaptur (D)	117,985	54.9
Frank Venner (R)	93,210	43.4
10 Clarence E. Miller (R)	149,337	73.0
John M. Buchanan (D)	55,172	27.0
11 Dennis E. Eckart (D)	133,096	66.8
Dean Beagle (R)	66,278	33.2
12 John R. Kasich (R)	148,899	69.5
Richard Sloan (D)	65,215	30.5
13 Don J. Pease (D)	131,923	66.4
William G. Schaffner (R)	59,610	30.0
14 John F. Seiberling (D)	155,729	71.4
Jean E. Bender (R)	62,366	28.6
15 Chalmers P. Wylie (R)	148,311	71.6
Duane Jager (D)	58,870	28.4

	Candidates	Votes	%
16	Ralph Regula (R)	152,399	72.4
	James Gwin (D)	58,048	27.6
17	James A. Traficant Jr. (D)	123,014	53.3
	Lyle Williams (R)	105,449	45.7
18	Douglas Applegate (D)	155,759	75.9
	Kenneth P. Burt Jr. (R)	49,356	24.1
19	Edward F. Feighan (D)	139,605	55.2
	Matthew J. Hatchadorian (R)	107,957	42.7
20	Mary Rose Oakar (D)	167,115	100.0
21	Louis Stokes (D)	165,247	82.4
	Robert L. Woodall (R)	29,500	14.7

OKLAHOMA

	Candidates	Votes	%
1	James R. Jones (D)	113,919	52.2
	Frank Keating (R)	103,098	47.3
2	Mike Synar (D)	148,124	74.1
	Gary K. Rice (R)	51,889	25.9
3	Wes Watkins (D)	137,964	77.8
	Patrick K. Miller (R)	39,454	22.2
4	Dave McCurdy (D)	109,447	63.6
	Jerry Smith (R)	60,844	35.4
5	Mickey Edwards (R)	135,167	75.6
	Allen Greeson (D)	39,089	21.9
6	Glenn English (D)	96,994	58.9
	Craig Dodd (R)	67,601	41.1

OREGON

	Candidates	Votes	%
1	Les AuCoin (D)	138,393	53.1
	Bill Moshofsky (R)	122,247	46.9
2	Robert F. Smith (R)	132,649	57.0
	Larryann C. Willis (D)	100,152	43.0
3	Ron Wyden (D)	173,438	72.3
	Drew Davis (R)	66,394	27.7
4	James Weaver (D)	134,190	58.2
	Bruce Long (R)	96,487	41.8
	Ruth McFarland (D)	108,919	45.5

PENNSYLVANIA

	Candidates	Votes	%
1	Thomas M. Foglietta (D)	148,123	74.9
	Carmine DiBiase (R)	49,559	25.1
2	William H. Gray III (D)	200,484	91.0
	Ronald J. Sharper (R)	18,224	8.3
3	Robert A. Borski (D)	152,598	63.9
	Flora L. Becker (R)	85,358	35.7
4	Joe Kolter (D)	114,040	56.8
	James Kunder (R)	86,769	43.2
5	Richard T. Schulze (R)	141,965	72.6
	Louis J. Fanti (D)	53,586	27.4
6	Gus Yatron (D)	181,165	100.0
7	Bob Edgar (D)	124,458	50.1
	Curt Weldon (R)	124,046	49.9
8	Peter H. Kostmayer (D)	112,648	50.9
	David A. Christian (R)	108,696	49.1
9	Bud Shuster (R)	118,437	66.5
	Nancy Kulp (D)	59,549	33.5
10	Joseph M. McDade (R)	150,166	77.1
	Gene Basalyga (D)	44,571	22.9
11	Paul E. Kanjorski (D)	108,430	58.6
	Robert P. Hudock (R)	76,692	41.4
12	John P. Murtha (D)	134,384	69.1
	Thomas J. Fullard III (R)	57,466	29.5
13	Lawrence Coughlin (R)	133,948	56.1
	Joseph M. Hoeffel (D)	104,756	43.9
14	William J. Coyne (D)	163,818	76.6
	John Robert Clark (R)	42,616	19.9
15	Don Ritter (R)	110,338	58.1
	Jane Wells-Schooley (D)	79,490	41.9
16	Robert S. Walker (R)	138,477	77.8
	Martin L. Bard (D)	39,515	22.2
17	George W. Gekas (R)	129,716	80.3
	Stephen A. Anderson (D)	31,770	19.7
18	Doug Walgren (D)	149,628	62.7
	John G. Maxwell (R)	87,521	36.7
19	Bill Goodling (R)	141,196	75.6
	F. John Rarig (D)	44,117	23.6
20	Joseph M. Gaydos (D)	158,751	76.0
	Daniel Lloyd (R)	50,247	24.0

	Candidates	Votes	%
21	Tom Ridge (R)	125,730	65.4
	James A. Young (D)	65,594	34.1
22	Austin J. Murphy (D)	153,514	79.0
	Nancy S. Pryor (R)	39,752	20.0
23	William F. Clinger Jr. (R)	94,952	51.6
	Bill Wachob (D)	88,957	48.4

RHODE ISLAND

	Candidates	Votes	%
1	Fernand J. St Germain (D)	130,584	68.5
	Alfred Rego Jr. (R)	60,026	31.5
2	Claudine Schneider (R)	135,161	67.7
	Richard Sinapi (D)	64,341	32.3

SOUTH CAROLINA

	Candidates	Votes	%
1	Thomas F. Hartnett (R)	103,288	61.7
	Ed Pendarvis (D)	64,022	38.3
2	Floyd Spence (R)	108,085	62.1
	Ken Mosely (D)	63,932	36.7
3	Butler Derrick (D)	88,917	58.4
	Clarence E. Taylor (R)	61,739	40.6
4	Carroll A. Campbell Jr. (R)	105,139	63.9
	Jeff Smith (D)	57,854	35.2
5	John M. Spratt Jr. (D)	98,513	96.3
6	Robin Tallon (D)	97,329	59.9
	Lois Eargle (R)	63,005	38.8

SOUTH DAKOTA

	Candidates	Votes	%
AL	Thomas A. Daschle (D)	181,401	57.4
	Dale Bell (R)	134,821	42.6

TENNESSEE

	Candidates	Votes	%
1	James H. Quillen (R)	113,407	100.0
2	John J. Duncan (R)	132,604	77.3
	John F. Bowen (D)	38,846	22.7
3	Marilyn Lloyd (D)	99,465	52.4
	John Davis (R)	90,216	47.6
4	Jim Cooper (D)	93,848	75.2
	James Beau Seigneur (R)	31,011	24.8
5	Bill Boner (D)	138,233	100.0
6	Bart Gordon (D)	103,989	62.8
	Joe Simpkins (R)	61,559	37.2
7	Don Sundquist (R)	107,257	100.0
8	Ed Jones (D)	118,653	100.0
9	Harold E. Ford (D)	133,428	71.5
	William B. Thompson Jr. (R)	53,064	28.5

TEXAS

	Candidates	Votes	%
1	Sam B. Hall Jr. (D)	139,829	100.0
2	Charles Wilson (D)	113,225	59.3
	Louis Dugas Jr. (R)	77,842	40.7
3	Steve Bartlett (R)	228,819	83.0
	Jim Westbrook (D)	46,890	17.0
4	Ralph M. Hall (D)	120,749	58.0
	Thomas Blow (R)	87,553	42.0
5	John Bryant (D)	94,391	100.0
6	Joe L. Barton (R)	131,482	56.6
	Dan Kubiak (D)	100,799	43.4
7	Bill Archer (R)	213,480	86.7
	Billy Willibey (D)	32,835	13.3
8	Jack Fields (R)	113,031	64.6
	Don Buford (D)	62,072	35.4
9	Jack Brooks (D)	120,559	58.9
	Jim Mahan (R)	84,306	41.2
10	J. J. Pickle (D)	186,447	99.8
11	Marvin Leath (D)	112,940	100.0
12	Jim Wright (D)	106,299	100.0
13	Beau Boulter (R)	107,600	53.0
	Jack Hightower (D)	95,367	47.0
14	Mac Sweeney (R)	104,181	51.3
	Bill Patman (D)	98,885	48.7
15	E. (Kika) de la Garza (D)	104,863	100.0
16	Ronald D. Coleman (D)	76,375	57.4
	Jack Hammond (R)	56,589	42.6

	Candidates	Votes	%
17	Charles W. Stenholm (D)	143,012	100.0
18	Mickey Leland (D)	109,626	78.8
	Glen E. Beaman (R)	26,400	19.0
19	Larry Combest (R)	102,805	58.1
	Don R. Richards (D)	74,044	41.9
20	Henry B. Gonzalez (D)	100,443	100.0
21	Tom Loeffler (R)	199,909	80.6
	Joe Sullivan (D)	48,039	19.4
22	Thomas D. DeLay (R)	125,225	65.3
	Doug Williams (D)	66,495	34.7
23	Albert G. Bustamante (D)	95,721	100.0
24	Martin Frost (D)	105,210	59.5
	Bob Burk (R)	71,703	40.5
25	Michael A. Andrews (D)	113,946	64.0
	Jerry Patterson (R)	63,974	36.0
26	Dick Armey (R)	126,641	51.3
	Tom Vandergriff (D)	120,484	48.7
27	Solomon P. Ortiz (D)	105,516	63.6
	Richard Moore (R)	60,283	36.4

UTAH

	Candidates	Votes	%
1	James V. Hansen (R)	142,952	71.2
	Milton C. Abrams (D)	56,619	28.2
2	David S. Monson (R)	105,540	49.4
	Frances Farley (D)	105,044	49.1
3	Howard C. Nielson (R)	138,918	74.5
	Bruce R. Baird (D)	46,560	25.0

VERMONT

	Candidates	Votes	%
AL	James M. Jeffords (R)	148,025	65.4
	Anthony Pollina (D)	60,360	26.7

VIRGINIA

	Candidates	Votes	%
1	Herbert H. Bateman (R)	118,085	59.1
	John McGlennon (D)	79,577	39.8
2	G. William Whitehurst (R)	136,632	99.8
3	Thomas J. Bliley Jr. (R)	169,987	85.6
	Roger L. Coffey (I)	28,556	14.4
4	Norman Sisisky (D)	120,093	99.9
5	Dan Daniel (D)	117,738	100.0
6	James R. Olin (D)	105,207	53.5
	Ray Garland (R)	91,344	46.5
7	D. French Slaughter Jr. (R)	109,110	56.5
	Lewis M. Costello (D)	77,624	40.2
8	Stan Parris (R)	125,015	55.8
	Richard L. Saslaw (D)	97,250	43.4
9	Frederick C. Boucher (D)	102,446	52.0
	Jefferson Stafford (R)	94,510	48.0
10	Frank R. Wolf (R)	158,528	62.5
	John P. Flannery II (D)	95,074	37.5

WASHINGTON

	Candidates	Votes	%
1	John R. Miller (R)	147,926	56.3
	Brock Evans (D)	115,001	43.7
2	Al Swift (D)	142,065	58.6
	Jim Klauder (R)	93,472	38.6
3	Don Bonker (D)	150,432	71.1
	Herb Elder (R)	61,219	28.9
4	Sid Morrison (R)	150,322	76.1
	Mark Epperson (D)	47,158	23.9
5	Thomas S. Foley (D)	154,988	69.7
	Jack Hebner (R)	67,438	30.3
6	Norman D. Dicks (D)	124,367	66.1
	Mike Lonergan (R)	60,721	32.3
7	Mike Lowry (D)	174,560	70.4
	Robert O. Dorse (R)	71,576	28.9
8	Rod Chandler (R)	146,891	62.4
	Bob Lamson (D)	88,379	37.6

WEST VIRGINIA

	Candidates	Votes	%
1	Alan B. Mollohan (D)	104,639	54.4
	James Altmeyer (R)	87,622	45.6
2	Harley O. Staggers Jr. (D)	100,345	56.0
	Cleve Benedict (R)	78,936	44.0

Candidates	Votes	%
3 Bob Wise (D)	125,306	*67.9*
Margaret Miller (R)	59,128	*32.1*
4 Nick J. Rahall II (D)	98,919	*66.7*
Jess T. Shumate (R)	49,474	*33.3*

WISCONSIN

1 Les Aspin (D)	127,184	*56.2*
Pete Jansson (R)	99,080	*43.8*
2 Robert W. Kastenmeier (D)	159,987	*63.6*
Albert E. Wiley Jr. (R)	91,345	*36.3*

Candidates	Votes	%
3 Steve Gunderson (R)	160,437	*68.4*
Charles F. Dahl (D)	74,253	*31.6*
4 Gerald D. Kleczka (D)	158,722	*66.6*
Robert V. Nolan (R)	78,056	*32.8*
5 Jim Moody (D)	175,243	*98.0*
6 Thomas E. Petri (R)	170,271	*75.8*
David L. Iaquinta (D)	54,266	*24.2*
7 David R. Obey (D)	146,131	*61.2*
Mark G. Michaelsen (R)	92,507	*38.8*
8 Toby Roth (R)	161,005	*67.9*
Paul Willems (D)	73,090	*30.8*

Candidates	Votes	%
9 F. James Sensenbrenner Jr. (R)	180,247	*73.4*
John Krause (D)	64,157	*26.1*

Special Election		
4 Gerald D. Kleczka (D)	76,384	*65.0*
Robert V. Nolan (R)	41,007	*34.9*

WYOMING

AL Dick Cheney (R)	138,234	*73.6*
Hugh B. McFadden Jr. (D)	45,857	*24.4*

1984 Elections

1. Contested election. A recount by a House Administration Committee task force determined that McCloskey defeated McIntyre by a four-vote margin, 116,645 (50.00085 percent) to 116,641 (49.99914 percent). On May 1, 1985, the House voted 236-190 to seat McCloskey.

2. A special election was held in conjunction with the November election. Perkins was elected to fill both the unexpired term of his father, Rep. Carl D. Perkins, D, who died Aug. 3, 1984, and the two-year term beginning Jan. 3, 1985.

3. For the 1984 House elections in Louisiana, an open primary election was held with candidates from all parties running on the same ballot. Any candidate who received a majority was elected unopposed, with no further appearance on the general election ballot. If no candidate received 50 percent, a runoff was held between the two top finishers.

4. In Minnesota the Democratic Party is known as the Democratic-Farmer-Labor Party and the Republican Party as the Independent-Republican Party; candidates appear on the ballot with these designations.

5. A special election was held in conjunction with the November election. Saxton was elected to serve both the unexpired term of Rep. Edwin B. Forsythe, R, who died March 29, 1984, and the two-year term beginning Jan. 3, 1985.

1985 House Elections

LOUISIANA

Special Election

Candidates	Votes	%
8[1] Cathy (Mrs. Gillis) Long (D)	52,684	*51.8*
John E. (Jock) Scott (D)	27,136	*26.7*
Clyde C. Holloway (R)	18,113	*17.8*

TEXAS

Special Election

Candidates	Votes	%
1[2] Edd Hargett (R)	29,814	*42.2*
Jim Chapman (D)	21,370	*30.2*
Sam Fussell (D)	13,099	*18.5*

Special Runoff Election

Candidates	Votes	%
1 Jim Chapman (D)	52,670	*50.9*
Edd Hargett (R)	50,737	*49.1*

1985 Elections

1. Long was elected to serve the unexpired term of her husband, Rep. Gillis W. Long, D, who died Jan. 20, 1985.

2. A special election was held to fill the unexpired term of Rep. Sam B. Hall Jr., D, who resigned May 27, 1985, to accept a federal judgeship.

House Returns: Other Sources

In the preceding pages of House popular election returns (701-1061) the symbol # is used to denote returns for the years 1824-1973 that were taken from a source other than the Inter-University Consortium for Political and Social Research (ICPSR). This page lists the source for each of those returns. *(For description of ICPSR data, see pp. xiv, 700.)*

The two most frequently used alternative sources were *Statistics of the Congressional Elections of ____*, published

by the Clerk of the House of Representatives for every general election year since 1920, and the Elections Research Center, which compiles the biennial *America Votes* series under the direction of Richard M. Scammon and Alice V. McGillivray.

For elections 1974-85, Congressional Quarterly obtained the returns from the state secretaries of state. Where discrepancies existed between these figures and *America Votes,* the latter's figures were used.

1840—Georgia (at-large special):
Georgia Secretary of State.

1844—Ohio (10th District special):
Ohio Historical Society Archives.

1845—Tennessee (8th District):
Tennessee Secretary of State.

1872—Georgia (4th District special):
Georgia Secretary of State.

1872—Pennsylvania (13th District special):
Pennsylvania Secretary of State.

1873—Louisiana (4th District special):
Louisiana State University Library.

1874—Tennessee (4th District special):
Tennessee Secretary of State.

1884—Pennsylvania (19th District special):
Pennsylvania Secretary of State.

1884—South Carolina (4th District special):
South Carolina Secretary of State.

1886—Louisiana (2nd District special):
Biographical Directory of the American Congress, 1774-1971 (Washington, D. C.: Government Printing Office, 1971).

1892—Texas (9th District special):
Official Texas Election Register.

1908—Nebraska (5th District):
1910 World Almanac, published by *The New York World* newspaper.

1922—New Jersey (8th District):
Statistics of the Congressional Election of Nov. 7, 1922.

1924—Georgia (9th District) **Ohio** (22nd District):
Statistics of the Congressional and Presidential Election of Nov. 4, 1924.

1926—Massachusetts (8th District special); **Minnesota** (4th District):
Statistics of the Congressional Election of Nov. 2, 1926.

1928—New Jersey (8th District); **Oregon** (3rd District); **Tennessee** (5th District):
Statistics of the Congressional and Presidential Election of Nov. 6, 1928.

1930—California (3rd District); **Georgia** (8th and 11th districts); **Kentucky** (2nd District special); **Wisconsin** (5th District):
Statistics of the Congressional Election of Nov. 4, 1930.

1937—New York (17th District special):
New York Secretary of State.

1944—Wisconsin (8th District):
Statistics of the Presidential and Congressional Election of Nov. 7, 1944.

1946—Georgia (5th District); **Nebraska** (3rd District):
Statistics of the Congressional Election of Nov. 5, 1946.

1950—Tennessee (5th District):
Statistics of the Congressional Election of Nov. 4, 1958.

1950—Texas (18th District special):
Texas Secretary of State.

1951—Missouri (11th District special):
Missouri Secretary of State.

1959—Iowa (4th District special):
Iowa Secretary of State.

1960—Indiana (5th District):
Richard M. Scammon (ed.), *America Votes 4* (Pittsburgh: University of Pittsburgh Press, 1962), p. 123

1961—Arizona, Arkansas, Michigan, Tennessee (special elections):
Elections Research Center.

1962—Michigan (14th District special); **New York** (6th District special); **South Carolina** (2nd District special):
Elections Research Center.

1963—North Dakota, Pennsylvania, Texas (special elections):
Elections Research Center.

1964—Pennsylvania (5th District special); **Tennessee** (2nd District special):
Elections Research Center.

1964—Pennsylvania (6th District):
Pennsylvania Secretary of State.

1965—South Carolina (special):
Elections Research Center.

1966—California (4th District special); **Texas** (8th District special):
Elections Research Center.

1967—California (11th District special primary):
California Secretary of State.

1967—California (11th District special):
Elections Research Center.

1967—New York; Rhode Island (special elections):
Elections Research Center.

1968—New York (7th District):
Richard M. Scammon (ed.), *America Votes 8* (Washington, D.C.: Congressional Quarterly, 1970), p. 274.

1968—New York (13th District special); **Texas** (3rd District special):
Elections Research Center.

1968—Mississippi (3rd District special):
Mississippi Secretary of State.

1969—California (27th District special primary):
California Secretary of State.

1969—Massachusetts; Montana; Tennessee (special elections):
Elections Research Center.

1970—Texas (2nd District):
Texas Secretary of State.

1971—Kentucky (special):
Kentucky Secretary of State.

1972—Pennsylvania (27th District special):
Pennsylvania Secretary of State.

1972—Vermont (special):
Elections Research Center.

1973—Illinois (special):
Illinois Secretary of State.

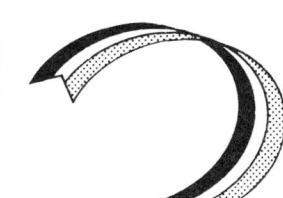
Southern Primaries

Georgia Gov. Eugene Talmadge Announces He Will Seek Re-election to a Fourth Term. July 1942.

Wide World Photos Inc.

Southern Primaries

Because of the overwhelming dominance of the Democratic Party in the South during the first half of the 20th century, the party's primaries became, in effect, the region's significant elections. The 11 states comprising the South — all members of the Civil War Confederacy — are Alabama, Arkansas, Florida, Georgia, Louisiana, Mississippi, North Carolina, South Carolina, Tennessee, Texas and Virginia.

In his classic study *Southern Politics in State and Nation,* V. O. Key Jr. concluded, "In fact, the Democratic primary is no nominating method at all. The primary is the election. . . ." That was in 1949, shortly before Republicans began seriously challenging Democrats for hegemony in the region.

But Key's observation holds true for the 20th century up through the time of his study and for much of the period since, depending on the particular state and election involved. Of the 114 gubernatorial elections held in the 11 former Confederate states in the period 1919-48, the Democratic nominee won 113 times. The exception was Tennessee's election of a Republican governor in the Harding presidential landslide of 1920. In the same period, the Democratic nominee won 131 of 132 elections to the Senate in these 11 states, the only exception being a special election in Arkansas in 1937 when the Democratic nominee lost to an independent Democrat.

Republican Party growth since 1948 has been steady though uneven. The first popularly elected Republican U.S. senator from the South, John G. Tower of Texas, won a special election in 1961. Thereafter, Republicans won Senate seats in South Carolina (1966), Tennessee (1966), Florida (1968), North Carolina and Virginia (1972), Mississippi (1978), and Alabama and Georgia (1980). Likewise, Republicans picked up governorships slowly after 1949, their first victories in the South coming in Arkansas and Florida in 1966.

But even in 1985 Republicans were a distinct minority in the South, on the state level. They were outnumbered 9 to 2 in governorships, 12 to 10 in Senate seats and 73 to 43 in U.S. House seats. Thus, the Democratic primaries continued to be the deciding election in most Southern states. (On the presidential level, the inroads on Democratic strength have gone much deeper, with Republican presidential nominee Richard Nixon carrying all 11 states of the Old South with at least 65 percent of the vote in 1972. In 1984 Ronald Reagan did almost as well, carrying every Southern state with 59 percent or more of the vote.)

Runoff Primaries

The South along with the rest of the nation instituted primaries during the first two decades of the 20th century. By 1920 all 11 Southern states were choosing their Democratic gubernatorial and senatorial nominees through the primary process.

But because the primaries were, for all practical purposes, the deciding election, many legislators began to doubt the effectiveness of a system that frequently allowed a candidate in a multi-candidate race to win a plurality of the popular vote — and thus the Democratic nomination that ensured election — even though he received only a small percentage of the total primary vote.

So, most Southern states adopted the runoff primary — a second election following the first primary, usually by two to four weeks — that matched only the top two contenders from the first primary. The runoff system was adopted in Alabama in 1931, Arkansas in 1939, Florida in 1929, Georgia in 1917 (with the county unit system, *see p. 1069)*, Louisiana in 1922, Mississippi in 1902, North Carolina in 1915, South Carolina in 1915, Texas in 1918 and Virginia in 1969. (Arkansas had adopted the runoff in 1933, abandoned it in 1935, then reinstituted it in 1939.)

After 1969 Tennessee remained the only Southern state to nominate by plurality. In that state's 1974 gubernatorial race, Ray Blanton won the Democratic nomination with only 22.7 percent of the vote in a field of 12 candidates. Blanton went on to win the governorship in November.

Runoffs are not always obligatory. In most states, if the second-place finisher in the primary does not want a

Sources

Heard, Alexander, and Donald S. Strong. *Southern Primaries and Elections, 1920-1949.* 1950. Reprint. Salem, N.H.: Ayers, 1970.

Key, V. O. Jr. *Southern Politics in State and Nation.* New York: Alfred A. Knopf, 1949.

Secretaries of state and state handbooks of the 11 Southern states.

runoff, the first-place candidate is then the winner without a runoff. In the North Carolina Democratic gubernatorial primary of 1968, for example, front-runner Robert W. Scott narrowly missed winning a majority of the vote in the first primary, winding up with 48.1 percent. However, the second-place candidate, J. Melville Broughton Jr., who received 33.4 percent, declined a runoff. None was held and Scott automatically became the Democratic nominee.

Jackson's Anti-runoff Campaign

Jesse L. Jackson, contender for the 1984 Democratic presidential nomination, mounted an attack against the runoff feature in the spring of that year. Jackson hoped to persuade the 10 other Southern states to join Tennessee in avoiding the runoff.

Jackson argued that runoffs injured black candidates' chances of victory because in the second election whites, who comprised the majority of registered voters, usually voted on the basis of race.

Jackson carried his plea to the Democratic National Convention, which defeated his move to abolish runoffs, 2,500.8 to 1,253.2. Supporters argued that runoffs prevented the election of fringe candidates when more qualified candidates split the vote in hotly contested primaries. In addition, conservative Southerners voiced opposition against having a national convention decide their own state election procedures.

Preferential Primaries

Three Southern states — Alabama, Florida and Louisiana — tried to avoid the effort and expense of runoff elections by experimenting with a preferential system of primary voting. All three later switched to the runoff system — Alabama after the election of 1930, Florida after the election of 1928 and Louisiana (whose system was similar to Alabama's) after the election of 1920. Louisiana modified its system yet again in 1975, this time to a two-step process: an initial non-partisan primary followed by a general election runoff between the two top finishers.

Under the preferential system a voter, instead of simply marking an X opposite one candidate's name, writes the digits 1 *or* 2, beside the names of two candidates. This indicates the "preference" order the voter gives each of the candidates, the number one indicating his first choice, the number two his second choice. To determine the winner, without a runoff, second-choice votes are added to the first-choice votes and the candidate with the highest combined total wins.

Alabama. Under the Alabama system, each voter expressed a first and second choice. If no candidate received a majority of the first choices, all but the two leaders were eliminated. All second choices expressed for the two leaders were then added to their first-choice totals, the candidate with the highest combined total winning.

In the Democratic primary for U.S. senator on May 13, 1920, for a special four-year term to fill a vacancy, the candidates were J. Thomas Heflin and three persons whose first names are not available: White, O'Neal and Rushton. Heflin, with 49,554 first-choice votes, led the field but received only 37.9 percent of the total. White ran second with 34,854 first-choice votes, or 26.6 percent; O'Neal had 33,174 first-choice votes or 25.4 percent, and Rushton was last with 13,232 first-choice votes, or 10.1 percent. Thus, in many Southern states a runoff would have been necessary. But instead of a runoff all second-choice votes cast for the two leaders — Heflin and White — were added to their

first-choice ballots. A total of 11,062 second-choice votes were cast for Heflin by voters whose first choice had gone to one of the other three candidates. Added to his first-choice vote of 49,554, this gave Heflin a grand total of 60,016 votes. White received 12,699 second-choice votes — more than Heflin — but the second-choice votes were not enough to raise his grand total above Heflin's. White thus wound up with a grand total of 47,553 votes, and Heflin was the winner.

Florida. The Florida system of preference voting differed somewhat from the Alabama system. In Florida, as in Alabama, each voter expressed a first and second choice. Also as in Alabama, if no candidate received a majority of first choices, all candidates but the two highest first-choice candidates were eliminated. To determine the winner, the second choices expressed for the two highest *on the ballots of eliminated candidates only* were added to the first-choice totals. (In Alabama, the second choices for the two leaders expressed on ballots for *all* candidates, including the two leaders, were added to the first-choice totals.)

For example, in the Florida Democratic gubernatorial election of 1924 there were five candidates. John W. Martin received 55,715 first-choice votes, to lead the field. His closest rival, Sidney J. Catts, received 43,230 votes. But a third major contender, Frank E. Jennings, received 37,962 first-choice votes, depriving either Martin or Catts of a majority. In addition, two other candidates also received first-choice votes — Worth W. Trammell with 8,381 and Charles H. Spencer with 1,408. The percentages stood Martin 38.0, Catts 29.5, Jennings 25.9, Trammell 5.7 and Spencer 0.9 percent.

To determine the winner, the second-choice votes cast for Martin (17,339) and Catts (6,067) by voters who had cast first-choice votes for Jennings, Trammell and Spencer were added to Martin's and Catts' first-choice totals. The result was Martin 73,054 and Catts 49,297, a clear win for Martin.

The preference system, however, did not prove useful. Apparently it was too confusing for voters, most of whom did not bother to cast second-choice votes. In the Alabama election discussed above, for example, there were 130,814 first-choice votes, but only 34,768 second-choice votes.

Louisiana. Not satisfied with either the partisan runoff or the preferential primary, Louisiana adopted a law in 1975 that allowed its voters to participate in an initial non-partisan primary followed by a general election runoff between the two top finishers. In the primary, all candidates of all parties were to be on the ballot, but party designations were optional and at the individual candidate's discretion. A candidate receiving more than 50 percent of the primary vote would be unopposed in the general election. If no candidate received more than 50 percent of the vote, the two candidates receiving the greatest number of votes — regardless of party — would oppose each other in the general election.

Thus, in 1975, when the governor was chosen under this new system, six candidates, all Democrats, entered the initial non-partisan primary held on Nov. 1. There were no Republican, independent or minor party candidates. Gov. Edwin W. Edwards, D, received 62.4 percent of the vote, and in accordance with the law only his name appeared on the Dec. 13 general election ballot. If Edwards had received less than 50 percent of the vote, but still remained in first or second place, the general election would have been a runoff between him and the other of the top two candidates, even though the other candidate was also a

Democrat. In 1978 the law went into effect for House and Senate races.

Georgia: County Unit System

Another variant of the primary system was Georgia's county unit system. Each county in the state was apportioned a certain number of unit votes. The candidate who received the largest number of popular votes in the county was awarded all the county's unit votes, even if he won only a plurality and not a majority. A candidate had to have a majority of the state's county unit votes to win the primary, otherwise a runoff became necessary. The runoff also was held on the basis of the county unit system.

For example, as of 1946, there were 410 county unit votes. The eight most populous counties had six unit votes each, the next 30 most populous counties had four each, and the remaining 121 counties two each. The system was heavily weighted toward rural and sparsely populated areas, because every county, no matter how small, had at least two unit votes.

The county unit system sometimes produced winners who received less than a majority of popular votes. Political scientist Key found that in two of 16 gubernatorial races between 1915 and 1948 the winner of a majority of county units received less than a majority of the popular votes. In a third case, that of 1946, the winner of the county unit vote, Eugene Talmadge, actually received fewer popular votes than his chief opponent, James V. Carmichael. The popular vote stood Carmichael 313,389 (45.3 percent), Talmadge 297,245 (43.0 percent), E. D. Rivers 69,489 (10.0 percent) and Hoke O'Kelly 11,758 (1.7 percent). But the county unit totals were Talmadge 244 (59.5 percent), Carmichael 144 (35.1 percent), Rivers 22 (5.4 percent) and O'Kelly (0.0 percent).

Talmadge's victory was attributable to the rural orientation of the county unit system. His popularity in farm areas gave him an almost clean sweep of the small counties, allowing him to amass more county unit votes than Carmichael, whose strength was centered in the underrepresented urban areas. However, Talmadge died shortly after the November election, precipitating a crisis in Georgia's gubernatorial succession.

The county unit system fell before the Supreme Court's "one-person, one-vote" doctrine. In the 1963 case, *Gray v. Sanders,* the court declared the Georgia county unit system unconstitutional because of the disparity in representation between the urban and rural areas.

Special Elections

As in other states, special elections in the South are held to fill vacancies for Senate seats or governorships when they occur. However, vacancies sometimes happen at times inconvenient for going through the lengthy runoff primary process prior to the special election. Either the filing deadline for the primaries has passed, or the vacancy occurs in a year when there is no regular primary scheduled. In such cases, the Democratic state committee sometimes selects the party nominee without holding a primary.

This process has led to unexpected results. In Arkansas in 1937, for example, a special election was held on Oct. 19 for the five years remaining in the term of Sen. Joseph T. Robinson, D, who had died in office. The Democratic state committee chose Gov. Carl E. Bailey as the party's official nominee. But Rep. John E. Miller of the 2nd District promptly jumped into the race as an independent Democrat, complaining that Democratic voters had not

---

Preference and Runoff Primaries

State	Preferential Primary	Runoff Primary Adopted
Alabama	Until 1931	1931
Arkansas	—	1939[1]
Florida	Until 1929	1929
Georgia	—	1917[2]
Louisiana[3]	Until 1922	1922
Mississippi	—	1902
North Carolina	—	1915
South Carolina	—	1915
Tennessee[4]	—	—
Texas	—	1918
Virginia[5]	—	—

1. Arkansas adopted the runoff in 1933, abandoned it in 1935 and reinstituted it in 1939.
2. Runoff held under county unit system; see text opposite.
3. Louisiana used the runoff "for a time prior to 1916," according to political scientist V. O. Key Jr.; in 1975 Louisiana adopted an initial non-partisan primary followed by a general election runoff.
4. Tennessee has never used the preferential or runoff primary. Candidates are nominated by winning a plurality; see text, p. 1067.
5. Virginia adopted the runoff primary in 1969 and repealed it in 1971.

Sources: Heard, Alexander, and Donald S. Strong. *Southern Primaries and Elections.* 1950. Reprint. Salem, N.H.: Ayers, 1970. Key, V. O. Jr. *Southern Politics in State and Nation.* New York: Alfred A. Knopf, 1949. Virginia secretary of state.

---

been given a choice of who their nominee should be. The result was a Miller victory, with 60.5 percent of the vote.

In an even more sensational case, this time in a regular election, the Democratic Party leadership in South Carolina found its wishes thwarted in 1954 when it nominated Edgar A. Brown following the death of Sen. Burnet R. Maybank, who had won renomination in the Democratic primary June 8. Former governor Strom Thurmond, feeling aggrieved that he had been deprived of a chance for the Senate nomination, entered the November election as a write-in candidate. With the backing of the outgoing governor, James F. Byrnes, Thurmond overwhelmingly won the race 143,444 to 83,525 — making him the only senator ever elected on a write-in vote.

Texas' Runoff Special Elections

To avoid the pitfalls sometimes encountered when candidates are chosen without a primary, Texas adopted a unique method of holding special elections for U.S. House and Senate seats. (Governors are not elected by special election. Instead, the lieutenant governor automatically becomes governor when a vacancy occurs.) All candidates, no matter which party they belong to, compete in a free-for-all first election. If no one receives a majority, a second election is held between the top two candidates, regardless of party. Thus, the second election could occur between two Democrats, between two Republicans, or between a Democrat and a Republican or even between third-party candidates. The system was used in the 1961 special Senate contest to fill the vacancy caused when Sen. Lyndon B. Johnson, D (1949-61), resigned to become vice president. In the first contest, there were 73 candidates competing, with Republican John G. Tower and Democrat William Blakley finishing first and second. The second election resulted in a

Tower victory, 448,217 to 437,874. The same system prevails for Texas' special U.S. House elections.

White Primaries

Closely connected with the history of Southern Democratic primaries is the issue of race. In many Southern states, blacks were long barred from participation in the Democratic primary, either on a statewide basis or in various counties. To exclude blacks from the primaries, the Democratic Party was designated as a private association or club. The practice was defended as constitutional because the 15th Amendment, ratified in 1870, only prohibited *states,* not private associations, from denying the right to vote to persons on account of race or color. However, in 1944 the Supreme Court, in the case of *Smith v. Allwright,* declared the white primary unconstitutional, holding that it was an integral part of the election machinery for choosing state and federal officials.

Poll Tax. Another device used in limiting both black and white voters was the poll tax, which required the payment of a fee before voting. The amount of the poll tax ranged from one to two dollars, but in Alabama, Mississippi, Virginia and Georgia before 1945 the tax was cumulative. Thus, a new voter in Georgia could face up to $47 in fees. Various regulations as to the time and manner of payment of the tax also substantially reduced the number of voters. In Mississippi, for example, a person wanting to vote in the Democratic primary (usually held in August) had to pay his poll tax on or before the first day of the two preceding Februarys — long before most voters had even begun to think about the election.

The poll tax was barred in federal elections by ratification of the 24th Amendment in January 1964. The amendment simply stated that the "right of citizens of the United States to vote in any primary or other election . . . shall not be denied or abridged by the United States or any other State by reason of failure to pay any poll tax or other tax."

Literacy Tests. The literacy test was another method used to limit the Southern franchise to whites. Voters were required to read and/or write correctly — usually a section of the state or federal Constitution. Sometimes, voters who could not pass the test could have the materials read to them, to see if they could "understand" or "interpret" it correctly. This allowed local voting officials, inevitably whites, to judge whether voters passed the tests and usually resulted in whites passing and blacks failing.

However, in his study of Southern politics, Key concluded that informal pressures — including economic reprisals and other sanctions — were more important in limiting the black franchise than were the official suffrage limitations.

By the 1970s most formal bars to voting in the South, and many informal ones, had been lifted, either by constitutional amendment, federal laws, state action or protest movements.

Bibliography

Books

Bartley, Numan V. *From Thurman to Wallace: Political Tendencies in Georgia 1948-1968.* Baltimore: Johns Hopkins Press, 1970.

——, and Hugh D. Graham. *Southern Elections: County and Precinct Data, 1950-1972.* Baton Rouge: Louisiana State University Press, 1977.

Bass, Jack, and Walter DeVries. *Transformation of Southern Politics: Social Change and Political Consequence Since 1945.* New York: New American Library, 1977.

Cosman, Bernard. *Five States for Goldwater: Continuity and Change in Southern Voting Patterns 1920-1964.* University, Ala.: University of Alabama Press, 1965.

Ewing, Cortez A. *Primary Elections in the South: Study in Uniparty Politics.* 1953. Reprint. Westport, Conn.: Greenwood Press, 1980.

Grantham, Dewey W. *Democratic South.* 1963. Reprint. New York: W. W. Norton, 1965.

Heard, Alexander, and Donald S. Strong. *Southern Primaries and Elections 1920-1949.* 1950. Reprint. Salem, N.H.: Ayers, 1970.

Hollingsworth, Harold M. *Essays on Recent Southern Politics.* Austin: University of Texas Press, 1970.

Jacobstein, Helen L. *The Segregation Factor in the Florida Gubernatorial Primary Election of 1956.* Gainesville: University of Florida Press, 1972.

Key, V. O. Jr. *Southern Politics in State and Nation.* New York: Alfred A. Knopf, 1949.

Kousser, J. Morgan. *The Shaping of Southern Politics: Suffrage Restrictions and the Establishment of the One Party South, 1880-1910.* New Haven, Conn.: Yale University Press, 1974.

Kurland, Gerald, *George Wallace: Southern Governor and Presidential Candidate.* Charlotteville, N.Y.: Sam Har Press, 1972.

Moreland, Laurence W., et al. *Contemporary Southern Political Attitudes and Behavior: Studies and Essays.* New York: Praeger Publishing, 1982.

Paolucci, Henry. *The South and the Presidency: From Reconstruction to Carter.* Whitestone, N.Y.: Griffon House Publishing, 1978.

Sale, Kirkpatrick. *Power Shift: The Rise of the Southern Rim and Its Challenge to the Eastern Establishment.* New York: Random House, 1975.

Sindler, Allan P., ed. *Change in the Contemporary South.* Durham, N.C.: Duke University Press, 1963.

——. *Huey Long's Louisiana: State Politics 1920-1952.* 1956. Reprint. Baltimore: Johns Hopkins University Press, 1980.

Spence, James R. *The Making of a Governor: The Moore-Preyer-Lake Primaries of 1964.* Winston-Salem, N.C.: John H. Blair, 1968.

Steed, Robert P., and Laurence W. Moreland, eds. *Party Politics in the South.* New York: Praeger, 1980.

Sydnor, Charles S. *The Development of Southern Sectionalism, 1819-1848.* Baton Rouge: Louisiana State University Press, 1968.

Tindale, George B. *The Disruption of the Solid South.* New York: W. W. Norton, 1972.

Woodward, C. Vann. *Origins of the New South, 1877-1913.* Baton Rouge: Louisiana State University Press, 1951.

——. *Reunion and Reaction: The Compromise of 1877 and the End to Reconstruction.* Boston: Little, Brown, 1966.

Articles

Alexander, H. M. "The Double Primary." *Arkansas Historical Quarterly* (Autumn 1944): 217-268.

"The American South, 1950-1970." *Journal of Politics* (February 1964).

Boyd, W. M. "Southern Politics, 1948-1952." *Phylon* (Third Quarter 1952): 226-235.

Black, Merle, and Earl Black. "Republican Party Development in the South: The Rise of the Contested Primary." *Social Science Quarterly* (December 1976): 566-578.

Burnham, Walter D. "The Alabama Senatorial Election of 1962: Return of Inter-Party Competition." *Journal of Politics* (November 1964): 798-829.

Carleton, William C. "The Southern Politician." *Journal of Politics* 13 (1951): 215-231.

Clark, E. P. "Solid South Dissolving." *Forum* (November 1896): 263-274.

Cosman, Bernard. "Republican in the South: Goldwater's Impact Upon Voting Alignment in Congressional, Gubernatorial and Senatorial Races." *Southwestern Social Science Quarterly* (June 1967): 13-23.

Eisenberg, Ralph. "1966 Politics in Virginia: The Democratic Senatorial Primary." *University of Virginia News Letter* (January 15, 1967).

Heberle, Rudolf. "Factors Motivating Voting Behavior in a One-Party State: A Case Study of the 1948 Louisiana Gubernatorial Primaries." *Social Forces* 27 (1948): 343-350.

Irish, M. D. "The Southern One-Party System and National Politics." *Journal of Politics* (February 1942): 80-94.

McCrary, Peyton, Clark Miller and Dale Baum. "Class and Party in Secession Crisis: Voting Behavior in the Deep South." *Journal of Interdisciplinary History* 8 (Winter 1977): 429-457.

Pettigrew, Thomas F. "Faubus and Segregation: An Analysis of Arkansas Voting." *Public Opinion Quarterly* (Fall 1960): 346-347.

"Post-Mortem of a Georgia Primary." *New South* (Summer 1969): 80-88.

Shannon, W. V. "Southern Sectionalism and National Politics." *Social Science* (June 1957): 135-141.

Weeks, O. D. "The White Primary: 1944-1948." *American Political Science Review* (June 1948): 500-510.

Worsnop, Richard L. "Changing Southern Politics." *Editorial Research Reports* 1 (January 19, 1966): 43-59.

Popular Vote Returns, 1919-1984

Sources: Southern Primary Returns

The Southern primary popular election returns presented in this section (pages 1075 to 1102) for the years 1919 through 1973 were obtained, except where indicted by a footnote, from the Inter-University Consortium for Political and Social Research (ICPSR) at the University of Michigan.

Major sources for returns since 1973 were Congressional Quarterly, which obtained them from the state secretaries of state, and the *America Votes* series, compiled biennially by Richard M. Scammon and Alice V. McGillivray of the Elections Research Center, Washington, D.C., and published by Congressional Quarterly.

Returns are listed for gubernatorial (pages 1075 to 1089) and senatorial (pages 1090 to 1102) primary elections in the 11 Southern states that were members of the Civil War Confederacy: Alabama, Arkansas, Florida, Georgia, Louisiana, Mississippi, North Carolina, South Carolina, Tennessee, Texas and Virginia. *(For gubernatorial primary returns of other states see p. 537; for other Senate primary returns see p. 638.)*

The vast majority of Southern primaries during the period were held to nominate candidates of the dominant Democratic Party. Returns for Republican primaries have been included, however, whenever available. Unless otherwise identified, all primaries in this section are Democratic.

Compilation of ICPSR Data File

Statewide candidate totals for Southern primary elections for governor and senator were prepared by the ICPSR staff from several sources. Election returns for the years prior to 1949 were obtained from *Southern Primaries and Elections* (University, Ala.: University of Alabama Press, 1950), edited by Alexander Heard and Donald S. Strong. It should be noted that, although they transcribed their data from official returns, Professors Heard and Strong found that many of the returns contained errors and discrepancies between the sum of county totals and the state total, or returns published as final in newspapers and secretary of state reports. No attempt was made by Heard and Strong to correct these discrepancies because the source of the error could not be determined.

For the period from 1949 to 1972, candidate totals were acquired from two sources. The first was a collection of Southern primary electoral statistics prepared from official returns by Hugh Davis Graham, chairman, division of social sciences, University of Maryland (Baltimore County), and Numan V. Bartley, department of history, University of Georgia (Athens). In addition, reference was made to official returns supplied to ICPSR by the various secretaries of state in conjunction with the ICPSR effort to maintain its continuing collection of election materials. The returns obtained from Bartley and Graham, and the secretary of state offices, were compared with published reports of the election outcomes (notably state manuals and the *America Votes* series) to verify the completeness and accuracy of the returns.

Presentation of Returns

The gubernatorial returns for Southern primaries are arranged alphabetically by state and in chronological order of election within each state listing. The Senate returns are arranged alphabetically by state and in chronological order by class of senator within each state listing. *(For an explanation of Senate classes, see p. 574.)*

Candidates are listed in descending order, with the candidate receiving the greatest number of popular votes listed first. Percentage of the total vote is listed for each candidate who received *at least 5 percent* of the total vote cast.

Primaries for special elections to fill vacancies and runoff primaries are designated in the returns. Republican primary results are labeled and appear in their proper chronological sequence within the primary returns listed for each state.

Names, Vote Totals and Percentages

The names of gubernatorial and senatorial Southern primary candidates are listed as they appeared in the source materials. In a few cases, first names are not known.

For pre-1976 primary elections included in this section, the ICPSR computed statewide vote totals for each candidate. (County-level returns are available from the ICPSR.) *(ICPSR collection, box, p. xiv.)*

Percentages of the total vote were calculated on the basis of each candidate's proportion of the *total number of votes cast* for all candidates. Percentages have been calculated to two decimal places and rounded to one place. Due to rounding and the scattered votes of minor candidates, percentages in individual primary races may not add up to 100.

If no vote is shown for a candidate but the percentage of total vote is listed as 100 percent, in most cases the candidates in question ran unopposed and state election officials either did not bother to put the candidate's name on the ballot or simply did not make an effort to record the total number of votes.

When Senate and gubernatorial primary elections were held under a preferential voting system and the use of second choice votes was required to determine a winner, the symbol ✔ appears next to the winner's name. *(Explanation of preferential voting, p. 1068.)*

There were a number of unusual cases in the history of Southern Senate primaries in which the nominee of one or both major parties was chosen by a party committee rather than in a primary, even though a primary would have been the normal method of selection. In these cases, the names of the nominees will appear in the primary returns along with a footnote indicating the particular circumstances. *(See, for example, the listing for Carl E. Bailey of Arkansas on p. 1091.)*

Southern Gubernatorial Primary Returns, 1919-1984

ALABAMA

	Candidates	Votes	%
1922	William W. Brandon (D)	163,217	78.7
	Bibb Graves (D)	44,151	21.3
1926	Bibb Graves (D)	61,493	27.6
	McDowell (D)	59,699	26.8
	Carmichael (D)	54,072	24.3
	Patterson (D)	47,411	21.3

Second Choice Votes

	Bibb Graves (D)	21,978	31.0
	Patterson (D)	20,893	29.5
	Carmichael (D)	20,061	28.3
	McDowell (D)	7,943	11.2
1930	B. M. Miller (D)	77,066	39.2
	W. C. Davis (D)	70,966	36.1
	W. Finnell (D)	19,320	9.8
	Charles C. McCall (D)	19,004	9.7

Second Choice Votes

	W. C. Davis (D)	10,673	25.8
	B. M. Miller (D)	9,994	24.2
	W. Finnell (D)	9,867	23.9
	Charles C. McCall (D)	6,467	15.7
	J. A. Carnley (D)	2,819	6.8
1934	Bibb Graves (D)	132,462	43.4
	Frank M. Dixon (D)	97,508	32.0
	Leon McCord (D)	75,208	24.6

Runoff

	Bibb Graves (D)	157,140	53.7
	Frank M. Dixon (D)	135,309	46.3
1938	Frank M. Dixon (D)	152,860	48.6
	Chauncey Sparks (D) [1]	74,554	23.7
	R. J. Goode (D)	70,287	22.4
1942	Chauncey Sparks (D)	145,798	52.2
	James E. Folsom (D)	73,306	26.2
	Chris J. Sherlock (D)	53,448	19.1
1946	James E. Folsom (D)	104,152	28.5
	Handy Ellis (D)	88,459	24.2
	Joe N. Poole (D)	70,925	19.4
	Elbert Boozer (D)	58,134	15.9
	Gordon Persons (D)	43,843	12.0

Runoff

	James E. Folsom (D)	205,168	58.7
	Handy Ellis (D)	144,126	41.3

	Candidates	Votes	%
1950	Gordon Persons (D)	137,055	34.1
	Philip J. Hamm (D) [2]	56,395	14.0
	Elbert Boozer (D)	48,021	11.9
	J. Bruce Henderson (D)	38,867	9.7
	Chauncey Sparks (D)	27,404	6.8
	Eugene (Bull) Connor (D)	20,629	5.1
	Robert K. (Buster) Bell (D)	20,171	5.0
1954	James E. Folsom (D)	305,384	51.4
	Jimmy Faulkner (D)	151,925	25.6
	Jim Allen (D)	61,530	10.4
	J. Bruce Henderson (D)	47,969	8.1
1958	John Patterson (D)	196,859	31.8
	George C. Wallace (D)	162,435	26.3
	Jimmy Faulkner (D)	91,512	14.8
	A. W. Todd (D)	59,240	9.6
	Laurie C. Battle (D)	38,955	6.3

Runoff

	John Patterson (D)	315,353	55.7
	George C. Wallace (D)	250,451	44.3
1962	George C. Wallace (D)	207,062	32.5
	Ryan deGraffenried (D)	160,704	25.2
	James E. Folsom (D)	159,640	25.1
	Macdonald Gallion (D)	80,374	12.6

Runoff

	George C. Wallace (D)	340,730	55.9
	Ryan deGraffenried (D)	269,122	44.1
1966	Lurleen B. Wallace (D)	480,841	54.1
	Richmond M. Flowers (D)	172,386	19.4
	Carl Elliott (D)	71,972	8.1
	Bob Gilchrist (D)	49,502	5.6
1970	Albert Brewer (D)	428,146	42.0
	George C. Wallace (D)	416,443	40.8
	Charles Woods (D)	149,887	14.7

Runoff

	George C. Wallace (D)	559,832	51.6
	Albert Brewer (D)	525,951	48.4
1974 [3]	George C. Wallace (D)	536,235	64.7
	Gene McLain (D)	249,695	30.1

Republican Primary

	Elvin McCary (R)		100.0

1. Sparks withdrew from the race May 11, 1938, declining a runoff with Dixon, who became the Democratic nominee.

2. Hamm withdrew May 12, 1950, declining a runoff with Persons, who became the Democratic nominee.

3. Returns from Elections Research Center, Washington, D.C. (The Elections Research Center, Richard M. Scammon, director, publishes the America Votes series.)

	Candidates	Votes	%
1978	Forrest (Fob) James (D)	256,196	*28.5*
	Bill Baxley (D)	210,089	*23.3*
	Albert Brewer (D)	193,479	*21.5*
	Sid McDonald (D)	143,930	*16.0*
	Jere Beasley (D)	77,202	*8.6*

Runoff

	Forrest (Fob) James (D)	515,520	*55.2*
	Bill Baxley (D)	418,932	*44.8*

Republican Primary

	Guy Hunt (R)	21,499	*83.2*
	Bert Hayes (R)	2,817	*10.9*
	Julian Elgin (R)	1,534	*5.9*
1982	George C. Wallace (D)	425,469	*42.5*
	George McMillan (D)	296,262	*29.6*
	Joe C. McCorquodale (D)	250,614	*25.1*

Runoff

	George C. Wallace (D)	512,203	*51.2*
	George McMillan (D)	488,444	*48.8*

Republican Primary

	Emory Folmar (R)		*100.0*

ARKANSAS

	Candidates	Votes	%
1920	Thomas C. McRae (D)	41,907	*26.9*
	Smead Powell (D)	32,263	*20.7*
	Thomas J. Terral (D)	29,303	*18.8*
	J. C. Floyd (D)	21,596	*13.9*
	G. R. Haynie (D)	16,747	*10.8*
1922	Thomas C. McRae (D)	127,728	*70.5*
	E. P. Toney (D)	53,572	*29.6*
1924	Thomas J. Terral (D)	54,533	*26.3*
	Lee Cazort (D)	43,466	*21.0*
	John E. Martineau (D)	35,438	*17.1*
	Jim G. Ferguson (D)	27,155	*13.1*
	Hamp Williams (D)	23,785	*11.5*
	Jacob R. Willson (D)	22,626	*10.9*
1926	John E. Martineau (D)	117,232	*53.5*
	Thomas J. Terral (D)	101,981	*46.5*
1928	Harvey J. Parnell (D)	94,207	*41.7*
	Brooks Hays (D)	57,497	*25.4*
	Thomas J. Terral (D)	34,476	*15.2*
	J. Carrol Cone (D)	31,786	*14.1*
1930	Harvey J. Parnell (D)	133,870	*54.2*
	Brooks Hays (D)	88,541	*35.8*
	J. C. Sheffield (D)	20,133	*8.2*
1932	J. Marion Futrell (D)	124,239	*44.0*
	Thomas J. Terral (D)	59,066	*21.0*
	A. B. Priddy (D)	37,134	*13.2*
	D. H. Blackwood (D)	33,147	*11.8*
1934	J. Marion Futrell (D)	167,917	*65.9*
	Howard Reed (D)	86,894	*34.1*
1936	Carl E. Bailey (D)	76,014	*32.0*
	Ed F. McDonald (D)	72,075	*30.3*
	R. A. Cook (D)	60,768	*25.6*
	Thomas J. Terral (D)	23,663	*10.0*
1938	Carl E. Bailey (D)	146,472	*51.5*
	R. A. Cook (D)	131,791	*46.3*

	Candidates	Votes	%
1940	Homer M. Adkins (D)	142,247	*56.2*
	Carl E. Bailey (D)	110,613	*43.7*
1942	Homer M. Adkins (D)	120,811	*71.8*
	Fred Keller (D)	44,304	*26.3*
1944	Ben Laney (D)	70,965	*38.6*
	J. Bryan Sims (D) [4]	63,454	*34.5*
	David L. Terry (D)	49,685	*27.0*
1946	Ben Laney (D)	125,444	*64.6*
	J. M. Malone (D)	63,601	*32.8*
1948	Sidney S. McMath (D)	87,829	*34.1*
	Jack Holt (D)	60,313	*23.4*
	James McKrell (D)	57,030	*22.1*
	Horace Thompson (D)	48,674	*18.9*

Runoff

	Sidney S. McMath (D)	157,137	*51.7*
	Jack Holt (D)	146,880	*48.3*
1950	Sidney S. McMath (D)	209,559	*64.0*
	Ben T. Laney (D)	112,651	*34.4*
1952	Sidney S. McMath (D)	100,858	*30.7*
	Francis Cherry (D)	91,195	*27.7*
	Tackett (D)	63,827	*19.4*
	Jack Holt (D)	45,233	*13.8*
	Murry (D)	27,937	*8.5*

Runoff

	Francis Cherry (D)	237,448	*63.1*
	Sidney S. McMath (D)	139,052	*36.9*
1954	Francis Cherry (D)	154,879	*47.7*
	Orval E. Faubus (D)	109,614	*33.8*
	Guy Jones (D)	41,249	*12.7*
	McMillan (D)	18,857	*5.8*

Runoff

	Orval E. Faubus (D)	191,328	*50.9*
	Francis Cherry (D)	184,509	*49.1*
1956	Orval E. Faubus (D)	180,760	*58.1*
	James Johnson (D)	83,856	*26.9*
	Jim Snoddy (D)	43,630	*14.0*
1958	Orval E. Faubus (D)	264,346	*68.9*
	Chris Finkbeiner (D)	60,173	*15.7*
	Lee Ward (D)	59,385	*15.5*

Republican Primary [5]

	George W. Johnson (R)	3,147	*72.7*
	Donald D. Layne (R)	1,273	*28.8*
1960	Orval E. Faubus (D)	238,997	*58.8*
	Joe C. Hardin (D)	66,499	*16.4*
	Bruce Bennett (D)	58,400	*14.4*
	H. E. Williams (D)	33,374	*8.2*

Republican Primary [6]

	Henry M. Britt (R)		*100.0*

4. Sims withdrew from a runoff, and Laney became the Democratic nominee.

5. Returns from Richard M. Scammon, *America Votes, 3* (Pittsburgh, 1959), p. 36.

6. Returns from Richard M. Scammon, *America Votes, 4* (Pittsburgh, 1962), p. 36.

	Candidates	Votes	%
1962	Orval E. Faubus (D)	208,996	*51.6*
	Sidney S. McMath (D)	83,473	*20.6*
	Dale Alford (D)	82,815	*20.4*
	Vernon H. Whitten (D)	22,377	*5.5*

Republican Primary [7]

	Candidates	Votes	%
	Willis Ricketts (R)		*100.0*
1964	Orval E. Faubus (D)	239,890	*65.7*
	Ervin Odell Dorsey (D)	69,638	*19.1*
	Joe Hubbard (D)	39,199	*10.7*

Republican Primary [8]

	Candidates	Votes	%
	Winthrop Rockefeller (R)		*100.0*
1966	James Johnson (D)	105,607	*25.1*
	Frank Holt (D)	92,711	*22.1*
	Brooks Hays (D)	64,814	*15.4*
	Dale Alford (D)	53,531	*12.7*
	Sam Boyce (D)	49,744	*11.8*
	Raymond Rebsamen (D)	35,607	*8.5*

Runoff

Candidates	Votes	%
James Johnson (D)	210,543	*51.9*
Frank Holt (D)	195,442	*48.1*

Republican Primary [9]

Candidates	Votes	%
Winthrop Rockefeller (R)	19,646	*98.5*

	Candidates	Votes	%
1968	Marion Crank (D)	106,092	*25.6*
	Virginia Johnson (D)	86,038	*20.7*
	Ted Boswell (D)	85,629	*20.6*
	Bruce Bennett (D)	65,095	*15.7*
	Frank Whitbeck (D)	61,758	*14.9*

Runoff

Candidates	Votes	%
Marion Crank (D)	215,087	*63.3*
Virginia Johnson (D)	124,880	*36.7*

Republican Primary [10]

Candidates	Votes	%
Winthrop Rockefeller (R)	27,913	*95.5*

	Candidates	Votes	%
1970	Orval E. Faubus (D)	156,578	*36.4*
	Dale Bumpers (D)	86,156	*20.0*
	Joe Purcell (D)	81,566	*18.9*
	Hayes C. McClerkin (D)	45,011	*10.5*
	Bill Wells (D)	32,543	*7.6*

Runoff

Candidates	Votes	%
Dale Bumpers (D)	259,780	*58.7*
Orval E. Faubus (D)	182,732	*41.3*

	Candidates	Votes	%
	Republican Primary [11]		
	Winthrop Rockefeller (R)	58,197	*96.8*
1972	Dale Bumpers (D)	330,088	*66.7*
	Q. Byrum Hurst (D)	81,239	*16.4*
	Mack Harbour (D)	55,172	*11.2*

Republican Primary [12]

Candidates	Votes	%
Len E. Blaylock (R)		*100.0*

	Candidates	Votes	%
1974 [13]	David Pryor (D)	297,673	*51.0*
	Orval E. Faubus (D)	193,105	*33.1*
	Bob Riley (D)	92,612	*15.9*

Republican Primary

Candidates	Votes	%
Ken Coon (R)	3,698	*81.9*
Joseph Weston (R)	815	*18.1*

	Candidates	Votes	%
1976	David Pryor (D)	312,865	*59.5*
	Jim Lindsey (D)	171,031	*32.5*
	Frank Lady (D)	36,832	*7.0*

Republican Primary

Candidates	Votes	%
Leon Griffith (R)	13,044	*57.2*
Joseph Weston (R)	9,753	*42.8*

	Candidates	Votes	%
1978	Bill Clinton (D)	341,118	*59.7*
	Joe D. Woodward (D)	123,674	*21.6*
	Frank Lady (D)	76,026	*13.1*

Republican Primary

Candidates	Votes	%
A. Lynn Lowe (R)		*100.0*

	Candidates	Votes	%
1980	Bill Clinton (D)	306,735	*68.9*
	Monroe A. Schwarzlose (D)	138,660	*31.1*

Republican Primary

Candidates	Votes	%
Frank D. White (R)	5,867	*71.8*
Marshall Chrisman (R)	2,310	*28.2*

	Candidates	Votes	%
1982	Bill Clinton (D)	236,961	*41.8*
	Joe Purcell (D)	166,066	*29.3*
	Jim Guy Tucker (D)	129,362	*22.8*

Runoff

Candidates	Votes	%
Bill Clinton (D)	239,209	*53.7*
Joe Purcell (D)	206,358	*46.3*

Republican Primary

Candidates	Votes	%
Frank D. White (R)	11,111	*83.2*
Marshall Chrisman (R)	1,410	*10.6*
Connie Voll (R)	826	*6.2*

7. *Returns from Richard M. Scammon,* America Votes, 5 *(Pittsburgh, 1964), p. 37.*

8. *Returns from Richard M. Scammon,* America Votes, 6 *(Washington, 1966), p. 40.*

9. *Returns from Richard M. Scammon,* America Votes, 7 *(Washington, 1968), p. 38.*

10. *Returns from Richard M. Scammon,* America Votes, 8 *(Washington, 1970), p. 32.*

11. *Returns from Richard M. Scammon,* America Votes, 9 *(Washington, 1972), p. 37.*

12. *Returns from Richard M. Scammon,* America Votes, 10 *(Washington, 1973), p. 48.*

13. *Returns from Elections Research Center, Washington, D.C.*

	Candidates	Votes	%
	Democratic Primary		
1984	Bill Clinton (D)	317,577	*64.4*
	Lonnie Turner (D)	119,266	*24.2*
	Kermit Moss (D)	31,727	*6.4*
	Republican Primary		
	Woody Freeman (R)	13,030	*68.4*
	Erwin Davis (R)	6,010	*31.2*

FLORIDA

	Candidates	Votes	%
1920	Cary E. Hardee (D)	52,591	*59.5*
	V. C. Swearingen (D)	30,240	*34.2*
	Lincoln Hulley (D)	5,591	*6.3*
	Second Choice Votes		
	Cary A. Hardee (D)	1,559	*51.7*
	V. C. Swearingen (D)	1,459	*48.3*
1924	John W. Martin (D)	55,715✔	*38.0*
	Sidney J. Catts (D)	43,230	*29.5*
	Frank E. Jennings (D)	37,962	*25.9*
	Worth W. Trammell (D)	8,381	*5.7*
	Second Choice Votes		
	John W. Martin (D)	17,339	*74.1*
	Sidney J. Catts (D)	6,067	*25.9*
1928	Doyle E. Carlton (D)	77,569✔	*30.4*
	Sidney J. Catts (D)	68,984	*27.1*
	Fons A. Hathaway (D)	67,849	*26.6*
	John S. Taylor (D)	37,304	*14.6*
	Second Choice Votes		
	Doyle E. Carlton (D)	28,471	*75.9*
	Sidney J. Catts (D)	9,066	*24.2*
1932	John W. Martin (D)	66,940	*24.2*
	David Sholtz (D)	55,406	*20.0*
	Cary A. Hardee (D)	50,427	*18.2*
	Stafford Caldwell (D)	44,938	*16.2*
	Charles M. Durrance (D)	36,291	*13.1*
	Runoff		
	David Sholtz (D)	173,540	*62.8*
	John W. Martin (D)	102,805	*37.2*
1936	Raleigh Pettaway (D)	51,705	*15.7*
	Fred P. Cone (D)	46,842	*14.3*
	William C. Hodges (D)	46,471	*14.1*
	Jerry W. Carter (D)	35,578	*10.8*
	B. F. Paty (D)	34,153	*10.4*
	Dan Chappell (D)	29,494	*9.0*
	Grady Burton (D)	24,985	*7.6*
	Peter Thomasello Jr. (D)	22,355	*6.8*
	Stafford Caldwell (D)	19,789	*6.0*
	Runoff		
	Fred P. Cone (D)	184,540	*58.8*
	Raleigh Pettaway (D)	129,150	*41.2*

	Candidates	Votes	%
1940	Spessard L. Holland (D)	118,962	*24.7*
	Francis P. Whitehair (D)	95,431	*19.8*
	Fuller Warren (D)	83,316	*17.3*
	B. F. Paty (D)	75,608	*15.7*
	W. B. Fraser (D)	36,855	*7.7*
	James Barbee (D)	33,699	*7.0*
	Runoff		
	Spessard L. Holland (D)	272,718	*57.0*
	Francis P. Whitehair (D)	206,158	*43.1*
1944	Millard F. Caldwell (D)	116,111	*28.6*
	Robert A. (Lex) Green (D)	113,300	*27.9*
	E. R. Graham (D)	91,174	*22.5*
	F. D. Upchurch (D)	30,524	*7.5*
	Raymond Sheldon (D)	27,940	*6.9*
	J. Edwin Baker (D)	27,028	*6.6*
	Runoff		
	Millard F. Caldwell (D)	215,485	*55.3*
	Robert A. (Lex) Green (D)	174,100	*44.7*
	Republican Primary		
	Bert L. Acker (R)	5,954	*61.3*
	Edward T. Keenan (R)	3,766	*38.7*
1948	Fuller Warren (D)	183,326	*32.7*
	Daniel T. McCarty (D)	161,788	*28.9*
	Colin English (D)	85,158	*15.2*
	W. A. Shands (D)	62,358	*11.1*
	J. Tom Watson (D)	51,505	*9.2*
	Runoff		
	Fuller Warren (D)	299,641	*52.0*
	Daniel T. McCarty (D)	276,425	*48.0*
	Republican Primary		
	Bert L. Acker (R)	10,807	*64.0*
	John L. Cogdill (R)	6,079	*36.0*
1952	Daniel T. McCarty (D)	316,427	*48.9*
	Brailey Odham (D)	232,565	*31.5*
	Alto Adams (D)	126,426	*17.1*
	Runoff		
	Daniel T. McCarty (D)	384,200	*53.3*
	Brailey Odham (D)	336,716	*46.7*
	Republican Primary [14]		
	Harry S. Swan (R)	11,148	*43.0*
	Bert L. Acker (R)	9,728	*37.5*
	Elmore F. Kitzmiller (R)	5,050	*19.5*
	Republican Runoff		
	Harry L. Swan (R)	10,217	*63.0*
	Bert L. Acker (R)	5,995	*37.0*

14. Returns from Florida Handbook, 1975-76, p. 534.

	Candidates	Votes	%
1954 [15]	**Special Primary**		
	Charley E. Johns (D)	255,787	38.4
	Leroy Collins (D)	222,791	33.4
	Brailey Odham (D)	187,782	28.2
	Special Runoff		
	Leroy Collins (D)	380,323	54.8
	Charley E. Johns (D)	314,198	45.2
	Republican Special Primary		
	J. Tom Watson (R)	24,429	68.0
	Charles E. Compton (R)	11,552	32.0
1956	Leroy Collins (D)	434,274	51.7
	Sumter L. Lowery (D)	179,019	21.3
	Farris Bryant (D)	110,469	13.2
	Fuller Warren (D)	107,990	12.9
	Republican Primary [16]		
	W. A. Washburn Jr. (R)		100.0
1960	Farris Bryant (D)	193,507	20.7
	Doyle E. Carlton Jr. (D)	186,228	19.9
	Haydon Burns (D)	166,352	17.8
	John M. McCarty (D)	144,750	15.5
	Fred Dickinson (D)	115,520	12.3
	Thomas E. David (D)	80,057	8.5
	Runoff		
	Farris Bryant (D)	512,757	55.2
	Doyle E. Carlton Jr. (D)	416,052	44.8
	Republican Primary [17]		
	George C. Peterson (R)	65,202	72.7
	Emerson H. Rupert (R)	24,484	27.3
1964	Haydon Burns (D)	312,453	27.5
	Robert King High (D)	207,280	18.3
	Scott Kelly (D)	205,078	18.1
	Fred Dickinson (D)	184,865	16.3
	John E. Mathews (D)	140,210	12.3
	Frederick B. Karl (D)	85,953	7.6
	Runoff		
	Haydon Burns (D)	648,093	58.2
	Robert King High (D)	465,547	41.8
	Republican Primary [18]		
	Charles R. Holley (R)	70,573	53.9
	H. B. Foster (R)	33,563	25.6
	Ken Folks (R)	26,815	20.5

	Candidates	Votes	%
1966	Haydon Burns (D)	372,451	35.4
	Robert King High (D)	338,281	32.1
	Scott Kelly (D)	331,580	31.5
	Runoff		
	Robert King High (D)	596,471	53.9
	Haydon Burns (D)	509,271	46.1
	Republican Primary [19]		
	Claude R. Kirk Jr. (R)	100,838	80.8
	Richard B. Muldrew (R)	23,953	19.2
1970	Earl Faircloth (D)	227,413	30.0
	Reubin Askew (D)	206,333	27.2
	John E. Matthews (D)	186,053	24.5
	Chuck Hall (D)	139,384	18.4
	Runoff		
	Reubin Askew (D)	447,025	57.7
	Earl Faircloth (D)	328,038	42.3
	Republican Primary [20]		
	Claude R. Kirk Jr. (R)	172,888	48.1
	Jack M. Eckerd (R)	137,731	38.4
	L. A. (Skip) Bafalis (R)	48,378	13.5
	Republican Runoff		
	Claude R. Kirk Jr. (R)	199,943	56.8
	Jack M. Eckerd (R)	152,327	43.2
1974 [21]	Reubin Askew (D)	597,137	68.8
	Ben Hill Griffin (D)	137,008	16.3
	Tom Adams (D)	85,557	10.2
	Republican Primary		
	Jerry Thomas (R)		100.0
1978	Robert L. Shevin (D)	364,732	35.2
	Robert Graham (D)	261,972	25.2
	Hans G. Tanzler (D)	124,706	12.0
	Jim Williams (D)	124,427	12.0
	Bruce A. Smathers (D)	85,298	8.2
	Claude R. Kirk Jr. (D)	62,534	6.0
	Runoff		
	Robert Graham (D)	482,535	53.5
	Robert L. Shevin (D)	418,636	46.5
	Republican Primary		
	Jack M. Eckerd (R)	244,394	63.8
	Louis Frey (R)	138,437	36.2

15. *Returns from Florida Handbook, 1975-76, p. 534.*
16. *Returns from Richard M. Scammon, America Votes, 2 (New York, 1958), p. 71.*
17. *Returns from Richard M. Scammon, America Votes, 4 (Pittsburgh, 1962), p. 77.*
18. *Returns from Richard M. Scammon, America Votes, 6 (Washington, 1966), p. 82.*

19. *Returns from Richard M. Scammon, America Votes, 7 (Washington, 1968), p. 81.*
20. *Returns from Richard M. Scammon, America Votes, 9 (Washington, 1972), p. 74.*
21. *Returns from Elections Research Center, Washington, D.C.*

1982	Candidates	Votes	%
	Robert Graham (D)	839,320	84.5
	Fred Kuhn (D)	93,078	9.4
	Robert P. Kunst (D)	61,136	6.2
	Republican Primary		
	L. A. (Skip) Bafalis (R)	325,108	86.4
	Vernon Davids (R)	51,340	13.6

GEORGIA

1920	Candidates	Votes	%
	Thomas W. Hardwick (D)	99,210	42.9
	Clifford M. Walker (D)	90,738	39.2
	John N. Holder (D)	37,957	16.4
	Runoff*		
	Thomas W. Hardwick (D)	84,257	55.3
	Clifford M. Walker (D)	68,234	44.8
1922	Clifford M. Walker (D)	123,784	58.1
	Thomas W. Hardwick (D)	86,389	40.6
1924	Clifford M. Walker (D)		100.0
1926	John N. Holder (D)	71,976	37.3
	Lamartine G. Hardman (D)	67,708	35.1
	George H. Carswell (D)	32,484	16.8
	J. O. Wood (D)	20,857	10.8
	Runoff*		
	Lamartine G. Hardman (D)	80,868	57.3
	John N. Holder (D)	60,197	42.7
1928	Lamartine G. Hardman (D)	137,430	58.5
	Eurith D. Rivers (D)	97,339	41.5
1930	Richard B. Russell (D)	56,177	27.3
	George H. Carswell (D)	51,851	25.2
	Eurith D. Rivers (D)	47,121	22.9
	John N. Holder (D)	44,318	21.5
	Runoff*		
	Richard B. Russell (D)	99,505	67.9
	George H. Carswell (D)	47,157	32.2
1932	Eugene Talmadge (D)	116,381	42.0
	Abit Nix (D)	78,588	28.4
	Thomas W. Hardwick (D)	35,252	12.7
	John N. Holder (D)	19,697	7.1
1934	Eugene Talmadge (D)	178,409	66.0
	Claude Pittman (D)	87,049	32.2
1936	Eurith D. Rivers (D)	233,503	60.0
	Charles D. Redwine (D)	123,095	31.6
	Blanton Fortson (D)	32,715	8.4
1938	Eurith D. Rivers (D)	160,459	51.1
	Hugh Howell (D)	134,121	42.7
	J. J. Mangham (D)	19,537	6.2

1940	Candidates	Votes	%
	Eugene Talmadge (D)	183,133	51.6
	Columbus Roberts (D)	127,653	36.0
	Abit Nix (D)	44,282	12.5
1942	Ellis Arnall (D)	174,757	57.7
	Eugene Talmadge (D)	128,394	42.4
1946	J. V. Carmichael (D)	313,389	45.3
	Eugene Talmadge (D) [22]	297,245	43.0
	Eurith D. Rivers (D)	69,489	10.0
1948	**Special Primary**		
	Herman E. Talmadge (D)	357,865	51.8
	M. E. Thompson (D)	312,035	45.1
1950	Herman E. Talmadge (D)	287,637	49.3
	M. E. Thompson (D)	279,137	47.9
1954	S. Marvin Griffin (D)	234,690	36.3
	M. E. Thompson (D)	162,007	25.1
	Tom Linder (D)	87,204	13.5
	Fred Hand (D)	78,125	12.1
	Charlie Gowen (D)	73,809	11.4
1958	S. Ernest Vandiver (D)	499,477	80.5
	William T. Bodenhamer (D)	87,830	14.2
	Lee Roy Abernathy (D)	33,099	5.3
1962	Carl E. Sanders (D)	494,978	58.1
	S. Marvin Griffin (D)	332,746	39.0
1966	Ellis Arnall (D)	231,480	29.4
	Lester Maddox (D)	185,672	23.6
	Jimmy Carter (D)	164,562	20.9
	James H. Gray (D)	152,973	19.4
	Garland T. Byrd (D)	39,994	5.1
	Runoff		
	Lester Maddox (D)	443,055	54.3
	Ellis Arnall (D)	373,004	45.7
1970	Jimmy Carter (D)	388,280	48.6
	Carl E. Sanders (D)	301,659	37.8
	C. B. King (D)	70,424	8.8
	Runoff		
	Jimmy Carter (D)	506,462	59.4
	Carl E. Sanders (D)	345,906	40.6
	Republican Primary [23]		
	Hal Suit (R)	62,868	58.5
	James L. Bentley (R)	40,251	37.4
1974 [24]	Lester Maddox (D)	310,384	36.3
	George Busbee (D)	177,997	20.8
	Bert Lance (D)	147,026	17.2
	David H. Gambrell (D)	66,000	7.7
	George T. Smith (D)	43,196	5.1

* In the Georgia primaries for the Democratic nomination for governor in 1920, 1926, 1930 and 1948, no candidate received a majority of the county unit votes. Thus, runoffs were necessary in each case between the two candidates who received the most county unit votes; these also happened to be the candidates who had the most popular votes.

In the runoffs, the candidate who achieved a county unit majority was the winner, regardless of whether he had a popular vote majority; but the county unit winner also finished first in the popular vote in each case. (For an explanation of the Georgia county unit system, see p. 1069.)

22. Under Georgia's county unit system, Talmadge actually won the primary easily even though he finished in second place in the popular vote. He received 244 county unit votes, 59.5 percent, to Carmichael's 144 votes, 35.1 percent. (Explanation of county unit system, p. 1069)

Talmadge later won the general election but died before his term was to begin, precipitating a famous crisis in Georgia's gubernatorial succession. (Footnote, p. 465)

23. Returns from Richard M. Scammon, America Votes, 9 (Washington, 1972), p. 81.

24. Returns from Elections Research Center, Washington, D.C.

Candidates	Votes	%
Runoff		
George Busbee (D)	551,106	59.9
Lester Maddox (D)	369,608	40.1
Republican Primary		
Ronnie Thompson (R)	19,691	41.0
Harold Dye (R)	10,912	22.7
George Lankford (R)	8,618	17.9
Harry Geisinger (R)	6,078	12.7
W. M. (Bill) Coolidge (R)	2,723	5.7
Republican Runoff		
Ronnie Thompson (R)	22,211	50.6
Harold Dye (R)	21,669	49.4

	Candidates	Votes	%
1978	George Busbee (D)	503,875	72.4
	Roscoe Emory Dean (D)	111,901	16.1
	J. B. Stoner (D)	37,654	5.4

Candidates	Votes	%
Republican Primary		
Rodney M. Cook (R)	23,231	87.3
Bud Herrin (R)	3,374	12.7

	Candidates	Votes	%
1982	Bo Ginn (D)	316,019	35.1
	Joe Frank Harris (D)	223,445	24.8
	Norman Underwood (D)	147,536	16.4
	Jack Watson (D)	114,533	12.7
	Billy Lovett (D)	62,341	6.9

Candidates	Votes	%
Runoff		
Joe Frank Harris (D)	500,765	55.0
Bo Ginn (D)	410,259	45.0
Republican Primary		
Bob Bell (R)	36,347	59.2
Ben Blackburn (R)	25,063	40.8

LOUISIANA

	Candidates	Votes	%
1920	John M. Parker (D)	77,868	54.2
	Frank P. Stubbs (D)	65,685	45.8
1924	Hewitt Bouanchaud (D)	84,162	35.1
	Henry L. Fuqua (D)	81,382	34.0
	Huey P. Long (D)	73,985	30.9

Candidates	Votes	%
Runoff		
Henry L. Fuqua (D)	125,880	57.8
Hewitt Bouanchaud (D)	92,006	42.2

	Candidates	Votes	%
1928	Huey P. Long (D)	126,842	43.9
	Riley J. Wilson (D) [25]	81,747	28.3
	O. H. Simpson (D)	80,326	27.8
1932	Oscar K. Allen (D)	214,699	56.5
	Dudley J. LeBlanc (D)	110,048	29.0
	George Seth Guion (D)	53,756	14.2

25. Wilson declined a runoff with Long, who became the Democratic nominee.

	Candidates	Votes	%
1936	Richard W. Leche (D)	362,502	67.1
	Cleveland Dear (D)	176,150	32.6
1940	Earl K. Long (D)	226,385	40.9
	Sam H. Jones (D)	154,936	28.0
	J. A. Noe (D)	116,564	21.1
	James H. Morrison (D)	48,243	8.7

Candidates	Votes	%
Runoff		
Sam H. Jones (D)	284,437	51.7
Earl K. Long (D)	265,403	48.3

	Candidates	Votes	%
1944	Jimmie H. Davis (D)	167,434	34.9
	Lewis L. Morgan (D)	131,682	27.5
	James H. Morrison (D)	76,081	15.9
	Dudley J. LeBlanc (D)	40,392	8.4
	Sam S. Caldwell (D)	34,335	7.2

Candidates	Votes	%
Runoff		
Jimmie H. Davis (D)	251,228	53.6
Lewis L. Morgan (D)	217,915	46.5

	Candidates	Votes	%
1948	Earl K. Long (D)	267,253	41.5
	Sam H. Jones (D)	147,329	22.9
	Robert F. Kennon (D)	127,569	19.8
	James H. Morrison (D)	101,754	15.8

Candidates	Votes	%
Runoff		
Earl K. Long (D)	432,528	65.9
Sam H. Jones (D)	223,971	34.1

	Candidates	Votes	%
1952	Carlos G. Spaht (D)	173,987	22.8
	Robert F. Kennon (D)	163,434	21.5
	Hale Boggs (D)	142,542	18.7
	James M. McLemore (D)	116,405	15.3
	William J. Dodd (D)	90,925	11.9
	Dudley J. LeBlanc (D)	62,906	8.3

Candidates	Votes	%
Runoff		
Robert F. Kennon (D)	482,302	61.4
Carlos G. Spaht (D)	302,743	38.6

	Candidates	Votes	%
1956	Earl K. Long (D)	421,681	51.4
	deLesseps S. Morrison (D)	191,576	23.4
	Frederick T. Preaus (D)	95,955	11.7
	Francis C. Grevemberg (D)	62,309	7.6
	James M. McLemore (D)	48,188	5.9
1959 [26]	deLesseps S. Morrison (D)	278,956	33.1
	Jimmie H. Davis (D)	213,551	25.3
	William M. Rainach (D)	143,095	17.0
	James A. Noe (D)	97,654	11.6
	William J. Dodd (D)	85,436	10.1

Candidates	Votes	%
Runoff		
Jimmie H. Davis (R)	487,681	54.1
deLesseps S. Morrison (D)	414,110	45.9
Republican Primary [27]		
F. C. Grevemberg (R)		100.0

26. The Democratic and Republican primaries were held Dec. 5, 1959; the Democratic runoff was held Jan. 9, 1960.

27. Returns from Richard M. Scammon, *America Votes, 4* (Pittsburgh, 1962), p. 162.

	Candidates	Votes	%
1963 [28]	deLesseps S. Morrison (D)	299,702	*33.1*
	John J. McKeithen (D)	157,304	*17.4*
	Gillis W. Long (D)	137,778	*15.2*
	Robert F. Kennon (D)	127,870	*14.1*
	Shelby M. Jackson (D)	103,949	*11.5*
	Runoff		
	John J. McKeithen (D)	492,905	*52.2*
	deLesseps S. Morrison (D)	451,161	*47.8*
	Republican Primary [29]		
	Charlton H. Lyons Sr. (R)		*100.0*
1967	John J. McKeithen (D)	836,304	*80.6*
	John R. Rarick (D)	179,846	*17.3*
1971	Edwin W. Edwards (D)	276,397	*23.5*
	J. Bennett Johnston (D)	208,830	*17.8*
	Gillis W. Long (D)	164,276	*14.0*
	Jimmie H. Davis (D)	138,756	*11.8*
	John G. Schwegmann (D)	92,072	*7.8*
	A. A. Aycock (D)	88,465	*7.5*
	Samuel Bell (D)	72,486	*6.2*
	Speedy O. Long (D)	61,359	*5.2*
	Runoff		
	Edwin W. Edwards (D)	584,262	*50.2*
	J. Bennett Johnston (D)	579,774	*49.8*
	Republican Primary [30]		
	David C. Treen (R)	9,732	*92.1*
	Robert Ross (R)	839	*7.9*
1975 [31]	Edwin W. Edwards (R)	750,107	*62.3*
	Robert C. Jones (D)	292,220	*24.3*
	Wade O. Martin (D)	146,368	*12.2*
1979 [31]	David C. Treen (R)	297,674	*21.8*
	Louis Lambert (D)	283,266	*20.7*
	James E. Fitzmorris (D)	280,760	*20.6*
	Paul Hardy (D)	227,026	*16.6*
	E. L. Henry (D)	135,769	*9.9*
	Edgar G. Mouton (D)	124,333	*9.1*

MISSISSIPPI

	Candidates	Votes	%
1919	Lee M. Russell (D)	48,348	*32.6*
	Oscar Johnston (D)	39,206	*26.4*
	A. H. Longino (D)	30,831	*20.8*
	Ross A. Collins (D)	30,026	*20.2*

28. The Democratic and Republican primaries were held Dec. 7, 1963; the Democratic runoff was held Jan. 11, 1964.

29. Returns from Richard M. Scammon, *America Votes, 6* (Washington, 1966), p. 166.

30. Returns from Richard M. Scammon, *America Votes, 10* (Washington, 1973), p. 160.

31. In 1975 Louisiana eliminated the partisan primary and instituted an open primary with candidates from all parties running on the same ballot. Any candidate who received a majority appeared in the general election unopposed. If no candidate received 50 percent, a runoff was held between the two top finishers. In 1979 there was a court-ordered recount of the votes for the top three candidates. Results were as follows: Treen: 297,469 votes, 34.6 per cent; Lambert: 282,708, 32.8; and Fitzmorris: 280,412, 32.6. Returns from Richard M. Scammon and Alice V. McGillivray, *America Votes, 14* (Washington, 1981), p. 181.

	Candidates	Votes	%
	Runoff		
	Lee M. Russell (D)	77,427	*52.7*
	Oscar Johnston (D)	69,565	*47.3*
1923	Henry L. Whitfield (D)	85,328	*33.6*
	Theodore G. Bilbo (D)	65,105	*25.6*
	Martin S. Conner (D)	48,739	*19.2*
	L. C. Franklin (D)	37,245	*14.7*
	Percey Bell (D)	17,724	*7.0*
	Runoff		
	Henry L. Whitfield (D)	134,715	*53.3*
	Theodore G. Bilbo (D)	118,143	*46.7*
1927	Theodore G. Bilbo (D)	135,065	*46.9*
	Dennis Murphree (D)	71,836	*25.0*
	Martin S. Conner (D)	57,402	*19.9*
	A. C. Anderson (D)	23,528	*8.2*
	Runoff		
	Theodore G. Bilbo (D)	153,669	*52.8*
	Dennis Murphree (D)	137,130	*47.2*
1931	Hugh L. White (D)	108,022	*34.5*
	Martin S. Conner (D)	92,089	*29.4*
	Paul B. Johnson (D)	58,668	*18.7*
	Mitchell (D)	54,202	*17.3*
	Runoff		
	Martin S. Conner (D)	170,690	*54.1*
	Hugh L. White (D)	144,918	*45.9*
1935	Paul B. Johnson (D)	111,523	*31.5*
	Hugh L. White (D)	110,825	*31.3*
	Dennis Murphree (D)	92,997	*26.2*
	Franklin (D)	34,700	*9.8*
	Runoff		
	Hugh L. White (D)	182,771	*51.7*
	Paul B. Johnson (D)	170,705	*48.3*
1939	Paul B. Johnson (D)	103,099	*33.5*
	Martin S. Conner (D)	79,305	*25.8*
	Thomas L. Bailey (D)	58,987	*19.2*
	Franklin (D)	31,845	*10.4*
	Snider (D)	24,244	*7.9*
	Runoff		
	Paul B. Johnson (D)	163,620	*54.7*
	Martin S. Conner (D)	135,724	*45.3*
1943	Martin S. Conner (D)	110,917	*38.8*
	Thomas L. Bailey (D)	68,963	*24.1*
	Dennis Murphree (D)	68,510	*24.0*
	Franklin (D)	37,240	*13.0*
	Runoff		
	Thomas L. Bailey (D)	143,153	*53.2*
	Martin S. Conner (D)	125,882	*46.8*
1947	Fielding L. Wright (D)	202,014	*55.3*
	Paul B. Johnson Jr. (D)	112,123	*30.7*
	Jesse M. Byrd (D)	37,997	*10.4*

	Candidates	Votes	%
1951	Hugh L. White (D)	94,820	*23.3*
	Paul B. Johnson Jr. (D)	86,150	*21.1*
	Sam Lumpkin (D)	84,451	*20.7*
	Ross R. Barnett (D)	81,674	*20.0*
	Mary D. Cain (D)	24,756	*6.1*
	Jesse M. Byrd (D)	22,783	*5.6*

Runoff

	Hugh L. White (D)	201,222	*51.2*
	Paul B. Johnson Jr. (D)	191,966	*48.8*

1955	Paul B. Johnson Jr. (D)	122,423	*28.1*
	James P. Coleman (D)	104,140	*23.9*
	Fielding L. Wright (D)	94,410	*21.6*
	Ross R. Barnett (D)	92,785	*21.3*
	Mary D. Cain (D)	22,469	*5.2*

Runoff

	James P. Coleman (D)	233,237	*55.6*
	Paul B. Johnson Jr. (D)	185,924	*44.4*

1959	Ross R. Barnett (D)	155,508	*35.3*
	Carroll Gartin (D)	151,043	*34.3*
	Charles L. Sullivan (D)	131,792	*29.9*

Runoff

	Ross R. Barnett (D)	230,557	*54.3*
	Carroll Gartin (D)	193,706	*45.7*

1963	Paul B. Johnson Jr. (D)	182,540	*38.5*
	James P. Coleman (D)	156,296	*33.0*
	Charles L. Sullivan (D)	132,321	*27.9*

Runoff

	Paul B. Johnson Jr. (D)	261,493	*57.3*
	James P. Coleman (D)	194,958	*42.7*

Republican Primary [32]

	Rubel L. Phillips (R)		*100.0*

1967	William Winter (D)	222,001	*32.5*
	John Bell Williams (D)	197,778	*28.9*
	James E. (Jimmy) Swan (D)	124,361	*18.2*
	Ross R. Barnett (D)	76,053	*11.1*
	William L. Waller (D)	60,090	*8.8*

Runoff

	John Bell Williams (D)	371,815	*54.5*
	William Winter (D)	310,527	*45.5*

Republican Primary [33]

	Rubel L. Phillips (R)		*100.0*

1971	Charles L. Sullivan (D)	288,219	*37.8*
	William L. Waller (D)	227,424	*29.8*
	James E. (Jimmy) Swan (D)	128,946	*16.9*

32. *Returns from Richard M. Scammon,* America Votes, 5 *(Pittsburgh, 1964), p. 225.*

33. *Returns from Richard M. Scammon.* America Votes, 7 *(Washington, 1968), p. 207.*

	Candidates	Votes	%
	Roy C. Adams (D)	45,445	*6.0*
	Ed Pittman (D)	38,170	*5.0*

Runoff

	William L. Waller (D)	389,952	*54.2*
	Charles L. Sullivan (D)	329,236	*45.8*

1975 [34]	William Winter (D)	286,652	*36.3*
	Cliff Finch (D)	253,829	*32.1*
	Maurice Dantin (D)	179,472	*22.7*
	John Arthur Eaves (D)	50,606	*6.4*

Runoff

	Cliff Finch (D)	442,865	*57.7*
	William Winter (D)	324,749	*42.3*

1979	Evelyn Gandy (D)	224,746	*30.5*
	William Winter (D)	183,944	*25.0*
	John A. Eaves (D)	143,411	*19.5*
	Jim Herring (D)	135,812	*18.4*

Runoff

	William Winter (D)	386,174	*56.6*
	Evelyn Gandy (D)	295,835	*43.4*

Republican Primary

	Gil Carmichael (R)	17,216	*53.1*
	Leon Bramlett (R)	15,236	*46.9*

1983	Evelyn Gandy (D)	316,304	*38.2*
	William A. Allain (D)	293,348	*35.4*
	Mike P. Sturdivant (D)	172,526	*21.0*

Runoff

	William A. Allain (D)	405,348	*52.4*
	Evelyn Gandy (D)	367,953	*47.5*

Republican Primary

	Leon Bramlett (R)		*100.0*

NORTH CAROLINA

	Candidates	Votes	%
1920	Cameron Morrison (D)	49,070	*38.3*
	O. Max Gardner (D)	48,983	*38.2*
	R. N. Page (D)	30,180	*23.5*

Runoff

	Cameron Morrison (D)	70,332	*53.5*
	O. Max Gardner (D)	61,073	*46.5*

1924	Angus Wilton McLean (D)	151,197	*64.4*
	Josiah W. Bailey (D)	83,573	*35.6*
1928	O. Max Gardner (D)		*100.0*
1932	J. C. B. Ehringhaus (D)	162,498	*42.8*
	R. T. Fountain (D)	115,127	*30.3*

34. *Returns from Mississippi Democratic State Committee.*

Candidates	Votes	%
Allen J. Maxwell (D)	102,032	*26.9*
Runoff		
J. C. B. Ehringhaus (D)	182,005	*51.9*
R. T. Fountain (D)	168,971	*48.1*
1936 Clyde R. Hoey (D)	193,972	*37.5*
Ralph McDonald (D)	189,504	*36.7*
A. H. Graham (D)	126,782	*24.5*
Runoff		
Clyde R. Hoey (D)	266,354	*55.4*
Ralph McDonald (D)	214,414	*44.6*
1940 J. Melville Broughton (D)	147,386	*31.4*
W. P. Horton (D) [35]	105,916	*22.6*
A. J. Maxwell (D)	102,095	*21.8*
Lee Gravely (D)	63,030	*13.4*
Thomas E. Cooper (D)	33,176	*7.1*
Republican Primary		
Robert H. McNeill (R)	13,190	*47.3*
Pritchard (R)	11,847	*42.7*
Hoffman (R)	2,773	*10.0*
1944 R. Gregg Cherry (D)	185,027	*57.5*
Ralph McDonald (D)	134,661	*41.9*
1948 Charles M. Johnson (D)	170,141	*40.2*
W. Kerr Scott (D)	161,293	*38.1*
R. Mayne Albright (D)	76,281	*18.0*
Runoff		
W. Kerr Scott (D)	217,620	*54.4*
Charles M. Johnson (D)	182,684	*45.6*
1952 William B. Ulmstead (D)	294,170	*52.1*
Hubert E. Olive (D)	265,675	*47.1*
1956 Luther H. Hodges (D)	401,082	*86.0*
Tom Sawyer (D)	29,248	*6.3*
Harry P. Stokely (D)	24,416	*5.2*
Republican Primary		
Kyle Hayes (R)		*100.0*
1960 Terry Sanford (D)	269,463	*41.3*
I. Beverly Lake (D)	181,692	*27.8*
Malcolm B. Seawell (D)	101,148	*15.5*
John D. Larkins (D)	100,757	*15.4*
Runoff		
Terry Sanford (D)	352,133	*56.1*
I. Beverly Lake (D)	275,905	*43.9*
Republican Primary [36]		
Robert L. Gavin (R)		*100.0*
1964 Richardson Preyer (D)	281,430	*36.6*
Dan K. Moore (D)	257,872	*33.5*

Candidates	Votes	%
I. Beverly Lake (D)	217,172	*28.2*
Runoff		
Dan K. Moore (D)	480,431	*62.1*
Richardson Preyer (D)	293,863	*38.0*
Republican Primary [37]		
Robert L. Gavin (R)	53,145	*83.3*
Charles W. Strong (R)	8,652	*13.6*
1968 Robert W. Scott (D)	337,368	*48.1*
J. Melville Broughton Jr. (D) [38]	233,924	*33.4*
Reginald A. Hawkins (D)	129,808	*18.5*
Republican Primary [39]		
James C. Gardner (R)	113,584	*72.7*
John L. Stikley (R)	42,483	*27.3*
1972 Hargrove (Skipper) Bowles Jr. (D)	367,433	*45.5*
H. P. (Pat) Taylor (D)	304,910	*37.7*
Reginald A. Hawkins (D)	65,950	*8.2*
Wilbur Hobby (D)	58,990	*7.3*
Runoff		
Hargrove (Skipper) Bowles Jr. (D)	336,034	*54.3*
H. P. (Pat) Taylor (D)	282,345	*45.7*
Republican Primary [40]		
James C. Gardner (R)	84,906	*49.8*
James E. Holshouser Jr. (R)	83,637	*49.0*
Republican Runoff		
James E. Holshouser Jr. (R)	69,916	*50.6*
James C. Gardner (R)	68,134	*49.4*
1976 James B. Hunt Jr. (D)	362,102	*53.4*
Edward M. O'Herron (D)	157,815	*23.2*
George Wood (D)	121,673	*17.9*
Republican Primary		
David T. Flaherty (R)	57,663	*49.8*
Coy C. Privette (R)	37,573	*32.4*
J. F. Alexander (R)	16,149	*13.9*
Republican Runoff		
David T. Flaherty (R)	45,661	*60.5*
Coy C. Privette (R)	29,810	*39.5*
1980 James B. Hunt Jr. (D)	524,844	*69.6*
Robert W. Scott (D)	217,289	*28.8*

35. *Horton declined a runoff with Broughton, who became the Democratic nominee.*

36. *Returns from Richard M. Scammon,* America Votes, 4 *(Pittsburgh, 1962), p. 306.*

37. *Returns from Richard M. Scammon,* America Votes, 6 *(Washington, 1966), p. 309.*

38. *J. Melville Broughton Jr. declined a runoff with Scott, who became the Democratic nominee.*

39. *Returns from Richard M. Scammon,* America Votes, 8 *(Washington, 1970), p. 288.*

40. *Returns from Richard M. Scammon,* America Votes, 10 *(Washington, 1973), p. 285.*

Candidates	Votes	%
Republican Primary		
I. Beverly Lake Jr. (R)	119,255	80.8
C. J. Carstens (R)	28,354	19.2
Democratic Primary		
1984 Rufus Edmisten (D)	295,051	30.9
H. Edward Knox (D)	249,286	26.1
D. M. Faircloth (D)	153,210	16.0
Thomas O. Gilmore (D)	82,299	8.6
James C. Green (D)	80,775	8.4
John Ingram (D)	75,248	7.9
Runoff		
Rufus Edmisten (D)	352,351	51.9
H. Edward Knox (D)	326,278	48.1
Republican Primary		
James G. Martin (R)	128,714	91.7
Ruby T. Hooper (R)	11,640	8.3

SOUTH CAROLINA

Candidates	Votes	%
1920 Robert A. Cooper (D)		100.0
1922 Coleman L. Blease (D)	77,798	44.8
Thomas G. McLeod (D)	65,768	37.9
George K. Laney (D)	23,164	13.4
Runoff		
Thomas G. McLeod (D)	100,114	53.8
Coleman L. Blease (D)	85,834	46.2
1924 [41] Thomas G. McLeod (D)	107,356	61.2
J. T. Duncan (D)	68,155	38.8
1926 John G. Richards (D)	44,806	25.8
Ibra C. Blackwood (D)	34,870	20.1
Edmund B. Jackson (D)	33,804	19.5
Carroll D. Nance (D)	16,970	9.8
George K. Laney (D)	13,386	7.7
Thomas H. Peeples (D)	10,636	6.1
D. A. G. Ouzts (D)	10,570	6.1
Runoff		
John G. Richards (D)	95,007	58.2
Ibra C. Blackwood (D)	68,224	41.8
1930 Olin D. Johnston (D)	58,653	24.9
Ibra C. Blackwood (D)	43,859	18.6
Lever (D)	39,477	16.8
Williams (D)	36,488	15.5
Keith (D)	28,780	12.2
Herbert (D)	17,102	7.3
Runoff		
Ibra C. Blackwood (D)	118,721	50.2
Olin D. Johnston (D)	117,752	49.8

Candidates	Votes	%
1934 Olin D. Johnston (D)	104,799	35.2
Coleman L. Blease (D)	85,795	28.9
Wyndham Manning (D)	55,767	18.8
Pearce (D)	36,328	12.2
Runoff		
Olin D. Johnston (D)	157,673	56.2
Coleman L. Blease (D)	122,876	43.8
1938 Burnet R. Maybank (D)	177,900	44.9
Wyndham Manning (D)	74,356	18.8
Coleman L. Blease (D)	60,823	15.4
Bennett (D)	47,882	12.1
Adams (D)	26,376	6.7
Runoff		
Burnet R. Maybank (D)	163,947	52.3
Wyndham Manning (D)	149,368	47.7
1942 Olin D. Johnston (D)	121,465	51.8
Manning (D)	113,014	48.2
1946 Strom Thurmond (D)	96,691	33.4
James C. McLeod (D)	83,464	28.9
Williams (D)	35,813	12.4
Taylor (D)	22,447	7.8
O'Neal (D)	16,574	5.7
Long (D)	16,503	5.7
Runoff		
Strom Thurmond (D)	144,420	57.0
James C. McLeod (D)	109,169	43.1
1950 James F. Byrnes (D)	248,069	71.6
Bates (D)	63,143	18.2
Pope (D)	29,622	8.6
1954 George Bell Timmerman Jr. (D)	185,541	61.3
Bates (D)	116,942	38.7
1958 Ernest F. Hollings (D)	158,159	41.9
Donald S. Russell (D)	132,099	35.0
William C. Johnston (D)	86,981	23.1
Runoff		
Ernest F. Hollings (D)	190,691	56.8
Donald S. Russell (D)	145,162	43.2
1962 Donald S. Russell (D)	199,619	60.8
Burnet R. Maybank (D)	103,015	31.4
A. W. Bethea (D)	17,251	5.3
1966 Robert E. McNair (D)		100.0
1970 John C. West (D)		100.0
1974 [42] Charles D. Ravenel (D)	107,345	33.6
William Jennings Bryan Dorn (D)	105,734	33.1
Earle E. Morris Jr. (D)	80,292	25.2
Runoff		
Charles D. Ravenel (D) [43]	186,985	54.8
William Jennings Bryan Dorn (D)	154,187	45.2

41. The New York Times of Aug. 28, 1924, provided the returns given for McLeod and Duncan. Gov. McLeod was renominated and subsequently re-elected to a second term.

42. Returns from Elections Research Center, Washington, D.C.

43. Charles D. Ravenel was ruled ineligible by the state Supreme Court because he did not meet the state's residency requirement for gubernatorial candidates. At a special state party convention, Dorn was designated to replace Ravenel as the Democratic candidate.

Candidates	Votes	%
Republican Primary		
James B. Edwards (R)	20,177	*57.7*
William C. Westmoreland (R)	14,777	*42.3*
1978 W. Brantley Harvey (D)	142,785	*37.5*
Richard Riley (D)	125,185	*32.9*
William Jennings Bryan Dorn (D)	112,793	*29.6*
Runoff		
Richard Riley (D)	180,882	*53.3*
W. Brantley Harvey (D)	158,665	*46.7*
Republican Primary		
Edward L. Young (R)	12,172	*51.4*
Raymond Finch (R)	11,499	*48.6*
1982 Richard Riley (D)		*100.0*
Republican Primary		
W. D. Workman (R)	17,128	*81.8*
Roddy T. Martin (R)	3,816	*18.2*

TENNESSEE

	Candidates	Votes	%
1920	Albert H. Roberts (D)	67,886	*59.6*
	W. R. Crabtree (D)	44,853	*39.4*
1922	Austin Peay (D)	63,940	*39.2*
	Benton McMillin (D)	59,922	*36.8*
	Harvey Hannah (D)	24,062	*14.8*
	L. E. Gwinn (D)	15,137	*9.3*
1924	Austin Peay (D)	125,031	*79.0*
	John R. Neal (D)	33,199	*21.0*
1926	Austin Peay (D)	96,545	*51.6*
	Hill McAlister (D)	88,488	*47.3*
1928	Henry H. Horton (D)	97,333	*44.7*
	Hill McAlister (D)	92,017	*42.3*
	Lewis S. Pope (D)	27,779	*12.8*
1930	Henry H. Horton (D)	144,990	*58.9*
	L. E. Gwinn (D)	101,285	*41.1*
1932	Hill McAlister (D)	116,020	*40.9*
	Lewis S. Pope (D)	106,450	*37.5*
	M. R. Patterson (D)	58,915	*20.8*
1934	Hill McAlister (D)	191,460	*58.3*
	Lewis S. Pope (D)	137,253	*41.8*
1936	Gordon Browning (D)	243,463	*68.0*
	Burgin E. Dossett (D)	109,170	*30.5*
1938	Prentice Cooper (D)	237,853	*59.5*
	Gordon Browning (D)	158,854	*39.7*
1940	Prentice Cooper (D)	240,427	*83.6*
	Dempster (D)	44,122	*15.3*
1942	Prentice Cooper (D)	171,259	*57.6*
	J. Ridley Mitchell (D)	124,037	*41.7*
1944	James N. McCord (D)	132,466	*87.4*
	John R. Neal (D)	11,659	*7.7*
	Republican Primary		
	John W. Kilgo (R)	33,979	*63.9*
	W. O. Lowe (R)	13,425	*25.2*
	H. C. Lowery (R)	3,681	*6.9*
1946	James N. McCord (D)	187,119	*59.8*
	Gordon Browning (D)	120,535	*38.5*

	Candidates	Votes	%
	Republican Primary		
	W. O. Lowe (R)	33,269	*100.0*
1948	Gordon Browning (D)	240,676	*55.8*
	James N. McCord (D)	183,948	*42.6*
	Republican Primary		
	Roy Acuff (R)	90,140	*80.6*
	Robert M. McMurry (R)	21,765	*19.5*
1950	Gordon Browning (D)	267,855	*55.7*
	Clifford R. Allen (D)	208,634	*43.4*
1952	Frank G. Clement (D)	302,491	*46.7*
	Gordon Browning (D)	245,166	*37.9*
	Clifford R. Allen (D)	75,269	*11.6*
1954	Frank G. Clement (D)	481,808	*68.2*
	Gordon Browning (D)	195,156	*27.6*
1958	Buford Ellington (D)	213,415	*31.1*
	Andrew T. Taylor (D)	204,629	*29.9*
	Edmund Orgill (D)	204,382	*29.8*
	Clifford R. Allen (D)	56,854	*8.3*
	Republican Primary [44]		
	Robert L. Peters (R)	18,323	*59.3*
	Hansell Proffitt (R)	12,565	*40.7*
1962	Frank G. Clement (D)	309,333	*42.5*
	P. R. Olgiati (D)	211,812	*29.1*
	William W. Farris (D)	202,813	*27.9*
	Republican Primary		
	Hubert D. Patty		*100.0*
1966	Buford Ellington (D)	413,950	*53.5*
	John J. Hooker (D)	360,105	*46.5*
1970	John J. Hooker (D)	261,580	*44.3*
	Stanley Snodgrass (D)	193,199	*32.7*
	Robert L. Taylor (D)	90,009	*15.3*
	Republican Primary [45]		
	Winfield Dunn (R)	81,475	*33.2*
	Maxey Jarman (R)	70,420	*28.7*
	William Jenkins (R)	50,910	*20.8*
	Claude Robertson (R)	40,547	*16.5*
1974 [46]	Ray Blanton (D)	148,062	*22.7*
	Jake Butcher (D)	131,412	*20.2*
	Tom Wiseman (D)	89,061	*13.7*
	Hudley Crockett (D)	86,852	*13.2*
	Franklin Haney (D)	84,155	*12.9*
	Stanley Snodgrass (D)	40,211	*6.2*
	Republican Primary		
	Lamar Alexander (R)	120,773	*48.5*
	Nat Winston (R)	90,980	*36.5*
	Dortch Oldham (R)	35,683	*14.3*
1978	Jake Butcher (D)	320,329	*40.9*

44. Returns from Richard M. Scammon, *America Votes, 3* (Pittsburgh, 1959), p. 392.

45. Returns from Richard M. Scammon, *America Votes, 9* (Washington, 1972), p. 320.

46. Returns from Elections Research Center, Washington, D.C.

Candidates	Votes	%
Bob Clement (D)	288,577	36.9
Richard Fulton (D)	122,101	15.6
Roger Murray (D)	40,871	5.2
Republican Primary		
Lamar Alexander (R)	230,922	86.0
Harold Sterling (R)	34,037	12.7

	Candidates	Votes	%
1982	Randy Tyree (D)	318,205	50.0
	Anna Belle Clement O'Brien (D)	254,500	40.0

Republican Primary		
Lamar Alexander (R)		100.0

TEXAS

	Candidates	Votes	%
1920	Joseph W. Bailey (D)	152,340	33.9
	Pat M. Neff (D)	149,818	33.3
	Robert E. Thomason (D)	99,002	22.0
	Ben F. Looney (D)	48,640	10.8

Runoff		
Pat M. Neff (D)	264,075	58.8
Joseph W. Bailey (D)	184,702	41.2

	Candidates	Votes	%
1922	Pat M. Neff (D)	318,000	53.9
	Fred S. Rogers (D)	195,941	33.2
	Harry T. Warner (D)	57,617	9.8
1924	F. D. Robertson (D)	193,508	27.5
	Miriam A. Ferguson (D)	146,424	20.8
	Lynch Davidson (D)	141,208	20.1
	T. W. Davidson (D)	125,011	17.8

Runoff		
Miriam A. Ferguson (D)	413,751	56.7
F. D. Robertson (D)	316,019	43.3

	Candidates	Votes	%
1926	Dan Moody (D)	409,732	49.9
	Miram A. Ferguson (D)	283,482	34.5
	Lynch Davidson (D)	122,449	14.9

Runoff		
Dan Moody (D)	495,723	64.7
Miriam A. Ferguson (D)	270,595	35.3

Republican Primary		
H. H. Haines (R)	11,215	73.4
E. P. Scott (R)	4,074	26.7

	Candidates	Votes	%
1928	Dan Moody (D)	442,080	59.9
	Louis J. Wardlaw (D)	245,508	33.3
1930	Miriam A. Ferguson (D)	242,959	29.2
	Ross S. Sterling (D)	170,754	20.5
	Clint C. Small (D)	138,934	16.7
	T. B. Love (D)	87,068	10.5
	James Young (D)	73,385	8.8
	Barry Miller (D)	54,652	6.6
	E. B. Mayfield (D)	54,459	6.5

Candidates	Votes	%
Runoff		
Ross S. Sterling (D)	473,371	55.2
Miriam A. Ferguson (D)	384,402	44.8
Republican Primary		
George C. Butte (R)	5,001	51.2
H. E. Exum (R)	2,773	28.4
John F. Grant (R)	1,800	18.4

	Candidates	Votes	%
1932	Miriam A. Ferguson (D)	402,238	41.8
	Ross S. Sterling (D)	296,383	30.8
	Tom F. Hunter (D)	220,391	22.9

Runoff		
Miriam A. Ferguson (D)	477,644	50.2
Ross S. Sterling (D)	473,846	49.8

	Candidates	Votes	%
1934	James V. Allred (D)	298,903	29.9
	Tom F. Hunter (D)	243,254	24.3
	C. C. McDonald (D)	207,200	20.7
	Clint C. Small (D)	125,324	12.5
	Edgar E. Witt (D)	62,476	6.2
	Maury Hughes (D)	58,815	5.9

Runoff		
James V. Allred (D)	499,343	52.1
Tom F. Hunter (D)	459,106	47.9

Republican Primary		
D. E. Waggoner (R)	13,043	100.0

	Candidates	Votes	%
1936	James V. Allred (D)	553,219	52.5
	Tom F. Hunter (D)	239,460	22.7
	F. W. Fischer (D)	145,877	13.9
	Roy Sanderford (D)	81,170	7.7
1938	W. Lee O'Daniel (D)	573,166	51.4
	Ernest O. Thompson (D)	231,630	20.8
	William McCraw (D)	152,278	13.7
	Tom F. Hunter (D)	117,634	10.6
1940	W. Lee O'Daniel (D)	645,646	54.3
	Ernest O. Thompson (D)	256,923	21.6
	Harry Hines (D)	119,121	10.0
	Miriam A. Ferguson (D)	100,578	8.5
	Jerry Sadler (D)	61,396	5.2
1942	Coke R. Stevenson (D)	651,218	68.5
	Hal H. Collins (D)	272,469	28.6
1944	Coke R. Stevenson (D)	696,586	84.6
	Minnie F. Cunningham (D)	48,039	5.8
1946	Beauford H. Jester (D)	443,804	38.2
	Homer P. Rainey (D)	291,282	25.0
	Grover Sellers (D)	162,431	14.0
	Jerry Sadler (D)	103,120	8.9
	John Lee Smith (D)	102,941	8.9

Runoff		
Beauford H. Jester (D)	701,018	66.3
Homer P. Rainey (D)	355,654	33.7

	Candidates	Votes	%
1948	Beauford H. Jester (D)	642,025	53.1
	Roger Q. Evans (D)	279,602	23.1
	Caso March (D)	187,658	15.5
1950	Allan Shivers (D)	829,730	76.4

	Candidates	Votes	%
1952	Caso March (D)	195,997	18.0
	Allan Shivers (D)	833,861	61.5
	Ralph Yarborough (D)	488,345	36.0
1954	Allan Shivers (D)	668,913	49.5
	Ralph Yarborough (D)	645,994	47.8

Runoff

	Allan Shivers (D)	775,088	53.2
	Ralph Yarborough (D)	683,132	46.9

1956	Price Daniel (D)	628,914	39.9
	Ralph Yarborough (D)	463,416	29.4
	W. Lee O'Daniel (D)	347,757	22.1
	J. Evetts Haley (D)	88,772	5.6

Runoff

	Price Daniel (D)	698,001	50.1
	Ralph Yarborough (D)	694,830	49.9

1958	Price Daniel (D)	799,107	60.7
	Henry B. Gonzalez (D)	245,969	18.7
	W. Lee O'Daniel (D)	238,767	18.1

Republican Primary [47]

	Edwin S. Mayer (R)		100.0

1960	Price Daniel (D)	908,992	59.5
	Jack Cox (D)	619,834	40.5
1962	John B. Connally (D)	431,498	29.8
	Don Yarborough (D)	317,986	22.0
	Price Daniel (D)	248,524	17.2
	Will Wilson (D)	171,617	11.9
	Marshall Formby (D)	139,094	9.6
	Edwin A. Walker (D)	138,387	9.6

Runoff

	John B. Connally (D)	565,174	51.2
	Don Yarborough (D)	538,924	48.8

Republican Primary [48]

	Jack Cox (R)	99,138	86.0
	Roy Whittenbury (R)	16,112	14.0

1964	John B. Connally (D)	1,125,884	69.1
	Don Yarborough (D)	471,411	28.9

Republican Primary [49]

	Jack Crichton (R)		100.0

1966	John B. Connally (D)	932,641	74.3
	Stanley C. Woods (D)	291,651	23.2

Republican Primary [50]

	T. E. Kennerly (R)		100.0

	Candidates	Votes	%
1968	Don Yarborough (D)	419,003	23.9
	Preston Smith (D)	389,564	22.3
	Waggoner Carr (D)	257,535	14.7
	Dolph Briscoe (D)	225,686	12.9
	Eugene Locke (D)	218,118	12.5
	John Hill (D)	154,908	8.9

Runoff

	Preston Smith (D)	767,490	55.3
	Don Yarborough (D)	621,226	44.7

Republican Primary [51]

	Paul W. Eggers (R)	65,501	62.5
	John R. Trice (R)	28,849	27.5
	Wallace Sisk (R)	10,415	10.0
1970	Preston Smith (D)		100.0

Republican Primary [52]

	Paul W. Eggers (R)	101,875	93.4
	Roger Martin (R)	7,146	6.6
1972	Dolph Briscoe (D)	963,397	43.9
	Frances Farenthold (D)	612,051	27.9
	Ben Barnes (D)	392,356	17.9
	Preston Smith (D)	190,709	8.7

Runoff

	Dolph Briscoe (D)	1,100,601	55.3
	Frances Farenthold (D)	889,544	44.7

Republican Primary [53]

	Henry C. Grover (R)	37,118	32.6
	Albert B. Fay (R)	24,329	21.3
	David Reagan (R)	20,119	17.6
	Tom McElroy (R)	19,559	17.2
	John Hall (R)	4,864	7.0

Republican Runoff

	Henry C. Grover (R)	37,842	66.4
	Albert B. Fay (R)	19,166	33.6
1974 [54]	Dolph Briscoe (D)	1,025,632	67.4
	Frances Farenthold (D)	437,287	28.7

Republican Primary

	Jim Granberry (R)	53,617	77.6
	Odell McBrayer (R)	15,484	22.4
1978	John Hill (D)	932,338	51.4
	Dolph Briscoe (D)	753,305	41.6
	Preston Smith (D)	92,088	5.1

47. Returns from Richard M. Scammon, America Votes, 3 *(Pittsburgh, 1959), p. 410.*

48. Returns from Richard M. Scammon, America Votes, 5 *(Pittsburgh, 1964), p. 403.*

49. Returns from Richard M. Scammon, America Votes, 6 *(Washington, 1966), p. 414.*

50. Returns from Richard M. Scammon, America Votes, 7 *(Washington, 1968), p. 392.*

51. Returns from Richard M. Scammon, America Votes, 8 *(Washington, 1970), p. 377.*

52. Returns from Richard M. Scammon, America Votes, 9 *(Washington, 1972), p. 332.*

53. Returns from Richard M. Scammon, America Votes, 10 *(Washington, 1973), p. 364.*

54. Returns from Elections Research Center, Washington, D.C.

Candidates	Votes	%
Republican Primary		
William P. Clements (R)	115,345	*72.8*
Ray Hutchison (R)	38,268	*24.2*

1982	Candidates	Votes	%
	Mark White (D)	592,210	*44.9*
	Buddy Temple [55] (D)	402,567	*30.5*
	Bob Armstrong (D)	261,940	*19.9*

Candidates	Votes	%
Republican Primary		
William P. Clements (R)	246,120	*92.6*
Lowell D. Embs (R)	19,731	*7.4*

VIRGINIA

	Candidates	Votes	%
1921	Elbert Lee Trinkle (D)	86,812	*57.5*
	Henry St. George Tucker (D)	64,286	*42.6*
1925	Harry F. Byrd (D)	107,317	*61.4*
	G. Walter Mapp (D)	67,579	*38.6*
1929	John Garland Pollard (D)	104,310	*75.5*
	G. Walter Mapp (D)	29,386	*21.3*
1933	George C. Peery (D)	116,837	*61.6*
	J. T. Deal (D)	40,268	*21.2*
	W. Worth Smith (D)	32,518	*17.2*
1937	James H. Price (D)	166,319	*86.1*
	Vivian L. Page (D)	26,955	*14.0*
1941	Colgate W. Darden Jr. (D)	105,655	*76.6*

55. Temple withdrew and no runoff was held. Returns from Richard M. Scammon and Alice V. McGillivray, *America Votes*, 15 *(Washington, 1983)*, p. 345.

	Candidates	Votes	%
	Vivian L. Page (D)	19,526	*14.2*
	Hudson Cary (D)	12,793	*9.3*
1945	William M. Tuck (D)	97,304	*70.1*
	Moss A. Plunkett (D)	41,484	*29.9*
1949	John S. Battle (D)	135,426	*42.8*
	Francis P. Miller (D)	111,697	*35.3*
	Horace H. Edwards (D)	47,435	*15.0*
	Remmie L. Arnold (D)	22,054	*7.0*
1953	Thomas B. Stanley (D)	150,499	*65.9*
	Charles R. Fenwick (D)	77,715	*34.1*
1957	J. Lindsay Almond Jr. (D)	119,307	*79.5*
	Howard H. Carwile (D)	30,794	*20.5*
1961	Albertis S. Harrison Jr. (D)	199,519	*56.7*
	A. E. S. Stephens (D)	152,639	*43.3*
1965	Mills E. Godwin Jr. (D)		*100.0*
1969	William C. Battle (D)	158,956	*38.9*
	Henry Howell (D)	154,617	*37.8*
	Fred G. Pollard (D)	95,057	*23.3*

Runoff		
William C. Battle (D)	226,108	*52.5*
Henry Howell (D)	207,505	*47.9*

1973 [56]			

1977 [57]	Henry Howell (D)	253,373	*51.4*
	Andrew P. Miller (D)	239,735	*48.6*

56. There were no candidates for the Democratic gubernatorial nomination in Virginia in 1973. Independent Henry Howell received the tacit support of the Democratic Party. See p. 532.

57. In subsequent years candidates were chosen by convention rather than through primaries.

Southern Senate Primary Returns, 1920-1984

ALABAMA

Candidates	Votes	%

Class 2

1920

Special Primary

J. Thomas Heflin (D)	49,554✔	37.9
White (D)	34,854	26.6
O'Neal (D)	33,174	25.4
Rushton (D)	13,232	10.1

Second Choice Votes

White (D)	12,699	36.5
J. Thomas Heflin (D)	11,062	31.8
Rushton (D)	7,316	21.0
O'Neal (D)	3,691	10.6

1924	J. Thomas Heflin (D)		100.0
1930	John H. Bankhead II (D)	102,462	63.9
	Fred I. Thompson (D)	57,809	36.1
1936	John H. Bankhead II (D)	178,500	81.1
	H. L. Anderton (D)	41,673	18.9
1942	John H. Bankhead II (D)		100.0

1946

Special Primary

John Sparkman (D)	85,049	50.1
James A. Simpson (D)	46,762	27.6
Frank W. Boykin (D)	35,982	21.2

1948	John Sparkman (D)	235,464	75.7
	Philip J. Hamm (D)	61,308	19.7
1954	John Sparkman (D)	323,877	58.3
	Laurie C. Battle (D)	208,166	37.4
1960	John Sparkman (D)	335,722	83.1
	John G. Crommelin Jr. (D)	51,571	12.8
1966	John J. Sparkman (D)	378,295	57.0
	Frank E. Dixon (D)	133,139	20.1
	John G. Crommelin Jr. (D)	114,622	17.3
	Mrs. Frank R. Stewart (D)	37,889	5.7
1972	John Sparkman (D)	331,818	50.3
	Melba T. Allen (D)	194,690	29.5
	Lambert C. Mims (D)	87,461	13.3

Republican Primary [1]

Winton M. (Red) Blount (R)	27,736	54.2
James D. Martin (R)	16,800	32.8
Bert Nettles (R)	5,765	11.3

1978	Howell Heflin (D)	369,270	43.3
	Walter Flowers (D)	236,894	27.8
	John Baker (D)	191,110	22.4

Candidates	Votes	%

Runoff

Howell Heflin (D)	556,685	64.9
Walter Flowers (D)	300,654	35.1

Republican Primary

James D. Martin (R) [2]		100.0

Democratic Primary

1984	Howell Heflin (D)	399,817	83.2
	Charles Wayne Borden (D)	47,462	9.9
	Mrs. Frank Ross Stewart (D)	33,114	6.9

Republican Primary

Albert Lee Smith Jr. (R)	27,304	61.8
Doug Carter (R)	8,067	18.3
Joseph Keith (R)	5,171	11.7
Clint Wilkes (R)	3,644	8.2

Class 3

1920	Oscar W. Underwood (D)	66,916	50.3
	Musgrove (D)	56,257	42.3
	Weakley (D)	9,766	7.4

Second Choice Votes

Weakley (D)	21,199	74.4
Musgrove (D)	5,172	18.2
Oscar W. Underwood (D)	2,129	7.5

1926	Hugo L. Black (D)	71,916✔	33.4
	John H. Bankhead II (D)	49,841	23.1
	Mayfield (D)	34,326	15.9
	Musgrove (D)	30,454	14.1
	Thomas E. Kilby (D)	29,123	13.5

Second Choice Votes

Mayfield (D)	16,668	24.9
John H. Bankhead II (D)	14,024	21.0
Hugo L. Black (D)	12,961	19.4
Musgrove (D)	12,598	18.9
Thomas E. Kilby (D)	10,587	15.8

1932	Hugo L. Black (D)	92,930	49.7
	Thomas E. Kilby (D)	57,875	30.9
	John Morgan Burns (D)	15,528	8.3
	Charles C. McCall (D)	11,376	6.1
	Henry L. Anderson (D)	9,467	5.1

Candidates	Votes	%
Runoff		
Hugo L. Black (D)	103,453	58.3
Thomas E. Kilby (D)	74,039	41.7

	Candidates	Votes	%
1938	**Special Primary**		
	Lister Hill (D)	90,601	61.8
	J. Thomas Heflin (D)	50,189	34.3
1938	Lister Hill (D)		100.0
1944	Lister Hill (D)	126,372	55.5
	James A. Simpson (D)	101,176	44.5
1950	Lister Hill (D)	✔	
1956	Lister Hill (D)	249,271	68.4
	John G. Crommelin Jr. (D)	115,440	31.7
1962	Lister Hill (D)	363,613	73.7
	Donald G. Hallmark (D)	72,855	14.8
	John G. Crommelin Jr. (D)	56,822	11.5
1968	James B. Allen (D)	224,483	41.9
	Armistead I. Selden (D)	190,283	35.5
	Bob Smith (D)	72,928	13.6
	James E. Folsom (D)	32,004	6.0
	Runoff		
	James B. Allen (D)	196,511	50.5
	Armistead I. Selden (D)	192,448	49.5
1974 [3]	James B. Allen (D)	572,584	82.8
	John Taylor (D)	118,848	17.2
1978	**Special Primary**		
	Maryon Pittman Allen (D)	334,758	44.6
	Donald W. Stewart (D)	259,795	34.6
	Ted Taylor (D)	70,894	9.4
	Dan Wiley (D)	66,689	8.9
	Special Runoff		
	Donald W. Stewart (D)	502,346	57.2
	Maryon Pittman Allen (D)	375,894	42.8
	Republican Special Primary		
	George Nichols (R) [4]	15,637	72.5
	Elvin McCary (R)	5,941	27.5
1980	Donald W. Stewart (D)	222,540	48.6
	Jim Folsom Jr. (D)	163,196	35.7
	Finis St. John (D)	51,260	11.2
	Runoff		
	Jim Folsom Jr. (D)	204,486	50.6
	Donald W. Stewart (D)	199,428	49.4
	Republican Primary		
	Jeremiah Denton (R)	73,708	63.8
	Armistead Selden (R)	41,825	36.2

1. Returns from Richard M. Scammon, America Votes, 10 (Washington, 1973), p. 28.

2. Martin withdrew after the primary to run for the short-term Senate seat. He was not replaced.

3. Returns from Elections Research Center, Washington, D.C. (The Elections Research Center, Richard M. Scammon, director, publishes the America Votes series.)

4. Nichols withdrew after the primary and James D. Martin was substituted by the state committee.

ARKANSAS

	Candidates	Votes	%
	Class 2		
1924	Joseph T. Robinson (D)		100.0
1930	Joseph T. Robinson (D)	167,167	76.6
	Tom W. Campbell (D)	51,085	23.4
1936	Joseph T. Robinson (D)	170,356	72.7
	Cleveland Holland (D)	42,541	18.2
	J. Rosser Venable (D)	21,352	9.1
1937	Carl E. Bailey (D) [5]		
1942	Jack Holt (D)	54,185	32.1
	John L. McClellan (D)	53,729	31.8
	Clyde Ellis (D)	34,264	20.3
	David D. Terry (D)	26,911	15.9
	Runoff		
	John L. McClellan (D)	134,277	61.7
	Jack Holt (D)	83,516	38.4
1948	John L. McClellan (D)		100.0
1954	John L. McClellan (D)		100.0
1960	John L. McClellan (D)		100.0
1966	John L. McClellan (D)	310,526	77.2
	Foster Johnson (D)	91,746	22.8
1972	John L. McClellan (D)	220,588	44.7
	David Pryor (D)	204,058	41.4
	Ted Boswell (D)	62,496	12.7
	Runoff		
	John L. McClellan (D)	242,983	52.0
	David Pryor (D)	224,262	48.0
	Republican Primary [6]		
	Wayne H. Babbitt (R)		100.0
1978	David Pryor (D)	198,039	34.3
	Jim Guy Tucker (D)	187,568	32.5
	Ray Thorton (D)	184,095	31.9
	Runoff		
	David Pryor (D)	265,525	54.9
	Jim Guy Tucker (D)	218,026	45.1
	Republican Primary		
	Tom Kelly (R)		100.0
	Democratic Primary		
1984	David Pryor (D)		100.0

Candidates	Votes	%
Republican Primary		
Ed Bethune (R)		*100.0*

Class 3

	Candidates	Votes	%
1920	Thaddeus H. Caraway (D)	92,411	*62.9*
	Charles F. Kirby (D)	54,527	*37.1*
1926	Thaddeus H. Caraway (D)		*100.0*
1932	Hattie W. Caraway (D)	127,702	*44.7*
	O. L. Bodenhamer (D)	63,858	*22.4*
	Vincent M. Miles (D)	30,423	*10.7*
	Charles H. Brough (D)	26,207	*9.2*
	William F. Kirby (D)	21,448	*7.5*
1938	Hattie W. Caraway (D)	145,472	*51.0*
	John L. McClellan (D)	134,708	*47.3*
1944	J. William Fulbright (D)	67,228	*36.2*
	Homer M. Adkins (D)	49,795	*26.8*
	T. H. Barton (D)	43,053	*23.2*
	Hattie W. Caraway (D)	24,881	*13.4*

Runoff		
J. William Fulbright (D)	117,121	*57.9*
Homer M. Adkins (D)	85,163	*42.1*

	Candidates	Votes	%
1950	J. William Fulbright (D)	189,200	*100.0*
1956	J. William Fulbright (D)		*100.0*
1962	J. William Fulbright (D)	253,751	*66.1*
	Winston G. Chandler (D)	129,987	*33.9*

Republican Primary [7]		
Kenneth G. Jones (R)		*100.0*

	Candidates	Votes	%
1968	J. William Fulbright (D)	220,684	*52.9*
	James Johnson (D)	132,038	*31.7*
	Bobby K. Hayes (D)	52,906	*12.7*

Republican Primary [8]		
Charles T. Bernard (R)		*100.0*

	Candidates	Votes	%
1974 [9]	Dale Bumpers (D)	380,748	*65.0*
	J. William Fulbright (D)	204,630	*35.0*

Republican Primary		
John H. Jones (R)		*100.0*

1980	Dale Bumpers (D)		*100.0*

Republican Primary		
Bill Clark (R)		*100.0*

5. *Robinson died July 14, 1937, a few months into his new six-year term. The state committee of the Democratic Party in Arkansas selected Gov. Carl E. Bailey as the Democratic nominee to run in an Oct. 19 special election; no Democratic primary was held. Bailey lost the special election to Rep. John E. Miller, a Democrat running as an Independent. (See p. 610)*

6. *Returns from Richard M. Scammon, America Votes, 10 (Washington, 1973), p. 48.*

7. *Returns from Richard M. Scammon, America Votes, 5 (Pittsburgh, 1964), p. 37.*

8. *Returns from Richard M. Scammon, America Votes, 8 (Washington, 1970), p. 32.*

9. *Returns from Elections Research Center, Washington, D.C.*

FLORIDA

	Candidates	Votes	%
	Class 1		
1922	Park Trammell (D)	59,232	*66.7*
	Albert W. Gilchrist (D)	29,527	*33.3*
1928	Park Trammell (D)	138,534	*58.0*
	John W. Martin (D)	100,454	*42.0*
1934	Park Trammell (D)	81,321	*38.0*
	Claude Pepper (D)	79,396	*37.1*
	Charles A. Mitchell (D)	30,455	*14.2*
	James F. Sikes (D)	14,558	*6.8*

Runoff		
Park Trammell (D)	103,028	*51.0*
Claude Pepper (D)	98,978	*49.0*

	Special Primary		
1936	Charles O. Andrews (D)	67,387	*51.9*
	Doyle E. Carlton (D)	62,530	*48.1*
1940	Charles O. Andrews (D)	179,195	*40.9*
	Jerry W. Carter (D)	80,869	*18.5*
	B. MacFadden (D)	71,487	*16.3*
	Fred P. Cone (D)	68,584	*15.7*
	Charles F. Coe (D)	33,463	*7.6*

Runoff		
Charles O. Andrews (D)	312,293	*69.4*
Jerry W. Carter (D)	137,641	*30.6*

	Candidates	Votes	%
1946	Spessard L. Holland (D)	204,352	*60.7*
	Robert A. (Lex) Green (D)	109,040	*32.4*
1952	Spessard L. Holland (D)	485,515	*84.2*
	William A. Gaston (D)	91,011	*15.8*
1958	Spessard L. Holland (D)	408,084	*55.9*
	Claude Pepper (D)	321,377	*44.1*

Republican Primary [10]		
Leland Hyzer (R)		*100.0*

1964	Spessard L. Holland (D)	676,014	*70.0*
	Brailey Odham (D)	289,454	*30.0*

Republican Primary [11]		
Claude R. Kirk Jr. (R)		*100.0*

1970	Farris Bryant (D)	240,222	*32.9*
	Lawton Chiles (D)	188,300	*25.8*
	Fred Schultz (D)	175,745	*24.1*
	Al Hastings (D)	91,948	*12.6*

Runoff		
Lawton Chiles (D)	474,420	*65.7*
Farris Bryant (D)	247,211	*34.3*

Republican Primary [12]		
William C. Cramer (R)	220,553	*62.5*
G. Harrold Carswell (R)	121,281	*34.4*

1976	Lawton Chiles (D)		*100.0*

Candidates	Votes	%
Republican Primary		
John Grady (R)	164,644	*54.5*
Walter Sims (R)	74,684	*24.7*
Helen S. Hansel (R)	62,718	*20.8*
Lawton Chiles (D)		*100.0*

1982

Candidates	Votes	%
Republican Primary		
Van B. Poole	154,158	*41.6*
David H. Bludworth	116,030	*31.3*
George Snyder	100,607	*27.1*
Runoff		
Van B. Poole	131,638	*58.1*
David H. Bludworth	95,024	*41.9*

Class 3

	Candidates	Votes	%
1920	Duncan U. Fletcher (D)	62,304	*71.4*
	Sidney J. Catts (D)	25,007	*28.6*
1926	Duncan U. Fletcher (D)	63,760	*59.5*
	Jerry W. Carter (D)	39,143	*36.5*
	Second Choice Votes		
	Jerry W. Carter (D)	932	*53.4*
	Duncan U. Fletcher (D)	812	*46.6*
1932	Duncan U. Fletcher (D)		*100.0*
1936	**Special Primary**		
	Claude Pepper (D)		*100.0*
1938	Claude Pepper (D)	242,350	*58.4*
	J. Mark Wilcox (D)	110,675	*26.7*
	David Sholtz (D)	52,785	*12.7*
1944	Claude Pepper (D)	194,445	*51.3*
	J. Ollie Edmunds (D)	127,158	*33.5*
	Millard B. Conklin (D)	33,317	*8.8*
	Republican Primary		
	Mlles H. Draper (R)	5,289	*53.3*
	H. K. Gibson (R)	4,628	*46.7*
1950	George A. Smathers (D)	387,215	*54.8*
	Claude Pepper (D)	319,754	*45.2*
1956	George A. Smathers (D)	614,663	*87.5*
	Erle Griffis (D)	87,525	*12.5*
1962	George A. Smathers (D)	587,562	*84.2*
	Roger L. Davis (D)	74,565	*10.7*
	Douglas Randolph Voorhees (D)	35,832	*5.1*
	Republican Primary [13]		
	Emerson H. Rupert (R)		*100.0*
1968	Leroy Collins (D)	426,096	*49.5*
	Earl Faircloth (D)	397,642	*46.2*
	Runoff		
	Leroy Collins (D)	410,689	*50.2*
	Earl Faircloth (D)	407,696	*49.8*

	Candidates	Votes	%
	Republican Primary [14]		
	Edward J. Gurney (R)	169,805	*80.0*
	Herman W. Goldner (R)	42,347	*20.0*
1974 [15]	William D. Gunter Jr. (D)	236,185	*29.8*
	Richard Stone (D)	157,301	*19.8*
	Richard A. Pettigrew (D)	146,728	*18.5*
	Mallory E. Horne (D)	90,684	*11.4*
	Glenn W. Turner (D)	51,326	*6.5*
	Runoff		
	Richard Stone (D)	321,683	*50.8*
	William D. Gunter Jr. (D)	311,044	*49.2*
	Republican Primary		
	Jack M. Eckerd (R)	186,897	*67.5*
	Paula Hawkins (R)	90,049	*32.5*
1980	Richard Stone (D)	355,287	*32.1*
	Bill Gunter (D)	335,859	*30.3*
	Buddy MacKay (D)	272,538	*24.6*
	Richard A. Pettigrew (D)	108,154	*9.8*
	Runoff		
	Bill Gunter (D)	594,676	*51.8*
	Richard Stone (D)	554,268	*48.2*
	Republican Primary		
	Paula Hawkins (R)	209,856	*48.1*
	Louis Frey (R)	119,834	*27.5*
	Ander Crenshaw (R)	54,767	*12.6*
	Republican Runoff		
	Paula Hawkins (R)	293,600	*61.6*
	Louis Frey (R)	182,911	*38.4*

10. *Returns from Richard M. Scammon,* America Votes, 3 *(Pittsburgh, 1959), p. 79.*

11. *Returns from Richard M. Scammon,* America Votes, 6 *(Washington, 1966), p. 82.*

12. *Returns from Richard M. Scammon,* America Votes, 9 *(Washington, 1972), p. 74.*

13. *Returns from Richard M. Scammon,* America Votes, 5 *(Pittsburgh, 1964), p. 81.*

14. *Returns from Richard M. Scammon,* America Votes, 8 *(Washington, 1970), p. 68.*

15. *Returns from Elections Research Center, Washington, D.C.*

GEORGIA

	Candidates	Votes	%
	Class 2		
1924	William J. Harris (D)	144,740	*65.7*
	Thomas W. Hardwick (D)	75,713	*34.3*
1930	William J. Harris (D)	162,169	*77.9*
	John M. Slaton (D)	46,095	*22.1*

	Candidates	Votes	%
1932	**Special Primary**		
	Richard B. Russell (D)	162,745	57.7
	Charles R. Crisp (D)	119,193	42.3
1936	Richard B. Russell (D)	256,154	65.5
	Eugene Talmadge (D)	134,695	34.5
1942	Richard B. Russell (D)	232,084	80.6
	Will D. Upshaw (D)	55,845	19.4
1948	Richard B. Russell (D)	703,048	100.0
1954	Richard B. Russell (D)	619,129	100.0
1960	Richard B. Russell (D)	560,256	100.0
1966	Richard B. Russell (D)	596,209	90.6
	Harry L. Hyde (D)	61,922	9.4
1972	David H. Gambrell (D)	225,470	31.5
	Sam Nunn (D)	166,035	23.2
	S. Ernest Vandiver (D)	147,135	20.5
	Hosea Williams (D)	46,153	6.4
	J. B. Stoner (D)	40,675	5.7
	Runoff		
	Sam Nunn (D)	334,670	54.2
	David H. Gambrell (D)	283,414	45.9
	Special Primary		
	David H. Gambrell (D)	258,216	34.3
	Sam Nunn (D)	170,689	22.7
	S. Ernest Vandiver (D)	151,908	20.2
	Hosea Williams (D)	45,613	6.1
	J. B. Stoner (D)	38,261	5.1
	Special Runoff		
	Sam Nunn (D)	326,186	52.1
	David H. Gambrell (D)	299,919	47.9
	Republican Primary [16]		
	Fletcher Thompson (R)	71,464	91.1
	Republican Special Primary [17]		
	Fletcher Thompson (R)	70,859	100.0
1978	Sam Nunn (D)	525,703	80.0
	Jack Dorsey (D)	71,223	10.8
	Republican Primary		
	John W. Stokes (R)	14,443	58.5
	Dean Parkison (R)	10,250	41.5
	Democratic Primary		
1984	Sam Nunn (D)	801,412	90.2
	Jim Boyd (D)	86,973	9.8
	Republican Primary		
	Mike Hicks (R)	27,547	41.1
	Kelly Stratton Brown (R)	26,657	39.7
	J. W. Tibbs Jr. (R)	12,849	19.2

	Candidates	Votes	%
	Republican Runoff		
	Mike Hicks (R)	16,987	67.1
	J. W. Tibbs Jr. (R)	8,336	32.9
	Class 3		
1920	Thomas Watson (D)	102,647	45.0
	Dorsey (D)	68,220	29.9
	Smith (D)	56,357	24.7
1922	**Special Primary**		
	Walter F. George (D)	60,436	54.6
	Thomas W. Hardwick (D)	36,328	32.9
	Wright (D)	12,820	11.6
1926	Walter F. George (D)	128,179	67.4
	Richard B. Russell (D)	61,911	32.6
1932	Walter F. George (D)		100.0
1938	Walter F. George (D)	141,235	44.0
	Eugene Talmadge (D)	103,075	32.1
	L. S. Camp (D)	76,778	23.9
1944	Walter F. George (D)	211,081	86.0
	John W. Goolsby (D)	34,465	14.0
1950	Walter F. George (D)	470,156	82.5
	Alex McLennan (D)	79,886	14.0
1956	Herman E. Talmadge (D)	498,327	80.3
	M. E. Thompson (D)	122,152	19.7
1962	Herman E. Talmadge (D)	673,782	88.0
	Henry M. Henderson (D)	91,664	12.0
1968	Herman E. Talmadge (D)	697,915	77.1
	Maynard H. Jackson Jr. (D)	207,171	22.9
	Republican Primary [18]		
	E. Earl Patton (R)	20,316	59.5
	Jack Sells (R)	13,805	40.5
1974	Herman E. Talmadge (D)	523,133	81.5
	Carlton Myers (D)	119,011	18.5
	Republican Primary		
	Jerry R. Johnson (R)		100.0
1980	Herman E. Talmadge (D)	432,215	42.0
	Zell Miller (D)	247,766	24.1
	Norman Underwood (D)	183,683	17.8
	Dawson Mathis (D)	133,729	13.0
	Runoff		
	Herman E. Talmadge (D)	559,615	58.6
	Zell Miller (D)	395,773	41.4
	Republican Primary		
	Mack Mattingly (R)	28,191	59.8
	E. J. Bagley (R)	6,082	12.9
	Hulon M. Madeley (R)	3,999	8.5
	Dean Parkison (R)	3,219	6.8
	Nick M. Belluso (R)	2,947	6.3
	J. W. Tibbs (R)	2,700	5.7

16. *Returns from Richard M. Scammon,* America Votes, 10 *(Washington, 1973), p. 88.*
17. *Returns from Elections Research Center, Washington, D.C.*
18. *Returns from Richard M. Scammon,* America Votes, 8 *(Washington, 1970), p. 79.*

LOUISIANA

Candidates	Votes	%
Class 2		
1924 Joseph E. Ransdell (D)	104,312	54.9
Lee E. Thomas (D)	85,547	45.1
1930 Huey P. Long (D)	149,640	57.3
Joseph E. Ransdell (D)	111,451	42.7
1936 [19] **Special Primary**		
Oscar K. Allen (D)	368,115	68.7
Frank J. Looney (D)	160,566	30.0
1936 Allen J. Ellender (D)	364,931	68.0
John N. Sandlin (D)	167,471	31.2
1942 Allen J. Ellender (D)	218,141	68.0
E. A. Stephens (D)	102,900	32.1
1948 Allen J. Ellender (D)	284,293	61.7
James Domengeaux (D)	119,459	25.9
Charles S. Gerth (D)	57,047	12.4
1954 Allen J. Ellender (D)	268,064	59.2
Frank B. Ellis (D)	162,775	35.9
1960 Allen J. Ellender (D)		100.0
Republican Primary [20]		
George W. Reese Jr. (R)	726	72.3
William Dane (R)	278	27.7
1966 Allen J. Ellender (D)	494,519	74.2
J. D. Deblieux (D)	94,154	14.1
Troyce E. Guice (D)	78,137	11.7
1972 J. Bennett Johnston (D)	623,078	79.4
Frank Tunney Allen (D)	88,198	11.2
Allen J. Ellender (D) [21]	73,088	9.3
Republican Primary [22]		
C. M. McLean (R)		100.0
1978 J. Bennett Johnston (D)	498,773	59.4
Louis (Woody) Jenkins (D)	340,896	40.6
Democratic Primary		
1984 J. Bennett Johnston Jr. (D)	838,181	100.0
Republican Primary		
Robert M. Ross (R)	86,546	62.1
Larry N. (Boo-ga-loo) Cooper (R)	52,746	37.8
Class 3		
1920 Edwin S. Broussard (D)	49,718	45.7
Jared Y. Sanders (D)	43,425	40.0
D. Caffery (D)	15,563	14.3
Second Choice Votes		
D. Caffery (D)	3,328	38.6
Edwin S. Broussard (D)	2,931	34.0
Jared Y. Sanders (D)	2,374	27.5
1926 Edwin S. Broussard (D)	84,041	51.1
Jared Y. Sanders (D)	80,562	48.9

Candidates	Votes	%
1932 John H. Overton (D)	181,464	59.2
Edwin S. Broussard (D)	124,935	40.8
1938 John H. Overton (D)		100.0
1944 John H. Overton (D)	151,886	61.6
E. A. Stephens (D)	68,408	27.8
Griffin T. Hawkins (D)	19,087	7.7
1948 **Special Primary**		
Russell B. Long (D)	264,143	51.0
Robert F. Kennon (D)	253,668	49.0
1950 Russell B. Long (D)	359,330	68.5
Malcolm E. LaFargue (D)	156,918	29.9
1956 Russell B. Long (D)		100.0
1962 Russell B. Long (D)	407,162	80.2
Philemon A. Stamant (D)	100,843	19.9
Republican Primary [23]		
Taylor W. O'Hearn (R)		100.0
1968 Russell B. Long (D)	494,467	87.0
Maurice P. Blanche (D)	73,791	13.0
Republican Primary [24]		
Richard H. Kilbourne (R)		100.0
1974 [25] Russell B. Long (D)	520,606	74.7
Sherman A. Bernard (D)	131,540	18.9
Annie Smart (D)	44,341	6.4
1980 Russell B. Long (D)	484,770	57.6
Louis (Woody) Jenkins (D)	325,922	38.8

19. Allen, the incumbent governor of Louisiana, died Jan. 28, 1936, just one week after winning the Democratic nomination for the Senate for the term ending Jan. 3, 1937. The Senate seat had been vacant since the assassination Sept. 10, 1935, of Sen. Huey P. Long, D (1932-35). The new governor appointed Long's widow, Rose McConnell Long, to the Senate seat and she took office Jan. 31, 1936. She was also designated the Democratic nominee to replace Allen in the April 20 special election, which she won without opposition. (See p. 618)

20. Returns from Richard M. Scammon, America Votes, 4 (Pittsburgh, 1962), p. 162.

21. Ellender died July 27, 1972, before the Aug. 19 primary in which he was a candidate for renomination to a seventh term. But Ellender's name remained on the ballot for the primary, which Johnston won without a runoff.

22. Returns from Richard M. Scammon, America Votes, 10 (Washington, 1973), p. 160. McLean withdrew from the race after the primary. The Republican state central committee substituted Ben C. Toledano as the candidate for the general election.

23. Returns from Richard M. Scammon, America Votes, 5 (Pittsburgh, 1964), p. 163.

24. Returns from Richard M. Scammon, America Votes, 8 (Washington, 1970), p. 157. Kilbourne withdrew from the race after the primary. The Republicans did not choose any substitute candidate, thus allowing Long to run unopposed in the November election.

25. Returns from Elections Research Center, Washington, D.C.

MISSISSIPPI

Candidates	Votes	%
Class 1		
1922 James K. Vardaman (D)	74,597	47.0
Hubert D. Stephens (D)	65,980	41.5
Bell Kearney (D)	18,303	11.5

Candidates	Votes	%
Runoff		
Hubert D. Stephens (D)	95,351	52.3
James K. Vardaman (D)	86,853	47.7
1928		
Hubert D. Stephens (D)	62,850	52.6
T. Webber Wilson (D)	56,641	47.4
1934 Hubert D. Stephens (D)	64,035	37.3
Theodore G. Bilbo (D)	63,752	37.2
Ross A. Collins (D)	42,209	24.6
Runoff		
Theodore G. Bilbo (D)	101,702	51.8
Hubert D. Stephens (D)	94,587	48.2
1940 Theodore G. Bilbo (D)	91,334	59.3
Hugh L. White (D)	62,641	40.7
1946 Theodore G. Bilbo (D)	97,820	51.0
Ellis (D)	58,005	30.2
Ross A. Collins (D)	18,875	9.8
Levings (D)	15,720	8.2
1952 John C. Stennis (D)	191,380	89.4
William P. Davis (D)	22,802	10.7
1958 John C. Stennis (D)		100.0
1964 John C. Stennis (D)	173,764	97.4
1970 John C. Stennis (D)		100.0
1976 John Stennis (D)	157,943	85.4
E. Michael Marks (D)	27,016	14.6
1982 John C. Stennis (D)	145,817	75.1
Charles Pittman (D)	33,651	17.3
Colon Johnston (D)	14,696	7.6
Republican Primary		
Haley Barbour (R)	30,636	74.2
Bobby Richard (R)	10,651	25.8

Class 2

	Candidates	Votes	%
1924	Pat Harrison (D)	80,371	82.1
	Earl Brewer (D)	17,496	17.9
1930	Pat Harrison (D)		100.0
1936	Pat Harrison (D)	128,729	65.5
	M. S. Conner (D)	65,296	33.2
1942	James O. Eastland (D)	50,112	37.6
	Wall Doxey (D)	37,756	28.3
	Ross A. Collins (D)	36,511	27.4
	Wall (D)	8,077	6.1
	Runoff		
	James O. Eastland (D)	74,747	56.8
	Wall Doxey (D)	56,748	43.2
1948	James O. Eastland (D)		100.0
1954	James O. Eastland (D)	136,836	62.0
	Carroll Gartin (D)	83,761	38.0
1960	James O. Eastland (D)	136,735	94.2
	Ance Blakeney (D)	8,397	5.8
1966	James O. Eastland (D)	240,171	83.1
	Clifton Whitley (D)	34,323	11.9
	Charles P. Mosby (D)	14,591	5.1

	Candidates	Votes	%
	Republican Primary [26]		
	Prentiss Walker (R)		100.0
1972	James O. Eastland (D)	203,847	70.2
	Taylor Webb (D)	67,656	23.3
	Louis Fondren (D)	18,753	6.5
	Republican Primary [27]		
	Gil Carmichael (R)	18,369	79.1
	James H. Meredith (R)	4,859	20.9
1978	Maurice Dantin (D)	102,968	27.2
	Cliff Finch (D)	98,751	26.1
	Charles Sullivan (D)	78,702	20.8
	William L. Waller (D)	74,465	19.7
	Runoff		
	Maurice Dantin (D)	235,904	65.3
	Cliff Finch (D)	125,109	34.7
	Republican Primary		
	Thad Cochran (R)	51,212	69.1
	Charles W. Pickering (R)	22,949	30.9
	Democratic Primary		
1984	William Winter (D)	88,883	69.5
	W. W. Easley III (D)	15,363	12.0
	William L. Gilbert (D)	13,843	10.8
	Billy Taylor (D)	9,786	7.6
	Republican Primary		
	Thad Cochran (R)		100.0

26. Returns from Richard M. Scammon, *America Votes, 7 (Washington, 1968), p. 212.*
27. Returns from Richard M. Scammon, *America Votes, 10 (Washington, 1973), p. 215.*

NORTH CAROLINA

Class 2

	Candidates	Votes	%
1924	Furnifold M. Simmons (D)		100.0
1930	Josiah W. Bailey (D)	200,242	60.2
	Furnifold M. Simmons (D)	129,875	39.0
	Republican Primary		
	George M. Pritchard (R)	22,287	56.9
	G. E. Butler (R)	9,098	23.2
	I. B. Tucker (R)	6,277	16.0
1936	Josiah W. Bailey (D)	247,365	52.5
	Richard T. Fountain (D)	184,197	39.1
	W. H. Griffin (D)	26,171	5.6
1942	Josiah W. Bailey (D)	211,038	65.8
	Richard T. Fountain (D)	94,581	29.5

	Candidates	Votes	%
1948	J. Melville Broughton (D)	207,981	*53.1*
	William B. Umstead (D)	183,865	*46.9*

Special Primary

	Candidates	Votes	%
	J. Melville Broughton (D)	206,605	*52.3*
	William B. Umstead (D)	188,420	*47.7*

1950	**Special Primary**		
	Frank P. Graham (D)	303,605	*49.1*
	Willis Smith (D)	250,222	*40.5*
	Robert R. Reynolds (D)	58,752	*9.5*

Special Runoff

	Candidates	Votes	%
	Willis Smith (D)	281,114	*51.8*
	Frank P. Graham (D)	261,789	*48.2*
1954	W. Kerr Scott (D)	312,053	*50.8*
	Alton Lennon (D)	286,730	*46.7*

1954	**Special Primary**		
	W. Kerr Scott (D)	274,674	*49.4*
	Alton Lennon (D)	264,265	*47.5*

1958 [28]	B. Everett Jordan (D)		
	Richard C. Clarke Jr. (R)		
1960	B. Everett Jordan (D)	324,188	*54.3*
	Addison Hewlett (D)	217,899	*36.5*
	Robert W. Gregory (D)	31,463	*5.3*

Republican Primary [29]

	Candidates	Votes	%
	Kyle Hayes (R)		*100.0*
1966	B. Everett Jordan (D)	445,454	*79.3*
	Hubert E. Seymour (D)	116,548	*20.7*

Republican Primary [30]

	Candidates	Votes	%
	John S. Shallcross (R)		*100.0*
1972	Nick Galifianakis (D)	377,993	*49.3*
	B. Everett Jordan (D)	340,391	*44.4*

Runoff

	Candidates	Votes	%
	Nick Galifianakis (D)	333,558	*55.5*
	B. Everett Jordan (D)	267,997	*44.6*

Republican Primary [31]

	Candidates	Votes	%
	Jesse Helms (R)	92,496	*60.1*
	James C. Johnson (R)	45,303	*29.5*
	William H. Booe (R)	16,032	*10.4*
1978	Luther H. Hodges Jr. (D)	260,868	*40.1*
	John Ingram (D)	170,715	*26.2*
	Lawrence Davis (D)	105,381	*16.2*
	McNeill Smith (D)	82,703	*12.7*

Runoff

	Candidates	Votes	%
	John Ingram (D)	244,469	*54.2*
	Luther H. Hodges Jr. (D)	206,223	*45.8*

Republican Primary

	Candidates	Votes	%
	Jesse Helms (R)		*100.0*

Democratic Primary

	Candidates	Votes	%
1984	James B. Hunt Jr. (D)	655,429	*77.5*
	Thomas L. Allred (D)	126,841	*15.0*
	Harrill Jones (D)	63,676	*7.5*

Republican Primary

	Candidates	Votes	%
	Jesse Helms (R)	134,675	*90.6*
	George Wimbish (R)	13,899	*9.4*

Class 3

	Candidates	Votes	%
1920	Lee S. Overman (D)	94,806	*79.9*
	A. L. Brooks (D)	23,869	*20.1*
1926	Lee S. Overman (D)	140,260	*60.4*
	Robert R. Reynolds (D)	91,914	*39.6*
1932	Robert R. Reynolds (D)	156,548	*42.5*
	Cameron Morrison (D)	143,179	*38.9*
	Bowie (D)	37,748	*10.2*
	Grist (D)	31,010	*8.4*

Runoff

	Candidates	Votes	%
	Robert R. Reynolds (D)	227,864	*65.4*
	Cameron Morrison (D)	120,428	*34.6*

Republican Primary

	Candidates	Votes	%
	Jake F. Newell (R)	29,906	*86.5*
	G. W. DePriest (R)	4,668	*13.5*
1938	Robert R. Reynolds (D)	315,316	*61.5*
	Frank Hancock (D)	197,154	*38.5*
1944	Clyde R. Hoey (D)	211,049	*68.9*
	Cameron Morrison (D)	80,154	*26.2*
1950	Clyde R. Hoey (D)		*100.0*
1954	Sam J. Ervin Jr. (D) [32]		
1956	Sam J. Ervin Jr. (D)	360,967	*84.6*
	Marshall C. Kurfees (D)	65,512	*15.4*

Republican Primary [33]

	Candidates	Votes	%
	Joel A. Johnson (R)		*100.0*
1962	Sam J. Ervin Jr. (D)		*100.0*

Republican Primary [34]

	Candidates	Votes	%
	Claude L. Greene Jr. (R)	31,756	*61.1*
	C. H. Babcock (R)	20,246	*38.9*
1968	Sam J. Ervin Jr. (D)	499,392	*78.3*
	Charles A. Pratt (D)	60,362	*9.5*
	John T. Gathings (D)	48,357	*7.6*

Candidates	Votes	%
Republican Primary [35]		
Robert V. Somers (R)	48,351	*36.6*
J. L. Zimmerman (R)	43,644	*33.1*
Edwin W. Tenney (R)	40,023	*30.3*
Republican Runoff		
Robert V. Somers (R)	8,816	*60.0*
J. L. Zimmerman (R)	5,734	*39.4*
1974 [36] Robert Morgan (D)	294,986	*50.4*
Nick Galifianakis (D)	189,815	*32.4*
Henry Hall Wilson (D)	67,247	*11.5*
Republican Primary		
William E. Stevens (R)	62,419	*65.1*
Wood Hall Young (R)	26,918	*28.1*
B. E. (Bee) Sweatt (R)	6,520	*6.8*
1980 Robert Morgan (D)		*100.0*
Republican Primary		
John P. East (R)		*100.0*

28. Sen. W. Kerr Scott (D 1954-58) died April 16, 1958. Jordan was appointed to succeed him. Jordan and Clarke were designated by the state committee of their respective parties to run in the Nov. 4 special election for the remaining two years of Scott's term. Jordan won. (See p. 626)

29. Returns from Richard M. Scammon, America Votes, 4 (Pittsburgh, 1962), p. 306.

30. Returns from Richard M. Scammon, America Votes, 7 (Washington, 1968), p. 296.

31. Returns from Richard M. Scammon, America Votes, 10 (Washington, 1973), p. 283.

32. Sen. Clyde R. Hoey (D 1945-54) died May 12, 1954. Ervin was appointed to replace him and was also named by the Democratic state executive committee to run in a Nov. 2 special election for the remaining two years of the term. (See p. 626)

33. Returns from Richard M. Scammon, America Votes, 2 (New York, 1958), p. 300.

34. Returns from Richard M. Scammon, America Votes, 5 (Pittsburgh, 1964), p. 303.

35. Returns from Richard M. Scammon, America Votes, 8 (Washington, 1970), p. 288.

36. Returns from Elections Research Center, Washington, D.C.

SOUTH CAROLINA

Candidates	Votes	%
Class 2		
1924 Coleman L. Blease (D)	83,738	*41.8*
James F. Byrnes (D)	67,727	*33.8*
Nathan B. Dial (D)	44,425	*22.2*
Runoff		
Coleman L. Blease (D)	100,686	*50.6*
James F. Byrnes (D)	98,465	*49.4*
1930 Coleman L. Blease (D)	111,989	*45.6*
James F. Byrnes (D)	94,242	*38.4*
Harris (D)	39,512	*16.1*

Candidates	Votes	%
Runoff		
James F. Byrnes (D)	120,755	*51.0*
Coleman L. Blease (D)	116,264	*49.1*
1936 James F. Byrnes (D)	257,247	*87.1*
Stoney (D)	25,672	*8.7*
1941 **Special Primary**		
Burnet R. Maybank (D)	59,017	*47.4*
Olin D. Johnston (D)	40,296	*32.4*
Bryson (D)	25,257	*20.3*
Special Runoff		
Burnet R. Maybank (D)	92,100	*56.6*
Olin D. Johnston (D)	70,687	*43.4*
1942 Burnet R. Maybank (D)	120,731	*51.4*
Eugene Blease (D)	114,241	*48.6*
1948 Burnet R. Maybank (D)	172,611	*51.6*
William Jennings Bryan Dorn (D)	83,068	*24.9*
Bennett (D)	45,068	*13.5*
Johnstone (D)	18,184	*5.4*
1954 Burnet R. Maybank (D) [37]		*100.0*
1956 **Special Primary**		
Strom Thurmond (D)		*100.0*
1960 Strom Thurmond (D)	273,795	*89.5*
R. B. Herbert (D)	32,136	*10.5*
1966 Bradley Morrah (D)	167,401	*55.9*
John B. Culbertson (D)	131,870	*44.1*
1972 Eugene N. Ziegler (D)	201,170	*58.7*
John B. Culbertson (D)	141,757	*41.3*
1978 Charles D. Ravenel (D)	205,348	*55.9*
John B. Culbertson (D)	69,184	*18.8*
James T. Triplett (D)	50,951	*13.9*
William T. McElveen (D)	41,550	*11.3*
Republican Primary		
Strom Thurmond (R)		*100.0*
Democratic Primary		
1984 Melvin Pervis Jr. (D)	149,730	*50.2*
Cecil J. Williams (D)	148,586	*49.8*
Republican Primary		
Strom Thurmond (R)	44,662	*94.3*
R. H. Cunningham (R)	2,693	*5.7*
Class 3		
1920 Ellison D. Smith (D)	57,423	*48.7*
George Warren (D)	36,272	*30.8*
W. P. Pollock (D)	15,678	*13.3*
W. C. Irby (D)	8,454	*7.2*
Runoff		
Ellison D. Smith (D)	65,880	*60.7*
George Warren (D)	42,735	*39.3*

TENNESSEE

	Candidates	Votes	%
1926	Ellison D. Smith (D)	72,015	*42.0*
	Edgar Brown (D)	65,331	*38.1*
	Nathan B. Dial (D)	34,114	*19.9*

Runoff

	Candidates	Votes	%
	Ellison D. Smith (D)	82,783	*51.6*
	Edgar Brown (D)	77,559	*48.4*
1932	Ellison D. Smith (D)	100,270	*37.0*
	Coleman L. Blease (D)	81,297	*30.0*
	Williams (D)	48,084	*17.7*
	Harris (D)	41,748	*15.4*

Runoff

	Candidates	Votes	%
	Ellison D. Smith (D)	150,468	*56.7*
	Coleman L. Blease (D)	114,840	*43.3*
1938	Ellison D. Smith (D)	186,519	*55.4*
	Olin D. Johnston (D)	150,437	*44.7*
1944	Olin D. Johnston (D)	138,440	*55.2*
	Ellison D. Smith (D)	88,045	*35.1*
	Daniel (D)	14,572	*5.8*
1950	Olin D. Johnston (D)	186,180	*54.0*
	Strom Thurmond (D)	158,904	*46.1*
1956	Olin D. Johnston (D)		*100.0*
1962	Olin D. Johnston (D)	210,918	*65.7*
	Ernest F. Hollings (D)	110,023	*34.3*

1966 Special Primary

	Candidates	Votes	%
	Ernest F. Hollings (D)	16,405	*60.8*
	Donald S. Russell (D)	126,595	*39.2*
1968	Ernest F. Hollings (D)	307,561	*78.3*
	John B. Culbertson (D)	85,219	*21.7*
1974 [38]	Ernest F. Hollings (D)		*100.0*

Republican Primary

	Candidates	Votes	%
	Gwenyfred Bush (R)		*100.0*
1980	Ernest F. Hollings (D)	266,796	*81.2*
	Nettie D. Dickerson (D)	34,720	*10.6*
	William P. Kreml (D)	27,049	*8.2*

Republican Primary

	Candidates	Votes	%
	Marshall T. Mays (R)	14,075	*42.6*
	Charles F. Rhodes (R)	11,395	*34.5*
	Robert K. Carley (R)	7,575	*22.9*

Republican Runoff

	Candidates	Votes	%
	Marshall T. Mays (R)	6,853	*64.8*
	Charles F. Rhodes (R)	3,717	*35.2*

---

37. Maybank had been renominated July 13, 1954, but died Sept. 1. Officials of the South Carolina Democratic Party, charged with replacing him on the ballot for the November general election, declined to order a new primary and selected state Sen. Edgar A. Brown as their candidate. He was defeated in the election by former governor Strom Thurmond (D 1947-51), who waged a successful write-in campaign.

38. Returns from Elections Research Center, Washington, D.C.

	Candidates	Votes	%

Class 1

	Candidates	Votes	%
1922	Kenneth D. McKellar (D)	102,692	*64.0*
	Fitzhugh (D)	47,627	*29.7*
	Cooper (D)	9,480	*5.9*
1928	Kenneth D. McKellar (D)	120,298	*63.3*
	Finis Garrett (D)	64,470	*33.9*
1934	Kenneth D. McKellar (D)	212,226	*84.0*
	John R. Neal (D)	40,463	*16.0*
1940	Kenneth D. McKellar (D)	230,033	*91.5*
	John R. Neal (D)	14,583	*5.8*
1946	Kenneth D. McKellar (D)	188,805	*62.0*
	Edward W. Carmack (D)	107,363	*35.2*

Republican Primary

	Candidates	Votes	%
	William B. Ladd (R)	30,954	*100.0*
1952	Albert Gore (D)	334,957	*56.5*
	Kenneth D. McKellar (D)	245,054	*41.4*
1958	Albert Gore (D)	375,439	*59.0*
	Prentice Cooper (D)	253,191	*39.8*

Republican Primary [39]

	Candidates	Votes	%
	Hobart F. Atkins (R)		*100.0*
1964	Albert Gore (D)	401,163	*84.7*
	Sam J. Galloway (D)	37,974	*8.0*

Republican Primary [40]

	Candidates	Votes	%
	Dan H. Kuykendall (R)		*100.0*
1970	Albert Gore (D)	269,770	*51.0*
	Hudley Crockett (D)	238,767	*45.2*

Republican Primary [41]

	Candidates	Votes	%
	Bill Brock (R)	176,703	*74.9*
	Tex Ritter (R)	54,401	*23.0*

1976 Democratic Primary

	Candidates	Votes	%
	James R. Sasser (D)	244,930	*44.2*
	John J. Hooker (D)	171,716	*31.0*
	Harry Sadler (D)	54,125	*9.8*
	David Bolin (D)	44,056	*8.0*
	Lester Kefauver (D)	29,864	*5.4*

Republican Primary

	Candidates	Votes	%
	William E. Brock (R)		*100.0*
1982	Jim Sasser (D)	511,059	*88.9*
	Charles G. Vick (D)	13,488	*11.1*

Republican Primary

	Candidates	Votes	%
	Robin L. Beard (R)	205,271	*91.4*
	William B. Thompson (R)	19,277	*8.6*

Class 2

	Candidates	Votes	%
1924	Lawrence D. Tyson (D)	72,496	*41.9*
	John K. Shields (D)	54,990	*31.8*
	Nathan L. Bachman (D)	44,946	*26.0*

	Candidates	Votes	%
1930	Cordell Hull (D)	140,802	*62.9*
	A. L. Todd (D)	79,649	*35.6*
	Special Primary		
	William E. Brock (D)	113,492	*70.7*
	John R. Neal (D)	47,110	*29.3*
1934	**Special Primary**		
	Nathan L. Bachman (D)	166,293	*57.9*
	Gordon Browning (D)	121,169	*42.2*
1936	Nathan L. Bachman (D)	217,531	*82.9*
	John R. Neal (D)	44,830	*17.1*
1938	**Special Primary**		
	A. Tom Stewart (D)	174,940	*49.3*
	George Berry (D)	101,966	*28.7*
	J. Ridley Mitchell (D)	70,393	*19.8*
1942	A. Tom Stewart (D)	136,415	*51.9*
	Edward W. Carmack (D)	116,841	*44.4*
1948	Estes Kefauver (D)	171,791	*42.4*
	A. Tom Stewart (D)	129,873	*32.1*
	John A. Mitchell (D)	96,192	*23.7*
	Republican Primary		
	B. Carroll Reece (R)	82,522	*81.7*
	Allen J. Strawbridge (R)	18,526	*18.3*
1954	Estes Kefauver (D)	440,497	*68.2*
	Pat Sutton (D)	186,363	*28.9*
1960	Estes Kefauver (D)	463,848	*64.6*
	Andrew T. Taylor (D)	249,336	*34.7*
	Republican Primary [42]		
	A. Bradley Frazier (R)	16,633	*58.8*
	Hansel Proffitt (R)	11,667	*41.2*
1964	**Special Primary**		
	Ross Bass (D)	330,213	*50.8*
	Frank G. Clement (D)	233,245	*35.9*
	M. M. Bullard (D)	86,718	*13.3*
	Republican Special Primary [43]		
	Howard H. Baker Jr. (R)	93,301	*85.0*
	Charles Moffett (R)	10,596	*9.6*
	Hubert D. Patty (R)	5,947	*5.4*
1966	Frank G. Clement (D)	384,322	*51.2*
	Ross Bass (D)	366,079	*48.8*
	Republican Primary [44]		
	Howard H. Baker Jr. (R)	112,617	*75.7*
	Kenneth Roberts (R)	36,043	*24.2*
1972	Ray Blanton (D)	292,249	*76.4*
	Don Palmer (D)	40,700	*10.6*

	Candidates	Votes	%
	Republican Primary [45]		
	Howard H. Baker Jr. (R)	242,373	*97.0*
1978	Jane Eskind (D)	196,156	*34.5*
	Bill Bruce (D)	170,795	*30.1*
	J. D. Lee (D)	89,939	*15.8*
	James Boyd (D)	48,458	*8.5*
	Republican Primary		
	Howard H. Baker Jr. (R)	205,680	*83.4*
	Harvey D. Howard (R)	21,154	*8.6*
	Democratic Primary		
1984	Albert Gore Jr. (D)	345,527	*100.0*
	Republican Primary		
	Victor Ashe (R)	145,774	*86.5*
	Jack McNeil (R)	17,970	*10.7*

39. Returns from *Richard M. Scammon, America Votes, 3* (Pittsburgh, 1959), p. 392.

40. Returns from *Richard M. Scammon, America Votes, 6* (Washington, 1966), p. 396.

41. Returns from *Richard M. Scammon, America Votes, 9* (Washington, 1972), p. 320.

42. Returns from *Richard M. Scammon, America Votes, 4* (Pittsburgh, 1962), p. 388.

43. Returns from *Richard M. Scammon, America Votes, 6* (Washington, 1966), p. 396.

44. Returns from *Richard M. Scammon, America Votes, 7* (Washington, 1968), p. 378.

45. Returns from *Richard M. Scammon, America Votes, 10* (Washington, 1973), p. 348.

TEXAS

	Candidates	Votes	%
	Class 1		
1922	Earle B. Mayfield (D)	153,538	*26.8*
	James E. Ferguson (D)	127,071	*22.2*
	Charles A. Culberson (D)	99,635	*17.4*
	Cullen F. Thomas (D)	88,026	*15.4*
	Clarence Ousley (D)	62,451	*10.9*
	Robert L. Henry (D)	41,567	*7.3*
	Runoff		
	Earle B. Mayfield (D)	273,308	*54.4*
	James E. Ferguson (D)	228,701	*45.6*
1928	Earle B. Mayfield (D)	200,246	*29.7*
	Tom Connally (D)	178,091	*26.4*
	Alvin Owsley (D)	131,755	*19.5*
	Thomas L. Blanton (D)	126,758	*18.8*
	Runoff		
	Tom Connally (D)	320,071	*55.4*
	Earle B. Mayfield (D)	257,747	*44.6*

	Candidates	Votes	%
1934	Tom Connally (D)	567,139	*58.8*
	J. W. Bailey (D)	355,963	*36.9*

Republican Primary

	Candidates	Votes	%
	U. S. Goen (R)	1,148	*100.0*

	Candidates	Votes	%
1940	Tom Connally (D)	923,219	*84.8*
	Guy B. Fisher (D)	98,125	*9.0*
	A. P. Belcher (D)	66,962	*6.2*
1946	Tom Connally (D)	823,818	*75.4*
	Floyd E. Ryan (D)	85,292	*7.8*
	Cyclone Davis (D)	74,252	*6.8*
	Terrell Sledge (D)	66,947	*6.1*
1952	Price Daniel (D)	940,770	*72.6*
	Lindley Beckworth (D)	285,842	*22.0*
	E. W. Napier (D)	70,132	*5.4*
1958	Ralph Yarborough (D)	761,511	*58.7*
	William A. Blakley (D)	535,418	*41.3*

Republican Primary [46]

	Candidates	Votes	%
	Roy Whittenburg (R)		*100.0*

	Candidates	Votes	%
1964	Ralph Yarborough (D)	904,811	*57.4*
	Gordon McLendon (D)	672,573	*42.6*

Republican Primary [47]

	Candidates	Votes	%
	George Bush (R)	62,985	*44.1*
	Jack Cox (R)	45,561	*31.9*
	Robert Morris (R)	28,279	*19.8*

Runoff

	Candidates	Votes	%
	George Bush (R)	49,751	*62.1*
	Jack Cox (R)	30,333	*37.9*

	Candidates	Votes	%
1970	Lloyd Bentsen (D)	816,641	*53.0*
	Ralph Yarborough (D)	724,122	*47.0*

Republican Primary [48]

	Candidates	Votes	%
	George Bush (R)	96,806	*87.6*
	Robert Morris (R)	13,654	*12.4*

1976	**Democratic Primary** [49]		
	Lloyd Bentsen (D)	970,983	*63.5*
	Phil Gramm (D)	427,597	*28.0*
	Hugh Wilson (D)	10,715	*7.2*

Republican Primary [49]

	Candidates	Votes	%
	Alan Steelman (R)	251,252	*70.5*
	Hugh Sweeney (R)	64,404	*18.1*
	Louis Leman (R)	40,651	*11.4*
1982	Lloyd Bentsen (D)	987,153	*78.1*
	Joe Sullivan (D)	276,314	*21.9*

Republican Primary

	Candidates	Votes	%
	James M. Collins (R)	152,469	*58.0*
	Walter H. Mengden (R)	91,780	*34.9*
	Don L. Richardson (R)	18,616	*7.1*

Class 2

	Candidates	Votes	%
1924	Morris Sheppard (D)	440,511	*64.8*
	Fred W. Davis (D)	159,663	*23.5*
	John F. Maddox (D)	80,070	*11.8*
1930	Morris Sheppard (D)	526,293	*71.1*
	Robert L. Henry (D)	174,260	*23.5*
	C. A. Mitchner (D)	40,130	*5.4*

Republican Primary

	Candidates	Votes	%
	Doran John Haesly (R)	3,645	*40.5*
	C. O. Harris (R)	2,784	*31.0*
	Harve H. Haines (R)	2,568	*28.5*
1936	Morris Sheppard (D)	616,293	*64.6*
	Joe H. Eagle (D)	136,718	*14.3*
	Guy B. Fisher (D)	89,215	*9.4*
1942	W. Lee O'Daniel (D)	475,541	*48.3*
	James Allred (D)	317,501	*32.3*
	Moody (D)	178,471	*18.1*

Runoff

	Candidates	Votes	%
	W. Lee O'Daniel (D)	451,359	*51.0*
	James Allred (D)	433,203	*49.0*
1948	Coke R. Stevenson (D)	477,077	*39.7*
	Lyndon B. Johnson (D)	405,617	*33.7*
	George Peddy (D)	237,195	*19.7*

Runoff

	Candidates	Votes	%
	Lyndon B. Johnson (D)	494,191	*50.0*
	Coke R. Stevenson (D)	494,104	*50.0*
1954	Lyndon B. Johnson (D)	883,264	*71.4*
	Dudley T. Dougherty (D)	354,188	*28.6*
1960	Lyndon B. Johnson (D)		*100.0*
1966	Waggoner Carr (D)	899,523	*79.9*
	John R. Willoughby (D)	226,598	*20.1*

Republican Primary [50]

	Candidates	Votes	%
	John Tower (R)		*100.0*

	Candidates	Votes	%
1972	Ralph Yarborough (D)	1,032,606	*50.0*
	Barefoot Sanders (D)	787,504	*38.1*
	Hugh Wilson (D)	125,460	*6.1*

Runoff

	Candidates	Votes	%
	Barefoot Sanders (D)	1,008,499	*52.1*
	Ralph Yarborough (D)	928,132	*47.9*

1972	**Republican Primary** [51]		
	John Tower (R)		*100.0*
1978	Robert Krueger (D)	853,460	*54.7*
	Joe Christie (D)	707,738	*45.3*

Republican Primary

	Candidates	Votes	%
	John Tower (R)		*100.0*

Democratic Primary

1984	Kent Hance (D)	456,446	*31.2*
	Lloyd Doggett (D)	456,173	*31.2*
	Robert Kreuger (D)	454,886	*31.1*

Democratic Runoff

Lloyd Doggett (D)	489,932	*50.0*
Kent Hance (D)	489,834	*50.0*

Democratic Runoff recount

Lloyd Doggett (D)	491,251	*50.1*
Kent Hance (D)	489,906	*50.0*

Republican Primary

Phil Gramm (R)	246,716	*73.2*
Ron Paul (R)	55,431	*16.4*
Rob Mosbacher (R)	26,279	*7.8*

46. *Returns from Richard M. Scammon,* America Votes, 3 *(Pittsburgh, 1959), p. 410.*
47. *Returns from Richard M. Scammon,* America Votes, 6 *(Washington, 1966), p. 414.*
48. *Returns from Richard M. Scammon,* America Votes, 9 *(Washington, 1972), p. 332.*
49. *Returns from Richard M. Scammon,* America Votes, 12 *(Washington, 1977), p. 361.*
50. *Returns from Richard M. Scammon,* America Votes, 7 *(Washington, 1968), p. 392.*
51. *Returns from Richard M. Scannon,* America Votes, 10 *(Washington, 1973), p. 365.*

VIRGINIA

Candidates	Votes	%

Class 1

1922	Claude A. Swanson (D)	102,045	*73.0*
	Davis (D)	37,671	*27.0*
1928	Claude A. Swanson (D)	✔	

1933	**Special Primary**		

	Harry F. Byrd (D)		*100.0*

1934	Harry F. Byrd (D)		*100.0*
1940	Harry F. Byrd (D)		*100.0*
1946	Harry F. Byrd (D)	141,923	*63.5*
	Martin A. Hutchinson (D)	81,605	*36.5*
1952	Harry F. Byrd (D)	216,438	*62.7*
	Francis Pickens Miller (D)	128,869	*37.3*
1958	Harry F. Byrd (D)		*100.0*
1964	Harry F. Byrd (D)		*100.0*

1966	**Special Primary**		

	Harry F. Byrd Jr. (D)	221,221	*51.0*
	Armistead L. Boothe (D)	212,996	*49.1*

1970 [52]	George C. Rawlings (D)	58,874	*45.7*
	Clive L. DuVal (D)	58,174	*45.1*
	Milton Colvin (D)	11,911	*9.2*
1976 [53]	Elmo R. Zumwalt (D)		*100.0*

Class 2

1920	**Special Primary**		

	Carter Glass (D)		*100.0*

1924	Carter Glass (D)		*100.0*
1930	Carter Glass (D)		*100.0*
1936	Carter Glass (D)		*100.0*
1942	Carter Glass (D)		*100.0*

1946	**Special Primary**		

	A. Willis Robertson (D)	✔	

1948	A. Willis Robertson (D)	80,340	*70.3*
	James P. Hart Jr. (D)	33,928	*29.7*
1954	A. Willis Robertson (D)		*100.0*
1960	A. Willis Robertson (D)		*100.0*
1966	William B. Spong Jr. (D)	216,885	*50.1*
	A. Willis Robertson (D)	216,274	*49.9*
1972	William B. Spong Jr. (D)		*100.0*

52. *DuVal did not request a runoff, so Rawlings became the Democratic nominee.*
53. *Following 1976, candidates were nominated by state party convention.*

Appendix

Sessions of the U.S. Congress, 1789-1985

Source: Official Congressional Directory

Congress	Session	Date of beginning[1]	Date of adjournment[2]	Length in days	President pro tempore of the Senate[3]	Speaker of the House of Representatives
1st	1	Mar. 4, 1789	Sept. 29, 1789	210	John Langdon of New Hampshire	Frederick A. C. Muhlenberg of Pennsylvania
	2	Jan. 4, 1790	Aug. 12, 1790	221		
	3	Dec. 6, 1790	Mar. 3, 1791	88		
2nd	1	Oct. 24, 1791	May 8, 1792	197	Richard Henry Lee of Virginia	Jonathan Trumbull of Connecticut
	2	Nov. 5, 1792	Mar. 2, 1793	119	John Langdon of New Hampshire	
3rd	1	Dec. 2, 1793	June 9, 1794	190	Langdon Ralph Izard of South Carolina	Frederick A. C. Muhlenberg of Pennsylvania
	2	Nov. 3, 1794	Mar. 3, 1795	121	Henry Tazewell of Virginia	
4th	1	Dec. 7, 1795	June 1, 1796	177	Tazewell Samuel Livermore of New Hampshire	Jonathan Dayton of New Jersey
	2	Dec. 5, 1796	Mar. 3, 1797	89	William Bingham of Pennsylvania	
5th	1	May 15, 1797	July 10, 1797	57	William Bradford of Rhode Island	Dayton
	2	Nov. 13, 1797	July 16, 1798	246	Jacob Read of South Carolina Theodore Sedgwick of Massachusetts	George Dent of Maryland[5]
	3	Dec. 3, 1798	Mar. 3, 1799	91	John Laurence of New York James Ross of Pennsylvania	
6th	1	Dec. 2, 1799	May 14, 1800	164	Samuel Livermore of New Hampshire Uriah Tracy of Connecticut	Theodore Sedgwick of Massachusetts
	2	Nov. 17, 1800	Mar. 3, 1801	107	John E. Howard of Maryland James Hillhouse of Connecticut	
7th	1	Dec. 7, 1801	May 3, 1802	148	Abraham Baldwin of Georgia	Nathaniel Macon of North Carolina
	2	Dec. 6, 1802	Mar. 3, 1803	88	Stephen R. Bradley of Vermont	
8th	1	Oct. 17, 1803	Mar. 27, 1804	163	John Brown of Kentucky Jesse Franklin of North Carolina	Macon
	2	Nov. 5, 1804	Mar. 3, 1805	119	Joseph Anderson of Tennessee	
9th	1	Dec. 2, 1805	Apr. 21, 1806	141	Samuel Smith of Maryland	Macon
	2	Dec. 1, 1806	Mar. 3, 1807	93		
10th	1	Oct. 26, 1807	Apr. 25, 1808	182	Smith	Joseph B. Varnum of Massachusetts

(Footnotes, p. 1111)

Congress	Session	Date of beginning[1]	Date of adjournment[2]	Length in days	President pro tempore of the Senate[3]	Speaker of the House of Representatives
	2	Nov. 7, 1808	Mar. 3, 1809	117	Stephen R. Bradley of Vermont	
					John Milledge of Georgia	
11th	1	May 22, 1809	June 28, 1809	38	Andrew Gregg of Pennsylvania	Varnum
	2	Nov. 27, 1809	May 1, 1810	156	John Gaillard of South Carolina	
	3	Dec. 3, 1810	Mar. 3, 1811	91	John Pope of Kentucky	
12th	1	Nov. 4, 1811	July 6, 1812	245	William H. Crawford of Georgia	Henry Clay of Kentucky
	2	Nov. 2, 1812	Mar. 3, 1813	122	Crawford	
13th	1	May 24, 1813	Aug. 2, 1813	71		Clay
	2	Dec. 6, 1813	Apr. 18, 1814	134	Joseph B. Varnum of Massachusetts	
	3	Sept. 19, 1814	Mar. 3, 1815	166	John Gaillard of South Carolina	Langdon Cheves of South Carolina[6]
14th	1	Dec. 4, 1815	Apr. 30, 1816	148	Gaillard	Henry Clay of Kentucky
	2	Dec. 2, 1816	Mar. 3, 1817	92	Gaillard	
15th	1	Dec. 1, 1817	Apr. 20, 1818	141	Gaillard	Clay
	2	Nov. 16, 1818	Mar. 3, 1819	108	James Barbour of Virginia	
16th	1	Dec. 6, 1819	May 15, 1820	162	John Gaillard of South Carolina	Clay
	2	Nov. 13, 1820	Mar. 3, 1821	111	Gaillard	John W. Taylor of New York[7]
17th	1	Dec. 3, 1821	May 8, 1822	157	Gaillard	Philip P. Barbour of Virginia
	2	Dec. 2, 1822	Mar. 3, 1823	92	Gaillard	
18th	1	Dec. 1, 1823	May 27, 1824	178	Gaillard	Henry Clay of Kentucky
	2	Dec. 6, 1824	Mar. 3, 1825	88	Gaillard	
19th	1	Dec. 5, 1825	May 22, 1826	169	Nathaniel Macon of North Carolina	John W. Taylor of New York
	2	Dec. 4, 1826	Mar. 3, 1827	90	Macon	
20th	1	Dec. 3, 1827	May 26, 1828	175	Samuel Smith of Maryland	Andrew Stevenson of Virginia
	2	Dec. 1, 1828	Mar. 3, 1829	93	Smith	
21st	1	Dec. 7, 1829	May 31, 1830	176	Smith	Stevenson
	2	Dec. 6, 1830	Mar. 3, 1831	88	Littleton Waller Tazewell of Virginia	
22nd	1	Dec. 5, 1831	July 16, 1832	225	Tazewell	Stevenson
	2	Dec. 3, 1832	Mar. 2, 1833	91	Hugh Lawson White of Tennessee	
23rd	1	Dec. 2, 1833	June 30, 1834	211	George Poindexter of Mississippi	Stevenson
	2	Dec. 1, 1834	Mar. 3, 1835	93	John Tyler of Virginia	John Bell of Tennessee[8]
24th	1	Dec. 7, 1835	July 4, 1836	211	William R. King of Alabama	James K. Polk of Tennessee
	2	Dec. 5, 1836	Mar. 3, 1837	89	King	
25th	1	Sept. 4, 1837	Oct. 16, 1837	43	King	Polk
	2	Dec. 4, 1837	July 9, 1838	218	King	
	3	Dec. 3, 1838	Mar. 3, 1839	91	King	
26th	1	Dec. 2, 1839	July 21, 1840	233	King	Robert M. T. Hunter of Virginia
	2	Dec. 7, 1840	Mar. 3, 1841	87		
27th	1	May 31, 1841	Sept. 13, 1841	106	Samuel L. Southard of New Jersey	John White of Kentucky
	2	Dec. 6, 1841	Aug. 31, 1842	269	Willie P. Mangum of North Carolina	
	3	Dec. 5, 1842	Mar. 3, 1843	89	Mangum	

(Footnotes, p. 1111)

Congress	Session	Date of beginning[1]	Date of adjournment[2]	Length in days	President pro tempore of the Senate[3]	Speaker of the House of Representatives
28th	1	Dec. 4, 1843	June 17, 1844	196	Mangum	John W. Jones of Virginia
	2	Dec. 2, 1844	Mar. 3, 1845	92	Mangum	
29th	1	Dec. 1, 1845	Aug. 10, 1846	253	David R. Atchison of Missouri	John W. Davis of Indiana
	2	Dec. 7, 1846	Mar. 3, 1847	87	Atchison	
30th	1	Dec. 6, 1847	Aug. 14, 1848	254	Atchison	Robert C. Winthrop of Massachusetts
	2	Dec. 4, 1848	Mar. 3, 1849	90	Atchison	
31st	1	Dec. 3, 1849	Sept. 30, 1850	302	William R. King of Alabama	Howell Cobb of Georgia
	2	Dec. 2, 1850	Mar. 3, 1851	92	King	
32nd	1	Dec. 1, 1851	Aug. 31, 1852	275	King	Linn Boyd of Kentucky
	2	Dec. 6, 1852	Mar. 3, 1853	88	David R. Atchison of Missouri	
33rd	1	Dec. 5, 1853	Aug. 7, 1854	246	Atchison	Boyd
	2	Dec. 4, 1854	Mar. 3, 1855	90	Jesse D. Bright of Indiana / Lewis Cass of Michigan	
34th	1	Dec. 3, 1855	Aug. 18, 1856	260	Jesse D. Bright of Indiana	Nathaniel P. Banks of Massachusetts
	2	Aug. 21, 1856	Aug. 30, 1856	10	Bright	
	3	Dec. 1, 1856	Mar. 3, 1857	93	James M. Mason of Virginia / Thomas J. Rusk of Texas	
35th	1	Dec. 7, 1857	June 14, 1858	189	Benjamin Fitzpatrick of Alabama	James L. Orr of South Carolina
	2	Dec. 6, 1858	Mar. 3, 1859	88	Fitzpatrick	
36th	1	Dec. 5, 1859	June 25, 1860	202	Fitzpatrick / Jesse D. Bright of Indiana	William Pennington of New Jersey
	2	Dec. 3, 1860	Mar. 3, 1861	93	Solomon Foot of Vermont	
37th	1	July 4, 1861	Aug. 6, 1861	34	Foot	Galusha A. Grow of Pennsylvania
	2	Dec. 2, 1861	July 17, 1862	228	Foot	
	3	Dec. 1, 1862	Mar. 3, 1863	93	Foot	
38th	1	Dec. 7, 1863	July 4, 1864	209	Foot / Daniel Clark of New Hampshire	Schuyler Colfax of Indiana
	2	Dec. 5, 1864	Mar. 3, 1865	89	Clark	
39th	1	Dec. 4, 1865	July 28, 1866	237	Lafayette S. Foster of Connecticut	Colfax
	2	Dec. 3, 1866	Mar. 3, 1867	91	Benjamin F. Wade of Ohio	
40th	1	Mar. 4, 1867[9]	Dec. 2, 1867	274	Wade	Colfax
	2	Dec. 2, 1867[10]	Nov. 10, 1868	345	Wade	
	3	Dec. 7, 1868	Mar. 3, 1869	87	Wade	Theodore M. Pomeroy of New York
41st	1	Mar. 4, 1869	Apr. 10, 1869	38	Henry B. Anthony of Rhode Island	James G. Blaine of Maine
	2	Dec. 6, 1869	July 15, 1870	222	Anthony	
	3	Dec. 5, 1870	Mar. 3, 1871	89	Anthony	
42nd	1	Mar. 4, 1871	Apr. 20, 1871	48	Anthony	Blaine
	2	Dec. 4, 1871	June 10, 1872	190	Anthony	
	3	Dec. 2, 1872	Mar. 3, 1873	92	Anthony	
43rd	1	Dec. 1, 1873	June 23, 1874	204	Matthew H. Carpenter of Wisconsin	Blaine
	2	Dec. 7, 1874	Mar. 3, 1875	87	Carpenter / Henry B. Anthony of Rhode Island	

(Footnotes, p. 1111)

Congress	Session	Date of beginning[1]	Date of adjournment[2]	Length in days	President pro tempore of the Senate[3]	Speaker of the House of Representatives
44th	1	Dec. 6, 1875	Aug. 15, 1876	254	Thomas W. Ferry of Michican	Michael C. Kerr of Indiana[12] Samuel S. Cox of New York, pro tempore[12] Milton Sayler of Ohio, pro tempore
	2	Dec. 4, 1876	Mar. 3, 1877	90	Ferry	Samuel J. Randall of Pennsylvania
45th	1	Oct. 15, 1877	Dec. 3, 1877	50	Ferry	Randall
	2	Dec. 3, 1877	June 20, 1878	200	Ferry	
	3	Dec. 2, 1878	Mar. 3, 1879	92	Ferry	
46th	1	Mar. 18, 1879	July 1, 1879	106	Allen G. Thurman of Ohio	Randall
	2	Dec. 1, 1879	June 16, 1880	199	Thurman	
	3	Dec. 6, 1880	Mar. 3, 1881	88	Thurman	
47th	1	Dec. 5, 1881	Aug. 8, 1882	247	Thomas F. Bayard of Delaware David Davis of Illinois	J. Warren Keifer of Ohio
	2	Dec. 4, 1882	Mar. 3, 1883	90	George F. Edmunds of Vermont	
48th	1	Dec. 3, 1883	July 7, 1884	218	Edmunds	John G. Carlisle of Kentucky
	2	Dec. 1, 1884	Mar. 3, 1885	93	Edmunds	
49th	1	Dec. 7, 1885	Aug. 5, 1886	242	John Sherman of Ohio	Carlisle
	2	Dec. 6, 1886	Mar. 3, 1887	88	John J. Ingalls of Kansas	
50th	1	Dec. 5, 1887	Oct. 20, 1888	321	Ingalls	Carlisle
	2	Dec. 3, 1888	Mar. 3, 1889	91	Ingalls	
51st	1	Dec. 2, 1889	Oct. 1, 1890	304	Ingalls	Thomas B. Reed of Maine
	2	Dec. 1, 1890	Mar. 3, 1891	93	Charles F. Manderson of Nebraska	
52nd	1	Dec. 7, 1891	Aug. 5, 1892	251	Manderson	Charles F. Crisp of Georgia
	2	Dec. 5, 1892	Mar. 3, 1893	89	Isham G. Harris of Tennessee	
53rd	1	Aug. 7, 1893	Nov. 3, 1893	89	Harris	Crisp
	2	Dec. 4, 1893	Aug. 28, 1894	268	Harris	
	3	Dec. 3, 1894	Mar. 3, 1895	97	Matt W. Ransom of North Carolina Isham G. Harris of Tennessee	
54th	1	Dec. 2, 1895	June 11, 1896	193	William P. Frye of Maine	Thomas B. Reed of Maine
	2	Dec. 7, 1896	Mar. 3, 1897	87	Frye	
55th	1	Mar. 15, 1897	July 24, 1897	131	Frye	Reed
	2	Dec. 6, 1897	July 8, 1898	215	Frye	
	3	Dec. 5, 1898	Mar. 3, 1899	89	Frye	
56th	1	Dec. 4, 1899	June 7, 1900	186	Frye	David B. Henderson of Iowa
	2	Dec. 3, 1900	Mar. 3, 1901	91	Frye	
57th	1	Dec. 2, 1901	July 1, 1902	212	Frye	Henderson
	2	Dec. 1, 1902	Mar. 3, 1903	93	Frye	
58th	1	Nov. 9, 1903	Dec. 7, 1903	29	Frye	Joseph G. Cannon of Illinois
	2	Dec. 7, 1903	Apr. 28, 1904	144	Frye	
	3	Dec. 5, 1904	Mar. 3, 1905	89	Frye	
59th	1	Dec. 4, 1905	June 30, 1906	209	Frye	Cannon
	2	Dec. 3, 1906	Mar. 3, 1907	91	Frye	
60th	1	Dec. 2, 1907	May 30, 1908	181	Frye	Cannon
	2	Dec. 7, 1908	Mar. 3, 1909	87	Frye	

(Footnotes, p. 1111)

Congress	Session	Date of beginning[1]	Date of adjournment[2]	Length in days	President pro tempore of the Senate[3]	Speaker of the House of Representatives
61st	1	Mar. 15, 1909	Aug. 5, 1909	144	Frye	Cannon
	2	Dec. 6, 1909	June 25, 1910	202	Frye	
	3	Dec. 5, 1910	Mar. 3, 1911	89	Frye	
62nd	1	Apr. 4, 1911	Aug. 22, 1911	141	Frye[15]	Champ Clark of Missouri
	2	Dec. 4, 1911	Aug. 26, 1912	267	Augustus O. Bacon of Georgia[16]; Frank B. Brandegee of Connecticut[17]; Charles Curtis of Kansas[18]; Jacob H. Gallinger of New Hampshire[19]; Henry Cabot Lodge of Mass.[20]	
	3	Dec. 2, 1912	Mar. 3, 1913	92	Bacon[21]; Gallinger[22]	
63rd	1	Apr. 7, 1913	Dec. 1, 1913	239	James P. Clarke of Arkansas	Clark
	2	Dec. 1, 1913	Oct. 24, 1914	328	Clarke	
	3	Dec. 7, 1914	Mar. 3, 1915	87	Clarke	
64th	1	Dec. 6, 1915	Sept. 8, 1916	278	Clarke[23]	Clark
	2	Dec. 4, 1916	Mar. 3, 1917	90	Willard Saulsbury of Delaware	
65th	1	Apr. 2, 1917	Oct. 6, 1917	188	Saulsbury	Clark
	2	Dec. 3, 1917	Nov. 21, 1918	354	Saulsbury	
	3	Dec. 2, 1918	Mar. 3, 1919	92	Saulsbury	
66th	1	May 19, 1919	Nov. 19, 1919	185	Albert B. Cummins of Iowa	Frederick H. Gillett of Massachusetts
	2	Dec. 1, 1919	June 5, 1920	188	Cummins	
	3	Dec. 6, 1920	Mar. 3, 1921	88	Cummins	
67th	1	Apr. 11, 1921	Nov. 23, 1921	227	Cummins	Gillett
	2	Dec. 5, 1921	Sept. 22, 1922	292	Cummins	
	3	Nov. 20, 1922	Dec. 4, 1922	15	Cummins	
	4	Dec. 4, 1922	Mar. 3, 1923	90	Cummins	
68th	1	Dec. 3, 1923	June 7, 1924	188	Cummins	Gillett
	2	Dec. 1, 1924	Mar. 3, 1925	93	Cummins	
69th	1	Dec. 7, 1925	July 3, 1926	209	George H. Moses of New Hampshire	Nicholas Longworth of Ohio
	2	Dec. 6, 1926	Mar. 3, 1927	88	Moses	
70th	1	Dec. 5, 1927	May 29, 1928	177	Moses	Longworth
	2	Dec. 3, 1928	Mar. 3, 1929	91	Moses	
71st	1	Apr. 15, 1929	Nov. 22, 1929	222	Moses	Longworth
	2	Dec. 2, 1929	July 3, 1930	214	Moses	
	3	Dec. 1, 1930	Mar. 3, 1931	93	Moses	
72nd	1	Dec. 7, 1931	July 16, 1932	223	Moses	John N. Garner of Texas
	2	Dec. 5, 1932	Mar. 3, 1933	89	Moses	
73rd	1	Mar. 9, 1933	June 15, 1933	99	Key Pittman of Nevada	Henry T. Rainey of Illinois[24]
	2	Jan. 3, 1934	June 18, 1934	167	Pittman	
74th	1	Jan. 3, 1935	Aug. 26, 1935	236	Pittman	Joseph W. Byrns of Tennessee[25]
	2	Jan. 3, 1936	June 20, 1936	170	Pittman	William B. Bankhead of Alabama[26]
75th	1	Jan. 5, 1937	Aug. 21, 1937	229	Pitman	Bankhead
	2	Nov. 15, 1937	Dec. 21, 1937	37	Pittman	
	3	Jan. 3, 1938	June 16, 1938	165	Pittman	
76th	1	Jan. 3, 1939	Aug. 5, 1939	215	Pittman	Bankhead[27]
	2	Sept. 21, 1939	Nov. 3, 1939	44	Pittman	
	3	Jan. 3, 1940	Jan. 3, 1941	366	Pittman[28] William H. King of Utah[30]	Sam Rayburn of Texas[29]

(Footnotes, p. 1111)

Congress	Session	Date of beginning[1]	Date of adjournment[2]	Length in days	President pro tempore of the Senate[3]	Speaker of the House of Representatives
77th	1	Jan. 3, 1941	Jan. 2, 1942	365	Pat Harrison of Mississippi[31]; Carter Glass of Virginia[32]	Rayburn
	2	Jan. 5, 1942	Dec. 16, 1942	346	Carter Glass of Virginia	
78th	1	Jan. 6, 1943[33]	Dec. 21, 1943	350	Glass	Rayburn
	2	Jan. 10, 1944[34]	Dec. 19, 1944	345	Glass	
79th	1	Jan. 3, 1945[35]	Dec. 21, 1945	353	Kenneth McKellar of Tennessee	Rayburn
	2	Jan. 14, 1946[36]	Aug. 2, 1946	201	McKellar	
80th	1	Jan. 3, 1947[37]	Dec. 19, 1947	351	Arthur H. Vandenberg of Michigan	Joseph W. Martin Jr. of Massachusetts
	2	Jan. 6, 1948[38]	Dec. 31, 1948	361	Vandenberg	
81st	1	Jan. 3, 1949	Oct. 19, 1949	290	Kenneth McKellar of Tennessee	Sam Rayburn of Texas
	2	Jan. 3, 1950[39]	Jan. 2, 1951	365	McKellar	
82nd	1	Jan. 3, 1951[40]	Oct. 20, 1951	291	McKellar	Rayburn
	2	Jan. 8, 1952[41]	July 7, 1952	182	McKellar	
83rd	1	Jan. 3, 1953[42]	Aug. 3, 1953	213	Styles Bridges of New Hampshire	Joseph W. Martin Jr. of Massachusetts
	2	Jan. 6, 1954[43]	Dec. 2, 1954	331	Bridges	
84th	1	Jan. 5, 1955[44]	Aug. 2, 1955	210	Walter F. George of Georgia	Sam Rayburn of Texas
	2	Jan. 3, 1956[45]	July 27, 1956	207	George	
85th	1	Jan. 3, 1957[46]	Aug. 30, 1957	239	Carl Hayden of Arizona	Rayburn
	2	Jan. 7, 1958[47]	Aug. 24, 1958	230	Hayden	
86th	1	Jan. 7, 1959[47]	Sept. 15, 1959	252	Hayden	Rayburn
	2	Jan. 6, 1960[49]	Sept. 1, 1960	240	Hayden	
87th	1	Jan. 3, 1961[50]	Sept. 27, 1961	268	Hayden	Rayburn[51]
	2	Jan. 10, 1962[52]	Oct. 13, 1962	277	Hayden	John W. McCormack of Massachusetts[53]
88th	1	Jan. 9, 1963[54]	Dec. 30, 1963	356	Hayden	McCormack
	2	Jan. 7, 1964[55]	Oct. 3, 1964	270	Hayden	
89th	1	Jan. 4, 1965	Oct. 23, 1965	293	Hayden	McCormack
	2	Jan. 10, 1966[56]	Oct. 22, 1966	286	Hayden	
90th	1	Jan. 10, 1967[57]	Dec. 15, 1967	340	Hayden	McCormack
	2	Jan. 15, 1968[58]	Oct. 14, 1968	274	Hayden	
91st	1	Jan. 3, 1969[59]	Dec. 23, 1969	355	Richard B. Russell of Georgia	McCormack
	2	Jan. 19, 1970[60]	Jan. 2, 1971	349	Russell	
92nd	1	Jan. 21, 1971[61]	Dec. 17, 1971	331	Russell[62]; Allen J. Ellender of Louisiana[63]	Carl Albert of Oklahoma
	2	Jan. 18, 1972[64]	Oct. 18, 1972	275	Ellender[65]; James O. Eastland of Mississippi[66]	
93rd	1	Jan. 3, 1973[67]	Dec. 22, 1973	354	Eastland	Albert
	2	Jan. 21, 1974[68]	Dec. 20, 1974	334	Eastland	
94th	1	Jan. 14, 1975[69]	Dec. 19, 1975	340	Eastland	Albert
	2	Jan. 19, 1976[70]	Oct. 2, 1976	258	Eastland	
95th	1	Jan. 4, 1977[71]	Dec. 15, 1977	346	Eastland	Thomas P. O'Neill Jr. of Massachusetts
	2	Jan. 19, 1978[72]	Oct. 15, 1978	270	Eastland	
96th	1	Jan. 15, 1979[73]	Jan. 3, 1980	354	Warren G. Magnuson of Washington	O'Neill
	2	Jan. 3, 1980[74]	Dec. 16, 1980	349	Magnuson	
97th	1	Jan. 5, 1981[75]	Dec. 16, 1981	347	Strom Thurmond of of South Carolina	O'Neill
	2	Jan. 25, 1982[76]	Dec. 23, 1982	333	Thurmond	
98th	1	Jan. 3, 1983[77]	Nov. 18, 1983	320	Thurmond	O'Neill
	2	Jan. 23, 1984[78]	Oct. 12, 1984	264	Thurmond	
99th	1	Jan. 3, 1985			Thurmond	O'Neill

(Footnotes, p. 1111)

1. The Constitution (art I, sec. 4) provided that "The Congress shall assemble at least once in every year ... on the first Monday in December, unless they shall by law appoint a different day." Pursuant to a resolution of the Continental Congress, the first session of the First Congress convened March 4, 1789. Up to and including May 20, 1820, 18 acts were passed providing for the meeting of Congress on other days in the year. After 1820 Congress met regularly on the first Monday in December until 1934, when the 20th Amendment to the Constitution became effective changing the meeting date to Jan. 3. [Until then, brief special sessions of the Senate only were held at the beginning of each presidential term to confirm Cabinet and other nominations—and occasionally at other times for other purposes. The Senate last met in special session from March 4 to March 6, 1933.]

The first and second sessions of the First Congress were held in New York City; subsequently, including the first session of the Sixth Congress, Philadelphia was the meeting place; since then, Congress has convened in Washington.

2. Until adoption of the 20th Amendment, the deadline for adjournment of Congress in odd-numbered years was March 3. However, the expiring Congress often extended the "legislative day" of March 3 up to noon of March 4, when the new Congress came officially into being. After ratification of the 20th Amendment, the deadline for adjournment of Congress in odd-numbered years was noon on Jan. 3.

3. Until recent years the appointment or election of a President pro tempore was considered by the Senate to be for the occasion only, so that more than one appears in several sessions and in others none was chosen. Since March 12, 1890, they have served until "the Senate otherwise ordered."

4. Elected to count the vote for President and Vice President, which was done April 6, 1789, because there was a quorum of the Senate for the first time. John Adams, Vice President, appeared April 21, 1789, and took his seat as president of the Senate.

5. Elected Speaker pro tempore for April 20, 1798, and again for May 28, 1798.

6. Elected Speaker Jan. 19, 1814, to succeed Henry Clay, who resigned Jan. 19, 1814.

7. Elected Speaker Nov. 15, 1820, to succeed Henry Clay, who resigned Oct. 28, 1820.

8. Elected Speaker June 2, 1834, to succeed Andrew Stevenson of Virginia, who resigned.

9. There were recesses in this session from Saturday, Mar. 30, to Wednesday, July 1, and from Saturday, July 20, to Thursday, Nov. 21.

10. There were recesses in this session from Monday, July 27, to Monday, Sept. 21, to Friday, Oct. 16, and to Tuesday, Nov. 10. No business was transacted subsequent to July 27.

11. Elected Speaker Mar. 3, 1869, and served one day.

12. Died Aug. 19, 1876.

13. Appointed Speaker pro tempore Feb. 17, May 12, June 19.

14. Appointed Speaker pro tempore June 4.

15. Resigned as President pro tempore Apr. 27, 1911.

16. Elected to serve Jan. 11-17, Mar. 11-12, Apr. 8, May 10, May 30 to June 1 and 3, June 13 to July 5, Aug. 1-10, and Aug. 27 to Dec. 15, 1912.

17. Elected to serve May 25, 1912.

18. Elected to serve Dec. 4-12, 1911.

19. Elected to serve Feb. 12-14, Apr. 26-27, May 7, July 6-31, Aug. 12-26, 1912.

20. Elected to serve Mar. 25-26, 1912.

21. Elected to serve Aug. 27 to Dec. 15, 1912, Jan. 5-18, and Feb. 2-15, 1913.

22. Elected to serve Dec. 16, 1912, to Jan. 4, 1913, Jan. 19 to Feb. 1, and Feb. 16 to Mar. 3, 1913.

23. Died Oct. 1, 1916.

24. Died Aug. 19, 1934.

25. Died June 4, 1936.

26. Elected June 4, 1936.

27. Died Sept. 15, 1940.

28. Died Nov. 10, 1940.

29. Elected Sept. 16, 1940.

30. Elected Nov. 19, 1940.

31. Elected Jan. 6, 1941; died June 22, 1941.

32. Elected July 10, 1941.

33. There was a recess in this session from Thursday, July 8, to Tuesday, Sept. 14.

34. There were recesses in this session from Saturday, Apr. 1, to Wednesday, Apr. 12; from Friday, June 23, to Tuesday, Aug. 1; and from Thursday, Sept. 21, to Tuesday, Nov. 14.

35. The House was in recess in this session from Saturday, July 21, 1945, to Wednesday, Sept. 5, 1945, and the Senate from Wednesday, Aug. 1, 1945, to Wednesday, Sept. 5, 1945.

36. The House was in recess in this session from Thursday, Apr. 18, 1946, to Tuesday, Apr. 30, 1946.

37. There was a recess in this session from Sunday, July 27, 1947, to Monday, Nov. 17, 1947.

38. There were recesses in this session from Sunday, June 20, 1948, to Monday, July 26, 1948, and from Saturday, Aug. 7, 1948, to Friday, Dec. 31, 1948.

39. The House was in recess in this session from Thursday, Apr. 6, 1950, to Tuesday, Apr. 18, 1950, and both the Senate and the House were in recess from Saturday, Sept. 23, 1950, to Monday, Nov. 27, 1950.

40. The House was in recess in this session from Thursday, Mar. 22, 1951, to Monday, Apr. 2, 1951, and from Thursday, Aug. 23, 1951, to Wednesday, Sept. 12, 1951.

41. The House was in recess in this session from Thursday, Apr. 10, 1952, to Tuesday, Apr. 22, 1952.

42. The House was in recess in this session from Thursday, Apr. 2, 1953, to Monday, Apr. 13, 1953.

43. The House was in recess in this session from Thursday, Apr. 15, 1954, to Monday, Apr. 26, 1954, and adjourned sine die Aug. 20, 1954. The Senate was in recess in this session from Friday, Aug. 20, 1954, to Monday, Nov. 8, 1954; from Thursday, Nov. 18, 1954, to Monday, Nov. 29, 1954, and adjourned sine die Dec. 2, 1954.

44. There was a recess in this session from Monday, Apr. 4, 1955, to Wednesday, Apr. 13, 1955.

45. There was a recess in this session from Thursday, Mar. 29, 1956, to Monday, Apr. 9, 1956.

46. There was a recess in this session from Thursday, Apr. 18, 1957, to Monday, Apr. 29, 1957.

47. There was a recess in this session from Thursday, Apr. 3, 1958, to Monday, Apr. 14, 1958.

48. There was a recess in this session from Thursday, Mar. 26, 1959, to Tuesday, Apr. 7, 1959.

49. The Senate was in recess in this session from Thursday, Apr. 14, 1960, to Monday, Apr. 18, 1960; from Friday, May 27, 1960, to Tuesday, May 31, 1960, and from Sunday, July 3, 1960, to Monday, Aug. 8, 1960. The House was in recess in this session from Thursday, Apr. 14, 1960, to Monday, Apr. 18, 1960; from Friday, May 27, 1960, to Tuesday, May 31, 1960, and from Sunday, July 3, 1960, to Monday, Aug. 15, 1960.

50. The House was in recess in this session from Thursday, Mar. 30, 1961, to Monday, Apr. 10, 1961.

51. Died Nov. 16, 1961.

52. The House was in recess in this session from Thursday, Apr. 19, 1962, to Monday, Apr. 30, 1962.

53. Elected Jan. 10, 1962.

54. The House was in recess in this session from Thursday, Apr. 11, 1963, to Monday, Apr. 22, 1963.

55. The House was in recess in this session from Thursday, Mar. 26, 1964, to Monday, Apr. 6, 1964; from Thursday, July 2, 1964, to Monday, July 20, 1964; from Friday, Aug. 21, 1964, to Monday, Aug. 31, 1964. The Senate was in recess in this session from Friday, July 10, 1964, to Monday, July 20, 1964; from Friday, Aug. 21, 1964, to Monday, Aug. 31, 1964.

56. The House was in recess in this session from Thursday, Apr. 7, 1966, to Monday, Apr. 18, 1966; from Thursday, June 30, 1966, to Monday, July 11, 1966. The Senate was in recess in this session from Thursday, Apr. 7, 1966, to Wednesday, Apr. 13, 1966; from Thursday, June 30, 1966, to Monday, July 11, 1966.

57. There was a recess in this session from Thursday, Mar. 23, 1967, to Monday, Apr. 3, 1967; from Thursday, June 29, 1967, to Monday, July 10, 1967; from Thursday, Aug. 31, 1967, to Monday, Sept. 11, 1967; and from Wednesday, Nov. 22, 1967, to Monday, Nov. 27, 1967.

58. The House was in recess this session from Thursday, Apr. 11, 1968, to Monday, Apr. 22, 1968; from Wednesday, May 29, 1968, to Monday, June 3, 1968; from Wednesday, July 3, 1968, to Monday, July 8, 1968; from Friday, Aug. 2, 1968, to Wednesday, Sept. 4, 1968. The Senate was in recess this session from Thursday, Apr. 11, 1968, to Wednesday, Apr. 17, 1968; from Wednesday, May 29, 1968, to Monday, June 3, 1968; from Wednesday, July 3, 1968, to Monday, July 8, 1968; from Friday, Aug. 2, 1968, to Wednesday, Sept. 4, 1968.

59. The House was in recess this session from Friday, Feb. 7, 1969, to Monday, Feb. 17, 1969; from Thursday, Apr. 3, 1969, to Monday, Apr. 14, 1969; from Wednesday, May 28, 1969, to Monday, June 2, 1969; from Wednesday, July 2, 1969, to Monday, July 7, 1969; from Wednesday, Aug. 13, 1969, to Wednesday, Sept. 3, 1969; from Thursday, Nov. 6, 1969, to Wednesday, Nov. 12, 1969; from Wednesday, Nov. 26, 1969, to Monday, Dec. 1, 1969. The Senate was in recess this session from Friday, Feb. 7, 1969, to Monday, Feb. 17, 1969; from Thursday, Apr. 3, 1969, to Monday, Apr. 14, 1969; from Wednesday, July 2, 1969, to Monday, July 7, 1969; from Wednesday, Aug. 13, 1969, to Wednesday, Sept. 3, 1969; from Wednesday, Nov. 26, 1969, to Monday, Dec. 1, 1969.

60. The House was in recess this session from Tuesday, Feb. 10, 1970, to Monday, Feb. 16, 1970; from Thursday, Mar. 26, 1970, to Tuesday, Mar. 31, 1970; from Wednesday, May 27, 1970, to Monday, June 1, 1970; from Wednesday, July 1, 1970, to Monday, July 6, 1970; from Friday, Aug. 14, 1970, to Wednesday, Sept. 9, 1970; from Wednesday, Oct. 14, 1970, to Monday, Nov. 16, 1970; from Wednesday, Nov. 25, 1970, to Monday, Nov. 30, 1970; from Tuesday, Dec. 22, 1970, to Tuesday, Dec. 29, 1970. The Senate was in recess this session from Tuesday, Feb. 10, 1970, to Monday, Feb. 16, 1970; from Thursday, Mar. 26, 1970, to Tuesday, Mar. 31, 1970; from Wednesday, Sept. 2, 1970, to Tuesday, Sept. 8, 1970; from Wednesday, Oct. 14, 1970, to Monday, Nov. 16, 1970; from Wednesday, Nov. 25, 1970, to Monday, Nov. 30, 1970; from Tuesday, Dec. 22, 1970, to Monday, Dec. 28, 1970.

61. The House was in recess this session from Wednesday, Feb. 10, 1971, to Wednesday, Feb. 17, 1971; from Wednesday, Apr. 7, 1971, to Monday, Apr. 19, 1971; from Thursday, May 27, 1971, to Tuesday, June 1, 1971; from Thursday, July 1, 1971, to Tuesday, July 6, 1971; from Friday, Aug. 6, 1971, to Wednesday, Sept. 8, 1971; from Thursday, Oct. 7, 1971, to Tuesday, Oct. 12, 1971; from Thursday, Oct. 21, 1971, to Tuesday, Oct. 26, 1971; from Friday, Nov. 19, 1971, to Monday, Nov. 29, 1971. The Senate was in recess this session from Thursday, Feb. 11, 1971, to Wednesday, Feb. 17, 1971; from Wednesday, Apr. 7, 1971, to Wednesday, Apr. 14, 1971; from Wednesday, May 26, 1971, to Tuesday, June 1, 1971; from Wednesday, June 30, 1971, to Tuesday, July 6, 1971; from Friday, Aug. 6, 1971, to Wednesday, Sept. 8, 1971; from Thursday, Oct. 21, 1971, to Tuesday, Oct. 26, 1971; from Wednesday, Nov. 24, 1971, to Monday, Nov. 29, 1971.

62. Died Jan. 21, 1971.

63. Elected Jan. 22, 1971.

64. The House was in recess this session from Wednesday, Feb. 9, 1972, to Wednesday, Feb. 16, 1972; from Wednesday, Mar. 29, 1972, to Monday, Apr. 10, 1972; from Wednesday, May 24, 1972, to Tuesday, May 30, 1972; from Friday, June 30, 1972, to Monday, July 17, 1972; from Friday, Aug. 18, 1972, to Tuesday, Sept. 5, 1972. The Senate was in recess this session from Wednesday, Feb. 9, 1972, to Monday, Feb. 14, 1972; from Thursday, Mar. 30, 1972, to Tuesday, Apr. 4, 1972; from Thursday, May 25, 1972, to Tuesday, May 30, 1972; from Friday, June 30, 1972, to Monday, July 17, 1972; from Friday, Aug. 18, 1972, to Tuesday, Sept. 5, 1972.

65. Died July 27, 1972.

66. Elected July 28, 1972.

67. The House was in recess this session from Thursday, Feb. 8, 1973, to Monday, Feb. 19, 1973; from Thursday, Apr. 19, 1973, to Monday, Apr. 30, 1973; from Thursday, May 24, 1973, to Tuesday, May 29, 1973; from Saturday, June 30, 1973, to Tuesday, July 10, 1973; from Friday, Aug. 3, 1973, to Wednesday, Sept. 5, 1973; from Thursday, Oct. 4, 1973, to Tuesday, Oct. 9, 1973; from Thursday, Oct. 18, 1973, to Tuesday, Oct. 23, 1973; from Thursday, Nov. 15, 1973 to Monday, Nov. 26, 1973. The Senate was in recess this session from Thursday, Feb. 8, 1973, to Thursday, Feb. 15, 1973;

from Wednesday, Apr. 18, 1973, to Monday, Apr. 30, 1973; from Wednesday, May 23, 1973, to Tuesday, May 29, 1973; from Saturday, June 30, 1973, to Monday, July 9, 1973; from Friday, Aug. 3, 1973, to Wednesday, Sept. 5, 1973; from Thursday, Oct. 18, 1973, to Tuesday, Oct. 23, 1973; from Wednesday, Nov. 21, 1973, to Monday, Nov. 26, 1973.

68. The House was in recess this session from Thursday, Feb. 7, 1974, to Wednesday, Feb. 13, 1974; from Thursday, Apr. 11, 1974, to Monday, Apr. 22, 1974; from Thursday, May 23, 1974, to Tuesday, May 28, 1974; from Thursday, Aug. 22, 1974, to Wednesday, Sept. 11, 1974; from Thursday, Oct. 17, 1974, to Monday, Nov. 18, 1974; from Tuesday, Nov. 26, 1974, to Tuesday, Dec. 3, 1974. The Senate was in recess this session from Friday, Feb. 8, 1974, to Monday, Feb. 18, 1974; from Wednesday, Mar. 13, 1974, to Tuesday, Mar. 19, 1974; from Thursday, Apr. 11, 1974, to Monday, Apr. 22, 1974; from Wednesday, May 23, 1974, to Tuesday, May 28, 1974; from Thursday, Aug. 22, 1974, to Wednesday, Sept. 4, 1974; from Thursday, Oct. 17, 1974, to Monday, Nov. 18, 1974; from Tuesday, Nov. 26, 1974, to Monday, Dec. 2, 1974.

69. The House was in recess this session from Wednesday, Mar. 26, 1975, to Monday, Apr. 7, 1975; from Thursday, May 22, 1975, to Monday, June 2, 1975; from Thursday, June 26, 1975, to Tuesday, July 8, 1975; from Friday, Aug. 1, 1975, to Wednesday, Sept. 3, 1975; from Thursday, Oct. 9, 1975, to Monday, Oct. 20, 1975; from Thursday, Oct. 23, 1975, to Tuesday, Oct. 28, 1975; from Thursday, Nov. 20, 1975, to Monday, Dec. 1, 1975. The Senate was in recess this session from Wednesday, Mar. 26, 1975, to Monday, Apr. 7, 1975; from Thursday, May 22, 1975, to Monday, June 2, 1975; from Friday, June 27, 1975, to Monday, July 7, 1975; from Friday, Aug. 1, 1975, to Wednesday, Sept. 3, 1975; from Thursday, Oct. 9, 1975, to Monday, Oct. 20, 1975; from Thursday, Oct. 23, 1975, to Tuesday, Oct. 28, 1975; from Thursday, Nov. 20, 1975, to Monday, Dec. 1, 1975.

70. The House was in recess this session from Wednesday, Feb. 11, 1976, to Monday, Feb. 16, 1976; from Wednesday, Apr. 14, 1976, to Monday, Apr. 26, 1976; from Thursday, May 27, 1976, to Tuesday, June 1, 1976; from Friday, July 2, 1976, to Monday, July 19, 1976; from Tuesday, Aug. 10, 1976, to Monday, Aug. 23, 1976; from Thursday, Sept. 2, 1976, to Wednesday, Sept. 8, 1976. The Senate was in recess this session from Friday, Feb. 6, 1976, to Monday, Feb. 16, 1976; from Wednesday, Apr. 14, 1976, to Monday, Apr. 26, 1976; from Friday, May 28, 1976, to Wednesday, June 2, 1976; from Friday, July 2, 1976, to Monday, July 19, 1976; from Tuesday, Aug. 10, 1976, to Monday, Aug. 23, 1976; from Wednesday, Sept. 1, 1976, to Tuesday, Sept. 7, 1976.

71. The House was in recess this session from Wednesday, Feb. 9, 1977, to Wednesday, Feb. 16, 1977; from Wednesday, Apr. 6, 1977, to Monday, Apr. 18, 1977; from Thursday, May 26, 1977, to Wednesday, June 1, 1977; from Thursday, June 30, 1977, to Monday, July 11, 1977; from Friday, Aug. 5, 1977, to Wednesday, Sept. 7, 1977; from Thursday, Oct. 6, 1977, to Tuesday, Oct. 11, 1977. The Senate was in recess this session from Friday, Feb. 11, 1977, to Monday, Feb. 21, 1977; from Thursday, Apr. 7, 1977, to Monday, Apr. 18, 1977; from Friday, May 27, 1977, to Monday, June 6, 1977; from Friday, July 1, 1977, to Monday, July 11, 1977; from Saturday, Aug. 6, 1977, to Wednesday, Sept. 7, 1977.

72. The House was in recess this session from Thursday, Feb. 9, 1978, to Tuesday, Feb. 14, 1978; from Wednesday, Mar. 22, 1978, to Monday, Apr. 3, 1978; from Thursday, May 25, 1978, to Wednesday, May 31, 1978; from Thursday, June 29, 1978, to Monday, July 10, 1978; from Thursday, Aug. 17, 1978, to Wednesday, Sept. 6, 1978. The Senate was in recess this session from Friday, Feb. 10, 1978, to Monday, Feb. 20, 1978; from Thursday, Mar. 23, 1978, to Monday, Apr. 3, 1978; from Friday, May 26, 1978, to Monday, June 5, 1978; from Thursday, June 29, 1978, to Monday, July 10, 1978; from Friday, Aug. 25, 1978, to Wednesday, Sept. 6, 1978.

73. The House was in recess this session from Thursday, Feb. 8, 1979, to Tuesday, Feb. 13, 1979; from Tuesday, Apr. 10, 1979, to Monday, Apr. 23, 1979; from Thursday, May 24, 1979, to Wednesday, May 30, 1979; from Friday, June 29, 1979, to Monday, July 9, 1979; from Thursday, Aug. 2, 1979, to Wednesday, Sept. 5, 1979; from Tuesday, Nov. 20, 1979, to Monday, Nov. 26, 1979. The Senate was in recess this session from Friday, Feb. 9, 1979, to

Monday, Feb. 19, 1979; from Tuesday, Apr. 10, 1979, to Monday, Apr. 23, 1979; from Friday, May 25, 1979, to Monday, June 4, 1979; from Friday, Aug. 3, 1979, to Wednesday, Sept. 5, 1979; from Tuesday, Nov. 20, 1979, to Monday, Nov. 26, 1979.

74. The House was in recess this session from Wednesday, Feb. 13, 1980, to Tuesday, Feb. 19, 1980; from Wednesday, Apr. 2, 1980, to Tuesday, Apr. 15, 1980; from Thursday, May 22, 1980, to Wednesday, May 28, 1980; from Wednesday, July 2, 1980, to Monday, July 21, 1980; from Friday, Aug. 1, 1980, to Monday, Aug. 18, 1980; from Thursday, Aug. 28, 1980, to Wednesday, Sept. 13, 1980. The Senate was in recess this session from Monday, Feb. 11, 1980, to Thursday, Feb. 14, 1980; from Thursday, Apr. 3, 1980, to Tuesday, Apr. 15, 1980; from Thursday, May 22, 1980, to Wednesday, May 28, 1980; from Wednesday, July 2, 1980, to Monday, July 21, 1980; from Wednesday, Aug. 6, 1980, to Monday, Aug. 18, 1980; from Wednesday, Aug. 27, 1980, to Wednesday, Sept. 3, 1980; from Wednesday, Oct. 1, 1980, to Wednesday, Nov. 12, 1980; from Monday, Nov. 24, 1980, to Monday, Dec. 1, 1980.

75. The House was in recess this session from Friday, Feb. 6, 1981 to Tuesday, Feb. 17, 1981; from Friday, Apr. 10, 1981, to Monday, Apr. 27, 1981; from Friday, June 26, 1981, to Wednesday, July 8, 1981; from Tuesday, Aug. 4, 1981, to Wednesday, Sept. 9, 1981; from Wednesday, Oct. 7, 1981, to Tuesday, Oct. 13, 1981; from Monday, Nov. 23, 1981, to Monday, Nov. 30, 1981. The Senate was in recess this session from Friday, Feb. 6, 1981, to Monday, Feb. 16, 1981; from Friday, Apr. 10, 1981, to Monday, Apr. 27, 1981; from Thursday, June 25, 1981, to Wednesday, July 8, 1981; from Monday, Aug. 3, 1981, to Wednesday, Sept. 9, 1981; from Wednesday, Oct. 7, 1981, to Wednesday, Oct. 14, 1981; from Tuesday, Nov. 24, 1981, to Monday, Nov. 30, 1981.

76. The House was in recess this session from Wednesday, Feb. 10, 1982, to Monday, Feb. 22, 1982; from Tuesday, Apr. 6, 1982, to Tuesday, Apr. 20, 1982; from Thursday, May 27, 1982, to Wednesday, June 2, 1982; from Thursday, July 1, 1982, to Monday, July 12, 1982; from Friday, Aug. 20, 1982, to Wednesday, Sept. 8, 1982; from Friday, Oct. 1, 1982, to Monday, Nov. 29, 1982. The Senate was in recess this session Thursday, Feb. 11, 1982, to Monday, Feb. 22, 1982; from Thursday, Apr. 1, 1982, to Tuesday, Apr. 13, 1982; from Thursday, May 27, 1982, to Tuesday, June 8, 1982; from Thursday, July 1, 1982, to Monday, July 12, 1982; from Friday, Aug. 20, 1982, to Wednesday, Sept. 8, 1982; from Friday, Oct. 1, 1982, to Monday, Nov. 29, 1982.

77. The House was in recess this session Friday, Jan. 7, 1983, to Tuesday, Jan. 25, 1983; Thursday, Feb. 17, 1983, to Tuesday, Feb. 22, 1983; from Thursday, March 24, 1983, to Tuesday, Apr. 5, 1983; from Thursday, May 26, 1983, to Wednesday, June 1, 1983; from Thursday, June 30, 1983, to Monday, July 11, 1983; from Friday, Aug. 5, 1983, to Monday, Sept. 12, 1983; from Friday, Oct. 7, 1983, to Monday, Oct. 17, 1983. The Senate was in recess this session Monday, Jan. 3, 1983, to Tuesday, Jan. 25, 1983; Friday, Feb. 4, 1983, to Monday, Feb. 14, 1983; from Friday, March 25, 1983, to Tuesday, Apr. 5, 1983; from Friday, May 27, 1983, to Monday, June 6, 1983; from Friday, July 1, 1983, to Monday, July 11, 1983; from Friday, Aug. 5, 1983, to Monday, Sept. 12, 1983; from Monday Oct. 10, 1983, to Monday, Oct. 17, 1983.

78. The House was in recess this session Thursday, Feb. 9, 1984, to Tuesday, Feb. 21, 1984; from Friday, Apr. 13, 1984, to Tuesday, Apr. 24, 1984; from Friday, May 25, 1984, to Wednesday, May 30, 1984; from Friday, June 29, 1984, to Monday, July 23, 1984; Friday, Aug. 10, 1984, to Wednesday, Sept. 5, 1984. The Senate was in recess this session Friday, Feb. 10, 1984, to Monday, Feb. 20, 1984; from Friday, Apr. 13, 1984, to Tuesday, Apr. 24, 1984; from Friday, May 25, 1984, to Thursday, May 31, 1984; from Friday, June 29, 1984, to Monday, July 23, 1984; from Friday, Aug. 10, 1984, to Wednesday, Sept. 5, 1984.

Leaders of the Senate and House

(For Presidents pro tempore of the Senate and Speakers of the House, see p. 1105)

Congress	Senate Floor Leaders		Senate Whips	
	Majority	**Minority**	**Majority**	**Minority**
62nd (1911-1913)	Shelby M. Cullom (R Ill.)	Thomas S. Martin (D Va.)	None	None
63rd (1913-1915)	John W. Kern (D Ind.)	Jacob H. Gallinger (R N.H.)	J. Hamilton Lewis (D Ill.)	None
64th (1915-1917)	Kern	Gallinger	Lewis	James W. Wadsworth Jr. (R N.Y.) Charles Curtis (R Kan.)[8]
65th (1917-1919)	Thomas S. Martin (D Va.)	Gallinger/Henry Cabot Lodge (R Mass.)[1]	Lewis	Curtis
66th (1919-1921)	Henry Cabot Lodge (R Mass.)	Martin/Oscar W. Underwood (D Ala.)[2]	Charles Curtis (R Kan.)	Peter G. Gerry (D R.I.)
67th (1921-1923)	Lodge	Underwood	Curtis	Gerry
68th (1923-1925)	Lodge/Charles Curtis (R Kan.)[3]	Joseph T. Robinson (D Ark.)	Curtis/Wesley L. Jones (R Wash.)[9]	Gerry
69th (1925-1927)	Curtis	Robinson	Jones	Gerry
70th (1927-1929)	Curtis	Robinson	Jones	Gerry
71st (1929-1931)	James E. Watson (R Ind.)	Robinson	Simeon D. Fess (R Ohio)	Morris Sheppard (D Texas)
72nd (1931-1933)	Watson	Robinson	Fess	Sheppard
73rd (1933-1935)	Joseph T. Robinson (D Ark.)	Charles L. McNary (R Ore.)	Lewis	Felix Hebert (R R.I.)
74th (1935-1937)	Robinson	McNary	Lewis	None
75th (1937-1939)	Robinson/Alben W. Barkley (D Ky.)[4]	McNary	Lewis	None
76th (1939-1941)	Barkley	McNary	Sherman Minton (D Ind.)	None
77th (1941-1943)	Barkley	McNary	Lister Hill (D Ala.)	None
78th (1943-1945)	Barkley	McNary	Hill	Kenneth Wherry (R Neb.)
79th (1945-1947)	Barkley	Wallace H. White Jr. (R Maine)	Hill	Wherry
80th (1947-1949)	Wallace H. White Jr. (R Maine)	Alben W. Barkley (D Ky.)	Kenneth Wherry (R Neb.)	Scott Lucas (D Ill.)
81st (1949-1951)	Scott W. Lucas (D Ill.)	Kenneth S. Wherry (R Neb.)	Francis Myers (D Pa.)	Leverett Saltonstall (R Mass.)
82nd (1951-1953)	Ernest W. McFarland (D Ariz.)	Wherry/Styles Bridges (R N.H.)[5]	Lyndon B. Johnson (D Texas)	Saltonstall
83rd (1953-1955)	Robert A. Taft (R Ohio)/ William F. Knowland (R Calif.)[6]	Lyndon B. Johnson (D Texas)	Leverett Saltonstall (R Mass.)	Earle Clements (D Ky.)
84th (1955-1957)	Lyndon B. Johnson (D Texas)	William F. Knowland (R Calif.)	Earle Clements (D Ky.)	Saltonstall
85th (1957-1959)	Johnson	Knowland	Mike Mansfield (D Mont.)	Everett McKinley Dirksen (R Ill.)
86th (1959-1961)	Johnson	Everett McKinley Dirksen (R Ill.)	Mansfield	Thomas H. Kuchel (R Calif.)
87th (1961-1963)	Mike Mansfield (D Mont.)	Dirksen	Hubert H. Humphrey (D Minn.)	Kuchel
88th (1963-1965)	Mansfield	Dirksen	Humphrey	Kuchel
89th (1965-1967)	Mansfield	Dirksen	Russell Long (D La.)	Kuchel
90th (1967-1969)	Mansfield	Dirksen	Long	Kuchel
91st (1969-1971)	Mansfield	Dirksen/Hugh Scott (R Pa.)[7]	Edward M. Kennedy (D Mass.)	Hugh Scott (R Pa.)/ Robert P. Griffin (R Mich.)[10]
92nd (1971-1973)	Mansfield	Scott	Robert C. Byrd (D W.Va.)	Griffin
93rd (1973-1975)	Mansfield	Scott	Byrd	Griffin
94th (1975-1977)	Mansfield	Scott	Byrd	Griffin
95th (1977-1979)	Robert C. Byrd (D W.Va.)	Howard H. Baker Jr. (R Tenn.)	Alan Cranston (D Calif.)	Ted Stevens (R Alaska)
96th (1979-1981)	Byrd	Baker	Cranston	Stevens
97th (1981-1983)	Howard H. Baker Jr. (R Tenn.)	Robert C. Byrd (D W.Va.)	Ted Stevens (R Alaska)	Alan Cranston (D Calif.)
98th (1983-1985)	Baker	Byrd	Stevens	Cranston
99th (1985-1987)	Robert J. Dole (R Kan.)	Byrd	Alan K. Simpson (R Wyo.)	Cranston

---

Senate Footnotes

1. Lodge became minority leader on Aug. 24, 1918, filling the vacancy caused by the death of Gallinger on Aug. 17, 1918.

2. Underwood became minority leader on April 27, 1920, filling the vacancy caused by the death of Martin on Nov. 12, 1919. Gilbert M. Hitchcock (D Neb.) served as acting minority leader in the interim.

3. Curtis became majority leader on Nov. 28, 1924, filling the vacancy caused by the death of Lodge on Nov. 9, 1924.

4. Barkley became majority leader on July 22, 1937, filling the vacancy caused by the death of Robinson on July 14, 1937.

5. Bridges became minority leader on Jan. 8, 1952, filling the vacancy caused by the death of Wherry on Nov. 29, 1951.

6. Knowland became majority leader on Aug. 4, 1953, filling the vacancy caused by the death of Taft on July 31, 1953. Taft's vacant seat was filled by a Democrat, Thomas Burke, on Nov. 10, 1953. The division of the Senate changed to 48 Democrats, 47 Republicans and 1 Independent, thus giving control of the Senate to the Democrats. However, Knowland remained as majority leader until the end of the 83rd Congress.

7. Scott became minority leader on Sept. 24, 1969, filling the vacancy caused by the death of Dirksen on Sept. 7, 1969.

8. Wadsworth served as minority whip for only one week, from Dec. 6 to Dec. 13, 1915.

9. Jones became majority whip filling the vacancy caused by the elevation of Curtis to the post of majority leader. *(Footnote 3)*

10. Griffin became minority whip on Sept. 24, 1969, filling the vacancy caused by the elevation of Scott to the post of minority leader. *(Footnote 7)*

House Floor Leaders | House Whips

Congress	Majority	Minority	Majority	Minority
56th (1899-1901)	Sereno E. Payne (R N.Y.)	James D. Richardson (D Tenn.)	James A. Tawney (R Minn.)	Oscar W. Underwood (D Ala.)[6]
57th (1901-1903)	Payne	Richardson	Tawney	James T. Lloyd (D Mo.)
58th (1903-1905)	Payne	John Sharp Williams (D Miss.)	Tawney	Lloyd
59th (1905-1907)	Payne	Williams	James E. Watson (R Ind.)	Lloyd
60th (1907-1909)	Payne	Williams/Champ Clark (D Mo.)[1]	Watson	Lloyd[7]
61st (1909-1911)	Payne	Clark	John W. Dwight (R N.Y.)	None
62nd (1911-1913)	Oscar W. Underwood (D Ala.)	James R. Mann (R Ill.)	None	John W. Dwight (R N.Y.)
63rd (1913-1915)	Underwood	Mann	Thomas M. Bell (D Ga.)	Charles H. Burke (R S.D.)
64th (1915-1917)	Claude Kitchin (D N.C.)	Mann	None	Charles M. Hamilton (R N.Y.)
65th (1917-1919)	Kitchin	Mann	None	Hamilton
66th (1919-1921)	Franklin W. Mondell (R Wyo.)	Clark	Harold Knutson (R Minn.)	None
67th (1921-1923)	Mondell	Claude Kitchin (D N.C.)	Knutson	William A. Oldfield (D Ark.)
68th (1923-1925)	Nicholas Longworth (R Ohio)	Finis J. Garrett (D Tenn.)	Albert H. Vetal (R Ind.)	Oldfield
69th (1925-1927)	John Q. Tilson (R Conn.)	Garrett	Vestal	Oldfield
70th (1927-1929)	Tilson	Garrett	Vestal	Oldfield/John McDuffie (D Ala.)[8]
71st (1929-1931)	Tilson	John N. Garner (D Texas)	Vestal	McDuffie
72nd (1931-1933)	Henry T. Rainey (D Ill.)	Bertrand H. Snell (R N.Y.)	John McDuffie (D Ala.)	Carl G. Bachmann (R W.Va.)
73rd (1933-1935)	Joseph W. Byrns (D Tenn.)	Snell	Arthur H. Greenwood (D Ind.)	Hary L. Englebright (R Calif.)
74th (1935-1937)	William B. Bankhead (D Ala.)[2]	Snell	Patrick J. Boland (D Pa.)	Englebright
75th (1937-1939)	Sam Rayburn (D Texas)	Snell	Boland	Englebright
76th (1939-1941)	Rayburn/John W. McCormack (D Mass.)[3]	Joseph W. Martin Jr. (R Mass.)	Boland	Englebright
77th (1941-1943)	McCormack	Martin	Boland/Robert Ramspeck (D Ga.)[9]	Englebright
78th (1943-1945)	McCormack	Martin	Ramspeck	Leslie C. Arends (R Ill.)
79th (1945-1947)	McCormack	Martin	Ramspeck/John J. Sparkman (D Ala.)[10]	Arends
80th (1947-1949)	Charles A. Halleck (R Ind.)	Sam Rayburn (D Texas)	Leslie C. Arends (R Ill.)	John W. McCormack (D Mass.)
81st (1949-1951)	McCormack	Martin	J. Percy Priest (D Tenn.)	Arends
82nd (1951-1953)	McCormack	Martin	Priest	Arends
83rd (1953-1955)	Halleck	Rayburn	Arends	McCormack
84th (1955-1957)	McCormack	Martin	Carl Albert (D Okla.)	Arends
85th (1957-1959)	McCormack	Martin	Albert	Arends
86th (1959-1961)	McCormack	Charles A. Halleck (R Ind.)	Albert	Arends
87th (1961-1963)	McCormack/Carl Albert (D Okla.)[4]	Halleck	Albert/Hale Boggs (D La.)[11]	Arends
88th (1963-1965)	Albert	Halleck	Boggs	Arends
89th (1965-1967)	Albert	Gerald R. Ford (R Mich.)	Boggs	Arends
90th (1967-1969)	Albert	Ford	Boggs	Arends
91st (1969-1971)	Albert	Ford	Boggs	Arends
92nd (1971-1973)	Hale Boggs (D La.)	Ford	Thomas P. O'Neill Jr. (D Mass.)	Arends
93rd (1973-1975)	Thomas P. O'Neill Jr. (D Mass.)	Ford/John J. Rhodes (R Ariz.)[5]	John J. McFall (D Calif.)	Arends
94th (1975-1977)	O'Neill	Rhodes	McFall	Robert H. Michel (R Ill.)
95th (1977-1979)	Jim Wright (D Texas)	Rhodes	John Brademas (D Ind.)	Michel
96th (1979-1981)	Wright	Rhodes	Brademas	Michel
97th (1981-1983)	Wright	Robert H. Michel (R Ill.)	Thomas S. Foley (D Wash.)	Trent Lott (R Miss.)
98th (1983-1985)	Wright	Michel	Foley	Lott
99th (1985-1987)	Wright	Michel	Foley	Lott

House Footnotes

1. Clark became minority leader in 1908.

2. Bankhead became Speaker of the House on June 4, 1936. The post of majority leader remained vacant until the next Congress.

3. McCormack became majority leader on Sept. 26, 1940, filling the vacancy caused by the elevation of Rayburn to the post of Speaker of the House on Sept. 16, 1940.

4. Albert became majority leader on Jan. 10, 1962, filling the vacancy caused by the elevation of McCormack to the post of Speaker of the House on Jan. 10, 1962.

5. Rhodes became minority leader on Dec. 7, 1973, filling the vacancy caused by the resignation of Ford on Dec. 6, 1973, to become Vice President.

6. Underwood did not become minority whip until 1901.

7. Lloyd resigned to become chairman of the Democratic Congressional Campaign Committee in 1908. The post of minority whip remained vacant until the beginning of the 62nd Congress.

8. John McDuffie became minority whip after the death of William Oldfield on Nov. 19, 1928.

9. Ramspeck became majority whip on June 8, 1942, filling the vacancy caused by the death of Boland on May 18, 1942.

10. Sparkman became majority whip on Jan. 14, 1946, filling the vacancy caused by the resignation of Ramspeck on Dec. 31, 1945.

11. Boggs became majority whip on Jan. 10, 1962, filling the vacancy caused by the elevation of Albert to the post of majority leader on Jan. 10, 1962.

Sources: Oleszek, Walter J. "Party Whips in the United States Senate." *Journal of Politics* 33 (November 1971): 955-979; Ripley, Randall B. *Party Leaders in the House of Representatives.* Washington, D.C.: Brookings Institution, 1967; U.S. Congress. Joint Committee on Printing. *Official Congressional Directory.* Washington, D.C.: Government Printing Office, 1967-—. U.S. Congress. Senate. *Biographical Directory of the American Congress, 1774-1971.* Compiled by Lawrence F. Kennedy. 92d Cong, 1st sess., 1971. S Doc. 8; U.S. Congress. Senate. *Majority and Minority Leaders of the Senate.* Compiled by Floyd M. Riddick. 94th Cong, 1st sess., 1975. S Doc. 66.

Political Party Affiliations in Congress...

(Letter symbols for political parties: Ad—Administration; AM—Anti-Masonic; C—Coalition; D—Democratic; DR—Democratic-Republican; F—Federalist; J—Jacksonian; NR—National Republican; Op—Opposition; R—Republican; U—Unionist; W—Whig. Figures are for the beginning of the first session of each Congress.)

Year	Congress	HOUSE Majority party	HOUSE Principal minority party	HOUSE Other (except vacancies)	SENATE Majority party	SENATE Principal minority party	SENATE Other (except vacancies)	President
1985-1987	99th	D-252	R-182	-	R-53	D-47	-	R (Reagan)
1983-1985	98th	D-269	R-165	-	R-54	D-46	-	R (Reagan)
1981-1983	97th	D-243	R-192	-	R-53	D-46	1	R (Reagan)
1979-1981	96th	D-276	R-157	-	D-58	R-41	1	D (Carter)
1977-1979	95th	D-292	R-143	-	D-61	R-38	1	D (Carter
1975-1977	94th	D-291	R-144	-	D-60	R-37	2	R (Ford)
1973-1975	93rd	D-239	R-192	1	D-56	R-42	2	R (Nixon-Ford)
1971-1973	92nd	D-254	R-180	-	D-54	R-44	2	R (Nixon)
1969-1971	91st	D-243	R-192	-	D-57	R-43	-	R (Nixon)
1967-1969	90th	D-247	R-187	-	D-64	R-36	-	D (L. Johnson)
1965-1967	89th	D-295	R-140	-	D-68	R-32	-	D (L. Johnson)
1963-1965	88th	D-258	R-177	-	D-67	R-33	-	D (L. Johnson)
								D (Kennedy)
1961-1963	87th	D-263	R-174	-	D-65	R-35	-	D (Kennedy)
1959-1961	86th	D-283	R-153	-	D-64	R-34	-	R (Eisenhower)
1957-1959	85th	D-233	R-200	-	D-49	R-47	-	R (Eisenhower)
1955-1957	84th	D-232	R-203	-	D-48	R-47	1	R (Eisenhower)
1953-1955	83rd	R-221	D-211	1	R-48	D-47	1	R (Eisenhower)
1951-1953	82nd	D-234	R-199	1	D-49	R-47	-	D (Truman)
1949-1951	81st	D-263	R-171	1	D-54	R-42	-	D (Truman)
1947-1949	80th	R-245	D-188	1	R-51	D-45	-	D (Truman)
1945-1947	79th	D-242	R-190	2	D-56	R-38	1	D (Truman)
1943-1945	78th	D-218	R-208	4	D-58	R-37	1	D (F. Roosevelt)
1941-1943	77th	D-268	R-162	5	D-66	R-28	2	D (F. Roosevelt)
1939-1941	76th	D-261	R-164	4	D-69	R-23	4	D (F. Roosevelt)
1937-1939	75th	D-331	R-89	13	D-76	R-16	4	D (F. Roosevelt)
1935-1937	74th	D-319	R-103	10	D-69	R-25	2	D (F. Roosevelt)
1933-1935	73rd	D-310	R-117	5	D-60	R-35	1	D (F. Roosevelt)
1931-1933	72nd	D-220	R-214	1	R-48	D-47	1	R (Hoover)
1929-1931	71st	R-267	D-167	1	R-56	D-39	1	R (Hoover)
1927-1929	70th	R-237	D-195	3	R-49	D-46	1	R (Coolidge)
1925-1927	69th	R-247	D-183	4	R-56	D-39	1	R (Coolidge)
1923-1925	68th	R-225	D-205	5	R-51	D-43	2	R (Coolidge)
1921-1923	67th	R-301	D-131	1	R-59	D-37	-	R (Harding)
1919-1921	66th	R-240	D-190	3	R-49	D-47	-	D (Wilson)
1917-1919	65th	D-216	R-210	6	D-53	R-42	-	D (Wilson)
1915-1917	64th	D-230	R-196	9	D-56	R-40	-	D (Wilson)
1913-1915	63rd	D-291	R-127	17	D-51	R-44	1	D (Wilson)
1911-1913	62nd	D-228	R-161	1	R-51	D-41	-	R (Taft)
1909-1911	61st	R-219	D-172	-	R-61	D-32	-	R (Taft)
1907-1909	60th	R-222	D-164	-	R-61	D-31	-	R (T. Roosevelt)
1905-1907	59th	R-250	D-136	-	R-57	D-33	-	R (T. Roosevelt)
1903-1905	58th	R-208	D-178	-	R-57	D-33	-	R (T. Roosevelt)
1901-1903	57th	R-197	D-151	9	R-55	D-31	4	R (T. Roosevelt)
								R (McKinley)
1899-1901	56th	R-185	D-163	9	R-53	D-26	8	R (McKinley)
1897-1899	55th	R-204	D-113	40	R-47	D-34	7	R (McKinley)
1895-1897	54th	R-244	D-105	7	R-43	D-39	6	R (McKinley)
1893-1895	53rd	D-218	R-127	11	D-44	R-38	3	D (Cleveland)
1891-1893	52nd	D-235	R-88	9	R-47	D-39	2	D (Cleveland)
1889-1891	51st	R-166	D-159	-	R-39	D-37	-	R (B. Harrison)
1887-1889	50th	D-169	R-152	4	R-39	D-37	-	R (B. Harrison)
1885-1887	49th	D-183	R-140	2	R-43	D-34	-	D (Cleveland)
1883-1885	48th	D-197	R-118	10	R-38	D-36	2	D (Cleveland)
1881-1883	47th	R-147	D-135	11	R-37	D-37	1	R (Arthur)
								R (Arthur)
								R (Garfield)

...and the Presidency: 1789 to 1985

(Letter symbols for political parties: Ad—Administration; AM—Anti-Masonic; C—Coalition; D—Democratic; DR—Democratic-Republican; F—Federalist; J—Jacksonian; NR—National Republican; Op—Opposition; R—Republican; U—Unionist; W—Whig. Figures are for the beginning of the first session of each Congress.)

Year	Congress	HOUSE Majority party	HOUSE Principal minority party	HOUSE Other (except vacancies)	SENATE Majority party	SENATE Principal minority party	SENATE Other (except vacancies)	President
1879-1881	46th	D-149	R-130	14	D-42	R-33	1	R (Hayes)
1877-1879	45th	D-153	R-140	-	R-39	D-36	1	R (Hayes)
1875-1877	44th	D-169	R-109	14	R-45	D-29	2	R (Grant)
1873-1875	43rd	R-194	D-92	14	R-49	D-19	5	R (Grant)
1871-1873	42nd	R-134	D-104	5	R-52	D-17	5	R (Grant)
1869-1871	41st	R-149	D-63	-	R-56	D-11	-	R (Grant)
1867-1869	40th	R-143	D-49	-	R-42	D-11	-	R (A. Johnson)
1865-1867	39th	U-149	D-42	-	U-42	D-10	-	R (A. Johnson)
								R (Lincoln)
1863-1865	38th	R-102	D-75	9	R-36	D-9	5	R (Lincoln)
1861-1863	37th	R-105	D-43	30	R-31	D-10	8	R (Lincoln)
1859-1861	36th	R-114	D-92	31	D-36	R-26	4	D (Buchanan)
1857-1859	35th	D-118	R-92	26	D-36	R-20	8	D (Buchanan)
1855-1857	34th	R-108	D-83	43	D-40	R-15	5	D (Pierce)
1853-1855	33rd	D-159	W-71	4	D-38	W-22	2	D (Pierce)
1851-1853	32nd	D-140	W-88	5	D-35	W-24	3	W (Fillmore)
1849-1851	31st	D-112	W-109	9	D-35	W-25	2	W (Fillmore)
								W (Taylor)
1847-1849	30th	W-115	D-108	4	D-36	W-21	1	D (Polk)
1845-1847	29th	D-143	W-77	6	D-31	W-25	-	D (Polk)
1843-1845	28th	D-142	W-79	1	W-28	D-25	1	W (Tyler)
1841-1843	27th	W-133	D-102	6	W-28	D-22	2	W (Tyler)
								W (W. Harrison)
1839-1841	26th	D-124	W-118	-	D-28	W-22	-	D (Van Buren)
1837-1839	25th	D-108	W-107	24	D-30	W-18	4	D (Van Buren)
1835-1837	24th	D-145	W-98	-	D-27	W-25	-	D (Jackson)
1833-1835	23rd	D-147	AM-53	60	D-20	NR-20	8	D (Jackson)
1831-1833	22nd	D-141	NR-58	14	D-25	NR-21	2	D (Jackson)
1829-1831	21st	D-139	NR-74	-	D-26	NR-22	-	D (Jackson)
1827-1829	20th	J-119	Ad-94	-	J-28	Ad-20	-	C (John Q. Adams)
1825-1827	19th	Ad-105	J-97	-	Ad-26	J-20	-	C (John Q. Adams)
1823-1825	18th	DR-187	F-26	-	DR-44	F-4	-	DR (Monroe)
1821-1823	17th	DR-158	F-25	-	DR-44	F-4	-	DR (Monroe)
1819-1821	16th	DR-156	F-27	-	DR-35	F-7	-	DR (Monroe)
1817-1819	15th	DR-141	F-42	-	DR-34	F-10	-	DR (Monroe)
1815-1817	14th	DR-117	F-65	-	DR-25	F-11	-	DR (Madison)
1813-1815	13th	DR-112	F-68	-	DR-27	F-9	-	DR (Madison)
1811-1813	12th	DR-108	F-36	-	DR-30	F-6	-	DR (Madison)
1809-1811	11th	DR-94	F-48	-	DR-28	F-6	-	DR (Madison)
1807-1809	10th	DR-118	F-24	-	DR-28	F-6	-	DR (Jefferson)
1805-1807	9th	DR-116	F-25	-	DR-27	F-7	-	DR (Jefferson)
1803-1805	8th	DR-102	F-39	-	DR-25	F-9	-	DR (Jefferson)
1801-1803	7th	DR-69	F-36	-	DR-18	F-13	-	DR (Jefferson)
1799-1801	6th	F-64	DR-42	-	F-19	DR-13	-	F (John Adams)
1797-1799	5th	F-58	DR-48	-	F-20	DR-12	-	F (John Adams)
1795-1797	4th	F-54	DR-52	-	F-19	DR-13	-	F (Washington)
1793-1795	3rd	DR-57	F-48	-	F-17	DR-13	-	F (Washington)
1791-1793	2nd	F-37	DR-33	-	F-16	DR-13	-	F (Washington)
1789-1791	1st	Ad-38	Op-26	-	Ad-17	Op-9	-	F (Washington)

Sources: U.S. Bureau of the Census. *Historical Statistics of the United States, Colonial Times to 1970.* Washington, D.C: Government Printing Office, 1975; U.S. Bureau of the Census. *Statistical Abstract of the United States, 1985.* Washington, D.C.: Government Printing Office, 1984; U.S. Congress. Joint Committee on Printing. *Official Congressional Directory.* Washington, D.C.: Government Printing Office, 1967- —.

Results of Elections in House . . .

	44	46	48	50	52	54	56	58	60	62	64	66	68	70	72	74	76	78	80	82	84
National Totals																					
Democrats	242	188	263	235	213	232	234	283	263	259	295	248	243	255	243	291	292	277	243[7]	269	253
Republicans	191	246	171	199	221	203	201	153	174	176	140	187	192	180	192	143	143	158	192	166	182
Alabama																					
Democrats	9	9	9	9	9	9	9	9	9	8[2]	3	5	5	5	4[2]	4	4	4	4	5	5
Republicans	0	0	0	0	0	0	0	0	0	0	5	3	3	3	3	3	3	3	3	2	2
Alaska																					
Democrats	—	—	—	—	—	—	—	1	1	1	1	0	0	1	1[4]	0	0	0	0	0	0
Republicans	—	—	—	—	—	—	—	0	0	0	0	1	1	0	0	1	1	1	1	1	1
Arizona																					
Democrats	2	2	2	2	1[1]	1	1	1	1	2[1]	2	1	1	1	1[1]	1	2	2	2	2[1]	1
Republicans	0	0	0	0	1[1]	1	1	1	1	1	1	2	2	2	3	3	2	2	2	3	4
Arkansas																					
Democrats	7	7	7	7	6	6	6	6	6	4[2]	4	3	3	3	3	3	3	2	2	2	3
Republicans	0	0	0	0	0	0	0	0	0	0	0	1	1	1	1	1	1	2	2	2	1
California																					
Democrats	16	9	10	10	11	11	13	16	16	25[1,4]	23	21	21	20	23[1]	28	29	26	22	28[1]	27
Republicans	7	14	13	13	19	19	17	14	13	15	17	17	18	20	15	14	17	21	17	17	18
Colorado																					
Democrats	0	1	3	2	2	2	2	3	2	2	4	3	3	2	2[1]	3	3	3	3	3[1]	2
Republicans	4	3	1	2	2	2	2	1	2	2	0	1	1	2	3	2	2	2	2	3	4
Connecticut																					
Democrats	4	0	3	2	1	1	0	6	4	5	6	5	4	4	3	4	4	5	4	4	3
Republicans	2	6	3	4	5	5	6	0	2	1	0	1	2	2	3	2	2	1	2	2	3
Delaware																					
Democrats	1	0	0	0	0	1	0	1	1	1	1	0	0	0	0	0	0	0	0	1	1
Republicans	0	1	1	1	1	0	1	0	0	0	0	1	1	1	1	1	1	1	1	0	0
Florida																					
Democrats	6	6	6	6	8	7	7	7	7	10[1]	10	9	9	9	11[1]	10	10	12	11	13[1]	12
Republicans	0	0	0	0	0	1	1	1	1	2	2	3	3	3	4	5	5	3	4	6	7
Georgia																					
Democrats	10	10	10	10	10	10	10	10	10	10	9	8	8	8	9	10	10	9	9	9	8
Republicans	0	0	0	0	0	0	0	0	0	0	1	2	2	2	1	0	0	1	1	1	2
Hawaii																					
Democrats	—	—	—	—	—	—	—	—	1	2[1]	2	2	2	2	2	2	2	2	2	2	2
Republicans	—	—	—	—	—	—	—	—	0	0	0	0	0	0	0	0	0	0	0	0	0
Idaho																					
Democrats	1	0	1	0	1	1	1	1	2	2	1	0	0	0	0	0	0	0	0	0	1
Republicans	1	2	1	2	1	1	1	1	0	0	1	2	2	2	2	2	2	2	2	2	1
Illinois																					
Democrats	11	6	12	8	9	12	11	14	14	12[2]	13	12	12	12	10	13	12	11	10	12[2]	13
Republicans	15	20	14	18	16	13	14	11	11	12	11	12	12	12	14	11	12	13	14	10	9
Indiana																					
Democrats	2	2	7	2	1	2	2	8	4[3]	4	6	5	4	5	4	9	8	7	6	5[2]	6[8]
Republicans	9	9	4	9	10	9	9	3	7	7	5	6	7	6	7	2	3	4	5	5	5
Iowa																					
Democrats	0	0	0	0	0	0	1	4	2	1[2]	6	2	2	2	3[2]	5	4	3	3	3	2
Republicans	8	8	8	8	8	8	7	4	6	6	1	5	5	5	3	1	3	3	3	3	4
Kansas																					
Democrats	0	0	0	0	1	0	1	3	1	0[2]	0	0	0	1	1	1	2	1	1	2	2
Republicans	6	6	6	6	5	6	5	3	5	5	5	5	5	4	4	4	3	4	4	3	3
Kentucky																					
Democrats	8	6	7	7	6	6	6	7	7	5[2]	6	4	4	5	5	5	5	4	4	4	4
Republicans	1	3	2	2	2	2	2	1	1	2	1	3	3	2	2	2	2	3	3	3	3
Louisiana																					
Democrats	8	8	8	8	8	8	8	8	8	8	8	8	8	7[4]	6[8]	6	5	6	6	6	6
Republicans	0	0	0	0	0	0	0	0	0	0	0	0	0	0	1	1	2	3	2	2	2
Maine																					
Democrats	0	0	0	0	0	0	1	2	0	0[2]	1	2	2	2	1	0	0	0	0	0	0
Republicans	3	3	3	3	3	3	2	1	3	2	1	0	0	0	1	2	2	2	2	2	2
Maryland																					
Democrats	5	4	4	3	3	4	4	7	6	6[1]	6	5	4	5	4	5	5	6	7	7	6
Republicans	1	2	2	3	4	3	3	0	1	2	2	3	4	3	4	3	3	2	1	1	2
Massachusetts																					
Democrats	4	5	6	6	6	7	7	8	8	7[2]	7	7	7	8	9[5]	10	10	10	10	10[2]	10
Republicans	10	9	8	8	8	7	7	6	6	5	5	5	5	4	3	2	2	2	2	1	1
Michigan																					
Democrats	6	3	5	5	5	7	6	7	7	8[1]	12	7	7	7	7	12	11	13	12	12[2]	11
Republicans	11	14	12	12	13	11	12	11	11	11	7	12	12	12	7	7	8	6	7	6	7
Minnesota																					
Democrats	2	1	4	4	4	5	5	4	3	4[2]	4	3	3	4	4	5	5	4	3	5	5
Republicans	7	8	5	5	5	4	4	5	6	4	4	5	5	4	4	3	3	4	5	3	3
Mississippi																					
Democrats	7	7	7	7	6	6	6	6	6	5[2]	4	5	5	5	3	3	3	3	3	3	3
Republicans	0	0	0	0	0	0	0	0	0	0	1	0	0	0	2	2	2	2	2	2	2
Missouri																					
Democrats	7	4	12	10	7	9	10	10	9	8[2]	8	8	9	9	9	9	8	8	6	6[2]	6
Republicans	6	9	1	3	4	2	1	1	2	2	2	2	1	1	1	1	2	2	4	3	3
Montana																					
Democrats	1	1	1	1	1	1	2	2	1	1	1	1	1	1	1	2	1	1	1	1	1
Republicans	1	1	1	1	1	1	0	0	1	1	1	1	1	1	1	0	1	1	1	1	1
Nebraska																					
Democrats	0	0	1	0	0	0	0	2	1	0[2]	1	0	0	0	0	1	1	0	0	0	0
Republicans	4	4	3	4	4	4	4	2	4	3	2	3	3	3	3	2	2	3	3	3	3

. . . of Representatives, 1944-1984

	44	46	48	50	52	54	56	58	60	62	64	66	68	70	72	74	76	78	80	82	84
National Totals																					
Democrats	242	188	263	235	213	232	234	283	263	259	295	248	243	255	243	291	292	277	243[7]	269	253
Republicans	191	246	171	199	221	203	201	153	174	176	140	187	192	180	192	143	143	158	192	166	182
Nevada																					
Democrats	1	0	1	1	0	0	1	1	1	1	1	1	1	1	1	0	1	1	1	1[1]	1
Republicans	0	1	0	0	1	1	0	0	0	0	0	0	0	0	0	1	0	0	0	0	1
New Hampshire																					
Democrats	0	0	0	0	0	0	0	0	0	0	1	0	0	0	0	1	1	1	1	1	0
Republicans	2	2	2	2	2	2	2	2	2	2	1	2	2	2	2	1	1	1	1	1	2
New Jersey																					
Democrats	2	2	5	5	5	6	4	5	6	7[1]	11	9	9	9	8	12	11	10	8	9[2]	8
Republicans	12	12	9	9	9	8	10	9	8	8	4	6	6	6	7	3	4	5	7	5	6
New Mexico																					
Democrats	2	2	2	2	2	2	2	2	2	2	2	2	0	1	1	1	1	1	1	1[1]	1
Republicans	0	0	0	0	0	0	0	0	0	0	0	0	2	1	1	1	1	1	1	2	2
New York																					
Democrats	22	16	24	23	16	17	17	19	22	20[2]	27	26	26	24	22[2]	27	28	26	22	20[2]	19
Republicans	22	28	20	22	27	26	26	24	21	21	14	15	15	17	17	12	11	13	17	14	15
North Carolina																					
Democrats	12	12	12	12	11	11	11	11	11	9[2]	9	8	7	7	7	9	9	9	7	9	6
Republicans	0	0	0	0	1	1	1	1	1	2	2	3	4	4	4	2	2	2	4	2	5
North Dakota																					
Democrats	0	0	0	0	0	0	0	1	0	0	1	0	0	1	0[2]	1	1	1	1	0	0
Republicans	2	2	2	2	2	2	2	1	2	2	1	2	2	1	1	0	0	0	0	1	1
Ohio																					
Democrats	6	4	12	7	6	6	6	9	7	6[1]	10	5	6	7	7[2]	8	10	10	11	10[2]	11
Republicans	17	19	11	15	16	17	17	14	16	18	14	19	18	17	16	15	13	13	12	11	10
Oklahoma																					
Democrats	6	6	8	6	5	5	5	5	5	5	5	4	4	4	5	6	5	5	5	5	5
Republicans	2	2	0	2	1	1	1	1	1	1	1	2	2	2	1	0	1	1	1	1	1
Oregon																					
Democrats	0	0	0	0	0	1	3	3	2	3	3	2	2	2	2	4	4	4	3	3[1]	3
Republicans	4	4	4	4	4	3	1	1	2	1	1	2	2	2	2	0	0	0	1	2	2
Pennsylvania																					
Democrats	15	5	16	13	11	14	13	16	14	13[2]	15	14	14	14	13[2]	14	17	15	13[7]	13[2]	13
Republicans	18	28	17	20	19	16	17	14	16	14	12	13	13	13	12	11	8	10	12	10	10
Rhode Island																					
Democrats	2	2	2	2	2	2	2	2	2	2	2	2	2	2	2	2	2	2	1	1	1
Republicans	0	0	0	0	0	0	0	0	0	0	0	0	0	0	0	0	0	0	1	1	1
South Carolina																					
Democrats	6	6	6	6	6	6	6	6	6	6	6	5	5	5	4	5	5	4	2	3	3
Republicans	0	0	0	0	0	0	0	0	0	0	0	1	1	1	2	1	1	2	4	3	3
South Dakota																					
Democrats	0	0	0	0	0	0	1	1	0	0	0	0	0	2	1	0	0	1	1	1[2]	1
Republicans	2	2	2	2	2	2	1	1	2	2	2	2	2	0	1	2	2	1	1	0	0
Tennessee																					
Democrats	8	8	8	8	7	7	7	7	7	6	6	5	5	5	3[2]	5	5	5	5	6[1]	6
Republicans	2	2	2	2	2	2	2	2	2	3	3	4	4	4	5	3	3	3	3	3	3
Texas																					
Democrats	21	21	21	21	22	21	21	21	21	21[1]	23	21	20	20	20[1]	21	22	20	19	22[1]	17
Republicans	0	0	0	0	0	1	1	1	1	2	0	2	3	3	4	3	2	4	5	5	10
Utah																					
Democrats	2	1	2	2	0	0	0	1	2	0	1	0	0	1	2	2	1	1	0	0[1]	0
Republicans	0	1	0	0	2	2	2	1	0	2	1	2	2	1	0	0	1	1	2	3	3
Vermont																					
Democrats	0	0	0	0	0	0	0	1	0	0	0	0	0	0	0	0	0	0	0	0	0
Republicans	1	1	1	1	1	1	1	0	1	1	1	1	1	1	1	1	1	1	1	1	1
Virginia																					
Democrats	9	9	9	9	7	8	8	8	8	8	8	6	5	4	3	5	4	4	1	4	4
Republicans	0	0	0	0	3	2	2	2	2	2	2	4	5	6	7	5	6	6	9	6	6
Washington																					
Democrats	4	1	2	2	1	1	1	1	2	1	5	5	5	6	6	6	6	6	5	5[1]	5
Republicans	2	5	4	4	6	6	6	6	5	6	2	2	2	1	1	1	1	1	2	3	3
West Virginia																					
Democrats	5	2	6	6	5	6	4	5	5	4[2]	4	4	5	5	4[2]	4	4	4	2	4	4
Republicans	1	4	0	0	1	0	2	1	1	1	1	1	0	0	0	0	0	0	2	0	0
Wisconsin																					
Democrats	2	0	2	1	1	3	3	5	4	4	5	3	3	5	5[2]	7	7	6	5	5	5
Republicans	7	10	8	9	9	7	7	5	6	6	5	7	7	5	4	2	2	3	4	4	4
Wyoming																					
Democrats	0	0	0	0	0	0	0	0	0	0	1	0	0	1	1	1	1	0	0	0	0
Republicans	1	1	1	1	1	1	1	1	1	1	0	1	1	0	0	0	0	1	1	1	1

1. State gained seats due to reapportionment.
2. State lost seats due to reapportionment.
3. Indiana 1960: Figures include final outcome of disputed election in 5th District where a Republican was at first certified the winner but the House decided to seat the Democrat. The 7-4 figure reflects the seating of the Democrat.
4. California 1962, Alaska and Louisiana 1972: Total includes one Democratic candidate who died before the election but his name remained on the ballot and he was re-elected. A special election was held the next year to fill the vacancy.
5. Massachusetts 1972: Democratic total includes Rep. Joe Moakley, elected as an Independent but served as a Democrat.
6. Louisiana 1974: One vacancy. There was no declared winner in the 6th District. A special election was held the next year to fill the vacancy.
7. Pennsylvania 1980: Includes Foglietta, Pa., elected as an Independant.
8. Indiana 1984: Figures include final outcome of disputed election in 8th District where a Republican was at first certified the winner but the House decided to seat the Democrat. The 6-5 figure reflects the seating of the Democrat.

Summary of American...

YEAR	NO OF STATES	CANDIDATES		ELECTORAL VOTE		POPULAR VOTE	
		DEM.	GOP	DEM.	GOP	DEM.	GOP
1860(a)	33	Stephen A. Douglas Herschel V. Johnson	Abraham Lincoln Hannibal Hamlin	12 4%	180 59%	1,380,202 29.5%	1,865,908 39.8%
1864(b)	36	George B. McClellan George H. Pendleton	Abraham Lincoln Andrew Johnson	21 9%	212 91%	1,812,807 45.0%	2,218,388 55.0%
1868(c)	37	Horatio Seymour Francis P. Blair Jr.	Ulysses S. Grant Schuyler Colfax	80 27%	214 73%	2,708,744 47.3%	3,013,650 52.7%
1872(d)	37	Horace Greeley Benjamin Gratz Brown	Ulysses S. Grant Henry Wilson	(d)	286 78%	2,834,761 43.8%	3,598,235 55.6%
1876	38	Samuel J. Tilden Thomas A. Hendricks	Rutherford B. Hayes William A. Wheeler	184 50%	185 50%	4,288,546 51.0%	4,034,311 47.9%
1880	38	Winfield S. Hancock William H. English	James A. Garfield Chester A. Arthur	155 42%	214 58%	4,444,260 48.2%	4,446,158 48.3%
1884	38	Grover Cleveland Thomas A. Hendricks	James G. Blaine John A. Logan	219 55%	182 45%	4,874,621 48.5%	4,848,936 48.2%
1888	38	Grover Cleveland Allen G. Thurman	Benjamin Harrison Levi P. Morton	168 42%	233 58%	5,534,488 48.6%	5,443,892 47.8%
1892(e)	44	Grover Cleveland Adlai E. Stevenson	Benjamin Harrison Whitelaw Reid	277 62%	145 33%	5,551,883 46.1%	5,179,244 43.0%
1896	45	William J. Bryan Arthur Sewall	William McKinley Garret A. Hobart	176 39%	271 61%	6,511,495 46.7%	7,108,480 51.0%
1900	45	William J. Bryan Adlai E. Stevenson	William McKinley Theodore Roosevelt	155 35%	292 65%	6,358,345 45.5%	7,218,039 51.7%
1904	45	Alton B. Parker Henry G. Davis	Theodore Roosevelt Charles W. Fairbanks	140 29%	336 71%	5,028,898 37.6%	7,626,593 56.4%
1908	46	William J. Bryan John W. Kern	William H. Taft James S. Sherman	162 34%	321 66%	6,406,801 43.0%	7,676,258 51.6%
1912(f)	48	Woodrow Wilson Thomas R. Marshall	William H. Taft James S. Sherman	435 82%	8 2%	6,293,152 41.8%	3,486,333 23.2%
1916	48	Woodrow Wilson Thomas R. Marshall	Charles E. Hughes Charles W. Fairbanks	277 52%	254 48%	9,126,300 49.2%	8,546,789 46.1%
1920	48	James M. Cox Franklin D. Roosevelt	Warren G. Harding Calvin Coolidge	127 24%	404 76%	9,140,884 34.2%	16,133,314 60.3%
1924(g)	48	John W. Davis Charles W. Bryant	Calvin Coolidge Charles G. Dawes	136 26%	382 72%	8,386,169 28.8%	15,717,553 54.1%
1928	48	Alfred E. Smith Joseph T. Robinson	Herbert C. Hoover Charles Curtis	87 16%	444 84%	15,000,185 40.8%	21,411,991 58.2%
1932	48	Franklin D. Roosevelt John N. Garner	Herbert C. Hoover Charles Curtis	472 89%	59 11%	22,825,016 57.4%	15,758,397 39.6%
1936	48	Franklin D. Roosevelt John N. Garner	Alfred M. London Frank Knox	523 98%	8 2%	27,747,636 60.8%	16,679,543 36.5%
1940	48	Franklin D. Roosevelt Henry A. Wallace	Wendell L. Willkie Charles L. McNary	449 85%	82 15%	27,263,448 54.7%	22,336,260 44.8%
1944	48	Franklin D. Roosevelt Harry S Truman	Thomas E. Dewey John W. Bricker	432 81%	99 19%	25,611,936 53.4%	22,013,372 45.9%
1948(h)	48	Harry S Truman Alben W. Barkley	Thomas E. Dewey Earl Warren	303 57%	189 36%	24,105,587 49.5%	21,970,017 45.1%
1952	48	Adlai E. Stevenson John J. Sparkman	Dwight D. Eisenhower Richard M. Nixon	89 17%	442 83%	27,314,649 44.4%	33,936,137 55.1%
1956(i)	48	Adlai E. Stevenson Estes Kefauver	Dwight D. Eisenhower Richard M. Nixon	73 14%	457 86%	26,030,172 42.0%	35,585,245 57.4%
1960(j)	50	John F. Kennedy Lyndon B. Johnson	Richard M. Nixon Henry Cabot Lodge	303 56%	219 41%	34,221,344 49.7%	34,106,671 49.5%
1964	50*	Lyndon B. Johnson Hubert H. Humphrey	Barry Goldwater William E. Miller	486 90%	52 10%	43,126,584 61.1%	27,177,838 38.5%
1968(k)	50*	Hubert H. Humphrey Edmund S. Muskie	Richard M. Nixon Spiro T. Agnew	191 36%	301 56%	31,274,503 42.7%	31,785,148 43.4%

...Presidential Elections, 1860-1984

YEAR	NO OF STATES	CANDIDATES		ELECTORAL VOTE		POPULAR VOTE	
		DEM.	GOP	DEM.	GOP	DEM.	GOP
1972[l]	50*	George McGovern Sargent Shriver	Richard M. Nixon Spiro T. Agnew	17 3%	520 97%	29,171,791 37.5%	47,170,179 60.7%
1976[m]	50*	Jimmy Carter Walter F. Mondale	Gerald R. Ford Robert Dole	297 55%	240 45%	40,830,763 50.1%	39,147,793 48.0%
1980	50*	Jimmy Carter Walter F. Mondale	Ronald Reagan George Bush	49 9%	489 91%	35,483,883 41.0%	43,904,153 50.7%
1984	50*	Walter F. Mondale Geraldine Ferraro	Ronald Reagan George Bush	13 2%	525 98%	37,577,137 40.6%	54,455,074 58.8%

(a) *1860: John C. Breckinridge, Southern Democrat, polled 72 electoral votes. John Bell, Constitutional Union, polled 39 electoral votes.*
(b) *1864: 81 electoral votes were not cast.*
(c) *1868: 23 electoral votes were not cast.*
(d) *1872: Horace Greeley died after election, 63 Democratic electoral votes were scattered, 17 were not voted.*
(e) *1892: James B. Weaver, People's Party, polled 22 electoral votes.*
(f) *1912: Theodore Roosevelt, Progressive Party, polled 86 electoral votes.*

(g) *1924: Robert M. LaFollette, Progressive Party, polled 13 electoral votes.*
(h) *1948: J. Strom Thurmond, States' Rights Party, polled 39 electoral votes.*
(i) *1956: Walter B. Jones, Democrat, polled 1 electoral vote.*
(j) *1960: Harry Flood Byrd, Democrat, polled 15 electoral votes.*
(k) *1968: George C. Wallace, American Independent, polled 46 electoral votes.*
(l) *1972: John Hospers, Libertarian Party, polled 1 electoral vote.*
(m) *1976: Ronald Reagan, Republican, polled 1 electoral vote.*
* *Fifty states plus District of Columbia.*

Changing Methods of Electing . . .

Note: The following chart shows the changing methods used by the states to elect presidential electors from 1788 to 1836. *(Additional detail, p. 254)*

State	1788-1789	1792	1796	1800	1804	1808
Alabama	-	-	-	-	-	-
Arkansas	-	-	-	-	-	-
Connecticut	L	L	L	L	L	L
Delaware	D(3) [1]	L	L	L	L	L
Georgia	L	L	GT	L	L	L
Illinois	-	-	-	-	-	-
Indiana	-	-	-	-	-	-
Kentucky	-	D(4)	D(4)	D(4)	D(2) [2]	D(2) [2]
Louisiana	-	-	-	-	-	-
Maine	-	-	-	-	-	-
Maryland	GT	GT	D(10)	D(10)	D(9) [4]	D(9) [4]
Massachusetts	D(8) and L [6]	D(4) and L [7]	D(14) and L [8]	L	D(17) and A(2)	L
Michigan	-	-	-	-	-	-
Mississippi	-	-	-	-	-	-
Missouri	-	-	-	-	-	-
New Hampshire	GT and L [10]	GT [11]	GT and L [10]	L	GT	GT
New Jersey	L	L	L	L	GT	GT
New York	-	L	L	L	L	L
North Carolina	-	L [13]	D(12)	D(12)	D(14)	D(14)
Ohio	-	-	-	-	GT	GT
Pennsylvania	GT	GT	GT	L	GT	GT
Rhode Island	-	L	L	GT	GT	GT
South Carolina	L	L	L	L	L	L
Tennessee	-	-	E [14]	E [14]	D(5)	D(5)
Vermont	-	L	L	L	L	L
Virginia	D(12)	D(21)	D(21)	GT	GT	GT

Explanation of Symbols: L—by Legislature; GT—by people, on general ticket; D—by people, in districts; A—by people, in the state at large; E—by electors. The number in parentheses following the symbol "D" is the number of districts into which the state was divided. As a rule, each district elected 1 elector. The number in parentheses following the symbol "A" is the number of electors elected at large.

1. Each qualified voter voted for 1 elector. The 3 electors who received most votes in the State were elected.
2. Each district elected 4 electors.
3. 2 districts chose 5 electors each, and 1 chose 4 electors.
4. During the years 1804-1828, Maryland chose 11 electors in 9 districts, 2 of the districts elected 2 members each.
5. 1 district chose 4 electors; 1, 3 electors; 1, 2 electors; 1, 1 elector.
6. Each of the 8 districts chose 2 electors, from which the General Court (i.e., the legislature) selected 1. It also elected 2 electors at large.
7. 2 of the districts voted for 5 members each, and 2 for 3 members each. A majority of votes was necessary for a choice. In case of a failure to elect by popular vote the General Court supplied the deficiency. In the election of 1792, the people chose 5 electors and the General Court, 11.

... Presidential Electors: 1788-1836

Source: Bureau of the Census, *Historical Statistics of the United States; Colonial Times to 1970* (Washington, D.C.: Government Printing Office, 1975).

	1812	1816	1820	1824	1828	1832	1836
Ala.	-	-	L	GT	GT	GT	GT
Ark.	-	-	-	-	-	-	GT
Conn.	L	L	GT	GT	GT	GT	GT
Del.	L	L	L	L	L	GT	GT
Ga.	L	L	L	L	GT	GT	GT
Ill.	-	-	D(3)	D(3)	GT	GT	GT
Ind.	-	L	L	GT	GT	GT	GT
Ky.	D(3) [2]	D(3) [2]	D(3) [2]	D(3) [3]	GT	GT	GT
La.	L	L	L	L	GT	GT	GT
Maine	-	-	D(7) and A(2)	D(7) and A(2)	D(7) and A(2)	GT	GT
Md.	D(9) [4]	D(9) [4]	D(9) [4]	D(9) [4]	D(9) [4]	D(4) [5]	GT
Mass.	D(6) [9]	L	D(13) and A(2)	GT	GT	GT	GT
Mich.	-	-	-	-	-	-	GT
Miss.	-	-	GT	GT	GT	GT	GT
Mo.	-	-	L	D(3)	GT	GT	GT
N.H.	GT	GT	GT	GT	GT	GT	GT
N.J.	L	GT	GT	GT	GT	GT	GT
N.Y.	L	L	L	L	D(30) and E [12]	GT	GT
N.C.	L	GT	GT	GT	GT	GT	GT
Ohio	GT	GT	GT	GT	GT	GT	GT
Pa.	GT	GT	GT	GT	GT	GT	GT
R.I.	GT	GT	GT	GT	GT	GT	GT
S.C.	L	L	L	L	L	L	L
Tenn.	D(8)	D(8)	D(8)	D(11)	D(11)	GT	GT
Vt.	L	L	L	L	GT	GT	GT
Va.	GT	GT	GT	GT	GT	GT	GT

8. A majority of votes was necessary for a popular choice. Deficiencies were filled by the General Court, as in 1792. It also chose 2 electors at large. In 1796 it chose 9 electors, and the people, 7.

9. 1 district chose 6 electors; 1, 5 electors; 1, 4 electors; 2, 3 electors each; and 1, 1 elector.

10. A majority of the popular vote was necessary for a choice. In case of a failure to elect, the legislature supplied the deficiency.

11. A majority of votes was necessary for a choice. In case of a failure to elect 1 or more electors a second election was held by the people, at which choice was made from the candidates in the first election who had the most votes. The

number of candidates in the second election was limited to twice the number of electors wanted.

12. 1 district elected 3 electors; 2, 2 electors each; and 27, 1 elector each. The 34 electors thus elected chose 2 presidential electors.

13. The State was divided into 4 districts, and the members of the legislature residing in each district chose 3 electors.

14. In 1796 and 1800, Tennilton choose 3 presidential electors—1 each for the districts of Washington, Hamilton, and Mero. 3 "electors" for each county in the State were appointed by the legislature, and the "electors" residing in each of the 3 districts chose 1 of the 3 presidential electors.

Election Results, Congress and Presidency, 1856-1984

Election Year	Congress Elected	HOUSE Members Elected Dem.	Rep.	Misc.	HOUSE Gains/Losses Dem.	Rep.	SENATE Members Elected Dem.	Rep.	Misc.	SENATE Gains/Losses Dem.	Rep.	PRESIDENCY Elected	Popular Vote Plurality
1856	35th	131	92	14	+ 48	− 16	39	20	5	− 3	+ 5	Buchanan (D)	498,209
1858	36th	101	113	23	− 30	+· 21	38	26	2	− 1	+ 6		
1860	37th	42	106	28	− 59	− 7	11	31	7	−27	+ 5	Lincoln (R)	487,764
1862	38th	80	103		+ 38	− 3	12	39		+ 1	+ 8		
1864	39th	46	145		− 34	+ 42	10	42		− 2	+ 3	Lincoln (R)	414,299
1866	40th	49	143		+ 3	− 2	11	42		+ 1	0	Johnson (R)	
1868	41st	73	170		+ 24	+ 27	11	61		0	+19	Grant (R)	309,380
1870	42nd	104	139		+ 31	− 31	17	57		+ 6	− 4		
1872	43rd	88	203		− 16	+ 64	19	54		+ 2	− 3	Grant (R)	763,664
1874	44th	181	107	3	+ 93	−96	29	46		+10	− 8		
1876	45th	156	137		− 25	+ 30	36	39	1	+ 7	− 7	Hayes (R)	−251,746
1878	46th	150	128	14	− 6	− 9	43	33		+ 7	− 6		
1880	47th	130	152	11	− 20	+ 24	37	37	2	− 6	+ 4	Garfield (R)	9,457
1882	48th	200	119	6	+ 70	− 33	36	40		− 1	+ 3	Arthur (R)	
1884	49th	182	140	2	− 18	+ 21	34	41		− 2	+ 2	Cleveland (D)	23,737
1886	50th	170	151	4	− 12	+ 11	37	39		+ 3	− 2		
1888	51st	156	173	1	− 14	+ 22	37	47		0	+ 8	Harrison (R)	−95,096
1890	52nd	231	88	14	+ 75	− 85	39	47	2	+ 2	0		
1892	53rd	220	126	8	− 11	+ 38	44	38	3	+ 5	− 9	Cleveland (D)	365,516
1894	54th	104	246	7	−116	+120	30	44	5	− 5	+ 6		
1896	55th	134	206	16	+ 30	− 40	34	46	10	− 5	+ 2	McKinley (R)	597,012
1898	56th	163	185	9	+ 29	− 21	26	53	11	− 8	+ 7		
1900	57th	153	198	5	− 10	+ 13	29	56	3	+ 3	+ 3	McKinley (R)	861,668
1902	58th	178	207		+ 25	+ 9	32	58		+ 3	+ 2	Roosevelt (R)	
1904	59th	136	250		− 42	+ 43	32	58		0	0	Roosevelt (R)	2,544,298
1906	60th	164	222		+ 28	− 28	29	61		− 3	− 3		
1908	61st	172	219		+ 8	− 3	32	59		+ 3	− 2	Taft (R)	1,268,449
1910	62nd	228	162	1	+ 56	− 57	42	49		+10	−10		
1912	63rd	290	127	18	+ 62	− 35	51	44	1	+ 9	− 5	Wilson (D)	2,173,466
1914	64th	231	193	8	− 59	+ 66	56	39	1	+ 5	− 5		
1916	65th	210	216	9	− 21	+ 23	53	42	1	− 3	+ 3	Wilson (D)	582,576
1918	66th	191	237	7	− 19	+ 21	47	48	1	− 6	+ 6		
1920	67th	132	300	1	− 59	+ 63	37	59		−10	+11	Harding (R)	7,020,023
1922	68th	207	225	3	+ 75	− 75	43	51	2	+ 6	− 8	Coolidge (R)	
1924	69th	183	247	5	− 24	+ 22	40	54	1	− 3	+ 3	Coolidge (R)	333,217
1926	70th	195	237	3	+ 12	− 10	47	48	1	+ 7	− 6		
1928	71st	163	267	1	− 32	+ 30	39	56	1	− 8	+ 8	Hoover (R)	6,429,579
1930	72nd	216	218	1	+ 53	− 49	47	48	1	+ 8	− 8		
1932	73rd	313	117	5	+ 97	−101	59	36	1	+12	−12	Roosevelt (D)	7,068,817
1934	74th	322	103	10	+ 9	− 14	69	25	2	+10	−11		
1936	75th	333	89	13	+ 11	− 14	75	17	4	+ 6	− 8	Roosevelt (D)	11,073,102
1938	76th	262	169	4	− 71	+ 80	69	23	4	− 6	+ 6		
1940	77th	267	162	6	+ 5	− 7	66	28	2	− 3	+ 5	Roosevelt (D)	4,964,561
1942	78th	222	209	4	− 45	+ 47	57	38	1	− 9	+ 10		
1944	79th	243	190	2	+ 21	− 19	57	38	1	0	0	Roosevelt (D)	3,594,993
1946	80th	188	246	1	− 55	+ 56	45	51		−12	+13	Truman	
1948	81st	263	171	1	+ 75	− 75	54	42		+ 9	− 9	Truman (D)	2,188,054
1950	82nd	234	199	2	− 29	+ 28	48	47	1	− 6	+ 5		
1952	83rd	213	221	1	− 21	+ 22	47	48	1	− 1	+ 1	Eisenhower (R)	6,621,242
1954	84th	232	203		+ 19	− 18	48	47	1	+ 1	− 1		
1956	85th	234	201		+ 2	− 2	49	47		+ 1	0	Eisenhower (R)	9,567,720
1958	86th	283	154		+ 49	− 47	64	34		+17	−13		
1960	87th	263	174		− 20	+ 20	64	36		− 2	+ 2	Kennedy (D)	118,574*
1962	88th	258	176	1**	− 4	+ 2	67	33		+ 4	− 4		
1964	89th	295	140		+ 38	− 38	68	32		+ 2	− 2	Johnson (D)	15,951,296
1966	90th	248	187		− 47	+ 47	64	36		− 3	+ 3		
1968	91st	243	192		− 4	+ 4	58	42		− 5	+ 5	Nixon (R)	510,314
1970	92nd	255	180		+ 12	− 12	55	45		− 4	+ 2		
1972	93rd	243	192		− 12	+ 12	57	43		+ 2	− 2	Nixon (R)	17,999,528
1974	94th	291	144		+ 43	− 43	61†	38		+ 3†	− 3		
1976	95th	292	143		+ 1	− 1	62	38		0	0	Carter (D)	1,682,970
1978	96th	277	158		− 11	+ 11	59	41		− 3	+ 3		
1980	97th	243	192		− 33	+ 33	47	53		−12	+12	Reagan (R)	8,420,270
1982	98th	269	166		+ 26	− 26	46	54		0	0		
1984	99th	253	182		− 14	+ 14	47	53		+ 2	− 2	Reagan (R)	16,877,937

* Includes divided Alabama elector slate votes.

** Vacancy — Rep. Clem Miller, D-Calif. (1959-62) died Oct. 6, 1962, but his name remained on the ballot and he received a plurality.

Distribution of House Seats and Electoral Votes

Based on Censuses of 1950, 1960, 1970 and 1980

	U.S. HOUSE SEATS							ELECTORAL VOTES		
	1953-1963	1960 Census Changes	1963-1973	1970 Census Changes	1973-1983	1980 Census Changes	1985	1952, 1956, 1960	1964, 1968	1972, 1976, 1980, 1984
Alabama	9	−1	8	−1	7	0	7	11	10	9
Alaska	1	—	1	—	1	0	1	3	3	3
Arizona	2	+1	3	+1	4	+1	5	4	5	6
Arkansas	6	−2	4	—	4	0	4	8	6	6
California	30	+8	38	+5	43	+2	45	32	40	45
Colorado	4	—	4	+1	5	+1	6	6	6	7
Connecticut	6	—	6	—	6	0	6	8	8	8
Delaware	1	—	1	—	1	0	1	3	3	3
District of Columbia	—	—	—	—	—	—	—	—	3	3
Florida	8	+4	12	+3	15	+4	19	10	14	17
Georgia	10	—	10	—	10	0	10	12	12	12
Hawaii	1	+1	2	—	2	0	2	3	4	4
Idaho	2	—	2	—	2	0	2	4	4	4
Illinois	25	−1	24	—	24	−2	22	27	26	26
Indiana	11	—	11	—	11	−1	10	13	13	13
Iowa	8	−1	7	−1	6	0	6	10	9	8
Kansas	6	−1	5	—	5	0	5	8	7	7
Kentucky	8	−1	7	—	7	0	7	10	9	9
Louisiana	8	—	8	—	8	0	8	10	10	10
Maine	3	−1	2	—	2	0	2	5	4	4
Maryland	7	+1	8	—	8	0	8	9	10	10
Massachusetts	14	−2	12	—	12	−1	11	16	14	14
Michigan	18	+1	19	—	19	−1	18	20	21	21
Minnesota	9	−1	8	—	8	0	8	11	10	10
Mississippi	6	−1	5	—	5	0	5	8	7	7
Missouri	11	−1	10	—	10	−1	9	13	12	12
Montana	2	—	2	—	2	0	2	4	4	4
Nebraska	4	−1	3	—	3	0	3	6	5	5
Nevada	1	—	1	—	1	+1	2	3	3	3
New Hampshire	2	—	2	—	2	0	2	4	4	4
New Jersey	14	+1	15	—	15	−1	14	16	17	17
New Mexico	2	—	2	—	2	+1	3	4	4	4
New York	43	−2	41	−2	39	−5	34	45	43	41
North Carolina	12	−1	11	—	11	0	11	14	13	13
North Dakota	2	—	2	−1	1	0	1	4	4	3
Ohio	23	+1	24	−1	23	−2	21	25	26	25
Oklahoma	6	—	6	—	6	0	6	8	8	8
Oregon	4	—	4	—	4	+1	5	6	6	6
Pennsylvania	30	−3	27	−2	25	−2	23	32	29	27
Rhode Island	2	—	2	—	2	0	2	4	4	4
South Carolina	6	—	6	—	6	0	6	8	8	8
South Dakota	2	—	2	—	2	−1	1	4	4	4
Tennessee	9	—	9	−1	8	+1	9	11	11	10
Texas	22	+1	23	+1	24	+3	27	24	25	26
Utah	2	—	2	—	2	+1	3	4	4	4
Vermont	1	—	1	—	1	0	1	3	3	3
Virginia	10	—	10	—	10	0	10	12	12	12
Washington	7	—	7	—	7	+1	8	9	9	9
West Virginia	6	−1	5	−1	4	0	4	8	7	6
Wisconsin	10	—	10	−1	9	0	9	12	12	11
Wyoming	1	—	1	—	1	0	1	3	3	3

Constitutional Provisions and Amendments on Elections

Article I

Section 2:

The House of Representatives shall be composed of Members chosen every second Year by the People of the several States, and the Electors in each State shall have the Qualifications requisite for Electors of the most numerous Branch of the State Legislature.

No Person shall be a Representative who shall not have attained to the age of twenty five Years, and been seven Years a Citizen of the United States, and who shall not, when elected, be an Inhabitant of that State in which he shall be chosen.

Representatives and direct Taxes shall be apportioned among the several States which may be included within this Union, according to their respective Numbers, which shall be determined by adding to the whole Number of free Persons, including those bound to Service for a Term of Years, and excluding Indians not taxed, three fifths of all other Persons. The actual Enumeration shall be made within three Years after the first Meeting of the Congress of the United States, and within every subsequent Term of ten Years, in such Manner as they shall by Law direct. The number of Representatives shall not exceed one for every thirty Thousand, but each State shall have at Least one Representative; and until such enumeration shall be made, the State of New Hampshire shall be entitled to chuse three, Massachusetts eight, Rhode-Island and Providence Plantations one, Connecticut five, New-York six, New Jersey four, Pennsylvania eight, Delaware one, Maryland six, Virginia ten, North Carolina five, South Carolina five, and Georgia three.

When vacancies happen in the Representation from any State, the Executive Authority thereof shall issue Writs of Election to fill such Vacancies....

Section 3:

The Senate of the United States shall be composed of two Senators from each State, chosen by the Legislature thereof, for six Years; and each Senator shall have one Vote.

Immediately after they shall be assembled in Consequence of the first Election, they shall be divided as equally as may be into three Classes. The Seats of the Senators of the first Class shall be vacated at the Expiration of the second Year, of the second Class at the Expiration of the fourth Year, and of the third Class at the Expiration of the sixth Year, so that one third may be chosen every second Year; and if Vacancies happen by Resignation, or pointments until the next Meeting of the Legislature, which shall then fill such Vacancies.

No Person shall be a Senator who shall not have attained to the Age of thirty Years, and been nine Years a Citizen of the United States, and who shall not, when elected, be an Inhabitant of that State for which he shall be chosen....

Section 4:

The Times, Places and Manner of holding Elections for Senators and Representatives, shall be prescribed in each State by the Legislature thereof; but the Congress may at any time by Law make or alter such Regulations, except as to the Places of chusing Senators.

The Congress shall assemble at least once in every Year, and such Meeting shall be on the first Monday in December, unless they shall by Law appoint a different Day.

Section 5:

Each House shall be the Judge of the Elections, Returns and Qualifications of its own Members, and a Majority of each shall constitute a Quorum to do Business; but a smaller Number may adjourn from day to day, and may be authorized to compel the Attendance of absent Members, in such Manner, and under such Penalties as each House may provide....

Article II

Section 1:

The executive Power shall be vested in a President of the United States of America. He shall hold his Office during the Term of four Years, and, together with the Vice President, chosen for the same Term, be elected, as follows:

Each State shall appoint, in such Manner as the Legislature thereof may direct, a Number of Electors, equal to the whole Number of Senators and Representatives to which the State may be entitled in the Congress: but no Senator or Representative, or Person holding an Office of Trust or Profit under the United States, shall be appointed an Elector.

[The Electors shall meet in their respective States, and vote by Ballot for two Persons, of whom one at least shall not be an Inhabitant of the same State with themselves. And they shall make a List of all the Persons voted for, and of the Number of Votes for each; which List they shall sign and certify, and transmit sealed to the Seat of the Government of the United States, directed to the President of the Senate. The President of the Senate shall, in the Presence of the Senate and House of Representatives, open all the Certificates, and the Votes shall then be counted. The Person having the greatest Number of Votes shall be the President, if such Number be a Majority of the whole Number of Electors appointed; and if there be more than one who have such Majority, and have an equal Number of Votes, then the House of Representatives shall immediately chuse by Ballot one of them for President; and if no Person have a Majority, then from the five highest on the List the said House shall in like Manner chuse the President. But in chusing the President, the Votes shall be taken by States, the Representation from each State having one Vote; a quorum for this Purpose shall consist of a Member or Members from two thirds of the States, and a Majority of all the States shall be necessary to a Choice. In every Case, after the Choice of the President, the Person having the greatest Number of Votes of the Electors shall be the Vice President. But if there should remain two or more who have equal Votes, the Senate shall chuse from them by Ballot the Vice-President.]*

The Congress may determine the Time of chusing the Electors, and the Day on which they shall give their Votes; which Day shall be the same throughout the United States.

No person except a natural born Citizen, or a Citizen of the United States, at the time of the Adoption of this Constitution, shall be eligible to the Office of President; neither shall any person be eligible to that Office who shall not have attained to the Age of thirty five Years, and been fourteen Years a Resident within the United States.

In Case of the Removal of the President from Office, or of his Death, Resignation, or Inability to discharge the Powers and Duties of the said Office, the Same shall devolve on the Vice President, and the Congress may by Law provide for the Case of Removal, Death, Resignation or Inability, both of the President and Vice President, declaring what Officer shall then act as President, and such Officer shall act accordingly, until the Disability be removed, or a President shall be elected....

Amendment XII

(Ratified July 27, 1804)

The Electors shall meet in their respective states and vote by ballot for President and Vice-President, one of whom, at least, shall not be an inhabitant of the same state with themselves; they shall name in their ballots the person voted for as President, and in distinct ballots the person voted for as Vice-President, and they shall make distinct lists of all persons voted for as President, and of all persons voted for as Vice-President, and of the number of votes for each, which lists they shall sign and certify, and transmit sealed to the seat of the government of the United States, directed to the President of the Senate;—The President of the Senate shall, in the presence of the Senate and House of Representatives, open all the certificates and the votes shall then be counted;—The person having the greatest number of votes for President, shall be the President, if such number be a majority of the whole number of Electors appointed; and if no person have such majority, then from

the persons having the highest numbers not exceeding three on the list of those voted for as President, the House of Representatives shall choose immediately, by ballot, the President. But in choosing the President, the votes shall be taken by states, the representation from each state having one vote; a quorum for this purpose shall consist of a member or members from two-thirds of the states, and a majority of all the states shall be necessary to a choice. [And if the House of Representatives shall not choose a President whenever the right of choice shall devolve upon them, before the fourth day of March next following, then the Vice-President shall act as President, as in the case of the death or other constitutional disability of the President.—]† The person having the greatest number of votes as Vice-President, shall be the Vice-President, if such number be a majority of the whole number of Electors appointed, and if no person have a majority, then from the two highest numbers on the list, the Senate shall choose the Vice President; a quorum for the purpose shall consist of two-thirds of the whole number of Senators, and a majority of the whole number shall be necessary to a choice. But no person constitutionally ineligible to the office of President shall be eligible to that of Vice-President of the United States.

Amendment XIV

(Ratified July 9, 1868)

Section 2:

Representatives shall be apportioned among the several States according to their respective numbers, counting the whole number of persons in each State, excluding Indians not taxed. But when the right to vote at any election for the choice of electors for President and Vice President of the United States, Representatives in Congress, the Executive and Judicial officers of a State, or the members of the Legislature thereof, is denied to any of the male inhabitants of such State, being twenty-one years of age, and citizens of the United States, or in any way abridged, except for participation in rebellion, or other crime, the basis of representation therein shall be reduced in the proportion which the number of such male citizens shall bear to the whole number of male citizens twenty-one years of age in such State.

Section 3:

No person shall be a Senator or Representative in Congress, or elector of President and Vice President, or hold any office, civil or military, under the United States, or under any State, who, having previously taken an oath, as a member of Congress, or as an officer of the United States, or as a member of any State legislature, or as an executive or judicial officer of any State, to support the Constitution of the United States, shall have engaged in insurrection or rebellion against the same, or given aid or comfort to the enemies thereof. But Congress may by a vote of two-thirds of each House, remove such disability.

Amendment XV

(Ratified February 3, 1870)

Section 1:

The right of citizens of the United States to vote shall not be denied or abridged by the United States or by any State on account of race, color, or previous condition of servitude.

Section 2:

The Congress shall have power to enforce this article by appropriate legislation.

Superseded by the 12th Amendment.
† *Changed to Jan. 20 by the 20th Amendment, ratified in 1933.*

Amendment XVII
(Ratified April 8, 1913)

The Senate of the United States shall be composed of two Senators from each State, elected by the people thereof, for six years; and each Senator shall have one vote. The electors in each State shall have the qualifications requisite for electors of the most numerous branch of the State legislatures.

When vacancies happen in the representation of any State in the Senate, the executive authority of such State shall issue writs of election to fill such vacancies: *Provided,* That the legislature of any State may empower the executive thereof to make temporary appointments until the people fill the vacancies by election as the legislature may direct.

This amendment shall not be so construed as to affect the election or term of any Senator chosen before it becomes valid as part of the Constitution.

Amendment XIX
(Ratified August 18, 1920)

The right of citizens of the United States to vote shall not be denied or abridged by the United States or by any State on account of sex.

Congress shall have power to enforce this article by appropriate legislation.

Amendment XX
(Ratified January 23, 1933)

Section 1:
The terms of the President and Vice President shall end at noon on the 20th day of January, and the terms of Senators and Representatives at noon on the 3d day of January, of the years in which such terms would have ended if this article had not been ratified; and the terms of their successors shall then begin.

Section 2:
The Congress shall assemble at least once in every year, and such meeting shall begin at noon on the 3d day of January, unless they shall by law appoint a different day.

Section 3:
If, at the time fixed for the beginning of the term of the President, the President elect shall have died, the Vice President elect shall become President. If a President shall not have been chosen before the time fixed for the beginning of his term, or if the President elect shall have failed to qualify, then the Vice President elect shall act as President until a President shall have qualified; and the Congress may be law provide for the case wherein neither a President elect nor a Vice President elect shall have qualified, declaring who shall then act as President, or the manner in which one who is to act shall be selected, and such person shall act accordingly until a President or Vice President shall have qualified.

Section 4:
The Congress may by law provide for the case of the death of any of the persons from whom the House of Representatives may choose a President whenever the right of choice shall have devolved upon them, and for the case of the death of any of the persons from whom the Senate may choose a Vice President whenever the right of choice shall have devolved upon them.

Section 5:
Sections 1 and 2 shall take effect on the 15th day of October following the ratification of this article.

Amendment XXII
(Ratified February 27, 1951)

Section 1:
No person shall be elected to the office of the President more than twice, and no person who has held the office of President, or acted as President, for more than two years of a term to which some other person was elected President shall be elected to the office of the President more than once. But this Article shall not apply to any person holding the office of President, when this Article was proposed by the Congress, and shall not prevent any person who may be holding the office of President, or acting as President, during the term within which this Article becomes operative from holding the office of President or acting as President during the remainder of such term.

Amendment XXIII
(Ratified March 29, 1961)

Section 1:
The District constituting the seat of Government of the United States shall appoint in such manner as the Congress may direct:

A number of electors of President and Vice President equal to the whole number of Senators and Representatives in Congress to which the District would be entitled if it were a State, but in no event more than the least populous State; they shall be in addition to those appointed by the States, but they shall be considered, for the purposes of the election of President and Vice President, to be electors appointed by a State; and they shall meet in the District and perform such duties as provided by the twelfth article of amendment.

Amendment XXIV
(Ratified January 23, 1964)

Section 1:
The right of citizens of the United States to vote in any primary or other election for President or Vice President, for electors for President or Vice President, or for Senator or Representative in Congress, shall not be denied or abridged by the United States or any State by reason of failure to pay any poll tax or other tax.

Amendment XXV
(Ratified February 10, 1967)

Section 1:
In case of the removal of the President from office or of his death or resignation, the Vice President shall become President.

Section 2:
Whenever there is a vacancy in the office of the Vice President, the President shall nominate a Vice President who shall take office upon confirmation by a majority vote of both Houses of Congress.

Section 3:
Whenever the President transmits to the President pro tempore of the Senate and the Speaker of the House of Representatives his written declaration that he is unable to discharge the powers and duties of his office, and until he transmits to them a written declaration to the contrary, such powers and duties shall be discharged by the Vice President as Acting President.

Section 4:
Whenever the Vice President and a majority of either the principal officers of the executive departments or of such other body as Congress may by law provide, transmit

to the President pro tempore of the Senate and the Speaker of the House of Representatives their written declaration that the President is unable to discharge the powers and duties of his office, the Vice President shall immediately assume the powers and duties of the office as Acting President.

Thereafter, when the President transmits to the President pro tempore of the Senate and the Speaker of the House of Representatives his written declaration that no inability exists, he shall resume the powers and duties of his office unless the Vice President and a majority of either the principal officers of the executive department or of such other body as Congress may by law provide, transmit within four days to the President pro tempore of the Senate and the Speaker of the House of Representatives their written declaration that the President is unable to discharge the powers and duties of his office. Thereupon

Congress shall decide the issue, assembling within forty-eight hours for that purpose if not in session. If the Congress, within twenty-one days after receipt of the latter written declaration, or, if Congress is not in session, within twenty-one days after Congress is required to assemble, determines by two-thirds vote of both Houses that the President is unable to discharge the powers and duties of his office, the Vice President shall continue to discharge the same as Acting President; otherwise, the President shall resume the powers and duties of his office.

Amendment XXVI
(Ratified July 1, 1971)
Section 1:
The right of citizens of the United States, who are eighteen years of age or older, to vote shall not be denied or abridged by the United States or by any State on account of age.

Population of the United States . . .

	1790	1800	1810	1820	1830	1840	1850	1860	1870	1880
Ala.	-	1,250[1]	9,046[1]	127,901	309,527	590,756	771,623	964,201	996,992	1,262,505
Alaska	-	-	-	-	-	-	-	-	-	33,426
Ariz.	-	-	-	-	-	-	-	-	9,658	40,440
Ark.	-	-	1,062	14,273	30,388	97,574	209,897	435,450	484,471	802,525
Calif.	-	-	-	-	-	-	92,597	379,994	560,247	864,694
Colo.	-	-	-	-	-	-	-	34,277	39,864	194,327
Conn.	237,946	251,002	261,942	275,248	297,675	309,978	370,792	460,147	537,454	622,700
Del.	59,096	64,273	72,674	72,749	76,748	78,085	91,532	112,216	125,015	146,608
D.C.	-	8,144	15,471	23,336	30,261	33,745	51,687	75,080	131,700	177,624
Fla.	-	-	-	-	34,730	54,477	87,445	140,424	187,748	269,493
Ga.	82,548	162,686	252,433	340,989	516,823	691,392	906,185	1,057,286	1,184,109	1,542,180
Hawaii	-	-	-	-	-	-	-	-	-	-
Idaho	-	-	-	-	-	-	-	-	14,999	32,610
Ill.	-	-	12,282[3]	55,211	157,445	476,183	851,470	1,711,951	2,539,891	3,077,871
Ind.	-	5,641[4]	24,520[4]	147,178	343,031	685,866	988,416	1,350,428	1,680,637	1,978,301
Iowa	-	-	-	-	-	43,112[5]	192,214	674,913	1,194,020	1,624,615
Kan.	-	-	-	-	-	-	-	107,206	364,399	996,096
Ky.	73,677	220,955	406,511	564,317	687,917	779,828	982,405	1,155,684	1,321,011	1,648,690
La.	-	-	76,556	153,407	215,739	352,411	517,762	708,002	726,915	939,946
Maine	96,540	151,719	228,705	298,335	399,455	501,793	583,169	628,279	626,915	648,936
Md.	319,728	341,548	380,546	407,350	447,040	470,019	583,034	687,049	780,894	934,943
Mass.	378,787	422,845	472,040	523,287	610,408	737,699	994,514	1,231,066	1,457,351	1,783,085
Mich.	-	-	4,762[6]	8,896[6]	31,639[6]	212,267	397,654	749,113	1,184,059	1,636,937
Minn.	-	-	-	-	-	-	6,077	172,023	439,706	780,773
Miss.	-	7,600[7]	31,306[7]	75,448	136,621	375,651	606,526	791,305	827,922	1,131,597
Mo.	-	-	19,783	66,586	140,455	383,702	682,044	1,182,012	1,721,295	2,168,380
Mont.	-	-	-	-	-	-	-	-	20,595	39,159
Neb.	-	-	-	-	-	-	-	28,841	122,993	452,402
Nev.	-	-	-	-	-	-	-	6,857[8]	42,491	62,266
N.H.	141,885	183,858	214,460	244,161	269,328	284,574	317,976	326,073	318,300	346,991
N.J.	184,139	211,149	245,562	277,575	320,823	373,306	489,555	672,035	906,096	1,131,116
N.M.	-	-	-	-	-	-	61,547[9]	93,516[9]	91,874	119,565
N.Y.	340,120	589,051	959,049	1,372,812	1,918,608	2,428,921	3,097,394	3,880,735	4,382,759	5,082,871
N.C.	393,751	478,103	555,500	638,829	737,987	753,419	869,039	992,622	1,071,361	1,399,750
N.D.	-	-	-	-	-	-	-	4,837[10]	2,405	36,909
Ohio	-	45,365[11]	230,760	581,434	937,903	1,519,467	1,980,329	2,339,511	2,665,260	3,198,062
Okla.	-	-	-	-	-	-	-	-	-	-
Ore.	-	-	-	-	-	-	12,093	52,465	90,923	174,768
Pa.	434,373	602,365	810,091	1,049,458	1,348,233	1,724,033	2,311,786	2,906,215	3,521,951	4,282,891
Puerto Rico	-	-	-	-	-	-	-	-	-	-
R.I.	68,825	69,122	76,931	83,059	97,199	108,830	147,545	174,620	217,353	276,531
S.C.	249,073	345,591	415,115	502,741	581,185	594,398	688,507	703,708	705,606	995,577
S.D.	-	-	-	-	-	-	-	4,837[10]	11,776	98,268
Tenn.	35,691	105,602	261,727	422,823	681,904	829,210	1,002,717	1,109,801	1,258,520	1,542,359
Texas	-	-	-	-	-	-	212,592	604,215	818,579	1,591,749
Utah	-	-	-	-	-	-	11,380	40,273[13]	86,786	143,963
Vt.	85,425	154,465	217,895	235,981	280,652	291,948	314,120	315,098	330,551	332,286
Va.	691,737	807,557	877,683	938,261	1,044,054	1,025,227	1,119,348	1,219,630	1,225,163	1,512,565
Wash.	-	-	-	-	-	-	1,201	11,594[14]	23,955	75,116
W.Va.	55,873	78,592	105,469	136,808	176,924	224,537	302,313	376,688	442,014	618,457
Wis.	-	-	-	-	-	30,945[15]	305,391	775,881	1,054,670	1,315,497
Wyo.	-	-	-	-	-	-	-	-	9,118	20,789
Total	3,929,214	5,308,483	7,239,881	9,638,453	12,866,020[16]	17,069,453[16]	23,191,876	31,443,321	38,558,371	50,189,209

1. Alabama. Population of those parts of Mississippi Territory now in Alabama.

2. Alaska. 1940 Census taken as of Oct. 1, 1939; 1930 Census, as of Oct. 1, 1929.

3. Illinois. Population of Illinois Territory, which comprised area constituting State of Illinois, almost all of Wisconsin, the western part of the upper peninsula of Michigan, and the northeastern part of Minnesota.

4. Indiana. 1810 figure includes population of area separated in 1816; 1800 figure includes population (3,124) of those portions of Indiana Territory which were taken to form Michigan and Illinois Territories in 1805 and 1809, respectively, and that portion which was separated in 1816.

5. Iowa. Includes population of area constituting that part of Minnesota lying west of the Mississippi River and a line drawn from it source northwards to the Canadian boundary.

6. Michigan. Population of Michigan Territory as then constituted; boundaries changed in 1816, 1818, 1834, and 1836.

7. Mississippi. Population of those parts of present state included in Mississippi Territory as then constituted.

8. Nevada. Population of Nevada Territory as organized in 1861.

9. New Mexico. 1860 figure includes population of area taken to form part of Arizona Territory in 1863. 1850 figure is for Territory of New Mexico which included greater parts of present states of Arizona and New Mexico and smaller parts of Colorado and Nevada.

10. Dakotas. Population of Dakota Territory.

11. Ohio. Population of Territory northwest of the River Ohio.

12. Puerto Rico. Census taken as of Nov. 10, 1899 by War Department.

. . . and Puerto Rico: 1790 to 1980

1890	1900	1910	1920	1930	1940	1950	1960	1970	1980
1,513,401	1,828,697	2,138,093	2,348,174	1,646,248	2,832,961	3,061,743	3,266,740	3,444,354	3,893,888
32,052	63,592	64,356	55,036	59,278[2]	72,524[2]	128,643	226,167	302,583	401,851
88,243	122,931	204,354	334,162	435,573	499,261	749,587	1,302,161	1,775,399	2,718,215
1,128,211	1,311,564	1,574,449	1,752,204	1,854,482	1,949,387	1,909,511	1,786,272	1,923,322	2,286,435
1,213,398	1,485,053	2,377,549	3,426,861	5,677,251	6,907,387	10,586,223	15,717,204	19,971,069	23,667,902
413,249	539,700	799,024	939,629	1,035,791	1,123,296	1,325,089	1,753,947	2,209,596	2,889,964
746,258	908,420	1,114,756	1,380,631	1,606,903	1,709,242	2,007,280	2,535,234	3,032,217	3,107,576
168,493	184,735	202,322	223,003	238,380	266,505	318,085	446,292	548,104	594,338
230,392	278,718	331,069	437,571	486,869	663,091	802,178	763,956	756,668	638,333
391,422	528,542	752,619	968,470	1,468,211	1,897,414	2,771,305	4,951,560	6,791,418	9,746,324
1,837,353	2,216,331	2,609,121	2,895,832	2,908,506	3,123,723	3,444,578	3,943,116	4,587,930	5,463,105
-	154,001	191,874	255,881	368,300	422,770	499,794	632,772	769,913	964,691
88,548	161,772	325,594	431,866	445,032	524,873	588,637	667,191	713,015	943,935
3,826,352	4,821,550	5,638,591	6,485,280	7,630,654	7,897,241	8,712,176	10,081,158	11,110,285	11,426,518
2,192,404	2,516,462	2,700,876	2,930,390	3,238,503	3,427,796	3,934,224	4,662,498	5,195,392	5,490,224
1,912,297	2,231,853	2,224,771	2,404,021	2,470,939	2,538,268	2,621,073	2,757,537	2,825,368	2,913,808
1,428,108	1,470,495	1,690,949	1,769,257	1,880,999	1,801,028	1,905,299	2,178,611	2,249,071	2,363,679
1,858,635	2,147,174	2,289,905	2,416,630	2,614,589	2,845,627	2,944,806	3,038,156	3,220,711	3,660,777
1,118,588	1,381,625	1,656,388	1,798,509	2,101,593	2,363,880	2,683,516	3,257,022	3,644,637	4,205,900
661,086	694,466	742,371	768,014	797,423	847,226	913,774	969,265	993,722	1,124,660
1,042,390	1,188,044	1,295,346	1,449,661	1,631,526	1,821,244	2,343,001	3,100,689	3,923,897	4,216,975
2,238,947	2,805,346	3,366,416	3,852,356	4,249,614	4,316,721	4,690,514	5,148,578	5,689,170	5,737,037
2,093,890	2,420,982	2,810,173	3,668,412	4,842,325	5,256,106	6,371,766	7,823,194	8,881,826	9,262,078
1,310,283	1,751,394	2,075,708	2,387,125	2,563,953	2,792,300	2,982,483	3,413,864	3,806,103	4,075,970
1,289,600	1,551,270	1,797,114	1,790,618	2,009,821	2,183,796	2,178,914	2,178,141	2,216,994	2,520,638
2,679,185	3,106,665	3,293,335	3,404,055	3,629,367	3,784,664	3,954,653	4,319,813	4,677,623	4,916,686
142,924	243,329	376,053	548,889	537,606	559,456	591,024	674,767	694,409	786,690
1,062,656	1,066,300	1,192,214	1,296,372	1,377,963	1,315,834	1,325,510	1,411,330	1,485,333	1,569,825
47,355	42,335	81,875	77,407	91,058	110,247	160,083	285,278	488,738	800,493
376,530	411,588	430,572	443,083	465,293	491,524	533,242	606,921	737,681	920,610
1,444,933	1,883,669	2,537,167	3,155,900	4,041,334	4,160,165	4,835,329	6,066,782	7,171,112	7,364,823
160,282	195,310	327,301	360,350	423,317	531,818	681,187	951,023	1,017,055	1,302,894
6,003,174	7,268,894	9,113,614	10,385,227	12,588,066	13,479,142	14,830,192	16,782,304	18,241,391	17,558,072
1,617,949	1,893,810	2,206,287	2,559,123	3,170,276	3,571,623	4,061,929	4,556,155	5,084,411	5,881,766
190,983	319,146	577,056	646,872	680,845	641,935	619,636	632,446	617,792	652,717
3,672,329	4,157,545	4,767,121	5,759,394	6,646,697	6,907,612	7,946,627	9,706,397	10,657,423	10,797,630
258,657	790,391	1,657,155	2,028,283	2,396,040	2,336,434	2,233,351	2,328,284	2,559,463	3,025,290
317,704	413,536	672,765	783,389	953,786	1,089,684	1,521,341	1,768,687	2,091,533	2,633,105
5,258,113	6,302,115	7,665,111	8,720,017	9,631,350	9,900,180	10,498,012	11,319,366	11,800,766	11,863,895
-	953,243[12]	1,118,012	1,299,809	1,543,913	1,869,255	2,210,703	2,349,544	2,712,033	3,196,520
345,506	428,556	542,610	604,397	687,497	713,346	791,896	859,488	949,723	947,154
1,151,149	1,340,316	1,515,400	1,683,724	1,738,765	1,899,804	2,117,027	2,382,594	2,590,713	3,121,820
348,600	401,570	583,888	636,547	692,849	642,961	652,740	680,514	666,257	690,768
1,767,518	2,020,616	2,184,789	2,337,885	2,616,556	2,915,841	3,291,718	3,567,089	3,926,018	4,591,120
2,235,527	3,048,710	3,896,542	4,663,228	5,824,715	6,414,824	7,711,194	9,579,677	11,198,655	14,229,191
210,779	276,749	373,351	449,396	507,847	550,310	688,862	890,627	1,059,273	1,461,037
332,422	343,641	355,956	352,428	359,611	359,231	377,747	389,881	444,732	511,456
1,655,980	1,854,184	2,061,612	2,309,187	2,421,851	2,677,773	3,318,680	3,966,949	4,651,448	5,346,818
357,232	518,103	1,141,990	1,356,621	1,563,396	1,736,191	2,378,963	2,853,214	3,413,244	4,132,156
762,794	958,800	1,221,119	1,463,701	1,729,205	1,901,974	2,005,552	1,860,421	1,744,237	1,949,644
1,693,330	2,069,042	2,333,860	2,632,067	2,939,006	3,137,587	3,434,575	3,951,777	4,417,821	4,705,767
62,555	92,531	145,965	194,402	225,565	250,742	290,529	330,066	332,416	469,557
62,979,766[17]	76,212,168	92,228,496	106,021,537	123,202,624	132,164,569	151,325,798	179,323,175	203,302,031	226,545,805

13. *Utah. Population of Utah Territory exclusive of that part of present state of Colorado taken to form Colorado Territory in 1861.*

14. *Washington. 1860 figure includes population of Idaho and parts of Montana and Wyoming. 1850 figure of population of those parts of Oregon Territory taken to form part of Washington Territory in 1853 and 1859.*

15. *Wisconsin. Includes population of that part of Minnesota northeast of the Mississippi River.*

16. *Includes persons (6,100 in 1840 and 5,318 in 1830) on public ships in the service of the United States, not credited to any region, division, or state.*

17. *Includes population (325,464) of Indian Territory and Indian reservations specially enumerated in 1890 but not included in general report on population for 1890.*

Source: Bureau of the Census, *Number of Inhabitants* (Washington, D.C.: Government Printing Office, 1981).

Immigrants, by Country (Europe: 1820-1980)

(For years ending June 30, except 1820-1831 and 1844-1849, years ending Sept. 30; 1833-1842 and 1851-1867, years ending Dec. 31; 1832 covers 15 months ending Dec. 31; 1843, 9 months ending Sept. 30; 1850, 15 months ending Dec. 31; 1868, 6 months ending June 30)

			Northwestern Europe				Central Europe			Eastern Europe		Southern Europe	
Year	All countries[1]	Total Europe	Great Britain	Ireland[2]	Scandinavia[3]	Other Northwestern[4]	Germany[5]	Poland	Other Central[6]	U.S.S.R. and Baltic States[7]	Other Eastern[8]	Italy	Other Southern[9]
1980	530,639	72,121	15,485	1,006	1,861	4,236	6,595	4,725	4,370	11,034	2,101	5,467	20,708
1979	460,348	60,845	13,907	982	1,735	3,930	6,314	4,418	4,164	3,018	1,742	6,174	20,635
1978	601,442	73,198	14,245	1,180	1,601	4,163	6,739	5,050	4,773	5,661	2,239	7,415	27,547
1977	462,315	70,010	12,477	1,238	1,475	3,650	6,372	4,010	4,619	6,154	2,221	7,510	27,794
1976	398,613	72,411	11,392	1,171	1,370	3,428	5,836	3,808	4,576	8,638	2,384	8,380	29,808
1975	386,194	73,996	10,807	1,285	1,337	3,068	5,154	3,947	5,333	5,485	2,580	11,552	36,274
1974	394,861	81,212	10,710	1,572	1,544	3,583	6,320	4,046	8,204	1,620	1,765	15,884	41,848
1973	400,063	92,870	10,638	2,000	1,524	3,786	6,600	4,927	11,286	1,735	1,973	22,151	48,401
1972	384,685	89,993	10,078	1,780	1,689	4,106	6,848	4,797	10,004	1,509	1,631	21,427	47,551
1971	370,478	96,498	10,787	1,614	1,699	4,439	7,519	2,883	10,039	1,274	1,926	22,137	54,304
1970	373,326	110,653	14,089	1,583	2,110	6,961	10,632	2,013	10,411	836	1,357	27,369	33,292
1969	358,579	114,052	15,072	1,981	2,149	5,944	10,380	2,115	8,889	574	1,158	27,033	38,757
1968	454,448	129,022	26,025	2,995	4,203	9,873	16,590	3,676	5,659	974	883	25,882	32,262
1967	361,972	128,775	23,004	2,765	4,230	9,881	16,595	4,356	5,116	876	899	28,487	32,566
1966	323,040	115,898	18,777	3,267	4,549	9,049	17,654	8,490	3,972	768	878	26,447	22,047
1965	296,697	101,468	24,135	5,187	5,853	11,526	22,432	7,093	3,693	632	859	10,874	9,184
1964	292,248	108,215	25,758	6,055	5,497	11,120	24,494	7,097	3,248	763	1,054	12,769	10,360
1963	306,260	109,066	22,708	5,746	5,208	11,938	24,727	6,785	3,244	591	996	16,175	10,948
1962	283,763	103,989	18,066	5,118	4,716	13,117	21,477	5,660	2,533	753	753	20,119	11,677
1961	271,344	108,532	18,719	5,738	4,943	14,635	25,815	6,254	2,911	996	620	18,956	8,945
1960	265,398	120,178	19,967	6,918	6,185	17,234	29,452	4,216	9,073	856	761	13,369	12,147
1959	260,686	138,191	18,325	6,595	6,100	14,217	32,039	2,800	30,738	775	726	16,804	9,072
1958	253,265	115,198	24,147	9,134	5,873	11,364	29,498	1,470	3,508	641	673	23,115	5,775
1957	326,867	169,625	24,020	8,227	6,189	25,109	60,353	571	15,498	663	558	19,624	8,813
1956	321,625	156,866	19,008	5,607	5,681	15,254	44,409	263	10,284	643	394	40,430	14,893
1955	237,790	110,591	15,761	5,222	5,159	10,707	29,596	129	4,133	523	134	30,272	8,955
1954	208,177	92,121	16,672	4,655	5,459	11,853	33,098	67	2,873	475	104	13,145	3,720
1953	170,434	82,352	16,639	4,304	5,537	11,145	27,329	136	2,885	609	86	8,432	5,250
1952	265,520	193,626	22,177	3,526	5,416	12,476	104,236	235	23,529	548	137	11,342	10,004
1951	205,717	149,545	14,898	3,144	5,502	10,973	87,755	98	10,365	555	223	8,958	7,074
1950	249,187	199,115	12,755	5,842	5,661	10,857	128,592	696	17,792	526	277	12,454	3,663
1949	188,317	129,592	21,149	8,678	6,665	12,288	55,284	1,673	7,411	694	246	11,695	3,809
1948	170,570	103,544	26,403	7,534	6,127	13,721	19,368	2,447	6,006	897	485	16,075	4,481
1947	147,292	83,535	23,788	2,574	4,918	14,562	13,900	745	4,622	761	249	13,866	3,550
1946	108,721	52,852	33,552	1,816	1,278	8,651	2,598	335	511	153	98	2,636	1,224
1945	38,119	5,943	3,029	427	224	365	172	195	206	98	97	213	917
1944	28,551	4,509	1,321	112	281	619	238	292	316	157	109	120	944
1943	23,725	4,920	974	165	239	1,531	248	394	206	159	54	49	901
1942	28,781	11,153	907	83	371	5,622	2,150	343	396	197	117	103	864
1941	51,776	26,541	7,714	272	1,137	9,009	4,028	451	786	665	299	450	1,730
1940	70,756	50,454	6,158	839	1,260	7,743	21,520	702	3,628	898	491	5,302	1,913
1939	82,998	63,138	3,058	1,189	1,178	5,214	33,515	3,072	5,334	1,021	620	6,570	2,367
1938	67,895	44,495	2,262	1,085	1,393	3,352	17,199	2,403	5,195	960	542	7,712	2,392
1937	50,244	31,863	1,726	531	971	2,512	10,895	1,212	3,763	629	533	7,192	1,899
1936	36,329	23,480	1,310	444	646	1,745	6,346	869	2,723	378	424	6,774	1,821
1935	34,956	22,778	1,413	454	688	1,808	5,201	1,504	2,357	418	453	6,566	1,916
1934	29,470	17,210	1,305	443	557	1,270	4,392	1,032	1,422	607	347	4,374	1,461
1933	28,068	12,383	979	338	511	1,045	1,919	1,332	981	458	352	3,477	991
1932	35,576	20,579	2,057	539	938	1,558	2,670	1,296	1,749	636	592	6,662	1,882
1931	97,139	61,909	9,110	7,305	3,144	4,420	10,401	3,604	4,500	1,396	1,192	13,399	3,438
1930	241,700	147,438	31,015	23,445	6,919	9,170	26,569	9,231	9,184	2,772	2,159	22,327	4,647
1929	279,678	158,598	21,327	19,921	17,379	9,091	46,751	9,002	8,081	2,450	2,153	18,008	4,435
1928	307,255	158,513	19,958	25,268	16,184	9,079	45,778	8,755	7,091	2,652	1,776	17,728	4,244
1927	335,175	168,368	23,669	28,545	16,860	9,134	48,513	9,211	6,559	2,933	1,708	17,297	3,939
1926	304,488	155,562	25,528	24,897	16,818	8,773	50,421	7,126	6,020	3,323	1,596	8,253	2,807
1925	294,314	148,366	27,172	26,650	16,810	8,548	46,068	5,341	4,701	3,121	1,566	6,203	2,186
1924	706,896	364,339	59,490	17,111	35,577	16,077	75,091	28,806	32,700	20,918	13,173	56,246	9,150
1923	522,919	307,920	45,759	15,740	34,184	12,469	48,277	26,538	34,038	21,151	16,082	46,674	7,008

Footnotes, see p. 1136.

Immigrants, by Country (Europe: 1820-1980)

(For years ending June 30, except 1820-1831 and 1844-1849, years ending Sept. 30; 1833-1842 and 1851-1867,
years ending Dec. 31; 1832 covers 15 months ending Dec. 31; 1843, 9 months ending Sept. 30;
1850, 15 months ending Dec. 31; 1868, 6 months ending June 30)

Year	All countries[1]	Total Europe	Northwestern Europe				Central Europe			Eastern Europe		Southern Europe	
			Great Britain	Ireland[2]	Scandi-navia[3]	Other North-western[4]	Germany[5]	Poland	Other Central[6]	U.S.S.R. and Baltic States[7]	Other Eastern[8]	Italy	Other Southern[9]
1922	309,556	216,385	25,153	10,579	14,625	11,149	17,931	28,635	29,363	19,910	12,244	40,319	6,477
1921	805,228	652,364	51,142	28,435	22,854	29,317	6,803	95,089	77,069	10,193	32,793	222,260	76,409
1920	430,001	246,295	38,471	9,591	13,444	24,491	1,001	4,813	5,666	1,751	3,913	95,145	48,009
1919	141,132	24,627	6,797	474	5,590	5,126	52	10	53	1,403	51	1,884	3,197
1918	110,618	31,063	2,516	331	6,506	3,146	447	10	61	4,242	93	5,250	8,471
1917	295,403	133,083	10,735	5,406	13,771	6,731	1,857	10	1,258	12,716	369	34,596	45,644
1916	298,826	145,699	16,063	8,639	14,761	8,715	2,877	10	5,191	7,842	1,167	33,665	46,779
1915	326,700	197,919	27,237	14,185	17,883	12,096	7,799	10	18,511	26,187	2,892	49,688	21,441
1914	1,218,480	1,058,391	48,729	24,688	29,391	25,591	35,734	10	278,152	255,660	21,420	283,738	55,288
1913	1,197,892	1,055,855	60,328	27,876	32,267	28,086	34,329	10	254,825	291,040	18,036	265,542	43,526
1912	838,172	718,875	57,148	25,879	27,554	22,921	27,788	10	178,882	162,395	20,925	157,134	38,249
1911	878,587	764,757	73,384	29,112	42,285	25,549	32,061	10	159,057	158,721	21,655	182,882	40,051
1910	1,041,570	926,291	68,941	29,855	48,267	23,852	21,283	10	258,737	186,792	25,287	215,537	37,740
1909	751,786	654,875	46,793	25,033	32,496	17,756	25,540	10	170,191	120,460	11,659	183,218	21,729
1908	782,870	691,901	62,824	30,556	30,175	22,177	32,309	10	168,509	156,711	27,345	128,503	32,792
1907	1,285,349	1,199,566	79,037	34,530	49,965	26,512	37,807	10	338,452	258,943	36,510	285,731	52,079
1906	1,100,735	1,018,365	67,198	34,995	52,781	23,277	37,564	10	265,138	215,665	18,652	273,120	29,975
1905	1,026,499	974,273	84,189	52,945	60,625	24,693	40,574	10	275,693	184,897	11,022	221,479	18,156
1904	812,870	767,933	51,448	36,142	60,096	23,321	46,380	10	177,156	145,141	12,756	193,296	22,197
1903	857,046	814,507	33,637	35,310	77,647	17,009	40,086	10	206,011	136,093	12,600	230,622	25,492
1902	648,743	619,068	16,898	29,138	54,038	10,322	28,304	10	171,989	107,347	8,234	178,375	14,423
1901	487,918	469,237	14,985	30,561	39,234	9,279	21,651	10	113,390	85,257	8,199	135,996	19,685
1900	448,572	424,700	12,509	35,730	31,151	5,822	18,507	10	114,847	90,787	6,852	100,135	8,360
1899	311,715	297,349	13,456	31,673	22,192	5,150	17,476	10	62,491	60,982	1,738	77,419	4,772
1898	229,299	217,786	12,894	25,128	19,282	4,698	17,111	4,726	39,797	29,828	1,076	58,613	4,633
1897	230,832	216,397	12,752	28,421	21,089	5,323	22,533	4,165	33,031	25,816	943	59,431	2,893
1896	343,267	329,067	24,565	40,262	33,199	7,611	31,885	691	65,103	51,445	954	68,060	5,292
1895	258,536	250,342	28,833	46,304	26,952	7,313	32,173	790	33,401	35,907	768	35,427	2,574
1894	285,631	277,052	22,520	30,231	32,400	9,514	53,989	1,941	38,638	39,278	1,027	42,977	4,537
1893	439,730	429,324	35,189	43,578	58,945	17,838	78,756	16,374	57,420	42,310	625	72,145	6,094
1892	579,663	570,876	42,215	51,383	66,295	21,731	119,168	40,536	76,937	81,511	1,331	61,631	8,138
1891	560,319	546,085	66,605	55,706	60,107	21,824	113,554	27,497	71,042	47,426	1,222	76,055	5,047
1890	455,302	445,680	69,730	53,024	50,368	20,575	92,427	11,073	56,199	35,598	723	52,003	3,960
1889	444,427	434,790	87,992	65,557	57,504	22,010	99,538	4,922	34,174	33,916	1,145	25,307	2,725
1888	546,889	538,131	108,692	73,513	81,924	23,251	109,717	5,826	45,811	33,487	1,393	51,558	2,959
1887	490,109	482,829	93,378	68,370	67,629	17,307	106,865	6,128	40,265	30,766	2,251	47,622	2,248
1886	334,203	329,529	62,929	49,619	46,735	11,737	84,403	3,939	28,680	17,800	670	21,315	1,702
1885	395,346	353,083	57,713	51,795	40,704	13,732	124,443	3,085	27,309	17,158	941	13,642	2,561
1884	518,592	453,686	65,950	63,344	52,728	18,768	179,676	4,536	36,571	12,689	388	16,510	2,526
1883	603,322	522,587	76,606	81,486	71,994	24,271	194,786	2,011	27,625	9,909	163	31,792	1,944
1882	788,992	648,186	102,991	76,432	105,326	27,796	250,630	4,672	29,150	16,918	134	32,159	1,978
1881	669,431	528,545	81,376	72,342	81,582	26,883	210,485	5,614	27,935	5,041	102	15,401	1,784
1880	457,257	348,691	73,273	71,603	65,657	15,042	84,638	2,177	17,267	5,014	35	12,354	1,631
1879	177,826	134,259	29,955	20,013	21,820	9,081	34,602	489	5,963	4,453	29	5,791	2,063
1878	138,469	101,612	22,150	15,932	12,254	6,929	29,313	547	5,150	3,048	29	4,344	1,916
1877	141,857	106,195	23,581	14,569	11,274	8,621	29,298	533	5,396	6,599	32	3,195	3,097
1876	169,986	120,920	29,291	19,575	12,323	10,923	31,937	925	6,276	4,775	38	3,015	1,842
1875	227,498	182,961	47,905	37,957	14,322	11,987	47,769	984	7,658	7,997	27	3,631	2,724
1874	313,339	262,783	62,021	53,707	19,178	15,998	87,291	1,795	8,850	4,073	62	7,666	2,142
1873	459,803	397,541	89,500	77,344	35,481	22,892	149,671	3,338	7,112	1,634	53	8,757	1,759
1872	404,806	352,155	84,912	68,732	28,575	15,614	141,109	1,647	4,410	1,018	20	4,190	1,928
1871	321,350	265,145	85,455	57,439	22,132	7,174	82,554	535	4,887	673	23	2,816	1,457
1870	387,203	328,626	103,677	56,996	30,742	9,152	118,225	223	4,425	907	6	2,891	1,382
1869	352,768	315,963	84,438	40,786	43,941	10,585	131,042	184	1,499	343	18	1,489	1,638
1868	138,840	130,090	24,127	32,068	11,985	4,293	55,831	-	192	141	4	891	558
1867	315,722	283,751	52,641	72,879	8,491	12,417	133,426	310	692	205	26	1,624	1,040

Footnotes, see p. 1136.

Immigrants, by Country (Europe: 1820-1980)

(For years ending June 30, except 1820-1831 and 1844-1849, years ending Sept. 30; 1833-1842 and 1851-1867, years ending Dec. 31; 1832 covers 15 months ending Dec. 31; 1843, 9 months ending Sept. 30; 1850, 15 months ending Dec. 31; 1868, 6 months ending June 30)

			Northwestern Europe				Central Europe			Eastern Europe		Southern Europe	
Year	All countries[1]	Total Europe	Great Britain	Ireland[2]	Scandi-navia[3]	Other North-western[4]	Germany[5]	Poland	Other Central[6]	U.S.S.R. and Baltic States[7]	Other Eastern[8]	Italy	Other Southern[9]
1866	318,568	278,916	94,924	36,690	14,495	13,648	115,892	412	93	287	18	1,382	1,075
1865	248,120	214,048	82,465	29,772	7,258	7,992	83,424	528	422	183	14	924	1,066
1864	193,418	185,233	53,428	63,523	2,961	5,621	57,276	165	230	256	11	600	1,162
1863	176,282	163,733	66,882	55,916	3,119	3,245	33,162	94	85	77	16	547	590
1862	91,985	83,710	24,639	23,351	2,550	4,386	27,529	63	111	79	11	566	425
1861	91,918	81,200	19,675	23,797	850	3,769	31,661	48	51	34	5	811	499
1860	153,640	141,209	29,737	48,637	840	5,278	54,491	82	-	65	4	1,019	1,056
1859	121,282	110,949	26,163	35,216	1,590	3,727	41,784	106	-	91	10	932	1,330
1858	123,126	111,354	28,956	26,873	2,662	4,580	45,310	9	-	246	17	1,240	1,461
1857	251,306	216,224	58,479	54,361	2,747	6,879	91,781	124	-	25	11	1,007	810
1856	200,436	186,083	44,658	54,349	1,330	12,403	71,028	20	-	9	5	1,365	916
1855	200,877	187,729	47,572	49,627	1,349	14,571	71,918	462	-	13	9	1,052	1,156
1854	427,833	405,542	58,647	101,606	4,222	23,070	215,009	208	-	2	7	1,263	1,508
1853	368,645	361,576	37,576	162,649	3,396	14,205	141,946	33	-	3	15	555	1,198
1852	371,603	362,484	40,699	159,548	4,106	11,278	145,918	110	-	2	3	351	469
1851	379,466	369,510	51,487	221,253	2,438	20,905	72,482	10	-	1	2	447	485
1850	369,980	308,323	51,085	164,004	1,589	11,470	78,896	5	-	31	15	431	797
1849	297,024	286,501	55,132	159,398	3,481	7,634	60,235	4	-	44	9	209	355
1848	226,527	218,025	35,159	112,934	1,113	9,877	58,465	-	-	1	3	241	232
1847	234,968	229,117	23,302	105,536	1,320	24,336	74,281	8	-	5	2	164	163
1846	154,416	146,315	22,180	51,752	2,030	12,303	57,561	4	-	248	4	151	82
1845	114,371	109,301	19,210	44,821	982	9,466	34,355	6	-	1	3	137	320
1844	78,615	74,745	14,353	33,490	1,336	4,343	20,731	36	-	13	10	141	292
1843	52,496	49,013	8,430	19,670	1,777	4,364	14,441	17	-	6	5	117	186
1842	104,565	99,945	22,005	51,342	588	5,361	20,370	10	-	28	2	100	139
1841	80,289	76,216	16,188	37,772	226	6,077	15,291	15	-	174	6	179	288
1840	84,066	80,126	2,613	39,430	207	7,978	29,704	5	-	-	1	37	151
1839	68,069	64,148	10,271	23,963	380	7,891	21,028	46	-	7	1	84	477
1838	38,914	34,070	5,420	12,645	112	3,839	11,683	41	-	13	-	86	231
1837	79,340	71,039	12,218	28,508	399	5,769	23,740	81	-	19	-	36	269
1836	76,242	70,465	13,106	30,578	473	5,189	20,707	53	-	2	3	115	239
1835	45,374	41,987	8,970	20,927	68	3,369	8,311	54	-	9	-	60	219
1834	65,365	57,510	10,490	24,474	66	4,468	17,686	54	-	15	1	105	151
1833	58,640	29,111	4,916	8,648	189	5,355	6,988	1	-	159	1	1,699	1,155
1832	60,482	34,193	5,331	12,436	334	5,695	10,194	34	-	52	-	3	114
1831	22,633	13,039	2,475	5,772	36	2,277	2,413	-	-	1	-	28	37
1830	23,322	7,217	1,153	2,721	19	1,305	1,976	2	-	3	2	9	27
1829	22,520	12,523	3,179	7,415	30	1,065	597	-	-	1	1	23	212
1828	27,382	24,729	5,352	12,488	60	4,700	1,851	1	-	7	6	34	230
1827	18,875	16,719	4,186	9,766	28	1,829	432	1	-	19	1	35	422
1826	10,837	9,751	2,319	5,408	26	968	511	-	-	4	2	57	456
1825	10,199	8,543	2,095	4,888	18	719	450	1	-	10	-	75	287
1824	7,912	4,965	1,264	2,345	20	671	230	4	-	7	2	45	377
1823	6,354	4,016	1,100	1,908	7	528	183	3	-	7	2	33	245
1822	6,911	4,418	1,221	2,267	28	522	148	3	-	10	4	35	180
1821	9,127	5,936	3,210	1,518	24	521	383	1	-	7	-	63	209
1820	8,385	7,691	2,410	3,614	23	452	968	5	-	14	1	30	174

- Represents zero.

[1] For 1820-1867 excludes returning citizens.
[2] Comprises Eire and Northern Ireland.
[3] Comprises Norway, Sweden, Denmark, and Iceland.
[4] Comprises Netherlands, Belgium, Luxembourg, Switzerland, and France.
[5] Includes Austria, 1938 to 1945.
[6] Comprises Czechoslovakia (since 1920), Yugoslavia (since 1920), Hungary (since 1861), and Austria (since 1861, except for the years 1938-1945, when Austria was included with Germany).
[7] Comprises U.S.S.R. (excluding Asian U.S.S.R. between 1931 and 1963, Latvia, Estonia, Lithuania, and Finland).
[8] Comprises Romania, Bulgaria, and Turkey in Europe.
[9] Comprises Spain, Portugal, Greece, and other Europe, not elsewhere classified.
[10] Between 1899 and 1919, included with Austria-Hungary, Germany, and Russia.

Immigrants, by Country (Asia, Americas: 1820-1980)

(For years ending June 30, except 1820-1831 and 1844-1849, years ending Sept. 30; 1833-1842 and 1851-1867, years ending Dec. 31; 1832 covers 15 months ending Dec. 31; 1843, 9 months ending Sept. 30; 1850, 15 months ending Dec. 31; 1868, 6 months ending June 30)

	Asia								Americas				
Year	Total	Turkey in Asia[11]	China[12]	India	Japan[13]	Korea[14]	Philippines	Other Asia	Total	Canada, Newfoundland and Greenland[15]	Mexico	West Indies	Other America
1980	236,097	2,233	27,651	22,607	4,225	32,320	42,316	104,745	204,489	13,622	56,680	73,296	60,891
1979	189,293	1,764	24,272	19,717	4,063	29,248	41,300	68,929	192,923	13,776	52,096	74,074	52,977
1978	249,776	1,578	21,331	20,772	4,028	29,288	37,216	135,563	262,548	16,877	92,367	91,361	61,943
1977	157,759	1,758	19,765	18,636	4,192	30,917	39,111	43,380	220,300	12,692	44,079	114,011	49,518
1976	149,881	1,676	18,824	17,500	4,275	30,803	37,281	39,522	165,006	7,639	57,863	66,839	32,665
1975	132,469	1,592	18,536	15,785	4,293	28,362	31,751	32,150	169,653	7,312	62,205	67,430	32,706
1974	130,662	1,867	18,056	12,795	4,917	28,028	32,857	50,198	173,752	7,661	71,586	62,959	31,546
1973	124,160	1,899	17,296	13,128	5,676	22,930	30,799	32,432	173,123	8,952	70,141	64,769	29,261
1972	121,058	1,986	17,339	16,929	5,777	18,876	29,376	30,775	163,736	10,778	64,040	61,373	27,545
1971	103,459	1,748	11,136	14,310	4,457	14,297	28,471	29,040	160,825	13,130	50,105	68,181	29,407
1970	90,215	495	6,427	8,795	4,731	8,888	30,507	30,372	161,727	26,850	44,821	56,614	33,442
1969	72,959	556	5,264	5,205	4,095	5,854	20,263	31,722	164,045	29,303	45,748	53,190	35,804
1968	56,298	325	4,851	4,165	3,810	3,592	16,086	23,469	262,736	41,716	44,716	140,827	35,477
1967	57,574	491	7,118	4,129	4,125	3,845	10,336	27,530	170,235	34,768	43,034	61,987	30,446
1966	40,113	365	2,948	2,293	3,468	2,414	5,894	22,731	162,551	37,273	47,217	37,999	40,062
1965	20,040	365	1,611	467	3,294	2,139	2,963	9,201	171,019	50,035	40,686	31,141	49,157
1964	21,279	331	2,684	488	3,774	2,329	2,862	8,811	158,644	51,114	34,448	24,067	49,015
1963	23,242	307	1,605	965	4,147	2,560	3,483	10,175	169,966	50,509	55,986	22,951	40,520
1962	20,249	304	1,356	390	4,054	1,463	3,354	9,328	155,871	44,272	55,805	20,917	34,877
1961	19,495	296	900	292	4,490	1,442	2,628	9,447	139,580	47,470	41,476	20,520	30,114
1960	21,604	200	1,380	244	5,699	1,410	2,791	9,880	119,525	46,668	32,708	13,636	26,513
1959	25,259	229	1,702	351	6,248	1,614	2,503	12,612	93,061	34,599	22,909	12,109	23,444
1958	20,870	197	1,143	323	6,847	1,470	2,034	8,856	113,132	45,143	26,791	16,983	24,215
1957	20,008	77	2,098	196	6,829	577	1,874	8,357	134,160	46,354	49,321	18,362	20,123
1956	17,327	48	1,386	185	5,967	579	1,792	7,370	144,713	42,363	61,320	19,512	21,518
1955	10,935	54	568	194	4,150	263	1,598	4,108	110,436	32,435	43,702	12,876	21,423
1954	9,970	33	254	144	3,846	175	1,234	4,284	95,587	34,873	30,645	8,411	21,658
1953	8,231	13	528	104	2,579	75	1,074	3,858	77,650	36,283	17,183	8,628	15,556
1952	9,328	12	263	123	3,814	47	1,179	3,890	61,049	33,354	9,079	6,672	11,944
1951	7,149	3	335	109	271	21	3,228	3,182	47,631	25,880	6,153	5,902	9,696
1950	4,508	13	1,280	121	100	24	729	2,241	44,191	21,885	6,744	6,206	9,356
1949	7,595	40	3,415	175	529	39	1,157	2,240	49,334	25,156	8,083	6,733	9,362
1948	11,907	16	7,203	263	423	44	1,168	2,790	52,746	25,485	8,384	6,932	11,945
1947	6,733	22	3,191	432	131	-	910	2,047	52,753	24,342	7,558	6,728	14,125
1946	2,108	16	252	425	14	-	475	926	46,066	21,344	7,146	5,878	11,698
1945	461	13	71	103	1	-	19	254	29,646	11,530	6,702	5,452	5,962
1944	231	15	50	41	4	-	4	117	23,084	10,143	6,598	3,198	3,145
1943	342	36	65	71	20	-	8	142	18,162	9,761	4,172	2,312	1,917
1942	615	31	179	36	44	-	51	274	16,377	10,599	2,378	1,599	1,801
1941	1,971	16	1,003	94	289	-	170	399	22,445	11,473	2,824	4,687	3,461
1940	2,050	7	643	52	102	-	137	1,109	17,822	11,078	2,313	2,675	1,756
1939	2,281	15	642	36	102	-	119	1,367	17,139	10,813	2,640	2,231	1,455
1938	2,492	11	613	34	93	-	116	1,625	20,486	14,404	2,502	2,110	1,470
1937	1,149	13	293	47	132	-	84	580	16,903	12,011	2,347	1,322	1,223
1936	793	20	273	13	91	-	72	324	11,786	8,121	1,716	985	964
1935	682	31	229	32	88	-	16	302	11,174	7,782	1,560	931	901
1934	597	22	187	28	86	-	-	274	11,409	7,945	1,801	861	802
1933	552	27	148	44	75	-	-	258	9,925	6,187	1,936	862	940
1932	1,931	43	750	87	526	-	-	525	12,577	8,003	2,171	1,029	1,374
1931	3,345	139	1,150	123	653	-	-	1,280	30,816	22,183	3,333	2,496	2,804

Footnotes, see p. 1139.

Immigrants, by Country (Asia, Americas: 1820-1980)

(For years ending June 30, except 1820-1831 and 1844-1849, years ending Sept. 30; 1833-1842 and 1851-1867, years ending Dec. 31; 1832 covers 15 months ending Dec. 31; 1843, 9 months ending Sept. 30; 1850, 15 months ending Dec. 31; 1868, 6 months ending June 30)

	Asia								Americas				
Year	Total	Turkey in Asia[11]	China[12]	India	Japan[13]	Korea[14]	Philippines	Other Asia	Total	Canada, Newfoundland and Greenland[15]	Mexico	West Indies	Other America
1930	4,535	118	1,589	110	837	-	-	1,881	88,104	65,254	12,703	5,225	4,922
1929	3,758	70	1,446	103	771	-	-	1,368	116,177	66,451	40,154	4,306	5,266
1928	3,380	80	1,320	102	550	-	-	1,328	144,281	75,281	59,016	4,058	5,926
1927	3,669	73	1,471	102	723	-	-	1,300	161,872	84,580	67,721	4,019	5,552
1926	3,413	37	1,751	93	654	-	-	878	144,393	93,368	43,316	3,222	4,487
1925	3,578	51	1,937	65	723	-	-	802	141,496	102,753	32,964	2,106	3,673
1924	22,065	2,820	6,992	183	8,801	-	-	3,269	318,855	200,690	89,336	17,559	11,270
1923	13,705	2,183	4,986	257	5,809	-	-	470	199,972	117,011	63,768	13,181	6,012
1922	14,263	1,998	4,406	360	6,716	-	-	783	77,448	46,810	19,551	7,449	3,638
1921	25,034	11,735	4,009	511	7,878	-	-	901	124,118	72,317	30,758	13,774	7,269
1920	17,505	5,033	2,330	300	9,432	-	-	410	162,666	90,025	52,361	13,808	6,472
1919	12,674	19	1,964	171	10,064	-	-	456	102,286	57,782	29,818	8,826	5,860
1918	12,701	43	1,795	130	10,213	-	-	520	65,418	32,452	18,524	8,879	5,563
1917	12,756	393	2,237	109	8,991	-	-	1,026	147,779	105,399	17,869	15,507	9,004
1916	13,204	1,670	2,460	112	8,680	-	-	282	137,424	101,551	18,425	12,027	5,421
1915	15,211	3,543	2,660	161	8,613	-	-	234	111,206	82,215	12,340	11,598	5,053
1914	34,273	21,716	2,502	221	8,929	-	-	905	122,695	86,139	14,614	14,451	7,491
1913	35,358	23,955	2,105	179	8,281	-	-	838	103,907	73,802	11,926	12,458	5,721
1912	21,449	12,788	1,765	175	6,114	-	-	607	95,926	55,990	23,238	12,467	4,231
1911	17,428	10,229	1,460	524	4,520	-	-	695	94,364	56,830	19,889	13,403	4,242
1910	23,533	15,212	1,968	1,696	2,720	-	-	1,937	89,534	56,555	18,691	11,244	3,044
1909	12,904	7,506	1,943	203	3,111	-	-	141	82,208	51,941	16,251	11,180	2,836
1908	28,365	9,753	1,397	1,040	15,803	-	-	372	59,997	38,510	6,067	11,888	3,532
1907	40,524	8,053	961	898	30,226	-	-	386	41,762	19,918	1,406	16,689	3,749
1906	22,300	6,354	1,544	216	13,835	-	-	351	24,613	5,063	1,997	13,656	3,897
1905	23,925	6,157	2,166	190	10,331	-	-	5,081	25,217	2,168	2,637	16,641	3,771
1904	26,186	5,235	4,309	261	14,264	-	-	2,117	16,420	2,837	1,009	10,193	2,381
1903	29,966	7,118	2,209	94	19,968	-	-	577	11,023	1,058	528	8,170	1,267
1902	22,271	6,223	1,649	93	14,270	-	-	36	6,698	636	709	4,711	642
1901	13,593	5,782	2,459	22	5,269	-	-	61	4,416	540	347	3,176	353
1900	17,946	3,962	1,247	9	12,635	-	-	93	5,455	396	237	4,656	166
1899	8,972	4,436	1,660	17	2,844	-	-	15	4,316	1,322	161	2,585	248
1898	8,637	4,275	2,071	-	2,230	-	-	61	2,627	352	107	2,124	44
1897	9,662	4,732	3,363	-	1,526	-	-	41	4,537	291	91	4,101	54
1896	6,764	4,139	1,441	-	1,110	-	-	74	7,303	278	150	6,828	47
1895	4,495	2,767	539	-	1,150	-	-	39	3,508	244	116	3,096	52
1894	4,690	-	1,170	-	1,931	-	-	1,589	3,551	194	109	2,177	71
1893	2,392	-	472	-	1,380	-	-	540	2,593	17	18	2,593	-
1892	17	-	-	-	-	-	-	-	17	17	18	17	17
1891	7,678	2,488	2,836	42	1,136	-	-	1,176	5,082	234	18	3,906	942
1890	4,448	1,126	1,716	43	691	-	-	872	3,833	183	18	3,070	580
1889	1,725	593	118	59	640	-	-	315	5,459	28	18	4,923	508
1888	843	273	26	20	404	-	-	120	5,402	15	18	4,880	507
1887	615	208	10	32	229	-	-	136	5,270	9	18	4,876	385
1886	317	15	40	17	194	-	-	51	3,026	17	18	2,734	275
1885	198	-	22	34	49	-	-	93	41,203	38,336	323	2,477	67
1884	510	-	279	12	20	-	-	199	63,339	60,626	430	2,208	75
1883	8,113	-	8,031	9	27	-	-	46	71,729	70,274	469	903	83
1882	39,629	-	39,579	10	5	-	-	35	100,129	98,366	366	1,291	106
1881	11,982	5	11,890	33	11	-	-	43	127,577	125,450	325	1,680	122

Footnotes, see p. 1139.

SOURCE: *Historical Statistics of the United States, Colonial Times to 1970*, Bureau of the Census (in press).

Immigrants, by Country (Asia, Americas: 1820-1980)

(For years ending June 30, except 1820-1831 and 1844-1849, years ending Sept. 30; 1833-1842 and 1851-1867,
years ending Dec. 31; 1832 covers 15 months ending Dec. 31; 1843, 9 months ending Sept. 30;
1850, 15 months ending Dec. 31; 1868, 6 months ending June 30)

| | Asia | | | | | | | | Americas | | | | |
Year	Total	Turkey in Asia[11]	China[12]	India	Japan[13]	Korea[14]	Philippines	Other Asia	Total	Canada, Newfoundland and Greenland[15]	Mexico	West Indies	Other America
1880	5,839	4	5,802	21	4	-	-	8	101,692	99,744	492	1,351	105
1879	9,660	31	9,604	15	4	-	-	6	33,043	31,286	556	1,123	78
1878	9,014	7	8,992	8	2	-	-	5	27,204	25,592	465	1,019	128
1877	10,640	3	10,594	17	7	-	-	19	24,065	22,137	445	1,390	93
1876	22,943	8	22,781	25	4	-	-	125	24,686	22,505	631	1,382	168
1875	16,499	1	16,437	19	3	-	-	39	26,640	24,097	610	1,790	143
1874	13,838	6	13,776	17	21	-	-	18	35,339	33,020	386	1,777	156
1873	20,325	3	20,292	15	9	-	-	6	40,335	37,891	606	1,634	204
1872	7,825	-	7,788	12	17	-	-	5	42,205	40,204	569	1,322	110
1871	7,240	4	7,135	14	78	-	-	9	48,835	47,164	402	1,169	100
1870	15,825	-	15,740	24	48	-	-	13	42,658	40,414	463	1,679	102
1869	12,949	2	12,874	3	63	-	-	7	23,767	21,120	320	2,233	94
1868	5,171	-	5,157	-	-	-	-	14	3,415	2,785	129	419	82
1867	3,961	-	3,863	2	67	-	-	29	24,715	23,379	292	817	227
1866	2,411	-	2,385	17	7	-	-	2	33,582	32,150	239	895	298
1865	2,947	-	2,942	5	-	-	-	-	22,778	21,586	193	851	148
1864	2,982	-	2,975	6	-	-	-	1	4,607	3,636	99	718	154
1863	7,216	-	7,214	1	-	-	-	1	4,147	3,464	96	491	96
1862	3,640	-	3,633	5	-	-	-	2	4,175	3,275	142	585	173
1861	7,528	-	7,518	6	1	-	-	3	2,763	2,069	218	358	118
1860	5,476	-	5,467	5	-	-	-	4	6,343	4,514	229	1,384	216
1859	3,461	-	3,457	2	-	-	-	2	5,466	4,163	265	879	159
1858	5,133	-	5,128	5	-	-	-	-	5,821	4,603	429	647	142
1857	5,945	-	5,944	1	-	-	-	-	6,811	5,670	133	923	85
1856	4,747	-	4,733	13	-	-	-	1	9,058	6,493	741	1,337	487
1855	3,540	-	3,526	6	-	-	-	8	9,260	7,761	420	887	192
1854	13,100	-	13,100	-	-	-	-	-	8,533	6,891	446	1,036	160
1853	47	-	42	5	-	-	-	-	6,030	5,424	162	406	38
1852	4	-	-	4	-	-	-	-	7,695	6,352	72	1,232	39
1851	2	-	-	2	-	-	-	-	9,703	7,438	181	1,929	155
1850	7	-	3	4	-	-	-	-	15,768	9,376	597	3,171	2,624
1849	11	-	3	8	-	-	-	-	8,904	6,890	518	1,073	423
1848	8	-	-	6	-	-	-	2	7,989	6,473	24	1,338	154
1847	12	-	4	8	-	-	-	-	5,231	3,827	62	1,251	91
1846	11	-	7	4	-	-	-	-	5,525	3,855	222	1,351	97
1845	6	-	6	-	-	-	-	-	5,035	3,195	498	1,241	101
1844	6	-	3	1	-	-	-	2	3,740	2,711	197	771	61
1843	11	-	3	2	-	-	-	6	2,854	1,502	398	880	74
1842	7	-	4	2	-	-	-	1	3,994	2,078	403	1,410	103
1841	3	-	2	1	-	-	-	-	3,429	1,816	352	1,042	219
1840	1	-	-	1	-	-	-	-	3,815	1,938	395	1,446	36
1839	-	-	-	-	-	-	-	-	3,617	1,926	353	1,289	49
1838	1	-	-	1	-	-	-	-	2,990	1,476	211	1,231	72
1837	11	-	-	11	-	-	-	-	3,628	1,279	627	1,627	95
1836	4	-	-	4	-	-	-	-	4,936	2,814	798	1,178	146
1835	17	-	8	8	-	-	-	1	3,312	1,193	1,032	938	149
1834	6	-	-	6	-	-	-	-	2,779	1,020	885	791	83
1833	3	-	-	3	-	-	-	-	3,282	1,194	779	1,264	45
1832	4	-	-	4	-	-	-	-	2,871	608	827	1,256	180
1831	1	-	-	1	-	-	-	-	2,194	176	692	1,281	45

Footnotes, see p. 1139.

Immigrants, by Country (Asia, Americas: 1820-1980)

(For years ending June 30, except 1820-1831 and 1844-1849, years ending Sept. 30; 1833-1842 and 1851-1867, years ending Dec. 31; 1832 covers 15 months ending Dec. 31; 1843, 9 months ending Sept. 30; 1850, 15 months ending Dec. 31; 1868, 6 months ending June 30)

	Asia								Americas				
Year	Total	Turkey in Asia[11]	China[12]	India	Japan[13]	Korea[14]	Philip-pines	Other Asia	Total	Canada, Newfound-land and Green-land[15]	Mexico	West Indies	Other Amer-ica
1830	-	-	-	-	-	-	-	-	2,296	189	983	937	187
1829	2	-	1	1	-	-	-	-	3,299	409	2,290	517	83
1828	3	-	-	3	-	-	-	-	2,090	267	1,089	652	82
1827	1	-	-	1	-	-	-	-	580	165	127	227	61
1826	1	-	-	1	-	-	-	-	831	223	106	427	75
1825	1	-	1	-	-	-	-	-	846	314	68	389	75
1824	1	-	-	1	-	-	-	-	559	155	110	259	35
1823	-	-	-	-	-	-	-	-	382	167	35	160	20
1822	-	-	-	1	-	-	-	-	378	204	5	159	10
1821	1	-	-	-	-	-	-	-	303	184	4	107	8
1820	5	-	1	1	-	-	-	3	387	209	1	164	13

Footnotes, see p. 1139.

Immigrants, by Country (Africa, Australasia: 1820-1980)

(For years ending June 30, except: 1820-1831 and 1844-1849, years ending Sept. 30; 1833-1842 and
1851-1867, years ending Dec. 31; 1832 covers 15 months ending Dec. 31; 1843, 9 months
ending Sept. 30; 1850, 15 months ending Dec. 31; 1868, 6 months ending June 30)

Year	Africa Total	Australasia Total	Australia and New Zealand	Other Pacific Islands	All Other Countries Total	Year	Africa Total	Australasia Total	Australia and New Zealand	Other Pacific Islands	All Other Countries Total
1980	13,981	3,951	2,209	1,742	-	1935	118	141	132	9	63
1979	12,838	4,449	1,999	2,450	-	1934	104	147	130	17	3
1978	11,524	4,396	2,184	2,212	-	1933	71	137	122	15	-
1977	10,155	4,091	1,986	2,105	-	1932	186	303	291	12	-
1976	7,723	3,591	1,796	1,795	1	1931	417	652	616	36	-
1975	6,729	3,346	1,500	1,846	1	1930	572	1,051	1,026	25	-
1974	6,182	3,051	1,645	1,406	2	1929	509	636	619	17	-
1973	6,655	3,255	1,890	1,365	-	1928	475	606	578	28	-
1972	6,612	3,284	2,048	1,236	2	1927	520	746	712	34	-
1971	6,772	2,922	1,870	1,052	2	1926	529	591	556	35	-
1970	7,099	3,632	2,693	939	-	1925	412	462	416	46	-
1969	4,460	3,061	2,278	783	2	1924	900	679	635	44	58
1968	3,220	3,172	2,374	798	-	1923	548	759	711	48	15
1967	2,577	2,811	2,128	683	-	1922	520	915	855	60	25
1966	1,967	2,500	1,894	606	11	1921	1,301	2,281	2,191	90	130
1965	1,949	2,199	1,803	396	22	1920	648	2,185	2,066	119	702
1964	2,015	2,070	1,767	303	25	1919	189	1,310	1,234	76	46
1963	1,982	1,977	1,642	335	27	1918	299	1,090	925	165	47
1962	1,834	1,819	1,427	392	1	1917	566	1,142	1,014	128	77
1961	1,851	1,881	1,556	325	5	1916	894	1,574	1,484	90	31
1960	1,925	2,140	1,892	248	26	1915	934	1,399	1,282	117	31
1959	1,992	2,162	1,878	284	21	1914	1,539	1,446	1,336	110	136
1958	2,008	2,045	1,783	262	12	1913	1,409	1,340	1,229	111	23
1957	1,600	1,458	1,228	230	16	1912	1,009	898	794	104	15
1956	1,351	1,346	1,171	175	22	1911	956	1,043	984	59	39
1955	1,203	1,028	932	96	3,597	1910	1,072	1,097	998	99	43
1954	1,248	910	845	65	8,341	1909	858	892	839	53	49
1953	989	782	742	40	430	1908	1,411	1,179	1,098	81	17
1952	931	578	545	33	8	1907	1,486	1,989	1,947	42	22
1951	845	527	490	37	20	1906	712	1,733	1,682	51	33,012[19]
1950	849	517	460	57	7	1905	757	2,166	2,091	75	161
1949	995	776	661	115	25	1904	686	1,555	1,461	94	90
1948	1,027	1,336	1,218	118	10	1903	176	1,349	1,150	199	25
1947	1,284	2,960	2,821	139	27	1902	37	566	384	182	103
1946	1,516	6,106	6,009	97	73	1901	173	498	325	173	1
1945	406	1,663	1,625	38	-	1900	30	428	214	214	13
1944	112	615	577	38	-	1899	51	810	456	354	217
1943	141	160	120	40	-	1898	48	201	153	48	-
1942	473	163	120	43	-	1897	37	199	139	60	-
1941	564	255	194	61	-	1896	21	112	87	25	-
1940	202	228	207	21	-	1895	36	155	155	-	-
1939	218	222	213	9	-	1894	24	244	244	-	70
1938	174	248	228	20	-	1893	[17]	248	248	[17]	5,173
1937	155	174	145	29	-	1892	[17]	267	267	[17]	8,520
1936	105	165	147	18	-	1891	103	1,301	777	524	70

- Represents zero.

[11] No record of immigration from Turkey in Asia until 1869.
[12] Beginning 1957, includes Taiwan.
[13] No record of immigration from Japan until 1861.
[14] No record of immigration from Korea prior to 1948.
[19] Includes 32,897 persons returning to their homes in the United States.

[15] Prior to 1920, Canada and Newfoundland were recorded as British North America.
[16] Philippines included in "All other countries" prior to 1936.
[17] Included in "All other countries."
[18] No record of immigration from Mexico for 1886 to 1893.

Immigrants, by Country (Africa, Australasia: 1820-1980)

(For years ending June 30, except: 1820-1831 and 1844-1849, years ending Sept. 30; 1833-1842 and
1851-1867, years ending Dec. 31; 1832 covers 15 months ending Dec. 31; 1843, 9 months
ending Sept. 30; 1850, 15 months ending Dec. 31; 1868, 6 months ending June 30)

Year	Africa Total	Australasia Total	Australia and New Zealand	Other Pacific Islands	All Other Countries Total	Year	Africa Total	Australasia Total	Australia and New Zealand	Other Pacific Islands	All Other Countries Total
1890	112	1,167	699	468	62	1855	14	-	-	-	334
1889	187	2,196	1,000	1,196	70	1854	-	-	-	-	658
1888	65	2,387	697	1,690	61	1853	8	-	-	-	984
1887	40	1,282	528	754	73	1852	-	-	-	-	1,420
1886	122	1,136	522	614	73	1851	3	-	-	-	248
1885	112	679	449	230	71	1850	-	-	-	-	45,882
1884	59	900	502	398	98	1849	3	-	-	-	1,605
1883	67	747	554	193	79	1848	10	-	-	-	495
1882	60	889	878	11	99	1847	-	-	-	-	608
1881	33	1,191	1,188	3	103	1846	1	-	-	-	2,564
1880	18	954	953	1	63	1845	4	-	-	-	25
1879	12	816	813	3	36	1844	14	-	-	-	110
1878	18	606	606	-	15	1843	6	-	-	-	612
1877	16	914	912	2	27	1842	3	-	-	-	616
1876	89	1,312	1,205	107	36	1841	14	-	-	-	627
1875	54	1,268	1,104	164	76	1840	6	-	-	-	118
1874	58	1,193	960	233	128	1839	10	-	-	-	294
1873	28	1,414	1,135	279	160	1838	10	-	-	-	1,843
1872	41	2,416	2,180	236	164	1837	2	-	-	-	4,660
1871	24	21	18	3	85	1836	6	-	-	-	831
1870	31	36	36	-	27	1835	14	-	-	-	44
1869	72	-	-	-	17	1834	1	-	-	-	5,069
1868	3	-	-	-	161	1833	1	-	-	-	26,243
1867	25	-	-	-	3,270	1832	2	-	-	-	23,412
1866	33	-	-	-	3,626	1831	2	-	-	-	7,397
1865	49	-	-	-	8,298	1830	2	-	-	-	13,807
1864	37	-	-	-	559	1829	1	-	-	-	6,695
1863	3	-	-	-	1,183	1828	6	-	-	-	554
1862	12	-	-	-	448	1827	4	-	-	-	1,571
1861	47	-	-	-	380	1826	-	-	-	-	254
1860	126	-	-	-	486	1825	1	-	-	-	808
1859	11	-	-	-	1,395	1824	-	-	-	-	2,387
1858	17	-	-	-	801	1823	-	-	-	-	1,956
1857	25	-	-	-	22,301	1822	-	-	-	-	2,114
1856	6	-	-	-	542	1821	2	-	-	-	2,886
						1820	1	-	-	-	301

Sources: Bureau of the Census, *Historical Statistics of the United States, Colonial Times to 1970*
(Washington, D.C.: Government Printing Office, 1975); Bureau of the Census, *1980 Census of
Population* (Washington, D.C.: Government Printing Office, 1983).

Party Abbreviations

The election data obtained from the Inter-University Consortium for Political and Social Research contain nearly 1,500 different party labels. In many cases the party labels represent combinations of multi-party support received by individual candidates. However, in preparing the returns for publication, approximately 1,000 of the party labels were eliminated because the candidate(s) did not receive at least 5 percent of the votes cast. The following list provides a key to the abbreviations developed by Congressional Quarterly from the original complete list of parties supplied by the ICPSR. The names of the parties appear below in the form they were obtained from ICPSR.

A-A	Anti-Adams	BC	Butter Congressional	D-HANKER	Democrat-Hanker
A-AK R	Anti-Addicks Republican	BENTON D	Benton Democrat	DI	Democratic-Independent
AB	Abolition	B MOOSE	Bull Moose	D & I	Democrat and Independent
A-BANK	Anti-Bank	BOLT D	Bolting Democrat	D & ID	Democrat and Independent
AB-D	Abolition-Democrat	BRECK D	Breckinridge Democrat		Democrat
A-BEN D	Anti-Benton Democrat	BROD D	Broderick Democrat	D IL	Democrat, Independent
A-BOSS	Anti-Boss	BRYAN	Bryan Party		League
A-BROD D	Anti-Broderick Democrat	BRYAN D	Bryan Democrat	D & IL	Democrat and Independence
A-CB	Anti Carpet-Baggers	B-T R	Brindle-Tail Republican		League
AD	Adams Democrat	B & T R	Black and Tan Republican	D IL A NP	Dem., Independent League,
A-D-FUS	Anti-Democrat-Fusion	BUSINESS	Business Med		Amer., Nat'l. Progressive
AG WHEEL	Agricultural Wheeler	BUT D & N	Butler Democrat	D IL ANPI	Democrat, Independent
A JAC	Andrew Jackson		and National		League, American, Nat'l
A-JAC	Anti-Jackson	BUT D & R	Butler Democrat		Progressive, Ind.
A-JAC D	Anti-Jackson Democrat		and Greenback	D IL NPR	Democrat, Independent
A-KN D	Anti-Know Nothing Democrat	BUT R	But. Republican		League, Nat'l Progressive
A-KN I	Anti-Know Nothing	C	Conservative	D-IP	Democrat-Independent
	Independent	CALH D	Calhoun Democrat		Progressive
A-KN I D	Anti-Know Nothing	CASS D	Cass Democrat	D & I POP	Democrat and Independent
	Independent Democrat	CD	Conservative Democrat		Populist
AK R	Addicks Republican	CI/IC	Citizen Independent or	DISS D	Dissident Democrat
A-LD D	Anti-Land Distribution		Independent Citizen	DISTRIB	Distributionist Candidate
	Democrat	CIT	Citizens	D & KEY	Democrat and Keystone
A-LEC D	Anti-Lecompton Democrat	CIT & CO D	Citizen and County Democrat	D K & PROG	Democrat, Keystone and
A-LEC DR	Anti-Lecompton Democrat	CITY	City Party		Progressive
	and Republican	CITY FUS	City Fusion	D & L	Democrat and Liberal
ALI	ALaskan Independent	CIV A	'Civ. A'	D & LAB	Democrat and Labor
ALL PP	All Peoples	CLAY D	Clay Democrat	D-LAB-PP	Democrat-Labor-Peoples
ALNC	Alliance	CLAY R	Clay Republican	D-LAF I	Democrat-La Follette
A-LOT D	Anti-Lottery Democrat	CLEAN GV	Clean Government		Independent
AM	American	CLINT R	Clinton Republican	D & LIBN	Democrat and Liberation
A-MACH	Anti-Machine	CLP	Commonwealth Land Party	D & LP	Democrat and Law
A-MAINE	Anti-Maine Law	CLUNEY	Cluney Taxpayers Good		Preservation
A-MAS	Anti-Mason		Government		and Liberty
A-MASC	Anti-Masonic	CNM	Cincinnatus Nonpartisan	D LP & L	Democrat, Law Preservation
A-MASDNR	Anti-Mason-Democrat-		Movement		and Liberty
	National Republican	COALIT	Coalition	DN	Democratic National
AM & EMANC	American	CO D	County Democrat	DN & FS	D.N. and F.S. (Free Silver)
	and Emancipationist	COLORED	Colored	D-NG LAB	Democrat-National Green
AM I	American Independent	COLOR R	Colored Republican		Labor
AM LAB	American Labor	COM	Communist	D NPR	Democrat National
AM MO	American Party of Missouri	CONST	Constitution		Progressive
AM NAT	American National	CONSU	Consumer	D & NS	Democrat and National Silver
A-MON D	Anti-Monopoly Democrat	CP	Commonwealth Party	DODD I	Dodd Independent
A-MONOP	Anti-Monopoly	CR	Conservative Republican	D-OP	Democrat-Other Parties
AM R	American Republican	CREOLE	Creole Faction	DOUG D	Douglas Democrat
AM&R	American and Republican	CSI	Civil Service Independents	D & P	Democrat and Prohibition
A-NEB	Anti-Nebraska	CSR & D	'CSR' and Democrat	D & POP	Democrat and Populist
A-NEB D	Anti-Nebraska Democrat	CST	Constitutional	D-POP I	Democrat-Populist
ANTI-CLINT	Anti-Clinton	CST U	Constitutional Union		Independent
ANTI-CL R	Anti-Clinton Republican	D	Democrat	DPOP PFS	Democrat, Populist,
ANTI-FED	Anti-Federalist	D & AM	Democrat and American		Prohibition & Free Silver
AP	Action Party	D & A-MASC	Democrat and Anti-Masonic	D-PP	Democrat-Peoples
APOLLO	Apollo Hall	D AM IL	Democrat, American,	DPPC	Direct People's Candidate
AR	Adams Republican		Independence League	D & PPI	Democratic and People's
A-RENT	Anti-Rent	D & A-RENT	Democrat and Anti-Rent		Independent
A-RPT D	Anti-Redemption Democrat	D & CD	Democrat and Co. Democrat	D PPI & PR	Democrat, People's
A-TAM	Anti-Tammany	D CIT	Democratic Citizen		Independent and
A-TARIFF	Anti-Tariff	D & CIT	Democrat and Citizen		Progressive
A-TAX	Anti-Tax	D & CST	Democrat and Constitution	D & PRI	Democrat and Progressive
A-TRUST	Anti-Trust (A.T.)	DENVER I	Denver Independent Party		Independent
A VB D	Anti-Van Buren Democrat	D & F ALNC	Democrat and Farmers	D PR & IL	Democrat, Progressive and
A-WOLF D	Anti-Wolf Democrat		Alliance		Independence League
BALLOT	Ballot Reform	DFL	Democrat Farmer-Labor	D & PROG	Democrat and Progressive
BARN D	Barnburner Democrat	D & G	Democrat and Greenback	D-PRO-TN	Democrat-Progressive-
					Townsend

---

* The party label D-R used in early 19th century returns refers to the party associated with Thomas Jefferson.

In California from 1913 to 1959, D-R refers to that state's system of crossfiling in primary elections for House, Senate and Governor. Democrats and Republicans would each run in the other party's primary in addition to their own. Frequently, the same candidate would win both nominations. In cases in which a Democrat won both primaries, the symbol D-R is used in the California vote returns in this book. Where a Republican won both primaries, the symbol R-D is used.

DPUS — D.P.U.S.
D-R* — Democratic-Republican
D & REC — Democrat and Recovery
D REF — Democrat Reform
D & RESUB — Democrat and Resubmission
D R & SOC — Democratic, Republican, Socialist
DR SOC P — Democratic, Republican, Socialist, Prohibition
D SIL — Democratic (Silver)
D & SILVER — Democrat and Silver
D SM — Democrat (S.M.)
D SOC — Democratic Socialist
D & SOC — Democrat & Socialist
D SOCIAL — Democratic Social
D & UN LAB — Democrat and Union Labor
D-WM — Democrat-Working Man
EMANCIP — Emancipation
ENVIRON — Environment
EP — Elec. Prog.
ER — Equal Right
E TAX — Equal Tax
FACP R — Father Coughlin's Principles, Republican
F ALNC — Farmers' Alliance
FB R — 'Free Bridge' Republican
FED — Federalist
FEDL — Federal
FEDL AB — Federal Abolition
FEDR LAB — Federated Labor
FF — Four Freedoms
FILL AM — Fillmore American
F-LAB — Farmer-Labor
FLA PP — Florida People's Party
F PLAY — Fair Play
FREM AM — Fremont American
FS CLN — Free Soil Coalition
F SIL — Free Silver
F SIL R — Free Silver Republican
F SOIL — Free Soil
F SOIL D — Free Soil Democrat
F SOIL W — Free Soil Whig
FS & SC — Free Soil and Scattering
FUS — Fusion
FUS-D-PO — Fusion-Democrat-Populist
FUS R — Fusion Republican
G — Greenback
GD — Greenback Democrat
G & D — Greenback and Democrat
G LAB — Greenback Labor
G LAB & P — Greenback Labor and Prohibition
G LAB R — Greenback Labor Republican
GOLD D — Gold Democrat
GOOD GOV — Good Government
G & P — Greenback and Prohibition
G & R — Greenback and Republican
G & TAM — Greenback and Tammany
HARD D — Hard Democratic
HARD D & AM — Hard Democrat and American
HC W — Henry Clay Whig
HE — Honest Elections
HG — Honest Government
HIG R — Higgins Republican
HL — High Life
H LIC — High License
HUNKER D — Hunker Democrat
I — Independent
IA — Independent American
I ALNC — Independent Alliance
IC — Independent Conservative
I CIT AL — Independent Citizens Alliance
ID — Independent Democrat
I & D — Independent and Democrat
I DEMOC — Independent Democracy
I D-R — Independent Democratic Republican
ID & OPP — Independent Democrat and Opposition
ID R & P — Independent Democratic Republican and Prohibition

IG — Independent Greenback
IG & R — Independent Greenback and Republican
I LEAGUE — Independence League
I LG — Independent League
IL & NPR — Independence League and National Progressive
I-N — Independent-National
IND CONG — 'Ind. Cong.'
INDEP — Independence
IND GOVT — Industrial Government
INDL — Industrialist
INDUST — Industrial
I N-PART — Independent Non-Partisan
I-PO — Independent-Public Ownership
IPP CH — Independent People's Choice
I PROG — Independent Progressive
I-PROG-R — Independent-Progressive-Republicans
I-PR-SOC — Independent-Progressive-Socialist
IR, I-R — Independent Republican
I.R. — I.R.
I RAD R — Independent Radical Republican
IR & D — Independent Republican and Democrat
I REF — Independent-Reform
I REF D — Independent Reform Democrat
IR & P — Independent Republican and Prohibition
IRR U — Irregular Union
IRR W — Irregular Whig
I SOC — Independent Socialist
I VT — Independent Vermonters Party
I W — Independent Whig
JAC — Jackson
JAC & AR — Jackson and Adams Republican
JAC D — Jackson Democrat
JAC R — Jackson Republican
JACS R — Jacksonian Republican
JEFF — Jefferson
JEFF D — Jefferson-Democrat
JEFFS — Jeffersonian
JOBLESS — Jobless
KEY — Keystone
KN — Know-Nothing
K POP — Kolbite Populist
L — Liberal
LAB — Labor
LAB & POP — Labor and Populist
LAB-R — Labor-Republican
LAB REF — Labor Reform
— Labor Reform and Prohibition
LAF — La Follette
LAF I — La Follette Independent
LANCAST — Lancaster
LAW ENF — Law Enforcement
LAW ORD — Law and Order
LAW PRES — Law Preservation
LD D — Land Distribution Democrat
LFD — Lincoln Fair Deal
LIB — Liberty
LIBER W — Liberation Whig
LIBERT — Libertarian
LIN — Lin.
LINCOLN — Lincoln
L-LAB D — Liberal-Labor-Democratic
LOCOFOCO — Locofoco
L & O W — Law and Order Whig
LOW TAX D — Low Tax Democrat
LR — Liberal Republican
LRU — La Raza Unida
LU — Liberty Union
LW & B — Light Wines and Beer
LW R — Lily-White Republican
MCK SM — McKinley Sound Money

MID ROAD — Middle of the Road Populist
MINN TAX — Minnesota Taxpayers
MLP — Municipal League Party (M.L.)
MOZART D — Mozart Democrat
MR — Minstrel Republican
N — National Party
NAM — Native American
N AM — National American
NC R — North Carolina Republican
ND — National Democrat
NDPA — National Democratic Party of Alabama
NEB — Nebraska
NEB D — Nebraska Democrat
NEIGH — Neighborhood
NEW DEAL — New Deal
NEW I — New Independent
NEW LEAD — New Leadership
NF — Nuclear Freeze
NG — National Greenback
NON PART — Non Partisan
NON PL — Nonpartisan League
NP — National Prohibition
N PROG — National Progressive
NR — National Republican
NR-A-MAS — National Republican-Anti-Mason
N SILVER — National Silver
N SR — National States Rights
NULL — Nullifier
NULL D — Nullifier Democrat
NULL NR — Nullification-National Republican
N UNION — National Union
OB — Open Book
OLD AGE — Old Age Pension
OLD R — Old Republican
OP — Occion Popular
OPP — Opposition
OPP D — Opposition Democrat
OPP R — Opposition Republican
OPP & SC — Opposition and Scattering
P — Prohibition
P & D — Prohibition and Democrat
P D-R & PR — Prohibition, Democrat-Republican and Progressive
P D SOC — Prohibition, Democrat, Socialist
PEACE D — Peace Democrat
PERS LIB — Personal Liberty
P & F ALNC — Prohibition and Farmer's Alliance
PFP — Peace and Freedom
P-LAB — Population-Labor
POP — Populist
POP & D — Populist and Democrat
POP I — Populist Independent
POP & R — Populist and Republican
POP SIL — Populist Silver
POP & SL D — Populist and Silver Democrat
POPU GOV — Popular Government
PP — People's
PP CAND — People's Candidate, The
PP & D — People's and Democrat
PP-D-S-R — Peoples-Democrat-Silver-Republican
PP I — People's Independent
PPL DR S — People's Party Labor, Democratic Republican, Silver
PP & R — Peoples and Republican
PRC TOWN — PRC, Townsend
PRI R — Primary Republican
PRO-BANK — Pro-Bank
PROG — Progressive
PROG-BMR — Progressive-Bull Moose-Roosevelt
PROG & BUS — Progressive and Businessmen's
PROG D — Progressive Democrat
PROG D & P — Progressive-Democrat and Prohibition

PROG & IL	Progressive and Independence League	R K & WASH	Republican, Keystone, and Washington	SR FT	State Rights Free Trader
PROG-P	Progressive-Prohibition	RKW & ROPR	Republican, Keystone, Washington and Roosevelt Progressive	SR W	State Rights Whig
PROG R	Progressive Republican			SSR D	State's Rights Democrat
PT	Protectionist			SSR NULL	State's Rights Nullifier
PUB OWN	Public Ownership	R & LAB	Republican and Labor	STAL D	Stalwart Democrat
PURE POL	Pure Politics	R & LP	Republican and Law Preservation	STAL SIL	Stalwart Silver
R	Republican			STATE D	State Democrat
RAD	Radical	R MCK CIT	Republican, McKinley Citizen	STC D	State Credit Democrat
RAD R	Radical Republican	R & ND	Republican and National Democrat	STICKER	Sticker
R AM	Republican American			TAFT	'Taft for President'
R & A-MONO	Republican and Anti-Monopoly	R & NG	Republican and National Greenback	TAM	Tammany
				TAM D	Tammany Democrat
R AM & PR	Republican, American and Progressive	R & NP	Republican and Nonpartisan	TAM D & UL	Tammany Democrat and Union Labor
		R NPR	Republican, Nat'l Progressive		
R & A-TAM	Republican and Anti-Tammany	R NPR AM	Republican, Nat'l Progressive, American	TAM & NY D	Tammany and New York Democracy
R & A-TR	Republican and Anti-Trust Republican	RO	Roosevelt	TAYLOR W	Taylor Whig
		ROBINSON	Robinson Citizens Party	TEMP	Temperance
R & BM	Republican and Bull Moose	ROB R	Rob. Republican	TEMP REF	Temperance Reform
RBM & PR	Republican, Bull Moose and Progressive	R-OP	Republican-Other Parties	THIRD	The Third Party
		RO PROG	Roosevelt Progressive	TOL	Toleration
R & CF	Republican and City Fusion	RO SOC D	Roosevelt Social Democrat	TOWN	Townsend
RCF & LP	Republican City Fusion and Law Preservation	ROYAL OAK	Royal Oak	TOWN-C-L	Townsend-Coughlin-Labor
		RP	Rate Payers Against LILCO	TOWN OAP	Townsend Old Age Pension
R CF & REC	Republican, City Fusion, and Recovery	R & P	Republican and Prohibition	TOWN SJ	Townsend Social Justice
		RP & DC	Republican Party and Delegate Convention	TOWN-SJD	Townsend-Social Justice, Democratic
RCI	Rich County Independent				
R CIT	Republican Citizens	R P NPR	Republican, Prohibition, Nat'l Progressive	TCPT	Taxpayers Party to Cut Taxes
R CST & CF	Republican, Constitutional, and City Fusion	R POP FU	Republican Populist Fusion	U	United
				U CIT	United Citizen
R-D*	Republican-Democrat	RP & PROG	Republican, Prohibition, and Progressive	U LAB	United Labor
RDC	Republican Delegate Convention	R PR IL	Republican, Progressive, Independence League	ULTRA AB	Ultra Abolitionist
				UN	Union
R-D-P	Republican-Democrat-Prohibition	R & PROG	Republican and Progressive	UN D	Union Democrat
		R-SIL R	Republican-Silver Republican	UN LAB	Union Labor
R-D-PR-C	Republican-Democrat-Progressive-Commonwealth	R & SOC	Republican and Socialist	UN LAB & D	Union Labor and Democrat
		R SOC & LP	Republican, Socialist, and Law Preservation	UNP R	Unpledged Republican
R-D-PROG	Republican-Democratic-Progressive			UN PROG	Union Progressive
		R & SQDEAL	Republican and Square Deal	UN R	Union Republican
R D P T	Republican, Democrat, Progressive, Townsend	RT	Republican, Townsend	UN & SQD	Union and Square Deal
		R & TEMP	Republican and Temperance	UNT	Unionist
R D T	Republican, Democrat, Townsend	RTL	Right to Life	UN W	Union Whig
		R & UL	Republican and Union Labor	USLP	U.S. Labor Party
READJ	Readjuster	R-UNION	Republican-Union	U TAX	United Taxpayers
REDEM D	Redemption Democrat	R & VIC	Republican and 'Vic'	UVD	Ultra-Veto Democrat
REF	Reform	R VIC & CF	Republican, 'Vic,' and City Fusion	VB D	Van Buren Democrat
REF D	Reform Democrat			VB R	Van Buren Republican
REG	Regular	R & WASH	Republican and Washington	VETS F	Veterans Farmer
REG D	Regular Democrat	R & YD	Republican and Young Democracy	VETS V	Veterans Victory
REPEAL	Repeal			VI	Voice of Independence
REPEAL L	Repeal League	SEC	Secessionist	VL	Voters League
R & F ALNC	Republican and Farmer's Alliance	SEC D	Secession Democrat	W	Whig
		SEC W	Secessionist Whig	W & AM	Whig and American
R-FF	Republican-Federalist Fusion	SILENT	Silent Majority	W & A-MASC	Whig and Anti-Masonic
R-F-LAB	Republican-Farmer Labor	SIL-R	Silver Republican	W-A-RENT	Whig Anti-Rent
R F-L-P	Republican, Farmer-Labor-Prohibition	SIL-R-D	Silver-Republican-Democrat	WASH	Washington
		SINGLE T	Single Tax	WCP AM	Workers (Communist) Party of America
RG	Republican Greenback	SM D	Sound Money Democrat		
R-G-FUS	Republican-Greenback-Fusion	SOC	Socialist	WELFARE	Welfare
		SOC & F-L	Socialist and Farmer-Labor	W FS	Whig Free Soil
R-GOLD D	Republican-Gold Democrat	SOCIAL D	Social Democrat	WILDCAT	Wildcat
R & ID	Republican and Independent Democrat	SOC LAB	Socialist Labor	WILSON I	Wilson Independent
		SOC & LP	Socialist and Law Preservation	WM	Workingmen
R & IL	Republican and Independence League			WM PENN	William Penn
		SOC & PROG	Socialist and Progressive	WMP/L	Workingman's Party or League
RIL A NP	Republican Ind League, Amer. Nat'l Progressive	SOC WORK	Socialist Workers		
		SO D	Southern Democrat	WOLF-D	Wolf Democrat
RIL & NPR	Republican, Independent League and National Progressive	SOFT D	Soft Democrat	WP AM	Workers Party of America
		SOFT D & AM	Soft Democrat and American	WRITE IN	Write In
		SOJ	Scales of Justice	YD	Young Democracy
RIL P NP	Republican, Independent League, Prohibition, Nat'l Progressive	SO RTS	Southern Rights	YD & R	Young Democrat and Republican
		SO RTS D	Southern Rights Democrat		
		SOR W	Southern Rights Whig	YOUNGMAN	Youngman
R IL PR	Republican, Independence League and Progressive	SPP	Straight People Party		
		SR	State Rights		
R & IV	Republican and Independent Voters	SR D	State Rights Democrat		

---

* *See footnote p. 1141.*

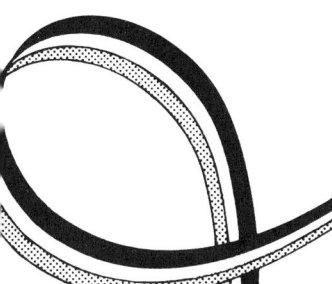

Presidential
Candidates Index

The Presidential Candidates Index includes all presidential candidates appearing in Presidential Elections, Popular Vote Returns, 1824-1984 (pp. 329-377).

The index includes candidates' names followed by the years of candidacy. To locate a candidate's returns, turn to pages 329-377 where the returns are arranged in chronological order. For major candidate returns, see pages 329-366; for minor candidate returns, see pages 367-377.

For other references to presidential candidates in the *Guide to U.S. Elections, Second Edition,* see the General Index, p. 1275.

Gubernatorial Candidates Index

The Gubernatorial Candidates Index includes all candidates appearing in Gubernatorial Elections: Popular Vote Returns, 1789-1984 (pp. 489-536).

The index includes candidates' names followed by state abbreviations and the years of candidacy. To locate a candidate's returns, turn to pages 489-536 where the returns are arranged alphabetically by state (State Abbreviations below) and in chronological order of election for each state.

For other references to gubernatorial candidates in the *Guide to U.S. Elections, Second Edition,* see the General Index, page 1275.

A

Aandahl, Fred G. (ND) - 1944, 1946, 1948
Abbett, Leon (NJ) - 1883, 1889
Abbott, Martha (VT) - 1974
Acker, Bert Lee (FL) - 1944, 1948
Abernethy, Tom (AL) - 1954
Ackerman, Lee (AZ) - 1960
Acuff, Roy (TN) - 1948
Adair, John (KY) - 1820
Adair, John A. M. (IN) - 1916
Adams, Alva (CO) - 1884, 1886, 1896, 1904, 1906
Adams, Charles Francis (MA) - 1876
Adams, Jewett W. (NV) - 1882, 1886
Adams, John Quincy (MA) - 1833, 1867, 1868, 1869, 1870, 1871
Adams, Paul L. (NY) - 1966, 1970
Adams, Samuel (MA) - 1794, 1795, 1796
Adams, Sherman (NH) - 1948, 1950
Adams, Spencer B. (NC) - 1900
Adams, Tod R. (TX) - 1954
Adams, William H. (CO) - 1926, 1928, 1930
Adkins, Homer M. (AR) - 1940, 1942
Agnew, Spiro T. (MD) - 1966
Aiken, George D. (VT) - 1936, 1938
Akin (GA) - 1859
Alcorn, Hugh Meade (CT) - 1934
Alcorn, James L. (MS) - 1869, 1873
Aldrich, Chester H. (NE) - 1910, 1912
Aldrich, Walter J. (VT) - 1914
Alexander (NJ) - 1856
Alexander, Archibald (DE) - 1795
Alexander, Lamar (TN) - 1974, 1978, 1982
Alexander, Moses (ID) - 1908, 1914, 1916, 1922
Alfange, Dean (NY) - 1942
Alger, Fred M. Jr. (MI) - 1952
Alger, Horace C. (WY) - 1898
Alger, Russell A. (MI) - 1884
Allain, Bill (MS) - 1983
Allen (MO) - 1844
Allen, Byron G. (MN) - 1944
Allen, Charles H. (MA) - 1891
Allen, Frank G. (MA) - 1928, 1930

Allen, G. H. (CO) - 1896
Allen, George W. (FL) - 1916
Allen, Heman (VT) - 1829, 1831
Allen, Henry J. (KS) - 1914, 1918, 1920
Allen, Henry W. (LA) - 1864, 1865
Allen, James C. (IL) - 1860
Allen, John (KY) - 1808
Allen, Oscar K. (LA) - 1932
Allen, Philip (RI) - 1851, 1852, 1853
Allen, Samuel L. (MA) - 1833
Allen, William (OH) - 1873, 1875
Allen, William C. (SD) - 1934
Allin, Roger (ND) - 1894
Allis, Edward P. (WI) - 1877
Allred, James V. (TX) - 1934, 1936
Almond, J. Lindsay Jr. (VA) - 1957
Almond, Lincoln (RI) - 1978
Alschuler, Samuel (IL) - 1900
Alsop, John P. (IL) - 1892, 1896
Altgeld, John P. (IL) - 1892, 1896
Ameringer, Oscar (WI) - 1914
Ames, A. A. (MN) - 1886
Ames, Adelbert (MS) - 1873
Ames, Alfred K. (ME) - 1934
Ames, Oliver (MA) - 1886, 1887, 1888
Ammons, Elias M. (CO) - 1912
Ammons, Teller (CO) - 1936, 1938
Amsden, Charles H. (NH) - 1888, 1890
Anaya, Toney (NM) - 1982
Anderson, D. G. (HI) - 1982
Andersen, Elmer L. (MN) - 1960, 1962
Anderson, C. Elmer (MN) - 1952, 1954
Anderson, Emmett T. (WA) - 1956
Anderson, Forrest H. (MT) - 1968
Anderson, Henry W. (VA) - 1921
Anderson, Hugh J. (ME) - 1843, 1844, 1845
Anderson, J. H. (ID) - 1898
Anderson, John Jr. (KS) - 1960, 1962
Anderson, Kenneth T. (KS) - 1950
Anderson, Sigurd (SD) - 1950, 1952
Anderson, T. J. (IA) - 1887
Anderson, Thomas J. (MN) - 1916
Anderson, Victor E. (NE) - 1954, 1956, 1958
Anderson, Wendell R. (MN) - 1970, 1974

Anderson, William R. (TN) - 1962
Andrew, John A. (MA) - 1860, 1861, 1862, 1863, 1864
Andrew, John F. (MA) - 1886
Andrews (GA) - 1855
Andrews, Charles B. (CT) - 1878
Andrews, Lloyd (WA) - 1960
Andrews, Mark (ND) - 1962
Andrews, Reddin (TX) - 1910, 1912
Andrus, Cecil D. (ID) - 1966, 1970, 1974
Ansel, Martin F. (SC) - 1906, 1908
Anthony, George T. (KS) - 1876
Anthony, Henry B. (RI) - 1849, 1850
Apodaca, Jerry (NM) - 1974
Appleton, James (ME) - 1842, 1843, 1844
Archambault, Alberic A. (RI) - 1918, 1928
Archambault, Raoul Jr. (RI) - 1952
Ariyoshi, George R. (HI) - 1974, 1978, 1982
Armstrong (TN) - 1837
Armstrong, Alexander (MD) - 1923
Armstrong, Charles M. (CO) - 1936
Arn, Edward F. (KS) - 1950, 1952
Arnall, Ellis (GA) - 1942
Arnold (WI) - 1904
Arnold, Lemuel H. (RI) - 1831, 1832, 1833
Arnold, Louis A. (WI) - 1922
Arnold, Olney (RI) - 1872, 1908, 1909
Arnold, Peleg (RI) - 1806, 1815
Aronson, John Hugo (MT) - 1952, 1956
Ashcroft, John (MO) - 1984
Ashe, Thomas S. (NC) - 1868
Ashelstrom, Charles A. (CO) - 1912
Ashley (MO) - 1836
Ashley, William H. (MO) - 1824
Askew, Reubin (FL) - 1970, 1974
Atiyeh, Victor G. (OR) - 1974, 1978, 1982
Atkinson (MO) - 1920
Atkinson, George W. (WV) - 1896
Atkinson, W. P. (OK) - 1962
Atkinson, William Y. (GA) - 1894, 1896
Atwater (CT) - 1878
Atwell, W. H. (TX) - 1922
Atwood, John (NH) - 1851, 1852
Austin, Horace (MN) - 1869, 1871
Austin, Richard B. (IL) - 1956
Auten, H. F. (AR) - 1898

Avery, Carlos (MN) - 1924
Avery, William H. (KS) - 1964, 1966
Aycock, Charles B. (NC) - 1900
Ayers, Roy E. (MT) - 1936, 1940
Aylward, John A. (WI) - 1906, 1908
Ayres, Tom (SD) - 1926

B

Babb, W. I. (IA) - 1895
Babbitt, Bruce (AZ) - 1978, 1980
Babcock, Tim (MT) - 1964, 1968
Bachelder, Nahum J. (NH) - 1902
Bacon, Gaspar G. (MA) - 1934
Bacon, Waler W. (DE) - 1940, 1944
Badger, William (NH) - 1834, 1835
Bafalis, L. A. (Skip) (DE) - 1982
Bagby, Arthur P. (AL) - 1837, 1839
Bagley, John J. (MI) - 1872, 1874
Bagwell, Paul D. (MI) - 1958, 1960
Bailey, Carl E. (AR) - 1936, 1938
Bailey, Ed F. (OR) - 1930
Bailey, Ernest H. (VT) - 1944
Bailey, John (MA) - 1834
Bailey, John W. (MI) - 1918
Bailey, M. S. (CO) - 1896
Bailey, Thomas L. (MS) - 1943
Bailey, W. (FL) - 1848
Bailey, W. J. (KS) - 1902
Baird (WI) - 1853
Baird, David Jr. (NJ) - 1931
Bakalis, Michael (IL) - 1978
Baker, Conrad (IN) - 1868
Baker, Davis S. Jr. (RI) - 1893, 1894
Baker, Howard H. (TN) - 1938
Baker, John I. (MA) - 1875
Baker, Nathaniel B. (NH) - 1854, 1855
Baker, R. Tarvin (KY) - 1868
Baker, Samuel Aaron (MO) - 1924
Baldridge, H. C. (ID) - 1926, 1928
Baldwin, Eli (OH) - 1836
Baldwin, Henry P. (MI) - 1868, 1870
Baldwin, Raymond E. (CT) - 1938, 1940, 1942, 1944

State Abbreviations

Alabama	AL	Illinois	IL	Montana	MT	Rhode Island	RI
Alaska	AK	Indiana	IN	Nebraska	NE	South Carolina	SC
Arizona	AZ	Iowa	IA	Nevada	NV	South Dakota	SD
Arkansas	AR	Kansas	KS	New Hampshire	NH	Tennessee	TN
California	CA	Kentucky	KY	New Jersey	NJ	Texas	TX
Colorado	CO	Louisiana	LA	New Mexico	NM	Utah	UT
Connecticut	CT	Maine	ME	New York	NY	Vermont	VT
Delaware	DE	Maryland	MD	North Carolina	NC	Virginia	VA
Florida	FL	Massachusetts	MA	North Dakota	ND	Washington	WA
Georgia	GA	Michigan	MI	Ohio	OH	West Virginia	WV
Hawaii	HI	Minnesota	MN	Oklahoma	OK	Wisconsin	WI
Idaho	ID	Mississippi	MS	Oregon	OR	Wyoming	WY
		Missouri	MO	Pennsylvania	PA		

Baldwin, Roger S. (CT) - 1843, 1844, 1845
Baldwin, Simeon E. (CT) - 1910, 1912
Ballantine, James W. (ID) - 1894
Ballou, Olney (RI) - 1847
Balzar, Fred B. (NV) - 1926, 1930
Bamberger, Simon (UT) - 1916
Bancroft, George (MA) - 1844
Bancroft, Joseph (DE) - 1924
Bangerter, Norman H. (UT) - 1984
Banks, John (PA) - 1841
Banks, Nathaniel P. (MA) - 1857, 1858, 1859
Banning, W. L. (MN) - 1877
Barker, D. E. (AR) - 1894
Barker, Harold H. (MN) - 1946
Barlocker, William A. (UT) - 1960
Barnaby, Jerothmul B. (RI) - 1877
Barnes (MI) - 1878
Barnes, Sidney M. (KY) - 1867
Barnett, Ross R. (MS) - 1959
Barnette, J. R. (AZ) - 1914
Barnum, E. M. (OR) - 1858
Barrere, Nelson (OH) - 1853
Barrett, Frank A. (WY) - 1950
Barrett, Jesse W. (MO) - 1936
Barron, W. W. (WV) - 1960
Barrows, Lewis O. (ME) - 1936, 1938
Barry (MI) - 1854, 1860
Barry, John S. (MI) - 1841, 1843, 1849
Barry, William T. (KY) - 1828
Barstow, Amos C. (RI) - 1864
Barstow, John L. (VT) - 1882
Barstow, William Augustus (WI) - 1853, 1855
Bartlett, Charles W. (MA) - 1905
Bartlett, Dewey F. (OK) - 1966, 1970
Bartlett, Ichabod (NH) - 1831, 1832
Bartlett, John H. (NH) - 1918
Bartlett, Josiah (NH) - 1789, 1790, 1791, 1792, 1793
Bartlett, Washington (CA) - 1886
Bartley, Mordecai (OH) - 1844
Barton (DE) - 1854
Barton, Ara (MN) - 1873
Barzee, C. W. (OR) - 1906
Bashford, Coles (WI) - 1855
Baskin, Alonzo P. (FL) - 1892
Bass, Robert P. (NH) - 1910
Bassett, Richard (DE) - 1798
Bate, William B. (TN) - 1882, 1884
Bateman, Raymond H. (NJ) - 1977
Bates, Curtis (IA) - 1854
Bates, Frederick (MO) - 1824
Bates, John L. (MA) - 1902, 1903, 1904
Bates, Mark P. (SD) - 1918, 1920
Batt, Philip (ID) - 1982
Battle, John S. (VA) - 1949
Battle, William C. (VA) - 1969
Baxter (TN) - 1890
Baxter, Elisha (AR) - 1872
Baxter, George W. (WY) - 1890
Baxter, Percival P. (ME) - 1922
Beach, Erasmus D. (MA) - 1855, 1856, 1857, 1858, 1860
Beach, William B. (RI) - 1876
Beall, J. Glenn (MD) - 1978
Beardsley (CT) - 1912
Beardsley, Morris (CT) - 1916
Beardsley, William (IA) - 1948, 1950, 1952
Beattie, Taylor (LA) - 1879
Beauvais, Arnaud (LA) - 1831
Beaver, James A. (PA) - 1882, 1886
Bebb, William (OH) - 1846
Beck, George T. (WY) - 1902
Becker, George L. (MN) - 1859, 1894
Beckham, John C. W. (KY) - 1900, 1903, 1927
Bedell, John (NH) - 1869, 1870
Bedford, Gunning Jr. (DE) - 1795
Bedford, Homer F. - (CO) - 1942
Bedle, Joseph D. (NJ) - 1874
Beeckman, R. Livingston (RI) - 1914, 1916, 1918
Beekman, C. C. (OR) - 1878
Beers, S. P. (CT) - 1838
Begole, Josiah W. (MI) - 1882, 1884
Behan, W. J. (LA) - 1904
Belknap (KY) - 1903
Bell, Bob (GA) - 1982
Bell, Charles H. (NH) - 1880
Bell, Charles J. (VT) - 1904
Bell, James (NH) - 1853, 1854, 1855
Bell, John (NH) - 1828, 1829
Bell, Joshua F. (KY) - 1859

Bell, P. Hansbrough (TX) - 1849, 1851
Bell, Samuel (NH) - 1819, 1820, 1821, 1822
Bell, Theodore A. (CA) - 1906, 1910, 1918
Bellmon, Henry (OK) - 1962
Bellotti, Francis X. (MA) - 1964
Benedict, Omer K. (OK) - 1926
Bennett (WV) - 1908
Bennett, Caleb P. (DE) - 1832
Bennett, John J. Jr. (NY) - 1942
Bennett, Robert F. (KS) - 1974, 1978
Benson, Elmer A. (MN) - 1936, 1938
Bentall, J. O. (MN) - 1916
Bentley, Arthur A. (WI) - 1922
Benton, Thomas H. (IA) - 1865
Benton, Thomas Hart (MO) - 1856
Benz (WI) - 1944
Berge, George W. (NE) - 1904
Berry, James H. (AR) - 1882
Berry, Nathaniel S. (NH) - 1846, 1847, 1848, 1849, 1850, 1861, 1862
Berry, Tom (SD) - 1932, 1934, 1936
Berry, William H. (PA) - 1910
Best, Roy (CT) - 1944
Beveridge, Albert J. (IN) - 1912
Bibb, William Wyatt (AL) - 1819
Bickett, Thomas W. (NC) - 1916
Bicknell, Lewis W. (SD) - 1940, 1942
Biddle, John (MI) - 1835
Bidwell, John (CA) - 1875
Bierman, A. (MN) - 1883
Bigelow, Hobart B. (CT) - 1880
Bigger, Samuel (IN) - 1840, 1843
Biggs, Benjamin T. (DE) - 1886
Bigler, John (CA) - 1851, 1853, 1855
Bigler, William (PA) - 1851, 1854
Bilbo, Theodore G. (MS) - 1915, 1927
Billard, J. B. (KS) - 1914
Billings, Franklin S. (VT) - 1924
Bingham, Arthur (AL) - 1886
Bingham, Hiram (CT) - 1924
Bingham, J. A. (AL) - 1926
Bingham, Kinsley S. (MI) - 1854, 1856
Bingham, Robert P. (NH) - 1950
Bingham, W. H. H. (VT) - 1874, 1876, 1878
Bird, Charles Sumner (MA) - 1912, 1913
Bird, Francis W. (MA) - 1872
Bird, James B. (SD) - 1918
Birney, James G. (MI) - 1843, 1845
Bishop (AR) - 1876
Bishop, Henry W. (MA) - 1852, 1853, 1854
Bishop, Neil (ME) - 1952
Bishop, Richard M. (OH) - 1877
Bishop, Robert R. (MA) - 1882
Bissell, Clark (CT) - 1846, 1847, 1848
Bissell, William H. (IL) - 1856
Black (NJ) - 1904
Black, C. R. (AR) - 1948
Black, Chauncey F. (PA) - 1886
Black, Frank S. (NY) - 1896
Black, J. D. (KY) - 1919
Black, W. W. (WA) - 1940
Blackburn, Luke P. (KY) - 1879
Blackford, Isaac (IN) - 1825
Blackmer, John (MA) - 1889
Blackwood, Ibra C. (SC) - 1930
Blaine, John J. (WI) - 1914, 1920, 1922, 1924
Blair (MI) - 1872
Blair, Austin (MI) - 1860, 1862
Blair, C. Stanley (MD) - 1970
Blair, James T. Jr. (MO) - 1956
Blair, John I. (NJ) - 1868
Blanchard, James J. (MI) - 1982
Blanchard, Newton C. (LA) - 1904
Blandin, Amos (NH) - 1936
Blanton, Ray (TN) - 1974
Blasdel, Henry G. (NV) - 1864, 1866
Blaylock, Len E. (AR) - 1972
Bleakley, William F. (NY) - 1936
Blease, Coleman L. (SC) - 1910, 1912
Blewett, Pierce (ND) - 1930
Bliss, Aaron T. (MI) - 1900, 1902
Blood, Henry H. (UT) - 1932, 1936
Blood, Robert O. (NH) - 1940, 1942
Blount, J. H. (AR) - 1920
Blount, Willie (TN) - 1809, 1811, 1813
Bloxham, William D. (FL) - 1872, 1880, 1896
Blue, Robert D. (IA) - 1944, 1946
Boardman, Elijah (CT) - 1812, 1813, 1814, 1815
Boatright, William L. (CO) - 1928
Bodwell, Joseph R. (ME) - 1886
Boe, Nils A. (SD) - 1964, 1966

Boggs, J. Caleb (DE) - 1952, 1956
Boggs, Lilburn W. (MO) - 1836
Boles, Horace (IA) - 1889, 1891, 1893
Boles, Thomas (AR) - 1884
Bolens (WI) - 1938
Bomrich, Louis G. (WI) - 1900
Bond, Christopher S. (MO) - 1972, 1976, 1980
Bond, Hugh L. (MD) - 1867
Bond, Shadrach (IL) - 1818
Bonner, John W. (MT) - 1948, 1952
Bonniwell, Eugene C. (PA) - 1918, 1926
Bookwalter, John W. (OH) - 1881
Booth, James (DE) - 1822
Booth, Newton (CA) - 1871
Bordelon, Louis (LA) - 1852
Boreman, Arthur I. (WV) - 1863, 1864, 1866
Boreman, Herbert S. (WV) - 1948
Boren, David L. (OK) - 1974
Botkin, Alexander C. (MT) - 1896
Botkin, Jeremiah D. (KS) - 1908
Bottolfsen, C. A. (ID) - 1938, 1940, 1942
Botts, Clarence M. (NM) - 1930
Bouck, William C. (NY) - 1840, 1842
Bourn, Augustus O. (RI) - 1883, 1884
Boutin, Bernard L. (NH) - 1958, 1960
Boutwell, George S. (MA) - 1849, 1850, 1851
Bowen, A. E. Jr. (ND) - 1912
Bowen, Otis R. (IN) - 1972, 1976
Bowerman, Jay (OR) - 1910
Bowers, M. D. (AR) - 1926, 1928
Bowie, G. W. (CA) - 1857
Bowie, Oden (MD) - 1867
Bowie, Richard J. (MD) - 1853
Bowles, Chester (CT) - 1948, 1950
Bowles, Hargrove Jr. (NC) - 1972
Boyce, D. A. Jelly (OK) - 1958
Boyd, James E. (NE) - 1890
Boyle, Emmet D. (NV) - 1914, 1918
Boynton, Charles A. (TX) - 1918
Brackett, John Q. A. (MA) - 1889, 1890
Bradbury, Bion (ME) - 1862, 1863
Bradford, Augustus W. (MD) - 1861
Bradford, Robert F. (MA) - 1946, 1948
Bradish, Luther (NY) - 1842
Bradley, L. R. (NV) - 1870, 1874, 1878
Bradley, Tom (CA) - 1982
Bradley, William C. (VT) - 1819, 1834, 1835, 1836, 1837, 1838
Bradley, William O. (KY) - 1887, 1895
Bradshaw, John Paul (MO) - 1944
Brady, James H. (ID) - 1908, 1910
Bragg, Thomas (NC) - 1854, 1856
Brainard, Lawrence (VT) - 1846, 1847, 1852, 1853
Bramlett, Leon (MS) - 1983
Bramlett, Thomas E. (KY) - 1863
Branch, John (NC) - 1838
Brandon, Gerald C. (MS) - 1827, 1829
Brandon, William W. (AL) - 1922
Branigin, Roger D. (IN) - 1964
Brann, Louis J. (ME) - 1932, 1934, 1936
Branon, E. Frank (VT) - 1954, 1956
Branson, L. C. (NV) - 1934
Branstad, Terry E. (IA) - 1982
Breathitt, Edward T. (KY) - 1963
Breathitt, John (KY) - 1832
Breaux, John E. (LA) - 1892
Breidenthal, John W. (KS) - 1900
Brennan, Joseph E. (ME) - 1978, 1982
Brewer, Earl (MS) - 1911
Brewster, Ralph O. (ME) - 1924, 1926
Bricker, John W. (OH) - 1936, 1938, 1940, 1942
Bridges, H. Styles (NH) - 1934
Bridges, Robert (WA) - 1920
Bridgham, Samuel W. (RI) - 1821
Briggs, Ansel (IA) - 1846
Briggs, Frank A. (ND) - 1896
Briggs, George N. (MA) - 1843, 1844, 1845, 1846, 1847, 1848, 1849, 1850, 1859
Brigham, Herbert F. (VT) - 1890
Brinkley, John R. (KS) - 1930, 1932
Briscoe, Dolph (TX) - 1972, 1974
Britt, Henry M. (AR) - 1960
Brockett, Bruce D. (AZ) - 1946, 1948
Broderick, Raymond J. (PA) - 1970
Broening, William F. (MD) - 1930
Bronson, David (ME) - 1846, 1847
Bronson, Greene C. (NY) - 1854
Bronson, S. L. (CT) - 1900

Brooks (MD) - 1887
Brooks, Bryant B. (WY) - 1904, 1906
Brooks, C. Wayland (IL) - 1936
Brooks, Erastus (NY) - 1856
Brooks, John (MA) - 1816, 1817, 1818, 1819, 1820, 1821, 1822
Brooks, Joseph (AR) - 1872
Brooks, Ralph G. (NE) - 1958
Broome, James E. (FL) - 1852
Brotzman, Donald G. (CO) - 1954, 1956
Brough, Charles H. (AR) - 1916, 1918
Brough, John (OH) - 1863
Broughton, J. Melville (NC) - 1940
Broward, Napoleon Bonaparte (FL) - 1904
Brown (MO) - 1880
Brown, Aaron V. (TN) - 1845, 1847
Brown, Albert G. (MS) - 1843, 1845
Brown, Albert O. (NH) - 1920
Brown, Arthur M. (CT) - 1936
Brown, Benjamin Gratz (MO) - 1870
Brown, Clarence J. (OH) - 1934
Brown, Clarence Jr. (OH) - 1982
Brown, D. Russell (RI) - 1892, 1893, 1894
Brown, Earl (MN) - 1932
Brown, Edmund G. (CA) - 1958, 1962, 1966
Brown, Edmund G. Jr. (CA) - 1974, 1978
Brown, Ethan A. (OH) - 1816, 1818, 1820
Brown, Frank (MD) - 1891
Brown, Fred H. (NH) - 1922, 1924
Brown, Harvey D. (WI) - 1908
Brown, J. Y. Jr. (KY) - 1979
Brown, John C. (TN) - 1870, 1872
Brown, John Young (KY) - 1891
Brown, Joseph Emerson (GA) - 1857, 1859
Brown, Joseph M. (GA) - 1908, 1910
Brown, Neill S. (TN) - 1847, 1849
Brown, Robert B. (OH) - 1912
Brown, Thomas S. (FL) - 1848
Brown, W. S. (NH) - 1879
Brown, William Moseley (VA) - 1929
Browne, George H. (RI) - 1864
Browne, Thomas C. (IL) - 1822
Browne, Thomas McClelland (IN) - 1872
Browning, Gordon (TN) - 1936, 1948, 1950
Brownlow, William G. (TN) - 1865, 1867
Bruce, Alexander B. (MA) - 1898
Bruce, C. Arthur (TN) - 1930, 1940
Brucker, Wilber M. (MI) - 1930, 1932
Brumbaugh, Martin G. (PA) - 1914
Brunsdale, Norman (ND) - 1950, 1952, 1954
Bryan, Charles W. (NE) - 1922, 1926, 1928, 1930, 1932, 1938, 1942
Bryan, Richard H. (NV) - 1982
Bryant, Farris (FL) - 1960
Bryant, William R. (TX) - 1956
Buchanan, John P. (TN) - 1890, 1892
Buchtel, Henry A. (CO) - 1906
Buck (KY) - 1832
Buck, Clayton Douglass (DE) - 1928, 1932
Buckalew, Charles B. (PA) - 1872
Buckingham, R. G. (CO) - 1878
Buckingham, William A. (CT) - 1858, 1859, 1860, 1861, 1862, 1863, 1864, 1865
Buckmaster (DE) - 1858
Buckner, Simon B. (KY) - 1887
Buckson, David P. (DE) - 1964
Budd, James H. (CA) - 1894
Budlong, David H. (ID) - 1896
Buehner, Carl W. (UT) - 1968
Buel, Jesse (NY) - 1836
Buell, David E. (NV) - 1864
Buell, David L. (MN) - 1875
Bugbee, Newton A. K. (NJ) - 1919
Bulger, Michael J. (AL) - 1865
Bulkeley, Morgan G. (CT) - 1882, 1888
Bull, John (MO) - 1832
Bull, Mansen (DE) - 1816, 1819
Bullington, Orville (TX) - 1932
Bullitt, Scott (WA) - 1928
Bullock, Alexander H. (MA) - 1865, 1866, 1867
Bullock, Nathaniel (RI) - 1839
Bullock, Rufus B. (GA) - 1868
Bulow, William J. (SD) - 1924, 1926, 1928
Bumpers, Dale L. (AR) - 1970, 1972
Bunning, Jim (KY) - 1983
Burch, Palmer L. (CO) - 1958
Burdick, Quentin (ND) - 1946
Burges, Tristam (RI) - 1836, 1839
Burgess, D. (WA) - 1904
Burke, Andrew H. (ND) - 1890, 1892
Burke, James E. (VT) - 1908

1149

Burke, John (ND) - 1906, 1908, 1910
Burke, John M. (ID) - 1892
Burke, William H. (KS) - 1940, 1942
Burkett, George W. (TX) - 1902
Burleigh, Edwin C. (ME) - 1888, 1890
Burnett, P. H. (CA) - 1849
Burney, Dwight W. (NE) - 1964
Burnquist, Joseph A. A. (MN) - 1916, 1918
Burns, Haydon (FL) - 1964
Burns, John A. (HI) - 1959, 1962, 1966, 1970
Burnside, Ambrose E. (RI) - 1866, 1867, 1868
Burr, Aaron (NY) - 1804
Burroughs, John (NM) - 1958, 1960
Burrows, Lorenzo (NY) - 1858
Bursum, Holm O. (NM) - 1911, 1916
Burt, Homer P. (UT) - 1912
Burt, Wellington R. (MI) - 1888
Burton, William (DE) - 1858
Busbee, George (GA) - 1974, 1978
Bushfield, Harlan J. (SD) - 1938, 1940
Bushnell, Asa S. (OH) - 1895, 1897
Busiel, Charles A. (NH) - 1894
Bussiere, Emile R. (NH) - 1968
Butcher, Jake (TN) - 1978
Butler (KY) - 1844
Butler, Anthony (KY) - 1820
Butler, Benjamin F. (MA) - 1859, 1878, 1879, 1882, 1883
Butler, Dan (NE) - 1924
Butler, David (NE) - 1866, 1868, 1870
Butler, Ezra (VT) - 1826, 1827
Butler, Thomas (LA) - 1828
Butrovich, John Jr. (AK) - 1958
Butte, George C. (TX) - 1924
Buxton, Ralph P. (NC) - 1880
Byerly, Clyde G. (ND) - 1950
Bymers, Cornelius (ND) - 1954
Byrd (AR) - 1844
Byrd, Harry Clifton (MD) - 1954
Byrd, Harry F. (VA) - 1925
Byrne, Brendan T. (NJ) - 1973, 1977
Byrne, Frank M. (SD) - 1912, 1914
Byrnes, James F. (SC) - 1950

C

Cady (CT) - 1894
Cady, Virgil H. (WI) - 1926
Caffery, Don Jr. (LA) - 1900
Cahill, Horace T. (MA) - 1944
Cahill, William T. (NJ) - 1969
Caine, J. T. (UT) - 1896
Calderwood, W. G. (MN) - 1914
Caldwell, Millard F. (FL) - 1944
Caldwell, Tod R. (NC) - 1872
Calkins, William H. (IN) - 1884
Callan, Luke H. (RI) - 1934
Callaway, E. E. (FL) - 1936
Callaway, Howard H. (GA) - 1966
Camden, James M. (WV) - 1868
Camden, Johnson N. (WV) - 1872
Cameron, Ralph H. (AZ) - 1914
Cameron, William E. (VA) - 1881
Campbell (TN) - 1902
Campbell, Alex (OH) - 1826
Campbell, C. (VA) - 1913
Campbell, Daniel (IA) - 1879
Campbell, E. L. (CO) - 1882
Campbell, Jack M. (NM) - 1962, 1964
Campbell, James E. (OH) - 1889, 1891, 1895
Campbell, John W. (OH) - 1828
Campbell, Thomas E. (AZ) - 1916, 1918, 1920, 1922, 1936
Campbell, Thomas F. (OR) - 1874
Campbell, Thomas M. (TX) - 1906, 1908
Campbell, William B. (TN) - 1851
Canby, Israel T. (IN) - 1828
Candler, Allen D. (GA) - 1898, 1900
Cannon, Harry L. (DE) - 1936
Cannon, Joseph D. (NY) - 1920
Cannon, Newton (TN) - 1827, 1835, 1837, 1839
Cannon, Paul (MT) - 1960
Cannon, William (DE) - 1862
Capers, H. (TX) - 1920
Capper, Arthur (KS) - 1912, 1914, 1916
Carey, Hugh L. (NY) - 1974, 1978

Carey, Joseph M. (WY) - 1910
Carey, Robert D. (WY) - 1918
Cargo, David F. (NM) - 1966, 1968
Carlin, John (KS) - 1978, 1982
Carlin, Thomas (IL) - 1838
Carlson, Frank (KS) - 1946, 1948
Carlson, George A. (CO) - 1914, 1916
Carlton, Doyle E. (FL) - 1928
Carmichael, Gil (MS) - 1975, 1979
Carnahan, J. P. (AR) - 1892
Carney, Thomas (KS) - 1862
Carpenter, Cyrus Clay (IA) - 1871, 1873
Carpenter, R. B. (SC) - 1870
Carpenter, Randolph (KS) - 1948
Carpenter, Terry (NE) - 1940
Carpenter, Thomas F. (RI) - 1840, 1842, 1843
Carr (MO) - 1825
Carr, Clarence E. (NH) - 1908, 1910
Carr, Elias (NC) - 1892
Carr, Ralph L. (CO) - 1938, 1940
Carroll (MD) - 1844
Carroll, Beryl F. (IA) - 1908, 1910
Carroll, John Lee (MD) - 1875
Carroll, Julian (KY) - 1975
Carroll, Robert P. (NY) - 1930
Carroll, William (TN) - 1821, 1823, 1825, 1829, 1831, 1833, 1835
Carruth, Walter L. (AR) - 1970
Carson, Joseph K. Jr. (OR) - 1954
Carter, Jimmy (GA) - 1970
Carter, Yancy (GA) - 1908
Caruthers, Robert L. (TN) - 1863
Carvel, Elbert N. (DE) - 1948, 1952, 1960
Carville, Edward P. (NV) - 1938, 1942
Cary, Melbert B. (CT) - 1902
Case, Norman S. (RI) - 1928, 1930, 1932
Casey, Thomas B. (NV) - 1906
Cashin, John Logan (AL) - 1970
Castle, Michael N. (DE) - 1984
Castro, Raul H. (AZ) - 1970, 1974
Cate, Asa P. (NH) - 1858, 1859, 1860
Catlin, George S. (CT) - 1848
Catts, Sidney J. (FL) - 1916
Caulfield, Henry Stewart (MO) - 1928
Causey, Peter F. (DE) - 1846, 1850, 1854
Celeste, Richard F. (OH) - 1978, 1982
Center, John H. (VT) - 1900
Chace, Benjamin G. (RI) - 1873
Chace, James H. (RI) - 1889
Chafee, John H. (RI) - 1962, 1964, 1966, 1968
Chamberlain, Abiram (CT) - 1902
Chamberlain, Daniel H. (SC) - 1874, 1876
Chamberlain, Edwin M. (MA) - 1869, 1871
Chamberlain, George E. (OR) - 1902, 1906
Chamberlain, Henry (MI) - 1874
Chamberlain, Joshua L. (ME) - 1866, 1867, 1868, 1869
Chamberlain, Levi (NH) - 1849, 1850
Chamberlin, Roscoe (SD) - 1966, 1968
Chambers, Dr. Henry (AL) - 1821, 1823
Chambers, E. F. (MD) - 1864
Chambers, Ernest W. (NE) - 1974
Chambers, J. J. (TX) - 1851
Chambers, T. J. (TX) - 1853, 1861, 1863
Chambers, William (TX) - 1875
Chandler, Albert B. (Happy) (KY) - 1935, 1955
Chandler, Anson G. (ME) - 1852
Chandler, Zacharaiah (MI) - 1852
Chanler, Lewis Stuyvesant (NY) - 1908
Chapin, Josiah (RI) - 1851
Chapman, Horace L. (OH) - 1897
Chapman, Reuben (AL) - 1847
Chapn (CT) - 1854
Chase (WI) - 1849
Chase, Dudley (VT) - 1823
Chase, Ira J. (IN) - 1892
Chase, John C. (MA) - 1902, 1903
Chase, Ray P. (MN) - 1930
Chase, Salmon P. (OH) - 1855, 1857
Chavez, Fabian Jr. (NM) - 1968
Cheney, John M. (FL) - 1908
Cheney, Person C. (NH) - 1875, 1876
Cherry, Francis (AR) - 1952
Cherry, R. Gregg (NC) - 1944
Chittenden, Martin (VT) - 1811, 1812, 1813, 1814, 1815
Chittenden, Thomas (VT) - 1791, 1792, 1793, 1794, 1795, 1796
Christiancy, Isaac P. (MI) - 1852
Christianson, Theodore (MN) - 1924, 1926, 1928

Church, Daniel T. (RI) - 1897, 1898
Churchill, Thomas J. (AR) - 1880
Churchill, Winston (NH) - 1912
Cianci, Vincent A. (RI) - 1980
Claflin, William (MA) - 1868, 1869, 1870
Claiborne, W. C. C. (LA) - 1812
Clardy, W. A. (AL) - 1938
Clark (KY) - 1855
Clark (MD) - 1850
Clark (MO) - 1840
Clark, A. M. (WY) - 1934
Clark, Barzilla W. (ID) - 1936
Clark, Charles (MS) - 1863
Clark, Chase A. (ID) - 1940, 1942
Clark, D. M. (IA) - 1881
Clark, E. S. (AZ) - 1926
Clark, Ed (CA) - 1978
Clark, Edward (TX) - 1861
Clark, F. Davis (ME) - 1946
Clark, George (TX) - 1892
Clark, James (KY) - 1836
Clark, John (GA) - 1825
Clark, Jonas (VT) - 1849
Clark, Merritt (VT) - 1854, 1855
Clark, Myron H. (NY) - 1854
Clark, Nehemiah (DE) - 1836
Clark, William (MO) - 1820
Clarke, George W. (IA) - 1912, 1914
Clarke, J. P. (AR) - 1894
Clarke, John (DE) - 1816
Clauson, Clinton A. (ME) - 1958
Clay, Clement Comer (AL) - 1835
Clay, Green (KY) - 1808
Clayton (MS) - 1843
Clayton, Joshua (DE) - 1792
Cleaves, Henry B. (ME) - 1892, 1894
Clee, Lester H. (NJ) - 1937
Clement, Frank G. (TN) - 1952, 1954, 1962
Clement, Percival W. (VT) - 1902, 1906, 1918
Clements, Earle C. (KY) - 1947
Clements, William P. (TX) - 1978, 1980
Cleveland (CT) - 1886
Cleveland, A. C. (NV) - 1894, 1902
Cleveland, Chauncey F. (CT) - 1842, 1843, 1844
Cleveland, Grover (NY) - 1882
Clifford, John H. (MA) - 1852
Clifford, Tom (OH) - 1910
Clinch (GA) - 1847
Clinton, Bill (AR) - 1978, 1980, 1982, 1984
Clinton, De Witt (NY) - 1817, 1820, 1824, 1826
Clinton, George (NY) - 1789, 1792, 1801
Cloud, Roger (OH) - 1970
Clough, David M. (MN) - 1896
Clyde, George Dewey (UT) - 1956, 1960
Clymer, Hiester (PA) - 1866
Cobb, Howell (GA) - 1851
Cobb, Osro (AR) - 1936
Cobb, Rufus W. (AL) - 1878, 1880
Cobb, William T. (ME) - 1904, 1906
Coblentz, L. A. (ID) - 1912, 1914
Cobo, Albert E. (MI) - 1956
Coburn, Abner (ME) - 1862
Coburn, Berthold C. (VT) - 1946
Cochran, A. M. (TN) - 1886
Cochran, John P. (DE) - 1874
Cochran, Robert L. (NE) - 1934, 1936, 1938
Cochrane, John (WI) - 1886
Cocke, Edmund R. (VA) - 1893
Cocke, William (TN) - 1807, 1809
Coffin, Frank M. (ME) - 1960
Coffin, O. Vincent (CT) - 1894
Cogswell (NH) - 1886
Coke, Richard (TX) - 1873, 1875
Colby, Anthony (NH) - 1843, 1844, 1845, 1846, 1847
Colby, Everett (NJ) - 1913
Colcord, R. K. (NV) - 1890
Cole, A. L. (MN) - 1906
Cole, Charles H. (MA) - 1928
Cole, Charles S. (AR) - 1938
Coleman (WI) - 1920
Coleman, J. Marshall (VA) - 1981
Coleman, J. P. (MS) - 1955
Coler, Bird S. (NY) - 1902
Coles, Edward (IL) - 1822
Collier, Henry Watkins (AL) - 1849, 1851
Collins (WI) - 1849
Collins, James M. (CO) - 1920
Collins, John (DE) - 1820
Collins, John (IL) - 1904

Collins, Leroy (FL) - 1954, 1956
Collins, Martha Layne (KY) - 1983
Collins, P. V. (MN) - 1912
Collins, Timothy E. (MT) - 1892
Colquitt, Alfred Holt (GA) - 1876, 1880
Colquitt, Oscar B. (TX) - 1910, 1912
Colt, Samuel Pomeroy (RI) - 1903
Colter, Fred T. (AZ) - 1918
Colton, Don B. (UT) - 1940
Combs, Bert T. (KY) - 1959
Comegys, Cornelius (DE) - 1836
Comer, B. B. (AL) - 1906
Comings, Herbert C. (VT) - 1926
Comstock, Charles C. (MI) - 1870
Comstock, William A. (MI) - 1926, 1928, 1930, 1932
Cone, Fred P. (FL) - 1936
Conley, William G. (WV) - 1928
Conlin, Roxanne (IA) - 1982
Connally, John B. (TX) - 1962, 1964, 1966
Conner, Martin S. (MS) - 1931
Conness, John (CA) - 1861
Connor, Selden (ME) - 1875, 1876, 1877, 1878
Conover, Simon B. (FL) - 1880
Conrad, Larry A. (IN) - 1976
Converse, Julius (VT) - 1872
Conway, Elias N. (AR) - 1852, 1856
Conway, James S. (AR) - 1836
Cony, Samuel (ME) - 1863, 1864, 1865
Cook, C. W. (KY) - 1879
Cook, Rodney M. (GA) - 1978
Cooke, Lorrin A. (CT) - 1896
Coolidge, Arthur W. (MA) - 1950
Coolidge, Calvin (MA) - 1918, 1919
Coolidge, Carlos (VT) - 1848, 1849
Coon, Ken (AR) - 1974
Cooper, Job A. (CO) - 1888
Cooper, John R. (NE) - 1960
Cooper, Mark A. (GA) - 1843
Cooper, Myers Y. (OH) - 1926, 1928, 1930
Cooper, Prentice (TN) - 1938, 1940, 1942
Cooper, Robert A. (SC) - 1918, 1920
Cooper, William B. (DE) - 1840
Coopwood (MS) - 1845
Corbet, Leo (AZ) - 1980
Cornelius, T. R. (OR) - 1886
Cornell, Alonzo B. (NY) - 1879
Cornwell, John J. (WV) - 1904, 1916
Corwin, Thomas (CH) - 1840, 1842
Cosgrove, Samuel G. (WA) - 1908
Costigan, Edw. P. (CO) - 1912, 1914
Couch, Darius N. (MA) - 1865
Couchman, Peter (SD) - 1892
Coursey, Thomas B. (DE) - 1870
Courtney, Thomas J. (IL) - 1944
Cowherd (MO) - 1908
Cox, Channing H. (MA) - 1920, 1922
Cox, J. E. (NC) - 1908
Cox, Jack (TX) - 1962
Cox, Jacob D. (OH) - 1865
Cox, James M. (OH) - 1912, 1914, 1916, 1918
Cox, Thomas W. (FL) - 1912
Coxey, Jacob S. (OH) - 1895
Coy, John G. (CO) - 1890
Cozzens, William C. (RI) - 1863
Craddock, W. H. (KS) - 1902
Crafts, Samuel C. (VT) - 1828, 1829, 1830, 1832
Cragin, Charles R. (ME) - 1982
Craig, George N. (IN) - 1952
Craig, Locke (NC) - 1912
Craig, William H. (NH) - 1952
Crane, Elvin W. (NJ) - 1898
Crane, S. B. (IA) - 1895
Crane, Winthrop Murray (MA) - 1899, 1900, 1901
Crank, Marion (AR) - 1968
Crapo, Henry H. (MI) - 1864, 1866
Crawford, Coe I. (SD) - 1906
Crawford, George Walker (GA) - 1843, 1845
Crawford, Joel (GA) - 1829, 1833
Crawford, Samuel J. (KS) - 1864, 1866
Creager, R. B. (TX) - 1916
Creighton, Hobart (IN) - 1948
Crichton, Jack (TX) - 1964
Crill, Louis N. (SD) - 1904, 1922
Crittenden, John J. (KY) - 1848
Crittenden, Thomas Theodore (MO) - 1880
Croft, Chancy (AK) - 1978
Cronan (ND) - 1902
Crook, Abraham J. (ID) - 1892

Ferguson, Miriam A. (TX) - 1924, 1932
Ferguson, Phil (OK) - 1958
Fernald, Bert M. (ME) - 1908, 1910
Ferris, Woodbridge N. (MI) - 1904, 1912, 1914, 1920
Ferry, Elisha P. (WA) - 1889
Ferry, William M. (UT) - 1904
Fessenden, Samuel (ME) - 1846, 1847, 1848
Fielder, James F. (NJ) - 1913
Fields, John (OK) - 1914, 1922
Fields, William J. (KY) - 1923
Fifer, Joseph W. (IL) - 1888, 1892
Fike, Ed (NV) - 1970
Files, A. W. (AR) - 1896
Files, J. R. (IA) - 1922
Fillmore, Millard (NY) - 1844
Finch, Cliff (MS) - 1975
Findlay, James (OH) - 1834
Findlay, William (PA) - 1817, 1820
Fine, John S. (PA) - 1950
Fink, Tom (AK) - 1982
Finkelnburg, Gustavus A. (MO) - 1876
Fish, Hamilton (NY) - 1848
Fishback, W. M. (AR) - 1892
Fisher, E. S. (MS) - 1865
Fisher, Jake (WV) - 1924
Fisher, John S. (PA) - 1926
Fisher, Spencer O. (MI) - 1894
Fisk (NJ) - 1886
Fitzgerald, David (CT) - 1922
Fitzgerald, Frank D. (MI) - 1934, 1936, 1938
Fitzgerald, Jerome D. (IA) - 1978
Fitzgerald, John F. (MA) - 1922
Fitzgerald, William (MI) - 1978
Fitzpatrick, Benjamin (AL) - 1841, 1843
Fizer, N. B. (AR) - 1890
Flaherty, David T. (NC) - 1976
Flaherty, Peter (PA) - 1978
Flanagan, Webster (TX) - 1890
Flandrau, Charles E. (MN) - 1867
Flegel, Austin F. (OR) - 1950
Fleming, A. Brooks (WV) - 1888
Fleming, Francis P. (FL) - 1888
Fletcher, Allen M. (VT) - 1912
Fletcher, Ryland (VT) - 1856, 1857
Fletcher, Thomas C. (MO) - 1864
Florio, James J. (NJ) - 1981
Flory (MO) - 1900
Flournoy (VA) - 1855, 1863
Flournoy, Houston I. (CA) - 1974
Flournoy, M. (KY) - 1836
Flower, Roswell P. (NY) - 1891
Floyd, Charles M. (NH) - 1906
Flynn, Olney R. (OK) - 1946
Flynn, William S. (RI) - 1922
Folger, Charles J. (NY) - 1882
Folk, Joseph Wingate (MO) - 1904
Folmar, Emory (AL) - 1982
Folsom, David S. (MT) - 1900
Folsom, James E. (AL) - 1946, 1954
Fontaine, C. D. (MS) - 1855
Foot, Samuel A. (CT) - 1834, 1835
Foote, Henry S. (MS) - 1851
Foote, Ralph A. (VT) - 1964
Foraker, Joseph B. (OH) - 1883, 1885, 1887, 1889
Forbes, Malcolm S. (NJ) - 1957
Ford, Nicholas (MO) - 1884
Ford, Peter J. (DE) - 1900
Ford, Samuel C. (MT) - 1940, 1944, 1948
Ford, Seabury (OH) - 1848
Ford, Thomas (IL) - 1842
Ford, Wendell H. (KY) - 1971
Forsyth, John (GA) - 1827
Fort, George F. (NJ) - 1850
Fort, John Franklin (NJ) - 1907
Fosheim, Oscar (SD) - 1938
Foss, Eugene N. (MA) - 1910, 1911, 1912
Foss, Joe (SD) - 1954, 1956
Foster (CT) - 1850, 1851
Foster (TN) - 1845
Foster, Charles (OH) - 1879, 1881
Foster, Henry D. (PA) - 1860
Foster, Murphy J. (LA) - 1892, 1896
Foster, Robert C. (TN) - 1815, 1817
Fowle, Daniel G. (NC) - 1888
Fowler (TN) - 1898
Fowler, Absalom (AR) - 1836
Francis, David Rowland (MO) - 1888
Francis, John Brown (R) - 1833, 1834, 1835, 1836, 1837, 1838
Frank, M. P. (ME) - 1896

Frankland, Herman C. (ME) - 1978
Frantz, Frank (OK) - 1907
Franzenburg, Paul (IA) - 1968, 1972
Fratt, Nicholas D. (WI) - 1881, 1884
Frazier, C. N. (TN) - 1942
Frazier, Clifford (NC) - 1932
Frazier, James B. (TN) - 1902, 1904
Frazier, Lynn J. (ND) - 1916, 1918, 1920, 1921
Fredericks, John D. (CA) - 1914
Freehafer, A. L. (ID) - 1924
Freeman (TN) - 1872
Freeman, Orville L. (MN) - 1952, 1954, 1956, 1958, 1960
Freeman, Woody (AR) - 1984
French (KY) - 1840
French, Augustus C. (IL) - 1846, 1848
French, N. B. (WV) - 1880
Frensdorf, Edward (MI) - 1924
Frink, J. M. (WA) - 1900
Frizzell, Kent (KS) - 1970
Frohmiller, Ana (AZ) - 1950
Frothingham, Louis A. (MA) - 1911
Fry, Edward J. (MI) - 1944
Fuhr, John D. (CO) - 1982
Fulks, Clay (AR) - 1918
Fuller, Alvan T. (MA) - 1924, 1926
Fuller, Levi K. (VT) - 1892
Fuller, Philo C. (MI) - 1841
Fulton, John A. (NV) - 1938
Fulton, Robert D. (IA) - 1970
Funk, Frank H. (IL) - 1912
Fuqua, Henry L. (LA) - 1924
Furches, David M. (NC) - 1892
Furcolo, Foster (MA) - 1956, 1958
Furnas, Robert W. (NE) - 1872
Furnish, W. J. (OR) - 1902
Futrell, Julius M. (AR) - 1932, 1934

G

Gable, Robert E. (KY) - 1975
Gage, Henry T. (CA) - 1898
Gage, Jack R. (WY) - 1962
Gainer, Joseph H. (RI) - 1926
Gaither (MD) - 1907
Gallagher, Thomas (MN) - 1938
Gallen, Hugh J. (NH) - 1978, 1980, 1982
Gallentine, P. W. (AZ) - 1911
Gallogly, Edward P. (RI) - 1964
Galloway, William (OR) - 1894
Galusha, Jonas (VT) - 1809, 1810, 1811, 1812, 1813, 1814, 1815, 1816, 1817, 1818, 1819
Garber, Silas (NE) - 1874, 1876
Garcelon, Alonzo (ME) - 1878, 1879
Garcia, Felix (NM) - 1918
Gardiner, William Tudor (ME) - 1928, 1930
Gardner, A. B. (VT) - 1872
Gardner, Augustus P. (MA) - 1913
Gardner, Booth (WA) - 1984
Gardner, Frederick Dozier (MO) - 1916
Gardner, H. P. (ME) - 1914
Gardner, Henry J. (MA) - 1854, 1855, 1856, 1857
Gardner, J. F. (NE) - 1874, 1876
Gardner, James C. (NC) - 1968
Gardner, O. Max (NC) - 1928
Gardner, Obadiah (ME) - 1908
Garey (MD) - 1879
Garfield, James R. (OH) - 1914
Garford, Arthur L. (OH) - 1912
Garland, A. H. (AR) - 1874
Garland, R. K. (AR) - 1882
Garrahy, Joseph J. (RI) - 1976, 1978, 1980, 1982
Garrard, James (KY) - 1800
Gartrell (GA) - 1882
Garvey, Dan E. (AZ) - 1948
Garvin, Lucius F. C. (RI) - 1901, 1902, 1903, 1904, 1905
Gary, Raymond (OK) - 1954
Gaston, William (MA) - 1873, 1874, 1875, 1877
Gaston, William A. (MA) - 1902, 1903, 1926
Gates, Charles W. (VT) - 1914
Gates, Ralph F. (IN) - 1944
Gavin, Robert L. (NC) - 1960, 1964
Gay, George E. (FL) - 1920
Gayle, John (AL) - 1831, 1833
Gaylord, Winfield R. (WI) - 1906

Gear, John Henry (IA) - 1877, 1879
Geary, J. W. (CA) - 1849
Geary, John White (PA) - 1866, 1869
Geer, Theodore Thurston (OR) - 1898
Gegax, Henry F. (NV) - 1910
Gellatly, John A. (WA) - 1932
Gengras, E. Clayton (CT) - 1966
Gentry (TN) - 1855
Gentry, William (MO) - 1874
George, Hyland P. (DE) - 1948
Gerry, Elbridge (MA) - 1800, 1801, 1802, 1803, 1810, 1811, 1812
Gibbons, Charles (MA) - 1958
Gibbs, A. C. (OR) - 1862
Gibbs, Barnett (TX) - 1898
Gibbs, William C. (RI) - 1821, 1822, 1823
Gibson (AR) - 1844
Gibson, Ernest W. (VT) - 1946, 1948
Gidley, Townsend E. (MI) - 1851
Gilchrist, Albert W. (FL) - 1908
Gillaspie, George (IA) - 1869
Gillett, James N. (CA) - 1906
Gillette (CT) - 1853
Gillette, Lester S. (IA) - 1950
Gilligan, John J. (OH) - 1970, 1974
Gilman, John T. (NH) - 1793, 1794, 1795, 1796, 1797, 1798, 1799, 1800, 1801, 1802, 1803, 1804, 1805, 1806, 1808, 1812, 1813, 1814, 1815
Gilmer, George R. (GA) - 1829, 1831, 1837
Gilmer, John A. (NC) - 1856
Gilmore, Joseph A. (NH) - 1863, 1864
Glade, Earl J. (UT) - 1952
Glasscock, William E. (WV) - 1908
Glenn, Hugh J. (CA) - 1879
Glenn, R. B. (NC) - 1904
Glick, George W. (KS) - 1868, 1882, 1884
Glynn, Martin H. (NY) - 1914
Goddard, Sam (AZ) - 1962, 1964, 1966, 1968
Godwin, Mills E. Jr. (VA) - 1965, 1973
Goebel, William (KY) - 1899
Goff, Nathan (WV) - 1876, 1888
Goggin (VA) - 1859
Goldberg, Arthur J. (NY) - 1970
Goldsborough (MD) - 1847
Goldsborough, Phillips Lee (MD) - 1911
Goodell, David H. (NH) - 1888
Goodenow, Daniel (ME) - 1831, 1832, 1833
Goodin, John R. (KS) - 1878
Gooding, Frank R. (ID) - 1904, 1906
Goodland, Walter S. (WI) - 1944, 1946
Goodnow, Windsor H. (NH) - 1922
Goodover, Pat M. (MT) - 1984
Goodrich, James P. (IN) - 1916
Goodwin (CT) - 1910
Goodwin, Frank A. (MA) - 1934
Goodwin, Ichabod (NH) - 1859, 1860
Goodwyn, Albert T. (AL) - 1896
Gordon (GA) - 1868
Gordon, George W. (MA) - 1856
Gordon, John B. (GA) - 1886, 1888
Gordy, William J. (DE) - 1980
Gore, Christopher (MA) - 1808, 1809, 1810, 1811
Gore, Howard M. (WV) - 1924
Gore, Louise (MD) - 1974
Gorman, Arthur Pue (MD) - 1911
Gossett, Charles C. (ID) - 1944
Goudy, Frank C. (CO) - 1900
Gould, Samuel W. (ME) - 1902
Gould, Vick (WA) - 1972
Grabiel, John W. (AR) - 1922, 1924
Gragson, Oran K. (NV) - 1962
Graham, Bob (FL) - 1978, 1982
Graham, Horace C. (VT) - 1916
Graham, William A. (NC) - 1844, 1846
Granai, Edwin C. (VT) - 1978
Granberry, Jim (TX) - 1974
Granger, Francis (NY) - 1830, 1832
Grant, Earle S. (ME) - 1950
Grant, James B. (CO) - 1882
Grantham, Everett (NM) - 1952
Grasso, Ella T. (CT) - 1974, 1978
Graves, Bibb (AL) - 1926, 1934
Graves, Richard Perrin (CA) - 1954
Gray, C. A. (TX) - 1906
Gray, Isaac P. (IN) - 1884
Gray, James (MN) - 1910
Grayson, Beverly R. (MS) - 1827
Grayson, William (MD) - 1838
Greaves, Charles D. (AR) - 1902
Green, Charles B. (MS) - 1821
Green, Dwight H. (IL) - 1940, 1944, 1948

Green, Fred W. (MI) - 1926, 1928
Green, J. A. (TX) - 1851
Green, Jesse (DE) - 1820
Green, John T. (SC) - 1874
Green, Robert S. (NJ) - 1886
Green, Theodore Francis (RI) - 1912, 1930, 1932, 1934
Green, Warren E. (SD) - 1930, 1932
Greene (CT) - 1875
Greene (WI) - 1934
Greene, George W. (RI) - 1899
Greene, William (RI) - 1802
Greenhalge, Frederic T. (MA) - 1893, 1894, 1895
Greenup, Christopher (KY) - 1800, 1804
Gregg, Andrew (PA) - 1823
Gregg, Hugh (NH) - 1952, 1966
Gregg, S. (AR) - 1886
Gregory, William (RI) - 1900, 1901
Grevemberg, F. C. (LA) - 1960
Griffen, Horace B. (AZ) - 1956
Griffin, S. Marvin (GA) - 1954
Griffith, Benjamin (CO) - 1922
Griffith, Leon (AR) - 1976
Griggs, John W. (NJ) - 1895
Grim, Webster (PA) - 1910
Grimball (MS) - 1837
Grimes, James W. (IA) - 1854
Grissom, Gilliam (NC) - 1936
Griswold, Dwight (NE) - 1932, 1934, 1936, 1940, 1942, 1944
Griswold, John A. (NY) - 1868
Griswold, Morley (NV) - 1934
Griswold, Roger (CT) - 1810, 1811, 1812
Groesbeck, Alexander J. (MI) - 1920, 1922, 1924
Groome, John C. (MD) - 1857
Gross, Harold J. (RI) - 1922
Grout, Josiah (VT) - 1896
Grover, Hank C. (TX) - 1972
Grover, LaFayette F. (OR) - 1870, 1874
Grubb (NJ) - 1889
Gubbrud, Archie M. (SD) - 1960, 1962
Guild, Curtis Jr. (MA) - 1905, 1906, 1907
Gunby, E. R. (FL) - 1896
Gunderson, Carl (SD) - 1924, 1926
Gunderson, Carroll G. (NM) - 1944
Gunter, Julius C. (CO) - 1916
Gurham, George C. (CA) - 1867
Gurney, Chester (MI) - 1847
Guthrie, William A. (NC) - 1896
Guy, William L. (ND) - 1960, 1962, 1964, 1968

H

Hackel, Stella B. (VT) - 1976
Hackett, Luther F. (VT) - 1972
Hadley, Herbert Spencer (MO) - 1908
Haeder, Richard (SD) - 1946
Hagan, John N. (ND) - 1938
Hageman, Fred P. (IA) - 1930
Hagen, Oscar M. (ND) - 1942
Hager (KY) - 1907
Hagood, Johnson (SC) - 1880
Haight, H. H. (CA) - 1867, 1871
Haight, Raymond L. (CA) - 1934
Haigis, John W. (MA) - 1936
Haile, William (NH) - 1857, 1858
Haile, William H. (MA) - 1892
Haines, Daniel (NJ) - 1847
Haines, H. H. (TX) - 1926
Haines, John M. (ID) - 1912, 1914
Haines, William T. (ME) - 1912, 1914
Halcrow, Don (ND) - 1964
Haldiman, Joe C. (AZ) - 1952
Hale, Samuel W. (NH) - 1882
Hale, William (NH) - 1817, 1818, 1819
Hall, David (DE) - 1798, 1801
Hall, David (OK) - 1970
Hall, Fred (KS) - 1954
Hall, Hiland (VT) - 1858, 1859
Hall, John W. (DE) - 1878
Hall, Luther E. (LA) - 1912
Hall, W. Scott (ID) - 1926
Halsey (NJ) - 1874
Halsted, Charles L. (MN) - 1948
Halvorson, Halvor L. (ND) - 1924
Hamil, David A. (CO) - 1948
Hamilton, A. J. (TX) - 1869
Hamilton, Clark (ID) - 1954
Hamilton, John T. (IA) - 1914

Jester, Beauford H. (TX) - 1946, 1948
Jewell, Marshall (CT) - 1868, 1869, 1870, 1871, 1872
Jewett, Hugh J. (OH) - 1861
Johnson (MD) - 1841
Johnson, Andrew (TN) - 1853, 1855
Johnson, C. A. (ND) - 1908, 1910
Johnson, C. W. (TX) - 1912
Johnson, Charles F. (ME) - 1892, 1894
Johnson, Edwin C. (CO) - 1932, 1934, 1954
Johnson, Edwin S. (SD) - 1912
Johnson, George W. (AR) - 1958
Johnson, Henry (LA) - 1824, 1842
Johnson, Hershel Vespasian (GA) - 1853, 1855
Johnson, Hiram W. (CA) - 1910, 1914
Johnson, Isaac (LA) - 1846
Johnson, J. N. (CA) - 1855
Johnson, James (AR) - 1966
Johnson, John A. (MN) - 1904, 1906, 1908
Johnson, John W. (MN) - 1974
Johnson, Joseph (VA) - 1851
Johnson, Joseph B. (VT) - 1954, 1956
Johnson, Keen (KY) - 1939
Johnson, M. T. (TX) - 1851
Johnson, Magnus (MN) - 1922, 1926
Johnson, Ole S. (ND) - 1952
Johnson, Paul B. (MS) - 1939, 1963
Johnson, R. H. (AR) - 1860
Johnson, R. W. (MN) - 1881
Johnson, Thomas (TN) - 1815
Johnson, Tom L. (OH) - 1903
Johnson, Walter (VA) - 1949
Johnson, Walter W. (CO) - 1950
Johnston, Henry S. (OK) - 1926
Johnston, Joseph F. (AL) - 1896, 1898
Johnston, Olin D. (SC) - 1934, 1942
Johnston, William (OH) - 1850
Johnston, William F. (PA) - 1849, 1851
Johnston, William J. (NC) - 1862
Jones, Buell F. (SD) - 1928
Jones, Charles Alvin (PA) - 1938
Jones, Daniel Webster (AR) - 1896, 1898
Jones, Dick (WY) - 1974
Jones, Frank (NY) - 1880
Jones, George W. (TX) - 1882, 1884
Jones, J. S. (NV) - 1894
Jones, James C. (TN) - 1841, 1843
Jones, Norman L. (IL) - 1924
Jones, R. T. (AZ) - 1938
Jones, Sam H. (LA) - 1940
Jones, Samuel M. (OH) - 1899
Jones, Thomas G. (AL) - 1890, 1892
Jones, William (RI) - 1811, 1812, 1813, 1814, 1815, 1816, 1817
Jordan, Chester B. (NH) - 1900
Jordan, Len B. (ID) - 1950
Joseph, J. M. (IA) - 1893
Judge, Thomas L. (MT) - 1972, 1976
Jullien, Paul J. (ME) - 1944
Jump (DE) - 1874
Jungert, Philip W. (ID) - 1966

K

Kanouse, Theodore D. (WI) - 1881
Karel, John C. (WI) - 1912, 1914
Katterfeld, L. E. (WA) - 1916
Katzenbach (NJ) - 1907
Kay, Morris (KS) - 1972
Kean, John Jr. (NJ) - 1892
Kean, Thomas H. (NJ) - 1981
Kearby, Jerome C. (TX) - 1896
Keefe, F. Clyde (NH) - 1940, 1946
Keister, Stephen A. D. (WY) - 1906
Kelley, Thomas F. (ID) - 1906
Kellogg, Daniel (VT) - 1843, 1844, 1845
Kellogg, William Pitt (LA) - 1872
Kelly (TN) - 1890
Kelly, Harry F. (MI) - 1942, 1944, 1950
Kelly, James K. (OR) - 1866
Kelly, John (NY) - 1879
Kelly, Tom (AK) - 1978
Kelly, William (NY) - 1860
Kemper, James L. (VA) - 1873
Kendall, Nathan E. (IA) - 1920, 1922
Kendrick (CT) - 1852
Kendrick, John B. (WY) - 1914
Kennedy, John C. (IL) - 1912
Kennedy, Walter L. (VT) - 1974
Kennedy, William (MT) - 1892

Kennerly, T. E. (TX) - 1966
Kennon, Robert F. (LA) - 1952
Kent, Edward (ME) - 1836, 1837, 1838, 1839, 1840, 1841
Kent, Henry O. (NH) - 1894, 1896
Kent, Herman O. (WI) - 1926
Kent, William P. (VA) - 1909
Kern, John W. (IN) - 1900, 1904
Kernan, Francis (NY) - 1872
Kerner, Otto (IL) - 1960, 1964
Kerr, John (NC) - 1852
Kerr, Robert S. (OK) - 1942
Kerrey, Robert F. (NE) - 1982
Ketchum, Omar B. (KS) - 1934
Keyes, Henry (VT) - 1856, 1857, 1858
Keyes, Henry W. (NH) - 1916
Keyser, F. Ray Jr. (VT) - 1960, 1962
Kilbourne, James (OH) - 1901
Kilby, Thomas E. (AL) - 1918
Kilgo, J. W. (TN) - 1944
Kilpatrick, Thomas M. (IL) - 1846
Kimball, Charles Dean (RI) - 1902
Kimball, Charles P. (ME) - 1871, 1872
Kimball, E. E. (MO) - 1888
Kimball, Horace A. (RI) - 1880, 1881, 1882
Kimberle, Charles H. (MI) - 1906
King (MS) - 1881
King, Austin A. (MO) - 1848
King, Bruce (NM) - 1970, 1978
King, Edward J. (MA) - 1978
King, John A. (NY) - 1856
King, John W. (NH) - 1962, 1964, 1966
King, Rufus (NY) - 1816
King, Sam (NV) - 1970
King, Samuel Ward (RI) - 1840, 1841, 1842
King, W. R. (OR) - 1898
King, William (ME) - 1820, 1835
Kinkead, John H. (NV) - 1878
Kinkead, William B. (KY) - 1867
Kinney, Audrey L. (AR) - 1914
Kinney, J. C. (AZ) - 1932
Kinney, William (IL) - 1830, 1834
Kinnie, L. G. (IA) - 1881, 1883
Kinter (ND) - 1894
Kirby, Ephraim (CT) - 1802, 1803
Kirk, Claude R. Jr. (FL) - 1966, 1970
Kirker, Thomas (OH) - 1808
Kirkwood, Samuel Jordan (IA) - 1859, 1861, 1875
Kirman, Richard Sr. (NV) - 1934
Kitchin, W. W. (NC) - 1908
Kleihege, George W. (KS) - 1912
Kleindienst, Richard (AZ) - 1964
Knapp, J. C. (IA) - 1871
Kneip, Richard Francis (SD) - 1970, 1972, 1974
Knight, Goodwin J. (CA) - 1954
Knight, Jesse William (UT) - 1908
Knight, Nehemiah R. (RI) - 1816, 1817, 1818, 1819, 1820, 1834, 1835
Knott, J. Procter (KY) - 1883
Knott, W. V. (FL) - 1916
Knous, Robert L. (CO) - 1966
Knous, William Lee (CO) - 1946, 1948
Knowland, William F. (CA) - 1958
Knowles, Warren P. (WI) - 1964, 1966, 1968
Knowlton, D. A. (IL) - 1852
Koener, Gust (IL) - 1872
Kohler, Terry J. (WI) - 1982
Kohler, Walter J. (WI) - 1928, 1932
Kohler, Walter J. Jr. (WI) - 1950, 1952, 1954
Kolb, R. F. (AL) - 1892, 1894
Koontz, Arthur B. (WV) - 1920
Kraschel, Nelson G. (IA) - 1936, 1938, 1942
Kuehn, Philip G. (WI) - 1960, 1962
Kulongoski, Ted (OR) - 1982
Kump, Herman G. (WV) - 1932
Kunin, Madeleine M. (VT) - 1982, 1984

L

Lachapelle, Eugene J. (RI) - 1950
Lacy, Arthur J. (MI) - 1934
Ladd, Herbert W. (RI) - 1889, 1890, 1891
LaFollette, Bronson C. (WI) - 1968
LaFollette, Philip F. (WI) - 1930, 1934, 1936, 1938
LaFollette, Robert M. (WI) - 1900, 1902, 1904

Lafoon, Ruby (KY) - 1931
Lake, Everett J. (CT) - 1920
Lake, I. Beverly Jr. (NC) - 1980
Lambert, Louis (LA) - 1979
Lamm (MO) - 1916
Lamm, Richard D. (CO) - 1974, 1978, 1982
Landers, Franklin (IN) - 1880
Landon, Alfred M. (KS) - 1932, 1934
Landreth, S. Lloyd (VA) - 1945
Lane, Alvin H. (TX) - 1948
Lane, Franklin K. (CA) - 1902
Lane, George W. Jr. (ME) - 1942
Lane, Henry S. (IN) - 1860
Lane, William Preston Jr. (MD) - 1946, 1950
Laney, Ben (AR) - 1944, 1946
Langdon, John (NH) - 1788, 1793, 1802, 1803, 1804, 1805, 1806, 1807, 1808, 1809, 1810, 1811
Langdon, W. H. (CA) - 1906
Langer, Lydia (ND) - 1934
Langer, William (ND) - 1932, 1936
Langlie, Arthur B. (WA) - 1940, 1944, 1948, 1952
Lanhan, Samuel W. T. (TX) - 1902, 1904
Lansdon, W. C. (KS) - 1916, 1918
Larrabee, William (IA) - 1885, 1887
Larrazolo, Octaviano A. (NM) - 1918
Larrow, Robert W. (VT) - 1952
Larsen, Allan (ID) - 1978
Larsen, Richard (ND) - 1972
Larson, Morgan F. (NJ) - 1928
Lasater, Ed C. (TX) - 1912
Lashkowitz, Herschel (ND) - 1960
Latham, M. S. (CA) - 1859
Lathrop, Samuel (MA) - 1824, 1831, 1832
Lattimore, William (MS) - 1823
Lausche, Frank J. (OH) - 1944, 1946, 1948, 1950, 1952, 1954
Lausier, Louis B. (ME) - 1948
Lavington, Leon E. (CO) - 1946
Law, Richard (CT) - 1796, 1801
Lawler, Daniel W. (MN) - 1892
Lawrence, Amos A. (MA) - 1858, 1860
Lawrence, David L. (PA) - 1958
Lawrence, Isaac (RI) - 1878
Laxalt, Paul (NV) - 1966
Layton, L. (DE) - 1932
Lea (MS) - 1849
Lea, Preston (DE) - 1904
Leader, George M. (PA) - 1954
Leake, Walter (MS) - 1821, 1823
Leamy, James P. (VT) - 1932, 1934
Leche, Richard W. (LA) - 1936
Ledbetter, C. C. (AR) - 1934
Leddy, Bernard J. (VT) - 1958
Ledoux, Henri (NH) - 1932
Lee, Andrew E. (SD) - 1896, 1898, 1908
Lee, Fitzhugh (VA) - 1885
Lee, J. Bracken (UT) - 1944, 1948, 1952, 1956
Lee, Jerrie W. (AZ) - 1938, 1940, 1942, 1944
Lee, William E. (MN) - 1914
Leedy, John W. (KS) - 1896, 1898
Leffler, Shepherd (IA) - 1875
Lehman, Herbert H. (NY) - 1932, 1934, 1936, 1938
Lehrman, Lew (NY) - 1980
Lemke, William (ND) - 1922
Lemon, Robert S. (KS) - 1944
Leonard, A. H. (LA) - 1892
Leonard, Donald S. (MI) - 1954
Leonard, L. (MO) - 1892
Leonard, Richard W. (NH) - 1974
Leopold, John (HI) - 1978
Leslie, Harry G. (IN) - 1928
Leslie, Preston H. (KY) - 1871
Lester, J. T. (MS) - 1915
Letcher, John (VA) - 1859, 1861
Letcher, Robert P. (KY) - 1840
Lett, H. C. (NE) - 1872
Levander, Harold (MN) - 1966
Levin, Sander (MI) - 1970, 1974
Lewelling, L. D. (KS) - 1892, 1894
Lewis, Andrew L. (Drew) Jr. (PA) - 1974
Lewis, Austin (CA) - 1906
Lewis, David P. (AL) - 1872, 1874
Lewis, Dean G. (RI) - 1954
Lewis, James Hamilton (IL) - 1920
Lewis, James T. (WI) - 1863
Lewis, Joshua (LA) - 1816
Lewis, Lunsford L. (VA) - 1905
Lewis, Morgan (NY) - 1804, 1807

Lewis, Robert E. (MO) - 1896
Lewis, Samuel (OH) - 1851, 1853
Lewis, Tom J. (MN) - 1914
Lewis, Vivian M. (NJ) - 1910
Licht, Frank (RI) - 1968, 1970
Lien, Burre H. (SD) - 1900
Ligon, Thomas Watkins (MD) - 1853
Lilley, George L. (CT) - 1908
Lincoln, Enoch (ME) - 1826, 1827, 1828
Lincoln, Levi (MA) - 1825, 1826, 1827, 1828, 1829, 1830, 1831, 1832
Lincoln, Levi I (MA) - 1809
Lind, John (MN) - 1896, 1898, 1900
Lindley, John F. (IL) - 1964
Lindsay, H. B. (TN) - 1918
Lindsay, Robert B. (AL) - 1870
Lindsay, William (MT) - 1904
Lindsay, Ben B. (CO) - 1906
Link, Arthur A. (ND) - 1972, 1976, 1980
Linney, Frank A. (NC) - 1916
Lippitt, Charles Warren (RI) - 1895, 1896
Lippitt, Henry (RI) - 1875, 1876
List, Robert F. (NV) - 1978, 1982
Lister, Ernest (WA) - 1912, 1916
Little, Chauncey B. (KS) - 1928
Little, John S. (AR) - 1906
Littlefield, Alfred H. (RI) - 1880, 1881, 1882
Littlefield, George L. (RI) - 1895, 1896
Littlefield, Nathan W. (RI) - 1900
Littlejohn, Flavius (MI) - 1849
Littleton (TN) - 1904
Livesay, J. O. (AR) - 1930, 1932
Livingston, Robert R. (NY) - 1798
Lloyd, James (MA) - 1826
Lobeck, E. E. (MN) - 1912
Locke, Hugh A. (AL) - 1930
Lodge, John D. (CT) - 1950, 1954
Logan, Benjamin (KY) - 1800
Logan, William (KY) - 1820
Long, Benjamin M. (AL) - 1890
Long, Earl K. (LA) - 1948, 1956
Long, Huey P. (LA) - 1928
Long, John D. (MA) - 1879, 1880, 1881
Long, Richard H. (MA) - 1918, 1919
Longino, Andrew H. (MS) - 1899
Longley, James B. (ME) - 1974
Longshore, William L. Jr. (AL) - 1958
Longstreth, Morris (PA) - 1848
Looker, Othniel (OH) - 1814
Loomis (CT) - 1861, 1862
Loomis, Orland S. (WI) - 1940, 1942
Lord, John F. (ND) - 1958
Lord, Samuel L. (ME) - 1898, 1900
Lord, William P. (OR) - 1894
Loucks, H. L. (SD) - 1890
Lounsbury, George E. (CT) - 1898
Lounsbury, Phineas C. (CT) - 1886
Love, John A. (CO) - 1962, 1966, 1970
Loveland, W. A. H. (CO) - 1878
Loveless, Herschel C. (IA) - 1952, 1956, 1958
Lovering, Henry B. (MA) - 1887
Low, Frederick F. (CA) - 1863
Lowden, Frank O. (IL) - 1916
Lowden, J. G. (TX) - 1904
Lowe, A. Lynn (AR) - 1978
Lowe, Enoch L. (MD) - 1850
Lowe, Ralph P. (IA) - 1857
Lowe, W. O. (TN) - 1946
Lowndes, Lloyd (MD) - 1895, 1899
Lowry, Robert (MS) - 1881, 1885
Lubbock, Francis R. (TX) - 1861
Lucas, Robert (OH) - 1830, 1832, 1834
Luce, Cyrus G. (MI) - 1886, 1888
Lucey, Patrick J. (WI) - 1966, 1970, 1974
Ludington, Harrison (WI) - 1875
Ludlow, George C. (NJ) - 1880
Lueck, Martin L. (WI) - 1924
Lueck, William L. (WI) - 1936
Lujan, Manuel (NM) - 1948
Lumpkin, Wilson (GA) - 1831, 1833
Lundeen, Ernest (MN) - 1928
Lusk, T. E. (NM) - 1966
Lyman, Darius (OH) - 1832
Lynch, Andrew J. (DE) - 1920
Lynch, Charles (MS) - 1831, 1835
Lynch, Walter A. (NY) - 1950
Lyons, Charlton H. Sr. (LA) - 1964

M

Mabey, Charles R. (UT) - 1920, 1924

Muir (ND) - 1890
Mullen, W. E. (WY) - 1910
Mullikin, Addison E. (MD) - 1926
Muncy, T. J. (VA) - 1917
Munford (VA) - 1863
Muniz, Ramsey (TX) - 1972, 1974
Munroe Addison P. (RI) - 1916
Munson, Henry C. (ME) - 1877
Murphy, Ed (MN) - 1940
Murphy, Francis P. (NH) - 1936, 1938
Murphy, Frank (MI) - 1936, 1938
Murphy, Franklin (NJ) - 1901
Murphy, George W. (AR) - 1913
Murphy, Jack M. (ID) - 1974
Murphy, John (AL) - 1825, 1827
Murphy, John G. (RI) - 1946
Murphy, Robert F. (MA) - 1954
Murphy, Vincent J. (NJ) - 1943
Murrah, Pendleton (TX) - 1863
Murray, Johnston (OK) - 1950
Murray, William G. (IA) - 1958, 1966
Murray, William H. (OK) - 1930
Murtagh, J. C. (IA) - 1924
Muse (VA) - 1941
Muskie, Edmund S. (ME) - 1954, 1956
Musselman, Amos S. (MI) - 1912
Myers, Harry H. (AR) - 1904

N

Nance, Albinus (NE) - 1878, 1880
Nash, George K. (OH) - 1899, 1901
Naudain, Arnold (DE) - 1832
Neal, John R. (TN) - 1950, 1954
Neal, Lawrence T. (OH) - 1893
Neal, William J. (NH) - 1942
Needham, Horatio (VT) - 1849
Neely, Harold E. (WV) - 1960
Neely, Matthew M. (WV) - 1940
Neff, Pat M. (TX) - 1920, 1922
Nelsen, Ancher (MN) - 1956
Nelson, A. T. (MO) - 1924
Nelson, Andrew (MN) - 1928
Nelson, Gaylord A. (WI) - 1958, 1960
Nelson, Knute (MN) - 1892, 1894
Nelson, Martin A. (MN) - 1934, 1936
Nestos, Ragnvald A. (ND) - 1921, 1922
Netherland (TN) - 1859
Neville, Keith (NE) - 1916, 1918
Newell (NJ) - 1877
Newell, William A. (NJ) - 1856
Nice, Harry W. (MD) - 1919, 1934, 1938
Nicholls, Francis T. (LA) - 1876, 1888
Nichols, Alva W. (MI) - 1894
Nicks (AL) - 1853
Nicoll (CT) - 1841
Nigh, George (OK) - 1978, 1982
Niles (CT) - 1839, 1840, 1849
Niquette, Russell F. (VT) - 1960
Nixon, Richard M. (CA) - 1962
Noble, Noah (IN) - 1831, 1834
Noel, Edmond F. (MS) - 1907
Noel, Philip W. (RI) - 1972, 1974
Nolte, Eugene Jr. (TX) - 1946
Noone, Albert W. (NH) - 1914, 1930
Norbeck, Peter (SD) - 1916, 1918
Norcross (GA) - 1876
Norris, Edwin L. (MT) - 1908
North, J. E. (NE) - 1886
Northen, William J. (GA) - 1890, 1892
Norton, A. B. (TX) - 1878, 1884
Norton, J. N. (NE) - 1924
Nortoni, Albert D. (MO) - 1912
Norwood (GA) - 1880
Norwood, C. M. (AR) - 1888
Notte, John A. Jr. (RI) - 1960, 1962
Noyes, Edward F. (OH) - 1871, 1873
Nugent, James W. (RI) - 1974
Nugent, Thomas L. (TX) - 1892, 1894
Nunn, Louie B. (KY) - 1979
Nunn, Louis B. (KY) - 1963, 1967
Nutter, Donald G. (MT) - 1960

O

Oates, W. C. (AL) - 1894
O'Brien, Leo Jr. (VT) - 1970
O'Callaghan, Mike (NV) - 1970, 1974
Ochiltree, W. B. (TX) - 1853
O'Connell, John J. (WA) - 1968

O'Conner, Frank (NY) - 1966
O'Connor, Herbert R. (MD) - 1938, 1942
O'Connor, J. F. T. (ND) - 1920
O'Connor, Michael J. (SD) - 1982
O'Daniel, W. Lee (TX) - 1938, 1940, 1956
Oddie, Tasker L. (NV) - 1910, 1914, 1918
Odell, Benjamin B. Jr. (NY) - 1900, 1902
O'Donnell, C. C. (CA) - 1886
O'Ferrall, Charles T. (VA) - 1893
Ogilvie, Richard B. (IL) - 1968, 1972
Oglesby, Richard J. (IL) - 1864, 1872, 1884
Olcott, Ben W. (OR) - 1922
Olden, Charles S. (NJ) - 1859
Oliver, James C. (ME) - 1952
Oliver, Samuel W. (AL) - 1837
Olsen, Arnold H. (MT) - 1956
Olsen, George W. (NE) - 1944
Olson, Allen I. (ND) - 1980, 1984
Olson, Culbert L. (CA) - 1938, 1942
Olson, Floyd B. (MN) - 1924, 1930, 1932, 1934
Olson, Jack B. (WI) - 1970
Olson, John E. (SD) - 1974
O'Malley, Malcolm A. (MT) - 1904
Oman, J. R. (WA) - 1924
O'Neal, Edward A. (AL) - 1882, 1884
O'Neal, Emmet (AL) - 1910
O'Neal, W. (FL) - 1924
O'Neal, William R. (FL) - 1912
O'Neill, C. William (OH) - 1956, 1958
O'Neill, William A. (CT) - 1982
Orear, E. C. (KY) - 1911
Orman, James B. (CO) - 1900
Ormsbee, Ebenezer J. (VT) - 1886
Orr, James L. (SC) - 1865
Orr, Robert D. (IN) - 1980, 1984
Orr, Sample (MO) - 1860
Osborn, Chase S. (MI) - 1910, 1914
Osborn, Sidney P. (AZ) - 1940, 1942, 1944, 1946
Osborn, Thomas A. (KS) - 1872, 1874
Osborne, John E. (WY) - 1892, 1904
Osgood, William N. (MA) - 1908
Ostlund, John C. (WY) - 1978
Otero, Manuel B. (NM) - 1924
Otis, George L. (MN) - 1869
Otis, Harrison G. (MA) - 1823
Otjen, William J. (OK) - 1942
Ottinger, Albert (NY) - 1928
Overall, John W. (TN) - 1916
Overby (GA) - 1855
Overmyer, David (KS) - 1894
Owen, Sidney M. (MN) - 1890, 1894
Owens, Wayne (UT) - 1984
Owsley, William (KY) - 1844

P

Packard, Stephen B. (LA) - 1876
Packer, Asa (PA) - 1869
Packer, William F. (PA) - 1857
Padelford, Seth (RI) - 1860, 1869, 1870, 1871, 1872
Page, Carroll S. (VT) - 1890
Page, John (NH) - 1839, 1840, 1841
Page, John B. (VT) - 1867, 1868
Paine, Charles (VT) - 1835, 1841, 1842
Paine, Henry W. (MA) - 1863, 1864
Paine, Robert Treat (MA) - 1899, 1900
Palfrey, John G. (MA) - 1851
Palmer, John M. (IL) - 1868, 1888
Palmer, Joel (OR) - 1870
Palmer, Linwood E. (ME) - 1978
Palmer, William A. (VT) - 1830, 1831, 1832, 1833, 1834, 1835
Pardee, George C. (CA) - 1902
Park, Guy Brasfield (MO) - 1932
Parker, Amasa J. (NY) - 1856, 1858
Parker, Crawford (IN) - 1960
Parker, Joel (NJ) - 1862, 1871
Parker, John C. (NC) - 1920
Parker, John M. (LA) - 1916, 1920
Parkhurst, Frederick H. (ME) - 1920
Parks (AR) - 1880
Parks, C. C. (CO) - 1912
Parks, Gorham (ME) - 1837
Parnell, Harvey J. (AR) - 1928, 1930
Parriott, James D. (CO) - 1932
Parris, Albion K. (ME) - 1821, 1822, 1823, 1824, 1825, 1854

Parsons, Enoch (AL) - 1835
Parsons, Enoch (TN) - 1819
Partridge, Azariah S. (MI) - 1890
Pascal, Robert A. (MD) - 1982
Pastore, John O. (RI) - 1946, 1948
Pattangall, William R. (ME) - 1922, 1924
Patten, George F. (ME) - 1856
Pattengill, Henry R. (MI) - 1914
Patterson, I. L. (OR) - 1926
Patterson, Jack A. (ND) - 1940
Patterson, John (AL) - 1958
Patterson, Malcolm R. (TN) - 1906, 1908
Patterson, Paul (OR) - 1954
Patterson, T. M. (CO) - 1888, 1914
Patteson, Okey L. (WV) - 1948
Pattison, John (WA) - 1908
Pattison, John M. (OH) - 1905
Pattison, Robert E. (PA) - 1882, 1890, 1902
Patton, Frank C. (NC) - 1944
Patton, Robert Miller (AL) - 1865
Patton, W. S. (MS) - 1865
Paulen, Ben S. (KS) - 1924, 1926
Payne, Frederick G. (ME) - 1948, 1950
Payne, H. B. (OH) - 1857
Paynter, Rowland G. (DE) - 1908
Paynter, Samuel (DE) - 1823
Peabody, Endicott (MA) - 1962
Peabody, James H. (CO) - 1902, 1904
Peabody, Oliver (NH) - 1798
Peabody, Thomas H. (RI) - 1887, 1896, 1897
Pearson, H. Clyde (VA) - 1961
Pease, Elisha M. (TX) - 1853, 1855, 1865, 1866
Peasley, B. J. (TX) - 1944
Peay, Austin (TN) - 1922, 1924, 1926
Peck (GA) - 1892
Peck, Asahel (VT) - 1874
Peck, George W. (WI) - 1890, 1892, 1894, 1904
Peck, Lucius B. (VT) - 1850
Peck, T. F. (TN) - 1924
Peckham, G. E. (NV) - 1894
Peckham, William (RI) - 1837
Peery, George C. (VA) - 1933
Peery, Harman W. (UT) - 1936
Pendleton, George H. (OH) - 1869
Pennewill, Caleb S. (DE) - 1904
Pennewill, Simeon S. (DE) - 1908
Pennoyer, Sylvester (OR) - 1886, 1890
Pennypacker, Samuel W. (PA) - 1902
Percy, Charles H. (IL) - 1964
Perham, Sidney (ME) - 1870, 1871, 1872
Perkins, George C. (CA) - 1879
Perkins, Jared (NH) - 1854
Perpich, Rudy (MN) - 1978, 1982
Perry, Charles B. (WI) - 1926
Perry, Edward A. (FL) - 1884
Perry, Madison S. (FL) - 1856
Pershing, Cyrus L. (PA) - 1875
Persons, Gordon (AL) - 1950
Peters, John S. (CT) - 1831, 1832, 1833
Petersen, George C. (FL) - 1960
Petersen, Hjalmar (MN) - 1940, 1942
Peterson, Harry H. (MN) - 1950
Peterson, Russell W. (DE) - 1968, 1972
Peterson, Val (NE) - 1946, 1948, 1950
Peterson, Walter (NH) - 1968, 1970
Pettigrew, A. J. (FL) - 1908
Pettus, John J. (MS) - 1859, 1861
Pharr, Henry N. (LA) - 1908
Pharr, John N. (LA) - 1896
Phelps, Edward J. (VT) - 1880
Phelps, John S. (MO) - 1868, 1876
Phelps, T. G. (CA) - 1869
Philipp, Emanuel L. (WI) - 1914, 1916, 1918
Phillip, Stephen L. (MA) - 1848
Phillips, John C. (AZ) - 1928, 1930
Phillips, Joseph B. (IL) - 1822
Phillips, Kirk G. (SD) - 1898
Phillips, Leon C. (OK) - 1938
Phillips, Rubel L. (MS) - 1963, 1967
Phillips, Stephen C. (MA) - 1849, 1850
Phillips, T. J. (IA) - 1901
Phillips, Wendell (MA) - 1870
Philp, John W. (TX) - 1914
Pickens (AL) - 1880
Pickens, Israel (AL) - 1821, 1823
Pickering, John (NH) - 1789, 1790
Pierce, Benjamin (NH) - 1826, 1827, 1828, 1829

Pierce, Lymon (RI) - 1866, 1867, 1868, 1869, 1870, 1874
Pierce, Nathan (OR) - 1894
Pierce, Walter M. (OR) - 1918, 1922, 1926
Pike, James (NH) - 1871
Pilcher, Zind (MI) - 1843
Pillsbury, Albert (ME) - 1853
Pillsbury, Eben F. (ME) - 1866, 1867, 1868
Pillsbury, John (NH) - 1962, 1964
Pillsbury, John S. (MN) - 1875, 1877, 1879
Pinchot, Gifford (PA) - 1922, 1930
Pine, William B. (OK) - 1934
Pingree, Hazen S. (MI) - 1896, 1898
Pingree, Samuel E. (VT) - 1884
Pitkin, Frederick W. (CO) - 1878, 1880
Pitkin, Timothy (CT) - 1824, 1825
Pitman, Robert C. (MA) - 1877
Pittman, Vail (NV) - 1946, 1950, 1954
Plaisted, Frederick W. (ME) - 1910, 1912
Plaisted, Harris M. (ME) - 1880, 1882
Platt, Jonas (NY) - 1810
Pleasant, Ruffin G. (LA) - 1916
Plumer, William (NH) - 1812, 1813, 1814, 1815, 1816, 1817, 1818
Poindexter, George (MS) - 1819
Polk, James K. (TN) - 1839, 1841, 1843
Polk, Trusten (MO) - 1856
Pollard, John Garland (VA) - 1929
Pollard, Park H. (VT) - 1930, 1942
Pollock, James (PA) - 1854
Pond, E. B. (CA) - 1890
Ponder, James (DE) - 1870
Pool, John (NC) - 1860
Pope (FL) - 1884
Pope, Lewis S. (TN) - 1932, 1934
Pope, Sampson (SC) - 1894, 1896
Porter, Albert Gallatin (IN) - 1880
Porter, Claude R. (IA) - 1906, 1910, 1918
Porter, David R. (PA) - 1838, 1841
Porter, Eli H. (VT) - 1904
Porter, James D. Jr. (TN) - 1874, 1876
Porter, T. R. (NE) - 1868
Porter, W. D. (SC) - 1868
Porter, Wilber E. (NY) - 1896
Posey, Thomas (IN) - 1816
Pothier, Aram J. (RI) - 1908, 1909, 1910, 1911, 1912, 1924, 1926
Potter, Americus V. (RI) - 1855, 1856, 1857
Potter, Elisha R. (RI) - 1818, 1858, 1859
Potter, Frederick E. (NH) - 1900
Potts (NJ) - 1880
Powell, D. Frank (WI) - 1894
Powell, Lazarus W. (KY) - 1848, 1851
Powell, Thomas E. (OH) - 1887
Powell, Wesley (NH) - 1958, 1960
Powers, J. H. (NE) - 1890
Powers, James J. (NH) - 1944
Powers, Llewellyn (ME) - 1896, 1898
Power, Thomas C. (MT) - 1889
Poynter, William A. (NE) - 1898, 1900
Pratt (CT) - 1858, 1859
Pratt, Thomas G. (MD) - 1844
Prescott, Benjamin F. (NH) - 1877, 1878
Pressman, Hyman A. (MD) - 1966
Preston, David (MI) - 1884
Preus, Jacob A. O. (MN) - 1920, 1922
Prewitt, R. K. (MS) - 1899
Price, James H. (VA) - 1937
Price, Rodman M. (NJ) - 1853
Price, Sterling (MO) - 1852
Price, Thomas L. (MO) - 1864
Prieur (LA) - 1838
Prince, Frederick O. (MA) - 1885
Pritchard, George M. (NC) - 1948
Proctor, Fletcher D. (VT) - 1906
Proctor, Mortimer R. (VT) - 1944
Proctor, Redfield (VT) - 1878, 1922
Prouty, George H. (VT) - 1908
Proxmire, William (WI) - 1952, 1954, 1956
Pryor, David (AR) - 1974, 1976
Putnam, A. L. (SD) - 1924
Putnam, Roger L. (MA) - 1942
Putnam, William L. (ME) - 1888
Pyle, Howard (AZ) - 1950, 1952, 1954

Q

Quick, Williamk F. (WI) - 1924
Quie, Albert H. (MN) - 1978
Quillen, William T. (DE) - 1984
Quimby, Smith (RI) - 1895
Quimby, Henry B. (NH) - 1908

Gubernatorial Primary Candidates Index

The Gubernatorial Primary Candidates Index includes all candidates appearing in Gubernatorial Elections: Primary Vote Returns, 1956-1984 (pp. 537-565).

The index includes candidates' names followed by state abbreviations and the years of candidacy. To locate a candidate's returns, turn to pages 537-565 where the re-

turns are arranged alphabetically by state *(State Abbreviations below)* and in chronological order of election for each state.

For other references to gubernatorial candidates in the *Guide to U.S. Elections, Second Edition,* see the General Index, page 1275.

A

Abel, Hazel (NE) - 1960
Ackerman, Lee (AZ) - 1960
Ackermann, Barbara (MA) - 1978
Adams, Paul L. (NY) - 1970
Addington, William H. (KS) - 1960
Agnew, Spiro T. (MD) - 1966
Albertazzie, Ralph D. (WV) - 1976
Alioto, Joseph L. (CA) - 1974
Allen, William C. (NV) - 1978
Almond, Lincoln (RI) - 1978
Altofer, John H. (IL) - 1968
Altvater, George (OR) - 1962
Amaimo, Morgan L. (MD) - 1958
Anaya, Toney (NM) - 1982
Andersen, Elmer L. (MN) - 1960, 1962
Anderson, D. G. (HI) - 1982
Anderson, Emmett T. (WA) - 1956
Anderson, Forrest H. (MT) - 1968
Anderson, John (KS) - 1960, 1962, 1972
Anderson, LeRoy (MT) - 1968
Anderson, Sigurd (SD) - 1964
Anderson, Victor E. (NE) - 1956, 1958
Anderson, Wendell R. (MN) - 1970, 1974
Andrews, Lloyd J. (WA) - 1960
Andrews, Mark (ND) - 1962
Andrus, Cecil D. (ID) - 1966, 1970, 1974
Annable, Robert W. (OH) - 1970
Apodaca, Jerry (NM) - 1974
Ariyoshi, George R. (HI) - 1974, 1978, 1982
Aronson, J. Hugo (MT) - 1956
Ashcroft, John (MO) - 1984
Ashworth, Emily (OR) - 1978
Atiyeh, Victor G. (OR) - 1974, 1978, 1982
Atkinson, W. P. (OK) - 1958
Austin, Gene (NV) - 1962
Avery, William H. (KS) - 1964, 1966

B

Babbitt, Bruce (AZ) - 1978, 1982
Babcock, Robert S. (VT) - 1960, 1964

Babcock, Tim M. (MT) - 1964, 1968
Badgett, Joseph M. (MO) - 1964
Baggett, Bryce (OK) - 1970
Bagwell, Paul D. (MI) - 1958, 1960
Bakalis, Michael (IL) - 1978
Balentine, Karla (MD) - 1962
Bangerter, Norman H. (UT) - 1984
Barlocker, W. A. (UT) - 1960
Barnes, Clarence E. (OK) - 1958
Barnes, Wallace (CT) - 1970
Barnes, Wilson K. (MD) - 1974
Barron, W. W. (WV) - 1960
Barry, James J. (NH) - 1966
Bartlett, Dewey F. (OK) - 1966, 1970
Batchelder, Clifton B. (NE) - 1970
Bateman, Raymond H. (NJ) - 1977
Bates, Charles A. (NE) - 1960, 1964
Batt, Phillip (ID) - 1982
Baum, Ted (NE) - 1956
Beall, Carlton (MD) - 1978
Beall, J. Glenn Jr. (MD) - 1978
Beck, Robert K. (IA) - 1966, 1968
Begley, Elmer (KY) - 1975
Bell, Howard L. (OK) - 1982
Bellmon, Harry (OK) - 1962
Bellotti, Francis X. (MA) - 1964, 1970
Bennett, Robert F. (KS) - 1974, 1978
Berentson, Duane (WA) - 1980
Berube, Georgette B. (ME) - 1982
Bickerstaff, William (NV) - 1974
Bishop, Al (MT) - 1980
Blackwell, Earl (MO) - 1972
Blair, C. Stanley (MD) - 1970
Blair, James T. (MO) - 1956
Blanchard, James J. (MI) - 1982
Blenski, Roman R. (WI) - 1970
Bloom, Jeremiah B. (NY) - 1978
Boe, Nils A. (SD) - 1964, 1966
Bohner, Robert J. (NY) - 1982
Bond, Christopher S. (Kit) (MO) - 1972, 1976, 1980
Bonner, John W. (MT) - 1956
Boren, David L. (OK) - 1974
Boucher, H. A. (AK) - 1982
Bourgois, Anna Belle (ND) - 1984
Boutin, Bernard L. (NH) - 1958, 1960
Bowen, Otis R. (IN) - 1976

Boyd, McDill (KS) - 1960, 1964
Boyden, John S. (UT) - 1956
Bradley, Tom (CA) - 1982
Branon, E. Frank (VT) - 1956
Branstad, Terry (IA) - 1982
Breathitt, Edward T. (KY) - 1963
Brennan, Joseph E. (ME) - 1974, 1978, 1982
Brett, George J. (PA) - 1966
Brickley, James H. (MI) - 1982
Brimmer, Clarence (WY) - 1974
Brock, Art (AZ) - 1964
Broderick, Raymond (PA) - 1970
Brooks, Mrs. Ralph G. (NE) - 1962
Brooks, Ralph G. (NE) - 1958
Brotzman, Donald G. (CO) - 1956
Brown, Bonn (WV) - 1964
Brown, Clarence Jr. (OH) - 1982
Brown, Edmund G. (CA) - 1958, 1962, 1966
Brown, Edmund G. Jr. (CA) - 1974, 1978
Brown, Glenn B. (MN) - 1958
Brown, John W. (OH) - 1956
Brown, John Y. (KY) - 1979
Brown, Paul W. (OH) - 1970
Brown, William J. (OH) - 1982
Browning, Chauncey H. (WV) - 1984
Bruce, Walter E. (NM) - 1974
Bryan, Richard (NV) - 1982
Buck, Gilbert (NV) - 1974
Buckley, Thomas H. (MA) - 1956
Buckson, David P. (DE) - 1972
Buehner, Carl W. (UT) - 1968
Bunning, Jim (KY) - 1983
Burbach, J. W. (NE) - 1966, 1970
Burch, Palmer L. (CO) - 1958
Burdett, Joe F. (WV) - 1956
Burke, Howard L. (WY) - 1966
Burke, Joe (WY) - 1966
Burney, Dwight W. (NE) - 1964
Burns, Brian D. (VT) - 1976
Burns, Edward P. (ND) - 1972
Burns, John A. (HI) - 1959, 1962, 1966, 1970
Burns, Lester (KY) - 1983
Burroughs, John (NM) - 1958, 1960, 1966
Burrows, George (NE) - 1982

Bursey, Joseph A. (NM) - 1958, 1960
Burton, Marvin L. (AZ) - 1958
Bush, Hilary A. (MO) - 1964
Bussey, Elmer E. (NH) - 1962
Bussiere, Emile R. (NH) - 1968
Butera, Bob (PA) - 1978
Butrovich, John (AK) - 1958
Byer, George H. (AK) - 1962
Byrne, Brendan T. (NJ) - 1973, 1977

C

Cahill, William T. (NJ) - 1969, 1973
Camp, John N. H. (OK) - 1966
Campbell, Bruce S. (MD) - 1958
Campbell, Edward L. (IA) - 1982
Campbell, Jack M. (NM) - 1962, 1964
Cannon, D. James (UT) - 1964
Cannon, Joe (OK) - 1970
Cannon, Paul (MT) - 1960
Card, Andrew (MA) - 1982
Carey, Hugh L. (NY) - 1974, 1978
Carey, Richard J. (ME) - 1978
Cargo, David F. (NM) - 1966, 1968
Carley, David (WI) - 1966, 1978
Carlin, John (KS) - 1978, 1982
Carnahan, Mel (MO) - 1984
Carpenter, Terry (NE) - 1960
Carr, Larry (AK) - 1970
Carroll, Julian (KY) - 1975
Cartwright, Wilburn (OK) - 1970
Casey, Robert P. (PA) - 1966, 1970, 1978
Cason, William (MO) - 1976
Castle, Michael N. (DE) - 1984
Castro, Raul H. (AZ) - 1970, 1974
Cavanagh, Jerome P. (MI) - 1974
Cecil, J. N. R. (KY) - 1963
Celebrezze, Anthony J. (OH) - 1958
Celeste, Richard F. (OH) - 1978, 1982
Chafee, John H. (RI) - 1962, 1964, 1966, 1968
Chamberlin, Robert (SD) - 1966, 1968
Champagne, Alfred J. (NH) - 1958
Chance, Simon W. (SD) - 1972

State Abbreviations

Alabama	AL	Illinois	IL	Montana	MT	Rhode Island	RI
Alaska	AK	Indiana	IN	Nebraska	NE	South Carolina	SC
Arizona	AZ	Iowa	IA	Nevada	NV	South Dakota	SD
Arkansas	AR	Kansas	KS	New Hampshire	NH	Tennessee	TN
California	CA	Kentucky	KY	New Jersey	NJ	Texas	TX
Colorado	CO	Louisiana	LA	New Mexico	NM	Utah	UT
Connecticut	CT	Maine	ME	New York	NY	Vermont	VT
Delaware	DE	Maryland	MD	North Carolina	NC	Virginia	VA
Florida	FL	Massachusetts	MA	North Dakota	ND	Washington	WA
Georgia	GA	Michigan	MI	Ohio	OH	West Virginia	WV
Hawaii	HI	Minnesota	MN	Oklahoma	OK	Wisconsin	WI
Idaho	ID	Mississippi	MS	Oregon	OR	Wyoming	WY
		Missouri	MO	Pennsylvania	PA		

J

Jack, William (WY) - 1962
Jackson, Clingan (OH) - 1958
Jackson, Larry (ID) - 1978
Jackson, Lowell B. (WI) - 1982
Jackvony, Louis (RI) - 1962
Jacobson, Alvin J. (PA) - 1974
Jacquin, William C. (AZ) - 1974
James, Peter (MD) - 1970
James, Ted (MT) - 1968
Jancek, Steve (AZ) - 1982
Janklow, William J. (SD) - 1978, 1982
Jeffords, James M. (VT) - 1972
Johnson, Carl A. (WY) - 1982
Johnson, Donald E. (IA) - 1968
Johnson, John W. (MN) - 1974
Johnson, Joseph B. (VT) - 1956
Johnson, Robert W. (MN) - 1978
Johnson, W. L. (MI) - 1958
Johnston, Harvey F. (PA) - 1962, 1974
Jones, Dick (WY) - 1974
Jones, Walter H. (NJ) - 1961
Judge, Thomas L. (MT) - 1972, 1976, 1980
Juelfs, Stanley R. (NE) - 1978

K

Kaiser, Edmon V. (CA) - 1974
Kasten, Bob (WI) - 1978
Kaufman, Paul J. (WV) - 1968
Kay, Morris (KS) - 1972
Kay, Wendell P. (AK) - 1966
Kealoha, James K. (HI) - 1962
Kean, Thomas H. (NJ) - 1977, 1981
Keathley, Elizabeth (CA) - 1974
Kecskemethy, Laszlo (CA) - 1978
Keith, A. M. (MN) - 1966
Kelleher, Robert Carlson (MT) - 1984
Kelley, Harry W. (MD) - 1982
Kelley, Peter S. (ME) - 1974
Kelley, V. A. (IL) - 1982
Kelly, Francis G. (MA) - 1960
Kelly, William F. (NJ) - 1969
Kendall, Bruce (AK) - 1966
Kenna, Lee M. (WV) - 1972
Kennedy, John F. (MA) - 1960
Kennedy, Walter L. (VT) - 1974
Kerner, Otto (IL) - 1960, 1964
Kerrey, Bob (NE) - 1982
Kerttula, Jalmar M. (AK) - 1978
Keyser, F. Ray (VT) - 1960, 1962
Kihei, David (HI) - 1959
Killian, Robert K. (CT) - 1978
King, Bruce (NM) - 1968, 1970, 1978
King, Edward F. (MA) - 1978
King, Edward J. (MA) - 1978, 1982
King, Jean (HI) - 1982
King, John W. (NH) - 1962, 1964, 1966
King, R. J. (MO) - 1972
King, Samuel P. (HI) - 1970
Klein, Ann (NJ) - 1973
Klein, T. William (KY) - 1975
Kleindienst, Richard (AZ) - 1964
Kline, Ernest P. (PA) - 1978
Kneip, Richard F. (SD) - 1970, 1972, 1974
Knight, Harold (KS) - 1978
Knous, Robert L. (CO) - 1966
Knowland, William F. (CA) - 1958
Knowles, Warren P. (WI) - 1964, 1966, 1968
Knox, Eugene (PA) - 1982
Knutson, Milo G. (WI) - 1964
Koch, Edward I. (NY) - 1982
Kohler, Terry J. (WI) - 1982
Kramer, Lawrence F. (NJ) - 1981
Krupsak, Mary Anne (NY) - 1978
Kryzan, Frank X. (OH) - 1956
Kuchera, Mike (MT) - 1960, 1964
Kuehn, Philip G. (WI) - 1960, 1962
Kuhlmann, Henry E. (NE) - 1966
Kulongowski, Ted (OR) - 1982
Kunin, Madeleine M. (VT) - 1982, 1984
Kurfess, Charles F. (OH) - 1978

L

Lacey, Charles (SD) - 1958
Lady, Wendell (KS) - 1982

LaFleur, Alexander A. (KY) - 1956
LaFollette, Bronson C. (WI) - 1968
LaFountain, Lloyd P. (ME) - 1974
Lakian, John R. (MA) - 1982
Lamm, Richard D. (CO) - 1974, 1978, 1982
Lannon, T. James (VT) - 1974
Larry, Jackson (ID) - 1978
Larsen, Allan (ID) - 1978
Larsen, Richard (ND) - 1972
Larsen, Richard R. (NE) - 1970
Lavelle, Edward P. (PA) - 1958
Lawrence, David (PA) - 1958
Lawton, Edwin G. (OH) - 1970
Laxalt, Paul (NV) - 1966
Leavitt, Dixie L. (UT) - 1976
Leavitt, Myron E. (NV) - 1982
Leddy, Bernard J. (VT) - 1958
Lee, Blair (MD) - 1978
Lee, Charles A. (MO) - 1956
Lee, J. Bracken (UT) - 1956
Lehrman, Lew (NY) - 1982
Leimback, Harry E. (WY) - 1974
Leinemann, Del (NE) - 1960
Leonard, Donald S. (MI) - 1956
Leonard, Frank J. (MO) - 1972
Leonard, Richard W. (NH) - 1974
Leopold, John (HI) - 1978
Leota, Alema (HI) - 1978
LeVander, Harold (MN) - 1966
Levin, Sander (MI) - 1970, 1974
Lewis, Andrew L. (PA) - 1974
Lewter, V. Gene (AZ) - 1978
Ley, Henry E. (NE) - 1966
Licht, Frank (RI) - 1968, 1970
Lindley, John F. (SD) - 1964
Lindquist, Elvin A. (ID) - 1962
Lindsay, Roderick (WA) - 1968
Link, Arthur A. (ND) - 1972, 1976, 1980
Lint, Lewis E. (IA) - 1962
List, Robert F. (NV) - 1978, 1982
Livengood, William S. (PA) - 1958
Loeta, Alema (HI) - 1978
Lohman, Joseph D. (IL) - 1960
Londen, Jack (AZ) - 1978
Lopez, Junio (NM) - 1970
Lord, John F. (ND) - 1958
Love, John A. (CO) - 1962, 1966, 1970
Loveless, Herschel C. (IA) - 1956, 1958
Loveless, James W. (ID) - 1978
Lucey, Patrick J. (WI) - 1966, 1970, 1974
Lukens, Donald E. (OH) - 1970
Lusk, Thomas E. (NM) - 1966

M

MacBride, Roger (VT) - 1964
MacKinnon, George (MN) - 1958
Maddy, Ken (CA) - 1978
Mahoney, Eugene H. (MT) - 1968
Mahoney, George P. (MD) - 1962, 1966
Mandel, Marvin (MD) - 1970
Mangiamelli, Tony (NE) - 1962
Mantooth, Donald W. (IN) - 1984
Marriott, Dan (UT) - 1984
Marshall, Edward G. (NV) - 1966
Marston, David W. (PA) - 1978
Martin, Ried (KY) - 1971
Martin, Roger (OR) - 1978
Martin, Verne O. (AK) - 1962
Martinez, Elizabeth (CA) - 1982
Marvel, Richard D. (NE) - 1974
Marzullo, Vincent (RI) - 1982
Mash, Jerry L. (OK) - 1978
Matheson, Scott M. (UT) - 1976
Mathis, John (IL) - 1972
Mayfield, Bobby M. (NM) - 1968, 1974
McBrayer, Terry (KY) - 1979
McCaleb, Neal A. (OK) - 1982
McCall, Tom (OR) - 1966, 1970, 1978
McCarney, Robert P. (ND) - 1964, 1968, 1972
McCarty, Virginia Dill (IN) - 1984
McCormack, Edward J. (MA) - 1966
McCormick, James L. (MI) - 1970
McCullough, Patrick (MI) - 1978
McDermott, Francis X. (NJ) - 1969
McDermott, James A. (WA) - 1972, 1980, 1984
McDonald, John K. (MT) - 1976
McDonald, Leo J. (WI) - 1970
McDonald, Thomas E. (MN) - 1974
McDonnell, Jessop (WA) - 1964

McDowell, Earl S. (PA) - 1982
McEachern, Paul (NH) - 1984
McElroy, Mark (OH) - 1962, 1970
McFarland, Ernest W. (AZ) - 1956
McGeever, Francis T. (PA) - 1970
McGonigle, A. T. (PA) - 1958
McGraw, Warren R. (WV) - 1984
McGuire, Pat (WY) - 1982
McGuirk, Harry J. (MD) - 1982
McIlwain, Harry H. (OH) - 1966
McKellips, Roger (SD) - 1978
McKinstry, Margaret (WY) - 1978
McManus, E. J. (IA) - 1960
McNary, Gene (MO) - 1972, 1984
McNichols, Stephen (CO) - 1956, 1958, 1962
McSpadden, Clem R. (OK) - 1974
McSparren, J. Collins (PA) - 1962
Mead, Ed V. (NM) - 1962
Mecham, Evan (AZ) - 1964, 1974, 1978, 1982
Mechem, Edwin L. (NM) - 1956, 1958, 1960, 1962
Melich, Mitchell (UT) - 1964
Merdes, Edward A. (AK) - 1978
Merlino, Joseph P. (NJ) - 1981
Merrell, Norman L. (MO) - 1984
Merrill, Philip L. (ME) - 1978
Meskill, Thomas J. (CT) - 1970
Meyner, Robert B. (NJ) - 1957, 1969
Miles, Clarence W. (MD) - 1966
Miller, Charles S. (MO) - 1972
Miller, Keith (AK) - 1970, 1974
Miller, O. D. (AZ) - 1956
Miller, Terry (AK) - 1982
Miller, Vern (KS) - 1974
Milliken, William G. (MI) - 1970, 1974, 1978
Miskovsky, George (OK) - 1958
Mitchell, George J. (ME) - 1974
Mitchell, James P. (NJ) - 1961
Mitchell, Stephen A. (IL) - 1960
Mollohan, Robert H. (WV) - 1956
Mongan, John C. (NH) - 1964
Monier, Robert B. (NH) - 1982
Montague, Harry R. (VT) - 1974
Montgomery, George F. (MI) - 1970
Montgomery, Jimmy D. (KS) - 1982
Moody, Mike (NV) - 1982
Moore, Arch A. Jr. (WV) - 1968, 1972, 1980, 1984
Moore, John (HI) - 1978
Moore, Preston (OK) - 1962, 1966
Moretti, Robert (CA) - 1974
Morris, J. M. (AZ) - 1962, 1964
Morris, Milton (MO) - 1968
Morris, William S. (MO) - 1972
Morrison, Edward (NY) - 1974
Morrison, Frank B. (NE) - 1960, 1962, 1964
Morrison, Robert (AZ) - 1958
Morton, Warren A. (WY) - 1982
Moss, David R. (AZ) - 1974, 1978
Mullen, Martin P. (PA) - 1974
Murphy, Jack M. (ID) - 1974
Murphy, Leo T. (NM) - 1964
Murphy, Robert F. (MA) - 1960
Murray, Erwin L. (PA) - 1966
Murray, William G. (IA) - 1958, 1966
Musa, Ben (OR) - 1966
Muskie, Edmund S. (ME) - 1956
Myers, Clay (OR) - 1974
Myers, J. Howard (WV) - 1956
Myers, Robert (WV) - 1972

N

Nader, George (AZ) - 1970
Nation, Bill (WY) - 1966
Neely, Harold E. (WV) - 1960
Nelsen, Ancher (MN) - 1956
Nelson, Donovan D. (IA) - 1978
Nelson, Gaylord (WI) - 1958, 1960
Nereim, Robert L. (IA) - 1974
Nesbitt, Charles (OK) - 1966
New, Jack L. (IN) - 1976
Nicholas, W. H. (IA) - 1956, 1960, 1962
Nielsen, Warren A. (CA) - 1970
Nigh, George (OK) - 1962, 1978, 1982
Niquette, Russell F. (VT) - 1960
Nixon, David L. (NH) - 1974
Nixon, Richard M. (CA) - 1962

Noel, Philip W. (RI) - 1972, 1974
Nolan, James D. (OH) - 1974
Nordhougen, Orris G. (ND) - 1960
Notte, John A. (RI) - 1960, 1962
Nugent, James W. (RI) - 1954
Nunn, Louie B. (KY) - 1963, 1967, 1979
Nutter, Donald G. (MT) - 1960

O

Oakes, James L. (VT) - 1968
O'Brien, Leo (VT) - 1970
O'Brien, Robert (VT) - 1976
O'Callaghan, Mike (NV) - 1970, 1974
O'Connell, John J. (WA) - 1968
O'Connor, Michael J. (SD) - 1982
O'Connor, Timothy J. (VT) - 1980
O'Donnell, Kenneth P. (MA) - 1966, 1970
Ogilvie, Richard B. (IL) - 1968, 1972
Olmstead, Ralph (ID) - 1982
Olsen, Arnold H. (MT) - 1956
Olson, Allen I. (ND) - 1980, 1984
Olson, Jack B. (WI) - 1970
Olson, John E. (SD) - 1974
O'Neill, C. William (OH) - 1956, 1958
O'Neill, Danny (MT) - 1956
Orr, Robert D. (IN) - 1980, 1984
O'Shea, Bernard G. (VT) - 1978
Ostlund, John C. (WY) - 1978
Otter, C. L. (ID) - 1978
Owen, Dave (KS) - 1982
Owens, Wayne (UT) - 1984

P

Palmer, Linwood E. (ME) - 1978
Parker, Barry T. (NJ) - 1981
Parris, George N. (MI) - 1970
Parsekian, Ned J. (NJ) - 1969
Pascal, Robert A. (MD) - 1982
Paschen, Herbert C. (IL) - 1956
Patric, John (WA) - 1960
Patterson, L. Brooks (MI) - 1982
Pavlock, Joseph L. (MD) - 1962
Peabody, Endicott (MA) - 1960, 1962, 1964
Pearl, Art (OR) - 1970
Pearson, Walter J. (OR) - 1962
Peck, Roy (WY) - 1974
Pedersen, Richard (MN) - 1978
Percy, Charles H. (IL) - 1964
Perpich, Rudy (MN) - 1978, 1982
Peterson, Donald O. (WI) - 1970
Peterson, John C. (MN) - 1960
Peterson, Russell W. (DE) - 1972
Peterson, Val (NE) - 1966
Peterson, Walter R. (NH) - 1968, 1970, 1972
Phares, Robert A. (NE) - 1978
Phelps, William (MO) - 1980
Phillips, Joseph A. (MD) - 1958
Pickett, Ingram B. (NM) - 1956, 1958
Pickrell, Robert W. (AZ) - 1966
Pierce, Edward C. (MI) - 1982
Pierce, Richard H. (ME) - 1982
Pierpont, Ross Z. (MD) - 1982
Pillsbury, John (NH) - 1962, 1964
Plawecki, David A. (MI) - 1982
Plock, Richard (CO) - 1978
Plummer, Lawrence E. (IA) - 1956
Pollock, Howard W. (AK) - 1962, 1970
Pore, Frank (NH) - 1978
Porter, Albert S. (OH) - 1958
Porteus, Hebden (HI) - 1970
Powell, Wesley (NH) - 1956, 1958, 1960, 1962, 1964, 1968, 1978
Price, BraDa Ji (HI) - 1982
Proxmire, William (WI) - 1956

Q

Quie, Albert H. (MN) - 1978
Quillen, William T. (DE) - 1984
Quinn, Robert (MA) - 1974
Quinn, William F. (HI) - 1959, 1962

Senate
Candidates Index

The Senate Candidates Index includes all candidates appearing in Senate Popular Vote Returns, 1913-1984 (pp. 609-637).

The index includes candidates' names followed by state abbreviations and the years of candidacy. To locate a candidate's returns, turn to pages 609-637 where the re-turns are arranged alphabetically by state *(State Abbreviations below)* and in chronological order of election for each state. For other references to Senate candidates in the *Guide to U.S. Elections, Second Edition,* see the Southern Senate Primary Candidates Index, page 1178, and the General Index, page 1275.

A

Aandahl, Fred G. (ND) - 1952
Abel, Hazel H. (NE) - 1954
Abdnor, James (SD) - 1980
Abourezk, James (SD) - 1972
Adams, Alva B. (CO) - 1924, 1932, 1938
Adams, Wilbur L. (DE) - 1934
Aiken, George D. (VT) - 1940, 1944, 1950, 1956, 1962, 1968
Aiken, Paul (KS) - 1950
Akins, Thomas J. (MO) - 1914
Alexander, Archibald S. (NJ) - 1948, 1952
Alexander, John G. (MN) - 1936
Alexander, Morton (CO) - 1924
Alexander, W. H. Bill (OK) - 1950
Allen, Henry J. (KS) - 1930
Allen, Jim (AL) - 1968, 1974
Allott, Gordon (CO) - 1954, 1960, 1966, 1972
Anaya, Toney (NM) - 1978
Anderson, Clinton P. (NM) - 1948, 1954, 1960, 1966
Anderson, Wendell R. (MN) - 1978
Andrews, Charles O. (FL) - 1936, 1940
Andrews, Lloyd J. (WA) - 1964
Andrews, Mark (ND) - 1980
Archambault, Raoul (RI) - 1960
Armstrong, William L. (CO) - 1978, 1984
Arndt, Raymond W. (NE) - 1964
Arnold, James W. (GA) - 1932
Ashe, Victor (TN) - 1984
Ashurst, Henry F. (AZ) - 1916, 1922, 1928, 1934
Atcheson, Alex W. (TX) - 1916
Atchley, Forrest S. (NM) - 1958
Atkins, Hobart F. (TN) - 1952, 1958
Atkinson, C. D. (AR) - 1938
Austin, Warren R. (VT) - 1931, 1934, 1940
Aylward Paul L. (KS) - 1962
Ayres, Tom (SD) - 1920, 1924

B

Babbitt, Wayne H. (AR) - 1972

Babcock, Howard C. (FL) - 1936
Babcock, Tim (MT) - 1966
Bachman, Nathan L. (TN) - 1934, 1936
Bailey, Carl E. (AR) - 1937
Bailey, John W. (MI) - 1928
Bailey, Josiah W. (ND) - 1930, 1936, 1942
Baird, David (NJ) - 1918
Baker, Howard (TN) - 1940
Baker, Howard H. Jr. (TN) - 1964, 1966, 1972, 1978
Baker, Ray T. (NV) - 1926
Baker, Stuart D. (VA) - 1960
Baldwin, Raymond E. (CT) - 1946
Baldwin, Simeon (CT) - 1914
Ball, Joseph H. (MN) - 1942, 1948
Ball, Lewis Heisler (DE) - 1918
Bamberger, Ernest (UT) - 1922, 1928
Bancroft, Philip (CA) - 1938
Bankhead, John H. (AL) - 1918, 1930, 1936, 1942
Banks, L. A. (OR) - 1930
Bantz, William B. (WA) - 1958
Barbour, Haley (MS) - 1982
Barbour, W. Warren (NJ) - 1932, 1936, 1938, 1940
Bard, Guy Kurtz (PA) - 1952
Barkley, Alben W. (KY) - 1926, 1932, 1938, 1944, 1954
Barnett, Don (SD) - 1978
Barrett, Frank A. (WY) - 1952, 1958
Barry, Alex G. (OR) - 1938
Barth, Adam H. (WA) - 1914
Bartlett, Dewey F. (OK) - 1972
Bartlett, E. L. (AK) - 1958, 1960, 1966
Barton, Bruce (NY) - 1940
Bass, Perkins (NH) - 1962
Bass, Ross (TN) - 1964
Baucus, Max (MT) - 1978, 1984
Baxter, James H. (DE) - 1978
Bayard, A. I. du Pont (DE) - 1952
Bayard, Thomas F. (DE) - 1922, 1928, 1930
Bayh, Birch (IN) - 1962, 1968, 1974, 1980
Beall, J. Glenn (MD) - 1952, 1958, 1964
Beall, J. Glenn Jr. (MD) - 1970, 1976
Bean, Martha E. (OR) - 1918
Beard, Robin L. (TN) - 1976
Beckham, John C. W. (KY) - 1914, 1920

Beeckman, R. Livingston (RI) - 1922
Bell, Jeffrey (NJ) - 1978
Bellmon, Henry (OK) - 1968, 1974
Bender, George H. (OH) - 1954, 1956
Benedict, Cleveland K. (WV) - 1982
Benedict, Cooper P. (WV) - 1964
Bennett, Wallace F. (UT) - 1950, 1956, 1962, 1968
Bennion, Adams S. (UT) - 1944
Benson, Elmer A. (MN) - 1940, 1942
Bentley, Alvin M. (MI) - 1960
Benton, William (CT) - 1950, 1952
Bentsen, Lloyd (TX) - 1970, 1976, 1982
Berger, Victor L. (WI) - 1918
Berkstresser, H. E. (AL) - 1936
Berl, E. Ennalls (DE) - 1942
Berman, Dan (UT) - 1980
Bernard, Charles (AR) - 1968
Berry, Tom (SD) - 1938, 1942
Bethune, Ed (AR) - 1984
Betley, Joseph J. (NH) - 1944
Betley, Stanley J. (NH) - 1954
Bettman, Gilbert (OH) - 1932
Betts, James E. (OH) - 1980
Beveridge, Albert J. (IN) - 1914, 1922
Bible, Alan (NV) - 1954, 1956, 1962, 1968
Biden, Joseph R. Jr. (DE) - 1972, 1978, 1984
Bigelow, James E. (VT) - 1950
Bilbo, Theodore G. (MS) - 1934, 1940, 1946
Bingaman, Jeff (NM) - 1982
Bingham, Hiram (CT) - 1924, 1926, 1932
Birch, Alex C. (AL) - 1914
Bishop, Neil S. (ME) - 1970
Bjornson, Val (MN) - 1954
Black, Hugo L. (AL) - 1926, 1932
Black, John G. (AR) - 1978
Black, W. W. (WA) - 1914
Blaine, John J. (WI) - 926
Blakley, William A. (TX) - 1961
Blanton, Ray (TN) - 1972
Blatt, Genevieve (PA) - 1964
Blease, Cole L. (SC) - 1924
Blewett, Alex (MT) - 1964
Blount, Winton M. (Red) (AL) - 1972
Boggs, J. Caleb (DE) - 1960, 1966, 1972
Bone, Homer T. (WA) - 1932, 1938

Bontrager, D. Russell (IN) - 1964
Boole, Ella A. (NY) - 1920
Booth, John P. (FL) - 1950
Booth, R. A. (OR) - 1914
Borah, William E. (ID) - 1918, 1924, 1930, 1936
Boren, David L. (OK) - 1978, 1984
Borough, Reuben W. (CA) - 1952
Boschwitz, Rudy (MN) - 1978, 1984
Bottolfsen, C. A. (ID) - 1944
Bottum, Joe (SD) - 1962
Bourne, Jonathan Jr. (OR) - 1912
Bourquin, George M. (MT) - 1934
Bradford, W. S. (AZ) - 1916
Bradley, Bill (NJ) - 1978, 1984
Bradshaw, George M. (SD) - 1944
Bradshaw, Jean Paul (MO) - 1964
Brady, James H. (ID) - 1914
Brandegee, Frank B. (CT) - 1914, 1920
Brann, Louis J. (ME) - 1936, 1940
Brannen, James H. (CT) - 1974
Bratton, Sam G. (NM) - 1924, 1930
Breeding, J. Floyd (KS) - 1966
Brekke, Gerald W. (MN) - 1976
Brennan, George E. (IL) - 1926
Brewster, Daniel B. (MD) - 1962, 1968
Brewster, R. R. (MO) - 1922
Brewster, Ralph O. (ME) - 1940, 1946
Bricker, John W. (OH) - 1946, 1952, 1958
Bridges, Styles (NH) - 1936, 1942, 1948, 1954, 1960
Briggs, Frank (MO) - 1946
Briggs, Ruth M. (RI) - 1966
Briley, John Marshall (OH) - 1962
Brock, Bill (TN) - 1970, 1976
Brock, William E. (TN) - 1930
Brockett, Bruce (AZ) - 1950
Brooke, Edward W. (MA) - 1966, 1972, 1978
Brookhart, Smith W. (IA) - 1922, 1924, 1926
Brooks, C. Wayland (IL) - 1940, 1942, 1948
Broughton, J. Melville (NC) - 1948
Broussard, Edwin S. (LA) - 1920, 1926
Broussard, Robert F. (LA) - 1914
Brown, Clarence H. (HI) - 1982
Brown, Cooper (HI) - 1980
Brown, Edgar A. (SC) - 1954

State Abbreviations

Alabama	AL	Illinois	IL	Montana	MT	Rhode Island	RI
Alaska	AK	Indiana	IN	Nebraska	NE	South Carolina	SC
Arizona	AZ	Iowa	IA	Nevada	NV	South Dakota	SD
Arkansas	AR	Kansas	KS	New Hampshire	NH	Tennessee	TN
California	CA	Kentucky	KY	New Jersey	NJ	Texas	TX
Colorado	CO	Louisiana	LA	New Mexico	NM	Utah	UT
Connecticut	CT	Maine	ME	New York	NY	Vermont	VT
Delaware	DE	Maryland	MD	North Carolina	NC	Virginia	VA
Florida	FL	Massachusetts	MA	North Dakota	ND	Washington	WA
Georgia	GA	Michigan	MI	Ohio	OH	West Virginia	WV
Hawaii	HI	Minnesota	MN	Oklahoma	OK	Wisconsin	WI
Idaho	ID	Mississippi	MS	Oregon	OR	Wyoming	WY
		Missouri	MO	Pennsylvania	PA		

Brown, Edmund G. Jr. (CA) - 1982
Brown, Ernest S. (NV) - 1954
Brown, Fred H. (NH) - 1932, 1938
Brown, George Alfred (KS) - 1932
Brown, George M. (WA) - 1976
Brown, John Young (KY) - 1946, 1966
Brown, Prentiss M. (MI) - 1936, 1942
Brown, W. H. (ND) - 1914
Bruce, William Cabell (MD) - 1922, 1928
Brucker, Wilber M. (MI) - 1936
Bruner, Ben L. (KY) - 1918
Brunner, George E. (NJ) - 1946
Buchanan, Mary E. (CO) - 1980
Buck, Clayton Douglass (DE) - 1942, 1948
Buckley, James L. (CT) - 1980
Buckley, James L. (NY) - 1968, 1970, 1976
Bulkley, Robert J. (OH) - 1930, 1932, 1938
Bullitt (KY) - 1914
Bullitt, A. Scott (WA) - 1926
Bulow, William J. (SD) - 1930, 1936
Bumpers, Dale (AR) - 1974, 1980
Bunker, Berkeley L. (NV) - 1946
Burchard, F. F. (ND) - 1926, 1928
Burdick, Quentin N. (ND) - 1956, 1960, 1964, 1970, 1976, 1982
Burditt, Goerge M. (IL) - 1974
Burford (OK) - 1914
Burger, Stanley C. (MT) - 1976
Burke, Charles H. (SD) - 1914
Burke, Edward R. (NE) - 1934
Burke, John (ND) - 1916
Burke, Thomas A. (OH) - 1954
Burke, William J. (PA) - 1922
Burris, John M. (DE) - 1984
Bursum, Holm O. (NM) - 1921, 1924
Burtenshaw, Claude J. (ID) - 1950
Burton, Harold H. (OH) - 1940
Burton, Laurence J. (UT) - 1970
Burton, Theodore E. (OH) - 1928
Busch, Peter M. (ID) - 1984
Bush, George (TX) - 1964, 1970
Bush, Gwenyfred (SC) - 1974
Bush, Prescott C. (CT) - 1950, 1952, 1956
Bushfield, Harlan J. (SD) - 1942
Butler, Hugh (NE) - 1940, 1946, 1952
Butler, John Marshall (MD) - 1950, 1956
Butler, William M. (MA) - 1926, 1930
Byars, J. Cloyd (VA) - 1930
Byrd, Harry F. (VA) - 1933, 1934, 1940, 1946, 1952, 1958, 1964
Byrd, Harry F. Jr. (VA) - 1966, 1970, 1976
Byrd, Robert C. (WV) - 1958, 1964, 1970, 1976, 1982
Byrnes, James F. (SC) - 1930, 1936

C

Cain, Harry P. (WA) - 1944, 1946, 1952
Cake, H. M. (OR) - 1908
Calder, William M. (NY) - 1916, 1922
Calderwood, W. G. (MN) - 1916, 1918
Callahan, Donald A. (ID) - 1938
Callahan, John M. (WI) - 1934
Camden, Johnson N. Jr. (KY) - 1914
Cameron, Ralph H. (AZ) - 1920, 1926, 1928, 1932
Campbell, Alex M. (IN) - 1950
Cannon, Howard W. (NV) - 1958, 1964, 1970, 1976, 1982
Capehart, Homer E. (IN) - 1944, 1950, 1956, 1962
Capper, Arthur (KS) - 1918, 1924, 1930, 1936, 1942
Caraway, Hattie W. (AR) - 1932, 1938
Caraway, Thaddeus H. (AR) - 1920, 1926
Carey, Robert D. (WY) - 1930, 1936
Carlson, Frank (KS) - 1950, 1956, 1962
Carlson, William E. (MN) - 1952
Carmichael, Gil (MS) - 1972
Carpenter, Terry (NE) - 1936, 1948, 1972
Carr, Ralph L. (CO) - 1942
Carr, Waggoner (TX) - 1966
Carrington, Edward C. Jr. (MD) - 1914
Carroll, John A. (CO) - 1950, 1954, 1956, 1962
Carter, Anderson (NM) - 1966, 1970
Carter, John W. (VA) - 1966
Carter, Vincent (WY) - 1934
Carvel, Elbert N. (DE) - 1958, 1964
Case, Clifford P. (NJ) - 1954, 1960, 1966, 1972
Case, Francis (SD) - 1950, 1956

Casey, Joseph E. (MA) - 1942
Cashmore, John (NY) - 1952
Catalfo, Alfred Jr. (NY) - 1962
Catlin, Frank D. (CO) - 1912
Caulfield, Henry S. (MO) - 1938
Celeste, Vincent J. (MA) - 1958
Cermak, A. J. (IL) - 1928
Chadwick, Stephen F. (WA) - 1940
Chafee, John H. (RI) - 1972, 1976, 1982
Chafin, Eugene W. (AZ) - 1914
Chamberlain, George E. (OR) - 1908, 1914, 1920
Chandler, Albert B. (KY) - 1940, 1942
Chandler, Charles S. (NV) - 1922
Chapman, Virgil (KY) - 1948
Chapple, Bia (WI) - 1932, 1934
Chavez, Dennis (NM) - 1934, 1936, 1940, 1946, 1952, 1958
Cheadle, E. K. (MT) - 1940
Cheney, John M. (FL) - 1920
Cherry, U. S. G. (SD) - 1920, 1924, 1932
Chiles, Lawton (FL) - 1970, 1976, 1980
Chilton, William E. (WV) - 1916, 1924
Chimento, Carmen C. (NH) - 1975
Christensen, Richard G. (WA) - 1962
Christianson, Theodore (MN) - 1936
Church, Frank (ID) - 1956, 1962, 1968, 1974, 1980
Clagstone, Paul (ID) - 1914
Clark, A. E. (OR) - 1912
Clark, Bill (AR) - 1980
Clark, Chase (ID) - 1928
Clark, Clarence D. (WY) - 1916
Clark, D. Worth (ID) - 1938, 1950
Clark, Dick (IA) - 1972, 1978
Clark, Joel Bennett (MO) - 1932, 1938
Clark, Joseph S. (PA) - 1956, 1962, 1968
Clark, Ramsey (NY) - 1974
Clark, William G. (IL) - 1968
Clarke, Clem S. (LA) - 1948
Clarke, James P. (AR) - 1914
Clarke, Richard C. Jr. (NC) - 1958
Clausen, Fred H. (WI) - 1940
Clement, Frank G. (TN) - 1966
Clements, Earle C. (KY) - 1950, 1956
Clingan, B. H. (AZ) - 1938
Cluett, E. Harold (NY) - 1934
Coats, Andrew (OK) - 1980
Cochran, R. L. (NE) - 1940
Cochran, Thad (MS) - 1978, 1984
Cohen, James M. (ME) - 1978, 1984
Colbert, Richard J. (KY) - 1942
Cole, Charles F. (AR) - 1920, 1924
Collins, James M. (TX) - 1982
Collins, Leroy (FL) - 1968
Collins, Ross (MS) - 1941
Colmer, W. M. (MS) - 1947
Colt, Lebaron B. (RI) - 1918
Colton, Don B. (UT) - 1934
Colvin, Ewing D. (WA) - 1938
Colwes, William (NM) - 1960
Comings, Herbert B. (VT) - 1940
Connally, Tom (TX) - 1928, 1934, 1940, 1946
Connolly (IA) - 1914
Conrad, Robert B. (NE) - 1960
Conroy, Edward T. (MD) - 1980
Cook, Marlow W. (KY) - 1968, 1974
Cook, Vernon (OR) - 1978
Cooke, Jay (PA) - 1940
Cooley, Mortimer E. (MI) - 1924
Coolidge, Marcus A. (MA) - 1930
Cooper, C. W. (ID) - 1914
Cooper, John Sherman (KY) - 1946, 1948, 1952, 1954, 1956, 1960, 1966
Copeland, Royal S. (NY) - 1922, 1928, 1934
Corcoran, John H. (MA) - 1944
Cordon, Guy (OR) - 1944, 1948, 1954
Cormier, Lucia M. (ME) - 1960
Cornell, Paul L. (CT) - 1940
Corsi, Edward F. (NY) - 1938
Costigan, Edward P. (CO) - 1930
Cotterill, George F. (WA) - 1920
Cotton, Norris (NH) - 1954, 1956, 1962, 1968
Couch, Jerome B. (AL) - 1978
Coulter, F. E. (OR) - 1924
Counts, George S. (NY) - 1952
Couzens, James (MI) - 1924, 1930
Cozzens, Chuck (MT) - 1984
Cramer, Bill (FL) - 1970
Cranston, Alan (CA) - 1968, 1974, 1980
Crawford, B. Hayden (OK) - 1960, 1962

Crawford, L. P. (SC) - 1956
Creel, Cecil W. (NV) - 1942
Cristman, F. W. (NY) - 1926
Crommelin, John G. Jr. (AL) - 1950
Cromwell, James. H. R. (NJ) - 1940
Cross, Wilbur L. (CT) - 1946
Crozier, Will E. (OK) - 1984
Culberson, Charles A. (TX) - 1916
Culver, John C. (IA) - 1974, 1980
Cummings, Homer (CT) - 1916
Cummins, Albert B. (IA) - 1914, 1920
Cunningham, George V. (SD) - 1984
Curley, James M. (MA) - 1936
Curran, Thomas J. (NY) - 1944
Curtis, Carl T. (NE) - 1954, 1960, 1966, 1972
Curtis, Charles (KS) - 1914, 1920, 1926
Curtis, O. C. (ME) - 1922
Curtis, Thomas B. (MO) - 1968, 1974
Cutting, Bronson M. (NM) - 1928, 1934

D

Dale, Porter H. (VT) - 1923, 1926, 1932
D'Alesandro, Thomas Jr. (MD) - 1958
D'Amato, Alphonse M. (NY) - 1980
D'Amours, Norman E. (NH) - 1984
Danaher, John A. (CT) - 1938, 1944
Danforth, John C. (MO) - 1970, 1976, 1982
Daniel, Price (TX) - 1952
Daniels, Jack (NM) - 1972
Dantin, Maurice (MS) - 1978
Davies, John (WI) - 1918
Davis, Bert (AZ) - 1914
Davis, James J. (PA) - 1930, 1932, 1938, 1944
Davis, John E. (ND) - 1960
Davis, Jonathan M. (KS) - 1930
Davis, Manvel H. (MO) - 1940
Davis, Richard (VA) - 1982
Davis, S. B. Jr. (NM) - 1922
Davis, Tom J. (MT) - 1948
Davis, William E. (Bud) (ID) - 1972
Dawson, Charles I. (KY) - 1950
Dawson, Clyde C. (CO) - 1912
Dayton, Mark (MN) - 1982
DeConcini, Dennis (AZ) - 1976, 1982
Deneen, Charles S. (IL) - 1924
Denton, Jeremiah (AL) - 1980
Devold, Andrew Olaf (MN) - 1936
D'Ewart, Wesley A. (MT) - 1954
Dial, Nathaniel B. (SC) - 1918
Dick, Nancy (CO) - 1984
Dickerson (OK) - 1912
Dickey (MS) - 1916
Dickinson, Lester J. (IA) - 1930, 1936, 1938
Dies, Martin (TX) - 1941, 1957
Dieterich, William H. (IL) - 1932
Dill, Clarence C. (WA) - 1922, 1928
Dillingham, Ben (HI) - 1962
Dillingham, William P. (VT) - 1914, 1920
Dillon, Richard C. (NM) - 1934
Dirksen, Everett McKinley (IL) - 1950, 1956, 1962,1968
DiSalle, Michael V. (OH) - 1952
Dithmar, Edward F. (WI) - 1925
Divine, Paul E. (TN) - 1930
Dixon, Alan J. (IL) - 1980
Dixon, Joseph M. (MT) - 1912, 1928
Dodd, Christopher J. (CT) - 1980
Dodd, Thomas J. (CT) - 1956, 1958, 1964, 1970
Dodson, Elmer H. (WV) - 1970
Doggett, Lloyd (TX) - 1984
Dole, Robert (KS) - 1968, 1974, 1980
Domenici, Pete V. (NM) - 1972, 1978, 1984
Dominick, Peter H. (CO) - 1962, 1968, 1974
Donahey, Vic (OH) - 1934
Donart, George E. (ID) - 1946
Donnell, Forrest C. (MO) - 1944, 1950
Donnelly, Frederick W. (NJ) - 1924
Donovan, James B. (NY) - 1962
Douglas, Helen Gahagan (CA) - 1950
Douglas, Herbert (MO) - 1956
Douglas, Paul H. (IL) - 1948, 1954, 1960, 1966
Downey, Sheridan (CA) - 1938, 1944
Doxey, Wall (MS) - 1941
Draper, Miles H. (FL) - 1944
Driscoll, Stephen M. (UT) - 1931
Droney, John J. (MA) - 1972

Dryer, E. H. (AL) - 1926
Dube, Roger P. (ME) - 1952
Dubord, F. H. (ME) - 1934
Duff, James H. (PA) - 1950, 1956
Duffey, Joseph D. (CT) - 1970
Duffy, F. Ryan (WI) - 1932, 1938
Dulles, John Foster (NY) - 1949
Duncan, James A. (WA) - 1922
Duncan, Robert B. (OR) - 1966
Dunn, Pete (AZ) - 1982
du Pont, Henry A. (DE) - 1916
du Pont, T. Coleman (DE) - 1922, 1924
Durenberger, Dave (MN) - 1978, 1982
Durkin, John A. (NH) - 1974, 1975, 1980
Dworshak, Henry C. (ID) - 1946, 1948, 1950, 1954, 1960
Dyer, W. Gurnee (RI) - 1946
Dyster, Fred (CA) - 1940

E

Eagleton, Thomas F. (MO) - 1968, 1974, 1980
Earle, George H. (PA) - 1938
East, John P. (NC) - 1980
Eastland, James O. (MS) - 1942, 1948, 1954, 1960, 1966, 1972
Eckerd, Jack (FL) - 1974
Ecton, Zales N. (MT) - 1946, 1952
Edge, Walter E. (NJ) - 1918, 1924
Edmondson, Ed (OK) - 1972, 1974
Edwards, Edward I. (NJ) - 1922, 1928
Edwards, Harvey S. (GA) - 1920
Edwards, James S. (CA) - 1920
Egan, George W. (SD) - 1924
Ekern, Herman L. (WI) - 1938
Elgin, Julian (AL) - 1960
Elicker, Charles W. (WA) - 1970
Elkins, Davis (WV) - 1918
Ellender, Allen J. (LA) - 1936, 1942, 1948, 1954, 1960, 1966
Elliott, John B. (CA) - 1926
Elsner, Richard (WI) - 1916
Elson, Roy (AZ) - 1964, 1968
Ely, William H. J. (NJ) - 1938
Emery, David F. (ME) - 1982
Engel, John A. (SD) - 1948, 1950
Engle, Clair (CA) - 1958
Erickson, John E. (WI) - 1970
Erickson, Leif (MT) - 1946
Ernst, Richard P. (KY) - 1920, 1926
Ervin, Sam J. Jr. (NC) - 1954, 1956, 1962, 1968
Esch, Marvin L. (MI) - 1976
Eskind, Jane (TN) - 1978
Evans, Daniel J. (WA) - 1983
Evans, H. Clay (TN) - 1918
Evans, R. M. (IA) - 1956
Everly, Ernest W. (NM) - 1936
Evers, Charles (MS) - 1978
Ewing, Bayard (RI) - 1952, 1958
Exon, J. James (NE) - 1978, 1984

F

Fairchild, Thomas E. (WI) - 1950, 1952
Fall, Albert B. (NM) - 1918
Fannin, Paul (AZ) - 1964, 1970
Farnsworth, Philo T. Jr. (UT) - 1940
Farrand, George E. (NH) - 1924
Farrell, John A. (PA) - 1920
Farrell, John J. (MN) - 1924
Fasi, Frank F. (HI) - 1959
Fayette, Frederick J. (VT) - 1958, 1964
Fenwick, Millicent (NJ) - 1982
Ferguson, Homer (MI) - 1942, 1948, 1954
Ferguson, Joseph T. (OH) - 1950
Fernald, Bert M. (ME) - 1916, 1918, 1924
Ferree, A. I. (NC) - 1944
Ferris, Scott (OK) - 1920
Ferris, Woodbridge N. (MI) - 1922
Fess, Simeon D. (OH) - 1922, 1928, 1934
Fickett, Fred W. (AZ) - 1944
Field, Henry (IA) - 1932
Fike, Ed (NV) - 1968
Finnegan, James E. (WI) - 1940
Fithian, Floyd (IN) - 1982
Fitzgerald, Frank (MI) - 1940
Fitzgerald, John F. (MA) - 1916
Fitzgerald, John I. (MA) - 1948

Senate Primary Candidates Index

The Senate Primary Candidates Index includes all candidates appearing in Senate Elections: Primary Vote Returns, 1956-1984 (pp. 638-672).

The index includes candidates' names followed by state abbreviations and the years of candidacy. To locate a candidate's returns, turn to pages 638-672 where the returns are arranged alphabetically by state (State Abbreviations below) and in chronological order of election for each state. For other references to Senate candidates in the *Guide to U.S. Elections, Second Edition,* see the Southern Senate Primary Candidates Index, page 1178, and the General Index, page 1275.

A

Abdnor, James (SD) - 1980
Abercrombie, Neil (HI) - 1970
Abourezk, James (SD) - 1972
Abzug, Bella (NY) - 1976
Adams, Thomas B. (MA) - 1966
Aiken, George D. (VT) - 1956, 1962, 1968
Airy, Frederic W. (NJ) - 1960
Albough, William A. (MD) - 1964, 1982
Albright, Ernest G. (OK) - 1956
Alderson, Fleming N. (WV) - 1958
Alexander, Lee (NY) - 1974
Alioto, Kathleen Sullivan (MA) - 1978
Allott, Gordon (CO) - 1960, 1966, 1972
Altvater, George (OR) - 1960
Anaya, Toney (NM) - 1972
Anderson, Anson (ND) - 1958
Anderson, Ava A. (KS) - 1966
Anderson, Blanche (MT) - 1958
Anderson, Clinton P. (NM) - 1960, 1966
Anderson, Fred (NV) - 1958
Anderson, Le Roy (MT) - 1960
Anderson, Mark E. (UT) - 1968
Anderson, Steve (OR) - 1978
Anderson, Tom (PA) - 1980
Anderson, Wendell R. (MN) - 1978
Andrews, Jackson M. (KY) - 1980
Andrews, Lloyd J. (WA) - 1964
Andrews, Mark (ND) - 1980
Angell, Wayne (KS) - 1978
Apodaca, Jerry (NM) - 1982
Aragona, Xavier A. (MD) - 1974
Archambault, Raoul (RI) - 1960
Armstrong, Hepburn T. (WY) - 1958
Armstrong, William L. (CO) - 1978, 1984
Arn, Edward F. (KS) - 1962
Arndt, Raymond W. (NE) - 1964, 1966
Arnold, Burleigh (MO) - 1982
Arvidson, Gene (OR) - 1980
Atchley, Forrest S. (NM) - 1958
Austin, Richard H. (MI) - 1976
Auvil, Ken (WV) - 1984
Avery, William (KS) - 1968
Aylward, Paul (KS) - 1956, 1962

B

Babb, Leslie R. (NH) - 1974
Babcock, Tim M. (MT) - 1966
Bacaloff, James (OR) - 1966
Baker, Albert J. (NE) - 1960
Baker, Deane (MI) - 1976, 1982
Baker, Gerald (IA) - 1978
Ball, Albert T. (OH) - 1962
Ballard, John S. (OH) - 1962
Ballenger, William S. (MI) - 1982
Bangerter, Bruce (UT) - 1974
Bantz, William B. (WA) - 1958
Barnes, John (KS) - 1980
Barnett, Don (SD) - 1978
Baron, Murray (NY) - 1968
Barrett, Frank A. (WY) - 1958, 1960
Barrows, Gordon H. (WY) - 1978
Bartlett, Dewey F. (OK) - 1972
Bartlett, E. L. (AK) - 1958, 1960, 1966
Bartlett, Roscoe G. (MD) - 1980
Bartley, David M. (MA) - 1984
Bass, Doris M. (MO) - 1970
Bass, Perkins (NH) - 1962
Batchelor, George M. (UT) - 1980
Bates, Joe B. (KY) - 1956
Baucom, John D. (MN) - 1970
Baucus, Max (MT) - 1978, 1984
Baxter, James H. (DE) - 1978
Bayh, Birch (IN) - 1980
Beall, Forest W. (OK) - 1964
Beall, J. Glenn (MD) - 1958, 1964, 1970, 1976
Beaseley, Michael (AK) - 1984
Beck, Paul V. (MN) - 1970
Beckjord, Walter E. (OH) - 1982
Beilenson, Anthony C. (CA) - 1968
Bell, Alphonzo E. (CA) - 1976
Bell, Dale (SD) - 1980
Bell, Jeffrey J. (NJ) - 1978, 1982
Bellmon, Henry (OK) - 1968, 1974
Bender, George H. (OH) - 1956
Benedict, Cleveland K. (WV) - 1982
Benedict, Cooper P. (WV) - 1964
Bennett, Wallace F. (UT) - 1956, 1962, 1968
Bennett, William M. (CA) - 1968
Bentley, Alvin M. (MI) - 1960
Bergeson, Rollo (IA) - 1960
Bergland, David (CA) - 1980
Beringer, Raymond Warren (OH) - 1962
Berman, Dan (UT) - 1980
Bernier-Nachtwey, E. F. (HI) - 1980, 1982
Bertroche, Joe (IA) - 1978
Betts, James E. (OH) - 1968
Bible, Alan (NV) - 1956, 1962, 1968
Bichsel, T. J. (AK) - 1966
Biddle, Walter I. (KS) - 1956
Biden, Joseph R. (DE) - 1984
Bingaman, Jeff (NM) - 1982
Binford, Hugh (WY) - 1978
Bishop, Neil S. (ME) - 1970
Blatt, Genevieve (PA) - 1964
Blauvelt, Ronald I. (NJ) - 1972
Blewett, Alex (MT) - 1964
Blue, George (SD) - 1972
Boe, Jason (OR) - 1974
Bolstridge, Charles (ID) - 1974
Bond, Michael A. (MT) - 1982
Bonner, John W. (MT) - 1960
Booras, Peter J. (NH) - 1972
Boren, David L. (OK) - 1978, 1984
Boschwitz, Rudy (MN) - 1978, 1984
Bouma, Ralph (MT) - 1984
Bove, Fiore L. (VT) - 1970
Bowers, Clarence P. (PA) - 1958
Bowman, Rose (ID) - 1972
Boyd, John S. (OR) - 1968
Bradley, Bill (NJ) - 1978, 1984
Bradley, David H. (NH) - 1980
Bradshaw, Jean P. (MO) - 1964
Brady, Lawrence J. (NH) - 1980
Brandborg, Gustav K. (OK) - 1966
Brannan, Charles (CO) - 1956
Brayton, Lawrence M. (AK) - 1960, 1966
Brazin, Harvey E. (KY) - 1974
Breeding, J. Floyd (KS) - 1966
Brekke, Gerald W. (MN) - 1976
Brennan, John M. (MD) - 1980
Brennan, Thomas E. (MI) - 1976
Brewer, Paul T. (WI) - 1982
Brewster, Daniel B. (MD) - 1962, 1968

Brewster, Lyman (MT) - 1964
Brian, Earl W. (CA) - 1974
Bricker, John W. (OH) - 1958
Bridges, Doloris (NH) - 1962, 1966
Bridges, Styles (NH) - 1960
Briggs, Ruth M. (RI) - 1966
Briley, John M. (OH) - 1962
Brock, David A. (NH) - 1972
Bromwell, James E. (IA) - 1968
Brooke, Edward W. (MA) - 1966, 1972, 1978
Brooks, Ralph G. (NE) - 1960
Broschart, Frank J. (MD) - 1980
Brown, Billy E. (OK) - 1962, 1966, 1968
Brown, Clarence J. (HI) - 1982
Brown, Cooper (HI) - 1980
Brown, Edmund G. Jr. (CA) - 1982
Brown, George E. (CA) - 1970
Brown, George M. (WA) - 1976
Brown, Jack A. (OR) - 1978
Brown, John Young (KY) - 1966, 1968
Brown, Kenneth A. (OR) - 1972, 1980
Brown, Mahlon (NV) - 1956
Brown, Ted W. (OH) - 1964
Bruce, James (MD) - 1958
Brunt, A. W. (ID) - 1960
Bryant, Alice F. (WA) - 1958, 1964
Buchanan, Mary E. (CO) - 1980
Buchanan, Walter R. (CA) - 1968
Buckley, Edmund C. (MA) - 1960
Buckley, James L. (CT) - 1980
Buckley, James L. (NY) - 1968, 1970, 1976
Buckley, T. Garry (VT) - 1980
Bullock, Dick (MN) - 1976
Burdick, Quentin N. (ND) - 1956, 1964, 1970, 1976, 1982
Burditt, George M. (IL) - 1974
Burger, Stanley C. (MT) - 1976
Burris, John M. (DE) - 1984
Burris, Roland W. (IL) - 1984
Burtenshaw, Claude (ID) - 1956
Burton, Laurence J. (UT) - 1970
Busch, Peter M. (ID) - 1984
Bussey, Woodrow W. (OK) - 1962
Butler, John Marshall (MD) - 1956
Buzzuto, Richard C. (CT) - 1980
Byrd, Elbert (MD) - 1962

State Abbreviations

Alabama	AL	Illinois	IL	Montana	MT
Alaska	AK	Indiana	IN	Nebraska	NE
Arizona	AZ	Iowa	IA	Nevada	NV
Arkansas	AR	Kansas	KS	New Hampshire	NH
California	CA	Kentucky	KY	New Jersey	NJ
Colorado	CO	Louisiana	LA	New Mexico	NM
Connecticut	CT	Maine	ME	New York	NY
Delaware	DE	Maryland	MD	North Carolina	NC
Florida	FL	Massachusetts	MA	North Dakota	ND
Georgia	GA	Michigan	MI	Ohio	OH
Hawaii	HI	Minnesota	MN	Oklahoma	OK
Idaho	ID	Mississippi	MS	Oregon	OR
		Missouri	MO	Pennsylvania	PA

Rhode Island	RI
South Carolina	SC
South Dakota	SD
Tennessee	TN
Texas	TX
Utah	UT
Vermont	VT
Virginia	VA
Washington	WA
West Virginia	WV
Wisconsin	WI
Wyoming	WY

V

Van Nostrand, Maurie (IA) - 1978
Van Taay, William E. (MO) - 1956
Van Zandt, James E. (PA) - 1962
Vance, Marion (KY) - 1962
Vander Veen, Richard F. (MI) - 1978
Vaught, DeSota (KY) - 1980
Veach, R. L. (AK) - 1962
Vendsel, Raymond (ND) - 1958
Venema, James E. (DE) - 1978
Vickers, Arnold M. (WV) - 1958
Vidal, Gore (CA) - 1982
Vinich, Mike (WY) - 1972
Violette, Elmer H. (ME) - 1966
Vollack, Anthony (CO) - 1972
Vorachek, Roger (ND) - 1962
Voss, Peter E. (OH) - 1974

W

Wald, David (CA) - 1976, 1980, 1982
Walker, E. S. (NM) - 1958
Wallace, Harold E. (MT) - 1970, 1972
Wallace, James E. (KY) - 1972
Wallace, Robert A. (IL) - 1980
Wallace, Wilson (OK) - 1962

Wallop, Malcolm (WY) - 1976, 1982
Walstead, Elliot N. (WI) - 1956
Warner, Carolyn (AZ) - 1976
Warner, Leigh (KS) - 1966
Washburn, James A. (WV) - 1982
Washington, George (OK) - 1968
Waterman, Frances A. (OH) - 1980
Watkins, Arthur V. (UT) - 1958
Watson, Andrew J. (PA) - 1976
Watson, Jack A. (KY) - 1978
Wattay, Paul F. (MD) - 1968
Wecht, Cyril H. (PA) - 1982
Wegner, Glen (ID) - 1972
Weicker, Lowell P. (CT) - 1970
Weiland, Frederick A. (WV) - 1982
Weilenmann, Milton (UT) - 1968
Weisman, Lawrence I. (HI) - 1980
Welch, John J. (VT) - 1976
Welch, Lou W. (MT) - 1958
Welker, Herman (ID) - 1956
Wendelken, Martin E. (NJ) - 1976
Westlake, Ralph O. (WA) - 1968
Whaley, Maxine B. (AK) - 1966
Wheeler, Norman C. (MT) - 1972
Whitaker, Raymond B. (WY) - 1960, 1978
Whitcomb, Edgar D. (IN) - 1976
White, Compton (ID) - 1960
White, Dorothy K. (KS) - 1978
White, William L. (OH) - 1968
Whitehurst, Daniel K. (CA) - 1982

Whitmore, Howard (MA) - 1964
Whitney, Wheelock (MN) - 1964
Wickstrom, James P. (WI) - 1980
Wilcox, Lumund (IA) - 1956
Wilentz, Warren W. (NJ) - 1966
Wiley, Alexander (WI) - 1956, 1962
Wilkinson, Bud (OK) - 1964
Wilkinson, Ernest L. (UT) - 1964
Williams, David J. (WA) - 1964
Williams, G. Mennen (MI) - 1966
Williams, Harrison A. Jr. (NJ) - 1958, 1964, 1970, 1976
Williams, James Malcolm (MN) - 1960
Williams, Larry (MT) - 1978, 1982
Williams, W. Dakin (IL) - 1972, 1974
Williamson, Ronald F. (SD) - 1978
Willner, Don (OR) - 1972
Wilson, Gaines P. (KY) - 1966
Wilson, Pete (CA) - 1982
Wilson, W. R. (WV) - 1958
Winberry, John J. (NJ) - 1966
Winder, Donald L. (ID) - 1974
Witwer, Samuel W. (IL) - 1960
Wold, James S. (WY) - 1964, 1970
Wollenburg, Arlyn F. (WI) - 1962, 1964
Wood, C. W. (OK) - 1972
Woodruff, Wilford Owen (NV) - 1970
Woods, Harriet (MO) - 1982
Wright, Donn H. (SD) - 1966
Wright, Lacy (WV) - 1984

Wright, Lloyd (CA) - 1962
Wright, Warren E. (IL) - 1960
Wright, William (NV) - 1962
Wyatt, Wilson W. (KY) - 1962
Wyman, Louis C. (NH) - 1974

Y

Yates, Sidney R. (IL) - 1962
York, Stanley (WI) - 1976
Yorty, Samuel W. (CA) - 1956, 1980
Yoshinaga, Nadao (HI) - 1964
Young, Clifton (NV) - 1956
Young, Kenneth E. (HI) - 1959
Young, Milton R. (ND) - 1956, 1962, 1968, 1974
Young, Stephen M. (OH) - 1958, 1964

Z

Zablocki, Clement J. (WI) - 1957
Zakhem, Sam (CO) - 1980
Ziebarth, Wayne W. (NE) - 1972
Zink, John (OK) - 1980
Zorinsky, Edward (NE) - 1976, 1982
Zych, Thomas E. (MO) - 1982

Southern Gubernatorial Primary Candidates Index

The Southern Gubernatorial Candidates Index includes all candidates appearing in Southern Gubernatorial Primary Returns, 1919-1984 (pp. 1075-1089).

The index includes candidates' names followed by state abbreviations and the years of candidacy. To locate a candidate's returns, turn to pages 1075-1089 where the returns are arranged alphabetically by state and in chronological order of election for each state. For State Abbreviations, see page 1180.

For other references to southern gubernatorial candidates in the *Guide to U.S. Elections, Second Edition,* see the General Index, page 1275.

Swan, Harry S. (FL) - 1952
Swan, James E. (Jimmy) (MS) - 1967, 1971
Swearingen, V. C. (FL) - 1920

T

Tackett (AR) - 1952
Talmadge, Eugene (GA) - 1932, 1934, 1940, 1942, 1946
Talmadge, Herman E. (GA) - 1948
Tanzler, Hans (FL) - 1978
Taylor (SC) - 1946
Taylor, Andrew T. (TN) - 1958
Taylor, H. P. (Pat) 1972
Taylor, John S. (FL) - 1928
Taylor, Robert L. (TN) - 1970
Temple, Buddy (TX) - 1982
Terral, Thomas J. (AR) - 1920, 1924, 1926, 1928, 1932, 1936
Terry, David L. (AR) - 1944
Thomas, Jerry (FL) - 1974
Thomasello, Peter Jr. (FL) - 1936
Thomason, Robert E. (TX) - 1920
Thompson, Ernest O. (TX) - 1938, 1940
Thompson, Horace (AR) - 1948

Thompson, M. E. (GA) - 1948, 1950, 1954
Thompson, Ronnie (GA) - 1974
Thurmond, J. Strom (SC) - 1946
Timmerman, George Bell Jr. (SC) - 1954
Todd, A. W. (AL) - 1958
Toney, E. P. (AR) - 1922
Trammell, Worth W. (FL) - 1924
Treen, David C. (LA) - 1971, 1979
Trice, John R. (TX) - 1968
Trinkle, Elbert Lee (VA) - 1921
Tuck, William M. (VA) - 1945
Tucker, Harry St. George (VA) - 1921
Tucker, Jim Guy (AR) - 1982
Turner, Lonnie (AR) - 1984
Tyree, Randy (TN) - 1982

U, V

Umstead, William B. (NC) - 1952
Underwood, Norman (GA) - 1982
Upchurch, F. D. (FL) - 1944
Vandiver, S. Ernest (GA) - 1958
Voll, Connie (AR) - 1982

W, Y

Waggoner, D. E. (TX) - 1934
Walker, Clifford M. (GA) - 1920, 1922, 1924
Walker, Edwin A. (TX) - 1962
Wallace, George C. (AL) - 1958, 1962, 1970, 1974, 1982
Wallace, Lurleen B. (AL) - 1966
Waller, William L. (MS) - 1967, 1971
Wardlaw, Louis J. (TX) - 1928
Ward, Lee (AR) - 1958
Warner, Harry T. (TX) - 1922
Warren, Fuller (FL) - 1940, 1948, 1956
Washburne, W. A. Jr. (FL) - 1956
Watson, J. Tom (FL) - 1948, 1954
Watson, Jack (GA) - 1982
Wells, Bill (AR) - 1970
West, John C. (SC) - 1970
Weston, Joseph H. (AR) - 1974, 1976
Westmoreland, William (SC) - 1974
Whitbeck, Frank (AR) - 1968
White, Frank D. (AR) - 1980, 1982
White, Hugh L. (MS) - 1931, 1935, 1951
White, Mark (TX) - 1982
Whitehair, Francis P. (FL) - 1940

Whitfield, Henry L. (MS) - 1923
Whitten, Vernon H. (AR) - 1962
Whittenburg, Roy (TX) - 1962
Williams (SC) - 1930, 1946
Williams, H. E. (AR) - 1960
Williams, Hamp (AR) - 1924
Williams, Jim (FL) - 1978
Williams, John Bell (MS) - 1967
Willson, Jacob R. (AR) - 1924
Wilson, Riley J. (LA) - 1928
Wilson, Will (TX) - 1962
Winston, Nat (TN) - 1974
Winter, William (MS) - 1967, 1975, 1979
Wiseman, Tom (TN) - 1974
Witt, Edgar E. (TX) - 1934
Wood, George (NC) - 1976
Wood, J. O. (GA) - 1926
Woods, Charles (AL) - 1970
Woods, Stanley C. (TX) - 1966
Woodward, Joe D. (AR) - 1978
Workman, W. D. (SC) - 1982
Wright, Fielding L. (MS) - 1947, 1955
Yarborough, Don (TX) - 1962, 1964, 1968
Yarborough, Ralph W. (TX) - 1952, 1954, 1956
Young, Edward L. (SC) - 1978
Young, James (TX) - 1930

Southern Senate Primary Candidates Index

The Southern Senate Primary Candidates Index includes all candidates appearing in Southern Senate Primary Returns, 1920-1984 (pp. 1090-1102).

The index includes candidates' names followed by state abbreviations and the years of candidacy. To locate a candidate's returns, turn to pages 1090-1102 where the returns are arranged alphabetically by state and in chronological order by class of senator for each state. *(Explanation of Senate classes, see p. 574; for State Abbreviations, see p. 1180.)* For other references to Southern Senate primary candidates in the *Guide to U.S. Elections, Second Edition*, see the General Index, page 1275.

House Candidates Index

The House Candidates Index includes all candidates appearing in House Popular Vote Returns, 1824-1985 (pp. 701-1062).

The index includes candidates' names followed by state abbreviations and the years of candidacy. To locate a candidate's returns, turn to pages 701-1062 where the returns are arranged chronologically by year and alphabetically by state for each year. State abbreviations appear below.

A

Aaker (MN) - 1900
Aandahl, Fred G. (ND) - 1950
Aaron, Samuel (NJ) - 1840
Aaron, Ward (NY) - 1824
Aarons, Morris (NY) - 1960
Abbett, Edwin L. (NY) - 1890
Abbey, Frank E. (IL) - 1914
Abbey, George W. (MI) - 1886
Abbey, James B. (CA) - 1942, 1944
Abbitt, Watkins M. (VA) - 1948, 1950, 1952, 1954, 1956, 1958, 1960, 1962, 1964, 1966, 1968, 1970
Abbot, William S. (MA) - 1968
Abbott (WI) - 1852
Abbott, Amos (MA) - 1842, 1844, 1846
Abbott, Burnett J. (MI) - 1928
Abbott, Israel B. (NC) - 1886
Abbott, Jo (TX) - 1886, 1888, 1890, 1892, 1894
Abbott, Josiah G. (MA) - 1862, 1864, 1874
Abbott, Nehemiah (ME) - 1856
Abdella, James (NY) - 1980
Abdnor, James (SD) - 1972, 1974, 1976, 1978
Abele, Homer E. (OH) - 1958, 1962, 1964
Abercrombie, C. H. (OR) - 1912
Abercrombie, James (AL) - 1851, 1853
Abercrombie, James F. (AL) - 1914
Abercrombie, John W. (AL) - 1912, 1914
Abernathy, Thomas G. (MS) - 1962
Abernethy, Charles L. (NC) - 1922, 1924, 1926, 1928, 1930, 1932
Abernethy, Thomas G. (MS) - 1942, 1944, 1946, 1948, 1950, 1952, 1954, 1956, 1958, 1960, 1964, 1966, 1968, 1970
Abernethy, Tom (AL) - 1962
Abourezk, James (SD) - 1970
Abrams, Milton C. (UT) - 1984
Abrams, Samuel (MA) - 1930
Abramson, Irving (NJ) - 1942
Abramson, R. S. (LA) - 1972
Abzug, Bella S. (NY) - 1970, 1972, 1974, 1978
Acee (MS) - 1837
Acer, Christopher T. (NY) - 1970, 1974
Acers, N. F. (KS) - 1882
Acheson, A. W. (TX) - 1898, 1920

Acheson, Ernest F. (PA) - 1892, 1894, 1896, 1898, 1900, 1902, 1904, 1906
Achison, A. W. (TX) - 1890
Acker, Bert L. (FL) - 1940, 1942
Acker, Ephraim L. (PA) - 1870, 1874
Ackerman, Edwin D. (NY) - 1908
Ackerman, Ernest R. (NJ) - 1918, 1920, 1922, 1924, 1926, 1928, 1930
Ackerman, Gary L. (NY) - 1983, 1984
Ackerman, J. Waldo Jr. (IL) - 1960
Ackerman, Johann S. (IL) - 1956
Ackerman, Luther H. (PA) - 1958
Ackerson, Nels J. (IN) - 1980
Ackerty, Merrick W. (IN) - 1892
Acklen, Joseph H. (LA) - 1876, 1878, 1882
Acklen, William (AL) - 1847
Ackley, Charles W. (NJ) - 1934
Acklin, George W. (PA) - 1998
Acklin, J. A. (LA) - 1884
Acuff, Judd (TN) - 1938
Adair, Charles R. (MI) - 1922, 1940
Adair, Clark W. (NE) - 1904
Adair, E. Ross (IN) - 1950, 1952, 1954, 1956, 1958, 1960, 1962, 1964, 1966, 1968, 1970
Adair, J. Carlton (NV) - 1962
Adair, J. Leroy (IL) - 1932, 1934
Adair, John (KY) - 1831
Adair, John A. M. (IN) - 1906, 1908, 1910, 1912, 1914, 1924
Adair, Verdell (MD) - 1972
Adamowski, Benjamin S. (IL) - 1942
Adams (GA) - 1916
Adams (MO) - 1858
Adams (NJ) - 1912
Adams (NY) - 1842, 1872
Adams (PA) - 1848, 1850
Adams (VT) - 1872
Adams, Alfred (TN) - 1972
Adams, Allen C. (OK) - 1916
Adams, Allison L. (NY) - 1918
Adams, Alva (CO) - 1902
Adams, Alva B. (CO) - 1954, 1956
Adams, Augustus (IL) - 1878
Adams, Billy (GA) - 1976
Adams, Brock (WA) - 1964, 1966, 1968, 1970, 1972, 1974, 1976
Adams, C. E. (NE) - 1898
Adams, C. P. (MN) - 1882
Adams, Charles D. (OH) - 1880

Adams, Charles F. (MA) - 1852, 1858, 1860
Adams, Charles H. (NY) - 1874
Adams, Clifford R. (MN) - 1970
Adams, Clyde (FL) - 1976
Adams, David (TN) - 1835
Adams, Dennis (NJ) - 1984
Adams, Dennis Sr. (NJ) - 1976
Adams, Edson (CA) - 1974
Adams, Francis A. (NY) - 1908
Adams, G. (KY) - 1845
Adams, George (OH) - 1892, 1900
Adams, George E. (IL) - 1882, 1884, 1886, 1888, 1890
Adams, George M. (KY) - 1867, 1868, 1870, 1872, 1882
Adams, Green (KY) - 1847, 1859
Adams, Henry C. (WI) - 1902, 1904
Adams, J. A. (WA) - 1900
Adams, J. M. (AL) - 1855
Adams, James A. (WI) - 1972
Adams, James F. (MO) - 1926
Adams, John (NH) - 1976
Adams, John (NY) 1832
Adams, John J. (NY) - 1882, 1884
Adams, John Q. (NY) - 1896
Adams, John Quincy (MA) - 1830, 1833, 1834, 1836, 1838, 1840, 1842, 1844, 1846
Adams, Joseph S. (NC) - 1896
Adams, L. S. (AZ) - 1954
Adams, Mike (TN) - 1980
Adams, Monroe (NC) - 1938, 1940
Adams, Norman W. (OH) - 1946
Adams, Parmenio (NY) - 1824
Adams, Paul L. (MI) - 1942
Adams, Percy D. (NY) - 1890
Adams, Robert Jr. (PA) - 1893, 1894, 1896, 1898, 1900, 1902, 1904
Adams, S. C. (VA) - 1890
Adams, Samuel (PA) - 1878
Adams, Seth (MA) - 1870
Adams, Sherman (NH) - 1944
Adams, Silas R. (KY) - 1892, 1894
Adams, Spencer B. (NC) - 1898
Adams, Stanley G. (VA) - 1948
Adams, Stephen (MS) - 1845
Adams, Thomas J. (NY) - 1968
Adams, W.P.C. (WA) - 1894
Adams, Wayne N. (WA) - 1968

Adams, Wilbur (DE) - 1932
Adams, William (PA) - 1908, 1916, 1922
Adamson, William C. (GA) - 1896, 1898, 1900, 1902, 1904, 1906, 1908, 1910, 1912, 1914, 1916
Adanti, Michael J. (CT) - 1976
Addabbo, Joseph P. (NY) - 1960, 1962, 1964, 1966, 1968, 1970, 1972, 1974, 1976, 1978, 1980, 1982, 1984
Addams, William (PA) - 1824, 1826, 1828
Addonizio, G. George (NJ) - 1956, 1958
Addonizio, Hugh J. (NJ) - 1948, 1950, 1952, 1954, 1956, 1958, 1960
Ade, William H. (IN) - 1914
Adelman, Daniel (NY) - 1932
Adelman Lynn S. (WI) - 1974
Adelman, William J. (IL) - 1970
Adkins, Charles (IL) - 1924, 1926, 1928, 1930, 1932
Adkins, James (GA) - 1868
Adkins, Stockton (TN) - 1972
Adkinson, Ray (CA) - 1946
Adler, Charles S. (NY) - 1902, 1906
Adler, John R. (CA) - 1980
Adler, Milton H. (NY) - 1956, 1958
Adney, Roy W. (IN) - 1926
Adrain, Garnett B. (NJ) - 1856, 1858
Afflis, Margaret A. (IN) - 1946
Africa, J. Murray (PA) - 1910
Agnew, Arnie W. (WI) - 1952
Agnew, Carroll J. (PA) - 1932
Agnew, Park (VA) - 1888
Ahearn, John (AZ) - 1964
Ahearn, Maurice F. (MA) - 1920
Ahern, D. Patrick (CA) - 1960
Ahl, John A. (PA) - 1856
Ahlgren, Oscar A. (IN) - 1932
Aigg (NJ) - 1838
Aiken, D. Wyatt (SC) - 1876, 1878, 1880, 1882, 1884
Aiken, Patricia O'Brien (MD) - 1982
Aiken, Robert K. (PA) - 1906
Aiken, William (SC) - 1850, 1853, 1854
Aiken, William A. (NY) - 1936
Aiken, Wyatt (SC) - 1902, 1904, 1906, 1908, 1910, 1912, 1914
Aikin (TN) - 1843
Ailman, Jerome T. (PA) - 1896
Aimee, Joseph M. (NY) - 1934, 1936
Ain, Stewart L. (NY) - 1978

State Abbreviations

Alabama	AL	Illinois	IL	Montana	MT	Rhode Island	RI
Alaska	AK	Indiana	IN	Nebraska	NE	South Carolina	SC
Arizona	AZ	Iowa	IA	Nevada	NV	South Dakota	SD
Arkansas	AR	Kansas	KS	New Hampshire	NH	Tennessee	TN
California	CA	Kentucky	KY	New Jersey	NJ	Texas	TX
Colorado	CO	Louisiana	LA	New Mexico	NM	Utah	UT
Connecticut	CT	Maine	ME	New York	NY	Vermont	VT
Delaware	DE	Maryland	MD	North Carolina	NC	Virginia	VA
Florida	FL	Massachusetts	MA	North Dakota	ND	Washington	WA
Georgia	GA	Michigan	MI	Ohio	OH	West Virginia	WV
Hawaii	HI	Minnesota	MN	Oklahoma	OK	Wisconsin	WI
Idaho	ID	Mississippi	MS	Oregon	OR	Wyoming	WY
		Missouri	MO	Pennsylvania	PA		

Bradley, David O. (NY) - 1868
Bradley, Edward (MI) - 1846
Bradley, Fred (MI) - 1938, 1940, 1942, 1944, 1946
Bradley, George (MI) - 1852
Bradley, Gerald A. (IL) - 1984
Bradley, J. M. (AR) - 1872
Bradley, James O. (OH) - 1958
Bradley, John F. (PA) - 1976
Bradley, Michael J. (PA) - 1934, 1936, 1938, 1940, 1942, 1944
Bradley, Nathan B. (MI) - 1872, 1874
Bradley, Paul (CO) - 1968
Bradley, Richard (NH) - 1837
Bradley, Thomas J. (NY) - 1896, 1898
Bradley, Thomas W. (NY) - 1902, 1904, 1906, 1908, 1910
Bradley, Vernon E. (MA) - 1954
Bradley, W. O. (KY) - 1872, 1876
Bradley, W. S. (IL) - 1926
Bradley, William C. (VT) - 1824
Bradley, Willis W. (CA) - 1946, 1948, 1952
Bradshaw, Charles (SC) - 1968
Bradshaw, James (MS) - 1982
Bradshaw, Jim (TX) - 1980, 1982
Bradshaw, Samuel C. (PA) - 1854, 1856
Bradstreet (CT) - 1912
Bradt, Mary A. (NY) - 1976
Brady, Chuck (CO) - 1972
Brady, David (CT) - 1954
Brady, Francis M. (KS) - 1904, 1906, 1912
Brady, Fred D. (SD) - 1970
Brady, Hugh E. (OR) - 1932
Brady, J. L. (KS) - 1912, 1914
Brady, J. T. (TX) - 1880
Brady, James D. (VA) - 1884
Brady, Jasper E. (PA) - 1846, 1848
Brady, Jim (TX) - 1972, 1974
Brady, John E. (NY) - 1912
Brady, Philip E. (MA) - 1898
Brady, S. (MD) - 1843
Brady, Thomas J. (MN) - 1920
Brady, William (NY) - 1833
Bragg (WI) - 1862
Bragg, Edward S. (WI) - 1876, 1878, 1880, 1884
Bragg, John (AL) - 1851
Bragg, Merl J. (OH) - 1946
Brainard, F. W. (CO) - 1912
Brainard, Robert L. (ID) - 1944
Brainerd, Clarence J. (MI) - 1936
Braman, Isaac G. (NY) - 1932
Bramback (OH) - 1856
Bramble, A. F. (KS) - 1968
Bramblett, Ernest K. (CA) - 1946, 1948, 1950, 1952
Bramhall, Ronald O. (IA) - 1956
Bramlage, Ervin L. (KY) - 1936
Bramlett, Lunsford M. (TN) - 1825, 1827
Bramlette, Thomas E. (KY) - 1853
Bramwell, Arthur (NY) - 1978
Branagan, W. J. (IA) - 1904
Branagan, William T. (IA) - 1932
Branch (MO) - 1862
Branch, H. B. (MO) - 1864
Branch, John (NC) - 1831
Branch, Lawrence Ob (NC) - 1855, 1857, 1859
Branch, William A. B. (NC) - 1890, 1892, 1884
Branch, William McKinley (AL) - 1968
Branch, Wilson (CA) - 1980
Brand, Charles (OH) - 1922, 1924, 1926, 1928, 1930
Brand, Charles H. (GA) - 1916, 1918, 1920, 1922, 1924, 1926, 1928, 1930, 1932
Brandau, John P. (MD) - 1928
Brandegee, Augustus (CT) - 1863, 1865
Brandegee, Frank B. (CT) - 1902, 1904
Brandenburg, C. W. (KS) - 1894
Brandenburg, Tony (CA) - 1982
Brandofino, Robert L. (NY) - 1984
Brandon, Doug (AR) - 1978
Brandon, Martin O. (MN) - 1934, 1936, 1938
Brandon, Rodney H. (IL) - 1926
Brandreth (NY) - 1876
Brandreth, George A. (NY) - 1892
Brandt (MO) - 1914
Brandt, Charles F. (NY) - 1896
Brandt, J. Seldon (NY) - 1926
Branham (GA) - 1832
Branine, Ezra (KS) - 1914
Brann, Louis J. (ME) - 1942

Brannan, Charles I. (GA) - 1900
Brannan, W. F. (IA) - 1878
Brannon, John (WV) - 1884
Branscum, Truman T. (OK) - 1966
Bransford (TN) - 1843
Branson, David (PA) - 1874
Bransrator, Charles W. (IN) - 1922, 1924
Branth (NY) - 1854
Brantley, Hobart (NC) - 1926, 1934
Brantley, William G. (GA) - 1896, 1898, 1900, 1902, 1904, 1906, 1908
Branyan, James C. (IN) - 1886
Brasco, Frank J. (NY) - 1966, 1968, 1970, 1972
Brasnears, J. (PA) - 1838
Brass, E. E. (IL) - 1912
Bratcher, Rhodes (KY) - 1964
Brathwaite, Peter L. W. (FL) - 1978
Bratten, Robert F. (MD) - 1892
Brattland, M. A. (MN) - 1912, 1914
Bratton, John (SC) - 1884
Bratton, U. S. (AR) - 1900
Braun, Ernst A. (WI) - 1924
Braun, Harry W. III (AZ) - 1984
Brauner, William J. (ID) - 1970
Braunstein, Alexander (NY) - 1916, 1923
Braver, Ruth C. (IL) - 1984
Brawley, William H. (SC) - 1890, 1892
Braxton (VA) - 1820, 1831, 1841
Braxton, Elliott M. (VA) - 1870, 1872
Braxton, Thomas N. (IN) - 1888
Bray (NY) - 1882
Bray, Everett L. (MI) - 1900
Bray, W. S. (SD) - 1908
Bray, William G. (IN) - 1950, 1952, 1954, 1956, 1958, 1960, 1962, 1964, 1966, 1968, 1970, 1972, 1974
Brayman, J. B. (VA) - 1960
Brayton (RI) - 1861
Brayton, Buell G. (NY) - 1934
Brayton, Dean F. (UT) - 1938
Brayton, E. M. (SC) - 1882
Brayton, E. W. (SC) - 1890
Brayton, William (CA) - 1934
Brayton, William D. (RI) - 1857, 1859
Bream, John H. (PA) - 1958
Breaux, John B. (LA) - 1972, 1974, 1976, 1978, 1980, 1982, 1984
Breazeale, Phanor (LA) - 1898, 1900, 1902
Brecht, John C. (PA) - 1942, 1944
Brecht, Milton J. (PA) - 1904
Breck, Daniel (KY) - 1849
Breck, Philip S. Jr. (CA) - 1976
Breck, S. (PA) - 1826
Breckenridge (PA) - 1843
Breckinridge, Clifton R. (AR) - 1882, 1884, 1886, 1888, 1890, 1892
Breckinridge, John (KY) - 1972, 1974, 1976
Breckinridge, John C. (KY) - 1851, 1853
Breckinridge, William C. P. (KY) - 1884, 1886, 1888, 1890, 1892, 1896
Breckon, Charles L. (IL) - 1906
Bredsteen, Joseph (CA) - 1912
Breed, Robert T. (MA) - 1956, 1958
Breed, William B. (MA) - 1833
Breeding, J. Floyd (KS) - 1956, 1958, 1960, 1962
Breen, Bartley (MI) - 1887
Breen, Edward (IA) - 1942
Breen, Edward (OH) - 1948, 1950
Breen, James W. (PA) - 1892
Breene, William J. (PA) - 1896, 1910
Breese, Sidney (IL) - 1831, 1832
Brehm, John W. (PA) - 1946
Brehm, Walter E. (OH) - 1942, 1944, 1946, 1948, 1950
Breill (KY) - 1902
Breitenbach, John R. (PA) - 1868
Breitenstein, Joseph C. (OH) - 1918
Breitung, Edward (MI) - 1882
Bremer, Al (IA) - 1982
Bremner, Robert G. (NJ) - 1912
Brengle, Francis (MD) - 1843
Brenholt, John Jacob (IL) - 1900
Brennan (MO) - 1916
Brennan (NJ) - 1916, 1918
Brennan, Charles F. (NY) - 1980
Brennan, James P. (MA) - 1928
Brennan, James T. (PA) - 1916
Brennan, John P. (MA) - 1926, 1930
Brennan, Martin A. (IL) - 1932, 1934
Brennan, Thomas F. (CT) - 1960
Brennan, Thomas M. (NY) - 1966
Brennan, Tim (ID) - 1958

Brennan, Vincent M. (MI) - 1920
Brennan, William J. (PA) - 1890
Brennan, William R. Jr. (NY) - 1954
Brennau (NY) - 1853
Brennen, Francis P. (NJ) - 1972
Brennen, Robert H. (NY) - 1938
Brenner, B. H. (PA) - 1916
Brenner, Benjamin (NY) - 1940
Brenner, George A. (NY) - 1950, 1952
Brenner, John L. (OH) - 1896, 1898
Brent, William L. (LA) - 1824, 1826
Brentano, Lorenzo (IL) - 1876
Brenton, Samuel (IN) - 1851, 1852, 1854, 1856
Breslin, John V. (NJ) - 1946
Breslin, Joseph R. (PA) - 1970
Breslin, William M. (PA) - 1874, 1892
Bresnahan, John M. (MA) - 1944
Bresnahan, Lawrence J. (MA) - 1938
Bressler, C. H. (PA) - 1876
Brett, R. Houston (VA) - 1930
Brettelle, James (OH) - 1894
Bretz, John L. (IN) - 1890, 1892, 1894
Bretz, Julian P. (NY) - 1930, 1932, 1934
Brevetti, Vincent P. (NY) - 1964
Brewer (OH) - 1852
Brewer, Emery L. (NY) - 1894
Brewer, Francis B. (NY) - 1882
Brewer, George D. (KS) - 1912
Brewer, George D. (MN) - 1924
Brewer, J. Hart (NJ) - 1880,, 1882
Brewer, Lafayette W. (IL) - 1888
Brewer, Mark S. (MI) - 1876, 1878, 1886, 1888
Brewer, Raleigh (MS) - 1898, 1900
Brewer, Thomas (IL) - 1868
Brewer, Willis (AL) - 1896, 1898
Brewer, Willis M. (MI) - 1924
Brewster (MO) - 1898, 1918
Brewster (PA) - 1848
Brewster, A. T. (MO) - 1920
Brewster, C. G. (TX) - 1892
Brewster, Calvin J. (TX) - 1888
Brewster, Daniel B. (MD) - 1958, 1960
Brewster, David (NY) - 1838, 1840
Brewster, Henry B. (NY) - 1927
Brewster, Henry C. (NY) - 1894, 1896
Brewster, Ralph O. (ME) - 1932, 1934, 1936, 1938
Brewster, S. A. (IA) - 1904
Brian, Hardy L. (LA) - 1898
Brice, Palestine (OK) - 1930
Brick (NJ) - 1834
Brick, Abraham L. (IN) - 1898, 1900, 1902, 1904, 1906
Bricker, W. B. (PA) - 1898
Brickett, George (MA) - 1908
Brickey, Preston P. (MO) - 1846
Brickhouse, Grady G. (PA) - 1980
Brickner, George H. (WI) - 1888, 1890, 1892
Bridge, Adam (OH) - 1900
Bridges, L. W. Dan (CO) - 1978
Bridges, Phil M. (TX) - 1964
Bridges, Samuel A. (PA) - 1848, 1852, 1854, 1876
Bridwell, John T. (OH) - 1904
Brien (TN) - 1872
Brier, David (IN) - 1847, 1851
Briggs (DE) - 1860
Briggs (NY) - 1856
Briggs (OH) - 1848
Briggs, Bruce B. (NC) - 1976
Briggs, C. M. (IL) - 1900
Briggs, Charles D. (MA) - 1958
Briggs, Clay S. (TX) - 1918, 1820, 1922, 1924, 1926, 1928, 1930, 1932
Briggs, Edward L. (MI) - 1886, 1890
Briggs, George (NY) - 1848, 1850, 1858
Briggs, George E. (PA) - 1916, 1920
Briggs, George N. (MA) - 1830, 1833, 1834, 1836, 1838, 1840
Briggs, George W. (MA) - 1828
Briggs, James A. (NY) - 1870
Briggs, James F. (NH) - 1877, 1878, 1880
Briggs, M. J. (WI) - 1916
Briggs, Warren (FL) - 1978, 1980
Briggs, Willis G. (NC) - 1908, 1938
Brigham (NJ) - 1884
Brigham (VT) - 1866
Brigham, Elbert S. (VT) - 1924, 1926, 1928
Brigham, Herbert F. (VT) - 1898
Brigham, Joseph H. (OH) - 1882, 1890
Brigham, Lewis A. (NJ) - 1878, 1880

Brigham, Waldo (VT) - 1868, 1886
Bright (NJ) - 1914
Bright (TN) - 1880
Bright, Arthur (TN) - 1948, 1952, 1954, 1956, 1960, 1964, 1968
Bright, Hiram (IL) - 1858
Bright, John M. (TN) - 1870, 1872, 1874, 1876, 1878
Bright, Robert S. (PA) - 1914
Bright, Temus (TN) - 1966
Bright, William H. (PA) - 1924
Brightwell, Charles O. (TX) - 1972
Brignall, James T. (MI) - 1972
Brill, Franklin P. (NY) - 1918
Brimberry (GA) - 1880
Brimmer (MA) - 1878
Brindle (NJ) - 1888
Bringham, Robert (PA) - 1900
Brink, Edward H. (OH) - 1916, 1932
Brinkerhoff, Henry R. (OH) - 1843
Brinkerhoff, Jacob (OH) - 1843, 1844, 1848, 1852
Brinkley, Jack (GA) - 1966, 1968, 1970, 1972, 1974, 1976, 1978, 1980
Brinkman, M. A. (KY) - 1912
Brinkman, William A. (PA) - 1930
Brinkmeier, Robert E. (IL) - 1964
Brinson, Jack D. (NC) - 1960
Brinson, James M. (MT) - 1914
Brinson, Samuel L. (NC) - 1918, 1920
Brinton (MD) - 1888
Brinton (PA) - 1860
Brisbane, W. (SC) - 1868
Brisbin, John (PA) - 1851
Briscoe, Frank (TX) - 1966
Bristor, Thomas G. (OH) - 1886
Bristow (KY) - 1908
Bristow (NY) - 1891
Bristow (VA) - 1906
Bristow, Francis M. (KY) - 1854, 1859
Bristow, Henry (NY) - 1900, 1902
Bristow, Joseph A. (VA) - 1898
Bristow, Louis L. (KY) - 1914
Britt, Charles Robin (NC) - 1982
Britt, James J. (NC) - 1906, 1914, 1916, 1918
Britt, Robin (NC) - 1984
Brittain, F. C. (PA) - 1916
Britten, Fred A. (IL) - 1912, 1914, 1916, 1918, 1920, 1922, 1924, 1926, 1928, 1930, 1932, 1934
Britton, Louis C. (NY) - 1956
Britton, Raymond P. (CA) - 1966, 1968
Brizzolara, James (AR) - 1904
Broaddus, E. J. (MO) - 1878
Broadhead, James O. (MO) - 1882
Broadhurst, Joseph J. (PA) - 1904
Broadt, Gerald C. (PA) - 1966
Broady, Jefferson H. (NE) - 1896
Brock (MO) - 1888
Brock (TN) - 1900
Brock, B. C. (NC) - 1944
Brock, Lawrence (NE) - 1956, 1958, 1960
Brock, Bill (TN) - 1962, 1964, 1966, 1968
Brockenbrough, William H. (FL) - 1845
Brockmeier, C. L. (MN) - 1880
Brockson, Franklin (DE) - 1912, 1914
Brockway (NY) - 1872
Brockway, Charles B. (PA) - 1870
Brockway, John (CT) - 1836, 1837, 1839, 1841
Brodbeck, Andrew R. (PA) - 1910, 1912, 1914, 1916, 1918
Broderick, Case (KS) - 1890, 1892, 1894, 1896
Broderick, David (NY) - 1846
Brodhd (NY) - 1856
Brodhead (PA) - 1860
Brodhead, J. Davis (PA) - 1904, 1906
Brodhead, John (NH) - 1829, 1831
Brodhead, John (MI) - 1830, 1836
Brodhead, Richard (PA) - 1843, 1844, 1846
Brodhead, William M. (MI) - 1974, 1976, 1978, 1980
Brodie, David C. (KY) - 1952
Brodsky (NY) - 1882
Brodsky, Louis B. (NY) - 1930
Brodsky, Rubin (NY) - 1954
Brogden, Curtis H. (NC) - 1876, 1884
Bromberg, Frederick G. (AL) - 1872, 1874, 1876
Bromberg, Mendel (NY) - 1926
Bromwell, Henry P. H. (IL) - 1856, 1864, 1866

Bryle (NY) - 1854
Bryson, Joseph R. (SC) - 1938, 1940, 1942, 1944, 1946, 1948, 1950, 1952
Bryson, Rodney G. (KY) - 1920
Bryton (MO) - 1872
Bualman, Bowen (MA) - 1854
Bubacz, S. Charles (IL) - 1954
Bubbett, Benjamin A. (PA) - 1900
Bube, J. O. (IA) - 1894
Bubel, Neil F. (NY) - 1964
Buchan (NY) - 1850
Buchanan (TN) - 1849
Buchanan, Andrew (PA) - 1834, 1836
Buchanan, Frank (IL) - 1906, 1908, 1910, 1912, 1914, 1916
Buchanan, Frank (PA) - 1946, 1948, 1950
Buchanan, George M. (MS) - 1880, 1890
Buchanan, Hugh (GA) - 1880, 1882
Buchanan, J. C. (PA) - 1916
Buchanan, James (NJ) - 1884, 1886, 1888, 1890
Buchanan, James (PA) - 1824, 1826, 1828
Buchanan, James P. (TX) - 1914, 1916, 1918, 1920, 1922, 1924, 1926, 1928, 1930, 1932, 1934, 1936
Buchanan, John (AL) - 1962, 1964, 1966, 1968, 1970, 1972, 1974, 1976, 1978
Buchanan, John A. (VA) - 1888, 1890
Buchanan, John M. (OH) - 1982, 1984
Buchanan, Tate C. (VA) - 1970
Buchanan, Vera D. (PA) - 1952, 1954
Bucher (PA) - 1834
Bucher, John C. (NY) - 1912
Bucher, John C. (PA) - 1830
Buchschacher, Lee (MO) - 1978
Buck (GA) - 1882
Buck (MN) - 1870, 1910
Buck (MO) - 1858
Buck (NY) - 1874
Buck, Alfred E. (AL) - 1869
Buck, Alfred E. (NY) - 1940
Buck, Charles F. (LA) - 1894
Buck, Chester (NY) - 1830
Buck, Daniel Azro Ashley (VT) - 1824, 1826, 1828
Buck, E. B. (IL) - 1882
Buck, Ellsworth B. (NY) - 1944, 1946
Buck, Frank H. (CA) - 1930, 1932, 1934, 1936, 1938, 1940
Buck, Frank H. (PA) - 1966
Buck, Frederick S. (NY) - 1950
Buck, John J. (TN) - 1868
Buck, John R. (CT) - 1880, 1882, 1884, 1886
Buck, S. C. (TX) - 1882
Buckalew, Charles R. (PA) - 1886, 1888, 1894
Buckbee, John T. (IL) - 1926, 1928, 1930, 1932, 1934
Buckel, Thomas C. Jr. (NY) - 1984
Buckingham, Edward T. (CT) - 1934
Buckland, Edward A. (MA) - 1898
Buckland, Ralph P. (OH) - 1864, 1866
Buckler, Bertram L. (NJ) - 1982
Buckler, Richard T. (MN) - 1934, 1936, 1938, 1940
Buckles (IN) - 1854
Buckley (AL) - 1888
Buckley, Bert B. (OH) - 1912
Buckley, Charles A. (NY) - 1934, 1936, 1938, 1940, 1942, 1944, 1946, 1948, 1950, 1952, 1954, 1956, 1958, 1960, 1962
Buckley, Charles W. (AL) - 1868, 1869, 1870
Buckley, Edgar T. (MN) - 1944
Buckley, Elliot Ross (LA) - 1960
Buckley, James P. (WI) - 1964, 1966
Buckley, James R. (IL) - 1922, 1924
Buckley, James V. (IL) - 1948, 1950
Buckley, John J. (MA) - 1978
Buckley, John J. (PA) - 1906
Buckley, John T. (NY) - 1936
Buckley, F. Mac (CT) - 1974
Buckley, Thomas (IL) - 1928
Buckley, Thomas H. (MA) - 1932
Buckman, Clarence B. (MN) - 1902, 1904
Buckner, Aylett (KY) - 1847, 1849
Buckner, Aylett H. (MO) - 1872, 1874, 1876, 1878, 1880, 1882
Buckner, Henry (NY) - 1914
Buckner, R. A. (KY) - 1863
Buckner, Richard A. (KY) - 1824, 1827
Buckwalter, A. M. (PA) - 1920
Buckwalter, Charles (PA) - 1864, 1866

Buckwoth, W. A. (IA) - 1894
Budd (NJ) - 1832
Budd, James H. (CA) - 1882
Budd, William H. (OH) - 1906
Buddington, Thomas C. (FL) - 1910
Buder, Eugene H. (MO) - 1954
Buder, William E. (MO) - 1938
Budge, Hamer H. (ID) - 1950, 1952, 1954, 1956, 1958, 1960
Budlong, Wilford S. (RI) - 1950
Buech, Robert (WI) - 1920
Buechner, John (MO) - 1984
Buechner, John C. (CO) - 1982
Buehman, Albert R. (AZ) - 1948
Buel, Alexander H. (NY) - 1850
Buel, Alexander W. (MI) - 1848, 1850
Buell, Carl Johnson (MN) - 1912
Buell, Lawrence L. (IN) - 1976
Buffett, Howard (NE) - 1942, 1944, 1946, 1948, 1950
Buffett, William (NY) - 1840
Buffington, Joseph (PA) - 1843, 1844
Buffinton, James (MA) - 1854, 1856, 1858, 1860, 1868, 1870, 1872, 1874
Buford, Don (TX) - 1984
Buford, J. Lester (IL) - 1934, 1946
Bugbee, T. S. (TX) - 1910
Bugg, Robert M. (TN) - 1853
Buggelli, Richard A. (NJ) - 1976
Buggles, Micah H. (MA) - 1830
Buhr, August (NY) - 1950
Buikema, Ronald (IL) - 1976
Buker, Howard E. (OH) - 1912
Buckley, Robert J. (OH) - 1910, 1912
Bull (RI) - 1893
Bull, Chipman C. (ME) - 1984
Bull, Clifford B. (CA) - 1960
Bull, George (PA) - 1880
Bull, Henry Adsit (NY) - 1932
Bull, John (MO) - 1833
Bull, Melville (RI) - 1892, 1894, 1896, 1898, 1900, 1902
Bull, Vernon (OR) - 1950
Bullard, Henry A. (LA) - 1830, 1832
Bullene (MO) - 1888
Bullis, A. H. (MN) - 1886
Bullitt, Stimson (WA) - 1952
Bullitt, William A. (KY) - 1867
Bullock (NY) - 1856
Bullock, George (PA) - 1864
Bullock, John (TN) - 1865
Bullock, Lynwood (NC) - 1970, 1972
Bullock, Robert (FL) - 1888, 1890
Bullock, William I. (AL) - 1896
Bullock, William J. (MA) - 1912
Bulthouse, Peter (IL) - 1910
Bulwinkle, Alfred L. (NC) - 1920, 1922, 1924, 1926, 1928, 1930, 1932, 1934, 1936, 1938, 1940, 1942, 1944, 1946, 1948
Bumgardner, James Jr. (VA) - 1886
Bumgardner, Rex Keith (WV) - 1958
Bumpas (MO) - 1912
Bumpass, H. Kent (OH) - 1974
Bunch, John T. (KY) - 1861
Bunch, Ralph E. (OR) - 1972
Bunch, Samuel (TN) - 1833, 1835, 1837
Bundy (IN) - 1866
Bundy, Hezekiah S. (OH) - 1862, 1864, 1872, 1874, 1893
Bundy, John J. (IL) - 1914
Bundy, Solomon (NY) - 1876
Bunick, Nick (OR) - 1978
Bunker (ME) - 1916
Bunker, Berkeley L. (NV) - 1944
Bunn, Benjamin H. (NC) - 1888, 1890, 1892
Bunn, Stanley (PA) - 1968
Bunnell, Frank C. (PA) - 1872, 1884, 1886
Bunner, Rudolph (NY) - 1826
Bunting, Thomas L. (NY) - 1890
Buonpane, Blase A. (OH) - 1936
Buram, Peter (TN) - 1835
Burch, Alvan V. (IN) - 1960
Burch, Edwin Whitney (OK) - 1952
Burch, George H. (VA) - 1876
Burch, John C. (CA) - 1858
Burch, Thomas G. (VA) - 1930, 1932, 1934, 1936, 1938, 1940, 1942, 1944
Burcham, John B. Jr. (MD) - 1974, 1976
Burchard (OH) - 1856
Burchard (RI) - 1914
Burchard, Horatio C. (IL) - 1869, 1870, 1872, 1874, 1876
Burchard, Samuel D. (WI) - 1874

Burchett, Drury J. (KY) - 1888
Burchill, Thomas F. (NY) - 1942
Burchinal, Warren S. (PA) - 1830, 1832
Burden, Carter (NY) - 1978
Burden, J. R. (PA) - 1832
Burden, Theron H. (NY) - 1916
Burdett (WV) - 1863
Burdett, Samuel S. (MO) - 1868, 1870, 1872
Burdette, Frank C. (WV) - 1934
Burdick, Clark (RI) - 1918, 1920, 1922, 1924, 1926, 1928, 1930, 1932
Burdick, Clayton E. (NJ) - 1954
Burdick, I. B. (AL) - 1944
Burdick, James W. (MI) - 1976
Burdick, Morton H. (MA) - 1914
Burdick, Quentin N. (ND) - 1958
Burdick, Theodore W. (IA) - 1876
Burdick, Usher L. (ND) - 1934, 1936, 1938, 1940, 1942, 1944, 1948, 1950, 1952, 1954, 1956
Burgener, Clair W. (CA) - 1972, 1974, 1976, 1978, 1980
Burger, Bob (PA) - 1982
Burger, James C. (CO) - 1908, 1910
Burger, Josef (WI) - 1974
Burges, Tristam (RI) - 1825, 1827, 1829, 1831, 1833, 1835
Burgeson, Floyd M. (IA) - 1960
Burgess, Charlie (AL) - 1968
Burgess, D. (WA) - 1902
Burgess, Duke (TX) - 1966
Burgess, G. L. (AZ) - 1936
Burgess, George F. (TX) - 1900, 1902, 1904, 1906, 1908, 1910, 1912, 1914
Burgess, Henry E. (IL) - 1914
Burgess, Jack (TX) - 1976, 1978
Burgess, John A. (VT) - 1976
Burgess, Peter D. (NC) - 1924
Burgin, William O. (NC) - 1938, 1940, 1942, 1944
Burham, L. Dewey (IN) - 1952
Burhans (NY) - 1862
Burk, Andrew C. (OR) - 1938
Burk, Bob (TX) - 1984
Burk, Henry (PA) - 1900, 1902
Burk, W. W. (PA) - 1900
Burke (LA) - 1857
Burke (NJ) - 1906
Burke (ND) - 1896
Burke (PA) - 1858
Burke, Charles A. (NY) - 1900
Burke, Charles H. (SD) - 1898, 1900, 1902, 1904, 1908, 1910, 1912
Burke, Daniel C. (NY) - 1923
Burke, Edmund (NH) - 1839, 1841, 1843
Burke, Edward R. (NE) - 1930, 1932
Burke, Frank B. (IN) - 1900
Burke, Frank W. (KY) - 1958, 1960, 1962
Burke, J. (AL) - 1841
Burke, J. Herbert (FL) - 1966, 1968, 1970, 1972, 1974, 1976, 1978
Burke, J. W. (AL) - 1868
Burke, James A. (MA) - 1958, 1960, 1962, 1964, 1966, 1968, 1970, 1972, 1974, 1976
Burke, James Francis (PA) - 1902, 1904, 1906, 1908, 1910, 1912
Burke, John H. (CA) - 1932
Burke, Joseph W. (TX) - 1908
Burke, Michael E. (WI) - 1910, 1912, 1914, 1916
Burke, Paul (NE) - 1946
Burke, Raymond H. (OH) - 1946, 1948
Burke, Richard K. (AZ) - 1962
Burke, Richard W. (WI) - 1910
Burke, Robert E. (TX) - 1896, 1898, 1900
Burke, Robert R. (PA) - 1980
Burke, Thomas H. (OH) - 1948, 1950, 1952
Burke, Thomas J. (NY) - 1928
Burke, Thomas J. (PA) - 1894
Burke, Timothy M. (OH) - 1978
Burke, W. J. (IA) - 1928
Burke, William H. (NY) - 1896
Burke, William J. (PA) - 1918, 1920
Burke, William J. (WI) - 1956
Burke, Yvonne Brathwaite (CA) - 1972, 1974, 1976
Burkett, Elmer J. (NE) - 1898, 1900, 1902, 1904, 1928
Burkhalter, Everett G. (CA) - 1946, 1952, 1962
Burkhart, A. G. (IN) - 1894
Burkholder (MO) - 1892
Burkholder, H. Clay (PA) - 1936, 1944

Burkholder, P. C. (NC) - 1946
Burkitt, Frank (MS) - 1892
Burkitt, James (MS) - 1892
Burkle, William Sr. (NY) - 1918, 1920
Burks, Jesse Rice (IN) - 1924
Burlage, L. Charles (VA) - 1972
Burleigh, Edwin C. (ME) - 1897, 1898, 1900, 1902, 1904, 1906, 1908, 1910
Burleigh, Henry G. (NY) - 1882, 1884, 1886
Burleigh, Henry M. (MA) - 1875
Burleigh, John H. (ME) - 1872, 1874
Burleigh, William (ME) - 1824, 1826
Burleson, Albert S. (TX) - 1898, 1900, 1902, 1904, 1906, 1908, 1910, 1912
Burleson, J. O. (TX) - 1920
Burleson, Omar (TX) - 1946, 1948, 1950, 1952, 1954, 1956, 1958, 1960, 1962, 1964, 1966, 1968, 1970, 1972, 1974, 1976
Burlingame, Ason (MA) - 1852, 1854, 1856, 1858, 1860
Burlison, Bill D. (MO) - 1968, 1970, 1972, 1974, 1976, 1978, 1980
Burman, E. P. (CA) - 1892
Burnell, Barker (MA) - 1824, 1840, 1842
Burnes, C. C. (KS) - 1880
Burnes, Daniel D. (MO) - 1892
Burnes, James N. (MO) - 1882, 1884, 1886, 1888
Burnet, A. Lining (NY) - 1968
Burnett, Carles C. (OH) - 1884
Burnett, Edward (MA) - 1886, 1888
Burnett, George (KS) - 1910
Burnett, George P. (GA) - 1870
Burnett, Hamilton S. (TN) - 1932
Burnett, Henry C. (KY) - 1855, 1857, 1859, 1861
Burnett, John (OR) - 1872
Burnett, John L. (AL) - 1898, 1900, 1902, 1904, 1906, 1908, 1910, 1912, 1914, 1916, 1918
Burnett, Mary (TN) - 1932
Burnett, R. L. (TN) - 1922
Burnett, Rad (IL) - 1936
Burney (GA) - 1838
Burney, William E. (CO) - 1940
Burnham, Alfred A. (CT) - 1859, 1861
Burnham, Edwin K. (NY) - 1890
Burnham, George (CA) - 1932, 1934
Burnham, John B. (NY) - 1912
Burnquist, J. A. A. (MN) - 1932
Burns (NH) - 1859, 1861, 1863
Burns (PA) - 1888
Burns, Bernard J. (CT) - 1964
Burns, Charles G. (MI) - 1948
Burns, Edward (MI) - 1960
Burns, Henry J. (PA) - 1920
Burns, J. M. (KY) - 1872
Burns, James (MA) - 1932, 1938, 1940, 1942
Burns, James Irving (NY) - 1898
Burns, James M. (MA) - 1958
Burns, John C. (OK) - 1936
Burns, John J. (NY) - 1922, 1933, 1950
Burns, John M. III (NY) - 1972
Burns, Joseph (OH) - 1856, 1858, 1860, 1868
Burns, Joseph R. (PA) - 1952, 1962
Burns, Lawrence (OH) - 1958
Burns, Louis Henry (LA) - 1914
Burns, R. F. (TX) - 1946
Burns, Robert (NH) - 1833, 1835
Burns, Thomas E. (KY) - 1880
Burns, W. Bruce (PA) - 1900
Burns, W. P. (TX) - 1884
Burns, William H. (MA) - 1952, 1960
Burns, William R. (VA) - 1956
Burnside, Ambrose E. (RI) - 1857
Burnside, Isaac M. (SD) - 1910
Burnside, Maurice G. (WV) - 1946, 1948, 1950, 1952, 1954, 1956
Burnside, Robert J. (CA) - 1980
Burnstein, Sidney (NY) - 1955
Buroker, Charles E. (OH) - 1914
Burow, B. R. (TX) - 1902
Burr (NY) - 1862
Burr, A. G. (ND) - 1904, 1906
Burr, Albert G. (IL) - 1866, 1868
Burr, F. A. (WV) - 1878
Burr, Herbert W. (MA) - 1928
Burr, Isaac (NY) - 1826
Burr, J. D. (CO) - 1890
Burr, Redmond M. (MI) - 1940, 1942, 1944
Burrell, Orlando (IL) - 1894, 1896
Burris, J. T. (KS) - 1888

Cameron, Don O. (OH) - 1944
Cameron, John A. (NC) - 1827, 1829
Cameron, Kenneth (NY) - 1934
Cameron, Ronald Brooks (CA) - 1962, 1964, 1966
Camerzell, Fritz (NJ) - 1982
Caminetti, Anthony (CA) - 1890, 1892, 1894, 1904
Cammarota, A. J. (PA) - 1956
Camp, A. Sidney (GA) - 1940, 1942, 1944, 1946, 1948, 1950, 1952
Camp, Billy Joe (AL) - 1982
Camp, Cyrus C. (PA) - 1878
Camp, Elisha (NY) - 1826, 1828
Camp, John G. (NY) - 1824, 1828
Camp, John H. (NY) - 1876, 1878, 1880
Camp, John N. Happy (OK) - 1968, 1970, 1972, 1974
Camp, Katherine L. (PA) - 1972
Camp, Silas (NY) - 1846
Camp, Thomas L. (GA) - 1946
Campbell (AL) - 1872
Campbell (GA) - 1840
Campbell (KY) - 1837
Campbell (NY) - 1844, 1848, 1874
Campbell (OK) - 1914
Campbell (PA) - 1848, 1862
Campbell (TN) - 1872
Campbell (VT) - 1880
Campbell (VA) - 1827
Campbell, Albert J. (MT) - 1898
Campbell, Alex (OH) - 1846
Campbell, Alexander (IL) - 1874, 1876, 1878
Campbell, Andrew J. (NY) - 1894
Campbell, B. C. (NC) - 1934
Campbell, Braxton W. (OH) - 1904
Campbell, Brookins (TN) - 1853
Campbell, Bruce A. (IL) - 1910
Campbell, Carroll A. Jr. (SC) - 1978, 1980, 1982, 1984
Campbell, Charles M. (OK) - 1912
Campbell, Courtney (FL) - 1952, 1954
Campbell, Daniel (IA) - 1880, 1892
Campbell, Daniel (TN) - 1980
Campbell, David C. (GA) - 1838
Campbell, Ed. H. (IA) - 1928, 1930, 1932
Campbell, Edgar (PA) - 1946
Campbell, Edmund D. (VA) - 1952
Campbell, Edward (NY) - 1966
Campbell, Edward E. (IL) - 1922, 1924
Campbell, Emerson (OH) - 1930
Campbell, Ethan H. (MO) - 1960, 1962
Campbell, Felix (NY) - 1882, 1884, 1886, 1888
Campbell, Frank T. (IA) - 1884
Campbell, George (OK) - 1950
Campbell, Guy E. (PA) - 1914, 1916, 1918, 1920, 1922, 1924, 1926, 1928, 1930, 1932, 1934
Campbell, Howard E. (PA) - 1944
Campbell, Howard O. (IN) - 1984
Campbell, J. B. (SC) - 1882
Campbell, J. C. (CA) - 1886
Campbell, J. E. (WA) - 1914
Campbell, J. Ike (NC) - 1920, 1922
Campbell, Jacob M. (PA) - 1876, 1878, 1880, 1882, 1884
Campbell, James (PA) - 1882
Campbell, James A. (NY) - 1930
Campbell, James E. (OH) - 1882, 1884, 1886, 1906
Campbell, James H. (PA) - 1854, 1856, 1858, 1860
Campbell, James R. (IL) - 1896, 1918
Campbell, John (SC) - 1828, 1830, 1836, 1838, 1840, 1843
Campbell, John A. (MA) - 1908
Campbell, John H. (PA) - 1844
Campbell, John P. (KY) - 1855
Campbell, John P. (MO) - 1842, 1846
Campbell, John W. (OH) - 1824
Campbell, John W. (OR) - 1912
Campbell, Joseph C. (IA) - 1918
Campbell, Julian H. (TN) - 1940
Campbell, Lee (OR) - 1912
Campbell, Lewis D. (OH) - 1840, 1842, 1844, 1848, 1850, 1852, 1854, 1856, 1858, 1870
Campbell, Lorne R. (VA) - 1953
Campbell, Neill (OR) - 1912
Campbell, Newman (IL) - 1852
Campbell, Nixon (MA) - 1920
Campbell, Philip P. (KS) - 1902, 1904,

1906, 1908, 1910, 1912, 1914, 1916, 1918, 1920
Campbell, Robert B. (SC) - 1826, 1834
Campbell, Stewart (IL) - 1932
Campbell, Terry L. (OK) - 1970
Campbell, Thomas (SC) - 1980
Campbell, Thomas E. (AZ) - 1912
Campbell, Thomas J. (TN) - 1841, 1843
Campbell, Thompson (IL) - 1850, 1852
Campbell, Timothy J. (NY) - 1886, 1888, 1890, 1892, 1894, 1896
Campbell, Val B. (IL) - 1928
Campbell, William (NY) - 1824, 1844, 1846
Campbell, William B. (TN) - 1837, 1839, 1841, 1865
Campbell, William C. (IA) - 1906
Campbell, William D. (CA) - 1932, 1934, 1936, 1938, 1944
Campbell, William J. (WI) - 1934
Campbell, William W. (OH) - 1904, 1906, 1908
Campenni, Anthony L. (NJ) - 1976
Camper, Frank Sneed (TX) - 1922
Camper, John E. T. (MD) - 1948
Campolo, Anthony (PA) - 1976
Canaday, Delmar A. (OH) - 1948, 1952
Canaday, R. O. (NE) - 1940
Canaday, William P. (NC) - 1876, 1880, 1882
Canade, Austen D. (NY) - 1974
Canary, Kathryn (NY) - 1980
Canby, Richard S. (OH) - 1846
Candee, George (OH) - 1894
Candler, Allen D. (GA) - 1882, 1884, 1886, 1888
Candler, Ezekiel S. Jr. (MS) - 1900, 1902, 1904, 1906, 1908, 1910, 1912, 1914, 1916, 1918
Candler, John W. (MA) - 1880, 1882, 1888, 1890
Candler, Milton A. (GA) - 1874, 1876
Candler, W. W. (NC) - 1948
Candler, William G. (NC) - 1872
Candon, John B. (VT) - 1936, 1942
Canfield, Clar W. (PA) - 1890
Canfield, Gordon (NJ) - 1940, 1942, 1944, 1946, 1948, 1950, 1952, 1954, 1956, 1958
Canfield, Harry C. (IN) - 1920, 1922, 1924, 1926, 1928, 1930
Canfield, Roger (CA) - 1982, 1984
Canning, Charles (MN) - 1888
Cannon (KS) - 1882
Cannon (LA) - 1859
Cannon, Arthur P. (FL) - 1938, 1940, 1942, 1944
Cannon, Clarence (MO) - 1922, 1924, 1926, 1928, 1930, 1932, 1934, 1936, 1938, 1940, 1942, 1944, 1946, 1948, 1950, 1952, 1954, 1956, 1958, 1960, 1962
Cannon, Francis A. (WI) - 1914
Cannon, James J. (NJ) - 1944
Cannon, John C. (KS) - 1882
Cannon, Joseph G. (IL) - 1872, 1874, 1876, 1878, 1880, 1882, 1884, 1886, 1888, 1890, 1892, 1894, 1896, 1898, 1900, 1902, 1904, 1906, 1908, 1910, 1912, 1914, 1916, 1918, 1920
Cannon, LeGrand B. (NY) - 1866
Cannon, Marion (CA) - 1892
Cannon, Michael D. (VA) - 1976
Cannon, Quayle Jr. (UT) - 1944
Cannon, Raymond J. (WI) - 1932, 1934, 1936, 1938
Cannon, Richard M. (CA) - 1932
Cannon, V. S. (OK) - 1936
Cannon, W. L. (KY) - 1902
Cantando, Leonard L. (CA) - 1962
Canter, Julius D. (NJ) - 1952
Cantor, Bernard (TN) - 1972
Cantor, Jacob A. (NY) - 1894, 1912, 1914
Cantrell, Harvey E. (TN) - 1928
Cantrell, J. C. (KY) - 1926
Cantrill, James C. (KY) - 1908, 1910, 1912, 1914, 1916, 1918, 1920, 1922
Cantu, Mitchell (GA) - 1984
Cantwell (NY) - 1872
Cantwell, John M. (NY) - 1924
Cantwell, Percy J. (RI) - 1922
Cantwell, Thomas (NY) - 1910
Canwell, Al (WA) - 1952, 1954
Capatosto, Alice A. (NY) - 1968
Capehart, James (WV) - 1892

Capehart, Jones (WV) - 1890
Caperton (VA) - 1841
Capozzi, Alvin D. (PA) - 1964
Capozzoli, Louis J. (NY) - 1940, 1942
Cappelli, Michael R. (NY) - 1960
Cappiello, O. Artur (PA) - 1954
Caprio, Frank (CA) - 1972
Capron, Adin B. (RI) - 1892, 1996, 1998, 1900, 1902, 1904, 1906, 1908
Capron, Wiley W. (NY) - 1912
Capstick, John H. (NJ) - 1914, 1916
Capua, S. Peter (FL) - 1974
Caputo, Bruce F. (NY) - 1976
Caputo, Vic (MI) - 1980
Capuzi, Louis F. (IL) - 1952
Car (MO) - 1852
Carasso, Max (NY) - 1978
Caraway, Thaddeus H. (AR) - 1912, 1914, 1916, 1918
Carbajal, Michael Jr. (NY) - 1974
Card (MI) - 1878
Carden, Cap R. (KY) - 1930, 1932, 1934
Carden, M. W. (AL) - 1902
Cardenas, Al (FL) - 1978
Carder (RI) - 1867
Carew, John F. (NY) - 1912, 1914, 1916, 1918, 1920, 1922, 1924, 1926, 1928
Carey, Archibald James Jr. (IL) - 1950
Carey, Daniel J. (NY) - 1954
Carey, Henry (NY) - 1904, 1906
Carey, Hugh L. (NY) - 1960, 1962, 1964, 1966, 1968, 1970, 1972
Carey, Jacob S. Sr. (OH) - 1922
Carey, James C. Jr. (CA) - 1984
Carey, James F. (MA) - 1904, 1910
Carey, John (OH) - 1858, 1860
Carey, John I. (GA) - 1848
Carey, John L. (MI) - 1938
Carey, Robert (NJ) - 1902
Carey, William A. (MA) - 1942, 1944
Carlan, Andrew E. (NY) - 1980
Carlebach, William D. (NY) - 1956
Carleton (MA) - 1878
Carleton, Ezra C. (MI) - 1882, 1894
Carley, Patrick J. (NY) - 1926, 1928, 1930, 1932
Carlin, Charles C. (VA) - 1908, 1910, 1912, 1914, 1916, 1918
Carlin, John J. (NJ) - 1948
Carlisle (VA) - 1857
Carlisle, Charles A. (IN) - 1912
Carlisle, John G. (KY) - 1876, 1878, 1880, 1882, 1884, 1886, 1888
Carlisle, John S. (VA) - 1855
Carllee, R. B. (AR) - 1886
Carlson, Anthony (WY) - 1912
Carlson, Clifford D. (IL) - 1972, 1974
Carlson, Dave (AK) - 1982
Carlson, Elmer G. (IA) - 1954
Carlson, Frank (KS) - 1934, 1936, 1938, 1940, 1942, 1944
Carlson, Gary K. (MT) - 1984
Carlson, Gerald R. (MI) - 1980, 1984
Carlson, Harry (NH) - 1944
Carlson, Lawrence M. (MN) - 1928
Carlson, Mrs. P. J. (IL) - 1926
Carlson, Peggy T. (OR) - 1948
Carlson, Ruth (Paula) (CA) - 1984
Carlson, Samuel A. (NY) - 1912, 1938
Carlson, William H. (CA) - 1896
Carlton (ME) - 1870
Carlton, Ezra C. (MI) - 1884
Carlton, Henry H. (GA) - 1886, 1888
Carlton, J. F. (AR) - 1912
Carlyle, F. Ertel (NC) - 1948, 1950, 1952, 1954
Carmack, Edward W. (TN) - 1896, 1898
Carman, E. Day (CA) - 1964
Carman, Gregory W. (NY) - 1978, 1980
Carmical (GA) - 1886
Carmichael (MD) - 1847
Carmichael, Archibald H. (AL) - 1934
Carmichael, James H. (MA) - 1910
Carmichael, Leander B. (NC) - 1855
Carmichael, Richard B. (MD) - 1833
Carmody, Dana Warren (CA) - 1978
Carmon, Henry P. (DE) - 1890
Carmony, Gerald C. (IN) - 1956
Carnahan, A. A. (KS) - 1884
Carnahan, A. S. J. (MO) - 1944, 1946, 1948, 1950, 1952, 1954, 1956, 1958
Carnahan, Charles C. (IL) - 1900
Carner, Grant C. (CA) - 1976
Carnes, Nicholas (NY) - 1948

Carney, Charles J. (OH) - 1970, 1972, 1974, 1976, 1978
Carney, Clarence S. (IA) - 1980
Carney, Claude S. (MI) - 1912, 1924
Carney, Cy Jr. (AR) - 1962
Carney, Herschel W. (MI) - 1946
Carney, J. J. (OK) - 1912
Carney, Joseph P. (WI) - 1910, 1918
Carney, William (NY) - 1978, 1980, 1982, 1984
Carnine, A. G. (IL) - 1938
Carnoy, Martin (CA) - 1984
Carns, William L. (NY) - 1932
Caron, Guy W. (AR) - 1908
Carothers, B. F. (TX) - 1853
Carothers, T. L. (CA) - 1884
Carp, Richard L. (Larry) (MO) - 1960
Carpenter (AL) - 1882
Carpenter (NY) - 1854
Carpenter, Alva (NY) - 1890
Carpenter, Charles T. (PA) - 1934
Carpenter, Cyrus C. (IA) - 1878, 1880
Carpenter, Edmund N. (PA) - 1918, 1824, 1826
Carpenter, Frank G. (OH) - 1914
Carpenter, G. J. (CA) - 1876
Carpenter, Lewis Cass (SC) - 1874, 1876
Carpenter, Noel (MO) - 1954
Carpenter, Oliver C. (NY) - 1936
Carpenter, Paul B. (CA) - 1964
Carpenter, R. R. (KY) - 1866
Carpenter, Raymond G. (NY) - 1966
Carpenter, Terry (NE) - 1932
Carpenter, W. H. (AR) - 1902
Carpenter, W. L. (IA) - 1886
Carpenter, William Randolph (KS) - 1932, 1934
Carpenter, Winfield S. (IN) - 1892
Carper, Thomas R. (DE) - 1982, 1984
Carr (IN) - 1870
Carr, Bob (MI) - 1974, 1976, 1978, 1980, 1982, 1984
Carr, D. R. (KY) - 1870, 1882
Carr, Edward Ellis (IL) - 1922
Carr, Edwin S. (IL) - 1930, 1932
Carr, Homer S. (MI) - 1922
Carr, John (IN) - 1831, 1833, 1835, 1839, 1841
Carr, John B. (MA) - 1950
Carr, John C. (MA) - 1952
Carr, M. Robert (MI) - 1972
Carr, Nathan Tracy (IN) - 1876
Carr, Samuel W. (NH) - 1835
Carr, Sherman S. (IL) - 1946
Carr, Thomas S. (MD) - 1950
Carr, William A. (PA) - 1904, 1910
Carr, Wooda N. (PA) - 1900, 1912, 1914
Carran, Edward F. (OH) - 1930
Carrano, Ralph J. (NY) - 1968
Carreau, Rene A. (NY) - 1942
Carrelas, Arthur (RI) - 1954
Carricarte, Michael A. (FL) - 1974
Carrick, Duncan (TX) - 1914
Carrick, Jonathan G. (ID) - 1912
Carrier, Chester O. (KY) - 1943, 1944
Carrigan, Charles E. (WV) - 1910
Carrigan, James D. (IL) - 1942
Carrigg, John J. (OH) - 1962
Carrigg, Joseph L. (PA) - 1952, 1954, 1956, 1958
Carrin (PA) - 1862
Carrol (NY) - 1882
Carroll (MO) - 1882
Carroll (WA) - 1890
Carroll, Charles H. (NY) - 1824, 1842, 1844
Carroll, Dennis M. (CT) - 1950
Carroll, Edward P. (PA) - 1922, 1924, 1930
Carroll, James (MD) - 1839
Carroll, James H. (WI) - 1938
Carroll, John A. (CO) - 1946, 1948
Carroll, John M. (NY) - 1870
Carroll, John S. (HI) - 1966
Carroll, John S. (CO) - 1974
Carroll, Michael A. (IN) - 1982
Carroll, Otis S. (NY) - 1924
Carroll, Patrick D. (IN) - 1980
Carroll, T. Francis (PA) - 1922
Carroll, Thomas (WA) - 1892
Carroll, Thomas J. (PA) - 1928, 1930
Carroll, William D. (WI) - 1942, 1944
Carron, Joe (MO) - 1976
Carrott, Montgomery B. (IL) - 1942, 1960
Carryl (NY) - 1862
Carson (NJ) - 1916, 1918

Cooper, Mark A. (GA) - 1838, 1840, 1842
Cooper, Richard M. (NJ) - 1828, 1830
Cooper, Samuel B. (TX) - 1892, 1894, 1896, 1898, 1900, 1902, 1906
Cooper, Thomas (IL) - 1904
Cooper, Thomas B. (PA) - 1860
Cooper, William C. (OH) - 1884, 1886, 1888
Cooper, William F. (IL) - 1952
Cooper, William R. (NJ) - 1838, 1840
Cooter, Charles S. (IA) - 1932
Coover, Morris (KS) - 1972
Copeland, Charles W. (MA) - 1908
Copeland, L. D. (TN) - 1926
Copeland, Oren S. (NE) - 1940
Copeland, Thomas (MA) - 1890
Copley, Ira C. (IL) - 1910, 1912, 1914, 1916, 1918, 1920
Copner (NY) - 1880
Copp, Belton A. (CT) - 1964
Copper, Luther S. (OH) - 1894
Coppinger (MO) - 1894
Coray, Carla W. (HI) - 1974
Corbett, Donald J. (NY) - 1936
Corbett, Frank E. (IN) - 1940
Corbett, Hal S. (MT) - 1894
Corbett, Robert J. (PA) - 1938, 1940, 1944, 1946, 1948, 1950, 1952, 1954, 1956, 1958, 1960, 1962, 1964, 1966, 1968, 1970
Corbett, William L. (PA) - 1864
Corbin (NY) - 1886
Corbin (VA) - 1841
Corbin, Orville F. (IL) - 1954
Corcoran, Dan (CA) - 1978
Corcoran, Lawrence E. (MA) - 1956
Corcoran, Tom (IL) - 1976, 1978, 1980, 1982
Corder, John F. (KS) - 1928
Cordill, H. H. (NV) - 1918
Cordill, William E. (OH) - 1914
Core, J. Calvin (PA) - 1928
Corey (NY) - 1888
Corker (GA) - 1878
Corkery, Thomas (WA) - 1914, 1916, 1928
Corley, B. W. F. (IL) - 1882
Corley, M. Simeon (SC) - 1868
Corliss, John B. (MI) - 1894, 1896, 1898, 1900, 1902
Corman, James C. (CA) - 1960, 1962, 1964, 1966, 1968, 1970, 1972, 1974, 1976, 1978, 1980
Corman, Patti Lear (CA) - 1976
Cormier, August J. (MA) - 1950
Corneck (MO) - 1854
Cornelius, Preston (NC) - 1982
Cornell (NY) - 1862
Cornell, A. M (PA) - 1918
Cornell, Burdett (CA) - 1894
Cornell, Dudley (NM) - 1956
Cornell, F. Shepard (NY) - 1940
Cornell, K. B. (OK) - 1950, 1952
Cornell, Orville J. (MI) - 1914
Cornell, Robert J. (WI) - 1970, 1972, 1974, 1976, 1978
Cornell, Thomas (NY) - 1866, 1868, 1880
Cornell, William B. (NY) - 1938
Cornett, George W. (VA) - 1894
Corning, Erastus (NY) - 1850, 1856, 1858, 1860, 1862
Corning, Parker (NY) - 1922, 1924, 1926, 1928, 1930, 1932, 1934
Corning, Paul E. Jr. (MO) - 1958
Cornish, Frank V. (CA) - 1932
Cornish, Johnston (NJ) - 1892, 1894
Cornman (PA) - 1852
Cornwall, Andrew (NY) - 1868, 1870
Cornwall, Andrew C. (NY) - 1908
Cornwell, David L. (IN) - 1976, 1978
Coronel, Jean Jacques (NY) - 1920
Correll, John P. (PA) - 1896
Corrigan, Edward (OH) - 1962
Corrigan, Walter D. (WI) - 1934, 1940
Corry, Robert M. (OH) - 1956
Corse, George (NY) - 1964
Corso, Frank M. (NY) - 1966
Corson, Charles P. (IL) - 1918
Cortese, Frank V. (CA) - 1972
Cortum, Don (CA) - 1966
Corwin, Franklin (IL) - 1872, 1874
Corwin, Jesse (OH) - 1836
Corwin, John A. (OH) - 1848, 1850
Corwin, Moses B. (OH) - 1848, 1852
Corwin, Thomas (OH) - 1830, 1832, 1834, 1836, 1838, 1858, 1860

Corwine, Herbert J. (KS) - 1916
Cory, David M. (NY) - 1932
Cosetti, Joseph L. (PA) - 1968
Cosgrave, Otway J. (OH) - 1888, 1890
Cosgrove, James (VT) - 1930
Cosgrove, John (MO) - 1882
Cosseboom, John C. (RI) - 1934
Costa, Catherine A. (NJ) - 1976
Costanza, Margaret (NY) - 1974
Costas, William (IN) - 1978
Costello, John M. (CA) - 1932, 1934, 1936, 1938, 1940, 1942
Costello, Lewis M. (VA) - 1984
Costello, Paul G. (NY) - 1982
Costello, Peter E. (PA) - 1914, 1916, 1918
Costello, Stephen V. (CA) - 1912
Costello, T. E. (PA) - 1928
Costello, Thomas P. (IL) - 1914
Costigan, Edward A. (NJ) - 1970
Costley, William (CA) - 1904
Costley, William M. (CA) - 1954
Cothran, James S. (SC) - 1886, 1888
Cothren (WI) - 1880
Cotter, William R. (CT) - 1970, 1972, 1974, 1976, 1978, 1980
Cotterill, George F. (WA) - 1902, 1916
Cottman (MD) - 1841
Cottman, Joseph S. (MD) - 1851
Cotton (MO) - 1912
Cotton, Aylett R. (IA) - 1870, 1872
Cotton, Homer S. (MO) - 1938
Cotton, Norris (NH) - 1946, 1948, 1950, 1952
Cottrell (IN) - 1870
Cottrell, James L. F. (AL) - 1846
Couch, C. F. (IA) - 1890
Couch, Natalie F. (NY) - 1934, 1936
Couch, Harry (CA) - 1976
Coudert, Frederic R. Jr. (NY) - 1946, 1948, 1950, 1952, 1954, 1956
Coudrey, Harry M. (MO) - 1904, 1906, 1908
Coughlin, Clarence D. (PA) - 1912, 1920, 1922
Coughlin, Daniel J. (MA) - 1936
Coughlin, Dennis O'Brien (PA) - 1914
Coughlin, Jerome W. (MN) - 1976
Coughlin, John P. (MN) - 1932
Coughlin, John W. (MA) - 1912
Coughlin, R. Lawrence (PA) - 1968, 1970, 1972, 1974, 1976, 1978, 1980, 1982, 1984
Coukling, James C. (IL) - 1859
Coulomb, Harry R. (NJ) - 1932
Coulter, Charles H. (MA) - 1904
Coulter, Joe (TX) - 1964
Coulter, Richard (PA) - 1826, 1828, 1830, 1932, 1934
Coumans, Lewis P. (MI) - 1908, 1912
Countie, David R. (MO) - 1972
Counts, Hubert (KY) - 1948
Coursen (NJ) - 1852
Courter, James A. (NJ) - 1978
Courter, Jim (NJ) - 1980, 1982, 1984
Courtht (PA) - 1862
Courtney (MO) - 1914
Courtney, H. E. (OR) - 1898
Courtney, Kent (LA) - 1976
Courtney, Thomas J. (IN) - 1952
Courtney, Wirt (TN) - 1940, 1942, 1944, 1946
Cousins, Robert G. (IA) - 1892, 1894, 1896, 1898, 1900, 1902, 1904, 1906
Coveleskie, Stanley R. (PA) - 1972
Coverdell, Paul D. (GA) - 1977
Covert, Anna (MO) - 1926
Covert, James W. (NY) - 1872, 1876, 1878, 1888, 1890, 1892
Covey, Winton G. Jr. (WV) - 1980
Covington, George W. (MD) - 1880, 1882
Covington, H. J. (SC) - 1868
Covington, James Harry (MD) - 1908, 1910, 1912
Covode, John (PA) - 1854, 1856, 1858, 1860, 1866, 1868
Cowan, Benjamin S. (OH) - 1840, 1846
Cowan, George R. (VA) - 1892
Covan, Homer (OK) - 1964
Cowan, Jacob B. (OH) - 1874
Cowan, Roger (TN) - 1970
Cowan, Stanley R. (IL) - 1962
Cowan, Stewart C. (PA) - 1910
Cowan, W. D. (TX) - 1920
Cowdin (NY) - 1862
Cowell, A. L. (CA) - 1910

Cowen (NY) - 1848
Cowen (OH) - 1843
Cowen, John K. (MD) - 1894
Cowen, T. (WA) - 1904
Cowger, William O. (KY) - 1966, 1968, 1970
Cowgill, Calvin (IN) - 1878
Cowherd, William S. (MO) - 1896, 1898, 1900, 1902, 1904
Cowles (NY) - 1850
Cowles, Calvin I. (NC) - 1868
Cowles, Charles H. (NC) - 1908, 1910
Cowles, George W. (NY) - 1868
Cowles, Henry B. (NY) - 1828, 1832
Cowles, Horace (CT) - 1834, 1835
Cowles, William H. H. (NC) - 1884, 1886, 1888, 1890
Cowper (VA) - 1851
Cox (IN) - 1874
Cox (KY) - 1847
Cox (MD) - 1859, 1874
Cox (MN) - 1874
Cox (TN) - 1876
Cox, Asher R. (IL) - 1920
Cox, Billie M. (IL) - 1970
Cox, Boyd W. (TN) - 1952
Cox, Delson Jr. (IN) - 1974
Cox, E. E. (GA) - 1916, 1924, 1926, 1928, 1930, 1932, 1934, 1936, 1938, 1940, 1942, 1944, 1946, 1948, 1950, 1952
Cox, Emery D. (CO) - 1916
Cox, Isaac N. (NY) - 1890, 1892
Cox, J. Clifford (IL) - 1910
Cox, J. Ray (ID) - 1974
Cox, Jacob D. (OH) - 1876
Cox, James A. (IN) - 1908
Cox, James B. (TN) - 1914
Cox, James M. (OH) - 1908, 1910
Cox, James O. (IN) - 1940, 1944
Cox, Julius W. (OK) - 1942
Cox, Leander M. (KY) - 1853, 1855, 1857
Cox, Levi (OH) - 1840
Cox, Linton A. (IN) - 1910
Cox, Micajah (NC) - 1837
Cox, Nicholas N. (TN) - 1890, 1892, 1894, 1896, 1898
Cox, Noel (MO) - 1958
Cox, Rosslyn M. (NY) - 1916, 1920, 1924, 1932
Cox, Sampson (IN) - 1890
Cox, Samuel S. (NY) - 1868, 1870, 1872, 1874, 1876, 1878, 1880, 1882, 1884, 1886, 1888
Cox, Samuel S. (OH) - 1856, 1858, 1860, 1862, 1864
Cox, Stanley R. Jr. (WV) - 1964
Cox, Thad A. (TX) - 1894
Cox, Theodore (NY) - 1900
Cox, Thomas W. (FL) - 1910
Cox, William E. (IN) - 1906, 1908, 1910, 1912, 1914, 1916, 1918
Cox, William H. (NC) - 1920
Cox, William R. (NC) - 1880, 1882, 1884
Coxe (PA) - 1830
Coxe (TN) - 1837
Coxey, Jacob S. (OH) - 1894
Coxhill, Arnold B. (MI) - 1942, 1944
Coyle, Alfred F. (OH) - 1924
Coyle, Francis I. J. (PA) - 1924
Coyle, John A. (PA) - 1894
Coyle, T. Burton (NJ) - 1938
Coyle, William R. (PA) - 1924, 1926, 1928, 1930, 1932, 1936, 1942
Coyne, Frederick E. (IL) - 1914
Coyne, Jim (PA) - 1980, 1982
Coyne, William J. (PA) - 1980, 1982, 1984
Cozad, Harry (CA) - 1984
Crabb (WI) - 1848
Crabb, George W. (AL) - 1839, 1841
Crabb, R. H. (TX) - 1908
Crabbe, William (OH) - 1976
Crabtree, Alva (OH) - 1898
Crachi, Domenico Jr. (NY) - 1966
Craddock, John D. (KY) - 1928, 1930
Craft, Scott (KY) - 1956
Crafts, Erastus (NY) - 1828
Cragin, Aaron H. (NH) - 1855, 1857
Crago, Thomas S. (PA) - 1912, 1914, 1916, 1918, 1921
Craig (MO) - 1880
Craig (PA) - 1843
Craig, Alexander K. (PA) - 1890
Craig, Allen E. R. (NY) - 1936
Craig, Charles C. (IL) - 1922
Craig, George H. (AL) - 1882, 1884, 1892

Craig, Hector (NY) - 1824, 1826, 1828
Craig, James (MO) - 1856, 1858
Craig, James A. (NC) - 1829
Craig, John E. (IA) - 1902, 1904
Craig, John Russell (PA) - 1952
Craig, Larry E. (ID) - 1980, 1982, 1984
Craig, Robert (VA) - 1829, 1831, 1833, 1835, 1837, 1839
Craig, Samuel A. (PA) - 1888
Craig, Thomas H. (OH) - 1900
Craig, William (CA) - 1898
Craig, William B. (AL) - 1906, 1908
Craige, F. Burton (NC) - 1835, 1843, 1853, 1855, 1857, 1859
Craighead (OH) - 1860
Crail, Joe (CA) - 1926, 1928, 1930
Crail, Joe S. (IA) - 1912
Crain (OK) - 1914
Crain, Cleo (OK) - 1950
Crain, William H. (TX) - 1884, 1886, 1888, 1890, 1892, 1894
Craley, N. Neiman Jr. (PA) - 1964, 1966
Crall, Don H. (OK) - 1960
Cramer (AL) - 1868
Cramer (MO) - 1884, 1892
Cramer (NY) - 1856
Cramer, Floyd (NY) - 1954
Cramer, James M. (PA) - 1922, 1930
Cramer, John (NY) - 1828, 1832, 1834, 1840
Cramer, Ward Collins (MA) - 1960
Cramer, William C. (FL) - 1952, 1954, 1956, 1958, 1960, 1962, 1964, 1966, 1968
Crampton, Lewis (MA) - 1984
Cramton, Louis C. (MI) - 1912, 1914, 1916, 1918, 1920, 1922, 1924, 1926, 1928
Crandall (AL) - 1894
Crandall, Phineas (MA) - 1842
Crane (MD) - 1878
Crane (VA) - 1857
Crane, A. M. (VA) - 1869
Crane, C. F. (WI) - 1904
Crane, Daniel B. (IL) - 1978, 1980, 1982, 1984
Crane, David G. (IN) - 1976, 1978, 1980
Crane, Edward H. (IA) - 1914
Crane, Irving M. (NY) - 1912
Crane, Isaac M. (IN) - 1868
Crane, Joseph H. (OH) - 1828, 1830, 1832, 1834
Crane, Michael A. (CA) - 1970
Crane, Philip M. (IL) - 1969, 1970, 1972, 1974, 1976, 1978, 1980, 1982, 1984
Crane, R. T. (IL) - 1914
Crane, Robert (PA) - 1868
Crane, Samuel (WV) - 1864
Crane, Thomas M. (IL) - 1920, 1922
Crane, William F. (WI) - 1938
Cranford, John W. (TX) - 1896
Crangle, Frank M. (IL) - 1918
Crangle, Roland (NY) - 1930
Crank, W. J. L. (CO) - 1912
Cranmer, Neil Dow (NY) - 1940
Cranmore, George (NY) - 1951
Cranston (RI) - 1833, 1835
Cranston, Henry Y. (RI) - 1843, 1845
Cranston, Robert B. (RI) - 1837, 1839, 1841, 1847
Crapo, William W. (MA) - 1875, 1876, 1878, 1880
Crary, H. L. (OH) - 1930
Crary, Isaac E. (MI) - 1835, 1837, 1838
Crasno, Joseph H. (IL) - 1892
Crass, Oliver H. (TX) - 1928
Craugh, Joseph P. (NY) - 1928, 1930
Craven (MN) - 1904
Craven (NJ) - 1912
Craven, James E. (IA) - 1922
Craven, Leslie W. (CA) - 1970, 1972
Cravens (IN) - 1874
Cravens (MO) - 1886
Cravens, Fadjo (AR) - 1940, 1942, 1944, 1946
Cravens, James A. (IN) - 1860, 1862
Cravens, James H. (IN) - 1841
Cravens, John O. (IN) - 1880, 1884
Cravens, Jordan E. (AR) - 1876, 1878, 1880
Cravens, Thomas C. (IN) - 1960
Cravens, William B. (AR) - 1906, 1908, 1910, 1932, 1934, 1936, 1938
Craver, John (IL) - 1976
Crawford (GA) - 1844, 1846
Crawford (MO) - 1916

Dempster, Milen C. (CA) - 1932
DeNardis, Lawrence J. (CT) - 1980, 1982, 1984
Denby, Edwin (MI) - 1904, 1906, 1908, 1910
Denholm, Frank E. (SD) - 1968, 1970, 1972, 1974
Denio, C. B. (CA) - 1875
Denison, Charles (PA) - 1862, 1864, 1866
Denison, Dudley C. (VT) - 1874, 1876
Denison, Edward E. (IL) - 1916, 1918, 1920, 1922, 1924, 1926, 1928, 1930, 1932
Denison, John D. Jr. (IA) - 1910
Denman, James (CA) - 1894
Denman, William F. (IA) - 1956
Denn, Gale A. (NY) - 1980
Dennerll, Norbert G. Jr. (OH) - 1964
Denney, Arthur J. (NE) - 1936
Denney, Robert V. (NE) - 1966, 1968
Dennis (MD) - 1855
Dennis, Andrew B. (IL) - 1922, 1924
Dennis, David W. (IN) - 1968, 1970, 1972, 1974
Dennis, Henry D. (IL) - 1892
Dennis, John (MD) - 1837, 1839
Dennis, John W. (NY) - 1918
Dennis, Littleton P. (MD) - 1833
Dennison, David (OH) - 1956, 1958, 1960
Dennison, Edward E. (IL) - 1914
Dennison, Fern Coste (NY) - 1972
Dennison, Margaret (OH) - 1970
Denny, George (KY) - 1878
Denny, George Jr. (KY) - 1894
Denny, George L. (IN) - 1948
Denny, Harmar (PA) - 1829, 1830, 1832, 1834
Denny, Harmar D. Jr. (PA) - 1950, 1952
Denny, Jacob F. (IN) - 1916
Denny, James W. (MD) - 1898, 1900, 1902
Denny, Walter McK. (MS) - 1894
Denson, William H. (AL) - 1892, 1894
Denston (NY) - 1858
Dent, Jerry A. (MO) - 1978
Dent, John H. (PA) - 1958, 1960, 1962, 1964, 1966, 1968, 1970, 1972, 1974, 1976
Dent, Lewis (CA) - 1849
Dent, M. H. (WV) - 1906
Dent, S. Hubert Jr. (AL) - 1908, 1910, 1912, 1914, 1916, 1918
Dent, Thomas A. (NY) - 1954
Dent, William B. W. (GA) - 1853
Denton, E. Brady (MI) - 1976
Denton, George K. (IN) - 1916, 1918
Denton, J. A. (TN) - 1894
Denton, Winfield K. (IN) - 1946, 1948, 1950, 1952, 1954, 1956, 1958, 1960, 1962, 1964, 1966
Denver, James W. (CA) - 1854
Denver, James W. (OH) - 1870, 1884, 1886
Denver, Matthew R. (OH) - 1906, 1908, 1910
Dergance, Philip A. (KS) - 1948
Derham, Donald A. (NY) - 1970
Dermody, Joseph (NY) - 1938
Dermond, Philip C. (IN) - 1952
DeRouen, Rene L. (LA) - 1927, 1928, 1930, 1932, 1934, 1936, 1938
Derounian, Steven B. (NY) - 1952, 1954, 1956, 1958, 1960, 1962, 1964, 1966
Derrick (NJ) - 1918
Derrick, Butler C. (SC) - 1976, 1978, 1974, 1980, 1982, 1984
Derrick, George H. (CA) - 1914
Derry, George H. (NY) - 1922
Dershem, Frank L. (PA) - 1912, 1914
Derwinski, Edward J. (IL) - 1958, 1960, 1962, 1964, 1966, 1968, 1970, 1972, 1974, 1976, 1978, 1980
Desantis, John B. (PA) - 1916
Desborough, E. G. (NY) - 1974
Desha, L. B. (KY) - 1847
Desha, Robert (TN) - 1827, 1829
Desmond, Andrew D. (NJ) - 1944
Desmond, John J. (IL) - 1964
Desmond, John J. (MA) - 1894
Dethloff, Edward C. (NY) - 1924
Detig, Robert H. (NY) - 1966
Dettry, William H. (PA) - 1906
Deupree, Harlan (OK) - 1937, 1938
Deuster, Peter V. (WI) - 1878, 1880, 1882, 1884
Devalle, A. F. (CA) - 1884

Devaney, Joe (TX) - 1982
Devany, John A. Jr. (NY) - 1944, 1946
Dever (GA) - 1872
Dever, John J. (IL) - 1926
Devereaux, Alvin (NY) - 1868
Devereaux, James P. (MI) - 1910
Devereux, James P. S. (MD) - 1950, 1952, 1954, 1956
Devereux, Thomas P. (NC) - 1882
Devery, John Patrick (NY) - 1944
Devine, Herbert W. (MI) - 1950
Devine, John E. Jr. (IL) - 1970, 1972
Devine, John M. (NE) - 1894
Devine, Samuel L. (OH) - 1958, 1960, 1962, 1964, 1966, 1968, 1970, 1972, 1974, 1976, 1978, 1980
Devine, Thomas C. (OH) - 1912, 1916
Devito, Anthony J. (NY) - 1968, 1970
Devitt, Edward J. (MN) - 1946, 1948
Devlin (IN) - 1858
Devlin, James (PA) - 1916
Devlin, William E. (NY) - 1924, 1930
DeVoe, Fred W. (NJ) - 1926
Devol (MO) - 1910
Dewalt, Arthur G. (PA) - 1914, 1916, 1918, 1926
Dewan, James T. (OH) - 1956
Dewar (GA) - 1914
Dewar (PA) - 1854, 1858
Dewart, Lewis (PA) - 1830
D'Ewart, Wesley A. (MT) - 1945, 1946, 1948, 1950, 1952
Dewart, William L. (PA) - 1856
Deweese, John T. (NC) - 1868
Dewey, Charles (IN) - 1835
Dewey, Charles S. (IL) - 1938, 1940, 1942, 1944
Dewey, Henry B. (WA) - 1912
DeWine, Michael (OH) - 1982, 1984
DeWitt, William C. (NY) - 1924
Dexter, Simon (NY) - 1830
Deyendorf, John F. (VA) - 1892
DeYoung, James E. (NY) - 1976
Dezendorf, John F. (VA) - 1878, 1880, 1882
Dial (OH) - 1854
Dial, A. Clayton (KS) - 1964
Diamond, Robert (NY) - 1950
Diamondstone, Peter (VT) - 1978, 1980
Dibble, A. B. (CA) - 1856
Dibble, Henry C. (LA) - 1876
Dibble, Samuel (SC) - 1882, 1884, 1886, 1888
DiBiase, Carmine (NY) - 1984
Dible, Samuel (PA) - 1914
Dibrell, Anthony (TN) - 1839
Dibrell, George G. (TN) - 1874, 1876, 1878, 1880, 1882
DiCarlo, David C. (PA) - 1980
Dichter, David (NJ) - 1968
Dick, Archibald T. (PA) - 1834
Dick, Charles (OH) - 1898, 1900, 1902, 1918
Dick, Chuck (IA) - 1974
Dick, David (PA) - 1838
Dick, John (PA) - 1852, 1854, 1856
Dick, Samuel B. (PA) - 1878
Dickens, E. Dana (NC) - 1930
Dickenson, A. C. (WA) - 1898
Dickenson, Edward (MA) - 1855
Dickenson, S. N. (WI) - 1886
Dicker, Herbert (NY) - 1970
Dickerman, Charles H. (PA) - 1902
Dickerson (NJ) - 1918
Dickerson, David W. (TN) - 1843
Dickerson, J. G. (ME) - 1854
Dickerson, Philemon (NJ) - 1832, 1834, 1838, 1840
Dickerson, William W. (KY) - 1890
Dickes, Louis (IL) - 1902
Dickey (VT) - 1876, 1878
Dickey, F. B. (TN) - 1894
Dickey, F. Lyle (IL) - 1862
Dickey, Frank P. (TN) - 1892
Dickey, H. G. (OK) - 1952
Dickey, Henry L. (OH) - 1876, 1878
Dickey, Howard A. Jr. (KY) - 1960
Dickey, J. T. (GA) - 1900
Dickey, Jesse C. (PA) - 1848, 1850
Dickey, John (PA) - 1843, 1846
Dickey, Oliver J. (PA) - 1868, 1870
Dickey, T. Lyle (IL) - 1866
Dickey, W. C. (KS) - 1928

Dickheiser, Saul J. (NY) - 1928
Dickie, Samuel (MI) - 1890
Dickinson (NJ) - 1864
Dickinson (PA) - 1886
Dickinson, A. C. (WA) - 1892
Dickinson, Clement C. (MO) - 1910, 1912, 1914, 1916, 1918, 1920, 1922, 1924, 1926, 1928, 1930, 1932
Dickinson, David W. (TN) - 1833
Dickinson, Edward (MA) - 1852, 1854
Dickinson, Edward F. (OH) - 1868, 1870
Dickinson, John (NY) - 1826, 1828, 1830, 1832
Dickinson, John Jr. (MA) - 1846
Dickinson, Lester J. (IA) - 1918, 1920, 1922, 1924, 1926, 1928
Dickinson, Rodolphus (MA) - 1839
Dickinson, Rodolphus (OH) - 1846, 1848
Dickinson, Samuel F. (MA) - 1828
Dickinson, Wiliam A. (VA) - 1936
Dickinson, William L. (AL) - 1964, 1966, 1968, 1970, 1972, 1974, 1976, 1978, 1980, 1982, 1984
Dickman, Charles C. (IL) - 1936
Dicks, Norman D. (WA) - 1976, 1978, 1980, 1982, 1984
Dickson, Charles A. (IA) - 1906
Dickson, David (MS) - 1829, 1831, 1835
Dickson, E. E. (SC) - 1868
Dickson, Frank L. (IL) - 1904
Dickson, Frank S. (IL) - 1906, 1908
Dickson, Hugh L. (CA) - 1920
Dickson, J. L. (IL) - 1920
Dickson, John (NY) - 1830, 1832
Dickson, Samuel (NY) - 1854
Dickson, William A. (MS) - 1908, 1910
Dickstein, Samuel (NY) - 1922, 1924, 1926, 1928, 1930, 1932, 1934, 1936, 1938, 1940, 1942, 1944
Diefenderfer, Flora J. (PA) - 1920
Diehl, Harry E. (PA) - 1942
Diehl, Julius F. (MD) - 1926
Diehl, W. D. (Bill) (MT) - 1976
Diekema, Gerrit J. (MI) - 1907, 1908, 1910
Dielman, Fred (TX) - 1964
Dielmann, Harold L. (MO) - 1982
Dielmann, Henry B. (TX) - 1930
Dierkes, Edward (IL) - 1904
Dies, Martin (TX) - 1908, 1910, 1912, 1914, 1916
Dies, Martin Jr. (TX) - 1930, 1932, 1934, 1936, 1938, 1940, 1942, 1952, 1954, 1956
Dieterich, William H. (IL) - 1930
Dietrich, C. Elmer (PA) - 1934, 1936
Dietz, Carl P. (WI) - 1936
Dietz, S. Marie (VT) - 1978
Dietz, Walter F. (LA) - 1914
DiFazio, Lucien P. Jr. (CT) - 1976
Difenderfer, Robert E. (PA) - 1910, 1912
Diffendorffer (MO) - 1914
Digennaro, Vincent (NY) - 1956
Diggs, Charles C. Jr. (MI) - 1954, 1956, 1958, 1960, 1962, 1964, 1966, 1968, 1970, 1972, 1974, 1976, 1978
Diggs, E. E. (TX) - 1906, 1914
DiGiovanni, John (NY) - 1974
Dignan, Thomas S. (NJ) - 1940
Diiorio, Ralph (NY) - 1956
Dike, George W. (MA) - 1846
Dikeman, John (NY) - 1836
Dill, Clarence C. (WA) - 1914, 1916, 1918, 1942
Dill, Charles C. (NY) - 1904
Dill, Harry V. (KY) - 1920
Dillard, Ann W. (OK) - 1930
Dillard, Barney E. Jr. (FL) - 1980
Dillemuth, Charles H. (LA) - 1960
Dillingham, Paul Jr. (VT) - 1843, 1844
Dillner, Arthur E. (IL) - 1952
Dillon (TN) - 1882
Dillon, Charles H. (SD) - 1912, 1914, 1916
Dillon, James C. (IL) - 1938
Dillon, Jim (Matt) (TX) - 1978
Dillon, John E. (IN) - 1904
Dillon, John J. (IL) - 1956
Dillon, M. J. (MN) - 1936
Dillon, Martin F. (NY) - 1902
Dillon, Walter K. (MO) - 1946, 1948
Dills, John (KY) - 1878
Dillw (DE) - 1846
Dilweg, LaVern R. (WI) - 1942, 1944
Dimarco, Antony (MD) — 1922
Di Micelli, Leonard (CA) - 1958

Dimitri, William A. Jr. (RI) - 1970
Dimk, E. S. (PA) - 1856
Dimmick, Milo M. (PA) - 1848, 1850
Dimmick, William H. (PA) - 1856, 1858, 1878
Dimmitt, James P. (IL) - 1878
Dimock, Davis Jr. (PA) - 1840
Dingell, John D. (MI) - 1932, 1934, 1936, 1938, 1940, 1942, 1944, 1946, 1948, 1950, 1952, 1954
Dingell, John D. Jr. (MI) - 1955, 1956, 1958, 1960, 1962, 1964, 1966, 1968, 1970, 1972, 1974, 1976, 1978, 1980, 1982, 1984
Dingeman, A. J. (CA) - 1942
Dingley, Edward N. (MI) - 1912, 1914
Dingley, Nelson Jr. (ME) - 1881, 1882, 1884, 1886, 1888, 1890, 1892, 1894, 1896, 1898
Dininny (NY) - 1888
Dinis, Edmund (MA) - 1968
Diniz, Jacinto F. (MA) - 1948
d'Innocenzo, Michael (NY) - 1984
Dinsmoor, James (IL) - 1872
Dinsmore, Hugh A. (AR) - 1892, 1894, 1896, 1898, 1900, 1902
Dinsmore, J. W. (KY) - 1912
DioGuardi, Joseph J. (NY) - 1984
Dirks, A. Stephen (UT) - 1982
Dirksen, Everett M. (IL) - 1932, 1934, 1936, 1938, 1940, 1942, 1944, 1946
DiSalle, Michael V. (OH) - 1946
Dishman (KY) - 1916
Dishongh, Lewis (NC) - 1833, 1835
Disney, David T. (OH) - 1848, 1850, 1852
Disney, Loren G. (OK) - 1907
Disney, Wesley E. (OK) - 1930, 1932, 1934, 1936, 1938, 1940, 1942
Disosway (NY) - 1854
Ditchen, John F. (OH) - 1904
Ditchey, Charles F. (PA) - 1922
Ditter, J. William (PA) - 1932, 1934, 1936, 1938, 1940, 1942
Ditucci, Cosmo J. (NY) - 1970
Ditus, Stan (NE) - 1980
Divelbiss, Carl W. (AZ) - 1950
Diven, Alexander S. (NY) - 1860
Dix, David (WV) - 1972
Dix, John W. (PA) - 1918
Dixon (CT) - 1869
Dixon (MD) - 1833
Dixon (RI) - 1833
Dixon (RI) - 1916
Dixon, Charles G. (IL) - 1894
Dixon, Emerald B. (MI) - 1930
Dixon, Henry Aldous (UT) - 1954, 1956, 1958
Dixon, J. N. (TX) - 1882
Dixon, James (CT) - 1845, 1847
Dixon, Joseph (NC) - 1870
Dixon, Joseph A. (OH) - 1936, 1938, 1940
Dixon, Joseph M. (MT) - 1902, 1904
Dixon, Julian C. (CA) - 1978, 1980, 1982, 1984
Dixon, Kelly (NC) - 1960
Dixon, L. P. (NC) - 1932
Dixon, Lincoln (IN) - 1904, 1906, 1908, 1910, 1912, 1914, 1916, 1918
Dixon, Moses (NY) - 1828
Dixon, Mott C. (NY) - 1890
Dixon, Nathan F. (RI) - 1849, 1863, 1865, 1867, 1868, 1885, 1886
Dixon, Oliver O. (IN) - 1946
Dixon, Robert H. (NC) - 1918
Dixon, Sherwood (IL) - 1886
Dixon, T. B. (KY) - 1912
Dixon, Thurman B. (KY) - 1926
Dixon, W. O. (NC) - 1914, 1916, 1920
Dixon, W. R. (NC) - 1906
Dixon, William C. (OH) - 1934
Dixon, William W. (MT) - 1890, 1892
Dizotell, Forest (IL) - 1940
Doah, W. M. (VA) - 1920
Doan, Robert E. (OH) - 1890
Doan, William (OH) - 1838, 1840
Doan, William H. (OH) - 1878, 1882
Doane, George W. (NE) - 1892
Doane, Josial (IA) - 1882
Doane, Paul V. (MA) - 1980
Dobbin, James C. (NC) - 1845
Dobbins, Donald C. (IL) - 1932, 1934
Dobbins, James (NJ) - 1960
Dobbins, Samuel A. (NJ) - 1872, 1874
Dobbs, Jim (TX) - 1962
Dobler, Henry G. (IL) - 1922

Dobosh, Jack N. (NY) - 1974, 1976
Dobsevage, George (NY) - 1926
Dobson, David M. (IN) - 1847
Dock (PA) - 1848
Dockery, Alexander M. (MO) - 1882, 1884, 1886, 1888, 1890, 1892, 1894, 1896
Dockery, Alfred (NC) - 1845, 1851
Dockery, Oliver H. (NC) - 1868, 1870, 1872, 1882, 1884, 1898, 1900
Dockweiler, John F. (CA) - 1930, 1932, 1934, 1936, 1938
Dodd (NJ) - 1856
Dodd (NY) - 1862
Dodd, Christopher J. (CT) - 1974, 1976, 1978
Dodd, Craig (OK) - 1984
Dodd, Edward (NY) - 1854, 1856
Dodd, Hiram (AL) - 1948
Dodd, J. W. (AL) - 1934
Dodd, Thomas J. (CT) - 1952, 1954
Doddridge (VA) - 1825
Doddridge, Philip (VA) - 1829, 1831
Dodds, Francis H. (MI) - 1908, 1910
Dodge (NY) - 1848, 1856, 1888
Dodge, Clarence (CO) - 1912
Dodge, Frank L. (MI) - 1908, 1914, 1920, 1926
Dodge, Grenville M. (IA) - 1866
Dodge, James S. (IN) - 1892
Dodge, N. A. (TX) - 1900
Dodge, Rufus B. (MA) - 1902
Dodge, W. A. (TX) - 1908
Dodge, William (NY) - 1824, 1828
Dodge, William E. (NY) - 1864
Dodson (PA) - 1886
Dodson, George H. (OK) - 1916
Doe, Joseph B. Jr. (WI) - 1888
Doerfler, Ernest (NY) - 1950, 1954
Doherty (NJ) - 1892
Doherty, A. B. C. (MN) - 1936, 1938
Doherty, George T. (WI) - 1940
Doherty, James L. (IL) - 1954
Doherty, John (MN) - 1980
Doherty, John F. (WI) - 1898
Doherty, Philip J. (MA) - 1896
Doherty, Thomas A. (PA) - 1920
Dohr, William F. (CA) - 1982
Doig, Andrew (NY) - 1838, 1840
Dolan, John P. J. (MN) - 1928
Dolan, Joseph C. (PA) - 1956
Dolan, Thomas F. (IL) - 1950
Dolan, Thomas P. (PA) - 1906
Dole, Robert (KS) - 1960, 1962, 1964, 1966
Dolezal, Gerald (IL) - 1968
Dolgaard, Keith (AZ) - 1974
Doll, Ken (WV) - 1970
Dollinger, Isidore (NY) - 1948, 1950, 1952, 1954, 1956, 1958
Dolliver, James I. (IA) - 1944, 1946, 1948, 1950, 1952, 1954, 1956
Dolliver, Jonathan P. (IA) - 1888, 1890, 1892, 1894, 1896, 1898
Dombrowski, Leon A. (NY) - 1944
Domengeaux, James (LA) - 1940, 1942, 1944, 1946
Dominick, Fred H. (SC) - 1916, 1918, 1920, 1922, 1924, 1926, 1928, 1930
Dominick, Peter H. (CO) - 1960
Domme, Robert W. (KS) - 1958
Donahoe, John T. (IL) - 1908
Donahue (CT) - 1906
Donahue, Edward M. (CT) - 1980
Donahue, Louis A. (ME) - 1922
Donald, Clark M. (KY) - 1928
Donaldson, C. M. (OR) - 1898
Donaldson, Curt (NE) - 1982
Donaldson, Frank (AL) - 1968
Donaldson, Michael C. (CA) - 1970
Donaldson, Presley G. (IL) - 1892
Donaugh, Carl C. (OR) - 1950
Dondero, George A. (MI) - 1932, 1934, 1936, 1938, 1940, 1942, 1944, 1946, 1948, 1950, 1952, 1954
Donelon, James (LA) - 1980
Donges, John W. (NJ) - 1948
Dongvillo, Henry J. (MI) - 1966
Donihi, Robert M. (TN) - 1954
Donlan, Fraser P. (PA) - 1950
Donley, Charles C. (OH) - 1892
Donley, Joseph B. (PA) - 1868, 1870
Donley, Willis E. (WI) - 1934
Donlin, Patrick J. (OH) - 1978, 1980
Donlon, Mary (NY) - 1940
Donnally, Andrew (VA) - 1837

Donnan, William G. (IA) - 1870, 1872
Donnaruma, Walter (NY) - 1952
Donnell, John A. (IA) - 1886
Donnell, Louis A. (KS) - 1950
Donnell, Richard S. (NC) - 1845, 1847
Donnelly (MN) - 1870, 1876, 1878
Donnelly (PA) - 1886, 1888
Donnelly, Brian J. (MA) - 1978, 1980, 1982, 1984
Donnelly, Edward L. (MA) - 1928, 1930
Donnelly, I. (MN) - 1884
Donnelly, Ignatius (MN) - 1862, 1864, 1866, 1868
Donnelly, Joseph G. (WI) - 1898, 1906
Donnelly, Neil (IL) - 1862
Donnelly, Thomas John (OH) - 1894, 1896
Donnelly, William M. (MI) - 1926, 1928, 1930
Donnelson (TN) - 1843
Donnohue (MO) - 1892
Donoghue, Arthur J. (IL) - 1906
Donoghue, Roger P. (MA) - 1897
Donohoe, Eugene G. (MI) - 1950
Donohoe, Michael (PA) - 1910, 1912, 1914, 1916
Donohue (MN) - 1916
Donohue, Charles (WI) - 1912
Donohue, Harold D. (MA) - 1946, 1948, 1950, 1952, 1954, 1956, 1958, 1960, 1962, 1964, 1966, 1968, 1970, 1972
Donohue, Michael (PA) - 1908
Donohue, Michael J. (IL) - 1984
Donovan (CT) - 1916
Donovan (MA) - 1886, 1888
Donovan (MO) - 1890
Donovan (NY) - 1886
Donovan, Andrew (IL) - 1912
Donovan, Cornelius (NY) - 1890
Donovan, Dennis D. (OH) - 1890, 1892
Donovan, James G. (NY) - 1950, 1952, 1954, 1956
Donovan, Jeremiah (CT) - 1912, 1914
Donovan, Jerome F. (NY) - 1918, 1920
Donovan, John C. (ME) - 1960
Donovan, John F. (WI) - 1902
Donovan, Joseph Francis (CA) - 1962
Donovan, Joseph O. (CA) - 1942
Donovan, Thomas F. (IL) - 1894
Donson, W. M. (KY) - 1898
Donworth, John P. (ME) - 1876
Doodridge (VA) - 1825
Doolan, Edward F. (MA) - 1952, 1954, 1956, 1958, 1960, 1962, 1964
Doole, D. (TX) - 1906
Dooley, Edwin B. (NY) - 1956, 1958, 1960
Dooling, Peter J. (NY) - 1912, 1914, 1916, 1918, 1920
Doolittle, Dudley (KS) - 1912, 1914, 1916, 1918, 1940
Doolittle, Harvey (NY) - 1840
Doolittle, James R. (IL) - 1878
Doolittle, James R. (WI) - 1886
Doolittle, M. B. (IA) - 1880
Doolittle, Richard L. (PA) - 1968
Doolittle, William H. (WA) - 1892, 1894, 1896
Doon, Aloysius J. (MA) - 1918
Dopp, Arthur (WI) - 1904
Doran, James P. (MA) - 1922
Dore, C. F. (IL) - 1972
Doremus, Frank E. (MI) - 1910, 1912, 1914, 1916, 1918
Dorfman, Henry D. (NY) - 1948, 1952, 1954, 1956
Dorgan, Byron L. (ND) - 1974, 1980, 1982, 1984
Dorland (NY) - 1882
Dorlon, Robert (NY) - 1838
Dorn, D. A. (PA) - 1926, 1932
Dorn, Francis E. (NY) - 1948, 1949, 1950, 1952, 1954, 1956, 1958, 1960, 1962
Dorn, Frank A. (NY) - 1930
Dorn, W. J. Bryan (SC) - 1946, 1950, 1952, 1954, 1956, 1958, 1960, 1962, 1964, 1966, 1968, 1970, 1972
Dornan, Bob (CA) - 1984
Dornan, Robert K. (CA) - 1976, 1978, 1980
Dornbach, George W. (PA) - 1912
Dornon, R. A. (PA) - 1908
Dorr (RI) - 1837
Dorr, Charles P. (WV) - 1896
Dorr, L. Bradley (NY) - 1908, 1912
Dorr, Thomas H. (WI) - 1924
Dorr, Thomas W. (RI) - 1839

Dorriblum, Jennie (PA) - 1924
Dorrier, Lindsay G. Jr. (VA) - 1982
Dorrity, Dan (MI) - 1980
Dorsett, James D. (NC) - 1924
Dorse, Bob (WA) - 1982
Dorse, Robert L. (WA) - 1984
Dorsey (MO) - 1882
Dorsey (OH) - 1854, 1856
Dorsey, Clement (MD) - 1824, 1826, 1829, 1833
Dorsey, Clinton G. (OH) - 1976
Dorsey, Frank J. G. (PA) - 1934, 1936, 1938
Dorsey, George W. E. (NE) - 1884, 1886, 1888, 1890
Dorsey, John L. Jr. (KY) - 1930
Dorsey, William (OH) - 1886
Dorsheimer, William (NY) - 1882
Dorwin (NY) - 1856
Dosland, Goodwin L. (IL) - 1938
Doss, Evan (MS) - 1978
Doss, W. G. (TN) - 1970
Dostal, Frank (NY) - 1916
Doster, F. (KS) - 1878
Doster, Robert M. (SC) - 1962, 1964
Doten, David C. (KS) - 1936
Dotson, Dalton (AR) - 1948
Dotts (PA) - 1884
Doty, Bessie (NJ) - 1976
Doty, Elizabeth G. (IL) - 1928
Doty, Ethan Allen (PA) - 1950
Doty, Foster W. (MA) - 1956
Doty, Harvey Walter (OH) - 1898
Doty, James Duane (WI) - 1848, 1850
Doty, Paul E. (MN) - 1922
Doubleday, Ulysses (NY) - 1830, 1834
Doud, A. J. (PA) - 1900
Doug (IL) - 1865
Doughan, John E. (CT) - 1926
Dougherty (PA) - 1888
Dougherty (RI) - 1936
Dougherty, Charles (FL) - 1884, 1886
Dougherty, Charles F. (PA) - 1970, 1978, 1980, 1982
Dougherty, Frank W. (PA) - 1930
Dougherty, Harry V. (PA) - 1932
Dougherty, James E. (PA) - 1950
Dougherty, James G. (MN) - 1892
Dougherty, John (MO) - 1898, 1900, 1902
Doughton, Robert L. (NC) - 1910, 1912, 1914, 1916, 1918, 1920, 1922, 1924, 1926, 1928, 1930, 1932, 1934, 1936, 1938, 1940, 1942, 1944, 1946, 1948, 1950
Doughton, Rufus A. (NC) - 1896
Doughty (PA) - 1843
Doughty, James C. (NV) - 1894, 1896
Douglas (CT) - 1878
Douglas (GA) - 1859
Douglas (MD) - 1888
Douglas (MO) - 1856
Douglas, Albert (OH) - 1906, 1908, 1910, 1912
Douglas, Ben E. (NC) - 1956
Douglas, Beverly B. (VA) - 1874, 1876
Douglas, Charles I. (UT) - 1908
Douglas, Curtis N. (NY) - 1910
Douglas, Earl (NM) - 1946
Douglas, Emily Taft (IL) - 1944, 1946
Douglas, Fred J. (NY) - 1936, 1938, 1940, 1942
Douglas, Helen Gahagan (CA) - 1944, 1946, 1948
Douglas, Mrs. Jett W. (IA) - 1922
Douglas, Lewis W. (AZ) - 1926, 1928, 1930, 1932
Douglas, Stephen A. (IL) - 1838, 1843, 1844, 1846
Douglas, Thomas H. (MO) - 1936
Douglas, Walter W. (VA) - 1870
Douglas, William H. (NY) - 1900
Douglass (OH) - 1843
Douglass, John J. (MA) - 1924, 1926, 1928, 1930, 1932
Douglass, Thomas E. (OH) - 1872
Douglass, William H. (NY) - 1902
Douthett, Russell M. (PA) - 1960
Douthitt, W. F. (TX) - 1896
Doutrich, Isaac H. (PA) - 1926, 1928, 1930, 1932, 1934, 1936
Dove, F. R. (IL) - 1916
Dovener, Blackburn B. (WV) - 1892, 1894, 1896, 1898, 1900, 1902, 1904
Dover, Floyd K. (OR) - 1944

Dow (NY) - 1860
Dow, John G. (NY) - 1964, 1966, 1968, 1970, 1972, 1974
Dow, L. F. (ND) - 1904
Dow, Michael F. (CA) - 1980
Dow, Warren O. (WA) - 1936
Dowd, Clement (NC) - 1880, 1882
Dowd, Harry J. (MA) - 1936
Dowd, Thomas M. (OH) - 1954
Dowd, William F. (NJ) - 1970, 1972
Dowda, F. William (GA) - 1980
Dowdall, John A. (IL) - 1922
Dowdell, James F. (AL) - 1853, 1855, 1857
Dowdell, Robert E. (SD) - 1908, 1912
Dowden, B. Tarkington (CA) - 1942
Dowdney, Abraham (NY) - 1884
Dowdy, John (TX) - 1952, 1954, 1956, 1958, 1960, 1962, 1964, 1966, 1968, 1970
Dowdy, Wayne (MS) - 1981, 1982, 1984
Dowe (NY) - 1860
Dowe, John M. (CT) - 1934
Dowell, Cassius C. (IA) - 1914, 1916, 1918, 1920, 1922, 1924, 1926, 1928, 1930, 1932, 1934, 1936, 1938
Dowell, George W. (IL) - 1914
Dowiat, Stan (FL) - 1980
Dowley, Levi A. (MA) - 1852
Dowling, D. J. (SC) - 1846
Dowling, Lamoine Montgomery (MN) - 1940
Downer, Sylvester S. (NV) - 1918
Downes, George (ME) - 1848
Downes, James E. (NJ) - 1940
Downes, John W. (IL) - 1882
Downey, James B. (NY) - 1946
Downey, O. P. (WV) - 1870
Downey, R. J. (ND) - 1940
Downey, Thomas J. (NY) - 1974, 1976, 1978, 1980, 1982, 1984
Downing (NY) - 1888
Downing, Charles E. (MI) - 1936
Downing, Erie Lee (GA) - 1984
Downing, Finis E. (IL) - 1894
Downing, Frank (GA) - 1954
Downing, Thomas N. (VA) - 1958, 1960, 1962, 1964, 1966, 1968, 1970, 1972, 1974
Downing, W. C. (NC) - 1928, 1936
Downs (NY) - 1886
Downs (SC) - 1843
Downs, Arthur W. (MD) - 1968
Downs, Caleb B. (OH) - 1886
Downs, LeRoy D. (CT) - 1940, 1942
Downs, Mary (CO) - 1984
Downs, Thomas J. (IL) - 1942, 1944
Dows, David (SC) - 1952
Dox, Peter M. (AL) - 1869, 1870
Doxey, Charles T. (IN) - 1882, 1884
Doxey, Wall (MS) - 1928, 1930, 1932, 1934, 1936, 1938, 1940
Doyle, Arthur W. (NY) - 1924
Doyle, Bernard W. (MA) - 1936
Doyle, Clyde (CA) - 1944, 1946, 1948, 1950, 1952, 1954, 1956, 1958, 1960, 1962
Doyle, Cornelius J. (IL) - 1904
Doyle, Helen Poppy (MN) - 1980
Doyle, James E. (IL) - 1972
Doyle, James F. (IL) - 1924, 1926
Doyle, James William III (TX) - 1976
Doyle, Jeremiah J. (NH) - 1932
Doyle, Joseph F. (GA) - 1896
Doyle, Laurence A. (MA) - 1950
Doyle, Lawrence E. (WA) - 1894
Doyle, Michael Francis (PA) - 1898, 1900
Doyle, Michael G. (GA) - 1890
Doyle, Michael J. (MI) - 1918
Doyle, Patrick A. (MA) - 1940
Doyle, Richard (CA) - 1981
Doyle, T. J. (NE) - 1906
Doyle, Thomas A. (IL) - 1923, 1924, 1926, 1928
Dozier, R. C. (NC) - 1934
Dozier, R. Clarence (NC) - 1944
Draffen, E. W. (KY) - 1926
Drake (TN) - 1876
Drake, C. C. (TX) - 1892, 1900
Drake, Frank (MS) - 1980
Drake, Frank M. (KY) - 1934
Drake, Frederick S. (PA) - 1912, 1914
Drake, Henry P. (OH) - 1952
Drake, Herbert L. (KS) - 1942, 1943

Drake, John A. (IL) - 1854
Drake, Robin (WA) - 1980
Drake, Thomas J. (MI) - 1843
Drake, William J. (NY) - 1942
Dramesi, John A. (NJ) - 1982
Drane, Herbert J. (FL) - 1916, 1918, 1920, 1922, 1924, 1926, 1928, 1930
Drane, S. T. (KY) - 1878
Draper, Dan M. (MO) - 1878
Draper, Edward (MO) - 1870
Draper, Frederick E. Jr. (NY) - 1912
Draper, Joseph (VA) - 1831
Draper, Robert M. (OH) - 1948
Draper, William F. (MA) - 1892, 1894
Draper, William H. (NY) - 1900, 1902, 1904, 1906, 1908, 1910
Draper, William H. III (CA) - 1967
Drath, Phillip (CA) - 1968
Dratz, Paul A. (IL) - 1906
Drayton, William (SC) - 1826, 1828, 1830
Dreger, Alvin (WI) - 1906
Dreier, David (CA) - 1978, 1980, 1982, 1984
Dreitzler, John (OH) - 1924
Drennan (MS) - 1880
Drenovac, Sam P. (IL) - 1976
Dresbach, Eli (OH) - 1846
Drescher, Alex S. (NY) - 1914
Dresser, Solomon R. (PA) - 1902, 1904
Dretzin, William (NY) - 1970
Drew (ME) - 1858
Drew, A. M. (CA) - 1914
Drew, Charles B. (MA) - 1908
Drew, Ira Walton (PA) - 1936, 1938
Drew, Thomas S. (AR) - 1858
Drewry, Patrick Henry (VA) - 1920, 1922, 1924, 1926, 1928, 1930, 1932, 1934, 1936, 1938, 1940, 1942, 1944, 1946
Drews, Gustav (NY) - 1938
Drexler, John (IL) - 1910
Drexler, John M. (MN) - 1964
Drexler, Louis A. (DE) - 1912
Dreyfus, Jules (LA) - 1910
Drezdzon, Joseph F. (WI) - 1922
Driehaus, Don (OH) - 1968
Driggs, C. M. (PA) - 1926
Driggs, Charles M. (PA) - 1924
Driggs, Edmund H. (NY) - 1897, 1898, 1900
Driggs, John F. (MI) - 1862, 1864, 1866, 1870
Driggs, Laurence L. (NY) - 1908
Drinan, Robert F. (MA) - 1970, 1972, 1974, 1976, 1978
Drinkle, H. C. (OH) - 1882
Drinnon, T. C. (TN) - 1934
Driscoll, D. J. (PA) - 1932, 1934, 1936
Driscoll, Daniel A. (NY) - 1908, 1910, 1912, 1914, 1916
Driscoll, Lee F. Jr. (PA) - 1962
Driscoll, Michael E. (NY) - 1898, 1900, 1902, 1904, 1906, 1908, 1910, 1912
Driscoll, Patrick J. (MI) - 1966, 1970
Driscoll, Timothy J. (MA) - 1924
Driver, William J. (AR) - 1920, 1922, 1924, 1926, 1928, 1930, 1932, 1934, 1936
Dromgoole, George C. (VA) - 1833, 1835, 1837, 1839, 1843, 1845, 1847
Drucker, Harvey (OH) - 1924
Drukker, Dow H. (NJ) - 1914, 1916
Drum, Augustus (PA) - 1852, 1854
Drumheller, Roscoe M. (WA) - 1912, 1914
Drummond, Dock (MS) - 1966
Drummond, J. H. (FL) - 1924, 1926
Drummond, Richard C. S. (NY) - 1912
Drummond, Robert L. (NY) - 1896, 1900
Drury, Charles (WA) - 1914
Drury, John J. (NY) - 1960
Dryden, A. L. (MD) - 1894
Dryden, A. Lincoln (MD) - 1910
Drye, Don V. (KY) - 1942
Drye, Don Victor Sr. (KY) - 1946
Drzazga, John (FL) - 1968
Du Pont, Elise R. W. (DE) - 1984
Duane, W. (PA) - 1826
Dubin, Melvin (NY) - 1968
Dubois (MN) - 1902, 1914
Dubois, George (IL) - 1968
Dubois, Jarvis F. (IL) - 1914
Dubois, John E. (NY) - 1936
Dubord, F. H. (ME) - 1938
DuBose, Dudley M. (GA) - 1870, 1872
Dubrow, Walter (NJ) - 1966
Duchesne, Leon C. (MS) - 1888

Ducote, James H. (LA) - 1900
Ducunha (NY) - 1876
Dudkin, Harry (NJ) - 1948, 1950
Dudley, C. W. (SC) - 1870
Dudley, Charles (NY) - 1828
Dudley, Dudley (NH) - 1984
Dudley, Edward B. (NC) - 1829
Dudley, F. P. (IL) - 1916
Dudley, John G. (VA) - 1924
Dudley, Robert (PA) - 1910
Dudley, W. L. (CA) - 1858
Dudley, William (MA) - 1910
Duell, R. Holland (NY) - 1858, 1860, 1870, 1872
Duenow, Gordon E. (MN) - 1960
Duer, Robert F. (MD) - 1914, 1916, 1940
Duer, William (NY) - 1842, 1846, 1848
Duff, F. Odair (WV) - 1958
Duff, James K. P. (PA) - 1878
Duff, John B. (NJ) - 1968
Duff, O. E. (OH) - 1908
Duffey, Warren J. (OH) - 1932, 1934
Duffie, Edward R. (NE) - 1896
Duffield (MI) - 1876
Duffield, Will Ward (KY) - 1930
Duffy (NY) - 1860, 1862
Duffy, Edward F. (PA) - 1908
Dugan, Steve (CA) - 1976
Dugas, Louis Jr. (TX) - 1984
Dugdale, Robert E. (OR) - 1970
Duggan (TN) - 1882
Duggan, Jerome F. (MO) - 1924
Dugro, Philip Henry (NY) - 1880
Duhe, J. Paulin (LA) - 1948
Duke, Richard T. W. (VA) - 1870
Dukehart, Edward C. (MD) - 1954
Dula, Thomas J. (NC) - 1876
Dulin, P. P. (NC) - 1932
Dulski, Thaddeus J. (NY) - 1958, 1960, 1962, 1964, 1966, 1968, 1970, 1972
Dumaine, Dudley B. (MA) - 1964
Dumont, Ebenezer (IN) - 1862, 1864
Dun, McEldin (OH) - 1896
Dunavant, Leonard (TN) - 1969
Dunaway (MO) - 1912
Dunaway, Dave (TN) - 1980
Dunaway, Osmer E. (CA) - 1968
Dunbar (MS) - 1843
Dunbar (OH) - 1854
Dunbar, Danius (MA) - 1856
Dunbar, David C. (UT) - 1922
Dunbar, James W. (IN) - 1918, 1920, 1928, 1930
Dunbar, John G. (IN) - 1890
Dunbar, William (LA) - 1853
Dunblazier, W. H. (AR) - 1920
Duncan (MD) - 1845
Duncan, Alexander (OH) - 1836, 1838, 1840, 1843
Duncan, B. Stiles (PA) - 1934
Duncan, Daniel (OH) - 1846, 1848
Duncan, Eugene J. (PA) - 1982
Duncan, George H. (NH) - 1926
Duncan, Henry C. (IN) - 1888
Duncan, J. D. (KY) - 1912
Duncan, James A. (WA) - 1920
Duncan, James H. (MA) - 1848, 1850
Duncan, John J. (TN) - 1964, 1966, 1968, 1970, 1972, 1974, 1976, 1978, 1980, 1982, 1984
Duncan, Joseph (IL) - 1826, 1828, 1831, 1832
Duncan, Lewis J. (MT) - 1908, 1914
Duncan, Richard M. (MO) - 1928, 1932, 1934, 1936, 1938, 1940, 1942
Duncan, Robert (OR) - 1976, 1978
Duncan, Robert B. (OR) - 1962, 1964, 1974
Duncan, Thomas (IN) - 1896, 1898
Duncan, W. Garnett (KY) - 1847
Duncan, William A. (PA) - 1882, 1884
Duncomb, John F. (IA) - 1862, 1872
Dundas, W. Wurt (PA) - 1882
Dungan, Harry S. (NE) - 1920
Dungan, Irvin (OH) - 1886
Dungan, James Irvine (OH) - 1890, 1892
Dunham (MA) - 1878
Dunham, Charles (IL) - 1876, 1878
Dunham, Cyrus L. (IN) - 1849, 1851, 1852
Dunham, Jarvis N. (MA) - 1884
Dunham, Ransom W. (IL) - 1882, 1884, 1886
Dunk, Edith (MI) - 1920
Dunkle, John C. (PA) - 1920
Dunlap (TN) - 1865

Dunlap, George W. (KY) - 1855, 1861
Dunlap, Harry B. (IA) - 1936
Dunlap, Renick W. (OH) - 1934
Dunlap, Robert P. (ME) - 1843, 1844
Dunlap, Ron (WA) - 1980
Dunlap, Tom (OK) - 1976
Dunlap, William C. (TN) - 1833, 1835, 1837, 1839
Dunlavy, D. F. (OH) - 1932
Dunleavy, James Patrick (ME) - 1982
Dunm (IN) - 1854
Dunn (AL) - 1845
Dunn (CT) - 1916
Dunn (IN) - 1870
Dunn (MO) - 1886
Dunn (RI) - 1936
Dunn (WI) - 1858
Dunn, Adolph G. (NY) - 1872
Dunn, Aubert C. (MS) - 1934
Dunn, Charles (IL) - 1832
Dunn, Charles W. (UT) - 1936
Dunn, Elijah T. (OH) - 1894
Dunn, Francis G. (SD) - 1954
Dunn, George G. (IN) - 1843, 1847, 1854
Dunn, George H. (IN) - 1835, 1837, 1839
Dunn, Harold H. (MI) - 1946
Dunn, Harry J. (PA) - 1920
Dunn, Jack B. (NJ) - 1958, 1960
Dunn, Jacob P. (IN) - 1902
Dunn, James (NY) - 1840
Dunn, James R. (CA) - 1968
Dunn, Jim (MI) - 1980, 1982
Dunn, Joe A. (NC) - 1958
Dunn, John T. (NJ) - 1892, 1894
Dunn, L. E. (TX) - 1894
Dunn, Laurel N. (TX) - 1966
Dunn, Matthew A. (PA) - 1932, 1934, 1936, 1938
Dunn, Poindexter (AR) - 1878, 1880, 1882, 1884, 1886
Dunn, Robert J. (CT) - 1970
Dunn, Robert W. (PA) - 1890
Dunn, Thomas B. (NY) - 1912, 1914, 1916, 1918, 1920
Dunn, William D. (AL) - 1841
Dunn, William McKee (IN) - 1849, 1858, 1860, 1862
Dunne, Robert L. (IL) - 1978
Dunnell, Mark H. (MN) - 1870, 1872, 1874, 1876, 1878, 1880, 1888, 1890
Dunngton (VA) - 1857
Dunning, A. J. Jr. (VA) - 1932
Dunning, A. R. (VA) - 1956
Dunning, Dow (ID) - 1922
Dunphy, Edward J. (NY) - 1888, 1890, 1892
Dunseath, James A. (AZ) - 1920
Dunstan, C. W. (AL) - 1869
Dunwell, Charles T. (NY) - 1902, 1904, 1906
Dupay, Robert L. (NH) - 1982
Duplantis, Floyd J. (LA) - 1960
Dupre, Gilbert L. (LA) - 1902
Dupre, H. Garland (LA) - 1910, 1912, 1914, 1916, 1918, 1920, 1922
Dupuis, Frederick G. (CA) - 1958, 1960
Dur (WI) - 1852
Durand (MI) - 1876
Durand, Charles A. (MI) - 1904
Durand, Edward G. (WI) - 1886
Durand, George H. (MI) - 1874
Durant, Richard (MI) - 1950, 1952
Duras, Victor H. (NY) - 1908, 1910
Durbin, Andrew T. (OH) - 1948
Durbin, Francis W. (OH) - 1940
Durbin, Richard J. (IL) - 1982, 1984
Durbin, W. W. (OH) - 1912
Durborow, Allan C. Jr. (IL) - 1890, 1892, 1902
Durell (LA) - 1862
Durey, Cyrus (NY) - 1906, 1908, 1910
Durfee, Job (RI) - 1825, 1829
Durfee, Nathaniel B. (RI) - 1855, 1857
Durgan, George R. (IN) - 1932, 1934, 1935
Durham, C. M. (IA) - 1882
Durham, Carl T. (NC) - 1938, 1940, 1942, 1944, 1946, 1948, 1950, 1952, 1954, 1956, 1958
Durham, Charles L. (NY) - 1920, 1924
Durham, Milton J. (KY) - 1872, 1874, 1876
Durham, Plato (NC) - 1868, 1874
Durham, W. R. (TX) - 1976

Durham, William J. (IN) - 1890
Durick, Jeremiah C. (VT) - 1920, 1928
Durkee, Charles (WI) - 1848, 1850
Durkee, Wilbur G. (CA) - 1966
Durkin, Roger P. (MA) - 1976
Durland, O. C. (NC) - 1926
Durland, William R. (VA) - 1972
Durner, Charles (PA) - 1914
Durning, Marvin (WA) - 1977
Durno, Edwin R. (OR) - 1960
Durston (NY) - 1878
Dusatko, Alan A. (NE) - 1952
Dusek, F. W. (TX) - 1936
Dustin, Charles W. (OH) - 1916, 1918
Dutcher, Henry R. Jr. (NY) - 1960
Dutcher, Silas B. (NY) - 1870
Dutton, Joseph F. (CT) - 1920, 1922
Duval, Claud (KS) - 1900
Duval, Clive L. III (VA) - 1966
Duval, Issac H. (WV) - 1868
Duval, William P. (FL) - 1848
Duvall (MD) - 1839
Duvall, Frank M. (MD) - 1918
Duvall, Jacob (PA) - 1876
Duy, Albert W. (PA) - 1918
D'Vries (NY) - 1878
Dwight, Henry W. (MA) - 1824, 1826, 1828, 1830
Dwight, Jeremiah W. (NY) - 1876, 1878, 1880
Dwight, John W. (NY) - 1902, 1904, 1906, 1908, 1910
Dwinal, Zelda M. (ME) - 1934
Dwinell, Wilbert Ormand (MA) - 1895
Dwolf, John Jr. (RI) - 1829
Dworkis, Martin B. (NY) - 1962
Dworshak, Henry C. (ID) - 1936, 1938, 1940, 1942, 1944
Dwyer (MN) - 1910
Dwyer (NJ) - 1908
Dwyer, Bernard J. (NJ) - 1980, 1982, 1984
Dwyer, Florence P. (NJ) - 1956, 1958, 1960, 1962, 1964, 1966, 1968, 1970
Dwyer, James E. (NY) - 1924
Dwyer, James M. (NY) - 1930
Dwyer, John J. (MA) - 1954
Dwyer, Marion D. (NJ) - 1968
Dwyer, Robert J. (WI) - 1968, 1970
Dwyer, Thomas P. (MN) - 1908, 1912
Dwyer, Vernon J. (IN) - 1950
Dyal, Kenneth W. (CA) - 1964, 1966
Dyas, Hess (NB) - 1974, 1978
Dye, Paul F. (OH) - 1920
Dyer (RI) - 1906
Dyer, David P. (MO) - 1868, 1870
Dyer, John N. (IN) - 1912
Dyer, Joseph A. (IA) - 1892
Dyer, Leonidas C. (MO) - 1910, 1912, 1914, 1916, 1918, 1920, 1922, 1924, 1926, 1928, 1930, 1932, 1934, 1936
Dyer, Napoleon J. (NH) - 1904, 1930
Dyer, Russell (KS) - 1924
Dyer, Thomas (IL) - 1858
Dyer, William H. (MA) - 1922, 1924
Dykema, Martin (IL) - 1940
Dykeman, David D. (IN) - 1878
Dykes, John B. (KS) - 1900, 1914
Dymally, Mervyn M. (CA) - 1980, 1982, 1984
Dyson, John S. (NY) - 1968
Dyson, Roy (MD) - 1976, 1980, 1982, 1984

E

Eads (MO) - 1908
Eads, Henry L. (AZ) - 1914, 1916
Eagan, John J. (NJ) - 1912, 1914, 1916, 1918, 1920, 1922
Eager, J. J. (TX) - 1898
Eager, Samuel (NY) - 1836
Eagle, Carl (NC) - 1976
Eagle, Joe (TX) - 1898
Eagle, Joe H. (TX) - 1896, 1912, 1914, 1916, 1918, 1934
Eagleton, Leander O. (IL) - 1918
Eagleton, William L. (OK) - 1907
Eagon, John A. - 1888
Eakin, Edgar O. (IL) - 1940
Eames, Benjamin T. (RI) - 1870, 1873, 1874, 1876

Forrester, E. L. (GA) - 1950, 1952, 1954, 1956, 1958, 1960, 1962
Forsberg (MN) - 1902
Forst (PA) - 1856
Forster, Benjamin L. (PA) - 1900, 1902
Forster, John M. (PA) - 1826
Forstner, Ernest W. (TN) - 1944
Forsyth (GA) - 1882
Forsyth, Alexander (MI) - 1894
Forsyth, John (GA) - 1824, 1826
Forsythe, Albert P. (IL) - 1878, 1880
Forsythe, Edwin B. (NJ) - 1970, 1972, 1974, 1976, 1978, 1980, 1982
Fort, Franklin W. (NJ) - 1924, 1926, 1928
Fort, Greenbury L. (IL) - 1872, 1874, 1876, 1878
Fort, Tomlinson (GA) - 1826
Forte, Jim (MA) - 1984
Fortney, Mrs. James G. (AL) - 1956
Forward, Chauncey (PA) - 1826, 1828
Forwood, J. S. (PA) - 1874
Fosdick, Nicolli (NY) - 1824, 1826
Fosgt (NY) - 1856
Fosheim, Oscar (SD) - 1940
Foss (ND) - 1892
Foss, Eugene N. (MA) - 1902, 1904
Foss, Frank H. (MA) - 1924, 1926, 1928, 1930, 1932, 1934
Foss, George Edmund (IL) - 1894, 1896, 1898, 1900, 1902, 1904, 1906, 1908, 1910, 1912, 1914, 1916
Foss, Horatio G. (ME) - 1902, 1904
Foss, Joe (SD) - 1958
Fossel, Jon S. (NY) - 1982
Foster (CT) - 1875
Foster (GA) - 1835
Foster (NY) - 1848, 1872
Foster (PA) - 1852, 1884
Foster, A. Lawrence (NY) - 1838, 1840
Foster, Benjamin L. (PA) - 1900
Foster, Charles (OH) - 1870, 1872, 1874, 1876, 1878, 1890
Foster, Charles D. (PA) - 1892
Foster, David J. (VT) - 1900, 1902, 1904, 1906, 1908, 1910
Foster, E. L. (TN) - 1906
Foster, George P. (IL) - 1898, 1900, 1902, 1904
Foster, George S. (IL) - 1904
Foster, Henry (NY) - 1836
Foster, Henry D. (PA) - 1843, 1844, 1858, 1868, 1870, 1872
Foster, Hervey C. (IL) - 1918
Foster, Israel M. (OH) - 1918, 1920, 1922
Foster, John H. (IN) - 1906, 1908
Foster, John W. (MA) - 1855
Foster, Martin D. (IL) - 1904, 1906, 1908, 1910, 1912, 1914, 1916, 1918
Foster, Morrison (PA) - 1890, 1896
Foster, Nathaniel G. (GA) - 1855
Foster, R. C. (KS) - 1870
Foster, R. C. (TX) - 1896
Foster, Stephen C. (ME) - 1850, 1856, 1858
Foster, Thomas J. (AL) - 1865
Foster, Thomas F. (GA) - 1828, 1830, 1832, 1834, 1840
Foster, Wilder (MI) - 1872
Foster, William (MA) - 1834
Foster, William (NY) - 1914
Fouke, Philip B. (IL) - 1854, 1858, 1860
Fouke, T. B. (IL) - 1852
Foulkes, George (MI) - 1932, 1934
Foulkrod, William W. (PA) - 1906, 1908, 1910
Foulois, Benjamin D. (NJ) - 1942
Fountain, L. H. (NC) - 1952, 1954, 1956, 1958, 1960, 1962, 1964, 1966, 1968, 1970, 1972, 1974, 1976, 1978, 1980
Fountain, William E. (NC) - 1898
Fournoy (MO) - 1854
Fow, John H. (PA) - 1904, 1912, 1914
Fowler (AR) - 1840, 1856
Fowler (KY) - 1916
Fowler (NH) - 1851
Fowler (NJ) - 1830
Fowler (NY) - 1856
Fowler, A. S. (AR) - 1904
Fowler, Charles N. (NJ) - 1894, 1896, 1898, 1900, 1902, 1904, 1906, 1908
Fowler, David (PA) - 1924
Fowler, Edward (DE) - 1900
Fowler, Edwin S. (IL) - 1866
Fowler, Frank L. (IL) - 1912
Fowler, Frank L. (MI) - 1900

Fowler, H. J. (OK) - 1918
Fowler, H. Robert (IL) - 1910, 1912, 1914, 1924
Fowler, J. Samuel (NY) - 1924
Fowler, James (MA) - 1824
Fowler, John E. (NC) - 1896, 1898, 1900
Fowler, Leonard B. (NV) - 1914
Fowler, Marilyn (NE) - 1978
Fowler, O. L. (WA) - 1902
Fowler, Orin (MA) - 1848, 1850
Fowler, Samuel (NJ) - 1828, 1832, 1834
Fowler, Samuel (NJ) - 1888, 1890
Fowler, Samuel (NY) - 1840
Fowler, Thomas P. (TN) - 1948
Fowler, W. T. (KY) - 1898
Fowler, Wade H. (WY) - 1920
Fowler, William C. (MA) - 1856
Fowler, Wyche Jr. (GA) - 1977, 1978, 1980, 1982, 1984
Fox (MA) - 1894
Fox (NY) - 1882
Fox, Andrew F. (MS) - 1896, 1898, 1900
Fox, Beech N. (NJ) - 1980
Fox, E. Frank (IA) - 1940, 1942
Fox, F. T. (KY) - 1855
Fox, George W. (PA) - 1910, 1912, 1916
Fox, Hamilton P. (MD) - 1956
Fox, Harry M. (PA) - 1974
Fox, Henry I. (KY) - 1912
Fox, J. Frank (MD) - 1916
Fox, James A. (MA) - 1890
Fox, John (NY) - 1866, 1868
Fox, John D. (MO) - 1962
Fox, John H. (NY) - 1978, 1984
Fox, L. R. (KY) - 1912
Fox, Leo P. (WI) - 1920
Fox, Martin S. (NJ) - 1952, 1954
Fox, Noel P. (MI) - 1938, 1940, 1950
Fox, Rosa Lee (IL) - 1970
Fox, William C. (CT) - 1930, 1932
Fox, William R. (OH) - 1894, 1902
Foxhall (NJ) - 1908
Foy, Francis H. (MA) - 1934, 1942
Frahn, Harry J. (AL) - 1948
Fraley, Elmer E. (WI) - 1946
Frambach, H. A. (WI) - 1892
France, James D. (IA) - 1948, 1950
Franchot, Richard (NY) - 1860
Francis, Clarence (NY) - 1952
Francis, Frank (UT) - 1924
Francis, George B. (NY) - 1914, 1916
Francis, James A. (NY) - 1916
Francis, John J. (NJ) - 1944
Francis, John T. (OH) - 1984
Francis, Margaret (TN) - 1978
Francis, William B. (OH) - 1910, 1912, 1914, 1916, 1918
Francisco (MO) - 1894
Francisco, Michael A. (IL) - 1946
Francke, Carrie (MO) - 1984
Franck, Augustus (NY) - 1858, 1860, 1862
Frank, Barney (MA) - 1980, 1982, 1984
Frank, David L. (NY) - 1926
Frank, E. L. (IL) - 1972, 1976
Frank, Gerry (CO) - 1978
Frank, Henry (NY) - 1922, 1924
Frank, M. P. (ME) - 1890
Frank, Nathan (MO) - 1886, 1888
Franke, Dorothy (OH) - 1972, 1974, 1976
Frankenfield, Robert F. (PA) - 1956
Frankhauser, William H. (MI) - 1920
Franklin (GA) - 1855
Franklin, Benjamin J. (MO) - 1874, 1876
Franklin, Brenda Lee (MA) - 1978
Franklin, Charles A. (CA) - 1956
Franklin, George T. (NY) - 1946
Franklin, J. H. (OK) - 1910
Franklin, John R. (MD) - 1853
Franklin, S. J. (NE) - 1922
Franklin, W. C. (VA) - 1908
Franklin, Webb (MS) - 1982, 1984
Franks, E. F. (KY) - 1890
Franks, E. T. (KY) - 1896
Franks, Richard L. (MO) - 1974
Frantz, Frank (OK) - 1932
Frantz, Robert A. (OH) - 1974
Franz, Ed. (TX) - 1924
Franz, William J. (OH) - 1974
Frappier, J. H. (MO) - 1976
Fraser, Archie C. (MI) - 1938, 1940
Fraser, Donald M. (MN) - 1962, 1964, 1966, 1968, 1970, 1972, 1974, 1976
Fraser, Robert (MI) - 1890
Fraser, Willard E. (MT) - 1948, 1952
Fratt (WI) - 1874

Frawley (WI) - 1918
Frazce, John (NY) - 1830
Frazee (MS) - 1884
Frazee, W. D. (MS) - 1900
Frazer, R. (PA) - 1838
Frazer, W. D. (MS) - 1890
Frazier, A. Bradley (TN) - 1944
Frazier, James A. (VA) - 1880
Frazier, James B. (TN) - 1954
Frazier, James B. Jr. (TN) - 1948, 1950, 1952, 1956, 1958, 1960
Frazier, William G. (IN) - 1976, 1978, 1980
Fream (NY) - 1856
Frear, James A. (WI) - 1912, 1914, 1916, 1918, 1920, 1922, 1924, 1926, 1928, 1930, 1932
Frederick, Benjamin Todd (IA) - 1882, 1884, 1886
Frederick, Theodore C. Jr. (PA) - 1948
Frederick, Walter E. (IN) - 1946
Fredericks, John D. (CA) - 1924
Fredericks, Thomas Jackson (PA) - 1912
Fredriksen, Arnold L. (MN) - 1956
Free, Arthur Monroe (CA) - 1920, 1922, 1924, 1926, 1928, 1930, 1932
Freed, C. William (PA) - 1922, 1924
Freedley, John (PA) - 1846, 1848, 1850
Freedom, John G. (OH) - 1958, 1960, 1974, 1976
Freehill, Joseph H. (VA) - 1958
Freeland, J. A. (TX) - 1912
Freeland, William B. (PA) - 1946
Freeman (TN) - 1855
Freeman, A. H. (GA) - 1896, 1900
Freeman, Alexander H. (NJ) - 1840
Freeman, Allan C. (MA) - 1968
Freeman, Allen A. (IL) - 1958
Freeman, Andrew Yates (NY) - 1894
Freeman, Chapman (PA) - 1874, 1876
Freeman, Debra Hanania (MD) - 1978
Freeman, Frank (CA) - 1900
Freeman, George (AL) - 1865
Freeman, Howard F. (NC) - 1894
Freeman, J. J. (Tiny) (WA) - 1972
Freeman, J. Y. (TN) - 1932
Freeman, James C. (GA) - 1872
Freeman, John D. (MS) - 1851
Freeman, Michael O. (MN) - 1978
Freeman, N. H. (AL) - 1908
Freeman, Newman H. (AL) - 1916
Freeman, Porter (TN) - 1958
Freeman, Richard C. (OK) - 1980, 1982
Freeman, Richard P. (CT) - 1914, 1916, 1918, 1920, 1922, 1924, 1926, 1928, 1930
Freeman, Robert D. (OH) - 1964, 1966
Freeman, Ross R. (KS) - 1976
Freeman, Samuel (NE) - 1952, 1956
Freeman, Terry (OH) - 1980
Freeman, William G. (NJ) - 1954
Freer, Romeo H. (WV) - 1898
Freese, Arnold E. (CT) - 1932, 1934
Freiday, William (NJ) - 1942
Freidheim, J. B. (AR) - 1896
Frelinghuysen, Peter H. B. Jr. (NJ) - 1952, 1954, 1956, 1958, 1960, 1962, 1964, 1966, 1968, 1970, 1972
French (KY) - 1837
French (MA) - 1886
French (MN) - 1906, 1908
French (NJ) - 1918
French (NY) - 1842, 1874, 1886
French, A. F. (NY) - 1916
French, Burton L. (ID) - 1902, 1904, 1906, 1910, 1912, 1916, 1918, 1920, 1922, 1924, 1926, 1928, 1930, 1932, 1934
French, Carlos (CT) - 1886
French, Charles J. (NH) - 1914, 1920
French, Eleanor C. (NY) - 1964
French, Ezra (ME) - 1858
French, James (NY) - 1840
French, John R. (NC) - 1868
French, Jonas H. (MA) - 1890
French, Richard (KY) - 1835, 1843, 1845, 1847
French, Robert (AL) - 1964
French, Samuel T. (NJ) - 1932
French, William H. (VT) - 1843, 1844
Frensdorf, Edward (MI) - 1912, 1930
Frenzel, Bill (MN) - 1970, 1972, 1974, 1976, 1978, 1980, 1982, 1984
Freschi, Raymond (CA) - 1966
Freshwater, Milton R. (IL) - 1888
Frethy, George C. (PA) - 1912
Frew (PA) - 1870

Frey (NY) - 1842
Frey, Louis Jr. (FL) - 1968, 1970, 1972, 1974, 1976
Frey, Louis G. (OH) - 1964
Frey, Oliver W. (PA) - 1934, 1936, 1938
Frey, William C. (AZ) - 1952
Frey, William J. (OH) - 1900
Frick, Henry (PA) - 1843
Friedel, Samuel N. (MD) - 1952, 1954, 1956, 1958, 1960, 1962, 1964, 1966, 1968
Friedman, Charles (FL) - 1974, 1976
Friedman, Don (CO) - 1976
Friedman, Esther (NY) - 1920, 1932
Friedman, Eugene M. (NJ) - 1962, 1964
Friedman, Herbert J. (IL) - 1906
Friedman, Nathaniel Jay (CA) - 1970
Friedman, Richard E. (IL) - 1962
Friedman, Samuel H. (NY) - 1934
Friend (FL) - 1868
Friend (NY) - 1858
Frierson, J. N. (SC) - 1868
Fries, Frank W. (IL) - 1936, 1938, 1940
Fries, George (OH) - 1844, 1846
Friloux, C. A. Jr. (TX) - 1956
Frink, Garry F. (MI) - 1968
Frisby (WI) - 1868, 1878
Frischer, Gerald G. (MO) - 1970
Fritsch, Joseph Jr. (NY) - 1936
Fritsche, Felix (NY) - 1912
Fritsche, L. A. (MN) - 1930
Frizell, William G. (OH) - 1908
Froehlich, Harold V. (WI) - 1972, 1974, 1976
Froehlich, William H. (WI) - 1902, 1910
Froehlicher, Hans Jr. (NJ) - 1930
Froeman (WI) - 1880
Fromowitz, Hyman (NY) - 1956
Frooks, Dorothy (NY) - 1934
Frost (MO) - 1918
Frost (WV) - 1863
Frost, Frank (CA) - 1982
Frost, Frank P. (NY) - 1902, 1904, 1906
Frost, Gene (MO) - 1936
Frost, J. E. (PA) - 1900
Frost, J. E. (WA) - 1912
Frost, Martin (TX) - 1978, 1980, 1982, 1984
Frost, Richard G. (MO) - 1876, 1878, 1880
Frost, Rufus S. (MA) - 1874, 1876
Frothingham (MA) - 1876
Frothingham, Louis A. (MA) - 1920, 1922, 1924, 1926
Frothingham, Richard Jr. (MA) - 1848, 1850
Fruchter, Henry (NY) - 1922
Frugone, Frank L. (NY) - 1904, 1906
Fry, Jacob Jr. (PA) - 1834, 1836
Fry, Joseph Jr. (PA) - 1826, 1828
Fry, Speed S. (KY) - 1865, 1880
Frye, Pliney S. (OK) - 1946
Frye, William P. (ME) - 1870, 1872, 1874, 1876, 1878, 1880
Fuchs, Joanne S. (NY) - 1976
Fugate, J. B. (KS) - 1878
Fugate, J. T. (TN) - 1908, 1922
Fugate, Thomas B. (VA) - 1948, 1950
Fuhrig, Joseph (CA) - 1980
Fulbright, J. William (AR) - 1942
Fulbright, James F. (MO) - 1922, 1924, 1926, 1928, 1930
Fulcrut, Vernon D. (MO) - 1946, 1950
Fulk, Kenneth R. (IA) - 1976
Fulkerson, Abram (VA) - 1880, 1882
Fulkerson, Frank B. (MO) - 1904, 1906
Fulkerson, George J. (MI) - 1962
Fullam, John P. (PA) - 1954, 1956
Fullard, Thomas L. III (PA) - 1984
Fullenweider, Robert (AL) - 1914
Fuller (CT) - 1888
Fuller (ME) - 1860
Fuller (PA) - 1852, 1860
Fuller, Alvan T. (MA) - 1916, 1918
Fuller, Benoni S. (IN) - 1874, 1876
Fuller, Cecil R. (WA) - 1934
Fuller, Charles E. (IL) - 1902, 1904, 1906, 1908, 1910, 1912, 1914, 1916, 1918, 1920, 1922, 1924
Fuller, Claude A. (AR) - 1928, 1930, 1932, 1934, 1936
Fuller, E. S. (GA) - 1920
Fuller, George (PA) - 1844
Fuller, H. A. (MN) - 1920
Fuller, Hadwen C. (NY) - 1944, 1946, 1948
Fuller, Henry M. (PA) - 1850, 1854
Fuller, Jesse Jr. (NY) - 1912

Fuller, John F. (MA) - 1950
Fuller, L. F. (KS) - 1914
Fuller, Luther E. (VA) - 1936
Fuller, Nelson M. (NY) - 1942
Fuller, Philo C. (NY) - 1832, 1834
Fuller, Smith (PA) - 1864
Fuller, Thomas C. (NC) - 1865, 1868
Fuller, Thomas J. D. (ME) - 1848, 1850, 1852, 1854
Fuller, William (NY) - 1846
Fuller, William Elijah (IA) - 1884, 1886
Fuller, William K. (NY) - 1832, 1834
Fullerton (NY) - 1862
Fullerton, Dick (GA) - 1970
Fullerton, Hugh (IL) - 1864
Fullerton, Reese P. (NM) - 1942
Fullinwider, Patricia (AZ) - 1974, 1976
Fulmer, Hampton P. (SC) - 1920, 1922, 1924, 1926, 1928, 1930, 1932, 1934, 1936, 1938, 1940, 1942
Fulton (VA) - 1843
Fulton (WI) - 1874
Fulton, Andrew S. (VA) - 1847
Fulton, Arthur W. (IL) - 1912, 1916
Fulton, Elmer L. (OK) - 1907, 1908, 1910
Fulton, Frank M. (IL) - 1934, 1936
Fulton, James G. (PA) - 1942, 1944, 1946, 1948, 1950, 1952, 1954, 1956, 1958, 1960, 1962, 1964, 1966, 1968, 1970
Fulton, John H. (VA) - 1833, 1835
Fulton, Richard (TN) - 1962, 1964, 1966, 1968, 1970, 1972, 1974
Funk, Benjamin F. (IL) - 1892
Funk, Frank H. (IL) - 1920, 1922, 1924
Funk, James W. (UT) - 1920
Funk, Robert S. (CA) - 1936
Funkhouser, Alexander M. (IL) - 1900
Funsch, Richard O. (MO) - 1972
Funston, Edward H. (KS) - 1883, 1884, 1886, 1888, 1890, 1892
Fuqua, Don (FL) - 1962, 1964, 1966, 1968, 1970, 1972, 1974, 1976, 1978, 1980, 1982, 1984
Fuqua, W. M. (KY) - 1882
Furber (NJ) - 1918
Furchess, David M. (NC) - 1872, 1880
Furcolo, Foster (MA) - 1946, 1948, 1950
Furgeson, Charles (KY) - 1912
Furlong, Grant (PA) - 1924, 1942
Furlow, Allen J. (MN) - 1924, 1926
Furlow, W. A. S. (TN) - 1934
Furman, Robert (NY) - 1840
Furman, Willis B. (NE) - 1944
Furst, Lyndon G. (MI) - 1980
Fusco, Dominick A. (NY) - 1960
Fussell, Sam (TX) - 1985
Fuzzell (TN) - 1900
Fyan, Robert W. (MO) - 1882, 1890, 1892

G

Gaarenstroom, C. F. (MN) - 1932, 1938
Gabbard, Elmer E. (KY) - 1942, 1944
Gabbert, L. C. (MO) - 1922
Gableman, William N. (OH) - 1922
Gabler, Ray (TX) - 1968
Gabriel, Charles J. (MA) - 1960
Gabriel, G. W. (KS) - 1884
Gadd, Cyrus H. (WV) - 1952
Gaddie, D. W. (KY) - 1910
Gaddis, Albert (PA) - 1918
Gaddie (KY) - 1908
Gadrix, Ed (GA) - 1976
Gadsden, James (SC) - 1856
Gaffner, Robert H. (IL) - 1982, 1984
Gaffney, Edward (ID) - 1940
Gaffney, Hubert J. (MI) - 1934
Gaffney, James J. III (MA) - 1978
Gaffney, James P. (IA) - 1938
Gaffney, Warren N. (NJ) - 1930
Gage (WI) - 1876
Gage, A. W. (FL) - 1924
Gage, Gary G. (WA) - 1974
Gagen, August M. (MN) - 1926
Gagne, W. E. (Ted) (CA) - 1980
Gahn, Harry C. (OH) - 1920, 1922, 1924, 1926, 1936, 1944
Gain, Charles E. (OH) - 1894
Gaines, Franklin D. (KS) - 1974
Gaines, John P. (KY) - 1833, 1845, 1847, 1849
Gaines, John W. (TN) - 1896, 1898, 1900, 1902, 1904, 1906

Gaines, Joseph Holt (WV) - 1900, 1902, 1904, 1906, 1908, 1910
Gaines, Theophilus (WV) - 1890
Gaines, William E. (VA) - 1886
Gaither, Burgess S. (NC) - 1851, 1853, 1865, 1868
Gaither, Nathan (KY) - 1829, 1831, 1833, 1841
Gaiton, William (MA) - 1870
Gaitskill, Joe E. (KS) - 1928, 1946
Galasso, M. S. (MT) - 1944
Galasso, Michael R. (IL) - 1972
Galbraith (TN) - 1876
Galbraith, John (PA) - 1832, 1834, 1838
Galbraith, W. J. (AZ) - 1924
Gale, E. (KS) - 1878
Gale, John (NY) - 1824
Gale, Levin (MD) - 1826
Gale, Richard P. (MN) - 1940, 1942, 1944
Galen, Joseph L. (PA) - 1904, 1906
Galetich, Lou (IA) - 1970
Galifianakis, Nick (NC) - 1966, 1968, 1970
Galighr (OH) - 1854
Gall, Charles (NY) - 1912
Gall, Samuel (MA) - 1846
Gallagher (MD) - 1841
Gallagher, Bernard J. (WA) - 1960, 1962
Gallagher, Buel G. (CA) - 1948
Gallagher, Charles T. (MA) - 1882
Gallagher, Cornelius E. (NJ) - 1958, 1960, 1962, 1964, 1966, 1968, 1970
Gallagher, Edward J. Jr. (IA) - 1960
Gallagher, Hugh J. (WI) - 1886
Gallagher, J. P. (IA) - 1926
Gallagher, J. S. G. (PA) - 1938
Gallagher, James (PA) - 1942, 1944, 1946
Gallagher, John T. (NY) - 1972
Gallagher, Joseph (PA) - 1912
Gallagher, Kenneth C. (MI) - 1974
Gallagher, Thomas (IL) - 1908, 1910, 1912, 1914, 1916, 1918
Gallagher, William J. (MN) - 1942, 1944
Gallant, David A. (WA) - 1962
Gallegos, Eugene (NM) - 1972
Gallegos, Louis H. (NM) - 1984
Gallemore, Johnnie L. Jr. (NC) - 1976
Gallinger, Jacob H. (NH) - 1884, 1886
Gallivan, James A. (MA) - 1898, 1914, 1916, 1918, 1920, 1922, 1924, 1926
Gallo, Dean A. (NJ) - 1984
Galloway, Barritt (OK) - 1926
Galloway, Ben (CO) - 1974
Galloway, Charles V. (OR) - 1906
Galloway, Samuel (OH) - 1850, 1852, 1854, 1856, 1860
Gallup, Albert (NY) - 1836, 1838
Galusha (VT) - 1830
Galvan, Jeremiah (TX) - 1874
Galvin, George W. (MA) - 1906
Galvin, J. Mitchell (MA) - 1908, 1910
Galvin, Thomas F. (NY) - 1962
Gambill, Walter R. (VA) - 1952
Gamble (GA) - 1835
Gamble (MN) - 1890
Gamble, George (WA) - 1970
Gamble, James (PA) - 1850, 1852
Gamble, John R. (SD) - 1890
Gamble, Ralph A. (NY) - 1938, 1940, 1942, 1944, 1946, 1948, 1950, 1952, 1954
Gamble, Robert J. (SD) - 1894, 1896, 1898
Gamble, Roger L. (GA) - 1830, 1832, 1834, 1840, 1842
Gamble, Tip (TN) - 1894
Gambrill, Stephen W. (MD) - 1924, 1926, 1928, 1930, 1932, 1934, 1936, 1938
Gammage, Bob (TX) - 1976, 1978
Gammell, Archibald B. (PA) - 1898
Gammell, Robert L. (RI) - 1958, 1960
Gandy, Harry L. (SD) - 1912, 1914, 1916, 1918, 1920
Gandy, Jesse (NE) - 1924
Gangemi, John F. (NY) - 1972
Ganly, James V. (NY) - 1918, 1920, 1922
Gannon, Charles W. (IN) - 1946
Gannon, Peter J. (NJ) - 1962
Gans, Charles L. (PA) - 1912
Gansbergen, Frederick H. (IL) - 1910
Ganson, John (NY) - 1862
Gants, Albert M. (NY) - 1966
Gantt (AR) - 1860
Gantt, Elbert (LA) - 1872
Gantz, Martin K. (OH) - 1890, 1892
Garber (MO) - 1904, 1906
Garber, George H. (PA) - 1898

Garber, Harvey C. (OH) - 1902, 1904
Garber, Jacob A. (VA) - 1928, 1930, 1932, 1940, 1950
Garber, Martin (OK) - 1948
Garber, Milton C. (OK) - 1922, 1924, 1926, 1928, 1930, 1932
Garbutt, Mary E. (CA) - 1920
Garcelon, Alonzo (ME) - 1868, 1872, 1886
Garcia, Faustino Louis (NY) - 1960
Garcia, Raymond (NM) - 1976
Garcia, Robert (NY) - 1978, 1980, 1982, 1984
Gard, Warren (OH) - 1912, 1914, 1916, 1918, 1922
Gardenhire (MO) - 1850
Gardiner, Addison (NY) - 1828
Gardiner, Charles T. (KY) - 1914
Gardiner, Curtiss C. (NY) - 1868
Gardiner, David (NY) - 1832
Gardiner, E. Watson (NY) - 1926, 1928
Gardiner, John H. (NY) - 1864
Gardiner, Marshall G. (KS) - 1960
Gardiner, Reece B. (NY) - 1966
Gardiner, Robert D. L. (NY) - 1972
Gardiner, William R. (IN) - 1898
Gardner (AL) - 1894
Gardner (TN) - 1853
Gardner, Augustus P. (MA) - 1902, 1904, 1906, 1908, 1910, 1912, 1914, 1916
Gardner, Barry L. (NC) - 1978, 1980
Gardner, Benjamin (AL) - 1865
Gardner, Carroll A. (NY) - 1934, 1946
Gardner, Edward J. (OH) - 1944, 1946
Gardner, Frank (IN) - 1922, 1924, 1926, 1928
Gardner, Jack (TX) - 1958
Gardner, James C. (NC) - 1964, 1966
Gardner, James F. (MA) - 1954
Gardner, John (TN) - 1847
Gardner, John F. (NJ) - 1924
Gardner, John J. (NJ) - 1892, 1894, 1896, 1898, 1900, 1902, 1904, 1906, 1908, 1910, 1912
Gardner, Kenneth (NY) - 1932, 1934
Gardner, M. R. (KY) - 1892
Gardner, Mills (OH) - 1876
Gardner, Ogburn (IL) - 1976
Gardner, Reece B. (NC) - 1968
Gardner, Steve (MO) - 1980
Gardner, Theodore R. (PA) - 1934, 1936
Gardner, Walter H. (MI) - 1956
Gardner, Washington (MI) - 1898, 1900, 1902, 1904, 1906, 1908
Garfield, Frederick (NY) - 1922
Garfield, James A. (OH) - 1862, 1864, 1866, 1868, 1870, 1872, 1874, 1876, 1878
Gargiulo, Frank X. (NY) - 1976
Garibaldi, Peter P. (NJ) - 1970, 1972
Garland (AR) - 1880
Garland, Charles H. (IL) - 1944
Garland, James (VA) - 1835, 1837, 1839, 1841
Garland, Mahlon M. (PA) - 1914, 1916, 1918, 1920
Garland, Peter A. (ME) - 1960, 1966
Garland, Ray (VA) - 1984
Garland, Rice (LA) - 1834, 1836, 1838
Garland, Robert (PA) - 1942
Garlghse (NY) - 1848
Garlington (SC) - 1854
Garman, Ira (PA) - 1948
Garman, John M. (PA) - 1896
Garmatz, Edward A. (MD) - 1948, 1950, 1952, 1954, 1956, 1958, 1960, 1962, 1964, 1966, 1968, 1970
Garner, Alfred B. (PA) - 1908, 1912
Garner, David (SD) - 1968
Garner, John N. (TX) - 1902, 1904, 1906, 1908, 1910, 1912, 1914, 1916, 1918, 1920, 1922, 1924, 1926, 1928, 1930, 1932
Garner, John Nance (WA) - 1976, 1978
Garner, Pal (KY) - 1926
Garner, Stanley S. (VA) - 1950
Garnett, Muscoe R. H. (VA) - 1857, 1859
Garnett, Robert S. (VA) - 1825
Garnsey, Daniel (NY) - 1824, 1826, 1828
Garnsey, David (NY) - 1830
Garrard (KY) - 1837
Garrard, Daniel (KY) - 1843
Garrard, T. T. (KY) - 1859, 1865
Garrard, Theodore T. (KY) - 1851
Garretson, Arthur S. (IA) - 1898

Garrett, A. B. (IL) - 1898
Garrett, Abraham E. (TN) - 1870, 1872
Garrett, Albin (PA) - 1912
Garrett, Clyde L. (TX) - 1936, 1938
Garrett, C. W. (TN) - 1890
Garrett, Daniel E. (TX) - 1912, 1916, 1920, 1922, 1924, 1926, 1928, 1930, 1932
Garrett, E. A. (TN) - 1868
Garrett, Finis J. (TN) - 1904, 1906, 1908, 1910, 1912, 1914, 1916, 1918, 1920, 1922, 1924, 1926
Garrett, George A. (CA) - 1910
Garrett, Henry V. (PA) - 1910, 1912
Garrett, Julian B. (IA) - 1978
Garrett, Robert (MD) - 1904, 1906, 1908
Garrett, Shirley S. (PA) - 1972
Garrett, T. G. (AL) - 1853
Garrett, Thomas (NY) - 1940
Garrettson, Theodore (PA) - 1874
Garrigan, P. C. (VA) - 1892
Garrison, Daniel (NJ) - 1824, 1826
Garrison, Denzil D. (OK) - 1966
Garrison, E. C. (VA) - 1914
Garrison, George T. (VA) - 1880, 1882
Garrison, Theodore E. (NY) - 1974
Garrow, Nathaniel (NY) - 1826
Garside, Charles (NY) - 1946
Garten, Z. M. (IN) - 1916
Gartenstein, Jacob (IL) - 1912, 1920, 1922
Gartern, C. A. (CA) - 1886
Garth (AL) - 1865, 1878
Garth, Jesse Winston (AL) - 1831
Garth, William W. (AL) - 1876
Gartland, James F. (CT) - 1954
Gartley, Markham L. (ME) - 1974, 1978
Gartner, Fred C. (PA) - 1938, 1940, 1958
Garton, Art (WA) - 1954
Garton, Robert D. (IN) - 1968
Gartrell, Lucius J. (GA) - 1857, 1859
Garver (IN) - 1856
Garvey, J. E. (ND) - 1930
Garvey, James S. (TX) - 1974
Garvin (RI) - 1894, 1896, 1898, 1900, 1906
Garvin, Thomas E. (IN) - 1878
Garvin, William S. (PA) - 1844
Gary, Algia (PA) - 1968
Gary, Holland M. (OH) - 1950
Gary, J. Vaughan (VA) - 1946, 1948, 1950, 1952, 1954, 1956, 1958, 1960, 1962
Gary, James A. (MD) - 1870
Gary, Roger V. (TX) - 1982
Gase, Virgil M. (OH) - 1958, 1960
Gash, Thomas A. (NJ) - 1902
Gaskill, J. R. (NC) - 1906
Gaskill, Julian T. (NC) - 1936, 1940
Gasque, Allard H. (SC) - 1922, 1924, 1926, 1928, 1930, 1932, 1934, 1936
Gassaway, P. L. (OK) - 1934
Gasser, Robert A. (NJ) - 1968
Gaston, Athelston (PA) - 1898, 1900
Gaston, James B. (SC) - 1948
Gaston, Matthew (OH) - 1848
Gaston, William (CT) - 1948
Gatch (OH) - 1862
Gatch, Thomas (OH) - 1848
Gatens, Peter R. (NY) - 1910
Gates, A. V. (TX) - 1894
Gates, Clinton H. (MO) - 1960
Gates, E. N. (IA) - 1874
Gates, Edward J. (IL) - 1928
Gates, John (AR) - 1888
Gates, Richard (IL) - 1854
Gates, Robert D. (PA) - 1968
Gates, Seth (NY) - 1838, 1840
Gates, Theodore B. (NY) - 1864
Gatewood, A. T. (NE) - 1892
Gatewood, William J. (IL) - 1836
Gathings, Ezekiel C. (AR) - 1938, 1940, 1942, 1944, 1946, 1948, 1950, 1952, 1954, 1956, 1958, 1960, 1962, 1964, 1966
Gatins, James L. (PA) - 1950
Gatliff, Ancil (KY) - 1906
Gatlin, Alfred M. (NC) - 1825
Gatling, Reddick (NC) - 1892
Gaudet, Larry (FL) - 1982
Gauer, Paul (WI) - 1936, 1938
Gauger, Carl F. (IL) - 1912
Gaul, Edward L. (NY) - 1880
Gault, Lillien Cox (MN) - 1922
Gaumer, Clay F. (IL) - 1934
Gauntt (NJ) - 1884
Gause, Lucien C. (AR) - 1872, 1874, 1876
Gause, Thomas E. (IL) - 1964

Hall, Edwin Arthur (NY) - 1940, 1942, 1944, 1946, 1948, 1950
Hall, Frank H. (IL) - 1920
Hall, Frederick (MI) - 1864
Hall, George C. (KS) - 1932
Hall, George H. (DE) - 1912
Hall, Henry L. (NY) - 1968
Hall, Hiland (VT) - 1832, 1834, 1836, 1838, 1840
Hall, Homer W. (IL) - 1926, 1928, 1930, 1932
Hall, J. T. (AR) - 1910
Hall, James K. P. (PA) - 1896, 1898, 1900
Hall, John (MA) - 1926
Hall, John (TN) - 1827, 1841
Hall, John E. (NY) - 1972
Hall, John F. (NJ) - 1898
Hall, John H. (PA) - 1912
Hall, John J. (IL) - 1894
Hall, John J. (OH) - 1876
Hall, John S. (IL) - 1926
Hall, John S. (MI) - 1928
Hall, John S. (NY) - 1966
Hall, Joseph (ME) - 1833, 1834
Hall, Joshua G. (NH) - 1878, 1880
Hall, Julian E. (CO) - 1942
Hall, Katie (IN) - 1982
Hall, Lawrence W. (OH) - 1856, 1858
Hall, Leonard W. (NY) - 1938, 1940, 1942, 1944, 1946, 1948, 1950
Hall, Lyman W. (OH) - 1844
Hall, Nathan (NY) - 1846
Hall, Norman (PA) - 1886
Hall, Osee M. (MN) - 1890, 1892, 1894
Hall, Philo (SD) - 1906
Hall, Prescott (NY) - 1840
Hall, Ralph M. (TX) - 1980, 1982, 1984
Hall, Robert B. (MA) - 1854, 1856
Hall, Robert G. (MI) - 1958
Hall, Robert S. (MS) - 1928, 1930
Hall, S. Evan (NC) - 1942, 1946
Hall, Sam B. Jr. (TX) - 1976, 1978, 1980, 1982, 1984
Hall, Thomas (ND) - 1924, 1926, 1928, 1930, 1940
Hall, Thomas H. (NC) - 1825, 1827, 1829, 1831, 1833, 1835, 1839
Hall, Tim L. (IL) - 1972, 1974, 1976, 1978, 1982
Hall, Tony P. (OH) - 1978, 1980, 1982, 1984
Hall, Uriel S. (MO) - 1892, 1894
Hall, Vivian (CA) - 1976
Hall, Willard P. (MO) - 1846, 1848, 1850
Hall, William (TN) - 1831
Hall, William A. (MO) - 1862
Hall, William R. (NC) - 1847
Hallam, J. W. (IA) - 1912
Halleck, Charles A. (IN) - 1935, 1936, 1938, 1940, 1942, 1944, 1946, 1948, 1950, 1952, 1954, 1956, 1958, 1960, 1962, 1964, 1966
Hallen (CT) - 1904
Haller, Bruce R. (IN) - 1972
Haller, Henry C. (MI) - 1916, 1918, 1930
Halleran, Thomas J. (NJ) - 1940
Hallett (NY) - 1856
Hallett, Benjamin F. (MA) - 1844, 1848
Halley, David A. (MD) - 1956
Halliday (MN) - 1908
Halligan, John J. (NY) - 1906
Hallin, Richard (CA) - 1974
Hallock, John Jr. (NY) - 1824, 1826
Halloran, Aaron J. (OH) - 1932
Halloran, Joseph M. (MA) - 1930
Halloway, Ransom (NY) - 1848
Hallowell (PA) - 1848
Hallowell, Edwin (PA) - 1890, 1892
Hallowell, J. R. (KS) - 1878
Hallowell, James R. (KS) - 1890
Hallstead, William F. (PA) - 1938
Hally, George (NE) - 1942, 1944
Halpern, Gerald P. (NY) - 1976
Halpern, Seymour (NY) - 1954, 1958, 1960, 1962, 1964, 1966, 1968, 1970
Halpin, Daniel K. (CA) - 1958
Halsell, John E. (KY) - 1882, 1884
Halsey (NY) - 1850
Halsey, George A. (NJ) - 1866, 1868, 1870
Halsey, Howard H. (PA) - 1960
Halsey, Jehiel (NY) - 1828, 1830
Halsey, Nicoll (NY) - 1832
Halsey, Thomas J. (MO) - 1928, 1930
Halstead, S. R. (TX) - 1926

Halstead, William (NJ) - 1836, 1840
Halsted, P. O. (CA) - 1849
Halter, Edward J. (NY) - 1920
Halterman, Frederick (PA) - 1894, 1896
Halvorsen, Hal (ND) - 1912
Halvorson, H. (ND) - 1906
Halvorson, Halvor (ND) - 1914, 1918
Halvorson, Halvor L. (ND) - 1942, 1944
Halvorson, Kittel (MN) - 1890, 1894
Ham (PA) - 1852, 1888
Ham, Benjamin F. (IN) - 1886
Hamblen, Carl Stuart (CA) - 1938
Hambleton, Samuel (MD) - 1868, 1870
Hamby, Tom (KY) - 1982
Hamer, Robert E. (NJ) - 1966
Hamer, Thomas L. (OH) - 1832, 1834, 1836, 1846
Hamer, Thomas R. (ID) - 1908
Hami (PA) - 1854
Hamill, E. (AL) - 1865
Hamill, Fred B. (IL) - 1908
Hamill, James A. (NJ) - 1906, 1908, 1910, 1912, 1914, 1916, 1918
Hamill, Patrick (MD) - 1868
Hamill, Samuel R. (IN) - 1898
Hamiln (MD) - 1855
Hamilton (MO) - 1896, 1914
Hamilton (NY) - 1854, 1856, 1858
Hamilton (PA) - 1862
Hamilton, Andrew H. (IN) - 1874, 1876
Hamilton, Andrew J. (TX) - 1859
Hamilton, Charles M. (FL) - 1868
Hamilton, Charles M. (NY) - 1912, 1914, 1916
Hamilton, Cornelius S. (OH) - 1866
Hamilton, Daniel W. (IA) - 1906, 1908, 1910
Hamilton, Edward L. (MI) - 1896, 1898, 1900, 1902, 1904, 1906, 1908, 1910, 1912, 1914, 1916, 1918
Hamilton, Finley (KY) - 1932
Hamilton, Frank I. Jr. (IN) - 1978
Hamilton, Hal A. (MO) - 1950
Hamilton, Hiram (CA) - 1892
Hamilton, J. J. (GA) - 1900
Hamilton, J. Kent (OH) - 1910
Hamilton, James Jr. (SC) - 1822, 1824, 1826
Hamilton, John M. (WV) - 1910, 1912, 1914
Hamilton, John T. (IA) - 1890, 1892
Hamilton, Lee H. (IN) - 1964, 1966, 1968, 1970, 1972, 1974, 1976, 1978, 1980, 1982, 1984
Hamilton, M. A. (WA) - 1898
Hamilton, Norman R. (VA) - 1936
Hamilton, Pat R. (WV) - 1980
Hamilton, Richard J. (PA) - 1926
Hamilton, Robert (KY) - 1888
Hamilton, Robert (NJ) - 1872, 1874
Hamilton, Roy L. (KS) - 1938
Hamilton, Samuel K. (MA) - 1894
Hamilton, Thomas H. (PA) - 1912
Hamilton, W. H. (IA) - 1914
Hamilton, William T. (MD) - 1849, 1851, 1853
Hamlen, James C. (ME) - 1906
Hamlin (OH) - 1843
Hamlin, Alanson (CT) - 1833
Hamlin, Courtney W. (MO) - 1902, 1904, 1906, 1908, 1910, 1912, 1914, 1916
Hamlin, Elijah (ME) - 1834
Hamlin, Hannibal (ME) - 1840, 1843, 1844
Hamlin, Howland J. (IL) - 1884
Hamlin, Lewis P. (NC) - 1924, 1944
Hamlin, Simon M. (ME) - 1934, 1936
Hamm, John (OH) - 1836
Hamm, John C. (WY) - 1906
Hammar, Conrad H. (MN) - 1958, 1962
Hammer, Joseph T. (NY) - 1948, 1950
Hammer, William C. (NC) - 1920, 1922, 1924, 1926, 1928
Hammerschlag (NJ) - 1886
Hammerschmidt, John Paul (AR) - 1966, 1968, 1970, 1972, 1974, 1976, 1978, 1980, 1982, 1984
Hammersley, Gary L. (OH) - 1980
Hammersley, William (CT) - 1847
Hammerstrom, Claus V. (MN) - 1930
Hammesfahr, E. J. (NJ) - 1974
Hammett, William H. (MS) - 1843
Hammond (NY) - 1848, 1882
Hammond (VA) - 1839
Hammond, A. B. (KY) - 1918

Hammond, Edward (MD) - 1849, 1851
Hammond, Edwin F. (KS) - 1926
Hammond, F. Eugene (NY) - 1892
Hammond, Jack (TX) - 1984
Hammond, James B. (PA) - 1914
Hammond, James H. (SC) - 1834
Hammond, James W. (NE) - 1934
Hammond, Jerry (KY) - 1984
Hammond, John (NY) - 1878, 1880
Hammond, Nathaniel J. (GA) - 1878, 1880, 1882, 1884
Hammond, Peter F. (OH) - 1936
Hammond, R. L. (NE) - 1896
Hammond, Robert (PA) - 1836, 1838
Hammond, Thomas (IN) - 1892
Hammond, Thomas T. (MD) - 1914
Hammond, Winfield S. (MN) - 1892, 1906, 1908, 1910, 1912
Hammons, David (ME) - 1847
Hammons, Joseph (NH) - 1829, 1831
Hamner, A. B. (VA) - 1912
Hamner, B. L. (FL) - 1936
Hampson, David F. (NY) - 1970
Hampson, L. F. (MN) - 1892
Hampton (NJ) - 1844, 1910
Hampton, Charles S. (MI) - 1896
Hampton, Charles V. (MI) - 1944
Hampton, Chester C. (PA) - 1960
Hampton, Erastus P. (NC) - 1876
Hampton, James G. (NJ) - 1846
Hampton, Mason L. Jr. (NY) - 1968
Hampton, Moses (PA) - 1846, 1848
Hampton, Vernon B. (NY) - 1934
Hamrle, Joseph (IL) - 1918
Hanahan, John J. (IL) - 1894
Hanback, Lewis (KS) - 1882, 1884
Hanbury, Harry A. (NY) - 1900, 1902
Hance, Kent (TX) - 1978, 1980, 1982
Hanchett, Luther (WI) - 1860, 1862
Hancock (MD) - 1872
Hancock (MS) - 1876
Hancock (TX) - 1855, 1878
Hancock, Clarence E. (NY) - 1927, 1928, 1930, 1932, 1934, 1936, 1938, 1940, 1942, 1944
Hancock, Clinton C. (PA) - 1898
Hancock, Franklin W. Jr. (NC) - 1930, 1932, 1934, 1936
Hancock, James Denton (PA) - 1892, 1894
Hancock, John (TX) - 1871, 1872, 1874, 1882
Hancock, Joseph G. (NJ) - 1957, 1958
Hancock, Stewart F. Jr. (NY) - 1966
Hand (NY) - 1860
Hand, Augustus (NY) - 1838, 1840
Hand, George F. (NY) - 1892
Hand, I. H. (GA) - 1892
Hand, Owen S. Jr. (OH) - 1978
Hand, Russell R. (CA) - 1938
Hand, T. Millet (NJ) - 1944, 1946, 1948, 1950, 1952, 1954, 1956
Hand, Thomas J. (IL) - 1980
Handerson, Phinchas (NH) - 1824
Handerson, P. (NH) - 1839
Handley, Lawrence A. (IN) - 1924
Handley, Lorin A. (CA) - 1910
Handley, William A. (AL) - 1870, 1872
Handloff, Norma (DE) - 1972
Handy (MO) - 1837
Handy, Bolling H. (VA) - 1920
Handy, Joseph B. (NY) - 1900, 1922
Handy, L. Irving (DE) - 1896, 1898, 1908
Haneke, Gottlieb (NY) - 1910
Hanes, Lewis (NC) - 1865
Haney, David J. (NJ) - 1912
Haney, Franklin (TN) - 1966
Haney, James W. (IL) - 1878
Haney, Jasper W. (TX) - 1908
Haney, Richard (IL) - 1882
Hank (TN) - 1865
Hankerd, Patrick (MI) - 1886
Hanks, Hardin E. (IL) - 1940
Hanks, Howard H. (NE) - 1902
Hanks, James M. (AR) - 1870
Hanlan (AL) - 1888
Hanlan, M.J. (PA) - 1920
Hanley, Charles P. (IA) - 1914
Hanley, James H. (NE) - 1922
Hanley, James M. (NY) - 1964, 1966, 1968, 1970, 1972, 1974, 1976, 1978
Hanley, James M. (ND) - 1946
Hanley, James W. (MI) - 1918
Hanlon, Neal B. (CT) - 1982
Hanlon, Thomas J. (PA) - 1974

Hanly, J. Frank (IN) - 1894
Hann, Yandell (TN) - 1906
Hanna (IN) - 1880
Hanna (OH) - 1843
Hanna, B. F. (TX) - 1950
Hanna, Charles (IA) - 1944
Hanna, Forest W. (MO) - 1940
Hanna, Harry A. (OH) - 1976
Hanna, John (IN) - 1876, 1878
Hanna, L. B. (MN) - 1924, 1926
Hanna, Louis B. (ND) - 1908, 1910
Hanna, Richard T. (CA) - 1962, 1964, 1966, 1968, 1970, 1972
Hanna, Robert B. (IN) - 1900
Hannaford, Peter (CA) - 1972
Hannaford, Mark W. (CA) - 1974, 1976, 1978
Hannah (MO) - 1888
Hannah (TN) - 1902
Hannah, H. H. (TN) - 1914
Hannegan, Edward A. (IN) - 1833, 1835, 1840
Hannis, Herbert E. (WV) - 1934
Hannon, Robert E. (CA) - 1960
Hanon, Jesse (IL) - 1890
Hanrahan, Edward V. (IL) - 1960, 1974
Hanrahan, Robert P. (IL) - 1972, 1974
Hanrick, R. A. (TX) - 1922
Hansbrough, Henry C. (ND) - 1889
Hanscom, Fred L. (MI) - 1950
Hansen, Diana (HI) - 1972
Hansen, George V. (ID) - 1964, 1966, 1974, 1976, 1978, 1980, 1982, 1984
Hansen, Hans A. (NY) - 1916
Hansen, J. W. (NM) - 1911
Hansen, James T. (NE) - 1976
Hansen, James V. (UT) - 1980, 1982, 1984
Hansen, Janine M. (NV) - 1976
Hansen, Joel F. (NV) - 1974
Hansen, John R. (IA) - 1964, 1966
Hansen, John S. (VA) - 1968
Hansen, Julia Butler (WA) - 1960, 1962, 1964, 1966, 1968, 1970, 1972
Hansen, Orval (ID) - 1962, 1968, 1970, 1972
Hansen, Richard C. (MN) - 1954
Hansen, Rudy (CA) - 1978
Hanson (VA) - 1906
Hanson, Charles (KY) - 1867
Hanson, George M. (IL) - 1848
Hanson, George M. (ME) - 1906, 1908, 1910
Hanson, J. Louis (WI) - 1962
Hanson, Max (ID) - 1974
Hanson, Moses P. (MA) - 1842
Hanson, Roger W. (KY) - 1857
Hanson, Royce (MD) - 1964, 1966
Hanson, Severin H. (IL) - 1936
Hanton, Henry B. (MA) - 1844
Hantusch, Rudolph (NY) - 1920
Haralson (AL) - 1876, 1878
Haralson, Hugh A. (GA) - 1842, 1844, 1846, 1848
Haralson, Jeremiah (AL) - 1874
Haralson, W. J. (AL) - 1869
Harberson, A. J. (KY) - 1854
Harbison, Robert C. (CA) - 1916
Harby, Harold (CA) - 1946
Harct (NY) - 1854
Hard, David (NY) - 1840
Hard, Gideon (NY) - 1832, 1834
Hard, Ron (TX) - 1982
Harueman, Thomas (GA) - 1882
Harden, Cecil M. (IN) - 1948, 1950, 1952, 1954, 1956, 1958
Harden, Junius H. (NC) - 1928
Harden, Mary M. (MI) - 1960
Hardenbergh, Augustus A. (NJ) - 1874, 1876, 1880
Harder (NY) - 1870
Hardesty, Thomas W. (KY) - 1950
Hardie (AL) - 1886
Hardiman, Francis X. (NY) - 1956
Hardin (KY) - 1837
Hardin, Benjamin (KY) - 1833, 1835
Hardin, John J. (IL) - 1843
Hardin, Justin (IL) - 1843
Hardin, T. J. (KY) - 1892, 1898
Harding, Aaron (KY) - 1861, 1863, 1865
Harding, Abner C. (IL) - 1864, 1866
Harding, Eva (KS) - 1916
Harding, F. D. B. (NC) - 1940, 1958
Harding, Harold H. (KS) - 1940
Harding, John Eugene (OH) - 1906

Harding, Philip L. (PA) - 1968
Harding, Ralph R. (ID) - 1960, 1962, 1964
Harding, Ralph W. (ID) - 1928
Harding, Reed (NY) - 1956
Hardman, George W. (WV) - 1906
Hardman, Thomas (GA) - 1859
Hardtner, Henry E. (LA) - 1900
Hardwick, Thomas W. (GA) - 1902, 1904, 1906, 1908, 1910, 1912
Hardy (AL) - 1888
Hardy (NY) - 1874, 1878, 1884
Hardy, Alexander M. (IN) - 1894, 1896
Hardy, Guy U. (CO) - 1918, 1920, 1922, 1924, 1926, 1928, 1930, 1932
Hardy, Jack W. (CA) - 1950
Hardy, John (NY) - 1871, 1872, 1874, 1880, 1882
Hardy, Lewis W. (IL) - 1906
Hardy, Porter Jr. (VA) - 1946, 1948, 1950, 1952, 1954, 1956, 1958, 1960, 1962, 1964, 1966
Hardy, Robert R. (VA) - 1972
Hardy, Rufus (TX) - 1906, 1908, 1910, 1912, 1914, 1916, 1918, 1920
Hare, Butler B. (SC) - 1924, 1926, 1928, 1930, 1938, 1940, 1942, 1944
Hare, Darius D. (OH) - 1890, 1892
Hare, James B. (SC) - 1948
Hare, Silas (TX) - 1886, 1888
Harger, Charles M. (KS) - 1916
Hargett, A. W. (AL) - 1940
Hargett, Edd (TX) - 1985
Hargett, John (MS) - 1984
Hargis, Denver D. (KS) - 1956, 1958, 1960
Hargis, H. C. (IA) - 1890
Hargraves, Homer P. Jr. (IL) - 1958
Hargraves, Z. B. (GA) - 1888
Hargreaves, John R. (MD) - 1972
Haring, Aarron (NY) - 1826
Harkavy, Bernard (NY) - 1940, 1950
Harkin, Joseph D. (IN) - 1974, 1980
Harkin, Tom (IA) - 1972, 1974, 1976, 1978, 1980, 1982
Harkness, J. C. (WA) - 1914
Harl, Hattie T. (IA) - 1920
Harlan, Aaron (OH) - 1852, 1854, 1856
Harlan, Andrew J. (IN) - 1849, 1852
Harlan, Byron B. (OH) - 1930, 1932, 1934, 1936, 1938
Harlan, Douglas S. (TX) - 1972, 1974
Harlan, Edwin (IL) - 1888
Harlan, Hal E. (KS) - 1934
Harlan, James (KY) - 1835, 1837
Harlan, John M. (KY) - 1859
Harlan, Levi P. (IN) - 1904
Harlan, Milton (CA) - 1920
Harlan, N. V. (NE) - 1890
Harless, Richard F. (AZ) - 1942, 1944, 1946, 1960
Harley, William (MS) - 1841
Harlin, Robert H. (WA) - 1944
Harlowe, Norman C. (NY) - 1966
Harman, C. Henry (VA) - 1924
Harman, Dale F. (IL) - 1984
Harman, F. A. (NE) - 1882
Harmanson, John H. (LA) - 1844, 1847, 1849
Harmer, Alfred C. (PA) - 1870, 1872, 1874, 1876, 1878, 1880, 1882, 1884, 1886, 1888, 1890, 1892, 1894, 1896, 1898
Harmon, James L. (IN) - 1924
Harmon, Lloyd V. (MO) - 1928
Harmon, Randall S. (IN) - 1958, 1960
Harmon, Roy A. (NC) - 1948
Harmsen, Stephen M. (UT) - 1974
Harner, Carol O. (CA) - 1972, 1974, 1976, 1984
Harness, Forest A. (IN) - 1938, 1940, 1942, 1944, 1946, 1948
Harney, C. L. (KY) - 1910
Harney, James F. (IN) - 1864
Harold, John R. (NY) - 1954, 1960
Haroldson, Clint (MN) - 1956
Harpel, John L. (CO) - 1958
Harpel, O. A. (SD) - 1900
Harpending, Harry B. (NY) - 1902
Harper (GA) - 1859
Harper, Alexander (OH) - 1836, 1838, 1843, 1844, 1850
Harper, Francis J. (PA) - 1836
Harper, Frank H. (MS) - 1950
Harper, Herbert (TN) - 1956
Harper, J. A. (TX) - 1908
Harper, J. C. (AL) - 1922
Harper, J. M. (NH) - 1839

Harper, James (PA) - 1832, 1834
Harper, James C. (NC) - 1870
Harper, Jesse (IL) - 1878, 1892
Harper, Joseph M. (NH) - 1831, 1833
Harper, R. L. (TN) - 1928
Harper, Robert M. (IL) - 1942
Harpster, David (OH) - 1886
Harrall (GA) - 1882
Harreld, John W. (OK) - 1919, 1940
Harrell, Jack E. Jr. (GA) - 1980
Harrelson, F. Marion (FL) - 1964
Harri, Jerry A. (MN) - 1934
Harrick, Adolph (IL) - 1904
Harries, William H. (MN) - 1890, 1892
Harrigan, Albert F. (IN) - 1966
Harrington (MO) - 1890
Harrington (VT) - 1849, 1850
Harrington, C. B. (VT) - 1843
Harrington, Cecil R. (PA) - 1970
Harrington, Conner (TX) - 1961, 1962
Harrington, Edward F. (MA) - 1960, 1966
Harrington, Edward W. (NH) - 1867, 1869
Harrington, Giles (VT) - 1863, 1864
Harrington, H. B. (OH) - 1894, 1900
Harrington, Henry W. (IN) - 1862, 1864
Harrington, John H. (MA) - 1896
Harrington, Jubal (MA) - 1836
Harrington, Michael J. (MA) - 1969, 1970, 1972, 1974, 1976
Harrington, Patrick H. Jr. (MA) - 1966
Harrington, Vincent F. (IA) - 1936, 1938, 1940
Harrington, William P. (MI) - 1964, 1966
Harris (GA) - 1832, 1878
Harris (MD) - 1861
Harris (MI) - 1876
Harris (MS) - 1849, 1880
Harris (NY) - 1876
Harris (TN) - 1874, 1884
Harris, A. M. S. (SC) - 1833
Harris, Abram J. (IL) - 1914
Harris, Addison C. (IN) - 1886
Harris, Andrew L. (OH) - 1894
Harris, Benjamin G. (MD) - 1863, 1864
Harris, Benjamin W. (MA) - 1872, 1874, 1876, 1878, 1880
Harris, C. O. (TX) - 1916
Harris, Carmon C. (OK) - 1946, 1948
Harris, Charles M. (IL) - 1862, 1864
Harris, Curtis W. (VA) - 1974
Harris, D. M. (IA) - 1888
Harris, Dave (CA) - 1968
Harris, David (CA) - 1976
Harris, David T. (CA) - 1964
Harris, Earl (NJ) - 1966
Harris, Ellen G. (CO) - 1954
Harris, Ellis B. (WI) - 1912
Harris, Fred L. (MI) - 1970
Harris, Geroge A. (PA) - 1916
Harris, George E. (MS) - 1869, 1870
Harris, Henry C. (KY) - 1855
Harris, Henry R. (GA) - 1872, 1874, 1876, 1884
Harris, Henry S. (NJ) - 1880, 1882
Harris, Herbert E. (VA) - 1974, 1976, 1978, 1980, 1982
Harris, Homer L. (WV) - 1982
Harris, Isham G. (TN) - 1849, 1851
Harris, J. G. (AL) - 1870
Harris, J. Morrison (MD) - 1855, 1857, 1859
Harris, James (NC) - 1870
Harris, James H. (NC) - 1878
Harris, James N. (NY) - 1968
Harris, James R. (AR) - 1946
Harris, James W. (GA) - 1848
Harris, John P. (KS) - 1896
Harris, John T. (VA) - 1859, 1869, 1870, 1872, 1874, 1876, 1878
Harris, John W. (TN) - 1847
Harris, Joseph K. (MA) - 1894
Harris, Josiah (OH) - 1846
Harris, L. E. (Larry) - 1980
Harris, Leodis (OH) - 1962
Harris, Lovell B. (OH) - 1882
Harris, Marsha A. (IL) - 1980
Harris, Max B. (MI) - 1968
Harris, Morrison J. (MD) - 1876
Harris, Morton (TX) - 1937
Harris, Moses S. (NY) - 1980
Harris, Oren (AR) - 1940, 1942, 1944, 1946, 1948, 1950, 1952, 1954, 1956, 1958, 1960, 1962, 1964

Harris, Ray (SC) - 1968
Harris, Robert (PA) - 1824
Harris, Robert O. (MA) - 1910, 1912
Harris, S. H. (IL) - 1866
Harris, Sampson W. (AL) - 1847, 1849, 1851, 1853, 1855
Harris, Saul J. (MD) - 1978
Harris, Stephen R. (OH) - 1894, 1896
Harris, Thomas L. (IL) - 1848, 1850, 1854, 1856, 1858
Harris, W. H. (CA) - 1886
Harris, W. S. (OH) - 1912, 1914
Harris, Walter H. (IL) - 1912
Harris, Wiley P. (MS) - 1853
Harris, William A. (KS) - 1892, 1894
Harris, William A. (VA) - 1841
Harris, Winder R. (VA) - 1942
Harris, Z. A. (OK) - 1916
Harris, Zach A. (OH) - 1920, 1922
Harrison (KY) - 1829
Harrison (MO) - 1886, 1916, 1932
Harrison (PA) - 1826
Harrison, Albert G. (MO) - 1835, 1836, 1838
Harrison, Burr P. (VA) - 1946, 1948, 1950, 1952, 1954, 1956, 1958, 1960
Harrison, C. S. (NE) - 1886
Harrison, Caleb (PA) - 1910
Harrison, Carter H. (IL) - 1872, 1874, 1876
Harrison, Charles D. (IL) - 1926
Harrison, Dabney C. (VA) - 1924, 1926
Harrison, E. M. (AR) - 1890
Harrison, Francis Burton (NY) - 1902, 1906, 1908, 1910, 1912
Harrison, Frank (PA) - 1982, 1984
Harrison, George A. (VA) - 1904
Harrison, George P. (AL) - 1894
Harrison, Horace H. (TN) - 1872, 1874
Harrison, J. P. (KY) - 1902
Harrison, James A. (MI) - 1968
Harrison, James O. (KY) - 1855
Harrison, John F. (OH) - 1908
Harrison, John Scott (OH) - 1852, 1854, 1856, 1860
Harrison, Joseph R. (IN) - 1920
Harrison, Pat (MS) - 1910, 1912, 1914, 1916
Harrison, R. B. (TX) - 1912
Harrison, Robert D. (NE) - 1951, 1952, 1954, 1956, 1958
Harrison, Samuel S. (PA) - 1832, 1834
Harrison, Thomas W. (VA) - 1916, 1918, 1920, 1922, 1924, 1926, 1928
Harrison, W. H. (LA) - 1888
Harrison, William (IL) - 1928
Harrison, William G. (MD) - 1859
Harrison, William H. (IN) - 1932
Harrison, William Henry (WY) - 1950, 1952, 1960, 1962, 1964, 1966
Harrison, William Preston (IL) - 1904
Harrison, William W. (NJ) - 1932
Harrop, Roy M. (NE) - 1922, 1924
Harry, David G. (MD) - 1946
Harry, Floyd (TX) - 1928, 1930, 1946
Harsha, William H. (OH) - 1960, 1962, 1964, 1966, 1968, 1970, 1972, 1974, 1976, 1978
Hart (NY) - 1848
Hart (OH) - 1860
Hart, Alphonso (OH) - 1880, 1882, 1884
Hart, Archibald C. (NJ) - 1912, 1914, 1930
Hart, Bernard E. (NY) - 1948, 1950
Hart, E. Kirke (NY) - 1876
Hart, Edward (PA) - 1914
Hart, Edward H. (CA) - 1912, 1914, 1916
Hart, Edward J. (NJ) - 1934, 1936, 1938, 1940, 1942, 1944, 1946, 1948, 1950, 1952
Hart, Emanuel B. (NY) - 1850
Hart, Fred J. (CA) - 1944
Hart, Gary K. (CA) - 1970
Hart, George (PA) - 1914, 1920
Hart, H. A. (KS) - 1888
Hart, H. L. (MT) - 1936
Hart, Henry A. (CA) - 1914
Hart, J. L. Jr. (OK) - 1942
Hart, James A. (IA) - 1950
Hart, James A. (NE) - 1952, 1954
Hart, Jerome T. (MI) - 1962, 1972
Hart, Joe Jr. (OK) - 1946
Hart, John C. (NY) - 1952
Hart, John J. Jr. (NY) - 1964
Hart, Joseph J. (PA) - 1894
Hart, Larry Joe (WY) - 1976

Hart, Mary Ward (IL) - 1924
Hart, Michael J. (MI) - 1930, 1932, 1934, 1936, 1942
Hart, Michael J. (MO) - 1924
Hart, Rawleigh K. (KY) - 1894
Hart, Roswell (NY) - 1864, 1866
Hart, Royal (MD) - 1970
Hart, Sheila M. (MI) - 1982
Hart, Simpson (MA) - 1848, 1850
Hart, Thomas P. (OH) - 1908, 1910
Hart, William J. (OH) - 1898
Hart, William R. (MI) - 1956
Harter, Dow W. (OH) - 1930, 1932, 1934, 1936, 1938, 1940, 1942
Harter, Eugene C. (KY) - 1966
Harter, J. Francis (NY) - 1938, 1940
Harter, Jerry K. (CA) - 1952
Harter, Michael D. (OH) - 1890, 1892
Harter, Theodore C. (PA) - 1910
Harter, William H. (NY) - 1976
Hartke, Jan Alan (NM) - 1982
Hartle, Russell Peter (MD) - 1950
Hartley, Fred A. Jr. (NJ) - 1928, 1930, 1932, 1934, 1936, 1938, 1940, 1942, 1944, 1946
Hartman, Charles S. (MT) - 1892, 1894, 1896, 1910
Hartman, David N. (CA) - 1970
Hartman, Gustave (NY) - 1908
Hartman, H. H. (OH) - 1922
Hartman, Jesse L. (PA) - 1910, 1912, 1914
Hartman, John D. (TX) - 1918
Hartman, M. (VA) - 1908
Hartman, Stanley E. (OR) - 1962
Hartman, W. D. (PA) - 1876
Hartman, William M. (PA) - 1918
Hartness, William (IL) - 1918
Hartnett, Thomas F. (SC) - 1980, 1982, 1984
Hartnett, William E. (IL) - 1952
Hartranft, A. S. (PA) - 1880
Hartranft, Marshall V. (CA) - 1932
Hartridge, Julian (GA) - 1874, 1876
Hartsell, Charles (CO) - 1898
Hartson, C. (CA) - 1867, 1868
Hartsuff, William (MI) - 1888
Hartwell, J. W. (VA) - 1884
Hartwig (MO) - 1888
Hartzell, Richard F. (PA) - 1944, 1946
Hartzell, William (IL) - 1870, 1874, 1876, 1880, 1886
Hartzell, William H. (IL) - 1928, 1930
Harvey (AL) - 1888
Harvey (NJ) - 1906
Harvey, A. M. (KS) - 1904
Harvey, J. Mark (MI) - 1914
Harvey, Jack (WI) - 1948, 1950
Harvey, James (MI) - 1960, 1962, 1964, 1966, 1968, 1970, 1972
Harvey, John (NH) - 1833
Harvey, Jonathan (NH) - 1824, 1827, 1829
Harvey, Peter (MA) - 1868
Harvey, Ralph (IN) - 1948, 1950, 1952, 1954, 1956, 1958, 1960, 1962, 1964
Harvey, Ruth L. (VA) - 1968
Harvey, Samuel (PA) - 1828
Harvey, Thomas H. (WV) - 1894
Harvey, W. H. (TX) - 1910
Harvey, W. Scott (NC) - 1966, 1968
Harwell, W. D. (AL) - 1916
Harwood (MO) - 1884, 1886
Harwood (VA) - 1837
Harwood, H. L. (KY) - 1932
Hasbrook, Stephen (NY) - 1836
Hasbrouck (NY) - 1844, 1848, 1878
Hasbrouck, Abraham (NY) - 1824
Hasbrouck, Anthony (NY) - 1838
Hascall, Asa (NY) - 1826, 1836
Hascall, Augustus P. (NY) - 1850
Hascall, Charles C. (MI) - 1850
Hascall, M. S. (IN) - 1870
Haseltine (MO) - 1882
Haseman, Paul (CA) - 1978
Haskell, Dudley C. (KS) - 1876, 1878, 1880, 1882
Haskell, F. H. (ME) - 1920
Haskell, Harry G. Jr. (DE) - 1956, 1958
Haskell, Reuben L. (NY) - 1912, 1914, 1916, 1918
Haskell, Robert H. (NY) - 1904
Haskell, William Henry (MA) - 1940
Haskell, William T. (TN) - 1847
Haskin, John B. (NY) - 1856, 1858
Haskins, Dave (Buster) (TX) - 1980

Kurtz, J. Banks (PA) - 1922, 1924, 1926, 1928, 1930, 1932, 1934
Kurtz, William H. (PA) - 1850, 1852
Kusek, Laurence A. (IL) - 1958
Kustermann, Gustav (WI) - 1888, 1906, 1908, 1910
Kuta, Matthew P. (CT) - 1956
Kutz, Charles (PA) - 1926
Kuykendall, Andrew J. (IL) - 1864
Kuykendall, Dan (TN) - 1966, 1968, 1970, 1972, 1974
Kuykendall, Hardy (AR) - 1926
Kvale, Ole J. (MN) - 1920, 1922, 1924, 1926, 1928
Kvale, Paul John (MN) - 1930, 1932, 1934, 1936, 1938
Kveton, W. J. (TX) - 1922
Kyl, John (IA) - 1958, 1959, 1960, 1962, 1964, 1966, 1968, 1970, 1972
Kyle, Dwight V. (TN) - 1948
Kyle, James B. (IL) - 1856
Kyle, John C. (MS) - 1890, 1892, 1894
Kyle, John K. (WI) - 1944
Kyle, Thomas B. (OH) - 1900, 1902
Kyne, Martin C. (NY) - 1938
Kyros, Peter N. (ME) - 1966, 1968, 1970, 1972, 1974

L

Labaff, Ernest J. (NY) - 1972
LaBeau, Henri (MT) - 1912
Labine, Lorenzo (MA) - 1852
LaBorde, Robert C. (NY) - 1968
LaBranche, Alcee (LA) - 1842
LaCaff (MO) - 1902
LaCapra, John R. (FL) - 1980
LaCaze, Jeff (LA) - 1974, 1975
Lacey, Edward S. (MI) - 1880, 1882
Lacey, John F. (IA) - 1888, 1890, 1892, 1894, 1896, 1898, 1900, 1902, 1904, 1906
Lackey, E. Dent (NY) - 1952, 1962
Lackner, Frank (PA) - 1906
Lackore, Frederick (MI) - 1894
Lacock, S. A. (PA) - 1912
Lacy, Arthur J. (MI) - 1906
Lacy, B. W. (VA) - 1880
Ladd (NY) - 1886
Ladd, George W. (ME) - 1868, 1878, 1880, 1882
Ladd, Joseph E. (ME) - 1882, 1886
Ladd, Roger B. (CT) - 1968
Laderman, Morris (OH) - 1962
La Dow, George A. (OR) - 1874
Laessig, James E. (WI) - 1966
LaFalce, John J. (NY) - 1974, 1976, 1978, 1980, 1982, 1984
LaFayette (OK) - 1914
Lafean, Daniel F. (PA) - 1902, 1904, 1906, 1908, 1910, 1912, 1914
Lafferty, Abraham W. (OR) - 1910, 1912, 1914, 1916, 1918
Laffoon, Polk (KY) - 1884, 1886
Lafin, Andrew (IL) - 1916, 1922
LaFlamme, Edward J. (IL) - 1984
Laflin, Addison H. (NY) - 1864, 1866, 1868
LaFollette, Charles M. (IN) - 1942, 1944
LaFollette, Latelle M. Jr. (WV) - 1950, 1952
LaFollette, Robert M. (WI) - 1884, 1886, 1888, 1890
LaFollette, William L. (WA) - 1910, 1912, 1914, 1916
Lafore, John A. Jr. (PA) - 1958
Lagan, Matthew D. (LA) - 1886, 1890
Lagomarsino, Robert J. (CA) - 1974, 1976, 1978, 1980, 1982, 1984
LaGuardia, Fiorello H. (NY) - 1914, 1916, 1918, 1922, 1924, 1926, 1928, 1930, 1932
Lahm (OH) - 1856
Lahm, Samuel (OH) - 1846
Lahr, Frederick W. (NY) - 1924
Lahtinen, Leonard L. (CA) - 1980
Laidlaw, William G. (NY) - 1886, 1888
Laidler, Harry W. (NY) - 1920, 1932
Laidley (VA) - 1859
Laimbeer, William (NY) - 1868
Laird, Carlton W. (NE) - 1954, 1956
Laird, James (NE) - 1882, 1884, 1886, 1888
Laird, Melvin R. (WI) - 1952, 1954, 1956, 1958, 1960, 1962, 1964, 1966, 1968

Laisi, Lauri T. (NY) - 1946
Lake, George B. (NE) - 1870
Lake, Harry F. (NH) - 1918
Lake, W. Mallam (KY) - 1948, 1952
Lake, William A. (MS) - 1855
Lake, William H. (MS) - 1857
Lakin, James O. (WV) - 1932
Lakritz, Simon (CA) - 1984
Lall, Betty G. (NY) - 1982
LaMagna, Frank (CA) - 1966
Lamar, Henry G. (GA) - 1829, 1830, 1832, 1834, 1855
Lamar, J. Robert (MO) - 1902, 1904, 1906, 1908
Lamar, John B. (GA) - 1842
Lamar, Lucius Q. C. (MS) - 1857, 1859, 1872, 1875
Lamar, Ward (WV) - 1872
Lamar, William B. (FL) - 1902, 1904, 1906
LaMaster, Hugh (NE) - 1904
LaMaster, Leroy (TX) - 1954
Lamb (IN) - 1868
Lamb (MA) - 1876
Lamb, Alfred W. (MO) - 1852
Lamb, G. F. (ND) - 1934
Lamb, John (VA) - 1896, 1898, 1900, 1902, 1904, 1906, 1908, 1910
Lamb, John Edward (IN) - 1882, 1884, 1886
Lamb, John M. (MI) - 1848
Lamb, W. R. (TX) - 1890
Lambdin, Samuel A. (IN) - 1922
Lamberry, W. N. (FL) - 1912
Lambert (PA) - 1852
Lambert, George H. (NJ) - 1900
Lambert, Walter Raymond (CA) - 1942
Lamberton (MN) - 1916
Lamberton (NY) - 1878
Lamberton, George D. (NY) - 1932
Lamberton, Henry W. (MN) - 1864
Lambertson, William P. (KS) - 1928, 1930, 1932, 1934, 1936, 1938, 1940, 1942
Lambeth, J. Walter (NC) - 1930, 1932, 1934, 1936
Lambirth, Harry W. (PA) - 1912
Lambros, C. D. (OH) - 1964
Lamison, Charles L. (OH) - 1870
Lamison, Charles N. (OH) - 1872
Lamkin, Robert B. (IL) - 1972
Lamm, Edwin S. (CO) - 1964
Lammers, Bernard J. (NY) - 1984
Lamneck, Arthur P. (OH) - 1920, 1930, 1932, 1934, 1936, 1938, 1940, 1942, 1946
Lamon, Ward H. (WV) - 1876
Lamond, Leo D. (ME) - 1930
Lamont, John F. (WI) - 1910
Lamoreaux, J. Neal (MI) - 1944
Lamoureux, Wilfrid J. (MA) - 1924
Lampert, Florian (WI) - 1918, 1920, 1922, 1924, 1926, 1928
Lampman, William W. (NY) - 1928
Lamport, William H. (NY) - 1870, 1872
Lamson, Bob (WA) - 1984
Lanagan, Frank R. (NY) - 1934
Lanborn, Levi L. (OH) - 1876
Lancaster, Carlyle J. (MD) - 1960
Lancaster, W. Emery (IL) - 1908
Land, Yates (OK) - 1960
Landau, Gustave J. (NY) - 1930
Landau, Sonia (NY) - 1976
Lander (AR) - 1874
Landers (CT) - 1878
Landers, Franklin (IN) - 1874, 1876
Landers, George M. (CT) - 1875, 1876
Landes, Carl K. (FL) - 1950
Landes, Silas Z. (IL) - 1884, 1886
Landgraf, Vernon H. (MO) - 1968
Landgrebe, Earl F. (IN) - 1968, 1970, 1972, 1974
Landi, P. Vincent (NY) - 1950, 1952
Landis, Charles B. (IN) - 1896, 1898, 1900, 1902, 1904, 1906, 1908
Landis, Frederick (IN) - 1902, 1904, 1906, 1934
Landis, Gerald W. (IN) - 1934, 1936, 1938, 1940, 1942, 1944, 1946, 1948
Landis, Milford (OH) - 1964
Lando (MN) - 1906
Landon (NY) - 1852
Landon, Daniel (WA) - 1912
Landram, B. S. (KY) - 1924
Landreth, S. Floyd (VA) - 1920
Landrum, John J. (KY) - 1876, 1884
Landrum, John M. (LA) - 1859

Landrum, Phil M. (GA) - 1952, 1954, 1956, 1958, 1960, 1962, 1964, 1966, 1968, 1970, 1972, 1974
Landrum, W. R. (TN) - 1910
Landry (LA) - 1847
Landry, J. Aristide (LA) - 1851
Landy (PA) - 1854, 1858
Landy, David P. (NY) - 1982
Landy, James (PA) - 1856
Landy, Robert J. (PA) - 1968
Lane (KY) - 1849
Lane, Amos (IN) - 1833, 1835, 1837
Lane, Benjamin C. (MA) - 1892
Lane, Charles R. (IN) - 1912, 1914
Lane, Clive R. (KS) - 1940
Lane, Dan (OK) - 1982
Lane, Daniel W. (MA) - 1906, 1908
Lane, Edward (IL) - 1886, 1888, 1890, 1892, 1894, 1895
Lane, Henry S. (IN) - 1840, 1841, 1849
Lane, James H. (IN) - 1852
Lane, Joseph R. (IA) - 1898
Lane, La Fayette (OR) - 1875, 1876
Lane, Layle (NY) - 1942
Lane, Millard E. (MO) - 1926
Lane, Thomas J. (MA) - 1942, 1944, 1946, 1948, 1950, 1952, 1954, 1956, 1958, 1960, 1962
Lane, William K. (NC) - 1847, 1849
Lang (ME) - 1872
Lang (MD) - 1882, 1888
Lang, George B. (MO) - 1928
Langan, John P. (NJ) - 1958
Langdon, Charles C. (AL) - 1851, 1865
Langdon, Lawrence K. (OH) - 1912
Lange, George L. (OK) - 1964
Lange, Joseph F. (OH) - 1928
Langelier, Louis F. R. (MA) - 1918
Langen, Odin (MN) - 1958, 1960, 1962, 1964, 1966, 1968, 1970
Langfitt (PA) - 1888
Langham, Jonathan N. (PA) - 1908, 1910, 1912
Langhorne (VA) - 1843
Langhorne, Maurice (WA) - 1910
Langley (MO) - 1932
Langley, Albert S. (NH) - 1902
Langley, C. W. (PA) - 1896
Langley, Fred (OK) - 1934
Langley, Isom P. (AR) - 1886, 1890
Langley, Jane P. (NY) - 1972
Langley, John N. (KY) - 1922
Langley, John W. (KY) - 1896, 1906, 1908, 1910, 1912, 1914, 1916, 1918, 1920, 1924
Langley, Katherine (KY) - 1926, 1928, 1930
Langley, Samuel W. (KY) - 1868
Langslet, Halvor (MN) - 1944
Langston, J. Luther (OK) - 1912
Langston, John M. (VA) - 1888, 1890
Langworthy, Lyman (NY) - 1840
Langworthy, Robert B. (MO) - 1964
Lanham, Fritz G. (TX) - 1920, 1922, 1924, 1926, 1928, 1930, 1932, 1934, 1936, 1938, 1940, 1942, 1944
Lanhan, Henderson (GA) - 1946, 1948, 1950, 1952, 1954, 1956
Lanham, Samuel W. T. (TX) - 1882, 1884, 1886, 1888, 1890, 1896, 1898, 1900
Lanier (VA) - 1825
Lanier, P. W. (ND) - 1930, 1954
Lanier, R. H. (LA) - 1880
Lanigan, Tom (NE) - 1942, 1944
Laning (NY) - 1854
Laning, J. Ford (OH) - 1906
Lankard, Fred W. (OK) - 1926
Lankford, Menalcus (VA) - 1920, 1924, 1928, 1930, 1932
Lankford, Richard E. (MD) - 1952, 1954, 1956, 1958, 1960, 1962
Lankford, William C. (GA) - 1918, 1920, 1922, 1924, 1926, 1928, 1930
Lanning, William M. (NJ) - 1902
Lannon, Thomas J. (PA) - 1902
Lansing (NY) - 1881
Lansing, Edward S. (NY) - 1866
Lansing, Frederick (NY) - 1888
Lansing, Gerrit (NY) - 1830, 1832, 1834
Lansing, I. D. (IL) - 1856
Lansing, William E. (NY) - 1860, 1870, 1872
Lantaff, Bill (FL) - 1950, 1952
Lantos, Tom (CA) - 1980, 1982, 1984
Lantz, Simon E. (IL) - 1938
Lanzetta, James J. (NY) - 1932, 1934, 1936, 1938, 1940

Laos, Roby B. (AZ) - 1982
Lapham, Elbridge G. (NY) - 1874, 1876, 1878, 1880
Lapham, Oscar (RI) - 1882, 1886, 1888, 1890, 1892, 1893, 1894
Laphani, Louis (MA) - 1874
La Pina, Frank A. (NY) - 1972
Laporte, B. (PA) - 1874
Laporte, John (PA) - 1832, 1834
Lapp, Charles W. (OH) - 1904, 1906, 1908
Larcade, Henry D. Jr. (LA) - 1942, 1944, 1946, 1948, 1950
Larcamp, William L. (WV) - 1974
Lardner, William (SD) - 1892
Larew, Jim (IA) - 1980
Larimer, Joseph H. (IN) - 1896
Larimore, W. L. (LA) - 1878
Larkenson, Rhodelphius (MA) - 1840
Larkin, Edwin J. (WI) - 1936
Larkin, Francis (NY) - 1864
Larkin, Thomas F. (NY) - 1896
Larkin, William T. (IL) - 1958, 1960
LaRocco, Larry (ID) - 1982
Larossa, Alfred A. (NY) - 1940
Larrabee (MN) - 1906
Larrabee, Charles H. (WI) - 1858, 1860
Larrabee, William H. (IN) - 1928, 1930, 1932, 1934, 1936, 1938, 1940, 1942
Larrison (NJ) - 1878
Larsen, Christian F. (WA) - 1900
Larsen, E. J. (MN) - 1942
Larsen, William C. (NY) - 1976, 1982
Larsen, William W. (GA) - 1916, 1918, 1920, 1922, 1924, 1926, 1928, 1930
Larson (UT) - 1914
Larson, A. William (NY) - 1958
Larson, Charles A. (IL) - 1912
Larson, Erwin (IA) - 1923
Larson, L. R. (WI) - 1884
Larson, Lewis (UT) - 1912
Larson, Oscar J. (MN) - 1920, 1922, 1926
LaRue (CT) - 1906
Laser, James C. (OH) - 1894
LaSere (LA) - 1859
LaSere, Emile (LA) - 1847, 1849
Lash, Eli Reynolds (OH) - 1894
Lash, Israel G. (NC) - 1868
Lasker, Morris E. (NY) - 1950
Lasky, Herbert (NY) - 1948
Lassalle, Joseph (LA) - 1904
Lassiter, Francis R. (VA) - 1900, 1906, 1908
Latady, Francis (AL) - 1916
Latham, Allen (OH) - 1838, 1840
Latham, George R. (WV) - 1864
Latham, Henry J. (NY) - 1944, 1946, 1948, 1950, 1952, 1954, 1956
Latham, Louis C. (NC) - 1880, 1882, 1886
Latham, Milton S. (CA) - 1852, 1854
Latham, Thomas J. (NC) - 1855
Lathrop (AL) - 1898
Lathrop (MA) - 1878
Lathrop, Frank H. (AL) - 1926
Lathrop, George V. N. (MI) - 1856, 1860
Lathrop, Horace (NY) - 1830
Lathrop, Lowell E. (CA) - 1946, 1948
Lathrop, Samuel C. (MA) - 1826, 1833
Lathrop, Tom (MA) - 1824
Lathrop, William (IL) - 1876
Lathrope (PA) - 1888
Latimer (MN) - 1916
Latimer, Asbury C. (SC) - 1892, 1894, 1896, 1898, 1900
Latimer, J. A. (MN) - 1882
Latimer, Thomas E. (MN) - 1912
Laton, Jesse J. (CO) - 1912
Latta, Bruce (CA) - 1976
Latta, Delbert L. (OH) - 1958, 1960, 1962, 1964, 1966, 1968, 1970, 1972, 1974, 1976, 1978, 1980, 1982, 1984
Latta, James P. (NE) - 1908, 1910
Lattin, G. W. (SD) - 1904
Lattin, Ralph W. (NV) - 1940
Laub, George R. (IA) - 1952, 1954
Laucks, Robert G. (CA) - 1906
Laudani, Angelo (MA) - 1982
Laudin, Donald M. (IL) - 1962
Laughlin, G. A. (WV) - 1912
Laughlin, John K. (PA) - 1918
Laughlin, L. W. (IA) - 1912
Laughlin, T. P. (KS) - 1916
Laughlin, W. R. (KS) - 1872
Laukaitis, William F. (MD) - 1952
Lauri, Carl E. (WI) - 1956, 1966

Laurisch, Christian J. (MN) - 1936
Laurita, Joe Jr. (WV) - 1974
Lausmann, Jerry (OR) - 1976, 1978
Lauve, John (MI) - 1984
Lavelle, Thomas D. (MA) - 1928
Laverty (NJ) - 1878
Laverty (PA) - 1886
Lavery, James F. (PA) - 1940, 1942, 1944
Lavery, Urban A. (IL) - 1924
Lavery, Vincent J. (CA) - 1972
Law (NY) - 1848
Law, Arthur J. (MI) - 1952
Law, Charles B. (NY) - 1904, 1906, 1908, 1910
Law, John (IN) - 1831, 1833, 1837, 1860, 1862
Law, Lyman (CT) - 1825, 1827
Lawler, Dan W. (MN) - 1924
Lawler, Frank (IL) - 1884, 1886, 1888, 1894
Lawler, Frank J. (MA) - 1906
Lawler, Joab (AL) - 1835, 1837
Lawler, Joseph V. (OH) - 1902
Lawlor, Francis X. (IL) - 1975
Lawn, Victor H. (NY) - 1920
Lawr (NY) - 1856
Lawrance, F. B. (KS) - 1906
Lawrence (NY) - 1844, 1848
Lawrence, Abbott (MA) - 1834, 1839
Lawrence, Abraham (NY) - 1830
Lawrence, Charles B. (IL) - 1862
Lawrence, Chester R. (MA) - 1914
Lawrence, Cornelius (NY) - 1832
Lawrence, Darius W. (NY) - 1866
Lawrence, E. J. (ME) - 1906
Lawrence, Edson (NY) - 1906
Lawrence, Edward I. (OH) - 1902
Lawrence, Edwin (MI) - 1844, 1846
Lawrence, Effingham (LA) - 1872
Lawrence, Frank B. (KS) - 1908
Lawrence, George N. (UT) - 1930
Lawrence, George P. (MA) - 1897, 1898, 1900, 1902, 1904, 1906, 1908, 1910
Lawrence, George V. (PA) - 1864, 1866, 1882
Lawrence, George W. (IL) - 1956
Lawrence, Henry F. (MO) - 1920, 1922, 1924, 1928, 1930
Lawrence, Isaac (RI) - 1880
Lawrence, James W. (MN) - 1892
Lawrence, John S. (MI) - 1891
Lawrence, John W. (NY) - 1844
Lawrence, Joseph (CA) - 1906
Lawrence, Joseph (PA) - 1824, 1846, 1838, 1840
Lawrence, L. L. (TN) - 1896
Lawrence, Luther (MA) - 1826
Lawrence, Sidney (NY) - 1846
Lawrence, William (NY) - 1846
Lawrence, William (OH) - 1856, 1864, 1866, 1868, 1872, 1874, 1876
Lawrence, William H. (MD) - 1916
Lawrence, William Jr. (OH) - 1888
Laws, Donald B. (OH) - 1970
Laws, Gilbert L. (NE) - 1889
Laws, R. Don (NC) - 1912
Lawson (AL) - 1896
Lawson (LA) - 1838
Lawson (MO) - 1862
Lawson (NY) - 1874, 1886
Lawson, A. M. (TX) - 1910
Lawson, Daniel T. (OH) - 1868, 1878
Lawson, Donald M. (MN) - 1946
Lawson, John D. (NY) - 1872
Lawson, John W. (VA) - 1890
Lawson, Joseph A. (NY) - 1918
Lawson, Thomas G. (GA) - 1890, 1892, 1894
Lawson, William C. (FL) - 1926, 1928
Lawton, Winburn J. (GA) - 1870
Lay (MO) - 1874
Lay, Alfred M. (MO) - 1878
Lay, George W. (NY) - 1832, 1834
Layne, Edythe (NY) - 1974
Layton, Caleb R. (DE) - 1918, 1920, 1922
Layton, Fernando C. (OH) - 1890, 1892, 1894
Layton, Roy E. (OH) - 1938
Lazaro, Ladislas (LA) - 1912, 1914, 1916, 1918, 1920, 1922, 1924, 1926
Lazear, Jesse (PA) - 1860, 1862, 1864
Le Blond, Frank C. (OH) - 1862, 1864
Le Bosky, Leo S. (IL) - 1918
Le Bourgeois, Louis (LA) - 1914
Le Claire, Berthelot (RI) - 1952

Le Clercq, Fred (SC) - 1966
Le Compte (KY) - 1843
Le Fevre, Benjamin (OH) - 1878, 1880, 1882, 1884
Le Grand, J. (MD) - 1843
Le Moyne (PA) - 1843
Le Moyne, John V. (IL) - 1872, 1874, 1876
Lea (AL) - 1843
Lea (MO) - 1910
Lea, Clarence F. (CA) - 1916, 1918, 1920, 1922, 1924, 1926, 1928, 1930, 1932, 1934, 1936, 1938, 1940, 1942, 1944, 1946
Lea, Luke (TN) - 1833, 1835
Lea, Pryor (TN) - 1827, 1829, 1831
Leach (KY) - 1837
Leach (NC) - 1843
Leach, Claude (Buddy) (LA) - 1978, 1980
Leach, D. D. (AR) - 1886
Leach, De Witt C. (MI) - 1856, 1858
Leach, Freeman (PA) - 1898
Leach, James A. S. (IA) - 1974, 1976
Leach, James M. (NC) - 1859, 1870, 1872
Leach, Jim (IA) - 1978, 1980, 1982, 1984
Leach, John B. (NY) - 1926
Leach, Robert E. (IA) - 1912
Leach, Robert Fulton Jr. (MD) - 1900
Leach, Wallace (CA) - 1879, 1880
Leadbetter, Daniel P. (OH) - 1836, 1838
Leaf, James P. (PA) - 1926
Leafdale, C. Edgar (NE) - 1948
Leahy, Daniel P. (MA) - 1924
Leak, Spencer (IL) - 1976
Leake (VA) - 1847
Leake, Eugene W. (NJ) - 1906
Leake, Shelton F. (VA) - 1845, 1859
Leake, Walter F. (NC) - 1847, 1853
Leaken, W. R. (GA) - 1900
Leaming (IL) - 1860
Leamy, James P. (VT) - 1938
Leap, Charles C. (VA) - 1938
Lear, Pat (CA) - 1978
Learnid, George (CT) - 1825
Leary, Cornelius L. L. (MD) - 1861
Leary, Daniel J. (MO) - 1950
Leath, J. Marvin (TX) - 1978
Leath, Marvin (TX) - 1980, 1982, 1984
Leathers, J. W. (KY) - 1863
Leatherwood (UT) - 1914
Leatherwood, Elmer O. (UT) - 1920, 1922, 1924, 1926, 1928
Leavenworth, Alson (NY) - 1832
Leavenworth, Elias W. (NY) - 1874
Leavitt, B. (MA) - 1860
Leavitt, F. A. (SD) - 1890
Leavitt, Halsey B. (NC) - 1934
Leavitt, Humphrey H. (OH) - 1830, 1832
Leavitt, Reuben H. (ND) - 1926, 1928, 1930
Leavitt, S. D. (ME) - 1892
Leavitt, Scott (MT) - 1922, 1924, 1926, 1928, 1930, 1932
Leavitt, Sheldon (CT) - 1834, 1835
Leavy, Charles H. (WA) - 1936, 1938, 1940
LeBoutillier, John (NY) - 1980, 1982
Lebson, Abram A. (NJ) - 1940
Lechner, Ira M. (VA) - 1982
Leckemby, J. C. (ME) - 1936, 1938
Lecompte, Joseph (KY) - 1824, 1827, 1829, 1831
LeCompte, Karl M. (IA) - 1938, 1940, 1942, 1944, 1946, 1950, 1952, 1954, 1956
Ledbetter, Jesse I. (NC) - 1972
Ledbetter, John Q. A. (IL) - 1908
Letbetter, W. E. (KD) - 1940
Leddy, James J. (IL) - 1920
Leder, Julius M. (NY) - 1918
Lederer, Raymond F. (PA) - 1976, 1978, 1980
Ledergerber (MO) - 1886
Ledgerwood (TN) - 1884
Ledgerwood, W. L. (TN) - 1896
Ledoux, Henri T. (NH) - 1906
Ledvina, J. P. (TX) - 1948
Ledyard, J. D. (NY) - 1834
Ledyd (NY) - 1844
Lee (MS) - 1876
Lee (NY) - 1860
Lee (OH) - 1852, 1854
Lee, A. L. (KS) - 1864
Lee, Algernon (NY) - 1912, 1918, 1920, 1926
Lee, Andrew E. (SD) - 1900
Lee, Baker R. (VA) - 1872

Lee, Benjamin F. (NJ) - 1870
Lee, Blair (MD) - 1896
Lee, C. W. (AL) - 1865
Lee, Charles R. (NY) - 1924
Lee, Charles W. (IN) - 1898
Lee, Daniel (NY) - 1832
Lee, Detroit (AL) - 1970
Lee, E. Brooke (MD) - 1942
Lee, Francis D. (ME) - 1952
Lee, Frank (TX) - 1902
Lee, Frank H. (MO) - 1922, 1930, 1932, 1934, 1938
Lee, Gary A. (NY) - 1978, 1980
Lee, Gideon (NY) - 1836
Lee, Gordon (GA) - 1904, 1906, 1908, 1910, 1912, 1914, 1916, 1918, 1920, 1922, 1924
Lee, Guy Jr. (NJ) - 1936
Lee, Henry (MA) - 1830
Lee, J. Bracken (UT) - 1942
Lee, J. Ira (NC) - 1944
Lee, James H. (MI) - 1920
Lee, Jason (OR) - 1956
Lee, John (MD) - 1824, 1826
Lee, John (NJ) - 1840
Lee, Larry (AL) - 1984
Lee, M. Lindley (NY) - 1858
Lee, Noble W. (IL) - 1938
Lee, Oliver (NY) - 1834, 1836
Lee, Mrs. R. Q. (TX) - 1930
Lee, Ray (MS) - 1970
Lee, Robert C. (NY) - 1926, 1928
Lee, Robert E. (LA) - 1902, 1970, 1973
Lee, Robert E. (PA) - 1908, 1910, 1912, 1914, 1916
Lee, Robert F. (MN) - 1950
Lee, Robert Q. (TX) - 1928
Lee, Samuel (SC) - 1874, 1882
Lee, Samuel J. (SC) - 1880
Lee, Thomas (NJ) - 1832, 1834
Lee, Timothy Jr. (NJ) - 1982
Lee, Wallace L. (OR) - 1960
Lee, Warren I. (NY) - 1910, 1920, 1922, 1924
Lee, William H. F. (VA) - 1886, 1888, 1890
Leech, J. Russell (PA) - 1926, 1928, 1930
Leedom, John P. (OH) - 1880, 1882
Leedom, John S. (OH) - 1868
Leedom, Walter F. (PA) - 1906
Leedy, C. B. (OK) - 1918
Leeman (MN) - 1908
Leeper (MO) - 1900
Leeper, Bob (OK) - 1968
Leeper, W. T. (MO) - 1864
Leet (PA) - 1843
Leet, Isaac (PA) - 1838
Leete, Ralph (OH) - 1870
Leevy, I. S. (SC) - 1916
LeFante Joseph A. (NJ) - 1976
Lefcourt, Harold (PA) - 1958
Leferre (PA) - 1854
LeFever, Jacob (NY) - 1892, 1894
Lefevre, Frank J. (NY) - 1904
LeFevre, Jay (NY) - 1942, 1944, 1946, 1948
LeFevre, John P. (DE) - 1930
Leffier, Elwood W. (PA) - 1916
Leffingwell, William E. (IA) - 1858, 1868, 1870, 1872
Leffler, Isaac (VA) - 1827
Leffler, Sheldon (NY) - 1983
Leffler, Shepherd (IA) - 1846, 1847, 1848, 1856
Lefkowitz, Abraham (NY) - 1922
Lefkowitz, Jacob P. (NY) - 1952, 1956
Lefler, Charles W. (NY) - 1906
Leftwich, J. (VA) - 1825
Leftwich, John W. (TN) - 1865, 1868
Leftwick, J. F. (TN) - 1867
Legace, Herve J. (RI) - 1920
Legare, George S. (SC) - 1902, 1904, 1906, 1908, 1910, 1912
Legare, Hugh S. (SC) - 1836, 1838, 1840
Legrndre, Edward F. (MI) - 1900
Legendre, James (LA) - 1896
Leggett, Robert L. (CA) - 1962, 1964, 1966, 1968, 1970, 1972, 1974, 1976
LeGore, Harry W. (MD) - 1936
Leguineche, Pete (ID) - 1946
Lehlbach, Frederick R. (NJ) - 1914, 1916, 1918, 1920, 1922, 1924, 1926, 1928, 1930, 1932, 1934, 1936
Lehlbach, Herman (NJ) - 1884, 1886, 1888
Lehman, M. J. (TX) - 1944
Lehman, Orin (NY) - 1966

Lehman, Richard H. (CA) - 1982, 1984
Lehman, Robert E. (OH) - 1978
Lehman, William (FL) - 1972, 1974, 1976, 1978, 1980, 1982, 1984
Lehman, William E. (PA) - 1860
Lehner, Philip (WI) - 1930
Lehr, John C. (MI) - 1932, 1934
Lehrfeld, William I. (NY) - 1944, 1946
Leib, Owen D. (PA) - 1844
Leiby, Scott S. (PA) - 1918
Leicester, Robert T. (NY) - 1950
Leick, Charles R. (MO) - 1976
Leidy, Paul (PA) - 1857
Leigh, J. (VA) - 1841
Leighton, M. R. (ME) - 1894
Leighty, Jacob D. (IN) - 1894, 1896
Leims, John L. (MO) - 1966
Leinbach, Thomas K. (PA) - 1956
Leiper, G. G. (PA) - 1838
Leiper, George C. (PA) - 1828
Leisenring, John (PA) - 1894
Leiseth Bob (MN) - 1976
Leiter, Benjamin F. (OH) - 1854, 1856
LeJeune, Paris T. (PA) - 1982
Lelack, John W. Jr. (OH) - 1972
Leland (KS) - 1882
Leland, Lorenzo (IL) - 1871
Leland, Mickey (TX) - 1978, 1980, 1982, 1984
Leland, Sher (MA) - 1824
Lelansky, George F. (OH) - 1912
Leman, Louis (TX) - 1966
Lemishow, Albert (NY) - 1974, 1976, 1978, 1980, 1982, 1983
Lemke, William (ND) - 1932, 1934, 1936, 1938, 1942, 1944, 1946, 1948
Lemon, G. L. (AL) - 1922
Lemon, Henry E. Jr. (MA) - 1884
Lemon, Thomas L. (IN) - 1958
Lemp (MO) - 1896
Lemucchi, Timothy (CA) - 1972
Lenahan, John T. (PA) - 1906
Lenci, Ivaldo (CA) - 1974
Lene, Jeremiah M. (OH) - 1836
L'Engle, Claude (FL) - 1912
Lenhart, C. S. (PA) - 1954
Lenhart, Thomas B. (CA) - 1966, 1968, 1970
Lennard, Melvin (CA) - 1958
Lennon, Alton (NC) - 1956, 1958, 1960, 1962, 1964, 1966, 1968, 1970
Lennon, Francis X. Jr. (CT) - 1962
Lennon, W. J. (TX) - 1916
Lenroot, Irvine L. (WI) - 1908, 1910, 1912, 1914, 1916
Lent, Frank B. (NY) - 1958
Lent, J. Milton (GA) - 1964
Lent, James (NY) - 1824, 1828, 1830
Lent, Norman F. (NY) - 1970, 1972, 1974, 1976, 1978, 1980, 1982, 1984
Lento, Thomas J. (IL) - 1968, 1970, 1972
Lentz, John J. (OH) - 1896, 1898, 1900
Leombruno, Salvatore J. (NY) - 1940
Leonard (LA) - 1840
Leonard (MO) - 1854
Leonard, Franklin Jr. (NY) - 1904, 1912
Leonard, Fred C. (PA) - 1894
Leonard, Henry (CO) - 1938, 1940
Leonard, Jane E. (PA) - 1922
Leonard, John Edwards (LA) - 1876
Leonard, John W. (IL) - 1898, 1900
Leonard, Moses G. (NY) - 1842, 1844
Leonard, Norman T. (MA) - 1860
Leonard, Raymond B. (MI) - 1964
Leonard, Richard W. (NH) - 1948
Leonard, Stephen B. (NY) - 1834, 1838
Lepley, Herman G. (PA) - 1922
Leppek, Harry Vincent (CA) - 1958
Leppert, George (CA) - 1966
Lequier, Fred (MN) - 1932
Leroux, Frank (WA) - 1956, 1958
Leroux, Howard M. (MI) - 1978
Leroy, Edison Jr. (NY) - 1966
LeRoy, Harvey C. (WI) - 1974
LeSage, Mike (CA) - 1984
Lesemann, Arthur J. (NJ) - 1970, 1972
Leseuer, Arthur (ND) - 1912
Lesher, John V. (PA) - 1912, 1914, 1916, 1918, 1920
Lesinski, John (MI) - 1932, 1934, 1936, 1938, 1940, 1942, 1944, 1946, 1948
Lesinski, John Jr. (MI) - 1950, 1952, 1954, 1956, 1958, 1960, 1962
Leslie, Bob (AR) - 1982

Leslie, Ronald E. (PA) - 1970
Less, Frank W. (IA) - 1962
Lesser, M. (CA) - 1904
Lessler, Montague (NY) - 1902, 1916
Lester (GA) - 1878
Lester, Ebenezer (NY) - 1846
Lester, Posey G. (VA) - 1888, 1890
Lester, Rufus E. (GA) - 1888, 1890, 1892, 1894, 1896, 1898, 1900, 1902, 1904
Leszynski, John H. (IL) - 1966
Letcher, John (VA) - 1851, 1853, 1855, 1857
Letcher, Robert P. (KY) - 1824, 1827, 1829, 1831, 1833, 1834, 1853
Letendre, Andre E. (WI) - 1970
LeTourneau, Dick (TX) - 1974
Letts, F. Dickinson (IA) - 1924, 1926, 1928, 1930
Leupp, Thomas A. (ID) - 1960
Levenhagen, Alvin W. (PA) - 1972
Levensaler, A. (ME) - 1896
Levensaler, Alfred W. (NH) - 1928
Levenson, Joseph (NY) - 1904
Levenworth, Seth M. (IN) - 1833
Lever, Asbury F. (SC) - 1902, 1904, 1906, 1908, 1910, 1912, 1914, 1916, 1918
Leveronne, Norbert D. (KY) - 1978
Levering, John C. (OH) - 1886
Levering, Robert W. (OH) - 1948, 1950, 1954, 1956, 1958, 1960, 1962, 1964, 1968
Levin (PA) - 1850, 1852
Levin, Adam K. (NJ) - 1974, 1982
Levin, Emanuel (NY) - 1934
Levin, Emil (NY) - 1962, 1964
Levin, Lew Y. (NY) - 1984
Levin, Lewis C. (PA) - 1844, 1846, 1848
Levin, Sander M. (MI) - 1982, 1984
Levine, Barry (NY) - 1970
Levine, Bruce M. (NY) - 1984
Levine, Joseph (NY) - 1936, 1940
Levine, Mel (CA) - 1982, 1984
Levinson, Bryan F. (NY) - 1976
Levis, George W. (WI) - 1894, 1906
Levis, Mahon M. (PA) - 1832
Levis, Robert P. (NY) - 1938
Levitas, Elliott H. (GA) - 1974, 1976, 1978, 1980, 1982, 1984
Levitin, Emil Z. (IL) - 1930
Levitt, William (NY) - 1966
Levy (SC) - 1824
Levy, Annette Flatto (NY) - 1972
Levy, Barnett (NY) - 1950
Levy, Bernard P. (NY) - 1944
Levy, Jefferson M. (NY) - 1898, 1910, 1912
Levy, William M. (LA) - 1874
Lewandowski, David S. (NY) - 1984
Lewis (CT) - 1886
Lewis (GA) - 1851
Lewis (LA) - 1855
Lewis (MI) - 1874
Lewis (MO) - 1890, 1894
Lewis (NY) - 1854, 1860, 1878
Lewis (RI) - 1893
Lewis (VA) - 1853, 1855, 1869
Lewis, Abiel L. (MA) - 1856
Lewis, Abner (NY) - 1844
Lewis, Augustus M. (NC) - 1853
Lewis, Austin (CA) - 1910
Lewis, Barbour (TN) - 1872, 1874
Lewis, Brian (WA) - 1970
Lewis, Burwell B. (AL) - 1874, 1878
Lewis, Charles D. (MA) - 1900
Lewis, Charles V. (NY) - 1868
Lewis, Clarke (MS) - 1888, 1890
Lewis, Daniel S. (VA) - 1876
Lewis, David J. (MD) - 1908, 1910, 1912, 1914, 1928, 1930, 1932, 1934, 1936
Lewis, David J. (OH) - 1932
Lewis, Dixon H. (AL) - 1829, 1831, 1833, 1835, 1837, 1839, 1841, 1843
Lewis, Donald J. (OH) - 1966, 1968
Lewis, Earl R. (OH) - 1936, 1938, 1940, 1942, 1944, 1946, 1948
Lewis, Edward (IN) - 1952
Lewis, Edward (NY) - 1902
Lewis, Edward M. (MA) - 1914
Lewis, Edward T. (LA) - 1883
Lewis, Elijah B. (GA) - 1896, 1898, 1900, 1902, 1904, 1906
Lewis, Frank H. (NY) - 1906
Lewis, Frederick E. (PA) - 1912
Lewis, G. K. (TX) - 1851, 1853

Lewis, J. A. (OK) - 1916
Lewis, J. R. C. (VA) - 1892
Lewis, J. W. (KY) - 1876
Lewis, James Hamilton (WA) - 1896, 1898
Lewis, Jerome (NY) - 1942
Lewis, Jerry (CA) - 1978, 1980, 1982, 1984
Lewis, John (GA) - 1977
Lewis, John F. (VA) - 1865, 1874
Lewis, John H. (IL) - 1880, 1882
Lewis, John M. (AL) - 1841
Lewis, John W. (IN) - 1908, 1966
Lewis, John W. (KY) - 1894, 1896
Lewis, John W. (TX) - 1982
Lewis, John W. Jr. (LA) - 1962
Lewis, Joseph D. (OH) - 1970
Lewis, Joseph H. (KY) - 1857, 1861, 1870
Lewis, K. (SD) - 1896
Lewis, Kendrick R. (KY) - 1922
Lewis, Knute (SD) - 1910
Lewis, L. L. (VA) - 1896
Lewis, Lawrence (CO) - 1930, 1932, 1934, 1936, 1938, 1940, 1942
Lewis, M. J. (PA) - 1916
Lewis, Marx (NY) - 1930
Lewis, N. (TX) - 1846
Lewis, Philip N. (IL) - 1924
Lewis, Robert J. (PA) - 1898, 1900
Lewis, Samuel (OH) - 1848
Lewis, Stillman E. (NY) - 1899, 1900
Lewis, T. N. (TN) - 1894
Lewis, Tom (FL) - 1982, 1984
Lewis, W. D. (TX) - 1920
Lewis, William (KY) - 1932
Lewis, William C. (IL) - 1914
Lewis, William T. (OH) - 1890
Lewis, Winfred D. (PA) - 1916
Lexow, Clarence (NY) - 1890
Ley, Albert S. (MI) - 1918
Leys, Helen Benson (IL) - 1956
Libbey (NJ) - 1910
Libbey, Harry (VA) - 1882, 1884
Libley, James (MA) - 1824
Libonati, Roland V. (IL) - 1956, 1958, 1960, 1962
Libous, Alfred J. (NY) - 1974
Licari, Jerome G. (NY) - 1936
Lichtenwalner, Norton L. (PA) - 1930, 1932
Lichtenwalter, Franklin H. (PA) - 1948
Lichtie, G. T. (PA) - 1894
Liddell (GA) - 1837
Liddle, Ray A. (PA) - 1944
Lieb, Charles (IN) - 1912, 1914
Liebel, Michael Jr. (PA) - 1914
Lieberg, Prescott O. (CA) - 1958
Lieberman, Joseph I. (CT) - 1980
Liebermann, William (NY) - 1908, 1912
Lieblong, Warren (AR) - 1962
Liebman, Walter H. (NY) - 1938
Liff, Joseph (NY) - 1952
Ligham, Chester K. (NJ) - 1956
Lightburn, Joseph B. (WV) - 1954
Lightfoot, Jim (IA) - 1984
Ligon (VA) - 1855
Ligon, Robert F. (AL) - 1865, 1876
Ligon, Thomas W. (MD) - 1845, 1847
Likins, William M. (KY) - 1934
Likins, William M. (PA) - 1908
Lillard (TN) - 1878
Lillard, R. Q. (TN) - 1908
Lilley, Charles S. (MA) - 1882, 1884
Lilley, George L. (CT) - 1902, 1904, 1906
Lilly, Mial E. (PA) - 1904, 1906
Lilly, Samuel (NJ) - 1852, 1854
Lilly, Thomas J. (WV) - 1922, 1924, 1930
Lilly, William (PA) - 1866, 1892
Lima, Albert J. (CA) - 1940, 1942
Limehouse, J. Sidi (SC) - 1972
Limes, Leonard L. (LA) - 1966
Liming, Richard E. (OH) - 1960
Lincoln, Abraham (IL) - 1846
Lincoln, D. J. (PA) - 1866
Lincoln, Enoch (ME) - 1824
Lincoln, Frederick (MA) - 1833
Lincoln, Harold T. (MO) - 1926
Lincoln, Herman (MA) - 1834
Lincoln, Isaac (ME) - 1848
Lincoln, Levi (MA) - 1834, 1836, 1838, 1840
Lincoln, R. V. B. (PA) - 1876
Lincoln, Ralph L. (VA) - 1944
Lincoln, Solomon (MA) - 1836
Lincoln, William S. (NY) - 1866
Lind, James F. (PA) - 1948, 1950, 1952
Lind, John (MN) - 1886, 1888, 1890, 1902

Lindauer, L. (WI) - 1908
Lindbergh, Charles A. (MN) - 1906, 1908, 1910, 1912, 1914, 1920
Lindbloom, Milton (MN) - 1936
Linder, Usher F. (IL) - 1844
Linderman, Frank B. (MT) - 1918
Lindgren, Don (CA) - 1968
Lindheim, Irma (NY) - 1948
Lindley (MO) - 1856
Lindley, Alfred D. (MN) - 1950
Lindley, Cicero J. (IL) - 1890
Lindley, Hervey (CA) - 1892
Lindley, James J. (MO) - 1853, 1854, 1868
Lindner, John (PA) - 1906
Lindquist, Francis O. (MI) - 1912
Lindquist, Leonard E. (MN) - 1958
Lindsay (MN) - 1910
Lindsay (MO) - 1863
Lindsay, George G. (PA) - 1956
Lindsay, George H. (NY) - 1900, 1902, 1904, 1906, 1908, 1910
Lindsay, George W. (NY) - 1922, 1924, 1926, 1928, 1930, 1932
Lindsay, John V. (NY) - 1958, 1960, 1962, 1964
Lindsay, William R. (NC) - 1892
Lindsey, Archie (GA) - 1966
Lindsey, D. H. (IL) - 1886
Lindsey, D. McDonald (NC) - 1876
Lindsey, D. W. (KY) - 1884
Lindsey, Jack B. (CA) - 1969
Lindsey, John L. (IL) - 1934
Lindsey, L. B. (TX) - 1912
Lindsey, Philip (TX) - 1901
Lindsey, Stephen D. (ME) - 1876, 1878, 1880
Lindsley (NY) - 1870
Lindsley (WI) - 1872
Lindsley, Charles (VT) - 1840
Lindsley, James G. (NY) - 1884
Lindsley, William D. (OH) - 1852
Lindy (OH) - 1854
Lineberger, Walter F. (CA) - 1922, 1924
Linehan, John J. (IA) - 1884
Linehan, Neil J. (IL) - 1948, 1950, 1952
Lines (PA) - 1888
Linford, Velma (WY) - 1968
Lingan, Arch (TX) - 1914, 1916
Lingle, James (IL) - 1902
Link, Arthur A. (ND) - 1970
Link, H. F. (WV) - 1914
Link, William U. (IL) - 1944, 1946
Linn (NJ) - 1862
Linn (NY) - 1842
Linn, Archibald (NY) - 1840
Linn, C. H. (KY) - 1902
Linnard (PA) - 1834
Linney, Frank A. (NC) - 1914, 1918
Linney, Romulus Z. (NC) - 1894, 1896, 1898
Linscott, Charles H. (IL) - 1932
Linsky, Martin A. (MA) - 1972
Linsley, Charles (VT) - 1838
Linthicum, J. Charles (MD) - 1910, 1912, 1914, 1916, 1918, 1920, 1922, 1924, 1926, 1928, 1930
Linton (MO) - 1896
Linton, John P. (PA) - 1868
Linton, William C. (IN) - 1833
Linton, William S. (MI) - 1892, 1894, 1896
Lionett, David J. (MA) - 1974
Lipes, J. Chante (NY) - 1914
Lipinski, William O. (IL) - 1982, 1984
Lippencott, Charles E. (IL) - 1866
Lippert, George W. (WI) - 1920
Lipscomb (MO) - 1874
Lipscomb, Glenard P. (CA) - 1954, 1956, 1958, 1960, 1962, 1964, 1966, 1968
Lipscomb, Martin (VA) - 1865
Lipsett, John (PA) - 1914
Lisle, Marcus C. (KY) - 1892
Lisoni, Joseph L. (CA) - 1980
Lisoski, Edward V. (NY) - 1958, 1960
Litchfield (NY) - 1858, 1878
Litchfield, Elisha (NY) - 1824
Litke, William W. (PA) - 1962
Litsey, James P. (KS) - 1978
Littauer, Lucius N. (NY) - 1896, 1898, 1900, 1902, 1904
Litell (PA) - 1850
Littell, E. S. (PA) - 1910
Littell, John S. (PA) - 1848
Little (ME) - 1856
Little (NJ) - 1864

Little, Alexander (NC) - 1865
Little, Charles A. (MD) - 1900
Little, Charles J. (PA) - 1880
Little, Chauncey B. (KS) - 1924, 1926, 1930
Little, Edward C. (KS) - 1916, 1918, 1920, 1922
Little, Edward P. (MA) - 1850, 1852
Little, Elijah (OH) - 1884
Little, Erick P. (NC) - 1972
Little, Henry B. (MA) - 1892, 1894
Little, James N. (NY) - 1924
Little, John (OH) - 1884, 1886
Little, John S. (AR) - 1894, 1896, 1898, 1900, 1902, 1904
Little, John T. (WA) - 1946
Little, Joseph J. (NY) - 1891
Little, Josiah S. (ME) - 1843, 1847
Little, P. (MD) - 1829
Little, Peter (MD) - 1824, 1826
Little, Ted (WA) - 1950
Littlefield, Charles A. (MA) - 1924
Littlefield, Charles E. (ME) - 1899, 1900, 1902, 1904, 1906
Littlefield, George E. (MA) - 1902
Littlefield, Nathaniel S. (ME) - 1840, 1848
Littlejohn, De Witt C. (NY) - 1862
Littlejohn, Flavius (MI) - 1856
Littlepage, Adam B. (WV) - 1910, 1912, 1914, 1916, 1918
Littleton, C. C. (TX) - 1910
Littleton, Jessie M. (TN) - 1916
Littleton, Martin W. (NY) - 1910
Littman, Louis N. (IN) - 1912
Litton, Jerry (MO) - 1972, 1974
Livaudais, Oliver S. (LA) - 1902
Livergood (PA) - 1848
Livermore (MI) - 1874, 1876
Livermore (NH) - 1824
Livernash, Edward J. (CA) - 1902, 1904
Livesay, J. O. (AR) - 1912
Livingston (MO) - 1894, 1896
Livingston (PA) - 1834
Livingston, Clyde B. (SC) - 1976
Livingston, Edward (LA) - 1824, 1826
Livingston, Hugh L. (IN) - 1833
Livingston, Jacob (NY) - 1828
Livingston, John Henry (NY) - 1898
Livingston, Leonidas F. (GA) - 1890, 1892, 1894, 1896, 1898, 1900, 1902, 1904, 1906, 1908
Livingston, Peter (NY) - 1824
Livingston, Robert (NY) - 1824
Livingston, Robert L. (Bob) (LA) - 1976, 1977, 1978, 1980, 1982, 1984
Livingston, Robert Le Roy (NY) - 1830
Livingston, Robert R. (NY) - 1928
Livingston, Robert W. (NY) - 1868
Livingston, Tally R. (TN) - 1962
Livingston, W. C. (PA) - 1838
Lloyd, Daniel (PA) - 1984
Lloyd, Henry D. (IL) - 1894
Lloyd, James B. (NC) - 1898
Lloyd, James T. (MO) - 1897, 1898, 1900, 1902, 1904, 1906, 1908, 1910, 1912, 1914
Lloyd, Jim (CA) - 1974, 1976, 1978, 1980
Lloyd, Joseph R. (NC) - 1831
Lloyd, Marilyn (TN) - 1974, 1976, 1978, 1980, 1982, 1984
Lloyd, O. Straughn (MD) - 1936
Lloyd, Robin (VT) - 1980
Lloyd, Sherman P. (UT) - 1960, 1962, 1966, 1968, 1970, 1972
Lloyd, Wesley (WA) - 1932, 1934
Lloyd, William H. (MD) - 1942
Loan, Benjamin F. (MO) - 1862, 1864, 1866, 1876
Lobeck (MN) - 1916, 1918
Lobeck, Charles O. (NE) - 1910, 1912, 1914, 1916, 1918
Lochrane (GA) - 1868
Lockard, Robert R. (IA) - 1984
Locke (FL) - 1884
Locke, Bobby (TX) - 1980
Locke, Bobby A. (TX) - 1976
Locke, Daniel W. (OH) - 1900
Locke, John (MA) - 1824, 1826
Locke, Thomas F. (ME) - 1930
Locker, Dale (OH) - 1981
Locket, H. E. (GA) - 1920
Lockey, Caleb P. (NC) - 1888
Lockhart, Andrew Francis (SD) - 1922
Lockhart, James (IN) - 1841, 1851, 1856

Luttrell, Hiram A. (CA) - 1912
Luttrell, John K. (CA) - 1872, 1875, 1876
Lutz, Earle (VA) - 1946
Lutz, Ralph C. (OH) - 1940
Luxford, Richard (CO) - 1950
Lybarger, Edwin L. (OH) - 1888
Lybrand, Archibald (OH) - 1896, 1898
Lybrand, Samuel (OH) - 1872
Lyerle, William D. (IL) - 1910
Lyford, Joseph P. (CT) - 1952, 1954
Lyle (TN) - 1882, 1902
Lyle, Cy H. (TN) - 1910, 1914
Lyle, John E. Jr. (TX) - 1944, 1946, 1948, 1950, 1952
Lyle, R. J. (MS) - 1894
Lyman (CT) - 1898, 1900
Lyman (GA) - 1824
Lyman (OH) - 1852
Lyman (VT) - 1850
Lyman, A. P. (VT) - 1850
Lyman, Arthur (MA) - 1902
Lyman, Asael (ID) - 1948
Lyman, Howard (MT) - 1982
Lyman, Joseph (IA) - 1884, 1886
Lyman, Theodore (MA) - 1833, 1882, 1884
Lynch (KY) - 1900
Lynch (MD) - 1841, 1851
Lynch (MS) - 1882, 1884, 1886
Lynch, Charles W. (PA) - 1942
Lynch, David J. (MI) - 1920
Lynch, Daniel C. (NB) - 1974
Lynch, Emmett (CA) - 1982
Lynch, Eugene A. (MA) - 1926
Lynch, J. Gregory (CT) - 1950
Lynch, James (NY) - 1824
Lynch, Joe D. (CA) - 1886
Lynch, John (ME) - 1864, 1866, 1868, 1870
Lynch, John (PA) - 1886, 1888
Lynch, John D. (MA) - 1920
Lynch, John F. (CT) - 1936
Lynch, John F. (ME) - 1884, 1886
Lynch, John J. (ME) - 1900
Lynch, John R. (MS) - 1872, 1875, 1876, 1880
Lynch, P. J. (IN) - 1914
Lynch, Patrick H. (PA) - 1914, 1916
Lynch, Ralph N. (IA) - 1944
Lynch, T. Joseph (NY) - 1956, 1958, 1960, 1962
Lynch, Thomas (WI) - 1890, 1892, 1894
Lynch, W. A. (SD) - 1904
Lynch, W. D. (ND) - 1932
Lynch, Walter A. (NY) - 1940, 1942, 1944, 1946, 1948
Lynch, Walter A. Jr. (NY) - 1958
Lynch, William A. (SD) - 1894
Lynch, William D. (ND) - 1934
Lynde, John (NY) - 1824
Lynde, Tilly (NY) - 1828, 1832
Lynde, William P. (WI) - 1848, 1874, 1876
Lynn, James F. (MN) - 1922, 1928
Lynn, John D. (NY) - 1894
Lynn, William H. (NY) - 1908
Lyon (AL) - 1839
Lyon (MS) - 1882
Lyon (NY) - 1858, 1878
Lyon (TN) - 1849
Lyon (WI) - 1870
Lyon, Caleb (NY) - 1852
Lyon, Chittenden (KY) - 1826, 1827, 1829, 1831, 1833
Lyon, David Greenhill (AL) - 1837
Lyon, Frances (AL) - 1835, 1837
Lyon, Frank (VA) - 1932
Lyon, Homer L. (NC) - 1920, 1922, 1924, 1926
Lyon, J. L. (CA) - 1892
Lyon, Judson W. (GA) - 1888
Lyon, Lucius (MI) - 1843
Lyon, T. J. (MS) - 1920
Lyons, Charlton H. (LA) - 1961
Lyons, Hall M. (LA) - 1966
Lyons, J. A. (IA) - 1898
Lyons, J. Walter (VT) - 1902
Lyons, James (VA) - 1902
Lytel, Elaine (NY) - 1982
Lytle (GA) - 1859
Lytle, Reynold K. (OH) - 1874
Lytle, Robert T. (OH) - 1832, 1834

M

Maas, Melvin J. (MN) - 1926, 1928, 1930, 1932, 1934, 1936, 1938, 1940, 1942, 1944

Mabee, Wallace F. (ME) - 1936
Mabey, Charles R. (UT) - 1916
Mabie, J. Frank (MT) - 1910, 1912
Mabry (TN) - 1874
Mabson (AL) - 1884
Mabson, A. A. (AL) - 1880
Macaluso, Michael (NY) - 1976
MacArthur, Walter (CA) - 1910
Macchio, Nicholas R. (NY) - 1972
MacCracken, Henry F. (OH) - 1904
MacCrate, John (NY) - 1918
MacDevitt, James C. (NY) - 1930
MacDonald, Marie (NY) - 1912, 1920
MacDonald, Moses (ME) - 1850
MacDonald, Torbert H. (MA) - 1954, 1956, 1958, 1960, 1962, 1964, 1966, 1968, 1970, 1972, 1974
MacDonald, William J. (MI) - 1914, 1916
MacDougall, Clinton D. (NY) - 1872, 1874
MacDougall, Curtis D. (IL) - 1944
Mace, Daniel (IN) - 1851, 1852, 1854
Mace, Lawson (IN) - 1914
Macey, C. C. (SC) - 1884
MacFarland, Grenville S. (MA) - 1902
MacFarlane, William (NY) - 1928
MacGregor, Clarence (NY) - 1918, 1920, 1922, 1924, 1926
MacGregor, Clark (MN) - 1960, 1962, 1964, 1966, 1968
Machen, Hervey G. (MD) - 1964, 1966, 1968
Machrowicz, Thaddeus M. (MI) - 1950, 1952, 1954, 1956, 1958, 1960
Maciejewski, A. F. (IL) - 1938, 1940
MacIntyre, N. J. (PA) - 1908
Maciora, Lucien J. (CT) - 1940, 1942
Mack, Bill (OH) - 1970, 1974, 1978
Mack, Charles C. (KS) - 1918
Mack, Connie (FL) - 1982, 1984
Mack, Edward J. (MI) - 1984
Mack, H. C. (TX) - 1886
Mack, Joseph S. (MI) - 1956, 1958
Mack, Mansfield E. (WA) - 1934
Mack, Peter F. Jr. (IL) - 1948, 1950, 1952, 1954, 1956, 1958, 1960, 1962, 1974, 1976
Mack, Russell V. (WA) - 1934, 1940, 1948, 1950, 1952, 1954, 1956, 1958
MacKaig, Milton R. (CA) - 1982
MacKay, Kenneth H. (Buddy) (FL) - 1982, 1984
MacKay, J. Alan (MA) - 1974
MacKay, James A. (GA) - 1964, 1966, 1968
Macken, Terry R. (CA) - 1966
MacKenzie, A. E. (NV) - 1950
MacKenzie, Charles S. (NJ) - 1934, 1936
MacKenzie, Ken (IN) - 1984
Mackey (NY) - 1888
Mackey (PA) - 1884, 1886
Mackey, Cyms H. (IA) - 1866, 1882
Mackey, Edmund W. M. (SC) - 1874, 1878, 1880, 1882
Mackey, Harry A. (PA) - 1912
Mackey, Levi A. (PA) - 1868, 1874, 1876
Mackie, John C. (MI) - 1964, 1966
Mackie, John G. (CO) - 1958
MacKinnon Daniel F. (CT) - 1978
MacKinnon, George (MN) - 1946, 1948
MacKintosh (MN) - 1914
MacKintosh, George L. (IN) - 1928
Macklin, Joseph (NC) - 1837
MacLafferty, James H. (CA) - 1922
MacLaren, Joseph R. (NY) - 1954
Maclay, William B. (NY) - 1842, 1844, 1846, 1848, 1856, 1858, 1864
MacLean, Andrew A. (NY) - 1930
MacLean, John P. (OH) - 1896
MacLeod, Charles Kevin (MA) - 1978
Macleod, Kenneth P. (ME) - 1964
Maclin, Earl (TN) - 1964
Macmillan, J. H. (NV) - 1886
Macmillan, Thomas C. (IL) - 1892
MacMullen, Arthur H. J. (NY) - 1938
MacMullen, Leon C. (PA) - 1950
MacNeil, L. W. (IL) - 1906
Macomber (NY) - 1854
Macon, Robert B. (AR) - 1902, 1904, 1906, 1908, 1910
Macon, Thomas (CO) - 1888
MacRae, Colin D. (NY) - 1936
MacVicar, James A. (ME) - 1948
Macy, John B. (WI) - 1852, 1854
Macy, W. Kingsland (NY) - 1946, 1948, 1950
Madden, Charles F. Jr. (OH) - 1966

Madden, John (KS) - 1896
Madden, Martin B. (IL) - 1904, 1906, 1908, 1910, 1912, 1914, 1916, 1918, 1920, 1922, 1924, 1926
Madden, Ray J. (IN) - 1942, 1944, 1946, 1948, 1950, 1952, 1954, 1956, 1958, 1960, 1962, 1964, 1966, 1968, 1970, 1972, 1974
Madden, Thomas M. (NJ) - 1938
Madden, William C. (MA) - 1960
Madden, William E. Jr. (PA) - 1928
Madden, William F. (MA) - 1936
Maddock, Thomas (AZ) - 1918
Maddox, Fletcher (MT) - 1914
Maddox, Henry J. (MS) - 1952
Maddox, John W. (GA) - 1892, 1894, 1896, 1898, 1900, 1902
Maddox, P. W. (TN) - 1942
Maddox, Samuel T. (NY) - 1864
Madigan (ME) - 1864
Madigan, Edward R. (IL) - 1972, 1974, 1976, 1978, 1980, 1982, 1984
Madison, Edmond H. (KS) - 1906, 1908, 1910
Madrid, Jim (CA) - 1976
Madoo, William (NY) - 1908
Maffett, James T. (PA) - 1886
Magee, Clare (MO) - 1948, 1950
Magee, David F. (PA) - 1890, 1920
Magee, Edward T. (NJ) - 1984
Magee, Hugh (NY) - 1846
Magee, James M. (PA) - 1922, 1924, 1926
Magee, John (NY) - 1826, 1828, 1830, 1864
Magee, John A. (PA) - 1872
Magee, Walter W. (NY) - 1914, 1916, 1918, 1920, 1922, 1924, 1926
Magill, Frank S. (PA) - 1936
Maginness, Edmund A. (IN) - 1902
Maginnis, John J. (MA) - 1948
Maginnis, Martin (MT) - 1889
Magisen, Robert C. (IL) - 1910
Magli, Vito (NY) - 1952
Magner, Thomas F. (NY) - 1888, 1890, 1892
Magnuson, Don (WA) - 1952, 1954, 1956, 1958, 1960, 1962
Magnuson, Warren G. (WA) - 1936, 1938, 1940, 1942
Magoon, Henry S. (WI) - 1874
Magove (NY) - 1876
Magrady, Frederick W. (PA) - 1924, 1926, 1928, 1930
Magrann, Thomas J. (PA) - 1980
Magraw, S. M. (MD) - 1849
Magruder, Bernard F. (WI) - 1942
Maguire, Andrew (NJ) - 1974, 1976, 1978, 1980
Maguire, Crispin M. (NY) - 1978
Maguire, Francis J. (WI) - 1906
Maguire, James E. (MA) - 1920, 1924
Maguire, James G. (CA) - 1892, 1894, 1896, 1908
Maguire, John A. (NE) - 1908, 1910, 1912, 1914, 1916
Maguire, Robert C. (MA) - 1968
Mahaffey, Dan (CA) - 1980
Mahan (MI) - 1872
Mahan, Bryan F. (CT) - 1912, 1914
Mahan, Jim (TX) - 1984
Mahany, Rowland B. (NY) - 1892, 1894, 1896, 1898, 1900
Maher, James P. (NY) - 1908, 1910, 1912, 1914, 1916, 1918, 1920
Maher, Michael E. (IL) - 1910
Maher, Phillip V. (MO) - 1962
Mahler, George (WA) - 1966
Mahon (PA) - 1831
Mahon, Don (IA) - 1966, 1968, 1970
Mahon, G. Heyward Jr. (SC) - 1936
Mahon, George (TX) - 1934, 1936, 1938, 1940, 1942, 1944, 1946, 1948, 1950, 1952, 1954, 1956, 1958, 1960, 1962, 1964, 1966, 1968, 1970, 1972, 1974, 1976
Mahon, Thaddeus M. (PA) - 1876, 1892, 1894, 1896, 1898, 1900, 1902, 1904
Mahon, Thomas C. (IN) - 1910
Mahon, William D. (MI) - 1908
Mahoney (MN) - 1914
Mahoney, Charles H. (MI) - 1932
Mahoney, Dennis A. (IA) - 1862
Mahoney, Elmo J. (KS) - 1954, 1956, 1958
Mahoney, Jeremiah L. (WI) - 1896
Mahoney, John E. (IL) - 1928

Mahoney, John J. (NJ) - 1982
Mahoney, Paul W. (WI) - 1910
Mahoney, Peter P. (NY) - 1884, 1886
Mahoney, Thomas R. (OR) - 1942
Mahoney, Walter T. (IA) - 1942
Mahoney, William (MN) - 1942
Mahoney, William F. (IL) - 1900, 1902
Mahoney, William P. Jr. (AZ) - 1956
Maickel, Aloysius J. (NY) - 1946
Maietta, Julia L. (PA) - 1948, 1958
Mailliard, William S. (CA) - 1948, 1952, 1954, 1956, 1958, 1960, 1962, 1964, 1966, 1968, 1970, 1972
Mailloux, Raymond A. (RI) - 1946
Mailly, Bertha H. (NY) - 1920
Main, Charles W. (MD) - 1910, 1916
Main, Claude E. (KS) - 1938, 1940
Main, George (PA) - 1900
Maish, David F. (IN) - 1916
Maish, Levi (PA) - 1874, 1876, 1886, 1888
Major, J. Earl (IL) - 1920, 1922, 1924, 1926, 1928, 1930, 1932
Major, O. G. (ND) - 1908
Major, Samuel C. (MO) - 1918, 1920, 1922, 1924, 1926, 1928, 1930
Major, Stan (IL) - 1968
Majors, Thomas J. (NE) - 1878
Makemson, W. K. (TX) - 1896
Malang, Robert J. (NY) - 1964
Malby, George R. (NY) - 1906, 1908, 1910
Malinowsky, Winifred H. (PA) - 1962
Malkiel, Theresa (NY) - 1918
Malkin, Herbert (NY) - 1942, 1944
Malkus, Frederick C. (MD) - 1973
Mallalieu, Joseph (MD) - 1894
Mallary, Richard W. (VT) - 1972
Mallary, Rollin C. (VT) - 1824, 1826, 1828, 1830
Mallery, Arlington H. (NY) - 1916
Mallett, J. M. (TX) - 1904
Mallon, J. W. (IA) - 1904
Mallonee, Walter L. (CA) - 1970
Mallory (MI) - 1878
Mallory (MN) - 1918
Mallory (VA) - 1839, 1849
Mallory, Francis (VA) - 1837, 1841
Mallory, Meredith (NY) - 1838
Mallory, Robert (KY) - 1859, 1861, 1863, 1865
Mallory, Rufus (OR) - 1866
Mallory, Stephen R. (FL) - 1890, 1892
Malone, George W. (NV) - 1960
Malone, John E. (PA) - 1892
Malone, Richard T. (MN) - 1952
Malone, William H. (NC) - 1886
Maloney (NY) - 1888
Maloney, David B. (IL) - 1934
Maloney, Francis T. (CT) - 1932
Maloney, Franklin J. (PA) - 1944, 1946, 1948
Maloney, John J. Jr. (ME) - 1950
Maloney, John R. (NY) - 1976
Maloney, Paul H. (LA) - 1930, 1932, 1934, 1936, 1938, 1942, 1944
Maloney, Robert S. (MA) - 1920
Malony, John J. (PA) - 1892
Malony, Richard S. S. (IL) - 1856
Malott, Ernest (IN) - 1912
Malpass, C. Dana (NC) - 1956, 1958
Maltby, W. J. (TX) - 1892
Maltese, Serphin R. (NY) - 1984
Maltz, Irving C. (NY) - 1932
Maltzberger, H. (PA) - 1878
Man, Edward A. S. (NJ) - 1900
Manahan, James (MN) - 1912
Manahan, William L. (OH) - 1932
Manasco, Carter (AL) - 1942, 1944, 1946
Manby (KY) - 1916
Mandable, Matthew L. (IL) - 1908
Mandel, William M. (NY) - 1950
Mandell, Alvin (MA) - 1974
Mandell, Luther (CA) - 1972
Manes, Panny (OH) - 1972
Maness, T. L. (VA) - 1958
Maney, Michael J. (NY) - 1924
Mangels, Louis A. (OH) - 1980, 1982
Manginelli, Emanuel A. (NY) - 1936
Mangum, Willie P. (NC) - 1825
Manion, Albert F. (IL) - 1966
Manistre (MO) - 1882
Mankin, Helen Douglas (GA) - 1946
Mankin, Jack H. (IN) - 1950, 1952
Mankus, Louis A. (WY) - 1962
Manley (PA) - 1858
Manley, Louis K. (PA) - 1922

Mastorelli, Nicholas S. (NJ) - 1978
Mata, Augustin (TX) - 1978
Matheny, M. F. (WV) - 1936
Mather, Lewis H. (KY) - 1940
Matherly, Clyde J. (OK) - 1936
Mathers, Albert N. (NE) - 1934
Mathers, Hugh T. (OH) - 1924
Mathers, John (IL) - 1878
Matheson, Mac C. (AZ) - 1960, 1961
Mathew, Hector (NY) - 1958, 1960
Mathew, S. D. (TN) - 1886
Mathews (AL) - 1865
Mathews (MN) - 1900
Mathews (OH) - 1826
Mathews, Arline (CA) - 1974
Mathews, Frank A. Jr. (NJ) - 1946
Mathews, James (OH) - 1843
Mathews, James E. (OH) - 1914
Mathews, James N. (IL) - 1858
Mathews, John R. (WI) - 1898
Mathews, Thomas B. (KY) - 1894
Mathews, William H. (MD) - 1974
Mathews, William W. (IL) - 1894
Mathewson, John J. (TN) - 1845
Mathias, Charles McC. J. (MD) - 1960,
  1962, 1964, 1966
Mathias, Robert B. (CA) - 1966, 1968,
  1970, 1972, 1974
Mathias, William G. (KS) - 1862
Mathiot, Joshua (OH) - 1840
Mathis, Dawson (GA) - 1970, 1972, 1974,
  1976, 1978
Mathison, Sonya (Sonny) (CA) - 1978
Mathna, Woodrow W. (OH) - 1976
Matlock (MO) - 1888
Matlock, Harry L. (IN) - 1930
Matlock, James T. (CA) - 1914, 1946
Matson, Courtland C. (IN) - 1880, 1882,
  1884, 1886
Matson, Dirk (PA) - 1980
Matson, James B. (OH) - 1894
Matson, John A. (IN) - 1843
Matson, M. L. (OK) - 1930
Matson, R. M. (PA) - 1914
Matsui, Robert T. (CA) - 1978, 1980, 1982,
  1984
Matsunaga, Spark M. (HI) - 1962, 1964,
  1966, 1968, 1970, 1972, 1974
Mattby, La Fayette (MA) - 1875
Matteo, Michael R. (NY) - 1930
Matter, Edward P. (NY) - 1968
Mattera, Lawrence C. (CA) - 1978
Matteson (NY) - 1850, 1876
Matteson, C. B. (GA) - 1890
Matteson, Orsamus B. (NY) - 1846, 1848,
  1852, 1854, 1856
Matthaei, W. H. (TX) - 1926
Matthai, W. A. (TX) - 1906
Matthews (NJ) - 1912, 1916
Matthews (TN) - 1904
Matthews, Asa C. (IL) - 1872
Matthews, Charles (PA) - 1910, 1912
Matthews, David W. (IL) - 1904, 1906
Matthews, Donald R. (FL) - 1952, 1954,
  1956, 1958, 1960, 1962, 1964
Matthews, George W. (MN) - 1960
Matthews, J. M. (MS) - 1890
Matthews, James (OH) - 1840
Matthews, John C. (NC) - 1930
Matthews, John W. (NY) - 1978
Matthews, Nelson E. (OH) - 1914, 1916
Matthews, Stanley (OH) - 1876
Matthews, Thomas (CO) - 1946
Mattingly, Mack F. (GA) - 1966
Mattingly, Robert L. (OH) - 1888
Mattis, Abraham (PA) - 1896
Mattison, Eugene L. (MI) - 1972
Mattmiller, John N. (ID) - 1964
Mattocks, John (IL) - 1880
Mattocks, John (VT) - 1824, 1840
Mattox, Jim (TX) - 1976, 1978, 1980
Mattox, Lucius C. (GA) - 1892
Matturri, Alexander J. (NJ) - 1952
Mau, Louis C. (IL) - 1918
Mauck, Harry H. (NE) - 1904
Maughan, Richard J. (UT) - 1968
Maughmer, Fred (MO) - 1938, 1940
Mauhs, Sharon J. (NY) - 1942, 1944
Mauk, C. S. (OH) - 1892
Mauldin, William H. (NY) - 1956
Maull, W. M. (PA) - 1882
Maultsby, Josiah A. (NC) - 1944
Maund (MD) - 1880
Maupin, Joseph H. (CO) - 1904

Maurer, Charles J. (MO) - 1910
Maurer, Theodore W. (NY) - 1962
Maurice, James (NY) - 1952
Maury, Abram P. (TN) - 1833, 1835, 1837
Mavroules, Nicholas (MA) - 1978, 1980,
  1982, 1984
Maverick, Maury (TX) - 1934, 1936
Max (NJ) - 1838
Max, Herbert J. (IL) - 1944
Max, Ralph C. (MO) - 1942
Maxey, B. M. (IL) - 1912
Maxey, F. E. (VA) - 1916
Maxfield, Morgan (MO) - 1976
Maxfield, Thomas (OH) - 1850
Maxson, H. B. (NV) - 1908
Maxwell (NY) - 1872
Maxwell (TN) - 1904
Maxwell (VA) - 1825, 1833, 1835
Maxwell, Allen B. (IN) - 1982, 1984
Maxwell, Andrew C. (MI) - 1882
Maxwell, Anita (NY) - 1976, 1982
Maxwell, Augustus E. (FL) - 1852, 1854
Maxwell, Charles (NC) - 1978
Maxwell, David O. (PA) - 1960
Maxwell, F. T. (MS) - 1918
Maxwell, George P. (OH) - 1912
Maxwell, Howard (IN) - 1908
Maxwell, J. W. (WV) - 1944
Maxwell, John G. (PA) - 1984
Maxwell, John P. B. (NJ) - 1836, 1840
Maxwell, Lewis (VA) - 1827, 1829, 1831
Maxwell, Milton F. (MN) - 1948
Maxwell, Robert L. (DE) - 1980
Maxwell, Samuel (NE) - 1896
Maxwell, Stephan (MN) - 1966
Maxwell, Thomas (NY) - 1828
Maxwell, Thomas L. (IA) - 1892
May (AL) - 1835
May (IN) - 1862
May (ME) - 1852
May (NJ) - 1914
May, Andrew J. (KY) - 1928, 1930, 1932,
  1934, 1936, 1938, 1940, 1942, 1944,
  1946
May, Catherine (WA) - 1958, 1960, 1962,
  1964, 1966, 1968, 1970
May, Edwin H. Jr. (CT) - 1956, 1958
May, Frank W. (MO) - 1956
May, George (SD) - 1964
May, George M. (PA) - 1940
May, Harry S. (CA) - 1958
May, Henry (MD) - 1853, 1855, 1861
May, Mitchell (NY) - 1898
May, Richard A. (VA) - 1960
May, Seth (ME) - 1843, 1850
May, William (IL) - 1834
May, William L. (IL) - 1834, 1836
Mayall, Samuel (ME) - 1852
Maybell, S. (CA) - 1882
Maybury (MI) - 1880
Maybury, William C. (MI) - 1882, 1884
Mayer, E. S. Jr. (TX) - 1962
Mayer, George (IL) - 1918, 1922
Mayer, James J. (OH) - 1952
Mayer, L. S. (IL) - 1922
Mayer, Leon (CA) - 1962
Mayes, J. F. (AR) - 1904
Mayes, Josephine U. (NY) - 1946
Mayes, Richard T. (NY) - 1948
Mayes, T. H. (AR) - 1920
Mayers, Lawrence S. (NY) - 1944
Mayfield, James L. (CA) - 1975
Mayhall, Don (AL) - 1966
Mayham, Stephen L. (NY) - 1868, 1876,
  1898
Mayhew, Alex E. (ID) - 1890
Mayhew, Stanley W. (CT) - 1946
Maynard (TN) - 1853
Maynard, Atlas A. (NC) - 1892
Maynard, Charles S. (MI) - 1888
Maynard, Harry L. (VA) - 1900, 1902, 1904,
  1906, 1908
Maynard, Horace (TN) - 1857, 1859, 1865,
  1867, 1868, 1870, 1872
Maynard, James E. (VA) - 1928
Maynard, John (NY) - 1824, 1826, 1836,
  1840
Mayne, Wiley (IA) - 1966, 1968, 1970,
  1972, 1974
Mayo, Edward L. (IL) - 1854
Mayo, Guy B. (PA) - 1914
Mayo, Jesse M. (CA) - 1944
Mayo, Robert M. (VA) - 1882, 1884
Mays, Dannitte H. (FL) - 1908, 1910

Mays, James H. (UT) - 1914, 1916, 1918
Mays, Robert (IL) - 1972
Mazar, Joseph JA. (NY) - 1964
Mazur, Stephen (PA) - 1978
Mazzoli, Romano L. (KY) - 1970, 1972,
  1974, 1976, 1978, 1980, 1982, 1984
McAbe, James L. (IL) - 1966
McAboy, Thomas Jr. (AL) - 1972
McAdoo, William (NJ) - 1882, 1884, 1886,
  1888
McAfee, Charles B. (MO) - 1868
McAffee (MO) - 1872
McAleer, B. A. (OK) - 1918
McAleer, William (PA) - 1890, 1892, 1896,
  1898, 1900
McAlilly, S. (SC) - 1868
McAllister (PA) - 1860
McAllister, Archibald (PA) - 1862
McAllister, L. L. Jr. (MS) - 1966
McAllister, Robert S. (MI) - 1954
McAllister, Thomas F. (MI) - 1934, 1936
McAlpin (TN) - 1870, 1884
McAnally (MO) - 1934
McAnarney, Art (KS) - 1952
McAndrews, James (IL) - 1896, 1900,
  1902, 1912, 1914, 1916, 1918, 1920,
  1932, 1934, 1936, 1938, 1940
McAndrews, James P. (MA) - 1944
McArdle, Francis J. (PA) - 1974
McArdle, Joseph A. (PA) - 1938, 1940
McArthur (OH) - 1832
McArthur, Clifton N. (OR) - 1914, 1916,
  1918, 1920, 1922
McArthur, E. W. (PA) - 1904
McAscliff, John (IL) - 1878
McAtee, Charles D. (KS) - 1972
McAuliffe, William (MA) - 1944, 1946, 1956
McAuslen, William C. (OH) - 1840
McAyeal, J. A. (TX) - 1898
McBride, Charles P. (MO) - 1948
McBride, Conrad L. (CO) - 1962
McBride, Eddie L. (MS) - 1972
McBride, Edward A. (WA) - 1970
McBride, George W. (MI) - 1886
McBride, J. C. (TX) - 1894
McBride, John K. (OH) - 1874
McBride, John R. (OR) - 1862
McBride, Thomas H. (IA) - 1934
McCabe (NY) - 1882
McCabe, Anthony M. (NY) - 1910
McCabe, Charles J. (NY) - 1960
McCabe, Charles P. (NY) - 1946
McCabe, George (CA) - 1964
McCabe, James (IN) - 1878, 1888
McCabe, Thomas J. (NY) - 1948
McCafferty (MA) - 1880
McCafferty, Thomas F. (OH) - 1938
McCaffery, Bernard (NE) - 1902
McCaffery, Robert E. (NY) - 1959
McCaffrey, James E. (PA) - 1964
McCain, A. J. (SD) - 1904
McCain, John (AZ) - 1982, 1984
McCall (PA) - 1862
McCall, Archie (IL) - 1912
McCall, Emory C. (NC) - 1944
McCall, G. (AL) - 1890
McCall, George E. (MI) - 1974
McCall, George T. (TN) - 1890
McCall, J. C. R. (TN) - 1906
McCall, James (NY) - 1834
McCall, John E. (TN) - 1894, 1896
McCall, Samuel K. (PA) - 1916
McCall, Samuel W. (MA) - 1892, 1894,
  1896, 1898, 1900, 1902, 1904, 1906
  1908, 1910
McCall, Tom Lawson (OR) - 1954
McCalmont, A. B. (PA) - 1866
McCalmont, S. P. (PA) - 1894
McCammon, Byron (IN) - 1960
McCandless, Al (CA) - 1982, 1984
McCandless, William P. (PA) - 1878
McCann, Charles P. (NJ) - 1934
McCann, Frank M. (VA) - 1958
McCann, T. A. (OH) - 1926
McCans (PA) - 1856
McCarney, Robert P. (ND) - 1970
McCarther (SD) - 1918
McCarthy, Charles F. (MA) - 1920
McCarthy, Dan M. (KS) - 1944
McCarthy, Dennis (NY) - 1866, 1868, 1870
McCarthy, Eugene J. (MN) - 1948, 1950,
  1952, 1954, 1956
McCarthy, James (IL) - 1906
McCarthy, John (NY) - 1898

McCarthy, John D. (MA) - 1976
McCarthy, John H. (NY) - 1888
McCarthy, John J. (NE) - 1902, 1904
McCarthy, Kathryn O'Loughlin (KS) - 1934
McCarthy, Richard D. (NY) - 1964, 1966,
  1968, 1972
McCarthy, Robert C. (MI) - 1960
McCarthy, Robert E. (NY) - 1980
McCarthy, Sean (CA) - 1974
McCartin, James M. (NY) - 1868
McCartney, David (IL) - 1980
McCartney, James (IL) - 1884
McCartney, John P. (KY) - 1892
McCartney, O. J. (MN) - 1922
McCarton, Dan (OH) - 1912
McCarty (VA) - 1845
McCarty, Andrew Z. (NY) - 1854
McCarty, Charles E. (MI) - 1914
McCarty, D. J. (UT) - 1976
McCarty, Elijah (IL) - 1862
McCarty, Enoch (IN) - 1833
McCarty, H. M. (KY) - 1851
McCarty, John (MA) - 1912
McCarty, Johnathan (IN) - 1828, 1831,
  1833, 1835, 1837, 1839, 1841
McCarty, Leeman C. (MI) - 1948
McCarty, Nicolas (IN) - 1847
McCarty, Paul J. (MA) - 1946
McCarty, Walter (MO) - 1962
McCarty, William M. (VA) - 1840
McCash, Buell (IA) - 1918
McCaskey, I. Willits (PA) - 1956
McCaskill, Alexander L. (NC) - 1916, 1918
McCaskill, J. (AL) - 1857
McCasland, Guy R. (IL) - 1920
McCauley (AL) - 1868
McCauley, Daniel J. Jr. (PA) - 1952
McCauley, Mike (MI) - 1984
McCaull, Patrick H. (VA) - 1894, 1896
McCauslin, William C. (OH) - 1843
McCawley, A. L. (MO) - 1944
McCay, Howard W. (FL) - 1922
McClain (TN) - 1880, 1900
McClain (KY) - 1922
McClammy, Charles W. (NC) - 1886, 1888
McClanahan, Donald (MO) - 1952
McClanahan, Fred C. (LA) - 1960
McClanahan, Sidney B. (MO) - 1964
McClannon, James C. (TN) - 1892
McClarg (IN) - 1874
McClarin, Jim (CA) - 1980
McClave (NJ) - 1910, 1912
McClean, Moses (PA) - 1844
McClean, William (PA) - 1902
McClear, James L. (ID) - 1908
McClear, Louis W. (MI) - 1918
McCleary, James T. (MN) - 1892, 1894,
  1896, 1898, 1900, 1902, 1904, 1906,
  1908
McCleary, Kenneth (IL) - 1966
McCleery, James (LA) - 1870
McCleery, John (PA) - 1882
McClellan (AL) - 1876, 1888
McClellan (NY) - 1854, 1858, 1884
McClellan, Abraham (TN) - 1837, 1839,
  1841
McClellan, Charles A. O. (IN) - 1888, 1890
McClellan, George (NY) - 1912, 1914
McClellan, George (ND) - 1944
McClellan, George B. (NY) - 1894, 1896,
  1898, 1900, 1902
McClellan, John L. (AR) - 1934, 1836
McClellan, Robert (NY) - 1836, 1840
McClelland, E. G. (OH) - 1906
McClelland, George E. (CO) - 1916
McClelland, J. F. (FL) - 1906
McClelland, Robert (MI) - 1843, 1844,
  1846
McClelland, T. E. (CO) - 1896
McClelland, Thomas Jefferson (PA) - 1938
McClelland, William (PA) - 1870, 1872
McClenathan, Coulson V. (IL) - 1904
McClernand, John A. (IL) - 1843, 1846,
  1848, 1859, 1860
McClintic, James V. (OK) - 1914, 1916,
  1918, 1920, 1922, 1924, 1926, 1928,
  1930, 1932
McClintock, C. B. (OH) - 1928, 1930, 1932,
  1934
McClintock, C. D. (OH) - 1926
McClintock, H. R. (OH) - 1930
McClory, Robert (IL) - 1962, 1964, 1966,
  1968, 1970, 1972, 1974, 1976, 1978,
  1980

McNalley, Pat (AR) - 1912
McNally, Miles H. (WI) - 1928, 1932
McNally, Pat (AR) - 1928
McNamara, A. R. (OH) - 1944
McNamara, Frank Luke Jr. (MA) - 1982
McNamara, James (IL) - 1886
McNamara, James Edward (MI) - 1972
McNamara, Joseph A. (VT) - 1930, 1932
McNamara, Robert C. (PA) - 1896
McNaron, Thomas G. (AL) - 1940
McNary, William S. (MA) - 1892, 1894, 1902, 1904
McNaught, C. E. (MN) - 1940
McNaughton, Coll (IL) - 1908
McNaughton, Donald (NY) - 1892
McNaughton, John T. (IL) - 1952
McNeal, W. W. (WV) - 1918, 1920
McNealy, Thompson W. (IL) - 1870
McNeece, John Henry (MA) - 1936
McNeel, Walter B. (NE) - 1904
McNeeley (MO) - 1918
McNeely, Thompson W. (IL) - 1868
McNees, James L. Jr. (TX) - 1982
McNeil, Archibald (CT) - 1922
McNeil, Ron (FL) - 1982
McNeill, Archibald (NC) - 1825
McNeill, Neil E. (OK) - 1910
McNeill, Mrs. Phronia A. (VA) - 1950
McNett, Andrew J. (NY) - 1864, 1892
McNight, Charles B. (PA) - 1874
McNinch, S. S. (NC) - 1910
McNulta, John (IL) - 1872, 1874
McNulty, Caleb J. (OH) - 1844
McNulty, Frank J. (NJ) - 1922, 1924
McNulty, Jim (AZ) - 1982, 1984
McNulty, William H. (NJ) - 1952
McNutt (IN) - 1872
McNutt (OH) - 1834
McNutt, Lawrence E. (CA) - 1964
McPherran, James E. (IL) - 1892
McPherson (MO) - 1912
McPherson, Edward (PA) - 1858, 1860, 1862
McPherson, Isaac V. (MO) - 1918, 1920
McPherson, James (MA) - 1926
McPherson, John H. (MI) - 1934
McPherson, Logan (TX) - 1904
McPherson, Smith (IA) - 1898
McPherson, W. L. (AR) - 1902
McPike, H. C. (CA) - 1886
McPike, Henry C. (CA) - 1904
McQuade, Marian (WV) - 1970
McQuaid, Dennis (CA) - 1980, 1982
McQuaid, Wilfred T. (MD) - 1944
McQueen, John (SC) - 1844, 1848, 1850, 1853, 1854, 1856, 1858, 1860
McQuigg, J. R. (OH) - 1914
McQuiston, H. L. (TX) - 1908
McRae, John L. (MS) - 1859
McRae, Taylor (TX) - 1896
McRae, Thomas C. (AR) - 1886, 1888, 1890, 1892, 1894, 1896, 1898, 1900
McReynold, J. C. (TN) - 1896
McReynolds (MI) - 1872
McReynolds (PA) - 1858
McReynolds, Sam D. (TN) - 1922, 1924, 1926, 1928, 1930, 1932, 1934, 1936, 1938
McRight, Frank (AL) - 1984
McRitchie, Tom P. (OH) - 1960
McRoberts, Samuel (IL) - 1838
McRuer, Donald C. (CA) - 1864
McShane, John A. (NE) - 1886
McSherry (PA) - 1831
McSherry, Charles T. (MI) - 1940
McSherry, Frank D. (OK) - 1938, 1940, 1942, 1952, 1964
McSherry, Michael J. (NY) - 1982
McSherry, Thomas R. (NJ) - 1966
McSherry, William (PA) - 1882, 1904
McSpadden, Clem Rogers (OK) - 1972
McSparran, James G. (PA) - 1910
McSparran, John A. (PA) - 1928
McSpedon, Richard W. (NY) - 1948, 1958
McSwain, John J. (SC) - 1920, 1922, 1924, 1926, 1928, 1930, 1932, 1934
McSween, Harold B. (LA) - 1958, 1960
McSween, W. J. (TN) - 1892
McSweeney, John (OH) - 1920, 1922, 1924, 1926, 1928, 1936, 1938, 1948, 1950, 1952, 1956
McVay, Gratton C. (OK) - 1916
McVean, Charles (NY) - 1832
McVeay, Jimmy (MS) - 1980

McVey, James J. (MA) - 1902
McVey, Walter L. (KS) - 1960
McVey, William E. (IL) - 1950, 1952, 1954, 1956
McVicar, James A. (ME) - 1952
McVicker, Roy H. (CO) - 1964, 1966, 1968
McWane, F. W. (VA) - 1924
McWane, Fred W. (VA) - 1932, 1938, 1940
McWane, J. W. (VA) - 1922
McWherter, George H. (PA) - 1918
McWhorter (GA) - 1838
McWilliams (PA) - 1888
McWilliams, Christian J. (NY) - 1920
McWilliams, Gordon S. (CA) - 1960
McWilliams, John D. (CT) - 1942, 1944
McWilliams, Robert (IL) - 1886
McWillie, William (MS) - 1849, 1851
Meacham, James (VT) - 1849, 1850, 1852, 1854
Meacham, Ozro (VT) - 1888, 1900
Mead (NY) - 1854
Mead, James M. (NY) - 1918, 1920, 1922, 1924, 1926, 1928, 1930, 1932, 1934, 1936
Mead, John (TX) - 1970
Mead, Larry E. (MO) - 1982
Meade (MI) - 1878
Meade, Clarence W. (NY) - 1896
Meade, Edwin R. (NY) - 1874
Meade, Gregory J. (PA) - 1968
Meade, Hugh A. (MD) - 1946
Meade, Richard K. (VA) - 1847, 1849, 1851
Meade, W. Howes (KY) - 1946, 1948
Meader, George (MI) - 1950, 1952, 1954, 1956, 1958, 1960, 1962, 1964
Meader, John D. (NY) - 1964
Meaker, W. Lathrop (MA) - 1910
Means, John (KY) - 1874
Means, Rice W. (CO) - 1912
Meares, Iredell (NC) - 1910
Meares, O. P. (NC) - 1857
Meares, Thomas D. (NC) - 1845
Mears, William C. (AR) - 1978
Meas, Augustus (NY) - 1920
Mebane, William G. (NC) - 1928, 1930
Mechem, Edwin (AR) - 1908
Medary, Samuel (OH) - 1846
Medill, William (OH) - 1838, 1840, 1843, 1856
Medina, James R. (WI) - 1978
Medonick, Carl (NY) - 1958
Mee, John William (OK) - 1936
Meech, Ezra (VT) - 1824, 1828
Meeds, Lloyd (WA) - 1964, 1966, 1968, 1970, 1972, 1974, 1976
Meehan, James (WI) - 1884
Meek, D. H. (TX) - 1902
Meek, Louis F. (IL) - 1906
Meeker, George W. (KS) - 1968
Meeker, Jacob E. (MO) - 1914, 1916
Meeker, Raymond D. (IL) - 1922
Meeker, T. B. (FL) - 1906
Meekins, Isaac M. (NC) - 1900, 1908
Meekins, J. C. Jr. (NC) - 1942
Meekison, David (OH) - 1896, 1898
Meeks, James A. (IL) - 1932, 1934, 1936, 1938, 1940
Megellas, James (WI) - 1958, 1960
Meggett (WI) - 1870
Megginson, Joseph C. (TX) - 1846
Mehler, John M. (NJ) - 1946
Meier, William H. (NE) - 1946
Meiers, Robert W. (IN) - 1900
Meighen (MN) - 1878
Meighen, Thomas G. (MN) - 1894
Meiklejohn, George D. (NE) - 1892, 1894
Meinel, H. G. (PA) - 1914, 1916
Meissener, Albert F. (MT) - 1916
Meissner, Joe B. (TX) - 1961, 1962
Meister, Robert (WI) - 1900
Meitzn, E. O. (TX) - 1892
Mekota, Joseph (IA) - 1914
Melani, Thomas (NJ) - 1978
Melcher, John (MT) - 1966, 1970, 1972, 1974
Meldahl, Andrew (MN) - 1944
Meldon, O. F. (CA) - 1914
Meldon, P. M. (VT) - 1910
Meldon, Patrick M. (VT) - 1912
Mellish, David B. (NY) - 1872
Mellon, Knos (CA) - 1962
Mellon, William J. (PA) - 1904, 1916
Melms (WI) - 1918
Melms, Edmund T. (WI) - 1906, 1908, 1922, 1926

Melson (MD) - 1886
Melton, E. J. (MO) - 1930
Melville, Frank (NJ) - 1926
Melville, J. Keith (UT) - 1966
Menard, J. W. (LA) - 1868
Menard, Perrie (IL) - 1834
Mendenhall, George C. (NC) - 1843
Mendenhall, L. D. (NC) - 1904
Mendonca, Joseph M. (MA) - 1948
Menees (TN) - 1859
Menefee, John N. (KY) - 1948
Menifee, Richard H. (KY) - 1837
Menkens, George C. (NE) - 1962
Menzies, Gustavus V. (IN) - 1906
Menzies, John W. (KY) - 1861, 1863
Mercer, Charles F. (VA) - 1825, 1827, 1829, 1831, 1833, 1835, 1837, 1839
Mercer, David H. (NE) - 1892, 1894, 1896, 1898, 1900, 1902
Mercer, Forrest (PA) - 1934
Mercer, Samuel C. (TN) - 1868
Mercer, Thomas H. (OR) - 1976
Merchant, W. B. (LA) - 1878
Mercogliano, Louis R. (NY) - 1966, 1968
Mercur, Ulysses (PA) - 1864, 1866, 1868, 1870
Merdinger, Brainard G. (CA) - 1974
Mereac (NY) - 1848
Meredith, Elisha E. (VA) - 1891, 1892, 1894
Mering, Luther M. (IN) - 1892
Meriwether, David (KY) - 1847
Meriwether, James (GA) - 1824
Meriwether, James A. (GA) - 1840
Merlino, Joseph P. (NJ) - 1982
Meroney, Ronald A. (MD) - 1976
Merriam, Chester C. (CA) - 1964
Merriam, Clinton L. (NY) - 1870, 1872
Merriam, Jonathan (IL) - 1870
Merriam, Nathan (NE) - 1914
Merrick (NY) - 1842
Merrick, A. C. (SC) - 1896
Merrick, Frank W. (MI) - 1926
Merrick, Fred H. (PA) - 1912
Merrick, Wayne R. (PA) - 1970
Merrick, William D. (MD) - 1837
Merrick, William M. (MD) - 1870, 1872
Merrifield, Edward (PA) - 1894, 1896
Merrill, D. Bailey (IN) - 1952, 1954, 1956
Merrill, D. H. (TX) - 1920, 1922
Merrill, Del (ME) - 1914
Merrill, Herbert M. (NY) - 1916, 1918
Merrill, James (PA) - 1838
Merrill, John (MA) - 1824
Merrill, Lot M. (ME) - 1850
Merrill, Orsamus C. (VT) - 1830
Merrill, William H. (MI) - 1966
Merriman, Matthew S. (OH) - 1904
Merriman, O. C. (MN) - 1884
Merriman, Truman A. (NY) - 1884, 1886
Merritt, Edwin A. Jr. (NY) - 1912, 1914
Merritt, Harry D. (WA) - 1910
Merritt, Henry W. (PA) - 1928
Merritt, Matthew J. (NY) - 1934, 1936, 1938, 1940, 1942
Merritt, Paul (TX) - 1972
Merritt, Schuyler (CT) - 1918, 1920, 1922, 1924, 1926, 1928, 1930, 1932, 1934, 1936
Merritt, Thomas Polk (PA) - 1892
Merritt, W. W. (IA) - 1872
Merritt, William (NC) - 1894
Merritt, William D. (NC) - 1920
Merriwether, David (KY) - 1851
Merrow, Chester E. (NH) - 1942, 1944, 1946, 1948, 1950, 1952, 1954, 1956, 1958, 1960, 1970, 1972
Merson, Alan (CO) - 1972
Merton, Ernst (WI) - 1884
Mertz, Claudia (MS) - 1974
Merwin (CT) - 1882
Merwin, Orange (CT) - 1825, 1827, 1829
Meshel, Harry (OH) - 1980
Mesick, William S. (MI) - 1896, 1898
Meskill, Thomas J. Jr. (CT) - 1964, 1966, 1968
Messenger, H. Burdett (MD) - 1934
Messinger, Charles (NY) - 1920
Metcalf, George R. (NY) - 1968
Metcalf, Harry B. (NH) - 1934
Metcalf, Henry H. (NH) - 1910
Metcalf, L. S. (MO) - 1878
Metcalf, Lee (MT) - 1952, 1954, 1956, 1958

Metcalf, Randall (OH) - 1964
Metcalf, Victor H. (CA) - 1898, 1900, 1902
Metcalfe, Henry B. (NY) - 1874
Metcalfe, Lyne S. (MO) - 1876
Metcalfe, Ralph H. (IL) - 1970, 1972, 1974, 1976
Metcalfe, Theodore W. (NE) - 1940
Metcalfe, Thomas (KY) - 1824, 1827
Metton, L. D. (SC) - 1894
Metz, Herman A. (NY) - 1912, 1922
Metzenbaum, James (OH) - 1942
Metzerott, Oliver (MD) - 1928
Metzger, Bruce A. (PA) - 1928
Metzger, Charles J. (IL) - 1924
Metzger, Donald L. (IL) - 1974
Metzger, Fraser (VT) - 1914
Metzger, Tom (CA) - 1980
Metzler, Gottfried (PA) - 1894
Mewboorne, James M. (NC) - 1890
Meyer, Adolph (LA) - 1890, 1892, 1894, 1896, 1898, 1900, 1902, 1904, 1906
Meyer, Alvin P. (IA) - 1952
Meyer, Ben F. (NM) - 1944, 1948
Meyer, Conrad J. (NY) - 1914
Meyer, Donald D. (MO) - 1978
Meyer, Ed J. (OH) - 1914
Meyer, F. B. (MO) - 1938, 1940
Meyer, Fred W. (NY) - 1926
Meyer, G. A. (IA) - 1912, 1914
Meyer, G. E. H. (TX) - 1920
Meyer, Henry (PA) - 1894
Meyer, Herbert A. (KS) - 1946, 1948
Meyer, Howard M. (IN) - 1942
Meyer, J. Edward (NY) - 1976
Meyer, John A. (MD) - 1940
Meyer, John H. (OH) - 1906
Meyer, Kathleen M. (PA) - 1978, 1980
Meyer, Lee S. (MD) - 1902, 1904
Meyer, William H. (VT) - 1958, 1960, 1972
Meyer, William X. (IL) - 1926
Meyerhoeffer (VA) - 1833
Meyers, Benjamin F. (PA) - 1870, 1872
Meyers, George Jr. (IN) - 1980
Meyers, Jan (KS) - 1984
Meyers, Joseph J. (IA) - 1934
Meyers, Jerome M. (PA) - 1960
Meyers, Leonard A. (PA) - 1872
Meyers, Mahlon (PA) - 1900
Meyers, Meredith (PA) - 1924, 1932
Meyers, O. P. (IA) - 1920
Meyers, Robert M. (PA) - 1954, 1960
Meyers, Victor A. (WA) - 1958
Meyner, Helen S. (NJ) - 1972, 1974, 1976, 1978
Meyner, Robert B. (NJ) - 1946
Mezger, Irving H. (MD) - 1938
Mezvinsky, Edward (IA) - 1970, 1972, 1974, 1976
Mgrath (NY) - 1850
Mica, Daniel A. (FL) - 1978, 1980, 1982, 1984
Michael, George W. (IN) - 1898
Michael, Lawrence (VA) - 1944, 1946
Michael, W. E. (TN) - 1948
Michaels, Ernest E. (IL) - 1962
Michaels, Mortimer H. (NY) - 1936
Michaelson, M. Alfred (IL) - 1920, 1922, 1924, 1926, 1928, 1932
Michaelson, Mark G. (WI) - 1984
Michal, Charles J. (IL) - 1950
Michalek, Anthony (IL) - 1904, 1906, 1908
Michales, William H. (NY) - 1918
Michalowski, Edward S. (PA) - 1928, 1930
Michaux, H. M. Jr. (NC) - 1982
Michel, Robert H. (IL) - 1956, 1958, 1960, 1962, 1964, 1966, 1968, 1970, 1972, 1974, 1976, 1978, 1980, 1982, 1984
Michelson, Adolph (ND) - 1940
Michener, Earl C. (MI) - 1918, 1920, 1922, 1924, 1926, 1928, 1930, 1932, 1934, 1936, 1938, 1940, 1942, 1944, 1946, 1948
Michener, James A. (PA) - 1962
Michener, Ross (OH) - 1944
Michler, P. S. (PA) - 1838
Micich, Michael (IA) - 1956, 1958
Mickelson, Grace (SD) - 1976
Mickey, J. Ross (IL) - 1900
Mickle (NJ) - 1830
Middleswarth, Ner (PA) - 1852
Middleton, Clyde (KY) - 1962, 1964
Middleton, George (NJ) - 1862, 1864
Middleton, J. O. (AL) - 1924
Middleton, J. Osmond (AL) - 1908

Morgan, William (NY) - 1890
Morgan, William M. (OH) - 1918, 1920, 1922, 1924, 1926, 1928, 1930, 1932
Morgan, William S. (VA) - 1833, 1835, 1837
Morgenstein, J. (NY) - 1894
Moriarity, Joseph J. (MN) - 1930
Moriarty, Daniel J. (NH) - 1940
Moriarty, John L. (OH) - 1936
Moriber, Joseph (NY) - 1954, 1956
Morin, J. S. (TX) - 1904
Morin, John M. (PA) - 1912, 1914, 1916, 1918, 1920, 1922, 1924, 1926
Morin, Richard W. (MN) - 1936
Morison, H. S. K. (VA) - 1894
Moritz, Christopher D. (IN) - 1948
Moritz, Theodore L. (PA) - 1934
Morian, Webster L. (NE) - 1900
Morley, Dean (MI) - 1942
Morphis, Joseph L. (MS) - 1869, 1870, 1880
Morphos, Diane (LA) - 1974
Morr, John W. (IN) - 1906
Morrell, Daniel J. (PA) - 1866, 1868, 1870
Morrell, Edward de V. (PA) - 1900, 1902, 1904
Morrell, Gerald (NY) - 1934, 1936
Morrill (ME) - 1866
Morrill, Anson P. (ME) - 1860
Morrill, Edmund N. (KS) - 1882, 1884, 1886, 1888
Morrill, Justin S. (VT) - 1854, 1856, 1858, 1860, 1863, 1864
Morrill, Milton L. (IL) - 1910
Morrill, Philip (ME) - 1836
Morrill, Samuel P. (ME) - 1868
Morries, Mildred A. (WI) - 1974
Morris (AL) - 1865
Morris (DE) - 1858
Morris (NY) - 1878
Morris (OH) - 1826, 1832
Morris (PA) - 1854, 1872
Morris (TN) - 1849, 1872
Morris, B. (MD) - 1894
Morris, Buckner S. (IL) - 1844
Morris, C. (OH) - 1946
Morris, Calvary (OH) - 1836, 1838, 1840
Morris, Christopher D. (NY) - 1958
Morris, D. (OH) - 1826
Morris, Daniel (NY) - 1862, 1864
Morris, David H. (TX) - 1916, 1928
Morris, Douglas (IN) - 1888
Morris, E. H. (NC) - 1902
Morris, Edward G. (MA) - 1930, 1932
Morris, Edward Joy (PA) - 1843, 1856, 1858, 1860
Morris, Ernest B. (NY) - 1942
Morris, Frank L. (NY) - 1928
Morris, Henry (MA) - 1854
Morris, Isaac N. (IL) - 1856, 1858
Morris, James F. (MA) - 1910, 1914
Morris, James Francis (MA) - 1896
Morris, James M. (OH) - 1864
Morris, James R. (OH) - 1860, 1862
Morris, John (NY) - 1832
Morris, John H. (OH) - 1900
Morris, Jonathan D. (OH) - 1848
Morris, Joseph (OH) - 1838, 1843, 1844
Morris, Mathias (PA) - 1834, 1836
Morris, Matthew (PA) - 1838
Morris, Monson (NY) - 1906, 1908
Morris, O. M. (OK) - 1916
Morris, R. P. W. (VA) - 1884
Morris, R. Page W. (MN) - 1896, 1898, 1900
Morris, Robert (PA) - 1978
Morris, Robert H. (PA) - 1980
Morris, Samuel W. (PA) - 1836, 1838
Morris, T. (OH) - 1826
Morris, Thomas (NM) - 1968
Morris, Thomas C. (NM) - 1960
Morris, Thomas G. (NM) - 1958, 1962, 1964, 1966
Morris, Toby (OK) - 1946, 1948, 1950, 1956, 1958
Morris, Truman A. (OH) - 1954
Morris, Walter E. (PA) - 1936
Morris, William A. (NC) - 1839
Morris, William S. (IL) - 1890
Morrison (MA) - 1888
Morrison (MO) - 1932
Morrison (NH) - 1851, 1855, 1857
Morrison, A. E. (IA) - 1888
Morrison, Bruce A. (CT) - 1982, 1984
Morrison, Cameron (NC) - 1942

Morrison, David A. (NY) - 1896
Morrison, Edward A. (NY) - 1964
Morrison, Elaine M. (NY) - 1966
Morrison, Frank B. (NE) - 1948, 1954
Morrison, Mrs. Frank B. (NE) - 1968
Morrison, George W. (NH) - 1853
Morrison, Herbert O. (PA) - 1954, 1956
Morrison, Howard L. (IN) - 1952
Morrison, I. L. D. (IL) - 1856
Morrison, Isaac L. (IL) - 1880
Morrison, J. J. (CA) - 1892
Morrison, J. L. D. (IL) - 1843
Morrison, J. T. (ID) - 1900
Morrison, James H. (LA) - 1942, 1944, 1946, 1948, 1950, 1952, 1954, 1956, 1958, 1960, 1962, 1964
Morrison, John A. (PA) - 1850
Morrison, John D. (OK) - 1934, 1936
Morrison, John E. (MI) - 1942
Morrison, John H. (ID) - 1904
Morrison, John H. (NY) - 1902
Morrison, John T. (ID) - 1896
Morrison, Kenneth (VA) - 1980
Morrison, Martin A. (IN) - 1908, 1910, 1912, 1914
Morrison, Robert S. (CO) - 1880
Morrison, Royd E. (PA) - 1916
Morrison, Sid (WA) - 1980, 1982, 1984
Morrison, Timothy A. (KY) - 1984
Morrison, William R. (IL) - 1862, 1864, 1866, 1872, 1874, 1876, 1878, 1880, 1882, 1884, 1886
Morrissey, John (NY) - 1866, 1868
Morrissey, John P. (NY) - 1948
Morrissey, Joseph F. (CT) - 1934
Morrissey, Patrick H. (IL) - 1924
Morrissey, Richard J. (MA) - 1912
Morrow (NJ) - 1886
Morrow, Jeremiah (OH) - 1840
Morrow, John (NM) - 1922, 1924, 1926, 1928
Morrow, Robert D. (MD) - 1972
Morrow, Thomas H. (OH) - 1920
Morrow, William (KY) - 1859
Morrow, William E. (NC) - 1958
Morrow, William W. (CA) - 1882, 1884, 1886, 1888
Morroway (MO) - 1912, 1914
Morse (CT) - 1902, 1904
Morse (MA) - 1886
Morse (MO) - 1884
Morse, Bushrod (MA) - 1890
Morse, Charles A. (NH) - 1906
Morse, D. A. (CA) - 1849
Morse, Elijah A. (MA) - 1888, 1890, 1892, 1894
Morse, Elmer A. (WI) - 1906, 1908, 1910, 1912
Morse, F. Bradford (MA) - 1960, 1962, 1964, 1966, 1968, 1970
Morse, Freeman H. (ME) - 1843, 1844, 1847, 1856, 1858
Morse, I. Porter (MA) - 1896, 1898
Morse, Isaac E. (LA) - 1847, 1849
Morse, Jenner E. (MI) - 1908
Morse, Leopold (MA) - 1870, 1872, 1876, 1878, 1880, 1882, 1886
Morse, Oliver A. (NY) - 1856
Morse, Roy L. (WI) - 1904
Morse, Issac E. (LA) - 1844, 1847, 1849, 1851
Morsey (MO) - 1892
Morss, Joseph B. (MA) - 1864
Morten, Stanley W. (IL) - 1952
Morton, Eskridge H. (WV) - 1922
Morton, Frank L. (PA) - 1916
Morton, Howard A. (MA) - 1924
Morton, Isaac (OH) - 1878
Morton, J. Sterling (NE) - 1888
Morton, Jeremiah (VA) - 1849
Morton, Levi P. (NY) - 1876, 1878, 1880
Morton, Minor G. (OH) - 1922
Morton, Nathaniel (MA) - 1848
Morton, Richard (NY) - 1906
Morton, Rogers C. B. (MD) - 1962, 1964, 1966, 1968, 1970
Morton, Thomas B. (AL) - 1900
Morton, Thruston B. (KY) - 1946, 1948, 1950
Morton, W. O. (CA) - 1904
Mosby (VA) - 1865
Moseley, Edna D. (NY) - 1948
Moseley, James Brady (MA) - 1972
Moseley, Nicholas (CT) - 1928
Moseley, Ralph S. (NE) - 1930

Moseley, William A. (NY) - 1842, 1844
Moseley, William D. (NC) - 1837
Moseley (VA) - 1853
Mosely, J. H. (WI) - 1888
Mosely, Ken (SC) - 1982, 1984
Moser, Guy L. (PA) - 1936, 1938, 1940
Moses (SC) - 1853
Moses, Charles L. (GA) - 1890, 1892, 1894
Moses, David (NY) - 1938, 1940
Moses, Halsey H. (OH) - 1864
Moses, Joel (NY) - 1922
Mosgrove, James (PA) - 1878, 1880
Mosher, Charles (MI) - 1884
Mosher, Charles A. (OH) - 1960, 1962, 1964, 1966, 1968, 1970, 1972, 1974
Mosher, H. S. (IA) - 1914
Mosher, Orris (IA) - 1912
Mosher, Richard T. (NY) - 1948
Mosier, Harold G. (OH) - 1936
Moskowitz, Henry (NY) - 1912
Mosley (GA) - 1846
Moss (MO) - 1856
Moss, C. V. (NC) - 1944
Moss, D. S. (NC) - 1896
Moss, David (IN) - 1878
Moss, Edward F. (NY) - 1940
Moss, Hunter H. Jr. (WV) - 1912, 1914
Moss, J. McKenzie (KY) - 1900, 1902
Moss, John E. (CA) - 1952, 1954, 1956, 1958, 1960, 1962, 1964, 1966, 1968, 1970, 1972, 1974, 1976
Moss, M. J. Jr. (FL) - 1946, 1948
Moss, Norman H. (IL) - 1892
Moss, Preston B. (MT) - 1922
Moss, Ralph W. (IN) - 1908, 1910, 1912, 1914, 1916, 1918
Moss, William R. (OH) - 1976
Moss, St. Clair Mrs. (MO) - 1922
Mosser, Charles M. (PA) - 1944
Mossholder, Max (TX) - 1960
Most, Amicus (NY) - 1942
Mostyn, William H. (NY) - 1956
Motley, Joseph (TN) - 1868
Motlow, George (TN) - 1930
Motsinger, Newel H. (IN) - 1896
Mott, Frank H. (NY) - 1918
Mott, George (NY) - 1870
Mott, James W. (OR) - 1932, 1934, 1936, 1938, 1940, 1942, 1944
Mott, Luther W. (NY) - 1910, 1912, 1914, 1916, 1918, 1920, 1922
Mott, Richard (OH) - 1854, 1856
Mottashed, J. Charles (MI) - 1946
Mottl, Ronald M. (OH) - 1970, 1974, 1976, 1978, 1980
Mottley, E. L. (KY) - 1876
Mottola, Rudolph E. (MA) - 1956
Mottola, Vincent (MA) - 1942
Moulder, Garret (PA) - 1898
Moulder, Morgan M. (MO) - 1948, 1950, 1952, 1954, 1956, 1958, 1960
Mouln (NY) - 1852
Moulton (MO) - 1916
Moulton (NH) - 1847
Moulton (NY) - 1882
Moulton, Arthur L. (OR) - 1914
Moulton, Mace (NH) - 1845
Moulton, Samuel W. (IL) - 1862, 1864, 1880, 1882
Mount, James A. (IN) - 1890
Mouser, Grant E. (OH) - 1904, 1906, 1908
Mouser, Grant E. Jr. (OH) - 1928, 1930, 1932, 1936
Mouton, Robert L. (LA) - 1936, 1938
Mowery, Jean D. (PA) - 1982
Mowery, Wes (TX) - 1976
Mowery, Wesley H. (TX) - 1978
Mowry (RI) - 1916
Mowry, Sumner (RI) - 1928
Moxley, William J. (IL) - 1909, 1910
Moye, Charles A. Jr. (GA) - 1954
Moye, James M. (MS) - 1966
Moyer, Charles W. (PA) - 1942
Moyer, William B. (PA) - 1944
Moynihan, James F. (IL) - 1982
Moynihan, Joseph A. Jr. (MI) - 1954
Moynihan, P. H. (IL) - 1932, 1934, 1936, 1940
Mozley (MO) - 1900
Mozley, Norman A. (MO) - 1894
Mrazek, Robert J. (NY) - 1982, 1984
Mrozinski, Phillip D. (WI) - 1970, 1972
Mruk, Joseph (NY) - 1942
Mton (VA) - 1851

Mucci, Henry A. (CT) - 1946
Mudd, John E. (MD) - 1968
Mudd, Sydney E. (MD) - 1888, 1890, 1896, 1898, 1900, 1902, 1904, 1906, 1908, 1914, 1916, 1918, 1920, 1922
Mudd, Thomas Brackett Reed (MD) - 1924, 1926
Mudd, W. S. (AL) - 1851
Mudge (NY) - 1878
Mudge, D. H. (IL) - 1916
Mudge, Ezra (MA) - 1828
Mueller, Alfred C. (IA) - 1938
Mufsey, Benjamin B. (MA) - 1850
Mugford, James E. (PA) - 1976
Muhlenberg, Francis S. (OH) - 1828
Muhlenberg, Frederick A. (PA) - 1946, 1948
Muhlenberg, H. A. (PA) - 1892
Muhlenberg, Henry A. (PA) - 1852
Muhlenberg, Henry A. P. (PA) - 1828, 1830, 1832, 1834, 1836
Muhler, Marie Sheehan (NJ) - 1980, 1982
Muir (ND) - 1894
Muir, Robert (NY) - 1836
Muldoon, Hugh (IL) - 1972
Muldowney, Michael J. (PA) - 1932, 1934
Muldrow, Henry L. (MS) - 1876, 1878, 1880, 1882
Mulford (NJ) - 1854
Mulhern, Joseph J. (MA) - 1960
Mulholland, Frank L. (OH) - 1916, 1934
Mulkey, William O. (AL) - 1900, 1914
Mullaney, T. W. (IA) - 1948, 1952
Mullen, C. N. (ME) - 1912
Mullen, C. W. (ME) - 1914
Mullen, John (NY) - 1910
Mullen, John F. (MA) - 1902
Muller, Gustav A. (PA) - 1894
Muller, Nicholas (NY) - 1876, 1878, 1880, 1882, 1884, 1898, 1900
Muller, Paul Jr. (NY) - 1910
Mullholland (NY) - 1884
Mulligan, Thomas J. (OH) - 1908
Mullikin, Addison E. (MD) - 1910
Mullin, Joseph (NY) - 1846
Mullins, Fenton P. F. (PA) - 1896
Mullins, James (TN) - 1867, 1870
Mulloy, William P. (KY) - 1984
Muloaney, William (IA) - 1900
Mulrenan, John P. (PA) - 1930
Multer, Abraham J. (NY) - 1947, 1948, 1950, 1952, 1954, 1956, 1958, 1960, 1962, 1964, 1966
Mulvaney, John T. (IA) - 1904, 1914
Mulvaney, M. F. (NE) - 1938
Mulvany (PA) - 1856
Mumma, Walter M. (PA) - 1950, 1952, 1954, 1956, 1958, 1960
Muncaster, Robert (CA) - 1964
Munday, James A. (WA) - 1892, 1913
Mundt, Karl E. (SD) - 1936, 1938, 1940, 1942, 1944, 1946
Mundy (NY) - 1852
Mundy, Roy (WA) - 1960
Mungen (OH) - 1858
Mungen, William (OH) - 1866, 1868
Munger, Frank Sr. (MN) - 1930
Munger, W. H. (NE) - 1882
Munly, M. G. (OR) - 1912
Munn, Charles (MN) - 1942
Munn, Daniel W. (IL) - 1870
Munn, James (WA) - 1966
Munro, Donald L. (PA) - 1898
Munro, William (WI) - 1894
Munroe, John H. (IA) - 1892
Muntzing, Melvin C. (WV) - 1944
Munyon, LeRoy (IA) - 1924
Mur (PA) - 1852
Murback, Jacob F. (MD) - 1912
Murch, Thompson H. (ME) - 1878, 1880, 1882
Murchison, Carmack (TN) - 1928
Murchison, Roderick (NC) - 1839, 1841
Murdock (WI) - 1892
Murdock, Abe (UT) - 1932, 1934, 1936, 1938
Murdock, Allen C. (WV) - 1904
Murdock, John R. (AZ) - 1936, 1938, 1940, 1942, 1944, 1946, 1948, 1950, 1952
Murdock, Norman A. (OH) - 1984
Murdock, Victor (KS) - 1904, 1906, 1908, 1910, 1912
Murer, Michael A. (IL) - 1980, 1982
Murkowski, Frank H. (AK) - 1970
Murphey (AL) - 1839

O'Brien, Walter A. (MA) - 1948
O'Brien, William A. (NJ) - 1922
O'Brien, William H. (MA) - 1910, 1920
O'Brien, William J. (MD) - 1872, 1874
O'Brien, William J. (PA) - 1906
O'Brien, William S. (WV) - 1926, 1928
O'Brien, William W. (IL) - 1868
O'Bryant, Henri Jr. (CA) - 1966
Obsuchowski, C. E. (TX) - 1912
O'Byrne (NJ) - 1914
O'Callaghan, Jeremiah J. (NJ) - 1954, 1968
O'Callaghan, Jerry A. (WY) - 1956
O'Callaghan, L. J. (GA) - 1962, 1964
O'Callaghan, Thomas P. (NY) - 1960
Ocamb, Faye B. (PA) - 1902
Ocasek, Oliver (OH) - 1962, 1968
Occhiogrosso, Frank J. (NY) - 1970
Ochenkowski, Edmund W. (IL) - 1970
O'Chiltree, Thomas P. (TX) - 1882
O'Chiltree, William B. (TX) - 1846, 1851, 1859
O'Connell, Bernard J. (NY) - 1952
O'Connell, D. J. (IA) - 1898, 1900
O'Connell, David J. (NY) - 1918, 1920, 1922, 1924, 1926, 1928, 1930
O'Connell, James E. (OH) - 1940
O'Connell, Jeremiah E. (RI) - 1922, 1924, 1926, 1928
O'Connell, Jerry J. (MT) - 1936, 1938, 1940
O'Connell, John A. (CA) - 1962
O'Connell, John J. (WA) - 1952
O'Connell, John M. (RI) - 1932, 1936
O'Connell, John M. (TX) - 1964
O'Connell, John Matthew (RI) - 1934
O'Connell, John P. (MA) - 1920
O'Connell, Joseph F. (MA) - 1906, 1908
O'Connell, M. Fred (MA) - 1912, 1922, 1932
O'Connell, Mort L. (NJ) - 1940
O'Connell, Walter J. (NJ) - 1954
O'Connor (MO) - 1912
O'Connor (NY) - 1886
O'Connor, Charles (OK) - 1928, 1930
O'Connor, Colleen M. (CA) - 1974
O'Connor, Donald J. (NY) - 1948, 1950, 1952
O'Connor, Ed (CA) - 1966
O'Connor, Eugene (NY) - 1968
O'Connor, Henry J. (NY) - 1920
O'Connor, Herman R. (NY) - 1912
O'Connor, Hugh T. (IN) - 1900
O'Connor, J. Joseph (MA) - 1914
O'Connor, J. L. (MN) - 1938, 1940
O'Connor, James (LA) - 1920, 1922, 1924, 1926, 1928
O'Connor, James F. (MT) - 1936, 1938, 1940, 1942, 1944
O'Connor, James H. (NY) - 1954
O'Connor, James K. (NY) - 1906
O'Connor, John (IA) - 1954
O'Connor, John C. (NY) - 1922, 1923
O'Connor, John D. (MA) - 1928
O'Connor, John F. (NY) - 1970
O'Connor, John J. (NY) - 1923, 1924, 1926, 1928, 1930, 1932, 1934, 1936, 1938
O'Connor, John T. (TN) - 1936, 1942
O'Connor, Joseph (TX) - 1882
O'Connor, Michael P. (SC) - 1876, 1878, 1880
O'Connor, R. E. (WV) - 1938, 1940
O'Day, Caroline (NY) - 1934, 1936, 1938, 1940
Oddo, Salvatore E. (IL) - 1974
Oddstad, Elma D. (CA) - 1958
Odegard, Robert J. (MN) - 1962, 1964
O'Dell (NY) - 1858
O'Dell, Benjamin B. Jr. (NY) - 1894, 1896
O'Dell, Moses F. (NY) - 1860, 1862
O'Dell, N. Holmes (NY) - 1874
O'Dell, Tracy (CA) - 1966
Oder, Henry A. Jr. (VA) - 1958
Odlum, Jacqueline Cochran (CA) - 1956
Odman, Robert (WA) - 1958
O'Doherty, Kieran (NY) - 1964
Odom, Archie C. (SC) - 1966
Odom, Christine P. (NC) - 1954
O'Donnall, Fred (IA) - 1878
O'Donnell, Daniel J. C. (PA) - 1924, 1926, 1942
O'Donnell, James (MI) - 1884, 1886, 1888, 1890, 1892
O'Donnell, P. M. (PA) - 1922, 1924
O'Donnell, Pierce (CA) - 1980
O'Donnell, Robert J. (OH) - 1924, 1926

O'Donnell, T. J. (CO) - 1890
O'Donovan, M. C. (PA) - 1906
Odum, Harry C. (IL) - 1942
Odum, J. T. (TN) - 1910
O'Dwyer, Paul (NY) - 1948
Oehmen, John S. (IL) - 1904
O'Ferrall, Charles T. (VA) - 1882, 1884, 1886, 1888, 1890, 1892
Offenhender, Jacob M. (NY) - 1940
Officer, Charles B. (NH) - 1964, 1972
Offner, Paul (WI) - 1982
O'Flaherty, D. C. (VA) - 1898
O'Flanagan (KS) - 1882
Ogara, John (MA) - 1896
Ogdahl, Harmon T. (MN) - 1968
Ogden (LA) - 1849
Ogden (NJ) - 1834
Ogden (NY) - 1828, 1856, 1858
Ogden, A. R. (VA) - 1974, 1976
Ogden, Alan R. (VA) - 1978
Ogden, Charles F. (KY) - 1918, 1920
Ogden, Dan (CO) - 1976
Ogden, David (NY) - 1832
Ogden, Henry W. (LA) - 1894, 1896
Ogden, Isaac (NY) - 1830
Ogden, William (MD) - 1896
Ogg, James B. (CA) - 1928
Ogier, Benson (OH) - 1936
Ogilivie, Thomas J. (TN) - 1892
Ogle (PA) - 1834
Ogle, Andrew Jackson (PA) - 1848, 1850
Ogle, Charles (PA) - 1836, 1838, 1840
Oglesby, Richard J. (IL) - 1858
Oglesby, Woodson R. (NY) - 1912, 1914, 1916
O'Grady, Jack J. (IN) - 1948
O'Grady, James M. E. (NY) - 1898
Ogren, Oscar (IL) - 1918
O'Hagan, C. J. (NC) - 1870
O'Hair, Frank T. (IL) - 1912, 1914
O'Halloran, Edward J. (PA) - 1968
O'Halloran, Richard J. (IL) - 1930
O'Hanlon, J. (SC) - 1848
O'Hara, Barnatt (IL) - 1923
O'Hara, Barratt (IL) - 1948, 1950, 1952, 1954, 1956, 1958, 1960, 1962, 1964, 1966
O'Hara, Frederic S. (IL) - 1956
O'Hara, James (MI) - 1918
O'Hara, James (NE) - 1920
O'Hara, James E. (NC) - 1878, 1882, 1884, 1886
O'Hara, James F. (NY) - 1950
O'Hara, James G. (MI) - 1958, 1960, 1962, 1964, 1966, 1968, 1970, 1972, 1974
O'Hara, John Grady (TN) - 1958
O'Hara, John J. (MI) - 1934
O'Hara, Joseph P. (MN) - 1938, 1940, 1942, 1944, 1946, 1948, 1950, 1952, 1954, 1956
O'Hara, Thomas (MI) - 1902
O'Hara, Thomas A. (PA) - 1924, 1928
O'Hare, Bernard V. (PA) - 1928
Ohlendorf, Howard C. (MO) - 1964, 1974
Ohliger, Lewis P. (OH) - 1892
Ohlis, G. W. (PA) - 1916
Ojala, William R. (MN) - 1975
Ojeda, Miriam (CA) - 1984
O'Keefe (CT) - 1918
O'Keefe, Dan (CA) - 1978
O'Keefe, Esther Kathleen (IN) - 1922
O'Keefe, John A. (MA) - 1906
O'Keefe, Maurice P. (KS) - 1928
O'Keefe, Richard B. (MA) - 1946
O'Keefe, William W. (WI) - 1896
Okicki, Joseph F. (PA) - 1970
Okonski, Alvin E. (WI) - 1942, 1944, 1946, 1948, 1950, 1952, 1954, 1956, 1958, 1960, 1962, 1964, 1966, 1968, 1970, 1972
Olcott (NY) - 1860
Olcott, Jacob Vanvechten (NY) - 1904, 1906, 1908
Oldfield, Pearl Peden Mrs. (AR) - 1928
Oldfield, William A. (AR) - 1908, 1910, 1912, 1914, 1916, 1918, 1920, 1922, 1924, 1926
Oldham, George W. (WV) - 1924, 1926
Oldham, Wiley H. (OH) - 1874
Olds (OH) - 1832, 1834
Olds, Edson B. (OH) - 1848, 1850, 1852, 1854
O'Leary, Arthur F. (CT) - 1926
O'Leary, Denis (NY) - 1912

O'Leary, James A. (NY) - 1934, 1936, 1938, 1940, 1942
O'Leary, Jeremiah A. (NY) - 1920
O'Leary, Mark B. (IL) - 1914
O'Leary, Richard A. (NY) - 1952
O'Leary, Thomas C. (NY) - 1938
O'Leen, O. Henry (OR) - 1944
Oleson, Ole B. (WI) - 1892
Olessker, Karl (IN) - 1964
Oley, John H. (WV) - 1866
Olin, Abram B. (NY) - 1856, 1858, 1860
Olin, James R. (VA) - 1982, 1984
Olin, John M. (WI) - 1884
Olin, Vernon E. (NY) - 1954
Olinger, Henry W. (IL) - 1922
Olinger, R. J. (WA) - 1916
Oliphant, H. (PA) - 1838
Oliver, Andrew (NY) - 1852, 1854, 1856
Oliver, Daniel C. (NY) - 1916
Oliver, David S. (OH) - 1896
Oliver, Frank (NY) - 1922, 1924, 1926, 1928, 1930, 1932
Oliver, James C. (ME) - 1936, 1938, 1940, 1954, 1956, 1958, 1960
Oliver, John A. (PA) - 1870
Oliver, John E. (TN) - 1906
Oliver, Mordecai (MO) - 1852, 1854, 1868
Oliver, Robert C. (IN) - 1948
Oliver, Samuel (AL) - 1829
Oliver, Samuel Addison (IA) - 1874, 1876
Oliver, Thomas J. (WI) - 1910
Oliver, William (NY) - 1840
Oliver, William B. (AL) - 1914, 1916, 1918, 1920, 1922, 1924, 1926, 1928, 1930, 1932, 1934
Olmsted, Marlin E. (PA) - 1896, 1898, 1900, 1902, 1904, 1906, 1908, 1910
Olney (NY) - 1848
Olney, Richard (MA) - 1914, 1916, 1918, 1920
O'Laughlin, Joseph M. (MA) - 1976
Oloughlin, Kathryn E. Miss (KS) - 1932
Olpp, Archibald E. (NJ) - 1920, 1922
Olsen, Arnold (MT) - 1960, 1962, 1964, 1966, 1968, 1970, 1972
Olsen, Bob (TN) - 1975
Olsen, John E. (MI) - 1976
Olsen, Jon D. (HI) - 1968
Olsen, Kirsten (CA) - 1978, 1980
Olsen, Leslie O. (MO) - 1970
Olsen, Martin (WA) - 1896
Olson, Alec G. (MN) - 1962, 1964, 1966
Olson, Andrew H. (SD) - 1908
Olson, Andrew (IL) - 1920
Olson, Curtiss T. (MN) - 1950, 1952
Olson, Dawn (WA) - 1962
Olson, Jonas W. (IL) - 1894, 1902
Olson, Larry H. (MI) - 1972
Olson, Leslie O. (MO) - 1968
Olson, O. Martin (NY) - 1932
Olson, Ole H. (ND) - 1920
Olson, Robert C. (MN) - 1954
Olson, Robert C. Jr. (MN) - 1976
Olson, Virgil L. (KS) - 1976
O'Malley (MO) - 1900
O'Malley, Matthew V. (NY) - 1931
O'Malley, Patrick J. (MA) - 1948
O'Malley, Thomas (WI) - 1928, 1930, 1932, 1934, 1936, 1938
O'Mara, Bill (NV) - 1978
O'Mara, Eugene J. (NJ) - 1928
O'Mauleby, William (MD) - 1866
Omdahl, John (ND) - 1940
Omdahl, Lloyd (ND) - 1976
O'Meara, John R. (MI) - 1958
O'Meara, Thomas J. (IA) - 1886
O'Merberg, Maynard J. (CA) - 1948
O'Neal (AL) - 1849
O'Neal (GA) - 1874
O'Neal, Emmet (KY) - 1934, 1936, 1938, 1940, 1942, 1944, 1946
O'Neal, H. F. (TX) - 1880
O'Neal, I. C. (VA) - 1876
O'Neal, James (NY) - 1918, 1920
O'Neal, John H. (IN) - 1886
O'Neal, Maston (GA) - 1964, 1966, 1968
O'Neal, Weden (KY) - 1890, 1892
O'Neal, William R. (FL) - 1908
O'Neall, John H. (IN) - 1888
O'Neil (CT) - 1902
O'Neil, A. F. (OH) - 1928
O'Neil, Frank M. (PA) - 1962
O'Neil, James F. (MI) - 1962
O'Neil, Joseph B. (CA) - 1942
O'Neil, Joseph H. (MA) - 1884, 1888, 1890, 1892

O'Neil, Patrick M. (NY) - 1972
O'Neil, Thomas J. (KS) - 1894
O'Neill (TX) - 1878
O'Neill, Charles (PA) - 1862, 1864, 1866, 1868, 1870, 1872, 1874, 1876, 1878, 1880, 1882, 1884, 1886, 1888, 1890, 1892
O'Neill, Edward L. (NJ) - 1934, 1936, 1938
O'Neill, Eugene T. (NY) - 1946
O'Neill, Francis A. (NY) - 1912
O'Neill, Francis G. (MA) - 1940
O'Neill, Francis P. (MA) - 1942
O'Neill, Harry P. (PA) - 1948, 1950, 1952
O'Neill, James F. (MA) - 1952, 1954
O'Neill, John (OH) - 1862
O'Neill, John J. (MO) - 1882, 1884, 1886, 1888, 1890, 1892
O'Neill, Paul J. (FL) - 1964
O'Neill, Thomas P. Jr. (MA) - 1952, 1954, 1956, 1958, 1960, 1962, 1964, 1966, 1968, 1972, 1974, 1976, 1978, 1980, 1982, 1984
O'Neill, Vincent E. (MI) - 1952
O'Neill, William E. (IL) - 1900
Oppenheim, J. Philip (IN) - 1978
Orchard, Ernest R. (MN) - 1952
Orchard, Ernie (MN) - 1954
Ordway, Albert (VA) - 1870
O'Reilly, Daniel (NY) - 1878, 1880
O'Reilly, Gerald (NY) - 1946
O'Reilly, Kathleen F. (MI) - 1980
O'Reilly, Maurice (PA) - 1950
O'Reilly, T. Bronson (NY) - 1956
O'Reilly, Timothy I. (CA) - 1954
Orenstein, Jeffrey R. (OH) - 1982
Organ, Rollin B. (IL) - 1898
Orlikoski, Walter J. (IL) - 1940
Orloski, Richard J. (PA) - 1982
Ormon, John M. (CT) - 1984
Ormsby, Caleb N. (MI) - 1848
Ormsby, Walter M. (NY) - 1962
Ornstein, Franklin (NY) - 1974
O'Rourke, Hugh (MA) - 1914
O'Rourke, James S. (IL) - 1926, 1928
O'Rourke, Jerome F. (MI) - 1960
O'Rourke, Peter (MI) - 1968
O'Rourke, Philip A. (CA) - 1954
O'Rourke, Vernon A. (PA) - 1942, 1944, 1946
O'Rourke, William J. (PA) - 1932
Orozco, Bill (CA) - 1966, 1968
Orr (MO) - 1914
Orr, Emmett (KY) - 1914
Orr, George (NY) - 1920
Orr, Jackson (IA) - 1870, 1872
Orr, James A. (CO) - 1910
Orr, James L. (SC) - 1848, 1850, 1853, 1854, 1856
Orr, James W. (TX) - 1964
Orr, Robert Jr. (PA) - 1826
Orr, Sample (MO) - 1864
Orr, Samuel (NY) - 1926, 1930, 1932, 1934
Orr, William (IL) - 1834
Orr, William P. (OH) - 1890
Orrick (MD) - 1841
Orth, Godlove S. (IN) - 1862, 1864, 1866, 1868, 1872, 1878, 1880, 1882
Ortiz, Solomon P. (TX) - 1982, 1984
Ortmeyer, D. H. (IN) - 1912
Orton (MO) - 1894, 1896
Orton (WI) - 1876
Orton, Duane (IA) - 1960
Orvis, E. E. (PA) - 1878
Orwig, Samuel H. (PA) - 1882
Osborn (NJ) - 1854
Osborn, Michael (TN) - 1970
Osborn, Robert A. (NY) - 1922
Osborne (NJ) - 1856
Osborne, A. B. (PA) - 1902
Osborne, Bartley P. (PA) - 1960
Osborne, Charles (NY) - 1942
Osborne, Edwin S. (PA) - 1884, 1886, 1888
Osborne, George (KY) - 1924
Osborne, Henry Z. (CA) - 1914, 1916, 1918, 1920, 1922
Osborne, James W. (NC) - 1853
Osborne, John E. (WY) - 1896
Osborne, Lithgow (NY) - 1932
Osborne, Thomas B. (CT) - 1839, 1841, 1843
Osborne, Thomas C. (NE) - 1926
Osborne, W. Ted (OH) - 1958, 1960
Osburn, Frank C. (PA) - 1892
O'Scannlain, Diarmuid (OR) - 1974
Osgood B. L. (TX) - 1904

Osgood, Charles (MA) - 1858
Osgood, Gayton P. (MA) - 1830, 1833, 1834, 1836, 1938, 1940, 1842
Osgood, Jason C. (MA) - 1868
Osgood, Jim (CA) - 1974
Osgood (IL) - 1856
Osgood, William N. (MA) - 1912, 1914
O'Shaunessy, George F. (RI) - 1910, 1912, 1914, 1916, 1922
O'Shea, Bernard (VT) - 1970
O'Shea, Bernard G. (VT) - 1964
O'Shea, George J. (MA) - 1962
O'Shea, Robert S. (IL) - 1972
Osheal, Shaemas (NY) - 1940
Oshel, Val (IL) - 1968, 1974
O'Shinskie, John (PA) - 1948
Oshlo, Richard (IA) - 1968
Osmer, James H. (PA) - 1878
Osmers, Frank C. Jr. (NJ) - 1938, 1940, 1952, 1954, 1956, 1958, 1960, 1962, 1964, 1966
Osser, Maurice S. (PA) - 1948, 1950
Osserman, Stanley (NY) - 1937
Osteen, William L. (NC) - 1968
Osterhaut, J. P. (TX) - 1876, 1884
Ostertag, Harold C. (NY) - 1950, 1952, 1954, 1956, 1958, 1960, 1962
Ostrander (NY) - 1874
O'Sullivan, Daniel E. (VT) - 1914
O'Sullivan, Eugene D. (NE) - 1948, 1950
O'Sullivan, Frank P. (CA) - 1954
O'Sullivan, Humphrey (MA) - 1912, 1924
O'Sullivan, Jeremiah J. (MA) - 1934
O'Sullivan, Jerry (IA) - 1968
O'Sullivan, Patrick B. (CT) - 1922, 1924
O'Sullivan, William Jr. (NJ) - 1980
Oswald, Louis William (IL) - 1946
Otero-Warren, Adelina (NM) - 1922
Otey, Peter J. (VA) - 1894, 1896, 1898, 1900
Otgen, Theobald (WI) - 1893
Otii, Joseph (OK) - 1916
Otis (MO) - 1914
Otis (NJ) - 1904
Otis (NY) - 1878
Otis, John (ME) - 1848
Otis, John G. (KS) - 1890
Otis, Lusien B. (IL) - 1872
Otis, Norton P. (NY) - 1900, 1902
Otjen, Theobald (WI) - 1892, 1894, 1896, 1898, 1900, 1902, 1904
O'Toole, Donald L. (NY) - 1936, 1938, 1940, 1942, 1944, 1946, 1948, 1950, 1952, 1954, 1956
O'Toole, Phelim (MO) - 1944
O'Toole, Thomas J. (PA) - 1952
O'Toole, Thomas P. (CA) - 1964
Otrich, Charles L. (IL) - 1904
Ott, Ed A. (IA) - 1892
Ottenberg, Irving (NY) - 1916
Ottinger, Albert (NY) - 1914
Ottinger, Richard L. (NY) - 1964, 1966, 1968, 1972, 1974, 1976, 1978, 1980, 1982
Otto, Carl (MO) - 1932
Outhwaite, Joseph H. (OH) - 1884, 1886, 1888, 1890, 1892, 1894
Outland, George E. (CA) - 1942, 1944, 1946, 1948
Outlaw, David (NC) - 1845, 1847, 1849, 1851, 1853
Outlaw, George Sr. (NC) - 1825
Overby, W. A. (KY) - 1904
Overcarsh, Orville G. (IN) - 1910
Overmeyer, Arthur W. (OH) - 1914, 1916, 1918, 1922
Overmeyer, D. (KS) - 1888
Overstreet, E. K. Jr. (GA) - 1932
Overstreet, James W. (GA) - 1916, 1918, 1920
Overstreet, Jesse (IN) - 1894, 1896, 1898, 1900, 1902, 1904, 1906, 1908
Overstreet, Russell (OK) - 1944, 1948
Overton, Archibald W. (TN) - 1833
Overton, Edward Jr. (PA) - 1876, 1878, 1882
Overton, John H. (LA) - 1931
Overton, Walter H. (LA) - 1828
Owen (MO) - 1912
Owen (RI) - 1904
Owen, Alfred Dale (IN) - 1900
Owen, Allen F. (GA) - 1848
Owen, Emmett M. (GA) - 1932, 1934, 1936, 1938

Owen, Frank V. (OH) - 1908
Owen, George (AL) - 1825, 1827
Owen, John L. (MI) - 1970
Owen, Marion R. (NJ) - 1902
Owen, Robert Dale (IN) - 1839, 1843, 1845, 1847
Owen, Ruth Bryan (FL) - 1928, 1930
Owen, S. M. (MN) - 1896
Owen, William D. (IN) - 1884, 1886, 1888, 1890
Owen, William E. (WI) - 1954
Owen, William L. (VA) - 1870
Owens (GA) - 1832
Owens (KY) - 1827, 1916
Owens, A. W. (SC) - 1853
Owens, David M. (MA) - 1940
Owens, Dusty (FL) - 1976
Owens, E.S. (IA) - 1892
Owens, George C. (NY) - 1936, 1938
Owens, George W. (GA) - 1834, 1836
Owens, J. Henry (MI) - 1954
Owens, James W. (OH) - 1888, 1890
Owens, John J. (PA) - 1936
Owens, John M. (NY) - 1980
Owens, Leon (VA) - 1962
Owens, Major R. (NY) - 1982, 1984
Owens, Millard M. (FL) - 1920
Owens, Marv (OR) - 1960
Owens, Thomas A. (PA) - 1946
Owens, Thomas L. (IL) - 1946
Owens, Wayne (UT) - 1972
Owens, William (KY) - 1829
Owens, William C. (KY) - 1894, 1904, 1906
Owensby, Don W. (MO) - 1958
Owings, Theodore R. (CA) - 1954
Ownbey, James A. (CO) - 1924
Owsley, Bryan Y. (KY) - 1841, 1843
Oxley, Michael G. (OH) - 1981, 1982, 1984
Oyster, Daniel C. (PA) - 1890
Ozols, Gunars (NY) - 1980
Ozols, Gunars M. (NY) - 1978

P

Pace, Stephen (GA) - 1936, 1938, 1940, 1942, 1944, 1946, 1948
Pacheco, Romualdo (CA) - 1876, 1879, 1880
Pachios, Harold C. (ME) - 1980
Pacht, Jerry (CA) - 1960
Packard, Eliot L. (MA) - 1908
Packard, Jasper (IN) - 1868, 1870, 1872, 1886
Packard, L. C. (AR) - 1914
Packard, Ron (CA) - 1982, 1984
Packard, William B. (PA) - 1900
Packer (PA) - 1834
Packer, Asa (PA) - 1852, 1854
Packer, Horace B. (PA) - 1896, 1898
Packer, John B. (PA) - 1868, 1870, 1872, 1874
Packer, Robert H. (PA) - 1880
Paczkowski, John M. (IL) - 1984
Padden, Frank M. (IL) - 1918, 1922
Padden, John W. (MN) - 1942
Paddock, A. S. (NE) - 1866
Paddock, Charles A. (IN) - 1920
Paddock, George A. (IL) - 1940
Paddock, Porter (IN) - 1914
Padgett, Lemuel P. (TN) - 1900, 1902, 1904, 1906, 1908, 1910, 1912, 1914, 1916, 1918, 1920
Padgett, William L. (NY) - 1931
Padrutt, Arthur L. (WI) - 1953
Padway, Joseph A. (WI) - 1932
Paecht (CT) - 1910
Paeirs, Herbert (TX) - 1922
Page (MO) - 1888
Page, Charles H. (RI) - 1876, 1884, 1887, 1890, 1891, 1892, 1893
Page, Demerville (NY) - 1890
Page, Douglas R. (CA) - 1960
Page, Heber (TX) - 1922
Page, Henry (MD) - 1890
Page, Horace F. (CA) - 1872, 1875, 1876, 1879, 1880, 1882
Page, L. A. (ND) - 1926, 1928
Page, Jay W. (WI) - 1916
Page, Mann (VA) - 1886
Page, Marguerite A. (NJ) - 1984
Page, Oliver J. (MO) - 1934
Page, Robert N. (NC) - 1902, 1904, 1906, 1908, 1910, 1912, 1914

Page, Ronnie (TN) - 1968
Page, Sherman (NY) - 1832, 1834
Page, William T. (MD) - 1902
Page, Winfield E. (MT) - 1954
Pagett, Alfred (MI) - 1892
Paige (OH) - 1862
Paige, Alonzo C. (NY) - 1864
Paige, Calvin D. (MA) - 1914, 1916, 1918, 1920, 1922
Paige, David R. (OH) - 1882, 1884
Paine (NY) - 1856
Paine, Halbert E. (WI) - 1864, 1866, 1868
Paine, Robert T. (NC) - 1855
Paine, Robert Trete Jr. (MA) - 1884
Painken, Louis (NY) - 1928
Painter (PA) - 1852
Painter, Carl F. (MO) - 1964
Palen (NY) - 1842
Palen, Rufus (NY) - 1838
Palestine, Ira J. (NY) - 1946
Palfrey, John G. (MA) - 1846, 1848, 1850
Pallison, John (IA) - 1890
Pallotti, Francis (CT) - 1936
Palm, Andrew J. (PA) - 1906
Palmason, Edward (WA) - 1964
Palmer (MO) - 1880
Palmer (NY) - 1854
Palmer (PA) - 1854
Palmer, A. F. (IA) - 1880
Palmer, A. Mitchell (PA) - 1908, 1910, 1912
Palmer, Clarence E. (RI) - 1926
Palmer, Cyrus M. (PA) - 1926
Palmer, E. C. (IA) - 1886
Palmer, Francis W. (IA) - 1868, 1870
Palmer, Frank M. (IL) - 1896
Palmer, Frederick W. (NY) - 1916, 1918
Palmer, George M. (NY) - 1910
Palmer, George W. (NY) - 1856, 1858
Palmer, Henry W. (PA) - 1900, 1902, 1904, 1908
Palmer, Jackson (MA) - 1920
Palmer, John (NY) - 1836
Palmer, John M. (IL) - 1859
Palmer, John W. (MO) - 1926, 1930, 1932
Palmer, Julian (TN) - 1940
Palmer, K. T. (AZ) - 1940
Palmer, L. T. (OH) - 1932
Palmer, Leroy G. (IA) - 1874
Palmer, Nathan B. (IN) - 1841
Palmer, Q. (IA) - 1872
Palmer, Robert M. (PA) - 1922
Palmieri, Frank A. (NJ) - 1960, 1962
Palmisano, Vincent L. (MD) - 1926, 1928, 1930, 1932, 1934, 1936
Panetti, Edward S. (MD) - 1942
Pangborn, Zebina K. (NJ) - 1898
Panken, Jacob (NY) - 1922, 1930
Panken, Rachel (NY) - 1934
Panneck, Walter (IL) - 1916
Pannill, F. H. Sr. (TX) - 1980
Panuccio, Anthony (SC) - 1978
Panzer, Michael G. (NY) - 1928
Paolino, Thomas J. (RI) - 1948
Paone, Arthur J. (NY) - 1976
Pape, G. Herbert (VT) - 1916
Pappas, Jordan E. (NY) - 1970
Paradis, Dorothy D. (CA) - 1974
Parburt (NY) - 1848
Pardue, George (TN) - 1912
Parent, Daniel L. (MI) - 1966
Parent, Gerald J. (MI) - 1970
Parenti, Michael (VT) - 1974
Pareti, Harold A. (NJ) - 1974
Parish (OH) - 1832, 1843
Parish, Lucian W. (TX) - 1920
Parish, Richard J. (MN) - 1964
Park (TN) - 1900
Park (WI) - 1866
Park, Frank (GA) - 1914, 1916, 1918, 1920, 1922
Park, G. L. (WI) - 1882
Park, Julian (NY) - 1942
Parke, Thomas E. (PA) - 1894
Parker (GA) - 1880
Parker (MO) - 1886
Parker (NJ) - 1830, 1886
Parker (NY) - 1858, 1862
Parker (OH) - 1852
Parker (PA) - 1848
Parker (TN) - 1902
Parker (WI) - 1878

Parker, Abraham X. (NY) - 1880, 1882, 1884, 1886
Parker, Amasa (NY) - 1836
Parker, Amasa J. (NY) - 1914
Parker, Andrew (PA) - 1850
Parker, B. F. (WI) - 1882
Parker, Billy (FL) - 1924
Parker, C. Alex Jr. (KY) - 1962
Parker, D. P. (ME) - 1900
Parker, Don (TX) - 1948
Parker, Ezra (NC) - 1940
Parker, Frederick B. (AL) - 1912
Parker, George H. (IA) - 1864
Parker, George W. (IL) - 1876
Parker, Homer G. (GA) - 1932
Parker, Hosea W. (NH) - 1869, 1871, 1873, 1892
Parker, Isaac C. (MO) - 1870, 1872
Parker, J. W. D. (VT) - 1854
Parker, James (NJ) - 1826, 1828, 1832, 1834
Parker, James D. (NC) - 1920
Parker, James S. (NY) - 1912, 1914, 1916, 1918, 1920, 1922, 1924, 1926, 1928, 1930, 1932
Parker, John J. (NY) - 1962
Parker, John J. (NC) - 1910
Parker, John M. (NY) - 1854, 1856
Parker, Joseph M. (TN) - 1952
Parker, Jr. (NJ) - 1882
Parker, Larry J. (NC) - 1980
Parker, Marshall (SC) - 1974, 1980
Parker, Orrin H. (NY) - 1944
Parker, Peter (MD) - 1970
Parker, Philip P. (IN) - 1960
Parker, Richard (VA) - 1849
Parker, Richard W. (NJ) - 1892, 1894, 1896, 1898, 1900, 1902, 1904, 1906, 1908, 1910, 1912, 1914, 1916, 1918, 1920, 1922
Parker, Robert A. (MA) - 1956
Parker, S. M. (MA) - 1828
Parker, Samuel W. (IN) - 1849, 1851, 1852
Parker, William (PA) - 1912
Parker, William H. (SD) - 1906
Parker, Young Z. (NC) - 1924
Parkhurst (MI) - 1872
Parkhurst (PA) - 1858
Parkins, Nathan (VA) - 1912
Parkinson (PA) - 1886, 1888
Parkinson, Henry D. (KS) - 1948
Parkinson, J. C. (AL) - 1869
Parkinson, John B. (WI) - 1888
Parks, Fred C. (IA) - 1934, 1940
Parks, G. D. A. (IL) - 1872
Parks, Gorham (ME) - 1833, 1834
Parks, Henry M. (WI) - 1910, 1916
Parks, John E. (CA) - 1970
Parks, Marshall (VA) - 1886
Parks, Roy C. (VA) - 1934
Parks, Tilman B. (AR) - 1920, 1922, 1924, 1926, 1928, 1930, 1932, 1934
Parmelee (MI) - 1878
Parment, W. L. (NY) - 1974
Parmenter (NY) - 1876
Parmenter, William (MA) - 1836, 1838, 1840, 1842, 1844, 1854
Parnell, Kevin (Pat) (AK) - 1980
Parr, E. (VA) - 1898
Parr, John (NY) - 1908
Parr, Norman M. (OH) - 1972
Parran, Thomas (MD) - 1910, 1912
Parrau, Thomas (MD) - 1892
Parrett, William F. (IN) - 1888, 1890
Parrillo, Dan (IL) - 1918, 1920
Parriott, James D. (CO) - 1940
Parris, Hollis B. (AL) - 1930
Parris, Stan (VA) - 1972, 1974, 1980, 1982, 1984
Parris, Virgil D. (ME) - 1838
Parrish (AL) - 1872
Parrish, Claude (CA) - 1984
Parrish, Isaac (OH) - 1838, 1840, 1844
Parrish, Lucian W. (TX) - 1918
Parrish, W. H. (KY) - 1882
Parrott, Marcus J. (KS) - 1862, 1874
Parsons (MO) - 1900
Parsons, A. C. (MN) - 1892
Parsons, Bill (FL) - 1968
Parsons, Claude V. (IL) - 1930, 1932, 1934, 1936, 1938, 1940
Parsons, D. C. M. (MO) - 1844
Parsons, Edward Y. (KY) - 1874
Parsons, Herbert (NY) - 1900, 1904, 1906, 1908, 1910

Perley (NY) - 1884
Perlman, Jesse B. (NY) - 1932
Perlman, Max (NY) - 1924
Perlman, Nathan D. (NY) - 1922, 1924, 1926
Perlman, Nathan S. (NY) - 1920
Perrill, Augustus L. (OH) - 1844, 1846
Perrin, Arthur R. (NY) - 1936
Perrin, J. Nick (IL) - 1904, 1918
Perrin, Solomon (NY) - 1934
Perrine, Lewis (NJ) - 1902
Perrini, Joseph J. (NY) - 1952, 1956, 1958
Perry (NJ) - 1904, 1906
Perry (NY) - 1856, 1858, 1872
Perry (SC) - 1834
Perry, Aaron F. (OH) - 1870
Perry, Albertus (NY) - 1864, 1866
Perry, Andrew J. (NY) - 1890
Perry, B. F. (SC) - 1848, 1872
Perry, Donald J. (PA) - 1962
Perry, Eli (NY) - 1870, 1972, 1874
Perry, Ernest B. (NE) - 1936
Perry, Gardner B. (MA) - 1842
Perry, George R. (MI) - 1898
Perry, James W. (NY) - 1898, 1902
Perry, Jesse L. (TN) - 1948
Perry, John J. (ME) - 1854, 1858
Perry, Joseph S. (IL) - 1942
Perry, Matthew J. (SC) - 1974
Perry, Nehemiah (NJ) - 1860, 1862
Perry, Oliver Hazzard (MA) - 1862
Perry, Thomas J. (MD) - 1845
Perry, W. T. (TN) - 1920
Perry, Walter Emmett (AL) - 1966
Perry, Will T. (TN) - 1946
Perry, William H. (SC) - 1884, 1886, 1888
Perryman (MO) - 1856, 1860
Pershing (PA) - 1856, 1858
Person, Henry (GA) - 1884
Person, Seymour H. (MI) - 1930, 1932
Person, Thomas (NC) - 1849
Persons, Henry (GA) - 1878
Persons, Richard S. (NY) - 1924
Persons, Thomas H. (TN) - 1825
Pert, William L. (NY) - 1900
Pestana, H. L. (KS) - 1892
Peter (MD) - 1878
Peter (VA) - 1827
Peter, George (MD) - 1824, 1826
Peter, Henry (PA) - 1914, 1918
Peter, William A. (WV) - 1912
Peters (MO) - 1912
Peters, Andrew J. (MA) - 1906, 1908, 1910, 1912
Peters, David W. (MO) - 1928
Peters, Edward J. (IA) - 1962
Peters, Henry Clay (MA) - 1914
Peters, Henry Clay (NY) - 1906
Peters, John A. (ME) - 1866, 1868, 1870, 1914, 1916, 1918, 1920
Peters, John M. (NY) - 1976
Peters, John Michael (NY) - 1978
Peters, Marvin J. (IL) - 1948
Peters, Mason S. (KS) - 1896, 1898, 1900, 1906
Peters, Mathews H. (IL) - 1886
Peters, Mel E. (TX) - 1926
Peters, Ralph A. (NY) - 1938
Peters, Samuel (LA) - 1872
Peters, Samuel R. (KS) - 1882, 1884, 1886, 1888
Petersen, Andrew N. (NY) - 1920, 1922, 1924
Petersen, Harold (CA) - 1962
Petersen, John C. (KS) - 1974
Peterson (MN) - 1906
Peterson, Arthur L. (WI) - 1956
Peterson, B. (AL) - 1857
Peterson, Bob (FL) - 1962
Peterson, Charles D. (MN) - 1941
Peterson, Collin C. (MN) - 1984
Peterson, Dave (MN) - 1984
Peterson, Duane K. (NE) - 1948, 1950
Peterson, Ed C. (NV) - 1936
Peterson, Everette L. (NC) - 1952
Peterson, F. H. (MN) - 1924
Peterson, Frank A. (NE) - 1918, 1920
Peterson, Geoffrey G. (CT) - 1976
Peterson, Gust C. (NY) - 1920
Peterson, Harold L. (MN) - 1940
Peterson, Henry K. (IA) - 1936
Peterson, Howard V. (AZ) - 1962
Peterson, Hugh (GA) - 1934, 1936, 1938, 1940, 1942, 1944
Peterson, J. E. (GA) - 1896

Peterson, J. Hardin (FL) - 1932, 1934, 1936, 1938, 1940, 1942, 1944, 1946, 1948
Peterson, J. L. (MN) - 1932
Peterson, John A. (CA) - 1950
Peterson, John B. (IN) - 1910, 1912, 1914
Peterson, John H. (NY) - 1950
Peterson, Morris Blaine (UT) - 1958, 1960, 1962
Peterson, Payson (WA) - 1934, 1936, 1940, 1942, 1944, 1946, 1948, 1956, 1960
Peterson, Stephen M. (IA) - 1964
Peterson, W. O. (CO) - 1934
Petito, Joseph J. (NY) - 1950
Petri, Kenneth M. (OH) - 1940
Petri, Thomas E. (WI) - 1979, 1980, 1982, 1984
Petrie, Alexander P. (IL) - 1884
Petrie, George (NY) - 1846
Petrie, William W. (WI) - 1976, 1978
Petrikin, David (PA) - 1836, 1838
Petro J. William (OH) - 1968, 1970
Petroni, Romeo G. (CT) - 1966
Pettengill, Samuel B. (IN) - 1930, 1932, 1934
Pettibone, Augustus H. (TN) - 1878, 1880, 1882, 1884
Pettibone, John S. (VT) - 1834
Pettigrew, Ebenezer (NC) - 1835
Pettingell, Charles I. (MA) - 1922
Pettingill, Samuel B. (IN) - 1936
Pettis, Andrew A. (ME) - 1944
Pettis, Jerry L. (CA) - 1964, 1966, 1968, 1970, 1972, 1974
Pettis, Ron (CA) - 1975
Pettis, Shirley N. (CA) - 1975, 1976
Pettis, Spencer D. (MO) - 1828, 1831
Pettit (AL) - 1843
Pettit (IN) - 1862
Pettit (PA) - 1841
Pettit, H. Frank (NJ) - 1948, 1952
Pettit, John (IN) - 1843, 1845, 1847
Pettit, John U. (IN) - 1854, 1856, 1858
Pettit, Thomas S. (KY) - 1892
Pettus, S. Newton (PA) - 1868
Petty, Emery S. (CA) - 1956, 1958
Petty, Judy (AR) - 1974, 1984
Pettyjohn (MO) - 1890
Peyser, Minna Post (NY) - 1976
Peyser, Peter A. (NY) - 1970, 1972, 1974, 1978, 1980, 1982
Peyser, Theodore A. (NY) - 1932, 1934, 1936
Peyton, Balie (TN) - 1833, 1835, 1867
Peyton, Joseph H. (TN) - 1843, 1845
Peyton, Samuel O. (KY) - 1847, 1849, 1855, 1857, 1859
Pfaff, Otto (NY) - 1916
Pfeifer, Herbert J. (OH) - 1968
Pfeifer, Joseph L. (NY) - 1934, 1936, 1938, 1940, 1942, 1944, 1946, 1948
Pfeiffer, George Jr. (NJ) - 1900
Pfeiffer, Rudolf (IL) - 1912
Pfeiffer, William L. (NY) - 1948
Pfender, William (PA) - 1972
Pflum, John E. (PA) - 1970
Pfost, Gracie B. Mrs. (ID) - 1950, 1952, 1954, 1956, 1958, 1960
Phair, Ronald E. (OR) - 1960
Pharr, Henry N. (LA) - 1904
Pheiffer, William T. (NY) - 1940, 1942
Phelan (TN) - 1902
Phelan, James (TN) - 1886, 1888
Phelan, John (NY) - 1892
Phelan, Michael F. (MA) - 1912, 1914, 1916, 1918, 1920
Phelan, Thomas H. (OR) - 1982
Phelen, Thomas C. (TN) - 1922
Phelps (KY) - 1837
Phelps (MO) - 1862
Phelps (PA) - 1860
Phelps (VA) - 1869
Phelps, Charles (CT) - 1839
Phelps, Charles E. (MD) - 1864, 1866
Phelps, Darwin (PA) - 1868
Phelps, Delos P. (IL) - 1878
Phelps, Early C. (IL) - 1944
Phelps, Elisha (CT) - 1825, 1827, 1829
Phelps, Horace (CO) - 1914
Phelps, Isaac H. (OH) - 1898
Phelps, J. Arthur (CO) - 1936
Phelps, James (CT) - 1875, 1876, 1878, 1880
Phelps, John M. (WV) - 1864

Phelps, John S. (MO) - 1844, 1846, 1848, 1850, 1852, 1854, 1856, 1858, 1860
Phelps, L. G. (CA) - 1888
Phelps, Lancelot (CT) - 1834, 1835, 1837
Phelps, Oliver (NY) - 1834
Phelps, Timothy G. (CA) - 1861, 1867
Phelps, Wallace H. (OH) - 1886
Phelps, William W. (MN) - 1857
Phelps, William W. (NJ) - 1872, 1874, 1882, 1884, 1886
Philbin, John J. (IL) - 1902
Philbin, Philip J. (MA) - 1942, 1944, 1946, 1948, 1950, 1952, 1954, 1956, 1958, 1960, 1962, 1964, 1966, 1968, 1970
Philbrick, O. H. (CA) - 1908
Philbrick, William (ME) - 1878, 1880
Philip (NY) - 1870
Philip, George (SD) - 1922
Philipbar, Charles W. (NY) - 1916
Philips, John F. (MO) - 1874, 1880
Phillips (AL) - 1847
Phillips (KS) - 1882
Phillips (MO) - 1886, 1932
Phillips (PA) - 1872
Phillips, Alfred J. (NY) - 1944
Phillips, Alfred N. Jr. (CT) - 1936, 1938
Phillips, B. Leonard (SC) - 1970, 1972
Phillips, David L. (IL) - 1858, 1876
Phillips, Dayton E. (TN) - 1946, 1948, 1950
Phillips, Fremont O. (OH) - 1898, 1900
Phillips, Hal (CA) - 1982
Phillips, Helen (NY) - 1950
Phillips, Henry M. (PA) - 1856, 1858
Phillips, Howard (NY) - 1904
Phillips, Hubert (CA) - 1946
Phillips, Isidor (NY) - 1904
Phillips, J. M. (WA) - 1922
Phillips, James A. (NY) - 1946
Phillips, James H. (CA) - 1954
Phillips, Joe B. (TX) - 1964
Phillips, John (CA) - 1942, 1944, 1946, 1948, 1950, 1952, 1954
Phillips, John A. (CT) - 1980, 1982
Phillips, John F. (MO) - 1868
Phillips, John R. Jr. (NJ) - 1928
Phillips, Len (SC) - 1974
Phillips, Philip (AL) - 1853
Phillips, Samuel (MA) - 1828
Phillips, Stephen C. (MA) - 1834, 1836
Phillips, Thomas W. (PA) - 1890, 1892, 1894
Phillips, Thomas W. Jr. (PA) - 1922, 1924
Phillips, W. N. (GA) - 1930
Phillips, W. W. (CA) - 1916
Phillips, William A. (KS) - 1872, 1874, 1876, 1890
Phillips, William J. (PA) - 1980
Philpot, S. B. (IA) - 1912
Philps (PA) - 1854
Philson (PA) - 1841, 1842
Phinney, Sylvanus B. (MA) - 1864
Phister, Elijah C. (KY) - 1878, 1880
Phlpa (OH) - 1862
Phoebus, Harry T. (MD) - 1924, 1932
Phoenix, J. Phillips (NY) - 1842, 1846, 1848
Piacentini, John (OR) - 1974
Piarulli, Michael J. (NJ) - 1966
Picall, William (NY) - 1846
Picken, George F. (NY) - 1942
Pickens, Francis W. (SC) - 1834, 1836, 1838, 1840, 1853
Pickering (TN) - 1904
Picket, Charles E. (IA) - 1912
Pickett (MO) - 1916
Pickett (NJ) - 1906
Pickett (TN) - 1857
Pickett, Charles E. (IA) - 1908, 1910
Pickett, Dovie T. (MI) - 1978
Pickett, C. Leon (TX) - 1982
Pickett, G. B. (TX) - 1886
Pickett, John F. (CT) - 1970
Pickett, Roscoe (GA) - 1942, 1964
Pickett, T. (GA) - 1890, 1904
Pickett, T. J. (KY) - 1874
Pickett, Thaddeus K. (GA) - 1888, 1892
Pickett, Tom (TX) - 1944, 1946, 1948, 1950
Pickle, J. J. (Jake) (TX) - 1964, 1966, 1968, 1970, 1972, 1974, 1976, 1978, 1980, 1982, 1984
Pickler (MO) - 1890
Pickler, John A. (SD) - 1889, 1890, 1892, 1894
Pickrel, William G. (OH) - 1920
Pickrell, James H. (IL) - 1874
Picone, Dominic E. (NY) - 1922
Pidcock, James N. (NJ) - 1884, 1886

Pierce (GA) - 1876
Pierce (ME) - 1916
Pierce (MS) - 1868
Pierce, Alfred R. (NJ) - 1952
Pierce, Charles W. (AL) - 1868
Pierce, Edward C. (MI) - 1976
Pierce, Edward L. (MA) - 1890
Pierce, Franklin (NH) - 1833, 1835
Pierce, George B. (MA) - 1900
Pierce, Henry H. Jr. (CT) - 1954
Pierce, Henry L. (MA) - 1874
Pierce, Isaac (NY) - 1830
Pierce, J. M. (VT) - 1872
Pierce, Jeremiah S. (KY) - 1853
Pierce, John (PA) - 1904
Pierce, John J. (PA) - 1854
Pierce, Orrin R. (MI) - 1898
Pierce, Ray V. (NY) - 1878
Pierce, Rice A. (TN) - 1882, 1888, 1890, 1896, 1898, 1900, 1902
Pierce, Thomas W. (PA) - 1890
Pierce, Wallace E. (NY) - 1938
Pierce, Walter M. (OR) - 1928, 1932, 1934, 1936, 1938, 1940, 1942
Pierce, William C. (IL) - 1912
Piercey, John H. (MI) - 1952
Piercy, Henry Clay (NY) - 1904
Pierpoint (VT) - 1852
Pierpont (NY) 1874, 1878, 1882, 1884
Pierpont, Robert (VT) - 1834
Pierpont, Ross Z. (MD) - 1970, 1984
Pierson, Atwood (TN) - 1894
Pierson, Charles T. (NY) - 1880
Pierson, Frederick T. (NY) - 1922
Pierson, Isaac (NJ) - 1826, 1828
Pierson, Job (NY) - 1830, 1832, 1834
Pierson, Oruan (IL) - 1886
Pierson, Stuart E. (IL) - 1938
Pierstorff, W. F. (WI) - 1914
Pigott, James P. (CT) - 1892, 1894
Pigott, Joe (MS) - 1968
Pike (ME) - 1847
Pike (MO) - 1872
Pike, Austin F. (NH) - 1873, 1875
Pike, B. R. (PA) - 1914
Pike, Frederick Augustus (ME) - 1860, 1862, 1864, 1866, 1872
Pike, James (NH) - 1855, 1857
Pike, James S. (ME) - 1850
Pike, Otis G. (NY) - 1958, 1960, 1962, 1964, 1966, 1968, 1970, 1972, 1974, 1976
Pikiel, Rena E. (IL) - 1938, 1942
Pilcher, John L. (GA) - 1953, 1954, 1956, 1958, 1960, 1962
Pile, C. E. (KS) - 1918
Pile, J. Charles (WI) - 1936
Pile, William A. (MO) - 1866, 1868
Pillart, Ignatius J. (PA) - 1946
Pilley, S. A. (AL) - 1890
Pillich, Walter J. (NY) - 1982
Pilliod, Gerard (OH) - 1932
Pillion, John R. (NY) - 1952, 1954, 1956, 1958, 1960, 1962, 1964, 1966
Pillion, Kieran E. (NJ) - 1980
Pillon, Gregory M. (MI) - 1952, 1954
Pillow, George W. (IL) - 1890
Pillsbury (ME) - 1856
Pillsbury, Kent L. (WI) - 1952
Pillsbury, Rosecrans W. (NH) - 1920
Pillsbury, Timothy (TX) - 1846
Pilsbury, Timothy (ME) - 1836
Pinchback, Pinckney B. S. (LA) - 1872
Pinchot, Amos R. E. (NY) - 1912
Pinchot, Cornelia Bryce (PA) - 1928
Pinckney, Henry L. (SC) - 1833, 1834, 1836
Pinckney, John M. (TX) - 1904
Pinckney, Joseph C. (NY) - 1868
Pindar, John S. (NY) - 1880, 1884, 1888, 1890
Pinkham (MO) - 1892
Pinkney, David J. (IL) - 1874
Pino, James O. (MI) - 1958
Pinson, Clyde B. (WV) - 1960, 1962
Pinto, Nicholas Howard (NY) - 1932
Piolet, Victor E. (PA) - 1864, 1868, 1886
Piolett, (PA) - 1872
Piper (NY) - 1842, 1844, 1850
Piper, William (PA) - 1826
Piper, William A. (CA) - 1872, 1875, 1876
Pipes, David W. Jr. (LA) - 1940
Pipkin, Isaac (NC) - 1835
Pirce, William A. (RI) - 1884, 1887
Pirnie, Alexander (NY) - 1958, 1960, 1962, 1964, 1966, 1968, 1970

Sauer, Mack (OH) - 1932
Sauerhering, Edward (WI) - 1894
Sauerhering, Edward (WI) - 1896
Saul, E. Adele Scott (PA) - 1940
Saund, Dalip S. (CA) - 1956, 1958, 1960, 1962
Saunders (LA) - 1847
Saunders (TN) - 1865
Saunders, Dave L. (CA) - 1938
Saunders, Edward W. (VA) - 1906, 1908, 1910, 1912, 1914, 1916, 1918
Saunders, Francis C. (NY) - 1970
Saunders, JoAnn (FL) - 1974, 1976
Saunders, John I. (KS) - 1912
Saunders, Romulus M. (NC) - 1825, 1841, 1843
Saunders, Vince (NV) - 1980
Saunders, Warren D. (VA) - 1974, 1976
Saussaman, Harry B. (PA) - 1916
Sauthoff, Harry (WI) - 1934, 1936, 1938, 1940, 1942
Savage (NY) - 1860
Savage (TN) - 1859
Savage, Carl (GA) - 1974
Savage, Charles R. (WA) - 1944, 1946, 1948
Savage, Gus (IL) - 1980, 1982, 1984
Savage, James W. (NE) - 1874
Savage, John (NY) - 1868
Savage, John H. (TN) - 1849, 1851, 1855, 1857
Savage, John S. (OH) - 1874, 1876
Savage, Wallace (TX) - 1954
Savery (PA) - 1850
Savin, Moses A. (CT) - 1962
Savino, Frank A. (WI) - 1976
Savoie, Gene (AZ) - 1972
Savory, George (MA) - 1828
Sawtelle, Cullen (ME) - 1844, 1848
Sawyer (CT) - 1880
Sawyer (NH) - 1845
Sawyer, Arthur T. (NY) - 1948
Sawyer, Charles (OH) - 1930
Sawyer, E. J. (SC) - 1892
Sawyer, Edward J. (MA) - 1882
Sawyer, Harold S. (MI) - 1976, 1978, 1980, 1982
Sawyer, John G. (NY) - 1884, 1886, 1888
Sawyer, Lemuel (NC) - 1825, 1827, 1829
Sawyer, Lewis E. (AR) - 1922
Sawyer, O. C. (VT) - 1912
Sawyer, Philetus (WI) - 1864, 1866, 1868, 1870, 1872
Sawyer, Samuel L. (MO) - 1878
Sawyer, Samuel T. (NC) - 1837, 1839
Sawyer, William (OH) - 1838, 1840, 1844, 1846
Sawyer, William C. (MA) - 1980
Sawyer, William T. (OH) - 1896
Sawyers, William Orr (Tom) (MO) - 1946
Saxton, H. James (NJ) - 1984
Sayers, James E. (PA) - 1880
Sayers, Joseph D. (TX) - 1884, 1886, 1888, 1890, 1892, 1894, 1896
Sayler, Henry B. (IN) - 1872
Sayler, Milton (OH) - 1870, 1872, 1874, 1876, 1878
Sayler, Walter B. (IL) - 1916
Sayles (MA) - 1888
Sayles, Lycurgus (RI) - 1878
Sayles, Stephen D. (IN) - 1888
Sayles, Welcome B. (RI) - 1851
Saylor, John L. (PA) - 1904
Saylor, John P. (PA) - 1950, 1952, 1954, 1956, 1958, 1960, 1962, 1964, 1966, 1968, 1970, 1972
Sayre, Mornell (NJ) - 1922, 1924, 1932
Sayre, Woodrow Wilson (CA) - 1952
Scaggs, Emmet F. (WV) - 1926
Scales, Alfred M. (NC) - 1855, 1857, 1859, 1874, 1876, 1878, 1880, 1882
Scalf, Charles E. (PA) - 1962
Scalf, W. D. (KY) - 1952, 1956, 1958
Scalzitti, Clement R. (PA) - 1974
Scamman, George (ME) - 1844
Scamman, John F. (ME) - 1844
Scammon, J. Young (IL) - 1848
Scammon, John (NH) - 1844
Scandrett, Richard B. Jr. (NY) - 1938
Scanlan, Charles V. (NY) - 1954, 1958
Scanlan, Martin J. (NV) - 1914, 1916
Scanlon, Michael A. (MA) - 1918
Scanlon, Michael T. (OH) - 1976
Scanlon, Thomas E. (PA) - 1940, 1942, 1944

Scannel, Joseph J. (DE) - 1952
Scannell, William F. (IL) - 1964
Scarborough, Robert B. (SC) - 1900, 1902
Scates, John C. (ME) - 1908, 1914
Schaap, Michael (NY) - 1916
Schaar, John G. (IL) - 1890
Schade, Terrence J. (PA) - 1976
Schade, W. John Jr. (IL) - 1974
Schadeberg, Henry C. (WI) - 1960, 1962, 1964, 1966, 1968, 1970
Schaefer, Dan L. (CO) - 1983, 1984
Schaefer, Edwin M. (IL) - 1932, 1934, 1936, 1938, 1940
Schaefer, Elmer P. (IL) - 1930
Schaefer, Howard G. (CA) - 1978
Schaefer, Louis (OH) - 1866
Schaefer, Mike (CA) - 1968
Schaefer, Walter (CA) - 1936
Schaeffer, Morris (NY) - 1944
Schaeffer, Tim (TN) - 1974
Schaeffer, William A. (IL) - 1924
Schaeffer, William R. Jr. (NY) - 1978
Schaeffler, Frank C. (NY) - 1902
Schafer, John C. (WI) - 1922, 1924, 1926, 1928, 1930, 1932, 1934, 1936, 1938, 1940, 1942, 1952, 1954
Schaffenegger, John (IL) - 1952
Schaffer, Max (NY) - 1914
Schaffer, Russell T. (MD) - 1980
Schaffner, William G. (OH) - 1984
Schall, Thomas D. (MN) - 1912, 1914, 1916, 1918, 1920, 1922
Schaller (MN) - 1900
Schallern, Eugene (WI) - 1942
Schanen, William F. (WI) - 1922
Schanke, A. M. (IA) - 1922
Schantz, Horace W. (PA) - 1916
Schaux, Nicolas (CT) - 1980
Schector, Morris S. (NY) - 1926
Scheenline, Isaiah (PA) - 1910
Scheftel, Stuart (NY) - 1942
Scheirer, Henry V. (PA) - 1940
Schell (PA) - 1860
Schell, John W. (AL) - 1900
Schell, Richard (NY) - 1874
Schellenger, Waldo E. (IL) - 1956
Schenck, Ferdinand S. (NJ) - 1832, 1834
Schenck, Paul F. (OH) - 1950, 1952, 1954, 1956, 1958, 1960, 1962, 1964
Shenck, Robert C. (OH) - 1843, 1844, 1846, 1848, 1862, 1864, 1866, 1868, 1870
Schendel, Harry (MO) - 1951
Schenk (NJ) - 1890
Schenk, Herbert C. (WI) - 1944
Schenken, Charles (TX) - 1902
Scher, David (NY) - 1946
Scherer, Gordon H. (OH) - 1952, 1954, 1956, 1958, 1960
Scherle, William J. (IA) - 1966, 1968, 1970, 1972, 1974
Schermerhorn, Abraham M. (NY) - 1848, 1850
Schermerhorn, Simon J. (NY) - 1892
Scherr, J. Robert (MD) - 1982
Scheuer, James H. (NY) - 1964, 1966, 1968, 1970, 1974, 1976, 1978, 1980, 1982, 1984
Scheuermann, David H. Sr. (LA) - 1976
Schiaffo, Alfred D. (NJ) - 1972
Schiemann, Fred E. (NY) - 1950
Schiff, Jacob R. (NY) - 1906
Schiffler, Andrew C. (WV) - 1938, 1940, 1942, 1944
Schiflersmith, Frank (IL) - 1912, 1914
Schifrin, Louis (NY) - 1952, 1954
Schilling, George A. (IL) - 1878
Schilling, Henry (IL) - 1920
Schilling, Robert (IL) - 1896, 1898
Schilson, Donald L. (IL) - 1968
Schirm, Charles R. (MD) - 1900, 1902
Schirmer, John G. (PA) - 1908
Schisler, Gale (IL) - 1964, 1966
Schissler, James J. (PA) - 1956
Schlaeger, Victor L. (IL) - 1932
Schlafly, Phyllis Stewart (IL) - 1952, 1960, 1970
Schlegel, Henry W. (PA) - 1918, 1920
Schleicher, Gustave (TX) - 1874, 1876, 1878
Schleper, Henry J. (MO) - 1924
Schlesinger, Bert (CA) - 1912
Schlessel, Bennett I. (NY) - 1950
Schlessinger, Gary (CA) - 1969
Schley (MD) - 1880
Schley, William (GA) - 1832, 1834

Schlingheyde, Leslie B. (CA) - 1952
Schlipf, William Jr. (PA) - 1908, 1912
Schlissel, Harry (NY) - 1924
Schlitz, Lester E. (VA) - 1974
Schlossberg, David A. (NY) - 1946
Schlossberg, Joseph (NY) - 1938
Schlosser, Chalmer (IN) - 1916, 1918
Schluter, William E. (NJ) - 1976
Schmarkey, John C. (AL) - 1970
Schmauch, Ray (KY) - 1946
Schmedeman, Albert C. (WI) - 1910
Schmidhauser, John R. (IA) - 1964, 1966, 1968
Schmidt, Albert C. (WI) - 1914
Schmidt, Edward (OH) - 1910
Schmidt, Herman (NJ) - 1974
Schmidt, John O. (NE) - 1922, 1924
Schmidt, John W. (MN) - 1934
Schmidt, Ludwig (NY) - 1914
Schmidt, William F. H. (IL) - 1958
Schmiedeskamp, Henry E. (IL) - 1924
Schmitt, Philip H. (NY) - 1908
Schmitt, William Patrick (OK) - 1972
Schmitz (MO) - 1902
Schmitz, J. B. (TX) - 1922
Schmitz, John G. (CA) - 1970
Schmudde, Henry F. (IL) - 1940
Schneck, Robert M. (NY) - 1970
Schneebeli, Gustav A. (PA) - 1904, 1906, 1908
Schneebeli, Herman T. (PA) - 1960, 1962, 1964, 1966, 1968, 1970, 1972, 1974
Schneid, Hyman (IL) - 1932
Schneider, C. S. (IL) - 1908, 1918, 1920, 1930
Schneider, Claudine (RI) - 1978, 1980, 1982, 1984
Schneider, E. B. (OH) - 1926
Schneider, Ernest B. (OH) - 1902, 1904
Schneider, George J. (WI) - 1922, 1924, 1926, 1928, 1930, 1932, 1934, 1936, 1938
Schneider, Jerome P. (NY) - 1958, 1960
Schneider, L. V. (SD) - 1908
Schneider, Robert (TX) - 1968
Schneir, Ned (NY) - 1976
Schnitzpan, William (NY) - 1902
Schnur, Frank (IL) - 1934
Schnur, Warren L. (NY) - 1954
Schoen, Douglas F. (NY) - 1983
Schoening, Robert W. (IL) - 1904
Schofield, George A. (MA) - 1906, 1912, 1914
Schofield, George S. (NY) - 1914
Scholl, Inez M. (IN) - 1954
Scholle (MN) - 1906
Scholle, August (MI) - 1970
Schonberg, Mary G. (NY) - 1916
School, J. T. (PA) - 1876
Schoolcraft, John L. (NY) - 1848, 1850
Schooley, Edward K. (IL) - 1936
Schooley, Herschel (MO) - 1936
Schooley, Thomas M. Jr. (PA) - 1964
Schoonard, Forest A. (MI) - 1950
Schoonmaker, Marius (NY) - 1850
Schrader, Digter J. (AL) - 1972
Schreiber, Ed (CO) - 1980
Schroeder, Anthony C. (MO) - 1958, 1960, 1962, 1964, 1966, 1970
Schroeder, Lou (OH) - 1978
Schroeder, Patricia (CO) - 1972, 1974, 1976, 1978, 1980, 1982, 1984
Schroeder, Raymond W. (NJ) - 1964
Schroyer, Richard L. (PA) - 1938
Schrump, Raymond C. (NC) - 1978
Schubert, A. H. (WI) - 1926, 1928
Schuck, Charles J. (WV) - 1918
Schuerman, William F. (KY) - 1906
Schuette, Bill (MI) - 1984
Schuetz, Leonard W. (IL) - 1930, 1932, 1934, 1936, 1938, 1940, 1942
Schuh, David W. (CA) - 1968
Schuler, Otto (NY) - 1944
Schulken, James B. (NC) - 1906
Schullman, Alexander H. (PA) - 1934
Schulte, William T. (IN) - 1932, 1934, 1936, 1938, 1940
Schultz, Edward A. (PA) - 1946
Schultz, Emanuel (OH) - 1878, 1880
Schultz, Fred F. (IN) - 1936
Schultz, Malvern E. (OH) - 1958
Schultz, Robert C. (WI) - 1952
Schulz, E. C. (KY) - 1932
Schulz, Frank F. (NY) - 1912
Schulz, William Adams (NY) - 1952

Schulze, Richard T. (PA) - 1974, 1976, 1978, 1980, 1982, 1984
Schumacher, Ervin (ND) - 1950
Schumacher, John G. (NY) - 1868
Schumaker, John G. (NY) - 1872, 1874
Schumer, Charles E. (NY) - 1980, 1982, 1984
Schuster, Bob (AZ) - 1984
Schutt, Garret J. (IL) - 1944
Schutz, Alvin (KY) - 1938
Schutz, Carl F. (IL) - 1918
Schutz, J. Raymond (IN) - 1932
Schwab, Frank X. (NY) - 1966
Schwabe, George B. (OK) - 1944, 1946, 1948, 1950
Schwabe, Max (MO) - 1942, 1944, 1946, 1948, 1950, 1952
Schwandt, Russel (MN) - 1960
Schwartz (NY) - 1888
Schwartz, Albert E. (NY) - 1922
Schwartz, Charles L. (IL) - 1946
Schwartz, Emmett A. (CA) - 1960
Schwartz, Irving A. (NY) - 1980
Schwartz, John (PA) - 1858
Schwartz, Morton L. (MO) - 1960
Schwartz, Ron (CA) - 1980
Schwartz, Sidney A. (PA) - 1912
Schwatka, J. (MD) - 1898
Schweiker, Richard S. (PA) - 1960, 1962, 1964, 1966
Schweikert (NJ) - 1916
Schweinhaut, Margaret C. (MD) - 1968
Schwendler, Louis J. (NY) - 1922
Schwengel, Fred (IA) - 1954, 1956, 1958, 1960, 1962, 1964, 1966, 1968, 1970, 1972
Schwenk, Ladislaus W. (NY) - 1910
Schweppe, Ernest (WI) - 1900
Schwerdtfeger, Carl R. (IL) - 1982, 1984
Schwert, Hattie E. (NY) - 1941
Schwert, Pius L. (NY) - 1938, 1940
Schwick, Charles (NY) - 1900
Schwiebert, Erwin H. (ID) - 1954, 1962
Schwinger, Louis C. (MI) - 1938, 1940, 1948
Schwolsky, Harry (CT) - 1950
Scialabba, Samuel R. (NY) - 1946
Scifres, Ben M. (IN) - 1920
Scimeca, Anthony (NY) - 1946
Scoblick, James P. (PA) - 1946
Scofield (NY) - 1878
Scofield, Glenni W. (PA) - 1862, 1864, 1866, 1868, 1870, 1972
Scoggin, J. L. (TX) - 1916
Scoggins, Dennis (TX) - 1982
Scola, Robert N. (MA) - 1960
Scoles (NY) - 1842
Sconing, C. L. (PA) - 1974
Scopes, J. T. (KY) - 1932
Scott (AL) - 1835
Scott (IN) - 1862
Scott (MO) - 1860
Scott (VA) - 1839, 1855
Scott, Anna Wall (IL) - 1976
Scott, Audrey (MD) - 1981
Scott, Byron N. (CA) - 1934, 1936, 1938, 1940
Scott, Charles F. (KS) - 1900, 1902, 1904, 1906, 1908
Scott, Charles L. (CA) - 1856, 1858
Scott, Donald E. (OH) - 1984
Scott, E. G. (PA) - 1870
Scott, Ed (CO) - 1976, 1978
Scott, Edward W. (MS) - 1960
Scott, Frank D. (MI) - 1914, 1916, 1918, 1920, 1922, 1924
Scott, G. F. (WV) - 1876
Scott, George (NE) - 1888
Scott, George C. (IA) - 1912, 1914, 1916
Scott, George Cole (VA) - 1932
Scott, George W. (WA) - 1902
Scott, Hardie (PA) - 1946, 1948, 1950
Scott, Harvey D. (IN) - 1854
Scott, Horace (KY) - 1878
Scott, Horace C. (PA) - 1956
Scott, Howard T. (PA) - 1942
Scott, Hugh (MO) - 1968
Scott, Hugh D. Jr. (PA) - 1940, 1942, 1944, 1946, 1948, 1950, 1952, 1954, 1956
Scott, James R. (IL) - 1880
Scott, Jerry C. (NC) - 1972
Scott, John (ME) - 1898, 1899
Scott, John (MO) - 1824, 1826
Scott, John (PA) - 1828
Scott, John C. (TX) - 1902

Swanjord, O. F. (MN) - 1924
Swank, Fletcher B. (OK) - 1920, 1922, 1924, 1926, 1928, 1930, 1932
Swank, Richard A. (PA) - 1954
Swank, Thomas P. (MA) - 1976, 1978, 1980, 1982, 1984
Swann, Edward (NY) - 1904
Swann, J. (MD) - 1898
Swann, J. C. Dr. (AL) - 1934
Swann, John S. (WV) - 1872
Swann, Thomas (MD) - 1868, 1870, 1872, 1874, 1876
Swanson (MN) - 1916
Swanson, Albert F. (IA) - 1938, 1940
Swanson, Charles E. (IA) - 1928, 1930, 1932, 1934
Swanson, Claude A. (VA) - 1892, 1894, 1896, 1898, 1900, 1902, 1904
Swanson, Thomas E. (FL) - 1936
Swanson, Walter A. (OR) - 1952
Swarr, Hiram B. (PA) - 1868
Swartz, Joshua W. (PA) - 1924
Swasey, George T. (VT) - 1900
Swasey, Horatio E. (MA) - 1882, 1884
Swasey, John P. (ME) - 1908, 1910
Swayne, John T. (TN) - 1847
Swayze, Ruth (NJ) - 1966
Swayzie, C. C. (LA) - 1884
Swearingen, Henry (OH) - 1838
Sweat, Lorenzo D. M. (ME) - 1862, 1864, 1866
Sweat, M. (ME) - 1850
Sweatland, A. E. (TX) - 1916, 1924
Sweeney (MO) - 1924
Sweeney, Arthur (OH) - 1926
Sweeney, George E. (NY) - 1970
Sweeney, James J. (PA) - 1922
Sweeney, John D. (WV) - 1926
Sweeney, Mac (TX) - 1984
Sweeney, Marie R. (OH) - 1942
Sweeney, Martin L. (OH) - 1932, 1934, 1936, 1938, 1940
Sweeney, Robert E. (OH) - 1964
Sweeney, Tom (WV) - 1968
Sweeney, William N. (KY) - 1868
Sweeny, George (OH) - 1838, 1840
Sweet (NY) - 1844, 1876
Sweet, Burton E. (IA) - 1914, 1916, 1918, 1920
Sweet, Edwin F. (MI) - 1908, 1910, 1912
Sweet, Ezra (NY) - 1840
Sweet, Martin P. (IL) - 1844, 1850
Sweet, Thaddeus C. (NY) - 1923, 1924, 1926
Sweet, Willis (ID) - 1890, 1892
Sweetser, Charles (OH) - 1850
Sweetser, Theodore H. (MA) - 1864
Sweetzer, Charles (OH) - 1848
Sweetzey, Claude B. (MD) - 1932
Sweney, Joseph H. (IA) - 1888
Swenson, Erling (MN) - 1914, 1930
Swenson, John Richard (NE) - 1964
Swett, L. B. (ME) - 1918
Swett, Leonard (IL) - 1862
Swick, J. Howard (PA) - 1926, 1928, 1930, 1932, 1934
Swift, Al (WA) - 1978, 1980, 1982, 1984
Swift, Benjamin (VT) - 1824, 1826, 1828
Swift, H. A. (MN) - 1857
Swift, John F. (CA) - 1875
Swift, Oscar W. (NY) - 1912, 1914, 1916, 1918
Swigert, Jack (CO) - 1982
Swinburne, John (NY) - 1884, 1886
Swindall, Charles (OK) - 1920
Swindall, Pat (GA) - 1984
Swing, Philip D. (CA) - 1920, 1922, 1924, 1926, 1928, 1930
Switzer, J. B. (PA) - 1866
Switzer, Robert M. (OH) - 1910, 1912, 1914, 1916
Switzler, William F. (MO) - 1866, 1868
Swonger, William B. (OH) - 1938
Swoope, William Irvin (PA) - 1922, 1924
Swope, Armstead M. (KY) - 1888
Swope, Guy J. (PA) - 1936, 1938, 1956
Swope, John Augustus (PA) - 1884
Swope, John W. (KY) - 1964
Swope, King (KY) - 1920
Swope, Samuel F. (KY) - 1855
Syester (MD) - 1864
Sykes, A. (IA) - 1924
Sykes, George (NJ) - 1843, 1844
Sylk, William H. (PA) - 1942
Sylvester (NY) - 1860
Sylvester, Fred H. (NY) - 1920

Sylvester, Peter (NY) - 1846
Syme, David A. (IL) - 1904
Symes, George G. (CO) - 1884, 1886
Symes, George G. (KY) - 1867
Symington, Fife (MD) - 1958, 1960
Symington, James W. (MO) - 1968, 1970, 1972, 1974
Symington, John Fife Jr. (MD) - 1962
Symms, Steven D. (ID) - 1972, 1974, 1976, 1978
Symons, T. W. Jr. (WA) - 1930
Synar, Mike (OK) - 1978, 1980, 1982, 1984
Synder, Oliver P. (AR) - 1870
Synnestvedt, John T. (PA) - 1958
Sypher, J. Hale (LA) - 1868, 1870, 1872
Szczerbinski, Anthony (WI) - 1916

T

Tabak, Fred N. (WI) - 1970
Tabbert, Don A. (IN) - 1964
Taber (MO) - 1892
Taber, John (NY) - 1922, 1924, 1926, 1928, 1930, 1932, 1934, 1936, 1938, 1940, 1942, 1944, 1946, 1948, 1950, 1952, 1954, 1956, 1958, 1960
Taber, Stephen (NY) - 1864, 1866
Taber, Stephen S. W. (MA) - 1846
Tablack, George D. (OH) - 1982
Tabor (NY) - 1850
Tabor, Edward O. (PA) - 1936
Tackett, Boyd (AR) - 1948, 1950
Tackett, Gene (CA) - 1982
Tackett, Roger D. (OH) - 1982
Tacy, John (NY) - 1840
Taffe, John (NE) - 1866, 1868, 1870
Taffe, John E. (MA) - 1936
Taft (OH) - 1856
Taft, Charles P. (OH) - 1894
Taft, F. W. (CA) - 1906
Taft, Frederick L. (OH) - 1912
Taft, Homes S. (OH) - 1978
Taft, Irving W. (NJ) - 1930
Taft, Marcus H. (IL) - 1904
Taft, Robert Jr. (OH) - 1962, 1966, 1968
Taft, W. N. (SC) - 1884
Taft, Walbridge S. (NY) - 1916
Taggart, David A. (NH) - 1890
Taggart, Harold F. (CA) - 1952, 1954
Taggart, Joseph (KS) - 1912, 1914, 1916
Tague, Peter F. (MA) - 1914, 1916, 1918, 1920, 1922, 1924
Taintor (NY) - 1888
Takaki, Melvin H. (CO) - 1976
Taketa, Grayson S. (CA) - 1968
Talbert, Harlin (OR) - 1918, 1920
Talbert, W. Jasper (SC) - 1892, 1894, 1896, 1898
Talbert, William J. (SC) - 1900
Talbot, Edmond P. (MA) - 1944
Talbot, Joseph E. (CT) - 1942, 1944
Talbot, Thomas B. (OH) - 1952, 1954, 1958
Talbot, Walter R. (VA) - 1926
Talbott, Albert G. (KY) - 1855, 1857, 1861
Talbott, J. Dan (KY) - 1943
Talbott, J. Fred C. (MD) - 1878, 1880, 1882, 1892, 1894, 1900, 1902, 1904, 1906, 1908
Talbott, John Sherman (OH) - 1920
Talbott, Joshua Frederick C. (MD) - 1910, 1912, 1914, 1916
Talbott, Walter S. (WA) - 1938
Talcott, Burt L. (CA) - 1962, 1964, 1966, 1968, 1970, 1972, 1974, 1976
Talcott, Charles A. (NY) - 1910, 1912, 1914, 1916
Talcott, James (NY) - 1880
Talcott, Wade (IL) 1846
Talento, R. Fred (NY) - 1926
Taliaferro, Eugene S. (NY) - 1932
Taliaferro, Henry B. (LA) - 1902
Taliaferro, J. G. (LA) - 1898
Taliaferro, John R. (NJ) - 1974
Taliaferro, T. S. Jr. (WY) - 1904
Talle, Henry O. (IA) - 1936, 1938, 1940, 1942, 1944, 1946, 1948, 1950, 1952, 1954
Talliaferro, John (VA) - 1825, 1827, 1829, 1831, 1833, 1835, 1837, 1839, 1841, 1856, 1858
Tallmadge, Frederick (NY) - 1846
Tallman, Clay (NV) - 1912
Tallman, Earl J. (MI) - 1946

Tallman, Henry (ME) - 1882
Tallon, Robert M. Jr. (SC) - 1982
Tallon, Robin (SC) - 1984
Talmage, D. W. (NY) - 1880
Talman, George (NY) - 1832
Tambling, Corydon L. (OH) - 1886
Tannehill, James B. (OH) - 1896
Tanner (CT) - 1904
Tanner, Adolphus H. (NY) - 1868
Tanner, Frederick C. (NY) - 1918
Tanner, H. B. (TX) - 1926
Tanton, William F. (OR) - 1948
Tappan, Mason W. (NH) - 1855, 1857, 1859
Tarbell (VT) - 1880
Tarbox, John K. (MA) - 1870, 1872, 1874, 1876, 1878
Tarbutton, George T. (OH) - 1952
Tarlowe, Joseph D. (NY) - 1926
Tarner, Samuel R. (PA) - 1918
Tarr, Curtis W. (CA) - 1958
Tarsney, John C. (MO) - 1888, 1890, 1892, 1894
Tarsney, Timothy E. (MI) - 1880, 1884, 1886, 1888
Tartaglia, Hugh M. (FL) - 1960
Tarver, Malcolm C. (GA) - 1926, 1928, 1930, 1932, 1934, 1936, 1938, 1940, 1942, 1944
Tate (PA) - 1886
Tate, Farish C. (GA) - 1892, 1894, 1896, 1898, 1900, 1902
Tate, Humphrey D. (PA) - 1908
Tate, James R. (VA) - 1976
Tate, J. F. (AL) - 1892
Tattnall, Edward F. (GA) - 1824, 1826
Tatum, Homer S. (TN) - 1922
Tatum, S. Homer (TN) - 1942, 1944, 1948
Tatum, Stewart L. (OH) - 1900
Taub, Jerome H. (NJ) - 1960
Tauber, Fred G. (NJ) - 1934, 1936
Tauke, Tom (IA) - 1978, 1980, 1982, 1984
Taulbee, William P. (KY) - 1884, 1886
Tauriello, Anthony F. (NY) - 1948, 1950, 1952
Tauzin, W. J. (Billy) (LA) - 1980, 1982, 1984
Tavenner, Clyde H. (IL) - 1910, 1912, 1914, 1916
Tawney, James A. (MN) - 1892, 1894, 1896, 1898, 1900, 1902, 1904, 1906, 1908
Tayler, Robert W. (OH) - 1894, 1896, 1898, 1900
Taylor (CT) - 1865, 1878
Taylor (IN) - 1874, 1880
Taylor (KY) - 1827, 1916
Taylor (NJ) - 1872
Taylor (NY) - 1828, 1854
Taylor (PA) - 1848, 1850, 1852, 1872
Taylor (TN) - 1849, 1855, 1857, 1880, 1882, 1900
Taylor (VA) - 1839
Taylor, A. A. (TN) - 1906
Taylor, A. J. (VA) - 1890
Taylor, Abner (IL) - 1888, 1890
Taylor, Alexander Jr. (NY) - 1880, 1890
Taylor, Alexander W. (PA) - 1872
Taylor, Alfred (KS) - 1882
Taylor, Alfred A. (TN) - 1888, 1890, 1892
Taylor, Arthur H. (IN) - 1892, 1894
Taylor, B. A. (MT) - 1928
Taylor, Benjamin Irving (NY) - 1912, 1914
Taylor, Benjamin W. (NY) - 1892
Taylor, C. Ed. (NC) - 1930
Taylor, Caleb N. (PA) - 1866, 1868
Taylor, Charles (NY) - 1970
Taylor, Charles E. (MT) - 1924
Taylor, Charles G. (IL) - 1906
Taylor, Clarence E. (SC) - 1984
Taylor, Claude O. (MI) - 1922
Taylor, Clifford W. (MI) - 1974, 1976
Taylor, D. F. (AR) - 1906
Taylor, Daniel (TX) - 1892
Taylor, David Jr. (OH) - 1874
Taylor, Dean P. (NY) - 1942, 1944, 1946, 1948, 1950, 1952, 1954, 1956, 1958
Taylor, Dennis (TX) - 1962
Taylor, Donald E. (IN) - 1968
Taylor, Edward L. (PA) - 1970
Taylor, Edward L. Jr. (OH) - 1904, 1906, 1908, 1910, 1912
Taylor, Edward T. (CO) - 1908, 1910, 1912, 1914, 1916, 1918, 1920, 1922, 1924, 1926, 1928, 1930, 1932, 1934, 1936, 1938, 1940

Taylor, Elmer A. (IL) - 1934
Taylor, Ezra B. (OH) - 1880, 1882, 1884, 1886, 1888, 1890
Taylor, Formington (NY) - 1954, 1956
Taylor, Frank J. (NE) - 1914
Taylor, Franklin (NY) - 1918
Taylor, Gene (MO) - 1972, 1974, 1976, 1978, 1980, 1982, 1984
Taylor, George (CT) - 1847
Taylor, George (NY) - 1856, 1858
Taylor, George E. (CA) - 1964
Taylor, George W. (AL) - 1896, 1898, 1900, 1902, 1904, 1906, 1908, 1910, 1912
Taylor, Henry W. (MI) - 1844
Taylor, Herbert W. (NJ) - 1920, 1924, 1926
Taylor, Howard S. (IL) - 1894
Taylor, Hugh S. (PA) - 1906
Taylor, Isaac H. (OH) - 1884
Taylor, J. (AL) - 1865
Taylor, J. Alfred (WV) - 1922, 1924, 1926
Taylor, J. B. (IL) - 1886
Taylor, J. F. (KY) - 1914
Taylor, J. H. R. (MS) - 1855
Taylor, J. Henry (PA) - 1890
Taylor, J. W. (MN) - 1860
Taylor, J. Will (TN) - 1918, 1920, 1922, 1924, 1926, 1928, 1930, 1932, 1934, 1936, 1938
Taylor, James (OH) - 1872
Taylor, James E. (CA) - 1976, 1978
Taylor, James M. (CO) - 1924
Taylor, James M. (IL) - 1884
Taylor, James M. (MO) - 1964
Taylor, Jerome (TN) - 1940
Taylor, Jesse (OH) - 1908, 1910
Taylor, Jim (AR) - 1984
Taylor, John (AL) - 1847
Taylor, John (NY) - 1836
Taylor, John C. (SC) - 1932, 1934, 1936
Taylor, John G. (CO) - 1892
Taylor, John J. (NY) - 1850, 1852
Taylor, John L. (OH) - 1846, 1848, 1850, 1852
Taylor, John M. (TN) - 1882, 1884
Taylor, John W. (KY) - 1934
Taylor, John W. (NY) - 1824, 1826, 1828, 1830, 1832
Taylor, Jonathan (OH) - 1838, 1840
Taylor, Jonathan B. (IL) - 1888
Taylor, Joseph D. (OH) - 1883, 1884, 1886, 1888, 1890
Taylor, Leighton C. (PA) - 1932
Taylor, Lyle D. (IA) - 1970, 1972
Taylor, M. A. (TX) - 1916
Taylor, Marion C. (KY) - 1865, 1867
Taylor, Miles (LA) - 1855, 1857, 1859
Taylor, N. G. (TN) - 1870
Taylor, Nathaniel G. (TN) - 1853, 1865
Taylor, Nelson (NY) - 1860, 1864, 1866
Taylor, Nelson E. (MS) - 1950
Taylor, Patrick H. (KY) - 1930
Taylor, Paul (CA) - 1948
Taylor, R. H. (TX) - 1869
Taylor, R. S. (OH) - 1916
Taylor, Robert (VA) - 1825
Taylor, Robert (WI) - 1964
Taylor, Robert L. (TN) - 1878
Taylor, Roy A. (NC) - 1960, 1962, 1964, 1966, 1968, 1970, 1972, 1974
Taylor, Samuel M. (AR) - 1912, 1914, 1916, 1918, 1920
Taylor, Stanley (KS) - 1938, 1940
Taylor, Thaddeus B. (MI) - 1914
Taylor, Vincent A. (OH) - 1890
Taylor, W. H. (IA) - 1894
Taylor, W. J. (NE) - 1912
Taylor, William (NY) - 1832, 1834, 1836
Taylor, William (VA) - 1843, 1845
Taylor, William A. (OH) - 1906
Taylor, William J. (NE) - 1910
Taylor, William P. (VA) - 1833, 1835
Taylor, Zachary (TN) - 1884, 1886
Tazewell (VA) - 1855
Tchon, Irvin R. (IL) - 1962
Teague, Charles M. (CA) - 1954, 1956, 1958, 1960, 1962, 1964, 1966, 1968, 1970, 1972
Teague, I. E. (TX) - 1916
Teague, Olin E. (TX) - 1946, 1948, 1950, 1952, 1954, 1956, 1958, 1960, 1962, 1964, 1966, 1968, 1970, 1972, 1974, 1976
Teague, William J. (CA) - 1968, 1970
Teale, Theodore C. (NY) - 1890
Tebben, Geraldine (OH) - 1980

Tebbetts, Leon O. (ME) - 1922, 1924
Teese, Frederick H. (NJ) - 1874
Teft (NY) - 1860
Teicher, Oren J. (NY) - 1984
Teichner, Irving (CA) - 1966, 1968
Teigan, Henry G. (MN) - 1932, 1936, 1938, 1940
Telfair (OH) - 1852, 1860
Telford, Erastus D. (IL) - 1926
Teller (NY) - 1856
Teller, James H. (IL) - 1896
Teller, Ludwig (NY) - 1956, 1958, 1960
Temple, Elam Reamuel Jr. (NC) - 1960
Temple, Henry W. (PA) - 1912, 1914, 1915, 1916, 1918, 1920, 1922, 1924, 1926, 1928, 1930, 1932
Temple, Jack (CA) - 1864
Temple, Josiah H. (MA) - 1858
Temple, M. D. (TX) - 1946, 1950
Temple, Oliver P. (TN) - 1847
Temple, William (DE) - 1862
Templeton, C. V. (SD) - 1906
Templeton, Leroy (IN) - 1876, 1878, 1890
Templeton, T. W. (PA) - 1916
Tenbrk (NY) - 1842
Tenck (NY) - 1852
Tener, John K. (PA) - 1908
Tenerowicz, Rudolph G. (MI) - 1938, 1940, 1948, 1950, 1952, 1954
Ten Eyck, Egbert (NY) - 1824
Ten Eyck, Peter G. (NY) - 1912, 1914, 1920
Tennelle (GA) - 1876
Tenney (WI) - 1878
Tenney, John S. (ME) - 1836, 1838
Tenney, M. D. (KS) - 1884
Tenzer, Herbert (NY) - 1964, 1966
Teommey, George H. Sr. (NY) - 1926
Terhunr, Edgar (IL) - 1886
Terrell (GA) - 1832
Terrell (MO) - 1882
Terrell, Ben (TX) - 1892
Terrell, Charles W. Jr. (CT) - 1964
Terrell, George B. (TX) - 1932
Terrell, Henry (TX) - 1892
Terrell, James C. (GA) - 1834
Terrell, John D. (AL) - 1825
Terrell, L. L. Dr. (KY) - 1934
Terrell, W. L. (TN) - 1908
Terry, David D. (AR) - 1934, 1936, 1938, 1940
Terry, Ira L. (NY) - 1924
Terry, John H. (NY) - 1970
Terry, Lee (NE) - 1976
Terry, R. B. (CA) - 1888
Terry, William (VA) - 1870, 1874
Terry, William L. (AR) - 1890, 1892, 1894, 1896
Terry, William T. (AR) - 1898
Test, Charles H. (IN) - 1843, 1847
Test, John (IN) - 1824, 1826, 1828, 1831, 1833
Teti, Dennis E. (NJ) - 1980
Tew (NJ) - 1912
Tew, Charles F. (CO) - 1906
Tewes, Donald E. (WI) - 1956, 1958, 1960
Thach, Pat H. (TN) - 1934
Thacher, Henry C. (MA) - 1892
Thacher, Moses (MA) - 1830
Thacher, Ned (OH) - 1930
Thacher, Thomas C. (MA) - 1910, 1912, 1914
Thackray, J. S. (PA) - 1876
Thakar, Rosemary (CA) - 1984
Thasler, Adam W. Jr. (MA) - 1852
Thatch (AL) - 1835
Thatcher, Maurice H. (KY) - 1922, 1924, 1926, 1928, 1930
Thayer (CT) - 1892, 1898
Thayer (MO) - 1932
Thayer (NY) - 1872
Thayer, Edward H. (IA) - 1862
Thayer, Eli (MA) - 1856, 1858, 1860, 1874, 1878
Thayer, Harry I. (MA) - 1924
Thayer, Henry (IN) - 1884
Thayer, John A. (MA) - 1910, 1912
Thayer, John R. (MA) - 1892, 1898, 1900, 1902
Thayer, M. Russell (PA) - 1862, 1864
Thayer, Robert H. (NY) - 1946
Theaker, Thomas C. (OH) - 1858, 1860
Theilmann (MO) - 1912, 1914
Theinert (RI) - 1898
Theusch, Charles J. (IL) - 1984
Thibodeaux, Bannon G. (LA) - 1844, 1847

Thiessen, Wayne C. (VA) - 1964
Thill, Lewis D. (WI) - 1938, 1940, 1942, 1944
Thing, Daniel H. (ME) - 1882, 1884
Thistlewood, Napoleon B. (IL) - 1908, 1910, 1912
Thobe, J. J. (KY) - 1932
Thoebe, George H. (KY) - 1886
Thom, William R. (OH) - 1930, 1932, 1934, 1936, 1938, 1940, 1942, 1944, 1946
Thoman, Leroy D. (OH) - 1880
Thomas (KY) - 1916
Thomas (MD) - 1853
Thomas (MI) - 1878
Thomas (MO) - 1882, 1884
Thomas (NY) - 1854
Thomas (VA) - 1859
Thomas, Albert (TX) - 1936, 1938, 1940, 1942, 1944, 1946, 1948, 1950, 1952, 1954, 1956, 1958, 1960, 1962, 1964
Thomas, Albert L. (PA) - 1928
Thomas, Andrew D. (IL) - 1978
Thomas, Arthur C. (PA) - 1962
Thomas, Benjamin F. (MA) - 1862
Thomas, C. W. (MO) - 1926
Thomas, Charles R. (NC) - 1870, 1872, 1898, 1900, 1902, 1904, 1906, 1908
Thomas, Charles R. (NC) - 1964
Thomas, Charles S. (CO) - 1884
Thomas, Christopher Y. (VA) - 1872, 1874
Thomas, Dan R. (IL) - 1914
Thomas, Daniel L. (IL) - 1912, 1922
Thomas, David (PA) - 1866
Thomas, Dorsey B. (IN) - 1865, 1867
Thomas, Elmer (OK) - 1920, 1922, 1924
Thomas, Enoch H. Jr. (PA) - 1956
Thomas, Francis (MD) - 1831, 1833, 1835, 1837, 1839, 1861, 1863, 1864, 1866
Thomas, Francis A. (NY) - 1868
Thomas, Frank B. (IL) - 1914
Thomas, Frank W. (OH) - 1946
Thomas, G. P. (KY) - 1896
Thomas, George (NY) - 1940
Thomas, George M. (KY) - 1870, 1880, 1886
Thomas, George S. (GA) - 1888
Thomas, George W. (NY) - 1952
Thomas, Grant (WI) - 1906
Thomas, Granville (KY) - 1974, 1976, 1978
Thomas, Harry D. (OH) - 1912
Thomas, Henry F. (MI) - 1892, 1894
Thomas, Henry P. (PA) - 1924
Thomas, Horatio W. (NY) - 1940
Thomas, J. J. (NE) - 1906
Thomas, J. Parnell (NJ) - 1936, 1938, 1940, 1942, 1944, 1946, 1948
Thomas, J. W. (TX) - 1888, 1900
Thomas, James H. (TN) - 1847, 1849, 1851, 1859
Thomas, Jim (MO) - 1962, 1964, 1978
Thomas, John (IL) - 1856
Thomas, John (MA) - 1836
Thomas, John H. (OH) - 1868
Thomas, John L. Jr. (MD) - 1865, 1866
Thomas, John R. (IL) - 1878, 1880, 1882, 1884, 1886
Thomas, John T. (IL) - 1954
Thomas, Josiah C. (MO) - 1958
Thomas, Lera M. (TX) - 1966
Thomas, Lindsay (GA) - 1982
Thomas, Lot (IA) - 1898, 1900, 1902
Thomas, Lowell Jr. (AK) - 1962, 1964
Thomas, Mathonihah (UT) - 1912, 1920
Thomas, Milo (NY) - 1966
Thomas, Norman (NY) - 1930
Thomas, O. D. (CA) - 1938
Thomas, Ormsby B. (WI) - 1884, 1886, 1888, 1890
Thomas, Otis C. (KY) - 1951
Thomas, Philip F. (MD) - 1839, 1874
Thomas, Pleasant C. (NC) - 1890
Thomas, R. S. (KS) - 1912
Thomas, Richard W. (NY) - 1932
Thomas, Robert Lindsay (GA) - 1984
Thomas, Robert Y. Jr. (KY) - 1908, 1910, 1912, 1914, 1916, 1918, 1920, 1922, 1924
Thomas, S. Crago (PA) - 1910
Thomas, S. M. (LA) - 1902
Thomas, Samuel Bell (NY) - 1910
Thomas, Stan (PA) - 1978, 1980
Thomas, Theodore M. (WI) - 1926
Thomas, W. Aubrey (OH) - 1904, 1906, 1908, 1910
Thomas, W. Larue (KY) - 1896

Thomas, Willard (OH) - 1946
Thomas, William (CA) - 1978
Thomas, William (MO) - 1972
Thomas, William B. (PA) - 1870
Thomas, William D. (NY) - 1934
Thomas, William D. (PA) - 1956
Thomas, William H. (PA) - 1900, 1912
Thomas, William M. (CA) - 1980, 1982, 1984
Thomas, William R. (CA) - 1962
Thomas, Philemon (LA) - 1830, 1832
Thomason (AR) - 1856
Thomason (MN) - 1914
Thomason, R. Ewing (TX) - 1930, 1932, 1934, 1936, 1938, 1940, 1942, 1944, 1946
Thomasson, William P. (KY) - 1843, 1845
Thompson (KY) - 1827
Thompson (MD) - 1878
Thompson (MI) - 1878
Thompson (MN) - 1916
Thompson (MO) - 1874, 1908
Thompson (NY) - 1850
Thompson (OH) - 1843
Thompson (OK) - 1908
Thompson (SC) - 1848
Thompson (VA) - 1827, 1849
Thompson (WI) - 1874, 1918, 1947
Thompson, A. M. (PA) - 1916
Thompson, Albert C. (OH) - 1884, 1886, 1888
Thompson, Alexander (PA) - 1824
Thompson, Anders (MN) - 1954
Thompson, Arad (MA) - 1830
Thompson, Arthur R. (FL) - 1932
Thompson, B. C. (AR) - 1910
Thompson, Benjamin (MA) - 1844, 1848, 1850
Thompson, C. K. (SD) - 1904
Thompson, Carl D. (IL) - 1914, 1916
Thompson, Charles J. (OH) - 1918, 1920, 1922, 1924, 1926, 1928, 1930
Thompson, Charles P. (MA) - 1872, 1874, 1876, 1882
Thompson, Charles S. (MN) - 1972
Thompson, Charles W. (AL) - 1900, 1902
Thompson, Chester (IL) - 1932, 1934, 1936, 1938
Thompson, Clark W. (TX) - 1948, 1950, 1952, 1954, 1956, 1958, 1960, 1962, 1964
Thompson, Cyrus (NC) - 1894
Thompson, D. O. Dr. (IL) - 1936
Thompson, David F. (IL) - 1894
Thompson, E. M. (ME) - 1914
Thompson, Edward (MI) - 1860
Thompson, Fletcher (GA) - 1966, 1968, 1970
Thompson, Frank (NC) - 1896
Thompson, Frank J. (AL) - 1924
Thompson, Frank Jr. (NJ) - 1954, 1956, 1958, 1960, 1962, 1964, 1966, 1968, 1970, 1972, 1974, 1976, 1978, 1980
Thompson, George W. (VA) - 1851
Thompson, Hagan (MS) - 1968
Thompson, Hedge (NJ) - 1826
Thompson, J. C. (TX) - 1914, 1916
Thompson, J. D. (IA) - 1866
Thompson, J. H. (WV) - 1878
Thompson, J. O. (AL) - 1918
Thompson, J. Q. (MO) - 1876
Thompson, J. S. (AR) - 1924, 1936
Thompson, J. S. (CA) - 1875
Thompson, Jacob (MS) - 1839, 1841, 1843, 1845, 1847, 1849, 1851
Thompson, James (PA) - 1844, 1846, 1848
Thompson, James H. (OH) - 1844
Thompson, John (NY) - 1856
Thompson, John B. (KY) - 1841, 1847, 1849, 1896
Thompson, John C. (KY) - 1912
Thompson, John Charles (WY) - 1900
Thompson, John H. (IN) - 1828, 1831
Thompson, John L. (IN) - 1910
Thompson, John M. (IL) - 1898
Thompson, John M. (PA) - 1876
Thompson, John S. (IL) - 1866
Thompson, Jonathan (NY) - 1832
Thompson, Joseph B. (OK) - 1912, 1914, 1916, 1918
Thompson, Ken (CA) - 1972
Thompson, Lemon (NY) - 1882
Thompson, Lewis G. (IN) - 1843, 1845
Thompson, Lynn (MN) - 1920
Thompson, Lynn (WI) - 1910

Thompscn, M. L. (PA) - 1904
Thompson, Mike (FL) - 1966, 1968
Thompson, N. A. (WA) - 1912
Thompson, Newell A. (MA) - 1858
Thompson, O. W. (KY) - 1950
Thompson, Olive T. (CA) - 1952
Thompson, Philip (KY) - 1833
Thompson, Philip B. Jr. (KY) - 1878, 1880, 1882
Thompson, R. C. (AR) - 1904, 1906
Thompson, Ralph W. (IA) - 1924
Thompson, Richard W. (IN) - 1841, 1847
Thompson, Robert A. (VA) - 1847
Thompson, Ronnie (GA) - 1972
Thompson, Roy Jr. (FL) - 1972
Thompson, Ruth (MI) - 1950, 1952, 1954
Thompson, Scott (IN) - 1930
Thompson, Smith (PA) - 1857
Thompson, Steve (MN) - 1972
Thompson, T. Ashton (LA) - 1952, 1954, 1956, 1958, 1960, 1962, 1964
Thompson, Thomas (MA) - 1912, 1914
Thompson, Thomas L. (CA) - 1886, 1888
Thompson, Tyler (IL) - 1960
Thompson, W. H. (NE) - 1890
Thompson, W. P. (ME) - 1892
Thompson, Waddy Jr. (SC) - 1836, 1838
Thompson, Wiley (GA) - 1824, 1826, 1828, 1830
Thompson, William (IN) - 1839
Thompson, William (IA) - 1847, 1848, 1850
Thompson, William A. (NM) - 1958
Thompson, William B. Jr. (TN) - 1984
Thompson, William D. (WI) - 1932
Thompson, William G. (IA) - 1880
Thompson, William G. (OH) - 1902
Thompson, William H. (KS) - 1922
Thompson, William H. Jr. (NJ) - 1942
Thompson, William M. (LA) - 1840
Thompson, William W. (MA) - 1833, 1838
Thompson, Mrs. Wilson (TN) - 1926
Thomson (NY) - 1878
Thomson, Charles M. (IL) - 1912, 1914
Thomson, E. Keith (WY) - 1954
Thomson, Frederick W. (NY) - 1922
Thomson, John (OH) - 1824, 1828, 1830, 1832, 1834
Thomson, Keith (WY) - 1956, 1958
Thomson, Vernon W. (WI) - 1960, 1962, 1964, 1966, 1968, 1970, 1972, 1974
Thomson, W. H. S. (PA) - 1904
Thone, Charles (NE) - 1970, 1972, 1974, 1976
Thongood, Charles (NY) - 1902
Thoren, Everett J. (OR) - 1964, 1966, 1970
Thorington, James (IA) - 1854
Thorkelson, Jacob (MT) - 1938
Thormodson, N. E. (MN) - 1920
Thorn (NJ) - 1914
Thorn, William W. (PA) - 1914
Thornberry, Homer (TX) - 1948, 1950, 1952, 1954, 1956, 1958, 1960, 1962
Thornburgh, Jacob M. (TN) - 1872, 1874, 1876
Thornburgh, Richard L. (PA) - 1966
Thorne, Edward A. (NC) - 1892
Thorne, George H. (OH) - 1918
Thorne, Guy (PA) - 1930
Thorne, Sanford N. (NY) - 1908
Thornley, Benjamin (NY) - 1960
Thornton, Anthony (IL) - 1864
Thornton, Carey (GA) - 1894
Thornton, J. (MO) - 1844
Thornton, J. J. (MN) - 1884
Thornton, Ray (AR) - 1972, 1974, 1976
Thornton, Robert Y. (OR) - 1958
Thornton, William J. (IL) - 1930, 1932
Thorp, John S. (NY) - 1944
Thorp, Robert T. (VA) - 1894, 1896, 1898
Thorpe, John J. (PA) - 1910
Thorpe, Roy H. (NE) - 1924
Thorsness, Leo K. (SD) - 1978
Thorson, Thomas L. (IN) - 1976, 1978
Thrasher (MO) - 1874
Thrasher, R. H. (TN) - 1908
Thrasher, Wilkes T. Jr. (TN) - 1962
Threasher, P. H. (TN) - 1892
Threatt, Frank H. (AL) - 1880, 1888, 1890, 1896
Throckmorton, James W. (TX) - 1874, 1876, 1882, 1884
Thropp, Joseph E. (PA) - 1896, 1898, 1904, 1906
Thrower, Randolph W. (GA) - 1956
Thum (NY) - 1884

Vandegrift, Charles S. (PA) - 1896
Vandenheuvel, William J. (NY) - 1960
Vander Jagt, Guy A. (MI) - 1966, 1968, 1970, 1972, 1974, 1976, 1978, 1980, 1982, 1984
Vander Laan, Robert (MI) - 1974
Vander Veen, Richard F. (MI) - 1958, 1974, 1976
Vanderbilt (NJ) - 1918
Vanderbilt (NY) - 1888
Vanderbilt, Andrew N. (NY) - 1890
Vanderburg, W. S. (OR) - 1896
Vanderlin, Joseph C. (PA) - 1894
Vanderploeg, Jan B. (MI) - 1958
Vanderpoel, Aaron (NY) - 1832, 1834, 1838
Vanderpoel, James (NY) - 1828
Vanderpoel, W. Irving (NY) - 1926
Vanderpool, S. O. (NY) - 1880
Vanderslice, Kathryn Z. (PA) - 1961
Vanderveer, Abraham (NY) - 1836
Vanderventer, Isaac (IL) - 1846
Vandervoort, Robert (PA) - 1942
Vandeventer, Judson W. (PA) - 1892
Vandever, William (CA) - 1886, 1888
Vandever, William (IA) - 1858, 1860
Vandillen, H. C. (MO) - 1878
Vandiver, Willard D. (MO) - 1896, 1898, 1900, 1902
Vandusen, W. W. (WA) - 1894
Vandyken, Sam (CA) - 1966, 1968, 1970
Vaneaton, Henry S. (MS) - 1882, 1884
Vaneschen, John E. (IA) - 1968
Vanet, Randall (MO) - 1970
Vanguilder, Harry P. (WI) - 1944
Vanhecke, Frederick (WI) - 1972
Vanheusen (NY) - 1882
Vanheyde, Robert L. (OH) - 1964, 1966
Vanhoesen, Walter H. (NJ) - 1944, 1946
Vanhoose, Walter Clay (KY) - 1964
Vanik, Charles A. (OH) - 1954, 1956, 1958, 1960, 1962, 1964, 1966, 1968, 1970, 1972, 1974, 1976, 1978
Vankennen, John D. (NY) - 1944
Vanlear (MN) - 1914
Vanmatre, Nelson B. (CA) - 1936
Vanmetre (KY) - 1837
Vanmeter, John I. (OH) - 1843, 1844
Vann, W. A. (CA) - 1894
Vannatto, J. L. (TX) - 1916
Vannoort, Frank J. (NJ) - 1934
Vannortwick, John (IL) - 1856
Vannostrand, Peter (WI) - 1940
Vanoosterhaut, P. D. (IA) - 1904
Vanpetten, H. O. (CA) - 1964
Vanrenr (NY) - 1852
Vanslyck (RI) - 1870
Van Slyke, Jim (KS) - 1984
Vantassel, A. T. (OH) - 1896
Vantuys, Ben (TX) - 1906
Vanwagenen, Gerret (NY) - 1846
Vanwagenen, A. (IA) - 1912
Vanwagenen, Hubert (NY) - 1832
Vanwagener, H. (IA) - 1896
Vanwagner, Karl D. (NJ) - 1950
Vanwinder (LA) - 1851
Vanwormer, A. (MO) - 1870
Vanworner, Clements H. (WI) - 1894
Vanwych (NY) - 1826
Vanwyck, Charles H. (NY) - 1858, 1860, 1866, 1868
Vanzandt, C. C. (RI) - 1881
Vare, William S. (PA) - 1912, 1914, 1916, 1918, 1920, 1922, 1924
Varian, Isaac (NY) - 1838
Varn, Wilfred C. (FL) - 1962
Varnadoe (GA) - 1855
Varnes, Blair L. (IL) - 1948
Varnum (NY) - 1852
Varnum, Charles W. (CO) - 1934
Varnum, John (MA) - 1824, 1826, 1828
Varon, Joe (FL) - 1966
Vatcher, William H. Jr. (CA) - 1956
Vaughan, Harry J. (WA) - 1922
Vaughan, Horace W. (TX) - 1912
Vaughan, John Charles (IL) - 1910, 1912, 1914
Vaughan, R. T. (VA) - 1902
Vaughan, Taylor G. (VA) - 1928, 1936
Vaughan, William W. (TN) - 1870
Vaughey, Alex (IL) - 1904
Vaughn, Albert C. (PA) - 1950
Vaughn, Frank B. (TX) - 1932

Vaughn, Harry T. (PA) - 1918
Vaughn, John L. (TX) - 1916
Vaughn, M. H. (Mike) (NC) - 1976
Vaux (PA) - 1928
Vaux, Richard (PA) - 1872, 1890
Vawter, W. R. (VA) - 1910
Veach (IN) - 1856
Veatch (IN) - 1868
Veatch, R. M. (OR) - 1892, 1898, 1904
Veazie, Samuel (ME) - 1848
Veeder William D. (NY) - 1876
Veghte (NJ) - 1876
Vehslage, John H. G. (NY) - 1896
Veile, P. (IA) - 1852
Velasquez, Waldo (CA) - 1968
Velazquez, Manuel (NY) - 1958
Velde, Harold H. (IL) - 1948, 1950, 1952, 1954
Veltre, Philip J. (PA) - 1984
Venable, Abraham W. (NC) - 1847, 1849, 1851, 1853
Venable, Edward C. (VA) - 1888
Venable, William W. (MS) - 1916, 1918
Vendsel, Raymond G. (ND) - 1954, 1960
Vener, Samuel S. (CA) - 1966
Vennard, George H. (LA) - 1904
Venner, Frank (OH) - 1888
Vento, Bruce F. (MN) - 1976, 1978, 1980, 1982, 1984
Venuti, Joseph E. (NY) - 1944
Verbofsky, Harry L. (PA) - 1958
Vergari, Carl A. (NY) - 1972
Verges, Frank G. (CA) - 1982
Verk (NY) - 1852
Vermilya, James I. (MN) - 1892
Vermorel, Dorothea M. B. (FL) - 1952
Vernon (TN) - 1898
Vernon, Thomas O. P. (SC) - 1858
Verplanck, Gulian (NY) - 1824, 1826, 1828, 1830, 1834
Verplanck, Isaac A. (NY) - 1868
Ver Ploeg, C. (IA) - 1928
Verree, John P. (PA) - 1858, 1860
Verreos, Nick A. (CA) - 1960, 1964
Verry (MA) - 1876
Verry, George F. (MA) - 1872
Vertrees (MO) - 1890
Vest, S. A. (TN) - 1922
Vesta, Vinton A. (WI) - 1978
Vestal, Albert H. (IN) - 1914, 1916, 1918, 1920, 1922, 1924, 1926, 1928, 1930
Vetterli, Reed E. (UT) - 1942
Veysey, Victor V. (CA) - 1970, 1972, 1974
Vibbard, Chauncey (NY) - 1860
Vick, M. R. (NC) - 1924
Vickerman, John (SD) - 1972
Vickers, Tom (NE) - 1984
Vickers, Robert L. (CA) - 1976
Vickery, Charles R. (MA) - 1854, 1856
Victor, Eugene (NY) - 1980
Victora, William (WI) - 1924, 1928
Vidal, Gore (NY) - 1960
Viele, Egbert L. (NY) - 1884, 1886
Vifquain, Victor (NE) - 1892
Vigelius, Anton (NY) - 1894
Vigorito, Joseph P. (PA) - 1964, 1966, 1968, 1970, 1972, 1974, 1976, 1978
Vilas (WI) - 1868
Vilas, Levi B. (VT) - 1844
Villiers (LA) - 1857
Vilt, Thomas E. (OH) - 1972
Vincent (CT) - 1912
Vincent, Beverly M. (KY) - 1938, 1940, 1942
Vincent, Bird J. (MI) - 1922, 1924, 1926, 1928, 1930
Vincent, Bobby Ray (CA) - 1974
Vincent, Lena Duell (IL) - 1940
Vincent, Merle D. (CO) - 1920, 1922
Vincent, William D. (KS) - 1896, 1898, 1900
Vinson, Carl (GA) - 1914, 1916, 1918, 1920, 1922, 1924, 1926, 1928, 1930, 1932, 1934, 1936, 1938, 1940, 1942, 1944, 1946, 1948, 1950, 1952, 1954, 1956, 1958, 1960, 1962
Vinson, Fred M. (KY) - 1924, 1926, 1928, 1930, 1932, 1934, 1936
Vinton (NY) - 1878
Vinton, Samuel F. (OH) - 1824, 1826, 1828, 1830, 1832, 1834, 1843, 1844, 1846, 1848
Vinton, William H. (ME) - 1848
Violette, Elmer H. (ME) - 1972
Virdone, James (NY) - 1932

Virgin (WI) - 1866
Virkus, Frederick A. (IL) - 1936
Visclosky, Peter J. (IN) - 1984
Visel, Jacob A. (NY) - 1928
Visnaw, Roy E. (MI) - 1950
Vista, Vinton A. (WI) - 1980
Vitell, Scott John (IL) - 1946
Vivian, Weston E. (MI) - 1964, 1966, 1968
Vladeck, Baruch C. (NY) - 1930, 1932, 1934
Vladeck, Stephen C. (NY) - 1948
Vocke, William (IL) - 1892
Voelkerding (MO) - 1934
Voelz, Peter M. (IL) - 1980
Vogel, Matt J. (IL) - 1926
Vogel, Robert (ND) - 1962
Vogel, Walter J. (OH) - 1978
Vogelbach (PA) - 1872
Vogler, John N. (NC) - 1847
Voigt, Edward (WI) - 1914, 1916, 1918, 1920, 1922, 1924
Volk, Lester D. (NY) - 1920, 1922
Volkel, William (NY) - 1898
Volkema, Russell H. (OH) - 1968
Volkel, William (NY) - 1898
Volkmer, Harold L. (MO) - 1976, 1978, 1980, 1982, 1984
Vollmer, Henry (IA) - 1900, 1914
Volstead, Andrew J. (MN) - 1902, 1904, 1906, 1908, 1910, 1912, 1914, 1916, 1918, 1920, 1922
Vonaxelson, Eric (FL) - 1910
Vontobel, George (NV) - 1964
Voorhees (NJ) - 1888
Voorhees, Daniel W. (IN) - 1856, 1860, 1862, 1864, 1868, 1870, 1872
Voorhees, William (IL) - 1886
Voorhis (NY) - 1878
Voorhis, Charles H. (NJ) - 1878
Voorhis, H. Jerry (CA) - 1936, 1938, 1940, 1942, 1944, 1946
Vopicka, Charles J. (IL) - 1904
Vorys, John M. (OH) - 1938, 1940, 1942, 1944, 1946, 1948, 1950, 1952, 1954, 1956
Vosbgh (NY) - 1842
Vose (NH) - 1849
Vose, Harry (MS) - 1835
Vosholl (MO) - 1898
Vosholl, W. J. (MO) - 1899
Vought, DeWitt (MI) - 1922
Voyles (IN) - 1872
Voyticky, Francis J. (NY) - 1972, 1974
Vreeland, Albert L. (NJ) - 1938, 1940, 1950
Vreeland, Edward B. (NY) - 1899, 1900, 1902, 1904, 1906, 1908, 1910
Vroom, Peter D. Jr. (NJ) - 1826, 1828, 1838, 1840
Vrooman, Carl (IL) - 1946, 1948
Vucanovich, Barbara F. (NV) - 1982, 1984
Vursell, Charles W. (IL) - 1942, 1944, 1946, 1948, 1950, 1952, 1954, 1956, 1958

W

Wabeke, Jay A. (MI) - 1968
Wachob, Bill (PA) - 1984
Wachter, Frank C. (MD) - 1898, 1900, 1902, 1904
Wacker, Leonard H. (NY) - 1941
Wacks, William (NY) - 1946
Waddell (LA) - 1847
Waddell (MS) - 1882
Waddell, Alfred M. (NC) - 1870, 1872, 1874, 1876, 1878
Waddill (KY) - 1847
Waddill, Edmond Jr. (VA) - 1886, 1888
Waddill, John S. (MO) - 1866
Waddill, James R. (MO) - 1878, 1880
Wade (GA) - 1878
Wade, C. T. (IL) - 1928
Wade, Edward (OH) - 1843, 1844, 1846, 1852, 1854, 1856, 1858
Wade, Henry (TX) - 1956
Wade, Herbert (NY) - 1908
Wade, Jeph H. (OH) - 1864
Wade, John (MA) - 1833
Wade, Martin J. (IA) - 1902, 1904
Wade, Roy J. (MI) - 1916
Wade, T. W. (TN) - 1906
Wade, William H. (MO) - 1884, 1886, 1888, 1890
Wade, William M. (IA) - 1924, 1926

Wadsworth (NY) - 1844, 1848, 1850, 1886
Wadsworth, David L. (OH) - 1880, 1888
Wadsworth, J. (NY) - 1870
Wadsworth, James S. (NY) - 1894
Wadsworth, James W. (NY) - 1881, 1882, 1890, 1892, 1896, 1898, 1900, 1902, 1904, 1906
Wadsworth, James W. Jr. (NY) - 1932, 1934, 1936, 1938, 1940, 1942, 1944, 1946, 1948
Wadsworth, Peter R. (IN) - 1900
Wadsworth, S. B. (IA) - 1900
Wadsworth, W. W. (AL) - 1908
Wadsworth, William H. (KY) - 1861, 1863, 1884
Wafford, Jefferson L. (MS) - 1869
Wagaman, Charles D. (MD) - 1912
Wagenen, Hubert (NY) - 1836
Wagener (NY) - 1886
Wagener, David D. (PA) - 1832, 1834, 1836, 1838
Wagenknecht, Alfred (WA) - 1906, 1912
Wager (NY) - 1860
Waggoner, Alfred (OH) - 1920
Waggoner, Peter J. (NY) - 1834
Waggoner, J. T. (Jabo) (AL) - 1984
Waggoner, Robert E. (IA) - 1958
Waggonner, Joe D. Jr. (LA) - 1961, 1962, 1964, 1966, 1968, 1970, 1972, 1974, 1976
Wagner, Albert A. (MI) - 1936, 1940
Wagner, Earl T. (OH) - 1948, 1950, 1952, 1954
Wagner, Edward J. (NY) - 1938
Wagner, Ernest C. (NY) - 1906, 1928
Wagner, Fred C. (CA) - 1938
Wagner, John A. (NC) - 1950
Wagner, John E. (KS) - 1902
Wagner, Joseph (IL) - 1940
Wagner, Peter (NY) - 1838
Wagner, Wayne E. (NY) - 1974
Wagner, William H. (IL) - 1898
Wagoner, Roy (TX) - 1968
Wagonseller (TX) - 1951
Wahl, Maurice (NY) - 1938
Wahlen, Frank (SD) - 1920
Waidelich, Jacob B. (PA) - 1916
Wainwright, J. Mayhew (NY) - 1922, 1924, 1926, 1928
Wainwright, Stuyvesant (NY) - 1952, 1954, 1956, 1958, 1960
Wait, A. E. (OR) - 1862
Wait, John T. (CT) - 1876, 1878, 1880, 1882, 1884
Waite (MN) - 1874
Waite (NY) - 1850
Waite (OH) - 1862
Waite, E. R. (OK) - 1918
Waite, L. Herman (WI) - 1934
Waite, Morrison R. (OH) - 1846
Wajerski, Thomas J. (IL) - 1976
Wakefield, E. F. (NC) - 1930
Wakefield, James A. (PA) - 1894, 1910
Wakefield, James B. (MN) - 1882, 1884
Wakeman (NJ) - 1864
Wakeman, Abram (NY) - 1854, 1856, 1860
Wakeman, Seth (NY) - 1870
Wakeman, Wilbur F. (NY) - 1920, 1930
Walaskay, James D. (MI) - 1976
Walbe (NY) - 1858
Walbridge, David S. (MI) - 1854, 1856
Walbridge, Henry S. (NY) - 1850
Walbridge, Hiram (NY) - 1852, 1862
Walda, John D. (IN) - 1978, 1980
Waldan (OH) - 1843
Waldby (MI) - 1880
Walden, Hiram (NY) - 1848
Walden, Madison M. (IA) - 1870
Waldie, Jerome R. (CA) - 1966, 1968, 1970, 1972
Waldman, Louis F. (PA) - 1966, 1970
Waldo (NY) - 1858, 1874
Waldo, George E. (NY) - 1904, 1906
Waldo, Loren P. (CT) - 1849, 1851
Waldo, Rhinelander (NY) - 1908
Waldor, Milton A. (NJ) - 1972
Waldow, William F. (NY) - 1916, 1918
Waldron, Alfred M. (PA) - 1932
Waldron, Henry (MI) - 1854, 1856, 1858, 1870, 1872, 1874
Waldron, Robert E. (MI) - 1962
Waldron, Samuel W. (MA) - 1858
Waldrop, John A. Jr. (VA) - 1982
Waldrop, Joseph (OR) - 1894

House Candidates Index

Willson, George B. (PA) - 1908
Willson, James C. (MI) - 1884
Willson, Jared (NY) - 1836, 1838, 1840
Willson, William C. D. (NY) - 1914
Willy, John F. (IN) - 1878
Willyard, S. L. (TX) - 1912
Wilmer (MD) - 1880
Wilmer, Joseph Allison (MD) - 1934
Wilmeth, Delbert O. (IN) - 1934
Wilmot, David (PA) - 1844, 1846, 1848
Wilmot, George (IA) - 1886
Wilshire, H. G. (NY) - 1902
Wilshire, William W. (AR) - 1872, 1874
Wilson (CT) - 1845, 1908, 1910
Wilson (IN) - 1856, 1858, 1860
Wilson (MO) - 1838, 1848, 1904
Wilson (NY) - 1854, 1874
Wilson (OH) - 1852, 1860
Wilson (PA) - 1860
Wilson (SC) - 1854
Wilson (SD) - 1902
Wilson (VA) - 1839
Wilson, A. E. (KY) - 1884
Wilson, A. L. (AR) - 1910
Wilson, A. S. (KS) - 1886
Wilson, Asher B. (ID) - 1924
Wilson, Augusta E. (AL) - 1974
Wilson, Ben F. (KS) - 1908
Wilson, Benjamin (WV) - 1872, 1874, 1876, 1878, 1880
Wilson, Bob (CA) - 1952, 1954, 1956, 1958, 1960, 1962, 1964, 1966, 1968, 1970, 1972, 1974, 1976, 1978, 1980
Wilson, Bob (IL) - 1962
Wilson, C. E. (VA) - 1900
Wilson, Calvert S. (CA) - 1942
Wilson, Charles (TX) - 1972, 1974, 1976, 1978, 1980, 1982, 1984
Wilson, Charles B. (LA) - 1888
Wilson, Charles E. (CO) - 1954
Wilson, Charles G. (VA) - 1936
Wilson, Charles H. (CA) - 1962, 1964, 1966, 1968, 1970, 1972, 1974, 1976, 1978
Wilson, Charles Ray (NY) - 1946, 1952
Wilson, Cora Pattleton (CA) - 1916
Wilson, David J. (UT) - 1946, 1948
Wilson, David M. (OH) - 1874
Wilson, Dick (CA) - 1962, 1964
Wilson, E. W. (WV) - 1896
Wilson, Earl (IN) - 1940, 1942, 1944, 1946, 1948, 1950, 1952, 1954, 1956, 1958, 1960, 1962, 1964
Wilson, Edgar (ID) - 1894, 1898
Wilson, Edgar C. (VA) - 1833, 1835
Wilson, Edward G. (PA) - 1954, 1956
Wilson, Edward H. (NY) - 1940
Wilson, Edwin L. (IL) - 1928
Wilson, Ellis E. (IA) - 1926
Wilson, Emmett (FL) - 1912, 1914
Wilson, Ephraim K. (MD) - 1826, 1829
Wilson, Ephraim K. (MD) - 1872
Wilson, Eugene M. (MN) - 1868, 1874
Wilson, Francis H. (NY) - 1896
Wilson, Frank E. (NY) - 1898, 1900, 1902, 1904, 1910, 1912
Wilson, Frank W. (TN) - 1950
Wilson, George A. (IL) - 1876, 1878, 1890
Wilson, George H. (OK) - 1948, 1950
Wilson, George P. R. (IN) - 1845
Wilson, George W. (OH) - 1892, 1894
Wilson, George W. (VA) - 1916
Wilson, Gill Robb (NJ) - 1950
Wilson, H. B. (IN) - 1890
Wilson, H. Clay (IL) - 1908, 1910, 1912
Wilson, Harrison (OH) - 1878
Wilson, Harry H. (KY) - 1938
Wilson, Henry (MA) - 1852
Wilson, Henry (PA) - 1824
Wilson, Henry E. (NY) - 1910
Wilson, Henry H. (PA) - 1910
Wilson, Herb (WA) - 1950
Wilson, I. (CT) - 1843
Wilson, Increase (CT) - 1847
Wilson, Isaac (NY) - 1824, 1830
Wilson, J. B. (IN) - 1914
Wilson, J. E. (SC) - 1894, 1896
Wilson, J. Frank (TX) - 1946, 1948, 1950, 1952
Wilson, J. Stanyarne (SC) - 1894
Wilson, J. Stitt (CA) - 1912, 1932
Wilson, Jack (FL) - 1984
Wilson, James (IN) - 1856, 1858
Wilson, James (IA) - 1872, 1874, 1882

Wilson, James (NH) - 1847, 1849
Wilson, James (NY) - 1846
Wilson, James (PA) - 1824, 1826
Wilson, James B. (WA) - 1956
Wilson, James C. (TX) - 1916, 1918
Wilson, James F. (IA) - 1861, 1862, 1864, 1866
Wilson, James Jr. (NH) - 1833, 1835, 1837
Wilson, James P. (IL) - 1906
Wilson, Jarad (NY) - 1830
Wilson, Jeremiah M. (IN) - 1870, 1872
Wilson, Jerome L. (NY) - 1966
Wilson, Jerome M. (NY) - 1960
Wilson, Jimmy (LA) - 1978
Wilson, John (MA) - 1858
Wilson, John (SC) - 1824, 1826
Wilson, John E. (MD) - 1890
Wilson, John H. (KY) - 1888, 1890, 1914
Wilson, John H. (PA) - 1919, 1920
Wilson, John J. (VT) - 1922
Wilson, John L. (WA) - 1889, 1890, 1892
Wilson, John T. (OH) - 1866, 1868, 1870, 1872
Wilson, Joseph G. (OR) - 1870, 1872
Wilson, Karl M. (AZ) - 1946
Wilson, Kirby L. Jr. (MI) - 1948, 1950
Wilson, Leonard (AL) - 1976
Wilson, Leroy S. (MI) - 1942
Wilson, Louis D. (NC) - 1837
Wilson, M. D. (IN) - 1914
Wilson, M. R. (LA) - 1894
Wilson, Manly D. (IN) - 1888
Wilson, Mauley D. (IN) - 1916
Wilson, R. R. (OK) - 1938
Wilson, Riley J. (LA) - 1914, 1916, 1918, 1920, 1922, 1924, 1926, 1928, 1930, 1932, 1934
Wilson, Robert P. C. (MO) - 1889, 1890
Wilson, Roderick J. (CA) - 1974
Wilson, Sam B. (PA) - 1932
Wilson, Stanyarne (SC) - 1896, 1898
Wilson, Stephen F. (PA) - 1864, 1866
Wilson, T. A. (TX) - 1892
Wilson, T. B. (OH) - 1890
Wilson, T. Webber (MS) - 1922, 1924, 1926
Wilson, Thomas (MN) - 1886, 1888
Wilson, Thomas A. (OH) - 1944
Wilson, Thomas C. (KS) - 1916
Wilson, Thomas J. Jr. (VA) - 1934
Wilson, Thomas P. (KY) - 1829
Wilson, W. B. (PA) - 1876
Wilson, W. H. (TX) - 1914
Wilson, W. R. (PA) - 1878
Wilson, Willett (TX) - 1922
Wilson, William (OH) - 1824, 1826
Wilson, William B. (PA) - 1906, 1908, 1910, 1912
Wilson, William E. (IN) - 1920, 1922, 1924, 1926
Wilson, William Edwin (WV) - 1920
Wilson, William H. (PA) - 1934, 1936
Wilson, William L. (CA) - 1912
Wilson, William L. (WV) - 1882, 1884, 1886, 1888, 1890, 1892, 1894
Wilson, William Warfield (IL) - 1902, 1904, 1906, 1908, 1910, 1912, 1914, 1916, 1918
Wilson, Willis Ray (IL) - 1940
Wiltermood, John A. (IN) - 1902
Wimberley, Jon (GA) - 1874
Wimberly, F. D. (GA) - 1892
Wimbush, L. (SC) - 1870
Wimmell, Arthur M. (CO) - 1944
Wimmer, D. F. (TX) - 1926
Wimmer, Ed (KY) - 1942
Wimpey, John A. (GA) - 1868, 1870
Winans (MS) - 1849
Winans (WI) - 1868
Winans, Edwin B. (MI) - 1880, 1882, 1884
Winans, George W. (WI) - 1896
Winans, James J. (OH) - 1868, 1872
Winans, John (WI) - 1882
Winant (NJ) - 1878
Winberry, John J. (NJ) - 1952
Winch (NY) - 1888
Winchester, Boyd (KY) - 1868, 1870
Winchester, Charles M. (NY) - 1922
Winchester, Henry M. (DE) - 1950
Winckler, F. C. (WI) - 1882
Wind (MO) - 1886
Winder, Dick (GA) - 1982
Windom, William (MN) - 1859, 1860, 1862, 1864, 1866

Winebrenner, David C. (MD) - 1924
Winegarner, E. H. (IL) - 1956
Wineland, Fred L. (MD) - 1974
Wineland, H. L. (OK) - 1926
Winfield, Charles H. (NY) - 1862, 1864
Winfield, Jack (AL) - 1970
Winfrey, Thomas C. (KY) - 1863
Wing, Charles G. (MI) - 1906
Wing, Halsey R. (NY) - 1865
Wingate (MO) - 1872
Wingate, H. L. Jr. (GA) - 1953
Wingate, John (NH) - 1833
Wingate, Joseph F. (ME) - 1826, 1828
Wingback, H. M. (TX) - 1916
Wingerd, Daniel H. (PA) - 1890
Wingo, Effiegene (AR) - 1930
Wingo, Otis T. (AR) - 1912, 1914, 1916, 1918, 1920, 1922, 1924, 1926, 1928
Winkler (WI) - 1872
Winkler, Robert (CA) - 1980
Winn (LA) - 1840
Winn, Henry (MA) - 1900
Winn, Larry Jr. (KS) - 1966, 1968, 1970, 1972, 1974, 1976, 1978, 1980, 1982
Winn, Thomas C. (GA) - 1896
Winn, Thomas E. (GA) - 1890
Winnell, William (OH) - 1852
Winnen, Jacob (IL) - 1902
Winnie, Charles O. (NY) - 1928
Winningham, Richard (TN) - 1970
Wirth, Timothy E. (CO) - 1980, 1982, 1984
Winslow (NY) - 1886
Winslow (WI) - 1876
Winslow, John (MA) - 1950
Winslow, Samuel E. (MA) - 1912, 1914, 1916, 1918, 1920, 1922
Winslow, Warren (NC) - 1855, 1857, 1859
Winstead, W. Arthur (MI) - 1942, 1944, 1946, 1948, 1950, 1952, 1954, 1956, 1958, 1960, 1962, 1964
Winston (MO) - 1848
Winston, Daniel (OH) - 1958, 1960
Winston, John R. (NC) - 1882
Winter, Charles E. (WY) - 1912, 1922, 1924, 1926, 1934
Winter, Thomas D. (KS) - 1938, 1940, 1942, 1944
Winterberg, Edward J. (KY) - 1976
Winterbotham (IN) - 1882
Winterbottom, James E. (NY) - 1908
Winterquist, A. L. (MN) - 1934
Wintersmith, C. G. (KY) - 1855
Winthrop, Robert (MA) - 1842
Winthrop, Robert C. (MA) - 1840, 1842, 1844, 1846, 1848
Wintringer, Margaret (IL) - 1920
Wire (OH) - 1854
Wirth, Russell Jr. (WI) - 1956
Wirth, Timothy E. (CO) - 1974, 1976, 1978, 1980, 1982, 1984
Wise, Bob (WV) - 1982, 1984
Wise, Frank J. (IL) - 1926
Wise, George A. (OH) - 1894
Wise, George D. (VA) - 1872, 1880, 1882, 1884, 1886, 1888, 1890, 1892
Wise, George N. (VA) - 1908, 1910, 1922
Wise, Henry A. (VA) - 1833, 1835, 1837, 1839, 1841, 1843, 1932
Wise, James W. (GA) - 1914, 1916, 1918, 1920, 1922
Wise, Jesse H. (PA) - 1910
Wise, John H. (PA) - 1824
Wise, John S. (VA) - 1880, 1882
Wise, Morgan R. (PA) - 1878, 1880
Wise, Richard A. (VA) - 1896, 1898, 1900
Wise, S. B. (MS) - 1966
Wisener (TN) - 1874
Wishnofsky, Helen (NY) - 1950
Wisner (MI) - 1872
Wisner (NY) - 1848
Wisner, George W. (MI) - 1844, 1846
Wisner, J. Nelson (WV) - 1872, 1892
Wisner, John (NY) - 1846
Wisner, Moses (MI) - 1854
Wister, Langhorne (PA) - 1874
Wiswell (ME) - 1856
Wiswell, Arno (ME) - 1868
Wiswell, T. C. (WA) - 1904
Witbeck, George H. Jr. (NY) - 1958
Witcher (VA) - 1839, 1841
Witcher, John S. (WV) - 1868, 1870, 1874
Witcher, W. C. (TX) - 1930
Witcher, William A. (VA) - 1878
Withers (MO) - 1892
Withers (VA) - 1865

Withers, Garrett L. (KY) - 1952
Withers, Harold J. Jr. (NY) - 1978
Withers, S. R. (TX) - 1880
Witherspoon (FL) - 1880
Witherspoon, Robert L. (MO) - 1976
Witherspoon, Samuel A. (MS) - 1910, 1912, 1914
Witherspoon, W. A. (TN) - 1892
Witherstine (MN) - 1914
Withhorn (NH) - 1875
Withington, Arthur (MA) - 1908
Withington, M. J. D. (PA) - 1878
Withrow, Gardner R. (WI) - 1930, 1932, 1934, 1936, 1938, 1940, 1942, 1948, 1950, 1952, 1954, 1956, 1958
Withrow, Pat B. Jr. (WV) - 1954
Witkin, Morton (PA) - 1952
Witmer, A. K. (PA) - 1870
Witmer, Ed (OH) - 1962
Witner, J. N. (SC) - 1838
Witt, Charles T. (MA) - 1900, 1902
Witt, Richard C. (PA) - 1956
Witte (PA) - 1872
Witte, William H. (PA) - 1852
Witteck, Charles Jr. (NY) - 1968
Witter, Lawrence O. (MA) - 1936
Witters, Harry W. (VT) - 1920, 1928
Wixson, Clarence T. (PA) - 1912
Wixson, Philip L. (MI) - 1892
Wofford (MS) - 1868
Wofford, Louise (GA) - 1976
Wofld (GA) - 1853
Wogan, John A. (LA) - 1910
Wognum, James (IL) - 1978
Wohlfarth, John R. (PA) - 1966
Wohlheter, Walter P. (SD) - 1924
Wojtkowiak, Bernard J. (NY) - 1954
Wolbank, Edward (IL) - 1970
Wolcott, Jesse P. (MI) - 1930, 1932, 1934, 1936, 1938, 1940, 1942, 1944, 1946, 1948, 1950, 1952, 1954
Wold, John (WY) - 1968
Wolf (WI) - 1936
Wolf, Alexander (NY) - 1912
Wolf, C. K. (OH) - 1924
Wolf, Frank R. (VA) - 1978, 1980, 1982, 1984
Wolf, Franz S. (NY) - 1892
Wolf, Fred B. (IA) - 1936
Wolf, George (PA) - 1824, 1826, 1828
Wolf, George W. (IN) - 1940
Wolf, Harry B. (MD) - 1906, 1908
Wolf, L. Edward (MD) - 1922
Wolf, Leonard G. (IA) - 1956, 1958, 1960
Wolf, William P. (IA) - 1870
Wolfe, Bruce P. (CA) - 1972
Wolfe, Charles P. (PA) - 1914
Wolfe, George E. (PA) - 1928, 1930
Wolfe, Louis E. (NY) - 1960
Wolfe, Nathaniel (KY) - 1863
Wolfe, Richard R. (IL) - 1966
Wolfe, Simeon K. (IN) - 1872
Wolfe, Thomas E. (OH) - 1966
Wolfenden, James (PA) - 1928, 1930, 1932, 1934, 1936, 1938, 1940, 1942, 1944
Wolff, Barnet (NY) - 1910, 1912
Wolff, J. Scott (MO) - 1922, 1924
Wolff, Lester L. (NY) - 1964, 1966, 1968, 1970, 1972, 1974, 1976, 1978, 1980
Wolff, Nelson W. (TX) - 1978
Wolford, Frank L. (KY) - 1882, 1884, 1888
Wolfram, Ray (IL) - 1964
Wolpe, Howard (MI) - 1976, 1978, 1980, 1982, 1984
Wolterman, Edward W. (OH) - 1974
Wolthuis, Robert K. (UT) - 1972
Woltz, John W. (VA) - 1880
Wolverton, Charles A. (NJ) - 1926, 1928, 1930, 1932, 1934, 1936, 1938, 1940, 1942, 1944, 1946, 1948, 1950, 1952, 1954, 1956
Wolverton, John M. (WV) - 1924, 1926, 1928, 1930, 1932, 1936
Wolverton, Simon P. (PA) - 1890, 1892
Womack, L. E. (FL) - 1930
Wood (AL) - 1849
Wood (NY) - 1848, 1856, 1874, 1886, 1888
Wood (OH) - 1828, 1832, 1862
Wood, Alfred M. (NY) - 1868
Wood, Allan P. (PA) - 1874
Wood, Amos E. (OH) - 1849
Wood, Benjamin (NY) - 1860, 1862, 1880
Wood, Benson (IL) - 1894, 1896

General Index

The General Index includes page references to all sections of the *Guide to U.S. Elections, Second Edition*, except the popular vote returns, which are indexed separately in candidate indexes. The eight candidates indexes are: Presidential Candidates Index, p. 1147; Gubernatorial Candidates Index, pp. 1148-1159; Gubernatorial Primary Candidates Index, pp. 1160-1163; Senate Candidates Index, pp. 1164-1169; Senate Primary Candidates Index, pp. 1170-1174; Southern Gubernatorial Primary Candidates Index, pp. 1175-1177; Southern Senate Primary Candidates Index, pp. 1178-1179; House Candidates Index, pp. 1180-1273.

A

Aandahl, Fred G.
Governor, North Dakota - 478
Abbett, Leon
Governor, New Jersey - 476
Abbott, Joseph C.
Senator, North Carolina - 597
Abdnor, James
Senator, South Dakota - 602
Abel, Hazel H.
Senator, Nebraska - 593
Abourezk, James
Senator, South Dakota - 601
Adair, John
Governor, Kentucky - 468
Senator, Kentucky - 587
Adams, Alva
Governor, Colorado - 463
Adams, Alva B.
Senator, Colorado - 581
Adams, Charles Francis
Biography - 442
Free Soil convention - **(1848)** 38
Liberal Republican convention - **(1872)** 52
Party VP nominee - **(1848)** 239
Adams, James H.
Governor, South Carolina - 481
Adams, Jewett W.
Governor, Nevada - 475
Adams, John
Background - 325
Biography - 442
Continental Congress - 680
Elections of - **(1789)** 8; **(1792, 1796, 1800)** 9
Electoral votes - **(1789)** 269; **(1792)** 270; **(1796)** 271; **(1800)** 272
Vice presidency - 383
Adams, John Quincy
Background - 322 (box), 325
Biography - 442
Election by House, 1825 - 259-260
Elections of - **(1824, 1828)** 11
Electoral votes, Pres. - **(1820)** 275; **(1824)** 275; **(1828)** 276
House election rules, 1825 - 257
House membership after presidency - 679, 680
Pres. popular votes - **(1824)** 329; **(1828)** 329
Redistricting law, 1842 - 690
Senator, Massachusetts - 590
Adams, John Quincy II
Party VP nominee - **(1872)** 240
Adams, Robert H.
Senator, Mississippi - 592
Adams, Samuel
Biography - 442
Electoral votes - **(1796)** 271
Governor, Massachusetts - 471
Adams, Samuel
Governor, Arkansas - 462
Adams, Sherman
Governor, New Hampshire - 475
Adams, Stephen
Senator, Mississippi - 592
Adams, William H.
Governor, Colorado - 463
Addams, Jane
Progressive convention - **(1912)** 77
Adkins, Homer M.
Governor, Arkansas - 462

Agnew, Spiro Theodore
Biography - 442
Electoral votes, VP - **(1968)** 315; **(1972)** 315
Governor, Maryland - 470, 471
Party VP nominee - **(1968, 1972)** 245
Presidential aspirations, 1976 - 323
Republican conventions - **(1968)** 117; **(1972)** 126, 127
Resignation - 264
Ahern, Frank
Presidential primaries - **(1976)** 428; **(1980)** 431, 435
Aiken, George D.
Governor, Vermont - 484
Senator, Vermont - 604
Aiken, John W.
Party Pres. nominee - **(1936, 1940)** 243
Party VP nominee - **(1932)** 243
Pres. popular votes - **(1936)** 371; **(1940)** 372
Aiken, William
Governor, South Carolina - 481
Alabama
Apportionment, Vinton method - 686
Preferential primaries - 1068
Albaugh, Arla A.
Party VP nominee - **(1944)** 243
Pres. popular votes - **(1944)** 372
Albert, Carl
Democratic conventions - **(1968)** 120; **(1976)** 130
Alcorn, James L.
Governor, Mississippi - 473
Senator, Mississippi - 592
Aldrich, Chester H.
Governor, Nebraska - 474
Aldrich, Nelson W.
Senator, Rhode Island - 600
Alexander, Lamar
Governor, Tennessee - 483
Alexander, Moses
Governor, Idaho - 466
Alexander, Nathaniel
Governor, North Carolina - 477
Alger, Russell A.
Convention balloting - **(1888)** 180
Governor, Michigan - 472
Republican convention - **(1888)** 62
Senator, Michigan - 591
Allee, James F.
Senator, Delaware - 582
Allen, Frank G.
Governor, Massachusetts - 471
Allen, H. C.
Presidential primaries - **(1940)** 403
Allen, Henry J.
Governor, Kansas - 468
Senator, Kansas - 587
Allen, Henry T.
Convention balloting - **(1924)** 195
Allen, Henry W.
Governor, Louisiana - 469
Allen, James B.
Senator, Alabama - 579
Allen, John B.
Senator, Washington - 605
Allen, Maryon Pittman
Senator, Alabama - 579
Allen, Oscar K.
Governor, Louisiana - 469
Allen, Philip
Governor, Rhode Island - 481
Senator, Rhode Island - 600

Allen, Seymour E.
Party Pres. nominee - **(1932)** 243
Allen, William
Convention balloting - **(1876)** 174
Governor, Ohio - 479
Senator, Ohio - 598
Allen, William V.
Senator, Nebraska - 593
Allen, Willis
Presidential primaries - **(1940)** 403
Allin, Roger
Governor, North Dakota - 478
Allison, William B.
Convention balloting - **(1888)** 180; **(1896)** 183
Senator, Iowa - 586
Allott, Gordon
Senator, Colorado - 581
Allred, James V.
Governor, Texas - 483
Almond, James Lindsay Jr.
Governor, Virginia - 485
Alston, Joseph
Governor, South Carolina - 481
Alston, Robert F. W.
Governor, South Carolina - 481
Altgeld, John P.
Governor, Illinois - 466
Amendments to the Constitution
12th - 9, 254, 259, 263, 383, 1127
14th - 319, 678, 680, 686, 692, 694, 1127
15th - 319, 677, 692, 1070, 1127
17th - 2, 573, 574, 1128
19th - 319, 677, 1128
20th - 256, 573, 575, 678, 680, 1128
22nd - 1128
23rd - 319, 677, 1128
24th - 319, 677, 1070, 1128
25th - 256, 263, 264, 1128-1129
26th - 319, 677, 1129
America First Party. *See also* Tax Cut Party.
Nominees - 243, 245
American Independent Party
National ticket, 1968 - 121
Nominees - 245, 246
Party history (chart) - 224
Percentage of vote (chart) - 23
Platform - **(1968)** 121-122
Profile - 225-226
American Labor Party
Nominees - 244
American National Party
Nominees - 240
American Party. *See also* Tax Cut Party.
Nominees - 240-242
American Party (American Independent)
Nominees - 245, 246
Profile - 225-226
American Party (Know-Nothings)
Convention - **(1856)** 43
Nominees - 240
Party history (chart) - 224
Percentage of vote (chart) - 23
Platform - **(1856)** 43
Profile - 226
American Prohibition Party
Nominees - 241
American Third Party
Nominees - 244
American Vegetarian Party
Nominees - 244
Ames, Adelbert
Governor, Mississippi - 473

Senator, Mississippi - 592
Ames, Benjamin
Governor, Maine - 470
Ames, Oliver
Governor, Massachusetts - 471
Ammons, Elias M.
Governor, Colorado - 463
Ammons, Teller
Governor, Colorado - 463
Anaya, Toney
Governor, New Mexico - 477
Andersen, Elmer L.
Governor, Minnesota - 472
Anderson, Alexander
Senator, Tennessee - 602
Anderson, C. Elmer
Governor, Minnesota - 472
Anderson, Charles
Governor, Ohio - 479
Anderson, Clinton P.
Senator, New Mexico - 596
Anderson, Forrest H.
Governor, Montana - 474
Anderson, Hugh J.
Governor, Maine - 470
Anderson, John B.
Biography - 442
Convention balloting - **(1980)** 218
National Unity candidate - **(1980)** 145
Party Pres. nominee - **(1980)** 246
Percentage of vote, 1980 (chart) - 23
Photograph - 137
Pres. popular votes - **(1980)** 365; **(1984)** 377
Presidential primaries - **(1980)** 429-435
Republican platform - **(1976)** 134
Anderson, John Jr.
Governor, Kansas - 468
Anderson, Joseph
Senator, Tennessee - 602
Anderson, Sigurd
Governor, South Dakota - 482
Anderson, Thomas Jefferson
Party Pres. nominee - **(1976)** 245
Party VP nominee - **(1972)** 245
Pres. popular votes - **(1976)** 374
Anderson, Victor E.
Governor, Nebraska - 474
Anderson, Wendell R.
Governor, Minnesota - 472
Senator, Minnesota - 591
Andrew, John A.
Governor, Massachusetts - 471
Andrews, Charles B.
Governor, Connecticut - 464
Andrews, Charles O.
Senator, Florida - 583
Andrews, Mark
Senator, North Dakota - 598
Andrews, Thomas Coleman
Party Pres. nominee - **(1956, 1964)** 244
Pres. popular votes - **(1956)** 359; **(1960)** 373
Andrus, Cecil D.
Governor, Idaho - 466
Angelo, Ernie
Republican primary rules (box) - 20
Ankeny, Levi
Senator, Washington - 605
Ansel, Martin F.
Governor, South Carolina - 482
Anthony, George T.
Governor, Kansas - 468
Anthony, Henry B.
Governor, Rhode Island - 481
Senator, Rhode Island - 600

M

JK
1967
.C662
1985

CANISIUS COLLEGE LIBRARY

3 5084 00266 4319

Book Shelves
JK1967 .C662 1985
Congressional Quarte   ,
Guide to U.S. electi

CANISIUS COLLEGE LIBRARY
BUFFALO, N. Y.